MW00698332

THE THREE-IN-ONE CONCISE

BIBLE REFERENCE COMPANION

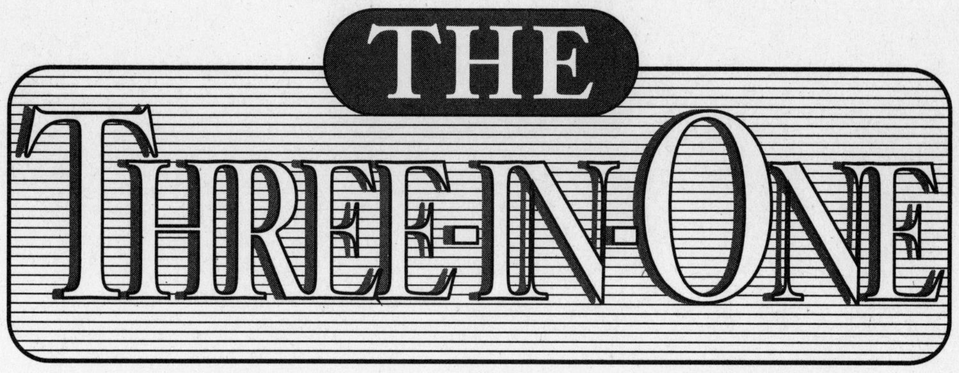

C·O·N·C·I·S·E

BIBLE REFERENCE COMPANION

THOMAS NELSON PUBLISHERS
NASHVILLE

Originally released as *Guideposts Family Topical Concordance to the Bible* and published jointly by Thomas Nelson Publishers and by Guideposts Associates, Inc.

Published in Nashville, Tennessee, by Thomas Nelson Publishers.

Library of Congress Cataloging-in-Publication Data

Three-in-one Bible reference companion / foreword by Lloyd John Ogilvie.
Originally published: Guideposts family topical concordance to the Bible. © 1982.
Includes index.
ISBN 0-7852-0972-7
Library of Congress has cataloged an earlier printing.
(ISBN 0-8407-6911-3)
1. Bible—Concordances, English. I. Thomas Nelson Publishers.
II. Title. III. Title: Three-in-one Bible reference companion.
BS425.G84 1993
220.5'2033—dc20 93-4593
CIP

Printed in the United States of America
11 12 13 14 15 – 05

FOREWORD

by Dr. Lloyd John Ogilvie

The Bible is my constant companion. It is a source of courage in my deepest needs and the answer to my most urgent questions. Daily devotions in God's Word gives me strength in the ups and downs of life. It is the basis of my teaching and preaching, the main resource in my work with people. Listening to people and then listening to God for His guidance for them in the Bible is the purpose and passion of my life.

In preparing my sermons, I ask people to share their hurts and hopes, joys and sorrows. I ask them to tell me the greatest challenges they are facing and the most frustrating stresses they are enduring. Then I turn to the Scriptures for the most salient verses and passages to help them live the abundant life.

On my desk in my study, I have dozens of books to help me find the rich treasures of the Bible. Though I have spent most of my life in studying the Scriptures, I have only begun to penetrate its limitless resources for living. And so I have found Bible dictionaries, biblical encyclopedias, and cross-reference books on the words and themes of the Word of God to be very helpful. So often, as I juggled these many books, I've said, "Why doesn't someone put them all together in one volume?!"

And here it is. That's why I am so excited about the publication of the *Three-in-One Bible Reference Companion.* When I search the Scriptures about a particular theme or word, I want to know all that is available in all the passages and verses of the Bible. Some concordances help with lists of references, but give little assistance in understanding what the Bible says about a theme, place, word, or idea. This new companion to the Bible provides us with the all-important, basic information about the Word of God in a way that no other book does. It defines the words the Bible uses. There is a convenient index to virtually every subject the Bible discusses. And it lists the places where we can find every word that is used in the King James Version. But whatever translation you use, you will find the references you need.

Because the *Three-in-One Bible Reference Companion* combines so many of the features of other books for help in Bible study, it will be an ideal volume for your home and library. You will find it so invaluable, you will want to keep it next to your Bible for ready reference in your daily devotions and study. With it you will be able to plumb the depths of what the Bible really says. Whether you want to know about a person, place, subject, doctrine, theme, or idea—you will find that the index information provided will lead you quickly to the references, definitions, and related subjects you need. You will feel the excitement of discovering how the words and ideas of Scripture are intertwined. Suddenly the treasure chest of the Bible will be open for you to understand and live.

But the *Three-in-One Bible Reference Companion* is more than just a reference book to aid in the study of the Scriptures. It will also be a lifeline in your devotional reading of the Bible. We all long to know God better and live life fully in fellowship with Him. He is the author of that need. It is His gift to draw us closer to Him. I find that this unique companion offers us practical help. Whatever problems we're confronting, or spiritual dilemmas we're feeling, this volume helps us identify what the Bible says about them. We can identify the word which expresses our condition, look in the companion, and then find the passages which will speak to our needs. Or when we feel gratitude, joy, or praise, we can find verses which maximize our thoughts and feelings. We can learn how to pray in the valleys and mountaintops of life. Our decisions will be guided by what the Bible actually says about the specific choices we have.

The great themes of the Christian life are included in this remarkable volume. Prayer. Worship. Repentance. Forgiveness. Thanksgiving. Salvation. The Bible's resources for facing life's bitterest moments are presented as well. Discouragement? Fear? Frustration? Sin and selfishness? Pride? Anxiety? Hopelessness? The Bible tells us what causes these painful times and what can be done to overcome them. This volume shows us what the Bible says and where it says it.

Whatever our problem or need, the Word of God points us to His power to live life triumphantly. And the *Three-in-One Bible Reference Companion* will help us discover exactly what the Bible teaches us about how to experience and live by His power.

You will cherish this volume as one of your most valued books. I am delighted that it is available to help us meet God, hear what He has to say to us, and live the many-splendored gift of life. I recommend it to you for your reading and study of the Word of God with enthusiasm!

Hollywood Presbyterian Church
Hollywood, California

INTRODUCTION

Welcome to the *Three-in-One Bible Reference Companion.* It is a unique book, totally unlike any other reference hitherto available to the student of the Bible; it results from the dedicated labor of a specially chosen team of scholars and researchers. Between the covers of this book readers will find guidance in studying the Word of God as in no other book. Here—in just one volume—are all the features of a Bible concordance, a comprehensive biblical index and a Bible dictionary.

WHAT IS THE THREE-IN-ONE COMPANION?

After a lifetime of experience in the fields of religious publishing and education, the editors of *Guideposts* and Thomas Nelson Publishers came to realize that many people tend to think of a concordance as a complicated, hard-to-use volume with small type, found only in pastors' offices, libraries or seminary classrooms.

While it is true that some concordances are baffling to the lay person, designed for use by only the serious scholar and theologian, the editors felt strongly that a great wellspring of spiritual guidance and inspiration was lying dormant. They determined to produce a clear and concise concordance that would be of everyday use to Bible readers everywhere. After years of meticulous, painstaking and devoted labor, the *Three-in-One Bible Reference Companion* is the result—a reference guide that will be forever treasured by people in all walks of life and in all countries the world over as they come to depend upon it for enriching and broadening their understanding of God's Word.

A Bible Concordance

Quite simply, the *Three-in-One Bible Reference Companion* is an alphabetical listing of all the words in the King James Version of the Bible,[1] most with the adjacent references that indicate in biblical order where each word can be found.

---

[1] Although this concordance is based on the King James Version of the Bible, it can be used with all Bible versions.

In the concordance, each reference cited is accompanied by a brief introductory phrase from the verse. For example, the entry *abroad* gives sixty cases of the use of the word in the Bible, beginning with Genesis 10:18 and ending with James 1:1.

ABROAD—*beyond the boundaries*
of the Canaanites spread ***a*** . . . .Gen 10:18
lest we be scattered ***a*** . . . . .Gen 11:4
the Lord scattered them ***a*** . . . . .Gen 11:8
the Lord scatter them ***a*** . . . . . . .Gen 11:9
he brought him forth ***a*** . . . . . . .Gen 15:5
people were scattered ***a*** . . . . . . .Ex 5:12
I will spread ***a*** my hands . . . . . .Ex 9:29
Pharaoh and spread ***a*** his . . . . .Ex 9:33
carry forth..of the flesh ***a*** . . . . .Ex 12:46
. . . .
love of God is shed ***a*** . . . . .Rom 5:5
He hath dispersed ***a*** he 2Cor 9:9
faith..God-ward is spread ***a*** 1Thess 1:8
tribes which..scattered ***a*** . . . . . .James 1:1

Not all references have been included. Actually, *abroad* appears eighty times in the King James Version of the Bible but because of the requirements of space, only those references that are the most widely known and familiar have been included. In addition, there are one hundred and thirty-two entry words in this concordance that carry no reference because they are in such common usage that students of the Bible are not likely to refer to them in searching for a particular Scripture passage. These words are:

a
about
according
after
again
against
all
also
am
among
amongst
an
and
any
are*
as
at
away
be
because
been
before
both
brought
but
by
came
cast
cause
children
days
did
do*
down
even
every
for
forth
from
given
go*
good
gotten
have*
he
her*
him
himself
his
how
I
if
in
into
is
it
let*
like*
many
may*
me
mine
more
my
neither
no
nor
not
now
O
of
off
on
one*
or
our*
over
own
part
people*
place*
same
say*
set*
shall
she
should*
so
sought
than
that
the
thee
their
them
themselves
then
there
therefore
therein
thereof
thereon
thereto
these
they
thine
thing*
this
those
thou
thus
thy
to
took*
unto
up
upon
us
was*
we
went*
were*
what
when
which
who
whom
with
ye
yea
yet
you

The asterisk (*) following certain words indicates that additional forms of the word are also not indexed in the concordance.

This unique companion is *also* a comprehensive biblical index *as well as* a Bible dictionary.

A Biblical Index

A comprehensive biblical index gathers together information in a very different way than that of a concordance. The index is more concerned with the *ideas* of Scripture than it is with the *words* of Scripture. It lists verses by subject matter rather than by specific words. For instance, although Genesis 2:18–24 is an important passage about marriage, it does not contain the word *marriage.*

Many of the concepts of the Bible, its most treasured theological and doctrinal teachings, can best be described by words that may not even appear in Scripture; yet the truths expressed by these words constitute the very essence of the Bible. While the word *miracle(s)* appears only thirty-seven times in the Bible, examples of God's *miracle-working* power are found throughout. Following true biblical-index procedure, the *Three-in-One Bible Reference Companion* lists one hundred and sixty-one *miracles* recorded in Scripture, regardless of whether the word *miracle* occurs in the text or not.

Another example is found in the word *divination,* an attempt to foretell the future by occult means. The practice is not mentioned by name in the Bible, yet accounts of it occur in Ezekiel 13:6, 7; Deuteronomy 18:11, 12; Leviticus 20:6, 27; and Acts 16:16. Other simple examples of words that do not actually appear in the Bible but which, as subjects, are dwelt upon are *intolerance, trinity* and *backsliding.*

Often a student of the Bible has experienced the frustration of trying to locate a particular verse without success. Perhaps he or she has been in a discussion and the verse was needed quickly to demonstrate a point. Or perhaps the reader has been intrigued by the power of certain words—*love, faith, hope* and *salvation,* for instance—but was unable to locate their usage in the Bible. In the easy-to-understand format of this unique companion, the answers are readily available; the student will never become discouraged by tiresome and fruitless search.

Further, the index is invaluable when one looks at whole categories such as *prophets,* illustrations of *faithfulness, animals,* or even a fascinating list of *first things.* And it proves that the mundane is not necessarily banal. What, for instance, do even the most devoted biblical students know about topics such as *wagons* and *waterproofing, shoes* and *seals, locks* and *lunatics, employment* and *excuses?*

In addition, a comprehensive biblical index functions as a guide to the basic principles of life that are rooted in the Bible. *Blessings of God, prayer, integrity* and the *character of God's people* can be traced through the Bible, using this companion.

Because the *Three-in-One Bible Reference Companion* contains all of the features of a comprehensive biblical index, it will serve as a constant companion to the Bible reader. Further, it invites one to undertake a journey of exploration wherein at random, or even unexpectedly, the student will discover that the treasures of God's Word are opening to him or her in new and enriched profusion.

A Bible Dictionary

A dictionary gives the background and meaning of words by providing their definitions, roots (etymologies) and pronunciation. The *Three-in-One Bible Reference Companion* does all of this.

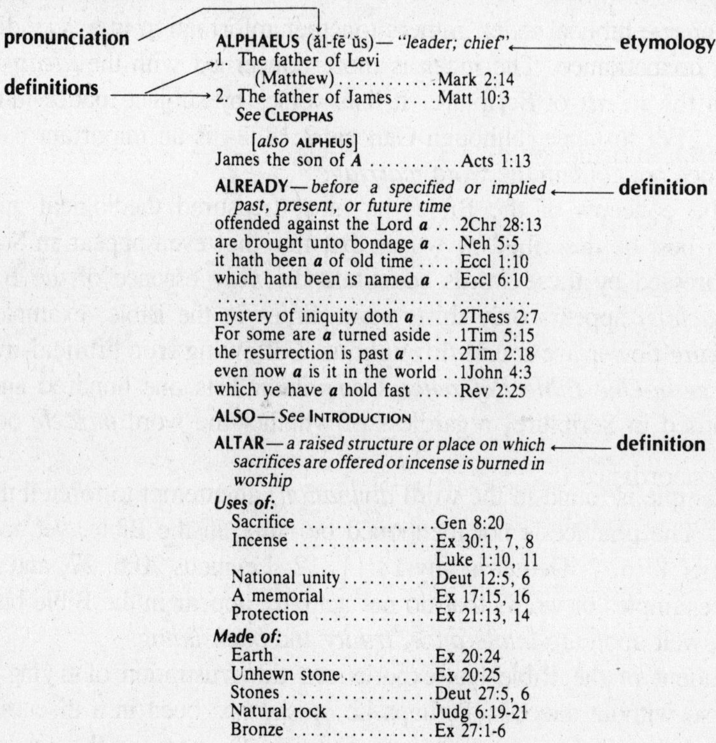

ALPHAEUS (ăl-fē'ŭs)—*"leader; chief"*
1. The father of Levi (Matthew) . . . . Mark 2:14
2. The father of James . . . . Matt 10:3
See CLEOPHAS

[*also* ALPHEUS]
James the son of *A* . . . . Acts 1:13

ALREADY—*before a specified or implied past, present, or future time*
offended against the Lord ***a*** . . . 2Chr 28:13
are brought unto bondage ***a*** . . . Neh 5:5
it hath been ***a*** of old time . . . . . Eccl 1:10
which hath been is named ***a*** . . . Eccl 6:10
. . . .
mystery of iniquity doth ***a*** 2Thess 2:7
For some are ***a*** turned aside . . . 1Tim 5:15
the resurrection is past ***a*** 2Tim 2:18
even now ***a*** is it in the world . . 1John 4:3
which ye have ***a*** hold fast . . . . . Rev 2:25

ALSO—*See* INTRODUCTION

ALTAR—*a raised structure or place on which sacrifices are offered or incense is burned in worship*
Uses of:
Sacrifice . . . . Gen 8:20
Incense . . . . Ex 30:1, 7, 8; Luke 1:10, 11
National unity . . . . Deut 12:5, 6
A memorial . . . . Ex 17:15, 16
Protection . . . . Ex 21:13, 14
Made of:
Earth . . . . Ex 20:24
Unhewn stone . . . . Ex 20:25
Stones . . . . Deut 27:5, 6
Natural rock . . . . Judg 6:19-21
Bronze . . . . Ex 27:1-6

The entry word is given first in all boldface capital letters. For proper names, this is followed by a pronunciation (See Guide to Pronunciation on page *xv*) in parentheses, and an etymology in quotation marks. The etymology gives the origin of the meaning of a proper name. When it is not included, the etymology of the word is not known. In the example above, the etymology of the name *Alphaeus* is "leader" or "chief," but that does not tell who Alphaeus was. The definition of the entry word can be found in either of two places: 1) in the biblical index portion. This is where definitions of proper names are usually placed, especially when one name designates more than one biblical character; 2) following the entry word itself and the pronunciation and etymology (if there is any). In this case the definition is set in italics.

With the concordance, index and dictionary features combined, this companion will help the student maintain a balance in his or her study of the Scriptures. By not limiting itself to the words of only one version of the Bible, the biblical index portion helps the reader to explore the nature and meaning of subjects of far-reaching interest. However, because the concordance portion is based on the King James Version of the Bible, it provides reference to the most familiar words of the Bible. These features have been deliberately incorporated in the belief that the student of God's Word will derive richer insights the closer he or she is to the long-beloved usage of biblical terminology.

THE ORGANIZATION OF THE COMPANION

The *Three-in-One Bible Reference Companion* consists of one alphabetical list of entry words. The list includes words found in the Bible (e.g., *Lord*) and index concepts that are not found as words in the Bible (e.g., *trinity*). Therefore, after giving the dictionary information (entry word, pronunciation, etymology and definition) an entry may contain index information only, concordance information only, or a combination.

Index information only:

GATES OF JERUSALEM—*the entries into the holy city*

1. Corner Gate 2Chr 26:9
2. Dung Gate ....Neh 12:31
3. Of Ephraim ....Neh 8:16
4. Fish Gate ....Zeph 1:10
5. Fountain Gate ....Neh 12:37
6. Horse Gate ....Jer 31:40
7. Benjamin's Gate ....Zech 14:10
8. Prison gate ....Neh 12:39
9. Sheep Gate ....Neh 3:1
10. Upper Benjamin Gate . .Jer 20:2
11. Valley Gate ....Neh 2:13
12. Water Gate ....Neh 8:16

Concordance information only:

HEIGHT—*the distance from the bottom to the top of something*

[*also* HEIGHTS]
and the ***h*** of it thirty.........Gen 6:15
cubit and a half the ***h***.........Ex 25:10
the ***h*** five cubits of fine ....Ex 27:18
a cubit and a half the ***h*** ....Ex 37:1
and two cubits was the ***h***......Ex 37:25
the ***h*** in the breadth was ......Ex 38:18
or on the ***h*** of his stature 1Sam 16:7
and the ***h*** thereof thirty 1Kin 6:2
The ***h*** of the one cherub 1Kin 6:26
the ***h*** of the one chapiter......1Kin 7:16
the ***h*** of the other chapiter 1Kin 7:16
all about, and his ***h*** was five. . .1Kin 7:23
the ***h*** of a wheel was a........1Kin 7:32
come up to the ***h*** of the.......2Kin 19:23
h of the one pillar was........2Kin 25:17

Both index and concordance information:

GARDEN—*a protected and cultivated place*
Notable examples of:
In Eden ....Gen 2:15
In Egypt................Deut 11:10
In Shushan..............Esth 1:5
In Gethsemane..........Mark 14:32
A royal.................2Kin 25:4
Used for:
Festivities ....Esth 1:5
Idolatry.................Is 65:3
Meditations ....Matt 26:36
Burial ....John 19:41
Figurative of:
Desolation ....Amos 4:9
Fruitfulness ....Is 51:3
Prosperity...............Is 58:11
Righteousness ....Is 61:11

[*also* GARDENS]
the Lord God planted a ***g***.....Gen 2:8
out of Eden to water the ***g***....Gen 2:10
g thou mayest freely eat ......Gen 2:16
fruit of the trees of the ***g*** .....Gen 3:2
Lord God walkng in the ***g*** ....Gen 3:8
I heard thy voice in the ***g*** .....Gen 3:10
the east of the ***g*** of Eden .....Gen 3:24
as ***g*** by the river's side ....Num 24:6
may have it for a ***g*** of herbs . . .1Kin 21:2

Notice that the index information is indented slightly while the concordance phrases are placed at the left margin. Moreover, the Bible references for the index portion are lined up farther to the left than those of the concordance references. The index portion always comes first when an entry includes both index and concordance information.

One especially helpful feature of the *Three-in-One Bible Reference Companion* is that a word and its cognates (related words) are listed together. For instance, *angel, angels, angel's* and *angels'*—or *look, looked, lookest, looketh, looking* and *looks*. The cognate words included in the concordance listing are indicated as follows:

GIRD—*to put on, as a belt*
Purposes of:
Strengthening ....Prov 31:17
Supporting clothing 2Kin 4:29
Figurative of:
Gladness................Ps 30:11
Truth...................Eph 6:14
Readiness...............1Pet 1:13
Those girding:
Priests ....Ex 28:4, 39
Warriors 1Sam 18:4
Jesus ....John 13:3, 4

cognates ——→ [*also* GIRDED, GIRDEDST, GIRDETH, GIRDING, GIRT]
eat it; with your loins ***g*** ....Ex 12:11
and ***g*** him with the curious ....Ex 29:5
shalt ***g*** them with girdles ......Ex 29:9
and ***g*** him with the girdle .....Lev 8:7

Because of this manner of listing related words, the Bible student does not have to check individual entries. In many concordances where cognates are not provided, the reader may look up a word but not succeed in locating the verse he or she wants because the verse actually contains not that word, but one related to it.

Still another unique feature of this concordance is the way in which it treats a word that has more than one meaning. Unless the various meanings are clearly differentiated, the Bible student may not gain the fullest appreciation of the truths they express. For instance, there is much difference between *fear* meaning "anxiety caused by approaching danger" and *fear* of God because of His majesty and holiness. This concordance, unlike others, separates the two usages. As another example, there are four specific *temples* mentioned in the Bible: Solomon's Temple, Zerubbabel's Temple, Herod's Temple and, metaphorically, the believer as the temple of God. Each of these temples is listed separately in this concordance.

Also, an extensive system of cross-references had been built into the *Three-in-One Bible Reference Companion*. This feature will enable the student to find information about a word that may not appear in its alphabetical order; sometimes the spelling that appears in the reader's Bible had been updated and the word therefore appears under another listing. For instance, older editions of the King James Version use the term *broidered* when the meaning is more accurately expressed by the spelling in modern editions *embroidered.* With the cross-reference, locating the proper listing is made simple.

PERSONAL BIBLE STUDY USING THIS COMPANION

Because the Bible is God's written Word, it is the believers' guide for life. A sincere study of the Bible deepens students' understandings of the God they love and worship and leads them to the highest appreciation of the salvation He has provided.

The *Three-in-One Bible Reference Companion* is the tool with which the Scriptures may be opened to the student's maturing comprehension and insight. It is not a replacement for the Bible itself. Every reference in this book refers to a specific passage in the Bible. It is wise to read the verses before and after the passage under study to gain an awareness of the historical background in which the text is set. "What did it mean then?" is a question every bit as important as "What does it mean to me today?"

Character Study

Since God works through the lives and deeds of His people, an in-depth study of the individuals in the Bible reveals many essential truths about standards of conduct. These truths are given directly or indirectly, and they are presented to the reader in various forms: as inspiration, as warnings, as depictions of Christian principles of forgiveness and charity or as examples of wrongdoing, to suggest but a few.

A specific individual such as David may be studied with great benefit. A quick glance at the concordance portion of the listing for David reveals that his name is mentioned throughout the Bible. But the index portion provides a comprehensive outline of the life of David that could form the basis of an excellent study: his early life, his life under King Saul, his life as a fugitive hero, as king over Judah, king over all Israel, and the spiritual significance of David himself to following generations of believers. The biblical references given in both the index and the concordance sections can be brought together to fuel the study of David's life so that the reader may draw applications to his or her own experience.

The same method could be used to study the lives of many of the characters of the Bible: Aaron, Abraham, Moses, Paul, Peter, Solomon, and even the Lord Jesus Christ.

Another approach to the character study of people in the Bible would be the study of a group of people such as kings, prophets, judges, priests and women. In each category there are some individuals who walked closely with God, obeying His voice, and others who went on their own way, exerting their own will. Any of these groups of people could form the basis of a series of Bible studies.

Furthermore, on almost any page of this companion reference is made to lesser-known personalities of the Bible. Diligent study of their lives, too, will be equally rewarding. Often they provide insights and encouragement that even the best-known characters do not. It is particularly interesting to study the etymologies of the names of these characters and compare those meanings with their actual lives.

Another interesting way to study the characters of the Bible is to consider those entries where a number of different people share the same name. For instance, nine men shared the name *Simon;* twenty-two men shared the name *Azariah;* fourteen men were named *Jonathan.*

Doctrinal Study

The words *doctrine* and *theology* frequently raise anxiety in the mind of the Bible student. They have become weighted words, words that bear overtones of complexity and controversy. Actually they are very helpful words when properly understood. Simply put, doctrine gives substance and order to faith. Most of the questions that are raised about Christian truths are doctrinal questions and they can be studied by a tracing of their appearance through the Bible. Great doctrines of the Christian faith are listed in this companion. For instance, the entry *salvation* identifies descriptions of the various kinds of salvation mentioned in Scripture; it lists the sources of salvation, gives a history of salvation throughout Scripture, shows the requirements of salvation, gives the blessings of salvation (both negative and positive), and shows the ways in which salvation affects the past, the present and the future. By consulting the index references *and* the concordance entries, the reader will be able to "flesh out" the bones of his or her understanding of the doctrine of salvation.

In the study of a given doctrine, the student will often find reference to other doctrines. For example, in the entry *grace,* the sources of grace are listed as salvation, the call of God, faith, justification, forgiveness and consolation. Most of these words are also entries in other parts of the companion.

Word Studies

A close examination of the words of Scripture will yield worthwhile fruit for the student's efforts. One interesting example is *long-suffering.* The index portion of this companion describes God's long-suffering and the way in which a Christian is to manifest long-suffering. In referring to Galatians 5:22, the reader will find a list of the fruits of the Spirit, and it would be helpful for him or her to look at the entries for the other fruits of the Spirit as well. Those who do so will discover much about the loving qualities that God's Holy Spirit makes available to the Christian believer.

Topics such as *confession, fasting, prayer, praise of God, teaching* and *worship* offer the opportunity for profitable study. An examination of *confession of sin* might be approached in a number of ways: manifestations of confession of sin, the results of confessions of sin, instances of confession of sin. A study of those individuals in the Bible who have confessed sin would be another exceedingly valuable project.

Many other programs of studies can be developed. Social customs, personal relationships, religious objects, and places of the Bible are examples of studies that one may pursue through the unique guidance of the *Three-in-One Bible Reference Companion.*

* * * * * * * * * * * * * *

The Publishers hope that the suggestions offered here will stimulate not only those students just beginning to study God's Word, but all believers everywhere. To fully understand God's Word requires a lifetime endeavor, and it is our prayer that the *Three-in-One Bible Reference Companion* will enrich every person who seeks to learn of Him and follow His way. If this companion introduces even one Christian to the comfort and joy that may be known through reading and studying the Bible, the labor of love that went into the volume will have been richly rewarded.

Nashville, Tennessee

GUIDE TO PRONUNCIATION

ā as in *fame*
ă as in *cat*
â as in *share, dare*
ä as in *farm, father*
ai as in *pail*
aw as in *ought*
ch as in *chicken*
ē as in *beat, street*
ĕ as in *jet, met*
er as in *further, operation*
ī as in *kite, shine*
ĭ as in *sit, dim*
ks as in *vex*
ō as in *bone, boat*
*ŏ*as in *bottle*
ô as in *shore*
oi as in *boy, toy*
o͞o as in *pool*
o͝o as in *foot*
ow as in *about*
sh as in *harsh*
ū as in *cute, tune*
ŭ as in *fuss*
û as in *turn*
zh as in *leisure*

ABBREVIATIONS

Old Testament:	
Gen	Genesis
Ex	Exodus
Lev	Leviticus
Num	Numbers
Deut	Deuteronomy
Josh	Joshua
Judg	Judges
Ruth	Ruth
1Sam	First Samuel
2Sam	Second Samuel
1Kin	First Kings
2Kin	Second Kings
1Chr	First Chronicles
2Chr	Second Chronicles
Ezra	Ezra
Neh	Nehemiah
Esth	Esther
Job	Job
Ps	Psalms
Prov	Proverbs
Eccl	Ecclesiastes
Song	Song of Solomon
Is	Isaiah
Jer	Jeremiah
Lam	Lamentations
Ezek	Ezekiel
Dan	Daniel
Hos	Hosea
Joel	Joel
Amos	Amos
Obad	Obadiah
Jon	Jonah
Mic	Micah
Nah	Nahum
Hab	Habakkuk
Zeph	Zephaniah
Hag	Haggai
Zech	Zechariah
Mal	Malachi

New Testament:	
Matt	Matthew
Mark	Mark
Luke	Luke
John	John
Acts	Acts
Rom	Romans
1Cor	First Corinthians
2Cor	Second Corinthians
Gal	Galatians
Eph	Ephesians
Phil	Philippians
Col	Colossians
1Thess	First Thessalonians
2Thess	Second Thessalonians
1Tim	First Timothy
2Tim	Second Timothy
Titus	Titus
Philem	Philemon
Heb	Hebrews
James	James
1Pet	First Peter
2Pet	Second Peter
1John	First John
2John	Second John
3John	Third John
Jude	Jude
Rev	Revelation

BIBLE REFERENCE COMPANION

A

A—*See* INTRODUCTION

AARON (âr´ŭn)—*"enlightened; rich; mountaineer"—the brother of Moses and first high priest of Israel*

Ancestry and family of:
Descendant of Levi ......Ex 6:16-20
Son of Amram and Jochebed ....Ex 6:20
Moses' older brother.....Ex 7:1, 7
Brother of Miriam ....Ex 15:20
Husband of Elisheba.....Ex 6:23
Father of Nadab, Abihu, Eleazar, and Ithamar ..Ex 6:23

Position of:
Moses' helper ....Ex 4:13-31
Becomes "prophet" to Moses ....Ex 7:1, 2
God inspired ....Ex 12:1
Commissioned, with Moses to deliver Israelites from Egypt { Ex 6:13, 26; Josh 24:5 }
Inferior to that of Melchizedek ....Heb 7:11-19

Special privileges of:
Appears before Pharaoh..Ex 5:1-4
Performs miracles ....Ex 7:9, 10, 19, 20
Supports Moses' hands...Ex 17:10-12
Ascends Mt. Sinai ....Ex 19:24; Ex 24:1, 9
Sees God's glory ....Ex 24:9, 10
Judges Israel in Moses' absence ....Ex 24:14
Allowed inside the veil...Lev 16:15
Blesses the people ....Lev 9:22
Intercedes for Miriam....Num 12:10-12

Sins of:
Tolerates idolatry........Ex 32:1-4
Permits evil ....Ex 32:21-25
Conspires against Moses..Num 12:1-16
With Moses, fails at Meribah .... { Num 20:1-13, 24 }

Character of:
A good speaker ....Ex 4:14
Weak in crises ....Ex 32:1-24
Subject to jealousy ......Num 12:1, 2
Conscious of guilt ....Num 12:11
Submissive ....Lev 10:1-7
A saint ....Ps 106:16

Priesthood of:
Chosen by God ....Ex 28:1
Sons, in office..........Lev 8:1-36
Anointed with oil........Ex 30:25, 30
Duties given ....Ex 30:7-10
Garments prescribed.....Ex 39:27-29
Ordained to teach ....Lev 10:8, 11
Set apart to offer sacrifices............. { Lev 9:1-24; Heb 5:1-4 }
Alone enters within the holy place .... { Ex 30:10; Heb 9:7, 25 }
Intercedes for others.....Num 16:46-48
Confirmed by God ......Num 17:8-10; Heb 9:4
Hereditary ....Num 20:23-28
For lifetime ....Heb 7:23
Inferior to Melchizedek's .Heb 7:11-19

Death and descendants of
Lives 123 years..........Num 33:39
Death ....Num 20:23, 24
Eleazar, son of, successor.Num 20:25-28; Deut 10:6

[*also* AARON'S]
A the Levite thy brother? .....Ex 4:14
Eleazar *A* son took him one...Ex 6:25
in the priest's office, even *A*...Ex 28:1
they may make *A* garments....Ex 28:3
they shall be upon *A* heart ....Ex 28:30
shall be upon *A* forehead .....Ex 28:38
for *A* sons..make coats........Ex 28:40
the ram of *A* consecration .....Ex 29:26
it shall be *A* and his sons' .....Ex 29:28
and brought them unto *A* .....Ex 32:3
when *A* saw..it he built an ....Ex 32:5
they made the calf, which *A*...Ex 32:35
priests, *A* sons, shall bring ....Lev 1:5
the priests, *A* sons, shall lay...Lev 1:8
priests, *A* sons..sprinkle ....Lev 1:11
he shall bring it to *A* sons .....Lev 2:2
meat offerings shall be *A* ......Lev 2:3
A sons the priests..sprinkle ....Lev 3:2
A sons shall burn it..altar .....Lev 3:5
A sons shall sprinkle the ......Lev 3:8
but the breast shall be *A* ......Lev 7:31
Take *A* and his sons with .....Lev 8:2
Moses brought *A* and his .....Lev 8:6
Moses brought *A* sons, and....Lev 8:13
upon the tip of *A* right ear ....Lev 8:23
brought *A* sons and Moses ....Lev 8:24
he put all upon *A* hands ......Lev 8:27
and *A* sons presented ....Lev 9:12
it shall be *A* and his sons' .....Lev 24:9
A and his sons shall go in .....Num 4:19
Moses and against *A* and.....Num 16:3
thou shalt write *A* name ......Num 17:3
Bring *A* rod again before......Num 17:10
spake unto Moses and *A* ......Num 20:12
and *A* died there in the top ...Num 20:28
But *A* and his sons offered 1Chr 6:49
He sent Moses..and *A* ....Ps 105:26
upon the beard, even *A* ....Ps 133:2
wife..the daughters of *A* ......Luke 1:5
unto *A*, Make us gods to......Acts 7:40
called after the order of *A*? ...Heb 7:11

AARONITES—*descendants of Aaron*
Fights with David 1Chr 12:27
Under Zadok 1Chr 27:17

AB—*fifth month of the Jewish year*
Aaron died in ....Num 33:38
See JEWISH CALENDAR

AB—*"father"*
A part of many Hebrew names (e.g., Abinadab, Abner, Abijah) 1Sam 7:1

ABADDON (ă-băd´ŭn)—*"place of destruction"*
Designates ruin in ....Job 31:12
Parallel with hell (Sheol) in ....Job 26:6
Refers to death ....Job 28:22
Personified..............Rev 9:11

ABAGTHA (ă-băg'thă)—*"happy; prosperous"*
A eunuch under King Ahasuerus .... Esth 1:10

ABANA (ăb'ä-nä)—*"stony"—a river that flows through Damascus*
Spoken of highly by Naaman ....2 Kin 5:12

ABANDON—*desert*

Required for:
Safety ....Gen 19:12-26; Acts 27:41-44
Salvation ....Phil 3:7-10
Service ....Matt 10:37-39
Sanctification............2Cor 6:14-18
Spiritual success ....Heb 11:24-27

Aspects of:
Land, commanded ....Gen 12:1-5
Idolaters, justified ....Ex 32:1-10
One's ministry, rebuked ..1Kin 19:3-18
Family, regretted 1Sam 30:1-6
The tabernacle, remembered ....Jer 7:12
Jerusalem, lamented .....Matt 23:37,38

Of men to judgment because of:
Sin.....................Gen 6:5-7
Rebellion 1Sam 15:16-26
Unbelief ....Matt 23:37-39
Rejecting God ....Rom 1:21-32
Fornication 1Cor 5:1-5
Apostasy ....Heb 10:26-29

ABARIM (ăb'ä-rĭm)—*"mountain beyond"—a large mountain range in Moab*
Moses sees the promised land from.............Num 27:12

pitched in the mountains of *A* .Num 33:47
departed..mountains of *A* .....Num 33:48
get thee up..mountain *A* ......Deut 32:49

ABASE—*to degrade; to humiliate*

As a judgment for:
Stubbornness 2Kin 14:8-14
Defaming God 2Chr 32:1-22
Pride . . . . . Is 14:12-17
Hating Jews . . . . . Esth 7:5-10
Arrogance . . . . . Dan 4:33, 37
Acts 12:20-23

As a virtue, seen in:
Nineveh's repentance . . . . John 3:1-10
Matt 12:41
A publican's unworthiness. Luke 18:13, 14
Paul's life 1Cor 9:19-23
Christ's humiliation . . . . . Phil 2:5-8

Rewards of, seen in:
Healing 2Kin 5:11-14
Elevation . . . . . Matt 23:12
Restoration . . . . . Luke 15:11-24
Renewed service 1Cor 15:9, 10

[*also* ABASED, ABASING]
one that is proud and *a* . . . . . Job 40:11
nor *a* himself for the noise . . . . Is 31:4
low, and *a* him that is high . . . . Ezek 21:26
exalteth himself shall be *a* . . . . . Luke 14:11
a myself that ye might be 2Cor 11:7
I know both how to be *a* . . . . . Phil 4:12

ABATE—*diminish; desist*
Flood waters . . . . . Gen 8:8, 11
Moses' natural force not. . Deut 34:7
Anger of Ephraim . . . . . Judg 8:3

[*also* ABATED]
fifty days the waters were *a* . . . Gen 8:3
a from thy estimation . . . . . Lev 27:18
nor his natural force *a* . . . . . Deut 34:7
their anger was *a* toward . . . . . Judg 8:3

ABBA (ăb'ä)—*"papa"—an Aramaic word meaning "father"*
Used by Christ . . . . . Mark 14:36
Expressive of sonship . . . . Rom 8:15

And he said, *A*, Father . . . . . Mark 14:36
adoption, whereby we cry, *A* . . Rom 8:15
hearts, crying, *A*, Father . . . . . Gal 4:6

ABDA (ăb'dä)—*"servant; worshiper"*
1. The father of Adoniram . 1Kin 4:6
2. A Levite, son of Shammua . . . . . Neh 11:17
Called Obadiah 1Chr 9:16

ABDEEL (ăb'dĕ-ĕl)—*"servant of God"*
The father of Shelemiah. . Jer 36:26

ABDI (ăb'dī)—*"servant of Jehovah"*
1. The grandfather of Ethan 1Chr 6:44
2. A Levite 2Chr 29:12
3. A Jew who divorced his foreign wife . . . . . Ezra 10:26

ABDIEL (ăb'dĭ-ĕl)—*"servant of God"*
A Gadite residing in Gilead 1Chr 5:15, 16

ABDON (ăb'dŏn)—*"service; servile"*
1. A minor judge . . . . . Judg 12:13-15
2. A Benjamite living in Jerusalem 1Chr 8:23, 28
3. A son of Jeiel 1Chr 8:30
4. A courtier of King Josiah 2Chr 34:20
5. A Levitical city . . . . . Josh 21:30
1Chr 6:74

ABED-NEGO (ä-bĕd'nĕ-gó)—*"servant of Nebo: servant of Ishtar"—the name given to Azariah, one of Daniel's three friends*
Name given to Azariah, a Hebrew captive . . . . . Dan 1:7
Appointed by Nebuchadnezzar . . . . . Dan 2:49
Accused of disobedience . Dan 3:12
Cast into furnace but delivered . . . . . Dan 3:13-27
Promoted by Nebuchadnezzar . . . . . Dan 3:28-30

ABEL (ā'bĕl)—*"a breath; vapor; shepherd"—the second son of Adam and Eve*
Adam's second son . . . . . Gen 4:2
The first shepherd . . . . . Gen 4:2
Offering of, accepted . . . . Gen 4:4
Hated and slain by Cain . Gen 4:8
Place of, filled by Seth . . . Gen 4:25
First martyr . . . . . Matt 23:35
Righteous . . . . . Matt 23:35
Sacrificed to God by faith. Heb 11:4
Christ's blood superior to . Heb 12:24

From the blood of *A* unto . . . . . Luke 11:51

ABEL (ā'bĕl)—*"meadow; brook; stream"*
A city involved in Sheba's rebellion 2Sam 20:14-18
Translated as "great stone of Abel" in 1Sam 6:18
Elsewhere in place names—See following entries

tribes of Israel unto *A* 2Sam 20:14
they..besieged him in *A* 2Sam 20:15
They..ask counsel at *A* 2Sam 20:18

ABEL-BETH-MAACHAH (à'bĕl-bĕth-mā'ä-kä)—*"meadow (brook) of the house of Maacah"*
Captured by Tiglath-pileser 2Kin 15:29
A town in North Palestine 2Sam 20:14, 15
Refuge of Sheba; saved from destruction 2Sam 20:14-22
Seized by Ben-hadad 1Kin 15:20

ABEL-MAIM (ā'bĕl-mā'ĭm)—*"meadow (brook) of waters"*
Another name for Abel-beth-maacah 2Chr. 16:4

ABEL-MEHOLAH (ā'bĕl-mĕ-hō'lä)—*"meadow (brook) of dancing"*
Midianites flee to . . . . . Judg 7:22
A few miles east of Jabesh-gilead 1Kin 4:12
Elisha's native city 1Kin 19:16

ABEL-MIZRAIM (ā'bĕl-mĭz'rā-ĭm)—*"meadow (brook) of the Egyptians"*
A place, east of Jordan, where Israelites mourned for Jacob . . . . Gen 50:10, 11

ABEL-SHITTIM (ā'bĕl-shĭt'ĭm)—*"meadow (brook) of the Acacias"*
A place in Moab . . . . . Num 33:49

ABEZ (ā'bĕz)—*"lofty"*
A town of Issachar . . . . . Josh 19:20

ABHOR—*to detest; loathe; hate*

Descriptive of:
Disliking God's laws . . . . . Lev 26:15
Prejudice toward non-Israelites . . . . . Deut 23:7
Right attitude toward idolatry . . . . . Deut 7:25, 26
Self-rejection . . . . . Job 42:6
Israel abhorred by Rezon. 1Kin 11:25
Israel's rejection by God . Ps 89:38, 39
Rejection by former friends . . . . . Job 19:19
Loss of appetite . . . . . Job 33:20
Rejecting false description Prov 24:24

Expressive of God's loathing of:
Israel's idolatry . . . . . Deut 32:17-19
Customs of other nations . Lev 20:23
Men of bloodshed . . . . . Ps 5:6

Expressive of Israel's rejection of God's:
Judgments . . . . . Lev 26:15
Ceremonies 1Sam 2:17
Promises . . . . . Is 7:16

Expressive of the believer's hatred of:
Lying . . . . . Ps 119:163
Evil . . . . . Rom 12:9

[*also* ABHORRED, ABHORREST, ABHORRETH, ABHORRING]
made our savor to be *a* . . . . . Ex 5:21
your idols..soul shall *a* . . . . . Lev 26:30
because their soul *a* my . . . . . Lev 26:43
neither will I *a* them . . . . . Lev 26:44
his..Israel utterly to *a* 1Sam 27:12
own clothes shall *a* me . . . . . Job 9:31
so that his life *a* bread . . . . . Job 33:20
the covetous..Lord *a* . . . . . Ps 10:3
hath not despised nor *a* . . . . . Ps 22:24
that is not good; he *a* . . . . . Ps 36:4
was wroth..*a* Israel . . . . . Ps 78:59
a his own inheritance . . . . . Ps 106:40
Their soul *a* all manner . . . . . Ps 107:18
he that is *a* of the Lord . . . . . Prov 22:14
to him..nation *a*. to a . . . . . Is 49:7
they shall be an *a* unto . . . . . Is 66:24
Do not *a* us, for..name's . . . . . Jer 14:21
he hath *a* his sanctuary . . . . . Lam 2:7
made thy beauty to be *a* . . . . . Ezek 16:25
and they *a* him that . . . . . Amos 5:10
I *a*..excellency of Jacob . . . . . Amos 6:8
and their soul also *a* . . . . . Zech 11:8
that *a* idols, dost thou . . . . . Rom 2:22

ABI (ā'bī)—*a contraction of Abijah, which means "Jehovah is father"*
King Hezekiah's mother . 2Kin 18:2
Also called Abijah 2Chr 29:1

ABIA, ABIAH—*See* ABIJAH

ABI-ALBON (ā'bī-ăl'bŏn)—*"father of strength"*
An Arbathite 2Sam 23:31
See ABIEL

ABIASAPH (ä-bí'ä-săf)—*"my father has gathered"*
A descendant of Levi through Korah . . . . . Ex 6:24
Called Ebiasaph 1Chr 6:23, 37
Descendants of, act as doorkeepers 1Chr 9:19

ABIATHAR (ä-bī'ä-thär)—*"father of preeminence"*
A priest who escapes Saul at Nob 1Sam 22:20-23
Becomes high priest under David 1Sam 23:6, 9-12
Shares high priesthood with Zadok 2Sam 8:17
Remains faithful to David. 2Sam 15:24-29
Informs David about Ahithophel 2Sam 15:34-36
Supports Adonijah's usurpation 1Kin 1:7, 9, 25
Deposed by Solomon 1Kin 2:26, 27, 35
Eli's line ends 1Sam 2:31-35
Referred by Christ . . . . . Mark 2:26

[*also* ABIATHAR'S]
And David said to *A* the 1Sam 30:7
And *A* brought thither the 1Sam 30:7
A went up, until all the 2Sam 15:24
and Jonathan the son of *A* 2Sam 15:27
Zadok therefore..*A* carried 2Sam 15:29
Zadok's son, and Jonathan *A* . . 2Sam 15:36
said Hushai unto Zadok..to *A* . 2Sam 17:15
David sent to Zadok..to *A* 2Sam 19:11
and Zadok and *A* were the 2Sam 20:25
sons of the king, and *A* the . . . 1Kin 1:19
Jonathan the son of *A* the 1Kin 1:42
for him..for *A* the priest 1Kin 2:22
Zadok..*A* were the priests 1Kin 4:4
And David..Zadok and *A* 1Chr 15:11
and Abimelech the son of *A* . . . 1Chr 18:16
Abimelech the son of *A* 1Chr 24:6
the son of Benaiah, and *A* 1Chr 27:34

ABIB (ā'bĭb)—*"ear of corn"—the Hebrew month in which the barley ripened*
First month in Hebrew year . . . . . Ex 12:1, 2
Commemorative of the Passover . . . . . Ex 12:1-28
Called Nisan in postexilic times . . . . . Neh 2:1

day came ye out..month *A* ....Ex 13:4
time appointed..month *A* ......Ex 23:15
in the time of the month *A* ....Ex 34:18
the month *A* thou camest ......Ex 34:18
Observe the month of *A* ......Deut 16:1
in the month of *A* the Lord ...Deut 16:1

ABIDA, ABIDAH (ä-bī'dä)—*"father of knowledge"*
A son of Midian;
grandson of Abraham
and Keturah ....Gen 25:4

and Epher..Henoch, and *A* 1Chr 1:33

ABIDAN (ä-bī'dăn)—*"father is judge; my father"*
Represents tribe of
Benjamin ....Num 1:11
Brings offering ....Num 7:60, 65
Leads Benjamites ....Num 10:24

ABIDE—*to continue in a state or place; to endure*

Applied to:
Earth's existence ....Ps 119:90
Believer's works 1Cor 3:14
Three graces 1Cor 13:13
God's faithfulness 2Tim 2:13
Christ's priesthood ....Heb 7:3
God's Word 1Pet 1:23
Believer's eternity 1John 2:17

Sphere of, in the Christian's life:
Christ ....John 15:4-6
Christ's words ....John 15:7
Christ's love ....John 15:10
Christ's doctrine 2John 9
The Holy Spirit ....John 14:16
God's Word 1John 2:14,24
One's earthly calling 1Cor 7:20, 24
The truth 2John 2

Descriptive of the believer's:
Protection ....Ps 91:1
Satisfaction ....Prov 19:23
Fruitfulness ....John 15:4, 5
Prayer life ....John 15:7
Assurance 1John 2:28

[*also* ABIDETH, ABIDING, ABODE, ABODEST]
we will *a* in the street all ......Gen 19:2
A ye here with the ass ....Gen 22:5
Let the damsel *a* with us ......Gen 24:55
a with him the space of a .....Gen 29:14
a with me...................Gen 29:19
let thy servant *a* instead of ....Gen 44:33
but his bow *a* in strength......Gen 49:24
a ye every man in his place ...Ex 16:29
glory of the Lord *a* upon......Ex 24:16
because..cloud *a* thereon ......Ex 40:35
Therefore shall ye *a* at the ....Lev 8:35
shall not *a*..thee all night......Lev 19:13
the place where the cloud *a* ...Num 9:17
as long as the cloud *a* upon ...Num 9:18
when the cloud *a* from even ...Num 9:21
they *a* over against me ....Num 22:5
he saw Israel *a* in his tents ....Num 24:2
a without..camp seven days ...Num 31:19
Every thing..may *a* the fire ....Num 31:23
all that *a* not the fire ye ......Num 31:23
he shall *a* in it..the death .....Num 35:25
a..your cities which I have ....Deut 3:19
So we *a* in the valley over ....Deut 3:29
I *a* in the mount forty days....Deut 9:9
a between Beth-el and Ai .....Josh 8:9
Judah shall *a* in their coast ....Josh 18:5
Joseph..*a* in their coasts on....Josh 18:5
a with her in the chamber .....Judg 16:9
a in the chamber ....Judg 16:12
a there till even before God ...Judg 21:2
a here fast by my maidens .....Ruth 2:8
and there *a* for ever 1Sam 1:22
God of Israel shall not *a* 1Sam 5:7
the ark *a* in Kirjath-jearim 1Sam 7:2
and *a* in a secret place 1Sam 19:2
A not in the hold 1Sam 22:5
A thou with me, fear not......1Sam 22:23
David *a* in the wilderness 1Sam 23:14
and David *a* in the wood 1Sam 23:18
a in the wilderness of Maon ...1Sam 23:25
two hundred *a* by the stuff 1Sam 25:13
David *a* in the wilderness 1Sam 26:3
whom they had..also to *a* at ...1Sam 30:21
ark..Israel, and Judah, *a* 2Sam 11:11
Uriah *a* in Jerusalem that 2Sam 11:12
return to thy place..*a* with 2Sam 15:19
he *a* at Jerusalem.............2Sam 16:3
with him will I *a* 2Sam 16:18
a settled place..thee to *a* 1Kin 8:13
up into a loft, where he *a* 1Kin 17:19
I know thy *a*, and thy going ...2Kin 19:27
there is none *a* 1Chr 29:15
a now at home 2Chr 25:19
ye *a*..siege in Jerusalem? 2Chr 32:10
there *a* we in tents three ......Ezra 8:15
nor *a* in the paths thereof. ....Job 24:13
a in the..to lie in wait? ....Job 38:40
serve thee, or *a* by thy crib ...Job 39:9
She dwelleth and *a* on the .....Job 39:28
who shall *a*..thy tabernacle? ...Ps 15:1
man being in honor *a* not .....Ps 49:12
even he that *a* of old ....Ps 55:19
I will *a* in thy tabernacle ......Ps 61:4
He..*a* before God for ever ....Ps 61:7
cannot be removed, but *a* for..Ps 125:1
her feet *a* not in her house ....Prov 7:11
reproof of life *a* among the....Prov 15:31
the earth *a* for ever...........Eccl 1:4
shall *a*..him of his labor ....Eccl 8:15
I know thy *a*, and thy going ...Is 37:28
nations shall not..able to *a* ....Jer 10:10
He that *a* in this city shall.....Jer 21:9
So Jeremiah *a* in the court ....Jer 38:28
If ye will still *a* in..land ....Jer 42:10
no man shall *a* there ....Jer 49:18
there shall no man *a* there ....Jer 49:33
so shall no man *a* there ....Jer 50:40
Thou..*a* for me many days ....Hos 3:3
children of Israel..*a* many .....Hos 3:4
sword shall *a* on his cities .....Hos 11:6
and who can *a* it? ....Joel 2:11
and they shall *a* ....Mic 5:4
who can *a* in the fierceness ....Nah 1:6
may *a*.. day of his coming? ....Mal 3:2
there *a* till ye go thence.......Matt 10:11
they *a* in Galilee, Jesus ....Matt 17:22
a till ye depart from..place ....Mark 6:10
a with her about three ....Luke 1:56
shepherds *a* in the field ....Luke 2:8
a in any house, but in the ....Luke 8:27
there *a*, and thence depart .....Luke 9:4
today I must *a* at thy house ...Luke 19:5
he went out, and *a* in the .....Luke 21:37
constrained him, saying, *A* ....Luke 24:29
like a dove, and it *a* upon.....John 1:32
saw where he dwelt, and *a* .....John 1:39
the wrath of God *a* on him....John 3:36
he *a* there two days ....John 4:40
ye have not his word *a* in .....John 5:38
servant *a* not in the house.....John 8:35
but the Son *a* ever ....John 8:35
a not in the truth, because ....John 8:44
ground and die, it *a* alone.....John 12:24
of the law that Christ *a* for ....John 12:34
believeth..me should not *a* ....John 12:46
and make our *a* with him .....John 14:23
except it *a* in the vine ....John 15:4
no more can ye, except ye *a* ..John 15:4
He that *a* in me, and I in .....John 15:5
Long time therefore *a* they ....Acts 14:3
it pleased Silas to *a* there .....Acts 15:34
were in that city *a* certain .....Acts 16:12
come into my house, and *a*....Acts 16:15
he *a*..them, and wrought ....Acts 18:3
where we *a* seven days ....Acts 20:6
and afflictions *a* me...........Acts 20:23
Except these *a* in the ship .....Acts 27:31
a not still in unbelief ....Rom 11:23
if they *a* even as I 1Cor 7:8
she is happier if she so *a* 1Cor 7:40
see Peter, and *a* with him .....Gal 1:18
to *a* in the flesh is more ......Phil 1:24
know that I shall *a* and ....Phil 1:25
to *a* still at Ephesus 1Tim 1:3
He that saith he *a* in him 1John 2:6
a in the light 1John 2:10
received of him *a* in you 1John 2:27
ye shall *a* in him 1John 2:27
Whosoever *a* in him sinneth ...1John 3:6
He..loveth not his brother *a* ...1John 3:14
no murderer..eternal life *a* 1John 3:15
hereby we know that he *a*.....1John 3:24

ABIEL (ā'bĭ-ĕl)—*"God is father"*
1. The grandfather of Saul
and Abner 1Sam 9:1
2. David's mighty man 1Chr 11:32
Also called Abi-albon ...2Sam 23:31

father of Abner..son of *A* 1Sam 14:51

ABIEZER (ā-bĭ-ē'zer)—*"father of help"*
1. A descendant of Joseph .Josh 17:1, 2
Called Jeezer ....Num 26:30
Family settles at Ophrah .Judg 6:34
Gideon belongs to ......Judg 6:11, 12
Family rallies to Gideon's
call ....Judg 6:34
2. A mighty man and
commander in David's
army 2Sam 23:27

better than the vintage..*A* .....Judg 8:2
Hammoleketh bare Ishod..*A* ...1Chr 7:18
Ikkesh the Tekoite, *A* the 1Chr 11:28
captain..ninth month was *A* ...1Chr 27:12

ABIEZRITE (ăb'ĭ-ē'zĕ-rīts)
A member of the family of Abiezer .... Judg 6:11; Judg 6:24, 34

ABIGAIL (ăb'ĭ-găl)—*"father (i.e., cause) of delight"*
1. Nabal's beautiful and
wise wife 1Sam 25:3
Appeases David's anger .1Sam 25:14-35
Becomes David's wife ...1Sam 25:36-42
Captured and rescued ...1Sam 30:5, 18
Mother of Chileab 2Sam 3:3
2. A stepsister of David....1Chr 2:16, 17

one of the young men told *A* ..1Sam 25:14
Then *A* made haste, and 1Sam 25:18
when *A* saw David, she 1Sam 25:23
David said to *A*, Blessed be ...1Sam 25:32
And *A* came to Nabal; and 1Sam 25:36
David sent and communed..*A* .1Sam 25:39
servants of David..to *A* 1Sam 25:40
And *A* hasted, and arose 1Sam 25:42
A the Carmelitess, Nabal's 1Sam 27:3
and *A* Nabal's wife the 2Sam 2:2
in to *A* the daughter of 2Sam 17:25
the second Daniel, of *A* 1Chr 3:1

ABIHAIL (ăb'ĭ-hāl)—*"father of might"*
1. A Levite head of the
house of Merari ......Num 3:35
2. Abishur's wife 1Chr 2:29
3. A Gadite chief in Bashan.1Chr 5:14
4. Wife of King Rehoboam .2Chr 11:18
5. Father of Queen Esther .Esth 2:15

Esther..the daughter of *A* .....Esth 9:29

ABIHU (ä-bī'hū)—*"he is my father"*
Second of Aaron's four
sons ....Ex 6:23
Ascends Mt. Sinai ....Ex 24:1, 9
Chosen as priest ....Ex 28:1
Offers, with Nadab,
strange fire ....Lev 10:1-7
Died in the presence of
the Lord..............Num 3:4
Dies with heirs 1Chr 24:2

Aaron was born Nadab ....Num 26:60
And Nadab and *A* died ....Num 26:61
sons of Aaron; Nadab..*A* 1Chr 24:1

ABIHUD (ä-bī'hŭd)—*"father of honor"*
A Benjamite 1Chr 8:3

ABIJAH, ABIA, ABIAH (ä-bī'jä)—*"the Lord is my father"*
1. Wife of Hezron...........1Chr 2:24
2. Son of Becher 1Chr 7:8

3. Samuel's second son; follows corrupt ways 1Sam 8:2
4. Descendant of Aaron; head of an office of priests 1Chr 24:3, 10
   Zechariah belongs to ......Luke 1:5
5. Son of Jeroboam I 1Kin 14: 1-18
6. Slays 500,000 Israelites 2Chr 13: 13-20
7. Fathers 38 children by 14 wives 2Chr 13:21
8. The mother of Hezekiah ..2Chr 29:1
   Called Abi 2Kin 18:2
9. A priest who signs the document ....Neh 10:7
10. A priest returning from Babylon with Zerubbabel Neh 12:1, 4, 17

time *A* the son of Jeroboam ...1Kin 14:1
which bare him *A*, and Attai ..2Chr 11:20
Rehoboam made *A* the son....2Chr 11:22
A his son reigned in his 2Chr 12:16
king Jeroboam began *A* to 2Chr 13:1
war between *A*..Jeroboam 2Chr 13:2
And *A* set the battle in 2Chr 13:3
A stood up upon mount 2Chr 13:4
Jeroboam..Israel before *A* 2Chr 13:15
And *A* and his people slew 2Chr 13:17
A pursued after Jeroboam 2Chr 13:19
strength..in the days of *A* 2Chr 13:20
But *A* waxed mighty, and 2Chr 13:21
rest of the acts of *A*, and 2Chr 13:22
So *A* slept with his fathers 2Chr 14:1

ABIJAM (ă-bī'jăm)—*"father of the sea (west)"—another form of "Abijah"*
King of Judah 1Kin 14:31
Son and successor of King Rehoboam 1Kin 15:1-7
Follows in his father's sins 1Kin 15:3, 4
Wars against King Jeroboam 1Kin 15:6, 7

ABILENE (ăb-ī-lē'nē)—*"stream; brook"*
A province or tetrarchy of Syria ....Luke 3:1

ABILITY—*power to perform*

Descriptive of:
Material prosperity ......Deut 16:17
Emotional strength ......Num 11:14
Military power ....Num 13:31
 1Kin 9:21
Physical strength ....Ex 18:18, 23
Mental power ....Gen 15:5
Moral power 1Cor 3:2
Spiritual power ....James 3:2
Divine power ....Rom 4:21

Of God's power to:
Deliver 1Cor 10:13
Humble men ....Dan 4:37
Create life ....Matt 3:9
Destroy.................Matt 10:28
Preserve believers ....John 10:28
Keep His promise ....Rom 4:21
Make us stand ....Rom 16:25
Supply grace 2Cor 9:8
Exceed our petitions .....Eph 3:20
Service 1Pet 4:11
Comfort others 2Cor 1:4
Keep what we have entrusted 2Tim 1:12
Save from death ....Heb 5:7
Resurrect men ....Heb 11:19
Keep from falling........Jude 24, 25

Of Christ's power to:
Heal ....Matt 9:28
Subdue all things ....Phil 3:21
Help His own ....Heb 2:18
Have compassion ....Heb 4:15, 16
Save completely ....Heb 7:25

Of the Christian's power to:
Speak for the Lord ......Luke 21:15
Admonish ....Rom 15:14
Survive testings..........1Cor 3:13
Withstand Satan ....Eph 6:11, 13
Convince opposition .....Titus 1:9
Bridle the whole body ...James 3:2

according to his *a* that ....Lev 27:8
They gave after their *a*........Ezra 2:69
We after our *a* have ....Neh 5:8
such as had *a* in them ....Dan 1:4
according to his several *a* .....Matt 25:15
every man according..his *a* ....Acts 11:29

ABIMAEL (ă-bĭm'ā-ĕl)—*"my father is God"*
A son of Joktan ....Gen 10:28

ABIMELECH (ă-bĭm'ĕ-lĕk)—*"father of the king"*
1. A Philistine king of Gerar ....Gen 20:1-18
   Makes treaty with Abraham ....Gen 21:22-34
2. A second king of Gerar .Gen 26:1-12
   Tells Isaac to go home ..Gen 26:13-16
   Makes a treaty with Isaac concerning certain wells ....Gen 26:17-33
3. A son of Gideon by a concubine ....Judg 8:31
   Conspires to become king ....Judg 9:1-4
   Slays his 70 brothers ....Judg 9:5
   Made king of Shechem ..Judg 9:6
   Rebuked by Jotham, lone survivor ....Judg 9:7-21
   Conspired against by Gaal ....Judg 9:22-29
   Captures Shechem and Thebez................Judg 9:41-50
   Death of ....Judg 9:51-57
4. A son of Abiathar the priest 1Chr 18:16
   Also called Ahimelech ..1Chr 24:6

But God came to *A* in a ......Gen 20:3
A rose early in the morning ...Gen 20:8
Then *A* called Abraham.......Gen 20:9
A said unto Abraham, What...Gen 20:10
And *A* took sheep, and oxen ..Gen 20:14
and God healed *A*, and his ....Gen 20:17
A king of the Philistines.......Gen 26:8
And *A* called Isaac, and said ..Gen 26:9
A said, What is this thou ......Gen 26:10
A charged all his people ......Gen 26:11
A hired vain and light.........Judg 9:4
and went, and made *A* king ...Judg 9:6
he sent messengers unto *A* ....Judg 9:31
And *A* rose up, and all the ....Judg 9:34
And *A* rose up, and the ....Judg 9:35
Who is *A*, that we should .....Judg 9:38
of Shechem..fought with *A* ....Judg 9:39
A chased him, and he fled ....Judg 9:40
men of Israel saw that *A* ......Judg 9:55
God rendered..wickedness..*A* ..Judg 9:56
after *A* there arose to defend ..Judg 10:1
A the son of Jerubbesheth?....2Sam 11:21
changed his behavior..*A* ....Ps 34:*title*

ABINADAB (ă-bĭn'ā-dăb)—*"father (source) of generosity (willingness)"*
1. A man of Kirjath-jearim whose house tabernacles the ark of the Lord 1Sam 7:1, 2
2. The second of Jesse's eight sons 1Sam 16:8
   A soldier in Saul's army .1Sam 17:13
3. A son of Saul slain at Mt. Gilboa 1Sam 31:1-8
   Bones of, buried by men of Jabesh.............1Chr 10:1-12
4. The father of one of Solomon's sons-in-law .1Kin 4:11

Philistines slew Jonathan..*A* ...1Sam 31:2
brought..out of the house..*A* ..2Sam 6:3
the sons of *A*, drove the 2Sam 6:3
brought it out..house of *A*.....2Sam 6:4
son of *A*, in all the region 1Kin 4:11
Malchishua, and *A*............1Chr 8:33
Philistines slew Jonathan..*A* ...1Chr 10:2
new cart out of..house of *A* ...1Chr 13:7

ABINOAM (ă-bĭn'ō-ăm)—*"father of pleasantness"*
Father of Barak ....Judg 4:6

that Barak the son of *A* ....Judg 4:12
Deborah and Barak..of *A* .....Judg 5:1
captivity captive, thou..*A* ......Judg 5:12

ABIRAM (ă-bī'răm)—*"father of elevation"*
1. Reubenite who conspired against Moses ....Num 16:1-50
2. The first-born son of Hiel.1Kin 16:34
 Josh 6:26

Dathan..*A*..sons of Eliab ......Num 16:1
Moses sent..call Dathan..*A* ....Num 16:12
tabernacle..Korah, Dathan..*A* ..Num 16:24
up and went unto Dathan..*A* ..Num 16:25
tabernacle..Korah, Dathan..*A* ..Num 16:27
Dathan and *A* came out.......Num 16:27
Eliab; Nemuel, and Dathan..*A* .Num 26:9
Dathan and *A*, which were ....Num 26:9
what he did unto Dathan..*A* ...Deut 11:6
he laid the foundations..*A* 1Kin 16:34
covered the company of *A* ....Ps 106:17

ABISHAG (ăb'ĭ-shăg)—*"my father was a wanderer"*
A Shunammite employed as David's nurse 1Kin 1:1-4, 15
Witnessed David's choice of Solomon as successor 1Kin 1:15-31
Adonijah slain for desiring to marry her ..1Kin 2:13-25

and found *A* a Shunammite ...1Kin 1:3
give me *A* the Shunammite 1Kin 2:17
Let *A* the Shunammite be 1Kin 2:21
dost thou ask *A* the...........1Kin 2:22

ABISHAI (ă-bĭsh'ā-ī)—*"my father is Jesse; source of wealth"*
A son of Zeruiah, David's sister 2Sam 2:18
Brother of Joab and Asahel 1Chr 2:16
Rebuked by David 1Sam 26:5-9
Serves under Joab in David's army..........2Sam 2:17, 18
Joins Joab in blood-revenge against Abner 2Sam 2:18-24
Co-commander of David's army 2Sam 10:9, 10
Loyal to David during Absalom's uprising 2Sam 16:9-12
Sternly rebuked by David.2Sam 19:21-23
Loyal to David during Sheba's rebellion 2Sam 20:1-6, 10
Slays 300 Philistines 2Sam 23:18
Slays 18,000 Edomites ...1Chr 18:12, 13
Saves David by killing a giant 2Sam 21:16, 17

and to *A* the son of Zeruiah ...1Sam 26:6
A said, I will go down with....1Sam 26:6
So David and *A* came to the ..1Sam 26:7
said *A* to David, God hath 1Sam 26:8
David said to *A*, Destroy......1Sam 26:9
A pursued after Abner 2Sam 2:24
Joab and *A* his brother slew ...2Sam 3:30
fled they also before *A*........2Sam 10:14
a third part..hand of *A*........2Sam 18:2
commanded Joab and *A*.......2Sam 18:5
king charged thee and *A* 2Sam 18:12
So Joab and *A* his brother ...2Sam 20:10
A the son of Zeruiah 2Sam 21:17
A the brother of Joab, he 1Chr 11:20
he delivered..hand of *A* 1Chr 19:11
likewise fled before *A* his 1Chr 19:15

ABISHALOM (ä-bĭsh'ä-lŏm)—*"father of peace"*
A variant form of
Absalom..............1Kin 15:2, 10

ABISHUA (ä-bĭsh'ū-ä)—*"father of safety (salvation)"*
1. A Benjamite 1Chr 8:3, 4
2. Phinehas' son 1Chr 6:4,5,50

ABISHUR (ä-bī'sher)—*"father of oxen; father is a wall"*
A Jerahmeelite 1Chr 2:28, 29

ABITAL (ä-bī'täl)—*"father (source) of dew"*
Wife of David...........2Sam 3:2, 4

ABITUB (ä-bī'tŭb)—*"father (source) of goodness"*
A Benjamite 1Chr 8:8-11

ABIUD (ă-bī'ŭd)—*"father of honor"—the Greek form of "Abihud"*
Ancestor of Jesus........Matt 1:13

ABJECTS—*the downcast*
a gathered themselves.........Ps 35:15

ABLE—*having sufficient resources to accomplish a goal*
if thou be *a* to number........Gen 15:5
and the children be *a* ....Gen 33:14
one cannot be *a* to see........Ex 10:5
provide out..people *a* men ....Ex 18:21
then thou shalt be *a* to........Ex 18:23
Moses chose *a* men out of .....Ex 18:25
Moses was not *a* to enter .....Ex 40:35
such as he is *a* to get ....Lev 14:22
himself be *a* to redeem it .....Lev 25:26
if he be not *a* to restore it ....Lev 25:28
he be *a*, he may redeem ......Lev 25:49
I am not *a* to bear all this.....Num 11:14
we are well *a* to overcome ....Num 13:30
not *a* to go up against the .....Num 13:31
the Lord was not *a* to bring ...Num 14:16
I shall be *a* to overcome ......Num 22:11
all that are *a* to go to war.....Num 26:2
no man be *a* to stand ....Deut 7:24
Lord was not *a* to bring.......Deut 9:28
no man be *a* to stand ....Deut 11:25
man shall give as he is *a* ......Deut 16:17
hath been *a* to stand..........Josh 23:9
shall not be *a* to deliver.......2Kin 18:29
a men for strength for 1Chr 26:8
is *a* to build him a house......2Chr 2:6
none is *a* to withstand 2Chr 20:6
Lord is *a* to give..much 2Chr 25:9
any ways *a* to deliver 2Chr 32:13
your God should be *a* to 2Chr 32:14
was *a* to deliver his people 2Chr 32:15
we are not *a* to stand ....Ezra 10:13
we are not *a* to build the .....Neh 4:10
who then is *a* to stand before ..Job 41:10
that they were not *a* to rise ...Ps 18:38
they are not *a* to perform .....Ps 21:11
shall not be *a* to rise..........Ps 36:12
I am not *a* to look up ....Ps 40:12
who is *a* to stand before ......Prov 27:4
yet shall he not be *a* to find ...Eccl 8:17
thou be *a* on thy part ....Is 36:8
shall not be *a* to deliver.......Is 36:14
thou shalt not be *a* to put .....Is 47:11
if so be thou shalt be *a* ....Is 47:12
the nations shall not be *a* .....Jer 10:10
shall not be *a* to escape ....Jer 11:11
he shall not be *a* to hide ......Jer 49:10
I am not *a* to rise up ....Lam 1:14
their gold shall not be *a*.......Ezek 7:19
shall the righteous be *a* ....Ezek 33:12
God whom we serve is *a* to ...Dan 3:17
walk in pride he is *a* to ....Dan 4:37
a to deliver thee from ....Dan 6:20
land is not *a* to bear ....Amos 7:10
God is *a* of these stones ......Matt 3:9
Believe ye that I am *a* ....Matt 9:28
are not *a* to kill the soul ......Matt 10:28
He that is *a* to receive it ......Matt 19:12
Are ye *a* to drink of..cup .....Matt 20:22
I am *a* to destroy the temple ..Matt 26:61
as they were *a* to hear ....Mark 4:33
God is *a* of these stones ......Luke 3:8
ye then be not *a* to do ....Luke 12:26
is not *a* to finish it, all ....Luke 14:29
no man is *a* to pluck them ....John 10:29
were not *a* to resist the ....Acts 6:10
word of..grace, which is *a* .....Acts 20:32
he had promised, he was *a* ....Rom 4:21
shall be *a* to separate us ......Rom 8:39
God is *a* to graft them in .....Rom 11:23
for God is *a* to make him .....Rom 14:4
hitherto ye were not *a* to 1Cor 3:2
neither yet now are ye *a* 1Cor 3:2
tempted above..ye are *a* 1Cor 10:13
hath made us *a* ministers 2Cor 3:6
God is *a* to make all grace 2Cor 9:8
a to comprehend with all......Eph 3:18
Now unto him that is *a* ....Eph 3:20
that ye may be *a* to stand .....Eph 6:11
ye shall be *a* to quench ....Eph 6:16
he is *a* even to subdue ....Phil 3:21
persuaded that he is *a* to.......2Tim 1:12
shall be *a* to teach others 2Tim 2:2
scriptures, which are *a* 2Tim 3:15
he is *a* to succor them ....Heb 2:18
was *a* to save him from ....Heb 5:7
Wherefore he is *a* also ....Heb 7:25
that God was *a* to raise ....Heb 11:19
which is *a* to save your ....James 1:21
a also to bridle the whole .....James 3:2
lawgiver, who is *a* to save .....James 4:12
Now unto him that is *a* ....Jude 24
was *a* to open the book ....Rev 5:3
who shall be *a* to stand? ......Rev 6:17

ABLUTION—*a ceremonial washing*
Of priests ....Ex 30:18-21
Ex 40:30, 31
Of ceremonially unclean. .Lev 14:7-9
Lev 15:5-10
Of a house..............Lev 14:52
By Pharisees ....Mark 7:1-5

ABNER (ăb'nĕr)—*"my father of light"*
Commands Saul's army ..1Sam 14:50, 51
Introduces David to Saul .1Sam 17:55-58
Rebuked by David 1Sam 26:5, 14-16
Saul's cousin 1Sam 14:50, 51
Supports Ish-bosheth as
Saul's successor 2Sam 2:8-10
Defeated by David's men.2Sam 2:12-17
Kills Asahel in
self-defense 2Sam 2:18-23
Pursued by Joab.........2Sam 2:24-32
Slain by Joab 2Sam 3:8-27
Death of, condemned by
David 2Sam 3:28-39

and Jonathan arose, and *A* 1Sam 20:25
A the son of Ner, and the 2Sam 2:12
A said to Joab, Let the 2Sam 2:14
A was beaten, and the men ...2Sam 2:17
Asahel pursued after *A* 2Sam 2:19
the left from following *A* 2Sam 2:19
A looked behind him, and.....2Sam 2:20
And *A* said to him, Turn 2Sam 2:21
A said again to Asahel 2Sam 2:22
A with the hinder end of 2Sam 2:23
Abishai pursued after *A* 2Sam 2:24
themselves together after *A* 2Sam 2:25
Then *A* called to Joab, and....2Sam 2:26
A and his men walked all 2Sam 2:29
Joab returned..following *A* 2Sam 2:30
that *A* made himself strong 2Sam 3:6
Ishbosheth said to *A* 2Sam 3:7
Then was *A* very wroth for 2Sam 3:8
So do God to *A*, and more 2Sam 3:9
And he could not answer *A* ...2Sam 3:11
And *A* sent messengers to 2Sam 3:12
Then said *A* unto him, Go 2Sam 3:16
And *A* had communication 2Sam 3:17
And *A* also spake in the 2Sam 3:19
A went also to speak in the ...2Sam 3:19
So *A* came to David to 2Sam 3:20
David made *A* and the men ...2Sam 3:20
A said unto David, I will 2Sam 3:21
David sent *A* away; and he 2Sam 3:21
A was not with David 2Sam 3:22
A the son of Ner came 2Sam 3:23
behold, *A* came unto thee 2Sam 3:24
Thou knowest *A* the son of....2Sam 3:25
he sent messengers after *A* 2Sam 3:26
when *A* was returned to.......2Sam 3:27
for ever from the blood of *A* ..2Sam 3:28
Abishai his brother slew *A* 2Sam 3:30
sackcloth..mourn before *A* 2Sam 3:31
And they buried *A* in 2Sam 3:32
wept at the grave of *A* 2Sam 3:32
the king lamented over *A* 2Sam 3:33
Died *A* as a fool dieth? 2Sam 3:33
not of the king to slay *A* 2Sam 3:37
Saul's son heard that *A* was ...2Sam 4:1
buried..sepulcher of *A* 2Sam 4:12
unto *A* the son of Ner, and ...1Kin 2:5
to wit, *A* the son of Ner 1Kin 2:32
Saul the son of Kish..*A* 1Chr 26:28
Benjamin, Jaasiel..of *A* 1Chr 27:21

ABOARD—*upon*
we went *a*, and set forth ......Acts 21:2

ABOLISH—*to do away with*
Of evil things:
Idolatry.................Is 2:18
Man-made ordinances ....Col 2:20-22
Death 1Cor 15:26
Evil works ....Ezek 6:6
Enmity ....Eph 2:15
Of things good for a while:
Old covenant 2Cor 3:13
Present world ....Heb 1:10-12
Temporal rule 1Cor 15:24
The partial..............1Cor 13:10
Of things not to be abolished:
God's righteousness......Is 51:6
God's Word ....Matt 5:18

[*also* ABOLISHED]
Christ, who hath *a* death ......2 Tim 1:10

ABOMINATION—*things utterly repulsive*
Descriptive of:
Hebrew eating with
Egyptians ....Gen 43:32
Undesirable social
relations ....Ex 8:26
Spiritist practices ....Deut 18:9-12
Heathen idolatry ....Deut 7:25, 26
Child-sacrifice ....Deut 12:31
Pagan gods 2Kin 23:13
Applied to perverse sexual relations:
Unnatural acts ....Lev 18:19-29
Wrong clothing..........Deut 22:5
Prostitution and sodomy. .Deut 23:17, 18
Reclaiming a defiled
woman ....Deut 24:4
In ceremonial matters, applied to:
Unclean animals.........Lev 11:10-23, 41-43
Deformed animals ....Deut 17:1
Heathen practices in
God's house 2Chr 36:14
Sinfulness of, seen in:
Being enticed 1Kin 11:5, 7
Delighting in ....Is 66:3
Rejecting admonitions
against ....Jer 44:4, 5
Defiling God's house ....Jer 7:30
Being polluted ....Ezek 20:7, 30-32
Judgments upon, manifested in:
Stoning to death.........Deut 17:2-5
Destroying a city ....Deut 13:13-17
Forfeiting God's mercy...Ezek 5:11-13
Experiencing God's fury .Ezek 20:7, 8
Things especially classed as:
Silver or gold from
graven images.........Deut 7:25

Perverse man .... Prov 3:32
Seven sins .... Prov 6:16-19
False balance .... Prov 11:1
Lying lips .... Prov 12:22
Sacrifices of the wicked .. Prov 15:8, 9
Proud in heart .... Prov 16:5
Justifying the wicked .... Prov 17:15
Scorner .... Prov 24:9
Prayer of one who turns away his ear .... Prov 28:9
False worship .... Is 1:13
Scant measures .... Mic 6:10
Self-righteousness .... Luke 16:15

[*also* ABOMINABLE, ABOMINABLY, ABOMINATIONS]

every shepherd is an *a* .... Gen 46:34
it shall be an *a* .... Lev 7:18
or any *a* unclean thing .... Lev 7:21
they shall be..*a* unto you .... Lev 11:10
be even an *a* unto you .... Lev 11:11
have their carcases in *a* .... Lev 11:11
that shall be an *a* .... Lev 11:12
shall have in *a* among the .... Lev 11:13
they are an *a* .... Lev 11:13
an *a* unto you .... Lev 11:20
four feet, shall be an *a* .... Lev 11:23
the earth shall be an *a* .... Lev 11:41
not eat; for they are an *a* .... Lev 11:42
shall not make yourselves *a* .... Lev 11:43
not any one of these *a* .... Lev 18:30
them have committed an *a* .... Lev 20:13
such *a* is wrought among .... Deut 13:14
after the *a* of those nations .... Deut 18:9
these things are an *a* unto .... Deut 18:12
and because of these *a* the .... Deut 18:12
not to do after all their *a* .... Deut 20:18
unrighteously, are an *a* .... Deut 25:16
molten image, an *a* unto .... Deut 27:15
have seen their *a*, and their .... Deut 29:17
a provoked they him to .... Deut 32:16
all the *a* of the nations 1Kin 14:24
he did very *a* in following 1Kin 21:26
according to the *a* of the 2Kin 16:3
after the *a* of the heathen 2Kin 21:2
Judah hath done these *a* 2Kin 21:11
Chemosh the *a* of the 2Kin 23:13
Milcom the *a* of the children 2Kin 23:13
the *a* that were spied in the 2Kin 23:24
king's word was *a* to Joab 1Chr 21:6
put away the *a* idols out of 2Chr 15:8
after the *a* of the heathen 2Chr 28:3
like unto the *a* of the 2Chr 33:2
Josiah took away all the *a* 2Chr 34:33
and his *a* which he did 2Chr 36:8
according to their *a* .... Ezra 9:1
with their *a*, which have .... Ezra 9:11
the people of these *a*? .... Ezra 9:14
How much more *a* and .... Job 15:16
they have done *a* works .... Ps 14:1
and have done *a* iniquity .... Ps 53:1
and wickedness is an *a* to .... Prov 8:7
it is *a* to fools to depart .... Prov 13:19
of the wicked are an *a* to .... Prov 15:26
a to kings to commit .... Prov 16:12
both of them are alike *a* .... Prov 20:10
Divers weights are an *a* .... Prov 20:23
sacrifice of the wicked is *a* .... Prov 21:27
for there are seven *a* in his .... Prov 26:25
An unjust man is an *a* to .... Prov 29:27
is upright in the way is *a* .... Prov 29:27
thy grave like an *a* branch .... Is 14:19
a is he that chooseth you .... Is 41:24
the residue thereof an *a*? .... Is 44:19
of *a* things is in their .... Is 65:4
eating swine's flesh..*a* .... Is 66:17
made mine heritage an *a* .... Jer 2:7
put away thine *a* out of my .... Jer 4:1
they had committed *a*? .... Jer 6:15
delivered to do all these *a*? .... Jer 7:10
set their *a* in the house .... Jer 7:30
they had committed *a*? .... Jer 8:12
whoredom, and thine *a* on .... Jer 13:27
detestable and *a* things .... Jer 16:18
set their *a* in the house .... Jer 32:34
do this *a*, to cause Judah to .... Jer 32:35
a which ye have committed .... Jer 44:22
because of all thine *a* .... Ezek 5:9
have committed..all their *a* .... Ezek 6:9
Alas for all the evil *a* of .... Ezek 6:11
recompense upon..thine *a* .... Ezek 7:3
a shall be in the midst of .... Ezek 7:4
recompense..all thine *a* .... Ezek 7:8
to thy ways and thine *a* .... Ezek 7:9
made the images of their *a* .... Ezek 7:20
a that the house of Israel .... Ezek 8:6
shalt see greater *a* .... Ezek 8:6
wicked *a* that they do here .... Ezek 8:9
Judah that..commit the *a* .... Ezek 8:17
that cry for all the *a* that .... Ezek 9:4
all the *a* thereof from .... Ezek 11:18
detestable things and their .... Ezek 11:21
may declare all their *a* .... Ezek 12:16
faces from all your *a* .... Ezek 14:6
Jerusalem to know her *a* .... Ezek 16:2
in all thine *a* and thy .... Ezek 16:22
with all the idols of thy *a* .... Ezek 16:36
lewdness above all thine *a* .... Ezek 16:43
nor done after their *a* .... Ezek 16:47
haughty, and committed a .... Ezek 16:50
hast multiplied thine a .... Ezek 16:51
in all thine *a* which thou .... Ezek 16:51
thy lewdness and thine *a* .... Ezek 16:58
idols, hath committed *a* .... Ezek 18:12
hath done all these *a* .... Ezek 18:13
doeth according to all the *a* .... Ezek 18:24
cause them to know the *a* .... Ezek 20:4
shalt show her all her *a* .... Ezek 22:2
a with his neighbor's wife .... Ezek 22:11
declare unto them their *a* .... Ezek 23:36
ye work *a*, and ye defile .... Ezek 33:26
desolate because..their *a* .... Ezek 33:29
iniquities and for your *a* .... Ezek 36:31
defiled..name by their *a* .... Ezek 43:8
suffice you of all your *a* .... Ezek 44:6
because of all your *a* .... Ezek 44:7
bear their shame, and..*a* .... Ezek 44:13
the *a* that maketh desolate .... Dan 12:11
a were according as they .... Hos 9:10
will cast *a* filth upon thee .... Nah 3:6
and his *a* from between his .... Zech 9:7
and an *a* is committed in .... Mal 2:11
see the *a* of desolation .... Mark 13:14
being *a*, and disobedient .... Titus 1:16
banquetings..*a* idolatries 1Pet 4:3
mother of harlots and *a* of .... Rev 17:5
unbelieving; and the *a* .... Rev 21:8
worketh *a*, or maketh a lie .... Rev 21:27

ABOMINATION OF DESOLATION—*the action of Antiochus Epiphanes in sacrificing a pig in the Temple in 168 B.C.*

Predicted by Daniel .... Dan 9:27
Cited by Christ .... Matt 24:15

ABORTION—*accidental or planned miscarriage*

Laws concerning .... Ex 21:22-25
Pronounced as a judgment .... Hos 9:14
Sought to relieve misery .... Job 3:16
Of animals, by thunder .... Ps 29:9
Figurative of abrupt conversion 1Cor 15:8

ABOUND—*to increase greatly*

Of good things:

God's truth .... Rom 3:7
God's grace .... Rom 5:15, 20
Hope .... Rom 15:13
God's work 1Cor 15:58
Suffering for Christ 2Cor 1:5
Joy in suffering 2Cor 8:2
Gracious works 2Cor 8:7
Good works 2Cor 9:8
Wisdom .... Eph 1:8
Love .... Phil 1:9
Fruitfulness .... Phil 4:17, 18
Faith .... Col 2:7
Pleasing God 1Thess 4:1
Christian qualities 2Pet 1:5-7
Blessings .... Prov 28:20
Charity 2Thess 1:3

Source of, in good things:

From God 2Cor 9:8
From Christian generosity 2Cor 8:2, 3
Faithfulness .... Prov 28:20
Generosity .... Phil 4:14-17

Of evil things:

Transgressions .... Prov 29:22
Lawlessness .... Matt 24:12
Increasing sins .... Rom 5:20

[*also* ABOUNDING]

no fountains *a* with water .... Prov 8:24
that grace may *a*? .... Rom 6:1
and I know how to *a* .... Phil 4:12
both to *a* and to suffer .... Phil 4:12
make you to increase and *a* 1Thess 3:12

ABOUT—*See* INTRODUCTION

ABOVE—*higher or earlier*

were *a* the firmament .... Gen 1:7
a the earth in the open .... Gen 1:20
cursed *a* all cattle, and *a* .... Gen 3:14
cubit shalt thou finish it *a* .... Gen 6:16
and it was lifted up *a* the .... Gen 7:17
Lord stood *a* it, and said .... Gen 28:13
dealt proudly he was *a* them .... Ex 18:11
thing that is in heaven *a* .... Ex 20:4
the mercy seat *a* upon the .... Ex 25:21
with thee from *a* the mercy .... Ex 25:22
covering of the tent *a* .... Ex 40:19
the mercy seat *a* upon the .... Ex 40:20
from sixty years old and *a* .... Lev 27:7
he is God in heaven *a* .... Deut 4:39
that is in heaven *a*, or .... Deut 5:8
Thou shalt be blessed *a* all .... Deut 7:14
even you *a* all people, as .... Deut 10:15
a all the nations that are .... Deut 14:2
high *a* all nations which he .... Deut 26:19
set thee on high *a* all .... Deut 28:1
he is God in heaven *a* .... Josh 2:11
that come down from *a* .... Josh 3:13
Blessed *a* women shall .... Judg 5:24
blessed shall she be *a* .... Judg 5:24
and honorest thy sons *a* 1Sam 2:29
hast lifted me up on high *a* 2Sam 22:49
God like thee, in heaven *a* 1Kin 8:23
Set his throne *a* the throne 2Kin 25:28
he also is to be feared *a* 1Chr 16:25
twenty years old and *a* 1Chr 23:27
for great is our God *a* all 2Chr 2:5
the sea was set *a* upon 2Chr 4:4
images, that were..high *a* 2Chr 34:4
man, and feared God *a* .... Neh 7:2
(for he was *a* all the people .... Neh 8:5
king loved Esther *a* all the .... Esth 2:17
not God regard it from *a* .... Job 3:4
set thy glory *a*..heavens .... Ps 8:1
sent from *a*, he took me .... Ps 18:16
call to the heavens from *a* .... Ps 50:4
exalted, O God, *a* the .... Ps 57:5
let thy glory be *a* all .... Ps 57:5
exalted, O God, *a* the .... Ps 57:11
commanded..clouds from *a* .... Ps 78:23
God, and a great King *a* all .... Ps 95:3
he is to be feared *a* all .... Ps 96:4
Lord, art high *a* all the .... Ps 97:9
thou art exalted far *a* all .... Ps 97:9
and he is high *a* all the .... Ps 99:2
as the heaven is high *a* .... Ps 103:11
thy mercy is great *a* the .... Ps 108:4
exalted, O God, *a* the .... Ps 108:5
and thy glory *a* all the .... Ps 108:5
the Lord is high *a* all .... Ps 113:4
and his glory *a* the .... Ps 113:4
and that our Lord is *a* all .... Ps 135:5
her price is far *a* rubies .... Prov 31:10
man hath no preeminence *a* .... Eccl 3:19
A it stood the seraphim .... Is 6:2
a the stars of God .... Is 14:13
The heart is deceitful *a* all .... Jer 17:9
If heaven *a*..be measured .... Jer 31:37
set his throne *a* the throne .... Jer 52:32
From *a* hath he sent fire .... Lam 1:13

God of Israel..over them *a* .... Ezek 11:22
a all thine abominations .... Ezek 16:43
itself any more *a* the .... Ezek 29:15
Daniel was preferred *a* the .... Dan 6:3
and it shall be exalted *a* .... Mic 4:1
merchants *a* the stars of .... Nah 3:16
The disciple is not *a* his .... Matt 10:24
nor the servant *a* his lord ..... Matt 10:24
Added yet this *a* all, that ..... Luke 3:20
The disciple is not *a* his .... Luke 6:40
sinners *a* all the Galileans ..... Luke 13:2
they were sinners *a* all .... Luke 13:4
cometh from *a* is *a* all .... John 3:31
cometh from heaven is *a* all ... John 3:31
beneath; I am from *a* .... John 8:23
except..given thee from *a* ..... John 19:11
I..wonders in heaven *a* .... Acts 2:19
bring Christ down from *a* ..... Rom 10:6
one day *a* another .... Rom 14:5
not to think of men *a* that 1Cor 4:6
to be tempted *a* that ye are ... 1Cor 10:13
seen of *a* five hundred 1Cor 15:6
a fourteen years ago 2Cor 12:2
a that which he seeth me 2Cor 12:6
Jews' religion *a* many my ..... Gal 1:14
Jerusalem which is *a* is .... Gal 4:26
Far *a* all principality, and ..... Eph 1:21
who is *a* all, and through ..... Eph 4:6
ascended up far *a* all .... Eph 4:10
a name which is *a* every ...... Phil 2:9
seek..things which are *a* .... Col 3:1
Set..affection on things *a* ...... Col 3:2
a all that is called God 2Thess 2:4
Not now as a servant, but *a* ... Philem 16
A when he said, Sacrifice ..... Heb 10:8
every perfect gift is from *a* .... James 1:17
descendeth not from *a*, but .... James 3:15
the wisdom that is from *a* ..... James 3:17
a all things have fervent 1Pet 4:8
I wish *a* all things that 3John 2

ABRAHAM (ā'brä-hăm)—*"father of multitudes"—the founder of the Jewish nation and an ancestor of Christ*

Ancestry and family:
- Descendant of Shem 1Chr 1:24-27
- Son of Terah .... Gen 11:26
- First named Abram ...... Gen 11:27
- A native of Ur .... Gen 11:28, 31
- Pagan ancestors .... John 24:2
- Weds Sarai .... Gen 11:29

Wanderings of:
- Goes to Haran .... Gen 11:31
- Receives God's call ...... Gen 12:1-3; Acts 7:2-4
- Prompted by faith .... Heb 11:8
- Enters Canaan .... Gen 12:4-6
- Canaan promised to, by God .... Gen 12:1, 7
- Pitched his tent at Beth-el Gen 12:8
- Famine sends him to Egypt .... Gen 12:10-20
- Returns to Canaan enriched .... Gen 13:1-5
- Chooses Hebron rather than strife .... Gen 13:6-12

Testing and victory of:
- Separates from Lot ...... Gen 13:8-12
- Rescues captured Lot .... Gen 14:14-16
- Receives Melchizedek's blessing .... Gen 14:18-20
- Covenant renewed; a son promised to .... Gen 15:1-21
- Justified by faith .... Gen 15:6; Rom 4:3
- Takes Hagar as concubine Gen 16:1-4
- Ishmael born .... Gen 16:5-16
- Covenant renewed; named Abraham ...... Gen 17:1-8
- Household of, circumcised .... Gen 17:9-14, 23-27
- Promised a son .... Gen 17:15-19
- Covenant in Isaac, not Ishmael .... Gen 17:20-22; Gal 4:22-31
- Receives messengers ..... Gen 18:1-15
- Intercedes concerning Sodom .... Gen 18:16-33
- Witnesses Sodom's doom . Gen 19:27, 28
- His faith saves Lot ...... Gen 19:29
- Sojourns at Gerar; deceives Abimelech .... Gen 20:1-18
- Isaac born to, and circumcised .... Gen 21:1-8
- Sends Hagar and Ishmael away .... Gen 21:9-21
- Makes covenant with Abimelech .... Gen 21:22-34
- Testing of, offering Isaac . Gen 22:1-19
- Receives news about Nahor .... Gen 22:20-24
- Buys burial place for Sarah .... Gen 23:1-20
- Obtains wife for Isaac ... Gen 24:1-67
- Marries Keturah; fathers other children; dies .... Gen 25:1-10

Characteristics of:
- Friend of God 2Chr 20:7
- Obedient .... Gen 22:1-18
- Tither .... Gen 14:20; Heb 7:1, 2, 4
- Generous .... Gen 13:8, 9
- Courageous .... Gen 14:13-16
- Independent .... Gen 14:21-23
- Man of prayer .... Gen 18:23-33
- Man of faith .... Gen 15:6
- Rich man .... Gen 13:2
- Mighty prince .... Gen 23:5, 6
- Good provider .... Gen 25:5, 6

References to, in the New Testament:
- In the line of faith .... Heb 11:8-10
- Christ the true seed of ... Matt 1:1
- Foresees Christ's day .... John 8:56
- Hears the Gospel preached .... Gal 3:8
- Justified by faith .... Rom 4:1-12
- Faith of, seen in works .. James 2:21-23
- Father of true believers .. Matt 8:11; Rom 4:11-25; Gal 3:7, 29
- Sees the eternal city ..... Heb 11:8-10, 13-16
- Covenant with, still valid . Luke 1:73; Acts 3:25
- Sons of, illustrate covenants .... Gal 4:22-31
- Tithing of, has deeper meaning .... Heb 7:9, 10
- Headship of, in marriage . 1Pet 3:6, 7
- Eternal home of, in heaven .... Luke 16:19-25

[*also* ABRAHAM'S, ABRAM]

A went up out of Egypt, he ... Gen 13:1
And *A* was very rich in .... Gen 13:2
and there *A* called on the ..... Gen 13:4
Lot also, which went with *A* ... Gen 13:5
A said unto Lot, Let there .... Gen 13:8
A dwelled in the land of ...... Gen 13:12
the Lord said unto *A*, after .... Gen 13:14
Then *A* removed his tent ...... Gen 13:18
of the Lord came unto *A* ...... Gen 15:1
vision, saying, Fear not, *A* .... Gen 15:1
A said, Lord God, what .... Gen 15:2
A said, Behold, to me thou ... Gen 15:3
came down..carcases, *A* ...... Gen 15:11
a deep sleep fell upon *A* ...... Gen 15:12
he said unto *A*, Know of a .... Gen 15:13
Sarai said unto *A*, My .... Gen 16:5
A said unto Sarai, Behold ..... Gen 16:6
Hagar bare *A* a son..*A* .... Gen 16:15
A was fourscore and six .... Gen 16:16
Hagar bare Ishmael to *A* ...... Gen 16:16
when *A* was ninety years ...... Gen 17:1
the Lord appeared to *A* .... Gen 17:1
A fell on his face; and God ... Gen 17:3
name any more..called *A* ...... Gen 17:5
but thy name shall be *A* .... Gen 17:5
God said unto *A*, Thou .... Gen 17:9
God said unto *A*, As for Sarai . Gen 17:15
A fell upon his face, and ...... Gen 17:17
A said unto God..Ishmael ..... Gen 17:18
A hastened into the tent ...... Gen 18:6
A ran unto the herd, and ..... Gen 18:7
A and Sarah were old and ..... Gen 18:11
the Lord said unto *A* .... Gen 18:13
A went with them to bring .... Gen 18:16
Shall I hide from *A* that .... Gen 18:17
Seeing that *A* shall surely ..... Gen 18:18
Lord may bring upon *A* .... Gen 18:19
but *A* stood yet before the .... Gen 18:22
A drew near, and said .... Gen 18:23
A answered and said .... Gen 18:27
left communing with *A* .... Gen 18:33
and *A* returned unto his .... Gen 18:33
A journeyed from thence ...... Gen 20:1
A said of Sarah his wife .... Gen 20:2
Abimelech called *A*, and ...... Gen 20:9
Abimelech said unto *A* .... Gen 20:10
A said, Because I thought ..... Gen 20:11
gave them unto *A*, and .... Gen 20:14
So *A* prayed unto God .... Gen 20:17
and bare *A* a son in his old ... Gen 21:2
A called the name of his ...... Gen 21:3
A circumcised..son Isaac ...... Gen 21:4
A..hundred years old, when ... Gen 21:5
Who would..said unto *A* .... Gen 21:7
A made a great feast the ...... Gen 21:8
which she had born unto *A* .... Gen 21:9
she said unto *A*, Cast out ..... Gen 21:10
God said unto *A*, Let it not ... Gen 21:12
A rose up early in the .... Gen 21:14
captain of his host spake..*A* ... Gen 21:22
And *A* said, I will swear ...... Gen 21:24
A reproved Abimelech .... Gen 21:25
A took sheep and oxen .... Gen 21:27
A set seven ewe lambs of ..... Gen 21:28
Abimelech said unto *A* .... Gen 21:29
A planted a grove in .... Gen 21:33
A sojourned..Philistines' .... Gen 21:34
that God did tempt *A*, and .... Gen 22:1
unto him, *A*; and he said ...... Gen 22:1
A rose up early..morning ...... Gen 22:3
A said..his young men .... Gen 22:5
A took the wood of the .... Gen 22:6
Isaac spake unto *A* his .... Gen 22:7
A said, My son, God will ...... Gen 22:8
A built an altar there .... Gen 22:9
A stretched forth his hand ..... Gen 22:10
out of heaven, and said *A*, *A* .. Gen 22:11
A lifted up his eyes, and ...... Gen 22:13
A went and took the ram ..... Gen 22:13
A called the name of that ..... Gen 22:14
angel..Lord called unto *A* ..... Gen 22:15
So *A* returned unto his .... Gen 22:19
and *A* dwelt at Beer-sheba .... Gen 22:19
it was told *A*, saying .... Gen 22:20
and *A* came to mourn for ..... Gen 23:2
A stood up from before his .... Gen 23:3
the children of Heth..*A* .... Gen 23:5
A stood up, and bowed .... Gen 23:7
Ephron the Hittite..*A* .... Gen 23:10
A bowed down himself .... Gen 23:12
Ephron answered *A* .... Gen 23:14
A hearkened unto Ephron ..... Gen 23:16
A weighed to Ephron the ..... Gen 23:16
Unto *A* for a possession in .... Gen 23:18
after this, *A* buried Sarah ..... Gen 23:19
unto *A* for a possession .... Gen 23:20
A was old..well stricken .... Gen 24:1
Lord had blessed *A* in all ..... Gen 24:1
A said..his eldest servant ...... Gen 24:2
A said unto him, Beware ...... Gen 24:6
hand under the thigh of *A* ..... Gen 24:9
O Lord God of my master *A* .. Gen 24:12
kindness unto..master *A* .... Gen 24:12
Lord God of my master *A* .... Gen 24:27
O Lord God..my master *A* .... Gen 24:42
Lord God of my master *A* .... Gen 24:48
Then again *A* took a wife ..... Gen 25:1
A gave all that he..Isaac ...... Gen 25:5
concubines, which *A*..*A* .... Gen 25:6
Then *A* gave up the ghost ..... Gen 25:8
field which *A* purchased .... Gen 25:10
A buried, and Sarah his .... Gen 25:10

the death of *A*, that God . . . . . .Gen 25:11
Sarah's handmaid, bare..*A* . . . .Gen 25:12
A begat Isaac . . . . .Gen 25:19
famine..in the days of *A* . . . . . .Gen 26:1
oath which I sware unto *A* . . . .Gen 26:3
Because that *A* obeyed . . . . .Gen 26:5
had digged..the days of *A* . . . . .Gen 26:15
digged in the days of *A* . . . . . . .Gen 26:18
stopped them..death of *A* . . . . .Gen 26:18
said, I am the God of *A* . . . . . .Gen 26:24
give thee..blessing of *A* . . . . . . .Gen 28:4
stranger, which God..unto *A* . .Gen 28:4
I am the Lord God of *A* . . . . . .Gen 28:13
God..father, the God of *A* . . . .Gen 31:42
The God of *A*, and the God . . .Gen 31:53
Jacob said, O God..father *A* . . .Gen 32:9
the land which I gave *A* . . . . . .Gen 35:12
which is Hebron, where *A* . . . . .Gen 35:27
before whom my fathers *A* . . . .Gen 48:15
name of my fathers *A* and . . . . .Gen 48:16
A bought with the field . . . . . . .Gen 49:30
they buried *A* and Sarah . . . . . .Gen 49:31
A bought with the field . . . . . . .Gen 50:13
land which he sware to *A* . . . . .Gen 50:24
remembered his covenant..*A* . . .Ex 2:24
thy father, the God of *A* . . . . . .Ex 3:6
God..fathers, the God of *A* . . .Ex 3:15
God of *A*, of Isaac, and of . . . .Ex 3:16
God..fathers, the God of *A* . . .Ex 4:5
I appeared unto *A*..Isaac . . . . . .Ex 6:3
I did swear to give it to *A* . . . . .Ex 6:8
Remember *A*, Isaac..Israel . . . .Ex 32:13
the land which I sware..*A* . . . . .Ex 33:1
also my covenant with *A* . . . . . .Lev 26:42
land which I sware unto *A* . . . . .Num 32:11
Lord sware..your fathers, *A* . . .Deut 1:8
land which I sware unto *A* . . . .Deut 34:4
Terah, the father of *A* . . . . .Josh 24:2
I took your father *A* from . . . . .Josh 24:3
came near..Lord God of *A* 1Kin 18:36
because of his covenant..*A* 2Kin 13:23
The sons of *A*; Isaac, and 1Chr 1:28
the sons of Keturah, *A* 1Chr 1:32
O Lord God of *A*, Isaac 1Chr 29:18
gavest him the name of *A* . . . . .Neh 9:7
the people of the God of *A* . . .Ps 47:9
O ye seed of *A* his servant . . . .Ps 105:6
Which covenant he..with *A* . . . .Ps 105:9
his holy promise, and *A* . . . . . . .Ps 105:42
the Lord, who redeemed *A* . . . .Is 29:22
the seed of *A* my friend . . . . . . .Is 41:8
Look unto *A* your father . . . . . .Is 51:2
rulers over the seed of *A* . . . . .Jer 33:26
A was one, and he inherited . . .Ezek 33:24
truth to Jacob..mercy to *A* . . . .Mic 7:20
A begat Isaac; and Isaac . . . . . .Matt 1:2
the generations from *A* to . . . . .Matt 1:17
We have *A* to our father . . . . . .Matt 3:9
raise up children unto *A* . . . . . .Matt 3:9
shall sit down with *A* . . . . .Matt 8:11
I am the God of *A* and the . . . .Matt 22:32
I am the God of *A* . . . . .Mark 12:26
spake to our fathers to *A* . . . . .Luke 1:55
We have *A* to our father . . . . . .Luke 3:8
raise up children unto *A* . . . . . .Luke 3:8
which was the son of *A* . . . . . . .Luke 3:34
this woman..daughter of *A* . . . .Luke 13:16
ye shall see *A* and Isaac . . . . . . .Luke 13:28
forsomuch as he..a son of *A* . . .Luke 19:9
calleth..Lord the God of *A* . . . .Luke 20:37
We be *A* seed and were . . . . . . .John 8:33
I know that ye are *A* seed . . . . .John 8:37
If ye were *A* children ye . . . . . .John 8:39
answered..unto him, *A* is . . . . . .John 8:39
would do the works of *A* . . . . . .John 8:39
this did not *A* . . . . .John 8:40
A is dead..the prophets . . . . . .John 8:52
Art thou greater..father *A* . . . . .John 8:53
and hast thou seen *A*? . . . . .John 8:57
Before *A* was, I am . . . . .John 8:58
The God of *A* and..Isaac . . . . . .Acts 3:13
circumcision; and so *A* . . . . .Acts 7:8
the sepulcher that *A* . . . . .Acts 7:16
which God had sworn to *A* . . . .Acts 7:17
God..fathers, the God of *A* . . .Acts 7:32
children of the stock of *A* . . . . .Acts 13:26
A our father as pertaining . . . . .Rom 4:1
if *A* were justified by . . . . .Rom 4:2
A believed God, and it was . . .Rom 4:3
faith was reckoned to *A* . . . . . . .Rom 4:9
that faith of our father *A* . . . . . .Rom 4:12
not to *A* or to his seed . . . . .Rom 4:13
which is of the faith of *A* . . . . .Rom 4:16
because they..the seed of *A* . . .Rom 9:7
seed of *A* of the tribe of . . . . . .Rom 11:1
Are they the seed of *A*? 2Cor 11:22
Even as *A* believed God . . . . . .Gal 3:6
blessed with faithful *A* . . . . .Gal 3:9
the blessing of *A* might . . . . . . .Gal 3:14
to *A* and his seed were the . . . .Gal 3:16
God gave it to *A* by . . . . .Gal 3:18
took on him the seed of *A* . . . .Heb 2:16
God made promise to *A* . . . . . .Heb 6:13
come out of the loins of *A* . . . .Heb 7:5
received tithes of *A* . . . . .Heb 7:6
By faith *A* when he was . . . . . . .Heb 11:17

ABRAHAM'S BOSOM—*a figurative expression for the state of bliss following death*
Expressive of heavenly status . . . . .Luke 16:22,23

ABRAM (ā'brăm)—*See* ABRAHAM

ABROAD—*beyond the boundaries*
of the Canaanites spread *a* . . . .Gen 10:18
lest we be scattered *a* . . . . .Gen 11:4
the Lord scattered them *a* . . . . .Gen 11:8
the Lord scatter them *a* . . . . . . .Gen 11:9
he brought him forth *a* . . . . .Gen 15:5
people were scattered *a* . . . . . . .Ex 5:12
I will spread *a* my hands . . . . . .Ex 9:29
Pharaoh and spread *a* his . . . . .Ex 9:33
carry forth..of the flesh *a* . . . . .Ex 12:46
walk *a* upon his staff . . . . .Ex 21:19
And he spread *a* the tent . . . . .Ex 40:19
a leprosy break out *a* in . . . . . . .Lev 13:12
tarry *a* out of his tent . . . . .Lev 14:8
at home or born *a* . . . . .Lev 18:9
they spread them all *a* for . . . . .Num 11:32
then shall he go *a* out of . . . . . .Deut 23:10
Thou shalt stand *a* and . . . . .Deut 24:11
bring out the pledge *a* . . . . .Deut 24:11
spreadeth *a* her wings . . . . .Deut 32:11
daughters, whom he sent *a* . . . .Judg 12:9
took in thirty daughters..*a* . . . . .Judg 12:9
he and Samuel *a* 1Sam 9:26
did spread them *a* 2Sam 22:43
and walkest *a*..whither 1Kin 2:42
vessels *a*..thy neighbors 2Kin 4:3
a unto our brethren every 1Chr 13:2
Uzziah..his name spread *a* 2Chr 26:8
I will scatter you *a* among . . . . .Neh 1:8
deed..queen shall come *a* . . . . .Esth 1:17
lion's whelps..scattered *a* . . . . . .Job 4:11
wandereth *a* for bread . . . . .Job 15:23
Cast *a* the rage of thy . . . . .Job 40:11
when he goeth *a* he telleth . . . .Ps 41:6
thine arrows also went *a* . . . . . .Ps 77:17
fountains be dispersed *a* . . . . . .Prov 5:16
a the inhabitants thereof . . . . . .Is 24:1
doth he not cast *a* the . . . . .Is 28:25
spreadeth *a* the earth by . . . . . .Is 44:24
pour it out..children *a* . . . . .Jer 6:11
a the sword bereaveth at . . . . . .Lam 1:20
ye have scattered them *a* . . . . . .Ezek 34:21
prosperity..yet be spread *a* . . . .Zech 1:17
spread you *a* as the four . . . . . .Zech 2:6
a his fame in all that . . . . .Matt 9:31
scattered *a*, as sheep . . . . .Matt 9:36
not with me scattereth *a* . . . . . .Matt 12:30
flock shall be scattered *a* . . . . . .Matt 26:31
fame spread *a* throughout . . . . .Mark 1:28
these sayings..noised *a* . . . . .Luke 1:65
more went there a fame *a* . . . . .Luke 5:15
be known and come *a* . . . . .Luke 8:17
God that were scattered *a* . . . . .John 11:52
went this saying *a* among . . . . .John 21:23
when this was noised *a* . . . . .Acts 2:6
all scattered *a* throughout . . . . .Acts 8:1
scattered *a*..persecution . . . . . . .Acts 11:19
love of God is shed *a* . . . . .Rom 5:5
He hath dispersed *a* he 2Cor 9:9
faith..God-ward is spread *a* 1Thess 1:8
tribes which..scattered *a* . . . . . .James 1:1

ABSALOM (ăb'sä-lŏm)—*"father of peace"—a son of David who tried to usurp the throne from his father*
Son of David 2Sam 3:3
A handsome man 2Sam 14:25
Receives Tamar after her rape by Ammon 2Sam 13:20
Slays Ammon for raping Tamar 2Sam 13:22-33
Flees from David 2Sam 13:34-39
Returns through Joab's intrigue 2Sam 14:1-24
Fathers children 2Sam 14:27
Reconciled to David 2Sam 14:28-33
Alienates the people from David 2Sam 15:1-6
Conspires against David . .2Sam 15:7-12
Takes Jerusalem 2Sam 15:13-29
Receives Hushai 2Sam 15:31-37
Hears Ahithophel's counsel 2Sam 16:20-23
Prefers Hushai's counsel .2Sam 17:5-14
Strategy of, revealed to David 2Sam 17:15-22
Masses his army against David 2Sam 17:24-26
Caught and slain by Joab .2Sam 18:9-18
Death of, brings sorrow to David 2Sam 18:19-33
Joab rebukes David for mourning over 2Sam 19:1-8
Death of, unites Israel again to David 2Sam 19:9-15
See ABISHALOM

[*also* ABSALOM'S]
that *A* the son of David had . . .2Sam 13:1
I love Tamar, my brother *A* . . .2Sam 13:4
And *A* spake unto his 2Sam 13:22
Amnon..good nor bad; for *A* . .2Sam 13:22
A had sheepshearers in 2Sam 13:23
and *A* invited all..king's 2Sam 13:23
And *A* came to the king 2Sam 13:24
the king said to *A* Nay 2Sam 13:25
Then said *A*, If not, I pray 2Sam 13:26
A pressed him..he let Amnon . .2Sam 13:27
Now *A* had commanded 2Sam 13:28
A hath slain all the king's 2Sam 13:30
But *A* fled..young man 2Sam 13:34
But *A* fled..to Talmai 2Sam 13:37
So *A* fled..went to Geshur 2Sam 13:38
So *A* returned to his own 2Sam 14:24
unto *A* there were born 2Sam 14:27
A dwelt..years in Jerusalem . . .2Sam 14:28
A sent for Joab to have 2Sam 14:29
A answered Joab, Behold 2Sam 14:32
A prepared him chariots 2Sam 15:1
And *A* rose up early and 2Sam 15:2
then *A* called unto him 2Sam 15:2
A said unto him, See thy 2Sam 15:3
A said moreover, Oh, that 2Sam 15:4
A said unto the king 2Sam 15:7
A sent spies throughout 2Sam 15:10
A sent for Ahithophel the 2Sam 15:12
increased continually with *A* . . .2Sam 15:12
came into the city and *A* 2Sam 15:37
the kingdom..hand of *A* 2Sam 16:8
And *A* and all the people 2Sam 16:15
David's friend..unto *A* 2Sam 16:16
Hushai said unto *A* God 2Sam 16:16
A said to Hushai, Is this 2Sam 16:17
said *A* to Ahithophel, Give 2Sam 16:20
So they spread *A* a tent 2Sam 16:22
and *A* went..his father's 2Sam 16:22
both with David..with *A* 2Sam 16:23
Ahithophel said unto *A* 2Sam 17:1
And the saying pleased *A* 2Sam 17:4
said *A*, Call now Hushai 2Sam 17:5
A and all the men of Israel 2Sam 17:14
the Lord..bring evil upon *A* . . .2Sam 17:14
And *A* passed over Jordan 2Sam 17:24

A made Amasa captain of 2Sam 17:25
Israel and *A* pitched in the 2Sam 17:26
young man, even with *A* 2Sam 18:5
the captains..concerning *A* 2Sam 18:5
And *A*..servants of David 2Sam 18:9
And *A* rode upon a mule 2Sam 18:9
said, Is the young man *A* 2Sam 18:29
Cushi, Is the young man *A* 2Sam 18:32
O my son *A*..my son *A*! 2Sam 18:33
died for thee, O *A* my son 2Sam 18:33
more harm than did *A* 2Sam 20:6
I fled because of *A* thy 1Kin 2:7
A the son of Maachah 2Chr 3:2
Maachah the daughter of *A* . . .2Chr 11:20
psalm of David..fled from *A* . . .Ps 3:*title*

ABSENCE—*not present*

Of physical relations:
A child from its father . . .Gen 37:32-35
Israel's ark 1Sam 4:21, 22
Israel from her land 2Chr 36:17-21
Believers from one another . . . . .Phil 1:25, 26
Believers from Christ 2Cor 5:6-9

Of God's Spirit as:
Judgment on the world . .Gen 6:3
Judgment on an individual 1Sam 16:14
Unable to flee . . . . .Ps 139:7-12

Of graces:
Holy Spirit . . . . .Jude 19
Faith 2Thess 3:2
Natural love 2Tim 3:2
Holiness . . . . .Rev 22:11
Righteousness . . . . .Rev 22:11

[*also* ABSENT]
we are *a* one from another . . . .Gen 31:49
in the *a* of the multitude . . . . . .Luke 22:6
For I verily, as *a* in body 1Cor 5:3
a am bold toward you 2Cor 10:1
by letters when we are *a* 2Cor 10:11
a now I write to them 2Cor 13:2
write these things being *a* 2Cor 13:10
and see you or else be *a* . . . . . .Phil 1:27
now much more in my *a* . . . . . .Phil 2:12
though I be *a* in the flesh . . . . .Col 2:5

ABSENTEEISM—*chronic absence from duty*
Work, condemned 2Thess 3:6-14
Church, rebuked . . . . .Heb 10:25

ABSTAIN—*to refrain from*

From moral evil:
Vindictiveness 2Sam 16:5-14
Idolatry . . . . .Acts 15:20, 29
Fornication . . . . .Acts 15:20
Sexual sins 1Thess 4:3
Fleshly lusts 1Pet 2:11
Evil appearances 1Thess 5:22

From things:
Food 2Sam 12:16, 23
Married relations . . . . .Ex 19:15; 1Cor 7:5
Meats . . . . .Rom 14:1-23; 1Cor 8:1-13

From unauthorized commands:
Forbidding to marry 1Tim 4:3
Requiring man-made ceremonies . . . . .Col 2:20-23
Abstaining from meats . . .1Tim 4:3

A from all appearance of evil . .1Thess 5:22

ABSTINENCE—*restraint*

Restraint from something
Blood . . . . .Acts 15:20
Evil 1Thess 5:22
Food . . . . .Acts 27:21
Fornication . . . . .Acts 15:20; 1Thess 4:3
Idolatry . . . . .Acts 15:20
Intoxicants . . . . .Prov 23:31
Lust 1Pet 2:11
Meats 1Tim 4:3
Things offered to idols . . .Acts 15:29
Meats contaminated . . . . .Acts 15:20

Restraint from strong drink
1. *Required of:*
Priests . . . . .Lev 10:9
Kings . . . . .Prov 31:4
Nazarites . . . . .Num 6:1-4

2. *Failure of, a cause of:*
Sudden death 1Sam 25:36-38
Delirium tremens . . . . .Prov 23:31-35
Insensibility to justice . . . .Is 5:11, 12, 22, 23
Error in judgment . . . . . . .Is 28:7
Moral callousness . . . . .Is 56:12
Revelry . . . . .Dan 5:2-4
Debauchery . . . . .Hab 2:15, 16
A weaker brother's stumble . . . . .Rom 14:20, 21
Excess . . . . .Eph 5:18

3. *Examples of:*
Manoah's wife . . . . .Judg 13:3, 4, 7
Samson . . . . .Judg 16:17
Hannah 1Sam 1:15
Rechabites . . . . .Jer 35:1-19
Daniel . . . . .Dan 1:8
John the Baptist . . . . .Luke 1:13-15

ABUNDANCE—*plentiful supply*

Of material things:
Wealth 1Kin 10:10
Rain 1Kin 18:41
Metals 1Chr 22:3, 14
Trees . . . . .1Chr 22:4; Neh 9:25
Sacrifices 1Chr 29:21
Camels 2Chr 14:15
Followers 2Chr 15:9
Flocks and herds 2Chr 18:2; 2Chr 32:29
Money 2Chr 24:11
Weapons 2Chr 32:5
Riches . . . . .Ps 52:7
Milk .Is 7:22
Wine . . . . .Is 56:12
Horses . . . . .Ezek 26:10
Labors 2Cor 11:23

Of God's spiritual blessings:
Goodness . . . . .Ex 34:6
Pardon . . . . .Is 55:7
Peace and truth . . . . .Jer 33:6
Answers to our prayers . .Eph 3:20
Grace 1Tim 1:14
Mercy 1Pet 1:3

Of spiritual things:
Predicted for Gospel times . . . . .Is 35:2
Realized in the Messiah . .Ps 72:7
Given to the meek . . . . . .Ps 37:11
Through Christ . . . . .Rom 5:17, 20
By grace 2Cor 4:15

Of good things for Christians:
Greater usefulness . . . . . . .Matt 13:12
Greater reward . . . . .Matt 25:29
Spiritual life . . . . .John 10:10
Grace . . . . .Rom 5:17; 2Cor 4:15
Christian service 1Cor 15:10
Joy 2Cor 8:2
Thanksgiving 2Cor 9:12
Rejoicing . . . . .Phil 1:26
Spiritual renewal . . . . .Titus 3:5, 6
Entrance in God's kingdom 2Pet 1:11

Of undesirable things:
Witchcraft . . . . .Is 47:9
Idleness . . . . .Ezek 16:49

Characteristics of:
Given to the obedient . . .Lev 26:3-13
Useful in God's work 2Chr 24:11
Cannot satisfy fully . . . . . .Eccl 5:10-12
Not to be trusted . . . . .Ps 52:7
Subject to conditions . . . .Mal 3:10-12; Matt 6:32, 33
Can be taken away . . . . . .Luke 12:13-21
Not a sign of real worth. .Luke 12:15

Obtained by:
Putting away sin 2Chr 15:9
Following God's commands 2Chr 17:5
Given by God . . . . .Job 36:31
Through Christ . . . . .John 10:10

[*also* ABUNDANT, ABUNDANTLY]
the waters bring forth *a* . . . . . . .Gen 1:20
the waters brought forth *a* . . . .Gen 1:21
they may breed *a* in the . . . . . . .Gen 8:17
bring forth *a* in the earth . . . . .Gen 9:7
fruitful and increased *a* . . . . . . .Ex 1:7
river..bring forth frogs *a* . . . . . .Ex 8:3
the water came out *a* . . . . .Num 20:11
for the *a* of all things . . . . .Deut 28:47
they shall suck of the *a* of . . . . .Deut 33:19
of the *a* of my complaint 1Sam 1:16
spoil..city in great *a* 2Sam 12:30
fat cattle and sheep in *a* 1Kin 1:19
fat cattle and sheep in *a* 1Kin 1:25
sycamore trees..for a 1Kin 10:27
oxen and sheep *a*; for 1Chr 12:40
David prepared *a* before 1Chr 22:5
Thou hast shed blood *a* 1Chr 22:8
marble stones in *a* 1Chr 29:2
sycamore trees..for *a* 2Chr 1:15
prepare me timber in *a* 2Chr 2:9
vessels in great *a* 2Chr 4:18
spices, and gold in *a* 2Chr 9:1
of spices great *a*..precious 2Chr 9:9
sycamore trees..in *a* 2Chr 9:27
gave them victual in *a* 2Chr 11:23
had riches and honor in *a* 2Chr 18:1
found among them..*a* both 2Chr 20:25
burnt offerings were in *a* 2Chr 29:35
children of Israel..in *a* 2Chr 31:5
things brought they in *a* 2Chr 31:5
royal wine in *a* according . . . . .Esth 1:7
hand God bringeth *a* . . . . .Job 12:6
and *a* of waters cover thee . . . .Job 22:11
distill upon man *a* . . . . .Job 36:28
that *a* of waters may cover . . . .Job 38:34
They shall be *a* satisfied . . . . . .Ps 36:8
waterest..ridges thereof *a* . . . . .Ps 65:10
brought forth frogs in *a* . . . . . . .Ps 105:30
I will *a* bless her provision . . . .Ps 132:15
They..*a* utter the memory . . . . .Ps 145:7
yea, drink *a* O beloved . . . . . . .Song 5:1
one shall howl, weeping *a* . . . . .Is 15:3
the *a* they have gotten . . . . .Is 15:7
a of the sea..be converted . . . . .Is 60:5
with the *a* of her glory . . . . .Is 66:11
silver, and apparel, in..*a* . . . . . .Zech 14:14
out of the *a* of the heart . . . . . .Matt 12:34
did cast in of their *a* . . . . .Mark 12:44
of the *a* of the heart his . . . . . . .Luke 6:45
these have of their *a* cast . . . . .Luke 21:4
we bestow more *a* honor 1Cor 12:23
have more *a* comeliness 1Cor 12:23
given more *a* honor 1Cor 12:24
and more *a* to you-ward 2Cor 1:12
I have more *a* unto you 2Cor 2:4
inward affection is more *a* 2Cor 7:15
your *a* may be a supply for 2Cor 8:14
that their *a* also may be 2Cor 8:14
blame us..this *a* which is 2Cor 8:20
according to our rule *a* 2Cor 10:15
the *a* of the revelations 2Cor 12:7
the more *a* I love you, the 2Cor 12:15
endeavored the more *a* to 1Thess 2:17
willing more *a* to shew . . . . .Heb 6:17

ABUSE—*application to a wrong purpose*

Of physical things:
Sexual perversions . . . . . . .Gen 19:5-9, 31-38
Immoral acts 1Cor 6:9
Torture . . . . .Judg 16:21

Of spiritual things:
Misuse of authority . . . . . .Num 20:10-13; 1Cor 9:18

Using the world wrongly. .1Cor 7:31
Perverting the truth 2Pet 2:10-22
Corrupting God's ordinances 1Sam 2:12-17; 1Cor 11:17-22

Manifested by:
Unbelieving . . . . .Mark 15:29-32

[*also* ABUSED, ABUSING]
they knew her, and *a* her . . . . .Judg 19:25
thrust me through and *a* 1Sam 31:4
uncircumcised come and *a*. 1Chr 10:4
use this world as not *a* it 1Cor 7:31

ABUSERS—*those who use themself wrongly*
a of themselves..mankind 1Cor 6:9

ABYSS—*"no bottom"*

Translated:
"deep" . . . . .Luke 8:31
"bottomless pit" . . . . .Rev 9:1,2,11
Rev 17:8

ACCAD—*"fortress"*
City in Shinar . . . . .Gen 10:10

ACCEPTANCE—*the reception of one's person or purpose*

Objects of, before God:
Righteousness and justice .Prov 21:3
Our words and meditations . . . . .Ps 19:14
Our dedication . . . . .Rom 12:1, 2
Service . . . . .Rom 14:18
Giving . . . . .Rom 15:16, 27
Offerings . . . . .Phil 4:18
Intercession 1Tim 2:1-3
Helping parents 1Tim 5:4
Spiritual sacrifices 1Pet 2:5
Suffering because of Christ 1Pet 2:20

Qualifications of, seen in:
Coming at God's time . . .Is 49:8
2Cor 6:2
Meeting God's requirements . . . . .Job 42:8, 9
Receiving divine sign . . . .Judg 6:9-21
Noting God's response . . .1Sam 7:8-10
John 12:28-30
Responding to God's renewal . . . . .Ezek 20:40-44
Manifesting spiritual rectitude . . . . .Mic 6:6-8

Persons disqualified for, such as:
The wicked . . . . .Ps 82:2
Blemished sacrifices . . . . .Mal 1:8, 10, 13
Man's person . . . . .Gal 2:6
Those who swear deceitfully . . . . .Ps 24:3-6

[*also* ACCEPT, ACCEPTABLE, ACCEPTABLY, ACCEPTATION, ACCEPTED, ACCEPTEST, ACCEPTETH, ACCEPTING]
shalt thou not be *a*? . . . . .Gen 4:7
I have *a* thee concerning . . . . . .Gen 19:21
preadventure he will *a* of . . . . .Gen 32:20
owner of it shall *a* thereof . . . . .Ex 22:11
may be *a* before the Lord . . . . .Ex 28:38
a in the sight of the Lord? . . . .Lev 10:19
abominable; it..not be *a* . . . . . .Lev 19:7
it shall not be *a* for you . . . . . . .Lev 22:20
shall be perfect to be *a* . . . . . . .Lev 22:21
they..*a* of the punishment . . . . .Lev 26:41
shall *a* of the punishment . . . . .Lev 26:43
a the work of his hands . . . . . . .Deut 33:11
him be *a* to his brethren . . . . . .Deut 33:24
and he was *a* in the sight 1Sam 18:5
me, let him *a* an offering 1Sam 26:19
The Lord thy God *a* thee 2Sam 24:23
and *a* of the multitude . . . . .Esth 10:3
Will ye *a* his person? . . . . .Job 13:8
ye do secretly *a* persons? . . . . . .Job 13:10
Let me not, I pray you, *a* . . . . .Job 32:21
him that *a* not the persons . . . .Job 34:19
a thy burnt sacrifice . . . . .Ps 20:3
thee, O Lord, in an *a* time . . . .Ps 69:13
A, I beseech..the freewill . . . . . .Ps 119:108
righteous know what is *a* . . . . . .Prov 10:32
to *a* the person..wicked . . . . . . .Prov 18:5
God now *a* thy works . . . . .Eccl 9:7
preacher sought to find..*a* . . . . .Eccl 12:10
their sacrifices shall be *a* . . . . . .Is 56:7
a fast..*a* day to the Lord? . . . . .Is 58:5
proclaim the *a* year..Lord . . . . .Is 61:2
burnt offerings are not *a* . . . . . .Jer 6:20
the Lord doth not *a* them . . . . .Jer 14:10
let my supplication..*a* . . . . .Jer 37:20
Let..supplication be *a* . . . . .Jer 42:2
there will I *a* them and . . . . . . .Ezek 20:40
will *a* you with your sweet . . . .Ezek 20:41
a you, saith the Lord God . . . .Ezek 43:27
O king, let my counsel be *a* . . .Dan 4:27
the Lord *a* them not . . . . .Hos 8:13
meat offerings, I will not *a* . . . .Amos 5:22
pleased with thee or *a* thy . . . . .Mal 1:8
should I *a* this..your hand? . . . .Mal 1:13
to preach the *a* year..Lord . . . .Luke 4:19
No prophet is *a* in his own . . . .Luke 4:24
neither *a* thou the person . . . . .Luke 20:21
worketh righteousness is *a* . . . . .Acts 10:35
We *a* it always and in all . . . . . .Acts 24:3
sacrifice, holy, *a* unto God . . . .Rom 12:1
may be *a* of the saints . . . . .Rom 15:31
we may be *a* of him 2Cor 5:9
I have heard thee..time *a* 2Cor 6:2
behold, now is the *a* time 2Cor 6:2
God *a* no man's person . . . . . . .Gal 2:6
wherein he hath made us *a* . . . .Eph 1:6
Proving what is *a*..Lord . . . . . . .Eph 5:10
worthy of all *a* that 1Tim 1:15
tortured, not *a* deliverance . . . .Heb 11:35
God *a* with reverence and . . . . .Heb 12:28

ACCESS TO GOD

By means of:
Christ . . . . .John 14:6
Christ's blood . . . . .Eph 2:13
Holy Spirit . . . . .Eph 2:18
Faith . . . . .Rom 5:2
Clean hands . . . . .Ps 24:3-5
God's grace . . . . .Eph 1:6
Prayer . . . . .Matt 6:6

Characteristics of:
On God's choosing . . . . . .Ps 64:4
Sinners commanded to seek . . . . Is 55:6; James 4:8
With confidence . . . . .Heb 4:16
Boldness . . . . .Eph 3:12
Results from reconciliation . . . . .Col 1:21, 22
Open to Gentiles . . . . .Acts 14:27
Experienced in Christ's priesthood . . . . .Heb 7:19-25
Sought by God's people . .Ps 27:4
Bold in prayer . . . . .Heb 4:16
A blessing to be chosen . .Ps 65:4

ACCHO (ăc'kō)—*"compressed"—a seacoast city located eight miles north of Mount Carmel*
Assigned to Asher . . . . . . .Judg 1:31
Called Ptolemais in the New Testament . . . . . . .Acts 21:7

ACCIDENT—*an unintended, unforeseen event*

Caused by:
An animal . . . . .Num 22:25
A fall 2Sam 4:4

Explanation of:
Known to God . . . . .Deut 29:29
Prov 16:9, 33
Misunderstood by men . . .Luke 13:4, 5
Subject to God's providence . . . . .Rom 8:28

ACCOMMODATION—*adapting oneself to limits or convenience*

Physically, caused by:
Age and sex . . . . .Gen 33:13-15
Strength and size 1Sam 17:38-40
Inability to repay . . . . .Luke 7:41, 42

Spiritually, caused by:
Man's blindness . . . . .Matt 13:10-14
Absence of the Spirit . . . .John 16:12, 13
Carnality 1Cor 3:1, 2
Spiritual immaturity . . . . .Rom 14:1-23
Man's present limitations .1Cor 2:7-16
Degrees of light . . . . .Heb 9:7-15

ACCOMPANY—*to go with*

[*also* ACCOMPANIED, ACCOMPANYING]
a the ark of God 2Sam 6:4
brethren from Joppa *a* . . . . .Acts 10:23
these six brethren *a* me . . . . . . .Acts 11:12
things that *a* salvation . . . . .Heb 6:9

ACCOMPLISH—*to fulfill*

Of God's Word concerning:
Judah's captivity 2Chr 36:23
Judah's return . . . . .Dan 9:2
God's sovereign plan . . . .Is 55:11
The Messiah's advent . . . .Dan 9:24-27
Christ's suffering . . . . .Luke 18:31
Christ's death . . . . .John 19:28-30
Final events . . . . .Dan 12:7

Of human things:
Food 1Kin 5:9
Purification rites . . . . .Esth 2:12
Priestly ministry . . . . .Luke 1:23
Time of pregnancy . . . . . .Luke 2:6
Afflictions 1Pet 5:9

[*also* ACCOMPLISHED, ACCOMPLISHING, ACCOMPLISHMENT]
to *a* his vow . . . . .Lev 22:21
of the Lord..might be *a* 2Chr 36:22
till he shall *a* as..hireling . . . . . .Job 14:6
shall be *a* before his time . . . . .Job 15:32
they *a* a diligent search . . . . . . .Ps 64:6
The desire *a* is sweet to the . . .Prov 13:19
her warfare is *a* that her . . . . . .Is 40:2
it shall *a* that which I . . . . .Is 55:11
when seventy years are *a* . . . . . .Jer 25:12
of your dispersions are *a* . . . . . .Jer 25:34
after seventy years be *a* . . . . . . .Jer 29:10
ye will surely *a* your vows . . . . .Jer 44:25
The Lord hath *a* his fury . . . . . .Lam 4:11
And when thou hast *a* . . . . .Ezek 4:6
Thus shall mine anger be *a* . . . .Ezek 5:13
when I have *a* my fury in . . . . .Ezek 5:13
thus will I *a* my fury upon . . . .Ezek 6:12
and *a* mine anger upon . . . . . . .Ezek 7:8
Thus will I *a* my wrath . . . . . . .Ezek 13:15
to *a* my anger against . . . . .Ezek 20:8
that he would *a* seventy . . . . . . .Dan 9:2
till the indignation be *a* . . . . . . .Dan 11:36
and when he shall have *a* . . . . .Dan 12:7
eight days were *a* . . . . .Luke 2:21
he should *a* at Jerusalem . . . . . .Luke 9:31
straitened till it be *a*! . . . . .Luke 12:50
the Son of man shall be *a* . . . . .Luke 18:31
all things were now *a* . . . . .John 19:28
when we had *a* those days . . . .Acts 21:5
a the service of God . . . . .Heb 9:6
are *a* in your brethren 1Pet 5:9

ACCORD—*united agreement*

Descriptive of:
A spontaneous response .Acts 12:10, 20
Voluntary action 2Cor 8:17
Single-mindedness . . . . . . .Josh 9:2
Spiritual unity . . . . .Acts 1:14

Manifested in:
Fellowship . . . . .Acts 2:46
Prayer . . . . .Acts 4:24
Opposition . . . . .Acts 7:57
Response . . . . .Acts 8:6
Decisions . . . . .Acts 15:25
Mind . . . . .Phil 2:2
which groweth..its own *a* . . . . . .Lev 25:5
were all with one *a* in one . . . .Acts 2:1
they were all with one *a* in . . . .Acts 5:12
insurrection with one *a* . . . . .Acts 18:12
rushed with one *a* into . . . . .Acts 19:29

ACCORDING—*See* INTRODUCTION

ACCORDINGLY—*consequently*
a he will repay, fury to his . . . .Is 59:18

ACCOUNT—*an explanation*

[*also* ACCOUNTED, ACCOUNTING, ACCOUNTS]

he giveth not *a* of any of ..... Job 33:13
shall be *a* to the Lord for a ... Ps 22:30
son of man..thou makest *a* .... Ps 144:3
by one, to find out the *a* ...... Eccl 7:27
the princes might give *a* .... Dan 6:2
they shall give *a* thereof ...... Matt 12:36
would..*a* of his servants .... Matt 18:23
an *a* of thy stewardship .... Luke 16:2
which shall be *a* worthy .... Luke 20:35
that ye may be *a* worthy ...... Luke 21:36
which of them should be *a* ..... Luke 22:24
we are *a* as sheep for the ..... Rom 8:36
a to him for righteousness ..... Gal 3:6
fruit..abound to your *a* .... Phil 4:17
A that God was able to .... Heb 11:19
as they that must give *a* .... Heb 13:17
shall give *a* to him that is 1Pet 4:5

ACCOUNTABILITY—*responsibility for one's own actions*

Kinds of:
Universal .... Rom 14:12
Personal 2Sam 12:1-15
Personal and family ...... Josh 7:1-26
Personal and national 2Sam 24:1-17
Delayed but exacted 2Sam 21:1-14
Final .... Rom 2:1-12

Determined by:
Federal headship .... Gen 3:1-24
Rom 5:12-21
Personal responsibility ... Ezek 18:1-32
Faithfulness .... Matt 25:14-30
Knowledge .... Luke 12:47, 48
Conscience .... Rom 2:12-16
Greater light .... Rom 2:17-29
Maturity of judgment 1Cor 8:1-13

ACCURSED—*under a curse*

Caused by:
Hanging on a tree .... Deut 21:23
Sin among God's people. . Josh 7:12
Possessing a banned thing. Josh 6:18
Preaching contrary to the Gospel .... Gal 1:8, 9
Blaspheming Christ 1Cor 12:3

Objects of being:
A city .... Josh 6:17
A forbidden thing .... Josh 22:20
An old sinner .... Is 65:20
Christ haters or nonbelievers 1Cor 16:22
Paul (for the sake of Israel) .... Rom 9:3

a trespass in the *a* thing .... Josh 7:1
took of the *a* thing .... Josh 7:1
have even taken of the *a* ...... Josh 7:11
an *a* thing in the midst of ..... Josh 7:13
until ye take away the *a* ...... Josh 7:13
taken with the *a* thing .... Josh 7:15
transgressed in the thing *a* 1Chr 2:7

ACCUSATION—*a charge of wrongdoing*

Kinds of:
Pagan .... Dan 3:8
Personal .... Dan 6:24
Public .... John 18:29
Perverted 1Pet 3:16

Sources of, in:
The devil .... Job 1:6-12
Rev 12:9, 10
Enemies .... Ezra 4:6
Man's conscience .... John 8:9
God's Word .... John 5:45
Hypocritical .... John 8:6, 10, 11
The last days 2Tim 3:1, 3
Apostates 2Pet 2:10, 11

Forbidden:
Against servants .... Prov 30:10
Falsely .... Luke 3:14
Among women .... Titus 2:3

False, examples of, against:
Jacob .... Gen 31:26-30
Joseph .... Gen 39:10-21
Ahimelech 1Sam 22:11-16
David 2Sam 10:3
Job .... Job 2:4, 5
Jeremiah .... Jer 26:8-11
Amos .... Amos 7:10, 11
Joshua .... Zech 3:1-5
Christ .... Matt 26:59-66
Stephen .... Acts 6:11-14
Paul and Silas .... Acts 16:19-21
Paul .... Acts 21:27-29
Christians 1Pet 2:12

[*also* ACCUSE, ACCUSED, ACCUSER, ACCUSETH, ACCUSING]

that they might *a* him .... Matt 12:10
he was *a* of the chief .... Matt 27:12
over..head his *a* written .... Matt 27:37
sabbath day..they might *a* ..... Mark 3:2
the chief priests *a* him of ...... Mark 15:3
his *a* was written over .... Mark 15:26
might find an *a* against .... Luke 6:7
mouth, that they might *a* ...... Luke 11:54
the same was *a* unto him ...... Luke 16:1
from any man by false *a* ...... Luke 19:8
stood and vehemently *a* .... Luke 23:10
there is one that *a* you .... John 5:45
that they might have to *a* ..... John 8:6
these things, whereof we *a* .... Acts 24:8
go down with me, and *a* ...... Acts 25:5
whereof these *a* me, no .... Acts 25:11
have the *a* face to face .... Acts 25:16
they brought none *a* of .... Acts 25:18
ought to *a* my nation of .... Acts 28:19
thoughts the mean while *a* .... Rom 2:15
receive not an *a* but 1Tim 5:19
children not *a* of riot or .... Titus 1:6
a railing *a*..said, the Lord ..... Jude 9
for the *a* of our brethren ...... Rev 12:10

ACCUSTOMED—*familiar*
that are *a* to do evil .... Jer 13:23

ACELDAMA (ä-kĕl'dä-mä)—*"field of blood"—a field purchased by the priests of Jerusalem from the 30 pieces of silver that bought the betrayal of Jesus*
Field called "field of blood" .... Acts 1:19

ACHAIA (ä-kā'yä)—*"trouble"—a region of Greece*
Visited by Paul .... Acts 18:1, 12
Gallio proconsul .... Acts 18:12
Apollos preaches in ...... Acts 18:24-28
Christians of, very generous .... Rom 15:26
Saints in all of 2Cor 1:1
Paul commends Christians of 2Cor 11:10
Gospel proclaimed throughout 1Thess 1:7, 8

through Macedonia and *A* ..... Acts 19:21
who is the firstfruits of *A* ..... Rom 16:5
first fruits of *A* and that 1Cor 16:15

ACHAICUS (ä-kā'ĭ-kŭs)—*"belonging to Achaia"*
A Corinthian Christian who visited Paul 1Cor 16:17, 18

ACHAN, ACHAR (ā'kăn; ā'kär)—*"trouble"*
A son of Carmi .... Josh 7:1
Sin of, caused Israel's defeat .... Josh 7:1-15
Stoned to death .... Josh 7:16-25
Sin of, recalled .... Josh 22:20
Also called Achar 1Chr 2:7

household man by man..*A* .... Josh 7:18
And Joshua said unto *A* ...... Josh 7:19
And *A* answered Joshua ...... Josh 7:20
Israel with him, took *A* .... Josh 7:24

ACHAZ (ā'kăz)—*the Greek word for "Ahaz"*
Ancestor of Jesus .... Matt 1:9

ACHBOR (ăk'bôr)—*"a mouse"*
1. Father of Edomite king. . Gen 36:36, 38
2. A courtier under Josiah. . 2Kin 22:12, 14
Called Abdon 2Chr 34:20

Baal-hanan the son of *A* ...... Gen 36:39
Baal-hanan the son of *A* 1Chr 1:49
Elnathan the son of *A* .... Jer 26:22
Elnathan the son of *A* .... Jer 36:12

ACHIM (ā'kĭm)—*"woes"—a shortened form of "Jehoiachim"*
Ancestor of Jesus .... Matt 1:14

ACHISH (ā'kĭsh)—*"serpent-charmer"*
A king of Gath 1Sam 21:10-15
David seeks refuge 1Sam 27:1-12
Forced to expel David by Philistine lords 1Sam 28:1, 2
Receives Shimei's servants 1Kin 2:39, 40

to *A* the king of Gath 1Sam 21:10
servants of *A* said unto 1Sam 21:11
was sore afraid of *A* the 1Sam 21:12
said *A* unto his servants 1Sam 21:14
unto *A* the son of Maoch 1Sam 27:2
David dwelt with *A*..Gath 1Sam 27:3
David said unto *A*, If I 1Sam 27:5
A gave him Ziklag that 1Sam 27:6
returned and came to *A* 1Sam 27:9
A said Whither have ye 1Sam 27:10
A believed David, saying 1Sam 27:12
passed on..rearward with *A* 1Sam 29:2
A said unto the princes 1Sam 29:3
A called David and said 1Sam 29:6
David said unto *A* But 1Sam 29:8
A answered..said to David 1Sam 29:9

ACHMETHA (ăk'mĕ-thä)—*"a place of horses"—the capital of Media (same as Ecbatana)*
Site of Persian archives . . Ezra 6:2

ACHOR (ā'kôr)—*"trouble"—a valley south of Jericho*
Site of Achan's stoning . . Josh 7:24-26
On Judah's boundary .... Josh 15:7
Promises concerning ..... Is 65:10

and the valley of *A* a place .... Is 65:10
and the valley of *A* for a ...... Hos 2:15

ACHSA, ACHSAH (ăk'sä)—*"serpent-charmer"*
A daughter of Caleb 1Chr 2:49
Given to Othniel .... Josh 15:16-19
Given springs of water . . . Judg 1:12-15

ACHSHAPH (ăk'shăf)—*"sorcery; dedicated"*
A royal city of Canaan . . . Josh 11:1
Captured by Joshua ..... Josh 12:7, 20
Assigned to Asher .... Josh 19:24, 25

ACHZIB (ăk'zĭb)—*"false"*
1. City of Judah .... Josh 15:44
Also called Chezib ...... Gen 38:5
2. Town of Asher .... Josh 19:29

nor of *A* nor of Helbah .... Judg 1:31
the houses of *A* shall be .... Mic 1:14

ACKNOWLEDGE—*to recognize*

Evil objects of:
Sin .... Ps 32:5
Transgressions .... Ps 51:3
Iniquity .... Jer 3:13
Wickedness .... Jer 14:20

Good objects of:
God .... Prov 3:6
God's might .... Is 33:13
God's people .... Is 61:9
God's mystery .... Col 2:2
God's truth 2Tim 2:25
The apostles 1Cor 14:37
Christian leaders 1Cor 16:18

[*also* ACKNOWLEDGED, ACKNOWLEDGETH, ACKNOWLEDGING, ACKNOWLEDGMENT]

And Judah *a* them .... Gen 38:26
he shall *a* the son of the ...... Deut 21:17
neither did he *a* his brethren . . Deut 33:9
Israel *a* us not .... Is 63:16

I *a* them that are carried ......Jer 24:5
a strange god..he shall *a* ......Dan 11:39
till they *a* their offense ....Hos 5:15
than what ye read or *a*........2Cor 1:13
ye shall *a* even to the end 2Cor 1:13
ye have *a* us in part 2Cor 1:14
the *a* of the truth which is ....Titus 1:1
by the *a* of every good thing ..Philem 6
a the Son hath the Father 1John 2:23

ACQUAINTANCE—*personal knowledge*
With God, gives peace ...Job 22:21
Deserted by............Ps 31:11
Made an abomination....Ps 88:8, 18
Jesus sought among......Luke 2:44
Stand afar off from Christ Luke 23:49
Come to Paul ....Acts 24:23
Of God, with man's ways.Ps 139:3

[*also* ACQUAINTED, ACQUAINTING]
them, every man of his *a* 2Kin 12:5
no more money of your *a* 2Kin 12:7
a are verily estranged ....Job 19:13
they that had been of his *a*....Job 42:11
my guide and mine *a* ....Ps 55:13
a mine heart..wisdom ....Eccl 2:3
sorrows, and *a* with grief......Is 53:3

ACQUIT—*to declare to be innocent*
Not possible with the
wicked ....Nah 1:3
Sought by the righteous ..Job 7:21
Difficulty of obtaining ...Job 9:28-31

thou wilt not *a* me from ......Job 10:14

ACRE—*a measurement of land*
Plowing of, by a yoke of
oxen 1Sam 14:14
Descriptive of barrenness .Is 5:10

ACROSTIC
A literary device using
the Hebrew alphabet;
illustrated best in
Hebrew..............Ps 119:1-176

ACT—*to do; take action*

[*also* ACTIONS, ACTIVITY, ACTS]
knowest any men of *a* ....Gen 47:6
all the great *a* of the Lord ....Deut 11:7
the righteous *a* of the Lord....Judg 5:11
even the righteous *a* ....Judg 5:11
by him *a* are weighed 1Sam 2:3
righteous *a* of the Lord 1Sam 12:7
who had done many *a* he 2Sam 23:20
in mine own land of..*a*........1Kin 10:6
rest of the *a* of Solomon 1Kin 11:41
book of the *a* of Solomon? 1Kin 11:41
rest of the *a* of Jeroboam 1Kin 14:19
of the *a* of Rehoboam 1Kin 14:29
rest of the *a* of Abijam 1Kin 15:7
rest of all the *a* of Asa........1Kin 15:23
the rest of the *a* of Nadab 1Kin 15:31
the rest of the *a* of Baasha 1Kin 16:5
the rest of the *a* of Elah 1Kin 16:14
the rest of the *a* of Zimri 1Kin 16:20
the rest of the *a* of Omri......1Kin 16:27
the rest of the *a* of Ahab 1Kin 22:39
of the *a* of Jehoshaphat 1Kin 22:45
of the *a* of Ahaziah which.....2Kin 1:18
the rest of the *a* of Joram 2Kin 8:23
the rest of the *a* of Jehu 2Kin 10:34
of the *a* of Joash and all 2Kin 12:19
rest of the *a* of Jehoahaz 2Kin 13:8
rest of the *a* of Joash 2Kin 13:12
rest of the *a* of Jehoash 2Kin 14:15
the rest of the *a* of Amaziah ..2Kin 14:18
of the *a* of Jeroboam, and 2Kin 14:28
the rest of the *a* of Azariah ...2Kin 15:6
rest of the *a* of Zachariah 2Kin 15:11
of the *a* of Shallum, and 2Kin 15:15
of the *a* of Menahem 2Kin 15:21
of the *a* of Pekahiah 2Kin 15:26
the rest of the *a* of Pekah 2Kin 15:31
the rest of the *a* of Jotham 2Kin 15:36
the rest of the *a* of Ahaz......2Kin 16:19
rest of the *a* of Hezekiah 2Kin 20:20
of the *a* of Manasseh, and 2Kin 21:17
the rest of the *a* of Amon 2Kin 21:25
a..he had done in Beth-el 2Kin 23:19
the rest of the *a* of Josiah 2Kin 23:28
who had done many *a* 1Chr 11:22
Now the *a* of David the king ..1Chr 29:29
in mine own land of thine *a* ...2Chr 9:5
the rest of the *a* of Solomon ..2Chr 9:29
Now the *a* of Rehoboam 2Chr 12:15
the rest of the *a* of Abijah 2Chr 13:22
behold, the *a* of Asa, first.....2Chr 16:11
of the *a* of Jehoshaphat 2Chr 20:34
of the *a* of Amaziah, first 2Chr 25:26
the rest of the *a* of Uzziah 2Chr 26:22
the rest of the *a* of Jotham 2Chr 27:7
Now the rest of his *a* 2Chr 28:26
of the *a* of Hezekiah, and 2Chr 32:32
of the *a* of Manasseh, and 2Chr 33:18
of the *a* of Josiah, and his 2Chr 35:26
of the *a* of Jehoiakim 2Chr 36:8
all the *a* of his power and .....Esth 10:2
his *a*..children of Israel ....Ps 103:7
Who can utter the mighty *a* ...Ps 106:2
shall declare thy mighty *a* .....Ps 145:4
the might of thy terrible *a*.....Ps 145:6
sons of men his mighty *a*......Ps 145:12
Praise him..his mighty *a* ......Ps 150:2
pass his *a*, his strange *a* ....Is 28:21
a of violence is in their ....Is 59:6
in adultery, in the very *a*......John 8:4

ACTS OF THE APOSTLES—*fifth book of the New Testament*
Written by Luke ....Luke 1:1-4
Acts 1:1, 2
Founding of the Church
at Jerusalem ....Acts 2:1-6:7
Stephen's Ministry ....Acts 6:8-8:3
Philip's Ministry ....Acts 8:4-40
Paul's Conversion ....Acts 9:1-31
Peter's Ministry at
Caesarea ....Acts 10:1-11:18
First Missionary Journey..Acts 13:1-14:28
Council at Jerusalem.....Acts 15:1-35
Second Missionary
Journey...............Acts 15:36-18:22
Third Missionary
Journey...............Acts 18:23-21:14
Paul's Arrest and
Defense ....Acts 21:15-28:31

ADADAH (ăd'ă-dä)—*"holiday"*
A city of Judah ....Josh 15:22

ADAH (ā'dä)—*"pleasure; beauty"*
1. One of Lamech's wives ..Gen 4:19
2. One of Esau's wives ....Gen 36:2, 4, 10, 12
Also called Bashemath ..Gen 26:34

and *A* bare Jabal; he was .....Gen 4:20
A and Zillah, Hear my........Gen 4:23
Edom; these..the sons of *A*....Gen 36:16

ADAIAH (ä-dā'yä)—*"pleasing to Jehovah; Jehovah has adorned"*
1. The maternal grandfather
of Josiah 2Kin 22:1
2. A Levite 1Chr 6:41
3. Son of Shimhi 1Chr 8:21
Called Shema...........1Chr 8:13
4. Aaronite priest 1Chr 9:10-12
5. The father of Maaseiah ..2Chr 23:1
6. A son of Bani ....Ezra 10:29
7. Another of a different
family of Bani ....Ezra 10:34, 39
8. A descendant of Judah ..Neh 11:4, 5

and *A* the son of Jeroham .....Neh 11:12

ADALIA (ä-dā'lĭ-ä)—*"honor of Ized"*
Haman's son ....Esth 9:8, 10

ADAM (ăd'ăm)—*"of the ground; firm; red earth man, mankind"—the first man*
Creation of:
In God's image..........Gen 1:26, 27
By God's breath.........Gen 2:7
A living soul 1Cor 15:45
From dust ....Gen 2:7
Before Eve 1Tim 2:13
Upright.................Eccl 7:29
Intelligent being ....Gen 2:19, 20
Position of, first:
Worker.................Gen 2:8, 15
To receive God's law ....Gen 2:16, 17
Husband................Gen 2:18-25
Man to sin ....Gen 3:6-12
To receive promise of the
Messiah ....Gen 3:15
Father..................Gen 4:1
Head of race ....Rom 5:12-14
Sin of:
Instigated by Satan ......Gen 3:1-5
Prompted by Eve........Gen 3:6
Done knowingly 1Tim 2:14
Resulted in broken
fellowship.............Gen 3:8
Brought God's curse .....Gen 3:14-19
Descendants of, are all:
Sinners ....Rom 5:12
Subject to death.........Rom 5:12-14
Scattered over the earth. .Deut 32:8
In need of salvation .....John 3:16

A called his wife's name Eve ..Gen 3:20
Unto *A* also and to his wife ...Gen 3:21
A knew his wife again ....Gen 4:25
the book..generations of *A* ....Gen 5:1
called their name *A* in the.....Gen 5:2
A lived a hundred and ....Gen 5:3
And the days of *A* after he....Gen 5:4
the days that *A* lived..........Gen 5:5
A, Sheth, Enosh..............1Chr 1:1
covered my transgressions..*A* ..Job 31:33
which was the son of *A* ....Luke 3:38
A all die, even so in Christ....1Cor 15:22
Enoch also, the seventh..*A* ....Jude 14

ADAM—*a city near Zaretan*
Site of Jordan's waters
rising to let Israel pass
over.................Josh 3:16

ADAM, LAST—a title of Christ
Prefigured in Adam .....Rom 5:14
Gift of, abound to many..Rom 5:15
A quickening spirit 1Cor 15:45
Spiritual and heavenly ...1Cor 15:46-48

ADAM, SECOND
Expressive of Christ 1Cor 15:20-24
1Cor 15:45

ADAMAH (ăd'ă-mä)—*"earth; red ground"*
City of Naphtali ....Josh 19:35, 36

ADAMANT (ăd'ă-mĕnt)—*a term that can refer to any number of hard gem stones*
As an *a* harder than flint......Ezek 3:9
made their hearts as an *a* .....Zech 7:12

ADAMI (ăd'ă-mī)—*"fortified"*
In Naphtali ....Josh 19:33

ADAR (ä-där')—*"height"*
A town of Judah ....Josh 15:1, 3

ADAR (ä-där)—*the twelfth month of the Hebrew year*
Date set by Haman for
massacre of Jews ......Esth 3:7, 13
Date adopted for Purim..Esth 9:19, 21, 26-28
Date of completion of
Temple ....Ezra 6:15

which is the month *A* ....Esth 8:12
that is the month *A* ....Esth 9:1
fourteenth day also..month *A* ..Esth 9:15
thirteenth day..month *A*.......Esth 9:17

A

ADBEEL (ăd'bĕ-ĕl)—*"languishing for God"*
A son of Ishmael . . . . Gen 25:13

Kedar, and *A* and Mibsam 1Chr 1:29

ADD—*to increase the sum*

Of material things:
Another child . . . . Gen 30:24
A population 2Sam 24:3
Heavy burdens 1Kin 12:11, 14
Years to life . . . . Prov 3:2
Kingly majesty . . . . Dan 4:36
Stature . . . . Matt 6:27

Of good things:
No sorrow . . . . Prov 10:22
Inspired words . . . . Jer 36:32
Learning . . . . Prov 16:23
Spiritual blessings . . . . Matt 6:33
Converts to Christ . . . . Acts 2:41, 47
A covenant . . . . Gal 3:15
The Law . . . . Gal 3:19

Of evil things:
Additions to God's Word . Deut 4:2
National sins 1Sam 12:19
Iniquity . . . . Ps 69:27
Sin to sin . . . . Is 30:1
Grief to sorrow . . . . Jer 45:3
Personal sin . . . . Luke 3:19, 20
Afflictions . . . . Phil 1:16

[*also* ADDED, ADDETH]
shall *a* the fifth part . . . . Lev 5:16
shall *a* the fifth part more . . . . . Lev 6:5
then he shall *a* a fifth part . . . . Lev 27:13
then he shall *a* the fifth . . . . . . Lev 27:15
and shall *a* a fifth part . . . . Lev 27:27
shall *a* thereto the fifth . . . . . . Lev 27:31
a unto it the fifth part . . . . Num 5:7
to them ye shall *a* forty . . . . Num 35:6
great voice; and he *a* no . . . . . . Deut 5:22
thou shalt not *a* thereto . . . . Deut 12:32
then shalt thou *a* three . . . . Deut 19:9
to *a* drunkenness to thirst . . . . . Deut 29:19
And I will *a* unto thy days 2Kin 20:6
thou mayest *a* thereto 1Chr 22:14
I will *a* thereto; my father 2Chr 10:14
ye intend to *a* more to our 2Chr 28:13
he *a* rebellion unto his sin . . . . . Job 34:37
peace, shall they *a* to thee . . . . Prov 3:2
a ye year to year . . . . Is 29:1
I will *a* unto thy days . . . . Is 38:5
a to his stature one cubit? . . . . . Luke 12:25
things shall be *a* unto you . . . . . Luke 12:31
he *a* and spake a parable . . . . . . Luke 19:11
believers were the more *a* . . . . . Acts 5:14
people was *a* unto the Lord . . . Acts 11:24
in conference *a* nothing to . . . . Gal 2:6
a to your faith virtue 2Pet 1:5
If any man shall *a* unto . . . . Rev 22:18
God shall *a* unto him the . . . . . Rev 22:18

ADDAN (ăd'ăn)—*"stony"*
A place in Babylonia whose returnees fail to prove Israelite ancestry . Ezra 2:59
See ADDON

ADDAR (ăd'är)—*"height; honor"*
A Benjamite 1Chr 8:3
Also called Ard . . . . Num 26:40

ADDER—*a venomous serpent*
Figurative of Dan's treachery . . . . Gen 49:17
Sting of wine . . . . Prov 23:31, 32
Wickedness of sinners . . . . Ps 58:3, 4
Triumph of saints . . . . Ps 91:13

ADDI (ăd'ī)—*"my witness"*
Ancestor of Jesus . . . . Luke 3:23, 28

ADDICTION—*a compulsion or habit*
To ministry of the saints. . 1Cor 16:15

ADDITION—*increase*

[*also* ADDITIONS]
certain *a* made..thin work 1Kin 7:29
at the side of every *a* 1Kin 7:30
and *a* round about 1Kin 7:36

ADDITIONS TO THE CHURCH

Manner and number of:
"The Lord added" . . . . . . Acts 2:47
"Believers..added to the Lord" . . . . Acts 5:14
"Disciples..multiplied" . . . Acts 6:1
"A great company of priests" . . . . Acts 6:7
"Churches..were multiplied" . . . . Acts 9:31
"A great number believed" . . . . Acts 11:21
"Much people added" . . . Acts 11:24
"Churches..increased in number" . . . . Acts 16:5

By means of:
Word preached . . . . Acts 2:14-41
The Spirit's convicting power . . . . John 16:7-11
The Gospel as God's power . . . . Rom 1:16
Responding faith . . . . Acts 14:1

ADDON (ăd'ŏn)
Tel-haresha, Cherub, *A* . . . . Neh 7:61

ADDRESS—*a public message*

In Old Testament:
Moses' expository . . . . Deut 1:1—4:40
Moses' second . . . . Deut 4:44—26:19
Moses' third . . . . Deut 27:1—30:20
Moses' fourth . . . . Deut 32:1-43
Moses' final . . . . Deut 33:1-29
Joshua's exhortation . . . . . Josh 23:2-16
Joshua's farewell . . . . Josh 24:1-25
Solomon's to God 1Kin 3:6-9
Ezra's expository . . . . Neh 8:1-8
Jeremiah's Temple sermon . . . . Jer 7:1—10:25

Of Paul:
First . . . . Acts 9:20-22
Second . . . . Acts 13:16-41
To Peter . . . . Gal 2:14-21
To women . . . . Acts 16:13
With Silas . . . . Acts 16:29-32
At Athens . . . . Acts 17:22-31
At Troas . . . . Acts 20:6, 7
To elders . . . . Acts 20:17-35
To the crowd . . . . Acts 22:1-21
Before Felix . . . . Acts 24:10-21
Before Agrippa . . . . Acts 26:1-29
On the ship . . . . Acts 27:21-26
Final recorded . . . . Acts 28:25-28

Of Peter:
In upper room . . . . Acts 1:13-22
Pentecost . . . . Acts 2:14-40
At Temple . . . . Acts 3:12-26
In house of Cornelius . . . . Acts 10:34-43
At Jerusalem council . . . . Acts 15:7-11

Of Others:
Stephen . . . . Acts 7:2-60
Herod . . . . Acts 12:21, 22
James . . . . Acts 15:13-21
Tertullus . . . . Acts 24:1-8

ADER (ā'dĕr)—*"a flock"—a son of Beriah*
Zebadiah, and Arad, and *A* . . . 1Chr 8:15

ADIEL (ā'dĭ-ĕl)—*"ornament of God"*
1. A Simeonite prince 1Chr 4:24, 36
2. Aaronite priest 1Chr 9:12, 13
3. Father of Azmaveth 1Chr 27:25

ADIN (ā'dĭn)—*"ornament"*
1. A man whose descendants return with Zerubbabel . . . . . . Ezra 2:2, 15
2. A man whose descendants return with Ezra . . . . Ezra 8:1, 6
3. Sealer of the covenant . . . Neh 10:1, 16

The children of *A* six . . . . Neh 7:20

ADINA (ăd'ĭ-nä)—*"ornament"*
A Reubenite captain under David 1Chr 11:42

ADINO (ăd'ĭ-nō)—*"ornament"*
A mighty man under David 2Sam 23:8
Compare parallel passage in 1Chr 11:11

ADITHAIM (ăd-ĭ-thā'ŭm)—*"double crossing; double ornaments"*
A city of Judah . . . . Josh 15:21, 36

ADJURATION—*placing under oath*
Joshua's, to Jericho . . . . . . Josh 6:26
Saul's, to those breaking a fast 1Sam 14:24-28
Ahab's, to the prophet Micaiah 1Kin 22:16
Caiaphas', by God . . . . Matt 26:63
Demon's, by God . . . . Mark 5:7
Exorcists', by Jesus . . . . . . Acts 19:13
Paul's charge, by the Lord 1Thess 5:27

ADLAI (ăd'lā-ī)—*"lax; weary"*
Father of Shaphat 1Chr 27:29

ADMAH (ăd'mä)—*"redness; red earth"*
A city near Sodom . . . . . . Gen 10:19
Joins other cities against Chedorlaomer . . . . Gen 14:1-4, 8
Destroyed with Sodom and Gomorrah . . . . Gen 19:24-28

A and Zeboim, which the . . . . . Deut 29:23
shall I make thee as *A*? . . . . Hos 11:8

ADMATHA (ăd'mä-thä)—*"God-given"*
One of Ahasuerus' chamberlains . . . . Esth 1:14, 15

ADMINISTER—*to serve*

Applied to:
Judgment 1Kin 3:28
Vengeance . . . . Jer 21:12
Justice 2Sam 8:15

[*also* ADMINISTERED]
abundance which is *a* by 2Cor 8:20

ADMINISTRATION—*the management or disposition of affairs*
Of gifts to Jerusalem saints 2Cor 8:19, 20
Of spiritual gifts 1Cor 12:5; 2Cor 9:12
Of government matters . . Rom 13:3-5
Of new covenant 2Cor 3:6

ADMIRATION—*high esteem*
Reserved for saints 2Thess 1:10
Flattering, shown by false teachers . . . . Jude 16
Astounding manifested by John . . . . Rev 17:6, 7

ADMONITION—*wise words spoken against wrong or foolish actions*

Performed by:
God . . . . Heb 8:5
Earthly fathers . . . . Eph 6:4
Leaders 1Thess 5:12
Christians . . . . Rom 15:14

Directed against:
A remnant . . . . Jer 42:19
Elders . . . . Acts 20:28-35
Those who will not work . . 2Thess 3:10, 15
Heretics . . . . Titus 3:10

Sources of in:
Scriptures 1Cor 10:11
Wise words . . . . Eccl 12:11, 12
Spiritual knowledge . . . . . . Col 3:16

[*also* ADMONISH, ADMONISHED, ADMONISHING]
who will no more be *a* . . . . Eccl 4:13
by these, my son, be *a* . . . . Eccl 12:12
certainly that I have *a* . . . . Jer 42:19

already past, Paul *a* them .....Acts 27:9
able also to *a* one another ....Rom 15:14
they are written for our *a* 1Cor 10:11
nurture and *a* of the Lord .....Eph 6:4
a one another in psalms ....Col 3:16
over you in the Lord and *a* ...1Thess5:12
but *a* him as a brother 2Thess3:15
after the first and second *a* ....Titus 3:10
as Moses was *a* of God ....Heb 8:5

ADNA (ăd'nä)—*"pleasure"*
1. Jew who divorced his foreign wife ....Ezra 10:18-30
2. Postexilic priest ....Neh 12:12-15

ADNAH (ăd'nä)—*"pleasure"*
1. Captain of Saul 1Chr 12:20
2. Chief Captain of Jehoshaphat 2Chr 17:14

ADO—*unnecessary bother over trivial things*
Not to make ....Mark 5:39

ADONAI (ä-dō'nī)—"Lord"
The Hebrew name for God (translated "Lord") expressing lordship (found in the following five compound words)

ADONI-BEZEK (ä-dō'nī-bē'zĕk)—*"lord of lightning (Bezek)"*
A king of Bezek ....Judg 1:3-7

ADONIJAH (ăd-ō-nī'jä)—*"Jehovah is my lord"*
1. David's fourth son 2Sam 3:2, 4
   Attempts to usurp throne.1Kin 1:5-53
   Desires Abishag as wife .1Kin 2:13-18
   Executed by Solomon ...1Kin 2:19-25
2. A teacher 2Chr 17:8, 9
3. A Jew who signed the document ....Neh 9:38; 10:16
   Probably the same as Adonikam in ....Ezra 2:13

A the son of Haggith 1Kin 1:5
they following *A* helped 1Kin 1:7
David, were not with *A* 1Kin 1:8
A slew sheep and oxen 1Kin 1:9
Hast thou not heard that *A* 1Kin 1:11
why then doth *A* reign? 1Kin 1:13
now, behold *A* reigneth 1Kin 1:18
hast thou said *A* shall 1Kin 1:24
and say, God save king *A* 1Kin 1:25
And *A* and all the guests 1Kin 1:41
A said unto him, Come in 1Kin 1:42
Jonathan answered..to *A* 1Kin 1:43
guests that were with *A* 1Kin 1:49
A feared because..Solomon 1Kin 1:50
Behold, *A* feareth..Solomon ...1Kin 1:51
And *A* the son of Haggith 1Kin 2:13
to speak unto him for *A* 1Kin 2:19
Shunammite be given to *A* 1Kin 2:21
Abishag the Shunammite for *A*.1Kin 2:22
if *A* have not spoken this 1Kin 2:23
A shall be put to death 1Kin 2:24
Joab had turned after *A* 1Kin 2:28
fourth, *A*..son of Haggith 1Chr 3:2

ADONIKAM (ăd-ō-nī'kăm)—*"my lord has risen"*
Descendants of, return from exile ....Ezra 2:13

And of the last sons of *A* .....Ezra 8:13
The children of *A*, six ....Neh 7:18

ADONIRAM, ADORAM (ăd-ō-nī'răm, ăd-ō'răm)—*"my lord is exalted"*
A son of Abda 1Kin 4:6
Official under David, Solomon, and Rehoboam...........{2Sam 20:24; 1Kin 5:14; 1Kin 12:18}
Stoned by angry Israelites.1Kin 12:18
Called Hadoram 2Chr 10:18

ADONI-ZEDEK (ä-dō'nī-zē'dĕk)—*"lord of justice (righteousness)"*
An Amorite king of Jerusalem ....Josh 10:1-5
Defeated and slain by Joshua ....Josh 10:6-27

when *A* king of Jerusalem .....Josh 10:1
A king of Jerusalem sent ......Josh 10:3

ADOPTION—*the legal act of taking by choice into a new relationship*
Used naturally of:
Eliezer under Abraham ..Gen 15:2-4
Joseph's sons under Jacob.Gen 48:5, 14, 16
Moses under Pharaoh's daughter ....{Ex 2:10; Acts 7:21}
Esther under Mordecai ..Esth 2:7
Used spiritually of Israel as:
Elected by God ....Deut 14:1, 2; Rom 11:1-32
Blessed by God ....Rom 9:4
Realized in history ......Ex 4:22, 23
Used spiritually of the Gentiles as:
Predicted in the prophets .Is 65:1
Confirmed by faith ......Rom 10:20
Realized in the new covenant............{Eph 2:12; Eph 3:1-6}
The time of:
Past, predestined to .....Rom 8:29
Present, regarded as sons .John 1:12, 13; John 3:1-11
Future, glorified as sons. .Rom 8:19, 23; 1John 3:2
The source of:
By God's grace..........Rom 4:16, 17
By faith ....Gal 3:7, 26
Through Christ ....Gal 4:4, 5
Assurances of, by:
Spirit's witness ....Rom 8:16
Spirit's leading ....Rom 8:14
"Abba, Father" ....Rom 8:15
Changed life 1John 3:9-17
Father's chastening ......Prov 3:11, 12; Heb 12:5-11
The blessings of:
A new nature 2Cor 5:17
A new name ....Is 62:2, 12; Rev 3:12
Access to God ....Eph 2:18
Fatherly love 1John 3:1
Help in prayer ....Matt 6:5-15
Spiritual unity ....John 17:11, 21; Eph 2:18-22
A glorious inheritance ...John 14:1-3; Rom 8:17, 18

the *a* of children by Jesus .....Eph 1:5

ADORAIM (ăd-ō-rā'ĭm)—*"two mounds"*
A city fortified by Rehoboam 2Chr 11:5, 9

ADORAM (ä-dō'răm)—*"the Lord is exalted"*
An official over forced labor 2Sam 20:24; 1Kin 12:18

See **Adoniram**

ADORATION—*reverental praise and admiration*
Rendered falsely to:
Idols ....Is 44:15, 17, 19
An image ....Dan 3:5-7
Heavenly hosts 2Kin 17:16
Satan ....Luke 4:8
Men ....Acts 10:25, 26
Angels ....Col 2:18, 23
Rendered properly to God:
Illustrated..............Is 6:1-5
Taught ....Ps 95—100
Proclaimed..............Rev 4:8-11
Rendered properly to Christ as God by:
Wise men...............Matt 2:1, 11
Leper ....Matt 8:2
Ruler...................Matt 9:18
Disciples................Matt 14:22, 33
Woman..................Matt 15:25
Mother ....Matt 20:20
Blind man ....John 9:1, 38
Every creature ....Phil 2:10, 11
See **Worship**

ADORNMENT—*a decoration*
Used literally of:
A ruler ....Gen 41:42-44
A harlot ....Gen 38:14, 15; Rev 17:3, 4
A woman ....Is 3:16-24; 1Tim 2:9
A building ....Luke 21:5
A bride.................Rev 21:2
Used spiritually of:
God....................Ps 104:1, 2
Messiah ....Ps 45:7, 8
Believer as justified......Is 61:10
Believer as sanctified ....Titus 2:10
Israel restored...........Jer 31:4
Saintly woman 1Tim 2:9
Saints in glory...........Rev 19:14
Guidelines for:
In modesty.............1Tim 2:9
Not external 1Pet 3:3-5

ADRAMMELECH (ä-drăm'ĕ-lĕk)—*"honor of the King; Adar is king"*
1. An Assyrian god worshiped by the Samarians 2Kin 17:31
2. Killed Sennacherib ......2Kin 19:36, 37; Is 37:38

ADRAMYTTIUM (ăd-rä-mĭt'ĭ-ŭm)—*a seaport in the northwestern part of the Roman province of Asia*
Travels of Paul ....Acts 27:2-6

ADRIATIC SEA
A part of the central Mediterranean Sea named after Adria, a city of Italy ....Acts 27:27

ADRIEL (ā'drĭ-ĕl)—*"honor of God; my help is God"*
Marries Saul's eldest daughter..............1Sam 18:19
Sons of, slain to atone Saul's crime...........2Sam 21:8, 9

ADULLAM (ä-dŭl'ăm)—*"refuge"*
A town of Canaan.......Gen 38:1, 12, 20
Conquered by Joshua ....Josh 12:7, 15
Assigned to Judah ....Josh 15:20, 35
Fortified by Rehoboam ..2Chr 11:5-7
Symbol of Israel's glory ..Mic 1:15
Reoccupied ....Neh 11:30
David seeks refuge in caves of 1Sam 22:1, 2
Exploits of mighty men while there 2Sam 23:13-17

David, into the cave of *A* 1Chr 11:15

ADULLAMITE—*a citizen of Adulla*
Judah's friend ....Gen 38:1, 12, 20

ADULTERER—*a man who commits adultery*
Punishment of...........Lev 20:10
Waits for the twilight ....Job 24:15
Offspring of.............Is 57:3
Land is full of...........Jer 23:10
Shall not inherit the kingdom of God 1Cor 6:9
God will judge ....Heb 13:4

[*also* ADULTERERS]
hast been partaker with *a* .....Ps 50:18
they be all *a* ....Jer 9:2
They are all *a* ....Hos 7:4
sorcerers..against the *a*........Mal 3:5
extortioners, unjust *a* ....Luke 18:11
Ye *a* and adulteresses.........James 4:4

ADULTERESS—*a woman who commits adultery*

Sin of:
Punished by death .... Lev 20:10
Ensnares the simple ..... Prov 7:6-23
Brings a man to poverty. . Prov 6:26
Leads to death .... Prov 2:16-19
Increases transgressors . . . Prov 23:27, 28
Defined by Christ .... Matt 5:32
Forgiven by Christ .... John 8:1-11

Examples of:
Tamar .... Gen 38:13-24
Potiphar's wife (attempted) .... Gen 39:7-20
Midianite women .... Num 25:6-8
Rahab .... Josh 2:1
Bath-sheba 2Sam 11:4, 5
Herodias .... Matt 14:3, 4
Unnamed woman .... John 8:1-11
See HARLOT

[*also* ADULTERESSES]
after the manner of *a* .... Ezek 23:45
because they are *a* .... Ezek 23:45
beloved of her friend..an *a* .... Hos 3:1
she shall be called an *a* .... Rom 7:3
so that she is no *a* .... Rom 7:3

ADULTERY—*voluntary sexual intercourse with someone other than one's husband or wife*

Defined:
In God's Law .... Ex 20:14
By Christ .... Matt 5:28, 32
By Paul .... Rom 7:3
In mental attitude .... Matt 5:28
As a work of the flesh . . . Gal 5:19

Sin of:
Breaks God's Law .... Deut 5:18
Punishable by death ..... Lev 20:10-12
Brings death .... Prov 2:18, 19
Makes one poor .... Prov 29:3
Produces moral insensibility .... Prov 30:20; 2Cor 12:21
Corrupts a land .... Hos 4:1, 2, 11
Justifies divorce .... Matt 19:7-9
Excludes from Christian fellowship 1Cor 5:1-13
Excludes from God's kingdom 1Cor 6:9, 10
Merits God's judgments . . Heb 13:4
Ends in hell (Sheol) ..... Prov 7:27
Rev 21:8

Forgiveness of, by:
Man .... Judg 19:1-4
Christ .... John 8:10, 11
Repentance 2Sam 12:7-14
Regeneration 1Cor 6:9-11

Examples of:
Lot .... Gen 19:31-38
Shechem .... Gen 34:2
Judah .... Gen 38:1-24
Eli's sons 1Sam 2:22
David 2Sam 11:1-5
Amnon 2Sam 13:1-20
The Samaritan woman . . John 4:17, 18

[*also* ADULTERIES, ADULTEROUS]
Thou shalt not commit *a* ...... Ex 20:14
committeth *a* with a .... Prov 6:32
backsliding Israel..*a* .... Jer 3:8
and committed *a* with .... Jer 3:9
they then committed *a* .... Jer 5:7
ye steal, murder,..commit *a* . . . Jer 7:9
I have seen thine *a* .... Jer 13:27
they commit *a* and walk ...... Jer 23:14
in Israel..committed *a* .... Jer 29:23
they have committed *a* .... Ezek 23:37
idols have they committed *a* . . . Ezek 23:37
her that was old in *a* .... Ezek 23:43
out of her sight, and her *a* .... Hos 2:2
your spouses shall commit *a* . . . Hos 4:13
when they commit *a* .... Hos 4:14
Thou shalt not commit *a* ...... Matt 5:27
an evil and *a* generation ...... Matt 12:39
murders, *a*, fornications .... Matt 15:19
A wicked and *a* generation .... Matt 16:4
Thou shalt not commit *a* ...... Matt 19:18
thoughts, *a*, fornications ...... Mark 7:21
a and sinful generation .... Mark 8:38
committeth *a* against her ...... Mark 10:11
another, she committeth *a* ..... Mark 10:12
Do not commit *a* .... Mark 10:19
another, committeth *a* .... Luke 16:18
husband committeth *a* .... Luke 16:18
Do not commit *a*, Do not ..... Luke 18:20
should not commit *a* .... Rom 2:22
dost thou commit *a*? .... Rom 2:22
Thou shalt not commit *a* ...... Rom 13:9
Do not commit *a*, said also .... James 2:11
Now if thou commit no *a* ..... James 2:11
Having eyes full of *a* 2Pet 2:14

ADULTERY, SPIRITUAL
Seen in Israel's idolatry . . Judg 2:11, 17
Described graphically .... Ezek 16
Symbolized in Hosea's marriage .... Hos 1:1-3
Symbolized in final apostasy .... Rev 17:1-5
Figurative of friendship with the world .... James 4:4
Figurative of false teaching .... Rev 2:14, 15, 20-22

ADUMMIM (ä-dŭm'ĭm)—*"bloody things; red spots"*
A hill between Jerusalem and Jericho .... Josh 15:5, 7, 8
The probable site of Good Samaritan parable in .... Luke 10:30-37

before the going up to *A* ...... Josh 15:7
against the going up of *A* ..... Josh 18:17

ADVANCEMENT—*progression*

Promotion to a higher office:
Moses and Aaron, by the Lord 1Sam 12:6
Promised to Balaam ..... Num 22:16, 17
Joseph, by true interpretation .... Gen 41:38-46
Levites, for loyalty ...... Ex 32:26-28
Phinehas, by decisive action .... Num 25:7-13
Haman, by intrigue ...... Esth 3:1, 2
Mordecai, by ability ..... Esth 10:2
Daniel, by fidelity .... Dan 2:48
Deacons, by faithfulness. . 1Tim 3:10, 13

Conditions of, seen in:
Humility .... Matt 18:4
Faithfulness .... Matt 25:14-30
Skilled in work .... Prov 22:29
Luke 22:24-30

Hindrances to, occasioned by:
Self-glory .... Is 14:12-15
1Cor 4:7-9
Pride .... Ezek 28:11-19
1Pet 5:5, 6

[*also* ADVANCED]
a him, and set his seat .... Esth 3:1
he had *a* him above the .... Esth 5:11
whereunto the king *a* him ..... Esth 10:2

ADVANTAGE—*superior circumstance or ability*

In God's kingdom, none by:
Birth .... Matt 3:8, 9
Race .... Gal 2:14-16
Position .... John 3:1-6
Works .... Matt 5:20
Wealth .... Luke 9:25

In God's kingdom, some by:
Industry 1Cor 15:10
Faithfulness .... Matt 25:14-30
Kindred spirit .... Phil 2:19-23
Works 1Cor 3:11-15
Dedication .... Rev 14:1-5

[*also* ADVANTAGETH]
thou saidst, What *a* will it ..... Job 35:3
What *a* then hath the Jew? .... Rom 3:1
what *a* it me, if the dead 1Cor 15:32
Lest Satan should get an *a* 2Cor 2:11
admiration because of *a* .... Jude 16

ADVENT OF CHRIST, THE FIRST

Announced in the Old Testament by:
Moses .... Deut 18:18, 19
Samuel .... Acts 3:24
David .... Ps 40:6-8
Heb 10:5-8
Prophets .... Luke 24:26, 27

Prophecies fulfilled by his:
Birth .... Is 7:14
Matt 1:23
Forerunner .... Mal 3:1, 2
Matt 3:1-3
Incarnation .... Is 9:6
Time of arrival .... Dan 9:24
Mark 1:15
Rejection .... Is 53:1-4
Rom 10:16-21
Crucifixion .... Ps 2:1, 2
Acts 4:24-28
Atonement .... Is 53:1-12
1Pet 1:18-21
Resurrection .... Ps 16:8-11
Acts 2:25-31
Priesthood .... Ps 110:4, 5
Heb 5:5, 6

His first coming:
Introduces Gospel age . . . Acts 3:24
Consummates new covenant .... Jer 31:31-34; Heb 8:6-13
Fulfills prophecy .... Luke 24:44, 45
Nullifies the ceremonial system .... Heb 9
Brings Gentiles in .... Acts 15:13-18

ADVENT OF CHRIST, THE SECOND—*See* SECOND COMING OF CHRIST

ADVENTS OF CHRIST, COMPARED

First Advent:
Prophesied .... Deut 18:18, 19
Is 7:14
Came as man .... Phil 2:5-7
Announced .... Luke 2:10-14
Time predicted .... Dan 9:25
To save the lost .... Matt 18:11
Subject to government . . . Matt 17:24-27

Second Advent:
Prophesied .... John 14:1-3
1Thess 4:16
Come as God 1Thess 4:16
As a thief 1Thess 5:2
At a time unknown ...... Matt 24:36
To judge the lost .... Matt 25:32-36
Source of government .... Rev 20:4-6
Rev 22:3-5

ADVENTURE—*a dangerous or exciting experience*

[*also* ADVENTURED]
would not *a* to set the .... Deut 28:56
fought for you, and *a* his ...... Judg 9:17
not *a* himself into the .... Acts 19:31

ADVERSARY—*one who actively opposes*

Descriptive of:
Satan 1Pet 5:8
Gospel's enemies 1Cor 16:9
Israel's enemies .... Josh 5:13
An enemy .... Esth 7:6
A rival 1Sam 1:6
God's agent 1Kin 11:14, 23
God's angel .... Num 22:22

Believer's attitude toward:
Pray for .... Ps 71:13
Use God's weapons against .... Luke 21:15
Not to be terrified by .... Phil 1:28
Not to give occasion to . . 1Tim 5:14
Remember God's judgment on .... Heb 10:27

[*also* ADVERSARIES]
a unto thine adversaries ....Ex 23:22
a..behave themselves ....Deut 32:27
render vengeance to his *a* .....Deut 32:43
a..Lord shall be broken to 1Sam 2:10
lest in the battle he be..*a* 1Sam 29:4
should this day be *a* unto 2Sam 19:22
is neither *a*..evil occurrent.....1Kin 5:4
he was an *a* to Israel all 1Kin 11:25
a of Judah and Benjamin .....Ezra 4:1
And our *a* said, They shall ....Neh 4:11
The *a* and enemy is this.......Esth 7:6
mine *a* had written a book ....Job 31:35
evil for good are mine *a* ......Ps 38:20
mine *a* are all before thee .....Ps 69:19
how long shall the *a* ....Ps 74:10
my hand against their *a* ....Ps 81:14
set the right hand of his *a* .....Ps 89:42
For my love they are my *a* ....Ps 109:4
the reward of mine *a* ....Ps 109:20
Let mine *a* be clothed ....Ps 109:29
I will ease me of mine *a* ......Is 1:24
shall set up the *a* of Rezin ....Is 9:11
and the *a* of Judah shall ......Is 11:13
who is mine *a*? ....Is 50:8
he will repay fury to his *a* .....Is 59:18
our *a* have trodden down .....Is 63:18
thy name known to thine *a* ....Is 64:2
devoured; and all thine *a* .....Jer 30:16
avenge him of his *a* ....Jer 46:10
Her *a* are the chief ....Lam 1:5
the *a* saw her, and did ....Lam 1:7
The *a* hath spread out his .....Lam 1:10
his *a*..be round about him .....Lam 1:17
with his right hand as an *a* ....Lam 2:4
set up the horn of thine *a* .....Lam 2:17
have believed that the *a* ....Lam 4:12
An *a* there shall be even ......Amos 3:11
lifted up upon thine *a*.........Mic 5:9
Lord..vengeance on his *a* .....Nah 1:2
Agree.thine *a* quickly ....Matt 5:25
at any time the *a* deliver ......Matt 5:25
thine *a* to the magistrate ......Luke 12:58
Avenge me of mine *a*.........Luke 18:3

ADVERSITY—*unfavorable circumstances*

Caused by:
Man's sin ....Gen 3:16, 17
Disobedience to God's Law ....Lev 26:14-20

Purposes of, to:
Punish for sin 2Sam 12:9-12
Humble us 2Chr 33:12
Lead us to God's Word ..Deut 8:2, 3
Chasten and correct .....Heb 12:5-11
Test our faith 1Pet 1:5-8
Give us final rest ....Ps 94:12, 13

Reactions to:
Rebellious ....Ex 14:4-8; Job 2:9
Distrustful ....Ex 6:8, 9
Complaining ....Ruth 1:20, 21
Questioning ....Jer 20:7-9
Fainting ....Prov 24:10
Arrogant ....Ps 10:6
Hopeful ....Lam 3:31-40
Submissive ....Job 5:17-22
Joyful ....James 1:2-4

God's relation to, He:
Troubles nations with 2Chr 15:5, 6
Knows the soul in ....Ps 31:7
Saves out of 1Sam 10:19
Redeems out of 2Sam 4:9

Helps under:
By prayer ....Jon 2:1-7
By understanding God's purpose ....Lam 3:31-39; Rom 5:3

[*also* ADVERSITIES]
in mine *a* they rejoiced ....Ps 35:15
a brother is born for *a* ....Prov 17:17
in the day of *a* consider ....Eccl 7:14
Lord give you the bread of *a* ..Is 30:20
and them which suffer *a* ......Heb 13:3

ADVERTISE—*to make publicly known*
Messiah's advent ....Num 24:14-19
A piece of property .....Ruth 4:4

ADVICE—*recommendation about a decision or conduct*

Sought by:
A king ....Esth 1:13-15
Another ruler ....Acts 25:13-27
A usurper 2Sam 16:20-23
Five men 2Kin 22:12-20

Sought from:
The ephod 1Sam 23:9-12
A prophet ....Jer 42:1-6
A dead prophet 1Sam 28:7-20
A council ....Acts 15:1-22
A grieving husband ......Judg 20:4-7

Kinds of:
Helpful ....Ex 18:12-25
Rejected 1Kin 12:6-8
Timely 1Sam 25:32-34
Good 2Kin 5:13, 14
God-inspired 2Sam 17:6-14
Foolish ....Job 2:9
Humiliating ....Esth 6:6-11
Fatal ....Esth 5:14
Ominous ....Matt 27:19
Accepted ....Acts 5:34-41

Sought from:
Congregation of Israel ...Judg 20:7

[*also* ADVISE, ADVISED, ADVISEMENT]
consider of it, take *a* ....Judg 19:30
give here your *a* and..........Judg 20:7
that our *a* should not be 2Sam 19:43
a and see what answer I 2Sam 24:13
Philistines upon *a* sent 1Chr 12:19
a thyself what word I 1Chr 21:12
What *a* give ye that we 2Chr 10:9
answered them after the *a*.....2Chr 10:14
Amaziah king of Judah..*a* 2Chr 25:17
with the well *a* is wisdom .....Prov 13:10
and with good *a* make ....Prov 20:18
the more part *a* to depart .....Acts 27:12
herein I give my *a*: for........2Cor 8:10

ADVOCATE, CHRIST OUR

His interest in believers, by right of:
Election ....John 15:16
Redemption ....Rev 1:5
Regeneration ....Col 1:27
Imputed righteousness ...2Cor 5:21; Phil 3:9

His defense of believers by:
Prayer ....Luke 22:31-34
Protection ....Heb 13:6
Provision ....Ps 23:1; John 10:28
Perseverance 2Tim 4:17, 18

His blessings upon believers:
Another Comforter ......John 14:16, 17
New commandment......John 13:34, 35
New nature 2Cor 5:17
New name ....Rev 2:17
New life ....John 4:14
New relationship ....John 15:15

Our duties prescribed by Him:
Our mission—world evangelization ....Matt 28:16-20
Our means—the Holy Spirit ....Acts 1:8
Our might—the Gospel ..Rom 1:16
Our motivation—the love of Christ 2Cor 5:14, 15

a with the Father, Jesus.......1John 2:1

AENEAS (ĕ-nē'ăs)—*"praise"*
A paralytic healed by Peter ....Acts 9:32-35

AENON (ē'nŏn)—*"fountains"*
A place near Salim where John the Baptist baptized ....John 3:22, 23

AFAR—*at a long distance*

Applied physically to:
Distance ....Gen 22:4
A journey ....Num 9:10
Sound of joy ....Ezra 3:13
Ostracism ....Luke 17:12

Applied spiritually to:
God's knowledge ....Ps 139:2
Unworthiness ....Luke 18:13
Eternal separation ....Luke 16:23
Backsliding ....Luke 22:54
Gentiles ....Acts 2:39
God's promises ....Heb 11:13
Consignment to doom ...Rev 17:10-17

Abraham saw the place *a* .....Gen 22:4
when they saw him *a* off ......Gen 37:18
his sister stood *a* off ....Ex 2:4
the people stood *a* off and ....Ex 20:21
I worship ye *a* off ....Ex 24:1
it without the camp *a* off......Ex 33:7
stood on the top of a hill *a*....1Sam 26:13
went, and stood to view *a* 2Kin 2:7
Jerusalem was heard..*a* off ....Neh 12:43
lifted up their eyes *a*..........Job 2:12
fetch my knowledge from *a* ...Job 36:3
man may behold it *a* off ......Job 36:25
he smelleth the battle *a* ....Job 39:25
her eyes behold *a* off ....Job 39:29
Why standest thou *a* off ......Ps 10:1
my kinsmen stand *a* off ....Ps 38:11
them that are *a* off upon ......Ps 65:5
the proud he knoweth *a* ....Ps 138:6
bringeth her food from *a*......Prov 31:14
feet shall carry her *a* off ......Is 23:7
justice standeth *a* off ....Is 59:14
isles *a* off that have not ....Is 66:19
saith the Lord..a God *a* ....Jer 23:23
I will save thee from *a*........Jer 30:10
declare it in the isles *a*........Jer 31:10
I will save thee from *a*........Jer 46:27
remember the Lord *a* off.......Jer 51:50
rebuke strong nations *a* ....Mic 4:3
Peter followed him *a* off ......Matt 26:58
women were..beholding *a* .....Matt 27:55
when he saw Jesus *a* off ......Mark 5:6
seeing a fig tree *a* off ....Mark 11:13
Peter followed him *a* off ......Mark 14:54
women looking on *a* off.......Mark 15:40
stood *a* off beholding ....Luke 23:49
is blind, and cannot see *a* 2Pet 1:9
Standing *a* off for the fear ....Rev 18:10
stand *a* off for the fear........Rev 18:15
as trade by sea, stood *a* ....Rev 18:17

AFFABILITY—*a state of being at ease with others*

Manifested in:
Cordiality ....Gen 18:1-8
Compassion ....Luke 10:33-37
Generosity ....Phil 4:10, 14-18
Unantagonizing speech ...1Sam 25:23-31

Examples of:
Jonathan 1Sam 18:1-4
Titus 2Cor 8:16-18
Timothy ....Phil 2:17-20
Gaius 3John 1-6
Demetrius 3John 12

AFFAIRS—*matters of business or concern*
pertaining to God and *a* 1Chr 26:32
he will guide his *a* ....Ps 112:5
the *a* of the province of.......Dan 2:49
thou hast set over the *a*.......Dan 3:12
also may know my *a*..........Eph 6:21
ye might know our *a* ....Eph 6:22
I may hear of your *a*, that ....Phil 1:27
entangleth himself..*a* of 2Tim 2:4

AFFECT—*an influence on emotions or actions*

[*also* AFFECTED, AFFECTETH]
Mine eye *a* mine heart ....Lam 3:51
made their minds evil *a* ....Acts 14:2
They zealously *a* you, but .....Gal 4:17
that ye might *a* them ....Gal 4:17
be zealously *a* always ....Gal 4:18

AFFECTATIONS—*an attitude or behavior not natural to one's person*
Parade of egotism ....Esth 6:6-9
Boast of the power ......Dan 4:29, 30
Sign of hypocrisy ....Matt 6:1,2,16
Outbreak of false teachers 2Pet 2:18, 19
Sign of antichrist 2Thess 2:4, 9
Proof of spiritual decay ..1Cor 4:6-8

AFFECTION—*inner feelings or emotions*
Kinds of:
Natural ....Rom 1:31
Paternal ....Luke 15:20
Maternal...............1Kin 3:16-27
Fraternal ....Gen 43:30-34
Filial ....Gen 49:29,30
National ....Ps 137:1-6
Racial ....Rom 9:1-3
For wife ....Eph 5:25-33
For husband ....Titus 2:4
Christian...............Rom 12:10
Heavenly ....Col 3:1, 2
Good, characteristics of:
Loyal, intense ....Ruth 1:14-18
Memorable 2Sam 1:17-27
Natural, normal 2Sam 13:37-39
Tested, tried ....Gen 22:1-19
Emotional ....John 11:33-36
Grateful ....Luke 7:36-50
Joyous.................Ps 126:1-6
Christ-centered ....Matt 10:37-42
Evil, characteristics of:
Unnatural..............Rom 1:18-32
Pretended..............Matt 26:47-49
Abnormal..............2Tim 3:3
Fleshly ....Rom 13:13, 14
Worldly 2Tim 4:10
Defiling, degrading 2Pet 2:10-12
Agonizing in hell ....Luke 16:23-28

[*also* AFFECTIONATELY, AFFECTIONED, AFFECTIONS]
because I have set my *a*.......1Chr 29:3
crucified..flesh with..*a* ....Gal 5:24
uncleanness, inordinate *a*......Col 3:5
So being *a* desirous of you 1Thess 2:8

AFFINITY—*having common interests*
Solomon..*a* with Pharaoh 1Kin 3:1
and joined *a* with Ahab 2Chr 18:1
and join in *a* with the.........Ezra 9:14

AFFIRM—*to state positively*

[*also* AFFIRMED]
another confidently *a* ....Luke 22:59
she constantly *a* that it........Acts 12:15
whom Paul *a* to be alive ......Acts 25:19
as some *a* that we say ....Rom 3:8
say, nor whereof they *a* 1Tim 1:7
I will..thou *a* constantly ....Titus 3:8

AFFLICTIONS—*hardships and trials*
Visited upon:
Israel in Egypt ....Gen 15:13
Samson by Philistines ....Judg 16:5,6,19
David by God...........Ps 88:7
Judah by God...........Lam 3:33
Israel by the world ......Ps 129:1, 2
The just by the wicked...Amos 5:12
Heb 11:37
Christians by the world ..2Cor 1:6
Design of, to:
Show God's mercy ......Is 63:9
Make us seek God ......Hos 5:15
Bring us back to God....Ps 119:67
Humble us..............2Chr 33:12
Test us ....Is 48:10
In the Christian's life:
A means of testing ......Mark 4:17
A part of life ....Matt 24:9
To be endured 2Tim 4:5
Part of Gospel 1Thess 1:6
Must not be disturbed by .1Thess 3:3
Commendable examples of 2Tim 3:11
Momentary 2Cor 4:17
Sometimes intense 2Cor 1:8-10
Must be shared..........Phil 4:14
Cannot separate from God ....Rom 8:35-39
Deliverance from, promised ....Ps 34:19
Need prayer in ....James 5:13
Terminated at Christ's return 2Thess 1:4-7
See also TRIALS

[*also* AFFLICT, AFFLICTED, AFFLICTEST, AFFLICTION]
the Lord hath heard thy *a*.....Gen 16:11
the Lord..looked upon my *a*...Gen 29:32
God hath seen mine *a* ....Gen 31:42
shalt *a* my daughters ....Gen 31:50
over them taskmasters to *a*....Exod 1:11
But the more they *a* them.....Exod 1:12
seen the *a* of my people ......Exod 3:7
out of the *a* of Egypt ....Exod 3:17
had looked upon their *a* ......Exod 4:31
Ye shall not *a* any widow .....Exod 22:22
thou *a* them in any wise ......Exod 22:23
ye shall *a* your souls ....Lev 16:29
you, and ye shall *a* your ......Lev 16:31
ye shall *a* your souls and ......Lev 23:27
shall not be *a* in that same ....Lev 23:29
a your souls; in the ninth .....Lev 23:32
Wherefore hast thou *a* thy ....Num 11:11
a Asshur and shall *a* Eber.....Num 24:24
and ye shall *a* your souls ......Num 29:7
binding oath to *a* the soul .....Num 30:13
the bread of *a*...............Deut 16:3
evil entreated us and *a*........Deut 26:6
and looked on our *a* ....Deut 26:7
the Almighty hath *a* me?......Ruth 1:21
the *a* of thine handmaid 1Sam 1:11
children of wickedness *a* 2Sam 7:10
Lord will look on mine *a* 2Sam 16:12
a people thou wilt save 2Sam 22:28
thou hast been *a* in all 1Kin 2:26
wherein my father was *a* 1Kin 2:26
their sin, when thou *a* 1Kin 8:35
I will..*a* the seed of David 1Kin 11:39
feed him with bread of *a*......1Kin 22:27
and with water of *a*...........1Kin 22:27
Lord saw the *a* of Israel 2Kin 14:26
seed of Israel, and *a* them 2Kin 17:20
when thou dost *a* them 2Chr 6:26
feed him with bread of *a*......2Chr 18:26
and with water of *a*...........2Chr 18:26
cry unto thee in our a 2Chr 20:9
a ourselves before..God ....Ezra 8:21
in great *a* and reproach ....Neh 1:3
see the *a* of our fathers ....Neh 9:9
a cometh not forth of the .....Job 5:6
To him that is *a* pity..........Job 6:14
see thou mine *a* ....Job 10:15
he..loosed my cord and *a* .....Job 30:11
days of *a* have taken hold .....Job 30:16
days of *a* prevented me ....Job 30:27
heareth the cry of the *a*.......Job 34:28
in cords of *a* ....Job 36:8
He delivered..poor in his *a*....Job 36:15
thou chosen rather than *a* .....Job 36:21
plenty of justice; he *a*.. ....Job 37:23
thou wilt save..*a* people ....Ps 18:27
the *a* of the afflicted ....Ps 22:24
for I am desolate and *a* ....Ps 25:16
Look upon mine *a* and my ....Ps 25:18
how thou didst *a*..people ......Ps 44:2
our *a* and our oppression .....Ps 44:24
God shall hear..*a* them ....Ps 55:19
laidst *a* upon our loins ....Ps 66:11
do justice to the *a* and ....Ps 82:3
hast *a* me with all thy.........Ps 88:7
mourneth by reason of *a* ......Ps 88:9
I am *a* and ready to die ....Ps 88:15
son of wickedness *a* him ......Ps 89:22
thou hast *a* us ....Ps 90:15
and *a* thine heritage ....Ps 94:5
A prayer of the *a* when he ....Ps 102: *title*
he regarded their *a* ....Ps 106:44
bound in *a* and iron ....Ps 107:10
because..iniquities are *a*.......Ps 107:17
through oppression, *a*.........Ps 107:39
poor on high from *a* ....Ps 107:41
I was greatly *a* ....Ps 116:10
my comfort in my *a* ....Ps 119:50
Before I..*a* I went astray ......Ps 119:67
good for me that I..been *a* ....Ps 119:71
thou in faithfulness hast *a* .....Ps 119:75
have perished in mine *a*.......Ps 119:92
I am *a* very much ....Ps 119:107
Consider mine *a*..............Ps 119:153
remember David..all his *a*.....Ps 132:1
maintain the cause of the *a*....Ps 140:12
destroy all them that *a* my ....Ps 143:12
All the days..*a* are evil........Prov 15:15
neither oppress the *a* in the ...Prov 22:22
hateth those that are *a* by .....Prov 26:28
judgment of any of the *a*......Prov 31:5
lightly a..land of Zebulun .....Is 9:1
afterward..grievously *a* ....Is 9:1
water of *a*, yet shall not.......Is 30:20
have mercy upon his *a* ....Is 49:13
hear now this, thou *a* ....Is 51:21
the hand of them that *a*.......Is 51:23
smitten of God, and *a* ....Is 53:4
He was oppressed..was *a*.......Is 53:7
a tossed with tempest, and ....Is 54:11
wherefore..we *a* our soul ......Is 58:3
for a man to *a* his soul?.......Is 58:5
satisfy the *a* soul ....Is 58:10
The sons also..that *a* thee .....Is 60:14
thy peace and *a* us very sore ..Is 64:12
a from mount Ephraim ....Jer 4:15
of evil and in the time of *a*....Jer 15:11
my refuge in the day of *a* .....Jer 16:19
criest thou for thine *a*?........Jer 30:15
and to destroy, and to *a* ......Jer 31:28
and his *a* hasteth fast ....Jer 48:16
priests sigh..virgins are *a* ......Lam 1:4
for the Lord hath *a* her for....Lam 1:5
wherewith..Lord hath *a* me....Lam 1:12
the man that hath seen *a*......Lam 3:1
remembering mine *a*..my ......Lam 3:19
not grieved..*a* of Joseph ......Amos 6:6
and they shall *a* you ....Amos 6:14
not have looked on their *a* ....Obad 13
reason of mine *a*..the Lord....Jon 2:2
her that I have *a* ....Mic 4:6
a..rise up the second time .....Nah 1:9
Though I have *a* thee ....Nah 1:12
I will *a* thee no more ....Nah 1:12
I saw..tents of Cushan in *a* ....Hab 3:7
an *a* and poor people ....Zeph 3:12
I will undo all that *a* thee .....Zeph 3:19
they helped forward the *a* .....Zech 1:15
came in because..the *a* ....Zech 8:10
pass through..sea with *a* ......Zech 10:11
in those days shall be *a* ....Mark 13:19
delivered him out of..his *a* ....Acts 7:10
Egypt and Canaan and..*a* .....Acts 7:11
I have seen the *a*..people .....Acts 7:34
bonds and *a* abide me ....Acts 20:23
out of much *a* and anguish 2Cor 2:4
in *a*, in necessities in 2Cor 6:4
How that..great trial of *a* 2Cor 8:2
to add *a* to my bonds ....Phil 1:16
our *a* and distress by your.....1Thess 3:7
if she have relieved the *a* 1Tim 5:10
partaker of the *a*..gospel 2Tim 1:8
Persecutions *a*..came 2Tim 3:11
endured a great fight of *a* .....Heb 10:32
both by reproaches and *a* .....Heb 10:33
Choosing rather to suffer *a*....Heb 11:25
and widows in their *a* ....James 1:27
Be a..mourn, and weep ....James 4:9
an example of suffering *a* .....James 5:10
same *a* are accomplished 1Pet 5:9

AFFORDING—*making available*
our garners may be full *a* .....Ps 144:13

AFFRIGHT—*to frighten*

[*also* AFFRIGHTED]
Thou shalt..*a* at them ....Deut 7:21

that went before were *a* .... Job 18:20
He mocketh at fear..not *a* ..... Job 39:22
fearfulness *a* me .... Is 21:4
and the men of war are *a* ..... Jer 51:32
garment; and they were *a* ..... Mark 16:5
And he saith..Be not *a* .... Mark 16:6
they were terrified and *a* ...... Luke 24:37
remnant were *a*..gave glory .... Rev 11:13

AFOOT—*under way, developing*
ran *a* thither out..cities .... Mark 6:33
minding himself to go *a* .... Acts 20:13

AFORE—*before*
to pass *a* Isaiah was gone 2Kin 20:4
withereth *a* it groweth up ..... Ps 129:6
a the harvest..bud is .... Is 18:5
a he that..escaped came .... Ezek 33:22
promised *a* by his prophets .... Rom 1:2
had *a* prepared unto glory ..... Rom 9:23
as I wrote *a* in few words ..... Eph 3:3

AFOREHAND—*before, earlier*
she is come *a* to anoint my .... Mark 14:8

AFORETIME—*previously*
a they laid..meat offerings ..... Neh 13:5
a I was as a tabret .... Job 17:6
My people went down *a* ...... Is 52:4
children..shall be as *a* .... Jer 30:20
his God, as he did *a* .... Dan 6:10
him that *a* was blind .... John 9:13
things were written *a* .... Rom 15:4

AFRAID—*overcome with fear*
Caused by:
Nakedness .... Gen 3:10
Unusual dream .... Gen 28:16, 17
God's presence .... Ex 3:6
Moses' approach .... Ex 34:30
A burning mountain ..... Deut 5:5
Giant's raging 1Sam 17:11, 24
A prophet's words 1Sam 28:20
Angel's sword 1Chr 21:30
God's judgments .... Ps 65:8
Gabriel's presence .... Dan 8:17
A terrifying storm .... Jon 1:5, 10
Peter's sinking .... Matt 14:30
Changed person .... Mark 5:15
Heavenly hosts .... Luke 2:9
Overcome by:
The Lord's presence ..... Ps 3:5, 6
Trusting God .... Ps 27:1-3
God's protection .... Ps 91:4, 5
Stability of heart .... Ps 112:7, 8
God's coming judgment .. Is 10:24-26
The Messiah's advent .... Is 40:9-11
God's sovereign power ... Is 51:12, 13
Christ's comforting words .... Matt 14:27

I laughed not; she was *a* ...... Gen 18:15
and the men were sore *a* ...... Gen 20:8
Because I was *a*: for I said .... Gen 31:31
Then Jacob was greatly *a* ..... Gen 32:7
failed them..they were *a* ...... Gen 42:28
And the men were *a* .... Gen 43:18
and they were sore *a*; and ..... Ex 14:10
people shall hear, and be *a* .... Ex 15:14
none shall make you *a* .... Lev 26:6
were ye not *a* to speak .... Num 12:8
Moab was sore *a* of the .... Num 22:3
shall not be *a* of the face ..... Deut 1:17
Dread not, neither be *a* of .... Deut 1:29
and they shall be *a* of you .... Deut 2:4
For I was *a* of the anger ...... Deut 9:19
thou shalt not be *a* of him .... Deut 18:22
be not *a* of them: for the ..... Deut 20:1
and they shall be *a* of thee .... Deut 28:10
which thou wast *a* of .... Deut 28:60
fear not, nor be *a* of them .... Deut 31:6
not *a*, neither be thou .... Josh 1:9
we were sore *a* of our .... Josh 9:24
Be not *a* because of them ..... Josh 11:6
Whosoever is fearful and *a* .... Judg 7:3
that the man was *a*, and ...... Ruth 3:8
And the Philistines were *a* 1Sam 4:7
they were *a*..Philistines 1Sam 7:7

And Saul was *a* of David 1Sam 18:12
very wisely, he was *a* of 1Sam 18:15
Saul was yet the more *a* of 1Sam 18:29
Ahimelech was *a* at the 1Sam 21:1
was sore *a*..the king of 1Sam 21:12
we be *a* here in Judah 1Sam 28:3
he was *a*, and his heart 1Sam 28:5
said unto her, Be not *a* 1Sam 28:13
thou not *a* to stretch 2Sam 1:14
David was *a* of the Lord 2Sam 6:9
the people have made me *a* ... 2Sam 14:15
and will make him *a* 2Sam 17:2
of ungodly men made me *a* ... 2Sam 22:5
they shall be *a* out of their 2Sam 22:46
were with Adonijah were *a* 1Kin 1:49
with him: be not *a* of him 2Kin 1:15
they were exceedingly *a* 2Kin 10:4
Be not *a*..the words which 2Kin 19:6
they were *a* of the Chaldees ... 2Kin 25:26
would not..he was sore *a* 1Chr 10:4
David was *a* of God that 1Chr 13:12
Be not *a* nor dismayed by 2Chr 20:15
be not *a* nor dismayed for 2Chr 32:7
Then I was very sore *a* .... Neh 2:2
Be not ye *a* of them .... Neh 4:14
they all made us *a*, saying ..... Neh 6:9
hired, that I should be *a* ...... Neh 6:13
Haman was *a* before the ...... Esth 7:6
which I was *a* of is come ..... Job 3:25
shalt thou be *a* of .... Job 5:21
neither shalt thou be *a* of .... Job 5:22
see my casting down..are *a* .... Job 6:21
I am *a* of all my sorrows ...... Job 9:28
none shall make thee *a* .... Job 11:19
his excellency make you *a* .... Job 13:11
not thy dread make me *a* ..... Job 13:21
anguish shall make him *a* ..... Job 15:24
Terrors shall make him *a* ..... Job 18:11
Be ye *a* of the sword .... Job 19:29
when I remember I am *a* ..... Job 21:6
when I consider, I am *a* of .... Job 23:15
wherefore I was *a*, and .... Job 32:6
terror shall not make..*a* .... Job 33:7
Canst thou make him *a* as .... Job 39:20
the mighty are *a* .... Job 41:25
floods of..men made me *a* .... Ps 18:4
shall fade away, and be *a* ..... Ps 18:45
Be not..*a* when one is made ... Ps 49:16
I am *a*, I will trust in thee .... Ps 56:3
not be *a* what..do unto me .... Ps 56:11
they were *a*..depths also ...... Ps 77:16
make them *a* with..storm ...... Ps 83:15
I am *a* of thy judgments ...... Ps 119:120
thou shalt not be *a* .... Prov 3:24
Be not *a* of sudden fear .... Prov 3:25
She is not *a* of the snow ...... Prov 31:21
they shall be *a* of that .... Eccl 12:5
fear..their fear, nor be *a* ...... Is 8:12
be not *a* of the Assyrian ...... Is 10:24
Ramah is *a*; Gibeah of .... Is 10:29
I will trust, and not be *a* ...... Is 12:2
And they shall be *a*; pangs .... Is 13:8
none shall make them *a* .... Is 17:2
and it shall be *a* and fear ..... Is 19:16
mention thereof shall be *a* .... Is 19:17
shall be *a* and ashamed .... Is 20:5
will not be *a* of their voice .... Is 31:4
shall be *a* of the ensign .... Is 31:9
The sinners in Zion are *a* ..... Is 33:14
Be not *a* of the words .... Is 37:6
ends of the earth were *a* ...... Is 41:5
Fear ye not, neither be *a* ..... Is 44:8
neither be ye *a* of their .... Is 51:7
of whom hast thou been *a* .... Is 57:11
Be not *a* of their faces .... Jer 1:8
be horribly *a*, be ye very .... Jer 2:12
none shall make him *a* .... Jer 30:10
all the words, they were *a* ..... Jer 36:16
Yet they were not *a* .... Jer 36:24
I am *a* of the Jews .... Jer 38:19
men of whom thou art *a* ...... Jer 39:17
of them, because of..*a* .... Jer 41:18
Be not *a*..king of Babylon ..... Jer 42:11
of whom ye are *a* .... Jer 42:11
Be not *a* of him saith the ..... Jer 42:11

the famine..ye were *a* .... Jer 42:16
none shall make him *a* .... Jer 46:27
son of man, be not *a* of .... Ezek 2:6
neither be *a* of their words .... Ezek 2:6
be not *a* of their words .... Ezek 2:6
their kings shall be sore *a* ..... Ezek 27:35
the careless Ethiopians *a* ...... Ezek 30:9
kings shall be horribly *a* ...... Ezek 32:10
none shall make them *a* .... Ezek 34:28
none made them *a* .... Ezek 39:26
a dream which made me *a* .... Dan 4:5
Be not *a*, ye beasts of the ..... Joel 2:22
the people not be *a* .... Amos 3:6
none shall make them *a* .... Mic 4:4
they shall be *a* of the Lord .... Mic 7:17
none made them *a* .... Nah 2:11
thy speech, and was *a* .... Hab 3:2
none shall make them *a* .... Zeph 3:13
was *a* before my name .... Mal 2:5
he was *a* to go thither .... Matt 2:22
fell..face, and were sore *a* ..... Matt 17:6
Arise, and be not *a* .... Matt 17:7
And I was *a*, and went and ... Matt 25:25
Be not *a*; go tell my .... Matt 28:10
Be not *a*, only believe .... Mark 5:36
It is I; be not *a* .... Mark 6:50
say; for they were sore *a* ...... Mark 9:6
and were *a* to ask him .... Mark 9:32
they followed, they were *a* .... Mark 10:32
any man; for they were *a* ..... Mark 16:8
they being *a* wondered .... Luke 8:25
and they were *a* .... Luke 8:35
Be not *a* of them that kill ..... Luke 12:4
as they were *a*, and bowed .... Luke 24:5
the ship; and they were *a* ..... John 6:19
It is I; be not *a* .... John 6:20
troubled, neither..be *a* .... John 14:27
he was the more *a* .... John 19:8
but they were all *a* of him .... Acts 9:26
looked on him, he was *a* ...... Acts 10:4
Be not *a*, but speak and ...... Acts 18:9
saw..the light, and were *a* ..... Acts 22:9
chief captain also was *a* .... Acts 22:29
Wilt thou then not be *a* of .... Rom 13:3
do that which is evil, be *a* ..... Rom 13:4
I am *a* of you, lest I have ..... Gal 4:11
were not *a* of the king's ...... Heb 11:23
not *a* with any amazement 1Pet 3:6
be not *a* of their terror 1Pet 3:14
they are not *a* to speak evil ... 2Pet 2:10

AFRESH—*a new beginning*
themselves the Son of God *a* .. Heb 6:6

AFTER—*See* INTRODUCTION

AFTERNOON—*the part of the day following noon*
Called cool of the day ... Gen 3:8

they tarried until *a*, and .... Judg 19:8

AFTERTHOUGHT—*a later reflection*
Of Esau .... Heb 12:16, 17
Of the Israelites .... Num 14:40-45
Of one of two sons ...... Matt 21:28-30
Of the prodigal son .... Luke 15:17
Of the unjust steward .... Luke 16:1-8
Of the rich man in hell .. Luke 16:23-31
Of Judas .... Matt 27:3-5

AFTERWARD—*at a later time*
Your hands will be ...... Judg 7:11
Those who are invited ... 1Sam 9:13
David's conscience bothered him 1Sam 24:5
His mouth shall .... Prov 20:17
Jesus findeth him .... John 5:14

[*also* AFTERWARDS]
and *a* were the families of ..... Gen 10:18
a shall they come out with .... Gen 15:14
And *a* she bare a daughter .... Gen 30:21
and *a* I will see his face .... Gen 32:20
And *a* came out his brother ... Gen 38:30
a Moses and Aaron went in ... Ex 5:1
a he will let you go hence ..... Ex 11:1
a all the children of Israel ..... Ex 34:32
a he shall kill the burnt .... Lev 14:19

a the priest shall go in to .....Lev 14:36
a come into the camp ....Lev 16:26
a he shall come into the ......Lev 16:28
and shall *a* eat of the holy ....Lev 22:7
a shall cause the woman to ....Num 5:26
a the people removed from....Num 12:16
a he shall come into the ......Num 19:7
a shalt thou be gathered ......Num 31:2
a ye shall come into the.......Num 31:24
a ye shall return, and be ......Num 32:22
and *a* the hand of..people ......Deut 13:9
a the hands of..the people ....Deut 17:7
thou shalt not glean it *a*.......Deut 24:21
and *a* may ye go your way ....Josh 2:16
a he read all the words of.....Josh 8:34
a Joshua smote them, and.....Josh 10:26
and *a* I brought you out ......Josh 24:5
a the children of Judah ....Judg 1:9
came to pass *a*..he loved ......Judg 16:4
and *a* go your way ....Judg 19:5
David..arose *a*, and went 1Sam 24:8
a when David heard it, he 2Sam 3:28
a Hezron went in..daughter ...1Chr 2:21
a they made ready for 2Chr 35:14
a offered..continual burnt .....Ezra 3:5
A I came unto the house of ...Neh 6:10
and *a* we will speak ....Job 18:2
and *a* receive me to glory .....Ps 73:24
a his mouth shall be filled .....Prov 20:17
a build thine house ....Prov 24:27
rebuketh a man *a* shall find ...Prov 28:23
a wise man keepeth..till *a* .....Prov 29:11
a thou shalt be called ....Is 1:26
a did..grievously afflict ....Is 9:1
a, saith the Lord, I will ....Jer 21:7
a they turned, and caused .....Jer 34:11
a it shall be inhabited ....Jer 46:26
a I will bring again the........Jer 49:6
A the spirit took me up ....Ezek 11:24
A he brought me..temple ......Ezek 41:1
A he brought me to the gate ..Ezek 43:1
A he brought me again unto ...Ezek 47:1
A he measured a thousand ....Ezek 47:5
a I rose up, and did..king's....Dan 8:27
A shall..children of Israel .....Hos 3:5
come to pass *a*, that I will ....Joel 2:28
he was *a* ahungered ....Matt 4:2
a he repented, and went ....Matt 21:29
seen it, repented not *a* ....Matt 21:32
A came..the other virgins .....Matt 25:11
a..affliction or persecution.....Mark 4:17
A he appeared unto..eleven ...Mark 16:14
were ended, he *a* hungered....Luke 4:2
It came to pass *a*..he went ....Luke 8:1
a thou shalt eat and drink?....Luke 17:8
a he said within himself ....Luke 18:4
but thou shalt follow me *a* ....John 13:36
And *a* they desired a king.....Acts 13:21
a they that are Christ's at 1Cor 15:23
a that which is spiritual 1Cor 15:46
A I came into the regions .....Gal 1:21
which should *a* be revealed ....Gal 3:23
would he not *a* have spoken ...Heb 4:8
a it yieldeth the..fruit ....Heb 12:11
ye know how that *a* when .....Heb 12:17
a destroyed them..believed ....Jude 5

AGABUS (ăg'ā-bŭs)—*"locust"*
A Christian prophet who foretells a famine and warns Paul .... {Acts 11:27, 28; Acts 21:10, 11}

AGAG (ā'găg)—*"high; warlike"*
1. A King of Amalek in Balaam's prophecy ....Num 24:7
2. Amalekite king spared by Saul, but slain by Samuel............ {1Sam 15:8, 9, 20-24, 32, 33}

have brought *A* the king 1Sam 15:20
hither to me *A* the king 1Sam 15:32

AGAGITE (ā'găg-īt)—*descendant of Agag*
A title applied to Haman, enemy of the Jews.....Esth 3:1, 10

AGAIN—*See* INTRODUCTION

AGAINST—*See* INTRODUCTION

AGAPE—*a Greek word translated both as "love" and "charity"*
Descriptive of God 1John 4:8
Demanded toward God ..Matt 22:37
Demanded toward neighbors ....Matt 22:39
Fulfills Law ....Matt 22:40
Activity of described.....1Cor 13:1-3

AGAR (ā'gär)—*"wandering"—the Greek word for Hagar*
to bondage, which is *A*........Gal 4:24
For this *A* is mount Sinai .....Gal 4:25
See HAGAR

AGATE—*a stone of translucent quartz*
Worn by the high priest..Ex 28:19
Sold by Syrians..........Ezek 27:16
Figurative of the new Israel.................Is 54:11, 12

AGE—*time counted by years; advanced years*

Handicaps of, seen in:
Physical infirmities.......Gen 48:10
Unwillingness to adventure.............2Sam 19:31-39
Declining strength ....Ps 71:9
Deterioration of body....Eccl 12:2-7

Glories of, manifested in:
Wisdom ....Job 12:12
Maturity ....Job 5:26
Spiritual beauty ....Prov 16:31
Fruitfulness ....Ps 92:12-15
Judgment 1Kin 12:6-8
Strong faith ....Josh 24:15

Attitude of others toward:
Respect.................Lev 19:32
Disrespect 2Chr 36:17
Insolence ....Is 3:5

Unusual things connected with:
Retaining physical vigor ..Deut 34:7
Becoming a father ....Gen 18:9-15; Luke 1:18, 36
Living to see Christ.....Luke 2:25-32
Knowing kind of death in.John 21:19

Attaining unto, by:
Honoring parents ....Ex 20:12; Eph 6:2, 3
Keeping God's law ......Prov 3:1, 2
Following wisdom ....Prov 3:13, 16
The fear of the Lord ....Ps 128:1, 6
Keeping from evil ....Ps 34:11-14
God's promise ....Gen 15:15

Those of Bible times who lived beyond age of one-hundred.
Methuselah ....Gen 5:27
Jared ....Gen 5:20
Noah ....Gen 9:29
Adam ....Gen 5:5
Seth ....Gen 5:8
Cainan ....Gen 5:14
Enos ....Gen 5:11
Mahalaleel ....Gen 5:17
Lamech ....Gen 5:31
Enoch ....Gen 5:23
Terah ....Gen 11:32
Isaac ....Gen 35:28
Abraham ....Gen 25:7
Jacob ....Gen 47:28
Ishmael ....Gen 25:17
Jehoiada 2Chr 24:15
Sarah ....Gen 23:1
Aaron ....Num 33:39
Moses ....Deut 34:7
Joseph ....Gen 50:26
Joshua ....Josh 24:29

[*also* AGED]
bare Abraham a son old *a* ....Gen 21:2
born him a son in his old *a* ...Gen 21:7
old, and well stricken in *a*.....Gen 24:1
Abraham..died..good old *a* ....Gen 25:8
he was the son of his old *a* ....Gen 37:3
child of his old *a*, a little ......Gen 44:20
from the *a* of fifty years.......Num 8:25
waxed old and stricken in *a* ...Josh 23:1
I am old and stricken in *a* .....Josh 23:2
Gideon..died..good old *a* ......Judg 8:32
a nourisher of thine old *a* .....Ruth 4:15
shall die..flower of their *a* 1Sam 2:33
eyes were set by reason..*a* 1Kin 14:4
in the time of his old *a* he 1Kin 15:23
from the *a* of thirty years 1Chr 23:3
from the *a* of twenty years 1Chr 23:24
died in a good old *a*, full 1Chr 29:28
come to..grave in a full *a* .....Job 5:26
pray thee, of the former *a* ....Job 8:8
and thine *a* shall be clearer....Job 11:17
the understanding of the *a* ....Job 12:20
grayheaded and very *a* men ...Job 15:10
the *a* arose, and stood up .....Job 29:8
whom old *a* was perished? ....Job 30:2
neither do..*a* understand ......Job 32:9
Mine *a* is departed, and is ....Is 38:12
even to your old *a* I am he....Is 46:4
a..him that is full of days .....Jer 6:11
his staff in..hand for very *a* ...Zech 8:4
was of the *a*..twelve years .....Mark 5:42
conceived a son in her old *a* ...Luke 1:36
was of a great *a*..had lived ....Luke 2:36
thirty years of *a*, being........Luke 3:23
we know not; he is of *a*........John 9:21
said his parents, He is of *a* ....John 9:23
she pass the flower of her *a* ...1Cor 7:36
That the *a* men be sober ......Titus 2:2
The *a* women likewise, that ...Titus 2:3
such an one as Paul the *a* .....Philem 9
to them that are of full *a* .....Heb 5:14
she was past *a*, because she ...Heb 11:11

AGEE (ā'gē)—*"fugitive"*
Shammah's father 2Sam 23:11

AGES—*extended periods of time*
Descriptive of the Old Testament period......Eph 3:5
Descriptive of eternity ...Eph 2:7

throughout..*a*, world without ..Eph 3:21
hid from *a*..generations ....Col 1:26

AGITATION—*disturbance*

Physically of:
Mountain ....Ex 19:16-18
The earth ....Matt 27:51-53
The world ....Ps 46:2-6
End-time events ....Luke 21:25-27
World's end.............2Pet 3:7-12

Emotionally of:
Extreme grief 2Sam 19:1-4
Remorse ....Matt 27:3, 4
Fear ....Matt 28:1-4

Figuratively of:
Messiah's advent ....Hag 2:6, 7
Enraged people ....Acts 4:25-28
The wicked ....Is 57:20
The drunkard ....Prov 23:29-35

AGO—*an earlier time*

[*also* AGONE]
asses were lost three days *a* ...1Sam 9:20
three days *a* I fell sick 1Sam 30:13
Hast thou not heard long *a*....2Kin 19:25
builded these many years *a* ....Ezra 5:11
him that fashioned it long *a* ....Is 22:11
repented long *a*..sackcloth .....Matt 11:21
How long is it *a* since this.....Mark 9:21
they had a great while *a* ......Luke 10:13
Cornelius said, Four days *a* ...Acts 10:30
a good while *a* God made .....Acts 15:7
also to be forward a year *a*....2Cor 8:10
in Christ..fourteen years *a*.....2Cor 12:2

AGONY—*extreme suffering*

Used literally of:
Christ in Gethsemane ....Luke 22:44
Christ on the cross ......Mark 15:34-37
Paul's sufferings 2Cor 1:8, 9

Used figuratively of:
Spiritual mastery 1Cor 9:25

Spiritual striving . . . . Col 1:29
Laborious prayer . . . . Col 4:12
Faithful conflict 1Tim 6:12

AGREE—*common consent*

Forbidden between:
Israel and pagans . . . . Ex 34:12-16
God and Baal 1Kin 18:21-40
Believers, unbelievers 1Cor 10:21
Truth, error 1John 4:1-6

Necessary between:
Prophecy, fulfillment . . . . . Acts 15:15
Doctrine, life . . . . James 2:14-21
Words, performance 2Cor 10:9-11
Believers in prayer . . . . . . Matt 18:19
Christian brothers . . . . Matt 5:24, 25
Christian workers . . . . Gal 2:7-9

Examples of:
Laban and Jacob . . . . Gen 31:43-53
God and Israel . . . . Ex 19:3-8
David and Jonathan 1Sam 18:1-4
The wicked and Sheol . . Is 28:15, 18
Employer and employees . Matt 20:10-13
Judas and the Sanhedrin. . Matt 26:14-16
Witnesses . . . . Mark 14:56, 59
Husband and wife . . . . Acts 5:9
The Jews and Gamaliel . . Acts 5:34-40
Conspiring Jews . . . . Acts 23:20
The people of antichrist . . Rev 17:17

[*also* AGREED, AGREEMENT, AGREETH]
an *a* with me by a present 2Kin 18:31
Assyria, Make an *a* with me . . . Is 36:16
king of..north to make an *a* . . . Dan 11:6
together, except they be *a*? . . . . Amos 3:3
A with thine adversary . . . . Matt 5:25
And when he had *a* with . . . . . . Matt 20:2
and thy speech *a* thereto . . . . . . Mark 14:70
a not with the old . . . . Luke 5:36
for the Jews had *a* already . . . . John 9:22
they *a* not..themselves . . . . Acts 28:25
what *a* hath the temple of 2Cor 6:16

AGRICULTURE—*the cultivation and harvesting of crops*

Terms and implements involved:
Binding . . . . Gen 37:7
Cultivating . . . . Luke 13:6-9
Fertilizing . . . . Is 25:10
Gleaning . . . . Ruth 2:3
Grafting . . . . Rom 11:17-19
Harrowing . . . . Is 28:24
Harvesting . . . . Matt 13:23
Mowing . . . . Amos 7:1
Planting . . . . Prov 31:16
Plowing . . . . Job 1:14
Pruning . . . . Is 5:6
Reaping . . . . Is 17:5
Removing stones . . . . Is 5:2
Rooting . . . . Matt 13:28, 29
Sowing . . . . Matt 13:3
Stacking . . . . Ex 22:6
Threshing . . . . Judg 6:11
Treading . . . . Neh 13:15
Watering 1Cor 3:6-8
Winnowing . . . . Ruth 3:2

Virtues required in:
Wisdom . . . . Is 28:24-29
Diligence . . . . Prov 27:23-27
Labor 2Tim 2:6
Patience . . . . James 5:7
Industry . . . . Prov 28:19
Faith . . . . Hab 3:17-19
Bountifulness 2Cor 9:6, 7
Hopefulness 1Cor 9:10

Enemies of:
War . . . . Jer 50:16
Pestilence . . . . Joel 1:9-12
Fire . . . . Joel 1:19
Animals . . . . Song 2:15
Dry seasons . . . . Jer 14:1, 4

Restrictions involving:
Coveting another's field . . Deut 5:21
Removing boundaries . . . . Deut 19:14
Roaming cattle . . . . Ex 22:5
Spreading fire . . . . Ex 22:6
Military service . . . . Deut 20:5, 6
Working on the Sabbath. . Ex 34:21
Complete harvest . . . . Lev 19:9, 10

God's part in:
Began in Eden . . . . Gen 2:15
Sin's penalty . . . . Gen 3:17
Providence of, impartial . . Matt 5:45
Goodness of, recognized. . Acts 14:16, 17
Judgments against, cited. . Hag 1:10, 11

Figurative of:
Gospel seed . . . . Matt 13:1-9
Gospel dispensation . . . . . Matt 13:24-30, 36-43
God's workers . . . . John 4:36-38
God's Word . . . . Is 55:10, 11
Spiritual barrenness . . . . . . Heb 6:7, 8
Spiritual bountifulness . . . 2Cor 9:9, 10
Final harvest . . . . Mark 4:28, 29

AGRIPPA (ă-grĭp'ä)—*the name of the Roman king of Judea of the Herod family*
king *A* and Bernice came . . . . . Acts 25:13
Then *A* said unto Festus . . . . . . Acts 25:22
when *A* was come . . . . Acts 25:23
And Festus said, King *A* . . . . . . Acts 25:24
before thee, O king *A* . . . . Acts 25:26
Then *A* said unto Paul . . . . Acts 26:1
think myself happy, king *A* . . . . Acts 26:2
which hope's sake, king *A* . . . . . Acts 26:7
whereupon, O king *A* . . . . Acts 26:19
King *A*, believest thou the . . . . Acts 26:27
Then *A* said unto Paul . . . . Acts 26:28
Then said *A* unto Festus . . . . . . Acts 26:32

AGROUND—*stranded in shallow water*
Ship carrying Paul . . . . Acts 27:41

AGUE—*a malarial fever; jaundice*
A divine punishment . . . . . Lev 26:16

AGUR (ā'gŭr)—*"gathered"*
Writer of proverbs . . . . Prov 30:1-33

AH—*expressions of delight, relief, surprise or derision*

[*also* AHA]
A, *a*, our eye hath seen it . . . . . Ps 35:21
A, so would we have it; let . . . . Ps 35:25
that say unto me, *A*, *a* . . . . Ps 40:15
their shame that say, *A*, *a* . . . . . Ps 70:3
A sinful nation, a people . . . . . . Is 1:4
A, I will ease me of mine . . . . . Is 1:24
saith, *A*, I am warm . . . . Is 44:16
Then said I, *A*, Lord God . . . . . Jer 1:6
A, Lord God! surely thou . . . . . Jer 4:10
A, Lord God! behold, the . . . . . Jer 14:13
A my brother! or, *A* sister . . . . . Jer 22:18
A lord! or *A* his glory . . . . Jer 22:18
A Lord God! behold, thou . . . . Jer 32:17
lament thee, saying, *A* lord! . . . Jer 34:5
Then said I, *A* Lord God . . . . . Ezek 4:14
cried, and said, *A* Lord God . . Ezek 9:8
and said, *A* Lord God . . . . Ezek 11:13
Then said I, *A* Lord God . . . . . Ezek 20:49
a! it is made bright . . . . Ezek 21:15
Because thou saidst, *A* . . . . Ezek 25:3
A, she is broken that was . . . . . Ezek 26:2
hath said against you, *A* . . . . . . Ezek 36:2
A, thou that destroyest the . . . . Mark 15:29

AHAB (ā'hăb)—*"father's brother"*
1. A wicked king of Israel . 1Kin 16:29
Marries Jezebel 1Kin 16:31
Introduces Baal worship . 1Kin 16:31-33
Denounced by Elijah 1Kin 17:1
Gathers prophets of Baal 1Kin 18:17-46
Wars against Ben-hadad. . 1Kin 20:1-43
Covets Naboth's vineyard 1Kin 21:1-16
Death of, predicted 1Kin 21:17-26
Repentance of, delays judgment 1Kin 21:27-29
Joins Jehoshaphat against Syrians 1Kin 22:1-4
Rejects Micaiah's warning 1Kin 22:5-33
Slain in battle 1Kin 22:34-38
Seventy sons of, slain . . . 2Kin 10:1-11
Prophecies concerning, fulfilled 1Kin 20:42
2. Lying prophet . . . . Jer 29:21-23

[*also* AHAB'S]
A his son reigned in his stead . . 1Kin 16:28
unto *A*, As the Lord God of . . 1Kin 17:1
Go, show thyself unto *A* 1Kin 18:1
went to show himself unto *A* . . 1Kin 18:2
A called Obadiah, which 1Kin 18:3
A said unto Obadiah, Go 1Kin 18:5
A went one way by himself 1Kin 18:6
servant into the hand of *A* 1Kin 18:9
so when I come and tell *A* 1Kin 18:12
So Obadiah went to meet *A* 1Kin 18:16
and *A* went to meet Elijah 1Kin 18:16
it came to pass, when *A* saw . . 1Kin 18:17
A said unto him Art thou 1Kin 18:17
A sent unto all the children . . . 1Kin 18:20
So *A* went up to eat and to . . . 1Kin 18:42
A rode, and went to Jezreel . . . 1Kin 18:45
a told Jezebel all..Elijah 1Kin 19:1
A said, By whom? And he 1Kin 20:14
said *A*, I will send thee 1Kin 20:34
A spake unto Naboth 1Kin 21:2
that *A* rose up 1Kin 21:16
go down to meet *A* king of 1Kin 21:18
A said to Elijah, Hast thou 1Kin 21:20
Seest thou how *A* humbleth . . . 1Kin 21:29
the rest of the acts of *A* 1Kin 22:39
So *A* slept with his fathers 1Kin 22:40
the fourth year of *A* king of . . . 1Kin 22:41
said Ahaziah the son of *A* 1Kin 22:49
Ahaziah the son of *A* began . . . 1Kin 22:51
Israel after the death of *A* 2Kin 1:1
Jehoram the son of *A* began . . . 2Kin 3:1
it came to pass, when *A* was . . 2Kin 3:5
year of Joram the son of *A* 2Kin 8:16
as did the house of *A* 2Kin 8:18
for the daughter of *A* was 2Kin 8:18
year of Joram the son of *A* 2Kin 8:25
walked in the way..house of *A* . . 2Kin 8:27
as did the house of *A*: for 2Kin 8:27
son in law of..house of *A* 2Kin 8:27
with Joram the son of *A* 2Kin 8:28
see Joram the son of *A* 2Kin 8:29
shalt smite the house of *A* 2Kin 9:7
the whole house of *A* shall 2Kin 9:8
and I will cut off from *A* 2Kin 9:8
I will make the house of *A* 2Kin 9:9
thou rode together after *A* 2Kin 9:25
year of Joram the son of *A* 2Kin 9:29
all that remained unto *A* 2Kin 10:17
unto them, *A* served Baal 2Kin 10:18
done unto the house of *A* 2Kin 10:30
and made a grove, as did *A* . . . 2Kin 21:3
plummet of the house of *A* 2Kin 21:13
and joined affinity with *A* 2Chr 18:1
years he went down to *A* 2Chr 18:2
A killed sheep and oxen for . . . 2Chr 18:2
A king of Israel said unto 2Chr 18:3
Who shall entice *A* king of 2Chr 18:19
like as did the house of *A* 2Chr 21:6
he had the daughter of *A* to . . . 2Chr 21:6
whoredoms of the house of *A* . 2Chr 21:13
the ways of the house of *A* 2Chr 22:3
the Lord like the house of *A* . . 2Chr 22:4
with Jehoram the son of *A* 2Chr 22:5
see Jehoram the son of *A* 2Chr 22:6
anointed to cut..house of *A* . . . 2Chr 22:7
judgment upon..house of *A* 2Chr 22:8
of *A* the son of Kolaiah . . . . Jer 29:21
the works of the house of *A* . . . Mic 6:16

AHARA (ă-hăr'ä)—*"brother's follower"*
Son of Benjamin 1Chr 8:1
Called Ahiram . . . . Num 26:38
Called Ehi . . . . Gen 46:21

AHARHEL (ă-här'hĕl)—*"brother of Rachel"*
A descendant of Judah . . . 1Chr 4:8

AHASAI (ă-hā'sī)—*"my holder; protector"*
A postexilic priest . . . . Neh 11:13
Also called Jahzerah 1Chr 9:12

AHASBAI (ă-hăs'bī)—*"blooming; shining"*
The father of Eliphelet...2Sam 23:34

AHASUERUS (ă-hăz-ū-ē'rŭs)
1. The father of Darius the Mede.................Dan 9:1
2. Persian king............Esth 1:1
Makes Esther queen ....Esth 2:16, 17
Follows Haman's intrigue.Esth 3:1, 8-12
Orders Jews annihilated..Esth 3:13-15
Responds to Esther's plea.................Esth 7:1-8
Orders Haman hanged ..Esth 7:9, 10
Promotes Mordecai .....Esth 8:1, 2
Reverses Haman's plot ..Esth 8:3-17
Exalts Mordecai ....Esth 10:1-3
3. A king of Persia; probably Xerxes, 486-465 B.C. ....Ezra 4:6

[*also* AHASUERUS']
when the king *A* sat on the....Esth 1:2
house..belonged to king *A*.....Esth 1:9
the presence of *A* the king ....Esth 1:10
commandment of the king *A* ..Esth 1:15
the provinces of the king *A*....Esth 1:16
king *A* commanded Vashti ....Esth 1:17
come no more before king *A* ..Esth 1:19
the wrath of king *A* was.......Esth 2:1
was come to go in to king *A* ..Esth 2:12
Esther..taken unto king *A*.....Esth 2:16
to lay hand on the king *A*.....Esth 2:21
throughout..kingdom of *A*.....Esth 3:6
the twelfth year of king *A*.....Esth 3:7
Haman said unto king *A*......Esth 3:8
in the name of king *A* was ....Esth 3:12
to lay hand on the king *A*.....Esth 6:2
Then the king *A* answered ....Esth 7:5
Then the king *A* said unto ....Esth 8:7
all the provinces of king *A* ....Esth 8:12
the provinces of the king *A*....Esth 9:2
the provinces of the king *A*....Esth 9:20
of the kingdom of *A*, with.....Esth 9:30

AHAVA (ă-hā'vä)—*"water"—a town in Babylonia*
Jewish exiles gather here .Ezra 8:15-31

AHAZ (ā'hăz)—*"he holds; he has grasped"*
1. A king of Judah; son of Jotham..............2Kin 16:1, 2
Pursues evil ways.......2Kin 16:3, 4
Defends Jerusalem against Rezin and Pekah................2Kin 16:5, 6
Refuses a divine sign....Is 7:1-16
Defeated with great loss .2Chr 28:5-15
Becomes subject to Assyria...............2Kin 16:7-9
Makes Damascus a pagan city...................2Kin 16:10-18
Erects sundial..........2Kin 20:11
Death of...............2Kin 16:19, 20
2. A descendant of Jonathan............1Chr 8:35, 36
1Chr 9:40-42
3. Ancestor of Jesus.......Matt 1:9

A the son of Jotham king 2Kin 16:1
Twenty years old was *A*......2Kin 16:2
So *A* sent messengers to 2Kin 16:7
A took the silver and gold.....2Kin 16:8
king *A* went to Damascus 2Kin 16:10
king *A* sent to Urijah the 2Kin 16:10
A had sent from Damascus 2Kin 16:11
made it against king *A*........2Kin 16:11
king *A* commanded Urijah 2Kin 16:15
all that king *A* commanded 2Kin 16:16
A cut off the borders of.......2Kin 16:17
In the twelfth year of *A*.......2Kin 17:1
of *A* king of Judah began 2Kin 18:1
A his son reigned in his.......2Chr 27:9
A was twenty years old 2Chr 28:1
that time did king *A* send 2Chr 28:16
Judah low because of *A*.......2Chr 28:19
A took away a portion out 2Chr 28:21
Lord; this is that king *A* 2Chr 28:22
A gathered..the vessels........2Chr 28:24
A slept with his fathers........2Chr 28:27
the vessels, which king *A*.......2Chr 29:19
days of Uzziah, Jotham, *A* ....Is 1:1
the days of *A* son of ....Is 7:1
Go forth now to meet *A*.......Is 7:3
Lord spake again unto *A*.......Is 7:10
But *A* said, I will not ask .....Is 7:12
that king *A* died was this......Is 14:28
down in the sun dial of *A*.....Is 38:8
A, and Hezekiah, kings of.....Hos 1:1
in the days of Jotham, *A*......Mic 1:1

AHAZIAH (ā-hä-zī'ä)—*"Jehovah holds (sustains)"*
1. A king of Israel; son of Ahab and Jezebel.....1Kin 22:40, 51
Worships Baal..........1Kin 22:52, 53
Seeks alliance with Jehoshaphat..........1Kin 22:48, 49
Falls through lattice; sends to Baal-zebub, the god of Ekron for help..................2Kin 1:2-16
Dies according to Elijah's word..................2Kin 1:17, 18
2. A king of Judah; son of Jehoram and Athaliah .2Kin 8:25, 26
Made king by Jerusalem inhabitants 2Chr 22:1, 2
Taught evil by his mother...............2Chr 22:2, 3
Follows Ahab's wickedness 2Chr 22:4
Joins Joram against the Syrians..............2Kin 8:28
Visits wounded Joram ...2Kin 9:16
Slain by Jehu...........2Kin 9:27, 28
Called Jehoahaz 2Chr 21:17
Called Azariah 2Chr 22:6

Then said *A*..son of Ahab 1Kin 22:49
A his son reigned in his.......2Kin 8:24
A the son of Jehoram king 2Kin 8:29
A king of Judah went out 2Kin 9:21
and fled, and said to *A* 2Kin 9:23
There is treachery, O *A*.......2Kin 9:23
A to reign over Judah..........2Kin 9:29
Jehu met..the brethren of *A*...2Kin 10:13
We are the brethren of *A* 2Kin 10:13
mother of *A* saw that her 2Kin 11:1
daughter of king..sister of *A*...2Kin 11:2
took Joash the son of *A*.......2Kin 11:2
and *A*, his fathers, kings 2Kin 12:18
year of Joash the son of *A* 2Kin 13:1
son of Jehoash the son of *A*...2Kin 14:13
Joram his son, *A* his son 1Chr 3:11
join himself with *A* king 2Chr 20:35
hast joined thyself with *A* 2Chr 20:37
destruction of *A* was of God...2Chr 22:7
sons of the brethren of *A* 2Chr 22:8
that ministered to *A* 2Chr 22:8
he sought *A*..they caught......2Chr 22:9
house of *A* had no power 2Chr 22:9
Athaliah the mother of *A* 2Chr 22:10
took Joash the son of *A*.......2Chr 22:11
(for she was the sister of *A*,) ..2Chr 22:11

AHBAN (ä'băn)—*"brother of intelligence"*.
A son of Abishur........1Chr 2:29

AHER (ā'her)—*"one that is behind"*
A Benjamite............1Chr 7:12

AHI (ā'hī)—*"my brother"*
1. Gadite chief...........1Chr 5:15
2. Asherite chief..........1Chr 7:34

AHIAH (ä-hī'ä)—*"Jehovah is brother"*
1. A priest during Saul's reign.................1Sam 14:3, 18
2. A secretary of Solomon .1Kin 4:3
3. A Benjamite 1Chr 8:7

AHIAM (ä-hī'ăm)—*"a mother's brother"*
One of David's mighty men..................2Sam 23:33

A the son of Sacar the 1Chr 11:35

AHIAN (ä-hī'ăn)—*"brother of day"*
A Manassite 1Chr 7:19

AHIEZER (ä-hī-ē'zer)—*"helping brother"*
1. Head of the tribe of Dan.Num 1:12
2. Benjamite chief, joined David at Ziklag.......1Chr 12:3

children of Dan shall be *A* ....Num 2:25
On the tenth day *A* the son ...Num 7:66
this was the offering of *A* .....Num 7:71
over his host was *A* son.......Num 10:25

AHIHUD (ä-hī'hŭd)—*"brother of honor"*
1. Asherite leader, helped Moses divide Canaan..Num 34:27
2. A Benjamite 1Chr 8:6, 7

AHIJAH (ä-hī'jä)—*"brother of Jehovah; Jehovah is brother"*
1. A great-grandson of Judah..................1Chr 2:25
2. One of David's warriors .1Chr 11:36
3. A Levite treasurer in David's reign 1Chr 26:20
4. A prophet of Shiloh who foretells division of Solomon's kingdom ...1Kin 11:29-39
Foretells elimination of Jeroboam's line 1Kin 14:1-18
A writer of prophecy 2Chr 9:29
5. The father of Baasha....1Kin 15:27, 33
6. A Jew who seals Nehemiah's covenant..Neh 10:26
See AHIAH

A the Shilonite found him.....1Kin 11:29
A caught the new garment 1Kin 11:30
which the Lord spake by *A*....1Kin 12:15
there is *A* the prophet 1Kin 14:2
and came to the house of *A*....1Kin 14:4
A could not see; for his eyes ..1Kin 14:4
Lord said unto *A*, Behold 1Kin 14:5
when *A* heard the sound 1Kin 14:6
spake..hand of his servant *A*...1Kin 14:18
house of Baasha..son of *A* 1Kin 21:22
house of Baasha..son of *A* 2Kin 9:9
the hand of *A* the Shilonite....2Chr 10:15

AHIKAM (ä-hī'kăm)—*"my brother has risen"*
A son of Shaphan the scribe 2Kin 22:12
Sent in Josiah's mission to Huldah 2Kin 22:12-14
Protects Jeremiah ....Jer 26:24
The father of Gedaliah, governor under Nebuchadnezzar 2Kin 25:22
Jer 39:14

commanded Hilkiah, and *A* ...2Chr 34:20
back..Gedaliah the son of *A*...Jer 40:5
unto Gedaliah the son of *A* ...Jer 40:6
Gedaliah the son of *A* ....Jer 40:7
the son of *A* the son of ....Jer 40:9
Gedaliah the son of *A* ....Jer 40:11
son of *A* believed them not....Jer 40:14
son of *A* said unto Johanan ...Jer 40:16
Gedaliah the son of *A* ....Jer 41:1
smote Gedaliah the son of *A* ..Jer 41:2
Gedaliah the son of *A* ....Jer 41:6
Gedaliah the son of *A* ....Jer 41:10
Gedaliah the son of *A* ....Jer 41:16
with Gedaliah the son of *A*....Jer 43:6

AHILUD (ä-hī'lŭd)—*"a child's brother; a brother born"*
1. The father of Jehoshaphat, the recorder under David and Solomon 2Sam 8:16
2. The father of Baana, a commissionary official .1Kin 4:7, 12

Jehoshaphat the son of *A* 2Sam 20:24
Jehoshaphat the son of *A* 1Kin 4:3

AHIMAAZ (ä-hĭm'ā-ăz)—*"powerful brother"*

1. The father of Ahinoam, wife of King Saul 1Sam 14:50
2. A son of Zadok the high priest 1Chr 6:8, 9
   Warns David of Absalom's plans 2Sam 15:27,36
   Good man 2Sam 18:27
   First to tell David of Absalom's defeat 2Sam 18:19-30
3. Solomon's son-in-law and commissioner in Naphtali 1Kin 4:15
   May be the same as 2.

Jonathan and *A* stayed by 2Sam 17:17
Where is *A* and Jonathan? 2Sam 17:20
Zadok his son, *A* his son 1Chr 6:53

AHIMAN (ä-hī'măn)—*"brother of fortune"*
1. A giant son of Anak seen by Israelite spies. .Num 13:22, 33
   Driven out of Hebron by Caleb ....Josh 15:13, 14
   Slain by tribe of Judah . . .Judg 1:10
2. A Levite gatekeeper 1Chr 9:17

Talmon, and *A*, and their 1Chr 9:17

AHIMELECH (ä-hĭm'e-lĕk)—*"brother of the king; my brother is king"*
1. The high priest at Nob during Saul's reign 1Sam 21:1
   Feeds David the showbread 1Sam 21:2-6
   Gives Goliath's sword to David 1Sam 21:8, 9
   Betrayed by Doeg 1Sam 22:9-16
   Slain by Doeg at Saul's command 1Sam 22:17-19
   Abiathar, son of, escapes. 1Sam 22:20
   David wrote concerning. .Ps 52 (title)
2. Abiathar's son 2Sam 8:17
   Co-priest with Zadok....1Chr 24:3, 6, 31
3. David's Hittite warrior . .1Sam 26:6

[*also* AHIMELECH'S]
came David to Nob to *A* 1Sam 21:1
A was afraid at the meeting . . .1Sam 21:1
said unto *A* the priest 1Sam 21:2
the king sent to call *A* 1Sam 22:11
Then *A* answered the king 1Sam 22:14
Thou shalt surely die, *A* 1Sam 22:16
to Abiathar the priest, *A* 1Sam 30:7

AHIMOTH (ä-hī'mŏth)—*"brother of death"*
A Kohathite Levite 1Chr 6:25

AHINADAB (ä-hĭn'ä-dăb)—*"brother of liberality (willingness)"*
One of Solomon's officers 1Kin 4:14

AHINOAM (ä-hĭn'ō-ăm)—*"pleasant brother"*
1. Wife of Saul...........1Sam 14:50
2. David's wife...........1Sam 25:43
   Lived with David at Gath................1Sam 27:3
   Captured by Amalekites at Ziklag............1Sam 30:5
   Rescued by David 1Sam 30:18
   Lived with David in Hebron 2Sam 2:1, 2
   Mother of Amnon 2Sam 3:2

AHIO (ä-hī'ō)—*"his brother"*
1. Abinadab's son 2Sam 6:3
2. A Benjamite 1Chr 8:14
3. A son of Jehiel 1Chr 8:31
   1Chr 9:37

and *A* went before the ark 2Sam 6:4

AHIRA (ä-hī'rä)—"brother of evil"
A tribal leader ....Num 1:15

Naphtali shall be *A* the son....Num 2:29
the twelfth day *A* the son .....Num 7:78
this was the offering of *A* .....Num 7:83
children of Naphtali was *A* ....Num 10:27

AHIRAM (ä-hī'răm)—*"exalted brother; any brother is exalted"*

[*also* AHIRAMITES]
Ahiram, the family of the *A* . . .Num 26:38

AHISAMACH (ä-hĭs'ä-măk)—*"supporting brother"*
A Danite ....Ex 31:6

and Aholiab, the son of *A* ....Ex 35:34
was Aholiab, son of *A* ....Ex 38:23

AHISHAHAR (ä-hĭsh'ä-här)—*"brother of the dawn"*
A Benjamite 1Chr 7:10

AHISHAR (ä-hī'shär)—*"brother of song; my brother has sung"*
A manager of Solomon's household 1Kin 4:6

AHITHOPHEL (ä-hĭth'ō-fĕl)—*"brother of foolishness"*
David's counselor 2Sam 15:12
Joins Absalom's insurrection 2Sam 15:31
Plans of, prepared against by David 2Sam 15:31-34
Counsels Absalom 2Sam 16:20-22
Reputed wise 2Sam 16:23
Counsel of, rejected by Absalom..............2Sam 17:1-22
Commits suicide 2Sam 17:23

A is among..conspirators 2Sam 15:31
the counsel of *A* into 2Sam 15:31
me defeat the counsel of *A* 2Sam 15:34
to Jerusalem, and *A* with 2Sam 16:15
A said into Absalom, Let 2Sam 17:1
A hath spoken after this 2Sam 17:6
The counsel that *A* hath 2Sam 17:7
better than the counsel of *A* . . .2Sam 17:14
defeat the good counsel of *A* . .2Sam 17:14
and thus did *A* counsel........2Sam 17:15
A counseled against you.......2Sam 17:21
Eliam the son of *A* the........2Sam 23:34
A was..king's counselor 1Chr 27:33
after *A* was Jehoida the 1Chr 27:34

AHITUB (ä-hī'tŭb)—*"a good brother; by brother is goodness"*
1. Phinehas' son 1Sam 14:3
2. The father of Zadok the priest 2Sam 8:17
3. The father of another Zadok 1Chr 6:11, 12

to Ahimelech the son of *A* 1Sam 22:9
the son of *A*, and all his 1Sam 22:11
Hear now, thou son of *A* 1Sam 22:12
of Ahimelech the son of *A* 1Sam 22:20
Amariah his son, *A* his son 1Chr 6:52
A, the ruler of the house of . . .1Chr 9:11
And Zadok the son of *A* 1Chr 18:16
son of Zadok, the son of *A* . . .Ezra 7:2
the son of *A*, was the ruler ....Neh 11:11

AHLAB (ä'lăb)—*"fertile"*
A city of Asher ....Judg 1:31

AHLAI (ä'lī)—*"Jehovah is staying"*
1. David's warrior 1Chr 11:41
2. Marries an Egyptian servant 1Chr 2:31-35

AHOAH (ä-hō'ä)—*"a brother's reed; brotherly"*
A son of Bela 1Chr 8:4

AHOHITE (ä hō'hīt)—*a descendant of Ahoah*
Applied to Dodo, Zalmon, and Ilai 2Sam 23:9, 28

the son of Dodo, the *A* 1Chr 11:12
the Hushathite, Ilai the *A* 1Chr 11:29
month was Dodai an *A* 1Chr 27:4

AHOLAH (ä-hō'lä)—*"tent-woman"*
Symbolic name of Samaria and Israel.....Ezek 23:4, 5, 36

AHOLIAB (ä-hō'lĭ-ăb)—*"a father's tent"*
Son of Ahisamach ....Ex 31:6

may teach, both he, and *A* ....Ex 35:34
wrought Bezaleel and *A* ....Ex 36:1
Moses called Bezaleel *A* ......Ex 36:2
And with him was *A*, son of. . .Ex 38:23

AHOLIBAH (ä-hō'lĭ-bä)—*"my tent is in her"*
the elder and *A* her sister .....Ezek 23:4
is Aholah, and Jerusalem *A* . . .Ezek 23:4
when her sister *A* saw this.....Ezek 23:11
Therefore, O *A*, thus saith ....Ezek 23:22
thou judge Aholah and *A*? ....Ezek 23:36
unto *A*, the lewd women ......Ezek 23:44

AHOLIBAMAH (ä-hōl-ĭ-bā'mä)—*"tent of the high place"*
and *A* the daughter of Anah. . .Gen 36:2
A bare Jeush, and Jaalam .....Gen 36:5
these were the sons of *A* ......Gen 36:14
the sons of *A* Esau's wife .....Gen 36:18
the dukes that came of *A* .....Gen 36:18
and *A* the daughter of Anah. . .Gen 36:25
Duke *A*, duke Elah, duke .....Gen 36:41
Duke *A*, duke Elah, duke 1Chr 1:52

AHUMAI (ä-hū'mī)—*"heated by Jehovah"*
A descendant of Judah. . .1Chr 4:2

and Jahath begat *A*, and 1Chr 4:2

AHUNGERED—*See* HUNGER, PHYSICAL

AHUZAM (ä-hŭz'ăm)—*"possession"*
A man of Judah 1Chr 4:6

AHUZZATH (ä-hŭz'ăth)—*"holding fast"*
A friend of Abimelech . . .Gen 26:26

AI (ā'ī)—*"heap of ruins"*
1. A city east of Beth-el in central Palestine ......Josh 7:2
   Abraham camps near....Gen 12:8
   A royal city of Canaan . .Josh 10:1
   Israel defeated at ....Josh 7:2-5
   Israel destroys completely ....Josh 8:1-28
   Occupied after exile .....Ezra 2:28
2. An Ammonite city near Heshbon ....Jer 49:3

sent men from Jericho to *A* . . .Josh 7:2
fled between the men of *A* ....Josh 7:4
and arise, go up to *A* ....Josh 8:1
into thy hand the king of *A* . . .Josh 8:1
abode between Beth-el and *A* .Josh 8:9
on the west side of *A*; but.....Josh 8:9
on the north side of *A* ....Josh 8:11
valley between them and *A* ....Josh 8:11
when the king of *A* saw it .....Josh 8:14
people that were in *A* were....Josh 8:16
was not a man left in *A* ....Josh 8:17
the men of *A* looked behind . . .Josh 8:20
and slew the men of *A* ....Josh 8:21
king of *A* they took alive......Josh 8:23
all the inhabitants of *A*........Josh 8:24
Israelites returned unto *A* .....Josh 8:24
destroyed..inhabitants of *A* ....Josh 8:26
Joshua burnt *A* and made .....Josh 8:28
the king of *A* he hanged on . . .Josh 8:29
done unto Jericho and to *A* . . .Josh 9:3
it was greater than *A* ....Josh 10:2
The men of Beth-el and *A* ....Neh 7:32

AIAH (ā-ī'ä)—*"a vulture"*
1. A Horite ....Gen 36:24
2. The father of Rizpah, Saul's concubine 2Sam 3:7

sons..the daughter of *A* 2Sam 21:8
Rizpah the daughter of *A* 2Sam 21:10
of *A*; the concubine of 2Sam 21:11
the sons of Zibeon, *A*. and 1Chr 1:40

AIATH (ā-ī'ăth)—*"heap of ruins"*
He is come to *A*, he is ....Is 10:28
See AI

AIDED—*helped*
which *a* him in the killing .....Judg 9:24

AIJA (ā-ī'jä)—*"heap of ruins"*
dwelt at Michmash and *A* .....Neh 11:31
See Ai

AIJALON (ā'jä-lŏn)—*"place of gazelles"*
1. A town assigned to Dan..Josh 19:42
   Amorites not driven from Judg 1:35
   Miracle there ....Josh 10:12
   Assigned to Kohathite Levites................Josh 21:24
   City of refuge 1Chr 6:66-69
   Included in Benjamin's territory..............1Chr 8:13
   Fortified by Rehoboam ..2Chr 11:10
   Captured by Philistines ..2Chr 28:18
2. The burial place of Elon, a judge ....Judg 12:12

A with her suburbs ....Josh 21:24
day from Michmash to *A* 1Sam 14:31

AIJELETH (ā'jĕ-lĕth)—*"gazelle of the morning"*
chief Musician upon *A* ....Ps 22:*title*

AILED—*to suffer*

[*also* AILETH]
said unto her, What ***a*** thee ....Gen 21:17
said unto Micah, What ***a*** ......Judg 18:23
ye say unto me, What ***a*** thee? .Judg 18:24
What ***a*** the people that they...1Sam 11:5
king said unto her, What ***a*** 2Sam 14:5
king said unto her, What ***a*** 2Kin 6:28
What ***a*** thee, O thou sea ......Ps 114:5
What ***a*** thee now, that thou ...Is 22:1

AIN (ä'ĕn)—*"eye; spring"*
1. A town near Riblah .....Num 34:11
2. Town of Judah ....Josh 15:32
   Transferred to Simeon...Josh 19:7
   Later assigned to the priests ....Josh 21:16
   Called Ashan 1Chr 6:59
3. Letter of the Hebrew alphabet ....Ps 119:121-136

villages were, Etam, and *A* 1Chr 4:32

AIR—*in the atmosphere*
   Man given dominion over.Gen 1:26-30
   Man names birds of .....Gen 2:19, 20
   God destroys birds of....Gen 6:7
   Mystery of eagle in ......Prov 30:19
   Satan, prince of ....Eph 2:2
   Believers meet Jesus in ..1Thess 4:17
   God's wrath poured out in ....Rev 9:2
   Figurative of emptiness ..1Cor 9:26

fowls also of the ***a*** by sevens ..Gen 7:3
upon every fowl of the ***a*** ......Gen 9:2
fowl that flieth in the ***a*** ....Deut 4:17
all fowls of the ***a*** and unto ....Deut 28:26
flesh unto the fowls of the ***a***...1Sam 17:44
unto the fowls of the ***a***........1Sam 17:46
birds of the ***a*** to rest on them .2Sam 21:10
shall the fowls of the ***a*** eat 1Kin 14:11
shall the fowls of the ***a*** eat 1Kin 16:4
field shall the fowls of the ***a***...1Kin 21:24
fowls of the ***a*** and they shall ..Job 12:7
close from the fowls of the ***a*** ..Job 28:21
no ***a*** can come between them..Job 41:16
fowl of the ***a*** and the fish .....Ps 8:8
bird of the ***a*** shall carry the ...Eccl 10:20
Behold the fowls of the ***a*** .....Matt 6:26
the birds of the ***a*** have nests ..Matt 8:20
birds of the ***a*** come and.......Matt 13:32
the fowls of the ***a*** came and ...Mark 4:4
fowls of the ***a*** may lodge ......Mark 4:32
fowls of the ***a*** devoured it .....Luke 8:5
birds of the ***a*** have nests ......Luke 9:58
fowls of the ***a*** lodged in the ...Luke 13:19
things, and fowls of the ***a*** .....Acts 10:12
and fowls of the ***a*** ....Acts 11:6
and threw dust into the ***a*** .....Acts 22:23
ye shall speak into the ***a*** 1Cor 14:9
poured out his vial into..***a*** .....Rev 16:17

AJAH (ā'jä)—*"a vulture"—an alternative spelling for "Aiah"*
children of Zibeon; both *A* ....Gen 36:24

AJALON (ā'jä-lŏn)—*"place of gazelles"—an alternate spelling for Aijalon*
Moon, in the valley of *A* ......Josh 10:12
taken Beth-shemesh, and *A* ...2Chr 28:18

AKAN (ā'kăn)—*"intelligent"*
Bilban, and Zaavan, and *A* ....Gen 36:27

AKKUB (ăk'ŭb)—*"lain in wait; pursuer"*
1. Elioenai's son 1Chr 3:24
2. A Levite head of a family of porters 1Chr 9:17
3. A family of Nethinim ...Ezra 2:45
4. A Levite interpreter.....Neh 8:7

Talmon, the children of *A* .....Ezra 2:42
children of *A*, the children ....Neh 7:45
Moreover the porters, *A* ......Neh 11:19
Talmon, *A* were porters ....Neh 12:25

AKRABBIM (ăk-răb'ĭm)—*"scorpions"*
   An "ascent" on the south of the Dead Sea.......Num 34:4
   One border of Judah—Acrabbim .....Josh 15:3

from the going up to *A* ....Judg 1:36

ALABASTER—*a white, translucent gypsum often made into containers*
   Used by woman anointing Jesus ....Matt 26:7

an ***a*** box of ointment ....Mark 14:3
an ***a*** box of ointment ....Luke 7:37

ALAMETH (ăl'ä-meth)
Abiah, and Anathoth, and *A* ..1Chr 7:8
See Alemeth

ALAMMELECH (ă-lăm'e-lĕk)—*"king's oak"*
   Village of Asher.........Josh 19:26

ALAMOTH (ăl'ä'mŏth)—*"virgins"*
   A musical term probably indicating a women's choir 1Chr 15:20

A song upon *A* ....Ps 46: *Title*

ALARM—*sudden and fearful surprise*

Caused physically by:
   Sudden attack ....Judg 7:20-23
   Death plague ....Ex 12:29-33
   A mysterious manifestation..........1Sam 28:11-14
   Prodigies of nature ......Matt 27:50-54

Caused spiritually by:
   Sin 1Sam 12:17-19
   Remorse................Gen 27:34-40
   Conscience.............Acts 24:24, 25
   Hopelessness in hell .....Luke 16:22-31

Shout of jubilee or warning:
   Instruction to Israel......Num 10:5, 6
   Causes anguish ....Jer 4:19
   Prophecy of judgment ...Jer 49:2
   See Agitation

ye shall not sound an ***a*** ....Num 10:7
an ***a*** with the trumpets ....Num 10:9
sounding trumpets to cry ***a*** 2Chr 13:12
sound an ***a*** in my holy ....Joel 2:1
A day of the trumpet and ***a*** ...Zeph 1:16

ALAS—*an intense emotional outcry*

Emotional outcry caused by:
   Israel's defeat ....Josh 7:7-9
   An angel's appearance ...Judg 6:22
   A vow's realization ......Judg 11:34, 35
   Army without water 2Kin 3:9, 10
   Loss of an ax 2Kin 6:5
   Servant's fear 2Kin 6:14, 15

Prophetic outcry caused by:
   Israel's future ....Num 24:23, 24
   Israel's punishment ......Amos 5:16-20
   Jacob's trouble ....Jer 30:7-9
   Babylon's fall ....Rev 18:10-19

Aaron said unto Moses, *A* ....Num 12:11
A who shall live when God....Num 24:23
mourned over him, saying, *A* ..1Kin 13:30
A for..the evil abominations ...Ezek 6:11
A for the day! for the day .....Joel 1:15
in all the highways, *A*! ***a***! .....Amos 5:16

ALBEIT—*although it be*
Lord saith it; ***a*** I have not ....Ezek 13:7
a I do not say to thee how ....Philem 19

ALEMETH (ăl'ĕ-mĕth)—*"hiding place"*
1. A Benjamite 1Chr 7:8
2. A descendant of Saul ...1Chr 8:36
3. A Levitical city 1Chr 6:60

See Alameth

Jarah begat *A* and 1Chr 9:42

ALEPH (ä'lef)
   The first letter in the Hebrew alphabet ......Ps 119:1-8

ALERT—*watchful*
   In battle ....Judg 7:15-22
   In personal safety 1Sam 19:9, 10
   In readiness for attack ...Neh 4:9-23
   In prayer ....Matt 26:41
   In spiritual combat ......Eph 6:18
   In waiting for Christ's return ....Matt 24:42-51
   Daily living 1Cor 16:13
   Times of testing ....Luke 21:34-36
   Against false teachers ....Acts 20:29-31

ALEXANDER (ăl-ĕg-zăn'der)—*"helper of men"*
1. A son of Simon of Cyrene...............Mark 15:21
2. A member of the high-priestly family....Acts 4:6
3. A Jew in Ephesus.......Acts 19:33, 34
4. An apostate condemned by Paul 1Tim 1:19, 20

A the coppersmith did me 2Tim 4:14

ALEXANDER THE GREAT—*Alexander III of Macedonia (356-323 B.C.)*

Not named in the Bible, but referred to as:
   The four-headed leopard..Dan 7:6
   The goat with a great horn ....Dan 8:5-9, 21
   A mighty king ....Dan 11:3

Rule of, described:
   His invasion of Palestine..Zech 9:1-8
   His kingdom being divided ....Dan 7:6

ALEXANDRIA (ăl-ĕg-zăn'drĭ-ä)—*a city of Egypt founded by Alexander the Great (332 B.C.)*
   Men of, persecute Stephen ....Acts 6:9
   Apollos, native of ....Acts 18:24
   Paul sails in ship ....Acts 27:6

we departed in a ship of *A* ....Acts 28:11

ALGUM—*a tree (probably the red sandalwood)*
   Imported from Ophir by Hiram's navy..........1Kin 10:11, 12
   Used in constructing the temple...............2Chr 9:10, 11
   Also imported from Lebanon 2Chr 2:8
   See Almug

ALIAH (ă-lī'ă)—*"sublimity"*
were; duke Timnah, Duke *A* ..1Chr 1:51
See Alvah

ALIAN (ă-lī'ăn)—*"sublime"*
Shobal; *A* and Manahath 1Chr 1:40
See Alvan

ALIENATE—*to deprive*

[*also* ALIENATED]
nor ***a*** the first fruits..land .....Ezek 48:14
that were sometime ***a*** and .....Col 1:21

ALIENS—*citizens of a foreign country*
Descriptive, naturally, of:
Israel in the Egyptian bondage ....Gen 15:13
Abraham in Canaan .....Gen 23:4
Moses in Egypt ....Ex 18:3
Israel in Babylon ....Ps 137:4
Descriptive, spiritually, of:
Estrangement from friends................Job 19:15
Israel's apostasy ....Ezek 23:17, 18, 22, 28
The condition of the Gentiles ....Eph 2:12
Spiritual deadness ....Eph 4:18
[*also* ALIEN]
mayest sell it unto an *a* ....Deut 14:21
a unto my mother's children...Ps 69:8
a shall be your plowmen ......Is 61:5
our houses to *a* ....Lam 5:2
to flight the armies of the *a* ...Heb 11:34

ALIKE—*exhibiting similarity*
clean shall eat of them *a* ......Deut 12:22
clean person shall eat it *a* .....Deut 15:22
they shall part *a*..............1Sam 30:24
They shall lie down *a* in ......Job 21:26
He fashioneth their hearts *a* ...Ps 33:15
darkness..light are both *a* .....Ps 139:12
both of them are *a* ....Prov 20:10
a contentious woman are *a* ....Prov 27:15
All things come *a* to all ....Eccl 9:2
whether they both shall be *a* ..Eccl 11:6
esteemeth every day *a* ....Rom 14:5

ALIVE—*having life; not dead*
Descriptive of:
Natural life ....Gen 43:7, 27, 28
Spiritual life ....Luke 15:24, 32
Restored physical life ....Acts 9:41
Christ's resurrected life ..Acts 1:3
The believer's glorified life 1Cor 15:22
The unbeliever's life in hell ....Num 16:33
The power of keeping:
Belongs to God ....Deut 32:39
Not in man's power .....Ps 22:29
Promised to the godly ...Ps 33:19
Gratefully acknowledged..Josh 14:10
Transformed by Christ's return 1Thess 4:15, 16
to keep them *a* with thee .....Gen 6:19
unto thee, to keep them *a* ....Gen 6:20
keep seed *a* upon the face ....Gen 7:3
and Noah only remained *a* ....Gen 7:23
but they will save thee *a* ......Gen 12:12
Is your father yet *a*? ....Gen 43:7
saying, Joseph is yet *a* ....Gen 45:26
Joseph my son is yet *a*........Gen 45:28
because thou art yet *a* ....Gen 46:30
to save much people *a* ....Gen 50:20
saved the men children *a*......Ex 1:17
saved the men children *a*?.....Ex 1:18
see whether they be yet *a* .....Ex 4:18
be..found in his hand *a* ....Ex 22:4
sons of Aaron which were left *a* Lev 10:16
cleansed two birds *a* and ......Lev 14:4
presented *a* before the Lord ...Lev 16:10
went down *a* into the pit ......Num 16:33
there was none left him *a* .....Num 21:35
slain thee, and saved her *a* ....Num 22:33
ye saved all the women *a*? ....Num 31:15
a every one of you this day ...Deut 4:4
who are all of us here *a* this...Deut 5:3
that he might preserve us alive.Deut 6:24
a nothing that breatheth ......Deut 20:16
while I am yet *a* with you .....Deut 31:27
I kill and I make *a*, I ....Deut 32:39
And that ye will save *a* my....Josh 2:13
saved Rahab the harlot *a* .....Josh 6:25
the king of Ai they took *a* ....Josh 8:23
the Lord hath kept me *a* .....Josh 14:10
if ye had saved them *a*, I .....Judg 8:19
Lord killeth, and maketh *a* 1Sam 2:6
Agag the king..Amalekites *a* ..1Sam 15:8
neither man nor woman *a* 1Sam 27:9
with one full line to keep *a* ...2Sam 8:2
while the child was yet *a* 2Sam 12:18
while he was yet *a* in the 2Sam 18:14
save the horses and mules *a* ...1Kin 18:5
come..for peace, take them *a*..1Kin 20:18
out for war, take them *a* 1Kin 20:18
said, Is he yet *a*? he is my 1Kin 20:32
Am I God, to kill..make *a* 2Kin 5:7
if they save us *a* we shall 2Kin 7:4
he said, Take them *a* 2Kin 10:14
And they took them *a* 2Kin 10:14
other ten thousand left *a* 2Chr 25:12
none can keep *a* his own ......Ps 22:29
thou hast kept me *a* ....Ps 30:3
to keep them *a* in famine .....Ps 33:19
preserve him and keep him *a* ..Ps 41:2
swallow them up *a* as the .....Prov 1:12
the living which are yet *a* .....Eccl 4:2
I will preserve them *a* ....Jer 49:11
although they were yet *a* ......Ezek 7:13
save the souls *a* that come ....Ezek 13:18
save the souls *a* that should ...Ezek 13:19
he shall save his soul *a*........Ezek 18:27
whom he would be kept *a*.....Dan 5:19
said, while he was yet *a*.......Matt 27:63
had heard that he was *a* ......Mark 16:11
son was dead and is *a* again ...Luke 15:24
brother was dead and is *a* .....Luke 15:32
which said that he was *a* ......Luke 24:23
he showed himself *a* after .....Acts 1:3
widows, presented her *a* ......Acts 9:41
brought the young man *a* .....Acts 20:12
whom Paul affirmed to be *a*...Acts 25:19
dead indeed unto sin, but *a* ...Rom 6:11
as those that are *a* from the ...Rom 6:13
I was *a* without the law ....Rom 7:9
in Christ shall all be made *a*...1Cor 15:22
we which are *a* and remain....1Thess 4:15
are *a* and remain shall be 1Thess 4:17
I am *a* for evermore ....Rev 1:18
which was dead and is *a* ......Rev 2:8
both were cast *a* into a lake ...Rev 19:20

ALL—*See* INTRODUCTION

ALLEGING—*asserting; proving*
Opening and *a* that Christ.....Acts 17:3

ALLEGORY—*an extended figure of speech using symbols*
Of natural things:
A king's doom ....Judg 9:8-15
Old age ....Eccl 12:3-7
Israel as a transplanted vine ....Ps 80:8-19
Of spiritual things:
Christian as sheep ....John 10:1-16
Two covenants ....Gal 4:21-31
Israel and the Gentiles ...Rom 11:15-24
Christ and His Church ...Eph 5:22-33
The Christian's armor ....Eph 6:11-17

ALLELUIA (ä-lai-lū'yă)—*"praise ye the Lord"*
The Greek form of the Hebrew Hallelujah ....Rev 19:1-6

ALLIANCE WITH EVIL
Forbidden to:
Israel ....Ex 34:11-16
Christians ....Rom 13:12
Christ ....Matt 4:1-11
Forbidden because:
Leads to idolatry ....Ex 23:32, 33
Deceives.................Num 25:1-3, 18
Enslaves 2Pet 2:18, 19
Defiles ....Ezra 9:1, 2
Brings God's anger ......Ezra 9:13-15
Corrupts 1Cor 15:33
Incompatible with Christ..2Cor 6:14-16
Pollutes.................Jude 23
The believer should:
Avoid ....Prov 1:10-15
Hate ....Ps 26:4, 5
Confess.................Ezra 10:9-11
Separate from 2Cor 6:17
Examples of:
Solomon 1Kin 11:1-11
Rehoboam 1Kin 12:25-33
Jehoshaphat.............2Chr 20:35-37
Judas Iscariot ....Matt 26:14-16
Heretics ....Rev 2:14-15, 20

See ASSOCIATION

ALLIANCES—*treaties between nations or individuals*
In the time of the patriarchs:
Abraham with Canaanite chiefs..................Gen 14:13
Abraham with Abimelech.Gen 21:22-34
Isaac with Abimelech ....Gen 26:26-33
Jacob with Laban........Gen 31:44-54
In the time of the wilderness:
Israel with Moab ....Num 25:1-3
In the time of the conquest:
Israel with Gibeonites....Judg 9:3-27
In the time of David:
David with Achish.......1Sam 27:2-12
In the time of Solomon:
Solomon with Hiram.....1Kin 5:12-18
Solomon with Egypt 1Kin 3:1
In the time of the divided kingdom:
Asa with Ben-hadad 1Kin 15:18-20
Ahab with Ben-hadad....1Kin 20:31-34
Israel with Syria 2Kin 16:5-9
Hoshea with Egypt 2Kin 17:1-6
In the time of Judah's sole kingdom:
Hezekiah with Egypt 2Kin 18:19-24
Josiah with Assyria 2Kin 23:29
Jehoiakim with Egypt 2Kin 23:31-35
[*also* ALLIED]
the priest..was *a* unto ....Neh 13:4

ALL IN ALL—*complete*
Descriptive of:
God 1Cor 15:28
Christ ....Eph 1:23

ALLON (ăl'ŏn)—*"an oak"*
1. A Simeonite prince 1Chr 4:37
2. A town in south Naphtali ....Josh 19:33

ALLON-BACHUTH (ăl'ŏn-băk'ŭth)—*"oak of weeping"*
A tree marking Deborah's grave.......Gen 35:8

ALLOW—*acknowledge; permit*
[*also* ALLOWED, ALLOWETH]
a the deeds of your fathers ....Luke 11:48
which they themselves..*a* ......Acts 24:15
that which I do I *a* not ....Rom 7:15
But as we were *a* of God to...1Thess 2:4

ALLOWANCE—*share or portion allotted or granted*
Daily to Jehoiachin 2Kin 25:27-30
Also called a diet........Jer 52:34

ALLURE—*to entice by charm or attraction*
I will *a* her, and bring her ....Hos 2:14
a through the lusts of the 2Pet 2:18

ALMIGHTY—*having absolute power over all; a title of God*
Applied to God ....Gen 17:1
2 Cor 6:18
Applied to Christ........Rev 1:8
And God *A* bless thee ....Gen 28:3
God said..him, I am God *A* ...Gen 35:11
God *A* appeared unto me at...Gen 48:3
by the *A*, who shall bless......Gen 49:25
by the name of God *A* ....Ex 6:3
saw the vision of the *A* ....Num 24:4

A hath dealt very bitterly .....Ruth 1:20
and the *A* hath afflicted me? ..Ruth 1:21
thou the chastening of the *A* ..Job 5:17
he forsaketh..fear of the *A* ....Job 6:14
doth the *A* pervert justice? ....Job 8:3
make..supplication to the *A* ...Job 8:5
find..*A* unto perfection? ....Job 11:7
I would speak to the *A* ....Job 13:3
himself against the *A* ....Job 15:25
What is the *A*, that we ....Job 21:15
drink of the wrath of the *A* ...Job 21:20
Is it any pleasure to the *A* ....Job 22:3
what can the *A* do for them? ..Job 22:17
If thou return to the *A* ....Job 22:23
The *A* shall be thy defense ....Job 22:25
have thy delight in the *A* ......Job 22:26
and the *A* troubleth me ....Job 23:16
are not hidden from the *A* ....Job 24:1
the *A* who hath vexed my .....Job 27:2
he delight himself in the *A*? ...Job 27:10
the *A* will I not conceal ....Job 27:11
they shall receive of the *A* ....Job 27:13
When the *A* was yet with .....Job 29:5
inheritance of the *A* from .....Job 31:2
the *A* would answer me ....Job 31:35
inspiration of the *A* giveth .....Job 32:8
breath of the *A* hath given ....Job 33:4
from the *A* that he should .....Job 34:10
will the *A* pervert judgment ...Job 34:12
neither will the *A* regard it ....Job 35:13
the *A*, we cannot find him ....Job 37:23
that contendeth with the *A* ....Job 40:2
the *A* scattered kings ....Ps 68:14
under the shadow of the *A* ....Ps 91:1
as a destruction from the *A* ...Is 13:6
as the voice of the *A* ....Ezek 1:24
A God when he speaketh .....Ezek 10:5
a destruction from the *A* ......Joel 1:15
holy, holy, Lord God *A* ......Rev 4:8
O Lord God *A* which art ......Rev 11:17
thy works Lord God *A* ....Rev 15:3
Lord God *A*, true and ....Rev 16:7
that great day of God *A* ......Rev 16:14
and wrath of *A* God ....Rev 19:15
Lord God *A* and the Lamb ....Rev 21:22

ALMODAD (ăl-mō'dăd)—*"the agitator"*
Eldest son of Joktan .....Gen 10:26

Joktan begat *A* and 1Chr 1:20

ALMON (ăl'mŏn)—*"covering"*
A with her suburbs; four ......Josh 21:18

ALMOND—*a small tree and its fruit*
Sent as a present to Pharaoh ....Gen 43:11
Used in the tabernacle ...Ex 25:33, 34
Aaron's rod produces ....Num 17:2, 3, 8
Used figuratively of old age ....Eccl 12:5
Translated "hazel" in ....Gen 30:37

[*also* ALMONDS]
made after the fashion of *a* ....Ex 37:19
three bowls made like *a* ....Ex 37:19
four bowls made like *a* ....Ex 37:20
the *a* tree shall flourish ....Eccl 12:5
I see a rod of an *a* tree ....Jer 1:11

ALMON-DIBLATHAIM (ăl'mŏn-dĭb-lä-thā'ĭm)—*"hiding place of two fig sacks"*
An Israelite encampment .Num 33:46, 47

ALMOST—*very nearly but not exactly or entirely*
they be *a* ready to stone me ...Ex 17:4
for me my feet were *a* gone ...Ps 73:2
soul had *a* dwelt in silence ....Ps 94:17
had *a* consumed me upon .....Ps 119:87
I was *a* in all evil ....Prov 5:14
came *a* the whole city ....Acts 13:44
but *a* throughout all Asia .....Acts 19:26
seven days were *a* ended ......Acts 21:27
A thou persuadest me to be ...Acts 26:28
a and altogether such as I .....Acts 26:29
a all things are by the law .....Heb 9:22

ALMS—*gifts given freely to help those in need*
Design of, to:
Help the poor ....Lev 25:35
Receive a blessing ....Deut 15:10, 11
Manner of bestowing with:
A willing spirit ....Deut 15:7-11
Simplicity ....Matt 6:1-4
Cheerfulness 2Cor 9:7
True love 1Cor 13:3
Fairness to all ....Acts 4:32-35
Regularity ....Acts 11:29, 30
Law of reciprocity ....Rom 15:25-27
Cautions concerning:
Not for man's honor .....Matt 6:1-4
Not for lazy 2Thess 3:10
Needful for the rich 1Tim 6:17, 18
Rewarded:
Now ....Deut 14:28, 29; 2Cor 9:9, 10
In heaven ....Matt 19:21
Examples of:
Zacchaeus ....Luke 19:8
Dorcas ....Acts 9:36
Cornelius ....Acts 10:2
The early Christians .....Acts 4:34-37

[*also* ALMSDEEDS]
give *a* of such things as ye ....Luke 11:41
Sell that ye have..give *a* ......Luke 12:33
ask *a* of them that entered ....Acts 3:2
into the temple asked an *a* ....Acts 3:3
it was he which sat for *a* ......Acts 3:10
full of good works and *a* ......Acts 9:36
prayers and thine *a* are ....Acts 10:4
a are had in remembrance ....Acts 10:31
I came to bring *a* to my.......Acts 24:17

ALMUG—*a tree (probably the red sandalwood)*
great plenty of *a* trees 1Kin 10:11
king made of the *a* trees 1Kin 10:12
there came no such *a* trees 1Kin 10:12
See ALGUM

ALOES—*perfume-bearing tree; dried juice therefrom*
Used on:
Beds ....Prov 7:17
The dead ....John 19:39
Figurative of:
Israel ....Num 24:5, 6
The Church ....Ps 45:8

a with all the chief spices .....Song 4:14

ALONE—*exclusive of anyone or anything else*
that the man should be *a* .....Gen 2:18
And Jacob was left *a* and .....Gen 32:24
brother is dead..is left *a* ......Gen 42:38
able to perform it thyself *a* ....Ex 18:18
And Moses *a* shall come ......Ex 24:2
shall dwell *a*; without the .....Lev 13:46
to bear all this people *a* ....Num 11:14
the Lord *a* did lead him.......Deut 32:12
man perished not *a* in his .....Josh 22:20
which he had for himself *a* ....Judg 3:20
art thou *a* and no man 1Sam 21:1
him *a*, and let him curse 2Sam 16:11
they two were *a* in the field ...1Kin 11:29
And he said, Let him *a* 2Kin 23:18
my son, whom *a* God hath 1Chr 29:1
the work..house of God *a* .....Ezra 6:7
even thou art Lord *a* ....Neh 9:6
lay hands on Mordecai *a* ......Esth 3:6
escaped *a* to tell.............Job 1:15
eaten my morsel myself *a* .....Job 31:17
whose name *a* is Jehovah .....Ps 83:18
things; thou art God *a* ....Ps 86:10
as a sparrow *a* upon the ......Ps 102:7
him who *a* doeth great ....Ps 136:4
Lord: for his name *a* is ....Ps 148:13
thou *a* shalt bear it ....Prov 9:12
There is one *a* and there is ....Eccl 4:8
him that is *a* when he.........Eccl 4:10
Lord *a* shall be exalted ....Is 2:11, 17
stretcheth..the heavens *a* ......Is 44:24
I called him *a* and blessed .....Is 51:2

sat *a* because of thy hand .....Jer 15:17
He sitteth *a* and keepeth ......Lam 3:28
I Daniel *a* saw the vision ......Dan 10:7
joined to idols; let him *a* ......Hos 4:17
Let them *a*: they be blind .....Matt 15:14
Saying, Let us *a* what have ....Mark 1:24
And when he was *a* ....Mark 4:10
and he *a* on the land ....Mark 6:47
not live by bread *a*, but by ....Luke 4:4
Saying, Let us *a*; what ....Luke 4:34
forgive sins, but God *a*? ......Luke 5:21
as he was *a* praying...........Luke 9:18
Jesus was found *a* ....Luke 9:36
hath left me to serve *a*? ....Luke 10:40
into a mountain himself *a* .....John 6:15
and Jesus was left *a* ....John 8:9
I am not *a*, but I and the .....John 8:16
Father hath not left me *a* .....John 8:29
If we let him thus *a*, all ....John 11:48
Then said Jesus, Let her *a* ....John 12:7
and die it abideth *a*...........John 12:24
and shall leave me *a* ....John 16:32
yet I am not *a* because........John 16:32
pray I for these *a*, but for.....John 17:20
these men, and let them *a* ....Acts 5:38
not *a* at Ephesus, but ....Acts 19:26
for his sake *a*, that it ....Rom 4:23
have rejoicing in himself *a* ....Gal 6:4
to be left at Athens *a*.........1Thess 3:1
went the high priest *a* once....Heb 9:7
not works, is dead, being *a*....James 2:17

ALONG—*beside*
walked *a* by the river's side ...Ex 2:5
fire ran *a* upon the ground ....Ex 9:23
will go *a* by the king's high....Num 21:22
wilderness of Zin *a* by the ....Num 34:3
I will go *a* by the highway ....Deut 2:27
and chased them *a* the way....Josh 10:10
and passed *a* to Zin ....Josh 15:3
and passed *a* to Hezron ......Josh 15:3
a by the north of Beth-arabah .Josh 15:6
a unto the side of mount......Josh 15:10
passed *a* to mount Baalah .....Josh 15:11
passeth *a* unto the borders ....Josh 16:2
border went *a* on the right ....Josh 17:7
passed *a* toward the side ......Josh 18:18
And the border passed *a* to ...Josh 18:19
from thence passeth on *a* .....Josh 19:13
east lay *a* in the valley ....Judg 7:12
it, that the tent lay *a* ....Judg 7:13
robbed all that came *a* that....Judg 9:25
a by the plain of Meonenim ...Judg 9:37
a through the wilderness ......Judg 11:18
cities that be *a* by the coasts ..Judg 11:26
in wait drew themselves *a* .....Judg 20:37
went *a* the highway, lowing ...1Sam 6:12
Saul fell straightway all *a* 1Sam 28:20
went with her *a* weeping 2Sam 3:16
Shimei went *a* on the hill's 2Sam 16:13
a by the altar..the temple 2Kin 11:11
a by the altar..the temple 2Chr 23:10
weeping all *a* as he went ......Jer 41:6

ALOOF—*at a distance; uninvolved*
friends stand *a* from my.......Ps 38:11

ALOTH (ā'lŏth)—*"ascents, steeps"*
A town in Asher 1Kin 4:16

ALOUD—*loudly; with a speaking voice*
And he wept *a* ....Gen 45:2
Cry *a* for he is a god 1Kin 18:27
they cried *a*, and cut 1Kin 18:28
many shouted *a* for joy ....Ezra 3:12
I cry *a*, but there is no........Job 19:7
my tongue shall sing *a* of .....Ps 51:14
will I pray and cry *a* and ......Ps 55:17
I will sing *a* of thy...........Ps 59:16
Sing *a* unto God our ....Ps 81:1
saints shall shout *a* for ....Ps 132:16
let them sing *a* upon their .....Ps 149:5
shall cry *a* from the sea ....Is 24:14
forth into singing and cry *a* ....Is 54:1
Cry *a*, spare not, lift up thy ...Is 58:1
Then an herald cried *a*, To ....Dan 3:4
He cried *a* and said thus ......Dan 4:14

The king cried *a* to bring in . . . Dan 5:7
cry *a* at Beth-aven . . . Hos 5:8
dost thou cry out *a* . . . Mic 4:9
multitude crying *a* began . . . Mark 15:8

ALPHA AND OMEGA—*first and last letters of the Greek alphabet*
Expressive of God and Christ's eternity . . . Rev 1:8, 17, 18; Rev 21:6, 7
I am *A* and Omega . . . Rev 22:13

ALPHABET—*the letters or characters of a language*
The Hebrew, seen in . . . Ps 119

ALPHAEUS (ăl-fē'ŭs)—*"leader; chief"*
1. The father of Levi (Matthew) . . . Mark 2:14
2. The father of James . . . Matt 10:3
See CLEOPHAS

[*also* ALPHEUS]
James the son of *A* . . . Acts 1:13

ALREADY—*before a specified or implied past, present, or future time*
offended against the Lord *a* . . . 2Chr 28:13
are brought unto bondage *a* . . . Neh 5:5
it hath been *a* of old time . . . Eccl 1:10
which hath been is named *a* . . . Eccl 6:10
I have cursed them *a* . . . Mal 2:2
adultery with her *a* . . . Matt 5:28
Elijah is come *a* and they . . . Matt 17:12
marveled if he were *a* dead . . . Mark 15:44
what will I, if..*a* kindled? . . . Luke 12:49
not is condemned *a* . . . John 3:18
they are white *a* to harvest . . . John 4:35
for the Jews had agreed *a* . . . John 9:22
in the grave four days *a* . . . John 11:17
saw that he was dead *a* . . . John 19:33
the fast was now *a* past . . . Acts 27:9
have judged *a* as though I . . . 1Cor 5:3
many which have sinned *a* . . . 2Cor 12:21
Not as though I had *a* . . . Phil 3:12
either were *a* perfect . . . Phil 3:12
whereto we have *a* attained . . . Phil 3:16
mystery of iniquity doth *a* . . . 2Thess 2:7
For some are *a* turned aside . . . 1Tim 5:15
the resurrection is past *a* . . . 2Tim 2:18
even now *a* is it in the world . . . 1John 4:3
which ye have *a* hold fast . . . Rev 2:25

ALSO—*See* INTRODUCTION

ALTAR—*a raised structure or place on which sacrifices are offered or incense is burned in worship*

Uses of:
Sacrifice . . . Gen 8:20
Incense . . . Ex 30:1, 7, 8; Luke 1:10, 11
National unity . . . Deut 12:5, 6
A memorial . . . Ex 17:15, 16
Protection . . . Ex 21:13, 14

Made of:
Earth . . . Ex 20:24
Unhewn stone . . . Ex 20:25
Stones . . . Deut 27:5, 6
Natural rock . . . Judg 6:19-21
Bronze . . . Ex 27:1-6

Built worthily by:
Noah . . . Gen 8:20
Abraham . . . Gen 12:7, 8
Isaac . . . Gen 26:25
Jacob . . . Gen 33:18, 20
Moses . . . Ex 17:15
Joshua . . . Deut 27:4-7
Eastern tribes . . . Josh 22:10, 34
Gideon . . . Judg 6:26, 27
Manoah . . . Judg 13:19, 20
Israelites . . . Judg 21:4
Samuel . . . 1Sam 7:17
Saul . . . 1Sam 14:35
David . . . 2Sam 24:18-25
Elijah . . . 1Kin 18:31, 32

Built unworthily* (for idolatry) *by:
Gideon's father . . . Judg 6:25-32
King Jeroboam . . . 1Kin 12:32, 33
King Ahab . . . 1Kin 18:25, 26
King Ahaz . . . 2Chr 28:1,3,5
Israelite people . . . Is 65:3
Athenians . . . Acts 17:23

Pagan altars destroyed by:
Gideon . . . Judg 6:25-29
King Asa . . . 2Chr 14:2, 3
Jehoiada . . . 2Kin 11:17, 18
King Hezekiah . . . 2Kin 18:22
King Josiah . . . 2Kin 23:12

Burnt offering:
1. *Of the tabernacle, features concerning:*
Specifications . . . Ex 27:1-9
Bezaleel, builder of . . . Ex 37:1
Place of, outside tabernacle . . . Ex 40:6, 29
Only priests allowed at . . . Num 18:3, 7
The defective not acceptable on . . . Lev 22:22
The putting on of blood . Ex 29:12
2. *Of Solomon's Temple:*
Described . . . 1Kin 8:63, 64
Renewed by King Asa . . . 2Chr 15:8
Cleansed by King Hezekiah . . . 2Chr 29:18-24
Repaired by King Manasseh . . . 2Chr 33:16
Vessels of, carried to Babylon . . . 2Kin 25:14
3. *Of the postexilic (Zerubbabel's) temple:*
Described . . . Ezra 3:1-6
Polluted . . . Mal 1:7, 8
4. *Of Ezekiel's vision:*
Described . . . Ezek 43:13-27

Incense:
In the tabernacle, described . . . Ex 30:1-10
Location of . . . Ex 30:6
Anointed with oil . . . Ex 30:26, 27
Annual atonement made at . . . Ex 30:10
In Solomon's Temple . . . 1Kin 7:48
In John's vision . . . Rev 8:3

New covenant:
A place of spiritual sacrifices . . . Rom 12:1, 2
Christ, our pattern . . . Heb 13:10-16

[*also* ALTARS]
burnt offerings on the *a* . . . Gen 8:20
there builded he an *a* . . . Gen 12:7
there he builded an *a* . . . Gen 12:8
Unto the place of the *a* . . . Gen 13:4
built..an *a* unto the Lord . . . Gen 13:18
Abraham built an *a* there . . . Gen 22:9
laid him on the *a* . . . Gen 22:9
he builded an *a* there . . . Gen 26:25
make there an *a* unto God . . . Gen 35:1
I will make there an *a* . . . Gen 35:3
he built there an *a* . . . Gen 35:7
And Moses built an *a* . . . Ex 17:15
a of earth thou shalt make . . . Ex 20:24
go up by steps unto mine *a* . . . Ex 20:26
builded an *a* under the hill . . . Ex 24:4
blood he sprinkled on the *a* . . . Ex 24:6
thou shalt make an *a* . . . Ex 27:1
compass of the *a* beneath . . . Ex 27:5
they come near unto the *a* . . . Ex 28:43
upon the horns of the *a* . . . Ex 29:12
burn them upon the *a* . . . Ex 29:13
sprinkle it round..the *a* . . . Ex 29:16
burn the..ram upon the *a* . . . Ex 29:18
sprinkle..upon the *a* . . . Ex 29:20
the blood..is upon the *a* . . . Ex 29:21
burn them upon the *a* . . . Ex 29:25
thou shalt cleanse the *a* . . . Ex 29:36
an atonement for the *a* and . . . Ex 29:37
it shall be an *a* most holy . . . Ex 29:37
toucheth the *a*..be holy . . . Ex 29:37
thou shalt offer upon the *a* . . . Ex 29:38
the congregation, and the *a* . . . Ex 29:44
the congregation and the *a* . . . Ex 30:18
they come near to the *a* . . . Ex 30:20
the *a* of burnt offering . . . Ex 30:28
the *a* of incense . . . Ex 31:8
the *a* of burnt offering . . . Ex 31:9
he built an *a* before it . . . Ex 32:5
ye shall destroy their *a* . . . Ex 34:13
the incense *a*, and his staves . . . Ex 35:15
The *a* of burnt offering . . . Ex 35:16
he made the incense *a* . . . Ex 37:25
made the *a* of burnt offering . . Ex 38:1
and the brazen *a* . . . Ex 38:30
all the vessels of the *a* . . . Ex 38:30
golden *a* and the anointing . . . Ex 39:38
The brazen *a* and his grate . . . Ex 39:39
thou shalt set the *a* of gold . . . Ex 40:5
congregation and the *a* . . . Ex 40:7
shalt anoint the *a* of the . . . Ex 40:10
vessels and sanctify the *a* . . . Ex 40:10
it shall be an *a* most holy . . . Ex 40:10
put the golden *a* in the tent . . . Ex 40:26
the congregation and the *a* . . . Ex 40:30
they came near unto the *a* . . . Ex 40:32
the tabernacle and the *a* . . . Ex 40:33
blood round about *a* . . . Lev 1:5
shall put fire upon the *a* . . . Lev 1:7
the fire which is upon the *a* . . . Lev 1:8
shall burn all on the *a* . . . Lev 1:9
kill it on the side of the *a* . . . Lev 1:11
blood round about..*a* . . . Lev 1:11
the fire which is upon the *a* . . . Lev 1:12
burn it upon the *a* . . . Lev 1:13
shall bring it unto the *a* . . . Lev 1:15
burn it on the *a*; and the . . . Lev 1:15
out at the side of the *a* . . . Lev 1:15
cast it beside the *a* . . . Lev 1:16
shall burn it upon the *a* . . . Lev 1:17
memorial of it upon the *a* . . . Lev 2:2
he shall bring it unto the *a* . . . Lev 2:8
shall burn it upon the *a* . . . Lev 2:9
shall not be burnt on the *a* . . . Lev 2:12
sprinkle the blood upon the *a* . Lev 3:2
shall burn it on the *a* . . . Lev 3:5
round about upon the *a* . . . Lev 3:8
shall burn it upon the *a* . . . Lev 3:11
upon the *a* round about . . . Lev 3:13
shall burn them upon the *a* . . . Lev 3:16
upon the horns of the *a* . . . Lev 4:7
at the bottom of the *a* . . . Lev 4:7
shall burn them upon the *a* . . . Lev 4:10
upon the horns of the *a* . . . Lev 4:18
blood at the bottom of the *a* . . Lev 4:18
burn it upon the *a* . . . Lev 4:19
it upon the horns of the *a* . . . Lev 4:25
blood at the bottom of the *a* . . Lev 4:25
burn all his fat upon the *a* . . . Lev 4:26
it upon the horns of the *a* . . . Lev 4:30
at the bottom of the *a* . . . Lev 4:30
shall burn it upon the *a* . . . Lev 4:31
it upon the horns of the *a* . . . Lev 4:34
at the bottom of the *a* . . . Lev 4:34
shall burn them upon the *a* . . . Lev 4:35
upon the side of the *a* . . . Lev 5:9
out at the bottom of the *a* . . . Lev 5:9
burn it on the *a* . . . Lev 5:12
the burning upon the *a* . . . Lev 6:9
fire of the *a*..burning . . . Lev 6:9
the burnt offering on the *a* . . . Lev 6:10
shall put them beside the *a* . . . Lev 6:10
the fire upon the *a* shall be . . . Lev 6:12
be burning upon the *a* . . . Lev 6:13
the Lord, before the *a* . . . Lev 6:14
shall burn it upon the *a* . . . Lev 6:15
round about upon the *a* . . . Lev 7:2
shall burn them upon the *a* . . . Lev 7:5
burn the fat upon the *a* . . . Lev 7:31
sprinkled..upon the *a* . . . Lev 8:11
and anointed the *a* and all . . . Lev 8:11
upon the horns of the *a* . . . Lev 8:15
purified the *a* and poured . . . Lev 8:15
blood at the bottom of the *a* . . Lev 8:15
Moses burnt it upon the *a* . . . Lev 8:16
sprinkled..upon the *a* . . . Lev 8:19
burnt the..ram upon the *a* . . . Lev 8:21
sprinkled..upon the *a* . . . Lev 8:24
burnt them on the *a* . . . Lev 8:28

blood which was upon the *a* . . . Lev 8:30
Go unto the *a* . . . Lev 9:7
therefore went unto the *a* . . . Lev 9:8
upon the horns of the *a* . . . Lev 9:9
at the bottom of the *a* . . . Lev 9:9
he burnt upon the *a* . . . Lev 9:10
round about upon the *a* . . . Lev 9:12
he burnt them upon the *a* . . . Lev 9:13
the burnt offering on the *a* . . . Lev 9:14
burnt it upon the *a* . . . Lev 9:17
he sprinkled upon the *a* . . . Lev 9:18
he burnt the fat upon the *a* . . . Lev 9:20
the *a* the burnt offering . . . Lev 9:24
without leaven beside the *a* . . . Lev 10:12
meat offering upon the *a* . . . Lev 14:20
coals of fire from off the *a* . . . Lev 16:12
he shall go out unto the *a* . . . Lev 16:18
upon the horns of the *a* . . . Lev 16:18
the *a*, he shall bring the . . . Lev 16:20
shall he burn upon the *a* . . . Lev 16:25
congregation and for the *a* . . . Lev 16:33
sprinkle..blood upon the *a* . . . Lev 17:6
to you upon the *a* . . . Lev 17:11
nor come nigh unto the *a* . . . Lev 21:23
by the *a* round about . . . Num 3:26
golden *a* they shall spread a . . . Num 4:11
take..the ashes from the *a* . . . Num 4:13
all the vessels of the *a* . . . Num 4:14
by the *a* round about . . . Num 4:26
offer it upon the *a* . . . Num 5:25
and burn it upon the *a* . . . Num 5:26
the *a* and all the vessels . . . Num 7:1
for dedicating of the *a* . . . Num 7:10
their offering before the *a* . . . Num 7:10
for the dedicating of the *a* . . . Num 7:11
was the dedication of the *a* . . . Num 7:84
dedication of the *a* after . . . Num 7:88
plates..a covering of the *a* . . . Num 16:38
fire therein from off the *a* . . . Num 16:46
the charge of the *a* . . . Num 18:5
their blood upon the *a* . . . Num 18:17
Build me here seven *a* . . . Num 23:1
on every *a* a bullock and a . . . Num 23:2
I have prepared seven *a* . . . Num 23:4
upon every *a* a bullock and a . . Num 23:4
and built seven *a* . . . Num 23:14
bullock..ram on every *a* . . . Num 23:14
Build me here seven *a* and . . . Num 23:29
a bullock..ram on every *a* . . . Num 23:30
ye shall destroy their *a* . . . Deut 7:5
ye shall overthrow their *a* . . . Deut 12:3
the *a* of the Lord thy God . . . Deut 12:27
be poured out upon the *a* . . . Deut 12:27
trees near unto the *a* of the . . . Deut 16:21
set it down before the *a* . . . Deut 26:4
burnt sacrifice upon thine *a* . . . Deut 33:10
Then Joshua built an *a* . . . Josh 8:30
an *a* of whole stones . . . Josh 8:31
and for the *a* of the Lord . . . Josh 9:27
built an *a* over against . . . Josh 22:11
ye have builded you an *a* . . . Josh 22:16
in building you an *a* . . . Josh 22:19
beside the *a* of the Lord . . . Josh 22:19
That we have built us an *a* . . . Josh 22:23
prepare to build us an *a* . . . Josh 22:26
Behold the pattern of the *a* . . . Josh 22:28
to build an *a* for burnt . . . Josh 22:29
beside the *a* of the Lord . . . Josh 22:29
ye shall throw down their *a* . . . Judg 2:2
to offer upon mine *a* . . . 1Sam 2:28
shall not cut off.mine *a* . . . 1Sam 2:33
the same was the first *a* . . . 1Sam 14:35
hold on the horns of the *a* . . . 1Kin 1:50
the horns of the *a*, saying . . . 1Kin 1:51
him down from the *a* . . . 1Kin 1:53
hold on the horns of the *a* . . . 1Kin 2:28
behold he is by the *a* . . . 1Kin 2:29
Solomon offer upon that *a* . . . 1Kin 3:4
and so covered the *a* . . . 1Kin 6:20
also the whole *a* . . . 1Kin 6:22
Solomon stood before the *a* . . . 1Kin 8:22
oath come before thine *a* . . . 1Kin 8:31
he arose from before the *a* . . . 1Kin 8:54
upon the *a* which he built . . . 1Kin 9:25
burnt incense upon the *a* . . . 1Kin 9:25
Jeroboam stood by the *a* . . . 1Kin 13:1
cried against the *a* in the . . . 1Kin 13:2
and said O *a*, *a* . . . 1Kin 13:2
the *a* shall be rent . . . 1Kin 13:3
had cried against the *a* . . . 1Kin 13:4
forth his hand from the *a* . . . 1Kin 13:4
the *a* also was rent, and . . . 1Kin 13:5
poured out from the *a* . . . 1Kin 13:5
against the *a* in Beth-el . . . 1Kin 13:32
he reared up an *a* for Baal . . . 1Kin 16:32
repaired the *a* of the Lord . . . 1Kin 18:30
the water ran round..the *a* . . . 1Kin 18:35
thrown down thine *a* . . . 1Kin 19:10
by the *a* and the temple . . . 2Kin 11:11
set it beside the *a* . . . 2Kin 12:9
saw an *a* that was at . . . 2Kin 16:10
the fashion of the *a* . . . 2Kin 16:10
the priest built an *a* . . . 2Kin 16:11
the king saw the *a* and . . . 2Kin 16:12
king approached to the *a* . . . 2Kin 16:12
peace offerings upon the *a* . . . 2Kin 16:13
brought also the brazen *a* . . . 2Kin 16:14
from between the *a* . . . 2Kin 16:14
put it..north side of the *a* . . . 2Kin 16:14
Upon the great *a* burn . . . 2Kin 16:15
brazen *a* shall be for me . . . 2Kin 16:15
shall worship before this *a* . . . 2Kin 18:22
he reared up *a* for Baal . . . 2Kin 21:3
he built *a* in the house of . . . 2Kin 21:4
built *a* for all the host of . . . 2Kin 21:5
came not up to the *a* of the . . . 2Kin 23:9
the *a* that was at Beth-el . . . 2Kin 23:15
both that *a* and the high . . . 2Kin 23:15
burned them upon the *a* . . . 2Kin 23:16
hast done against the *a* of . . . 2Kin 23:17
that were there upon the *a* . . . 2Kin 23:20
his sons offered upon the *a* . . . 1Chr 6:49
and on the *a* of incense . . . 1Chr 6:49
the *a* of the burnt offering . . . 1Chr 16:40
set up an *a* unto the Lord . . . 1Chr 21:18
that I may build an *a* . . . 1Chr 21:22
built there an *a* unto the . . . 1Chr 21:26
fire upon the *a* of burnt . . . 1Chr 21:26
the *a* of the burnt offering . . . 1Chr 21:29
the *a* of the burnt offering . . . 1Chr 22:1
And for the *a* of incense . . . 1Chr 28:18
the brazen *a* that Bezaleel . . . 2Chr 1:5
up thither to the brazen *a* . . . 2Chr 1:6
he made an *a* of brass . . . 2Chr 4:1
the golden *a* also . . . 2Chr 4:19
stood at..end of the *a* . . . 2Chr 5:12
he stood before the *a* of the . . . 2Chr 6:12
oath come before thine *a* . . . 2Chr 6:22
brazen *a* which Solomon . . . 2Chr 7:7
kept the dedication of the *a* . . . 2Chr 7:9
on the *a* of the Lord . . . 2Chr 8:12
by the *a* and the temple . . . 2Chr 23:10
brake his *a* and his images . . . 2Chr 23:17
priest of Baal before the *a* . . . 2Chr 23:17
incense upon the *a* of . . . 2Chr 26:16
from beside the incense *a* . . . 2Chr 26:19
a in every corner . . . 2Chr 28:24
burnt offering upon the *a* . . . 2Chr 29:27
arose and took away the *a* . . . 2Chr 30:14
the *a* for incense took they . . . 2Chr 30:14
the *a* out of all Judah . . . 2Chr 31:1
his high places and his *a* . . . 2Chr 32:12
shall worship before one *a* . . . 2Chr 32:12
he reared up *a* for Baalim . . . 2Chr 33:3
he built *a* in the house . . . 2Chr 33:4
built *a* for all the host of . . . 2Chr 33:5
all the *a* that he had built . . . 2Chr 33:15
brake down the *a* of Baalim . . . 2Chr 34:4
bones..priests upon their *a* . . . 2Chr 34:5
he had broken down the *a* . . . 2Chr 34:7
burnt offerings upon the *a* . . . 2Chr 35:16
builded the *a* of the God of . . . Ezra 3:2
set the *a* upon his bases . . . Ezra 3:3
and offer them upon the *a* . . . Ezra 7:17
burn upon the *a* of the Lord . . Neh 10:34
so will I compass thine *a* . . . Ps 26:6
I go unto the *a* of God . . . Ps 43:4
offer bullocks upon thine *a* . . . Ps 51:19
thine *a*, O Lord of hosts . . . Ps 84:3
unto the horns of the *a* . . . Ps 118:27
the tongs from off the *a* . . . Is 6:6
he shall not look to the *a* . . . Is 17:8
day shall there be an *a* . . . Is 19:19
all the stones of the *a* . . . Is 27:9
whose *a* Hezekiah hath . . . Is 36:7
worship before this *a*? . . . Is 36:7
accepted upon mine *a* . . . Is 56:7
with acceptance on mine *a* . . . Is 60:7
set up *a* to that shameful . . . Jer 11:13
a to burn incense unto Baal . . . Jer 11:13
upon the horns of your *a* . . . Jer 17:1
children remember their *a* . . . Jer 17:2
The Lord hath cast off his *a* . . . Lam 2:7
your *a* shall be desolate . . . Ezek 6:4
bones round about your *a* . . . Ezek 6:5
your *a* may be laid waste . . . Ezek 6:6
round about their *a* . . . Ezek 6:13
the gate of the *a* this image . . . Ezek 8:5
between the porch and the *a* . . Ezek 8:16
stood beside the brazen *a* . . . Ezek 9:2
keepers..of the *a* . . . Ezek 40:46
a that was before the house . . . Ezek 40:47
a of wood was three cubits . . . Ezek 41:22
of the settle of the *a* . . . Ezek 45:19
at the south side of the *a* . . . Ezek 47:1
Ephraim hath made many *a* . . . Hos 8:11
a shall be unto him to sin . . . Hos 8:11
he hath increased the *a* . . . Hos 10:1
he shall break down their *a* . . . Hos 10:2
shall come up on their *a* . . . Hos 10:8
their *a* are as heaps . . . Hos 12:11
howl, ye ministers of the *a* . . . Joel 1:13
weep between..the *a* . . . Joel 2:17
laid to pledge by every *a* . . . Amos 2:8
I will also visit the *a* of . . . Amos 3:14
horns of the *a* shall be cut . . . Amos 3:14
Lord standing upon the *a* . . . Amos 9:1
as the corners of the *a* . . . Zech 9:15
like the bowls before the *a* . . . Zech 14:20
do ye kindle fire on mine *a* . . . Mal 1:10
covering the *a* of the Lord . . . Mal 2:13
bring thy gift to the *a* . . . Matt 5:23
thy gift before the *a* . . . Matt 5:24
shall swear by the *a* . . . Matt 23:18
the gift, or the *a* . . . Matt 23:19
shall swear by the *a* . . . Matt 23:20
the temple and the *a* . . . Matt 23:35
the *a* and the temple . . . Luke 11:51
and digged down thine *a* . . . Rom 11:3
they which wait at the *a* . . . 1Cor 9:13
partakers with the *a*? . . . 1Cor 9:13
partakers of the *a*? . . . 1Cor 10:18
gave attendance at the *a* . . . Heb 7:13
offered Isaac..upon the *a*? . . . James 2:21
under the *a* the souls . . . Rev 6:9
saints upon the golden *a* . . . Rev 8:3
filled it with fire of the *a* . . . Rev 8:5
horns of the golden *a* . . . Rev 9:13
temple of God, and the *a* . . . Rev 11:1
angel came out from the *a* . . . Rev 14:18
I heard another out of the *a* . . . Rev 16:7

ALTASCHITH (ăl-tăs'kĭth)—*"destroy not"*
A term found in the title of . . . Ps 57; 59; 75

chief musician, *A* . . . Ps 58:*title*

ALTER—*to make different*

[*also* ALTERED, ALTERETH]
shall not *a* it, nor change . . . Lev 27:10
whosoever shall *a* this . . . Ezra 6:11
put to their hand to *a* . . . Ezra 6:12
it..not *a*, That Vashti . . . Esth 1:19
will I not break, nor *a* . . . Ps 89:34
Persians, which *a* not . . . Dan 6:8
of his countenance was *a* . . . Luke 9:29

ALTHOUGH—*in spite of the fact that*
a that was near; for God . . . Ex 13:17
a there was a plague in the . . . Josh 22:17
A my house be not so with . . . 2Sam 23:5
a he make it not to grow . . . 2Sam 23:5
A I have sent unto thee . . . 1Kin 20:5
held my tongue, *a* the . . . Esth 7:4
integrity, *a* thou movedst . . . Job 2:3

A affliction cometh not........Job 5:6
a I was a husband unto.......Jer 31:32
is sold, *a* they were yet.......Ezek 7:13
A the fig tree shall not........Hab 3:17
A all shall be offended........Mark 14:29
a the works were finished.....Heb 4:3

ALTOGETHER—*on the whole: thoroughly*
whether they have done *a*.....Gen 18:21
And mount Sinai was *a* on a..Ex 19:18
make thyself *a* a prince.......Num 16:13
her husband *a* hold his........Num 30:14
is *a* just shalt thou follow.....Deut 16:20
he would not destroy him *a*...2Chr 12:12
if thou *a* holdest thy peace....Esth 4:14
O that ye would *a* hold your..Job 13:5
are true and righteous *a*......Ps 19:9
man at his best state is *a*......Ps 39:5
thoughtest that I was *a*........Ps 50:21
they are *a* become filthy......Ps 53:3
they are *a* lighter than........Ps 62:9
O Lord, thou knowest it *a*....Ps 139:4
most sweet..he is *a* lovely.....Song 5:16
Are not my princes *a* kings?...Is 10:8
these have *a* broken the......Jer 5:5
Thou wast *a* born in sins......John 9:34
both almost, and *a* such as....Acts 26:29
Yet not *a* with the............1Cor 5:10
Or saith he it *a* for our.......1Cor 9:10

ALTRUISM—*unselfish devotion to the welfare of others*

Manifested in:
- Service.................Matt 20:26-28
- Doing good.............Acts 10:38
- Seeking the welfare of others................Gal 6:1, 2, 10
- Helping the weak........Acts 20:35

Examples of:
- Moses..................Ex 32:30-32
- Samuel.................1Sam 12:1-5
- Jonathan................1Sam 18:1-4
- Christ..................John 13:4-17
- Paul...................1Cor 9:19-22

ALUSH (ā'lŭsh)—*"crowd"*
- An Israelite encampment.Num 33:13, 14

ALVAH (ăl'vä)—*"sublimity"*
- An Edomite chief.......Gen 36:40
- Also called Aliah........1Chr 1:51

ALVAN (ăl'văn)—*"sublime"*
- A son of Shobal the Horite...............Gen 36:23
- Also called Alian........1Chr 1:40

ALWAYS—*at all times; forever*

Of God's:
- Care...................Deut 11:12
- Covenant...............1Chr 16:15
- Chide..................Ps 103:9

Of Christ's:
- Determination...........Ps 16:8-11; Acts 2:25
- Delight.................Prov 8:30-31
- Presence................Matt 28:20
- Desire..................John 8:29
- Prayer..................John 11:42

Of the believer's:
- Prayer..................Luke 21:36
- Peace...................2Thess 3:16
- Obedience...............Phil 2:12
- Work....................1Cor 15:58
- Defense.................1Pet 3:15
- Rejoicing...............Phil 4:4
- Thanksgiving............1Thess 1:2
- Victory.................2Cor 2:14
- Conscience..............Acts 24:16
- Confidence..............2Cor 5:6
- Sufficiency.............2Cor 9:8

Of the unbeliever's:
- Probation...............Gen 6:3
- Turmoil.................Mark 5:5
- Rebellion...............Acts 7:51
- Lying...................Titus 1:12

showbread before me *a*.......Ex 25:30
cause the lamp to burn *a*.......Ex 27:20
be *a* upon his forehead.......Ex 28:38
So it was *a*; the cloud.........Num 9:16
all my commandments *a*......Deut 5:29
for our good *a*..............Deut 6:24
his commandments *a*..........Deut 11:1
fear the Lord thy God *a*......Deut 14:23
oppressed and crushed *a*......Deut 28:33
eat bread *a* at my table.......2Sam 9:10
have a light *a* before me......1Kin 11:36
to give him *a* a light..........2Kin 8:19
good unto me, but *a* evil......2Chr 18:7
I would not live *a*............Job 7:16
will he *a* call upon God?......Job 27:10
needy..not *a* be forgotten.....Ps 9:18
His ways are *a* grievous.......Ps 10:5
perform thy statutes *a*........Ps 119:112
ravished *a* with her love......Prov 5:19
Happy..man that feareth *a*....Prov 28:14
Let..garments be *a* white......Eccl 9:8
neither will I be *a* wroth......Is 57:16
her womb to be *a* great.......Jer 20:17
which have been *a* waste......Ezek 38:8
their angels do *a* behold......Matt 18:10
have the poor *a* with you......Matt 26:11
but me ye have not *a*.........Matt 26:11
ye have the poor with you *a*...Mark 14:7
but me ye have not *a*.........Mark 14:7
that men ought *a* to pray.....Luke 18:1
but your time is *a* ready......John 7:6
the poor *a* ye have with you...John 12:8
but me ye have not *a*.........John 12:8
whither the Jews *a* resort.....John 18:20
and prayed to God *a*..........Acts 10:2
We accept it *a* and in all......Acts 24:3
mention of you *a* in my.......Rom 1:9
bow down their back *a*........Rom 11:10
thank my God *a* on your......1Cor 1:4
A bearing about in the.......2Cor 4:10
we which live are *a*...........2Cor 4:11
sorrowful, yet *a* rejoicing......2Cor 6:10
affected *a* in a good thing.....Gal 4:18
Giving thanks *a* for all........Eph 5:20
Praying *a* with all............Eph 6:18
A in every prayer of mine.....Phil 1:4
with all boldness as *a*.........Phil 1:20
Rejoice in the Lord *a*.........Phil 4:4
praying *a* for you............Col 1:3
your speech be *a*..grace.......Col 4:6
a laboring fervently for.......Col 4:12
to fill up their sins *a*..........1Thess 2:16
good remembrance of us *a*....1Thess 3:6
bound to thank God *a* for....2Thess 1:3
we pray *a* for you............2Thess 1:11
give thanks *a* to God.........2Thess 2:13
mention of thee *a* in my......Philem 4
do *a* err in their heart.......Heb 3:10
a into the first tabernacle.....Heb 9:6
a in remembrance of these....2Pet 1:12
things *a* in remembrance......2Pet 1:15

AM—*See* INTRODUCTION

AMAD (ā'măd)—*"enduring"*
- A city of Asher.........Josh 19:26

AMAL (ā'măl)—*"laboring"*
- Asher's descendant......1Chr 7:35

AMALEK (ăm'ä-lĕk)—*"warlike; dweller in the vale"*
- A son of Eliphaz........1Chr 1:36
- Grandson of Esau.......Gen 36:11, 12
- A duke of Edom........Gen 36:16
- Founder of first nation...Num 24:20

and go out fight with *A*.......Ex 17:9
to him, and fought with *A*.....Ex 17:10
let down his hand *A*..........Ex 17:11
Lord will have war with *A*....Ex 17:16
a root of them against *A*......Judg 5:14
that which *A* did to Israel.....1Sam 15:2
Now go and smite *A* and......1Sam 15:3
Saul came to a city of *A*......1Sam 15:5
brought Agag the king of *A*...1Sam 15:20
his fierce wrath upon *A*.......1Sam 28:18
and of *A* and of the spoil.....2Sam 8:12
the Philistines and from *A*.....1Chr 18:11
Gebal and Ammon and *A*.....Ps 83:7

AMALEKITES (ăm-ä'lĕk-īts)—*a people against whom the Israelites often fought*

Defeated by:
- Chedorlaomer..........Gen 14:5-7
- Joshua.................Ex 17:8, 13
- Gideon.................Judg 7:12-25
- Saul...................1Sam 14:47, 48
- David..................1Sam 27:8, 9
- Simeonites.............1Chr 4:42, 43

Overcame Israel during:
- Wilderness.............Num 14:39-45
- Judges.................Judg 3:13

Destruction of:
- Predicted..............Ex 17:14
- Reaffirmed.............Deut 25:17-19
- Fulfilled in part by David.1Sam 27:8, 9; 2Sam 1:1-16
- Fulfilled by the Simeonites...........1Chr 4:42, 43

[*also* AMALEKITE]

A dwell in the land of........Num 13:29
A and the Canaanites.........Num 14:25
A and the children of.........Judg 6:3
the Midianites and the *A*......Judg 6:33
Zidonians also and the *A*......Judg 10:12
in the mount of the *A*........Judg 12:15
down from among the *A*......1Sam 15:6
departed from among the *A*...1Sam 15:6
Saul smote the *A* from........1Sam 15:7
Agag the king of the *A*.......1Sam 15:8
brought them from the *A*.....1Sam 15:15
destroy the sinners the *A*.....1Sam 15:18
utterly destroyed the *A*........1Sam 15:20
Agag the king of the *A*.......1Sam 15:32
A had invaded the south......1Sam 30:1
Egypt, servant to an *A*........1Sam 30:13
all that the *A* had carried.....1Sam 30:18
I answered him, I am an *A*....2Sam 1:8
son of a stranger, an *A*.......2Sam 1:13

AMAM (ā'măm)—*"gathering place"*
- A city of Judah.........Josh 15:26

AMANA (ă-mā'nä)—*"forth"*
- A summit in the Anti-Lebanon mountain range................Song 4:8

AMARIAH (ăm-ä-rī'ä)—*"Jehovah has said"*
1. The grandfather of Zadok the priest......1Chr 6:7-8, 52
2. A priest...............1Chr 6:11
3. Levite in David's time...1Chr 23:19
4. A high priest...........2Chr 19:11
5. A Levite in Hezekiah's reign..................2Chr 31:14, 15
6. Son of King Hezekiah...Zeph 1:1
7. One who divorced his foreign wife..........Ezra 10:42, 44
8. A signer of Nehemiah's document............Neh 10:3
9. A postexilic chief priest.Neh 12:1, 2, 7

Meraioth his son, *A* his son...1Chr 6:52
A the second, Jahaziel the.....1Chr 24:23
The son of *A*, the son of......Ezra 7:3
Shallum, *A*, and Joseph.......Ezra 10:42
son of *A*, the son of..........Neh 11:4
of *A*, Jehohanan..............Neh 12:13

AMASA (ăm'ä-sä)—*"burden-bearer; people of Jesse"*
1. The son of Ithra; David's nephew.............2Sam 17:25
   - Commands Absalom's rebels...............2Sam 17:25
   - Made David's commander..........2Sam 19:13
   - Treacherously killed by Joab..............2Sam 20:9-12
   - Death avenged.........1Kin 2:28-34
2. An Ephraimite leader...2Chr 28:9-12

Then said the king to *A* 2Sam 20:4
A went to assemble the men...2Sam 20:5
which is in Gibeon *A* went 2Sam 20:8
unto *A* the son of Jether 1Kin 2:5
And Abigail bare *A* 1Chr 2:17
father of *A* was Jether 1Chr 2:17

AMASAI (ä-măs'ā-ī)—*"burden-bearer"*
1. A Kohathite Levite 1Chr 6:25, 35
2. David's officer 1Chr 12:18
3. A priestly trumpeter in David's time..........1Chr 15:24
4. A Kohathite Levite 2Chr 29:12

AMASHAI (ä-măsh'ī)—*"carrying spoil"*
A priest ....Neh 11:13

AMASIAH (ăm-ä-sī'ä)—*"Jehovah bears; Jehovah has strength"*
One of Jehoshaphat's commanders 2Chr 17:16

AMAZEMENT—*strong emotional reaction, especially to the unusual or miraculous*

Caused by:
Christ's miracles ....Matt 12:22, 23; Luke 5:25, 26
Christ's teaching..........Matt 19:25
God's power ....Luke 9:43
Apostolic miracle ....Acts 3:7-10

Manifested by:
Christ's parents..........Luke 2:48
Christ's disciples.........Matt 19:25
The Jews ....Mark 9:15
Jesus ....Mark 14:33
The early Christians .....Acts 9:19-21

[*also* AMAZED]
dukes of Edom shall be *a* .....Ex 15:15
men of Benjamin were *a* ......Judg 20:41
were *a*, they answered ....Job 32:15
shall be *a* one at another......Is 13:8
make many people *a* at thee ..Ezek 32:10
And they were all *a* ....Mark 1:27
that they were all *a*...........Mark 2:12
were sore *a* in themselves .....Mark 6:51
and they were *a* ....Mark 10:32
they trembled and were *a* .....Mark 16:8
And they were all *a* ....Luke 4:36
were all *a* and marveled ......Acts 2:7
were all *a*, and were in ....Acts 2:12
not afraid with any *a* 1Pet 3:6

AMAZIAH (ăm-ä-zī'ä)—*"Jehovah has strength"*
1. King of Judah 2Kin 14:1-4
   Kills his father's assassinators 2Kin 14:5, 6
   Raises a large army 2Chr 25:5
   Employs troops from Israel 2Chr 25:6
   Rebuked by a man of God 2Chr 25:7-10
   Defeats Edomites 2Kin 14:7
   Worships Edomite gods .2Chr 25:14
   Rebuked by a prophet ..2Chr 25:15, 16
   Defeated by Israel 2Kin 14:8-14
   Killed by conspirators ...2Chr 25:25-28
2. A priest of Bethel ......Amos 7:10-17
3. A Simeonite 1Chr 4:34, 42-44
4. A Merarite Levite 1Chr 6:45

A his son reigned in his 2Kin 12:21
he fought against *A* 2Kin 13:12
how he fought with *A* 2Kin 14:15
A the son of Joash king 2Kin 14:17
the rest of the acts of *A* 2Kin 14:18
instead of his father *A* 2Kin 14:21
In the fifteenth year of *A* 2Kin 14:23
Azariah son of *A* king of 2Kin 15:1
to all that his father *A* 2Kin 15:3
A his son, Azariah his son 1Chr 3:12
Hashabiah, the son of *A* 1Chr 6:45
A his son reigned in his 2Chr 24:27
A was twenty and five years ...2Chr 25:1
A said to the man of God 2Chr 25:9
A strengthened himself........2Chr 25:11
army which *A* sent back.......2Chr 25:13
A king of Judah took 2Chr 25:17
Joash king..sent to *A* 2Chr 25:18
But *A* would not hear for 2Chr 25:20
he and *A* king of Judah 2Chr 25:21
the king of Israel took *A* 2Chr 25:23
in the room of his father *A* 2Chr 26:1
to all..his father *A* did 2Chr 26:4

AMBASSADOR—*an authorized representative or messenger*

Some purposes of, to:
Grant safe passage ......Num 20:14-21
Settle disputes...........Judg 11:12-28
Arrange business 1Kin 5:1-12
Stir up trouble 1Kin 20:1-12
Issue an ultimatum 2Kin 19:9-14
Spy 2Kin 20:12-19
Learn God's will ....Jer 37:6-10

Some examples of:
Judah to Egypt..........Is 30:1-4
Babylonians to Judah 2Chr 32:31
Necho to Josiah 2Chr 35:20, 21

Used figuratively of:
Christ's ministers 2Cor 5:20
Paul in particular ....Eph 5:20

[*also* AMBASSADORS]
made as if they had been *a*....Josh 9:4
but a faithful *a* is health ......Prov 13:17
That sendeth *a* by the sea .....Is 18:2
the *a* of peace shall weep .....Is 33:7
a is sent unto the heathen .....Jer 49:14
in sending his *a* into Egypt ....Ezek 17:15
an *a* is sent among the ....Obad 1

AMBASSAGE—*an official commission*
Coming to seek peace ...Luke 14:32

AMBER—*a yellow, fossilized resin*
Descriptive of the divine glory ....Ezek 1:4, 27
as the color of *a*..............Ezek 8:2

AMBIDEXTROUS—*using either hand with equal skill*
True of some of David's warriors 1Chr 12:1, 2

AMBITION, CHRISTIAN

Good, if for:
The best gifts 1Cor 12:31
Spiritual growth ....Phil 3:12-14
The Gospel's extension ..Rom 15:17-20
Acceptance before God ..2Cor 5:7
Quietness 1Thess 4:11

Evil, if it leads to:
Strife ....Matt 20:20-28
Sinful superiority ....Matt 18:1-6
A Pharisaical spirit ......Matt 12:38-40
Contention about gifts ...1Cor 3:3-8
Selfish ambition ....Phil 1:14-17

AMBITION, WORLDLY

Inspired by:
Satan ....Gen 3:1-6; Luke 4:5-8
Pride ....Is 14:12-15; 1Tim 3:6
Jealousy ....Num 12:2

Leads to:
Sin ....Acts 8:18-24
Strife ....James 4:1, 2
Suicide 2Sam 17:23
Self-glory ....Hab 2:4, 5

Examples of:
Builders of Babel........Gen 11:4
Korah's company ....Num 16:3-35
Abimelech ....Judg 9:1-6
Absalom 2Sam 15:1-13
Adonijah 1Kin 1:5-7
Haman ....Esth 5:9-13
Nebuchadnezzar ....Dan 3:1-7
James and John ....Mark 10:35-37
The antichrist 2Thess 2:4
Diotrephes 3John 9, 10

AMBUSH—*strategic concealment for surprise attack*
Joshua at Ai ....Josh 8:2-22
Abimelech against Shechem..............Judg 9:31-40
Israel at Gibeah ....Judg 20:29-41
David against the Philistines..............2Sam 5:23-25
Jehoshaphat against the Ammonites 2Chr 20:22

[*also* AMBUSHES, AMBUSHMENT, AMBUSHMENTS]
Jeroboam caused an *a* 2Chr 13:13
and the *a* was behind them....2Chr 13:13
watchmen, prepare the *a* ......Jer 51:12

AMEN (ā'mĕn)—*"verily; so be it"—used to express assent or approval*

Used in the Old Testament to:
Confirm a statement .....Num 5:22
Close a doxology 1Chr 16:36
Confirm an oath.........Neh 5:13
Give assent to laws ......Deut 27:15-26

Used in the New Testament to:
Close a doxology ....Rom 9:5
Close epistle ....Rom 16:27
Personalize Christ 2Cor 1:20
Close prayer 1Cor 14:16
Give assent ....Rev 1:7
Emphasize a truth (translated "verily") ..John 3:3, 5, 11

shall answer and say *A* ....Deut 27:15
answered the king, and said *A* .1Kin 1:36
the people answered, *A*, *A* ....Neh 8:6
to everlasting..*A*, and *A* ....Ps 41:13
filled with..glory; *A*, and *A* ....Ps 72:19
for evermore; *A*, and *A* ....Ps 89:52
A, Praise ye the Lord ....Ps 106:48
prophet Jeremiah said, *A*......Jer 28:6
the glory, for ever. *A* ....Matt 6:13
end of the world. *A* ....Matt 28:20
with signs following. *A* ....Mark 16:20
and blessing God. *A* ....Luke 24:53
books be written. *A* ....John 21:25
who is blessed for ever. *A*.....Rom 1:25
be glory for ever. *A* ....Rom 11:36
peace be with you all. *A* ......Rom 15:33
Christ be with you. *A* ....Rom 16:20
Christ be with you all. *A* ......Rom 16:24
you all in Christ Jesus. *A* 1Cor 16:24
Ghost be with you all. *A*.......2Cor 13:14
be glory for ever. *A* ....Gal 1:5
Christ be..spirit. *A*............Gal 6:18
world without end. *A* ....Eph 3:21
Jesus Christ in sincerity. *A* ....Eph 6:24
for ever and ever. *A* ....Phil 4:20
Christ be with you all. *A* ......Phil 4:23
Grace be with you. *A* ....Col 4:18
Jesus Christ be with you. *A* ...1Thess 5:28
Christ be with you all. *A* 2Thess 3:18
glory for ever and ever. *A*.....1Tim 1:17
and power everlasting. *A* 1Tim 6:16
Grace be with thee. *A* 1Tim 6:21
for ever and ever. *A* 2Tim 4:18
Grace be with you. *A* 2Tim 4:22
Grace be with you all. *A* ......Titus 3:15
be with your spirit. *A* ....Philem 25
for ever and ever. *A* ....Heb 13:21
dominion..and ever. *A* 1Pet 4:11
dominion..and ever. *A* 1Pet 5:11
are in Christ Jesus. *A* 1Pet 5:14
for ever and ever. *A* ....Rev 1:6
I am alive for evermore, *A* ....Rev 1:18
These things saith the *A* ......Rev 3:14
the four beasts said, *A* ....Rev 5:14
Saying, *A*..Blessing and ....Rev 7:12
God for ever and ever. *A* .....Rev 7:12
sat on the throne, saying, *A* ...Rev 19:4
A Even so, come, Lord ....Rev 22:20
Christ be with you all. *A* ......Rev 22:21

AMEND—*put right; change for the better*

[*also* AMENDS]
shall make *a* for.. ....Lev 5:16

repair and *a* the house 2Chr 34:10
A your ways..doings . . . . .Jer 7:3
if ye thoroughly *a*..ways . . . . . . .Jer 7:5
a your ways and..doings . . . . . .Jer 26:13
and *a* your doings . . . . .Jer 35:15
hour when he began to *a* . . . . .John 4:52

AMERCE—*to inflict a penalty*
For false charges . . . . .Deut 22:19

AMETHYST—*purple to blue-violet quartz often made into jewelry*
Worn by the high priest . .Ex 28:19
Ex 39:12
In the New Jerusalem . . . .Rev 21:20

AMI (ā'mī)—*(meaning uncertain)*
Head of a family of
Solomon's servants . . . .Ezra 2:57
Called Amon . . . . .Neh 7:59

AMIABLE—*pleasing, admirable*
God's tabernacles . . . . . . .Ps 84:1

AMINADAB (ă-mĭn'ä-dăb)—*"my people are willing (noble)"—the Greek form of Amminadab*
Nahshon the son of *A* shall . . . .Num 2:3
the son of *A* of the tribe . . . . . .Num 7:12
Nahshon the son of *A* . . . . .Num 7:17
was Nahshon the son of *A* . . . .Num 10:14
and *A* begat Nahshon 1Chr 2:10
Which was the son of *A* . . . . . . .Luke 3:33

AMISS—*wrongly; mistakenly*
sinned we have done *a* 2Chr 6:37
speak anything *a* against . . . . . .Dan 3:29
man hath done nothing *a* . . . . .Luke 23:41
not, because ye ask *a* . . . . .James 4:3

AMITTAI (a-mit'i)—*"truthful"*
The father of Jonah the
prophet . . . . .Jon 1:1

Jonah the son of *A* the 2Kin 14:25

AMMAH (ăm'ä)—*"head"*
A hill near Gish 2Sam 2:24

AMMI (ăm'ī)—*"my people"*
A symbolic name of
Israel . . . . .Hos 2:1

AMMIEL (ăm'ĭ-ĕl)—*"my people are strong; my kinsman is God"*
1. A spy representing the
tribe of Dan . . . . .Num 13:12
2. The father of Machir 2Sam 9:4, 5
3. The father of Bath-shua
(Bath-sheba), one of
David's wives 1Chr 3:5
Called Eliam 2Sam 11:3
4. A son of Obed-edom 1Chr 26:4-5

Machir the son of *A* of 2Sam 17:27

AMMIHUD (ă-mī'hŭd)—*"my people are honorable or glorious"*
1. An Ephraimite . . . . .Num 1:10
2. A Simeonite, father of
Shemuel . . . . .Num 34:20
3. A Naphtalite . . . . .Num 34:28
4. The father of king of
Geshur 2Sam 13:37
5. A Judahite 1Chr 9:4

be Elishama the son of *A* . . . . .Num 2:18
Elishama the son of *A* . . . . .Num 7:48
of Elishama the son of *A* . . . . . .Num 7:53
Elishama the son of *A* . . . . .Num 10:22
Laadan his son, *A* his son 1Chr 7:26

AMMINADAB (ă-mĭn'ä-dăb)—*"my people are willing or noble"*
1. Man of Judah 1Chr 2:10
The father of Nashon . . .Num 1:7
Aaron's father-in-law . . . .Ex 6:23
An ancestor of David . . .Ruth 4:19, 20
An ancestor of Christ . . .Matt 1:4
2. Chief of a Levitical
house 1Chr 15:10, 11
3. Son of Kohath 1Chr 6:22

AMMINADIB (ă-mĭn'ä-dĭb)—*"my people are liberal"*
Should probably be
translated "my princely
(or willing) people" . . . .Song 6:12

AMMISHADDAI (ăm-ĭ-shăd'ī)—*"the Almighty is my kinsman; my people are mighty"*
A captain representing
the Danites . . . . .Num 1:12

be Ahiezer the son of *A* . . . . . .Num 2:25
day Ahiezer the son of *A* . . . . .Num 7:66
of Ahiezer the son of *A* . . . . . . .Num 7:71
was Ahiezer the son of *A* . . . . .Num 10:25

AMMIZABAD (ă-mĭz'ä-băd)—*"my people are endowed; my kinsman has a present"*
A son of Benaiah 1Chr 27:6

AMMON (ăm'ŏn)—*"a people"*
A son of Lot by his
youngest daughter . . . . .Gen 19:38

even unto the children of *A* . . .Num 21:24
children of *A* was strong . . . . . .Num 21:24
against the children of *A* . . . . . .Deut 2:19
the children of *A* any . . . . .Deut 2:19
of the children of *A* thou . . . . . .Deut 2:37
of the children of *A* . . . . .Deut 3:11
border of the children of *A* . . . .Deut 3:16
border of the children of *A* . . . .Josh 12:2
border of the children of *A* . . . .Josh 13:10
land of the children of *A* . . . . . .Josh 13:25
unto him the children of *A* . . . .Judg 3:13
gods of the children of *A* . . . . . .Judg 10:6
hands of the children of *A* . . . .Judg 10:7
children of *A* passed over . . . . .Judg 10:9
from the children of *A* . . . . .Judg 10:11
the children of *A* were . . . . .Judg 10:17
against the children of *A* . . . . . .Judg 10:18
children of *A* made against . . . .Judg 11:4
the children of *A* made . . . . . . .Judg 11:5
fight with the children of *A* . . . .Judg 11:6
against the children of *A* . . . . . .Judg 11:8, 9
king of the children of *A* . . . . . .Judg 11:12
king of the children of *A* . . . . . .Judg 11:13
king of the children of *A* . . . . . .Judg 11:14
land of the children of *A* . . . . . .Judg 11:15
and the children of *A* . . . . .Judg 11:27
king of the children of *A* . . . . . .Judg 11:28
over unto the children of *A* . . .Judg 11:29
children of *A* into mine . . . . . . .Judg 11:30
from the children of *A* . . . . .Judg 11:31
unto the children of *A* . . . . .Judg 11:32
children of *A* were subdued . . .Judg 11:33
even of the children of *A* . . . . .Judg 11:36
against the children of *A* . . . . . . .Judg 12:1
strife with the children of *A* . . . .Judg 12:2
against the children of *A* . . . . . . .Judg 12:3
king of the children of *A* 1Sam 12:12
against the children of *A* 1Sam 14:47
and of the children of *A* 2Sam 8:12
king of the children of *A* 2Sam 10:1
land of the children of *A* 2Sam 10:2
princes of the children of *A* 2Sam 10:3
when the children of *A* saw 2Sam 10:6
the children of *A* sent and 2Sam 10:6
children of *A* came out 2Sam 10:8
against the children of *A* 2Sam 10:10
children of *A* be too strong 2Sam 10:11
when the children of *A* saw 2Sam 10:14
help the children of *A* 2Sam 10:19
destroyed the children of *A* 2Sam 11:1
sword of the children of *A* 2Sam 12:9
of *A* and took the royal 2Sam 12:26
cities of the children of *A* 2Sam 12:31
of the children of *A* 2Sam 17:27
of the children of *A* 1Kin 11:7
god of the children of *A* 1Kin 11:33
of the children of *A* 2Kin 23:13
bands of the children of *A* 2Kin 24:2
and from the children of *A* 1Chr 18:11
king of the children of *A* 1Chr 19:1
land of the children of *A* 1Chr 19:2
princes of the children of *A* . . .1Chr 19:3

A saw that they had made 1Chr 19:6
A sent a thousand talents 1Chr 19:6
of *A* gathered themselves 1Chr 19:7
of *A* came out and put the 1Chr 19:9
against the children of *A* 1Chr 19:11
of *A* be too strong for thee 1Chr 19:12
of *A* saw that the Syrians 1Chr 19:15
help the children of *A* 1Chr 19:19
A and came and besieged 1Chr 20:1
cities of the children of *A* 1Chr 20:3
of *A* and with them other 2Chr 20:1
the children of *A* and Moab . . .2Chr 20:10
against the children of *A* 2Chr 20:22
children of *A* and Moab 2Chr 20:23
A gave him the same year 2Chr 27:5
did the children of *A* pay 2Chr 27:5
wives of Ashdod, of *A* . . . . .Neh 13:23
Gebal, and *A*, and Amalek . . . .Ps 83:7
children of *A* shall obey . . . . . . .Is 11:14
A, and Moab, and all that . . . . .Jer 9:26
and the children of *A* . . . . .Jer 25:21
captivity..children of *A* . . . . .Jer 49:6
chief of the children of *A* . . . . .Dan 11:41
of the children of *A* . . . . .Amos 1:13
of the children of *A* . . . . .Zeph 2:8
of *A* as Gomorrah, even the . . .Zeph 2:9

AMMONITES (ăm'ŏn-īts)—*descendants of Ammon*

Characterized by:
Cruelty . . . . .Amos 1:13
Pride . . . . .Zeph 2:9, 10
Callousness . . . . .Ezek 25:3, 6
Idolatry 1Kin 11:7, 33

Hostility toward Israel, seen in:
Aiding the Moabites . . . . .Deut 23:3, 4
Helping the Amalekites . .Judg 3:13
Proposing a cruel treaty . .1Sam 11:1-3
Abusing David's
ambassadors 2Sam 10:1-4
Hiring Syrians against
David 2Sam 10:6
Assisting the Chaldeans . .2Kin 24:2
Harassing postexilic Jews .Neh 4:3, 7, 8

Defeated by:
Jephthah . . . . .Judg 11:4-33
Saul 1Sam 11:11
David 2Sam 10:7-14
Jehoshaphat 2Chr 20:1-25
Jotham 2Chr 27:5

Prohibitions concerning:
Exclusion from worship . .Deut 23:3-6
No intermarriage with . . .Ezra 9:1-3

Prophecies concerning their:
Captivity . . . . .Amos 1:13-15
Subjection . . . . .Jer 25:9-21
Destruction . . . . .Ps 83:1-18

[*also* AMMONITE]
A call them Zamzummims . . . . .Deut 2:20
Zelek the *A* Naharai the 2Sam 23:37
women of the Moabites, *A* 1Kin 11:1
abomination of the *A* 1Kin 11:5
Zelek the *A* Naharai the 1Chr 11:39
the *A* gave gifts to Uzziah 2Chr 26:8
Tobiah the servant, the *A* . . . . .Neh 2:10
the *A* and Geshem the . . . . .Neh 2:19
A and the Moabite should . . . . .Neh 13:1
to the king of the *A* and . . . . . .Jer 27:3
among the *A* and in Edom . . . .Jer 40:11
Baalis the king of the *A* . . . . . . .Jer 40:14
departed to go over to the *A* . .Jer 41:10
men and went to the *A* . . . . . . .Jer 41:15
Concerning the *A*, thus . . . . . . .Jer 49:1

AMMONITESS (ăm'ŏn-īt-ĕs)—*a female Ammonite*
Naamah 1Kin 14:21, 31
Shimeath 2Chr 24:26

AMNESTY—*a pardon given to political offenders*
To Shimei 2Sam 19:16-23
To Amasa 2Sam 17:25
2Sam 19:13

AMNON (ăm'nŏn)—*"upbringing; faithful"*
1. A son of David 2Sam 3:2
   Rapes his half sister 2Sam 13:1-18
   Killed by Absalom 2Sam 13:19-29
2. Son of Shimon 1Chr 4:20

[*also* AMMON'S]
Go now to thy brother *A* 2Sam 13:7
went to her brother *A* 2Sam 13:8
when *A* heart is merry with ...2Sam 13:28
for *A* only is dead: for by 2Sam 13:32
A only is dead 2Sam 13:33
comforted concerning *A* 2Sam 13:39
the firstborn *A*, of Ahinoam ...1Chr 3:1

AMOK (ā'mŏk)—*"deep"*
A chief priest ....Neh 12:7, 20

AMON (ā'mŏn)—*"workman"*
1. King of Judah 2Kin 21:18, 19
   Follows evil 2Chr 33:22, 23
   Killed by conspiracy 2Kin 21:23, 24
2. A governor of Samaria ..1Kin 22:10, 26

the rest of the acts of *A* 2Kin 21:25
A his son, Josiah his son 1Chr 3:14
carry him back to *A* the 2Chr 18:25
A his son reigned in his 2Chr 33:20
A was two and twenty years ...2Chr 33:21
A sacrificed unto all the 2Chr 33:22
but *A* trespassed more and 2Chr 33:23
conspired against king *A* 2Chr 33:25
Zebaim, the children of *A* .....Neh 7:59
days of Josiah the son of *A* ....Jer 1:2
year of Josiah the son of *A* ....Jer 25:3
the son of *A*, king of Judah ...Zeph 1:1
Manasseh begat *A* ....Matt 1:10
and *A* begat Josiah ....Matt 1:10

AMONG, AMONGST—*See* INTRODUCTION

AMORITES (ăm'ŏ-rīts)—*"mountain dwellers"*

Described as:
Descendants of Canaan ..Gen 10:15, 16
Original inhabitants of Palestine ....Ezek 16:3
One of seven nations ....Gen 15:19-21
A confederation ....Josh 10:1-5
Ruled by great kings .....Ps 136:18, 19
Of great size ....Amos 2:9
Very wicked ....Gen 15:16
Worshipers of idols ......Judg 6:10

Contacts of, with Israel:
Their defeat by Joshua ...Josh 10:1-43
Their not being destroyed.Judg 1:34-36
Peace with 1Sam 7:14
Their being taxed by Solomon 1Kin 9:20, 21
Intermarriage with ....Judg 3:5, 6

[*also* AMORITE]
and also the *A* that dwelt .....Gen 14:7
the plain of Mamre the *A* .....Gen 14:13
the *A* and the Canaanites .....Gen 15:21
out of the hand of the *A* ......Gen 48:22
the Hittites and the *A* ....Ex 3:8
the *A* and the Perizzites ....Ex 3:17
and the *A* and the Hivites .....Ex 13:5
bring thee in unto the *A* ......Ex 23:23
will drive out the *A* ....Ex 33:2
drive out before thee the *A* ...Ex 34:11
A dwell in the mountains ......Num 13:29
out of the coasts of the *A* .....Num 21:13
between Moab and the *A* .....Num 21:13
unto Sihon king of the *A* ......Num 21:21
in all the cities of the *A* ....Num 21:25
Sihon the king of the *A* ....Num 21:26
unto Sihon king of the *A* ......Num 21:29
dwelt in the land of the *A* .....Num 21:31
drove out the *A* that were .....Num 21:32
unto Sihon king of the *A* ......Num 21:34
Israel had done to the *A* ......Num 22:2
dispossessed the *A* which ......Num 32:39
Sihon the king of the *A* ....Deut 1:4
go to the mount of the *A* .....Deut 1:7
of the mountain of the *A* ......Deut 1:19
the mountain of the *A* ....Deut 1:20
into the hand of the *A* ....Deut 1:27
A, which dwelt in that ....Deut 1:44
thine hand Sihon the *A* ....Deut 2:24
of the *A*, which dwelt at ....Deut 3:2
of the two kings of the *A* .....Deut 3:8
the A call it Shenir ....Deut 3:9
land of Sihon king of the *A* ...Deut 4:46
two kings of the *A*, which .....Deut 4:47
Girgashites and the *A* ....Deut 7:1
the Hittites and the *A* ....Deut 20:17
and to Og, kings of the *A* .....Deut 31:4
the two kings of the *A* ....Josh 2:10
the *A* and the Jebusites ....Josh 3:10
when all the kings of the *A* ....Josh 5:1
us into the hand of the *A* .....Josh 7:7
and the *A*, the Canaanite .....Josh 9:1
two kings of the *A* that ....Josh 9:10
on the west and to the *A* ......Josh 11:3
Sihon king of the *A*, who .....Josh 12:2
the *A* and the Canaanites .....Josh 12:8
to the borders of the *A* ....Josh 13:4
Sihon king of the *A*, which ....Josh 13:10
of Sihon king of the *A* ....Josh 13:21
into the land of the *A* ....Josh 24:8
fought against you, the *A* .....Josh 24:11
even the two kings of the *A* ...Josh 24:12
the gods of the *A* in ....Josh 24:15
even the *A* which dwelt in .....Josh 24:18
Jordan in the land of the *A* ...Judg 10:8
Egyptians and from the *A* .....Judg 10:11
Sihon king of the *A* ....Judg 11:19
A, the inhabitants of that .....Judg 11:21
all the coasts of the *A* ....Judg 11:22
hath dispossessed the *A* ....Judg 11:23
of the remnant of the *A* 2Sam 21:2
of Sihon king of the *A* 1Kin 4:19
all things as did the *A* 1Kin 21:26
wickedly..that the *A* did 2Kin 21:11
Jebusite also and the *A* 1Chr 1:14
of the Hittites and the *A* 2Chr 8:7
the Egyptians and the *A* ......Ezra 9:1
the *A* and the Perizzites ....Neh 9:8
Sihon king of the *A* and ....Ps 135:11
and your father an *A* ....Ezek 16:45
possess the land of the *A* ......Amos 2:10

AMOS (ā'mŏs)—*"burden-bearer; burden-some"*
1. A prophet of Israel .....Amos 1:1
   Pronounces judgment against nations ....Amos 1:1-3, 15
   Denounces Israel's sins ..Amos 4:1—7:9
   Condemns Amaziah, the priest of Beth-el ....Amos 7:10-17
   Predicts Israel's downfall .Amos 9:1-10
   Foretells great blessings ..Amos 9:11-15
2. An ancestor of Christ ...Luke 3:25

the Lord said unto me *A* ......Amos 7:8
said, *A*, what seest thou? ......Amos 8:2

AMOUNTING—*adding up to*
gold *a* to six hundred 2Chr 3:8

AMOZ (ā'mŏz)—*"strong"*
The father of Isaiah the prophet ....Is 1:1

the prophet the son of *A* 2Kin 19:2
the son of *A* sent to 2Kin 19:20
the son of *A* came to him 2Kin 20:1
the prophet, the son of *A* 2Chr 26:22
the son of *A* prayed and 2Chr 32:20
prophet, the son of *A* 2Chr 32:32
that Isaiah the son of *A* ....Is 2:1
which Isaiah the son of *A* .....Is 13:1
by Isaiah the son of *A* ....Is 20:2
the prophet the son of *A* ......Is 37:2
the son of *A* sent unto ....Is 37:21
son of *A* came unto him .....Is 38:1

AMPHIPOLIS (ăm-fĭp'ō-lĭs)—*"surrounded city"*
Visited by Paul ....Acts 17:1

AMPLIAS (ăm'plĭ-ăs)—*"large"*
Christian at Rome ....Rom 16:8

AMRAM (ăm'răm)—*"people exalted; red"*
1. Son of Kohath ....Num 3:17-19
   The father of Aaron, Moses and Miriam .. { Ex 6:18-20; 1Chr 6:3 }
2. Jew who divorced his foreign wife ....Ezra 10:34

[*also* AMRAM'S]
And Kohath begat *A* ....Num 26:58
name of *A* wife was ....Num 26:59
and she bare unto *A* Aaron ...Num 26:59
A, and Eshban, and Ithran 1Chr 1:41
A, Izhar, and Hebron and 1Chr 6:2
children of *A*, Aaron and 1Chr 6:3
sons of Kohath were *A* and ...1Chr 6:18
sons of Kohath *A* Izhar 1Chr 23:12
sons of *A*; Aaron and 1Chr 23:13
sons of *A*; Shubael of the 1Chr 24:20

AMRAMITES (ăm'răm-īts)—*descendants of Amram*
A subdivision of the Levites ....Num 3:27

Of the *A* and the Izharites 1Chr 26:23

AMRAPHEL (ăm'ră-fĕl—*"powerful people"*
A king of Shinar who invaded Canaan during Abraham's time; identified by some as the Hammurabi of the monuments ....Gen 14:1, 9

AMULET—*charm worn to protect wearer against evil or to aid him.*
Condemned ....Is 3:18-23

AMUSEMENTS—*entertainments; pleasurable diversions*

Found in:
Dancing ....Ex 32:18, 19, 25
Music 1Sam 18:6, 7
Earthly pleasures ....Eccl 2:1-8
Drunkenness ....Amos 6:1-6; 1Pet 4:3
Feasting ....Mark 6:21, 22
Games ....Luke 7:32
Gossip ....Acts 17:21

Productive of:
Sorrow ....Prov 14:13
Poverty ....Prov 21:17
Vanity ....Eccl 2:1-11
Immorality 1Cor 10:6-8
Spiritual deadness 1Tim 5:6

Prevalence of:
In the last days 2Tim 3:1, 4
In Babylon ....Rev 18:21-24
At Christ's return ....Matt 24:38, 39

AMZI (ăm'zī)—*"my strength"*
1. A Merarite Levite 1Chr 6:46
2. A priest ....Neh 11:12

AN—*See* INTRODUCTION

ANAB (ā'năb)—*"grape"*
A town of Judah ....Josh 11:21

ANAH (ā'nä)—*"answering"*
1. Father of Esau's wife ....Gen 36:2, 14, 18
2. A Horite chief ....Gen 36:20, 29
3. Son of Zibeon ....Gen 36:24

And the children of *A* were ...Gen 36:25
the daughter of *A* ....Gen 36:25
and Zibeon, and *A*, and 1Chr 1:38
of Zibeon; Ajah, and *A* 1Chr 1:40
The sons of *A*; Dishon 1Chr 1:41

ANAHARATH (ă-nā'hă-răth)—*"gorge"*
A city in the valley of Jezreel ....Josh 19:19

ANAIAH (ă-nī'ä) —*"Jehovah has covered; Jehovah answers"*
1. A Levite assistant ....Neh 8:4
2. One who sealed the new covenant ....Neh 10:22

ANAK (ā'năk)—*"giant; long necked"*
Descendant of Arba .....Josh 15:13
Father of three sons .....Num 13:22

We saw the children of *A* ......Num 13:28
the giants, the sons of *A* ....Num 13:33
before the children of *A* ....Deut 9:2
thence the three sons of *A* .....Josh 15:14
Talmai, the children of *A* ......Josh 15:14
city of Arba the father of *A* ...Josh 21:11
thence the three sons of *A* .....Judg 1:20

ANAKIM (ăn'ā-kĭm)—*descendants of Anak; a race of giants*

Described as:
Giants ....Num 13:28-33
Very strong ....Deut 2:10-11, 21

Defeated by:
Joshua..................Josh 10:36-39
Caleb ....Josh 14:6-15

A remnant left:
Among the Philistines....Josh 11:22
Possibly in Gath.........1Sam 17:4-7

seen the sons of the *A* there...Deut 1:28
the children of the *A* ....Deut 9:2
cut off the *A* from the ....Josh 11:21

ANAMIM (ă'ä-mĭm)—*"rockmen"*
A tribe of people listed among Mizraim's (Egypt's) descendants ..Gen 10:13

ANAMMELECH (ăn-ăm'ĕ-lĕk)—*"Anu is king"*
A god worshiped at Samaria 2Kin 17:24, 31

ANAN (ā'năn)—*"he beclouds; cloud"*
A signer of Nehemiah's document ....Neh 10:26

ANANI (ă-nā'nī)—*"my cloud"*
Son of Elioenai 1Chr 3:24

ANANIAH (ăn-ä-nī'ä)—*"Jehovah is a cloud"*
1. The father of Maaseiah ..Neh 3:23
2. A town inhabited by Benjamite returnees...Neh 11:32

ANANIAS (ăn-ä-nī'ăs)—*"Jehovah is gracious"*
1. Disciple at Jerusalem slain for lying to God .Acts 5:1-11
2. A Christian disciple at Damascus ....Acts 9:10-19; Acts 22:12-16
3. A Jewish high priest ....Acts 23:1-5

after five days *A* the high .....Acts 24:1

ANARCHY—*state of lawlessness or disorder due to the absence of governmental authority*

Manifested in:
Moral looseness ....Ex 32:1-8, 25
Idolatry.................Judg 17:1-13
Religious syncretism 2Kin 17:27-41
A reign of terror ....Jer 40:13-16
Perversion of justice .....Hab 1:1-4

Instances of:
At Kadesh ....Num 14:1-10
During the judges ....Judg 18:1-31
In the northern kingdom..1Kin 12:26-33
At the crucifixion........Matt 27:15-31
At Stephen's death ......Acts 7:54, 57-58
At Ephesus ....Acts 19:28-34
In the time of Antichrist..2Thess 2:3-12

ANATH (ā'năth)—*"answer"*
Father of Shamgar.......Judg 3:31

of Shamgar the son of *A* ......Judg 5:6

ANATHEMA (ă-năth'ĭ-mă)—*denunciation of something as accursed*
Applied to non-believers or Christ haters .....1Cor 16:22; Gal 1:8, 9
Translated "accursed" ...Rom 9:3; 1Cor 12:3

See ACCURSED

ANATHOTH (ăn'ä-thŏth)—*"answers"*
1. A Benjamite, son of Becher 1Chr 7:8
2. A leader who signed the document ....Neh 10:19
3. A Levitical city in Benjamin ....Josh 21:18
Birthplace of Jeremiah ..Jer 1:1
Citizens of, hate Jeremiah ....Jer 11:21, 23
Jeremiah bought property there ....Jer 32:6-15
Home of famous mighty man 2Sam 23:27
Home of Abiathar, the high priest 1Kin 2:26
Reoccupied after exile ...Ezra 2:1, 23
Go to, to die 1Kin 2:26
Wretched place ....Is 10:30
Reproved Jeremiah of...Jer 29:27

and *A* with her suburbs 1Chr 6:60
A, a hundred twenty and......Neh 7:27
And at *A*, Nob, Ananiah......Neh 11:32

ANCESTORS—*those from whom a person is descended*
the covenant of their *a*........Lev 26:45

ANCHOR—*a weight used to hold a ship in place*
Literally, of Paul's ship ..Acts 27: 29-30, 40
Figuratively of the believer's hope ....Heb 6:19

ANCIENT—*of or relating to a remote period; aged person*
Applied to the beginning (eternity) ....Is 45:21
Applied to something very old ....1Sam 24:13; Prov 22:28
Applied to old men (elders) ....Ps 119:100; Jer 19:1

[*also* ANCIENTS]
chief things of..*a* mountains ...Deut 33:15
a river, the river Kishon ....Judg 5:21
Hast thou not heard..of *a* 2Kin 19:25
And these are *a* things 1Chr 4:22
of the fathers, who were *a*......Ezra 3:12
With the *a* is wisdom ....Job 12:12
the years of *a* times ....Ps 77:5
and the prudent, and the *a* ....Is 3:2
himself proudly against..*a*......Is 3:5
enter into judgment..the *a* .....Is 3:14
a and honorable, he is the .....Is 9:15
son of the wise, the son of *a*...Is 19:11
Whose antiquity is *a* of days ...Is 23:7
and before his *a* gloriously .....Is 24:23
Hast thou not heard..of *a* ......Is 37:26
I appointed the *a* people? .....Is 44:7
a times the things that are .....Is 46:10
upon the *a* hast thou very .....Is 47:6
a days, in the generations......Is 51:9
mighty nation, it is an *a* ....Jer 5:15
in their ways from the *a* ....Jer 18:15
priest..counsel from the *a*.......Ezek 7:26
seventy men of the *a* of the.....Ezek 8:11
the *a* of the house of Israel ....Ezek 8:12
then they began at the *a* ......Ezek 9:6
a of Gebal and the wise ....Ezek 27:9
the *a* high places are ours .....Ezek 36:2

ANCIENT OF DAYS
Title applied to God .....Dan 7:9, 13, 22

ANCLE—*See* ANKLE

AND—*See* INTRODUCTION

ANDREW (ăn'drōō)—*"manly, conqueror"*
A fisherman ....Matt 4:18
A disciple of John the Baptist ....John 1:40
Brought Peter to Christ ..John 1:40-42
Called to Christ's discipleship ....Matt 4:18, 19
Enrolled among the Twelve ....Matt 10:2
Told Jesus about a lad's lunch ....John 6:8, 9
Carried a request to Jesus..John 12:20-22
Sought further light on Jesus' words ....Mark 13:3, 4
Met in the upper room ..Acts 1:13

Simon and *A* his brother ......Mark 1:16
the house of Simon and *A*.....Mark 1:29
A and Philip..Bartholomew ....Mark 3:18
named Peter,) and *A* his ......Luke 6:14

ANDRONICUS (ăn-drō-nī'kŭs)—*"conqueror"*
A notable Christian at Rome ....Rom 16:7

ANEM (ā'nĕm)—*"two fountains"*
Levitical city 1Chr 6:73

ANER (ā'ner)—*"sprout; waterfall"*
1. Amorite chief ....Gen 14:13, 24
2. A Levitical city 1Chr 6:70

ANETHOTHITE (ăn'ĕ-thŏth-īt)—*a native of Anathoth*
Abiezer thus called 2Sam 23:27

Abiezer the *A*, of the 1Chr 27:12

ANGEL—*"agent; messenger"—Supernatural being created by God before mankind*

Described as:
Created.................Ps 148:2, 5; Col 1:16
Spiritual beings ....Heb 1:14
Immortal ....Luke 20:36
Holy ....Matt 25:31
Innumerable ....Heb 12:22
Wise 2Sam 14:17, 20
Powerful................Ps 103:20
Elect 1Tim 5:21
Meek....................Jude 9
Sexless ....Matt 22:30
Invisible.................Num 22:22-31
Obedient ....Ps 103:20
Possessing emotions .....Luke 15:10
Concerned in human things 1Pet 1:12
Incarnate in human form at times ....Gen 18:2-8
Not perfect ....Job 4:18
Organized in ranks or orders ....Is 6:2; 1Thess 4:16

Ministry of, toward believers:
Guide ....Gen 24:7, 40
Provide for 1Kin 19:5-8
Protect ....Ps 34:7
Deliver ....Dan 6:22; Acts 12:7-10
Gather ....Matt 24:31
Direct activities ....Acts 8:26
Comfort.................Acts 27:23, 24
Minister to..............Heb 1:14

Ministry of, toward unbelievers:
A destruction ....Gen 19:13
A curse.................Judg 5:23
A pestilence 2Sam 24:15-17
Sudden death ....Acts 12:23
Persecution ....Ps 35:5, 6

Ministry of, in Christ's life, to:
Announce His conception..Matt 1:20, 21
Herald His birth.........Luke 2:10-12
Sustain Him ....Matt 4:11
Witness His resurrection. .1Tim 3:16
Proclaim His resurrection..Matt 28:5-7
Accompany Him to heaven ....Acts 1:9-11

Ministry of, on special occasions, at:
The world's creation .....Job 38:7
Sinai ....Acts 7:38, 53
Satan's binding ....Rev 20:1-3
Christ's return...........Matt 13:41, 49; 1Thess 4:16

Appearance of, during the Old Testament, to:
Abraham ....Gen 18:2-15

Hagar ... Gen 16:7-14
Lot ... Gen 19:1-22
Jacob ... Gen 28:12
Moses ... Ex 3:2
Balaam ... Num 22:31-35
Joshua ... Josh 5:13-15
All Israel ... Judg 2:1-4
Gideon ... Judg 6:11-24
Manoah ... Judg 13:6-21
David ... 2Sam 24:16, 17
Elijah ... 1Kin 19:5-7
Daniel ... Dan 6:22
Zechariah ... Zech 2:3

Appearances of, during the New Testament, to:

Zechariah ... Luke 1:11-20
The virgin Mary ... Luke 1:26-38
Joseph ... Matt 1:20-25
Shepherds ... Luke 2:9-14
Certain women ... Matt 28:1-7
Mary Magdalene ... John 20:12, 13
The apostles ... Acts 1:10, 11
Peter ... Acts 5:19, 20
Philip ... Acts 8:26
Cornelius ... Acts 10:3-32
Paul ... Acts 27:23, 24
John ... Rev 1:1
Seven churches ... Rev 1:20

[*also* ANGEL'S, ANGELS, ANGELS']

a of the Lord called unto ... Gen 22:15
way, and the **a** of God met ... Gen 32:1
The **a** which redeemed me ... Gen 48:16
mine **a** shall go before ... Ex 23:23
mine **a** shall go before ... Ex 32:34
I will send an **a** before ... Ex 33:2
he heard our voice..an **a** ... Num 20:16
the **a** of the Lord stood ... Num 22:22
the ass saw the **a** of the ... Num 22:23
the **a** of the Lord stood ... Num 22:24
And when the ass saw the **a** ... Num 22:25
the **a** of the Lord went ... Num 22:26
the **a** of the Lord, she fell ... Num 22:27
he saw the **a** of the Lord ... Num 22:31
the **a** of the Lord said unto ... Num 22:32
Balaam said unto the **a** of ... Num 22:34
a of the Lord said unto ... Num 22:35
there came an **a** of the ... Judg 6:11
a of the Lord appeared ... Judg 6:12
the **a** of God said unto him ... Judg 6:20
a of the Lord put forth ... Judg 6:21
Then the **a** of the Lord ... Judg 6:21
perceived that he was an **a** ... Judg 6:22
I have seen an **a** of the ... Judg 6:22
the **a** of the Lord appeared ... Judg 13:3
the countenance of an **a** ... Judg 13:6
the **a** of God came again ... Judg 13:9
the **a** of the Lord said ... Judg 13:13
Manoah said unto the **a** ... Judg 13:15
Manoah knew..he was an **a** ... Judg 13:16
And the **a** of the Lord said ... Judg 13:18
and the **a** did wondrously ... Judg 13:19
the **a** of the Lord ascended ... Judg 13:20
a of the Lord did no more ... Judg 13:21
Manoah knew that he..**a** ... Judg 13:21
good in my sight, as an **a** ... 1Sam 29:9
the king is as an **a** of God ... 2Sam 19:27
and an **a** spake unto me ... 1Kin 13:18
the **a** of the Lord said to ... 2Kin 1:3
the **a** of the Lord said unto ... 2Kin 1:15
the **a** of the Lord went out ... 2Kin 19:35
a of the Lord destroying ... 1Chr 21:12
God sent an **a**..Jerusalem ... 1Chr 21:15
a that destroyed, It is ... 1Chr 21:15
And the **a** of the Lord stood ... 1Chr 21:15
Ornan turned back..the **a** ... 1Chr 21:20
Lord commanded the **a** ... 1Chr 21:27
the sword of the **a**, of the ... 1Chr 21:30
the Lord sent an **a**, which ... 2Chr 32:21
him a little lower than..**a** ... Ps 8:5
thousand..thousands of **a** ... Ps 68:17
by sending evil **a** among ... Ps 78:49
give his **a** charge over ... Ps 91:11
who maketh his **a** spirits ... Ps 104:4
neither say thou before the **a** ... Eccl 5:6
a of the Lord went forth ... Is 37:36
the **a** of his presence saved ... Is 63:9
who hath sent his **a**, and ... Dan 3:28
My God hath sent his **a** ... Dan 6:22
he had power over the **a** ... Hos 12:4
the **a** that talked with me ... Zech 1:9
they answered the **a** of the ... Zech 1:11
a of the Lord answered ... Zech 1:12
the Lord answered the **a** ... Zech 1:13
the **a** that communed with ... Zech 1:14
I said unto the **a**..talked ... Zech 1:19
a of the Lord, and Satan ... Zech 3:1
stood before the **a** ... Zech 3:3
the **a** of the Lord stood ... Zech 3:5
the **a** of the Lord protested ... Zech 3:6
a that talked with me came ... Zech 4:1
spake to the **a** that talked ... Zech 4:4
a that talked with me ... Zech 4:5
a that talked with me went ... Zech 5:5
said I to the **a** that talked ... Zech 5:10
answered and said unto the **a** ... Zech 6:4
the **a** answered and said ... Zech 6:5
as the **a** of the Lord before ... Zech 12:8
a of the Lord appeared ... Matt 1:20
did as the **a** of the Lord ... Matt 1:24
a of the Lord appeareth to ... Matt 2:13
behold, an **a** of the Lord ... Matt 2:19
He shall give his **a** charge ... Matt 4:6
and the reapers are the **a** ... Matt 13:39
the glory of his Father..**a** ... Matt 16:27
That in heaven their **a** do ... Matt 18:10
no, not the **a** of heaven ... Matt 24:36
than twelve legions of **a** ... Matt 26:53
and the **a** ministered unto ... Mark 1:13
glory of his Father..holy **a** ... Mark 8:38
are as the **a** which are in ... Mark 12:25
then shall he send his **a** ... Mark 13:27
not the **a** which are in ... Mark 13:32
appeared unto him an **a** of ... Luke 1:11
the **a** said unto him, Fear ... Luke 1:13
Zachariah said unto the **a** ... Luke 1:18
the **a** answering said unto ... Luke 1:19
as the **a** were gone away ... Luke 2:15
which was so named..**a** ... Luke 2:21
He shall give his **a** charge ... Luke 4:10
in his Father's..holy **a** ... Luke 9:26
confess before the **a**..God ... Luke 12:8
denied before the **a** of God ... Luke 12:9
carried..**a** into Abraham's ... Luke 16:22
there appeared an **a** unto ... Luke 22:43
had also seen a vision of **a** ... Luke 24:23
a of God ascending and ... John 1:51
a went down at a certain ... John 5:4
others said, An **a** spake to ... John 12:29
had been the face of an **a** ... Acts 6:15
an **a** of the Lord in a flame ... Acts 7:30
the hand of the **a** which ... Acts 7:35
an **a** of God coming in to ... Acts 10:3
a which spake unto Cornelius ... Acts 10:7
warned from God by a holy **a**. ... Acts 10:22
how he had seen an **a** in ... Acts 11:13
the Lord hath sent his **a** ... Acts 12:11
said they, It is his **a** ... Acts 12:15
resurrection, neither **a** ... Acts 23:8
if a spirit or an **a** hath ... Acts 23:9
nor life, nor **a**, nor ... Rom 8:38
world, and to **a**, and to ... 1Cor 4:9
know ye not..shall judge **a** ... 1Cor 6:3
her head because of the **a** ... 1Cor 11:10
tongues of men and of **a** ... 1Cor 13:1
transformed into an **a** of ... 2Cor 11:14
we, or an **a** from heaven ... Gal 1:8
and it was ordained by **a** ... Gal 3:19
received me as an **a** of God ... Gal 4:14
humility and worshiping of **a** ... Col 2:18
heaven with his mighty **a** ... 2Thess 1:7
so much better than the **a** ... Heb 1:4
unto which of the **a** said he ... Heb 1:5
let all the **a** of God worship ... Heb 1:6
of the **a** he said ... Heb 1:7
Who maketh his **a** spirits ... Heb 1:7
to which of the **a** said he ... Heb 1:13
if the word spoken by **a** ... Heb 2:2
unto the **a** hath he not put ... Heb 2:5
a little lower than the **a** ... Heb 2:7
a little lower than the **a** ... Heb 2:9
not on him the nature of **a** ... Heb 2:16
entertained **a** unawares ... Heb 13:2
a and authorities and ... 1Pet 3:22
Whereas **a**, which are ... 2Pet 2:11
the **a** of the church of ... Rev 2:1
the **a** of the church in ... Rev 2:8
to the **a** of the church in ... Rev 2:12
the **a** of the church in ... Rev 2:18
unto the **a** of the church in ... Rev 3:1
my Father, and before his **a** ... Rev 3:5
the **a** of the church in ... Rev 3:7
unto the **a** of the church ... Rev 3:14
I saw a strong **a** ... Rev 5:2
I heard the voice of many **a** ... Rev 5:11
I saw four **a** standing on ... Rev 7:1
all the **a** stood round about ... Rev 7:11
I saw the seven **a** which ... Rev 8:2
a came and stood at the ... Rev 8:3
before God out of the **a** ... Rev 8:4
the **a** took the censer, and ... Rev 8:5
a which had the seven ... Rev 8:6
The first **a** sounded, and ... Rev 8:7
the second **a** sounded, and ... Rev 8:8
the third **a** sounded, and ... Rev 8:10
the fourth **a** sounded, and ... Rev 8:12
an **a** flying through the ... Rev 8:13
the trumpet of the three **a** ... Rev 8:13
the fifth **a** sounded, and I ... Rev 9:1
which is the **a**..bottomless ... Rev 9:11
and the sixth **a** sounded ... Rev 9:13
saying to the sixth **a** ... Rev 9:14
Loose the four **a** which are ... Rev 9:14
and the four **a** were loosed ... Rev 9:15
I saw another mighty **a** ... Rev 10:1
a which I saw stand upon ... Rev 10:5
voice of the seventh **a** ... Rev 10:7
open in the hand of the **a** ... Rev 10:8
I went unto the **a**, and said ... Rev 10:9
little book out of the **a** ... Rev 10:10
and the **a** stood, saying ... Rev 11:1
the seventh **a** sounded ... Rev 11:15
I saw another **a** fly in the ... Rev 14:6
there followed another **a** ... Rev 14:8
the third **a** followed them ... Rev 14:9
the presence of the holy **a** ... Rev 14:10
a came out of the ... Rev 14:15
another **a** come out from ... Rev 14:18
a thrust in his sickle ... Rev 14:19
seven **a** having the seven ... Rev 15:1
seven **a** came out of the ... Rev 15:6
gave unto the seven **a** ... Rev 15:7
the seven **a** were fulfilled ... Rev 15:8
saying to the seven **a**, Go ... Rev 17:1
and the **a** said unto me ... Rev 17:7
I saw another **a** come down ... Rev 18:1
a mighty **a** took up a stone ... Rev 18:21
I saw an **a** standing in the ... Rev 19:17
and I saw an **a** come down ... Rev 20:1
unto me one of the seven **a** ... Rev 21:9
at the gates twelve **a** ... Rev 21:12
measure of a man, that..**a** ... Rev 21:17
his **a** to show unto his ... Rev 22:6
before the feet of the **a** ... Rev 22:8
have sent mine **a** to testify ... Rev 22:16

ANGEL OF GOD, THE—*a heavenly being sent by God as his personal agent or spokesman*

Names of:

Angel of God ... Gen 21:17
Angel of the Lord ... Gen 22:11
Captain of host of the Lord ... Josh 5:14

Appearances of, to:

Hagar ... Gen 16:7, 8; Gen 21:17
Abraham ... Gen 22:11, 15; Gen 18:1-33
Eliezer ... Gen 24:7, 40
Jacob ... Gen 31:11-13; Gen 32:24-30
Moses ... Ex 3:2

Children of Israel........Ex 13:21, 22
Ex 14:19
Balaam.................Num 22:22-35
Joshua..................Judg 2:1
David..................1Chr 21:16-18

Divine characteristics:
Deliver Israel..........Judg 2:1-3
Extend blessings........Gen 16:7-12
Pardon sin.............Ex 23:20-22

ANGELS, FALLEN—*supernatural opponents of God and man*
Fall of, by pride.........Is 14:12-15
Jude 6
Seen by Christ.........Luke 10:18
Make war on saints......Rev 12:7-17
Imprisoned............2Pet 2:4
Everlasting fire prepared for.................Matt 25:41

ANGELS' FOOD—*meaning is uncertain*
Eaten by men...........Ps 78:25
Eaten by Elijah.........1Kin 19:5-8

ANGER—*a strong feeling of displeasure*

[*also* ANGERED, ANGRY]
Oh let not the Lord be *a*.....Gen 18:30
Oh let not the Lord be *a*.....Gen 18:32
thine *a* burn against thy.......Gen 44:18
the *a* of the Lord was.........Ex 4:14
Balak's *a* was kindled.........Num 24:10
was *a* with me for your.......Deut 1:37
was *a* with me for your.......Deut 4:21
lest the *a* of the Lord thy.....Deut 6:15
will the *a* of the Lord be......Deut 7:4
Lord, to provoke him to *a*....Deut 9:18
a of the Lord and his........Deut 29:20
Then my *a* shall be...........Deut 31:17
provoke him to *a* through.....Deut 31:29
provoked they him to *a*.......Deut 32:16
they..provoked me to *a*.......Deut 32:21
I will provoke them to *a*......Deut 32:21
fire is kindled in mine *a*.......Deut 32:22
then shall the *a* of the........Josh 23:16
And the *a* of the Lord was....Judg 2:20
a of the Lord was hot........Judg 3:8
not thine *a* be hot against.....Judg 6:39
the *a* of the Lord was hot.....Judg 10:7
David's *a* was greatly.........2Sam 12:5
provoking the Lord to *a*......1Kin 14:15
Lord God of Israel to *a*.......1Kin 15:30
provoke me to *a* with their....1Kin 16:2
provoking him to *a* with......1Kin 16:7
Lord God of Israel to *a*.......1Kin 16:13
Lord God of Israel to *a*.......1Kin 16:26
thou hast provoked me to *a*...1Kin 21:22
and provoked to *a* the Lord...1Kin 22:53
the *a* of the Lord was.........2Kin 13:3
to provoke the Lord to *a*.....2Kin 17:11
Lord to provoke him to *a*.....2Kin 17:17
to provoke him to *a*..........2Kin 21:6
provoked me to *a*, since......2Kin 21:15
might provoke me to *a*........2Kin 22:17
to provoke the Lord to *a*.....2Kin 23:19
through the *a* of the Lord.....2Kin 24:20
the *a* of the Lord was.........1Chr 13:10
wherefore their *a* was.........2Chr 25:10
and provoked to *a* the........2Chr 28:25
to provoke him to *a*..........2Chr 33:6
might provoke me to *a*........2Chr 34:25
they provoked thee to *a*......Neh 4:5
God..not withdraw his *a*......Job 9:13
teareth himself..his *a*.........Job 18:4
distributeth sorrows in his *a*...Job 21:17
he hath visited in his *a*........Job 35:15
Kiss the Son, lest he be *a*.....Ps 2:12
O Lord, rebuke me not in *a*...Ps 6:1
Arise, O Lord in thine *a*......Ps 7:6
God is *a* with the wicked.....Ps 7:11
oven in the time of thine *a*....Ps 21:9
put not thy servant away in *a*..Ps 27:9
Cease from *a*, and forsake....Ps 37:8
flesh because of thine *a*.......Ps 38:3
in thine *a* cast down the......Ps 56:7
let thy wrathful *a* take........Ps 69:24
doth thine *a* smoke against....Ps 74:1
in *a* shut up his tender........Ps 77:9
For they provoked him to *a*...Ps 78:58
Wilt thou be *a* for ever?......Ps 79:5
how long wilt thou be *a*.......Ps 80:4
the fierceness of thine *a*.......Ps 85:3
Wilt thou be *a* with us for....Ps 85:5
gracious slow to *a*............Ps 103:8
they provoked him to *a*.......Ps 106:29
a him also at the waters.......Ps 106:32
slow to *a*, and of great........Ps 145:8
that is slow to *a* appeaseth....Prov 15:18
slow to *a* is better than the....Prov 16:32
discretion..deferreth his *a*.....Prov 19:11
whoso provoketh him to *a*....Prov 20:2
A gift in secret pacifieth *a*....Prov 21:14
a contentious and an *a*........Prov 21:19
the rod of his *a* shall fail......Prov 22:8
no friendship with an *a*.......Prov 22:24
so doth an *a* countenance.....Prov 25:23
cruel, and *a* is outrageous.....Prov 27:4
An *a* man stirreth up.........Prov 29:22
Be not hasty..spirit to be *a*....Eccl 7:9
a resteth..bosom of fools......Eccl 7:9
mother's children were *a*......Song 1:6
Holy One of Israel unto *a*.....Is 1:4
the *a* of the Lord kindled.....Is 5:25
all this his *a* is not turned.....Is 5:25
the fierce *a* of Rezin with.....Is 7:4
all this his *a* is not turned.....Is 9:12
slain. For all this his *a*.......Is 10:4
though thou wast *a* with......Is 12:1
thine *a* is turned away and....Is 12:1
mighty ones for mine *a*.......Is 13:3
ruled the nations in *a*.........Is 14:6
far burning with his *a*.........Is 30:27
upon him the fury of his *a*....Is 42:25
sake will I defer mine *a*.......Is 48:9
A people..provoketh me to *a*..Is 65:3
to render his *a* with fury......Is 66:15
surely his *a* shall turn.........Jer 2:35
Will he reserve his *a*..........Jer 3:5
for the fierce *a* of..Lord......Jer 4:8
may provoke me to *a*.........Jer 7:18
not in thine *a*, lest thou.......Jer 10:24
to provoke me to *a* in.........Jer 11:17
because of the fierce *a* of.....Jer 12:13
fire is kindled in mine *a*.......Jer 15:14
kindled a fire in mine *a*.......Jer 17:4
them in the time of thine *a*....Jer 18:23
a, and in fury, and in great...Jer 21:5
The *a* of the Lord shall not...Jer 23:20
provoke me not to *a* with.....Jer 25:6
a of the Lord shall not........Jer 30:24
gods, to provoke me to *a*.....Jer 32:29
I have slain in mine *a*.........Jer 33:5
for great is the *a* and the.....Jer 36:7
As mine *a* and my fury........Jer 42:18
provoke me to *a*, in that......Jer 44:3
them, even my fierce *a*........Jer 49:37
the fierce *a* of the Lord.......Jer 51:45
through the *a* of the Lord.....Jer 52:3
in the day of his fierce *a*......Lam 1:12
with a cloud in his *a*..........Lam 2:1
footstool in..day of his *a*......Lam 2:1
covered with *a*, and...........Lam 3:43
poured out his fierce *a*........Lam 4:11
mine *a* be accomplished.......Ezek 5:13
I will send mine *a* upon.......Ezek 7:3
returned to provoke me to *a*..Ezek 8:17
overflowing shower in mine *a*..Ezek 13:13
to provoke me to *a*...........Ezek 16:26
to accomplish my *a* against....Ezek 20:8
will I gather you in mine *a*....Ezek 22:20
Edom according to mine *a*.....Ezek 25:14
I will..according to thine *a*....Ezek 35:11
I have consumed..mine *a*.......Ezek 43:8
let thine *a* and thy fury be....Dan 9:16
neither in *a*, nor in battle.....Dan 11:20
mine *a* is kindled against......Hos 8:5
the fierceness of mine *a*.......Hos 11:9
provoked him to *a* most.......Hos 12:14
gave thee a king in mine *a*....Hos 13:11
for mine *a* is turned away.....Hos 14:4
slow to *a*, and of great........Joel 2:13
his *a* did tear perpetually......Amos 1:11
turn away from his fierce *a*....Jon 3:9
will execute vengeance in *a*....Mic 5:15
The Lord is slow to *a* and.....Nah 1:3
thine *a* against the rivers......Hab 3:8
before the fierce *a* of the.....Zeph 2:2
even all my fierce *a*..........Zeph 3:8
Mine *a* was kindled against....Zech 10:3
whosoever is *a* with his.......Matt 5:22
the master..house being *a*.....Luke 14:21
by a foolish nation I will *a*....Rom 10:19
put off all these, *a*, wrath,....Col 3:8
not soon *a*, not given to......Titus 1:7
nations were *a*, and thy.......Rev 11:18

ANGER OF GOD—*righteous, unerring; directed against evil*

Caused by man's:
Sin.....................Num 32:10-15
Unbelief................Ps 78:21, 22
Error..................2Sam 6:7
Disobedience............Josh 7:1, 11, 12
Idolatry................Judg 2:11-14

Described as:
Sometimes delayed......2Kin 23:25-27
Slow...................Neh 9:17
Brief...................Ps 30:5
Restrained..............Ps 78:38
Fierceness..............Ps 78:49, 50
Consuming..............Ps 90:7
Powerful...............Ps 90:11
Not forever.............Mic 7:18
To be feared............Ps 76:7

Visitation of, upon:
Miriam and Aaron.......Num 12:9-15
Israelites...............Num 11:4-10
Balaam.................Num 22:21, 22
Moses..................Deut 4:21, 22
Israel..................Deut 9:8
Aaron..................Deut 9:20
Wicked cities...........Deut 29:23
A land.................Deut 29:24-28
A king.................2Chr 25:15, 16

Deliverance from, by:
Intercessory prayer......Num 11:1, 2
Deut 9:19, 20
Decisive action..........Num 25:3-12
Obedience..............Deut 13:16-18
Executing the guilty.....Josh 7:1, 10-26
Atonement.............Is 63:1-6
See WRATH OF GOD

ANGER OF JESUS—*reflects character and nature of God*
Provoked by unbelievers .Mark 3:5
In the Temple...........Matt 21:12
Mark 11:15

ANGER OF MAN—*sometimes righteous, but often mixed with hatred and rage*

Caused by:
A brother's deception....Gen 27:45
A wife's complaint......Gen 30:1, 2
Rape..................Gen 34:1, 7
Inhuman crimes.........Gen 49:6, 7
A leader's indignation...Ex 11:8
A people's idolatry......Ex 32:19, 22
Disobedience............Num 31:14-18
The Spirit's arousal......1Sam 11:6
A brother's jealousy.....1Sam 17:28
Luke 15:28
A king's jealousy........1Sam 20:30
Righteous indignation....1Sam 20:34
Priestly rebuke.........2Chr 26:19
Unrighteous dealings.....Neh 5:6, 7
Wife's disobedience......Esth 1:12
Lack of respect.........Esth 3:5
Failure of astrologers....Dan 2:12
Flesh..................Gal 5:19, 20
Harsh treatment.........Eph 6:4

Justifiable, seen in:
Jacob..................Gen 31:36
Moses..................Ex 32:19
Samson.................Judg 14:1, 19
Saul...................1Sam 11:6
Samuel.................1Sam 15:16-31

Jonathan................1Sam 20:34
Christ....................Mark 3:5

Unjustifiable, seen in:

Cain......................Gen 4:5, 6
Simeon and Levi........Gen 49:5-7
Potiphar.................Gen 39:1, 19
Moses....................Num 20:10-12
Balaam...................Num 22:27, 28
Saul......................1Sam 20:30
Naaman..................2Kin 5:11, 12
Asa.......................2Chr 16:10
Uzziah...................2Chr 26:19
Ahasuerus...............Esth 1:9, 12
Haman...................Esth 3:5
Nebuchadnezzar.........Dan 3:13
Jonah....................Jon 4:1-9
Herod....................Matt 2:16
The Jews.................Luke 4:28
Jewish officialdom.......Acts 5:17

The Christian attitude toward:

To be slow in...........Prov 14:17
Not to sin in............Eph 4:26
To put away.............Eph 4:31

Effects of, seen in:

Attempted assassination..Esth 2:21
Punishment..............Prov 19:19
Mob action..............Acts 19:28, 29

Pacified by:

Kindly suggestion........2Kin 5:10-14
Righteous execution.....Esth 7:10
Gentle answer...........Prov 15:1

ANGLE—*a fishing instrument*

Of Egyptian fishermen...Is 19:8

take..them with the ***a***........Hab 1:15

ANGUISH—*extreme pain or distress of body or mind*

Caused by:

Physical hardships.......Gen 6:9
Physical pain............2Sam 1:9
Impending destruction...Deut 2:25
Conflict of soul..........Job 7:11
National distress.........Is 8:21, 22
Childbirth................John 16:21
A spiritual problem......2Cor 2:4

Reserved for:

People who refuse wisdom...............Prov 1:20-27
The wicked..............Job 15:20, 24
Those in Hell............Luke 16:23, 24

we saw the ***a*** of his soul......Gen 42:21
hearkened not...for ***a*** of......Ex 6:9
Trouble and ***a*** have taken.....Ps 119:143
and ***a***, upon every soul of.....Rom 2:9

ANIAM (ă-nī'ăm)—*"lamentation of the people"*

A Manassite.............1Chr 7:19

ANIM (ā'nĭm)—*"fountains"*

A city in south Judah....Josh 15:50

ANIMALS—*living creatures other than humans*

Described as:

Domesticated and wild...2Sam 12:3
Clean and unclean.......Lev 11:1-31
Deut 14:1-20
For sacrifices............Ex 12:3-14
Lev 16:3, 5

List of, in the Bible:

Antelope.................Deut 14:5
Ape......................1Kin 10:22
Asp......................Is 11:8
Ass......................Gen 22:3
Badger...................Ex 25:5
Bats.....................Deut 14:18
Bear.....................1Sam 17:34
Bittern...................Is 14:23
Boar.....................Ps 80:13
Bulls.....................Jer 52:20
Calf......................Gen 18:7
Camel....................Gen 12:16
Cattle....................Gen 1:25
Chameleon...............Lev 11:30
Chamois.................Deut 14:5
Cockatrice (adder).......Is 11:8
Colt......................Zech 9:9
Coney....................Lev 11:5
Crocodile (Leviathan)....Job 41:1
Deer.....................Deut 14:5
Dog......................Deut 23:18
Dragon...................Is 51:9
Elephant ("ivory").......1Kin 10:22
Ewe lambs...............Gen 21:30
Ferret....................Lev 11:30
Fox......................Judg 15:4
Frogs.....................Ex 8:2-14
Goat.....................Gen 27:9
Greyhound...............Prov 30:31
Hare.....................Deut 14:7
Hart......................Ps 42:1
Heifer....................Gen 15:9
Hind.....................Hab 3:19
Hippopotamus (Behemoth)...........Job 40:15
Horse....................Gen 47:17
Jackal ("Dragons").......Is 13:22
Kine.....................Gen 32:15
Lamb.....................Ex 29:39
Leopard..................Rev 13:2
Lion......................1Sam 17:34
Lizard....................Lev 11:30
Mole.....................Is 2:20
Mouse....................Lev 11:29
Mule.....................2Sam 13:29
Ox.......................Ex 21:28
Pygarg...................Deut 14:5
Ram......................Gen 15:9
Roebuck..................Deut 14:5
Satyr.....................Is 13:21
Scorpion.................Deut 8:15
Serpents.................Matt 10:16
Sheep....................Gen 4:2
Snail.....................Lev 11:30
Spider....................Prov 30:28
Swine....................Is 65:2-4
Tortoise..................Lev 11:29
Unicorn..................Num 23:22
Weasel...................Lev 11:29
Whale (sea monster).....Gen 1:21
Wolf.....................Is 11:6

Used figuratively of:

Human traits.............Gen 49:9-14, 21
Universal peace..........Is 11:6-9
Man's innate nature.....Jer 13:23
World empires...........Dan 7:2-8
Satanic powers..........Rev 12:4, 9
Christ's sacrifice........1Pet 1:18-20

ANISE—*a plant used for seasoning and medicinal purposes; dill*

Tithed by the Jews......Matt 23:23

ANKLE—*joint connecting foot and leg*

Lame man's healed......Acts 3:7

the waters were to the ***a***......Ezek 47:3
feet and ***a*** bones received.....Acts 3:7

ANKLET—*ornament worn by women on the ankles*

Included in Isaiah's denunciation..........Is 3:16, 18

ANNA (ăn'ä)—*"grace"*

Aged prophetess........Luke 2:36-38

ANNAS (ăn'ăs)—*"grace of Jehovah"*

A Jewish high priest.....Luke 3:2
Christ appeared before..John 18:12-24
Peter and John appeared before.................Acts 4:6

ANOINTING—*applying or pouring oil upon*

Performed upon:

The patriarchs...........1Chr 16:22
Priest....................Ex 29:7
Prophets.................1Kin 19:16
Israel's kings............1Sam 10:1
Foreign kings............1Kin 19:15
The Messianic King......Ps 2:2
Sacred objects...........Ex 30:26-28

Ordinary, purposes of, for:

Adornment...............Ruth 3:3
Invigoration.............2Sam 12:20
Hospitality..............Luke 7:38, 46
Purification..............Esth 2:12
Battle....................Is 21:5
Burial....................Matt 26:12
Sanctifying..............Ex 30:29

Medicinal, purposes of, for:

Wound...................Luke 10:34
Healing..................Mark 6:13
James 5:14

Sacred, purposes of, to:

Memoralize an event....Gen 28:18
Confirm a covenant......Gen 35:14
Set apart................Ex 30:22-29
Institute into office......1Sam 16:12, 13

Absence of:

Sign of judgment........Deut 28:40
Fasting..................2Sam 12:16, 20
Mourning.................2Sam 14:2

Of Christ the Messiah "the Anointed One," as:

Predicted................Ps 45:7
Is 61:1
Fulfilled.................Luke 4:18
Heb 1:9
Interpreted..............Acts 4:27
Symbolized in His name ("the Christ")....... Matt 16:16, 20; Acts 9:22
Typical of the believer's anointing.............1John 2:27

Significance of, as indicating:

Divine appointment......2Chr 22:7
Special honor...........1Sam 24:6, 10
Special privilege.........Ps 105:15
God's blessing...........Ps 23:5

[*also* ANOINT, ANOINTED, ANOINTEST]

Bethel, where thou ***a*** the......Gen 31:13
spices for ***a*** oil, and for.......Ex 25:6
a them, and consecrate.......Ex 28:41
wafers unleavened ***a*** with.....Ex 29:2
it upon his head, and ***a***.......Ex 29:7
of the ***a*** oil, and sprinkle......Ex 29:21
a..and to be consecrated......Ex 29:29
thou shalt ***a*** Aaron and his....Ex 30:30
This shall be a holy ***a*** oil......Ex 30:31
And the ***a*** oil, and sweet......Ex 31:11
light, and spices for the ***a***.....Ex 35:8
he made the holy ***a*** oil........Ex 37:29
golden altar and the ***a*** oil.....Ex 39:38
thou shalt take the ***a*** oil.......Ex 40:9
a the tabernacle, and all......Ex 40:9
a shall surely be an...........Ex 40:15
unleavened wafers ***a*** with.....Lev 2:4
If the priest that is ***a*** do.......Lev 4:3
And the priest that is ***a***.......Lev 4:5
is ***a*** shall bring of the.........Lev 4:16
the Lord..day when he is ***a***....Lev 6:20
a with oil, and cakes..........Lev 7:12
is the portion of the ***a*** of......Lev 7:35
the ***a*** oil, and a bullock.......Lev 8:2
a the tabernacle and all.......Lev 8:10
Moses took the ***a*** oil, and.....Lev 8:10
he poured of the ***a*** oil upon...Lev 8:12
Moses took of the ***a*** oil.......Lev 8:30
the ***a*** oil of the Lord is.......Lev 10:7
whose head the ***a*** oil was.....Lev 21:10
crown of the ***a*** oil of..........Lev 21:12
of Aaron, the priests..***a***.......Num 3:3
daily meat offering..the ***a***.....Num 4:16
wafers..unleavened bread ***a***....Num 6:15
set up the tabernacle..***a***.......Num 7:1
given them by reason..***a***.......Num 18:8
and exalt..horn of his ***a***.......1Sam 2:10
shall walk before mine ***a***......1Sam 2:35
a him to be captain over......1Sam 9:16
the Lord, and before his ***a***....1Sam 12:3
The Lord sent me to ***a*** thee...1Sam 15:1
the Lord ***a*** thee king over.....1Sam 15:17
Surely the Lord's ***a*** is........1Sam 16:6

my master, the Lord's *a* 1Sam 24:6
he is the Lord's *a* 1Sam 24:10
hand against the Lord's *a* 1Sam 26:9
to destroy the Lord's *a*........2Sam 1:14
and there they *a* David 2Sam 2:4
this day weak, though *a*.......2Sam 3:39
they *a* David king over 2Sam 5:3
I *a* thee king over Israel 2Sam 12:7
Absalom, whom we *a* over 2Sam 19:10
showeth mercy to his *a* 2Sam 22:51
the tabernacle, and *a* 1Kin 1:39
a him king in the room of.....1Kin 5:1
I have *a* thee king over 2Kin 9:3
they made him king, and *a* 2Kin 11:12
and *a* him, and made him 2Kin 23:30
they *a* David king over 1Chr 11:3
David was *a* king over 1Chr 14:8
turn not away the face..*a* 2Chr 6:42
Jehoiada and his sons *a* 2Chr 23:11
to eat and to drink, and *a*.....2Chr 23:15
the Lord saveth his *a* ....Ps 20:6
he is the saving strength..*a* ....Ps 28:8
upon the face of thine *a* ......Ps 84:9
been wroth with thine *a*.......Ps 89:38
I shall be *a* with fresh oil .....Ps 92:10
I have ordained a lamp..*a* .....Ps 132:17
be destroyed because *a* ....Is 10:27
Thus saith the Lord..his *a* .....Is 45:1
art the *a* cherub that..........Ezek 28:14
thou shalt not *a* thee with .....Mic 6:15
for salvation with thine *a*......Hab 3:13
the two *a* ones, that stand.....Zech 4:14
a thine head, and wash thy....Matt 6:17
a my body to the burying .....Mark 14:8
they might come and *a*........Mark 16:1
a them with the ointment .....Luke 7:38
hath *a* my feet with...........Luke 7:46
a the eyes of the blind man ...John 9:6
made clay and *a* mine eyes ....John 9:11
was that Mary which *a* the ....John 11:2
a the feet of Jesus, and ....John 12:3
How God *a* Jesus of..........Acts 10:38
a thine eyes with eyesalve .....Rev 3:18

ANOINTING OF THE HOLY SPIRIT—*endowment with the Spirit of God*

Of Christ:
Predicted ....Is 61:1
Fulfilled ....John 1:32-34
Explained...............Luke 4:18

Of Christians:
Predicted ....Ezek 47:1-12
Foretold by Christ ....John 7:38, 39
Fulfilled at Pentecost ....Acts 2:1-41
Fulfilled at conversion ...2 Cor 1:21
1John 2:20, 27

ANON—*at once; immediately*
and *a* with joy receiveth it ....Matt 13:20
a they tell him of her ....Mark 1:30

ANOTHER—*one that is different from the first thing considered; one more*

[*also* ANOTHER'S]
not understand one *a* ....Gen 11:7
if one man's ox hurt *a*, that ...Ex 21:35
shalt be turned into *a* man 1Sam 10:6
eyes shall behold..not *a* ....Job 19:27
let *a* take his office ....Ps 109:8
discover not a secret to *a* .....Prov 25:9
Let *a* man praise thee ....Prov 27:2
glory will I not give to *a* ......Is 42:8
call his servants by *a* name ....Is 65:15
thou shalt not be for *a* man ...Hos 3:3
man strive, nor reprove *a* ....Hos 4:4
come, or do we look for *a* ....Matt 11:3
Is it I? and *a* said, Is it I?.....Mark 14:19
said he to *a*, And how ....Luke 16:7
ye also ought to wash one *a*...John 13:14
give you *a* Comforter ....John 14:16
but every man *a* wealth 1Cor 10:24
a Jesus whom we have 2Cor 11:4
Which is not *a*, but there ......Gal 1:7
Bear ye one *a* burdens, and ...Gal 6:2
himself alone, and not in *a*....Gal 6:4
exhort one *a* daily, while ......Heb 3:13

ANSWER—*a reply*

Good:
Soft ....Prov 15:1
Confident ....Dan 3:16-18
Convicting ....Dan 5:17-28
Astonished..............Luke 2:47
Unanswerable ....Luke 20:3-8
Spontaneous ....Luke 21:14, 15
Spirit-directed ....Luke 12:11, 12
Ready 1Pet 3:15

Evil:
Unwise 1Kin 12:12-15
Incriminating............2Sam 1:5-16
Insolent 2Kin 18:27-36
Humiliating ....Esth 6:6-11
Satanic ....Job 1:8-11

[*also* ANSWERABLE, ANSWERED, ANSWEREST, ANSWERETH, ANSWERING, ANSWERS]
And Abraham *a* and said .....Gen 18:27
the children of Heth *a* ....Gen 23:5
Laban and Bethuel *a* ....Gen 24:50
And Isaac *a* and said unto ....Gen 27:37
shall my righteousness *a* ......Gen 30:33
And Rachel and Leah *a* ......Gen 31:14
And the sons of Jacob *a* ......Gen 34:13
unto God, who *a* me in the ...Gen 35:3
And Joseph *a* and said........Gen 40:18
God shall give Pharaoh an *a* ..Gen 41:16
And Joseph *a* Pharaoh ....Gen 41:16
And Reuben *a* them ....Gen 42:22
they *a*, Thy servant our ....Gen 43:28
Moses *a* and said, But ....Ex 4:1
And Miriam *a* them ....Ex 15:21
And all the people *a*..........Ex 19:8
and all the people *a* with......Ex 24:3
Joshua the son of Nun..*a* .....Num 11:28
And Balaam *a* and said ....Num 22:18
and he *a* and said ....Num 23:12
the children of Reuben *a*......Num 32:31
And ye *a* me, and said........Deut 1:14
if it make thee *a* of peace .....Deut 20:11
And they *a* Joshua, saying ....Josh 1:16
And Achan *a* Joshua ....Josh 7:20
And they *a* Joshua ....Josh 9:24
Who *a*, Give me a blessing....Josh 15:19
Joshua *a* them, If thou be .....Josh 17:15
half tribe of Manasseh *a* .....Josh 22:21
the people *a* and said, God ...Josh 24:16
Her wise ladies *a* her ....Judg 5:29
and his fellow *a* and said .....Judg 7:14
and the men of Penuel *a* .....Judg 8:8
of Ammon *a* unto the ....Judg 11:13
they *a* Samson, the son-in ....Judg 15:6
a the five men that went .....Judg 18:14
be going. But none *a* ....Judg 19:28
the Levite..*a* and said ....Judg 20:4
they *a* him, The Lord bless....Ruth 2:4
and Boaz *a* and said unto .....Ruth 2:11
she *a*, I am Ruth thine........Ruth 3:9
Hannah *a* and said, No 1Sam 1:15
and he *a*, Here am I..........1Sam 3:4
And the messenger *a* and 1Sam 4:17
And they *a*, Let the ark of....1Sam 5:8
They *a*, Five golden 1Sam 6:4
the servant *a* Saul again 1Sam 9:8
one of the same place *a*........1Sam 10:12
Nahash the Ammonite *a* 1Sam 11:2
And they *a*, He is witness.....1Sam 12:5
men of the garrison *a*.........1Sam 14:12
Then *a* one of the servants 1Sam 16:18
people *a* him after this 1Sam 17:27
the women *a* one another 1Sam 18:7
Michal *a* Saul, He said........1Sam 19:17
And Jonathan *a* Saul 1Sam 20:28
And the priest *a* David 1Sam 21:4
Then *a* Doeg the Edomite 1Sam 22:9
the Lord *a* him and said 1Sam 23:4
And Nabal *a* David's 1Sam 25:10
a David and said to 1Sam 26:6
Abner *a* and said, Who art....1Sam 26:14
the Lord *a* him not, neither ...1Sam 28:6
Saul *a*, I am sore distressed ...1Sam 28:15
And Achish *a* and said to 1Sam 29:9
And he *a* him, Pursue 1Sam 30:8
Art thou Ashel? And he *a* 2Sam 2:20
David *a* Rechab and..........2Sam 4:9
And he *a*, Behold thy 2Sam 9:6
she *a* him, Nay my 2Sam 13:12
she *a*, I am indeed a widow ...2Sam 14:5
And Ittai *a* the king, and 2Sam 15:21
people *a*, Thou shalt not 2Sam 18:3
But Abishai the son of..*a* 2Sam 19:21
he *a*, I am he. Then she 2Sam 20:17
And the Lord *a*, It is for......2Sam 21:1
the Lord, but he *a* them 2Sam 22:42
Then king David *a* and 1Kin 1:28
And king Solomon *a* and 1Kin 2:22
Then the king *a* and said......1Kin 3:27
he *a*, Nothing: howbeit let 1Kin 11:22
the king *a* the people 1Kin 12:13
king *a* and said unto the 1Kin 13:6
And he *a* him, I am 1Kin 18:8
the God that *a* by fire let 1Kin 18:24
neither voice, nor any to *a* 1Kin 18:29
And the king of Israel *a* 1Kin 20:4
a I will not give thee my 1Kin 21:6
he *a* him, Go, and prosper 1Kin 22:15
they *a* him, He was a hairy ...2Kin 1:8
And he *a*, Yea, I know it 2Kin 2:5
a The way through the........2Kin 3:8
she *a*, I dwell among mine 2Kin 4:13
And he *a*, Go ye 2Kin 6:2
king leaned *a* the man of 2Kin 7:2
he *a*, Because I know the 2Kin 8:12
And Jehu *a*, What hast 2Kin 9:19
And they *a*, We are the........2Kin 10:13
and *a* him not a word.........2Kin 18:36
Hezekiah *a*, It is a light.......2Kin 20:10
David went out..and *a* 1Chr 12:17
And Joab *a*, The Lord........1Chr 21:3
the king of Tyre *a* in 2Chr 2:11
And it shall be *a*, Because 2Chr 7:22
And the king *a* them 2Chr 10:13
And he *a* him, I am as thou...2Chr 18:3
the man of God *a*, The 2Chr 25:9
Then Hezekiah *a* and said......2Chr 29:31
of the house of Zadok *a* 2Chr 31:10
Hilkiah *a* and said to 2Chr 34:15
sons of Elam, *a* and said ......Ezra 10:2
Then *a* I them, and said ......Neh 2:20
a them after the same ....Neh 6:4
all the people *a*, Amen ....Neh 8:6
And Memucan *a* before........Esth 1:16
Esther *a*, If it seem good .....Esth 5:4
And Haman *a* the king ....Esth 6:7
Esther the queen *a* and ....Esth 7:3
Satan *a* the Lord and ....Job 1:7, 9
Satan *a* the Lord, and ....Job 2:2, 4
Eliphaz the Temanite *a* ....Job 4:1
But Job *a* and said ....Job 6:1
Then *a* Bildad the Shuhite ....Job 8:1
Then Job *a* and said ....Job 9:1
cannot *a* him one of a ....Job 9:3
a Zophar the Naamathite .....Job 11:1
And Job *a* and said...........Job 12:1
upon God, and he *a* him ......Job 12:4
Then call thou..I will *a* ....Job 13:22
Thou shalt call and I will *a*....Job 14:15
Then *a* Eliphaz the ....Job 15:1
Then Job *a* and said ....Job 16:1
emboldeneth thee that..*a?* .....Job 16:3
Then *a* Bildad the Shuhite ....Job 18:1
Then Job *a* and said ....Job 19:1
servant, and he gave me no *a* .Job 19:16
Then *a* Zophar the ....Job 20:1
But Job *a* and said ....Job 21:1
a..remaineth falsehood? ....Job 21:34
Then Eliphaz the..*a* ....Job 22:1
Then Job *a* and said ....Job 23:1
Then *a* Bildad the Shuhite ....Job 25:1
But Job *a* and said ....Job 26:1
that the Almighty would *a* ....Job 31:35
they had found no *a*, and .....Job 32:3
the son of Barachel the..*a*.....Job 32:6
Furthermore Elihu *a* and.......Job 34:1
of his *a* for wicked men ......Job 34:36
there they cry, but none.. *a* ...Job 35:12
Lord *a* Job out of the.........Job 38:1
demand of thee, and *a* thou ..Job 38:3

Moreover the Lord *a* Job ... Job 40:1
vile; what shall I *a* thee ... Job 40:4
I spoken; but I will not *a* ... Job 40:5
Then Job *a* the Lord ... Job 42:1
the Lord, but he *a* them ... Ps 18:41
also upon me, and *a* me ... Ps 27:7
wilt thou *a* us, O God ... Ps 65:5
I *a* thee in the secret place ... Ps 81:7
thee; for thou wilt *a* me ... Ps 86:7
call upon me, and I will *a* ... Ps 91:15
upon the Lord, and he *a* ... Ps 99:6
Thou *a* them, O Lord our ... Ps 99:8
the day when I call *a* me ... Ps 102:2
Lord *a* me, and set me ... Ps 118:5
day when I cried thou *a* me ... Ps 138:3
in thy faithfulness *a* me ... Ps 143:1
upon me, but I will not *a* ... Prov 1:28
a of the tongue, is from ... Prov 16:1
He that *a* a matter before ... Prov 18:13
entreaties; but the rich *a* ... Prov 18:23
A not a fool according to ... Prov 26:4
A a fool according to his ... Prov 26:5
understand he will not *a* ... Prov 29:19
God *a* him in the joy of his ... Eccl 5:20
him, but he gave me no *a* ... Song 5:6
And he *a,* Until the cities ... Is 6:11
shall one then *a* the ... Is 14:32
he *a* and said, Babylon is ... Is 21:9
peace, and *a* him not a ... Is 36:21
Hezekiah *a,* All that is in ... Is 39:4
call, and the Lord shall *a* ... Is 58:9
when I called, ye did not *a* ... Is 65:12
before they call, I will *a* ... Is 65:24
when I called, none did *a* ... Is 66:4
I called you, but ye *a* not ... Jer 7:13
Then *a* I, and said, So be it ... Jer 11:5
What hath the Lord *a?* ... Jer 23:35
Call unto me, and I will *a* ... Jer 33:3
them, but they have not *a* ... Jer 35:17
Then Baruch *a* them ... Jer 36:18
all the men..*a* Jeremiah ... Jer 44:15
I the Lord will *a* him that ... Ezek 14:4
the Lord will *a* him by ... Ezek 14:7
I *a* them, The word of the ... Ezek 24:20
I *a,* O Lord God, thou ... Ezek 37:3
king *a* and said to the ... Dan 2:5
a and said to the king ... Dan 3:16
Belteshazzar *a* and said ... Dan 4:19
Daniel *a* and said before ... Dan 5:17
king *a* and said, The thing ... Dan 6:12
a Amos, and said to ... Amos 7:14
for there is no *a* of God ... Mic 3:7
Balaam the son of Beor *a* ... Mic 6:5
And the Lord *a* me, and ... Hab 2:2
And the priests *a* and said ... Hag 2:12
the man that stood..*a* ... Zech 1:10
And he *a* and spake ... Zech 3:4
So I *a* and spake to the ... Zech 4:4
And I *a,* I see a flying roll ... Zech 5:2
Then I *a* and said unto the ... Zech 6:4
Jesus *a* said unto him ... Matt 3:15
he *a* and said, It is written ... Matt 4:4
Jesus *a* and said unto ... Matt 11:4
and of the Pharisees *a* ... Matt 12:38
He *a* and said unto ... Matt 13:11
Peter *a* him and said, Lord ... Matt 14:28
he *a* and said unto them ... Matt 15:3
he *a* and said, Every plant ... Matt 15:13
He *a* and said unto them ... Matt 16:2
Simon Peter *a* and said ... Matt 16:16
Jesus *a* and said unto ... Matt 16:17
Then *a* Peter, and said ... Matt 17:4
he *a* and said, unto them ... Matt 19:4
he *a* one of them, and said ... Matt 20:13
Jesus *a* and said unto ... Matt 21:21
Jesus *a* and spake unto ... Matt 22:1
no man was able to *a* him ... Matt 22:46
Jesus *a* and said unto them ... Matt 24:4
the wise *a,* saying, Not so ... Matt 25:9
Then shall the righteous *a* ... Matt 25:37
he *a* and said, He that ... Matt 26:23
unto him, *A* thou nothing? ... Matt 26:62
priests and elders, he *a* ... Matt 27:12
the angel *a* and said unto ... Matt 28:5
he *a* them, saying, Who is ... Mark 3:33
he *a* saying, My name is ... Mark 5:9
He *a* and said unto them ... Mark 6:37
He *a* and said unto them ... Mark 7:6
his disciples *a* him ... Mark 8:4
And Peter *a* and saith ... Mark 8:29
Peter *a* and said to Jesus ... Mark 9:5
he *a* and said unto them ... Mark 10:3
Jesus *a* and said unto it ... Mark 11:14
Jesus *a* and saith unto ... Mark 11:22
Jesus *a* said unto them ... Mark 12:17
perceiving that he had *a* ... Mark 12:28
Jesus *a* said unto them ... Mark 13:2
he *a* and said unto them ... Mark 14:20
saying, *A* thou nothing ... Mark 14:60
he *a* said unto him, Thou ... Mark 15:2
many things: but he *a* ... Mark 15:3
Jesus yet *a* nothing; so ... Mark 15:5
Pilate *a* them, saying ... Mark 15:9
Pilate *a* and said again ... Mark 15:12
the angel *a* said unto him ... Luke 1:19
the angel *a* and said unto ... Luke 1:35
He *a* and saith unto them ... Luke 3:11
John *a,* saying unto them ... Luke 3:16
Jesus *a* him, saying ... Luke 4:4
Jesus *a* said unto him ... Luke 4:12
Simon *a* said unto him ... Luke 5:5
Jesus *a* them said, Have ... Luke 6:3
Then Jesus *a* said unto ... Luke 7:22
Simon *a* and said, I ... Luke 7:43
he *a* and said unto them ... Luke 8:21
They *a* said, John the ... Luke 9:19
John *a* and said, Master ... Luke 9:49
he *a* said, Thou shalt love ... Luke 10:27
unto him, Thou has *a* ... Luke 10:28
Then *a* one of the lawyers ... Luke 11:45
Jesus *a* said unto them ... Luke 13:2
ruler of the synagogue *a* ... Luke 13:14
he shall *a* and say unto ... Luke 13:25
Jesus *a* spake unto the ... Luke 14:3
a them, saying, Which of ... Luke 14:5
he *a* said to his father ... Luke 15:29
Jesus *a* said, Were there ... Luke 17:17
he *a* them, and said ... Luke 17:20
he *a* and said unto them ... Luke 19:40
Jesus *a* said unto them ... Luke 20:34
Jesus *a* and said, Suffer ye ... Luke 22:51
he *a* him and said, Thou ... Luke 23:3
the other *a* rebuked him ... Luke 23:40
Cleopas, *a* said unto him ... Luke 24:18
prophet? And he *a,* No ... John 1:21
give an *a* to them that sent ... John 1:22
John *a* them, saying, I ... John 1:26
Then *a* the Jews and said ... John 2:18
Jesus *a* and said unto him ... John 3:3
Jesus *a,* Verily, verily, ... John 3:5
Nicodemus *a* and said ... John 3:9
Jesus *a* and said unto ... John 4:10
The impotent man *a* ... John 5:7
Philip *a* him, Two hundred ... John 6:7
Jesus *a* them, and said ... John 7:16
Jesus *a* and said unto ... John 8:14
Jesus *a,* Neither hath this ... John 9:3
Jesus *a* them, I told you ... John 10:25
Jesus *a,* Are there not ... John 11:9
Jesus *a* them saying ... John 12:23
Jesus *a* and said unto him ... John 13:7
Jesus *a* and said unto him ... John 14:23
Jesus *a* them, Do ye now ... John 16:31
They *a* him, Jesus of ... John 18:5
The Jews *a* him, We have ... John 19:7
Jesus gave him no *a* ... John 19:9
Thomas *a* and said unto ... John 20:28
They *a* him, No ... John 21:5
he *a* unto the people ... Acts 3:12
Peter and John *a* and said ... Acts 4:19
Peter *a* unto her, Tell me ... Acts 5:8
Then *a* Simon, and said ... Acts 8:24
Ananias *a,* Lord, I have ... Acts 9:13
magnify God. Then *a* ... Acts 10:46
the voice *a* me again from ... Acts 11:9
James *a,* saying, Men ... Acts 15:13
the evil spirit *a* and said ... Acts 19:15
Then Paul *a,* What mean ... Acts 21:13
I *a,* Who art thou, Lord? ... Acts 22:8
answered, Forasmuch as I ... Acts 24:10
Festus *a,* that Paul should ... Acts 25:4
hand, and *a* for himself ... Acts 26:1
what saith the *a* of God ... Rom 11:4
a to them that do ... 1Cor 9:3
somewhat to *a* them ... 2Cor 5:12
and *a* to Jerusalem which ... Gal 4:25
how ye ought to *a* every ... Col 4:6
first *a* no man stood with ... 2Tim 4:16
well in *a* things; not *a* ... Titus 2:9
a of a good conscience ... 1Pet 3:21
one of the elders *a,* saying ... Rev 7:13

ANT—*a small insect*
An example industry ... Prov 6:6-8; Prov 30:24

ANTAGONISM—*actively expressed opposition*

Of men, against:
God's people ... Ex 5:1-19; Deut 2:26-33
The prophets ... Amos 7:10-17; Zech 1:2-6
The light ... John 3:19, 20
The truth ... John 8:12-47; Acts 7:54-60
Christians ... Acts 16:16-24

Of Satan, against:
Job ... Job 2:9-12
Christ ... Luke 4:1-13
Peter ... Luke 22:31-34
Paul ... 1Thess 2:18
Christians ... Eph 6:11-18

ANTEDILUVIANS—*those who lived before the flood*

Described as:
Long-lived ... Gen 5:3-32
Very wicked ... Gen 6:5
A mixed race ... Gen 6:1-4; Jude 6, 7
Of great size ... Gen 6:4

Warnings against, made by:
Enoch ... Jude 14, 15
Noah ... 2Pet 2:5
Christ ... 1Pet 3:19, 20

Destruction of:
Only Noah's family escaped ... Gen 7:21-23
Predicted ... Gen 6:5-7
Comparable to Christ's return ... Matt 24:37-39; Luke 17:26, 27
Comparable to the world's end ... 2Pet 3:3-7

ANTHROPOMORPHISMS—*human attributes ascribed to God*

Physical likenesses, such as:
Feet ... Ex 24:10
Hands ... Ex 24:11
Mouth ... Num 12:8
Eyes ... Hab 1:13
Arms ... Ex 6:6

Non-physical characteristics, such as:
Memory ... Gen 9:16
Anger ... Ex 22:24
Jealousy ... Ps 78:58
Repentance ... Jon 3:10

ANTICHRIST—*one who is against or is a substitute for Christ; Satan's final opponent of Christ and Christians.*

Called:
Man of sin ... 2Thess 2:3
Son of perdition ... 2Thess 2:3
Wicked one ... 2Thess 2:8
Antichrist ... 1John 2:18, 22
Beast ... Rev 11:7

Described as:
Lawless ... 2Thess 2:3-12
Opposing Christ ... 2Thess 2:4
Working wonders ... 2Thess 2:9
Deceiving the world ... 2John 7; Rev 19:20

Persecuting Christians ....Rev 13:7
Satan-inspired 2Thess 2:9
Denying Christ's incarnation 1John 4:3; 2John 7
One and many 1John 2:18-22
A person and a system ...2Thess 2:3, 7
Seeking man's worship ...2Thess 2:4

Coming of:
Foretold 2Thess 2:5
In the last time 1John 2:18
Now restrained 2Thess 2:6
Follows removal of hindrance 2Thess 2:7, 8
Before Christ's return 2Thess 2:8
By Satan's deception 2Thess 2:9, 10

Destruction of:
At Christ's return ....2Thess 2:8; Rev 19:20
Eternal in lake of fire ....Rev 20:10

[*also* ANTICHRISTS]
heard that *a* shall come 1John 2:18
even now are there many *a* 1John 2:18
He is *a*, that denieth 1John 2:22
this is that spirit of *a* 1John 4:3
deceiver and an *a* 2John 7

ANTIDOTE—*a remedy given to counteract poison*

Literal:
A tree ....Ex 15:23-25
Meal 2Kin 4:38-41

Figurative and spiritual, for:
Sin, Christ ....Num 21:8, 9; John 3:14, 15
Christ's absence, the Holy Spirit ....John 14:16-18
Sorrow, joy ....John 16:20-22
Satan's lies, God's truth ..1John 4:1-6
Earth's trials, faith 1Pet 1:6-8
Testings, God's grace 1Cor 10:13; 2Cor 12:7-9
Suffering, heaven's glory ..Rom 8:18; 2Cor 5:1-10

ANTINOMINISM—*the idea that grace, or Christian liberty, exempts one from the moral law*

Prevalence of, among:
Christians ....Rom 6:1-23
False teachers ....2Pet 2:19; Jude 4

Based on error, that:
Grace allows sin ....Rom 6:1, 2
Moral law is abolished ...Rom 7:1-14
Liberty has no bounds ...1Cor 10:23-33

Corrected by remembering, that liberty is:
Not a license to sin ......Rom 6:1-23
Limited by moral law ....Rom 8:1-4
Controlled by Holy Spirit .Rom 8:5-14
Not to be a stumbling block .... Rom 14:1-23; 1Cor 8:1-13
Motivated by love ....Gal 5:13-15

ANTIOCH OF PISIDIA (ăn'tĭ-ŏk) (pĭ-sĭd'ĭ-ä)—*"speedy as a chariot"—a city in Pisidia*
Jewish synagogue ....Acts 13:14
Paul visits...............Acts 13:14, 42
Jews of, reject the Gospel ....Acts 13:45-51
Paul revisits.............Acts 14:21
Paul recalls persecution at 2Tim 3:11

certain Jews from *A* ....Acts 14:19

ANTIOCH OF SYRIA (ăn'tĭ-ŏk; sĭr'ĭ-ä)—*"speedy as a chariot"—a city in Syria*
Home of Nicolas ....Acts 6:5
Haven of persecuted Christians............Acts 11:19
Home of first Gentile church................Acts 11:20, 21
Name "Christian" originated in ....Acts 11:26
Barnabas ministered here .Acts 11:22-24
Barnabas and Paul minister in church of...Acts 11:25-30
Paul commissioned by church of .... Acts 13:1-4; Acts 15:35-41
Paul reports to ....Acts 14:26-28
Church of, troubled by Judaizers .... Acts 15:1-4; Gal 2:11-21

their own company to *A* ......Acts 15:22
Gentiles in *A* and Syria ....Acts 15:23
dismissed, they came to *A* .....Acts 15:30
the church, down to *A* ....Acts 18:22

ANTIPAS (ăn'tĭ păs)
A Christian martyr of Pergamum ....Rev 2:13

ANTIPATRIS (ăn-tĭp'ä-trĭs)—*"for his father"*
A city between Jerusalem and Caesarea ....Acts 23:31

ANTIQUITY—*pertaining to ancient times*
whose *a* is of ancient days?....Is 23:7

ANTITYPE—*the fulfillment of a type*
The Greek word translated "figure" in Heb 9:24; 1Pet 3:21
Generally, a fulfillment of an Old Testament type .... Matt 12:39, 40; John 1:29

ANTONIA, TOWER OF (ăn-tō'nĭ-ä)—*fortress built by Herod the Great, not mentioned by name in Scripture*
Called "castle" ....Acts 21:30-40
Possible site of Jesus' trial, called "the Pavement" ....John 19:13

ANTOTHIJAH (ăn-thō-thī'jä)—*"answers"*
A Benjamite 1Chr 8:24

ANTOTHITE—*a native of Anathoth of Jehovah; belonging to Anathoth*
Home of famous soldiers. .1Chr 11:28; 1Chr 12:3

ANUB (a'nub)—*"strong; high"*
A man of Judah 1Chr 4:8

ANVIL—*an iron block used in forging hot metals*
Used figuratively in ......Is 41:7

ANXIETY—*an agitated state of mind produced by real or imaginary fears*

Caused by:
Brother's hatred ....Gen 32:6-12
Son's rebellion 2Sam 18:24-33
King's decree ....Esth 4:1-17
Child's absence ....Luke 2:48
Son's sickness ....John 4:46-49
Friend's delay 2Cor 2:12, 13

Overcome by:
Trust ....Ps 37:1-5
Reliance upon the Holy Spirit ....Mark 13:11
God's provision ....Luke 12:22-30
Upward look ....Luke 21:25-28
Assurance of God's sovereignty ....Rom 8:28
Angel's word ....Acts 27:21-25
Prayer ....Phil 4:6
God's care 1Pet 5:6, 7
See CARES, WORLDLY

ANY—*See* INTRODUCTION

APACE—*quickly*
And he came *a* and drew 2Sam 18:25
Kings of armies did flee *a* .....Ps 68:12
their mighty ones..*a* ....Jer 46:5

APART—*at some distance; away from others*
thou shalt set *a* unto the ......Ex 13:12
she shall be put *a* seven ....Lev 15:19
as long as she is put *a* ....Lev 18:19
the Lord hath set *a* him ....Ps 4:3
humbled her that was set *a* ....Ezek 22:10
mourn, every family *a* ....Zech 12:12
of the house of David *a* ....Zech 12:12
and their wives *a* ....Zech 12:12
of the house of Nathan *a* .....Zech 12:12
and their wives *a* ....Zech 12:12
The family of..Levi *a* ....Zech 12:13
and their wives *a* ....Zech 12:13
the family of Shimei *a* ....Zech 12:13
and their wives *a* ....Zech 12:13
every family *a* ....Zech 12:14
and their wives *a* ....Zech 12:14
into a desert place *a* ....Matt 14:13
into a mountain *a* to pray .....Matt 14:23
into a high mountain *a* ....Matt 17:1
the disciples to Jesus *a* ....Matt 17:19
took the twelve disciples *a* ....Matt 20:17
mountain *a* by themselves .....Mark 9:2
Wherefore lay *a* all ....James 1:21

APE—*a short-tailed primate; a monkey*
Article of trade 1Kin 10:22

[*also* APES]
ivory, and *a*, and peacocks 2Chr 9:21

APELLES (ä-pĕl'ēz)—*meaning uncertain*
A Christian in Rome ....Rom 16:10

APHARSACHITES (a-făr'sa-kīts)—"investigator"—*an unknown people, possibly part of an Assyrian tribe that settled in Samaria*
his companions the *A*, ...Ezra 5:6
your companions the *A* ....Ezra 5:6

APHARSITES (ă-făr-sīts)
Assyrian colonists in Samaria opposing Zerubbabel's work.....Ezra 4:9

APHEK (ā'fĕk)—*"strength"*
1. A town in Plain of Sharon ....Josh 12:18
Site of Philistine camp...1Sam 4:1; 1Sam 29:1
2. A city assigned to Asher .Josh 19:30
3. Border city ....Josh 13:4
4. A city in Jezreel 1Kin 20:26-30
Syria's defeat prophesied here 2Kin 13:14-19

APHEKAH (ä-fē'kä)—*"fortress"*
A city of Judah ....Josh 15:53

APHIAH (ä-fī'ä)—*"striving"*
An ancestor of King Saul..1Sam 9:1

APHIK (ā'fĭk)—*"strength"*
Spared by Asher ....Judg 1:31
See APHEK 2

APHRAH (ăf'ră)—*"house of dust"*
A Philistine city; symbolic of doom ....Mic 1:10

APHSES (ăf'sēz)—*"the dispersed"*
Chief of a priestly course .1Chr 24:15

APIECE—*for each one; individually*
take five shekels *a* by ....Num 3:47
ten shekels *a*, after the........Num 7:86
princes gave him a rod *a* ......Num 17:6
eighteen cubits high *a* 1Kin 7:15
Every one had four faces *a* ....Ezek 10:21
doors had two leaves *a*........Ezek 41:24
neither have two coats *a* ......Luke 9:3
two or three firkins *a* ....John 2:6

APOCALYPSE (ă-pŏk'ă-lĭps)—*an unveiling of the truth or of something unknown*
The Greek word usually translated "revelation" Rom 16:25; Gal 1:12

APOCRYPHA (ă-pŏk'rĭ-fă)—*"hidden; secret things"*
Writings in Greek written during the period between the testaments

APOLLONIA (ăp-ŏ-lō'nĭ-ä)—*"city of Apollo"*
A town between Amphipolis and Thessalonica ....Acts 17:1

APOLLOS (ă-pŏl'ŏs)—*"a destroyer"*
An Alexandrian Jew
mighty in the Scriptures ... Acts 18:24, 25
Receives further instruction ... Acts 18:26
Sent to preach in Achaia ... Acts 18:27, 28
A minister in Corinth ... 1Cor 1:12
1Cor 3:4, 22
Cited by Paul ... 1Cor 4:6
Urged to revisit Corinth ... 1Cor 16:12
Journey of, noted by Paul ... Titus 3:13

while *A* was at Corinth ... Acts 19:1
I of *A*; and I of Cephas ... 1Cor 1:12
another, I am of *A*; are ye ... 1Cor 3:4
Who then is Paul..who is *A* ... 1Cor 3:5
A watered; but God gave ... 1Cor 3:6
Whether Paul, or *A*, or ... 1Cor 3:22
and to *A* for your sakes ... 1Cor 4:6
touching our brother *A* ... 1Cor 16:12
Bring Zenas the lawyer..*A* ... Titus 3:13

APOLLYON (ă-pŏl'yŭn)—*"the destroyer"*
Angel of the bottomless pit ... Rev 9:11

APOSTASY—*renunciation or falling away from the truth*

Kinds of:
National ... 1Kin 12:26-33
Individual ... 2Kin 21:1-9
Heb 3:12
Satanic ... Rev 12:7-9
Angelic ... 2Pet 2:4
General ... 2Tim 3:1-5
Imputed ... Acts 21:21
Final ... 2Thess 2:3
Irremedial ... Heb 6:1-8

Caused by:
Satan ... Luke 22:31
False teachers ... Acts 20:29, 30
Perversion of Scripture ... 2Tim 4:3, 4
Persecution ... Matt 13:21
Unbelief ... Heb 4:9-11
Love of world ... 2Tim 4:10
Hardened heart ... Acts 7:54, 57
Spiritual blindness ... Acts 28:25-27

Manifested in:
Resisting truth ... 2Tim 3:7, 8
Resorting to deception ... 2Cor 11:13-15
Reverting to immorality ... 2Pet 2:14, 19-22

Safeguards against, found in:
God's Word ... 2Tim 3:13-17
Spiritual growth ... 2Pet 1:5-11
Indoctrination ... Acts 20:29-31
Faithfulness ... Matt 24:42-51
Spiritual perception ... 1John 4:1-6
Being grounded in the truth ... Eph 4:13-16
Using God's armor ... Eph 6:10-20
Preaching the Word ... 2Tim 4:2, 5

Examples of, seen in:
Israelites ... Ex 32:1-35
Saul ... 1Sam 15:11
Solomon ... 1Kin 11:1-10
Amaziah ... 2Chr 25:14-16
Judas ... Matt 26:14-16
Hymenaeus and Philetus ... 2Tim 2:17, 18
Demas ... 2Tim 4:10
Certain men ... Jude 4

APOSTLE—*"send forth"—men personally commissioned by Christ to represent Him.*

Descriptive of:
Christ ... Heb 3:1
The twelve ... Matt 10:2
Others (Barnabas, James, etc.) ... Acts 14:4; Gal 1:19
Messengers ... 2Cor 8:23
False teachers ... 2Cor 11:13
Simon Peter ... Matt 10:2
Andrew ... Matt 10:2
James, son of Zebedee ... Matt 10:2
John ... Matt 10:2
Philip ... Matt 10:3
Bartholomew (Nathanael) ... Matt 10:3
John 1:45
Thomas ... Matt 10:3
Matthew (Levi) ... Matt 10:3
Luke 5:27
James, son of Alphaeus ... Matt 10:3
Thaddaeus (Judas) ... Matt 10:3
John 14:22
Simon the Zealot ... Luke 6:15
Judas Iscariot ... Matt 10:4
Matthias ... Acts 1:26
Paul ... 2Cor 1:1
Barnabas ... Acts 14:14
James, the Lord's brother ... Gal 1:19
Silvanus and Timothy ... 1Thess 1:1
1Thess 2:9
Andronicus and Junias ... Rom 16:7

Mission of, to:
Perform miracles ... Matt 10:1, 8
Preach Gospel ... Matt 28:19, 20
Witness Christ's resurrection ... Acts 1:22; Acts 10:40-42
Write Scripture ... Eph 3:5
Establish the Church ... Eph 2:20

Limitations of, before Pentecost:
Lowly in position ... Matt 4:18
Unlearned ... Acts 4:13
Subject to disputes ... Matt 20:20-28
Faith often obscure ... Matt 16:21-23
Need of instruction ... Matt 17:4, 9-13

Position of, after Pentecost:
Interpreted prophecy ... Acts 2:14-36
Defended truth ... Phil 1:7, 17
Exposed heretics ... Gal 1:6-9
Upheld discipline ... 2Cor 13:1-6
Established churches ... Rom 15:17-20

[*also* APOSTLE'S, APOSTLES, APOSTLESHIP]
the *a* gathered themselves ... Mark 6:30
whom also he named *a* ... Luke 6:13
the *a*, when they were ... Luke 9:10
send them prophets and *a* ... Luke 11:49
the *a* said unto the Lord ... Luke 17:5
the twelve *a* with him ... Luke 22:14
these things unto the *a* ... Luke 24:10
commandments unto the *a* ... Acts 1:2
take part of this ministry..*a* ... Acts 1:25
Peter, and to the rest..*a* ... Acts 2:37
in the *a* doctrine and ... Acts 2:42
and signs were done..*a* ... Acts 2:43
the *a* witness of the ... Acts 4:33
laid them down at the *a* ... Acts 4:35
by the *a* was surnamed ... Acts 4:36
the money, and laid it..*a* ... Acts 4:37
part, and laid it at the *a* ... Acts 5:2
hands of the *a* were many ... Acts 5:12
laid their hands on the *a* ... Acts 5:18
Peter and the other *a* ... Acts 5:29
to put the *a* forth a little ... Acts 5:34
called the *a*, and beaten ... Acts 5:40
Whom they set before..*a* ... Acts 6:6
Judea and Samaria..*a* ... Acts 8:1
the *a* which were at ... Acts 8:14
through laying on of the *a* ... Acts 8:18
him and brought him to the *a* ... Acts 9:27
a and brethren that were ... Acts 11:1
unto the *a* and elders ... Acts 15:2
of the *a* and elders, and ... Acts 15:4
the *a* and elders came ... Acts 15:6
Then pleased it the *a* and ... Acts 15:22
The *a* and elders and ... Acts 15:23
the brethren unto the *a* ... Acts 15:33
were ordained of the *a* and ... Acts 16:4
called to be an *a* separated ... Rom 1:1
received grace and *a*, for ... Rom 1:5
am the *a* of the Gentiles ... Rom 11:13
called to be an *a* of Jesus ... 1Cor 1:1
Am I not an *a*? am I not ... 1Cor 9:1
If I be not an *a* unto others ... 1Cor 9:2
seal of mine *a* are ye in ... 1Cor 9:2
as well as other *a*, and as ... 1Cor 9:5
first *a*, secondarily ... 1Cor 12:28
Are all *a*?..all prophets? ... 1Cor 12:29
of James; then of all the *a* ... 1Cor 15:7
I am the least of the *a* ... 1Cor 15:9
not meet to be called an *a* ... 1Cor 15:9
a whit behind the very..*a* ... 2Cor 11:5
the very chiefest *a*, though ... 2Cor 12:11
the signs of an *a* were ... 2Cor 12:12
Paul, an *a*, (not of men ... Gal 1:1
a of the circumcision ... Gal 2:8
Paul, an *a* of Jesus Christ ... Eph 1:1
gave some, *a*, and some ... Eph 4:11
Paul, an *a* of Jesus Christ ... Col 1:1
burdensome, as the *a* of ... 1Thess 2:6
Paul, an *a* of Jesus Christ ... 1Tim 1:1
am ordained a preacher..*a* ... 1Tim 2:7
Paul, an *a* of Jesus Christ ... 2Tim 1:1
appointed a preacher..*a* ... 2Tim 1:11
an *a* of Jesus Christ ... Titus 1:1
Peter, an *a* of Jesus Christ ... 1Pet 1:1
a servant and an *a* of Jesus ... 2Pet 1:1
ye holy *a* and prophets ... Rev 18:20
names of the twelve *a* of ... Rev 21:14

APOTHECARY—*"pharmacist," "perfumer"*
Used in tabernacle ... Ex 30:25, 35
Used in embalming ... 2Chr 16:14
A maker of ointment ... Eccl 10:1
Among returnees ... Neh 3:8

according to the work..*a* ... Ex 37:29

APPAIM (ăp'ā-ĭm)—*"face; presence; nostrils"*
A man of Judah ... 1Chr 2:30, 31

APPAREL—*that which clothes or adorns*

Kinds of:
Harlot's ... Gen 38:14
Virgin's ... 2Sam 13:18
Mourner's ... 2Sam 12:20
Splendid ... Luke 7:25
Rich ... Ezek 27:24
Worldly ... 1Pet 3:3
Showy ... Luke 16:19
Official ... 1Kin 10:5
Royal ... Esth 6:8
Priestly ... Ezra 3:10
Angelic ... Acts 1:10
Heavenly ... Rev 19:8

Attitude toward:
Not to covet ... Acts 20:33
Without show ... 1Pet 3:3
Be modest in ... 1Tim 2:9

Figurative of:
Christ's blood ... Is 63:1-3
Christ's righteousness ... Zech 3:1-5
The Church's purity ... Ps 45:13, 14

and a suit of *a*, and thy ... Judg 17:10
the camels, and the *a* ... 1Sam 27:9
ornaments of gold..your *a* ... 2Sam 1:24
put on now mourning *a* ... 2Sam 14:2
his ministers, and their *a* ... 2Chr 9:4
cupbearers..and their *a* ... 2Chr 9:4
Esther put on her royal *a* ... Esth 5:1
let this *a* and horse be ... Esth 6:9
take the *a* and the horse ... Esth 6:10
Then took Haman the *a* ... Esth 6:11
in royal *a* of blue and ... Esth 8:15
The changeable suits of *a* ... Is 3:22
own bread, and wear..*a* ... Is 4:1
clothed with strange *a* ... Zeph 1:8
gold, and silver, and *a* ... Zech 14:14
Herod, arrayed in royal *a* ... Acts 12:21
themselves in modest *a* ... 1Tim 2:9
gold ring, in goodly *a* ... James 2:2

APPARENTLY—*clearly; plainly*
mouth to mouth, even *a* ... Num 12:8

APPARITION—*appearance of ghost or disembodied spirit*
Samuel ... 1Sam 28:12-14
Christ mistaken for ... Matt 14:26
Luke 24:37, 39

APPEAL—*petition for higher judgment*
To Christ ....Luke 12:13, 14
Of Paul, to Caesar ......Acts 25:11, 25-28

[*also* APPEALED]
Hast thou *a* unto Caesar ......Acts 25:12
when Paul had *a* to be ....Acts 25:21
constrained to *a* unto ....Acts 28:19

APPEARANCE—*that which is seen; image; arriving*
Can conceal:
Deception ....Josh 9:3-16
Hypocrisy...............Matt 23:25-28
Rottenness..............Acts 12:21-23
Rebellion 2Sam 15:7-13
False apostles 2Cor 11:13-15
Inner glory.............Is 53:1-3
Matt 17:1, 2
Can be:
Misunderstood ....Josh 22:10-31
Mistaken 1Sam 1:12-18
Misleading 2Cor 10:7-11
Misjudged ....John 7:24
Misinterpreted ....Matt 11:16-19
Of the Lord in the Old Testament:
To Abraham ....Gen 12:7
To Isaac ....Gen 26:2, 24
To Jacob ....Gen 35:1, 9
To Moses ....Ex 3:2, 16
To Israel ....Ex 16:10
In mercy seat ....Lev 16:2
In tabernacle............Num 14:10
To Gideon ....Judg 6:11, 12
To Manoah ....Judg 13:3, 10, 21
To Samuel 1Sam 3:21
To David 2Chr 3:1
To Solomon 1Kin 3:5
Of Christ's first advent, in:
Nativity.................2Tim 1:10
Transfiguration ....Luke 9:30, 31
Resurrected form ....Luke 24:34
Priestly intercession ......Heb 9:24
Return ....Col 3:4
Of Christ resurrected, to, at:
Mary Magdalene ....John 20:11-18
Other women ....Matt 28:9-10
Disciples on road to Emmaus ....Luke 24:13-35
Ten disciples ....John 20:19-25
Thomas.................John 20:26-31
Sea of Galilee...........John 21:1-25
Give great commission ...Matt 28:16-20
Five hundred brethren ...1Cor 15:6
His ascension ....Acts 1:4-11
Paul....................Acts 9:3-6
John ....Rev 1:10-18
Of Christ's second advent, a time of:
Salvation ....Heb 9:28
Confidence..............1John 2:28
Judgment 2Tim 4:1
Reward.................2Tim 4:8
Blessedness ....Titus 2:13
Joy.....................1Pet 1:7, 8
Rulership 1Tim 6:14, 15
See THEOPHANY

[*also* APPEAR, APPEARANCE, APPEARANCES APPEARED, APPEARETH, APPEARING]
let the dry land *a*; and it ......Gen 1:9
And when..the Lord *a* to .....Gen 17:1
And the Lord *a* unto him .....Gen 18:1
made the white *a* which ....Gen 30:37
God Almighty *a* unto me .....Gen 48:3
The Lord hath not *a* unto .....Ex 4:1
And I *a* unto Abraham ....Ex 6:3
strength when the morning *a* ..Ex 14:27
all thy males shall *a* before ....Ex 23:17
none shall *a* before me........Ex 34:20
men children *a* before the .....Ex 34:23
to *a* before the Lord thy ......Ex 34:24
today the Lord will *a* unto ....Lev 9:4
glory of the Lord shall *a* ......Lev 9:6
and the glory of the Lord *a* ...Lev 9:23
when raw flesh *a* in him ......Lev 13:14
if it *a* still in the garment .....Lev 13:57
as it were the *a* of fire ....Num 9:15
and the *a* of fire by night .....Num 9:16
Lord *a* unto all the ....Num 16:19
the glory of the Lord *a* ....Num 20:6
into thy hand, as *a* this ....Deut 2:30
males *a* before the Lord ......Deut 16:16
shall not *a* before the Lord....Deut 16:16
Israel is come to *a* before .....Deut 31:11
And the Lord *a* in the ....Deut 31:15
angel of the Lord did..*a* ......Judg 13:21
that he may *a* before the 1Sam 1:22
Did I plainly *a* unto the.......1Sam 2:27
looketh on the outward *a* 1Sam 16:7
channels of the sea *a* 2Sam 22:16
the Lord *a* to Solomon the 1Kin 9:2
Lord God of Israel..*a*.........1Kin 11:9
behold, there *a* a chariot 2Kin 2:11
night did God *a* unto 2Chr 1:7
the Lord *a* to Solomon.........2Chr 7:12
morning till the stars *a*........Neh 4:21
shall I come and *a* before .....Ps 42:2
every one of them in Zion *a* ..Ps 84:7
thy work *a* unto thy ....Ps 90:16
he shall *a* in his glory ....Ps 102:16
The hay *a*, and the tender ....Prov 27:25
the flowers *a* on the earth.....Song 2:12
goats, that *a* from mount.......Song 4:1
goats that *a* from Gilead ......Song 6:5
whether the tender grape *a*....Song 7:12
When ye come to *a* before ....Is 1:12
but he shall *a* to your joy .....Is 66:5
evil *a* out of the north ....Jer 6:1
that thy shame may *a*.........Jer 13:26
The Lord hath *a* of old ....Jer 31:3
this was their *a*; they had .....Ezek 1:5
their *a* was like burning ....Ezek 1:13
and like the *a* of lamps ....Ezek 1:13
as the *a* of a flash of ....Ezek 1:14
The *a* of the wheels ....Ezek 1:16
and their *a* and their work ....Ezek 1:16
as the *a* of a sapphire.........Ezek 1:26
as the *a* of a man above it ....Ezek 1:26
as the *a* of fire round about ...Ezek 1:27
the *a*..loins even upward ......Ezek 1:27
the *a*..loins even downward ...Ezek 1:27
as it were the *a* of fire ....Ezek 1:27
a of the bow that is in the ....Ezek 1:28
a of the brightness round .....Ezek 1:28
This was the *a* of the ....Ezek 1:28
a likeness as the *a* of fire .....Ezek 8:2
from the *a* of his loins ....Ezek 8:2
as the *a* of brightness ....Ezek 8:2
there *a* over them as it........Ezek 10:1
the *a* of the likeness of a......Ezek 10:1
and there *a* in the ....Ezek 10:8
and the *a* of the wheels ....Ezek 10:9
as for the..*a*, they four........Ezek 10:10
Chebar, their *a* and...........Ezek 10:22
and she *a* in her height ....Ezek 19:11
so that..your sins do *a* ....Ezek 21:24
whose *a* was like the *a* of .....Ezek 40:3
a of the one as the *a* of.......Ezek 41:21
like the *a* of the chambers ....Ezek 42:11
according to the *a* of the .....Ezek 43:3
countenances *a* fairer and .....Dan 1:15
a unto me,..which *a* unto me ..Dan 8:1
as the *a* of a man ....Dan 8:15
his face as the *a* of ....Dan 10:6
like the *a* of a man, and he ...Dan 10:18
a of them is as the *a* of ....Joel 2:4
shall stand when he *a*.........Mal 3:2
the angel of the Lord *a* ....Matt 1:20
what time the star *a* ....Matt 2:7
angel of the Lord *a* to ....Matt 2:13
a in a dream to Joseph ....Matt 2:19
they may *a* unto men to ......Matt 6:16
thou *a* not unto men to ....Matt 6:18
then *a* the tares also ....Matt 13:26
a unto them Moses and ....Matt 17:3
shall *a* the sign of the Son ....Matt 24:30
into the holy city, and *a* ......Matt 27:53
a unto them Elijah with.......Mark 9:4
he *a* first to Mary ....Mark 16:9
there *a* unto him an angel.....Luke 1:11
of some, that Elijah had *a* ....Luke 9:8
are as graves which *a* not .....Luke 11:44
God should immediately *a* ....Luke 19:11
And there *a* an angel unto ....Luke 22:43
there *a* unto them cloven .....Acts 2:3
God of glory *a* unto our ......Acts 7:2
Jesus, that *a* unto thee in .....Acts 9:17
a vision *a* to Paul in the ......Acts 16:9
and all their council to *a* ......Acts 22:30
I have *a* unto thee for this ....Acts 26:16
in the which I will *a* unto ....Acts 26:16
nor stars in many days *a* ......Acts 27:20
all *a* before the judgment 2Cor 5:10
glory in *a*, and not in heart ...2Cor 5:12
sight of God might *a* unto.....2Cor 7:12
not that we should *a*..........2Cor 13:7
Abstain from all *a* of evil 1Thess 5:22
that thy profiting may *a*.......1Tim 4:15
the *a* of our Savior Jesus......2Tim 1:10
at his *a* and his kingdom 2Tim 4:1
salvation hath *a* to all men ....Titus 2:11
of God our Savior..man *a* .....Titus 3:4
hath he *a* to put away sin .....Heb 9:26
made of things which do *a* ....Heb 11:3
vapor, that *a* for a little ....James 4:14
ungodly and the sinner *a*......1Pet 4:18
chief Shepherd shall *a* 1Pet 5:4
doth not yet *a* what we 1John 3:2
when he shall *a* we shall 1John 3:2
of thy nakedness do not *a*.....Rev 3:18
a a great wonder..heaven .....Rev 12:1

APPEASEMENT—*pacification; reconciliation of opposing parties*
Kinds of, between:
Brothers ....Gen 32:20
Nations 1Kin 20:31-34
Tribes ....Josh 22:10-34
Jews and Gentiles ....Eph 2:11-17
Means of, by:
Gifts ....Gen 43:11-16
Special pleading 1Sam 25:17-35
Correcting an abuse .....Acts 6:1-6
Slowness to anger ....Prov 15:18
Wisdom ....Prov 16:14
None allowed between:
Righteousness, evil 2Cor 6:14-17
Truth, error.............Gal 1:7-9
Faith, works ....Gal 5:1-10
Flesh, Spirit.............Gal 5:16-26
Christ, Satan ....Matt 4:1-11
Heaven, Sheol ....Is 28:18
Of God's wrath, by:
Righteous action ....Num 16:44-50
Repentance 2Sam 12:10-14
Atoning for an evil 2Sam 21:1-14
Christ's death ....Is 63:1-7
Christ's righteousness ....Zech 3:1-5
2Cor 5:18-21

[*also* APPEASE, APPEASED, APPEASETH]
of king Ahasuerus was *a* ......Esth 2:1
the townclerk had *a* the ......Acts 19:35

APPERTAIN—*belonging to*

[*also* APPERTAINED, APPERTAINETH]
it unto him to whom it *a*......Lev 6:5
with all that *a* unto them......Num 16:30
all the men that *a* unto ....Num 16:32
It *a* not unto thee, Uzziah 2Chr 26:18
palace which *a* to the house ...Neh 2:8
for to thee doth it *a* ....Jer 10:7

APPETITE—*necessary desires which sustain life*
Kinds of:
Physical 1Sam 14:31-33
Sexual..................1Cor 7:1-9
Lustful ....Matt 5:28
Insatiable ....Prov 27:20
Spiritual ....Ps 119:20, 131
Perversion of, by:
Gluttony ....Prov 23:1, 2

Wine ... Prov 23:29-35
Adultery ... Prov 6:24-29
Ezek 23:1-49
Impurity ... Rom 1:24-31

Loss of, by:
Age ... 2Sam 19:35
Trouble ... 1Sam 28:22, 23
Visions ... Dan 10:3-16
Deep concern ... John 4:31-34

Spiritual, characteristics of:
Satisfying ... Is 55:1, 2
Sufficient ... Matt 5:6
Spontaneous ... John 7:38, 39
Sanctifying ... 1Pet 2:2
Sublime ... Col 3:1-3

See GLUTTONY; HUNGER; TEMPERANCE

or fill the *a* of the young ... Job 38:39
faint, and his soul hath *a* ... Is 29:8

APPHIA (ăf'ĭ-ä)
Christian lady of Colossae ... Philem 2

APPII FORUM (ăp'i-i fōr'rŭm)—*"market-place of Appius"—a town about 40 miles south of Rome*
Paul meets Christians here ... Acts 28:15

APPLAUSE—*a visible expression of public approval*
Men seek after ... Matt 6:1-5

APPLE—*red or yellow edible fruit*

[*also* APPLES]
as the *a* tree among the ... Song 2:3
flagons, comfort me..*a* ... Song 2:5
smell of thy nose like *a* ... Song 7:8
I raised thee up under the *a* ... Song 8:5
palm tree also, and the *a* ... Joel 1:12

"APPLE OF THE EYE"—*a figurative expression for something very valuable*

Translated as:
"The pupil of his eye" ... Deut 32:10
"The apple of his eye" ... Zech 2:8

Figurative of:
God's care ... Deut 32:10
God's Law ... Prov 7:2
The saint's security ... Ps 17:8
Abundance of sorrow ... Lam 2:18

APPLES OF GOLD—*something of great value*
A word fitly spoken ... Prov 25:11

APPLY—*to employ diligently or with close attention*

[*also* APPLIED]
may *a* our hearts unto ... Ps 90:12
a thine heart to ... Prov 2:2
a thine heart unto my ... Prov 22:17
A thine heart unto ... Prov 23:12
I *a* mine heart to know ... Eccl 7:25
and *a* my heart unto every ... Eccl 8:9

APPOINT—*to designate; set in an official position or relationship*

Descriptive of ordination, to:
Priesthood ... Num 3:10
Prophetic office ... Heb 3:2
Ruler ... 2Sam 6:21
Apostleship ... Luke 10:1
Deacon's office ... Acts 6:3

Descriptive of God's rule, over:
Earth ... Ps 104:20
World history ... Acts 17:26
Israel's history ... 2Chr 33:8
Nations ... Jer 47:7
Man's plans ... 2Sam 17:14
Man's life ... Job 14:5
Death ... Heb 9:27
Final judgment ... Acts 17:31
Man's destiny ... Matt 24:51

Descriptive of the believer's life:
Trials ... 1Thess 3:3
Service ... Acts 22:10
Salvation ... 1Thess 5:9

[*also* APPOINTED, APPOINTETH, APPOINTMENT]
she, hath *a* me another ... Gen 4:25
At the time *a* I will return ... Gen 18:14
hast *a* for thy servant ... Gen 24:14
A me thy wages, and I will ... Gen 30:28
him *a* officers over the ... Gen 41:34
And the Lord *a* a set time ... Ex 9:5
then I will *a* thee a place ... Ex 21:13
the time *a* of the month ... Ex 23:15
shalt *a* it for the service ... Ex 30:16
I will even *a* over you ... Lev 26:16
thou shalt *a* the Levites ... Num 1:50
and *a* them every one to ... Num 4:19
At the *a* of Aaron and his ... Num 4:27
keep the passover at his *a* ... Num 9:2
shall *a* for the manslayer ... Num 35:6
time *a* before the plain ... Josh 8:14
A out for you cities of ... Josh 20:2
and *a* them for himself, for ... 1Sam 8:11
And he will *a* him captains ... 1Sam 8:12
time that Samuel had *a* ... 1Sam 13:8
Samuel standing as *a* over ... 1Sam 19:20
field at the time *a* with ... 1Sam 20:35
I have *a* my servants to ... 1Sam 21:2
and shall have *a* thee ruler ... 1Sam 25:30
place which thou has *a* ... 1Sam 29:4
I will *a* a place for my ... 2Sam 7:10
by the *a* of Absalom this ... 2Sam 13:32
my lord the king shall *a* ... 2Sam 15:15
set time which he had *a* ... 2Sam 20:5
morning even to the time *a* ... 2Sam 24:15
I have *a* him to be ruler ... 1Kin 1:35
all that thou shalt *a* ... 1Kin 5:6
a him victuals and gave ... 1Kin 11:18
as the king had *a*, saying ... 1Kin 12:12
whom I *a* to utter ... 1Kin 20:42
king *a* the lord on whose ... 2Kin 7:17
king *a* unto her a certain ... 2Kin 8:6
Jehu *a* fourscore men ... 2Kin 10:24
And the priest *a* officers ... 2Kin 11:18
the king of Assyria *a* unto ... 2Kin 18:14
Levites were *a* unto all ... 1Chr 6:48
and were *a* for all the ... 1Chr 6:49
were *a* to oversee the ... 1Chr 9:29
the Levites to *a* their ... 1Chr 15:16
So the Levites *a* Heman ... 1Chr 15:17
And he *a* certain of the ... 1Chr 16:4
And he *a*, according to the ... 2Chr 8:14
he *a* singers unto the Lord ... 2Chr 20:21
Jehoiada *a* the officers of ... 2Chr 23:18
And Hezekiah *a* the ... 2Chr 31:2
king had *a* went to ... 2Chr 34:22
and *a* the Levites, from ... Ezra 3:8
according to the *a* of the ... Ezra 6:9
David and the princes had *a* ... Ezra 8:20
come at *a* time, and with ... Ezra 10:14
I was *a*..their governor ... Neh 5:14
thou has also *a* prophets ... Neh 6:7
singers and the Levites..*a* ... Neh 7:1
a watches of the ... Neh 7:3
in their rebellion *a* ... Neh 9:17
at time *a* year by year ... Neh 10:34
a two great companies ... Neh 12:31
and *a* the wards of the ... Neh 13:30
king had *a* to all..officers ... Esth 1:8
And let the king *a* officers ... Esth 2:3
keeper of the women *a* ... Esth 2:15
whom he had *a* to attend ... Esth 4:5
and according to their *a* ... Esth 9:27
for they had made an *a* ... Job 2:11
a time to man upon the ... Job 7:1
thou wouldst *a* me a set ... Job 14:13
the heritage *a* unto him by ... Job 20:29
the thing that is *a* for me ... Job 23:14
the house *a* for all living ... Job 30:23
given us like sheep *a* for ... Ps 44:11
preserve thou those..*a* ... Ps 79:11
new moon, in the time *a* ... Ps 81:3
loose those that are *a* to ... Ps 102:20
He *a*..moon for seasons ... Ps 104:19
come home at the day *a* ... Prov 7:20
when he *a* the foundations ... Prov 8:29
as are *a* to destruction ... Prov 31:8
new moons and your *a* ... Is 1:14
shall be alone in his *a* ... Is 14:31
salvation will God *a* for ... Is 26:1
wheat and the *a* barley ... Is 28:25
since I *a* the ancient ... Is 44:7
To *a* unto them that mourn ... Is 61:3
reserveth unto us the *a* ... Jer 5:24
the stork..knoweth her *a* ... Jer 8:7
I will *a* over them four ... Jer 15:3
he hath passed the time *a* ... Jer 46:17
that I may *a* over her? ... Jer 49:19
man, that I may *a* over her ... Jer 50:44
a a captain against her ... Jer 51:27
have *a* thee each day for a ... Ezek 4:6
son of man, *a* thee two ... Ezek 21:19
he shall burn it in the *a* ... Ezek 43:21
ye shall *a* the possession ... Ezek 45:6
the king *a* them a daily ... Dan 1:5
who hath *a* your meat ... Dan 1:10
he *a* over it whomsoever ... Dan 5:21
but the time *a* was long ... Dan 10:1
end shall be at the time *a* ... Dan 11:27
a themselves one head ... Hos 1:11
the rod, and who hath *a* it ... Mic 6:9
the vision is yet for an *a* ... Hab 2:3
and *a* him his portion with ... Matt 24:51
disciples did as Jesus had *a* ... Matt 26:19
as the Lord *a* me ... Matt 27:10
where Jesus had *a* them ... Matt 28:16
than that which is *a* you ... Luke 3:13
and will *a* him his portion ... Luke 12:46
I *a* unto you a kingdom ... Luke 22:29
as my Father hath *a* unto ... Luke 22:29
a two, Joseph called ... Acts 1:23
as he had *a*, speaking unto ... Acts 7:44
for so he had *a* minding ... Acts 20:13
And when they had *a* him ... Acts 28:23
as it were *a* to death ... 1Cor 4:9
until the time *a* of the ... Gal 4:2
Whereunto I am *a* a ... 2Tim 1:11
as I had *a* thee ... Titus 1:5
hath *a* heir of all things ... Heb 1:2

APPRECIATION—*favorable recognition of blessings*
Sought for among men ... Ps 107:8-21
Of favors, rebuffed ... 2Sam 10:1-5
Of blessings, unnoticed ... Acts 14:15-18

APPREHENSION—*the ability to understand*
God ... Job 11:7
God's Word ... Acts 17:11
Prophecy ... 1Pet 1:10-12
Parables ... Matt 13:10-17
Spiritual truths ... 1Cor 2:7-16
Christ ... Phil 3:12-14

[*also* APPREHEND, APPREHENDED]
desirous to *a* me ... 2Cor 11:32
if that I may *a* that for ... Phil 3:12

APPROACH—*come near to*

[*also* APPROACHED, APPROACHETH, APPROACHING]
None of you shall *a* to any ... Lev 18:6
thou shalt not *a* to his wife ... Lev 18:14
thou shalt not *a* unto a ... Lev 18:19
if a woman *a* unto ... Lev 20:16
let him not *a* to offer the ... Lev 21:17
a blemish, he shall not *a* ... Lev 21:18
they *a* unto the most holy ... Num 4:19
that the priest shall *a* and ... Deut 20:2
Israel, ye *a* this day unto ... Deut 20:3
thy days *a* that thou must ... Deut 31:14
that are with me will *a* ... Josh 8:5
Wherefore *a* ye so nigh ... 2Sam 11:20
and the king *a* to the altar ... 2Kin 16:12
make his sword to *a* unto ... Job 40:19
choosest and causest to *a* ... Ps 65:4
they take delight in *a* to ... Is 58:2
and he shall *a* unto me ... Jer 30:21
engaged his heart to *a* ... Jer 30:21
the priests that *a* unto the ... Ezek 42:13
shall *a* to those things ... Ezek 42:14
the Levites..which *a* ... Ezek 43:19
where no thief *a*, neither ... Luke 12:33
light which no man can *a* ... 1Tim 6:16
more, as ye see the day *a* ... Heb 10:25

APPROPRIATION—*possessing for one's use*
God's promises ....Heb 11:8-16
God's Word ....Ps 119:11
Salvation ....Acts 16:30-34

APPROVAL—*favorable opinion or acceptance of*

Means of, by:
God ....Acts 2:22
The Lord 2Cor 10:18
The Jews ....Rom 2:18
A church 1Cor 16:3
Man ....Rom 14:18

Obtained by:
Endurance 2Cor 6:4
Innocence 2Cor 7:11
Spiritual examination 2Cor 13:5-8
Spiritual judgment ....Phil 1:9, 10
Diligence 2Tim 2:15

[*also* APPROVE, APPROVED, APPROVEST, APPROVETH, APPROVING]
their posterity *a* their ....Ps 49:13
in his cause, the Lord *a* ....Lam 3:36
a the things that are more .....Hos 2:18
Salute Apelles *a* in Christ .....Rom 16:10
which..*a* may be made 1Cor 11:19
may *a* things that are ....Phil 1:10

APRONS—*articles of clothing*
Item of miraculous healing ....Acts 19:12

and made themselves *a* ....Gen 3:7

APT—*ready; qualified*
all that were strong and *a* 2Kin 24:16
that were *a* to the war and 1Chr 7:40
given to hospitality, *a* to 1Tim 3:2
unto all men, *a* to teach 2Tim 2:24

AQUILA (ăk'wy-lä)—*"eagle"—Jewish Christian; husband of Priscilla and friend of Paul*
Jewish tentmaker ....Acts 18:2, 3
Paul stays with ....Acts 18:3
Visits Syria ....Acts 18:18
Resides in Ephesus ......Acts 18:19
Instructs Apollos ....Acts 18:24-26
Esteemed by Paul ....Rom 16:3, 4

A and Priscilla salute you 1Cor 16:19
Salute Prisca and *A* 2Tim 4:19

AR—*"city"*
A chief Moabite city .....Num 21:15
On Israel's route ....Deut 2:18
Destroyed by Sihon ......Num 21:28
Destroyed by God ....Is 15:1

I have given *A* unto the ....Deut 2:9
Moabites which dwell in *A* ....Deut 2:29

ARA (ā'rä)—*"strong"*
A descendant of Asher ..1Chr 7:38

ARAB (âr'ăb)
A mountain city of Judah.Josh 15:52

ARABAH (ăr'ä-bä)—*"desert plain; steppe"*
A district east of Jordan. .2Sam 2:29
A major natural division of Palestine .... Josh 11:16; Josh 12:8
Opposite Gilgal ....Deut 11:30
Restoration of, predicted .Ezek 47:1-12
Referred by "desert" in ..Is 35:1

over against *A* northward .....Josh 18:18
and went down unto *A* ....Josh 18:18

ARABIA (ä-rā'bĭ-ä)—*"desert"—a large peninsula bounded on the east by the Persian Gulf and the Gulf of Oman, on the West by the Red Sea, and on the south by the Indian Ocean*

A Place of:
Mount Sinai ....Gal 4:25
Gold mines 2Chr 9:14
Paul visited ....Gal 1:17

People of:
Lustful ....Is 13:20
Paid tribute to Solomon . .1Kin 10:14, 15
Plundered Jerusalem 2Chr 21:16, 17
Defeated by Uzziah 2Chr 26:7
Sold sheep and goats to Tyre ....Ezek 27:21
Opposed Nehemiah ......Neh 2:19
Denounced by prophets . .Is 21:13-17
Visited Jerusalem at Pentecost ....Acts 2:11

[*also* ARABIAN, ARABIANS]
and the *A* brought him 2Chr 17:11
band of men that came *A* 2Chr 22:1
and the *A*..Ammonites ....Neh 4:7
Geshem the *A*, and the ....Neh 6:1
thou sat for them, as the *A* ....Jer 3:2
And all the kings of *A*, and ...Jer 25:24

ARAD (ā'răd)—*"fugitive; wild ass"*
1. A Benjamite 1Chr 8:15
2. A city south of Hebron . .Num 21:1-3
Defeated by Joshua .....Josh 12:14
Kenites settled near .....Judg 1:16

A the Canaanite, which ....Num 33:40

ARAH (ā'rä)—*"wayfarer"*
1. A descendant of Asher . .1Chr 7:39
2. A family of returnees ...Ezra 2:5

Shechaniah the son of *A* ......Neh 6:18
the children of *A*, six hundred. .Neh 7:10

ARAM (ā'răm)—*"high; exalted"*
1. A son of Shem ....Gen 10:22, 23
2. A grandson of Nahor ...Gen 22:21
3. A descendant of Asher . .1Chr 7:34
4. A district in Gilead 1Chr 2:23
5. An ancestor of Christ ...Matt 1:3, 4

[*also* ARAMITESS]
Moab hath brought me from *A*.Num 23:7
Arphaxad, and Lud, and *A* 1Chr 1:17
his concubine the *A* bare 1Chr 7:14
which was the son of *A* ....Luke 3:33

ARAMAIC (ăr'ä-mā'ĭk)—*Semitic language related to Hebrew*
Used by the Syrians 2Kin 18:26
The language of the postexilic period ..... Ezra 4:7; Dan 2:4
Portions of the Bible written in, include .... Dan 2:4—7:28; Ezra 4:8—6:18; Ezra 7:12-26
The same as "Hebrew" in ....John 19:20

Words and phrases of, found in .... Matt 27:46; Mark 5:41; Mark 7:34

ARAM-NAHARIM (ā'răm-nā-hä-rā'ĭm)—*an area in northern Mesopotamia*
when he strove with *A* ....Ps 60: title

ARAM-ZOBAH (ăr'ăm-zō'bä)
and with *A* ....Ps 60:*title*

ARAN (ā'răn)—*"firmness"*
Esau's descendant ....Gen 36:28

ARARAT (ăr'ä-răt)—*"high land"—mountainous land in eastern Armenia (modern Turkey)*
Site of ark's landing .....Gen 8:4
Assassins flee to ....2Kin 19:37; Is 37:38

against her the kingdoms of *A*. .Jer 51:27

ARATUS (ăr'ä-toos)—*a Greek poet who lived about 270 B.C.*
Paul quotes from his *Phaenomena* ....Acts 17:28

ARAUNAH (ä-rô'nä)—*"Jehovah is firm"*
A Jebusite 2Sam 24:15-25
His threshing floor bought by David 2Sam 24:18-25
Became site of Temple . . .2Chr 3:1
Also called Ornan 1Chr 21:18-28

A said unto the king, The 2Sam 24:23
the king said unto *A*, Nay 2Sam 24:24

ARBA (är'bä)—*"four; strength of Baal"*
The father of the Anakim ....Josh 14:15

the city of *A* the father ....Josh 15:13
gave them the city of *A* ....Josh 21:11

ARBAH (är'bä)—*a region in early Palestine*
the city of *A*, which is ....Gen 35:27

ARBATHITE (är'bä-thīt)—*a native of Beth-arabah*
Two of David's mighty men 2Sam 23:31

ARBITE (är'bīt)—*a native of Arab*
In Judah 2Sam 23:35

ARBITRATOR—*one authorized to settle disputes*

Exercised by:
Judges ....Ex 18:18-27
Priests ....Deut 17:8-13
Kings 2Kin 3:9, 16-28
Christ ....Matt 22:17-33
Apostles ....Acts 6:1-6
Church ....Acts 15:1-29

Purposes of:
Determine the Lord's will .... Lev 24:11-16; Num 15:32-36
Settle disputes ....Josh 22:9-34
Settle labor disputes .....Matt 18:23-35; Matt 20:1-16

ARCHAEOLOGY—*the study of material remains of past civilizations*
Truth springs out of the earth ....Ps 85:11
The stones cry out ....Luke 19:40

ARCHANGEL—*a chief, or specially designated, angel*
Contends with Satan .....Jude 9
Will herald the Lord's return 1Thess 4:16

ARCHELAUS (är-kĕ-lā'ŭs)—*"people's chief"*
Son of Herod the Great. .Matt 2:22

ARCHER—*those proficient with the bow and arrow*

Descriptive of:
Ishmael ....Gen 21:20
Jonathan 1Sam 20:34-39
Sons of Ulam 1Chr 8:40

Instrumental in the death of:
Saul 1Sam 31:3
Uriah the Hittite 2Sam 11:24
Josiah 2Chr 35:23, 24

Figurative of:
Invincibility ....Gen 49:23
The Lord's chastisements .Job 16:13
Loss of glory ....Is 21:17
Divine judgment ....Jer 50:29

[*also* ARCHERS]
are delivered..noise of *a* ......Judg 5:11
the *a* hit him 1Chr 10:3
he was wounded of the *a* 1Chr 10:3

ARCHES—*curved structures spanning an opening and providing support*
about and likewise to the *a* ....Ezek 40:16
posts thereof and the *a* ....Ezek 40:21
their windows and their *a* .....Ezek 40:22
the *a* thereof according to .....Ezek 40:24
windows in it and in the *a* ....Ezek 40:25
a thereof were before them ...Ezek 40:26
the posts thereof and the *a* ....Ezek 40:29
the *a* thereof round about .....Ezek 40:29
a..were five and twenty ....Ezek 40:30
a.. were toward the outer .....Ezek 40:31
a..were according to these .....Ezek 40:33
windows..and in the *a* ....Ezek 40:33
the *a*..were toward the ....Ezek 40:34
and the *a*..and the windows ...Ezek 40:36

ARCHEVITES (är'kĕ-vīts)—*people settled in Samaria during exile*
Opposed rebuilding of Jerusalem ....Ezra 4:9-16

ARCHI—*See* ARCHITE

ARCHIPPUS (är-kĭp'ŭs)—*"chief groom"*
A church worker ....Col 4:17

A our fellowsoldier ....Philem 2

ARCHITE (är'kīt)—*"the long"*
Canaanite tribe..........Josh 16:2
David's friend 2Sam 15:32

the *A*, David's friend 2Sam 16:16
Call now Hushai the *A* also ...2Sam 17:5
the *A* was the king's 1Chr 27:33

ARCHITECT—*one who designs plans for a building*
Plan of, given to Noah ...Gen 6:14-16
Plan of, shown to Moses .Ex 25:8, 9, 40
Bezaleel, an inspired......Ex 35:30-35
Plan of, given to Solomon 1Chr 28:11-21
Seen in Ezekiel's vision ..Ezek 40-42

ARCHIVES—*place where public and historical documents are preserved*
The book of the law found in 2Kin 22:8
Jeremiah's roll placed in .Jer 36:20, 21
Record book kept in.....Ezra 4:15
Genealogies kept in .....Neh 7:5, 64

ARCTURUS (ärk-tūr'ŭs)—*a constellation called the Bear*
Cited as evidence of God's sovereignty .....Job 9:9

thou guide *A* with his sons ....Job 38:32

ARD (ärd)—*"sprout; descent"*
A son of Benjamin ......Gen 46:21
Progenitor of the Ardites .Num 26:40
Also called Addar 1Chr 8:3

ARDON (är'dŏn)—*"descendant"*
A son of Caleb..........1Chr 2:18

ARE—*See* INTRODUCTION

ARELI (ä-rē'lī)—*"valiant; heroic; God's hearth"*
A son of Gad ....Gen 46:16

of *A*..family of the Arelites ....Num 26:17

ARELITES (ä-rē'līts)—*of the family of Areli*
Areli, the family of the *A* .....Num 26:17

AREOPAGITE (ăr-ĕ-ŏp'ä-gīt)—*a member of the court*
A convert..............Acts 17:34

AREOPAGUS (ăr-ĕ-ŏp'ä-gŭs)—*"hill of Ares" (Mars)—a hill west of the Acropolis in Athens*
Paul preached ....Acts 17:18-34
Called "Mars' Hill"......Acts 17:22

ARETAS (ăr'ĕ-tăs)—*"pleasing; virtuous"*
The title borne by four Nabataean rulers, the last of whom Paul mentions (Aretas IV, Philopatris, 9 B.C.-A.D. 40) 2Cor 11:32, 33

ARGOB (är'gŏb)—*"region of clods"*
1. District of Bashan with 60 fortified cities ..... {Deut 3:4, 1Kin 4:13}
2. Guard killed by Pekah ..2Kin 15:25

region of *A* with all Bashan ...Deut 3:13
Manasseh took..country of *A* ..Deut 3:14

ARGUING—*reasons given in proof or rebuttal*

[*also* ARGUMENTS]
what doth your *a* reprove? ....Job 6:25
fill my mouth with *a* ....Job 23:4

ARIDAI (ä-rĭd'ā-ī)—*"delight of Hari"*
A son of Haman ....Esth 9:9

ARIDATHA (ä-rĭd'ä-thä)—*"given by Hari"*
A son of Haman ....Esth 9:8

ARIEH (ä-rī'ĕ)—*"lion of Jehovah"*
Guard killed by Pekah ...2Kin 15:25

ARIEL (âr'ĭ-ĕl)—*"lion of God"*
1. Ezra's friend ....Ezra 8:15-17
2. Name applied to Jerusalem ....Is 29:1, 2, 7

ARIGHT—*correctly; exactly*
ordereth his conversation ***a*** ....Ps 50:23
that set not their heart ***a*** ......Ps 78:8
the wise useth knowledge ***a*** ...Prov 15:2
the cup..it moveth itself ***a*** .....Prov 23:31
heard, but they spake not ***a*** ...Jer 8:6

ARIMATHEA (ăr-ĭ-mä-thē'ä)—*"heights"—city believed to have been located in western Ephraim*
Joseph's native city ....John 19:38

there came a rich man of *A* ...Matt 27:57
Joseph of *A*, an honorable ....Mark 15:43
A, a city of the Jews..........Luke 23:51
Joseph of *A*..a disciple of .....John 19:38

ARIOCH (ăr'ĭ-ŏk)—*"lion-like"*
1. King of Ellasar ....Gen 14:1, 9
2. Captain of Nebuchadnezzar ......Dan 2:14, 15

Daniel went in unto *A* ....Dan 2:24
A brought in Daniel ....Dan 2:25

ARISAI (ä-rĭs'ā-ī)—*(meaning uncertain)*
A son of Haman ....Esth 9:9

ARISE—*to get up; to come into being or to one's attention*

Descriptive of:
Natural events ....Eccl 1:5
Standing up 1Sam 28:23
Regeneration ....Luke 15:18, 20
Resurrection ....Matt 9:25
A miracle...............Luke 4:39

Descriptive of prophetic events:
World kingdoms..........Dan 2:39
The Messiah's advent ....Is 60:1-3
Persecution ....Mark 4:17
False Christs ....Matt 24:24

[*also* ARISETH, ARISING, AROSE]
A, walk through the land......Gen 13:17
when..morning ***a*** then.........Gen 19:15
A, take thy wife ....Gen 19:15
A, lift up the lad ....Gen 21:18
a, I pray thee, sit and eat .....Gen 27:19
Let my father ***a*** and eat.......Gen 27:31
a, flee thou to Laban ....Gen 27:43
A, go to Padan-aram ....Gen 28:2
a, get thee out from this land. .Gen 31:13
A, go up to Beth-el and dwell. .Gen 35:1
let us ***a***, and go up to Bethel ..Gen 35:3
there shall ***a*** after them ....Gen 41:30
and we will ***a*** and go ....Gen 43:8
Take..your brother, and ***a*****.....Gen 43:13
there ***a*** up a new king ....Ex 1:8
A, get thee down quickly......Deut 9:12
A, take thy journey............Deut 10:11
If there ***a*** among you ....Deut 13:1
there ***a*** a matter too hard .....Deut 17:8
shalt thou ***a*** and get thee......Deut 17:8
there ***a*** not a prophet since ....Deut 34:10
a, go over this Jordan ....Josh 1:2
a, go..to Ai; see, I have ......Josh 8:1
Joshua ***a***, and..the people .....Josh 8:3
the men ***a*** and went away .....Josh 18:8
a and warred against Israel ....Josh 24:9
a another generation ....Judg 2:10
And he ***a*** out of his seat ......Judg 3:20
Deborah ***a*** and went with .....Judg 4:9
until that I Deborah ***a*** ....Judg 5:7
a Barak..lead thy captivity ....Judg 5:12
the men of the city ***a*** early ....Judg 6:28
A get thee..unto the host.......Judg 7:9
A..the Lord hath delivered ....Judg 7:15
Gideon ***a*** and slew Zebah .....Judg 8:21
after Abimelech there ***a*** to ....Judg 10:1
Manoah ***a*** and went after .....Judg 13:11
lay till midnight and ***a*** at ......Judg 16:3
A that we may go..against .....Judg 18:9
her husband ***a*** and went ......Judg 19:3
all the people ***a*** as one man ...Judg 20:8
when the flame began to ***a*** ....Judg 20:40
a with her daughters-in-law ....Ruth 1:6
Samuel ***a*** and went to Eli 1Sam 3:6
when they of Ashdod ***a*** early ..1Sam 5:3
and ***a***, go seek the asses 1Sam 9:3
they ***a*** early and it came 1Sam 9:26
Samuel ***a*** and got him up 1Sam 13:15
A, anoint him..this is he 1Sam 16:12
he ***a*** against me, I caught 1Sam 17:35
David ***a*** and went 1Sam 18:27
Jonathan ***a***..Abner sat by 1Sam 20:25
David ***a*** and fled that day 1Sam 21:10
A, go down to Keilah 1Sam 23:4
David..***a*** and departed out 1Sam 23:13
David ***a*** and cut..the skirt 1Sam 24:4
David ***a*** and went down to 1Sam 25:1
Saul ***a*** and went down 1Sam 26:2
David ***a*** and..passed over 1Sam 27:2
All the valiant men ***a*** 1Sam 31:12
Let the young men now ***a*****.....2Sam 2:14
And Joab said, Let them ***a*** 2Sam 2:14
Then there ***a*** and went over ...2Sam 2:15
said unto David, I will ***a*** 2Sam 3:21
And David ***a*** and went with 2Sam 6:2
that David ***a*** from..his bed 2Sam 11:2
if..the king's wrath ***a***..........2Sam 11:20
the elders of his house ***a*** 2Sam 12:17
Ammon said unto her, *A*......2Sam 13:15
Then all the king's sons ***a*** 2Sam 13:29
Joab ***a*** and went to Geshur....2Sam 14:23
he ***a*** and went to Hebron 2Sam 15:9
A and let us flee 2Sam 15:14
I will ***a*** and pursue after 2Sam 17:1
A and pass quickly over.......2Sam 17:21
David ***a*** and all the people 2Sam 17:22
Now therefore ***a***, go forth 2Sam 19:7
the king ***a*** and sat in the 2Sam 19:8
them that they could not ***a*** 2Sam 22:39
He ***a*** and smote the 2Sam 23:10
Shimel ***a*** and saddled his 1Kin 2:40
after thee shall any ***a*** like 1Kin 3:12
And she ***a*** at midnight 1Kin 3:20
he ***a*** from..the altar...........1Kin 8:54
And they ***a*** out of Midian 1Kin 11:18
A, I pray thee, and disguise ...1Kin 14:2
Jeroboam's wife did..and ***a*** 1Kin 14:4
A, get thee to Zarephath 1Kin 17:9
he ***a*** and went to Zarephath ...1Kin 17:10
a a..cloud out of the sea 1Kin 18:44
And when he saw that, he ***a*** ..1Kin 19:3
said unto him, *A* and eat 1Kin 19:5
a and eat..the journey is 1Kin 19:7
a and eat bread..let thine 1Kin 21:7
A, take possession of the 1Kin 21:15
A, go down to meet Ahab 1Kin 21:18
A, go..meet the messengers ...2Kin 1:3
he ***a*** and went..with him 2Kin 1:15
And he ***a*** and followed her....2Kin 4:30
they ***a*** and fled in the 2Kin 7:7
A, and go thou and thine 2Kin 8:1
woman ***a*** and did after the 2Kin 8:2
a..from among his brethren ...2Kin 9:2
he ***a***..went into the house 2Kin 9:6
And he ***a*** and departed 2Kin 10:12
she ***a*** and destroyed..seed 2Kin 11:1
a and made a conspiracy 2Kin 12:20
they ***a*** early in the morning ...2Kin 19:35
after him ***a*** any like him 2Kin 23:25
captains of the armies ***a*** 2Kin 25:26
They ***a***, all the valiant men 1Chr 10:12
a war at Gezer with the 1Chr 20:4
A therefore, and be doing 1Chr 22:16
a..and build ye the 1Chr 22:19
Now..***a***, O Lord God 2Chr 6:41
the Levites ***a***, Mahath the 2Chr 29:12
they ***a*** and took..the altars 2Chr 30:14
wrath of the Lord ***a*** against ...2Chr 36:16
I ***a*** up from my heaviness .....Ezra 9:5
A..this matter belongeth .....Ezra 10:4
a..made the chief priest ....Ezra 10:5

And I *a* in the night ....Neh 2:12
we his servants will *a* ....Neh 2:20
a too much contempt ....Esth 1:18
deliverance *a* to the Jews .....Esth 4:14
king *a* from the banquet of ....Esth 7:7
Esther *a* and stood before .....Esth 8:4
Job *a* and rent his mantle .....Job 1:20
When shall I *a* and the ....Job 7:4
I *a*..they spake against me ....Job 19:18
doth not his light *a*? ....Job 25:3
the aged *a* and stood up ......Job 29:8
A, O Lord, save me ....Ps 3:7
A, O Lord, in thine anger .....Ps 7:6
A, O Lord, let not man ....Ps 9:19
A, O Lord, O God, lift up ....Ps 10:12
now will I *a* saith the Lord ....Ps 12:5
A, O Lord, disappoint him ....Ps 17:13
why sleepest thou..*A* ....Ps 44:23
A, for our help..redeem us ....Ps 44:26
Let God *a*, let his enemies ....Ps 68:1
A, O God, plead thine own ...Ps 74:22
when God *a* to judgment .....Ps 76:9
who should *a* and declare .....Ps 78:6
A, O God, judge the earth ....Ps 82:8
Shall the dead *a* and praise ....Ps 88:10
when the waves thereof *a* .....Ps 89:9
shalt *a* and have mercy ....Ps 102:13
sun *a*..gather themselves ......Ps 104:22
they *a*, let them be ashamed ..Ps 109:28
Unto..upright there *a* light ....Ps 112:4
A, O Lord, into thy rest ......Ps 132:8
thou *a* out of thy sleep........Prov 6:9
children *a* up and call her .....Prov 31:28
The sun also *a* and the sun ....Eccl 1:5
to his place where he *a* ....Eccl 1:5
A, my love, my fair one.......Song 2:13
when he *a* to shake ....Is 2:19
a, ye princes, and anoint .....Is 21:5
a, pass over to Chittim........Is 23:12
dead body shall they *a* ....Is 26:19
will *a* against the house of ....Is 31:2
Kings shall see and *a* ....Is 49:7
a..sit down, O Jerusalem ......Is 52:2
gird up thy loins and *a* ....Jer 1:17
they will say, *A*..save us ......Jer 2:27
let them *a* if they can save ....Jer 2:28
a, and let us go up at noon ....Jer 6:4
A, and let us go by night......Jer 6:5
Shall they fall and not *a*? .....Jer 8:4
and *a*, go to Euphrates ....Jer 13:4
A, go to Euphrates ....Jer 13:6
A, and go..to the potter's .....Jer 18:2
A ye, and let us to..to Zion ...Jer 31:6
a Ishmael..son of Nethaniah ...Jer 41:2
A, and let us go..to our own ..Jer 46:16
A ye, go up to Kedar ....Jer 49:28
A, get you..unto the wealthy ..Jer 49:31
A, cry out in the night ....Lam 2:19
A, go forth into the plain .....Ezek 3:22
Then I *a* and went forth ......Ezek 3:23
king *a* very early in...........Dan 6:19
A, devour much flesh ....Dan 7:5
shall *a* out of the earth ....Dan 7:17
ten kings that shall arise ......Dan 7:24
tumult *a* among thy people ....Hos 10:14
by whom shall Jacob *a*? for ...Amos 7:2
A ye,..let us rise up ....Obad 1
A, go to Nineveh............Jon 1:2
a, call upon thy God ....Jon 1:6
A, go unto Nineveh..........Jon 3:2
Jonah *a*..went unto Nineveh ..Jon 3:3
when the sun did *a* ....Jon 4:8
A ye..depart for this is ....Mic 2:10
A and thresh, O daughter ......Mic 4:13
A, contend thou before the ....Mic 6:1
when I fall, I shall *a* ....Mic 7:8
when the sun *a* they flee ......Nah 3:17
A, it shall teach! Behold ......Hab 2:19
the Sun of righteousness *a* ....Mal 4:2
A, and take the young child ...Matt 2:13
a he took the young child .....Matt 2:14
A, and take the young child ...Matt 2:20
she *a* and ministered unto .....Matt 8:15
or to say *A* and walk? ....Matt 9:5
A, take up thy bed, and go....Matt 9:6
he *a* and departed ....Matt 9:7
tribulation or persecution *a* ....Matt 13:21
said, *A*, and be not afraid .....Matt 17:7
those virgins *a* and trimmed ...Matt 25:7
the high priest *a* and said .....Matt 26:62
of the saints which slept *a* .....Matt 27:52
to say, *A*..take up thy bed ....Mark 2:9
thee, *A*..take up thy bed ......Mark 2:11
he *a*, took up the bed ....Mark 2:12
Damsel, I say unto thee, *a* ....Mark 5:41
the damsel *a* and walked ....Mark 5:42
he *a*..went into the borders....Mark 7:24
lifted him up; and he *a* ....Mark 9:27
a from thence and cometh ....Mark 10:1
a..and bare false witness ......Mark 14:57
And Mary *a* in those days.....Luke 1:39
he *a* out of the synagogue .....Luke 4:38
I say unto thee, *A*, and take...Luke 5:24
he *a* and stood forth ....Luke 6:8
I say unto thee, *A* ....Luke 7:14
he *a* and rebuked the wind ....Luke 8:24
called saying, Maid, *a*.........Luke 8:54
a a reasoning among them ....Luke 9:46
a a..famine in that land ....Luke 15:14
said unto him, *A*, go thy way ..Luke 17:19
whole multitude of them *a* ....Luke 23:1
a Peter, and ran unto ....Luke 24:12
thoughts *a* in your hearts?.....Luke 24:38
there *a* a question between ....John 3:25
sea *a* by..a great wind ....John 6:18
out of Galilee *a* no prophet ..John 7:52
she *a* quickly..unto him ....John 11:29
even so I do. *A*, let us go .....John 14:31
young men *a*, wound him .....Acts 5:6
a a murmuring of..Grecians ...Acts 6:1
king *a*..knew not Joseph ......Acts 7:18
A, and go toward the south ...Acts 8:26
he *a* and went; and behold ...Acts 8:27
A, and go into the city ....Acts 9:6
Saul *a* from the earth ....Acts 9:8
A, and go into the street ......Acts 9:11
a, and make thy bed..........Acts 9:34
to the body said, Tabitha, *a* ..Acts 9:40
A therefore..get thee down ....Acts 10:20
A, Peter; slay and eat.........Acts 11:7
persecution that *a* about ......Acts 11:19
your own selves..men *a* ....Acts 20:30
A, and go into Damascus ......Acts 22:10
a..be baptized..wash away .....Acts 22:16
a a dissension between the ....Acts 23:7
a against it a tempestuous .....Acts 27:14
a from the dead and Christ....Eph 5:14
there *a* another priest ....Heb 7:15
day star *a* in your hearts 2Pet 1:19
a a smoke out of the pit ......Rev 9:2

ARISTARCHUS (ăr-ĭs-tär′kŭs)—*"the best ruler"*
A Macedonian Christian .Acts 19:29
Accompanied Paul.......Acts 20:4
Imprisoned with Paul ....Col 4:10

A, a Macedonian ....Acts 27:2
Marcus, *A*, Demas.............Philem 24

ARISTOBULUS (ă-rĭs-tō-bū′lŭs)—*"the best counselor"*
A Christian at Rome ....Rom 16:10

ARK OF BULRUSHES—*a small boat in which Moses' mother hid him*
Moses placed in ....Ex 2:3-6
Made by faith ....Heb 11:23

ARK OF THE COVENANT—*wooden chest containing the tablets of the law; a visible symbol of God's presence and power*

Called:
Ark of the covenant .....Num 10:33
Ark of the testimony ....Ex 30:6
Ark of the Lord.........Josh 4:11
Ark of God............1Sam 3:3
Ark of God's strength ...2Chr 6:41

Construction of:
Described..............Ex 25:10-22
Executed ....Ex 37:1-5

Contained:
The Ten Commandments .Deut 10:4
Aaron's rod ....Num 17:10; Heb 9:4
Pot of manna ....Ex 16:33, 34

Conveyed:
By Levites ....Num 3:30, 31
Before Israel ....Josh 3:3-17
Into battle 1Sam 4:4, 5
On a cart 1Sam 6:7-15

Purposes of:
Symbol of God's Law ....Ex 25:16, 21
Memorial of God's provision ....Ex 16:33, 34
Place to know God's will .Ex 25:22; Ex 30:6, 36
Place of entreaty ....Josh 7:6-15
Symbol of God's holiness .1Sam 6:19; 2Sam 6:6, 7
Place of atonement ......Lev 16:2, 14-17
Type of Christ ....Rom 3:25-31
Symbol of heaven ....Rev 11:19

History of:
Carried across Jordan ....Josh 3:16, 14-17
Caused Jordan's stoppage..Josh 4:5-11, 18
Carried around Jericho ...Josh 6:6-20
At Mt. Ebal ceremony ...Josh 8:30-33
Set up at Shiloh ....Josh 18:1
Moved to house of God. .Judg 20:26, 27
Returned to Shiloh 1Sam 1:3
Carried into battle.......1Sam 4:3-22
Captured 1Sam 4:10-21
Caused Dagon's fall 1Sam 5:1-4
Brought a plague 1Sam 5:6-12
Returned to Israel 1Sam 6:1-21
Set in Abinadab's house .1Sam 7:1, 2
In Obed-edom's house ...2Sam 6:10-12
Established in Jerusalem .2Sam 6:12-17
During Absalom's rebellion 2Sam 15:24-29
Placed in Temple 1Kin 8:1-11
Restored by Josiah 2Chr 35:3
Carried to Babylon 2Chr 36:6, 18
Prophetic fulfillment .....Jer 3:16, 17; Acts 15:13-18

within the veil the *a* of the ....Ex 26:33
upon the *a* of the testimony ...Ex 26:34
therewith and the *a* of the ....Ex 30:26
the *a* of the testimony ....Ex 31:7
The *a* and the staves..........Ex 35:12
The *a* of the testimony, and ...Ex 39:35
the *a* of the testimony ....Ex 40:3
cover the *a* with the veil ......Ex 40:3
the *a* of the testimony ....Ex 40:5
put the testimony into the *a* ...Ex 40:20
and set the staves on the *a* ....Ex 40:20
mercy seat..upon the *a*........Ex 40:20
the *a* into the tabernacle ......Ex 40:21
the *a* of the testimony ....Ex 40:21
cover the *a* of testimony ......Num 4:5
mercy seat..upon the *a*........Num 7:89
when the *a* set forward ....Num 10:35
the *a* of the covenant ....Num 14:44
make thee an *a* of wood ....Deut 10:1
shalt put them in the *a*.......Deut 10:2
made an *a* of shittim wood ....Deut 10:3
put the tables in the *a* ....Deut 10:5
bear the *a* of the covenant ....Deut 10:8
sons of Levi..bare the *a*.......Deut 31:9
bare the *a* of the covenant ....Deut 31:25
side of the *a* of the covenant ..Deut 31:26
the priests that bear the *a* .....Josh 4:16
shall bear before the *a* ....Josh 6:4
Let us fetch the *a* of the 1Sam 4:3
they set down the *a* of 1Sam 6:18
Bring hither the *a* of God 1Sam 14:18
the *a* of God was at that 1Sam 14:18
bring up from..the *a* of God ...2Sam 6:2
they set the *a* of God upon 2Sam 6:3
accompanying the *a* of God 2Sam 6:4
and Ahio went before the *a* ...2Sam 6:4
How shall the *a* of the Lord ...2Sam 6:9
but the *a* of God dwelleth 2Sam 7:2

The *a*, and Israel, and 2Sam 11:11
because thou barest the *a*......1Kin 2:26
before the *a* of the covenant ...1Kin 3:15
set..the *a* of the covenant......1Kin 6:19
set there a place for the *a* 1Kin 8:21
after that the *a* had rest 1Chr 6:31
bring again the *a* of our God ..1Chr 13:3
bring the *a* of God from 1Chr 13:5
to bring up..the *a* of God 1Chr 13:6
carried the *a* of God in a new .1Chr 13:7
forth his hand to hold the *a* ...1Chr 13:9
he put his hand to the *a*.......1Chr 13:10
How shall I bring the *a* of 1Chr 13:12
David brought not the *a*.......1Chr 13:13
the *a* of God remained 1Chr 13:14
a place for the *a* of God 1Chr 15:1
ought to carry the *a* of God ...1Chr 15:2
chosen to carry the *a* of 1Chr 15:2
bring up the *a* of the Lord.....1Chr 15:3
bring up the *a* of the Lord.....1Chr 15:12
Levites bare the *a* of God 1Chr 15:15
doorkeepers for the *a* 1Chr 15:23
trumpets before the *a* of.......1Chr 15:24
the *a* of the covenant 1Chr 15:25
the Levites that bare the *a*.....1Chr 15:26
the Levites that bare the *a*.....1Chr 15:27
all Israel brought up the *a* 1Chr 15:28
a of the covenant of the 1Chr 15:29
they brought the *a* of God.....1Chr 16:1
to minister before the *a* 1Chr 16:4
he left..before the *a* of 1Chr 16:37
minister before the *a*..........1Chr 16:37
a of the covenant of 1Chr 17:1
bring the *a* of the covenant 1Chr 22:19
house of rest for the *a* of......1Chr 28:2
the *a* of the covenant 1Chr 28:18
But the *a* of God had David ...2Chr 1:4
bring..*a* of the covenant 2Chr 5:2
the Levites took up the *a*......2Chr 5:4
they brought up the *a*.........2Chr 5:5
unto him before the *a*.........2Chr 5:6
priests brought in the *a*........2Chr 5:7
wings over the place of the *a* ..2Chr 5:8
cherubim covered the *a* 2Chr 5:8
drew out the staves of the *a* ...2Chr 5:9
were seen from the *a* before ...2Chr 5:9
nothing in the *a* save the 2Chr 5:10
in it have I put the *a*.........2Chr 6:11
and the *a* of thy strength 2Chr 6:41
a of the Lord hath come 2Chr 8:11
Put the holy *a* in the house 2Chr 35:3
and the *a* of thy strength ......Ps 132:8

ARK OF NOAH—*large wooden ship in which Noah, his family, and pairs of living creatures were preserved during the Flood*
Construction ....Gen 6:14-16
Cargo ....Gen 6:19-21
Ready for the flood .....Matt 24:38, 39
Rested on Mt. Ararat....Gen 8:1-16
A type of baptism 1Pet 3:20, 21

all thy house into the *a* ....Gen 7:1
wives with him, into the *a*.....Gen 7:7
two unto Noah into the *a* .....Gen 7:9
sons with them into the *a* .....Gen 7:13
went..unto Noah into the *a*....Gen 7:15
increased..bare up the *a* ......Gen 7:17
the *a* went upon the face of ...Gen 7:18
that were with him in the *a* ...Gen 7:23
went forth out of the *a* ....Gen 8:19
all that go out of the *a*........Gen 9:10
that went forth of the *a* ....Gen 9:18
Noah entered into the *a* ......Luke 17:27
prepared an *a* to the saving ...Heb 11:7

ARKITE (är'kīt)—*belonging to Arka*
Canaan's descendants ....Gen 10:17
1Chr 1:15

ARM—*an appendage of the body used for lifting or carrying*
[*also* ARMS]
a of his hands were made .....Gen 49:24
by the greatness of thine *a* ....Ex 15:16
A some..yourselves unto ......Num 31:3
and by thy stretched out *a* ....Deut 9:29
and his stretched out *a*........Deut 11:2
and with an outstretched *a* ....Deut 26:8
teareth the *a*..crown of........Deut 33:20
are the everlasting *a* ....Deut 33:27
cords that were upon his *a* ....Judg 15:14
brake them..off his *a* like .....Judg 16:12
a of thy father's house 1Sam 2:31
bracelet that was on his *a* 2Sam 1:10
bow..is broken by mine *a* 2Sam 22:35
and of thy stretched out *a*.....1Kin 8:42
smote..between his *a* 2Kin 9:24
and a stretched out *a* 2Kin 17:36
and thy stretched out *a* 2Chr 6:32
With him is an *a* of flesh......2Chr 32:8
a of the fatherless have ....Job 22:9
a fall from my shoulder ....Job 31:22
a be broken from the bone ....Job 31:22
by reason of the *a* of the......Job 35:9
the high *a* shall be broken ....Job 38:15
Hast thou an *a* like God? .....Job 40:9
bow..is broken by mine *a* .....Ps 18:34
a of the wicked shall be.......Ps 37:17
a redeemed thy people........Ps 77:15
and with a stretched out *a* ....Ps 136:12
and strengtheneth her *a* ....Prov 31:17
as a seal upon thine *a* ....Song 8:6
man the flesh of his own *a* ....Is 9:20
reapeth the ears with his *a* ....Is 17:5
be..their *a* every morning .....Is 33:2
gather the lambs with his *a*....Is 40:11
with the strength of his *a* .....Is 44:12
his *a*..be on the Chaldeans ...Is 48:14
bring thy sons in their *a*......Is 49:22
a shall judge the people.......Is 51:5
on mine *a* shall they trust .....Is 51:5
put on strength, O *a* of the ...Is 51:9
Lord..made bare his holy *a*....Is 52:10
whom is the *a* of the Lord ....Is 53:1
a brought salvation unto ......Is 59:16
by the *a* of his strength ....Is 62:8
a brought salvation unto ......Is 63:5
and maketh flesh his *a* ....Jer 17:5
and with a strong *a*..........Jer 21:5
and by my outstretched *a* .....Jer 27:5
power and stretched out *a*.....Jer 32:17
and with a stretched out *a* ....Jer 32:21
a is broken saith the Lord.....Jer 48:25
will tear them from your *a* ....Ezek 13:20
with a stretched out *a* and ....Ezek 20:33
and with a stretched out *a* ....Ezek 20:34
broken the *a* of Pharaoh ......Ezek 30:21
and they that were his *a* ......Ezek 31:17
a and his feet like in color ....Dan 10:6
retain not the power of..*a* .....Dan 11:6
shall he stand, nor his *a*.......Dan 11:6
a of the south shall not ....Dan 11:15
and strengthened their *a* ......Hos 7:15
taking them by their *a* ....Hos 11:3
sword shall be upon his *a* .....Zech 11:17
a shall be clean dried up ......Zech 11:17
he had taken him in his *a* .....Mark 9:36
he took them up in his *a*.......Mark 10:16
hath the *a* of the Lord ....John 12:38
an high *a* brought he them ....Acts 13:17
a yourselves likewise with 1Pet 4:1

ARM OF GOD—*symbolizes strength or power of God*

Described as:
Stretched out ....Deut 4:34
Everlasting.............Deut 33:27
Strong, mighty ....Ps 89:10, 13
Holy ....Ps 98:1
Glorious ....Is 63:12

Descriptive of, God's:
Redeeming..............Ex 6:6
Saving ....Ps 44:3
Victorious ....Ps 98:1
Ruling ....Is 40:10
Strengthening ....Ps 89:21
Protecting..............Deut 7:19
Destroying ....Is 30:30

ARM OF THE WICKED—*expression for harassment by enemies*
Shall be broken ....Ps 10:15

ARMAGEDDON (är-mä-gĕd'ŭn)—*"hill of Megiddo"*
Historic wars ....Judg 5:19
Notable deaths 1Sam 31:8
Final battle ....Rev 16:16

ARMED—*furnished or equipped with weapons*
he *a* his trained servants ......Gen 14:14
twelve thousand *a* for war.....Num 31:5
we..will go ready *a* ....Num 32:17
ye will go *a* before the Lord...Num 32:20
go all of you *a* over Jordan ...Num 32:21
every man *a* for war ....Num 32:27
every man *a* to battle ....Num 32:29
not pass over with you *a* ......Num 32:30
pass over *a* before the Lord ...Num 32:32
pass over *a* before your ....Deut 3:18
Manasseh, passed over *a* ......Josh 4:12
is *a* pass on before the ark ....Josh 6:7
the *a* men went before ....Josh 6:9
a men went before them ....Josh 6:13
a men that were in the host ...Judg 7:11
was *a* with a coat of mail 1Sam 17:5
Saul *a* David with..armor 1Sam 17:38
he *a* him with a coat of mail ..1Sam 17:38
They were *a* with bows 1Chr 12:2
were ready *a* to the war.......1Chr 12:23
ready *a* to the war............1Chr 12:24
a men with bow and shield 2Chr 17:17
the *a* men left the captives 2Chr 28:14
goeth on to meet the *a* men...Job 39:21
children of Ephraim being *a* ...Ps 78:9
and thy want as an *a* man.....Prov 6:11
and thy want as an *a* man.....Prov 24:34
a soldiers of Moab shall.......Is 15:4
strong man *a* keepeth his .....Luke 11:21

ARMENIA (är-mē'nĭ-ä)—*land southeast of the Black Sea; Ararat*
Assassins flee to.........2Kin 19:37
See ARARAT

escaped into the land of *A* ....Is 37:38

ARMHOLES—*openings in clothing for the arms*
Armpits, protected with rags ....Jer 38:12
Articles of alluring dress. .Ezek 13:18

ARMONI (är-mō'nī)—*"of the palace"*
A son of Saul 2Sam 21:8-11

ARMOR—*defensive covering used in battle*

As a protective weapon:
Shield 1Sam 17:7, 41
Helmet 1Sam 17:38
Scale-armor 1Sam 17:5, 38
1Kin 22:34
Greaves 1Sam 17:6
Girdle 1Sam 18:4
Body armor 2Chr 26:14

As an aggressive weapon:
Rod ....Ps 2:9
Sling 1Sam 17:40
Bow and arrow 2Sam 1:18
Spear..................Is 2:4
Sword 1Sam 17:51

young man that bare his *a*.....1Sam 14:1
head, and stripped off his *a*....1Sam 31:9
take thee his *a*. But Asahel 2Sam 2:21
garments and *a* and 1Kin 10:25
that were able to put on *a*.....2Kin 3:21
took his head and his *a* 1Chr 10:9
a of the house of the forest ....Is 22:8
clothed with all sorts of *a*......Ezek 38:4
his *a* wherein he trusted ....Luke 11:22
let us put on the *a* of light ....Rom 13:12
by the *a* of righteousness 2Cor 6:7

ARMOR, SPIRITUAL—*that which gives the Christian protection and confidence*

The Christian's, complete . Eph 6:11-17; 1Thess 5:8
Of light . Rom 13:12
Of righteousness . 2Cor 6:7
The Bible, the sword . Eph 6:17
Not of flesh . 2Cor 10:4, 5

ARMOR-BEARER—*one who bears the arms of another*
Assists kings in battle . Judg 9:54
David serves Saul as . 1Sam 16:21
Jonathan's, a man of courage . 1Sam 14:7, 12
Saul's, dies with him . 1Sam 31:4-6
Goliath's, precedes him . 1Sam 17:7, 41

a to Joab the son of Zeruiah . 2Sam 23:37
Then said Saul to his ***a*** . 1Chr 10:4
his ***a*** would not . 1Chr 10:4
a saw that Saul was dead . 1Chr 10:5
a of Joab..son of Zeruiah . 1Chr 11:39

ARMORY—*storage place for military equipment*
Armor stored in . Neh 3:19
God's, opened for war . Jer 50:25
David's, well stocked . Song 4:4

up to the ***a*** at the turning . Neh 3:19

ARMY—*those organized and disciplined for battle*

Consisted of:
Men over 20 . Num 1:3
Infantrymen . 2Chr 25:5
Archers . 1Chr 5:18
Sling stones . 2Chr 26:14
Chariots . 1Kin 4:26
Foreigners . 2Sam 15:18
Choice men . 2Sam 10:7-9

Commanded by:
God . Josh 5:14
Judges . Judg 11:1, 6, 32
Captain . 2Sam 2:8
Kings . 2Sam 12:28, 29

Commands regarding:
Use of chariots . Deut 17:16
Deferred certain classes . Num 2:33; Deut 20:1-9
Division of spoil . 1Sam 30:21-25
Fearfulness . Deut 20:1

Units of:
Fifties . 2Kin 1:9
Hundreds . Num 31:14, 48
Legions . Matt 26:53
Bands . Acts 21:31
Guards . Acts 28:16
Quaternions . Acts 12:4
Thousands . Num 31:14, 48

Of Israel, conquered:
Egyptians . Ex 14:19-31
Jericho . Josh 6:1-25
Midianites . Judg 7:1-23
Philistines . 1Sam 14:14-23
Syrians . 2Kin 7:1-15
Assyrians . 2Kin 19:35, 36

[*also* ARMIES]
the chief captain of his ***a*** . Gen 26:26
Egypt according to their ***a*** . Ex 6:26
mine ***a*** and my people . Ex 7:4
your ***a*** out of..Egypt . Ex 12:17
land of Egypt by their ***a*** . Ex 12:51
his horsemen and his ***a*** . Ex 14:9
pitch throughout their ***a*** . Num 2:3
throughout their ***a***. These . Num 2:9
the north side by their ***a*** . Num 2:25
according to their ***a*** and . Num 10:14
according to his ***a***; and over . Num 10:22
Israel according to their ***a*** . Num 10:28
a under the hand of Moses . Num 33:1
he did unto the ***a*** of Egypt . Deut 11:4
the captain of Jabin's ***a*** . Judg 4:7
slew of the ***a*** in the field . 1Sam 4:2
he that came out of the ***a*** . 1Sam 4:16
I fled today out of the ***a*** . 1Sam 4:16
together their ***a*** to battle . 1Sam 17:1
battle in array ***a*** against ***a*** . 1Sam 17:21
the ***a*** of the Philistines? . 1Sam 23:3
Philistines gathered..***a*** . 1Sam 28:1
all their ***a*** to Aphek . 1Sam 29:1
the ***a*** which followed them . 1Kin 20:19
a of the Chaldees pursued . 2Kin 25:5
a were scattered from him . 2Kin 25:5
the captains of the ***a***, they . 2Kin 25:23
captains of the ***a*** arose . 2Kin 25:26
the valiant men of the ***a*** . 1Chr 11:26
Joab led..power of the ***a*** . 1Chr 20:1
the general of the king's ***a*** . 1Chr 27:34
array with an ***a*** of valiant . 2Chr 13:3
Asa had an ***a*** of men that . 2Chr 14:8
of his ***a*** against the cities . 2Chr 16:4
they went out before the ***a*** . 2Chr 20:21
a of the Syrians came with . 2Chr 24:24
let not the ***a*** of Israel go . 2Chr 25:7
given to the ***a*** of Israel? . 2Chr 25:9
under their hand was an ***a*** . 2Chr 26:13
had sent captains of the ***a*** . Neh 2:9
there any number of his ***a***? . Job 25:3
dwelt as a king in the ***a*** . Job 29:25
goest not forth with our ***a*** . Ps 44:9
not go out with our ***a***? . Ps 60:10
Kings of ***a*** did flee space . Ps 68:12
terrible as an ***a*** with . Song 6:4
his fury upon all their ***a*** . Is 34:2
Hezekiah with a great ***a*** . Is 36:2
horse, the ***a*** and the power . Is 43:17
Babylon's ***a*** besieged . Jer 32:2
king of Babylon..all his ***a*** . Jer 34:1
for fear of the ***a*** of the . Jer 35:11
Pharaoh's ***a*** was come forth . Jer 37:5
the king of Babylon's ***a*** . Jer 38:3
all his ***a*** against Jerusalem . Jer 39:1
the ***a*** of Pharaoh-necho . Jer 46:2
all his ***a*** against Jerusalem . Jer 52:4
Pharaoh with his mighty ***a*** . Ezek 17:17
Lud and Phut..in thine ***a*** . Ezek 27:10
his ***a*** to serve a great . Ezek 29:18
Pharaoh and all his ***a*** slain . Ezek 32:31
an exceeding great ***a*** . Ezek 37:10
al thine ***a***, horses and . Ezek 38:4
men that were in his ***a*** . Dan 3:20
according..his will in..***a*** . Dan 4:35
which shall come with an ***a*** . Dan 11:7
utter his voice before his ***a*** . Joel 2:11
mine house because of the ***a*** . Zech 9:8
he sent forth his ***a*** and . Matt 22:7
compassed with ***a*** . Luke 21:20
then came I with an ***a*** and . Acts 23:27
of the ***a*** of the horsemen . Rev 9:16
their ***a*** gathered together . Rev 19:19
horse, and against his ***a*** . Rev 19:19

ARMY, CHRISTIAN—*expression applied to believers*

Warfare against:
The world . James 4:4; 1John 2:15-17
The flesh . Gal 5:17-21
Satan . 1Pet 5:8, 9
Evil men . 2Tim 3:8
False teachers . Jude 3, 4
Spiritual wickedness . Eph 6:12
Worldly "vain babblings" . 1Tim 6:20

Equipment for:
Sufficient for total war . Eph 6:12-17; 1Thess 5:8
Spiritual in nature . 2Cor 10:3, 4
Sharper than any sword . Heb 4:12

The soldier in, must:
Enlist . Matt 28:18-20
Obey . 2Cor 10:5, 6
Please captain . 2Tim 2:4
Use self-control . 1Cor 9:25-27
Stand firm . Eph 6:13-17
Endure hardship . 2Tim 2:3
Show courage . 2Tim 4:7-18
Fight hard . 1Tim 6:12
Be pure . 1Pet 2:11, 12
Be alert . 1Pet 5:8
Be faithful . 1Tim 1:18-20

Jesus Christ, the Captain of, is:
Perfect . Heb 2:10
Undefiled . Heb 7:26
Powerful . 2Thess 2:8

ARNAN (är'năn)—*"joyous; strong"*
A descendant of David . 1Chr 3:21

the sons of ***A***, the sons of . 1Chr 3:21

ARNON (är'nŏn)—*"rushing water"—a river that pours into the Dead Sea*
Boundary between Moab and Ammon . Num 21:13, 26
Border of Reuben . Deut 3:12, 16
Ammonites reminded of . Judg 11:18-26

which is in the border of ***A*** . Num 22:36
and pass over the river ***A*** . Deut 2:24
of ***A*** unto mount Hermon . Deut 3:8
upon the bank of the river ***A*** . Josh 13:9
from ***A*** even unto Jabbok . Judg 11:13
by the river ***A***, even Gilead . 2Kin 10:33
shall be at the fords of ***A*** . Is 16:2
tell ye it in ***A*** that Moab . Jer 48:20

AROD (ā'rŏd)—*"descent; posterity"*
A son of Gad . Num 26:17
Called Arodi . Gen 46:16

AROER (ă-rō'er)—*"naked"*
1. A town in east Jordan . Deut 2:36
An Amorite boundary city . Josh 13:9, 10, 16
Sihon ruled . Josh 12:2
Assigned to Reuben . Deut 3:12
Rebuilt by Gadites . Num 32:34
Beginning of David's census . 2Sam 24:5
Taken by Hazael . 2Kin 10:32
Possessed by Moab . Jer 48:19
2. A city of Judah . 1Sam 30:28
3. A city of Gad . Josh 13:25

[*also* AROERITE]
From ***A***..by the bank of . Deut 4:48
and in ***A*** and her towns . Judg 11:26
A which is by the river . 2Kin 10:33
son of Joel..dwelt in ***A*** . 1Chr 5:8
cities of ***A*** are forsaken . Is 17:2

AROERITE (ă-rō'ĕr-īte)—*a descendant of Aroer*
the sons of Hothan the ***A*** . 1Chr 11:44

AROMA—*a distinctive, pervasive, and usually pleasant smell*
Of sacrifices . Lev 26:31
Figurative of gifts . Phil 4:18

AROSE—*See* **ARISE**

ARPAD (är'păd)—*"strong"*
A town in Samaria . 2Kin 18:34
End of, predicted . Jer 49:23

[*also* ARPHAD]
Hamath and the king of ***A*** . 2Kin 19:13
not Hamath as ***A***? is not . Is 10:9
the gods of Hamath and ***A***? . Is 36:19
Hamath and the king of ***A*** . Is 37:13

ARPHAXAD (är'făk'săd)—*(meaning uncertain)*
A son of Shem . Gen. 10:22, 24
Born two years after the flood . Gen 11:10-13
An ancestor of Christ . Luke 3:36

begat ***A*** two years after the . Gen 11:10
A, and Lud, and Aram . 1Chr 1:17

ARRAY—*to arrange; to clothe; clothing*

[*also* ARRAYED]
a him in vestures of..linen . Gen 41:42
put themselves in ***a*** . Judg 20:20
put themselve in ***a*** . 1Sam 4:2
and set the battle in ***a*** . 1Sam 17:2
battle in ***a*** at the entering . 2Sam 10:8
servants, Set yourselves..***a*** . 1Kin 20:12
and put the battle in ***a*** . 1Chr 19:9

a in white linen, having 2Chr 5:12
Abijah set the battle in ***a*** 2Chr 13:3
and ***a*** them, and shod them ...2Chr 28:15
a the man withal whom the ...Esth 6:9
a Mordecai and brought ......Esth 6:11
set themselves in ***a*** against ....Job 6:4
set themselves in ***a*** at the .....Is 22:7
ride upon horses set, in ***a*** .....Jer 6:23
and he shall ***a*** himself with ....Jer 43:12
shall set themselves in ***a*** ......Jer 50:9
strong people set in battle ***a*** ...Joel 2:5
was not ***a*** like one of these ....Matt 6:29
was not ***a*** like one of these ....Luke 12:27
a him in a gorgeous robe .....Luke 23:11
Herod, ***a*** in royal apparel .....Acts 12:21
gold, or pearls or costly ***a*** 1Tim 2:9
these which are ***a*** in white ....Rev 7:13
woman was ***a*** in purple ....Rev 17:4
she should be ***a*** in fine linen ..Rev 19:8

ARRIVED
a at the country of the ....Luke 8:26
the next day we ***a*** at Samos ...Acts 20:15

ARROGANCE—*overbearing pride or presumption*
Mentioned with other evils ....Prov 8:13
To be punished by God ..Is 13:11
Seen in haughtiness ......Jer 48:29

[*also* ARROGANCY]
not ***a*** come out of your 1Sam 2:3

ARROW—*slender-shafted weapon shot from a bow*
Uses of:
Hunting ....Gen 27:3
Send message 1Sam 20:20-22
Divination ....Ezek 21:21
Prophecy 2Kin 13:14-19
War 2Kin 19:32
Described as:
Deadly ....Prov 26:18
Sharp ....Ps 120:4
Bright ....Jer 51:11
Like lightning ....Zech 9:14
Figurative of:
God's judgments ....Deut 32:23, 42
Intense affliction ....Job 6:4
Wicked intentions ....Ps 11:2
Messiah's mission........Ps 45:5
Bitter words ....Ps 64:3
God's power ....Ps 76:3
Daily hazards ....Ps 91:5
Children ....Ps 127:4
A false witness ....Prov 25:18
A deceitful tongue.......Jer 9:8

[*also* ARROWS]
pierce them..with his ***a***........Num 24:8
now the ***a*** which I shoot 1Sam 20:36
he shot an ***a*** beyond him 1Sam 20:36
lad gathered up the ***a*** 1Sam 20:38
he sent out ***a*** and scattered 2Sam 22:15
the ***a*** went out at his heart 2Kin 9:24
a of the Lord's deliverance 2Kin 13:17
in..stones and shooting ***a*** 1Chr 12:2
to shoot ***a*** and great stones 2Chr 26:15
a cannot make him flee ....Job 41:28
he ordaineth his ***a*** against .....Ps 7:13
Yea, he sent out his ***a*** ....Ps 18:14
thine ***a*** upon thy strings ....Ps 21:12
thine ***a*** stick fast in me........Ps 38:2
teeth are spears and ***a*** ....Ps 57:4
bendeth..bow to shoot his ***a*** ...Ps 58:7
shoot at them with an ***a*******.......Ps 64:7
shoot out thine ***a*** and ....Ps 144:6
Whose ***a*** are sharp ....Is 5:28
nor shoot an ***a*** there ....Is 37:33
a shall be as of a mighty ......Jer 50:9
shoot at her spare no ***a*** ....Jer 50:14
set me as a mark for the ***a*** ....Lam 3:12
caused the ***a*** of his quiver .....Lam 3:13
send upon them the evil ***a*******.....Ezek 5:16
will cause thine ***a*** to fall......Ezek 39:3
light of thine ***a*** they went .....Hab 3:11

ARSON—*maliciously setting fire to property*
Features concerning:
A law forbidding ....Ex 22:6
A means of revenge .....Judg 12:1
Instances of, by:
Samson ....Judg 15:4, 5
Danites ....Judg 18:27
Absalom 2Sam 14:30
Enemies ....Ps 74:7, 8

ART—*task requiring knowledge or skill*
Ointment after the ......Ex 30:25
Spices prepared by 2Chr 16:14
Stones graven by ....Acts 17:29

ART—*See* INTRODUCTION

ARTAXERXES (är-tŭk-sûrk'sēz)—*"fervent to spoil"*
Artaxerxes I, king of Persia (465-425 B.C.), authorizes Ezra's mission to Jerusalem ...Ezra 7:1-28
Temporarily halts rebuilding program at Jerusalem ....Ezra 4:7-23
Commissions Nehemiah's mission ....Neh 2:1-10
Permits Nehemiah to return ....Neh 13:6

Darius..***A*** kings of Persia ......Ezra 6:14
In the reign of ***A*** the king .....Ezra 8:1
two and thirtieth year of ***A*** ....Neh 5:14

ARTEMAS (är-tĕ'măs)—*"whole, sound"*
Paul's companion at Nicopolis ....Titus 3:12

ARTEMIS (är'tĕ-mĭs)—*the mother-goddess of Asia Minor*
Worship of, at Ephesus, creates uproar.........Acts 19:23-41

ARTIFICERS—*skilled or artistic workmen*
Tubal-cain, the earliest...Gen 4:22
Employed in temple construction 1Chr 29:5
Removed in judgment ...Is 3:1-3

Even to the ***a*** and builders 2Chr 34:11

ARTILLERY—*weapons that hurl projectiles*
gave his ***a*** unto his lad 1Sam 20:40

ARTS—*magical works*
also which used curious ***a*** .....Acts 19:19

ARTS AND CRAFTS IN THE BIBLE
Apothecary ....Ex 30:25, 35
Armorer 1Sam 8:12
Artificer ....Gen 4:22
Baker ....Gen 40:1
Barber ....Ezek 5:1
Brickmaker ....Ex 5:7
Calker ....Ezek 27:9
Carpenter ....Mark 6:3
Carver ....Ex 31:5
Confectioner 1Sam 8:13
Cook 1Sam 8:13
Coppersmith 2Tim 4:14
Draftsman ....Ezek 4:1
Dyer ....Ex 25:5
Embalmer ....Gen 50:2, 3
Embroiderer ....Ex 35:35
Engraver ....Ex 28:11
Fisherman ....Matt 4:18
Fuller ....Mark 9:3
Gardener ....John 20:15
Goldsmith ....Is 40:19
Husbandman ....Gen 4:2
Jeweler ....Ex 28:17-21
Lapidary ....Ex 35:33
Mariner ....Ezek 27:8, 9
Mason 2Sam 5:11
Moulder ....Ex 32:4
Musician 2Sam 6:5
Needleworker ....Ex 26:36
Painting ....Jer 22:14
Potter ....Jer 18:3
Porter 2Sam 18:26
Refiner ....Mal 3:2, 3
Ropemaker ....Judg 16:11
Sewing ....Ezek 13:18
Ship building...........1Kin 9:26
Silversmith ....Acts 19:24
Smelter ....Job 28:1, 2
Smith 1Sam 13:19
Spinner ....Prov 31:19
Stonecutter ....Ex 31:5
Tailor ....Ex 28:3, 4
Tanner ....Acts 10:6
Tentmaking ....Acts 18:3
Watchman 2Sam 18:26
Weaver ....Ex 35:35
Winemaker ....Neh 13:15
Worker in metal.........Ex 31:3, 4
Writer ....Judg 5:14

ARUBOTH (ä-rŭb'ŏth)—*"windows"*
A town in one of Solomon's districts.....1Kin 4:10

ARUMAH (ä-rōō'mä)—*"heights"*
A village near Shechem; Abimelech's refuge ....Judg 9:41

ARVAD (är'văd)—*"wandering"*
A Phoenician city built on an island north of Tyre ....Ezek 27:8, 11

ARVADITES (är'văd-īts)—*inhabitants of Arvad*
Of Canaanite ancestry ...Gen 10:18
1Chr 1:16

ARZA (är'zä)—*"firm"*
King Elah's steward in Tirzah 1Kin 16:9

AS—*See* INTRODUCTION

ASA (ā'sä)—*"physician; healer"*
1. Third king of Judah 1Kin 15:8-10
Reigns 10 years in peace .2Chr 14:1
Overthrows idolatry 2Chr 14:2-5
Removes his mother 1Kin 15:13
Fortifies Judah..........2Chr 14:6-8
Defeats the Ethiopians ..2Chr 14:9-15
Leads in national revival .2Chr 15:1-15
Hires Ben-hadad against Baasha 2Chr 16:1-6
Reproved by a prophet ..2Chr 16:7-10
Diseased, seeks physicians rather than the Lord 2Chr 16:12
Buried in Jerusalem 2Chr 16:13, 14
An ancestor of Christ ...Matt 1:7
2. A Levite among returnees 1Chr 9:16

[*also* ASA'S]
And ***A*** did..which was right ...1Kin 15:11
A heart was perfect 1Kin 15:14
war between ***A*** and Baasha....1Kin 15:16
to go out or come in to ***A***.....1Kin 15:17
A took..silver and..gold 1Kin 15:18
A sent them to Ben-hadad 1Kin 15:18
hearkened unto king ***A***........1Kin 15:20
king ***A*** made a proclamation...1Kin 15:22
and king ***A*** built with them 1Kin 15:22
rest of all the acts of ***A*** 1Kin 15:23
A slept with his fathers........1Kin 15:24
Israel..second year of ***A***.......1Kin 15:25
Even in the third year of ***A*** ...1Kin 15:28
war between ***A*** and Baasha....1Kin 15:32
In the third year of ***A*** king 1Kin 15:33
twenty and sixth year of ***A*** 1Kin 16:8
and seventh year of ***A*** 1Kin 16:10
thirty and first year of ***A*** 1Kin 16:23
thirty and eighth year of ***A*** 1Kin 16:29
the son of ***A*** began to reign ...1Kin 22:41
he walked in..the ways of ***A***...1Kin 22:43
in the days of his father ***A*** 1Kin 22:46
Abia his son, ***A*** his son 1Chr 3:10
the mother of ***A*** the king......2Chr 15:16
A cut down her idol and 2Chr 15:16
A was perfect all his days 2Chr 15:17

year of the reign of *A*.........2Chr 15:19
the acts of *A*, first and last 2Chr 16:11
A his father had taken 2Chr 17:2
walked in the way of *A* 2Chr 20:32
ways of *A* king of Judah 2Chr 21:12
which *A* the king had made ...Jer 41:9
and *A* begat Johoshaphat......Matt 1:8

ASAHEL (ăs'ä-hĕl)—*"God is doer; God has made"*
1. A son of Zeruiah, David's sister 1Chr 2:16
   Noted for valor 2Sam 2:18; 2Sam 23:24
   Pursues Abner..........2Sam 2:19
   Killed by Abner 2Sam 2:23
   Avenged by Joab 2Sam 3:27, 30
   Made a commander in David's army 1Chr 27:7
2. A Levite teacher........2Chr 17:8
3. A collector of tithes.....2Chr 31:13
4. A priest who opposes Ezra's reforms........Ezra 10:15

him and said, Art thou *A*? 2Sam 2:20
But *A* would not turn aside ...2Sam 2:21
And Abner said again to *A*....2Sam 2:22
nineteen men and *A* 2Sam 2:30
they took up *A* and buried 2Sam 2:32
were, *A* the brother of Joab ...1Chr 11:26

ASAIAH (ä-sā'yä)—*"Jehovah is doer; Jehovah has made"*
1. A Simeonite chief.......1Chr 4:36
2. A Levite during David's reign.................1Chr 6:30
   Helps restore ark to Jerusalem 1Chr 15:6, 11
3. An officer sent to Huldah 2Chr 34:20-22
4. Called Asahiah 2Kin 22:12-14
5. The first-born of the Shilonites 1Chr 9:5
   Probably called Maaseiah.Neh 11:5

ASAPH (ā'săf)—*"collector; gatherer"*
1. A Gershonite Levite choir leader in the time of David and Solomon...........1Chr 15:16-19; 1Chr 16:4-7; 2Chr 5:12
   Called a seer............2Chr 29:30
   Sons of, made musicians .1Chr 25:1-9
   Twelve Psalms assigned to.................Ps 50—83; 2Chr 29:30
   Descendants of, among returnees ....Ezra 2:41; Neh 7:44
   In dedication ceremony ..Ezra 3:10
2. The father of Hezekiah's recorder.............2Kin 18:18, 37
3. A chief forester whom Artaxerxes commands to supply timber to Nehemiah ....Neh 2:8
4. A Korhite Levite 1Chr 26:1
Also called Ebiasaph.......1Chr 9:19

[*also* ASAPH'S]
his brother *A*, who stood on...1Chr 6:39
right hand, even *A* the son 1Chr 6:39
the son of Zichri..son of *A* 1Chr 9:15
A..brethren, to minister 1Chr 16:37
son of Kore..sons of *A*........1Chr 26:1
a Levite of the sons of *A*......2Chr 20:14
of the sons of *A*; Zechariah ...2Chr 29:13
the sons of *A* were in their 2Chr 35:15
of David, and *A*..............2Chr 35:15
the son of *A* was..principal ....Neh 11:17
the sons of *A*, the singers .....Neh 11:22
son of Zaccur, the son of *A* ...Neh 12:35
days of David and *A* of old ...Neh 12:46
the scribe, and Joah *A* son ....Is 36:3
Joah, the son of *A* the ....Is 36:22

ASAREEL (ăs'ă-rēl)—*"God is joined or ruler"*
A son of Jehaleleel 1Chr 4:16

ASARELAH (ăs'ă-rē-lä)—*"Jehovah is joined; whom God has bound"*
A son of Asaph in David's time 1Chr 25:2
Called Jesharelah 1Chr 25:14

ASCENSION—*rising upward*

Descriptive of:
Physical rising of smoke ..Ex 19:18; Josh 8:20, 21
Going uphill ....Luke 19:28
Rising to heaven.........Ps 139:8
Christ's ascension ....John 6:62
Sinful ambition ....Is 14:13, 14

Of saints:
Enoch, translation of .....Gen 5:24; Heb 11:5
Elijah, translation of .....2Kin 2:11; Matt 17:1-9
Christians, at Christ's return 1Thess 4:13-18; 1Cor 15:51, 52

Of Christ:
Foretold in the Old Testament...........Ps 68:18; Eph 4:8-10
Announced by Christ ....Luke 9:51; John 20:17
Forty days after His resurrection ....Luke 24:48-51; Acts 1:1-12
Necessary for the Spirit's coming ....John 16:7
Enters heaven by redemption ....Heb 6:19, 20; Heb 9:12, 24
Crowned with glory and honor ....Heb 2:9
Rules from David's throne.................Acts 2:29-36
Sits at the Father's side ..Eph 1:20; Heb 1:3
Intercedes for the saints ..Rom 8:34
Preparing place of His people................John 14:2
Highly exalted ....Acts 5:31; Phil 2:9
Reigns triumphantly .....1Cor 15:24-28; Heb 10:12, 13
Exercises priestly ministry.Heb 4:14-16; Heb 8:1, 2

[*also* ASCEND, ASCENDED, ASCENDETH, ASCENDING, ASCENT]
angels of God *a* and ....Gen 28:12
And they *a* by the south ......Num 13:22
to the *a* of Akrabbim ....Num 34:4
and the people shall *a* up .....Josh 6:5
So Joshua *a* from Gilgal ......Josh 10:7
and *a* up on the south side ....Josh 15:3
the angel of the Lord *a* in.....Judg 13:20
flame of the city *a* up to .....Judg 20:40
I saw gods *a* out of the 1Sam 28:13
up by the *a* of Mount Olivet ..2Sam 15:30
and his *a* by which he went ...1Kin 10:5
and his *a* by which he went ...2Chr 9:4
Who shall *a* into the hill ......Ps 24:3
causeth the vapors to *a* ....Ps 135:7
a up into heaven ....Ps 139:8
Who hath *a* up into heaven ...Prov 30:4
causeth the vapors to *a* ....Jer 10:13
causeth the vapors to *a* ....Jer 51:16
the angels of God *a* and ......John 1:51
no man hath *a* up to heaven ..John 3:13
a from Caesarea to ....Acts 25:1
Who shall *a* into heaven? .....Rom 10:6
another angel *a* from the......Rev 7:2
a up before God out of ....Rev 8:4
a out of..bottomless pit ....Rev 11:7
their torment *a* up for ever....Rev 14:11
a out of..bottomless pit ....Rev 17:8

ASCETICISM—*strict self-discipline; denial of bodily appetites*

Forms of, seen in:
Nazarite vow...........Num 6:1-21
Manoah's wife ....Judg 13:3-14
Samson ....Judg 16:16, 17
Elijah's life 1Kin 19:4-9
The Rechabites..........Jer 35:1-19
John the Baptist.........Matt 3:4; Matt 11:18
Jesus Christ ....Matt 4:2
Paul....................1Cor 9:27

Teaching concerning:
Extreme, repudiated .....Luke 7:33-36
False, rejected ....Col 2:20-23; 1Tim 4:3, 4
Some necessary 1Cor 9:26, 27; 2Tim 2:3, 4
Temporary helpful.......Ezra 8:21-23; 1Cor 7:3-9
Figurative of complete consecration ....Matt 19:12; Rev 14:1-5

ASCRIBE—*to relate to a cause, source, or author*

[*also* ASCRIBED]
a ye greatness unto our God ..Deut 32:3
They have *a* unto David 1Sam 18:8
a righteousness to my.........Job 36:3
A ye strength unto God ....Ps 68:34

ASENATH (ăs'ĕ-năth)—*"dedicated to (the deity) Neith"*
Daughter of Potiphera and wife of Joseph ....Gen 41:45
Mother of Manasseh and Ephraim ....Gen 41:50-52; Gen 46:20

ASER—*See* ASHER

ASH—*a tree of the olive family*
Idols made from.........Is 44:14

ASHAMED—*feeling of shame, guilt, or disgrace*

Caused by:
Mistreatment............2Sam 10:4, 5
Sad tidings..............2Kin 8:11-13
Transgression ....Ps 25:3
Inconsistent action.......Ezra 8:22
Idolatry.................Is 44:9-17
Rebellion against God ...Is 45:24
Lewdness ....Ezek 16:27
False prophecy ....Zech 13:3, 4
Rejecting God's mercy ...Is 65:13
Unbelief................Mark 8:38
Unpreparedness 2Cor 9:4

Avoidance of, by:
Waiting for the Lord ....Ps 34:5; Is 49:23
Regarding God's commands ....Ps 119:6
Sound in statutes ....Ps 119:80
Trusting God ....Ps 25:20
Believing in Christ.......Rom 9:33; Rom 10:11
Christian diligence 2Tim 2:15
Assurance of faith 2Tim 1:12
Abiding in Christ 1John 2:28

Possible objects of, in the Christian's life:
Life's plans ....Phil 1:20
God's message 2Tim 1:8
The Gospel ....Rom 1:16
The old life ....Rom 6:21
One's faith..............1Pet 4:16

and were not *a*..............Gen 2:25
should she not be *a* seven .....Num 12:14
tarried till they were *a* ....Judg 3:25
people being *a* steal away 2Sam 19:3
urged him till he was *a* 2Kin 2:17
the men were greatly *a* 1Chr 19:5
and the Levites were *a*........2Chr 30:15
I am *a* and blush to lift up ....Ezra 9:6
came thither, and were *a*......Job 6:20
shall no man make thee *a*? ....Job 11:3
ye are not *a* that ye make .....Job 19:3
Let all mine enemies be *a*.....Ps 6:10
return and be *a* suddenly......Ps 6:10
in thee; let me not be *a*.......Ps 25:2
let them be *a* which ....Ps 25:3
let me never be *a* ....Ps 31:1
Let me not be *a*, O Lord .....Ps 31:17
let the wicked be *a* ....Ps 31:17
a and brought to confusion ....Ps 35:26
not be *a* in the evil time ......Ps 37:19

them be *a* and confounded ....Ps 40:14
that wait on thee..be *a*........Ps 69:6
them be *a* and confounded ....Ps 70:2
not the oppressed return *a* ....Ps 74:21
may see it and be *a* ....Ps 86:17
them be *a*..let thy servant .....Ps 109:28
and will not be *a* ....Ps 119:46
Let the proud be *a* ....Ps 119:78
let me not be *a* of my hope ...Ps 119:116
they shall not be *a* ....Ps 127:5
she that maketh *a* is as ....Prov 12:4
they shall be *a* of the oaks ....Is 1:29
be afraid and *a* of Ethiopia....Is 20:5
Be thou *a*, O Zidon ....Is 23:4
and the sun *a* ....Is 24:23
be *a* for their envy at the .....Is 26:11
Jacob shall not now be *a*......Is 29:22
They were all *a* of a people ...Is 30:5
Lebanon is *a* and hewn ....Is 33:9
shall be *a* and confounded ....Is 41:11
they shall be greatly *a* ....Is 42:17
shall be *a* and..confounded ....Is 45:16
not be *a* nor confounded ......Is 45:17
that I shall not be *a* ....Is 50:7
for thou shalt not be *a*........Is 54:4
they shall be *a* ....Is 66:5
thief is *a* when he is found ....Jer 2:26
so is the house of Israel *a*.....Jer 2:26
thou..shalt be *a* of Egypt......Jer 2:36
as thou wast *a* of Assyria .....Jer 2:36
thou refusedst to be *a* ....Jer 3:3
Were they *a* when they had ...Jer 6:15
they were not at all *a*.........Jer 6:15
The wise men are *a* ....Jer 8:9
Were they *a* when they ....Jer 8:12
a, neither could they blush ....Jer 8:12
shall be *a* of your enemies ....Jer 12:13
were *a* and confounded ....Jer 14:3
the plowmen were *a* ....Jer 14:4
been *a* and confounded ....Jer 15:9
all that forsake..be *a*.........Jer 17:13
they shall be greatly *a* ....Jer 20:11
surely then shalt thou be *a* ....Jer 22:22
I was *a*..even confounded .....Jer 31:19
Moab shall be *a* of Chemosh ..Jer 48:13
house of Israel was *a* of.......Jer 48:13
she that bare you shall be *a* ...Jer 50:12
remember thy ways, and be *a*. .Ezek 16:61
they are *a* of their might ......Ezek 32:30
be *a* and confounded for ......Ezek 36:32
be *a* of their iniquities ....Ezek 43:10
if they be *a* of all that ....Ezek 43:11
and they shall be *a* ....Hos 4:19
be *a* of his own counsel ....Hos 10:6
Be ye *a*, O ye husbandmen ...Joel 1:11
My people shall never be *a*....Joel 2:26
seers be *a* and the diviners ....Mic 3:7
that day shalt thou not be *a* ...Zeph 3:11
her expectation shall be *a* .....Zech 9:5
whosoever shall be *a* of me ....Luke 9:26
shall the Son of man be *a* ....Luke 9:26
all his adversaries were *a*......Luke 13:17
I cannot dig; to beg I am *a* ...Luke 16:3
maketh not *a*; because ....Rom 5:5
I am not *a* 2Cor 7:14
destruction..not be *a*..........2Cor 10:8
with him that he may be *a* 2Thess 3:14
and was not *a* of my chain 2Tim 1:16
the contrary part may be *a* ....Titus 2:8
not *a* to call them brethren....Heb 2:11
a to be called their God ......Heb 11:16
of evildoers, they may be *a* ...1Pet 3:16

ASHAN (ā'shăn)—*"smoke"—a town probably located northwest of Beersheba*
A city of Judah ....Josh 15:42
Later allotted to Judah...Josh 19:7
Assigned to the Levites ..1Chr 6:50

Rimmon, and Tochen, and *A* ..1Chr 4:32

ASHBEA (ăsh'bĕ-ä)—*"man of Baal"*
A descendant of Shelah ..1Chr 4:21

ASHBEL (ăsh'bĕl)—*"man of Baal"*
A son of Benjamin ......Gen 46:21; 1Chr 8:1
Progenitor of the Ashbelites ....Num 26:38

ASHCHENAZ (ăsh'kĕ-năz)—*"a fire that spreads"*
sons of Gomer, *A* and 1Chr 1:6
of Ararat, Minni, and *A* ......Jer 51:27
See ASHKENAZ

ASHDOD (ăsh'dŏd)—*"stronghold"*
One of five Philistine cities ....Josh 13:3
Anakim refuge ....Josh 11:22
Assigned to Judah ....Josh 15:46, 47
Seat of Dagon worship...1Sam 5:1-8
Captured by Tartan......Is 20:1
Opposed Nehemiah......Neh 4:7
Women of, marry Jews ..Neh 13:23, 24
Called a mingled people. .Jer 25:20
Called Azotus ....Acts 8:40

for *A* one, for Gaza one 1Sam 6:17
of *A*..built cities about *A* 2Chr 26:6
cut..the inhabitant from *A*.....Amos 1:8
Publish in the palaces at *A* ....Amos 3:9
drive out *A* at the noonday ....Zeph 2:4
a bastard shall dwell in *A* .....Zech 9:6

ASHDOTH-PISGAH (ăsh'dŏth-pĭz'gä)—*"springs of Pisgah; springs of the fortress"*
The slopes of Mount Pisgah .... Deut 3:17; Josh 12:3
Translated "springs" in. ..Deut 4:49

And Beth-peor, and *A* and ....Josh 13:20

ASHER, ASER (ăsh'er)—*"happy"*
1. Jacob's second son by Zilpah ....Gen 30:12, 13
   Goes to Egypt with Jacob ....Gen 46:17
   Father of five children...Gen 46:17
   Blessed by Jacob........Gen 49:20
2. The tribe fathered by Asher, Jacob's son ....Deut 33:24
   Census of ....Num 1:41; Num 26:47
   Tolerant of Canaanites ..Judg 1:31, 32
   Failure of, in national crisis................Judg 5:17
   Among Gideon's army ..Judg 6:35; Judg 7:23
   A godly remnant among .2Chr 30:11
   Anna, descendant of ....Luke 2:36-38
3. A town in Manasseh ....Josh 17:7

Leah's handmaid..and *A* ......Gen 35:26
Dan, and Naphtali..and *A* .....Ex 1:4
A, Pagiel the son of Ocran ....Num 1:13
of *A*, by their generations .....Num 1:40
shall be the tribe of *A* ....Num 2:27
captain of..children of *A* ......Num 2:27
prince of the children of *A* ....Num 7:72
tribe of the children of *A* .....Num 10:26
of *A*, Sethur the son of ....Num 13:13
children of *A* after their ....Num 26:44
daughter of *A* was Sarah ......Num 26:46
of *A*, Ahihud the son of ......Num 34:27
Reuben, Gad and *A* and ......Deut 27:13
Manasseh was from *A* to ......Josh 17:7
met together in *A* on the ......Josh 17:10
had in Issachar and in *A*.......Josh 17:11
tribe of the children of *A* .....Josh 19:24
tribe of the children of *A* .....Josh 19:31
reacheth to *A* on the west .....Josh 19:34
out of the tribe of *A* and ......Josh 21:6
A Mishal with her suburbs .....Josh 21:30
son of Hushai was in *A* and....1Kin 4:16
Benjamin, Naphtali..and *A*.....1Chr 2:2
out of the tribe of *A* 1Chr 6:62
of *A*; Mashal with her 1Chr 6:74
of *A*; Imnah and Isuah 1Chr 7:30
these..children of *A* 1Chr 7:40
of *A* such as went forth to 1Chr 12:36
west side a portion for *A* ......Ezek 48:2
of *A* from the east side ....Ezek 48:3
of *A*, one gate of Naphtali .....Ezek 48:34
of the tribe of *A*..............Luke 2:36
the tribe of *A* were sealed.....Rev 7:6

ASHERAH (ăsh'ē-räh)—*a goddess of the Phoenicians and Arameans*
1. Translated "groves," the female counterpart of Baal .... Judg 3:7; 1Kin 18:19
   Translated "Ashtaroth" (plural) in ....Judg 2:13
   Asa's mother worships ..1Kin 15:13
   Curtains for, made by women...............2Kin 23:7
   Vessels of, destroyed by Josiah...............2Kin 23:4
2. Translated "groves," the images (idols) made to Asherah...............2Kin 23:6
   Erected by Manasseh in the temple 2Kin 21:7
   Set up by Ahab in Samaria 1Kin 16:32, 33
3. Translated "groves," the trees or poles symbolizing the worship of Asherah.. Ex 34:13; Deut 12:3; Deut 16:21

ASHES
Used for:
A miracle...............Ex 9:8-10
Purification ....Num 19:1-10; Heb 9:13
A disguise 1Kin 20:38, 41
Symbolic of:
Mourning ....2Sam 13:19; Esth 4:1, 3
Dejection ....Job 2:8
Repentance ....Job 42:6; Matt 11:21
Fasting ....Dan 9:3
Figurative of:
Frailty ....Gen 18:27
Destruction ....Ezek 28:18
Victory ....Mal 4:3
Worthlessness ....Job 13:12
Transformation ....Is 61:3
Deceit ....Is 44:20
Afflictions ....Ps 102:9
Destruction ....Jer 6:26

pans to receive his *a* ....Ex 27:3
by the place of the *a* ....Lev 1:16
where the *a* are poured out ...Lev 4:12
where the *a* are poured out ...Lev 4:12
take up the *a* ....Lev 6:10
carry forth the *a*.............Lev 6:11
they shall take away the *a*.....Num 4:13
they shall take of the *a* ....Num 4:17
the *a* that are upon it 1Kin 13:3
a poured out from the altar ...1Kin 13:5
the *a* of them unto Beth-el 2Kin 23:4
I am become like dust and *a* ..Job 30:19
sackcloth and *a* under him ....Is 58:5
wallow yourselves in the *a* ....Jer 25:34
of the *a* and all the fields .....Jer 31:40
he hath covered me with *a* ....Lam 3:16
wallow themselves in the *a* ....Ezek 27:30
and sat in *a* ....Jon 3:6
sitting in sackcloth and *a*......Luke 10:13
Sodom and Gomorrah into *a* ..2Pet 2:6

ASHIMA (ä'shĭ-mă)—*"heaven"*
A god or idol worshiped by Assyrian colonists at Samaria 2Kin 17:30

ASHKELON (ăsh'kĕ-lŏn)—*"wandering"*
One of five Philistine cities .... Josh 13:3; Jer 47:5, 7
Captured by Judah .....Judg 1:18
Men of, killed by Samson.Judg 14:19
Repossessed by Philistines.1Sam 6:17; 2Sam 1:20
Doom of, pronounced by the prophets.......... Jer 47:5, 7; Amos 1:8; Zeph 2:4, 7; Zech 9:5

[*also* ASKELON]
A with the coast thereof .....Judg 1:18

for Gaza one, and *A* one for . . 1Sam 6:17
publish..not..streets of *A* 2Sam 1:20
A, and Azzah, and Ekron . . . . . Jer 25:20

ASHKENAZ (ăsh'kĕ-năz)—*"a fire that spreads"*
1. A descendant of Noah through Japheth . . . . {Gen 10:3 1Chr 1:6}
2. A nation (probably descendants of 1) associated with Ararat, Minni . . . . Jer 51:27
See ASCHENAZ

ASHNAH (ăsh'nä)—*"hard, firm"*
1. A village of Judah near Zorah . . . . Josh 15:33
2. Another village of Judah . Josh 15:43

ASHPENAZ (ăsh'pē-năz)
The chief of Nebuchadnezzar's eunuchs . . . . Dan 1:3

ASHRIEL (ăsh'rĭ-ĕl)—*"God is joined; vow of God"*
Manasseh; *A* whom she bare . . 1Chr 7:14

ASHTAROTH, ASTAROTH (ăsh'tä-rŏth; ăs'tä-rŏth)—*plural of Ashtoreth*
A city in Bashan; residence of King Og {Deut. 1:4 Josh 12:4}
Captured by Israel . . . . Josh 9:10
Assigned to Manasseh . . . Josh 13:31
Made a Levitical city ("Beeshterah") . . . . Josh 21:27
Uzzia, a native of 1Chr 11:44

Gilead, and *A* and Edrei . . . . . . Josh 13:31
have served Baalim and *A* 1Sam 12:10
and *A* with her suburbs 1Chr 6:71

ASHTEROTH-KARMAIN (ăsh'tĕ-rŏth-kär-nā'ĭm)—*"Ashtaroth of the two horns"*
A fortified city in Gilead occupied by the Rephaims . . . . Gen 14:5

ASHTORETH (ăsh'tō-rĕth)—*name given by the Hebrews to the goddess Ashtart (Astarte)*
A mother goddess of love, fertility and war worshiped by:
Philistines 1Sam 31:10
Sidonians 1Kin 11:5, 33
Israel's relation to:
Ensnared by . . . . Judg 2:13
Judg 10:6
Repent of, in Samuel's time 1Sam 7:3, 4
Worship of, by Solomon . 1Kin 11:5, 33
Destroyed by Josiah 2Kin 23:13
See ASHERAH

ASHUR (ăsh'ŭr)—*"free man; man of Horus"*
A descendant of Judah . . . 1Chr 2:24
1Chr 4:5-7

ASHURITES (ăsh-ŭr-ītes)
A people belonging to Ish-bosheth's kingdom . . 2Sam 2:8, 9

A have made thy benches . . . . . Ezek 27:6

ASHVATH (ăsh'văth)—*"made; wrought"*
An Asherite 1Chr 7:33

and *A*. These are the children. . 1Chr 7:33

ASIA—*in New Testament times, referred to Roman province incorporating the countries of western Asia Minor*
People from, at Pentecost. Acts 2:9, 10
Paul forbidden to preach in . . . . Acts 16:6
Paul's later ministry in . . . Acts 19:1-26
Paul plans to pass by . . . . Acts 20:16, 17
Converts in, greeted by Paul . . . . Rom 16:5
Paul's great conflict in . . . 2Cor 1:8
Paul writes to saints of . . . 1Pet 1:1
Seven churches of . . . . Rev 1:4, 11

all *A* and the world . . . . Acts 19:27
certain of the chief of *A* . . . . Acts 19:31
accompanied him into *A* . . . . . . Acts 20:4
A, Tychicus and Trophimus . . . Acts 20:4
the Jews which were of *A* . . . . . Acts 21:27
certain Jews from *A* . . . . Acts 24:18
by the coasts of *A* . . . . Acts 27:2
churches of *A* salute you 1Cor 16:19
which came to us in *A* 2Cor 1:8
all they which are in *A* 2Tim 1:15

ASIDE—*to one side*
the Lord saw..he turned *a* . . . . . Ex 3:4
have turned *a* quickly out . . . . . Ex 32:8
if thou hast not gone *a* . . . . Num 5:19
if thou hast gone *a* . . . . Num 5:20
when a wife goeth *a* . . . . Num 5:29
and the ass turned *a* . . . . Num 22:23
are quickly turned *a* out of . . . . Deut 9:12
had turned *a* quickly out of . . . Deut 9:16
ye turn *a*..serve other gods . . . . Deut 11:16
but turn *a* out of the way . . . . . Deut 11:28
that he turn not *a* from the . . . Deut 17:20
shalt not go *a* from any . . . . Deut 28:14
corrupt yourselves..turn *a* . . . . . Deut 31:29
ye turn not *a* therefrom . . . . Josh 23:6
turned *a* to see the carcase . . . . Judg 14:8
We will not turn *a* hither . . . . . Judg 19:12
they turned *a* thither to go . . . . Judg 19:15
Ho, such a one! turn *a*, sit . . . . Ruth 4:1
he turned *a* and sat down . . . . . Ruth 4:1
but turned *a* after lucre 1Sam 8:3
turn not *a* from following 1Sam 12:20
turn ye not *a*: for then 1Sam 12:21
Turn..*a* to thy right hand 2Sam 2:21
Asahel would not turn *a* 2Sam 2:21
Turn thee *a* from following 2Sam 2:22
he refused to turn *a* 2Sam 2:23
when..Joab took him *a* in 2Sam 3:27
but David carried it *a* 2Sam 6:10
Turn *a* and stand there 2Sam 18:30
turned *a* and stood still 2Sam 18:30
behold, a man turned *a* 1Kin 20:39
And they turned *a* to fight 1Kin 22:32
he turned not *a* from it 1Kin 22:43
shalt set *a* that which is 2Kin 4:4
carried it *a* into the house 1Chr 13:13
of their way are turned *a* . . . . . Job 6:18
They are all gone *a* . . . . Ps 14:3
nor such as turn *a* to lies . . . . . . Ps 40:4
turned *a* like a deceitful . . . . Ps 78:57
work of them that turn *a* . . . . . . Ps 101:3
is thy beloved turned *a*? . . . . . . Song 6:1
turn *a* the just for a thing . . . . . Is 29:21
turn *a* out of the path . . . . Is 30:11
heart hath turned him *a* . . . . Is 44:20
a wayfaring man..turneth *a* . . . . Jer 14:8
shall go *a* to ask how thou . . . . Jer 15:5
turn *a* the right of a man . . . . . Lam 3:35
turn *a* the way of the meek . . . Amos 2:7
they turn *a* the poor . . . . Amos 5:12
that turn *a* the stranger . . . . Mal 3:5
turned *a* into the parts of . . . . . Matt 2:22
laying *a* the commandment . . . . Mark 7:8
a from the multitude . . . . Mark 7:33
and went *a* privately . . . . Luke 9:10
went with him *a* privately . . . . . Acts 23:19
when they were gone *a* . . . . Acts 26:31
turned *a* unto vain jangling 1Tim 1:6
let us lay *a* every weight . . . . . . Heb 12:1

ASIEL (ā'sĭ-ĕl)—*"God is doer or maker"*
A Simeonite 1Chr 4:35

ASK—*to question; make a request of*
[*also* ASKED, ASKEST, ASKETH, ASKING]
And I *a* her and said . . . . Gen 24:47
the men of the place *a* him . . . . Gen 26:7
my brother meeteth thee..*a* . . . Gen 32:17
thou dost *a* after my name . . . . Gen 32:29
And Jacob *a* him . . . . Gen 32:29
A me never so much dowry . . . Gen 34:12
and the man *a* him . . . . Gen 37:15
he *a* the men of that place . . . . Gen 38:21
And he *a* Pharaoh's officers . . . Gen 40:7
The man *a* us straitly . . . . Gen 43:7

My lord *a* his servants . . . . Gen 44:19
when thy son *a* thee . . . . Ex 13:14
a each..of their welfare . . . . Ex 18:7
who shall *a* counsel for him . . . Num 27:21
a now of the days that are . . . . Deut 4:32
thy son *a* thee in time to . . . . . . Deut 6:20
and make search, and *a* . . . . Deut 13:14
a thy father, and he will . . . . . . Deut 32:7
children *a* their fathers . . . . Josh 4:6
a not counsel at the mouth . . . . Josh 9:14
she moved him to *a* of her . . . . Josh 15:18
gave him the city which he *a* . . Josh 19:50
that..children of Israel *a* . . . . . . Judg 1:1
she moved him to *a* of her . . . . Judg 1:14
a water and she gave him . . . . . Judg 5:25
when they inquired and *a* . . . . . Judg 6:29
I *a* him not whence he was . . . . Judg 13:6
Why *a* thou thus after my . . . . . Judg 13:18
A counsel, we pray thee, of . . . Judg 18:5
and *a* counsel of God . . . . Judg 20:18
thy petition..thou hast *a* 1Sam 1:17
the people that *a* of him 1Sam 8:10
in *a* you a king 1Sam 12:17
sins this evil, to *a* us a king . . . 1Sam 12:19
And Saul *a* counsel of God . . . 1Sam 14:37
and he *a* and said 1Sam 19:22
David earnestly *a* leave 1Sam 20:6
A thy young men, and they . . . 1Sam 25:8
thing that I shall *a* thee 2Sam 14:18
surely *a* counsel at Abel 2Sam 20:18
I *a* one petition of thee 1Kin 2:16
A what I shall give thee 1Kin 3:5
Solomon had *a* this thing 1Kin 3:10
whatsoever she *a* 1Kin 10:13
cometh to *a* a thing of thee . . . 1Kin 14:5
A what I shall do for thee 2Kin 2:9
Thou hast *a* a hard thing 2Kin 2:10
when the king *a* the woman . . . 2Kin 8:6
a counsel of one that had 1Chr 10:13
thou hast not *a* riches 2Chr 1:11
neither yet hast *a* long life 2Chr 1:11
a wisdom and knowledge 2Chr 1:11
her desire, whatsoever she *a* . . . 2Chr 9:12
to *a* help of the Lord 2Chr 20:4
Then *a* we those elders . . . . Ezra 5:9
a them concerning the Jews . . . Neh 1:2
a now the beasts and they . . . . . Job 12:7
Have ye not *a* them that go . . . Job 21:29
A of me and I shall give . . . . . . Ps 2:8
He *a* life of thee . . . . Ps 21:4
tempted God..by *a* meat . . . . . . Ps 78:18
people *a* and he brought . . . . . . Ps 105:40
A thee a sign of the Lord . . . . . Is 7:11
have not *a* at my mouth . . . . . . Is 30:2
I *a* of them, could answer . . . . . Is 41:28
A me of things to come . . . . Is 45:11
a of me the ordinances of . . . . . Is 58:2
sought of them that *a* not . . . . . Is 65:1
and *a* for the old paths . . . . Jer 6:16
who shall go aside to *a* how . . Jer 15:5
A ye..among the heathen . . . . . . Jer 18:13
prophet..priest, shall *a* . . . . Jer 23:33
A ye now, and see . . . . Jer 30:6
they *a* Baruch . . . . Jer 36:17
the king *a* him secretly in . . . . . Jer 37:17
I will *a* thee a thing . . . . Jer 38:14
princes unto Jeremiah, and *a* . . Jer 38:27
a him that fleeth . . . . Jer 48:19
shall *a* the way to Zion . . . . Jer 50:5
the young children *a* bread . . . . Lam 4:4
a..things at any magician . . . . . . Dan 2:10
whosoever shall *a* a petition . . . Dan 6:7
a him the truth of all this . . . . . Dan 7:16
people *a* counsel at their . . . . . . Hos 4:12
earnestly, the prince *a* . . . . Mic 7:3
A ye of the Lord rain . . . . Zech 10:1
Give to him that *a* thee . . . . Matt 5:42
need of, before ye *a* him . . . . . . Matt 6:8
A, and it shall be given . . . . Matt 7:7
they *a* him, saying . . . . Mat 12:10
give..whatsoever she would *a* . . Matt 14:7
he *a* his disciples, saying . . . . . . Matt 16:13
his disciples *a* him, saying . . . . . Matt 17:10
any thing that they shall *a* . . . . . Matt 18:19
said, Ye know not what ye *a* . . Matt 20:22

whatsoever ye..**a** in prayer ... Matt 21:22
no resurrection, and **a** him ... Matt 22:23
a him any more questions ... Matt 22:46
the governor **a** him, saying ... Matt 27:11
they should **a** Barabbas ... Matt 27:20
about him with the twelve **a** ... Mark 4:10
And he **a** him, What is thy ... Mark 5:9
A of me whatsoever thou ... Mark 6:22
the king, and **a** saying ... Mark 6:25
Pharisees and scribes **a** him ... Mark 7:5
a them, How many loaves ... Mark 8:5
they **a** him saying, Why say ... Mark 9:11
and were afraid to **a** him ... Mark 9:32
came to him, and **a** him ... Mark 10:2
Ye know not what ye **a** ... Mark 10:38
I will..**a** of you one question ... Mark 11:29
no resurrection; and they **a** ... Mark 12:18
no man after that durst **a** ... Mark 12:34
John and Andrew **a** him ... Mark 13:3
the midst, and **a** Jesus ... Mark 14:60
And Pilate **a** him, Art thou ... Mark 15:2
he **a** for a writing table and ... Luke 1:63
them, and **a** them questions ... Luke 2:46
the people **a** him saying ... Luke 3:10
I will **a** you one thing; Is ... Luke 6:9
Give to every man that **a** of ... Luke 6:30
his disciples **a** him saying ... Luke 8:9
he **a** them, saying, Whom ... Luke 9:18
they feared to **a** him of that ... Luke 9:45
A and it shall be given you ... Luke 11:9
of him they will **a** the more ... Luke 12:48
a what these things meant ... Luke 15:26
certain ruler **a** him, saying ... Luke 18:18
if any man **a** you ... Luke 19:31
I will also **a** you one thing ... Luke 20:3
they **a** him, saying, Master ... Luke 20:21
they **a** him, saying, Master ... Luke 21:7
a him, saying, Prophesy ... Luke 22:64
And if I also **a** you ... Luke 22:68
Pilate **a** him, saying, Art ... Luke 23:3
from Jerusalem to **a** him ... John 1:19
And they **a** him, What then ... John 1:21
being a Jew, **a** drink of me ... John 4:9
wouldest have **a** of him ... John 4:10
a they him, What man is ... John 5:12
So when they continued **a** ... John 8:7
his disciples **a** him ... John 9:2
is of age, **a** him, he shall ... John 9:21
parents, He is of age, **a** ... John 9:23
whatsoever thou wilt **a** of ... John 11:22
that he should **a** who it ... John 13:24
none of you **a** me ... John 16:5
they were desirous to **a** him ... John 16:19
ye **a** nothing in my name ... John 16:24
Then **a** he them again ... John 18:7
Why **a** thou me? ask them ... John 18:21
none..disciples durst **a** ... John 21:12
they **a** of him, saying, Lord ... Acts 1:6
to **a** alms of them that ... Acts 3:2
to go into the temple **a** an ... Acts 3:3
they **a**, By what power, or ... Acts 4:7
and the high priest **a** them ... Acts 5:27
and **a** whether Simon ... Acts 10:18
a therefore for what intent ... Acts 10:29
aside privately, and **a** him ... Acts 23:19
I **a** him whether he would ... Acts 25:20
unto them that **a** not after ... Rom 10:20
a no question for conscience ... 1Cor 10:25
let them **a** their husbands ... 1Cor 14:35
above all that we **a** or think ... Eph 3:20
every man that **a** you ... 1Pet 3:15
not unto death, he shall **a** ... 1John 5:16

ASKELON—*See* ASHKELON

ASKING IN PRAYER

Based upon:
God's foreknowledge ... Matt 6:8
God's willingness ... Luke 11:11-13
God's love ... John 16:23-27
Abiding in Christ ... John 15:7

Receiving of answer, based upon:
Having faith ... James 1:5, 6
Keeping God's commands. 1John 3:22
Regarding God's will ... 1John 5:14, 15
Believing trust ... Matt 21:22
Unselfishness ... James 4:2, 3
In Christ's name ... John 14:13, 14; John 15:16

ASLEEP—*a state of sleep or death*
he was fast **a** and weary ... Judg 4:21
for they were all **a** ... 1Sam 26:12
those that are **a** to speak ... Song 7:9
and he lay, and was fast **a** ... Jon 1:5
but he was **a** ... Matt 8:24
and findeth them **a** ... Matt 26:40
a on a pillow; and they ... Mark 4:38
as they sailed he fell **a** ... Luke 8:23
he had said this, he fell **a** ... Acts 7:60
but some are fallen **a** ... 1Cor 15:6
them which are **a** ... 1Thess 4:13
since the fathers fell **a**, all ... 2Pet 3:4

ASNAH (ăs′nä)—*"thornbush"*
The head of a family of Nethinims ... Ezra 2:50

ASNAPPER (ăs-năp′pĕr)—*believed to have been Ashurbanipal, king of Assyria*
Called "the great and noble" ... Ezra 4:10

ASP—*a deadly snake*
Figurative of man's evil nature ... Deut 32:33; Rom 3:13
Figurative of man's changed nature ... Is 11:8

[*also* ASPS]
the cruel venom of **a** ... Deut 32:33
the gall of **a** within him ... Job 20:14
shall suck the poison of **a** ... Job 20:16
play on the hole of the **a** ... Is 11:8
poison of **a** is under their lips. . Rom 3:13

ASPATHA (ăs-pā′thä)—*"horse-given"*
A son of Haman ... Esth 9:7

ASPIRATION—*exalted desire combined with holy zeal*

Centered in:
God Himself ... Ps 42:1, 2
God's kingdom ... Matt 6:33
The high calling ... Phil 3:10-14
Heaven ... Col 3:1, 2
Acceptableness with Christ ... 2Tim 2:4

Inspired by:
Christ's love ... 2Cor 5:14-16
Work yet to be done ... Rom 15:18-20; 2Cor 10:13-18
Christ's grace ... 2Cor 12:9-15
The reward ... 2Tim 4:7, 8
The Lord's return ... Matt 24:42-47; 1John 3:1-3
World's end ... 2Pet 3:11-14

ASRIEL (ăs′rĭ-ĕl)—*"God is joined; vow of God"*
A descendant of Manasseh and progenitor of the Asrielites ... Num 26:31; Josh 17:2; 1Chr 7:14

ASS—*donkey*

Used for:
Riding ... Gen 22:3
Carrying burdens ... Gen 42:26
Food ... 2Kin 6:25
Royalty ... Judg 5:10

Regulations concerning:
Not to be yoked with an ox ... Deut 22:10
To be rested on Sabbath. . Ex 23:12; Luke 13:15
To be redeemed with a lamb ... Ex 34:20

Special features regarding:
Spoke to Balaam ... Num 22:28-31
Knowing his owner ... Is 1:3
Jawbone kills many ... Judg 15:15-17
Jesus rides upon one ... Zech 9:9; Matt 21:2, 5
All cared for by God ... Ps 104:11

Figurative of:
Wildness (in Hebrew, "wild ass") ... Gen 16:12
Stubbornness ... Hos 8:9
Promiscuity ... Jer 2:24

[*also* ASSES, ASS'S]
he **a**, and menservants ... Gen 12:16
maidservants..and **a** ... Gen 24:35
menservants..and **a** ... Gen 30:43
I have oxen, and **a**, flocks ... Gen 32:5
their oxen, and their **a** ... Gen 34:28
as he fed the **a** of Zibeon ... Gen 36:24
give his **a** provender in the ... Gen 42:27
for bondmen, and our **a** ... Gen 43:18
sent away, they and their **a** ... Gen 44:3
laded every man his **a** ... Gen 44:13
ten **a** laden with the good ... Gen 45:23
herds, and for the **a** ... Gen 47:17
his **a** colt unto the choice ... Gen 49:11
is a strong **a** couching ... Gen 49:14
set them upon an **a** ... Ex 4:20
upon the horses, upon the **a** ... Ex 9:3
firstling of an **a** thou shalt ... Ex 13:13
nor his ox, nor his **a**, nor ... Ex 20:17
an ox or an **a** fall therein ... Ex 21:33
whether it be ox, or **a**, or ... Ex 22:4
enemy's ox or his **a** going ... Ex 23:4
firstling of an **a** thou shalt ... Ex 34:20
I have not taken one **a** from ... Num 16:15
and saddled his **a** and went ... Num 22:21
of the beeves, and of the **a** ... Num 31:28
nor thine ox, nor thine **a** ... Deut 5:14
shalt thou do with his **a** ... Deut 22:3
thine **a** shall be violently ... Deut 28:31
ox and sheep, and **a** with ... Josh 6:21
his oxen, and his **a** ... Josh 7:24
took old sacks upon their **a** ... Josh 9:4
she lighted from off her **a** ... Judg 1:14
sons that rode on thirty **a** ... Judg 10:4
threescore and ten **a** colts ... Judg 12:14
with him, and a couple of **a** ... Judg 19:3
man took her up upon an **a** ... Judg 19:28
young men, and your **a** ... 1Sam 8:16
a of Kish, Saul's father were ... 1Sam 9:3
a which thou wentest to ... 1Sam 10:2
or whose **a** have I taken? ... 1Sam 12:3
ox and sheep, camel and **a** ... 1Sam 15:3
Jesse took an **a** laden with ... 1Sam 16:20
oxen, and **a**, and sheep ... 1Sam 22:19
laid them on **a** ... 1Sam 25:18
she rode on the **a** ... 1Sam 25:20
oxen, and the **a**, and the ... 1Sam 27:9
with a couple of **a** saddled ... 2Sam 16:1
he saddled his **a**, and arose ... 2Sam 17:23
I will saddle me an **a** ... 2Sam 19:26
Shimel arose..saddled his **a** ... 1Kin 2:40
Saddle me the **a** ... 1Kin 13:13
young men, and one of the **a** ... 2Kin 4:22
Then she saddled an **a** ... 2Kin 4:24
their horses, and their **a** ... 2Kin 7:7
and of **a** two thousand ... 1Chr 5:21
brought bread on **a** ... 1Chr 12:40
and over the **a** was Jehdeiah ... 1Chr 27:30
all the feeble of them upon **a** ... 2Chr 28:15
a, six thousand seven hundred . Ezra 2:67
seven hundred and twenty **a** ... Neh 7:69
in sheaves, and lading **a** ... Neh 13:15
five hundred she **a** ... Job 1:3
Doth the wild **a** bray ... Job 6:5
be born like a wild **a** colt ... Job 11:12
away the **a** of the fatherless ... Job 24:3
as wild **a** in the desert ... Job 24:5
sent out the wild **a** free? ... Job 39:5
a thousand she **a** ... Job 42:12
wild **a** quench their thirst ... Ps 104:11
a bridle for the **a** ... Prov 26:3
a chariot of **a**, and a chariot ... Is 21:7
the shoulders of young **a** ... Is 30:6
wild **a**, a pasture of flocks ... Is 32:14
feet of the ox and the **a** ... Is 32:20
a did stand in the high ... Jer 14:6

with the burial of an *a* . . . . Jer 22:19
flesh is as the flesh of *a* . . . . . . Ezek 23:20
dwelling was with the wild *a* . . . Dan 5:21
of the camel, and of the *a* . . . . Zech 14:15
you shall have an *a* or . . . . Luke 14:5
he had found a young *a* . . . . . . John 12:14
cometh, sitting on an *a* colt . . John 12:15
a speaking with man's 2Pet 2:16

ASSASSINATION—*to murder by sudden or secret attack*

Actual cases of:
Eglon by Ehud . . . . Judg 3:21
Sisera by Jael . . . . Judg 4:17-21
Abner by Joab 2Sam 3:27
Ish-bosheth by sons of Rimmon 2Sam 4:5-8
Amnon by Absalom 2Sam 13:28, 29
Absalom by Joab 2Sam 18:14
Amasa by Joab 2Sam 20:10
Elah by Zimri 1Kin 16:10
Ben-hadad by Hazael 2Kin 8:7, 15
Jehoram by Jehu 2Kin 9:24
Ahaziah by Jehu 2Kin 9:27
Jezebel by Jehu 2Kin 9:30-37
Joash by servants 2Kin 12:20, 21
Zechariah by Shallum 2Kin 15:10
Shallum by Menahem 2Kin 15:14
Pekahiah by Pekah 2Kin 15:25
Pekah by Hoshea 2Kin 15:30
Amon by servants 2Kin 21:23
Gedaliah by Ishmael 2Kin 25:25
Sennacherib by his sons . . 2Kin 19:37

Attempted cases of:
Jacob by Esau . . . . Gen 27:41-45
Joseph by his brothers . . . Gen 37:18-22
David by Saul 1Sam 19:10-18
David by Absalom 2Sam 15:10-14
Joash by Athaliah 2Kin 11:1-3
Ahasuerus by servants . . . Esth 2:21-23
Jesus by the Jews . . . . Luke 4:28-30; John 7:1
Paul by the Jews . . . . Acts 9:23-25; Acts 23:12-31

Crime of:
Against God's image in man . . . . Gen 9:6
Punishable by death . . . . . Ex 21:12-15; Num 35:33
Not to be condoned . . . . . Deut 19:11-13
Puts the guilty under a curse . . . . Deut 27:24
Abhorred by the righteous 2Sam 4:4-12

ASSAULT—*a violent attack; to make attack on*

[*also* ASSAULTED]
people..that would *a* them . . . . Esth 8:11
when there was an *a* made . . . . Acts 14:5
a the house of Jason, and . . . . . Acts 17:5

ASSAY—*to attempt; an attempt*

[*also* ASSAYED, ASSAYING]
hath God *a* to go and take . . . . Deut 4:34
he *a* to go; for he had not 1Sam 17:39
If we *a* to commune with . . . . . Job 4:2
a to join himself to the . . . . Acts 9:26
they *a* to go into Bithynia . . . . . Acts 16:7
Egyptians *a* to do were . . . . . . Heb 11:29

ASSEMBLY—*a gathering of people*

Descriptive of:
Israel as a people . . . . Num 10:2-8
Israel as a nation . . . . Judg 20:2; 2Chr 30:23
God's elect people . . . . Ps 111:1
A civil court . . . . Acts 19:32-41
A church gathering . . . . . . James 2:2

Purposes of:
Proclaim war . . . . Judg 10:17, 18; 1Sam 14:20
Establish the ark in Zion . 1Kin 8:1-6
Institute reforms . . . . Ezra 9:4-15; Neh 9:1, 2
Celebrate victory . . . . Esth 9:17, 18
Condemn Christ . . . . Matt 26:3, 4, 57
Worship God . . . . Acts 4:31; Heb 10:25

Significant ones, at:
Sinai . . . . Ex 19:1-19
Joshua's farewell . . . . Josh 23:1-16; Josh 24:1-28
David's coronation 2Sam 5:1-3
The Temple's dedication . 2Chr 5:1-14
Josiah's reformation 2Kin 23:1-3, 21, 22
Ezra's reading the Law. . . Neh 8:1-18
Jesus' trial . . . . Matt 27:11-26
Pentecost . . . . Acts 2:1-21
The Jerusalem Council . . . Acts 15:5-21

[*also* ASSEMBLE, ASSEMBLED, ASSEMBLIES, ASSEMBLING]
their secret; unto their *a* . . . . . Gen 49:6
a of the congregation of . . . . . . Ex 12:6
this whole *a* with hunger . . . . . . Ex 16:3
glasses of the women *a* . . . . Ex 38:8
a at the door of the . . . . Ex 38:8
hid from the eyes of the *a* . . . . Lev 4:13
a was gathered together . . . . Lev 8:4
it is a solemn *a* . . . . Lev 23:36
they *a* all the congregation . . . . Num 1:18
shalt gather the whole *a* . . . . . . Num 8:9
shall *a* themselves to thee . . . . . Num 10:3
their faces before all the *a* . . . . Num 14:5
princes of the *a* famous . . . . Num 16:2
from the presence of the *a* . . . . Num 20:6
ye shall have a solemn *a* . . . . . . Num 29:35
Lord spake unto all your *a* . . . . Deut 5:22
fire in the day of the *a* . . . . Deut 9:10
fire in the day of the *a* . . . . Deut 10:4
a solemn *a* to the Lord thy . . . . Deut 16:8
Horeb in the day of the *a* . . . . . Deut 18:16
congregation..*a* together . . . . . . Josh 18:1
a at the door of the 1Sam 2:22
the people..*a* themselves 1Sam 14:20
this *a* shall know that the 1Sam 17:47
A me the men of Judah 2Sam 20:4
he *a* all the house of Judah . . . 1Kin 12:21
Proclaim a solemn *a* for 2Kin 10:20
David *a* the children 1Chr 15:4
David *a* all the princes of 1Chr 28:1
they made a solemn *a* 2Chr 7:9
they *a* themselves in the 2Chr 20:26
a at Jerusalem much 2Chr 30:13
there *a* unto him..a very . . . . . . Ezra 10:1
And I set a great *a* against . . . . Neh 5:7
children of Israel were *a* . . . . . . Neh 9:1
a of the wicked have . . . . Ps 22:16
kings were *a*, they passed . . . . . Ps 48:4
and the *a* of violent men . . . . . . Ps 86:14
feared in the *a* of the saints . . . Ps 89:7
praise him in the *a* of the . . . . . Ps 107:32
of the congregation and *a* . . . . . Prov 5:14
fastened by the masters of *a* . . . Eccl 12:11
calling of *a*, I cannot away . . . . Is 1:13
her *a*, a cloud and smoke by . . Is 4:5
a the outcasts of Israel . . . . Is 11:12
and let the people be *a* . . . . Is 43:9
A yourselves and come . . . . Is 45:20
All ye, *a* yourselves, and . . . . . . Is 48:14
A yourselves and let us . . . . Jer 4:5
and *a* themselves by troops . . . . Jer 5:7
do we sit still? *a* yourselves . . . Jer 8:14
an *a* of treacherous men . . . . . . Jer 9:2
a all the beasts of the field . . . . Jer 12:9
I sat not in the *a* of the . . . . Jer 15:17
and I will *a* them into the . . . . . Jer 21:4
to all the *a* of the people . . . . . Jer 26:17
Babylon an *a* of great . . . . Jer 50:9
he hath called an *a* against . . . . Lam 1:15
destroyed his places of the *a* . . Lam 2:6
a you out of the countries . . . . . Ezek 11:17
not be in the *a* of my people . . Ezek 13:9
and with an *a* of people . . . . Ezek 23:24
company that are *a* unto . . . . . . Ezek 38:7
A yourselves, and come . . . . Ezek 39:17
my statutes in all mine *a* . . . . . . Ezek 44:24
presidents and princes *a* . . . . Dan 6:6
a a multitude of great . . . . Dan 11:10
they *a* themselves for corn . . . . Hos 7:14
call a solemn *a*, gather the . . . . Joel 1:14
a fast, call a solemn *a* . . . . Joel 2:15
Gather the people..*a* the . . . . . . Joel 2:16
A yourselves, and come, all . . . Joel 3:11
A yourselves upon the . . . . Amos 3:9
not smell in your solemn *a* . . . . Amos 5:21
a, O Jacob, all of thee . . . . Mic 2:12
will I *a* her that halteth . . . . Mic 4:6
that I may *a* the kingdoms . . . . Zeph 3:8
sorrowful for the solemn *a* . . . . Zeph 3:18
they were *a* with the elders . . . . Matt 28:12
were *a* all the chief priests . . . . Mark 14:53
where the disciples were *a* . . . . John 20:19
And being *a* together with . . . . Acts 1:4
a themselves with the . . . . Acts 11:26
being *a* with one accord . . . . Acts 15:25
a and church of..firstborn . . . . . Heb 12:23

ASSENT—*to agree to the truth of a statement or fact; act of assenting*

Concerning good things:
Accepting God's covenant . . . . Ex 19:7, 8
Agreeing to reforms . . . . . 1Sam 7:3, 4; Ezra 10:1-12, 19
Accepting a Scriptural decision . . . . Acts 15:13-22
Receiving Christ as Savior . . . . Rom 10:9, 10

Concerning evil things:
Tolerating idolatry . . . . Jer 44:15-19
Condemning Christ to death . . . . Matt 27:17-25
Putting Stephen to death. . Acts 7:51-60
Refusing to hear the Gospel . . . . Acts 13:44-51

[*also* ASSENTED]
good to the king with one *a* . . . 2Chr 18:12
And the Jews also *a* saying . . . . Acts 24:9

ASSHUR (äs'shŏŏr)—*"level plain"*

1. One of the sons of Shem; progenitor of the Assyrians . . . . Gen 10:22; 1Chr 1:17
2. The chief god of the Assyrians; seen in names like Ashurbanipal (Asnapper) . . . . Ezra 4:10
3. A city in Assyria or the nation of Assyria . . . . Num 24:22, 24; Ps 83:8; Ezek 27:23; Ezek 32:22

[*also* ASSUR]
of that land went forth *A* . . . . . Gen 10:11
of Esar-haddon king of *A* . . . . . Ezra 4:2
A shall not save us; we will . . . Hos 14:3

ASSHURIM (ă-shŏŏ'rĭm)—*"mighty ones"*
Descendants of Abraham by Keturah . . . . Gen 25:3

ASSIGNED—*transferred or given to another*
priests had a portion *a* them . . . Gen 47:22
a Bezer in the wilderness . . . . . Josh 20:8
that he *a* Uriah unto a place . . 2Sam 11:16

ASSIR (ăs'er)—*"prisoner"*

1. A son of Korah . . . . Ex 6:24; 1Chr 6:22
2. A son of Ebiasaph 1Chr 6:23, 37
3. A son of King Jeconiah. . 1Chr 3:17

ASSIST—*to give help or aid*
and that ye *a* her in . . . . Rom 16:2

ASSISTANCE, DIVINE

Offered, in:
Battle 2Chr 20:5-15
Trouble . . . . Ps 50:15
Crises . . . . Luke 21:14, 15
Prayer . . . . Rom 8:16-27

Testimony 2Tim 4:17
Guidance ....James 1:5-8

Given:
Internally ....Phil 2:13
Heb 13:21
By God 2Cor 8:9
By Christ ....Phil 4:13
By the Spirit ....Zech 4:6
By God's Word 1Thess 2:13
By grace 1Cor 15:10
By prayer ....James 5:15-18
By trusting God ....Ps 37:3-7
By God's providence ....Rom 8:28

ASSOCIATE—*to keep company with; join together*
A yourselves, O ye people ....Is 8:9

ASSOCIATION—*joining together for mutually beneficial purposes*

Among believers, hindered by:
Sin ....Acts 5:1-11
Friction ....Acts 6:1-6
Inconsistency ....Gal 2:11-14
Disagreement ....Acts 15:36-40
Selfishness 3John 9-11
Ambition ....Matt 20:20-24
Error 2John 7-11
Partiality ....James 2:1-5

Among believers, helped by:
Common faith ....Acts 2:42-47
Mutual helpfulness ......Gal 6:1-5
United prayer ....Matt 18:19, 20
Impending dangers ......Neh 4:1-23
Grateful praise ....Acts 4:23-33
See Alliance with Evil; Fellowship

ASSOS (ăs'ŏs)—*"approaching"—a seaport of Mysia in Asia Minor*
Paul walks to, from Troas ....Acts 20:13, 14

ASSUAGE—*lessen the intensity of*
[*also* ASSUAGED]
the waters *a* ....Gen 8:1
my lips should *a* your grief ....Job 16:5
my grief is not *a* ....Job 16:6

ASSUR—*See* Asshur

ASSURANCE—*security; trust; complete confidence*

Objects of, one's:
Election 1Thess 1:4
Adoption ....Eph 1:4, 5
Union with Christ 1Cor 6:15
Possession of eternal life. .John 5:24
1John 5:13
Peace ....Rom 5:1

Steps in:
Believing God's Word ...1Thess 2:13
Accepting Christ as Savior ....Rom 10:9, 10
Standing upon the promises ....John 10:28-30
Desiring spiritual things . .1Pet 2:2
Growing in grace 2Pet 1:5-11
Knowing life is changed . .2Cor 5:17
1John 3:14-22
Having inner peace and joy ....Rom 15:12, 13; Phil 4:7
Victorious living 1John 5:4, 5
The Spirit's testimony ....Rom 8:15, 16
Absolute assurance ......Rom 8:33-39
2Tim 1:12

Compatible with:
A nature still subject to sin 1John 1:8-10; 1John 2:1
Imperfection of life ......Gal 6:1
Limited knowledge 1Cor 13:9-12
Fatherly chastisement ....Heb 12:5-11

[*also* ASSURE, ASSURED, ASSUREDLY]
and it shall be *a* to him ....Lev 27:19
shalt have none *a* of thy life . . .Deut 28:66
Know thou *a*, that thou 1Sam 28:1
A Solomon thy son shall 1Kin 1:13
quietness and *a* for ever ......Is 32:17
a peace in this place ....Jer 14:13
a with my whole heart ....Jer 32:41
a go forth unto the king ......Jer 38:17
of the cup have *a* drunken ....Jer 49:12
house of Israel know *a* ....Acts 2:36
a gathering that the Lord .....Acts 16:10
hath given *a* unto all men .....Acts 17:31
the full *a* of understanding ....Col 2:2
and in much *a*, as ye know 1Thess 1:5
and hast been *a* of 2Tim 3:14
full *a* of hope unto the end....Heb 6:11
in full *a* of faith, having.......Heb 10:22

ASSWAGE—*See* Assuage

ASSYRIA (ă-sĭr'ĭ-ä)—*"country of Assur"—a Semitic nation on the Tigris River, whose capital was Nineveh*

Significant facts regarding:
Of remote antiquity .....Gen 2:14
Of Shem's ancestry ......Gen 10:22
Founded by Nimrod .....Gen 10:8-12
Mic 5:6
Nineveh, chief city of ....Gen 10:11
Tigris river flows through .Gen 2:14
Proud nation ....Is 10:5-15
A cruel military power . . .Nah 3:1-19
Agent of God's purposes .Is 7:17-20
Is 10:5, 6

Contacts of, with Israel:
Pul (Tiglath-pileser III, 745-727 B.C.) captures Damascus ....Is 8:4
Puts Menahem under tribute 2Kin 15:19, 20
Occasions Isaiah's prophesy ....Is 7—8
Puts Pekah under tribute .2Kin 15:29
Shalmaneser (727-722 B.C.) besieges Samaria .2Kin 17:3-5
Sargon II (722-705 B.C.) captures Israel 2Kin 17:6-41

Contacts of, with Judah:
Sargon's general takes Ashdod (in Philistia) . . .Is 20:1-6
Sennacherib (704-681 B.C.) invades Judah 2Kin 18:13
Puts Hezekiah under tribute 2Kin 18:14-16
Threatens Hezekiah through Rabshakeh 2Kin 18:17-37
Army of, miraculously slain 2Kin 19:35
Assassination of, by his sons 2Kin 19:37

Prophecies concerning:
Destruction of, anciently foretold ....Num 24:22-24
Israel captive in land of . .Hos 10:6
Hos 11:5
Doom of, mentioned ....Is 10:12, 19
Is 14:24, 25
End eulogized ....Nah 3:1-19
Shares, figuratively, in Gospel blessings ....Is 19:23-25

[*also* ASSYRIAN, ASSYRIANS]
to Tiglath-pileser king of *A* 2Kin 16:7
for a present to the king of *A* .2Kin 16:8
king of *A* hearkened unto 2Kin 16:9
of *A* went up against 2Kin 16:9
Tiglath-pileser king of *A* 2Kin 16:10
the Lord for the king of *A* 2Kin 16:18
rebelled against..king of *A* 2Kin 18:7
Shalmaneser king of *A* 2Kin 18:9
king of *A* did carry away 2Kin 18:11
carry away Israel unto *A* 2Kin 18:11
whom the king of *A* his 2Kin 19:4
servants of the king of *A* 2Kin 19:6
and found the king of *A* 2Kin 19:8
the hand of the king of *A* 2Kin 19:10
the kings of *A* have done 2Kin 19:11
kings of *A* have destroyed 2Kin 19:17
Sennacherib king of *A* 2Kin 19:20
concerning the king of *A* 2Kin 19:32
smote in the camp of the *A* . . .2Kin 19:35
Sennacherib king of *A* 2Kin 19:36
went up against the king of *A* .2Kin 23:29
Tilgath-pileser king of *A* 1Chr 5:6
send unto the kings of *A* 2Chr 28:16
the hand of the kings of *A* 2Chr 30:6
Sennacherib king of *A* 2Chr 32:1
Why should the kings of *A* 2Chr 32:4
dismayed for the king of *A* 2Chr 32:7
did Sennacherib king of *A* 2Chr 32:9
saith Sennacherib king..*A* 2Chr 32:10
the hand of the king of *A*? 2Chr 32:11
camp of the king of *A* 2Chr 32:21
Sennacherib the king of *A* 2Chr 32:22
host of the king of *A* 2Chr 33:11
heart of the king of *A* ....Ezra 6:22
the time of the kings of *A* .....Neh 9:32
O *A*, the rod of mine anger . . .Is 10:5
Zion be not afraid of the *A* . . .Is 10:24
which shall be left from *A* .....Is 11:11
which shall be left from *A* .....Is 11:16
break the *A* in my land ....Is 14:25
A shall come into Egypt ......Is 19:23
shall serve with the *A* ....Is 19:23
the king of *A* sent him ....Is 20:1
So shall the king of *A* lead ....Is 20:4
delivered from the king of *A* . . .Is 20:6
the *A* founded it for them .....Is 23:13
to perish in the land of *A* .....Is 27:13
shall the *A* be beaten down . . .Is 30:31
the *A* fall with the sword ......Is 31:8
that Sennacherib king of *A* ....Is 36:1
king of *A* sent Rabshakeh .....Is 36:2
king of *A* what confidence .....Is 36:4
to my master the king of *A* .....Is 36:8
great king, the king of *A* ......Is 36:13
the hand of the king of *A* .....Is 36:15
thus saith the king of *A* ....Is 36:16
the hand of the king of *A*? ....Is 36:18
the king of *A* his master ......Is 37:4
servants of the king of *A* ......Is 37:6
and found the king of *A* ......Is 37:8
the hand of the king of *A* .....Is 37:10
the kings of *A* have done .....Is 37:11
kings of *A* have laid waste ....Is 37:18
Sennacherib king of *A* ....Is 37:21
concerning the king of *A* ......Is 37:33
smote in the camp of the *A* . . .Is 37:36
Sennacherib king of *A* ....Is 37:37
the hand of the king of *A* .....Is 38:6
A oppressed them without .....Is 52:4
thou to do in the way of *A* ....Jer 2:18
as thou wast ashamed of *A* ....Jer 2:36
king of *A* hath devoured ......Jer 50:17
punished the king of *A* ....Jer 50:18
and to the *A*, to be satisfied . . .Lam 5:6
the whore also with the *A* .....Ezek 16:28
her lovers on the *A* her ....Ezek 23:5
were the chosen men of *A* ....Ezek 23:7
into the hand of the *A*, upon . .Ezek 23:9
upon the *A* her neighbors .....Ezek 23:12
and Koa, and all the *A* with . . .Ezek 23:23
A was a cedar in Lebanon .....Ezek 31:3
then went Ephraim to the *A* . . .Hos 5:13
to Egypt, they go to *A* ....Hos 7:11
For they are gone up to *A* ....Hos 8:9
shall eat unclean things in *A* . . .Hos 9:3
a dove out of the land of *A* . . .Hos 11:11
make a covenant with the *A* . . .Hos 12:1
A shall come into our land ....Mic 5:5
shall come..to thee from *A* ....Mic 7:12
the north, and destroy *A* ......Zeph 2:13
and gather them out of *A* .....Zech 10:10
pride of *A* shall be brought ....Zech 10:11

ASTAROTH—*See* Ashtaroth

ASTONIED—*See* Astonished

ASTONISHMENT—*an emotion of perplexed amazement*

Caused by:
God's judgments 1Kin 9:8, 9
Jer 18:16
Racial intermarriage .....Ezra 9:2-4

Utter desolation ....Jer 50:13
Urgent message ....Ezek 3:15
A miracle ....Dan 3:24
King's dream ....Dan 4:19
An unexplained vision ...Dan 8:27
Christ's knowledge ......Luke 2:47
Christ's teaching ....Luke 4:32
Christ's miracles ....Mark 5:42
Luke 5:9
Gentile conversions ......Acts 10:45
Miracles ....Acts 12:16
Acts 13:6-12

Applied figuratively to:
God ....Jer 14:9
Babylon ....Jer 51:37, 41
Jerusalem ....Ezek 4:16, 17
Ezek 5:5, 15
Priests ....Jer 4:9

[*also* ASTONISHED]
your enemies..shall be *a* ......Lev 26:32
and *a* of heart ....Deut 28:28
shall be an *a* to every one 2Chr 7:21
trouble, to *a* and to hissing 2Chr 29:8
my beard and sat down *a* .....Ezra 9:3
men shall be *a* at this ....Job 17:8
come after him shall be *a* .....Job 18:20
Mark me, and be *a*, and lay ...Job 21:5
and are *a* at his reproof ....Job 26:11
to drink the wine of *a* ....Ps 60:3
As many were *a* at thee ....Is 52:14
Be *a* O ye heavens, at this ....Jer 2:12
a hath taken hold on me ......Jer 8:21
passeth thereby shall be *a* .....Jer 19:8
make them an *a* and an ....Jer 25:9
a curse, and an *a* ....Jer 29:18
execration and an *a* ....Jer 42:18
an *a*, and a curse ....Jer 44:12
that goeth by it shall be *a* .....Jer 49:17
drink their water with *a* ....Ezek 12:19
the cup of *a* and desolation ...Ezek 23:33
every moment, and be *a* at ....Ezek 26:16
inhabitants..shall be *a* ....Ezek 27:35
people shall be *a* at thee ......Ezek 28:19
him, and his lords were *a* .....Dan 5:9
smite every horse with *a* ......Zech 12:4
the people were *a* at his ......Matt 7:28
insomuch that they were *a* ....Matt 13:54
they were *a* at his doctrine ....Matt 22:33
they were *a* at his doctrine ....Mark 1:22
many hearing him were *a* .....Mark 6:2
were beyond measure *a* ....Mark 7:37
disciples were *a* at his ....Mark 10:24
a at his understanding ....Luke 2:47
her parents were *a* ....Luke 8:56
made us *a* which were ....Luke 24:22
he trembling and *a* said ....Acts 9:6

ASTRAY—*off the correct road; away from the truth*
ox or his ass going *a* ....Ex 23:4
see thy brother's ox..go *a* .....Deut 22:1
they go *a* as soon as they .....Ps 58:3
I was afflicted I went *a* ....Ps 119:67
of his folly he shall go *a* ......Prov 5:23
go not *a* in her paths ....Prov 7:25
the righteous to go *a* ....Prov 28:10
we like sheep have gone *a* ....Is 53:6
have caused them to go *a* .....Jer 50:6
may go no more *a* from me ...Ezek 14:11
when Israel went *a* ....Ezek 44:10
which went not *a* ....Ezek 48:11
and one of them be gone *a* ....Matt 18:12
ye were as sheep going *a* 1Pet 2:25
and are gone *a*, following 2Pet 2:15

ASTROLOGER—*one who studies the supposed influences of the stars and planets on human affairs*
Cannot save Babylon ....Is 47:1, 12-15
Cannot interpret dreams. .Dan 2:2, 10-13
Dan 4:7
Cannot decipher handwriting ....Dan 5:7, 8
Daniel surpasses ....Dan 1:20
Daniel made master of ...Dan 5:11
God does not speak through ....Dan 2:27, 28

[*also* ASTROLOGERS]
things at any magician or *a* ....Dan 2:10

ASUNDER—*into parts; apart from one another*
shall not divide it *a* ....Lev 1:17
but shall not divide it *a* ....Lev 5:8
and parted them both *a* 2Kin 2:11
but he hath broken me *a* ......Job 16:12
Let us break their bands *a* ....Ps 2:3
he hath cut *a* the cords of .....Ps 129:4
of the whole earth cut *a* ......Jer 50:23
No shall be rent *a* ....Ezek 30:16
and drove *a* the nations ....Hab 3:6
and cut it *a*, that I might ......Zech 11:10
together let not man put *a* ....Matt 19:6
cut him *a* and appoint him ....Matt 24:51
had been plucked *a* by him ....Mark 5:4
let not man put *a* ....Mark 10:9
he burst *a* in the midst ....Acts 1:18
they departed *a* one from .....Acts 15:39
to the dividing *a* of soul ......Heb 4:12
were sawn *a*, were tempted ...Heb 11:37

ASUPPIM (ă-sŭp'ĭm)—*"gatherings; stores"*
Should be rendered as "storehouse" in 1Chr 26:15, 17
Same word translated "thresholds" in ....Neh 12:25

ASYLUM—*protection; refuge*
Afforded by altar 1Kin 1:50-53
1Kin 2:28
Cities of refuge ....Ex 21:12-14
Deut 19:1-13

ASYNCRITUS (ä-sĭn'krĭ-tŭs)—*"incomparable"*
A Christian at Rome ....Rom 16:14

AT—*See* INTRODUCTION

ATAD (ā'tăd)—*"a thorn"*
A mourning site east of Jordan ....Gen 50:9-13

ATARAH (ăt'ä-rä)—*"crown; ornament"*
A wife of Jerahmeel 1Chr 2:26

ATAROTH (ăt'ä-rŏth)—*"crown"*
1. Town of Gad ....Num 32:3, 34
2. A town of Ephraim .....Josh 16:7
3. A town between Ephraim and Benjamin ....Josh 16:2
Probably the same as Ataroth-addar .... Josh 16:5; Josh 18:13
4. A village near Bethlehem 1Chr 2:54

ATAROTH-ADDAR (ăt'ä-rŏth-ā'där)—*"crown of Addar"*
A frontier town of Ephraim ....Josh 16:5
See ATAROTH

ATE—*See* EAT

ATER (ā'ter)—*"bound; lame"*
1. The ancestors of a family of returnees .. Ezra 2:16; Neh 7:21
2. The ancestor of a family of porters Ezra 2:42; Neh 7:45
3. A signer of Nehemiah's document ....Neh 10:17

ATHACH (ā'thăk)—*"stopping place"*
A town in south Judah ...1Sam 30:30

ATHAIAH (ä-thā'yä)—*"Jehovah is helper"*
A Judahite in Nehemiah's time ....Neh 11:4

ATHALIAH (ăth-ä-lī'ä)—*"whom Jehovah has afflicted; Jehovah is strong"*
1. The daughter of Ahab and Jezebel 2Kin 8:18, 26; 2Chr 22:2, 3
Destroys all the royal seed except Joash ... 2Kin 11:1, 2; 2Chr 22:10, 11
Usurps throne for six years 2Kin 11:3
Killed by priestly uprising 2Kin 11:4-16; 2Chr 23:1-21
Called wicked 2Chr 24:7
2. A Benjamite 1Chr 8:26, 27
3. The father of Jeshaiah ...Ezra 8:7

they slew *A* with the sword 2Kin 11:20
and Shehariah, and *A* 1Chr 8:26
of God in six years: and *A* 2Chr 22:12
sons of *A* that wicked 2Chr 24:7
of Elam..the son of *A* ....Ezra 8:7

ATHARIM (ăth'är-ĭm)—*"spies"*
Israel attacked there .....Num 21:1

ATHEISM—*the denial of God's existence*
Defined as:
The fool's philosophy ....Ps 14:1
Ps 53:1
Living without God ......Rom 1:20-32
Eph 2:12

Manifestations of, seen in:
Defiance of God ....Ex 5:2
2Kin 18:19-35
Irreligion ....Titus 1:16
Corrupt morals ....Rom 13:12, 13
1Pet 4:3

Evidences against, seen in:
Man's inner conscience ...Rom 2:14, 15
Design in nature ....Job 38:1-41
Job 39:1-30
God's works ....Ps 19:1-6
God's providence ....Ps 104:1-35
Acts 14:17
Clear evidence ....Rom 1:19, 20
The testimony of pagans .Dan 4:24-37
Fulfillment of prophecy ..Is 41:20-23
Is 46:8-11

ATHENS (ăth'ĕnz)—*"city of Athena"—greatest city of Classical Greece; named for the goddess Athena*
Paul preaches in ....Acts 17:15-34
Paul resides in 1Thess 3:1

Paul departed from *A* ....Acts 18:1

ATHIRST—*thirsty*
was sore *a*, and called on .....Judg 15:18
thou art *a*, go unto the ....Ruth 2:9
thee ahungered, or *a* ....Matt 25:44
I will give unto him that is *a* ..Rev 21:6
let him that is *a* come ....Rev 22:17

ATHLAI (ăth'lā-ī)—*"Jehovah is strong"*
A Jew who divorced his foreign wife ....Ezra 10:28

ATHLETES
Discipline 1Cor 9:24-27
Removal of weights ......Heb 12:1
Prize ....Phil 3:14

ATONEMENT—*reconciliation of God and man through divine sacrifice*
Elements involved in, seen in:
Man's sin ....Ex 32:30
Ps 51:3, 4
The blood sacrificed .....Lev 16:11, 14-20
Heb 9:13-22
Guilt transferred ....Lev 1:3, 4
2Cor 5:21
Guilt removed ....Lev 16:21
1Cor 6:11
Forgiveness granted ......Lev 5:10, 11
Rom 4:6, 7
Righteousness given .....Rom 10:3, 4
Phil 3:9

Fulfilled by Christ:
Predicted ....Is 53:10-12
Dan 9:24-26
Symbolized ....Is 63:1-9
Zech 3:3-9
Realized ....Rom 3:23-26
1Pet 1:18-21

wherewith the *a* was made ... Ex 29:33
for a sin offering for *a* ... Ex 29:36
when thou hast made an *a* ... Ex 29:36
make an *a* for the altar ... Ex 29:37
an *a* upon the horns ... Ex 30:10
the sin offering of *a* ... Ex 30:10
shall make an *a* for them ... Lev 4:20
the priest shall make an *a* ... Lev 4:26
shall make an *a* for him ... Lev 4:31
shall make an *a* for his sin ... Lev 4:35
shall make an *a* for him ... Lev 5:6
a for him before the Lord ... Lev 6:7
the priest that maketh *a* ... Lev 7:7
to make an *a* for you ... Lev 8:34
and make an *a* for thyself ... Lev 9:7
a for them before the Lord ... Lev 10:17
and make an *a* for her ... Lev 12:7
the priest shall make an *a* ... Lev 14:18
and the priest..make an *a* ... Lev 15:15
priest..shall make the *a* ... Lev 16:32
a for the holy sanctuary ... Lev 16:33
make an *a* for..tabernacle ... Lev 16:33
he shall make an *a* for the ... Lev 16:33
make an *a* for your souls ... Lev 17:11
blood that maketh an *a* ... Lev 17:11
the priest shall make an *a* ... Lev 19:22
the day of *a* shall ye make ... Lev 25:9
the ram of the *a* ... Num 5:8
and make an *a* for him ... Num 6:11
make an a for the Levites ... Num 8:12
the priest shall make an *a* ... Num 15:25
and make an *a* for them ... Num 16:46
a for the children of Israel ... Num 25:13
offering to make an *a* for ... Num 28:22
offering to make an *a* for ... Num 29:5
to make an *a* for our souls ... Num 31:50
shall I make the *a* ... 2Sam 21:3
and to make an *a* for Israel ... 1Chr 6:49
to make an *a* for all Israel ... 2Chr 29:24
to make an *a* for Israel ... Neh 10:33
we have now received the *a* ... Rom 5:11

ATONEMENT OF CHRIST—*reconciliation of God and man through Christ's sacrificial death on the cross*

Typified by:
The paschal lamb ... Ex 12:5, 11, 14; John 1:29; 1Cor 5:7
The Day of Atonement ... Lev 16:30, 34; Heb 9:8-28

What man is:
A sinner ... Rom 5:8
Alienated in mind ... Col 1:21
Strangers ... Eph 2:12

What God does:
Loves us ... John 3:16
Commends His love to us ... Rom 5:8
Sends Christ to save us ... Gal 4:4
Spared not His own Son ... Rom 8:32

What Christ does:
Takes our nature ... Heb 2:14
Becomes our ransom ... Matt 20:28
Dies in our place ... 1Pet 3:18
Dies for our sins ... 1Pet 2:24
Dies as a sacrifice ... Eph 5:2
Dies willingly ... John 10:18
Reconciles us to God ... Rom 5:10
Brings us to God ... 1Pet 3:18
Restores our fellowship ... 1Thess 5:10
See BLOOD OF CHRIST

What the believer receives:
Forgiveness ... Eph 1:7
Peace ... Rom 5:1
Reconciliation ... 2Cor 5:19
Righteousness ... 2Cor 5:21
Justification ... Rom 3:24-26
Access to God ... Eph 2:18
Cleansing ... 1John 1:7
Liberty ... Gal 5:1
Freedom from the devil's power ... Heb 2:14
Christ's intercession ... Heb 2:17, 18

ATONEMENT, DAY OF—*Jewish holy day on which atonement was made on behalf of the entire nation of Israel*

Features regarding:
Time specified ... Lev 23:26, 27
The ritual involved in ... Lev 16:3, 5-15
A time of humiliation ... Lev 16:29, 31
Exclusive ministry of the high priest in ... Lev 16:2, 3; Heb 9:7

Benefits of, for:
The holy place ... Lev 16:15, 16
The people ... Lev 16:17, 24
The high priest ... Lev 16:11; Heb 9:7

Result of, seen in:
Atonement for sin ... Rom 3:25
Removal of sin ... Heb 9:8-28; Heb 13:10-13

ATROTH-SHOPHAN (ă'trŏth-shō'făn)
A city built by the Gadites ... Num 32:35

ATTAI (ăt'ā-ī)—*"timely"*
1. A half-Egyptian Judahite ... 1Chr 2:35, 36
2. A Gadite in David's army ... 1Chr 12:11
3. Rehoboam's son ... 2Chr 11:20

ATTAIN—*to gain or achieve; to possess*

[*also* ATTAINED]
not *a* unto the days of the ... Gen 47:9
he *a* not unto the first three ... 2Sam 23:19
he *a* not to the first ... 2Sam 23:23
he *a* not to the first three ... 1Chr 11:21
but *a* not to the first three ... 1Chr 11:25
is high, I cannot *a* unto it ... Ps 139:6
of understanding shall *a* ... Prov 1:5
as his hand shall *a* unto ... Ezek 46:7
be ere they *a* to innocency ... Hos 8:5
means they might *a* to ... Acts 27:12
have *a* to righteousness ... Rom 9:30
not *a* to the law of ... Rom 9:31
I might *a* unto the ... Phil 3:11
as though I had already *a* ... Phil 3:12
whereto we have already *a* ... Phil 3:16
whereunto thou hast *a* ... 1Tim 4:6

ATTALIA (ăt-ä-lī-ä)—*seaport town of Pamphylia named after Attalus II*
Paul sails from, to Antioch ... Acts 14:25, 26

ATTEND—*to give heed to; be present with*
To care for ... Esth 4:5

[*also* ATTENDANCE, ATTENDED, ATTENDING]
and the *a* of his ministers ... 1Kin 10:5
and the *a* of his ministers ... 2Chr 9:4
Yea, I *a* unto you, and ... Job 32:12
a unto my cry, give ear ... Ps 17:1
A unto me, and hear me ... Ps 55:2
a unto my prayer ... Ps 61:1
hath *a* to the voice of my ... Ps 66:19
a to the voice of my ... Ps 86:6
A unto my cry; for I am ... Ps 142:6
a to know understanding ... Prov 4:1
My son, *a* to my words ... Prov 4:20
My son, *a* unto my wisdom ... Prov 5:1
and *a* to the words of my ... Prov 7:24
she *a* unto the things which ... Acts 16:14
a continually upon this very ... Rom 13:6
ye may *a* upon the Lord ... 1Cor 7:35

ATTENDANCE, CHURCH
Taught by example ... Acts 11:25-26; Acts 14:27
Not to be neglected ... Heb 10:25

ATTENT—*mindful; observant*

[*also* ATTENTIVE, ATTENTIVELY]
ears be *a* unto the prayer ... 2Chr 6:40
ears *a* unto the prayer ... 2Chr 7:15
let thine ear now be *a* ... Neh 1:6
were *a* unto the book of the ... Neh 8:3
a the noise of his voice ... Job 37:2
let thine ears be *a* to the ... Ps 130:2
were very *a* to hear him ... Luke 19:48

ATTIRE—*clothing, clothed*

[*also* ATTIRED]
linen mitre shall he be *a* ... Lev 16:4
the *a* of a harlot ... Prov 7:10
ornaments, or a bride her *a*? ... Jer 2:32
in dyed *a* upon their heads ... Ezek 23:15

ATTITUDE—*the state of mind toward something*

Of Christians toward Christ, must:
Confess ... Rom 10:9, 10
Obey ... John 14:15, 23
Follow ... Matt 16:24
Imitate ... 1Pet 2:21

Of Christians toward the world, not to:
Conform to ... Rom 12:2
Abuse ... 1Cor 7:31
Love ... 1John 2:15
Be friend of ... James 4:4
Be entangled with ... 2Tim 2:4
Be polluted with ... Jude 23

Of Christians toward sinners:
Seek their salvation ... 1Cor 9:22
Pray for ... Rom 9:1-3
Plead with ... Acts 17:22-31
Rebuke ... Titus 1:10-13
Persuade ... 2Cor 5:11

AUDIENCE—*an assembly of hearers*
Disturbed ... Neh 13:1-3
Attentive ... Luke 7:1
Hostile ... Luke 4:28-30
Receptive ... Acts 2:1-40
Menacing ... Acts 7:54-60
Rejecting ... Acts 13:44-51
Critical ... Acts 17:22-34
Sympathetic ... Acts 20:17-38
Vast ... Rev 5:9; Rev 7:9, 10

See ASSEMBLY

in the *a* of the children of ... Gen 23:10
read in the *a* of the people ... Ex 24:7
in thine *a*, and hear the ... 1Sam 25:24
and in the *a* of our God ... 1Chr 28:8
in the *a* of the people ... Neh 13:1
sayings in the *a* of the ... Luke 7:1
in the *a* of all the people he ... Luke 20:45
ye that fear God, give *a* ... Acts 13:16
gave *a* to Barnabas and ... Acts 15:12
they gave him *a* unto this ... Acts 22:22

AUDITORIUM—*a room for assembly*
Hearing ... Acts 25:23

AUGHT—*See* NAUGHT, OUGHT

AUGMENT—*to increase*
a yet the fierce anger of ... Num 32:14

AUGUSTUS (ô-gŭs'tŭs)—*emperor of Rome at time of Christ's birth*

[*also* AUGUSTUS']
a decree from Caesar *A* ... Luke 2:1
unto the hearing of *A* ... Acts 25:21
a centurion of *A* band ... Acts 27:1

AUGUSTUS' BAND—*a battalion of Roman soldiers*
Paul placed in custody of ... Acts 27:1

AUL—*See* AWL

AUNT—*the sister of a parent*
she is thine *a* ... Lev 18:14

AUSTERE—*hard; severe*
because thou art an *a* man ... Luke 19:21
that I was an *a* man ... Luke 19:22

AUTHOR—*creator; originator; writer*
God of peace ... 1Cor 14:33
Christ of salvation ... Heb 5:9
Christ of faith ... Heb 12:2
Solomon of many writings ... 1Kin 4:32

AUTHORITY—*the lawful power or right to enforce obedience*

As rulers:
Governor ....Acts 23:24, 26
Matt 10:18

Delegated to, man as:
Created ....Gen 1:26-31
A legal state ....Esth 9:29
Luke 22:25
Agent of the state ....Matt 8:9
Rom 13:1-6
Husband 1Cor 14:35
Agent of religious leaders ....Acts 26:10, 12

Christ's, seen in His power:
Over demons ....Mark 1:27
In teaching.............Matt 7:29
To forgive ....Luke 5:24
To judge ....John 5:22, 27
To rule..............Matt 2:6; 1Cor 15:24; 1Pet 3:22
To commission ....Matt 28:18-20

Purpose:
Protection ....Heb 13:17
Instruction 1Pet 5:2, 3
Example of Christ's power ....Matt 8:5-13
Testimony to unbelievers .1Tim 6:1
1Pet 3:13-15

Of Christians, given to:
Apostles 2Cor 10:8
Ministers ....Titus 2:15
The righteous ....Prov 29:2

taught..as one having *a* ....Matt 7:29
that are great exercise *a* ......Matt 20:25
what *a* doest thou these ....Matt 21:23
and who gave thee this *a*......Matt 21:23
by what *a* I do these things ...Matt 21:24
as one that had *a*............Mark 1:22
for with *a* commandeth he ....Mark 1:27
their great ones exercise *a*.....Mark 10:42
what *a* doest thou these ....Mark 11:28
and who gave thee this *a*......Mark 11:28
by what *a* I do these..........Mark 11:29
with *a* and power he ....Luke 4:36
I am a man set under *a* ....Luke 7:8
gave them power and *a* ....Luke 9:1
have thou *a* over ten cities ....Luke 19:17
what *a* doest thou these ....Luke 20:2
is he that gave thee this *a*? ....Luke 20:2
by what *a* I do these things ...Luke 20:8
and *a* of the governor ....Luke 20:20
given him *a* to execute ....John 5:27
eunuch of great *a* under ......Acts 8:27
he hath *a* from the chief ......Acts 9:14
and for all that are in *a* 1Tim 2:2
and his seat, and great *a* ......Rev 13:2

AVA (ā'vä)—*"legion"—Assyrian city*
Colonists from, brought to Samaria by Sargon ..2Kin 17:24
Worshipers of Nibhaz and Tartak 2Kin 17:31

AVAILETH—*of use or advantage to*
all this *a* me nothing ....Esth 5:13
neither circumcision *a* any .....Gal 5:6
prayer of a righteous man *a* ...James 5:16

AVARICE—*covetousness; greed*

Productive of:
Defeat.................Josh 7:11, 21
Death 1Kin 21:5-16
Discontent ....James 4:1-4

Examples of:
Balaam 2Pet 2:15
Achan ....Josh 7:20, 21
Ahab 1Kin 21:1-4
Judas Iscariot ....Matt 26:15, 16
Ananias and Sapphira ....Acts 5:1-10
Rich men ....Luke 12:16-21
James 5:1-6

AVEN (ā'vĕn)—*"nothingness"*
1. The city of On in Egypt near Cairo; known as Heliopolis ....Gen 41:45; Ezek 30:17
2. A name contemptuously applied to Bethel .....Hos 10:5, 8
3. Valley in Syria..........Amos 1:5

AVENGE—*to take vengeance; exact satisfaction for a wrong by punishing evildoer*

Kinds of:
Commanded by God.....Num 31:1, 2
Given strength for ....Judg 16:28-30
Sought maliciously 1Sam 18:25
Possible but not done 1Sam 24:12
Attempted but hindered. .1Sam 25:26-33
Obtained in self-defense. .Esth 8:12, 13

Sought because of:
A murdered neighbor ....Num 35:12
Josh 20:5
A wife's mistreatment....Judg 15:6-8
Judah's sins ....Jer 5:9
Mistreatment ....Acts 7:24, 25
Impurity 1Thess 4:5-7

Performed by:
God Himself ....Lev 26:25
Luke 18:7, 8
Wicked men 2Sam 4:8-12
Impetuous general 2Sam 18:18, 19, 31
An anointed king........2Kin 9:6, 7
A judge ....Luke 18:3, 5
Jesus Christ ....Rev 19:2

Restrictions on:
Personal, prohibited .....Lev 19:17, 18
Christians prohibited.....Rev 12:9

[*also* AVENGED, AVENGER, AVENGETH, AVENGING]
If Cain shall be *a* sevenfold ...Gen 4:24
the *a* of the blood pursue .....Deut 19:6
into the hand of the *a* of......Deut 19:12
a the blood of his servants ....Deut 32:43
the people had *a* themselves ..Josh 10:13
your refuge from the *a*........Josh 20:3
the hand of the *a* of blood ....Josh 20:9
Praise ye the Lord for the *a* ..Judg 5:2
that I may be *a* on mine 1Sam 14:24
and the Lord *a* me of thee 1Sam 24:12
from *a* thyself with thine 1Sam 25:26
from *a* myself with mine 1Sam 25:33
It is God that *a* me 2Sam 22:48
I may *a* the blood of my 2Kin 9:7
to *a* themselves on their ......Esth 8:13
It is God that *a* me ....Ps 18:47
reason of the enemy and *a* ....Ps 44:16
and *a* me of mine enemies ....Is 1:24
shall not my soul be *a* on .....Jer 9:9
he may *a* him of his ....Jer 46:10
and I will *a* the blood of ......Hos 1:4
beloved, *a* not yourselves .....Rom 12:19
dost thou not judge and *a*.....Rev 6:10
God hath *a* you on her ....Rev 18:20

AVENGER OF BLOOD—*closest of kin to slain person; was expected to kill person's slayer*
An ancient practice ......Gen 4:14
Seen in kinsman as "redeemer" of enslaved relative.....Lev 25:25, 47-49; Ruth 4:1-10
Seen also in kinsman as "avenger" of a murdered relative .....Num 35:11-34
Avenger alone must kill murderer ....Deut 19:6, 11-13
Practice, of set aside by David 2Sam 14:4-11
Same word translated "kinsman" and "redeemer" ....Ruth 4:1; Job 19:25
Figurative of a violent person ....Ps 8:2

AVERSE—*opposed; disinclined, unwilling*
securely as men *a* from war ...Mic 2:8

AVIM, AVITES (ăv'ĭm; ăv'īts)—*"villagers"*
1. A tribe of early Canaanites living near Gaza; absorbed by the Caphtorim (Philistines).Deut 2:23
2. A city of Benjamin near Beth-el ....Josh 18:23
3. Colonists brought from Ava in Assyria 2Kin 17:24, 31

AVITH (ā'vĭth)—*"ruins"*
An Edomite city ....Gen 36:35

AVOID—*to keep away from*

[*also* AVOIDED, AVOIDING]
David *a* out of his presence ...1Sam 18:11
A it, pass not by it, turn ......Prov 4:15
ye have learned, and *a* ....Rom 16:17
to *a* fornication...............1Cor 7:2
A this, that no man should 2Cor 8:20
a profane and vain 1Tim 6:20
and unlearned questions *a* 2Tim 2:23
But *a* foolish questions ....Titus 3:9

AVOUCHED—*guaranteed; affirmed*
hast *a* the Lord this day to ....Deut 26:17
the Lord hath *a* thee this .....Deut 26:18

AWAIT—*to wait for*
laying *a* was known of Saul ...Acts 9:24

AWAKE—*to wake up; become aware of something*

[*also* AWAKED, AWAKEST, AWAKETH, AWAKING, AWOKE]
And Noah *a* from his wine ....Gen 9:24
And Jacob *a* out of his sleep ..Gen 28:16
So Pharaoh *a* and, behold .....Gen 41:4
Pharaoh *a*, and behold it ......Gen 41:7
as at the beginning. So I *a* ....Gen 41:21
A, *a* Deborah; *a*, *a*, utter a ....Judg 5:12
And he *a* out of his sleep .....Judg 16:14
And he *a* out of his sleep .....Judg 16:20
nor knew it, neither *a* 1Sam 26:12
Solomon *a*; and behold, it.....1Kin 3:15
he sleepeth, and must be *a* 1Kin 18:27
The child is not *a* 2Kin 4:31
now he would *a* for thee ......Job 8:6
shall not *a*, nor be raised ......Job 14:12
I *a*, for the Lord sustained ....Ps 3:5
a for me to the judgment .....Ps 7:6
I shall be satisfied, when I *a* ..Ps 17:15
Stir up thyself, and *a* to my ..Ps 35:23
A, why sleepest thou..........Ps 44:23
A up, my glory ....Ps 57:8
a, psaltery and harp ....Ps 57:8
I myself will *a* early ....Ps 57:8
A to help me, and behold .....Ps 59:4
a to visit all the heathen ......Ps 59:5
when thou *a*, thou shalt ....Ps 73:20
Lord *a* as one out of sleep ....Ps 78:65
A, psaltery and harp ....Ps 108:2
I *a*, I am still with thee ....Ps 139:18
when thou *a*, it shall talk .....Prov 6:22
when shall I *a*? I will seek ....Prov 23:35
a my love, till he please.........Song 2:7
not up, nor *a* my love, till he..Song 3:5
A, O north wind; and come ..Song 4:16
ye stir not up, nor *a* my love ..Song 8:4
A and sing, ye that dwell in ...Is 26:19
A, *a*, put on strength ....Is 51:9
the Lord; *a*, as in the ....Is 51:9
A, *a*..O Jerusalem ....Is 51:17
A, *a*; put on thy strength ......Is 52:1
Upon this I *a*, and beheld .....Jer 31:26
dust of the earth shall *a*......Dan 12:2
A, ye drunkards, and weep ....Joel 1:5
and *a* that shall vex thee ......Hab 2:7
that saith to the wood, *A* .....Hab 2:19
A, O sword against my........Zech 13:7
a him, saying, Lord, save us...Matt 8:25
a him, and say unto him ......Mark 4:38
they came to him, and *a* ......Luke 8:24
when they were *a*, they saw ...Luke 9:32
that I may *a* him out of......John 11:11
a out of his sleep, and ....Acts 16:27

is high time to *a* out of ....Rom 13:11
A to righteousness, and 1Cor 15:34
A thou that sleepest, and......Eph 5:14

AWAKENING, SPIRITUAL—*a movement in which people become more deeply aware of and open to God's working in their lives*
Produced by:
Returning to Beth-el.....Gen 35:1-7
Discovering God's Word. .2Kin 22:8-11
Reading God's Word ....Neh 8:2-18
Confessing sin...........Ezra 10:1-17
Receiving the Spirit......John 7:38, 39
Acts 2:1-47
Old Testament examples of, under:
Joshua..................Josh 24:1-31
Samuel 1Sam 7:3-6
Elijah 1Kin 18:21-40
Hezekiah 2Chr 30:1-27
Josiah 2Kin 23:1-3
Ezra...................Ezra 10:1-17
New Testament examples of:
John the Baptist.........Luke 3:2-14
Jesus in Samaria.........John 4:28-42
Philip in Samaria ....Acts 8:5-12
Peter at Lydda ....Acts 9:32-35
Peter with Cornelius .....Acts 10:34-48
Paul at Antioch in Pisidia.Acts 13:14-52
Paul at Thessalonica .....Acts 17:11, 12
1Thess 1:1-10
Paul at Corinth..........2Cor 7:1-16

AWARE—*having or showing perception or knowledge*
Or ever I was *a*, my soul .....Song 6:12
thou wast not *a*: thou art .....Jer 50:24
an hour that he is not *a* of ....Matt 24:50
over them are not *a* of them . .Luke 11:44
at an hour when he is not *a* . . .Luke 12:46

AWAY—*See* INTRODUCTION

AWE—*fear mingled with reverence*
A restraint on sin ....Ps 4:4
Proper attitude toward God.................Ps 33:8
Also toward God's Word .Ps 119:161

AWL—*a sharp, pointed tool for piercing*
Used on the ear as a symbol of perpetual obedience........... { Ex 21:6; Deut 15:17 }

AXE—*a sharp tool for cutting wood*
Used in:
Cutting timber ....Judg 9:48
War 1Chr 20:3
Malicious destruction ....Ps 74:5-7
A miracle; floated in water.................2Kin 6:5, 6
As a figure of:
Judgment ....Matt 3:10
Wrath ....Jer 51:20-24
God's sovereignty ....Is 10:15

[*also* AX, AXES]
the *a* to cut down the tree ....Deut 19:5
by forcing an *a* against them . .Deut 20:19
to sharpen every man.. his *a* . .1Sam 13:20
for the forks, and for the *a*....1Sam 13:21
and under *a* of iron...........2Sam 12:31
neither hammer nor *a* nor 1Kin 6:7
harrows of iron, and with *a* . . .1Chr 20:3
he had lifted up *a* upon the . . .Ps 74:5
with *a* and hammers ....Ps 74:6
of the workman with the *a* ....Jer 10:3
come against her with *a* ....Jer 46:22
now also the *a* is laid unto ....Luke 3:9

AXLETREE—*shaft on which a wheel is mounted*
Used in the temple 1Kin 7:32, 33

AZAL (ā'zăl)—*"noble; slope"*
1. A descendant of Jonathan 1Chr 8:37, 38
2. A place near Jerusalem. .Zech 14:5

AZALIAH (ăz-ä-lī'ä)—*"Jehovah is noble"*
Father of Shaphan 2Kin 22:3

the son of *A*, and Maaseiah . . .2Chr 34:8

AZANIAH (ăs-ä-nī'ä)—*"Jehovah is hearer"*
A Levite who signs the document ....Neh 10:9

AZAREEL, AZAREL (ăz'ä-rēl, ăz'ä-rĕl)—*"God is helper"*
1. A Levite in David's army at Ziklag 1Chr 12:6
2. A musician in David's time 1Chr 25:18
3. A prince of Dan under David 1Chr 27:22
4. A Jew who divorced his foreign wife ....Ezra 10:41
5. A postexilic priest.......Neh 11:13
6. A musician in dedication service ....Neh 12:36

AZARIAH (ăz-ä-rī'ä)—*"Jehovah has helped"*
1. Man of Judah 1Chr 2:8
2. A Kohathite Levite 1Chr 6:36
3. A son of Zadok the high priest 1Kin 4:2
4. A son of Ahimaaz 1Chr 6:9
5. A great-grandson of Ahimaaz 1Chr 6:9-10
6. Son of Nathan 1Kin 4:5
7. A son of Jehu, with Egyptian ancestry 1Chr 2:34-38
8. A prophet who encourages King Asa .2Chr 15:1-8
9. Son of King Jehoshaphat 2Chr 21:2
10. A captain under Jehoiada 2Chr 23:1
11. Another under Jehoiada.2Chr 23:1
12. A head of Ephraim 2Chr 28:12
13. King of Judah 2Kin 15:1
14. A high priest who rebukes King Uzziah. .2Chr 26:16-20
15. Kohathite, father of Joel 2Chr 29:12
16. A reforming Levite 2Chr 29:12
17. Chief priest in time of Hezekiah............2Chr 31:9, 10
18. A high priest, son of Hilkiah 1Chr 6:13, 14
19. Ancestor of Ezra ......Ezra 7:1-3
20. An opponent of Jeremiah ....Jer 43:2
21. The Hebrew name of Abednego ....Dan 1:7
22. Postexilic Jew ....Neh 7:6, 7
23. A workman under Nehemiah ....Neh 3:23, 24
24. A prince of Judah .....Neh 12:32, 33
25. An expounder of the law ....Neh 8:7
26. A signer of the covenant ....Neh 10:1, 2
27. A descendant of Hilkiah 1Chr 9:11

See AHAZIAH

the people of Judah took *A* . . .2Kin 14:21
the rest of the acts of *A*........2Kin 15:6
So *A* slept with his fathers 2Kin 15:7
thirty and eighth year of *A* 2Kin 15:8
nine and thirtieth year of *A* . . .2Kin 15:17
the fiftieth year of *A* king of . .2Kin 15:23
two and fiftieth year of *A* 2Kin 15:27
Jehu, and Jehu begat *A* 1Chr 2:38
A begat Helez, and Helez 1Chr 2:39
Amaziah his son, *A* his son....1Chr 3:12
And *A* begat Amariah, and . . .1Chr 6:11
Spirit of God came upon *A*....2Chr 15:1
A the son of Jeboram king 2Chr 22:6
A the priest went in after 2Chr 26:17
And *A* the chief priest, and . . .2Chr 26:20
A the ruler of the house of....2Chr 31:13
son of Seraiah, the son of *A*. . .Ezra 7:1
son of Amariah, the son of *A* .Ezra 7:3

Hananiah, Mishael, and *A*.....Dan 1:6
Hananiah, Mishael, and *A*.....Dan 1:11
and *A*: therefore stood they . . .Dan 1:19
and *A*, his companions ....Dan 2:17

AZAZ (ā'zăz)—*"strong; powerful"*
A Reubenite 1Chr 5:8

AZAZIAH (ăz-ä-zī'ä)—*"Jehovah is strong"*
1. A musician 1Chr 15:21
2. Father of Hoshea 1Chr 27:20
3. A temple overseer 2Chr 31:13

AZBUK (ăz'bŭk)—*"pardon"*
Father of a certain Nehemiah; but not the celebrated one ....Neh 3:16

AZEKAH (ä-zē'kä)—*"dug up place"—city southwest of Jerusalem*
Great stones cast upon. . .Josh 10:11
Camp of Goliath 1Sam 17:1, 4, 17
Fortified by Rehoboam . .2Chr 11:9
Reoccupied after exile . . .Neh 11:30
Besieged by Nebuchadnezzar ....Jer 34:7

smote them to *A*, and unto....Josh 10:10
and Adullam, Socoh, and A . . .Josh 15:35

AZEL (ā'zĕl)—*"noble"—a descendant of King Saul*
Eleasah his son, *A* his son.....1Chr 8:37
A had six sons, whose 1Chr 8:38
All these were the sons of *A* . .1Chr 8:38
Eleasah his son, *A* his son.....1Chr 9:43
A had six sons, whose names . .1Chr 9:44
these were the sons of *A* 1Chr 9:44

AZEM, EZEM (ă'zĕm, ē'zĕm)—*"bone"*
A town of Judah ....Josh 15:29
Allotted to Simeon ......Josh 19:3
Also called Ezem........1Chr 4:29

AZGAD (ăz'găd)—*"worship; supplication; God is strong"*
Head of exile family .....Ezra 2:12
Ezra 8:12
Among document signers .Neh 10:15

AZIEL (ā'zĭ-ĕl)—*"God is determining"*
A Levite musician 1Chr 15:20
Called Jaaziel 1Chr 15:18

AZIZA (ä-zī'zä)—*"strong"*
Divorced foreign wife ....Ezra 10:27

AZMAVETH (ăz-mā'vĕth)—*"council or strength of death"*
1. One of David's mighty men 2Sam 23:31
2. A Benjamite 2Chr 12:3
3. David's treasurer........1Chr 27:25
4. A son of Jehoaddah.....1Chr 8:36
5. A village near Jerusalem .Neh 12:29
Also called Beth-azmaveth........Neh 7:28

Jarah begat Alemeth, and *A* . . .1Chr 9:42
A the Baharumite, Eliahba 1Chr 11:33
Jeziel, and Pelet the sons of *A* .1Chr 12:3
children of *A*, forty and two . . .Ezra 2:24

AZMON (ăz'mŏn)—*"strong"*
A place in south Canaan. .Num 34:4, 5

thence it passed toward *A* .....Josh 15:4

AZNOTH-TABOR (ăz'nŏth-tā'bôr)—*"Peaks (ears) of Tabor"*
Place in Naphtali ....Josh 19:34

AZOR (ā'zor)—*"helper"*
Ancestor of Christ ....Matt 1:13, 14

AZOTUS (ä-zō'tŭs)—*"stronghold"*
Philip went there ....Acts 8:40
Same as Ashdod 1Sam 6:17

AZRIEL (ăz'rĭ-ĕl)—*"God is helper"*
1. A chief of Manasseh 1Chr 5:24
2. Father of Jerimoth 1Chr 27:19
3. Father of Seraiah ....Jer 36:26

AZRIKAM (ăz'rĭ-kăm)—*"my help has risen"*
1. Son of Neariah 1Chr 3:23
2. A son of Aziel 1Chr 8:38
3. A Merarite Levite 1Chr 9:14
4. Governor under King Ahaz 2Chr 28:7

sons, whose names are these *A*.1Chr 9:44
son of Hashub, the son of *A*...Neh 11:15

AZUBAH (ä-zū'bä)—*"forsaken"*
1. Wife of Caleb 1Chr 2:18, 19
2. Mother of Jehoshaphat ..1Kin 22:42

his mother's name was *A*......2Chr 20:31

AZUR, AZZUR (ā'zŭr, ăz'ŭr)—*helper; helpful*
1. Father of Hananiah .....Jer 28:1
2. Father of Jaazaniah .....Ezek 11:1
3. A covenant signer.......Neh 10:17

AZZAH (ăz'ă)—*"strong"—southernmost of five chief Philistine cities; same as Gaza*
in Hazerim, even unto *A*......Deut 2:23
from Tiphsah even to *A*.......1Kin 4:24
and Ashkelon, and *A*, and ....Jer 25:20

AZZAN (ăz'ăn)—*"sharp; thorn"*
Father of Paltiel.........Num 34:26

B

BAAL (bā'ăl)—*"master; lord"—the most important of the Canaanite gods; male counterpart to Ashtaroth*

The nature of:
The male god of the Phoenicians and Canaanites; the counterpart of the female Ashtaroth .. {Judg 10:6; 1 Sam 7:4}
Connected with immorality .... {Num 25:3, 5; Hos 9:10}
Incense burned to ....Jer 7:9
Kissing the image of .....1 Kin 19:18; Hos 13:1, 2
Dervish rites by priests of.1Kin 18:26, 28
Children burned in fire of.Jer 19:5
Eating sacrifices ....Ps 106:28

History of:
Among Moabites in Moses' time...........Num 22:41
Altars built to, during time of judges....... {Judg 2:11-14; Judg 6:28-32}
Jezebel introduces into Israel.................1Kin 16:31, 32
Elijah's overthrow of, on Mt. Carmel 1Kin 18:17-40
Athaliah introduces it into Judah .... {2Kin 11:17-20; 2 Chr 22:2-4}
Revived again in Israel and Judah .... {Hos 2:8; Amos 5:26}
Ahaz makes images to ...2 Chr 28:2-4
Manasseh worships ......2 Kin 21:3
Altars everywhere ....Jer 11:13
Overthrown by Josiah....2 Kin 23:4, 5
Denounced by prophets ..Jer 19:4, 5; Ezek 16:20, 21
Historic retrospect ....Rom 11:4

[*also* BAAL'S]
Lord, and served *B* and.......Judg 2:13
altar of *B* was cast down ......Judg 6:28
cast down the altar of *B* ......Judg 6:30
Will ye plead for *B*? ....Judg 6:31
Let *B* plead against him.......Judg 6:32
prophets of *B* four hundred ...1Kin 18:19
but if *B*, then follow him......1Kin 18:21
but *B* prophets are four.......1Kin 18:22
unto the prophets of *B*........1Kin 18:25
called on the name of *B* 1Kin 18:26
saying, O *B*, hear us..........1Kin 18:26
Take the prophets of *B* 1Kin 18:40
For he served *B*, and 1Kin 22:53
put away the image of *B* 2Kin 3:2
Ahab served *B* a little 2Kin 10:18
all the prophets of *B*.........2Kin 10:19
great sacrifice to do to *B* 2Kin 10:19
the worshipers of *B* 2Kin 10:19
solemn assembly for *B* 2Kin 10:20
the worshipers of *B* came 2Kin 10:21
came into the house of *B* 2Kin 10:21
house of *B* was full 2Kin 10:21
all the worshipers of *B* 2Kin 10:22
into the house of *B* 2Kin 10:23
unto the worshipers of *B* 2Kin 10:23
but the worshipers of *B* 2Kin 10:23
city of the house of *B*.........2Kin 10:25
out of the house of *B* 2Kin 10:26
brake down the image of *B* ...2Kin 10:27
brake down the house of *B*....2Kin 10:27
Jehu destroyed *B* out 2Kin 10:28
went into the house of *B*......2Kin 11:18
Mattan the priest of *B* 2Kin 11:18
of heaven, and served *B* 2Kin 17:16
went to the house of *B* 2Chr 23:17
slew Mattan the priest of *B* ...2Chr 23:17
prophets prophesied by *B* .....Jer 2:8
offering incense unto *B* ....Jer 11:17
my people to swear by *B*.......Jer 12:16
they prophesied in *B*, and .....Jer 23:13
forgotten my name for *B*......Jer 23:27
offered incense unto *B* ....Jer 32:29
built the high places of *B* .....Jer 32:35
cut off the remnant of *B* ......Zeph 1:4

BAAL (bā'ăl)—*"master; lord"*
1. A Benjamite, from Gideon 1Chr 8:30
2. A descendant of Reuben.1Chr 5:5, 6
3. A village of Simeon 1Chr 4:33
Also called Baalath-beer .Josh 19:8

Kish, and *B* and Ner, and 1Chr 9:36

BAALAH (bā'ăl-ä)—*"mistress"*
1. A town also known as Kirjathjearim ....Josh 15:9,10
2. A hill in Judah ....Josh 15:11
3. A town in South Judah ..Josh 15:29
Probably the same as Bilhah 1Chr 4:29
May be the same as Balah ....Josh 19:3

went up..Israel, to *B*..........1Chr 13:6

BAALATH (bā'ăl-ăth)—*"mistress"*
A village of Dan ....Josh 19:44
Fortified by Solomon 1Kin 9:18

B, and all the store cities 2Chr 8:6

BAALATH-BEER (bā'ă-lăth-bē'er)—*"mistress of a well"*
A border town of Simeon.Josh 19:8
Called Ramath of the south ....Josh 19:8
Also called Baal.........1Chr 4:33

BAAL-BERITH (bā'ăl-bĕ-rĭth')—*"lord of the covenant"*
A god (Baal) of Shechem.Judg 8:33; Judg 9:4
Also called El-berith.....Judg 9:46

BAALE (bā'ă-lē)—*"mistress"*
A town of Judah 2Sam 6:2
Also called Baalah and Kirjathjearim ....Josh 15:9, 10

BAAL-GAD (bā'ăl-găd)—*"the lord of fortune; Gad is Lord"*
A place in the valley of Lebanon ....Josh 11:17

west, from *B* in the valley .....Josh 12:7
from *B* under mount..........Josh 13:5

BAAL-HAMON (bā'ăl-hā'mŏn)—*"lord of a multitude"*
Site of Solomon's vineyard ....Song 8:11

BAAL-HANAN (bā'ăl-hā'năn)—*"the lord is gracious"*
1. Edomite king ....Gen 36:38
2. David's gardener........1Chr 27:28

B the son of Achbor died .....Gen 36:39
Shaul was dead, *B* 1Chr 1:49
when *B* was dead, Hadad 1Chr 1:50

BAAL-HAZOR (bā'ăl-hā'zôr)—*"lord of Hazor (enclosure)"*
A place near Ephraim ...2Sam 13:23

BAAL-HERMON (bā'ăl-hûr'mŏn)—*"lord of Hermon"*
A mountain east of Jordan................Judg 3:3

from Bashan unto *B* and 1Chr 5:23

BAALI (bā'ă-lī)—*"my master (lord)"*
A title rejected by Jehovah ....Hos 2:16

BAALIM (bā'ă-lĭm)—*"lords"—plural of Baal*
Dieties of Canaanite polytheism ....Judg 10:10-14
Ensnared Israelites ......Judg 2:11; Judg 3:7
Rejected in Samuel's time.1Sam 7:4
Historic reminder........1Sam 12:10

went a whoring after *B* ....Judg 8:33
served *B*, and Ashtaroth ......Judg 10:6
God, and also served *B* ....Judg 10:10
and thou hast followed *B* 1Kin 18:18
and sought not unto *B* 2Chr 17:3
did they bestow upon *B* 2Chr 24:7
also molten images for *B* 2Chr 28:2
reared up altars for *B* 2Chr 33:3
brake down..altars of *B* 2Chr 34:4
I have not gone after *B* ....Jer 2:23
after *B*, which their ....Jer 9:14
visit upon her..days of *B* ......Hos 2:13
take away the names of *B*.....Hos 2:17
sacrificed unto *B*, and.........Hos 11:2

BAALIS (bā'ă-lĭs)
An Ammonite king ......Jer 40:14

BAAL-MEON (bā'ăl-mē'ŏn)—*"lord of the house"*
An Amorite city on the Moabite boundary .....Ezek 25:9
Rebuilt by Reubenites ...Num 32:38; Josh 13:17

even unto Nebo and *B* 1Chr 5:8

BAAL-PEOR (bā'ăl-pē'ŏr)—*"lord of Mount Peor"*
A Moabite god..........Num 25:1-5
Infected Israel; 24,000 died ....Num 25:1-9
Vengeance taken on .....Num 31:1-18
Sin long remembered... {Deut 4:3, 4; Josh 22:17; Ps 106:28, 29}
Historic reminder........1Cor 10:8

Israel joined himself unto *B* ...Num 25:3
that were joined unto *B*.......Num 25:5
went to *B*, and separated .....Hos 9:10

BAAL-PERAZIM (bā'ăl-pĕ-rā'zĭm)—*"lord of breaches"*
Where David defeated the Philistines 2Sam 5:18-20
Same as Perazim ....Is 28:21

David came to *B*, and 2Sam 5:20
the name of that place *B*......2Sam 5:20
So they came up to *B*; and 1Chr 14:11
the name of that place *B*......1Chr 14:11

BAAL-SHALISHA (Bā'ăl-shăl'ĭ-shä)—*"lord of a third part"*
A place from which Elisha received food ...2Kin 4:42-44

BAAL-TAMAR (bā'ăl-tāmär)—*"lord of palms"*
A place in Benjamin.....Judg 20:33

BAAL-ZEBUB ((bā'ăl-zē'bŭb)—*"lord of the flies"*
A Philistine god at Ekron.2Kin 1:2

Ahaziah inquired of 2Kin 1:2, 6, 16
Also called Beelzebub ...Matt 10:25
Matt 12:24

BAAL-ZEPHON (bā´ăl-zē´fŏn)—*"lord of the North"*
Israelite camp site ....Ex 14:2, 9
Num 33:7

BAANA (bā´ä-hä)—*"son of grief; patient"*
1. Supply officer 1Kin 4:12
2. Zadok's father ....Neh 3:4

BAANAH (bā´ä-nä)—*"son of grief; affliction"*
1. A murderer of Ish-bosheth 2Sam 4:1-12
2. Heled's father 1Chr 11:30
3. A returning exile ....Ezra 2:2
Neh 7:7
Signs document ....Neh 10:27
4. Supply officer 1Kin 4:16

name of the one was *B* 2Sam 4:2
Rechab and *B*, went, and 2Sam 4:5
Rechab and *B* his brother 2Sam 4:6
answered Rechab and *B* 2Sam 4:9
Heleb the son of *B*, a.........2Sam 23:29

BAARA (bā´ä-rä)—*"a wood; the burning one"*
Shaharaim's wife 1Chr 8:8

BAASEIAH (bā-ä-sē´yä)—*"Jehovah is bold"*
A Levite ancestor of Asaph 1Chr 6:40

BAASHA (bā´ä-shä)—*"boldness"*
Gains throne by murder. .1Kin 15:27, 28
Kills Jeroboam's household 1Kin 15:29, 30
Wars against Asa 1Kin 15:16, 32
Restricts access to Judah. .1Kin 15:17
Contravened by Asa's league with Benhadad. .1Kin 15:18-22
Evil reign 1Kin 15:33, 34

break thy league with *B* 1Kin 15:19
to pass, when *B* heard 1Kin 15:21
wherewith *B* had builded 1Kin 15:22
son of Hanani against *B* 1Kin 16:1
away the posterity of *B* 1Kin 16:3
Him that dieth of *B* 1Kin 16:4
rest of the acts of *B* 1Kin 16:5
B slept with his fathers.........1Kin 16:6
word of the Lord against *B*....1Kin 16:7
Elah the son of *B* to reign 1Kin 16:8
slew all the house of *B*.........1Kin 16:11
destroy all the house of *B*.....1Kin 16:12
which he spake against *B* 1Kin 16:12
all the sins of *B*, and the 1Kin 16:13
like the house of *B* 1Kin 21:22
B king of Israel came up 2Chr 16:1
break thy league with *B*.......2Chr 16:3
it came to pass, when *B*.......2Chr 16:5
wherewith *B* was building 2Chr 16:6
king..made for fear of *B* ......Jer 41:9

BABBLER—*an inane prattler*
The mumblings of drunkards ....Prov 23:29-35
Like a serpent ....Eccl 10:11
Paul called such ....Acts 17:18
Paul's warnings against ...1Tim 6:20
2 Tim 2:16

BABBLING—*inane prattling*
who hath *b*? who hath ....Prov 23:29

BABE—*an infant*

Natural:
Moses ....Ex 2:6
John Baptist ....Luke 1:41, 44
Christ ....Luke 2:12, 16
Timothy ....2 Tim 3:15
Offspring ....Ps 17:14

Figurative of:
Unenlightened ....Rom 2:20
True believers ....Matt 11:25
Matt 21:16
New Christians 1Pet 2:2
Carnal Christians 1Cor 3:1
Heb 5:13

[*also* BABES]
of the mouth of *b* and ....Ps 8:2
their substance to their *b*......Ps 17:14
and *b* shall rule over them ....Is 3:4
hast revealed them unto *b*.....Luke 10:21

BABEL (bā´bĕl)—*"gate of God"*
A city built by Nimrod in the plain of Shinar ....Gen 10:10

BABEL, TOWER OF
A huge brick structure intended to magnify man and preserve the unity of the race ......Gen 11:1-4
Objectives thwarted by God ....Gen 11:5-9

BABYLON (băb´ĭ-lŏn)—*a city situated on banks of the Euphrates river; capital of Babylonian empire*

History of:
Built by Nimrod ....Gen 10:9, 10
Tower built there ....Gen 11:1-9
Amraphel's capital ....Gen 14:1
Once the capital of Assyria 2Chr 33:11
Greatest power under Nebuchadnezzar ....Dan 4:30
A magnificent city ....Is 13:19
Is 14:4
Wide walls of ....Jer 51:44
Gates of ....Is 45:1, 2
Bel, god of ....Is 46:1
Jews carried captive to ...2Kin 25:1-21
2 Chr 36:5-21

Inhabitants, described as:
Idolatrous ....Jer 50:35, 38
Dan 3:18
Enslaved by magic ....Is 47:1, 9-13
Sacrilegious ....Dan 5:1-3

Prophecies concerning:
Babylon, God's agent ....Jer 25:9
Jer 27:5-8
God fights with ....Jer 21:1-7
Jews, 70 years in ....Jer 25:12
Jer 29:10
First of great empires ....Dan 2:31-38
Dan 7:2-4
Downfall of ....Is 13:1-22
Jer 50:1-46
Cyrus, God's agent ......Is 45:1-4
Perpetual desolation of...Is 13:19-22
Jer 50:13, 39

[*also* BABYLON'S]
brought men from *B* 2Kin 17:24
men of *B* made Succoth.......2Kin 17:30
son of Baladan, king of *B*.....2Kin 20:12
far country, even from *B*......2Kin 20:14
shall be carried unto *B*........2Kin 20:17
palace of the king of *B* 2Kin 20:18
king of *B* came up, and 2Kin 24:1
the king of *B* had taken.......2Kin 24:7
of *B* came up against 2Kin 24:10
king of *B* came against........2Kin 24:11
went out to the king of *B*.....2Kin 24:12
king of *B* took him in the 2Kin 24:12
away Jehoiachin to *B* 2Kin 24:15
from Jerusalem to *B* 2Kin 24:15
of *B* brought captive to *B* 2Kin 24:16
the king of *B* made 2Kin 24:17
rebelled against..of *B* 2Kin 24:20
of *B* came, he, and all 2Kin 25:1
him up to the king of *B* 2Kin 25:6
and carried him to *B* 2Kin 25:7
Nebuchadnezzar king of *B* 2Kin 25:8
servant of the king of *B*.......2Kin 25:8
fell away to the king of *B* 2Kin 25:11
the brass of them to *B* 2Kin 25:13
them to the king of *B* to 2Kin 25:20
king of *B* smote them, and 2Kin 25:21
Nebuchadnezzar king of *B* 2Kin 25:22
of *B* had made Gedaliah 2Kin 25:23
and serve the king of *B* 2Kin 25:24
Evil-merodach king of *B* 2Kin 25:27
that were with him in *B*.......2Kin 25:28
away to *B* for their 1Chr 9:1
of the princes of *B* 2Chr 32:31
up from *B* unto Jerusalem.....Ezra 1:11
B had carried away unto *B*....Ezra 2:1
king of *B*, the Chaldean ......Ezra 5:12
the people away into *B* ....Ezra 5:12
of Cyrus the king of *B* ....Ezra 5:13
brought them..temple of *B* ....Ezra 5:14
take out of the temple of *B* ...Ezra 5:14
house, which is there at *B*.....Ezra 5:17
treasures were laid up in *B* ....Ezra 6:1
and brought unto *B*, be ....Ezra 6:5
This Ezra went up from *B* ....Ezra 7:6
began he to go up from *B*.....Ezra 7:9
in all the province of *B* ....Ezra 7:16
went up with me from *B* ......Ezra 8:1
king of *B* had carried away....Neh 7:6
of Artaxerxes king of *B* ....Neh 13:6
king of *B* had carried away....Esth 2:6
mention of Rahab and *B* ......Ps 87:4
the rivers of *B*..we sat ....Ps 137:1
O daughter of *B*, who art .....Ps 137:8
cut off from *B* the name ......Is 14:22
B is fallen, is fallen ....Is 21:9
king of *B*, sent letters..........Is 39:1
unto me, even from *B* ....Is 39:3
day, shall be carried to *B* .....Is 39:6
palace of the king of *B* ....Is 39:7
your sake I have sent to *B* ....Is 43:14
will do his pleasure on *B*......Is 48:14
Go ye forth of *B*, flee ye .....Is 48:20
the hand of the king of *B* .....Jer 20:4
carry them captive into *B* .....Jer 20:4
and carry them to *B* ....Jer 20:5
and thou shalt come to *B* .....Jer 20:6
the hand of the king of *B* .....Jer 21:10
king of *B*, and into the ....Jer 22:25
king of *B* had carried away....Jer 24:1
and had brought them to *B* ...Jer 24:1
Nebuchadnezzar king of *B* ....Jer 25:1
serve the king of *B* seventy....Jer 25:11
not serve the king of *B* ....Jer 27:9
yoke of the king of *B*.........Jer 27:11
not serve the king of *B* ....Jer 27:13
not serve the king of *B* ....Jer 27:14
be brought again from *B* ......Jer 27:16
serve the king of *B*, and ......Jer 27:17
at Jerusalem, go not to *B* .....Jer 27:18
Nebuchadnezzar king of *B* ....Jer 27:20
from Jerusalem to *B*, and .....Jer 27:20
They shall be carried to *B*.....Jer 27:22
the yoke of the king of *B* ....Jer 28:2
Nebuchadnezzar king of *B* ....Jer 28:3
and carried them to *B* ....Jer 28:3
Judah, that went into *B* ....Jer 28:4
the yoke of the king of *B* .....Jer 28:4
from *B* into this place.........Jer 28:6
king of *B* from the neck ......Jer 28:11
Nebuchadnezzar king of *B* ....Jer 28:14
from Jerusalem to *B* ....Jer 29:1
king of Judah sent unto *B*.....Jer 29:3
Nebuchadnezzar king of *B* ....Jer 29:3
from Jerusalem unto *B*........Jer 29:4
raised us up prophets in *B* ....Jer 29:15
sent from Jerusalem to *B* .....Jer 29:20
king of *B* and he shall slay ....Jer 29:21
of Judah which are in *B*........Jer 29:22
king of *B* roasted..fire ....Jer 29:22
he sent unto us in *B* ....Jer 29:28
king of *B* army besieged ......Jer 32:2
king of *B*, and he shall.......Jer 32:3
the king of *B* and shall........Jer 32:4
shall lead Zedekiah to *B* ......Jer 32:5
Nebuchadrezzar king of *B*.....Jer 32:28
king of *B* by the sword ....Jer 32:36
king of *B*, and all his army....Jer 34:1
king of *B*, and he shall........Jer 34:2
the eyes of the king of *B*......Jer 34:3
and thou shalt go to *B* ....Jer 34:3
When the king of *B* army .....Jer 34:7
the hand of the king of *B* .....Jer 34:21

Nebuchadrezzar king of ***B*** ..... Jer 35:11
king of ***B*** shall certainly .... Jer 36:29
Nebuchadrezzar king of ***B*** ..... Jer 37:1
the hand of the king of ***B*** ..... Jer 37:17
king of ***B*** shall not come ...... Jer 37:19
B army, which shall take ...... Jer 38:3
forth unto the king of ***B*** ...... Jer 38:17
to the king of ***B*** princes .... Jer 38:18
forth to the king of ***B*** .... Jer 38:22
hand of the king of ***B*** .... Jer 38:23
Nebuchadrezzar king of ***B*** ..... Jer 39:1
princes of the king of ***B*** .... Jer 39:3
princes of the king of ***B*** .... Jer 39:3
Nebuchadrezzar king of ***B*** ..... Jer 39:5
king of ***B*** slew the sons .... Jer 39:6
the king of ***B*** slew all .... Jer 39:6
chains, to carry him to ***B*** ...... Jer 39:7
away captive into ***B*** .... Jer 39:9
king of ***B*** gave charge .... Jer 39:11
and all the king of ***B*** .... Jer 39:13
carried..captive unto ***B*** .... Jer 40:1
to come with me into ***B*** .... Jer 40:4
to come with me into ***B*** .... Jer 40:4
the king of ***B*** hath made ...... Jer 40:5
the king of ***B*** had made .... Jer 40:7
carried away captive to ***B*** ..... Jer 40:7
and serve the king of ***B*** .... Jer 40:9
king of ***B*** had left a remnant .. Jer 40:11
him, whom the king of ***B*** ..... Jer 41:2
whom the king of ***B*** made ..... Jer 41:18
not afraid of the king of ***B*** .... Jer 42:11
us away captives into ***B*** .... Jer 43:3
the king of ***B*** .... Jer 43:10
king of ***B***, his enemy .... Jer 44:30
king of ***B*** smote in the .... Jer 46:2
Nebuchadrezzar king of ***B*** ..... Jer 46:13
Nebuchadrezzar king of ***B*** ..... Jer 46:26
Nebuchadrezzar king of ***B*** ..... Jer 49:28
king of ***B*** hath taken .... Jer 49:30
I will raise up against ***B*** ...... Jer 51:1
will send unto ***B*** fanners ...... Jer 51:2
Flee out of the midst of ***B*** .... Jer 51:6
B hath been a golden cup ..... Jer 51:7
B is suddenly fallen and .... Jer 51:8
We would have healed ***B*** ...... Jer 51:9
his device is against ***B*** .... Jer 51:11
upon the walls of ***B*** .... Jer 51:12
the inhabitants of ***B*** .... Jer 51:12
I will render unto ***B*** and ...... Jer 51:24
be performed against ***B*** .... Jer 51:29
make the land of ***B*** a .... Jer 51:29
mighty men of ***B*** have .... Jer 51:30
shew the king of ***B*** that .... Jer 51:31
B is like a threshing .... Jer 51:33
king of ***B*** hath devoured ...... Jer 51:34
to my flesh be upon ***B*** .... Jer 51:35
B shall become heaps, a ...... Jer 51:37
how is ***B*** become an .... Jer 51:41
The sea is come up upon ***B*** ... Jer 51:42
the graven images of ***B*** .... Jer 51:47
therein, shall sing for ***B*** .... Jer 51:48
As ***B*** hath caused..slain .... Jer 51:49
at ***B*** shall fall the slain .... Jer 51:49
B should mount up to .... Jer 51:53
of a cry cometh from ***B*** .... Jer 51:54
the Lord hath spoiled ***B*** .... Jer 51:55
upon her, even upon ***B*** .... Jer 51:56
walls of ***B*** shall be utterly ..... Jer 51:58
B in the fourth year of his .... Jer 51:59
that should come upon ***B*** ..... Jer 51:60
are written against ***B*** .... Jer 51:60
When thou comest to ***B*** .... Jer 51:61
Thus shall ***B*** sink, and .... Jer 51:64
against the king of ***B*** .... Jer 52:3
king of ***B*** came, he and all ... Jer 52:4
up unto the king of ***B*** .... Jer 52:9
king of ***B*** slew the sons .... Jer 52:10
the king of ***B*** bound him ...... Jer 52:11
and carried him to ***B*** .... Jer 52:11
Nebuchadrezzar king of ***B*** ..... Jer 52:12
served the king of ***B*** .... Jer 52:12
fell to the king of ***B*** .... Jer 52:15
the brass of them to ***B*** .... Jer 52:17
them to the king of ***B*** to ...... Jer 52:26
the king of ***B*** smote them ..... Jer 52:27
Evil-merodach king of ***B*** ...... Jer 52:31
kings..with him in ***B*** .... Jer 52:32
given him of..king of ***B*** ...... Jer 52:34
I will bring him to ***B*** .... Ezek 12:13
Behold, the king of ***B*** .... Ezek 17:12
led them with him to ***B*** .... Ezek 17:12
midst of ***B*** he shall die .... Ezek 17:16
I will bring him to ***B***, and ..... Ezek 17:20
him to the king of ***B*** .... Ezek 19:9
sword of the king of ***B*** .... Ezek 21:19
the king of ***B*** stood at .... Ezek 21:21
the king of ***B*** set himself ...... Ezek 24:2
Nebuchadrezzar king of ***B*** ..... Ezek 26:7
Nebuchadrezzar king of ***B*** ..... Ezek 29:18
Nebuchadrezzar king of ***B*** ..... Ezek 29:19
Nebuchadrezzar king of ***B*** ..... Ezek 30:10
the arms of the king of ***B*** ..... Ezek 30:24
king of ***B***, and the arms ...... Ezek 30:25
the king of ***B***, and he shall ... Ezek 30:25
the sword of the king of ***B*** .... Ezek 32:11
Nebuchadrezzar king of ***B*** ..... Dan 1:1
all the wise men of ***B*** .... Dan 2:12
to slay the wise men of ***B*** ..... Dan 2:14
rest of the wise men of ***B*** ..... Dan 2:18
Destroy the wise men of ***B*** .... Dan 2:24
not the wise men of ***B*** .... Dan 2:24
over..whole province of ***B*** ..... Dan 2:48
over all the wise men of ***B*** .... Dan 2:48
affairs of the province of ***B*** .... Dan 2:49
Dura, in..the province of ***B*** ... Dan 3:1
affairs of the province of ***B*** .... Dan 3:12
in the province of ***B*** .... Dan 3:30
in all the wise men of ***B*** ...... Dan 4:6
palace of the kingdom of ***B*** ... Dan 4:29
Is not this great ***B*** .... Dan 4:30
said to the wise man of ***B*** ..... Dan 5:7
year of Belshazzar..of ***B*** ...... Dan 7:1
thou shalt go even..***B*** .... Mic 4:10
with the daughter of ***B*** .... Zech 2:7
which are come from ***B*** .... Zech 6:10

BABYLON IN THE NEW TESTAMENT

The city on the Euphrates

Listed as a point of reference .... Matt 1:11, 12, 17
As the place of Israel's exile .... Acts 7:43
As the place of Peter's residence 1Pet 5:13

The prophetic city

Fall predicted .... Rev 14:8
Wrath taken on .... Rev 16:19
Called "the Mother of Harlots" .... Rev 17:1-18
Fall described .... Rev 18:1-24

BABYLONIANS (bab-i-lo'ni-ans)
Inhabitants of Babylonia. . Ezra 4:9; Ezek 23:15-23

BABYLONISH GARMENT—*a valuable robe worn in Babylon*
Coveted by Achan .... Josh 7:21

BACA (bā'kä)—*"weeping"*
Figurative of sorrow ..... Ps 84:6

BACHELOR—*an unmarried man*
Described literally 1Cor 7:26-33
Described figuratively . . . Is 56:3, 4; Matt 19:12; Rev 14:1-5
Not for elders .... Titus 1:5, 6

BACHRITES
Family of Becher .... Num 26:35

BACK—*the rear; rearward; return*

[also BACKS]

he brought ***b*** all the goods .... Gen 14:16
they said, Stand ***b*** .... Gen 19:9
his wife looked ***b*** from .... Gen 19:26
as he drew ***b*** his hand .... Gen 38:29
neither hath he kept ***b*** .... Gen 39:9
Lord caused..sea to go ***b*** ...... Ex 14:21
after he had sent her ***b*** .... Ex 18:2
surely bring it ***b*** to him .... Ex 23:4
thou shalt see my ***b*** parts ..... Ex 33:23
wherefore are we kept ***b*** ...... Num 9:7
brought ***b*** word unto them .... Num 13:26
I will get me ***b*** again .... Num 22:34
hath kept thee ***b*** from .... Num 24:11
shalt turn ***b*** and cover .... Deut 23:13
Joshua drew not his hand ***b*** ... Josh 8:26
at that time turned ***b*** .... Josh 11:10
if ye do in any wise go ***b*** ...... Josh 23:12
he turned and went ***b*** unto .... Judg 18:26
they turned their ***b*** .... Judg 20:42
damsel that came ***b*** .... Ruth 2:6
he is turned ***b*** from 1Sam 15:11
hath kept me ***b*** from 1Sam 25:34
can I bring him ***b*** again? 2Sam 12:23
and take ***b*** thy brethren 2Sam 15:20
Carry ***b*** the ark of God into ... 2Sam 15:25
I will bring ***b*** all..people 2Sam 17:3
Joab held ***b*** the people 2Sam 18:16
word of bringing..king ***b*** 2Sam 19:10
Bring him ***b*** with thee 1Kin 13:18
hast cast me behind thy ***b*** 1Kin 14:9
turned their heart ***b*** 1Kin 18:37
Go ***b*** again; for what 1Kin 19:20
carry him ***b*** unto Amon 1Kin 22:26
the messengers turned ***b*** 2Kin 1:5
and went ***b***, and stood by 2Kin 2:13
king Joram went ***b*** to be 2Kin 8:29
king of Assyria turned ***b*** 2Kin 15:20
I will turn thee ***b*** by the 2Kin 19:28
ten degrees, or go ***b*** ten 2Kin 20:9
And Ornan turned ***b***, and 1Chr 21:20
when Judah looked ***b*** 2Chr 13:14
and carry him ***b*** to Amon 2Chr 18:25
brought them ***b*** unto the 2Chr 19:4
which Amaziah sent ***b*** 2Chr 25:13
Lord, and turned their ***b*** 2Chr 29:6
brought the king word ***b*** 2Chr 34:16
the wall, and turned ***b*** .... Neh 2:15
cast..law behind their ***b*** .... Neh 9:26
I gone ***b*** from the .... Job 23:12
He holdeth ***b*** the face of ...... Job 26:9
He keepeth ***b*** his soul .... Job 33:18
they turned ***b*** from him .... Job 34:27
neither turneth he ***b*** from ..... Job 39:22
enemies are turned ***b*** .... Ps 9:3
the Lord bringeth ***b*** the .... Ps 14:7
Keep ***b*** thy servant also .... Ps 19:13
make them turn their ***b*** .... Ps 21:12
let them be turned ***b*** and ...... Ps 35:4
makest us to turn ***b*** from ...... Ps 44:10
Every one of them is gone ***b*** .. Ps 53:3
shall mine enemies turn ***b*** ..... Ps 56:9
Let them be turned ***b*** .... Ps 70:3
turned ***b*** in..day of battle ...... Ps 78:9
will not we go ***b*** from .... Ps 80:18
brought ***b*** the captivity .... Ps 85:1
fled: Jordan was driven ***b*** ..... Ps 114:3
plowed upon my ***b***; they .... Ps 129:3
a rod is for the ***b*** of him ..... Prov 10:13
stripes for the ***b*** of fools ...... Prov 19:29
a rod for the fool's ***b*** .... Prov 26:3
and who shall turn it ***b*** .... Is 14:27
will not call ***b*** his words .... Is 31:2
and I will turn thee ***b*** .... Is 37:29
all my sins behind thy ***b*** .... Is 38:17
They shall be turned ***b*** .... Is 42:17
to the south. Keep not ***b*** ...... Is 43:6
neither turned away ***b*** .... Is 50:5
turned their ***b*** unto me .... Jer 2:27
the Lord is not turned ***b*** ...... Jer 4:8
turn ***b*** thine hand as a .... Jer 6:9
Jerusalem slidden ***b*** by a ...... Jer 8:5
They are turned ***b*** to the ...... Jer 11:10
show them the ***b***, and not ..... Jer 18:17
I will turn ***b*** the weapons ..... Jer 21:4
have turned unto me the ***b*** ... Jer 32:33
and they are turned away ***b*** .. Jer 38:22
he was not yet gone ***b*** .... Jer 40:5
I will keep nothing ***b*** .... Jer 42:4
and turned away ***b***? .... Jer 46:5
fathers shall not look ***b*** .... Jer 47:3
he..keepeth ***b*** his sword .... Jer 48:10
Flee ye, turn ***b***, dwell deep .... Jer 49:8
he hath turned me ***b***; he ...... Lam 1:13
their ***b*** toward the temple ..... Ezek 8:16

their *b*, and their hands . . . . . . .Ezek 10:12
me behind thy *b*, therefore . . . .Ezek 23:35
I will not go *b*, neither . . . . .Ezek 24:14
And I will turn thee *b* . . . . .Ezek 38:4
I will turn thee *b*, ...Ezek 39:2
Then he brought me *b* the . . . .Ezek 44:1
which had upon the *b* of . . . . . .Dan 7:6
Israel slideth *b* as a . . . . .Hos 4:16
cry; but none shall look *b* . . . . .Nah 2:8
them that are turned *b* . . . . . .Zeph 1:6
I turn *b* your captivity . . . . .Zeph 3:20
return *b* to take..clothes . . . . . .Matt 24:18
came..rolled *b* the stone . . . . . .Matt 28:2
in the field not turn *b* . . . . .Mark 13:16
b again to Jerusalem . . . . .Luke 2:45
ship..returned *b* again . . . . .Luke 8:37
looking *b*, is fit for . . . . .Luke 9:62
turned *b*, and with a loud . . . . .Luke 17:15
his disciples went *b* . . . . .John 6:66
turned herself *b*..saw . . . . .John 20:14
kept *b* part of the price . . . . . . .Acts 5:2
hearts turned *b* again . . . . .Acts 7:39
how I kept *b* nothing that . . . . .Acts 20:20
bow down their *b* always . . . . . .Rom 11:10
but if any man draw *b*, my . . . .Heb 10:38
is of you kept *b* by fraud . . . . . .James 5:4

BACKBITING—*reviling another in secret; slander*
A fruit of sin . . . . .Rom 1:30
Expressed by the mouth. .Ps 50:20
An offspring of anger . . . .Prov 25:23
Merits punishment . . . . . . .Ps 101:5
Keeps from God . . . . .Ps 15:1, 3
To be laid aside 1Pet 2:1
Unworthy of Christians . .2Cor 12:20

BACKBONE—*spinal column*
take off hard by the *b* . . . . .Lev 3:9

BACKSIDE—*in or on the back of*
flock to the *b* of..desert . . . . . . .Ex 3:1
over the *b* of..tabernacle . . . . . .Ex 26:12
written within..on the *b* . . . . . . .Rev 5:1

BACKSLIDING—*forgetting good resolutions; turning away from God after conversion*

Described as:
Turning from God 1Kin 11:9
Turning to evil . . . . .Ps 125:5
Turning to Satan . . . . .1 Tim 5:15
Turning back to the world 2Tim 4:10
Tempting Christ 1Cor 10:9
Turning from first love . . .Rev 2:4
Turning from the Gospel .Gal 3:1-5

Prompted by:
Haughty spirit . . . . .Prov 16:18
Spiritual blindness 2Pet 1:9; Rev.3:17
Murmuring . . . . .Ex 17:3
Lusting after evil . . . . .Ps 106:14
Material things . . . . .Mark 4:18, 19; 1Tim 6:10
Prosperity . . . . .Deut 8:11-14
Tribulation . . . . .Matt 13:20, 21

Results:
Displeases God . . . . .Ps 78:56-59
Punishment . . . . .Num 14:43-45; Jer 8:5-13
Blessings withheld . . . . . .Is 59:2
Unworthiness . . . . .Luke 9:62

Examples of Israel's:
At Meribah . . . . .Ex 17:1-7
At Sinai . . . . .Ex 32:1-35
In wilderness . . . . .Ps 106:14-33
After Joshua's death . . . . .Judg 2:8-23; Ps 106:34-43
In Solomon's life . . . . .1Kin 11:4-40; Neh 13:26
During Asa's reign 2Chr 15:3, 4
During Manasseh's reign. .2 Chr 33:1-10

Examples of, among believers:
Lot . . . . .Gen 19:1-22
David . . . . .2Sam 11:1-5; Ps 51:1-19
Peter . . . . .Matt 26:69-75; Luke 22:31, 32
Galatians . . . . .Gal 1:6; Gal 4:9-11
Corinthians 1Cor 5:1-13
Churches of Asia . . . . .2Tim 1:15; Rev 2, 3

See APOSTASY

[*also* BACKSLIDER, BACKSLIDINGS]
b in heart shall be filled . . . . . . .Prov 14:14
thy *b* shall reprove thee . . . . . . .Jer 2:19
which *b* israel hath done? . . . . .Jer 3:6
b Israel committed . . . . .Jer 3:8
b Israel hath justified . . . . .Jer 3:11
Return, thou *b* Israel . . . . .Jer 3:12
Turn, O *b* children, saith . . . . . .Jer 3:14
Return, ye *b* children . . . . .Jer 3:22
and I will heal your *b* . . . . .Jer 3:22
their *b* are increased . . . . .Jer 5:6
our *b* are many . . . . .Jer 14:7
O thou *b* daughter? . . . . .Jer 31:22
thy flowing valley, O *b* . . . . .Jer 49:4
Israel slideth back as..*b* . . . . . .Hos 4:16
my people are bent to *b* . . . . . .Hos 11:7
I will heal their *b* . . . . .Hos 14:4

BACKWARD—*toward the back*
shoulders, and went *b* . . . . .Gen 9:23
his rider shall fall *b* . . . . .Gen 49:17
fell from off the seat *b* 1Sam 4:18
shadow return *b* ten degrees . . .2Kin 20:10
b; but I cannot perceive . . . . . . .Job 23:8
them be driven *b* and put . . . . .Ps 40:14
be turned *b*, and put to . . . . . . .Ps 70:2
they are gone away *b* . . . . .Is 1:4
might go, and fall *b* . . . . .Is 28:13
sun dial ten degrees *b* . . . . .Is 38:8
that turneth wise men *b* . . . . . . .Is 44:25
judgment is turned away *b* . . . .Is 59:14
went *b*, and not forward . . . . . .Jer 7:24
sigheth, and turneth *b* . . . . .Lam 1:8
they went *b*, and fell to . . . . . . .John 18:6

BAD—*not good in any way*

[*also* BADNESS]
cannot speak unto thee *b* . . . . .Gen 24:50
Jacob either good or *b* . . . . .Gen 31:24
nor change..good for a *b* . . . . . .Lev 27:10
whether it be good or *b* . . . . . . .Num 18:19
good or *b* of mine own . . . . . . .Num 24:13
Amnon neither good nor *b* 2Sam 13:22
king to discern good and *b* 2Sam 14:17
discern good and *b* 1Kin 3:9
rebellious and the *b* city . . . . . .Ezra 4:12
not..eaten, they were so *b* . . . . .Jer 24:2
vessels, but cast the *b* . . . . .Matt 13:48
as they found, both *b* . . . . .Matt 22:10

BADE—*commanded to*

[*also* BADEST]
done according as thou *b* . . . . . .Gen 27:19
did as Joseph *b*; and the . . . . . .Gen 43:17
the morning as Moses *b* . . . . . . .Ex 16:24
congregation *b* stone them . . . .Num 14:10
unto them as the Lord *b* . . . . . .Josh 11:9
all..her mother in law *b* . . . . . . .Ruth 3:6
and some *b* me kill 1Sam 24:10
b them teach the children 2Sam 1:18
thy servant Joab, he *b* me 2Sam 14:19
the king *b*, saying, Come 2Chr 10:12
Then Esther *b* them return . . . .Esth 4:15
they how that he *b* them . . . . . .Matt 16:12
he that *b* thee and him . . . . .Luke 14:9
spirit *b* me go with them . . . . . .Acts 11:12
b them farewell, saying . . . . . . .Acts 18:21
b that he should be . . . . .Acts 22:24

BADGER—*believed to refer to a dolphin or porpoise*
Skins of, used in tabernacle coverings . . . . .Ex 26:14; Ex 35:7
Used for sandals . . . . .Ezek 16:10

[*also* BADGERS']
b skins, and shittim wood . . . . .Ex 25:5
skins of rams, and *b* skins . . . . .Ex 35:23
covering of *b* skins above . . . . .Ex 36:19
the covering of *b* skins . . . . .Ex 39:34
the covering of *b* skins . . . . .Num 4:6
shod thee with *b* skin . . . . .Ezek 16:10

BAG—*a purse or pouch*

Used for:
Money . . . . .2Kin 12:10; John 12:6
Stones 1Sam 17:40, 49
Weights . . . . .Deut 25:13; Prov 16:11
Food ("vessels") . . . . .1 Sam 9:7

Figurative of:
Forgiveness . . . . .Job 14:17
True righteousness . . . . . . .Prov 16:11
True riches . . . . .Luke 17:33
Insecure riches . . . . .Hag 1:6

[*also* BAGS]
talents of silver in two *b* 2Kin 5:23
taken a *b* of money with . . . . . .Prov 7:20
lavish gold out of the *b* . . . . . . .Is 46:6
b of deceitful weights? . . . . .Mic 6:11
provide yourselves *b* which . . . .Luke 12:33
because Judas had the *b* . . . . . .John 13:29

BAHUMITE (bä-hū´mīt)
Applied to Azmaveth 2Sam 23:31

Azmaveth the *b*, Eliahba 1Chr 11:33
See BARHUMITE

BAHURIM (bä-hū´rĭm)—*"low ground"*
A village near Jerusalem. .2Sam 3:16
Where Shimei cursed David 2Sam 16:5
Where two men hid in a well 2Sam 17:18

Benjamite, which was of *B* 2Sam 19:16
a Benjamite of *B*, which 1Kin 2:8

BAJITH (bā´jĭth)—*"house"*
A derisive reference to the temple of Moabite gods . . . . .Is 15:2

BAKBAKKAR (băk-băk´er)—*"diligent; searcher"*
A Levite 1Chr 9:15

BAKBUK (băk´bŭk)—*"waste; hollow"*
Head of postexilic family. .Ezra 2:51; Neh 7:53

BAKBUKIAH (băk-bū-kī´ä)—*"wasted by Jehovah"*
1. A Levite of high position.Neh 11:17
2. Levite porter . . . . .Neh 12:25

BAKE—*to prepare food in an oven*

[*also* BAKED, BAKEN, BAKETH]
did *b* unleavened bread . . . . . . .Gen 19:3
they *b* unleavened cakes . . . . . .Ex 12:39
b that which ye will *b* . . . . .Ex 16:23
a meat offering *b* in the . . . . . . .Lev 2:4
a meat offering *b* in a pan . . . .Lev 2:5
offering *b* in..frying pan . . . . . . .Lev 2:7
shall not be *b* with leaven . . . . .Lev 6:17
when it is *b*, thou shalt . . . . . . .Lev 6:21
the *b* pieces of the meat . . . . . .Lev 6:21
meat offering that is *b* . . . . .Lev 7:9
shall be *b* with leaven . . . . .Lev 23:17
and *b* twelve cakes thereof . . . .Lev 24:5
ten women shall *b* your . . . . . . .Lev 26:26
b it in pans, and made cakes . .Num 11:8
did *b* unleavened bread 1Sam 28:24
sight, and did *b* the cakes 2Sam 13:8
was a cake *b* on the coals 1Kin 19:6
that which is *b* in the pan 1Chr 23:29
kindleth it, and *b* bread . . . . . . .Is 44:15
I have *b* bread upon the . . . . . .Is 44:19
shall *b* the meat offering . . . . . .Ezek 46:20

BAKEMEATS—*baked goods prepared for the pharaoh*
of *b* for Pharaoh . . . . .Gen 40:17

BAKER—*one who cooks food (bread)*

Kinds of:
Household ....Gen 18:6
Public ....Jer 37:21
Royal ....Gen 40:1, 2

[*also* **BAKERS**]
the *b* of the king of Egypt ....Gen 40:5
When the chief *b* saw that ....Gen 40:16
of the chief *b* among his ......Gen 40:20
But he hanged the chief *b*.....Gen 40:22
both me and the chief *b*.......Gen 41:10
as an oven heated by the *b*....Hos 7:4
b sleepeth all the night........Hos 7:6

BALAAM (bā'lăm)—*"a pilgrim; lord (Baal) of the people"—a prophet under the king of Moab*

Information concerning:
A son of Beor ....Num 22:5
From Mesopotamia ......Deut 23:4
A soothsayer ....Josh 13:22
A prophet 2Pet 2:15
A Midianite.............Num 31:8
Killed because of his sin. .Num 31:1-8

Mission of:
Balak sent to curse Israel.Num 22:5-7
Josh 24:9
Hindered by speaking ass.Num 22:22-35
2Pet 2:16
Curse becomes a blessing.Deut 23:4, 5
Josh 24:10

Prophecies of:
Under divine control.....Num22:18, 38
Num23:16, 20, 26
By the Spirit's prompting..Num 24:2
Blessed Israel three times.Num 24:10
Spoke of the Messiah in final message..........Num 24:14-19

Nature of:
"Unrighteousness"—greed.................2Pet 2:14, 15
"Error"—rebellion ......Jude 11

[*also* **BALAAM'S**]
of Moab abode with *B* ....Num 22:8
God came unto *B*, and........Num 22:9
And *B* said unto God.........Num 22:10
God said unto *B*, Thou ....Num 22:12
B rose up in the morning .....Num 22:13
said, *B* refuseth to come ......Num 22:14
they came to *B*, and said......Num 22:16
God came unto *B* at night ....Num 22:20
B rose up in the morning .....Num 22:21
Balak heard that *B* was ....Num 22:36
Balak said unto *B*, Did ....Num 22:37
sent to *B* and to the ....Num 22:40
Balak took *B*, and brought ....Num 22:41
And *B* said unto Balak ....Num 23:1
Balak did as *B* had spoken ....Num 23:2
Balak and *B* offered on ....Num 23:2
B said unto Balak, Stand......Num 23:3
And God met *B*; and he ......Num 23:4
the Lord put a word in *B* .....Num 23:5
Balak said unto *B*, What .....Num 23:11
Balak said unto *B*, Neither ....Num 23:25
Balak said unto *B*, Come, I ...Num 23:27
brought *B* unto the top of.....Num 23:28
B said unto Balak, Build ......Num 23:29
Balak did as *B* had said ....Num 23:30
B saw that it pleased the ....Num 24:1
B said unto Balak, Spake I....Num 24:12
B rose up, and went and ......Num 24:25
through the counsel of *B* ......Num 31:16
but hired *B* against them ......Neh 13:2
what *B* the son of Beor ....Mic 6:5
doctrine of *B*, who taught .....Rev 2:14

BALAC—*See* **BALAK**

BALADAN (băl'ā-dăn)—*"having power"*
Father of Merodach-baladan (*also spelled* Berodach-baladan).....2Kin 20:12

BALAH (bā'lä)—*"mistress"*
Hazar-shual, and *B*, and ......Josh 19:3
See **BAALAH**

BALAK, BALAC (bā'lăk)—*"void; empty"*
A Moabite king ....Num 22:4
Hired Balaam to curse Israel...................Num 22-24

[*also* **BALAK'S**]
B the son of Zippor saw all ...Num 22:2
unto him the words of *B* ......Num 22:7
B the son of Zippor, king .....Num 22:10
said unto the princes of *B* .....Num 22:13
went unto *B*, and said ....Num 22:14
B sent yet again princes.......Num 22:15
saith *B* the son of Zippor .....Num 22:16
unto the servants of *B* ....Num 22:18
If *B* would give me ....Num 22:18
went with the princes of *B* ....Num 22:35
B heard that Baalam was .....Num 22:36
B said unto Balaam, Did I ....Num 22:37
Balaam said unto *B*, Lo, I ....Num 22:38
Balaam went with *B*, and .....Num 22:39
B offered oxen and sheep .....Num 22:40
B took Balaam, and ....Num 22:41
Balaam said unto *B*, Build ....Num 23:1
B did as Balaam had ....Num 23:2
B and Balaam offered on .....Num 23:2
Balaam said unto *B*, Stand ....Num 23:3
Return unto *B*, and thus ......Num 23:5
said, *B* the king of Moab .....Num 23:7
B said unto Balaam, What ....Num 23:11
B said unto him, Come, I.....Num 23:13
said unto *B*, Stand here ....Num 23:15
Go again unto *B*, and say .....Num 23:16
B said unto him, What hath ...Num 23:17
said, Rise up, *B*, and hear ....Num 23:18
And *B* said unto Balaam ......Num 23:25
said unto *B*, Told not ....Num 23:26
B said unto Balaam, Come ....Num 23:27
B brought Balaam unto the ...Num 23:28
Balaam said unto *B*, Build ....Num 23:29
B did as Baalam had said .....Num 23:30
And *B* anger was kindled .....Num 24:10
B said unto Balaam, I ....Num 24:10
Balaam said unto *B*, Spake....Num 24:12
to his place; and *B* also ....Num 24:25
Then *B* the son of Zippor .....Josh 24:9
anything better than *B* ....Judg 11:25
taught *B* to cast a ....Rev 2:14

BALANCES—*an instrument for weighing; scales*

Used for weighing:
Things ....Lev 19:36
Money ....Jer 32:10

Laws concerning:
Must be just ....Lev 19:36
False, an abomination ...Prov 11:1
Deceit, condemned ......Amos 8:5

Figurative of:
God's justice ....Job 31:6
Man's smallness ....Ps 62:9
Is 40:12, 15
God's judgment ....Dan 5:27
Man's tribulation ....Rev 6:5

[*also* **BALANCE, BALANCINGS**]
my calamity laid in the *b*......Job 6:2
thou know the *b* of the ....Job 37:16
just weight and *b* are the......Prov 16:11
and a false *b* is not good ......Prov 20:23
weigh silver in the *b* and ......Is 46:6
then take thee *b* to weigh .....Ezek 5:1
Ye shall have just *b* ....Ezek 45:10
b of deceit are in his hand ....Hos 12:7
pure with the wicked *b*........Mic 6:11

BALD—*without hair or natural covering*

Natural:
Not a sign of leprosy ....Lev 13:40, 41
Elijah mocked for 2Kin 2:23, 24

Artificial:
A sign of mourning ......Is 22:12
An idolatrous practice ...Lev 21:5
Deut 14:1
Inflicted upon captives ...Deut 21:12
Forbidden to priests .....Ezek 44:20
A part of Nazarite vow ..Num 6:9, 18

Figurative of judgment, upon:
Israel...................Is 3:24
Amos 8:10
Moab ....Is 15:2
Philistia................Jer 47:5
Tyre....................Ezek 27:31

if there be in the *b* head ......Lev 13:42
or *b* forehead, a white ....Lev 13:42
leprosy sprung up in the *b* ....Lev 13:42
head or his *b* forehead ....Lev 13:42
reddish in his *b* head ....Lev 13:43
or in his *b* forehead ....Lev 13:43
make themselves *b* for ....Jer 16:6
every head shall be *b* ....Jer 48:37
b upon all their heads.........Ezek 7:18
every head was made *b* ....Ezek 29:18
Make thee *b*, and poll thee....Mic 1:16
enlarge thy *b* as the eagle .....Mic 1:16

BALD LOCUST—*a common insect in arid regions*
A specie of edible locust. .Lev 11:22
See **LOCUST**

BALL—*a spherical object*
Prophetic ....Is 22:18

BALLAD SINGERS
Rendered "they that speak proverbs" ....Num 21:27

BALM—*an aromatic resin or gum*
A product of Gilead .....Jer 8:22
Sent to Joseph ....Gen 43:11
Exported to Tyre ....Ezek 27:17
Healing qualities of ......Jer 46:11
Jer 51:8

spicery and *b* and myrrh ......Gen 37:25

BAMAH (bā'mä)—*"high place"*
A place of idolatry ......Ezek 20:29

BAMOTH (bā-mōth)—*"high places"*
Encampment site Num21:19, 20
Also called Bamoth-baal. .Josh 13:17

BAMOTH-BAAL (bā'mōth-bā'ăl)—*"high places"—same as Bamoth*
Assigned to Reuben .....Josh 13:17

BAND—*something which confines or constricts movement; a group of people*
[*also* **BANDED, BANDS**]
the camels, into two *b* ....Gen 32:7
now I am become two *b* ......Gen 32:10
a *b* round about the hole......Ex 39:23
broken the *b* of your yoke ....Lev 26:13
b loosed from off his ....Judg 15:14
him a *b* of men, whose 1Sam 10:26
that were captains of *b*........2Sam 4:2
captain over a *b*, when........1Kin 11:24
So the *b* of Syria came no 2Kin 6:23
And the *b* of the Moabites 2Kin 13:20
they spied a *b* of men; and 2Kin 13:21
put him in *b* at 2Kin 23:33
against him *b* of the 2Kin 24:2
and *b* of the Syrians 2Kin 24:2
and *b* of the Moabites 2Kin 24:2
b of the children of Ammon ...2Kin 24:2
were *b* of soldiers for war 1Chr 7:4
them captains of the *b* 1Chr 12:18
David against the *b* of 1Chr 12:21
b, that were ready armed 1Chr 12:23
b of men that came with 2Chr 22:1
went out to war by *b* 2Chr 26:11
the king a *b* of soldiers ....Ezra 8:22
made out three *b*, and ....Job 1:17
Pleiades, or loose the *b* ....Job 38:31
loosed the *b* of the wild.......Job 39:5
unicorn with his *b* in the ......Job 39:10
break their *b* asunder, and ....Ps 2:3
are no *b* in their death........Ps 73:4
break their *b* in sunder........Ps 107:14

The ***b*** of the wicked have ..... Ps 119:61
forth all of them by ***b*** .... Prov 30:27
nets, and her hands as ***b*** ...... Eccl 7:26
lest your ***b*** be made strong .... Is 28:22
loose thyself from the ***b*** .... Is 52:2
thy yoke, and burst thy ***b*** ..... Jer 2:20
they shall put ***b*** upon thee .... Ezek 3:25
to help him, and all his ***b*** ..... Ezek 12:14
with all his ***b*** shall fall .... Ezek 17:21
have broken the ***b*** of their .... Ezek 34:27
Gomer, and all his ***b*** .... Ezek 38:6
quarters, and all his ***b*** .... Ezek 38:6
land, thou, and all thy ***b*** ...... Ezek 38:9
upon him, upon his ***b*** .... Ezek 38:22
Israel, thou..all thy ***b*** .... Ezek 39:4
even with a ***b*** of iron .... Dan 4:15
earth, even with a ***b*** .... Dan 4:23
of a man, with ***b*** of love ...... Hos 11:4
Beauty..other I called ***B*** ...... Zech 11:7
mine other staff, even ***B*** ...... Zech 11:14
unto him the whole ***b*** .... Matt 27:27
call together the whole ***b*** ...... Mark 15:16
he brake the ***b***, and was ...... Luke 8:29
having received a ***b*** of men .... John 18:3
Then the ***b*** and the captain .... John 18:12
b called the Italian ***b*** .... Acts 10:1
every one's ***b*** were loosed ..... Acts 16:26
chief captain of the ***b*** .... Acts 21:31
he loosed him from his ***b*** ...... Acts 22:30
of the Jews ***b*** together .... Acts 23:12
a centurion of Augustus' ***b*** ...... Acts 27:1
loosed the rudder ***b***, and ...... Acts 27:40
body by joints and ***b*** .... Col 2:19

BANDAGE
Used as disguise 1Kin 20:37-41
In prophecy against Egypt .... Ezek 30:20-22

BANI (bā'nī)—*"posterity"*
1. Gadite warrior 2Sam 23:36
2. A Judahite 1Chr 9:4
3. A postexilic family ...... Ezra 2:10; Neh 10:14
4. A Merarite Levite 1Chr 6:46
5. A Levite; father of Rehum .... Neh 3:17
6. Signed document .... Neh 10:13
7. Head of Levitical family. . Ezra 10:34
8. A postexilic Levite ...... Ezra 10:38
9. A descendant of Asaph . . Neh 11:22

sons of ***B***; Meshullam .... Ezra 10:29
Jeshua and ***B***, and .... Neh 8:7
Levites, Jeshua, and ***B*** .... Neh 9:4
B and Chenani, and cried ..... Neh 9:4
Kadmiel, ***B***, Hashabniah ...... Neh 9:5

BANISHMENT—*forceful expulsion from one's place*

Political, of:
Absalom by David 2Sam 14:13, 14
The Jews into exile 2Chr 36:20, 21
The Jews from Rome .... Acts 18:2

Moral and spiritual, of:
Adam from Eden .... Gen 3:22-24
Cain from others .... Gen 4:12, 14
Lawbreaker .... Ezra 7:26
John to Patmos .... Rev 1:9
Satan from heaven ...... Rev 12:7-9
The wicked to lake of fire .... Rev 20:15; Rev 21:8

burdens and causes of ***b*** ...... Lam 2:14

BANK

A mound:
Raised against a besieged city .... 2Sam 20:15; Is 37:33

A place for money:
Exchange charges .... John 2:15
Interest paid on deposits. . Matt 25:27; Luke 19:23

[*also* BANKS]
I stood upon the ***b*** of the ..... Gen 41:17
is by the ***b*** of the river .... Deut 4:48
overfloweth all his ***b*** all .... Josh 3:15
flowed over all his ***b***, as .... Josh 4:18
upon the ***b*** of the river .... Josh 12:2
is upon the ***b*** of the river ..... Josh 13:9
is on the ***b*** of the river .... Josh 13:16
stood by the ***b*** of Jordan 2Kin 2:13
nor cast a ***b*** against it 2Kin 19:32
it had overflown all his ***b*** 1Chr 12:15
and go over all his ***b*** .... Is 8:7
at the ***b*** of the river were ..... Ezek 47:7
by the river upon the ***b*** .... Ezek 47:12
man's voice between the ***b*** .... Dan 8:16
this side of the ***b*** of the .... Dan 12:5
other on that side of the ***b*** .... Dan 12:5

BANKRUPTCY—*state of financial ruin; inability to pay debts*

Literal:
Condition of David's men. 1Sam 22:2
Unjust steward .... Matt 18:25

Moral and spiritual:
Israel's condition .... Hos 4:1-5
Mankind's condition ..... Rom 1:20-32; Rom 3:9-19
Individual's condition .... Phil 3:4-8; 1Tim 1:13

BANNER—*a flag or cloth standard*

Literal:
Used by armies .... Num 2:2, 3
Signal for blowing trumpet .... Is 18:3

Figurative of:
Jehovah's name ("Jehovah is my banner") .... Ex 17:15
God's salvation .... Ps 20:5; Ps 60:4
God's protection .... Song 2:4
God's power .... Song 6:4, 10

Lift ye up a ***b*** upon the .... Is 13:2

BANQUET—*an elaborate and sumptuous feast*

Reasons for:
Birthday .... Gen 40:20
Marriage .... Gen 29:22
Reunion .... Luke 15:22-25
State affairs .... Esth 1:3, 5; Dan 5:1

Features of:
Invitations sent .... Esth 5:8, 9; Luke 14:16, 17
Non-acceptance merits censure .... Luke 14:18-24
Courtesies to guests ..... Luke 7:40-46
Special garment .... Matt 22:11; Rev 3:4, 5
A presiding governor .... John 2:8
Protocol of seating ...... Gen 43:33; Prov 25:6, 7
Anointing oil .... Ps 45:7
Honor guest noted 1Sam 9:22-24

[*also* BANQUETING, BANQUETINGS]
Haman come..unto the ***b*** ...... Esth 5:4
Haman came to the ***b*** .... Esth 5:5
said unto Esther at the ***b*** ...... Esth 5:6
with the king unto the ***b*** ...... Esth 5:12
with the king unto the ***b*** ...... Esth 5:14
to bring Haman unto the ***b*** .... Esth 6:14
and Haman came to ***b*** .... Esth 7:1
on the second day at the ***b*** .... Esth 7:2
the king arising from the ***b*** .... Esth 7:7
into the place of the ***b*** of ..... Esth 7:8
the companions make a ***b*** ..... Job 41:6
He brought me to the ***b*** .... Song 2:4
his lords, came into the ***b*** ..... Dan 5:10
b of them that stretched ...... Amos 6:7
b, and abominable 1Pet 4:3

BAPTISM, CHRISTIAN—*a rite signifying one's cleansing from sin through Christ's sacrifice*

Commanded by:
Christ .... Matt 28:19, 20; Mark 16:15, 16
Peter .... Acts 10:46-48
Christian ministers .... Acts 22:12-16

Administered by:
The apostles .... Acts 2:1, 41
Ananias .... Acts 9:17, 18
Philip .... Acts 8:12; Acts 8:36-38
Peter .... Acts 10:44-48
Paul .... Acts 18:8; 1Cor 1:14-17

Places:
Jordan .... Matt 3:13-16; Mark 1:5-10
Jerusalem .... Acts 2:5, 41
Samaria .... Acts 8:12
A house .... Acts 10:44-48
A jail .... Acts 16:25-33

Subjects of:
Believing Jews .... Acts 2:41
Believing Gentiles .... Acts 10:44-48; Acts 18:8
Households .... Acts 16:15, 33; 1Cor 1:16

Characteristics of:
By water .... Acts 10:47
Only one .... Eph 4:5
Necessary .... Acts 2:38, 41
Source of power .... Acts 1:5
Follows faith .... Acts 2:41; Acts 18:8

Symbolism of:
Forecast in prophecy ..... Joel 2:28, 29; Acts 2:16-21
Prefigured in types ...... 1 Cor 10:2; 1Pet 3:20, 21
Visualized by the Spirit's descent .... John 1:32, 33; Acts 2:3,4,41; Acts 10:44-48
Expressive of spiritual unity .... 1Cor 12:13; Gal 3:27, 28
Figurative of regeneration. John 3:3, 5,6; Rom 6:3, 4, 11
Illustrative of cleansing . . . Acts 22:16; Titus 3:5

[*also* BAPTISMS, BAPTIZE, BAPTIZED, BAPTIZEST, BAPTIZING]
I indeed ***b*** you with water ..... Matt 3:11
shall ***b*** you with the Holy ..... Matt 3:11
the ***b*** that I am baptized ...... Matt 20:22
the baptism that I am ***b*** with?. . Matt 20:22
I shall drink of, and to be ***b*** . . . Matt 20:22
baptized with the ***b*** that .... Matt 20:23
and be ***b*** with the baptism ..... Matt 20:23
that I am ***b*** with .... Matt 20:23
preach the ***b*** of repentance .... Mark 1:4
shall ***b*** you with the Holy ..... Mark 1:8
and be ***b*** with the baptism ..... Mark 10:38
the ***b*** that I am baptized ..... Mark 10:38
that I am ***b*** with? .... Mark 10:38
the ***b*** that I am baptized ...... Mark 10:39
the baptism that I am ***b*** .... Mark 10:39
withal shall ye be ***b*** .... Mark 10:39
the ***b*** of John, was it from .... Mark 11:30
shall ***b*** you with the Holy ..... Luke 3:16
that Jesus also being ***b*** .... Luke 3:21
I have a ***b*** to be baptized ..... Luke 12:50
I have a baptism to be ***b*** ...... Luke 12:50
the ***b*** of John, was it from .... Luke 20:4
tarried with them, and ***b*** ..... John 3:22
and they came, and were ***b*** . . . John 3:23
the same ***b***, and all men ...... John 3:26
Jesus made and ***b*** more .... John 4:1
(Though Jesus himself ***b*** .... John 4:2
place where John at first ***b*** .... John 10:40
he was ***b***, he continued with . . . Acts 8:13
they were ***b*** in the name ...... Acts 8:16
or were ye ***b*** in the name of . . . 1Cor 1:13
Christ sent me not to ***b*** 1Cor 1:17
they do which are ***b*** for the . . . 1Cor 15:29

why are they then *b* for the . . .1Cor 15:29
Buried with him in *b* . . . . .Col 2:12
Of the doctrine of *b*, and of . . .Heb 6:2

BAPTISM, JOHN'S
Administrator—John . . . . .Matt 3:7
Place—at Jordan . . . . .Matt 3:6, 13, 16
in Aenon . . . . .John 3:23
Persons—people and Jesus . . . . .Mark 1:5, 9
Acts 13:24
Character—repentance . . .Luke 3:3
Reception—rejected by some . . . . .Luke 7:29, 30
Nature—of God . . . . .Matt 21:25, 27
Insufficiency—rebaptism. . .Acts 19:1-7
Intent—to prepare . . . . . Matt 3:11, 12; Acts 11:16; Acts 19:4
Jesus' submission to—fulfilling all righteousness . . . . .Matt 3:13-17

[*also* BAPTIST, BAPTIST'S]
days came John the *B* . . . . .Matt 3:1
greater than John the *B* . . . . . . .Matt 11:11
from the days of John the *B* . . .Matt 11:12
This is John the *B*; he is . . . . . .Matt 14:2
Give me here John *B* head . . . .Matt 14:8
that thou art John the *B* . . . . . .Matt 16:14
unto them of John the *B* . . . . . .Matt 17:13
John did *b* in..wilderness . . . . . .Mark 1:4
That John the *B* was risen . . . .Mark 6:14
The head of John the *B* . . . . . . .Mark 6:24
the head of John the *B* . . . . . . .Mark 6:25
they answered, John the *B* . . . .Mark 8:28
came forth to be *b* of him . . . . .Luke 3:7
also publicans to be *b* . . . . .Luke 3:12
I indeed *b* you with water . . . .Luke 3:16
When all the people were *b* . . .Luke 3:21
John *B* hath sent us unto . . . . .Luke 7:20
prophet than John the *B* . . . . . .Luke 7:28
John the *B* came neither . . . . . .Luke 7:33
answering said, John the *B* . . . .Luke 9:19
said unto him, Why *b* thou . . . .John 1:25
saying, I *b* with water; but . . . .John 1:26
Jordan, where John was *b* . . . . .John 1:28
am I come *b* with water . . . . . . .John 1:31
Beginning from the *b* of . . . . . .Acts 1:22
after the *b* which John . . . . .Acts 10:37
knowing only the *b* of John . . .Acts 18:25

BAR
the middle *b* in the midst . . . . .Ex 26:28
and shall put it upon a *b* . . . . . .Num 4:10
and shall put them on a *b* . . . .Num 4:12
away with them, *b* and all . . . . .Judg 16:3
them shut the doors, and *b* . . . .Neh 7:3
break also the *b* . . . . .Amos 1:5

BARABBAS (bär-ăb'ăs)—*"father's son"*
A murderer released in place of Jesus . . . . Matt 27:16-26; Acts 3:14, 15

there was one named *B* . . . . . . .Mark 15:7
he should rather release *B* . . . .Mark 15:11
released *B* unto them, and . . . .Mark 15:15
and release unto us *B* . . . . .Luke 23:18
Not this man, but *B* . . . . .John 18:40
Now *B* was a robber . . . . .John 18:40

BARACHEL (băr'ä-kĕl)—*"blessed of God"*
Father of Elihu . . . . .Job 32:2, 6

BARACHIAS (băr'ă-kī'ăs)—*"blessed of Jehovah"*
Father of Zechariah . . . . .Matt 23:35

BARAK (bâr'ăk)—*"lightening"—the judge Deborah's general*
Defeats Jabin . . . . .Judg 4:1-24
A man of faith . . . . .Heb 11:32

Then sang Deborah and *B* . . . .Judg 5:1
arise, *B*, and lead thy . . . . .Judg 5:12
even Issachar, and also *B* . . . . .Judg 5:15

BARBARIAN—*non-Greek speaking people*

[*also* BARBARIANS, BARBAROUS]
the *b* people showed us . . . . . .Acts 28:2
when the *b* saw the . . . . .Acts 28:4
to the Greeks, and to the *B* . . .Rom 1:14
unto him that speaketh a *b* 1Cor 14:11
B, Scythian, bond . . . . .Col 3:11

BARBED—*sharply pointed*
fill his skin with *b* irons? . . . . . .Job 41:7

BARBER'S—*belonging to a hair cutter*
take thee a *b* razor . . . . .Ezek 5:1

BARE—*uncovered, naked; past tense of "bear"*

Figurative of:
Destitution . . . . .Ezek 16:22, 39
Uncleanness . . . . .Lev 13:45
Undeveloped state, immaturity . . . . Ezek 16:7; 1Cor 15:37
Power revealed . . . . .Is 52:10
Destruction . . . . .Joel 1:7
Mourning . . . . .Is 32:9-11

[*also* BAREST]
she conceived, and *b* Cain . . . . .Gen 4:1
she again *b* his brother . . . . .Gen 4:2
she conceived, and *b* Enoch . . .Gen 4:17
Adah *b* Jabal: he was the . . . . .Gen 4:20
and Zillah, she also *b* . . . . .Gen 4:22
b a son, and called his . . . . .Gen 4:25
they *b* children to them . . . . . . .Gen 6:4
increased, and *b* up the . . . . . . .Gen 7:17
Abram's wife, *b* him no . . . . . . .Gen 16:1
And Hagar *b* Abram a son . . . .Gen 16:15
name, which Hagar *b* . . . . .Gen 16:15
when Hagar *b* Ishmael to . . . . .Gen 16:16
the firstborn *b* a son, and . . . . .Gen 19:37
the younger, she also *b* . . . . . . .Gen 19:38
maidservants; and they *b* . . . . . .Gen 20:17
Sarah conceived, and *b* . . . . . . .Gen 21:2
Sarah *b* to him, Isaac . . . . .Gen 21:3
she *b* also Tebah and . . . . .Gen 22:24
Milcah, which she *b* unto . . . . .Gen 24:24
wife *b* a son to my master . . . . .Gen 24:36
son, whom Milcah *b* unto . . . . .Gen 24:47
she *b* him Zimran, and . . . . .Gen 25:2
handmaid *b* unto Abraham . . . .Gen 25:12
years old when she *b* . . . . .Gen 25:26
And Leah conceived, and *b* . . .Gen 29:32
again, and *b* a . . . . .Gen 29:33
I saw that she *b* Jacob no . . . . .Gen 30:1
conceived, and *b* Jacob a . . . . . .Gen 30:5
maid conceived again, and *b* . . .Gen 30:7
Zilpah Leah's maid *b* Jacob . . .Gen 30:10
Leah's maid *b* Jacob . . . . .Gen 30:12
she conceived and *b* Jacob . . . .Gen 30:17
again, and *b* Jacob the sixth . . .Gen 30:19
And afterwards she *b* a . . . . . . .Gen 30:21
she conceived, and *b* a son . . . .Gen 30:23
all the cattle *b* speckled . . . . . . .Gen 31:8
then *b* all the cattle . . . . .Gen 31:8
I *b* the loss of it; of my . . . . . . .Gen 31:39
which she *b* unto Jacob . . . . . . .Gen 34:1
Adah *b* to Esau Eliphaz . . . . . .Gen 36:4
and Bashemath *b* Reuel . . . . . . .Gen 36:4
Aholibamah *b* Jeush, and . . . . .Gen 36:5
she *b* to Eliphaz Amalek . . . . . .Gen 36:12
she *b* to Esau Jeush, and . . . . . .Gen 36:14
she conceived, and *b* a son . . . .Gen 38:3
she conceived again, and *b* . . . .Gen 38:4
yet again conceived, and *b* . . . .Gen 38:5
was at Chezib, when she *b* . . . .Gen 38:5
Poti-pherah priest of On *b* . . . .Gen 41:50
Ye know that my wife *b* me . . .Gen 44:27
she *b* unto Jacob in Padan . . . .Gen 46:15
and these she *b* unto Jacob . . . .Gen 46:18
priest of On *b* unto him . . . . . . .Gen 46:20
and she *b* these unto Jacob . . . .Gen 46:25
woman conceived and *b* . . . . . . .Ex 2:2
And she *b* him a son, and . . . . .Ex 2:22
and she *b* him Aaron and . . . . .Ex 6:20
and she *b* him Nadab, and . . . .Ex 6:23
and she *b* him Phinehas . . . . . . .Ex 6:25
whether it be *b* within or . . . . . .Lev 13:55
and they *b* it between two . . . . .Num 13:23
her mother *b* to Levi in . . . . . . .Num 26:59
she *b* unto Amram Aaron . . . . .Num 26:59
that the Lord thy God *b* . . . . . .Deut 1:31
the sons of Levi, which *b* . . . . .Deut 31:9
Levites, which *b* the ark . . . . . .Deut 31:25
they that *b* the ark were . . . . . .Josh 3:15
feet of the priests that *b* . . . . . .Josh 3:15
the priests that *b* the ark . . . . . .Josh 3:17
which *b* the ark of . . . . .Josh 4:9
priests that *b* the ark . . . . .Josh 4:10
priests that *b* the ark . . . . .Josh 4:18
Levites, which *b* the ark . . . . . .Josh 8:33
people that *b* the present . . . . . .Judg 3:18
she also *b* him a son . . . . .Judg 8:31
Gilead's wife *b* him sons . . . . . .Judg 11:2
wife was barren, and *b* . . . . .Judg 13:2
And the woman *b* a son . . . . . . .Judg 13:24
Pharez, whom Tamar *b* . . . . . . .Ruth 4:12
her conception, and she *b* . . . . .Ruth 4:13
had conceived, that she *b* 1Sam 1:20
she conceived, and *b* three 1Sam 2:21
unto the young man that *b* 1Sam 14:1
the young man that *b* his 1Sam 14:6
man that *b* the shield went 1Sam 17:41
that *b* the ark of the Lord 2Sam 6:13
became his wife, and *b* him . . .2Sam 11:27
child that Uriah's wife *b* 2Sam 12:15
and she *b* a son, and he 2Sam 12:24
ten young men that *b* 2Sam 18:15
Aiah, whom she *b* unto 2Sam 21:8
his mother *b* him after 1Kin 1:6
because thou *b* the ark 1Kin 2:26
and ten thousand that *b* 1Kin 5:15
and fifty, which *b* 1Kin 9:23
camels that *b* spices, and 1Kin 10:2
the sister of Tahpenes *b* 1Kin 11:20
the guard *b* them, and 1Kin 14:28
woman conceived, and *b* 2Kin 4:17
and they *b* them before him . . .2Kin 5:23
she *b* Zimran, and Jokshan 1Chr 1:32
his daughter-in-law *b* him 1Chr 2:4
Abigail *b* Amasa: and the 1Chr 2:17
Ephrath, which *b* him Hur 1Chr 2:19
and she *b* him Segub 1Chr 2:21
Abiah Hezron's wife *b* him 1Chr 2:24
and she *b* him Ahban, and 1Chr 2:29
servant to wife; and she *b* 1Chr 2:35
Caleb's concubine *b* 1Chr 2:46
Caleb's concubine *b* 1Chr 2:48
she *b* also Shaaph the 1Chr 2:49
Naarah *b* him Ahuzam 1Chr 4:6
saying, Because I *b* him 1Chr 4:9
and she *b* Miriam and 1Chr 4:17
And his wife Jehudijah *b* 1Chr 4:18
Ashriel, whom she *b*; but 1Chr 7:14
concubine the Aramitess *b* 1Chr 7:14
the wife of Machir *b* a 1Chr 7:16
his sister Hammoleketh *b* 1Chr 7:18
she conceived, and *b* a son 1Chr 7:23
children of Judah that *b* 1Chr 12:24
children of the Levites *b* 1Chr 15:15
the Levites that *b* the ark 1Chr 15:26
and all the Levites that *b* 1Chr 15:27
two hundred and fifty, that *b* . .2Chr 8:10
camels that *b* spices and 2Chr 9:1
Which *b* him children 2Chr 11:19
which *b* him Abijah, and 2Chr 11:20
an army of men that *b* 2Chr 14:8
out of Benjamin, that *b* 2Chr 14:8
and they that *b* burdens . . . . . . .Neh 4:17
even their servants *b* rule . . . . .Neh 5:15
and bitterness to her that *b* . . . .Prov 17:25
she that *b* thee shall rejoice . . .Prov 23:25
choice one of her that *b* . . . . . . .Song 6:9
brought thee forth that *b* . . . . . .Song 8:5
she conceived, and *b* a son . . . .Is 8:3
Elam *b* the quiver with . . . . . . .Is 22:6
make *b* the leg, uncover the . . .Is 47:2
father unto Sarah that *b* . . . . . .Is 51:2
and he *b* the sin of many . . . . .Is 53:12
and he *b* them, and carried . . . . .Is 63:9
thou never *b* rule over them . . .Is 63:19
their mothers that *b* . . . . .Jer 16:3
day wherein my mother *b* . . . . .Jer 20:14

out, and thy mother that ***b*** . . . .Jer 22:26
I have made Esau ***b***, I have . . .Jer 49:10
b it upon my shoulder in . . . . . .Ezek 12:7
the scepters of them that ***b*** . . . .Ezek 19:11
they ***b*** sons and daughters . . . . .Ezek 23:4
leave thee naked and ***b*** . . . . . . .Ezek 23:29
their sons, whom they ***b*** . . . . . .Ezek 23:37
which conceived, and ***b*** him . . .Hos 1:3
she conceived again, and ***b*** . . . .Hos 1:6
she conceived, and ***b*** a son . . . .Hos 1:8
our infirmities, and ***b*** our . . . . .Matt 8:17
For many ***b*** false witness . . . . . .Mark 14:56
and ***b*** false witness against . . . .Mark 14:57
all ***b*** him witness and . . . . .Luke 4:22
they that ***b*** him stood still . . . . .Luke 7:14
and sprang up, and ***b*** fruit . . . .Luke 8:8
Blessed is the womb that ***b*** . . . .Luke 11:27
the wombs that never ***b*** . . . . . . .Luke 23:29
John ***b*** witness of him, and . . . .John 1:15
of the feast. And they ***b*** it . . . .John 2:8
to whom thou ***b*** witness . . . . . . .John 3:26
and he ***b*** witness unto the . . . . .John 5:33
had the bag and ***b*** what . . . . . . .John 12:6
he that saw it ***b*** record, and . . .John 19:35
b them witness giving . . . . .Acts 15:8
who his own self ***b*** our sins 1Pet 2:24
b record of the word of . . . . . . .Rev 1:2
which ***b*** twelve manner of . . . . .Rev 22:2

BAREFOOT—*without covering for one's feet*
Expression of great distress 2Sam 15:30
Forewarning of judgment .Is 20:2-4
Indicative of reverence . . .Ex 3:5

BARGAIN—*agreement between persons in a transaction*
A disastrous . . . . .Gen 25:29-34
A blessed . . . . .Gen 28:20-22
Involving a wife . . . . .Gen 29:15-20
Deception of . . . . .Prov 20:14
Resulting in death . . . . . . .Matt 14:7-10
History's most notorious .Matt 26:14-16

BARHUMITE (bär-hū'mīt)—*another form of Baharumite; an inhabitant of Bahurim*
One of David's mighty men 2Sam 23:31
See BAHUMITE

BARIAH (bä-rī'ä)—*"fugitive"*
A descendant of David . .1Chr 3:22

BAR-JESUS, ELYMAS (bär-jē'zŭs)—*"a son of Joshua"—a sorcerer*
A Jewish imposter . . . . . . .Acts 13:6-12

BAR-JONA (bär-jō'nä)—*"son of Jonah"*
Surname of Peter . . . . .Matt 16:17

BARK—*short, loud cry of a dog*
dumb dogs, they cannot ***b*** . . . . .Is 56:10

BARKOS (bär'kŏs)—*"partly colored"*
Postexilic family . . . . .Ezra 2:53

The children of ***B*** . . . . .Neh 7:55

BARLEY—*a cereal grass*
A product of Palestine . . .Deut 8:8
Ruth 1:22
Food for animals 1Kin 4:28
Used by the poor . . . . .Ruth 2:17
Used in trade 2Chr 2:10
In a miracle . . . . .John 6:9, 13

flax and the ***b*** was smitten . . . .Ex 9:31
for the ***b*** was in the ear . . . . . . .Ex 9:31
a homer of ***b*** seed shall be . . . .Lev 27:16
tenth part of an ephah of ***b*** . . .Num 5:15
and, lo, a cake of ***b*** bread . . . .Judg 7:13
he winnoweth ***b*** tonight in . . . . .Ruth 3:2
he hath ***b*** there; go and set 2Sam 14:30
wheat, and ***b*** and flour 2Sam 17:28
beginning of ***b*** harvest 2Sam 21:9
twenty loaves of ***b*** and full 2Kin 4:42
two measures of ***b*** for a 2Kin 7:1
and ten thousand of ***b*** 2Chr 27:5
cockle instead of ***b***. The . . . . . .Job 31:40
and the appointed ***b*** and . . . . . .Is 28:25
of wheat and of ***b*** and of . . . . . .Jer 41:8
for handfuls of ***b*** and for . . . . . .Ezek 13:19
an ephah of a homer of ***b*** . . . . .Ezek 45:13
and for a homer of ***b*** . . . . .Hos 3:2
for the wheat and for the ***b*** . . .Joel 1:11
three measures of ***b*** for a . . . . .Rev 6:6

BARN—*a storehouse*
Literal:
A place of storage . . . . . . .Deut 28:8
Joel 1:17

Spiritual, of:
God's blessings . . . . .Prov 3:10
Mal 3:10
Man's vanity . . . . .Luke 12:16-19
Heaven itself . . . . .Matt 13:30, 43

[*also* BARNFLOOR, BARNS]
b, or out of the winepress? 2Kin 6:27
and gather it into thy ***b***? . . . . . .Job 39:12
reap, nor gather into ***b*** . . . . .Matt 6:26
have storehouse nor ***b*** . . . . .Luke 12:24

BARNABAS (bär'nä'băs)—*"son of consolation"—Jewish Christian who traveled widely with Paul*
Gives property . . . . .Acts 4:36, 37
Supports Paul . . . . .Acts 9:27
Assists in Antioch . . . . . . .Acts 11:22-24
Brings Paul from Tarsus. .Acts 11:25, 26
Carries relief to Jerusalem . . . . .Acts 11:27-30
Travels with Paul . . . . .Acts 13:2
Called Jupiter by the multitudes . . . . .Acts 14:12
Speaks before Jerusalem Council . . . . {Acts 15:1, 2, 12}
With Paul, takes decree to churches . . . . .Acts 15:22-31
Breaks with Paul over John Mark . . . . .Acts 15:36-39
Highly regarded by Paul. .1Cor 9:6
Gal 2:1, 9
Not always steady . . . . . . .Gal 2:13

And ***B*** and Saul returned . . . . .Acts 12:25
as ***B***, and Simeon that was . . . .Acts 13:1
called for ***B*** and Saul, and . . . .Acts 13:7
followed Paul and ***B*** . . . . .Acts 13:43
Paul and ***B*** waxed bold . . . . . . .Acts 13:46
persecution against..***B*** . . . . .Acts 13:50
when the apostles, ***B*** and . . . . .Acts 14:14
he departed with ***B*** to Derbe . .Acts 14:20
B continued in Antioch . . . . . . .Acts 15:35
Marcus, sister's son to ***B*** . . . . . .Col 4:10

BARREL—*a round wooden container*
For food storage 1Kin 17:12-16
For water 1Kin 18:33

BARREN—*unable to reproduce*
Physically of:
Unproductive soil . . . . . . .Ps 107:34
Joel 2:20
Trees . . . . .Luke 13:6-9
Females . . . . .Prov 30:16

Significance of:
A reproach . . . . .Gen 16:2
A judgment 2Sam 6:23
Absence of God's blessing . . . . .Ex 23:26
Deut 7:14
Removal of, from the Lord . . . . .Ps 113:9

Spiritually:
Removal of, in new Israel . . . . {Is 54:1, Gal 4:27}
Remedy against 2Pet 1:8

Examples of:
Sarah . . . . .Gen 21:2
Rebekah . . . . .Gen 25:21
Rachel . . . . .Gen 30:22
Manoah's wife . . . . .Judg 13:2, 3, 24
Hannah 1Sam 1:18-20
The Shunammite woman. .2Kin 4:14-17
Elizabeth . . . . .Luke 1:7, 13, 57

but Rachel was ***b*** . . . . .Gen 29:31
the ***b*** hath born seven 1Sam 2:5
is naught, and the ground ***b*** . . .2Kin 2:19
the ***b*** land his dwellings . . . . . . .Job 39:6
and none is ***b*** among them . . . .Song 4:2
is not one ***b*** among them . . . . . .Song 6:6
Blessed are the ***b*** and the . . . . .Luke 23:29

BARS—*poles or rods*
make ***b*** of shittim wood . . . . . . .Ex 26:26
his ***b***, his pillars, and his . . . . . .Ex 35:11
he made ***b*** of shittim wood . . . .Ex 36:31
his ***b***, and his pillars, and . . . . .Ex 39:33
put in the ***b*** thereof, and . . . . . .Ex 40:18
and the ***b*** thereof, and the . . . .Num 3:36
the tabernacle, and the ***b*** . . . . . .Num 4:31
high walls, gates, and ***b*** . . . . . . .Deut 3:5
that hath gates and ***b*** 1Sam 23:7
with walls and brazen ***b*** 1Kin 4:13
with walls, gates, and ***b*** 2Chr 8:5
and towers, gates, and ***b*** 2Chr 14:7
locks thereof, and the ***b*** . . . . . . .Neh 3:3
shall go down to the ***b*** of . . . . .Job 17:16
place, and set ***b*** and doors . . . .Job 38:10
bones are like ***b*** of iron . . . . . . .Job 40:18
cut the ***b*** of iron in sunder . . . .Ps 107:16
strengthened the ***b*** of thy . . . . .Ps 147:13
are like the ***b*** of a castle . . . . . .Prov 18:19
cut in sunder the ***b*** of iron . . . .Is 45:2
have neither gates nor ***b*** . . . . . .Jer 49:31
her ***b*** are broken . . . . .Jer 51:30
destroyed and broken her ***b*** . . .Lam 2:9
having neither ***b*** nor gates . . . . .Ezek 38:11
the earth with her ***b*** was . . . . . .Jon 2:6
the fire shall devour thy ***b*** . . . . .Nah 3:13

BARSABAS (bär-săb'ăs)—*"son of Saba"*
1. Nominated to replace Judas . . . . .Acts 1:23
2. Sent to Antioch . . . . .Acts 15:22

BARTER—*to trade by exchanging*
Between Joseph and the Egyptians . . . . .Gen 47:17
Between Solomon and Hiram 1Kin 5:10, 11

BARTHOLOMEW (bär-thŏl'ō-mū)—*"son of Tolmai"—one of Jesus' twelve apostles*
One of Christ's apostles . .Matt 10:3
Acts 1:13
Called Nathanael . . . . .John 1:45, 46

Philip, and ***B***, and Matthew . . .Mark 3:18
Philip and ***B*** . . . . .Luke 6:14

BARTIMAEUS (bär-tī-mē'ŭs)—*"honorable son"*
Blind beggar healed by Jesus . . . . .Mark 10:46-52

BARUCH (bâr'ŭk)—*"blessed"*
1. Son of Neriah . . . . .Jer 32:12, 13
Jeremiah's faithful friend .Jer 36:4-32
The Jewish remnant takes him to Egypt . . . .Jer 43:1-7
2. Son of Zabbai . . . . .Neh 3:20
Signs document . . . . .Neh 10:6
3. A Shilonite of Judah . . . .Neh 11:5

After him ***B*** the son of . . . . . . .Neh 3:20
Daniel, Ginnethon, ***B*** . . . . .Neh 10:6
Maaseiah the son of ***B***, the . . . .Neh 11:5
the purchase unto ***B*** . . . . .Jer 32:16
Then Jeremiah called ***B*** the . . .Jer 36:4
B wrote from the mouth . . . . . .Jer 36:4
Jeremiah commanded ***B*** . . . . . . .Jer 36:5
B the son of Neriah did . . . . . . .Jer 36:8
Then read ***B*** in the book . . . . . .Jer 36:10
when ***B*** read the book in . . . . . .Jer 36:13
unto ***B***, saying, Take in . . . . . . .Jer 36:14
B the son of Neriah took . . . . .Jer 36:14
So ***B*** read it in their ears . . . . . .Jer 36:15
said unto ***B***, We will . . . . .Jer 36:16
they asked ***B***, saying, Tell . . . . .Jer 36:17
B answered them, He . . . . .Jer 36:18
said the princes unto ***B***, Go . . .Jer 36:19
to take ***B*** the scribe and . . . . . .Jer 36:26
the words which ***B*** wrote . . . . . .Jer 36:27

gave it to ***B*** the scribe ....Jer 36:32
the prophet spake unto ***B*** ......Jer 45:1
of Israel, unto thee, O ***B*** ......Jer 45:2

BARZILLAI (bär-zĭl'ā-ī)—*"strong"*
1. Helps David with food ..2Sam 17:27-29
   Age restrains him from following David 2Sam 19:31-39
2. Father of Adriel 2Sam 21:8
3. A postexilic priest.......Ezra 2:61

wife of the daughters of ***B*** ....Ezra 2:61
children of ***B***, which took .....Neh 7:63
one of the daughters of ***B*** .....Neh 7:63

BASE—*low in place or character; foundation*
As a foundation 1Kin 7:27-43
Of lowly estate 2Sam 6:22
Of evil character 1Cor 1:28
Of humble nature 2Cor 10:1

[*also* BASER, BASES, BASEST]
And he made ten ***b*** of brass ...1Kin 7:27
the work of the ***b*** was on 1Kin 7:28
manner he made the ten ***b*** 1Kin 7:37
upon every one of the ten ***b*** ...1Kin 7:38
he put five ***b*** on the right 1Kin 7:39
And the ten ***b***...............1Kin 7:43
and ten layers on the ***b*** 1Kin 7:43
cut off the borders of the ***b*** ...2Kin 16:17
and the ***b*** and the brazen 2Kin 25:13
the ***b*** which Solomon had 2Kin 25:16
He made also ***b*** 2Chr 4:14
layers made he upon the ***b*** 2Chr 4:14
set the altar upon his ***b*** ....Ezra 3:3
yea, children, of ***b*** men ....Job 30:8
b against the honorable ....Is 3:5
concerning the ***b***, and ....Jer 27:19
and the ***b***, and the brazen .....Jer 52:17
bulls that were under the ***b***....Jer 52:20
the kingdom might be ***b***.......Ezek 17:14
shall be there a ***b*** kingdom ....Ezek 29:14
be the ***b*** of the kingdoms .....Ezek 29:15
setteth up over it the ***b*** ....Dan 4:17
set there upon her own ***b*** .....Zech 5:11
and ***b*** before all the people ....Mal 2:9
lewd fellows of the ***b*** sort .....Acts 17:5

BASHAN (bā'shăn)—*"fertile plain"—district stretching from the Upper Jordan Valley to the Arabian Desert*
A vast highland east of the Sea of Chinnereth (Galilee).............Num 21:33-35
Ruled by Og ....Deut 29:7
Conquered by Israel .....Neh 9:22
Assigned to Manasseh ...Deut 3:13
Smitten by Hazael 2Kin 10:32, 33
Fine cattle ....Ezek 39:18
Typical of cruelty........Ps 22:12; Amos 4:1

kingdom of Og king of ***B*** .....Num 32:33
Og the king of ***B***, which ......Deut 1:4
up the way to ***B***.............Deut 3:1
Og the king of ***B*** came out ....Deut 3:1
Og also, the king of ***B*** ....Deut 3:3
the kingdom of Og in ***B***.......Deut 3:4
all Gilead, and all ***B***, unto ....Deut 3:10
of the kingdom of Og in ***B*** ....Deut 3:10
For only Og king of ***B*** ....Deut 3:11
in ***B***, of the Manassites ....Deut 4:43
the land of Og king of ***B***......Deut 4:47
and rams of the breed of ***B*** ...Deut 32:14
he shall leap from ***B*** ....Deut 33:22
and to Og king of ***B***, which ...Josh 9:10
the coast of Og king of ***B*** ....Josh 12:4
and in Salcah, and in all ***B*** ....Josh 12:5
mount Hermon, and all ***B*** .....Josh 13:11
All the kingdom of Og in ***B*** ...Josh 13:12
from Mahanaim, all ***B*** ....Josh 13:30
kingdom of Og king of ***B*** .....Josh 13:30
of Jair, which are in ***B*** ....Josh 13:30
the kingdom of Og in ***B***.......Josh 13:31
he had Gilead and ***B*** ....Josh 17:1
the land of Gilead and ***B***......Josh 17:5
tribe of..and Golan in ***B*** ....Josh 20:8
half tribe of Manasseh in ***B*** ...Josh 21:6
they gave Golan in ***B*** ....Josh 21:27
given possession in ***B*** ....Josh 22:7
of Argob, which is in ***B*** 1Kin 4:13
and of Og king of ***B***..........1Kin 4:19
them, in the land of ***B*** unto ...1Chr 5:11
Jaanai, and Shaphat in ***B***.......1Chr 5:12
dwelt in Gilead in ***B***, and in ...1Chr 5:16
they increased from ***B*** unto....1Chr 5:23
the tribe of Manasseh in ***B*** 1Chr 6:62
Golan in ***B*** with her 1Chr 6:71
of God is as the hill of ***B*** .....Ps 68:15
high hill as the hill of ***B***.......Ps 68:15
I will bring again from ***B***, I ...Ps 68:22
Amorites, and Og king of ***B***...Ps 135:11
Og the king of ***B***: for his.....Ps 136:20
and upon all the oaks of ***B*** ....Is 2:13
like a wilderness: and ***B***.......Is 33:9
and lift up thy voice in ***B*** .....Jer 22:20
feed on Carmel and ***B***, and ...Jer 50:19
of ***B*** have they made thine ....Ezek 27:6
let them feed in ***B*** and ....Mic 7:14
B languisheth, and Carmel ....Nah 1:4
howl, O ye oaks of ***B***; for.....Zech 11:2

BASHAN-HAVOTH-JAIR (bā'shăn hā'vŏth-jā'ĭr)
A district named after Jair ....Deut 3:14

BASHEMATH (băsh'ĕ-măth)—*"fragrant"*
1. Wife of Esau ....Gen 26:34
   Called Adah ....Gen 36:2, 3
2. Wife of Esau ....Gen 36:3, 4, 13
   Called Mahalath ....Gen 28:9
3. A daughter of Solomon. .1Kin 4:15

son of ***B*** the wife of Esau .....Gen 36:10
are the sons of ***B*** Esau's ......Gen 36:17

BASIN—*cup or bowl for containing liquids*
Moses used ....Ex 24:6
Made for the altar.......Ex 38:3; Ex 27:3
Brought for David.......2Sam 17:28, 29
Hiram made 1Kin 7:40

[*also* BASON, BASONS]
blood that is in the ***b*** ....Ex 12:22
shovels, and the ***b***, all ....Num 4:14
and the ***b***: and all these 1Kin 7:45
the snuffers, and the ***b***........1Kin 7:50
bowls of silver, snuffers, ***b*** 2Kin 12:13
for the golden ***b*** he gave 1Chr 28:17
gold by weight for every ***b*** 1Chr 28:17
silver by weight by every ***b***....1Chr 28:17
he made an hundred ***b*** of 2Chr 4:8
and the shovels, and the ***b*** 2Chr 4:11
the snuffers, and the ***b***........2Chr 4:22
Thirty ***b*** of gold ....Ezra 1:10
silver ***b*** of a second sort.......Ezra 1:10
Also twenty ***b*** of gold, of a....Ezra 8:27
drams of gold, fifty ***b*** ....Neh 7:70
the ***b***, and the firepans ....Jer 52:19
he poureth water into a ***b*** .....John 13:5

BASKET—*light woven or wooden containers*
Used for carrying:
Produce ....Deut 26:2
Food ....Matt 14:20
Ceremonial offerings.....Ex 29:3, 23
Paul ....Acts 9:24, 25
Other objects (heads) 2Kin 10:7
Symbolic of:
Approaching death ......Gen 40:16-19
Israel's judgment ....Amos 8:1-3
Judah's judgment........Jer 24:1-3

[*also* BASKETS]
the bread that is in the ***b***......Ex 29:32
a ***b*** of unleavened bread ......Lev 8:2
out of the ***b*** of unleavened .....Lev 8:26
is in the ***b*** of consecrations ....Lev 8:31
a ***b*** of unleavened bread ......Num 6:15
the ***b*** of unleavened bread.....Num 6:17
cake out of the ***b***............Num 6:19
put it in a ***b*** and shalt.........Deut 26:2
the priest shall take the ***b*** .....Deut 26:4
Blessed shall be thy ***b*** and.....Deut 28:5
Cursed shall be thy ***b*** and .....Deut 28:17
the flesh he put in a ***b*** and ....Judg 6:19
a grape gatherer into the ***b*** ....Jer 6:9
two ***b*** of figs were set ....Jer 24:1
meat that was left seven ***b***.....Matt 15:37
and how many ***b*** ye took up? ..Matt 16:9
and how many ***b*** ye took up? ..Matt 16:10
twelve ***b*** full of the ....Mark 6:43
meat that was left seven ***b***.....Mark 8:8
how many ***b*** full of ....Mark 8:19
how many ***b*** full of ....Mark 8:20
remained to them twelve ***b*** ....Luke 9:17
and filled twelve ***b*** with ....John 6:13
in a ***b*** was I let down by 2Cor 11:33

BASMATH (băs'măth)—*"fragrant"—same as Bashemath (3)*
took ***B*** the daughter of........1Kin 4:15
See BASHEMATH

BASON—*See* BASIN

BASTARD—*an illegitimate child*
Penalty attached to ....Deut 23:2
Examples of:
Ishmael.................Gen 16:3, 15; Gal 4:22
Moab and Ammon ......Gen 19:36, 37
Sons of Tamar by Judah. .Gen 38:12-30
Jephthah................Judg 11:1
Figurative of:
A mixed race ....Zech 9:6
The unregenerate state...Heb 12:8

[*also* BASTARDS]
then are ye ***b***, and not sons ...Heb 12:8

BAT—*a nocturnal flying mammal*
Listed among unclean birds ....Lev 11:19; Deut 14:18
Lives in dark places .....Is 2:19, 20

BATH—*a liquid measure (about nine gallons)*
A tenth of a homer......Ezek 45:10, 11
For measuring oil and wine ....2Chr 2:10; Is 5:10

[*also* BATHS]
contained two thousand ***b*** 1Kin 7:26
one laver contained forty ***b***....1Kin 7:38
twenty thousand ***b*** of wine 2Chr 2:10
twenty thousand ***b*** of oil 2Chr 2:10
and held three thousand ***b***.....2Chr 4:5
to a hundred ***b*** of wine ....Ezra 7:22
and to a hundred ***b*** of oil .....Ezra 7:22
the ***b*** of oil, ye shall ....Ezek 45:14
offer the tenth part of a ***b***.....Ezek 45:14
a homer of ten ***b*** ....Ezek 45:14
for ten ***b*** are a homer..........Ezek 45:14

BATHING—*a washing*
For pleasure:
Pharaoh's daughter ......Ex 2:5
Bath-sheba..............2Sam 11:2, 3
For purification:
Cleansing the feet ....Gen 24:32; John 13:10
Ceremonial cleansing ....Lev 14:8; 2Kin 5:10-14
Before performing priestly duties ....Ex 30:19-21; Lev 16:4, 24
Jewish rituals ....Mark 7:2

[*also* BATHE, BATHED]
and ***b*** himself in water ....Lev 15:5
wash his clothes, and ***b*** ....Lev 15:6
b himself in water, and be ....Lev 15:7
wash his clothes, and ***b*** ....Lev 15:8
b himself in water, and ***b***......Lev 15:10
wash his clothes, and ***b*** ....Lev 15:11
and ***b*** his flesh in running .....Lev 15:13
shall both ***b*** themselves in .....Lev 15:18
wash his clothes, and ***b*** ....Lev 15:21
b himself in water, and be ....Lev 15:22
wash his clothes, and ***b*** ....Lev 15:27
b his flesh in water, and ....Lev 16:26
clothes, and ***b*** his flesh........Lev 16:28
b himself in water, and be ....Lev 17:15
nor ***b*** his flesh.................Lev 17:16

shall *b* his flesh in water ......Num 19:7
b his flesh in water, and ......Num 19:8
and *b* himself in water ....Num 19:19
sword shall be *b* in heaven ....Is 34:5

BATH-RABBIM (băth-răb´ĭm)—*"daughter of multitudes"*
Gate of Heshbon ....Song 7:4

BATH-SHEBA (băth-shē´bä)—*"the seventh daughter; daughter of the oath"*
Wife of Uriah 2Sam 11:2, 3
Commits adultery with David 2Sam 11:4, 5
Husband's death contrived by David 2Sam 11:6-25
Mourns husband's death. .2Sam 11:26
Becomes David's wife....2Sam 11:27
Her first child dies 2Sam 12:14-19
Solomon's mother 2Sam 12:24
Secures throne for Solomon 1Kin 1:15-31
Deceived by Adonijah ...1Kin 2:13-25

BATH-SHUA (băth´shōō-ä)—*"daughter of prosperity"*
Same as Bath-sheba 1Chr 3:5

BATTERED—*beaten; destroyed*
b the wall, to throw it down...2Sam 20:15

BATTERING RAM—*large wooden beam used to beat down walls*
Used in destroying walls. .Ezek 4:2
Ezek 21:22

BATTLE—*encounter between antagonists*

[also BATTLES]
they joined *b* with them in ....Gen 14:8
people, to the *b* at Edrei ......Num 21:33
which came from the *b*........Num 31:14
before the Lord to *b*, as my ...Num 32:27
contend with them in *b* ....Deut 2:9
and all his people, to *b* at .....Deut 3:1
When thou goest out to *b* .....Deut 20:1
came out against us unto *b* ....Deut 29:7
unto *b*, to the plains of ....Josh 4:13
went out against Israel to *b* ...Josh 8:14
all other they took in *b* ....Josh 11:19
to go up against them in *b* ....Josh 22:33
Joash returned from *b* ....Judg 8:13
unto Gibeah, to go out to *b* ...Judg 20:14
shall go up first to the *b* ......Judg 20:18
men of Israel went out to *b* ...Judg 20:20
set their *b* again in array ......Judg 20:22
Shall I go up again to *b*.......Judg 20:23
Shall I yet again go out to *b*...Judg 20:28
of all Israel, and the *b* ....Judg 20:34
of Israel retired in the *b* ......Judg 20:39
as in the first *b*...............Judg 20:39
but the *b* overtook them ......Judg 20:42
against..Philistines to *b*........1Sam 4:1
Philistines drew near to *b* 1Sam 7:10
before us, and fight our *b* 1Sam 8:20
to pass in the day of *b* 1Sam 13:22
and they came to the *b* 1Sam 14:20
together their armies to *b* 1Sam 17:1
set the *b* in array against 1Sam 17:2
come out to set your *b* in 1Sam 17:8
and followed Saul to the *b* 1Sam 17:13
sons that went to the *b* 1Sam 17:13
and shouted for the *b*.........1Sam 17:20
had put the *b* in array 1Sam 17:21
thou mightest see the *b* 1Sam 17:28
the *b* is the Lord's, and 1Sam 17:47
fight the Lord's *b*. For 1Sam 18:17
fighteth the *b* of the Lord 1Sam 25:28
he shall descend into *b*.........1Sam 26:10
shalt go out with me to *b* 1Sam 28:1
not go down with us to *b* 1Sam 29:4
that goeth down to the *b*......1Sam 30:24
b went sore against Saul 1Sam 31:3
people are fled from the *b* 2Sam 1:4
there was a very sore *b* 2Sam 2:17
Asahel at Gibeon in the *b*.....2Sam 3:30
put the *b* in array at the 2Sam 10:8
when kings go forth to *b* 2Sam 11:1
to *b* in thine own person 2Sam 17:11
b was in the wood of 2Sam 18:6
away when they flee in *b*......2Sam 19:3
go no more out with us to *b*...2Sam 21:17
with strength to *b* 2Sam 22:40
gathered together to *b* 2Sam 23:9
go out to *b* against their 1Kin 8:44
Who shall order the *b*? 1Kin 20:14
Wilt thou go with me to *b* 1Kin 22:4
with me against Moab to *b*? ...2Kin 3:7
they cried to God in the *b* 1Chr 5:20
fit to go out for war and *b* 1Chr 7:11
b went sore against Saul 1Chr 10:3
were gathered together to *b* ...1Chr 11:13
men of war fit for the *b*.......1Chr 12:8
then thou shalt go out to *b*....1Chr 14:15
their cities, and came to *b*.....1Chr 19:7
time that kings go out to *b* 1Chr 20:1
spoils won in *b* did they.......1Chr 26:27
Abijah set the *b* in array 2Chr 13:3
set the *b* in array in the.......2Chr 14:10
go to Ramoth-gilead to *b* 2Chr 18:5
against Jehoshaphat to *b* 2Chr 20:1
b is not yours, but God's......2Chr 20:15
not need to fight in this *b* 2Chr 20:17
do it, be strong for the *b*......2Chr 25:8
to fight our *b*. And the 2Chr 32:8
as a king ready to the *b*.......Job 15:24
against the day of *b* and ......Job 38:23
he smelleth the *b* afar off .....Job 39:25
remember the *b*, do no ....Job 41:8
me with strength unto the *b* ...Ps 18:39
the Lord mighty in *b* ....Ps 24:8
my soul in peace from the *b*...Ps 55:18
and the sword, and the *b* .....Ps 76:3
turned back in the day of *b* ...Ps 78:9
him to stand in the *b* ....Ps 89:43
my head in the day of *b* ......Ps 140:7
against the day of *b* ....Prov 21:31
nor the *b* to the strong........Eccl 9:11
For every *b* of the warrior ....Is 9:5
mustereth the host of the *b*....Is 13:4
the sword, nor dead in *b*......Is 22:2
and thorns against me in *b*? ...Is 27:4
to them that turn the *b* ....Is 28:6
and in *b* of shaking will he ....Is 30:32
the strength of *b*; and it.......Is 42:25
horse rusheth into the *b*.......Jer 8:6
slain by the sword in *b*........Jer 18:21
and draw near to *b* ....Jer 46:3
and rise up to the *b* ....Jer 49:14
A sound of *b* is in the land....Jer 50:22
Thou art my *b* axe and ....Jer 51:20
none goeth to the *b*: for my ...Ezek 7:14
stand in the *b* in the day ......Ezek 13:5
neither in anger, nor in *b* .....Dan 11:20
nor by sword, nor by *b* ....Hos 1:7
and the sword and the *b* ......Hos 2:18
b in Gibeah against the ....Hos 10:9
a strong people set in *b* ....Joel 2:5
shouting in the day of *b*.......Amos 1:14
rise up against her in *b* ....Obad 1
and the *b* bow shall be cut ....Zech 9:10
his goodly horse in the *b*......Zech 10:3
against Jerusalem to *b* ....Zech 14:2
prepare himself to the *b*? 1Cor 14:8
horses prepared unto *b*........Rev 9:7
to the *b* of that great day .....Rev 16:14
gather them together to *b* .....Rev 20:8
See WARS

BATTLE-AXE—*broadaxe used as instrument of war*
Applied to Israel ....Jer 51:19, 20

BATTLEMENT—*parapet surmounting a wall, used for defense*
A protective ....Deut 22:8
Figurative of partial destruction ....Jer 5:10

BAVAI (băv´ā-ī)—*"wisher"*
Postexilic worker ....Neh 3:18

BAY—*inlet; reddish-brown horse*
1. Dead Sea's cove at Jordan's mouth ....Josh 15:5
Used also of the Nile ...Is 11:15
2. Color of a horse ....Zech 6:2
3. Name of a tree; figurative of pride.....Ps 37:35

b that looketh southward......Josh 15:2
the north *b* of the salt sea.....Josh 18:19
chariot grizzled and *b* ....Zech 6:3
And the *b* went forth, and ....Zech 6:7

BAZLUTH (băz´lŭth)—*"asking"*
Head of a family ....Ezra 2:52
Called Bazlith in ....Neh 7:54

BDELLIUM—*gum resin similar to myrrh; a white pearl*
A valuable mineral of Havilah...............Gen 2:12
Manna colored like ......Num 11:7

BE—*See* INTRODUCTION

BEACH—*shore of an ocean, sea, or lake*

Place of:
Jesus' preaching ....Matt 13:2
Fisherman's task.........Matt 13:48
Jesus' meal with disciples .John 21:9
A prayer meeting........Acts 21:5
A notable shipwreck .....Acts 27:39-44
A miracle...............Acts 28:1-6

BEACON—*a signal fire*
Figurative, a warning to others ....Is 30:17

BEALIAH (bē-ä-lī´ä)—*"Jehovah is lord"*
A warrior...............1Chr 12:5

BEALOTH (bē´ä-lŏth)—*"mistresses; possessors"*
Village of Judah.........Josh 15:24

BEAM—*long piece of heavy timber used in construction*

Physical:
Wood undergirding floors.1Kin 7:2
Part of weaver's frame ...1Sam 17:7

Figurative of:
The cry of vengeance ....Hab 2:11
God's power ....Ps 104:3
Notorious faults ....Matt 7:3-5

[*also* BEAMS]
away with the pin of the *b* ....Judg 16:14
spear was like a weaver's *b*....2Sam 21:19
that the *b* should not be 1Kin 6:6
thick *b* were before them 1Kin 7:6
take thence every man a *b* 2Kin 6:2
a spear like a weaver's *b* 1Chr 11:23
the *b*, the posts, and the 2Chr 3:7
give me timber to make *b*.....Neh 2:8
b of our house are cedar ......Song 1:17
perceivest not the *b* that ......Luke 6:41

BEAN—*refers to the horse bean*
Brought to David by friends.................2Sam 17:27, 28
Mixed with grain for bread................Ezek 4:9

BEAR—*a wild animal*

Natural:
Killed by David 1Sam 17:34, 35
Two tore up forty-two lads 2Kin 2:23, 24

Figurative of:
Fierce revenge 2Sam 17:8
Fool's folly.............Prov 17:12
Wicked rulers ....Prov 28:15
World empire ....Dan 7:5
Final antichrist ....Rev 13:2
Messianic times ....Is 11:7

[*also* BEARS]
two she *b* out of the wood 2Kin 2:24
We roar all like *b*, and........Is 59:11
He was unto me as a *b* ....Lam 3:10
I will meet them as a *b* that ...Hos 13:8
from a lion, and a *b* met ......Amos 5:19

BEAR—*to carry; to yield*

Used literally of:

Giving birth ... Gen 17:19
Carrying a load ... Josh 3:13
Jer 17:21
Cross ... Matt 27:32

Used figuratively of:

Excessive punishment ... Gen 4:13
Divine deliverance ... Ex 19:4
Responsibility for sin ... Lev 5:17
Lev 24:15
Burden of leadership ... Deut 1:9, 12
Personal shame ... Ezek 16:54
Evangelism ... Acts 9:15
Spiritual help ... Gal 6:1, 2
Spiritual productivity ... John 15:2, 4, 8

[*also* BEARERS, BEAREST, BEARETH, BEARING, BORNE]

the land was not able to *b* ... Gen 13:6
hath restrained me from *b* ... Gen 16:2
art with child and shalt *b* ... Gen 16:11
that is ninety years old, *b*? ... Gen 17:17
Shall I of a surety *b* a ... Gen 18:13
these eight Milcah did *b* to ... Gen 22:23
his name Judah; and left *b* ... Gen 29:35
she shall *b* upon my knees ... Gen 30:3
Leah saw that she had left *b* ... Gen 30:9
were strangers could not *b* ... Gen 36:7
b spicery and balm and ... Gen 37:25
then let me *b* the blame ... Gen 43:9
then I shall *b* the blame ... Gen 44:32
bowed his shoulder to *b* ... Gen 49:15
shall *b* the burden with ... Ex 18:22
shalt not *b* false witness ... Ex 20:16
the ark may be *b* with ... Ex 25:14
places of the staves to *b* ... Ex 25:27
two sides of the altar to *b* ... Ex 27:7
Aaron shall *b* their names ... Ex 28:12
for the staves to *b* it ... Ex 30:4
the sides of the ark, to *b* ... Ex 37:5
sides of the altar, to *b* it ... Ex 38:7
he shall *b* his iniquity ... Lev 5:1
eateth of it shall *b* his ... Lev 7:18
b the iniquity of the ... Lev 10:17
whosoever *b* aught of the ... Lev 11:25
he that *b* the carcase of ... Lev 11:28
he also that *b* the carcase ... Lev 11:40
But if she *b* a maid child ... Lev 12:5
and he that *b* any of those ... Lev 15:10
And the goat shall *b* upon ... Lev 16:22
flesh; then he shall *b* his ... Lev 17:16
that eateth it shall *b* his ... Lev 19:8
nakedness: he shall *b* his ... Lev 20:17
lest they *b* sin for it and ... Lev 22:9
they shall *b* the tabernacle ... Num 1:50
of Kohath shall come to *b* ... Num 4:15
they shall *b* the curtains ... Num 4:25
this woman shall *b* her ... Num 5:31
should *b* upon their ... Num 7:9
that man shall *b* his sin ... Num 9:13
forward, *b* the tabernacle ... Num 10:17
a nursing father *b* the ... Num 11:12
I am not able to *b* all this ... Num 11:14
shall *b* the burden of the ... Num 11:17
that thou *b* it not thyself ... Num 11:17
long shall I *b* with this ... Num 14:27
b the iniquity of the ... Num 18:1
them; then he shall *b* her ... Num 30:15
Neither shalt thou *b* false ... Deut 5:20
b the ark of the covenant ... Deut 10:8
the firstborn which she *b* ... Deut 25:6
children which she shall *b* ... Deut 28:57
a root that *b* gall and ... Deut 29:18
is not sown, nor *b*, nor any ... Deut 29:23
b them on her wings ... Deut 32:11
the priests the Levites *b* ... Josh 3:3
command the priests that *b* ... Josh 3:8
the priests that *b* the ark ... Josh 4:16
seven priests shall *b* ... Josh 6:4
seven priests *b* the seven ... Josh 6:8
thou art barren and *b* not ... Judg 13:3
thou shalt conceive, and *b* ... Judg 13:3
and on which it was *b* up ... Judg 16:29
tonight, and should also *b* ... Ruth 1:12
one *b* a shield went before ... 1Sam 17:7
and *b* the king tidings, how ... 2Sam 18:19
not my son, which I did *b* ... 1Kin 3:21
before him, to *b* witness ... 1Kin 21:10
thou puttest on me will I *b* ... 2Kin 18:14
root downward, and *b* fruit ... 2Kin 19:30
men able to *b* buckler and ... 1Chr 5:18
ten thousand men to *b* ... 2Chr 2:2
of them to be *b* of burdens ... 2Chr 2:18
they were over the *b* of ... 2Chr 34:13
the *b* of burdens is decayed ... Neh 4:10
every man should *b* rule in ... Esth 1:22
rising up in me *b* witness ... Job 16:8
entreateth the barren that *b* ... Job 24:21
I have *b* chastisement, I ... Job 34:31
then I could have *b* it ... Ps 55:12
I have *b* reproach; shame ... Ps 69:7
dissolved; I *b* up the pillars ... Ps 75:3
how I do *b* in my bosom the ... Ps 89:50
shall *b* thee up in their ... Ps 91:12
the favor that thou *b* unto ... Ps 106:4
b precious seed, shall ... Ps 126:6
scornest thou alone shalt *b* ... Prov 9:12
of the diligent shall *b* ... Prov 12:24
wounded spirit who can *b*? ... Prov 18:14
A man that *b* false witness ... Prov 25:18
but when the wicked *b* rule ... Prov 29:2
for four which it cannot *b* ... Prov 30:21
whereof every one *b* twins ... Song 4:2
every one *b* twins, and ... Song 6:6
unto me; I am weary to *b* ... Is 1:14
virgin shall conceive and *b* ... Is 7:14
and *b* fruit upward ... Is 37:31
are *b* by me from the belly ... Is 46:3
I have made, and I will *b* ... Is 46:4
Surely he hath *b* our griefs ... Is 53:4
clean, that *b* the vessels ... Is 52:11
he shall *b* their iniquities ... Is 53:11
thou that didst not *b* ... Is 54:1
ye shall be *b* upon her ... Is 66:12
the priests *b* rule ... Jer 5:31
they must needs be *b* ... Jer 10:5
is a grief, and I must *b* ... Jer 10:19
hath *b* seven languisheth ... Jer 15:9
may *b* sons and daughters ... Jer 29:6
I did *b* the reproach of my ... Jer 31:19
Lord could no longer *b* ... Jer 44:22
because he hath *b* it upon ... Lam 3:28
we have *b* their iniquities ... Lam 5:7
thou shalt *b* their iniquity ... Ezek 4:4
In their sight shalt thou *b* ... Ezek 12:6
And they shall *b* the ... Ezek 14:10
daughters, whom..hast *b* ... Ezek 16:20
b thine own shame for thy ... Ezek 16:52
and that it might *b* fruit ... Ezek 17:8
doth not the son *b* the ... Ezek 18:19
b thou also thy lewdness ... Ezek 23:35
yet have they *b* their ... Ezek 32:24
yet have they *b* their ... Ezek 32:25
b their shame with them ... Ezek 32:30
neither *b* the shame of the ... Ezek 34:29
ye have *b* the shame of the ... Ezek 36:6
they shall *b* their shame ... Ezek 36:7
that they have *b* their ... Ezek 39:26
shall even *b* their iniquity ... Ezek 44:10
they *b* them not out into ... Ezek 46:20
which shall *b* rule over all ... Dan 2:39
dried up, they shall *b* no ... Hos 9:16
tree *b* her fruit, the ... Joel 2:22
b the tabernacle of your ... Amos 5:26
land is not able to *b* all ... Amos 7:10
ye shall *b* the reproach of ... Mic 6:16
I will *b* the indignation of ... Mic 7:9
they that *b* silver are cut ... Zeph 1:11
If one *b* holy flesh in the ... Hag 2:12
Whither do these *b* the ... Zech 5:10
he shall *b* the glory, and ... Zech 6:13
shoes I am not worthy to *b* ... Matt 3:11
their hands they shall *b* ... Matt 4:6
also *b* fruit, and bringeth ... Matt 13:23
shalt not *b* false witness ... Matt 19:18
which have *b* the burden ... Matt 20:12
burdens..grievous to be *b* ... Matt 23:4
the palsy, which was *b* ... Mark 2:3
Do not *b* false witness ... Mark 10:19
a man *b* a pitcher of water ... Mark 14:13
Alexander and Rufus, to *b* ... Mark 15:21
wife Elisabeth shall *b* thee ... Luke 1:13
their hands they shall *b* ... Luke 4:11
burdens grievous to be *b* ... Luke 11:46
Truly ye *b* witness that ye ... Luke 11:48
And if it *b* fruit, well ... Luke 13:9
whosoever doth not *b* his ... Luke 14:27
though he *b* long with them? ... Luke 18:7
he might *b* it after Jesus ... Luke 23:26
to *b* witness of the Light ... John 1:7
b unto the governor of the ... John 2:8
yourselves *b* me witness ... John 3:28
If I *b* witness of myself ... John 5:31
another that *b* witness of ... John 5:32
hath sent me, hath *b* ... John 5:37
Thou *b* record of thyself ... John 8:13
Though I *b* record of ... John 8:14
that sent me *b* witness of ... John 8:18
they *b* witness of ... John 10:25
branch in me that *b* not ... John 15:2
but ye cannot *b* them now ... John 16:12
b witness of the evil: but ... John 18:23
b his cross went forth ... John 19:17
Sir, if thou have *b* him ... John 20:15
nor we were able to *b*? ... Acts 15:10
would that I should *b* with ... Acts 18:14
that he was *b* of the ... Acts 21:35
doth *b* me witness, and all ... Acts 22:5
must thou *b* witness, also ... Acts 23:11
could not *b* up in the wind ... Acts 27:15
conscience also *b* witness ... Rom 2:15
The Spirit itself *b* witness ... Rom 8:16
conscience also *b* me ... Rom 9:1
For I *b* them record that ... Rom 10:2
thou *b* not the root, but ... Rom 11:18
he *b* not the sword in vain ... Rom 13:4
shalt not *b* false witness ... Rom 13:9
to *b* the infirmities of the ... Rom 15:1
ye were not able to *b* it ... 1Cor 3:2
that ye may be able to *b* it ... 1Cor 10:13
B all things, believeth all ... 1Cor 13:7
b the image of the heavenly ... 1Cor 15:49
b the image of the earthy ... 1Cor 15:49
Always *b* about in the body ... 2Cor 4:10
I *b* record, yea, and beyond ... 2Cor 8:3
b with me a little in my ... 2Cor 11:1
for I *b* you record, that ... Gal 4:15
Rejoice, thou barren that *b* ... Gal 4:27
shall *b* his judgment ... Gal 5:10
For I *b* him record, that he ... Col 4:13
women marry, *b* children ... 1Tim 5:14
God also *b* them witness ... Heb 2:4
that which *b* thorns and ... Heb 6:8
offered to *b* the sins of ... Heb 9:28
without the camp, *b* his ... Heb 13:13
brethren, *b* olive berries? ... James 3:12
and *b* witness and show ... 1John 1:2
the Spirit that *b* witness ... 1John 5:6
three that *b* record in ... 1John 5:7
b witness of thy charity ... 3John 6
yea, and we also *b* record ... 3John 12
canst not *b* them which are ... Rev 2:2

BEARD—*hair grown on the face*

Long, worn by:

Aaron ... Ps 133:2
Samson ... Judg 16:17
David ... 1Sam 21:13

In mourning:

Left untrimmed ... 2Sam 19:24
Plucked ... Ezra 9:3
Cut ... Jer 48:37, 38

Features regarding:

Leper's must be shaven ... Lev 13:29-33
Half-shaven, an indignity ... 2Sam 10:4, 5
Marring of, forbidden ... Lev 19:27
Shaven, by Egyptians ... Gen 41:14
Spittle on, sign of lunacy ... 1Sam 21:13
Holding to, a token of respect ... 2Sam 20:9

[*also* BEARDS]

and his *b* and his eyebrows ... Lev 14:9
shave..the corner of their *b* ... Lev 21:5

by his *b*, and smote him 1Sam 17:35
shaved..one half of their *b* 2Sam 10:4
until your *b* be grown..........2Sam 10:5
until your *b* be grown..........1Chr 19:5
it shall also consume the *b* ....Is 7:20
be baldness and every *b* cut ...Is 15:2
b shaven..their clothes ....Jer 41:5

BEAST—*four-footed animal; mammal*

Characteristics of:

God-created ....Gen 1:21
Of their own order 1Cor 15:39
Named by Adam ....Gen 2:20
Suffer in man's sin ......Rom 8:20-22
Perish at death ....Ps 49:12-15
Follow instincts..........Is 1:3; Jude 10
Under God's control.....1Sam 6:7-14
Wild ....Mark 1:13
For man's food..........Gen 9:3; Acts 10:12, 13
Eat people.............1Sam 17:46; 1Cor 15:32
Used in sacrifices........Lev 27:26-29
Spiritual lessons from ....1Kin 4:33; Job 12:7

Treatment of:

No sexual relation with ..Lev 20:15, 16
Proper care of, sign of a righteous man.......Gen 33:13, 14; Prov 12:10
Abuse of, rebuked ......Num 22:28-32
Extra food for, while working ....Deut 25:4; 1 Tim 5:18

Typical of:

Man's folly..............Ps 73:22
Unregenerate men ....Titus 1:12
False prophets 2Pet 2:12
Antichrist ....Rev 13:1-4

See ANIMALS

[*also* BEASTS]

and *b* of the earth after his ....Gen 1:24
God formed every *b* of the ....Gen 2:19
subtil than any *b* of..field .....Gen 3:1
and *b*, and the creeping ....Gen 6:7
Of every clean *b* thou shalt....Gen 7:2
b that are not clean by two ....Gen 7:2
Every *b*, every creeping ....Gen 8:19
upon every *b* of the earth .....Gen 9:2
That which was torn of *b* I .....Gen 31:39
every *b* of theirs be ours? .....Gen 34:23
and all his *b*, and all his ......Gen 36:6
Some evil *b* hath devoured ....Gen 37:20
lade your *b*, and go, get you ..Gen 45:17
became lice in man..in *b* ......Ex 8:17
blains upon man..upon *b* ......Ex 9:9
and all the firstborn of *b* ......Ex 11:5
tongue, against man or *b* ......Ex 11:7
of Egypt, both man and *b* ......Ex 12:12
of man and of *b*; it is mine ....Ex 13:2
whether it be *b* or man ....Ex 19:13
and the dead *b* shall be ....Ex 21:34
shall put in his *b* and shall ....Ex 22:25
is torn of *b* in the field........Ex 22:31
they leave the *b* of the field ...Ex 23:11
the *b* of the field multiply .....Ex 23:29
unclean *b*..any abominable .....Lev 7:21
that which is torn with *b* ......Lev 7:24
are the *b* which ye shall.......Lev 11:2
every *b* which divideth the ....Lev 11:26
hunteth and catcheth any *b* ....Lev 17:13
that which was torn with *b* ....Lev 17:15
shalt thou lie with any *b* ......Lev 18:23
between clean *b* and ....Lev 20:25
is torn with *b*, he shall not ....Lev 22:8
that killeth a *b* shall make.....Lev 24:18
cattle, and for..*b* that are .....Lev 25:7
I will rid evil *b* out of.........Lev 26:6
if it be a *b*, whereof men .....Lev 27:9
in Israel, both man and *b* .....Num 3:13
Israel are mine..man and *b* ....Num 8:17
whether it be of men or *b*.....Num 18:15
congregation and their *b* ......Num 20:8
prey, both of men and of *b* ...Num 31:11
man and of *b*, thou, and ......Num 31:26
goods, and for all their *b*......Num 35:3
of any *b*..on the earth ....Deut 4:17
the *b* of the field increase .....Deut 7:22
are the *b* which ye shall.......Deut 14:4
every *b* that parteth the hoof ..Deut 14:6
lieth with any manner of *b* ....Deut 27:21
and unto the *b* of the earth ...Deut 28:26
also send the teeth of *b* ....Deut 32:24
men of every city, as the *b* ....Judg 20:48
air..the *b* of the field 1Sam 17:44
the *b* of the field by night 2Sam 21:10
he spake also of *b*, and of.....1Kin 4:33
that we lose not all the *b* 1Kin 18:5
and your cattle, and your *b* ...2Kin 3:17
passed by a wild *b* that was ...2Kin 14:9
passed by a wild *b* that was ...2Chr 25:18
stalls for all manner of *b* 2Chr 32:28
with goods, and with *b*........Ezra 1:4
was there any *b* with me ......Neh 2:12
save the *b* that I rode upon ...Neh 2:12
ask now the *b*..they shall ......Job 12:7
are we counted as *b* ....Job 18:3
teacheth..more than the *b* of ..Job 35:11
Then the *b* go into dens.......Job 37:8
the wild *b* may break them ....Job 39:15
where all the *b* of the field ....Job 40:20
oxen..and the *b* of the field ...Ps 8:7
thou preservest man and *b* ....Ps 36:6
every *b* of the forest is mine...Ps 50:10
wild *b* of the field are mine ...Ps 50:11
I was as a *b* before thee ......Ps 73:22
unto the *b* of the earth........Ps 79:2
b of the field doth devour it...Ps 80:13
drink to every *b* of the field ...Ps 104:11
the *b* of the forest do creep ...Ps 104:20
of Egypt, both of man and *b* ..Ps 135:8
He giveth to the *b* his food....Ps 147:9
b, and all cattle; creeping .....Ps 148:10
she hath killed her *b* ....Prov 9:2
regardeth the life of his *b* .....Prov 12:10
which is strongest among *b* ....Prov 30:30
that they themselves are *b*.....Eccl 3:18
no preeminence above a *b* ....Eccl 3:19
fat of fed *b*; and I delight .....Is 1:11
b of the desert shall lie ....Is 13:21
and to the *b* of the earth.......Is 18:6
The burden of the beasts of ...Is 30:6
wild *b* of the desert shall ......Is 34:14
nor any ravenous *b* shall go ...Is 35:9
nor the *b* thereof sufficient ....Is 40:16
b of the field shall honor......Is 43:20
their idols were upon the *b*....Is 46:1
are a burden to the weary *b*...Is 46:1
ye *b* of the field, come to .....Is 56:9
As a *b* goeth down into the ...Is 63:14
mules, and upon swift *b*........Is 66:20
upon man, and upon *b*, and ...Jer 7:20
fowl of..heavens and the *b* ....Jer 9:10
b are consumed, and the ......Jer 12:4
b of the earth, to devour......Jer 15:3
and for the *b* of the earth .....Jer 16:4
for the *b* of the earth ....Jer 19:7
of this city, both man and *b* ...Jer 21:6
b that are upon the ground....Jer 27:5
b of the field have I given.....Jer 27:6
given him the *b* of the field ....Jer 28:14
man, and with the seed of *b*...Jer 31:27
desolate without man or *b*.....Jer 32:43
without man and without *b* ....Jer 33:10
inhabitant, and without *b* .....Jer 33:10
and to the *b* of the earth......Jer 34:20
cease from thence man and *b*..Jer 36:29
shall depart..man and *b* ....Jer 50:3
Therefore the wild *b* of the....Jer 50:39
neither man nor *b*, but that ...Jer 51:62
upon you famine and evil *b* ...Ezek 5:17
abominable *b*, and all the .....Ezek 8:10
cut off man and *b* from it .....Ezek 14:13
cause noisome *b* to pass.......Ezek 14:15
through because of the *b* ......Ezek 14:15
and will cut off man and *b* ....Ezek 25:13
meat to..*b* of the field ....Ezek 29:5
cut off man and *b* out of ......Ezek 29:8
his branches did all the *b* .....Ezek 31:6
I will fill the *b* of..earth.......Ezek 32:4
I give to..*b* to be devoured ....Ezek 33:27
became meat to all the *b* of ...Ezek 34:5
meat to every *b* of the field ...Ezek 34:8
multiply upon..man and *b* .....Ezek 36:11
and the *b* of the field ....Ezek 38:20
to the *b* of the field ....Ezek 39:4
to every *b* of the field ....Ezek 39:17
torn..it be fowl or *b* ....Ezek 44:31
b of the field and..fowls.......Dan 2:38
b of the field had shadow .....Dan 4:12
heart was made like the *b*.....Dan 5:21
four great *b* came up from ....Dan 7:3
And behold another *b* ....Dan 7:5
no *b* might stand before him ..Dan 8:4
b of the field shall eat ....Hos 2:12
with the *b* of the field and ....Hos 4:3
the wild *b* shall tear them .....Hos 13:8
How do the *b* groan! the......Joel 1:18
Be not afraid, ye *b* of the .....Joel 2:22
offerings of your fat *b* ....Amos 5:22
Let neither man nor *b*, herd...Jon 3:7
bind the chariot to the..*b* .....Mic 1:13
among the *b* of the forest .....Mic 5:8
spoil of *b*, which made them ..Hab 2:17
I will consume man and *b*.....Zeph 1:3
all the *b* of the nations........Zeph 2:14
for man, nor any hire for *b* ...Zech 8:10
the *b* that shall be in these ....Zech 14:15
and set him on his own *b* .....Luke 10:34
ye offered to me slain *b*.......Acts 7:42
and saw fourfooted *b* of the ...Acts 11:6
provide them *b*, that they .....Acts 23:24
the venomous *b* hang on his...Acts 28:4
fourfooted *b*, and creeping ....Rom 1:23
if so much as a *b* touch the ...Heb 12:20
of those *b* whose blood is .....Heb 13:11
every kind of *b*, and of ....James 3:7
were four *b* full of eyes ....Rev 4:6
the first *b* was like a lion......Rev 4:7
throne and of the four *b* ......Rev 5:6
of the four *b* saying, Come ....Rev 6:1
I heard the second *b* say ......Rev 6:3
the elders and the four *b*......Rev 7:11
the *b* that ascendeth out of....Rev 11:7
I beheld another *b* coming ....Rev 13:11
before the four *b*, and the.....Rev 14:3
If any man worship the *b* ......Rev 14:9
the victory over the *b* and.....Rev 15:2
one of the four *b* gave unto ...Rev 15:7
mark of the *b*, and upon ......Rev 16:2
out of the mouth of the *b* .....Rev 16:13
upon a scarlet-colored *b*.......Rev 17:3
the *b* that thou sawest was ....Rev 17:8
the *b* that was, and is not .....Rev 17:8
b, and sheep, and horses ......Rev 18:13
and the four *b* fell down ......Rev 19:4
I saw the *b*, and the kings.....Rev 19:19
had not worshiped the *b* ......Rev 20:4
the *b* and the false prophet....Rev 20:10

BEAT—*to flog; to pound; strike; hammer*

Inflicted on:

The wicked ....Deut 25:3
The guilty ....Lev 19:20
Children ....Prov 22:15
The disobedient ....Prov 26:3; Luke 12:47, 48

Victims of unjust beatings:

A servant..............Luke 20:10, 11
Christ ....Is 50:6; Mark 15:19
The apostles ....Acts 5:40
Paul...................Acts 16:19-24

[*also* BEATEN, BEATEST, BEATETH, BEATING]

had set over them, were *b* ....Ex 5:14
of *b* work shalt thou make ....Ex 25:18
olive oil *b* for the light........Ex 27:20
shalt *b* some of it very ....Ex 30:36
of gold, *b* out of one piece ....Ex 37:7
b the gold into thin plates .....Ex 39:3
even corn *b* out of full ears ...Lev 2:14
full of sweet incense *b* ....Lev 16:12
candlestick was of *b* gold......Num 8:4
mills, or *b* it in a mortar ......Num 11:8

fourth part..hin of **b** oil ....Num 28:5
When thou **b** thine olive tree . . Deut 24:20
wicked man be worthy to be **b** . Deut 25:2
made as if they were **b** ....Josh 8:15
be **b** down the tower of ....Judg 8:17
and **b** down the city; and ......Judg 9:45
b at the door, and spake to . . .Judg 19:22
b out that she had gleaned ....Ruth 2:17
on **b** down one another 1Sam 14:16
and Abner was **b**, and the 2Sam 2:17
Then did I **b** them as small....2Sam 22:43
they **b** down the cities and 2Kin 3:25
Three times did Joash **b** 2Kin 13:25
did the king **b** down, and 2Kin 23:12
measures of **b** wheat 2Chr 2:10
b..graven images into powder . .2Chr 34:7
did I **b** them small as the .....Ps 18:42
b down his foes before his .....Ps 89:23
if thou **b** him with the rod ....Prov 23:13
shalt **b** him with the rod ......Prov 23:14
have **b** me and I felt it ....Prov 23:35
b their swords into plowshares. .Is 2:4
ye **b** my people to pieces ......Is 3:15
chalkstones that are **b** in ......Is 27:9
Lord shall **b** off from the ......Is 27:12
fitches..**b** out with a staff ......Is 28:27
the Assyrian be **b** down ....Is 30:31
and **b** them small, and shalt . . .Is 41:15
their mighty ones are **b** ....Jer 46:5
B your plowshares into........Joel 3:10
the sun **b** upon the head of....Jon 4:8
images..shall be **b** to pieces....Mic 1:7
b their swords into plowshares .Mic 4:3
winds blew, and **b** upon ....Matt 7:25
took his servants, and **b** one . . .Matt 21:35
the waves **b** into the ship......Mark 4:37
they caught him, and **b** him . . .Mark 12:3
b some, and killing some ......Mark 12:5
synagogues ye shall be **b** ......Mark 13:9
stream **b** vehemently upon ....Luke 6:48
begin to **b** the menservants ....Luke 12:45
the husbandmen **b** him and ....Luke 20:10
and commanded to **b** them ....Acts 16:22
b him before the judgment ....Acts 18:17
soldiers, they left **b** of Paul ....Acts 21:32
and **b** in every synagogue .....Acts 22:19
not as one that **b** the air 1Cor 9:26
Thrice was I **b** with rods 2Cor 11:25

BEATEN GOLD—*gold shaped by hammering*
Ornamental shields 1Kin 10:16, 17
2Chr 9:15, 16

BEATEN OIL —*highest quality of olive oil*
In sacrifices ....Ex 29:39, 40
In tent of meeting lamp . . Lev 24:2

BEATEN SILVER—*silver shaped by hammering*
Overlaid idols ....Is 30:22
Hab 2:19
In trade ....Jer 10:9

BEATITUDES—*pronouncements of blessings*
Jesus begins His sermon with .... Matt 5:3-12 / Luke 6:20-22

BEAUTIFUL GATE—*gate at East of Temple area*
Lame man healed there . . Acts 3:1-10

BEAUTY, PHYSICAL

Temporal:
Seen in nature ....Hos 14:6
Matt 6:28, 29
Consumed in dissipation .Is 28:1
Contest, Abishag winner of 1Kin 1:1-4
Esther, winner of ....Esth 2:1-17
Destroyed by sin ....Ps 39:11
Ends in grave ....Ps 49:14

In Women:
Vain ....Prov 31:30
Without discretion ....Prov 11:22
Enticements of ....Prov 6:25
Source of temptation ....Gen 6:2
2Sam 11:2-5
Leads to marriage ....Deut 21:11
A bride's ....Ps 45:11
Sarah's ....Gen 12:11
Rebekah's ....Gen 24:15, 16
Rachel's ....Gen 29:17
Daughters of Job ....Job 42:15
Abigail's 1Sam 25:3
Bath-sheba's 2Sam 11:2, 3
Tamar's 2Sam 13:1
Abishag's 1Kin 1:3, 4
Vashti's ....Esth 1:11
Esther's ....Esth 2:7

In Men:
Of man ....Is 44:13
Of the aged ....Prov 20:29
Joseph's ....Gen 39:6
David's 1Sam 16:12, 13
Absalom's 2Sam 14:25

[*also* BEAUTIFUL, BEAUTIFY]
brother, for glory and for **b** . . .Ex 28:2
b of Israel is slain upon 2Sam 1:19
the Lord in the **b** of holiness . . 1Chr 16:29
with precious stones for **b** 2Chr 3:6
to **b** the house of the Lord ....Ezra 7:27
people and..princes her **b** .....Esth 1:11
the maid was fair and **b** ....Esth 2:7
array..with glory and **b** ....Job 40:10
to behold the **b** of the Lord . . .Ps 27:4
Lord in the **b** of holiness ......Ps 29:2
B for situation, the joy of .....Ps 48:2
out of Zion..perfection of **b** . . .Ps 50:2
the **b** of the Lord our God ....Ps 90:17
and **b** are in his sanctuary .....Ps 96:6
the Lord in the **b** of holiness . .Ps 96:9
he will **b** the meek with ....Ps 149:4
every thing **b** in his time ....Eccl 3:11
Thou are **b**, O my love ....Song 6:4
How **b** are thy feet with.......Song 7:1
burning instead of **b** ....Is 3:24
the branch of the Lord be **b** . . .Is 4:2
shall see the king in his **b** .....Is 33:17
no **b** that we should desire ....Is 53:2
b the place of my sanctuary . . .Is 60:13
give unto them **b** for ashes ....Is 61:3
Our holy and our **b** house .....Is 64:11
was given thee, thy **b** flock? . . .Jer 13:20
staff broken, and the **b** rod! . . .Jer 48:17
b is departed; her princes .....Lam 1:6
the **b** of Israel..remembered . . .Lam 2:1
As for the **b** of his ornament . .Ezek 7:20
a **b** crown upon thine head ....Ezek 16:12
among the heathen for thy **b** . .Ezek 16:14
b crowns upon their heads ....Ezek 23:42
hast said, I am of perfect **b**....Ezek 27:3
against the **b** of thy wisdom . . .Ezek 28:7
God was like..him in his **b** ....Ezek 31:8
Whom dost thou pass in **b**? . . .Ezek 32:19
goodness..how great is his **b** . . .Zech 9:17
indeed appear **b** outward ......Matt 23:27

BEAUTY, SPIRITUAL
The Messiah ....Ps 110:3
Is 52:7
The true Israel ....Ps 45:8-11
Song 1:8
The meek ....Ps 149:4
Spiritual worship 2Chr 20:21
Christian ministers ....Rom 10:15
Holy garments ....Is 52:1
Christ's rejection by Israel ....Zech 11:7-14

BEBAI (bē´bā-ī)—*"fatherly"*
1. Family head ....Ezra 2:11
2. One who signs document. Neh 10:15

And of the sons of **B** ....Ezra 8:11

BECAME—*See* BECOME

BECAUSE—*See* INTRODUCTION

BECHER (bē´ker)—*"youthful; firstborn"*
1. Benjamin's son ....Gen 46:21
2. Son of Ephraim.........Num 26:35
Called Bered 1Chr 7:20

Bela, and **B** and Jediael.......1Chr 7:6

BECHORATH (bĕ-kō´răth)—*"first birth"*
Ancestor of Saul 1Sam 9:1

BECKONED—*summoned with wave or nod*

[*also* BECKONING]
b unto them, and remained....Luke 1:22
they **b** unto their partners .....Luke 5:7
Peter therefore **b** to him ......John 13:24
b unto them with the hand ....Acts 12:17
and **b** with his hand, said .....Acts 13:16
Alexander **b** with the hand ....Acts 19:33
b with the hand unto the ......Acts 21:40
that the governor had **b** ....Acts 24:10

BECOME—*to come into existence; to change or develop*

[*also* BECAME, BECAMEST, BECOMETH]
of life..man **b** a living soul ....Gen 2:7
the man is **b** as one of us .....Gen 3:22
same **b** mighty men which .....Gen 6:4
Abraham shall surely **b** a ......Gen 18:18
and she **b** a pillar of salt ......Gen 19:26
my mother..she **b** my wife .....Gen 20:12
and he is **b** great; and he .....Gen 24:35
Rebekah and she **b** his wife . . .Gen 24:67
grew until he **b** very great .....Gen 26:13
We shall see what will **b** of....Gen 37:20
servant **b** surety for the lad....Gen 44:32
so the land **b** Pharaoh's ....Gen 47:20
also shall **b** a people and he . . .Gen 48:19
b a multitude of nations ....Gen 48:19
and **b** a servant unto tribute . . .Gen 49:15
daughter and he **b** her son ....Ex 2:10
b a serpent and Moses fled ....Ex 4:3
of the river shall **b** blood ......Ex 4:9
and it shall **b** a serpent........Ex 7:9
servants, and it **b** a serpent....Ex 7:10
it may **b** lice throughout all....Ex 8:16
b lice in man and in beast.....Ex 8:17
it shall **b** small dust in all .....Ex 9:9
it **b** a boil breaking forth ......Ex 9:10
he is **b** my salvation; he is.....Ex 15:2
so it **b** one tabernacle ....Ex 36:13
land **b** full of wickedness ......Lev 19:29
enter into her and **b** bitter ....Num 5:24
Miriam **b** leprous, white as ....Num 12:10
art **b** the people of the Lord . . .Deut 27:9
of the people melted, and **b** . . .Josh 7:5
b old by reason of the very....Josh 9:13
therefore **b** the inheritance ....Josh 14:14
and it **b** the inheritance of.....Josh 24:32
them, and **b** tributaries........Judg 1:30
thing **b** a snare unto Gideon . . .Judg 8:27
b as flax..burnt with fire ......Judg 15:14
I shall **b** weak, and be like ....Judg 16:17
one of his sons, who **b** his.....Judg 17:5
in her bosom, and **b** nurse .....Ruth 4:16
b a proverb, Is Saul also 1Sam 10:12
and he **b** his armor bearer.....1Sam 16:21
b David's enemy continually . . .1Sam 18:29
he **b** a captain over them......1Sam 22:2
and he **b** as a stone 1Sam 25:37
from thee, and is **b** thine 1Sam 28:16
and **b** one troop, and stood . . .2Sam 2:25
he fell and **b** lame. And.......2Sam 4:4
thou, Lord, art **b** their God . . .2Sam 7:24
the Moabites **b** David's 2Sam 8:2
she **b** his wife, and bare him . .2Sam 11:27
and is **b** my brother's 1Kin 2:15
and **b** captain over a band.....1Kin 11:24
And this thing **b** a sin.........1Kin 12:30
again, and **b** as it was before . .1Kin 13:6
and Hoshea **b** his servant 2Kin 17:3
shall **b** a prey and a spoil 2Kin 21:14
Jehoiakim **b** his servant 2Kin 24:1
and thou, Lord, **b** their God . .1Chr 17:22
Moabites **b** David's servants . . .1Chr 18:2
David, and **b** his servants 1Chr 19:19
Jotham **b** mighty, because 2Chr 27:6
what should **b** of her..........Esth 2:11
people of the land **b** Jews .....Esth 8:17
do the wicked live, **b** old ......Job 21:7
I am **b** like dust and ashes ....Job 30:19
are all together **b** filthy ....Ps 14:3
I **b** like them that go down....Ps 28:1

they are altogether *b* filthy ....Ps 53:3
b not vain in robbery; if ......Ps 62:10
I am *b* a stranger unto my ....Ps 69:8
my garment..I *b* a proverb ....Ps 69:11
b a reproach to our ....Ps 79:4
perished at Endor: they *b* .....Ps 83:10
holiness *b* thine house, O .....Ps 93:5
and let his prayer *b* sin ....Ps 109:7
I *b* also a reproach unto ......Ps 109:25
and song and is *b* my ....Ps 118:14
For I am *b* like a bottle in ....Ps 119:83
He *b* poor that dealeth with ...Prov 10:4
Excellent speech *b* not a ......Prov 17:7
born in his kingdom *b* poor ...Eccl 4:14
faithful city *b* an harlot! ....Is 1:21
shall *b* briers and thorns ......Is 7:24
he also is *b* my salvation ......Is 12:2
Art thou also *b* weak as we ...Is 14:10
Of Pharaoh is *b* brutish ....Is 19:11
the vision of all is *b* unto .....Is 29:11
shall *b* burning pitch ....Is 34:9
ground shall *b* a pool ....Is 35:7
webs shall not *b* garments .....Is 59:6
little one shall *b* a thousand ...Is 60:22
after vanity and are *b* vain ....Jer 2:5
him, and *b* another man's .....Jer 3:1
the prophets shall *b* wind .....Jer 5:13
b a den of robbers in your ....Jer 7:11
the pastors are *b* brutish .....Jer 10:21
house shall *b* a desolation .....Jer 22:5
Jerusalem shall *b* heaps ....Jer 26:18
Bozrah shall *b* a desolation ....Jer 49:13
is Babylon *b* a desolation .....Jer 50:23
and they shall *b* as women ....Jer 50:37
they *b* as women; they have ...Jer 51:30
And Babylon shall *b* heaps ....Jer 51:37
how is she *b* as a widow ......Lam 1:1
How is the gold *b* dim! ....Lam 4:1
b a spreading vine of low .....Ezek 17:6
b a vine, and brought forth ....Ezek 17:6
whelps; it *b* a young lion ......Ezek 19:3
Thou are *b* guilty in thy.......Ezek 22:4
she *b* famous among women ...Ezek 23:10
shall *b* a spoil to the nations ...Ezek 26:5
and his branches *b* long ....Ezek 31:5
they *b* meat to all the beasts ..Ezek 34:5
are forsaken which *b* a prey ...Ezek 36:4
land that was desolate is *b* ....Ezek 36:35
shall *b* one in thine hand ......Ezek 37:17
b like the chaff of..summer ....Dan 2:35
that art grown and *b* strong ...Dan 4:22
according to his will, and *b* ...Dan 8:4
people are *b* a reproach to ....Dan 9:16
the ground, and I *b* dumb .....Dan 10:15
come up, and shall *b* strong ...Dan 11:23
Ephraim said, Yet I am *b* .....Hos 12:8
and his spring shall *b* dry .....Hos 13:15
the day that he *b* a stranger ...Obad 12
see what would *b* of the city ..Jon 4:5
Jerusalem shall *b* heaps ....Mic 3:12
their goods shall *b* a booty ....Zeph 1:13
is she *b* a desolation ....Zeph 2:15
Zerubbabel thou shalt *b*.......Zech 4:7
for thus it *b* us to fulfill ....Matt 3:15
word and he *b* unfruitful ......Matt 13:22
converted and *b* as little ......Matt 18:3
is *b* the head of the corner ....Matt 21:42
did shake and *b* as dead ......Matt 28:4
you to *b* fishers of men ....Mark 1:17
word, and it *b* unfruitful ......Mark 4:19
his raiment *b* shining..........Mark 9:3
is *b* the head of the corner ....Mark 12:10
is *b* the head of the corner? ...Luke 20:17
power to *b* the sons of God ...John 1:12
is *b* the head of the corner ....Acts 4:11
we wot not what is *b* of him ...Acts 7:40
he *b* very hungry, and would ..Acts 10:10
the soldiers, what was *b* of ....Acts 12:18
but *b* vain in their ....Rom 1:21
are together *b* unprofitable ....Rom 3:12
might *b* the father of many ....Rom 4:18
b..servants of righteousness....Rom 6:18
b servants to God, ye have ....Rom 6:22
ye also are *b* dead to..law .....Rom 7:4
her in the Lord, as *b* saints....Rom 16:2
b a fool, that he may be 1Cor 3:18
b a stumbling block to them ...1Cor 8:9
unto the Jews I *b* as a Jew 1Cor 9:20
I am *b* as sounding brass 1Cor 13:1
when I *b* a man, I put away ...1Cor 13:11
b the firstfruits of them 1Cor 15:20
behold, all things are *b* new ...2Cor 5:17
yet for your sakes he *b* poor ..2Cor 8:9
I am *b* a fool in glorying 2Cor 12:11
I therefore *b* your enemy .....Gal 4:16
Christ is *b* of no effect ....Gal 5:4
among you as *b* saints ....Eph 5:3
as it *b* the gospel of Christ ....Phil 1:27
b obedient unto death, even ...Phil 2:8
ye *b* followers of us, and of ...1Thess 1:6
ye, brethren, *b* followers of ...1Thess 2:14
b women professing..........1Tim 2:10
which *b* sound doctrine ....Titus 2:1
in behavior as *b* holiness ......Titus 2:3
thy faith may *b* effectual ......Philem 6
For it *b* him, for whom are....Heb 2:10
b the author of..salvation .....Heb 5:9
an high priest *b* us who is .....Heb 7:26
whilst ye *b* companions of .....Heb 10:33
b heir of the righteousness ....Heb 11:7
b judges of evil thoughts? .....James 2:4
sun *b* black as sackcloth.......Rev 6:12
and the moon *b* as blood......Rev 6:12
third part of the sea *b* blood ..Rev 8:8
kingdoms of this world are *b* ..Rev 11:15
b as the blood of a dead ......Rev 16:3
b the habitation of devils ......Rev 18:2

BED—*an article of furniture for rest or sleep*

Made of:
The ground ....Gen 28:11
Iron, 13½ feet long .....Deut 3:11
Ivory ....Amos 6:4
Gold and silver..........Esth 1:6

Used for:
Sleep ....Luke 11:7
Rest...................2Sam 4:5-7
Sickness ....Gen 49:33
Meals ....Amos 6:4
Prostitution ....Prov 7:16, 17
Evil ....Ps 36:4
Marriage...............Song 3:1
Heb 13:4
Singing ....Ps 149:5

Figurative of:
The grave..............Job 17:13-16
Divine support ....Ps 41:3
Worldly security ....Is 57:7

[*also* BED'S, BEDS, BEDSTEAD]

bowed himself upon the *b* .....Gen 47:31
himself and sat upon the *b* .....Gen 48:2
wentest up to thy father's *b* ...Gen 49:4
bedchamber and upon thy *b* ...Ex 8:3
he die not, but keepeth his *b* ..Ex 21:18
Every *b*, whereon he lieth .....Lev 15:4
his *b* was a *b* of iron ....Deut 3:11
image, and laid it in the *b* 1Sam 19:13
David arose from off his *b* 2Sam 11:2
Lay thee down on thy *b*.........2Sam 13:5
b, and basons, and earthen 2Sam 17:28
bowed himself upon the *b* 1Kin 1:47
and laid him upon his own *b* ..1Kin 17:19
he laid him down upon his *b* ..1Kin 21:4
b on which thou art gone up ..2Kin 1:4
let us set for him there a *b* 2Kin 4:10
defiled his father's *b*, his 1Chr 5:1
laid him in the *b* which was ...2Chr 16:14
slew him on his *b*, and he 2Chr 24:25
was fallen upon the *b* ....Esth 7:8
My *b* shall comfort me ....Job 7:13
in slumberings upon the *b* .....Job 33:15
your own heart upon your *b* ...Ps 4:4
night make I my *b* to swim ....Ps 6:6
I remember thee upon my *b* ...Ps 63:6
house, nor go up into my *b* ...Ps 132:3
if I make my *b* in hell ....Ps 139:8
should he take away thy *b* ....Prov 22:27
the slothful upon his *b* ....Prov 26:14
also our *b* is green............Song 1:16
b is shorter than that a man ...Is 28:20
they shall rest in their *b*.......Is 57:2
came to her into the *b* of .....Ezek 23:17
of thy head upon thy *b* ....Dan 2:28
and the thoughts upon my *b* ...Dan 4:5
of his head upon his *b* ....Dan 7:1
they howled upon their *b* .....Hos 7:14
Samaria in the corner of a *b* ...Amos 3:12
and work evil upon their *b*! ...Mic 2:1
of the palsy, lying on a *b* .....Matt 9:2
they let down the *b* wherein ...Mark 2:4
a bushel, or under a *b*? ....Mark 4:21
began to carry about in *b* .....Mark 6:55
daughter laid upon the *b* ......Mark 7:30
men brought in a *b* a man ....Luke 5:18
putteth it under a *b* but ....Luke 8:16
shall be two men in one *b*.....Luke 17:34
take up thy *b* and walk ....John 5:8
laid them on *b* and couches ...Acts 5:15
Aeneas, which had kept his *b* .Acts 9:33
I will cast her into a *b* ....Rev 2:22

BED—*a garden plot*
Used literally ....Song 6:2
Used figuratively ....Song 5:13

BEDAD (bē´dăd)—*"alone"*
Father of Hadad ....Gen 36:35

BEDAN (bē´dăn)—*"son of judgment"*
1. Judge of Israel.........1Sam 12:11
2. Descendant of Manasseh .1Chr 7:17

BEDCHAMBER—*bedroom*
A place of sleep.........2Sam 4:7
Elijah's special 2Kin 4:8, 10
Secrets of 2Kin 6:12
Joash hidden in 2Kin 11:2

into thy *b* and upon thy bed ...Ex 8:3
put him and his nurse in a *b*...2Chr 22:11
curse not the rich in thy *b*.....Eccl 10:20

BEDEIAH (bĕ-dē´yä)—*"servant of Jehovah"*
Son of Bani.............Ezra 10:34, 35

BEDFELLOWS—*those who share a bed*
Provide mutual warmth ..Eccl 4:11

BEE—*an insect*
Abundant in Canaan.....Judg 14:8
Amorites compared to ...Deut 1:44
David's enemies
compared to ....Ps 118:12
Assyria compared to .....Is 7:18
See HONEY

BEEF, BOILED
Elisha gives people 1Kin 19:21

BEELIADA (bē-ĕ-lī´ä-dä)—*"the Lord knows"*
Son of David 1Chr 14:7
Called Eliada 2Sam 5:14-16

BEELZEBUB—*chief of the devils*
Prince of demons ....Matt 12:24
Identified as Satan.......Matt 12:26
Jesus thus called.........Matt 10:25

BEEN—*See* INTRODUCTION

BEER (bē´er)—*"a well"*
1. Moab station ....Num 21:16-18
2. Jotham's place of refuge .Judg 9:21

BEERA (bĕ-ē´rä)—*"expounder"*
An Asherite 1Chr 7:37

BEERAH (bĕ-ē´rä)—*"expounder"*
Reubenite prince 1Chr 5:6

BEERI (bĕ-ē´rī)—*"man of the springs; expounder"*
1. Esau's father-in-law .....Gen 26:34
2. Hosea's father ....Hos 1:1
3. Well dug by leaders of
Israel ....Is 15:8
(Also spelled Beer-elim)

BEER-LAHAI-ROI (bē´er-lä-hī´roi)—*"well of the living one who sees me"*
Angel met Hagar there ..Gen 16:7-14
Isaac dwelt in ....Gen 24:62

BEEROTH (bĕ-ē´rŏth)—*"wells"*
1. Edom station ....Deut 10:6
2. Gibeonite city ....Josh 9:17

Kirjath-arim..and *B* ....Ezra 2:25
Kirjath-jearim..and *B* ....Neh 7:29

BEEROTHITE (bĕ-ē´rŏth-īt)
An inhabitant of Beeroth .2Sam 4:2
1Chr 11:39

[*also* BEEROTHITES, BEROTHITE]
the *B* fled to Gittaim and 2Sam 4:3
Nahari the *B* armorbearer 2Sam 23:37

BEER-SHEBA (bē´er-shē´bä)—*"well of oaths"—city in southern Judah*

God appeared to:
Hagar ....Gen 21:14, 17-19
Isaac ....Gen 26:23, 24
Jacob ....Gen 46:1-5
Elijah 1Kin 19:3-7

Other features of:
Named after an oath.....Gen 21:31-33
Gen 26:26-33
Isaac's residence at ......Gen 26:23-25
Jacob's departure from ...Gen 28:10
Assigned to Judah ....Josh 15:20, 28
Later assigned to Simeon .Josh 19:1, 2, 9
Judgeship of Samuel's sons 1Sam 8:2
Became seat of idolatry ..Amos 5:5
Amos 8:14
"From Dan even to Beer-sheba" 2Sam 17:11

up and went together to *B* ....Gen 22:19
Abraham dwelt at *B* ....Gen 22:19
the name of the city is *B* ......Gen 26:33
one man, from Dan even to *B* .Judg 20:1
Israel from Dan even to *B* 1Sam 3:20
Judah, from Dan even to *B* ...2Sam 3:10
Israel, from Dan even to *B*....2Sam 24:2
south of Judah, even to *B* 2Sam 24:7
Dan even to *B*, seventy 2Sam 24:15
even to *B*, all the days of 1Kin 4:25
name was Zibiah of *B* 2Kin 12:1
Geba to *B*, and brake down ...2Kin 23:8
dwelt at *B* and Moladah 1Chr 4:28
Israel from *B* even to Dan 1Chr 21:2
from *B* to mount Ephraim 2Chr 19:4
name also was Zibiah of *B* 2Chr 24:1
Israel, from *B* even to Dan....2Chr 30:5
at *B*, and in the villages.......Neh 11:27

BEESHTERAH (bē-ĕsh´tē-rǎ)—*"temple of Ashterah"*
A Levitical city.........Josh 21:27
Same as Ashtaroth 1Chr 6:71

BEETLE—*four-winged insect*
the *b* after his kind, and the...Lev 11:22

BEEVES—*cattle; oxen*
blemish of the *b* of the........Lev 22:19
of persons, and of the *b*.......Num 31:28

BEFALL—*to happen to*
[*also* BEFALLEN, BEFALLETH, BEFELL]
peradventure mischief *b* ....Gen 42:4
told him all that *b* unto ....Gen 42:29
mischief *b* him by the way ....Gen 42:38
mischief *b* him, ye shall ....Gen 44:29
tell you that which shall *b* .....Gen 49:1
and such things have *b* me ....Lev 10:19
travail that hath *b* us ....Num 20:14
evils and troubles shall *b* ......Deut 31:17
evils and troubles are *b* ....Deut 31:21
b you in the latter days ....Deut 31:29
told him all things that *b* ......Josh 2:23
why then is all this *b* us? ......Judg 6:13
Something hath *b* him 1Sam 20:26
evil that *b* thee from thy 2Sam 19:7
every thing that had *b* him ....Esth 6:13
shall be no evil *b* thee ....Ps 91:10
b the sons of men *b* beasts ....Eccl 3:19
even one thing *b* them ....Eccl 3:19
what shall *b* thy people ....Dan 10:14
b to the possessed of the ......Matt 8:33
b to him that was possessed ...Mark 5:16
temptations, which *b* me by ...Acts 20:19
the things that shall *b* me .....Acts 20:22

BEFORE—*See* INTRODUCTION

BEFOREHAND—*in anticipation; in advance*
take no thought *b* what ye ....Mark 13:11
and make up *b* your bounty ...2Cor 9:5
Some men's sins are open *b* ...1Tim 5:24
of some are manifest *b*........1Tim 5:25
testified *b* the sufferings 1Pet 1:11

BEFORETIME—*formerly*
Horims also dwelt in Seir *b* ...Deut 2:12
for Hazor *b* was the head .....Josh 11:10
and hated him not *b* ....Josh 20:5
B in Israel, when a man 1Sam 9:9
Prophet was *b* called a Seer ...1Sam 9:9
when all that knew him *b* 1Sam 10:11
afflict them any more, as *b* 2Sam 7:10

BEGAT—*See* BEGOTTEN

BEGET—*See* BEGOTTEN

BEGGAR—*needy person; one who lives by begging for gifts*

Statements concerning:
Shame of ....Luke 16:3
Seed of righteous, kept from ....Ps 37:25
Punishment of...........Ps 109:10
Object of prayer 1Sam 2:1, 8

Examples of:
Bartimaeus..............Mark 10:46
Lazarus.................Luke 16:20-22
Blind man ....Luke 18:35
Lame man ....Acts 3:2-6

[*also* BEG, BEGGARLY, BEGGED, BEGGING]
shall he *b* in the harvest.......Prov 20:4
and *b* the body of Jesus ....Matt 27:58
certain *b* named Lazarus ......Luke 16:20
that the *b* died and was ....Luke 16:22
and *b* the body of Jesus ....Luke 23:52
Is not this he..sat and *b* ....John 9:8
the weak and *b* elements ......Gal 4:9

BEGINNING—*the origin of; the starting point*
Creation ....Gen 1:1
John 1:1-3
Sin ....Gen 3:1-6
Rom 5:12-21
Death ....Gen 3:3, 22-24
Salvation ....Eph 1:4
Satan ....John 8:44
The Gospel ....Gen 3:15
Gal 3:8
The old covenant ....Ex 19:5
Heb 8:9
The new covenant......Jer. 31:31-34; Matt 26:28; Heb 9:14-28

[*also* BEGAN, BEGIN, BEGINNEST, BEGINNINGS, BEGUN]
b men to call upon the name ..Gen 4:26
when men *b* to multiply on....Gen 6:1
Noah *b* to be an husbandman .Gen 9:20
b to be a mighty one in the ...Gen 10:8
b of his kingdom was Babel ...Gen 10:10
this they *b* to do, and now ....Gen 11:6
his tent had been at the *b*.....Gen 13:3
ill favored, as at the *b* ....Gen 41:21
seven years of dearth *b* to .....Gen 41:54
he searched, and *b* at the .....Gen 44:12
and the *b* of my strength ......Gen 49:3
the *b* of months; it shall be....Ex 12:2
the Lord; the plague is *b*......Num 16:46
b to commit whoredom ....Num 25:1
in the *b* of your months ....Num 28:11
b Moses to declare this law....Deut 1:5
b to possess it, and contend ...Deut 2:24
will I *b* to put the dread ......Deut 2:25
I have *b* to give Sihon and ....Deut 2:31
his land before thee; *b* ....Deut 2:31
the *b* of the year even unto ...Deut 11:12
b to number the seven ....Deut 16:9
he is the *b* of his strength .....Deut 21:17
b of revenges upon the........Deut 32:42
This day will I *b* to magnify ...Josh 3:7
the *b* of the middle watch .....Judg 7:19
What man is he that will *b* ....Judg 10:18
he shall *b* to deliver Israel....Judg 13:5
Spirit of the Lord *b* to move ..Judg 13:25
and she *b* to afflict him, and ..Judg 16:19
when the day *b* to spring......Judg 19:25
b to smite of the people.......Judg 20:31
in the *b* of barley ....Ruth 1:22
latter end than at the *b* ....Ruth 3:10
his eyes *b* to wax dim, that.....1Sam 3:2
I *b*, I will also make an end ...1Sam 3:12
I then *b* to enquire of God 1Sam 22:15
old when he *b* to reign over ...2Sam 2:10
old when he *b* to reign 2Sam 5:4
in the *b* of barley harvest 2Sam 21:9
the *b* of harvest until water....2Sam 21:10
b to build the house of the 1Kin 6:1
when he *b* to reign, and he....1Kin 14:21
son of Jeroboam *b* to reign....1Kin 15:25
b Elah the son of Baasha 1Kin 16:8
son of Asa *b* to reign over 1Kin 22:41
the son of Ahab *b* to reign 2Kin 3:1
king of Judah *b* to reign 2Kin 8:16
Jeroham..*b* to reign...........2Kin 8:25
b Ahaziah to reign over 2Kin 9:29
Lord *b* to cut Israel short 2Kin 10:32
Jehoash when he *b* to reign ...2Kin 11:21
Jehoash *b* to reign; and 2Kin 12:1
the son of Jehu *b* to reign.....2Kin 13:1
he *b* to reign, and reigned.....2Kin 14:2
b Azariah son of Amaziah 2Kin 15:1
Jotham..*b* to reign 2Kin 16:1
b Hoshea the son of Elah 2Kin 17:1
at the *b* of their dwelling......2Kin 17:25
of Ahaz king of Judah *b* 2Kin 18:1
old when he *b* to reign........2Kin 22:1
old when he *b* to reign........2Kin 23:31
old when he *b* to reign........2Kin 24:8
year that he *b* to reign did ...2Kin 25:27
b to be mighty upon the earth. .1Chr 1:10
them any more as at the *b* 1Chr 17:9
son of Zeruiah *b* to number ...1Chr 27:24
Solomon *b* to build the 2Chr 3:1
old when he *b* to reign........2Chr 12:13
b Abijah to reign over 2Chr 13:1
when they *b* to sing and to 2Chr 20:22
old when he *b* to reign........2Chr 21:5
Ahaziah when he *b* to reign ...2Chr 22:2
years old when he *b* to reign ..2Chr 24:1
old when he *b* to reign........2Chr 25:1
was Uzziah when he *b* to 2Chr 26:3
five years old when he *b* 2Chr 27:1
old when he *b* to reign........2Chr 28:1
Hezekiah *b* to reign when he ..2Chr 29:1
b to lay the foundation of 2Chr 31:7
twelve years old when he *b*....2Chr 33:1
eight years old when he *b* 2Chr 34:1
three years old when he *b* 2Chr 36:2
b..to offer burnt offerings .....Ezra 3:6
Ahasuerus, in the *b* of his .....Ezra 4:6
b to build the house of God ...Ezra 5:2
the first month *b* he to go .....Ezra 7:9
the breaches *b* to be stopped ..Neh 4:7
to *b* the thanksgiving in ....Neh 11:17
gates of Jerusalem *b* to be ....Neh 13:19
whom thou hast *b* to fall ......Esth 6:13
to do as they had *b* ....Esth 9:23
Though thy *b* was small ....Job 8:7
end of Job more than his *b*....Job 42:12
the Lord is the *b* of wisdom ...Ps 111:10
is true from the *b*; and ....Ps 119:160
the *b* of knowledge; but.......Prov 1:7
possessed me in the *b* of ......Prov 8:22
from everlasting, from the *b*...Prov 8:23
fear of the Lord is the *b* of....Prov 9:10
The *b* of strife is as when .....Prov 17:14
hastily at the *b*; but the end ...Prov 20:21
God maketh from the *b* ....Eccl 3:11
end of a thing than the *b* .....Eccl 7:8

the *b* of the words of his ......Eccl 10:13
thy counsellers as at the *b* .....Is 1:26
from their *b* hitherto; a ....Is 18:2
people terrible from their *b* ...Is 18:7
from the *b*? have ye not ....Is 40:21
the generations from the *b* ....Is 41:4
hath declared from the *b* ......Is 41:26
the end from the *b* ....Is 46:10
former things from the *b* ......Is 48:3
even from the *b* declared ......Is 48:5
and not from the *b*; even .....Is 48:7
spoken in secret from the *b* ...Is 48:16
For since the *b* of the world ...Is 64:4
high throne from the *b* ....Jer 17:12
I *b* to bring evil on the city ...Jer 25:29
the *b* of the reign of ....Jer 26:1
b of the reign of Jehoiakim....Jer 27:1
b of the reign of Zedekiah ....Jer 28:1
Elam in the *b* of the reign ....Jer 49:34
years old when he *b* to reign ..Jer 52:1
b of the watches pour out .....Lam 2:19
and *b* at my sanctuary ....Ezek 9:6
they *b* at the ancient men .....Ezek 9:6
unto you than at your *b* ....Ezek 36:11
in the *b* of the year of our ....Ezek 40:1
seen in the vision at the *b* .....Dan 9:21
the *b* of thy supplications .....Dan 9:23
b of the word of the Lord .....Hos 1:2
grasshoppers in the *b* of.......Amos 7:1
b of the sin to the daughter ...Mic 1:13
Jesus *b* to preach, and to .....Matt 4:17
Jesus *b* to say unto the........Matt 11:7
b to pluck the ears of corn ....Matt 12:1
b to sink, he cried, saying .....Matt 14:30
when he had *b* to reckon ......Matt 18:24
which made them at the *b* .....Matt 19:4
from the *b* it was not so ......Matt 19:8
b from the last unto the ....Matt 20:8
these are the *b* of sorrows .....Matt 24:8
since the *b* of the world ....Matt 24:21
b to smite his ....Matt 24:49
b every one of them to say ....Matt 26:22
as it *b* to dawn toward the ....Matt 28:1
The *b* of the gospel of Jesus ...Mark 1:1
b to publish it much, and to ...Mark 1:45
disciples *b*, as they went ......Mark 2:23
he *b* again to teach by the ....Mark 4:1
they *b* to pray him to depart ..Mark 5:17
b to teach in the synagogue ...Mark 6:2
b to question with him ....Mark 8:11
from the *b* of the creation .....Mark 10:6
Peter *b* to say unto him ....Mark 10:28
b to cast out them..sold ....Mark 11:15
b to speak unto them by ......Mark 12:1
Jesus answering them *b* to.....Mark 13:5
these are the *b* of sorrows .....Mark 13:8
such as was not from the *b* ....Mark 13:19
they *b* to be sorrowful, and ...Mark 14:19
crying aloud, *b* to desire ......Mark 15:8
the *b* were eyewitnesses ....Luke 1:2
been since the world *b* ....Luke 1:70
b not to say within ....Luke 3:8
Jesus himself *b* to be about....Luke 3:23
he *b* to say unto them. This ...Luke 4:21
ships, so..they *b* to sink ....Luke 5:7
was dead sat up, and *b* to .....Luke 7:15
the day *b* to wear away ....Luke 9:12
thick together, he *b* to ....Luke 11:29
b to say unto his disciples .....Luke 12:1
b to beat the menservants .....Luke 12:45
ye *b* to stand without and .....Luke 13:25
thou *b* with shame to take ....Luke 14:9
with one consent *b* to make ...Luke 14:18
behold it *b* to mock him ......Luke 14:29
in that land, and he *b* to be ...Luke 15:14
b he to speak to the people ...Luke 20:9
things *b* to come to pass ......Luke 21:28
they *b* to enquire among ......Luke 22:23
b to accuse him, saying ....Luke 23:2
b to say to the mountains .....Luke 23:30
b at Moses and all the ....Luke 24:27
In the *b* was the Word and ....John 1:1
man at the *b* doth set forth....John 2:10
This *b* of miracles did..........John 2:11
when he *b* to amend. And ....John 4:52
Jesus knew from the *b* who ...John 6:64
b at the eldest, even unto .....John 8:9
Since the world *b* was it not ...John 9:32
b to wash..disciples' feet ......John 13:5
been with me from the *b* ....John 15:27
not unto you at the *b* ....John 16:4
B from the baptism of John ...Acts 1:22
b to speak with..tongues ......Acts 2:4
prophets since the world *b* ....Acts 3:21
b at the same scripture ....Acts 8:35
b from Galilee, after the ......Acts 10:37
rehearsed..matter from the *b* ..Acts 11:4
I *b* to speak, the Holy ....Acts 11:15
his works from the *b* of the ....Acts 15:18
he *b* to speak boldly in the ....Acts 18:26
Tertullus *b* to accuse him .....Acts 24:2
Which knew me from the *b* ...Acts 26:5
when he had broken it, he *b* ..Acts 27:35
secret since the world *b* ....Rom 16:25
Do we *b* again? commend 2Cor 3:1
as he had *b*, so he would 2Cor 8:6
who have *b* before, not only ...2Cor 8:10
having *b* in the Spirit, are .....Gal 3:3
from the *b* of the world ....Eph 3:9
that he which hath *b* a good ...Phil 1:6
that in the *b* of the gospel.....Phil 4:15
who is the *b*, the firstborn.....Col 1:18
hath from the *b* chosen you ...2Thess 2:13
when they have *b* to wax 1Tim 5:11
Jesus before the world *b* 2Tim 1:9
Thou..in the *b* hast laid ....Heb 1:10
which at the first *b* to be ......Heb 2:3
hold the *b* of our confidence ..Heb 3:14
having neither *b* of days ......Heb 7:3
must *b* at the house of God ...1Pet 4:17
and if it first *b* at us what 1Pet 4:17
worse with them than the *b* ...2Pet 2:20
from the *b* of the creation 2Pet 3:4
That which was from the *b* 1John 1:1
which ye had from the *b* 1John 2:7
the devil sinneth from the *b* ...1John 3:8
which we had from the *b*.......2John 5
as ye have heard from the *b*...2John 6
the *b* and the ending..........Rev 1:8
the *b* of the creation of God ..Rev 3:14
shall *b* to sound the mystery...Rev 10:7
the *b* and the end. I will ......Rev 21:6
Alpha and Omega, the *b* ......Rev 22:13

BEGOTTEN—*from "beget"; to procreate as the father; to bring into being*

Applied to Christ:
Predicted ....Ps 2:7
Acts 13:33
Prefigured ....Heb 11:17
Proclaimed.............John 1:14
Proffered ....John 3:16
Professed ....Heb 1:6

Applied to Christians:
By the Gospel 1Cor 4:15
In bonds...............Philem 10
Unto hope 1Pet 1:3
For safekeeping 1John 5:18

[*also* BEGAT, BEGET, BEGETTEST, BEGETTETH]
Irad *b* Mehujael ....Gen 4:18
b a son in his own likeness ....Gen 5:3
of Adam after he had *b* Seth ..Gen 5:4
Noah *b* three sons, Shem .....Gen 6:10
Cush *b* Nimrod; he began .....Gen 10:8
and *b* Arphaxed two years ....Gen 11:10
Terah *b* Abram, Nahor and ...Gen 11:27
Haran; and Haran *b* Lot ......Gen 11:27
twelve princes shall he *b* ......Gen 17:20
b of thy father, she is thy .....Lev 18:11
with you, which they *b* in .....Lev 25:45
I *b* them, that thou ....Num 11:12
Machir *b* Gilead; of Gilead ....Num 26:29
When thou shalt *b* children ....Deut 4:25
children that are *b* of them ....Deut 23:8
Thou shalt *b* sons and ....Deut 28:41
Rock that *b* thee thou art .....Deut 32:18
and ten sons of his body *b* ....Judg 8:30
Salmon *b* Boaz, and Boaz *b* ...Ruth 4:21
Obed *b* Jesse, and Jesse *b* .....Ruth 4:22
thou shalt *b*, shall they 2Kin 20:18
hath *b* the drops of dew? ......Job 38:28
He that *b* a fool doeth it ......Prov 17:21
unto thy father that *b* thee ....Prov 23:22
and he that *b* a wise child .....Prov 23:24
he *b* a son, and there is ....Eccl 5:14
If a man *b* a hundred ....Eccl 6:3
thee, which thou shalt *b* ......Is 39:7
unto his father, What *b* ....Is 45:10
Who hath *b* me these ....Is 49:21
their fathers that *b* them ......Jer 16:3
Take ye wives, and *b* sons ....Jer 29:6
he *b* a son that is a robber ....Ezek 18:10
if he *b* a son, that seeth all ....Ezek 18:14
shall *b* children among you ....Ezek 47:22
brought her, and he that *b* ....Dan 11:6
for they have *b* strange ....Hos 5:7
father..mother that *b* ....Zech 13:3
Jacob *b* Joseph the husband ...Matt 1:16
Abraham *b* Isaac and ....Acts 7:8
Isaac *b* Jacob, and Jacob *b* ....Acts 7:8
Midian, where he *b* two........Acts 7:29
my Son, this day have I *b* .....Heb 1:5
Son, to day have I *b* thee .....Heb 5:5
own will *b* he us with the .....James 1:18
God sent his only *b* Son 1John 4:9
that loveth him that *b*.........1John 5:1
loveth him also that is *b* 1John 5:1
first *b* of the dead, and the ....Rev 1:5

BEGUILE—*to deceive or mislead*

In Old Testament:
Eve, by Satan ....Gen 3:13
Israel, by the Midianites .Num 25:18
Joshua, by the Gibeonites.Josh 9:22

Of Christians:
By flattering words ......Rom 16:18
By false reasoning ....Col 2:4

[*also* BEGUILED, BEGUILING]
wherefore then hast thou *b* ....Gen 29:25
the serpent *b* Eve through.....2Cor 11:3
Let no man *b* you of your.....Col 2:18
b unstable souls; an heart 2Pet 2:14

BEHALF—*for one's interest, benefit, support, defense*
on the *b* of the children of ....Ex 27:21
to David on his *b*.............2Sam 3:12
shew himself strong in the *b* ...2Chr 16:9
yet to speak on God's *b*.......Job 36:2
but a prince for his own *b*.....Dan 11:18
glad therefore on your *b* ......Rom 16:19
thank..God always on your *b* ..1Cor 1:4
be given by many on our *b*....2Cor 1:11
occasion to glory on our *b* 2Cor 5:12
of our boasting on your *b* 2Cor 8:24
should be in vain in this *b*.....2Cor 9:3
given in the *b* of Christ ....Phil 1:29
him glorify God on this *b* 1Pet 4:16

BEHAVIOR—*one's conduct*

Strange:
Feigned insanity 1Sam 21:13
Supposed drunkenness ...1Sam 1:12-16
Pretended grief..........2Sam 14:1-8
Professed loyalty ....Matt 26:48, 49
Insipid hypocrisy ....Esth 6:5-11
Counterfeit religion 2Cor 11:13-15

True:
Reverent ....Titus 2:7
Orderly.................2Thess 3:7
Good...................1Tim 3:2
Without blame 1Thess 2:10

[*also* BEHAVE, BEHAVED, BEHAVETH]
their adversaries should *b* ......Deut 32:27
him, and *b* himself wisely 1Sam 18:5
let us *b* ourselves valiantly 1Chr 19:13
when he changed his *b* ....Ps 34:*title*
I *b* myself as though he had ...Ps 35:14
I will *b* myself wisely in a .....Ps 101:2
I have *b* and quieted myself ...Ps 131:2
the child shall *b* himself ....Is 3:5
as they have *b* themselves .....Mic 3:4
that he *b* himself uncomely 1Cor 7:36
Doth not *b* itself unseemly 1Cor 13:5

to ***b*** thyself in the house 1Tim 3:15
they be in ***b*** as becometh .....Titus 2:3

BEHEADING—*to cut off one's head; a form of capital punishment*
Ish-bosheth 2Sam 4:5-7
John the Baptist.........Matt 14:10
James ....Acts 12:2
Martyrs.................Rev 20:4

[*also* BEHEADED]
the heifer that is ***b*** in the .....Deut 21:6
It is John, whom I ***b***..........Mark 6:16
Herod said, John have I ***b*** ....Luke 9:9

BEHEMOTH—*a colossal beast*
Described..............Job 40:15-24

BEHIND—*in back of or to the rear of*
the tent door, which was ***b***....Gen 18:10
look not ***b*** thee neither stay ...Gen 19:17
b him a ram, caught in a ....Gen 22:13
and behold, also he is ***b*** us ....Gen 32:18
shall not an hoof be left ***b*****.....Ex 10:26
the maidservant that is ***b***......Ex 11:5
removed and went ***b*** them.....Ex 14:19
there be yet many years ***b***.....Lev 25:51
b the tabernacle westward .....Num 3:23
even all that were feeble ***b***....Deut 25:18
an ambush for the city ***b***......Josh 8:2
it is ***b*** Kirjath-jearim..........Judg 18:12
Benjamites looked ***b*** them.....Judg 20:40
wrapped in a cloth ***b*** the 1Sam 21:9
when Saul looked ***b*** him 1Sam 24:8
that were left ***b*** stayed 1Sam 30:9
when he looked ***b*** him, he 2Sam 1:7
Then Abner looked ***b*** him.....2Sam 2:20
weeping ***b*** her to Bahurim.....2Sam 3:16
fetch a compass ***b*** them 2Sam 5:23
against him before and ***b***......2Sam 10:9
by..way of the hillside ***b*** 2Sam 13:34
the throne was round ***b***........1Kin 10:19
hast cast me ***b*** thy back 1Kin 14:9
sound of his master's feet ***b*** ...2Kin 6:32
with peace? turn thee ***b*** me ...2Kin 9:18
third part at the gate ***b***........2Kin 11:6
against him before and ***b***......1Chr 19:10
ambushment to come about ***b*** .2Chr 13:13
the lower places ***b*** the wall ....Neh 4:13
cast thy law ***b*** their backs ....Neh 9:26
castest my words ***b*** thee ....Ps 50:17
Thou hast beset me ***b*** and.....Ps 139:5
he standeth ***b*** our wall, he ....Song 2:9
before..the Philistines ***b*******.......Is 9:12
Ears shall hear a word ***b***......Is 30:21
hast cast all my sins ***b*** thy .....Is 38:17
B the doors also and the ......Is 57:8
b one tree in the midst........Is 66:17
I heard ***b*** me a voice of a .....Ezek 3:12
and cast me ***b*** thy back ....Ezek 23:35
separate place which was ***b***....Ezek 41:15
and ***b*** them a flame burneth ...Joel 2:3
and ***b*** him were there red .....Zech 1:8
b him, and touched the hem...Matt 9:20
Get thee ***b*** me, Satan; thou ...Matt 16:23
came in the press ***b***, and ......Mark 5:27
Get thee ***b*** me, Satan; for .....Mark 8:33
die, and leave his wife ***b***.....Mark 12:19
tarried ***b*** in Jerusalem.........Luke 2:43
Get thee ***b*** me Satan; for it ...Luke 4:8
And stood at his feet ***b*** him ...Luke 7:38
Came ***b*** him and touched .....Luke 8:44
So that ye come ***b*** in no gift...1Cor 1:7
suppose I was not a whit ***b***....2Cor 11:5
for in nothing am I ***b*** the 2Cor 12:11
those things which are ***b***......Phil 3:13
is ***b*** of the afflictions..........Col 1:24
and heard ***b*** me a great ....Rev 1:10
full of eyes before and ***b***......Rev 4:6

BEHOLD—*to see; to gaze upon; to observe*

[*also* BEHELD, BEHOLDEST, BEHOLDETH, BEHOLDING]
had made, and ***b*** it was ....Gen 1:31
the Egyptians ***b*** the woman....Gen 12:14
b all the plain of Jordan ......Gen 13:10
and ***b***, and lo, the smoke of...Gen 19:28
And ***b***, I am with thee, and ...Gen 28:15
Jacob ***b*** the countenance ......Gen 31:2
And Israel ***b*** Joseph's sons ....Gen 48:8
he ***b*** the serpent of brass ......Num 21:9
He hath not ***b*** iniquity in......Num 23:21
men and women that ***b*** ......Judg 16:27
David ***b*** the place where 1Sam 26:5
Lord ***b***, and he repented him ..1Chr 21:15
B, all that he hath is in ....Job 1:12
b not the way of the ....Job 24:18
B, the fear of the Lord ....Job 28:28
b the sun when it shined ....Job 31:26
He ***b*** all high things; he is.....Job 41:34
man may see it; man may ***b***...Job 36:25
B, I am vile..................Job 40:4
thou ***b*** mischief and spite......Ps 10:14
heaven; he ***b*** all the sons of ...Ps 33:13
Turn..mine eyes from ***b*** ....Ps 119:37
I ***b*** the transgressors, and .....Ps 119:158
b, thou art there ....Ps 139:8
b, but there was no man ......Ps 142:4
b among the simple ones ....Prov 7:7
every place, ***b*** the evil and ....Prov 15:3
the ***b*** of them with their.......Eccl 5:11
I ***b*** all the work of God ....Eccl 8:17
B, a virgin shall conceive......Is 7:14
B, I and the children whom ...Is 8:18
B, God is my salvation........Is 12:2
B your God!..................Is 40:9
shall say to Zion ***B***, ***b*** them ...Is 41:27
I ***b***, and there was no man ....Is 41:28
b, it is I ....Is 52:6
I said ***B*** me, ***b*** me, unto a.....Is 65:1
I ***b*** the earth, and lo, it ....Jer 4:23
I awaked and ***b***, and my ....Jer 31:26
B, I am the Lord.............Jer 32:27
b..see if there be any sorrow ..Lam 1:12
as I ***b*** the living creatures .....Ezek 1:15
Then I ***b*** and lo a likeness ....Ezek 8:2
when I ***b*** lo, the sinews and ...Ezek 37:8
b till the wings thereof ....Dan 7:4
he ***b***, and drove asunder the...Hab 3:6
b..king cometh unto thee......Zech 9:9
B, a virgin shall be with.......Matt 1:23
why ***b*** thou the mote that is ...Matt 7:3
b them, and said unto them ...Matt 19:26
B thy King cometh unto ......Matt 21:5
women were there ***b*** afar.......Matt 27:55
the people, when they ***b*** him ..Mark 9:15
Jesus ***b*** him loved him ....Mark 10:21
b the place where they laid....Mark 16:6
And ***b*** thou shalt conceive.....Luke 1:31
b, I bring you good tidings ....Luke 2:10
And why ***b*** thou the mote .....Luke 6:41
b Satan as lightning fall ....Luke 10:18
the people stood ***b***............Luke 23:35
B my hands and my feet ......Luke 24:39
b, I send the promise of ......Luke 24:49
we ***b*** his glory, the glory as....John 1:14
B the Lamb of God, which....John 1:29
b thy King cometh, sitting.....John 12:15
Pilate saith unto them, ***B***......John 19:5
while they ***b***, he was taken ....Acts 1:9
b the man which was healed...Acts 4:14
B, I see the heavens opened...Acts 7:56
b the miracles and signs ....Acts 8:13
Saul, of Tarsus, for ***b***, he .....Acts 9:11
who steadfastly ***b*** him and.....Acts 14:9
passed by, and ***b*** your ....Acts 17:23
Paul, earnestly ***b*** the ....Acts 23:1
b as in a glass the glory of 2Cor 3:18
b, all things are become new ..2Cor 5:17
b, now is the accepted time ...2Cor 6:2
b, now is the day of 2Cor 6:2
joying and ***b*** your order ....Col 2:5
unto a man ***b*** his natural ......James 1:23
For he ***b*** himself, and goeth ...James 1:24
B, I come quickly; hold that...Rev 3:11
I ***b***, and lo, in the midst of....Rev 5:6
I ***b***, and lo a black horse ......Rev 6:5
After this I ***b***, and lo ....Rev 7:9
I ***b***, and heard an angel ....Rev 8:13
and their enemies ***b*** them .....Rev 11:12
I ***b*** another beast coming......Rev 13:11
B, I come as a thief. Blessed ..Rev 16:15
B, the tabernacle of God is ...Rev 21:3
B, I come quickly; blessed ....Rev 22:7

BEHOOVED—*was necessary for*
thus it ***b*** Christ to suffer ......Luke 24:46
in all things it ***b*** him to be ....Heb 2:17

BEING—*existing; becoming*
I have pleasure, my lord ***b***....Gen 18:12
the Lord ***b*** merciful unto ......Gen 19:16
Isaac ***b*** eight days old ....Gen 21:4
I ***b*** in the way, the Lord led...Gen 24:27
and I ***b*** few in number, they...Gen 34:30
gathered unto his people, ***b*** ...Gen 35:29
Joseph, ***b*** seventeen years .....Gen 37:2
Joseph died, ***b*** an hundred ....Gen 50:26
kneading troughs ***b*** bound .....Ex 12:34
that openeth the matrix ***b*** .....Ex 13:15
the owner thereof ***b*** not.......Ex 22:14
shall be ***b*** doubled, a span ....Ex 28:16
of them that cry for ***b***.........Ex 32:18
span the breadth thereof, ***b***....Ex 39:9
b a chief man among his ......Lev 21:4
b taken from the children .....Lev 24:8
princes of Israel ***b*** twelve......Num 1:44
of the vineyards a wall ***b***......Num 22:24
bond, ***b*** in her father's house ..Num 30:3
And the booty, ***b*** the rest of ..Num 31:32
Baal-meon (their names ***b*** .....Num 32:38
all Bashan, ***b*** the kingdom ....Deut 3:13
b matters of controversy ......Deut 17:8
because she cried not, ***b*** in ....Deut 22:24
our enemies themselves ***b*** ....Deut 32:31
be freed from ***b*** bondmen .....Josh 9:23
of Aaron, ***b*** of the family of...Josh 21:10
b an hundred and ten years ...Josh 24:29
servant of the Lord died, ***b***....Judg 2:8
Jerubbaal, ***b*** threescore and ...Judg 9:5
before the Lord ***b*** a 1Sam 2:18
rejected thee from ***b*** king 1Sam 15:23
great space ***b*** between them ...1Sam 26:13
b eighteen thousand men 2Sam 8:13
Why art thou, ***b*** the king's 2Sam 13:4
as people ***b*** ashamed steal.....2Sam 19:3
b girded with a new sword 2Sam 21:16
noise of the city, ***b*** in an 1Kin 1:41
thrust out Abiathar from ***b***....1Kin 2:27
Hadad ***b*** yet a little child......1Kin 11:17
he removed from ***b*** queen 1Kin 15:13
b like the house of Jeroboam ..1Kin 16:7
of Israel ***b*** seven thousand.....1Kin 20:15
Jehoshaphat ***b***..King of Judah .2Kin 8:16
king's sons, ***b*** seventy 2Kin 10:6
gave the money, ***b*** told into ...2Kin 12:11
fathers, ***b*** over the host 1Chr 9:19
household ***b*** taken for.........1Chr 24:6
b arrayed in white linen 2Chr 5:12
thousand chosen men, ***b*** 2Chr 13:3
removed her from ***b*** queen 2Chr 15:16
departed without ***b*** desired 2Chr 21:20
a several house, ***b*** a leper 2Chr 26:21
down from his house, and ***b***...Ezra 6:11
and ***b*** guilty, they offered a ...Ezra 10:19
and who is there, that ***b*** as ....Neh 6:11
provinces, ***b*** before him ....Esth 1:3
b hastened by the king's ......Esth 3:15
b hastened and pressed on ....Esth 8:14
ever perished, ***b*** innocent? ....Job 4:7
b wholly at ease and quiet ....Job 21:23
died, ***b*** old and full of days....Job 42:17
man ***b*** in honor abideth ....Ps 49:12
mountains; ***b*** girded with ......Ps 65:6
children of Ephraim, ***b***.........Ps 78:9
cut them off from ***b*** ....Ps 83:4
my God while I have my ***b***....Ps 104:33
b bound in affliction and ......Ps 107:10
substance, yet ***b*** unperfect ......Ps 139:16
unto..God while I have any ***b***. .Ps 146:2
keep thy foot from ***b*** taken....Prov 3:26
b often reproved hardeneth....Prov 29:1
hold swords, ***b*** expert in ......Song 3:8
and she ***b*** desolate shall sit ....Is 3:26
is taken away from ***b*** a city....Is 17:1
b his counselor hath taught.....Is 40:13
b a hundred years old shall....Is 65:20
Withhold thy foot from ***b*** .....Jer 2:25

b desolate it mourneth unto . . .Jer 12:11
not hastened from *b* a . . . . .Jer 17:16
shall cease from *b* a nation . . . .Jer 31:36
maidservant *b* a Hebrew . . . . . .Jer 34:9
him *b* bound in chains . . . . .Jer 40:1
cut it off from *b* a nation . . . . .Jer 48:2
behold, *b* planted, shall it . . . . .Ezek 17:10
voice of the multitude *b* at . . . .Ezek 23:42
b in the midst of that which . . .Ezek 48:22
counselors, *b* gathered . . . . .Dan 3:27
b about threescore and two . . . .Dan 5:31
his windows *b* open in his . . . . .Dan 6:10
Now that *b* broken, whereas . . .Dan 8:22
b caused to fly swiftly . . . . .Dan 9:21
Joseph her husband, *b* . . . . .Matt 1:19
b warned of God in a dream . .Matt 2:12
if ye then, *b* evil know . . . . .Matt 7:11
b evil, speak good things . . . . . .Matt 12:34
b..instructed of her mother . . . .Matt 14:8
with anger, *b* grieved for . . . . . .Mark 3:5
which is, *b* interpreted . . . . .Mark 5:41
the multitude *b* very great . . . . .Mark 8:1
b in the house he asked . . . . . . .Mark 9:33
b in Bethany in the house . . . . .Mark 14:3
Golgotha..*b* interpreted . . . . . . .Mark 15:22
that we, *b* delivered out of . . . .Luke 1:74
wife, *b* great with child . . . . . . .Luke 2:5
Pontius Pilate *b* governor of . . .Luke 3:1
Jesus *b* full of the Holy . . . . . . .Luke 4:1
justified God, *b* baptized . . . . . .Luke 7:29
And they *b* afraid wondered . . .Luke 8:25
If ye then, *b* evil know how . . .Luke 11:13
this woman, *b* a daughter of . . .Luke 13:16
master of the house *b* angry . . .Luke 14:21
lift up his eyes, *b* in . . . . .Luke 16:23
children of God, *b* the . . . . .Luke 20:36
b brought before kings and . . . .Luke 21:12
Iscariot, *b* of the number . . . . . .Luke 22:3
to say, *b* interpreted, Master . .John 1:38
Jesus therefore, *b* wearied . . . . .John 4:6
a multitude *b* in that place . . . .John 5:13
betray him, *b* one of the . . . . . .John 6:71
Jesus by night, *b* one . . . . .John 7:50
b convicted by their own . . . . . .John 8:9
that thou, *b* a man, makest . . . .John 10:33
Caiaphas, *b* the high priest . . . .John 11:49
supper *b* ended, the devil . . . . .John 13:2
you, *b* yet present with you . . .John 14:25
high priest, *b* his kinsman . . . . .John 18:26
Joseph of Arimathea, *b* . . . . . . .John 19:38
evening, *b* the first day of . . . . .John 20:19
b seen of them forty days . . . . .Acts 1:3
b delivered by the . . . . .Acts 2:23
of prayer, *b* the ninth hour . . . .Acts 3:1
b grieved that they taught . . . . .Acts 4:2
his wife also *b* privy to it . . . . . .Acts 5:2
b full of the Holy Ghost . . . . . .Acts 7:55
b sent forth by the Holy . . . . . .Acts 13:4
in his feet, *b* a cripple . . . . .Acts 14:8
And *b* brought on their way . . .Acts 15:3
These men, *b* Jews do . . . . .Acts 16:20
and move, and have our *b* . . . .Acts 17:28
and *b* fervent in the Spirit . . . . .Acts 18:25
there *b* no cause whereby . . . . .Acts 19:40
b fallen into a deep sleep . . . . .Acts 20:9
glory of that light *b* . . . . .Acts 22:11
b exceedingly mad against . . . . .Acts 26:11
of Thessalonica *b* . . . . .Acts 27:2
b understood by the things . . . .Rom 1:20
b instructed out of the law . . . .Rom 2:18
b witnessed by the law and . . . .Rom 3:21
he had yet *b* uncircumcised . . . .Rom 4:11
b justified by faith . . . . .Rom 5:1
that Christ *b* raised from . . . . . .Rom 6:9
b dead wherein we were . . . . . .Rom 7:6
For the children *b* not yet . . . . .Rom 9:11
b ignorant of God's . . . . .Rom 10:3
thou, *b* a wild olive tree . . . . . .Rom 11:17
we, *b* many, are one body . . . .Rom 12:5
b sanctified by the Holy . . . . . . .Rom 15:16
b reviled, we bless 1Cor 4:12
any man called *b* circumcised? .1Cor 7:18
conscience *b* weak is defiled . . .1Cor 8:7
(*b* not without law to God 1Cor 9:21
we *b* many are one bread 1Cor 10:17
of that one body, *b* many 1Cor 12:12
If so be that *b* clothed we 2Cor 5:3
b more forward, of his own . . .2Cor 8:17
B enriched in every thing 2Cor 9:11
b absent am bold toward 2Cor 10:1
myself from *b* burdensome 2Cor 11:9
nevertheless, *b* crafty, I 2Cor 12:16
and *b* absent now I write 2Cor 13:2
b more exceedingly zealous . . . .Gal 1:14
was with me, *b* a Greek . . . . . . .Gal 2:3
curse of the law, *b* made . . . . . .Gal 3:13
inheritance, *b* predestinated . . .Eph 1:11
ye *b* in time past Gentiles . . . . .Eph 2:11
b rooted and grounded in . . . . .Eph 3:17
b alienated from the life . . . . . .Eph 4:18
B confident of this very . . . . . . .Phil 1:6
same love, *b* of one accord . . . .Phil 2:2
b made conformable unto . . . . .Phil 3:10
b fruitful in every good . . . . . . .Col 1:10
might be comforted, *b* knit . . . .Col 2:2
b..desirous of you, we were . . .1Thess 2:8
but the woman *b* deceived 1Tim 2:14
novice, lest *b* lifted up 1Tim 3:6
b mindful of thy tears, that 2Tim 1:4
deceiving and *b* deceived 2Tim 3:13
deny him, *b* abominable . . . . . .Titus 1:16
b justified by his grace . . . . .Titus 3:7
b such a one as Paul the . . . . . .Philem 9
Who *b* the brightness of his . . .Heb 1:3
b tempted, he is able to . . . . . . .Heb 2:18
fear, lest a promise *b* left . . . . .Heb 4:1
b made perfect, he became . . . .Heb 5:9
b by interpretation King . . . . . .Heb 7:2
Christ *b* come a high priest . . . .Heb 9:11
by it he *b* dead yet speaketh . .Heb 11:4
as *b* yourselves also in the . . . . .Heb 13:3
he *b* not a forgetful hearer . . . .James 1:25
not works, is dead, *b* alone . . . .James 2:17
your faith, *b*..more precious . . .1Pet 1:7
stumble at the word, *b* 1Pet 2:8
b in subjection unto their 1Pet 3:5
b lords over God's heritage 1Pet 5:3
b overflowed with water 2Pet 3:6
b turned, I saw seven . . . . .Rev 1:12
And she *b* with child cried . . . .Rev 12:2
b the first-fruits unto God . . . . .Rev 14:4

BEKAH (bē´kä)
Half a shekel . . . . .Ex 38:26
See Jewish Measures

BEL (bĕl)—*name for Babylonian sun god Marduk*
Patron god of Babylon . . .Is 46:1
Jer 51:44
Merodach title . . . . .Jer 50:2

BELA, BELAH (bē´lä)—*"destroying"*
1. King of Edom . . . . .Gen 36:32
2. Reubenite chief 1Chr 5:8
3. Benjamin's son . . . . .Gen 46:21
4. A city . . . . .Gen 14:2, 8

[*also* BELAITES]
family of the *B*: of Ashbel . . . .Num 26:38
B the son of Beor; and the 1Chr 1:43
sons of Benjamin; *B* and 1Chr 7:6
Benjamin begat *B* his 1Chr 8:1

BELCH—*to burp*
b out with their mouth . . . . .Ps 59:7

BELIAL (bē´lĭ-ăl)—*"useless; without worth"*
Applied properly to:
Seducers . . . . .Deut 13:13
The profligate . . . . .Judg 19:22
Eli's sons 1Sam 2:12
Rebels 1Sam 10:27
A fool 1Sam 25:25
The wicked 1Sam 30:22
Liars 1Kin 21:10, 13
Satan 2Cor 6:15
Applied improperly to:
Hannah 1Sam 1:16
David 2Sam 16:7

children of *B*, which are in . . . .Judg 20:13
for he is such a son of *B* 1Sam 25:17
a man of *B*, whose name 2Sam 20:1
the sons of *B* shall be all 2Sam 23:6
vain men, the children of *B* . . .2Chr 13:7

BELIED—*misrepresented*
They have *b* the Lord, and . . . .Jer 5:12

BELIEVE—*to accept trustfully; to have faith*
[*also* BELIEF, BELIEVED, BELIEVEST, BELIEVETH, BELIEVING]
he *b* in the Lord; and . . . . .Gen 15:6
heart fainted, for he *b* . . . . .Gen 45:26
will not *b* me, nor hearken . . . .Ex 4:1
And the people *b*; and when . .Ex 4:31
b the Lord, and his servant . . . .Ex 14:31
with thee, and *b* thee for . . . . . .Ex 19:9
will it be ere they *b* me . . . . . . .Num 14:11
Because ye *b* me not . . . . .Num 20:12
ye did not *b* the Lord your . . . .Deut 1:32
ye *b* him not, nor hearkened . .Deut 9:23
Achish *b* David, saying, He . . .1Sam 27:12
Howbeit I *b* not the words 1Kin 10:7
that did not *b* in the Lord 2Kin 17:14
Howbeit I *b* not their words . . .2Chr 9:6
B in the Lord your God, so . . .2Chr 20:20
b his prophets, so shall ye 2Chr 20:20
manner, neither yet *b* him 2Chr 32:15
b that he had hearkened . . . . . .Job 9:16
He *b* not that he shall . . . . .Job 15:22
I laughed on them, they *b* . . . . .Job 29:24
Wilt thou *b* him, that he . . . . . .Job 39:12
neither *b* he that it is . . . . .Job 39:24
unless I had *b* to see the . . . . . .Ps 27:13
Because they *b* not in God . . . .Ps 78:22
b not for his wondrous . . . . .Ps 78:32
Then *b* they his words; they . . .Ps 106:12
pleasant land they *b* not . . . . . .Ps 106:24
I *b*, therefore have I spoken . . .Ps 116:10
I have *b* thy commandments . . .Ps 119:66
The simple *b* every word . . . . . .Prov 14:15
When he speaketh fair, *b* . . . . .Prov 26:25
If ye will not *b*, surely ye . . . . .Is 7:9
he that *b* shall not make . . . . . .Is 28:16
that ye may know and *b* me . . .Is 43:10
Who hath *b* our report? and . . .Is 53:1
b them not, though they . . . . . .Jer 12:6
son of Ahikam *b* them not . . . .Jer 40:14
world, would not have *b* that . .Lam 4:12
upon him, because he *b* in . . . .Dan 6:23
people of Nineveh *b* God . . . . .Jon 3:5
ye will not *b*, though it be . . . .Hab 1:5
as thou hast *b*, so be it . . . . . . .Matt 8:13
B ye that I am able to do . . . . .Matt 9:28
little ones which *b* in me . . . . . .Matt 18:6
shall ask in prayer, *b* ye . . . . . . .Matt 21:22
Why did ye not then *b* him? . . .Matt 21:25
and ye *b* him not, but the . . . . .Matt 21:32
publicans and the harlots *b* . . . .Matt 21:32
here is Christ or there *b* it . . . .Matt 24:26
and we will *b* him . . . . .Matt 27:42
repent ye, and *b* the gospel . . .Mark 1:15
Be not afraid, only *b* . . . . .Mark 5:36
If thou canst *b*, all things . . . . .Mark 9:23
are possible to him that *b* . . . . .Mark 9:23
Lord, I *b*; help thou mine . . . . .Mark 9:24
shall *b* that those things . . . . . . .Mark 11:23
b that ye receive them, and . . .Mark 11:24
lo, he is there; *b* him not . . . . .Mark 13:21
that we may see and *b* . . . . .Mark 15:32
had been seen of her, *b* . . . . . . .Mark 16:11
He that *b* and is baptized . . . . .Mark 16:16
shall follow them that *b* . . . . . . .Mark 16:17
which are most surely *b* . . . . . . .Luke 1:1
because thou *b* not my . . . . .Luke 1:20
lest they should *b* and be . . . . .Luke 8:12
which for a while *b*, and . . . . . .Luke 8:13
say, Why then *b* ye him not . . .Luke 20:5
ye will not *b* . . . . .Luke 22:67
idle tales, and they *b* them . . . .Luke 24:11
fools, and slow of heart to *b* . .Luke 24:25
while they yet *b* not for joy . . .Luke 24:41
men through him might *b* . . . . .John 1:7
even to them that *b* on his . . . .John 1:12
under the fig tree, *b* thou? . . . .John 1:50
his disciples *b* on him . . . . .John 2:11
and ye *b* not . . . . .John 3:12

whosoever *b* in him should . . . .John 3:16
He that *b* on him is not . . . . . . .John 3:18
he that *b* not is condemned . . .John 3:18
because he hath not *b* . . . . .John 3:18
He that *b* on the Son hath . . . .John 3:36
b not the Son shall not . . . . .John 3:36
Woman, *b* me, the hour . . . . . .John 4:21
Samaritans of that city *b* . . . . . .John 4:39
and wonders ye will not *b* . . . . .John 4:48
himself *b*, and his whole . . . . . .John 4:53
and *b* on him that sent me . . . .John 5:24
whom he hath sent, him ye *b* . .John 5:38
had ye *b* Moses . . . . .John 5:46
ye *b* on him whom he hath . . . .John 6:29
he that *b* on me shall never . . .John 6:35
and *b* on him, may have . . . . . .John 6:40
He that *b* on me hath . . . . .John 6:47
who they were that *b* not . . . . .John 6:64
neither did his brethren *b* . . . . .John 7:5
many of the people *b* on him . .John 7:31
He that *b* on me, as the . . . . . .John 7:38
they that *b* on him should . . . . .John 7:39
or of the Pharisees *b* on him . .John 7:48
if ye *b* not that I am he, ye . . .John 8:24
spake these words, many *b* . . . .John 8:30
Jews did not *b* concerning . . . . .John 9:18
b not: the works that I do . . . . .John 10:25
But ye *b* not, because ye are . .John 10:26
intent ye may *b*; nevertheless . .John 11:15
he that *b* in me, though he . . . .John 11:25
in me shall never die. *B* . . . . . . .John 11:26
b that thou art the Christ . . . . .John 11:27
wouldest *b*; thou shouldest . . . .John 11:40
I said it that they may *b* . . . . . .John 11:42
things which Jesus did *b* . . . . . .John 11:45
Jews went away and *b* on . . . . .John 12:11
b in the light, that ye may . . . .John 12:36
Therefore they could not *b* . . . .John 12:39
He that *b* on me, *b* not on . . . .John 12:44
that whosoever *b* on me . . . . . .John 12:46
come to pass, ye may *b* that . . .John 13:19
ye *b* in God, *b* also in me . . . . .John 14:1
B thou not that I am in the . . .John 14:10
He that *b* on me, the works . . .John 14:12
because they *b* not on me . . . . .John 16:9
have *b* that I came out from . . .John 16:27
they have *b* that thou didst . . . .John 17:8
for them also which shall *b* . . . .John 17:20
saith true, that ye might *b* . . . . .John 19:35
sepulcher and he saw, and *b* . . .John 20:8
hand..his side I will not *b* . . . . .John 20:25
and be not faithless, but *b* . . . .John 20:27
b that Jesus is the Christ . . . . . .John 20:31
that *b* ye might have life . . . . . .John 20:31
And all that *b* were together . . .Acts 2:44
them which heard the word *b* . .Acts 4:4
of them that *b* were of one . . . .Acts 4:32
But when they *b* Philip . . . . . . .Acts 8:12
Then Simon himself *b* also . . . .Acts 8:13
If thou *b* with all thine . . . . .Acts 8:37
I *b* that Jesus Christ is . . . . .Acts 8:37
b not that he was a disciple . . .Acts 9:26
Joppa, and many *b* in the . . . . .Acts 9:42
whosoever *b* in him shall . . . . . .Acts 10:43
of the circumcision which *b* . . . .Acts 10:45
who *b* on the Lord Jesus . . . . . .Acts 11:17
a great number *b*, and turned .Acts 11:21
he saw what was done *b* . . . . . .Acts 13:12
him all that *b* are justified . . . . .Acts 13:39
ordained to eternal life *b* . . . . . .Acts 13:48
and also of the Greeks *b* . . . . . .Acts 14:1
of the Pharisees which *b* . . . . . .Acts 15:5
word of the gospel, and *b* . . . . .Acts 15:7
which was a Jewess, and *b* . . . .Acts 16:1
B on the Lord Jesus Christ . . . .Acts 16:31
rejoiced, *b* in God with all . . . .Acts 16:34
And some of them *b* and . . . . .Acts 17:4
b on the Lord with all his . . . . .Acts 18:8
the Holy Ghost since ye *b*? . . . .Acts 19:2
that they should *b* on him . . . . .Acts 19:4
of Jews there are which *b* . . . . .Acts 21:20
synagogue them that *b* on . . . . .Acts 22:19
b all things which are . . . . .Acts 24:14
King Agrippa, *b* thou the . . . . .Acts 26:27
I know that thou *b* . . . . .Acts 26:27
the centurion *b* the master . . . .Acts 27:11
for I *b* God, that it shall be . . .Acts 27:25
some *b* the things which . . . . . .Acts 28:24
salvation to every one..*b* . . . . . .Rom 1:16
For what if some did not *b*? . . .Rom 3:3
and upon all them that *b* . . . . . .Rom 3:22
justifier of him which *b* . . . . . . .Rom 3:26
Abraham *b* God, and it was . . .Rom 4:3
but *b* on him that justifieth . . . .Rom 4:5
father of all them that *b* . . . . . .Rom 4:11
who against hope *b* in hope . . .Rom 4:18
we *b* that we shall also live . . . .Rom 6:8
whosoever *b* on him shall . . . . .Rom 9:33
to every one that *b* . . . . .Rom 10:4
shalt *b* in thine heart that . . . . .Rom 10:9
and how shall they *b* . . . . .Rom 10:14
ye in times past have not *b* . . . .Rom 11:30
nearer than when we *b* . . . . .Rom 13:11
one *b* that he may eat all . . . . .Rom 14:2
with all joy and peace in *b* . . . .Rom 15:13
them that do not *b* in Judea . . .Rom 15:31
to save them that *b* 1Cor 1:21
ministers by whom ye *b* 1Cor 3:5
hath a wife, that *b* not, and . . .1Cor 7:12
hath a husband that *b* not 1Cor 7:13
any of them that *b* not bid 1Cor 10:27
and I partly *b* it 1Cor 11:18
b all things, hopeth all 1Cor 13:7
not to them that *b* 1Cor 14:22
there come in one that *b* not . .1Cor 14:24
unless ye have *b* in vain 1Cor 15:2
minds of them which *b* not 2Cor 4:4
I *b*, and therefore have I 2Cor 4:13
we also *b* and therefore 2Cor 4:13
he that *b* with an infidel? 2Cor 6:15
we have *b* in Jesus Christ . . . . .Gal 2:16
as Abraham *b* God, and it . . . .Gal 3:6
be given to them that *b* . . . . . . .Gal 3:22
in whom also after that ye *b* . . .Eph 1:13
to us-ward who *b*, according . . .Eph 1:19
only to *b* on him, but also to . .Phil 1:29
were examples to all that *b* 1Thess 1:7
ourselves among you that *b* . . .1Thess 2:10
if we *b* that Jesus died and 1Thess 4:14
admired in all them that *b* 2Thess 1:10
testimony among you was *b* . . .2Thess 1:10
who *b* not the truth, but had . .2Thess 2:12
the Spirit and *b* of the truth . . .2Thess 2:13
should hereafter *b* on him 1Tim 1:16
b on in the world, received 1Tim 3:16
them which *b* and know the . . .1Tim 4:3
specially of those that *b* 1Tim 4:10
If any man or woman that *b* . . .1Tim 5:16
they that have *b* masters 1Tim 6:2
I know whom I have *b*, and . . .2Tim 1:12
if we *b* not yet he abideth 2Tim 2:13
that they which have *b* in . . . . .Titus 3:8
his rest, but to them that *b* . . . .Heb 3:18
which have *b* do enter into . . . .Heb 4:3
of them that *b* to the saving . . .Heb 10:39
must *b* that he is, and that . . . .Heb 11:6
not with them that *b* . . . . .Heb 11:31
b that there is one God . . . . . . .James 2:19
devils also *b*, and tremble . . . . .James 2:19
Abraham *b* God, and it was . . .James 2:23
yet *b*, ye rejoice with joy 1Pet 1:8
by him do *b* in God, that 1Pet 1:21
and he that *b* on him shall 1Pet 2:6
Unto you therefore which *b* . . .1Pet 2:7
That we should *b* on the 1John 3:23
Beloved, *b* not every spirit 1John 4:1
we have known and *b* the 1John 4:16
Whosoever *b* that Jesus is the .1John 5:1
that *b* that Jesus is the Son . . .1John 5:5
He that *b* on the Son of God . .1John 5:10
he that *b* not God hath 1John 5:10
because he *b* not the record . . .1John 5:10
you that *b* on the name of 1John 5:13
ye may *b* on the name of the . .1John 5:13
destroyed them that *b* not . . . . .Jude 5

BELIEVERS—*synonymous with "Christians"*
Applied to converts . . . . . .Acts 5:14
1Tim 4:12

BELL—*tassel*
On Aaron's garment . . . . .Ex 28:33, 34
Ex 39:25, 26
Attention-getters . . . . .Is 3:16, 18
Symbols of consecration . .Zech 14:20

[*also* BELLS]
b and a pomegranate . . . . .Ex 28:34
b and a pomegranate, a *b* . . . . .Ex 39:26

BELLOW—*to moo like a cow*
the heifer at grass, and *b* . . . . . .Jer 50:11

BELLOWS—*an instrument used in forcing air at a fire*
A figure of affliction . . . . .Jer 6:29
Descriptive of God's judgment . . . . .Jer 6:27-30

BELLY—*stomach; underside of an animal*

[*also* BELLIES]
upon thy *b* shalt thou go . . . . . .Gen 3:14
against the *b* which was by 1Kin 7:20
when I came out of the *b* . . . . .Job 3:11
fill his *b* with..east wind . . . . . . .Job 15:2
and their *b* prepareth . . . . .Job 15:35
shall cast them out..his *b* . . . . . .Job 20:15
b thou fillest with thy hid . . . . .Ps 17:14
my God from my mother's *b* . . .Ps 22:10
to the dust, our *b* cleaveth . . . .Ps 44:25
the inward parts of the *b* . . . . . .Prov 20:27
borne by me from the *b* . . . . . . .Is 46:3
in the *b* of the fish three . . . . . .Jon 1:17
his God out of the fish's *b* . . . .Jon 2:1
out of the *b* of hell cried I . . . .Jon 2:2
my *b* trembled; my lips . . . . . . .Hab 3:16
would fain have filled his *b* . . . .Luke 15:16
his *b* shall flow rivers of . . . . . . .John 7:38
Meats for the *b* 1Cor 6:13
and the *b* for meats 1Cor 6:13
whose God is their *b* and . . . . .Phil 3:19
liars, evil beasts, slow *b* . . . . . . .Titus 1:12

BELONG—*to be the property of a person, group of people, or God*

[*also* BELONGED, BELONGEST, BELONGETH, BELONGING]
Do not interpretations *b* . . . . . .Gen 40:8
possession of the land did *b* . . .Lev 27:24
and over all things that *b* . . . . .Num 1:50
service of the sanctuary *b* . . . . .Num 7:9
The secret things *b* unto . . . . . .Deut 29:29
things which are revealed *b* . . . .Deut 29:29
b to the children of . . . . .Josh 17:8
a part of the field *b* unto . . . . . .Ruth 2:3
of the Philistines *b* to 1Sam 6:18
the herdmen that *b* to Saul 1Sam 21:7
unto him, To whom *b* thou? . . .1Sam 30:13
mighty men which *b* to 1Kin 1:8
which *b* to the Philistines 1Kin 15:27
which *b* to the Philistines 1Kin 16:15
and Hamath, which *b* to 2Kin 14:28
these *b* to the sons of 1Chr 2:23
Kirjath-jearim, which *b* to 1Chr 13:6
this matter *b* unto thee . . . . .Ezra 10:4
which *b* to king Ahasuerus . . . .Esth 1:9
things as *b* to her, and . . . . .Esth 2:9
Salvation *b* unto the Lord . . . . .Ps 3:8
shields of the earth *b* unto . . . .Ps 47:9
that power *b* unto God . . . . . . .Ps 62:11
the Lord *b* the issues from . . . .Ps 68:20
These things also *b* to the . . . . .Prov 24:23
strife *b* not to him, is like . . . . .Prov 26:17
O Lord, righteousness *b* . . . . . .Dan 9:7
To the Lord our God *b* . . . . . . .Dan 9:9
because ye *b* to Christ . . . . .Mark 9:41
desert place *b* to the city . . . . . .Luke 9:10
things which *b* unto thy . . . . . . .Luke 19:42
b unto Herod's jurisdiction . . . .Luke 23:7
careth for the things that *b* 1Cor 7:32
But strong meat *b* to them . . . .Heb 5:14

BELOVED—*dearly loved; one dearly loved*
Applied naturally to:
A wife . . . . .Deut 21:15, 16
A husband . . . . .Song 6:1-3

Applied spiritually to:
Christ ....Matt 3:17
Spiritual Israel ....Rom 9:25
Believers ....Col 3:12
Christian friends.........Rom 16:8, 9
New Jerusalem ....Rev 21:9, 10

[*also* BELOVED'S]
b of the Lord shall dwell ......Deut 33:12
was *b* of his God, and God ...Neh 13:26
thy *b* may be delivered........Ps 60:5
thy *b* may be delivered........Ps 108:6
so he giveth his *b* sleep ....Ps 127:2
My *b* is unto me as a cluster ..Song 1:14
so is my *b* among the sons ....Song 2:3
My *b* is like a roe or a........Song 2:9
My *b* is mine, and I am his ...Song 2:16
turn, my *b*, and be thou like ..Song 2:17
b come into his garden, and ...Song 4:16
voice of my *b* that knocketh...Song 5:2
My *b* put in his hand by the...Song 5:4
to open to my *b*, and my .....Song 5:5
to my *b*; but my *b* had ....Song 5:6
if ye find my *b*, that ye ....Song 5:8
thy *b* more than another *b* ....Song 5:9
thy *b* more than another *b* ....Song 5:9
my *b* is white and ruddy ......Song 5:10
This is my *b*, and this is.......Song 5:16
b, and my beloved is mine ....Song 6:3
I am my *b*, and his desire .....Song 7:10
well-beloved a song of my *b*...Is 5:1
my *b* to do in mine house .....Jer 11:15
greatly *b*, understand the ......Dan 10:11
said, O man greatly *b*, fear....Dan 10:19
yet, love a woman *b* of her....Hos 3:1
said, This is my *b* Son ....Matt 17:5
Thou art my *b* Son, in ....Mark 1:11
said, Thou art my *b* Son ......Luke 3:22
men unto you with our *b*......Acts 15:25
the election, they are *b* ....Rom 11:28
as my *b* sons I warn you 1Cor 4:14
my *b* son, and faithful in 1Cor 4:17
dearly *b*, let us cleanse........2Cor 7:1
made us accepted in the *b*.....Eph 1:6
dearly *b* and longed for ....Phil 4:1
in the Lord, my dearly *b* ......Phil 4:1
Luke, the *b* physician, and ....Col 4:14
Knowing, brethren *b*, your 1Thess 1:4
brethren *b* of the Lord 2Thess 2:13
they are faithful and *b* 1Tim 6:2
Timothy, my dearly *b* son 2Tim 1:2
Philemon our dearly *b*, and ...Philem 1
b, we are persuaded better ....Heb 6:9
Do not err, my *b* brethren ....James 1:16
b, I beseech you as 1Pet 2:11
our *b* brother Paul also 2Pet 3:15
B, now are we the sons 1John 3:2
B, I wish above all things 3John 2
B, when I gave all diligence ....Jude 3
saints about, and the *b* city....Rev 20:9

BELSHAZZAR (bĕl-shăz'er)—*"Bel has protected the king(ship)"*
Son of Nebuchadnezzar ..Dan 5:2
Gives feast..............Dan 5:1, 4
Disturbed by handwriting.Dan 5:5-12
Seeks Daniel's aid ....Dan 5:13-16
Daniel interprets for him .Dan 5:17-29
Last Chaldean king ......Dan 5:30, 31

B king of Babylon Daniel .....Dan 7:1
B a vision appeared unto......Dan 8:1

BELTESHAZZAR (bĕl-tĕ-shăz'er)—*"protect his life"*
Daniel's Babylonian name Dan 1:7

unto Daniel the name of *B*....Dan 1:7
Daniel, whose name was *B*....Dan 2:26
me, whose name was *B* ....Dan 4:8
B, master of the magicians ....Dan 4:9
B, declare the ....Dan 4:18
whose name was *B*, was ....Dan 4:19
said, *B*, let not the dream .....Dan 4:19
B answered and said, My .....Dan 4:19
whom the king named *B* ......Dan 5:12
whose name was called *B* .....Dan 10:1

BEMOAN—*to express deep grief or distress over*

[*also* BEMOANED, BEMOANING]
they *b* him, and comforted ....Job 42:11
who shall *b* thee? or who .....Jer 15:5
neither go to lament nor *b* ....Jer 16:5
for the dead, neither *b* him....Jer 22:10
heard Ephraim *b* himself ......Jer 31:18
All ye that are about him, *b*...Jer 48:17
is laid waste: who will *b*.......Nah 3:7

BEN (bĕn)—*"son"*
Levite porter 1Chr 15:18

BENAIAH (bĕ-nā'yă)—*"Jehovah has built"*
1. Jehoiada's son 2Sam 23:20
A mighty man 2Sam 23:20, 21
David's bodyguard 2Sam 8:18
Faithful to David 2Sam 15:18; 2Sam 20:23
Escorts Solomon to the throne 1Kin 1:38-40
Executes Adonijah, Joab and Shimei.... { 1Kin 2:25, 29-34; 1Kin 2:46 }
Commander-in-chief.....1Kin 2:35
2. One of David's mighty men 2Sam 23:30
Divisional commander...1Chr 27:14
3. Levite musician 1Chr 15:18-20
4. Priestly trumpeter 1Chr 15:24; 1Chr 16:6
5. Levite of Asaph's family .2Chr 20:14
6. Simeonite 1Chr 4:36
7. Levite overseer 2Chr 31:13
8. Father of leader Pelatiah .Ezek 11:1, 13
9-12. Four postexilic Jews who divorced their foreign wives ....Ezra 10:25-43

B the son of Jehoiada was 2Sam 20:23
These things did *B* the son 2Sam 23:22
and *B* the son of Jehoiada 1Kin 1:8
Nathan the prophet, and *B*....1Kin 1:10
and Zadok the priest, and *B* ..1Kin 1:26
and *B* the son of Jehoiada 1Kin 1:32
B the son of Jehoiada.........1Kin 1:36
B the son of Jehoiada, and 1Kin 1:44
B the son of Jehoiada was 1Kin 4:4
B the son of Jehoiada.........1Chr 11:22
These things did *B* the son 1Chr 11:24
of Benjamin, *B* the 1Chr 11:31
and Eliab, and *B*, and 1Chr 16:5
And *B* the son of Jehoiada 1Chr 18:17
third month was *B* the son 1Chr 27:5
This is that *B*, who was 1Chr 27:6
was Jehoiada the son of *B* 1Chr 27:34

BEN-AMMI (bĕn-ăm'ī)—*"son of my people"*
Son of Lot; father of the Ammonites ....Gen 19:38

BENCHES—*deck of a ship*
Made of ivory ....Ezek 27:6

BEND—*to force or turn from being straight or proper; to curve*

[*also* BENDETH, BENDING, BENT]
hath *b* his bow, and made .....Ps 7:12
wicked *b* their bow, they ......Ps 11:2
have *b* their bow, to cast......Ps 37:14
he *b* his bow to shoot his .....Ps 58:7
b their bows to shoot their ....Ps 64:3
their bows *b*, their horses .....Is 5:28
sword, and from the *b* bow....Is 21:15
thee shall come *b* unto thee ...Is 60:14
they *b* their tongues like ......Jer 9:3
Lydians, that handle and *b* ....Jer 46:9
all ye that *b* the bow ....Jer 50:14
Babylon; all ye that *b* the .....Jer 50:29
let the archer *b* his bow ....Jer 51:3
He hath *b* his bow like an......Lam 2:4
He hath *b* his bow, and set....Lam 3:12
vine did *b* her roots toward ...Ezek 17:7
my people are *b* to ....Hos 11:7
I have *b* Judah for me ....Zech 9:13

BENEATH—*below; underneath*
she was buried *b* Beth-el ......Gen 35:8
or that is in the earth *b* ....Ex 20:4
shall be coupled together *b*....Ex 26:24
the compass of the altar *b*.....Ex 27:5
b upon the hem of it thou.....Ex 28:33
brake them *b* the mount ......Ex 32:19
they were coupled *b*, and ......Ex 36:29
b unto the midst of it ....Ex 38:4
that is in the waters *b* the .....Deut 4:18
or that is in the earth *b* ....Deut 5:8
only, thou shalt not be *b* ......Deut 28:13
the deep that coucheth *b* .....Deut 33:13
heaven above, and in earth *b*..Josh 2:11
the host of Midian was *b* ......Judg 7:8
is by Zartanah *b* Jezreel 1Kin 4:12
and *b* the lions and oxen 1Kin 7:29
heaven above, or on earth *b*...1Kin 8:23
roots shall be dried up *b* ......Job 18:16
he may depart from hell *b* ....Prov 15:24
Hell from *b* is moved for......Is 14:9
and look upon the earth *b* ....Is 51:6
of the earth searched out *b*....Jer 31:37
above, and his roots from *b* ...Amos 2:9
Peter was *b* in the palace .....Mark 14:66
Ye are from *b*, I am from.....John 8:23
and signs in the earth *b* ....Acts 2:19

BENE-BERAK (bĕn'ĕ-ber'ăk)—*"sons of lightning"*
A town of Dan..........Josh 19:45

BENEDICTION—*an act of blessing*
Characteristics of:
Instituted by God ....Gen 1:22, 28
Divinely approved ....Deut 10:8
Aaronic form ....Num 6:23-26
Apostolic form 2Cor 13:14
Jesus' last words.........Luke 24:50, 51
Pronounced upon:
Creation ....Gen 1:22, 28
New world ....Gen 9:1, 2
Abraham ....Gen 14:19, 20
Marriage...............Gen 24:60
Son (Jacob) ....Gen 27:28, 29
Monarch (Pharaoh) ......Gen 47:7, 10
Sons (Joseph's) ....Gen 48:15, 16, 20
Tribes (Israel's) ....Deut 33:1-29
Foreigner ....Ruth 1:8, 9
People..................2Sam 6:18
Jesus ....Luke 2:34
Song of Zecharias ....Luke 1:68-79
Children's blessing ....Mark 10:16

BENEFACTOR—*one who bestows benefits*
Materially, God as:
Israel's ....Deut 7:6-26
Unbeliever's ....Acts 14:15-18
Christian's ....Phil 4:19
Spiritually:
By God ....Eph 1:3-6
Through Christ ....Eph 2:13-22
For enrichment..........Eph 1:16-19
Attitudes toward:
Murmuring.............Num 11:1-10
Forgetfulness ....Ps 106:13
Rejection ....Acts 13:44-47
Remembrance ....Luke 7:1-5
Gratefulness ....Acts 13:48

upon them are called *b* ....Luke 22:25

BENEFICE—*an enriching act or gift*
Manifested by a church ..Phil 4:15-17
Encouraged in a friend...Philem 17-22
Justified in works.......James 2:14-17
Remembered in heaven ..1Tim 6:18, 19

BENEFIT—*something that promotes well being; to be useful or profitable to*

[*also* BENEFITS]
according to the *b* done 2Chr 32:25
who daily loadeth us with *b* ...Ps 68:19
and forget not all his *b*........Ps 103:2
Lord for all his *b* toward me ..Ps 116:12

wherewith I said I would *b* .... Jer 18:10
ye might have a second *b* 2Cor 1:15
beloved, partakers of the *b* 1Tim 6:2
that thy *b* should not be as .... Philem 14

BENE-JAAKAN (bĕn-ĕ-jā´ă-kăn)—*"the children of Jaakan"*
A wilderness station ..... Num 33:31

BENEVOLENCE—*generosity towards others*
Exercised toward:
The poor .... Gal 2:10
The needy .... Eph 4:28
Enemies .... Prov 25:21
God's servant .... Phil 4:14-17
Measured by:
Ability .... Acts 11:29
Love 1Cor 13:3
Sacrifice .... Mark 12:41-44
Bountifulness 2Cor 9:6-15
Blessings of:
Fulfills a grace .... Rom 12:6, 13
Performs a spiritual sacrifice .... Heb 13:16
Makes us "more blessed". Acts 20:35
Enriches the giver .... Prov 11:25; Is 58:10, 11
Reward 1Tim 6:18, 19
render unto the wife due *b* 1Cor 7:3

BEN-HADAD (bĕn-hā´dăd)—*"son of (the god) Hadad"*
1. Ben-hadad I, king of Damascus.
Hired by Asa, king of Judah, to attack Baasha, king of Israel . 1Kin 15:18-21
2. Ben-hadad II, king of Damascus. Makes war on Ahab, king of Israel 1Kin 20:1-21
Defeated by Israel 1Kin 20:26-34
Fails in siege against Samaria 2Kin 6:24-33; 2Kin 7:6-20
Killed by Hazael 2Kin 8:7-15
3. Ben-hadad III, king of Damascus. Loses all Israelite conquests made by Hazael, his father 2Kin 13:3-25

and sent to *B* king of Syria 2Chr 16:2
And *B* hearkened unto king ... 2Chr 16:4
consume the palaces of *B* ..... Jer 49:27
devour the palaces of *B* .... Amos 1:4

BEN-HAIL (bĕn-hāl´)—*"strong; son of strength"*
A teacher 2Chr 17:7

BEN-HANAN (Bĕn-hā´năn)—*"son of grace"*
A son of Shimon 1Chr 4:20

BENINU (bĕ-nī´nū)—*"our son"*
A Levite document signer. Neh 10:13

BENJAMIN (bĕn´jă-mĭn)—*"son of the right hand"*
1. A son of Bilhan 1Chr 7:10
2. Son of Harim .... Ezra 10:18, 31, 32
Same as in .... Neh 3:23

BENJAMIN (bĕn´jă-mĭn)—*"son of the right hand"—the youngest son of Jacob and progenitor of the tribe of Benjamin*
Jacob's youngest son ..... Gen 35:16-20
Jacob's favorite son ...... Gen 42:4; Gen 43:1-14
Loved by Joseph .... Gen 43:29-34
Judah intercedes for ..... Gen 44:18-34
Joseph's gifts to .... Gen 45:22
Father of five sons 1Chr 8:1, 2
Head of a tribe .... Num 26:38-41
Jacob's prophecy concerning .... Gen 49:27

[*also* BENJAMIN'S]
of Rachel; Joseph, and *B* ..... Gen 35:24
B, Joseph's brother, Jacob .... Gen 42:4
and ye will take *B* away .... Gen 42:36
money in their hand, and *B* ... Gen 43:15
Joseph saw *B* with them, he ... Gen 43:16
but *B* mess was five times ..... Gen 43:34
cup was found in *B* sack ...... Gen 44:12
the eyes of my brother *B* ..... Gen 45:12
upon his brother *B* .... Gen 45:14
and wept; and *B* wept upon ... Gen 45:14
Jacob's wife; Joseph and *B* .... Gen 46:19
sons of *B* were Belah, and .... Gen 46:21
Issachar, Zebulun, and *B* ..... Ex 1:3

BENJAMIN, TRIBE OF
Background features of:
Descendants of Jacob's youngest son .... Gen 35:18
Family divisions of ...... Num 26:38-41
Strength of .... Num 1:36, 37
Bounds of .... Josh 18:11-28
Prophecies respecting .... Gen 49:27; Deut 33:12
Memorable events of:
Almost destroyed for protecting men of Gibeah .... Judg 20:12-48
Wives provided for, to preserve the tribe ..... Judg 21:1-23
Furnished Israel her first king 1Sam 9:1-17
Hailed David's return 2Sam 19:16, 17
Celebrities belonging to:
Ehud, a judge .... Judg 3:15
Saul, Israel's first king ... 1Sam 9:1
Abner, David's general .. 1Sam 17:55
Mordecai .... Esth 2:5
The apostle Paul .... Phil 3:5

[*also* BENJAMINITE, BENJAMINITES]
of *B*; Abidan the son of .... Num 1:11
Then the tribe of *B* .... Num 2:22
the captain of the sons of *B* ... Num 2:22
prince of the children of *B* .... Num 7:60
children of *B* was Abidan ..... Num 10:24
tribe of *B*, Palti the son .... Num 13:9
Of the tribe of *B*, Elidad ...... Num 34:21
Issachar, and Joseph, and *B* ... Deut 27:12
tribe of *B*, thirteen cities ...... Josh 21:4
of *B*, Gibeon with her .... Josh 21:17
B did not drive out the .... Judg 1:21
of *B* in Jerusalem unto this .... Judg 1:21
Ehud the son of Gera, a *B* .... Judg 3:15
after thee, *B* among thy .... Judg 5:14
Judah, and against *B* .... Judg 10:9
which belongeth to *B* .... Judg 19:14
men of the place were *B* ...... Judg 19:16
children of *B* heard that the ... Judg 20:3
belongeth to *B*, I and my ..... Judg 20:4
Gibeah of *B* according to ..... Judg 20:10
B would not hearken to the ... Judg 20:13
went out to battle against *B* .. Judg 20:20
of *B* my brother? And the .... Judg 20:23
B said, They are smitten ...... Judg 20:32
the Lord smote *B* before ...... Judg 20:35
Israel destroyed of the *B* ...... Judg 20:35
So the children of *B* saw ...... Judg 20:36
in the battle, *B* began to ...... Judg 20:39
upon the children of *B* .... Judg 20:48
give his daughter unto *B* to ... Judg 21:1
Israel repented them for *B* .... Judg 21:6
B came again at that time ..... Judg 21:14
are destroyed out of *B* .... Judg 21:16
through the land of the *B* 1Sam 9:4
tribe of *B* to come near by 1Sam 10:21
Jonathan in Gibeah of *B* 1Sam 13:2
of Saul in Gibeah of *B* 1Sam 14:16
Hear now, ye *B*; will the 1Sam 22:7
over Ephraim, and over *B* 2Sam 2:9
Abner..spake in..ears of *B* 2Sam 3:19
of the children of *B* 2Sam 4:2
Beeroth..was reckoned to *B* ... 2Sam 4:2
more now may this *B* do it 2Sam 16:11
Shimei the son of Gera, a *B* ... 2Sam 19:16
men of *B* with him 2Sam 19:17
the son of Bichri, a *B* 2Sam 20:1
in the country of *B* in Zelah ... 2Sam 21:14
Gibeah of the children of *B* .. 2Sam 23:29
the son of Gera, a *B* of 1Kin 2:8
Shimei..son of Elah, in *B* 1Kin 4:18
Judah, with the tribe of *B* 1Kin 12:21
built with them Geba of *B* 1Kin 15:22
The sons of *B*; Bela, and 1Chr 7:6
children of *B*, and of the 1Chr 9:3
the children of *B*, Benaiah 1Chr 11:31
of Saul's brethren of *B* 1Chr 12:2
But Levi and *B* counted he 1Chr 21:6
the Anetothite, of the *B* 1Chr 27:12
B, Jaasiel the son of Abner ... 1Chr 27:21
house of Judah and *B* a 2Chr 11:1
out of *B*, that bare shields 2Chr 14:8
Asa and all Judah and *B* 2Chr 15:2
And of *B*; Eliada a mighty 2Chr 17:17
throughout all Judah and *B* ... 2Chr 25:5
altars out of..Judah and *B* 2Chr 31:1
all Judah and *B*; and they 2Chr 34:9
fathers of Judah and *B* .... Ezra 1:5
adversaries of Judah and *B* .... Ezra 4:1
men of Judah and *B* .... Ezra 10:9
After him repaired *B* and ..... Neh 3:23
and of the children of *B* ...... Neh 11:4
and *B*, and Shemaiah .... Neh 12:34
Shimei..son of Kish, a *B* ...... Esth 2:5
the words of Cush the *B* ...... Ps 7 title
There is little *B* with .... Ps 68:27
Before Ephraim and *B* and .... Ps 80:2
Anathoth in the land of *B* ..... Jer 1:1
O ye children of *B*, gather .... Jer 6:1
and from the land of *B* .... Jer 17:26
were in the high gate of *B* .... Jer 20:2
which is in..country of *B* ...... Jer 32:8
and in the land of *B* and in ... Jer 33:13
to go into the land of *B* .... Jer 37:12
sitting in the gate of *B* .... Jer 38:7
Judah and the border of *B* .... Ezek 48:22
Beth-aven, after thee, O *B* .... Hos 5:8
Samaria; and *B* shall .... Obad 19
in her place, from *B* .... Zech 14:10
a man of the tribe of *B* .... Acts 13:21
Abraham, of the tribe of *B* .... Rom 11:1
the tribe of *B*, an Hebrew ..... Phil 3:5
the tribe of *B* were sealed ..... Rev 7:8

BENO (bē´nō)—*"his son"*
A Merarite Levite 1Chr 24:26, 27

BEN-ONI (bĕn-ō´nī)—*"son of my sorrow"*
Rachel's name for Benjamin .... Gen 35:16-18

BEN-ZOHETH (bĕn-zō´-hĕth)—*"son of Zoheth; corpulent; strong"*
A man of Judah 1Chr 4:20

BEON (bē´ŏn)—*"house of On"*
A locality east of Jordan . Num 32:3
Same as Baal-meon ...... Num 32:37, 38

BEOR, BOSOR (bē´ôr)—*"shepherd"*
1. Father of Bela .... Gen 36:32
2. Father of Balaam .... Num 22:5; 2Pet 2:15

Balaam the son of *B* hath ..... Num 24:3
Balaam also the son of *B* ..... Num 31:8
thee Balaam the son of *B* ..... Deut 23:4
Balaam also the son of *B* ..... Josh 13:22
called Balaam the son of *B* .... Josh 24:9
Bela the son of *B*: and the 1Chr 1:43
Balaam the son of *B* .... Mic 6:5

BERA (bē´rä)—*"gift"*
A king of Sodom .... Gen 14:2

BERACHAH (bĕr´-ā-kä)—*"blessing"*
1. David's warrior 1Chr 12:3
2. A valley in Judah near Tekoa 2Chr 20:26

BERACHIAH—*See* BERECHIAH

BERAIAH (bĕr-ā-ī´ä)—*"unfortunate"*
A Benjamite chief 1Chr 8:21

BEREA (be´rē-ă)—*"watered"*
A city of Macedonia visited by Paul .... Acts 17:10-15

BEREAVEMENT
General attitudes in:
Horror . . . . .Ex 12:29, 30
Great emotion 2Sam 18:33
Complaint . . . . .Ruth 1:20, 21
Genuine sorrow . . . . .Gen 37:33-35
Submission . . . . .Job 1:18-21
Christian attitudes in:
Unlike world's 1Thess 4:13-18
Yet sorrow allowed . . . . . .John 11:35
Acts 9:39
With hope of reunion . . . .John 11:20-27
Unusual circumstances of, mourning:
Forbidden . . . . .Lev 10:6
Of great length . . . . .Gen 50:1-11
Turned to joy . . . . .John 11:41-44

[*also* BEREAVE, BEREAVED, BEREAVETH]
have ye ***b*** of my children . . . . . .Gen 42:36
b of my children, I am ***b*** . . . . . .Gen 43:14
I labor and ***b*** my soul of . . . . . .Eccl 4:8
I will ***b*** them of children . . . . . .Jer 15:7
wives be ***b*** of their children . . .Jer 18:21
abroad the sword ***b***, at . . . . .Lam 1:20
beasts, and they shall ***b*** . . . . . . .Ezek 5:17
no more henceforth ***b*** them . . .Ezek 36:12
up men, and hast ***b*** thy . . . . . . .Ezek 36:13
neither ***b*** thy nations any . . . . . .Ezek 36:14
yet will I ***b*** them, that there . . .Hos 9:12
as a bear that is ***b*** of her . . . . . .Hos 13:8

BERECHIAH (bĕr-ĕ-kī´ä)—*"Jehovah is blessing"*
1. Asaph's father 1Chr 6:39
2. Levite doorkeepers 1Chr 15:23, 24
3. Head man of Ephraim . .2Chr 28:12
4. Son of Zerubbabel 1Chr 3:20
5. Levite 1Chr 9:16
6. Postexilic workman . . . . .Neh 3:4, 30
7. Father of Zechariah . . . . .Zech 1:1, 7
Matt 23:35

[*also* BERACHIAH]
even Asaph the son of ***B*** 1Chr 6:39
brethren, Asaph the son of ***B***. .1Chr 15:17
of Meshullam the son of ***B*** . . . .Neh 6:18

BERED (bē´rĕd)—*"hail"*
1. A place in the wilderness of Shur . . . . .Gen 16:7, 14
2. An Ephraimite 1Chr 7:20

BERI (bē´rī)—*"expounded"*
An Asherite 1Chr 7:36

BERIAH (bĕ-rī´ä)—*"unfortunate"*
1. Son of Asher . . . . .Gen 46:17
2. Ephraim's son 1Chr 7:22, 23
3. Chief of Benjamin 1Chr 8:13, 16
4. Levite 1Chr 23:10, 11

Jesuites: of ***B***, the family of . . .Num 26:44
Of the sons of ***B***, of Heber . . . .Num 26:45
B, and Serah their sister 1Chr 7:30
of ***B***; Heber, and Malchiel 1Chr 7:31

BERIITES (bĕ-rī´-īts)
Descendants of Beriah (No. 1) . . . . .Num 26:44

BERITES (bĕr´īts)
A people in northern Palestine 2Sam 20:14, 15

BERITH (bē´-rĭth)—*"covenant"*
Shechem idol . . . . .Judg 9:46
Same as Baal-berith . . . . .Judg 8:33
Judg 9:4

BERNICE (ber-nī´sē)—*"victorious"*
Sister of Herod Agrippa II . . . . .Acts 25:13, 23
Hears Paul's defense . . . . .Acts 26:1-30

BERODACH-BALADAN (bĕr´ŏ-dăk-băl´ă-dăn)—*same as Merodach-baladan*
A king of Babylon 2Kin 20:12-19
Also called Merodach-baladan . . . . .Is 39:1

BEROTHAH, BEROTHAI (bĕ-rō´thä)—*"of a well"*
City of Syria taken by David 2Sam 8:8
Boundary in the ideal kingdom . . . . .Ezek 47:16

BEROTHITE—*See* BEEROTHITE

BERRIES
two or three ***b*** in the top of . . .Is 17:6
my brethren, bear olive ***b*** . . . . .James 3:12

BERYL—*a precious stone*
In breastplate of high priest . . . . Ex 28:20; Ex 39:13
Ornament of a king . . . . .Ezek 28:12, 13
Describes a lover . . . . .Song 5:14
Applied to an angel . . . . .Dan 10:5, 6
Wheels like color of . . . . .Ezek 1:16
In New Jerusalem . . . . . . .Rev 21:20

was the color of a ***b*** . . . . .Ezek 10:9

BESAI (bē´sī)—*"treading down"*
A family head . . . . .Ezra 2:49

of ***B***, the children of Meunim . .Neh 7:52

BESEECH—*to request earnestly; make supplication*
[*also* BESEECHING, BESOUGHT]
when he ***b*** us, and we would . .Gen 42:21
and now let us go, we ***b*** thee . .Ex 3:18
Moses ***b*** the Lord his God . . . . . .Ex 32:11
I ***b*** thee, show me thy glory . . . .Ex 33:18
I ***b*** thee, lay not the sin . . . . . . .Num 12:11
now, I ***b*** thee, let..power . . . . . .Num 14:17
I ***b*** the Lord at that time . . . . . .Deut 3:23
I ***b*** thee, tell thy servant 1Sam 23:11
David therefore ***b*** God for 2Sam 12:16
let the king, I ***b*** thee, and 2Sam 13:24
I humbly ***b*** thee that I may 2Sam 16:4
and now I ***b*** thee, O Lord 2Sam 24:10
I ***b*** thee, save thou us out 2Kin 19:19
I ***b*** thee, O Lord, remember . .2Kin 20:3
I ***b*** thee, do away the 1Chr 21:8
Now, my God, let I ***b*** thee 2Chr 6:40
he ***b*** the Lord his God 2Chr 33:12
fasted and ***b*** our God for . . . . .Ezra 8:23
And said, I ***b*** thee, O Lord . . .Neh 1:5
and ***b*** him with tears to put . . .Esth 8:3
Remember, I ***b*** thee that . . . . . .Job 10:9
Hear, I ***b*** thee, and I will . . . . .Job 42:4
Return, we ***b*** thee, O God of . .Ps 80:14
O Lord, I ***b*** thee, deliver my . .Ps 116:4
Save now, I ***b*** thee, O Lord . . .Ps 118:25
Accept, I ***b*** thee..freewill . . . . . .Ps 119:108
Remember now, O Lord, I ***b*** . .Is 38:3
we ***b*** thee, we are all thy . . . . . .Is 64:9
fear the Lord, and ***b*** the . . . . . .Jer 26:19
We ***b*** thee, let this man be . . . .Jer 38:4
we ***b*** thee, our supplication . . . .Jer 42:2
Prove thy servants, I ***b*** thee . . .Dan 1:12
I ***b*** thee, let thine anger . . . . . . .Dan 9:16
God, forgive, I ***b*** thee; by . . . . .Amos 7:2
O Lord God, cease, I ***b*** thee . .Amos 7:5
We ***b*** thee, O Lord, we ***b*** . . . .Jon 1:14
take, I ***b*** thee, my life from . . .Jon 4:3
b God that he..be gracious . . . .Mal 1:9
unto him a centurion, ***b*** him . . .Matt 8:5
the devils ***b*** him, saying, If . . . .Matt 8:31
And ***b*** him that they might . . . .Matt 14:36
his disciples came and ***b*** . . . . . . .Matt 15:23
b him..Have patience . . . . .Matt 18:29
there came a leper to him ***b*** . . .Mark 1:40
And he ***b*** him much that he . . .Mark 5:10
streets, and ***b*** him that . . . . .Mark 6:56
and she ***b*** him that he . . . . .Mark 7:26
b him to put his hand upon . . .Mark 7:32
him, and ***b*** him to touch . . . . . .Mark 8:22
and they ***b*** him for her . . . . .Luke 4:38
Jesus fell on his face, and ***b*** . . .Luke 5:12
b him that he would come . . . .Luke 7:3
they ***b*** him instantly, ...Luke 7:4
high? I ***b*** thee, torment me . . . .Luke 8:28
And they ***b*** him that he . . . . . . .Luke 8:31
I ***b*** thee, look upon my son . . .Luke 9:38
I ***b*** thy disciples to cast . . . . . .Luke 9:40
certain Pharisee ***b*** him to . . . . . .Luke 11:37
they ***b*** him that he would . . . . .John 4:40
b Pilate that their legs . . . . .John 19:31
the Gentiles ***b*** that these . . . . . .Acts 13:42
she ***b*** us, saying, If ye have . . .Acts 16:15
b him not to go up to . . . . .Acts 21:12
I ***b*** thee, suffer me to speak . . .Acts 21:39
him against Paul, and ***b*** him . . .Acts 25:2
b thee to hear me patiently . . . .Acts 26:3
Paul ***b*** them all to take meat . .Acts 27:33
I ***b*** you therefore, brethren . . . .Rom 12:1
Now I ***b*** you, brethren, for . . . . .Rom 15:30
Now I ***b*** you, brethren . . . . .Rom 16:17
Now I ***b*** you, brethren, by 1Cor 1:10
I ***b*** you, be ye followers 1Cor 4:16
I ***b*** you, brethren, (ye know . . .1Cor 16:15
Wherefore I ***b*** you that ye 2Cor 2:8
as though God did ***b*** you 2Cor 5:20
b you also that ye receive 2Cor 6:1
I Paul myself ***b*** you by the 2Cor 10:1
Brethren, I ***b*** you, be as I . . . . .Gal 4:12
b you that ye walk worthy . . . .Eph 4:1
b Euodias, and ***b*** Syntyche . . . .Phil 4:2
we ***b*** you, brethren, and 1Thess 4:1
And we ***b*** you, brethren, to . . .1Thess 5:12
Now we ***b*** you, brethren, by . . .2Thess 2:1
As I ***b*** thee to abide still 1Tim 1:3
for love's sake I rather ***b*** . . . . . .Philem 9
I ***b*** you the rather to do . . . . . . .Heb 13:19
I ***b*** you as strangers 1Pet 2:11
I ***b*** thee, lady, not as though . .2John 5

BESET—*harass; assail; surround*
Belial, ***b*** the house round . . . . .Judg 19:22
and ***b*** the house round . . . . .Judg 20:5
of Bashan have ***b*** me round . . .Ps 22:12
hast ***b*** me behind and . . . . .Ps 139:5
own doings have ***b*** them . . . . . .Hos 7:2
which doth so easily ***b*** us . . . . . .Heb 12:1

BESIDE—*by the side of; in addition to*
[*also* BESIDES]
Lot, Hast thou here any ***b*** . . . .Gen 19:12
b the first famine that was . . . .Gen 26:1
take other wives ***b*** my . . . . .Gen 31:50
b Jacob's sons' wives, all . . . . . .Gen 46:26
that were men ***b*** children . . . . . .Ex 12:37
the sea, ***b*** Pi-hahiroth . . . . .Ex 14:9
blood ***b*** the bottom of the . . . . .Ex 29:12
he shall put them ***b*** the . . . . . . .Lev 6:10
B the cakes, he shall offer . . . .Lev 7:13
b the burnt sacrifice of . . . . .Lev 9:17
eat it without leaven ***b*** the . . . .Lev 10:12
b the other in her life time . . . .Lev 18:18
B the sabbaths of the Lord . . . .Lev 23:38
b the ram of the atonement . . .Num 5:8
b that that his hand shall . . . . . .Num 6:21
at all, ***b*** this manna, before . . . .Num 11:6
b them that died about the . . . .Num 16:49
and as cedar trees ***b*** the . . . . . .Num 24:6
b the continual burnt . . . . .Num 28:10
B the burnt offering of the . . . .Num 29:6
b..continual burnt offering . . . . .Num 29:34
b..rest of them that were . . . . . .Num 31:8
b unwalled towns a great . . . . . .Deut 3:5
God; there is none else ***b*** . . . . .Deut 4:35
b the plains of Moreh? . . . . .Deut 11:30
to eat, ***b*** that which cometh . . .Deut 18:8
more for thee, ***b*** these three . . .Deut 19:9
the land of Moab ***b*** the . . . . . . .Deut 29:1
city Adam, that is ***b*** Zaretan . .Josh 3:16
to Ai, which is ***b*** Beth-aven . . .Josh 7:2
of Ai, which is ***b*** Beth-el . . . . . .Josh 12:9
that is ***b*** the Sidonians . . . . .Josh 13:4
b the land of Gilead . . . . .Josh 17:5
building you an altar ***b*** . . . . .Josh 22:19
be dry upon all the earth ***b*** . . . .Judg 6:37
and pitched ***b*** the well of . . . . . .Judg 7:1
of gold; ***b*** ornaments . . . . .Judg 8:26
was his only child; ***b*** her . . . . . .Judg 11:34
sword, ***b*** the inhabitants . . . . . . .Judg 20:15
she sat ***b*** the reapers . . . . .Ruth 2:14
there is none to redeem it ***b*** . . .Ruth 4:4
for there is none ***b*** thee 1Sam 2:2
battle, and pitched ***b*** 1Sam 4:1
go out and stand ***b*** my 1Sam 19:3

neither is there any God *b* 2Sam 7:22
Baal-hazor, which is *b* 2Sam 13:23
stood *b* the way of the gate ... 2Sam 15:2
my son from *b* me, while 1Kin 3:20
b harts, and roebucks 1Kin 4:23
B the chief of Solomon's 1Kin 5:16
Ezion-geber, which is *b* 1Kin 9:26
asked, *b* that which 1Kin 10:13
b the mischief that Hadad 1Kin 11:25
lay my bones *b* his bones 1Kin 13:31
a prophet of the Lord *b* 1Kin 22:7
sword *b* the king's house 2Kin 11:20
it *b* the altar, on the right 2Kin 12:9
b his sin wherewith he 2Kin 21:16
sons of David, *b* the sons 1Chr 3:9
neither is there any God *b* 1Chr 17:20
b that which she had 2Chr 9:12
waited on the king *b* those 2Chr 17:19
a prophet of the Lord *b* 2Chr 18:6
other *b* the Ammonites 2Chr 20:1
Lord, from *b* the incense 2Chr 26:19
B their genealogy of males 2Chr 31:16
b the freewill offering .... Ezra 1:4
B their servants and their ..... Ezra 2:65
b forty shekels of silver .... Neh 5:15
B their manservants and ...... Neh 7:67
b him stood Mattithiah .... Neh 8:4
the asses feeding *b* them ...... Job 1:14
leadeth me *b* the still .... Ps 23:2
upon earth that I desire *b* ..... Ps 73:25
thy kids *b* the shepherds ...... Song 1:8
our God, other lords *b* thee ... Is 26:13
Blessed are ye that sow *b* ..... Is 32:20
b me there is no savior .... Is 43:11
and *b* me there is no God ..... Is 44:6
else, there is no God *b* me .... Is 45:5
I am, and none else *b* me ..... Is 47:8
others to him, *b* those that ... Is 56:8
the eye seen, O God, *b* thee .. Is 64:4
princes which stood *b* the ..... Jer 36:21
and there were added *b* .... Jer 36:32
stood *b* the brazen altar .... Ezek 9:2
went in, and stood *b* the ...... Ezek 10:6
wings and the wheels *b* .... Ezek 11:22
even for others *b* those .... Dan 11:4
there is no savior *b* me .... Hos 13:4
there is none *b* me; how is .... Zeph 2:15
men, *b* women and children ... Matt 14:21
b women and children .... Matt 15:38
I have gained *b* them five ..... Matt 25:20
they said, He is *b* himself ..... Mark 3:21
b all this, between us and ..... Luke 16:26
and *b* all this, to day .... Luke 24:21
Paul, thou art *b* thyself .... Acts 26:24
b, I know not whether I 1Cor 1:16
whether we be *b* ourselves 2Cor 5:13
B those things that are 2Cor 11:28
me even thine own self *b* ..... Philem 19
And *b* this, giving all 2Pet 1:5

BESIEGE—*to surround with armed forces*
[*also* BESIEGED]
thee, then thou shalt *b* it ...... Deut 20:12
And he shall *b* thee in all ..... Deut 28:52
b David and his men 1Sam 23:8
of Ammon, and *b* Rabbah 2Sam 11:1
And they came and *b* him 2Sam 20:15
if their enemy *b* them in 1Kin 8:37
with him, and they *b* Tirzah ... 1Kin 16:17
he went up and *b* Samaria 1Kin 20:1
went up and *b* Samaria 2Kin 6:24
they *b* Ahaz, but could not 2Kin 16:5
Samaria, and *b* it three 2Kin 17:5
against Samaria, and *b* 2Kin 18:9
up all the rivers of *b* places ... 2Kin 19:24
and the city was *b* 2Kin 24:10
city, and his servants did *b* 2Kin 24:11
And the city was *b* unto 2Kin 25:2
and came and *b* Rabbah 1Chr 20:1
if their enemies *b* them in 2Chr 6:28
and *b* it, and built great .... Eccl 9:14
of cucumbers, as a *b* city .... Is 1:8
Go up, O Elam: *b*, O Media .. Is 21:2
all the rivers of the *b* places ... Is 37:25
the Chaldeans, which *b* you ... Jer 21:4
king of Babylon's army *b* ...... Jer 32:2
Chaldeans that *b* Jerusalem .... Jer 37:5
Jerusalem, and they *b* it ...... Jer 39:1
city was *b* unto the eleventh ... Jer 52:5
it shall be *b*, and thou shalt ... Ezek 4:3
he that remaineth and is *b* .... Ezek 6:12
unto Jerusalem, and *b* it ...... Dan 1:1

BESODEIAH (bĕs-ō-dē´yä)—*"given to trust in Jehovah"*
Father of Meshullam ..... Neh 3:6

BESOM (bē´zŏm)—*a broom made of twigs*
Symbol of destruction .... Is 14:23

BESOR (bē´sôr)—*"cold"*
A brook south of Ziklag. . 1Sam 30:9, 10, 21

BEST—*excelling all others*
take of the *b* fruits in the ..... Gen 43:11
the *b* of the land make thy .... Gen 47:6
of the *b* of his own field ...... Ex 22:5
All the *b* of the oil .... Num 18:12
to whom they think *b* .... Num 36:6
where it liketh him *b*: thou .... Deut 23:16
your oliveyards, even the *b* 1Sam 8:14
the *b* of the sheep, and of 1Sam 15:9
What seemeth you *b* I will 2Sam 18:4
and overlaid it with the *b* 1Kin 10:18
Look even out the *b* and 2Kin 10:3
her maids unto the *b* place .... Esth 2:9
at his *b* state is altogether ..... Ps 39:5
roof of thy mouth like the *b* ... Song 7:9
choice and *b* of Lebanon ...... Ezek 31:16
The *b* of them is as a brier .... Mic 7:4
Bring forth the *b* robe, and ... Luke 15:22
covet earnestly the *b* gifts 1Cor 12:31

BESTEAD—*distressed*
pass through it, hardly *b* ...... Is 8:21

BESTIAL—*beast-like*
Condemned .... Ex 22:19
Punishment of .... Lev 20:13-21

BESTIR—*to rouse to action*
then thou shalt *b* thyself 2Sam 5:24

BESTOW—*to convey as a gift; store*
[*also* BESTOWED]
may *b* upon you a blessing .... Ex 32:29
thou shalt *b* that money .... Deut 14:26
horsemen, whom he *b* in 1Kin 10:26
their hand, and *b* them in 2Kin 5:24
money to be *b* on workmen ... 2Kin 12:15
b upon him such royal 1Chr 29:25
whom he *b* in the chariot 2Chr 9:25
of the Lord did they *b* 2Chr 24:7
shalt have occasion to *b* .... Ezra 7:20
to all that the Lord hath *b* .... Is 63:7
no more room where to *b* ..... Luke 12:17
whereon ye *b* no labor .... John 4:38
Mary, who *b* much labor ...... Rom 16:6
these we *b* more abundant 1Cor 12:23
though I *b* all my goods 1Cor 13:3
his grace which was *b* 1Cor 15:10
that for the gift *b* upon 2Cor 1:11
of God *b* on the churches 2Cor 8:1
lest I have *b* upon you .... Gal 4:11
of love the Father hath *b* 1John 3:1

BETAH (bē´tä)—*"confidence"*
Cities of Hadadezer 2Sam 8:8
Called Tibhath 1Chr 18:8

BETEN (bē´tĕn)—*"valley"*
City of Asher .... Josh 19:25

BETH—*"house"*
Second letter of the Hebrew alphabet ...... Ps 119:9-16

BETHABARA (bĕth-ăb´ä-rä)—*"house at the ford"*
A place beyond Jordan where John baptized .. John 1:28

BETH-ANATH (bĕth-ā´năth)—*"house of reply; house of Anath"*
A town of Naphtali ..... Josh 19:38, 39
Canaanites remain in .... Judg 1:33

BETH-ANOTH (bĕth-ā´nŏth)—*"house of reply; house of Anoth"*
A town of Judah .... Josh 15:59

BETHANY (bĕth´ă-nĭ)—*"house of affliction; place of unripe figs"*
A town on Mt. of Olives . Luke 19:29
Home of Lazarus .... John 11:1
Home of Simon, the leper .... Matt 26:6
Jesus visits there .... Mark 11:1, 11, 12
Scene, Ascension .... Luke 24:50, 51

went out of..city into *B* .... Matt 21:17
being in *B* in the house .... Mark 14:3
Now *B* was nigh unto .... John 11:18
the passover came to *B* .... John 12:1

BETH-ARABAH (bĕth-är´ă-bă)—*"house of the desert"*
A village of Judah .... Josh 15:6, 61
Assigned to Benjamin ... Josh 18:21, 22

BETH-ARAM (bĕth-ā´răm)—*"house of the heights"*
A town of Gad .... Josh 13:27
Probably same as Beth-haran .... Num 32:36

BETH-ARBEL (bĕth-är´bĕl)—*"house of ambush"*
A town destroyed by Shalman .... Hos 10:14

BETH-AVEN (bĕth-ā´vĕn)—*"house of idols"*
A town of Benjamin ..... Josh 7:2
Israel defeated Philistines there 1Sam 13:5

were at..wilderness of *B* ...... Josh 18:12
Michmash, eastward from *B* ... 1Sam 13:5
battle passed over unto *B* 1Sam 14:23
neither go ye up to *B*, nor ..... Hos 4:15
cry aloud at *B*, after thee ..... Hos 5:8
because of the calves of *B* ..... Hos 10:5

BETH-AZMAVETH (bĕth-ăz-mā´vĕth)—*"house of Azmaveth"*
The men of *B*, forty and ...... Neh 7:28

BETH-BAAL-MEON (bĕth-bā´ăl-mē´ŏn)
City of Reuben .... Josh 13:17

BETH-BARAH (bĕth-bâr´ä)—*"house of the ford"*
A passage over Jordan .. Judg 7:24

BETH-BIREI (bĕth-bĭr´ĕ-ī)—*"house of my creation"*
A town of Simeon 1Chr 4:31
Probably same as Bethlebaoth .... Josh 19:6

BETH-CAR (bĕth-kär)—*"house of the lamb"*
Site of Philistines' retreat . 1Sam 7:11

BETH-DAGON (bĕth-dā´gŏn)—*"house of Dagon"*
1. Village of Judah .... Josh 15:41
2. Town of Asher .... Josh 19:27

BETH-DIBLATHAIM (bĕth-dĭb-lä-thā´ĭm)—*"house of fig cakes"*
A Moabite town .... Jer 48:21, 22

BETH-EL (bĕth´ĕl)—*"house of God"*
1. A town of Benjamin .... Judg 21:19
Abraham settles near .... Gen 12:8
Site of Abraham's altar .. Gen 13:3, 4
Scene of Jacob's ladder .. Gen 28:10-18
Luz becomes Bethel ..... Gen 28:19
Jacob returns to .... Gen 35:1-15
On Ephraim's border .... Josh 16:2
Samuel judged there 1Sam 7:15, 16
Site of worship and sacrifice 1Sam 10:3
Center of idolatry 1Kin 12:28-33
School of prophets 2Kin 2:1, 3
Youths from, mock Elisha 2Kin 2:23, 24
Denounced by a man of God 1Kin 13:1-10

Denounced by Amos . . . . Amos 7:10-13
Josiah destroys altars of. . 2Kin 23:4, 15-20
Denounced by Jeremiah . Jer 48:13
Denounced by Hosea . . . Hos 10:15
2. Simeonite town 1Sam 30:27
Called Bethul and Bethuel . . . . Josh 19:4; 1Chr 4:30

[*also* BETHELITE]
Jacob, Arise, go up to ***B*** . . . . . . Gen 35:1
let us arise..go up to ***B*** . . . . Gen 35:3
land of Canaan, that is ***B*** . . . . . Gen 35:6
she was buried beneath ***B*** . . . . . Gen 35:8
on the east side of ***B*** . . . . Josh 7:2
abode between ***B*** and Ai . . . . . . Josh 8:9
lie in ambush between ***B*** . . . . . . Josh 8:12
not a man left in Ai or ***B*** . . . . . Josh 8:17
of Ai, which is beside ***B*** . . . . . . Josh 12:9
the king of ***B***, one . . . . Josh 12:16
Jericho throughout mount ***B*** . . . Josh 16:1
side of Luz, which is ***B*** . . . . Josh 18:13
Zemaraim, and ***B*** . . . . Josh 18:22
also went up against ***B*** . . . . Judg 1:22
Joseph sent to descry ***B*** . . . . . . Judg 1:23
Ramah and ***B*** in mount . . . . Judg 4:5
and in mount ***B*** 1Sam 13:2
he set the one in ***B***, and 1Kin 12:29
So did he in ***B***, sacrificing 1Kin 12:32
and he placed in ***B*** the 1Kin 12:32
which he had made in ***B*** 1Kin 12:33
dwelt an old prophet in ***B*** 1Kin 13:11
God had done that day in ***B*** . . 1Kin 13:11
Lord against..altar in ***B*** 1Kin 13:32
Hiel the ***B*** build Jericho 1Kin 16:34
Lord hath sent me to ***B*** 2Kin 2:2
So they went down to ***B*** 2Kin 2:2
up from thence unto ***B*** 2Kin 2:23
golden calves..were in ***B*** 2Kin 10:29
came and dwelt in ***B*** and 2Kin 17:28
B and the towns thereof 1Chr 7:28
B with the towns thereof 2Chr 13:19
of ***B*** and Ai, two hundred . . . . . Ezra 2:28
of ***B*** and Ai, a hundred . . . . Neh 7:32
and Aiji and ***B***, and in . . . . Neh 11:31
he found him in ***B***, and . . . . Hos 12:4
also visit..altars of ***B*** . . . . Amos 3:14
Come to ***B***, and transgress . . . . Amos 4:4
But seek not ***B***, nor enter . . . . . Amos 5:5
captivity, and ***B*** shall come . . . . Amos 5:5
be none to quench it in ***B*** . . . . . Amos 5:6

BETH-EMEK (bĕth-ē´mĕk)—*"house of the valley"*
A town of Asher . . . . Josh 19:27

BETHER (bē´ther)—*"separation"*
Designates mountains . . . . Song 2:17

BETHESDA (bĕ-thĕz´dă)—*"house of outpouring or overflowing water"*
Jerusalem pool . . . . John 5:2-4

BETH-EZEL (bĕth-ē´zĕl)—*"a place near"*
A town of Judah . . . . Mic 1:11

BETH-GADER (bĕth-gā´der)—*"house of walls"*
A town of Judah 1Chr 2:51
Probably same as Geder. . Josh 12:13

BETH-GAMUL (bĕth-gā´mŭl)—*"camel house"*
A Moabite town . . . . Jer 48:23

BETH-HACCEREM (bĕth-hăk´sĕ-rĕm)—*"house of vines"*
Town of Judah . . . . Jer 6:1

BETH-HARAM (bĕth-hā´răm)—*"mountain house"*
A town of Gad . . . . Josh 13:27
Same as Beth-haran . . . . . Num 32:36

BETH-HOGLA, BETH-HOGLAH (bĕth-hŏg´lă)—*"partridge house"*
A village of Benjamin . . . Josh 15:6; Josh 18:19, 21

BETH-HORON (bĕth-hō´rŏn)—*"cave house"*
Twin towns of Ephraim . . Josh 16:3, 5
The nether, built by Sherah, a woman 1Chr 7:24
Assigned to Kohathite Levites . . . . Josh 21:20, 22
Fortified by Solomon 2Chr 8:5
Prominent in battles . . . . . Josh 10:10-14; 1Sam 13:18

south side of the nether ***B*** . . . . . Josh 18:13
hill that lieth before ***B*** . . . . Josh 18:14
Gezer, and ***B*** the nether 1Kin 9:17
B with her suburbs 1Chr 6:68
from Samaria even unto ***B*** 2Chr 25:13

BETHINK—*to remember; recall*
b themselves in the 1Kin 8:47
b themselves in the 2Chr 6:37

BETH-JESHIMOTH (bĕth-jĕsh´ĭ-mŏth)—*"house of deserts"*
A town near Pisgah . . . . . Josh 12:3
Israel camps near . . . . Num 33:49
Assigned to Reubenites . . Josh 13:20
Later a town of Moab . . . Ezek 25:9

BETH-LEBAOTH (bĕth-lĕ-bā´ŏth)—*"house of lionesses"*
A town in southern Judah; assigned to Simeonites . . . . Josh 19:6
Called Lebaoth . . . . Josh 15:32

BETH-LEHEM (JUDAH) (bĕth´lĕ-hĕm)—*"house of bread"—birthplace of Jesus Christ*

Significant features of:
Built by Salma 1Chr 2:51
Originally called Ephrath . Gen 35:16
Burial of Rachel . . . . Gen 35:19
Two wandering Levites of . . . . Judg 17:1-13; Judg 19:1-30
Naomi's home . . . . Ruth 1:1, 19
Home of Boaz . . . . Ruth 4:9-11
Home of David 1Sam 16:1-18
Stronghold of Philistines. . 2Sam 23:14, 15
Fortified by Rehoboam. . . 2Chr 11:6
Refuge of Gedaliah's murderers . . . . Jer 41:17

Messianic features of:
Sought for the tabernacle . Ps 132:6
Predicted place of the Messiah's birth . . . . Mic 5:2
Fulfillment cited . . . . Matt 2:1, 5
Infants of, slain by Herod . . . . Jer 31:15; Matt 2:16-18

[*also* BETH-LEMITE, BETH-LEHEM-JUDAH]
Ephrath; the same is ***B*** . . . . Gen 48:7
Shimron..Idaliah, and ***B*** . . . . Josh 19:15
after him Ibzan of ***B*** judged . . . Judg 12:8
Ibzan, and was buried at ***B*** . . . . Judg 12:10
Chilion, Ephrathites of ***B*** . . . . . Ruth 1:2
came to ***B*** in the beginning . . . . Ruth 1:22
Boaz came from ***B*** . . . . Ruth 2:4
send thee to Jesse the ***B*** 1Sam 16:1
seen a son of Jesse the ***B*** 1Sam 16:18
son of..Ephrathite of ***B*** 1Sam 17:12
his father's sheep at ***B*** 1Sam 17:15
son of thy servant..the ***B*** 1Sam 17:58
that he might run to ***B*** 1Sam 20:6
leave of me to go to ***B*** 1Sam 20:28
father, which was in ***B*** 2Sam 2:32
son of Jaare-oregim, a ***B*** 2Sam 21:19
water of the well of ***B*** 2Sam 23:15
water out of the well of ***B*** 2Sam 23:16
the son of Dodo of ***B*** 2Sam 23:24
B, and the Netophathites 1Chr 2:54
Ephratah, the father of ***B*** 1Chr 4:4
garrison was then at ***B*** 1Chr 11:16
of ***B***, that is at the gate 1Chr 11:17
water out of the well of ***B*** 1Chr 11:18
the son of Dodo of ***B*** 1Chr 11:26
children of ***B***, a hundred . . . . . . Ezra 2:21
The men of ***B*** and Netophah . . Neh 7:26
B, in the land of Judah . . . . Matt 2:6
And he sent them to ***B***, and . . . Matt 2:8
David, which is called ***B*** . . . . . . Luke 2:4
now go even unto ***B*** . . . . Luke 2:15
and out of the town of ***B*** . . . . . John 7:42

BETH-LEHEM (ZEBULUN) (bĕth´lĕ-hĕm)
Town assigned to Zebulun . . . . Josh 19:15, 16
Home of Judge Ibzan . . . . Judg 12:8-11

BETH-MAACHAH (bĕth-mā´ă-kă)—*"house of Maacah"*
Tribe of Israel 2Sam 20:14, 15

BETH-MARCABOTH (bĕth-mär´kă-bŏth)—*"house of chariots"*
Town of Simeon . . . . Josh 19:5

BETH-MEON (bĕth-mē´ŏn)—*"house of habitation"*
Moabite town . . . . Jer 48:23

BETH-NIMRAH (bĕth-nĭm´ră)—*"house of leopardess"*
Town of Gad . . . . Num 32:3, 36

BETH-PALET (bĕth-pā´lĕt)—*"house of escape"*
Town of Judah . . . . Josh 15:27

BETH-PAZZEZ (bĕth-păz´ĕz)—*"house of dispersion"*
Town of Issachar . . . . Josh 19:21

BETH-PEOR (bĕth-pē´ôr)—*"house of Peor"*
Town near Pisgah . . . . Deut 3:29
Valley of Moses' burial place . . . . Deut 34:6
Assigned to Reubenites . . Josh 13:15, 20

BETHPHAGE (bĕth´fă-jē)—*"house of unripe figs"*
Village near Bethany . . . . Mark 11:1
Near Mt. of Olives . . . . . . Matt 21:1

was come nigh to ***B*** and . . . . . . Luke 19:29

BETH-PHELET (bĕth-fē´lĕt)—*"house of escape"*
and at Moladah, and at ***B*** . . . . . Neh 11:26

BETH-RAPHA (bĕth-ra´fă)—*"house of a giant"*
A town or family of Judah 1Chr 4:12

BETH-REHOB (bĕth-rē´hŏb)—*"house of Rehob (breath)"*
A town in northern Palestine . . . . Judg 18:28
Inhabited by Syrians 2Sam 10:6

BETHSAIDA (bĕth-sā´ĭ-dă)—*"fish house"*
A city of Galilee . . . . Mark 6:45
Home of Andrew, Peter and Philip . . . . John 1:44; John 12:21
Blind man healed . . . . Mark 8:22, 23
Near feeding of 5,000 . . . . Luke 9:10-17
Unbelief of, denounced . . Matt 11:21; Luke 10:13

BETH-SHAN, BETH-SHEAN (bĕth-shăn, bĕth-shē´ăn)
A town in Issachar . . . . . . Josh 17:11
Assigned to Manasseh . . . 1Chr 7:29
Tribute paid by . . . . Josh 17:12-16
Users of iron chariots . . . . Josh 17:16
Saul's corpse hung up at. . 1Sam 31:10-13; 2Sam 21:12-14

out the inhabitants of ***B*** . . . . . . Judg 1:27
all ***B***, which..by Zartanah 1Kin 4:12
from ***B*** to Abel-meholah 1Kin 4:12

BETH-SHEMESH (bĕth-shē´mĕsh)—*"house of the sun"*
1. A border town between Judah and Dan . . . . Josh 15:10
Also called Ir-shemesh . . Josh 19:41
Assigned to priests . . . . . . Josh 21:16
Ark brought to 1Sam 6:12-19
Joash defeats Amaziah at 2Kin 14:11
Taken by Philistines 2Chr 28:18
2. A town of Naphtali . . . . . Josh 19:38

3. A town of Issachar . . . . . . Josh 19:22
4. Egyptian city . . . . Jer 43:13

[*also* BETH-SHEMITE]
the inhabitants of ***B*** . . . . Judg 1:33
the field of Joshua, a ***B*** 1Sam 6:14
field of Joshua, the ***B*** 1Sam 6:18
the men of ***B*** said, Who is 1Sam 6:20
and in Shaalbim, and ***B*** 1Kin 4:9
the son of Ahaziah at ***B*** 2Kin 14:13
with her suburbs, and ***B*** 1Chr 6:59
king of Judah, at ***B*** 2Chr 25:21
the son of Jehoahaz, at ***B*** 2Chr 25:23

BETH-SHITTAH (bĕth-shĭt'ä)—*"house of acacia"*
A town in the Jordan valley . . . . Judg 7:22

BETH-TAPPUAH (bĕth-tăp'ū-ä)—*"house of apricots"*
A town of Judah . . . . Josh 15:53

BETHUEL (bĕ-thū'ĕl)—*"dweller of God"*
1. Father of Laban and Rebekah . . . . Gen 22:20-23; Gen 24:29
2. Simeonite town 1Chr 4:30
Called Bethul . . . . Josh 19:4

who was born to ***B***, son of . . . . Gen 24:15
I am the daughter of ***B*** the . . . . Gen 24:24
she said..daughter of ***B*** . . . . Gen 24:47
Laban and ***B*** answered . . . . Gen 24:50
daughter of ***B*** the Syrian of . . . Gen 25:20
the house of ***B*** thy mother's . . . Gen 28:2
unto Laban, son of ***B*** the . . . . . Gen 28:5

BETH-ZUR (bĕth-zûr)—*"house of rock"*
A town of Judah . . . . Josh 15:58
Fortified by Rehoboam . . 2Chr 11:7
Help to rebuild . . . . Neh 3:16

Maon was the father of ***B*** 1Chr 2:45

BETIMES—*in good time; in a short time; at times*
And they rose up ***b*** in the . . . . . Gen 26:31
rising up ***b*** and sending 2Chr 36:15
wouldest seek unto God ***b*** . . . . . Job 8:5
rising ***b*** for a prey; the . . . . Job 24:5
him chasteneth him ***b*** . . . . Prov 13:24

BETONIM (bĕt'ō-nĭm)—*"bellies; pistachio nuts"*
A town of Gad . . . . Josh 13:26

BETRAYAL—*deliver to an enemy by treachery*
Of Christ:
Predicted . . . . Ps 41:9
Frequently mentioned . . . . Matt 17:22; John 13:21
Betrayer identified . . . . John 13:26
Sign of, a kiss . . . . Matt 26:48, 49
Guilt of . . . . Matt 27:3, 4
Supper before 1Cor 11:23
Jewish nation guilty of . . . Matt 27:9, 10; Acts 7:52, 53

Examples of:
Israelites by Gibeonites . . Josh 9:22
Samson by Delilah . . . . . . Judg 16:18-20
The woman of En-dor by Saul 1Sam 28:9-12
Jesus by Judas . . . . Matt 26:14, 15
Christians . . . . Matt 10:21

[*also* BETRAY, BETRAYED, BETRAYEST, BETRAYETH]
Judas Iscariot, who also ***b*** . . . . Matt 10:4
Son of man shall be ***b*** unto . . . . Matt 20:18
and shall ***b*** one another . . . . Matt 24:10
Son of man is ***b*** to be . . . . Matt 26:2
sought opportunity to ***b*** . . . . Matt 26:16
one of you shall ***b*** me . . . . Matt 26:21
dish, the same shall ***b*** . . . . Matt 26:23
Then Judas, which ***b*** him . . . . . . Matt 26:25
Son of man is ***b*** into the . . . . . . Matt 26:45
is at hand that doth ***b*** me . . . . . Matt 26:46
Judas, which had ***b*** him . . . . Matt 27:3
Judas Iscariot, which..***b*** . . . . Mark 3:19
brother shall ***b***..brother . . . . Mark 13:12
chief priests, to ***b*** him . . . . Mark 14:10
he might conveniently ***b*** . . . . Mark 14:11
eateth with me shall ***b*** me . . . . . Mark 14:18
whom the Son of man is ***b*** . . . . Mark 14:21
the Son of man is ***b*** into . . . . . . Mark 14:41
lo, he that ***b*** me..at hand . . . . . Mark 14:42
he that ***b*** him had given . . . . Mark 14:44
And ye shall be ***b*** both by . . . . Luke 21:16
how he might ***b*** him unto . . . . . Luke 22:4
sought opportunity to ***b*** . . . . Luke 22:6
hand of him that ***b*** me is . . . . . . Luke 22:21
that man by whom he is ***b*** . . . . . Luke 22:22
b thou the Son of man with . . . Luke 22:48
not, and who should ***b*** him . . . . John 6:64
he it was that should ***b*** him . . . John 6:71
Simon's son..should ***b*** . . . . John 12:4
Iscariot, Simon's son..***b*** . . . . John 13:2
For he knew who should ***b*** . . . . John 13:11
that one of you shall ***b*** . . . . John 13:21
Judas also, which ***b*** him . . . . John 18:2
Judas also, which ***b*** him . . . . John 18:5
which is he that ***b*** thee . . . . John 21:20
in which he was ***b*** took 1Cor 11:23

BETROTHED—*promised in marriage*
Treatment of . . . . Ex 21:8, 9

maid that is not ***b*** and lie . . . . . Ex 22:16
that is a bondsmaid, ***b*** to . . . . . . Lev 19:20
that hath ***b*** a wife . . . . Deut 20:7
is a virgin be ***b*** unto . . . . Deut 22:23
if a man find a ***b*** damsel . . . . Deut 22:25
b damsel cried, and there . . . . . Deut 22:27
is not ***b*** and lay hold . . . . Deut 22:28
Thou shalt ***b*** a wife, and . . . . . . Deut 28:30
And I will ***b*** thee unto me . . . . Hos 2:19
I will even ***b*** thee unto me . . . . Hos 2:20

BETTER—*superior to good*

[*also* BETTERED]
b that I give her to thee . . . . . . Gen 29:19
been ***b*** for us to serve . . . . Ex 14:12
not ***b*** for us to return . . . . Num 14:3
the grapes of Ephraim ***b*** . . . . . . Judg 8:2
Whether is ***b*** for you . . . . Judg 9:2
now art thou any thing ***b*** . . . . . Judg 11:25
is it ***b*** for thee to be . . . . Judg 18:19
is ***b*** to thee than seven . . . . Ruth 4:15
not I ***b*** to thee than ten 1Sam 1:8
nothing ***b***..me than that 1Sam 27:1
b than the counsel of 2Sam 17:14
b that thou succor us 2Sam 18:3
make the name of Solomon ***b*** . 1Kin 1:47
more righteous and ***b*** 1Kin 2:32
for I am not ***b*** than my 1Kin 19:4
I will give thee..a ***b*** 1Kin 21:2
b than all the waters of 2Kin 5:12
which were ***b*** than thyself 2Chr 21:13
unto another that is ***b*** than . . . . Esth 1:19
b than the riches of many . . . . . Ps 37:16
loving-kindness is ***b*** than . . . . . . Ps 63:3
shall please the Lord ***b*** . . . . Ps 69:31
day in thy courts..***b*** than . . . . . . Ps 84:10
b to trust in the Lord . . . . Ps 118:8
the law of thy mouth is ***b*** . . . . . Ps 119:72
b than the merchandise of . . . . . Prov 3:14
wisdom is ***b*** than rubies . . . . Prov 8:11
My fruit is ***b*** than gold . . . . Prov 8:19
b than he that honoreth . . . . Prov 12:9
B is little with the fear . . . . Prov 15:16
B is a dinner of herbs . . . . Prov 15:17
B is a little with . . . . Prov 16:8
how much ***b*** is it to get . . . . Prov 16:16
B it is to be..humble . . . . Prov 16:19
slow to anger is ***b*** than . . . . Prov 16:32
B is a dry morsel, and . . . . Prov 17:1
B is..poor that walketh . . . . Prov 19:1
b to dwell in a corner . . . . Prov 21:9
b to dwell in..wilderness . . . . . Prov 21:19
b it is that it be said . . . . Prov 25:7
b is a neighbor that is . . . . Prov 27:10
B is the poor that walketh . . . . . Prov 28:6
nothing ***b*** for a man, than . . . . . Eccl 2:24
that there is nothing ***b*** . . . . Eccl 3:22
Yea, ***b*** is he than both . . . . Eccl 4:3
B is a handful with . . . . Eccl 4:6
are ***b*** than one; because . . . . Eccl 4:9
B is a poor and a wise . . . . Eccl 4:13
B is it..thou shouldest . . . . Eccl 5:5
an untimely birth is ***b*** . . . . Eccl 6:3
B is the sight of the eyes . . . . . . Eccl 6:9
what is man the ***b***? . . . . Eccl 6:11
A good name is ***b*** than . . . . Eccl 7:1
b to go to the house of . . . . Eccl 7:2
Sorrow is ***b*** than laughter . . . . . Eccl 7:3
the heart is made ***b*** . . . . Eccl 7:3
b to hear the rebuke of . . . . Eccl 7:5
B is the end of a thing . . . . Eccl 7:8
spirit is ***b*** than the proud . . . . Eccl 7:8
the former days were ***b*** . . . . Eccl 7:10
hath no ***b*** thing under the . . . . . Eccl 8:15
dog is ***b*** than a dead lion . . . . . . Eccl 9:4
Wisdom is ***b*** than strength . . . . . Eccl 9:16
Wisdom is ***b*** than weapons . . . . Eccl 9:18
and a babbler is no ***b*** . . . . Eccl 10:11
thy love is ***b*** than wine . . . . Song 1:2
much ***b*** is thy love than . . . . Song 4:10
b than of sons and of . . . . Is 56:5
b than they that be slain . . . . . . Lam 4:9
will do ***b*** unto you than . . . . Ezek 36:11
ten times ***b*** than all the . . . . Dan 1:20
then was it ***b*** with me than . . . . Hos 2:7
be they ***b*** than these . . . . Amos 6:2
it is ***b*** for me to die than . . . . . . Jon 4:3
Art thou ***b*** than populous . . . . . Nah 3:8
ye not much ***b*** than they? . . . . . Matt 6:26
then is a man ***b*** than a . . . . Matt 12:12
b for him that a millstone . . . . . Matt 18:6
it is ***b*** for thee to enter . . . . Matt 18:8
nothing ***b***, but rather grew . . . . Mark 5:26
b for him that a millstone . . . . . Mark 9:42
is ***b*** for thee to enter . . . . Mark 9:43
is ***b*** for thee to enter . . . . Mark 9:45
is ***b*** for thee to enter . . . . Mark 9:47
for he saith, The old is ***b*** . . . . . . Luke 5:39
are ye ***b*** than the fowls . . . . Luke 12:24
b for him that a millstone . . . . . Luke 17:2
What then? are we ***b*** than . . . . . Rom 3:9
b to marry than to burn 1Cor 7:9
her not in marriage doeth ***b*** . . . 1Cor 7:38
if we eat, are we the ***b*** 1Cor 8:8
it were ***b*** for me to die 1Cor 9:15
not for the ***b***, but for the 1Cor 11:17
with Christ; which is far ***b*** . . . . . Phil 1:23
esteem other ***b*** than . . . . Phil 2:3
made so much ***b*** than the . . . . . . Heb 1:4
we are persuaded ***b*** things . . . . . Heb 6:9
less is blessed of the ***b*** . . . . Heb 7:7
a surety of a ***b*** testament . . . . . . Heb 7:22
mediator of a ***b*** covenant . . . . Heb 8:6
was established upon ***b*** . . . . Heb 8:6
b sacrifices than these . . . . Heb 9:23
in heaven a ***b*** and an . . . . Heb 10:34
But now they desire a ***b*** . . . . Heb 11:16
they might obtain a ***b*** . . . . Heb 11:35
b thing for us . . . . Heb 11:40
b things than that of Abel . . . . . Heb 12:24
it is ***b***, if the will of God 1Pet 3:17
For it had been ***b*** for them 2Pet 2:21

BETWEEN

[*also* BETWIXT]
enmity ***b*** thee and the . . . . Gen 3:15
which I make ***b*** me and . . . . Gen 9:12
And Resen ***b*** Nineveh, and . . . . Gen 10:12
beginning ***b*** Bethel and . . . . Gen 13:3
lamp that passed ***b*** those . . . . . . Gen 15:17
the Lord judge ***b*** me, and . . . . . Gen 16:5
make my covenant ***b*** me . . . . Gen 17:2
token of the covenant ***b*** . . . . Gen 17:11
and dwelt ***b*** Kadesh and . . . . . . Gen 20:1
what is that ***b*** me and thee . . . . Gen 23:15
an oath ***b*** us, even ***b*** us . . . . . . Gen 26:28
set three days' journey . . . . Gen 30:36
that they may judge ***b*** us . . . . Gen 31:37
be for a witness ***b*** me and . . . . . Gen 31:44
put a space ***b*** drove and . . . . Gen 32:16
them out from ***b*** his knees . . . . Gen 48:12
nor a lawgiver from ***b*** his . . . . . Gen 49:10
I will put a division ***b*** my . . . . . Ex 8:23

difference *b* the Egyptians ..... Ex 11:7
and for a memorial *b* thine .... Ex 13:9
b Migdol and the sea over .... Ex 14:2
wilderness of Sin..is *b* .... Ex 16:1
and I judge *b* one and .... Ex 18:16
oath of the Lord be *b* them ... Ex 22:11
from *b* the two cherubim ...... Ex 25:22
shall divide unto you *b* .... Ex 26:33
bells of gold *b* them round .... Ex 28:33
put it *b* the tabernacle .... Ex 30:18
it is a sign *b* me and you ...... Ex 31:13
put the bells *b* the .... Ex 39:25
set the laver *b* the tent .... Ex 40:7
ye may put difference *b* .... Lev 10:10
make a difference *b* the .... Lev 11:47
therefore put difference *b* ..... Lev 20:25
which the Lord made *b* him ... Lev 26:46
from *b* the two cherubim ...... Num 7:89
flesh was..*b* their teeth .... Num 11:33
they bare it *b* two upon .... Num 13:23
stood *b* the dead and the ...... Num 16:48
border of Moab, *b* .... Num 21:13
thereof be divided *b* many .... Num 26:56
b a man and his wife .... Num 30:16
prey into two parts; *b* .... Num 31:27
congregation shall judge *b* ..... Num 35:24
over against the Red Sea, *b* ... Deut 1:1
I stood *b* the Lord and you ... Deut 5:5
shall be as frontlets *b* .... Deut 6:8
may be as frontlets *b* your .... Deut 11:18
baldness *b* your eyes for the ... Deut 14:1
blood and blood, *b* plea .... Deut 17:8
b whom the controversy is .... Deut 19:17
If there be a controversy ...... Deut 25:1
one that cometh out from *b* ... Deut 28:57
shall dwell *b* his shoulders ..... Deut 33:12
there shall be a space *b* ...... Josh 3:4
in ambush, and abode .... Josh 8:9
their lot came forth *b* .... Josh 18:11
made Jordan a border *b* .... Josh 22:25
b you and the Egyptians ...... Josh 24:7
b Ramah and Beth-el in ...... Judg 4:5
God sent an evil spirit *b* ...... Judg 9:23
The Lord be witness *b* us ..... Judg 11:10
camp of Dan *b* Zorah and .... Judg 13:25
firebrand in the midst *b* ...... Judg 15:4
they set him *b* the pillars ..... Judg 16:25
an appointed sign *b* the .... Judg 20:38
which dwelleth *b* the 1Sam 4:4
took a stone, and set it *b* 1Sam 7:12
And *b* the passages, by 1Sam 14:4
b Shochah and Azekah 1Sam 17:1
there is but a step *b* me 1Sam 20:3
The Lord judge *b* me and 1Sam 24:12
a great space being *b* them 1Sam 26:13
was long war *b* the house 2Sam 3:1
b the heaven and the earth 2Sam 18:9
can I discern *b* good and 2Sam 19:35
oath that was *b* them, *b* 2Sam 21:7
discern *b* good and bad 1Kin 3:9
b Hiram and Solomon 1Kin 5:12
the borders were *b* the 1Kin 7:28
b Rehoboam and Jeroboam ... 1Kin 14:30
b Rehoboam and Jeroboam ... 1Kin 15:6
divided the land *b* them to 1Kin 18:6
without war *b* Syria and 1Kin 22:1
and smote Jehoram *b* his 2Kin 9:24
a covenant *b* the Lord 2Kin 11:17
from *b* the altar and the 2Kin 16:14
God..which dwellest *b* 2Kin 19:15
way of..gate *b* two walls 2Kin 25:4
dwelleth *b* the cherubim 1Chr 13:6
angel of the Lord stand *b* 1Chr 21:16
the clay ground *b* Succoth 2Chr 4:17
b Rehoboam and Jeroboam ... 2Chr 12:15
there was war *b* Abijah 2Chr 13:2
is a league *b* me and thee 2Chr 16:3
smote..king of Israel *b* 2Chr 18:33
b blood and blood, *b* law 2Chr 19:10
Jehoiada made..covenant *b* 2Chr 23:16
And *b* the going up of the .... Neh 3:32
is there any daysman *b* us ..... Job 9:33
the cloud that cometh *b* .... Job 36:32
that no air can come *b* .... Job 41:16
that dwellest *b* the .... Ps 80:1
cease, and parteth *b* the ...... Prov 18:18
he shall lie all night *b* my ..... Song 1:13
pray you, *b* me and my .... Is 5:3
Ye made also a ditch *b* the .... Is 22:11
God..that dwellest *b* .... Is 37:16
b you and your God, and ..... Is 59:2
b a man and his neighbor ..... Jer 7:5
passed *b* the parts thereof ..... Jer 34:18
the gate *b* the two walls .... Jer 39:4
faithful witness *b* us, if .... Jer 42:5
way of the gate *b* the two ..... Jer 52:7
persecutors overtook her *b* .... Lam 1:3
wall of iron *b* thee and .... Ezek 4:3
lifted me up *b* the earth .... Ezek 8:3
in *b* the wheels, even under ... Ezek 10:2
coals of fire from *b* the .... Ezek 10:2
executed true judgment *b* ..... Ezek 18:8
to be a sign *b* me and them ... Ezek 20:12
difference *b* the holy and ...... Ezek 22:26
I judge *b* cattle..cattle .... Ezek 34:17
b the little chambers were ..... Ezek 40:7
b the chambers was the .... Ezek 41:10
separation *b* the sanctuary ..... Ezek 42:20
and the wall *b* me and them ... Ezek 43:8
difference *b* the holy and ...... Ezek 44:23
b the border of Damascus ..... Ezek 47:16
b the border of Judah and .... Ezek 48:22
ribs in the mouth of it *b* ...... Dan 7:5
had a notable horn *b* his ...... Dan 8:5
tabernacles..his palace *b* ...... Dan 11:45
her adulteries from *b* her ...... Hos 2:2
b the porch and the altar ..... Joel 2:17
that cannot discern *b* .... Jon 4:11
lifted up the ephah *b* the ...... Zech 5:9
out from *b* two mountains ..... Zech 6:1
abominations from *b* his .... Zech 9:7
brotherhood *b* Judah and ..... Zech 11:14
Lord hath been witness *b* ..... Mal 2:14
ye return, and discern *b* .... Mal 3:18
fault *b* thee and him alone .... Matt 18:15
b the temple and the altar .... Matt 23:35
b the altar and the temple ..... Luke 11:51
b us and you there is a .... Luke 16:26
at enmity *b* themselves .... Luke 23:12
b some of John's disciples ..... John 3:25
sleeping *b* two soldiers .... Acts 12:6
no difference *b* us and them ... Acts 15:9
dissension *b* the Pharisees ..... Acts 23:7
they talked *b* themselves ...... Acts 26:31
their own bodies *b* .... Rom 1:24
there is no difference *b* .... Rom 10:12
able to judge *b* his 1Cor 6:5
There is difference also *b* 1Cor 7:34
middle wall of partition *b* ..... Eph 2:14
I am in a strait *b* two .... Phil 1:23
and one mediator *b* God 1Tim 2:5

BEULAH (bū'lä)—*"married"*
A symbol of true Israel .. Is 62:4, 5

BEVERAGE—*a drink*

Literal:
Milk .... Judg 4:19
Judg 5:25
Strong drink .... Prov 31:6
Water .... Matt 10:42
Wine 1Tim 5:23

Figurative:
Christ's blood .... John 6:53
Cup of suffering .... John 18:11
Living water .... John 4:10
Water of life .... Rev 22:17

BEWAIL—*to wail over*
[*also* BEWAILED, BEWAILETH]
whole house of Israel, *b* ...... Lev 10:6
and *b* her father and her ...... Deut 21:13
and *b* my virginity, I and ...... Judg 11:37
companions, and *b* her .... Judg 11:38
I will *b* with the weeping ...... Is 16:9
daughter of Zion, that *b* ...... Jer 4:31
all wept, and *b* her; but .... Luke 8:52
which also *b* and lamented .... Luke 23:27
that I shall *b* many which 2Cor 12:21
shall *b* her, and lament .... Rev 18:9

BEWARE—*be wary of; guard against*

Of evil things:
Strong drink .... Judg 13:4
False prophets .... Matt 7:15
Evil men .... Matt 10:17
Covetousness .... Luke 12:15
Dogs (figurative) .... Phil 3:2

Of possibilities:
Disobeying God .... Ex 23:20, 21
Forgetting God .... Deut 6:12
Being led away 2Pet 3:17

B thou that thou bring not .... Gen 24:6
B of him, and obey his .... Ex 23:21
Then *b* lest thou forget .... Deut 6:12
B that thou forget not the ..... Deut 8:11
B that there be not a .... Deut 15:9
Now therefore *b*, I pray .... Judg 13:4
B that none touch the 2Sam 18:12
B that thou pass not such 2Kin 6:9
Because there is wrath, *b* ..... Job 36:18
and the simple will *b* .... Prov 19:25
B lest Hezekiah persuade ..... Is 36:18
B of false prophets which ..... Matt 7:15
b of men; for they will .... Matt 10:17
Take heed and *b* of the .... Matt 16:6
Take heed and *b* of the .... Mark 8:15
B of the scribes, which .... Mark 12:38
B ye of the leaven of the ..... Luke 12:1
B of the scribes, which .... Luke 20:46
B therefore lest that come ..... Acts 13:40
B of dogs, *b* of evil workers ... Phil 3:2
B lest any man spoil you ...... Col 2:8
know these things before, *b* ... 2Pet 3:17

BEWITCH—*to cast a spell over; charm; astound*
Activity of Simon .... Acts 8:9-11
Descriptive of legalism ... Gal 3:1

BEWRAY—*divulge; betray*
[*also* BEWRAYETH]
right hand, which *b* itself ...... Prov 27:16
heareth cursing and *b* it .... Prov 29:24
outcasts; *b* not him that .... Is 16:3
for thy speech *b* thee .... Matt 26:73

BEYOND—*on the farther side of; out of reach*
spread his tent *b* the tower .... Gen 35:21
of Atad, which is *b* Jordan .... Gen 50:10
b the time..of her separation .. Lev 15:25
I cannot go *b* the word of ..... Num 22:18
go *b* the commandment of .... Num 24:13
God hath given them *b* .... Deut 3:20
Neither is it *b* the sea .... Deut 30:13
the Amorites, that were *b* ..... Josh 9:10
Moses gave them, *b* Jordan ... Josh 13:8
their inheritance *b* .... Josh 18:7
and passed *b* the quarries ..... Judg 3:26
Gilead abode *b* Jordan .... Judg 5:17
the arrows are *b* thee 1Sam 20:22
the Syrians that were *b* the 2Sam 10:16
unto the place that is *b* 1Kin 4:12
scatter them *b* the river 1Kin 14:15
the Syrians that were *b* 1Chr 19:16
from *b* the sea on this 2Chr 20:2
unto the rest *b* the river .... Ezra 4:17
Tatnai, governor *b* the .... Ezra 6:6
treasurers which are *b* the ..... Ezra 7:21
b the tower of the furnaces .... Neh 12:38
by them *b* the river, by .... Is 7:20
b the rivers of Ethiopia .... Is 18:1
cast forth *b* the gates .... Jer 22:19
the isles which are *b* the ...... Jer 25:22
you to go into captivity *b* ..... Amos 5:27
b the rivers of Ethiopia .... Zeph 3:10
way of the sea, *b* Jordan ...... Matt 4:15
coasts of Judea, *b* Jordan ..... Matt 19:1
Idumea, and from *b* Jordan ... Mark 3:8
in themselves *b* measure ...... Mark 6:51
were *b* measure, astonished ... Mark 7:37
in Bethabara *b* Jordan .... John 1:28
he that was with thee *b* .... John 3:26
went away again *b* Jordan ..... John 10:40
carry you away *b* Babylon ..... Acts 7:43
yea, and *b* their power they ... 2Cor 8:3

we stretch not ourselves *b* 2Cor 10:14
b measure I persecuted ....Gal 1:13
no man go *b* and defraud 1Thess 4:6

BEZAI (bē'zā-ī)—*"shining; high"*
Postexilic family head ....Ezra 2:17
Neh 7:23
Signs document ....Neh 10:18

The children of *B*, three ......Ezra 2:17
children of *B*, three..........Neh 7:23
Hodijah, Hashum, *B*..........Neh 10:18

BEZALEEL (bĕz'ä-lēl)—*"God is protection"*
1. Hur's grandson 1Chr 2:20
Tabernacle builder ......Ex 31:1-11
Ex 35:30-35
2. Divorced foreign wife ...Ezra 10:18, 30

I have called by name *B* ......Ex 31:2
hath called by name *B* ....Ex 35:30
wrought *B* and Aholiab ....Ex 36:1
B made the ark of shittim .....Ex 37:1
B the son of Uri, the son .....Ex 38:22
begat Uri, and Uri begat *B*....1Chr 2:20
the brazen altar, that *B* 2Chr 1:5
Mattaniah, *B*, and Binnui .....Ezra 10:30

BEZEK (bē'zĕk)—*"sowing"*
1. Town near Jerusalem....Judg 1:4, 5
2. Saul's army gathered there 1Sam 11:8

BEZER (bē'zer)—*"fortress"*
1. An Asherite 1Chr 7:37
2. City of Reuben ....Deut 4:43
Place of refuge ....Josh 20:8

Reuben, *B* with her ....Josh 21:36
B in the wilderness with 1Chr 6:78
B, and Hod, and Shamma.....1Chr 7:37

BIBLE HISTORY, OUTLINED

Pre-patriarchal period, the
Creation ....Gen 1:1—2:25
Fall of man ....Gen 3:1-24
Development of wickedness............Gen 4:1—6:8
Flood ....Gen 6:9—8:22
Establishment of nations. .Gen 9:1—10:32
Confusion of tongues ....Gen 11:1-32

Patriarchal period:
Abraham ....Gen 12:1—25:11
Isaac.................Gen 21:1—28:9; Gen 35:27-29
Jacob.................Gen 25:19—37:36; Gen 45:21—46:7; Gen 49:1-33
Joseph..................Gen 37:1—50:26

Egypt and the Exodus:
Preparation of Moses ....Ex 1:1—7:7
Plagues and Passover ....Ex 7:8—12:36
From Egypt to Sinai .....Ex 12:37—18:27
The Law and tabernacle. .Ex 19:1—40:38

Wilderness:
Spies at Kadesh-Barnea ..Num 13:1—14:38
Fiery serpents ....Num 21:4-9
Balak and Balaam ....Num 22:1—24:25
Appointment of Joshua ..Num 27:18-23
Death of Moses ....Deut 34:1-8

Conquest and settlement:
Spies received by Rahab. .Josh 2:1-21
Crossing Jordan ....Josh 3:14-17
Fall of Jericho ....Josh 6:1-27
Southern and central mountains ....Josh 7:1-11
Victory at Merom ....Josh 11:1-14
Division of the land .....Josh 14:1—21:45

Period of the judges:
Later conquests ....Judg 1:1—2:23
Othniel ....Judg 3:8-11
Ehud ....Judg 3:12-30
Shamgar ....Judg 3:31
Deborah and Barak .....Judg 4:1—5:31
Gideon ....Judg 6:11—8:35
Abimelech ....Judg 9:1-57
Tola and Jair ....Judg 10:1-5
Jephthah................Judg 11:1—12:7
Ibzan, Elon, and Abdon. .Judg 12:8-15
Samson ....Judg 13:1—16:31
Tribal wars ....Judg 17:1—21:25

From Samuel to David:
Eli and Samuel..........1Sam 1:1—4:22
Samuel as judge ....1Sam 5:1—8:22
The first king ....1Sam 9:1—12:25
Battle of Michmash......1Sam 13:1—14:52
Saul and the Amalekites. .1Sam 15:1-35
David chosen 1Sam 16:1-13
David and Goliath.......1Sam 17:1-58
David in exile ....1Sam 18:5—31:13

Kingdom united:
David's reign at Hebron. .2Sam 2:1—4:12
David's reign at Jerusalem ....2Sam 5:1—10:19
David's sin..............2Sam 11:1-25
Absalom's rebellion......2Sam 15:1—18:33
David's death 1Kin 2:10-12
Accession of Solomon ...1Kin 1:32-53
1Chr 29:20-25
The Temple ....1Kin 6:1—9:9
2Chr 2:1—7:22
Death of Solomon 1Kin 11:41-43
2Chr 9:29-31

Kingdom divided:
Rebellion of Israel.......2Chr 10:1-19
Rehoboam and Abijah ...2Chr 10:1—13:22
Jeroboam and Nadab ....1Kin 12:25—14:20
1Kin 15:25-31
Asa 1Kin 15:9-24
1Chr 14:1—16:14
Baasha, Elah, Zimri and Omri ....1Kin 15:32—16:27

Mutual alliance:
Ahab and Elijah ....1Kin 16:28—18:19
Contest on Mount Carmel 1Kin 18:20-40
Ahab and Ben-hadad 1Kin 20:1-34
Murder of Naboth 1Kin 21:1-29
Revival under Jehoshaphat.........1Kin 22:41-50; 2Chr 17:1-19
Battle of Ramoth-gilead ..1Kin 22:1-40
2Chr 18:1-34
Wars of Jehoshaphat.....2Chr 19:1—20:30
Translation of Elijah.....2Kin 2:1-11
Jehoshaphat and Jehoram.2Kin 3:1-27
Ministry of Elisha ....2Kin 4:1—6:23
2Kin 8:1-15
Siege of Samaria ....2Kin 6:24—7:20
Death of Elisha 2Kin 13:14-20

Decline of both kingdoms:
Accession of Jehu ....2Kin 9:1—10:31
Athaliah and Joash ......2Kin 11:1—12:21
Amaziah and Jeroboam ..2Kin 14:1-29
Captivity of Israel 2Kin 15:1-23
Reign of Hezekiah ......2Kin 18:1—20:21
2Chr 29:1—32:33
Reign of Manasseh 2Kin 29:1-18
2Chr 33:1-20
Josiah's reforms ....2Kin 22:1—23:30
2Chr 34:1—35:27
Captivity of Judah ....2Kin 24:1—25:30
2Chr 36:5-21

Captivity:
Daniel and Nebuchadnezzer ....Dan 1:1—4:37
Belshazzar and Darius ...Dan 5:1—6:28
Rebuilding the Temple...Ezra 1:1—6:15
Rebuilding Jerusalem ....Neh 1:1—6:19
Esther and Mordecai ....Esth 2:1-10:3

Ministry of Christ:
Birth ....Matt 1:18-25
Luke 2:1-20
Childhood ....Luke 2:40-52
Baptism ....Matt 3:13-17
Luke 3:21-23
Temptation ....Matt 4:1-11
Luke 4:1-13
First miracle ....John 2:1-11
With Nicodemus.........John 3:1-21
The Samaritan woman ...John 4:5-42
Healing................Luke 4:31-41
Controversy on the Sabbath ....Luke 6:1-11
Apostles chosen ....Mark 3:13-19
Luke 6:12-16
Sermon on the Mount ...Matt 5:1—7:29
Luke 6:20-49
Raises dead son ....Luke 7:11-17
Anointed ....Luke 7:36-50
Accused of blasphemy ...Matt 12:22-37
Mark 3:19-30
Calms the sea ....Matt 8:23-27
Mark 4:35-41
Demoniac healed ....Matt 8:28-34
Mark 5:1-20
Daughter of Jairus healed ....Matt 9:18-26; Luke 8:41-56
Feeds 5,000 ....Matt 14:13-21
Mark 6:30-44
Feeds 4,000 ....Matt 15:32-39
Peter confesses Jesus is Christ ....Matt 16:5-16; Mark 8:27-29
Foretells death ....Matt 16:21-26
Luke 9:22-25
Transfiguration ....Matt 17:1-13
Luke 9:28-36
Forgiving of adulteress ...John 7:53—8:11
Resurrection of Lazarus ..John 11:1-44
Blesses the children......Matt 19:13-15
Mark 10:13-16
Bartimaeus healed ......Matt 20:29-34
Mark 10:46-52
Meets Zacchaeus ....Luke 19:1-10
Triumphant entry........Matt 21:1-9
Luke 19:29-44
Anointed ....Matt 26:6-13
Mark 14:3-9
The Passover...........Matt 26:17-19
Luke 22:7-13
The Lord's Supper .....Matt 26:26-29
Mark 14:22-25
Gethsemane ....Luke 22:39-46

Betrayal and arrest ......Matt 26:47-56
John 18:3-12
Before the Sanhedrin ....Matt 26:57-68
Luke 22:54-65
Denied by Peter ....John 18:15-27
Before Pilate ....Matt 27:2-14
Luke 23:1-7
Before Herod ....Luke 23:6-12
Returns to Pilate ....Matt 27:15-26
Luke 23:13-25
Crucifixion ....Matt 27:35-56
Luke 23:33-49
Burial ....Matt 27:57-66
Luke 23:50-56
Resurrection ....Matt 28:1-15
John 20:1-18
Appearance to disciples ..Luke 24:36-43
John 20:19-25
Appearance to Thomas ..John 20:26-31
Great commission ....Matt 28:16-20
Ascension ....Luke 24:50-53

The early church:
Pentecost ....Acts 2:1-42
In Jerusalem ....Acts 2:3—6:7
Martyrdom of Stephen ...Acts 6:8—7:60
In Judaea and Samaria ...Acts 8:1—12:25
Conversion of Saul ......Acts 9:1-18
First missionary journey ..Acts 13:1—14:28
Jerusalem conference ....Acts 15:1-35
Second missionary journey .... Acts 15:36—18:22
Third missionary journey .Acts 18:23—21:16
Captivity of Paul ....Acts 21:27—28:31

BICHRI (bĭk'rī)—*"youth; firstborn"*
Father of Sheba 2Sam 20:1

BID—*to beseech; order; request*
[*also* BIDDEN, BIDDETH, BIDDING]
b them that they make ....Num 15:38
until..day I ***b*** you shout ....Josh 6:10
they eat that be ***b*** 1Sam 9:13
among them that were ***b*** 1Sam 9:22
B the servant pass on 1Sam 9:27
goeth at thy ***b***, and is 1Sam 22:14
it be then, ere thou ***b*** 2Sam 2:26
for the Lord hath ***b*** him 2Sam 16:11
riding for me, except I ***b*** 2Kin 4:24
the prophet had ***b*** thee do 2Kin 5:13
do all that thou shalt ***b*** 2Kin 10:5
the preaching that I ***b*** thee ....Jon 3:2
a sacrifice, he hath ***b*** ....Zeph 1:7
angel of the Lord had ***b*** ....Matt 1:24
b me come unto thee on ......Matt 14:28
to call them that were ***b*** ....Matt 22:3
Tell them which are ***b*** ....Matt 22:4
which were ***b*** were not ....Matt 22:8
ye shall find, ***b*** to the ....Matt 22:9
whatsoever they ***b*** ....Matt 23:3
the Pharisee which had ***b*** ......Luke 7:39
let me first go ***b*** them ....Luke 9:61
b her..that she help me ....Luke 10:40
to those which were ***b*** ....Luke 14:7
when thou art ***b*** of..man ......Luke 14:8
man than thou be ***b*** of him ....Luke 14:8
when thou art ***b***, go ....Luke 14:10
lest they also ***b*** thee again .....Luke 14:12
say to them that were ***b*** ....Luke 14:17
those men which were ***b*** ......Luke 14:24
them that believe not ***b*** 1Cor 10:27
house, neither ***b*** him God 2John 10
he that ***b*** him God speed 2John 11

BIDKAR (bĭd'kär)—*"servant of Ker (Kar)"*
Captain under Jehu 2Kin 9:25

BIER—*a frame for carrying a corpse*
Abner's body borne on ..2Sam 3:31
he came and touched the ***b*** ....Luke 7:14

BIGAMIST—*one who has more than one wife*
First, Lamech ....Gen 4:19

BIGAMY—*See* MARRIAGE

BIGOTRY—*excessive intolerance, prejudice, or fanaticism*

Characteristics of:
Name-calling ....John 8:48, 49
Spiritual blindness ....John 9:39-41
Hatred ....Acts 7:54-58
Self-righteousness ....Phil 3:4-6
Ignorance 1Tim 1:13

Examples of:
Haman ....Esth 3:8-10
The Pharisees ....John 8:33-48
The Jews 1Thess 2:14-16
Saul (Paul) ....Acts 9:1, 2
Peter ....Acts 10:14, 28
See INTOLERANCE; PERSECUTION

BIGTHA (bĭg'thä)—*"given by fortune"*
An officer of Ahasuerus. .Esth 1:10

BIGTHAN, BIGTHANA (bĭg'thăn, bĭg-thā'nä)—*"given by fortune"*
Conspired against Ahasuerus. .... Esth 2:21; Esth 6:2

BIGVAI (bĭg'vā-ī)—*"happy; of the people"*
1. Zerubbabel's companion. .Ezra 2:2
Neh 7:7, 19
2. One who signs covenant. .Neh 10:16

The children of ***B*** two ....Ezra 2:14
Of..sons also of ***B***; Uthai ......Ezra 8:14

BILDAD (bĭl'dăd)—*"lord Adad; son of contention"*
One of Job's friends .....Job 2:11
Makes three speeches .. Job 8:1-22; Job 18:1-21; Job 25:1-6

Temanite and ***B*** the ....Job 42:9

BILEAM (bĭl'ĕ-ăm)—*"foreigners"*
A town of Manasseh 1Chr 6:70

BILGAH (bĭl'gä)—*"bursting forth; first-born"*
1. A descendant of Aaron ..1Chr 24:1, 6, 14
2. A chief of the priests ....Neh 12:5, 7, 18
Same as Bilgai; signs document ....Neh 10:8
Called Bilgai ....Neh 10:8

BILGAI (bĭl'gā-ī)—*"bursting forth"*
One who sealed the covenant after the Exile ....Neh 10:8
See BILGAH

BILHAH (bĭl'hä)—*"tender"*
1. Rachel's maid ....Gen 29:29
The mother of Dan and Naphtali ....Gen 30:1-8
Commits incest with Reuben ....Gen 35:22
2. Simeonite town 1Chr 4:29
Same as Baalah ....Josh 15:29

the sons of ***B***, Rachel's ....Gen 35:25
lad was with..sons of ***B*** ....Gen 37:2
These are the sons of ***B*** ....Gen 46:25
And at ***B***, and at Ezem 1Chr 4:29
Shallum, the sons of ***B*** 1Chr 7:13

BILHAN (bĭl'hăn)—*"tender"*
1. A Horite chief; son of Ezer .... Gen 36:27; 1Chr 1:42
2. A Benjamite family head.1Chr 7:10

BILL—*a written document*
her a ***b*** of divorcement ....Deut 24:1
her a ***b*** of divorcement ....Deut 24:3
is the ***b*** of your mother's ......Is 50:1
given her a ***b*** of divorce ....Jer 3:8
write a ***b*** of divorcement ......Mark 10:4
said unto him, Take thy ***b*** .....Luke 16:6

BILLOWS—*great wave or surge of water*
all thy waves and thy ***b*** ....Ps 42:7
b and thy waves passed ....Jon 2:3

BILSHAN (bĭl'shăn)—*"searcher"*
A postexilic leader ......Ezra 2:2
Neh 7:7

BIMHAL (bĭm'hăl)—*"circumcised"*
An Asherite 1Chr 7:33

BINDING—*restraining; typing together; making firm or sure*

Used literally of:
Tying a man ....Gen 22:9
Imprisonment 2Kin 17:4
Acts 22:4
Ocean's shores ....Prov 30:4

Used figuratively of:
A fixed agreement ....Num 30:2
God's Word ....Prov 3:3
The brokenhearted ......Is 61:1
Satan ....Luke 13:16
The wicked ....Matt 13:30
Ceremonialism ....Matt 23:4
The keys ....Matt 16:19
A determined plan ......Acts 20:22
Marriage ....Rom 7:2

[*also* BIND, BINDETH, BOUND]
and ***b*** Isaac his son, and ......Gen 22:9
For, behold, we were ***b*** ....Gen 37:7
b upon his hand a scarlet .....Gen 38:28
king's prisoners were ***b*** ....Gen 39:20
place where Joseph was ***b*** .....Gen 40:3
let one of..brethren be ***b*** ......Gen 42:19
seeing..his life is ***b*** ....Gen 44:30
B his foal unto the vine ....Gen 49:11
utmost ***b*** of the everlasting ....Gen 49:26
kneading troughs being ***b*** ......Ex 12:34
shall ***b*** the breastplate ....Ex 28:28
it shall have a ***b*** of woven ......Ex 28:32
they did ***b*** the breastplate .....Ex 39:21
b it unto him herewith ....Lev 8:7
which hath no covering ***b*** .....Num 19:15
Lord, and ***b*** herself by a ......Num 30:3
bond wherewith she hath ***b*** ....Num 30:4
wherewith she hath ***b*** her .....Num 30:4
b oath to afflict the soul ......Num 30:13
thou shalt ***b*** them for a ....Deut 6:8
and ***b*** them for a sign upon ...Deut 11:18
b up the money in thine ......Deut 14:25
thou shalt ***b*** this line of ....Josh 2:18
she ***b*** the scarlet line ....Josh 2:21
bottles, old, and rent..***b*** ....Josh 9:4
To ***b*** Samson are we come ....Judg 15:10
We are come down to ***b*** thee . Judg 15:12
but we will ***b*** thee fast ....Judg 15:13
b him with two new cords .....Judg 15:13
we may ***b*** him to afflict ....Judg 16:5
thou mightest be ***b*** to ....Judg 16:6
they ***b*** me with seven green ...Judg 16:7
b me fast with new ropes .....Judg 16:11
soul of my lord shall be ***b*** in ..1Sam 25:29
Thy hands were not ***b***, nor 2Sam 3:34
b two talents of silver 2Kin 5:23
shut him up, and ***b*** him 2Kin 17:4
and ***b*** him with fetters of 2Kin 25:7
and ***b*** him with fetters 2Chr 33:11
and ***b*** him in fetters, to 2Chr 36:6
he maketh sore, and ***b*** up .....Job 5:18
He ***b*** up the waters in his .....Job 26:8
b the floods from ....Job 28:11
b me about as the collar ......Job 30:18
and ***b*** it as a crown to me .....Job 31:36
they cry not when he ***b*** ....Job 36:13
to the ***b*** thereof, and that .....Job 38:20
Canst thou ***b*** the sweet ....Job 38:31
Canst thou ***b*** the unicorn ......Job 39:10
b their faces in secret ....Job 40:13
or wilt thou ***b*** him for thy .....Job 41:5
out those which are ***b*** ....Ps 68:6
Thou hast set a ***b*** that ....Ps 104:9
to ***b*** his princes at his ....Ps 105:22
b the sacrifice with cords ......Ps 118:27
nor he that ***b*** sheaves his ......Ps 129:7
in heart, and ***b*** up their ....Ps 147:3
b their kings with chains ......Ps 149:8
b them continually upon ......Prov 6:21
B them upon thy fingers ......Prov 7:3

Foolishness is *b* in the ....Prov 22:15
As he that *b* a stone in a .....Prov 26:8
Who hath *b* the waters in .....Prov 30:4
B up the testimony, seal ......Is 8:16
they are *b* by the archers......Is 22:3
that the Lord *b* up the ....Is 30:26
and *b* them on thee, as a .....Is 49:18
prison to them that are *b* .....Is 61:1
b of..the sea by a perpetual ...Jer 5:22
that thou mayest be *b*.........Jer 30:13
being *b* in chains among ......Jer 40:1
thou shalt *b* a stone to it ......Jer 51:63
and the king of Babylon *b* ....Jer 52:11
my transgressions is *b* ....Lam 1:14
and shall *b* thee with them ....Ezek 3:25
and *b* them to thy skirts.......Ezek 5:3
b the tire of thine head ....Ezek 24:17
apparel, *b* with cords ....Ezek 27:24
to put a roller to *b* it to.......Ezek 30:21
b up that which was broken ...Ezek 34:16
were in his army to *b* ....Dan 3:20
Then these men were *b* in.....Dan 3:21
The wind hath *b* her up in ....Hos 4:19
them that remove the *b* ....Hos 5:10
I have *b* and strengthened.....Hos 7:15
when they shall *b*.............Hos 10:10
iniquity of Ephraim is *b* ....Hos 13:12
b the chariot to the swift ......Mic 1:13
all her great men were *b* ......Nah 3:10
he first *b* the strong ....Matt 12:29
laid hold on John, and *b* ......Matt 14:3
earth shall be *b* in heaven .....Matt 16:19
shall *b* on earth shall be.......Matt 18:18
earth shall be *b* in heaven .....Matt 18:18
B him hand and foot, and .....Matt 22:13
when they had *b* him, they ....Matt 27:2
first *b* the strong man ....Mark 3:27
no man could *b* him, no, not ..Mark 5:3
been often *b* with fetters ......Mark 5:4
laid hold upon John, and *b*....Mark 6:17
and *b* Jesus, and carried ......Mark 15:1
he was kept *b* with chains .....Luke 8:29
And went to him, and *b* up ...Luke 10:34
Satan hath *b*, lo, these ....Luke 13:16
b hand and foot with ....John 11:44
the Jews took Jesus and *b*.....John 18:12
he might bring them *b* unto ...Acts 9:2
to *b* all that call on thy ....Acts 9:14
b with two chains; and the ....Acts 12:6
and *b* on thy sandals...........Acts 12:8
I go *b* in the spirit unto ....Acts 20:22
b his own hands and feet......Acts 21:11
the Jews at Jerusalem *b* ....Acts 21:11
I am ready not to be *b*........Acts 21:13
b unto Jerusalem for to be ....Acts 22:5
and *b* themselves under a .....Acts 23:12
a pleasure, left Paul *b* ....Acts 24:27
hope of Israel I am *b* with ....Acts 28:20
which hath a husband is *b*.....Rom 7:2
thou *b* unto a wife? Seek 1Cor 7:27
We are *b* to thank God 2Thess 1:3
we are *b* to give thanks 2Thess 2:13
the word of God is not *b* 2Tim 2:9
that are in bonds, as *b* ....Heb 13:3
four angels which are *b* ....Rev 9:14
and *b* him a thousand.........Rev 20:2

BINEA (bĭn'ĕ-ä)—*"wanderer"*
A son of Moza..........1Chr 8:37

Moza begat *B*; and 1Chr 9:43

BINNUI (bĭn'ū-ī)—*"being a family"*
1. Head of postexilic family...............Neh 7:15
Called Bani ....Ezra 2:10
2. Son of Pahath-moab ....Ezra 10:30
3. Son of Bani ....Ezra 10:38
4. Postexilic Levite ....Neh 12:8
Henadad's son ....Neh 10:9
Family of, builds wall ...Neh 3:24

Noadiah the son of *B* ....Ezra 8:33
the son of Azaniah, *B* ....Neh 10:9
the Levites; Jeshua, *B* ....Neh 12:8

BIRD—*a vertebrate with feathers and wings*
List of:
Cock................Matt 26:34, 74; Mark 14:30; John 18:27; Luke 22:61
Cormorant ....Lev 11:17
Crane ....Jer 8:7
Cuckoo ....Lev 11:16
Dove ....Gen 8:8
Eagle...................Job 39:27
Glede ....Deut 14:13
Hawk ....Job 39:26
Hen ....Matt 23:37
Heron ....Lev 11:19
Kite ....Deut 14:13
Lapwing ....Lev 11:19
Ossifrage ....Lev 11:13
Ostrich ....Lev 11:16
Owls ....Job 30:29
Desert ....Ps 102:6
Great ....Lev 11:17
Little ....Lev 11:17
Partridge 1Sam 26:20
Peacock 1Kin 10:22
Pelican ....Ps 102:6
Pigeon..................Lev 12:6
Quail ....Num 11:31, 32
Raven ....Job 38:41
Sparrow ....Matt 10:29-31
Stork ....Ps 104:17
Swallow ....Ps 84:3
Turtledove ....Song 2:12
Vulture ....Lev 11:13
Features regarding:
Created by God ....Gen 1:20, 21
Named by Adam ....Gen 2:19, 20
Clean, unclean ....Gen 8:20
Differ from animals......1Cor 15:39
Under man's dominion ...Ps 8:8
For food ....Gen 9:2, 3
Belong to God ....Ps 50:11
God provides for ....Ps 104:10-12; Luke 12:23, 24
Can be tamed ....James 3:7
Differ in singing ....Song 2:12
Some migratory ....Jer 8:7
Solomon writes of 1Kin 4:33
Clean, used in sacrifices ..Lev 1:14; Luke 2:24
Worshiped by man ......Rom 1:23
Figurative of:
Escape from evil ....Ps 124:7
A wanderer ....Prov 27:8
Snares of death ....Eccl 9:12
Cruel kings ....Is 46:11
Hostile nations ....Jer 12:9
Wicked rich.............Jer 17:11
Kingdom of heaven......Matt 13:32
Maternal love ....Matt 23:37

[*also* BIRD'S, BIRDS, BIRDS']
kind, every *b* of every ....Gen 7:14
but the *b* divided he not ......Gen 15:10
and the *b* did eat them.........Gen 40:17
b shall eat thy flesh from......Gen 40:19
cleansed two *b* alive and ......Lev 14:4
one of the *b* be killed.........Lev 14:5
As for the living *b*, he ....Lev 14:6
b in the blood of the *b*.......Lev 14:6
shall let the living *b* ....Lev 14:7
cleanse the house two *b*.......Lev 14:49
kill the one of the *b* ....Lev 14:50
scarlet, and the living *b* ......Lev 14:51
in the blood of the slain *b*.....Lev 14:51
with the blood of the *b* ....Lev 14:52
living *b*, and with..cedar ....Lev 14:52
he shall let go..the living *b* ....Lev 14:53
Of all clean *b* ye shall eat .....Deut 14:11
b nest chance to be before ....Deut 22:6
neither the *b* of the air........2Sam 21:10
play with him as with a *b*? ....Job 41:5
Flee as a *b* to..mountain ......Ps 11:1
where the *b* make their ....Ps 104:17
b out of the snare of..........Ps 124:7
in the sight of any *b* ....Prov 1:17
a *b* from the hand of the ......Prov 6:5
as a *b* hasteth to the snare ....Prov 7:23
As the *b* by wandering, as ....Prov 26:2
As a *b* that wandereth from ...Prov 27:8
as the *b* that are caught ....Eccl 9:12
b of the air shall carry ....Eccl 10:20
voice of the *b*, and all ....Eccl 12:4
time of the singing of *b* ....Song 2:12
wandering *b* cast out of ....Is 16:2
As *b* flying, so will the ....Is 31:5
ravenous *b* from the east ......Is 46:11
the *b* of the heavens were .....Jer 4:25
are consumed, and the *b* ......Jer 12:4
as a speckled *b*, the *b*.........Jer 12:9
chased me sore, like a *b* ......Lam 3:52
thee unto the ravenous *b*......Ezek 39:4
and his nails like *b* claws ......Dan 4:33
shall fly away like a *b*.........Hos 9:11
shall tremble as a *b* out ....Hos 11:11
Can a *b* fall in a snare........Amos 3:5
the *b* of the air have..........Matt 8:20
so that the *b* of the air ....Matt 13:32
b of the air have nests ....Luke 9:58
corruptible man, and to *b* .....Rom 1:23
fishes, and another of *b* 1Cor 15:39
kind of beasts, and of *b*.......James 3:7
every unclean and hateful *b* ...Rev 18:2

BIRD CAGE
Used figuratively ....Jer 5:27

BIRSHA (bĭr'shä)—*"thick; strong"*
A king of Gomorrah.....Gen 14:2, 8, 10

BIRTH—*the act of coming into life*
Kinds of:
Natural ....Eccl 7:1
Figurative...............Is 37:3
Supernatural ....Matt 1:18-25
The new ....John 3:5
See New Birth
Natural, features regarding:
Pain of, results from sin. .Gen 3:16
Produces a sinful being. ..Ps 51:5
Makes ceremonially unclean ....Lev 12:2, 5; Luke 2:22
Affliction from ....John 9:1
Twins of, differ ....Gen 25:21-23
Sometimes brings death ..Gen 35:16-20
Pain of, forgotten ....John 16:21

stone, according to..*b* ....Ex 28:10
children are come to..*b* 2Kin 19:3
untimely *b* I had not..........Job 3:16
untimely *b* of a woman ....Ps 58:8
an untimely *b* is better ....Eccl 6:3
to the *b*, and not cause ....Is 66:9
Thy *b* and thy nativity is ......Ezek 16:3
from the *b*, and from the .....Hos 9:11
many shall rejoice at his *b* ....Luke 1:14
I travail in *b* again until.......Gal 4:19
cried, travailing in *b* ....Rev 12:2

BIRTHDAY—*date of one's birth*
Job and Jeremiah curse theirs...............Job 3:1-11; Jer 20:14, 15
Celebration:
Pharaoh's ....Gen 40:20
Herod's.................Mark 6:21

when Herod's *b* was kept .....Matt 14:6

BIRTHRIGHT—*legal rights inherited by birth*
Blessings of:
Seniority................Gen 43:33
Double portion ....Deut 21:15-17
Royal succession 2Chr 21:3
Loss of:
Esau's—by sale..........Gen 25:29-34; Rom 9:12
Reuben's—as a punishment ....Gen 49:3, 4; 1Chr 5:1, 2
Manasseh's—by Jacob's will..................Gen 48:15-20; 1Chr 5:1, 2
David's brother—by divine will 1Sam 16:2-22
Adonijah's—by the Lord. .1Kin 2:15

Hosah's son's—by his father's will ... 1Chr 26:10
Transferred to:
Jacob ... Gen 27:6-46
Judah ... Gen 49:8-10
Solomon ... 1Chr 28:5-7
See **First-born**

first-born according to..***b*** ... Gen 43:33
morsel of meat sold his ***b*** ... Heb 12:16

BIRTHS, FORETOLD
Over a short period:
Ishmael's ... Gen 16:11
Isaac's ... Gen 18:10
Samson's ... Judg 13:3, 24
Samuel's ... 1Sam 1:11, 20
Shunammite's son's ... 2Kin 4:16, 17
John the Baptist's ... Luke 1:13
Over a longer period:
Josiah's ... 1Kin 13:2
Cyrus' ... Is 45:1-4
Christ's ... Gen 3:15; Mic 5:1-3

BIRZAVITH (bĭr-zā'vĭth)—*"olive well"*
An Asherite ... 1Chr 7:31

BISHLAM (bĭsh'lăm)—*"peaceful"*
A Persian officer ... Ezra 4:7

BISHOP—*an overseer; elder*
Qualifications of, given by:
Paul ... 1Tim 3:1-7
Peter, called "elder" ... 1Pet 5:1-4
Duties of:
Oversee the church ... Acts 20:17, 28-31
Feed God's flock ... 1Pet 5:2
Watch over men's souls ... Heb 13:17
Teach ... 1Tim 5:17
Office of:
Same as elder ... Acts 20:17, 28
Several in a church ... Acts 20:17, 28; Phil 1:1
Follows ordination ... Titus 1:5, 7
Held by Christ ... 1Pet 2:25

BISHOPRIC—*the office of a bishop*
and his ***b*** let another ... Acts 1:20

BIT—*the part of a bridle inserted into a horse's mouth*
Figurative, of man's stubborn nature ... Ps 32:9; James 3:3

BITE—*to seize with the teeth or jaws*
[*also* **bit, biteth, bitten**]
path, that ***b*** the horse ... Gen 49:17
and they ***b*** the people ... Num 21:6
every one that is ***b*** ... Num 21:8
if a serpent had ***b*** any ... Num 21:9
it ***b*** like a serpent, and ... Prov 23:32
hedge, a serpent shall ***b*** ... Eccl 10:8
b without enchantment ... Eccl 10:11
charmed..they shall ***b*** ... Jer 8:17
the wall, and a serpent ***b*** ... Amos 5:19
serpent, and he shall ***b*** ... Amos 9:3
that ***b*** with their teeth ... Mic 3:5
up suddenly that shall ***b*** ... Hab 2:7
if ye ***b*** and devour one ... Gal 5:15

BITHIAH (bĭ-thī'ä)—*"daughter of Jehovah"*
Pharaoh's daughter; wife of Mered ... 1Chr 4:18

BITH-RON (bĭth'rŏn)—*"ravine"*
A district east of Jordan. . 2Sam 2:29

BITHYNIA (bĭ-thĭn'ĭ-ä)—*"violent rainfall"*
The Spirit keeps Paul from ... Acts 16:7
Peter writes to Christians of ... 1Pet 1:1

BITTER—*distasteful and distressing; astringent taste; expressive of severe pain, grief, or regret*
[*also* **bitterly**]
great and exceeding ***b*** cry ... Gen 27:34
made their lives ***b*** with ... Ex 1:14
b herbs they shall eat it ... Ex 12:8
of Marah, for they were ***b*** ... Ex 15:23
b water that causeth the ... Num 5:18
free from this ***b*** water ... Num 5:19
blot them out with the ***b*** ... Num 5:23
into her, and become ***b*** ... Num 5:27
unleavened bread and ***b*** ... Num 9:11
and with ***b*** destruction ... Deut 32:24
gall, their clusters are ***b*** ... Deut 32:32
curse ye ***b*** the inhabitants ... Judg 5:23
Almighty hath dealt very ***b*** ... Ruth 1:20
Israel, that it was very ***b*** ... 2Kin 14:26
cried with a loud and a ***b*** ... Esth 4:1
life unto the ***b*** in soul ... Job 3:20
writest ***b*** things against me ... Job 13:26
today is my complaint ... Job 23:2
to the hungry soul every ***b*** ... Prov 27:7
more ***b*** than death the ... Eccl 7:26
b for sweet..sweet for ***b*** ... Is 5:20
I will weep ***b***, labor not ... Is 22:4
strong drink shall be ***b*** ... Is 24:9
of peace shall weep ***b*** ... Is 33:7
is an evil thing and ***b*** ... Jer 2:19
wickedness, because it is ***b*** ... Jer 4:18
and only son, most ***b*** ... Jer 6:26
and shall cry ***b***, and shall ... Ezek 27:30
bitterness of heart and ***b*** ... Ezek 27:31
him to anger most ***b*** ... Hos 12:14
and the end thereof as a ***b*** ... Amos 8:10
Chaldeans, that ***b*** and hasty ... Hab 1:6
man shall cry there ***b*** ... Zeph 1:14
he went out, and wept ***b*** ... Matt 26:75
Peter went out, and wept ***b*** ... Luke 22:62
place sweet water and ***b***? ... James 3:11
because they were made ***b*** ... Rev 8:11
it shall make thy belly ***b*** ... Rev 10:9
eaten it, my belly was ***b*** ... Rev 10:10

BITTER HERBS
Part of Passover meal ... Ex 12:8; Num 9:11
Descriptive of sorrow ... Lam 3:15

"BITTER IS SWEET"
Descriptive of man's hunger ... Prov 27:7

BITTER WATERS
Made sweet by a tree ... Ex 15:23-25
Swallowed by suspected wife ... Num 5:11-31

BITTERN—*a nocturnal member of the heron family*
Sings in desolate windows . Zeph 2:14

it a possession for the ***b*** ... Is 14:23
cormorant and the ***b*** shall ... Is 34:11

BITTERNESS—*extreme enmity; sour temper*
Kinds of:
The soul ... Job 3:20
The heart ... Prov 14:10
Words ... Ps 64:3
Death ... 1Sam 15:32
"Water of" ... Num 5:24
Causes of:
Childlessness ... 1Sam 1:10
A foolish son ... Prov 17:25
Demanding woman ... Eccl 7:26
Sickness ... Is 38:17
Sin ... Prov 5:4
Death ... Jer 31:15
Apostasy ... Acts 8:23
Avoidance of:
Toward others ... Eph 4:31
Toward a wife ... Col 3:19
As a source of defilement . Heb 12:15
As contrary to the truth . . James 3:14

will be ***b*** in the latter end ... 2Sam 2:26
I will complain in the ***b*** ... Job 7:11
but filleth me with ***b*** ... Job 9:18
I will speak in the ***b*** ... Job 10:1
dieth in the ***b*** of his soul ... Job 21:25
years in the ***b*** of my soul ... Is 38:15
for peace I had great ***b*** ... Is 38:17
afflicted, and she is in ***b*** ... Lam 1:4
He hath filled me with ***b*** ... Lam 3:15
me away, and I went in ***b*** ... Ezek 3:14
with ***b*** sigh before their ... Ezek 21:6
shall weep for thee with ***b*** ... Ezek 27:31
shall be in ***b*** for him ... Zech 12:10
as one that is in ***b*** ... Zech 12:10
is full of cursing and ***b*** ... Rom 3:14

BIZJOTHJAH (bĭz-jōth'jă)—*"contempt of Jehovah"*
A town in south Judah . . . Josh 15:28

BIZTHA (bĭz'thä)—*"eunuch"*
An officer under Ahasuerus ... Esth 1:10

BLACK—*destitute of light*
Literally of:
Hair ... Song 5:11
Skin ... Song 1:5
Horse ... Zech 6:2
Sky ... 1Kin 18:45
Mountain ... Heb 12:18
Night ... Prov 7:9
Figuratively of:
Affliction ... Job 30:30
Mourning ... Jer 8:21
Foreboding evil ... Joel 2:6; Nah 2:10
Hell ... Jude 13
Specifically:
Let blackness of the day . Job 3:5
Clothe heaven with ... Is 50:3
Shall gather ... Joel 2:6

[*also* **blacker, blackish**]
that there is no ***b*** hair in it ... Lev 13:31
and blue, and white, and ***b*** ... Esth 1:6
are ***b*** by reason of the ice ... Job 6:16
in the evening, in the ***b*** and ... Prov 7:9
not upon me, because I am ***b*** . . Song 1:6
and the heavens above be ***b*** ... Jer 4:28
they are ***b*** unto the ground ... Jer 14:2
visage is ***b*** than a coal ... Lam 4:8
Our skin was ***b*** like an oven ... Lam 5:10
b horses which are therein ... Zech 6:6
make one hair white or ***b*** ... Matt 5:36
I beheld, and lo a ***b*** horse ... Rev 6:5
became ***b*** as sackcloth of ... Rev 6:12

BLADE—*edge of a knife; scapula; leaf of grass or herb*
haft also went in after the ***b*** ... Judg 3:22
the fat closed upon the ***b*** ... Judg 3:22
fall from my shoulder ***b*** ... Job 31:22
when the ***b*** was sprung up ... Matt 13:26
first the ***b***, then the ear ... Mark 4:28

BLAINS—*blisters full of pus*
The sixth plague on Egypt ... Ex 9:8-11

BLAME—*to find fault with; responsibility; reproach*
[*also* **blamed**]
let me bear the ***b*** for ever ... Gen 43:9
I shall bear the ***b*** to my ... Gen 44:32
that the ministry be not ***b*** ... 2Cor 6:3
no man should ***b*** us in this ... 2Cor 8:20
face, because he was to be ***b*** . . Gal 2:11
be holy and without ***b*** ... Eph 1:4

BLAMELESS—*innocent*
servant; and ye shall be ***b*** ... Gen 44:10
We will be ***b*** of this thine ... Josh 2:17
Now shall I be more ***b*** than . . Judg 15:3

BLAMELESSNESS—*freedom from fault; innocence*
Used ritualistically of:
Priests ... Matt 12:5
Proper observance ... Luke 1:6
Works, righteousness ... Phil 3:6
Desirable in:
Bishops (elders) ... 1Tim 3:2; Titus 1:6, 7

Deacons................1Tim 3:10
Widows.................1Tim 5:7

Attainment of:
Desirable now...........Phil 2:15
At Christ's return..... 1Cor 1:8; 1Thess 5:23; 2Pet 3:14

BLASPHEMY—*insulting, cursing, lacking reverence for God; claiming deity*

Arises out of:
Pride...................Ps 73:9, 11; Ezek 35:12, 13
Hatred..................Ps 74:18
Affliction..............Is 8:21
Injustice...............Is 52:5
Defiance................Is 36:15, 18, 20
Scepticism..............Ezek 9:8; Mal 3:13, 14
Self-deification........Dan 11:36, 37; 2Thess 2:4
Unworthy conduct........2Sam 12:14; Rom 2:24

Instances of:
Job's wife..............Job 2:9
Shelomith's son.........Lev 24:11-16, 23
Sennacherib.............2Kin 19:4, 10, 22
The beast...............Dan 7:25; Rev 13:1, 5, 6
The Jews................Luke 22:65
Saul of Tarsus..........1Tim 1:13
Ephesians...............Rom 2:9
Hymenaeus...............1Tim 1:20

Those falsely accused of:
Naboth..................1Kin 21:12, 13
Jesus...................Matt 9:3; Matt 26:65
Stephen.................Acts 6:11, 13

Guilt of:
Punishable by death.....Lev 24:11, 16
Christ accused of.......John 10:33, 36

See Revile

[*also* BLASPHEME, BLASPHEMED, BLASPHEMER, BLASPHEMERS, BLASPHEMEST, BLASPHEMETH, BLASPHEMIES, BLASPHEMING, BLASPHEMOUS, BLASPHEMOUSLY]

he that *b* the name of the.....Lev 24:16
when he *b* the name of the....Lev 24:16
didst *b* God and the king.....1Kin 21:10
Naboth did *b* God and the....1Kin 21:13
trouble, and of rebuke, and *b*..2Kin 19:3
king of Assyria have *b* me....2Kin 19:6
that reproacheth and *b*........Ps 44:16
shall the enemy *b* thy name...Ps 74:10
and of rebuke, and of *b*.......Is 37:3
king of Assyria have *b* me....Is 37:6
hast thou reproached and *b*...Is 37:23
continually every day is *b*.....Is 52:5
the mountains, and *b* me......Is 65:7
in this your fathers have *b*....Ezek 20:27
I have heard all thy *b* which...Ezek 35:12
themselves, This man *b*.......Matt 9:3
thefts, false witness, *b*........Matt 15:19
saying, He hath spoken *b*.....Matt 26:65
Why doth this man..speak *b*...Mark 2:7
an evil eye, *b*, pride..........Mark 7:22
Ye have heard the *b*; what....Mark 14:64
is this which speaketh *b*?......Luke 5:21
unto him that *b* against.......Luke 12:10
things *b* spake they against....Luke 22:65
b; because I said I am the.....John 10:36
Paul, contradicting and *b*......Acts 13:45
opposed themselves, and *b*....Acts 18:6
churches, nor yet *b* of........Acts 19:37
and compelled them to *b*......Acts 26:11
anger, wrath, malice, *b*.......Col 3:8
Who was before a *b*, and a....1Tim 1:13
they may learn not to *b*.......1Tim 1:20
and his doctrine be not *b*.....1Tim 6:1
covetous, boasters, proud, *b*...2Tim 3:2
the word of God be not *b*.....Titus 2:5
Do not they *b* that worthy....James 2:7
I know the *b* of them which...Rev 2:9
upon his heads the name of *b*.Rev 13:1
he opened his mouth in *b*.....Rev 13:6
to *b* his name, and his.......Rev 13:6
and *b* the name of God.......Rev 16:9
b the God of heaven..........Rev 16:11
men *b* God because of the....Rev 16:21
full of names of *b*, having.....Rev 17:3

BLASPHEMY AGAINST THE HOLY SPIRIT
Attributing Christ's miracles to Satan......Matt 12:22-32
Never forgiveable.......Mark 3:28-30

BLASTING—*blighting, withering; injuring severely*
Shows God's power......Ex 15:8
Sent as judgment........Deut 28:22; Amos 4:9
Figurative of death......Job 4:9

[*also* BLAST, BLASTED]

seven thin ears and *b* with....Gen 41:6
ears, withered, thin, and *b*....Gen 41:23
seven empty ears *b* with the...Gen 41:27
when they make a long *b*.....Josh 6:5
at the *b* of the breath of......2Sam 22:16
if there be pestilence, *b*.......1Kin 8:37
I will send a *b* upon him......2Kin 19:7
and as corn *b* before it be.....2Kin 19:26
if there be *b*, or mildew,......2Chr 6:28
at the *b* of the breath of thy...Ps 18:15
when the *b* of the terrible.....Is 25:4
I will send a *b* upon him......Is 37:7
and as corn *b* before it be.....Is 37:27
I smote you with *b* and.......Hag 2:17

BLASTUS (blăs'tŭs)—*"a bud"*
Herod's chamberlain.....Acts 12:20

BLAZE—*synonym for "proclaim"*
and to *b* abroad the matter....Mark 1:45

BLEATINGS—*calling of sheep*
to hear the *b* of the flocks?...Judg 5:16

BLEMISH—*any deformity or injury*

Those without physical:
Priests.................Lev 21:17-24
Absalom.................2Sam 14:25
Animals used in sacrifices.Lev 22:19-25; Mal 1:8

Those without moral:
Christ..................Heb 9:14
The Church..............Eph 5:27

Those with:
Apostates...............2Pet 2:13

[*also* BLEMISHES]

lamb shall be without *b*, a.....Ex 12:5
and two rams without *b*.......Ex 29:1
him offer a male without *b*....Lev 1:3
bring it a male without *b*.....Lev 1:10
offer it without *b* before......Lev 3:1
he shall offer it without *b*.....Lev 3:6
a young bullock without *b*.....Lev 4:3
goats, a male without *b*.......Lev 4:23
goats, a female without *b*.....Lev 4:28
bring it a female without *b*....Lev 4:32
a ram without *b* out of the....Lev 5:15
shall bring a ram without *b*....Lev 5:18
a ram without *b* out of the....Lev 6:6
burnt offering without *b*.......Lev 9:2
two he lambs without *b*.......Lev 14:10
of the first year without *b*.....Lev 14:10
generations that hath any *b*....Lev 21:17
own will a male without *b*.....Lev 22:19
corruption is in them and *b*...Lev 22:25
he lamb without *b* of the......Lev 23:12
And if a man cause a *b* in....Lev 24:19
of the first year without *b*.....Num 6:14
and one ram without *b* for....Num 6:14
spot, wherein is no *b*.........Num 19:2
be unto you without *b*.........Num 28:19
of the first year without *b*.....Num 29:2
any *b* therein, as if it be......Deut 15:21
or sheep, wherein is *b*.........Deut 17:1
kid of the goats without *b*.....Ezek 43:22
young bullock without *b*......Ezek 45:18
six lambs without *b*...........Ezek 46:4
and a ram without *b*..........Ezek 46:4
Children in whom was no *b*...Dan 1:4
as of a lamb without *b* and....1Pet 1:19
Spots they are and *b*..........2Pet 2:13

BLESS—*to bestow happiness or prosperity upon; praise and glorify*
To give divine blessings..Gen 1:22; Gen 9:1-7
To adore God for His blessings............Gen 24:48; Ps 103:1
To invoke blessings upon another.............Gen 24:60; Gen 27:4, 27

[*also* BLESSEST, BLESSETH]

I will *b* her, and give thee a...Gen 17:16
son also of her:..I will *b*......Gen 17:16
blessing I will *b* thee and......Gen 22:17
be with thee, and will *b* thee..Gen 26:3
and blessed be he that *b* thee..Gen 27:29
God Almighty *b* thee, and....Gen 28:3
let thee go, except thou *b*.....Gen 32:26
thee, unto me, and I will *b*....Gen 48:9
the Almighty, who shall *b*.....Gen 49:25
and be gone; and *b* me also...Ex 12:32
unto thee, and I will *b*........Ex 20:24
and he shall *b* thy bread......Ex 23:25
on this wise ye shall *b*........Num 6:23
that he whom thou *b* is.......Num 22:6
received commandment to *b*...Num 23:20
Blessed is he that *b* thee......Num 24:9
and *b* you, as he hath.........Deut 1:11
will love thee, and *b* thee.....Deut 7:13
then thou shalt *b* the Lord....Deut 8:10
thy God may *b* thee in all.....Deut 14:29
shall greatly *b* thee in.........Deut 15:4
Lord thy God *b* thee, as he...Deut 15:6
the Lord thy God shall *b*......Deut 16:15
unto him, and to *b* in the.....Deut 21:5
the Lord thy God may *b*......Deut 23:20
in his own raiment, and *b*.....Deut 24:13
from heaven, and *b* thy.......Deut 26:15
upon mount Gerizim to *b*.....Deut 27:12
and he shall *b* thee in the.....Deut 28:8
he *b* himself in his heart......Deut 29:19
the Lord thy God shall *b*......Deut 30:16
B, Lord, his substance, and...Deut 33:11
they should *b* the people of...Josh 8:33
among the people, *B* ye the...Judg 5:9
answered him, The Lord *b*.....Ruth 2:4
because he doth *b* the.........1Sam 9:13
Then David returned to *b*.....2Sam 6:20
let it please thee to *b* the.....2Sam 7:29
to salute him, and to *b* him...2Sam 8:10
ye may *b* the inheritance of...2Sam 21:3
servants came to *b* our lord...1Kin 1:47
Oh that thou wouldest *b* me...1Chr 4:10
and David returned to *b*......1Chr 16:43
b the house of thy servant.....1Chr 17:27
minister unto him, and to *b*...1Chr 23:13
the congregation, Now *b* the..1Chr 29:20
b the Lord your God for ever.Neh 9:5
For thou, Lord, wilt *b* the.....Ps 5:12
b the covetous, whom the.....Ps 10:3
I will *b* the Lord who hath....Ps 16:7
congregations will I *b* the.....Ps 26:12
thy people, and *b* thine.......Ps 28:9
the Lord will *b* his people.....Ps 29:11
I will *b* the Lord..all times....Ps 34:1
they *b* with their mouth.......Ps 62:4
will I *b* thee while I live......Ps 63:4
O *b* our God, ye people, and..Ps 66:8
be merciful unto us and *b*.....Ps 67:1
B ye God in the..............Ps 68:26
Sing unto the Lord, *b* his.....Ps 96:2
be thankful unto him, and *b*...Ps 100:4
B the Lord, O my soul........Ps 104:1
He *b* them also, so that.......Ps 107:38
Let them curse, but *b* thou....Ps 109:28
he will *b* us; he will *b* the.....Ps 115:12
he will *b* the house of.........Ps 115:12
The Lord shall *b* thee out of..Ps 128:5
upon you; we *b* you in the....Ps 129:8
I will abundantly *b* her........Ps 132:15

b ye the Lord, all ye servants . . Ps 134:1
b ye the Lord, all ye servants . . Ps 135:19
I will *b* thy name for ever . . . . . Ps 145:1
but he *b* the habitation of . . . . . Prov 3:33
b his friend with a loud . . . . Prov 27:14
and doth not *b* their mother . . . Prov 30:11
the Lord of hosts shall *b* . . . . . . Is 19:25
That he who *b* himself in the . . Is 65:16
shall *b* himself in the God . . . . . Is 65:16
and the nations shall *b* . . . . Jer 4:2
The Lord *b* thee, O . . . . Jer 31:23
from this day will I *b* you . . . . . Hag 2:19
b them that curse you, do . . . . . Matt 5:44
B them that curse you, and . . . Luke 6:28
him to *b* you, in turning . . . . . . Acts 3:26
B them which persecute you; *b*. Rom 12:14
being reviled, we *b*; being 1Cor 4:12
cup of blessing which we *b* 1Cor 10:16
Else when thou shalt *b* 1Cor 14:16
Surely blessing I will *b* . . . . Heb 6:14
Therewith *b* we God, even . . . . James 3:9

BLESSED—*past tense of "bless," the objects of God's favor*

Reasons for, they:
Are chosen . . . . Eph 1:3, 4
Believe . . . . Gal 3:9
Are forgiven . . . . Ps 32:1, 2
Are justified . . . . Rom 4:6-9
Are chastened . . . . Ps 94:12
Keep God's Word . . . . Rev 1:3

Time of:
Eternal past . . . . Eph 1:3, 4
Present . . . . Luke 6:22
Eternal future . . . . Matt 25:34

[*also* BLESSEDNESS]
And God *b* the seventh day . . . Gen 2:3
he them; and *b* them . . . . Gen 5:2
And God *b* Noah and his . . . . . Gen 9:1
families of the earth be *b* . . . . . Gen 12:3
B be Abram of the most . . . . . . Gen 14:19
Behold, I have *b* him, and . . . . Gen 17:20
nations of the earth shall be *b* . Gen 18:18
nations of the earth be *b* . . . . . . Gen 22:18
the Lord had *b* Abraham in . . . Gen 24:1
Abraham, that God *b* his son . . Gen 25:11
nations of the earth be *b* . . . . . . Gen 26:4
Esau's hands; so he *b* him . . . . . Gen 27:23
Isaac called Jacob, and *b* . . . . . . Gen 28:1
the daughters will call me *b* . . . Gen 30:13
b them; and Laban . . . . Gen 31:55
my name? And he *b* him . . . . . . Gen 32:29
out of Padan-aram, and *b* . . . . . Gen 35:9
the Lord *b* the Egyptian's . . . . . Gen 39:5
Pharaoh; and Jacob *b* . . . . Gen 47:7
land of Canaan, and *b* me . . . . . Gen 48:3
spake unto them, and *b* . . . . Gen 49:28
Jethro said, *B* be the Lord . . . . Ex 18:10
the Lord *b* the sabbath day . . . . Ex 20:11
they done it: and Moses *b* . . . . . Ex 39:43
toward the people, and *b* . . . . . Lev 9:22
he whom thou blessest is *b* . . . . Num 22:6
hast *b* them altogether . . . . Num 23:11
B is he that blesseth thee . . . . . Num 24:9
Lord thy God hath *b* thee in . . . Deut 2:7
Thou shalt be *b* above all . . . . . Deut 7:14
Lord thy God hath *b* thee . . . . . Deut 12:7
Lord thy God hath *b* thee . . . . . Deut 14:24
Lord thy God hath *b* thee . . . . . Deut 15:14
Lord thy God hath *b* thee . . . . . Deut 16:10
B shalt thou be in the city . . . . Deut 28:3
Moses the man of God *b* the . . Deut 33:1
Joshua *b* him, and gave . . . . Josh 14:13
as the Lord hath *b* me . . . . Josh 17:14
So Joshua *b* them, and sent . . . Josh 22:6
Balaam: therefore he *b* you . . . Josh 24:10
B above women shall Jael . . . . . Judg 5:24
child grew, and the Lord *b* . . . . Judg 13:24
B be thou of the Lord, my . . . . Judg 17:2
b be he that did take . . . . Ruth 2:19
B be thou of the Lord, my . . . . Ruth 3:10
B be the Lord, which hath . . . . Ruth 4:14
And Eli *b* Elkanah and his 1Sam 2:20
B be thou of the Lord; I 1Sam 15:13
B be ye of the Lord, for ye . . . 1Sam 23:21
B be the Lord God of Israel . . 1Sam 25:32
B be thou, my son David 1Sam 26:25
B be ye of the Lord, that ye . . 2Sam 2:5
and the Lord *b* Obed-edom . . . 2Sam 6:11
house of thy servant be *b* 2Sam 7:29
he would not go, but *b* him . . . 2Sam 13:25
B be the Lord thy God 2Sam 18:28
king kissed Barzillai, and *b* 2Sam 19:39
Lord liveth; and *b* be my 2Sam 22:47
B be the Lord God of Israel . . 1Kin 1:48
king Solomon shall be *b* 1Kin 2:45
B be the Lord this day 1Kin 5:7
and *b* all the congregation 1Kin 8:14
B be the Lord thy God 1Kin 10:9
And the Lord *b* the house of . . 1Chr 13:14
he *b* the people in the name . . . 1Chr 16:2
B be the Lord God of Israel . . 1Chr 16:36
O Lord, and it shall be *b* 1Chr 17:27
the eighth: for God *b* him 1Chr 26:5
Wherefore David *b* the Lord . . 1Chr 29:10
B be the Lord God of Israel . . 2Chr 2:12
b the whole congregation of . . . 2Chr 6:3
B be the Lord thy God 2Chr 9:8
for there they *b* the Lord 2Chr 20:26
Levites arose and *b* the 2Chr 30:27
they *b* the Lord, and his 2Chr 31:8
B be the Lord God of our . . . . Ezra 7:27
Ezra *b* the Lord, the great . . . . Neh 8:6
and *b* be thy glorious name . . . . Neh 9:5
the people *b* all the men . . . . . . Neh 11:2
b the work of his hands . . . . Job 1:10
the ear heard me, then it *b* . . . . Job 29:11
If his loins have not *b* me . . . . . Job 31:20
So the Lord *b* the latter end . . . Job 42:12
B is the man that walketh . . . . . Ps 1:1
B are all they that put their . . . Ps 2:12
Lord liveth; and *b* be my . . . . . Ps 18:46
hast made him most *b* for . . . . . Ps 21:6
B be the Lord, because he . . . . Ps 28:6
B be the Lord; for he hath . . . . Ps 31:21
B is he whose transgression . . . Ps 32:1
B is the man unto whom . . . . . . Ps 32:2
B is the nation whose God . . . . Ps 33:12
b is the man that trusteth . . . . . Ps 34:8
For such as be *b* of him . . . . Ps 37:22
b is that man that maketh . . . . . Ps 40:4
B is he that considereth the . . . Ps 41:1
B be the Lord God of Israel . . Ps 41:13
God hath *b* thee for ever . . . . . Ps 45:2
while he lived he *b* his soul . . . Ps 49:18
B is the man whom thou . . . . . . Ps 65:4
B be God, which hath not . . . . Ps 66:20
B be the Lord, who daily . . . . . Ps 68:19
sun: and men shall be *b* in . . . . Ps 72:17
all nations shall call him *b* . . . . . Ps 72:17
B are they that dwell in thy . . . Ps 84:4
B is the people that know . . . . . Ps 89:15
B is the man whom thou . . . . . . Ps 94:12
B are they that keep . . . . Ps 106:3
B is the man that feareth . . . . . Ps 112:1
B be the name of the Lord . . . . Ps 113:2
Ye are *b* of the Lord which . . . Ps 115:15
B be he that cometh in the . . . . Ps 118:26
B are the undefiled in the . . . . . Ps 119:1
B be the Lord, who hath . . . . . . Ps 124:6
B is every one that feareth . . . . Ps 128:1
B be the Lord out of Zion . . . . Ps 135:21
B be the Lord my strength . . . . Ps 144:1
he hath *b* thy children . . . . Ps 147:13
Let thy fountain be *b*; and . . . . Prov 5:18
for *b* are they that keep my . . . Prov 8:32
B is the man that heareth . . . . . Prov 8:34
The memory of the just is *b* . . . Prov 10:7
his children are *b* after him . . . . Prov 20:7
bountiful eye shall be *b* . . . . Prov 22:9
children arise up, and call . . . . . Prov 31:28
B art thou, O land, when . . . . . Eccl 10:17
daughters saw her, and *b* . . . . . . Song 6:9
B be Egypt my people . . . . Is 19:25
b are all they that wait . . . . Is 30:18
B are ye that sow beside all . . . Is 32:20
I called him alone, and *b* . . . . . Is 51:2
B is the man that doeth this . . . Is 56:2
seed which the Lord hath *b* . . . Is 61:9
seed of the *b* of the Lord . . . . . Is 65:23
incense, as if he *b* an idol . . . . . Is 66:3
B is the man that trusteth . . . . . Jer 17:7
my mother bare me be *b* . . . . . . Jer 20:14
B be the glory of the Lord . . . . Ezek 3:12
Then Daniel *b* the God of . . . . Dan 2:19
B be the God of Shadrach . . . . Dan 3:28
I *b* the most High, and I . . . . . . Dan 4:34
B is he that waiteth, and . . . . . . Dan 12:12
that sell them say, *B* be . . . . Zech 11:5
nations shall call you *b* . . . . Mal 3:12
B are the poor in spirit . . . . Matt 5:3
B are they that mourn; for . . . . Matt 5:4
B are the meek; for they . . . . . . Matt 5:5
B are they which do hunger . . . Matt 5:6
B are the merciful; for they . . . Matt 5:7
B are the pure in heart: for . . . Matt 5:8
B are the peacemakers; for . . . . Matt 5:9
B are they..are persecuted . . . . Matt 5:10
B are ye, when men shall . . . . . Matt 5:11
And *b* is he, whosoever shall . . Matt 11:6
But *b* are your eyes, for . . . . . . Matt 13:16
he *b*, and brake, and gave . . . . Matt 14:19
said unto him, *B* art thou, ... Matt 16:17
B is he that cometh in the . . . . Matt 21:9
B is he that cometh in the . . . . Matt 23:39
B is that servant, whom . . . . Matt 24:46
ye *b* of my Father, inherit . . . . Matt 25:34
b it, and brake it, and gave . . . Matt 26:26
looked up to heaven, and *b* . . . Mark 6:41
and he *b*, and commanded . . . . Mark 8:7
B is he that cometh in the . . . . Mark 11:9
and *b*, and brake it, and . . . . . . Mark 14:22
thee; *b* art thou among . . . . Luke 1:28
B art thou among women . . . . . Luke 1:42
and *b* is the fruit of thy . . . . Luke 1:42
B be the Lord God of Israel . . Luke 1:68
him up in his arms, and *b* . . . . . Luke 2:28
disciples, and said, *B* be ye . . . . Luke 6:20
B are ye that hunger now . . . . . Luke 6:21
B are ye that weep now . . . . Luke 6:21
And *b* is he, whosoever shall . . Luke 7:23
he *b* them, and brake, and . . . . Luke 9:16
B are the eyes which see . . . . . . Luke 10:23
B is the womb that bare . . . . . . Luke 11:27
Yea..*b* are they that hear . . . . . Luke 11:28
B are those servants whom . . . . Luke 12:37
b are those servants . . . . Luke 12:38
B is he that cometh in the . . . . Luke 13:35
thou shalt be *b*; for they . . . . . . Luke 14:14
B be the King that cometh . . . . Luke 19:38
they shall say, *B* are the . . . . . . Luke 23:29
took bread, and *b* it, and . . . . . Luke 24:30
B is the King of Israel that . . . . John 12:13
b are they that have not . . . . . . John 20:29
kindreds of the earth be *b* . . . . . Acts 3:25
b to give than to receive . . . . . . Acts 20:35
the Creator, who is *b* for . . . . . Rom 1:25
also describeth the *b* of . . . . Rom 4:6
B are they whose iniquities . . . . Rom 4:7
B be God, even the Father of . 2Cor 1:3
Jesus Christ, which is *b* for 2Cor 11:31
In thee shall all nations be *b* . . Gal 3:8
Where is then the *b* ye spake . . Gal 4:15
B be the God and Father of . . . Eph 1:3
glorious gospel of the *b* God . . 1Tim 1:11
b and only Potentate, the 1Tim 6:15
Looking for that *b* hope, and . . Tit 2:13
slaughter of the kings, and *b* . . Heb 7:1
By faith Isaac *b* Jacob and . . . . Heb 11:20
B is the man that endureth . . . . James 1:12
B be the God and Father of . . . 1Pet 1:3
B is he that readeth, and . . . . . . Rev 1:3
B are the dead which die in . . . Rev 14:13
B is he that watcheth, and . . . . Rev 16:15
B are they which are called . . . Rev 19:9

BLESSING—*the gift and approval of God; one who is a helper, encourager, giver of good gifts*

Physical and temporal:
Prosperity . . . . Mal 3:10-12
Food, clothing . . . . Matt 6:26, 30-33
Sowing, harvest . . . . Acts 14:17

Longevity ... Ex 20:12
Children ... Ps 127:3-5

National and Israelitish:
General ... Gen 12:1-3
Specific ... Rom 9:4, 5
Fulfilled ... Rom 11:1-36
Perverted ... Rom 2:17-29
Rejected ... Acts 13:46-52

Spiritual and eternal:
Salvation ... John 3:16
Election ... Eph 1:3-5
Regeneration ... 2Cor 5:17
Forgiveness ... Col 1:14
Adoption ... Rom 8:15-17
No condemnation ... Rom 8:1
Holy Spirit ... Acts 1:8
Justification ... Acts 13:38, 39
New covenant ... Heb 8:6-13
Fatherly chastisement ... Heb 12:5-11
Christ's intercession ... Rom 8:34
Sanctification ... Rom 8:3-14
Perseverance ... John 10:27-29
Glorification ... Rom 8:30

[*also* BLESSINGS]
great; and thou shalt be a ***b*** ... Gen 12:2
That in ***b*** I will bless thee ... Gen 22:17
curse upon me, and not a ***b*** ... Gen 27:12
hath taken away my ***b***, ... Gen 27:36
Hast thou not reserved a ***b*** ... Gen 27:36
give thee the ***b*** of Abraham ... Gen 28:4
Take, I pray thee, my ***b*** ... Gen 33:11
the ***b*** of the Lord was upon ... Gen 39:5
bless thee with ***b*** of heaven ... Gen 49:25
b of the deep that lieth ... Gen 49:25
b of the breasts, and of the ... Gen 49:25
every one according to his ***b*** ... Gen 49:28
may bestow upon you a ***b*** ... Ex 32:29
I will command my ***b*** upon ... Lev 25:21
this day a ***b*** and a curse ... Deut 11:26
according to the ***b*** of the ... Deut 12:15
according to the ***b*** of the ... Deut 16:17
God turned the curse into..***b*** ... Deut 23:5
these ***b*** shall come on thee ... Deut 28:2
Lord shall command the ***b*** ... Deut 28:8
the ***b*** and the curse, which ... Deut 30:1
this is the ***b*** wherewith ... Deut 33:1
the ***b*** and cursings ... Josh 8:34
Who answered, Give me a ***b*** ... Josh 15:19
Give me a ***b***: for thou hast ... Judg 1:15
now this ***b*** which thine ... 1Sam 25:27
and with thy ***b*** let the ... 2Sam 7:29
thee, take a ***b*** of..servant ... 2Kin 5:15
is exalted above all ***b*** and ... Neh 9:5
b of him that was ready to ... Job 29:13
thy ***b*** is upon thy people ... Ps 3:8
preventest him with the ***b*** of ... Ps 21:3
shall receive the ***b*** from the ... Ps 24:5
as he delighted not in ***b***, so ... Ps 109:17
The ***b*** of the Lord be upon ... Ps 129:8
the Lord commanded the ***b*** ... Ps 133:3
B are upon the head of ... Prov 10:6
b of the Lord, it maketh ... Prov 10:22
By the ***b*** of the upright the ... Prov 11:11
a good ***b*** shall come upon ... Prov 24:25
man shall abound with ***b*** ... Prov 28:20
even a ***b*** in the midst of the ... Is 19:24
my ***b*** upon thine offspring ... Is 44:3
Destroy it not; for a ***b*** is in ... Is 65:8
round about my hill a ***b*** ... Ezek 34:26
that he may cause the ***b*** ... Ezek 44:30
you, and ye shall be a ***b*** ... Zech 8:13
I will curse your ***b***; yea ... Mal 2:2
pour you out a ***b***, that ... Mal 3:10
the temple, praising and ***b*** ... Luke 24:53
the fullness of the ***b*** of the ... Rom 15:29
The cup of ***b*** which we bless ... 1Cor 10:16
b of Abraham might come ... Gal 3:14
is dressed, receiveth ***b*** ... Heb 6:7
would have inherited the ***b*** ... Heb 12:17
mouth proceedeth ***b*** and ... James 3:10
but contrariwise ***b*** ... 1Pet 3:9
honor, and glory, and ***b*** ... Rev 5:12
B, and glory, and wisdom ... Rev 7:12

BLIND—*unable to see*

[*also* BLINDED, BLINDETH]
deaf, or the seeing, or the ***b***? ... Ex 4:11
b the wise, and perverteth ... Ex 23:8
it be lame, or ***b***, or have any ... Deut 15:21
a gift doth ***b*** the eyes of the ... Deut 16:19
maketh the ***b*** to wander ... Deut 27:18
bribe to ***b*** mine eyes ... 1Sam 12:3
was eyes to the ***b***, and feet ... Job 29:15
openeth the eyes of the ***b*** ... Ps 146:8
the ***b*** shall see out of ... Is 29:18
eyes of the ***b*** shall be ... Is 35:5
Who is ***b***, but my servant? ... Is 42:19
is ***b*** as he that is perfect ... Is 42:19
b as the Lord's servant? ... Is 42:19
forth the ***b*** people that have ... Is 43:8
His watchmen are ***b***; they ... Is 56:10
for the wall like the ***b***, and ... Is 59:10
and with them the ***b*** and ... Jer 31:8
wandered as ***b*** men in the ... Lam 4:14
walk like ***b*** men, because ... Zeph 1:17
horse of the people with ***b*** ... Zech 12:4
two ***b*** men followed him ... Matt 9:27
the house, the ***b*** men came ... Matt 9:28
The ***b*** receive their sight ... Matt 11:5
possessed with a devil, ***b*** ... Matt 12:22
that the ***b*** and dumb both ... Matt 12:22
Let them alone; they be ***b*** ... Matt 15:14
if the ***b*** lead the ***b*** ... Matt 15:14
And, behold, two ***b*** men ... Matt 20:30
the ***b*** and the lame came to ... Matt 21:14
Woe unto you, ye blind ... Matt 23:16
and they bring a ***b*** man ... Mark 8:22
b Bartimeus, the son of ... Mark 10:46
Can the ***b*** lead the ***b***? ... Luke 6:39
many that were ***b*** he gave ... Luke 7:21
maimed, the lame, the ***b*** ... Luke 14:13
a certain ***b*** man sat by the ... Luke 18:35
b, halt, withered, waiting ... John 5:3
open the eyes of the ***b***? ... John 10:21
opened the eyes of the ***b*** ... John 11:37
He hath ***b*** their eyes, and ... John 12:40
shalt be ***b***, not seeing the ... Acts 13:11
thyself art a guide of the ***b*** ... Rom 2:19
it, and the rest were ***b*** ... Rom 11:7
b in part is happened to ... Rom 11:25
But their minds were ***b*** ... 2Cor 3:14
of this world hath ***b*** the ... 2Cor 4:4
because of the ***b*** of their ... Eph 4:18
lacketh these things is ***b*** ... 2Pet 1:9
that darkness hath ***b*** his ... 1John 2:11
poor, and ***b***, and naked ... Rev 3:17

BLINDFOLD—*a covering over the eyes*
A prelude to execution ... Esth 7:8
Put on Jesus ... Luke 22:63, 64

BLINDNESS—*destitute of sight (physically or spiritually)*

Causes of:
Old age ... Gen 27:1
Disobedience ... Deut 28:28, 29
Miracle ... 2Kin 6:18-20
Judgment ... Gen 19:11
Captivity ... Judg 16:20, 21
Condition of servitude ... 1Sam 11:2
Defeat in war ... 2Kin 25:7
Unbelief ... Acts 9: 8, 9
God's glory ... John 9:1-3

Disabilities of:
Keep from priesthood ... Lev 21:18
Offerings unacceptable ... Lev 22:22; Mal 1:8
Make protection ... Lev 19:14
Helplessness ... Judg 16:26
Occasional derision ... 2Sam 5:6-8

Remedies for:
Promised in Christ ... Is 42:7, 16
Proclaimed in the Gospel ... Luke 4:18-21; Acts 26:18
Portrayed in a miracle ... John 9:1-41; Acts 9:1-18
Perfected in faith ... John 11:37; Eph 1:18

Perverted by disobedience ... 1John 2:11

BLOCK—*an obstruction*
take up the stumbling ***b*** ... Is 57:14

BLOOD—*life-sustaining fluid in the arteries of animals and humans*

Used to designate:
Unity of mankind ... Acts 17:26
Human nature ... John 1:13
Human depravity ... Ezek 16:6, 22
The individual soul ... Ezek 33:8
The essence of life ... Gen 9:4; Lev 17:11, 14
The sacredness of life ... Gen 9:5, 6
Means of atonement ... Lev 17:10-14
Regeneration ... Is 4:4; Ezek 16:9; Joel 3:21
New covenant ... Matt 26:28
The new life ... John 6:53-56
Christ's atonement ... Heb 9:14
Redemption ... Zech 9:11

Miracles connected with:
Water turns to ... Ex 7:20, 21
Water appears like ... 2Kin 3:22, 23
The moon turns to ... Acts 2:20; Rev 6:12
Flow of, stops ... Mark 5:25, 29
Sea becomes ... Rev 11:6
Believers become white in ... Rev 7:14

Figurative of:
Sin ... Is 59:3
Cruelty ... Hab 2:12
Abominations ... Is 66:3
Guilt ... 2Sam 1:16; Matt 27:25
Inherited guilt ... Matt 23:35
Vengeance ... Ezek 35:6
Retribution ... Is 49:25, 26
Slaughter ... Is 34:6-8
Judgment ... Rev 16:6
Victory ... Ps 58:10

of thy brother's ***b*** crieth ... Gen 4:10
thy brother's ***b*** from thy ... Gen 4:11
Shed no ***b***, but cast him ... Gen 37:22
also his ***b*** is required ... Gen 42:22
and his clothes in the ***b*** ... Gen 49:11
become ***b*** upon the dry ... Ex 4:9
they shall be turned to ***b*** ... Ex 7:17
shall take of the ***b***, and ... Ex 12:7
shall no ***b*** be shed for him ... Ex 22:2
offer the ***b*** of my sacrifice ... Ex 23:18
took half of the ***b*** and put ... Ex 24:6
half of the ***b*** he sprinkled ... Ex 24:6
thou shalt take the ***b*** of ... Ex 29:12
with the ***b*** of the sin ... Ex 30:10
not offer the ***b*** of my ... Ex 34:25
the ***b***, and sprinkle the ***b*** ... Lev 1:5
sprinkle the ***b*** upon ... Lev 3:2
shall take of..bullock's ***b*** ... Lev 4:5
he shall sprinkle of the ***b*** ... Lev 5:9
is sprinkled of the ***b*** ... Lev 6:27
the ***b*** thereof shall he ... Lev 7:2
Moses took the ***b***, and put ... Lev 8:15
brought the ***b*** unto him ... Lev 9:9
dipped his finger in the ***b*** ... Lev 9:9
poured out the ***b*** at the ... Lev 9:9
Behold, the ***b*** of it was not ... Lev 10:18
shall then continue in the ***b*** ... Lev 12:4
the living bird in the ***b*** of ... Lev 14:6
her issue in her flesh be ***b*** ... Lev 15:19
shall take of the ***b*** of the ... Lev 16:14
shall he sprinkle of the ***b*** ... Lev 16:14
b shall be imputed unto ... Lev 17:4
he hath shed ***b***; and that ... Lev 17:4
life of the flesh is in..***b*** ... Lev 17:11
b that maketh an atonement ... Lev 17:11
against the ***b***..neighbor ... Lev 19:16
his ***b*** shall be upon him ... Lev 20:9
thou shalt sprinkle their ***b*** ... Num 18:17
take..her ***b*** with his finger ... Num 19:4
and sprinkle of her ***b*** ... Num 19:4

prey, and drink the ***b*** of the . . Num 23:24
The revenger of ***b*** himself . . . . . Num 35:19
Only ye shall not eat the ***b*** . . . . Deut 12:16
thou shalt not eat the ***b*** . . . . Deut 15:23
between ***b*** and ***b***, between . . . . . Deut 17:8
Lest the avenger of the ***b*** . . . . . Deut 19:6
Our hands..not shed this ***b*** . . . . Deut 21:7
that thou bring not ***b*** upon . . . . Deut 22:8
drink the pure ***b*** of the . . . . Deut 32:14
his ***b*** shall be upon his head . . . Josh 2:19
his ***b*** shall be on our head . . . . . Josh 2:19
refuge from the avenger of ***b*** . . Josh 20:3
their ***b*** be laid upon . . . . Judg 9:24
people did eat them..***b*** 1Sam 14:32
sin against innocent ***b*** 1Sam 19:5
thee from coming to shed ***b*** . . . 1Sam 25:26
let not my ***b*** fall to the 1Sam 26:20
he died, for the ***b*** of Asahel . . . 2Sam 3:27
therefore now require his ***b*** . . . 2Sam 4:11
the revengers of ***b*** to 2Sam 14:11
all the ***b*** of the house of 2Sam 16:8
Amasa wallowed in ***b*** in 2Sam 20:12
the ***b*** of the men that went 2Sam 23:17
shed the ***b*** of war in peace 1Kin 2:5
lancets, till the ***b*** gushed 1Kin 18:28
dogs licked the ***b*** of Naboth . . . 1Kin 21:19
shall dogs lick thy ***b*** 1Kin 21:19
and the ***b*** ran out of the 1Kin 22:35
avenge the ***b*** of my 2Kin 9:7
and the ***b*** of all the 2Kin 9:7
sprinkled the ***b*** of his 2Kin 16:13
shed innocent ***b*** very much 2Kin 21:16
for the innocent ***b*** that he 2Kin 24:4
Jerusalem with innocent ***b*** 2Kin 24:4
shall I drink the ***b*** of these 1Chr 11:19
hast shed ***b*** abundantly 1Chr 22:8
thou hast shed much ***b*** 1Chr 22:8
man of war, and hast shed ***b*** . . 1Chr 28:3
between ***b*** and ***b***, between 2Chr 19:10
conspired against him..***b*** 2Chr 24:25
the priests received the ***b*** 2Chr 29:22
sprinkled the ***b*** upon the 2Chr 29:22
lambs..sprinkled the ***b*** 2Chr 29:22
the priests sprinkled the ***b*** 2Chr 30:16
the priests sprinkled the ***b*** 2Chr 35:11
earth, cover not thou my ***b*** . . . . Job 16:18
he maketh inquisition for ***b*** . . . . Ps 9:12
their drink offerings of ***b*** . . . . . Ps 16:4
What profit is there in my ***b*** . . . Ps 30:9
of bulls, or drink the ***b*** of . . . . . Ps 50:13
dipped in the ***b*** of thine . . . . Ps 68:23
precious shall their ***b*** be . . . . Ps 72:14
had turned their rivers into ***b*** . . Ps 78:44
Their ***b*** have they shed like . . . Ps 79:3
condemn the innocent ***b*** . . . . Ps 94:21
shed innocent ***b***, even . . . . Ps 106:38
even the ***b*** of their sons . . . . . . Ps 106:38
land was polluted with ***b*** . . . . . . Ps 106:38
let us lay wait for ***b***, let us . . . . Prov 1:11
hands that shed innocent ***b*** . . . . Prov 6:17
to lie in wait for ***b***; but the . . . . Prov 12:6
violence to the ***b*** of any . . . . Prov 28:17
the nose bringeth forth ***b*** . . . . . . Prov 30:33
delight not in the ***b*** of . . . . Is 1:11
and garments rolled in ***b*** . . . . . . Is 9:5
of Dimon shall be full of ***b*** . . . . Is 15:9
the earth..disclose her ***b*** . . . . . . Is 26:21
his ears from hearing of ***b*** . . . . . Is 33:15
be melted with their ***b*** . . . . Is 34:3
their ***b*** shall be sprinkled . . . . . . Is 63:3
skirts is found the ***b*** of . . . . Jer 2:34
shed not innocent ***b*** in this . . . . Jer 7:6
pour out their ***b*** by the . . . . Jer 18:21
this place with the ***b*** of . . . . Jer 19:4
neither shed innocent ***b*** in . . . . . Jer 22:3
surely bring innocent ***b*** . . . . Jer 26:15
made drunk with their ***b*** . . . . . . Jer 46:10
back his sword from ***b*** . . . . Jer 48:10
b upon the inhabitants of . . . . . Jer 51:35
that have shed the ***b*** of the . . . . Lam 4:13
but his ***b*** will I require . . . . Ezek 3:18
but his ***b*** will I require . . . . Ezek 3:20
pestilence and ***b*** shall pass . . . . . Ezek 5:17
the land is full of ***b***, and . . . . . . Ezek 9:9
pour out my fury..it in ***b*** . . . . . . Ezek 14:19
is a robber, a shedder of ***b*** . . . . Ezek 18:10
mother is like a vine..***b*** . . . . Ezek 19:10
thy ***b*** shall be in the midst . . . . Ezek 21:32
The city sheddeth ***b*** in . . . . Ezek 22:3
b is in their hands, and . . . . Ezek 23:37
For her ***b*** is in the midst of . . . Ezek 24:7
her pestilence, and ***b*** into . . . . . Ezek 28:23
I will also water with thy ***b*** . . . . Ezek 32:6
his ***b*** shall be upon his own . . . Ezek 33:4
shed the ***b*** of the children . . . . . Ezek 35:5
the ***b*** that they had shed . . . . . . Ezek 36:18
with pestilence and with ***b*** . . . . . Ezek 38:22
ye may eat flesh, and drink ***b*** . . Ezek 39:17
thereon, and to sprinkle ***b*** . . . . . Ezek 43:18
my bread, the fat and the ***b*** . . . Ezek 44:7
priest shall take of the ***b*** . . . . . . Ezek 45:19
I will avenge the ***b*** of . . . . Hos 1:4
break out..***b*** toucheth ***b*** . . . . Hos 4:2
and is polluted with ***b*** . . . . Hos 6:8
shall he leave his ***b*** upon . . . . . . Hos 12:14
b, and fire, and pillars of . . . . . Joel 2:30
they have shed innocent ***b*** . . . . . Joel 3:19
not upon us innocent ***b*** . . . . Jon 1:14
They build up Zion with ***b*** . . . . Mic 3:10
they all lie in wait for ***b*** . . . . Mic 7:2
because of men's ***b***, and . . . . . . Hab 2:8
and their ***b*** shall be poured . . . . Zeph 1:17
I will take away his ***b*** out . . . . . Zech 9:7
diseased with an issue of ***b*** . . . . Matt 9:20
for flesh and ***b*** hath not . . . . Matt 16:17
with them in the ***b*** of the . . . . . . Matt 23:30
was called, The field of ***b*** . . . . . Matt 27:8
This is my ***b*** of the new . . . . Mark 14:24
having an issue of ***b*** twelve . . . . Luke 8:43
the ***b*** of all the prophets . . . . . . Luke 11:50
whose ***b*** Pilate had mingled . . . Luke 13:1
new testament in my ***b*** . . . . Luke 22:20
forthwith came there out ***b*** . . . . John 19:34
is to say, The field of ***b*** . . . . Acts 1:19
b, and fire, and vapor of . . . . . . Acts 2:19
intend to bring this man's ***b*** . . . Acts 5:28
from things strangled..***b*** . . . . Acts 15:20
Your ***b*** be upon your own . . . . . Acts 18:6
that I am pure from the ***b*** . . . . . Acts 20:26
b, and from strangled . . . . Acts 21:25
b of thy martyr Stephen . . . . Acts 22:20
feet are swift to shed ***b*** . . . . Rom 3:15
the communion of the ***b*** of 1Cor 10:16
the new testament in my ***b*** 1Cor 11:25
of the body and ***b*** of the 1Cor 11:27
I conferred not with..***b*** . . . . Gal 1:16
made peace through the ***b*** . . . . . Col 1:20
partakers of flesh and ***b*** . . . . Heb 2:14
every year, not without ***b*** . . . . . Heb 9:7
Saying, This is the ***b*** of the . . . . Heb 9:20
that the ***b*** of bulls and of . . . . . Heb 10:4
into the holiest by the ***b*** . . . . Heb 10:19
and the sprinkling of ***b*** . . . . Heb 11:28
not yet resisted unto ***b*** . . . . Heb 12:4
to the ***b*** of sprinkling, that . . . . Heb 12:24
those beasts, whose ***b*** is . . . . Heb 13:11
sprinkling of the ***b*** of Jesus 1Pet 1:2
water and ***b***, even Jesus 1John 5:6
from our sins in his own ***b*** . . . . Rev 1:5
redeemed..God by thy ***b*** . . . . . . Rev 5:9
judge and avenge our ***b*** . . . . Rev 6:10
the city, and ***b*** came out of . . . . Rev 14:20
it became as the ***b*** of a dead . . Rev 16:3
drunken with the ***b*** of the . . . . . Rev 17:6
And in her was found the ***b*** . . . Rev 18:24
avenged the ***b*** of his . . . . Rev 19:2

BLOOD MONEY
Payment made to Judas . . Matt 26:14-16

BLOOD OF CHRIST—*the sacrifice Jesus made on the cross*

Described as:
Innocent . . . . Matt 27:4
Precious 1Pet 1:19
Necessary . . . . Heb 9:22, 23
Sufficient . . . . Heb 9:13, 14
Final . . . . Heb 9:24-28
Cleansing 1John 1:7
Conquering . . . . Rev 12:11

Basis of:
Reconciliation . . . . Eph 2:13-16
Redemption . . . . Rom 3:24, 25
Justification . . . . Rom 5:9
Sanctification . . . . Heb 10:29
Communion . . . . Matt 26:26-29
Victory . . . . Rev 12:11
Eternal life . . . . John 6:53-56

BLOODGUILTINESS—*guilt incurred by murder*
Incurred by willful murder . . . . Ex 21:14
Not saved by altar 1Kin 2:29
Provision for innocent . . . Ex 21:13; 1Kin 1:50-53
David's prayer concerning Ps 51:14
Judas' guilt in . . . . Matt 27:4
The Jews' admission of . . Matt 27:25
Figurative, of individual responsibility . . . . Ezek 37:1-9
Of Christ-rejectors . . . . Acts 18:6

BLOODTHIRSTY
the ***b*** hate the upright . . . . Prov 29:10

BLOODY—*smeared or stained with blood*
Saul's house 2Sam 21:1
Crimes . . . . Ezek 7:23
Cities . . . . Ezek 22:2; Ezek 24:6, 9
David 2Sam 16:7

Surely a ***b*** husband art . . . . Ex 4:25
Lord will abhor the ***b*** . . . . Ps 5:6
sinners, nor my life with ***b*** . . . . Ps 26:9
b and deceitful men shall . . . . . . Ps 55:23
iniquity, and save me from ***b*** . . Ps 59:2
from me therefore, ye ***b*** . . . . . . Ps 139:19
Woe to the ***b*** city! it is all . . . . . Nah 3:1
sick of a fever and of a ***b*** . . . . . Acts 28:8

BLOODY SWEAT—*(believed to be caused by agony or stress)*
Agony in Gethsemane . . . Luke 22:44

BLOOMED—*to have put forth flowers*
b blossoms, and yielded . . . . Num 17:8

BLOSSOM—*to open into blossoms; to flower*
Aaron's rod . . . . Num 17:5, 8
A fig tree . . . . Hab 3:17
A desert . . . . Is 35:1, 2
Israel . . . . Is 27:6

[*also* BLOSSOMED, BLOSSOMS]
and their ***b*** shall go up as . . . . . Is 5:24
rod hath ***b***, pride hath . . . . Ezek 7:10

BLOT—*to rub or wipe out*
One's name in God's Book . . . . Ex 32:32, 33
One's sins . . . . Ps 51:1, 9; Acts 4:19
Legal ordinances . . . . Col 2:14
Amalek . . . . Deut 25:19
Israel as a nation 2Kin 14:27

[*also* BLOTTED, BLOTTETH, BLOTTING]
and he shall ***b*** them out . . . . Num 5:23
and ***b*** out their name from . . . . Deut 9:14
the Lord shall ***b*** out his . . . . Deut 29:20
let not their sin be ***b*** out . . . . . . Neh 4:5
if any ***b*** hath cleaved to . . . . Job 31:7
Let them be ***b*** out of the . . . . . . Ps 69:28
let their name be ***b*** . . . . Ps 109:13
the sin of his mother be ***b*** . . . . . Ps 109:14
man getteth himself a ***b*** . . . . Prov 9:7
he that ***b*** out thy . . . . Is 43:25
b out, as a thick cloud, thy . . . . Is 44:22
neither ***b*** out their sin from . . . Jer 18:23

BLOW—*to exhale forcefully*

[*also* BLEW, BLOWETH, BLOWING, BLOWN]
Thou didst ***b*** with thy wind . . . . Ex 15:10
a memorial of ***b*** of trumpets . . . Lev 23:24
a day of ***b*** the trumpets . . . . Num 29:1
the trumpets to ***b*** in his . . . . Num 31:6
priests shall ***b*** with the . . . . Josh 6:4
Lord, and ***b*** with the . . . . Josh 6:8

on, and *b* with the trumpets . . .Josh 6:9
on, and *b* with the trumpets . . .Josh 6:13
he *b* a trumpet in the . . . . .Judg 3:27
upon Gideon, and he *b* a . . . . .Judg 6:34
When I *b* with a trumpet . . . . .Judg 7:18
with me, then *b* ye the . . . . .Judg 7:18
they *b* the trumpets, and . . . . . .Judg 7:19
b the trumpet throughout 1Sam 13:3
So Joab *b* a trumpet, and 2Sam 2:28
And Joab *b* the trumpet 2Sam 18:16
and he *b* a trumpet 2Sam 20:1
and *b* ye with the trumpet 1Kin 1:34
And they *b* the trumpet 1Kin 1:39
of the stairs, and *b* with 2Kin 9:13
rejoiced, and *b* with 2Kin 11:14
did *b* with the trumpets 1Chr 15:24
a fire not *b* shall consume . . . . .Job 20:26
I am consumed by the *b* . . . . . .Ps 39:10
He caused an east wind to *b* . .Ps 78:26
B up the trumpet in the . . . . . . .Ps 81:3
he causeth his wind to *b* . . . . . .Ps 147:18
b upon my garden, that . . . . . . .Song 4:16
when he *b* a trumpet, hear . . . .Is 18:3
great trumpet shall be *b* . . . . . . .Is 27:13
the spirit of the Lord *b* . . . . . . .Is 40:7
he shall also *b* upon them . . . . .Is 40:24
the smith that *b* the coals . . . . .Is 54:16
B ye the trumpet in the . . . . . . .Jer 4:5
b the trumpet in Tekoa . . . . .Jer 6:1
with a very grievous *b* . . . . .Jer 14:17
b the trumpet among the . . . . . . .Jer 51:27
They have *b* the trumpet . . . . . .Ezek 7:14
I will *b* against thee in the . . . .Ezek 21:31
to *b* the fire upon it, to . . . . . . .Ezek 22:20
upon the land, he *b* the . . . . . . .Ezek 33:3
B ye the cornet in Gibeah . . . . .Hos 5:8
B ye the trumpet in . . . . .Joel 2:1
Shall a trumpet be *b* in the . . . .Amos 3:6
brought it home, I did *b* . . . . . .Hag 1:9
Lord God shall *b* the . . . . .Zech 9:14
winds *b*, and beat upon . . . . . . .Matt 7:25
ye see the south wind *b* . . . . . . .Luke 12:55
wind *b* where it listeth . . . . .John 3:8
reason of a great wind..*b* . . . . . .John 6:18
south wind *b* softly . . . . .Acts 27:13
one day the south wind *b* . . . . .Acts 28:13
wind should not *b* on the . . . . .Rev 7:1

BLUE—*color of the sky*
Often used in tabernacle. .Ex 25:4
Ex 28:15
Used by royalty . . . . .Esth 8:15
Imported . . . . .Ezek 27:7, 24

twined linen, and *b*, and . . . . . .Ex 26:1
hanging of twenty cubits, of *b*. .Ex 27:16
shall take gold, and *b* and . . . . .Ex 28:5
And *b*, and purple, and . . . . . . .Ex 35:6
twined linen, and *b*, and . . . . . .Ex 36:8
court was needlework, of *b* . . . .Ex 38:18
of the *b* and purple, and . . . . . .Ex 39:1
over it a cloth wholly of *b* . . . . .Num 4:6
borders a ribband of *b* . . . . .Num 15:38
in purple..crimson, and *b* 2Chr 2:7
he made the veil of *b*, and 2Chr 3:14
white, green, and *b* . . . . .Esth 1:6
b, and white, and black . . . . . . .Esth 1:6
b of a wound cleanseth . . . . . . .Prov 20:30
b and purple is their . . . . .Jer 10:9
were clothed with *b* . . . . .Ezek 23:6

BLUNT—*dull; not sharp*
If the iron be *b*, and he do . . . .Eccl 10:10

BLUSH—*to redden in the cheeks*
Sin makes impossible . . . .Jer 6:15
Jer 8:12
Sin causes saints to . . . . . .Ezra 9:6

BOANERGES (bō-ă-nûr'jēz)—*"sons of thunder"*
Surname of James and John . . . . .Mark 3:17

BOAR—*male wild hog*
Descriptive of Israel's enemies . . . . .Ps 80:13

BOARD—*long piece of sawn lumber used in construction*

[*also* BOARDS]
shalt make *b* for the . . . . .Ex 26:15
shall be the length of a *b* . . . . .Ex 26:16
half..the breadth of one *b* . . . . .Ex 26:16
with *b* shalt thou make it . . . . .Ex 27:8
his *b*, his bars..pillars . . . . .Ex 35:11
he made *b*..tabernacle . . . . .Ex 36:20
b was ten cubits . . . . .Ex 36:21
the altar, hollow with *b* . . . . . . .Ex 38:7
his taches, his *b*, his bars . . . . . .Ex 39:33
set up the *b* thereof . . . . .Ex 40:18
b of the tabernacle . . . . .Num 3:36
b of the tabernacle . . . . .Num 4:31
we will inclose her with *b* . . . . .Song 8:9
thy ship *b* of fir trees . . . . .Ezek 27:5
And the rest, some on *b* . . . . . .Acts 27:44

BOASTING—*to speak of with pride; to brag*
Excluded because of:
Man's limited knowledge .Prov 27:1, 2
Uncertain issues 1Kin 20:11
Evil incurred thereby . . . .Luke 12:19-21
James 3:5
Salvation by grace . . . . . . .Eph 2:9
God's sovereignty . . . . . . .Rom 11:17-21
Examples of:
Goliath 1Sam 17:44
Ben-hadad 1Kin 20:10
Rabshakeh 2Kin 18:27, 34
Satan . . . . .Is 14:12-15
Ezek 28:12-19
See **HAUGHTINESS; PRIDE**

[*also* BOAST, BOASTED, BOASTERS, BOASTEST, BOASTETH, BOASTING, BOASTINGS]
wicked *b* of his heart's . . . . .Ps 10:3
In God we *b* all the day . . . . . .Ps 44:8
trust in their wealth, and *b* . . . .Ps 49:6
Why *b* thou thyself in . . . . .Ps 52:1
workers of iniquity *b* . . . . .Ps 94:4
images, that *b* themselves . . . . .Ps 97:7
gone his way, then he *b* . . . . . . .Prov 20:4
Whoso *b* himself of a false . . . .Prov 25:14
their glory shall ye *b* . . . . .Is 61:6
with your mouth ye have *b* . . . .Ezek 35:13
Theudas *b* himself to be . . . . . .Acts 5:36
despiteful, proud, *b* . . . . .Rom 1:30
law, and makest thy *b* . . . . .Rom 2:17
Where is *b* then? It is . . . . .Rom 3:27
I have *b* any thing to him 2Cor 7:14
even so our *b*, which I 2Cor 7:14
love, and of our *b* on your 2Cor 8:24
for which I *b* of you to 2Cor 9:2
lest our *b* of you should be 2Cor 9:3
though I should *b* 2Cor 10:8
Not *b* of things without our . . .2Cor 10:15
covetous, *b*, proud 2Tim 3:2

BOASTING IN GOD—*giving the credit for accomplishments to the Lord*
Continual duty . . . . .Ps 34:2
Always in the Lord 2Cor 10:13-18
Necessary to refute the wayward 2Cor 11:5-33
Of spiritual rather than natural . . . . .Phil 3:3-14

BOAT—*a small vessel used for transportation over water*
In Christ's time . . . . .John 6:22, 23
In Paul's travel to Rome .Acts 27:16
Lifeboats . . . . .Acts 27:30
Ferryboats 2Sam 19:18

there went over a ferry *b* 2Sam 19:18
that there was none other *b* . . .John 6:22
his disciples into the *b* . . . . .John 6:22

BOAZ (bō'ăz)—*"fleetness; strength"*
1. A wealthy Beth-lehemite .Ruth 2:1, 4-18
Husband of Ruth . . . . . . .Ruth 4:10-13
Ancestor of Christ . . . . . .Matt 1:5
2. Pillar of Temple 1Kin 7:21

[*also* BOOZ]
behold *B* came from . . . . .Ruth 2:4
Then said *B* unto his . . . . .Ruth 2:5
Then said *B* unto Ruth . . . . . . .Ruth 2:8
B answered and said unto . . . . .Ruth 2:11
B said unto her, At . . . . .Ruth 2:14
B commanded his young . . . . . .Ruth 2:15
I wrought today is *B* . . . . .Ruth 2:19
she kept fast..maidens of *B* . . . .Ruth 2:23
is not *B* of our kindred . . . . . . .Ruth 3:2
Then went *B* up to the gate . . .Ruth 4:1
called the name thereof *B* 1Kin 7:21
Salma, and Salma begat *B* 1Chr 2:11
name of that on the left *B* 2Chr 3:17
And Salmon begat *B* of . . . . . . .Matt 1:5
and *B* begat Obed of Ruth . . . .Matt 1:5
which was the son of *B* . . . . . . .Luke 3:32

BOCHERU (bō'kĕ-rōō)—*"youth"*
A son of Azel 1Chr 8:38

BOCHIM (bō'kĭm)—*"weepers"*
A place near Gilgal . . . . . .Judg 2:1-5

BODY—*The material part of man; the main part of anything; the most common figure of speech used to indicate the church*

[*also* BODIES, BODILY, BODY'S]
lord, but our *b*, and our . . . . . .Gen 47:18
as it were the *b* of heaven . . . . .Ex 24:10
any dead *b*, nor defile . . . . .Lev 21:11
shall come at no dead *b* . . . . . . .Num 6:6
defiled by the dead *b* of a . . . . .Num 9:6
He that toucheth the dead *b* . . .Num 9:11
His *b* shall not remain all . . . . .Deut 21:23
Blessed..fruit of thy *b* . . . . .Deut 28:4
in the fruit of thy *b* . . . . .Deut 28:11
Cursed shall..fruit of thy *b* . . . .Deut 28:18
the fruit of thine own *b* . . . . . . .Deut 28:53
in the fruit of thy *b*, and . . . . . .Deut 30:9
threescore and ten sons..*b* . . . . .Judg 8:30
they fastened his *b* to the 1Sam 31:10
took the *b* of Saul and the 1Sam 31:12
he had restored a dead *b* 2Kin 8:5
took away the *b* of Saul..*b* 1Chr 10:12
they were dead *b* fallen to 2Chr 20:24
have dominion over our *b* . . . . .Neh 9:37
children's sake of mine..*b* . . . . .Job 19:17
drawn, and cometh out..*b* . . . . .Job 20:25
The dead *b* of thy servants . . . .Ps 79:2
the places with the dead *b* . . . .Ps 110:6
fruit of thy *b*, will I set . . . . . . .Ps 132:11
when thy flesh and thy *b* . . . . . .Prov 5:11
both soul and *b*: and they . . . . .Is 10:18
with my dead *b* shall they . . . . .Is 26:19
thou hast laid thy *b* as the . . . .Is 51:23
and cast his dead *b* into . . . . . . .Jer 26:23
whole valley of the dead *b* . . . .Jer 31:40
the dead *b* of men, whom I . . .Jer 33:5
and their dead *b* shall be . . . . . .Jer 34:20
and his dead *b* shall be cast . . .Jer 36:30
dead *b* of the men, whom . . . . .Jer 41:9
they were more ruddy in *b* . . . .Lam 4:7
another..covered their *b* . . . . . . .Ezek 1:11
And their whole *b*, and . . . . . . .Ezek 10:12
upon whose *b* the fire had . . . .Dan 3:27
his *b* was wet with the dew . . . .Dan 4:33
his *b* was wet with the dew . . . .Dan 5:21
and his *b* destroyed, and . . . . . .Dan 7:11
His *b* also was like the . . . . .Dan 10:6
there shall be many dead *b* . . . .Amos 8:3
fruit of my *b* for the sin . . . . . . .Mic 6:7
unclean by a dead *b* touch . . . .Hag 2:13
not that thy whole *b* should . . .Matt 5:29
The light of the *b* is the eye . . .Matt 6:22
not them which kill the *b* . . . . .Matt 10:28
came, and took up the *b* . . . . . .Matt 14:12
Take, eat; this is my *b* . . . . .Matt 26:26
and many *b* of the saints . . . . . .Matt 27:52
begged the *b* of Jesus . . . . .Matt 27:58
Pilate commanded the *b* to . . . .Matt 27:58
felt in her *b* that she . . . . .Mark 5:29
aforehand to anoint my *b* . . . . .Mark 14:8
Pilate, and craved the *b* . . . . . . .Mark 15:43
Holy Ghost descended in a *b* . .Luke 3:22
light of the *b* is the eye . . . . . . .Luke 11:34
is single, thy whole *b* also . . . .Luke 11:34

evil, thy *b* also is full of....... Luke 11:34
afraid of them..kill the *b* ...... Luke 12:4
Wheresoever the *b* is .... Luke 17:37
This is my *b* which is given .... Luke 22:19
Pilate, and begged the *b* of.... Luke 23:52
and found not the *b* of the .... Luke 24:3
he spake..temple of his *b* ..... John 2:21
the *b* should not remain .... John 19:31
might take away the *b* .... John 19:38
therefore, and took the *b* ..... John 19:38
the feet, where the *b* of ...... John 20:12
and turning him to the *b* ...... Acts 9:40
So that from his *b* were .... Acts 19:12
considered not his own *b* ...... Rom 4:19
b of sin might be destroyed ... Rom 6:6
quicken your mortal *b* .... Rom 8:11
do mortify the deeds..*b* .... Rom 8:13
the redemption of our *b* ...... Rom 8:23
many members in one *b* ...... Rom 12:4
For I verily, as absent in *b* 1Cor 5:3
But I keep under my *b*, and ... 1Cor 9:27
the communion of the *b* 1Cor 10:16
Take, eat; this is my *b* 1Cor 11:24
discerning the Lord's *b* 1Cor 11:29
For as the *b* is one, and 1Cor 12:12
the members of that one *b* 1Cor 12:12
are one *b*; so also is Christ 1Cor 12:12
all baptized into one *b* 1Cor 12:13
the *b* is not one member 1Cor 12:14
I am not of the *b*; is it 1Cor 12:15
therefore not of the *b* 1Cor 12:15
I am not of the *b*; is it 1Cor 12:16
therefore not of the *b*? 1Cor 12:16
If the whole *b* were an eye 1Cor 12:17
every one of them in the *b* 1Cor 12:18
member, where were the *b*? ... 1Cor 12:19
members, yet but one *b* 1Cor 12:20
those members of the *b* 1Cor 12:22
those members of the *b* 1Cor 12:23
God hath tempered the *b* 1Cor 12:24
be no schism in the *b* 1Cor 12:25
now ye are the *b* of Christ 1Cor 12:27
though I give my *b* to be 1Cor 13:3
and with what *b* do they 1Cor 15:35
thou sowest not that *b* 1Cor 15:37
But God giveth it a *b* as it 1Cor 15:38
to every seed his own *b* 1Cor 15:38
also celestial *b*, and *b* 1Cor 15:40
It is sown a natural *b* 1Cor 15:44
It is raised a spiritual *b* 1Cor 15:44
There is a natural *b* 1Cor 15:44
and there is a spiritual *b* 1Cor 15:44
bearing about in the *b* the 2Cor 4:10
be made manifest in our *b* 2Cor 4:10
we are at home in the *b* 2Cor 5:6
but his *b* presence is weak 2Cor 10:10
or whether out of the *b* 2Cor 12:2
in the *b*, or out of the *b*, I 2Cor 12:3
I bear in my *b* the marks ..... Gal 6:17
heirs, and of the same *b* ...... Eph 3:6
There is one *b*, and one .... Eph 4:4
edifying of the *b* of Christ ..... Eph 4:12
is the savior of the *b* .... Eph 5:23
their wives as their own *b* ..... Eph 5:28
And he is the head of the *b* ... Col 1:18
fullness of the Godhead *b* ..... Col 2:9
putting off the *b* of the sins ... Col 2:11
also ye are called in one *b* .... Col 3:15
For *b* exercise profiteth 1Tim 4:8
and our *b* washed with .... Heb 10:22
yourselves also in the *b* .... Heb 13:3
For the *b* of those beasts ...... Heb 13:11
which are needful to the *b* .... James 2:16
also to bridle the whole *b* ..... James 3:2
that it defileth the whole *b* .... James 3:6
bare our sins in his own *b* 1Pet 2:24
he disputed about the *b* of .... Jude 9
And their dead *b* shall lie ..... Rev 11:8

BODY OF CHRIST—*the physical form of Christ; the church*

Descriptive of His own body:
Prepared by God .... Heb 10:5
Conceived by the Holy Spirit .... Luke 1:34, 35
Subject to growth .... Luke 2:40, 52; Heb 5:8, 9
Part of our nature .... Heb 2:14
Without sin 2Cor 5:21
Subject to human emotions .... Heb 5:7
Raised without corruption. Acts 2:31
Glorified by resurrection . Phil 3:21
Communion with 1Cor 11:27

Descriptive of the true church:
Identified .... Col 1:24
Described .... Eph 2:16
Christ, the head of ...... Eph 1:22
Christ dwells in .... Eph 1:23

BODY OF MAN—*the physical substance of a human being*

By creation:
Made by God .... Gen 2:7, 21
Various organs of 1Cor 12:12-25
Bears God's image ...... Gen 9:6; Col 3:10
Wonderfully made .... Ps 139:14

By sin:
Subject to death .... Rom 5:12
Destroyed .... Job 19:26
Instrument of evil .... Rom 1:24-32

By salvation:
A Temple of the Holy Spirit 1Cor 6:19
A living sacrifice .... Rom 12:1
Dead to the Law .... Rom 7:4
Dead to sin .... Rom 8:10
Control over .... Rom 6:12-23
Christ, the center of ..... Rom 6:8-11; Phil 1:20
Sins against, forbidden ... 1Cor 6:13, 18
Needful requirements of. . 1Cor 7:4; Col 2:23

By resurrection, to be:
Redeemed .... Rom 8:23
Raised .... John 5:28, 29
Changed .... Phil 3:21
Glorified .... Rom 8:29, 30
Judged 2Cor 5:10-14
Perfected 1Thess 5:23

Figurative descriptions of:
House 2Cor 5:1
House of clay .... Job 4:19
Earthen vessel 2Cor 4:7
Tabernacle 2Pet 1:13
Temple of God 1Cor 3:16, 17
Members of Christ 1Cor 6:15

BOHAN (bō'hăn)—*"stumpy"*
1. Reuben's son .... Josh 15:6
2. Border mark .... Josh 18:17

BOIL—*an inflamed ulcer*
Sixth Egyptian plague .... Ex 9:8-11
A symptom of leprosy ... Lev 13:18-20
Satan afflicts Job with ... Job 2:7
Hezekiah's life endangered by 2Kin 20:7

BOIL—*to generate bubbles of water by heating*
A part of cooking 1Kin 19:21
Of a child, in famine 2Kin 6:29
Figurative, of trouble .... Job 30:27

[*also* BOILING]
B the flesh at the door .... Lev 8:31
He maketh the deep to *b* ..... Job 41:31
causeth the waters to *b* .... Is 64:2
make it *b* well, and let .... Ezek 24:5
the priests shall *b* the .... Ezek 46:20
and it was made with *b* .... Ezek 46:23

BOISTEROUS—*agitated*
when he saw the wind *b* ...... Matt 14:30

BOLDNESS—*courage; bravery; confidence*

Comes from:
Righteousness .... Prov 28:1
Prayer .... Eph 6:19
Fearless preaching .... Acts 9:27-29
Christ .... Eph 3:12; Phil 1:20
Testimony .... Phil 1:14
Communion with God ... Heb 4:16
Perfect love 1John 4:17

Examples of:
Tribe of Levi .... Ex 32:26-28
David 1Sam 17:45-49
Three Hebrew men ...... Dan 3:8-18
Daniel .... Dan 6:10-23
The apostles .... Acts 4:13-31
Paul .... Acts 9:27-29
Paul, Barnabas .... Acts 13:46

See COURAGE; FEARLESSNESS

[*also* BOLD, BOLDLY]
came upon the city *b*, and ..... Gen 34:25
but the righteous are *b* .... Prov 28:1
the *b* of his face shall be ...... Eccl 8:1
and went in *b* unto Pilate ..... Mark 15:43
But, lo he speaketh *b* and ..... John 7:26
speaking *b* in the Lord .... Acts 14:3
to speak *b* in the synagogue ... Acts 18:26
spake *b* for the space of .... Acts 19:8
Isaiah is very *b*, and saith ..... Rom 10:20
I have written the more *b* ..... Rom 15:15
Great is my *b* of speech 2Cor 7:4
being absent am *b* toward 2Cor 10:1
whereinsoever any is *b* 2Cor 11:21
foolishly, I am *b* also 2Cor 11:21
we were *b* in our God unto ... 1Thess 2:2
great *b* in the faith which 1Tim 3:13
I might be..*b* in Christ .... Philem 8
Let us therefore come *b* .... Heb 4:16
b to enter into the holiest ..... Heb 10:19
So that we may *b* say, The .... Heb 13:6

BOLLED—*in bud; in seed*
Flax of Egypt .... Ex 9:31

BOLSTER—*a long pillow or cushion*
of goats' hair for his *b* 1Sam 19:13
of goats' hair for his *b* 1Sam 19:16
stuck in the ground..*b* 1Sam 26:7

BOLT—*to attach or fasten*
woman out from me, and *b* ... 2Sam 13:17

BOND—*a fetter; in slavery; agreement*

[*also* BONDS]
an oath to bind his soul..*b* .... Num 30:2
or of her *b* wherewith she ..... Num 30:5
He looseth the *b* of kings ..... Job 12:18
handmaid..loosed my *b* .... Ps 116:16
the yoke, and burst the *b* ..... Jer 5:5
Make thee *b* and yokes .... Jer 27:2
burst thy *b*, and strangers ..... Jer 30:8
I will bring you into the *b* ..... Ezek 20:37
and will burst thy *b* in .... Nah 1:13
be loosed from this *b* on ...... Luke 13:16
that *b* and afflictions .... Acts 20:23
charge worthy of death..*b* ..... Acts 23:29
a certain man left in *b* by ..... Acts 25:14
such..I am, except these *b* ..... Acts 26:29
of the Spirit in the *b* of .... Eph 4:3
Lord, whether he be *b* or ..... Eph 6:8
I am an ambassador in *b* .... Eph 6:20
as both in my *b* and in the .... Phil 1:7
Barbarian, Scythian, *b* nor .... Col 3:11
is the *b* of perfectness .... Col 3:14
for which I am also in *b* ...... Col 4:3
an evil doer, even unto *b* 2Tim 2:9
I have begotten in my *b* .... Philem 10
compassion of me in my *b* ...... Heb 10:34
of *b* and imprisonment .... Heb 11:36
Remember them that..*b* .... Heb 13:3
rich and poor, free and *b* ..... Rev 13:16
of all men, both free and *b* .... Rev 19:18

BONDAGE—*subjection to an oppressor*
Israel in Egypt .... Ex 1:7-22
Gibeonites to Israel ...... Josh 9:23
Israel in Assyria 2Kin 17:6, 20, 23
Judah in Babylon 2Kin 25:1-21
Denied by Jews .... John 8:33

sighed by reason of the *b* ..... Ex 2:23

up unto God by reason..*b* .....Ex 2:23
the Egyptians keep in *b* ....Ex 6:5
out of the house of *b*; for .....Ex 13:3
of Egypt, out..house of *b* .....Ex 20:2
Egypt, from the house of *b*....Deut 5:6
Egypt, from the house of *b*....Deut 6:12
Egypt, from the house of *b*....Deut 8:14
you out of the house of *b* .....Deut 13:5
and laid upon us hard *b*.......Deut 26:6
from the house of *b*, and......Josh 24:17
you forth..the house of *b*......Judg 6:8
a little reviving in our *b*.......Ezra 9:8
we bring into *b* our sons ......Neh 5:5
daughters are brought unto *b* . .Neh 5:5
captain to return to their *b* ....Neh 9:17
the hard *b* wherein thou ....Is 14:3
should bring them into *b* ......Acts 7:6
received the spirit of *b*........Rom 8:15
a sister is not under *b* in 1Cor 7:15
if a man bring you into *b* 2Cor 11:20
might bring us into *b* ....Gal 2:4
in *b* under the elements ....Gal 4:3
which gendereth to *b* ....Gal 4:24
again with the yoke of *b* ......Gal 5:1

BONDAGE, SPIRITUAL—*captivity to forces that are not from God*

Subjection to:
The devil 2Tim 2:26
Sin ....John 8:34
Fear of death ....Heb 2:14, 15
Death ....Rom 7:24
Corruption 2Pet 2:19

Deliverance from:
Promised ....Is 42:6, 7
Proclaimed ....Luke 4:18, 21
Through Christ ....John 8:36
By obedience ....Rom 6:17-19
By the truth ....John 8:32

BONDMAID—*female slave or bondservant*

[*also* BONDMAIDS, BONDWOMAN, BONDWOMEN]
Cast out this *b* and her ....Gen 21:10
the son of this *b* shall not .....Gen 21:10
is a *b*, betrothed to a ....Lev 19:20
thy bondmen, and thy *b* ....Lev 25:44
shall ye buy bondmen and *b* ...Lev 25:44
for bondmen, and *b*, and no ...Deut 28:68
for bondmen and *b* unto 2Chr 28:10
bondmen and *b*, I had held ....Esth 7:4
two sons, the one by a *b* ......Gal 4:22
he who was of the *b* was ......Gal 4:23

BONDMAN—*male slave or bondservant*

[*also* BONDMEN]
and take us for *b*, and our ....Gen 43:18
also will be my lord's *b* ....Gen 44:9
instead of the lad a *b* to my ...Gen 44:33
they shall not be sold as *b* ....Lev 25:42
ye should not be their *b*.......Lev 26:13
We were Pharaoh's *b* in.......Deut 6:21
you out of the house of *b* .....Deut 7:8
thou wast a *b* in the land .....Deut 15:15
thou wast a *b* in Egypt........Deut 16:12
thou wast a *b* in Egypt........Deut 24:18
sold unto your enemies for *b* . .Deut 28:68
none of you be freed..*b* ....Josh 9:23
did Solomon make no *b*.......1Kin 9:22
him my two sons to be *b* 2Kin 4:1
and Jerusalem for *b* 2Chr 28:10
For we were *b*; yet our God ...Ezra 9:9
if we had been sold for *b* .....Esth 7:4
Egypt, out of the house of *b* . .Jer 34:13
every *b*, and every free ....Rev 6:15

BONDSERVANT—*one bound to service without wages*

[*also* BONDSERVICE]
compel him to serve as a *b* ....Lev 25:39
Solomon levy a tribute of *b* ...1Kin 9:21

BONE—*part of a skeleton*

Descriptive of:
Unity of male and female.Gen 2:23
Human nature ....Luke 24:39
Family unity ....Gen 29:14
Tribal unity ....1 Chr 11:1

Prophecies concerning:
The paschal lamb's ......Ex 12:46
John 19:36
Jacob's ....Gen 50:25
Heb 11:22
Valley of dry...........Ezek 37:1-14

Figurative of health, affected by:
Shameful wife ....Prov 12:4
Good report ....Prov 15:30
Broken spirit............Prov 17:22

[*also* BONES]
took the *b* of Joseph with .....Ex 13:19
ye shall carry up my *b* away ...Ex 13:19
nor break any *b* of it ....Num 9:12
a dead body, or a *b* of........Num 19:16
break their *b*, and pierce ......Num 24:8
b of Joseph, which the ....Josh 24:32
that I am your *b* and your ....Judg 9:2
her, together with her *b*.......Judg 19:29
took their *b* and buried 1Sam 31:13
Behold, we are thy *b* and 2Sam 5:1
ye are my *b* and my flesh 2Sam 19:12
Art thou not of my *b*, and 2Sam 19:13
went and took the *b* 2Sam 21:12
and the *b* of Jonathan 2Sam 21:12
men's *b* shall be burnt 1Kin 13:2
and touched the *b* of 2Kin 13:21
their places with the *b* of......2Kin 23:14
buried their *b* under the 1Chr 10:12
b of the priests upon their.....2Chr 34:5
touch his *b* and his flesh ......Job 2:5
which made all my *b* to ....Job 4:14
fenced me with *b* and ....Job 10:11
My *b* cleaveth to my skin .....Job 19:20
His *b* are full of the sin ......Job 20:11
his *b* are moistened with ......Job 21:24
My *b* are pierced in me in ....Job 30:17
arm be broken from the *b*.....Job 31:22
of his *b* with strong pain ......Job 33:19
b are as strong pieces ....Job 40:18
his *b* are like bars of..........Job 40:18
enemies upon the cheek *b*.....Ps 3:7
heal me; for my *b* are ....Ps 6:2
all my *b* are out of joint ......Ps 22:14
and my *b* are consumed ....Ps 31:10
b waxed old through my ....Ps 32:3
He keepeth all his *b*: not ......Ps 34:20
All my *b* shall say, Lord ......Ps 35:10
is there any rest in my *b* ......Ps 38:3
with a sword in my *b* ....Ps 42:10
the *b* which thou hast ....Ps 51:8
God hath scattered the *b*......Ps 53:5
my *b* are burned as a ....Ps 102:3
water..like oil into his *b*......Ps 109:18
Our *b* are scattered at the .....Ps 141:7
navel..marrow to thy *b*........Prov 3:8
the rottenness of the *b*........Prov 14:30
soul and health to the *b*.......Prov 16:24
tongue breaketh the *b* ....Prov 25:15
how the *b* do grow in the .....Eccl 11:5
so will he break all my *b*.......Is 38:13
drought..make fat thy *b* ....Is 58:11
and your *b* shall flourish ....Is 66:14
the *b* of the kings of Judah ....Jer 8:1
and the *b* of his princes ....Jer 8:1
and the *b* of the priests ....Jer 8:1
and the *b* of the prophets .....Jer 8:1
b of the inhabitants ....Jer 8:1
burning fire shut..my *b*........Jer 20:9
all my *b* shake: I am like .....Jer 23:9
king of Babylon hath..*b* ....Jer 50:17
he sent fire into my *b* ....Lam 1:13
old; he hath broken my *b* .....Lam 3:4
skin cleaveth to their *b*........Lam 4:8
scatter your *b* round about ....Ezek 6:5
fill it with the choice *b* ....Ezek 24:4
shall be upon their *b*..........Ezek 32:27
valley which was full of *b* .....Ezek 37:1
Son of man..these *b* live? .....Ezek 37:3
upon these *b*, and say unto ....Ezek 37:4
O ye dry *b*, hear the word ....Ezek 37:4
Lord God unto these *b* ....Ezek 37:5
b came together, *b* to his *b* ....Ezek 37:7
b are the whole house ....Ezek 37:11
Our *b* are dried, and our......Ezek 37:11
when any seeth a man's *b* .....Ezek 39:15
and brake all their *b* in ....Dan 6:24
he burned the *b* of the king ...Amos 2:1
to bring out the *b* out of ......Amos 6:10
flesh from off their *b* ....Mic 3:2
rottenness..into my *b*, and.....Hab 3:16
gnaw not the *b* till the ....Zeph 3:3
full of dead men's *b*, and .....Matt 23:27
feet and ankle *b* received .....Acts 3:7

BONNET—*a headdress*
Used by priests..........Ex 28:40
Worn by women ....Is 3:20
Used by sons of Zadok ..Ezek 44:18

[*also* BONNETS]
and *b* shalt thou make for.....Ex 28:40
put the *b* on them; and the....Ex 29:9
goodly *b* of fine linen, and ....Ex 39:28
put *b* upon them; as the ......Lev 8:13

BOOK—*a set of written sheets of skin, paper, or tablets*

Features of:
Old ....Job 19:23, 24
Made of paper reeds.....Is 19:7
Made of parchment......2Tim 4:13
Made in a roll ....Jer 36:2
Written with ink.........3John 13
Dedicated..............Luke 1:3
Sealed ....Rev 5:1
Many...................Eccl 12:12
Quotations in ....Matt 21:4, 5
Written by secretary .....Jer 36:4, 18

Contents of:
Genealogies ....Gen 5:1
Law of Moses ....Deut 31:9, 24, 26
Geography ....Josh 18:9
Wars ....Num 21:14
Records ....Ezra 4:15
Miracles ....Josh 10:13
Legislation 1Sam 10:25
Lamentations 2Chr 35:25
Proverbs ....Prov 25:1
Prophecies ....Jer 51:60-64
Symbols ....Rev 1:1
The Messiah ....Luke 24:27, 44
Heb 10:7

Mentioned but not preserved:
Book of wars ....Num 21:14
Book of Jasher ....Josh 10:13
Chronicles of David 1Chr 27:24
Book of Gad............1Chr 29:29
Story of prophet Iddo....2Chr 13:22
Book of Nathan 1Chr 29:29
Book of Jehu 2Chr 20:34

[*also* BOOKS]
this for a memorial in a *b* .....Ex 17:14
the *b* of the covenant, and ....Ex 24:7
I pray thee, out of thy *b* ......Ex 32:32
write these curses in a *b* ......Num 5:23
curses..written in this *b* ....Deut 29:20
which are written in this *b* ....Deut 30:10
cities..seven parts in a *b* ......Josh 18:9
that is written in the *b* ....Josh 23:6
wrote these words in the *b* ....Josh 24:26
they not written in the *b* 1Kin 11:41
b of the chronicles of 2Kin 1:18
they not written in the *b* 2Kin 24:5
I were written in the *b* of 1Chr 9:1
in the *b* of Nathan the 2Chr 9:29
in the *b* of Shemaiah the 2Chr 12:15
are written in the *b* of the......2Chr 16:11
had the *b* of the law of the 2Chr 17:9
in the story of the *b* of the 2Chr 24:27
in the law in the *b* of Moses...2Chr 25:4
they are written in the *b* of....2Chr 27:7
in the *b* of the kings of 2Chr 28:26
in the *b* of the kings of 2Chr 32:32
written in the *b* of the 2Chr 33:18
Hilkiah the priest found a *b* ...2Chr 34:14

as it is written in the *b* 2Chr 35:12
they are written in the *b* of. . . .2Chr 36:8
as it is written in the *b* of . . . . .Ezra 6:18
bring the *b* of the law of . . . . . .Neh 8:1
read in the *b* of the law of . . . .Neh 9:3
written in the *b* of the . . . . .Neh 12:23
they read in the *b* of Moses . . .Neh 13:1
written in the *b* of the . . . . .Esth 2:23
commanded to bring the *b* . . . .Esth 6:1
Purim; and it was written..*b* . . .Esth 9:32
in the *b* of chronicles . . . . .Esth 10:2
adversary had written a *b* . . . . .Job 31:35
in the volume of the *b* it is . . . .Ps 40:7
are they not in thy *b*? . . . . .Ps 56:8
Let them be blotted out..*b* . . . .Ps 69:28
in thy *b* all my members . . . . . .Ps 139:16
making many *b* there is no . . . .Eccl 12:12
the words of a *b* that is . . . . . . .Is 29:11
and note it in a *b* that it . . . . . .Is 30:8
Seek ye out of the *b* of the . . . .Is 34:16
all that is written in this *b* . . . . .Jer 25:13
I have spoken.. in a *b* . . . . .Jer 30:2
subscribed the *b* of the . . . . .Jer 32:12
Take thee a roll of a *b* . . . . .Jer 36:2
reading in the *b* the words . . . .Jer 36:8
Then read Baruch in the *b* . . . .Jer 36:10
out of the *b* all the words . . . . .Jer 36:11
Baruch read the *b* in the . . . . .Jer 36:13
all the words of the *b* which . . .Jer 36:32
written these words in a *b* . . . . .Jer 45:1
and, lo, a roll of a *b* was . . . . . .Ezek 2:9
Daniel understood by *b* . . . . . .Dan 9:2
be found written in the *b* . . . . .Dan 12:1
The *b* of the vision of. . . . . .Nah 1:1
The *b* of the generation of . . . .Matt 1:1
have ye not read in the *b* . . . . .Mark 12:26
As it is written in the *b* of . . . .Luke 3:4
delivered unto him the *b* . . . . . .Luke 4:17
David himself saith..*b* . . . . .Luke 20:42
which are not written..*b* . . . . . . .John 20:30
could not contain the *b* . . . . . . .John 21:25
For it is written in the *b* . . . . . .Acts 1:20
as it is written in the *b* . . . . .Acts 7:42
brought their *b* together . . . . . . .Acts 19:19
things which are written..*b* . . . .Gal 3:10
sprinkled both the *b*, and . . . . .Heb 9:19
thou seest, write in a *b* . . . . . . .Rev 1:11
blot out his name out..*b* . . . . . .Rev 3:5
on the throne a *b* written . . . . .Rev 5:1
Who is worthy to open..*b* . . . . .Rev 5:2
was able to open the *b* . . . . .Rev 5:3
to open and to read the *b* . . . . .Rev 5:4
prevailed to open the *b* . . . . . . .Rev 5:5
he came and took the *b* out . . .Rev 5:7
when he had taken the *b* . . . . . .Rev 5:8
art worthy to take the *b* . . . . . . .Rev 5:9
had in his hand a little *b* . . . . . .Rev 10:2
written in the Lamb's *b* of . . . .Rev 21:27
of the prophecy of this *b* . . . . .Rev 22:7
keep the sayings of this *b* . . . . .Rev 22:9
of the prophecy of this *b* . . . . . .Rev 22:10
of the prophecy of this *b* . . . . . .Rev 22:18
that are written in this *b* . . . . . .Rev 22:18
from the words of the *b* . . . . .Rev 22:19
away his part out of the *b* . . . . .Rev 22:19
which are written in this *b* . . . .Rev 22:19

BOOK OF GOD'S JUDGMENT
In visions of Daniel and John . . . . {Dan. 7:10; Rev. 20:12}

BOOK OF THE LAW
Called "the law of Moses" . . . . .Josh 8:31, 32
Copied .Deut 17:18
Placed in the ark . . . . .Deut 31:26
Foundation of Israel's religion . . . . .Deut 28:58
Lost and found 2Kin 22:8
Produces reformation 2Kin 23:2-14
Produces revival . . . . .Neh 8:2, 8-18
Quoted 2Kin 14:6
To be remembered . . . . . .Josh 1:7, 8
Mal 4:4
Prophetic of Christ . . . . . .Luke 24:27, 44

BOOK OF LIFE—*a figurative expression for God's special care for His people*
Contains:
The names of the saved . .Phil 4:3
The deed of the righteous.Mal 3:16-18
Excludes:
Renegades . . . . .Ex 32:33
Ps 69:28
Apostates . . . . .Rev 13:8
Rev 17:8
Affords, basis of:
Joy . . . . .Luke 10:20
Hope . . . . .Heb 12:23
Judgment . . . . .Dan 7:10
Rev 20:12-15

BOOTH—*stall made of branches*
Used for cattle . . . . .Gen 33:17
Required in feast of tabernacle . . . . {Lev 23:40-43; Neh 8:14-17}

[*also* BOOTHS]
and as a *b* that the keeper . . . .Job 27:18
and there made him a *b* . . . . . . .Jon 4:5

BOOTY—*spoils taken in war*
Stipulations concerning:
No Canaanites . . . . .Deut 20:14-17
No cursed thing . . . . .Josh 6:17-19
Destruction of Amalek . . .1Sam 15:2, 3
Destruction of Arad . . . . .Num 21:1-3
The Lord's judgment . . . .Jer 49:30-32
Division of:
On percentage basis . . . . .Num 31:26-47
Rear troops share in 1Sam 30:24, 25

[*also* BOOTIES]
the *b* being the rest of the . . . .Num 31:32
thou shalt be for *b* unto . . . . . .Hab 2:7
goods shall become a *b* . . . . . . .Zeph 1:13

BOOZ—*See* BOAZ

BORDER—*boundary; ornamental design at edge of a fabric or rug*
Marked by:
Natural landmarks . . . . . . .Josh 18:16
Rivers . . . . .Josh 18:19
Markers . . . . .Deut 19:14
Enlargement of:
By God's power . . . . .Ex 34:24
A blessing 1Chr 4:10

[*also* BORDERS]
the *b* of the Canaanites was . . .Gen 10:19
in all the *b* round about . . . . . . .Gen 23:17
from one end of the *b* of . . . . .Gen 47:21
and his *b* shall be unto . . . . .Gen 49:13
I will smite all thy *b* with . . . . .Ex 8:2
unto the *b* of the land of . . . . . .Ex 16:35
or touch the *b* of it . . . . .Ex 19:12
make unto it a *b* of a . . . . .Ex 25:25
a golden crown to the *b* . . . . . . .Ex 25:25
breastplate in the *b* thereof . . . .Ex 28:26
made thereunto a *b* of an . . . . .Ex 37:12
a crown of gold for the *b* . . . . .Ex 37:12
b of it, which was on the . . . . . .Ex 39:19
in the *b* of their garments . . . . .Num 15:38
fringe of the *b* a ribband . . . . . .Num 15:38
city..uttermost of thy *b* . . . . .Num 20:16
until we have passed thy *b* . . . .Num 20:17
for Arnon is the *b* of Moab . . .Num 21:13
until we be past thy *b* . . . . .Num 21:22
which is in the *b* of Arnon . . . .Num 22:36
in Ije-abarim, in the *b* of . . . . . .Num 33:44
and your south *b* shall be . . . . .Num 34:3
the *b* of the city of his . . . . .Num 35:26
without the *b* of the city . . . . . .Num 35:27
the *b* even unto the river . . . . . .Deut 3:16
the *b* of the children of . . . . . . .Deut 3:16
God shall enlarge thy *b* . . . . . . .Deut 12:20
in the east *b* of Jericho . . . . . . .Josh 4:19
and in the *b* of Dor on the . . . .Josh 11:2
is the *b* of the children of . . . . .Josh 12:2
all the *b* of the Philistines . . . . .Josh 13:2
the *b* of the children of . . . . .Josh 13:10
b of Edom the wilderness . . . . .Josh 15:1
unto the *b* of Archi to . . . . .Josh 16:2
b..children of Ephraim . . . . .Josh 16:5
the *b* of their inheritance . . . . . .Josh 16:5
b went along on the right . . . . .Josh 17:7
And their *b* on the north . . . . . .Josh 18:12
b went up to the side of . . . . . .Josh 18:12
the *b* of their inheritance . . . . . .Josh 19:10
came unto the *b* of Jordan . . . .Josh 22:10
Lord hath made Jordan a *b* . . .Josh 22:25
in the *b* of his inheritance . . . . .Josh 24:30
in the *b* of his inheritance . . . . .Judg 2:9
to the *b* of Abel-meholah . . . . .Judg 7:22
within the *b* of Moab . . . . .Judg 11:18
unto the *b* of Beth-shemesh . . .1Sam 6:12
b of Benjamin at 1Sam 10:2
way of the *b* that looketh 1Sam 13:18
recover his *b* at the river 2Sam 8:3
and unto the *b* of Egypt 1Kin 4:21
they had *b*, and 1Kin 7:28
the *b* were between the 1Kin 7:28
upward..stood in the *b* 2Kin 3:21
Ahaz cut off the *b* of the 2Kin 16:17
the *b* thereof, from the 2Kin 18:8
into the lodgings of his *b* 2Kin 19:23
of Sharon, upon their *b* 1Chr 5:16
b..children of Manasseh 1Chr 7:29
Philistines, and to the *b* 2Chr 9:26
hast set all the *b* of the . . . . . . .Ps 74:17
he brought them to the *b* . . . . .Ps 78:54
maketh peace in thy *b*, and . . .Ps 147:14
will establish the *b* of . . . . .Prov 15:25
b of gold with studs of . . . . .Song 1:11
round about..*b* of Moab . . . . . .Is 15:8
b thereof to the Lord . . . . .Is 19:19
into the height of his *b* . . . . .Is 37:24
and all thy *b* of pleasant . . . . . .Is 54:12
destruction within thy *b* . . . . . . .Is 60:18
thy sins, even in all thy *b* . . . . .Jer 15:13
sin, throughout all thy *b* . . . . . .Jer 17:3
come again to their own *b* . . . .Jer 31:17
will judge you in the *b* of . . . . .Ezek 11:10
Thy *b* are in the midst of . . . . .Ezek 27:4
unto the *b* of Ethiopia . . . . .Ezek 29:10
and the *b* thereof by the . . . . . .Ezek 43:13
holy in all the *b* thereof . . . . . . .Ezek 45:1
the west *b* unto the east *b* . . . . .Ezek 45:7
This shall be the *b* . . . . .Ezek 47:13
b of Damascus northward . . . . .Ezek 48:1
them far from their *b* . . . . .Joel 3:6
might enlarge their *b* . . . . .Amos 1:13
b greater than your *b*? . . . . .Amos 6:2
brought thee even to the *b* . . . .Obad 7
he treadeth within our *b* . . . . . .Mic 5:6
themselves against their *b* . . . . .Zeph 2:8
Hamath also shall *b* . . . . .Zech 9:2
the *b* of wickedness, and . . . . . .Mal 1:4
the *b* of Zebulun and . . . . .Matt 4:13
enlarge the *b* of their . . . . .Matt 23:5
but the *b* of his garment . . . . . .Mark 6:56
into the *b* of Tyre and . . . . .Mark 7:24
touched the *b*..garment . . . . . . .Luke 8:44

BORE—*to pierce*

[*also* BORED]
master shall *b* his ear . . . . .Ex 21:6
and *b* a hole in the lid of 2Kin 12:9
b his jaw through with a . . . . . .Job 41:2

BORN—*to have come into existence through birth*
And unto Enoch was *b* . . . . . . .Gen 4:18
and daughters were *b* unto . . . .Gen 6:1
them were sons *b* after . . . . .Gen 10:1
b in his own house, three . . . . .Gen 14:14
one *b* in my house is mine . . . .Gen 15:3
he that is *b* in the house . . . . . .Gen 17:12
his son that was *b* unto him . . .Gen 21:3
she hath also *b* children . . . . . . .Gen 22:20
was *b* to Bethuel, son of . . . . . .Gen 24:15
because I have *b* him three . . . .Gen 29:34
I have *b* him six sons; and . . . .Gen 30:20
children which they..*b*? . . . . . . .Gen 31:43
were *b* to him in Padan . . . . . . .Gen 35:26
b unto him..land of Canaan . . .Gen 36:5
And unto Joseph were *b* . . . . . .Gen 41:50

land of Egypt..*b* Manasseh ....Gen 46:20
Manasseh, which were *b* ......Gen 48:5
Every son that is *b* ye shall....Ex 1:22
be a stranger, or *b* in the .....Ex 12:19
b him sons or daughters ....Ex 21:4
and *b* a man child, then.......Lev 12:2
whether she be *b* at home .....Lev 18:9
or *b* abroad ....Lev 18:9
unto you as one *b* among .....Lev 19:34
and he that is *b* in his ....Lev 22:11
all that are Israelites *b* ....Lev 23:42
as he that is *b* in the land .....Lev 24:16
him that was *b* in the land ....Num 9:14
that are *b* of the country ......Num 15:13
unto Aaron was *b* Nadab .....Num 26:60
they have *b* him children .....Deut 21:15
the people that were *b* in .....Josh 5:5
as he that was *b* among ....Josh 8:33
do..child that shall be *b* ....Judg 13:8
father, who was *b* unto ....Judg 18:29
than seven sons, hath *b* ....Ruth 4:15
so that the barren hath *b*......1Sam 2:5
Fear not, for thou hast *b* a 1Sam 4:20
David..sons *b* in Hebron 2Sam 3:2
sons and daughters *b* to 2Sam 5:13
the child also that is *b* 2Sam 12:14
Absalom there were *b* 2Sam 14:27
and he also was *b* 2Sam 21:20
be *b* unto the house of........1Kin 13:2
And unto Eber were *b* two....1Chr 1:19
which three were *b* unto 1Chr 2:3
were *b* unto him in Hebron ...1Chr 3:1
of Gath that were *b* in that....1Chr 7:21
b unto the giant in Gath 1Chr 20:8
a son shall be *b* to thee 1Chr 22:9
Shemaiah his son..sons *b* 1Chr 26:6
such as are *b* of them ....Ezra 10:3
there were *b* unto him ....Job 1:2
day perish wherein I was *b* ....Job 3:3
man is *b* unto trouble, as .....Job 5:7
man be *b* like a wild ass's .....Job 11:12
Man that is *b* of a woman.....Job 14:1
Art thou the first man..*b*? .....Job 15:7
he which is *b* of a woman .....Job 15:14
he be clean that is *b* of a .....Job 25:4
because thou wast then *b*? ....Job 38:21
a people that shall be *b* ....Ps 22:31
go astray..as they be *b* ....Ps 58:3
children..should be *b* ....Ps 78:6
Ethiopia; this man was *b* ......Ps 87:4
brother is *b* for adversity ......Prov 17:17
and had servants *b* in my .....Eccl 2:7
A time to be *b*, and a time....Eccl 3:2
is *b*..kingdom becometh ....Eccl 4:14
unto us a child is *b*, unto .....Is 9:6
shall a nation be *b* at ....Is 66:8
daughters that are *b* in........Jer 13:8
the day wherein I was *b*........Jer 20:14
country, where..not *b* ....Jer 22:26
in the day thou wast *b* thy ....Ezek 16:4
shall be unto you as *b* in ....Ezek 47:22
her as..that she was *b* ....Hos 2:3
of whom was *b* Jesus, who ....Matt 1:16
Jesus was *b* in Bethlehem .....Matt 2:1
Among them that are *b* of .....Matt 11:11
so *b* from their mother's ......Matt 19:12
man if he had not been *b* .....Matt 26:24
man if he had never..*b*........Mark 14:21
holy thing which shall..*b* ......Luke 1:35
For unto you is *b* this day.....Luke 2:11
Among those that are *b* of ....Luke 7:28
Which were *b*, not of blood ...John 1:13
can a man be *b* when he is ....John 3:4
mother's womb, and be *b*? ....John 3:4
unto thee, Ye must be *b* ....John 3:7
We be not *b* of fornication ....John 8:41
his parents, that he was *b* .....John 9:2
joy that a man is *b* into the ...John 16:21
To this end was I *b*, and ......John 18:37
tongue, wherein we..*b*? ....Acts 2:8
In which time Moses was *b*....Acts 7:20
Aquila, *b* in Pontus, lately .....Acts 18:2
am a Jew, *b* in Tarsus ....Acts 22:3
children being not yet *b* ....Rom 9:11
also, as of one *b* out of 1Cor 15:8
bondwoman was *b* after the ...Gal 4:23
By faith Moses, when..*b* ......Heb 11:23
child as soon as it was *b* ......Rev 12:4

BORN AGAIN—*new birth, regeneration; one who has become a Christian*

Necessity of, because of:
Inability ....John 3:3, 5
The flesh ....John 3:6
Deadness ....Eph 2:1

Produced by:
The Holy Spirit ....John 3:5, 8; Titus 3:5
The Word of God ....James 1:18; 1Pet 1:23
Faith 1John 5:1

Results of:
New creature 2Cor 5:17
Changed life ....Rom 6:4-11
Holy life................1John 3:9
Righteousness 1John 2:29
Love 1John 3:10
Victory 1John 5:4

BORROW—*to receive with the intention of returning*

Regulations regarding:
From other nations, forbidden ....Deut 15:6; Deut 28:12
Obligation to repay ......Ex 22:14, 15
Non-payment, wicked ....Ps 37:21
Involves servitude ....Prov 22:7
Evils of, corrected ....Neh 5:1-13
Christ's words on ....Matt 5:42

Examples of:
Jewels ....Ex 11:2
A widow's vessels 2Kin 4:3
A woodsman's axe 2Kin 6:5
Christ's transportation ...Matt 21:2, 3

[*also* BORROWED, BORROWER, BORROWETH]
they *b* of the Egyptians ....Ex 12:35
so with the *b*; as with the .....Is 24:2
from him that would *b* of .....Matt 5:42

BOSCATH—*See* BOZCATH

BOSOM—*breast as center of affections*

Expressive of:
Procreation ....Gen 16:5
Prostitution ....Prov 6:26, 27
Anger ....Eccl 7:9
Procrastination ....Prov 19:24
Protection ....Is 40:11
Iniquity.................Job 31:33

Symbolic of:
Man's impatience ....Ps 74:11
Christ's deity ....John 1:18
Eternal peace ....Luke 16:22, 23

Put now thine hand into thy *b*..Ex 4:6
he put his hand into his *b* ......Ex 4:6
Carry them in thy *b*, as a .....Num 11:12
or the wife of thy *b*, or thy....Deut 13:6
toward the wife of his *b*.......Deut 28:54
let her lie in thy *b*, that 1Kin 1:2
and laid it in her *b*, and.......1Kin 3:20
he took him out of her *b*......1Kin 17:19
returned into mine own *b* .....Ps 35:13
sevenfold into their *b* their ....Ps 79:12
I do bear in my *b* the ....Ps 89:50
that bindeth sheaves his *b* .....Ps 129:7
and embrace the *b* of a ....Prov 5:20
taketh a gift out of the *b*......Prov 17:23
a reward in the *b* strong ......Prov 21:14
hideth his hand in his *b* ....Prov 26:15
recompense..into their *b* ......Is 65:6
former work into their *b* ....Is 65:7
the *b* of their children ....Jer 32:18
out into their mother's *b* ......Lam 2:12
her that lieth in thy *b* ....Mic 7:5
shall men give into your *b*.....Luke 6:38
leaning on Jesus' *b* one of.....John 13:23

BOSOR (bō'sôr)—*"a lamp"*
Father of Balaam........2Pet 2:15
Same as Beor ....Num 22:5

BOSSES—*knobs that made a shield a strong weapon*
upon the thick *b* of his........Job 15:26

BOTCH—*a boil*
A punishment of disobedience ....Deut 28:27

BOTH—*See* INTRODUCTION

BOTTLE—*a vessel for carrying liquids*

Used for:
Milk....................Judg 4:19
Water ....Gen 21:14
Wine ....Hab 2:15

Made of:
Clay....................Jer 19:1, 10, 11
Skins ....Matt 9:17; Mark 2:22

Figurative of:
God's remembrance .....Ps 56:8
God's judgments ....Jer 13:12-14
Sorrow ....Ps 119:83
Impatience ....Job 32:19
Clouds of rain............Job 38:37
Old and new covenants ..Matt 9:17

[*also* BOTTLES]
and wine *b*, old, and rent .....Josh 9:4
one ephah of flour, and a *b* ...1Sam 1:24
another carrying a *b* of........1Sam 10:3
and a *b* of wine, and a kid 1Sam 16:20
two *b* of wine, and five 1Sam 25:18
summer fruits, and a *b* of 2Sam 16:1
vessels, and break their *b* .....Jer 48:12
have made him sick with *b* ....Hos 7:5
putteth new wine into old *b* ...Luke 5:37
new wine will burst the *b* .....Luke 5:37
and the *b* shall perish ....Luke 5:37

BOTTOM—*lowest part or place*

[*also* BOTTOMS]
they sank into the *b* as a ......Ex 15:5
blood beside the *b* of the .....Ex 29:12
blood of the bullock at the *b* ..Lev 4:7
shall be wrung out at the *b*....Lev 5:9
blood at the *b* of the altar.....Lev 8:15
out the blood at the *b* ....Lev 9:9
covereth the *b* of the sea.....Job 36:30
b thereof of gold, the ....Song 3:10
even the *b* shall be a cubit ....Ezek 43:13
or ever they came at the *b* ....Dan 6:24
in the *b* of the sea, thence ....Amos 9:3
I went down to the *b* of the ...Jon 2:6
trees that were in the *b* ....Zech 1:8
from the top to the *b*; and ....Matt 27:51
twain from the top to the *b* ...Mark 15:38

BOTTOMLESS PIT—*the literal translation of "Abyss"*
Apollyon, king of ....Rev 9:11
Beast comes from ....Rev 11:7; Rev 17:8
Devil, cast into..........Rev 20:1-3
A prison................Rev 20:7

I was given the key of the *b*...Rev 9:1

BOUGH—*branch of a tree*

Used:
To make ceremonial booths...............Lev 23:39-43
In siege of Shechem .....Judg 9:45-49

Figurative of:
Joseph's offspring ....Gen 49:22
Judgment ....Is 17:1-11
Israel...................Ps 80:8-11
Nebuchadnezzar's kingdom ....Dan 4:10-12

[*also* BOUGHS]
shalt not go over the *b*.......Deut 24:20
the thick *b* of a great oak 2Sam 18:9
will bud and bring forth *b* .....Job 14:9
I will take hold of the *b*.......Song 7:8
of hosts, shall lop the *b* ....Is 10:33
When the *b* thereof are ....Is 27:11

it shall bring forth *b*, and .....Ezek 17:23
top was among the thick *b* ....Ezek 31:3

BOUNDS—*boundaries; limits*
thou shalt set *b* unto the ......Ex 19:12
set thy *b* from the Red Sea....Ex 23:31
he set the *b* of the people .....Deut 32:8
hast appointed his *b* that ......Job 14:5
waters with *b*, until the ....Job 26:10
removed the *b* of the ....Is 10:13
the *b* of their habitation.......Acts 17:26

BOUNTIFUL—*liberal; abundant*

[*also* BOUNTIFULLY, BOUNTIFULNESS, BOUNTY]
gave her of his royal *b* 1Kin 10:13
he hath dealt *b* with me ....Ps 13:6
the Lord hath dealt *b* with ....Ps 116:7
Deal *b* with thy servant ....Ps 119:17
thou shalt deal *b* with me .....Ps 142:7
hath a *b* eye shall be ....Prov 22:9
nor the churl said to be *b* .....Is 32:5
your *b*, whereof ye had 2Cor 9:5
be ready, as a matter of *b*.....2Cor 9:5
soweth *b* shall reap also *b* 2Cor 9:6
thing to all *b*, which 2Cor 9:11

BOW—*an instrument for shooting arrows*

Uses of:
For hunting ....Gen 27:3
For war ....Is 7:24
As a token of friendship. .1Sam 18:4
As a commemorative song..................2Sam 1:18

Illustrative of:
Strength ....Job 29:20
The tongue ....Ps 11:2
Defeat..................Hos 1:5
Peace ....Hos 2:18, 19

[*also* BOWMEN, BOWS, BOWSHOT]
way off, as it were a *b* ....Gen 21:16
my sword and with my *b* ......Gen 48:22
thy sword, nor with thy *b* .....Josh 24:12
b of the mighty men are 1Sam 2:4
a *b* of steel is broken by 2Sam 22:35
certain man drew a *b* at a 1Kin 22:34
thy sword and with thy *b*......2Kin 6:22
drew a *b* with his full 2Kin 9:24
said unto him, Take *b* and 2Kin 13:15
shoot with *b*, and skillful 1Chr 5:18
They were armed with *b* 1Chr 12:2
arrows out of a *b*, even of 2Chr 12:2
bare shields and drew *b* 2Chr 14:8
armed men with *b* and 2Chr 17:17
certain man drew a *b* at a 2Chr 18:33
and habergeons, and *b* 2Chr 26:14
their spears, and their *b*.......Neh 4:13
b of steel shall strike him .....Job 20:24
bent his *b*, and made it ....Ps 7:12
a *b* of steel is broken by ......Ps 18:34
have bent their *b*, to cast .....Ps 37:14
and their *b* shall be broken....Ps 37:15
I will not trust in my *b*........Ps 44:6
he breaketh the *b* and ....Ps 46:9
bendeth his *b* to shoot his .....Ps 58:7
and bend their *b* to shoot .....Ps 64:3
the arrows of the *b*, the ....Ps 76:3
armed, and carrying *b* ....Ps 78:9
all their *b* bent, their ....Is 5:28
Their *b* also shall dash the ....Is 13:18
sword, and from the bent *b* ...Is 21:15
as driven stubble to his *b* .....Is 41:2
and Lud, that draw the *b* .....Is 66:19
of the horsemen and *b* ....Jer 4:29
lay hold on *b* and spear ....Jer 6:23
their tongues like their *b* ......Jer 9:3
that handle and bend the *b*....Jer 46:9
I will break the *b* of Elam ....Jer 49:35
all ye that bend the *b* ....Jer 50:14
bend his *b*, and against him ...Jer 51:3
every one of their *b* is ....Jer 51:56
hath bent his *b* like an ....Lam 2:4
He hath bent his *b*, and set ...Lam 3:12
As the appearance of the *b*....Ezek 1:28
smite thy *b* out of thy left .....Ezek 39:3
bucklers, the *b* and the ....Ezek 39:9
not save them by *b*, nor by....Hos 1:7
they are like a deceitful *b* .....Hos 7:16
stand that handleth the *b*......Amos 2:15
the battle *b* shall be cut ....Zech 9:10
out of him the battle *b*, out ...Zech 10:4
he that sat on him had a *b* ....Rev 6:2

BOW—*to bend the head, body, or knee in reverence, submission, or shame*

[*also* BOWED, BOWETH, BOWING]
and *b* himself toward the ......Gen 18:2
b himself with his face ....Gen 19:1
and *b* himself to the people ...Gen 23:7
b down himself before the.....Gen 23:12
the man *b* down his head .....Gen 24:26
worshipped the Lord, *b* ....Gen 24:52
and *b* himself to the ground ...Gen 33:3
come to *b* down ourselves .....Gen 37:10
cried before him, *B* the ....Gen 41:43
and *b* down themselves ....Gen 42:6
and *b* themselves to him to....Gen 43:26
Israel *b* himself upon the ......Gen 47:31
b himself with his face to .....Gen 48:12
children shall *b* down before...Gen 49:8
and *b* his shoulder to bear ....Gen 49:15
b their heads and ....Ex 4:31
and *b* down themselves ....Ex 11:8
b the head and worshiped .....Ex 12:27
Thou shalt not *b* down ....Ex 23:24
Moses made haste, and *b* .....Ex 34:8
in your land, to *b* down ....Lev 26:1
he *b* down his head, and ......Num 22:31
and *b* down to their gods .....Num 25:2
Thou shalt not *b* down ....Deut 5:9
nor *b* yourselves unto them....Josh 23:7
gods, and *b* yourselves to .....Josh 23:16
b themselves unto them ....Judg 2:12
and to *b* down unto them .....Judg 2:19
he *b*, he fell, he lay down .....Judg 5:27
at her feet he *b*, he fell ....Judg 5:27
where he *b*, there he fell ......Judg 5:27
every one that *b* down upon...Judg 7:5
people *b* down upon their .....Judg 7:6
he *b* himself with all his ....Judg 16:30
and *b* herself to the ground ...Ruth 2:10
she *b* herself and travailed 1Sam 4:19
and *b* himself three times 1Sam 20:41
face to the earth, and *b* 1Sam 24:8
and *b* herself to the ground ...1Sam 25:23
to the ground, and *b*..........1Sam 28:14
And he *b* himself, and said 2Sam 9:8
b himself and thanked the 2Sam 14:22
And Cushi *b* himself unto 2Sam 18:21
And he *b* the heart of all 2Sam 19:14
He *b* the heavens also, and....2Sam 22:10
b himself before the king......2Sam 24:20
Bath-sheba *b*..did obeisance ...1Kin 1:16
to meet her, and *b* himself 1Kin 2:19
which have not *b* unto Baal ...1Kin 19:18
b themselves to the ground 2Kin 2:15
and *b* herself to the ground ...2Kin 4:37
b myself in the house of 2Kin 5:18
other gods, nor *b* yourselves ...2Kin 17:35
Lord, *b* down thine ear and ...2Kin 19:16
b himself to David with his....1Chr 21:21
and *b* down their heads 1Chr 29:20
house, they *b* themselves 2Chr 7:3
Jehoshaphat *b* his head 2Chr 20:18
b down himself before 2Chr 25:14
present with him *b* 2Chr 29:29
b their heads, and ....Neh 8:6
b, and reverenced Haman .....Esth 3:2
Mordecai *b* not, nor did him ..Esth 3:2
and let others *b* down upon ....Job 31:10
They *b* themselves, they .....Job 39:3
have set their eyes *b* down ....Ps 17:11
He *b* the heavens also, and....Ps 18:9
go down to the dust shall *b* ...Ps 22:29
B down thine ear to me.......Ps 31:2
I *b* down heavily, as one ......Ps 35:14
b down greatly; I go ....Ps 38:6
our soul is *b* down to the .....Ps 44:25
my soul is *b* down; they.......Ps 57:6
as a *b* wall shall ye be, and ...Ps 62:3
wilderness shall *b* before ......Ps 72:9
all those that be *b* down ......Ps 145:14
raiseth them that are *b*........Ps 146:8
And the mean man *b* down ...Is 2:9
of men shall be *b* down ....Is 2:11
I was *b* down at..hearing of ...Is 21:3
unto me every knee shall *b*....Is 45:23
Bel *b* down, Nebo stoopeth ...Is 46:1
stoop, they *b* down together...Is 46:2
b down to thee with their .....Is 49:23
B down, that we may go over. .Is 51:23
b down his head as a ....Is 58:5
shall *b* themselves down at ....Is 60:14
all *b* down to the slaughter ....Is 65:12
b myself before the high ......Mic 6:6
the perpetual hills did *b*.......Hab 3:6
was *b* together, and could .....Luke 13:11
and *b* down their faces ....Luke 24:5
b his head, and gave up the ...John 19:30
have not *b* the knee to the ....Rom 11:4
and *b* down their back ....Rom 11:10
every knee shall *b* to me ......Rom 14:11

BOWELS—*intestines; seat of pity, tenderness, or courage*

Used literally of:
Intestines ....Num 5:22
Source of offspring ......Gen 15:4
Source of descendants ...Gen 25:23
Source of the Messiah ...2Sam 7:12
Amasa's—shed out 2Sam 20:10
Jehoram's—fell out 2Chr 21:14-19
Judas'—gushed out ......Acts 1:16-18

Used figuratively of:
Natural love ....Gen 43:30
Deep emotion...........Job 30:27
Intense suffering.........Ps 22:14
Great concern..........Jer 31:20
Spiritual distress ....Lam 1:20

be separated from thy *b*.......Gen 25:23
which came forth of my *b*......2Sam 16:11
her *b* yearned upon her son ...1Kin 3:26
came forth of his own *b*.......2Chr 32:21
his meat in his *b* is turned.....Job 20:14
out of my mother's *b* ....Ps 71:6
into his *b* like water, and .....Ps 109:18
and my *b* were moved for .....Song 5:4
my *b* shall sound like a ....Is 16:11
the offspring of thy *b* like .....Is 48:19
from the *b* of my mother.......Is 49:1
the sounding of thy *b* and of ..Is 63:15
My *b*, my *b* I am pained at....Jer 4:19
my *b* are troubled, my liver ...Lam 2:11
and fill thy *b* with this ....Ezek 3:3
souls, neither fill their *b* ......Ezek 7:19
straitened in your own *b* 2Cor 6:12
you all in the *b* of Jesus.......Phil 1:8
Spirit, if any *b* and mercies....Phil 2:1
b of mercies, kindness ....Col 3:12
the *b* of the saints are ....Philem 7
refresh my *b* in the Lord ......Philem 20

BOWING THE KNEE—*expression of reverence or submission*

Wrong:
Before idols............Ex 20:5
In mockery ....Matt 27:29
Before an angel ....Rev 22:8, 9

True, in:
Prayer 1Kin 8:54
Homage 2Kin 1:13
Repentance ....Ezra 9:5, 6
Worship ....Ps 95:6
Submission..............Eph 3:14
Phil 2:10

BOWL—*open vessel used for containing liquids*

[*also* BOWLS]
covers thereof, and *b* ....Ex 25:29
his spoons, and his *b*, and.....Ex 37:16
the spoons, and the *b*, and ....Num 4:7
one silver *b* of seventy ....Num 7:13
twelve silver *b*, twelve ....Num 7:84
fleece, a *b* full of water ....Judg 6:38

the two *b* of the chapiters 1Kin 7:41
house of the Lord *b* of........2Kin 12:13
firepans, and the *b*, and.......2Kin 25:15
the fleshhooks, and the *b* 1Chr 28:17
or the golden *b* be broken ....Eccl 12:6
the snuffers, and the *b* and ....Jer 52:18
That drink wine in *b*, and .....Amos 6:6
with a *b* upon the top of it ....Zech 4:2
upon the right side of the *b* ....Zech 4:3
they shall be filled like *b* ....Zech 9:15
shall be like *b* before the......Zech 14:20

BOWSHOT—*See* Bow

BOX—*a covered case*
Used for oil or perfume..2Kin 9:1
Matt 26:7

and the *b* together, to ....Is 60:13
having an alabaster *b* of.......Matt 26:7
having an alabaster *b* of.......Mark 14:3
brought an alabaster *b* of .....Luke 7:37

BOX TREE—*an evergreen tree*
Descriptive of Messianic times.................Is 41:19, 20

BOY—*male child*
Esau and Jacob ....Gen 25:27
Payment for a harlot.....Joel 3:3
Play in streets ....Zech 8:5
See Children; Young men

given a *b* for a harlot, and ....Joel 3:3

BOZEZ (bō'zĕz)—*"shining"*
Rock of Michmash 1Sam 14:4, 5

BOZKATH, BOSCATH (bŏz'kăth)—*"craggy"*
A town in south Judah...Josh 15:39
Home of Jedidah 2Kin 22:1

BOZRAH (bŏz'rä)—*"stronghold"*
1. City of Edom...........Gen 36:33
Destruction of, foretold. .Amos 1:12
Figurative, of Messiah's victory ....Is 63:1
2. City of Moab ....Jer 48:24
Jobab the son of Zerah of *B* ..1Chr 1:44
that *B* shall become a.........Jer 49:13
together as the sheep of *B* ....Mic 2:12

BRACELET—*ornamental band or chain worn around the wrist*
Worn by both sexes .....Ezek 16:11
Given to Rebekah ....Gen 24:22
In tabernacle offerings ...Ex 35:22
Worn by King Saul 2Sam 1:10
A sign of worldliness ....Is 3:19

[*also* bracelets]
Thy signet, and thy *b*, and ....Gen 38:18
jewels of gold, chains, and *b* ..Num 31:50
b upon their hands, and.......Ezek 23:42

BRAIDED HAIR
Contrasted to spiritual adornment 1Tim 2:9, 10

BRAKE—*See* Break

BRAMBLE—*a thorny bush*
Emblem of a tyrant......Judg 9:8-15
Used for fuel ....Ps 58:9
Symbol of destruction....Is 34:13

BRANCH—*a limb*
Used naturally of:
Limbs of tree ....Num 13:23
Used figuratively of:
A king ....Ezek 17:3-10
Israel...................Rom 11:16, 21
The Messiah ....Is 11:1
Christians..............John 15:5, 6
Prosperity..............Prov 11:28
Adversity ....Job 15:32

[*also* branches]
in the vine were three *b*.......Gen 40:10
a well; whose *b* run over ......Gen 49:22
his shaft, and his *b*, his ....Ex 25:31
in one *b*; and three bowls .....Ex 25:33
like almonds in the other *b*....Ex 25:33
his shaft, and his *b*, his ....Ex 37:17
six *b* going out of the sides ....Ex 37:18
b of palm trees, and the ......Lev 23:40
fetch olive *b*, and pine *b* ......Neh 8:15
and myrtle *b*, and palm *b* .....Neh 8:15
and *b* of thick trees...........Neh 8:15
b shooteth forth in his ....Job 8:16
tender *b* thereof will not ......Job 14:7
the flame shall dry up his *b* ...Job 15:30
above shall his *b* be cut off....Job 18:16
lay all night upon my *b* ....Job 29:19
unto the sea, and her *b* ....Ps 80:11
the *b* that thou madest ....Ps 80:15
which sing among the *b* ....Ps 104:12
day shall the *b* of the Lord ....Is 4:2
head and tail, *b* and rush .....Is 9:14
like an abominable *b*, and.....Is 14:19
her *b* are stretched out ....Is 16:8
in the outmost fruitful *b* ......Is 17:6
bough, and an uppermost *b* ...Is 17:9
and cut down the *b* ....Is 18:5
the head or tail, *b* or rush.....Is 19:15
the *b* of the terrible ones......Is 25:5
and consume the *b* thereof ....Is 27:10
the *b* of my planting, the......Is 60:21
and the *b* of it are broken.....Jer 11:16
unto David a righteous *B* .....Jer 23:5
time, will I cause the *B* ....Jer 33:15
and, lo, they put the *b* to .....Ezek 8:17
a *b* which is among the ....Ezek 15:2
whose *b* turned toward him ...Ezek 17:6
brought forth *b*, and shot .....Ezek 17:6
fruitful and full of *b* by ....Ezek 19:10
in Lebanon with fair *b* ....Ezek 31:3
ye shall shoot forth your *b* ....Ezek 36:8
cut off his *b*, shake off his ....Dan 4:14
and the fowls from his *b* ......Dan 4:14
out of a *b* of her roots shall ...Dan 11:7
consume his *b*, and devour ....Hos 11:6
b thereof are made white .....Joel 1:7
and marred their vine *b* ....Nah 2:2
my servant the *B* ....Zech 3:8
these two olive *b* which ....Zech 4:12
man whose name is The *B* ....Zech 6:12
leave..neither root nor *b* ......Mal 4:1
come and lodge in the *b* ......Matt 13:32
others cut down *b* from the ...Matt 21:8
When his *b* is yet tender ......Matt 24:32
shooteth out great *b*; so ....Mark 4:32
others cut down *b* off the .....Mark 11:8
When her *b* is yet tender......Mark 13:28
fowls..lodged in the *b* ....Luke 13:19
Took *b* of palm trees, and ....John 12:13
Every *b* in me that beareth ....John 15:2
every *b* that beareth fruit .....John 15:2
As the *b* cannot bear fruit.....John 15:4
if some of the *b* be broken ....Rom 11:17
Boast not against the *b* ....Rom 11:18

BRAND—*torch; charred piece of wood*

[*also* brands]
he had set the *b* on fire ....Judg 15:5
is not this a *b* plucked out ....Zech 3:2

BRANDISH—*to shake or wave menacingly*
I shall *b* my sword before .....Ezek 32:10

BRASEN—*See* Brazen

BRASS—*an alloy of copper and zinc (tin)*
Used for:
Tabernacle vessels ....Ex 38:2-31
Temple vessels 1Kin 7:41-46
Armor...................2Chr 12:10
Mirrors, etc. ....Ex 38:8
Is 45:2
Money ....Matt 10:9
Workers in:
Tubal-cain ....Gen 4:22
Hiram 1Kin 7:14
Alexander 2Tim 4:14
Figurative of:
Grecian Empire ....Dan 2:39
Obstinate sinners ....Is 48:4
Endurance ....Jer 15:20
God's decrees ....Zech 6:1
Christ's glory............Dan 10:6
Rev 1:15

gold, and silver, and *b* ....Ex 25:3
shalt make fifty taches of *b*....Ex 26:11
shalt overlay it with *b*.........Ex 27:2
also make a layer of *b* ....Ex 30:18
and his foot also of *b* ....Ex 30:18
and in silver, and in *b* ....Ex 31:4
gold, and silver, and *b* ....Ex 35:5
he made fifty taches of *b*......Ex 36:18
and his grate of *b* ....Ex 39:39
as iron, and your earth as *b* ...Lev 26:19
Moses made a serpent of *b* ....Num 21:9
beheld the serpent of *b* ....Num 21:9
gold, and the silver, the *b* .....Num 31:22
hills thou mayest dig *b* ....Deut 8:9
over thy head shall be *b* ......Deut 28:23
shoes shall be iron and *b*......Deut 33:25
vessels of *b* and iron are ......Josh 6:19
with gold, and with *b*, and ....Josh 22:8
bound him with fetters of *b* ...Judg 16:21
had an helmet of *b* upon 1Sam 17:5
five thousand shekels of *b*.....1Sam 17:5
took exceeding much *b*.........2Sam 8:8
three hundred shekels of *b* 2Sam 21:16
bound him with fetters of *b* ...2Kin 25:7
to sound with cymbals of *b*....1Chr 15:19
brought David very much *b* ...1Chr 18:8
b in abundance without 1Chr 22:3
the *b* for things of *b*, the 1Chr 29:2
the silver, and in *b*, and in 2Chr 2:7
made an altar of *b*, twenty 2Chr 4:1
as wrought iron and *b* 2Chr 24:12
stones? or is my flesh of *b*? ...Job 6:12
b is molten out of the stone ...Job 28:2
are as strong pieces of *b* ......Job 40:18
as straw and *b* as rotten.......Job 41:27
hath broken the gates of *b* ....Ps 107:16
For *b* I will bring gold, and ...Is 60:17
bring silver, and for wood *b* ...Is 60:17
they are *b* and iron; they......Jer 6:28
Also the pillars of *b* that ......Jer 52:17
and carried all the *b* of ....Jer 52:17
the color of burnished *b* ....Ezek 1:7
all they are *b*, and tin, and ....Ezek 22:18
that the *b* of it may be hot ....Ezek 24:11
of men and vessels of *b* ....Ezek 27:13
like the appearance of *b* ....Ezek 40:3
belly and his thighs of *b*.......Dan 2:32
a band of iron and *b*...........Dan 4:15
a band of iron and *b*...........Dan 4:23
gods of gold, and..of *b*........Dan 5:4
of iron, and his nails of *b* .....Dan 7:19
I will make thy hoofs *b*: and ..Mic 4:13
I am become as sounding *b* ...1Cor 13:1
his feet are like fine *b* ....Rev 2:18
idols of gold..and *b* ....Rev 9:20
and of *b*, and iron, and ....Rev 18:12

BRAVERY, MORAL
Condemning sin 2Sam 12:1-14
Denouncing hypocrisy....Matt 23:1-39
Opposing enemies ....Phil 1:28
Exposing inconsistency ...Gal 2:11-15
Uncovering false teachers.2Pet 2:1-22
Rebuking Christians 1Cor 6:1-8
James 4:1-11

BRAWLER—*fighter; wrangler*
Descriptive of certain women ....Prov 21:9
Disqualifies bishops 1Tim 3:3

[*also* brawlers, brawling]
with a *b* woman..in a wide ....Prov 25:24
evil of no man, to be no *b* ....Titus 3:2

BRAY—*loud, harsh cry of a donkey; to crush or grind fine*

[*also* brayed]
Doth the wild ass *b* when .....Job 6:5
Among the bushes they *b* .....Job 30:7
shouldest *b* a fool in a ....Prov 27:22

BRAZEN—*the color of polished brass*
make four ***b*** rings in the ......Ex 27:4
burnt offering with his ***b*** ......Ex 35:16
he made for the altar a ***b*** .....Ex 38:4
b altar, and his grate of ....Ex 39:39
sodden in a ***b*** pot, it shall .....Lev 6:28
priest took the ***b*** censers ......Num 16:39
cities with walls and ***b*** bars 1Kin 4:13
base had four ***b*** wheels........1Kin 7:30
b altar that was before the 1Kin 8:64
made in their stead ***b*** 1Kin 14:27
he brought also the ***b*** altar 2Kin 16:14
the ***b*** sea that was in the 2Kin 25:13
Solomon made the ***b***..........1Chr 18:8
Moreover the ***b*** altar, that.....2Chr 1:5
had made a ***b*** scaffold 2Chr 6:13
b altar which Solomon had 2Chr 7:7
an iron pillar, and ***b*** walls .....Jer 1:18
unto this people a fenced ***b***....Jer 15:20
the ***b*** sea that was in the ......Jer 52:17
stood beside the ***b*** altar ....Ezek 9:2
cups, and pots, ***b*** vessels ......Mark 7:4

BRAZEN SERPENT—*raised up by Moses as instrument of healing*
Occasion of ruin.........2Kin 18:4

BREACH—*a break; an infraction or violation of a law or obligation*

Used literally of:
Jerusalem's walls ....Neh 4:7

Used figuratively of:
Sin ....Is 30:13

[*also* BREACHES]
this ***b*** be upon thee ....Gen 38:29
B for ***b***, eye for eye, tooth ....Lev 24:20
ye shall know my ***b*** of ....Num 14:34
and abode in his ***b***............Judg 5:17
made a ***b*** in the tribes of......Judg 21:15
before me, as the ***b*** of 2Sam 5:20
Lord had made a ***b*** upon......2Sam 6:8
repaired the ***b*** of the city......1Kin 11:27
them repair the ***b*** of the 2Kin 12:5
wheresoever any ***b*** shall be 2Kin 12:5
Lord, to repair the ***b*** of the ...2Kin 22:5
Lord had made a ***b*** upon.....1Chr 13:11
our God made a ***b*** upon us....1Chr 15:13
the ***b*** began to be stopped.....Neh 4:7
there was no ***b*** left therein ....Neh 6:1
me with ***b*** upon ***b*** ....Job 16:14
heal the ***b*** thereof; for it ......Ps 60:2
stood before him in the ***b*** .....Ps 106:23
therein is a ***b*** in the spirit .....Prov 15:4
let us make a ***b*** therein for ....Is 7:6
b of the city of David, that....Is 22:9
a ***b*** ready to fall, swelling .....Is 30:13
bindeth up the ***b*** of his........Is 30:26
repairer of the ***b***, the ....Is 58:12
is broken with a great ***b***.......Jer 14:17
thy ***b*** is great like the sea .....Lam 2:13
city wherein is made a ***b*** ......Ezek 26:10
ye shall go out at the ***b*** ....Amos 4:3
smite the..house with ***b*** ....Amos 6:11
and close up the ***b*** thereof ....Amos 9:11

BREAD—*food; livelihood*

God's provision for:
A gift ....Ruth 1:6
2Cor 9:10
Earned by sweat ....Gen 3:19
Object of prayer ....Matt 6:11
Without work, condemned 2Thess 3:8, 12

Uses of unleavened, for:
Heavenly visitors ....Gen 19:3
The Passover............Ex 12:8
Priests 2Kin 23:9
Nazarites ....Num 6:13, 15
Lord's Supper ....Luke 22:7-19

Special uses of:
Provided by ravens 1Kin 17:6
Strength 1Kin 19:6-8
Satan's ....Matt 4:3
Miracle ....Matt 14:19-21
Insight..................Luke 24:35

Figurative of:
Adversity ....Is 30:20
Christ ....John 6:33-35
Christ's death 1Cor 11:23-28
Communion with Christ ..Acts 2:46
1Cor 10:17
Extreme poverty ....Ps 37:25
Prodigality ....Ezek 16:49
Wickedness ....Prov 4:17
Idleness ....Prov 31:27

Bread of life:
Christ is ....John 6:32-35
Same as manna ....Ex 16:4, 5
Fulfilled in Lord's Supper.1Cor 11:23, 24

Salem brought forth ***b*** and ....Gen 14:18
I will fetch a morsel of ***b***......Gen 18:5
and took ***b***, and a bottle of....Gen 21:14
Jacob gave Esau ***b*** and........Gen 25:34
gave..meat and the ***b*** ....Gen 27:17
and will give me ***b*** to eat......Gen 28:20
called his brethren to eat ***b***....Gen 31:54
and they did eat ***b*** ....Gen 31:54
they sat down to eat ***b*** ....Gen 37:25
save the ***b*** which he did ....Gen 39:6
land of Egypt there was ***b*** .....Gen 41:54
that they should eat ***b***.........Gen 43:25
laden with corn and ***b*** and ....Gen 45:23
with ***b***, according to their .....Gen 47:12
call him, that he may eat ***b***....Ex 2:20
shall ye eat unleavened ***b*** .....Ex 12:15
eateth leavened ***b***.............Ex 12:15
feast of unleavened ***b*** ....Ex 12:17
ye shall eat unleavened ***b*** .....Ex 12:18
shall ye eat unleavened ***b*** .....Ex 12:20
shall no leavened ***b*** be ....Ex 13:3
shalt eat unleavened ***b*** ....Ex 13:6
Unleavened ***b*** shall be ....Ex 13:7
there shall no leavened ***b***......Ex 13:7
when we did eat ***b*** to the .....Ex 16:3
to eat ***b*** with Moses' ....Ex 18:12
the feast of unleavened ***b*** .....Ex 23:15
unleavened ***b***, and cakes ......Ex 29:2
The feast of unleavened ***b***.....Ex 34:18
he set the ***b*** in order upon ....Ex 40:23
with unleavened ***b*** shall it .....Lev 6:16
leavened ***b*** with the ....Lev 7:13
a basket of unleavened ***b***......Lev 8:2
and the ***b*** of their God........Lev 21:6
the ***b*** of your God of any of...Lev 22:25
the feast of unleavened ***b*** .....Lev 23:6
ye must eat unleavened ***b*** .....Lev 23:6
may be on the ***b*** for a ....Lev 24:7
ye shall eat your ***b*** to the .....Lev 26:5
the staff of your ***b*** ....Lev 26:26
women shall bake your ***b***......Lev 26:26
shall deliver you your ***b*** ....Lev 26:26
the continual ***b*** shall be ....Num 4:7
eat it with unleavened ***b*** ......Num 9:11
they are ***b*** for us; their........Num 14:9
when ye eat of the ***b*** of the ...Num 15:19
for there is no ***b***, neither is....Num 21:5
soul loatheth this light ***b*** ......Num 21:5
my ***b*** for my sacrifices ....Num 28:2
shall unleavened ***b*** be ....Num 28:17
man doth not live by ***b***........Deut 8:3
neither did eat ***b*** nor drink ....Deut 9:9
shalt eat no leavened ***b*** ....Deut 16:3
thou eat unleavened ***b*** ....Deut 16:3
even the ***b*** of affliction; for....Deut 16:3
they met you not with ***b*** ......Deut 23:4
Ye have not eaten ***b*** ....Deut 29:6
all the ***b*** of their provision ....Josh 9:5
and, lo, a cake of barley ***b*** ....Judg 7:13
I pray you, loaves of ***b***........Judg 8:5
I will not eat of thy ***b***.........Judg 13:16
heart with a morsel of ***b*** ......Judg 19:5
eat of the ***b***, and dip thy ......Ruth 2:14
hired out themselves for ***b***.....1Sam 2:5
and a morsel of ***b***, and shall...1Sam 2:36
that I may eat a piece of ***b***....1Sam 2:36
b is spent in our vessels 1Sam 9:7
carrying three loaves of ***b*** 1Sam 10:3
an ass laden with ***b***, and a 1Sam 16:20
give me five loaves of ***b*** in 1Sam 21:3
thou hast given him ***b*** 1Sam 22:13
Shall I then take my ***b***, and ...1Sam 25:11
he had eaten no ***b*** all the 1Sam 28:20
to David, and gave him ***b*** 1Sam 30:11
sword, or that lacketh ***b***.......2Sam 3:29
to every one a cake of ***b*** 2Sam 6:19
shalt eat ***b*** at my table 2Sam 9:7
neither did he eat ***b*** with 2Sam 12:17
two hundred loaves of ***b*** 2Sam 16:1
neither will I eat ***b*** nor........1Kin 13:8
fed them with ***b*** and water 1Kin 18:4
face, and would eat no ***b***......1Kin 21:4
feed him with ***b*** of affliction...1Kin 22:27
constrained him to eat ***b*** 2Kin 4:8
set ***b*** and water before 2Kin 6:22
a land of ***b*** and vineyards, a...2Kin 18:32
there was no ***b*** for the 2Kin 25:3
b on asses, and on camels 1Chr 12:40
in the feast of unleavened ***b*** ...2Chr 8:13
feed him with ***b*** of affliction ...2Chr 18:26
the feast of unleavened ***b*** 2Chr 30:13
feast of unleavened ***b*** 2Chr 35:17
feast of unleavened ***b*** ....Ezra 6:22
he did eat no ***b***, nor drink ....Ezra 10:6
have not eaten the ***b*** of ....Neh 5:14
gavest them ***b*** from heaven ....Neh 9:15
children of Israel with ***b***.......Neh 13:2
wandereth abroad for ***b*** ....Job 15:23
thou hast withholden ***b***.........Job 22:7
shall not be satisfied with ***b*** ...Job 27:14
earth, out of it cometh ***b*** ......Job 28:5
his life abhorreth ***b***, and ......Job 33:20
and did eat ***b*** with him in ......Job 42:11
up my people as they eat ***b***....Ps 14:4
which did eat of my ***b***, hath ...Ps 41:9
my people as they eat ***b***.......Ps 53:4
he give ***b*** also? Can he........Ps 78:20
feedest them with the ***b*** of ....Ps 80:5
that I forget to eat my ***b*** ......Ps 102:4
I have eaten ashes like ***b*** ......Ps 102:9
and ***b*** which strengtheneth.....Ps 104:15
brake the whole staff of ***b*****.....Ps 105:16
let them seek their ***b*** also .....Ps 109:10
to eat the ***b*** of sorrows; for....Ps 127:2
satisfy her poor with ***b*** ....Ps 132:15
is brought to a piece of ***b*** .....Prov 6:26
Come, eat of my ***b***, and.......Prov 9:5
are sweet, and ***b*** eaten in .....Prov 9:17
honoreth..lacketh ***b*** ....Prov 12:9
shalt be satisfied with ***b*** ....Prov 20:13
B of deceit is sweet to a ......Prov 20:17
giveth of his ***b*** to the poor ....Prov 22:9
the ***b*** of him that hath an .....Prov 23:6
be hungry, give him ***b*** to .....Prov 25:21
land shall have plenty of ***b*** .....Prov 28:19
for a piece of ***b*** that man .....Prov 28:21
eat thy ***b*** with joy, and........Eccl 9:7
neither yet ***b*** to the wise ......Eccl 9:11
Cast thy ***b*** upon the waters ....Eccl 11:1
the whole stay of ***b***, and the...Is 3:1
We will eat our own ***b***, and ...Is 4:1
they prevented with their ***b***....Is 21:14
B corn is bruised; because.....Is 28:28
of rocks; ***b*** shall be given .....Is 33:16
a land of ***b*** and vineyards .....Is 36:17
he kindleth it and baketh ***b***....Is 44:15
nor that his ***b*** should fail ......Is 51:14
for that which is not ***b***? ....Is 55:2
seed to the sower, and ***b*** to ...Is 55:10
to deal thy ***b*** to the hungry....Is 58:7
thine harvest, and thy ***b***.......Jer 5:17
give him daily a piece of ***b*** ....Jer 37:21
is no more ***b*** in the city ....Jer 38:9
they did eat ***b*** together in .....Jer 41:1
nor have hunger of ***b***; and ....Jer 42:14
there was no ***b*** for the ....Jer 52:6
people sigh, they seek ***b*** ......Lam 1:11
the young children ask ***b*** ......Lam 4:4
to be satisfied with ***b*** ....Lam 5:6
make thee ***b*** thereof ....Ezek 4:9
I will break the staff of ***b*** .....Ezek 4:16

they shall eat *b* by weight ..... Ezek 4:16
will break your staff of *b* ..... Ezek 5:16
eat thy *b* with quaking ..... Ezek 12:18
barley and for pieces of *b* ..... Ezek 13:19
will break the staff of the *b* ..... Ezek 14:13
given his *b* to the hungry ..... Ezek 18:7
thy lips, and eat not the *b* ..... Ezek 24:17
sit in it to eat *b* before the ..... Ezek 44:3
unleavened *b* shall be ..... Ezek 45:21
I ate no pleasant *b*, neither ..... Dan 10:3
give me my *b* and my water ..... Hos 2:5
unto them as the *b* of ..... Hos 9:4
their *b* for their soul shall ..... Hos 9:4
want of *b* in all your places ..... Amos 4:6
there eat *b*, and prophesy ..... Amos 7:12
not a famine of *b*, nor a ..... Amos 8:11
they that eat thy *b* have ..... Obad 7
with his skirt do touch *b* ..... Hag 2:12
Ye offer polluted *b* upon ..... Mal 1:7
Man shall not live by *b* ..... Matt 4:4
whom if his son ask *b*, will ..... Matt 7:9
hands when they eat *b* ..... Matt 15:2
to take the children's *b* ..... Matt 15:26
had forgotten to take *b* ..... Matt 16:5
the feast of unleavened *b* ..... Matt 26:17
Jesus took *b*, and blessed it ..... Matt 26:26
could not so much as eat *b* ..... Mark 3:20
no scrip, no *b*, no money ..... Mark 6:8
of his disciples eat *b* ..... Mark 7:2
but eat *b* with unwashen ..... Mark 7:5
satisfy these men with *b* ..... Mark 8:4
and of unleavened *b* ..... Mark 14:1
first day of unleavened *b* ..... Mark 14:12
neither eating *b* nor ..... Luke 7:33
he that shall eat *b* in the ..... Luke 14:15
of my father's have *b* ..... Luke 15:17
he took *b*, and blessed it ..... Luke 24:30
Whence shall we buy *b* ..... John 6:5
I am that *b* of life ..... John 6:48
This is the *b* which cometh ..... John 6:50
He that eateth *b* with me ..... John 13:18
fish laid thereon, and *b* ..... John 21:9
the days of unleavened *b* ..... Acts 12:3
the days of unleavened *b* ..... Acts 20:6
came together to break *b* ..... Acts 20:7
he took *b*, and gave thanks ..... Acts 27:35
unleavened *b* of sincerity 1Cor 5:8
The *b* which we break, is it 1Cor 10:16

BREADTH—*width*

the *b* of it fifty cubits, and ..... Gen 6:15
length of it and in the *b* ..... Gen 13:17
a cubit and a half the *b* ..... Ex 25:10
and the *b* of one curtain ..... Ex 26:2
And for the *b* of the court ..... Ex 27:12
and a span shall be the *b* ..... Ex 28:16
and the *b* of one curtain ..... Ex 36:9
a cubit and a half the *b* of ..... Ex 37:1
five cubits the *b* thereof; it ..... Ex 38:1
thereof, and a span the *b* ..... Ex 39:9
so much as a foot *b* ..... Deut 2:5
four cubits the *b* of it, after ..... Deut 3:11
sling stones at an hair *b* ..... Judg 20:16
the *b* thereof twenty cubits 1Kin 6:2
the *b* thereof fifty cubits 1Kin 7:2
threescore cubits, and..*b* 2Chr 3:3
twenty cubits the *b* thereof 2Chr 4:1
the *b* thereof threescore ..... Ezra 6:3
and the *b* of the waters is ..... Job 37:10
Hast thou perceived the *b* ..... Job 38:18
shall fill the *b* of thy land ..... Is 8:8
by the cubit and a hand *b* ..... Ezek 40:5
other side, which was the *b* ..... Ezek 41:1
door, and the *b* was fifty ..... Ezek 42:2
is a cubit and a hand *b* ..... Ezek 43:13
b shall be ten thousand ..... Ezek 45:1
twenty thousand reeds in *b* ..... Ezek 48:8
threescore cubits, and the *b* ..... Dan 3:1
through the *b* of the land ..... Hab 1:6
to see what is the *b* thereof ..... Zech 2:2
twenty cubits and the *b* ..... Zech 5:2
what is the *b*, and length ..... Eph 3:18
they went up on the *b* of ..... Rev 20:9
length is as large as the *b* ..... Rev 21:16
and the *b* and the height of ..... Rev 21:16

BREAK—*to disrupt; divide*

[*also* BRAKE, BREAKER, BREAKEST, BREAKETH, BREAKING, BREAKINGS, BROKEN]

fountains..deep *b* up ..... Gen 7:11
he hath *b* my covenant ..... Gen 17:14
even Lot, came near to *b* ..... Gen 19:9
that thou shalt *b* his yoke ..... Gen 27:40
a man with him until the *b* ..... Gen 32:24
Let me go, for the day *b* ..... Gen 32:26
a boil *b* forth with blains ..... Ex 9:9
b every tree of the field ..... Ex 9:25
neither shall ye *b* a bone ..... Ex 12:46
then thou shalt *b* his neck ..... Ex 13:13
lest they *b* through unto ..... Ex 19:21
If a thief be found *b* up, and ..... Ex 22:2
If fire *b* out, and catch in ..... Ex 22:6
them, and quite *b* ..... Ex 23:24
B off the golden earrings ..... Ex 32:2
people *b* off the golden ..... Ex 32:3
first tables, which thou *b* ..... Ex 34:1
b their images, and cut ..... Ex 34:13
it is sodden shall be *b* ..... Lev 6:28
unclean; and ye shall *b* ..... Lev 11:33
if a leprosy *b* out abroad in ..... Lev 13:12
a plague of leprosy *b* out ..... Lev 13:20
and *b* out in the house ..... Lev 14:43
I have *b* the bands of your ..... Lev 26:13
but that ye *b* my covenant ..... Lev 26:15
unto the morning, nor *b* ..... Num 9:12
hath *b* his commandment ..... Num 15:31
shall *b* their bones, and ..... Num 24:8
he shall not *b* his word, he ..... Num 30:2
b down their images, and ..... Deut 7:5
b them before your eyes ..... Deut 9:17
first tables which thou *b* ..... Deut 10:2
and *b* their pillars, and ..... Deut 12:3
I will never *b* my covenant ..... Judg 2:1
were the horsehoofs *b* ..... Judg 5:22
again in peace, I will *b* ..... Judg 8:9
head, and all to *b* his skull ..... Judg 9:53
And he *b* the withes, as a ..... Judg 16:9
of the mighty men are *b* 1Sam 2:4
and his neck *b*, and he died 1Sam 4:18
servants now a days that *b* 1Sam 25:10
they came to Hebron at *b* 2Sam 2:32
hath *b* forth upon mine 2Sam 5:20
three mighty men *b* 2Sam 23:16
b thy league with Baasha 1Kin 15:19
altar of the Lord that was *b* 1Kin 18:30
and *b* in pieces the rocks 1Kin 19:11
that drew swords, to *b* 2Kin 3:26
they *b* down the image of 2Kin 10:27
the house, that it be not *b* 2Kin 11:6
house of Baal, and *b* it 2Kin 11:18
b down the wall of 2Kin 14:13
and *b* the images, and cut 2Kin 18:4
And he *b* down the houses 2Kin 23:7
b down the walls of 2Kin 25:10
did the Chaldees *b* in pieces 2Kin 25:13
And the three *b* through 1Chr 11:18
God hath *b* in upon mine 1Chr 14:11
like the *b* forth of waters 1Chr 14:11
and *b* down the images 2Chr 14:3
b thy league with Baasha 2Chr 16:3
the Lord hath *b* thy works 2Chr 20:37
and *b* into it, and carried 2Chr 21:17
the house of Baal, and *b* it 2Chr 23:17
that wicked woman had *b* 2Chr 24:7
that they all were *b* in 2Chr 25:12
b down the wall of 2Chr 25:23
b down the wall of Gath 2Chr 26:6
and *b* the images in pieces 2Chr 31:1
they *b* down the altars of 2Chr 34:4
b down the wall of 2Chr 36:19
Should we again *b* thy ..... Ezra 9:14
wall of Jerusalem also is *b* ..... Neh 1:3
he shall even *b* down their ..... Neh 4:3
teeth of..lions, are *b* ..... Job 4:10
my skin is *b*, and become ..... Job 7:5
he *b* me with a tempest ..... Job 9:17
Behold, he *b* down ..... Job 12:14
Wilt thou *b* a leaf driven to ..... Job 13:25
but he hath *b* me asunder ..... Job 16:12
He *b* me with breach upon ..... Job 16:14
my purposes are *b* off, even ..... Job 17:11
vex my soul, and *b* me in ..... Job 19:2
wickedness shall be *b* as a ..... Job 24:20
The flood *b* out from the ..... Job 28:4
I *b* the jaws of the wicked ..... Job 29:17
me as a wide *b* in of waters ..... Job 30:14
He shall *b* in pieces mighty ..... Job 34:24
when it *b* forth, as if it had ..... Job 38:8
that the wild beast may *b* ..... Job 39:15
by reason of *b* they purify ..... Job 41:25
Let us *b* their bands ..... Ps 2:3
hast *b* the teeth of the ..... Ps 3:7
B thou the arm of the ..... Ps 10:15
The voice of the Lord *b* the ..... Ps 29:5
I am like a *b* vessel ..... Ps 31:12
them that are of a *b* heart ..... Ps 34:18
though thou hast sore *b* ..... Ps 44:19
he *b* the bow, and cutteth ..... Ps 46:9
Thou *b* the ships of ..... Ps 48:7
bones which thou hast *b* ..... Ps 51:8
sacrifices of God are a *b* ..... Ps 51:17
a *b* and a contrite heart ..... Ps 51:17
he hath *b* his covenant ..... Ps 55:20
B their teeth, O God, in ..... Ps 58:6
b out the great teeth of ..... Ps 58:6
Reproach hath *b* my heart ..... Ps 69:20
b in pieces the oppressor ..... Ps 72:4
But now they *b* down the ..... Ps 74:6
b the heads of the dragons ..... Ps 74:13
b he the arrows of the bow ..... Ps 76:3
If they *b* my statutes and ..... Ps 89:31
My covenant will I not *b* ..... Ps 89:34
They *b* in pieces thy people ..... Ps 94:5
b the whole staff of bread ..... Ps 105:16
and the plague *b* in ..... Ps 106:29
b their bands in sunder ..... Ps 107:14
might even slay the *b* in ..... Ps 109:16
My soul *b* for the longing ..... Ps 119:20
shall not *b* my head; forget ..... Ps 141:5
that there be no *b* in nor ..... Ps 144:14
He healeth the *b* in heart ..... Ps 147:3
knowledge the depths are *b* ..... Prov 3:20
suddenly shall he be *b* ..... Prov 6:15
of the heart the spirit is *b* ..... Prov 15:13
a soft tongue *b* the bone ..... Prov 25:15
a time to *b* down and a ..... Eccl 3:3
a..cord is not quickly *b* ..... Eccl 4:12
whoso *b* a hedge a ..... Eccl 10:8
or the golden bowl be *b* ..... Eccl 12:6
the pitcher be *b* at the ..... Eccl 12:6
the wheel *b* at the cistern ..... Eccl 12:6
Until the day *b*, and the ..... Song 2:17
day *b*, and the shadows flee ..... Song 4:6
and *b* down the wall ..... Is 5:5
latchet of their shoes be *b* ..... Is 5:27
ye shall be *b* in pieces ..... Is 8:9
hath *b* the staff of the ..... Is 14:5
is quiet; they *b* forth into ..... Is 14:7
of her gods he hath *b* ..... Is 21:9
b down the walls, and of ..... Is 22:5
b the everlasting covenant ..... Is 24:5
he open and *b* the clods ..... Is 28:24
whose *b* cometh suddenly ..... Is 30:13
And he shall *b* it as the ..... Is 30:14
he hath *b* the covenant, he ..... Is 33:8
wilderness shall waters *b* ..... Is 35:6
staff of this *b* reed, on ..... Is 36:6
as a lion, so will he *b* all my ..... Is 38:13
bruised reed shall he not *b* ..... Is 42:3
b forth into singing, ye ..... Is 44:23
I will *b* in pieces the gates of ..... Is 45:2
and *b* forth into singing, O ..... Is 49:13
B forth into joy, sing ..... Is 52:9
b forth into singing, and ..... Is 54:1
and the hills shall *b* ..... Is 55:12
go free, and that ye *b* every ..... Is 58:6
crushed *b* out into a viper ..... Is 59:5
an evil shall *b* forth upon ..... Jer 1:14
b cisterns, that can hold no ..... Jer 2:13
B up your fallow ground ..... Jer 4:3
have altogether *b* the yoke ..... Jer 5:5
Judah have *b* my covenant ..... Jer 11:10
daughter of my people is *b* ..... Jer 14:17
b not thy covenant ..... Jer 14:21
Shall iron *b* the northern ..... Jer 15:12

shalt thou *b* the bottle ....Jer 19:10
as one *b* a potter's vessel......Jer 19:11
like a hammer that *b* the ......Jer 23:29
b the yoke of the king of .....Jer 28:2
I will *b* the yoke of the ....Jer 28:4
Jeremiah's neck, and *b* it......Jer 28:10
I will *b* his yoke from off thy ..Jer 30:8
to pluck up, and to *b* down ...Jer 31:28
my covenant they *b*...........Jer 31:32
If ye can *b* my covenant of ....Jer 33:20
also my covenant be *b* ....Jer 33:21
month, the city was *b* up ......Jer 39:2
b down the walls of...........Jer 39:8
He shall *b* also the images ....Jer 43:13
which I have built will I *b*.....Jer 45:4
empty his vessels, and *b* ......Jer 48:12
I will *b* the bow of Elam ......Jer 49:35
Merodach is *b* in pieces ....Jer 50:2
her images are *b* in pieces .....Jer 50:2
with thee will I *b* in pieces ....Jer 51:20
with thee will I *b* in pieces ....Jer 51:21
thee also will I *b* in pieces ....Jer 51:22
b down all the walls of.........Jer 52:14
destroyed and *b* her bars ......Lam 2:9
ask bread, and no man *b* it.....Lam 4:4
I will *b* the staff of bread in ...Ezek 4:16
will *b* your staff of bread ......Ezek 5:16
and your images shall be *b* ....Ezek 6:4
So will I *b* down the wall .....Ezek 13:14
will *b* the staff of the bread ...Ezek 14:13
women that *b* wedlock and ....Ezek 16:38
despised the oath in *b* the .....Ezek 16:59
or shall he *b* the covenant .....Ezek 17:15
whose covenant he *b*, even ....Ezek 17:16
by *b* the covenant, when lo....Ezek 17:18
covenant that he hath *b* ....Ezek 17:19
with the *b* of thy loins; and ...Ezek 21:6
thou shalt *b* the sherds ....Ezek 23:34
and *b* down her towers.........Ezek 26:4
thou didst *b* and rend all ......Ezek 29:7
leaned upon thee, thou *b* .....Ezek 29:7
her foundations shall be *b*.....Ezek 30:4
when I shall *b* there the ....Ezek 30:18
bound up that which was *b*....Ezek 34:4
they have *b* my covenant ......Ezek 44:7
and his sleep *b* from him ......Dan 2:1
the gold, *b* to pieces ....Dan 2:35
as iron *b* in pieces ....Dan 2:40
as iron that *b* all these ....Dan 2:40
all these shall it *b* in pieces ....Dan 2:40
partly strong, and partly *b*.....Dan 2:42
b off thy sins by ....Dan 4:27
b all their bones in pieces .....Dan 6:24
it devoured and *b* in pieces ....Dan 7:7
shall tread it down, and *b* it ...Dan 7:23
ram, and *b* his two horns .....Dan 8:7
I will *b* the bow Israel ....Hos 1:5
I will *b* the bow and ....Hos 2:18
they *b* out, and blood ....Hos 4:2
is oppressed and *b*............Hos 5:11
he shall *b* down their altars....Hos 10:2
in the place of the *b* forth of ..Hos 13:13
the barns are *b* down; for .....Joel 1:17
they shall not *b* their ranks ....Joel 2:7
I will *b* also the bar of ....Amos 1:5
lest he *b* out like fire in the ...Amos 5:6
the ship was like to be *b* ......Jon 1:4
The *b* is come up before ......Mic 2:13
they have *b* up, and have ......Mic 2:13
they *b* their bones, and chop ..Mic 3:3
now will I *b* his yoke from ....Nah 1:13
that I might *b* my covenant....Zech 11:10
And it was *b* in that day ......Zech 11:11
where thieves *b* through ....Matt 6:19
else the bottles *b*, and the.....Matt 9:17
bruised reed shall he not *b* ....Matt 12:20
he blessed, and *b* them, and...Matt 14:19
gave thanks, and *b* them ......Matt 15:36
they took up of the *b* meat.....Matt 15:37
fall on this stone shall be *b*....Matt 21:44
bread, and blessed it, and *b* ...Matt 26:26
when they had *b* it up, they ...Mark 2:4
and *b* the loaves, and gave ....Mark 6:41
and gave thanks, and *b* ....Mark 8:6
and she *b* the box, and ....Mark 14:3
of fishes; and their net *b* ......Luke 5:6
he *b* the bands, and was ......Luke 8:29
he blessed them, and *b* ....Luke 9:16
suffered his house to be *b* .....Luke 12:39
and gave thanks, and *b* it .....Luke 22:19
blessed it, and *b*, and ....Luke 24:30
known of them in *b* of ....Luke 24:35
not only had *b* the sabbath ....John 5:18
and *b* the legs of the first .....John 19:32
b of bread, and in prayers.....Acts 2:42
the congregation was *b*........Acts 13:43
came together to *b* bread .....Acts 20:7
mean ye to weep and to *b* ....Acts 21:13
b the law dishonorest ....Rom 2:23
if thou be a *b* of the law ....Rom 2:25
some of the branches be *b* .....Rom 11:17
The bread which we *b*, is it ...1Cor 10:16
my body, which is *b* for you...1Cor 11:24
he *b* it, and said, Take........1Cor 11:24
b forth and cry, thou that .....Gal 4:27
b down the middle wall ....Eph 2:14
the potter shall they be *b* .....Rev 2:27

BREAKING OF BREAD—*a meal*
Prayer before ....Matt 14:19
Insight through ....Luke 24:35
Fellowship thereby ......Acts 2:42
Strength gained by ......Acts 20:11
See LORD'S SUPPER

BREAST—*part of the body between the neck and the abdomen; mammary gland*

Literally of:
Married love ....Prov 5:19
Song 1:13
An infant's life ....Job 3:12
Ps 22:9
Posterity ....Gen 49:25

Figuratively, of:
Health..................Job 21:24
Mother Jerusalem ....Is 66:10, 11

[*also* BREASTS]
thou shalt take the *b* of the ...Ex 29:26
fat with the *b*, it shall he......Lev 7:30
that the *b* may be waved ......Lev 7:30
Moses took the *b*, and ....Lev 8:29
they put the fat upon the *b*....Lev 9:20
the wave *b* and heave..........Lev 10:14
priest, with the wave *b* and....Num 6:20
fatherless from the *b*..........Job 24:9
Thy two *b* are like two........Song 4:5
thy two *b* are like two ....Song 7:3
and thy *b* to clusters of ....Song 7:7
sucked the *b* of my mother! ...Song 8:1
sister, and she hath no *b* ......Song 8:8
and my *b* like towers; then ....Song 8:10
and drawn from the *b*.........Is 28:9
shalt suck the *b* of kings ......Is 60:16
monsters draw out the *b* ......Lam 4:3
thy *b* are fashioned, and ......Ezek 16:7
there were their *b* pressed.....Ezek 23:3
bruised the *b* of her ....Ezek 23:8
his *b* and his arms of silver ....Dan 2:32
from between her *b*...........Hos 2:2
womb and dry *b*..............Hos 9:14
and those that suck the *b* .....Joel 2:16
tabering upon their *b* ....Nah 2:7
but smote upon his *b* ....Luke 18:13
smote their *b*, and returned ...Luke 23:48
He then lying on Jesus' *b* .....John 13:25
their *b* girded with golden .....Rev 15:6

BREASTPLATE—*defensive armor for the breast: vestment worn by Jewish high priest*

Worn by:
High priest.............Ex 28:4, 15-20
Soldiers................1Sam 17:5, 38
"Locusts" ....Rev 9:7, 9

Figurative of:
Christ's righteousness ....Is 59:17
Faith's righteousness .....Eph 6:14

be set..and in the *b*...........Ex 25:7
the ephod, and the *b*, and.....Ex 29:5
set..and for the *b*............Ex 35:9
he made the *b* of cunning .....Ex 39:8
he put the *b* upon him ....Lev 8:8
he put in the *b* the Urim......Lev 8:8
putting on the *b* of faith 1Thess 5:8

BREATH—*life-giving force*
Comes from God ....Gen 2:7
Necessary for all ....Eccl 3:19
Held by God............Dan 5:23
Absence of, death ....Ps 146:4
Taken by God ....Ps 104:29
Figurative, of new life ...Ezek 37:5-10

[*also* BREATHE, BREATHED, BREATHETH, BREATHING]
and *b* into his nostrils the .....Gen 2:7
wherein is the *b* of life ....Gen 6:17
wherein is the *b* of life ....Gen 7:15
in whose nostrils was the *b* ....Gen 7:22
save alive nothing that *b* ......Deut 20:16
utterly destroyed all that *b* ....Josh 10:40
there was not any left to *b* ....Josh 11:11
to Jeroboam any that *b* 1Kin 15:29
that there was no *b* left in.....1Kin 17:17
not suffer me to take my *b* ....Job 9:18
and the *b* of all mankind .....Job 12:10
by the *b* of his mouth shall.....Job 15:30
My *b* is corrupt, my days .....Job 17:1
My *b* is strange to my wife ....Job 19:17
while my *b* is in me, and the ..Job 27:3
unto himself..and his *b*........Job 34:14
the *b* of God frost is given ....Job 37:10
His *b* kindleth coals, and a ....Job 41:21
the blast of the *b* of thy........Ps 18:15
and such as *b* out cruelty......Ps 27:12
the host of them by the *b* .....Ps 33:6
neither is there any *b* in.......Ps 135:17
everything that hath *b* ....Ps 150:6
from man, whose *b* is in his ...Is 2:22
his *b*, as an overflowing ....Is 30:28
the *b* of the Lord, like a ......Is 30:33
your *b*, as fire, shall devour ...Is 33:11
he that giveth *b* unto the......Is 42:5
and there is no *b* in ....Jer 10:14
and there is no *b* in ....Jer 51:17
hide not thine ear at my *b* ....Lam 3:56
b of our nostrils, the..........Lam 4:20
b upon these slain, that ....Ezek 37:9
neither is there *b* left ....Dan 10:17
there is no *b* at all in the .....Hab 2:19
said this, he *b* on them and ...John 20:22
Saul, yet *b* out threatenings ...Acts 9:1
he giveth to all life, and *b*.....Acts 17:25

BREATH OF GOD—*life-giving force*

Cause of:
Creation 2Sam 22:16
Life ....Job 33:4
Destruction ....Is 11:4
Death ....Job 4:9

BREECHES—*a garment*
Worn by priests ....Ex 28:42

linen *b* of fine twined ....Ex 39:28
and his linen *b* shall he put....Lev 6:10
he shall have the linen *b* ......Lev 16:4
and shall have linen *b* upon ...Ezek 44:18

BREED—*to beget; engender; produce*

[*also* BRED, BREEDING]
that they may *b* abundantly ...Gen 8:17
morning, and it *b* worms ......Ex 16:20
rams of the *b* of Bashan ......Deut 32:14
the *b* of nettles, and salt ......Zeph 2:9

BREVITY OF HUMAN LIFE

Compared to:
Pilgrimage ....Gen 47:9
A tale ....Ps 90:9
Sleep ....Ps 90:5
Flower ....Job 14:2
Grass..................1Pet 1:24
Vapor ....James 4:14
Shadow................Eccl 6:12
Moment 2Cor 4:17
A weaver's shuttle.......Job 7:6

Truths arising from:
Prayer can prolong ......Is 38:2-5
Incentive to improvement.Ps 90:12
Some kept from old age. .1Sam 2:32, 33
Some know their end 2Pet 1:13, 14
Hope regarding ....Phil 1:21-25
Life's completion 2Tim 4:6-8

BRIBERY—*giving gifts to influence others*
The effects of:
Makes sinners ....Ps 26:10
Corrupts conscience .....Ex 23:8
Perverts justice ....Is 1:23
Brings chaos ....Amos 5:12
Merits punishment ....Amos 2:6
Examples of:
Balak ....Num 22:17, 37
Delilah ....Judg 16:5
Samuel's sons 1Sam 8:3
Ben-hadad 1Kin 15:18, 19
Shemaiah ....Neh 6:10-13
Haman ....Esth 3:8, 9
Judas and priests ....Matt 27:3-9
Soldiers.................Matt 28:12-15
Simon ....Acts 8:18
Felix ....Acts 24:26

[*also* BRIBE, BRIBES]
hand have I received any *b*....Is 33:15
his hands from holding of *b* ...1Sam 12:3

BRICK—*building material made of baked clay*
Babel built of ....Gen 11:3
Israel forced to make ....Ex 1:14
Altars made of ....Is 65:3
Forts made of ....Is 9:10
Made in kiln 2Sam 12:31

[*also* BRICKS]
people straw to make *b* ....Ex 5:7
the tale of the *b*, which they ..Ex 5:8
task in making *b* ....Ex 5:14
and they say to us, Make *b* ...Ex 5:16
ye deliver the tale of *b*........Ex 5:18
from your *b* of your daily .....Ex 5:19

BRICKKILN—*place for making bricks*
Forced labor in..........2Sam 12:31

the clay in the *b*, which is .....Jer 43:9
mortar, make strong the *b* ....Nah 3:14

BRIDAL—*pertaining to a newly married woman*
Gift:
A burned city 1Kin 9:16
Veil:
Rebekah wears first .....Gen 26:64-67

BRIDE—*newlywed woman*
Wears adornments ....Is 61:10
Receives presents........Gen 24:53
Has damsels ....Gen 24:59, 61
Adorned for husband ....Rev 19:7, 8
Rejoices in her husband .Is 62:5
Stands near husband .....Ps 45:9
Receives benediction.....Ruth 4:11, 12
Must forget father's house Ruth 1:8-17
Must be chaste 2Cor 11:2
Figurative of Israel ......Ezek 16:8-14
Figurative of Church .....Rev 21:2, 9

bind them on thee, as a *b* .....Is 49:18
her ornaments, or a *b*.........Jer 2:32
and the voice of the *b* ....Jer 7:34
and the voice of the *b* ....Jer 16:9
the voice of the *b*, the ....Jer 25:10
the voice of the *b*, the voice ..Jer 33:11
and the *b* out of her closet ....Joel 2:16
that hath the *b* is the ....John 3:29
of the *b* shall be heard no .....Rev 18:23
the Spirit and the *b* say ....Rev 22:17

BRIDECHAMBER—*the place where newlyweds consummate their marriage*
Can the children of the *b* .....Matt 9:15
Can the children of the *b* .....Mark 2:19
make the children of the *b* ....Luke 5:34

BRIDEGROOM—*newlywed man*
Wears special garments ..Is 61:10
Attended by friends ......John 3:29
Adorned with garlands ...Song 3:11
Rejoices over bride ......Is 62:5
Returns with bride ......Matt 25:1-6
Exempted from military service................Deut 24:5
Figurative of God ....Ezek 16:8-14
Figurative of Christ ......John 3:29

[*also* BRIDEGROOM'S]
a *b* coming out of his ....Ps 19:5
the voice of the *b*, and the ....Jer 7:34
the voice of the *b* ....Jer 16:9
the voice of the *b*, and the ....Jer 25:10
the voice of the *b*, and the ....Jer 33:11
let the *b* go forth of his ....Joel 2:16
as long as the *b* is with ....Matt 9:15
when the *b* shall be taken .....Matt 9:15
while the *b* is with them? .....Mark 2:19
as long as they have the *b*.....Mark 2:19
fast, while the *b* is with ....Luke 5:34
of the feast called the *b* ....John 2:9
that hath the bride is the *b* ....John 3:29
but the friend of the *b* ....John 3:29
and the voice of the *b* and ....Rev 18:23

BRIDLE—*headgear of a horse; to restrain*
Used literally of:
An ass ....Prov 26:3
Used figuratively of:
God's control ....Is 30:28
Self-control ....James 1:26
Imposed control ....Ps 32:9

[*also* BRIDLES, BRIDLETH]
my *b* in thy lips, and I will 2Kin 19:28
have also let loose the *b* ......Job 30:11
him with his double *b*? ....Job 41:13
keep my mouth with a *b* ....Ps 39:1
be a *b* in the jaws of the ......Is 30:28
and my *b* in thy lips ....Is 37:29
able also to *b* the whole.......James 3:2
even unto the horse *b*, by .....Rev 14:20

BRIEFLY—*succinctly*
b comprehended in this ....Rom 13:9
I have written *b*, exhorting 1Pet 5:12

BRIER—*thorny shrub*
Used literally of:
Thorns ....Judg 8:7, 16
Used figuratively of:
Sinful nature ....Mic 7:4
Change of nature ....Is 55:13
Rejection ....Is 5:6

[*also* BRIERS]
it shall even be for *b* and .....Is 7:23
it shall devour the *b* and ......Is 9:18
devour..and his *b*.............Is 10:17
who would set the *b* and ......Is 27:4
shall come up thorns and *b*....Is 32:13
b and thorns be with thee .....Ezek 2:6
be no more a pricking *b* ......Ezek 28:24
which beareth thorns and *b*....Heb 6:8

BRIGANDINE—*a coat of mail*
Used as armor ....Jer 46:4

lifteth himself up in his *b* .....Jer 51:3

BRIGHT—*radiating or reflecting light*

[*also* BRIGHTNESS]
rising, a scab, or *b* spot ....Lev 13:2
If the *b* spot be white in ......Lev 13:4
or a *b* spot, white, and........Lev 13:19
if the *b* spot stay in his ....Lev 13:23
have a white *b* spot...........Lev 13:24
the hair in the *b* spot be ......Lev 13:25
no white hair in the *b* spot ....Lev 13:26
if the *b* spot stay in his ....Lev 13:28
in the skin of their flesh *b*.....Lev 13:38
even white *b* spots ....Lev 13:38
the *b* spots in the skin of.......Lev 13:39
Through the *b* before him 2Sam 22:13
the Lord, were of *b* brass 1Kin 7:45
the house of the Lord of *b* 2Chr 4:16
or the moon walking in *b* .....Job 31:26
he scattereth his *b* cloud ......Job 37:11
men see not the *b* light ....Job 37:21
the *b* that was before him .....Ps 18:12
his belly is as *b* ivory ....Song 5:14
b, but we walk in darkness ....Is 59:9
kings to the *b* of thy rising ....Is 60:3
thereof go forth as *b*..........Is 62:1
Make *b* the arrows; gather ....Jer 51:11
and a *b* was about it, and .....Ezek 1:4
and the fire was *b*, and out....Ezek 1:13
of fire, and it had *b* round ....Ezek 1:27
the appearance of the *b*.......Ezek 1:28
as the appearance of *b* ....Ezek 8:2
the court was full of the *b*.....Ezek 10:4
it is made *b*, it is wrapped ....Ezek 21:15
b iron, cassia, and ....Ezek 27:19
they shall defile thy *b*.........Ezek 28:7
by reason of thy *b* ....Ezek 28:17
All the *b* lights of heaven .....Ezek 32:8
This great image, whose *b*.....Dan 2:31
mine honor and *b* ....Dan 4:36
shall shine as the *b* of the .....Dan 12:3
even very dark, and no *b* .....Amos 5:20
both the *b* sword and the .....Nah 3:3
And his *b* was as the light.....Hab 3:4
Lord shall make *b* clouds .....Zech 10:1
a *b* cloud overshadowed.......Matt 17:5
as when the *b* shining of a ....Luke 11:36
stood before me in *b* ....Acts 10:30
from heaven, above the *b* of ..Acts 26:13
with the *b* of his coming 2Thess 2:8
Who being the *b* of his ....Heb 1:3
the *b* and morning star........Rev 22:16

BRIM—*edge*
were dipped in the *b* of the ...Josh 3:15
ten cubits from the one *b* to...1Kin 7:23
and the *b* thereof was.........1Kin 7:26
like the *b* of a cup............1Kin 7:26
from *b* to *b*, round in 2Chr 4:2
and the *b* of it like the work ..2Chr 4:5
the work of the *b* of a cup 2Chr 4:5
they filled them up to the *b* ...John 2:7

BRIMSTONE—*sulphur*
Falls upon Sodom ....Gen 19:24
Sent as judgment ....Deut 29:23
State of wicked..........Ps 11:6
Condition of hell ....Rev 14:10

b shall be scattered upon......Job 18:15
like a stream of *b*, doth ....Is 30:33
the dust thereof into *b*, and ...Is 34:9
hailstones, fire and *b* ....Ezek 38:22
fire and *b* from heaven, and ...Luke 17:29
fire, and of jacinth, and *b*.....Rev 9:17
issued fire and smoke and *b* ...Rev 9:17
lake of fire burning with *b* ....Rev 19:20
the lake of fire and *b* ....Rev 20:10
burneth with fire and *b* ....Rev 21:8

BRING—*to deliver; cause*

[*also* BRINGEST, BRINGETH, BRINGING, BROUGHT, BROUGHTEST]
of every sort shall thou *b* .....Gen 6:19
when I *b* a cloud over the .....Gen 9:14
went with them to *b* them ....Gen 18:16
b them out unto us, that we ....Gen 19:5
I shall *b* a curse upon me .....Gen 27:12
b your youngest brother.......Gen 42:20
and for your wives, and *b* .....Gen 45:19
B them, I pray thee, unto .....Gen 48:9
b you out from under the .....Ex 6:7
for *b* them out from the.......Ex 12:42
the Lord shall *b* thee into .....Ex 13:5
thou shalt *b* into the house ....Ex 23:19
thy people, which thou *b*.......Ex 32:7
let him *b* it, an offering ....Ex 35:5
The people *b* much more .....Ex 36:5
I am the Lord that *b* you .....Lev 11:45
b it not unto the door of the ..Lev 17:4
b iniquity to remembrance ....Num 5:15
he will *b* us into this land .....Num 14:8
thou *b* up this people in.......Num 14:13

by *b* up a slander upon the....Num 14:36
therefore ye shall not *b* ....Num 20:12
b it unto me, and I will ....Deut 1:17
shall *b* thee into the land.......Deut 7:1
the Lord thy God *b* thee ....Deut 8:7
land whence thou *b* us out ....Deut 9:28
the field *b* forth year by........Deut 14:22
Then thou shalt *b* her.........Deut 21:12
us to heaven, and *b* it unto....Deut 30:12
and *b* him unto his people ....Deut 33:7
and then I will *b* him, that 1Sam 1:22
he *b* down to the grave 1Sam 2:6
to the grave, and *b* up 1Sam 2:6
what shall we *b* the man? 1Sam 9:7
why shouldest thou *b* me 1Sam 20:8
to *b* about all Israel unto 2Sam 3:12
that leddest out and *b* in 2Sam 5:2
b him to me, and he shall 2Sam 14:10
He also *b* tidings 2Sam 18:26
speak ye not a word of *b* 2Sam 19:10
the last to *b* the king back 2Sam 19:11
and that *b* down the people 2Sam 22:48
art a valiant man, and *b* 1Kin 1:42
to *b* his way upon his head 1Kin 8:32
thou *b* forth out of Egypt 1Kin 8:51
b gold, and silver, ivory 1Kin 10:22
B me a new curse, and put 2Kin 2:20
and I will *b* you to the man ...2Kin 6:19
the *b* up of the children.......2Kin 10:5
am *b* such evil upon 2Kin 21:12
b in Israel; and the Lord 1Chr 11:2
b an offering, and come.......1Chr 16:29
the ships of Tarshish *b* 2Chr 9:21
and *b* him forth out of Ur.....Neh 9:7
b in sheaves, and lading.......Neh 13:15
and did not our God *b* all.....Neh 13:18
Did I say, *B* unto me? or, ...Job 6:22
and wilt thou *b* me into ....Job 10:9
into whose hand God *b* ....Job 12:6
b me into judgment with ......Job 14:3
Who can *b* a clean thing ......Job 14:4
wrath *b* the punishments ......Job 19:29
is hid *b* he forth to light ......Job 28:11
thou wilt *b* me to death ....Job 30:23
To *b* back his soul from the ...Job 33:30
b forth his fruit in his ....Ps 1:3
when the Lord *b* back the .....Ps 14:7
The Lord *b* the counsel of ....Ps 33:10
and he shall *b* it to pass ....Ps 37:5
of the man who *b* wicked .....Ps 37:7
let them *b* me unto thy ....Ps 43:3
When God *b* back the ....Ps 53:6
Who will *b* me into the ....Ps 60:9
Thou *b* us into the net ....Ps 66:11
he *b* out those which are ......Ps 68:6
mountains shall *b* peace ....Ps 72:3
And he shall *b* upon them ....Ps 94:23
he *b* them out of their ....Ps 107:28
rejoicing, *b* his sheaves........Ps 126:6
b the wind out of his ....Ps 135:7
The mouth of the just *b*.......Prov 10:31
moving his lips he *b* evil ......Prov 16:30
b him before great men ....Prov 18:16
causeth shame, and *b* ....Prov 19:26
and *b* the wheel over them ....Prov 20:26
he *b* it with a wicked mind? ..Prov 21:27
Scornful men *b* a city into a ...Prov 29:8
himself *b* his mother to ....Prov 29:15
churning of milk *b* forth ......Prov 30:33
she *b* her food from afar ......Prov 31:14
the wood that *b* forth trees ....Eccl 2:6
for who shall *b* him to see ....Eccl 3:22
God will *b* thee into ....Eccl 11:9
God shall *b* every work ....Eccl 12:14
I would lead thee, and *b* ......Song 8:2
The Lord shall *b* upon thee ...Is 7:17
the Lord *b* up upon them .....Is 8:7
and *b* them to their place .....Is 14:2
lay low, and *b* to the ....Is 25:12
he *b* down them that dwell ....Is 26:5
O Zion, that *b* good tidings ...Is 40:9
O Jerusalem, that *b* good .....Is 40:9
That *b* the princes to ....Is 40:23
Jerusalem one that *b* good ....Is 41:27
Which *b* forth the chariot .....Is 43:17
Tell ye and *b* them near ......Is 45:21
I *b* near my righteousness .....Is 46:13
the feet of him that *b* good....Is 52:7
b forth an instrument for.......Is 54:16
Even them will I *b* to my .....Is 56:7
that thou *b* the poor that......Is 58:7
For brass I will *b* gold ....Is 60:17
the earth *b* forth her bud .....Is 61:11
And I will *b* forth a seed......Is 65:9
will *b* their fears upon ....Is 66:4
and I will *b* you to Zion ......Jer 3:14
that *b* forth her first child .....Jer 4:31
and *b* forth the wind out of ...Jer 10:13
anger, lest thou *b* me to ......Jer 10:24
therefore I will *b* upon........Jer 11:8
b upon them the day of evil ...Jer 17:18
b burnt offerings, and.........Jer 17:26
and *b* sacrifices of praise ......Jer 17:26
I will *b* them from the ....Jer 31:8
so will I *b* upon them all......Jer 32:42
I will *b* it health and cure .....Jer 33:6
I will *b* a fear upon thee ......Jer 49:5
and *b* forth the wind out of ...Jer 51:16
will *b* a sword upon you ......Ezek 6:3
And I will *b* you out of the ...Ezek 11:9
b them forth out of the ....Ezek 20:9
I would not *b* them into the ...Ezek 20:15
to *b* thee upon the necks of ...Ezek 21:29
and I will *b* them against......Ezek 23:22
which *b* their iniquity to ......Ezek 29:16
will *b* them out from the ......Ezek 34:13
I would *b* thee against ....Ezek 38:17
by *b* upon us a great evil......Dan 9:12
b her into the wilderness ......Hos 2:14
he *b* forth fruit unto ....Hos 10:1
masters, *B*, and let us drink ...Amos 4:1
Yet will I *b* an heir unto ......Mic 1:15
feet of him that *b* good ....Nah 1:15
that which the ground *b*.......Hag 1:11
And I will *b* them, and they ...Zech 8:8
B ye all the tithes into the ....Mal 3:10
And she shall *b* forth a son ...Matt 1:21
until I *b* thee word: for ....Matt 2:13
tree which *b* not forth good ...Matt 3:10
if thou *b* thy gift to the ....Matt 5:23
good tree *b* forth good fruit ...Matt 7:17
a corrupt tree *b* forth evil .....Matt 7:17
of the heart *b* forth good......Matt 12:35
evil treasure *b* forth evil ......Matt 12:35
and *b* forth some a ....Matt 13:23
b them up into a high.........Matt 17:1
suffer you? *b* him hither to ....Matt 17:17
loose them and *b* them........Matt 21:2
a nation *b* forth the fruits .....Matt 21:43
b one sick of the palsy ....Mark 2:3
earth *b* forth fruit of..........Mark 4:28
And they *b* unto him one .....Mark 7:32
shall I suffer you? *b* him ......Mark 9:19
man sat; loose him, and *b* .....Mark 11:2
and *b* forth a son, and shalt ...Luke 1:31
I *b* you good tidings of........Luke 2:10
which *b* not forth good........Luke 3:9
b not forth corrupt fruit.......Luke 6:43
pleasures of this life, and *b*....Luke 8:14
when they *b* you unto the .....Luke 12:11
B forth the best robe, and ....Luke 15:22
sat: loose him, and *b* him .....Luke 19:30
b the spices which they had ...Luke 24:1
this fold: them also I must *b* ..John 10:16
if it die, it *b* forth much.......John 12:24
teach you all things, and *b* ....John 14:26
same *b* forth much fruit ....John 15:5
What accusation *b* ye ....John 18:29
unto Jerusalem, *b* sick ....Acts 5:16
and intend to *b* this man's.....Acts 5:28
they should *b* them into ....Acts 7:6
he might *b* them bound ....Acts 9:2
thou *b* certain strange ....Acts 17:20
to *b* them which were there ...Acts 22:5
them, and to *b* him into the ...Acts 23:10
b me into captivity to the .....Rom 7:23
b to nothing the 1Cor 1:19
b you into remembrance of....1Cor 4:17
under my body, and *b* it 1Cor 9:27
may *b* me on my journey 1Cor 16:6
b into captivity every 2Cor 10:5
if any man *b* you into 2Cor 11:20
schoolmaster to *b* us unto .....Gal 3:24
b them up in the nurture ......Eph 6:4
and *b* forth fruit, as it doth....Col 1:6
in Jesus will God *b* with 1Thess 4:14
grace of God that *b* ....Titus 2:11
he *b* in the first begotten......Heb 1:6
b many sons unto glory, to ....Heb 2:10
b forth herbs meet for them ...Heb 6:7
the *b* in of a better hope ......Heb 7:19
that he might *b* us to God 1Pet 3:18
b in the flood upon 2Pet 2:5
and *b* not this doctrine 2John 10
thou *b* forward on their 3John 6
do *b* their glory and honor ....Rev 21:24

BRINGERS
the *b* up of the children.......2Kin 10:5

BRINK—*edge; side of*
kine upon the *b* of the river ...Gen 41:3
in the flags by the river's *b* ....Ex 2:3
stand by the river's *b* ....Ex 7:15
by the *b* of the river of Arnon .Deut 2:36
When ye are come to the *b* ...Josh 3:8
return to the *b* of the river ....Ezek 47:6

BROAD—*width; wide, open*

[*also* BROADER]
long, and five cubits *b* ....Ex 27:1
them make them *b* plates .....Num 16:38
chamber was five cubits *b* 1Kin 6:6
middle was six cubits *b*........1Kin 6:6
third was seven cubits *b* 1Kin 6:6
long, and five cubits *b* 2Chr 6:13
Jerusalem unto the *b* wall .....Neh 3:8
furnaces even unto the *b* ......Neh 12:38
the earth, and *b* than the .....Job 11:9
out of the strait into a *b* ......Job 36:16
is exceeding *b* ....Ps 119:96
in the streets, and in the *b* ....Song 3:2
of *b* rivers and streams.........Is 33:21
seek in the *b* places thereof ...Jer 5:1
threshold..one reed *b* ....Ezek 40:6
six cubits *b* on the one side ....Ezek 41:1
six cubits *b* on the other .....Ezek 41:1
long as they, and as *b* as ......Ezek 42:11
cubits long, twelve *b* ....Ezek 43:16
of the city five thousand *b* ....Ezek 45:6
cubits long and thirty *b* ....Ezek 46:22
against another in the *b* ....Nah 2:4
b is the way, that leadeth .....Matt 7:13
they make *b* their ....Matt 23:5

BROIDED—*See* BRAIDED HAIR

BROIDERED—*See* EMBROIDERED

BROILED FISH
Eaten by Jesus ....Luke 24:42, 43

BROKEN-FOOTED—*disqualifies for the priesthood*
Or a man that is *b* ....Lev 21:19

BROKEN-HANDED—*disqualifies for the priesthood*
that is brokenfooted, or *b* .....Lev 21:19

BROKEN-HEARTED—*overcome by grief or despair*
Christ's mission to ....Is 61:1

hath sent me to heal the *b* ....Luke 4:18

BROOD—*the young of an animal*
as a hen doth gather her *b* ....Luke 13:34

BROOK—*creek, stream*

Characteristics of:
Numerous ....Deut 8:7
Produce grass 1Kin 18:5
Abound in fish ....Is 19:8
Afford protection........Is 9:6

Names of:
Arnon ....Num 21:14, 15
Besor 1Sam 30:9
Gaash 2Sam 23:30
Cherith 1Kin 17:3, 5
Eschol..................Num 13:23, 24

Kidron 2Sam 15:23
Kishon ....Ps 83:9
Zered ....Deut 2:13

Figurative of:
Wisdom ....Prov 18:4
Prosperity...............Job 20:17
Deception ....Job 6:15
Refreshment ....Ps 110:7

[*also* BROOKS]
and sent them over the *b* .....Gen 32:23
willows of the *b*; and ye.......Lev 23:40
they came unto the *b* of.......Num 13:23
in the *b* of Arnon ....Num 21:14
you over the *b* Zered ....Deut 2:13
smooth stones out of the *b* 1Sam 17:40
himself passed over the *b* 2Sam 15:23
Hiddai of the *b* of Gaash 2Sam 23:30
out and passest over the *b* 1Kin 2:37
unto all *b*: peradventure 1Kin 18:5
unto the *b* Kidron, and 2Kin 23:6
burned it at the *b* Kidron 2Kin 23:6
Hurai of the *b* of Gaash 1Chr 11:32
burnt it at the *b* Kidron.......2Chr 15:16
up in the night by the *b*.......Neh 2:15
dealt deceitfully as a *b* ....Job 6:15
and as the stream of *b* they ...Job 6:15
the *b* of honey and butter .....Job 20:17
panteth after the water *b*......Ps 42:1
as to Jabin, at the *b* of........Ps 83:9
He shall drink of the *b* in .....Ps 110:7
of wisdom as a flowing *b*......Prov 18:4
away to the *b* of the ....Is 15:7
the fields unto the *b* of ....Jer 31:40
over the *b* Cedron, where .....John 18:1

BROTH—*thin, watery soup*
Served by Gideon ....Judg 6:19, 20
Figurative of evil ....Is 65:4

BROTHER—*male sibling; fellow Christian*

Used naturally of:
Sons of same parents ....Gen 42:4
Common ancestry ....Gen 14:16
Same race ....Deut 23:7
Same humanity..........Gen 9:5

Used figuratively of:
An ally ....Amos 1:9
Christian disciples ....Matt 23:8
A spiritual companion ...1Cor 1:1

Characteristics of Christian brothers:
One Father ....Matt 23:8, 9
Believe ....Luke 8:21
Some weak 1Cor 8:11-13
In need..................James 2:15
Of low degree...........James 1:9
Disorderly 2Thess 3:6
Evil ....James 4:11
Falsely judge............Rom 14:10-21
Need admonishment 2Thess 3:15

[*also* BRETHREN]
she again bare his *b* Abel .....Gen 4:2
Cain talked with Abel his *b* ...Gen 4:8
rose up against Abel his *b*.....Gen 4:8
Where is Abel thy *b*? ....Gen 4:9
I know not; Am I my *b*.......Gen 4:9
voice of thy *b* blood crieth ....Gen 4:10
her mouth to receive thy *b* ....Gen 4:11
the hand of every man's *b*.....Gen 9:5
father, and told his two *b* .....Gen 9:22
the *b* of Japheth the elder .....Gen 10:21
and his *b* name was Joktan ....Gen 10:25
his wife, and Lot his *b* son ....Gen 12:5
thy herdmen; for we be *b* .....Gen 13:8
took Lot, Abram's *b* son ......Gen 14:12
b of Eschol, and *b* of Aner ....Gen 14:13
in the presence of all his *b* ....Gen 16:12
pray you, *b*, do not so ....Gen 19:7
she herself said, He is my *b* ...Gen 20:5
born children unto thy *b* ......Gen 22:20
wife of Nahor, Abraham's *b* ...Gen 24:15
house of my master's *b* ....Gen 24:27
to take my master's *b*.........Gen 24:48
the presence of all his *b*.......Gen 25:18
after that came his *b* out ......Gen 25:26
speak unto Esau thy *b* ....Gen 27:6
Esau my *b* is a hairy man .....Gen 27:11
as his *b* Esau's hands; so ......Gen 27:23
be lord over thy *b*, and let ....Gen 27:29
Esau his *b* came in from his ...Gen 27:30
Thy *b* came with subtilty ......Gen 27:35
and shalt serve thy *b*..........Gen 27:40
then will I slay my *b* Jacob ....Gen 27:41
Behold, thy *b* Esau, as........Gen 27:42
flee thou to Laban my *b* to....Gen 27:43
until thy *b* fury turn away .....Gen 27:44
Laban thy mother's *b* ....Gen 28:2
unto them, My *b*, whence .....Gen 29:4
of Laban his mother's *b*.......Gen 29:10
Laban his mother's *b* ....Gen 29:10
that he was her father's *b* .....Gen 29:12
he took his *b* with him, and ...Gen 31:23
before him to Esau his *b*......Gen 32:3
until he came near to his *b*....Gen 33:3
father and unto her *b* ....Gen 34:11
from the face of Esau thy *b* ...Gen 35:1
from the face of his *b*.........Gen 36:6
feeding the flock with his *b*....Gen 37:2
is it if we slay our *b*, and .....Gen 37:26
went down from his *b*.........Gen 38:1
in unto thy *b* wife, and ....Gen 38:8
and raise up seed to thy *b*.....Gen 38:8
Joseph's ten *b* went down to ..Gen 42:3
Joseph's *b* came, and ....Gen 42:6
bring your youngest *b* unto ....Gen 42:34
except your *b* be with you.....Gen 43:3
Judah and his *b* came to ......Gen 44:14
Have ye a father, or a *b*? .....Gen 44:19
himself known unto his *b* ......Gen 45:1
said, I am Joseph your *b*? .....Gen 45:4
Joseph's *b* are come; and it ...Gen 45:16
Joseph said unto his *b*, and....Gen 46:31
My *b*, and my father's ....Gen 46:31
My father and my *b*, and .....Gen 47:1
the name of their *b* in their ...Gen 48:6
younger *b* shall be greater.....Gen 48:19
Simeon and Levi are *b*........Gen 49:5
was separate from his *b* ....Gen 49:26
house of Joseph, and his *b* ....Gen 50:8
Joseph died, and all his *b* .....Ex 1:6
that he went out unto his *b* ...Ex 2:11
not Aaron the Levite thy *b*? ...Ex 4:14
unto my *b* which are in ....Ex 4:18
Aaron thy *b* shall be thy ......Ex 7:1
unto thee Aaron thy *b* ....Ex 28:1
slay every man his *b*, and .....Ex 32:27
carry your *b* from before ......Lev 10:4
Speak unto Aaron thy *b* ....Lev 16:2
nakedness of thy father's *b* ....Lev 18:14
the nakedness of thy *b* wife ...Lev 18:16
Thou shalt not hate thy *b* .....Lev 19:17
a man shall take his *b* wife ....Lev 20:21
his daughter, and for his *b*.....Lev 21:2
high priest among his *b* ....Lev 21:10
If thy *b* be waxen poor, and...Lev 25:25
over your *b* the children of....Lev 25:46
for his *b*, or for his sister .....Num 6:7
their *b* in the tabernacle ......Num 8:26
thy *b* the sons of Levi with ....Num 16:10
b also of the tribe of Levi .....Num 18:2
our *b* died before the Lord! .....Num 20:3
thou, and Aaron thy *b*, and ...Num 20:8
brought unto his *b* a ....Num 25:6
possession among the *b* of.....Num 27:4
If he have no *b*, then ye ......Num 27:10
Aaron thy *b* was gathered ......Num 27:13
Shall your *b* go to war, and ...Num 32:6
our *b* unto his daughters ......Num 36:2
unto their father's *b* sons.....Num 36:11
the causes between your *b* ....Deut 1:16
every man and his *b* ....Deut 1:16
the coast of your *b* ....Deut 2:4
armed before your *b* ....Deut 3:18
inheritance with his *b* ....Deut 10:9
If thy *b*, the son of thy ....Deut 13:6
of his neighbor, or of his *b* ....Deut 15:2
a poor man of one of thy *b* ...Deut 15:7
from among thy *b* shalt ....Deut 17:15
thee, which is not thy *b* ....Deut 17:15
inheritance among their *b* .....Deut 18:2
falsely against his *b* ....Deut 19:18
lest his *b* heart faint as well ...Deut 20:8
again unto thy *b*..............Deut 22:1
Thou shalt not see thy *b* ox ...Deut 22:1
any of his *b* of the children....Deut 24:7
When thou dost lend thy *b* ....Deut 24:10
thy *b* should seem vile unto ...Deut 25:3
If *b* dwell together, and ....Deut 25:5
like not to take his *b* wife .....Deut 25:7
then let his *b* wife go up to ...Deut 25:7
shall be evil toward his *b*......Deut 28:54
Aaron thy *b* died in mount ....Deut 32:50
did he acknowledge his *b* .....Deut 33:9
ye shall pass before your *b* ....Josh 1:14
my mother, and my *b*.........Josh 2:13
her mother, and her *b* ....Josh 6:23
Nevertheless my *b* that........Josh 14:8
son of Kenaz, the *b* of ....Josh 15:17
inheritance among our *b* ......Josh 17:4
among the *b* of their father....Josh 17:4
Ye have not left your *b* ....Josh 22:3
said unto Simeon his *b*........Judg 1:3
Kenaz, Caleb's younger *b* .....Judg 3:9
They were my *b*, even the ....Judg 8:19
unto his mother's *b* ....Judg 9:1
for they said, He is our *b* .....Judg 9:3
Jepthah fled from his *b* ....Judg 11:3
the daughters of thy *b* ....Judg 14:3
Then his *b* and all the ....Judg 16:31
they came unto their *b* to .....Judg 18:8
and their *b* said unto them ....Judg 18:8
said unto them, Nay, my *b* ....Judg 19:23
the voice of their *b* ....Judg 20:13
children of Benjamin my *b*? ...Judg 20:23
for Benjamin their *b* ....Judg 21:6
their *b* come unto us to ....Judg 21:22
was our *b* Elimelech's ....Ruth 4:3
cut off from among his *b*......Ruth 4:10
son of Ahitub, Ichabod's *b* 1Sam 14:3
in the midst of his *b* 1Sam 16:13
Take now for thy *b* an 1Sam 17:17
run to the camp to thy *b* 1Sam 17:17
Eliab his eldest *b* heard 1Sam 17:28
my *b*, he hath commanded 1Sam 20:29
I pray thee, and see my *b* 1Sam 20:29
his *b* and all his father's.......1Sam 22:1
son of Zeruiah, *b* of Joab 1Sam 26:6
Ye shall not do so, my *b* 1Sam 30:23
distressed for thee, my *b* 2Sam 1:26
my face to Joab thy *b*.........2Sam 2:22
return from following their *b* ..2Sam 2:26
to his *b*, and to his friends 2Sam 3:8
the blood of Asahel his *b* 2Sam 3:27
Rechab and Baanah his *b* 2Sam 4:6
hand of Abishai his *b* 2Sam 10:10
son of Shimeah David's *b* 2Sam 13:3
him that smote his *b* 2Sam 14:7
life of his *b* whom he slew 2Sam 14:7
take back thy *b*: mercy and ...2Sam 15:20
the son of Zeruiah, Joab's *b*...2Sam 18:2
Ye are my *b*, ye are my.......2Sam 19:12
Art thou in health, my *b*? 2Sam 20:9
slew the *b* of Goliath the.......2Sam 21:19
Abishai, the *b* of Joab 2Sam 23:18
called all his *b* the king's 1Kin 1:9
Solomon his *b*, he called 1Kin 1:10
because of Absalom thy *b*.....1Kin 2:7
and is become my *b* 1Kin 2:15
hast given me, my *b*? 1Kin 9:13
nor fight against your *b* the ...1Kin 12:24
saying, Alas, my *b*............1Kin 13:30
Is he yet alive? he is my *b* 1Kin 20:32
arise up from among his *b* 2Kin 9:2
Jehu met with the *b* of........2Kin 10:13
We are the *b* of Ahaziah 2Kin 10:13
bread among their *b* 2Kin 23:9
Mattaniah his father's *b* 2Kin 24:17
and his *b* name was Joktan 1Chr 1:19
sons of Jada the *b* of 1Chr 2:32
honorable than his *b* 1Chr 4:9
Chelub the *b* of Shuah 1Chr 4:11
prevailed above his *b* 1Chr 5:2
And his *b* Asaph, who stood ..1Chr 6:39
And their *b* the sons..........1Chr 6:44
And their *b* among all the.....1Chr 7:5

the name of his *b* was 1Chr 7:16
dwelt with their *b* in 1Chr 8:32
sons of Eshek his *b* were 1Chr 8:39
Zerah; Jeuel, and their *b*.......1Chr 9:6
Abishai the *b* of Joab, he 1Chr 11:20
of Saul's *b* of Benjamin 1Chr 12:2
us send abroad unto our *b* 1Chr 13:2
and his *b* hundred and 1Chr 15:5
the son of Joel; and of his *b*...1Chr 15:17
of the sons of Merari their *b* ..1Chr 15:17
hand of Asaph and his *b* 1Chr 16:7
hand of Abishai his *b* 1Chr 19:11
Jair slew Lahmi the *b* of 1Chr 20:5
and their *b* the sons of Kish ...1Chr 23:22
b of Michah was Isshiah 1Chr 24:25
lots over against their *b* 1Chr 24:31
against their younger *b* 1Chr 24:31
their *b* that were instructed 1Chr 25:7
whose *b* were strong men 1Chr 26:7
Zetham, and Joel his *b* 1Chr 26:22
Asahel the *b* of Joab, and 1Chr 27:7
Elihu, one of the *b* of David ..1Chr 27:18
Hear me, my *b*, and my 1Chr 28:2
with their sons and their *b* 2Chr 5:12
nor fight against your *b* 2Chr 11:4
shall come to you of your *b* ...2Chr 19:10
he had *b* the sons of...........2Chr 21:2
sons of the *b* of Ahaziah 2Chr 22:8
away captive of their *b*.........2Chr 28:8
they gathered their *b*, and 2Chr 29:15
and like your *b*, which 2Chr 30:7
your *b* and your children 2Chr 30:9
and Shimei his *b* was the 2Chr 31:12
give to their *b* by courses 2Chr 31:15
of the fathers of your *b* 2Chr 35:5
prepare your *b*, that they 2Chr 35:6
Eliakim his *b* king over 2Chr 36:4
his *b* the priests, and ....Ezra 3:2
son of Shealtiel, and his *b*......Ezra 3:2
for their *b* the priests, and ....Ezra 6:20
good to thee, and to thy *b* ....Ezra 7:18
to his *b* the Nethinim, at ....Ezra 8:17
son of Jozadak, and his *b* .....Ezra 10:18
That Hanani, one of my *b* ....Neh 1:2
with his *b* the priests, and .....Neh 3:1
he spake before his *b* and .....Neh 4:2
wives against their *b* the ......Neh 5:1
usury, every one of his *b*......Neh 5:7
That I gave my *b* Hanani ......Neh 7:2
And their *b*, Shebaniah ....Neh 10:10
And their *b* that did the ......Neh 11:12
of their *b* in the days of.......Neh 12:7
to distribute unto their *b* ......Neh 13:13
the multitude of his *b* ....Esth 10:3
wine in their eldest *b* ....Job 1:13
My *b* have dealt deceitfully....Job 6:15
He hath put my *b* far from.....Job 19:13
taken a pledge from thy *b*.....Job 22:6
I am a *b* to dragons, and a ....Job 30:29
there unto him all his *b* ....Job 42:11
declare thy name unto my *b* ...Ps 22:22
had been my friend or *b* ......Ps 35:14
by any means redeem his *b*....Ps 49:7
speakest against thy *b*.........Ps 50:20
a stranger unto my *b* ....Ps 69:8
my *b* and companions..........Ps 122:8
b to dwell together in unity! ...Ps 133:1
soweth discord among *b* ....Prov 6:19
inheritance among the *b* ......Prov 17:2
a *b* is born for adversity.......Prov 17:17
is *b* to him that is a great .....Prov 18:9
A *b* offended is harder........Prov 18:19
sticketh closer than a *b* ......Prov 18:24
All the *b* of the poor do hate..Prov 19:7
neither go into thy *b* house....Prov 27:10
that is near than a *b* far......Prov 27:10
he hath neither child nor *b* ....Eccl 4:8
O that thou wert as my *b* .....Song 8:1
shall take hold of his *b*........Is 3:6
no man shall spare his *b* ......Is 9:19
every one against his *b*.........Is 19:2
said to his *b*, Be of good......Is 41:6
Your *b* that hated you ....Is 66:5
I have cast out all your *b* .....Jer 7:15
trust ye not in any *b*.........Jer 9:4
even thy *b*, and the house .....Jer 12:6
saying, Ah my *b*..............Jer 22:18
one to his *b*, What hath........Jer 23:35
b that are not gone forth ......Jer 29:16
his *b*, saying, Know the ....Jer 31:34
of them,..of a Jew his *b*.......Jer 34:9
Habaziniah, and his *b*..........Jer 35:3
slew them not among their *b* ..Jer 41:8
b, and his neighbors ....Jer 49:10
Son of man, thy *b*, even thy...Ezek 11:15
spoiled his *b* by violence ......Ezek 18:18
every one to his *b*, saying .....Ezek 33:30
shall be against his *b*..........Ezek 38:21
son, or for daughter, for *b* ....Ezek 44:25
Say ye unto your *b*, Ammi ....Hos 2:1
He took his *b* by the heel in ..Hos 12:3
he be fruitful among his *b*.....Hos 13:15
because he did pursue his *b* ...Amos 1:11
thy violence against thy *b* .....Obad 10
the remnant of his *b* shall .....Mic 5:3
hunt every man his *b* with......Mic 7:2
by the sword of his *b* ....Hag 2:22
every man to his *b* ....Zech 7:9
Was not Esau Jacob's *b*? ......Mal 1:2
begat Judas and his *b* ....Matt 1:2
sea of Galilee, saw two *b* .....Matt 4:18
called..Andrew his *b*..........Matt 4:18
is angry with his *b* ....Matt 5:22
whosoever shall say to his *b* ...Matt 5:22
thy *b* hath aught against ......Matt 5:23
first be reconciled to thy *b* ....Matt 5:24
if ye salute your *b* only ....Matt 5:47
the mote that is in thy *b* eye ..Matt 7:3
wilt thou say to thy *b*, Let me .Matt 7:4
called Peter, and Andrew his *b*.Matt 10:2
b shall deliver up the *b* to .....Matt 10:21
his mother and his *b* stood ....Matt 12:46
the same is my *b*, and sister ...Matt 12:50
his *b* Philip's wife............Matt 14:3
James, and John his *b* ....Matt 17:1
thy *b* shall trespass ....Matt 18:15
thou hast gained thy *b* ....Matt 18:15
shall my *b* sin against me .....Matt 18:21
b, or sisters, or father.........Matt 19:29
indignation against..two *b* .....Matt 20:24
his *b* shall marry his wife......Matt 22:24
raise up seed unto his *b*.......Matt 22:24
were with us seven *b* ....Matt 22:25
Christ; and all ye are *b* ....Matt 23:8
the least of these my *b*........Matt 25:40
go tell my *b* that they.........Matt 28:10
saw Simon and Andrew his *b* ..Mark 1:16
and John the *b* of James ......Mark 3:17
came then his *b* ....Mark 3:31
son of Mary, the *b* of James...Mark 6:3
thee to have thy *b* wife ....Mark 6:18
left house, or *b*, or sisters ....Mark 10:29
If a man's *b* die, and leave ....Mark 12:19
b should take his wife.........Mark 12:19
raise up seed unto his *b*.......Mark 12:19
Now there were seven *b* ......Mark 12:20
the *b* shall betray the *b* ....Mark 13:12
b Philip tetrarch of Ituraea ....Luke 3:1
named Peter and Andrew..*b*...Luke 6:14
mote in thy *b* eye ....Luke 6:41
his mother and his *b* ....Luke 8:19
Master, speak to my *b* ....Luke 12:13
not thy friends, nor thy *b* .....Luke 14:12
children, and *b*, and ....Luke 14:26
Thy *b* is come ....Luke 15:27
I have five *b*; that he may.....Luke 16:28
If thy *b* trespass against ....Luke 17:3
parents, or *b*, or wife ....Luke 18:29
If any man's *b* die, having a ...Luke 20:28
his *b* should take his wife .....Luke 20:28
raise up seed unto his *b*.......Luke 20:28
were therefore seven *b* ....Luke 20:29
by parents, and *b*, and ....Luke 21:16
converted, strengthen thy *b*....Luke 22:32
Andrew, Simon Peter's *b*.......John 1:40
his mother, and his *b* and .....John 2:12
Andrew, Simon Peter's *b*......John 6:8
His *b* therefore said unto......John 7:3
neither did his *b* believe in ....John 7:5
whose *b* Lazarus was sick .....John 11:2
go to my *b*, and say unto .....John 20:17
saying abroad among the *b* ....John 21:23
Zelotes, and Judas the *b* of ...Acts 1:13
Men and *b*, let me freely......Acts 2:29
b, I wot that through ....Acts 3:17
unto you of your *b*, like.......Acts 3:22
Wherefore, *b*, look ye out.....Acts 6:3
said, Men, *b*, fathers..........Acts 7:2
saying, Sirs, ye are *b*: why ....Acts 7:26
unto you of your *b*, like.......Acts 7:37
said *b* Saul, the Lord, even....Acts 9:17
Which when the *b* knew ......Acts 9:30
b from Joppa accompanied ....Acts 10:23
apostles and *b* that were in....Acts 11:1
these six *b* accompanied.......Acts 11:12
send relief unto the *b* which ...Acts 11:29
he killed James the *b* of.......Acts 12:2
saying, Ye men and *b*, if ye ...Acts 13:15
evil affected against the *b* .....Acts 14:2
from Judea taught the *b* ......Acts 15:1
great joy unto all the *b* ....Acts 15:3
chief men among the *b*........Acts 15:22
exhorted the *b* with many .....Acts 15:32
recommended by the *b*........Acts 15:40
b that were at Lystra and .....Acts 16:2
drew Jason and certain *b*......Acts 17:6
took his leave of the *b* and ....Acts 18:18
b, I commend you to God .....Acts 20:32
saluted the *b*, and abode ......Acts 21:7
Thou seest *b*, how many ......Acts 21:20
Men, *b*, and fathers, hear ye ..Acts 22:1
unto me, *B* Saul, receive ......Acts 22:13
Men and *b*, I have lived in ....Acts 23:1
Men and *b*, I am a Pharisee ...Acts 23:6
we found *b* and were ....Acts 28:14
you ignorant, *b*, that I ....Rom 1:13
Know ye not, *b*, (for I speak ..Rom 7:1
Therefore, *b*, we are..........Rom 8:12
firstborn among many *b*.......Rom 8:29
from Christ for my *b* ....Rom 9:3
B, my heart's desire and ......Rom 10:1
not, *b*, that ye should be ......Rom 11:25
I beseech you therefore, *b* ....Rom 12:1
an occasion to fall in his *b* ....Rom 14:13
persuaded of you, my *b*.......Rom 15:14
and the *b* which are with......Rom 16:14
city saluteth you..a *b* ....Rom 16:23
I beseech you, *b*, by the 1Cor 1:10
I *b*, when I came to you 1Cor 2:1
I *b*, could not speak unto 1Cor 3:1
these things *b*, I have in a.....1Cor 4:6
that is called a *b* be a.........1Cor 5:11
judge between his *b*? 1Cor 6:5
b goeth to law with *b*, and 1Cor 6:6
If any *b* hath a wife that 1Cor 7:12
A *b* or a sister is not under ...1Cor 7:15
B, let every man, wherein.....1Cor 7:24
ye sin so against the *b*, and ...1Cor 8:12
b, I would not that ye 1Cor 10:1
praise you, *b*, that ye 1Cor 11:2
concerning spiritual gifts, *b* 1Cor 12:1
b, if I come unto you 1Cor 14:6
Moreover, *b*, I declare unto ..1Cor 15:1
of above five hundred *b* at 1Cor 15:6
I look for him with the *b* 1Cor 16:11
As touching our *b* Apollos 1Cor 16:12
God, and Timothy our *b* 2Cor 1:1
b, have you ignorant of 2Cor 1:8
I found not Titus my *b*........2Cor 2:13
Moreover, *b*, we do you to....2Cor 8:1
I have sent with him the *b* 2Cor 8:18
Yet have I sent the *b*, lest 2Cor 9:3
the *b* which came from........2Cor 11:9
and with him I sent a *b* 2Cor 12:18
Finally, *b*, farewell, Be........2Cor 13:11
And all the *b* which are ....Gal 1:2
save James the Lord's *b*.......Gal 1:19
that because of false *b* ....Gal 2:4
B, I speak after the manner ...Gal 3:15
B, I beseech you, be as I .....Gal 4:12
I, *b*, if I yet preach ....Gal 5:11
B, if a man be overtaken in ...Gal 6:1
Finally, my *b*, be strong in ....Eph 6:10
a beloved *b* and faithful ....Eph 6:21
ye should understand, *b* ....Phil 1:12

to you Epaphroditus, my *b* .... Phil 2:25
my *b*, rejoice in the Lord ..... Phil 3:1
my *b* dearly beloved and ...... Phil 4:1
God, and Timothy our *b* ...... Col 1:1
saints and faithful *b* .... Col 1:2
you, who is a beloved *b* .... Col 4:7
Salute the *b* which are in ...... Col 4:15
Knowing, *b* beloved, your 1Thess 1:4
yourselves, *b*, know our 1Thess 2:1
sent Timothy, our *b*, and 1Thess 3:2
b, we were comforted 1Thess 3:7
we beseech you, *b*, and 1Thess 4:1
end defraud his *b* in any 1Thess 4:6
times and the seasons, *b* 1Thess 5:1
God always for you, *b* 2Thess 1:3
we beseech you, *b*, by the 2Thess 2:1
Finally, *b*, pray for us that 2Thess 3:1
put the *b* in remembrance 1Tim 4:6
the younger men as *b* 1Tim 5:1
because they are *b* 1Tim 6:2
Claudia, and all the *b* 2Tim 4:21
above a servant, a *b* .... Philem 16
not ashamed to call them *b* .... Heb 2:11
holy *b*, partakers .... Heb 3:1
that is, of their *b*, though ..... Heb 7:5
and every man his *b* .... Heb 8:11
Having therefore, *b* .... Heb 10:19
I beseech you, *b*, suffer the ... Heb 13:22
Know ye that our *b* .... Heb 13:23
My *b*, count it all joy when ... James 1:2
My *b*, have not the faith of ... James 2:1
My *b*, be not many masters ... James 3:1
not evil one of another *b* ...... James 4:11
Be patient therefore, *b* .... James 5:7
unfeigned love of the *b* 1Pet 1:22
love as *b*, be pitiful, be 1Pet 3:8
accomplished in your *b* 1Pet 5:9
a faithful *b* unto you, as I 1Pet 5:12
B, I write no new 1John 2:7
the light, and hateth his *b* 1John 2:9
He that loveth his *b* 1John 2:10
he that hateth his *b* is in 1John 2:11
he that loveth not his *b* 1John 3:10
were evil, and his *b* 1John 3:12
Marvel not, my *b*, if the 1John 3:13
because we love the *b*, He 1John 3:14
loveth not his *b* abideth 1John 3:14
Whosoever hateth his *b* is a ... 1John 3:15
our lives for the *b* 1John 3:16
seeth his *b* have need, and 1John 3:17
who loveth God, love his *b* 1John 4:21
any man see his *b* sin a sin 1John 5:16
when the *b* came and 3John 3
he himself receive the *b* 3John 10
of Jesus Christ, and *b* of ...... Jude 1
I John who also am your *b* .... Rev 1:9
also and their *b* .... Rev 6:11
the accuser of our *b* is cast .... Rev 12:10
of thy *b* that have the .... Rev 19:10
of thy *b* the prophets, and .... Rev 22:9

BROTHERHOOD—*the sharing of common origin*

Based on common:
Creation .... Gen 1:27, 28
Blood .... Acts 17:26
Needs .... Prov 22:2; Mal 2:10

Disrupted by:
Sin 1John 3:12
Satan .... John 8:44

the *b* between Judah and ...... Zech 11:14
Love the *b*. Fear God 1Pet 2:17

BROTHERLY KINDNESS

Toward Christians:
Taught by God 1Thess 4:9
Commanded .... Rom 12:10
Explained 1John 4:7-21
Fulfills the Law .... Rom 13:8-10
Badge of new birth ...... John 13:34
A Christian grace 2Pet 1:5-7
Must continue .... Heb 13:1

Toward others:
Neighbors .... Matt 22:39
Enemies .... Matt 5:44

BROTHERS OF CHRIST
Four: James, Joses, Simon, Judas (Jude) .. Matt 13:55; Mark 6:3
Born after Christ .... Matt 1:25; Luke 2:7
Travel with Mary .... Matt 12:47-50
Disbelieve Christ .... John 7:4, 5
Become believers .... Acts 1:14
Work for Christ 1Cor 9:5
One (James) becomes prominent .... Acts 12:17
Wrote an epistle .... James 1:1
Another (Jude) wrote an epistle .... Jude 1

BROTHERS, TWIN
Figureheads on Paul's ship to Rome, called Castor and Pollux ..... Acts 28:11

BROUGHT—*See* INTRODUCTION

BROUGHT UP—*reared*
Ephraim's children—by Joseph .... Gen 50:23
Esther—by Mordecai .... Esth 2:5-7, 20
Wisdom (Christ)—by the Lord .... Prov 8:30
Jesus—at Nazareth ...... Luke 4:16
Paul—at Gamaliel's feet. . Acts 22:3

BROW
The forehead .... Is 48:4
Top of hill .... Luke 4:29

BROWN—*color of earth*
b cattle among..sheep .... Gen 30:32

BRUISED—*disabled; broken down by pounding; wounded*

Used literally of:
Physical injuries .... Luke 9:39

Used figuratively of:
Evils .... Is 1:6
The Messiah's pains ..... Is 53:5
Satan's defeat .... Gen 3:15; Rom 16:20

[*also* BRUISE, BRUISES, BRUISING]
it shall *b* thy head .... Gen 3:15
and thou shalt *b* his heel ...... Gen 3:15
the Lord that which is *b* ...... Lev 22:24
the staff of this *b* reed 2Kin 18:21
Bread corn is *b*, because ...... Is 28:28
nor *b* it with his horsemen .... Is 28:28
A *b* reed shall he not break ... Is 42:3
Yet it pleased the Lord to *b* .. Is 53:10
Thy *b* is incurable and thy .... Jer 30:12
they *b* the teats of their .... Ezek 23:3
in *b* thy teats by the .... Ezek 23:21
it break in pieces and *b* .... Dan 2:40
no healing of thy *b*; thy .... Nah 3:19
A *b* reed shall he not break ... Matt 12:20
at liberty them that are *b* ..... Luke 4:18

BRUIT—*rumor; noise*
the noise of the *b* is come ..... Jer 10:22
that hear the *b* of thee shall ... Nah 3:19

BRUTE—*strongly and grossly sensual; befitting beasts*

[*also* BRUTISH]
the fool and the *b* person ..... Ps 49:10
A *b* man knoweth not .... Ps 92:6
ye *b* among the people .... Ps 94:8
that hateth reproof is *b* .... Prov 12:1
Surely I am more *b* than ...... Prov 30:2
of Pharaoh is become *b* .... Is 19:11
they are altogether *b* and ...... Jer 10:8
Every man is *b* in his .... Jer 10:14
Every man is *b* by his .... Jer 51:17
into the hand of *b* men and ... Ezek 21:31
these, as natural *b* beasts 2Pet 2:12
know naturally, as *b* .... Jude 10

BUCKET—*container for water*
Figurative of blessing .... Num 24:7
Pictures God's magnitude . Is 40:15

BUCKLER—*small round shield held at arm's length*

[*also* BUCKLERS]
a *b* to all them that trust in ... 2Sam 22:31
men able to bear *b* and 1Chr 5:18
could handle shield and *b* 1Chr 12:8
spears, and *b*, and shields 2Chr 23:9
the thick bosses of his *b* .... Job 15:26
my *b*, and the horn of my ..... Ps 18:2
Take hold of shield and *b* ..... Ps 35:2
truth shall be thy..*b* .... Ps 91:4
a *b* to them that walk .... Prov 2:7
there hang a thousand *b* ...... Song 4:4
Order ye the *b* and shield ..... Jer 46:3
set against thee *b* and .... Ezek 23:24
and lift up the *b* against .... Ezek 26:8
company with *b* and .... Ezek 38:4
the shields and the *b*, the ..... Ezek 39:9

BUD—*the earliest stage of growth; to begin to grow*

[*also* BUDDED, BUDS]
it was as though it *b*, and ..... Gen 40:10
the house of Levi was *b* .... Num 17:8
budded, and brought forth *b* .. Num 17:8
the scent of water it will *b* .... Job 14:9
to cause the *b* of the tender ... Job 38:27
the horn of David to *b* .... Ps 132:17
and the pomegranates *b* .... Song 6:11
the pomegranates *b* forth ...... Song 7:12
when the *b* is perfect, and ..... Is 18:5
Israel shall blossom and *b* ..... Is 27:6
maketh it bring forth and *b* ... Is 55:10
earth bringeth forth her *b* ..... Is 61:11
blossomed, pride hath *b* .... Ezek 7:10
to multiply as the *b* of the .... Ezek 16:7
of the house of Israel to *b* .... Ezek 29:21
the *b* shall yield no meal ...... Hos 8:7
Aaron's rod that *b*, and the ... Heb 9:4

BUFFET—*to strike repeatedly; batter*
Jesus subjected to .... Matt 26:67; Mark 14:65
Descriptive of Paul 2Cor 12:7
Figurative of self-discipline 1Cor 9:27

[*also* BUFFETED]
and are *b*, and have no 1Cor 4:11
messenger of Satan to *b* 2Cor 12:7
ye..*b* for your faults 1Pet 2:20

BUILD—*to construct or erect*

Used literally, of:
City .... Gen 4:17
Altar .... Gen 8:20
Tower .... Gen 11:4
House .... Gen 33:17
Sheepfolds .... Num 32:16
Fortifications .... Deut 20:20; Ezek 4:2
Temple .... 1Kin 6:1, 14; Ezra 4:1
High place 1Kin 11:7
Walls .... Neh 4:6
Tombs .... Matt 23:29; Luke 11:47
Synagogue .... Luke 7:2-5

Used figuratively, of:
Obeying Christ .... Matt 7:24-27
Church .... Matt 16:18
Christ's resurrection ..... Matt 26:61; John 2:19
Return to legalism .... Gal 2:16-20
Christian unity .... Eph 2:19-22
Spiritual growth .... Acts 20:32; Col 2:7; 1Pet 2:5

See EDIFICATION

[*also* BUILDED, BUILDEST, BUILDETH, BUILDING, BUILDINGS, BUILT]
and *b* Nineveh, and the city ... Gen 10:11

which the children of men **b** ... Gen 11:5
b he an altar unto the Lord ... Gen 12:7
b..an altar unto the Lord ... Gen 13:18
Abraham **b** an altar there ... Gen 22:9
And he **b** an altar there ... Gen 26:25
b him a house, and made ... Gen 33:17
And he **b** there an altar ... Gen 35:7
b for Pharaoh..cities ... Ex 1:11
And Moses **b** an altar, and ... Ex 17:15
shalt not **b**..of hewn stone ... Ex 20:25
b an altar under the hill ... Ex 24:4
he **b** an altar before it; and ... Ex 32:5
Hebron was **b** seven years ... Num 13:22
let the city of Sihon be **b** ... Num 21:27
B me here seven altars ... Num 23:1
and **b** seven altars and ... Num 23:14
children of Gad **b** ... Num 32:34
unto the cities which they **b** ... Num 32:38
goodly cities..thou **b** not ... Deut 6:10
and hast **b** goodly houses ... Deut 8:12
it shall not be **b** again ... Deut 13:16
that hath **b** a new house ... Deut 20:5
When thou **b** a new house ... Deut 22:8
not **b** up his brother's house ... Deut 25:9
shalt thou **b** a house and ... Deut 28:30
and **b** this city Jericho; he ... Josh 6:26
Joshua **b** an altar unto..Lord ... Josh 8:30
Ephraim; and he **b** the city ... Josh 19:5
Manasseh **b** there an altar ... Josh 22:10
ye have **b** you an altar ... Josh 22:16
in **b** you an altar beside the ... Josh 22:19
Let us now prepare to **b** us ... Josh 22:26
cities which ye **b** not, and ... Josh 24:13
b a city, and called the name ... Judg 1:26
Gideon **b** an altar there ... Judg 6:24
b an altar unto the Lord ... Judg 6:26
they **b** a city, and dwelt ... Judg 18:28
b there an altar, and offered ... Judg 21:4
did **b** the house of Israel ... Ruth 4:11
I will **b** him a sure house ... 1Sam 2:35
b an altar unto the Lord ... 1Sam 7:17
Saul **b** an altar unto the Lord ... 1Sam 14:35
was the first altar that he **b** ... 1Sam 14:35
And David **b** round about ... 2Sam 5:9
Shalt thou **b** me a house ... 2Sam 7:5
to **b** an altar unto the Lord ... 2Sam 24:21
And David **b** there an altar ... 2Sam 24:25
B thee a house in Jerusalem ... 1Kin 2:36
an end of **b** his own house ... 1Kin 3:1
b unto the name of the Lord ... 1Kin 3:2
father could not **b** an house ... 1Kin 5:3
house which..Solomon **b** ... 1Kin 6:2
when it was in **b**, was built ... 1Kin 6:7
Solomon was **b** his own house ... 1Kin 7:1
b also..house of the forest ... 1Kin 7:2
have surely **b** thee a house ... 1Kin 8:13
tribes of Israel **b** a house ... 1Kin 8:16
this house that I have **b**? ... 1Kin 8:27
Solomon had finished the **b** ... 1Kin 9:1
hast **b**, to put my name ... 1Kin 9:3
to **b** the house of the Lord ... 1Kin 9:15
the house that he had **b** ... 1Kin 10:4
Solomon **b** Millo, and ... 1Kin 11:27
Then Jeroboam **b** Shechem ... 1Kin 12:25
from thence, and **b** Penuel ... 1Kin 12:25
also **b** them high places ... 1Kin 14:23
against Judah, and **b** Ramah ... 1Kin 15:17
that he left off **b** of Ramah ... 1Kin 15:21
wherewith Baasha had **b** ... 1Kin 15:22
and **b** on the hill, and called ... 1Kin 16:24
Hiel the Beth-elite **b** Jericho ... 1Kin 16:34
with the stones he **b** an altar ... 1Kin 18:32
He **b** Elath, and restored it ... 2Kin 14:22
Urijah the priest **b** an altar ... 2Kin 16:11
b them high places in all ... 2Kin 17:9
b up again the high places ... 2Kin 21:3
the king of Israel had **b** ... 2Kin 23:13
they **b** forts against it round ... 2Kin 25:1
Solomon **b** in Jerusalem ... 1Chr 6:10
b Beth-horon the nether ... 1Chr 7:24
who **b** Ono and Lod, with ... 1Chr 8:12
he **b** the city round about ... 1Chr 11:8
carpenters, to **b** him an house ... 1Chr 14:1
shalt not **b** me an house ... 1Chr 17:4
Why..ye not **b** me an house ... 1Chr 17:6
I may **b** an altar therein ... 1Chr 21:22
And David **b** there an altar ... 1Chr 21:26
stones to **b** the house of God ... 1Chr 22:2
be **b** for the Lord must be ... 1Chr 22:5
house that is to be **b** to ... 1Chr 22:19
in mine heart to **b** an house ... 1Chr 28:2
had made ready for the **b** ... 1Chr 28:2
to **b**..an house for thine holy ... 1Chr 29:16
Solomon determined to **b** an ... 2Chr 2:1
send him cedars to **b** him an ... 2Chr 2:3
Behold, I **b** an house to the ... 2Chr 2:4
house which I **b** is great ... 2Chr 2:5
is able to **b** him an house ... 2Chr 2:6
I should **b** him an house ... 2Chr 2:6
house which I am about to **b** ... 2Chr 2:9
b an house for the Lord ... 2Chr 2:12
Solomon began to **b** the ... 2Chr 3:1
the **b** of the house of God ... 2Chr 3:3
have **b** a house of habitation ... 2Chr 6:2
b an house in, that my name ... 2Chr 6:5
David my father to **b** an ... 2Chr 6:7
to **b** an house for my name ... 2Chr 6:8
thou shalt not **b** the house ... 2Chr 6:9
he shall **b** the house for my ... 2Chr 6:9
Solomon had **b** the house of ... 2Chr 8:1
desired to **b** in Jerusalem ... 2Chr 8:6
and the house that he had **b** ... 2Chr 9:3
b cities for defense in ... 2Chr 11:5
he **b** fenced cities in Judah ... 2Chr 14:6
Let us **b** these cities, and ... 2Chr 14:7
b Ramah, to the intent that ... 2Chr 16:1
that he left off **b** of Ramah ... 2Chr 16:5
he **b** in Judah castles, and ... 2Chr 17:12
b thee a sanctuary therein ... 2Chr 20:8
He **b** Eloth, and restored it ... 2Chr 26:2
He **b** the high gate of the ... 2Chr 27:3
on the wall of Ophel he **b** ... 2Chr 27:3
b up all the wall that was ... 2Chr 32:5
he **b** again the high places ... 2Chr 33:3
son of David..did **b** ... 2Chr 35:3
b him a house in Jerusalem ... 2Chr 36:23
b him a house at Jerusalem ... Ezra 1:2
b the altar of the God ... Ezra 3:2
Let us **b** with you ... Ezra 4:2
began to **b** the house of God ... Ezra 5:2
who hath commanded you to **b**. Ezra 5:3
the men that make this **b**? ... Ezra 5:4
made a decree to **b** this house ... Ezra 5:13
until now hath it been in **b** ... Ezra 5:16
made of Cyrus the king to **b** ... Ezra 5:17
Let the house be **b** ... Ezra 6:3
the **b** of this house of God ... Ezra 6:8
sepulchers, that I may **b** it ... Neh 2:5
b up the wall of Jerusalem ... Neh 2:17
and they **b** the sheep gate ... Neh 3:1
the sons of Hassenaah **b** ... Neh 3:3
b it, and set up the doors ... Neh 3:13
heard that we **b** the wall ... Neh 4:1
that which they **b**, if a fox ... Neh 4:3
So **b** we the wall; and all ... Neh 4:6
heard that I had **b** the wall ... Neh 6:1
cause thou **b** the wall ... Neh 6:6
when the wall was **b**, and I ... Neh 7:1
and the houses were not **b** ... Neh 7:4
singers had **b** them villages ... Neh 12:29
b desolate places for ... Job 3:14
and it cannot be **b** again ... Job 12:14
a house which he **b** not ... Job 20:19
thou shalt be **b** up, thou ... Job 22:23
he **b** his house as a moth ... Job 27:18
destroy them, and not **b** them. Ps 28:5
b thou..walls of Jerusalem ... Ps 51:18
will **b** the cities of Judah ... Ps 69:35
b his sanctuary like high ... Ps 78:69
Mercy shall be **b** up for ever ... Ps 89:2
b up thy throne to all ... Ps 89:4
the Lord shall **b** up Zion ... Ps 102:16
Jerusalem is **b** as a city ... Ps 122:3
the Lord **b** the house ... Ps 127:1
they labor in vain that **b** it ... Ps 127:1
Lord doth **b** up Jerusalem ... Ps 147:2
Wisdom hath **b** her house ... Prov 9:1
wise woman **b** her house ... Prov 14:1
wisdom is an house **b** ... Prov 24:3
afterwards **b** thine house ... Prov 24:27
I **b** me houses; I planted ... Eccl 2:4
break down and a time to **b** ... Eccl 3:3
and **b** great bulwarks ... Eccl 9:14
By much slothfulness the **b** ... Eccl 10:18
tower of David **b** for an ... Song 4:4
b upon her palace of silver ... Song 8:9
and **b** a tower in the midst ... Is 5:2
we will **b** with hewn stones ... Is 9:10
city; it shall never be **b** ... Is 25:2
Ye shall be **b**..I will raise ... Is 44:26
he shall **b** my city, and he ... Is 45:13
shall be of thee shall **b** ... Is 58:12
sons of strangers shall **b** ... Is 60:10
they shall **b** the old wastes ... Is 61:4
shall **b** houses, and inhabit ... Is 65:21
where is the house that ye **b** ... Is 66:1
throw down, to **b**, and plant ... Jer 1:10
concerning a kingdom, to **b** ... Jer 18:9
have **b** also the high places ... Jer 19:5
Woe unto him that **b** his ... Jer 22:13
I will **b** me a wide house ... Jer 22:14
I will **b** them, and not pull ... Jer 24:6
B ye houses, and dwell ... Jer 29:5
b ye houses, and dwell ... Jer 29:28
the city shall be **b** upon ... Jer 30:18
Again I will **b** thee, and ... Jer 31:4
thou shalt be **b**, O virgin of ... Jer 31:4
b the high places of Baal ... Jer 32:35
will **b** them, as at the first ... Jer 33:7
Neither shall ye **b** house ... Jer 35:7
will I **b** you, and not pull ... Jer 42:10
which I have **b** will I break ... Jer 45:4
He hath **b** against me, and ... Lam 3:5
let us **b** houses; this city is ... Ezek 11:3
b up a wall, and, lo others ... Ezek 13:10
b unto thee an eminent place ... Ezek 16:24
that thou **b** thine eminent ... Ezek 16:31
and **b** forts, to cut off many ... Ezek 17:17
cast a mount, and to **b** a fort ... Ezek 21:22
thou shalt be **b** no more ... Ezek 26:14
shall **b** houses, and plant ... Ezek 28:26
and the wastes shall be **b** ... Ezek 36:10
I the Lord **b** the ruined ... Ezek 36:36
breadth of the **b**, one reed ... Ezek 40:5
the **b** that was before the ... Ezek 41:12
and the wall of the **b** ... Ezek 41:12
before the **b** toward..north ... Ezek 42:1
the **b** was straitened ... Ezek 42:6
was a row of **b** round about ... Ezek 46:23
I have **b** for the house of ... Dan 4:30
restore and to **b** Jerusalem ... Dan 9:25
the street shall be **b** again ... Dan 9:25
and **b** temples; and Judah ... Hos 8:14
ye have **b** houses of hewn ... Amos 5:11
b his stories in the heaven ... Amos 9:6
I will **b** it as..days of old ... Amos 9:11
They **b** up Zion with blood ... Mic 3:10
day thy walls are to be **b** ... Mic 7:11
Woe to him that **b** a town ... Hab 2:12
they shall also **b** houses ... Zeph 1:13
Lord's house should be **b** ... Hag 1:2
and **b** the house; and I will ... Hag 1:8
my house shall be **b** in it ... Zech 1:16
b it a house in the land of ... Zech 5:11
he shall **b** the temple of ... Zech 6:12
that the temple might be **b** ... Zech 8:9
Tyrus did **b**..a strong hold ... Zech 9:3
return and **b** the desolate ... Mal 1:4
b, but I will throw down ... Mal 1:4
winepress in it, and **b** a ... Matt 21:33
show him the **b** of the temple. Matt 24:1
and **b** it in three days ... Matt 27:40
and **b** a tower, and let it ... Mark 12:1
stones and what **b** are here ... Mark 13:1
within three days I will **b** ... Mark 14:58
and **b** it in three days ... Mark 15:29
whereon their city was **b** ... Luke 4:29
a man which **b** an house ... Luke 6:48
pull down my barns, and **b** ... Luke 12:18
intending to **b** a tower ... Luke 14:28
sold, they planted, they **b** ... Luke 17:28
Solomon **b** him an house ... Acts 7:47
what house will ye **b** me? ... Acts 7:49
b again the tabernacle of ... Acts 15:16
I should **b** upon another ... Rom 15:20

husbandry, ye are God's ***b*** 1Cor 3:9
foundation, and another ***b*** 1Cor 3:10
take heed how he ***b*** 1Cor 3:10
if any man ***b*** upon this 1Cor 3:12
abide which he hath ***b*** 1Cor 3:14
have a ***b*** of God, a house 2Cor 5:1
if I ***b*** again the things ....Gal 2:18
are ***b*** upon the foundation .....Eph 2:20
as he who hath ***b*** the house ...Heb 3:3
he that ***b*** all things is God ....Heb 3:4
is to say, not of this ***b*** ....Heb 9:11
b up yourselves on your ....Jude 20
the ***b*** of the wall of it was .....Rev 21:18

BUILDER—*one who constructs, erects, or makes*

[*also* BUILDERS]
Solomon's ***b*** and Hiram's ***b*** 1Kin 5:18
to the carpenters and ***b*** 2Kin 12:11
Upon carpenters, and ***b*** 2Kin 22:6
to the artificers and ***b*** gave 2Chr 34:11
the ***b*** laid the foundation ......Ezra 3:10
thee to anger before the ***b*** ....Neh 4:5
stone which the ***b*** refused ......Ps 118:22
b have perfected thy beauty ...Ezek 27:4
stone which the ***b*** rejected ....Matt 21:42
stone which the ***b*** rejected ....Mark 12:10
stone which the ***b*** rejected ....Luke 20:17
was set at nought of you ***b*** ....Acts 4:11
whose ***b*** and maker is God ....Heb 11:10
stone which the ***b*** disallowed ..1Pet 2:7

BUKKI (bŭk'ī)—*"proved of Jehovah; mouth of Jehovah"*
1. Danite chief ....Num 34:22
2. A descendant of Aaron..1Chr 6:5, 51

BUKKIAH (bŭ-kī'ä)—*"proved of Jehovah; mouth of Jehovah"*
A Levite musician 1Chr 25:4, 13

BUL (bo͞ol)—*"growth"*
Eighth Hebrew month ...1Kin 6:38

BULL—*male of any bovine animal*
Used in sacrifices ....Heb 9:13
Blood of, insufficient ....Heb 10:4
Wild, trapped ....Is 51:20
Symbol of evil men ......Ps 22:12
Symbol of mighty men ...Ps 68:30
Restrictions on ....Deut 15:19, 20
Sacrifices of, inadequate. .Ps 69:30, 31
Blood of, unacceptable ...Is 1:11
Figurative of the Lord's sacrifice ....Is 34:6, 7
Figurative of strength ....Deut 33:17

[*also* BULLS]
forty kine, and ten ***b*** ....Gen 32:15
Will I eat the flesh of ***b***, or ...Ps 50:13
the bullocks with the ***b*** ....Is 34:7
heifer at grass..bellow as ***b*** ....Jer 50:11
twelve brazen ***b*** that were .....Jer 52:20

BULLOCK—*young bull*
Used in sacrifices ....Ex 29:1, 10-14
Restrictions on ....Deut 15:19, 20
Sacrifices of, inadequate. .Ps 69:30, 31
Blood of, unacceptable ...Is 1:11
Figurative of the Lord's sacrifice ....Is 34:6, 7
Figurative of strength ....Deut 33:17

[*also* BULLOCKS]
one young ***b*** and two rams ....Ex 29:1
with the ***b*** and two rams ......Ex 29:3
thou shalt cause a ***b*** to be .....Ex 29:10
upon the head of the ***b*** ....Ex 29:10
kill the ***b*** before the Lord .....Ex 29:11
take of the blood of the ***b***.....Ex 29:12
flesh of the ***b***, and his skin ....Ex 29:14
shalt offer every day a ***b*** ......Ex 29:36
kill the ***b*** before the Lord .....Lev 1:5
a young ***b*** without blemish ....Lev 4:3
bring the ***b*** unto the door .....Lev 4:4
head, and kill the ***b***...........Lev 4:4
blood of the ***b*** at the bottom ..Lev 4:7
b for the sin offering...........Lev 4:8
the ***b*** of the sacrifice ....Lev 4:10
skin of the ***b*** all his flesh ......Lev 4:11
Even the whole ***b*** shall he .....Lev 4:12
shall offer a young ***b***..........Lev 4:14
upon the head of the ***b*** ....Lev 4:15
Lord the ***b*** shall be killed .....Lev 4:15
And he shall do with the ***b*** ....Lev 4:20
as he did with the ***b*** for ....Lev 4:20
he shall carry forth the ***b*** ......Lev 4:21
as he burned the first ***b*** ....Lev 4:21
a ***b*** for the sin offering ....Lev 8:2
a ***b*** and a ram for peace ......Lev 9:4
a young ***b*** for a sin offering ...Lev 16:3
shall offer his ***b*** of the sin .....Lev 16:6
Aaron shall bring the ***b*** of .....Lev 16:11
kill the ***b***..sin offering ....Lev 16:11
take of the blood of the ***b*** .....Lev 16:14
did with the blood of the ***b*** ....Lev 16:15
take of the blood of the ***b*** .....Lev 16:18
the ***b*** for the sin offering ......Lev 16:27
Either a ***b*** or a lamb, that .....Lev 22:23
one young ***b***, and two rams ...Lev 23:18
One young ***b***, one ram, one ...Num 7:15
were twelve ***b***, the rams ....Num 7:87
let them take a young ***b*** ....Num 8:8
young ***b*** shalt thou take ....Num 8:8
upon the heads of the ***b*** ....Num 8:12
when thou preparest a ***b*** for ...Num 15:8
offered on every altar a ***b*** .....Num 23:2
prepare me here seven ***b*** ......Num 23:29
unto the Lord; two young ***b*** ...Num 28:11
mingled with oil, for one ***b*** ....Num 28:12
one young ***b***, one ram, and....Num 29:2
thirteen young ***b***, two rams ....Num 29:13
the firstling of thy ***b***, nor ......Deut 15:19
any ***b***, or sheep, wherein is ....Deut 17:1
like the firstling of his ***b*** ....Deut 33:17
Take thy father's young ***b*** .....Judg 6:25
even the second ***b*** of seven ....Judg 6:25
up with her, with three ***b*** 1Sam 1:24
they slew a ***b***, and brought 1Sam 1:25
therefore give us two ***b*** 1Kin 18:23
let them choose one ***b*** for 1Kin 18:23
I will dress the other ***b***.........1Kin 18:23
they offered seven ***b***, and 1Chr 15:26
a thousand ***b***, a thousand 1Chr 29:21
consecrate..with a young ***b*** 2Chr 13:9
they brought seven ***b*** 2Chr 29:21
thousand ***b*** and seven 2Chr 30:24
congregation a thousand ***b***.....2Chr 30:24
three thousand ***b***: these 2Chr 35:7
both young ***b***, and rams ....Ezra 6:9
buy speedily with..money ***b***....Ezra 7:17
twelve ***b*** for all Israel ....Ezra 8:35
take unto you now seven ***b*** ...Job 42:8
take no ***b*** out of thy house ....Ps 50:9
then shall they offer ***b*** upon ...Ps 51:19
I will offer ***b*** with goats ....Ps 66:15
lion shall eat straw like..***b*** .....Is 65:25
a ***b*** unaccustomed to..yoke ....Jer 31:18
midst of her like fatted ***b***......Jer 46:21
Slay all her ***b***; let them go ....Jer 50:27
of lambs, and of goats, of ***b*** ...Ezek 39:18
a young ***b*** for a sin offering ...Ezek 43:19
a young ***b*** without blemish ....Ezek 45:18
seven ***b*** and seven rams ....Ezek 45:23
a young ***b*** without blemish ....Ezek 46:6
they sacrifice ***b*** in Gilgal ......Hos 12:11

BULRUSH—*a large rush or reed growing in wetlands*
Used in Moses' ark ......Ex 2:3
Found in river banks ....Job 8:11
Figurative of judgment ...Is 9:14

[*also* BULRUSHES]
vessels of ***b*** upon the waters ...Is 18:2
bow down his head as a ***b*** .....Is 58:5

BULWARK—*defensive wall*
Around Jerusalem ....Ps 48:13
Used in wars ....Eccl 9:14
Made of logs ....Deut 20:20
Foundation of weapons ..2Chr 26:15

[*also* BULWARKS]
build ***b*** against the city ....Deut 20:20
towers and upon the ***b*** 2Chr 26:15
Mark ye well her ***b*** ....Ps 48:13
built great ***b*** against it ....Eccl 9:14
God appoint for walls and ***b***...Is 26:1

BUNAH (bū'nä)—*"understanding"*
A descendant of Judah...1Chr 2:25

BUNCH—*a cluster*

[*also* BUNCHES]
a hundred ***b*** of raisins.........2Sam 16:1
figs, and ***b*** of raisins 1Chr 12:40
upon the ***b*** of camels, to a ....Is 30:6

BUNDLE—*a group of objects fastened together*

[*also* BUNDLES]
bound in the ***b*** of life 1Sam 25:29
a ***b*** of myrrh is my ....Song 1:13
gathered a ***b*** of sticks ....Acts 28:3

BUNNI (bŭn'ī)—*"my understanding"*
1. A pre-exilic Levite ......Neh 11:15
2. A postexilic Levite ......Neh 9:4
3. Signer of document .....Neh 10:15

BURDEN—*a load; responsibility; something oppressive or worrisome*

Used physically of:
Load, cargo ....Neh 4:17

Used figuratively of:
Care ....Ps 55:22
Prophet's message ....Hab 1:1
Rules, rites ....Luke 11:46
Sin ....Ps 38:4
Responsibility ....Gal 6:2, 5
Christ's law ....Matt 11:30

[*also* BURDENED, BURDENS, BURDENSOME]
crouching..between two ***b*** ... .Gen 49:14
afflict them with their ***b*** ....Ex 1:11
looked on their ***b***; and he .....Ex 2:11
works? get you unto your ***b*** ...Ex 5:4
the ***b*** of the Egyptians ....Ex 6:6
they shall bear the ***b***..........Ex 18:22
lying under his ***b***, and.........Ex 23:5
b of the sons of Kohath ....Num 4:15
to serve, and for ***b*** ....Num 4:24
b of all this people upon ......Num 11:11
they shall bear the ***b*** of ......Num 11:17
your ***b***, and your strife? ....Deut 1:12
thou shalt be a ***b*** unto me 2Sam 15:33
thy servant be yet a ***b***.........2Sam 19:35
ten thousand that bare ***b*** 1Kin 5:15
two mules ***b*** of earth?.........2Kin 5:17
forty camels ***b***, and came......2Kin 8:9
Lord laid this ***b*** upon him 2Kin 9:25
ten thousand men..bear ***b*** 2Chr 2:2
the greatness of the ***b*** laid 2Chr 24:27
over the bearers of ***b***, and.....2Chr 34:13
not be a ***b*** upon your 2Chr 35:3
strength of the bearers of ***b*** ...Neh 4:10
all manner of ***b***, which ....Neh 13:15
should no ***b*** be brought in.....Neh 13:19
so that I am a ***b*** to myself?....Job 7:20
removed..shoulder from..***b*** ....Ps 81:6
grasshopper shall be a ***b*** ......Eccl 12:5
broken the yoke of his ***b*** ......Is 9:4
his ***b*** shall be taken away .....Is 10:27
b of Babylon, which Isaiah ....Is 13:1
his ***b*** depart from off their ....Is 14:25
king Ahaz died was this ***b*** .....Is 14:28
The ***b*** of Moab. Because in ...Is 15:1
The ***b*** of Damascus ....Is 17:1
The ***b*** of Egypt. Behold ....Is 19:1
b of the desert of the sea .....Is 21:1
The ***b*** of Dumah. He calleth ..Is 21:11
The ***b*** upon Arabia. In the ....Is 21:13
The ***b*** of..valley of vision ......Is 22:1
The ***b*** of Tyre. Howl, ye ......Is 23:1
The ***b*** of the beasts of the.....Is 30:6
the ***b*** thereof is heavy; his.....Is 30:27
they are a ***b*** to the weary .....Is 46:1
to undo the heavy ***b***, and to ...Is 58:6
bear no ***b*** on the sabbath .....Jer 17:21
Neither carry forth a ***b*** out ....Jer 17:22
to bring in no ***b*** through ......Jer 17:24
not to bear a ***b***, even ....Jer 17:27

What is the *b* of the Lord? ....Jer 23:33
say unto them. What *b*? ......Jer 23:33
false *b* and causes of.........Lam 2:14
b concerneth the prince ......Ezek 12:10
the *b* of the king of princes ...Hos 8:10
take from him *b* of wheat .....Amos 5:11
b which Habakkuk the prophet.Hab 1:1
the reproach of it was a *b* .....Zeph 3:18
b of the word of the Lord .....Zech 9:1
b of the word of the Lord .....Zech 12:1
all that *b* themselves ....Zech 12:3
will I make Jerusalem a *b* .....Zech 12:3
b of the word of the Lord .....Mal 1:1
which have borne the *b* and ...Matt 20:12
For they bind heavy *b* and ....Matt 23:4
with *b* grievous to be borne ...Luke 11:46
upon you no greater *b* than ...Acts 15:28
ship was to unlade her *b* ......Acts 21:3
do groan, being *b*; not for.....2Cor 5:4
men be eased, and ye *b* 2Cor 8:13
kept myself from being *b*......2Cor 11:9
I myself was not *b* to you? 2Cor 12:13
I did not *b* you 2Cor 12:16
Bear ye one another's *b*.......Gal 6:2
we might have been *b*; as 1Thess 2:6
put upon you none other *b* ....Rev 2:24

BURDEN-BEARER—*one who carries a load*
Christ is the believer's ...Ps 55:22

BURGLARIZING—*stealing*
Severe penalty for ....Ex 21:16
See STEALING; THEFT, THIEF

BURIAL—*dispose of by depositing in the ground or in a tomb; figurative of spiritual death*

Features regarding:
Body washed............Acts 9:37
Ointment used ....Matt 26:12
Embalm sometimes ....Gen 50:26
Body wrapped ....John 11:44
Placed in coffin ....Gen 50:26
Carried on a bier ....Luke 7:14
Mourners attend.........John 11:19
Graves provided.........Gen 23:5-20
Tombs erected ....Matt 23:27-29

Places of:
Abraham and Sarah .....Gen 25:7-10
Deborah ....Gen 35:8
Rachel ....Gen 35:19, 20
Miriam ....Num 20:1
Moses ....Deut 34:5, 6
Gideon ....Judg 8:32
Samson and Manoah.....Judg 16:30, 31
Saul and his sons 1Sam 31:12, 13
David 1Kin 2:10
Joab....................1Kin 2:33, 34
Solomon 1Kin 11:43
Rehoboam 1Kin 14:31
Asa 1Kin 15:24
Manasseh 2Kin 21:18
Amon 2Kin 21:23-26
Josiah 2Chr 35:23, 24
Jesus ....Luke 23:50-53
Lazarus ....John 11:14, 38

in the field of *b* which 2Chr 26:23
and also that ye have no *b* ....Eccl 6:3
not be joined with them in *b* ..Is 14:20
with the *b* of an ass drawn ....Jer 22:19
body, she did it for my *b* .....Matt 26:12
carried Stephen to his *b* ....Acts 8:2

BURIED—*See* BURY

BURIED ALIVE
Two rebellious families...Num 16:27-34
Desire of some ....Rev 6:15, 16

BURIERS—*those who bury*
till the *b* have buried it in the. .Ezek 39:15

BURN—*to consume by fire; a fire*

[*also* BURNED, BURNETH, BURNING, BURNINGS, BURNT]

b offerings on the altar........Gen 8:20
let us make brick, and *b* ......Gen 11:3
b lamp that passed between ...Gen 15:17
offer him there for a *b* ....Gen 22:2
and let her be *b* ....Gen 38:24
let not thine anger *b* ....Gen 44:18
why the bush is not *b* ....Ex 3:3
b offerings that we may ....Ex 10:25
until..morning ye shall *b* ....Ex 12:10
father-in-law took a *b* ....Ex 18:12
sacrifice thereon thy *b* ....Ex 20:24
B for *b*, wound for wound ....Ex 21:25
of Israel, which offered *b* .....Ex 24:5
and *b* them upon the altar .....Ex 29:13
thou shalt *b* the whole ram ....Ex 29:18
b offering unto the Lord ....Ex 29:18
and *b* them upon the altar ....Ex 29:25
make an altar to *b* incense ....Ex 30:1
nor *b* sacrifice, nor meat ......Ex 30:9
b offering with..furniture ....Ex 31:9
offered *b* offerings, and ....Ex 32:6
b offering with his brazen .....Ex 35:16
made the altar of *b* offering ...Ex 38:1
set the altar of..*b* offering ....Ex 40:6
offering be a *b* sacrifice ....Lev 1:3
priest..*b* all on the altar ....Lev 1:9
b it on the altar; and the ......Lev 1:15
priest shall *b* the memorial ....Lev 2:2
shall not be *b* on the altar.....Lev 2:12
upon the *b* sacrifice, which ....Lev 3:5
And Aaron's sons shall *b* .....Lev 3:5
And the priest shall *b* it.......Lev 3:11
And the priest shall *b* them ...Lev 3:16
altar of the *b* offering ....Lev 4:7
and the priest shall *b* them ....Lev 4:10
as he *b* the first bullock ....Lev 4:21
the other for a *b* offering .....Lev 5:7
b it on the altar according.....Lev 5:12
the law of the *b* offering ......Lev 6:9
It is the *b* offering ....Lev 6:9
because..*b* upon the altar .....Lev 6:9
fire of the altar shall be *b* .....Lev 6:9
and the priest shall *b* wood ....Lev 6:12
shall *b* it upon the altar ....Lev 6:15
they kill the *b* offering ....Lev 7:2
priest shall *b* them upon ....Lev 7:5
he *b* with fire without the .....Lev 8:17
bread shall ye *b* with fire......Lev 8:32
ram for..*b* offering without ....Lev 9:2
Moses *b* it upon the altar .....Lev 8:16
b which the Lord..kindled ......Lev 10:6
it was *b*; and he was angry ....Lev 10:16
first year for a *b* offering......Lev 12:6
b have a white bright spot.....Lev 13:24
is a *b* boil; and the priest .....Lev 13:23
therefore *b* that garment ....Lev 13:52
leprosy..be *b* in the fire ....Lev 13:52
sin offering..*b* offering ....Lev 14:13
the other for a *b* offering .....Lev 15:15
a ram for a *b* offering.........Lev 16:3
censer full of *b* coals ....Lev 16:12
offering shall he *b* upon ....Lev 16:25
he that *b* them shall wash .....Lev 16:28
b the fat for a sweet savor ....Lev 17:6
a *b* offering or sacrifice ....Lev 17:8
it shall be *b* in the fire ....Lev 19:6
they shall be *b* with fire.......Lev 20:14
she shall be *b* with fire........Lev 21:9
unto the Lord for a *b*..........Lev 22:18
a *b* offering unto the Lord ....Lev 23:12
the lamps to *b* continually .....Lev 24:2
consumption, and..*b* ague .....Lev 26:16
and *b* it upon the altar ....Num 5:26
the other for a *b* offering .....Num 6:11
a *b* offering unto the Lord ....Num 8:12
over your *b* offerings and .....Num 10:10
fire of the Lord *b* among......Num 11:1
b offering or a sacrifice ....Num 15:3
the censers out of the *b* ....Num 16:37
that were *b* had offered ....Num 16:39
b..fat for an offering ....Num 18:17
And one shall *b* the heifer ....Num 19:5
with her dung, shall he *b*......Num 19:5
into the midst of the *b* ....Num 19:6
he that *b* her shall wash.......Num 19:8
take..ashes of the *b* heifer.....Num 19:17
Stand by thy *b* offering ....Num 23:3
for a continual *b* offering......Num 28:3
ye shall offer a *b* offering .....Num 29:2
they *b* all their cities ....Num 31:10
the mountain *b* with fire ....Deut 4:11
mountain did *b* with fire ....Deut 5:23
b their graven images with .....Deut 7:5
and the mount *b* with fire .....Deut 9:15
b their groves with fire........Deut 12:3
shall bring your *b* offerings ....Deut 12:6
shalt *b* with fire the city.......Deut 13:16
offer *b* offerings thereon ....Deut 27:6
and with an extreme *b* ....Deut 28:22
brimstone, and salt, and *b*.....Deut 29:23
shall be *b* with hunger ....Deut 32:24
devoured with *b* heat, and .....Deut 32:24
b sacrifice upon thine altar ....Deut 33:10
they *b* the city with fire ....Josh 6:24
accursed thing shall be *b* ......Josh 7:15
and *b* them with fire, after ....Josh 7:25
And Joshua *b* Ai, and made...Josh 8:28
b their chariots with fire ......Josh 11:6
b their chariots with fire ......Josh 11:9
Israel *b* none of them save ....Josh 11:13
to offer thereon *b* offering ....Josh 22:23
offer a *b* sacrifice with the ....Judg 6:26
door of the tower to *b* it ......Judg 9:52
offer it up for a *b* offering ....Judg 11:31
we will *b* thine house upon ....Judg 12:1
thou wilt offer a *b* offering ....Judg 13:16
we *b* thee and thy father's.....Judg 14:15
and *b* up both the shocks .....Judg 15:5
and *b* the city with fire........Judg 18:27
and offered *b* offerings ....Judg 20:26
and offered *b* offerings ....Judg 21:4
before they *b* the fat, the 1Sam 2:15
Let them not fail to *b*.........1Sam 2:16
a *b* offering unto the Lord 1Sam 6:14
b offering wholly unto the 1Sam 7:9
thee to offer *b* offerings 1Sam 10:8
Bring hither a *b* offering 1Sam 13:9
he offered the *b* offering 1Sam 13:9
delight in *b* offerings 1Sam 15:22
Ziklag, and *b* it with fire 1Sam 30:1
Jabesh, and *b* them there 1Sam 31:12
and David and his men *b* 2Sam 5:21
David offered *b* offerings......2Sam 6:17
be oxen for *b* sacrifice 2Sam 24:22
b incense in high places 1Kin 3:3
he offered *b* offerings 1Kin 8:64
b it with fire and slain 1Kin 9:16
b incense and sacrificed 1Kin 11:8
upon the altar..*b* incense 1Kin 12:33
bones shall be *b* upon thee 1Kin 13:2
her idol..*b* it by the brook 1Kin 15:13
b the king's house over him ...1Kin 16:18
pour it on the *b* sacrifice 1Kin 18:33
people offered and *b* incense ..1Kin 22:43
and *b* up the two captains 2Kin 1:14
offered him for a *b* offering ...2Kin 3:27
neither *b* offering nor 2Kin 5:17
to offer sacrifices and *b* 2Kin 10:24
sacrificed and *b* incense 2Kin 12:3
b incense on..high places 2Kin 14:4
sacrificed and *b* incense 2Kin 15:4
b incense..the high places 2Kin 15:35
he sacrificed and *b* incense 2Kin 16:4
Upon the great altar *b* the 2Kin 16:15
And there they *b* incense 2Kin 17:11
children of Israel did *b*........2Kin 18:4
b incense unto other gods 2Kin 22:17
b them without Jerusalem 2Kin 23:4
ordained to *b* incense in 2Kin 23:5
he *b* the house of the Lord....2Kin 25:9
altar of the *b* offering 1Chr 6:49
and they were *b* with fire 1Chr 14:12
they offered *b* sacrifices 1Chr 16:1
oxen also for *b* offerings 1Chr 21:23
altar of the *b* offering 1Chr 22:1
b incense before the Lord 1Chr 28:18
offer all *b* sacrifices unto 1Chr 28:31
offered *b* offerings unto 1Chr 29:21
offered a thousand *b* 2Chr 1:6
b before him sweet incense 2Chr 2:4
for the *b* offerings morning 2Chr 2:4
offered for the *b* offering......2Chr 4:6

that they should *b* after 2Chr 4:20
consumed the *b* offering 2Chr 7:1
Solomon offered *b* offerings ...2Chr 8:12
And they *b* unto the Lord 2Chr 13:11
b sacrifices..sweet incense 2Chr 13:11
to *b* every evening; for we 2Chr 13:11
b it at the brook Kidron 2Chr 15:16
made a very great *b* for him ...2Chr 16:14
people made no *b* for him 2Chr 21:19
like the *b* of his fathers 2Chr 21:19
the *b* offerings of the Lord 2Chr 23:18
they offered *b* offerings 2Chr 24:14
them *b* incense unto them 2Chr 25:14
the temple of the Lord to *b* ...2Chr 26:16
he *b* incense in the valley 2Chr 28:3
b his children in the fire 2Chr 28:3
places to *b* incense unto 2Chr 28:25
not *b* incense nor offered 2Chr 29:7
nor offered *b* offerings in 2Chr 29:7
unto him, and *b* incense 2Chr 29:11
brought in the *b* offerings 2Chr 30:15
priests and Levites for *b* 2Chr 31:2
altar, and *b* incense upon 2Chr 32:12
b the bones of the priests 2Chr 34:5
removed the *b* offerings 2Chr 35:12
they *b* the house of God 2Chr 36:19
offer *b* offerings thereon ......Ezra 3:2
b offerings of the God ....Ezra 6:9
b offerings unto the God ......Ezra 8:35
a *b* offering unto the Lord ....Ezra 8:35
gates thereof are *b* with ....Neh 1:3
gates thereof are *b* with ....Neh 2:17
heaps of rubbish..are *b*? ......Neh 4:2
for the continual *b* offering ....Neh 10:33
b upon the altar of the Lord ..Neh 10:34
wroth..his anger *b* in him .....Esth 1:12
and offered *b* offerings ....Job 1:5
and hath *b* up the sheep ......Job 1:16
my bones are *b* with heat .....Job 30:30
Out of his mouth go *b* ....Job 41:19
for yourselves a *b* offering .....Job 42:8
and accept thy *b* sacrifice .....Ps 20:3
while I was musing..fire *b* .....Ps 39:3
b offering and sin offering .....Ps 40:6
he *b* the chariot in the fire ....Ps 46:9
sacrifices or..*b* offerings ....Ps 50:8
delightest not in *b* offering ....Ps 51:16
go into thy house with *b* ......Ps 66:13
have *b* up..the synagogues .....Ps 74:8
thy jealousy *b* like fire? ....Ps 79:5
It is *b* with fire, it is cut ......Ps 80:16
As the fire *b* a wood, and .....Ps 83:14
Shall thy wrath *b* like fire? ....Ps 89:46
fire goeth before him, and *b*...Ps 97:3
bones are *b* as a hearth ....Ps 102:3
the flame *b* up the wicked .....Ps 106:18
Let *b* coals fall upon them ....Ps 140:10
and his clothes not be *b*? ......Prov 6:27
his lips there is as a *b* fire .....Prov 16:27
As coals are to *b* coals ....Prov 26:21
your cities are *b* with fire .....Is 1:7
I am full of the *b* offerings ....Is 1:11
they shall both *b* together .....Is 1:31
and *b* instead of beauty ....Is 3:24
and by the spirit of *b* ....Is 4:4
shall be with *b* and fuel ....Is 9:5
For wickedness *b* as the fire ...Is 9:18
kindle a *b* like..*b* of a fire .....Is 10:16
it shall *b* and devour his ......Is 10:17
inhabitants of..earth are *b* .....Is 24:6
I would *b* them together ....Is 27:4
b with his anger, and the ......Is 30:27
land thereof shall become *b* ...Is 34:9
people shall be as the *b* of ....Is 33:12
as thorns cut up..they be *b* ....Is 33:12
dwell with everlasting *b*? ......Is 38:14
Lebanon..not sufficient to *b* ...Is 40:16
sufficient for a *b* offering ......Is 40:16
it *b* him, yet he laid it not ....Is 42:25
thou shalt not be *b* ....Is 43:2
cattle of thy *b* offerings ....Is 43:23
shall it be for a man to *b* .....Is 44:15
b part thereof in the fire ......Is 44:16
I have *b* part of it in..........Is 44:19
the fire shall *b* them; they .....Is 47:14

b offerings and..sacrifices ......Is 56:7
hate robbery for *b* offering ....Is 61:8
thereof as a lamp that *b*.......Is 62:1
As when the melting fire *b* ....Is 64:2
is *b* up with fire; and all ......Is 64:11
b incense upon altars of.......Is 65:3
b incense upon..mountains ....Is 65:7
he that *b* incense, as if he .....Is 66:3
b incense unto other gods .....Jer 1:16
cities are *b* without ....Jer 2:15
b that none can quench it ......Jer 4:4
b offerings..not acceptable .....Jer 6:20
The bellows are *b*, the lead ...Jer 6:29
and *b* incense unto Baal ......Jer 7:9
Put your *b* offerings unto .....Jer 7:21
they are *b* up, so that none ...Jer 9:10
altars..*b* incense unto Baal ....Jer 11:13
when they offer *b* offering.....Jer 14:12
anger, which shall *b* upon .....Jer 15:14
anger, which shall *b* for ....Jer 17:4
bringing *b* offerings, and ......Jer 17:26
have *b* incense to vanity ......Jer 18:15
b incense..unto other gods ....Jer 19:4
b their sons with fire..........Jer 19:5
burn..sons with fire for *b*.......Jer 19:5
in mine heart as a *b* fire ......Jer 20:9
and he shall *b* it with fire .....Jer 21:10
and *b* that none can quench ...Jer 21:12
and *b* it with the houses.......Jer 32:29
before me to offer *b* ....Jer 33:18
and he shall *b* it with fire .....Jer 34:2
with the *b* of thy fathers ......Jer 34:5
fire on the hearth *b* before ....Jer 36:22
he would not *b* the roll ....Jer 36:25
the king had *b* the roll ....Jer 36:27
take it, and *b* it with fire ......Jer 37:8
city shall not be *b*..fire ....Jer 38:17
they shall *b* it with fire........Jer 38:18
the Chaldeans *b* the king's ....Jer 39:8
he shall *b* them, and carry ....Jer 43:12
that they went to *b* incense ....Jer 44:3
b incense unto other gods .....Jer 44:8
wives had *b* incense unto ......Jer 44:15
b incense to his gods..........Jer 48:35
daughters..be *b* with fire ......Jer 49:2
make thee a *b* mountain ......Jer 51:25
have *b* her dwelling places ....Jer 51:30
b the house of the Lord........Jer 52:13
he *b* against Jacob like a ......Lam 2:3
b coals of fire, and like ....Ezek 1:13
shalt *b* with fire a third ....Ezek 5:2
and the midst of it is *b*........Ezek 15:4
they shall *b* thine houses ......Ezek 16:41
south to..north shall be *b* .....Ezek 20:47
b up their houses with fire ....Ezek 23:47
b also the bones under it.......Ezek 24:5
well, and let the bones be *b* ...Ezek 24:10
set on fire..*b* the weapons .....Ezek 39:9
they washed the *b* offering ....Ezek 40:38
to offer *b* offerings thereon ....Ezek 43:18
shall *b* it in the appointed .....Ezek 43:21
shall slay the *b* offering ....Ezek 44:11
for a *b* offering, and for.......Ezek 45:15
priests shall prepare his *b* .....Ezek 46:2
midst..*b* fiery furnace ....Dan 3:6
flame..wheels as *b* fire ....Dan 7:9
wherein she *b* incense to ....Hos 2:13
b incense upon the hills ....Hos 4:13
God more than *b* offerings ....Hos 6:6
morning it *b* as a flaming .....Hos 7:6
b incense to graven images ....Hos 11:2
flame hath *b* all the trees .....Joel 1:19
behind them a flame *b*; the....Joel 2:3
b the bones of the king ....Amos 2:1
firebrand plucked out..*b* ......Amos 4:11
ye offer me *b* offerings.........Amos 5:22
b him, to bring out..bones ....Amos 6:10
hires thereof shall be *b*........Mic 1:7
come before him with *b* ....Mic 6:6
earth is *b* at his presence ......Nah 1:5
and I will *b* her chariots........Nah 2:13
b incense unto their drag ......Hab 1:16
b coals went..at his feet ....Hab 3:5
that shall *b* as an oven ....Mal 4:1
day that cometh shall *b* ....Mal 4:1

but he will *b* up the chaff .....Matt 3:12
bind them in bundles to *b* .....Matt 13:30
tares are gathered and *b* ......Matt 13:40
murderers..*b* up their city .....Matt 22:7
his lot was to *b* incense ....Luke 1:9
chaff he will *b* with fire ....Luke 3:17
girded about..your lights *b* ....Luke 12:35
Did not our heart *b* within ....Luke 24:32
a *b* and a shining light ....John 5:35
into the fire, and they are *b* ...John 15:6
and *b* them before all men ....Acts 19:19
b in their lust one toward .....Rom 1:27
any man's work shall be *b*.....1Cor 3:15
better to marry than to *b* 1Cor 7:9
give my body to be *b*, and 1Cor 13:3
is offended, and I *b* not?......2Cor 11:29
whose end is to be *b*..........Heb 6:8
In *b* offerings and sacrifices ...Heb 10:6
and that *b* with fire, nor ......Heb 12:18
high priest for sin, are *b* .....Heb 13:11
sooner risen with a *b* heat.....James 1:11
works..therein shall be *b* 2Pet 3:10
as if they *b* in a furnace; ......Rev 1:15
lamps of fire *b* before the .....Rev 4:5
third part of trees was *b* ......Rev 8:7
all green grass was *b* up.......Rev 8:7
great mountain *b* with fire.....Rev 8:8
and *b* her with fire ....Rev 17:16
be utterly *b* with fire..........Rev 18:8
see the smoke of her *b*.........Rev 18:9
lake of fire *b* with brimstone ..Rev 19:20
lake which *b* with fire ....Rev 21:8

BURNING BUSH—*where the angel of the Lord appeared to Moses*
God speaks from ....Ex 3:2

BURNISHED—*shiny or lustrous*
like the color of *b* brass ....Ezek 1:7

BURST—*to be broken apart from within*
[*also* BURSTING]
ready to *b* like new bottles ....Job 32:19
and thy presses shall *b* ....Prov 3:10
shall not be found in the *b* ....Is 30:14
thy yoke and *b* thy bands .....Jer 2:20
broken the yoke, and *b* the ...Jer 5:5
and will *b* thy bonds, and .....Jer 30:8
will *b* thy bonds in sunder.....Nah 1:13
b the bottles, and the wine ....Mark 2:22
new wine will *b* the bottles ....Luke 5:37
he *b* asunder in the midst .....Acts 1:18

BURY—*to dispose of a body in the ground or tomb*
[*also* BURIED, BURYING, BURYINGPLACE]
shalt be *b* in a good old age ...Gen 15:15
give me a possession of a *b* ...Gen 23:4
I may *b* my dead out of my ...Gen 23:4
b me not, I pray thee in ......Gen 47:29
b me in their *b* place ....Gen 47:30
I *b* her there in the way........Gen 48:7
b me with my fathers in........Gen 49:29
for a possession of a *b* ....Gen 49:30
There they *b* Abraham and....Gen 49:31
there they *b* Isaac and ....Gen 49:31
and there I *b* Leah ....Gen 49:31
there shalt thou *b* me ....Gen 50:5
and *b* my father, and I will....Gen 50:5
for a possession of a *b* of .....Gen 50:13
b him in the cave of the ......Gen 50:13
Miriam died there, and..*b* .....Num 20:1
the Egyptians *b* all their ....Num 33:4
Aaron died..there he was *b* ...Deut 10:6
shalt in any wise *b* him ....Deut 21:23
they *b* him in the border ....Josh 24:30
they *b* him in the border ......Judg 2:9
died, and was *b* in Shamir.....Judg 10:2
the Gileadite and was *b* ....Judg 12:7
there will I be *b*; the Lord ....Ruth 1:17
and *b* him in his house at 1Sam 25:1
b him in Ramah, even in.......1Sam 28:3
Jabesh-gilead..they that *b* 2Sam 2:4
they *b* Abner in Hebron 2Sam 3:32

head of Ish-bosheth, and *b* 2Sam 4:12
and was *b* in the sepulcher 2Sam 17:23
be *b* by the grave of my 2Sam 19:37
Jonathan his son *b* they 2Sam 21:14
fall upon him, and *b* him......1Kin 2:31
was gone up to *b* the slain 1Kin 11:15
city, to mourn and to *b* him ...1Kin 13:29
after he had *b* him that he 1Kin 13:31
wherein..man of God is *b* 1Kin 13:31
shall mourn for him, and *b* 1Kin 14:13
they *b* him; and all Israel 1Kin 14:18
b him in the city of David.....1Kin 15:8
his fathers and was *b* 1Kin 16:6
his fathers, and was *b*.........1Kin 16:28
they *b* the king in Samaria 1Kin 22:37
with his fathers, and was *b* 2Kin 8:24
shall be none to *b* her 2Kin 9:10
b him in his sepulcher with 2Kin 9:28
fathers; and they *b* him in.....2Kin 10:35
they *b* him with his fathers 2Kin 12:21
and they *b* him in Samaria 2Kin 13:9
as they were *b* a man that.....2Kin 13:21
with his fathers, and was *b* 2Kin 14:16
they *b* him with his fathers 2Kin 15:7
with his fathers, and was *b* 2Kin 16:20
b him in his own sepulcher 2Kin 23:30
b their bones under the oak ...1Chr 10:12
was *b* in the city of David.....2Chr 9:31
with his fathers, and was *b* 2Chr 12:16
b him in the city of David.....2Chr 14:1
b him in his..sepulchers 2Chr 16:14
with his fathers, and was *b* 2Chr 21:1
had slain him, they *b* him 2Chr 22:9
b him in the city of David.....2Chr 24:16
b him with his fathers in 2Chr 25:28
b him with his fathers in 2Chr 26:23
b him in the city of David.....2Chr 27:9
and they *b* him in the city.....2Chr 28:27
they *b* him in the chiefest 2Chr 32:33
b him in his own house 2Chr 33:20
remain of him shall be *b* ......Job 27:15
there was none to *b* them .....Ps 79:3
And so I saw the wicked *b* ....Eccl 8:10
for they shall *b* in Tophet .....Jer 7:32
not be gathered, nor be *b* .....Jer 8:2
shall have none to *b* them .....Jer 14:16
neither shall they be *b* ....Jer 16:4
shall *b* them in Tophet.........Jer 19:11
shalt die, and shalt be *b*.......Jer 20:6
shall be *b* with the burial......Jer 22:19
neither gathered, nor *b* ....Jer 25:33
there shall they *b* Gog and ....Ezek 39:11
house of Israel be *b* of.........Ezek 39:12
till the buriers have *b* it ....Ezek 39:15
Memphis shall *b* them ....Hos 9:6
first to go and *b* my father ....Matt 8:21
b it..went and told Jesus ......Matt 14:12
potter's field, to *b* ....Matt 27:7
to anoint my body to the *b*....Mark 14:8
first to go and *b* my father ....Luke 9:59
rich man..died and was *b* .....Luke 16:22
against the day of my *b* ....John 12:7
manner of the Jews is to *b* ....John 19:40
he is both dead and *b*, and ....Acts 2:29
carried him out, and *b* him....Acts 5:6
are *b* with him by baptism ....Rom 6:4
that he was *b*, and that he 1Cor 15:4
B with him in baptism ....Col 2:12

BUSH—*low, spreading woody plant*

[*also* BUSHES, BUSHY]

out of the midst of a *b*........Ex 3:2
the *b* burned with fire ....Ex 3:2
the *b* was not consumed ......Ex 3:2
him that dwelt in the *b* ....Deut 33:16
cut up mallows by the *b*........Job 30:4
locks are *b*, and black ....Song 5:11
all thorns, and upon all *b* .....Is 7:19
how in the *b* God spake ......Mark 12:26
of a bramble *b* gather they ....Luke 6:44
even Moses shewed at the *b*...Luke 20:37
in a flame of fire in a *b*.......Acts 7:30

BUSHEL—*a measurement*

Mentioned by Christ.....Matt 5:15

BUSINESS—*one's work; concern or affair(s)*

Attitudes toward:

See God's hand ....James 4:13
Be diligent..............Prov 22:29
Be industrious...........Rom 12:8, 11
Be honest...............2Cor 8:20-22
Put God's first ....Matt 6:33, 34
Keep heaven in mind ....Matt 6:19-21
Give portion ....Mal 3:8-12
Avoid anxiety ....Luke 12:22-30
Remember the fool ......Luke 12:15-21

Those diligent in:

Joseph..................Gen 39:11
Moses ....Heb 3:5
Officers in Israel 2Chr 34:11, 12
Daniel...................Dan 6:4
Mordecai ....Esth 10:2, 3
Paul.....................Acts 20:17-35

into the house to do..*b*........Gen 39:11
he be charged with any *b* .....Deut 24:5
if ye utter not this our *b* ......Josh 2:14
had no *b* with any man ....Judg 18:7
when the *b* was in hand.......1Sam 20:19
know any thing of the *b*.......1Sam 21:2
the king's *b* required haste 1Sam 21:8
sons..for the outward *b* 1Chr 26:29
westward in..*b* of the Lord 1Chr 26:30
Levites wait upon their *b*......2Chr 13:10
b in the cities of Judah........2Chr 17:13
the *b* of the ambassadors......2Chr 32:31
outward *b* of..house of God ...Neh 11:16
the *b* of the house of God ....Neh 11:22
Levites, every one in his *b* ....Neh 13:30
have the charge of the *b* .....Esth 3:9
ships..*b* in great waters........Ps 107:23
through the multitude of *b* ....Eccl 5:3
b that is done upon..earth .....Eccl 8:16
rose up..did the king's *b* ......Dan 8:27
be about my Father's *b*? ......Luke 2:49
we may appoint over this *b*....Acts 6:3
Not slothful in *b*; fervent......Rom 12:11
in whatsoever *b* she hath ......Rom 16:2
do your own *b*, and to work...1Thess 4:11

BUSY—*to be occupied*

servant was *b* here and........1Kin 20:40
the sons of Aaron were *b* 2Chr 35:14

BUSYBODIES—*meddlers*

Women guilty of 1Tim 5:13
Some Christians 2Thess 3:11, 12
Admonitions against 1Pet 4:15
See SLANDER; WHISPERER

BUT—*See* INTRODUCTION

BUTLER—*an officer of Pharaoh*

Imprisonment of Pharaoh's.............Gen 40:1-13
Same as "cupbearer" 1Kin 10:5

[*also* BUTLERSHIP]

lifted..head of the chief *b* .....Gen 40:20
restored the chief *b* unto ......Gen 40:21
the chief butler unto his *b*......Gen 40:21
did not the chief *b* remember..Gen 40:23
spake..chief *b* unto Pharaoh ...Gen 41:9

BUTTER—*a milk product*

Article of diet...........2Sam 17:29
Set before visitors ....Gen 18:8
Got by churning.........Prov 30:33
Fed to infants ....Is 7:15, 22
Illustrative of prosperity..Deut 32:14
Figurative of smooth words ....Ps 55:21

brought forth *b* in a lordly ....Judg 5:25
the brooks of honey and *b* ....Job 20:17
I washed my steps with *b* .....Job 29:6

BUTTOCKS—*the rump*

the middle, even to their *b*....2Sam 10:4
the midst hard by their *b*.......1Chr 19:4
with their *b* uncovered, to.....Is 20:4

BUY—*to purchase something*

[*also* BOUGHT, BUYER, BUYEST, BUYETH]

b with money of any..........Gen 17:12
he *b* a parcel of a field........Gen 33:19
b him of the hands of the .....Gen 39:1
to Joseph for to *b* corn ....Gen 41:57
b for us from thence; that.....Gen 42:2
went down to *b* corn in ....Gen 42:3
sons of Israel came to *b*.......Gen 42:5
From..land of Canaan to *b* ....Gen 42:7
to *b* food are thy servants .....Gen 42:10
Go again, *b* us a little food....Gen 43:2
go down and *b* thee food .....Gen 43:4
the first time to *b* food........Gen 43:20
money have we..to *b* ....Gen 43:22
and *b* us a little food ....Gen 44:25
for the corn which they *b* .....Gen 47:14
b us..our land for bread.......Gen 47:19
Abraham *b* with the field ......Gen 49:30
Abraham *b* with the field .....Gen 50:13
man's servant that is *b* ....Ex 12:44
thou *b* a Hebrew servant ......Ex 21:2
But if the priest *b* any soul....Lev 22:11
b aught of thy neighbor's......Lev 25:14
shalt *b* of thy neighbor ....Lev 25:15
hand of him that hath *b* it.....Lev 25:28
them shall ye *b* bondmen .....Lev 25:44
of them shall ye *b*, and of.....Lev 25:45
field which he hath *b* ....Lev 27:22
shall *b* meat of them for ......Deut 2:6
shall also *b* water of them .....Deut 2:6
and no man shall *b* ....Deut 28:68
father that hath *b* thee? ....Deut 32:6
Jacob *b* of the sons of ....Josh 24:32
B it before the inhabitants ....Ruth 4:4
What day thou *b* the field.....Ruth 4:5
b it also of Ruth the..........Ruth 4:5
said unto Boaz, *b* it for ....Ruth 4:8
that I have *b* all that was .....Ruth 4:9
he had *b* and nourished up 2Sam 12:3
b the threshing floor of thee...2Sam 24:21
b it of thee at a price 2Sam 24:24
And he *b* the hill Samaria.....1Kin 16:24
b timber and hewed stone 2Kin 12:12
to *b* timber and hewn stone ...2Kin 22:6
b it for the full price..........1Chr 21:24
b hewn stone, and timber 2Chr 34:11
b speedily with this money ....Ezra 7:17
we might *b* corn, because .....Neh 5:3
of this wall, neither *b* we......Neh 5:16
not *b* it..on the sabbath ....Neh 10:31
it is naught, saith the *b* ....Prov 20:14
B the truth and sell it not ....Prov 23:23
considereth a field, and *b* .....Prov 31:16
the *b*, so with the seller.......Is 24:2
hast *b* me no sweet cane ......Is 43:24
come ye, *b* and eat ....Is 55:1
yea, come, *b* wine and milk ...Is 55:1
B thee my field that is in .....Jer 32:7
of redemption is thine to *b* ....Jer 32:7
B my field, I pray thee ....Jer 32:8
is thine; *b* it for thyself ....Jer 32:8
I *b* the field of Hanameel ......Jer 32:9
B thee the field for money ....Jer 32:25
shall *b* fields for money ....Jer 32:44
let not the *b* rejoice, nor ......Ezek 7:12
So I *b* her to me for fifteen ...Hos 3:2
may *b* the poor for silver......Amos 8:6
all that he hath, and *b* ....Matt 13:44
sold all that he had, and *b* ....Matt 13:46
and *b* themselves victuals......Matt 14:15
sold and *b* in the temple ......Matt 21:12
sell, and *b* for yourselves......Matt 25:9
while they went to *b* the ......Matt 25:10
b with them the potter's ......Matt 27:7
and *b* themselves bread ....Mark 6:36
b two hundred pennyworth ....Mark 6:37
cast out..that sold and *b* ......Mark 11:15
b fine linen, and took him ....Mark 15:46
had *b* sweet spices, that.......Mark 16:1
b meat for all this people .....Luke 9:13
I have *b* a piece of ground ....Luke 14:18
eat, they drank, they *b*........Luke 17:28
therein, and them that *b* ......Luke 19:45
sell his garment, and *b*........Luke 22:36
unto the city to *b* meat ....John 4:8
Whence shall we *b* bread......John 6:5
B..things that we have need ...John 13:29

Abraham *b* for a sum of ......Acts 7:16
For ye are *b* with a price......1Cor 6:20
Ye are *b* with a price; be 1Cor 7:23
they that *b*, as though they 1Cor 7:30
b and sell, and get gain ....James 4:13
denying the Lord that *b*.......2Pet 2:1
counsel thee to *b* of me gold ..Rev 3:18
no man might *b* or sell........Rev 13:17
no man *b* their merchandise ...Rev 18:11

BUYER—*one who purchases an item*
it is naught, saith the *b* ....Prov 20:14
the *b*, so with the seller ....Is 24:2
let not the *b* rejoice, nor ......Ezek 7:12

BUZ (bŭz)—*"contempt"*
1. A Gadite..............1Chr 5:14
2. An Aramean tribe descending from Nahor.Gen 22:20,21

Dedan, and Tema, and *B* .....Jer 25:23

BUZI (bū'zī)—*"despised by Jehovah"*
Father of Ezekiel........Ezek 1:3

BUZITE (bū'zīt)—*belonging to Buz*
Of the tribe of Buz......Job 32:2

the son of Barachel the *B* .....Job 32:6

BY—*See* INTRODUCTION

BY AND BY—*archaic expression meaning "immediately" or "right away"*
Quickly offended ....Matt 13:21
Rapid granting of a wish..Mark 6:25
Servant's duty..........Luke 7:7
Signs of Christ's return...Luke 21:9

BYWAY—*winding or secluded path*
Used by travelers.........Judg 5:6
Figurative of error.......Jer 18:15

BYWORD—*saying; remark*
Predicted as a taunt .....Deut 28:37
Job describes himself ....Job 17:6

and a *b* among all people 1Kin 9:7
and a *b* among all nations 2Chr 7:20
song, yea, I am their *b*........Job 30:9
us a *b* among the heathen .....Ps 44:14

C

CAB
A measure for dry things .2Kin 6:25

CABBON (kăb'ŏn)—*"understanding"*
Village of Judah.........Josh 15:40

CABIN—*a dungeon*
Jeremiah's imprisonment in...................Jer 37:16

CABUL (kā'bŭl)—*"displeasing; obscurity"*
1. Town of Asher ....Josh 19:27
2. A district of Galilee offered to Hiram 1Kin 9:12, 13
Solomon placed people in 2Chr 8:2

CAESAR (sē'zer)—*formal title for Roman emperors*

Used in reference to:
1. Augustus Caesar (31 B.C.—A.D. 14) Decree of brings Joseph and Mary to Bethelehm ....Luke 2:1
2. Tiberius Caesar (A.D. 14-37) Christ's ministry dated by.............Luke 3:1-23
Tribute paid to..........Matt 22:17-21
Jews side with...........John 19:12
3. Claudius Caesar (A.D. 41-54) Famine in time of....................Acts 11:28
Banished Jews from Rome ....Acts 18:2
4. Nero Caesar (A.D. 54—68) Paul appealed to ....Acts 25:8-12
Converts in household of .Phil 4:22
Paul before 2Tim 4:16-18
Called Augustus ....Acts 25:21

Represented Roman authority:
Image on coins ....Matt 22:19-21; Mark 12:15-16; Luke 20:24
Received tax ....Matt 22:19,21; Mark 12:14,17; Luke 20:25
Jesus called threat to ....Luke 23:2; John 19:12
Pilate's loyalty to, questioned ....John 19:12
Chosen over Jesus ....John 19:12

[*also* CAESAR'S]
To give tribute to *C* or not? ...Mark 12:14
And they said unto him, *C* ....Mark 12:16
They answered and said, *C* ....Luke 20:24
C..the things which be *C* .....Luke 20:25
thou art not *C* friend ....John 19:12
We have no king but *C* ....John 19:15
contrary to the decrees of *C* ...Acts 17:7
till I might send him to *C* .....Acts 25:21
had not appealed unto *C* ......Acts 26:32

CAESAR'S HOUSEHOLD—*the imperial staff*
Greeted the Philippians ..Phil 4:22

CAESAREA (sĕs-ä-rē'ä)—*"city of Caesar"*
Roman capital of Palestine............Acts 12:19; Acts 23:33
Home of Philip..........Acts 8:40
Home of Cornelius ......Acts 10:1
Peter preached at........Acts 10:34-43
Paul preached here three times ....Acts 9:30; Acts 18:22; Acts 21:8
Paul escorted to.........Acts 23:23, 33
Paul imprisoned at ......Acts 25:4
Paul appealed to Caesar at ....Acts 25:8-13

the towns of *C* Philippi ....Mark 8:27
after they entered into *C* ......Acts 10:24
I was sent from *C* unto me ....Acts 11:11
of the disciples of *C* and ......Acts 21:16
ascended from *C* to Jerusalem .Acts 25:1
days he went down unto *C* ....Acts 25:6

CAESAREA PHILIPPI (sĕs-ä-rē'ä fĭ-lĭp'ī)—*"Caesar's city of Philippi"*
A city in north Palestine; scene of Peter's great confession ....Matt 16:13-20
Probable place of the transfiguration.........Matt 17:1-13

CAGE—*a barred cell for confining prisoners*
Judah compared to ......Jer 5:27
Figurative of captivity....Ezek 19:9
Babylon called ....Rev 18:2

CAIAPHAS (kā'yä-făs)—*"depression"*
Son-in-law of Annas; high priest ....John 18:13
Makes prophecy ....John 11:49-52
Jesus before ....John 18:23, 24
Apostles before ....Acts 4:1-22

priest, who was called *C* ......Matt 26:3
led him away to *C* the high ...Matt 26:37
Annas and *C* being the high ...Luke 3:2
C was he, which gave counsel .John 18:14
Then led they Jesus from *C* ...John 18:28

CAIN (kān)—*"acquired; spear"*
Adam's son ....Gen 4:1
Offering rejected ....Gen 4:2-7; Heb 11:4
Was of the evil one......1 John 3:12
Murders Abel ....Gen 4:8
Becomes a vagabond ....Gen 4:9-15
Builds city ....Gen 4:16, 17
A type of evil ....Jude 11

she conceived and bare *C* .....Gen 4:1
but *C* was a tiller of the.......Gen 4:2
unto *C* and to his offering .....Gen 4:5
whosoever slayeth *C* ....Gen 4:15
Lord set a mark upon *C* ......Gen 4:15
C went out from the ....Gen 4:16
And *C* knew his wife; and ....Gen 4:17
If *C* shall be avenged seven ...Gen 4:24
instead of Abel whom *C* ......Gen 4:25

CAINAN (kā-ī'năn)—*"acquired"*
A son of Arphaxad......Luke 3:36

ninety years and begat *C* ......Gen 5:9
Enos lived after he begat *C* ...Gen 5:10
C lived seventy years and .....Gen 5:12
C lived after he begat.........Gen 5:13

CAKE—*usually small round cooked bread*

Kinds of:
Bread ....Ex 29:23
Unleavened ....Num 6:19
Fig 1Sam 30:12
Raisin 1Chr 16:3
Barley ....Ezek 4:12
Of fine flour ....Lev 2:4
Leavened ....Lev 7:13
Baked with oil ....Num 11:8

Used literally of:
Food 2Sam 13:6
Idolatry.................Jer 44:19
Food prepared for Elijah .1Kin 17:13

Used figuratively of:
Defeat..................Judg 7:13
Weak religion ....Hos 7:8

[*also* CAKES]
it and make *c* upon the ....Gen 18:6
bread and *c* unleavened ....Ex 29:2
unleavened *c* mingled with ....Lev 7:12
he took one unleavened *c* .....Lev 8:26
bake twelve *c* thereof ....Lev 24:5
two tenth deals shall be..*c*.....Lev 24:5
c of fine flour mingled ....Num 6:15
Ye shall offer up a *c*..........Num 15:20
unleavened *c*, and parched ....Josh 5:11
unleavened *c* of an ephah .....Judg 6:19
flesh and the unleavened *c* ....Judg 6:20
made *c* in his sight 2Sam 13:8
and did bake the *c* 2Sam 13:8
I have not a *c* but an 1Kin 17:12
meal, *c* of figs, and bunches ...1Chr 12:40

CALAH (kā'lä)—*"old age"*
A great city of Assyria built by Nimrod ....Gen 10:11, 12

CALAMITIES—*disasters*

Kinds of:
Personal ....Job 6:2
Tribal ....Judg 20:34-48
National ....Lam 1:1-22
Punitive ....Num 16:12-35
Judicial ....Deut 32:35
World-wide ....Luke 21:25-28
Sudden ....Prov 6:15; 1 Thess 5:3

Attitudes toward:
Unrepentance ....Prov 1:24-26
Repentance ....Jer 18:8
Hardness of heart ....Ex 14:8, 17
Bitterness...............Ruth 1:20, 21
Defeat..................1Sam 4:15-18
Submission..............Job 2:9, 10
Prayerfulness............Ps 141:5
Hopefulness.............Ps 27:1-3

[*also* CALAMITY]
prevented me..day of my *c* 2Sam 22:19
they set forward my *c*, they ...Job 30:13
prevented me..day of my *c* ....Ps 18:18
refuge, until these *c* be ....Ps 57:1
he that is glad at *c* shall.......Prov 17:5
foolish son is the *c* of his .....Prov 19:13
For their *c* shall rise ....Prov 24:22
brother's house..day of thy *c* ..Prov 27:10
face in the day of their *c*......Jer 18:17

the day of their *c* was come . . .Jer 46:21
The *c* of Moab is near to . . . . .Jer 48:16
will bring the *c* of Esau . . . . . . .Jer 49:8
bring their *c* from all sides . . . .Jer 49:23
in the day of their *c*; yea . . . . . .Obad 13
affliction in the day of their *c* .Obad 13

CALAMUS—*sweet cane*
Used in holy oil . . . . .Ex 30:23
Figurative of love . . . . .Song 4:14
Rendered "sweet cane" . .Jer 6:20

cassia and *c* were in thy . . . . . . .Ezek 27:19

CALCOL (kăl´kŏl)—*"sustaining; nourishment"*
A son of Zerah 1Chr 2:6
Famous for wisdom 1Kin 4:31

CALDRON—*a large kettle*
Used literally of:
Temple vessels 2Chr 35:13
Used figuratively of:
Leviathan's smoke . . . . . . .Job 41:20
Safety . . . . .Ezek 11:3, 7, 11
Oppression . . . . .Mic 3:3

[*also* CALDRONS]
the pan, or kettle, or *c*, or 1Sam 2:14
The *c* also and the shovels . . . .Jer 52:18
the *c*, and the candlesticks . . . .Jer 52:19

CALEB (kā´lĕb)—*"impetuous; raging with madness"*
1. Son of Jephunneh . . . . . . .Josh 15:13
Sent as spy . . . . .Num 13:2, 6
Gave good report . . . . . . .Num 13:27, 30
His life saved . . . . .Num 14:10-12
Told to divide Canaan . . .Num 34:17, 19
Entered Canaan . . . . .Num 14:24-38
Eighty-five at end of conquest . . . . .Josh 14:6-13
Given Hebron . . . . .Josh 14:14, 15
Josh 15:13-16
Gave daughter to Othniel . . . . .Judg 1:12-15
Descendants of 1Chr 4:15
2. Son of Hezron 1Chr 2:18, 42
3. A son of Hur 1Chr 2:50

[*also* CALEB'S]
Joshua the son of Nun, and *C* .Num 14:6
left a man of them, save *C* . . . .Num 26:65
Save *C* the son of Jephunneh . .Num 32:12
Save *C* the son of Jephunneh . .Deut 1:36
Kenaz the brother of *C* . . . . . . .Josh 15:17
C said unto her, What . . . . .Josh 15:18
they gave Hebron unto *C* . . . . .Judg 1:20
son of Kenaz, *C* younger . . . . . .Judg 3:9
he was of the house of *C* 1Sam 25:3
and upon the south of *C* 1Sam 30:14
Azubah was dead, *C* took 1Chr 2:19
Ephah, *C* concubine, bare 1Chr 2:46
Maachah, *C* concubine 1Chr 2:48
and the daughter of *C* was 1Chr 2:49
villages thereof, they..to *C* 1Chr 6:56

CELEB-EPHRATAH (kā´lĕb-ĕf´rä-tä)
Hezron died at 1Chr 2:24

CALENDAR—*a system of dating*
Year divided 1Chr 27:1-15
Determined by moon . . . .Ps 104:19
See JEWISH CALENDAR

CALF—*the young of a cow*
Characteristics of:
Playfulness of . . . . .Ps 29:6
Used for food . . . . .Amos 6:4
A delicacy . . . . .Luke 15:23, 27
In sacrifice . . . . .Lev 9:2, 3
Redeemed, if first-born . .Num 18:17
Figurative of:
Praise . . . . .Hos 14:2
Saints sanctified . . . . .Mal 4:2
Patience . . . . .Ezek 1:7

[*also* CALVES]
fetched a *c* tender and good . . .Gen 18:7
he saw the *c*, and the . . . . .Ex 32:19
made the *c*, which Aaron . . . . .Ex 32:35
had made you a molten *c* . . . . .Deut 9:16
bring their *c* home from 1Sam 6:7
woman had a fat *c* in the 1Sam 28:24
made two *c* of gold and said . .1Kin 12:28
golden *c* that were in Beth-el . .2Kin 10:29
and for the *c* which he had 2Chr 11:15
had made them a molten *c* . . . .Neh 9:18
cow calveth, and casteth..*c* . . . .Job 21:10
They made a *c* in Horeb . . . . . .Ps 106:19
between the parts of the *c* . . . .Jer 34:19
Thy *c*, O Samaria, hath cast . . .Hos 8:5
the *c* of Samaria, shall be . . . . .Hos 8:6
the *c* out of the midst . . . . .Amos 6:4
offerings, with *c* of a year . . . . .Mic 6:6
grow up as *c* of the stall . . . . . .Mal 4:2
killed for him the fatted *c* . . . . .Luke 15:30
they made a *c* in those days . . .Acts 7:41
the second beast like a *c* . . . . . .Rev 4:7

CALF, GOLDEN
Making of:
Inspired by Moses' delay . .Ex 32:1-4
Repeated by Jeroboam . . .1Kin 12:25-28
To represent God . . . . . . .Ex 32:4, 5
To replace Temple worship 1Kin 12:26, 27
Priests appointed for 1Kin 12:31
Sacrifices offered to . . . . .Ex 32:6
1Kin 12:32, 33
Sin of:
Immorality 1Cor 10:7
Great . . . . .Ex 32:21, 30, 31
An apostasy . . . . .Ex 32:8
Wrathful . . . . .Deut. 9:14-20
Brings punishment . . . . . . .Ex 32:26-29, 35
Repeated by Jeroboam . . .Hos 8:5, 6

CALKER—*a sealer*
Used on Tyrian vessels . . .Ezek 27:9, 27

CALL—*to shout; talk loudly; summon; convoke; a claim; vocation*
To:
Name . . . . .Gen 1:5
Pray . . . . .Gen 4:26
Be in reality . . . . .Luke 1:35
Set in office . . . . .Ex 31:2
Is 22:20
Give privileges . . . . .Luke 14:16, 17
Offer salvation . . . . .Matt 9:13
Engage in work 1Cor 7:20

[*also* CALLED, CALLEDST, CALLEST, CALLETH]
Adam *c* every living creature . .Gen 2:19
therefore is the name of it *c* . . .Gen 11:9
shalt *c* his name Ishmael . . . . . .Gen 16:11
thy name any more be *c* . . . . . .Gen 17:5
shalt not *c* her name Sarai . . . .Gen 17:15
angel of the Lord *c* unto . . . . . .Gen 22:11
We will *c* the damsel, and . . . . .Gen 24:57
the daughters will *c* me . . . . . . .Gen 30:13
not be *c* any more Jacob . . . . . .Gen 35:10
and he *c* his name Israel . . . . . .Gen 35:10
when Pharaoh shall *c* you . . . . .Gen 46:33
c unto him out..mountain . . . . .Ex 19:3
for the *c* of the assembly . . . . . .Num 10:2
Moabites *c* them Emim . . . . . . .Deut 2:11
I *c* heaven and earth to . . . . . . .Deut 4:26
c all Israel, and said unto . . . . .Deut 5:1
elders of his city shall *c* . . . . . .Deut 25:8
art *c*..name of the Lord . . . . . . .Deut 28:10
I *c* heaven and earth to . . . . . . .Deut 30:19
that thou *c* us not, when . . . . . .Judg 8:1
That the Lord *c* Samuel 1Sam 3:4
for thou *c* me. And he said . . .1Sam 3:5
I will *c* unto the Lord, and 1Sam 12:17
I will *c* on the Lord, who is . . .2Sam 22:4
c all his brethren the king's . . .1Kin 1:9
that the stranger *c* to thee 1Kin 8:43
c ye on the name of your 1Kin 18:24
and *c* on the name of Baal 1Kin 18:26
messenger that was gone to *c* . .1Kin 22:13
c on the name of the Lord 2Kin 5:11
Jabez *c* on the God of Israel . .1Chr 4:10
that the stranger *c* to thee 2Chr 6:33
people, which are *c* by my 2Chr 7:14
that she were *c* by name . . . . . .Esth 2:14
c upon God..he answereth . . . .Job 12:4
Thou shalt *c*, and I will . . . . . . .Job 14:15
bread, and *c* not upon the . . . .Ps 14:4
I have *c* upon thee, for thou . .Ps 17:6
I will *c* upon the Lord, who . . .Ps 18:3
king hear us when we *c* . . . . . . .Ps 20:9
Deep *c* unto deep at the . . . . . .Ps 42:7
c their lands after their . . . . . . .Ps 49:11
I *c* to remembrance my . . . . . . .Ps 77:6
we will *c* upon thy name . . . . . .Ps 80:18
unto all them that *c* upon . . . . .Ps 86:5
day of my trouble I will *c* . . . . .Ps 86:7
He shall *c* upon me, and I . . . .Ps 91:15
day when I *c* answer me . . . . . .Ps 102:2
c upon his name, make . . . . . . .Ps 105:1
c upon the name of the Lord . .Ps 116:13
c upon the name of the Lord . .Ps 116:17
unto all them that *c* upon . . . . .Ps 145:18
Then shall they *c* upon me . . . .Prov 1:28
c understanding thy . . . . .Prov 7:4
Unto you, O men, I *c* and . . . .Prov 8:4
To *c* passengers who go . . . . . . .Prov 9:15
arise up, and *c* her blessed . . . .Prov 31:28
that *c* evil good, and good . . . .Is 5:20
to me, *c* his name . . . . .Is 8:3
name shall be *c* Wonderful . . . .Is 9:6
will not *c* back his words . . . . . .Is 31:2
They shall *c* the nobles . . . . . . .Is 34:12
be *c* The way of holiness . . . . . .Is 35:8
he *c* them all by names by . . . .Is 40:26
shall he *c* upon my name . . . . .Is 41:25
hast not *c* upon me, O Jacob . .Is 43:22
Lord, which *c* thee by thy . . . . .Is 45:3
they *c* themselves of the . . . . . .Is 48:2
mine house shall be *c* . . . . .Is 56:7
wilt thou *c* this a fast . . . . .Is 58:5
thou *c*, and the Lord shall . . . .Is 58:9
c his servants by another . . . . . .Is 65:15
that before they *c*, I will . . . . . .Is 65:24
I will *c* all the families . . . . . . .Jer 1:15
c Jerusalem the throne of . . . . .Jer 3:17
I will *c* for a sword . . . . .Jer 25:29
Then shall ye *c* upon me . . . . . .Jer 29:12
c unto me, and I will . . . . .Jer 33:3
c together the archers . . . . .Jer 50:29
c together against her the . . . . .Jer 51:27
that men *c* The perfection . . . . .Lam 2:15
Thou hast *c* as in a solemn . . . .Lam 2:22
name thereof is *c* Bamah . . . . . .Ezek 20:29
c to remembrance the . . . . .Ezek 21:23
in *c* to remembrance the . . . . . .Ezek 23:19
shall *c* it The valley of . . . . .Ezek 39:11
is none among them that *c* . . . .Hos 7:7
thou shalt *c* me Ishi . . . . .Hos 2:16
whosoever shall *c* on the . . . . . .Joel 2:32
remnant..Lord shall *c* . . . . .Joel 2:32
shall *c* the husbandman . . . . . . .Amos 5:16
he that *c* for the waters . . . . . . .Amos 9:6
arise, *c* upon thy God, if so . . .Jon 1:6
now we *c* the proud happy . . . .Mal 3:15
they..*c* the children of God . . . .Matt 5:9
is not his mother *c* Mary? . . . . .Matt 13:55
Jesus *c* a little child unto . . . . . .Matt 18:2
Why *c* thou me good? there . . .Matt 19:17
c the laborers, and give . . . . . . .Matt 20:8
My house shall be *c* the . . . . . . .Matt 21:13
to *c* them that were bidden . . . .Matt 22:3
be not ye *c* Rabbi for one . . . . .Matt 23:8
And *c* no man your father . . . .Matt 23:9
or Jesus which *c* Christ . . . . . . .Matt 27:17
without, sent unto him, *c* . . . . . .Mark 3:31
they *c* the blind man, saying . . .Mark 10:49
and commanded him to be *c* . .Mark 10:49
of good comfort, rise; he *c* . . . .Mark 10:49
therefore himself..*c* Lord . . . . . .Mark 12:37
Peter *c* to mind the word . . . . .Mark 14:72
ye *c* the King of the Jews? . . . .Mark 15:12
heard it, said, Behold, he *c* . . .Mark 15:35
c the Son of the Highest . . . . . .Luke 1:32
generations shall *c* me . . . . .Luke 1:48

his name was *c* Jesus, which . . .Luke 2:21
I came not to *c* the righteous . .Luke 5:32
no more worthy to be *c* thy . . .Luke 15:19
these servants to be *c* unto . . . .Luke 19:15
c the Lord..God of Abraham . .Luke 20:37
place which is *c* Calvary . . . . . .Luke 23:33
Before that Philip *c* thee . . . . . .John 1:48
Go, *c* thy husband, and come. .John 4:16
Messiah cometh which is *c* . . . .John 4:25
A man that is *c* Jesus made . . .John 9:11
and he *c* his own sheep by . . . .John 10:3
as the Lord our God shall *c* . . .Acts 2:39
stoned Stephen, *c* upon God . .Acts 7:59
street which is *c* Straight . . . . . .Acts 9:11
that *c* not thou common . . . . . .Acts 11:9
the disciples..*c* Christians . . . . . .Acts 11:26
c for Barnabas and Saul . . . . . .Acts 13:7
upon whom my name is *c* . . . . .Acts 15:17
c over them which had evil . . . .Acts 19:13
we are in danger to be *c* in . . .Acts 19:40
sins, *c* on the name..Lord . . . . .Acts 22:16
I am *c* in question . . . . .Acts 23:6
c heresy, so worship I..God . . .Acts 24:14
c to be an apostle, separated . .Rom 1:1
Behold, thou art *c* a Jew . . . . . .Rom 2:17
c those things which be not . . .Rom 4:17
who are the *c* according . . . . . . .Rom 8:28
I will *c* them my people . . . . . . .Rom 9:25
rich unto all that *c* upon . . . . . .Rom 10:12
in every place *c* upon the 1Cor 1:2
For ye see your *c*, brethren . . .1Cor 1:26
mighty..many noble, are *c* 1Cor 1:26
if any man..is *c* a brother 1Cor 5:11
is any man *c* being 1Cor 7:18
wherein he is *c*, therein 1Cor 7:24
c Jesus accursed: and that 1Cor 12:3
I *c* God for a record upon 2Cor 1:23
from him that *c* you into . . . . . .Gal 1:6
ye have been *c* unto liberty . . .Gal 5:13
what is the hope of his *c* . . . . . .Eph 1:18
c in one hope of your *c* . . . . . . .Eph 4:4
to the which also ye are *c* . . . . .Col 3:15
himself above all..is *c* God 2Thess 2:4
When I *c* to remembrance 2Tim 1:5
called us with a holy *c* 2Tim 1:9
with them that *c* on the Lord . .2Tim 2:22
not ashamed to *c* them . . . . .Heb 2:11
while it is *c* Today; lest any . . .Heb 3:13
but he that is *c* of God, as . . . .Heb 5:4
c to remembrance the . . . . .Heb 10:32
ashamed to be *c* their God . . . .Heb 11:16
name by the which ye are *c* . . .James 2:7
c for the elders of the . . . . .James 5:14
And if ye *c* on the Father 1Pet 1:17
hath *c* you out of darkness 1Pet 2:9
hereunto were ye *c*; because . . .1Pet 2:21
as Sarah obeyed Abraham, *c* . .1Pet 3:6
who hath *c* us to glory 2Pet 1:3
should be *c* the sons of God . . .1John 3:1
c herself a prophetess, to . . . . .Rev 2:20
name..star is *c* Wormwood . . . .Rev 8:11
spiritually is *c* Sodom and . . . . .Rev 11:8
they that are with him are *c* . . .Rev 17:14

CALLING—*one's vocation*
Faith and one's 1Cor 7:20-22

CALLING, THE CHRISTIAN

Manifested through:
Christ . . . . .Matt 9:13
Holy Spirit . . . . .Rev 22:17
Gospel 2Thess 2:14

Described as:
Heavenly . . . . .Heb 3:1
Holy 2Tim 1:9
High . . . . .Phil 3:14
Unchangeable . . . . .Rom 11:29
By grace . . . . .Gal 1:15
2Tim 1:9
According to God's purpose 2Tim 1:9

Goals of:
Fellowship with Christ . . .1Cor 1:9
Holiness 1Thess 4:7
Liberty . . . . .Gal 5:13
Peace 1Cor 7:15
Glory and virtue 2Pet 1:3
Eternal glory 2Thess 2:14
Eternal life 1Tim 6:12

Attitudes toward:
Walk worthy of . . . . .Eph 4:1
Make it sure 2Pet 1:10
Of Gentiles . . . . .Eph 4:19

CALM—*absence of storms or rough water*
He maketh the storm a *c*, so . .Ps 107:29
ceased..there was a great *c* . . . .Mark 4:39
they ceased..there was a *c* . . . . .Luke 8:24

CALNEH (kăl'nĕ)—*"fortress"*
1. Nimrod's city . . . . .Gen 10:9, 10
2. A city linked with Hamath and Gath . . . . . . .Amos 6:2
Same as Calno . . . . .Is 10:9

CALVARY—*from the Latin "calvaria" (skull)*
Christ was crucified there .Luke 23:33
Same as "Golgotha" in Hebrew . . . . .John 19:17

CALVE—*give birth to a calf; produce offspring*

[*also* CALVED, CALVETH]
their cow *c*, and casteth not . . .Job 21:10
mark when the hinds do *c*? . . . .Job 39:1
Lord maketh the hinds to *c* . . .Ps 29:9

CAME—*See* INTRODUCTION

CAMEL—*humpbacked animal used as draft and saddle beast*

Used for:
Riding . . . . .Gen 24:61, 64
Trade . . . . .Gen 37:25
War . . . . .Judg 7:12
Hair of, for clothing . . . . .Matt 3:4
Used for garment worn by John the Baptist . . . .Matt 3:4
Wealth . . . . .Job 42:12

Features of:
Swift . . . . .Jer 2:23
Docile . . . . .Gen 24:11
Unclean . . . . .Lev 11:4
Adorned . . . . .Judg 8:21, 26
Prize for booty . . . . .Job 1:17
Treated well . . . . .Gen 24:31, 32
Illustrative of the impossible . . . . .Matt 19:24

[*also* CAMEL'S, CAMELS, CAMELS']
menservants, and *c*, and . . . . . .Gen 30:43
sons and his wives upon *c* . . . . .Gen 31:17
put them in the *c* furniture . . . .Gen 31:34
herds, and the *c*, into two . . . . .Gen 32:7
upon the asses, upon the *c* . . . .Ex 9:3
the *c*, and the hare, and the . . .Deut 14:7
suckling, ox and sheep, *c* 1Sam 15:3
the asses, and the *c*, and the . .1Sam 27:9
with *c* that bare spices, and . . .1Kin 10:2
of Damascus, forty *c* burden . .2Kin 8:9
cattle; of their *c* fifty 1Chr 5:21
company, and *c* that bare 2Chr 9:1
c, four hundred thirty and . . . . .Neh 7:69
three thousand *c*, and five . . . . .Job 1:3
all their vessels, and their *c* . . .Jer 49:29
make Rabbah a stable for *c* . . .Ezek 25:5
of the mule, of the *c* . . . . .Zech 14:15
at a gnat, and swallow a *c* . . . .Matt 23:24
clothed with *c* hair, and . . . . . . .Mark 1:6
easier for a *c* to go through . . .Mark 10:25
easier for a *c* to go through . . .Luke 18:25

CAMON (kā'mŏn)—*"elevation"*
Jair was buried there . . . .Judg 10:5

CAMP—*to pitch a tent; site on which tents are erected*

The Lord's guidance of, by:
An angel . . . . .Ex 14:19
Ex 32:34
His presence . . . . .Ex 33:14
A cloud . . . . .Ps 105:39

Israel's:
On leaving Egypt . . . . .Ex 13:20
At Sinai . . . . .Ex 18:5
Orderly . . . . .Num 2:2-34
Tabernacle in center of . .Num 2:17
Exclusion of:
Unclean . . . . .Deut 23:10-12
Lepers . . . . .Lev 13:46
Dead . . . . .Lev 10:4, 5
Executions outside . . . . .Lev 24:23
Log kept of . . . . .Num 33:1-49
In battle . . . . .Josh 10:5, 31, 34

Spiritual significance of:
Christ's crucifixion outside . . . . .Heb 13:13
God's people . . . . .Rev 20:9

[*also* CAMPED, CAMPS]
came up, and covered the *c* . . .Ex 16:13
and there Israel *c* before . . . . . .Ex 19:2
without the *c*, afar off from *c* . .Ex 33:7
which was without the *c* . . . . . .Ex 33:7
proclaimed throughout the *c* . . .Ex 36:6
he carry forth without the *c* . . .Lev 4:12
the ashes without the *c* unto . . .Lev 6:11
he burnt with fire without *c* . . .Lev 8:17
shall go forth out of the *c* . . . . .Lev 14:3
afterward come into the *c* . . . . .Lev 16:26
lamb, or goat, in the *c* or . . . . .Lev 17:3
killeth it out of the *c* . . . . .Lev 17:3
strove together in the *c* . . . . . . .Lev 24:10
every man by his own *c*, and . .Num 1:52
that were numbered of the *c* . .Num 2:32
when the *c* setteth forward . . . .Num 4:5
put out of the *c* every leper . . .Num 5:2
bring her forth without the *c* . .Num 19:3
God walketh..midst of thy *c* . . .Deut 23:14
the *c*, and lodged in the *c* . . . . .Josh 6:11
unto Joshua to the *c* to . . . . . . .Josh 10:6
come to the outside of the *c* . . .Judg 7:17
him at times in the *c* of Dan . .Judg 13:25
there came none to the *c* . . . . . .Judg 21:8
people were come into the *c* . .1Sam 4:3
out *c* of the Philistines 1Sam 13:17
went up with them into the *c* . .1Sam 14:21
the *c* of the Philistines 1Sam 17:4
over Israel that day in the *c* . . .1Kin 16:16
they came to the *c* of Israel . . .2Kin 3:24
such a place shall be my *c* 2Kin 6:8
the uttermost part of the *c* 2Kin 7:5
smote in the *c*..Assyrians 2Kin 19:35
envied Moses also in the *c* . . . .Ps 106:16
smote in the *c*..Assyrians . . . . . .Is 37:36
sin, are burned without the *c* . .Heb 13:11

CAMPHIRE—*henna; a fragrant shrub*
Illustrative of beauty . . . . .Song 1:14

c, with spikenard . . . . .Song 4:13

CAN—*to be able to*

[*also* CANNOT, CANST, COULD, COULDEST]
punishment is greater..*c* . . . . . . .Gen 4:13
they *c* not dwell together . . . . . .Gen 13:6
c number the dust of the . . . . . .Gen 13:16
eyes were dim, so that he *c* . . .Gen 27:1
were strangers *c* not bear . . . . .Gen 36:7
they hated him, and *c* not . . . . .Gen 37:4
c I do this great wickedness . . .Gen 39:9
was none that *c* interpret . . . . . .Gen 41:8
is none that *c* interpret it . . . . .Gen 41:15
thou *c* understand a dream . . . .Gen 41:15
c we find such a one as . . . . . . .Gen 41:38
as much as they *c* carry . . . . . . .Gen 44:1
Then Joseph *c* not refrain . . . . .Gen 45:1
dim for age, so that he *c* . . . . . .Gen 48:10
when she *c* not longer hide . . . .Ex 2:3
I know that he *c* speak well . . .Ex 4:14
out of Egypt, and *c* not tarry . .Ex 12:39
c not drink of the waters . . . . . .Ex 15:23
c not keep the passover on . . . .Num 9:6
the itch, whereof thou *c* not . . .Deut 28:27
children of Israel *c* not . . . . . . .Josh 7:12
thou *c* not stand before . . . . . . .Josh 7:13
children of Manasseh *c* not . . . .Josh 17:12

c not drive out..inhabitants....Judg 1:19
if ye *c* certainly declare it.....Judg 14:12
unto him, How *c* thou say....Judg 16:15
one *c* sling stones at..hair.....Judg 20:16
rose up before one *c* know....Ruth 3:14
to wax dim, that he *c* not.....1Sam 3:2
peradventure he *c* show us.....1Sam 9:6
they *c* not go over the brook..1Sam 30:10
I was sure that he *c* not live...2Sam 1:10
And what *c* David say more...2Sam 7:20
Who *c* tell whether God will..2Sam 12:22
every thing that ye *c* hear.....2Sam 15:36
c thy servant taste what I.....2Sam 19:35
c I hear any more the voice...2Sam 19:35
wounded them that they *c*.....2Sam 22:39
David my father *c* not build...1Kin 5:3
But Ahijah *c* not see; for.....1Kin 14:4
king of Edom; but they *c*.....2Kin 3:26
and *c* use both the right.......1Chr 12:2
What *c* David speak more to..1Chr 17:18
But David *c* not go before....1Chr 21:30
who *c* judge this thy people...2Chr 1:10
weight of the brass *c* not be...2Chr 4:18
that *c* skill of instruments.....2Chr 34:12
c not show their father's......Ezra 2:59
they *c* not cause them to......Ezra 5:5
c not show their father's......Neh 7:61
c not speak in the Jews'.......Neh 13:24
that night *c* not the king......Esth 6:1
people? or how *c* I endure....Esth 8:6
when they *c* find the grave?...Job 3:22
It stood still, but I *c* not......Job 4:16
C that which is unsavory......Job 6:6
C the rush grow up without...Job 8:11
c the flag grow without.......Job 8:11
c thou find out the Almighty..Job 11:7
or darkness, that thou *c* not...Job 22:11
one mind and who *c* turn.....Job 23:13
his highness I *c* not endure....Job 31:23
his face, who then *c* behold...Job 34:29
or *c* thou mark when the......Job 39:1
Who *c* discover the face of....Job 41:13
no thought *c* be withholden...Job 42:2
Who *c* understand his errors?..Ps 19:12
I sought him, but he *c* not....Ps 37:36
their floods, that they *c* not...Ps 78:44
Who *c* utter the mighty acts...Ps 106:2
c a man take fire in his.......Prov 6:27
but a wounded spirit who *c*...Prov 18:14
but a faithful man who *c*......Prov 20:6
seven men that *c* render a.....Prov 26:16
no man *c* find out the work...Eccl 3:11
for who *c* tell him when it....Eccl 8:7
after him, who *c* tell him?.....Eccl 10:14
I sought him, but I *c* not......Song 5:6
neither *c* the floods drown.....Song 8:7
c have been done more to my.Is 5:4
tongue that thou *c* not........Is 33:19
among them *c* declare this....Is 43:9
they *c* not deliver the burden..Is 46:2
unto him, yet *c* he not........Is 46:7
cisterns that *c* hold no........Jer 2:13
done evil things as thou *c*.....Jer 3:5
ashamed, neither *c* they.......Jer 6:15
how *c* thou contend with......Jer 12:5
burn that none *c* quench it....Jer 21:12
If ye *c* break my covenant....Jer 33:20
So that the Lord *c* no longer..Jer 44:22
How *c* it be quiet, seeing.....Jer 47:7
like the sea; who *c* heal.......Lam 2:13
men *c* not touch their..........Lam 4:14
for a nation that *c* not save...Lam 4:17
and yet *c* not be satisfied.....Ezek 16:28
no secret that they *c* hide.....Ezek 28:3
in the garden of God *c* not....Ezek 31:8
c play well on instrument.....Ezek 33:32
a river that I *c* not pass.......Ezek 47:5
river that *c* not be passed.....Ezek 47:5
know that ye *c* show me the...Dan 2:9
seeing thou *c* reveal this......Dan 2:47
God that *c* deliver after.......Dan 3:29
none *c* stay his hand..........Dan 4:35
they *c* not read the writing....Dan 5:8
thou *c* make interpretations...Dan 5:16
any that *c* deliver out of his...Dan 8:4
c the servant of this my lord..Dan 10:17
c he not heal you, nor cure...Hos 5:13
terrible; and who *c* abide it?..Joel 2:11
they *c* not: for the sea wrought.Jon 1:13
Who *c* tell if God will turn....Jon 3:9
none evil *c* come upon us.....Mic 3:11
Who *c* stand before his.......Nah 1:6
neither *c* a corrupt tree.......Matt 7:18
ye *c* discern the face of.......Matt 16:3
and they *c* not cure him.......Matt 17:16
When Pilate saw that he *c*....Matt 27:24
way, make it as sure as ye *c*...Matt 27:65
insomuch that Jesus *c* no......Mark 1:45
How *c* Satan cast out Satan?..Mark 3:23
and no man *c* bind him, no...Mark 5:3
he *c* there do no mighty......Mark 6:5
but if thou *c* do any thing.....Mark 9:22
themselves, Who then *c* be....Mark 10:26
She hath done what she *c*.....Mark 14:8
c not thou watch one hour?...Mark 14:37
he came out, he *c* not speak..Luke 1:22
if thou wilt, thou *c* make......Luke 5:12
c the blind lead the blind?....Luke 6:39
No servant *c* serve two........Luke 16:13
it said, Who then *c* be saved?.Luke 18:26
that they *c* not tell whence....Luke 20:7
c there any good thing........John 1:46
cometh, when no man *c*......John 9:4
were not of God, he *c* do......John 9:33
c a devil open the eyes of.....John 10:21
how *c* we know the way?......John 14:5
no more *c* ye, except ye......John 15:4
Thou *c* have no power at all..John 19:11
even the world itself *c* not....John 21:25
they *c* say nothing against.....Acts 4:14
How *c* I, except some man....Acts 8:31
c any man forbid water.......Acts 10:47
Neither *c* they prove the......Acts 24:13
and *c* not bear up into the....Acts 27:15
For what the law *c* not do....Rom 8:3
law of God, neither indeed *c*..Rom 8:7
For I *c* wish that myself.......Rom 9:3
neither *c* he know them, for...1Cor 2:14
And I, brethren, *c* not speak..1Cor 3:1
other foundation *c* no man....1Cor 3:11
no man *c* say that Jesus is.....1Cor 12:3
all faith, so that I *c* remove...1Cor 13:2
Israel *c* not steadfastly.......2Cor 3:7
Would to God ye *c* bear......2Cor 11:1
a law given which *c* have......Gal 3:21
when we *c* no longer forbear..1Thess 3:1
So we see that they *c* not.....Heb 3:19
for they *c* not endure that.....Heb 12:20
But the tongue *c* no man.....James 3:8
how *c* he love God whom he..1John 4:20
multitude, which no man *c*....Rev 7:9
neither *c* see, nor hear, nor...Rev 9:20
and no man *c* learn that......Rev 14:3

CANA OF GALILEE—*"reeds"*

A village of upper Galilee; home of Nathanael...........John 21:2
Christ's first miracle at...John 2:1-11
Healing at.............John 4:46-54

CANAAN (kā'năn)—*"low"*

1. A son of Ham.........Gen 10:6
   Cursed by Noah........Gen 9:20-25
2. Promised land.........Gen 12:5

and Ham is the father of *C*....Gen 9:18
tents of Shem; and *C* shall....Gen 9:27
C begat Sidon his firstborn....Gen 10:15

CANAAN, LAND OF—*"purple"—native name of Palestine*

Specifications regarding:

Boundaries.............Gen 10:19
Fertility................Ex 3:8, 17
Seven nations...........Deut 7:1
Language...............Is 19:18

God's promises concerning, given to:

Abraham...............Gen 12:1-3
Isaac..................Gen 26:2, 3
Jacob..................Gen 28:13
Israel..................Ex 3:8

Conquest of:

Announced.............Gen 15:7-21
Preceded by spies........Num 13:1-33
Delayed by unbelief.....Num 14:1-35
Accomplished by the Lord...............Josh 23:1-16
Done only in part.......Judg 1:21, 27-36

Names of:

Canaan.................Gen 11:31
Land of Hebrews........Gen 40:15
Palestine...............Ex 15:14
Land of Israel...........1Sam 13:19
Immanuel's land.........Is 8:8
Beulah.................Is 62:4
Pleasant...............Dan 8:9
The Lord's land.........Hos 9:3
Holy land..............Zech 2:12
Land of the Jews........Acts 10:39
Land of promise.........Heb 11:9

[*also* CHANAAN]

Chaldees..into the land of *C*...Gen 11:31
Abram dwelled..land of *C*.....Gen 13:12
ten years in the land of *C*.....Gen 16:3
land of *C* for an everlasting...Gen 17:8
Hebron in the land of *C*.....Gen 23:2
wife of the daughters of *C*....Gen 28:1
which is in the land of *C*......Gen 33:18
to Luz..in the land of *C*.......Gen 35:6
wives of the daughters of *C*...Gen 36:2
stranger, in the land of *C*.....Gen 37:1
thee out of the land of *C*.....Gen 44:8
go, get you..the land of *C*.....Gen 45:17
had gotten in the land of *C*...Gen 46:6
come out of the land of *C*....Gen 47:1
at Luz in the land of *C*.......Gen 48:3
Mamre, in the land of *C*......Gen 49:30
digged for me..land of *C*......Gen 50:5
inhabitants of *C* shall melt....Ex 15:15
Onan died in the land of *C*....Num 26:19
among you in the land of *C*...Num 32:30
in the south in the land of *C*..Num 33:40
When ye come..the land of *C*.Num 34:2
Jordan into the land of *C*.....Num 35:10
the land of *C*, which I give....Deut 32:49
the fruit of the land of *C*......Josh 5:12
Israel inherited..land of *C*.....Josh 14:1
at Shiloh in the land of *C*.....Josh 21:2
Shiloh, which..the land of *C*...Josh 22:9
throughout all the land of *C*...Josh 24:3
Mizraim, Put, and *C*..........1Chr 1:8
they sacrificed..idols of *C*.....Ps 106:38
O *C* the land..Philistines......Zeph 2:5
over..land of Egypt and *C*.....Acts 7:11
seven nations..land of *C*......Acts 13:19

CANAANITES (kā'năn-īts)—*original inhabitants of Canaan*

Described as:

Descendants of Ham.....Gen 10:5, 6
Under a curse...........Gen 9:25, 26
Amorites...............Gen 15:16
Seven nations...........Deut 7:1
Fortified...............Num 13:28
Idolatrous..............Deut 29:17
Defiled................Lev 18:24-27

Destruction of:

Commanded by God.....Ex 23:23, 28-33
Caused by wickedness...Deut 9:4
In God's time...........Gen 15:13-16
Done in degrees.........Ex 23:29, 30

Commands prohibiting:

Common league with....Deut 7:2
Intermarriage with.......Deut 7:3
Idolatry of..............Ex 23:24
Customs of.............Lev 18:24-27

[*also* CANAANITESS, CANAANITISH]

families of the *C* spread.......Gen 10:18
And the *C* was then in the....Gen 12:6
my son of the daughters..*C*....Gen 24:3

Shaul the son of a *C* woman . . Gen 46:10
and I will drive out the *C* . . . . . Ex 33:2
before thee the Amorite..*C* . . . . Ex 34:11
and the *C* dwell by the sea . . . . Num 13:29
and delivered up the *C*; and . . . Num 21:3
sea side, to the land of the *C* . . Deut 1:7
down in the land of the *C* . . . . . Deut 11:30
and the Amorites the *C* . . . . . . Deut 20:17
drive out from before you..*C* . . Josh 3:10
C and all the inhabitants . . . . . . Josh 7:9
Hittite, and the Amorite..*C* . . . Josh 9:1
C on the east and on the . . . . . . Josh 11:3
the Amorites, and the *C* . . . . . . Josh 12:8
which is counted to the *C* . . . . . Josh 13:3
they drove not out the *C* . . . . . . Josh 16:10
the Perizzites, and the *C* . . . . . Josh 24:11
go up for us against the *C* . . . . . Judg 1:1
Philistines, and all the *C* . . . . . Judg 3:3
of the Hivites, and of the *C* . . . 2Sam 24:7
daughter of Shua the *C* 1Chr 2:3
their abominations even..*C* . . . . Ezra 9:1
to give the land of the *C* . . . . . . Neh 9:8
C in the house of the Lord . . . . Zech 14:21

CANAANITES—*a Jewish Sect*
"Simon the Canaanite" . . Matt 10:4
Woman from that region. . Matt 15:22
Called Zelotes . . . . Luke 6:15

CANDACE (kăn′dä-sē)—*"contrite one"—dynastic title of Ethiopian queens*
Conversion of eunuch of. . Acts 8:27-39

CANDLE—*a light; lamp*

Used literally of:
Household lights . . . . Matt 5:15

Used figuratively of:
Conscience . . . . Prov 20:27
Prosperity . . . . Job 29:3
Industry . . . . Prov 31:18
Death . . . . Job 18:6
God's justice . . . . Zeph 1:12

is the *c* of the wicked put . . . . . Job 21:17
For thou wilt light my *c* . . . . Ps 18:28
c of the wicked shall be put . . . Prov 24:20
and the light of the *c* . . . . Jer 25:10
men light a *c*, and put it . . . . . . Matt 5:15
doth not light a *c*, and sweep . . Luke 15:8

CANDLESTICK—*a stand for lamps; the Menorah*

[*also* CANDLESTICKS]
and not to be set on a *c*? . . . . . Mark 4:21
but setteth it on a *c* that . . . . . . Luke 8:16
but on a *c* that they which . . . . Luke 11:33
in the midst of the seven *c* . . . . Rev 1:13
and the seven *c* which thou . . . Rev 1:20
remove thy *c* out of his place . . Rev 2:5
and the two *c* standing . . . . Rev 11:4

CANDLESTICK, THE GOLDEN

Specifications regarding:
Made of gold . . . . Ex 25:31
After a divine model . . . . Ex 25:31-40
Set in holy place . . . . Heb 9:2
Continual burning of . . . . . Ex 27:20, 21
Carried by Kohathites . . . Num 4:4, 15
Temple's ten branches of . 1Kin 7:49, 50
Taken to Babylon . . . . Jer 52:19

Used figuratively of:
Christ . . . . Zech 4:2, 11
The church . . . . Rev 1:13, 20

[*also* CANDLESTICKS]
the *c* over against the table . . . . Ex 26:35
the *c* and his vessels, and . . . . . Ex 30:27
the pure *c*..his furniture . . . . Ex 31:8
The *c* also for the light . . . . Ex 35:14
of beaten work made..*c* . . . . Ex 37:17
And in the *c* were four . . . . Ex 37:20
The pure *c*, with the lamps . . . . Ex 39:37
thou shalt bring in the *c* . . . . . . Ex 40:4
the lamps upon the pure *c* . . . . . Lev 24:4
c, and the altars, and the . . . . . Num 3:31
and cover the *c* of the light . . . Num 4:9
give light over against the *c* . . . Num 8:2
a table,..a stool, and a *c* 2Kin 4:10
the weight for the *c* of gold . . . 1Chr 28:15
by weight for every *c*, and 1Chr 28:15
c, and also for the lamps 1Chr 28:15
he made ten *c* of gold 2Chr 4:7
and the *c* of gold with the 2Chr 13:11
and wrote over against the *c* . . Dan 5:5
a *c* all of gold with a bowl . . . . Zech 4:2
midst of the seven golden *c* . . . Rev 2:1

CANE—*a tall, sedgy grass*
Used in sacrifices . . . . Is 43:24
Jer 6:20
Used in holy oil . . . . Ex 30:23
Trading city . . . . Ezek 27:23

CANKER—*a spreading sore; an erosion*

[*also* CANKERED]
word will eat as doth a *c* 2Tim 2:17
Your gold and silver is *c* . . . . . . James 5:3

CANKERWORM—*insect larvae that destroys plants by feeding on them*
Sent as judgment . . . . Joel 1:4
Large appetite of . . . . Nah 3:15

the *c*, and the caterpillar . . . . . . Joel 2:25

CANNEH (kăn′ĕ)—*"distinguished"—a town on the southern coast of Arabia*
as *C*, and Eden...merchants . . . Ezek 27:23

CANNIBALISM—*using human flesh as food*
Predicted as a judgment. . Deut 28:53-57
Fulfilled in a siege 2Kin 6:28, 29

CANNOT—*to be unable to*
I *c* escape to the mountain . . . . Gen 19:19
we *c* speak unto thee bad or . . Gen 24:50
We *c*, until all the flocks . . . . . . Gen 29:8
I *c* rise up before thee . . . . Gen 31:35
sand of the sea, which *c* . . . . . . Gen 32:12
and said, I *c* find her and . . . . . Gen 38:22
The lad *c* leave his father . . . . . Gen 44:22
one *c* be able to see the . . . . . . Ex 10:5
mouth unto the Lord..*c* . . . . Judg 11:35
if ye *c* declare it me then . . . . . Judg 14:13
I *c* redeem it for myself . . . . Ruth 4:6
things, which *c* profit nor 1Sam 12:21
I *c* go with these for I 1Sam 17:39
that a man *c* speak to him 1Sam 25:17
which *c* be gathered up 2Sam 14:14
heaven of heavens *c* contain . . . 1Kin 8:27
heaven of heavens *c* contain . . . 2Chr 2:6
we *c* stand before thee . . . . Ezra 9:15
so that I *c* come down . . . . Neh 6:3
c my taste discern perverse . . . . Job 6:30
c answer him one of a . . . . Job 9:3
c be built again; he . . . . Job 12:14
his bounds that he *c* . . . . Job 14:5
c find one wise man among . . . Job 17:10
backward, but I *c* perceive . . . . Job 23:8
It *c* be gotten for gold . . . . Job 28:15
flesh! we *c* be satisfied . . . . Job 31:31
that it *c* be seen and his . . . . . . Job 33:21
then a great ransom *c* . . . . Job 36:18
which we *c* comprehend . . . . Job 37:5
stick together, that they *c* . . . . . Job 41:17
they *c* be reckoned up in . . . . . . Ps 40:5
I am so troubled that I *c* . . . . . . Ps 77:4
mount Zion, which *c* be . . . . . . Ps 125:1
man *c* find out the work . . . . . . Eccl 8:17
and he saith, I *c*; for it is . . . . . Is 29:11
go down into the pit *c* hope . . . Is 38:18
that he *c* deliver his soul . . . . . . Is 44:20
and pray unto a god that *c* . . . . Is 45:20
shortened at all, that it *c* . . . . . Is 50:2
troubled sea, when it *c* rest . . . Is 57:20
Ah! Lord God! behold I *c* . . . . Jer 1:6
noise in me; I *c* hold my . . . . . . Jer 4:19
trust in lying words that *c* . . . . . Jer 7:8
for they *c* do evil . . . . Jer 10:5
them like vile figs that *c* be . . . Jer 29:17
I *c* get out; he hath made . . . . . Lam 3:7
that we *c* go in our streets . . . . Lam 4:18
c the wise men, the . . . . Dan 2:27
sea, which *c* be measured . . . . . Hos 1:10
that *c* discern between . . . . Jon 4:11
All men *c* receive this . . . . Matt 19:11
We *c* tell. And he said . . . . Matt 21:27
Thinkest thou that I *c* now . . . . Matt 26:53
bridegroom..them they *c* . . . . . . Mark 2:19
it *c* defile him . . . . Mark 7:18
c tell..Jesus answering . . . . Mark 11:33
in bed; I *c* rise and give . . . . Luke 11:7
also, he *c* be my disciple . . . . . . Luke 14:26
I *c* dig..beg I am ashamed . . . . Luke 16:3
I am, thither ye *c* come . . . . John 7:34
whither I go ye *c* come . . . . John 8:21
because ye *c* hear my word . . . . John 8:43
the scripture *c* be broken . . . . . John 10:35
Whither I go, ye *c* come . . . . . . John 13:33
whom the world *c* receive . . . . . John 14:17
As the branch *c* bear fruit . . . . . John 15:4
but ye *c* bear them now . . . . John 16:12
we *c* but speak the things . . . . . Acts 4:20
c overthrow it lest; haply . . . . . . Acts 5:39
of Moses, ye *c* be saved . . . . Acts 15:1
these things *c* be spoken . . . . . . Acts 19:36
in the ship, ye *c* be saved . . . . . Acts 27:31
are in the flesh *c* please God . . Rom 8:8
ye *c* be partakers of the 1Cor 10:21
the eye *c* say unto the hand . . . 1Cor 12:21
flesh and blood *c* inherit the . . . 1Cor 15:50
I *c* tell; or whether out 2Cor 12:2
of the body, I *c* tell 2Cor 12:2
c disannul, that it should . . . . . . Gal 3:17
speech that *c* be condemned . . . Titus 2:8
for God *c* be tempted with . . . . James 1:13
desire to have and *c* obtain . . . . James 4:2
is blind and *c* see afar off 2Pet 1:9
that *c* cease from sin 2Pet 2:14
he *c* sin, because he is born . . . 1John 3:9

CANST—*See* CAN

CAPACITY—*ability to perform*
Hindered by sin . . . . Gal 5:17
Fulfilled in Christ . . . . Phil 4:13

CAPERNAUM (kä-pûr′nā-ŭm)—*"village of Nahum"—a town on the northwest shore of the Sea of Galilee*

Scene of Christ's healing of:
Centurion's servant . . . . . . Matt 8:5-13
Nobleman's son . . . . John 4:46-54
Peter's mother-in-law . . . . Matt 8:14-17
The demoniac . . . . Mark 1:21-28
The paralytic . . . . Matt 9:1-8
Various diseases . . . . Matt 8:16, 17

Other events connected with:
Jesus' headquarters . . . . . . Matt 4:13-17
Simon Peter's home . . . . . Mark 1:21, 29
Jesus' sermon on the Bread of Life . . . . John 6:24-71
Other important messages. Mark 9:33-50
Judgment pronounced upon . . . . Matt 11:23, 24

were come to *C* they that . . . . . Matt 17:24
entered into *C* after some . . . . . Mark 2:1
people, he entered into *C* . . . . . Luke 7:1
And thou, *C* which art . . . . Luke 10:15
After this he went down..*C* . . . John 2:12
went over the sea toward *C* . . . John 6:17

CAPH (kăf)
Eleventh letter of Hebrew alphabet . . . . Ps 119:81-88

CAPHTOR (kăf′tôr)—*"isle"*
The place (probably Crete) from which the Philistines came to Palestine . . . . Jer 47:4

which came forth out of *C* . . . . Deut 2:23
the Philistines from *C* and . . . . . Amos 9:7

CAPHTORIM (kăf′tō-rĭm)
Those of Caphtor . . . . Deut 2:23
Descendants of Mizraim. . Gen 10:13, 14
Conquerors of the Avim. . Deut 2:23

[*also* CAPHTHORIM]
came the Philistines and *C* 1Chr 1:12

CAPITAL PUNISHMENT—*the death penalty*

Institution of:

By God . . . . Gen 9:5, 6
Ex 21:12-17

Crimes punished by:

Murder . . . . Gen 9:5, 6
Adultery . . . . Lev 20:10
Incest . . . . Lev 20:11-14
Sodomy . . . . Lev 20:13
Rape . . . . Deut 22:25
Witchcraft . . . . Ex 22:18
Disobedience to parents . . Ex 21:18-21
Blasphemy . . . . Lev 24:11-16, 23
False doctrines . . . . Deut 13:1-10

CAPPADOCIA (kăp-ă-dō´shĭ-ă)—*"five horses"—a province of Asia Minor*

Natives of, at Pentecost . . Acts 2:1, 9
Christians of, addressed by Peter 1Pet 1:1

CAPTAIN—*a civil or military officer*

Applied literally to:

Tribal heads . . . . Num 2:3, 5
Military leader . . . . Judg 4:2
King Saul 1Sam 9:15, 16
Potiphar . . . . Gen 37:36
David as leader 1Sam 22:2
David as king 2Sam 5:2
Temple police head . . . . . . Luke 22:4
Roman officer . . . . Acts 21:31

Applied spiritually to:

Angel of the Lord . . . . Josh 5:14

[*also* CAPTAINS]

c of his host spake unto . . . . Gen 21:22
Phichol, the chief *c* of his . . . . . Gen 26:26
c of the guard, an Egyptian . . . Gen 39:1
the house of the *c* of the . . . . . Gen 40:3
c of the guard's house, both . . . Gen 41:10
c over every one of them . . . . . Ex 14:7
Let us make a *c*, and let us . . . Num 14:4
the *c* over thousands . . . . Num 31:14
and *c* over hundreds . . . . Num 31:14
c over thousands . . . . Deut 1:15
and *c* over hundreds . . . . Deut 1:15
and *c* over fifties . . . . Deut 1:15
and *c* over tens . . . . Deut 1:15
c of the armies to lead the . . . . Deut 20:9
your *c* of your tribes, your . . . . Deut 29:10
c of the Lord's host said . . . . . . Josh 5:15
unto the *c* of the men of . . . . . . Josh 10:24
c over thousands 1Sam 8:12
be *c* over his inheritance? 1Sam 10:1
c of the host of Hazor and 1Sam 12:9
to be *c* over his people 1Sam 13:14
the name of the *c* of his 1Sam 14:50
the *c* of their thousand 1Sam 17:18
him his *c* over a thousand 1Sam 18:13
and *c* of hundreds 1Sam 22:7
Abner the son of Ner, the *c* . . . 1Sam 26:5
two men that were *c* of 2Sam 4:2
Shobach the *c* of the host 2Sam 10:16
And Absalom made Amasa *c* . . 2Sam 17:25
and *c* of hundreds 2Sam 18:1
c of the host before me 2Sam 19:13
chief among the *c* the 2Sam 23:8
therefore he was their *c* 2Sam 23:19
against the *c* of the host 2Sam 24:4
Joab the *c* of the host 1Kin 1:19
c of the host of Israel and 1Kin 2:32
Jether, *c* of the host 1Kin 2:32
his princes, and his *c*, and 1Kin 9:22
Joab the *c* of the host was 1Kin 11:15
the *c* of the hosts which he 1Kin 15:20
c of half his chariots 1Kin 16:9
and put *c* in their rooms 1Kin 20:24
unto him a *c* of fifty with 2Kin 1:9
the two *c* of the former 2Kin 1:14
the *c* of the host? And she 2Kin 4:13
And he said, To thee, O *c* 2Kin 9:5
to the guard and to the *c* 2Kin 10:25
guard and the *c* cast them 2Kin 10:25
with the *c* and the guard 2Kin 11:4
the son of Remaliah, a *c* 2Kin 15:25
c of the least of my master's . . 2Kin 18:24
Hezekiah the *c* of my people . . 2Kin 20:5
all the *c* of the armies 2Kin 25:23
having for their *c* Pelatiah 1Chr 4:42
first shall be chief and *c* 1Chr 11:6
c of thousands and hundreds . . 1Chr 13:1
c of the host of Hadarezer . . . 1Chr 19:16
The third *c* of the host for 1Chr 27:5
and *c* over hundreds 1Chr 28:1
and chief of his *c* 2Chr 8:9
himself is with us for..*c* 2Chr 13:12
Jehohanan the *c* and with 2Chr 17:15
and the *c* of the chariots 2Chr 21:9
the *c* of hundreds, Azariah 2Chr 23:1
c over thousands 2Chr 25:5
Hananiah one of the king's *c* . . 2Chr 26:11
set *c* of war over the people . . . 2Chr 32:6
the *c* of the host of the king . . . 2Chr 33:11
king had sent *c* of the army . . . Neh 2:9
rebellion appointed a *c* . . . . Neh 9:17
c of fifty..the honorable . . . . Is 3:3
c of the least of my . . . . Is 36:9
hast taught them to be *c* . . . . . . Jer 13:21
a *c* of the ward was there . . . . . Jer 37:13
the *c* of the guard carried . . . . . Jer 39:9
Nebuzar-adan, the *c* of the . . . . Jer 39:11
Now when all the *c* of the . . . . Jer 40:7
Nebuzar-adan the *c* of the . . . . . Jer 41:10
all the *c* of the forces . . . . Jer 41:11
Then all the *c* of the forces . . . Jer 42:1
all the *c* of the forces and . . . . . Jer 43:4
person..Nebuzar-adan the *c* . . . Jer 43:6
appoint a *c* against her . . . . Jer 51:27
c and rulers, all of them . . . . . . Ezek 23:6
the *c* of the king's guard . . . . . . Dan 2:14
and the *c* the judges, the . . . . . . Dan 3:2
counselors and the *c* have . . . . . Dan 6:7
locusts, and thy *c* as the . . . . . . Nah 3:17
supper to his lords, high *c* . . . . . Mark 6:21
band and the *c* and officers . . . John 18:12
and the *c* of the temple . . . . Acts 4:1
But the chief *c* Lysias came . . . Acts 24:7
the chief *c* and principal . . . . . . Acts 25:23
rich men and the chief *c* . . . . . . Rev 6:15

CAPTAIN, CHIEF OF THE TEMPLE—*priest who kept order*

Conspired with Judas . . . . Luke 22:3, 4
Arrested Jesus . . . . Luke 22:52-54
Arrested apostles . . . . Acts 5:24-26

CAPTIVE—*one who is enslaved or involuntarily held*

Good treatment of:

Compassion . . . . Ex 6:4-8
Kindness 2Chr 28:15
Mercy 2Kin 6:21-23

Bad treatment of:

Tortured 2Sam 12:31
Blinded . . . . Judg 16:21
Maimed . . . . Judg 1:6, 7
Ravished . . . . Lam 5:11-13
Enslaved 2Kin 5:2
Killed 1Sam 15:32, 33

Applied figuratively to those:

Under Satan 2Tim 2:26
Under sin 2Tim 3:6
Liberated by Christ . . . . . . Luke 4:18

[*also* CAPTIVES]

his brother was taken *c* . . . . Gen 14:14
away my daughters as *c* . . . . Gen 31:26
the firstborn of the *c* that . . . . . Ex 12:29
all the women of Midian *c* . . . . Num 31:9
And seest among the *c* a . . . . . . Deut 21:11
blood..slain and of the *c* . . . . . . Deut 32:42
And had taken the women *c* . . 1Sam 30:2
they carry them away *c* 1Kin 8:46
enemies..led them away *c* 1Kin 8:48
carried them *c* to Assyria 2Kin 15:29
ten thousand *c* and all the 2Kin 24:14
children of Judah carry..*c* 2Chr 25:12
them that lead them *c* so 2Chr 30:9
those that carried them *c* . . . . . . Ps 106:46
the Ethiopians *c*, young . . . . Is 20:4
and he shall let go my *c* . . . . . . Is 45:13
The *c* exile hasteneth that . . . . . Is 51:14
neck, O *c* daughter of Zion . . . Is 52:2
flock..carried away *c* . . . . Jer 13:17
and he shall carry them *c* . . . . . Jer 20:4
they have led him *c* and . . . . . . Jer 22:12
carried away *c* Jeconiah . . . . . . Jer 24:1
he carried away *c* Jeconiah . . . . Jer 27:20
all that is carried away *c* . . . . . . Jer 28:6
carried away *c* into Babylon . . . Jer 39:9
all that were carried away *c* . . . Jer 40:1
which were carried away *c* . . . . Jer 40:1
Ishmael carried away *c* . . . . Jer 41:10
carried them away *c*, and . . . . . Jer 41:10
death and carry us away *c* . . . . . Jer 43:3
thy sons are taken *c*, and . . . . . Jer 48:46
carried away *c* certain of . . . . . . Jer 52:15
as I was among the *c* by . . . . . . Ezek 1:1
shall also carry *c* into . . . . Dan 11:8
they carried away *c* the . . . . Amos 1:6
therefore..shall they go *c* . . . . . . Amos 6:7
Israel shall surely..away *c* . . . . . Amos 7:11
Huzzab shall be led away *c* . . . . Nah 2:7
high, he led captivity *c* . . . . Eph 4:8
lead *c* silly women laden 2Tim 3:6

CAPTIVITY—*a state of bondage; enslavement*

Foretold regarding:

Hebrews in Egypt . . . . Gen 15:13, 14
Israelites . . . . Deut 28:36-41
Ten tribes (Israel) . . . . Amos 7:11
Judah . . . . Is 39:6

Fulfilled:

In Egypt . . . . Ex 1:11-14
In many captivities . . . . . . Judg 2:14-23
In Assyria 2Kin 17:6-24
In Babylon 2Kin 24:11-16
Under Rome . . . . John 19:15

Causes of:

Disobedience . . . . Deut 28:36-68
Idolatry . . . . Amos 5:26, 27
Breaking Sabbatic law . . . 2Chr 36:20, 21

and his daughters into *c* . . . . Num 21:29
the raiment of her *c* from . . . . . Deut 21:13
thy God will turn thy *c* . . . . Deut 30:3
and lead thy *c* captive, thou . . . Judg 5:12
Dan until the day of the *c* . . . . Judg 18:30
And Jehozadak went into *c* . . . 1Chr 6:15
daughters..wives are in *c* 2Chr 29:9
bring up with them of the *c* . . . . Ezra 1:11
that went up out of the *c* . . . . . Ezra 2:1
that were come out of the *c* . . . Ezra 3:8
which were come out..*c* . . . . Ezra 8:35
to the sword to *c* and to a . . . . Ezra 9:7
all the children of the *c* . . . . Ezra 10:7
which were left of the *c* . . . . Neh 1:2
for a prey in the land of *c* . . . . Neh 4:4
went up out of the *c* of . . . . Neh 7:6
from Jerusalem with the *c* . . . . . Esth 2:6
Lord turned the *c* of Job . . . . . . Job 42:10
Lord bringeth back the *c* . . . . . . Ps 14:7
God bringeth back the *c* . . . . . . Ps 53:6
high..hast led *c* captive . . . . Ps 68:18
delivered his strength into *c* . . . Ps 78:61
brought back the *c* of Jacob . . . Ps 85:1
the Lord turned again the *c* . . . Ps 126:1
my people are gone into *c* . . . . Is 5:13
thee away with a mighty *c* . . . . Is 22:17
such as are for the *c*, to the *c* . Jer 15:2
thine house shall go into *c* . . . . Jer 20:6
and I will turn away your *c* . . . Jer 29:14
I will bring again the *c* of . . . . . Jer 30:3
will cause their *c* to return . . . . Jer 32:44
I will cause their *c* to . . . . Jer 33:26
Chemosh shall go forth..*c* . . . . . Jer 48:7
their king shall go into *c* . . . . . . Jer 49:3
and thirtieth year of the *c* . . . . . Jer 52:31
Judah is gone..*c* because . . . . . . Lam 1:3
to turn away thy *c*; but . . . . Lam 2:14
carry thee away into *c* . . . . Lam 4:22
year of king Jehoiachin's *c* . . . . Ezek 1:2
get thee to them of the *c* . . . . . Ezek 3:11
as they that go forth into *c* . . . . Ezek 12:4

I shall bring again their *c* .....Ezek 16:53
Judah, when they went..*c* .....Ezek 25:3
these cities shall go..*c* ....Ezek 30:17
year of our *c*..beginning ....Ezek 40:1
Gilgal shall surely go into *c* ...Amos 5:5
Israel shall surely go into *c* ....Amos 7:17
when I turn back your *c* ......Zeph 3:20
Take of them of the *c*, even ...Zech 6:10
city shall go forth into *c* ....Zech 14:2
bringing into *c* every 2Cor 10:5
he led *c* captive and gave .....Eph 4:8

CARAVAN—*a company of travelers*
Ishmaelite traders ....Gen 37:25
Jacob's family ....Gen. 46:5, 6
Jacob's funeral ....Gen 50:7-14
Queen of Sheba 1Kin 10:1, 2
Returnees from exile ....Ezra 8:31

CARBUNCLE—*a precious gem*
In high priest's garment ..Ex 28:17
Figuratively of glory .....Is 54:12
Descriptive of Tyre's beauty ....Ezek 28:12, 13

topaz and a *c*: this shall be ....Ex 28:17
emerald, and the *c*, and ....Ezek 28:13

CARCAS (kär'kăs)—*"severe"*
Eunuch under Ahsauerus .Esth 1:10

CARCASE—*a dead body*
Used literally of:
Sacrificial animals ....Gen 15:9, 11
Unclean beasts ....Lev 5:2
Lion ....Judg 14:8
Men ....Deut 28:25, 26
Idols ....Jer 16:18
Aspects of:
Makes unclean ....Lev 11:39
Food for birds ....Jer 16:4

[*also* CARCASES]
and their *c* shall ye not ....Lev 11:8
have their *c* in abomination ...Lev 11:11
Your *c* shall fall..wilderness ...Num 14:29
nor touch their dead *c* ....Deut 14:8
c of the host..Philistines 1Sam 17:46
thy *c* shall not come unto 1Kin 13:22
their *c* were torn in the ....Is 5:25
as a *c* trodden under feet .....Is 14:19
stink shall come up..*c* ....Is 34:3
upon the *c* of the men that ....Is 66:24
the *c* of men shall fall as .....Jer 9:22
their *c* will I give to be meat ..Jer 19:7
dead *c* of the children ....Ezek 6:5
nor by the *c* of their kings ....Ezek 43:7
slain..great number of *c* ....Nah 3:3
For wheresoever the *c* is ......Matt 24:28
whose *c* fell in the wilderness? .Heb 3:17

CARCHEMISH (kär'kĕ-mĭsh)—*"city (fortress) of Chemosh"*
Eastern capital of Hittites on the Euphrates 2Chr 35:20
Conquered by Sargon II .Is 10:9
Josiah wounded there 2Chr 35:20-24

[*also* CHARCHEMISH]
against *C* by Euphrates 2Chr 35:20

CARE—*wise and provident concern*
Natural concern for:
Children ....Luke 2:44-49
Duties ....Luke 10:40
Mate 1Cor 7:32-34
Health ....Is 38:1-22
Life ....Mark 4:38
Possessions ....Gen 33:12-17
Spiritual concern for:
Duties ....Phil 2:20
Office 1Tim 3:6-8
A minister's needs ....Phil 4:10-12
The flock of God ....John 10:11; 1Pet 5:2, 3
Churches 2Cor 11:28
Christians 1Cor 12:25
Spiritual things ....Acts 18:17

[*also* CARED, CAREFUL, CAREFULLY, CAREFULNESS, CAREST, CARETH, CARING]
which the Lord thy God *c* .....Deut 11:12
Only if thou *c* hearken unto ...Deut 15:5
lest my father leave *c* for 1Sam 9:5
left the *c* of the asses 1Sam 10:2
they will not *c* for us 2Sam 18:3
of us die, will they *c* for us 2Sam 18:3
thou hast been *c* for us 2Kin 4:13
failed me; no man *c* for my ...Ps 142:4
not be *c* in the year of ....Jer 17:8
water with trembling..*c* ....Ezek 12:18
we are not *c* to answer thee ...Dan 3:16
inhabitant..Maroth waited *c* ...Mic 1:12
neither *c* thou for any man ....Matt 22:16
the *c* of this world and the ....Mark 4:19
Martha, thou art *c* and ....Luke 10:41
hireling and *c* not for the .....John 10:13
not that he *c* for the poor .....John 12:6
being a servant? *c* not for 1Cor 7:21
Doth God take *c* for oxen? ...1Cor 9:9
sort, what *c* it wrought in 2Cor 7:11
our *c* for you in the sight 2Cor 7:12
him therefore the more *c* .....Phil 2:28
Be *c* for nothing but in ....Phil 4:6
shall he take *c* of the 1Tim 3:5
be *c* to maintain good works ..Titus 3:8
though he sought it *c* with ....Heb 12:17
upon him, for he *c* for you 1Pet 5:7

CARE, DIVINE—*God's concern for His creatures*
For the world ....Ps 104:1-10
For animals ....Ps 104:11-30
For pagans ....Jon 4:11
For Christians ....Matt 6:25-34
Babylon ....Is 47:1, 8-11
Ethiopians ....Ezek 30:9
Gallio ....Acts 18:17
Inhabitants of coastlands. .Ezek 39:6
Moab ....Jer 48:10-17
Nineveh ....Zeph 2:10-15
Those at ease in Zion ....Amos 6:1
Women of Jerusalem ....Is 32:9-11

CAREAH (kä-rē'ä)—*"bald head"*
Father of Johanan 2Kin 25:23
Same as Kareah ....Jer 40:8

CARELESSNESS—*lack of proper concern*
Babylon ....Is 47:8-11
Ethiopians ....Ezek 30:9
Islanders ....Ezek 39:6
Nineveh ....Zeph 2:15
Women of Jerusalem ....Is 32:9-11

CARES, WORLDLY—*overmuch concern for earthly things*
Evils of:
Chokes the Word ....Matt 13:7, 22
Gluts the soul ....Luke 21:34
Obstructs the Gospel ....Luke 14:18-20
Hinders Christ's work 2Tim 2:4
Manifests unbelief ....Matt 6:25-32
Antidotes for God's:
Protection ....Ps 37:5-11
Provision ....Matt 6:25-34
Promises ....Phil 4:6, 7

[*also* CARES]
the *c* of this world ....Mark 4:19
are choked with *c* ....Luke 8:14

CARMEL (kär'mĕl)—*"orchard"*
1. Rendered as:
"Fruitful field" ....Is 10:18
"Plentiful field" ....Is 16:10
"Plentiful country" ......Jer 2:7
2. City of Judah ....Josh 15:55
Site of Saul's victory 1Sam 15:12
Home of David's wife ...1Sam 27:3
3. A mountain of Palestine .Josh 19:26
Joshua defeated king there ....Josh 12:22
Scene of Elijah's triumph.1Kin 18:19-45
Elisha visits 2Kin 2:25
Place of beauty ....Song 7:5
Figurative of strength ...Jer 46:18
Barrenness foretold .....Amos 1:2

possessions were in *C* 1Sam 25:2
man of God to mount *C* 2Kin 4:25
into the forest of his *C* 2Kin 19:23
in the mountains and in *C* 2Chr 26:10
C shake off their fruits ....Is 33:9
and the forests of his *C* ....Is 37:24
he shall feed on *C* and ....Jer 50:19
themselves in the top of *C* ....Amos 9:3
wood, in the midst of *C* ....Mic 7:14
Bashan languisheth, and *C* ....Nah 1:4

CARMELITE (kär'mĕ-līt)—*natives of Judean Carmel*
Nabal 1Sam 30:5; 2Sam 2:2
Hezro 2Sam 23:35
Abigail 1Sam 27:3

[*also* CARMELITES, CARMELITESS]
the wife of Nabal the *C* 2Sam 3:3
Daniel of Abigail the *C* 1Chr 3:1
Hezro the *C*, Naarai the 1Chr 11:37

CARMI (kär'mī)—*"fruitful; noble"*
1. Son of Reuben ....Gen 46:9
2. Father of Achan ....Josh 7:1

Hanoch and Pallu, Hezron..*C*. .Ex 6:14
Hezronites: of *C*, the family ...Num 26:6
And the sons of *C* Achar 1Chr 2:7
Judah; Pharez, Hezron..*C* 1Chr 4:1

CARMITES (kär'mīts)—*family of Judah whose head was Carmi*
Carmi, the family of the *C* ....Num 26:6

CARNAL—*fleshly; worldly*
Used literally of:
Sexual relations ....Lev 19:20
Paul calls himself ....Rom 7:14
Gentiles ministered in ....Rom 15:27
Paul calls brethren at Corinth 1Cor 3:1, 3
Things not spiritual called.1Cor 9:11

[*also* CARNALLY]
thou shalt not lie *c* with thy ...Lev 18:20
to be *c* minded is death ....Rom 8:6
Because the *c* mind is ....Rom 8:7
weapons of our warfare..*c* 2Cor 10:4
law of a *c* commandment .....Heb 7:16

CAROB POD—*seedcase of the carob; locust tree*
Rendered "husk"; fed to swine ....Luke 15:16

CARPENTER—*a skilled woodworker*
David's house built by ...2Sam 5:11
Temple repaired by 2Chr 24:12
Idols made by ....Is 44:13
Temple restored by ......Ezra 3:7
Joseph works as ....Matt 13:55

[*also* CARPENTERS]
they laid it out to the *c* and ...2Kin 12:11
the *c* encouraged the ....Is 41:7
and the *c* and the smiths ......Jer 29:2
Is not this the *c*, the son of ...Mark 6:3

CARPENTER TOOLS—*implements for the carpenter's trade*
Axe ....Deut 19:5
Hammer ....Jer 23:29
Line ....Zech 2:1
Nail ....Jer 10:4
Saw 1Kin 7:9

CARPUS (kär'pŭs)—*"fruit; wrist"*
Paul's friend at Troas 2Tim 4:13

CARRIAGE—*ancient means of transportation; archaic word for baggage*
Goods, provisions 1Sam 17:22
An army's baggage ......Is 10:28
Heavy goods ....Judg 18:21
A vehicle ....Is 46:1

we took up our *c* and went ....Acts 21:15

CARRION VULTURE
Unclean bird ....Lev 11:18

CARRY—*to haul; force*

[*also* CARRIED, CARRIEST, CARRIETH, CARRYING]
going to *c* it down to Egypt ...Gen 37:25
go ye, *c* corn for the famine ...Gen 42:19
and *c* down the man a ....Gen 43:11
as much as they can *c* and ....Gen 44:1
which Joseph had sent to *c* ....Gen 45:27
which Pharaoh had sent to *c* ..Gen 46:5
and thou shalt *c* me out of ....Gen 47:30
shall *c* up my bones from .....Gen 50:25
thou shalt not *c* forth aught ...Ex 12:46
shall *c* up my bones away .....Ex 13:19
with me *c* us not up hence ....Ex 33:15
whole bullock shall be *c* ......Lev 4:12
c forth the ashes without ......Lev 6:11
c your brethren from before ...Lev 10:4
and he shall *c* them forth .....Lev 14:45
shall one *c* forth without ......Lev 16:27
C them in thy bosom as a .....Num 11:12
thou art not able to *c* it ....Deut 14:24
ye shall *c* them over with .....Josh 4:3
one *c* three kids and 1Sam 10:3
another *c* three loaves of 1Sam 10:3
and another *c* a bottle of 1Sam 10:3
And *c* these ten cheeses 1Sam 17:18
or small but *c* them away 1Sam 30:2
them that *c* them captives 1Kin 8:47
and *c* him up into a loft 1Kin 17:19
C him to his mother 2Kin 4:19
c them captive to Assyria 2Kin 15:29
shall be *c* into Babylon 2Kin 20:17
c the ashes of..Beth-el 2Kin 23:4
c tidings unto their idols 1Chr 10:9
he *c* away also the shields 2Chr 12:9
c away the stones of Ramah ...2Chr 16:6
more than they could *c* 2Chr 20:25
c away all the substance 2Chr 21:17
and *c* it to his place again 2Chr 24:11
the children of Judah *c* 2Chr 25:12
and they smote him and *c* 2Chr 28:5
and *c* forth the filthiness 2Chr 29:5
fetters, and *c* him to Babylon..2Chr 33:11
c the people away..Babylon ...Ezra 5:12
of those that had been *c* ......Neh 7:6
king of Babylon had *c* away ...Neh 7:6
captivity which had been *c* ....Esth 2:6
king of Babylon had *c* away ...Esth 2:6
and have *c* them away yea ....Job 1:17
I should have been *c* from ....Job 10:19
chaff that the storm *c* away ...Job 21:18
c bows turned back in the .....Ps 78:9
c them away as with a ....Ps 90:5
laid up, shall they *c* away .....Is 15:7
the Lord will *c* thee away .....Is 22:17
her own feet shall *c* her ....Is 23:7
griefs and *c* our sorrows ......Is 53:4
the wind shall *c* them all ......Is 57:13
had *c* away captive Jeconiah ...Jer 24:1
which were *c* away captive ....Jer 40:1
Then Ishmael *c* away ....Jer 41:10
c them away captive ....Jer 41:10
Thus Judah was *c* away ....Jer 52:27
they shall be *c* captives ....Ezek 6:9
thee are men that *c* tales to ...Ezek 22:9
to *c* away silver and gold......Ezek 38:13
he *c* into the land of Shinar ...Dan 1:2
And shall also *c* captives ......Dan 11:8
It shall be also *c*..Assyria .....Hos 10:6
because they *c* away captive ...Amos 1:6
the *c* away into Babylon ......Matt 1:17
to *c* about in beds those ......Mark 6:55
C neither purse nor scrip ......Luke 10:4
was *c* by the angels into.......Luke 16:22
not lawful for thee to *c* ....John 5:10
c away unto these dumb 1Cor 12:2
that are *c* with a tempest......2Pet 2:17
So he *c* me away in the spirit..Rev 17:3

CARSHENA (kär'shĕ-nä)—*"distinguished; lean"*
Prince of Persia ....Esth 1:14

CART—*a wagon*
Made of wood 1Sam 6:14
Sometimes covered ......Num 7:3
Drawn by cows..........1Sam 6:7
Used in threshing........Is 28:28
Used for hauling ....Amos 2:13
Ark carried by 2Sam 6:3
Figurative of sin ....Is 5:18

the ark of God in a new *c* 1Chr 13:7
Uzza and Ahio drove the *c*....1Chr 13:7

CARVING—*cutting figures in wood or stone*
Used in worship ....Ex 31:1-7
Found in homes 1Kin 6:18
Employed by idolators ...Judg 18:18
Used in the Temple 1Kin 6:35

[*also* CARVED, CARVINGS]
c of cherubims and palm 1Kin 6:32
he set a *c* image, the idol 2Chr 33:7
the *c* images and the..........2Chr 34:3
now they break down the *c* ...Ps 74:6
with *c* works, with fine.......Prov 7:16

CASE—*situations or conditions*

[*also* CASES]
see that they were in evil *c* ....Ex 5:19
this is the *c* of the slayer ......Deut 19:4
thou shalt in any *c* bring ......Deut 22:1
people that is in such a *c* .....Ps 144:15
long time in that *c* he ....John 5:6
under bondage in such *c* 1Cor 7:15

CASEMENT—*lattice; criss-crossed strips of wood or metal*
Looked through ....Prov 7:6

CASIPHIA (kä-sĭf'ĭ-ä)—*"silvery"*
Home of exiled Levites ..Ezra 8:17

CASLUHIM (kăs'lū-hĭm)
A tribe descended from Mizraim ....Gen 10:14
Descendant of Ham 1Chr 1:8, 12

CASSIA—*amber; an aromatic wood*
An ingredient of holy oil .Ex 30:24, 25
An article of commerce ..Ezek 27:19
Noted for fragrance......Ps 45:8

CAST—*See* INTRODUCTION

CASTAWAY—*worthless; reprobate*
The rejected ....Matt 25:30
2Pet 2:4
Warning concerning 1Cor 9:27

CASTE—*divisions of society*
Some leaders of low ....Judg 11:1-11
David aware of..........1Sam 18:18, 23
Jews and Samaritans observe ....John 4:9
Abolished...............Acts 10:28-35

CASTING—*throwing; discarding*

[*also* CASTEDST, CASTEST, CASTETH]
c them down to the ground ...2Sam 8:2
all of them had one *c*, one 1Kin 7:37
thou *c* off fear..restrainest.....Job 15:4
their cow calveth and *c* not....Job 21:10
c them down..destruction .....Ps 73:18
he *c* the wicked down to ......Ps 147:6
Slothfulness *c* into a deep .....Prov 19:15
and *c* down the strength of ....Prov 21:22
so she *c* out her wickedness ...Jer 6:7
parted his garments, *c* lots ....Matt 27:35
we saw one *c* out devils in ....Mark 9:38
he *c* away his garment, rose ...Mark 10:50
we saw one *c* out devils in ....Luke 9:49
he was *c* out a devil, and it ...Luke 11:14
the rich men *c* their gifts ......Luke 21:1
For if the *c* away of them be ..Rom 11:15
C all your care upon him 1Pet 5:7

CASTLE—*fortress; tower*

Used literally of:
King's residence 2Kin 15:25
An encampment.........Gen 25:16
A tower for guards 1Chr 6:54
Barracks for soldiers .....Acts 21:34
A fortress...............1Chr 11:7
David conquers Jebusite. .1Chr 11:5, 7

Used figuratively of:
Offended brother........Prov 18:19

[*also* CASTLES]
their towns and by their *c* .....Gen 25:16
they dwelt..their goodly *c* .....Num 31:10
to be brought into the *c* and ..Acts 22:24

CASTOR AND POLLUX (kăs'ter) (pŏl'ŭks)—*sons of Jupiter*
Gods in Greek and Roman mythology; figureheads on Paul's ship to Rome ....Acts 28:11

CASTRATION—*Removal of male testicles*
Disqualified for congregation ....Deut 23:1
Rights restored in new covenant..............Is 56:3-5
Figurative of absolute devotion ....Matt 19:12

CATCH—*to snare*

[*also* CATCHETH, CAUGHT]
ram *c* in a thicket by his ......Gen 22:13
put forth his hand and *c* it ....Ex 4:4
If fire break out and *c* in .....Ex 22:6
which hunteth and *c* any ......Lev 17:13
which the men of war had *c* ...Num 31:32
pursued after him and *c*.......Judg 1:6
And *c* a young man of the ....Judg 8:14
went and *c* three hundred .....Judg 15:4
whom they *c*: and they went ..Judg 21:23
he arose against me, I *c* 1Sam 17:35
And they *c* every one his 2Sam 2:16
and *c* hold on the horns of 1Kin 1:50
let his net that he hath hid *c* ..Ps 35:8
snares..set a trap they *c* ....Jer 5:26
they *c* them in their net and...Hab 1:15
they *c* him and cast him.......Matt 21:39
And they *c* him and beat .....Mark 12:3
the wolf *c* them and ....John 10:12
c him and brought him to .....Acts 6:12
Spirit of the Lord *c* away .....Acts 8:39
c up to the third heaven 2Cor 12:2
shall be *c* up together with 1Thess 4:17

CATERPILLAR—*insect larva which feeds on vegetation*
Works with locust ....Is 33:4
Devours land ....Amos 4:9

[*also* CATERPILLARS]
if there be *c*, if their enemy ...1Kin 8:37
mildew, locusts or *c* if 2Chr 6:28
their increase unto the *c* ......Ps 78:46
the locusts came and *c* and ....Ps 105:34
fill thee with men as with *c* ...Jer 51:14
cankerworm hath left.. *c* ......Joel 1:4
cankerworm and the *c*, and ...Joel 2:25

CATTLE—*domesticated animals held collectively; group of bovines*
Created by God ....Gen 1:24
Adam named ....Gen 2:20
Entered the ark ....Gen 7:13, 14
Struck by God ....Ex 12:29
Firstborn of, belong to God..................Ex 34:19
Can be unclean ....Lev 5:2
Taken as plunder ....Josh 8:2, 27
Belong to God ....Ps 50:10
Nebuchadnezzar eats like .Dan. 4:33
Pastureless ....Joel 1:18
East of Jordan good for ..Num 32:1, 4
Given as ransom ....Num 3:45

thou are cursed above all *c*....Gen 3:14
in tents..such as have *c* ....Gen 4:20
c after their kind, of every ....Gen 6:20
all the *c* that was with him ....Gen 8:1
neither is it time that the *c* ....Gen 29:7
according as the *c* that ....Gen 33:14
his sons were with his *c* in ....Gen 34:5
his *c* and all his beasts and ....Gen 36:6

And they took their *c* and ....Gen 46:6
make them rulers over my *c*...Gen 47:6
hand..Lord is upon thy *c*......Ex 9:3
Our *c* also shall go with us ....Ex 10:26
kill us..children and our *c*.....Ex 17:3
thy maidservant nor thy *c*.....Ex 20:10
bring your offering of the *c*...Lev 1:2
Thou shalt not let thy *c*.......Lev 19:19
And for thy *c* and for the .....Lev 25:7
and destroy your *c* and ....Lev 26:22
the *c* of the Levites, instead...Num 3:41
that we and all our *c* should...Num 20:4
the spoil of their *c* and........Num 31:9
shall be for their *c* and for ....Num 35:3
But all the *c* and the spoil ....Deut 3:7
nor any of thy *c*, nor thy......Deut 5:14
in the fruit of thy *c* and in ....Deut 30:9
their suburbs for their *c*.......Josh 14:4
suburbs thereof for our *c*......Josh 21:2
with very much *c*, with silver..Josh 22:8
and brought away their *c*.....1Sam 23:5
sheep and oxen and fat *c* 1Kin 1:9
down to take away their *c*.....1Chr 7:21
the tents of *c* and carried 2Chr 14:15
for he had much *c* both in 2Chr 26:10
small *c* and three hundred.....2Chr 35:8
our bodies, and over our *c*....Neh 9:37
of our *c* as it is written ....Neh 10:36
the *c* also concerning the......Job 36:33
He gave up their *c* also to ....Ps 78:48
the grass to grow for the *c*....Ps 104:14
Beasts and all *c*; creeping .....Ps 148:10
the beasts and upon the *c*.....Is 46:1
can men hear the voice.. *c*....Jer 9:10
between *c* and *c*, between.....Ezek 34:17
nations, which have gotten *c*..Ezek 38:12
herds of *c* are perplexed ....Joel 1:18
left hand, and also much *c*?...Jon 4:11
upon men and upon *c* and ....Hag 1:11
multitude of men and *c*.......Zech 2:4
to keep *c* from my youth......Zech 13:5
servant plowing or feeding *c*...Luke 17:7
and his children and his *c*.....John 4:12

CAUGHT—*See* CATCH

CAUL
1. A lining surrounding the stomach..............Ex 29:13,22
2. A hair net worn by women................Is 3:18

c above the liver with the .....Lev 3:4
c above the liver with the .....Lev 4:9

CAUSE—*See* INTRODUCTION

CAUSEWAY—*a road or passage*
Steps leading into temple .1Chr 26:16, 18

CAUTION—*provident care; alertness*
For safety...............Acts 23:10, 16-24
For defense ....Neh 4:12-23
For attack 1Sam 20:1-17
A principle ....Prov 14:15, 16
Neglect of 1Sam 26:4-16

CAVE—*natural passageway within the earth*
Used for:
Habitation ....Gen 19:30
Refuge 1Kin 18:4
Burial ....John 11:38
Concealment 1Sam 22:1
Protection ....Is 2:19
Rev 6:15

Mentioned in Scripture:
Machpelah ....Gen 23:9
Makkedah ....Josh 10:16, 17
Adullam 1Sam 22:1
Engedi 1Sam 24:1, 3

[*also* CAVE'S, CAVES]
c of the field of Machpelah....Gen 23:19
buried him..*c* of Machpelah...Gen 25:9
the *c* that is in the field ....Gen 49:29
buried him in the *c* of the .....Gen 50:13
laid great stones in the *c*......Josh 10:27
the mountains and *c* and ......Judg 6:2
people..themselves in *c* 1Sam 13:6
harvest time unto the *c* 2Sam 23:13
he came thither unto a *c*......1Kin 19:9
into the *c* of Adullam and.....1Chr 11:15
cliffs of the valleys, in *c*.......Job 30:6
he fled from Saul in the *c*.....Ps 57:*title*

CEASE—*to come to an end*
[*also*, CEASED, CEASETH, CEASING]
day and night shall not *c*......Gen 8:22
it *c* to be with Sarah after.....Gen 18:11
the thunder shall *c*, neither....Ex 9:29
and the thunders and hail *c*...Ex 9:33
years they shall *c* waiting......Num 8:25
and the manna *c* on the.......Josh 5:12
c not from their own doings...Judg 2:19
the villages *c*, they *c* in ....Judg 5:7
and after that I will *c*.........Judg 15:7
C not to cry unto the Lord....1Sam 7:8
Lord in *c* to pray for you 1Sam 12:23
Ramah, and let his work *c*....2Chr 16:5
to cause these men to *c*.......Ezra 4:21
So it *c* unto the second year...Ezra 4:24
could not cause them to *c*.....Ezra 5:5
and cause the work to *c*.......Neh 4:11
the wicked *c* from troubling...Job 3:17
these three men *c* to answer...Job 32:1
Help, Lord..godly man *c*......Ps 12:1
they did tear me and *c* not....Ps 35:15
C from anger and forsake .....Ps 37:8
precious and it *c* for ever .....Ps 49:8
sore ran in the night..*c*.......Ps 77:2
causeth contentions to *c*.......Prov 18:18
before mine eyes *c* to do......Is 1:16
How hath the oppressor *c*! ....Is 14:4
the golden city *c*!.............Is 14:4
spoiler *c*, the oppressors ....Is 16:4
their vintage shouting to *c*.....Is 16:10
The fortress also shall *c*.......Is 17:3
The mirth of tabrets *c* the.....Is 24:8
the joy of the harp *c* ....Is 24:8
eye trickleth down and *c*......Lam 3:49
The elders have *c* from the....Lam 5:14
idols may be broken and *c*....Ezek 6:6
The pomp of the strong to *c*..Ezek 7:24
will make this proverb to *c*....Ezek 12:23
and I will cause thee to *c*.....Ezek 16:41
I make thy lewdness to *c*......Ezek 23:27
the noise of thy songs to *c*....Ezek 26:13
the multitude of Egypt to *c*...Ezek 30:10
pomp of her strength..*c*.......Ezek 33:28
and cause them to *c* from .....Ezek 34:10
sacrifice and the oblation..*c*...Dan 9:27
and will cause to *c* the ....Hos 1:4
O Lord God, *c*, I beseech.....Amos 7:5
and the sea *c* from her........Jon 1:15
into the ship, the wind *c*......Matt 14:32
the wind *c*, and there was a...Mark 4:39
they *c*, and there was a ....Luke 8:24
they *c* not to teach and ....Acts 5:42
prayer was made without *c*....Acts 12:5
not be persuaded we *c*........Acts 21:14
that without *c* I make.........Rom 1:9
Remembering without *c*.......1Thess 1:3
thank we God without *c* 1Thess 2:13
would they not have *c* to be...Heb 10:2

CEDAR—*an evergreen tree*
Used in:
Ceremonial cleansing ....Lev 14:4-7
Building Temple.........1Kin 5:5, 6
Building palaces 2Sam 5:11
Gifts 1Chr 22:4
Making idols ....Is 44:14, 17

Figurative of:
Israel's glory ....Num 24:6
Christ's glory...........Ezek 17:22, 23
Growth of saints ....Ps 92:12
Mighty nations ....Amos 2:9
Arrogant rulers..........Is 2:13

[*also* CEDARS]
priest shall take *c* wood.......Num 19:6
devour the *c* of Lebanon......Judg 9:15
I dwell in an house of *c*.......2Sam 7:2
from the *c* tree that is in......1Kin 4:33
upon four rows of *c* pillars....1Kin 7:2
with *c* beams upon the........1Kin 7:2
measures of hewed stones..*c*...1Kin 7:11
furnished Solomon with *c* 1Kin 9:11
c made he to be as the 1Kin 10:27
sent to the *c* that was in 2Kin 14:9
timber of *c* with masons 1Chr 14:1
I dwell in an house of *c*.......1Chr 17:1
c trees made he as the 2Chr 1:15
send him *c* to build him an....2Chr 2:3
He moveth his tail like a *c*....Job 40:17
the Lord breaketh the *c* of....Ps 29:5
thereof were like..goodly *c*....Ps 80:10
beams of our house are *c* .....Song 1:17
excellent as the *c*.............Song 5:15
enclose her with boards of *c*...Song 8:9
we will change them into *c*....Is 9:10
cut down the tall *c* thereof ....Is 37:24
shall cut down thy choice *c*....Jer 22:7
ceiled with *c*, and painted .....Jer 22:14
highest branch of the *c*........Ezek 17:3
have taken *c* from Lebanon...Ezek 27:5
the Assyrian was a *c* in ....Ezek 31:3
the *c* in the garden of God....Ezek 31:8
for he shall uncover the *c*.....Zeph 2:14
the fire may devour thy *c*.....Zech 11:1

CEDAR CHESTS
Sold by traders..........Ezek 27:23, 24

CEDRON (sĕd´rŏn)—*"obscure; making black or sad"—a valley in Jerusalem*
over the brook *C* where.......John 18:1

CEILED—*sealed*
greater house he *c* with 2Chr 3:5
it is *c* with cedar and ....Jer 22:14
c with wood round ....Ezek 41:16
to dwell in your *c* houses .....Hag 1:4

CEILING—*top enclosure*
Temple's................1Kin 6:15

and the walls of the *c*.........1Kin 6:15

CELEBRATE—*commemorate with appropriate rites or ceremonies*
Feast of Weeks..........Ex 34:22
Feast of Ingathering .....Ex 34:22
The Sabbath ....Lev 23:32, 41
Passover 2Kin 23:21
Feast of Unleavened Bread 2Chr 30:13
Feast of Tabernacles.....Zech 14:16

CELESTIAL—*heavenly*
Bodies called............1Cor 15:40

CELIBACY—*the unmarried state*
Useful sometimes........Matt 19:10, 12
Not for bishops 1Tim 3:2
Requiring, a sign of apostasy 1Tim 4:1-3
Figurative of absolute devotion ....Rev 14:4

CELLARS—*places for storage*
Wines stored in 1Chr 27:27

CEMETERY—*place of burial*
Bought by Abraham .....Gen 23:15, 16
Pharisees compared to ...Matt 23:27
Man dwelt in ....Mark 5:2, 3
A resurrection from .....Matt 27:52

CENCHREA (sĕn´krē-ă)—*"millet"*
A harbor of Corinth .....Acts 18:18
A church near ....Rom 16:1

CENSER—*firepan; vessel for burning incense*
Used for incense ....Num 16:6, 7, 39
Made of bronze ....Num 16:39
Used in idol worship.....Ezek 8:11
Typical of Christ's intercession ....Rev 8:3, 5

[*also* CENSERS]
take a *c* full of burning ....Lev 16:12
the *c*, the fleshhooks, and .....Num 4:14

take every man his *c* and .....Num 16:17
the Lord every man his *c* .....Num 16:17
and Aaron each of you his *c* ..Num 16:17
spoons and the *c* of pure 1Kin 7:50
a *c* in his hand to burn 2Chr 26:19
Which had the golden *c* and...Heb 9:4

CENSORIOUSNESS—*a critical spirit*
Rebuked by Jesus ....Matt 7:1-5
Diotrephes..............3John 9, 10
Apostates...............Jude 10-16

CENSUS—*a count of the population*
At Sinai ....Ex 38:26
In Moab ....Num 26:1-64
By David 2Sam 24:1-9
Provoked by Satan 1Chr 21:1
Completed by Solomon ..2Chr 2:17
Of exiles................Ezra 2:1-70
By Rome ....Luke 2:1

CENTURION—*a Roman military officer*
Servant of, healed ....Matt 8:5-13
Watches crucifixion ......Matt 27:54
Is converted ....Acts 10:1-48
Protects Paul ....Acts 22:25-28
Takes Paul to Rome .....Acts 27:1

[*also* CENTURION'S, CENTURIONS]
c, and they that were with ....Matt 27:54
c which stood over against ....Mark 15:39
a certain *c* servant, who ....Luke 7:2
the *c* sent friends to him ......Luke 7:6
when the *c* saw what was .....Luke 23:47
immediately took solders..*c*....Acts 21:32
Paul called one of the *c* ....Acts 23:17
commanded a *c* to keep.......Acts 24:23
c delivered the prisoners ......Acts 28:16

CEPHAS (sē´fās)—*"the stone"*
Name of Peter ....John 1:42

Whether Paul or Apollos..*C* ...1Cor 3:22
brethren of the Lord and *C* ...1Cor 9:5
he was seen of *C*, then of 1Cor 15:5
And when James, *C*, and .....Gal 2:9

CEREMONIALISM—*adherence to forms and rites*
Jews guilty of ....Is 1:11-15
Christ condemns.........Matt 15:1-9
Apostles reject ....Acts 15:12-28
Sign of apostasy 1Tim 4:1-3
Exhortations against .....Col 2:14-23

CEREMONIES—*rites; ritual actions*
all the *c* thereof shall ye ......Num 9:3

CERTAIN—*specific*
And he lighted upon a *c* ......Gen 28:11
And a *c* man found him ......Gen 37:15
turned in to a *c* Adullamite ...Gen 38:1
there were *c* men who were ...Num 9:6
C men..children of Belial .....Deut 13:13
it be true and the thing *c* .....Deut 17:4
a *c* woman cast a piece of a ...Judg 9:53
And a *c* man of Beth-lehem ...Ruth 1:1
c man of the sons of the 1Kin 20:35
And a *c* man drew a bow at...1Kin 22:34
Now there cried a *c* woman ...2Kin 4:1
Even after a *c* rate every......2Chr 8:13
c chief of the fathers..........Ezra 10:16
came he and *c* men of ....Neh 1:2
And at Jerusalem dwelt *c* .....Neh 11:4
and *c* of the priests' sons......Neh 12:35
after *c* days obtained I ....Neh 13:6
for *c* that if ye put me to .....Jer 26:15
there came *c* from Shechem ...Jer 41:5
away captive *c* of the poor ....Jer 52:15
bring *c* of the children of .....Dan 1:3
and the dream is *c* and the ....Dan 2:45
that time *c* Chaldeans came ...Dan 3:8
another saint..unto that *c* .....Dan 8:13
and desiring a *c* thing ....Matt 20:20
c woman, which had an issue ..Mark 5:25
and *c* of the scribes which.....Mark 7:1
And *c* of them that stood .....Mark 11:5
A *c* man planted a vineyard ...Mark 12:1
c priest named Zechariah .....Luke 1:5
when he was in a *c* city ....Luke 5:12
And a *c* centurion's servant ...Luke 7:2
c women which had been .....Luke 8:2
c man said unto him, Lord ....Luke 9:57
a *c* lawyer stood up and.......Luke 10:25
ground of a *c* rich man ....Luke 12:16
A *c* man had two sons ....Luke 15:11
he entered into a *c* village.....Luke 17:12
there was a *c* nobleman ....John 4:46
angel went down at a *c* ....John 5:4
Now a *c* man was sick ....John 11:1
And a *c* man lame from his ...Acts 3:2
But a *c* man named Ananias ..Acts 5:1
arose *c* of the synagogue ......Acts 6:9
was a *c* man called Simon .....Acts 8:9
c disciple at Damascus ....Acts 9:10
a *c* man in Caesarea called ....Acts 10:1
A *c* vessel descend as it.......Acts 11:5
And there sat a *c* man at .....Acts 14:8
And *c* men which came ....Acts 15:1
a *c* disciple was there ....Acts 16:1
Timothy the son of a *c*.........Acts 16:1
Ephesus: and finding *c* ....Acts 19:1
c of the Jews banded ....Acts 23:12
c orator named Tertullus ......Acts 24:1
a *c* contribution for the ....Rom 15:26
have no *c* dwelling place 1Cor 4:11
one in a *c* place testified ......Heb 2:6
spake in a *c* place of the ......Heb 4:4
c fearful looking for of........Heb 10:27

CERTAINLY—*beyond doubt*
We saw *c* that the Lord.......Gen 26:28
a man as I can *c* divine? ......Gen 44:15
thy servant hath *c* heard 1Sam 23:10
him, Thou mayest *c* recover ...2Kin 8:10
Lord of hosts, Ye shall *c*......Jer 25:28
king of Babylon shall *c* ....Jer 36:29
Dost thou *c* know that ....Jer 40:14
we will *c* do whatsoever.......Jer 44:17
c this is the day that we.......Lam 2:16
shall *c* come and overflow .....Dan 11:10
C this was a righteous man ....Luke 23:47

CERTAINTY—*that which is true*
Sin's exposure ....Num 32:23
The Gospel ....Luke 1:4
Jesus' claims ....Acts 1:3
Apostolic testimony......2Pet 1:16-21
Death's approach........Heb 9:27
Ultimate judgment ....Acts 17:31

Know for a *c* that the Lord ...Josh 23:13

CERTIFY—*to authorize; make authentic*

[*also* CERTIFIED]
have we sent and *c* the ....Ezra 4:14
Also we *c* you that touching...Ezra 7:24

CHAFED—*angered*
be *c* in their minds 2Sam 17:8

CHAFF—*the husk of threshed grain*
Describes the ungodly ...Ps 1:4
Emptiness ....Is 33:11
False doctrine ....Jer 23:28
God's judgment ....Is 17:13
Punishment ....Matt 3:12

c that the storm carrieth ......Job 21:18
Let them be as *c* before the ...Ps 35:5
flame consumeth the *c* ....Is 5:24
terrible ones shall be as *c* .....Is 29:5
shalt make the hills as *c*.......Is 41:15
the *c* he will burn with fire ....Luke 3:17

CHAIN—*a series of links fitted together*

A badge of office:
On Joseph's neck........Gen 41:42
Promised to Daniel ......Dan 5:7

An ornament:
Worn by women ....Is 3:20

A means of confinement of:
Prisoners ....Judg 16:21
Paul....................Eph 6:20
Manasseh bound 2Chr 33:12

Used figuratively of:
Oppression..............Lam 3:7
Sin's bondage ....Jer 40:3, 4
Punishment ....Jude 6
Satan's defeat ....Rev 20:1

[*also* CHAINS]
two *c* of pure gold at the .....Ex 28:14
upon the breastplate *c* at......Ex 39:15
of gold, *c*, and bracelets ......Num 31:50
c that were about their........Judg 8:26
made a partition by the *c* 1Kin 6:21
wreaths of *c* work for the 1Kin 7:17
thereon palm trees and *c*......2Chr 3:5
compasseth them about..*c* .....Ps 73:6
To bind their kings with *c*.....Ps 149:8
Babylon bound him in *c* ....Jer 52:11
Make a *c* for the land is ......Ezek 7:23

CHALCEDONY—*"from Chalcedon"*
Variegated stone ....Rev 21:19

CHALCOL (kăl´kŏl)—*"sustaining"—a wise man with whom Solomon was compared*
Ezrahite, and Heman, and *C* ..1Kin 4:31

CHALDEA (kăl-dē´ä)—*"demons"*
Originally, the south portion of Babylonia...Gen 11:31
Applied later to all Babylonia.............Is 13:19
Abraham came from.....Gen 11:28, 31
Ezekiel prophesies in ....Ezek 1:3

And *C* shall be a spoil; all ....Jer 50:10
the inhabitants of *C* all.........Jer 51:24
by the Spirit of God into *C* ...Ezek 11:24
land of Canaan unto *C*........Ezek 16:29
manner..Babylonians of *C* .....Ezek 23:15

CHALDEANS, CHALDEES (kăl-dē´äns; kăl-dēs)—*those living in Chaldea*
Abraham, a native ......Gen 11:31
Ur, a city of ....Neh 9:7
Babylon, "the glory of" ..Is 13:19
Attack Job..............Job 1:17
Nebuchadnezzar, king of .2Kin 24:1
God's agent.............Hab 1:6
Predicted captivity of Jews among...........Jer 25:1-26
Jerusalem defeated by ...2Kin 25:1-21
Noted for astrologers ....Dan 2:2, 5, 10

[*also* CHALDEAN, CHALDEANS', CHALDEES']
brought thee out of Ur..*C*.....Gen 15:7
sent against him bands..*C* 2Kin 24:2
upon them the king..*C*........2Chr 36:17
Behold the land of the *C*......Is 23:13
nobles and the *C* whose ....Is 43:14
throne, O daughter of the *C*...Is 47:1
his arm shall be on the *C* .....Is 48:14
against the *C* which besiege ....Jer 21:4
and into the hand of the *C* ....Jer 22:25
the land of the *C* for their .....Jer 24:5
out of the hand of the *C* ......Jer 32:4
They come to fight..with *C*....Jer 33:5
for fear of the army of..*C* .....Jer 35:11
the *C* army pursued after .....Jer 39:5
and the *C* that were found ....Jer 41:3
deliver us into the hand..*C*....Jer 43:3
against the land of the *C*......Jer 50:1
shall fall in..land of the *C*.....Jer 51:4
C were by the city round......Jer 52:7
to Babylon to the land..*C* .....Ezek 12:13
images of the *C* portrayed.....Ezek 23:14
learning and the tongue..*C* ....Dan 1:4
at that time certain *C* came ...Dan 3:8
to bring..astrologers, the *C*....Dan 5:7
king over the realm..*C* ....Dan 9:1
out of the land of the *C*.......Acts 7:4

CHALKSTONE—*limestone*
Used figuratively ....Is 27:9

CHALLENGETH—*to dispute or defy*
which another *c* to be his .....Ex 22:9

CHAMBER—*inner room; enclosed place*

Used literally of:
Elisha's room 2Kin 4:10
Guest room.............Mark 14:14
Upper room ....Acts 9:37
Place of idolatry.........2Kin 23:12

Used figuratively of:
Heavens ....Ps 104:3, 13
Death ....Prov 7:27

[*also* CHAMBERS]
he entered into his *c* ....Gen 43:30
his feet in his summer *c* ....Judg 3:24
abiding with her in the *c* ......Judg 16:9
Bring the meat into the *c* 2Sam 13:10
brought them into the *c* to 2Sam 13:10
the *c* over the gate and 2Sam 18:33
in unto the king into the *c* 1Kin 1:15
oracle; and he made *c* 1Kin 6:5
The nethermost *c* was five 1Kin 6:6
them back into the guard *c* 1Kin 14:28
brought him down out of the *c*.1Kin 17:23
the city, into an inner *c* 1Kin 20:30
a lattice, in his upper *c* 2Kin 1:2
and carry him to an inner *c* ...2Kin 9:2
were over the *c* and treasuries .1Chr 9:26
in the courts, and in the *c*.....1Chr 23:28
and of the upper *c* thereof 1Chr 28:11
he overlaid the upper *c* 2Chr 3:9
them again into the guard *c* ...2Chr 12:11
shalt go into an inner *c* 2Chr 18:24
to prepare *c* in the house 2Chr 31:11
the *c* of the house of the ......Ezra 8:29
Berechiah over against his *c* ...Neh 3:30
the *c* for the treasures for .....Neh 12:44
bridegroom coming out..*c* .....Ps 19:5
abundance, in the *c* of ....Ps 105:30
by knowledge shall the *c* be ...Prov 24:4
hath brought me into his *c* ....Song 1:4
the *c* of her that conceived ....Song 3:4
people, enter thou into thy *c* ..Is 26:20
into one of the *c* and give them.Jer 35:2
entereth into their privy *c* .....Ezek 21:14
every little *c* was one reed ....Ezek 40:7
between the little *c* were ......Ezek 40:7
breadth of every side *c*........Ezek 41:5
the side *c* were three, one......Ezek 41:6
into the *c* that was over ....Ezek 42:1
before the *c* was a walk of ....Ezek 42:4
windows being open in his *c*...Dan 6:10
bridegroom go forth..his *c*.....Joel 2:16
he is in the secret *c*...........Matt 24:26
many lights in the upper *c* ....Acts 20:8

CHAMBERING—*sexual excesses*
not in *c* and wantonness ......Rom 13:13

CHAMBERLAIN—*chief officer in the home of a king or nobleman*
Seven, serving Ahasuerus.Esth 1:10, 15
Blastus, serving Herod ...Acts 12:20
Erastus, at Corinth ......Rom 16:23
See Eunuch

[*also* CHAMBERLAINS]
of Nathan-melech the *c* 2Kin 23:11
custody of Hege..king's *c* .....Esth 2:3
two of the king's *c*, Bigthan ...Esth 2:21
Harbonah, one of the *c*, said ..Esth 7:9

CHAMELEON—*a lizard-like reptile*
Unclean ....Lev 11:30

CHAMOIS—*probably a wild sheep*
Permitted for food.......Deut 14:4, 5

CHAMPAIGN—*campaign*
in the *c* over against Gilgal....Deut 11:30

CHAMPION—*a mighty one; a winner*
Goliath 1Sam 17:23, 51
David 1Sam 17:45-54
went out a *c* out of the 1Sam 17:4

CHANAAN—*See* CANAAN

CHANCE—*unpredictable occurrence; to happen*

[*also* CHANCETH]
If a bird's nest *c* to be ....Deut 22:6
reason of uncleanness that..*c* ..Deut 23:10
it was a *c* that happened to ...1Sam 6:9
I happened by *c* upon mount ..2Sam 1:6
time and *c* happeneth to ......Eccl 9:11
by *c* there came down a.......Luke 10:31
grain, it may *c* of wheat.......1Cor 15:37

CHANCE, SECOND
Not given to:
Angels 2Pet 2:4
Noah's world...........2Pet 2:5
Esau ....Heb 12:16, 17
Israelites...............Num 14:26-45
Saul 1Sam 16:1, 14
Judas ....John 13:26-30
Apostates ....Heb 10:26-31
Those in hell...........Luke 16:19-31

CHANCELLOR
Persian official ....Ezra 4:8
Rehum the *c* and Shimshai ....Ezra 4:8

CHANGE—*to alter*

[*also* CHANGEABLE, CHANGED, CHANGES CHANGEST, CHANGETH, CHANGING]
and *c* my wages ten times .....Gen 31:7
be clean and *c* your ....Gen 35:2
c his raiment and came in .....Gen 41:14
he gave each man *c* of ....Gen 45:22
turn again, and be *c* unto .....Lev 13:16
nor *c* it, a good for a bad .....Lev 27:10
and if he shall at all *c* ....Lev 27:10
(their names being *c*) and .....Num 32:38
redeeming..concerning *c* ......Ruth 4:7
he *c* his behavior before 1Sam 21:13
c his apparel and came........2Sam 12:20
gold and ten *c* of raiment 2Kin 5:5
c his prison garments; and 2Kin 25:29
me; *c* and war are against ....Job 10:17
time will I wait, till my *c*.....Job 14:14
thou *c* his countenance.......Job 14:20
disease is my garment *c* ....Job 30:18
to his own hurt, and *c* not ....Ps 15:4
when he *c* his behavior ....Ps 34:*title*
and they shall be *c* ....Ps 102:26
boldness..face shall be *c* ......Eccl 8:1
The *c* suits of apparel and.....Is 3:22
transgressed the laws *c* ....Is 24:5
Hath a nation *c* their gods ....Jer 2:11
my people have *c* their........Jer 2:11
about so much to *c* thy ....Jer 2:36
Can the Ethiopian *c* his ....Jer 13:23
and his scent is not *c* ....Jer 48:11
and *c* his prison garments .....Jer 52:33
the form of his visage was *c* ...Dan 3:19
neither were their coats *c* .....Dan 3:27
his heart be *c* from man's .....Dan 4:16
king's countenance was *c*......Dan 5:6
that it be not *c* according .....Dan 6:8
and thing to *c* times and ......Dan 7:25
my countenance *c* in me ......Dan 7:28
hath *c* the portion of my ......Mic 2:4
Then shall his mind *c* and .....Hab 1:11
clothe thee with *c* of..........Zech 3:4
I am the Lord, I *c* not ....Mal 3:6
shall *c* the customs which .....Acts 6:14
they *c* their minds and said.....Acts 28:6
Who *c* the truth of God into ..Rom 1:25
their women did *c* the ....Rom 1:26
sleep, but we shall all be *c* 1Cor 15:51
with you now and to *c* my ....Gal 4:20
Who shall *c* our vile body .....Phil 3:21
of necessity a *c* also of ....Heb 7:12

CHANGE OF CLOTHES—*gala, festal garments*
A gift ....Gen 45:22
A wager ....Judg 14:12-19
From a king 2Kin 5:5

CHANGERS—*money changers*
doves, and the *c* of money ....John 2:14

CHANNEL—*bed where stream of water flows*

[*also* CHANNELS]
the *c* of the sea appeared 2Sam 22:16
Then the *c* of waters were ....Ps 18:15
from the *c* of the river ....Is 27:12

CHANT—*to sing*
That *c* to the sound of the ....Amos 6:5

CHAPEL—*sanctuary*
it is the king's *c*, and it ....Amos 7:13

CHAPITER—*top of a post or column*
Variegated decorations of.Ex 36:38
Part of temple 1Kin 7:16, 19, 20

[*also* CHAPITERS]
the height of the other *c* 1Kin 7:16
the height of the *c* three 2Kin 25:17
pomegranates upon the *c*......2Kin 25:17
the *c* that was on the top 2Chr 3:15
the *c* which were on the top ...2Chr 4:12
the two pommels of the *c* 2Chr 4:12
a *c* of brass was upon it.......Jer 52:22
and the height of one *c* was ...Jer 52:22

CHAPMAN—*a merchant*
Sells gold to Solomon 2Chr 9:14
Same as "merchantmen"..1Kin 10:15

CHAPT—*parched; cracked*
Because the ground is *c* ....Jer 14:4

CHARACTER—*one's complete personality*
Traits of:
Described prophetically ..Gen 49:1-28
Indicated before birth....Gen 25:21-34
Seen in childhood ....Prov 20:11
Fixed in hell ....Rev 22:11, 15
Manifested by:
Decisions (Esau) ....Gen 25:29-34
Destiny (Judas) ....John 6:70, 71
Desires (Demas) 2Tim 4:10
Deeds (Saul) 1Sam 15:1-35

CHARACTER OF GOD'S PEOPLE
Their dedication:
Hear Christ ....John 10:3, 4
Follow Christ ....John 10:4, 5, 27
Receive Christ ....John 1:12
Their standing before God:
Blameless ....Phil 2:15
Faithful.................Rev 17:14
Godly 2Pet 2:9
Holy ....Col 3:12
Their graces:
Humble 1Pet 5:5
Loving 1Thess 4:9
Humility ....Phil 2:3, 4
Meek...................Matt 5:5
Merciful ....Matt 5:7
Obedient ....Rom 16:19
Pure...................Matt 5:8
Sincere 2Cor 1:12
Zealous................Titus 2:14
Courteous 1Pet 3:8
Unity of mind..........Rom 15:5-7
Hospitable 1Pet 4:9
Generous 2Cor 8:1-7
Peaceable ....Heb 12:14
Patient ....James 5:7, 8
Content ....Heb 13:5
Steadfast 1Cor 15:58

CHARACTER OF THE WICKED
Their attitude toward God:
Hostile ....Rom 8:7
Denial..................Ps 14:1
Disobedience...........Titus 1:16
Their spiritual state:
Blindness 2Cor 4:4
Slavery to sin 2Pet 2:14, 19
Deadness ....Eph 2:1
Inability ....Rom 8:8
Their works:
Boastful ....Ps 10:3-6
Full of evil.............Rom 1:29-32
Haters of the Gospel ....John 3:19, 20
Sensual 2Pet 2:12-22

CHARASHIM (kär´ă-shĭm)—*"ravine of craftsmen"*
Valley near Jerusalem ...1Chr 4:14

Called a "valley of craftsmen" ....Neh 11:35

CHARCHEMISH—*See* CARCHEMISH

CHARGE—*give responsibility or instructions to; a responsibility or obligation*

[*also* CHARGEABLE, CHARGED, CHARGEDST, CHARGES, CHARGEST, CHARGING]

my voice, and kept my *c* ......Gen 26:5
And Abimelech *c* all his ......Gen 26:11
thou *c* us, saying, Set ....Ex 19:23
keep the *c* of the Lord........Lev 8:35
c of the whole congregation ...Num 3:7
unto them in *c* all their ....Num 4:27
and give him a *c* in their ......Num 27:19
c Joshua, and encourage ......Deut 3:28
and Joshua *c* them that ....Josh 18:8
father *c* the people with.......1Sam 14:27
thou *c* me today with a 2Sam 3:8
c the messenger, saying 2Sam 11:19
now go, lest we be *c*..........2Sam 13:25
I will give *c* concerning 2Sam 14:8
keep the *c* of the Lord.........1Kin 2:3
man according to his *c* 1Kin 4:28
c of the house of Joseph 1Kin 11:28
he leaned to have the *c* 2Kin 7:17
the Lord had *c* them, that.....2Kin 17:15
because the *c* was upon 1Chr 9:27
thee *c* concerning Israel.......1Chr 22:12
the Levites to their *c* 2Chr 8:14
service in their *c* 2Chr 31:16
the priests in their *c* 2Chr 35:2
and he hath *c* me to build.....Ezra 1:2
before me were *c* unto the ....Neh 5:15
palace, *c* over Jerusalem ......Neh 7:2
c that they should not be .....Neh 13:19
Mordecai had *c* her that ......Esth 2:10
that have the *c* of the.........Esth 3:9
sinned not, nor *c* God ....Job 1:22
and his angels he *c* with.......Job 4:18
Who hath given him a *c* ....Job 34:13
shall give his angels *c* ....Ps 91:11
I *c* Baruch before them ....Jer 32:13
he hath *c* us, to drink.........Jer 35:8
Lord hath given it a *c* ....Jer 47:7
which had the *c* of the men ...Jer 52:25
kept the *c* of mine holy ....Ezek 44:8
which have kept my *c*..........Ezek 48:11
keep my *c*, then thou shalt ....Zech 3:7
Jesus straitly *c* them ....Matt 9:30
c them that they should ....Matt 12:16
Then *c* he his disciples ....Matt 16:20
Jesus *c* them, saying, Tell .....Matt 17:9
he straitly *c* him, and ....Mark 1:43
straitly *c* them that they.......Mark 3:12
c them straitly that no ....Mark 5:43
c them..they should tell ....Mark 7:36
but the more he *c* them ....Mark 7:36
he *c* them, saying, Take ......Mark 8:15
c them..should tell no..........Mark 9:9
And many *c* him that he ....Mark 10:48
he *c* him to tell no man ....Luke 5:14
c of all her treasure ....Acts 8:27
c the jailor to keep them......Acts 16:23
c with them, that they may ....Acts 21:24
c..See thou tell no man ....Acts 23:22
not be *c* unto any of you......1Thess 2:9
that we might not be *c*........2Thess 3:8
these things give in *c* 1Tim 5:7
give thee *c* in the sight........1Tim 6:13
c them that are rich 1Tim 6:17
I *c* thee therefore before 2Tim 4:1
not be laid to their *c* 2Tim 4:16

CHARGER—*a dish or platter*
- In tribal offerings........Num 7:13
- Translated "dish" ....Ex 25:29
- Used for a dead man's head ....Matt 14:8, 11
- Used figuratively ("platter") ....Luke 11:39

[*also* CHARGERS]

c of silver, twelve silver ....Num 7:84
thirty *c* of gold, and a ....Ezra 1:9
by and by in a *c* the head of ..Mark 6:25

CHARIOT—*two-wheeled horse-drawn carriage*

Used for:
- Travel ....Gen 46:29
- War 1Kin 20:25

Employed by:
- Kings......................1Kin 22:35
- Persons of distinction ....Gen 41:43
- God 2Kin 2:11, 12

Illustrative of:
- Clouds ....Ps 104:3
- God's judgments ....Is 66:15
- Angels 2Kin 6:16, 17

Used by:
- Egyptians ....Ex 14:7
- Canaanites ....Josh 17:16
- Philistines...............1Sam 13:5
- Syrians 2Sam 10:18
- Assyrians 2Kin 19:23
- Jews......................2Kin 8:21

Numbers employed by:
- Pharaoh—600 ....Ex 14:7
- Jabin—900 ....Judg 4:3
- Philistines—30,000 ....1Sam 13:5

[*also* CHARIOTS]

went up with him both *c* ......Gen 50:9
ready his *c*, and took his ......Ex 14:6
their *c* wheels that they ....Ex 14:25
Pharaoh's *c* and his host ......Ex 15:4
seest horses, and *c* ....Deut 20:1
with horses and *c* very ....Josh 11:4
c and horsemen unto the ......Josh 24:6
because they had *c* of iron ....Judg 1:19
Sisera lighted..off his *c*........Judg 4:15
Why is his *c* so long ....Judg 5:28
tarry the wheels of his *c*? .....Judg 5:28
for himself, for his *c* 1Sam 8:11
c and horsemen followed 2Sam 1:6
from him a thousand *c* 2Sam 8:4
of them for a hundred *c* 2Sam 8:4
prepared him *c* and horses 2Sam 15:1
prepared him *c*..horsemen.....1Kin 1:5
stalls of horses for his *c* 1Kin 4:26
like the work of a *c* wheel 1Kin 7:33
thousand..four hundred *c* 1Kin 10:26
he bestowed..cities for *c* 1Kin 10:26
c came up and went out of 1Kin 10:29
speed..him up to his *c* 1Kin 12:18
Zimri, captain of half his *c* 1Kin 16:9
say..Ahab, Prepare thy *c*......1Kin 18:44
him, and horses, and *c*.........1Kin 20:1
unto the driver of his *c* 1Kin 22:34
appeared a *c* of fire 2Kin 2:11
horses and with his *c* 2Kin 5:9
noise of *c*, and a noise 2Kin 7:6
therefore two *c* horses 2Kin 7:14
Jehu rode in a *c*, and went 2Kin 9:16
fifty horsemen and ten *c* 2Kin 13:7
c of Israel, and the 2Kin 13:14
servants carried him in a *c* 2Kin 23:30
also houghed all the *c* 1Chr 18:4
hire them *c* and horsemen 1Chr 19:6
c of the cherubim, that 1Chr 28:18
gathered *c* and horsemen.......2Chr 1:14
thousand..four hundred *c* 2Chr 1:14
which he placed in the *c* 2Chr 1:14
princes, and all his *c* 2Chr 21:9
him..captains of the *c*..........2Chr 21:9
trust in *c*..some in horses .....Ps 20:7
burneth the *c* in the fire ......Ps 46:9
the *c* and horse are cast.......Ps 76:6
King Solomon..himself a *c* ....Song 3:9
soul made me like the *c*........Song 6:12
is there any end of their *c*......Is 2:7
a *c*..a couple of horsemen .....Is 21:7
a *c* of asses, and a *c* of ....Is 21:7
Elam bare the quiver with *c* ...Is 22:6
c of thy glory shall be ....Is 22:18
trust in *c*, because they ....Is 31:1
thy trust on Egypt for *c*........Is 36:9
By the multitude of my *c* ......Is 37:24
his *c* shall, be..whirlwind ......Jer 4:13
riding in *c* and on horses.......Jer 17:25
David, riding in *c* and on ......Jer 22:4
rage, ye *c*; and let the ....Jer 46:9
the rushing of his *c* ....Jer 47:3
will I break in pieces the *c* ....Jer 51:21
precious clothes for *c* ....Ezek 27:20
with *c*, and with horsemen .....Dan 11:40
bind..*c* to the swift beast ......Mic 1:13
c shall be with flaming ....Nah 2:3
thine horses and thy *c* ....Hab 3:8
I will overthrow the *c*..........Hag 2:22
came four *c* out from ....Zech 6:1
first *c* were red horses ....Zech 6:2
and in the second *c* black .....Zech 6:2
will cut off the *c* from ....Zech 9:10
and sitting in his *c* read ....Acts 8:28
as the sound of *c* of many......Rev 9:9
and horses, and *c*, and ....Rev 18:13

CHARIOT CITIES
Many in Solomon's time. .1Kin 9:19

CHARIOT HORSES
Hamstrung..............1Chr 18:4

CHARIOT OF FIRE
Used in Elijah's exit from earth 2Kin 2:11

CHARIOTS OF THE SUN—*used in sun worship*
Destroyed 2Kin 23:11

CHARITABLENESS—*a generous spirit toward others*
- Bearing burdens.........Gal 6:2-4
- Showing forgiveness 2Cor 2:1-10
- Seeking concord ....Phil 4:1-3
- Helping the tempted .....Gal 6:1
- Encouraging the weak ...Rom 14:1-15
- Not finding fault ....Matt 7:1-3

CHARITY—*alms giving; a synonym for "love"*
- From within ....Luke 11:41
- Given freely ....Luke 12:33
- Of Dorcas ....Acts 9:36

mountains and have not *c* 1Cor 13:2
c suffereth long, and is........1Cor 13:4
envieth not; *c* vaunteth 1Cor 13:4
now abideth faith, hope, *c* 1Cor 13:13
Follow after *c*, and desire 1Cor 14:1
your things be done with *c* 1Cor 16:14
these things put on *c* ....Col 3:14
good tidings of..and *c*.........1Thess 3:6
faith and *c* and holiness 1Tim 2:15
another with a kiss of *c* 1Pet 5:14
borne witness of thy *c* 3John 6
spots in your feasts of *c* ......Jude 12

CHARMED—*cast a spell on*

[*also* CHARMING]

to the voice of charmers, *c*....Ps 58:5
which will not be *c*, and ......Jer 8:17

CHARMERS—*practitioners of magic*
Falsified by God ....Ps 58:4, 5

[*also* CHARMER]

Or a *c*, or a consulter.........Deut 18:11
the idols, and to the *c* ....Is 19:3

CHARRAN (kär'än)—*"mountains"—Mesopotamian city; same as Haran*
before he dwelt in *C* ....Acts 7:2

CHASE—*to pursue*

[*also* CHASED, CHASETH, CHASING]

ye shall *c* your enemies ......Lev 26:7
out against you, and *c* ....Deut 1:44
should one *c* a thousand ......Deut 32:30
they *c* them from before ......Josh 7:5
man of you shall *c* a ....Josh 23:10
Israel returned from *c* 1Sam 17:53
into darkness, and *c* out ......Job 18:18
let the angel of the Lord *c* ....Ps 35:5
Mine enemies *c* me sore ......Lam 3:52

CHASTISEMENT—*punishment; berated*
Sign of:
Sonship ....Prov 3:11, 12
God's love ....Deut 8:5
Design of, to:
Correct ....Jer 24:5, 6
Prevent sin 2Cor 12:7-9
Bless ....Ps 94:12, 13
Response to:
Penitence 2Chr 6:24-31
Submission 2Cor 12:7-10

[*also* CHASTEN, CHASTENED, CHASTENEST, CHASTENETH, CHASTENING, CHASTISE, CHASTISED, CHASTISETH]
and I, even I will *c* you ....Lev 26:28
as a man *c* his son, so ....Deut 8:5
the Lord thy God *c* thee ......Deut 8:5
not seen the *c* of the Lord ....Deut 11:2
when they have *c* him, will ....Deut 21:18
shall take that man and *c* .....Deut 22:18
I will *c* him with the rod 2Sam 7:14
my father hath *c* you with 1Kin 12:11
but I will *c* you with 1Kin 12:11
I will *c* you with scorpions 2Chr 10:11
I will *c* you with scorpions 2Chr 10:14
despise not thou the *c* ....Job 5:17
He is *c* also with pain ....Job 33:19
I have borne *c*, I will ....Job 34:31
neither *c* me in thy hot ....Ps 6:1
c me in thy..displeasures .....Ps 38:1
When I wept, and *c* my ....Ps 69:10
have I been plagued, and *c* ....Ps 73:14
He that *c* the heathen ....Ps 94:10
is the man whom thou *c* ......Ps 94:12
The Lord hath *c* me sore ......Ps 118:18
despise not the *c* of the ....Prov 3:11
he that loveth him *c* him ......Prov 13:24
c thy son while there is ....Prov 19:18
a prayer when thy *c* was ....Is 26:16
the *c* of our peace was ....Is 53:5
the *c* of a cruel one ....Jer 30:14
hast *c* me, and I was *c* ....Jer 31:18
to *c* thyself before thy God ....Dan 10:12
I will *c* them, as their ....Hos 7:12
my desire that I should *c* ......Hos 10:10
I will therefore *c* him ....Luke 23:16
we are *c* of the Lord that 1Cor 11:32
as *c*, and not killed 2Cor 6:9
despise not thou the *c* of......Heb 12:5
the Lord loveth he *c* ....Heb 12:6
If ye endure *c*, God dealeth ...Heb 12:7
But if ye be without *c* ....Heb 12:8
Now no *c* for the present .....Heb 12:11
as I love, I rebuke and *c* ......Rev 3:19

CHASTITY—*sexual purity; pure behavior*
Manifested in:
Dress 1Pet 3:1-6
Looks ....Matt 5:28, 29
Speech ....Eph 5:4
Intentions ....Gen 39:7-12
Aids to:
Shun the unchaste 1Cor 5:11
Consider your sainthood .Eph 5:3, 4
Dangers of unchastity ....Prov 6:24-35
Let marriage suffice 1Cor 7:1-7
"Keep thyself pure" 1Tim 5:22
Examples of:
Job ....Job 31:1, 9-12
Joseph ....Gen 39:7-20
Ruth ....Ruth 3:10, 11
Boaz ....Ruth 3:13, 14
Saints ....Rev 14:4

[*also* CHASTE]
present you as a *c* virgin 2Cor 11:2
discreet *c* keepers at ....Titus 2:5
they behold your *c* 1Pet 3:2

CHATTER—*to talk idly or incessantly*
so did I *c*; I did mourn as .....Is 38:14

CHEATING—*defrauding by deceitful means*
The Lord ....Mal 3:8, 9
One's soul ....Matt 16:26
The needy ....Amos 8:4, 5
Others 1Cor 7:5
See DISHONESTY

CHEBAR (kē´bär)—*"strength"*
River in Babylonia ......Ezek 1:3
Site of Ezekiel's visions
and Jewish captives ....Ezek 10:15, 20
captives by the river of *C* .....Ezek 1:1
dwelt by the river of *C* ....Ezek 3:15
I saw by the river *C* ....Ezek 43:3

CHECK—*censure*
heard the *c* of my reproach ...Job 20:3

CHECKER—*a criss cross design on the pillars of the temple*
nets of *c* work, and wreaths ...1Kin 7:17

CHEDORLAOMER (kĕd-ŏr-lā-ō´mer)—*"servant of (the goddess) Lakamar"*
A king of Elam; invaded
Canaan ....Gen 14:1-16

CHEEK—*area of face below eyes*
Micaiah struck on 1Kin 22:24
Slapped on ....Job 16:10
Messiah's plucked ....Is 50:6
Description of:
Beauty ....Song 5:13
Patience ....Matt 5:39
Victory ....Ps 3:7
Attack ....Mic 5:1

[*also* CHEEKS]
shoulder, and the two *c* ....Deut 18:3
smote Micaiah upon the *c* 2Chr 18:23
Thy *c* are comely with ....Song 1:10
her tears are on her *c* ....Lam 1:2
He giveth his *c* to him ....Lam 3:30
hath the *c* teeth of a great ....Joel 1:6
smite thee upon thy right *c* ....Matt 5:39
smiteth thee on..one *c* ....Luke 6:29

CHEERFULNESS—*full of good feeling*
Caused by:
A merry heart ....Prov 15:13
The Lord's goodness .....Zech 9:16, 17
The Lord's presence .....Mark 6:54, 55
Victory ....John 16:33
Confidence ....Acts 24:10
Manifested in:
Giving 2Cor 9:7
Christian graces ....Rom 12:8
Times of danger ....Acts 27:22-36

[*also* CHEER, CHEERETH, CHEERFUL, CHEERFULLY]
shall *c* up his wife which ....Deut 24:5
which *c* God and man, and ....Judg 9:13
and let thy heart *c* thee ....Eccl 11:9
gladness and *c* feasts; ....Zech 8:19
be of good *c*; thy sins be ......Matt 9:2
Be of good *c*; it is I ....Matt 14:27
unto them, Be of good *c* ......Mark 6:50
Be of good *c*, Paul; for ....Acts 23:11

CHEESE—*a milk product*
Used for food 1Sam 17:18
Received by David 2Sam 17:20
Figurative of trials ....Job 10:10
sheep, and *c* of kine, for 2Sam 17:29

CHELAL (kē´lăl)—*"completeness"*
A son of Pahath-moab ...Ezra 10:30

CHELLUH (kĕl´ū)—*"robust"*
A son of Bani ....Ezra 10:35

CHELUB (kē´lŭb)—*"boldness"*
1. A brother of Shuah 1Chr 4:11
2. Father of Ezri 1Chr 27:26

CHELUBAI (kĕ-lo͞o´bī)—*"impetuous; raging with madness"*
A son of Hezron 1Chr 2:9
Another form of Caleb ..1Chr 2:18, 42

CHEMARIM (kĕm´ä-rĭm)—*"servants; priests"*
Denounced ....Zeph 1:4
Translated "idolatrous
priests" 2Kin 23:5
Translated "priests" .....Hos 10:5

CHEMOSH (kē´mŏsh)—*"fire; hearth"—a god of Moab*
The god of the
Moabites ....Num 21:29
Children sacrificed to 2Kin 3:27
Solomon builds altars to. .1Kin 11:7
Josiah destroys altars of ..2Kin 23:13
which *C* thy god giveth ....Judg 11:24
and *C* shall go forth into ......Jer 48:7

CHENAANAH (kĕ-nā´ä-nä)—*"flat; low"*
1. A Benjamite 1Chr 7:10
2. Father of Zedekiah 2Chr 18:10
C made him horns of iron 1Kin 22:11

CHENANI (kĕ-nā´nī)—*"Jehovah; creator"*
A reforming Levite ......Neh 9:4

CHENANIAH (kĕn-ä-nī´ä)—*"established by Jehovah"*
1. A chief Levite in David's
reign 1Chr 15:22, 27
2. A reforming Levite;
contracted to Chenani..Neh 9:4
C and his sons were for 1Chr 26:29

CHEPHAR-HAAMMONAI (kē-fär-hā-ăm´ō-nī)—*"village of the Ammonites"*
A village of Benjamin ...Josh 18:24

CHEPHIRAH (kĕ-fī´rä)—*"town"*
A city of the Gibeonites. .Josh 9:17
Assigned to Benjamin ...Josh 18:26
Residence of exiles ......Ezra 2:25
of Kirjath-jearim, *C* and ......Neh 7:29

CHERAN (kē´răn)—*"lyre; lamb; union"*
A Horite, son of Dishon..1Chr 1:41
Eshban, and Ithran, and *C* ....Gen 36:26

CHERETHITES (kĕr´ĕ-thīts)—*Cretans in southwest Palestine*
Tribes in southwest
Canaan 1Sam 30:14
Identified with Philistines .Ezek 25:16
In David's bodyguard 2Sam 8:18
Serve Solomon 1Kin 1:38
all the *C* and all the 2Sam 15:18
and the *C* and the 2Sam 20:7
was over the *C* and the 1Chr 18:17
I will cut off the *C* and ....Ezek 25:16
the nation of the *C* ....Zeph 2:5

CHERISH—*to hold dear*

[*also* CHERISHED, CHERISHETH]
let her *c* him..let her 1Kin 1:2
was very fair, and *c* 1Kin 1:4
but nourisheth and *c* it ....Eph 5:29
as a nurse *c* her children 1Thess 2:7

CHERITH (kē´rĭth)—*"trench"—a brook in the Transjordan*
Elijah hid there 1Kin 17:3-6

CHERUB—*(the town)*
A district in Babylonia ...Ezra 2:59
Neh 7:61

CHERUBIM (chĕr´ŭb-ĭm)—*an angelic order*
Appearances of:
Fully described ....Ezek 1:5-14
Functions of:
Guard ....Gen 3:22-24
Fulfill God's purposes ....Ezek 10:9-16
Show God's majesty 2Sam 22:11
Images of:
On the mercy seat ....Ex 25:18-22
On the veil ....Ex 26:31
On curtains ....Ex 36:8
In the Temple 1Kin 8:6, 7

[*also* CHERUB, CHERUBIM'S]
of the garden of Eden *c* ....Gen 3:24
shalt make two *c* of gold ......Ex 25:18

c of cunning work shalt ....Ex 26:1
c of cunning work made he ...Ex 36:8
he made two *c* of gold ....Ex 37:7
One *c* on the end of this ......Ex 37:8
another *c* on the other ....Ex 37:8
from between the two *c* ....Num 7:89
dwelleth between the *c* 1Sam 4:4
dwelleth between the *c* 2Sam 6:2
oracle he made two *c* of 1Kin 6:23
the one wing of the *c* 1Kin 6:24
the other wing of the *c* 1Kin 6:24
ledges were..and *c* 1Kin 7:29
under the wings of the *c* 1Kin 8:6
dwellest between the *c* 2Kin 19:15
dwelleth between the *c* 1Chr 13:6
the chariot of the *c* 1Chr 28:18
and graved *c* on the walls 2Chr 3:7
one wing of the one *c* 2Chr 3:11
the wing of the other *c* 2Chr 3:11
under the wings of the *c* 2Chr 5:7
he rode upon a *c* and did .....Ps 18:10
dwellest between the *c* ....Ps 80:1
sitteth between the *c* ....Ps 99:1
dwellest between the *c* ....Is 37:16
was gone up from the *c* ....Ezek 9:3
head of the *c* there ....Ezek 10:1
under the *c* and fill ....Ezek 10:2
sound of the *c* wings ....Ezek 10:5
from between the *c* unto ......Ezek 10:7
fire that was between the *c* ....Ezek 10:7
c lift up their wings ....Ezek 11:22
Thou art the anointed *c* ....Ezek 28:14
was made with *c* and palm ....Ezek 41:18
between a *c* and a *c*; and .....Ezek 41:18
every *c* had two faces ....Ezek 41:18

CHESALON (kĕs´ä-lŏn)—*"hopes"*
A town of Judah ....Josh 15:10

CHESED (kē´sĕd)—*"gain"*
Fourth son of Nahor .....Gen 22:22

CHESIL (kē´sĭl)—*"fool"*
A village of Judah ....Josh 15:30
Probably same as Bethul and Bethuel......... { Josh 19:4; 1Chr 4:30 }

CHEST—*a case or box*
For offering 2Kin 12:9, 10
For money ("treasures")..Esth 3:9
For levy fixed by Moses. .2Chr 24:8, 9

[*also* CHESTS]
cast into the *c*, until 2Chr 24:10
c was brought unto the 2Chr 24:11
came and emptied the *c* 2Chr 24:11
c of rich apparel, bound ......Ezek 27:24

CHESTNUT TREE
Used by Jacob ....Gen 30:37
In Eden, God's garden...Ezek 31:8, 9

CHESULLOTH (kĕ-sŭl´ŏth)—*"loins"*
A border town of Issachar ....Josh 19:18

CHETH (kēth)
Eighth letter in Hebrew alphabet ....Ps 119:57-64

CHEW—*to grind or gnaw food with the teeth*

[*also* CHEWED, CHEWETH]
and *c* the cud, among the .....Lev 11:3
ye not eat of them that *c* .....Lev 11:4
he *c* the cud, but divideth .....Lev 11:4
the coney, because he *c* ....Lev 11:5
because he *c* the cud ....Lev 11:6
he *c* not the cud; he is ....Lev 11:7
not clovenfooted, nor *c* ....Lev 11:26
and *c* the cud among the ......Deut 14:6
of them that *c* the cud ....Deut 14:7
c the cud, but divide not ......Deut 14:7
yet *c* not the cud, it is ....Deut 14:8

CHEZIB (kē´zĭb)—*"false"*
Same as Achzib; birthplace of Shelah ...Gen 38:5

CHICKEN—*a domestic fowl*
Hen and brood..........Luke 13:34
Rooster (cock) ....Luke 22:34

CHICKS—*the young of a hen*
Figurative of Israel ......Matt 23:37

CHIDING—*reproving; rebuking*
Between men:
Jacob with Laban........Gen 31:36
Israelites with Moses.....Ex 17:2
Ephraimites with Gideon .Judg 8:1
Paul with Peter..........Gal 2:11, 14
By Christ, because of:
Unbelief ....Matt 11:20-24
Spiritual dullness ....Matt 16:8-12
Censoriousness ....Mark 10:13-16
Sluggishness.............Matt 26:40

[*also* CHIDE, CHODE]
was wroth and *c* with ....Gen 31:36
of the *c* of the children of .....Ex 17:7
the people *c* with Moses ......Num 20:3
He will not always *c* ....Ps 103:9

CHIDON (kī´dŏn)—*"javelin"*
Where Uzza was struck dead 1Chr 13:9, 10
Called Nahon 2Sam 6:6

CHIEF—*pertaining to highest rank or office*

[*also* CHIEFEST, CHIEFLY]
Phichol the *c* captain of ....Gen 21:22
Phichol the *c* captain of ....Gen 26:26
against the *c* of the butlers ....Gen 40:2
against the *c* of the bakers ....Gen 40:2
c butler told his dream ....Gen 40:9
When the *c* baker saw that ....Gen 40:16
the *c* butler..the *c* ....Gen 40:20
restored the *c* butler ....Gen 40:21
he hanged the *c* baker ....Gen 40:22
Yet did not the *c* butler.......Gen 40:23
spake the *c* butler unto ....Gen 41:9
a *c* man among his people ......Lev 21:4
the *c* of the house of the ......Num 3:24
the *c* of the congregation......Num 4:34
prince of a *c* house among ....Num 25:14
c fathers of the ....Num 31:26
c fathers of the tribes ....Num 32:28
c fathers of the families ....Num 36:1
I took the *c* of your tribes ....Deut 1:15
c things of the ancient ....Deut 33:15
c house a prince ....Josh 22:14
c of all the people ....Judg 20:2
c of all the offerings 1Sam 2:29
in the *c* place among them 1Sam 9:22
Draw ye..all the *c* 1Sam 14:38
c of the things which 1Sam 15:21
Edomite, the *c* of the 1Sam 21:7
David's soul, he shall be *c* 2Sam 5:8
David's sons were *c* rulers.....2Sam 8:18
was a *c* ruler about David.....2Sam 20:26
c among the captains; the 2Sam 23:8
Beside the *c* of Solomon's 1Kin 5:16
c of the fathers of the 1Kin 8:1
the *c* of the officers............1Kin 9:23
c of the guard, which kept 1Kin 14:27
guard took Seraiah the *c* 2Kin 25:18
of him came the *c* ruler 1Chr 5:2
five; all of them *c* men.........1Chr 7:3
their generations, *c* men 1Chr 8:28
men where *c* of the fathers 1Chr 9:9
Shallum was the *c* 1Chr 9:17
Jebusites first shall be *c* 1Chr 11:6
The *c* was Ahiezer then 1Chr 12:3
of Kohath; Uriel the *c* 1Chr 15:5
of Merari; Asaiah the *c* 1Chr 15:6
of Gershom; Joel the *c* 1Chr 15:7
Shemaiah the *c*...............1Chr 15:8
of Hebron; Eliel the *c* 1Chr 15:9
Uzziel; Amminadab, the *c* 1Chr 15:10
Chenaniah, *c* of the Levites ...1Chr 15:22
Asaph the *c* and, next 1Chr 16:5
sons of David were *c* 1Chr 18:17
the *c* was Jehiel, and 1Chr 23:8
more *c* men found of the 1Chr 24:4
Simri the *c* (for though 1Chr 26:10
c fathers and captains 1Chr 27:1
the *c* of the fathers and 1Chr 29:6
Israel, the *c* of the fathers.....2Chr 1:2
c of the fathers of the 2Chr 5:2
c of his captains, and 2Chr 8:9
c to be ruler among his 2Chr 11:22
c of the guard, that kept 2Chr 12:10
Aduah the *c*, and with 2Chr 17:14
c of the fathers of Israel 2Chr 19:8
c of the fathers of Israel 2Chr 23:2
called for Jehoiada the *c* 2Chr 24:6
c of the fathers of the 2Chr 26:12
Azariah the *c* priest of 2Chr 31:10
they buried him in the *c* 2Chr 32:33
Jozabad, *c* of the Levites......2Chr 35:9
c of the priests and the 2Chr 36:14
the *c* of the fathers of ....Ezra 1:5
some of the *c* of the fathers ...Ezra 2:68
c of the fathers, who ....Ezra 3:12
c of the fathers, and ....Ezra 4:2
men that were the *c* of........Ezra 5:10
son of Aaron the *c* priest .....Ezra 7:5
now the *c* of their fathers .....Ezra 8:1
been *c* in this trespass ....Ezra 9:2
and made the *c* priests ....Ezra 10:5
of the *c* of the fathers ....Neh 7:70
c of the fathers of all ....Neh 8:13
The *c* of the people ....Neh 10:14
These were the *c* of the ......Neh 12:7
the *c* of the people of.........Job 12:24
out their way, and sat *c* ....Job 29:25
the *c* of the ways of God .....Job 40:19
To the *c* Musician on ....Ps 4 *title*
To the *c* Musician upon ....Ps 8 *title*
c Musician upon Muth ....Ps 9 *title*
c Musician, A Psalm of ....Ps 11:*title*
the *c* Musician upon ....Ps 12:*title*
c Musician upon Aijeleth .....Ps 22:*title*
c Musician even to Jeduthun ..Ps 39:*title*
the *c* Musician, Maschil ....Ps 42:*title*
To the *c* Musician for..........Ps 44:*title*
c Musician upon...............Ps 45:*title*
the *c* Musician upon ....Ps 53:*title*
c Musician, Altaschith ....Ps 57:*title*
c Musician upon Shushan .....Ps 60:*title*
the *c* of their strength.........Ps 78:51
To the *c* Musician upon.......Ps 81:*title*
Jerusalem above my *c* joy .....Ps 137:6
the *c* place of concourse ......Prov 1:21
a whisperer separateth *c* ......Prov 16:28
with all the *c* spices...........Song 4:14
the *c* among ten thousand .....Song 5:10
even all the *c* ones of.........Is 14:9
thee from the *c* men ....Is 41:9
to be captains, and as *c* ....Jer 13:21
c governor in the house ....Jer 20:1
among the *c* of the nations ....Jer 31:7
of Elam, the *c* of their ....Jer 49:35
guard took Seraiah the *c* ....Jer 52:24
Her adversaries are the *c* .....Lam 1:5
in thy fairs with *c* of all ....Ezek 27:22
c prince of Meshech and ......Ezek 38:2
against thee, O Gog, the *c* ....Ezek 38:3
c prince of Meshech and ......Ezek 39:1
c of the governors over ....Dan 2:48
lo, Michael, one of the *c* ......Dan 10:13
the *c* of the children of ....Dan 11:41
which are named *c* of the .....Amos 6:1
themselves with the *c* ....Amos 6:6
to the *c* singer on my ....Hab 3:19
the *c* priests and scribes ....Matt 2:4
elders and *c* priests ....Matt 16:21
betrayed unto the *c* priests ....Matt 20:18
whosoever will be *c* among ....Matt 20:27
the *c* priests and scribes ....Matt 21:15
c priests and the elders ....Matt 21:23
c priests and Pharisees ....Matt 21:45
assembled together the *c* ......Matt 26:3
went unto the *c* priests........Matt 26:14
the *c* priests and elders ....Matt 26:47
c priests and elders of ....Matt 27:1
the *c* priests and elders ....Matt 27:3
c priests took the silver ....Matt 27:6
he was accused of the *c* ....Matt 27:12
the *c* priests and elders ....Matt 27:20
also the *c* priests mocking .....Matt 27:41
c priests and Pharisees ....Matt 27:62
showed unto the *c* priests .....Matt 28:11

captains, and *c* estates ....Mark 6:21
the *c* priests and scribes ....Mark 8:31
be delivered unto the *c* ....Mark 10:33
the *c*, shall be servant ....Mark 10:44
the scribes and *c* priests ....Mark 11:18
c seats in the synagogues ......Mark 12:39
c priests and the scribes ....Mark 14:1
the *c* priests held a ....Mark 15:1
c priests had delivered ....Mark 15:10
c priests and scribes ....Luke 9:22
through Beelzebub the *c* ......Luke 11:15
of one of the *c* Pharisees ......Luke 14:1
chose out the *c* rooms ....Luke 14:7
was the *c* among the ....Luke 19:2
c priests and the scribes ....Luke 20:1
and the *c* rooms at feasts .....Luke 20:46
the *c* priests and scribes ....Luke 22:2
that is *c*, as he that doth ......Luke 22:26
Pilate to the *c* priests ....Luke 23:4
how the *c* priests and our .....Luke 24:20
Pharisees and the *c* priests ....John 7:32
c priests and the Pharisees ....John 11:47
c priests consulted that ....John 12:10
c priests and Pharisees ....John 18:3
c priests therefore and ....John 19:6
c priests and elders had ....Acts 4:23
c priests heard these ....Acts 5:24
authority from the *c* priests ....Acts 9:14
and the *c* men of the city .....Acts 13:50
he was the *c* speaker ....Acts 14:12
c men among the brethren ....Acts 15:22
c city of that part of ....Acts 16:12
of the *c* women not a few .....Acts 17:4
c ruler of the synagogue ....Acts 18:8
a Jew, and *c* of the priests ....Acts 19:14
certain of the *c* of Asia ....Acts 19:31
unto the *c* captain of ....Acts 21:31
The *c* captain commanded .....Acts 22:24
c captain, fearing lest ....Acts 23:10
But the *c* captain Lysias ......Acts 24:7
c of the Jews informed ....Acts 25:2
authority from the *c* ....Acts 26:10
the *c* man of the island ....Acts 28:7
c because that unto them .....Rom 3:2
behind the very *c* apostles 2Cor 11:5
behind the very *c* apostles 2Cor 12:11
being the *c* corner stone ....Eph 2:20
c they that are of Caesar's ....Phil 4:22
sinners; of whom I am *c* 1Tim 1:15
I lay in Zion a *c* corner 1Pet 2:6
when the *c* Shepherd shall 1Pet 5:4
c them that walk after the 2Pet 2:10
c captains, and the mighty ....Rev 6:15

CHIEF SEATS—*seats or places of honor*
Sought by scribes and Pharisees .... { Matt 23:1, 6 / Mark 12:38, 39 }
Not to be sought ....Luke 14:7-11

CHILD—*young offspring*
[*also* CHILD'S]
was barren; she had no *c* .....Gen 11:30
Behold, thou art with *c* ....Gen 16:11
Every man *c* among you ......Gen 17:10
daughters of Lot with *c* ....Gen 19:36
c grew, and was weaned ......Gen 21:8
c is not; and I, whither ....Gen 37:30
she is with *c* by whoredom ....Gen 38:24
Do not sin against the *c* ....Gen 42:22
and a *c* of his old age ....Gen 44:20
that he was a goodly *c* ....Ex 2:2
and called the *c* mother ....Ex 2:8
hurt a woman with *c*, so ......Ex 21:22
afflict..or fatherless *c* ....Ex 22:22
born a man *c*; then she ....Lev 12:2
have no *c*, and is returned ....Lev 22:13
beareth the sucking *c* ....Num 11:12
and have no *c*, the wife ....Deut 25:5
c shall be a Nazarite ....Judg 13:5
Naomi took the *c* and laid ....Ruth 4:16
thine handmaid a man *c* 1Sam 1:11
the *c* did minister unto 1Sam 2:11
c Samuel grew before 1Sam 2:21
the *c* Samuel ministered 1Sam 3:1
Phinehas' wife was with *c* 1Sam 4:19
daughter of Saul had no *c* 2Sam 6:23
and said, I am with *c* 2Sam 11:5
the *c* also that is born 2Sam 12:14
I am but a little *c*; I know 1Kin 3:7
Hadad being yet a little *c* 1Kin 11:17
a *c* shall be born unto 1Kin 13:2
shall become of the *c* 1Kin 14:3
himself upon the *c* 1Kin 17:21
let this *c* soul come 1Kin 17:21
Verily she hath no *c* 2Kin 4:14
unto the flesh of a little *c* 2Kin 5:14
rip up their women with *c* 2Kin 8:12
therein that were with *c* 2Kin 15:16
said, There is a man *c* ....Job 3:3
shall be fresher than a *c* ......Job 33:25
c that is weaned of his ....Ps 131:2
soul is even as a weaned *c* ....Ps 131:2
c is known by his doings ......Prov 20:11
Train up a *c* in the way ....Prov 22:6
not correction from the *c* .....Prov 23:13
but a *c* left to himself ....Prov 29:15
he hath neither *c* nor ....Eccl 4:8
Better is a poor and a wise *c* ..Eccl 4:13
O land when thy king is a *c* ...Eccl 10:16
womb of her that is with *c* ....Eccl 11:5
the *c* shall behave himself .....Is 3:5
before the *c* shall know ....Is 7:16
the *c* shall have knowledge ....Is 8:4
unto us a *c* is born, unto ......Is 9:6
shall be few, that a *c* may .....Is 10:19
a little *c* shall lead them ......Is 11:6
Like as a woman with *c* ....Is 26:17
forget her sucking *c* ....Is 49:15
didst not travail with *c* ....Is 54:1
c shall die a hundred ....Is 65:20
was delivered of a man *c* ......Is 66:7
I cannot speak for I am a *c* ...Jer 1:6
bringeth forth her first *c* ......Jer 4:31
man *c* is born unto thee ....Jer 20:15
man doth travail with *c*? ......Jer 30:6
lame, the woman with *c* ......Jer 31:8
son? Is he a pleasant *c*? ....Jer 31:20
you man and woman, *c* ....Jer 44:7
tongue of the suckling *c* ....Lam 4:4
When Israel was a *c*, then .....Hos 11:1
women with *c* shall be ....Hos 13:16
ripped up the women with *c* ...Amos 1:13
with *c* of the Holy Ghost .....Matt 1:18
diligently for the young *c* .....Matt 2:8
sought the young *c* life ....Matt 2:20
and the father the *c* ....Matt 10:21
c was cured from that ....Matt 17:18
Jesus called a little *c* ....Matt 18:2
receive one such little *c* ....Matt 18:5
twofold more the *c* of hell ....Matt 23:15
them that are with *c* ....Matt 24:19
And he said, Of a *c* ....Mark 9:21
them that are with *c* ....Mark 13:17
And they had no *c*, because ...Luke 1:7
wife, being great with *c* ....Luke 2:5
for he is mine only *c* ....Luke 9:38
shall receive this *c* ....Luke 9:48
kingdom of God as a little *c* ...Luke 18:17
them that are with *c* ....Luke 21:23
Sir, come down ere my *c* .....John 4:49
she is delivered of the *c* ....John 16:21
against thy holy *c* Jesus ....Acts 4:27
when as yet he had no *c* ....Acts 7:5
thou *c* of the devil, thou ......Acts 13:10
I was a *c*, I spake as a *c* 1Cor 13:11
heir, as long as he is a *c* ......Gal 4:1
upon a woman with *c* 1Thess 5:3
from a *c* thou hast known 2Tim 3:15
and was delivered of a *c* ....Heb 11:11
they saw he was a proper *c* ...Heb 11:23
And she being with *c* ....Rev 12:2

CHILDBEARING—*the act of giving birth to children*
Agreeable to God's command ....Gen 1:28
Result of marriage 1Tim 5:14
Attended with pain ......Gen 3:16
Productive of joy ....John 16:21
Productive of the Messiah. Luke 2:7
Means of salvation 1Tim 2:15
Expressed in symbols ....Rev 12:2, 5

CHILDHOOD, CHARACTERISTICS OF
Dependence 1Thess 2:7
Immaturity 1Cor 13:11
Foolishness ....Prov 22:15
Unstableness ....Eph 4:14
Humility ....Matt 18:1-5
Need for instruction .....Prov 22:6
Influence on adults ......Is 49:15

before you from my *c* 1Sam 12:2
evil from thy flesh; for *c* ......Eccl 11:10

CHILDISHNESS—*an immature spirit*
Manifested by Saul 1Sam 18:8
Seen in Haman ....Esth 6:6-9
[*also* CHILDISH]
a man, I put away *c* things 1Cor 13:11

CHILDLESS—*being without children*
give me, seeing I go *c* ....Gen 15:2
sin; they shall die *c* ....Lev 20:20
nakedness; they shall be *c* .....Lev 20:21
sword hath made women *c* 1Sam 15:33
so shall thy mother be *c* 1Sam 15:33
Write ye this man *c*, a man ...Jer 22:30
to wife, and he died *c* ....Luke 20:30

CHILDLIKENESS—*marked by innocence and trust*
Requirement of God's kingdom ....Mark 10:15
An element in spiritual growth 1Pet 2:2
A model to be followed ..1Cor 14:20

CHILDREN—*See* INTRODUCTION

CHILDREN, FIGURATIVE
Disciples of a teacher ....Mark 10:24
God's own ....Rom 8:16, 17
Christians ....Eph 5:8
Devil's own 1John 3:10
Those who show such trait ....Matt 11:16-19

CHILDREN, ILLEGITIMATE—*those born outside marriage*
No inheritance ....Gal 4:30
No fatherly care ....Heb 12:8
Not in congregation .....Deut 23:2
Despised ....Judg 11:2

CHILDREN, NATURAL
Right estimate of:
God's gifts ....Gen 33:5
God's heritage ....Ps 127:3-5
Crown of age ....Prov 17:6
Characteristics of:
Imitate parents 1Kin 15:11, 26
Diverse in nature ....Gen 25:27
Playful ....Matt 11:16-19
Capacities of:
Glorify God ....Matt 21:15, 16
Come to Christ ....Mark 10:13-16
Understand Scripture 2Tim 3:15
Receive the promises ....Acts 2:39
Believe ....Matt 18:6
Receive training ....Eph 6:4
Worship in God's house. .1Sam 1:24, 28
Parental obligations toward:
Nourishment 1Sam 1:22
Discipline ....Eph 6:4
Instruction ....Gal 4:1, 2
Employment 1Sam 17:15
Inheritance ....Luke 12:13, 14
Duties of:
Obedience ....Eph 6:1-3
Honor to parents ....Heb 12:9
Respect for age 1Pet 5:5
Care for parents 1Tim 5:4
Obedience to God ....Deut 30:2
Remembering God ......Eccl 12:1
Description of ungrateful:
Stubborn ....Deut 21:18-21
Scorners ....Prov 30:17

Robbers ....Prov 28:24
Strikers ....Ex 21:15
Cursers ....Lev 20:9

Examples of good:
Isaac ....Gen 22:6-10
Joseph ....Gen 45:9, 10
Jephthah's daughter .....Judg 11:34-36
Samuel 1Sam 2:26
David 1Sam 17:20
Josiah 2Chr 34:3
Esther ....Esth 2:20
Daniel ....Dan 1:6
John the Baptist ....Luke 1:80
Jesus ....Luke 2:51
In the Temple ....Matt 21:15, 16
Timothy 2Tim 3:15

Examples of bad:
Esau ....Gen 26:34, 35
Job's haters ....Job 19:18
Sons of Eli.............1Sam 2:12, 17
Sons of Samuel..........1Sam 8:3
Absalom 2Sam 15:10
Adonijah 1Kin 1:5, 6
Elisha's mockers.........2Kin 2:23
Adrammelech 2Kin 19:37

Acts performed upon:
Naming ....Ruth 4:17
Blessing ....Luke 1:67, 76-79
Circumcision ....Luke 2:21

Murder of:
By Pharaoh ....Ex 1:16
By Herod the Great .....Matt 2:16-18
In war ....Num 31:17

CHILEAB (kĭl'ĕ-ăb)—*"restraint of father"*
A son of David 2Sam 3:3
Also called Daniel 1Chr 3:1

CHILION (kĭl'ĭ-ŏn)—*"pining"*
Elimelech's son..........Ruth 1:2
Orpah's deceased husband ....Ruth 1:4, 5
Boaz redeems his estate . .Ruth 4:9

CHILMAD (kĭl'măd)—*"closed"*
A town or country trading with Tyre ......Ezek 27:23

CHIMHAM (kĭm'hăm)—*"pining"*
A son of Barzillai 2Sam 19:37-40
Inn bearing his name ....Jer 41:17

CHIMNEY—*passageway for escaping smoke*
Smoke out of the *c* ....Hos 13:3

CHINNERETH (kĭn'ĕ-rĕth)—*"harps"*
1. A city of Naphtali ......Deut 3:17
2. The region of Chinneroth 1Kin 15:20
Same as plain of Gennesaret ....Matt 14:34
3. The Old Testament name for Sea of Galilee .....Num 34:11
Also called Lake of Gennesaret and Sea of Galilee ....Luke 5:1

[*also* CINNEROTH]
the plains south of *C* ....Josh 11:2
plain to the Sea of *C* ....Josh 12:3
the edge of the Sea of *C* .....Josh 13:27
Hammath, Rakkath, and *C* ....Josh 19:35
all *C*, with all the land 1Kin 15:20

CHIOS (kī'ŏs)—*"open"*
An island of the Aegean Sea; on Paul's voyage . .Acts 20:15

CHISLEU (kĭs'lū)
Ninth month of Hebrew year ....Neh 1:1
ninth month, even in *C* ....Zech 7:1

CHISLON (kĭs'lŏn)—*"strength"*
Father of Elidad.........Num 34:21

CHISLOTH-TABOR (kĭs'lŏth-tā'ber)—*"loins of tabor"*
A locality near Mt. Tabor.Josh 19:12
Probably same as Chesulloth ....Josh 19:18

CHITTIM, KITTIM (kĭt'ĭm)
The island of Cyprus; inhabited by descendants of Japheth (through Javan) ....Gen 10:4
Ships of, in Balaam's prophecy ....Num 24:24
A haven for Tyre's ships. .Is 23:1-12
Mentioned in the prophets ....Jer 2:10
out of the isles of *C* ....Ezek 27:6
ships of *C* shall come ....Dan 11:30

CHIUN (kī'ŭn)—*"detestable thing"*
Astral images made by Israel.................Amos 5:26

CHLOE (klō'ē)—*"a tender sprout"*
Woman of Corinth 1Cor 1:11

CHOICE—*selection*

Of human things:
Wives ....Gen 6:2
Land ....Gen 13:11
Soldiers................Ex 17:9
King 1Sam 8:18
Disciples ....Luke 6:13
Church officers ....Acts 6:5
Missionaries............Acts 15:40
Delegates ....Acts 15:22, 25

Of God's choice:
Moses as leader ....Num 16:28
Levites to priesthood 1Sam 2:28
Kings..................1Sam 10:24
Jerusalem ....Deut 12:5
Israel as His people .....Deut 7:6-8
Cyrus as deliverer ....Is 45:1-4
The Servant (the Messiah)..............Is 42:1-7
The new Israel (the Church) 1Pet 2:9
The weak as God's own. .1Cor 1:27, 28
The elect ....Matt 20:16

Kind of:
God and the Devil ......Gen 3:1-11
Life and death ....Deut 30:19, 20
God and idols ....Josh 24:15-28
Obedience and disobedience 1Sam 15:1-35
God and Baal 1Kin 18:21-40
Wisdom and folly........Prov 8:1-21
Obedience and sin 2Pet 2:4
Christ and antichrist 1John 2:18, 19

Factors determining choice, man's:
First choice ....Rom 5:12
Depraved nature ....John 3:19-21
Spiritual deadness ....Eph 4:17-19
Blindness ....John 9:39-41
Inability ....Rom 8:7, 8

Bad choice made by:
Disobeying God ....Num 14:1-45
Putting the flesh first ....Gen 25:29-34
Following a false prophet .Matt 24:11, 24
Letting the world overcome ....Matt 19:16-22
Rejecting God's promises .Acts 13:44-48

Good choice made by:
Using God's Word ......Ps 119:9-11
Believing God..........Heb 11:24-27
Obedience ....Acts 26:19-23
Prayer ....Eph 1:16-19
Faith ....Heb 11:8-10

[*also* CHOICEST, CHOOSE, CHOOSEST, CHOOSETH, CHOOSING, CHOSE, CHOSEN]
wives of all which they *c* ......Gen 6:2
Lot *c* him all the plain of .....Gen 13:11
c of our sepulchers bury thy . . .Gen 23:6
his ass's colt unto the *c* vine . . .Gen 49:11
he took six hundred *c*.........Ex 14:7
his *c* captains also are.........Ex 15:4
Moses *c* able men out of all . . .Ex 18:25
even him whom he hath *c* .....Num 16:5
the man whom the Lord doth *c*.Num 16:7
the man's rod, whom I shall *c* .Num 17:5
therefore he *c* their seed ......Deut 4:37
and he *c* their seed after ......Deut 10:15
God shall *c* to cause his ....Deut 12:11
your *c* vows which ye vow ....Deut 12:11
which the Lord shall *c* ....Deut 12:14
the Lord thy God shall *c* ......Deut 12:18
the Lord thy God hath *c* ......Deut 12:21
which the Lord shall *c* ....Deut 12:26
the Lord hath *c* thee to be ....Deut 14:2
the place which he shall *c* .....Deut 14:23
the Lord thy God shall *c* ......Deut 14:24
the Lord thy God shall *c* ......Deut 14:25
which the Lord shall *c* ....Deut 15:20
which the Lord shall *c* ....Deut 16:2
the Lord thy God shall *c* ......Deut 16:6
the Lord thy God shall *c* ......Deut 16:7
the Lord thy God hath *c* to . . .Deut 16:11
which the Lord shall *c* ....Deut 16:15
the place which he shall *c* .....Deut 16:16
the Lord thy God shall *c* ......Deut 17:8
which the Lord shall *c* ....Deut 17:10
the Lord thy God shall *c* ......Deut 17:15
the Lord thy God hath *c* ......Deut 18:5
which the Lord shall *c* ....Deut 18:6
Lord thy God hath *c* to ....Deut 21:5
that place which he shall *c* ....Deut 23:16
God shall *c* to place his ....Deut 26:2
therefore *c* life that both ......Deut 30:19
the place which he shall *c* .....Deut 31:11
Joshua *c* out thirty ....Josh 8:3
place which he should *c* ....Josh 9:27
c you this day whom ye will . . .Josh 24:15
that ye have *c* you the Lord . . .Josh 24:22
They *c* new gods; then was ....Judg 5:8
the gods which ye have *c* .....Judg 10:14
numbered seven hundred *c* ....Judg 20:15
there were seven hundred *c* . . .Judg 20:16
ten thousand *c* men out of ....Judg 20:34
king which ye shall have *c* 1Sam 8:18
c young man, and a goodly....1Sam 9:2
the king whom ye have *c* 1Sam 12:13
Saul *c* him three thousand.....1Sam 13:2
Neither hath the Lord *c*.......1Sam 16:8
Jesse, the Lord hath not *c* 1Sam 16:10
c you a man for you, and let . .1Sam 17:8
that thou hast *c* the son of 1Sam 20:30
Saul took three thousand *c* 1Sam 24:2
having three thousand *c*.......1Sam 26:2
all the *c* men of Israel 2Sam 6:1
c me before thy father 2Sam 6:21
chose of all the *c* men of......2Sam 10:9
and all the men of Israel, *c* . . .2Sam 16:18
let me now *c* out twelve 2Sam 17:1
Saul, whom the Lord did *c* 2Sam 21:6
c thee one of them, that I.....2Sam 24:12
people which thou hast *c* 1Kin 3:8
I *c* no city out of all the 1Kin 8:16
the city which thou hast *c* 1Kin 8:44
the city which thou hast *c* 1Kin 8:48
sake which I have *c* 1Kin 11:13
the city which I have *c*........1Kin 11:32
my servant's sake whom I *c* . . .1Kin 11:34
the city which I have *c*........1Kin 11:36
and fourscore thousand *c*......1Kin 12:21
which the Lord did *c* out of . . .1Kin 14:21
city and every *c* city 2Kin 3:19
and the *c* fir trees thereof 2Kin 19:23
which I have *c* out of all 2Kin 21:7
Jerusalem which I have *c* 2Kin 23:27
c and mighty men of valor 1Chr 7:40
c to be porters in the gates 1Chr 9:22
them hath the Lord *c* to 1Chr 15:2
ye children of Jacob his *c* 1Chr 16:13
the rest that were *c* who 1Chr 16:41
c out of all the choice of......1Chr 19:10
c thee one of them, that I.....1Chr 21:10
Thus saith the Lord, *C* thee . . .1Chr 21:11
the Lord God of Israel *c* me . . .1Chr 28:4
he hath *c* Judah to be the 1Chr 28:4
he hath *c* Solomon my son 1Chr 28:5

I have *c* him to be my son 1Chr 28:6
for the Lord hath *c* thee 1Chr 28:10
whom alone God hath *c*, is....1Chr 29:1
I *c* no city among all the 2Chr 6:5
neither *c* I any man to be 2Chr 6:5
But I have *c* Jerusalem 2Chr 6:6
and have *c* David to be over ..2Chr 6:6
city which thou hast *c*.........2Chr 6:34
city which thou hast *c*.........2Chr 6:38
have *c* this place to myself 2Chr 7:12
For now have I *c* and 2Chr 7:16
fourscore thousand *c* men 2Chr 11:1
which the Lord had *c* out 2Chr 12:13
four hundred thousand *c* 2Chr 13:3
eight hundred thousand *c* 2Chr 13:3
five hundred thousand *c* 2Chr 13:17
three hundred thousand *c* 2Chr 25:5
Lord hath *c* you to stand......2Chr 29:11
which I have *c* before all......2Chr 33:7
the place that I have *c*.........Neh 1:9
one ox and six *c* sheep.........Neh 5:18
the God who didst *c* Abram ...Neh 9:7
that my soul *c* strangling ......Job 7:15
c out my words to reason .....Job 9:14
thou *c* the tongue of ....Job 15:5
I *c* out their way, and sat .....Job 29:25
Let us *c* to us judgment.......Job 34:4
refuse, or whether thou *c* ......Job 34:33
for this hast thou *c* rather .....Job 36:21
in the way that he shall *c* .....Ps 25:12
the people whom he hath *c* ...Ps 33:12
He shall *c* our inheritance .....Ps 47:4
the man whom thou *c* ....Ps 65:4
smote down the *c* men of .....Ps 78:31
and *c* not the tribe of.........Ps 78:67
But *c* the tribe of Judah ......Ps 78:68
He *c* David also his servant ...Ps 78:70
made a covenant with my *c* ...Ps 89:3
children of Jacob his *c* ....Ps 105:6
I may see the good of thy *c* ...Ps 106:5
I have *c* the way of truth .....Ps 119:30
the Lord hath *c* Zion; he .....Ps 132:13
the Lord hath *c* Jacob unto ...Ps 135:4
not *c* the fear of the Lord .....Prov 1:29
oppressor, and *c* none of his ..Prov 3:31
tongue of the just is as *c* ......Prov 10:20
rather to be *c* than silver! .....Prov 16:16
good name is rather to be *c* ...Prov 22:1
the *c* one of her that bare .....Song 6:9
gardens that ye have *c* ....Is 1:29
planted it with the *c* vine .....Is 5:2
refuse the evil and *c* the ......Is 7:15
and will yet *c* Israel and ......Is 14:1
c valleys shall be full of ....Is 22:7
the *c* fir trees thereof; and I ...Is 37:24
he hath no obligation *c* a tree .Is 40:20
Jacob whom I have *c* ....Is 41:8
I have *c* thee and not cast......Is 41:9
an abomination is he that *c* ...Is 41:24
servant whom I have *c*.........Is 43:10
drink to my people my *c* ......Is 43:20
Israel, whom I have *c*.........Is 44:1
c thee in the furnace of ....Is 48:10
Israel, and he shall *c* thee .....Is 49:7
c the things that please ....Is 56:4
such a fast that I have *c*? .....Is 58:5
this the fast that I have *c*? ....Is 58:6
c that wherein I delighted .....Is 65:12
for a curse unto my *c* ....Is 65:15
they have *c* their own ways....Is 66:3
I also will *c* their delusions ....Is 66:4
and *c* that in which I ....Is 66:4
death shall be *c* rather ....Jer 8:3
shall cut down thy *c* cedars ...Jer 22:7
which the Lord hath *c* ....Jer 33:24
and his *c* young men are ......Jer 48:15
and who is a *c* man, that I ....Jer 49:19
from her; and who is a *c* ......Jer 50:44
In the day when I *c* Israel.....Ezek 20:5
c thou a place, *c* it at the .....Ezek 21:19
fill it with the *c* bones ....Ezek 24:4
Take the c of the flock, and...Ezek 24:5
Eden, the *c* and best of ....Ezek 31:16
neither his *c* people, neither ...Dan 11:15
for I have *c* thee saith the.....Hag 2:23
and shall yet *c* Jerusalem......Zech 1:17
the Lord that hath *c* ....Zech 3:2
my servant, whom I have *c*....Matt 12:18
are called, but few are chosen .Matt 22:14
sake, whom he hath *c* ....Mark 13:20
of them he *c* twelve whom ....Luke 6:13
Mary hath *c* that good part....Luke 10:42
they *c* out the chief rooms ....Luke 14:7
if he be Christ, the *c* of God ..Luke 23:35
Have not I *c* you twelve ......John 6:70
I know whom I have *c*........John 13:18
Ye have not *c* me ....John 15:16
but I have *c* you and ....John 15:16
I have *c* you out of the ....John 15:19
the apostles whom he had *c* ...Acts 1:2
they *c* Stephen, a man full ....Acts 6:5
he is a *c* vessel unto me, to ...Acts 9:15
unto witnesses *c* before of.....Acts 10:41
c our fathers, and exalted .....Acts 13:17
God made *c* among us, that ...Acts 15:7
to send *c* men of their own....Acts 15:22
And Paul *c* Silas, and.........Acts 15:40
hath *c* thee, that thou.........Acts 22:14
Salute Rufus *c* in the Lord ....Rom 16:13
who was also *c* of the.........2Cor 8:19
he hath *c* us in him before ....Eph 1:4
yet what I shall *c* I wot not ...Phil 1:22
hath from the beginning *c* 2Thess 2:13
please him who hath *c* 2Tim 2:4
C rather to suffer affliction ....Heb 11:25
Hath not God *c* the poor of ...James 2:5
but *c* of God and precious 1Pet 2:4
him are called and *c* and ......Rev 17:14

CHOIR—*musicians trained to sing together*
Appointed by Nehemiah. .Neh 12:31
In house of God ....Neh 12:40
Under instructor.........1Chr 15:22, 27

CHOKE—*to block a passage*

[*also* CHOKED]
thorns sprung up, and *c*.......Matt 13:7
of riches, *c* the ....Matt 13:22
c it, and it yielded no fruit ....Mark 4:7
entering in, *c* the word........Mark 4:19
sprang up with it, and *c* it.....Luke 8:7
are *c* with cares and riches ....Luke 8:14
into the lake, and were *c* .....Luke 8:33

CHOLER—*anger*
moved with *c* against ....Dan 8:7
shall be moved with *c*.........Dan 11:11

CHOP—*to cut*
their bones, and *c* them.......Mic 3:3

CHOR-ASHAN (kôr-a'shăn)—*"smoking furnace"—town in Judah given to Simeon*
them which were in *C* 1Sam 30:30

CHORAZIN (kō-rā'zĭn)—*"secret"—a coastal city of the Sea of Galilee*
Woe unto thee *C*! woe ....Matt 11:21
Woe unto thee *C*! woe ....Luke 10:13

CHOZEBA (kō-zē'bă)—*"untruthful"*
Town of Judah 1Chr 4:22

CHRIST—*the Anointed One*

Pre-existence of:
Affirmed in Old Testament ....Ps 2:7
Confirmed by Christ .....John 8:58
Proclaimed by apostles ...Col 1:15-19

Birth of:
Predicted ....Is 7:14
Fulfilled ....Matt 1:18-25
In the fullness of time ...Gal 4:4

Deity of:
Prophecy ....Is 9:6
Acknowledged by Christ. .John 20:28, 29
Acclaimed by witnesses ..John 1:14, 18
Affirmed by apostles.....Rom 9:5
Heb 1:8

Attributes of:
All-powerful ....Matt 28:18
All-knowing............Col 2:3
Ever-present ....Matt 18:20
Eternal ....John 1:1, 2, 15

Humanity of:
Foretold ....Gen 3:15
1Cor 15:45-47
Took man's nature ......John 1:14
Heb 2:9-18
Seed of woman..........Gal 4:4
A son of man ....Luke 3:38
Of David's line..........Matt 22:45
A man 1Tim 2:5
Four brothers ....Mark 6:3

Mission of:
Do God's will ....John 6:38
Save sinners ....Luke 19:10
Bring in everlasting righteousness..........Dan 9:24
Destroy Satan's works ...Heb 2:14
1John 3:8
Fulfill the Old Testament .Matt 5:17
Give life ....John 10:10, 28
Abolish ceremonialism ...Dan 9:27
Complete revelation .....Heb 1:1

Worship of, by:
Old Testament saints ....Josh 5:13-15
Demons................Mark 5:6
Men...................John 9:38
Angels ....Heb 1:6
Disciples...............Luke 24:52
Saints in glory...........Rev 7:9, 10
All ....Phil 2:10, 11

Character of:
Holy ....Luke 1:35
Righteous..............Is 53:11
Just ....Zech 9:9
Guileless...............1Pet 2:22
Sinless 2Cor 5:21
Spotless 1Pet 1:19
Innocent...............Matt 27:4
Meek..................Matt 11:29
Merciful ....Heb 2:17
Humble ....Phil 2:8
Forgiving ....Luke 23:34

Types of:
Adam ....Rom 5:14
Abel ....Heb 12:24
Moses ....Deut 18:15
Passover 1Cor 5:7
Manna ....John 6:32
Brazen serpent ....John 3:14

Other names for:
Adam, the second 1Cor 15:45-47
Advocate 1John 2:1
Almighty ....Rev 19:15
Alpha and Omega ....Rev 21:6
Amen ....Rev 3:14
Ancient of Days.........Dan 7:9
Angel of his presence ....Is 63:9
Anointed above His fellows ....Ps 45:7
Anointed of the Lord ....Ps 2:2
Apostle of our profession.Heb 3:1
Arm of the Lord ....Is 51:9, 10
Author and finisher of our faith..............Heb 12:2
Babe ....Luke 2:16
Beginning and end ......Rev 21:6
Beloved ....Eph 1:6
Beloved of God ....Matt 12:18
Beloved Son ....Mark 1:11
Blessed and only Potentate 1Tim 6:15
Born of God 1John 5:18
Branch ....Zech 3:8
Branch, a righteous ......Jer 23:5
Branch of righteousness ..Jer 33:15
Bread ....John 6:41
Bread of Life ....John 6:35
Bridegroom ....John 3:29
Bright morning star ......Rev 22:16
Captain of salvation .....Heb 2:10
Carpenter..............Mark 6:3
Carpenter's son ....Matt 13:55

Chief corner stone ....Ps 118:22, Mark 12:10
Chief Shepherd..........1Pet 5:4
Child..................Is 9:6
Child Jesus ....Luke 2:27
Chosen of God..........1Pet 2:4
Christ, the ....John 1:41, Acts 9:22
Christ a King ....Luke 23:2
Christ, Jesus ....Rom 8:2
Christ Jesus our Lord ....Rom 8:39
Christ of God, the.......Luke 9:20
Christ, of God, His Chosen One ....Luke 23:35
Christ, the Lord ....Luke 2:11
Christ, the power of God.1Cor 1:24
Christ, the Son of the Blessed ....Mark 14:61
Commander.............Is 55:4
Consolation of Israel.....Luke 2:25
Costly cornerstone ....Is 28:16
Counselor..............Is 9:6
Covenant of the people ..Is 42:6
Dayspring...............Luke 1:78
Day star 2Pet 1:19
Deity...................Col 2:9
Deliverer ....Rom 11:26
Desire of all nations .....Hag 2:7
Diadem.................Is 28:5
Door ....John 10:2
Door of the sheep ....John 10:1
Emmanuel ....Matt 1:23
Ensign of the people.....Is 11:10
Eternal life 1John 5:20
Everlasting Father ....Is 9:6
Faithful and True........Rev 19:11
Faithful witness ....Rev 1:5
Firmly placed foundation .Is 28:16
First-begotten ....Heb 1:6
First-born from the dead .Col 1:18
First-born of the dead ...Rev 1:5
First-born of every creature ....Col 1:15
First-born among many brethren ....Rom 8:29
First fruits 1Cor 15:23
First and last............Rev 22:13
Forerunner..............Heb 6:20
Foundation laid in Zion ..Is 28:16
Friend of publicans and sinners ....Luke 7:34
Glorious Lord ....Is 33:21
God...................John 20:28
God blessed forever .....Rom 9:5
God of Israel ....Is 45:15
God, our Savior 1Tim 2:3
God with us ....Matt 1:23
Good Master............Mark 10:17
Governor ....Matt 2:6
Great God ....Titus 2:13
Great High Priest ....Heb 4:14
Great Shepherd ....Heb 13:20
Guardian of souls 1Pet 2:25
Head, even Christ ....Eph 4:15
Head of all ....Col 2:10
Head of every man 1Cor 11:3
Head of the body, the church ....Col 1:18
Head over all things .....Eph 1:22
Heir of all things ....Heb 1:2
High Priest ....Heb 4:14
His beloved Son.........Col 1:13
Holy One..............1John 2:20
Holy and Righteous One .Acts 3:14
Holy One of God ....Luke 4:34
Holy One of Israel ......Is 37:23
Holy Child.............Acts 4:27
Hope of glory ....Col 1:27
Horn of salvation........Luke 1:69
Husband...............2Cor 11:2
I Am ....John 8:58
Image of God 2Cor 4:4
Image of the Invisible God ....Col 1:15
Jesus ....Luke 1:31
Jesus Christ ....Rom 1:4
Jesus Christ our Lord ....Rom 6:23
Jesus Christ our Savior...Titus 3:6
Jesus of Nazareth........Luke 24:19
Jesus, the Son of God ...Heb 4:14
Jesus, the (supposed) son of Joseph ....Luke 3:23
Judge of Israel ....Mic 5:1
Judge of the quick and the dead ....Acts 10:42
Just man...............Matt 27:19
King ....John 12:13
King eternal 1Tim 1:17
King of glory ....Ps 24:7
King of Israel ....John 12:13
King of kings 1Tim 6:15
King of the Jews ....Matt 27:37
King of Zion ....Zech 9:9
King over all the earth...Zech 14:9
Lamb ....Rev 13:8
Lamb of God ....John 1:36
Leader ....Is 55:4
Life ....John 14:6
Light ....John 1:9
Light of the Gentiles ....Acts 13:47
Light of the World ......John 9:5
Lily of the valleys ....Song 2:1
Lion of the tribe of Judah ....Rev 5:5
Living bread ....John 6:51
Living stone 1Pet 2:4
Lord..................John 21:7
Lord Christ ....Col 3:24
Lord God Almighty .....Rev 4:8
Lord Jesus ....Acts 19:17
Lord Jesus Christ........2Thess 2:1
Lord and Savior Jesus Christ 2Pet 2:20
Lord both of dead and living ....Rom 14:9
Lord of all.............Acts 10:36, Rom 10:12
Lord of glory 1Cor 2:8
Lord of hosts ....Is 54:5
Lord of lords 1Tim 6:15
Lord of Sabbath ....Luke 6:5
Lord our righteousness...Jer 23:6
Lord, your redeemer ....Is 43:14
Man of peace ....Luke 10:6
Man of sorrows ....Is 53:3
Master ....Mark 12:14
Mediator ....Heb 12:24
Messenger of the covenant.............Mal 3:1
Messiah ....John 4:25, 26
Mighty God............Is 9:6
Mighty One of Jacob ....Is 60:16
Minister of the circumcision...........Rom 15:8
Minister of the sanctuary .Heb 8:1, 2
Morning star ....Rev 22:16
Most Mighty ....Ps 45:3
Nazarene ....Matt 2:23
Only begotten of the Father ....John 1:14
Only begotten Son ......John 1:18
Only wise God 1Tim 1:17
Our Passover 1Cor 5:7
Our peace ....Eph 2:14
Physician ....Luke 4:23
Power of God..........1Cor 1:24
Precious cornerstone 1Pet 2:6
Priest.................Heb 5:6
Prince ....Acts 5:31
Prince of life ....Acts 3:15
Prince of peace..........Is 9:6
Prince of the kings of the earth ....Rev 1:5
Prophet...............Deut 18:15, 18
Propitiation ....Rom 3:25
Purifier and refiner ......Mal 3:3
Rabbi ....John 6:25
Rabboni ....John 20:16
Ransom 1Tim 2:6
Redeemer ....Is 59:20
Resurrection and the life .John 11:25
Righteous Judge 2Tim 4:8
Righteous One ....Is 53:11
Rock 1Cor 10:4
Rock of offense ....Rom 9:33
Rod of the stem of Jesse .Is 11:1
Root of David ....Rev 22:16
Root of Jesse ....Is 11:10
Rose of Sharon ....Song 2:1
Ruler in Israel ....Mic 5:2
Salvation ....Luke 2:30
Savior 1Tim 4:10
Savior, Jesus Christ.....2Pet 2:20
Savior, God our ....Titus 1:3
Savior of the world 1John 4:14
Scepter out of Israel .....Num 24:17
Second man............1Cor 15:47
Seed of David..........John 7:42
Seed of the woman ......Gen 3:15
Shepherd ....John 10:11
Shepherd of souls 1Pet 2:25
Shoot of the stem of Jesse ....Is 11:1
Son of the Blessed ......Mark 14:61
Son of David ....Matt 9:27
Son of God ....Rom 1:4
Son of Man ....Acts 7:56
Son of Mary ....Mark 6:3
Son of the Father 2John 3
Son of the Most High....Luke 1:32
Source of eternal salvation ....Heb 5:9
Sower ....Matt 13:3, 37
"Star out of Jacob"......Num 24:17
Stone.................Dan 2:45
Stone rejected..........Luke 20:17
Stone of stumbling ......Rom 9:32, 33
Sun of righteousness .....Mal 4:2
Teacher from God.......John 3:2
Tried stone ....Is 28:16
True vine ....John 15:1
Truth.................John 14:6
Unspeakable gift 2Cor 9:15
Way..................John 14:6
Wonderful ....Is 9:6
Word.................1John 1:1
Word of God ....Rev 19:13
Word of Life..........1John 1:1

[*also* CHRIST'S, CHRISTS]

where *C* should be born ......Matt 2:4
Thou art the *C*, the Son .....Matt 16:16
is your Master, even *C*......Matt 23:8
name, saying I am *C*.........Matt 24:5
there shall arise false *C* .....Matt 24:24
Prophesy unto us, thou *C* .....Matt 26:68
because ye belong to *C* ....Mark 9:41
false *C* and false.............Mark 13:22
Let *C* the King of Israel ......Mark 15:32
had seen the Lord's *C* ....Luke 2:26
Thou art *C* the Son of God ...Luke 4:41
Ought not *C* to have..........Luke 24:26
When *C* cometh, no man .....John 7:27
Shall *C* come out of ....John 7:41
C cometh of the seed of ......John 7:42
confess that he was *C*.........John 9:22
believe that thou art the *C* ....John 11:27
the law that *C* abideth ....John 12:34
raise up *C* to sit on his........Acts 2:30
prophets that *C* should ....Acts 3:18
Samaria, and preached *C*......Acts 8:5
preached *C* in the ....Acts 9:20
C must needs have ....Acts 17:3
That *C* should suffer ....Acts 26:23
in due time *C* died for ....Rom 5:6
were yet sinners *C* died ....Rom 5:8
as *C* was raised up from ......Rom 6:4
the law by the body of *C* .....Rom 7:4
have not the Spirit of *C* ......Rom 8:9
if *C* be in you, the body is ....Rom 8:10
accursed from *C* for my ....Rom 9:3
C is the end of the law for ....Rom 10:4
For even *C* pleased not ....Rom 15:3
the Lord Jesus *C* sake ....Rom 15:30
firstfruits of Achaia unto *C*....Rom 16:5

But we preach *C* crucified 1Cor 1:23
ye are Christ's; and *C* is 1Cor 3:23
for *C* sake, but ye are 1Cor 4:10
called, being free, is *C* 1Cor 7:22
Jesus *C*, by whom are all 1Cor 8:6
under the law to *C*) that 1Cor 9:21
and that rock was *C* 1Cor 10:4
C died for our sins 1Cor 15:3
then is not *C* raised 1Cor 15:16
afterward they that are *C* 1Cor 15:23
C gospel, and a door 2Cor 2:12
we through *C* to God 2Cor 3:4
we have known *C* after 2Cor 5:16
if any man be in *C*, he is 2Cor 5:17
was in *C*, reconciling 2Cor 5:19
in *C* stead, be ye 2Cor 5:20
what concord hath *C* 2Cor 6:15
to himself that he is *C* 2Cor 10:7
again, that, as he is *C* 2Cor 10:7
even so are we *C* 2Cor 10:7
you as a chaste virgin to *C* 2Cor 11:2
in distresses for *C* sake 2Cor 12:10
by the faith of Jesus *C* .... Gal 2:16
I am crucified with *C* .... Gal 2:20
not I, but *C* liveth in me ...... Gal 2:20
C hath redeemed us from ..... Gal 3:13
if ye be *C*, then are ye .... Gal 3:29
heir of God through *C* .... Gal 4:7
in birth again until *C* be ...... Gal 4:19
wherewith *C* hath made .... Gal 5:1
of our Lord Jesus *C* .... Gal 6:14
without *C*, being aliens .... Eph 2:12
C may dwell in your .... Eph 3:17
ye have not so learned *C* ...... Eph 4:20
God for *C* sake hath .... Eph 4:32
C shall give thee light .... Eph 5:14
church is subject unto *C* ...... Eph 5:24
C also loved the church .... Eph 5:25
concerning *C* and the .... Eph 5:32
of your heart, as unto *C* ...... Eph 6:5
indeed preach *C* even .... Phil 1:15
For me to live is *C*, and ...... Phil 1:21
knowledge of *C* Jesus .... Phil 3:8
C which strengtheneth me ..... Phil 4:13
world, and not after *C* .... Col 2:8
C, who is our life, shall ...... Col 3:4
for ye serve the Lord *C* .... Col 3:24
dead in *C* shall rise first 1Thess 4:16
C as a son over his own .... Heb 3:6
C glorified not himself .... Heb 5:5
C being come a high .... Heb 9:11
Jesus *C* the same yesterday .... Heb 13:8
because *C* also suffered 1Pet 2:21
as ye are partakers of *C* 1Pet 4:13
that Jesus is the *C*? 1John 2:22
of our Lord, and of his *C* ..... Rev 11:15
and the power of his *C* .... Rev 12:10

CHRISTIAN ATTRIBUTES

Manifested toward God:
Belief .... Heb 11:6
Holiness .... Heb 12:10, 14
Godliness .... Titus 2:12
Love .... Matt 22:36, 37
Faith .... Mark 11:22
Joy .... Phil 4:4

Manifested toward Christ:
Faith 2Tim 1:12
Worship .... Phil 2:4-11
Obedience 2Thess 1:8
Imitation 1Cor 11:1
Fellowship 1John 1:3

Manifested toward the Holy Spirit:
Walking in .... Gal 5:16
Filled with .... Eph 5:18
Guided by .... John 16:13
Praying in .... Jude 20
Quench not 1Thess 5:19
Taught by .... John 14:26
Living in .... Gal 5:25
Grieve not .... Eph 4:30

Manifested in the world:
Chastity 1Tim 5:22
Contentment .... Heb 13:5
Diligence 1Thess 3:7
Forbearance .... Eph 4:2
Honesty .... Rom 12:17
Industry 1Thess 4:11, 12
Love toward enemies .... Matt 5:44
Peacefulness .... Rom 14:17-19
Temperance 1Cor 9:25
Tolerance .... Rom 14:1-23
Zealous for good deeds .. Titus 2:14

Manifested toward other Christians:
Bearing burdens .... Gal 6:2
Helping the needy ...... Acts 11:14, 30
Fellowship .... Acts 2:42
Brotherly kindness 1Pet 4:7-11
Mutual edification 1Thess 5:11

Manifested as signs of faith:
Spiritual growth 2Pet 3:18
Fruitfulness .... John 15:1-6
Perseverance 1Cor 15:58
Persecution 2Tim 3:9-12
Obedience .... Phil 2:12
Good works .... James 2:14-26

Manifested as internal graces:
Kindness .... Col 3:12, 13
Humility 1Pet 5:5, 6
Gentleness .... James 3:17, 18
Love 1Cor 13:1-13
Self-control .... Gal 5:23
Peace .... Phil 4:7

CHRISTIANITY, A WAY OF LIFE
Founded on Christ 1Cor 3:10, 12
Based on doctrines 1Cor 15:1-4
Designed for all .... Matt 28:18-20
Centers in salvation ..... Acts 4:12
Produces change 1Cor 6:11

CHRISTIANS—*believers in Jesus Christ*
First applied at Antioch .. Acts 11:26
Agrippa almost becomes. . Acts 26:28
Proof of, by suffering 1Pet 4:16

Sometimes referred to as:
Believers .... Acts 5:14
Brethren .... Rom 7:1
Brethren, beloved 1Thess 1:4
Brethren, holy .... Heb 3:1
Children 2Cor 6:13
Children of God .... Rom 8:16
Children of Light .... Eph 5:8
Dear children .... Eph 5:1
Disciples .... Acts 9:25
Elect, the .... Rom 8:33
Friends .... John 15:14
Heirs of God and joint heirs with Christ ...... Rom 8:17
Light in the Lord .... Eph 5:8
Light of the world .... Matt 5:14
Little children 1John 2:1
Members 1Cor 12:18, 25
Priests .... Rev 1:6
Saints .... Rom 8:27
Salt of the earth .... Matt 5:13
Servants of God .... Acts 16:17
Sheep .... John 10:27
Soldier 2Tim 2:4
Sons of God .... Rom 8:14
Strangers 1Pet 2:11
Vessels of honor 2Tim 2:21
Witnesses .... Acts 1:8

CHRISTLIKENESS—*having qualities and character like Jesus Christ*
Model 2Cor 3:18
Motivation 2Cor 5:14-17
Manifestation .... Gal 5:22, 23
Means .... Rom 8:1-17
Mystery .... Phil 3:20, 21

CHRONICLES—*"the word of the days"—two books of the Old Testament*
c of the kings of Israel? 1Kin 14:19
c of the kings of Israel? 2Kin 1:18
c of king David 1Chr 27:24
book of the *c* even until ...... Neh 12:23
book of the *c* before the ...... Esth 2:23

CHRYSOLITE—*gold stone*
In New Jerusalem .... Rev 21:20

CHRYSOPRASUS—*golden-green stone*
In New Jerusalem .... Rev 21:20

CHUB (kŭb)—*a textual variant of Lub (Libya)*
Desolation of, predicted. . Ezek 30:5

CHUN (kŭn)—*"founding"*
A town of Syria 1Chr 18:8
Called Berothah .... Ezek 47:16

CHURCH—*all who have been redeemed; also refers to groups of Christians assembled for worship*

Descriptive of:
Local church .... Acts 8:1
Churches generally ...... Rom 16:4
Believers gathered .... Rom 16:5
The body of believers 1Cor 12:28
Body of Christ .... Eph 1:22, 23

Titled applied to:
The Bride of Christ ...... Eph 5:22-32
The body .... Col 1:18
One body 1Cor 12:18-24
Body of Christ .... Eph 4:12
The Church .... Eph 3:21
Church of the first-born . . Heb 12:23
Church of God 1Cor 1:2
Church of the Living God 1Tim 3:15
Churches of Christ ...... Rom 16:16
Churches of the Gentiles . Rom 16:4
City of God .... Heb 12:22
Flock .... Acts 20:28
Flock of God 1Pet 5:2
God's building 1Cor 3:9
God's husbandry 1Cor 3:9
Habitation of God .... Eph 2:22
Household of God .... Eph 2:19
Israel of God .... Gal 6:16
Jerusalem .... Gal 4:26
Kingdom .... Heb 12:28
Kingdom of God's dear Son .... Col 1:13
Lamb's wife .... Rev 19:7
Mount Zion .... Heb 12:22
People of God 1Pet 2:10
Spiritual house 1Pet 2:5
Temple of God 1Cor 3:16

Relation to Christ:
Saved by .... Eph 5:25-29
Purchased by .... Acts 20:28
Sanctified by .... Eph 5:26, 27
Founded on .... Eph 2:19, 20
Built by .... Matt 16:18
Loved by .... Eph 5:25
Subject to .... Rom 7:4

Members of:
Added by faith .... Acts 2:41
Added by the Lord ...... Acts 2:47
Baptized into one Spirit . . 1Cor 12:13
Edified by the Word ..... Eph 4:15, 16
Persecuted .... Acts 8:1-3
Disciplined .... Matt 18:15-17
Worship .... Acts 20:7
Fellowship together ...... Acts 2:42-46
Urged to attend .... Heb 10:25
Subject to pastoral oversight 1Pet 5:1-3
Unified in Christ .... Gal 3:28

Organization of:
Under bishops 1Tim 3:1-7
Function of deacons ..... Acts 6:3-6
Place of evangelists ...... Eph 4:11
Official assemblies .... Acts 15:1-31
Function of the presbytery 1Tim 4:14

Mission of:
Evangelize the world .... Matt 28:18-20
Guard the truth 2Tim 2:1-2
Edify the saints .... Eph 4:11-15
Discipline unruly 2Cor 13:1-10

Local, examples of:
Antioch ....Acts 11:26
Asia 1Cor 16:19
Rev 1:11
Babylon 1Pet 5:13
Caesarea...............Acts 18:22
Cenchrea ....Rom 16:1
Colossae ....Col 1:2
Corinth 1Cor 1:2
Ephesus ....Acts 20:17
Galatia ....Gal 1:2
Jerusalem ....Acts 8:1
Judea ....Gal 1:22
Laodicea...............Col 4:15
Macedonia 2Cor 8:1
Pergamos ....Rev 2:12
Philadelphia............Rev 3:7
Philippi ....Phil 1:1
Rome ....Rom 1:7
Sardis ....Rev 3:1
Smyrna ....Rev 2:8
Thyatira ....Rev 2:18
Thessalonica 1Thess 1:1

[*also* CHURCHES]
tell it unto the *c*.............Matt 18:17
he neglect to hear the *c*.......Matt 18:17
Lord added to the *c* ....Acts 2:47
fear came upon all the *c* ......Acts 5:11
he, that was in the *c* in ....Acts 7:38
Then had the *c* rest..........Acts 9:31
the *c* which was in...........Acts 11:22
themselves with the *c* ....Acts 11:26
to vex certain of the *c* ....Acts 12:1
Now there were in the *c* ......Acts 13:1
them elders in every *c* ....Acts 14:23
and had gathered the *c* ....Acts 14:27
confirming the *c*.............Acts 15:41
so were the *c* established ......Acts 16:5
up, and saluted the *c* ....Acts 18:22
neither robbers of *c* ....Acts 19:37
called the elders of the *c* ......Acts 20:17
is a servant of the *c* ....Rom 16:1
every where in every *c*........1Cor 4:17
least esteemed in the *c*........1Cor 6:4
And so ordain I in all *c*.......1Cor 7:17
nor to the *c* of God 1Cor 10:32
neither the *c* of God 1Cor 11:16
come together in the *c*........1Cor 11:18
edifieth the *c*...............1Cor 14:4
as in all *c* of the.............1Cor 14:33
keep silence in the *c*.........1Cor 14:34
I persecuted the *c* of God 1Cor 15:9
given order to the *c* 1Cor 16:1
with the *c* that is in their......1Cor 16:19
The *c* of Asia salute you 1Cor 16:19
unto the *c* of God which is 2Cor 1:1
bestowed on the *c* of 2Cor 8:1
throughout all the *c* 2Cor 8:18
also chosen of the *c* 2Cor 8:19
messengers of the *c*...........2Cor 8:23
to them, and before the *c* 2Cor 8:24
I robbed other *c* taking 2Cor 11:8
the care of all the *c* 2Cor 11:28
ye were inferior to other *c* 2Cor 12:13
unto the *c* of Galatia ....Gal 1:2
I persecuted the *c* of God .....Gal 1:13
unto the *c* of Judaea..........Gal 1:22
be known by the *c* ....Eph 3:10
zeal, persecuting the *c* ....Phil 3:6
no *c* communicated with ......Phil 4:15
sake, which is the *c*...........Col 1:24
and the *c* which is in ....Col 4:15
it be read also in the *c*........Col 4:16
unto the *c* of the 1Thess 1:1
followers of the *c* of God 1Thess 2:14
unto the *c* of the 2Thess 1:1
glory in you in the *c*..........2Thess 1:4
to the *c* in thy house ....Philem 2
in the midst of the *c*..........Heb 2:12
for the elders of the *c* ....James 5:14
c that is at Babylon...........1Pet 5:13
charity before the *c*...........3John 6
I wrote unto the *c* but 3John 9
them out of the *c*.............3John 10
John to the seven *c*...........Rev 1:4
send it unto the seven *c*.......Rev 1:11
angels of the seven *c* ....Rev 1:20
sawest are the seven *c* ....Rev 1:20
the angel of the *c* ....Rev 2:1
Spirit saith unto the *c*.........Rev 2:7
the angel of the *c* in ....Rev 2:8
Spirit saith unto the *c*.........Rev 2:11
to the angel of the *c* in ....Rev 2:12
Spirit saith unto the *c*.........Rev 2:17
the angel of the *c* in ....Rev 2:18
all the *c* shall know ....Rev 2:23
Spirit saith unto the *c*.........Rev 2:29
the angel of the *c* in ....Rev 3:1
saith unto the *c* ....Rev 3:6
the angel of the *c* in ....Rev 3:7
the angel of the *c* of the ......Rev 3:14
these things in the *c* ....Rev 22:16

CHURCH SLEEPER
Falls from window during
Paul's sermon ....Acts 20:7-12

CHURL—*a rude, surly person*
Nabal 1Sam 25:3
Descriptive of the
fraudulent ....Is 32:5, 7

CHUSAN-RISHATHAIM (kū'shăn-rĭsh-ă-thā'ĭm)—*"man of Cush; he of twofold crime"*
A Mesopotamian king;
oppressed Israel ....Judg 3:8
Othniel delivers Israel
from ....Judg 3:9, 10

CHUZA (kū'zä)—*"seer"*
Herod's steward ....Luke 8:3

CIELDED—*See* CEILED

CIELING—*See* CEILING

CILICIA (sĭ-lĭsh'ĭ-ä)—*"rolling"—a province of Asia Minor*
Paul's country ....Acts 21:39
Students from, argued
with Stephen..........Acts 6:9
Paul labors in ....Gal 1:21

and Syria and *C* ....Acts 15:23
through Syria and *C* ....Acts 15:41
born in Tarsus, a city in *C* ....Acts 22:3
that he was of *C* ....Acts 23:34
sailed over the sea of *C* ....Acts 27:5

CINNAMON—*a laurel-like spicy plant*
Used in holy oil ....Ex 30:23
A perfume ....Prov 7:17
In Babylon's trade ....Rev 18:13
Figurative of a lover .....Song 4:12, 14

CIRCLE—*a ring or round object*
Used of the earth ....Is 40:22

CIRCUIT—*circle; regular course*
Judge's itinerary 1Sam 7:16
Sun's orbit ....Ps 19:6

[*also* CIRCUITS]
he walketh in the *c* of ....Job 22:14

CIRCUMCISION—*rite in which foreskin of male infant is removed*
The physical rite:
Instituted by God ....Gen 17:10-14
A seal of righteousness ..Rom 2:25-29
Performed on the eighth
day...................Luke 1:59
Child named when
performed ....Luke 1:59
Allowed right to Passover.Ex 12:48
Neglect of, punished .....Ex 4:24
Neglected during
wilderness ....Josh 5:7
A sign of covenant
relation ....Rom 4:11
Necessity of:
Asserted in old
dispensation..........Gen 17:10-14
Abolished by the Gospel .Gal 5:1-4
Eph 2:11, 15
Avails nothing ....Gal 5:6
Col 3:11
Avowed by false teachers.Acts 15:1
Acclaimed a yoke ....Acts 15:10
Abrogated by apostles ...Acts 15:5-29
1Cor 7:18, 19
Spiritual significance of:
Regeneration.......... { Deut 10:16; Deut 30:6; Jer 4:4 }
The true Jew (Christian)..Rom 2:29
The Christian ....Phil 3:3
Col 2:11

[*also* CIRCUMCISE, CIRCUMCISED, CIRCUMCISING]
and *c* the flesh of their........Gen 17:23
was *c* in the flesh of his.......Gen 17:24
when he was *c* in the ....Gen 17:25
day was Abraham *c* ....Gen 17:26
the stranger, were *c* ....Gen 17:27
Abraham *c* his son ....Gen 21:4
male of you be *c* ....Gen 34:15
hearken unto us, to be *c* ......Gen 34:17
male among us be *c* ....Gen 34:22
as they are *c* ....Gen 34:22
and every male was *c* ....Gen 34:24
art, because of the *c* ....Ex 4:26
when thou hast *c* him ....Ex 12:44
his foreskin shall be *c*.........Lev 12:3
C therefore the foreskin.......Deut 10:16
Lord thy God will *c* ....Deut 30:6
c again the children of ....Josh 5:2
c the children of Israel ....Josh 5:3
cause why Joshua did *c* ....Josh 5:4
that came out were *c* ....Josh 5:5
them they had not *c* ....Josh 5:5
they had done *c* all the ....Josh 5:8
all them which are *c* ....Jer 9:25
accomplished for the *c* ....Luke 2:21
gave unto you *c* ....John 7:22
ye on the sabbath day *c*.......John 7:22
sabbath day receive *c* ....John 7:23
the covenant of *c*.............Acts 7:8
Isaac, and *c* him the ....Acts 7:8
they of the *c* which ....Acts 10:45
they that were of the *c*........Acts 11:2
be *c* after the manner..........Acts 15:1
and took and *c* him............Acts 16:3
they ought not to *c* ....Acts 21:21
what profit is there of *c*?......Rom 3:1
justify the *c* by faith ....Rom 3:30
then upon the *c* ....Rom 4:9
when he was in *c*, or in ....Rom 4:10
Not in *c*, but in ....Rom 4:10
the father of *c* to them........Rom 4:12
who are not of the *c*..........Rom 4:12
a minister of the *c* for ....Rom 15:8
was compelled to be *c* ....Gal 2:3
gospel of the *c* was ....Gal 2:7
apostleship of the *c* ....Gal 2:8
and they unto the *c*...........Gal 2:9
which were of the *c* ....Gal 2:12
if I yet preach *c*, why ....Gal 5:11
constrain you to be *c* ....Gal 6:12
themselves who are *c* ....Gal 6:13
desire to have you *c* ....Gal 6:13
neither *c* availeth any ....Gal 6:15
C the eighth day, of ....Phil 3:5
who are of the *c* ....Col 4:11
specially they of the *c*.........Titus 1:10

CIRCUMSPECT—*prudent; carefully considering all courses of action*

[*also* CIRCUMSPECTLY]
I have said unto you be *c* .....Ex 23:13
ye walk *c* not as fools.........Eph 5:15

CIRCUMSTANCES—*the situation; limitations*
Relationship to Christian:
Work for good ....Rom 8:28
Produce perseverance ....Rom 5:3

Not cause for anxiety . . . . Phil 4:6
Test and purify 1Pet 1:5-7
To be met with thanksgiving . . . . Eph 5:20; Phil 4:6
Can be overcome . . . . Phil 4:11-13

Examples, victory over:
Moses . . . . Ex 14:10-31
Joshua . . . . Josh 6:8-21
Shamgar . . . . Judg 3:31
Gideon . . . . Judg 7:19-23
Hannah 1Sam 1:9-19
David 1Sam 17:40-51
Widow of Zarephath 1Kin 17:8-16
Hezekiah 2Kin 20:1-11
Peter . . . . Acts 12:5-17
Paul . . . . Acts 14:19-20; Acts 16:19-26

CIS (sĭs)—*Greek form of Kish, father of King Saul*
Saul the son of *C* . . . . Acts 13:21

CISTERN—*an underground reservoir for water*

Literal uses of:
Water 2Kin 18:31
Imprisonment (when empty) . . . . Jer 38:6

Figurative uses of:
Wife . . . . Prov 5:15
Heart . . . . Eccl 12:6
False religion . . . . Jer 2:13

Kinds of:
Family cisterns . . . . Is 36:16
Garden ponds . . . . Eccl 2:6

CITIES, LEVITICAL
Forty-eight . . . . Num 35:7
Six designed for refuge . . . Deut 19:1-13

CITIES OF REFUGE
Given to Levites . . . . Num 35:6
For the manslayer . . . . Num 35:11

CITIES OF THE MOUNTAINS
Avoided by Israel . . . . Deut 2:37

CITIES OF THE PLAIN
Admah . . . . Gen 14:8
Bela . . . . Gen 14:2
Gomorrah . . . . Gen 19:28; Jude 7
Sodom . . . . Gen 19:28-29
Zeboiim . . . . Gen 14:8
Dibon, Bamoth-baal, Beth-baal-meon . . . . Josh 13:17

CITIES OF THE VALLEY
Restored . . . . Jer 32:44
Taken by Israel . . . . Deut 3:8, 10

CITIZEN—*a resident; a freeman; a member of a state*

Kinds of:
Hebrew . . . . Eph 2:12
Roman . . . . Acts 21:39
Spiritual . . . . Phil 3:20
Christian (see below)

Duties of Christian citizens:
Be subject to rulers . . . . . . Rom 13:1-7
Pray for rulers 1Tim 2:1, 2
Honor rulers 1Pet 2:17
Seek peace . . . . Jer 29:7
Pay taxes . . . . Matt 22:21
Obey God first . . . . Acts 5:27-29
Love one's nation . . . . Neh 2:3
Live righteously 1Pet 3:8-17

[*also* CITIZENS]
to a *c* of that country . . . . Luke 15:15
But his *c* hated him . . . . Luke 19:14
a *c* of no mean city . . . . Acts 21:39

CITY—*large organized community*

Features regarding:
Earliest . . . . Gen 4:17
Walled . . . . Lev 25:29-31; Deut 3:5
Often built on hills . . . . . . Matt 5:14
Gates guarded . . . . Acts 9:24
Guard posted . . . . 2Kin 7:10; Neh 13:19
Difficult to attack . . . . Prov 16:32
Business at gate . . . . Gen 23:10; Ruth 4:1-11

Descriptions of:
Sodom—wicked . . . . Gen 13:13
Jerusalem—like Sodom . . Is 1:10
Nineveh—repentant . . . . . Jon 3:5-10
Capernaum—arrogant . . . Matt 11:23
Athens—idolatrous . . . . . . Acts 17:16

[*also* CITIES]
Lot dwelled in the *c* . . . . Gen 13:12
overthrew those *c* and . . . . Gen 19:25
the inhabitants of the *c* . . . . Gen 19:25
them keep food in the *c* . . . . . . Gen 41:35
up the food in the *c* . . . . Gen 41:48
removed them to *c* from . . . . . . Gen 47:21
Pharaoh treasure *c* . . . . Ex 1:11
the houses of the *c* . . . . Lev 25:32
houses of the *c* of the . . . . Lev 25:33
the suburbs of their *c* . . . . Lev 25:34
together within your *c* . . . . Lev 26:25
I will make your *c* . . . . Lev 26:31
desolate, and your *c* . . . . Lev 26:33
what *c* they be that . . . . Num 13:19
and the *c* are walled . . . . Num 13:28
utterly destroy their *c* . . . . Num 21:2
them and their *c* . . . . Num 21:3
Israel took all these *c* . . . . Num 21:25
dwelt in all the *c* of . . . . Num 21:25
burnt all their *c* wherein . . . . . Num 31:10
cattle, and *c* for our . . . . Num 32:16
dwell in the fenced *c* . . . . Num 32:17
Build you *c* for your . . . . Num 32:24
shall be there in the *c* . . . . Num 32:26
with the *c* thereof in . . . . Num 32:33
the *c* of the country . . . . Num 32:33
Beth-haran, fenced *c* . . . . Num 32:36
unto the *c* which they . . . . Num 32:38
of their possessions *c* . . . . Num 35:2
suburbs for the *c* . . . . Num 35:2
the *c* shall they have to . . . . . . Num 35:3
the suburbs of the *c* . . . . Num 35:4
the suburbs of the *c* . . . . Num 35:5
And the *c* which ye . . . . Num 35:8
give of his *c* unto the . . . . Num 35:8
shall be unto you *c* . . . . Num 35:12
And of these *c* which . . . . Num 35:13
six *c* shall ye have for . . . . Num 35:13
give three *c* on this . . . . Num 35:14
three *c* shall ye give . . . . Num 35:14
which shall be *c* of refuge . . . . . Num 35:14
These six *c* shall be a . . . . Num 35:15
into what *c* we shall . . . . Deut 1:22
the *c* are great and walled . . . . . Deut 1:28
took all his *c* at that time . . . . . Deut 2:34
the spoil of the *c* which . . . . Deut 2:35
we took all his *c* . . . . Deut 3:4
them, threescore *c* . . . . Deut 3:4
spoil of the *c*, we took . . . . Deut 3:7
Gilead, and the *c* . . . . Deut 3:12
abide in your *c* which . . . . Deut 3:19
Moses severed three *c* . . . . Deut 4:41
unto one of these *c* . . . . Deut 4:42
c great and fenced up to . . . . . . Deut 9:1
say in one of thy *c* . . . . Deut 13:12
do unto all the *c* . . . . Deut 20:15
are not of the *c* of these . . . . . . Deut 20:15
But of the *c* of these people . . . Deut 20:16
measure unto the *c* . . . . Deut 21:2
came unto their *c* . . . . Josh 9:17
c were Gibeon and . . . . Josh 9:17
as one of the royal *c* . . . . Josh 10:2
not to enter into their *c* . . . . Josh 10:19
entered into fenced *c* . . . . Josh 10:20
all the *c* thereof, and all . . . . . . Josh 10:37
and all the *c* . . . . Josh 10:39
all the *c* of those kings . . . . Josh 11:12
c of Sihon king of the . . . . Josh 13:10
c to dwell in, with . . . . Josh 14:4
out to the *c* of mount . . . . Josh 15:9
uttermost *c* of the tribe . . . . Josh 15:21
separate *c* for the . . . . Josh 16:9
these *c* of Ephraim . . . . Josh 17:9
described it by *c* . . . . Josh 18:9
thirteen *c* with their . . . . Josh 19:6
Appoint out for you *c* . . . . Josh 20:2
to give us *c* to dwell in . . . . Josh 21:2
they had thirty *c* which . . . . Judg 10:4
the *c* that be along by . . . . Judg 11:26
buried in one of the *c* . . . . Judg 12:7
together out of the *c* . . . . Judg 20:14
that time out of the *c* . . . . Judg 20:15
came out of the *c* . . . . Judg 20:42
set on fire all the *c* . . . . Judg 20:48
number of all the *c* 1Sam 6:18
the *c* which the 1Sam 7:14
came out of all *c* 1Sam 18:6
the *c* of the Jerahmeelites 1Sam 30:29
they forsook the *c* 1Sam 31:7
go up into any of the *c* 2Sam 2:1
and from Berothai, *c* 2Sam 8:8
people, and for the *c* 2Sam 10:12
the *c* of the children 2Sam 12:31
he get him fenced *c* 2Sam 20:6
all the *c* of the Hivites 2Sam 24:7
threescore great *c* with 1Kin 4:13
in the land of their *c* 1Kin 8:37
gave Hiram twenty *c* 1Kin 9:11
Tyre to see the *c* 1Kin 9:12
he bestowed in the *c* 1Kin 10:26
which dwelt in the *c* 1Kin 12:17
which are in the *c* 1Kin 13:32
he had against the *c* 1Kin 15:20
The *c*, which my father 1Kin 20:34
all the *c* that he built 1Kin 22:39
they beat down the *c* 2Kin 3:25
son of Hazael the *c* 2Kin 13:25
Gozan, and in the *c* 2Kin 17:6
places in all their *c* 2Kin 17:9
placed them in the *c* 2Kin 17:24
and dwelt in the *c* 2Kin 17:24
and placed in the *c* of 2Kin 17:26
every nation in their *c* 2Kin 17:29
and in the *c* of the Medes 2Kin 18:11
to lay waste fenced *c* 2Kin 19:25
the high places in the *c* 2Kin 23:5
three and twenty *c* 1Chr 2:22
These were their *c* unto 1Chr 4:31
Aaron they gave the *c* 1Chr 6:57
possessions in their *c* 1Chr 9:2
they forsook their *c*, and 1Chr 10:7
which are in their *c* 1Chr 13:2
and from Chun, *c* of 1Chr 18:8
together from their *c* 1Chr 19:7
David with all the *c* 1Chr 20:3
the fields, in the *c*, and 1Chr 27:25
placed in the chariot *c* 2Chr 1:14
besiege them in the *c* 2Chr 6:28
c which Huram had 2Chr 8:2
in the chariot *c* 2Chr 9:25
that dwelt in the *c* of 2Chr 10:17
Jerusalem, and built *c* 2Chr 11:5
he took the fenced *c* 2Chr 12:4
and took *c* from him 2Chr 13:19
out of all the *c* of Judah 2Chr 14:5
built fenced *c* in Judah 2Chr 14:6
Let us build these *c* 2Chr 14:7
smote all the *c* round 2Chr 14:14
they spoiled all the *c* 2Chr 14:14
c which he had taken 2Chr 15:8
armies against the *c* 2Chr 16:4
in all the fenced *c* 2Chr 17:2
fenced *c* of Judah 2Chr 19:5
out of all the *c* of Judah 2Chr 20:4
with fenced *c* in 2Chr 21:3
Levites out of all the *c* 2Chr 23:2
Go out unto the *c* of 2Chr 24:5
and built *c* about Ashdod 2Chr 26:6
he built *c* in the mountains 2Chr 27:4
invaded the *c* of the 2Chr 28:18
went out to the *c* of Judah 2Chr 31:1
into their own *c* 2Chr 31:1
that dwelt in the *c* 2Chr 31:6
in the *c* of the priests 2Chr 31:15
the suburbs of their *c* 2Chr 31:19
against the fenced *c* 2Chr 32:1

war in all the fenced *c* 2Chr 33:14
so did he in the *c* of..........2Chr 34:6
dwelt in their *c*...............Ezra 2:70
and all Israel in their *c*........Ezra 2:70
Israel were in the *c*............Ezra 3:1
set in the *c* of Samaria ....Ezra 4:10
strange wives in our *c*.........Ezra 10:14
Israel, dwelt in their *c* ....Neh 7:73
proclaim in all their *c*.........Neh 8:15
took strong *c* and a fat........Neh 9:25
tithes in all the *c* of ....Neh 10:37
to dwell in other *c*............Neh 11:1
of the fields of the *c* ....Neh 12:44
together in their *c* ....Esth 9:2
dwelleth in desolate *c* ....Job 15:28
thou hast destroyed *c* ....Ps 9:6
and will build the *c*...........Ps 69:35
c are burned with fire.........Is 1:7
c be wasted without ....Is 6:11
and destroyed the *c*............Is 14:17
The *c* of Aroer are forsaken...Is 17:2
hath despised the *c* ....Is 33:8
all the defenced *c* ....Is 36:1
be to lay waste defenced *c* ....Is 37:26
say unto the *c* of Judah ....Is 40:9
wilderness and the *c* ....Is 42:11
and to the *c* of Judah ....Is 44:26
desolate *c* to be inhabited .....Is 54:3
repair the waste *c* ....Is 61:4
and against all the *c* ....Jer 1:15
c are burned without ....Jer 2:15
the number of thy *c* ....Jer 2:28
go into the defenced *c* ....Jer 4:5
c shall be laid waste ....Jer 4:7
their voice against the *c*.......Jer 4:16
c thereof were broken ....Jer 4:26
watch over their *c* ....Jer 5:6
what they do in the *c*...........Jer 7:17
to cease from the *c* of ....Jer 7:34
into the defenced *c* ....Jer 8:14
make the *c* of Judah ....Jer 9:11
to make the *c* of Judah ....Jer 10:22
all these words in the *c* ....Jer 11:6
shall the *c* of Judah...........Jer 11:12
number of thy *c* were ....Jer 11:13
c of the south shall be ....Jer 13:19
shall come from the *c*..........Jer 17:26
the *c* which the Lord ....Jer 20:16
and *c* which are not ....Jer 22:6
Jerusalem, and the *c*...........Jer 25:18
speak unto all the *c* ....Jer 26:2
turn again to these thy *c* ......Jer 31:21
c of Judah and in the ....Jer 33:10
and against all the *c* ....Jer 34:1
come out of their *c*............Jer 36:6
the *c* of Judah unto............Jer 36:9
governor over the *c*............Jer 40:5
in your *c* that ye have ....Jer 40:10
upon all the *c* of Judah ....Jer 44:2
was kindled in the *c* ....Jer 44:6
our princes, in the *c* ....Jer 44:17
ye burned in the *c*.............Jer 44:21
for the *c* thereof shall.........Jer 48:9
gone up out of her *c*...........Jer 48:15
all the *c* of the land of ....Jer 48:24
people dwell in his *c*? ....Jer 49:1
the *c* thereof shall be ....Jer 49:13
and the neighbor *c* ....Jer 49:18
kindle a fire in his *c* ....Jer 50:32
c are a desolation, a dry ....Jer 51:43
and the maids in the *c* ....Lam 5:11
the *c* shall be laid waste.......Ezek 6:6
And the *c* that are ....Ezek 12:20
laid waste their *c* ....Ezek 19:7
of Moab from the *c* ....Ezek 25:9
his *c* which are on ....Ezek 25:9
like the *c* that are ....Ezek 26:19
are desolate and her *c* ....Ezek 29:12
among the *c* that are ....Ezek 29:12
and her *c* shall be in...........Ezek 30:7
of the *c* that are wasted ....Ezek 30:7
and these *c* shall go ....Ezek 30:17
I will lay thy *c* waste ....Ezek 35:4
and to the *c* that are...........Ezek 36:4
in the *c* of Israel shall ....Ezek 39:9
the most fenced *c* ....Dan 11:15
multiplied fenced *c* ....Hos 8:14
send a fire upon his *c*..........Hos 8:14
shall abide on his *c* ....Hos 11:6
save thee in all thy *c*? ....Hos 13:10
teeth in all your *c* ....Amos 4:6
build the waste *c* ....Amos 9:14
shall possess the *c* of ....Obad 20
I will cut off the *c* ....Mic 5:11
from the fortified *c* ....Mic 7:12
against the fenced *c* ....Zeph 1:16
their *c* are destroyed............Zeph 3:6
Jerusalem and on the *c* ....Zech 1:12
prosperity, and the *c*............Zech 7:7
inhabitants of many *c* ....Zech 8:20
went about all the *c* ....Matt 9:35
over the *c* of Israel, till ....Matt 10:23
to preach in their *c* ....Matt 11:1
on foot out of the *c* ....Matt 14:13
thither out of all *c* ....Mark 6:33
of God to other *c* ....Luke 4:43
went through the *c* ....Luke 13:22
authority over ten *c* ....Luke 19:17
out of the *c* round about.........Acts 5:16
he preached in all the *c*.........Acts 8:40
Lystra and Derbe, *c* of...........Acts 14:6
through the *c*, they ....Acts 16:4
them even unto strange *c* ....Acts 26:11
c of Sodom and 2Pet 2:6
parts, and the *c* of the ....Rev 16:19

CITY BUILDER
Cain builds first ....Gen 4:17
Woe to, who uses bloodshed ....Hab 2:12

CITY, HOLY
Applied to Jerusalem ....Dan 9:24
Rev 11:2
Prophecy concerning .....Joel 3:17
Clothed with beautiful garments ....Is 52:1
New Jerusalem ....Rev 21:2

CITY OF DAVID
Applied to the castle of Zion 1Chr 11:5
Taken by David from Jebusites.............1Chr 11:4-8
Ark brought to..........1Chr 15:1-29
Bethelehem called ....Luke 2:4

CITY OF DESTRUCTION
Prophecy concerning an Egyptian city..........Is 19:18

CITY OF GOD
Prophetic description of Zion ....Ps 48:1-14
Dwelling place of God ...Ps 46:4, 5
Sought by the saints .....Heb 11:9, 10, 16
Descriptive of the heavenly Jerusalem ....Rev 21:2

CITY OF MOAB
Where Balak met Balaam.Num 22:36

CITY OF PALM TREES
Seen by Moses ....Deut 34:1-3
Occupied by Kenites.....Judg 1:16
Captured by Eglon ......Judg 3:12-14

CITY OF SALT
Near the Dead Sea ......Josh 15:62

CITY OF WATERS
Applied to Rabbah 2Sam 12:26, 27

CIVIL—*public*

Righteousness
Principle of ....Prov 14:34
Precepts of.............Prov 14:34
Practice of ....Zech 8:16, 17
Perversion of...........Mic 4:2
Service ....Mic 7:1-4

1. ***Characteristics of:***
Loyalty ....Neh 2:3
Industry ....Gen 41:37-57
Esteem ....Esth 10:3

2. ***Examples of:***
Joseph..................Gen 39:1-6
Daniel..................Dan 1:17-21
Mordecai ....Esth 8:1, 2, 9
Nehemiah...............Neh 2:1-8

Authority:
Obedience to commanded.Eccl 8:2-7
Rom 13:1-7
Submit for Christ's sake ..1Pet 2:13-15

CIVILITY—*good breeding; courtesy*
Shown by Joseph ....Gen 47:1-10
Taught by Christ ....Luke 14:8-10
Shown by Timothy ......Phil 2:19-23
Shown by Gaius 3John 1-6

CLAMOR—*confused din or outcry*

[*also* CLAMOROUS]
foolish woman is *c*; she is .....Prov 9:13
anger, and *c*, and evil.........Eph 4:31

CLAP—*to strike one's palms together*

[*also* CLAPPED, CLAPPETH]
and they *c* their hands 2Kin 11:12
Men shall *c* their hands ....Job 27:23
he *c* his hands among ....Job 34:37
O *c* your hands, all ye ....Ps 47:1
Let the floods *c* their hands ...Ps 98:8
of the field shall *c* ....Is 55:12
pass by *c* their hands ....Lam 2:15
thou hast *c* thine hands ....Ezek 25:6
shall *c* the hands ....Nah 3:19

CLASS DISTINCTION
Egyptians—against Hebrews..............Gen 43:32
Haman—against Hebrews.Esth 3:8, 9
Jews—against Samaritans .John 4:9
Jews—against Gentiles ...Acts 22:12, 22
Forbidden ....Ex 12:48, 49

CLAUDA (klô'dä)—*"lamentable"*
Small island southeast of Crete.................Acts 27:16

CLAUDIA (klô'dĭ-ä)—*"lame"*
Disciple at Rome 2Tim 4:21

CLAUDIUS (klô'dĭ-ŭs)—*"lame ruler"—a Roman emperor (reigned 41-54 A.D.)*
pass in the days of *C* ....Acts 11:28
C had commanded all.........Acts 18:2
C Lysias unto the.............Acts 23:26

CLAUDIUS LYSIAS (klô'dĭ-ŭs lĭs'ĭ-äs)—*"lame dissolution"*
Roman commander who protected Paul ....Acts 24:22-24

CLAWS—*hooked paw or foot*
the cleft into two *c* ....Deut 14:6
his nails like birds *c* ....Dan 4:33
tear their *c* in pieces ....Zech 11:16

CLAY—*earth that is pliable when moist but hard when fired*

Uses of:
Making bricks 2Sam 12:31
Making pottery..........Is 41:25
Sealing ....Job 38:14
Miracle ....John 9:6, 15

Figurative of:
Man's weakness ....Is 64:8
Unstable kingdom ....Dan 2:33-35, 42
Trouble.................Ps 40:2
Wealth ....Hab 2:6

king cast them in the *c*........1Kin 7:46
the *c* ground between 2Chr 4:17
dwell in houses of *c* ....Job 4:19
hast made me as the *c* ....Job 10:9
bodies to bodies of *c* ....Job 13:12
raiment as the *c* ....Job 27:16
formed out of the *c*...........Job 33:6
as the potter's *c* ....Is 29:16
c say to him that ....Is 45:9
that he made of *c* ....Jer 18:4

them in the *c* in the ....Jer 43:9
go into *c*, and tread ....Nah 3:14
potter power over the *c* ....Rom 9:21

CLEAN—*pure; innocent*

Used physically:
Outward purity..........Matt 23:26

Used ceremonially of:
Clean animals...........Gen 7:2
Freedom from defilement.Luke 5:14, 15

Used spiritually of:
Men's nature...........Job 9:30, 31
Repentance.............Gen 35:2
Regeneration...........Ezek 36:25
Sanctification..........Ps 24:4
Glorification...........Rev 19:8, 14

c beast and of every *c* ....Gen 8:20
c a place where the..........Lev 4:12
the camp unto a *c*...........Lev 6:11
all that be *c* shall eat ....Lev 7:19
between unclean and *c*........Lev 10:10
of water shall be *c*...........Lev 11:36
unclean and the *c* ....Lev 11:47
for her and she shall be *c* .....Lev 12:8
shall pronounce him *c* ....Lev 13:6
two birds alive and *c* ....Lev 14:4
spit upon him that is *c*........Lev 15:8
ye may be *c* from all ....Lev 16:30
then shall he be *c* ....Lev 17:15
between *c* beasts and ....Lev 20:25
unclean fowls and *c*...........Lev 20:25
things until he be *c* ....Lev 22:4
shalt not make *c* ....Lev 23:22
not defiled but be *c* ....Num 5:28
and so make themselves *c*.....Num 8:7
But the man that is *c* ....Num 9:13
every one that is *c* in ....Num 18:11
a man that is *c* shall ....Num 19:9
without the camp in a *c*......Num 19:9
fire and it shall be *c*..........Num 31:23
the unclean and the *c*.........Deut 12:15
all *c* birds ye shall eat ....Deut 14:11
unclean and the *c* person......Deut 15:22
not *c* by reason of............Deut 23:10
people were passed *c* ....Josh 3:17
people were *c* passed ....Josh 4:1
c; surely he is not *c* 1Sam 20:26
and thou shalt be *c*............2Kin 5:10
every one that was not *c*......2Chr 30:17
is pure, and I am *c*...........Job 11:4
Who can bring a *c* thing ......Job 14:4
that he should be *c*? ....Job 15:14
he that hath *c* hands..........Job 17:9
how can he be *c* that ....Job 25:4
I am *c* without ....Job 33:9
The fear of the Lord is *c*......Ps 19:9
He that hath *c* hands ....Ps 24:4
and I shall be *c* ....Ps 51:7
such as are of a *c* ....Ps 73:1
Is his mercy *c* gone for ....Ps 77:8
oxen are, the crib is *c* ....Prov 14:4
ways of a man are *c* in........Prov 16:2
I have made my heart *c*.......Prov 20:9
to the good and to the *c* ......Eccl 9:2
Wash you, make you *c*........Is 1:16
down, the earth is *c*...........Is 24:19
that there is no place *c* ....Is 28:8
the ground shall eat *c*.........Is 30;24
bring an offering in a *c* ....Is 66:20
wilt thou not be made *c*? .....Jer 13:27
the unclean and the *c*.........Ezek 22:26
the unclean and the *c*.........Ezek 44:23
he hath made it *c* bare........Joel 1:7
his arm shall be *c* dried ....Zech 11:17
thou canst make me *c* ....Matt 8:2
I will; be thou *c*..............Matt 8:3
he wrapped it in a *c* ....Matt 27:59
thou canst make me *c* ....Mark 1:40
thou canst make me *c* ....Luke 5:12
I will; be thou *c*.............Luke 5:13
ye Pharisees make *c* ....Luke 11:39
behold all things are *c* ....Luke 11:41
but is *c* every whit............John 13:10
and ye are *c* but not all ......John 13:10
ye are *c* through the word.....John 15:3
own heads; I am *c*............Acts 18:6
those that were *c* 2Pet 2:18

CLEANLINESS—*state of being pure*
Required of priests ......Is 52:11
Acceptability of worship. .Heb 10:22
Inner, better than outward ....Matt 23:25-28

[*also* CLEANNESS]
to the *c* of my hands 2Sam 22:21
to the *c* of my hands ....Ps 18:20
the *c* of my hands in..........Ps 18:24
also have given you *c* ....Amos 4:6

CLEANSE—*to wash; purify*

[*also* CLEANSED, CLEANSETH, CLEANSING]
thou shalt *c* the altar ....Ex 29:36
even so it shall be *c* ....Lev 11:32
and she shall be *c* from ....Lev 12:7
been seen..for his *c*...........Lev 13:7
leper in the day of his *c*.......Lev 14:2
for him that is to be *c* ....Lev 14:4
he shall take to *c* the ....Lev 14:49
hath an issue is *c*.............Lev 15:13
seven days for his *c*...........Lev 15:13
seven times and *c* it ....Lev 16:19
in the day of his *c*............Num 6:9
children of Israel and *c* ....Num 8:6
tha land cannot be *c* of ....Num 35:33
which we are not *c* until ......Josh 22:17
of the Lord to *c* the 2Chr 29:15
have *c* all the house 2Chr 29:18
not *c* themselves, yet 2Chr 30:18
altars and *c* Judah 2Chr 34:5
and they *c* the chambers ......Neh 13:9
that they should *c* ....Neh 13:22
I have if I be *c* from..........Job 35:3
wind passeth and *c* ....Job 37:21
c thou me from secret ....Ps 19:12
mine iniquity and *c* ....Ps 51:2
I have *c* my heart ....Ps 73:13
shall a young man *c* ....Ps 119:9
blueness of a wound *c* ....Prov 20:30
not to fan nor to *c* ....Jer 4:11
the land that is not *c* ....Ezek 22:24
that I shall have *c* ....Ezek 36:33
have sinned and will *c* ....Ezek 37:23
them, that they may *c* ....Ezek 39:12
thus shalt thou *c* and ....Ezek 43:20
made an end of *c*.............Ezek 43:23
after he is *c*, they shall.......Ezek 44:26
blemish and *c* the ....Ezek 45:18
the sanctuary be *c* ....Dan 8:14
For I will *c* their blood ....Joel 3:21
that I have not *c* ....Joel 3:21
his leprosy was *c* ....Matt 8:3
c the lepers, raise the ....Matt 10:8
lepers are *c* and the ....Matt 11:5
from him and he was *c* ....Mark 1:42
and offer for thy *c*............Mark 1:44
none of them was *c*...........Luke 4:27
and offer for thy *c*............Luke 5:14
the lepers are *c*, the ....Luke 7:22
as they went, they were *c* .....Luke 17:14
What God hath *c*, that........Acts 10:15
What God hath *c*, that........Acts 11:9
C your hands, ye ....James 4:8

CLEANSING, SPIRITUAL
Promise of..............Jer 33:8
Need of ....Ps 51:2
Extent of ....Ps 19:12
Command regarding 2Cor 7:1
Means of 1John 1:7, 9
Perfection of ....Eph 5:26

CLEANTHES (klē'ăn-thēs)—*Stoic teacher not mentioned by name in the Bible*
Quoted by Paul ....Acts 17:28

CLEAR—*to open up; to make good; apparent*

[*also* CLEARER, CLEARING, CLEARLY, CLEARNESS]
shalt be *c* from this ....Gen 24:8
or how shall we *c* ....Gen 44:16
body of heaven in his *c* ....Ex 24:10
will by no means *c* ....Ex 34:7
no means *c* the guilty ....Num 14:18
the earth by *c* shining.........2Sam 23:4
age shall be *c* than the ....Job 11:17
utter knowledge *c* ....Job 33:3
speakest and be *c* when ....Ps 51:4
fair as the moon *c* as ....Song 6:10
a *c* heat upon herbs ....Is 18:4
the earth in the *c* day.........Amos 8:9
the light shall not be *c* ....Zech 14:6
then shalt thou see *c* to ....Matt 7:5
and saw every man *c* ....Mark 8:25
then shalt thou see *c* to ....Luke 6:42
are *c* seen being..............Rom 1:20
in you, yea, what *c* of 2Cor 7:11
yourselves to be *c* 2Cor 7:11
like a jasper stone, *c* ....Rev 21:11
river of water of life, *c*........Rev 22:1

CLEAVE—*to adhere firmly; split*

[*also* CLAVE, CLEAVED, CLEAVETH, CLEFT, CLEFTS, CLOVEN]
shall *c* unto his wife ....Gen 2:24
and *c* the wood for ....Gen 22:3
his soul *c* unto Dinah ....Gen 34:3
shall *c* it with the............Lev 1:17
ground *c* asunder that.........Num 16:31
But ye that did *c* unto ....Deut 4:4
to him shalt thou *c* ....Deut 10:20
serve him and *c* ....Deut 13:4
c the *c* into two claws.........Deut 14:6
make the pestilence *c* ....Deut 28:21
that thou mayest *c*............Deut 30:20
to *c* unto him and to ....Josh 22:5
But *c* unto the Lord ....Josh 23:8
But God *c* a hollow ....Judg 15:19
but Ruth *c* unto her ....Ruth 1:14
and they *c* the wood 1Sam 6:14
men of Judah *c* unto..........2Sam 20;2
and his hand *c* unto 2Sam 23:10
Solomon *c* unto these 1Kin 11:2
Nevertheless he *c* unto 2Kin 3:3
Naaman shall *c* unto 2Kin 5:27
be *c* to the Lord, and.........2Kin 18:6
c to their brethren............Neh 10:29
he *c* my reins asunder ....Job 16:13
My bone *c* to my skin ....Job 19:20
tongue *c* to the roof ....Job 29:10
and the clods *c* fast ....Job 38:38
and my tongue *c* to............Ps 22:15
disease, say they, *c* fast ......Ps 41:8
our belly *c* unto the earth .....Ps 44:25
c the fountain and the ....Ps 74:15
He *c* the rocks in.............Ps 78:15
it shall not *c* to me ....Ps 101:3
groaning my bones *c*..........Ps 102:5
My soul *c* unto the dust.......Ps 119:25
tongue *c* to the roof of........Ps 137:6
one cutteth and *c*.............Ps 141:7
that *c* wood shall be ....Eccl 10:9
in the *c* of the rock in ....Song 2:14
To go into the *c* of the ....Is 2:21
they shall *c* to the house .....Is 14:1
he *c* the rock also and ....Is 48:21
the girdle *c* to the loins ......Jer 13:11
so have I caused to *c* ....Jer 13:11
that dwellest in the *c* ....Jer 49:16
of the sucking child *c* ....Lam 4:4
tongue..*c* to the roof..........Ezek 3:26
they shall not *c* one ....Dan 2:43
shall *c* to them with ....Dan 11:34
and the little house with *c*.....Amos 6:11
that dwelleth in the *c* of ......Obad 3
the valleys shall be *c*..........Mic 1:4
didst *c* the earth with ....Hab 3:9
of Olives shall *c* in the ....Zech 14:4
c to his wife: and they ....Matt 19:5
and *c* to his wife ....Mark 10:7
dust of your city, which *c* Luke10:11
appeared unto them *c*..........Acts 2:3
would *c* unto the Lord ....Acts 11:23
men *c* unto him and ....Acts 17:34
c to that which is good........Rom 12:9

CLEMENCY—*disposition to be merciful*
hear us of thy *c* a few ....Acts 24:4

CLEMENT (klĕm'ĕnt)—*"mild"*
Paul's companion ....Phil 4:3

CLEOPAS (klē'ō-păs)—*"renowned father"*
Christ appeared to ....Luke 24:18

CLEOPHAS (klē'ō-făs)—*"renowned"*
Husband of Mary ....John 19:25
Called Alphaeus ....Matt 10:3

Mary the wife of *C* and ....John 19:25

CLIFF—*high rock embankments*

[*also* CLIFFS]
they come up by the *c* 2Chr 20:26
in the *c* of the valleys ....Job 30:6

CLIFT—*cleft (as of a rock)*

[*also* CLIFTS]
put thee in a *c* of the rock ...Ex 33:22
under the *c* of the rocks? .....Is 57:5

CLIMATE—*temperature and weather conditions*

Elements of
Cold ....Job 37:9; Acts 28:2
Clouds ....Job 35:5
Thirsty ground ....Deut 8:15
Heat ....Is 49:10
Rain ....Ezra 10:13
Snow 1Chr 11:22
Sunshine ....Ex 16:21
Wind ....Matt 14:24

Order of:
Promised ....Gen 8:22
Controlled by God ......Job 37:5-13
Used in judgment ....Jer 50:38; Hag 1:10-11
Tool of correction ....Jon 1:3, 4
Shows deity of Christ ....Mark 4:37-39

CLIMB—*to scale*

[*also* CLIMBED, CLIMBETH]
Jonathan *c* up upon 1Sam 14:13
and *c* up upon the rocks ......Jer 4:29
shall *c* the wall like men ......Joel 2:7
though they *c* up to ....Amos 9:2
c up into a sycamore ....Luke 19:4
c up some other way ....John 10:1

CLIPPED—*cut; trimmed*
bald and every beard *c*........Jer 48:37

CLOAK—*outer garment*

Used literally of:
Outer garment ....Matt 5:40

Used figuratively of:
Covering for sin ....John 15:22
Covering for license 1Pet 2:16

[*also* CLOKE]
was clad with zeal as a *c* ......Is 59:17
that taketh away thy *c* ....Luke 6:29
nor a *c* of covetousness 1Thess 2:5
c that I left at Troas 2Tim 4:13

CLODS—*lumps of earth or clay*
with worms and *c* of dust .....Job 7:5
The *c* of the valley ....Job 21:33
and the *c* cleave fast ....Job 38:38
and break the *c* of his ....Is 28:24
Jacob shall break his *c* ....Hos 10:11
is rotten under their *c* ....Joel 1:17

CLOKE—*See* CLOAK

CLOSE—*be near; shut*

[*also* CLOSED, CLOSEST]
c up the flesh instead ....Gen 2:21
the Lord had fast *c* up ....Gen 20:18
husband and be kept *c* ....Num 5:13
and the earth *c* upon ....Num 16:33
and the fat *c* upon the ....Judg 3:22
be afraid out of their *c* 2Sam 22:46
he yet kept himself *c* 1Chr 12:1
kept *c* from the fowls of ......Job 28:21
up together as with a *c* ....Job 41:15
be afraid out of their *c* ....Ps 18:45
they have not been *c* ....Is 1:6
and hath *c* your eyes ....Is 29:10
because thou *c* thyself ....Jer 22:15
c after you there in Egypt .....Jer 42:16
saw him come *c* unto ....Dan 8:7
the words are *c* up ....Dan 12:9
and *c* up the breaches ....Amos 9:11
the depth *c* me round ....Jon 2:5
their eyes they have *c* ....Matt 13:15
c the book and he gave ....Luke 4:20
And they kept it *c* and........Luke 9:36
they sailed *c* by Crete ....Acts 27:13
their eyes have they *c* ....Acts 28:27

CLOSER—*nearer*
sticketh *c* than a brother ......Prov 18:24

CLOSET—*a small storage area*
A place of prayer ....Matt 6:6

[*also* CLOSETS]
and the bride out of her *c* .....Joel 2:16
spoken in the ear in *c* ....Luke 12:3

CLOTH—*material of interwoven fibers*

[*also* CLOTHS]
the *c* of service and ....Ex 31:10
The *c* of service, to do ....Ex 35:19
made *c* of service ....Ex 39:1
spread over it a *c* ....Num 4:6
spread the *c* before ....Deut 22:17
covered it with a *c* 1Sam 19:13
wrapped in a *c* behind 1Sam 21:9
cast a *c* upon him 2Sam 20:12
he took a thick *c* and 2Kin 8:15
as a menstruous *c* ....Is 30:22
of new *c* unto an old ....Matt 9:16
in a clean linen *c* ....Matt 27:59
of new *c* on an old ....Mark 2:21
linen *c* cast about his ....Mark 14:51

CLOTHING

Need of:
Cover nakedness ....Gen 3:10, 11
Maintain modesty 1Pet 3:1-5
Keep warm 2Tim 4:13
Remove anguish ....Esth 4:3, 4

Unusual features regarding:
Lasted forty years ....Deut 8:4
Torn into twelve pieces ..1Kin 11:29, 30
Borrowed from enemies ..Ex 12:35
Some stripped of ....Luke 10:30

Regulations concerning:
Wearing opposite sex's, forbidden ....Deut 22:5
Gaudy, denounced ......Is 3:16-24
Ostentatious, prohibited ..1Tim 2:9
Warnings concerning .....Matt 7:15
Judgments by, deceptive. .Luke 16:19
Proper sign of Christian sanity ....Mark 5:15

[*also* CLAD, CLOTHE, CLOTHED, CLOTHES, CLOTHEST]
make coats of skins, and *c* ....Gen 3:21
Then they rent their *c* ....Gen 44:13
in wine and his *c* in ....Gen 49:11
bound up in their *c* ....Ex 12:34
let them wash their *c* ....Ex 19:10
his sons and *c* them ....Ex 40:14
c him with the robe ....Lev 8:7
shall wash his *c* ....Lev 11:25
shall wash his *c* and ....Lev 13:6
wash his *c* and shave ....Lev 14:8
wash his *c*, and bathe ....Lev 15:5
wash his *c*, and bathe ....Lev 15:11
shall wash his *c* and ....Lev 16:26
shall both wash his *c* ....Lev 17:15
his head, nor rend his *c* ....Lev 21:10
let them wash their *c* ....Num 8:7
the land, rent their *c* ....Num 14:6
priest shall wash his *c* ....Num 19:7
wash your *c* on the ....Num 31:24
c are not waxen old ....Deut 29:5
that he rent his *c* and ....Judg 11:35
with his *c* rent and 1Sam 4:12
he stripped off his *c* 1Sam 19:24
from Saul with his *c* 2Sam 1:2
over Saul, who *c* you 2Sam 1:24
Rend your *c* and gird 2Sam 3:31
stood by with their *c* 2Sam 13:31
nor washed his *c* from 2Sam 19:24
covered him with *c* 1Kin 1:1
c himself with a new 1Kin 11:29
that he rent his *c* and put 1Kin 21:27
he took hold of his own *c* 2Kin 2:12
that he rent his *c* and 2Kin 5:7
that he rent his *c* 2Kin 6:30
Athaliah rent her *c* and 2Kin 11:14
to Hezekiah with their *c* 2Kin 18:37
rent his *c* and covered 2Kin 19:1
law that he rent his *c* 2Kin 22:11
was *c* with a robe of 1Chr 15:27
of Israel, who were *c* 1Chr 21:16
be *c* with salvation 2Chr 6:41
c in their robes and 2Chr 18:9
Athaliah rent her *c* 2Chr 23:13
c all that were naked 2Chr 28:15
law, that he rent his *c* 2Chr 34:19
none of us put off our *c* ......Neh 4:23
their *c* waxed not old ....Neh 9:21
Mordecai rent his *c* ....Esth 4:1
the king's gate *c* with ....Esth 4:2
she sent raiment to *c* ....Esth 4:4
My flesh is *c* with ....Job 7:5
hate thee shall be *c* ....Job 8:22
and mine own *c* shall ....Job 9:31
hast *c* me with skin ....Job 10:11
the naked of their *c* ....Job 22:6
naked to lodge without *c* ......Job 24:7
righteousness, and it *c* ....Job 29:14
perish for want of *c* ....Job 31:19
thou *c* his neck with ....Job 39:19
my *c* was sackcloth ....Ps 35:13
let them be *c* with ....Ps 35:26
her *c* is of wrought gold ....Ps 45:13
The pastures are *c* ....Ps 65:13
he is *c* with majesty ....Ps 93:1
Lord is *c* with strength ....Ps 93:1
art *c* with honor and ....Ps 104:1
As he *c* himself with ....Ps 109:18
priests be *c* with ....Ps 132:9
also *c* her priests with ....Ps 132:16
his *c* not be burned? ....Prov 6:27
shall *c* a man with rags ....Prov 23:21
lambs are for thy *c* and ....Prov 27:26
her household are *c* ....Prov 31:21
her *c* is silk and purple ....Prov 31:22
Thou hast *c*, be thou ....Is 3:6
And I will *c* him with ....Is 22:21
and for durable *c* ....Is 23:18
Hezekiah with their *c* ....Is 36:22
heard it, that he rent his *c* ....Is 37:1
shalt surely *c* thee with ....Is 49:18
c the heavens with ....Is 50:3
of vengeance for *c* ....Is 59:17
and was *c* with zeal ....Is 59:17
he hath *c* me with the ....Is 61:10
c thyself with crimson ....Jer 4:30
blue and purple is their *c* .....Jer 10:9
and their *c* rent and ....Jer 41:5
prince shall be *c* with ....Ezek 7:27
among them was *c* with ....Ezek 9:2
spake unto the man *c* ....Ezek 10:2
c thee also with embroidered ..Ezek 16:10
thee also of thy *c* ....Ezek 16:39
c with blue, captains ....Ezek 23:6
strip thee out of thy *c* ....Ezek 26:16
c themselves with ....Ezek 26:16
in precious *c* for chariots ......Ezek 27:20
ye *c* you with the wool, ye ....Ezek 34:3
c with all sorts of armor ......Ezek 38:4
shall be *c* with linen ....Ezek 44:17
shall be *c* with scarlet ....Dan 5:7
behold a certain man *c* ....Dan 10:5
one said to the man *c* ....Dan 12:6
themselves down upon *c* ......Amos 2:8
as are *c* with strange ....Zeph 1:8
ye *c* you, but there is ....Hag 1:6
Joshua was *c* with filthy ....Zech 3:3

c thee with change ....Zech 3:4
if God so *c* the grass ....Matt 6:30
he not much more *c* you ......Matt 6:30
shall we be *c*? ....Matt 6:31
A man *c* in soft raiment? .....Matt 11:8
wear soft *c* are in kings' ....Matt 11:8
put on them their *c* ....Matt 21:7
return back to take his *c* ......Matt 24:18
Naked, and ye *c* me ....Matt 25:36
high priest rent his *c* ....Matt 26:65
And John was *c* with ....Mark 1:6
may but touch his *c* ....Mark 5:28
love to go in long *c* ....Mark 12:38
c him with purple ....Mark 15:17
and put his own *c* on him .....Mark 15:20
c in a long white garment .....Mark 16:5
him in swaddling *c* ....Luke 2:7
A man *c* in soft raiment? .....Luke 7:25
and ware no *c*, neither ....Luke 8:27
at the feet of Jesus, *c* ....Luke 8:35
then God so *c* the grass ....Luke 12:28
much more will he *c* you ......Luke 12:28
they spread their *c* in ....Luke 19:36
the linen *c* laid by ....Luke 24:12
and wound it in linen *c* ....John 19:40
saw the linen *c* ....John 20:5
laid down their *c* ....Acts 7:58
before me in bright *c* ....Acts 10:30
rent off their *c* ....Acts 16:22
cast off their *c* and ....Acts 22:23
desiring to be *c* 2Cor 5:2
that weareth the gay *c* ....James 2:3
be *c* with humility for 1Pet 5:5
c with a garment down ....Rev 1:13
shall be *c* in white ....Rev 3:5
c in white raiment ....Rev 4:4
c with white robes and ....Rev 7:9
from heaven, *c* with ....Rev 10:1
days, *c* in sackcloth ....Rev 11:3
woman *c* with the sun ....Rev 12:1
c in pure and white ....Rev 15:6
that was *c* in fine ....Rev 18:16
c with a vesture dipped ....Rev 19:13
c in fine linen, white ....Rev 19:14

CLOTHING, TEARING OF—*symbolic expression of grief; reaction to blasphemy*
By Reuben ....Gen 37:29, 34
By Joshua ....Josh 7:6
By Tamar...............2Sam 13:19
By Job ....Job 1:20
By Ezra ....Ezra 9:3
By high priest ....Mark 14:63
By Paul and Barnabas ...Acts 14:14
Forbidden to Aaron .....Lev 10:6

CLOUD—*visible mass of vapor or smoke; that which lowers menancingly*

Miraculous uses of:
Israel's guidance ....Ex 13:21, 22
Manifesting the divine glory ....Ex 16:10
Manifesting the divine presence 2Chr 5:13
Jesus' transfiguration.....Luke 9:34, 35
Jesus' ascension ....Acts 1:9-11
Jesus' return ....Matt 24:30

Figurative of:
God's unsearchableness ..Ps 97:2
Sins ....Is 44:22
Witnesses ....Heb 12:1
False teachers 2Pet 2:17
Baptism 1Cor 10:1, 2
Boasting ....Prob 25:14

[*also* CLOUDS, CLOUDY]
I do set my bow in the *c* ......Gen 9:13
a *c* covered the mount ....Ex 24:15
c pillar descended ....Ex 33:9
descended in the *c* ....Ex 34:5
in the *c* upon the ....Lev 16:2
the *c* covered the ....Num 9:15
that the *c* was taken up ....Num 10:11
Lord came down in a *c* ....Num 11:25
that thy *c* standeth ....Num 14:14
ye should go and in a *c* ....Deut 1:33
darkness, *c*, and thick ....Deut 4:11
the *c* and of the thick ....Deut 5:22
in a pillar of a *c* ....Deut 31:15
the *c* also dropped water ......Judg 5:4
waters, and thick *c* of the 2Sam 22:12
even a morning without *c* 2Sam 23:4
the *c* filled the house 1Kin 8:10
ariseth a little *c* out 1Kin 18:44
was black with *c* and wind 1Kin 18:45
them in the day be a *c* ....Neh 9:12
the pillar of the *c* ....Neh 9:19
let a *c* dwell upon it ....Job 3:5
head reach unto the *c* ....Job 20:6
through the dark *c*? ....Job 22:13
Thick *c* are a covering ....Job 20:14
waters in his thick *c* ....Job 26:8
the *c* is not rent under ....Job 26:8
passeth away as a *c* ....Job 30:15
c which are higher than ....Job 35:5
c do drop and distill ....Job 36:28
by the *c* that cometh ....Job 36:32
he wearieth the thick *c* ....Job 37:11
the balancings of the *c* ....Job 37:16
made the *c* the garment ....Job 38:9
thy voice to the *c* ....Job 38:34
waters and thick *c* of ....Ps 18:11
reacheth unto the *c* ....Ps 36:5
and thy truth unto the *c* ......Ps 57:10
his strength is in the *c* ....Ps 68:34
The *c* poured out water ....Ps 77:17
he led them with a *c* ....Ps 78:14
commanded the *c* from ....Ps 78:23
unto them in the *c* ....Ps 99:7
who maketh the *c* his ....Ps 104:3
He spread a *c* for a ....Ps 105:39
reacheth unto the *c* ....Ps 108:4
the heaven with *c* ....Ps 147:8
and the *c* drop down ....Prov 3:20
he established the *c* ....Prov 8:28
favor is as a *c* of the ....Prov 16:15
If the *c* be full of rain ....Eccl 11:3
regardeth the *c* shall ....Eccl 11:4
nor the *c* return after ....Eccl 12:2
a *c* and smoke by day ....Is 4:5
also command the *c* ....Is 5:6
the heights of the *c* ....Is 14:14
a *c* of dew in the heat ....Is 18:4
rideth upon a swift *c* ....Is 19:1
the shadow of a *c* ....Is 25:5
these that fly as a *c* ....Is 60:8
he shall come up as *c* ....Jer 4:13
of Zion with a *c* ....Lam 2:1
thyself with a *c* ....Lam 3:44
a great *c* and a fire ....Ezek 1:4
a thick *c* of incense ....Ezek 8:11
and the *c* filled the inner ......Ezek 10:3
the Lord is near, a *c* ....Ezek 30:3
as for her, a *c* shall ....Ezek 30:18
cover the sun with a *c* ....Ezek 32:7
scattered in the *c* ....Ezek 34:12
shalt be like a *c* to cover ......Ezek 38:9
of man came with the *c* ....Dan 7:13
is as a morning *c* ....Hos 6:4
be as the morning *c* ....Hos 13:3
a day of *c* and of thick ....Joel 2:2
and the *c* are the dust ....Nah 1:3
a day of *c* and thick ....Zeph 1:15
shall make bright *c* ....Zech 10:1
bright *c* overshadowed ....Matt 17:5
voice out of the *c* ....Matt 17:5
and coming in the *c* ....Matt 26:64
c that overshadowed ....Mark 9:7
voice came out of the *c* ....Mark 9:7
man coming in the *c* ....Mark 13:26
and coming in the *c* of ....Mark 14:62
ye see a *c* rise out of ....Luke 12:54
in a *c* with power and ....Luke 21:27
with them in the *c* 1Thess 4:17
c they are without water.......Jude 12
he cometh with *c* ....Rev 1:7
clothed with a *c* ....Rev 10:1
to heaven in a *c* ....Rev 11:12
and behold a white *c* ....Rev 14:14
upon the *c* one sat like ....Rev 14:14

CLOUD, PILLAR OF

Designed to:
Regulate Israel's movements ....Ex 40:36, 37
Guide Israel ....Ex 13:21
Defend Israel ....Ex 14:19
Cover the tabernacle.....Ex 40:34

Special manifestations of, at:
Time of murmuring......Ex 16:9, 10
Giving of Law ....Ex 19:9, 16
Rebellion of Aaron and Miriam ....Num 12:5
Korah's rebellion ....Num 16:19, 42

CLOUDBURST—*a sudden downpour of rain*
Sent as punishment ......Ezra 10:9-14

CLOUTED—*a piece of cloth or leather; a rag*

[*also* CLOUTS]
old shoes and *c* upon ....Josh 9:5
old cast *c* and old ....Jer 38:11

CLOVEN FOOTED—*foot divided into two parts*
the hoof and is *c* ....Lev 11:3

CLUSTERS—*groups of similar things growing together*

Kinds of:
Grapes ....Num 13:23
Henna blossoms ....Song 1:14
Raisins 1Sam 25:18
Dates ....Song 5:11

[*also* CLUSTER]
the *c* thereof brought ....Gen 40:10
grapes of gall, their *c* ....Deut 32:32
cake of figs and two *c* 1Sam 30:12
and thy breasts to *c* ....Song 7:7
is found in the *c* ....Is 65:8
there is no *c* to eat ....Mic 7:1
the *c* of the vine of ....Rev 14:18

CNIDUS (nī'dŭs)—*"age"*
City of Asia Minor on Paul's voyage ....Acts 27:7

COAL—*ember; glowing carbon or charred wood*

Uses of:
Heating.................John 18:18
Cooking ....John 21:9
By smiths ....Is 44:11, 12

Figurative of:
Lust....................Prov 6:25-28
Purification ....Is 6:6
Good deeds ....Rom 12:20
Posterity 2Sam 14:7

[*also* COALS]
censer full of burning *c* ....Lev 16:12
c were kindled by it 2Sam 22:9
cake baked on the *c* 1Kin 19:6
His breath kindleth *c* ....Job 41:21
c were kindled by it ....Ps 18:8
hail stones and *c* ....Ps 18:12
of the mighty with *c* ....Ps 120:4
let burning *c* fall upon ....Ps 140:10
thou shalt heap *c* of ....Prov 25:22
As *c* are to burning *c* ....Prov 26:21
the *c* thereof are *c* of ....Song 8:6
there shall not be a *c* ....Is 47:14
that bloweth the *c* ....Is 54:16
is blacker than a *c* ....Lam 4:8
was like burning *c* of fire .....Ezek 1:13
fill thine hand with *c* of ....Ezek 10:2
it empty upon the *c* ....Ezek 24:11
and burning *c* went ....Hab 3:5

COAST—*the land alongside a large lake or sea; border*

[*also* COASTS]
locusts into thy *c* ....Ex 10:4
and rested in all the *c* ....Ex 10:14
the sea, and by the *c* ....Num 13:29
by the *c* of the land ....Num 20:23
out of the *c* of the ....Num 21:13
is in the utmost *c* ....Num 22:36

shall come from the *c* ....Num 24:24
cities thereof in the *c* ....Num 32:33
of Canaan with the *c* ....Num 34:2
of Zin along by the *c* ....Num 34:3
the outmost *c* of..............Num 34:3
through the *c* of your ....Deut 2:4
of Argob unto the *c* ....Deut 3:14
Jordan and the *c* thereof ......Deut 3:17
sea shall your *c* be ....Deut 11:24
with thee in all thy *c* ....Deut 16:4
divide the *c* of thy land ....Deut 19:3
enlarge thy *c* ....Deut 19:8
throughout all thy *c* ....Deut 28:40
shall be your *c* ....Josh 1:4
in all the *c* of the great ....Josh 9:1
And the *c* of Og king..........Josh 12:4
their *c* was from Aroer ....Josh 13:16
part of the south *c* ....Josh 15:1
c of Japhleti unto the *c* ......Josh 16:3
the *c* of Manasseh ....Josh 17:7
shall abide in their *c* ....Josh 18:5
shall abide in their *c* ....Josh 18:5
the *c* reacheth to Tabor ....Josh 19:22
Gaza with the *c* thereof ....Judg 1:18
to pass through his *c*..........Judg 11:20
all the *c* of the Amorites .....Judg 11:22
five men from their *c* ....Judg 18:2
sent her into all the *c* ....Judg 19:29
Ashdod and the *c* 1Sam 5:6
by the way of his own *c* to 1Sam 6:9
no more into the *c* 1Sam 7:13
the *c* thereof did Israel........1Sam 7:14
unto all the *c* of Israel 1Sam 11:3
any more in any *c* 1Sam 27:1
the *c* which belongeth..........1Sam 30:14
in any of the *c* of Israel 2Sam 21:5
all the *c* of Israel 1Kin 1:3
smote them in all the *c* 2Kin 10:32
He restored the *c* of 2Kin 14:25
and the *c* thereof 2Kin 15:16
and enlarge my *c* 1Chr 4:10
their castles in their *c* 1Chr 6:54
throughout all the *c* of 1Chr 21:12
him out of all their *c* 2Chr 11:13
flies, and lice in all their *c* ....Ps 105:31
up from the *c* of the earth ....Jer 25:32
from the *c* of the earth ....Jer 31:8
up from the *c* of the earth ....Jer 50:41
remnant of the sea *c* ....Ezek 25:16
take a man of their *c* ....Ezek 33:2
is by the *c* of Hauran ....Ezek 47:16
the *c* of the way of ....Ezek 48:1
Zidon and all the *c* of ....Joel 3:4
inhabitants of the sea *c* ....Zeph 2:5
in all the *c* thereof ....Matt 2:16
which is upon the sea *c* ....Matt 4:13
depart out of their *c* ....Mat 8:34
departed into the *c* ....Matt 15:21
Jesus came into the *c* ....Matt 16:13
and came into the *c* ....Matt 19:1
to depart out of their *c* ....Mark 5:17
departing from the *c* ....Mark 7:31
and cometh into the *c* ....Mark 10:1
them out of their *c* ....Acts 13:50
passed through the upper *c*....Acts 19:1
throughout all the *c* ....Acts 26:20
meaning to sail by the *c*........Acts 27:2

COAT—*an outer garment*
Makers of:
God—for man ....Gen 3:21
Jacob—for Joseph ....Gen 37:3
Hannah—for Samuel.....2Sam 2:18, 19
Dorcas—for wearing .....Acts 9:39

[*also* COATS]
and an embroidered *c*, ...Ex 28:4
thou shalt make *c* ....Ex 28:40
put upon Aaron the *c*, and ....Ex 29:5
sons, and put *c* upon them ....Ex 29:8
they made *c* of fine linen .....Ex 39:27
and clothe them with *c*........Ex 40:14
he put upon him the *c* ....Lev 8:7
put *c* upon them and girded ...Lev 8:13
mother made him a little *c* 1Sam 2:19
was armed with a *c* of mail....1Sam 17:5
to meet him with his *c* 2Sam 15:32
as the collar of my *c*...........Job 30:18
I have put off my *c*; how .....Song 5:3
bound in their *c*, their ....Dan 3:21
the law, and take away thy *c* ..Matt 5:40
neither two *c*, neither ....Matt 10:10
sandals..not put on two *c* .....Mark 6:9
He that hath two *c*, let ....Luke 3:11
forbid not to take thy *c* ....Luke 6:29
money; neither have two *c* ....Luke 9:3
and also his *c*; now the *c*.....John 19:23
he girt his fisher's *c*...........John 21:7

COCK—*rooster*
night, before the *c* crow ......Matt 26:34
before the *c* crow twice ....Mark 14:30
c shall not crow this day ....Luke 22:34
The *c* shall not crow ....John 13:38
immediately the *c* crew ....John 18:27

COCKATRICE—*type of venomous snake*
Figurative of evil deeds ..Is 11:8
Figurative of man's evil nature ....Deut 32:33

[*also* COCKATRICES]
shall come forth a *c*, and......Is 14:29
I will send serpents, *c*.........Jer 8:17

COCKCROWING—*a rooster's shrill calling*
Announced the dawn ....Mark 13:35
Reminded Peter ....Matt 26:34, 74

COCKLE—*stinging weeds*
Obnoxious among barley..Job 31:40

COFFER—*a strongbox; a chest*
Used to safeguard jewels .1Sam 6:8-15

COFFIN—*a box-like container for a corpse*
In Joseph's burial.........Gen 50:26
Jesus touched ....Luke 7:14

COGITATIONS—*meditations*
my *c* much troubled me ....Dan 7:28

COINS
Beckah (½ shekel) ......Ex 38:26
Brass ....Matt 10:9
Dram ....Ezra 2:69
Farthing ....Matt 10:29
Gerah ....Ex 30:13
Maneh ....Ezek 45:12
Mite....................Mark 12:42
Penny ....Matt 20:2
Piece of gold 2Kin 5:5
Piece of money..........Matt 17:27
Piece of silver ....Matt 26:15

COLD—*low temperature*
Used literally of:
Winter ....Gen 8:22
Cold weather ....John 18:18
Used figuratively of:
God's power ....Ps 147:17
Indolence ....Prov 20:4
Good news ....Prov 25:25
Apostasy ....Jer 18:14
Spiritual decay ....Matt 24:12

have no covering in the *c* .....Job 24:7
whirlwind: and *c* out of ....Job 37:9
the *c* of snow in the time .....Prov 25:13
the hedges in the *c* day ....Nah 3:17
little ones a cup of *c*..........Matt 10:42
rain, and because of the *c*.....Acts 28:2
fastings often, in *c* and 2Cor 11:27
thou art neither *c* nor hot .....Rev 3:15
I would thou wert *c* or hot ....Rev 3:15
neither *c* nor hot, I ....Rev 3:16

COL-HOZEH (kŏl-hō'zĕ)—*"wholly a seer"*
A man of Judah ....Neh 3:15
Neh 11:5

COLLABORATORS—*those who assist an enemy*
Delilah ....Judg 16:4-21
Doeg 1Sam 21:7
Judas ....Matt 26:14-16

COLLAR—*band worn around the neck*

[*also* COLLARS]
and *c*, and purple raiment .....Judg 8:26
about as the *c* of my coat .....Job 30:18

COLLECTION BOX
For Temple offerings 2Kin 12:9

COLLECTION OF MONEY
The Temple tax 2Chr 24:6, 9
For saints ....Rom 15:25, 26

COLLEGE—*dwelling*
Huldah's dwelling 2Kin 22:14

dwelt in Jerusalem in the *c* 2Chr 34:22

COLLOPS—*a slice of meat*
Maketh *c* of fat on his ....Job 15:27

COLONY—*citizens transported to another land*
Illustrated by:
Israel in Egypt ....Gen 46:28
Israel in Assyria 2Kin 17:6, 24
Judah in Babylon 2Kin 25:8-12
Applied to:
Philippi as a Roman colony ....Acts 16:12
Philippian Christians .....Phil 3:20

COLOR—*hue; pigment*
White, descriptive of:
Glory and majesty ....Dan 7:9
Rev 20:11
Purity, glory ....Rev 1:14
Victory ....Rev 6:2
Completion ....John 4:35
Black, descriptive of:
Sorrow, calamity ....Rev 6-12
Hell ....Jude 13
Green, descriptive of:
Spiritual privileges ....Jer 11:16
Spiritual life ....Ps 52:8
Ps 92:12-15
Red (crimson), descriptive of:
Atonement..............Is 63:2
Military might...........Nah 2:3
Persecution ....Rev 12:3
Drunkenness ....Prov 23:29
Sinfulness ....Is 1:18
Purple, descriptive of:
Royalty.................Judg 8:26
Wealth ....Luke 16:19
Luxury ....Rev 17:4
Blue, descriptive of:
Heavenly character ......Ex 28:31

[*also* COLORED, COLORS]
made him a coat of many *c* ...Gen 37:3
have not changed his *c*........Lev 13:55
thereof as the *c* of ....Num 11:7
Sisera a prey of divers *c* ......Judg 5:30
of divers *c* of needlework .....Judg 5:30
a garment of divers *c* upon 2Sam 13:18
stones, and of divers *c* 1Chr 29:2
giveth his *c* in the cup ....Prov 23:31
lay thy stones with fair *c* ......Is 54:11
thereof as the *c* of amber .....Ezek 1:4
of brightness, as the *c* ....Ezek 8:2
was as the *c* of a beryl ....Ezek 10:9
high places with divers *c* ......Ezek 16:16
feathers which had divers *c*....Ezek 17:3
like in *c* to polished brass .....Dan 10:6
under *c* as though they.........Acts 27:30
sit upon a scarlet-*c* beast ......Rev 17:3
in purple and scarlet *c* ....Rev 17:4

COLOSSAE (kō-lŏs'ē)—*"punishment"*
A city in Asia Minor ....Col 1:2
Evangelized by Epaphras .Col 1:7
Not visited by Paul ......Col 2:1
Paul writes against errors of ....Col 2:16-23

COLOSSIANS, THE EPISTLE OF THE—*an epistle of the New Testament*
Written by Paul ....Col 1:1

COLT—*young beast of burden*
Descriptive of Messiah . . . Gen 49:10, 11
Christ rides on . . . . Matt 21:2, 5, 7
Of camel, as gift . . . . Gen 32:13, 15

[*also* COLTS]
that rode on thirty ass *c* . . . . Judg 10:4
threescore and ten ass *c* . . . . Judg 12:14
born like a wild ass's *c* . . . . Job 11:12
upon a *c* the foal of an ass . . . . Zech 9:9
shall find a *c* tied . . . . Mark 11:2
ye shall find a *c* tied . . . . Luke 19:30
sitting on an ass's *c* . . . . John 12:15

COME—*to go forward*
Of invitation . . . . Is 1:18
Of salvation . . . . Matt 18:11
Of rest . . . . Matt 11:28
Of promise . . . . John 14:3
Of prayer . . . . Heb 4:16
The final . . . . Rev 22:17, 20
See INTRODUCTION

COMELY—*having a pleasing appearance*

[*also* COMELINESS]
in matters, and a *c* person 1Sam 16:18
power, nor his *c* proportion . . . Job 41:12
praise is *c* for the upright . . . . . Ps 33:1
pleasant; and praise is *c* . . . . Ps 147:1
go well, yea, four are *c* . . . . Prov 30:29
It is good and *c* for one . . . . Eccl 5:18
I am black, but *c*, O ye . . . . Song 1:5
and thy countenance is *c* . . . . . . Song 2:14
speech is *c*..temples . . . . Song 4:3
as Tirzah, *c* as Jerusalem . . . . . . Song 6:4
shall be excellent and *c* . . . . Is 4:2
he hath no form nor *c* . . . . Is 53:2
daughter of Zion to a *c* . . . . Jer 6:2
was perfect through my *c* . . . . . Ezek 16:14
they set forth thy *c* . . . . Ezek 27:10
for my *c* was turned in me . . . . Dan 10:8
but for that which is *c* 1Cor 7:35
Is it *c* that a woman pray 1Cor 11:13
parts have more abundant *c* . . . 1Cor 12:23
our *c* parts have no need 1Cor 12:24

COMERS—*those who draw near*
continually make the *c* . . . . Heb 10:1

COMFORT—*to strengthen; aid; relieve distress; console*
Sources of:
God 2Cor 1:3, 4
Christ . . . . Matt 9:22
Holy Spirit . . . . Acts 9:31
The Scriptures . . . . Rom 15:4
Christian friends 2Cor 7:6
Those in need of:
Afflicted . . . . Is 40:1, 2
Sorrowful 2Cor 2:7
Weak 1Thess 5:14
Discouraged 2Cor 2:7
Troubled 2Cor 7:5-7
One another 1Thess 4:18

[*also* COMFORTABLE, COMFORTABLY, COMFORTED, COMFORTEDST, COMFORTETH, COMFORTS]
shall *c* us concerning our . . . . . . Gen 5:29
and *c* ye your hearts . . . . Gen 18:5
Isaac was *c* after his . . . . Gen 24:67
c himself, purposing to . . . . Gen 27:42
daughters rose up to *c* . . . . Gen 37:35
he refused to be *c*; and . . . . Gen 37:35
wife died; and Judah was *c* . . . . Gen 38:12
And he *c* them, and spake . . . . Gen 50:21
C thine heart with a morsel . . . Judg 19:5
for that thou hast *c* me . . . . Ruth 2:13
David sent to *c* him by 2Sam 10:2
he hath sent *c* unto thee? 2Sam 10:3
And David *c* Bath-sheba his . . . 2Sam 12:24
he was *c* concerning Amnon . . . 2Sam 13:39
the king shall now be *c* 2Sam 14:17
speak *c* unto thy servants 2Sam 19:7
his brethren came to *c* him 1Chr 7:22
David sent messengers to *c* 1Chr 19:2
he hath sent *c* unto thee? 1Chr 19:3
spake *c* unto all the Levites . . . 2Chr 30:22
spake *c* to them, saying 2Chr 32:6
mourn with him and to *c* . . . . . . Job 2:11
should I yet have *c*; yea . . . . Job 6:10
bed shall *c* me, my couch . . . . . Job 7:13
my heaviness, and *c* myself . . . . Job 9:27
that I may take *c* a little . . . . . . Job 10:20
miserable *c* are ye all . . . . Job 16:2
How then *c* ye me in vain . . . . . Job 21:34
as one that *c* the mourners . . . . Job 29:25
they bemoaned him, and *c* . . . . Job 42:11
rod and thy staff they *c* . . . . Ps 23:4
for *c*, but I found none . . . . Ps 69:20
and *c* me on every side . . . . Ps 71:21
my soul refused to be *c* . . . . Ps 77:2
hast helped me, and *c* . . . . Ps 86:17
within me thy *c* delight . . . . Ps 94:19
is my *c* in my affliction . . . . Ps 119:50
O Lord; and have *c* myself . . . . Ps 119:52
flagons, *c* me with apples . . . . . Song 2:5
turned away, and thou *c* . . . . . . Is 12:1
to *c* me, because of the . . . . Is 22:4
Speak ye *c* to Jerusalem . . . . . . Is 40:2
the Lord hath *c* his people . . . . Is 49:13
the Lord shall *c* Zion . . . . Is 51:3
I, even I, am he that *c* . . . . Is 51:12
the Lord hath *c* his people . . . . Is 52:9
with tempest, and not *c* . . . . Is 54:11
And restore *c* unto him . . . . Is 57:18
to *c* all that mourn . . . . Is 61:2
As one whom his mother *c* . . . . Is 66:13
comforteth, so will I *c* . . . . Is 66:13
ye shall be *c* in Jerusalem . . . . . Is 66:13
I would *c* myself against . . . . . . Jer 8:18
to *c* them for the dead . . . . Jer 16:7
into joy, and will *c* them . . . . . . Jer 31:13
children refused to be *c* . . . . . . Jer 31:15
none to *c* her: all her . . . . Lam 1:2
I may *c* thee, O virgin . . . . Lam 2:13
upon them, and I will be *c* . . . . Ezek 5:13
ye shall be *c* concerning . . . . Ezek 14:22
And they shall *c* you, when . . . Ezek 14:23
in that thou art a *c* unto . . . . . . Ezek 16:54
be *c* in the nether parts . . . . Ezek 31:16
be *c* over all his multitude . . . . Ezek 32:31
speak *c* unto her . . . . Hos 2:14
whence shall I seek *c* for . . . . . . Nah 3:7
good words and *c* words . . . . . . Zech 1:13
the Lord shall yet *c* Zion . . . . . Zech 1:17
they *c* in vain: therefore . . . . . . Zech 10:2
would not be *c*, because . . . . . . Matt 2:18
mourn for they shall be *c* . . . . . Matt 5:4
of good *c*, rise; he calleth . . . . . Mark 10:49
Daughter, be of good *c* . . . . Luke 8:48
but now he is *c*, and thou . . . . . Luke 16:25
to Martha and Mary, to *c* . . . . . John 11:19
in the house, and *c* her . . . . John 11:31
the brethren, they *c* them . . . . . Acts 16:40
and were not a little *c* . . . . Acts 20:12
I may be *c* together with you . . Rom 1:12
and exhortation, and *c* 1Cor 14:3
learn, and all may be *c* 1Cor 14:31
c us in all our tribulation 2Cor 1:4
I am filled with *c*, I am 2Cor 7:4
that *c* those that are cast 2Cor 7:6
Be perfect, be of good *c* 2Cor 13:11
that he might *c* your hearts . . . . Eph 6:22
if any *c* of love, if any . . . . Phil 2:1
their hearts might be *c* . . . . Col 2:2
estate, and *c* your hearts . . . . . . Col 4:8
how we exhorted and *c* 1Thess 2:11
to *c* you concerning your 1Thess 3:2
we were *c* over you in all 1Thess 3:7
c yourselves together, and 1Thess 5:11
c your hearts and establish 2Thess 2:17

COMFORTER—*the Spirit; a helper*
Abides with believers . . . . John 14:16
Teaches . . . . John 14:26
Testifies of Christ . . . . John 15:26
Convicts . . . . John 16:7-11
Guides into truth . . . . John 16:13
Glorifies Christ . . . . John 16:14, 15

oppressed, and they had no *c* . . Eccl 4:1
was power; but they had no *c* . Eccl 4:1
down wonderfully: she had no *c* . . . . Lam 1:9
c that should relieve my soul . . Lam 1:6

COMFORTLESS—*absence of consolation*
I will not leave you *c* . . . . John 14:18

COMING—*arriving*

[*also* COMEST, COMETH, COMINGS]
behold, the camels were *c* . . . . . Gen 24:63
blessed thee since my *c* . . . . Gen 30:30
hinder thee from *c* unto me . . . Num 22:16
of the *c* of the children . . . . Num 33:40
his chariot so long in *c*? . . . . Judg 5:28
a company of prophets *c* 1Sam 10:5
c thou peaceably? 1Sam 16:4
saw the son of Jesse *c* to 1Sam 22:9
withholden thee from *c* to 1Sam 25:26
thy going out and thy *c* 1Sam 29:6
thy going out and thy *c* 2Sam 3:25
king and his servants *c* 2Sam 24:20
son of Rechab *c* to meet 2Kin 10:15
thy going out, and they *c* 2Kin 19:27
was of God by *c* to Joram 2Chr 22:7
second year of their *c* . . . . Ezra 3:8
bridegroom *c* out of his . . . . Ps 19:5
he seeth that his day is *c* . . . . . . Ps 37:13
thy *c* in from this time . . . . Ps 121:8
city, at the *c* in at the . . . . Prov 8:3
to meet thee at thy *c*: it . . . . Is 14:9
When it shall hail, *c* down . . . . Is 32:19
and thy *c* in, and thy rage . . . . . Is 37:28
and the things that are *c* . . . . . . Is 44:7
observe..time of their *c* . . . . Jer 8:7
When thou *c* to Babylon . . . . . . Jer 51:61
and the *c* in thereof, and . . . . . . Ezek 43:11
watcher and an holy one *c* . . . . Dan 4:23
to the days of thy *c* . . . . Mic 7:15
he *c* up unto the people . . . . Hab 3:16
abide the day of his *c*? . . . . Mal 3:2
before the *c* of the great . . . . . . Mal 4:5
devils, *c* out of the tombs . . . . . Matt 8:28
Son..man *c* in his kingdom . . . . Matt 16:28
shall be the sign of thy *c* . . . . . . Matt 24:3
at my *c* I should have . . . . Matt 25:27
c in the clouds of heaven . . . . . Matt 26:64
straightway *c* up out of . . . . Mark 1:10
for there were many *c* and . . . . Mark 6:31
see the Son of man *c* in . . . . Mark 13:26
c in the clouds of heaven . . . . . Mark 14:62
passed by, *c* out of the . . . . Mark 15:21
but one mightier than I *c* . . . . . Luke 3:16
c to me, and heareth my . . . . . . Luke 6:47
to another, Come, and he *c* . . . Luke 7:8
then *c* the devil..taketh . . . . Luke 8:12
when he *c*, he findeth it . . . . Luke 11:25
When he *c* and knocketh . . . . . . Luke 12:36
Blessed is he that *c* in . . . . Luke 13:35
he that bade thee *c*, he . . . . Luke 14:10
he *c* home, he calleth . . . . Luke 15:6
God *c* not with observation . . . . Luke 17:20
Son of man *c*, shall he find . . . Luke 18:8
c in the name of the Lord . . . . . Luke 19:38
c after me is preferred . . . . John 1:27
but while I am *c*, another . . . . . John 5:7
seeth..wolf *c*, and leaveth . . . . . John 10:12
she heard that Jesus was *c* . . . . John 11:20
Jesus was *c* to Jerusalem . . . . . . John 12:12
before of the *c* of the Just . . . . . Acts 7:52
a man named Ananias *c* in . . . . Acts 9:12
an angel of God *c* in to . . . . Acts 10:3
first preached before..*c* . . . . Acts 13:24
who *c* thither went into . . . . Acts 17:10
while the day was *c* on . . . . Acts 27:33
much hindered from *c* to . . . . . . Rom 15:22
waiting for the *c* of..Lord 1Cor 1:7
are Christ's at his *c* 1Cor 15:23
glad of the *c* of Stephanus 1Cor 16:17
comforted us by the *c* of 2Cor 7:6
This is..third time I am *c* 2Cor 13:1
for me by my *c* to you . . . . Phil 1:26
Lord Jesus Christ..his *c*? 1Thess 2:19
at the *c* of..Lord Jesus 1Thess 3:13

remain unto the *c* of the 1Thess 4:15
the *c* of our Lord Jesus 1Thess 5:23
by..*c* of our Lord Jesus 2Thess 2:1
unto the *c* of the Lord ....James 5:7
To whom *c*, as unto a living ...1Pet 2:4
power and *c* of our Lord 2Pet 1:16
is the promise of his *c*? 2Pet 3:4
unto the *c* of..day of God 2Pet 3:12
ashamed before him at..*c* 1John 2:28
beast *c* up out of..earth ....Rev 13:11
Jerusalem, *c* down from God ..Rev 21:2

COMING OF CHRIST—*See* SECOND COMING OF CHRIST

COMMAND—*to order; direct*

[*also* COMMANDED, COMMANDEST, COMMANDETH, COMMANDING]

the Lord God *c* the man ......Gen 2:16
the tree, whereof I *c* thee .....Gen 3:11
all that God *c* him, so did .....Gen 6:22
unto all that the Lord *c* ....Gen 7:5
Pharaoh *c* his men ....Gen 12:20
c his children and his ....Gen 18:19
eight days old, as God had *c* ..Gen 21:4
according to that which I *c* ....Gen 27:8
And he *c* them, saying ....Gen 32:4
Then Joseph *c* to fill their .....Gen 42:25
he *c* the steward of his ....Gen 44:1
Now thou art *c*, this do ye ....Gen 45:19
Rameses, as Pharaoh had *c* ...Gen 47:11
had made an end of *c* his .....Gen 49:33
And Joseph *c* his servants .....Gen 50:2
Thy father did *c* before he ....Gen 50:16
the signs which he had *c* ......Ex 4:28
Pharaoh *c* the same day the ...Ex 5:6
shalt speak all that I *c* ....Ex 7:2
as the Lord *c* them, so did ...Ex 7:6
Lord our God, as he shall *c* ...Ex 8:27
and did as the Lord had *c* .....Ex 12:28
Lord hath *c*, Gather of it .....Ex 16:16
the thing which the Lord *c* ....Ex 16:32
do this thing, and God *c* ......Ex 18:23
words which the Lord *c* him ...Ex 19:7
as I *c* thee, in the time ....Ex 23:15
thou shalt *c* the children ......Ex 27:20
which I have *c* thee: seven ....Ex 29:35
all that I have *c* thee ....Ex 31:6
out of the way which I *c* ......Ex 32:8
as the Lord had *c* him, and ...Ex 34:4
which I *c* thee this day ....Ex 34:11
which the Lord hath *c* ....Ex 35:1
all that the Lord had *c* ....Ex 36:1
made all that the Lord *c* ......Ex 38:22
for Aaron; as the Lord *c* ......Ex 39:1
Lord *c* Moses, so did they ....Ex 39:32
the Lord *c* him, so did ....Ex 40:16
C Aaron and his sons ....Lev 6:9
the Lord *c* to be given ....Lev 7:36
the Lord *c* Moses in mount ...Lev 7:38
in the day that he *c* the ....Lev 7:38
Moses did as the Lord *c* ......Lev 8:4
Moses *c* before the ....Lev 9:5
the Lord, which he *c* them ....Lev 10:1
priest shall *c* that they ....Lev 13:54
Then shall the priest *c* ....Lev 14:4
he did as the Lord *c* Moses ...Lev 16:34
the Lord hath *c*, saying ....Lev 17:2
C the children of Israel ....Lev 24:2
Israel did as the Lord *c* ....Lev 24:23
I will *c* my blessing upon ......Lev 25:21
the Lord *c* Moses for the .....Lev 27:34
the Lord *c* Moses, so he ......Num 1:19
Israel; as the Lord *c* Moses ...Num 2:33
of the Lord, as he was *c* ......Num 3:16
him, as the Lord *c* Moses .....Num 4:49
C the children of Israel ....Num 5:2
candlestick, as the Lord *c* .....Num 8:3
Lord *c* Moses, so did the .....Num 9:5
Lord will *c* concerning ....Num 9:8
the Lord hath *c* you by ....Num 15:23
Aaron took as Moses *c* ....Num 16:47
as the Lord *c* him, so did .....Num 17:11
the Lord hath *c*, saying ....Num 19:2
before the Lord, as he *c* ......Num 20:9
the Lord *c* Moses and the .....Num 26:4
of judgment, as the Lord *c* ....Num 27:11
C the children of Israel ....Num 28:2
according to all..Lord *c* ....Num 29:40
thing which the Lord hath *c* ...Num 30:1
Lord *c* Moses; and they ....Num 31:7
servants..do as my lord *c* ......Num 32:25
concerning them Moses *c* .....Num 32:28
C the children of Israel ....Num 34:2
c the children of Israel ....Num 34:13
C the children of Israel ....Num 35:2
Lord *c* my lord to give ....Num 36:2
Lord doth *c* concerning ....Num 36:6
I *c* you at that time all ....Deut 1:18
c thou the people, saying .....Deut 2:4
And I *c* you at that time ......Deut 3:18
add unto the word which I *c* ..Deut 4:2
as the Lord my God *c* me .....Deut 4:5
the Lord thy God hath *c* ......Deut 5:12
Lord your God hath *c* you ....Deut 5:32
Lord your God *c* to teach .....Deut 6:1
commandments, which I *c* .....Deut 6:2
judgments, which I *c* thee .....Deut 7:11
commandments which I *c* .....Deut 8:1
of the way which I *c* them ....Deut 9:12
they be, as the Lord *c* me .....Deut 10:5
his statutes, which I *c* ....Deut 10:13
commandments which I *c* .....Deut 11:8
shall ye bring all that I *c* ......Deut 12:11
as I have *c* thee, and thou ....Deut 12:21
the Lord thy God *c* thee ......Deut 13:5
commandments which I *c* .....Deut 13:18
commandments which I *c* .....Deut 15:5
heaven, which I have not *c* ....Deut 17:3
unto them all..I shall *c* ....Deut 18:18
I have not *c* him to speak .....Deut 18:20
Wherefore I *c* thee, saying ....Deut 19:7
Lord thy God hath *c* thee .....Deut 20:17
as I *c* them, so ye shall ....Deut 24:8
I *c* thee to do this thing ....Deut 24:18
I *c* thee to do this thing ....Deut 24:22
which thou hast *c* me: I ....Deut 26:13
c..people, saying, Keep ....Deut 27:1
which I *c* you this day ....Deut 27:1
I *c* thee this day, that ....Deut 28:1
his statutes which he *c* ....Deut 28:45
the Lord *c* Moses to make ....Deut 29:1
all that I *c* thee this day ......Deut 30:2
which I have *c* you ....Deut 31:5
Moses *c* us a law, even the ....Deut 33:4
and did as the Lord *c* Moses ..Deut 34:9
Moses my servant *c* thee ......Josh 1:7
c..people, saying, Prepare .....Josh 1:11
All that thou *c* us we will .....Josh 1:16
they *c* the people, saying ......Josh 3:3
c the priests that bear ....Josh 3:8
c ye them, saying, Take ....Josh 4:3
us Joshua *c*, and took up .....Josh 4:8
Joshua had *c* the people ......Josh 6:10
my covenant which I *c* them ...Josh 7:11
he *c* them, saying, Behold .....Josh 8:4
Lord thy God *c* his servant ....Josh 9:24
Joshua *c*, and they took ....Josh 10:27
the servant of the Lord *c* .....Josh 11:12
so did Moses *c* Joshua, and ...Josh 11:15
inheritance, as I have *c* ....Josh 13:6
as the Lord *c* by the hand .....Josh 14:2
Lord *c* Moses to give us ......Josh 17:4
The Lord *c* by the hand of ....Josh 21:2
servant of the Lord *c* you .....Josh 22:2
which he *c* you, and have .....Josh 23:16
covenant which I *c* their ......Judg 2:20
the Lord God of Israel *c* ......Judg 4:6
all that I *c* her let her ....Judg 13:14
and *c* them, saying, Go and ...Judg 21:10
Boaz *c* his young men ....Ruth 2:15
I have *c* in my habitation 1Sam 2:29
which he *c* thee: for now 1Sam 13:13
Let our lord now *c* thy 1Sam 16:16
went, as Jesse had *c* him 1Sam 17:20
And Saul *c* his servants 1Sam 18:22
he hath *c* me to be there 1Sam 20:29
king hath *c* me a business 1Sam 21:2
And David *c* his young men ...2Sam 4:12
did so, as the Lord had *c* 2Sam 5:25
whom I *c* to feed my people ..2Sam 7:7
my lord the king hath *c* 2Sam 9:11
Now Absalom had *c* his 2Sam 13:28
And the king *c* Joab and 2Sam 18:5
performed all..the king *c* 2Sam 21:14
Gad, went up as the Lord *c* ...2Sam 24:19
So the king *c* Benaiah the 1Kin 2:46
c thou that they hew me 1Kin 5:6
And the king *c*, and they 1Kin 5:17
judgments, which he *c* our 1Kin 8:58
all that I have *c* thee 1Kin 9:4
had *c* him concerning this 1Kin 11:10
hearken unto all that I *c* 1Kin 11:38
which the Lord thy God *c* 1Kin 13:21
any thing that he *c* him 1Kin 15:5
I have *c* the ravens to feed 1Kin 17:4
king of Syria *c* his thirty 1Kin 22:31
And he *c* them, saying 2Kin 11:5
wherein the Lord *c*, saying 2Kin 14:6
And king Ahaz *c* Urijah the ...2Kin 16:15
law which I *c* your fathers 2Kin 17:13
which the Lord *c* Moses 2Kin 18:6
all that I have *c* them 2Kin 21:8
And the king *c* Hilkiah 2Kin 22:12
And the king *c* Hilkiah 2Kin 23:4
the servant of God had *c* 1Chr 6:49
therefore did as God *c* him 1Chr 14:16
as Moses *c* according to 1Chr 15:15
which he *c* to a thousand 1Chr 16:15
whom I *c* to feed my people ..1Chr 17:6
Is it not I that *c* the people ...1Chr 21:17
David *c* to gather together 1Chr 22:2
according to the order *c* 1Chr 23:31
Lord God of Israel had *c* 1Chr 24:19
I *c* the locusts to devour 2Chr 7:13
I have *c* thee, and shalt 2Chr 7:17
had David the man of God *c* ..2Chr 8:14
c Judah to seek the Lord 2Chr 14:4
king of Syria had *c* the 2Chr 18:30
Jehoiada the priest had *c* 2Chr 23:8
Lord *c*, saying, The fathers 2Chr 25:4
he *c* the priests the sons 2Chr 29:21
Moreover he *c* the people 2Chr 31:4
c Judah and Jerusalem 2Chr 32:12
do all that I have *c* them 2Chr 33:8
king *c* Hilkiah, and Ahikam ...2Chr 34:20
God *c* me to make haste 2Chr 35:21
king of Persia hath *c* us ....Ezra 4:3
Who hath *c* you to build ......Ezra 5:3
Whatsoever is *c* by the God ...Ezra 7:23
Which thou hast *c* by thy .....Ezra 9:11
thou *c* thy servant Moses......Neh 1:7
which the Lord had *c* to ......Neh 8:1
c them precepts, statutes ......Neh 9:14
which was *c* to be given ....Neh 13:5
he *c* Mehuman, Biztha ....Esth 1:10
king had so *c* concerning ......Esth 3:2
Mordecai *c* to answer ....Esth 4:13
he *c* to bring the book of .....Esth 6:1
Mordecai *c* unto the Jews .....Esth 8:9
And the king *c* it so to be ....Esth 9:14
c the sun, and it riseth ....Job 9:7
c that they return from ....Job 36:10
may do whatsoever he *c* ....Job 37:12
Hast thou *c* the morning ......Job 38:12
eagle mount up at thy *c* ....Job 39:27
according as the Lord *c* ....Job 42:9
judgment that thou hast *c* .....Ps 7:6
done; he *c*, and it stood ....Ps 33:9
will *c* his lovingkindness ....Ps 42:8
c deliverances for Jacob ....Ps 44:4
God hath *c* thy strength ....Ps 68:28
he *c* our fathers, that they ....Ps 78:5
the word which he *c* to a ....Ps 105:8
whom the Lord *c* ....Ps 106:34
For he *c*, and raiseth the ......Ps 107:25
he hath *c* his covenant ....Ps 111:9
c us to keep thy precepts .....Ps 119:4
the Lord *c* the blessing ....Ps 133:3
c, and they were created ......Ps 148:5
also *c* the clouds that ....Is 5:6
I have *c* my sanctified ....Is 13:3
my mouth it hath *c*, and ......Is 34:16
the work of my hands *c* ye ....Is 45:11
all their host have I *c* ....Is 45:12

my molten image, hath *c* ......Is 48:5
I *c* thee thou shalt speak ......Jer 1:7
c them in the day that I.......Jer 7:22
I *c* your fathers in the day ....Jer 11:4
according to all which I *c* .....Jer 11:4
Euphrates, as the Lord *c* me ..Jer 13:5
neither have I *c* them.........Jer 14:14
sabbath day, as I *c* your ......Jer 17:22
unto Baal, which I *c* not ......Jer 19:5
nor *c* them: therefore they ....Jer 23:32
the words that I *c* thee........Jer 26:2
Lord had *c* him to speak ......Jer 26:8
c them to say unto their ......Jer 27:4
I have not *c* them; even I .....Jer 29:23
of all that thou *c* them to .....Jer 32:23
I *c* them not, neither came ....Jer 32:35
I will *c*, saith the Lord........Jer 34:22
of Rechab our father *c* us .....Jer 35:6
And Jeremiah *c* Baruch ....Jer 36:5
Then Zedekiah the king *c* .....Jer 37:21
the king *c* Ebed-melech ....Jer 38:10
to all that I have *c* thee ....Jer 50:21
Jeremiah the prophet *c* ....Jer 51:59
whom thou didst *c* that they...Lam 1:10
the Lord hath *c* concerning....Lam 1:17
his word that he had *c* in .....Lam 2:17
to pass, when the Lord *c*......Lam 3:37
I have done as thou hast *c* ....Ezek 9:11
when he had *c* the man ....Ezek 10:6
And I did so as I was *c* ....Ezek 12:7
in the morning as I was *c* .....Ezek 24:18
I prophesied as I was *c* ....Ezek 37:7
king *c* to call the magicians....Dan 2:2
To you it is *c*, O people ......Dan 3:4
whereas they *c* to leave ....Dan 4:26
c to bring the golden and .....Dan 5:2
Then the king *c*, and they .....Dan 6:16
c the prophets, saying.........Amos 2:12
Lord *c*, and he will smite .....Amos 6:11
thence will I *c* the serpent.....Amos 9:3
I *c* my servants the ....Zech 1:6
which I *c* unto him in Horeb ..Mal 4:4
c that these stones be.........Matt 4:3
offer the gift that Moses *c*.....Matt 8:4
and *c* them, saying, Go not ...Matt 10:5
an end of *c* his twelve ....Matt 11:1
he *c* it to be given her ....Matt 14:9
For God *c*, saying, Honor .....Matt 15:4
his lord *c* him to be sold ......Matt 18:25
Why did Moses then *c* to .....Matt 19:7
and did as Jesus *c* them ....Matt 21:6
Pilate *c* the body to be........Matt 27:58
C therefore that the ....Matt 27:64
whatsoever I have *c* you ....Matt 28:20
c he even the unclean.........Mark 1:27
those things which Moses *c*....Mark 1:44
c that something should ....Mark 5:43
c them that they should ....Mark 6:8
c the people to sit down ......Mark 8:6
them, What did Moses *c* you? .Mark 10:3
stood still, and *c* him to.......Mark 10:49
even as Jesus had *c*: and ......Mark 11:6
and *c* the porter to watch .....Mark 13:34
c this stone that it be ....Luke 4:3
he *c* the unclean spirits ....Luke 4:36
according as Moses *c*, for a ...Luke 5:14
he *c* even the winds and ......Luke 8:25
For he had *c* the unclean .....Luke 8:29
he would not *c* them to go ....Luke 8:31
and *c* them to tell no man ....Luke 9:21
wilt thou that we *c* fire ....Luke 9:54
it is done as thou hast *c*......Luke 14:22
he did..things that were *c* ....Luke 17:9
c him to be brought unto .....Luke 18:40
c these servants..called ....Luke 19:15
Now Moses in the law *c* us....John 8:5
if ye do whatsoever I *c* ....John 15:14
c them that they should ....Acts 1:4
when they had *c* them to go...Acts 4:15
Did not we straitly *c* you......Acts 5:28
c to put the apostles forth .....Acts 5:34
c the chariot to stand still .....Acts 8:38
all things that are *c* thee ......Acts 10:33
c that they should be put .....Acts 12:19
Lord *c* us, saying, I have......Acts 13:47
c them to keep the law of.....Acts 15:5
I *c* thee in the name of ....Acts 16:18
their clothes, and *c* to beat ....Acts 16:22
but now *c* all men every ......Acts 17:30
Claudius had *c* all Jews to.....Acts 18:2
and *c* him to be bound with ...Acts 21:33
chief captain *c* him to be ......Acts 22:24
Ananias *c* them that stood ....Acts 23:2
c me to be smitten contrary ...Acts 23:3
C his accusers to come ....Acts 24:8
c a centurion to keep Paul ....Acts 24:23
seat *c* Paul to be brought .....Acts 25:6
c that they which could ....Acts 27:43
the married I *c*, yet not I 1Cor 7:10
c to be under obedience 1Cor 14:34
For God, who *c* the light 2Cor 4:6
your own hands, as we *c*......1Thess 4:11
do the things which we *c*......2Thess 3:4
this we *c* you, that if any 2Thess 3:10
c to abstain from meats 1Tim 4:3
These things *c* and teach 1Tim 4:11
endure that which was *c* ......Heb 12:20
was *c* them that they ....Rev 9:4

COMMANDER—*one in an official position of command or control*

Names of:
Phichol ....Gen 21:32
Sisera ....Judg 4:7
Abner 1Sam 17:55
Shobach 2Sam 10:16
Joab.....................2Sam 24:2
Amasa 1Kin 2:32
Zimri....................1Kin 16:9
Omri 1Kin 16:16
Shophach 1Chr 19:16
Adnah....................2Chr 17:14
Jehohanan 2Chr 17:15
Rehum ....Ezra 4:8
Hanniah ....Neh 7:2
Arioch ....Dan 2:15
Lysias ....Acts 24:7

a leader and *c* to the people...Is 55:4

COMMANDMENT—*a rule imposed by authority*

God's, described as:
Faithful.................Ps 119:86
Broad ....Ps 119:96
A lamp ....Prov 6:23
Holy ....Rom 7:12
Not burdensome.........1John 5:3

Christ's, described as:
New.....................John 13:34
Obligatory ....Matt 5:19, 20
Promissory..............John 15:10, 12
Eternal life ....John 12:49, 50

[*also* COMMANDMENTS]

my *c*, my statutes and my .....Gen 26:5
according to the *c* of..........Gen 45:21
and wilt give ear to his *c*......Ex 15:26
refuse ye to keep my *c* and ...Ex 16:28
according to the *c* of..........Ex 17:1
that love me, and keep my *c* ..Ex 20:6
and *c* which I have written ....Ex 24:12
give thee in *c* unto the ....Ex 25:22
of the covenant, the ten *c*.....Ex 34:28
gave them in *c* all the.........Ex 34:32
Moses gave *c* and they ....Ex 36:6
counted according to the *c* ....Ex 38:21
against any of the *c* of the ....Lev 4:2
to be done by the *c* of the ....Lev 5:17
shall ye keep my *c* ....Lev 22:31
keep my *c*, and do them ......Lev 26:3
These are the *c*, which the ....Lev 27:34
numbered at the *c* of the......Num 3:39
according to the *c* of..........Num 4:37
At the *c* of the Lord, the .....Num 9:18
journeyed, and at the *c* of ....Num 9:18
according to the *c* ....Num 9:20
journey according to the *c* ....Num 10:13
by the *c* of the Lord sent .....Num 13:3
transgress the *c* of the Lord ...Num 14:41
all these *c*, which the Lord ....Num 15:22
hath broken his *c*, that soul ...Num 15:31
I have received *c* to bless .....Num 23:20
c of the Lord to do either.....Num 24:13
ye rebelled against my *c* in ....Num 27:14
journeys by the *c* of the Lord .Num 33:2
These are the *c* and the ....Num 36:13
the Lord had given him in *c*...Deut 1:3
rebelled against the *c* of ......Deut 1:26
ye may keep the *c* of the .....Deut 4:2
that love me and keep my *c*...Deut 5:10
Now these are the *c*, the ......Deut 6:1
and keep his *c* to a thousand ..Deut 7:9
All the *c* which I command ...Deut 8:1
the *c* of the Lord your God ...Deut 9:23
the ten *c* which the Lord......Deut 10:4
his judgments, and his *c* ......Deut 11:1
his *c*, and obey his voice ......Deut 13:4
observe to do all these *c* ......Deut 15:5
turn not aside from the *c* .....Deut 17:20
shalt keep all these *c* to do....Deut 19:9
to all thy *c* which thou hast ...Deut 26:13
all the *c* which I command ....Deut 27:1
to do all his *c* which I ....Deut 28:1
his *c* which I command thee...Deut 30:8
For this *c* which I command ...Deut 30:11
unto all the *c* which I have....Deut 31:5
doth rebel against thy *c* ....Josh 1:18
on fire; according to the *c*.......Josh 8:8
the *c* of the Lord to Joshua ...Josh 15:13
to the *c* of the Lord, he.......Josh 17:4
at the *c* of the Lord, these ....Josh 21:3
at the *c* of the Lord your .....Josh 22:3
and to keep his *c*, and to .....Josh 22:5
walked in, obeying the *c* of ...Judg 2:17
would hearken unto the *c* .....Judg 3:4
and not rebel against the *c* 1Sam 12:14
hast not kept the *c* of the 1Sam 13:13
hath not performed my *c*.......1Sam 15:11
have performed the *c* of the ...1Sam 15:13
despised the *c* of the Lord 2Sam 12:9
his statutes, and his *c*, and 1Kin 2:3
c that I have charged thee 1Kin 2:43
my statutes and my *c* 1Kin 3:14
and keep all my *c* to walk in ..1Kin 6:12
keep his *c*, and his statutes 1Kin 8:58
keep my *c* and my statutes 1Kin 9:6
kept my *c* and my statutes 1Kin 11:34
kept the *c* which the Lord.....1Kin 13:21
David, who kept my *c*, and ...1Kin 14:8
forsaken the *c* of the Lord 1Kin 18:18
evil ways, and keep my *c* 2Kin 17:13
after the law and *c* which 2Kin 17:34
but kept his *c*, which the 2Kin 18:6
c was, saying, Answer him 2Kin 18:36
to keep his *c* and his 2Kin 23:3
according to the *c* of..........1Kin 23:35
c of the Lord came this upon...2Kin 24:3
brethren were at their *c*.......1Chr 12:32
David gave a *c*, and they 1Chr 14:12
if he be constant to do my *c* ..1Chr 28:7
will be wholly at thy *c* 1Chr 28:21
perfect heart, to keep thy *c* ...1Chr 29:19
statutes and my *c*, which I 2Chr 7:19
according to the *c* of Moses ...2Chr 8:13
and to do the law and the *c* ...2Chr 14:4
and walked in his *c* and 2Chr 17:4
between law and *c*, statutes ...2Chr 19:10
according to the *c* of Moses ...2Chr 24:6
Why transgress ye the *c* of 2Chr 24:20
to the *c* of the king by 2Chr 29:15
and according to the *c* 2Chr 30:6
as soon as the *c* came.........2Chr 31:5
in the *c*, to seek his God, he ..2Chr 31:21
the Lord, and to keep his *c* ..2Chr 34:31
according to the king's *c* 2Chr 35:10
now *c* to cause these men .....Ezra 4:21
another *c* shall be given ....Ezra 4:21
according to the *c* of the ......Ezra 6:14
of the words of the *c* of the ...Ezra 7:11
And I sent them with *c* ....Ezra 8:17
for we have forsaken thy *c*....Ezra 9:10
tremble at the *c* of our.......Ezra 10:3
love him, and observe his *c* ...Neh 1:5
laws, good statutes and *c*.....Neh 9:13
do all the *c* of the Lord our ...Neh 10:29

king's *c* concerning them ......Neh 11:23
c of David the man of God ...Neh 12:24
to come at the king's *c*........Esth 1:12
when the king's *c* and his .....Esth 2:8
transgressest..the king's *c*? ....Esth 3:3
the king's *c* and his decree ....Esth 4:3
the writing for a *c* to be ......Esth 8:13
when the king's *c* and his .....Esth 9:1
gone back from the *c* of his ...Job 23:12
c of the Lord is pure ....Ps 19:8
thou hast given *c* to save ......Ps 71:3
works of God, but keep his *c*..Ps 78:7
statutes, and keep not my *c*...Ps 89:31
those that remember his *c*.....Ps 103:18
judgment; all his *c* are sure ...Ps 111:7
delighteth greatly in his *c* .....Ps 112:1
I have respect unto all thy *c*...Ps 119:6
sendeth forth his *c* upon ......Ps 147:15
and hide my *c* with thee ......Prov 2:1
let thine heart keep my *c* .....Prov 3:1
my words; keep my *c*, and ....Prov 4:4
keep thy father's *c*, and ....Prov 6:20
c is a lamp; and the law is ....Prov 6:23
and lay up my *c* with thee ....Prov 7:1
waters should not pass his *c*...Prov 8:29
wise in heart will receive *c* ....Prov 10:8
feareth the *c* shall be ....Prov 13:13
keepeth the *c* keepeth his .....Prov 19:16
thee to keep the king's *c*......Eccl 8:2
Fear God, and keep his *c* .....Eccl 12:13
Lord hath given a *c* against ...Is 23:11
not a word for the king's *c*....Is 36:21
hadst hearkened to my *c*! .....Is 48:18
but obey their father's *c* ......Jer 35:14
have rebelled against his *c* ....Lam 1:18
the king's *c* was urgent........Dan 3:22
and to them that keep his *c*...Dan 9:4
the *c* came forth, and I am....Dan 9:23
willingly walked after the *c*....Hos 5:11
and have not kept his *c*........Amos 2:4
hath given a *c* concerning .....Nah 1:14
O ye priests, this *c* is for......Mal 2:1
break one of these least *c*.....Matt 5:19
he gave *c* to depart unto the ..Matt 8:18
do ye also transgress the *c* ....Matt 15:3
made the *c* of God of none ...Matt 15:6
teaching for doctrines the *c*....Matt 15:9
enter into life, keep the *c* .....Matt 19:17
On these two *c* hang all the ...Matt 22:40
teaching for doctrines the *c*....Mark 7:7
laying aside the *c* of God .....Mark 7:8
Full well ye reject the *c*.......Mark 7:9
Thou knowest the *c*. Do not ..Mark 10:19
Which is the first *c* of all?.....Mark 12:28
all the *c* is Hear, O Israel .....Mark 12:29
in all the *c* and ordinances ....Luke 1:6
I at any time thy *c* ....Luke 15:29
Thou knowest the *c*, Do not ..Luke 18:20
sabbath..according to the *c*....Luke 23:56
This *c* have I received of ....John 10:18
the Pharisees had given a *c*....John 11:57
If ye love me, keep my *c* .....John 14:15
as the Father gave me *c*.......John 14:31
given *c* unto the apostles ......Acts 1:2
to whom we gave no such *c*...Acts 15:24
and receiving a *c* unto Silas ...Acts 17:15
c to his accusers also to say ...Acts 23:30
at Festus' *c* Paul was ....Acts 25:23
taking occasion by the *c* ......Rom 7:8
c of the everlasting God ....Rom 16:26
by permission, and not of *c*...1Cor 7:6
the keeping of the *c* of God...1Cor 7:19
I write unto you are the *c*.....1Cor 14:37
I speak not by *c*, but by 2Cor 8:8
of *c* contained in ordinances...Eph 2:15
which is the first *c* with ....Eph 6:2
after the *c* and doctrines ......Col 2:22
whom ye received *c* ....Col 4:10
ye know what *c* we gave 1Thess 4:2
by the *c* of God our Savior....1Tim 1:1
the end of the *c* is charity.....1Tim 1:5
That thou keep this *c* 1Tim 6:14
according to the *c* of God .....Titus 1:3
Jewish fables, and *c* of men ...Titus 1:14
priesthood, have a *c* to take...Heb 7:5
and gave *c* concerning his .....Heb 11:22
to turn from the holy *c* 2Pet 2:21
of the *c* of us the apostles.....2Pet 3:2
know him, if we keep his *c*....1John 2:3
I write no new *c* unto you 1John 2:7
because we keep his *c*, and....1John 3:22
And this is his *c*. That we 1John 3:23
this *c* have we from him 1John 4:21
love God, and keep his *c* 1John 5:2
have received a *c* from the 2John 4
This is the *c*, That, as ye......2John 6
love that we walk after his *c* ..2John 6
seed, which keep the *c* of .....Rev 12:17
here are that keep the *c* of....Rev 14:12
are they that do his *c* ....Rev 22:14

COMMANDMENT, THE NEW

Given by Christ ....John 13:34, 35
Based on old............1John 2:7-11
2John 5
Fulfulls the Law ....Matt 22:34-40

COMMANDMENTS, DIVINE

Sought by men ....Phil 3:6-15
Not material ....Rom 14:1-23
Lives an epistle of 2Cor 3:1-3
Revealed at judgment....Matt 25:20, 21

COMMANDMENTS, THE TEN

Divine origin............Ex 20:1
Written by God ....Ex 32:16
Described...............Ex 20:3-17
Christ sums up ....Matt 22:35-40
Spiritual nature..........Matt 5:28
Love fulfills ....Rom 13:8-10

COMMEND—*to entrust to; recommend as worthy of notice; praise*

[*also* COMMENDATION, COMMENDED, COMMENDETH, COMMENDING]

and *c* her before Pharaoh .....Gen 12:15
be *c* according to his..........Prov 12:8
Then I *c* mirth, because a .....Eccl 8:15
lord *c* the unjust steward......Luke 16:8
into thy hands I *c* my spirit ...Luke 23:46
they *c* them to the Lord, on...Acts 14:23
I *c* you to God, and to ....Acts 20:32
if our unrighteousness *c* ....Rom 3:5
But God *c* his love toward ....Rom 5:8
I *c* unto you Phoebe our ......Rom 16:1
But meat *c* us not to God 1Cor 8:8
Do we begin again to *c* 2Cor 3:1
some others, epistles of *c* 2Cor 3:1
or letters of *c* from you? 2Cor 3:1
truth *c* ourselves to every 2Cor 4:2
c not ourselves again unto.....2Cor 5:12
some that *c* themselves.........2Cor 10:12
that *c* himself is approved 2Cor 10:18
but whom the Lord *c* 2Cor 10:18
I ought to have been *c* of 2Cor 12:11

COMMERCE—*buying and selling on a large scale*

Engaged in:

Locally ....Prov 31:14-18
Nationally 2Chr 9:21
Internationally ....Rev 18:10-24

Abuses of:

Sabbath trading ....Neh 13:15-22
Temple business ....John 2:13-16
Ignoring the Lord ....James 4:13-17
Pride ....Ezek 28:2-18

COMMISSION—*a special assignment*

Kinds of:

Christ's—to mankind ....John 3:16-18
Israel's—to the Gentiles..Acts 13:47
The Church's—to the world................Matt 28:19, 20

Requirements of:

Faithfulness 2Tim 4:1-8
Diligence ....Rom 15:15-32
Willingness..............1Sam 3:9, 10

[*also* COMMISSIONS]

they delivered the king's *c* ....Ezra 8:36
with authority and *c* from .....Acts 26:12

COMMIT—*to perform*

[*also* COMMITTED, COMMITTEST, COMMITTETH, COMMITTING]

he hath *c* all that he hath .....Gen 39:8
Thou shalt not *c* adultery .....Ex 20:14
for his sin that he hath *c*......Lev 4:35
trespass, which he hath *c*......Lev 5:7
If a soul *c* a trespass, and .....Lev 5:15
If a soul sin and *c* a ....Lev 6:2
and shall not *c* any of these ...Lev 18:26
which were *c* before you ......Lev 18:30
to *c* whoredom with Molech ...Lev 20:5
man that *c* adultery with ......Lev 20:10
have *c* an abomination ....Lev 20:13
a man or woman shall *c*.......Num 5:6
be *c* by ignorance without .....Num 15:24
people began to *c* whoredom ..Num 25:1
to *c* trespass against the ....Num 31:16
Neither shall thou *c* ....Deut 5:18
that woman, which have *c*.....Deut 17:5
c no more any such evil.......Deut 19:20
man have *c* a sin worthy of ...Deut 21:22
children of Israel *c* a..........Josh 7:1
ye have *c* against the God.....Josh 22:16
son of Zerah *c* a trespass .....Josh 22:20
c lewdness and folly in ....Judg 20:6
If he *c* iniquity, I will 2Sam 7:14
we have *c* wickedness 1Kin 8:47
their sins which they had *c* 1Kin 14:22
transgression which he *c* 1Chr 10:13
shields of brass, and *c* 2Chr 12:10
Jerusalem to *c* fornication 2Chr 21:11
that was *c* to thy servants 2Chr 34:16
unto God would I *c* my ....Job 5:8
Almighty, that he should *c* ....Job 34:10
the poor *c* himself unto thee ..Ps 10:14
Into thine hand I *c* my........Ps 31:5
C thy way unto the Lord ......Ps 37:5
we have *c* iniquity, we have ...Ps 106:6
whose *c* adultery with a ....Prov 6:32
C thy works unto the Lord ....Prov 16:3
c thy government into his .....Is 22:21
shall *c* fornication with ....Is 23:17
For my people have *c* two ....Jer 2:13
backsliding Israel *c* ....Jer 3:8
then *c* adultery, and ....Jer 5:7
they had *c* abomination? ......Jer 6:15
murder, and *c* adultery........Jer 7:9
they had *c* abomination? ......Jer 8:12
weary themselves to *c*.........Jer 9:5
that we have *c* against the.....Jer 16:10
they *c* adultery, and walk in ..Jer 23:14
they have *c* villany in Israel ..Jer 29:23
c Jeremiah into the court .....Jer 37:21
c him unto Gedaliah the ......Jer 39:14
c unto him men, and ....Jer 40:7
guard had *c* to Gedaliah ......Jer 41:10
which they have *c* to..........Jer 44:3
Wherefore *c* ye this great .....Jer 44:7
his righteousness, and *c* ....Ezek 3:20
the evils which they have *c*....Ezek 6:9
that the house of Israel *c* .....Ezek 8:6
they *c* the abominations ....Ezek 8:17
which they *c* here? ....Ezek 8:17
have *c* a trespass, saith the ....Ezek 15:8
didst *c* whoredom with them ..Ezek 16:17
c fornication with the ....Ezek 16:26
as a wife that *c* adultery ......Ezek 16:32
idols, hath *c* abomination .....Ezek 18:12
c iniquity, and doeth..........Ezek 18:24
have *c* a trespass against ......Ezek 20:27
c ye whoredom after their .....Ezek 20:30
of thee they *c* lewdness ....Ezek 22:9
one hath *c* abomination ....Ezek 22:11
they *c* whoredoms in Egypt ...Ezek 23:3
Will they now *c* whoredoms ...Ezek 23:43
and *c* iniquity, all his ....Ezek 33:13
his iniquity that he hath *c*.....Ezek 33:13
without *c* iniquity, he shall ....Ezek 33:15
c iniquity, he shall..die ....Ezek 33:18
abominations..they have *c*.....Ezek 43:8
abominations..they have *c*.....Ezek 44:13
sinned, and have *c* iniquity ....Dan 9:5
land hath *c* great whoredom ...Hos 1:2

stealing, and *c* adultery ....Hos 4:2
they shall *c* whoredom, and ...Hos 4:10
c whoredom continually ....Hos 4:18
O Ephraim, thou *c* ....Hos 5:3
for they *c* lewdness ....Hos 6:9
they *c* falsehood; and the .....Hos 7:1
abomination is *c* in Israel .....Mal 2:11
Thou shalt not *c* adultery .....Matt 5:27
c adultery with her already ....Matt 5:28
that is divorced *c* adultery .....Matt 5:32
marry another, *c* adultery .....Matt 19:9
is put away doth *c* adultery....Matt 19:9
another, *c* adultery against ....Mark 10:11
Do not *c* adultery ....Mark 10:19
c murder in the ....Mark 15:7
did *c* things worthy of ....Luke 12:48
to whom men have *c* much ....Luke 12:48
c to your trust the true ....Luke 16:11
marrieth another *c*...........Luke 16:18
Do not *c* adultery ....Luke 18:20
Jesus did not *c* himself unto ...John 2:24
c all judgment unto the Son ...John 5:22
c sin is the servant of sin......John 8:34
men and women *c* them to ....Acts 8:3
or have *c* any thing worthy ....Acts 25:11
they *c* themselves unto the ....Acts 27:40
c nothing against the..........Acts 28:17
c such things are worthy ......Rom 1:32
them which *c* such things......Rom 2:2
were *c* the oracles of God .....Rom 3:2
Thou shalt not *c* adultery .....Rom 13:9
but he that *c* fornication 1Cor 6:18
of the gospel is *c* 1Cor 9:17
Neither let us *c* fornication 1Cor 10:8
as some of them *c* 1Cor 10:8
and hath *c* unto us the word ..2Cor 5:19
I *c* an offense in abasing 2Cor 11:7
which they have *c* 2Cor 12:21
uncircumcision was *c* unto me. .Gal 2:7
which was *c* to my trust 1Tim 1:11
This charge I *c* unto thee 1Tim 1:18
keep that which is *c* to thy 1Tim 6:20
to keep that which I have *c* ...2Tim 1:12
the same *c* thou to faithful 2Tim 2:2
preaching, which is *c* unto.....Titus 1:3
ye *c* sin, and are convinced....James 2:9
If he have *c* sins, they shall ...James 5:15
but *c* himself to him that 1Pet 2:23
c the keeping of their souls....1Pet 4:19
c sin transgresseth 1John 3:4
born of God doth not *c* sin....1John 3:9
which they have ungodly *c* ....Jude 15
idols, and to *c* fornication .....Rev 2:14
earth have *c* fornication ....Rev 17:2
have *c* fornication with her ....Rev 18:3

COMMODIOUS—*serviceable*
haven was not *c* to winter in ..Acts 27:12

COMMON—*public; general*
Normal, natural 1Cor 10:13
Ceremonially unclean ....Acts 10:14
Ordinary people ....Jer 26:23
Shared togetherness .....Acts 2:44
Things believed alike ....Titus 1:4

[*also* COMMONLY]
c people sin through ....Lev 4:27
If these men die the *c* death ...Num 16:29
no *c* bread under mine hand ..1Sam 21:4
and it is *c* among men ....Eccl 6:1
the graves of the *c* people .....Jer 26:23
shall eat them as *c* things .....Jer 31:5
of the *c* sort were brought ....Ezek 23:42
took Jesus into the *c* hall .....Matt 27:27
is *c* reported among the ....Matt 28:15
c people heard him gladly .....Mark 12:37
and had all things *c* ....Acts 2:44
but they had all things *c* ......Acts 4:32
put them in the *c* prison ......Acts 5:18
thing that is *c* or unclean......Acts 10:14
for nothing *c* or unclean ......Acts 11:8
It is reported *c* that there 1Cor 5:1
you but such as is *c* to man ...1Cor 10:13
mine own son after the *c*......Titus 1:4
write..you of the *c* salvation ..Jude 3

COMMON PEOPLE—*the impoverished of Judah*
Burial place of ....Jer 26:23

COMMONWEALTH—*a nation*
Descriptive of Israel .....Eph 2:12

being aliens from the *c* of .....Eph 2:12

COMMOTION—*civil unrest or insurrection*

[*also* COMMOTIONS]
great *c* out of the north ....Jer 10:22
ye shall hear of wars and *c* ....Luke 21:9

COMMUNE—*intimate fellowship or rapport*

[*also* COMMUNED, COMMUNING, COMMUNION]
he had left *c* with Abraham ...Gen 18:33
And he *c* with them, saying ...Gen 23:8
out unto Jacob to *c* with ......Gen 34:6
Hamor *c* with them, saying ....Gen 34:8
and *c* with them and took .....Gen 42:24
they *c* with him at the door ...Gen 43:19
and I will *c* with thee from ....Ex 25:22
made an end of *c* with him ....Ex 31:18
and *c* with them, and with ....Judg 9:1
Samuel *c* with Saul upon the ..1Sam 9:25
C with David secretly and 1Sam 18:22
I will *c* with my father of 1Sam 19:3
was come to Solomon, she *c* ..1Kin 10:2
and they *c* with her 2Kin 22:14
was come to Solomon, she *c* ..2Chr 9:1
we assay to *c* with thee, wilt ..Job 4:2
c with your own heart upon ...Ps 4:4
c of laying snares privily ......Ps 64:5
I *c* with mine own heart ......Ps 77:6
I *c* with mine own heart ......Eccl 1:16
And the king *c* with them .....Dan 1:19
c with me said unto me ....Zech 1:14
c one with another what ....Luke 6:11
and *c* with the chief priests .....Luke 22:4
c together and reasoned ....Luke 24:15
him the oftener, and *c* with ...Acts 24:26
the *c* of the blood of Christ ...1Cor 10:16
it not the *c* of the body of 1Cor 10:16
c hath light with darkness? 2Cor 6:14
the *c* of the Holy Ghost, be ...2Cor 13:14

COMMUNICATE—*to share; make known*

[*also* COMMUNICATED, COMMUNICATION, COMMUNICATIONS]
And Abner had *c* with this 2Sam 3:17
Ye know the man and his *c* ...2Kin 9:11
your *c* be, Yea, yea; Nay .....Matt 5:37
What manner of *c* are these ...Luke 24:17
evil *c* corrupt good manners ...1Cor 15:33
c unto them that gospel ....Gal 2:2
c unto him that teacheth ......Gal 6:6
Let no corrupt *c* proceed......Eph 4:29
ye did *c* with my affliction .....Phil 4:14
c with me as concerning ......Phil 4:15
filthy *c* out of your mouth.....Col 3:8
to distribute, willing to *c* 1Tim 6:18
c of thy faith may become ....Philem 6
to do good and to *c* forget ....Heb 13:16

COMMUNION—*See* LORD'S SUPPER

COMMUNION OF THE SAINTS—*See* FELLOWSHIP

COMMUNION WITH CHRIST

Based on:
Redemption.............Heb 2:10-13
Regeneration............1Cor 6:14-17
Resurrection (Spiritual) ..Col 3:1-3

Identifies Christians, in:
Name 1Pet 4:12-16
Character ....John 14:23
Hope 1John 3:1-3

COMMUNION WITH GOD

Prerequisites of:
Reconciliation 2Cor 5:18, 19
Acceptance of Christ ....John 14:6
Obedience ....John 14:23
Holiness 2Cor 6:14-18

Saints:
Desire such ....Heb 11:10
Seek it through prayer ...Matt 6:6-15
Realized fully in eternity..Rev 7:13-17

COMPACT—*to knit or draw together*

[*also* COMPACTED]
as a city that is *c* together.....Ps 122:3
and *c* by that which every .....Eph 4:16

COMPANIED—*accompanied*
men which have *c* with us .....Acts 1:21

COMPANION—*a fellow worker*
Wife ....Mal 2:14
Companion in tribulation .Rev 1:9
Co-worker ....Ezra 4:7, 9, 11
Fellow fool ....Prov 13:20
Fellow believer ....Ps 119:63
Fellow worker..........Phil 2:23, 25

[*also* COMPANIONS, COMPANIONS']
and every man his *c* ....Ex 32:27
she went with her *c* and.......Judg 11:38
they brought thirty *c* to be ....Judg 14:11
wife was given to his *c* ....Judg 14:20
I gave her to thy *c*; is not .....Judg 15:2
the Archite was the king's *c* ...1Chr 27:33
Shethar-boznai and their *c* ....Ezra 5:3
Shethar-boznai, and your *c* ....Ezra 6:6
brother to dragons, and a *c* ...Job 30:29
will answer thee, and thy *c* ....Job 35:4
Shall the *c* make a banquet ...Job 41:6
virgins her *c* that follow her ...Ps 45:14
am a *c* of all them that fear ...Ps 119:63
my brethren and *c* sakes ......Ps 122:8
c of fools shall be destroyed ...Prov 13:20
he that is a *c* of riotous men ..Prov 28:7
aside by the flocks of thy *c*....Song 1:7
the *c* hearken to thy voice ....Song 8:13
rebellious and *c* of thieves.....Is 1:23
the children of Israel his *c* ....Ezek 37:16
Mishael and Azariah, his *c* ....Dan 2:17
of Macedonia, Paul's *c* in .....Acts 19:29
ye became *c* of them that .....Heb 10:33

COMPANIONS, EVIL

Cause:
Rebellion ....Num 16:1-50
Idolatry.................Ex 32:1-8
Violence, death ....Acts 23:12-22
Persecution ....Acts 17:5-9

Warnings against:
Do not consent with
them ....Prov 1:10-19
Avoid them 1Cor 5:9-11
Remember their end.....Rev 22:11, 15

COMPANY—*a group of persons; a body of soldiers*

[*also* COMPANIES]
If Esau come to the one *c* ....Gen 32:8
c of nations shall be of thee ...Gen 35:11
c of Ishmaelites came from ....Gen 37:25
and it was a very great *c* ......Gen 50:9
they spake unto all the *c* of ...Num 14:7
unto all his *c* saying, Even ....Num 16:5
Now shall this *c* lick up all ....Num 22:4
the *c* of Korah, when they ....Num 26:9
the *c* of them that gathered ...Num 27:3
hundred men into three *c* .....Judg 7:16
against Shechem in four *c* .....Judg 9:34
another *c* come along by the ..Judg 9:37
thou comest with such a *c*?....Judg 18:23
shalt meet a *c* of prophets.....1Sam 10:5
put the people in three *c* 1Sam 11:11
the Philistines in three *c* 1Sam 13:17
one *c* turned unto the way 1Sam 13:17
saw the *c* of the prophets 1Sam 19:20
bring me down to this *c*? 1Sam 30:15
Syrians had gone out by *c* 2Kin 5:2
he and all his *c* and came 2Kin 5:15
he spied the *c* of Jehu as he ...2Kin 9:17

were porters in the *c* ... 1Chr 9:18
c that ministered to the ... 1Chr 28:1
with a very great *c*, and ... 2Chr 9:1
no might against this great *c* ... 2Chr 20:12
Syrians came with a small *c* ... 2Chr 24:24
two great *c* of them that ... Neh 12:31
the other *c* of them that ... Neh 12:38
the *c* of Sheba waited for ... Job 6:19
hast made desolate all my *c* ... Job 16:7
which goeth in *c* with the ... Job 34:8
unto the house of God in *c* ... Ps 55:14
great was the *c* of those ... Ps 68:11
covered the *c* of Abiram ... Ps 106:17
that keepeth *c* with harlots ... Prov 29:3
c of horses in Pharaoh's ... Song 1:9
ye traveling *c* of Dedanim ... Is 21:13
let thy *c* deliver thee ... Is 57:13
a great *c* shall return ... Jer 31:8
They shall also bring up a *c* ... Ezek 16:40
his mighty army and great *c* ... Ezek 17:17
I will bring up a *c* upon ... Ezek 23:46
with horsemen, and *c*, and ... Ezek 26:7
the *c* of the Ashurites have ... Ezek 27:6
my net over thee with a *c* of ... Ezek 32:3
great *c* with bucklers and ... Ezek 38:4
c of priests murder in the ... Hos 6:9
sit down by *c* upon the ... Mark 6:39
him to have been in the *c* ... Luke 2:44
c of publicans and of others ... Luke 5:29
and the *c* of his disciples ... Luke 6:17
sit down by fifties in a *c* ... Luke 9:14
woman of the *c* lifted up ... Luke 11:27
one of the *c* said unto him ... Luke 12:13
great *c* of people, and of ... Luke 23:27
certain women also of our *c* ... Luke 24:22
saw a great *c* come unto ... John 6:5
they went to their own *c* ... Acts 4:23
great *c* of the priests were ... Acts 6:7
is a Jew to keep *c* or come ... Acts 10:28
when Paul and his *c* loosed ... Acts 13:13
chosen men of their own *c* ... Acts 15:22
gathered a *c* and set all the ... Acts 17:5
day we that were of Paul's *c* ... Acts 21:8
somewhat filled with your *c* ... Rom 15:24
not to *c* with fornicators ... 1Cor 5:9
that man, and have no *c* ... 2Thess 3:14
an innumerable *c* of angels ... Heb 12:22
all the *c* in ships ... Rev 18:17

COMPARISON—*likeness; similarity*

Worthy comparisons, between:
God's greatness and man's littleness ... Is 46:12, 13
Christ's glory and humiliation ... Phil 2:5-11
Israel's call and responsibility ... Rom 2:17-29
Gentile faith and Jewish unbelief ... Matt 12:41, 42
Former and present unbelief ... Matt 11:20-24
Old and new covenants ... 2Cor 3:6-18
The believer's status now and hereafter ... 1John 3:1-3

Unworthy comparisons, based on:
Position ... Num 16:3
Privileges ... 1Cor 3:1-9
Ancestry ... James 2:1-9

[*also* COMPARABLE, COMPARE, COMPARED, COMPARING]
have I done now in *c* of you ... Judg 8:2
who in the heaven can be *c* ... Ps 89:6
canst desire are not to be *c* ... Prov 3:15
desired are not to be *c* to ... Prov 8:11
I have *c* thee, O my love ... Song 1:9
what likeness will ye *c* unto ... Is 40:18
c me that we may be like? ... Is 46:5
precious sons of Zion, *c* ... Lam 4:2
is it not in your eyes in *c* ... Hag 2:3
or with what *c* shall we *c* it? ... Mark 4:30
not worthy to be *c* with the ... Rom 8:18
c spiritual things with ... 1Cor 2:13
c ourselves with some that ... 2Cor 10:12
c themselves among ... 2Cor 10:12

COMPASS—*to encircle; travel around; surround; a circle*

[*also* COMPASSED, COMPASSEST, COMPASSETH, COMPASSING]
c the whole land of Havilah ... Gen 2:11
c the house round, both old ... Gen 19:4
put it under the *c* of the ... Ex 27:5
we *c* mount Seir many days ... Deut 2:1
And ye shall *c* the city all ... Josh 6:3
ark of the Lord *c* the city ... Josh 6:11
and fetched a *c* to Karkaa ... Josh 15:3
the border *c* from Baalah ... Josh 15:10
and *c* the corner of the sea ... Josh 18:14
border *c* it on the north ... Josh 19:14
and *c* the land of Edom ... Judg 11:18
they *c* him in, and laid wait ... Judg 16:2
Saul and his men *c* David ... 1Sam 23:26
fetch a *c* behind them and ... 2Sam 5:23
c about and smote Absalom ... 2Sam 18:15
waves of death *c* me, the ... 2Sam 22:5
line of twelve cubits did *c* ... 1Kin 7:15
knobs *c* it, ten in a cubit ... 1Kin 7:24
fetched a *c* of seven days' ... 2Kin 3:9
they came by night and *c* ... 2Kin 6:14
smote the Edomites which *c* ... 2Kin 8:21
ye shall *c* the king round ... 2Kin 11:8
brim to brim, round in *c* ... 2Chr 4:2
c the sea round about ... 2Chr 4:3
Therefore they *c* about him ... 2Chr 18:31
smote the Edomites which *c* ... 2Chr 21:9
Levites shall *c* the king ... 2Chr 23:7
c about Ophel and raised ... 2Chr 33:14
archers *c* me round about ... Job 16:13
and hath *c* me with his net ... Job 19:6
c the waters with bounds ... Job 26:10
willows of the brook *c* him ... Job 40:22
with favor wilt thou *c* him ... Ps 5:12
congregation of the people *c* ... Ps 7:7
my deadly enemies who *c* ... Ps 17:9
They have now *c* us in our ... Ps 17:11
The sorrows of death *c* me ... Ps 18:4
Many bulls have *c* me ... Ps 22:12
I *c* thine altar, O Lord ... Ps 26:6
thou shalt *c* me about with ... Ps 32:7
innumerable evils have *c* ... Ps 40:12
iniquity of my heels shall *c* ... Ps 49:5
pride *c* them about as a ... Ps 73:6
they *c* me about together ... Ps 88:17
They *c* me about also with ... Ps 109:3
Sorrows of death *c* me ... Ps 116:3
All nations *c* me about; but ... Ps 118:10
Thou *c* my path and my ... Ps 139:3
the head of those that *c* me ... Ps 140:9
righteous shall *c* me about ... Ps 142:7
marketh it out with the *c* ... Is 44:13
c yourselves about with ... Is 50:11
earth, A woman shall *c* ... Jer 31:22
a fillet of twelve cubits..*c* ... Jer 52:21
me, and *c* me with gall and ... Lam 3:5
Ephraim *c* me about with ... Hos 11:12
the floods *c* me about; all ... Jon 2:3
for the wicked doth *c* about ... Hab 1:4
c sea and land to make one ... Matt 23:15
a trench about thee and *c* ... Luke 19:43
shall see Jerusalem *c* with ... Luke 21:20
thence we fetched a *c* and ... Acts 28:13
also is *c* with infirmity ... Heb 5:2
they were *c* about seven ... Heb 11:30
are *c* about with so great a ... Heb 12:1
and *c* the camp of the saints ... Rev 20:9

COMPASSION—*suffering with another; desire to relieve another's distress*

God's, described as:
From of old ... Ps 26:6
New every morning ... Lam 3:22, 23
Great ... Is 54:7
Kindled ... Hos 11:8

God's, expressed:
Fully ... Ps 78:38
Sovereignly ... Rom 9:15
Unfailingly ... Lam 3:22
Willingly ... Luke 15:20

Christ's, expressed toward the:
Weary ... Matt 11:28-30
Tempted ... Heb 2:18
Helpless ... Mark 9:20-22
Ignorant ... Heb 5:2
Sorrowful ... Luke 7:13, 14
Multitude ... Matt 15:32

Examples of:
David in sorrow ... Ps 51:1-12
God to Israel ... Hos 11:8
Christ to sinners ... Matt 9:13

Christian's:
Commanded ... Zech 7:9; Col 3:12; Jude 22
Expressed ... Heb 10:34; 1Pet 3:8
Illustrated ... Luke 10:33
Unified ... Phil 2:1, 2

[*also* COMPASSIONS]
And she had *c* on him, and ... Ex 2:6
thee mercy and have *c* upon ... Deut 13:17
captivity and have *c* upon ... Deut 30:3
Lord; for ye have *c* on me ... 1Sam 23:21
c before them who carried ... 1Kin 8:50
that they may have *c* on ... 1Kin 8:50
had *c* on them and had ... 2Kin 13:23
children shall find *c* ... 2Chr 30:9
because he had *c* on his ... 2Chr 36:15
God full of *c* and gracious ... Ps 86:15
is gracious and full of *c* ... Ps 111:4
and full of *c* and righteous ... Ps 112:4
is gracious and full of *c* ... Ps 145:8
should not have *c* on the ... Is 49:15
I will return and have *c* ... Jer 12:15
will he have *c* according ... Lam 3:32
to have *c* upon thee; but ... Ezek 16:5
he will have *c* upon us ... Mic 7:19
show mercy and *c* every ... Zech 7:9
he was moved with *c* on ... Matt 9:36
was moved with *c* toward ... Matt 14:14
moved with *c* and loosed ... Matt 18:27
Jesus had *c* on them and ... Matt 20:34
Jesus, moved with *c*, put ... Mark 1:41
and hath had *c* on thee ... Mark 5:19
was moved with *c* toward ... Mark 6:34
I have *c* on the multitude ... Mark 8:2
have *c* on us, and help us ... Mark 9:22
shutteth up his bowels of *c* ... 1John 3:17
have *c*, making a difference ... Jude 22

COMPEL—*to cause or force one to act*

[*also* COMPELLED, COMPELLEST]
shalt not *c* him to serve as ... Lev 25:39
with the woman, *c* him ... 1Sam 28:23
fornication, and *c* Judah ... 2Chr 21:11
none did *c*; for so the king ... Esth 1:8
shall *c* thee to go a mile ... Matt 5:41
they *c* to bear his cross ... Matt 27:32
c one Simon a Cyrenian who ... Mark 15:21
c them to come in, that my ... Luke 14:23
and *c* them to blaspheme ... Acts 26:11
fool in glorying; ye have *c* ... 2Cor 12:11
was *c* to be circumcised ... Gal 2:3
why *c* thou the Gentiles to ... Gal 2:14

COMPLAINERS—*those who protest*
are murmurers, *c*, walking ... Jude 16

COMPLAINT—*expression of grief or pain; something which causes outcry or protest*

[*also* COMPLAIN, COMPLAINED, COMPLAINERS, COMPLAINING, COMPLAINTS]
the people *c*, it displeased ... Num 11:1
come unto us to *c*, that we ... Judg 21:22
abundance of my *c* and grief ... 1Sam 1:16
c in the bitterness of my ... Job 7:11
my couch shall ease my *c* ... Job 7:13
forget my *c*, I will leave ... Job 9:27
leave my *c* upon myself ... Job 10:1
is my *c* to man? And if it ... Job 21:4
to day is my *c* bitter; my ... Job 23:2
furrows likewise thereof *c* ... Job 31:38
I mourn in my *c* and make ... Ps 55:2

I *c*, and my spirit was . . . . Ps 77:3
poureth out his *c* before . . . . . . Ps 102: *title*
I poured out my *c* before . . . . . Ps 142:2
That there be no *c* in our . . . . . Ps 144:14
doth a living man *c* . . . . Lam 3:39
and grievous *c* against . . . . Acts 25:7
are murmurers, *c*, walking . . . . Jude 16

COMPLETE—*total; absolute*
seven sabbaths shall be *c* . . . . . . Lev 23:15
c in him, which is the head . . . . Col 2:10
perfect and *c* in all the will . . . . Col 4:12

COMPLICITY—*association or participation in a wrongful act*
In Adam's sin . . . . Rom 5:12
In the sins of others . . . . . Ps 50:18
In national guilt . . . . Matt 27:25

COMPOSITION—*arrangement*
other like it after the *c* . . . . Ex 30:32

COMPOSURE—*calmness; tranquility; self-possession*
Before enemies . . . . Neh 4:1-23
Under great strain . . . . Acts 27:21-26
Facing death . . . . Acts 7:59, 60
Lack of . . . . Dan 6:18-20

COMPOUND—*put or mixed together*

[*also* COMPOUNDETH]
an ointment *c* after the art . . . . Ex 30:25
Whosoever *c* any like it, or . . . Ex 30:33

COMPREHEND—*to overcome; encompass; understand*

[*also* COMPREHENDED]
doeth he; which we cannot *c* . . Job 37:5
and *c* the dust of the earth . . . . Is 40:12
and the darkness *c* it not . . . . . . John 1:5
briefly *c* in this saying . . . . Rom 13:9
able to *c* with all saints . . . . Eph 3:18

COMPROMISE—*agreement by concession*
Forbidden with:
Ungodly . . . . Ps 1:1
Evil . . . . Rom 12:9
Unbelievers 2Cor 6:14-18
False teachers . . . . Gal 1:8-10
2John 7-11
Spiritual darkness . . . . Eph 5:11
Examples:
Lot . . . . Gen 13:12, 13
Gen 19:1-29
Samson . . . . Judg 16:1-21
Solomon 1Kin 11:1-14
Asa 2Chr 16:1-9
Jehoshaphat . . . . { 2Chr 18:1-3; 2Chr 19:1, 2; 2Chr 20:35-37 }

CONANIAH (kō-nä-nī'ä)—*"Jehovah has founded"—a Levite appointed to be overseer of tithes and offerings at the temple*
C also, and Shemaiah, and 2Chr 35:9

CONCEALMENT—*keeping something secret*
Of sin, impossible . . . . Is 29:15
Of intrigue, exposed . . . . . Esth 2:21-23
Of intentions, revealed . . . Acts 23:12-22

[*also* CONCEAL, CONCEALED, CONCEALETH]
slay our brother and *c* his . . . . . Gen 37:26
neither shalt thou *c* him . . . . Deut 13:8
c the words of the Holy One . . Job 6:10
the Almighty will I not *c* . . . . . . Job 27:11
I will not *c* his parts nor . . . . . . Job 41:12
is of a faithful spirit *c* the . . . . . Prov 11:13
prudent man *c* knowledge . . . . . Prov 12:23
It is the glory of God to *c* . . . . Prov 25:2
publish and *c* not; say . . . . Jer 50:2

CONCEIT—*self-flattery*
Of persons:
Goliath 1Sam 17:42-44
Sanballat . . . . Neh 4:1-3
Haman . . . . Esth 6:6-9
The wicked . . . . Prov 6:12-17
Christians, deplored . . . . . Rom 12:16
Characteristic of:
False teachers 1Tim 6:3, 4
New convert 1Tim 3:6

[*also* CONCEITS]
as a high wall in his own *c* . . . . Prov 18:11
lest he be wise in his own *c* . . . Prov 26:5
rich man is wise in his own *c* . . Prov 28:11
be wise in your own *c* . . . . Rom 11:25

CONCEITED—*a self-righteous spirit*
Christians warned against . Rom 11:20
Rich tempted to 1Tim 6:17
To prevail in last days . . . 2Tim 3:1-5

CONCEPTION—*the act of becoming pregnant*
In marriage . . . . Gen 21:1-3
In adultery 2Sam 11:2-5
In virginity . . . . Matt 1:18-21

[*also* CONCEIVE, CONCEIVED, CONCEIVING]
multiply thy sorrow and..*c* . . . . Gen 3:16
and she *c* and bare Cain . . . . . . Gen 4:1
went in unto Hagar, and she *c* . Gen 16:4
and Rebekah his wife *c* . . . . Gen 25:21
And Leah *c* and bare a son . . . . Gen 29:32
Bilhah *c* and bare Jacob a . . . . Gen 30:5
should *c* when they came to . . . Gen 30:38
at the time that the cattle *c* . . . Gen 31:10
And she *c* and bare a son . . . . . Gen 38:3
woman *c* and bare a son . . . . . . Ex 2:2
If a woman have *c* seed . . . . Lev 12:2
shall be free and shall *c* . . . . Num 5:28
Have I *c* all this people? . . . . . . Num 11:12
but thou shalt *c* and bear . . . . . Judg 13:3
the Lord gave her *c* and she . . . Ruth 4:13
after Hannah had *c* that 1Sam 1:20
she *c* and bare three sons 1Sam 2:21
And the woman *c* and sent 2Sam 11:5
And the woman *c* and bare . . . 2Kin 4:17
c, and bare a son, and he 1Chr 7:23
There is a man child *c* . . . . Job 3:3
They *c* mischief and bring . . . . . Job 15:35
and hath *c* mischief and . . . . Ps 7:14
and in sin did my mother *c* . . . . Ps 51:5
chamber of her that *c* me . . . . . Song 3:4
a virgin shall *c* and bear a . . . . . Is 7:14
and she *c* and bare a son . . . . . Is 8:3
c chaff, ye shall bring . . . . Is 33:11
c mischief, and bring forth . . . . Is 59:4
c..uttering from the heart . . . . . Is 59:13
c a purpose against you . . . . Jer 49:30
which *c* and bare him a son . . . Hos 1:3
she that *c* them hath done . . . . Hos 2:5
the womb and from the *c* . . . . . Hos 9:11
that which is *c* in her is . . . . Matt 1:20
his wife Elisabeth *c* and . . . . Luke 1:24
thou shalt *c* in thy womb . . . . . . Luke 1:31
before he was *c* in the . . . . Luke 2:21
why hast thou *c* this thing . . . . . Acts 5:4
when Rebecca also had *c* . . . . . Rom 9:10
received strength to *c* . . . . Heb 11:11
Then when lust hath *c*, it . . . . . James 1:15

CONCERN—*to relate to; bear on; have an influence on*

[*also* CONCERNETH, CONCERNING]
comfort us *c* our work and . . . . Gen 5:29
accepted thee *c* this thing . . . . . Gen 19:21
sware to him *c* that matter . . . . Gen 24:9
c the well which they had . . . . . Gen 26:32
verily guilty *c* our brother . . . . . Gen 42:21
the land *c* the which I did . . . . . Ex 6:8
made with you *c* all these . . . . . Ex 24:8
the Lord *c* things which . . . . Lev 4:2
atonement for him *c* his sin . . . Lev 5:6
which was lost and lieth *c* . . . . . Lev 6:3
C the feasts of the Lord . . . . Lev 23:2
And *c* the tithe of the herd . . . Lev 27:32
Lord commanded Moses *c* . . . . Num 8:20
Lord will command *c* you . . . . . Num 9:8
hath spoken good *c* Israel . . . . . Num 10:29
the land, *c* which I sware . . . . . Num 14:30
tribes *c* the children of . . . . Num 30:1
c them Moses commanded . . . . Num 32:28
c the daughters of . . . . Num 36:6
man of God *c* me and thee . . . . Josh 14:6
Lord your God spake *c* you . . . Josh 23:14
Samson said *c* them, Now . . . . . Judg 15:3
oath *c* him that came not . . . . . Judg 21:5
c redeeming and *c* . . . . Ruth 4:7
which I have spoken *c* his 1Sam 3:12
with a fault *c* this woman? 2Sam 3:8
c thy servant and *c* his 2Sam 7:25
David all the things *c* the 2Sam 11:18
he was comforted *c* Amnon . . . 2Sam 13:39
I will give charge *c* thee 2Sam 14:8
captains charge *c* Absalom 2Sam 18:5
word which he spake *c* me 1Kin 2:4
will do all thy desire *c* 1Kin 5:8
C this house which thou art . . . 1Kin 6:12
Moreover *c* a stranger, that . . . 1Kin 8:41
c the name of the Lord, she . . . 1Kin 10:1
nations *c* which the Lord 1Kin 11:2
not prophesy good *c* me 1Kin 22:8
spake *c* the house of Ahab 2Kin 10:10
c whom the Lord hath 2Kin 17:15
that the Lord hath spoken *c* . . . 2Kin 19:21
c the words of this book 2Kin 22:13
that thou hast spoken *c* thy . . . 1Chr 17:23
to comfort him *c* his father 1Chr 19:2
give thee charge *c* Israel 1Chr 22:12
c Moses the man of God 1Chr 23:14
C Rehabiah: of the sons of 1Chr 24:21
C the divisions of the 1Chr 26:1
Moreover *c* the stranger 2Chr 6:32
c any matter or *c* the 2Chr 8:15
the seer *c* genealogies? 2Chr 12:15
c Maachah the mother of 2Chr 15:16
Now *c* his sons and the 2Chr 24:27
c the children of Israel 2Chr 31:6
c the words of the book 2Chr 34:21
answer by letter *c* this . . . . Ezra 5:5
a decree *c* the house of God . . Ezra 6:3
c Judah and Jerusalem . . . . Ezra 7:14
hope in Israel *c* this thing . . . . . Ezra 10:2
I asked them *c* the Jews . . . . . . Neh 1:2
them into the land *c* which . . . . Neh 9:23
king's commandment *c* . . . . Neh 11:23
Remember me..*c* this . . . . Neh 13:14
had so commanded *c* him . . . . . Esth 3:2
which they had seen *c* this . . . . Esth 9:26
C the works of men, by the . . . Ps 17:4
speak..*c* oppression . . . . Ps 73:8
let it repent thee *c* thy . . . . Ps 90:13
not destroy the nations, *c* . . . . . Ps 106:34
I esteem all thy precepts *c* . . . . Ps 119:128
repent himself *c* his . . . . Ps 135:14
that which *c* me: thy mercy . . . Ps 138:8
search out by wisdom *c* . . . . Eccl 1:13
I said in mine heart *c* . . . . Eccl 3:18
dost not inquire wisely *c* . . . . . . Eccl 7:10
of Amoz, which he saw *c* . . . . . Is 1:1
Amoz saw *c* Judah and . . . . Is 2:1
in it with a man's pen *c* . . . . Is 8:1
Lord hath spoken *c* Moab . . . . . Is 16:13
As at the report *c* Egypt . . . . . . Is 23:5
Abraham, *c* the house of . . . . . . Is 29:22
therefore have I cried *c* . . . . Is 30:7
he heard say *c* Tirhakah . . . . . . Is 37:9
c my sons and *c* the work . . . . . Is 45:11
c burnt offerings or . . . . Jer 7:22
to Jeremiah *c* the dearth . . . . . . Jer 14:1
c the sons and *c* the . . . . Jer 16:3
c a nation and *c* a . . . . Jer 18:7
saith the Lord *c* Jehoiakim . . . . Jer 22:18
the Lord of hosts *c* the . . . . Jer 23:15
came to Jeremiah *c* all the . . . . Jer 25:1
c..the pillars and *c* the . . . . Jer 27:19
c the bases and *c* the . . . . Jer 27:19
saith the Lord *c* Shemaiah . . . . Jer 29:31
Lord spake *c* Israel and *c* . . . . . Jer 30:4
c this city, whereof ye say . . . . . Jer 32:36
of Israel *c* the houses of . . . . . . Jer 33:4
c the houses of the kings . . . . . . Jer 33:4
gave charge *c* Jeremiah to . . . . . Jer 39:11
The Lord hath said *c* you . . . . . Jer 42:19
c all the Jews which dwell . . . . . Jer 44:1
C the Ammonites thus . . . . Jer 49:1
c the pillars, the height . . . . Jer 52:21

Lord..commanded *c* Jacob ....Lam 1:17
This burden *c* the prince in....Ezek 12:10
prophesy *c* Jerusalem ....Ezek 13:16
to inquire of him *c* me ....Ezek 14:7
proverb *c* the land of Israel ...Ezek 18:2
Lord God *c* the Ammonites ...Ezek 21:28
Prophesy therefore *c* the ......Ezek 36:6
I say unto thee *c* all the......Ezek 44:5
C the ordinance of oil ....Ezek 45:14
c the which I lifted up ....Ezek 47:14
God of heaven *c* this secret ...Dan 2:18
made a proclamation *c* him....Dan 5:29
against Daniel *c* the ....Dan 6:4
As *c* the rest of the beasts ....Dan 7:12
vision *c* the daily sacrifice .....Dan 8:13
which he saw *c* Israel in the ...Amos 1:1
saith the Lord God *c* Edom ...Obad 1
c Samaria and Jerusalem ......Mic 1:1
saith the Lord *c* the ....Mic 3:5
a commandment *c* thee ....Nah 1:14
now the priests *c* the law......Hag 2:11
give his angels charge *c* ....Matt 4:6
say unto the multitudes *c* .....Matt 11:7
spake it not to you *c* bread....Matt 16:11
and also *c* the swine ....Mark 5:16
disciples asked him *c* the ......Mark 7:17
which was told them *c* this ....Luke 2:17
to speak unto the people *c* ....Luke 7:24
by the prophets *c* the Son .....Luke 18:31
the things *c* me have an end...Luke 22:37
C Jesus of Nazareth, which ....Luke 24:19
among the people *c* him ......John 7:12
believe *c* him that he had .....John 9:18
to comfort them *c* their ....John 11:19
c Judas which was guide to....Acts 1:16
David speaketh *c* him.........Acts 2:25
things *c* the kingdom of God ..Acts 8:12
as *c* that he raised him up.....Acts 13:34
things *c* the kingdom of God ..Acts 19:8
they were informed *c* thee ....Acts 21:24
not receive thy testimony *c*....Acts 22:18
something more perfectly *c*....Acts 23:15
and heard him *c* the faith .....Acts 24:24
himself *c* the crime laid ....Acts 25:16
letters out of Judea *c* thee ....Acts 28:21
things which *c* the Lord ....Acts 28:31
C his son Jesus Christ our .....Rom 1:3
as *c* the flesh Christ came .....Rom 9:5
As *c* the gospel, they are .....Rom 11:28
is good and simple *c* evil ......Rom 16:19
c him that hath so done.......1Cor 5:3
Now *c* the things whereof ye ..1Cor 7:1
As *c* therefore the eating of ...1Cor 8:4
c spiritual gifts, brethren, I ...1Cor 12:1
c the collection for the saints ..1Cor 16:1
and fellow helper *c* you 2Cor 8:23
I speak as *c* reproach 2Cor 11:21
glory of the things which *c* 2Cor 11:30
c for former conversation .....Eph 4:22
I speak *c* Christ and the ......Eph 5:32
C zeal, persecuting the........Phil 3:6
with me as *c* giving and ....Phil 4:15
and to comfort you *c* your 1Thess 3:2
c them which are asleep 1Thess 4:13
of God in Christ Jesus *c* 1Thess 5:18
c faith have made shipwreck...1Tim 1:19
professing have erred *c* the 1Tim 6:21
Who *c* the truth have erred ...2Tim 2:18
minds, reprobate *c* the 2Tim 3:8
spake nothing *c* priesthood ......Heb 7:14
blessed Jacob and Esau *c* .....Heb 11:20
c the fiery trial which is 1Pet 4:12
is not slack *c* his promise 2Pet 3:9
have I written unto you *c* 1John 2:26

CONCISION—*mutilation*
Used of legalistic
circumcision...........Phil 3:2

CONCLUDE—*to bring to an end; decide; infer*
The main issue *c* ....Eccl 12:13

[*also* CONCLUDED]
we have written and *c* that ....Acts 21:25
Therefore we *c* that a man ....Rom 3:28
For God hath *c* them all in....Rom 11:32
scripture hath *c* all under .....Gal 3:22

CONCORD—*agreement*
And what *c* hath Christ with ..2Cor 6:15

CONCOURSE—*meeting; place where roads come together*
in the chief place of *c*.........Prov 1:21
give an account of this *c* ......Acts 19:40

CONCUBINE—*a mistress; a "wife" who is not legally a wife*

Features regarding:
Could be divorced ....Gen 21:10-14
Has certain rights........Deut 21:10-14
Children of, legitimate ...Gen 22:24
Unfaithfulness of ....Judg 19:9
Source of trouble ....Gen 21:10-14
Incompatible with
Christianity ....Matt 19:5

Men who had:
Abraham ....Gen 25:6
Nahor ....Gen 22:24
Jacob..................Gen 30:1, 4
Eliphaz ....Gen 36:12
Gideon ....Judg 8:30, 31
Saul 2Sam 3:7
David 2Sam 5:13
Solomon 1Kin 11:3
Caleb 1Chr 2:46
Manasseh 1Chr 7:14
Rehoboam 2Chr 11:21
Abijah 2Chr 13:21
Belshazzar ....Dan 5:2

[*also* CONCUBINES]
Bilhah his father's *c*; and......Gen 35:22
who took to him a *c* out of ...Judg 19:1
I and my *c* to lodge ....Judg 20:4
ten women which were *c* to ...2Sam 15:16
Go in unto thy father's *c*......2Sam 16:21
wives and the lives of thy *c* ...2Sam 19:5
the ten women his *c*, whom ...2Sam 20:3
the daughter of Aiah, the *c* ...2Sam 21:11
of Keturah, Abraham's *c*......1Chr 1:32
beside the sons of the *c* 1Chr 3:9
all his wives and his *c*.........2Chr 11:21
which kept the *c* ....Esth 2:14
fourscore *c* and virgins ....Song 6:8

CONCUPISCENCE—*sinful desire*

Causes of:
Learning evil ....Rom 16:19
Making provision for
flesh ....Rom 13:14
Not fearing God.........Prov 8:13
Prov 9:10
Not seeing consequences of sin.............. { Ex 34:6, 7 / Rom 6:23 / Heb 11:25 }

Fruits of:
Evil inclinations ....Rom 7:7, 8
Temptations ....James 1:14
Unchastity 1Thess 4:5
Reprobation ....Rom 1:21-32

Remedy for:
Repentance 2Cor 7:9, 10
James 4:9, 10
Submitting to God.......Rom 12:1, 2
James 4:7
Resisting the devil ....James 4:7
Drawing near to God ....James 4:8
Walking in the Spirit ....Rom 8:1-8

evil *c* and covetousness ....Col 3:5

CONDEMNATION—*the judicial act of declaring one guilty*

Causes of:
Adam's sin.............Rom 5:16-18
Actual sin ....Matt 27:3
Our words ....Matt 12:37
Self-judgment ....Rom 2:1
Titus 3:11
Legal requirements 2Cor 3:9
Rejection of Christ .....John 3:18, 19

Escape from:
In Christ................Rom 8:1, 3
By faith ....John 3:18, 19

[*also* CONDEMN, CONDEMNED, CONDEMNETH, CONDEMNING]
righteous, and *c* the wicked ...Deut 25:1
c the land in a hundred 2Chr 36:3
mine own mouth shall *c* me ...Job 9:20
Do not *c* me; show me ....Job 10:2
wilt thou *c* me, that thou .....Job 40:8
in his hand, no *c* him when ...Ps 37:33
the righteous and *c* the ....Ps 94:21
from those that *c* his soul .....Ps 109:31
of wicked devices will he *c* ....Prov 12:2
and he that *c* the just even ....Prov 17:15
who is he that shall *c* me? ....Is 50:9
in judgment thou shalt *c* ......Is 54:17
drink the wine of the *c* in .....Amos 2:8
not have *c* the guiltless.........Matt 12:7
and shall *c* it; because ....Matt 12:41
they shall *c* him to death ......Matt 20:18
c not, and ye shall not be .....Luke 6:37
thou art in the same *c*? ....Luke 23:40
delivered him to be *c* to ......Luke 24:20
Son into the world to *c* the....John 3:17
this is the *c* that light is ....John 3:19
shall not come into *c*; but .....John 5:24
Neither do I *c* thee; go and ...John 8:11
is he that *c*? It is Christ.......Rom 8:34
Happy is he that *c* not ....Rom 14:22
that we should not be *c* 1Cor 11:32
ye come not together unto *c*...1Cor 11:34
he fall into the *c* of the 1Tim 3:6
by the which he *c* the world ...Heb 11:7
shall receive the greater *c* .....James 3:1
lest ye be *c*; behold the ....James 5:9
nay; lest ye fall into *c*.........James 5:12
of old ordained to this *c* ......Jude 4

CONDESCEND—*to descend to or humble oneself to the level of others*
Christ's example.........John 13:3-5
The believer's practice ...Rom 12:16
The divine model........Phil 2:3-11

CONDITION—*terms of agreement*

[*also* CONDITIONS]
On this *c* will I make a 1Sam 11:2
and desireth *c* of peace ....Luke 14:32

CONDOLENCE—*an expression of sympathy*

Received by:
Job from friends.........Job 2:11
Hanun from David 2Sam 10:2
Hezekiah from a king....2Kin 20:12
Mary from Jesus ....John 11:23-35

Helps in expressing, assurance of:
Trust ....Ps 23:1-6
Hope ....John 14:1-4
Resurrection 1Thess 4:13-18
Help ....Is 40:10, 11

CONDUCT—*to lead*

[*also* CONDUCTED]
to *c* the king over Jordan 2Sam 19:15
the people of Judah *c* the 2Sam 19:40
c Paul brought him unto ......Acts 17:15
but *c* him forth in peace 1Cor 16:11

CONDUIT—*channel through which water is conducted*
stood by the *c* of the upper ...2Kin 18:17
he made a pool, and a *c* 2Kin 20:20
end of the *c* of the upper .....Is 7:3
stood by the *c* of the upper ...Is 36:2

CONEY—*a type of rabbit*
Listed as unclean ....Lev 11:5
Lives among rocks.......Ps 104:18
Likened to people ....Prov 30:26

[*also* CONIES]
and the hare and the *c*........Deut 14:7
and the rocks for the *c*........Ps 104:18
c are but a feeble folk ....Prov 30:26

CONFECTIONARIES—*perfume makers*
A female occupation 1Sam 8:13

[*also* CONFECTION]
c after the art of the ....Ex 30:35

CONFEDERACY—*an alliance*
Denounced ....Is 8:12

[*also* CONFEDERATE]
these were *c* with Abram .....Gen 14:13
they are *c* against thee ....Ps 83:5
Syria is *c* with Ephraim ....Is 7:2
All the men of thy *c* have .....Obad 7

CONFERENCE—*counsel*
in *c* added nothing to me .....Gal 2:6

CONFERRED—*to take counsel with*
And he *c* with Joab the son ...1Kin 1:7
they *c* among themselves ......Acts 4:15
Then Festus when he had *c* ...Acts 25:12
c not with flesh and blood ....Gal 1:16

CONFESS—*to make known; acknowledge sin*

[*also* CONFESSED, CONFESSETH, CONFESSING, CONFESSION]
shall *c* that he hath sinned ....Lev 5:5
and *c* over him all the ....Lev 16:21
they shall *c* their iniquity ....Lev 26:40
make *c* unto him; and tell .....Josh 7:19
and *c* thy name and pray 1Kin 8:33
c thy name and pray and 2Chr 6:24
and making *c* to the Lord 2Chr 30:22
when he had *c*, weeping and ..Ezra 10:1
make *c* unto the Lord God ....Ezra 10:11
c the sins of the children ......Neh 1:6
stood and *c* their sins and .....Neh 9:2
Then will I also *c* unto ....Job 40:14
my God and made my *c* ......Dan 9:4
praying and *c* my sin and .....Dan 9:20
of him in Jordan, *c* their ......Matt 3:6
shall *c* me before men, him ...Matt 10:32
river of Jordan, *c* their sins ....Mark 1:5
shall *c* me before men, him ...Luke 12:8
shall the Son of man also *c* ....Luke 12:8
he *c* and denied not, but ......John 1:20
c, I am not the Christ ....John 1:20
any man did *c* that he was ....John 9:22
the Pharisees they did not *c* ...John 12:42
c, and showed their deeds .....Acts 19:18
but the Pharisees *c* both ......Acts 23:8
But this I *c* unto thee, that ....Acts 24:14
c is made unto salvation ......Rom 10:10
and every tongue shall *c* to ....Rom 14:11
c to thee among the ....Rom 15:9
Pilate witnessed a good *c* 1Tim 6:13
c that they were strangers .....Heb 11:13
will *c* his name before my .....Rev 3:5

CONFESSING CHRIST—*acknowledging His lordship*

Necessity of:
For salvation ....Rom 10:9, 10
A test of faith 1John 2:23
An evidence of spiritual
union 1John 4:15
His confessing us ....Matt 10:32

Content of:
Christ's incarnation 1John 4:2, 3
Christ's Lordship ....Phil 2:11

Prompted by:
Holy Spirit 1Cor 12:3
Faith ....Rom 10:9

Hindrances to:
Fear of men ....John 7:13
Persecution ....Mark 8:34, 35
False teachers 2John 7

CONFESSION OF SIN

Manifested by:
Repentance ....Ps 51:1-19
Self-abasement ....Jer 3:25
Godly sorrow ....Ps 38:18
Turning from sin ....Prov 28:13
Restitution ....Num 5:6, 7

Results in:
Forgiveness 1John 1:9, 10
Pardon ....Ps 32:1-5
Renewed fellowship .....Ps 51:12-19
Healing ....James 5:16

Instances of:
Aaron ....Num 12:11
Israelites 1Sam 12:19
David 2Sam 24:10
Ezra ....Ezra 9:6
Nehemiah ....Neh 1:6, 7
Daniel ....Dan 9:4
Peter ....Luke 5:8
Thief ....Luke 23:41

CONFIDENCE—*assurance*

True, based upon:
God's Word ....Acts 27:22-25
Assurance 2Tim 1:12
Trust ....Hab 3:17-19
Christ's promise ....Phil 1:6
Illustrated 1Sam 17:45-50

False, based upon:
Unwarranted use of
sacred things 1Sam 4:5-11
Presumption ....Num 14:40-45
Pride 1Sam 17:43, 44

The believer's:
Source of 1John 3:21, 22
In prayer 1John 5:14, 15
In testimony ....Acts 28:31
In others 2Cor 2:3
2Cor 7:16
Of God's will ....Phil 1:25
Of faith's finality ....Phil 1:6
Of future things 2Cor 5:6, 8
Must be held ....Heb 10:35

[*also* CONFIDENCES, CONFIDENT, CONFIDENTLY]
men of Shechem put their *c* ...Judg 9:26
c is this wherein thou 2Kin 18:19
not this thy fear, thy *c* ....Job 4:6
His *c* shall be rooted out of ...Job 18:14
fine gold. Thou art my *c* ....Job 31:24
me, in this will I be *c* ....Ps 27:3
the *c* of all the ends of........Ps 65:5
in the Lord that to put *c* ......Ps 118:8
the Lord shall be thy *c* and ...Prov 3:26
the fool rageth and is *c* ....Prov 14:16
fear of the Lord is strong *c* ....Prov 14:26
strength of the *c* thereof ......Prov 21:22
C in an unfaithful man in .....Prov 25:19
in *c* shall be your strength .....Is 30:15
c is wherein thou ....Is 36:4
Lord hath rejected thy *c* ......Jer 2:37
ashamed of Beth-el their *c* ....Jer 48:13
they shall dwell with *c* ....Ezek 28:26
be no more the *c* of the ....Ezek 29:16
a friend, put ye not *c* in a .....Mic 7:5
c that thou thyself art a ....Rom 2:19
in this *c* I was minded to 2Cor 1:15
the great *c* which I have in 2Cor 8:22
in this same *c* boasting 2Cor 9:4
c wherewith I think to be 2Cor 10:2
in this *c* of boasting 2Cor 11:17
have *c* in you through the .....Gal 5:10
and access with *c* by the ......Eph 3:12
And having this *c*, I know ....Phil 1:25
and have no *c* in the flesh .....Phil 3:3
might have also *c* in the ....Phil 3:4
have *c* in the Lord touching ...2Thess 3:4
Having *c* in thy obedience I ...Philem 21
if we hold fast the *c* and ......Heb 3:6
we may have *c* and not be 1John 2:28

CONFIRMATION—*making something steadfast and sure*
Human things ....Ruth 4:7
Esth 9:31, 32
A kingdom 2Kin 14:5
An oath ....Heb 6:17
A covenant ....Gal 3:17
Prophecy ....Dan 9:12, 27
Promises ....Rom 15:8
Defense of faith ....Phil 1:7
Establishing faith ....Acts 14:22
Acts 15:32, 41

[*also* CONFIRM, CONFIRMED, CONFIRMETH, CONFIRMING]
he *c* them, because he held ...Num 30:14
Cursed be he that *c* not all ....Deut 27:26
c to thyself thy people 2Sam 7:24
in after thee, and *c* thy 1Kin 1:14
with him to *c* the kingdom 2Kin 15:19
Lord had *c* him king over 1Chr 14:2
hath *c* the same to Jacob 1Chr 16:17
to *c* this second letter of ......Esth 9:29
Esther *c* these matters of......Esth 9:32
didst *c* thine inheritance ....Ps 68:9
c the same unto Jacob for a ...Ps 105:10
and *c* the feeble knees ....Is 35:3
c the word of his servant ......Is 44:26
hope that they would *c* the .....Ezek 13:6
stood to *c* and to strengthen ...Dan 11:1
c the word with signs ....Mark 16:20
Syria and Cilicia, *c* the ....Acts 15:41
testimony of Christ was *c* 1Cor 1:6
Who shall also *c* you unto 1Cor 1:8
c your love toward him 2Cor 2:8
covenant, yet if it be *c* ....Gal 3:15
c unto us by them that ....Heb 2:3
an oath for *c* is to them an ....Heb 6:16

CONFISCATION—*seizure by authority*
c of goods or to ....Ezra 7:26

CONFLICT—*struggle*
the same *c* which ye ....Phil 3:20
ye knew what great *c* ....Col 2:1

CONFORMITY—*likeness of one thing to another*
To the world, forbidden. .Rom 12:2

[*also* CONFORMABLE, CONFORMED]
to be *c* to the image of his ....Rom 8:29
made *c* unto his death ....Phil 3:10

CONFOUND—*to confuse*

[*also* CONFOUNDED]
and there *c* their language .....Gen 11:7
they were dismayed and *c* 2Kin 19:26
were *c* because they had ......Job 6:20
in thee, and were not *c* ....Ps 22:5
Let them be *c* and put to ......Ps 35:4
Let them be ashamed and *c* ...Ps 40:14
those that seek thee be *c* .....Ps 69:6
Let them be ashamed and *c* ...Ps 70:2
them be *c* and consumed ......Ps 71:13
Let them be *c* and troubled ...Ps 83:17
C be all they that serve ....Ps 97:7
Let them all be *c* and ....Ps 129:5
shall be *c* for the gardens .....Is 1:29
weave networks shall be *c* .....Is 19:9
Then the moon shall be *c* .....Is 24:23
they were dismayed and *c* .....Is 37:27
shall be ashamed and *c* ....Is 41:11
be ashamed and also *c* ....Is 45:16
therefore shall I not be *c* ......Is 50:7
neither be thou *c*; for thou ....Is 54:4
lest I *c* thee before them ......Jer 1:17
we are greatly *c* because we ...Jer 9:19
founder is *c* by the graven ....Jer 10:14
they were ashamed and *c* ......Jer 14:3
hath been ashamed and *c* ......Jer 15:9
be *c* that persecute me ....Jer 17:18
shalt thou be ashamed and *c* ..Jer 22:22
I was ashamed, yea, even *c* ...Jer 31:19
daughter of Egypt shall be *c* ...Jer 46:24
Kiriathaim is *c* and taken .....Jer 48:1
Misgab is *c* and dismayed .....Jer 48:1
Hamath is *c* and Arpad; for ...Jer 49:23
Bel is *c*; Merodach is broken ..Jer 50:2
founder is *c* by the graven ....Jer 51:17
be thou *c* also and bear thy ...Ezek 16:52
be ashamed and *c* for your ....Ezek 36:32
ashamed and the diviners *c* ....Mic 3:7
nations shall see and be *c* .....Mic 7:16
riders on horses shall be *c* .....Zech 10:5
came together and were *c* .....Acts 2:6

things of the world to *c* 1Cor 1:27
c the things which are 1Cor 1:27
believeth..shall not be *c* 1Pet 2:6

CONFUSED—*disorderly; perplexed*

Concerning:
God's will 1Sam 23:1-12
The Messiah ....Matt 11:3
A great event ....Acts 2:1-6

of the warrior is with *c* ....Is 9:5
for the assembly was *c* ....Acts 19:32

CONFUSION—*bewilderment*

Aspects of:
God not author of 1Cor 14:33
Typical of evil..........James 3:16
Prayer concerning ....Ps 70:2
Illustrations of ....Acts 19:29

Examples of:
Babel ....Gen 11:9
Philistines...............1Sam 7:10
Egyptians ....Ex 14:24
City of Shushan ....Esth 3:15
Jerusalem...............Acts 21:31

to lie down thereto; it is *c* ....Lev 18:23
they have wrought *c*; their ....Lev 20:12
thine own *c*, and unto the *c* ...1Sam 20:30
to *c* of face, as it is this ....Ezra 9:7
I am full of *c*, therefore ....Job 10:15
back and brought to *c* ....Ps 35:4
My *c* is continually before .....Ps 44:15
let me never be put to *c* ......Ps 71:1
themselves with their own *c* ...Ps 109:29
city of *c* is broken down ......Is 24:10
the shadow of Egypt your *c* ...Is 30:3
stretch..upon it the line of *c* ...Is 34:11
images are wind and *c* ....Is 41:29
they shall go to *c* together ....Is 45:16
for *c* they shall rejoice ....Is 61:7
c covereth us; for we have ....Jer 3:25
to the *c* of their own faces? ...Jer 7:19
everlasting *c* shall never ....Jer 20:11
but unto us *c* of faces as ......Dan 9:7

CONGEALED—*coagulated or changed to a solid state*
the depths were *c* in the heart..Ex 15:8

CONGRATULATE—*to express pleasure on account of success or good fortune*
King Tou to David 1Chr 18:9, 10

to *c* him, because he had 1Chr 18:10

CONGREGATION—*an assembly of people*

Used of:
The political Israel ......Ex 12:3, 19, 47
A religious assembly .....Acts 13:43
The tent of meeting .....Ex 27:21

Regulations concerning:
Ruled by representatives..Num 16:6
Summoned by trumpets ..Num 10:3, 4, 7
Bound by decisions of representatives ....Josh 9:15-21
Atonement of sin of .....Lev 4:13-21
Exclusion of certain ones from ....Deut 23:1-8

[*also* CONGREGATIONS]
c of the children of Israel .....Ex 16:1
all the *c* of the children ....Ex 17:1
the tabernacle of the *c* ....Ex 28:43
of the tabernacle of the *c* .....Ex 29:4
the tabernacle of the *c* ....Ex 30:16
of the tabernacle of the *c* .....Ex 31:7
Tabernacle of the *c* ....Ex 33:7
rulers of the *c* returned ....Ex 34:31
Moses gathered all the *c* ......Ex 35:1
of the tabernacle of the *c* .....Ex 38:8
of the tent of the *c* ....Ex 39:32
of the tent of the *c* ....Ex 40:2
of the tabernacle of the *c* .....Lev 1:1
of the tabernacle of the *c* .....Lev 3:2
tabernacle of the *c* before .....Lev 4:4
of the *c* they shall eat.........Lev 6:16
gather thou all the *c* ....Lev 8:3
the tabernacle of the *c* ....Lev 9:5
the *c* drew near and stood ....Lev 9:5
of the tabernacle of the *c* .....Lev 10:7
the iniquity of the *c* to ....Lev 10:17
the tabernacle of the *c* ....Lev 12:6
the tabernacle of the *c* ....Lev 14:11
the tabernacle of the *c* ....Lev 15:14
shall take of the *c* of the ......Lev 16:5
of the tabernacle of the *c* .....Lev 17:4
Speak unto all the *c* of the ....Lev 19:2
in the tabernacle of the *c* .....Lev 24:3
and let all the *c* stone him ....Lev 24:14
in the tabernacle of the *c* .....Num 1:1
Take ye the sum of all the *c* ..Num 1:2
were the renowned of the *c* ...Num 1:16
the tabernacle of the *c* ....Num 2:2
the charge of the whole *c* .....Num 3:7
in the tabernacle of the *c* .....Num 4:3
door of the tabernacle of *c* ....Num 6:10
door of the tabernacle of..*c* ...Num 6:13
of the tabernacle of the *c* .....Num 7:5
the tabernacle of the *c* ....Num 8:9
the tabernacle of the *c* ....Num 11:16
the tabernacle of the *c* ....Num 12:4
c of the children of Israel .....Num 13:26
And all the *c* lifted up their ...Num 14:1
be both for you of the *c* ......Num 15:15
assembly, famous in the *c* .....Num 16:2
seeing all the *c* are holy.......Num 16:3
separated you from the *c* of ...Num 16:9
to stand before the *c* to ....Num 16:9
Korah gathered all the *c* ......Num 16:19
be wroth with all the *c* ....Num 16:22
perished from among the *c* ....Num 16:33
when the *c* was gathered ......Num 16:42
the tabernacle of the *c* ....Num 16:42
in the tabernacle of the *c* .....Num 17:4
of the tabernacle of the *c* .....Num 18:4
tabernacle of the *c* seven ......Num 19:4
the whole *c* into the desert ....Num 20:1
in the sight of all the *c*........Num 25:6
Take the sum of all the *c* .....Num 26:2
the princes and all the *c* ......Num 27:2
unto the *c* of the children .....Num 31:12
unto the princes of the *c* ....Num 32:2
until he stand before the *c* ....Num 35:12
in the tabernacle of the *c* .....Deut 31:14
the inheritance of the *c* ....Deut 33:4
Joshua read not before..the *c*..Josh 8:35
c of the children of Israel .....Josh 18:1
of the tabernacle of the *c* .....Josh 19:51
until he stand before the *c* ....Josh 20:6
c of the children of Israel .....Josh 22:12
the princes of the *c* and ....Josh 22:30
c was gathered together as ....Judg 20:1
came not up with the *c* unto ..Judg 21:5
whole *c* sent some to speak ...Judg 21:13
elders of the *c* said, How .....Judg 21:16
of the tabernacle of the *c* 1Sam 2:22
tabernacle of the *c* and all 1Kin 8:4
Jeroboam and all the *c* of 1Kin 12:3
of the tabernacle of the *c* 1Chr 6:32
of the tabernacle of the *c* 1Chr 9:21
David said unto all the *c* 1Chr 13:2
of the tabernacle of the *c* 1Chr 23:32
Israel the *c* of the Lord 1Chr 28:8
king said unto all the *c* 1Chr 29:1
David said to..the *c*, Now 1Chr 29:20
the *c* blessed the Lord God ...1Chr 29:20
Solomon and all the *c* with 2Chr 1:3
and the tabernacle of the *c* 2Chr 5:5
blessed the..*c* of Israel 2Chr 6:3
Israel with him, a..great *c* 2Chr 7:8
stood in the *c* of Judah and ...2Chr 20:5
Lord in the midst of the *c* 2Chr 20:14
all the *c* made a covenant 2Chr 23:3
and of the *c* of Israel for 2Chr 24:6
the princes and all the *c* 2Chr 28:14
before the king and the *c* 2Chr 29:23
all the *c* worshiped and 2Chr 29:28
all the *c* in Jerusalem to 2Chr 30:2
daughters, through..the *c* 2Chr 31:18
whole *c* together was forty ....Ezra 2:64
great *c* of men and women ....Ezra 10:1
all the *c* said, Amen, and .....Neh 5:13
c together was forty and two ..Neh 7:66
brought the law before the *c* ..Neh 8:2
not come into the *c* of God ...Neh 13:1
c of hypocrites shall be ....Job 15:34
stood up..cried in the *c* ....Job 30:28
in the *c* of the righteous ......Ps 1:5
of the *c* will I praise ....Ps 22:22
hated the *c* of evildoers ....Ps 26:5
the *c* will I bless the Lord .....Ps 26:12
thee thanks in the great *c* .....Ps 35:18
righteousness in..great *c* ....Ps 40:9
speak righteousness , O *c*? ....Ps 58:1
Thy *c* hath dwelt therein ......Ps 68:10
Bless ye God in the *c* even ....Ps 68:26
Remember thy *c*, which thou ..Ps 74:2
roar in the midst of thy *c* .....Ps 74:4
When I shall receive the *c* .....Ps 75:2
God standeth in the *c* of ......Ps 82:1
faithfulness also in the *c* ......Ps 89:5
also in the *c* of the people ....Ps 107:32
of the upright and in the *c* ....Ps 111:1
praise in the *c* of saints ....Ps 149:1
evil in the midst of the *c* ......Prov 5:14
shall remain in the *c* of the....Prov 21:16
showed before the whole *c* ....Prov 26:26
sit..the mount of the *c* ....Is 14:13
know, O *c*, what is among ....Jer 6:18
c shall be established ....Jer 30:20
should not enter into thy *c* ....Lam 1:10
chastise them, as their *c* ......Hos 7:12
the people, sanctify the *c* .....Joel 2:16
a cord by lot in the *c* of ......Mic 2:5
Now when the *c* was broken ..Acts 13:43

CONIAH (kōn-ī'ä)—*"Jehovah establishes"*
King of Judah...........Jer 22:24, 28
Same as Jehoiachin 2Kin 24:8

C the son of Jehoiakim ....Jer 22:24

CONNIVANCE AT WRONG—*tacit approval of evil*
Involves guilt ....Ps 50:18-22
Aaron's, at Sinai ....Ex 32:1, 2, 22
Pilate's, at Jesus' trial....Matt 27:17-26
Saul's (Paul's) at Stephen's death ....Acts 8:1

CONONIAH (kōn-ō-nī'ä)—*"Jehovah has founded"*
1. A Levite 2Chr 31:11, 12, 13
2. A Levite official 2Chr 35:9

CONQUER—*to overcome; vanquish*

[*also* CONQUERING, CONQUERORS]
more than *c* through him......Rom 8:37
he went forth *c* and to *c* ......Rev 6:2

CONSCIENCE—*the inner judge of moral issues*

Described as:
Good...................Acts 23:1
Pure....................1Tim 3:9
Evil ....Heb 10:22
Defiled 1Cor 8:7
Seared..................1Tim 4:2

Functions of:
A witness ....Rom 2:15
An accuser.............John 8:9
An upholder 1Tim 1:19
Server of good ....Rom 13:5
Source of joy 2Cor 1:12
Dead ....Prov 30:20

Limitations of:
Needs cleansing ....Heb 9:14
Subject to others 1Cor 10:28, 29
Differs 1Cor 8:7-13
Fallible ....Prov 16:25

[*also* CONSCIENCES]
c also bearing me witness .....Rom 9:1
asking no question for *c* sake ..1Cor 10:25
ourselves to every man's *c* 2Cor 4:2
made manifest in your *c* 2Cor 5:11
my forefathers with pure *c* 2Tim 1:3
their mind and *c* is defiled ....Titus 1:15
as pertaining to the *c* ....Heb 9:9

should have had no more *c*....Heb 10:2
we trust we have a good *c* ....Heb 13:18

CONSCIENCE, CLEAR—*freedom from guilt or guilt feelings*

Necessary for:
Freedom from legalism...Heb 9:13, 14
Access to God ....Heb 10:21, 22
Liberty in witnessing.....1Pet 3:15, 16
Christian love 1Tim 1:5
Confidence in prayer 1John 3:21, 22
Proud confidence 2Cor 1:12

Requirements for:
Doctrinal purity....... 1Tim 1:3-5, 18—2:1; 1Tim 4:1, 2
Proper conduct........ Acts 24:10-13, 16; Rom 9:14
Faith in Christ's blood ...Heb 9:14; Heb 10:19-22
Knowledge..............1Cor 8:7
Belief ....Titus 1:15
Submissive spirit.........1Pet 2:18, 19
Faith in God's greatness .1John 3:20
Consideration of others ..1Cor 10:28, 29
Seeking forgiveness ......Prov 28:13; Matt 5:23, 24

CONSCRIPTION—*enrollment for compulsory service*
Employed by Solomon ...1Kin 7:13, 14; 1Kin 9:20, 21
To build Temple 1Kin 5:2, 3, 18
To restore cities 1Kin 9:15-17
Led to revolt............1Kin 12:3-16
See LEVY

CONSECRATION—*dedication to God's service*

Applied to:
Israel...................Ex 19:6
Priests..................Lev 8:1-13
Levites ....Num 8:5, 6
Individuals 1Sam 1:11
First-born ....Ex 13:2, 12
Possessions..............Lev 27:28, 29
Christ ....Heb 2:10

The Christian's:
By Christ ....John 17:23
Complete and entire .....Rom 12:1, 2
Separation from world ...2Cor 6:14-18
Devotion to Christ ......Rev 14:1-6
Sacred anointing.........1John 2:20, 27
New priesthood 1Pet 2:5, 9

[*also* CONSECRATE, CONSECRATED, CONSECRATIONS]
make Aaron's garments to *c*...Ex 28:3
shalt *c* Aaron and his sons ....Ex 29:9
for it is a ram of *c* ....Ex 29:22
anointed therein..to be *c* ......Ex 29:29
aught of the flesh of the *c*.....Ex 29:34
Aaron and his sons, and *c* ....Ex 30:30
C yourselves today to the .....Ex 32:29
the *c*, and of the sacrifice .....Lev 7:37
other ram, the ram of *c*.......Lev 8:22
were *c* for a sweet savor .....Lev 8:28
seven days shall he *c* you .....Lev 8:33
he shall *c* to minister in ....Lev 16:32
and that is *c* to put on ....Lev 21:10
whom he *c* to minister in .....Num 3:3
because the *c* of his God is....Num 6:7
shall *c* unto the Lord the......Num 6:12
of brass and iron, are *c* ....Josh 6:19
and *c* one of his sons ....Judg 17:5
c him, and he became one 1Kin 13:33
c his service this day unto 1Chr 29:5
to *c* himself with a young 2Chr 13:9
Aaron, that are *c* to burn 2Chr 26:18
have *c* yourselves unto the 2Chr 29:31
which were *c* unto the Lord ...2Chr 31:6
feasts of the Lord..were *c* .....Ezra 3:5
they shall *c* themselves ....Ezek 43:26
I will *c* their gain unto ....Mic 4:13
Son, who is *c* for evermore ....Heb 7:28
which he hath *c* for us ....Heb 10:20

CONSENT—*to be in accord in opinion or sentiment*

[*also* CONSENTED, CONSENTEDST, CONSENTING]
in this will we *c* unto you .....Gen 34:15
Thou shalt not *c* unto him ....Deut 13:8
but he would not *c* ....Judg 11:17
they came out with one *c* 1Sam 11:7
Hearken not unto him, nor *c* ..1Kin 20:8
priests *c* to receive no more ...2Kin 12:8
thou *c* with him, and hast .....Ps 50:18
consulted..with one *c* ....Ps 83:5
entice thee, *c* thou not ....Prov 1:10
he *c* to them in this matter ....Dan 1:14
murder in the way by *c* ....Hos 6:9
to serve him with one *c* ....Zeph 3:9
one *c* began to make excuse ...Luke 14:18
had not *c* to the counsel ......Luke 23:51
Saul was *c* unto his death .....Acts 8:1
time with them, he *c* not.......Acts 18:20
by, and *c* unto his death ......Acts 22:20
I *c* unto the law..is good ......Rom 7:16
it be with *c* for a time 1Cor 7:5
c not to wholesome words.....1Tim 6:3

CONSERVATION—*preserving worthwhile things*
Material things ....John 6:12, 13
Spiritual things ....Rev 3:2, 3
Good ....Acts 26:22, 23
Unwise ....Luke 5:36, 37

CONSIDER—*to regard; think about; reflect on; study; contemplate*

[*also* CONSIDERED, CONSIDEREST, CONSIDERETH, CONSIDERING]
c that this nation is thy ....Ex 33:13
Then the priest shall *c* ....Lev 13:13
Know..this day, and *c* ....Deut 4:39
shalt also *c* in thine heart .....Deut 8:5
c the years of..generations ....Deut 32:7
therefore *c* what ye have ......Judg 18:14
c of it, take advice and speak. .Judg 19:30
c how great things he hath 1Sam 12:24
therefore know and *c* what 1Sam 25:17
I had *c* it in the morning......1Kin 3:21
I have *c* the things which 1Kin 5:8
c, I pray you, and see 2Kin 5:7
Hast thou *c* my servant Job ...Job 1:8
Hast thou *c* my servant Job ...Job 2:3
also; will he not then *c* ....Job 11:11
when I *c*, I am afraid of ......Job 23:15
would not *c* any of his ways ...Job 34:27
c..wondrous works of God ....Job 37:14
O Lord, *c* my meditation .....Ps 5:1
I *c* thy heavens, the work .....Ps 8:3
c my trouble which I suffer....Ps 9:13
C and hear me, O Lord my ...Ps 13:3
C mine enemies; for they .....Ps 25:19
thou hast *c* my trouble ....Ps 31:7
hearts alike; he *c* all their .....Ps 33:15
shalt diligently *c* his place .....Ps 37:10
Blessed is he..*c* the poor ......Ps 41:1
Hearken, O daughter, and *c*...Ps 45:10
her bulwarks, *c* her palaces....Ps 48:13
c this, ye that forget God .....Ps 50:22
shall wisely *c* of his doing .....Ps 64:9
have *c* the days of old ....Ps 77:5
I will *c* thy testimonies ....Ps 119:95
the ant, thou sluggard; *c* ......Prov 6:6
c the house of the wicked .....Prov 21:12
c diligently what is before .....Prov 23:1
pondereth the heart *c* it?......Prov 24:12
saw, and *c* it well; I looked ...Prov 24:32
c not..poverty shall come .....Prov 28:22
The righteous *c* the cause .....Prov 29:7
She *c* a field, and buyeth it ...Prov 31:16
and *c* all the oppressions ......Eccl 4:1
they *c* not that they do evil ...Eccl 5:1
C the work of God: for ....Eccl 7:13
I *c* in my heart even to ....Eccl 9:1
my people doth not *c* ....Is 1:3
neither *c* the operation of .....Is 5:12
look upon thee, and *c* thee....Is 14:16
will *c* in my dwelling place ....Is 18:4
may see, and know, and *c* ....Is 41:20
neither *c* the things of old.....Is 43:18
none *c* in his heart, neither....Is 44:19
had not heard shall they *c*.....Is 52:15
none *c* that the righteous is ...Is 57:1
c diligently..see if there ....Jer 2:10
C ye..call for the mourning....Jer 9:17
latter days ye shall *c* it........Jer 23:20
the latter days ye shall *c* ......Jer 30:24
C thou not what this people ...Jer 33:24
see, O Lord, and *c*; for I am ..Lam 1:11
Behold, O Lord, and *c* to .....Lam 2:20
c, and behold our reproach....Lam 5:1
may be they will *c*, though ....Ezek 12:3
and *c*, and doeth not such.....Ezek 18:14
c the horns, and, behold ......Dan 7:8
I was *c*, behold, a he goat ....Dan 8:5
the matter, and *c* the vision ...Dan 9:23
they *c* not in their hearts......Hos 7:2
hosts; *C* your ways ....Hag 1:5
c from this day and upward ...Hag 2:15
C the lilies of the field ....Matt 6:28
but *c* not the beam that is.....Matt 7:3
For they *c* not the miracle ....Mark 6:52
C the ravens: for they ....Luke 12:24
Nor *c* that it is expedient .....John 11:50
came together for to *c* of .....Acts 15:6
he *c* not his own body now....Rom 4:19
c thyself, lest thou also be ....Gal 6:1
C what I say..the Lord.......2Tim 2:7
c the Apostle and High ....Heb 3:1
c how great this man was .....Heb 7:4
c one another to provoke .....Heb 10:24
c him that endured such ......Heb 12:3
c the end..conversation ....Heb 13:7

CONSIST—*to comprise; hold together*

[*also* CONSISTETH]
life *c* not in the abundance ....Luke 12:15
things..by him all things *c* .....Col 1:17

CONSOLATION—*comfort fortified with encouragement*
God, source of ....Rom 15:5
Simeon waits for ....Luke 2:25
Source of joy ....Acts 15:31
To be shared............2Cor 1:4-11

[*also* CONSOLATIONS]
Are the *c* of God small with ..Job 15:11
and let this be your *c* ....Job 21:2
satisfied..breasts of her *c* ......Is 66:11
the cup of *c* to drink ....Jer 16:7
waiting for the *c* of Israel .....Luke 2:25
for ye have received your *c* ...Luke 6:24
interpreted, The son of *c*......Acts 4:36
but by the *c* wherewith he 2Cor 7:7
any *c* in Christ, if any ....Phil 2:1
given us everlasting *c* and 2Thess 2:16
we have great joy and *c*.......Philem 7
we might have a strong *c* .....Heb 6:18

CONSORTED—*associated*
believed, and *c* with Paul .....Acts 17:4

CONSPIRACY—*plot secretly to commit unlawful or wrongful act*

Against:
Joseph..................Gen 37:18-20
Moses ....Num 16:1-35
Samson ....Judg 16:4-21
Daniel..................Dan 6:4-17
Jesus ....Matt 12:14
Paul ....Acts 23:12-15

[*also* CONSPIRATORS, CONSPIRED]
all of you..*c* against me 1Sam 22:8
the *c* was strong; for the 2Sam 15:12
Ahithophel is among the *c* 2Sam 15:31
c against him, and Baasha.....1Kin 15:27
c against him, as he was 1Kin 16:9
the son of Nimshi *c*..........2Kin 9:14
servants arose..made a *c* 2Kin 12:20
Now they made a *c* against....2Kin 14:19

acts of Shallum, and his *c* 2Kin 15:15
the king of Assyria found *c* ... 2Kin 17:4
And they *c* against him 2Chr 24:21
they made a *c* against him 2Chr 25:27
c all of them together to ...... Neh 4:8
Lord said unto me, A *c* is ..... Jer 11:9
There is a *c* of her prophets ... Ezek 22:25
Amos hath *c* against thee ..... Amos 7:10

CONSTANCY—*firmness of purpose*
Ruth's, to Naomi .... Ruth 1:16
Jonathan's, to David 1Sam 20:17
Virgins, to Christ .... Rev 14:4, 5

[*also* CONSTANT, CONSTANTLY]
c to do my commandments 1Chr 28:7
man that heareth speaketh *c* ... Prov 21:28
she *c* affirmed that it was ..... Acts 12:15
I will that thou affirm *c* .... Titus 3:8

CONSTELLATION—*a group of stars*
Arcturus .... Job 9:9
Job 38:32
The Serpent .... Job 26:13
Orion .... Job 38:31
Amos 5:8
Pleiades (seven stars) .... Job 9:9
Job 38:31
Castor and Pollux .... Acts 28:11
Judgment on .... Is 13:10, 11
Incense burned to 2Kin 23:5

CONSTRAINT—*state of being restricted or compelled*

[*also* CONSTRAIN, CONSTRAINED, CONSTRAINETH]
she *c* him to eat bread 2Kin 4:8
the spirit within me *c* me ..... Job 32:18
Jesus *c* his disciples to get ..... Matt 14:22
straightway..*c* his disciples ..... Mark 6:45
they *c* him, saying, Abide ..... Luke 24:29
And she *c* us .... Acts 16:15
was *c* to appeal unto Caesar ... Acts 28:19
love of Christ *c* us; because ... 2Cor 5:14
c you to be circumcised .... Gal 6:12
not by *c*, but willingly 1Pet 5:2

CONSULTATION—*seeking advice from others*
Demonical 1Sam 28:7-25
Divided 1Kin 12:6, 8
Determined .... Dan 6:7
Devilish .... Matt 26:4
John 12:10, 11

[*also* CONSULT, CONSULTED, CONSULTETH]
David *c* with the captains 1Chr 13:1
he had *c* with the people 2Chr 20:21
Then I *c* with myself, and I ... Neh 5:7
only *c* to cast him down .... Ps 62:4
c against thy hidden ones ...... Ps 83:3
c with images, he looked in ... Ezek 21:21
Balak, king of Moab *c* .... Mic 6:5
hast *c* shame to thy house ..... Hab 2:10
priests held a *c* with..elders ... Mark 15:1
c whether..be able with ten ... Luke 14:31
chief priests *c* that they .... John 12:10

CONSULTER—*a medium; seer*
or a *c* with familiar spirits ..... Deut 18:11

CONSUME—*to devour; destroy*

[*also* CONSUMED, CONSUMETH, CONSUMING, CONSUMPTION]
lest thou be *c* in..iniquity ..... Gen 19:15
the famine shall *c* the land .... Gen 41:30
and the bush was not *c* .... Ex 3:2
that I may *c* them, and I ...... Ex 32:10
people: lest I *c* thee in .... Ex 33:3
which the fire hath *c* with ..... Lev 6:10
terror, *c*, and the burning ..... Lev 26:16
shall *c* the eyes, and cause .... Lev 26:16
and *c* them, that were in ...... Num 11:1
I may *c* them in a moment .... Num 16:21
the host, until they were *c* .... Deut 2:15
Lord thy God is a *c* fire ...... Deut 4:24
this great fire will *c* us .... Deut 5:25
thou shalt *c* all the people ..... Deut 7:16
Lord..smite thee with a *c* ...... Deut 28:22
for the locust shall *c* it .... Deut 28:38
came out of Egypt, were *c* .... Josh 5:6
turn and do you hurt, and *c* ... Josh 24:20
c the flesh and..unleavened .... Judg 6:21
c thine eyes, and to grieve 1Sam 2:33
ye shall be *c*, both ye and 1Sam 12:25
The man that *c* us, and 2Sam 21:5
c the burnt sacrifice, and 1Kin 18:38
and *c* thee and thy fifty 2Kin 1:10
heaven, and *c* him and his 2Kin 1:10
c the burnt offering and 2Chr 7:1
till thou hadst *c* us, so that .... Ezra 9:14
gates thereof..*c* with fire? ..... Neh 2:3
didst not utterly *c* them .... Neh 9:31
c them, and to destroy them .. Esth 9:24
sheep, and..servants, and *c* .... Job 1:16
cloud is *c* and vanisheth .... Job 7:9
he, as a rotten thing, *c*, as .... Job 13:28
c the tabernacles of bribery ... Job 15:34
eye is *c* because of grief .... Ps 6:7
c; into smoke shall they *c* ..... Ps 37:20
C them in wrath, *c* them ...... Ps 59:13
are utterly *c* with terrors ...... Ps 73:19
days did he *c* in vanity .... Ps 78:33
The fire *c* their young men .... Ps 78:63
we are *c* by thine anger .... Ps 90:7
Let the sinners be *c* out .... Ps 104:35
My zeal hath *c* me, because ... Ps 119:139
flesh and thy body are *c* ...... Prov 5:11
forsake the Lord shall be *c* .... Is 1:28
flame *c* the chaff, so their ..... Is 5:24
it shall also *c* the beard .... Is 7:20
c the glory of his forest .... Is 10:18
c decreed shall overflow ...... Is 10:22
God of hosts shall make a *c* ... Is 10:23
a *c*, even determined upon .... Is 28:22
scorner is *c*..all that watch .... Is 29:20
c us, because of..iniquities .... Is 64:7
thou hast *c* them, but they .... Jer 5:3
c them, saith the Lord .... Jer 8:13
up hath mine enemy *c* .... Lam 2:22
mercies that we are not *c* ..... Lam 3:22
c away for their iniquity ...... Ezek 4:17
with famine shall they be *c* .... Ezek 5:12
and *c* all these kingdoms ...... Dan 2:44
by his hand shall be *c* .... Dan 11:16
and shall *c* his branches .... Hos 11:6
c all things from off the .... Zeph 1:2
shall *c* it with the timber ...... Zech 5:4
ye sons of Jacob are not *c* .... Mal 3:6
from heaven, and *c* them ..... Luke 9:54
take heed that ye be not *c* .... Gal 5:15
Lord shall *c* with the spirit 2Thess 2:8
For our God is a *c* fire .... Heb 12:29
ye may *c* it upon your lusts ... James 4:3

CONSUMMATION—*completion*
until the *c*..that determined ... Dan 9:27

CONTAIN—*to limit; control; enclose; restrain*

[*also* CONTAINED, CONTAINETH, CONTAINING]
it *c* two thousand baths 1Kin 7:26
of heavens cannot *c* thee 1Kin 8:27
of heavens cannot *c* him? 2Chr 2:6
had in derision; it *c* much ..... Ezek 23:32
the bath may *c* the tenth ...... Ezek 45:11
Jews, *c* two or three firkins .. John 2:6
the world itself could not *c* .... John 21:25
by nature..things *c* in..law ..... Rom 2:14
cannot *c*, let them marry 1Cor 7:9
also it is *c* in the scripture 1Pet 2:6

CONTEMN—*to condemn*

[*also* CONTEMNED, CONTEMNETH]
doth the wicked *c* God? ...... Ps 10:13
eyes a vile person is *c* .... Ps 15:4
c..counsel of the Most High .. Ps 107:11
love, it would utterly be *c* ..... Song 8:7
glory of Moab shall be *c* ...... Is 16:14
c the rod of my son, as .... Ezek 21:10
the sword *c* even the rod? ..... Ezek 21:13

CONTEMPT—*scorn compounded with disrespect*

Forbidden toward:
Parents .... Prov 23:22
Weak Christians .... Matt 18:10
Rom 14:3
Believing masters 1Tim 6:2
The poor .... James 2:1-3

Objects of:
The righteous .... Ps 80:6
Spiritual things .... Matt 22:2-6
Christ .... John 9:28, 29

Examples of:
Nabal 1Sam 25:10, 11
Michal 2Sam 6:16
Sanballat .... Neh 2:19
Jews .... Matt 26:67, 68
False teachers 2Cor 10:10
The wicked .... Prov 18:3

[*also* CONTEMPTIBLE, CONTEMPTUOUSLY]
there arise too much *c* .... Esth 1:18
He poureth *c* upon princes .... Job 12:21
and *c* against the righteous .... Ps 31:18
He poureth *c* upon princes .... Ps 107:40
Remove..reproach and *c* ...... Ps 119:22
exceedingly filled with *c* .... Ps 123:3
bring into *c*..the honorable .... Is 23:9
to shame and everlasting *c* .... Dan 12:2
The table of the Lord is *c* ..... Mal 1:7
fruit..even his meat, is *c* ...... Mal 1:12
I also made you *c* and base ... Mal 2:9

CONTENTION—*severe disagreement; quarrelsomeness*

Caused by:
Pride .... Prov 13:10
Disagreement .... Acts 15:36-41
Divisions 1Cor 1:11-13
A quarrelsome spirit ..... Gal 5:15

Antidotes:
Avoid the contentious ... Prov 21:19
Avoid controversies ...... Titus 3:9
Abandon the quarrel .... Prov 17:14
Follow peace .... Rom 12:18-21

[*also* CONTEND, CONTENDED, CONTENDEST, CONTENDETH, CONTENDING, CONTENTIONS, CONTENTIOUS]
c with them in battle .... Deut 2:9
Then *c* I with the rulers .... Neh 13:11
If he will *c* with him, he ...... Job 9:3
me wherefore thou *c* with ..... Job 10:2
person? will ye *c* for God? .... Job 13:8
when they *c* with me .... Job 31:13
he that *c* with the Almighty .. Job 40:2
leave off *c*, before it be .... Prov 17:14
A fool's lips enter into *c* ...... Prov 18:6
c and an angry woman .... Prov 21:19
out the scorner, and *c* shall ... Prov 22:10
a *c* man to kindle strife .... Prov 26:21
rainy day and a *c* woman ..... Prov 27:15
such as keep the law *c* with .. Prov 28:4
wise man *c* with a foolish ..... Prov 29:9
neither may he *c* with him .... Eccl 6:10
even them that *c* with thee .... Is 41:12
c with him that contendeth .... Is 49:25
who will *c* with me? let us .... Is 50:8
I will not *c* for ever .... Is 57:16
canst thou *c* with horses? ..... Jer 12:5
man of *c* to..whole earth! ..... Jer 15:10
Lord God called to *c* by fire .. Amos 7:4
c thou before..mountains ...... Mic 6:1
that raise up strife and *c* ...... Hab 1:3
of the circumcision *c* with ..... Acts 11:2
c was so sharp between .... Acts 15:39
But unto them that are *c* ...... Rom 2:8
if any man seem to be *c* 1Cor 11:16
The one preach Christ of *c* .... Phil 1:16
gospel of God with much *c* 1Thess 2:2
earnestly *c* for the faith .... Jude 3
c with the devil he disputed .. Jude 9

CONTENTMENT—*an uncomplaining acceptance of one's life*

Opposed to:
Anxiety . . . . . Matt 6:25, 34
Murmuring 1Cor 10:10
Greed . . . . . Heb 13:5
Envy . . . . . James 3:16

Shown by our recognition of:
Our unworthiness . . . . . Gen 32:10
Our trust . . . . . Hab 3:17-19
God's care . . . . . Ps 145:7-21
God's provisions 1Tim 6:6-8
God's promises . . . . . Heb 13:5

[*also* CONTENT]
And his brethren were *c* . . . . . Gen 37:27
And Moses was *c* to dwell . . . . Ex 2:21
Moses heard that he was *c* . . . . Lev 10:20
to God we had been *c* . . . . . Josh 7:7
the Levite was *c* to dwell . . . . . Judg 17:11
Naaman said, Be *c*, take 2Kin 5:23
Now therefore be *c*, look . . . . . Job 6:28
neither will he rest *c* . . . . . Prov 6:35
and be *c* with your wages . . . . . Luke 3:14
I am, therewith to be *c* . . . . . Phil 4:11
let us be therewith *c* 1Tim 6:8
malicious words: and not *c* 3John 10

CONTINUAL—*incessant*

[*also* CONTINUALLY, CONTINUANCE, CONTINUE, CONTINUED, CONTINUETH, CONTINUING]
of his heart was only evil *c* . . . . Gen 6:5
they *c* a season in ward . . . . . Gen 40:4
if he *c* a day or two, he . . . . . Ex 21:21
memorial before..Lord *c* . . . . . Ex 28:29
be a *c* burnt offering . . . . . Ex 29:42
shall then *c* in the blood . . . . . Lev 12:4
cause the lamps to burn *c* . . . . . Lev 24:2
c bread shall be thereon . . . . . Num 4:7
great plagues, and of long *c* . . . Deut 28:59
went on *c*, and blew with . . . . . Josh 6:13
Asher *c* on the seashore . . . . . Judg 5:17
Moab, and *c* there . . . . . Ruth 1:2
she *c* praying before..Lord 1Sam 1:12
c following the Lord your 1Sam 12:14
became David's enemy *c* 1Sam 18:29
ark of the Lord *c* in 2Sam 6:11
may *c* for ever before thee 2Sam 7:29
eat bread at my table *c* 2Sam 9:7
the Lord may *c* his word 1Kin 2:4
which stand *c* before thee 1Kin 10:8
c three years without war 1Kin 22:1
God, which passeth by us *c* . . . 2Kin 4:9
his allowance was a *c* 2Kin 25:30
trumpets *c* before the ark 1Chr 16:6
strength, seek his face *c* 1Chr 16:11
for the *c* showbread, and 2Chr 2:4
which stand *c* before thee 2Chr 9:7
c until the burnt offering 2Chr 29:28
the *c* burnt offering, both . . . . . Ezra 3:5
I *c* in the work of this wall . . . . Neh 5:16
for the *c* meat offering . . . . . Neh 10:33
Thus did Job *c* . . . . . Job 1:5
also as a shadow, and *c* not . . . Job 14:2
shall his substance *c* . . . . . Job 15:29
Moreover Job *c* his parable . . . Job 27:1
praise..*c* be in my mouth . . . . . Ps 34:1
c thy loving-kindness unto . . . . . Ps 36:10
thy truth *c* preserve me . . . . . Ps 40:11
My confusion is *c* before . . . . . Ps 44:15
goodness of God endureth *c* . . . Ps 52:1
whereunto I may *c* resort . . . . . Ps 71:3
shall be made for him *c* . . . . . Ps 72:15
be *c* as long as the sun . . . . . Ps 72:17
I am *c* with thee . . . . . Ps 73:23
So shall I keep thy law *c* . . . . . Ps 119:44
which in *c* were fashioned . . . . . Ps 139:16
he deviseth mischief *c* . . . . . Prov 6:14
Bind..*c* upon thine heart . . . . . Prov 6:21
merry heart hath a *c* feast . . . . Prov 15:15
it whirleth about *c*, and . . . . . Eccl 1:6
c until night, till wine . . . . . Is 5:11
wrath with a *c* stroke . . . . . Is 14:6
Lord shall guide thee *c* . . . . . Is 58:11
in those is *c*, and we shall . . . . Is 64:5
before me *c* is grief and . . . . . Jer 6:7
a *c* whirlwind: it shall fall . . . . . Jer 30:23
that they may *c* many days . . . . Jer 32:14
c weeping shall go up; for . . . . . Jer 48:5
c diet given him of the . . . . . Jer 52:34
sever out men of *c* . . . . . Ezek 39:14
c by a perpetual ordinance . . . . Ezek 46:14
And Daniel *c* even unto the . . . Dan 1:21
God whom thou servest *c* . . . . . Dan 6:16
God, whom thou servest *c* . . . . . Dan 6:20
c more years than the king . . . . Dan 11:8
committed whoredom *c* . . . . . Hos 4:18
and wait on thy God *c* . . . . . Hos 12:6
all the heathen drink *c* . . . . . Obad 16
thy wickedness passed *c*? . . . . . Nah 3:19
c with me now three days . . . . . Matt 15:32
c all night in prayer to God . . . Luke 6:12
lest by her *c* coming . . . . . Luke 18:5
they *c* there not many days . . . . John 2:12
If ye *c* in my word, then . . . . . John 8:31
I loved you: *c* ye in my love . . . John 15:9
c with one accord in prayer . . . Acts 1:14
c daily with one accord . . . . . Acts 2:46
to *c* in the grace of God . . . . . Acts 13:43
exhorting them to *c* in the . . . . Acts 14:22
c unto this day, witnessing . . . . Acts 26:22
by patient *c* in well doing . . . . . Rom 2:7
we *c* in sin, that grace . . . . . Rom 6:1
heaviness and *c* sorrow . . . . . Rom 9:2
c instant in prayer . . . . . Rom 12:12
of the gospel might *c* with . . . . . Gal 2:5
every one that *c* not in all . . . . . Gal 3:10
shall abide and *c* with you . . . . Phil 1:25
ye *c* in the faith grounded . . . . . Col 1:23
they *c* in faith and charity 1Tim 2:15
c in supplications and 1Tim 5:5
of God; abideth a priest *c* . . . . . Heb 7:3
to *c* by reason of death . . . . . Heb 7:23
man, because he *c* ever . . . . . Heb 7:24
they *c* not in my covenant . . . . . Heb 8:9
offered year by year *c*..make . . Heb 10:1
here have we no *c* city, but . . . Heb 13:14
sacrifice of praise to God *c* . . . . Heb 13:15
law of liberty, and *c* . . . . . James 1:25
and *c* there a year, and buy . . . James 4:13
all things *c* as they were 2Pet 3:4
no doubt have *c* with us 1John 2:19
remain in you..also shall *c* 1John 2:24
to *c* forty and two months . . . . . Rev 13:5

CONTRACTS—*covenants legally binding*

Ratified by:
Giving presents . . . . . Gen 21:25-30
Public witness . . . . . Ruth 4:1-11
Oaths . . . . . Josh 9:15, 20
Joining hands . . . . . Prov 17:18
Pierced ear . . . . . Ex 21:2-6

Examples of:
Abraham and Abimelech . Gen 21:25-32
Solomon and Hiram 1Kin 5:8-12

CONTRADICTION—*resisting or opposing in argument; denying the truth of something*
without all *c*..less is blessed . . . Heb 7:7

CONTRARIWISE—*in distinction; opposite*
c ye ought rather to forgive . . . 2Cor 2:7
But *c*, when they saw that . . . . Gal 2:7
for railing: but *c* blessing 1Pet 3:9

CONTRARY—*opposite in character; antagonistic*

if ye walk *c* unto me, and . . . . . Lev 26:21
it was turned to the *c* . . . . . Esth 9:1
c is in thee from other women . Ezek 16:34
for the wind was *c* . . . . . Matt 14:24
the wind was *c* unto them . . . . . Mark 6:48
these all do *c* to the decrees . . . Acts 17:7
men to worship God *c* to . . . . . Acts 18:13
commandest me..smitten *c* . . . . Acts 23:3
many things *c* to the name . . . . Acts 26:9
grafted *c* to nature into . . . . . Rom 11:24
these are *c* the one to the . . . . . Gal 5:17
which was *c* to us, and took . . . Col 2:14
not God, and are *c* to all 1Thess 2:15
that is *c* to sound doctrine 1Tim 1:10
the *c* part may be ashamed . . . . Titus 2:8

CONTRIBUTION—*a gift*
a certain *c* for the poor . . . . . Rom 15:26

CONTRITION—*grief over sins or shortcomings*
Of the heart . . . . . Ps 51:17
The publican . . . . . Luke 18:13
Peter's example . . . . . Matt 26:75

[*also* CONTRITE]
such as be of a *c* spirit . . . . . Ps 34:18
that is of a *c* and humble . . . . . Is 57:15
is poor and of a *c* spirit . . . . . Is 66:2

CONTROVERSY—*dispute between people*
Between men . . . . . Deut 25:1
Between God and men . . Hos 4:1
A public . . . . . Acts 15:1-35
A private . . . . . Gal 2:11-15

[*also* CONTROVERSIES]
being matters of *c* within . . . . . Deut 17:8
men, between whom the *c* . . . . Deut 19:17
by their word shall every *c* . . . . Deut 21:5
any man that had a *c* came 2Sam 15:2
judgment of the Lord..for *c* . . . 2Chr 19:8
year of recompenses for..*c* . . . . Is 34:8
Lord hath a *c* with..nations . . . . Jer 25:31
in *c*..stand in judgment . . . . . Ezek 44:24
the Lord hath a *c* with the . . . . Hos 4:1
Lord hath..a *c* with Judah . . . . . Hos 12:2
O mountains, the Lord's *c* . . . . Mic 6:2
c great is the mystery 1Tim 3:16

CONVENIENT—*suitable; proper; appropriate*

[*also* CONVENIENTLY]
feed me with food *c* for me . . . Prov 30:8
it seemeth good and *c* . . . . . Jer 40:4
when a *c* day was come . . . . . Mark 6:21
how he might *c* betray . . . . . Mark 14:11
when I have a *c* season, I . . . . . Acts 24:25
things which are not *c* . . . . . Rom 1:28
when he shall have *c* time 1Cor 16:12
nor jesting..are not *c* . . . . . Eph 5:4
enjoin thee that which is *c* . . . . Philem 8

CONVERSANT—*having association with*
strangers that were *c* among . . . Josh 8:35
as long as we were *c* with 1Sam 25:15

CONVERSATION—*behavior; talk*
slay such as be of upright *c* . . . Ps 37:14
him that ordereth his *c* . . . . . Ps 50:23
had our *c* in the world 2Cor 1:12
have heard of my *c* in time . . . . Gal 1:13
all had our *c* in times past . . . . Eph 2:3
concerning the former *c* . . . . . Eph 4:22
let your *c* be as it becometh . . . Phil 1:27
our *c* is in heaven; from . . . . . Phil 3:20
in word, in *c*, in charity 1Tim 4:12
c be without covetousness . . . . . Heb 13:5
considering..end of their *c* . . . . . Heb 13:7
show out of a good *c* his . . . . . James 3:13
ye holy in all manner of *c* 1Pet 1:15
Having your *c* honest 1Pet 2:12
won by the *c* of the wives 1Pet 3:1
the filthy *c* of the wicked 2Pet 2:7
in all holy *c* and godliness 2Pet 3:11

CONVERSION—*turning to God from sin*

Produced by:
God . . . . . Acts 21:19
Christ . . . . . Acts 3:26
Holy Spirit 1Cor 2:13
The Scriptures . . . . . Ps 19:7
Preaching . . . . . Rom 10:14

Of Gentiles:
Foretold . . . . . Is 60:1-5
Explained . . . . . Rom 15:8-18; Acts 15:3
Illustrated . . . . . Acts 10:1-48; Acts 16:25-34
Confirmed . . . . . Acts 15:1-31
Defended . . . . . Gal 3:1-29

Results in:
Repentance ..... Acts 26:20
New creation 2Cor 5:17
Transformation 1Thess 1:9, 10

Fruits of:
Faithfulness ..... Matt 24:45-47
Gentleness 1Thess 2:7
Patience ..... Col 1:10-12
Love 1John 3:14
Obedience ..... Rom 15:18
Peacefulness ..... James 3:17, 18
Self-control 2Pet 1:6
Self-denial ..... John 12:25

[*also* CONVERT, CONVERTED, CONVERTETH, CONVERTING, CONVERTS]
Lord is perfect, *c* the soul ..... Ps 19:7
sinners shall be *c* unto thee ..... Ps 51:13
with judgment, and her *c* ..... Is 1:27
with their heart, and *c*, and ..... Is 6:10
should be *c*, and I should ..... Matt 13:15
Except ye be *c*, and become ..... Matt 18:3
should be *c*, and their sins ..... Mark 4:12
when thou art *c*, strengthen ..... Luke 22:32
be *c*, and I should heal them ..... John 12:40
Repent ye therefore..be *c* ..... Acts 3:19
declaring the *c* of..Gentiles ..... Acts 15:3
be *c*, and I should heal ..... Acts 28:27
from the truth, and one *c* ..... James 5:19
he which *c* the sinner from ..... James 5:20

CONVEY—*to transport*

[*also* CONVEYED]
will *c* them by sea in floats 1Kin 5:9
river, that they may *c* me ..... Neh 2:7
for Jesus had *c* himself ..... John 5:13

CONVICTION—*making one conscious of his guilt*

Produced by:
Holy Spirit ..... John 16:7-11
The Gospel ..... Acts 2:37
Conscience ..... Rom 2:15
The Law ..... James 2:9

Instances of:
Adam ..... Gen 3:8-10
Joseph's brothers ..... Gen 42:21, 22
Israel ..... Ex 33:4
David ..... Ps 51:1-17
Isaiah ..... Is 6:5
Men of Nineveh ..... Matt 12:41
Peter ..... Luke 5:8
Saul of Tarsus ..... Acts 9:4-18
Philippian jailer ..... Acts 16:29, 30

[*also* CONVICTED]
c by their own conscience ..... John 8:9

CONVINCE—*to demonstrate; prove*

[*also* CONVINCED, CONVINCETH]
was none of you that *c* Job ..... Job 32:12
Which of you *c* me of sin? ..... John 8:46
For he mightily *c* the Jews ..... Acts 18:28
unlearned, he is *c* of all, he 1Cor 14:24
exhort..to *c* the gainsayers ..... Titus 1:9
c of..law as transgressors ..... James 2:9
to *c* all that are ungodly ..... Jude 15

CONVOCATION—*a gathering for worship*

Applied to:
Sabbaths ..... Lev 23:2, 3
Passover ..... Ex 12:16
Pentecost ..... Lev 23:21
Feast of Trumpets ..... Num 29:1
Feast of Weeks ..... Num 28:26
Feast of Tabernacles ..... Lev 23:34-36
Day of Atonement ..... Lev 23:27

Designed to:
Gather the people ..... Josh 23:1-16
Worship God 2Kin 23:21, 22

[*also* CONVOCATIONS]
blowing of trumpets..holy *c* ..... Lev 23:24
first day shall be a holy *c* ..... Num 28:18

COOKING—*preparing food*
Carefully performed ..... Gen 27:3-10
Savory dish ..... Gen 27:4
Vegetables ..... Gen 25:29
Forbidden on the Sabbath ..... Ex 35:3
Fish ..... Luke 24:42

[*also* COOK, COOKS]
be confectionaries, and..be *c* 1Sam 8:13
Samuel said unto the *c*, Bring 1Sam 9:23

COOL—*moderately cold; to take away warmth*
garden in the *c* of the day ..... Gen 3:8
finger in water..*c* my tongue ..... Luke 16:24

CO-OPERATION—*working together*

Kinds of:
Man with man ..... Ex 17:12
God with man ..... Phil 2:12, 13

Needed to:
Complete job ..... Neh 4:16, 17
Secure results ..... Matt 18:19
Win converts ..... John 1:40-51
Maintain peace ..... Mark 9:50

Basis:
Obedience to God ..... Ps 119:63
Faith ..... Rom 14:1

COOS (kū'ŏs)
An island between Rhodes and Miletus ..... Acts 21:1

COPING—*covering course of a wall*
the foundation unto the *c* 1Kin 7:9

COPPER—*a reddish, metallic element*

[*also* COPPERSMITH]
vessels of fine *c*, precious ..... Ezra 8:27
Alexander the *c* did me 2Tim 4:14

COPULATION—*sexual intercourse*
if any man's seed of *c* go ..... Lev 15:16

COPY—*to duplicate*

[*also* COPIED]
write him a *c* of this law ..... Deut 17:18
c of the law of Moses ..... Josh 8:32
c of the letter that Tatnai ..... Ezra 5:6
this is the *c* of the letter ..... Ezra 7:11
The *c* of the writing for a ..... Esth 3:14
c of..writing of the decree ..... Esth 4:8
The *c* of the writing for a ..... Esth 8:13
king of Judah *c* out ..... Prov 25:1

COR—*a large measure of undetermined quantity*
part of a bath out of the *c* ..... Ezek 45:14

CORAL—*a rock-like substance formed from skeletons of sea creatures*
Wisdom more valuable than ..... Job 28:18
Bought by traders ..... Ezek 27:16

CORBAN (kôr'băn)—*an offering*
Money dedicated ..... Mark 7:11

CORD—*rope*

[*also* CORDS]
pins of..court and their *c* ..... Ex 35:18
his *c*, and his pins, and all ..... Ex 39:40
c of it for all the service ..... Num 3:26
c, and all the instruments ..... Num 4:26
by a *c* through the window ..... Josh 2:15
bound him with two new *c* ..... Judg 15:13
fastened with *c* of fine linen ..... Esth 1:6
loosed my *c*, and afflicted ..... Job 30:11
be holden in *c* of affliction ..... Job 36:8
or his tongue with a *c* ..... Job 41:1
cast away their *c* from us ..... Ps 2:3
with *c*, even unto the horns ..... Ps 118:27
cut asunder the *c* of..wicked ..... Ps 129:4
hid a snare for me, and *c* ..... Ps 140:5
with the *c* of his sins ..... Prov 5:22
c is not quickly broken ..... Eccl 4:12
ever the silver *c* be loosed ..... Eccl 12:6
that draw iniquity with *c* ..... Is 5:18
of the *c* thereof be broken ..... Is 33:20
lengthen thy *c*, and ..... Is 54:2
all my *c* are broken ..... Jer 10:20
let down Jeremiah with *c* ..... Jer 38:6
down by *c* into the dungeon ..... Jer 38:11
rich apparel, bound with *c* ..... Ezek 27:24
drew them with *c* of a man ..... Hos 11:4
c by lot in the congregation ..... Mic 2:5
made a scourge of small *c* ..... John 2:15

CORDIALITY—*sincere affection and kindness*
Abraham's ..... Gen 18:1-8
Seen in Jonathan 1Sam 20:11-23
Lacking in Nabal 1Sam 25:9-13

CORE (kô'rē)—*the Greek form of "Korah"*
perished..gainsaying of *C* ..... Jude 11

CORIANDER (kôr-ē-ăn'der)
A plant whose seed is compared to manna ..... Ex 16:31

manna was as *c* seed, and ..... Num 11:7

CORINTH (kôr'ĭnth)—*a city in Greece*
Paul labors at ..... Acts 18:1-18
Site of church 1Cor 1:2
Visited by Apollos ..... Acts 19:1
Abode of Erastus 2Tim 4:20

[*also* CORINTHIANS]
O ye *C*, our mouth is open 2Cor 6:11

CORINTHIANS, EPISTLES TO THE—*two books of the New Testament*
Written by Paul 1Cor 1:1; 2Cor 1:1

CORMORANT (kôr'môrănt)
An unclean bird ..... Lev 11:17

the gier-eagle, and the *c* ..... Deut 14:17
c and the bittern shall possess ..... Is 34:11
c and the bittern shall lodge ..... Zeph 2:14

CORN—*the generic term for cereal grasses*

Features regarding:
Grown in Palestine 2Kin 18:32
Chaff blown from ..... Matt 3:12
Article of food ..... Gen 42:1, 2, 19
Eaten with oil ..... Lev 2:14, 15
Parched ..... Ruth 2:14

Figurative of:
Blessings ..... Ezek 36:29
Heavenly food ..... Ps 78:24
Christ ..... John 12:24
Life's maturity ..... Job 5:26

and plenty of *c* and wine ..... Gen 27:28
seven ears of *c* came up ..... Gen 41:5
c which they had brought ..... Gen 43:2
and his *c* money. And he ..... Gen 44:2
ten she asses laden with *c* ..... Gen 45:23
c which they had bought ..... Gen 47:14
so that the stacks of *c* ..... Ex 22:6
neither bread, nor parched *c* ..... Lev 23:14
the *c* of the threshing floor ..... Num 18:27
land, thy *c*, and thy wine ..... Deut 7:13
gather in thy *c*..thy wine ..... Deut 11:14
tithe of thy *c*, or of thy wine ..... Deut 12:17
tithe of thy *c*, of thy wine ..... Deut 14:23
to put the sickle to the *c* ..... Deut 16:9
also of thy *c*, of thy wine ..... Deut 18:4
standing *c* of thy neighbor ..... Deut 23:25
ox when he treadeth out..*c* ..... Deut 25:4
leave thee either *c*, wine ..... Deut 28:51
upon a land of *c* and wine ..... Deut 33:28
eat of the old *c* of the land ..... Josh 5:11
standing *c* of the Philistines ..... Judg 15:5
glean ears of *c* after him ..... Ruth 2:2
an ephah of this parched *c* 1Sam 17:17
five measures of parched *c* 1Sam 25:18
spread ground *c* thereon 2Sam 17:19
full ears of *c* in the husk 2Kin 4:42
land of *c* and wine, a land 2Kin 18:32
c blasted before it be grown 2Kin 19:26
the first fruits of *c* 2Chr 31:5
for the increase of *c*, and 2Chr 32:28
offering of the *c*, of the new ..... Neh 10:39
and the tithes of the *c* ..... Neh 13:5
age, like as a shock of *c* ..... Job 5:26

reap every one his *c* in the ....Job 24:6
up with *c*; they go forth.......Job 39:4
in the time that their *c*........Ps 4:7
thou preparest them *c* ....Ps 65:9
are covered over with *c* ....Ps 65:13
handful of *c* in the earth ......Ps 72:16
them of the *c* of heaven.......Ps 78:24
He that withholdeth *c*, the ....Prov 11:26
harvestman gathereth the *c*....Is 17:5
threshing, and the *c* of my ....Is 21:10
Bread *c* is bruised; because....Is 28:28
own land, a land of *c* and .....Is 36:17
as *c* blasted before it be.......Is 37:27
give thy *c* to be meat ....Is 62:8
Where is *c* and wine? ....Lam 2:12
call for the *c*, and will ....Ezek 36:29
I gave her *c*, and wine, and ...Hos 2:8
assemble themselves for *c* .....Hos 7:14
loveth to tread out the *c* ......Hos 10:11
they shall revive as the *c* ......Hos 14:7
I will send you *c*, and wine....Joel 2:19
be gone, that we may sell *c* ...Amos 8:5
as *c* is sifted in a sieve ....Amos 9:9
the mountains, and upon the *c*.Hag 1:11
c shall make the young men ...Zech 9:17
sabbath day through the *c*.....Matt 12:1
began to pluck the ears of *c*...Matt 12:1
went through the *c* fields ......Mark 2:23
went to pluck the ears of *c* ....Mark 2:23
ear, after that the full *c* ....Mark 4:28
he went through the *c* fields ...Luke 6:1
disciples plucked..ears of *c* ....Luke 6:1
heard..there was *c* in Egypt ...Acts 7:12
ox that treadeth out the *c* 1Cor 9:9
ox that treadeth out the *c* 1Tim 5:18

CORNELIUS (kôr-nēl'yŭs)
A religious Gentile ......Acts 10:1-48

were sent unto him from *C* ....Acts 10:21

CORNER—*angular junction*

[*also* CORNERS]

put them in the four *c* ....Ex 25:12
for the *c* of the tabernacle ....Ex 26:23
horns of it upon the four *c* ....Ex 27:2
by the two *c* thereof, upon ....Ex 30:4
north *c*, he made twenty ......Ex 36:25
for the *c* of the tabernacle ....Ex 36:28
gold, to be set by the four *c*...Ex 37:3
horns thereof on the four *c*....Ex 38:2
not wholly reap the *c* of thy...Lev 19:9
off the *c* of their beard ....Lev 21:5
riddance of..*c* of thy field .....Lev 23:22
shall smite the *c* of Moab .....Num 24:17
I would scatter them into *c*....Deut 32:26
the *c* of the sea southward ....Josh 18:14
c thereof had undersetters.....1Kin 7:30
the right *c* of the temple 2Kin 11:11
to the left *c* of the temple.....2Kin 11:11
gate of Ephraim unto the *c*....2Kin 14:13
gate of Ephraim to the *c*......2Chr 25:23
in Jerusalem at the *c* gate 2Chr 26:9
in every *c* of Jerusalem 2Chr 28:24
the wall, even unto the *c*......Neh 3:24
didst divide them into *c*.......Neh 9:22
smote the four *c* of the house. .Job 1:19
or who laid the *c* stone ....Job 38:6
daughters..be as *c* stones ......Ps 144:12
through..street near her *c* .....Prov 7:8
dwell in a *c* of the housetop ...Prov 21:9
dwell in the *c* of..housetop ....Prov 25:24
the four *c* of the earth ....Is 11:12
precious *c* stone, a sure ....Is 28:16
teachers be removed into..*c* ...Is 30:20
in the utmost *c*, that dwell ....Jer 9:26
all that are in the utmost *c* ....Jer 25:23
unto the gate of the *c*.........Jer 31:38
shall devour the *c* of Moab ....Jer 48:45
that are in the utmost *c* ....Jer 49:32
take of thee a stone for a *c* ...Jer 51:26
upon the four *c* of the land ...Ezek 7:2
c thereof, and the length ......Ezek 41:22
the four *c* of the settle ....Ezek 43:20
the four *c* of the settle of ....Ezek 45:19
by the four *c* of the court .....Ezek 46:21
in every *c* of the court ....Ezek 46:21
Samaria in the *c* of a bed ......Amos 3:12
and as the *c* of the altar ......Zech 9:15
Out of him came..the *c* ....Zech 10:4
c gate, and from the tower ....Zech 14:10
in the *c* of the streets ....Matt 6:5
become the head of the *c* .....Matt 21:42
become the head of the *c* .....Mark 12:10
become the head of the *c*? ....Luke 20:17
knit at the four *c*, and let .....Acts 10:11
from heaven by four *c* ....Acts 11:5
thing was not done in a *c* .....Acts 26:26
standing on the four *c* of......Rev 7:1

CORNER STONE—*a stone placed to bind two walls together*
Laid in Zion ....Is 28:16
Rejected.................Ps 118:22
Christ is 1Pet 2:6, 8
Christ promised as.......Zech 4:7
Christ fulfills ....Acts 4:11
1Pet 2:7

Christ..being the chief *c s* .....Eph 2:20
I lay in Zion a chief *c s*.......1Pet 2:6

CORNET—*a musical instrument*
Used on occasions 1Chr 15:28
A part of worship 2Sam 6:5
Used in Babylon ....Dan 3:7, 10

with trumpets, and with *c* 2Chr 15:14
trumpets and sound of *c* ....Ps 98:6
ye hear the sound of the *c* ....Dan 3:5
Blow ye the *c* in Gibeah ......Hos 5:8

CORNFLOOR—*threshing floor*
a reward upon every *c* ....Hos 9:1

CORPSE—*a dead body*
Laws regarding:
Dwelling made unclean by...................Num 19:11-22
Contact with, makes unclean...............Lev 11:39
Food made unclean ......Lev 11:40
Used figuratively of:
Those in hell............Is 66:24
Idolatrous kings ....Ezek 43:7, 9
Attraction ....Matt 24:28

[*also* CORPSES]

they were all dead *c* 2Kin 19:35
they were all dead *c* ....Is 37:36
stumble upon their *c*..........Nah 3:3
came and took up his *c* ....Mark 6:29

CORRECTION—*punishment designed to restore*
Means of:
God's judgments ....Jer 46:28
The rod ....Prov 22:15
Wickedness ....Jer 2:19
Prayer...................Jer 10:24
Scriptures...............2Tim 3:16
Benefits of:
Needed for children .....Prov 23:13
Sign of sonship ....Prov 3:12
Brings rest ....Prov 29:17
Makes happy............Job 5:17

[*also* CORRECT, CORRECTED, CORRECTETH]

for *c*, or for his land.........Job 37:13
with rebukes dost *c* man ......Ps 39:11
heathen, shall not he *c*?.......Ps 94:10
neither be weary of his *c*.......Prov 3:11
fool to the *c* of the stocks .....Prov 7:22
C is grievous unto him ....Prov 15:10
A servant will not be *c* by ....Prov 29:19
they received no *c*: your ......Jer 2:30
have refused to receive *c*......Jer 5:3
nor receiveth *c*: truth is ....Jer 7:28
O Lord, *c* me, but with ....Jer 10:24
I will *c* thee in measure ....Jer 30:11
established them for *c* ....Hab 1:12
she received not *c*; she ....Zeph 3:2
fathers of our flesh which *c* ...Heb 12:9

CORRUPTION—*rottenness; depravity*
Descriptive of:
Physical blemishes ....Mal 1:14
Physical decay...........Matt 6:19, 20
Moral decay ....Gen 6:12
Eternal ruin.............Gal 6:8
Characteristics of:
Unregenerate men ....Luke 6:43, 44
Apostates 2Cor 2:7
2Pet 2:12, 19
Deliverance from:
By Christ ....Acts 2:27, 31
Promised ....Rom 8:21
Through conversion......1Pet 1:18, 23
Perfected in heaven......1Cor 15:42,50

[*also* CORRUPT, CORRUPTED, CORRUPTERS, CORRUPTETH, CORRUPTIBLE, CORRUPTING, CORRUPTLY]

earth also was *c* before God...Gen 6:11
flesh had *c* his way upon the ..Gen 6:12
land was *c* by reason of the ...Ex 8:24
out of Egypt, have *c*..........Ex 32:7
c is in them, and blemishes....Lev 22:25
Lest ye *c* yourselves, and .....Deut 4:16
the land of Egypt have *c*......Deut 9:12
ye will utterly *c* yourselves ....Deut 31:29
They have *c* themselves ....Deut 32:5
c themselves more than ....Judg 2:19
right hand of..mount of *c* 2Kin 23:13
And the people did yet *c* 2Chr 27:2
have dealt very *c* against ......Neh 1:7
breath is *c*, my days are.......Job 17:1
said to *c*, Thou art my father ..Job 17:14
They are *c*, they have done ...Ps 14:1
thine Holy One to see *c* ......Ps 16:10
My wounds stink and are *c*....Ps 38:5
live for ever, and not see *c*....Ps 49:9
C are they, and have done ....Ps 53:1
are *c*, and speak wickedly .....Ps 73:8
troubled fountain, and a *c*.....Prov 25:26
children that are *c*: they ......Is 1:4
delivered it from..pit of *c* .....Is 38:17
brass and iron;..are all *c* ......Jer 6:28
wast *c* more than they in......Ezek 16:47
according to your *c* doings ....Ezek 20:44
c in her inordinate love ....Ezek 23:11
thou hast *c* thy wisdom by ....Ezek 28:17
prepared lying and *c* words....Dan 2:9
was turned in me into *c*.......Dan 10:8
daughter of women, *c* her.....Dan 11:17
shall he *c* by flatteries ....Dan 11:32
have deeply *c* themselves......Hos 9:9
brought up my life from *c*.....Jon 2:6
rose early, and *c* all their .....Zeph 3:7
I will *c* your seed, and ....Mal 2:3
ye have *c* the covenant of .....Mal 2:8
c tree bringeth forth evil ......Matt 7:17
tree *c*, and his fruit *c* ....Matt 12:33
approacheth, neither moth *c*...Luke 12:33
to return to *c*, he said on .....Acts 13:34
God raised..saw no *c* ....Acts 13:37
image made like to *c* man .....Rom 1:23
do it to obtain a *c* crown......1Cor 9:25
evil communications *c*.........1Cor 15:33
c must put on incorruption 1Cor 15:53
which *c* the word of God 2Cor 2:17
we have *c* no man, we have ...2Cor 7:2
your minds should be *c* 2Cor 11:3
old man, which is *c*...........Eph 4:22
disputings of men of *c* 1Tim 6:5
men of *c* minds, reprobate 2Tim 3:8
Your riches are *c*, and your ...James 5:2
in that which is not *c*, even ...1Pet 3:4
escaped the *c*..in the world 2Pet 1:4
perish in their own *c*..........2Pet 2:12
things they *c* themselves ......Jude 10
which did *c* the earth with ....Rev 19:2

CORRUPTION, MOUNT OF
Site of pagan altars 1Kin 11:7
Altars of, destroyed 2Kin 23:13

CORRUPTION OF BODY
Results from Adam's sin..Rom 8:21
Begins in this life 2Cor 5:4

Consummated by death . .John 11:39
Freedom from, promised .Rom 8:21
Freedom from, accomplished 1Cor 15:42

COSAM (kō'săm)—*"a diviner"*
Father of Addi . . . . .Luke 3:28

COSMETICS—*preparations which improves physical appearance*
Used by Jezebel 2Kin 9:30
Futility of . . . . .Jer 4:30

COSMIC CONFLAGRATION—*destruction of the heavens and the earth by fire*
Day of judgment 2Pet 3:7-10

COST—*something given in exchange*

[*also* COSTLINESS, COSTLY]
eaten at all of the king's *c* 2Sam 19:42
which doth *c* me nothing 2Sam 24:24
c stones, and hewed stones 1Kin 5:17
All these were of *c* stones 1Kin 7:9
burnt offerings without *c* 1Chr 21:24
first, and counteth the *c* . . . . . .Luke 14:28
of spikenard, very *c* . . . . .John 12:3
or gold, or pearls, or *c* 1Tim 2:9
in the sea by reason of her *c* . .Rev 18:19

COTES—*a small coop or shed for keeping domestic animals*
of beasts, and *c* for flocks 2Chr 32:28

COTTAGE—*a booth; hut*

[*also* COTTAGES]
of Zion is left as a *c* in . . . . . . .Is 1:8
and shall be removed like a *c* .Is 24:20
c for shepherds, and folds . . . . .Zeph 2:6

COUCH—*article of furniture; to lie down*

[*also* COUCHED, COUCHES, COUCHETH, COUCHING, COUCHING PLACE]
thou it; he went up to my *c* . . .Gen 49:4
he *c* as a lion, and as an old . .Gen 49:9
Issachar is a strong ass *c* . . . . . .Gen 49:14
He *c*, he lay down as a lion . . .Num 24:9
for the deep that *c* beneath . . .Deut 33:13
c shall ease my complaint . . . . .Job 7:13
When they *c* in their dens . . . . .Job 38:40
I water my *c* with my tears . . . .Ps 6:6
Ammonites a *c*..for flocks . . . . .Ezek 25:5
and in Damascus in a *c* . . . . . .Amos 3:12
themselves upon their *c* . . . . . . .Amos 6:4
The tiling with his *c* . . . . .Luke 5:19
take up thy *c*, and go into . . . .Luke 5:24
laid them on beds and *c* . . . . . .Acts 5:15

COULD—*possibly able to*

[*also* COULDEST]
They *c* not dwell together . . . . .Gen 13:6
eyes were dim, so..he *c* not . . .Gen 27:1
were strangers *c* not bear . . . . .Gen 36:7
hated him, and *c* not speak . . .Gen 37:4
was none that *c* interpret . . . . . .Gen 41:8
Joseph *c* not refrain himself . . .Gen 45:1
dim for age, so that he *c* . . . . . .Gen 48:10
she *c* not longer hide him . . . . .Ex 2:3
out of Egypt, and *c* not . . . . . . .Ex 12:39
c not drink of the waters of . . .Ex 15:23
c not keep the passover on . . . .Num 9:6
the children of Israel *c* not . . . .Josh 7:12
children of Manasseh *c* not . . . .Josh 17:12
c not drive out..inhabitants . . . .Judg 1:19
c sling stones at a hair . . . . .Judg 20:16
rose up before one *c* know . . . .Ruth 3:14
wax dim, that he *c* not see 1Sam 3:2
c not go over the brook 1Sam 30:10
was sure that he *c* not live 2Sam 1:10
wounded them, that they *c* 2Sam 22:39
David my father *c* not build . . .1Kin 5:3
But Ahijah *c* not see; for 1Kin 14:4
king of Edom; but they *c* 2Kin 3:26
c use both the right hand 1Chr 12:2
But David *c* not go before it . .1Chr 21:30
weight of the brass *c* not be . . .2Chr 4:18
that *c* skill of instruments 2Chr 34:12
c not show their father's . . . . . .Ezra 2:59
c not cause them to cease . . . . .Ezra 5:5
c not show their father's . . . . . .Neh 7:61
c not speak in the Jews' . . . . . . .Neh 13:24
night *c* not the king sleep . . . . .Esth 6:1
still, but I *c* not discern . . . . . . .Job 4:16
his highness I *c* not endure . . . .Job 31:23
I sought him, but he *c* not . . . .Ps 37:36
their floods, that they *c* not . . .Ps 78:44
sought him, but I *c* not find . . .Song 5:6
c have been done more to . . . . .Is 5:4
c not deliver the burden . . . . . .Is 46:2
done evil things as thou *c* . . . . .Jer 3:5
ashamed, neither *c* they blush .Jer 6:15
So that the Lord *c* no . . . . .Jer 44:22
c not touch their garments . . . .Lam 4:14
nation that *c* not save us . . . . . .Lam 4:17
yet *c* not be satisfied . . . . .Ezek 16:28
garden of God *c* not hide . . . . .Ezek 31:8
a river that I *c* not pass . . . . . . .Ezek 47:5
river that *c* not be passed . . . . .Ezek 47:5
thou *c* reveal this secret . . . . . . .Dan 2:47
they *c* not read the writing . . . .Dan 5:8
that *c* deliver out of his . . . . . . .Dan 8:4
c he not heal you, nor cure . . .Hos 5:13
c not: for the sea wrought . . . . .Jon 1:13
and they *c* not cure him . . . . . . .Matt 17:16
Pilate saw that he *c* prevail . . . .Matt 27:24
that Jesus *c* no more . . . . .Mark 1:45
and no man *c* bind him, no . . .Mark 5:3
c there do no mighty work . . . .Mark 6:5
She hath done what she *c* . . . . .Mark 14:8
c not thou watch one hour . . . .Mark 14:37
came out, he *c* not speak . . . . .Luke 1:22
that they *c* not tell . . . . .Luke 20:7
not of God, he *c* do nothing . .John 9:33
Thou *c* have no power at . . . . .John 19:11
the world..*c* not contain . . . . . . .John 21:25
they *c* say nothing against . . . . .Acts 4:14
c not bear up into the wind . . .Acts 27:15
For what the law *c* not do . . . .Rom 8:3
For I *c* wish that myself . . . . . . .Rom 9:3
brethren, *c* not speak unto 1Cor 3:1
all faith, so..I *c* remove 1Cor 13:2
Israel *c* not steadfastly 2Cor 3:7
Would to God ye *c* bear 2Cor 11:1
a law given which *c* have . . . . . .Gal 3:21
we *c* no longer forbear 1Thess 3:1
we see that they *c* not enter . . .Heb 3:19
(For they *c* not endure . . . . .Heb 12:20
multitude, which no man *c* . . . .Rev 7:9
no man *c* learn that song . . . . . .Rev 14:3

COULTER—*a mattock or plowshare*

[*also* COULTERS]
man his share, and his *c* 1Sam 13:20
for the *c*, and for the forks 1Sam 13:21

COUNCIL—*Jewish Sanhedrin*
A judicial court . . . . .Matt 5:22
Christ's trial . . . . .Matt 26:57-59
Powers of, limited . . . . . . .John 18:31
Apostles before . . . . .Acts 4:5-30
Stephen before . . . . .Acts 6:12-15
Paul before . . . . .Acts 23:1-5

[*also* COUNCILS]
princes of Judah and..*c* . . . . . . .Ps 68:27
deliver you up to the *c* . . . . .Matt 10:17
Pharisees..held a *c* . . . . .Matt 12:14
shall deliver you up to *c* . . . . . .Mark 13:9
chief priests and all the *c* . . . . .Mark 14:55
and led him into their *c* . . . . . . .Luke 22:66
and the Pharisees a *c* . . . . .John 11:47
and called the *c* together . . . . . .Acts 5:21
and all their *c* to appear . . . . . .Acts 22:30

COUNSEL—*to advise; consult; plan*

[*also* COUNSELED, COUNSELS]
the priests, who shall ask *c* . . . .Num 27:21
through the *c* of Balaam . . . . . .Num 31:16
are a nation void of *c* . . . . .Deut 32:28
asked not *c* at the mouth . . . . .Josh 9:14
Ask *c*, we pray thee, of God . .Judg 18:5
give your advice and *c* . . . . .Judg 20:7
and asked *c* of God, and . . . . . .Judg 20:18
And Saul asked *c* of God 1Sam 14:37
turn the *c* of Ahithophel into . .2Sam 15:31
he *c* in those days, was as 2Sam 16:23
The *c* that Ahithophel hath . . .2Sam 17:7
I pray thee, give thee *c* 1Kin 1:12
took *c* with his servants 2Kin 6:8
asking *c* of one that had a 1Chr 10:13
Rehoboam took *c* with the 2Chr 10:6
were his *c* after the death 2Chr 22:4
according to the *c* of my lord . .Ezra 10:3
God had brought their *c* to . . . .Neh 4:15
c of the froward is carried . . . . .Job 5:13
strength, he hath *c* and . . . . . .Job 12:13
the *c* of the wicked is far . . . . .Job 21:16
How hast thou *c* him that . . . . .Job 26:3
Who is..that darkeneth *c* by . . .Job 38:2
not in the *c* of the ungodly . . . .Ps 1:1
Lord, who hath given me *c* . . . .Ps 16:7
The Lord bringeth the *c* . . . . . .Ps 33:10
We took sweet *c* together . . . . .Ps 55:14
shalt guide me with thy *c* . . . . .Ps 73:24
provoked him with their *c* . . . . .Ps 106:43
contemned the *c* of..Most . . . . .Ps 107:11
have set at nought all my *c* . . . .Prov 1:25
Where no *c* is..people fall . . . . .Prov 11:14
hearkeneth unto *c* is wise . . . . .Prov 12:15
without *c* purposes are . . . . .Prov 15:22
Hear *c*..receive instruction . . . .Prov 19:20
the *c* of the Lord . . . . .Prov 19:21
C in the heart of man is . . . . . .Prov 20:5
nor *c* against the Lord . . . . .Prov 21:30
wise *c* thou shalt make thy . . . .Prov 24:6
a man's friend by hearty *c* . . . .Prov 27:9
I *c* thee to keep the king's . . . .Eccl 8:2
the *c*, and the cunning . . . . .Is 3:3
taken evil *c* against . . . . .Is 7:5
Take *c* together, and it . . . . . . .Is 8:10
the spirit of *c* and might . . . . . .Is 11:2
because of the *c* of the Lord . .Is 19:17
c of old are faithfulness . . . . . . .Is 25:1
which is wonderful in *c* . . . . . . .Is 28:29
hide their *c* from the Lord . . . . .Is 29:15
Lord, that take *c*, but not . . . . .Is 30:1
there was no *c*, that, when I . .Is 41:28
c and in the imagination . . . . . .Jer 7:24
nor *c* from the wise, nor the . .Jer 18:18
stood in the *c* of the Lord . . . . .Jer 23:18
and *c* from the ancients . . . . . . .Ezek 7:26
with *c* and wisdom . . . . .Dan 2:14
My people ask *c* at their . . . . . .Hos 4:12
because of their own *c* . . . . .Hos 11:6
understand they his *c* . . . . .Mic 4:12
ye walk in their *c*; that I . . . . . .Mic 6:16
c of peace shall be between . . .Zech 6:13
c how they might entangle . . . .Matt 22:15
took *c* with the Herodians . . . . .Mark 3:6
they took *c* together for to . . . .John 11:53
and took *c* to slay them . . . . . . .Acts 5:33
c or this work be of men . . . . . .Acts 5:38
the *c* of the hearts 1Cor 4:5
after the *c* of his own will . . . . .Eph 1:11
the immutability of his *c* . . . . . .Heb 6:17
I *c* thee to buy of me gold . . . .Rev 3:18

COUNSEL, GOD'S

Called:
Immutable . . . . .Heb 6:17
Faithful . . . . .Is 25:1
Wonderful . . . . .Is 28:29
Great . . . . .Jer 32:19
Sovereign . . . . .Dan 4:35
Eternal . . . . .Eph 3:11

Events determined by:
History . . . . .Is 46:10, 11
Christ's death . . . . .Acts 2:23
Salvation . . . . .Rom 8:28-30
Union in Christ . . . . .Eph 1:9, 10

Attitudes toward:
Christians declare . . . . . . .Acts 20:27
Proper reserve . . . . .Acts 1:7
Wicked despise . . . . .Is 5:19
They reject . . . . .Luke 7:30

COUNSEL, MAN'S
Jethro's, accepted . . . . . . .Ex 18:13-27
Hushai's followed 2Sam 17:14

Of a woman, brings peace 2Sam 20:16-20
David's dying 1Kin 2:1-10
Of old men, rejected 1Kin 12:8, 13
Of friends, avenged......Esth 5:14

COUNSELOR—*an advisor*
Christ is ....Is 9:6
Thy testimonies are ......Ps 119:24
Safety in many ....Prov 11:14
Brings security ....Prov 15:22
Jonathan, a 1Chr 27:32
Gamaliel................Acts 5:33-40

[*also* COUNSELORS]
David's *c*, from his city 2Sam 15:12
Zechariah his son, a wise *c*....1Chr 26:14
mother was his *c* to do........2Chr 22:3
hired *c* against them, to ....Ezra 4:5
kings and *c* of the earth.......Job 3:14
turned round about by his *c*...Job 37:12
let them fall by..own *c*........Ps 5:10
shall attain unto wise *c*........Prov 1:5
c of the wicked are deceit .....Prov 12:5
but to the *c* of peace is joy....Prov 12:20
thy *c* as at the beginning ......Is 1:26
treasurers, the *c*, the..........Dan 3:2
thy *c* perished? for pangs .....Mic 4:9
against the Lord..wicked *c* ....Nah 1:11
an honorable *c* ....Mark 15:43
man named Joseph, a *c*.......Luke 23:50
or who hath been his *c*? ......Rom 11:34

COUNT—*to number*
Stars ....Gen 15:5
Days ....Lev 15:13
Years ....Lev 25:8
Booty ....Num 31:26
Weeks..................Deut 16:9
Money 2Kin 22:4
People.................1Chr 21:17
Bones ....Ps 22:17
Towers ....Ps 48:12
Houses ....Is 22:10

[*also* COUNTED, COUNTETH, COUNTING]
c it..for righteousness ....Gen 15:6
make your *c* for the lamb .....Ex 12:4
as it was *c*, according to ....Ex 38:21
c the fruit thereof as..........Lev 19:23
shall be *c* as the fields of......Lev 25:31
shall be *c* unto the Levites ....Num 18:30
can *c* the dust of Jacob ....Num 23:10
c to the Canaanite; five ....Josh 13:3
C not thine handmaid for a ...1Sam 1:16
son Solomon shall be *c* 1Kin 1:21
Levi and Benjamin *c* he 1Chr 21:6
they were *c* faithful, and ......Neh 13:13
are we *c* as beasts ....Job 18:3
he *c* me unto him as one of ...Job 19:11
maids, *c* me for a stranger ....Job 19:15
my ways, and *c* all my steps? ..Job 31:4
c as sheep for the slaughter ...Ps 44:22
The Lord shall *c*, when he ....Ps 87:6
If I should *c* them, they are ...Ps 139:18
I *c* them mine enemies.........Ps 139:22
holdeth his peace, is *c* wise....Prov 17:28
saith the preacher, *c* one by ...Eccl 7:27
horses' hoofs shall be *c* like ...Is 5:28
are *c* as the small dust of .....Is 40:15
were *c* as a strange thing......Hos 8:12
Shall I *c* them pure with ......Mic 6:11
they *c* him as a prophet.......Matt 14:5
men *c* John, that he was a ....Mark 11:32
c the cost, whether he hath ...Luke 14:28
were *c* worthy to suffer ....Acts 5:41
neither *c* I my life dear ....Acts 20:24
not his uncircumcision be *c*....Rom 2:26
c unto him for righteousness...Rom 4:3
gain to me, those I *c* loss .....Phil 3:7
I *c* all things but loss for ......Phil 3:8
be *c* worthy of the kingdom ...2Thess 1:5
God would *c* you worthy of ...2Thess 1:11
he *c* me faithful, putting me ...1Tim 1:12
c their own masters worthy 1Tim 6:1
c me therefore a partner ......Philem 17
c the blood of the covenant ...Heb 10:29
c it all joy when ye fall ....James 1:2
c them happy which endure ...James 5:11
hath understanding *c* the ......Rev 13:18

COUNTENANCE—*face; expression*
Kinds of:
Unfriendly ....Gen 31:1, 2
Fierce ....Deut 28:50
Terrible ....Judg 13:6
Sad ....Neh 2:2, 3
Beautiful 1Sam 16:12
Cheerful ....Prov 15:13
Angry ....Prov 25:23
Hatred ....Prov 10:18
Transfigured:
Moses' 2Cor 3:7
Christ's ....Matt 17:2
The believer's 2Cor 3:18

[*also* COUNTENANCES]
Cain was..wroth, his *c* fell.....Gen 4:5
Why is thy *c* fallen ....Gen 4:6
Neither shalt thou *c* a poor....Ex 23:3
The Lord lift up his *c* upon ...Num 6:26
and her *c* was no more sad....1Sam 1:18
Look not on his *c*, or on the ..1Sam 16:7
and ruddy, and of a fair *c*.....1Sam 17:42
was a woman of a fair *c* 2Sam 14:27
he settled his *c* steadfastly 2Kin 8:11
changest his *c*, and sendest ....Job 14:20
lift..up the light of thy *c* ......Ps 4:6
exceeding glad with thy *c* .....Ps 21:6
health of my *c*, and my God ..Ps 42:11
heart maketh a cheerful *c* .....Prov 15:13
the *c* of his friend ....Prov 27:17
sadness of the *c* the heart .....Eccl 7:3
let me see thy *c*, let me hear ..Song 2:14
c is as Lebanon, excellent as ..Song 5:15
The show of their *c* doth ......Is 3:9
shall be troubled in their *c* ....Ezek 27:35
let our *c* be looked upon......Dan 1:13
and the *c* of the children ......Dan 1:13
the hypocrites, of a sad *c* .....Matt 6:16
His *c* was like lightning ....Matt 28:3
his *c* was altered, and.........Luke 9:29
me full of joy with thy *c* ......Acts 2:28
Moses for the glory of his *c* ...2Cor 3:7
his *c* was as the sun shineth ...Rev 1:16

COUNTERFEIT—*a spurious imitation of the real thing*
Applied to persons:
Christ ....Matt 24:4,5,24
Apostles 2Cor 11:13
Ministers 2Cor 11:14,15
Christians ....Gal 2:3, 4
Teachers 2Pet 2:1
Prophets ....John 4:1
The antichrist ....Rev 19:20
Applied to things:
Worship ....Matt 15:8, 9
Gospel ....Gal 1:6-12
Miracles 2Thess 2:7-12
Science 1Tim 6:20
Commandments ....Titus 1:13, 14
Doctrines ....Heb 13:9
Religion ....James 1:26
Prayers ....James 4:3

COUNTERVAIL—*to counteract*
enemy could not *c* the king's ..Esth 7:4

COUNTRY—*the land of a nation*
Commanded to leave ....Gen 12:1-4
Love of native ....Gen 30:25
Exiled from ....Ps 137:1-6
A prophet in his own ....Luke 4:24
A heavenly ....Heb 11:16

[*also* COUNTRIES, COUNTRYMEN]
their tongues, in their *c* ....Gen 10:20
smote all the *c* of the ....Gen 14:7
give all these *c*, and I will.....Gen 26:3
it be one of your own *c*.......Lev 16:29
as for one of your own *c*......Lev 24:22
All that are born of the *c* .....Num 15:13
the *c* which the Lord smote ...Num 32:4
Manasseh took all the *c* of ....Deut 3:14
plain *c*, of the Reubenites .....Deut 4:43
come unto the *c* which the ....Deut 26:3
Israel to search out the *c*.....Josh 2:2
men that had spied out the *c* ..Josh 6:22
Go up and view the *c*.........Josh 7:2
We be come from a far *c* .....Josh 9:6
Joshua smote all the *c* of......Josh 10:40
all the south *c*, and all ....Josh 11:16
kings of the *c* which Joshua ...Josh 12:7
of the hill *c* from Lebanon ....Josh 13:6
are the *c* which Moses did ....Josh 13:32
get thee up to the wood *c*.....Josh 17:15
an end of dividing the *c*.......Josh 19:51
Hebron, in the hill *c* of ....Josh 21:11
to go unto the *c* of Gilead ....Josh 22:9
c was in quietness forty ....Judg 8:28
the inhabitants of that *c*.......Judg 11:21
Aijalon in the *c* of Zebulun ...Judg 12:12
the destroyer of our *c*.........Judg 16:24
to spy out the *c* of Laish ......Judg 18:14
the *c* of the inheritance of......Judg 20:6
to sojourn in the *c* of Moab ...Ruth 1:1
Naomi out of the *c* of Moab ..Ruth 2:6
come again out of the *c* of ....Ruth 4:3
c of the Philistines seven 1Sam 6:1
the camp from the *c* round 1Sam 14:21
place in some town in the *c* ...1Sam 27:5
all the *c* wept with a loud 2Sam 15:23
over the face of all the *c*......2Sam 18:8
c of Benjamin in Zelah 2Sam 21:14
the son of Uri was in the *c*....1Kin 4:19
a far *c* for thy name's sake 1Kin 8:41
and went to her own *c*........1Kin 10:13
I may go to mine own *c* 1Kin 11:21
the Syrians filled the *c* 1Kin 20:27
every man to his own *c* 1Kin 22:36
the *c* was filled with water 2Kin 3:20
gods of the *c*, that have 2Kin 18:35
delivered their *c* out of 2Kin 18:35
are come from a far *c* 2Kin 20:14
begat children in the *c* of 1Chr 8:8
the *c* of the children of 1Chr 20:1
of glory throughout all *c* 1Chr 22:5
a far *c* for thy great name's ...2Chr 6:32
governors of the *c* brought 2Chr 9:14
all the *c* of Judah and 2Chr 11:23
the low *c*, and in the plains ...2Chr 26:10
invaded..cities of the low *c*....2Chr 28:18
the *c* of Ephraim and 2Chr 30:10
of the people of those *c*.......Ezra 3:3
c round about Jerusalem ......Neh 12:28
the heads over many *c*.........Ps 110:6
so is good news from a far *c* ..Prov 25:25
Your *c* is desolate, your ......Is 1:7
give ear, all ye of far *c* ....Is 8:9
They come from a far *c*........Is 13:5
like a ball into a large *c*.......Is 22:18
are come from a far *c* unto....Is 39:3
my counsel from a far *c*.......Is 46:11
you into a plentiful *c* ....Jer 2:7
watchers come from a far *c* ...Jer 4:16
sweet cane from a far *c* ....Jer 6:20
them that dwell in a far *c* .....Jer 8:19
commotion out of the north *c* .Jer 10:22
more, nor see his native *c*.....Jer 22:10
flock out of all *c* whither......Jer 23:3
out of the north *c*, and from ..Jer 23:8
bring them from the north *c*...Jer 31:8
is in the *c* of Benjamin ....Jer 32:8
and in the *c* of Pathros ....Jer 44:1
a sacrifice in the north *c* ......Jer 46:10
remnant of the *c* of Caphtor...Jer 47:4
upon the plain *c*; upon........Jer 48:21
nations from the north *c* ......Jer 50:9
go every one into his own *c* ...Jer 51:9
the nations and *c* that are .....Ezek 5:5
scattered them among the *c* ....Ezek 11:16
the *c* where they sojourn ......Ezek 20:38
the glory of the *c*............Ezek 25:9
and the *c* shall be destitute ....Ezek 32:15
inhabited places of the *c* ......Ezek 34:13
issue out toward the east *c* ....Ezek 47:8
all the *c* whither thou hast ....Dan 9:7
fled into the *c* of Syria ....Hos 12:12

what is thy *c*? and of what ....Jon 1:8
when I was yet in my *c*? ......Jon 4:2
go forth into the north *c* ......Zech 6:6
go forth toward the south *c* ...Zech 6:6
people from the east *c* ....Zech 8:7
and from the west *c* ....Zech 8:7
shall remember me in far *c* ....Zech 10:9
into their own *c* another ......Matt 2:12
side into the *c* of the ....Matt 8:28
his fame in all that *c*.........Matt 9:31
was come into his own *c* ......Matt 13:54
all that *c* round about, and ....Matt 14:35
and went into a far *c* ....Matt 21:33
man traveling into a far *c* .....Matt 25:14
into the *c* of the Gadarenes ...Mark 5:1
and came into his own *c* ......Mark 6:1
and went into a far *c* ....Mark 12:1
coming out of the *c*, the ......Mark 15:21
walked, went into the *c* ....Mark 16:12
into the hill *c* with haste ......Luke 1:39
in the same *c* shepherds.......Luke 2:8
into all the *c* about Jordan ....Luke 3:3
do also here in thy *c*..........Luke 4:23
at the *c* of the Gadarenes .....Luke 8:26
go into the towns and *c* ....Luke 9:12
his journey into a far *c* ....Luke 15:13
went into a far *c* to receive....Luke 19:12
into a far *c* for a long time ....Luke 20:9
that are in the *c* enter ....Luke 21:21
coming out of the *c*...........Luke 23:26
no honor in his own *c* ....John 4:44
c near to the wilderness ......John 11:54
a..and of the *c* of Cyprus .....Acts 4:36
Get thee out of thy *c*, and ....Acts 7:3
c..nourished by..king's *c* ......Acts 12:20
deputy of the *c*, Sergius ....Acts 13:7
drew near to some *c* ....Acts 27:27
promise, as in a strange *c* .....Heb 11:9
mindful of that *c* from ....Heb 11:15

COUNTRYMEN—*natives of specified countries; compatriots*
in perils by mine own *c* 2Cor 11:26
suffered like things of your..*c*..1Thess 2:14

COUPLE—*to link together; a pair*
[*also* COUPLED, COUPLETH, COUPLING, COUPLINGS]
five curtains shall be *c* ....Ex 26:3
c one to another ....Ex 26:3
from the selvedge in the *c*.....Ex 26:4
in the *c* of the second.........Ex 26:4
and *c* the curtains together ....Ex 26:6
edge of the curtain which *c*....Ex 26:10
over against the other *c* ....Ex 28:27
And he *c* the five curtains.....Ex 36:10
from the selvedge in the *c*.....Ex 36:11
another curtain, in the *c* ......Ex 36:11
curtain which *c* the second ....Ex 36:17
brass to *c* the tent together....Ex 36:18
shoulderpieces for it, to *c* .....Ex 39:4
by the two edges was it *c* .....Ex 39:4
over against the other *c* ....Ex 39:20
servant with him, and a *c* .....Judg 19:3
make me a *c* of cakes in my...2Sam 13:6
with a *c* of asses saddled 2Sam 16:1
stone, and timber for *c* 2Chr 34:11
will a *c* of horsemen ....Is 21:7
chaste conversation *c* with.....1Pe 3:2

COURAGE—*fearlessness in the face of danger*

Manifested:
Among enemies ....Ezra 5:11
In battle 1Sam 17:46
Against great foes ....Judg 7:7-23
Against great odds 1Sam 17:32,50
When threatened ....Dan 3:16-18
When intimidated ....Dan 6:10
When facing death ......Judg 16:28
In youth 1Sam 14:6-45
In old age ....Josh 14:10-12
Before a king ....Esth 4:8, 16
In moral crises ....Neh 13:1-31
In preaching Christ ......Acts 3:12-26
In rebuking ....Gal 2:11-15

Men encouraged to:
Leaders.................Deut 31:7
Joshua..................Josh 1:5-7
Gideon ....Judg 7:11
Philistines..............1Sam 4:9
Zerubbabel ....Hag 2:4
Solomon 1Chr 28:20

[*also* COURAGEOUS, COURAGEOUSLY]
And be ye of good *c*, and .....Num 13:20
Be strong and of a good *c* ....Deut 31:6
there remain any more *c* ......Josh 2:11
be strong and of good *c*.......Josh 10:25
Be ye therefore very *c* to .....Josh 23:6
of good *c*, and let us play 2Sam 10:12
I commanded you? be *c* 2Sam 13:28
Be of good *c*, and let us 1Chr 19:13
be strong, and of good *c* 1Chr 22:13
Oded the prophet, he took *c* ..2Chr 15:8
Be strong and *c*, be not 2Chr 32:7
with thee; be of good *c* ....Ezra 10:4
Wait..Lord; be of good *c* .....Ps 27:14
Be of good *c*, and he shall ....Ps 31:24
his brother, Be of good *c* .....Is 41:6
stir up his power and his *c* ....Dan 11:25
And he that is *c* among the ...Amos 2:16
he thanked God, and took *c* ..Acts 28:15

COURSE—*onward movement; advance*
A ship's direction........Acts 16:11
A prescribed path ....Judg 5:20
One's life 2Tim 4:7
The age ....Eph 2:2
The cycle of life ....James 3:6
Orderly arrangement.....1Chr 27:1-15

[*also* COURSES]
ten thousand a month by *c* 1Kin 5:14
divided them into *c* among 1Chr 23:6
king in any matter of the *c* 1Chr 27:1
ministered to the king by *c* 1Chr 28:1
for the *c* of the priests 1Chr 28:13
did not then wait by *c* 2Chr 5:11
c of the priests to their 2Chr 8:14
porters also by their *c* 2Chr 8:14
priest dismissed not the *c* 2Chr 23:8
appointed the *c*..priests 2Chr 31:2
the Levites after their *c* 2Chr 31:2
fathers, after your *c* 2Chr 35:4
they sang together by *c* ....Ezra 3:11
and the Levites in their *c* .....Ezra 6:18
of the earth are out of *c* ......Ps 82:5
as willows by the water *c* .....Is 44:4
their *c* is evil, and their ....Jer 23:10
Zechariah, of the *c* of Abijah. .Luke 1:5
as John fulfilled his *c*, he .....Acts 13:25
that I might finish my *c* ....Acts 20:24
we came with a straight *c* .....Acts 21:1
three, and that by *c*; and......1Cor 14:27
word..Lord may have free *c* ...2Thess 3:1

COURTESY—*visible signs of respect*

Shown in:
Manner of address.......Gen 18:3
Gestures of bowing ......Gen 19:1
Rising before superiors...Lev 19:32
Well-wishing remarks ....Gen 43:29
Expressions of blessing...Ruth 2:4

Among Christians:
Taught ....Rom 12:9-21
Illustrated..............3John 1-6, 12

[*also* COURTEOUS, COURTEOUSLY]
Julius *c* entreated Paul ....Acts 27:3
and lodged us three days *c* ....Acts 28:7
brethren, be pitiful, be *c* 1Pet 3:8

COURTS—*institutions for administering justice*

Kinds of:
Circuit.................1Sam 7:15-17
Superior and inferior ....Ex 18:21-26
Ecclesiastical ....Matt 18:15-18

Places held:
At the tabernacle........Num 27:2
Outside the camp........Lev 24:14
At the city's gates ....Ruth 4:1, 2
Under a tree ....Judg 4:5

Features of:
Witness examined ....Deut 19:15-21
Accused speaks ....Mark 15:3-5
Sentence of, final.......Deut 17:8-13
Contempt of, forbidden ..Acts 23:1-5
Corruption of, deplored..Matt 26:59-62

COURTSHIP—*the period leading to marriage*
Isaac and Rebekah ......Gen 24:1-67
Jacob and Rachel........Gen 29:9-30
Samson ....Judg 14:1-7
Boaz and Ruth ....Ruth 3:4-13
Ahasuerus and Esther ...Esth 2:17

COURTYARD—*an enclosed area*
Tabernacle..............Ex 27:9
Temple 1Kin 6:36
Prison ....Jer 32:2
House 2Sam 17:18
Garden place ....Esth 1:5

[*also* COURT, COURTS]
thou shalt make the *c* of ......Ex 27:9
hangings for the *c* of fine .....Ex 27:9
The hangings of the *c*, his.....Ex 35:17
hanging..door of the *c* ....Ex 35:17
he made the *c*; on the south...Ex 38:9
The hangings of the *c*, his .....Ex 39:40
the hanging for the *c* gate .....Ex 39:40
thou shalt set up the *c* ....Ex 40:8
hang up the hanging..*c*........Ex 40:8
place; in the *c* of the ....Lev 6:16
the hangings of the *c*, and.....Num 3:26
curtain for the door of the *c*...Num 3:26
And the hangings of the *c*.....Num 4:26
door of the gate of the *c* ......Num 4:26
which had a well in his *c* 2Sam 17:18
he built the inner *c* with 1Kin 6:36
another *c* within the porch 1Kin 7:8
hallow the middle of the *c* 1Kin 8:64
gone out into the middle *c* 2Kin 20:4
two *c* of the house..Lord......2Kin 21:5
Manasseh had made..two *c*....2Kin 23:12
c and in the chambers 1Chr 23:28
build my house and my *c* 1Chr 28:6
he made the *c* of the priests...2Chr 4:9
and the great *c* 2Chr 4:9
and doors for the *c* 2Chr 4:9
set it in the midst of the *c* 2Chr 6:13
hallowed the middle of the *c* ..2Chr 7:7
house..Lord, before the new *c* .2Chr 20:5
people shall be in the *c* 2Chr 23:5
in the *c* of the house..Lord 2Chr 24:21
c of the house of the Lord 2Chr 29:16
two *c* of the house..Lord 2Chr 33:5
was by the *c* of the prison.....Neh 3:25
roof of his house..their *c* ......Neh 8:16
the *c* of the house of God .....Neh 8:16
preparing him a chamber..*c* ...Neh 13:7
in the *c* of the garden of ......Esth 1:5
before the *c* of the women's...Esth 2:11
unto the king into..inner *c* ....Esth 4:11
stood in the inner *c* of the ....Esth 5:1
king said. Who is in the *c*? ....Esth 6:4
that he may dwell in thy *c* ....Ps 65:4
even fainteth for the *c*..Lord ..Ps 84:2
shall flourish in the *c*..God ....Ps 92:13
offering..come into his *c* ......Ps 96:8
into his *c* with praise; be ......Ps 100:4
In the *c* of the Lord's house...Ps 116:19
c of the house of our God ....Ps 135:2
your hand, to tread my *c*? ....Is 1:12
of dragons, and a *c* for owls...Is 34:13
drink it in the *c* of my ....Is 62:9
he stood in the *c*..Lord's ......Jer 19:14
Stand in the *c* of the Lord's ...Jer 26:2
was shut up in the *c* of the ....Jer 32:2
yet shut up in the *c* of the ....Jer 33:1
the higher *c*, at the entry .....Jer 36:10
Jeremiah into the *c* of the.....Jer 37:21
remained in the *c* of the ......Jer 37:21
that was in the *c* of the ....Jer 38:6
Jeremiah out of the *c* of ......Jer 39:14
me to the door of the *c* ....Ezek 8:7

and fill the *c* with the slain . . . . Ezek 9:7
the cloud filled the inner *c* . . . . Ezek 10:3
unto the post of the *c* round . . Ezek 40:14
temple..porches of the *c* . . . . . . Ezek 41:15
brought me forth..outer *c* . . . . . Ezek 42:1
not pillars as the pillars..*c* . . . . . Ezek 42:6
brought me into the inner *c* . . . Ezek 43:5
the gates of the inner *c* . . . . Ezek 44:17
minister in..the inner *c* . . . . Ezek 44:17
posts..gate of the inner *c* . . . . . . Ezek 45:19
gate of the inner *c* that . . . . Ezek 46:1
c joined of forty cubits . . . . Ezek 46:22
chapel..it is the king's *c* . . . . Amos 7:13
and shalt also keep my *c* . . . . . . Zech 3:7
the *c* which is without the . . . . . Rev 11:2

COUSIN—*kinsman; relative*
behold, thy *c* Elizabeth . . . . Luke 1:36

COVENANT—*an agreement*

Between humans
Designed for:
Mutual protection . . . . Gen 31:50-52
Securing peace . . . . Josh 9:15, 21
Friendship 1Sam 18:3
Promoting commerce 1Kin 5:6-11

Requirements of:
Witnessed . . . . Gen 23:16-18
Confirmed by an oath . . . Gen 21:23,31
Specified 1Sam 11:1, 2
Written and sealed . . . . . . Neh 9:38

Examples of:
Abraham and Abimelech . Gen 21:27-32
Laban and Jacob . . . . Gen 31:43-55
David and elders 2Sam 5:1-3
Ahab and Ben-hadad 1Kin 20:34
New covenant . . . . Matt 26:28
New Testament dispensation 2Cor 3:6
Superiority of the new . . . Heb 8:6-13
Descriptive of a person's will . . . . Heb 9:15-17

Spiritual covenants
Between a leader and people:
Joshua's . . . . Josh 24:1-28
Jehoiada's 2Kin 11:17
Hezekiah's 2Chr 29:10
Josiah's 2Kin 23:3
Ezra's . . . . Ezra 10:3

Between God and man:
Adam . . . . Gen 2:16, 17
Noah . . . . Gen 9:1-17
Abraham . . . . Gen 15:18
Isaac . . . . Gen 26:3-5
Jacob . . . . Gen 28:13-22
Israel . . . . Ex 19:5
Levi . . . . Mal 2:4-10
Phinehas . . . . Num 25:11-13
David . . . . Ps 89:3, 28,34

The old (Sinaitic):
Instituted at Sinai . . . . Ex 19:5
Ratified by sacrifice . . . . . Ex 24:6-8
Heb 9:16
Does not annul the Abrahamic . . . . Gal 3:16-18
Designed to lead to Christ . . . . Gal 3:17-25
Consists of outward rites . . Heb 9:1-13
Sealed by circumcision . . . Gen 17:9-14
Prefigures the Gospel . . . . Heb 9:8-28

The new (evangelical):
Promised in Eden . . . . . . Gen 3:15
Proclaimed to Abraham . . Gen 12:3
Dated in prophecy . . . . Dan 9:24-27
Fulfilled in Christ . . . . Luke 1:68-79
Ratified by His blood . . . . Heb 9:11-23
Remembered in the Lord's Supper 1Cor 11:25
Called everlasting . . . . Heb 13:20

[*also* COVENANTED, COVENANTS]
thee will I establish my *c* . . . . . . Gen 6:18
I will make my *c* between . . . . . Gen 17:2
my *c* will I establish..Isaac . . . . Gen 17:21
and both of them made a *c* . . . Gen 21:27
and let us make a *c* with . . . . . . Gen 26:28
God remembered his *c* . . . . Ex 2:24
I have also established my *c* . . . Ex 6:4
Thou shalt make no *c* with . . . . Ex 23:32
he took the book of the *c* . . . . Ex 24:7
Behold, the blood of the *c* . . . . . Ex 24:8
generations..perpetual *c* . . . . . . Ex 31:16
Behold, I make a *c*; before . . . . Ex 34:10
tables the words of the *c* . . . . . . Ex 34:28
the salt of the *c* of thy God . . . Lev 2:13
Israel by an everlasting *c* . . . . . . Lev 24:8
and establish my *c* with . . . . Lev 26:9
the ark of the *c* of the Lord . . . Num 10:33
the ark of the *c* of the Lord . . . Num 14:44
it is a *c* of salt for ever . . . . . . Num 18:19
I give unto him my *c* of . . . . Num 25:12
he declared unto you his *c* . . . . Deut 4:13
lest ye forget the *c*..Lord . . . . . . Deut 4:23
Lord our God made a *c* . . . . Deut 5:2
thou shalt make no *c* with . . . . . Deut 7:2
keepeth *c* and mercy with . . . . . Deut 7:9
that he may establish his *c* . . . . Deut 8:18
the tables..*c* which the Lord . . . Deut 9:9
the two tables of the *c* were . . . Deut 9:15
bear the ark of the *c*..Lord . . . . Deut 10:8
in transgressing his *c* . . . . Deut 17:2
These are the words of the *c* . . Deut 29:1
which bare the ark of the *c* . . . Deut 31:9
thy word, and kept thy *c* . . . . . . Deut 33:9
When ye see the ark of the *c* . . Josh 3:3
cut off before the ark..*c* . . . . . . Josh 4:7
Take up the ark of the *c* . . . . . . Josh 6:6
also transgressed my *c* . . . . Josh 7:11
which bare the ark of the *c* . . . Josh 8:33
ye have transgressed the *c* . . . . . Josh 23:16
I will never break my *c* with . . Judg 2:1
the ark of the *c* of God was . . . Judg 20:27
Let us fetch..the ark of the *c* . . 1Sam 4:3
Make a *c* with us, and we 1Sam 11:1
brought thy servant into a *c* . . . 1Sam 20:8
made a *c* before the Lord 1Sam 23:18
the ark of the *c* of God 2Sam 15:24
with me an everlasting *c* 2Sam 23:5
stood before the ark of the *c* . . 1Kin 3:15
ark of the *c* of the Lord 1Kin 6:19
bring up the ark of the *c* 1Kin 8:1
thou hast not kept my *c* 1Kin 11:11
Israel have forsaken thy *c* 1Kin 19:10
Israel have forsaken thy *c* 1Kin 19:14
and made a *c* with them 2Kin 11:4
his *c* with Abraham 2Kin 13:23
c that he made..their fathers . . 2Kin 17:15
but transgressed his *c*, and . . . 2Kin 18:12
words of the book of the *c* 2Kin 23:2
David made a *c* with them 1Chr 11:3
bring up the ark of the *c* 1Chr 15:25
the ark of the *c* of God 1Chr 16:6
mindful always of his *c* 1Chr 16:15
Even of the *c* which he made . . 1Chr 16:16
Israel for an everlasting *c* 1Chr 16:17
the ark of the *c* of the Lord . . . 1Chr 17:1
the ark of the *c* of the Lord . . . 1Chr 22:19
rest for the ark of the *c* 1Chr 28:2
the ark of the *c* of the Lord . . . 2Chr 5:2
wherein is the *c* of the Lord . . . 2Chr 6:11
as I have *c* with David thy 2Chr 7:18
Into a *c* to seek the Lord 2Chr 15:12
because of the *c* that he had . . 2Chr 21:7
son of Zichri, into *c* with 2Chr 23:1
the book of the *c* that was 2Chr 34:30
that keepeth *c* and mercy . . . . . Neh 1:5
madest a *c* with him to give . . . Neh 9:8
and the *c* of the priesthood . . . . Neh 13:29
I made a *c* with mine eyes . . . . Job 31:1
Will he make a *c* with thee? . . . Job 41:4
as keep his *c* and his . . . . Ps 25:10
we dealt falsely in thy *c* . . . . . . Ps 44:17
a *c* with me by sacrifice . . . . Ps 50:5
him; he hath broken his *c* . . . . . Ps 55:20
have respect unto the *c* . . . . Ps 74:20
They kept not the *c* of God . . . . Ps 78:10
To such as keep his *c*, and . . . . Ps 103:18
hath remembered his *c* for . . . . Ps 105:8
remembered for them his *c* . . . . Ps 106:45
ever be mindful of his *c* . . . . Ps 111:5
children will keep my *c* . . . . Ps 132:12
forgetteth the *c* of her God . . . Prov 2:17
ordinance..the everlasting *c* . . . . Is 24:5
We have made a *c* with . . . . Is 28:15
he hath broken the *c*, he . . . . . . Is 33:8
give thee for a *c* of the . . . . Is 42:6
give thee for a *c* of the . . . . Is 49:8
neither shall the *c* of my . . . . . . Is 54:10
make an everlasting *c* with . . . . Is 55:3
me, and take hold of my *c* . . . . Is 56:4
and made thee a *c* with . . . . Is 57:8
As for me, this is my *c* with . . Is 59:21
make an everlasting *c* with . . . . Is 61:8
The ark of the *c* of the Lord . . Jer 3:16
Hear ye the words of this *c* . . Jer 11:2
of Judah having broken my *c* . . Jer 11:10
remember, break not thy *c* . . . . Jer 14:21
they have forsaken the *c* . . . . . . Jer 22:9
make a new *c* with the house . . Jer 31:31
I will make an everlasting *c* . . Jer 32:40
If ye can break my *c* of the . . Jer 33:20
and my *c* of the night . . . . Jer 33:20
had made a *c* with all the . . . . . Jer 34:8
to the Lord in a perpetual *c* . . Jer 50:5
and entered into a *c* with . . . . . Ezek 16:8
and made a *c* with him, and . . . Ezek 17:13
by keeping of his *c* it might . . . Ezek 17:14
into the bond of the *c* . . . . Ezek 20:37
will make with them a *c* of . . . . Ezek 34:25
will make a *c* of peace with . . . Ezek 37:26
keeping the *c* and mercy to . . . Dan 9:4
also the prince of the *c* . . . . Dan 11:22
in that day will I make a *c* . . . . Hos 2:18
men have transgressed the *c* . . Hos 6:7
have transgressed my *c* . . . . Hos 8:1
swearing falsely in..a *c* . . . . Hos 10:4
make a *c* with the Assyrians . . . Hos 12:1
remembered..brotherly *c* . . . . . . Amos 1:9
by the blood of thy *c* I have . . . Zech 9:11
that I might break my *c* . . . . Zech 11:10
the messenger of the *c* . . . . Mal 3:1
and *c* to give him money . . . . . . Luke 22:5
c which God made with our . . . Acts 3:25
And he gave him the *c* of . . . . . Acts 7:8
glory, and the *c*, and the . . . . . . Rom 9:4
this is my *c* unto them . . . . Rom 11:27
Though it be but a man's *c* . . . . Gal 3:15
This is the *c* that I will . . . . Heb 10:16
the blood of the *c*, where . . . . . Heb 10:29
strangers from the *c* of . . . . Eph 2:12
Jesus the mediator..new *c* . . . . . Heb 12:24

COVENANT OF SALT
Descriptive of Levites . . . . Num 18:19
Descriptive of David 2Chr 13:5
Used figuratively . . . . Mark 9:50

COVENANT-BREAKERS—*the unfaithful*
Under God's judgment . . . Is 24:5
By abominations . . . . Ezek 44:7

c, without natural affection . . . . Rom 1:31

COVENANT-KEEPERS—*the faithful*
God's blessing upon . . . . . Ex 19:5

COVER—*to conceal; protect*

[*also* COVERED, COVEREDST, COVEREST, COVERETH]
the whole heaven, were *c* . . . . . Gen 7:19
and the mountains were *c* . . . . . Gen 7:20
c the nakedness..father . . . . Gen 9:23
took a veil, and *c* herself . . . . . . Gen 24:65
and *c* her with a veil, and . . . . . Gen 38:14
the frogs came up, and *c* . . . . . . Ex 8:6
they shall *c* the face..earth . . . . Ex 10:5
For they *c* the face of the . . . . . Ex 10:15
waters returned, and *c* the . . . . Ex 14:28
depths have *c* them; they . . . . . Ex 15:5
quails came up, and *c* the . . . . . Ex 16:13
man shall dig a pit..not *c* . . . . . Ex 21:33
and a cloud *c* the mount . . . . . . Ex 24:15
bowls thereof, to *c* withal . . . . . Ex 25:29
and on that side, to *c* it . . . . Ex 26:13
to *c* their nakedness . . . . Ex 28:42
the fat that *c* the inwards . . . . . Ex 29:13
and will *c* thee with my hand . . Ex 33:22

and *c* with their wings over....Ex 37:9
bowls, and his covers to *c*.....Ex 37:16
and *c* the ark with the veil....Ex 40:3
c the ark of the testimony.....Ex 40:21
the fat that *c* the............Lev 3:3
the fat that *c* the inwards.....Lev 4:8
and the fat that *c* the........Lev 7:3
and that which *c* the..........Lev 9:19
the leprosy *c* all the skin......Lev 13:12
if the leprosy have *c* all.......Lev 13:13
incense may *c* the mercy......Lev 16:13
blood thereof, and *c* it with...Lev 17:13
c the ark of testimony with....Num 4:5
when the holy things are *c*....Num 4:20
cloud *c* the tabernacle........Num 9:15
cloud *c* it, and the glory......Num 16:42
they *c* the face of the earth...Num 22:5
c the face of the earth........Num 22:11
vesture, wherewith thou *c*.....Deut 22:12
and *c* that which cometh......Deut 23:13
thick, thou art *c* with.........Deut 32:15
the sea upon them, and *c*.....Josh 24:7
he *c* his feet in his summer....Judg 3:24
she *c* him with a mantle.......Judg 4:18
for his bolster, and *c* it.......1Sam 19:13
Saul went in to *c* his feet.....1Sam 24:3
the king *c* his face, and the...2Sam 19:4
and they *c* him with clothes...1Kin 1:1
And it was *c* with cedar.......1Kin 7:3
to *c* the chapiters that were...1Kin 7:18
and the cherubim *c* the ark....1Kin 8:7
c himself with sackcloth.......2Kin 19:1
two wreaths to *c* the two......2Chr 4:12
and the cherubim *c* the.......2Chr 5:8
built it, and *c* it, and set.....Neh 3:15
And *c* not their iniquity.......Neh 4:5
mourning..having his head *c*...Esth 6:12
he *c* the faces of the judges...Job 9:24
Because he *c* his face with....Job 15:27
c not thou my blood, and let..Job 16:18
and the worms shall *c* them...Job 21:26
and abundance of waters *c*....Job 22:11
hath he *c* the darkness........Job 23:17
c my transgressions as Adam..Job 31:33
it, and *c* the bottom of the....Job 36:30
abundance of waters may *c*....Job 38:34
trees *c* him with their.........Job 40:22
is forgiven, whose sin is *c*.....Ps 32:1
shame of my face hath *c*......Ps 44:15
valleys also are *c* over with....Ps 65:13
the wings of a dove *c* with....Ps 68:13
reproach; shame hath *c* my....Ps 69:7
let them be *c* with reproach...Ps 71:13
violence *c* them as a..........Ps 73:6
The hills were *c* with the......Ps 80:10
people, thou hast *c* all their...Ps 85:2
hast *c* him with shame........Ps 89:45
Who *c* thyself with light as....Ps 104:2
Thou *c* it with the deep as....Ps 104:6
they turn not again to *c*.......Ps 104:9
And the waters *c* their........Ps 106:11
him as the garment which *c*...Ps 109:19
them *c* themselves with.......Ps 109:29
Surely the darkness shall *c*....Ps 139:11
hast *c* me in my mother's.....Ps 139:13
thou hast *c* my head in the....Ps 140:7
mischief of their own lips *c*....Ps 140:9
Who *c* the heaven with.......Ps 147:8
but violence *c* the mouth......Prov 10:6
but violence *c* the mouth......Prov 10:11
up strifes; but love *c* all.......Prov 10:12
but a prudent man *c* shame...Prov 12:16
He that *c* a transgression......Prov 17:9
nettles had *c* the face........Prov 24:31
a potsherd *c* with silver.......Prov 26:23
that *c* his sins shall not........Prov 28:13
his name shall be *c* with......Eccl 6:4
with twain he *c* his face.......Is 6:2
the Lord, as the waters *c*.....Is 11:9
under thee, and the worms *c*..Is 14:11
captivity, and will surely *c*.....Is 22:17
shall no more *c* her slain......Is 26:21
rulers, the seers hath he *c*.....Is 29:10
that *c* with a covering but.....Is 30:1
c himself with sackcloth.......Is 37:1
I have *c* thee in the shadow...Is 51:16
seest the naked, that thou *c*...Is 58:7
neither..they *c* themselves.....Is 59:6
darkness shall *c* the earth.....Is 60:2
he hath *c* me with the robe...Is 61:10
and our confusion *c* us; for....Jer 3:25
confounded, and *c* their.......Jer 14:3
I will go up..will *c* the........Jer 46:8
she is *c* with the multitude....Jer 51:42
Lord *c* the daughter of Zion...Lam 2:1
stones, he hath *c* me with.....Lam 3:16
Thou hast *c* thyself with a.....Lam 3:44
and two *c* their bodies........Ezek 1:11
and horror shall *c* them.......Ezek 7:18
thou shalt *c* thy face, that.....Ezek 12:6
thee, and *c* thy nakedness.....Ezek 16:8
embroidered garments, and *c*..Ezek 16:18
c the naked with a garment...Ezek 18:7
ground, to *c* it with dust......Ezek 24:7
that it should not be *c*........Ezek 24:8
horses their dust shall *c*.......Ezek 26:10
Elishah was that which *c*......Ezek 27:7
the anointed cherub that *c*....Ezek 28:14
a cloud shall *c* her, and her...Ezek 30:18
I *c* the deep for him, and I....Ezek 31:15
I will *c* the heaven, and.......Ezek 32:7
I will *c* the sun with a cloud..Ezek 32:7
and *c* you with skin, and......Ezek 37:6
them and the skin *c* them.....Ezek 37:8
like a cloud to *c* the land.....Ezek 38:9
and the windows were *c*......Ezek 41:16
given to *c* her nakedness......Hos 2:9
say to the mountains, *C*.......Hos 10:8
shame shall *c* thee, and......Obad 10
and *c* him with sackcloth......Jon 3:6
yea, they shall all *c* their......Mic 3:7
and shame shall *c* her which...Mic 7:10
glory..Lord, as the waters *c*...Hab 2:14
His glory *c* the heavens.......Hab 3:3
one *c* violence with his........Mal 2:16
the ship was *c* with the.......Matt 8:24
to spit on him, and to *c* his...Mark 14:65
a candle, *c* it with a vessel....Luke 8:16
is nothing *c*, that shall.......Luke 12:2
Fall on us..to the hills, *C*.....Luke 23:30
forgiven..whose sins are *c*.....Rom 4:7
..his head *c*, dishonoreth......1Cor 11:4
the woman be not *c*, let her...1Cor 11:6
shorn or shaven, let her be *c*..1Cor 11:6
man indeed ought not to *c*....1Cor 11:7
charity shall *c* the multitude...1Pet 4:8

COVERED CARTS

Used as offerings........Num 7:3

COVERING—*clothing; shelter; something that conceals*

Symbolic of:

Immorality.............Prov 7:16
Diligence..............Prov 31:22

[*also* COVERINGS]

Noah removed the *c* of the....Gen 8:13
is to thee a *c* of the eyes......Gen 20:16
For that is his *c* only, it.......Ex 22:27
c the mercy seat with their....Ex 25:20
a *c* upon the tabernacle.......Ex 26:7
tabernacle, his tent..his *c*......Ex 35:11
a *c* for the tent of rams'......Ex 36:19
a *c* of badgers' skins above....Ex 36:19
the *c* of rams' skins dyed......Ex 39:34
and the *c* of badgers' skins....Ex 39:34
and the veil of the *c*..........Ex 39:34
c of the tent above upon......Ex 40:19
shall put a *c* upon his upper...Lev 13:45
the tent, the *c* thereof........Num 3:25
they shall take down the *c*....Num 4:5
plates for a *c* of the altar.....Num 16:38
no *c* bound upon it, is.........Num 19:15
spread a *c* over the well's.....2Sam 17:19
Thick clouds are a *c* to him...Job 22:14
that they have no *c* in the....Job 24:7
and destruction hath no *c*.....Job 26:6
clothing, or any poor..*c*.......Job 31:19
He spread a cloud for a *c*.....Ps 105:39
the *c* of it of purple, the......Song 3:10
discovered the *c* of Judah.....Is 22:8
face of the *c* cast over all.....Is 25:7
and the *c* narrower than......Is 28:20
that cover with a *c*, but not...Is 30:1
I make sackcloth their *c*......Is 50:3
precious stone was thy *c*......Ezek 28:13
c the altar of the Lord with...Mal 2:13
hair is given her for a *c*.......1Cor 11:15

COVERT—*hiding place*

Used by Abigail.........1Sam 25:20
Destroyed by Ahaz......2Kin 16:18
Figurative of protection..Is 32:2

and abide in the *c* to lie......Job 38:40
I will trust in the *c* of thy.....Ps 61:4
a *c* from storm and from......Is 4:6
be thou a *c* to them from.....Is 16:4
hath forsaken his *c*, as the....Jer 25:38

COVETOUSNESS—*an insatiable desire for worldly gain*

Described as:

Idolatry.................Col 3:5
Root of evil.............1Tim 6:9-11
Never satisfied..........Hab 2:9
Vanity..................Ps 39:6

Productive of:

Theft...................Josh 7:21
Lying...................2Kin 5:20-27
Murder.................Prov 1:18, 19
Falsehood..............Acts 5:1-10
Hurtful lusts............1Tim 6:9
Apostasy...............1Tim 6:10

Excludes from:

God's kingdom..........1Cor 6:10
Eph 5:5
Sacred offices..........1Tim 3:3
Heaven.................Eph 5:5

Examples of:

Achan..................Josh 7:21
Saul...................1Sam 15:9, 19
Judas..................Matt 26:14, 15
Ananias................Acts 5:1-11

See AVARICE

[*also* COVET, COVETED, COVETETH, COVETOUS]

God, men of truth, hating *c*...Ex 18:21
shalt not *c* thy neighbor's.....Ex 20:17
shalt not *c* thy neighbor's.....Ex 20:17
shalt thou *c* thy neighbor's....Deut 5:21
blesseth the *c*..Lord..........Ps 10:3
testimonies, and not to *c*......Ps 119:36
He *c* greedily all the day......Prov 21:26
hateth *c* shall prolong his.....Prov 28:16
the iniquity of his *c* was I.....Is 57:17
them every one is given to *c*..Jer 6:13
the greatest is given to *c*......Jer 8:10
are not but for *c*, and for.....Jer 22:17
is come, and the measure..*c*...Jer 51:13
heart goeth after their *c*.......Ezek 33:31
And they *c* fields, and take...Mic 2:2
that *c* an evil covetousness....Hab 2:9
Thefts, *c*, wickedness, deceit..Mark 7:22
Take heed, and beware of *c*...Luke 12:15
Pharisees also, who were *c*....Luke 16:14
I have *c* no man's silver, or...Acts 20:33
wickedness, *c*...............Rom 1:29
had said. Thou shall not *c*.....Rom 7:7
Thou shalt not *c*; and if.......Rom 13:9
with the *c*, or extortioners.....1Cor 5:10
But *c* earnestly the best.......1Cor 12:31
c to prophesy, and forbid.....1Cor 14:39
of bounty, and not as of *c*....2Cor 9:5
all uncleanness, or *c*, let......Eph 5:3
ye know, nor a cloke of *c*.....1Thess 2:5
lovers of their..selves, *c*.......2Tim 3:2
conversation be without *c*.....Heb 13:5
through *c* shall they with......2Pet 2:3
have exercised with *c*.........2Pet 2:14

COW—*milk-giving bovine animal*

Jacob's possessions......Gen 32:15
Found in Egypt.........Gen 41:2
Use of milk.............2Sam 17:29
Used in rituals..........Lev 3:1

[*also* COWS]
And whether it be *c* or ewe ...Lev 22:28
But the firstling of a *c* ....Num 18:17
their *c* calveth, and casteth ....Job 21:10
shall nourish a young *c* ....Is 7:21
And the *c* and the bear shall ..Is 11:7
me, Lo, I have given thee *c* ...Ezek 4:15
every *c* at that which is ....Amos 4:3

COWARDICE, SPIRITUAL
Causes of:
Fear of life ....Gen 12:11-13
Fear of others..........Ex 32:22-24
Unbelief................Num 13:28-33
Fear of rulers ....John 9:22
Results in:
Defeat..................Num 14:40-45
Escape 2Sam 15:13-17
Compromise ....John 19:12-16
Denial..................Matt 26:69-74
Guilty conscience makes:
Joseph's brothers ....Gen 42:21-28
David 2Sam 12:1-14
Pharisees ....John 8:1-11

COZ (kŏs)—*"thorn; nimble"*
Father of Anub 1Chr 4:8

COZBI (kŏs'bī)—*"deceitful"*
Slain by Phinehas........Num 25:6-18

CRACKLING—*crunching*
as the *c* of thorns under a .....Eccl 7:6

CRACKNELS—*hard, brittle biscuit*
with thee ten loaves and *c* 1Kin 14:3

CRAFT
Ships of Tarshish ....Is 2:16
A trade................Rev 18:22

cause *c* to prosper in his ......Dan 8:25
they might take him by *c* .....Mark 14:1
because he was..same *c* ....Acts 18:3
by this *c* we have our ....Acts 19:25

CRAFTINESS—*cunning deception*
Man's, known by God ...1Cor 3:19
Enemies', perceived by Christ ....Luke 20:23
Use of, rejected 2Cor 4:2
Warning against ....Eph 4:14

[*also* CRAFTY]
the devices of the *c*..........Job 5:12
the wise in their own *c*........Job 5:13
choosest the tongue of the *c*...Job 15:5
They have taken *c* counsel ....Ps 83:3
being *c*, I caught you with 2Cor 12:16

CRAFTSMEN—*men who work at a trade*
Makers of idols ....Deut 27:15
Destroyed in Babylon....Rev 18:21, 22

and all the *c* and smiths.......2Kin 24:14
Charashim; for they were *c*....1Chr 4:14
Lod, and Ono..valley of *c*.....Neh 11:35
all of it the work of the *c* .....Hos 13:2
brought no small gain..*c* ......Acts 19:24

CRAG—*abrupt rock formation*
upon the *c* of the rock, and ...Job 39:28

CRANE—*a migratory bird*
Chatters ....Is 38:14

c and the swallow observe.....Jer 8:7

CRASHING
and a great *c* from the hills ...Zeph 1:10

CRAVED—*asked for; wanted greatly*

[*also* CRAVETH]
for his mouth *c* it of him......Prov 16:26
and *c* the body of Jesus ....Mark 15:43

CREATION—*causing what did not exist to exist; that which has been created*
Author of:
God....................Heb 11:3
Jesus Christ............Col 1:16, 17
Holy Spirit.............Ps 104:30
Objects of:
Heaven, earth..........Gen 1:1-13
Vegetation ....Gen 1:11, 12
Animals ....Gen 1:21
Man....................Gen 1:26-28
Stars ....Is 40:26
Expressive of God's:
Deity...................Rom 1:20
Power ....Is 40:26, 28
Glory ....Ps 19:1
Goodness ....Ps 33:5-6
Wisdom ....Ps 104:24
Sovereignty ....Rev 4:11
Illustrative of:
The new birth...........2Cor 5:17
Renewal of believers.....Ps 51:10
The eternal world ....Is 65:17
2Pet 3:11, 13

[*also* CREATE, CREATED, CREATETH]
his work which God *c* and ....Gen 2:3
destroy man whom I have *c* ...Gen 6:7
C in me a clean heart O God .Ps 51:10
and the south thou hast *c* .....Ps 89:12
the people which shall be *c*....Ps 102:18
commanded; and they were *c*..Ps 148:5
Lord will *c* upon every........Is 4:5
Holy One of Israel hath *c* .....Is 41:20
he that *c* the heavens, and ....Is 42:5
thus saith the Lord that *c* .....Is 43:1
I have *c* him for my glory.....Is 43:7
I form the light, and *c* ....Is 45:7
I make peace, and *c* evil ......Is 45:7
I the Lord have *c* it ....Is 45:8
made the earth, and *c* man....Is 45:12
They are *c* now, and not ......Is 48:7
c the smith that bloweth ......Is 54:16
I *c* the fruit of the lips ....Is 57:19
I *c* new heavens and a new....Is 65:17
hath *c* a new thing in the .....Jer 31:22
place where thou wast *c* ......Ezek 21:30
thee..day that thou wast *c*.....Ezek 28:13
hath not one God *c* us? why ..Mal 2:10
from the beginning of the *c* ...Mark 10:6
from the beginning of the *c* ...Mark 13:19
which God *c* unto this time ...Mark 13:19
c of the world are clearly .....Rom 1:20
that the whole *c* groaneth .....Rom 8:22
man *c* for the woman 1Cor 11:9
c in Christ Jesus unto good....Eph 2:10
in God, who *c* all..by Jesus ...Eph 3:9
God is *c* in righteousness......Eph 4:24
image of him that *c* him ......Col 3:10
which God hath *c* to be 1Tim 4:3
were from the beginning..*c* 2Pet 3:4
beginning of the *c* of God.....Rev 3:14
for thou hast *c* all things ......Rev 4:11
thy pleasure they are..*c* ....Rev 4:11
c heaven, and the things ......Rev 10:6

CREATOR—*the Supreme Being*
A title of God ....Is 40:28
Man's disrespect of ......Rom 1:25
To be remembered ......Eccl 12:1

Holy One, the *c* of Israel .....Is 43:15
doing, as unto a faithful *C* 1Pet 4:19

CREATURE—*that which has been given life*
Subject to vanity ....Rom 8:19, 20
Will be delivered ....Rom 8:21
Believer, a new 2Cor 5:17

[*also* CREATURES]
the moving *c* that hath life ....Gen 1:20
called every living *c*, that .....Gen 2:19
every living *c* that is with .....Gen 9:10
every living *c* that moveth.....Lev 11:46
full of doleful *c* ....Is 13:21
likeness of four living *c* ....Ezek 1:5
spirit of the living *c* was.......Ezek 1:20
spirit of the living *c* was.......Ezek 1:21
wings of the living *c* ....Ezek 3:13
This is the living *c* that I ......Ezek 10:15
preach the gospel to every *c*...Mark 16:15
and served the *c* more than ...Rom 1:25
uncircumcision but a new *c*....Gal 6:15
God..firstborn of every *c* ......Col 1:15
was preached to every *c* ......Col 1:23
For every *c* of God is good ...1Tim 4:4
Neither is there any *c* that ....Heb 4:13
kind of firstfruits of his *c*......James 1:18
every *c* which is in heaven ....Rev 5:13
third part of the *c* which ......Rev 8:9

CREDITOR—*one to whom a debt is payable*
Interest, forbidden.......Ex 22:25
Debts remitted ....Neh 5:10-12
Some very cruel.........Matt 18:28-30
Christian principle ....Rom 13:8

[*also* CREDITORS]
Every *c* that lendeth ....Deut 15:2
and the *c* is come to take 2Kin 4:1
which of my *c* is it to whom...Is 50:1
There was a certain *c* which ..Luke 7:41

CREEK—*minor stream of water*
they discovered a certain *c* ....Acts 27:39

CREEP—*to crawl*

[*also* CREEPETH, CREEPING, CREPT]
cattle, and *c* thing, and ....Gen 1:24
and every thing that *c* upon ...Gen 1:25
the *c* thing, and the fowls .....Gen 6:7
and of every thing that *c*......Gen 7:8
every *c* thing that creepeth ....Gen 7:14
of every *c* thing..creepeth .....Gen 8:17
every creeping thing that *c* ....Gen 8:17
carcase of unclean *c* things ....Lev 5:2
All fowls that *c*, going upon ...Lev 11:20
every flying *c* thing that.......Lev 11:21
every creeping thing that *c* ....Lev 11:41
manner of living..that *c* ....Lev 20:25
whosoever toucheth any *c* .....Lev 22:5
likeness of any thing that *c*....Deut 4:18
every *c* thing that flieth is .....Deut 14:19
of fowl, and of *c* things 1Kin 4:33
beasts of the forest do *c* ......Ps 104:20
things *c* innumerable, both ....Ps 104:25
c things, and flying fowl ......Ps 148:10
and behold every form of *c* ...Ezek 8:10
field, and all *c* things that .....Ezek 38:20
all creeping things that *c* ......Ezek 38:20
with the *c* things of the ....Hos 2:18
as the *c* things, that have .....Hab 1:14
and wild beasts, and *c* ....Acts 10:12
and wild beasts, and *c* ....Acts 11:6
fourfooted beasts, and *c* ......Rom 1:23
they which *c* into houses 2Tim 3:6
For there are certain men *c* ...Jude 4

CREMATION—*burning a body*
Two hundred fifty were consumed ....Num 16:35
Zimri's end 1Kin 16:15-19

CRESCENS (krĕs'ĕnz)—*"increasing"*
Paul's assistant 2Tim 4:10

CRETE (krēt)—*"carnal"—an island in the Mediterranean Sea*
Some from, at Pentecost..Acts 2:11
Paul visits...............Acts 27:7-21
Titus dispatched to ......Titus 1:5
Inhabitants of, evil and lazy ....Titus 1:12

CRIB—*manger*
Animals feed from ......Is 1:3
A stall..................Prov 14:4

serve thee, or abide by thy *c*?. .Job 39:9

CRIMINAL—*a lawbreaker*
Paul considered a........Acts 25:16, 27
Christ accused of ....John 18:30
Christ crucified between. .Luke 23:32, 33
One unrepentant; one repentant ....Luke 23:39-43

[*also* CRIME, CRIMES]
For this is a heinous *c* ....Job 31:11
land is full of bloody *c*........Ezek 7:23

CRIMSON—*deep red*
in purple, and *c*, and blue.....2Chr 2:7
purple, and *c*, and fine........2Chr 3:14

though they be red like *c* .....Is 1:18
clothest thyself with *c* ....Jer 4:30

CRIPPLE—*one physically impaired*
Mephibosheth, by a fall ..2Sam 4:4
Paul's healing of.........Acts 14:8-10
Jesus heals ....Matt 15:30, 31

CRISIS—*the crest of human endurance*
Bad advice in ....Job 2:9, 10
God's advice in ....Luke 21:25-28

CRISPING PIN—*a hair curler ("handbag" may be a more accurate description)*
the wimples, and the *c* ....Is 3:22

CRISPUS (krĭs'pŭs)—*"curled"*
Chief ruler of synagogue at Corinth ....Acts 18:8
Baptized by Paul 1Cor 1:14

CROOKBACK—*one with a crooked back*
Barred from priesthood ..Lev 21:20, 21

CROOKED—*bent; perverse*
perverse and *c* generation .....Deut 32:5
hand hath formed the *c* ....Job 26:13
turn aside unto their *c* ....Ps 125:5
Whose ways are *c*, and they ...Prov 2:15
c cannot be made straight ....Eccl 1:15
straight..he hath made *c*? .....Eccl 7:13
leviathan that *c* serpent ....Is 27:1
c shall be made straight ....Is 40:4
them, and *c* things straight ....Is 42:16
make the *c* places straight .....Is 45:2
they have made them *c* ....Is 59:8
he hath made my paths *c* .....Lam 3:9
c shall be made straight ....Luke 3:5
midst of a *c* and perverse .....Phil 2:15

CROP—*craw of a bird; to chop*
Removed by priest ......Lev 1:16

[*also* CROPPED]
c off the top of his young .....Ezek 17:4
I will *c* off from the top of ....Ezek 17:22

CROSS—*an instrument of execution*
Used literally of:
Christ's death ....Matt 27:32
Used figuratively of:
Duty ....Matt 10:38
Christ's sufferings 1Cor 1:17
The Christian faith 1Cor 1:18
Reconciliation ....Eph 2:16

deny himself, and take..*c* .....Matt 16:24
deny himself, and take..*c* .....Mark 8:34
take up the *c*, and follow .....Mark 10:21
and Rufus, to bear his *c* ......Mark 15:21
himself, and take up his *c* .....Luke 9:23
whosoever doth..bear his *c* ....Luke 14:27
and on him they laid the *c* ....Luke 23:26
And he bearing his *c* went ....John 19:17
wrote a title, and put it..*c* .....John 19:19
then is the offense of the *c* ....Gal 5:11
save..*c* of our Lord Jesus .....Gal 6:14
unto God in one body..*c* ......Eph 2:16
death, even the death..*c* ......Phil 2:8
through the blood of his *c* .....Col 1:20
endured the *c*, despising ......Heb 12:2

CROSSWAY—*crossroad*
thou have stood in the *c* ......Obad 14

CROUCH—*to implore; stoop*

[*also* CROUCHETH]
c to him for a piece of silver ..1Sam 2:36
He *c*, and humbleth himself ...Ps 10:10

CROW—*to make loud, shrill sound of a cock*

[*also* CREW]
this night, before the cock *c* ...Matt 26:34
And immediately the cock *c* ...Matt 26:74
Before the cock *c*, thou ....Matt 26:75
before the cock *c* twice ....Mark 14:30
out into the porch..cock *c* .....Mark 14:68
him, Before the *c* crow ....Mark 14:72
cock shall not *c* this day ......Luke 22:34
him, Before the cock *c*........Luke 22:61
The cock shall not *c*, till ......John 13:38

CROWN—*an emblem of glory; to place a crown on the head*
Worn by:
High priest.............Lev 8:9
Kings..................2Sam 12:30
Queens ....Esth 2:17
Ministers of state ....Esth 8:15
Applied figuratively to:
A good wife ....Prov 12:4
Old age ....Prov 16:31
Grandchildren ....Prov 17:6
Honor ....Prov 27:24
Material blessings ....Ps 65:11
Applied spiritually to:
Christ ....Ps 132:18
Christ at His return ......Rev 19:12
Christ glorified ....Heb 2:7-9
The church ....Is 62:3
The Christian's reward ...2Tim 2:5
The minister's reward ....Phil 4:1
Soul winners 1Thess 2:19
The Christian's incorruptible prize 1Cor 9:25

[*also* CROWNED, CROWNEST, CROWNETH, CROWNING, CROWNS]
and on the *c* of the head ......Gen 49:26
put the holy *c* upon the ....Ex 29:6
shalt make unto it a *c* of ......Ex 30:3
and made a *c* of gold to it ....Ex 37:2
made the plate of the holy *c* ..Ex 39:30
golden plate, the holy *c* ....Lev 8:9
c of the anointing oil ....Lev 21:12
arm with the *c* of the head ....Deut 33:20
the *c* that was upon his head ..2Sam 1:10
his foot even to the *c* of his ...2Sam 14:25
and put the *c* upon him 2Kin 11:12
David took the *c* of their 1Chr 20:2
son, and put upon him the *c* ..2Chr 23:11
before the king with the *c* .....Esth 1:11
c royal which is set upon ......Esth 6:8
sole of his foot unto his *c* .....Job 2:7
and taken the *c* from my ......Job 19:9
and bind it as a *c* to me ......Job 31:36
c him with glory and honor ...Ps 8:5
a *c* of pure gold on his head ..Ps 21:3
hast profaned his *c* by ....Ps 89:39
c thee with lovingkindness.....Ps 103:4
c of glory shall she deliver ....Prov 4:9
prudent are *c* with knowledge. .Prov 14:18
The *c* of the wise is their .....Prov 14:24
king Solomon with the *c* ......Song 3:11
wherewith his mother *c* ....Song 3:11
will smite with a scab the *c*....Is 3:17
counsel against Tyre, the *c* ....Is 23:8
the *c* of pride..drunkards ......Is 28:1
have broken the *c* of thy ......Jer 2:16
down even the *c* of your ......Jer 13:18
c of the head..tumultuous .....Jer 48:45
The *c* is fallen from our ....Lam 5:16
and a beautiful *c* upon ....Ezek 16:12
diadem, and take off the *c* ....Ezek 21:26
and beautiful *c* upon their .....Ezek 23:42
Thy *c* are as the locusts ....Nah 3:17
silver and gold, and make *c* ...Zech 6:11
And the *c* shall be to Helem ..Zech 6:14
shall be as the stones of a *c* ...Zech 9:16
and plaited a *c* of thorns ......Mark 15:17
and I will give thee a *c* of.....Rev 2:10
hast, that no man take thy *c* ..Rev 3:11
they had on their heads *c* of...Rev 4:4
a *c* was given unto him ....Rev 6:2
heads were as it were *c* like ...Rev 9:7
upon her head a *c* of twelve...Rev 12:1
and seven *c* upon his heads ...Rev 12:3
and upon his horns ten *c* ......Rev 13:1
on his head a golden *c* ....Rev 14:14

CROWN OF THORNS
Placed on Christ.........Matt 27:29
John 19:2

CROWNS OF CHRISTIANS
Joy.....................1Thess 2:19
Righteousness 2Tim 4:8
Life ....James 1:12
Glory 1Pet 5:4
Incorruptible 1Cor 9:25

CRUCIFIXION—*death on a cross*
Jesus' death by:
Predicted ....Matt 20:19
Demanded ....Mark 15:13, 14
Gentiles ....Matt 20:19
Jews....................Acts 2:23, 36
Between thieves ....Matt 27:38
Nature of, unrecognized. .1Cor 2:8
Figurative of:
Utter rejection ....Heb 6:6
Apostasy ....Rev 11:8
Union with Christ ....Gal 2:20
Separation ....Gal 6:14
Sanctification............Rom 6:6
Dedication 1Cor 2:2

[*also* CRUCIFIED, CRUCIFY]
them ye shall kill and *c* ....Matt 23:34
Son of man is betrayed..*c* .....Matt 26:2
say unto him, Let him be *c* ...Matt 27:22
saying, Let him be *c* ....Matt 27:23
he delivered him to be *c* ......Matt 27:26
and led him away to *c* him ....Matt 27:31
Ye seek Jesus, which was *c* ...Matt 28:5
had scourged him to be *c* .....Mark 15:15
And with him they *c* two .....Mark 15:27
Jesus of Nazareth, which was *c*.Mark 16:6
they cried, saying, *C* him, *c* ...Luke 23:21
requiring that he might be *c* ..Luke 23:23
to death, and have *c* him .....Luke 24:20
cried out, saying, *C* him, *c* ...John 19:6
therefore unto them to be *c* ...John 19:16
Where they *c* him, and two ...John 19:18
Jesus, whom ye have *c*........Acts 2:36
Christ of Nazareth..ye *c*.......Acts 4:10
that our old man is *c* with.....Rom 6:6
was Paul *c* for you? or 1Cor 1:13
he was *c* through weakness 2Cor 13:4
I am *c* with Christ ....Gal 2:20
evidently set forth, *c* among ..Gal 3:1
have *c* the flesh with the ......Gal 5:24
by whom the world is *c* ....Gal 6:14

CRUELTY—*to cause suffering or fear*
Descriptive of the wicked.Ps 74:20
To animals, forbidden ...Num 22:27-35

[*also* CRUEL, CRUELLY]
instruments of *c* are ....Gen 49:5
their wrath, for it was *c*........Gen 49:7
of spirit and for *c* bondage ....Ex 6:9
dragons, and the *c* venom .....Deut 32:33
the *c* done to the threescore ...Judg 9:24
Thou art become *c* to me .....Job 30:21
and they hate me with *c* ......Ps 25:19
against me, and breathe out *c* .Ps 27:12
of the unrighteous and *c* ......Ps 71:4
others, and thy years..*c* ....Prov 5:9
he that is *c* troubleth his .....Prov 11:17
tender mercies..wicked are *c* ..Prov 12:10
a *c* messenger shall be sent....Prov 17:11
c and anger is outrageous .....Prov 27:4
Lord cometh *c* both with ......Is 13:9
over into the hand of a *c* .....Is 19:4
they are *c*, and have no ....Jer 6:23
the chastisement of a *c* one ...Jer 30:14
they are *c* and will not show ..Jer 50:42
daughter..people is become *c* ..Lam 4:3
father, because he *c* ....Ezek 18:18
and with *c* have ye ruled ......Ezek 34:4
others had trial of *c* ....Heb 11:36

CRUMBS—*fragments of bread*
Dogs eat of ....Matt 15:27
Lazarus begs for.........Luke 16:20, 21

table eat of the children's *c* ...Mark 7:28

CRUSE—*a small earthen vessel*
For water 1Sam 26:11, 12
For oil 1Kin 17:12, 14

and a *c* of honey, and go to ...1Kin 14:3
a *c* of water at his head 1Kin 19:6
Bring me a new *c* and put 2Kin 2:20

CRUSH—*to break; squeeze*

[*also* CRUSHED]
bruised, or *c*, or broken ......Lev 22:24
c Balaam's foot against the ....Num 22:25
be only oppressed and *c* ......Deut 28:33
are *c* before the moth? ....Job 4:19
they are *c* in the gate ....Job 5:4
that the foot may *c* them ......Job 39:15
is *c* breaketh out into a ....Is 59:5
he hath *c* me, he hath ....Jer 51:34
against me to *c* my young .....Lam 1:15
c under his feet all the ....Lam 3:34
which *c* the needy, which .....Amos 4:1

CRY—*wailing; calling out*
Accusation ....Gen 4:10
Remorse ....Heb 12:17
Pretense ....Judg 14:15-18
Sorrow 2Sam 18:33
Others' sins ....Ps 119:136
Pain ....Heb 5:7
None in heaven ....Rev 21:4

[*also* CRIED, CRIES, CRIEST, CRIETH]
c of Sodom and Gomorrah ....Gen 18:20
the *c* of them is waxen ....Gen 19:13
he *c* with a great and ....Gen 27:34
and exceeding bitter *c* ....Gen 27:34
me, and I *c* with a loud ....Gen 39:14
they *c* before him, Bow the ...Gen 41:43
and he *c*, Cause every man....Gen 45:1
and they *c*, and their cry ......Ex 2:23
their *c* came up unto God .....Ex 2:23
and have heard their *c* by .....Ex 3:7
they *c*, saying, Let us go ......Ex 5:8
children of Israel came and *c* ..Ex 5:15
Moses *c* unto the Lord ....Ex 8:12
shall be great *c* throughout ....Ex 11:6
was a great *c* in Egypt ....Ex 12:30
and the children of Israel *c* ....Ex 14:10
Wherefore *c* thou unto me? ...Ex 14:15
And he *c* unto the Lord ......Ex 15:25
And Moses *c* unto the Lord ...Ex 17:4
and they *c* at all unto me .....Ex 22:23
the voice of them that *c* ....Ex 32:18
and shall *c*, Unclean ....Lev 13:45
the people *c* unto Moses ......Num 11:2
And Moses *c* unto the Lord ...Num 12:13
lifted up their voice, and *c* ....Num 14:1
about them fled at the *c* of....Num 16:34
when we *c* unto the Lord .....Num 20:16
he *c* unto the Lord against ....Deut 15:9
the damsel, because she *c* .....Deut 22:24
he *c* against thee..Lord ....Deut 24:15
we *c* unto the Lord God ....Deut 26:7
when they *c* unto the Lord ....Josh 24:7
the children of Israel *c* ....Judg 3:9
And the children of Israel *c* ...Judg 4:3
and *c* through the lattice ......Judg 5:28
and the children of Israel *c* ....Judg 6:6
c, The sword of the Lord .....Judg 7:20
lifted up his voice, and *c* ......Judg 9:7
and the children of Israel *c* ....Judg 10:10
Go and *c* unto the gods ....Judg 10:14
c unto the children of Dan ....Judg 18:23
and told it, all the city *c* 1Sam 4:13
Eli heard the noise of the *c* ...1Sam 4:14
that the Ekronites *c* out 1Sam 5:10
c of the city went up to 1Sam 5:12
Cease not to *c* unto the Lord ..1Sam 7:8
and Samuel *c* unto the Lord ...1Sam 7:9
And ye shall *c* out in that 1Sam 8:18
because their *c* is come 1Sam 9:16
and he *c* unto the Lord all 1Sam 15:11
c unto the armies of Israel 1Sam 17:8
Jonathan *c* after the lad 1Sam 20:37
the cave, and *c* after Saul 1Sam 24:8
And David *c* to the people 1Sam 26:14
Who art thou that *c* to the 1Sam 26:14
woman saw Samuel, she *c* 1Sam 28:12
on her head, and went on *c* ...2Sam 13:19
watchman *c* and told the 2Sam 18:25
and the king *c* with a loud 2Sam 19:4
have I yet to *c* any more 2Sam 19:28
Then *c* a wise woman out 2Sam 20:16
and *c* to my God; and he 2Sam 22:7
and my *c* did enter into his....2Sam 22:7
the *c* and to the prayer 1Kin 8:28
he *c* against the altar in the ...1Kin 13:2
he *c* unto the Lord and 1Kin 17:20
C aloud; for he is a god.......1Kin 18:27
they *c* aloud and cut 1Kin 18:28
he *c* unto the king; and he ...1Kin 20:39
him; and Jehoshaphat *c* 1Kin 22:32
and he *c*, My father, my 2Kin 2:12
Now there *c* a certain woman .2Kin 4:1
c, and said, Alas, master! 2Kin 6:5
she went forth to *c* unto the ...2Kin 8:3
c to the king for her house 2Kin 8:5
Athaliah rent her clothes..*c* ...2Kin 11:14
Rab-shakeh stood and *c* 2Kin 18:28
And Isaiah the prophet *c* 2Kin 20:11
they *c* to God in the battle 1Chr 5:20
to hearken unto the *c* and 2Chr 6:19
sounding trumpets to *c* 2Chr 13:12
and they *c* unto the Lord 2Chr 13:14
Asa *c* unto the Lord his God ..2Chr 14:11
Jehoshaphat *c* out..Lord 2Chr 18:31
c unto thee in our affliction ...2Chr 20:9
Then they *c* with a loud 2Chr 32:18
there was a great *c* of the .....Neh 5:1
and *c* with a loud voice unto ..Neh 9:4
heardest their *c* by the Red ...Neh 9:9
c with a loud and a bitter *c* ...Esth 4:1
fastings and their *c* ....Esth 9:31
and let my *c* have no place ....Job 16:18
I *c* out of wrong, but I am ....Job 19:7
I *c* aloud, but there is no .....Job 19:7
the soul of the wounded *c* .....Job 24:12
Will God hear his *c* when .....Job 27:9
I delivered the poor that *c* ....Job 29:12
c after them as after a ....Job 30:5
I *c* unto thee and thou dost ...Job 30:20
If my land *c* against me, or ...Job 31:38
c of the poor to come unto ....Job 34:28
and he heareth the *c* of the ...Job 34:28
they make..oppressed to *c* .....Job 35:9
they *c* out by reason of the....Job 35:9
they *c* not when he bindeth ...Job 36:13
his young ones *c* unto God ....Job 38:41
regardeth he the *c*..driver .....Job 39:7
I *c* unto the Lord with my .....Ps 3:4
voice of my *c*, my King ....Ps 5:2
forgetteth not the *c*..humble ...Ps 9:12
attend unto my *c*, give ear ....Ps 17:1
and *c* unto my God; he ....Ps 18:6
and my *c* came before him ....Ps 18:6
O my God, I *c*..daytime ......Ps 22:2
They *c* unto thee, and were ...Ps 22:5
Hear, O Lord, when I *c* with ..Ps 27:7
Unto thee will I *c* O Lord ....Ps 28:1
O Lord my God, I *c* unto .....Ps 30:2
supplications when I *c* unto ...Ps 31:22
This poor man *c*..Lord ....Ps 34:6
his ears..open unto their *c* ....Ps 34:15
and give ear unto my *c*; hold ..Ps 39:12
inclined..and heard my *c* ......Ps 40:1
at noon; will I pray, and *c* ....Ps 55:17
I *c* unto thee, then shall ......Ps 56:9
I will *c* unto God most high ...Ps 57:2
Hear my *c* O God; attend......Ps 61:1
I *c* unto him with my mouth ..Ps 66:17
I am weary of my *c*; my ......Ps 69:3
deliver the needy when he *c* ...Ps 72:12
I *c* unto God with my voice ...Ps 77:1
my heart and my flesh *c* ......Ps 84:2
O Lord, for I *c* unto thee .....Ps 86:3
I have *c* day and night before. .Ps 88:1
incline thine ear unto my *c* ....Ps 88:2
He shall *c* unto me, Thou .....Ps 89:26
and let my *c* come unto ....Ps 102:1
affliction..he heard their *c* .....Ps 106:44
Then they *c* unto the Lord ....Ps 107:6
c unto the Lord in their ....Ps 107:19
I *c* with my whole heart.......Ps 119:145
Let my *c* come near before ....Ps 119:169
In my distress I *c*..Lord ....Ps 120:1
Out of the depths have I *c* ....Ps 130:1
day..I *c* thou answered ....Ps 138:3
Lord, I *c* unto thee; make ....Ps 141:1
my voice, when I *c* unto ......Ps 141:1
I *c* unto the Lord with my ....Ps 142:1
Attend unto my *c*; for I am ...Ps 142:6
hear their *c*, and will save .....Ps 145:19
the young ravens which *c* .....Ps 147:9
Wisdom *c* without; she ....Prov 1:20
Yea, if thou *c* after ....Prov 2:3
Doth not wisdom *c*? and ......Prov 8:1
She *c* at the gates at the ......Prov 8:3
she *c* upon the highest ....Prov 9:3
thy soul spare for his *c* ....Prov 19:18
his ears at the *c* of the poor ...Prov 21:13
hath two daughters, *c*, Give ...Prov 30:15
c of him that ruleth among ....Eccl 9:17
righteousness, but behold a *c* ..Is 5:7
And one *c* unto another, and ..Is 6:3
shall have knowledge to *c* .....Is 8:4
C..shout, thou inhabitant ......Is 12:6
wild beasts of the islands..*c* ...Is 13:22
Howl, O gate; *c*, O city ....Is 14:31
Heshbon shall *c* and ....Is 15:4
soldiers of Moab shall *c* ....Is 15:4
shall *c* unto the Lord ....Is 19:20
And he *c*, A lion; My lord ....Is 21:8
walls..*c* to the mountains ......Is 22:5
is a *c* for wine in the streets ...Is 24:11
they shall *c* aloud from the ....Is 24:14
wonder; *c* ye out, and *c* ....Is 29:9
therefore..I *c* concerning ......Is 30:7
thee at the voice of thy *c* .....Is 30:19
their valiant ones shall *c* ......Is 33:7
the satyr shall *c* to his ....Is 34:14
Rabshakeh stood, and *c* ....Is 36:13
and *c* unto her, that her ....Is 40:2
of him that *c* in the wilderness .Is 40:3
He shall not *c*, nor lift up .....Is 42:2
the Chaldeans, whose *c* is .....Is 43:14
yea one shall *c* unto him ......Is 46:7
forth into singing, and *c* ......Is 54:1
When thou *c*, let thy ....Is 57:13
C aloud, spare not, lift ....Is 58:1
ye shall *c* for sorrow, of........Is 65:14
in her, nor the voice of *c* .....Is 65:19
c in the ears of Jerusalem .....Jer 2:2
thou not from this time *c* .....Jer 3:4
land; *c* gather together ....Jer 4:5
Destruction..destruction is *c* ...Jer 4:20
lift up *c* nor prayer for ....Jer 7:16
c..daughter of my people ......Jer 8:19
though they shall *c* unto ......Jer 11:11
it *c* out against me ....Jer 12:8
the *c* of Jerusalem is gone .....Jer 14:2
a *c* be heard from their ....Jer 18:22
For since I spake, I *c* out .....Jer 20:8
let him hear the *c* in the ......Jer 20:16
Go up to Lebanon, and *c* ......Jer 22:20
Howl, ye shepherds, and *c* ....Jer 25:34
Why *c* thou for thine ....Jer 30:15
shall *c*, Arise ye and let us ....Jer 31:6
and thy *c* hath filled the ......Jer 46:12
then the men shall *c* and ......Jer 47:2
c shall be from Horonaim .....Jer 48:3
little ones have caused a *c* ....Jer 48:4
c ye daughters of Rabbah .....Jer 49:3
c is heard among the ....Jer 50:46
sound of a *c* cometh ....Jer 51:54
Their heart *c* unto the Lord ...Lam 2:18
Arise, *c* out in the night ......Lam 2:19
Also when I *c* and shout he ...Lam 3:8
they *c* unto them, Depart .....Lam 4:15
though, they *c* in mine ears ...Ezek 8:18
He *c* also in mine ears with ...Ezek 9:1
c for all the abominations .....Ezek 9:4
As for the wheels, it was *c* ....Ezek 10:13
upon my face, and *c* ....Ezek 11:13
C and howl, son of man ......Ezek 21:12
Forbear to *c* make no ....Ezek 24:17
wounded *c*..the slaughter ......Ezek 26:15
the sound of the *c* of thy ......Ezek 27:28
He *c* aloud and said thus ......Dan 4:14
The king *c* aloud to bring .....Dan 5:7
he *c* with a lamentable voice ..Dan 6:20

Ramah, *c* aloud at Beth ......Hos 5:8
And they have not *c* unto .....Hos 7:14
Israel..*c* unto me, My God ....Hos 8:2
and *c* unto the Lord ....Joel 1:14
young lion *c* out of his den ....Amos 3:4
great city and *c* against ....Jon 1:2
and *c* every man unto his ....Jon 1:5
said, I *c* by reason of mine ....Jon 2:2
he *c* and said, Yet forty days ..Jon 3:4
and *c* mightily unto God ......Jon 3:8
Then shall they *c*..Lord ....Mic 3:4
why dost thou *c* out aloud ....Mic 4:9
The Lord's voice *c* unto the ...Mic 6:9
Stand, stand, shall they *c* .....Nah 2:8
O Lord, how long shall I *c* ....Hab 1:2
the stone shall *c* out of the ....Hab 2:11
noise from a *c* from the fish ...Zeph 1:10
former prophets have *c* ....Zech 1:4
C thou, saying, Thus saith .....Zech 1:14
thereof with shoutings *c* ....Zech 4:7
Then *c* he unto me and ....Zech 6:8
the Lord hath *c* by the ....Zech 7:7
with weeping and with *c* ......Mal 2:13
voice of one *c*..wilderness .....Matt 3:3
behold, they *c* out saying .....Matt 8:29
c..saying, Thou son of David ..Matt 9:27
He shall not strive, nor *c* .....Matt 12:19
is a spirit and they *c* out ......Matt 14:26
c unto him, saying, Have .....Matt 15:22
for she *c* after us ....Matt 15:23
c out saying, Have mercy .....Matt 20:30
but they *c* the more, saying ...Matt 20:31
c saying, Hosanna to the ......Matt 21:9
and the children *c* in the ......Matt 21:15
at midnight there was a *c* .....Matt 25:6
But they *c* out the more ......Matt 27:23
Jesus, *c* with a loud voice .....Matt 27:46
Jesus, when he had *c* again....Matt 27:50
one *c* in the wilderness........Mark 1:3
an unclean spirit; and he *c* ....Mark 1:23
c..Thou art the Son of God ...Mark 3:11
and in the tombs *c* and ....Mark 5:5
c with a loud voice and ....Mark 5:7
it had been a spirit, and *c*.....Mark 6:49
c out, and said with tears .....Mark 9:24
he began to *c* out and say .....Mark 10:47
but he *c* the more a great .....Mark 10:48
and they that followed *c* ......Mark 11:9
the multitude *c* aloud ....Mark 15:8
they *c* out again, Crucify ......Mark 15:13
voice of one *c*..wilderness .....Luke 3:4
unclean devil and *c* out ....Luke 4:33
out of many, *c* out, and.......Luke 4:41
said these things, he *c* ....Luke 8:8
a man of the company *c* out...Luke 9:38
him and he suddenly *c* out ....Luke 9:39
c and said, Father Abraham ...Luke 16:24
own elect, which *c* day and....Luke 18:7
he *c* saying, Jesus, thou ....Luke 18:38
stones would immediately *c* ...Luke 19:40
they *c* out all at once ....Luke 23:18
and *c* saying, This was he .....John 1:15
one *c* in the wilderness........John 1:23
Then *c* Jesus in the temple ....John 7:28
c with a loud voice, Lazarus ...John 11:43
meet him and *c* Hosanna......John 12:13
Then *c* they all again ....John 18:40
saw him, they *c* out, saying ...John 19:6
they *c* out with a loud voice ...Acts 7:57
unclean spirits, *c* with loud ....Acts 8:7
ran in among the people, *c*....Acts 14:14
and *c* saying, These men ......Acts 16:17
unto the rulers of the city *c* ...Acts 17:6
c out saying, Great is Diana ...Acts 19:28
Some therefore *c* one thing....Acts 19:32
C out, Men of Israel, help ....Acts 21:28
some *c* one thing, some ....Acts 21:34
And as they *c* out and cast ....Acts 22:23
he *c* out in the council, Men ..Acts 23:6
And there arose a great *c* .....Acts 23:9
I *c* standing among them ......Acts 24:21
whereby we *c*, Abba, Father ..Rom 8:15
Isaiah also *c* concerning ....Rom 9:27
into your hearts, *c* Abba ......Gal 4:6
and *c* thou that travailest......Gal 4:27
you kept back by fraud, *c* .....James 5:4
the *c* of them which ....James 5:4
they *c* with a loud voice.......Rev 6:10
and he *c* with a loud voice ....Rev 7:2
And *c* with a loud voice ......Rev 7:10
And *c* with a loud voice ......Rev 10:3
And she being with child *c* .....Rev 12:2
c with a loud voice to him ....Rev 14:15
and cried with a loud *c* to......Rev 14:18
c with a loud cry to him that ..Rev 14:18
And he *c* mightily with a......Rev 18:2
and he *c* with a loud voice ....Rev 19:17

CRYSTAL—*rock crystal*
Wisdom surpasses ....Job 28:17-20
Gates of Zion ....Is 54:12
Descriptive of heaven ....Rev 4:6

color of the terrible *c* ....Ezek 1:22
a jasper stone, clear as *c* ......Rev 21:11
water of life, clear as *c* ....Rev 22:1

CUBIT—*a measurement; approximately 18 inches long*

[*also* CUBITS]
ark shall be three hundred *c*...Gen 6:15
the breadth of it fifty *c* ....Gen 6:15
and the height of it thirty *c* ...Gen 6:15
c shalt thou finish it above ....Gen 6:16
Fifteen *c* upward did the ......Gen 7:20
two *c* and a half shall be ......Ex 25:10
a *c* and a half the breadth.....Ex 25:10
c and a half the height ....Ex 25:10
two *c* and a half shall be ......Ex 25:17
shall be eight and twenty *c* ....Ex 26:2
the breadth..curtain four *c* ....Ex 26:2
And a *c* on one side ....Ex 26:13
wood, five *c* long..five *c* ......Ex 27:1
height thereof..three *c* ....Ex 27:1
A *c* shall be the length........Ex 30:2
a *c* the breadth thereof ....Ex 30:2
two *c* shall be the height ......Ex 30:2
was twenty and eight *c*........Ex 36:9
the breadth..curtain four *c* ....Ex 36:9
breadth of a board one *c*.......Ex 36:21
two *c* and a half was the ......Ex 37:1
and a *c* and a half the ....Ex 37:1
and a *c* and a half the height ..Ex 37:1
five *c* was the length..........Ex 38:1
and five *c* the breadth ....Ex 38:1
and three *c* the height ....Ex 38:1
and as it were two *c* high .....Num 11:31
and outward a thousand *c* .....Num 35:4
nine *c* was the length ....Deut 3:11
and four *c* the breadth of it ...Deut 3:11
breadth of it, after the *c* ......Deut 3:11
about two thousand *c* by ......Josh 3:4
had two edges of a *c* length ...Judg 3:16
whose height was six *c* and 1Sam 17:4
thereof was threescore *c* 1Kin 6:2
breadth thereof twenty *c* 1Kin 6:2
height thereof thirty *c*.........1Kin 6:2
length thereof..hundred *c* 1Kin 7:2
breadth thereof fifty *c* 1Kin 7:2
height thereof thirty *c*.........1Kin 7:2
knobs compassing it, ten..*c* 1Kin 7:24
corner gate, four hundred *c* ...2Kin 14:13
one pillar was eighteen *c* 2Kin 25:17
height of the chapiter three *c* ..2Kin 25:17
man of great stature, five *c*....1Chr 11:23
The length, by *c* after the 2Chr 3:3
measure was threescore *c* 2Chr 3:3
and the breadth twenty *c*......2Chr 3:3
twenty *c* the length thereof 2Chr 4:1
and twenty *c* the breadth......2Chr 4:1
and ten *c* the height thereof ...2Chr 4:1
a brazen scaffold of five *c* 2Chr 6:13
and five *c* broad and three *c* ..2Chr 6:13
corner gate, four hundred *c* ...2Chr 25:23
height thereof threescore *c* ....Ezra 6:3
breadth thereof threescore *c* ....Ezra 6:3
and a thousand *c* on the ......Neh 3:13
gallows be made of fifty *c* .....Esth 5:14
also, the gallows fifty *c* high ...Esth 7:9
of one pillar was eighteen *c* ...Jer 52:21
and a fillet of twelve *c* did ....Jer 52:21
a measuring reed of six *c* .....Ezek 40:5
six cubits long by the *c* ....Ezek 40:5
posts, six *c* broad on the ......Ezek 41:1
six *c* broad on the other ......Ezek 41:1
length of an hundred *c*........Ezek 42:2
and the breadth was fifty *c* ....Ezek 42:2
inward, a way of one *c* ....Ezek 42:4
of the altar after the *c* ....Ezek 43:13
The *c* is a *c* and a hand ....Ezek 43:13
even the bottom shall be a *c* ..Ezek 43:13
fifty *c* round about for the ....Ezek 45:2
were courts joined of forty *c* ..Ezek 46:22
he measured a thousand *c*.....Ezek 47:3
height was threescore *c* ....Dan 3:1
breadth thereof six *c*..........Dan 3:1
length thereof is twenty *c* .....Zech 5:2
breadth thereof ten *c* ....Zech 5:2
can add one *c* unto his........Matt 6:27
as it were two hundred *c*......John 21:8
hundred and forty and four *c* ..Rev 21:17

CUBS—*offspring of beasts*

Figurative of:
Babylonians ....Jer 51:38
Assyrians ....Nah 2:11, 12
Princes of Israel ....Ezek 19:2-9

CUCUMBER—*an edible fruit grown on a vine*
Lusted after.............Num 11:5
Grown in gardens ....Is 1:8

CUCKOW—*a bird considered unclean*
Probably refers to sea gull ....Lev 11:16

CUD—*partly digested food*
Animals chew again .....Lev 11:3-8

cheweth the *c* among the......Deut 14:6

CUMBERED—*encumbered*

[*also* CUMBERETH, CUMBRANCE]
I myself alone bear your *c* ....Deut 1:12
But Martha was *c* about ......Luke 10:40
cut it down; why *c* it the ......Luke 13:7

CUMI (kū'mī)—*an Aramaic word meaning "arise"*
unto her, Talitha *c* which .....Mark 5:41

CUMMIN—*an annual of the parsley family*
Seeds threshed by a rod. .Is 28:25, 27
A trifle of tithing ....Matt 23:23

CUNNING—*sly; clever*

Used in a good sense:
David 1Sam 23:19-22
Jehu....................2Kin 10:19

Used in a bad sense:
Thwarted by God ....Job 5:13
Of harlot's heart ....Prov 7:10

[*also* CUNNINGLY]
Esau was a *c* hunter ....Gen 25:27
cherubim of *c* work shalt......Ex 26:1
fine twined linen, with *c* ......Ex 28:6
devise *c* works, to work in ....Ex 31:4
to make any manner of *c* .....Ex 35:33
cherubim of *c* work made .....Ex 36:8
an engraver and a *c* ....Ex 38:23
in the fine linen with *c*........Ex 39:3
a man, who is a *c* player 1Sam 16:16
c to work all works in 1Kin 7:14
c men for every manner of 1Chr 22:15
were *c*, was two hundred......1Chr 25:7
c to work in gold, and in 2Chr 2:7
skill to grave with the *c* 2Chr 2:7
engines, invented by *c* men....2Chr 26:15
right hand forget her *c*........Ps 137:5
hands of a *c* workman ....Song 7:1
counselor, and the *c* artificer ..Is 3:3
seeketh unto him a *c* ....Is 40:20
may come; and send for *c*.....Jer 9:17
they are all the work of *c* .....Jer 10:9
and *c* in knowledge, and ......Dan 1:4
sleight of men, and *c* ....Eph 4:14
have not followed *c* devised ...2Pet 1:16

CUP—*drinking utensil*
Literal use of:
For drinking 2Sam 12:3
Figurative uses of:
One's portion ....Ps 11:6
Blessings...............Ps 23:5
Suffering...............Matt 20:23
Hypocrisy...............Matt 23:25, 26
New covenant 1Cor 10:16

[*also* CUPS]
and Pharaoh's *c* was in my ....Gen 40:11
pressed..Pharaoh's *c* ....Gen 40:11
gave the *c* into Pharaoh's .....Gen 40:11
And put my *c*, the silver *c*,....Gen 44:2
wrought like the brim of a *c*...1Kin 7:26
and the bowls and the *c*.......1Chr 28:17
the work of the brim of a *c* ...2Chr 4:5
inheritance and of my *c* ....Ps 16:5
and waters of a full *c* are .....Ps 73:10
hand of the Lord there is a *c*..Ps 75:8
I will take the *c* of salvation...Ps 116:13
it giveth his color in the *c* .....Prov 23:31
from the vessels of *c* even .....Is 22:24
the Lord the *c* of his fury .....Is 51:17
dregs of the *c* of trembling ....Is 51:17
c of consolation to drink ....Jer 16:7
wine *c* of this fury at my ......Jer 25:15
pots full of wine and *c* ....Jer 35:5
judgment was not to drink..*c* ..Jer 49:12
Babylon..been a golden *c* .....Jer 51:7
and the spoons, and the *c* .....Jer 52:19
the *c* also shall pass ....Lam 4:21
will I give her *c* into thine ....Ezek 23:31
c of the Lord's right hand .....Hab 2:16
make Jerusalem a *c* of ....Zech 12:2
c of cold water only in the ....Matt 10:42
drink of the *c* that I shall .....Matt 20:22
he took the *c*, and gave ....Matt 26:27
as the washing of *c* and ....Mark 7:4
give you a *c* of water to.......Mark 9:41
ye drink of the *c* that I ....Mark 10:38
he took the *c*, and when he ...Mark 14:23
make clean the outside..*c* .....Luke 11:39
he took the *c*, and gave ....Luke 22:17
Likewise also the *c* after ......Luke 22:20
This *c* is the new testament ...Luke 22:20
be willing, remove this *c* ......Luke 22:42
c which my Father hath ....John 18:11
Ye cannot drink the *c* of the ..1Cor 10:21
and the *c* of devils............1Cor 10:21
manner also he took the *c* 1Cor 11:25
This *c* is the new testament ...1Cor 11:25
into the *c* of his indignation ...Rev 14:10
c of the wine of the fierceness .Rev 16:19
having a golden *c* in her ....Rev 17:4
c which she hath filled, fill ....Rev 18:6

CUPBEARER—*one who handles and fills cups; a high court official*
Many under Solomon 1Kin 10:5
Nehemiah, a faithful .....Neh 1:11

[*also* CUPBEARERS]
their apparel; his *c* also 2Chr 9:4

CURDLED—*spoiled; soured*
as milk and *c* me like ....Job 10:10

CURE—*to restore to health*
Of the body ....Matt 17:16
Of the mind ....Mark 5:15
Of the demonized ....Matt 12:22
With means ....Is 38:21
By faith ....Num 21:8, 9
By prayer...............James 5:14, 15
By God's mercy ....Phil 2:27
Hindered 2Kin 8:7-15

[*also* CURED, CURES]
I will bring it health and *c* ....Jer 33:6
I will *c* them, and will ....Jer 33:6
for thou shalt not be *c* ....Jer 46:11
you, nor *c* you of your........Hos 5:13
child was *c* from that very.....Matt 17:18
c many of their infirmities.....Luke 7:21
over all devils, and to *c* ....Luke 9:1
said unto him that was *c* ......John 5:10

CURIOSITY—*inquisitive interest; nosiness*
Into God's secrets,
forbidden ....John 21:21, 22
Leads 50,070 to death ...1Sam 6:19

CURIOSITY SEEKERS—*those with an uncommitted interest in the affairs of others*
Eve ....Gen 3:6
Israelites ....Ex 19:21, 24
Babylonians 2Kin 20:13
Herod ....Matt 2:4-8
Zacchaeus ....Luke 19:1-6
Certain Greeks ....John 12:20, 21
Lazarus' visitors ....John 12:9
Peter ....Matt 26:58
At the crucifixion........Matt 27:46-49
Athenians...............Acts 17:21

CURIOUS—*artistically designed; magical*

[*also* CURIOUSLY]
the *c* girdle of the ephod ......Ex 28:8
the *c* girdle of the ephod ......Ex 29:5
devise *c* works to work in .....Ex 35:32
the *c* girdle of his ephod ......Ex 39:5
the *c* girdle of the ephod ......Lev 8:7
c wrought in the lowest ....Ps 139:15
used *c* arts brought their ......Acts 19:19

CURRENT—*a monetary measure of unknown value*
c money with the merchant....Gen 23:16

CURSE—*to call down evil upon others violently; a call for evil to rest on someone*
Pronounced upon:
The earth ....Gen 3:17
Cain....................Gen 4:11
Canaan ....Gen 9:25
Two sons ....Gen 49:7
Disobedient ....Deut 28:15-45
Meroz ....Judg 5:23
Jericho's rebuilders ......Josh 6:26
Forbidden upon:
Parents ....Ex 21:17
Ruler...................Ex 22:28
Deaf ....Lev 19:14
Enemies ....Luke 6:28
God ....Job 2:9
God's people ....Gen 12:3
Instances of:
Goliath's................1Sam 17:43
Balaam's attempted ......Num 22:1-12
The fig tree ....Mark 11:21
Peter's..................Matt 26:74
The crucified ....Gal 3:10, 13
Manifested by:
Rebellious 2Sam 16:5-8

[*also* CURSED, CURSEDST, CURSES, CURSEST, CURSETH, CURSING, CURSINGS]
thou art *c* above all cattle .....Gen 3:14
ground which the Lord hath *c* .Gen 5:29
I..not again *c* the ground......Gen 8:21
and curse him that *c* thee .....Gen 12:3
I shall bring a *c* upon me .....Gen 27:12
Upon me be thy *c*, my son ....Gen 27:13
c be every one that *c* ....Gen 27:29
everyone that *c* his father .....Lev 20:9
hath *c* his father or his ....Lev 20:9
name of the Lord and *c*.......Lev 24:11
Whosoever *c* his God shall ....Lev 24:15
water that causeth the *c*.......Num 5:18
water that causeth the *c*.......Num 5:19
woman with an oath of *c*......Num 5:21
priest shall write these *c* ......Num 5:23
he whom thou *c* is............Num 22:6
Come, *c* me Jacob and.......Num 23:7
I *c*, whom God hath not *c*? ...Num 23:8
thee and *c* is he that *c* ....Num 24:9
I called thee to *c* mine ....Num 24:10
lest thou be a *c* thing like .....Deut 7:26
abhor it; for it is a *c* thing ....Deut 7:26
day a blessing and a *c* ....Deut 11:26
cleave nought of the *c* ....Deut 13:17
Pethor of Mesopotamia, to *c* ..Deut 23:4
stand upon mount Ebal to *c*...Deut 27:13
C be the man that maketh .....Deut 27:15
C be he that confirmeth not ...Deut 27:26
Lord shall send upon thee *c* ...Deut 28:20
he heareth the words..*c* ....Deut 29:19
all the *c* that are written ......Deut 29:20
according to all the *c* of the ...Deut 29:21
to bring upon it all the *c* ......Deut 29:27
the blessing and the *c*.........Deut 30:1
put all these *c* upon thine .....Deut 30:7
and death, blessing and *c* .....Deut 30:19
make the camp of Israel a *c*...Josh 6:18
therefore ye are *c* and there ..Josh 9:23
Balaam the son of Beor to *c* ..Josh 24:9
drink, and *c* Abimelech ....Judg 9:27
them came the *c* of Jotham ...Judg 9:57
about which thou *c* and ....Judg 17:2
C be he that giveth a wife.....Judg 21:18
C be the man that eateth 1Sam 14:24
c be they before the Lord 1Sam 26:19
should this dead dog *c* my 2Sam 16:9
requite me good for his *c* 2Sam 16:12
because he *c* the Lord's 2Sam 19:21
which *c* me with a grievous....1Kin 2:8
a grievous *c* in the day........1Kin 2:8
c them in the name..Lord 2Kin 2:24
now this *c* woman, and bury ..2Kin 9:34
become a desolation and a *c* ..2Kin 22:19
all the *c* that are written 2Chr 34:24
entered into a *c* and into......Neh 10:29
against them..he should *c* .....Neh 13:2
God turned the *c* into a........Neh 13:2
contended with them, and *c* ...Neh 13:25
sinned, and *c* God in their ....Job 1:5
and he will *c* thee to thy ......Job 1:11
and he will *c* thee to thy ......Job 2:5
Job his mouth and *c* his.......Job 3:1
Let them *c* it that ....Job 3:8
that *c* the day, who are ....Job 3:8
suddenly I *c* his habitation ....Job 5:3
their portion is *c*..earth ....Job 24:18
to sin by wishing a *c* to his ....Job 31:30
His mouth is full of *c* ....Ps 10:7
they that be *c* of him shall ....Ps 37:22
for *c* and lying which they.....Ps 59:12
their mouth, but they *c* ....Ps 62:4
As he loved *c*, so let it come ..Ps 109:17
Let them *c*, but bless thou ....Ps 109:28
rebuked the proud that are *c* ..Ps 119:21
The *c* of the Lord is in the ....Prov 3:33
corn, the people shall *c* him ...Prov 11:26
Whoso *c* his father or his .....Prov 20:20
him shall the people *c* ....Prov 24:24
the *c* causeless shall not ....Prov 26:2
morning it..counted a *c* ....Prov 27:14
his eyes..many a *c* ....Prov 28:27
he heareth *c*, and bewrayeth it .Prov 29:24
lest he *c* thee, and thou be ....Prov 30:10
There is a generation that *c* ...Prov 30:11
lest thou hear thy servant *c* ...Eccl 7:21
thyself likewise hast *c*.........Eccl 7:22
C not the king, no not in .....Eccl 10:20
c not the rich in thy ....Eccl 10:20
c their king and their God ....Is 8:21
the *c* devoured the earth ......Is 24:6
upon the people of my *c* ......Is 34:5
Jacob to the *c* and Israel ......Is 43:28
leave your name for a *c*......Is 65:15
C be the man that obeyeth ....Jer 11:3
every one of them doth *c* .....Jer 15:10
C be the man that trusteth ....Jer 17:5
C be the day wherein I was ...Jer 20:14
a proverb, a taunt and a *c* ....Jer 24:9
a hissing, and a *c*............Jer 25:18
will make this city a *c* to ......Jer 26:6
a *c* and an astonishment ....Jer 29:18
them shall be taken up a *c* ...Jer 29:22
an astonishment and a *c* ......Jer 42:18
ye might be a *c* and a ....Jer 44:8
C be he that doeth the work ..Jer 48:10
c be he that keepeth back.....Jer 48:10
a reproach, a waste and a *c* ...Jer 49:13
sorrow of heart, thy *c* unto....Lam 3:65
the *c* is poured upon us ....Dan 9:11
is the *c* that goeth forth ....Zech 5:3
ye were a *c* among the........Zech 8:13

c be the deceiver, which . . . . . .Mal 1:14
I will even send a *c* upon . . . . .Mal 2:2
and I will *c* your blessings . . . . .Mal 2:2
yea, I have *c* them already . . . .Mal 2:2
Ye are *c* with a curse; for . . . . .Mal 3:9
are cursed with a *c* for ye . . . . .Mal 3:9
and smite the earth with a *c* . . .Mal 4:6
bless them that *c* you, do . . . . .Matt 5:44
He that *c* father or mother . . . .Matt 15:4
Depart from me, ye *c* into . . . .Matt 25:41
Whoso *c* father or mother . . . . .Mark 7:10
But he began to *c* and to . . . . .Mark 14:71
knoweth not the law are *c* . . . .John 7:49
bound themselves under a *c* . . .Acts 23:12
Whose mouth is full of *c* . . . . . .Rom 3:14
persecute you; bless, and *c* . . . .Rom 12:14
C is every one that hangeth . . .Gal 3:13
nigh unto *c*; whose end is . . . . .Heb 6:8
therewith *c* we men, which . . . .James 3:9
proceedeth blessing and *c* . . . . .James 3:10
covetous practices; *c* 2Pet 2:14
there shall be no more *c* . . . . . .Rev 22:3

CURTAIN—*an awning-like screen*
Ten, in tabernacle . . . . . . .Ex 26:1-13
Figurative of the heavens .Ps 104:2

[*also* CURTAINS]
ten *c* of fine twined linen . . . . .Ex 36:8
length of one *c* was twenty . . . .Ex 36:9
the *c* for the door of the . . . . . .Num 3:26
bear the *c* of the tabernacle . . .Num 4:25
ark of God dwelleth within *c* . .2Sam 7:2
Lord remaineth under *c* 1Chr 17:1
Kedar, as the *c* of Solomon . . .Song 1:5
stretcheth..heavens as a *c* . . . . .Is 40:22
let them stretch forth the *c* . . . .Is 54:2
spoiled, and my *c* in a . . . . .Jer 4:20
and to set up my *c* . . . . .Jer 10:20
take to themselves their *c* . . . . .Jer 49:29
the *c* of the land of Midian . . . .Hab 3:7

CUSH (kŭsh)—*"black"*
1. Ham's oldest son 1Chr 1:8-10
2. Means Ethiopia . . . . .Is 18:1
3. A Benjamite . . . . .Ps 7:*title*

sons of Ham; *C* and Mizraim . .Gen 10:6
from Pathros, and from *C* . . . . .Is 11:11

CUSHAN (kū'shăn)
Probably same as Cush. . .Hab 3:7

CUSHAN-RISHATHAIM (kū-shăn-rĭsh-ä-thā'ĭm)

Mesopotamian King
Oppressed Israel . . . . .Judg 3:8
Othniel delivers Israel from . . . . .Judg 3:9, 10

CUSHI (kū'shī)—*"black"*
1. Ancestor of Jehudi . . . . . .Jer 36:14
2. Father of Zephaniah . . . .Zeph 1:1

Joab to *C*, Go tell the King . . .2Sam 18:21
C bowed himself unto Joab 2Sam 18:21

CUSHITE (kū'shīt)
1. David's servant 2Sam 18:21-32
2. Moses' wife . . . . .Num 12:1

CUSTODY—*charge; control*
under the *c* and charge . . . . . . .Num 3:36
women, unto the *c* of Hege . . .Esth 2:3

CUSTOM—*tax; usage or practice*

As a tax:
Matthew collected . . . . . . .Matt 9:9
Kings require . . . . .Matt 17:25
Christians give . . . . .Rom 13:6, 7

As a common practice:
Abominable . . . . .Lev 18:30
Vain . . . . .Jer 10:3
Worthy . . . . .Luke 4:16
Traditional . . . . .Acts 21:21
A woman's menstruation .Gen 31:35

[*also* CUSTOMS]
And it was a *c* in Israel . . . . . . .Judg 11:39
priest's *c* with the people 1Sam 2:13
according to the *c*, as the . . . . .Ezra 3:4
not pay toll, tribute, and *c* . . . .Ezra 4:13
toll, tribute, or *c* upon . . . . .Ezra 7:24
sealed according..law and *c* . . . .Jer 32:11
sitting at the receipt of *c* . . . . . .Mark 2:14
c of the priest's office, his . . . . .Luke 1:9
do for him after the *c*..law . . . .Luke 2:27
as his *c* was, he went into . . . . .Luke 4:16
Levi sitting..receipt of *c* . . . . . . .Luke 5:27
ye have a *c* that I should . . . . . .John 18:39
the *c* which Moses delivered . . .Acts 6:14
teach *c* which are not lawful . . .Acts 16:21
neither to walk after the *c* . . . .Acts 21:21
to be expert in all *c* and . . . . . .Acts 26:3
people, or *c* of our fathers . . . .Acts 28:17
we have no such *c*, neither 1Cor 11:16

CUT—*to divide with a sharp instrument*

[*also* CUTTEST, CUTTETH, CUTTING, CUTTINGS]
neither shall all flesh be *c* . . . . .Gen 9:11
be *c* off from his people . . . . . .Gen 17:14
and *c* off the foreskin of . . . . . .Ex 4:25
shalt be *c* off from..earth . . . . .Ex 9:15
soul..*c* off from Israel . . . . .Ex 12:15
Jebusites; and I will *c* . . . . .Ex 23:23
thou shalt *c* the ram in . . . . .Ex 29:17
even be *c* off from his . . . . .Ex 30:33
even be *c* off from his . . . . .Ex 30:38
in *c* of stones, to set them . . . .Ex 31:5
that soul shall be *c* off from . . .Ex 31:14
images, and *c* down their . . . . .Ex 34:13
the *c* of stones, to set them . . .Ex 35:33
and *c* it into wires, to work . . .Ex 39:3
offering, and *c* it into his . . . . . .Lev 1:6
even that soul shall be *c* . . . . . .Lev 7:20
even that soul shall be *c* . . . . . .Lev 7:21
And he *c* the ram into pieces . .Lev 8:20
and that man shall be *c* off . . . .Lev 17:4
commit them shall be *c* . . . . . . .Lev 18:29
and that soul shall be *c* off . . . .Lev 19:8
make any *c* in your flesh . . . . . .Lev 19:28
c him off from among his . . . . .Lev 20:3
make any *c* in their flesh . . . . . .Lev 21:5
be *c* off from my presence . . . .Lev 22:3
day, he shall be *c* off from . . . .Lev 23:29
places, and *c* down your . . . . . .Lev 26:30
C ye not off the tribe of the . . .Num 4:18
same soul shall be *c* off . . . . . . .Num 9:13
and *c* down from thence . . . . . .Num 13:23
that soul shall be *c* off from . . .Num 15:30
soul shall be *c* off..Israel . . . . . .Num 19:13
c down their groves, and . . . . . .Deut 7:5
thy God shall *c* off the . . . . .Deut 12:29
ye shall not *c* yourselves . . . . . .Deut 14:1
thy God hath *c* off the . . . . .Deut 19:1
and thou shalt not *c* them . . . . .Deut 20:19
or hath his privy member *c* . . . .Deut 23:1
thou *c* down thine harvest . . . . .Deut 24:19
Then thou shalt *c* off her . . . . . .Deut 25:12
c off his thumbs..his great . . . . .Judg 1:6
c down the grove that is by . . .Judg 6:25
c down a bough from the . . . . .Judg 9:48
and *c* her in pieces and . . . . . . .Judg 20:6
is one tribe *c* off..Israel . . . . . . .Judg 21:6
name of the dead be not *c* . . . .Ruth 4:10
palms of his hands were *c* 1Sam 5:4
him and *c* off his head 1Sam 17:51
thou shalt not *c* off thy 1Sam 20:15
and *c* off the skirt of Saul's . . .1Sam 24:4
thou wilt not *c* off my seed 1Sam 24:21
he hath *c* off those that 1Sam 28:9
they *c* off his head, and 1Sam 31:9
c off their hands and their 2Sam 4:12
have *c* off all thine enemies . . .2Sam 7:9
and *c* off their garments in 2Sam 10:4
they *c* off the head of Sheba . .2Sam 20:22
will I *c* off Israel out of the . . .1Kin 9:7
he had *c* off every male 1Kin 11:16
to *c* it off and to destroy 1Kin 13:34
will *c* off from Jeroboam 1Kin 14:10
Jezebel *c* off the prophets 1Kin 18:4
cried aloud..*c* themselves 1Kin 18:28
and will *c* off from Ahab 1Kin 21:21
they came to Jordan, they *c* . . .2Kin 6:4
and I will *c* off from Ahab 2Kin 9:8
the Lord began to *c* Israel 2Kin 10:32
And king Ahaz *c*..borders 2Kin 16:17
c down the groves and 2Kin 18:4
will *c* down the tall cedar 2Kin 19:23
and *c* down the groves 2Kin 23:14
c in pieces all the vessels 2Kin 24:13
have *c* off all thine enemies . . .1Chr 17:8
and *c* off their garments in 1Chr 19:4
and *c* them with saws, and 1Chr 20:3
skill to *c* timber in Lebanon . . .2Chr 2:8
images and *c* down the 2Chr 14:3
Asa *c* down her idol and 2Chr 15:16
anointed to *c*..house of Ahab . .2Chr 22:7
c off from the house..Lord 2Chr 26:21
and *c* in pieces the vessels 2Chr 28:24
and *c* down the groves and 2Chr 31:1
Lord sent an angel which *c* 2Chr 32:21
on high above them, he *c* 2Chr 34:4
where were the righteous *c* . . . .Job 4:7
loose his hand, and *c* me off . .Job 6:9
in his greenness and not *c* . . . . .Job 8:12
Whose hope shall be *c* off . . . . .Job 8:14
If he *c* off, and shut up, or . . . .Job 11:10
flower, and is *c* down; he . . . . .Job 14:2
is hope of a tree, if it be *c* . . . .Job 14:7
above shall his branch be *c* . . . .Job 18:16
his months is *c* off in the . . . . . .Job 21:21
Which were *c* down out of . . . .Job 22:16
was not *c* off before the . . . . . . .Job 23:17
and *c* off as the tops of . . . . . . .Job 24:24
c out of rivers among the . . . . .Job 28:10
Who *c* up mallows by the . . . . .Job 30:4
people are *c* off in their . . . . . . .Job 36:20
Lord shall *c* off all flattering . . .Ps 12:3
I am *c* off from before thine . .Ps 31:22
to *c* off the remembrance of . . .Ps 34:16
they shall soon be *c* down . . . . .Ps 37:2
bow and *c* the spear in . . . . .Ps 46:9
enemies: *c* them off in thy . . . .Ps 54:5
let them be as *c* in pieces . . . . .Ps 58:7
of the wicked also will I *c* . . . . .Ps 75:10
He shall *c* off the spirit of . . . . .Ps 76:12
is burned with fire, it is *c* . . . . .Ps 80:16
Come, and let us *c* them off . . .Ps 83:4
and they are *c* off from thy . . .Ps 88:5
it is *c* down and withereth . . . . .Ps 90:6
it is soon *c* off, and we fly . . . .Ps 90:10
c them off in their own . . . . . . .Ps 94:23
his neighbor, him will I *c* . . . . .Ps 101:5
and *c* the bars of iron in . . . . . .Ps 107:16
Let his posterity be *c* off . . . . . .Ps 109:13
c asunder the cords of the . . . . .Ps 129:4
when one *c* and cleaveth . . . . . .Ps 141:7
of thy mercy *c* off mine . . . . . . .Ps 143:12
be *c* off from the earth . . . . . . .Prov 2:22
froward tongue shall be *c* . . . . .Prov 10:31
expectation shall not be *c* . . . . .Prov 23:18
expectation shall not be *c* . . . . .Prov 24:14
hand of the fool *c* off . . . . .Prov 26:6
the sycamores are *c* down . . . . . .Is 9:10
Lord will *c* off from Israel . . . . .Is 9:14
destroy and *c* off nations . . . . . .Is 10:7
adversaries of Judah..be *c* . . . . .Is 11:13
art thou *c* down..ground . . . . . .Is 14:12
and *c* off from Babylon the . . .Is 14:22
baldness, and every beard *c* . . .Is 15:2
both *c* off the sprigs with . . . . .Is 18:5
removed, and be *c* down, and. .Is 22:25
watch for iniquity are *c* . . . . . . .Is 29:20
thorns *c* up shall they be . . . . . .Is 33:12
c down the tall cedars . . . . .Is 37:24
I said in the *c* off of my . . . . . .Is 38:10
have *c* off like a weaver my . . .Is 38:12
and *c* in sunder the bars of . . . .Is 45:2
for thee, that I *c* thee not . . . . .Is 48:9
Art thou..that hath *c* Rahab . . .Is 51:9
c off out of the land of the . . . .Is 53:8
sign that shall not be *c* off . . . .Is 55:13
name, that shall not be *c* . . . . . .Is 56:5
lamb, as if he *c* off a dog's . . . .Is 66:3
and is *c* off from their . . . . .Jer 7:28
to *c* off the children from . . . . .Jer 9:21
for one *c* a tree out of the . . . .Jer 10:3
and let us *c* him off from . . . . .Jer 11:19
nor *c* themselves, nor make . . .Jer 16:6
shall *c* down thy choice . . . . . . .Jer 22:7

and *c* him out windows . . . . . . .Jer 22:14
peaceable habitations are *c* . . . .Jer 25:37
c the calf in twain and . . . . .Jer 34:18
he *c* it with the penknife . . . . . .Jer 36:23
and having *c* themselves . . . . . .Jer 41:5
c off from you man and . . . . . . .Jer 44:7
They shall *c* down her . . . . .Jer 46:23
c off from Tyrus and Zidon . . .Jer 47:4
let us *c* it off from being a . . . .Jer 48:2
shalt be *c* down, O Madmen . .Jer 48:2
all the hands shall be *c* . . . . . . .Jer 48:37
men of war shall be *c* off in . . .Jer 49:26
C off the sower from Babylon .Jer 50:16
soul; be not *c* off in her . . . . . . .Jer 51:6
He hath *c* off in his fierce . . . . .Lam 2:3
have *c* off my life..dungeon . . .Lam 3:53
and your images may be *c* . . . .Ezek 6:6
c him off from the midst . . . . . .Ezek 14:8
thy navel was not *c*, neither . . .Ezek 16:4
and *c* off the fruit thereof . . . . .Ezek 17:9
c off..thee the righteous . . . . . . .Ezek 21:3
I will *c* thee off from the . . . . . .Ezek 25:7
and *c* off man and beast out . . .Ezek 29:8
I will *c* off the multitude of . . .Ezek 30:15
of the nations, have *c* him . . . .Ezek 31:12
c off from it him that . . . . .Ezek 35:7
is lost; we are *c* off for our . . . .Ezek 37:11
out of the field, neither *c* . . . . .Ezek 39:10
ye shall be *c* in pieces and . . . .Dan 2:5
shall be *c* in pieces and . . . . . . .Dan 3:29
and *c* off his branches . . . . .Dan 4:14
shall Messiah be *c* off but . . . . .Dan 9:26
idols that they may be *c* off . . .Hos 8:4
her king is *c* off as the foam . .Hos 10:7
for it is *c* off from your . . . . . . .Joel 1:5
and *c* off the inhabitant . . . . . . .Amos 1:5
c off the judge from the . . . . . .Amos 2:3
horns..altar shall be *c* . . . . .Amos 3:14
c them in the head, all of . . . . .Amos 9:1
(how art thou *c* off!) would . . .Obad 5
all thine enemies shall be *c* . . .Mic 5:9
shall they be *c* down, when . . .Nah 1:12
I will *c* off thy prey from . . . . .Nah 2:13
thy house be *c* off many . . . . . .Hab 2:10
the sword shall *c* thee off . . . . .Nah 3:15
flock shall be *c* off from the . . .Hab 3:17
I will *c* off man from off the . .Zeph 1:3
I have *c* off the nations . . . . . . .Zeph 3:6
one that stealeth shall be *c* . . . .Zech 5:3
c off the pride..Philistines . . . . .Zech 9:6
Three shepherds also I *c* . . . . . .Zech 11:8
to be *c* off, let it be *c* off . . . . .Zech 11:9
with it shall be *c* in pieces . . . . .Zech 12:3
will *c* off the names of the . . . .Zech 13:2
of the people shall not be *c* . . .Zech 14:2
c it off, and cast it from . . . . . .Matt 5:30
c them off, and cast them . . . . .Matt 18:8
c down branches from the . . . . .Matt 21:8
shall *c* him asunder and . . . . . .Matt 24:51
crying and *c* himself with . . . . . .Mark 5:5
if thy hand offend thee, *c* . . . . .Mark 9:43
c down branches off the . . . . . .Mark 11:8
the high priest, and *c* of . . . . . .Mark 14:47
will *c* him in sunder, and . . . . . .Luke 12:46
c it down; why cumbereth . . . . .Luke 13:7
priest, and *c* off his right . . . . . .Luke 22:50
servant, and *c* off his right . . . .John 18:10
that they were *c* to the . . . . .Acts 5:33
they were *c* to the heart . . . . . .Acts 7:54
soldiers *c* off the ropes of . . . . .Acts 27:32
c it short in righteousness . . . . .Rom 9:28
otherwise thou..shalt be *c* . . . . .Rom 11:22
c out of the olive tree . . . . .Rom 11:24
I may *c* off occasion from 2Cor 11:12
were even *c* off which trouble. .Gal 5:12

CUTH, CUTHAH (kŭth, kū'-thăh)—*"burning"*
People from, brought to
Samaria 2Kin 17:24, 30

CYMBAL—*one of a pair of concave brass plates*
A musical instrument 1Chr 13:8
Figurative of pretense 1Cor 13:1

[*also* CYMBALS]
and on cornets, and on *c* 2Sam 6:5
psalteries and harps and *c* 1Chr 15:16
Asaph made a sound with *c* . . .1Chr 16:5
with psalteries and with *c* 1Chr 25:1
having *c* and psalteries and 2Chr 5:12
trumpets and *c* and 2Chr 5:13
the Lord with *c* with 2Chr 29:25
the sons of Asaph with *c* . . . . . .Ezra 3:10
with singing, with *c* . . . . .Neh 12:27
Praise him upon the loud *c* . . . .Ps 150:5

CYPRESS—*a hardwood tree*
Used by idol-makers . . . . .Is 44:14-17

CYPRUS (sī'prŭs)—*"fairness"*
A large Mediterranean island; home of Barnabas . . . . .Acts 4:36
Christians reach . . . . .Acts 11:19, 20
Paul visits . . . . .Acts 13:4-13
Barnabas visits . . . . .Acts 15:39
Paul twice sails past . . . . .Acts 21:3

we sailed under *C*, because . . . .Acts 27:4

CYRENE (sī-rē'nē)—*"wall"*
A Greek colonial city in North Africa; home of Simon . . . . .Matt 27:32
People from, at Pentecost.Acts 2:10
Synagogue of . . . . .Acts 6:9
Some from, become missionaries . . . . .Acts 11:20

[*also* CYRENIAN]
compel one Simon a *C* . . . . .Mark 15:21
hold upon one Simon, a *C* . . . .Luke 23:26
Lucius of *C* and Manaen . . . . . .Acts 13:1

CYRENIUS (sī-rē'nĕ-ŭs)—*of Cyrene*
Roman governor of Syria Luke 2:1-4

CYRUS (sī'rŭs)—*sun; throne*
Prophecies concerning, God's:
"Anointed" . . . . .Is 45:1
Liberator . . . . .Is 45:1
Rebuilder . . . . .Is 44:28

the first year of *C* king of 2Chr 36:22
Lord stirred..spirit of *C* 2Chr 36:22
year of *C* king of Persia . . . . . . .Ezra 1:1
the Lord stirred..spirit of *C* . . . .Ezra 1:1
grant that they had of *C* . . . . .Ezra 3:7
as king *C* the king of Persia . . .Ezra 4:3
year of *C* the king of Babylon .Ezra 5:13
the same king *C* made a . . . . . .Ezra 5:13
of *C* the king the same *C* . . . . .Ezra 6:3
of *C* He is my shepherd . . . . . . .Is 44:28
Lord to his anointed, to *C* . . . .Is 45:1
the first year of king *C* . . . . .Dan 1:21
reign of *C* the Persian . . . . .Dan 6:28
year of *C* king of Persia . . . . . . .Dan 10:1

D

DABAREH (dăb'ă-rĕ)—*"pasture"—a city of Issachar*
D with her suburbs . . . . .Josh 21:28

DABBASHETH (dăb'ă-shĕth)—*"camel hump"*
Town of Zebulun . . . . .Josh 19:10, 11

DABERATH (dăb'ĕ-răth)—*"pasture"—a city of Issachar*
Correct rendering of Dabareh . . . . .Josh 21:28
Assigned to Gershomites .1Chr 6:71, 72

and then goeth out to *D* . . . . . .Josh 19:12

DAGGER—*a short weapon for stabbing*
Ehud made him a *d* which . . . .Judg 3:16

DAGON (dā'gŏn)—*"fish"*
The national god of the Philistines . . . . .Judg 16:23
Falls before ark 1Sam 5:1-5

his head in the temple of *D* . . .1Chr 10:10

DAILY—*occurring every day*
Fulfill your works your *d* . . . . . . .Ex 5:13
as much as they gather *d* . . . . . .Ex 16:5
the *d* meat offering and the . . .Num 4:16
manner ye shall offer *d* . . . . . . .Num 28:24
d burnt offering and his . . . . . . .Num 29:6
pressed him *d* with her . . . . .Judg 16:16
a *d* rate for every day 2Kin 25:30
his *d* portion for their 2Chr 31:16
the *d* burnt offerings by . . . . . . .Ezra 3:4
prepared for me *d* was one . . . .Neh 5:18
when they spake *d* unto . . . . . . .Esth 3:4
having sorrow in my heart *d*? . . .Ps 13:2
while they say *d* unto me . . . . .Ps 42:10
he fighting *d* oppresseth . . . . . . .Ps 56:1
enemies would *d* swallow . . . . . .Ps 56:2
I may *d* perform my vows . . . . .Ps 61:8
who *d* loadeth us with . . . . .Ps 68:19
and *d* shall he be praised . . . . . .Ps 72:15
foolish..reproacheth thee *d* . . . .Ps 74:22
Lord *d* for I cry unto thee *d* . . .Ps 86:3
Lord, I..called *d* upon thee . . . .Ps 88:9
and I was *d* his delight . . . . .Prov 8:30
Yet they seek me *d*, and . . . . . . .Is 58:2
d rising up early and . . . . .Jer 7:25
I am in derision *d*, every . . . . . .Jer 20:7
d a piece of bread out of . . . . . .Jer 37:21
shall have distresses *d* . . . . .Ezek 30:16
without blemish *d* the seven . . .Ezek 45:23
shalt *d* prepare a burnt . . . . .Ezek 46:13
appointed them a *d* . . . . .Dan 1:5
the *d* sacrifice was taken . . . . . .Dan 8:11
shall take away the *d* . . . . .Dan 11:31
d sacrifice shall be taken . . . . . .Dan 12:11
d increaseth lies and . . . . .Hos 12:1
Give us this day our *d* . . . . .Matt 6:11
I sat *d* with you teaching . . . . . .Matt 26:55
was *d* with you in the . . . . .Mark 14:49
and take up his cross *d* . . . . . . .Luke 9:23
us day by day our *d* bread . . . .Luke 11:3
he taught *d* in the temple . . . . .Luke 19:47
d with you in the temple . . . . . .Luke 22:53
continuing *d* with one . . . . .Acts 2:46
Lord added to the church *d* . . .Acts 2:47
whom they laid *d* at the . . . . . . .Acts 3:2
And *d* in the temple, and in . . .Acts 5:42
neglected..*d* ministration . . . . . .Acts 6:1
increased in number *d* . . . . .Acts 16:5
searched the scriptures *d* . . . . . .Acts 17:11
disputing *d* in the school . . . . . .Acts 19:9
Jesus our Lord, I die *d* 1Cor 15:31
which cometh upon me *d* 2Cor 11:28
exhort one another *d* . . . . .Heb 3:13
Who needeth not *d*, as . . . . .Heb 7:27
naked, and destitute of *d* . . . . . .James 2:15

DAINTIES—*savory food; delicacies*
Used as a warning . . . . . . .Prov 23:3-6
Unrighteous fellowship . . .Ps 141:4

[*also* DAINTY]
and he shall yield royal *d* . . . . .Gen 49:20
abhorreth bread..soul *d* . . . . . . .Job 33:20
things which were *d* and . . . . . .Rev 18:14

DALAIAH (dă-lā'yă)—*"Jehovah is deliverer"—a descendant of Judah*
Johanan, and *D*, and Anani . . .1Chr 3:24

DALE, THE KING'S
A valley near Jerusalem. .Gen 14:17-20
Site of Absalom's monument 2Sam 18:18

DALETH (dä'lĭth)
The fourth letter in the Hebrew alphabet . . . . . .Ps 119:25-32

DALMANUTHA (dăl-mă-nū'thă)—*"bucket"*
A place near the Sea of Galilee . . . . .Mark 8:10

DALMATIA (dăl-mā'shĭ-ă)—*"deceitful"*
A region east of the Adriatic Sea; Titus departs to 2Tim 4:10

DALPHON (dăl'fŏn)—*"swift"*
A son of Haman . . . . .Esth 9:7-10

DAM—*mother (used of a domestic animal)*
Laws concerning:
Animals . . . . Ex 22:30
Birds . . . . Deut 22:6, 7
be seven days under the ***d*** . . . . Lev 22:27

DAMAGE—*loss; harm; injury*
why should ***d*** grow to the . . . . Ezra 4:22
countervail the king's ***d*** . . . . Esth 7:4
off the feet, and drinketh ***d*** . . . Prov 26:6
king should have no ***d*** . . . . Dan 6:2
with hurt and much ***d*** . . . . Acts 27:10
that ye might receive ***d*** by 2Cor 7:9

DAMAGES AND REMUNERATION
In law for:
Personal injury . . . . Ex 21:18, 19
Causing miscarriage . . . . Ex 21:22
Injuries by animals . . . . Ex 21:28-32
Injuries to animals . . . . Ex 21:33-35
Losses . . . . Ex 22:1-15
Stealing . . . . Lev 6:1-7
Defaming a wife . . . . Deut 22:13-19
Rape . . . . Deut 22:28, 29
In practice:
Jacob's . . . . Gen 31:38-42
Samson's . . . . Judg 16:28-30
Tamar's 2Sam 13:22-32
Zacchaeus' . . . . Luke 19:8
Paul's . . . . Acts 16:35-39
Philemon's . . . . Philem 10-18

DAMARIS (dăm′ă-rĭs)—*"heifer"*
An Athenian woman converted by Paul . . . . Acts 17:33, 34

DAMASCUS (dă-măs′kŭs)—*"sackful of blood"—chief city of Aram*
In the Old Testament:
Abram passed through . . . Gen 14:15
Abram heir from . . . . Gen 15:2
Captured by David 2Sam 8:5, 6
Rezon, king of 1Kin 11:23, 24
Ben-hadad, king of 1Kin 15:18
Rivers of, mentioned 2Kin 5:12
Elisha's prophecy in 2Kin 8:7-15
Taken by Assyrians 2Kin 16:9
Prophecies concerning . . . Is 8:4
In the New Testament, Paul:
Journeys to . . . . Acts 9:1-9
Is converted near . . . . Acts 9:3-19
First preaches at . . . . Acts 9:20-22
Escapes from 2Cor 11:32, 33
Revisits . . . . Gal 1:17

Syrians of ***D*** came to 2Sam 8:5
put garrisons in Syria of ***D*** 2Sam 8:6
way to the wilderness of ***D*** 1Kin 19:15
make streets for thee in ***D*** 1Kin 20:34
he recovered ***D***, and Hamath . . 2Kin 14:28
king Ahaz went to ***D*** to 2Kin 16:10
an altar that was at ***D*** 2Kin 16:10
king Ahaz had sent from ***D*** . . . 2Kin 16:11
king Ahaz came from ***D*** 2Kin 16:11
king was come from ***D*** 2Kin 16:12
when the Syrians of ***D*** 1Chr 18:5
king of Syria, that dwelt at ***D*** . . 2Chr 16:2
spoil of them..king of ***D*** 2Chr 24:23
captives, and..them to ***D*** 2Chr 28:5
he sacrificed..gods of ***D*** 2Chr 28:23
Lebanon..looketh toward ***D*** . . . Song 7:4
the head of Syria is ***D*** . . . . Is 7:8
and the head of ***D*** is Rezin . . . . Is 7:8
is not Samaria as ***D***? . . . . Is 10:9
The burden of ***D***, Behold . . . . Is 17:1
D is taken away from being . . . Is 17:1
and the kingdom from ***D*** . . . . Is 17:8
Concerning ***D***, Hamath is . . . . Jer 49:23
D is waxed feeble, and . . . . Jer 49:24
kindle a fire in the wall of ***D*** . . Jer 49:27
D was thy merchant in the . . . . Ezek 27:18
is between the border of ***D*** . . . . Ezek 47:16
the border of ***D***, and the . . . . Ezek 47:17
from ***D***, and from Gilead . . . . Ezek 47:18
the border of ***D*** northward . . . . Ezek 48:1
three transgressions of ***D*** . . . . Amos 1:3
I will break..the bar of ***D*** . . . . Amos 1:5
and in ***D*** in a couch . . . . Amos 3:12
into captivity beyond ***D*** . . . . Amos 5:27
and ***D*** shall be the rest . . . . Zech 9:1
how..preached boldly at ***D*** . . . . Acts 9:27
and went to ***D***, to bring . . . . Acts 22:5
and was come nigh unto ***D*** . . . . Acts 22:6
Arise, and go into ***D***; and . . . . Acts 22:10
with me, I came into ***D*** . . . . Acts 22:11
Whereupon as I went to ***D*** . . . . Acts 26:12
But showed first..of ***D*** . . . . Acts 26:20

DAMNATION—*condemnatory judgment*
Described as:
Having degrees . . . . Matt 23:14
Just . . . . Rom 3:8
Justified . . . . Rom 13:2
Self-inflicted 1Cor 11:29
Merited 1Tim 5:12
Inflicted:
Now . . . . Rom 14:23
In eternity . . . . Matt 23:33

[*also* DAMNABLE, DAMNED]
is in danger of eternal ***d*** . . . . Mark 3:29
shall receive greater ***d*** . . . . Mark 12:40
believeth not shall be ***d*** . . . . Mark 16:16
shall receive greater ***d*** . . . . Luke 20:47
unto the resurrection of ***d*** . . . . John 5:29
That they all might be ***d*** 2Thess 2:12
privily shall bring in ***d*** 2Pet 2:1
not, and their ***d*** slumbereth . . . 2Pet 2:3

DAMSEL—*a young woman*
Rebekah . . . . Gen 24:57
Ruth . . . . Ruth 2:5, 6
Raised by Jesus . . . . Mark 5:39-42
Demands John's head . . . . Matt 14:10, 11
Questions Peter . . . . John 18:17
Is disbelieved . . . . Acts 12:13-17
Healed by Paul . . . . Acts 16:16-18

[*also* DAMSEL'S, DAMSELS]
the ***d*** to whom I shall say . . . . Gen 24:14
And the ***d*** was very fair to . . . . Gen 24:16
And the ***d*** ran, and told . . . . Gen 24:28
Let the ***d*** abide with us a . . . . Gen 24:55
Rebekah arose, and her ***d*** . . . . Gen 24:61
and he loved the ***d***, and . . . . Gen 34:3
spake kindly unto the ***d*** . . . . Gen 34:3
saying, Get me this ***d*** to . . . . Gen 34:4
unto me; but give me the ***d*** . . . Gen 34:12
father of the ***d***, and her . . . . Deut 22:15
bring forth the tokens..***d*** . . . . Deut 22:15
And the ***d*** father shall say . . . . Deut 22:16
unto the father of the ***d*** . . . . Deut 22:19
of virginity be not found..***d*** . . . . Deut 22:20
they shall bring out the ***d*** . . . . Deut 22:21
a ***d*** that is a virgin be . . . . Deut 22:23
the ***d***, because she cried . . . . Deut 22:24
if a man find a betrothed ***d*** . . . . Deut 22:25
unto the ***d*** thou shalt do . . . . Deut 22:26
there is in the ***d*** no sin . . . . Deut 22:26
the betrothed ***d*** cried, and . . . . Deut 22:27
If a man find a ***d*** that is a . . . . Deut 22:28
shall give unto the ***d*** father . . . . Deut 22:29
to every man a ***d*** or two . . . . Judg 5:30
the father of the ***d*** saw him . . . Judg 19:3
the ***d*** father, retained him . . . . Judg 19:4
d father said unto his son . . . . Judg 19:5
the ***d*** father had said unto . . . . Judg 19:6
and the ***d*** father said . . . . Judg 19:8
his father-in-law, the ***d*** . . . . Judg 19:9
with five ***d*** of hers that went . . 1Sam 25:42
So they sought for a fair ***d*** 1Kin 1:3
And the ***d*** was very fair 1Kin 1:4
were the ***d*** playing with . . . . Ps 68:25
and a ***d*** came unto him . . . . Matt 26:69
the king said unto the ***d*** . . . . Mark 6:22
and gave it to the ***d***: and . . . . Mark 6:28
the ***d*** gave it to her mother . . . . Mark 6:28

DAN (dăn)—*"judge"*
1. Jacob's son by Bilhah . . . Gen 30:6
Prophecy concerning . . . . Gen 49:16, 17
2. *Tribe of:*
Census of . . . . Num 1:38, 39
Position of . . . . Num 2:25, 31
Blessing of . . . . Deut 33:22
Inheritance of . . . . Josh 19:40-47
Conquest by . . . . Josh 19:47
Failure of . . . . Judg 1:34, 35
Idolatry of . . . . Judg 18:1-31
3. *Town of:*
Called Leshem . . . . Josh 19:47
Captured by Danites . . . . Josh 19:47
Northern boundary of Israel . . . . Judg 20:1
Center of idolatry 1Kin 12:28-30
Destroyed by Ben-hadad . 1Kin 15:20
Later references to . . . . Jer 4:15

and pursued them unto ***D*** . . . . Gen 14:14
Rachel's handmaid; ***D*** . . . . Gen 35:25
And the sons of ***D***; Hushim . . . Gen 46:23
D, and Naphtali, Gad, and . . . . Ex 1:4
of Ahisamach..tribe of ***D*** . . . . Ex 31:6
Ahisamach..tribe of ***D*** . . . . Ex 35:34
tribe of ***D***, an engraver . . . . Ex 38:23
of Dibri, of the tribe of ***D*** . . . . Lev 24:11
Of ***D***; Ahiezer the son of . . . . Num 1:12
prince of the children of ***D*** . . . . Num 7:66
camp of the children of ***D*** . . . . Num 10:25
tribe of ***D***, Ammiel the son . . . Num 13:12
the sons of ***D*** after their . . . . Num 26:42
families of ***D*** after their . . . . Num 26:42
tribe of the children of ***D*** . . . . Num 34:22
Asher, and Zebulun, ***D*** . . . . Deut 27:13
land of Gilead, unto ***D*** . . . . Deut 34:1
tribe of the children of ***D*** . . . . Josh 19:48
and out of the tribe of ***D*** . . . . Josh 21:5
of the tribe of ***D***, Eltekeh . . . . Josh 21:23
and why did ***D*** remain in . . . . Judg 5:17
times in the camp of ***D*** . . . . Judg 13:25
from ***D*** even to Beer-sheba 1Sam 3:20
from ***D*** even to Beer-sheba 2Sam 3:10
from ***D*** even to Beer-sheba 2Sam 17:11
from ***D*** even to Beer-sheba 2Sam 24:2
from ***D*** even to Beer-sheba 2Sam 24:15
from ***D***, even to Beer-sheba . . . 1Kin 4:25
in Beth-el..were in ***D*** 2Kin 10:29
D, Joseph, and Benjamin 1Chr 2:2
from Beer-sheba even to ***D*** 1Chr 21:2
Of ***D***, Azareel the son of 1Chr 27:22
a woman..daughters of ***D*** 2Chr 2:14
smote Ijon, and ***D***, and Abel . . 2Chr 16:4
from Beer-sheba even to ***D*** 2Chr 30:5
horses was heard from ***D*** . . . . Jer 8:16
D also and Javan going to . . . . Ezek 27:19
west; a portion for ***D*** . . . . Ezek 48:1
border of ***D***, from the . . . . Ezek 48:2
Benjamin, one gate of ***D*** . . . . Ezek 48:32
and say, Thy god, O ***D*** . . . . Amos 8:14

DANCE—*series of rhythmic, patterned body movements usually set to music*
Kinds of:
Joyful . . . . Ps 30:11
Evil . . . . Ex 32:19
Designed to:
Express joy in victory 1Sam 18:6, 7
Greet a returning son . . . . Luke 15:23-25
Rejoice in the Lord 2Sam 6:14-16
Inflame lust . . . . Matt 14:6
Performed by:
Children . . . . Matt 11:16,17
Women . . . . Judg 11:34
David 2Sam 6:14,16
Worshipers . . . . Ps 149:3

[*also* DANCED, DANCES]
with timbrels, and with ***d*** . . . . Ex 15:20
Shiloh come out to ***d*** in ***d*** . . . . Judg 21:21
number, of them, that ***d*** . . . . Judg 21:23
one to another of him in ***d*** 1Sam 21:11
sang one to another in ***d*** 1Sam 29:5
flock, and their children ***d*** . . . . Job 21:11
Praise him..timbrel and ***d*** . . . . Ps 150:4
there, and satyrs shall ***d*** . . . . Is 13:21
go forth in the ***d*** of them . . . . Jer 31:4
the virgin rejoice in the ***d*** . . . . Jer 31:13
d is turned into mourning . . . . Lam 5:15
you, and ye have not ***d*** . . . . Luke 7:32

DANCING—*rhythmic movement of the feet and body*
David only 2Sam 6:14-16
Greeting a prodigal . . . . . Luke 15:20, 23-25
Lustful exhibition . . . . . Mark 6:22
Religious exercise 1Chr 15:25-29
Time of rejoicing 1Sam 18:6, 7
Time to dance . . . . . Eccl 3:4
Young women alone . . . . . Judg 21:20, 21
eating and drinking, and *d* 1Sam 30:16

DANDLED—*move up and down (as with baby) in affectionate play*
and be *d* upon her knees . . . . . Is 66:12

DANGER—*risk; peril*
Physical . . . . . Acts 27:9-44
Spiritual . . . . . Heb 2:1-3
Comfort in . . . . . Acts 27:22-25
Jesus sought in . . . . . Luke 8:22-24
Of many kinds 2Cor 11:23-33
Paul's escape from . . . . . Acts 9:22-25
in *d* of the judgment . . . . . Matt 5:21
shall be in *d* of the council . . . . Matt 5:22
thou fool, shall be in *d* of . . . . . Matt 5:22
d of eternal damnation . . . . . Mark 3:29
only this our craft is in *d* . . . . . Acts 19:27
we are in *d* to be called . . . . . Acts 19:40

DANIEL (dăn'yĕl)—*"God is my judge"*
1. Son of David 1Chr 3:1
Called Chileab 2Sam 3:2, 3
2. Postexilic priest . . . . . Ezra 8:1, 2
Signs covenant . . . . . Neh 10:6
3. Taken to Babylon . . . . . Dan 1:1-7
Refuses king's choice foods . . . . . Dan 1:8
Interprets dreams . . . . . Dan 2:1-45
Honored by Nebuchadnezzar . . . . . Dan 2:46-49
Interprets handwriting . . . Dan 5:10-29
Made a high official . . . . . Dan 6:1-3
Conspired against . . . . . Dan 6:4-15
Cast into lion's den . . . . Dan 6:16-22
Honored by Belshazzar . . Dan 5:29
Vision of beasts . . . . . Dan 7:1-28
Vision of ram and goat . . Dan 8:1-27
Great confession of . . . . . Dan 9:1-19
Vision of the seventy weeks . . . . . Dan 9:20-27
Vision by the great river . Dan 10:1-21
Vision of the kings . . . . . Dan 11:1-45
Vision of the two men . . Dan 12:1-13
three men, Noah, *D*, and Job. . Ezek 14:14
Noah, *D*, and Job, were . . . . . Ezek 14:20
Behold, thou art wiser than *D* . Ezek 28:3
children of Judah, *D* . . . . . Dan 1:6
God had brought *D* into . . . . . Dan 1:9
of the eunuchs said unto *D* . . . . Dan 1:10
D to Melzar, whom the..prince . Dan 1:11
eunuchs had set over *D* . . . . . Dan 1:11
D had understanding in all . . . . Dan 1:17
all was found none like *D* . . . . . Dan 1:19
D continued even unto the . . . . Dan 1:21
the last *D* came in before . . . . . Dan 4:8
in the same *D*, whom the . . . . . Dan 5:12
and they clothed *D* with . . . . . Dan 5:29
that they should take *D* up . . . . Dan 6:23
the den. So *D* was taken . . . . . Dan 6:23
men which had accused *D* . . . . . Dan 6:24
fear before the God of *D* . . . . . Dan 6:26
hath delivered *D* from the . . . . . Dan 6:27
D prospered in the reign . . . . . Dan 6:28
D had a dream and visions . . . . Dan 7:1
said he unto me, Fear not, *D* . . Dan 10:12
spoken of by *D* the prophet . . . Matt 24:15
spoken of by *D* the prophet . . . Mark 13:14

DANIEL—*book of the Old Testament*
History in Babylon . . . . . Dan 1—6
Prophecy of nations . . . . . Dan 2:4-45
Visions . . . . . Dan 7, 8
Kingdom . . . . . Dan 9—12

DANITES (dăn'īts)
Descendants of Dan . . . . . Judg 13:2
Zorah..the family of the *D* . . . . Judg 13:2
tribe of the *D* sought . . . . . Judg 18:1
of the family of the *D* . . . . . Judg 18:11
And of the *D* expert in war . . . 1Chr 12:35

DAN-JAAN (dăn-jā'ăn)—*"judgment"*
Town near Zidon 2Sam 24:6

DANNAH (dăn'ä)—*"judging"*
A city of Judah . . . . . Josh 15:49

DARDA (dâr'ä)—*"bearer (pearl) of wisdom"*
Famed for wisdom 1Kin 4:31
Also called Dara 1Chr 2:6

DARE—*to challenge; presume; have courage*

[*also* DURST]

that *d* presume in his heart . . . . Esth 7:5
and *d* not show you mine . . . . . Job 32:6
None is so fierce that *d* stir . . . Job 41:10
neither *d* any man from . . . . . Matt 22:46
no man after that *d* ask . . . . . Mark 12:34
they *d* did ask him any . . . . . Luke 20:40
none of the disciples *d* ask . . . . John 21:12
And of the rest *d* no man . . . . . Acts 5:13
Moses trembled, and *d* not . . . . Acts 7:32
man some would even *d* to . . . . Rom 5:7
For I will not *d* to speak . . . . . Rom 15:18
D any of you, having a 1Cor 6:1
For we *d* not make 2Cor 10:12
d not bring against him a . . . . . Jude 9

DARIUS (dä-rī'ŭs)—*"he that informs himself"*
1. *Darius the Mede:*
Son of Ahasuerus . . . . . Dan 9:1
Succeeds Belshazzar . . . . . Dan 5:30, 31
Co-ruler with Cyrus . . . . . Dan 6:28
Made king of the Chaldeans . . . . . Dan 9:1
2. *Darius Hystaspis* (521-486 B.C.)
King of all Persia . . . . . Ezra 4:5
Confirms Cyrus' royal edict . . . . . Ezra 6:1-14
Temple work dated by his reign . . . . . Ezra 4:24
Prophets during his reign . Hag 1:1
3. *Darius the Persian* (424-404 B.C.)
Priestly records to reign. . Neh 12:22
till the matter came to *D* . . . . . Ezra 5:5
on the river, sent unto *D* . . . . . Ezra 5:6
thus; Unto *D* the king, all . . . . . Ezra 5:7
sixth year of the reign of *D* . . . Ezra 6:15
It pleased *D* to set over the . . . Dan 6:1
thus unto him, King *D*, live . . Dan 6:6
Wherefore king *D* signed . . . . . Dan 6:9
Then king *D* wrote unto all . . . Dan 6:25
I in the first year of *D* . . . . . Dan 11:1
in the second year of *D* the . . . Hag 1:15
in the second year of *D* . . . . . Hag 2:10
in the second year of *D* . . . . . Zech 1:1
Sebat, in the second year of *D* . Zech 1:7
fourth year of king *D* . . . . . Zech 7:1

DARK SAYINGS—*riddles; secrets*
Speaks openly . . . . . Num 12:8
Utter of old . . . . . Ps 78:2

DARKNESS—*absence of light; nightfall; ignorance; moral or spiritual destitution*

Kinds of:
Pre-creational . . . . . Gen 1:2-4
Natural . . . . . Gen 15:17
Miraculous . . . . . Ex 10:21, 22
Supernatural . . . . . Matt 27:45
Spiritual . . . . . Acts 13:8-11
Eternal . . . . . Matt 8:12

Illustrative of:
God's unsearchableness . . Ps 97:2
The way of sin . . . . . Eph 5:11
Afflictions . . . . . Ps 112:4
Moral depravity . . . . . Rom 13:12
Ignorance 1John 2:8-11
Death . . . . . Job 10:21, 22
Hell . . . . . Matt 22:13

[*also* DARK, DARKEN, DARKENED, DARKENETH, DARKISH, DARKLY, DARKNESS]

horror of great *d* fell upon . . . . Gen 15:12
earth, so that the land..*d* . . . . . Ex 10:15
it was a cloud and *d* to . . . . . Ex 14:20
drew near unto the thick *d* . . . . Ex 20:21
plague be somewhat *d* . . . . . Lev 13:6
skin, but be somewhat *d* . . . . . Lev 13:21
skin, but be somewhat *d* . . . . . Lev 13:26
skin, but it be somewhat *d* . . . . Lev 13:28
skin of their flesh be *d* . . . . . Lev 13:39
the plague be somewhat *d* . . . . . Lev 13:56
midst of heaven, with *d* . . . . . Deut 4:11
clouds, and thick *d* . . . . . Deut 4:11
cloud, and of the thick *d* . . . . . Deut 5:22
as the blind gropeth in *d* . . . . . Deut 28:29
when it was *d*, that the men . . . Josh 2:5
d between you..Egyptians . . . . . Josh 24:7
the wicked..silent in *d* 1Sam 2:9
and *d* was under his feet 2Sam 22:10
round about him, *d* waters 2Sam 22:12
Lord will lighten my *d* 2Sam 22:29
would dwell in the thick *d* 1Kin 8:12
would dwell in the thick *d* 2Chr 6:1
gates of Jerusalem began..*d* . . . Neh 13:19
Let..day be *d*; let not God . . . . Job 3:4
Let *d* and the shadow of . . . . . Job 3:5
stars..twilight thereof be *d* . . . . Job 3:9
discovereth deep things..*d* . . . . . Job 12:22
grope in the *d* without light . . . Job 12:25
he shall return out of *d* . . . . . Job 15:22
light is short because of *d* . . . . . Job 17:12
I have made my bed..*d* . . . . . Job 17:13
light..*d* in his tabernacle . . . . . Job 18:6
be driven from light unto *d* . . . . Job 18:18
he hath set *d* in my paths . . . . . Job 19:8
d shall be hid in his secret . . . . Job 20:26
Or *d*, that thou canst not . . . . . Job 22:11
he judge through the *d* . . . . . Job 22:13
not cut off before the *d* . . . . . Job 23:17
neither..he covered the *d* . . . . . Job 23:17
In the *d* they dig through . . . . . Job 24:16
He setteth an end of *d*, and . . . Job 28:3
the stones of *d*, and the . . . . . Job 28:3
light I walked through *d* . . . . . Job 29:3
I waited for light..came *d* . . . . . Job 30:26
There is no *d*, nor shadow . . . . Job 34:22
our speech by reason of *d* . . . . . Job 37:19
Who is this that *d* counsel . . . . . Job 38:2
thick *d* a swaddling band . . . . . Job 38:9
and as for *d*, where is the . . . . . Job 38:19
and *d* was under his feet . . . . . Ps 18:9
He made *d* his secret place . . . . Ps 18:11
round about him were *d* . . . . . Ps 18:11
my God will enlighten my *d* . . . Ps 18:28
Let their way be *d* and . . . . . Ps 35:6
open my *d* saying upon . . . . . Ps 49:4
Let their eyes be *d*, that . . . . . Ps 69:23
the *d* places of the earth . . . . . Ps 74:20
understand; they walk..*d* . . . . . Ps 82:5
lowest pit, in *d*, in the deeps . . Ps 88:6
wonders, be known in the *d*? . . Ps 88:12
pestilence..walketh in *d* . . . . . Ps 91:6
d are round about him . . . . . Ps 97:2
Thou makest *d*, and it is . . . . . Ps 104:20
He sent *d* and made it *d* . . . . . Ps 105:28
Such as sit in *d* and in the . . . . Ps 107:10
there ariseth light in the *d* . . . . Ps 112:4
Yea, the *d* hideth not from . . . . Ps 139:12
he hath..me to dwell in *d* . . . . . Ps 143:3
of the wise, and their *d* . . . . . Prov 1:6
to walk in the ways of *d* . . . . . Prov 2:13
The way..wicked is as *d* . . . . . Prov 4:19
evening in the black and *d* . . . . Prov 7:9
be put out in obscure *d* . . . . . Prov 20:20
as far as light excelleth *d* . . . . . Eccl 2:13
All his days..eateth in *d* . . . . . Eccl 5:17
vanity, and departeth in *d* . . . . . Eccl 6:4
be not *d*, nor the clouds . . . . . Eccl 12:2
d for light, and light for *d* . . . . Is 5:20
light is *d* in the heavens . . . . . Is 5:30

trouble and *d*, dimness ....Is 8:22
The people that walked in *d*...Is 9:2
Lord of hosts is the land *d* ....Is 9:19
sun..*d* in his going forth ....Is 13:10
all joy is *d*, the mirth of ......Is 24:11
their works are in the *d* ....Is 29:15
obscurity, and out of *d*........Is 29:18
them that sit in *d* out of the...Is 42:7
I will..the treasures of *d* ......Is 45:3
secret, in a *d* place of the .....Is 45:19
Sit thou silent, and..into *d* ....Is 47:5
to them that are in *d*, Show ...Is 49:9
walketh in *d*, and hath no .....Is 50:10
and thy *d* be as the noon .....Is 58:10
brightness..we walk in *d* ......Is 59:9
the *d* shall cover the earth ....Is 60:2
unto Israel? a land of *d*? ......Jer 2:31
before he cause *d*, and ....Jer 13:16
stumble..*d* mountains ....Jer 13:16
led me, and brought..*d*.........Lam 3:2
He hath sent me in *d* places ...Lam 3:6
the house of Israel do..*d* ......Ezek 8:12
shall be *d* when I shall ....Ezek 30:18
make the stars thereof *d* ......Ezek 32:7
over thee, and set *d* upon .....Ezek 32:8
scattered in..cloudy and *d* .....Ezek 34:12
knoweth what is in the *d*......Dan 2:22
and understanding *d* ....Dan 8:23
A day of *d*..gloominess ....Joel 2:2
sun..the moon shall be *d* ......Joel 2:10
sun..moon shall be *d*..........Joel 3:15
that maketh the morning *d* ....Amos 4:13
maketh the day *d* with ....Amos 5:8
the day of the Lord is *d*.......Amos 5:18
and it shall be *d* unto you .....Mic 3:6
and the day shall be *d* over ...Mic 3:6
I sit in *d*, the Lord shall ......Mic 7:8
and *d* shall pursue his ....Nah 1:8
a day of *d* and gloominess .....Zeph 1:15
a day of clouds and thick *d*....Zeph 1:15
his right eye..utterly *d* ....Zech 11:17
The people which sat in *d* .....Matt 4:16
thy whole body..full of *d* ......Matt 6:23
be *d*, how great is that *d*! .....Matt 6:23
What I tell you in *d*, that .....Matt 10:27
of those days..sun be *d* ....Matt 24:29
unprofitable servant..outer *d*...Matt 25:30
the sun shall be *d*, and the ....Mark 13:24
there was *d* over the whole ....Mark 15:33
give light..that sit in *d* ....Luke 1:79
evil, thy body..full of *d* ....Luke 11:34
full of light..no part *d*.........Luke 11:36
whatsoever..spoken in *d*.......Luke 12:3
hour, and the power of *d* .....Luke 22:53
there was a *d* over all the .....Luke 23:44
And the sun was *d*..veil ....Luke 23:45
And the light shineth in *d* .....John 1:5
the *d* comprehended it not ....John 1:5
men loved *d* rather than ......John 3:19
it was now *d*, and Jesus ....John 6:17
followeth me..walk in *d* ....John 8:12
the light, lest *d* come upon ....John 12:35
for he that walketh in *d*.......John 12:35
Magdalene early..was yet *d*....John 20:1
sun shall be turned..*d*.........Acts 2:20
to turn them from *d* to........Acts 26:18
their foolish heart was *d* ......Rom 1:21
of them which are in *d*.......Rom 2:19
Let their eyes be *d*, that ......Rom 11:10
the hidden things of *d* 1Cor 4:5
we see through a glass *d* 1Cor 13:12
the light to shine out of *d* 2Cor 4:6
communion hath light..*d*? 2Cor 6:14
Having the understanding *d* ...Eph 4:18
ye were sometimes *d*, but .....Eph 5:8
the rulers of the *d* of this .....Eph 6:12
delivered us..power of *d* ......Col 1:13
ye, brethren, are not in *d* 1Thess 5:4
nor unto blackness, and *d* .....Heb 12:18
hath called you out of *d*.......1Pet 2:9
light that shineth in a *d* 2Pet 1:19
delivered them..chains of *d* 2Pet 2:4
light, and in him is no *d* 1John 1:5
everlasting chains under *d* .....Jude 6
third part of them was *d* ......Rev 8:12
sun and the air were *d* ....Rev 9:2
kingdom was full of *d*.........Rev 16:10

DARKON (där'kŏn)—*"carrier"*
Founder of a family .....Neh 7:58

of Jaalah, the children of *D* ...Ezra 2:56

DARLING—*"only one"*
Used poetically of the soul ....Ps 35:17

my *d* from the power of the ...Ps 22:20

DART—*short spear*
Absalom slain by 2Sam 18:14
Figurative of sin's penalty.Prov 7:23
Figurative of Satan's weapons ....Eph 6:16

[*also* DARTS]
he took three *d* in his hand ...2Sam 18:14
d and shields in abundance 2Chr 32:5
the *d*, nor the habergeon ......Job 41:26
D are counted as stubble ......Job 41:29
Till a *d* strike through his .....Prov 7:23
the fiery *d* of the wicked ......Eph 6:16
or thrust through with a *d*.....Heb 12:20

DASH—*to hurl; destroy*

[*also* DASHED, DASHETH]
hand, O Lord, hath *d* in ......Ex 15:6
wilt *d* their children, and 2Kin 8:12
thou shalt *d* them in pieces ....Ps 2:9
thou *d* thy foot against a ......Ps 91:12
taketh and *d* thy little ....Ps 137:9
children also shall be *d* to .....Is 13:16
shall *d* the young men to ......Is 13:18
d them one against another....Jer 13:14
the mother was *d* in pieces ....Hos 10:14
their infants shall be *d* in......Hos 13:16
He that *d* in pieces is come ...Nah 2:1
children also were *d* in ....Nah 3:10
thou *d* thy foot against a ......Matt 4:6
thou *d* thy foot against a ......Luke 4:11

DATHAN (dā'thăn)—*"front"*
A Reubenite ....Num 26:7-11
Joins Korah's rebellion...Num 16:1-35
Swallowed up by the earth ....Ps 106:17

he did unto *D* and Abiram ....Deut 11:6

DAUB—*to cover or coat*

[*also* DAUBED, DAUBING]
d it with slime and with ....Ex 2:3
d it with untempered ....Ezek 13:10
d it with untempered ....Ezek 13:11
Where is the *d* wherewith .....Ezek 13:12
And her prophets have *d*......Ezek 22:28

DAUGHTER—*female offspring*
Applied to:
Female child ....Gen 20:12
Female inhabitants of a city ....Judg 21:1
Female worshipers of God.................Is 43:6
Citizens of a town ....Ps 9:14
Described as:
Licentious ....Gen 19:30-38
Dutiful ....Judg 11:36-39
Ideal ....Prov 31:29
Beautiful ....Ps 45:9-13
Careless ....Is 32:9-11
Prophesy ....Joel 2:28

[*also* DAUGHTER'S, DAUGHTERS]
years..begat sons and *d* ....Gen 5:4
earth, and *d* were born ....Gen 6:1
the sons of God saw the *d* ....Gen 6:2
and begat sons and *d* ....Gen 11:11
Milcah, the *d* of Haran, the ...Gen 11:29
have two *d* which have not ....Gen 19:8
she is not the *d* of my father ..Gen 20:12
but not the *d* of my mother ...Gen 20:12
of the *d* of the Canaanites.....Gen 24:3
Whose *d* art thou: tell me .....Gen 24:23
the *d* of Bethuel the Syrian....Gen 25:20
Judith the *d* of Beeri the ......Gen 26:34
because of the *d* of Heth ......Gen 27:46
Jacob take a wife..*d* of Heth ..Gen 27:46
these which are of the *d* of....Gen 27:46
a wife of the *d* of Canaan .....Gen 28:1
Mahalath the *d* of Ishmael ....Gen 28:9
his *d* cometh with ....Gen 29:6
Laban had two *d*: the name ...Gen 29:16
d will call me blessed ....Gen 30:13
afterwards she bare a *d* ....Gen 30:21
away my *d*, as captives ....Gen 31:26
And Dinah the *d* of Leah .....Gen 34:1
went out to see the *d* of ......Gen 34:1
wives of the *d* of Canaan......Gen 36:2
the *d* of Elon the Hittite ......Gen 36:2
his *d* rose up to comfort ......Gen 37:35
a *d* of a certain Canaanite .....Gen 38:2
him to wife Asenath the *d* ....Gen 41:45
his *d*, and his sons' *d*, and.....Gen 46:7
with his *d* Dinah: all the ......Gen 46:15
but if it be a *d*, then she ......Ex 1:16
took to wife a *d* of Levi.......Ex 2:1
And the *d* of Pharaoh came ...Ex 2:5
priest of Midian had seven *d* ..Ex 2:16
sons, and upon your *d* ....Ex 3:22
Elisheba, *d* of Amminadab ....Ex 6:23
one of the *d* of Putiel to ......Ex 6:25
our sons and with our *d*.......Ex 10:9
thou, nor thy son, nor thy *d*...Ex 20:10
have born him sons or *d* ......Ex 21:4
man sell his *d* to be a.........Ex 21:7
of your sons, and of your *d* ...Ex 32:2
take of their *d* unto thy ....Ex 34:16
and thy sons, and thy *d* ....Lev 10:14
or for a *d*, she shall bring .....Lev 12:6
d of thy father, or *d* of........Lev 18:9
thy son's *d*, or of thy *d d*......Lev 18:10
Do not prostitute thy *d*, to ....Lev 19:29
man lie with his *d*-in-law ......Lev 20:12
for his son and for his *d* ......Lev 21:2
priest's *d* also be married .....Lev 22:12
Shelomith, the *d* of Dibri .....Lev 24:11
the flesh of your *d* shall.......Lev 26:29
to thy sons and to thy *d*.......Num 18:11
and his *d*, into captivity ....Num 21:29
whoredom with the *d* of ....Num 25:1
slain..Cozbi, the *d* of Zur .....Num 25:15
Hepner had no sons, but *d* ....Num 26:33
the *d* of Zelophehad were .....Num 26:33
d of Asher was Sarah ....Num 26:46
came the *d* of Zelophehad ....Num 27:1
are the names of his *d* ....Num 27:1
inheritance to pass..his *d* ......Num 27:8
between the father..*d* ....Num 30:16
Zelophehad our brother..*d* ....Num 36:2
every *d*, that possesseth an ....Num 36:8
thou, nor thy son, nor..*d*......Deut 5:14
d thou shalt not give unto .....Deut 7:3
d shalt thou take unto thy.....Deut 7:3
and your sons, and your *d* ....Deut 12:12
and thy son, and thy *d*........Deut 12:18
or thy son, or thy *d* ....Deut 13:6
thy *d*, and thy manservant.....Deut 16:11
his son or his *d* to pass ....Deut 18:10
I gave my *d* unto this man ....Deut 22:16
tokens of my *d* virginity ....Deut 22:17
whore of the *d* of Israel.......Deut 23:17
the *d* of his father, or the *d* ...Deut 27:22
Thy sons and thy *d* shall ......Deut 28:32
her son, and toward her *d*.....Deut 28:56
and his sons, and his *d*.........Josh 7:24
will I give Achsah my *d* to ....Josh 15:16
had no sons, but *d*: and ....Josh 17:3
are the names of his *d* ....Josh 17:3
will I give Achsah my *d* to ....Judg 1:12
they took their *d* to be ....Judg 3:6
and gave their *d* to their ......Judg 3:6
his *d* came out to meet him ...Judg 11:34
d of Israel went yearly to .....Judg 11:40
thirty sons, and thirty *d* ....Judg 12:9
thirty *d* from abroad for ......Judg 12:9
of the *d* of the Philistines .....Judg 14:2
Behold, here is my *d* a.........Judg 19:24
give his *d* unto Benjamin......Judg 21:1
them of our *d* to wives?.......Judg 21:7

D

she said unto her, Go, my ***d***...Ruth 2:2
My ***d***, shall I not seek rest ....Ruth 3:1
to all her sons and her ***d***......1Sam 1:4
handmaid for a ***d*** of Belial 1Sam 1:16
bare three sons and two ***d***.....1Sam 2:21
And his ***d*** in law, Phinehas' ...1Sam 4:19
names of his two ***d*** were 1Sam 14:49
Ahinoam, the ***d*** of Ahimaaz ...1Sam 14:50
and will give him his ***d***.........1Sam 17:25
Behold my elder ***d*** Merab 1Sam 18:17
Saul had given Michal his ***d*** ...1Sam 25:44
their sons, and their ***d*** 1Sam 30:3
the ***d*** of the Philistines 2Sam 1:20
d of the uncircumcised 2Sam 1:20
Maacah the ***d*** of Talmai.......2Sam 3:3
sons and ***d*** born to David 2Sam 5:13
Michal Saul's ***d*** looked 2Sam 6:16
Bath-sheba, the ***d*** of Eliam 2Sam 11:3
and was unto him as a ***d*** 2Sam 12:3
with such robes..king's ***d*** 2Sam 13:18
three sons, and one ***d***.........2Sam 14:27
Abigail the ***d*** of Nahash.......2Sam 17:25
lives of thy sons and of thy ***d***..2Sam 19:5
the ***d*** of Aiah, whom she......2Sam 21:8
Pharaoh's ***d***, and brought 1Kin 3:1
Taphath the ***d*** of Solomon 1Kin 4:11
an house for Pharaoh's ***d***......1Kin 7:8
for a present unto his ***d***........1Kin 9:16
together ***d*** of Pharaoh.........1Kin 11:1
Maachah, the ***d*** of............1Kin 15:2
Jezebel the ***d*** of Ethbaal 1Kin 16:31
was Azubah the ***d*** of Shilhi 1Kin 22:42
for the ***d*** of Ahab was his 2Kin 8:18
her for she is a king's ***d***.......2Kin 9:34
Jehosheba the ***d*** of king 2Kin 11:2
Give thy ***d*** to my son to 2Kin 14:9
Jerusha the ***d*** of Zadok 2Kin 15:33
their ***d*** to pass through the 2Kin 17:17
Abi, the ***d*** of Zachariah 2Kin 18:2
virgin the ***d*** of Zion hath.......2Kin 19:21
the ***d*** of Jerusalem hath 2Kin 19:21
Meshullemeth..***d*** of Haruz 2Kin 21:19
Jedidah, the ***d*** of Adaiah of ...2Kin 22:1
or his ***d*** to pass through.......2Kin 23:10
Nehushta..***d*** of Elnathan 2Kin 24:8
d of Matred..***d*** of Mezahab 1Chr 1:50
d of Shua the Canaanitess 1Chr 2:3
Sheshan had no sons, but ***d*** ...1Chr 2:34
of Maachah the ***d*** of Talmai ...1Chr 3:2
d of Pharaoh, which Mered ...1Chr 4:18
Shimei..sons and six ***d*** 1Chr 4:27
and Zelophehad had ***d***.........1Chr 7:15
And his ***d*** was Sherah.........1Chr 7:24
and David..sons and ***d*** 1Chr 14:3
Michal the ***d*** of Saul 1Chr 15:29
and had no sons, but ***d*** 1Chr 23:22
Heman fourteen sons..***d***........1Chr 25:5
son of a woman..***d*** of Dan 2Chr 2:14
Solomon brought up the ***d*** 2Chr 8:11
Mahalath the ***d*** of Jerimoth ...2Chr 11:18
eight sons, and threescore ***d*** ...2Chr 11:21
Michaiah the ***d*** of Uriel of 2Chr 13:2
twenty and two sons..***d***.........2Chr 13:21
was Azubah the ***d*** of Shilhi 2Chr 20:31
he had the ***d*** of Ahab to 2Chr 21:6
Athaliah the ***d*** of Omri 2Chr 22:2
wives..begat sons and ***d*** 2Chr 24:3
Give thy ***d*** to my son to 2Chr 25:18
Jerushah, the ***d*** of Zadok 2Chr 27:1
women, sons, and ***d*** and 2Chr 28:8
Abijah, the ***d*** of Zechariah 2Chr 29:1
our sons and our ***d*** and our ...2Chr 29:9
their sons, and their ***d*** 2Chr 31:18
d of Barzillai the Gileadite ....Ezra 2:61
of their ***d*** for themselves ......Ezra 9:2
Jerusalem, he and his ***d***.......Neh 3:12
your sons, and your ***d***, your ....Neh 4:14
our sons, and our ***d***, are ......Neh 5:2
taken the ***d*** of Meshullam .....Neh 6:18
one of the ***d*** of Barzillai.......Neh 7:63
their sons, and their ***d***........Neh 10:28
not give your ***d*** unto their .....Neh 13:25
nor take their ***d*** unto your ....Neh 13:25
is Esther, his uncle's ***d***........Esth 2:7
dead, took for his own ***d***......Esth 2:7

Esther the queen, the ***d*** of ....Esth 9:29
him seven sons and three ***d***....Job 1:2
also seven sons and three ***d*** ...Job 42:13
Kings' ***d*** were among thy......Ps 45:9
Hearken, O ***d***, and consider ...Ps 45:10
let the ***d*** of Judah be glad .....Ps 48:11
the ***d*** of Judah rejoiced ....Ps 97:8
sacrificed their sons..***d*** ....Ps 106:37
O ***d*** of Babylon, who art to ...Ps 137:8
that our ***d*** may be as corner ...Ps 144:12
horseleech hath two ***d***.........Prov 30:15
Many ***d*** have done virtuously ..Prov 31:29
d of music shall be ....Eccl 12:4
O ye ***d*** of Jerusalem, as the ...Song 1:5
so is my love among the ***d*** ....Song 2:2
you, O ye ***d*** of Jerusalem .....Song 3:5
you, O ***d*** of Jerusalem ....Song 5:8
The ***d*** saw her, and blessed....Song 6:9
O prince's ***d***! the joints of.....Song 7:1
you, O ***d*** of Jerusalem ....Song 8:4
Because the ***d*** of Zion are.....Is 3:16
the filth of the ***d*** of Zion ......Is 4:4
Lift..voice, O ***d*** of Gallim .....Is 10:30
the mount of the ***d*** of Zion....Is 16:1
the ***d*** of Moab shall be at .....Is 16:2
the spoiling of the ***d*** of my ....Is 22:4
d of Tarshish; there is no .....Is 23:10
my voice, ye careless ***d***........Is 32:9
virgin, the ***d*** of Zion hath .....Is 37:22
and my ***d*** from the ends of ....Is 43:6
O virgin ***d*** of Babylon, sit .....Is 47:1
thy ***d*** shall be carried upon ....Is 49:22
neck, O captive ***d*** of Zion......Is 52:2
than of sons and of ***d*** ....Is 56:5
Say ye to the ***d*** of Zion ....Is 62:11
herds, their sons and their ***d***..Jer 3:24
wilderness toward the ***d*** ....Jer 4:11
which thy sons and thy ***d***......Jer 5:17
have likened the ***d*** of Zion ....Jer 6:2
their sons and their ***d*** in.......Jer 7:31
hurt of the ***d*** of my people ....Jer 8:11
the hurt of the ***d*** of my ....Jer 8:21
the health of the ***d*** of my .....Jer 8:22
the slain of the ***d*** of my ....Jer 9:1
teach your ***d*** wailing, and .....Jer 9:20
d shall die by famine ....Jer 11:22
wives, nor their sons..***d*** ....Jer 14:16
for the virgin ***d*** of my.........Jer 14:17
shalt thou have sons or ***d*** .....Jer 16:2
flesh of their ***d***, and they.......Jer 19:9
beget sons and ***d***, and take ....Jer 29:6
give your ***d*** to husbands.......Jer 29:6
they may bear sons and ***d*** .....Jer 29:6
O thou backsliding ***d***?.........Jer 31:22
their ***d*** to pass through the ....Jer 32:35
wives, our sons, nor our ***d*** ....Jer 35:8
the king's ***d***, and all the ....Jer 41:10
and the king's ***d***, and every....Jer 43:6
O virgin, the ***d*** of Egypt ......Jer 46:11
d that dost inhabit Dibon ......Jer 48:18
taken captives, and thy ***d***......Jer 48:46
her ***d*** shall be burned with ....Jer 49:2
O backsliding ***d***? that ....Jer 49:4
thee, O ***d*** of Babylon ....Jer 50:42
The ***d*** of Babylon is like a ....Jer 51:33
d of Jeremiah of Libnah ......Jer 52:1
from the ***d*** of Zion all her.....Lam 1:6
Lord covered the ***d*** of Zion ...Lam 2:1
destruction of the ***d*** of my.....Lam 2:11
destruction of the ***d*** of my.....Lam 3:48
because of all the ***d*** of my.....Lam 3:51
d of my people is become .....Lam 4:3
against the ***d*** of thy people ....Ezek 13:17
deliver neither sons nor ***d*** .....Ezek 14:16
deliver neither son nor ***d*** ......Ezek 14:20
taken thy sons and thy ***d*** ......Ezek 16:20
is the mother, so is her ***d*** .....Ezek 16:44
hath lewdly defiled his ***d*** ......Ezek 22:11
sister, his father's ***d***..........Ezek 22:11
women, the ***d***..mother ....Ezek 23:2
your sons and your ***d*** ....Ezek 24:21
And her ***d*** which are in the ...Ezek 26:6
her ***d*** shall go into captivity ...Ezek 30:18
d of the nations..lament ....Ezek 32:16
the king's ***d*** of the south ......Dan 11:6

Gomer the ***d*** of Diblaim ......Hos 1:3
d shall commit whoredom .....Hos 4:13
I will sell your sons and ***d*** .....Joel 3:8
d shall fall by the sword.......Amos 7:17
of the sin to the ***d*** of Zion ....Mic 1:13
strong hold..***d*** of Zion ....Mic 4:8
thyself in troops, O ***d*** of ......Mic 5:1
d riseth up against her ....Mic 7:6
even the ***d*** of my dispersed ....Zeph 3:10
dwellest..***d*** of Babylon ....Zech 2:7
Rejoice greatly, O ***d***..Zion ....Zech 9:9
shout, O ***d*** of Jerusalem ......Zech 9:9
married the ***d*** of a strange.....Mal 2:11
My ***d*** is even now dead: but ...Matt 9:18
the ***d*** of Herodias danced .....Matt 14:6
my ***d*** is grievously vexed ......Matt 15:22
little ***d*** lieth at the point.......Mark 5:23
D, thy faith hath made thee ...Mark 5:34
d is dead: why troublest.......Mark 5:35
the ***d*** of the said Herodias......Mark 6:22
young ***d*** had an unclean ....Mark 7:25
wife was of the ***d*** of Aaron....Luke 1:5
the ***d*** of Phanuel, of the tribe..Luke 2:36
one only ***d***, about twelve ......Luke 8:42
D, be of good comfort: thy ....Luke 8:48
Thy ***d*** is dead; trouble not ....Luke 8:49
against the ***d***, and the ***d*** ....Luke 12:53
a ***d*** of Abraham..Satan ....Luke 13:16
D of Jerusalem, weep not ....Luke 23:28
Fear not, ***d*** of Zion: behold ...John 12:15
sons and your ***d***..prophesy.....Acts 2:17
Pharaoh's ***d*** took him up ......Acts 7:21
four ***d***, virgins..prophesy ......Acts 21:9
shall be my sons..***d***, saith 2Cor 6:18
called..son of Pharaoh's ***d*** .....Heb 11:24
whose ***d*** ye are, as long as 1Pet 3:6

DAUGHTER OF ZION—*a name referring to Jerusalem and the inhabitants therein*
Show praise to ....Ps 9:14
Gaze on Solomon ....Song 3:11
Left desolate ....Is 1:8
The King comes to ......Matt 21:5

DAUGHTER-IN-LAW—*wife of one's son*
and Sarai his ***d-in-l*** ....Gen 11:31
Judah to Tamar his ***d-in-l*** .....Gen 38:11
nakedness of thy ***d-in-l***.........Lev 18:15
said unto Ruth her ***d-in-l***......Ruth 2:22
Tamar his ***d-in-l*** bare 1Chr 2:4
lewdly defiled his ***d-in-l*** ....Ezek 22:11
the ***d-in-l*** against her..........Matt 10:35

DAVID (dā'vĭd)—*"beloved"*

Early life of:
Born at Bethlehem 1Sam 17:12
Son of Jesse ....Ruth 4:17, 22
Genealogy of 1Chr 2:3-15
Of tribe of Judah........1Chr 28:4
Youngest son 1Sam 16:10-13
Handsome 1Sam 17:42
A shepherd 1Sam 16:11
Strong..................1Sam 17:34-36
Chosen by God 1Sam 16:1, 13

His life under King Saul:
Royal harpist 1Sam 16:14-23
Armor bearer 1Sam 16:21
Kills Goliath 1Sam 17:4-49
Subdues Philistines 1Sam 17:32-54
Loved by Jonathan 1Sam 18:1-4
Wise behavior of 1Sam 18:5-30
Writes a Psalm ....Ps 59:*title*

The fugitive hero:
Flees from Saul 1Sam 19:1-18
Takes refuge with Samuel.1Sam 19:20-24
Makes covenant with
Jonathan 1Sam 20:1-42
Eats showbread ....Matt 12:3, 4
Feigns insanity in Gath ..1Sam 21:10-15
Dwells in cave 1Sam 22:1-8
Saves Keilah 1Sam 23:1-13
God delivers 1Sam 23:14, 15
Second covenant with
Jonathan 1Sam 23:16-18
Betrayed but saved 1Sam 23:19-29
Writes a Psalm ....Ps 54:*title*

Spares Saul's life ... 1Sam 24:1-22
Scorned by Nabal ... 1Sam 25:1-38
Marries Nabal's widow ... 1Sam 25:39-42
Again spares Saul's life ... 1Sam 26:1-25
Dwells in Ziklag ... 1Sam 27:5-7
Rejected by Philistines ... 1Sam 29:1-11
Smites the Amalekites ... 1Sam 30:1-31
Kills Saul's murderer ... 2Sam 1:1-16
Laments Saul's death ... 2Sam 1:17-27

King over Judah:
Anointed at Hebron ... 2Sam 2:1-4, 11
List of supporters ... 1Chr 12:23-40
Long war with Saul's house ... 2Sam 3:1
Abner, rebuffed, makes covenant with David ... 2Sam 3:6-21
Mourns Abner's death ... 2Sam 3:28-39
Punishes Ish-bosheth's murderers ... 2Sam 4:1-12

King over all Israel:
Recognized as king ... 2Sam 5:1-5
Takes Zion from Jebusites ... 2Sam 5:6-10
Builds a house ... 2Sam 5:11
Strengthens kingdom ... 2Sam 5:11-16
Strikes down the Philistines ... 2Sam 5:17-25
Escorts ark to Jerusalem ... 2Sam 6:1-16
Organizes worship ... 1Chr 15:1-29
Organizes musicians ... 1Chr 25:1-31
Blesses the people ... 2Sam 6:17-19
Upbraided by Michal ... 2Sam 6:20-23
Receives eternal covenant ... 2Sam 7:1-29
Subdues many nations ... 2Sam 8:1-18; 2Sam 10:1-19
Commits adultery ... 2Sam 11:1-27
Rebuked by Nathan ... 2Sam 12:1-14
Repents ... Ps 32:1-11; Ps 51:1-19
Afflictions follow ... 2Sam 12:15-23
Family strife ... 2Sam 13:1-39
Absalom's rebellion ... 2Sam 15:1-31
Flees from Jerusalem ... 2Sam 15:13-37
Mourns Absalom's death ... 2Sam 19:1-10
Returns to Jerusalem ... 2Sam 19:15-43
Sheba's conspiracy ... 2Sam 20:1-26
Atones for Saul's crime ... 2Sam 21:1-14
Further conflicts ... 2Sam 21:15-22
Song of deliverance ... 2Sam 22:1-51
Last words of ... 2Sam 23:1-7
His mighty men ... 2Sam 23:8-39
Sins by numbering people ... 2Sam 24:1-17
Buys Araunah's threshing floor ... 2Sam 24:18-25
Secures Solomon's succession ... 1Kin 1:5-53
Gives dying charge to Solomon ... 1Kin 2:1-11
Reign of forty years ... 1Kin 2:11

Spiritual significance of:
Prophet ... Acts 2:30
Musician ... 2Sam 23:1
Inspired man ... Matt 22:43
Type of Christ ... Jer 23:5, 6
Name designates Christ ... Ezek 34:23, 24
Christ, son of ... Matt 1:1
"Kingdom of" ... Mark 11:10
"Throne of" ... Luke 1:32
"Tabernacle of" ... Acts 15:16
"Key of" ... Is 22:22
Faith ... Heb 11:32, 33
Covenant with ... 2Sam 7:4-17

[*also* DAVID'S]
D wife, to Phalti the son of ... 1Sam 25:44
of ***D*** servants, nineteen ... 2Sam 2:30
sixth, Ithream, by Eglah ***D*** ... 2Sam 3:5
stones; and it was set on ***D*** ... 2Sam 12:30
Hushai the Archite, ***D*** ... 2Sam 16:16
unto the prophet Gad, ***D*** ... 2Sam 24:11
one tribe for my servant ***D*** ... 1Kin 11:32
for ***D*** sake did the Lord ... 1Kin 15:4
give king ***D*** spears and ... 2Kin 11:10
sake, and for my servant ***D*** ... 2Kin 19:34
sake, and for my servant ***D*** ... 2Kin 20:6
the Moabites became ***D*** ... 1Chr 18:2
the Syrians became ***D*** ... 1Chr 18:6
the Edomites became ***D*** ... 1Chr 18:13
D reigned over all Israel ... 1Chr 18:14
Wherefore Hanun took ***D*** ... 1Chr 19:4
it: and it was set upon ***D*** ... 1Chr 20:2
of Shimea ***D*** brother slew ... 1Chr 20:7
the Lord spake unto Gad, ***D*** ... 1Chr 21:9
substance..was king ***D*** ... 1Chr 27:31
D uncle was a counselor ... 1Chr 27:32
and shields..been king ***D*** ... 2Chr 23:9
For thy servant ***D*** sake ... Ps 132:10
D Psalm of praise ... Ps 146:*title*
sake, and for my servant ***D*** ... Is 37:35
kings that sit upon ***D*** ... Jer 13:13
covenant be broken with ***D*** ... Jer 33:21
I multiply the seed of ***D*** ... Jer 33:22
Thou son of ***D***, have mercy ... Matt 9:27
Is not this the son of ***D***? ... Matt 12:23
Hosanna to the son of ***D*** ... Matt 21:9
Thou son of ***D***, have mercy ... Mark 10:48
was..house and lineage of ***D*** ... Luke 2:4
say they that Christ is ***D*** ... Luke 20:41
Christ cometh..seed of ***D*** ... John 7:42
For ***D*** speaketh concerning ... Acts 2:25
Christ of the seed of ***D*** ... 2Tim 2:8

DAVID, ROOT OF—*a title of Christ*
Opens sealed book ... Rev 5:5
Jesus describes Himself as ... Rev 22:16

DAVID, TOWER OF—*fortress built by David; location now unknown*
Symbolic of strength ... Song 4:4

DAWN—*the break of day*
Not even one remained ... 2Sam 17:22
Worked from ... Neh 4:21
See the breaking ... Job 3:9
Continually tossing until ... Job 7:4
Murderer arises at ... Job 24:14
Mary came to the grave at ... Matt 28:1; Luke 24:1

[*also* DAWNING]
rose early about the ***d*** of ... Josh 6:15
the woman in the ***d*** of the ... Judg 19:26
neither let it see the ***d*** of ... Job 3:9
prevented the ***d*** of the ... Ps 119:147
until the day ***d***..day star ... 2Pet 1:19

DAY—*the time between sunup and sundown*

Natural uses of:
The daylight ... Gen 1:5, 16
Twelve hours ... John 11:9
Opposite of night ... Mark 5:5
The civil day (24 hours) ... Luke 13:14
Divisions of ... Neh 9:3
Security of ... Gen 8:22

Extended uses of:
Noah's time ... Matt 24:37
Gospel age ... John 9:4
Long period ... 2Pet 3:8

Descriptive of:
Believers ... 1Thess 5:5, 8
Christ's return ... 1Thess 5:2
Prophetic period ... Dan 12:11; Rev 2:10
Eternity ... Dan 7:9, 13
Present age ... Heb 1:2

[*also* DAY'S, DAYS', DAYTIME]
morning were the first ***d*** ... Gen 1:5
morning were the second ***d*** ... Gen 1:8
morning were the third ***d*** ... Gen 1:13
divide the ***d*** from the night ... Gen 1:14
rule over the ***d*** and over ... Gen 1:18
morning were the fourth ***d*** ... Gen 1:19
morning were the fifth ***d*** ... Gen 1:23
morning were the sixth ***d*** ... Gen 1:31
the seventh ***d*** God ended ... Gen 2:2
rested on the seventh ***d*** ... Gen 2:2
God blessed the seventh ***d*** ... Gen 2:3
in the ***d*** that the Lord God ... Gen 2:4
three ***d*** journey betwixt ... Gen 30:36
pursued after him seven ***d*** ... Gen 31:23
we beseech thee, three ***d*** ... Ex 3:18
we pray thee, three ***d*** ... Ex 5:3
d journey..wilderness ... Ex 8:27
Remember the sabbath ***d***, to ... Ex 20:8
Lord three ***d*** journey ... Num 10:33
in the three ***d*** journey ... Num 10:33
it were a ***d*** journey on this ... Num 11:31
were a ***d*** journey on the other ... Num 11:31
three ***d*** journey..wilderness ... Num 33:8
eleven ***d*** journey..Horeb ... Deut 1:2
Keep the sabbath ***d*** to ... Deut 5:12
Give us seven ***d*** respite ... 1Sam 11:3
three ***d*** pestilence..land? ... 2Sam 24:13
himself went a ***d*** journey ... 1Kin 19:4
a compass of seven ***d*** ... 2Kin 3:9
continually, as every ***d*** ... 1Chr 16:37
according..this ***d*** decree ... Esth 9:13
They meet with darkness..***d*** ... Job 5:14
marked for themselves..***d*** ... Job 24:16
O my God, I cry in the ***d*** ... Ps 22:2
his lovingkindness in the ***d*** ... Ps 42:8
d also he led them with a ... Ps 78:14
a ***d*** in thy courts is better ... Ps 84:10
knowest not what a ***d*** may ... Prov 27:1
a shadow in the ***d*** from the ... Is 4:6
the watchtower in the ***d*** ... Is 21:8
Behold the ***d***, behold, it is ... Ezek 7:10
city of three ***d*** journey ... Jon 3:3
a ***d*** journey, and he cried ... Jon 3:4
that ***d*** when I make up my ... Mal 3:17
Give us..***d*** our daily bread ... Matt 6:11
raised again the third ***d*** ... Matt 16:21
third ***d*** he shall be raised ... Matt 17:23
the third ***d*** he shall rise ... Matt 20:19
d and hour knoweth no ... Matt 24:36
know neither the ***d*** nor the ... Matt 25:13
he shall rise..third ***d*** ... Mark 9:31
third ***d*** he shall rise again ... Mark 10:34
of that ***d*** and that hour ... Mark 13:32
unto you is born this ***d*** in ... Luke 2:11
a ***d*** journey..they sought ... Luke 2:44
third ***d*** he shall rise again ... Luke 18:33
d is salvation come..house ... Luke 19:9
d come..you unawares ... Luke 21:34
and the third ***d*** rise again ... Luke 24:7
from the dead the third ***d*** ... Luke 24:46
raise it up..at the last ***d*** ... John 6:39
raise him up..last ***d*** ... John 6:40
At that ***d*** ye shall know ... John 14:20
Jerusalem a sabbath ***d*** ... Acts 1:12
Him God raised..third ***d*** ... Acts 10:40
in question..this ***d*** uproar ... Acts 19:40
the ***d*** when God shall judge ... Rom 2:16
we are killed all the ***d*** ... Rom 8:36
he rose again the third ***d*** ... 1Cor 15:4
now is the ***d*** of salvation ... 2Cor 6:2
saith, To ***d*** if ye will hear ... Heb 3:7
d is with the Lord as a ... 2Pet 3:8

DAY, JOSHUA'S LONG
Described ... Josh 10:12-14

DAY OF THE LORD—*the ultimate day of judgment*

In Old Testament:
Punishment of faithless ... Is 13:6-13; Amos 5:18-20
Day of wrath ... Is 2:6-22
Restoration of remnant ... Is 10:20-22; Hos 2:16-20

In New Testament:
The last times ... Matt 24:29; 2Pet 3:10
The great day ... Rev 16:14

DAY'S JOURNEY

Described as:
A distance ... Gen 30:36; Gen 31:23
Traveled to make a sacrifice ... Ex 3:18; Ex 5:3; Ex 8:27

DAYS—*See* INTRODUCTION

DAYSMAN—*mediator or umpire*
Desired by Job ... Job 9:33

DAYSPRING—*dawn or sunrise*
the *d* to know his place .... Job 38:12
d from on high hath visited .... Luke 1:78

DAYTIME—*See* DAY

DEACONESS—*a female helper in the Church*
Phoebe thus called ("a servant") .... Rom 16:1

DEACONS—*church officers*
Ordained by the apostles . Acts 6:1-6
Stephen, the first martyr of .... Acts 6:5-15
Named with bishops ..... Phil 1:1
Qualifications of 1Tim 3:8-13

DEAD—*no longer living*

Used literally of:
Lost physical functions ... Rom 4:19
Those in the other world . Rev 20:12

Used figuratively of:
Unregenerate .... Eph 2:1
Unreal faith .... James 2:17, 19
Decadent church .... Rev 3:1
Legal requirements ...... Heb 9:14
Freedom from sin's power .... Rom 6:2, 8, 11
Freedom from the Law .. Rom 7:4

[*also* DEADLY, DEADNESS, DIE, DIED, DIEST, DIETH, DYING]
but a *d* man, for the woman ... Gen 20:3
stood up from before his *d* ... Gen 23:3
his brother is *d*, and he ...... Gen 42:38
his brother is *d*, and he .... Gen 44:20
that their father was *d* .... Gen 50:15
men are *d* which sought .... Ex 4:19
cattle of the Israelites *d* .... Ex 9:7
house where..was not one *d* ... Ex 12:30
Israel saw the Egyptians *d* ..... Ex 14:30
and the *d* beast shall be his ... Ex 21:34
they be *d*, shall be unclean ... Lev 11:31
cuttings in..flesh for the *d* ..... Lev 19:28
none be defiled for the *d* ...... Lev 21:1
thing..unclean by the *d* .... Lev 22:4
whosoever..defiled by the *d* ... Num 5:2
he shall come at no *d* body .... Num 6:6
defiled..*d* body of a man ...... Num 9:6, 7
Let her not be as one *d* .... Num 12:12
stood between the *d* and ...... Num 16:48
that toucheth the *d* body ...... Num 19:11
Aaron was *d*, they mourned ... Num 20:29
men..were consumed and *d* .... Deut 2:16
between your eyes for..*d* ...... Deut 14:1
wife of the *d*..not marry ...... Deut 25:5
nor given..for the *d* .... Deut 26:14
Moses my servant is *d* .... Josh 1:2
the judge was *d*, that they ..... Judg 2:19
lord was fallen down *d* .... Judg 3:25
the Lord, when Ehud was *d* ... Judg 4:1
bowed, there he fell down *d* ... Judg 5:27
as soon as Gideon was *d* ...... Judg 8:33
saw that Abimelech was *d* ..... Judg 9:55
the *d* which he slew at his ..... Judg 16:30
they forced, that she is *d* ...... Judg 20:5
as ye have dealt with the *d* .... Ruth 1:8
to the living and to the *d* ..... Ruth 2:20
d, to raise..name of the *d* ..... Ruth 4:5
Hophni and Phinehas..*d* 1Sam 4:17
a *d* destruction throughout 1Sam 5:11
saw their champion was *d* 1Sam 17:51
after a *d* dog, after a flea 1Sam 24:14
heard that Nabal was *d* 1Sam 25:39
Now Samuel was *d*, and all 1Sam 28:3
saw that Saul was *d* 1Sam 31:5
people also are fallen and *d* ... 2Sam 1:4
Jonathan his son are *d* 2Sam 1:4
your master Saul is *d*, and 2Sam 2:7
Abner was *d* in Hebron, his ... 2Sam 4:1
such a *d* dog as I am? 2Sam 9:8
Uriah the Hittite is *d* 2Sam 11:21
tell him that..the child was *d* .. 2Sam 12:18
tell him that..the child is *d*? ... 2Sam 12:18
Amnon only is *d*: for by the ... 2Sam 13:32
time mourned for the *d* 2Sam 14:2
this *d* dog curse my lord 2Sam 16:9
because the king's son is *d* 2Sam 18:20
we anointed over us, is *d* 2Sam 19:10
laid her *d* child..my bosom 1Kin 3:20
captain of the host was *d* 1Kin 11:21
When I am *d*, then bury me ... 1Kin 13:31
Naboth is stoned, and is *d* 1Kin 21:14
Ahab was *d*, that the king 2Kin 3:5
servant my husband is *d* 2Kin 4:1
child was *d*, and laid upon 2Kin 4:32
he had restored a *d* body to ... 2Kin 8:5
saw that her son was *d* 2Kin 11:1
behold, they were all *d* 2Kin 19:35
carried him in a chariot *d* 2Kin 23:30
Bela was *d*, Jobab the son 1Chr 1:44
And when Azubah was *d* 1Chr 2:19
saw that Saul was *d*, he fell ... 1Chr 10:5
they were *d* bodies fallen 2Chr 20:24
Ahaziah saw..son was *d* 2Chr 22:10
father and mother were *d* ..... Esth 2:7
young men, and they are *d* .... Job 1:19
D things are formed from ..... Job 26:5
d enemies, who compass ...... Ps 17:9
I am forgotten as a *d* man .... Ps 31:12
are cast into a *d* sleep .... Ps 76:6
d bodies of thy servants .... Ps 79:2
Free among the *d*, like the .... Ps 88:5
show wonders to the *d*? .... Ps 88:10
shall the *d* arise and praise .... Ps 88:10
ate the sacrifices of the *d* ..... Ps 106:28
fill..places with..*d* bodies ...... Ps 110:6
The *d* praise not the Lord ..... Ps 115:17
that have been long *d* .... Ps 143:3
and her paths unto the *d* .... Prov 2:18
knoweth not that the *d* are .... Prov 9:18
the congregation of the *d* ..... Prov 21:16
praised the *d*..already *d* .... Eccl 4:2
after that they go to the *d* ..... Eccl 9:3
the *d* know not any thing ...... Eccl 9:5
D flies cause the ointment ..... Eccl 10:1
for the living to the *d*? .... Is 8:19
stirreth up the *d* for thee ...... Is 14:9
slain with the sword, nor *d* .... Is 22:2
are *d*, they shall not live ...... Is 26:14
in desolate places as *d* men .... Is 59:10
to comfort them for the *d* ..... Jer 16:7
Weep ye not for the *d* .... Jer 22:10
cast his *d* body into the .... Jer 26:23
valley of the *d* bodies .... Jer 31:40
fill them with the *d* bodies .... Jer 33:5
d bodies shall be for meat ..... Jer 34:20
his *d* body shall be cast .... Jer 36:30
all the *d* bodies of the men .... Jer 41:9
as they that be *d* of old .... Lam 3:6
I will lay the *d* carcases .... Ezek 6:5
groanings of a *d* wounded ..... Ezek 30:24
shall be many *d* bodies .... Amos 8:3
unclean by a *d* body touch ..... Hag 2:13
But when Herod was *d* .... Matt 2:19
My daughter is even now *d* .... Matt 9:18
maid is not *d*, but sleepeth .... Matt 9:24
lepers, raise the *d*, cast .... Matt 10:8
d are not raised up, and the ... Matt 11:5
the resurrection of the *d* ...... Matt 22:31
God is not the God of the *d* .. Matt 22:32
full of *d* men's bones .... Matt 23:27
He is risen from the *d* .... Matt 27:64
shake, and became as *d* men .. Matt 28:4
that he is risen from the *d* .... Matt 28:7
said, Thy daughter is *d* .... Mark 5:35
Baptist..risen from the *d* ...... Mark 6:14
Son of man..risen from..*d* ..... Mark 9:9
they shall rise from the *d* ..... Mark 12:25
if he were already *d* .... Mark 15:44
if they drink any *d* thing ...... Mark 16:18
was a *d* man carried out ...... Luke 7:12
Thy daughter is *d*; trouble .... Luke 8:49
John was risen from the *d* ..... Luke 9:7
departed, leaving him half *d* .. Luke 10:30
For this my son was *d*, and .... Luke 15:24
went unto them from the *d* .... Luke 16:30
resurrection from the *d* .... Luke 20:35
seek..living among the *d*? ..... Luke 24:5
he was risen from the *d* .... John 2:22
the Father raiseth up the *d* .... John 5:21
the *d* shall hear the voice ..... John 5:25
the wilderness, and are *d* ...... John 6:49
Abraham is *d*, and the .... John 8:52
Lazarus was which had been *d* . John 12:1
that he was *d* already, they .... John 19:33
must rise again from the *d* .... John 20:9
he was risen from the *d* .... John 21:14
he is both *d* and buried .... Acts 2:29
God hath raised from the *d* ... Acts 3:15
came in and found her *d* ...... Acts 5:10
when his father was *d* .... Acts 7:4
after he rose from the *d* .... Acts 10:41
the Judge of quick and *d* .... Acts 10:42
God raised him from the *d* .... Acts 13:30
supposing he had been *d* ...... Acts 14:19
risen again from the *d* .... Acts 17:3
loft, and was taken up *d* ...... Acts 20:9
hope..resurrection of the *d* .... Acts 23:6
of one Jesus, which was *d* ..... Acts 25:19
God should raise the *d*? .... Acts 26:8
or fallen down *d* suddenly ..... Acts 28:6
resurrection from the *d* .... Rom 1:4
God, who quickeneth the *d* ... Rom 4:17
yet the *d* of Sarah's womb .... Rom 4:19
offense of one many be *d* ..... Rom 5:15
raised from the *d*, *d* no more .. Rom 6:9
husband be *d*, she is loosed ... Rom 7:2
body is *d* because of sin .... Rom 8:10
Christ again from the *d* .... Rom 10:7
be, but life from the *d*? .... Rom 11:15
Lord..of the *d* and living ...... Rom 14:9
preached..he rose from the *d* .. 1Cor 15:12
no resurrection of the *d*? 1Cor 15:12
is Christ risen from the *d* 1Cor 15:20
are baptized for the *d* 1Cor 15:29
if the *d* rise not at all? why ... 1Cor 15:29
then baptized for the *d*? 1Cor 15:29
it me, if the *d* rise not? 1Cor 15:32
How are the *d* raised up? 1Cor 15:35
God which raiseth the *d* 2Cor 1:9
d for all, then were all *d* 2Cor 5:14
who raised him from the *d* .... Gal 1:1
I through the law am *d* to ..... Gal 2:19
then Christ is *d* in vain .... Gal 2:21
he raised him from the *d* ...... Eph 1:20
arise from..*d*, and Christ ...... Eph 5:14
the resurrection of the *d* ...... Phil 3:11
the firstborn from the *d* .... Col 1:18
raised him from the *d* .... Col 2:12
being *d* in your sins .... Col 2:13
if ye be *d* with Christ from .... Col 2:20
For ye are *d*, and your life .... Col 3:3
the *d* in Christ shall rise 1Thess 4:16
in pleasure is *d* while she 1Tim 5:6
was raised from the *d* 2Tim 2:8
For if we be *d* with him, we ... 2Tim 2:11
judge the quick and the *d* 2Tim 4:1
repentance from *d* works ...... Heb 6:1
he being *d* yet speaketh .... Heb 11:4
brought again from the *d* ...... Heb 13:20
faith without works is *d*? ...... James 2:20
unruly evil, full of *d* poison ... James 3:8
of Jesus Christ from the *d* 1Pet 1:3
raised him up from the *d* 1Pet 1:21
I fell at his feet as *d* .... Rev 1:17
he that liveth, and was *d* ...... Rev 1:18
which was *d*, and is alive ...... Rev 2:8
that thou livest, and art *d* ..... Rev 3:1
d wound was healed; and ...... Rev 13:3
Blessed are the *d* which die ... Rev 14:13
dead which *d* in the Lord ..... Rev 14:13
as the blood of a *d* man .... Rev 16:3
every..soul *d* in the sea .... Rev 16:3
rest of the *d* lived not again ... Rev 20:5
and hell delivered up the *d* .... Rev 20:13

DEAD SEA—*salt lake located east of Jerusalem*

Called the:
Salt Sea .... Gen 14:3
Sea of the Plain .... Deut 3:17

DEAF—*unable to hear*
Protection afforded ...... Lev 19:14
Healing of .... Matt 11:5

Figurative of spiritual inability ....Is 42:18, 19
Figurative of patience ....Ps 38:13
maketh the dumb, or **d** ....Ex 4:11
d adder that stoppeth her .....Ps 58:4
in that day shall the **d** hear ....Is 29:18
ears of the **d** shall be ....Is 35:5
and the **d** that have ears ......Is 43:8
mouth, their ears shall be **d** ...Mic 7:16
d, and had an impediment ....Mark 7:32
maketh both the **d** to hear ....Mark 7:37
Thou dumb and **d** spirit, I .....Mark 9:25
the **d** hear, the dead are ......Luke 7:22

DEAL—*to act; do business; a measure*

[*also* DEALEST, DEALETH, DEALING, DEALINGS, DEALS, DEALT]
Sarai **d** hardly with her........Gen 16:6
will we **d** worse with thee .....Gen 19:9
wilt not **d** falsely with me .....Gen 21:23
If ye will **d** kindly and truly ...Gen 24:49
and I will **d** well with thee ....Gen 32:9
God hath **d** graciously ....Gen 33:11
Should he **d** with our sister ....Gen 34:31
Wherefore **d** ye so ill with .....Gen 43:6
d kindly and truly with me .....Gen 47:29
let us **d** wisely with them ......Ex 1:10
God **d** well with..midwives ....Ex 1:20
d thou thus with..servants? ....Ex 5:15
not Pharaoh **d** deceitfully ......Ex 8:29
wherefore hast thou **d** thus ....Ex 14:11
wherein they **d** proudly ....Ex 18:11
seeing he..**d** deceitfully ....Ex 21:8
d with her after..manner ......Ex 21:9
the one lamb a tenth **d** of .....Ex 29:40
three tenth **d** of fine flour .....Lev 14:10
one tenth **d** of fine flour ......Lev 14:21
two tenth **d** of fine flour ......Lev 23:13
if thou **d** thus with me, kill ....Num 11:15
two tenth **d** of flour ....Num 15:6
two tenth **d** of flour for ....Num 28:9
a several tenth **d** of flour ......Num 28:13
three tenth **d** for a bullock ....Num 29:3
and two tenth **d** for a ram .....Num 29:3
one tenth **d** for one lamb .....Num 29:4
shall ye **d** with them; ye ....Deut 7:5
d kindly and truly with........Josh 2:14
have **d** well with Jerubbaal ....Judg 9:16
d Micah with me, and hath ....Judg 18:4
the Lord **d** kindly with you ....Ruth 1:8
as ye have **d** with the dead ....Ruth 1:8
evil **d** by all this people 1Sam 2:23
d kindly with thy servant 1Sam 20:8
told me..he **d** very subtilly 1Sam 23:22
hast **d** well with me; for 1Sam 24:18
the Lord shall have **d** well 1Sam 25:31
he **d** among all the people 2Sam 6:19
D gently for my sake with 2Sam 18:5
workmen..they **d** faithfully 2Kin 12:15
and **d** with familiar spirits 2Kin 21:6
because they **d** faithfully 2Kin 22:7
d to every one of Israel 1Chr 16:3
d David with all the cities 1Chr 20:3
didst **d** with David my 2Chr 2:3
dwell therein, even so **d**.......2Chr 2:3
amiss..have **d** wickedly 2Chr 6:37
he **d** wisely, and dispersed 2Chr 11:23
D courageously, and..Lord 2Chr 19:11
d with a familiar spirit 2Chr 33:6
d very corruptly against ....Neh 1:7
they **d** proudly against them ...Neh 9:10
brethren have **d** deceitfully ....Job 6:15
d with you after your folly ....Job 42:8
violent **d** shall come down .....Ps 7:16
hath **d** bountifully with me ....Ps 13:6
D not foolishly; and to the ....Ps 75:4
d unfaithfully like their........Ps 78:57
not **d** with us after our sins ....Ps 103:10
d subtilly with..servants ....Ps 105:25
d bountifully with thee ....Ps 116:7
D bountifully with..servant ....Ps 119:17
hast **d** well with..servant .....Ps 119:65
shalt **d** bountifully with........Ps 142:7
not **d** so with any nation ......Ps 147:20
He becometh poor that **d** .....Prov 10:4
that **d** truly are his delight.....Prov 12:22
prudent man **d** with...........Prov 13:16
He..soon angry **d** foolishly ....Prov 14:17
his name, who **d** in proud .....Prov 21:24
the treacherous **d**.............Is 21:2
treacherous **d** have **d**.........Is 24:16
have **d** treacherously ....Is 24:16
will he **d** unjustly ....Is 26:10
d treacherously, and they .....Is 33:1
an end to **d** treacherously .....Is 33:1
shall **d** treacherously with .....Is 33:1
d very treacherously ....Is 48:8
servant shall **d** prudently ......Is 52:13
d thy bread to the hungry .....Is 58:7
have ye **d** treacherously ....Jer 3:20
d very treacherously ....Jer 5:11
priest every one **d** falsely ....Jer 6:13
unto the priest every one **d**....Jer 8:10
that **d** very treacherously? .....Jer 12:1
d treacherously with thee......Jer 12:6
d thus with them in the ....Jer 18:23
Lord will **d** with us ....Jer 21:2
d treacherously with her ......Lam 1:2
will I also **d** in fury ....Ezek 8:18
d with thee as thou hast.......Ezek 16:59
kept my judgments to **d**........Ezek 18:9
have they **d** by oppression .....Ezek 22:7
days that I shall **d** with........Ezek 22:14
d against the house of ....Ezek 25:12
he shall surely **d** with him .....Ezek 31:11
seest, **d** with thy servants......Dan 1:13
and shall **d** against them ......Dan 11:7
d treacherously against ....Hos 5:7
d treacherously against ....Hos 6:7
your God that hath **d** ....Joel 2:26
them that **d** treacherously .....Hab 1:13
so hath he **d** with us ....Zech 1:6
why do we **d** treacherously ....Mal 2:10
Judah..**d** treacherously ....Mal 2:11
much the more a great **d**......Mark 7:36
cried the more a great **d** ......Mark 10:48
Thus hath the Lord **d** with ....Luke 1:25
why hast thou thus **d** with ....Luke 2:48
no **d** with the Samaritans ......John 4:9
The same **d** subtilly with ......Acts 7:19
God hath **d** to every man .....Rom 12:3
God **d** with you as..sons ......Heb 12:7

DEALER—*trader; businessperson*

[*also* DEALERS]
the treacherous **d** dealeth ......Is 21:2
the treacherous **d** have dealt ...Is 24:16

DEAR—*beloved; precious*

[*also* DEARLY]
the **d** beloved of my soul......Jer 12:7
Is Ephraim my **d** son? is he ...Jer 31:20
who was **d** unto him, was .....Luke 7:2
count I my life **d** unto myself ..Acts 20:24
D beloved, avenge not ....Rom 12:19
Wherefore, my **d** beloved 1Cor 10:14
these promises **d** beloved 2Cor 7:1
followers of God, as **d** ....Eph 5:1
my brethren **d** beloved and ....Phil 4:1
in the Lord, my **d** beloved ....Phil 4:1
our **d** fellow servant who is....Col 1:7
souls, because ye were **d** 1Thess 2:8
To Timothy my **d** beloved 2Tim 1:2
D beloved, I beseech you 1Pet 2:11

DEARTH—*a famine*
Visited upon Egypt ......Acts 7:11
Agabus predicts ....Acts 11:28
See FAMINE

seven years of **d** began to .....Gen 41:54
there was a **d** in the land......2Kin 4:38
If there be **d** in the land 2Chr 6:28
Jeremiah concerning the **d**.....Jer 14:1

DEATH—*the absence of life*

[*also* DEATHS]
not see the **d** of the child .....Gen 21:16
comforted after..mother's **d**....Gen 24:67
after the **d** of Abraham, that ..Gen 25:11
his wife shall..be put to **d** .....Gen 26:11
I know not the day of my **d** ...Gen 27:2
take away from me this **d** .....Ex 10:17
shall be surely put to **d** ....Ex 19:12
shall be surely put to **d** ....Ex 21:12
a beast shall..be put to **d**......Ex 22:19
defileth it..be put to **d** ....Ex 31:14
therein shall be put to **d** ......Ex 35:2
after the **d** of the two sons .....Lev 16:1
they shall not be put to **d** .....Lev 19:20
he shall surely be put to **d** ....Lev 20:2
he shall surely be put to **d** ....Lev 24:16
but shall surely be put to **d**....Lev 27:29
that cometh nigh..put to **d** ....Num 1:51
cometh nigh..put to **d**.........Num 3:10
The man shall be..put to **d**....Num 15:35
these men die the common **d** ..Num 16:29
cometh nigh..be put to **d**......Num 18:7
die the **d** of the righteous .....Num 23:10
murderer..put to **d**............Num 35:16
murderer shall be put to **d** ....Num 35:30
of dreams, shall be put to **d** ...Deut 13:5
shall he that is worthy of **d** ....Deut 17:6
put to **d**; but at the mouth ....Deut 17:6
he shall not be put to **d** ....Deut 17:6
he was not worthy of **d** ....Deut 19:6
a sin worthy of **d** ....Deut 21:22
and he be to be put to **d** ......Deut 21:22
damsel no sin worthy of **d**.....Deut 22:26
fathers..not be put to **d** ....Deut 24:16
and good, and **d** and evil......Deut 30:15
much more after my **d**? ....Deut 31:27
children of Israel before..**d** ....Deut 33:1
after the **d** of Moses the ......Josh 1:1
deliver our lives from **d** ....Josh 2:13
the **d** of the high priest ....Josh 20:6
after the **d** of Joshua it........Judg 1:1
that we may put them to **d** ....Judg 20:13
He shall surely be put to **d** ....Judg 21:5
if aught but **d** part thee and ...Ruth 1:17
that we may put them to **d** 1Sam 11:12
the bitterness of **d** is past 1Sam 15:32
a step between me and **d**......1Sam 20:3
I have occasioned the **d** of 1Sam 22:22
shut up unto the day of..**d** 2Sam 20:3
I will not put thee to **d** 1Kin 2:8
Egypt until..**d** of Solomon 1Kin 11:40
against Israel after the **d** 2Kin 1:1
any more **d** or barren land 2Kin 2:21
man of God, there is **d** in 2Kin 4:40
fathers..not be put to **d** 2Kin 14:6
leper unto the day of his **d** 2Kin 15:5
prepared..before his **d** 1Chr 22:5
God of Israel..put to **d**........2Chr 15:13
after the **d** of his father 2Chr 22:4
house, he shall be put to **d** 2Chr 23:7
after the **d** of Jehoiada 2Chr 24:17
after the death of Joash 2Chr 25:25
whether it be unto **d**, or to ....Ezra 7:26
law of his to put him to **d** .....Esth 4:11
darkness and..shadow of **d** ....Job 3:5
eyelids is the shadow of **d** .....Job 16:16
first-born of **d** shall devour ....Job 18:13
even as the shadow of **d** ....Job 24:17
terrors of the shadow of **d**.....Job 24:17
him shall be buried in **d**.......Job 27:15
and the shadow of **d** ....Job 28:3
thou wilt bring me to **d** ....Job 30:23
darkness, nor shadow of **d** ....Job 34:22
Have the gates of **d** been ......Job 38:17
doors of the shadow of **d**? .....Job 38:17
d there is no remembrance ....Ps 6:5
for him the instruments of **d**..Ps 7:13
liftest..from the gates of **d**.....Ps 9:13
lest I sleep the sleep of **d** .....Ps 13:3
sorrows of **d** compassed ....Ps 18:4
me into the dust of **d** ....Ps 22:15
valley of the shadow of **d** .....Ps 23:4
deliver their soul from **d** ......Ps 33:19
covered..the shadow of **d**......Ps 44:19
be our guide even unto **d** .....Ps 48:14
d shall feed on them; and .....Ps 49:14
terrors of **d** are fallen upon....Ps 55:4
delivered my soul from **d**......Ps 56:13
belong the issues from **d** ......Ps 68:20
are no bands in their **d**........Ps 73:4

spared not..soul from *d* ....Ps 78:50
liveth, and shall not see *d*? ....Ps 89:48
those..appointed to *d* ....Ps 102:20
and in the shadow of *d* ....Ps 107:10
sorrows of *d* compassed ....Ps 116:3
not given me over unto *d* .....Ps 118:18
her house inclineth unto *d*.....Prov 2:18
Her feet go down to *d*; her....Prov 5:5
delivereth from *d*............Prov 10:2
delivereth from *d*............Prov 11:4
pathway..there is no *d* ....Prov 12:28
depart from the snares of *d* ...Prov 13:14
end..are the ways of *d* ....Prov 14:12
king is as messengers of *d*.....Prov 16:14
D and life are in the power ...Prov 18:21
of them that seek *d*...........Prov 21:6
them..drawn unto *d*...........Prov 24:11
firebrands, arrows, and *d*......Prov 26:18
d than the day of..birth ....Eccl 7:1
power in the day of *d*.........Eccl 8:8
love is strong as *d* ....Song 8:6
the land of the shadow of *d* ...Is 9:2
swallow up *d* in victory ....Is 25:8
made a covenant with *d*.......Is 28:15
Hezekiah sick unto *d* ....Is 38:1
with the rich in his *d* ....Is 53:9
and of the shadow of *d* ....Jer 2:6
d shall be chosen rather.......Jer 8:3
d is come up into our.........Jer 9:21
into the shadow of *d*..........Jer 13:16
Such as are for *d*, to *d* ....Jer 15:2
shall die of grievous *d* ....Jer 16:4
let their men be put to *d*......Jer 18:21
of life, and the way of *d* ......Jer 21:8
put me to *d*, ye shall surely ...Jer 26:15
let this man be put to *d*.......Jer 38:4
that they might put us to *d*....Jer 43:3
prison till the day of his *d*....Jer 52:11
at home there is as *d* ....Lam 1:20
pleasure in the *d* of him.......Ezek 18:32
d of them that are slain ....Ezek 28:8
are all delivered unto *d* ....Ezek 31:14
I will redeem them from *d* ....Hos 13:14
turneth the shadow of *d*.......Amos 5:8
to be angry, even unto *d*......Jon 4:9
desire as hell, and is as *d* .....Hab 2:5
there until the *d* of Herod.....Matt 2:15
region and shadow of *d* ....Matt 4:16
deliver up the brother to *d* ....Matt 10:21
cause them to be put to *d* .....Matt 10:21
would have put him to *d* ......Matt 14:5
or mother, let him die the *d*...Matt 15:4
not taste of *d*, till they ....Matt 16:28
shall condemn him to *d* ....Matt 20:18
sorrowful, even unto *d* ....Matt 26:38
against Jesus..him to *d* ....Matt 27:1
daughter..the point of *d*.......Mark 5:23
let him die the *d* ....Mark 7:10
not taste of *d*, till they ....Mark 9:1
shall condemn him to *d* ....Mark 10:33
betray the brother to *d*........Mark 13:12
cause them to be put to *d* .....Mark 13:12
by craft, and put him to *d*.....Mark 14:1
and in the shadow of *d*, to ....Luke 1:79
that he should not see *d* ......Luke 2:26
which shall not taste of *d* .....Luke 9:27
scourge..and put him to *d* .....Luke 18:33
they cause to be put to *d* .....Luke 21:16
both into prison, and to *d*.....Luke 22:33
nothing worthy of *d* is done ...Luke 23:15
to be condemned to *d*, and ....Luke 24:20
for he was at the point of *d* ...John 4:47
passed from *d* unto life ....John 5:24
he shall never see *d* ....John 8:51
This sickness is not unto *d* ....John 11:4
put Lazarus also to *d* ....John 12:10
lawful..put any man to *d* ......John 18:31
by what *d* he..glorify God .....John 21:19
loosed the pains of *d* ....Acts 2:24
Saul was consenting..his *d*.....Acts 8:1
they should be put to *d* ....Acts 12:19
found no cause of *d* in him....Acts 13:28
persecuted..way unto the *d*....Acts 22:4
charge worthy of *d* or of ......Acts 23:29
any thing worthy of *d*.........Acts 25:11
when they were put to *d*, I ....Acts 26:10
was no cause of *d* in me ....Acts 28:18
such things are worthy of *d*....Rom 1:32
by the *d* of his Son, much.....Rom 5:10
were baptized into his *d*?.....Rom 6:3
to bring forth fruit unto *d* .....Rom 7:5
free from..law of sin and *d* ....Rom 8:2
life or *d*, or things present 1Cor 3:22
as it were appointed to *d*......1Cor 4:9
ye do show the Lord's *d* till ...1Cor 11:26
by man came *d*, by man 1Cor 15:21
had the sentence of *d* in 2Cor 1:9
us from so great a *d* 2Cor 1:10
are the savor of *d* unto *d*......2Cor 2:16
the ministration of *d* 2Cor 3:7
delivered unto *d* for Jesus' 2Cor 4:11
sorrow..world worketh *d* 2Cor 7:10
prisons more frequent in *d* 2Cor 11:23
it be by life, or by *d* ....Phil 1:20
became obedient unto *d*.......Phil 2:8
even the *d* of the cross........Phil 2:8
conformable unto his *d*........Phil 3:10
body of his flesh through *d* ....Col 1:22
who hath abolished *d*, and 2Tim 1:10
the suffering of *d*, crowned ....Heb 2:9
God should taste *d*, for ....Heb 2:9
save him from *d*, and was .....Heb 5:7
to continue by reason of *d* ....Heb 7:23
by means of *d*, for the ....Heb 9:15
that he should not see *d* ......Heb 11:5
finished, bringeth forth *d*......James 1:15
save a soul from *d*, and ....James 5:20
being put to *d* in the flesh.....1Pet 3:18
passed from *d* unto life 1John 3:14
a sin which is not unto *d*......1John 5:16
them that sin not unto *d* 1John 5:16
the keys of hell and of *d* ......Rev 1:18
be thou faithful unto *d*........Rev 2:10
name that sat on him was *D*...Rev 6:8
with hunger, and with *d*.......Rev 6:8
men seek *d*..shall not find .....Rev 9:6
and *d* shall flee from them ....Rev 9:6
loved not..lives unto the *d* ....Rev 12:11
no more *d*, neither sorrow ....Rev 21:4

DEATH, ETERNAL—*God's punishment for the sinner*

Described as:
Everlasting punishment ..Matt 25:46
Resurrection of damnation ....John 5:29
God's wrath 1Thess 1:10
Destruction 2Thess 1:9; 2Pet 2:12
Second death ....Rev 20:14

Truths regarding:
A consequence of man's sin ....Gen 3:17-19
The punishment of the wicked ....Matt 25:41, 46
Separates from God 2Thess 1:9
Christ saves from........John 3:16
Saints shall escape from ..1Cor 15:54-58; Rev 2:11
Vividly described ....Luke 16:23-26

DEATH, NATURAL—*the end of human existence*

Features regarding:
Consequence of sin ......Rom 5:12
Lot of all ....Heb 9:27
Ends earthly life.........Eccl 9:10
Christ delivers from fear of ....Heb 2:15
Some escaped from ......Gen 5:24
Some will escape 1Cor 15:51, 52
All to be raised from ....Acts 24:15
Illustrates regeneration...Rom 6:2

Described as:
Return to dust ....Gen 3:19
Removal of breath ......Gen 25:8
Removal from tabernacle .2Cor 5:1
Naked 2Cor 5:3, 4
Sleep ....John 11:11-14
Departure ....Phil 1:23
Yielded up the ghost ....Acts 5:10

Recognition after:
Departed saints recognized by the living.Matt 17:1-8
Greater knowledge in future world 1Cor 13:12
The truth illustrated .....Luke 16:19-24

DEATH OF SAINTS

Described as:
Asleep in Jesus..........1Thess 4:14
Blessed ....Rev 14:13
A gain ....Phil 1:21
Peace ....Is 57:1, 2
Crown of righteousness ..2Tim 4:8

Exemplified in:
Abraham ....Gen 25:8
Isaac ....Gen 35:28, 29
Jacob...................Gen 49:33
Elisha 2Kin 13:14, 20
The criminal ....Luke 23:39-43

DEATH OF THE WICKED
Result of sin ....Rom 5:12
Often punishment ....Ex 23:25-29; Is 65:11, 12
Unpleasant for God .....Ezek 33:11
Without hope.........1Thess 4:13; Rev 20:10, 14, 15

DEATH PENALTY—*legal execution*
By stoning ....Deut 13:6-10; Deut 17:5

DEBASE—*to lower in status or relationship*
d thyself even unto hell ....Is 57:9

DEBATE—*discussion; contention*
With a neighbor.........Prov 25:9
Wicked, full of..........Rom 1:29
Saints must avoid........2Cor 12:20

forth, thou wilt *d* with it ......Is 27:8
fast for strife and *d*, and ......Is 58:4

DEBIR (dē'ber)—*"oracle"*
1. King of Eglon ....Josh 10:3-26
2. City of Judah...........Josh 15:15
   Also called Kirjath-sepher ....Josh 15:15
   Captured by Joshua .....Josh 10:38,39
   Recaptured by Othniel ..Josh 15:15-17; Judg 1:11-13
   Assigned to priests.......Josh 21:13,15
3. A place east of the Jordan ....Josh 13:26
4. Town of Judah ....Josh 15:7

Hebron, from *D*, from Anab ..Josh 11:21
king of *D*, one; the king of....Josh 12:13
Hilen with her suburbs, *D*.....1Chr 6:58

DEBORAH (děb'ô-rä)—*"bee"*
1. Rebekah's nurse ....Gen 35:8
2. A prophetess and judge..Judg 4:4-14
   Composed song of triumph ....Judg 5:1-31

DEBT—*that which is owed*

Safeguards regarding:
No oppression allowed ...Deut 23:19, 20
Collateral protected......Ex 22:25-27
Time limitation of ....Deut 15:1-18
Non-payment forbidden ..Neh 5:5
Debts to be honored.....Rom 13:6
Interest (usury) forbidden.Ezek 18:8-17
Love, the unpayable .....Rom 13:8
Parable concerning ......Matt 18:23-35

Evils of:
Brings slavery ....Lev 25:39, 47
Causes complaint 2Kin 4:1-7
Produces strife ....Jer 15:10
Makes outlaws 1Sam 22:2
Endangers property......Prov 6:1-5

Figurative of:
Sins ....Matt 6:12
Works ....Rom 4:4

Moral obligation.........Rom 1:14
God's mercy ....Ps 37:26

[*also* DEBTOR, DEBTORS, DEBTS]
and the exaction of every *d* ...Neh 10:31
that are sureties for *d*.........Prov 22:26
him, and forgave him the *d* ...Matt 18:27
the temple, he is a *d*..........Matt 23:16
creditor which had two *d*......Luke 7:41
every one of his lord's *d* ......Luke 16:5
we are *d*, not to the flesh .....Rom 8:12
them verily; and their *d*.......Rom 15:27
is a *d* to do the whole law ....Gal 5:3

DECALOGUE—*See* THE TEN COMMANDMENTS

DECAPOLIS (dĕ-kăp'ō-lĭs)—*"ten cities"*
Multitudes from, follow Jesus ....Matt 4:25
Healed demon-possessed, preaches in ....Mark 5:20

midst of the coasts of *D*.......Mark 7:31

DECAY—*to fall into ruin; rot*

[*also* DECAYED, DECAYETH]
and fallen in *d* with thee ......Lev 25:35
the bearers of burdens is *d* ....Neh 4:10
the flood *d* and drieth up .....Job 14:11
slothfulness the building *d*.....Eccl 10:18
raise up the *d* places ....Is 44:26
which *d* and waxeth old ....Heb 8:13

DECEASE—*one's death*

[*also* DECEASED]
are *d*, they shall not rise ......Is 26:14
he had married a wife, *d*......Matt 22:25
spake of his *d* which he ....Luke 9:31
be able after my *d* to have 2Pet 1:15

DECEIT—*that which deludes or misleads*

The wicked:
Devise..................Ps 35:20
Speaks ....Jer 9:8
Are full of ....Rom 1:29
Increase in.............2Tim 3:13

Agents of:
Satan 2Cor 11:14
Sin.....................Rom 7:11
Self ....1Cor 3:18; James 1:22
Others..................2Thess 2:3

Warnings against:
Among religious workers .2Cor 11:3-15
As a sign of apostasy 2Thess 2:10
As a sign of the antichrist.1John 4:1-6

Examples of:
Eve 1Tim 2:14
Abram ....Gen 12:11-13
Isaac ....Gen 26:6, 7
Jacob...................Gen 27:18-27
Joseph's brothers ....Gen 37:31, 32
Pharaoh ....Ex 8:29
David 1Sam 21:12, 13
Amnon 2Sam 13:6-14
Gehazi 2Kin 5:20-27
Elisha 2Kin 6:19-23
Herod ....Matt 2:7, 8
Pharisees ....Matt 22:15,16
Peter ....Mark 14:70, 71
Ananias ....Acts 5:1-11
The earth ....Rev 13:14

[*also* DECEITFUL, DECEITFULLY, DECEITFULNESS, DECEITS]
and Hamor his father *d* ....Gen 34:13
let not Pharaoh deal *d* any ....Ex 8:29
seeing he hath dealt *d* with....Ex 21:8
which he hath *d* gotten........Lev 6:4
brethren have dealt *d* as a.....Job 6:15
for God? and talk *d* for ....Job 13:7
their belly prepareth *d* ....Job 15:35
nor my tongue utter *d* ....Job 27:4
my foot hath hasted to *d* ......Job 31:5
abhor the bloody and *d* ....Ps 5:6
is full of cursing and *d* ....Ps 10:7
unto vanity, nor sworn *d* ......Ps 24:4
mouth are iniquity and *d* ......Ps 36:3
imagine *d* all the day long .....Ps 38:12
me from the *d* and unjust .....Ps 43:1
and thy tongue frameth *d* ......Ps 50:19
a sharp razor, working *d* ......Ps 52:2
words, O thou *d* tongue.......Ps 52:4
d and guile depart not ....Ps 55:11
bloody and *d* men..not live ....Ps 55:23
redeem their soul from *d*......Ps 72:14
turned aside like a *d* bow .....Ps 78:57
d shall not dwell within my....Ps 101:7
d are opened against me ......Ps 109:2
for their *d* is falsehood ....Ps 119:118
lying lips, and from a *d* ....Ps 120:2
wicked worketh a *d* work .....Prov 11:18
counsels of..wicked are *d*......Prov 12:5
the folly of fools is *d* ....Prov 14:8
d witness speaketh lies ....Prov 14:25
Bread of *d* is sweet to a.......Prov 20:17
for they are *d* meat ....Prov 23:3
layeth up *d* within him ....Prov 26:24
hatred is covered by *d* ....Prov 26:26
kisses of an enemy are *d* ......Prov 27:6
d man meet together..........Prov 29:13
Favor is *d*..beauty is vain .....Prov 31:30
smooth things, prophesy *d*.....Is 30:10
was any *d* in his mouth ....Is 53:9
their houses full of *d*..........Jer 5:27
hold fast *d*, they refuse ....Jer 8:5
habitation..the midst of *d* .....Jer 9:6
through *d* they refuse to ......Jer 9:6
and the *d* of their heart ....Jer 14:14
heart is *d* above all things .....Jer 17:9
of the *d* of their own heart ....Jer 23:26
the work of the Lord *d* ....Jer 48:10
shall work *d*: for he shall......Dan 11:23
they are like a *d* bow ....Hos 7:16
house of Israel with *d*.........Hos 11:12
balances of *d*..in his hand .....Hos 12:7
falsifying..balances by *d* ....Amos 8:5
with the bag of *d* weights .....Mic 6:11
houses with violence and *d* ....Zeph 1:9
d tongue be found in their ....Zeph 3:13
d of riches, choke the word ...Matt 13:22
d of riches, and the lusts ......Mark 4:19
wickedness, *d*, lasciviousness...Mark 7:22
tongues they have used *d* .....Rom 3:13
the word of God *d* 2Cor 4:2
good report: as *d*, and yet.....2Cor 6:8
false apostles, *d* workers 2Cor 11:13
corrupt according to the *d*.....Eph 4:22
philosophy and vain *d*.........Col 2:8
exhortation was not of *d* 1Thess 2:3
all *d* of unrighteousness 2Thess 2:10
through the *d* of sin ....Heb 3:13
own *d* while they feast 2Pet 2:13
many *d* are entered into 2John 7

DECEIVE—*to delude or mislead*

In Old Testament:
Eve, by Satan ....Gen 3:13
Israel, by the Midianites. .Num 25:18
Joshua, by the Gibeonites.Josh 9:22

Of Christians:
By flattering words ......Rom 16:18
By false report 2Thess 2:3
By false reasoning ....Col 2:4

[*also* DECEIVED, DECEIVETH, DECEIVING, DECEIVINGS]
your father hath *d* me, and....Gen 31:7
or hath *d* his neighbor ....Lev 6:2
he came to *d* thee, and 2Sam 3:25
I not say, Do not *d* me? 2Kin 4:28
Let not Hezekiah *d* you 2Kin 18:29
let not Hezekiah *d* you........2Chr 32:15
whosoever is *d* thereby is .....Prov 20:1
and *d* not with thy lips ....Prov 24:28
man that *d* his neighbor ....Prov 26:19
the princes of Noph are *d* .....Is 19:13
Let not Hezekiah *d* you ....Is 36:14
God..thou trustest, *d* ....Is 37:10
a *d* heart had turned him .....Is 44:20
d every one his neighbor ......Jer 9:5
hast *d* me, and I was *d*........Jer 20:7
be in the midst of you *d* ......Jer 29:8
D not yourselves, saying ......Jer 37:9
terribleness hath *d* thee ....Jer 49:16
called..lovers, but they *d*......Lam 1:19
if the prophet be *d* when ......Ezek 14:9
Lord have *d* that prophet .....Ezek 14:9
pride of thine heart hath *d* ....Obad 3
wear a rough garment to *d* ....Zech 13:4
Take heed that no man *d* .....Matt 24:4
Take heed lest any man *d*......Mark 13:5
Take heed that ye be not *d* ...Luke 21:8
said, Nay; but he *d* the ....John 7:12
Pharisees, Are ye also *d*? .....John 7:47
not *d*: neither fornicators 1Cor 6:9
not *d*: evil communications 1Cor 15:33
he is nothing, he *d* himself ....Gal 6:3
not *d*; God is not mocked .....Gal 6:7
they lie in wait to *d* ....Eph 4:14
worse and worse, *d*, and 2Tim 3:13
d, serving divers lusts and .....Titus 3:3
but *d* his own heart...........James 1:26
their own *d* while they 2Pet 2:13
let no man *d* you: he that 1John 3:7
Satan, which *d* the..world .....Rev 12:9
were all nations *d* ....Rev 18:23
with which he *d* them that ....Rev 19:20
he should *d* the nations no ....Rev 20:3
devil that *d* them was cast.....Rev 20:10

DECEIVER—*one who misleads others*

[*also* DECEIVERS]
I shall seem to him as a *d*.....Gen 27:12
deceived and the *d* are his ....Job 12:16
cursed be the *d*, which ....Mal 1:14
remember what that *d* said ....Matt 27:63
and vain talkers and *d* ....Titus 1:10
is a *d* and an antichrist........2John 7

DECENTLY—*appropriately*
all things be done *d* and in 1Cor 14:40

DECISION—*determination to follow a course of action*

Sources of:
Loyalty ....Ruth 1:16
Prayer 1Sam 23:1-13
The Lord 1Kin 12:15
Satan 1Chr 21:1
The world ....Luke 14:16-24
Human need ....Acts 11:27-30
Disagreement ....Acts 15:36-41
Faith ....Heb 11:2-28

Wrong, leading to:
Spiritual decline ....Gen 13:7-11
Repentance ....Heb 12:16, 17
Defeat..................Num 14:40-45
Rejection 1Sam 15:6-26
Apostasy 1Kin 11:1-13
Division 1Kin 12:12-20
Death ....Acts 1:16-20

Good, manifested in:
Siding with the Lord .....Ex 32:26
Following God ....Num 14:24; Josh 14:8
Loving God.............Deut 6:5
Seeking God 2Chr 15:12
Obeying God ....Neh 10:28-30

[*also* DECIDED]
thyself hast *d* it...............1Kin 20:40

DECISION, VALLEY OF—*(location unknown)*
Called 'Valley of Jehoshaphat' ....Joel 3:2, 12, 14
Refers to final judgment. .Joel 3:1-21

DECISIVENESS—*showing firmness of decision*
In serving God ....Josh 24:15,16; Heb 11:24,25
Toward family ....Ruth 1:15-18
Toward a leader.........2Kin 2:1-6
To complete a task ......Neh 4:14-23
In morality.............Gen 39:10-12; Dan 1:8
In prayer ....Dan 6:1-16

DECK—*to cover; array*

[*also* DECKED, DECKEDST, DECKEST, DECKETH]
D thyself now with majesty....Job 40:10
d my bed with coverings ......Prov 7:16
as a bridegroom *d* himself.....Is 61:10
d thee with ornaments ....Jer 4:30
d it with silver and with ....Jer 10:4
d thee also with ornaments ....Ezek 16:11
and *d* thy high places with ....Ezek 16:16
d thyself with ornaments ......Ezek 23:40
d herself with her earrings.....Hos 2:13
d with gold and precious ......Rev 17:4
d with gold, and precious .....Rev 18:16

DECK—*the top side of a ship*
Made of ivory...........Ezek 27:6

DECLARATION—*proclamation; making known*

[*also* DECLARE, DECLARED, DECLARETH, DECLARING]
was none that could *d* it ......Gen 41:24
name may be *d* throughout ....Ex 9:16
Moses *d* unto the children .....Lev 23:44
they *d* their pedigrees ....Num 1:18
d unto you his covenant.......Deut 4:13
thou hast *d* this day, that 2Sam 19:6
prophets *d* good unto the 1Kin 22:13
D his glory among the 1Chr 16:24
words of the prophets *d*.......2Chr 18:12
the words that were *d* unto....Neh 8:12
d..unto her, and to charge ....Esth 4:8
d of the greatness of ....Esth 10:2
fishes of the sea shall *d* ....Job 12:8
and my *d* with your ears ......Job 13:17
Who shall *d* his way to his ......Job 21:31
hast thou plentifully *d* the .....Job 26:3
d unto him the number ....Job 31:37
thee, and *d* thou unto me .....Job 40:7
will *d* the decree: the Lord ....Ps 2:7
heavens *d* the glory of God ...Ps 19:1
shall it *d* thy truth? ....Ps 30:9
if I would *d* and speak of .....Ps 40:5
I have *d* thy faithfulness ......Ps 40:10
shall *d* the work of God.......Ps 64:9
that I may *d* all thy works.....Ps 73:28
d thy strength among the......Ps 77:14
d them to their children ....Ps 78:6
d his righteousness............Ps 97:6
With my lips have I *d* all......Ps 119:13
shall *d* thy mighty acts ....Ps 145:4
d all this, that..righteous ......Eccl 9:1
they *d* their sin as Sodom .....Is 3:9
A grievous vision is *d* unto ....Is 21:2
let him *d* what he seeth ....Is 21:6
there is none that *d*, yea ......Is 41:26
new things do I *d*: before .....Is 42:9
I have *d*, and have saved......Is 43:12
I shall call, and shall *d*........Is 44:7
who hath *d* this from ancient ..Is 45:21
D the end from..beginning ....Is 46:10
this; and will not ye *d* it? .....Is 48:6
I will *d* thy righteousness......Is 57:12
D ye in Judah, and publish ....Jer 4:5
For a voice *d* from Dan ....Jer 4:15
d it..the land perisheth ....Jer 9:12
Michaiah *d* unto ....Jer 36:13
If I *d* it unto thee, wilt........Jer 38:15
I will *d* it unto you; I will .....Jer 42:4
d all their abominations ....Ezek 12:16
d all that thou seest to ....Ezek 40:4
d the interpretation ....Dan 4:18
their staff *d* unto them ....Hos 4:12
d unto man..his thought.......Amos 4:13
D ye it not at Gath, weep .....Mic 1:10
to day do I *d* that I will.......Zech 9:12
D unto us the parable of ......Matt 13:36
to set forth in order a *d*.......Luke 1:1
d unto him before..people .....Luke 8:47
the Father, he hath *d* him .....John 1:18
thy name, and will *d* it.........John 17:26
who shall *d* his generation.....Acts 8:33
d unto them how he had ......Acts 9:27
d the conversion of the ....Acts 15:3
d all things that God had .....Acts 15:4
worship, him *d* I unto you .....Acts 17:23
d Paul's cause unto the ....Acts 25:14
d to be the Son of God ....Rom 1:4
to *d* his righteousness for......Rom 3:25
hath been *d* unto me of you ...1Cor 1:11
d..the testimony of God.......1Cor 2:1
for the day shall *d* it..........1Cor 3:13
I *d* unto you the gospel 1Cor 15:1
d to be the epistle of 2Cor 3:3
and *d* of your ready mind 2Cor 8:19
also *d* unto us your love ......Col 1:8
will *d* thy name unto my ......Heb 2:12
seen and heard *d* we unto 1John 1:3
d to his servants the ....Rev 10:7

DECLINE—*to turn away from; gradual lowering*

[*also* DECLINED, DECLINETH]
d..many to wrest judgment ....Ex 23:2
not *d* from the sentence ....Deut 17:11
d neither to the right hand 2Chr 34:2
way have I kept and not *d* ....Job 23:11
our steps *d* from thy way......Ps 44:18
days..a shadow that *d*.........Ps 102:11
like the shadow when it *d*.....Ps 109:23
not *d* from thy testimonies ....Ps 119:157
neither *d* from the words......Prov 4:5
not thine heart *d* to...........Prov 7:25

DECREASE—*to grow progressively less*

[*also* DECREASED]
waters *d* continually until......Gen 8:5
suffereth not..cattle to *d* ......Ps 107:38
increase, but I must *d*........Job 3:30

DECREE—*a course of action authoritatively determined*

As a human edict:
Issued by kings..........Dan 6:7-14
Considered inflexible ....Dan 6:15-17
Published widely ....Esth 3:13-15
Providentially nullified ...Esth 8:3-17
Sometimes beneficial.....Dan 4:25-28

As a divine edict, to:
Govern nature ....Jer 5:22

[*also* DECREED, DECREES]
So they established a *d* to 2Chr 30:5
Cyrus made a *d* to build ......Ezra 5:13
I make a *d*, that all they ......Ezra 7:13
the king's *d* which he shall ....Esth 1:20
what was *d* against her ....Esth 2:1
commandment..his *d* came ....Esth 4:3
his *d* drew near to be ....Esth 9:1
Thou shalt also *d* a thing......Job 22:28
brake up for it my *d* place ....Job 38:10
declare the *d*: the Lord ....Ps 2:7
and princes *d* justice ....Prov 8:15
that decree unrighteous *d* .....Is 10:1
them that *d* unrighteous ....Is 10:1
the consumption *d* shall ....Is 10:22
there is but one *d* for you .....Dan 2:9
made I a *d* to bring in ....Dan 4:6
d of the king and his ....Jon 3:7
shall the *d* be far removed ....Mic 7:11
Before the *d* bring forth ......Zeph 2:2
went out a *d* from Caesar .....Luke 2:1
delivered them the *d* for ......Acts 16:4
hath so *d* in his heart that 1Cor 7:37

DEDAN (dē'dăn)—*"low"*
1. Raamah's son ....Gen 10:7
2. Jokshan's son ....Gen 25:3
3. Descendants of Raamah; a commercial people . { Ezek 27:15, 20 / Ezek 38:13

[*also* DEDANIM]
of Raamah; Sheba, and *D*.....1Chr 1:9
traveling companies of *D*......Is 21:13
deep, O inhabitants of *D*......Jer 49:8
D shall fall by the sword ......Ezek 25:13

DEDICATION—*setting apart for a sacred use*

Of things:
Tabernacle...............Ex 40:34-38
Solomon's Temple 1Kin 8:12-66
Second Temple..........Ezra 6:1-22

Offerings in, must be:
Voluntary...............Lev 22:18-25
Without blemish.........Lev 1:3
Unredeemable ....Lev 27:28, 29

Examples of:
Samuel 1Sam 1:11, 22
The believer ....Rom 12:1, 2

[*also* DEDICATE, DEDICATED, DEDICATING]
princes offered for *d* of ....Num 7:10
d of the altar, in the day......Num 7:84
house, and hath not *d* it? .....Deut 20:5
battle, and another man *d*.....Deut 20:5
d the silver unto the Lord .....Judg 17:3
and gold that he had *d*........2Sam 8:11
also king David did *d*.........2Sam 8:11
David his father had *d*........1Kin 7:51
things..his father had *d*........1Kin 15:15
money of the *d* things that 2Kin 12:4
David *d* unto the Lord 1Chr 18:11
d to maintain the house 1Chr 26:27
treasuries of the *d* things 1Chr 28:12
to *d* it to him, and to burn 2Chr 2:4
David his father had *d* 2Chr 5:1
they kept the *d* of the altar....2Chr 7:9
things..his father had *d*........2Chr 15:18
and the *d* things faithfully 2Chr 31:12
d of the wall of Jerusalem .....Neh 12:27
keep the *d* with gladness ......Neh 12:27
d of the house of David.......Ps 30:*title*
every *d* thing in Israel ....Ezek 44:29
come to the *d* of the image....Dan 3:2
the feast of the *d*.............John 10:22
testament was *d* without ......Heb 9:18

DEDICATION, FEAST OF—*Hanukkah; commemorates the victories of Judas Maccabeus and the purification and rededication of the Temple. Also known as "lights"*
Jesus attended ....John 10:22, 23

DEED—*a thing done*

Descriptive of one's:
Past record ....Luke 11:48
Present achievements ....Acts 7:22
Future action 2Cor 10:11

Expressive of one's:
Evil nature..............2Pet 2:8
Parentage ....John 8:41
Record ....Luke 24:19
Profession 3John 10
Love 1John 3:18
Judgment ....Rom 2:6

Toward God:
Weighed 1Sam 2:3
Wrong punished.........Luke 23:41

Lord's are:
Righteous...............Judg 5:11; 1Sam 12:7
Mighty ....Ps 106:2
Beyond description ......Ps 106:2

Considered positively:
Example of ....Titus 2:7
Zealous for ....Titus 2:14
Careful to engage in .....Titus 3:8, 14
Stimulate to.............Heb 10:24
In heaven...............Rev 14:13

[*also* DEEDS]
thou hast done *d* unto me .....Gen 20:9
What *d* is this that ye have ....Gen 44:15
And in very *d* for this cause ....Ex 9:16
There was no such *d* done ....Judg 19:30
For..very *d*, as the Lord God ..1Sam 25:34
by this *d* thou hast given 2Sam 12:14
make known his *d* among 1Chr 16:8
will God in very *d* dwell 2Chr 6:18
his *d*, first and last 2Chr 35:27
for our evil *d*, and for our ....Ezra 9:13
reported his good *d* before ....Neh 6:19
this *d* of the queen shall ......Esth 1:17
Give..according to their *d* .....Ps 28:4
According to their *d* ....Is 59:18
the *d* of the wicked ....Jer 5:28
the counsel and *d* of them.....Luke 23:51

because their ***d*** were evil ......John 3:19
d done to the impotent ....Acts 4:9
and showed their ***d*** ....Acts 19:18
very worthy ***d*** are done ....Acts 24:2
d of the law there shall no ....Rom 3:20
mortify the ***d*** of the body .....Rom 8:13
obedient, by word and ***d*** ......Rom 15:18
hath done this ***d*** might be 1Cor 5:2
wonders, and mighty ***d*** 2Cor 12:12
put off..man with his ***d***.........Col 3:9
ye do in word or ***d***, do all.....Col 3:17
shall be blessed in his ***d*** ....James 1:25
is partaker of his evil ***d*** 2John 11
all their ungodly ***d*** which ......Jude 15
the ***d*** of the Nicolaitans ....Rev 2:6
repented not of their ***d***........Rev 16:11

DEEDS, THE UNBELIEVER'S—*disobedient acts*

Described as:
Evil ....Col 1:21
Done in dark place ......Is 29:15
Abominable ....Ps 14:1
Unfruitful ....Eph 5:11

God's attitude toward, will:
Never forget ....Amos 8:7
Render according to ......Prov 24:12
Bring to judgment ....Rev 20:12, 13

Believer's relation to:
Lay aside ....Rom 13:12
Not participate in........Eph 5:11
Be delivered from 2Tim 4:18

DEEMED—*ascertained*
shipmen ***d*** that they drew .....Acts 27:27

DEEP—*far downward; difficult to understand; ocean; abyss*

[*also* DEEPER, DEEPLY, DEEPNESS, DEEPS]
was upon the face of the ***d*** ....Gen 1:2
fountains of the great ***d*** ....Gen 7:11
a ***d*** sleep fell upon Abram ....Gen 15:12
in sight be ***d*** than the skin ....Lev 13:3
d that coucheth beneath.......Deut 33:13
d sleep from the Lord was 1Sam 26:12
thou threwest into the ***d*** ......Neh 9:11
d sleep falleth on men ....Job 4:13
d than hell; what canst ....Job 11:8
d sleep falleth upon men ......Job 33:15
the ***d*** to boil like a pot........Job 41:31
judgments are a great ***d***.......Ps 36:6
them, and the heart, is ***d***......Ps 64:6
cause it to take ***d*** root ....Ps 80:9
pit, in darkness, in the ***d***......Ps 88:6
In his hand are..***d*** places ......Ps 95:4
and his wonders in the ***d*** ......Ps 107:24
into the fire; into ***d*** pits ....Ps 140:10
ye dragons, and all ***d*** ....Ps 148:7
the fountains of the ***d***.........Prov 8:28
casteth into a ***d*** sleep; and ....Prov 19:15
mouth of..women is a ***d*** pit....Prov 22:14
the spirit of ***d*** sleep, and ......Is 29:10
children of Israel have ***d*** ....Is 31:6
a people of ***d*** speech than .....Is 33:19
That saith to the ***d***, Be dry ....Is 44:27
led them through the ***d*** ....Is 63:13
dwell ***d***, O inhabitants of......Jer 49:8
drink..thy sister's cup ***d*** ....Ezek 23:32
the ***d*** set him up on high ......Ezek 31:4
have drunk of the ***d*** waters ....Ezek 34:18
the ***d*** and secret things ....Dan 2:22
then was I in a ***d*** sleep on.....Dan 10:9
They have ***d*** corrupted ....Hos 9:9
it devoured the great ***d***........Amos 7:4
hadst cast me into the ***d***.......Jon 2:3
d uttered his voice, and ....Hab 3:10
d of the river shall dry ....Zech 10:11
they had no ***d*** of earth ....Matt 13:5
he sighed ***d*** in his spirit ....Mark 8:12
Launch out into the ***d***, and ....Luke 5:4
built a house..digged ***d***........Luke 6:48
them to go out into the ***d*** .....Luke 8:31
and the well is ***d*** ....John 4:11
being fallen into a ***d*** sleep .....Acts 20:9
shall descend into the ***d***? ......Rom 10:7

yea, the ***d*** things of God 1Cor 2:10
their ***d*** poverty abounded 2Cor 8:2
day I have been in the ***d*** 2Cor 11:25

DEER—*a hoofed cud-chewing animal*
roebuck, and the fallow ***d*** .....Deut 14:5

DEFAMED—*slandered*

[*also* DEFAMING]
For I heard the ***d*** of many ....Jer 20:10
Being ***d***, we entreat: we are ...1Cor 4:13

DEFEAT—*to destroy; nullify*
me ***d*** the counsel of 2Sam 15:34
d the good counsel of.........2Sam 17:14

DEFENSE—*protection during attack*
Of a city................2Kin 19:34
Of Israel................Judg 10:1
Of a plot 2Sam 23:11, 12
Of the upright ....Ps 7:10
Of one accused..........Acts 22:1
Of the Gospel...........Phil 1:7, 16

[*also* DEFENCED, DEFEND, DEFENDED, DEFENDEST, DEFENDING, DEFENSED]
d is departed from them ......Num 14:9
I arose to ***d*** Israel Tola ....Judg 10:1
d it..slew the Philistines 2Sam 23:12
I will ***d*** this city, to save 2Kin 19:34
d this city for mine own 2Kin 20:6
and built cities for ***d*** 2Chr 11:5
the Almighty shall be thy ***d*** ...Job 22:25
because thou ***d*** them: let ....Ps 5:11
name of the God of Jacob ***d***...Ps 20:1
a house of ***d*** to save me........Ps 31:2
d me from them that rise .....Ps 59:1
wait..for God is my ***d*** ....Ps 59:9
salvation; he is my ***d***..........Ps 62:2
D the poor and fatherless .....Ps 82:3
For the Lord is our ***d*** ....Ps 89:18
Lord is my ***d***; and my God ....Ps 94:22
wisdom..and money is a ***d***.....Eccl 7:12
the glory shall be a ***d*** ....Is 4:5
brooks of ***d***..be emptied.......Is 19:6
of a ***d*** city a ruin: a palace ....Is 25:2
d city shall be desolate ....Is 27:10
Lord of hosts ***d*** Jerusalem .....Is 31:5
d also he will deliver it........Is 31:5
place of ***d***..the munition ....Is 33:16
against all the ***d*** cities of ......Is 36:1
to lay waste ***d*** cities into ......Is 37:26
will ***d*** this city to save it.......Is 37:35
and I will ***d*** this city ....Is 38:6
made thee this day a ***d*** city....Jer 1:18
let us go into the ***d*** cities ......Jer 4:5
us enter into the ***d*** cities ....Jer 8:14
for these ***d*** cities remained ....Jer 34:7
Judah in Jerusalem the ***d***......Ezek 21:20
the ***d*** shall be prepared ....Nah 2:5
Lord of hosts shall ***d*** them ....Zech 9:15
that day shall the Lord ***d***......Zech 12:8
suffer wrong, he ***d*** him; and ...Acts 7:24
made his ***d*** unto the people ...Acts 19:33

DEFERENCE—*respectful yielding to another*
To a woman's entreaty...Ruth 1:15-18
To an old man's wish 2Sam 19:31-40
Results in exaltation .....Matt 23:12
Commanded ....Heb 13:17

[*also* DEFER, DEFERRED, DEFERRETH]
man ***d*** not to do the thing.....Gen 34:19
Hope ***d*** maketh..heart sick ....Prov 13:12
discretion of a man ***d*** his ......Prov 19:11
d not to pay it; for he ....Eccl 5:4
I ***d*** mine anger, and for ....Is 48:9
d not, for thine own sake .....Dan 9:19
of that way, he ***d*** them, and ...Acts 24:22

DEFILEMENT—*making the pure impure*

Ceremonial causes of:
Childbirth...............Lev 12:2-8
Leprosy ....Lev 13:3, 44-46
Bodily discharge.........Lev 15:1-15
Copulation ....Lev 15:17
Menstruation ....Lev 15:19-33
Touching the dead.......Lev 21:1-4, 11

Spiritual manifestations of:
Abominations ....Jer 32:34

Objects of:
Conscience 1Cor 8:7
Fellowship ....Heb 12:15
Flesh ....Jude 8

[*also* DEFILE, DEFILED, DEFILEDST, DEFILETH]
and lay with her, and ***d*** her ...Gen 34:2
then ***d*** thou it: he went up ....Gen 49:4
every one that ***d*** it shall ....Ex 31:14
a man shall be ***d*** withal ....Lev 5:3
them, that ye should be ***d*** .....Lev 11:43
neither shall ye ***d*** ....Lev 11:44
be in him he shall be ***d*** ....Lev 13:46
from him, and is ***d*** ....Lev 15:32
neighbor's wife, to ***d***..........Lev 18:20
all these the nations are ***d*****.....Lev 18:24
wizards, to be ***d*** by them......Lev 19:31
to ***d*** my sanctuary, and to .....Lev 20:3
There shall none be ***d*** for .....Lev 21:1
not eat to ***d*** himself...........Lev 22:8
whosoever is ***d*** by the dead....Num 5:2
that they ***d*** not their camps....Num 5:3
he hath ***d*** the head of his .....Num 6:9
who were ***d*** by the dead ......Num 9:6
d the tabernacle of..Lord......Num 19:13
hath ***d*** the sanctuary of the ....Num 19:20
for blood it ***d*** the land ....Num 35:33
D not therefore the land ....Num 35:34
that thy land be not ***d*** ....Deut 21:23
fruit of thy vineyard, be ***d*****.....Deut 22:9
after that she is ***d***; for ....Deut 24:4
d the high places where 2Kin 23:8
of Ammon, did the king ***d*** 2Kin 23:13
as he ***d*** his father's 1Chr 5:1
they have ***d*** the priesthood ....Neh 13:29
and ***d*** my horn in the dust ....Job 16:15
have ***d*** by casting down ....Ps 74:7
holy temple have they ***d*** ......Ps 79:1
were they ***d*** with their own ....Ps 106:39
feet; how shall I ***d*** them? ....Song 5:3
The earth also is ***d*** under .....Is 24:5
Ye shall ***d*** also the covering ...Is 30:22
hands are ***d*** with blood........Is 59:3
ye entered, ye ***d*** my land......Jer 2:7
d the land, and committed ....Jer 3:9
they have ***d*** my land ....Jer 16:18
d as the place of Tophet ......Jer 19:13
Israel eat their ***d*** bread........Ezek 4:13
thou hast ***d*** my sanctuary......Ezek 5:11
enter into it, and ***d*** ....Ezek 7:22
their holy places shall be ***d*** ....Ezek 7:24
he said..***D*** the house ....Ezek 9:7
hath ***d*** his neighbor's wife .....Ezek 18:6
d not..with the idols of........Ezek 20:7
wherein ye have been ***d*** ....Ezek 20:43
idols against herself to ***d*** ......Ezek 22:3
d thyself in thine idols ....Ezek 22:4
their idols..***d*** herself ....Ezek 23:7
they shall ***d*** thy brightness.....Ezek 28:7
hast ***d*** thy sanctuaries ....Ezek 28:18
d every one his neighbor's.....Ezek 33:26
their own land, they ***d*** it ......Ezek 36:17
Neither shall they ***d***...........Ezek 37:23
house of Israel no more ***d*** .....Ezek 43:7
even ***d*** my holy name ....Ezek 43:8
no dead person to ***d*** ....Ezek 44:25
they may ***d*** themselves ....Ezek 44:25
would not ***d*** himself with ......Dan 1:8
he might not ***d*** himself ....Dan 1:8
whoredom, and Israel is ***d*****.....Hos 5:3
whoredom..Israel is ***d*** ....Hos 6:10
that say, Let her be ***d***.........Mic 4:11
into the mouth ***d*** a man ....Matt 15:11
out of the mouth, this ***d*** a.....Matt 15:11
heart: and they ***d*** the man.....Matt 15:18
eat bread with ***d***, that is.......Mark 7:2
entering into him can ***d*** ....Mark 7:15
are they that ***d*** the man ....Mark 7:15
of the man, that ***d*** the man....Mark 7:20

D

lest they should be *d*; but .....John 18:28
If any man *d* the temple of....1Cor 3:17
d themselves with mankind 1Tim 1:10
but unto them that are *d*......Titus 1:15
mind and conscience is *d*......Titus 1:15
that it *d* the whole body ......James 3:6
not *d* their garments ....Rev 3:4
were not *d* with women ....Rev 14:4
into it any thing that *d*........Rev 21:27

DEFRAUDING—*depriving others by deceit*
Forbidden ....Mark 10:19
To be accepted..........1Cor 6:5-8
In marriage 1Cor 7:3-5
Paul, not guilty of 2Cor 7:2
Product of sexual immorality 1Thess 4:3-6

[*also* DEFRAUD, DEFRAUDED]
shalt not *d* thy neighbor.......Lev 19:13
I taken? or whom have I *d*....1Sam 12:3
no man, we have *d* no man ...2Cor 7:2

DEFY—*to challenge; disregard*

[*also* DEFIED]
Jacob, and come, *d* Israel .....Num 23:7
whom the Lord hath not *d*? ...Num 23:8
I *d* the armies of Israel 1Sam 17:10
seeing he hath *d* the armies ...1Sam 17:36
when he *d* Israel, Jonathan 2Sam 21:21
when they *d* the Philistines 2Sam 23:9
But when he *d* Israel 1Chr 20:7

DEGENERATE—*degraded*
thou turned into the *d* plant ....Jer 2:21

DEGREES—*ascents; steps; rank*
The sun dial 2Kin 20:9-11
Movement toward Jerusalem.............Ps 120—134: *titles*
Order of work 1Chr 15:18
Rank in society ....Luke 1:52
Advancement in service ..1Tim 3:13

[*also* DEGREE]
the shadow go forward ten *d* ..2Kin 20:9
or go back ten *d*? 2Kin 20:9
of the second *d*, Zechariah 1Chr 15:18
estate of a man of high *d* 1Chr 17:17
d are vanity..men of high *d*....Ps 62:9
the shadow of the *d* ....Is 38:8
Ahaz, ten *d* backward ....Is 38:8
ten *d*, by which *d* it was.......Is 38:8
and exalted them of low *d* ....Luke 1:52
to themselves a good *d*........1Tim 3:13
the brother of low *d* rejoice ...James 1:9

DEGREES, SONGS OF—*songs during Feast of Tabernacles*
"Songs of Ascent".......Ps 120—134

DEHAVITES (dē-hā'vīts)—*people who settled in Samaria during the exile*
Opposed rebuilding of Jerusalem.............Ezra 4:9-16

DEITY OF CHRIST—*See* CHRIST

DEKAR (dē'kär)—*"lancer"*
Father of one of Solomon's officers 1Kin 4:9

DELAIAH (dē-lā'yä)—*"Jehovah has raised; Jehovah is deliverer"*
1. Descendant of Aaron ...1Chr 24:18
2. Son of Shemaiah; urges Jehoiakim not to burn Jeremiah's roll..........Jer 36:12, 25
3. Founder of a family .....Eza 2:60
4. A son of Elioenai 1Chr 3:24

children of *D*, the children ....Ezra 2:60
of Shemaiah the son of *D* .....Neh 6:10
The children of *D*, the ....Neh 7:62

DELAY—*to hinder; postpone*

[*also* DELAYED, DELAYETH]
Thou shalt not *d* to offer......Ex 22:29
Moses *d* to come down out....Ex 32:1
I made haste, and *d* not to ....Ps 119:60
My lord *d* his coming ....Matt 24:48
My lord *d* his coming; and ....Luke 12:45
he would not *d* to come.......Acts 9:38
any *d* on the morrow ....Acts 25:17

DELECTABLE—*delightful*
d things shall not profit ....Is 44:9

DELIBERATION—*careful consideration of elements involved in a decision*
Necessary in life.........Luke 14:28-32
Illustrated in Jacob ......Gen 32:1-23

DELICATE—*luxurious; tender; fragile*

[*also* DELICACIES, DELICATELY, DELICATENESS, DELICATES]
is tender..and very *d*.........Deut 28:54
foot upon the ground for *d*....Deut 28:56
And Agag came unto him *d*...1Sam 15:32
d bringeth up his servant ......Prov 29:21
be called tender and *d* ....Is 47:1
to a comely and *d* woman .....Jer 6:2
filled his belly with my *d*......Jer 51:34
that..feed *d* are desolate ......Lam 4:5
poll thee..thy *d* children.......Mic 1:16
live *d*..in kings' courts ....Luke 7:25
the abundance of her *d* ....Rev 18:3

DELICIOUSLY—*luxuriously*
glorified herself..lived *d*.......Rev 18:7

DELIGHT—*great pleasure in something*
Wrong kind of:
Showy display ....Esth 6:6-11
Physical strength ....Ps 147:10
Sacrifices ....Ps 51:16; Is 1:11
Abominations ....Is 66:3
Right kind of:
God's will ....Ps 40:8
God's commandments....Ps 112:1
God's goodness ....Neh 9:25
Lord Himself ....Is 58:14

[*also* DELIGHTED, DELIGHTEST, DELIGHTETH, DELIGHTS, DELIGHTSOME]
d in Jacob's daughter ....Gen 34:19
If the Lord *d* in us, then he ...Num 14:8
Lord had a *d* in thy fathers....Deut 10:15
Hath the Lord as great *d* in ...1Sam 15:22
Saul's son *d* much in David ...1Sam 19:2
in scarlet, with other *d*........2Sam 1:24
I have no *d* in thee, behold ...2Sam 15:26
delivered me, because he *d*....2Sam 22:20
which *d* in thee, to set thee ...1Kin 10:9
which *d* in thee to set thee 2Chr 9:8
d themselves in thy great......Neh 9:25
except the king *d* in her.......Esth 2:14
To whom would the king *d*....Esth 6:6
then shalt thou have thy *d* ....Job 22:26
should *d* himself with God ....Job 34:9
d is in the law of the Lord ....Ps 1:2
in whom is all my *d* ....Ps 16:3
delivered me, because he *d*....Ps 18:19
D thyself also in the Lord .....Ps 37:4
Lord: and he *d* in his way.....Ps 37:23
d not in burnt offering ....Ps 51:16
they *d* in lies: they bless ......Ps 62:4
the people that *d* in war ......Ps 68:30
me thy comforts *d* my soul ....Ps 94:19
as he *d* not in blessing ....Ps 109:17
d myself in thy statutes ....Ps 119:16
testimonies also are my *d* .....Ps 119:24
thy law had been my *d*........Ps 119:92
d in their scorning ....Prov 1:22
and *d* in the forwardness ......Prov 2:14
the son in whom he *d*.........Prov 3:12
I was daily his *d* rejoicing .....Prov 8:30
my *d* were with the sons of....Prov 8:31
that deal truly are his *d* ....Prov 12:22
prayer of..upright is his *d* .....Prov 15:8
Righteous lips are the *d* of ....Prov 16:13
D is not seemly for a fool ....Prov 19:10
that rebuke him shall be *d* ....Prov 24:25
shall give *d* unto thy soul .....Prov 29:17
the *d* of the sons of men ......Eccl 2:8
his shadow with great *d*.......Song 2:3
art thou, O Love, for *d*! ......Song 7:6
d not in..blood of bullocks ....Is 1:11
for gold, they shall not *d*......Is 13:17
elect, in whom my soul *d* .....Is 42:1
your soul *d* itself in fatness ....Is 55:2
and *d* to know my ways.......Is 58:2
d in approaching to God ......Is 58:2
choose that wherein I *d* not ...Is 65:12
they have no *d* in it ....Jer 6:10
because he *d* in mercy ....Mic 7:18
and he *d* in them; or ....Mal 2:17
of the covenant, whom ye *d*...Mal 3:1
for ye shall be a *d* ....Mal 3:12
For I *d* in the law of God.....Rom 7:22

DELILAH (dē-lī'lä)—*"longing; dainty one"—a Philistine woman*
Deceives Samson ....Judg 16:4-22

DELIVER—*to rescue; save from evil*
By Christ, from:
Trials...................2Tim 3:11
Evil 2Tim 4:18; 2Pet 2:9
Death 2Cor 1:10
Power of darkness ....Col 1:13
God's wrath 1Thess 1:10
Examples of, by God:
Noah ....Gen 8:1-22
Lot.....................Gen 19:29,30
Jacob...................Gen 33:1-16
Israel...................Ex 12:29-51
David 1Sam 23:1-29
Jews....................Esth 9:1-19
Daniel..................Dan 6:13-27
Jesus ....Matt 2:13-23
Apostles ....Acts 5:17-26
Paul....................2Cor 1:10

[*also* DELIVERANCE, DELIVERANCES, DELIVERED, DELIVEREDST, DELIVEREST, DELIVERETH, DELIVERING, DELIVERY]
into your hand are they *d* .....Gen 9:2
hath *d* thine enemies into .....Gen 14:20
days to be *d* were fulfilled.....Gen 25:24
D me, I pray thee, from ......Gen 32:11
he *d* them into the hand ......Gen 32:16
he *d* him out of their hands ...Gen 37:21
d him to his father again ......Gen 37:22
d Pharaoh's cup into his ......Gen 40:13
will I *d* you your brother......Gen 42:34
save..lives by a great *d*........Gen 45:7
d ere the midwives come ......Ex 1:19
Egyptian *d* us out of the ......Ex 2:19
I am come down to *d* them ...Ex 3:8
shall ye *d* the tale of bricks....Ex 5:18
hast thou *d* thy people ....Ex 5:23
and *d* our houses ....Ex 12:27
d me from the sword of.......Ex 18:4
God *d* him into his hand ......Ex 21:13
shall *d* unto his neighbor .....Ex 22:7
d the inhabitants of the land...Ex 23:31
which was *d* him to keep......Lev 6:2
and ye shall be *d* into the .....Lev 26:25
shall *d* you your bread ....Lev 26:26
wilt indeed *d* this people ......Num 21:2
and *d* up the Canaanites ......Num 21:3
d out of the thousands ....Num 31:5
congregation shall *d* the ....Num 35:25
to *d* us into the hand of.......Deut 1:27
might *d* him into thy hand ....Deut 2:30
the Lord our God *d* him ......Deut 2:33
d him, and all his people .....Deut 3:2
So the Lord our God *d* into ...Deut 3:3
stone and *d* them unto me ....Deut 5:22
Lord thy God shall *d* them ....Deut 7:9
Lord *d* unto me two tables ....Deut 9:10
d him..hand of the avenger....Deut 19:12
God hath *d* it into thine.......Deut 20:13
Lord thy God hath *d* them ....Deut 21:10
the midst of thy camp, to *d* ..Deut 23:14
d him the pledge again........Deut 24:13
to *d* her husband out of the ...Deut 25:11
d it unto the priests the ....Deut 31:9
can *d* out of my hand ....Deut 32:39

and ***d*** our lives from death .... Josh 2:13
Lord hath ***d*** into our hands .... Josh 2:24
d us into the hand of the .... Josh 7:7
the Lord your God will ***d*** it .... Josh 8:7
d them out of the hand .... Josh 9:26
d them into thine hand .... Josh 10:8
this time will I ***d*** them up .... Josh 11:6
d them into the hand of Israel .... Josh 11:8
d the slayer up into his .... Josh 20:5
Lord ***d*** all their enemies .... Josh 21:44
d the children of Israel .... Josh 22:31
so I ***d*** you out of his hand .... Josh 24:10
d the land into his hand .... Judg 1:2
he ***d*** them into the hands .... Judg 2:14
children of Israel who ***d*** .... Judg 3:9
will ***d*** him into thine hand .... Judg 4:7
d Sisera into thine hand .... Judg 4:14
d from the noise of archers .... Judg 5:11
d them into the hand of .... Judg 6:1
and ***d*** the Midianites .... Judg 7:7
I have ***d*** it into thine hand .... Judg 7:9
God hath ***d*** into your .... Judg 8:3
d you out of the hand of .... Judg 9:17
d you from the Egyptians .... Judg 10:11
I ***d*** you out of their hand .... Judg 10:12
Lord ***d*** them before me .... Judg 11:9
Lord God of Israel ***d*** Sihon .... Judg 11:21
d me not out of their hands .... Judg 12:2
Lord ***d*** them into the hand .... Judg 13:1
shall begin to ***d*** Israel out .... Judg 13:5
we may ***d*** thee into the hand .... Judg 15:12
hast given this great ***d*** .... Judg 15:18
d Samson our enemy into .... Judg 16:23
Now therefore ***d*** us the men .... Judg 20:13
who shall ***d*** us out of the 1Sam 4:8
with child, near to be ***d*** 1Sam 4:19
d you out of the hand of 1Sam 7:3
d you out of the hand of 1Sam 10:18
d us out of the hand of 1Sam 12:10
d you out of the hand of 1Sam 12:11
d them into the hand of 1Sam 14:37
and ***d*** it out of his mouth 1Sam 17:35
d me out of the hand of 1Sam 17:37
d the Philistines into thine 1Sam 23:4
d thine enemy into thine 1Sam 24:4
the Lord had ***d*** thee today 1Sam 24:10
d thine enemy into thine 1Sam 26:8
d me out of all tribulation 1Sam 26:24
Lord will also ***d*** Israel 1Sam 28:19
nor ***d*** me into the hands of 1Sam 30:15
d the company that came 1Sam 30:23
not ***d*** thee..hand of David 2Sam 3:8
D me my wife Michal 2Sam 3:14
wilt thou ***d*** them into mine 2Sam 5:19
rest of the people he ***d*** 2Sam 10:10
I ***d*** thee..hand of Saul 2Sam 12:7
D him that smote his 2Sam 14:7
Lord hath ***d*** the kingdom 2Sam 16:8
hath ***d*** up the men that 2Sam 18:28
he ***d*** us out of the hand 2Sam 19:9
d him only..I will depart 2Sam 20:21
seven men of his sons be ***d*** 2Sam 21:6
the Lord had ***d*** him out of 2Sam 22:1
d of a child with her in 1Kin 3:17
d them to the enemy so 1Kin 8:46
thou wouldst ***d*** thy servant 1Kin 18:9
Thou shalt ***d*** me thy silver 1Kin 20:5
d it..hand of the king 1Kin 22:6
d them..hand of Moab 2Kin 3:10
Lord had given ***d*** unto 2Kin 5:1
d it for the breaches of 2Kin 12:7
d the money to be bestowed 2Kin 12:15
d them..hand of Hazael 2Kin 13:3
The arrow of the Lord's ***d*** 2Kin 13:17
the arrow of ***d*** from Syria 2Kin 13:17
Lord..***d*** him unto the lion 2Kin 13:26
and ***d*** them into the hand 2Kin 15:18
d them..hand of spoilers 2Kin 17:20
d you out of the hand of 2Kin 17:39
d thee two thousand horses 2Kin 18:23
not be ***d*** into the hand 2Kin 18:30
Jerusalem shall not be ***d*** 2Kin 19:10
I will ***d*** thee and this city 2Kin 20:6
d them into the hand of 2Kin 21:14
let them ***d*** it into the hand 2Kin 22:5

the money that was ***d*** into 2Kin 22:7
Hagarites were ***d*** into their 1Chr 5:20
d it..slew the Philistines 1Chr 11:14
Lord saved them by..***d*** 1Chr 11:14
d them into mine hand? 1Chr 14:10
David ***d*** first this psalm to 1Chr 16:7
and ***d*** us from the heathen 1Chr 16:35
the rest of the people he ***d*** 1Chr 19:11
angry with them and ***d*** 2Chr 6:36
I will grant them some ***d*** 2Chr 12:7
God ***d*** them into their hand 2Chr 13:16
Lord, he ***d*** them into thine 2Chr 16:8
God will ***d*** it into..the king's 2Chr 18:5
shall be ***d*** into your hand 2Chr 18:14
Jehoiada the priest ***d*** to 2Chr 23:9
d a very great host into 2Chr 24:24
not ***d*** their own people 2Chr 25:15
Lord his God ***d*** him into 2Chr 28:5
he was also ***d*** into the hand 2Chr 28:5
d the captives again, which 2Chr 28:11
he hath ***d*** them to trouble 2Chr 29:8
Lord our God shall ***d*** us 2Chr 32:11
not ***d*** their people out of 2Chr 32:17
priest, they ***d*** the money 2Chr 34:9
and they were ***d*** unto one .... Ezra 5:14
d thou before the God .... Ezra 7:19
d us from..hand of the enemy .... Ezra 8:31
our priests, been ***d*** into .... Ezra 9:7
given us such ***d*** as this .... Ezra 9:13
Therefore thou ***d*** them into .... Neh 9:27
many times didst thou ***d*** .... Neh 9:28
enlargement and ***d*** arise to .... Esth 4:14
let..apparel and horse be ***d*** .... Esth 6:9
neither is there any to ***d*** .... Job 5:4
D me from the enemy's .... Job 6:23
none that can ***d*** out of .... Job 10:7
God hath ***d*** me to the .... Job 16:11
d the island of the innocent .... Job 22:30
d by the pureness of thine .... Job 22:30
d for ever from my judge .... Job 23:7
I ***d*** the poor that cried and .... Job 29:12
D him from going down to .... Job 33:24
d the poor in his affliction .... Job 36:15
a great ransom cannot ***d*** .... Job 36:18
Return, O Lord, ***d*** my soul .... Ps 6:4
persecute me, and ***d*** me .... Ps 7:1
d him that without cause .... Ps 7:4
d my soul from the wicked .... Ps 17:13
Lord ***d*** him from the hand .... Ps 18:*title*
d me from mine enemies .... Ps 18:48
d giveth he to his king .... Ps 18:50
trusted and thou didst ***d*** .... Ps 22:4
cried unto thee and were ***d*** .... Ps 22:5
O keep my soul and ***d*** me .... Ps 25:20
D me not over unto the will .... Ps 27:12
d me in thy righteousness .... Ps 31:1
about with the songs of ***d*** .... Ps 32:7
man is not ***d*** by much .... Ps 33:16
d any by his great strength .... Ps 33:17
and ***d*** me from all my fears .... Ps 34:4
that fear him and ***d*** them .... Ps 34:7
which ***d*** the poor from him .... Ps 35:10
d them; he shall ***d*** them .... Ps 37:40
D me from..transgressions .... Ps 39:8
Be pleased, O Lord, to ***d*** me .... Ps 40:13
Lord will ***d*** him in time of .... Ps 41:1
O ***d*** me from the deceitful .... Ps 43:1
God; command ***d*** for Jacob .... Ps 44:4
the day of trouble, I will ***d*** .... Ps 50:15
D me from bloodguiltiness .... Ps 51:14
d me out of all trouble .... Ps 54:7
He hath ***d*** my soul in peace .... Ps 55:18
d my soul from death .... Ps 56:13
d my feet from falling .... Ps 56:13
D me from mine enemies .... Ps 59:1
That thy beloved may be ***d*** .... Ps 60:5
D me out of the mire and .... Ps 69:14
d from them that hate me .... Ps 69:14
Make haste, O God, to ***d*** me .... Ps 70:1
D me in thy righteousness .... Ps 71:2
d the needy when he crieth .... Ps 72:12
d not the soul..turtledove .... Ps 74:19
he ***d*** them from the enemy .... Ps 78:42
d us..purge away our sins .... Ps 79:9
hands were ***d*** from the pots .... Ps 81:6

D the poor and needy; rid .... Ps 82:4
and thou hast ***d*** my soul .... Ps 86:13
d his soul from the hand .... Ps 89:48
shall ***d*** thee from the snare .... Ps 91:3
he ***d*** them out of the hand .... Ps 97:10
Many times did he ***d*** them .... Ps 106:43
d them..their distresses .... Ps 107:6
That thy beloved may be ***d*** .... Ps 108:6
mercy is good ***d*** thou me .... Ps 109:21
I beseech thee, ***d*** my soul .... Ps 116:4
d my soul from death .... Ps 116:8
D me from the oppression .... Ps 119:134
mine affliction and ***d*** me .... Ps 119:153
D my soul, O Lord, from .... Ps 120:2
D me, O Lord, from the evil .... Ps 140:1
d me from my persecutors .... Ps 142:6
D me, O Lord, from mine .... Ps 143:9
d me out of great waters .... Ps 144:7
who ***d*** David his servant .... Ps 144:10
To ***d*** thee..way of the evil .... Prov 2:12
crown of glory shall she ***d*** .... Prov 4:9
now, my son, and ***d*** thyself .... Prov 6:3
but righteousness ***d*** from .... Prov 10:2
but righteousness ***d*** from .... Prov 11:4
the upright shall ***d*** them .... Prov 11:6
righteous..***d*** out of trouble .... Prov 11:8
of the upright shall ***d*** .... Prov 12:6
A true witness ***d*** souls: but .... Prov 14:25
if thou ***d*** him yet thou .... Prov 19:19
shall ***d*** his soul from hell .... Prov 23:14
If thou forbear to ***d*** them .... Prov 24:11
wisely, he shall be ***d*** .... Prov 28:26
d girdles unto the merchant .... Prov 31:24
neither shall wickedness ***d*** .... Eccl 8:8
by his widsom ***d*** the city .... Eccl 9:15
safe, and none shall ***d*** .... Is 5:29
a great one and he shall ***d*** .... Is 19:20
to be ***d*** from the king of .... Is 20:6
near the time of her ***d*** .... Is 26:17
we have not wrought any ***d*** .... Is 26:18
d to one that is learned .... Is 29:11
book is ***d*** to him that is .... Is 29:12
defending also he will ***d*** .... Is 31:5
d them to the slaughter .... Is 34:2
shall not be able to ***d*** you .... Is 36:14
this city shall not be ***d*** .... Is 36:15
utterly..shalt thou be ***d*** .... Is 37:11
I will ***d*** thee and this city .... Is 38:6
hast in love to my soul ***d*** it .... Is 38:17
prey, and none ***d***; for a spoil .... Is 42:22
is none that can ***d*** out of .... Is 43:13
D me, for thou art my god .... Is 44:17
could not ***d*** the burden .... Is 46:2
not ***d*** themselves from .... Is 47:14
or the lawful captive ***d***? .... Is 49:24
or have I no power to ***d***? .... Is 50:2
let thy companies ***d*** thee .... Is 57:13
she was ***d*** of a man child .... Is 66:7
I am with thee to ***d*** thee .... Jer 1:8
d to..these abominations .... Jer 7:10
residue of them will I ***d*** .... Jer 15:9
d up their children to the .... Jer 18:21
will ***d*** all the strength of .... Jer 20:5
d the soul of the poor .... Jer 20:13
I will ***d*** Zedekiah king of .... Jer 21:7
d the spoiled out of the .... Jer 22:3
will ***d*** them to be removed .... Jer 24:9
d them to be removed .... Jer 29:18
surely he ***d*** into the hand .... Jer 32:4
shalt surely be taken and ***d*** .... Jer 34:3
shalt be ***d*** into the hand .... Jer 37:17
d me into their hand .... Jer 38:19
will ***d*** thee in that day .... Jer 39:17
d you from his hand .... Jer 42:11
to ***d*** us into the hand of the .... Jer 43:3
shall be ***d*** into the hand .... Jer 46:24
will ***d*** them into the hand .... Jer 46:26
and ***d*** every man his soul .... Jer 51:6
Lord hath ***d*** me into their .... Lam 1:14
there is none that doth ***d*** us .... Lam 5:8
but thou hast ***d*** thy soul .... Ezek 3:19
gold shall not be able to ***d*** .... Ezek 7:19
and ***d*** you into the hands .... Ezek 11:9
d my people out of your .... Ezek 13:21
should ***d*** but their own souls .... Ezek 14:14

only shall be *d* but the land ...Ezek 14:16
d them to cause them to ......Ezek 16:21
break..covenant, and be *d*? ....Ezek 17:15
and *d* thee into the hand of ...Ezek 21:31
I have *d* her into the hand ....Ezek 23:9
I will *d* thee into the hand ....Ezek 23:28
I will *d* thee to the men of ....Ezek 25:4
I have therefore *d* him into ....Ezek 31:11
she is *d* to the sword: draw ....Ezek 32:20
warning shall *d* his soul ....Ezek 33:5
but thou hast *d* thy soul.......Ezek 33:9
d my flock from their mouth ..Ezek 34:10
and *d* them out of the hand ...Ezek 34:27
who is that God that..*d* you ...Dan 3:15
hath sent his angel and *d*.......Dan 3:28
set his heart on Daniel to *d* ...Dan 6:14
He *d* and rescueth and he ....Dan 6:27
who hath *d* Daniel from the ...Dan 6:27
was there any that could *d* ....Dan 8:4
people shall be *d*, every ....Dan 12:1
d her out of mine hand ....Hos 2:10
how shall I *d* thee, Israel?.....Hos 11:8
name of the Lord..be *d* ....Joel 2:32
and in Jerusalem shall be *d*....Joel 2:32
to *d* them up to Edom ....Amos 1:6
d up the whole captivity ......Amos 1:9
shall the mighty *d* himself .....Amos 2:14
will I *d* up the city ....Amos 6:5
escapeth of them..not be *d* ....Amos 9:1
shouldest thou have *d*.........Obad 14
upon Mount Zion shall be *d*...Obad 17
to *d* him from his grief........Jon 4:6
shalt thou be *d* ....Mic 4:10
d us from the Assyrian........Mic 5:6
take hold, but shalt not *d* .....Mic 6:14
which thou *d* will I give up ....Mic 6:14
may be *d* from the power .....Hab 2:9
able to *d* them in the day .....Zeph 1:18
D thyself, O Zion, that ....Zech 2:7
I will *d* the men every one ....Zech 11:6
that tempt God are even *d* ....Mal 3:15
d thee to the judge ....Matt 5:25
but *d* us from evil ....Matt 6:13
d you up to the councils ......Matt 10:17
All things are *d* unto me ......Matt 11:27
d him to the tormentors.......Matt 18:34
d him to the Gentiles ....Matt 20:19
shall they *d* you up to ....Matt 24:9
and *d* unto them his goods ....Matt 25:14
thou *d* unto me five talents....Matt 25:20
and I will *d* him unto you? ....Matt 26:15
and *d* him to Pontius Pilate ...Matt 27:2
let him *d* him now, if he ......Matt 27:43
tradition, which ye have *d*.....Mark 7:13
is *d* into the hands of men ....Mark 9:31
shall *d* him to the Gentiles ....Mark 10:33
the Son of man shall be *d*.....Mark 10:33
shall *d* you up to councils .....Mark 13:9
away and *d* him to Pilate......Mark 15:1
as they *d* them unto us........Luke 1:2
that she should be *d* ....Luke 2:6
for that is *d* unto me ....Luke 4:6
to preach *d* to the captives ....Luke 4:18
he *d* him to his mother ....Luke 7:15
d him again to his father ......Luke 9:42
are *d* to me of my Father .....Luke 10:22
but *d* us from evil ....Luke 11:4
mayest be *d* from him ....Luke 12:58
judge *d* thee to the officer ....Luke 12:58
be *d* unto the Gentiles ....Luke 18:32
d them ten pounds and ....Luke 19:13
that so they might *d* him ......Luke 20:20
d you up to the synagogues ...Luke 21:12
he *d* Jesus to their will........Luke 23:25
d into the hands of sinful .....Luke 24:7
as she is *d* of the child ....John 16:21
would not have *d* him up .....John 18:30
he that *d* me unto thee ....John 19:11
d by the determinate..........Acts 2:23
whom ye *d* up and denied.....Acts 3:13
customs which Moses *d* ....Acts 6:14
d him..his afflictions ....Acts 7:10
God by his hand would *d* .....Acts 7:25
d him to four quaternion ......Acts 12:4
they *d* the epistle ....Acts 15:30
d them the decrees for ....Acts 16:4
shall *d* him into the hands .....Acts 21:11
d into prisons both men ....Acts 22:4
d the epistle to..governor .....Acts 23:33
no man may *d* me unto ....Acts 25:11
D thee from the people ....Acts 26:17
d Paul and certain other ......Acts 27:1
centurion *d* the prisoners......Acts 28:16
was *d* for our offences ....Rom 4:25
doctrine which was *d* of you ...Rom 6:17
now we are *d* of the law ......Rom 7:6
shall *d* me from the body .....Rom 7:24
be *d* from the bondage........Rom 8:21
That I may be *d* from them ...Rom 15:31
d such a one unto Satan 1Cor 5:5
ordinances, as I *d* them to 1Cor 11:2
I *d* unto you first of all 1Cor 15:3
d unto death for Jesus 2Cor 4:11
he might *d* us from this ....Gal 1:4
be *d* from unreasonable 2Thess 3:2
whom I have *d* unto Satan 1Tim 1:20
was *d* out of the mouth of 2Tim 4:17
d them who through fear......Heb 2:15
and was *d* of a child when ....Heb 11:11
tortured, not accepting *d* ......Heb 11:35
d them..chains of darkness 2Pet 2:4
Lord knoweth how to *d*........2Pet 2:9
faith which was once *d*........Jude 3
birth, and pained to be *d* .....Rev 12:2
woman..was ready to be *d* ....Rev 12:4
death and hell *d* up the ....Rev 20:13

DELIVERER—*one who saves others from distress*

Lord raised up a *d* to the .....Judg 3:9
there was no *d* because it .....Judg 18:28
and my fortress and my *d* 2Sam 22:2
thou art my help and my *d*....Ps 40:17
my high tower, and my *d* .....Ps 144:2
send to be a ruler and a *d* ....Acts 7:35
come out of Zion the *D*......Rom 11:26

DELUGE, THE—*the Flood*

Warnings of:
Believed by Noah ....Heb 11:7
Disbelieved by the world .2Pet 2:5

Coming of:
Announced ....Gen 6:5-7
Dated ....Gen 7:11
Sudden ....Matt 24:38, 39

Purpose of:
Punish sin ....Gen 6:1-7
Destroy the world 2Pet 3:5, 6

Its non-repetition based on God's:
Promise ....Gen 8:21, 22
Covenant..............Gen 9:9-11
Token (the rainbow).....Gen 9:12-17
Pledge.................Is 54:9, 10

Type of:
Baptism 1Pet 3:20, 21
Christ's coming.........Matt 24:36-39
Destruction ....Is 28:2, 18
The end 2Pet 3:5-15

DELUSIONS, COMMON—*self-deception*
Rejecting God's existence.Ps 14:1
Supposing God does not see ....Ps 10:1-11
Trusting in one's heritage.Matt 3:9
Living for time alone ....Luke 12:17-19
Presuming on time ......Luke 13:23-30
Believing antichrist 2Thess 2:1-12
Denying facts 2Pet 3:5, 16, 17

I also will choose their *d* ......Is 66:4

DEMAGOGUE—*one who becomes a leader by exploiting mass prejudice or sentiment*
Absalom................2Sam 15:2-6
Haman ....Esth 3:1-11
Judas of Galilee ....Acts 5:37

DEMAND—*to claim as a right*

[*also* DEMANDED]
were beaten and *d*...........Ex 5:14
David *d* of him how Joab 2Sam 11:7
I will *d* of thee, and answer ...Job 38:3
like a man: I will *d* of thee ....Job 40:7
will speak: I will *d* of thee ....Job 42:4
secret..the king hath *d* ....Dan 2:27
d by the word of the holy .....Dan 4:17
he *d* of them where Christ ....Matt 2:4
soldiers likewise *d* of him .....Luke 3:14
he was *d* of the Pharisees .....Luke 17:20
d who he was, and what ......Acts 21:33

DEMAS (dē'măs)—*"popular"*
Follows Paul ....Col 4:14
Forsakes Paul 2Tim 4:10

beloved physician..*D* ....Col 4:14
For *D* hath forsaken me 2Tim 4:10
Marcus, Aristarchus, *D* ....Philem 24

DEMETRIUS (dĕ-mē'trĭ-ŭs)—*"belonging to Demeter"*
1. A silversmith at Ephesus.Acts 19:24-31
2. A good Christian 3John 12

a certain man named *D*.......Acts 19:24
if *D* and the craftsmen ....Acts 19:38
D hath good report of all 2John 12

DEMON—*an evil spirit*

Nature of:
Evil ....Luke 10:17, 18
Powerful................Luke 8:29
Numerous ....Mark 5:8, 9
Unclean ....Matt 10:1
Under Satan ....Matt 12:24-30

Ability of:
Recognize Christ ....Mark 1:23, 24
Possess human beings ....Matt 8:29
Overcome men ....Acts 19:13-16
Know their destiny ......Matt 8:29-33
Receive sacrifice.........1Cor 10:20
Instigate deceit 1Tim 4:1

DEMON POSSESSION

Recognized as:
Not insanity.............Matt 4:24
Not disease ....Mark 1:32
Productive harm.........Mark 5:1-5

Instances of:
Man in the synagogue ...Mark 1:23-26
Blind and dumb man ....Matt 12:22, 23
Two men of the Gergesenes ....Matt 8:28-34
Dumb man ....Matt 9:32, 33
Canaanite woman's daughter..............Matt 15:22-28
Epileptic child...........Matt 17:14-21
Mary Magdalene ....Mark 16:9

DEMONSTRATION—*proof; evidence*
d of the Spirit and of power...1Cor 2:4

DEN—*lair of an animal; cave*

[*also* DENS]
of Israel made them the *d*.....Judg 6:2
Then the beasts go into *d* .....Job 37:8
they couch in their *d*..........Job 38:40
secretly as a lion in his *d*......Ps 10:9
lay them down in their *d*......Ps 104:22
from the lions *d*, from the.....Song 4:8
hand on the cockatrice *d*......Is 11:8
and towers shall be for *d*......Is 32:14
d of robbers in your eyes? ....Jer 7:11
heaps and a *d* of dragons .....Jer 9:11
and a *d* of dragons ....Jer 10:22
be cast into the *d* of lions .....Dan 6:7
young lion cry out of his *d* ....Amos 3:4
prey and his *d* with ravin.....Nah 2:12
have made it a *d* of thieves....Matt 21:13
have made it a *d* of thieves....Mark 11:17
have made it a *d* of thieves....Luke 19:46
in *d* and caves of the earth ....Heb 11:38
hid themselves in the *d* ....Rev 6:15

DEN OF LIONS—*place of execution*
Daniel placed in.........Dan 6:16-24

DENIAL OF CHRIST—*rejection of the Lordship of Jesus*

The realm of:
Doctrine ....Mark 8:38
2Tim 1:8
Practice ....Titus 1:16
The agents of:
Individuals ....Matt 26:69-75
Jews ....John 18:40
False teachers 2Pet 2:1
Antichrist 1John 2:22, 23
The consequences of:
Christ denies them ......Matt 10:33
They merit destruction ...2Pet 2:1

DENOUNCE—*to reject openly*
I *d* unto you this day ....Deut 30:18

DENY—*to declare untrue; disavow*

[*also* DENIED, DENIETH, DENYING]
Sarah *d*, saying, I laughed .....Gen 18:15
you, lest ye *d* your God ....Josh 24:27
petition of thee, *d* me not 1Kin 2:16
my gold; and I *d* him not 1Kin 20:7
then it shall *d* him, saying .....Job 8:18
d the God that is above ....Job 31:28
d me them not before I die ...Prov 30:7
come after me, let him *d* ......Matt 16:24
cock crow, thou shalt *d* me ....Matt 26:34
let him *d* himself, and take ....Mark 8:34
crow twice, thou shalt *d* ....Mark 14:30
he *d* saying, I know not ....Mark 14:68
When all *d*, Peter and they ....Luke 8:45
after me, let him *d* himself ....Luke 9:23
he that *d* me before men ....Luke 12:9
d..there is any resurrection ....Luke 20:27
thrice *d* that thou knowest ....Luke 22:34
he *d* him, saying, Woman, I ...Luke 22:57
he confessed, and *d* not ....John 1:20
till thou hast *d* me thrice ......John 13:38
He *d* it, and said, I am not ....John 18:25
d him in the presence ....Acts 3:13
Jerusalem..we cannot *d* it .....Acts 4:16
he hath *d* the faith and is 1Tim 5:8
d him, he also will *d* us 2Tim 2:12
godliness but *d* the power 2Tim 3:5
d ungodliness and worldly .....Titus 2:12
d that Jesus is the Christ? 1John 2:22
d the Father and the Son 1John 2:22
d the only Lord God, and .....Jude 4
hast not *d* my faith, even .....Rev 2:13
and hast not *d* my name ......Rev 3:8

DEPART—*to leave; go away*

[*also* DEPARTED, DEPARTETH, DEPARTING, DEPARTURE]
Abram *d* as the Lord had .....Gen 12:4
thou *d* to the right hand ......Gen 13:9
and his goods, and *d* ....Gen 14:12
camels of his master and *d* ....Gen 24:10
sleep *d* from mine eyes ....Gen 31:40
soul was in *d* for she died .....Gen 35:18
asses with the corn and *d* .....Gen 42:26
scepter shall not *d* from ....Gen 49:10
frogs shall *d* from thee ....Ex 8:11
after their *d* out of the land ...Ex 16:1
Moses let..father in law *d* .....Ex 18:27
they were *d* from Rephidim ...Ex 19:2
that her fruit *d* from her ......Ex 21:22
D and go up hence, thou ......Ex 33:1
if the plague be *d* from ....Lev 13:58
then shall he *d* from thee .....Lev 25:41
I will *d* to mine own land .....Num 10:30
d from..mount of the Lord ....Num 10:33
cloud *d* from..tabernacle ......Num 12:10
their defence is *d* from ....Num 14:9
D, I pray you, from..tents .....Num 16:26
they *d* from Rameses in the ...Num 33:3
when we *d* from Horeb, we ...Deut 1:19
lest they *d* from thy heart .....Deut 4:9
the day that thou didst *d* ......Deut 9:7
book of the law shall not *d* ....Josh 1:8
sent..away and they *d* ....Josh 2:21
So Joshua let the people *d* ....Josh 24:28
D not hence, I pray thee ......Judg 6:18
angel of the Lord *d* out of ....Judg 6:21
let him return and *d* early .....Judg 7:3
not that the Lord was *d* ....Judg 16:20
the five men *d* and came ......Judg 18:7
he rose up to *d* and the ....Judg 19:5
the children of Israel *d* ....Judg 21:24
The glory is *d* from Israel 1Sam 4:21
thou art *d* from me to day 1Sam 10:2
d, get you down from 1Sam 15:6
the Spirit of the Lord *d* 1Sam 16:14
arose and *d*: and Jonathan 1Sam 20:42
d..get thee into the land 1Sam 22:5
hundred, *d* out of Keilah 1Sam 23:13
may lead them away and *d* 1Sam 30:22
So all the people *d* every 2Sam 6:19
mercy shall not *d* away 2Sam 7:15
never *d* from thine house 2Sam 12:10
Nathan *d* unto his house 2Sam 12:15
day the king *d* until the day ...2Sam 19:24
and I will *d* from the city 2Sam 20:21
wickedly *d* from my God 2Sam 22:22
Let me *d* that I may go to 1Kin 11:21
to me. And the people *d* 1Kin 12:5
Israel *d* unto their tents 1Kin 12:16
king..that he may *d* from 1Kin 15:19
d thence, and found Elisha 1Kin 19:19
surely die. And Elijah *d* 2Kin 1:4
d and took with him ten 2Kin 5:5
he arose and *d* and came 2Kin 10:12
d not from all the sins of 2Kin 14:24
they *d* not from them 2Kin 17:22
he was *d* from Lachish 2Kin 19:8
the people *d* every man 1Chr 16:43
d not from..commandment 2Chr 8:15
king..that he may *d* from 2Chr 16:3
d not from it, doing that 2Chr 20:32
when they were *d* from him ...2Chr 24:25
not *d* from their service 2Chr 35:15
d from the river of Ahava ....Ezra 8:31
cloud *d* not from them by .....Neh 9:19
long wilt thou not *d* from .....Job 7:19
of his house shall *d* ....Job 20:28
say unto God, *D* from ....Job 21:14
Which said unto God, *D* ......Job 22:17
carrieth him away..he *d* ....Job 27:21
to *d* from evil is ....Job 28:28
D from me, all ye workers ....Ps 6:8
wickedly *d* from my God ......Ps 18:21
D from evil, and do good ......Ps 34:14
D from evil, and do good .....Ps 37:27
froward heart shall *d* from ....Ps 101:4
Egypt was glad when they *d* ...Ps 105:38
d from me therefore, ye ......Ps 139:19
fear the Lord, and *d* from .....Prov 3:7
not *d* from thine eyes ....Prov 4:21
d from the snares of death ....Prov 13:14
A wise man feareth and *d* .....Prov 14:16
may *d* from hell beneath ....Prov 15:24
evil shall not *d* from his ....Prov 17:13
is old, he will not *d* from .....Prov 22:6
his foolishness *d* from him .....Prov 27:22
d in darkness..his name ....Eccl 6:4
the day that Ephraim *d* ....Is 7:17
envy..of Ephraim shall *d* ......Is 11:13
age is *d* and is removed ....Is 38:12
D ye, *d* ye, go ye out from ....Is 52:11
the mountains shall *d* and ....Is 54:10
my kindness shall not *d* ....Is 54:10
d away from our God ....Is 59:13
he that *d* from evil maketh ....Is 59:15
in thy mouth, shall not *d* ......Is 59:21
wife treacherously *d* from .....Jer 3:20
lest my soul *d* from thee ....Jer 6:8
were *d* from Jerusalem ....Jer 29:2
ordinances *d* from before ....Jer 31:36
Chaldeans shall surely *d* ....Jer 37:9
d to..the Ammonites ....Jer 41:10
d both man and beast ....Jer 50:3
of Zion all her beauty is *d* ....Lam 1:6
cried unto them, *D* ye ....Lam 4:15
unclean; *d*, *d*, touch not ....Lam 4:15
whorish heart, which..*d* ....Ezek 6:9
glory of the Lord *d* from ......Ezek 10:18
jealously shall *d* from ....Ezek 16:42
sea..be troubled at thy *d* ......Ezek 26:18
kingdom is *d* from thee ....Dan 4:31
by *d* from thy precepts ....Dan 9:5
whoredom *d* from the Lord ...Hos 1:2
woe also to them when I *d* ....Hos 9:12
because it is *d* from it ....Hos 10:5
Arise ye, and *d* for this is .....Mic 2:10
and robbery; the prey *d* not ...Nah 3:1
scepter of Egypt shall *d* ....Zech 10:11
ye are *d* out of the way ....Mal 2:8
they *d*; and, lo, the star ....Matt 2:9
d from me, ye that work ....Matt 7:23
the commandment to *d* ....Matt 8:18
would *d* out of their coasts ....Matt 8:34
he arose and *d* to his house ...Matt 9:7
d out of that house or city ....Matt 10:14
And when he was *d* thence ....Matt 12:9
d..by ship into a desert ....Matt 14:13
them, They need not *d* ....Matt 14:16
Jonah..left them and *d* ....Matt 16:4
d from Galilee and came ......Matt 19:1
d from the temple: and ....Matt 24:1
D from me, ye cursed, into ....Matt 25:41
out, and *d* into a solitary ......Mark 1:35
him to *d* out of their coasts ...Mark 5:17
ye *d* thence, shake off the .....Mark 6:11
d into a desert place ....Mark 6:32
And the people saw them *d* ...Mark 6:33
they *d* thence and passed ......Mark 9:30
he *d* to his own house ....Luke 1:23
thou thy servant *d* in peace ....Luke 2:29
saying, *D* from me for I ....Luke 5:8
messengers of John were *d* ....Luke 7:24
besought him to *d* from ....Luke 8:37
there abide, and thence *d* .....Luke 9:4
d..through the towns ....Luke 9:6
bruising him hardly *d* from ....Luke 9:39
d from me, all ye workers .....Luke 13:27
laid by themselves and *d* .....Luke 24:12
and *d* again into Galilee .....John 4:3
D hence..go into Judea ....John 7:3
should *d* out of this world .....John 13:1
but if I *d*, I will send ....John 16:7
not *d* from Jerusalem ....Acts 1:4
they *d* from the presence ......Acts 5:41
d Barnabas to Tarsus ....Acts 11:25
d unto Seleucia; and from .....Acts 13:4
John *d* from them returned ....Acts 13:13
d..from Pamphylia ....Acts 15:38
d and go in peace ....Acts 16:36
him with all speed they *d* .....Acts 17:15
all Jews to *d* from Rome ......Acts 18:2
d from them and separated ....Acts 19:9
know this, that after my *d* .....Acts 20:29
we *d* and went our way ....Acts 21:5
D; for I will send thee far .....Acts 22:21
then let the young man *d* .....Acts 23:22
himself would *d* shortly ....Acts 25:4
when we *d* they laded us ......Acts 28:10
wife *d* from her husband 1Cor 7:10
unbelieving *d*, let him *d* 1Cor 7:15
that it might *d* from me 2Cor 12:8
having a desire to *d* and ......Phil 1:23
when I *d* from Macedonia .....Phil 4:15
some shall *d* from the faith 1Tim 4:1
name of Christ *d* from 2Tim 2:19
time of my *d* is at hand 2Tim 4:6
is *d* unto Thessalonica 2Tim 4:10
For perhaps he therefore *d* ....Philem 15
in *d* from the living God ......Heb 3:12
say unto them, *D* in peace ....James 2:16
heaven *d* as a scroll when .....Rev 6:14

DEPORTATION—*exile from a nation*
Captives carried into 2Kin 15:29
To Babylon 2Kin 24:8-17

DEPOSED—*cast down*
d from his kingly throne ......Dan 5:20

DEPRAVITY OF MAN—*the sinful state of humanity*
Extent of:
Universal ....Gen 6:5
In the heart ....Jer 17:9
Man's whole being ......Rom 3:9-19
From birth ....Ps 51:5
Effects of:
Hardness ....Rom 2:5

Inability to listen ....Jer 17:23
2Pet 2:14, 19
Lovers of evil ....John 3:19
Defilement of conscience .Titus 1:15, 16

DEPRIVED—*taken away*
why should I be ***d*** also of .....Gen 27:45
God hath ***d*** her of wisdom ....Job 39:17
d of the residue of my years...Is 38:10

DEPTH—*distance downward; profundity*
[*also* DEPTHS]
The ***d*** have covered them .....Ex 15:5
d..congealed in the heart ......Ex 15:8
fountains and ***d*** that spring ....Deut 8:7
d saith, It is not in me ....Job 28:14
the ***d*** in storehouses ....Ps 33:7
again from the ***d*** of the sea....Ps 68:22
the ***d*** also were troubled ......Ps 77:16
he led them through the ***d*** ....Ps 106:9
go down again to the ***d*** ....Ps 107:26
Out of the ***d*** have I cried .....Ps 130:1
By his knowledge the ***d*** ....Prov 3:20
When there were no ***d***, I ......Prov 8:24
upon the face of the ***d*** ....Prov 8:27
guests are in the ***d*** of hell .....Prov 9:18
height, and the earth for ***d*** ....Prov 25:3
ask it either in the ***d*** or ....Is 7:11
made the ***d*** of the sea.........Is 51:10
seas in the ***d*** of the waters ....Ezek 27:34
d closed me round about ......Jon 2:5
sins into the ***d*** of the sea ......Mic 7:19
drowned in the ***d*** of the ....Matt 18:6
it had no ***d*** of earth ....Mark 4:5
Nor height, nor ***d***, nor any ....Rom 8:39
O the ***d*** of the riches both ....Rom 11:33
breadth, and length, and ***d*** ....Eph 3:18
not known the ***d*** of Satan .....Rev 2:24

DEPUTED—*assigned*
no man ***d*** of the king to.......2Sam 15:3

DEPUTY—*a person empowered to act for another*
King 1Kin 22:47
[*also* DEPUTIES]
d and rulers of..provinces .....Esth 8:9
with the ***d*** of the country......Acts 13:7
away the ***d*** from the faith .....Acts 13:8
Gallio was ***d*** of Achaia........Acts 18:12
law is open..there are ***d*** ....Acts 19:38

DERBE (dûr'bĕ)—*"sting"—a city of Lycaonia*
Paul visits...............Acts 14:6, 20
Paul meets Timothy here .Acts 16:1
Gaius, native of ....Acts 20:4

DERISION—*contempt manifested by laughter*
Heaped on God's people .Jer 20:7, 8
[*also* DERIDE, DERIDED, DERISION]
than I have me in ***d*** ....Job 30:1
Lord shall have them in ***d***.....Ps 2:4
a scorn and a ***d*** to them.......Ps 44:13
have all the heathen in ***d***......Ps 59:8
a scorn and ***d*** to them that ....Ps 79:4
have had me greatly in ***d***......Ps 119:51
reproach unto me and a ***d***.....Jer 20:8
and he also shall be in ***d*** ......Jer 48:26
I was a ***d*** to all my people ....Lam 3:14
to scorn and had in ***d***.........Ezek 23:32
which became a prey and ***d*** ...Ezek 36:4
their ***d*** in..land of Egypt ......Hos 7:16
shall ***d*** every strong hold ......Hab 1:10
these things and they ***d*** ....Luke 16:14

DESCEND—*to go down*
As a dove ....Matt 3:16
John 1:32
The angels of God ......John 1:51
[*also* DESCENDED, DESCENDETH, DESCENDING]
angels..ascending and ***d*** ....Gen 28:12
the Lord ***d*** upon it in fire .....Ex 19:18
the Lord ***d*** in the cloud ....Ex 34:5
and the border shall ***d*** and ....Num 34:11
brook that ***d***..the mount ......Deut 9:21
d from the mountain..........Josh 2:23
border ***d*** to Ataroth-adar ......Josh 18:13
d into battle and perish 1Sam 26:10
his glory shall not ***d*** ....Ps 49:17
d upon the mountains of ......Ps 133:3
up into heaven or ***d***? ....Prov 30:4
he that rejoiceth, shall ***d*** ......Is 5:14
them that ***d*** into the pit ....Ezek 26:20
rain ***d*** and the floods ....Matt 7:25
rain ***d*** and the floods ....Matt 7:27
the angel of the Lord ***d*** ....Matt 28:2
the Spirit like a dove ***d*** ....Mark 1:10
Christ the king of Israel ***d*** .....Mark 15:32
Holy Ghost ***d*** in a bodily......Luke 3:22
the Spirit ***d*** from heaven ......John 1:32
shalt see the Spirit ***d***..........John 1:33
angels..ascending and ***d*** ....John 1:51
certain vessel ***d*** unto him......Acts 10:11
A certain vessel ***d*** as it........Acts 11:5
priest ***d*** with the elders........Acts 24:1
Who shall ***d*** into the deep?....Rom 10:7
but that he also ***d*** first ....Eph 4:9
He that ***d*** is the same also ....Eph 4:10
Lord himself shall ***d*** from 1Thess 4:16
wisdom ***d*** not from above .....James 3:15
Jerusalem, ***d*** out of heaven....Rev 21:10

DESCENT—*coming down*
d of the mount of Olives ......Luke 19:37
without mother, without ***d***.....Heb 7:3
whose ***d*** is not counted.......Heb 7:6

DESCRIBE—*to give an account of*
[*also* DESCRIBED, DESCRIBETH, DESCRIPTION]
through the land and ***d***........Josh 18:4
bring the ***d*** hither to me ......Josh 18:6
d it be cities into seven ....Josh 18:9
he ***d*** unto him the princes .....Judg 8:14
David..***d*** the blessedness ......Rom 4:6
Moses ***d*** the righteousness .....Rom 10:5

DESCRY—*discover*
house of Joseph sent to ***d*** .....Judg 1:23

DESERT—*a wilderness place*
Israel journeys through ..Is 48:21
Place of great temptation .Ps 106:14
Rejoicing of, predicted...Is 35:1
A highway in ....Is 40:3
John's home in ....Luke 1:80
Israel received manna in. .John 6:31
[*also* DESERTS]
to the backside of the ***d***.......Ex 3:1
days' journey into the ***d***.......Ex 5:3
were come to the ***d*** of Sinai ...Ex 19:2
into the ***d*** of Zin in the ....Num 20:1
from the ***d*** of Sinai ....Num 33:16
He found him in a ***d*** land .....Deut 32:10
he built towers in the ***d*** 2Chr 26:10
wild asses in the ***d***, go ....Job 24:5
and grieve him in the ***d***! ....Ps 78:40
I am like an owl of the ***d*** .....Ps 102:6
and tempted God in the ***d***.....Ps 106:14
beasts of the ***d***..lie there ......Is 13:21
wild beasts of the ***d*** shall ......Is 34:14
d shall rejoice and blossom....Is 35:1
and streams in the ***d***..........Is 35:6
make straight in the ***d*** a.......Is 40:3
set in the ***d*** the fir tree.........Is 41:19
and rivers in the ***d***...........Is 43:19
he led them through the ***d*** ....Is 48:21
d like..garden of the Lord.....Is 51:3
a land of ***d*** and of pits ....Jer 2:6
like the heath in the ***d*** and ....Jer 17:6
people that dwell in the ***d*** .....Jer 25:24
a dry land and a ***d***...........Jer 50:12
the wild beasts of the ***d*** ....Jer 50:39
are like the foxes in the ***d***.....Ezek 13:4
go down into the ***d*** and go ....Ezek 47:8
ship into a ***d*** place apart .....Matt 14:13
Behold, he is in the ***d***; go .....Matt 24:26
was without in ***d*** places ....Mark 1:45
yourselves apart into a ***d*** ......Mark 6:31
departed into a ***d*** place by ....Mark 6:32
was in the ***d*** till the day ....Luke 1:80
departed and went into a ***d***....Luke 4:42
into a ***d*** place belonging to ....Luke 9:10
did eat manna in the ***d***........John 6:31
unto Gaza, which is ***d***.........Acts 8:26

DESERT—*just reward*
[*also* DESERTS]
render to them their ***d*** ....Ps 28:4
and according to their ***d***.......Ezek 7:27

DESERTION—*forsaking a person or thing*
Jesus, by His disciples ...Matt 26:56
Jesus, by God ....Matt 27:46
Paul, by others 2Tim 4:16
Christ, by professed
disciples 2Pet 2:15

DESERVE—*to have as a rightful reward*
[*also* DESERVETH]
less than our iniquities ***d*** ......Ezra 9:13
less than thine iniquity ***d*** ......Job 11:6

DESIRE—*to long for; request*
[*also* DESIRABLE, DESIRED, DESIRES, DESIREST, DESIRETH, DESIRING, DESIROUS]
tree to be ***d*** to make one .....Gen 3:6
d shall be to thy husband .....Gen 3:16
serve the Lord..ye did ***d*** ......Ex 10:11
d thy neighbor's wife ....Deut 5:21
not ***d*** the silver or gold ....Deut 7:25
whatsoever thy soul ***d***.........Deut 14:26
with all the ***d*** of his mind .....Deut 18:6
According to all that thou ***d***...Deut 18:16
I would ***d*** a request of you ....Judg 8:24
take as much as thy soul ***d*** 1Sam 2:16
whom is all the ***d*** of Israel? ...1Sam 9:20
and whom ye have ***d***! 1Sam 12:13
Whatsoever thy soul ***d*** 1Sam 20:4
reign over..thine heart ***d*** 2Sam 3:21
my salvation and all my ***d*** 2Sam 23:5
d one small petition of thee ...1Kin 2:20
all Solomon's ***d*** which he 1Kin 9:1
which Solomon ***d*** to build 1Kin 9:19
queen of Sheba all her ***d*** 1Kin 10:13
to all that thy soul ***d***..........1Kin 11:37
Did I ***d*** a son of my lord?.....2Kin 4:28
all that Solomon ***d*** to build 2Chr 8:6
queen of Sheba all her ***d*** 2Chr 9:12
sought him with..***d***............2Chr 15:15
departed without being ***d***......2Chr 21:20
who ***d*** to fear thy name ....Neh 1:11
she ***d*** was given her...........Esth 2:13
As a servant earnestly ***d*** ......Job 7:2
wilt have a ***d*** to the work .....Job 14:15
save of that which he ***d*** ....Job 20:20
the poor from their ***d*** ....Job 31:16
d is, that the Almighty ....Job 31:35
speak, for I ***d*** to justify ....Job 33:32
D not the night, when ....Job 36:20
boasteth of his heart's ***d***.......Ps 10:3
heard the ***d*** of the humble ....Ps 10:17
to be ***d*** are they than gold ....Ps 19:10
given him his heart's ***d***........Ps 21:2
thing have I ***d*** of the Lord ....Ps 27:4
What man is he that ***d*** life ....Ps 34:12
give..***d*** of thine heart ....Ps 37:4
all my ***d*** is before thee ....Ps 38:9
king greatly ***d*** thy beauty......Ps 45:11
d truth in the inward parts ....Ps 51:6
mine eye hath seen his ***d***......Ps 54:7
let me see my ***d*** upon mine ...Ps 59:10
upon earth that I ***d*** besides....Ps 73:25
my ***d*** upon mine enemies......Ps 92:11
them unto their ***d*** haven ......Ps 107:30
d of the wicked shall perish ...Ps 112:10
therefore shall I see my ***d***.....Ps 118:7
satisfiest the ***d*** of every ......Ps 145:16
He will fulfill the ***d*** of ....Ps 145:19
all the things that canst ***d*** .....Prov 3:15
the things that may be ***d*** ......Prov 8:11
d of the righteous shall........Prov 10:24
d..righteous is only good ......Prov 11:23
wicked ***d*** the net of evil ......Prov 12:12
The soul of the sluggard ***d*** ....Prov 13:4
the ***d*** cometh, it is a tree ......Prov 13:12
d accomplished is sweet ....Prov 13:19

Through *d* a man, having .....Prov 18:1
soul of the wicked *d* evil ......Prov 21:10
d of the slothful killeth........Prov 21:25
Be not *d* of his dainties ....Prov 23:3
neither *d* to be with them .....Prov 24:1
whatsoever mine eyes *d* ....Eccl 2:10
his soul of all that he *d* ....Eccl 6:2
the wandering of the *d* ....Eccl 6:9
a burden, and *d* shall fail .....Eccl 12:5
and his *d* is toward me ....Song 7:10
the oaks which ye have *d* .....Is 1:29
d of our soul is to thy name ...Is 26:8
no beauty that we should *d*....Is 53:2
have I *d* the woeful day.......Jer 17:16
whereunto they *d* to return ....Jer 22:27
they have a *d* to return ....Jer 44:14
all of them *d* young men ....Ezek 23:6
away from thee the *d* of ......Ezek 24:16
went in and *d* of the king .....Dan 2:16
That they would *d* mercies ....Dan 2:18
Nor the *d* of women ....Dan 11:37
d mercy and not sacrifice......Hos 6:6
my *d* that I should chastise ....Hos 10:10
Woe unto you that *d* of the ...Amos 5:18
soul *d* the first-ripe fruit ......Mic 7:1
uttereth..mischievous *d*........Mic 7:3
who enlargeth his *d* as hell ....Hab 2:5
together, O nation not *d* ......Zeph 2:1
d of all nations shall come ....Hag 2:7
d to speak with him ....Matt 12:46
righteous men..*d* to see ....Matt 13:17
d him that he would show .....Matt 16:1
debt, because thou *d* me ......Matt 18:32
d a certain thing of him ....Matt 20:20
If any man *d* to be first ....Mark 9:35
do for us..we shall *d* ....Mark 10:35
What things soever ye *d* ......Mark 11:24
one prisoner..they *d* ....Mark 15:6
drunk old wine..*d* new ....Luke 5:39
one of the Pharisees *d* him ....Luke 7:36
without *d* to see thee ....Luke 8:20
prophets and kings have *d*.....Luke 10:24
d to be fed with..crumbs ......Luke 16:21
ye shall *d* to see one of ....Luke 17:22
scribes, which *d* to walk ....Luke 20:46
d I have desired to eat ....Luke 22:15
Satan hath *d* to have you .....Luke 22:31
he was *d* to see him of a long .Luke 23:8
prison, whom they had *d*......Luke 23:25
d of him, saying, Sir, we ......John 12:21
they were *d* to ask him ....John 16:19
the Just, and *d* a murderer ....Acts 3:14
And he *d* Philip that he ....Acts 8:31
d him..he would not delay .....Acts 9:38
their friend, *d* peace ....Acts 12:20
d to hear the word of God ....Acts 13:7
out, and *d* them to depart .....Acts 16:39
d him that he would not ......Acts 19:31
The Jews have agreed to *d* ....Acts 23:20
d favor against him that ....Acts 25:3
d to have judgment against ....Acts 25:15
my heart's *d* and prayer ....Rom 10:1
having a great *d* these ....Rom 15:23
d spiritual gifts, but 1Cor 14:1
I greatly *d* him to come 1Cor 16:12
earnestly *d* to be clothed 2Cor 5:2
he told us your earnest *d*......2Cor 7:7
Insomuch that we *d* Titus 2Cor 8:6
d to apprehend me 2Cor 11:32
though I would *d* to glory 2Cor 12:6
d again to be in bondage?.....Gal 4:9
d to present with you ....Gal 4:20
Tell me, ye that *d* to be.......Gal 4:21
not be *d* of vain glory.........Gal 5:26
d to make a fair show ....Gal 6:12
fulfilling the *d* of the flesh.....Eph 2:3
I *d* that ye faint not at my ....Eph 3:13
having a *d* to depart and ......Phil 1:23
Not because I *d* a gift.........Phil 4:17
I *d* fruit that may abound .....Phil 4:17
d that ye might be filled ......Col 1:9
affectionately *d* of you 1Thess 2:8
d greatly to see us, as we 1Thess 3:6
D to be teachers of..law 1Tim 1:7
bishop, he *d* a good work 1Tim 3:1
Greatly *d* to see thee 2Tim 1:4
we *d* that every one of you ....Heb 6:11
they *d* a better country........Heb 11:16
and *d* to have and cannot .....James 4:2
which things the angels *d*......1Pet 1:12
d the sincere milk of the 1Pet 2:2
petitions that we *d* of him 1John 5:15
d to die and death shall ....Rev 9:6

DESIRE OF ALL NATIONS

A title descriptive of the Messiah ....Hag 2:6, 7

DESIRE, SPIRITUAL

Renewed fellowship 1Thess 2:17
Church office 1Tim 3:1
Spiritual knowledge 1Pet 2:2
Spiritual gifts............1Cor 14:1

DESOLATE—*deserted; joyless; barren*

[*also* DESOLATION, DESOLATIONS]

that the land be not *d* ....Gen 47:19
lest the land become *d*........Ex 23:29
your high ways shall be *d* .....Lev 26:22
your sanctuaries unto *d* ....Lev 26:31
your land shall be *d* and ......Lev 26:33
even a *d* unto this day ....Josh 8:28
Tamar remained *d* in her......2Sam 13:20
become a *d* and a curse 2Kin 22:19
gave them up to *d* as ye 2Chr 30:7
as long as she lay *d* she 2Chr 36:21
to repair the *d* thereof, and ...Ezra 9:9
built *d* places for ....Job 3:14
made *d* all my company.......Job 16:7
in the *d* they rolled ....Job 30:14
the *d* and waste ground ....Job 38:27
for I am *d* and ....Ps 25:16
trust in him shall be *d* ....Ps 34:22
Let them be *d* for a reward ...Ps 40:15
what *d* he hath made in the ...Ps 46:8
are they brought into *d* ....Ps 73:19
feet unto the perpetual *d*......Ps 74:3
also out of their *d* places ......Ps 109:10
your fear cometh as *d*.........Prov 1:27
of the *d* of the wicked ....Prov 3:25
Your country is *d*, your ....Is 1:7
many houses shall be *d* ....Is 5:9
all of them in the *d* valleys ....Is 7:19
in the *d* which shall come .....Is 10:3
waters of Nimrim..be *d* ....Is 15:6
and there shall be *d* ....Is 17:9
that dwell therein are *d* ....Is 24:6
city is left *d* and the gate......Is 24:12
defenced city shall be *d* ....Is 27:10
d shall come upon thee ....Is 47:11
to inherit the *d* heritages ......Is 49:8
thy waste and thy *d* places ....Is 49:19
and am *d*, a captive ....Is 49:21
d and destruction and ....Is 51:19
the children of the *d* than .....Is 54:1
d cities to be inhabited........Is 54:3
in *d* places as dead men.......Is 59:10
raise up the former *d* ....Is 61:4
land..be termed *D* ....Is 62:4
be..*d* saith the Lord ....Jer 2:12
place to make thy land *d*......Jer 4:7
The whole land shall be........Jer 4:27
lest I make thee *d* a land .....Jer 6:8
the cities of Judah *d* ....Jer 9:11
portion a *d* wilderness ....Jer 12:10
To make their land *d* and .....Jer 18:16
I will make this city *d* and ....Jer 19:8
house shall become a *d* ....Jer 22:5
hissing and perpetual *d*........Jer 25:9
whole land shall be a *d* ....Jer 25:11
will make it perpetual *d*.......Jer 25:12
this city shall be *d* without ....Jer 26:9
d without man or beast ....Jer 32:43
which ye say shall be *d* ....Jer 33:10
Judah a *d* without an ....Jer 34:22
Noph shall be waste and *d* ....Jer 46:19
shall be a *d* heap and her .....Jer 49:2
Bozrah shall become a *d* ......Jer 49:13
Babylon become a *d* ....Jer 50:23
thou shalt be *d* for ever ....Jer 51:26
Babylon a *d* without an ....Jer 51:29
feasts: all her gates are *d*......Lam 1:4
upon us, *d* and destruction ....Lam 3:47
did feed delicately are *d* ......Lam 4:5
And your altars shall be *d*.....Ezek 6:4
the high places shall be *d* .....Ezek 6:6
laid waste and made *d* ....Ezek 6:6
prince..be clothed with *d* ......Ezek 7:27
spoil it, so that it be *d* ....Ezek 14:15
I will make the land *d* ....Ezek 15:8
he knew their *d* places ....Ezek 19:7
of astonishment and *d* ....Ezek 23:33
land of Israel when it was *d* ...Ezek 25:3
land of Egypt shall be *d*.......Ezek 29:9
make the land of Egypt *d* .....Ezek 32:15
will lay the land most *d* ....Ezek 33:28
I will make thee most *d*.......Ezek 35:3
will make thee perpetual *d* ....Ezek 35:9
hand upon the *d* places ....Ezek 38:12
transgression of *d* to give ......Dan 8:13
in the *d* of Jerusalem ....Dan 9:2
thy sanctuary that is *d* ....Dan 9:17
eyes, and behold our *d*........Dan 9:18
end of the war *d* are ....Dan 9:26
abomination..maketh *d*........Dan 11:31
abomination that maketh *d* ....Dan 12:11
Ephraim shall be *d* in the .....Hos 5:9
daily increaseth lies and *d* .....Hos 12:1
Samaria shall become *d* ....Hos 13:16
the garners are laid *d* the .....Joel 1:17
behind..a *d* wilderness ....Joel 2:3
Egypt shall be a *d* and ....Joel 3:19
Edom..a *d* wilderness ....Joel 3:19
places of Isaac shall be *d*......Amos 7:9
idols thereof will I lay *d*.......Mic 1:7
thee *d* because of thy sins .....Mic 6:13
I should make thee a *d* ....Mic 6:16
land shall be *d* because of .....Mic 7:13
and their houses a *d* ....Zeph 1:13
a day of wasteness and *d*......Zeph 1:15
and Ashkelon a *d* ....Zeph 2:4
their towers are *d*; I made ....Zeph 3:6
the land was *d* after them .....Zech 7:14
and build the *d* places ....Mal 1:4
itself is brought to *d* ....Matt 12:25
house is left unto you *d* ....Matt 23:38
the abomination of *d* ....Matt 24:15
see the abomination of *d*......Mark 13:14
itself it brought to *d* ....Luke 11:17
house is left unto you *d* ....Luke 13:35
that the *d* thereof is nigh......Luke 21:20
Let his habitation be *d* and....Acts 1:20
d hath many more children ....Gal 4:27
a widow indeed and *d* 1Tim 5:5
make her *d* and naked ....Rev 17:16
in one hour is she made *d*.....Rev 18:19

DESPAIR—*a hopeless state*

Results from:

Heavy burdens ....Num 11:10-15
Disobedience............1Sam 28:16-25
Disappointment 2Sam 17:23
Impending death ....Esth 7:7-10
Futility of human things..Eccl 6:1-12
Rejection ....Matt 27:3-5
Rebellion against God ...Rev 9:6
Hopelessness............Luke 16:23-31

Remedies against:

Hope in God ....Ps 42:5, 11
God's faithfulness 1Cor 10:13
Accept God's chastening..Heb 12:5-11
Cast your care upon the Lord 1Pet 5:7

[*also* DESPAIRED]

Saul shall *d* of me to seek 1Sam 27:1
heart to *d* of all the labor .....Eccl 2:20
that we *d* even of life 2Cor 1:8
are perplexed, but not in *d* 2Cor 4:8

DESPERATE—*despairing recklessness*

[*also* DESPERATELY]

speeches of one that is *d* ......Job 6:26
day of grief..*d* sorrow ....Is 17:11
all things, and *d* wicked ....Jer 17:9

DESPISE—*to scorn; loathe*

[*also* DESPISED, DESPISEST, DESPISETH, DESPISING]

mistress was *d* in her eyes .....Gen 16:4
if ye shall *d* my statutes ....Lev 26:15
they *d* my judgments ....Lev 26:43
ye have *d* the Lord which .....Num 11:20
d the word of the Lord ....Num 15:31
people that thou hast *d*? ......Judg 9:38
that *d* me shall be lightly 1Sam 2:30
And they *d* him and 1Sam 10:27
and she *d* him in her heart 2Sam 6:16
why then did ye *d* us, that 2Sam 19:43
daughter of Zion hath *d* 2Kin 19:21
and she *d* him in her heart 1Chr 15:29
d his words and misused 2Chr 36:16
d us and said, What is ....Neh 2:19
O our God, for we are *d*......Neh 4:4
d not thou the chastening .....Job 5:17
d the work of thine hands .....Job 10:3
d in the thought of him ....Job 12:5
children *d* me; I arose ....Job 19:18
God is mighty and *d* not ......Job 36:5
men and *d* of the people ......Ps 22:6
O God thou wilt not *d*........Ps 51:17
because God hath *d* them .....Ps 53:5
and *d* not his prisoners........Ps 69:33
thou shalt *d* their image ....Ps 73:20
and not *d* their prayer ....Ps 102:17
they *d* the pleasant land.......Ps 106:24
fools *d* wisdom and ....Prov 1:7
they *d* all my reproof ....Prov 1:30
d not the chastening of the ....Prov 3:11
and my heart *d* reproof ....Prov 5:12
Men do not *d* a thief, if he ....Prov 6:30
void of wisdom *d* his..........Prov 11:12
perverse heart shall be *d* ......Prov 12:8
that is *d*..hath a servant ....Prov 12:9
Whoso *d* the word shall be ....Prov 13:13
perverse in his ways *d* him ....Prov 14:2
He that *d* his neighbor ....Prov 14:21
foolish man *d* his mother......Prov 15:20
refuseth instruction *d* his ......Prov 15:32
that *d* his ways shall die.......Prov 19:16
d not thy mother when she ....Prov 23:22
and *d* to obey his mother .....Prov 30:17
poor man's wisdom is *d* ....Eccl 9:16
yea, I should not be *d* ....Song 8:1
d the word of the Holy One ...Is 5:24
Because ye *d* this word ....Is 30:12
d the gain of oppressions ......Is 33:15
d thee and laughed thee to ....Is 37:22
He is *d* and rejected of men...Is 53:3
they that *d* thee shall bow .....Is 60:14
lovers will *d* thee, they.......Jer 4:30
they have *d* my people ....Jer 33:24
heathen, and *d* among men....Jer 49:15
that honored her *d* her........Lam 1:8
d in the indigation of his ......Lam 2:6
Philistines, which *d* thee ......Ezek 16:57
hast *d* the oath in breaking ....Ezek 16:59
they *d* my judgments ....Ezek 20:13
hast *d* mine holy things ....Ezek 22:8
round about them that *d* ......Ezek 28:24
have *d* the law of the Lord ....Amos 2:4
I hate, I *d* your feast days.....Amos 5:21
heathen..art greatly *d* ....Obad 2
d the day of small things? .....Zech 4:10
O priests, that *d* my name ....Mal 1:6
have we *d* thy name? ....Mal 1:6
hold to the one and *d* the .....Matt 6:24
ye *d* not one of these little ....Matt 18:10
he that *d* you *d* me ....Luke 10:16
he that *d* me *d* him that.......Luke 10:16
hold to the one and *d*..other ..Luke 16:13
righteous and *d* others ....Luke 18:9
Behold ye *d* and wonder ......Acts 13:41
Diana should be *d*............Acts 19:27
d thou the riches of his ....Rom 2:4
Let not him that eateth *d* .....Rom 14:3
things..*d* hath God 1Cor 1:28
honorable, but we are *d* 1Cor 4:10
or *d* ye the church of God 1Cor 11:22
no man therefore *d* him 1Cor 16:11
in my flesh ye *d* not, nor ......Gal 4:14
He..that *d*, *d* not man 1Thess 4:8
D not prophesyings 1Thess 5:20
Let no man *d* thy youth.......1Tim 4:12
masters, let them not *d* 1Tim 6:2
Let no man *d* thee ....Titus 2:15
He that *d* Moses law died .....Heb 10:28
the cross, *d* the shame ....Heb 12:2
d not thou the chastening .....Heb 12:5
But ye have *d* the poor ....James 2:6
and *d* government 2Pet 2:10
d dominion and speak evil ....Jude 8

DESPISERS—*those who loathe others*

Behold, ye *d*, and wonder.....Acts 13:41
d of those that are good 2Tim 3:3

DESPITE—*contempt*

[*also* DESPITEFUL, DESPITEFULLY]

rejoiced in heart with..*d* ......Ezek 25:6
vengeance with a *d* heart......Ezek 25:15
pray for them which *d* use ....Matt 5:44
pray for them which *d* use ....Luke 6:28
to use them *d* and to stone ....Acts 14:5
haters of God *d* ....Rom 1:30
done *d* unto the Spirit ....Heb 10:29

DESPONDENCY—*discouragement; dejection*

Causes of:

Mourning ....Gen 37:34,35
Sickness ....Is 38:9-12
Sorrow 2Sam 18:32,33
2Cor 2:7
Adversity ....Job 9:16-35
Fears 2Cor 7:5, 6

Examples of:

Moses ....Ex 14:15
Joshua..................Josh 7:7-9
Elijah 1Kin 19:2, 4
David ....Ps 42:6
Jonah ....Jon 4:3, 8
Two disciples ....Luke 24:13-17

DESTITUTE—*a state of extreme need*

The soul................Ps 102:17
The body ....James 2:14-17
Spiritual realities ....Prov 15:21

not..*d* my master of his mercy .Gen 24:27
my trust; leave not my soul *d*. .Ps 141:8
country shall be *d* of that .....Ezek 32:15
corrupt minds and *d* of..truth ..1Tim 6:5
d, afflicted, tormented ....Heb 11:37

DESTRUCTION—*a state of ruin*

Past:

Cities...................Gen 19:29
People..................1Cor 10:9, 10
Nations ....Jer 48:42

Present:

Satan's power of 1Cor 5:5
Power of lusts...........1Tim 6:9
Wicked on way to ....Rom 3:16

Future:

Men appointed to ....Prov 31:8
2Pet 2:12
Men fitted for...........Rom 9:22
End of the enemies of
Christ ....Phil 3:19
Sudden 1Thess 5:3
Swift 2Pet 2:1
Everlasting.............2Thess 1:9

[*also* DESTROY, DESTROYED, DESTROYEST, DESTROYETH, DESTROYING, DESTRUCTIONS]

Lord said, I will *d* man ....Gen 6:7
I will *d* them with ....Gen 6:13
I have made will I *d* from off. .Gen 7:4
every living substance..*d* ......Gen 7:23
before the Lord *d* Sodom .....Gen 13:10
d the righteous with the ....Gen 18:23
I will not *d* it for ten's sake ...Gen 18:32
when God *d* the cities of......Gen 19:29
to *d* the frogs from thee......Ex 8:9
thou not yet that Egypt is *d*? ..Ex 10:7
my sword, my hand shall *d*....Ex 15:9
Lord only..be utterly *d*........Ex 22:20
d all the people to whom .....Ex 23:27
But ye shall *d* their altars .....Ex 34:13
soul..I *d* from among his ......Lev 23:30
I will utterly *d* their cities .....Num 21:2
they utterly *d* them ....Num 21:3
ye shall *d* all this people ......Num 32:15
d all their pictures ....Num 33:52
d all their molten images ......Num 33:52
hand of the Amorites, to *d*....Deut 1:27
d you in Seir, even unto ....Deut 1:44
the Lord *d* them before ....Deut 2:21
we utterly *d* them ....Deut 3:6
utterly *d* the men, women .....Deut 3:6
d thee nor forget ....Deut 4:31
and utterly *d* them............Deut 7:2
themselves from thee be *d* ....Deut 7:20
d them with a mighty *d* ....Deut 7:23
nations which the Lord *d*......Deut 8:20
Let me alone..I may *d* them...Deut 9:14
God, *d* not thy people..thine ..Deut 9:26
Lord would not *d* thee ....Deut 10:10
Lord hath *d* them unto........Deut 11:4
Ye shall utterly *d*..places ......Deut 12:2
thou shalt utterly *d* them ......Deut 20:17
until thou be *d*..until thou.....Deut 28:20
d these nations from before ...Deut 31:3
burning heat..with bitter *d* ....Deut 32:24
and shall say, *D* them ....Deut 33:27
Og whom ye utterly *d* ....Josh 2:10
hand of..Amorites, to *d* us? ...Josh 7:7
d the accursed from among....Josh 7:12
until he had utterly *d* all ......Josh 8:26
edge..sword, utterly *d* them ...Josh 11:11
he utterly *d* them, as Moses ...Josh 11:12
he might *d* them utterly ....Josh 11:20
Zepath, and utterly *d* it ....Judg 1:17
d the increase of the earth ....Judg 6:4
entered into..land to *d* it ......Judg 6:5
seeing the women are *d*.......Judg 21:16
Benjamin..a tribe be not *d* ....Judg 21:17
Ashdod and he *d* them..smote .1Sam 5:6
city with a very great *d* 1Sam 5:9
smite Amalek and utterly *d* ...1Sam 15:3
Amalekites, lest I *d* you 1Sam 15:6
thou wilt not *d* my name 1Sam 24:21
hand to *d*..Lord's anointed? ...2Sam 1:14
they *d*..children of Ammon....2Sam 11:1
seekest to *d* a city..a mother ..2Sam 20:19
pursued mine enemies..*d* them .2Sam 22:38
might *d* them that hate me 2Sam 22:41
hand upon Jerusalem to *d*.....2Sam 24:16
were not able utterly to *d* 1Kin 9:21
Asa *d* her idol..burnt it 1Kin 15:13
Zimri *d* all..house Baasha 1Kin 16:12
I appointed to utter *d*........1Kin 20:42
Lord would not *d* Judah 2Kin 8:19
Samaria till he had *d* him 2Kin 10:17
Jehu *d* Baal out of Israel......2Kin 10:28
king of Syria had *d* them.......2Kin 13:7
would not *d*..neither cast.......2Kin 13:23
Lord against this place to *d* ...2Kin 18:25
against this land, and *d* 2Kin 18:25
to all lands, by *d* them 2Kin 19:11
Hezekiah his father had *d*......2Kin 21:3
sent..against Judah to *d* it 2Kin 24:2
d them utterly unto 1Chr 4:41
Joab smote Rabbah, and *d* 1Chr 20:1
angel of the Lord *d*...........1Chr 21:12
unto Jerusalem to *d* it 1Chr 21:15
will not *d* them..I will grant ...2Chr 12:7
they were *d* before..Lord.......2Chr 14:13
turned from them and *d* 2Chr 20:10
would not *d*..house of David ..2Chr 21:7
death of his father to his *d* 2Chr 22:4
d all the princes of 2Chr 24:23
heart was lifted up to his *d*....2Chr 26:16
nations..my fathers utterly *d*...2Chr 32:14
kings of Judah had *d* 2Chr 34:11
who is with me that he *d*......2Chr 35:21
cause was this city *d* ....Ezra 4:15
d all kings and people ....Ezra 6:12
Haman sought to *d* all ....Esth 3:6
be written..they may be *d* .....Esth 3:9
d, to be slain..to perish ....Esth 7:4

he wrote to ***d*** the Jews .... Esth 8:5
how can I endure to see..***d*** .... Esth 8:6
d him without cause .... Job 2:3
are ***d*** from morning to .... Job 4:20
neither..thou be afraid of ***d***.... Job 5:21
would please God to ***d*** me .... Job 6:9
If he ***d*** him from his place .... Job 8:18
d the perfect and .... Job 9:22
yet thou dost ***d*** me .... Job 10:8
and thou ***d*** the hope of .... Job 14:19
d shall be ready at his side .... Job 18:12
hath ***d*** me on every side ..... Job 19:10
my skin worms ***d*** this body .... Job 19:26
oft cometh their ***d*** upon .... Job 21:17
His eyes shall see his ***d*** .... Job 21:20
is reserved to the day of ***d***? ... Job 21:30
d hath no covering .... Job 26:6
D and death say We have ..... Job 28:22
Is not ***d*** to the wicked? ...... Job 31:3
d from God was a terror to ... Job 31:23
rejoiced at the ***d*** of him ...... Job 31:29
night, so that they are ***d*** ...... Job 34:25
d them that speak leasing ..... Ps 5:6
D thou them, O God .... Ps 5:10
d the wicked thou hast .... Ps 9:5
d are come to a perpetual ..... Ps 9:6
foundations be ***d***, what .... Ps 11:3
might ***d*** them that hate me .... Ps 18:40
fruit shalt thou ***d*** from .... Ps 21:10
d come upon him at .... Ps 35:8
transgressors shall be ***d***........ Ps 37:38
seek after my soul to ***d*** .... Ps 40:14
D, O Lord, and divide their ... Ps 55:9
down into the pit of ***d*** .... Ps 55:23
that seek my soul, to ***d*** .... Ps 63:9
they that would ***d*** me .... Ps 69:4
castedst them down into ***d***..... Ps 73:18
their iniquity and ***d*** them ...... Ps 78:38
he ***d*** their vines with hail ...... Ps 78:47
thy faithfulness in ***d***? .... Ps 88:11
turnest man to ***d*** .... Ps 90:3
d that wasteth at noonday ..... Ps 91:6
d all the wicked of .... Ps 101:8
redeemeth thy life from ***d*** ..... Ps 103:4
of the Lord will I ***d*** them ..... Ps 118:10
of the Lord will I ***d*** them ..... Ps 118:11
of the Lord will I ***d*** them ..... Ps 118:12
of Babylon, who art to be ***d***... Ps 137:8
and ***d*** all them that afflict ..... Ps 143:12
but all the wicked will he ***d*** ... Ps 145:20
d cometh as a whirlwind ...... Prov 1:27
prosperity of fools shall ***d*** ..... Prov 1:32
he that doeth it ***d*** his own ..... Prov 6:32
of the foolish is near ***d*** .... Prov 10:14
d of the poor is their .... Prov 10:15
d shall be to the workers ...... Prov 10:29
his mouth ***d*** his neighbor ...... Prov 11:9
openeth wide his lips..***d*** ...... Prov 13:3
despiseth..word shall be ***d***..... Prov 13:13
companion of fools..be ***d*** ...... Prov 13:20
there is that the ***d*** for want .... Prov 13:23
want of people is the ***d*** .... Prov 14:28
will ***d*** the house of .... Prov 15:25
Pride goeth before ***d*** .... Prov 16:18
exalteth his gate seeketh ***d*** .... Prov 17:19
A fool's mouth is his ***d***........ Prov 18:7
Before ***d*** the heart of man .... Prov 18:12
of the wicked shall ***d*** them .... Prov 21:7
heart studieth ***d*** and their ..... Prov 24:2
Hell and ***d*** are never full ...... Prov 27:20
shall suddenly be ***d*** .... Prov 29:1
ways to that which ***d*** kings .... Prov 31:3
such as are appointed to ***d*** .... Prov 31:8
d the work of thine hands? .... Eccl 5:6
and a gift ***d*** the heart .... Eccl 7:7
one sinner ***d*** much good .... Eccl 9:18
the ***d*** of the transgressors ..... Is 1:28
and ***d*** the way of thy paths .... Is 3:12
that are led of them are ***d***..... Is 9:16
not hurt nor ***d*** in all my .... Is 11:9
as a ***d*** from the Almighty ..... Is 13:6
d the sinners thereof out of ... Is 13:9
and ***d*** the cities thereof .... Is 14:17
sweep it with the besom of ***d*** .. Is 14:23
shall raise up a cry..***d*** .... Is 15:5
I will ***d*** the counsel thereof .... Is 19:3
be called the city of ***d*** .... Is 19:18
the gate is smitten with ***d*** ..... Is 24:12
he will ***d*** in this mountain ..... Is 25:7
of hail and a ***d*** storm .... Is 28:2
hath utterly ***d*** them .... Is 34:2
Lord against this land to ***d*** .... Is 36:10
not have been cut off nor ***d*** ... Is 48:19
of thy ***d***, shall even now ...... Is 49:19
as if he were ready to ***d***? ...... Is 51:13
and ***d*** and the famine .... Is 51:19
wasting and ***d*** are in .... Is 59:7
wasting nor ***d*** within .... Is 60:18
D it not for a blessing .... Is 65:8
I may not ***d*** them all .... Is 65:8
shall not hurt nor ***d*** in all ..... Is 65:25
to pull down and to ***d*** .... Jer 1:10
your prophets, like a ***d*** lion ... Jer 2:30
from the north..a great ***d***...... Jer 4:6
D upon ***d*** is cried; the whole .. Jer 4:20
let us ***d*** her palaces .... Jer 6:5
pastors have ***d*** my vineyard .... Jer 12:10
pluck up and ***d*** that nation .... Jer 12:17
of the earth, to devour and ***d***.. Jer 15:3
I will ***d*** my people .... Jer 15:7
d them with double .... Jer 17:18
to pull down, and to ***d*** it .... Jer 18:7
Woe be unto..pastors that ***d***... Jer 23:1
utterly ***d*** them and make them . Jer 25:9
certainly come and ***d*** .... Jer 36:29
d cometh, it cometh out of .... Jer 46:20
Horonaim, spoiling..great ***d*** ... Jer 48:3
Moab is ***d*** her little ones ...... Jer 48:4
he shall ***d*** thy strongholds ..... Jer 48:18
Moab shall be ***d*** from .... Jer 48:42
waste and utterly ***d*** after ...... Jer 50:21
Lord, which ***d*** all the earth .... Jer 51:25
great ***d*** from the land of ...... Jer 51:54
Babylon..***d*** out of .... Jer 51:55
he hath ***d*** his strong holds ..... Lam 2:5
Lord hath purposed to ***d*** ...... Lam 2:8
not withdrawn..hand from ***d***... Lam 2:8
d of the daughter of my .... Lam 2:11
d of the daughter of my .... Lam 3:48
d of the daughter of my .... Lam 4:10
which shall be for their ***d*** ..... Ezek 5:16
which I will send to ***d*** you ..... Ezek 5:16
D cometh..they shall seek ..... Ezek 7:25
man with his ***d*** weapon .... Ezek 9:1
d all..residue of Israel .... Ezek 9:8
brutish men..skillful to ***d*** ...... Ezek 21:31
shed blood and to ***d*** souls ..... Ezek 22:27
I will ***d***..thou shalt know ...... Ezek 25:7
How art thou ***d***, that wast ..... Ezek 26:17
I will ***d*** thee; O..cherub .... Ezek 28:16
all her helpers shall be ***d*** ...... Ezek 30:8
bring thy ***d*** among..nations .... Ezek 32:9
d also all the beasts .... Ezek 32:13
d the fat and the strong .... Ezek 34:16
saw when I came to ***d*** .... Ezek 43:3
d all..wise men of Babylon .... Dan 2:12
kingdom, which..never be ***d*** ... Dan 2:44
was slain and his body ***d*** ...... Dan 7:11
consume and to ***d*** .... Dan 7:26
d wonderfully..prosper .... Dan 8:24
shall ***d*** the city and .... Dan 9:26
d her vines and her fig .... Hos 2:12
people are ***d*** for lack of .... Hos 4:6
d unto them .... Hos 7:13
not return to ***d*** Ephraim ...... Hos 11:9
Israel thou hast ***d*** .... Hos 13:9
O grave, I will be thy ***d*** .... Hos 13:14
as a ***d*** from the Almighty ..... Joel 1:15
d I the Amorite before .... Amos 2:9
d it from off .... Amos 9:8
will not utterly ***d*** the house .... Amos 9:8
even ***d*** the wise men out ...... Obad 8
of Judah in..day of their ***d*** .... Obad 12
is polluted, it shall ***d*** you ...... Mic 2:10
destroy you..with a sore ***d***..... Mic 2:10
Philistines, I will..***d*** thee ...... Zeph 2:5
passeth by..cities are ***d*** .... Zeph 3:6
d the strength of..kingdoms ... Hag 2:22
seek to ***d*** all the nations .... Zech 12:9
shall be no more utter ***d*** ...... Zech 14:11
shall not ***d*** the fruits .... Mal 3:11
seek the young child to ***d*** ..... Matt 2:13
the way that leadeth to ***d*** ..... Matt 7:13
to ***d*** both soul and body in .... Matt 10:28
against him, how..might ***d***..... Matt 12:14
miserably ***d*** those wicked ...... Matt 21:41
and ***d*** those murderers .... Matt 22:7
I am able to ***d*** the temple ..... Matt 26:61
ask Barabbas and ***d*** Jesus ..... Matt 27:20
Thou that ***d*** the temple .... Matt 27:40
come to ***d*** us..know thee ...... Mark 1:24
into the waters, to ***d*** him ...... Mark 9:22
sought how they might ***d*** ...... Mark 11:18
will come and ***d***..husbandmen . Mark 12:9
will ***d*** this temple that is ...... Mark 14:58
thou that ***d*** the temple .... Mark 15:29
art thou come to ***d*** us? .... Luke 4:34
not come to ***d*** men's lives ..... Luke 9:56
flood came, and ***d*** them all .... Luke 17:27
people sought to ***d*** him .... Luke 19:47
come and ***d*** these .... Luke 20:16
D this temple..in three days ... John 2:19
d from among the people ..... Acts 3:23
Jesus of Nazareth..***d*** this ...... Acts 6:14
is not this he that ***d*** them ..... Acts 9:21
when..had ***d*** seven nations .... Acts 13:19
the body of sin might be ***d*** .... Rom 6:6
vessels..wrath fitted to ***d*** ..... Rom 9:22
D not him with thy meat ...... Rom 14:15
d the wisdom of..wise 1Cor 1:19
him shall God ***d*** 1Cor 3:17
God shall ***d*** both it and 1Cor 6:13
and were destroyed of the ***d***... 1Cor 10:10
last enemy that shall be ***d*** 1Cor 15:26
edification..not for your ***d*** 2Cor 10:8
edification, and not to ***d*** 2Cor 13:10
the faith which once he ***d*** ..... Gal 1:23
again the things which I ***d***..... Gal 2:18
d cometh upon them 1Thess 5:3
d with the brightness 2Thess 2:8
through death he might ***d*** ..... Heb 2:14
lest he that ***d*** the first born .... Heb 11:28
who is able to save and to ***d***.. James 4:12
scriptures, unto their own ***d*** ... 2Pet 3:16
he might ***d*** the works of 1John 3:8
d them that believed .... Jude 5
part of the ships were ***d*** .... Rev 8:9
d them which ***d*** the earth ..... Rev 11:18

DESTROYER—*one who oppresses; pillager*

[*also* DESTROYERS]
d of our country, which slew .. Judg 16:24
d shall come upon him .... Job 15:21
and his life to the ***d*** .... Job 33:22
from the paths of the ***d*** .... Ps 17:4
is the companion of a ***d*** .... Prov 28:24
d and they that made thee .... Is 49:17
I will prepare ***d*** against thee ... Jer 22:7

DETAIN—*to hold back*

[*also* DETAINED]
I pray thee, let us ***d*** thee 1Sam 21:7
that day, ***d*** before the Lord ... Judg 13:15

DETERMINATE COUNSEL
God's fixed purpose ..... Acts 2:23

DETERMINATION—*resolute persistence*
Against popular opposition .... Num 13:26-31; Num 14:1-9
Against great numbers ... 1Sam 14:1-5
Beyond human advice ... 2Kin 2:1-6
In perilous situation ..... Esth 4:10-16
In spite of persecution ... Acts 6:8—7:60

[*also* DETERMINE, DETERMINED]
shall pay as the judges ***d*** ...... Ex 21:22
sure that evil is ***d*** by him 1Sam 20:7
knew that it was ***d*** of 1Sam 20:33
hath been ***d*** from the day 2Sam 13:32
d to build a house for 2Chr 2:1
God hath ***d*** to destroy 2Chr 25:16
was evil ***d*** against him by ..... Esth 7:7
Seeing his days are ***d*** .... Job 14:5
consumption..***d***, in the midst .. Is 10:23
hosts..he hath ***d*** against it ..... Is 19:17
Seventy weeks are ***d*** upon ..... Dan 9:24

D

for that that is ***d*** shall be . . . . . .Dan 11:36
d is to gather the nations . . . . . .Zeph 3:8
Son of man goeth, as..was ***d***. . .Luke 22:22
Pilate, when he was ***d***. . . . . .Acts 3:13
counsel ***d*** before to be done . . .Acts 4:28
d to send relief unto . . . . .Acts 11:29
d that Paul and Barnabas . . . . .Acts 15:2
Barnabas ***d*** to take with . . . . . . .Acts 15:37
d the times..appointed . . . . .Acts 17:26
shall be ***d*** in a lawful . . . . .Acts 19:39
Paul had ***d*** to sail by. . . . . .Acts 20:16
I ***d*** not to know any thing 1Cor 2:2
But I ***d*** this with myself 2Cor 2:1
for I have ***d*** there to winter . . .Titus 3:12

DETEST—*to loathe*

[*also* DETESTABLE]
thou shalt utterly ***d*** . . . . .Deut 7:26
their ***d*** and abominable . . . . . . .Jer 16:18
sanctuary with all thy ***d*** . . . . . . .Ezek 5:11
all the ***d*** things thereof and . . . .Ezek 11:18
idols, nor with their ***d*** things . .Ezek 37:23

DEUEL (dū'ĕl)—*"knowledge of God"*
Father of Eliasaph . . . . . . .Num 1:14

Gad was Eliasaph..son of ***D*** . . .Num 10:20

DEUTERONOMY—*book of the Old Testament containing the farewell speeches of Moses*
Written and spoken by Moses . . . . Deut 31:9, 22, 24

DEVICE—*scheme; something contrived*

[*also* DEVICES]
d that he had devised . . . . .Esth 8:3
letters that his wicked ***d*** . . . . . . .Esth 9:25
He disappointeth the ***d***. . . . . . . .Job 5:12
d which ye wrongfully. . . . . .Job 21:27
let them be taken in the ***d*** . . . . .Ps 10:2
imagined a michievous ***d*** . . . . . .Ps 21:11
maketh the ***d*** of..people . . . . . . .Ps 33:10
bringeth wicked ***d*** to pass . . . . .Ps 37:7
further not his wicked ***d***. . . . . . .Ps 140:8
be filled with their own ***d*** . . . . .Prov 1:31
man of wicked ***d*** will he. . . . . . .Prov 12:2
man of wicked ***d*** is hated . . . . . .Prov 14:17
are many ***d*** in a man's heart . . .Prov 19:21
there is no work, nor ***d*** . . . . . . .Eccl 9:10
deviseth wicked ***d***..destroy . . . . .Is 32:7
had devised ***d*** against me . . . . . .Jer 11:19
devise a ***d*** against you . . . . .Jer 18:11
will walk after our own ***d*** . . . . .Jer 18:12
d is against Babylon . . . . .Jer 51:11
d against me all the day. . . . . . .Lam 3:62
forecast..***d*** against the strong . .Dan 11:24
graven by art and man's ***d***. . . . .Acts 17:29
are not ignorant of his ***d*** 2Cor 2:11

DEVIL—*the chief opponent of God*

Titles of:
Abaddon . . . . .Rev 9:11
Accuser . . . . .Rev 12:10
Adversary 1Pet 5:8
Angel of the bottomless pit . . . . .Rev 9:11
Apollyon . . . . .Rev 9:11
Beelzebub . . . . .Matt 12:24
Belial 2Cor 6:15
God of this world 2Cor 4:4
Murderer . . . . .John 8:44
Old serpent . . . . .Rev 20:2
Prince of demons . . . . .Matt 12:24
Prince of the power of the air . . . . .Eph 2:2
Prince of this world . . . . . .John 14:30
Ruler of darkness . . . . . . .Eph 6:12
Satan . . . . .Luke 10:18
Serpent . . . . .Gen 3:4
Wicked one . . . . .Matt 13:19

Origin of:
Heart lifted up in pride . .Is 14:12-20
Perfect until sin came . . . .Ezek 28:14-19
Greatest of fallen angels . .Rev 12:7-9
Tempts man to sin . . . . . .Gen 3:1-7
Father of lies . . . . .John 8:44

Character of:
Subtle . . . . .Gen 3:1; 2Cor 11:3
Slanderous . . . . .Job 1:9
Fierce . . . . .Luke 8:29
Deceitful 2Cor 11:14
Powerful . . . . .Eph 2:2
Proud 1Tim 3:6
Cowardly . . . . .James 4:7
Wicked 1John 2:13

Power of, over the wicked:
They are his children . . . .Acts 13:10; 1John 3:10
They do his will . . . . .John 8:44
He possesses . . . . .Luke 22:3
He blinds 2Cor 4:4
He deceives . . . . .Rev 20:7, 8
He ensnares 1Tim 3:7
He troubles 1Sam 16:14
They are punished with him . . . . .Matt 25:41

Power of, over God's people:
Tempt 1Chr 21:1
Afflict . . . . .Job 2:7
Accuse . . . . .Zech 3:1
Sift .Luke 22:31
Beguile 2Cor 11:3
Disguise 2Cor 11:14, 15

The believer's power over:
Watch against 2Cor 2:11
Fight against . . . . .Eph 6:11-16
Resist . . . . .James 4:7; 1Pet 5:9
Overcome . . . . .1John 2:13; Rev 12:10, 11

Christ's triumph over:
Predicted . . . . .Gen 3:15
Portrayed . . . . .Matt 4:1-11
Proclaimed . . . . .Luke 10:18
Perfected . . . . .Mark 3:27, 28

[*also* DEVILISH, DEVILS]
offer their sacrifices unto ***d*** . . . .Lev 17:7
sacrificed unto ***d***, not to God . .Deut 32:17
for the ***d***..for the calves 2Chr 11:15
sons..their daughters unto ***d*** . . .Ps 106:37
to be tempted of the ***d*** . . . . . . .Matt 4:1
d taketh him up into . . . . .Matt 4:5
Then the ***d*** leaveth him . . . . . . .Matt 4:11
were possessed with ***d***. . . . . .Matt 4:24
name have cast out ***d***? . . . . .Matt 7:22
were possessed with ***d***. . . . . .Matt 8:16
d besought him, saying, If . . . . .Matt 8:31
dumb man possessed with..***d***. . .Matt 9:32
Pharisees said..casteth out ***d*** . . .Matt 9:34
raise the dead, cast out ***d*** . . . . .Matt 10:8
they say, He hath a ***d***. . . . . .Matt 11:18
one possessed with a ***d***. . . . . . . .Matt 12:22
is grievously vexed with a ***d*** . . .Matt 15:22
that were possessed with ***d*** . . . .Mark 1:32
and cast out many ***d*** . . . . .Mark 1:34
suffered not the ***d*** to speak . . . .Mark 1:34
sicknesses..to cast out ***d*** . . . . . . .Mark 3:15
by the prince of the ***d***. . . . . .Mark 3:22
casteth he out ***d*** . . . . .Mark 3:22
d besought him, saying. . . . . . . .Mark 5:12
was possessed with the ***d*** . . . . . .Mark 5:15
they cast out many ***d*** . . . . .Mark 6:13
casting out ***d*** in thy name . . . . .Mark 9:38
out of whom..cast seven ***d***. . . . .Mark 16:9
my name shall..cast out ***d*** . . . . .Mark 16:17
forty days tempted of the ***d*** . . .Luke 4:2
a spirit of an unclean ***d*** . . . . . .Luke 4:33
d also came out of many . . . . . .Luke 4:41
wine..ye say, He hath a ***d*** . . . . .Luke 7:33
cometh the ***d*** and taketh . . . . . .Luke 8:12
certain man..had ***d*** long . . . . . .Luke 8:27
of the ***d*** into..wilderness . . . . . .Luke 8:29
Then went the ***d*** out of . . . . . . .Luke 8:33
possessed of..***d*** was healed . . . .Luke 8:36
power..authority over all ***d*** . . . .Luke 9:1
d threw him down..tare him . . .Luke 9:42
even the ***d*** are subject unto . . .Luke 10:17
out ***d*** through Beelzebub . . . . . .Luke 11:15
out ***d*** through Beelzebub . . . . . .Luke 11:18
finger of God cast out ***d*** . . . . . .Luke 11:20
one of you is a ***d***? . . . . .John 6:70
and said, Thou hast a ***d*** . . . . . . .John 7:20
Ye are of your father the ***d*** . . .John 8:44
art a Samaritan..hast a ***d***? . . . . .John 8:48
many..said, He hath a ***d*** . . . . . .John 10:20
d..now put into the heart . . . . .John 13:2
that were oppressed of the ***d*** . .Acts 10:38
thou child of the ***d*** . . . . .Acts 13:10
sacrifice to ***d***..not to God 1Cor 10:20
should..fellowship with ***d*** 1Cor 10:20
Neither give place to the ***d*** . . . .Eph 4:27
against the wiles of..***d*** . . . . .Eph 6:11
spirits and doctrines of ***d*** 1Tim 4:1
power of death, that is the ***d*** . .Heb 2:14
d also believe, and tremble . . . .James 2:19
earthly, sensual, ***d*** . . . . .James 3:15
that committeth sin is..***d*** 1John 3:8
d sinneth from..beginning 1John 3:8
destroy the works of the ***d*** . . .1John 3:8
when contending with the ***d*** . . .Jude 9
d shall cast some . . . . .Rev 2:10
they should not worship ***d*** . . . . .Rev 9:20
old serpent, called the ***D*** . . . . . .Rev 12:9
For they are the spirits of ***d*** . . .Rev 16:14
become the habitation of ***d*** . . . .Rev 18:2

DEVISE—*to form in the mind; to create*

[*also* DEVISED, DEVISETH]
d cunning works to work . . . . . .Ex 31:4
to ***d*** curious works to work . . . .Ex 35:32
those that ***d*** cunning work . . . . .Ex 35:35
doth he ***d*** means, that his 2Sam 14:14
d against us that we should 2Sam 21:5
mouth which he had ***d*** 1Kin 12:33
he had ***d*** against the Jews . . . . .Esth 8:3
d against..Jews to destroy . . . . .Esth 9:24
they ***d*** to take away my life . . .Ps 31:13
confusion that ***d*** my hurt . . . . . .Ps 35:4
d mischief upon his bed . . . . . .Ps 36:4
D not evil against. . . . . .Prov 3:29
d mischief continually . . . . .Prov 6:14
heart that ***d***..imaginations . . . . .Prov 6:18
Do they not err that ***d*** evil? . . .Prov 14:22
be to them that ***d*** good . . . . . . .Prov 14:22
man's heart ***d*** his ways . . . . . . .Prov 16:9
d wicked devices to destroy . . .Is 32:7
liberal ***d*** liberal things . . . . .Is 32:8
had ***d*** devices against me . . . . . .Jer 11:19
d a device against you . . . . .Jer 18:11
d devices against Jeremiah . . . .Jer 18:18
Lord hath both ***d*** and done . . . .Jer 51:12
done that which he had ***d*** . . . . .Lam 2:17
men that ***d*** mischief . . . . .Ezek 11:2
Woe to them that ***d*** iniquity . . .Mic 2:1
not followed..***d*** fables 2Pet 1:16

DEVOTION TO GOD—*devout attitude toward God*

How?:
With our whole selves . . Prov 3:9; Rom 12:1; 1Cor 6:20

Why? Because of:
God's goodness 1Sam 12:24; 1Thess 2:12
Christ's death 2Cor 5:15
Our redemption 1Cor 6:19, 20

[*also* DEVOTE, DEVOTED, DEVOTIONS]
unto the Lord, as a field ***d*** . . . .Lev 27:21
no ***d*** thing, that a man shall . . .Lev 27:28
man shall ***d*** unto the Lord . . . .Lev 27:28
every ***d*** thing is..holy unto . . . .Lev 27:28
None ***d***, which shall be. . . . . . . .Lev 27:29
which shall be ***d*** of men . . . . . . .Lev 27:29
Every thing ***d*** in Israel . . . . .Num 18:14
servant, who is ***d*** to thy fear . . .Ps 119:38
I passed by..beheld your ***d*** . . . .Acts 17:23

DEVOTION TO THE MINISTRY OF SAINTS
Household of Stephanas. .1Cor 16:15

DEVOTIONS, MORNING—*prayers at the beginning of the day*
Jacob's . . . . .Gen 28:16-18
Samuel's parents' 1Sam 1:19

Hezekiah's 2Chr 29:20-31
Job's ....Job 1:5
Jesus' ....Mark 1:35

DEVOUR—*to consume*

[*also* DEVOURED, DEVOUREST, DEVOURETH, DEVOURING]

hath quite ***d*** also..money ......Gen 31:15
evil beast hath ***d*** him ....Gen 37:20
beast hath ***d*** him; Joseph ......Gen 37:33
the seven thin ears ***d*** the ......Gen 41:7
the thin ears ***d*** the seven ......Gen 41:24
morning he shall ***d***..prey ......Gen 49:27
d fire on the top..mount ......Ex 24:17
d them..they died before ......Lev 10:2
fire ***d*** two hundred..fifty ......Num 26:10
they shall be ***d***, and many .....Deut 31:17
d with burning heat ....Deut 32:24
blood, and my sword shall ***d***...Deut 32:42
d the cedars of Lebanon ......Judg 9:15
Shall the sword ***d*** for ever?....2Sam 2:26
sword ***d*** one..as another 2Sam 11:25
wood ***d*** more people 2Sam 18:8
fire out of his mouth ***d***........2Sam 22:9
command the locusts to ***d*** 2Chr 7:13
shall ***d*** the strength of.........Job 18:13
born of death shall ***d*** ....Job 18:13
fire out of his mouth ***d***........Ps 18:8
wrath..fire shall ***d*** them ....Ps 21:9
silence..fire shall ***d***............Ps 50:3
Thou lovest all ***d*** words ....Ps 52:4
they have ***d*** Jacob ....Ps 79:7
d the fruit of their ground .....Ps 105:35
of the wicked ***d*** iniquity ....Prov 19:28
who ***d*** that which is holy ......Prov 20:25
to ***d*** the poor from..earth .....Prov 30:14
strangers ***d*** it in..presence .....Is 1:7
ye shall be ***d*** with the sword...Is 1:20
as the fire ***d*** the stubble .....Is 5:24
shall ***d*** Israel with..mouth .....Is 9:12
shall ***d*** the briers and thorns ...Is 9:18
thine enemies shall ***d*** them ....Is 26:11
tempest, and the flame of ***d***...Is 29:6
with the flame of a ***d*** fire .....Is 30:30
breath, as fire, shall ***d*** you ....Is 33:11
will destroy and ***d*** at once .....Is 42:14
beasts of the field, come to ***d***..Is 56:9
all that ***d*** him shall offend .....Jer 2:3
own sword..***d*** your prophets ...Jer 2:30
shame hath ***d*** the labor of .....Jer 3:24
come and have ***d*** ....Jer 8:16
beasts of..field, come to ***d***.....Jer 12:9
earth, to ***d*** and destroy........Jer 15:3
it shall ***d*** all things round......Jer 21:14
that ***d*** thee shall be ***d*** ....Jer 30:16
the sword shall ***d*** ....Jer 46:10
shall ***d*** the corner of Moab ....Jer 48:45
king of Assyria hath ***d*** him ....Jer 50:17
flaming fire, which ***d*** round....Lam 2:3
hath ***d***..foundations thereof....Lam 4:11
famine and pestilence..***d*** ......Ezek 7:15
fire ***d*** both the ends of it ......Ezek 15:4
when the fire hath ***d*** it ....Ezek 15:5
fire, and another fire shall ***d***...Ezek 15:7
hath ***d*** her fruit...............Ezek 19:14
d every green tree in thee .....Ezek 20:47
residue shall be ***d*** by the fire ..Ezek 23:25
through the fire to ***d*** them ....Ezek 23:37
shall ***d*** thee..I will bring.......Ezek 28:18
Thou land ***d*** up men ....Ezek 36:13
thou shalt ***d*** men ....Ezek 36:14
Arise, ***d*** much flesh ....Dan 7:5
d and brake in pieces ....Dan 7:7
a month ***d*** them with ....Hos 5:7
have ***d*** their judges ....Hos 7:7
it shall ***d*** the palaces thereof...Hos 8:14
d them, because of their ......Hos 11:6
will I ***d*** them like a lion ....Hos 13:8
cry for the fire hath ***d***.........Joel 1:19
A fire ***d*** before them ....Joel 2:3
d the palaces of Ben-hadad ....Amos 1:4
Tyrus, which shall ***d*** the........Amos 1:10
shall ***d*** the palaces thereof.....Amos 1:14
d the palaces of Jerusalem ....Amos 2:5
increased..palmerworm ***d***......Amos 4:9
it ***d*** the great deep, and did ...Amos 7:4
kindle in them..***d*** them ....Obad 18
shall be ***d*** as stubble fully .....Nah 1:10
sword shall ***d***..young lions .....Nah 2:13
There shall the fire ***d*** thee.....Nah 3:15
when the wicked ***d*** the man ...Hab 1:13
as to ***d*** the poor secretly ......Hab 3:14
d with..fire of my jealousy ....Zeph 3:8
she shall be ***d*** with fire ....Zech 9:4
they shall ***d***..subdue with ......Zech 9:15
they shall ***d*** all the people .....Zech 12:6
fowls came and ***d*** them up ....Matt 13:4
ye ***d*** widows' houses ....Matt 23:14
fowls of the air came and ***d*** ...Mark 4:4
which ***d*** widows' houses ....Mark 12:40
fowls of the air ***d*** it ....Luke 8:5
hath ***d***..living with harlots .....Luke 15:30
Which ***d*** widows' houses ......Luke 20:47
if ye bite and ***d*** one another ...Gal 5:15
shall ***d*** the adversaries ....Heb 10:27
seeking whom he may ***d*** 1Pet 5:8
their mouth..***d*** their enemies...Rev 11:5
for to ***d*** her child as soon as ...Rev 12:4
out of heaven, and ***d*** them ....Rev 20:9

DEVOURER—*locust*

will rebuke the ***d*** for..........Mal 3:11

DEVOUT—*pious; religious; sincere*

Simeon ....Luke 2:25
Cornelius ....Acts 10:1, 2,7
Ananias ....Acts 22:12
Those who buried
Stephen ....Acts 8:2
Converts...............Acts 13:43
Women of Antioch ......Acts 13:50
Greeks in Thessalonica...Acts 17:4
Gentiles ....Acts 17:17
Men...................Is 57:1

Jews, ***d*** men, out of ....Acts 2:5

DEW—*moisture condensed on the earth*

Used literally of:

Natural dew ....Ex 16:13, 14
A miraculous test........Judg 6:37-40
A curse.................1Kin 17:1
Hag 1:10

Used figuratively of:

God's blessings ....Gen 27:28
God's truth ....Deut 32:2
The Messiah ....Is 26:19
Man's fickleness ....Hos 6:4
Peace and harmony ......Ps 133:3

when ***d*** fell upon the camp ....Num 11:9
for the ***d***, and for the deep ....Deut 33:13
his heavens shall drop down ***d*** .Deut 33:28
let there be no ***d***, neither 2Sam 1:21
light upon him as..***d*** falleth 2Sam 17:12
d lay all night upon my ....Job 29:19
begotten the drops of ***d***? ......Job 38:28
thou hast the ***d*** of thy youth ...Ps 110:3
clouds drop down the ***d*** ....Prov 3:20
favor is as ***d*** upon..grass ......Prov 19:12
for my head is filled with ***d***....Song 5:2
like a cloud of ***d*** in the heat ...Is 18:4
it be wet with the ***d*** of heaven .Dan 4:15
wet with the ***d*** of heaven ......Dan 4:23
early ***d*** that passeth ....Hos 13:3
heavens shall give their ***d*** .....Zech 8:12

DEXTERITY—*skill in using one's hand or body*

Of 700 men ....Judg 20:16
David's 1Sam 17:40-50

DIADEM—*a crown*

Removed by judgment ...Ezek 21:25-27
Reserved for God's
people ....Is 28:5
Restored by grace ......Is 62:3

was as a robe and a ***d*** ....Job 29:14

DIAL—*an instrument for telling time*

Miraculous movement of .Is 38:8

it had gone down in..***d***.......2Kin 20:11

DIAMOND—*precious jewel made of crystallized carbon*

Sacred ....Ex 28:18
Precious ....Ezek 28:13

sapphire, and a ***d***............Ex 39:11
with the point of a ***d***.........Jer 17:1

DIANA (dī-ă'nȧ)

A pagan goddess ....Acts 19:24-34

DIBLAIM (dĭb-lā'ĭm)—*"two cakes; double embrace"*

Hosea's father-in-law ....Hos 1:3

DIBLATH (dĭb'lăth)—*"round cake"*

An unidentified place ....Ezek 6:14

DIBON (dī'bŏn)—*"wasting"*

1. Amorite town ....Num 21:30
Taken by Israel ....Num 32:3
Rebuilt by Gadites ......Num 32:34
Called Dibon-gad ....Num 33:45, 46
Later given to
Reubenites ....Josh 13:9, 17
Destruction of, foretold. .Jer 48:18, 22
2. A village of Judah ......Neh 11:25

gone up to Bajith, and to ***D***...Is 15:2

DIBON-GAD (dī'bŏn-găd)—*"wasting of God"—a halting place of the Israelites leaving Egypt*

from Iim and pitched in ***D*** ....Num 33:45

DIBRI (dĭb'rī)—*"eloquent; on the pasture born"*

A Danite ....Lev 24:11-14

DICTATOR—*ruler with absolute authority*

Powers of, to:

Take life................1Kin 2:46
Judge 1Kin 10:9
Tax 2Kin 15:19
Levy labor 1Kin 5:13-15
Make war..............1Kin 20:1
Form alliances 1Kin 15:18, 19

Examples, evil:

Pharaoh ....Ex 1:8-22
Ahab 1Kin 16:28-33
Herod ....Matt 2:16

Examples, benevolent:

Solomon 1Kin 8:12-21
1Kin 10:23-24
Cyrus ....Ezra 1:1-4

DID—*See* INTRODUCTION

DIDYMYS (dĭd'ĭ-mŭs)—*"twin"*

Surname of Thomas .....John 11:16

one of the twelve, call ***D***......John 20:24
Peter, and Thomas called ***D***...John 21:2

DIE—*to cease to live*

[*also* DIED, DIEST, DIETH, DYING]

eatest..shalt surely ***d***.........Gen 2:17
Ye shall not surely ***d***..........Gen 3:4
and thirty years: and he ***d***.....Gen 5:5
and five years: and he ***d***......Gen 5:11
and five years: and he ***d***......Gen 5:17
and nine years: and he ***d***......Gen 5:27
And all flesh ***d*** that moved ....Gen 7:21
and fifty years: and he ***d***......Gen 9:29
five years: and Terah ***d*** in .....Gen 11:32
some evil take me, and I ***d***....Gen 19:19
he ***d*** in the presence of all ....Gen 25:18
I am at the point to ***d***........Gen 25:32
may bless thee before I ***d***.....Gen 27:4
day, all the flock will ***d***.......Gen 33:13
soul..departing, (for she ***d***)....Gen 35:18
Rachel ***d***, and was buried .....Gen 35:19
And Bela ***d***, and Jobab the....Gen 36:33
And Husham ***d***, and Hadad ...Gen 36:35
Samlah ***d***, and Saul of ....Gen 36:37
the son of Achbor ***d***..........Gen 36:39
that we may live, and not ***d***...Gen 42:2
that we may live, and not ***d***...Gen 43:8
leave..his father would ***d***......Gen 44:22
go and see him before I ***d***.....Gen 45:28

Onan *d* in..Canaan ....Gen 46:12
why..*d* in thy presence? ....Gen 47:15
shall we *d* before thine ....Gen 47:19
that we may live, and not *d* . . .Gen 47:19
said unto Joseph..I *d* ....Gen 48:21
did command before he *d* .....Gen 50:16
Joseph said..I *d* ....Gen 50:24
Joseph *d*, and all his ....Ex 1:6
fish..in the river shall *d* ....Ex 7:18
fish that was in the river *d* ....Ex 7:21
there shall nothing *d* of all ....Ex 9:4
all the cattle of Egypt *d* ....Ex 9:6
children of Israel *d* not one ...Ex 9:6
them, and they shall *d* ....Ex 9:19
in the land of Egypt shall *d* ...Ex 11:5
to *d* in the wilderness? ....Ex 14:11
we..*d* in the wilderness ....Ex 14:12
not God speak..lest we *d* ......Ex 20:19
smiteth a man, so that he *d* ...Ex 21:12
with his fist, and he *d* not .....Ex 21:18
or a woman, that they *d* ......Ex 21:28
be smitten that he *d* ....Ex 22:2
it be hurt, or *d*, the owner ....Ex 22:14
bear not iniquity, and *d* ....Ex 28:43
wash..that they *d* not ....Ex 30:20
their feet, that they *d* not .....Ex 30:21
fat of the beast that *d*.........Lev 7:24
of the Lord, that ye *d* not .....Lev 8:35
and they *d* before the Lord....Lev 10:2
the congregation, lest ye *d* ....Lev 10:7
beast of which ye..eat, *d* ......Lev 11:39
d not in their uncleanness .....Lev 15:31
upon the ark; that he *d* not ...Lev 16:2
soul..eateth that which *d* ......Lev 17:15
sin; they shall *d* childless ......Lev 20:20
lest..bear sin for it, and *d* .....Lev 22:9
Abihu *d* before the Lord ......Num 3:4
any holy thing, lest they *d*.....Num 4:15
holy things..lest they *d*.......Num 4:20
man *d* very suddenly by him...Num 6:9
had *d* in this wilderness! ....Num 14:2
and there they shall *d*.........Num 14:35
stoned him..and he *d* ....Num 15:36
men *d* the common death .....Num 16:29
they that *d* in the plague ......Num 16:49
that *d* about the..Korah ....Num 16:49
Behold we *d*, we perish ....Num 17:12
tabernacle of..Lord shall *d* ....Num 17:13
we be consumed with *d*? ....Num 17:13
neither they, nor ye..*d* ....Num 18:3
children of Israel, lest ye *d* ....Num 18:32
when a man *d* in a tent ....Num 19:14
Would God that we had *d* ....Num 20:3
brethren *d* before the Lord ....Num 20:3
unto his people, and shall *d* ..Num 20:26
much people of Israel *d* ....Num 21:6
d the death of..righteous ......Num 23:10
when that company *d* ....Num 26:10
Onan *d* in..land of Canaan ....Num 26:19
They shall surely *d* in the .....Num 26:65
father *d* in the wilderness .....Num 27:3
If a man *d*..have no son.......Num 27:8
of the Lord, and *d* there ......Num 33:38
manslayer *d* not, until he.......Num 35:12
instrument of iron, so..he *d* ...Num 35:16
laying of wait, that he *d*.......Num 35:20
a man may *d*, seeing...........Num 35:23
person to cause him to *d* ......Num 35:30
I must *d* in this land, I........Deut 4:22
Now..why should we *d*? ....Deut 5:25
God anymore..we shall *d*......Deut 5:25
Aaron *d*, and..he was buried ..Deut 10:6
stone him..that he *d* ....Deut 13:10
eat of any thing that *d* of .....Deut 14:21
even that man shall *d* ....Deut 17:12
even that prophet shall *d* ......Deut 18:20
smite..mortally that he *d* ......Deut 19:11
he *d* in the battle, and ....Deut 20:5
stone her..that she *d* ....Deut 22:21
stone them..that they *d* ....Deut 22:24
if the latter husband *d* ....Deut 24:3
together, and one of them *d*...Deut 25:5
d in the mount whither ....Deut 32:50
the servant of the Lord *d* .....Deut 34:5
d in the wilderness by the .....Josh 5:4

not *d* by..hand of the avenger .Josh 20:9
Nun..servant of the Lord, *d* ...Josh 24:29
Jerusalem, and there he *d* .....Judg 1:7
Joshua left when he *d*..........Judg 2:21
asleep and weary. So he *d* ....Judg 4:21
fear not: thou shalt not *d* .....Judg 6:23
men of..tower of Shechem *d*...Judg 9:49
twenty..three years, and *d*.....Judg 10:2
d Jephthah the Gileadite ......Judg 12:7
And Elon the Zebulonite *d*....Judg 12:12
We shall surely *d*, because ....Judg 13:22
me *d* with the Philistines ......Judg 16:30
Naomi's husband *d* ....Ruth 1:3
Where thou *d*, will I *d* ....Ruth 1:17
increase of thine house..*d* 1Sam 2:33
his neck brake, and he *d* 1Sam 4:18
Lord thy God, that we *d* not ..1Sam 12:19
hand, and lo, I must *d* 1Sam 14:43
Shall Jonathan *d*, who 1Sam 14:45
rescued Jonathan..he *d* not 1Sam 14:45
the Lord, that I *d* not.........1Sam 20:14
shalt surely *d*, Ahimelech 1Sam 22:16
that his heart *d* within him 1Sam 25:37
ye are worthy to *d*, because ...1Sam 26:16
his sword, and *d* with him.....1Sam 31:5
he smote him that he *d* 2Sam 1:15
and *d* in the same place 2Sam 2:23
Asahel fell down and *d* 2Sam 2:23
under..fifth rib, that he *d* 2Sam 3:27
Died Abner as a fool *d*? 2Sam 3:33
there he *d* by the ark of God ..2Sam 6:7
he may be smitten, and *d* 2Sam 11:15
Uriah the Hittite *d* also 2Sam 11:17
away..sin; thou shalt not *d* 2Sam 12:13
seventh day, that the child *d* ..2Sam 12:18
For we must needs *d*, and.....2Sam 14:14
would God I had *d* for thee ...2Sam 18:33
Shimei, Thou shalt not *d* 2Sam 19:23
struck him not..and he *d* 2Sam 20:10
found in him, he shall *d*.......1Kin 1:52
fell upon him that he *d* 1Kin 2:25
Nay: but I will *d* here 1Kin 2:30
that thou shalt surely *d*? 1Kin 2:42
child *d* in the night 1Kin 3:19
Him that *d* of Jeroboam in 1Kin 14:11
of the door, the child *d* 1Kin 14:17
Him that *d* of Baasha in 1Kin 16:4
that *d* of his in the fields 1Kin 16:4
that we may eat it, and *d* 1Kin 17:12
himself that he might *d* 1Kin 19:4
stone him, that he may *d* 1Kin 21:10
stoned him..that he *d* 1Kin 21:13
that *d* of Ahab in the city 1Kin 21:24
against the Syrians, and *d* 1Kin 22:35
but shalt surely *d* 2Kin 1:4
he *d* according to the word 2Kin 1:17
Why sit we here until we *d*? ...2Kin 7:3
city and we shall *d* there 2Kin 7:4
if we sit still here, we *d* 2Kin 7:4
they kill us, we shall but *d* 2Kin 7:4
him in the gate, and he *d* 2Kin 7:17
that he shall surely *d* 2Kin 8:10
on his face, so that he *d* 2Kin 8:15
smote him, and he *d*...........2Kin 12:21
thou shalt *d*, and not live 2Kin 20:1
he came to Egypt, and *d*.......2Kin 23:34
Hadad *d* also..................1Chr 1:51
Jether *d* without children......1Chr 2:32
Saul *d*, and his three sons 1Chr 10:6
all his house *d* together 1Chr 10:6
Saul *d* for..transgression.......1Chr 10:13
and there he *d* before God 1Chr 13:10
Eleazar *d*, and had no sons....1Chr 23:22
And he *d* in a good old age ...1Chr 29:28
stoned him..that he *d* 2Chr 10:18
d in the one and fortieth 2Chr 16:13
so he *d* of sore diseases 2Chr 21:19
full of days when he *d* 2Chr 24:15
years old was he when he *d* ...2Chr 24:15
slew him on his bed..he *d* 2Chr 24:25
The fathers shall not *d* for 2Chr 25:4
neither shall the children *d* 2Chr 25:4
but every man shall *d* for 2Chr 25:4
integrity? curse God, and *d* ...Job 2:9
d I not from the womb? ......Job 3:11

d, even without wisdom ....Job 4:21
wisdom shall *d* with you ......Job 12:2
man *d*, and wasteth away ......Job 14:10
If a man *d*, shall he live ......Job 14:14
d in the bitterness of his ......Job 21:25
I said, I shall *d* in my nest ....Job 29:18
shall *d* without knowledge .....Job 36:12
shall he *d*, and his name ......Ps 41:5
he seeth that wise men *d*......Ps 49:10
when he *d* he shall carry ......Ps 49:17
those..appointed to *d* ....Ps 79:11
But ye shall *d* like men ....Ps 82:7
am afflicted and ready to *d*....Ps 88:15
they *d*, and return to their ....Ps 104:29
I shall not *d*, but live, and ....Ps 118:17
He shall *d* without............Prov 5:23
fools *d* for want of wisdom ....Prov 10:21
a wicked man *d*, his ....Prov 11:7
that hateth reproof shall *d*.....Prov 15:10
despiseth his ways shall *d* .....Prov 19:16
with the rod, he shall not *d* ...Prov 23:13
And how *d* the wise man? ......Eccl 2:16
to be born, and a time to *d* ...Eccl 3:2
shouldest thou *d* before ....Eccl 7:17
know that they shall *d* ....Eccl 9:5
year that king Uzziah *d* ....Is 6:1
for tomorrow we shall *d* ....Is 22:13
there shalt thou *d*, and ....Is 22:18
thou shalt *d*, and not live .....Is 38:1
no water, and *d* for thirst .....Is 50:2
that dwell therein shall *d* .....Is 51:6
he should not *d* in the pit .....Is 51:14
that eateth of their eggs *d*.....Is 59:5
child shall *d* a hundred........Is 65:20
their worm shall not *d* ....Is 66:24
Lord, that thou *d* not by ......Jer 11:21
men shall *d* by the sword .....Jer 11:22
their daughters shall *d* ....Jer 11:22
shall *d* of grievous deaths .....Jer 16:4
great and the small shall *d* ....Jer 16:6
and there thou shalt *d* ....Jer 20:6
abideth in this city shall *d* ....Jer 21:9
and there shall ye *d* ....Jer 22:26
This man is worthy to *d*.......Jer 26:11
ye *d*, thou and thy people .....Jer 27:13
this year thou shalt *d* ....Jer 28:16
So Hananiah the prophet *d*....Jer 28:17
But every one shall *d* for......Jer 31:30
Thou shalt *d* in peace ....Jer 34:5
the scribe, lest I *d* there.......Jer 37:20
he is like to *d* for hunger .....Jer 38:9
words, and thou shalt not *d* ...Jer 38:24
Egypt..there ye shall *d* ....Jer 42:16
know..that ye shall *d* by ......Jer 42:22
they shall *d*, from the least ....Jer 44:12
Thou shalt surely *d*; and ......Ezek 3:18
he shall *d* in his iniquity.......Ezek 3:19
eaten of that which *d* of.......Ezek 4:14
shall *d* with the pestilence .....Ezek 5:12
He that is far off shall *d* ......Ezek 6:12
and is besieged shall *d* ....Ezek 6:12
the son of Benaiah *d* ....Ezek 11:13
not see it..he shall *d* there ....Ezek 12:13
the souls that should not *d* ....Ezek 13:19
midst of Babylon he shall *d* ...Ezek 17:16
soul that sinneth, it shall *d* ....Ezek 18:4
he shall surely *d*; his blood ....Ezek 18:13
shall not *d* for the iniquity ....Ezek 18:17
he shall *d* in his iniquity.......Ezek 18:18
that sinneth, it shall *d*.........Ezek 18:20
surely live, he shall not *d* .....Ezek 18:21
that the wicked should *d*? .....Ezek 18:23
sinned, in them shall he *d*.....Ezek 18:24
surely live, he shall not *d* .....Ezek 18:28
in the death of him that *d*.....Ezek 18:32
and thou shalt *d* the deaths....Ezek 28:8
shalt surely *d*; if thou ....Ezek 33:8
he shall *d* in his iniquity.......Ezek 33:9
ye *d*, O house of Israel? ......Ezek 33:11
committed, he shall *d* for .....Ezek 33:13
surely live, he shall not *d* .....Ezek 33:15
shall *d* of the pestilence ....Ezek 33:27
he offended in Baal, he *d* .....Hos 13:1
Moab shall *d* with tumult .....Amos 2:2
house, that they shall *d* ....Amos 6:9

Jeroboam shall *d* by the ....Amos 7:11
sinners of..people shall *d* ......Amos 9:10
is better for me to *d* than .....Jon 4:3
Holy One? we shall not *d* .....Hab 1:12
that that *d*, let it *d* ....Zech 11:9
mother, let him *d* the death ...Matt 15:4
Moses said, If a man *d*........Matt 22:24
last of all the woman *d* ....Matt 22:27
Though I should *d* with ....Matt 26:35
let him *d* the death; But ......Mark 7:10
Where their worm *d* not ....Mark 9:44
If a man's brother *d*, and .....Mark 12:19
the first took a wife, and *d*....Mark 12:20
the second took her, and *d*....Mark 12:21
last of all the woman *d* also ...Mark 12:22
If I should *d* with thee, I......Mark 14:31
was sick, and ready to *d* ......Luke 7:2
of age, and she lay a *d*........Luke 8:42
her to wife, and he *d* childless .Luke 20:30
Last of all the woman *d*.......Luke 20:32
Neither can they *d* any.........Luke 20:36
come down ere my child *d* ....John 4:49
may eat thereof, and not *d*....John 6:50
and shall *d* in your sins ....John 8:21
go, that we may *d* with him ...John 11:16
my brother had not *d*.........John 11:21
believeth in me..never *d* ......John 11:26
man should *d* for..people ......John 11:50
that Jesus should *d* for that....John 11:51
wheat fall..and *d* ....John 12:24
abideth alone; but if it *d* .....John 12:24
what death he should *d* ....John 12:33
one man should *d* for the .....John 18:14
by our law he ought to *d*......John 19:7
and *d*, he, and our fathers ....Acts 7:15
also to *d* at Jerusalem for .....Acts 21:13
to deliver any man to *d* ....Acts 25:16
Christ *d* for the ungodly ......Rom 5:6
righteous man will one *d* ......Rom 5:7
some would even dare to *d*....Rom 5:7
he *d*, he *d* unto sin once ......Rom 6:10
It is Christ that *d*, yea ....Rom 8:34
we *d*, we *d* unto the Lord .....Rom 14:8
or *d*, we are the Lord's ....Rom 14:8
meat, for whom Christ *d* ......Rom 14:15
if her husband be *d*, she 1Cor 7:39
perish, for whom Christ *d* 1Cor 8:11
better for me to *d*, than.......1Cor 9:15
Jesus our Lord, I *d* daily 1Cor 15:31
not quickened, except it *d*.....1Cor 15:36
about in the body the *d* 2Cor 4:10
our hearts to *d* and live 2Cor 7:3
Jesus *d* and rose again 1Thess 4:14
Who *d* for us, that, whether ...1Thess 5:10
men that *d* receive tithes ......Heb 7:8
Moses, law *d* without mercy ...Heb 10:28
Jacob, when he was a *d*........Heb 11:21
By faith Joseph when he *d* ....Heb 11:22
remain, that are ready to *d*....Rev 3:2
in the sea, and had life, *d*.....Rev 8:9

DIET—*food normally eaten*
Of the Hebrews ....Lev 11:1-47

And for his *d*, there was a ....Jer 52:34
there was a continual *d* ....Jer 52:34

DIFFER—*to distinguish between; distinctions*

[*also* DIFFERENCE, DIFFERENCES, DIFFERETH, DIFFERING]
Lord doth put a *d* between ....Ex 11:7
that ye may put *d* between ....Lev 10:10
shall..put *d* between ....Lev 20:25
they have put no *d* between ...Ezek 22:26
d between the holy and ....Ezek 44:23
no *d* between us and them ....Acts 15:9
for there is no *d*.............Rom 3:22
gifts *d* according to..grace .....Rom 12:6
maketh..to *d* from another? ...1Cor 4:7
is *d* also between a wife 1Cor 7:34
are *d* of administrations 1Cor 12:5
star *d* from another star 1Cor 15:41
d nothing from a servant ......Gal 4:1
compassion, making a *d*.......Jude 22

DIFFERING WEIGHTS
Prohibited ....Deut 25:13, 14

DIFFICULTIES—*problems hard to solve*

Kinds of:
Mental ....Ps 139:6, 14
Moral ....Ps 38:1-22
Theological ....John 6:48-60

Examples of:
Birth of a child in old age Gen 18:9-15
Testing of Abraham .....Gen 22:1-14
Slaughter of Canaanites ..Ex 23:27-33
God's providence ....Ps 44:1-26
Prosperity of wicked .....Ps 73:1-28
Israel's unbelief ....John 12:39-41

Negative attitudes toward:
Rebellion against ....Num 21:4, 5
Unbelief under ....Heb 3:12-19

Positive attitudes toward:
Submission under........Num 14:7-9
Prayer concerning ....Mark 11:23, 24
Admission of............2Pet 3:16

DIG—*to break up and remove earth*

[*also* DIGGED, DIGGEDST, DIGGETH]
that I have *d* this well ....Gen 21:30
Isaac *d* again..wells of water ...Gen 26:18
which they had *d* in..days .....Gen 26:18
servants *d* in the valley........Gen 26:19
d another well................Gen 26:22
well which they had *d*.........Gen 26:32
in my grave which I have *d* ...Gen 50:5
Egyptians *d* round about ......Ex 7:24
man shall *d* a pit ....Ex 21:33
The princes *d* the well ....Num 21:18
wells digged which thou *d* .....Deut 6:11
hills thou mayest *d* brass ......Deut 8:9
d and drunk strange waters 2Kin 19:24
in desert and *d* many wells 2Chr 26:10
houses full..goods, wells *d*.....Neh 9:25
d for it more than..treasures ..Job 3:21
thou shalt *d* about thee ....Job 11:18
made a pit..*d* it, and is........Ps 7:15
they have *d* a pit before me ...Ps 57:6
proud have *d* pits for me......Ps 119:85
ungodly man *d* up evil ....Prov 16:27
He that *d* a pit shall fall ......Eccl 10:8
shall not be pruned, nor *d* .....Is 5:6
I have *d* and drunk water .....Is 37:25
I went to Euphrates, and *d*....Jer 13:7
they have *d* a pit to take me ..Jer 18:22
Son of man, *d* now in.........Ezek 8:8
when I had *d* in the wall ......Ezek 8:8
d through the wall to carry ....Ezek 12:12
they *d* into hell, thence ....Amos 9:2
d a winepress in it ....Matt 21:33
d a place for the winevat ......Mark 12:1
d deep and laid..foundation ...Luke 6:48
I shall *d* about it and dung ....Luke 13:8
and *d* down thine altars ....Rom 11:3

DIGNITY—*worthiness; honor*

[*also* DIGNITIES]
excellency of *d*, and ....Gen 49:3
honor and *d* has been done ...Esth 6:3
Fully is set in great *d* ....Eccl 10:6
d..proceed of themselves ......Hab 1:7
not afraid to speak evil of *d* ...2Pet 2:10
and speak evil of *d* ....Jude 8

DIKLAH (dĭk'lä)—*"place of palms"*
Son of Joktan ....Gen 10:27

Hadoram also, and Uzal..*D* ...1Chr 1:21

DILEAN (dĭl'ĕ-ăn)—*"cucumber"*
Town of Judah ....Josh 15:38

DILEMMA—*perplexing alternatives*
Given to David 1Chr 21:9-17
Presented to Jews ....Matt 21:23-27

DILIGENCE—*faithful application to one's work*

Manifested in:
A child's education ......Deut 6:7
Dedicated service........Rom 12:11
A minister's task 2Tim 4:1-5

Special objects of:
The soul.................Deut 4:9
God's commandments....Deut 6:17
The heart ....Prov 4:23
Christian qualities 2Pet 1:5-9
One's calling 2Pet 1:10

Rewards of:
Prosperity...............Prov 10:4
Ruling hand ....Prov 12:24
Perseverance 2Pet 1:10

[*also* DILIGENT, DILIGENTLY]
thou will *d* hearken to ....Ex 15:26
Moses *d* sought the goat of.....Lev 10:16
hearken *d* unto my ....Deut 11:13
make search and ask *d*........Deut 13:14
judges shall make *d*...........Deut 19:18
leprosy that thou observe *d*....Deut 24:8
d heed to do..commandment ..Josh 22:5
d observe whether 1Kin 20:33
it be *d* done for the house of ..Ezra 7:23
Hear *d* my speech ....Job 13:17
shalt *d* consider his place ......Ps 37:10
they accomplish a *d* search ....Ps 64:6
Keep thy heart with all *d* .....Prov 4:23
d to seek thy face ....Prov 7:15
d man is precious............Prov 12:27
thoughts of the *d* tend only....Prov 21:5
ruler, consider *d* what is ......Prov 23:1
Be thou *d* to know the state ...Prov 27:23
hearkened *d* with ....Is 21:7
consider *d*..see if there ....Jer 2:10
if ye *d* hearken unto me ......Jer 17:24
d obey the voice..Lord ....Zech 6:15
them *d* what time the star.....Matt 2:7
search *d* for the young child ...Matt 2:8
had *d* enquired of the wise ....Matt 2:16
give *d* that thou mayest be ....Luke 12:58
seek *d* till she find it?.........Luke 15:8
spake and taught *d* ....Acts 18:25
that ruleth, with *d*; he that ....Rom 12:8
knowledge, and in all *d* 2Cor 8:7
proved *d* in many things 2Cor 8:22
d followed every good work ...1Tim 5:10
he sought me out very *d* 2Tim 1:17
d to come shortly unto me 2Tim 4:9
d..come unto me to Nicopolis. .Titus 3:12
Apollos on their journey *d* ....Titus 3:13
same *d* to the full assurance ...Heb 6:11
rewarder of them that *d* seek ..Heb 11:6
inquired and searched *d*.......1Pet 1:10
giving all *d*, add to..faith 2Pet 1:5
d that ye may be found of 2Pet 3:14
I gave all *d* to write unto .....Jude 3

DIM—*indistinct; not clear*

[*also* DIMNESS]
was old..his eyes were *d* ......Gen 27:1
eye was not *d*, nor his ....Deut 34:7
eyes were *d*, that he could 1Sam 4:15
is *d* by reason of sorrow ......Job 17:7
darkness *d* of anguish ....Is 8:22
d shall not be such as was .....Is 9:1
them that see shall not be *d*...Is 32:3
How is the gold become *d* ....Lam 4:1

DIMINISH—*to grow less; wane*

[*also* DIMINISHED, DIMINISHING]
shall not *d* aught thereof ......Ex 5:8
of your work shall be *d* ....Ex 5:11
thou shalt *d* the price of it ....Lev 25:16
neither shall ye *d* aught ....Deut 4:2
by vanity shall be *d*...........Prov 13:11
children of Kedar shall be *d* ...Is 21:17
speak unto..*d* not a word .....Jer 26:2
increased there and not *d* .....Jer 29:6
therefore will I also *d*.........Ezek 5:11
have *d* thine ordinary food ....Ezek 16:27
d of them the riches of........Rom 11:12

DIMNAH (dĭm'nä)—*"dung heap"*
City of Zebulun ....Josh 21:35
Same as Rimmon........1Chr 6:77

D with her suburbs ....Job 21:35

DIMON (dī'mŏn)—*river bed*
Place in Moab ....Is 15:9

DIMONAH (dī-mō'nä)—*"wasting"*
Town in Judah . . . . Josh 15:22
Same as Dibon . . . . Neh 11:25

DINAH (dī'nä)—*"judgment"*
Daughter of Leah . . . . Gen 30:21
Defiled by Shechem . . . . . Gen 34:1-24
Avenged by brothers . . . . Gen 34:25-31
Guilt concerning . . . . Gen 49:5-7

DINAITES
Foreigners who settled in Samaria . . . . Ezra 4:9

DINE—*to eat*
[*also* DINED]
men shall *d* with me at noon . . Gen 43:16
besought him to *d* with him . . . Luke 11:37
saith unto them, Come and *d*. . John 21:12
when they..*d*, Jesus saith . . . . . John 21:15

DINHABAH (dĭn'hä-bä)—*"give judgment"*
City of Edom . . . . Gen 36:32

name of his city was *D* 1Chr 1:43

DINNER—*a meal*
d of herbs where love is . . . . Prov 15:17
I have prepared my *d* . . . . Matt 22:4
had not..washed before *d* . . . . . Luke 11:38

DIONYSIUS (dī-ŏ-nĭ'sē-ŭs)—*"of the (god) Dionysos"*
Prominent Athenian; converted by Paul . . . . . Acts 17:34

DIOTREPHES (dī-ŏt'rĕ-fēz)—*"nourished by Jupiter"*
Unruly church member . . 3John 9, 10

DIP—*to plunge beneath*
[*also* DIPPED, DIPPETH]
d..coat in the blood . . . . Gen 37:31
d it in the blood . . . . Ex 12:22
shall *d* his finger in..blood . . . . . Lev 4:6
d them and the living bird . . . . . Lev 14:6
d it in the water . . . . Num 19:18
d in the brim . . . . Josh 3:15
d thy morsel in the vinegar . . . . Ruth 2:14
d it in a honeycomb 1Sam 14:27
d..seven times in Jordan 2Kin 5:14
foot may be *d* in the blood . . . . Ps 68:23
d his hand with me in . . . . Matt 26:23
d with me in the dish . . . . Mark 14:20
may *d* the tip of his finger . . . . Luke 16:24
give a sop when I have *d* it . . . John 13:26
d the sop he gave..to Judas . . . John 13:26

DIPLOMACY—*the art of managing affairs of state*
Joseph, an example in . . . Gen 41:33-46
Mordecai's advancement in . . . . Esth 10:1-3
Daniel's ability in . . . . Dan 2:48, 49
Paul's resort to . . . . Acts 21:20-25

DIRECT—*to point toward*
[*also* DIRECTED, DIRECTETH, DIRECTION, DIRECTLY]
d his face unto Goshen . . . . Gen 46:28
blood *d* before the tabernacle . . Num 19:4
by the *d* of the lawgiver . . . . Num 21:18
not *d* his words against me . . . . Job 32:14
d it under the whole heaven . . . Job 37:3
I *d* my prayer unto thee . . . . Ps 5:3
d to keep thy statutes . . . . Ps 119:5
he shall *d* thy paths . . . . Prov 3:6
the perfect shall *d* his way . . . . . Prov 11:5
but the Lord *d*..steps . . . . Prov 16:9
for the upright, he *d* his way . . Prov 21:29
wisdom is profitable to *d* . . . . . . Eccl 10:10
hath *d* the spirit of the . . . . Is 40:13
I will *d* all his ways . . . . Is 45:13
I will *d*..work in truth . . . . Is 61:8
man walketh to *d* his steps . . . . Jer 10:23
way *d* before the wall . . . . Ezek 42:12
Christ, *d* our way unto you 1Thess 3:11
d your hearts..love of God 2Thess 3:5

DIRT—*loose earth*
out as the *d* in the streets . . . . . Ps 18:42
waters cast up mire and *d* . . . . . Is 57:20

DISALLOW—*to deny the truth of; refuse to allow*
[*also* DISALLOWED]
father *d* her in the day . . . . Num 30:5
because her father *d* her . . . . . . Num 30:5
husband *d* her on the day . . . . . Num 30:8
d..of men but chosen of 1Pet 2:4
stone which the builders *d* 1Pet 2:7

DISANNUL—*to annul; cancel*
[*also* DISANNULLED, DISANNULLETH, DISANNULLING]
thou also *d* my judgment? . . . . . Job 40:8
purposed and who shall *d* . . . . . Is 14:27
covenant with death..be *d* . . . . . Is 28:18
no man *d* or addeth thereto . . . Gal 3:15
years after, cannot *d* . . . . Gal 3:17
a *d* of the commandment . . . . . . Heb 7:18

DISAPPOINT—*to thwart expectations*
Concerning one's:
Sons 1Sam 2:12-17
Mate 1Sam 25:23-31
Failure 2Sam 17:23
Wisdom . . . . Eccl 1:12-18
Acceptance . . . . Jer 20:7-9
Mission . . . . Jon 4:1-9
Hopes . . . . Luke 24:17-24
Antidotes against:
Let trust prevail . . . . Hab 3:17-19
Put God first . . . . Hag 1:2-14
Accept God's plan . . . . Rom 8:28
Remember God's promises . . . . Heb 6:10-12
[*also* DISAPPOINTED, DISAPPOINTETH]
d the devices of the crafty . . . . . Job 5:12
O Lord, *d* him, cast him . . . . . . Ps 17:13
Without counsel purposes..*d* . . Prov 15:22

DISARMAMENT—*abolishing weapons of war*
Imposed upon Israel 1Sam 13:19-22
Figurative of peace . . . . . . Is 2:4

DISCERN—*to distinguish; detect; discriminate; come to know*
[*also* DISCERNED, DISCERNETH, DISCERNING]
he *d* him not..his hands . . . . Gen 27:23
d..what is thine with me . . . . . . Gen 31:32
D I pray thee, whose are . . . . . . Gen 38:25
lord the king to *d* good 2Sam 14:17
I *d* between good and evil? 2Sam 19:35
people could not *d* the noise . . Ezra 3:13
could not *d* the form thereof . . Job 4:16
my taste *d* perverse things? . . . . Job 6:30
d among the youths a young . . . Prov 7:7
a wise man's heart *d* both . . . . . Eccl 8:5
them to *d* between..unclean . . . Ezek 44:23
cannot *d* between . . . . Jon 4:11
d between the righteous . . . . Mal 3:18
ye can *d* the face of the sky . . . Matt 16:3
can ye not *d*..signs of . . . . Matt 16:3
ye can *d* the face of the sky . . . Luke 12:56
that ye do not *d* this time? . . . . Luke 12:56
himself, not *d*..Lord's body 1Cor 11:29
to another *d* of spirits 1Cor 12:10
exercised to *d*..good and evil . . Heb 5:14

DISCERNER—*a judge*
is a *d* of the thoughts . . . . Heb 4:12

DISCERNMENT, SPIRITUAL
Requested by Solomon . . . 1Kin 3:9-14
Prayed for by David . . . . . Ps 119:18
Sought by Daniel . . . . Dan 7:15, 16
Denied to the unregenerate 1Cor 2:14
Necessity of 1John 4:1-6

DISCHARGE—*to shoot; release*
[*also* DISCHARGED]
cause them to be *d* there 1Kin 5:9
there is no *d* in that war . . . . . . Eccl 8:8

DISCIPLE—*follower of a teacher*
John the Baptist's . . . . John 1:35
Jesus' . . . . John 2:2
Moses' . . . . John 9:28
False teachers' . . . . Acts 20:30
[*also* DISCIPLES, DISCIPLES']
seal the law among my *d* . . . . . . Is 8:16
d came unto him . . . . Matt 5:1
of his *d* said unto him . . . . Matt 8:21
sat down with him and his *d* . . . Matt 9:10
came to him the *d* of John . . . . Matt 9:14
fast oft, but thy *d* fast not? . . . . Matt 9:14
called unto him his twelve *d* . . . Matt 10:1
is enough for the *d* . . . . Matt 10:25
water only in..name of a *d* . . . . Matt 10:42
commanding his twelve *d* . . . . . . Matt 11:1
of Christ he sent two of..*d* . . . . Matt 11:2
d were ahungered . . . . Matt 12:1
the *d* came..said unto him . . . . . Matt 13:10
d came and took up the body . Matt 14:12
loaves to his *d* and the *d* . . . . . Matt 14:19
d saw him walking on . . . . Matt 14:26
Why do thy *d* transgress . . . . . . Matt 15:2
d came and besought him . . . . . Matt 15:23
d say unto him, Whence . . . . . . Matt 15:33
brake them..gave to his *d* . . . . . Matt 15:36
the *d* to the multitude . . . . Matt 15:36
d were come to the other . . . . . Matt 16:5
asked his *d*, saying, Whom . . . . Matt 16:13
show unto his *d*, how that . . . . . Matt 16:21
brought him to thy *d* . . . . Matt 17:16
d unto Jesus, saying . . . . Matt 18:1
d say unto him, If the case . . . . Matt 19:10
pray; and the *d* rebuked . . . . . . Matt 19:13
When his *d* heard..they were . . Matt 19:25
twelve *d* apart in the way . . . . . Matt 20:17
of Olives..sent Jesus two *d* . . . . Matt 21:1
sent out unto him their *d* . . . . . Matt 22:16
multitude, and to his *d* . . . . Matt 23:1
d came..to show him . . . . Matt 24:1
d came unto him privately . . . . . Matt 24:3
said unto..*d*, Ye know that . . . . Matt 26:1
d saw it they had indignation . . Matt 26:8
at thy house with my *d* . . . . Matt 26:18
gave it to the *d*, and said . . . . . Matt 26:26
saith unto the *d*, Sit ye here . . . Matt 26:36
Then cometh he to his *d* . . . . . . Matt 26:45
Then all the *d* forsook him . . . . Matt 26:56
himself was Jesus' *d* . . . . Matt 27:57
d come by night and steal . . . . . Matt 27:64
d that he is risen from . . . . Matt 28:7
as they went to tell his *d* . . . . . . Matt 28:9
eleven *d* went..into Galilee . . . . Matt 28:16
together with Jesus and..*d* . . . . . Mark 2:15
the *d* of John and of the . . . . . . Mark 2:18
Why do..*d* of John and of . . . . . Mark 2:18
fast, but thy *d* fast not? . . . . Mark 2:18
d began, as they went . . . . Mark 2:23
himself with his *d* to the sea . . . Mark 3:7
expounded all things to..*d* . . . . . Mark 4:34
d said unto him, Thou seest . . . Mark 5:31
own country..*d* follow him . . . . Mark 6:1
d to set before them . . . . Mark 6:41
saw some of his *d* eat bread . . . Mark 7:2
Why walk not thy *d* according . Mark 7:5
Jesus called his *d* unto him . . . . Mark 8:1
to his *d* to set before them . . . . Mark 8:6
d had forgotten to take . . . . Mark 8:14
out, and his *d*, into . . . . Mark 8:27
by the way he asked his *d* . . . . . Mark 8:27
he came to his *d*, he saw . . . . . . Mark 9:14
spake to thy *d*..they should . . . . Mark 9:18
taught his *d*..said unto . . . . Mark 9:31
in the house..*d* asked him . . . . . Mark 10:10
d rebuked those that . . . . Mark 10:13
d were astonished at..words . . . Mark 10:24
sendeth forth two of his *d* . . . . . Mark 11:1
called unto him his *d* . . . . Mark 12:43
one of his *d* saith unto him . . . . Mark 13:1
d said..Where wilt thou . . . . Mark 14:12
eat..passover with my *d*? . . . . . . Mark 14:14
tell his *d* and Peter . . . . Mark 16:7
murmured against his *d* . . . . Luke 5:30
d plucked the ears of corn . . . . Luke 6:1

he called unto him his ***d*** ...... Luke 6:13
lifted up his eyes on..***d*** .... Luke 6:20
d is not above his master ...... Luke 6:40
many of his ***d*** went with ...... Luke 7:11
John calling unto him two..***d*** .. Luke 7:19
d asked him, saying, What .... Luke 8:9
called..twelve ***d*** together ...... Luke 9:1
besought thy ***d*** to cast him .... Luke 9:40
he turned him unto his ***d*** ...... Luke 10:23
d said unto him, Lord .... Luke 11:1
began to say unto his ***d*** .... Luke 12:1
come after me, cannot be..***d***... Luke 14:27
said also unto his ***d***, There .... Luke 16:1
said he unto the ***d***, It is .... Luke 17:1
d saw it, they rebuked .... Luke 18:15
of Olives, he sent two of..***d*** ... Luke 19:29
d..rejoice and praise God ..... Luke 19:37
d, Beware of the scribes ...... Luke 20:45
eat the passover with my ***d***? ... Luke 22:11
two ***d*** heard him speak .... John 1:37
and his ***d*** believed on him ..... John 2:11
d remembered that it was ..... John 2:17
came Jesus and his ***d*** .... John 3:22
between some of John's ***d*** ..... John 3:25
baptized more ***d*** than John .... John 4:1
d were gone away into .... John 4:8
meanwhile..***d*** prayed him...... John 4:31
he sat with his ***d*** .... John 6:3
distributed to the ***d*** .... John 6:11
d went down unto..sea .... John 6:16
whereinto..***d*** were entered ..... John 6:22
Jesus went not with..***d*** into .... John 6:22
d were gone away alone ...... John 6:22
Many..of his ***d***, when they .... John 6:60
many of his ***d*** went back ...... John 6:66
d also may see the works ..... John 7:3
d asked him..Master .... John 9:2
to his ***d***, Let us go into .... John 11:7
said his ***d***, Lord, if he sleep ... John 11:12
saith one of his ***d***, Judas ...... John 12:4
d looked one on another ...... John 13:22
so shall ye be my ***d*** .... John 15:8
said some of his ***d*** among ..... John 16:17
d said unto him, Lo, now ..... John 16:29
went forth with his ***d*** over ..... John 18:1
which he entered, and his ***d*** .. John 18:1
another ***d***..***d*** was known .... John 18:15
not thou also one..man's ***d***? ... John 18:17
not thou also one..man's ***d***? ... John 18:25
d standing by, whom he .... John 19:26
saith he to the ***d***, Behold ...... John 19:27
from that hour..***d*** took her .... John 19:27
Arimathea..a ***d*** of Jesus .... John 19:38
d, whom Jesus loved .... John 20:2
other ***d*** did outrun Peter ...... John 20:4
d went away unto their .... John 20:10
Magdalene came and told..***d***... John 20:18
the ***d*** glad, when they saw..... John 20:20
d were within, and Thomas.... John 20:26
again to the ***d*** at the sea ...... John 21:1
d knew not that it was Jesus... John 21:4
that ***d*** whom Jesus loved ...... John 21:7
none of the ***d*** durst ask him ... John 21:12
that ***d*** should not die .... John 21:23
in the midst of..***d*** .... Acts 1:15
number of..***d*** was multiplied ... Acts 6:1
multitude of the ***d*** unto .... Acts 6:2
against the ***d*** of the Lord ...... Acts 9:1
d at Damascus..Ananias .... Acts 9:10
d took him by night .... Acts 9:25
believed not that he was a ***d***... Acts 9:26
d had heard that Peter .... Acts 9:38
d were called Christians .... Acts 11:26
d, every man according .... Acts 11:29
d were filled with joy .... Acts 13:52
as the ***d*** stood round .... Acts 14:20
abode long time with the ***d***.... Acts 14:28
yoke upon the neck of..***d*** ..... Acts 15:10
d..named Timothy .... Acts 16:1
in order, strengthening..***d*** ..... Acts 18:23
Ephesus; and finding..***d*** .... Acts 19:1
people..***d*** suffered him not .... Acts 19:30
d came together to break ..... Acts 20:7
finding ***d*** we tarried .... Acts 21:4
d, with whom we..lodge .... Acts 21:16

DISCIPLESHIP—*adherence to a teacher's faith and instructions*

Tests of:
Obedience .... John 14:15
Faithfulness .... John 15:8
Perseverance .... John 8:31
Love .... John 13:35
Humility .... Matt 10:24, 25
Surrender of all .... Luke 14:26, 33
Bearing the cross .... Matt 16:25

Rewards of:
Acknowledged by Christ.. Matt 12:49, 50
Enlightened by Christ .... John 8:12
Guided by the Spirit ..... John 16:13
Honored by the Father .. John 12:26

DISCIPLINE—*reproof; correction*
openeth also their ear to ***d*** .... Job 36:10

DISCIPLINE OF THE CHURCH—*rules of practice among a community of believers*

Needed to:
Maintain sound faith ..... Titus 1:13
Correct disorder 2Thess 3:6-15
Remove the wicked 1Cor 5:3-5, 13

How performed:
In meekness .... Gal 6:1
In love 2Cor 2:6-8
In submission .... Heb 13:17
For edification 2Cor 10:8

DISCIPLINE, PARENTAL

Needed to:
Produce understanding ... Prov 10:13
Drive out foolishness .... Prov 22:15
Deliver from Sheol ...... Prov 23:13, 14
Produce obedience ...... Prov 19:18
Develop reverence .... Heb 12:8-10

How performed:
Without anger .... Eph 6:4
In love .... Heb 12:5-7

DISCLOSURE—*unfolding of the unknown*
A person's identity ...... Gen 45:1-5
Desirable information 1Sam 23:10-12
God's plan .... Rom 16:25-27

[*also* DISCLOSE]
earth also shall ***d*** her blood .. Is 26:21

DISCOMFITED—*defeated; frustrated*

[*also* DISCOMFITURE]
Joshua ***d*** Amalek and his ..... Ex 17:13
smote them..***d*** them, even ..... Num 14:45
Lord ***d*** them before .... Josh 10:10
Lord ***d*** Sisera, and all his ..... Judg 4:15
Philistines, and ***d*** them 1Sam 7:10
there was a very great ***d*** 1Sam 14:20
lightning, and ***d*** them 2Sam 22:15
shot out lightnings and ***d*** ...... Ps 18:14
his young men shall be ***d*** ...... Is 31:8

DISCONTENTMENT—*unhappiness at the condition of things*
Between Jacob and Laban .... Gen 31:1-16
Between Moses and Miriam .... Num 12:1-16
Among soldiers .... Luke 3:14

[*also* DISCONTENTED]
every one that was ***d*** 1Sam 22:2

DISCONTINUE—*to terminate*
even thyself, shalt ***d*** .... Jer 17:4

DISCORD—*lack of love; disagreement*
Caused by contention .... Prov 26:20, 21
Envy 1Cor 3:3
Caused by lies .... Prov 6:16-19
Among Jews .... John 6:43

continually; he soweth ***d*** ...... Prov 6:14

DISCOURAGEMENT—*depression of one's spirits*

Causes of:
Heavy burden .... Num 11:10-15
Defeat .... Josh 7:7-9
Apparent failure 1Kin 19:4
Sickness .... Is 38:9-20

Remedies against:
"What doest thou here?". 1Kin 19:9-18
"Cast thy burden upon the Lord" .... Ps 55:22
"Come ye apart" .... Mark 6:31
"Lift up your heads" .... Luke 21:28

[*also* DISCOURAGE, DISCOURAGED]
soul of the people was much ***d***. Num 21:4
d ye the heart of the children.. Num 32:7
fear not, neither be ***d*** .... Deut 1:21
shall not fail nor be ***d*** .... Is 42:4
children to anger..they be ***d*** ... Col 3:21

DISCOURTESY—*rudeness in manners*
Nabal's 1Sam 25:3, 14
Hanun's 2Sam 10:1-5
Simon's .... Luke 7:44

DISCOVER—*to know for the first time*

[*also* DISCOVERED, DISCOVERETH, DISCOVERING]
that thy nakedness be not ***d*** ... Ex 20:26
hath ***d*** her fountain .... Lev 20:18
nor ***d*** his father's skirt .... Deut 22:30
we will ***d*** ourselves 1Sam 14:8
both of them ***d*** themselves 1Sam 14:11
foundations..world were ***d***..... 2Sam 22:16
d..things out of darkness ...... Job 12:22
d the face of his garment? ..... Job 41:13
foundations of..world were ***d*** .. Ps 18:15
d the forests and in his .... Ps 29:9
his heart may ***d*** itself .... Prov 18:2
Lord will ***d***..secret parts .... Is 3:17
d the covering of Judah .... Is 22:8
iniquity are thy skirts ***d*** .... Jer 13:22
will I ***d*** thy skirts .... Jer 13:26
have not ***d*** thine iniquity ...... Lam 2:14
he will ***d*** thy sins .... Lam 4:22
foundation..shall be ***d*** .... Ezek 13:14
d thy nakedness unto them .... Ezek 16:37
wickedness was ***d***, as at .... Ezek 16:57
your transgressions are ***d*** ...... Ezek 21:24
In thee have they ***d***..fathers'... Ezek 22:10
d her whoredoms..***d*** her .... Ezek 23:18
I ***d*** her lewdness in the .... Hos 2:10
iniquity of Ephraim was ***d***..... Hos 7:1
d the foundations thereof ..... Mic 1:6
d thy skirts upon thy face ..... Nah 3:5
d..foundation unto the neck ... Hab 3:13
when we had ***d*** Cyprus .... Acts 21:3
they ***d*** a certain creek with .... Acts 27:39

DISCRETION—*action based upon caution*
Joseph chosen for .... Gen 41:33, 39
The value of .... Prov 2:11
A woman without .... Prov 11:22
A woman with .... Titus 2:5
God teaches .... Is 28:26
Trait of a good man ..... Ps 112:5

[*also* DISCREET, DISCREETLY]
look out a man ***d*** and wise .... Gen 41:33
man knowledge and ***d*** .... Prov 1:4
keep sound wisdom and ***d***..... Prov 3:21
thou mayest regard ***d*** .... Prov 5:2
d of a man deferreth..anger ... Prov 19:11
out the heavens by his ***d*** ...... Jer 10:12
saw that he answered ***d*** .... Mark 12:34
be ***d***, chaste, keepers .... Titus 2:5

DISCRIMINATION—*making distinctions*

Forbidden, on basis of:
Wealth .... James 2:1-9
Personal righteousness ... Rom 3:10, 23

Between truth and error:
Test the spirits 1John 4:1-6
Spirit of truth .... John 14:17
Word is truth .... Ps 119:160; John 17:17
Satan, father of lies ...... John 8:44

Between God's Word and man's:
Paul preached 1Thess 2:13
God's Word inspired 2Tim 3:16
By Spirit 1Cor 2:10-16

DISDAINED—*looked with scorn*
saw David, he *d* him 1Sam 17:42
fathers I would have *d* ....Job 80:1

DISEASES—*physical impairments of health*
Kinds of:
Ague ....Lev 26:16
Boil 2Kin 20:7
Atrophy ....Job 16:8
Blindness ....Matt 9:27
Boils and blains ....Ex 9:10
Consumption ....Deut 28:22
Deafness ....Mark 7:32
Weakness ....Ps 102:23
Dropsy ....Luke 14:2
Dumbness ....Matt 9:32
Dysentery 2Chr 21:12-19
Emerods 1Sam 5:6, 12
Epilepsy ....Matt 4:24
Fever ....Matt 8:14, 15
Inflammation ....Deut 28:22
Insanity ....Dan 4:33
Issue of blood ....Matt 9:20
Itch ....Deut 28:27
Leprosy 2Kin 5:1
Palsy ....Matt 4:24
Plague 2Sam 24:15-25
Scab ....Deut 28:27
Sores ....Luke 16:20
Causes of:
Man's original sin ....Gen 3:16-19
Man's actual sin 2Kin 5:27
2Chr 21:12-19
Satan's afflictions ....Job 2:7
Luke 13:16
God's sovereign will .....John 9:1-3
2Cor 12:7-10
Cures of:
From God 2Chr 16:12
Ps 103:3
By Jesus ....Matt 4:23, 24
By prayer ....Acts 28:8, 9
James 5:14, 15
By the use of means .....Is 38:21
Luke 10:34
See SICKNESS

[*also* DISEASE, DISEASED]
none of these *d* ....Ex 15:26
the evil *d* of Egypt ....Deut 7:15
he was *d* in his feet 1Kin 15:23
I shall recover of this *d* 2Kin 1:2
Shall I recover of this *d* 2Kin 8:8, 9
an incurable *d* 2Chr 21:18
they left him in great *d* 2Chr 24:25
By the great force of my *d* ....Job 30:18
filled with a loathsome *d* ......Ps 38:7
it is an evil *d* ....Eccl 6:2
d have..not strengthened ......Ezek 34:4
all manner of *d* among the ....Matt 4:23
all manner of *d* ....Matt 10:1
unto him all that were *d* ......Matt 14:35
unto him all that were *d* ......Mark 1:32
sick of divers *d* ....Mark 1:34
any sick with divers *d* ....Luke 4:40
to be healed of their *d* ....Luke 6:17
and to cure *d* ....Luke 9:1
whatsoever *d* he had ....John 5:4
on them that were *d* ....John 6:2
d departed from them ....Acts 19:12

DISFIGURE—*to deface*
for they *d* their faces ....Matt 6:16

DISFIGURED FACES—*mutilated, blemished faces*
Disqualifies for service ...Lev 21:18

DISGRACE—*shame produced by evil conduct*
Treachery 2Sam 10:4
Private 2Sam 13:6-20
Public ....Esth 6:6-13
Posthumous ....Jer 8:1-3
Permanent ....Matt 27:21-25
Paramount ....Matt 27:26-44
do not *d* the throne ....Jer 14:21

DISGRACEFUL—*contemptuous or shameful conduct*
Immorality ....Gen 34:7
Transgression ....Josh 7:15
Rape 2Sam 13:12

DISGUISE—*a false appearance; to conceal*

[*also* DISGUISED, DISGUISETH]
And Saul *d* himself 1Sam 28:8
Arise..and *d* thyself 1Kin 14:2
and *d* himself with ashes 1Kin 20:38
I will *d* myself and will go 2Chr 18:29
king of Israel *d* himself 2Chr 18:29
shall see me: and *d* his face ..Job 24:15

DISH—*platter used for food*
Tabernacle implement ...Ex 25:29
Figurative of annihilating Jerusalem 2Kin 21:13
In the tabernacle ....Ex 25:29
A common ....Matt 26:23
Man washing 2Kin 21:13

[*also* DISHES]
the table, his *d*..his spoons ....Ex 37:16
put thereon the *d* ....Num 4:7
brought..in a lordly *d* ....Judg 5:25
dippeth with me in the *d* ......Mark 14:20

DISHAN (dī'shăn)—*"antelope; leaping"*
Son of Seir ....Gen 36:21, 28

Dishon, and Ezar, and *D* 1Chr 1:38

DISHON (dī'shŏn)—*"antelope; leaping"*
1. Son of Seir ....Gen 36:21-30
2. Grandson of Seir ....Gen 36:25

and *D*, and Ezar 1Chr 1:38

DISHONESTY—*untruthfulness*
Manifested in:
Half-truths ....Gen 12:11-20
Trickery ....Gen 27:6-29
Falsifying one's word ....Gen 34:15-31
Wicked devices ....Prov 1:10-19
Theft ....John 12:6
Unpaid wages ....James 5:4
Consequences of:
Uncovered by God 1Kin 21:17-26
Uncovered by men ......Josh 9:3-22
Condemned by conscience Matt 27:3-5

[*also* DISHONEST]
at thy *d* gain ....Ezek 22:13
hidden things of *d* 2Cor 4:2

DISHONOR—*lack or loss of honor; to bring shame on*

[*also* DISHONOREST, DISHONORETH]
to see the king's *d* ....Ezra 4:14
clothed with..*d* that ....Ps 35:26
and my shame, and my *d* .....Ps 69:19
be covered with..*d* ....Ps 71:13
A wound and *d* shall he get ...Prov 6:33
son *d* the father ....Mic 7:6
ye do *d* me ....John 8:49
to *d* their own bodies ....Rom 1:24
breaking..law *d* thou God? ....Rom 2:23
head covered, *d* his head 1Cor 11:4
is sown in *d*; it is raised 1Cor 15:43
By honor and *d* 2Cor 6:8
some to *d* 2Tim 2:20

DISINHERIT—*to prevent from inheriting*
the pestilence..*d* them ....Num 14:12

DISMAYED—*caused to fear*

[*also* DISMAYING]
thee: fear not, neither be *d* ....Deut 31:8
neither be thou *d* ....Josh 1:9
neither be thou *d* ....Josh 8:1
Fear not, nor be *d* ....Josh 10:25
Philistine, they were *d* 1Sam 17:11
they were *d* 2Kin 19:26
dread not, nor be *d* 1Chr 22:13
Be not afraid nor *d* 2Chr 20:15
be not afraid nor *d* 2Chr 32:7
I was *d* at the seeing of it .....Is 21:3
be not *d*; for I am thy God ...Is 41:10
be not *d* at their faces ....Jer 1:17
be not *d* at the signs ....Jer 10:2
let them be *d* ....Jer 17:18
fear no more, nor be *d* ....Jer 23:4
neither be *d*, O Israel ....Jer 30:10
have I seen them *d* ....Jer 46:5
Misgab is confounded and *d* ..Jer 48:1
a derision and a *d* to ....Jer 48:39
they shall be *d* ....Jer 50:36
nor be *d* at their ....Ezek 2:6
mighty men..shall be *d* ....Obad 9

DISMISSED—*discharged; allowed to leave*
Jehoiada the priest *d* not 2Chr 23:8
when they were *d* ....Acts 15:30

DISOBEDIENCE—*rebellion against recognized authority*
Sources of:
Satan's temptations ......Gen 3:1-13
Lust ....James 1:13-15
Rebellion ....Num 20:10-24
1Sam 15:16-23
Consequences of:
Death ....Rom 5:12-19
The flood 1Pet 3:20
Exclusion from the promised land ....Num 14:26-39
Defeat ....Judg 2:2, 11-15
Doom 1Pet 2:7, 8

[*also* DISOBEDIENT, DISOBEYED]
d the mouth of the Lord 1Kin 13:21
the man of God, who was *d* ...1Kin 13:26
Nevertheless they were *d* ......Neh 9:26
d to..wisdom of the just ....Luke 1:17
not *d*..to the heavenly ....Acts 26:19
of evil things, *d* to parents ....Rom 1:30
d and gainsaying people ....Rom 10:21
to revenge all *d*, when your ...2Cor 10:6
in the children of *d* ....Eph 2:2
upon the children of *d* ....Eph 5:6
on the children of *d* ....Col 3:6
but for the lawless and *d* 1Tim 1:9
blasphemers, *d* to parents 2Tim 3:2
being abominable, and *d* ......Titus 1:16
d received a ....Heb 2:2

DISORDERLY—*unruly and irregular*
Paul not guilty 1Thess 5:14
Some guilty 2Thess 3:6-11

DISPATCH—*to do away with*
d them with their swords ......Ezek 23:47

DISPENSATION—*a stewardship entrusted to one*
Of divine working ....Eph 1:10
Of the Gospel 1Cor 9:17
Paul's special privilege in .Eph 3:2

according to the *d* of God .....Col 1:25

DISPERSION—*a scattering abroad*
Of Noah's generation ....Gen 11:8
Of Israelites 2Kin 17:5, 6
Because of disobedience. .Hos 9:1-12
Of the early Christians ...1Pet 1:1

[*also* DISPERSE, DISPERSED, DISPERSIONS]
D yourselves among the 1Sam 14:34
d of all his children 2Chr 11:23
and *d* among the people ......Esth 3:8
He hath *d*, he hath given .....Ps 112:9
thy fountains be *d* abroad .....Prov 5:16
lips of..wise *d* knowledge ......Prov 15:7
gather..the *d* of Judah ....Is 11:12
of your *d* ....Jer 25:34
d them in the countries ....Ezek 12:15
d thee in the countries ....Ezek 22:15
will *d* them through the ....Ezek 30:23
d through the countries ....Ezek 36:19
the daughter of my *d* ....Zeph 3:10
the *d* among the Gentiles .....John 7:35
as obeyed him, were *d* ....Acts 5:37
He hath *d* abroad 2Cor 9:9

DISPLAY—*an unusual exhibition*

Of God's:
Power ....Ex 14:23-31
Glory ....Ex 33:18-23
Wrath ....Num 16:23-35
Universe ....Job 38:1-41
Holiness ....Is 6:1-10

Of man's:
Kingdom ....Esth 1:2-7
Pride ....Esth 5:11
Wealth ....Is 39:2
Hypocrisy ....Luke 20:46, 47

[*also* DISPLAYED]
d because of the truth ....Ps 60:4

DISPLEASURE—*disapproval*
God's, at man...........1Chr 21:7
Man's, at God 2Sam 6:8
Man's, at men ....Acts 12:20

[*also* DISPLEASE, DISPLEASED]
Let it not ***d*** my lord ....Gen 31:35
which he did ***d*** the Lord ......Gen 38:10
when Joseph..it ***d*** him ....Gen 48:17
complained, it ***d*** the Lord .....Num 11:1
d thee, I will get me back .....Num 22:34
was afraid of the..hot ***d*** ....Deut 9:19
though I do them a ***d*** ....Judg 15:3
But the thing ***d*** Samuel 1Sam 8:6
thou ***d*** not the lords of........1Sam 29:7
Let not this thing ***d*** thee 2Sam 11:25
his father had not ***d*** him 1Kin 1:6
came into his house..***d*** 1Kin 21:4
And David was ***d***, because 1Chr 13:11
and vex them in his sore ***d*** ....Ps 2:5
neither chasten me in thy hot ***d*** Ps 38:1
thou hast been ***d***; O turn......Ps 60:1
the Lord see it..it ***d*** him ......Prov 24:18
it ***d*** him that there was no.....Is 59:15
was sore ***d*** with himself ....Dan 6:14
But it ***d*** Jonah exceedingly ....Jon 4:1
Lord ***d*** against the rivers? .....Hab 3:8
The Lord hath been sore ***d***....Zech 1:2
I am very sore ***d*** with the .....Zech 1:15
for I was but a little ***d*** ....Zech 1:15
they were sore ***d*** ....Matt 21:15
Jesus saw it, he was..***d*** ....Mark 10:14

DISPOSITION—*natural temperament*
Ambitious Absalom 2Sam 15:1-6
Boastful Nebuchadnezzar .Dan 4:30
Cowardly Peter..........Matt 26:58
Devilish Judas...........John 13:20-30
Envious Saul............1Sam 18:6-12
Foolish Nabal 1Sam 25:10-25
Gullible Haman ....Esth 6:6-11
Humble Job ....Job 1:20-22

[*also* DISPOSED, DISPOSING]
who hath ***d*** the..world? ....Job 34:13
d thereof is of the Lord ....Prov 16:33
the law by the ***d*** of angels.....Acts 7:53
he was ***d***..into Achaia ....Acts 18:27
and ye be ***d*** to go 1Cor 10:27

DISPOSSESS—*to take away one's possession of something*

[*also* DISPOSSESSED]
and ***d*** the Amorite............Num 32:39
ye shall ***d*** the inhabitants ......Num 33:53
how can I ***d*** them? ....Deut 7:17
God..hath ***d*** the Amorites .....Judg 11:23

DISPUTATION—*arguments, dissensions, debates*

[*also* DISPUTATINGS, DISPUTATIONS, DISPUTE, DISPUTED, DISPUTER, DISPUTING]
the righteous..***d*** with him......Job 23:7
ye ***d*** among yourselves ....Mark 9:33
d with Stephen ....Acts 6:9
and ***d*** against the Grecians ....Acts 9:29
no small dissension and ***d*** .....Acts 15:2
there had been much ***d*** ....Acts 15:7
d daily in the school of one ...Acts 19:9
but not to doubtful ***d*** ....Rom 14:1
where is the ***d*** of..world? 1Cor 1:20
without murmurings and ***d*** ....Phil 2:14
d of men of corrupt 1Tim 6:5
he ***d*** about the body ....Jude 9

DISQUIET—*to disturb; alarm*

[*also* DISQUIETED, DISQUIETNESS]
Why hast thou ***d*** me 1Sam 28:15
I..roared by reason of the ***d***...Ps 38:8
surely they are ***d*** in vain ......Ps 39:6
and why art thou ***d*** in me? ....Ps 42:5
why art thou ***d*** within me? ....Ps 42:11
why art thou ***d*** within me? ....Ps 43:5
the earth is ***d*** ....Prov 30:21
and ***d*** the inhabitants ....Jer 50:34

DISSEMBLERS—*liars*

[*also* DISSEMBLED, DISSEMBLETH]
and have also stolen, and ***d*** ...Josh 7:11
neither will I go in with ***d*** .....Ps 26:4
he that hateth ***d*** ....Prov 26:24
For ye ***d*** in your hearts ....Jer 42:20
other Jews ***d*** likewise ....Gal 2:13

DISSENSION—*contentious disagreement*
had no small ***d*** ....Acts 15:2
there arose a great ***d***..........Acts 23:10

DISSIMULATION—*the act of dissembling*
Let love be without ***d***.........Rom 12:9
carried away with..***d*** ....Gal 2:13

DISSOLVE—*to cause to disperse or disappear*

[*also* DISSOLVED, DISSOLVEST, DISSOLVING]
and ***d*** my substance ....Job 30:22
the inhabitants..are ***d*** ....Ps 75:3
thou..Palestina, art ***d*** ....Is 14:31
the earth is clean ***d*** ....Is 24:19
host of heaven shall be ***d***......Is 34:4
d of doubts ....Dan 5:12
and ***d*** doubts ....Dan 5:16
and the palace shall be ***d***......Nah 2:6
this tabernacle were ***d***.........2Cor 5:1
these things shall be ***d*** 2Pet 3:11

DISTAFF—*staff used in spinning*
and her hands hold the ***d*** .....Prov 31:19

DISTANT—*remote; far apart*
equally ***d*** one from another....Ex 36:22

DISTILL—*to precipitate*
speech shall ***d*** as the dew .....Deut 32:2
clouds do drop and ***d*** upon ....Job 36:28

DISTINCTION—*clearness; clearly*

[*also* DISTINCTLY]
in the law of God ***d*** ....Neh 8:8
they give a ***d*** in the sounds 1Cor 14:7

DISTRACTED—*diverted; confused*

[*also* DISTRACTION]
while I suffer..terrors I am ***d*** ..Ps 88:15
attend..the Lord without ***d*** 1Cor 7:35

DISTRESS—*affliction; suffering*

[*also* DISTRESSED, DISTRESSES]
Jacob was..afraid and ***d*** ....Gen 32:7
in the day of my ***d*** ....Gen 35:3
therefore is this ***d*** come ....Gen 42:21
and Moab was ***d*** because of ...Num 22:3
D not the Moabites ....Deut 2:9
thine enemies shall ***d*** thee .....Deut 28:53
enemy shall ***d*** thee in..gates ...Deut 28:57
and they were greatly ***d*** ....Judg 2:15
when ye are in ***d***? ....Judg 11:7
for the people were ***d*** 1Sam 13:6
every one that was in ***d*** 1Sam 22:2
Saul answered, I am sore ***d***....1Sam 28:15
I am ***d*** for thee, my brother ...2Sam 1:26
In my ***d*** I called upon the 2Sam 22:7
redeemed my soul..of all ***d*** 1Kin 1:29
d him, but strengthened 2Chr 28:20
And in the time of his ***d*** did...2Chr 28:22
Ye see the ***d*** that we are in ...Neh 2:17
and we are in great ***d***.........Neh 9:37
when I was in ***d*** ....Ps 4:1
bring thou me out of my ***d*** ....Ps 25:17
delivered them out of..***d*** ......Ps 107:6
he saved them..of their ***d*** .....Ps 107:13
he saveth them..of their ***d*** .....Ps 107:19
he bringeth them out of..***d*** ....Ps 107:28
I called upon the Lord in ***d*** ...Ps 118:5
d and anguish cometh upon ...Prov 1:27
Yet I will ***d*** Ariel, and there ..Is 29:2
and will ***d*** them, that they.....Jer 10:18
O Lord; for I am in ***d*** ....Lam 1:20
Noph shall have ***d*** daily ....Ezek 30:16
spoken..in the day of ***d*** ....Obah 12
a day of trouble and ***d***........Zeph 1:15
shall be great ***d*** in the land ....Luke 21:23
tribulation, or ***d*** ....Rom 8:35
this is good for..***d*** 1Cor 7:26
troubled..yet not ***d*** 2Cor 4:8
in necessities, in ***d*** 2Cor 6:4
d by your faith 1Thess 3:7

DISTRIBUTE—*to give out portions*

[*also* DISTRIBUTED, DISTRIBUTETH, DISTRIBUTING, DISTRIBUTION]
Moses did ***d*** for inheritance ...Josh 13:32
Israel, ***d*** for inheritance to ....Josh 14:1
David ***d*** them, both Zadok 1Chr 24:3
David had ***d*** in..house of......2Chr 23:18
d..oblations of the Lord 2Chr 31:14
was to ***d*** unto..brethren ....Neh 13:13
God ***d*** sorrows in his anger....Job 21:17
d unto the poor ....Luke 18:22
he ***d*** to the disciples ....John 6:11
and ***d*** was made unto every ...Acts 4:35
D to the..saints ....Rom 12:13
God hath ***d*** to every man 1Cor 7:17
and for your liberal ***d*** unto 2Cor 9:13
rule which God..***d*** to us 2Cor 10:13
ready to ***d***, willing to 1Tim 6:18

DITCH—*channel dug in the ground*
Miraculously filled 2Kin 3:16-20
Wicked fall into ....Ps 7:15
Blind leaders fall into ....Luke 6:39

thou plunge me in the ***d*** ......Job 9:31
For a whore is a deep ***d***.......Prov 23:27
Ye made also a ***d*** between ....Is 22:11
both shall fall into the ***d*** ......Matt 15:14

DIVERS—*various kinds*
Colors ....Ezek 17:3
Diseases ....Luke 4:40
Doctrines ....Heb 13:9
Flies....................Ps 78:45
Lusts ....Titus 3:3
Manners ....Heb 1:1
Measures ....Prov 20:10
Miracles ....Heb 2:4
Seeds...................Deut 22:9
Temptations ....James 1:2
Tongues 1Cor 12:10
Vanities ....Eccl 5:7
Washings ....Heb 9:10
Weights ....Prov 20:10, 23

shalt not have..***d*** weights ......Deut 25:13
of ***d*** colors of needlework .....Judg 5:30
a garment of ***d*** colors 2Sam 13:18
and of ***d*** colors 1Chr 29:2
with sweet odors and ***d*** 2Chr 16:14
d of Asher and Manasseh 2Chr 30:11
came ***d*** sorts of flies ....Ps 105:31
high places with ***d*** colors .....Ezek 16:16
with ***d*** diseases ....Matt 4:24
many..sick of ***d*** diseases ....Mark 1:34
earthquakes in ***d*** places ....Mark 13:8
earthquakes shall be in ***d***......Luke 21:11
But when ***d*** were hardened ....Acts 19:9
led away with ***d*** lusts 2Tim 3:6

DIVERSITY—*variety*
Among hearts ....Mark 13:3-8
Of Gods's gifts 1Cor 12:4-11
Of God's times ....Heb 1:1

[*also* DIVERSE, DIVERSITIES]
cattle..with a ***d*** kind ....Lev 19:19
vessels being ***d*** one from ......Esth 1:7
the sea, ***d*** one from another ...Dan 7:3

d from all the others ....Dan 7:19
he shall be *d* from the ....Dan 7:24
governments, *d* of tongues 1Cor 12:28

DIVIDE—*to separate*

[*also* DIVIDED, DIVIDETH, DIVIDING]
God *d*..light from..darkness ...Gen 1:4
let it *d* the waters from the ....Gen 1:6
d the light from the darkness ..Gen 1:18
the isles of the Gentiles *d* .....Gen 10:5
by these were the nations *d* ...Gen 10:32
and *d* them in the midst.......Gen 15:10
he *d* the people that was ......Gen 32:7
at night he shall *d* the spoil ...Gen 49:27
over the sea, and *d* it ....Ex 14:16
and the waters were *d* ....Ex 14:21
and *d* the money of it.........Ex 21:35
the vail shall *d* unto you ......Ex 26:33
thereof, but shall not *d* it .....Lev 1:17
or of them that *d* the hoof ....Lev 11:4
but *d* not the hoof............Lev 11:5
beast which *d* the hoof........Lev 11:26
the land shall be *d*............Num 26:53
shall the possession..be *d*......Num 26:56
d the prey into two parts ......Num 31:27
shall *d* the land unto you ......Num 34:17
Lord commanded to *d* the .....Num 34:29
the Lord thy God hath *d*......Deut 4:19
that *d* the cloven hoof ....Deut 14:7
because it *d* the hoof ....Deut 14:8
d the coasts..three parts ....Deut 19:3
shalt thou *d* for..inheritance ...Josh 1:6
d this land for..inheritance ....Josh 13:7
Israel did..they *d* the land .....Josh 14:5
end of *d* the land ....Josh 19:49
d for an inheritance by lot ....Josh 19:51
d the spoil of your enemies....Josh 22:8
have they not *d* the prey ......Judg 5:30
d them into..companies ....Judg 9:43
in..death they were not *d* 2Sam 1:23
Thou and Ziba *d* the land 2Sam 19:29
D the living child in two 1Kin 3:25
were the people of Israel *d* 1Kin 16:21
they were *d* hither and 2Kin 2:8
in his days the earth was *d* 1Chr 1:19
and thus were they *d* 1Chr 24:4
Thus were they *d* by lot.......1Chr 24:5
d them speedily among all.....2Chr 35:13
thou didst *d* the sea ....Neh 9:11
He *d* the sea with his power...Job 26:12
innocent shall *d* the silver .....Job 27:17
Who hath *d* a watercourse ....Job 38:25
Lord *d* the flames of fire ......Ps 29:7
Destroy, O Lord..*d* their ......Ps 55:9
tarried at home *d* the spoil ....Ps 68:12
Thou didst *d* the sea by thy ...Ps 74:13
and *d* them an inheritance .....Ps 78:55
d the spoil with the proud .....Prov 16:19
when they *d* the spoil ....Is 9:3
the prey of a great spoil *d*.....Is 33:23
the Lord..that *d* the sea ....Is 51:15
will I *d* him a portion ....Is 53:12
he shall *d* the spoil with ....Is 53:12
d the water before them ......Is 63:12
which *d* the sea ....Jer 31:35
anger of the Lord hath *d*......Lam 4:16
and *d* the hair................Ezek 5:1
neither shall they be *d* into ....Ezek 37:22
shall ye *d*..land unto you ......Ezek 47:21
ye shall *d* by lot unto the .....Ezek 48:29
the kingdom shall be *d*........Dan 2:41
and times and the *d* of........Dan 7:25
shall be *d* toward the four .....Dan 11:4
shall *d* the land for gain.......Dan 11:39
Their heart is *d* ....Hos 10:2
thy land shall be *d*............Amos 7:17
away he hath *d* our fields .....Mic 2:4
thy spoil shall be *d* ....Zech 14:1
kingdom *d* against itself ....Matt 12:25
house *d* against itself..........Matt 12:25
he is *d* against himself ....Matt 12:26
kingdom be *d* against itself ....Mark 3:24
and be *d*, he cannot stand ....Mark 3:26
the two fishes *d* he among ....Mark 6:41
kingdom *d* against itself ....Luke 11:17
Satan..be *d* against himself ....Luke 11:18
that he *d* the inheritance .....Luke 12:13
be five in one house *d* ....Luke 12:52
he *d* their land to them ....Acts 13:19
and the multitude was *d* ......Acts 23:7
Is Christ *d*? was Paul 1Cor 1:13
d to every man severally as 1Cor 12:11
rightly *d* the word of truth 2Tim 2:15
to the *d* asunder of soul.......Heb 4:12
great city was *d* into three.....Rev 16:19

DIVIDER—*a judge*
made me a judge or a *d* ......Luke 12:14

DIVINATION—*attempt to foretell the unknown by occult means*

Considered as:
System of fraud ....Ezek 13:6, 7
Lucrative employment ...Acts 16:16
Abomination ....Deut 18:11, 12
Punishable by death .....Lev 20:6, 27

Practiced by:
Astrologers ....Is 47:13
Charmers ....Deut 18:11
Consulters ....Deut 18:14
Enchanter ....Deut 18:10
False prophets ....Jer 14:14
Magicians ....Gen 41:8
Necromancer............Deut 18:11
Soothsayers ....Is 2:6
Sorcerers ....Acts 13:6, 8
Witch ....Ex 22:18
Wizard ....Deut 18:11

[*also* DIVINATIONS, DIVINE, DIVINERS, DIVINETH, DIVINING]
and whereby indeed he *d*? ....Gen 44:5
such a man as I can..*d*? ....Gen 44:15
with the rewards of *d* ....Num 22:7
is there..*d* against Israel ....Num 23:23
called for the..*d* 1Sam 6:2
d unto me by the..spirit 1Sam 28:8
used *d* and enchantments......2Kin 17:17
A *d* sentence is in the lips.....Prov 16:10
and maketh *d* mad ....Is 44:25
to your *d*, nor to..dreamers ...Jer 27:9
vain vision nor flattering *d* ....Ezek 12:24
vanity and lying *d*, saying .....Ezek 13:6
and that *d* lies...............Ezek 13:9
see no more vanity, nor..*d* ....Ezek 13:23
to use *d* ....Ezek 21:21
hand was..*d* for Jerusalem.....Ezek 21:22
be unto them as a false *d* .....Ezek 21:23
they *d* a lie unto thee ....Ezek 21:29
and *d* lies unto ....Ezek 22:28
that ye shall not *d* ....Mic 3:6
and the *d* confounded.........Mic 3:7
and the *d* have seen a lie .....Zech 10:2
had..ordinances of *d* service ..Heb 9:1
According as his *d* power 2Pet 1:3

DIVISION—*diversity; discord*

Causes of:
Real faith...............Luke 12:51-53
Carnal spirit 1Cor 3:3

Opposed to:
Prayer of Christ ....John 17:21-23
Unity of Christ..........1Cor 1:13
Unity of the church......John 10:16
1Cor 12:13-25

I will put a *d* between my .....Ex 8:23
to their *d* by their tribes ......Josh 11:23
Israel according to their *d* .....Josh 18:10
For the *d* of Reuben ....Judg 5:15
the *d* of the sons of Aaron 1Chr 24:1
to the *d* of the families........2Chr 35:5
after the *d* of the families 2Chr 35:5
they set the priests in..*d* ......Ezra 6:18
Levites were *d* in Judah ....Neh 11:36
there was a *d* among the ......John 7:43
There was a *d* again ....John 10:19
them which cause *d*...........Rom 16:17
there be no *d* among you 1Cor 1:10
there be *d* among you 1Cor 11:18

DIVISION OF PRIESTS
Outlined by David 1Chr 24:1-19
Determined by casting lots..................1Chr 24:5, 7
Of Zacharias ....Luke 1:5

DIVORCE—*breaking of the marriage tie*

The Old Testament teaching:
Permitted ....Deut 24:1-3
Divorced may not return to first husband ....Deut 24:4
Denied to those making false claims ....Deut 22:13-19
Denied to those seducing a virgin ....Deut 22:28,29
Unjust, reproved ....Mal 2:14-16
Required, foreign wives put away ....Ezra 10:1-16
Disobedience, a cause among heathen ....Esth 1:10-22
A prophet's concern with .Hos 2:1-22

In the New Testament:
Marriage binding as long as life .... Mark 10:2-9; Rom 7:2, 3
Divorce allowed because of adultery............Matt 5:27-32
Marriage of the divorced constitutes adultery ....Luke 16:18
Reconciliation encouraged.1Cor 7:10-17

[*also* DIVORCED, DIVORCEMENT]
widow, or a *d* woman ....Lev 21:14
daughter be a widow, or *d* ....Lev 22:13
and of her that is *d*...........Num 30:9
the bill of your mother's *d* ....Is 50:1
and given her a bill of *d* ......Jer 3:8
to give a writing of *d* ....Matt 19:7

DIZAHAB (dī'zä-hăb)—*"have gold"*
Location of Moses' farewell addresses .....Deut 1:1

DO—*See* INTRODUCTION

DOCTORS—*teachers*
Christ questions ....Luke 2:46
They hear Christ ....Luke 5:17
Gamaliel, a famous doctor ....Acts 5:34

DOCTRINE—*teaching*

Statements of:
Foundational ....Heb 6:1, 2
Traditional 1Cor 15:1-4
Creedal.................2Tim 3:16

Essentials of:
The Bible's inspiration ...2Tim 3:16
Christ's deity 1Cor 12:3
Christ's incarnation 1John 4:1-6
Christ's resurrection 1Cor 15:12-20
Christ's return...........2Pet 3:3-13
Salvation by faith........Acts 2:38

Attitudes toward:
Obey ....Rom 6:17
Receive.................1Cor 15:1-4
Devote ....Acts 2:42
Hold fast 2Tim 1:13
Adorn ....Titus 2:10

[*also* DOCTRINES]
My *d* shall drop as the rain....Deut 32:2
My *d* is pure..I am clean .....Job 11:4
I give you good *d* ....Prov 4:2
he make to understand *d*? .....Is 28:9
stock is a *d* of vanities ....Jer 10:8
people..astonished at his *d* ....Matt 7:28
for *d* the commandments ......Matt 15:9
were astonished at his *d*.......Matt 22:33
were astonished at his *d*.......Mark 1:22
said unto them in his *d* ....Mark 4:2
for *d* the commandments ......Mark 7:7
he said unto them in his *d* ....Mark 12:38
were astonished at his *d*.......Luke 4:32
My *d* is not mine, but his .....John 7:16
disciples, and of his *d*........John 18:19
filled Jerusalem with..*d* ....Acts 5:28
astonished at..*d* of..Lord ......Acts 13:12
what this new *d* ....Acts 17:19

offenses contrary to the ***d*** .....Rom 16:17
by prophesying, or by ***d***? 1Cor 14:6
about with every wind of ***d*** ....Eph 4:14
the commandments and ***d*** .....Col 2:22
they teach no other ***d*** 1Tim 1:3
that is contrary to sound ***d*** 1Tim 1:10
and ***d*** of devils 1Tim 4:1
words of faith and..good ***d*** 1Tim 4:6
to exhortation, to ***d***...........1Tim 4:13
unto thyself, and unto the ***d*** ...1Tim 4:16
labor in the word and ***d***.......1Tim 5:17
his ***d*** be not blasphemed 1Tim 6:1
to the ***d*** which is according 1Tim 6:3
thou hast fully known my ***d*** ...2Tim 3:10
with..longsuffering and ***d*** 2Tim 4:2
able by sound ***d*** both to.......Titus 1:9
things..become sound ***d*** ....Titus 2:1
d showing uncorruptness ......Titus 2:7
with divers and strange ***d***......Heb 13:9
not in the ***d*** of Christ 2John 9
abideth in the ***d*** of Christ 2John 9
bring not this ***d***...............2John 10
that hold the ***d*** of Balaam .....Rev 2:14

DOCTRINE, FALSE—*erroneous teaching*

What constitutes:
Perverting the Gospel....Gal 1:6, 7; 1John 4:1-6
Satanic deception........2Cor 11:13-15

Teachers of:
Deceive many...........Matt 24:5, 24
Attract many...........2Pet 2:2
Speak perverse things....Acts 20:30
Are savage..............Acts 20:29
Deceitful 2Cor 11:13
Ungodly ....Jude 4, 8
Proud 1Tim 6:3, 4
Corrupt.................2Tim 3:8
Love error 2Tim 4:3, 4

Christian attitude toward:
Avoid ....Rom 16:17, 18
Test 1John 4:1
Detest..................Jude 23

DODAI (dō'dī)—*"beloved"*
An Ahohite 1Chr 27:4
See DODO 2

DODANIM (dō'dä-nĭm)
Descendants of Javan ....Gen 10:4

Tarshish, Kittim, and ***D*** 1Chr 1:7

DODAVAH (dō-dä'vä)—*"loved of Jehovah"*
Eliezer's father 2Chr 20:37

DODO (dō'dō)—*"beloved"*
1. A descendant of Issachar.Judg 10:1
2. A mighty man of David's.2Sam 23:9
   Called Dodai 1Chr 27:4
3. Father of Elhanan 2Sam 23:24

Eleazar the son of ***D***..........1Chr 11:12

DOEG (dō'ĕg)—*"anxious; cared for"*
An Edomite; chief of Saul's herdsmen 1Sam 21:7
Betrays David...........1Sam 22:9, 10
Kills 85 priests 1Sam 22:18, 19

when ***D*** the Edomite came ....Ps 52 *title*

DOER—*See* INTRODUCTION

DOG—*canine mammal*

Described as:
Carnivorous.............1Kin 14:11
Blood-eating 1Kin 21:19
Dangerous ....Ps 22:16
Domesticated ....Matt 15:26, 27
Unclean ....Is 66:3

Figurative of:
Promiscuity ....Deut 23:18
Contempt 1Sam 17:43
Worthlessness 2Sam 9:8
Satan ....Ps 22:20
Hypocrite ....Matt 7:6
Gentiles ....Matt 15:26
False teachers 2Pet 2:22
The unsaved ....Rev 22:15

[*also* DOG'S, DOGS]
shall not a ***d*** move..tongue ....Ex 11:7
ye shall cast it to the ***d***........Ex 22:31
his tongue, as a ***d*** lappeth .....Judg 7:5
after a dead ***d***, after a flea 1Sam 24:14
Am I a ***d*** head, which 2Sam 3:8
should this dead ***d*** curse 2Sam 16:9
in the city shall the ***d*** eat......1Kin 16:4
The ***d*** shall eat Jezebel........1Kin 21:23
the ***d*** licked up his blood......1Kin 22:38
is thy servant a ***d***, that 2Kin 8:13
the ***d*** shall eat Jezebel in 2Kin 9:10
to have set with the ***d***.........Job 30:1
For ***d*** have compassed me .....Ps 22:16
they make a noise like a ***d*** ....Ps 59:6
a ***d*** returneth to his vomit .....Prov 26:11
living ***d*** is better than a ....Eccl 9:4
they are all dumb ***d***...........Is 56:10
they are greedy ***d*** which.......Is 56:11
as if he cut off a ***d*** neck.......Is 66:3
the ***d*** to tear, and the fowls ...Jer 15:3
and to cast it unto the ***d*** .....Mark 7:27
d under the table eat ....Mark 7:28
d came and licked his sores ...Luke 16:21
Beware of ***d***, beware of evil ...Phil 3:2

DOLEFUL—*full of sadness*
houses..full of ***d*** creatures .....Is 13:21
with a ***d*** lamentation ....Mic 2:4

DOMINION—*supreme authority to govern*

Man's:
Delegated by God ....Gen 1:26-28
Under God's control.....Jer 25:12-33
Misused ....Dan 5:18-23

Satan's:
Secured by rebellion .....Is 14:12-16
Offered to Christ ....Luke 4:6
Destroyed by Christ 1John 3:8
Abolished at Christ's return 2Thess 2:8, 9

Christ's:
Predicted ....Is 11:1-10
Announced ....Luke 1:32, 33
Secured by His resurrection ....Acts 2:24-36; Rev 1:18
Perfected at His return...1Cor 15:24-28

[*also* DOMINIONS]
let them have ***d*** over the ......Gen 1:26
thou shalt have the ***d*** ....Gen 27:40
shalt thou..have ***d*** over us? ....Gen 37:8
he that shall have ***d***...........Num 24:19
him that remaineth have ***d*** ....Judg 5:13
Philistines had ***d*** over ....Judg 14:4
he had ***d*** over..the region 1Kin 4:24
nor in all his ***d*** 2Kin 20:13
Saraph..had the ***d*** in Moab 1Chr 4:22
throughout..land of his ***d*** 2Chr 8:6
they had the ***d*** over them .....Neh 9:28
they have ***d*** over our bodies ...Neh 9:37
D and fear are with him ......Job 25:2
Thou madest him to have ***d*** ...Ps 8:6
them not have ***d*** over me .....Ps 19:13
upright shall have ***d*** over......Ps 49:14
He shall have ***d***..from sea .....Ps 72:8
in all places of his ***d*** ....Ps 103:22
and Israel his ***d***...............Ps 114:2
let not any iniquity have ***d*** ....Ps 119:133
thy ***d*** endureth ....Ps 145:13
thee have had ***d*** over us.......Is 26:13
the kingdoms..of his ***d*** ....Jer 34:1
his ***d*** is from generation ....Dan 4:3
whose ***d*** is..everlasting ***d*** ......Dan 4:34
in every ***d*** of my kingdom .....Dan 6:26
d shall be..unto the end ....Dan 6:26
they had..***d*** taken away ....Dan 7:12
there was given him ***d*** ....Dan 7:14
his ***d*** is an everlasting ***d*** ....Dan 7:14
And the kingdom and ***d***.......Dan 7:27
d shall serve and obey him ....Dan 7:27
according to his ***d*** ....Dan 11:4
above him, and have ***d***........Dan 11:5
his ***d*** shall be a great ....Dan 11:5
shall be a great ***d***.............Dan 11:5
even the first ***d***..............Mic 4:8
his ***d*** shall be from sea to .....Zech 9:10
princes..exercise ***d*** ....Matt 20:25
death hath no..***d*** over him......Rom 6:9
sin shall not have ***d*** over ......Rom 6:14
the law hath ***d*** over a man ....Rom 7:1
we have ***d*** over your faith 2Cor 1:24
might..***d*** and every name ......Eph 1:21
d for ever and ever 1Pet 4:11
To him be glory and ***d*** for 1Pet 5:11
despise ***d***, and speak evil ......Jude 8
d and power, both now and ...Jude 25
to him be glory and ***d*** for .....Rev 1:6

DONE—*See* INTRODUCTION

DOOR—*an entrance*

Used literally of:
City gates...............Neh 3:1-6
Prison gates.............Acts 5:19

Used figuratively of:
Christ ....John 10:7, 9
Christ's return...........Matt 24:33
Day of salvation.........Matt 25:10
Inclusion of Gentiles.....Acts 14:27
Opportunity.............2Cor 2:12

[*also* DOORS]
sin lieth at the ***d***..............Gen 4:7
he sat in the tent ***d*** ....Gen 18:1
Sarah heard it in the tent ***d*** ...Gen 18:10
Lot went out at the ***d*** unto ....Gen 19:6
and shut the ***d*** after him ......Gen 19:6
and shut to the ***d***.............Gen 19:10
the men that were at the ***d***....Gen 19:11
wearied..to find the ***d***.........Gen 19:11
on the ***d*** post of the houses ...Ex 12:7
Lord will pass over the ***d***......Ex 12:23
he shall..bring him to the ***d*** ...Ex 21:6
unto the ***d*** post...............Ex 21:6
make an hanging for..***d***........Ex 26:36
by the ***d*** of the tabernacle .....Ex 29:11
at the ***d*** of the tabernacle .....Ex 29:42
at the ***d*** of..tabernacle ....Ex 33:9
pillar stand..tabernacle ***d*** ......Ex 33:10
every man in his tent ***d*** ....Ex 33:10
the hanging for the ***d*** ....Ex 35:15
the tabernacle ***d*** of blue.......Ex 36:37
the sockets to the ***d*** of the ......Ex 38:30
put the hanging of the ***d*** ......Ex 40:5
his sons unto the ***d*** ....Ex 40:12
by the ***d*** of the tabernacle .....Ex 40:29
voluntary will at the ***d*** of......Lev 1:3
kill it at the ***d***..tabernacle .....Lev 3:2
is at the ***d*** of..tabernacle ....Lev 4:7
together unto the ***d*** ....Lev 8:3
flesh at the ***d***..tabernacle ......Lev 8:31
shall ye abide at the ***d*** ....Lev 8:35
sin offering unto..***d*** of the .....Lev 12:6
the priest, unto the ***d*** of the ...Lev 14:23
Lord unto..***d*** of..tabernacle ....Lev 15:14
at the ***d*** of the tabernacle .....Lev 16:7
unto the Lord, unto the ***d***.....Lev 17:5
bringeth it not unto the ***d*** .....Lev 17:9
for the ***d*** of the tabernacle ....Num 3:25
for the ***d*** of the tabernacle ....Num 4:25
to the ***d*** of..tabernacle ....Num 6:10
his separation at the ***d*** of......Num 6:18
every man in the ***d*** of..tent ....Num 11:10
stood in the ***d***..tabernacle .....Num 16:18
stood in..***d*** of their tents ......Num 16:27
unto..***d*** of the tabernacle ......Num 20:6
congregation, by the ***d*** ....Num 27:2
upon the ***d*** posts of..house ....Deut 11:20
the ***d*** of her father's house ....Deut 22:21
go out of the ***d*** of thy house...Josh 2:19
Lord, at..***d*** of..tabernacle .....Josh 19:51
d of the parlor upon him ......Judg 3:23
opened not the ***d*** of..parlor....Judg 3:25
hard..to the ***d*** of the tower ....Judg 9:52
took the ***d*** of the gate ....Judg 16:3
at the ***d*** of the man's house ...Judg 19:26
assembled at the ***d*** of the 1Sam 2:22
d of the house of the Lord 1Sam 3:15
and bolt the ***d*** after her 2Sam 13:17
d for..middle chamber 1Kin 6:8
he made ***d*** of olive tree 1Kin 6:31

the two *d* were of fir tree 1Kin 6:34
leaves of..*d* were folding 1Kin 6:34
of the *d* of the inner house 1Kin 7:50
and for the *d* of the house 1Kin 7:50
as she came in at the *d* 1Kin 14:6
kept the *d* of..king's house 1Kin 14:27
thou shalt shut the *d* upon 2Kin 4:4
she stood in the *d* 2Kin 4:15
shut the *d* upon them twain ...2Kin 4:33
d and hold him..at the *d* 2Kin 6:32
he opened the *d*, and fled 2Kin 9:10
the *d* of the temple 2Kin 18:16
keepers of the *d* have 2Kin 22:4
three keepers of the *d* 2Kin 25:18
the nails for the *d* 1Chr 22:3
and the *d* thereof.............2Chr 3:7
and *d* for the court 2Chr 4:9
overlaid the *d* of them 2Chr 4:9
the inner *d*..for the most 2Chr 4:22
and the *d* of the house 2Chr 4:22
up the *d* of the house 2Chr 28:24
shut..the *d* of the porch 2Chr 29:7
and set up the *d* thereof ......Neh 3:3
the *d* of..house of Eliashib ....Neh 3:20
shut the *d* of the temple ......Neh 6:10
let them shut the *d* ....Neh 7:3
which kept..*d*, were wroth.....Esth 2:21
the *d* of my mother's womb ...Job 3:10
laid wait at..neighbor's *d* ......Job 31:9
who shut..the sea with *d* ......Job 38:8
thou seen the *d* ....Job 38:17
lifted up, ye everlasting *d* .....Ps 24:7
opened the *d* of heaven ....Ps 78:23
keep the *d* of my lips ....Ps 141:3
at the coming in at the *d*......Prov 8:3
she sitteth at the *d* of her .....Prov 9:14
d shall be shut in..streets......Eccl 12:4
the hole of the *d* ....Song 5:4
posts of the *d* moved at the ...Is 6:4
shut thy *d* about thee: hide....Is 26:20
to the *d* of the inner gate .....Ezek 8:3
in the wall, behold a *d*........Ezek 8:8
d of the temple of the Lord ...Ezek 8:16
behold at the *d* of the gate ....Ezek 11:1
and in the *d* of the houses ....Ezek 33:30
breadth of the *d* was ten ....Ezek 41:2
the sides of the *d* were five....Ezek 41:2
measured..post of the *d* ....Ezek 41:3
and the *d*, six cubits ....Ezek 41:3
the breadth of the *d*, seven....Ezek 41:3
one *d* toward the north ....Ezek 41:11
d toward the south ....Ezek 41:11
The *d* posts..the narrow ....Ezek 41:16
against the *d*, cieled with ......Ezek 41:16
unto above the *d* ....Ezek 41:20
sanctuary had two *d* ....Ezek 41:23
for the one *d*, and..other *d* ....Ezek 41:24
on the *d* of the temple ....Ezek 41:25
cubits was the north *d* ....Ezek 42:2
and according to their *d*.......Ezek 42:11
worship at the *d* of..gate ......Ezek 46:3
for a *d* of hope...............Hos 2:15
Smite the lintel of the *d*.......Amos 9:1
keep the *d* of thy mouth ......Mic 7:5
Open thy *d*, O Lebanon ......Zech 11:1
that would shut the *d* for......Mal 1:10
when thou hast shut thy *d*.....Matt 6:6
to the *d* of the sepulcher ......Matt 27:60
rolled..stone from the *d* ....Matt 28:2
was gathered..at the *d* ....Mark 1:33
not so much..about the *d* .....Mark 2:2
colt tied by the *d* without .....Mark 11:4
it is nigh, even at the *d* ....Mark 13:29
stone from the *d* of the ....Mark 16:3
the *d* is now shut ....Luke 11:7
by the *d* into the sheepfold ....John 10:1
d is the shepherd of..sheep ....John 10:2
Peter stood at the *d* ....John 18:16
the damsel that kept the *d* ....John 18:17
when the *d* were shut ....John 20:19
at the *d*, and shall carry.......Acts 5:9
Peter knocked at the *d*........Acts 12:13
all the *d* were opened.........Acts 16:26
the *d* were shut ....Acts 21:30
a great *d* and effectual is 1Cor 16:9
open..a *d* of utterance ....Col 4:3
judge standeth before the *d* ...James 5:9
set before thee an open *d* .....Rev 3:8
I stand at the *d*, and knock ...Rev 3:20
hear my voice..open the *d*.....Rev 3:20

DOORKEEPER—*guardian of an entrance*

Descriptive of:
Maaseiah ....Jer 35:4
Good shepherd..........John 10:3
One who was spoken to by a disciple ....John 18:16

[*also* DOORKEEPERS]
Elkanah were *d* for..ark 1Chr 15:23
rather be a *d* in the house.....Ps 84:10

DOORPOST—*support posts to which the door is attached*
Servant's ears pierced at. .Ex 21:6

DOPHKAH (dŏf'kä)—*"drover"*
A desert encampment....Num 33:12, 13

DOR (dôr)—*"dwelling"*
Jabin's ally.............Josh 11:1, 2
Taken by Joshua ....Josh 12:23
Assigned to Manasseh ...Josh 17:11
Inhabitants unexpelled ..Judg 1:27

D and her towns 1Chr 7:29

DORCAS (dôr'kăs)—*"gazelle"*
Good woman ....Acts 9:36
Raised to life ....Acts 9:37-42
Called Tabitha ....Acts 9:36, 40

DOTE—*show excessive or foolish affection*

[*also* DOTED, DOTING]
they shall *d*; a sword is ....Jer 50:36
and she *d* on her lovers ....Ezek 23:5
Assyrians, upon whom she *d* ..Ezek 23:9
with her eyes, she *d* ....Ezek 23:16
but *d* about questions 1Tim 6:4

DOTHAN (dō'thăn)—*"two wells"*
Ancient town ....Gen 37:14-25
Joseph sold there........Gen 37:17-28
Elisha strikes Syrians at ..2Kin 6:8-23

DOUBLE—*twice as much; two of a kind*

[*also* DOUBLED]
that the dream was *d* unto ....Gen 41:32
take *d* money in your hand....Gen 43:12
and he shall restore *d*.........Ex 22:4
pay *d* unto his neighbor ....Ex 22:9
it shall be being *d* ....Ex 28:16
made the breastplate *d*........Ex 39:9
worth a *d* hired servant ....Deut 15:18
d portion of thy spirit 2Kin 2:9
they were not of *d* heart 1Chr 12:33
of wisdom, that they are *d* ....Job 11:6
and with a *d* heart do they ....Ps 12:2
of the Lord's hand *d* for ......Is 40:2
shall have *d*; and for..........Is 61:7
they shall possess the *d* ....Is 61:7
iniquity and their sin *d*........Jer 16:18
the sword be *d* the third ......Ezek 21:14
I will render *d* unto thee ......Zech 9:12
worthy of *d* honor 1Tim 5:17
A *d* minded man is unstable ...James 1:8
rewarded you, and *d* unto .....Rev 18:6
d according to her works......Rev 18:6
hath filled fill to her *d* ....Rev 18:6

DOUBLE-MINDEDNESS—*inability to hold a fixed belief*
Makes one unstable .....James 1:8

DOUBLE-TONGUED—*two-faced; hypocritical*
Condemned in deacons ..1Tim 3:8

DOUBT—*uncertainty of mind*

Objects of, Christ's:
Miracles ....Matt 12:24-30
Resurrection ....John 20:24-29
Messiahship ....Luke 7:19-23
Return 2Pet 3:4

Causes of:
Satan..................Gen 3:4
Unbelief ....Luke 1:18-20
Worldly wisdom 1Cor 1:18-25
Spiritual instability.......James 1:6, 7

Removal of, by:
Putting God to the test...Judg 6:36-40; John 7:17
Searching the Scriptures..Acts 17:11, 12
Believing God's Word ...Luke 16:27-31

[*also* DOUBTED, DOUBTETH, DOUBTFUL, DOUBTING, DOUBTLESS, DOUBTS]
Joseph is without *d* rent.......Gen 37:33
D ye shall not come into ......Num 14:30
shall hang in *d* before.........Deut 28:66
I will *d* deliver the............2Sam 5:19
No *d* but ye are the people....Job 12:2
d come again with rejoicing ...Ps 126:6
D thou art our father ....Is 63:16
dissolving of *d* were found ....Dan 5:12
wherefore didst thou *d*? ....Matt 14:31
worshiped him..some *d*........Matt 28:17
shall not *d* in his heart ....Mark 11:23
no *d* the kingdom of God .....Luke 11:20
neither be ye of *d* mind ....Luke 12:29
dost thou make us to *d*? ......John 10:24
on another *d* of whom he .....John 13:22
all amazed and were in *d* .....Acts 2:12
they *d* of them whereunto .....Acts 5:24
go with them, *d* nothing ......Acts 10:20
d of such manner of ....Acts 25:20
but not to *d* disputations ......Rom 14:1
he that *d* is damned if ....Rom 14:23
unto others yet *d* I am 1Cor 9:2
our sakes, no *d* this is 1Cor 9:10
not expedient for me *d*........2Cor 12:1
for I stand in *d* of you ....Gal 4:20
Yea *d*, and I count all ....Phil 3:8
hands, without wrath and *d* ...1Tim 2:8
would no *d* have continued 1John 2:19

DOUGH—*mixture of flour and water for baking*
people took their *d* before ....Ex 12:34
cake of the first of your *d*.....Num 15:20
first fruits of your *d* and ......Neh 10:37
the women knead their *d*......Jer 7:18
first of your *d* that he.........Ezek 44:30
he hath kneaded the *d* ....Hos 7:4

DOVE—*pigeon*

Features regarding:
Sent from ark ....Gen 8:8, 10, 12
Offered in sacrifice ......Gen 15:9
Habits of, migratory .....Jer 8:7
Sold in Temple..........Matt 21:12

Figurative of:
Loveliness ....Song 2:14
Desperate mourning .....Is 38:14
Foolish insecurity........Hos 7:11
Israel's restoration ....Hos 11:11
Holy Spirit..............Matt 3:16
Harmlessness............Matt 10:16

[*also* DOVE'S, DOVES, DOVES']
d found no rest for the.......Gen 8:9
d came in to him in the ....Gen 8:11
fourth part of a cab of *d* 2Kin 6:25
O that I..wings like a *d*! ......Ps 55:6
thou art fair; thou hast *d*......Song 1:15
my sister, my love, my *d*......Song 5:2
eyes are as the eyes of *d* ......Song 5:12
and mourn sore like *d* ....Is 59:11
be like the *d* that maketh .....Jer 48:28
be on the mountains like *d* ....Ezek 7:16
as with the voice of *d*.........Nah 2:7
and the Spirit like a *d* ....Mark 1:10
seats of them that sold *d* ......Mark 11:15
bodily shape like a *d* upon ....Luke 3:22
descending..like a *d*...........John 1:32
sold oxen and sheep and *d* ....John 2:14

DOVE'S DUNG—*an edible plant bulb*
Sold in Samaria 2Kin 6:25

DOWN—*See* INTRODUCTION

DOWNSITTING—*sitting down*
Thou knowest my *d* and ......Ps 139:2

DOWNWARD—*in a descending direction*
shall yet..take root ***d***..........2Kin 19:30
spirit of the beast..goeth ***d***....Eccl 3:21
shall again take root ***d***........Is 37:31
appearance..loins even ***d***......Ezek 1:27
appearance..loins even ***d***......Ezek 8:2

DOWRY—*gifts given to the bride's father for the bride*
Regulations regarding:
Sanctioned in the Law...Ex 22:17
Amount of, specified....Deut 22:29
Sometimes given by bride's father.........Josh 15:16-19
Instances of:
Abraham (Isaac) for Rebekah..............Gen 24:22-53
Jacob for Rachel........Gen 29:15-20
Shechem for Dinah......Gen 34:12
David for Michal........1Sam 18:20-25

endued me with a good ***d***.....Gen 30:20

DRAG—*a net dragged on the bottom of a river or lake or, sometimes, on the ground*

[*also* DRAGGING]
gather them in their ***d***........Hab 1:15
d the net with fishes..........John 21:8

DRAGON—*vicious sea creature*
Applied (Heb., tan) to:
Some wild asses.........Jer 14:6
Wicked men............Is 43:19, 20
Applied (Heb., tannin) to:
Sea monster............Gen 1:21
Great serpents..........Ex 7:9,10,12
Cruel tyrants............Is 51:9
Applied (Gr., dragon) to:
Satan...................Rev 12:9
Antichrist...............Rev 12:3

[*also* DRAGONS]
wine is the poison of ***d***........Deut 32:33
I am a brother to ***d***, and a....Job 30:29
broken us in the place of ***d***....Ps 44:19
breakest..heads of the ***d***.......Ps 74:13
young lion and the ***d*** shalt.....Ps 91:13
the earth, ye ***d***, and all.......Ps 148:7
d in their pleasant palaces.....Is 13:22
he shall slay the ***d*** that........Is 27:1
shall be an habitation of ***d***....Is 34:13
in the habitation of ***d***.........Is 35:7
honor me, the ***d*** and the......Is 43:20
heaps and a den of ***d***.........Jer 9:11
desolate and a den of ***d***.......Jer 10:22
shall be a dwelling for ***d***......Jer 49:33
swallowed me up like a ***d***......Jer 51:34
the great ***d*** that lieth in......Ezek 29:3
make a wailing like the ***d***.....Mic 1:8
the ***d*** of the wilderness........Mal 1:3
out of the mouth of the ***d***.....Rev 16:13
laid hold on the ***d***, that old....Rev 20:2

DRAGON WELL
In Jerusalem............Neh 2:13

DRAMS—*gold coins of Persia, weighing about 3.4 grams*
talents and ten thousand ***d***....1Chr 29:7
and one thousand ***d*** of gold...Ezra 2:69
thousand ***d*** of gold, fifty......Neh 7:70
was twenty thousand ***d***........Neh 7:72

DRAUGHT—*that which is drawn out*
Excrement..............Matt 15:17
Catch of fish............Luke 5:9

made it a ***d*** house unto this...2Kin 10:27
goeth out into the ***d***..........Mark 7:19
let down your nets for a ***d***....Luke 5:4

DRAW—*to come; pull toward*

[*also* DRAWETH, DRAWING, DRAWN, DREW, DREWEST]
And Abraham ***d*** near and.....Gen 18:23
women go out to ***d*** water.....Gen 24:11
d water for thy camels also....Gen 24:19
virgin cometh forth to ***d***.......Gen 24:43
down unto the well and ***d***.....Gen 24:45
to pass, as he ***d*** back his......Gen 38:29
Because I ***d*** him out of the....Ex 2:10
also ***d*** water enough for us....Ex 2:19
D not nigh hither; put off.....Ex 3:5
I will ***d*** my sword, mine.......Ex 15:9
d near unto the thick.........Ex 20:21
and all the congregation ***d***.....Lev 9:5
will ***d*** out a sword after.......Lev 26:33
his sword ***d*** in his hand.......Num 22:23
his sword ***d*** in his hand.......Num 22:31
which hath not ***d*** in the.......Deut 21:3
the wife of the one ***d*** near....Deut 25:11
him with his sword ***d***.........Josh 5:13
were ***d*** away from the city.....Josh 8:16
Joshua ***d*** not his hand back....Josh 8:26
the border was ***d*** from the....Josh 15:9
the border was ***d*** to Baalah....Josh 15:9
the border was ***d*** thence......Josh 18:14
could not ***d*** the dagger out....Judg 3:22
I will ***d*** unto thee to the.....Judg 4:7
in the places of ***d*** water.......Judg 5:11
thousand men that ***d*** sword....Judg 8:10
the day ***d*** toward evening.....Judg 19:9
us ***d*** near to one of these.....Judg 19:13
thousand footmen that ***d***......Judg 20:2
thousand men that ***d*** sword....Judg 20:17
were ***d*** away from the city.....Judg 20:31
liers in wait ***d*** themselves.....Judg 20:37
which the young men have ***d***..Ruth 2:9
for thee. So he ***d*** off his......Ruth 4:8
together to Mizpeh and ***d*****.....1Sam 7:6
d near to Samuel in..gate.....1Sam 9:18
Let us ***d*** near hither unto.....1Sam 14:36
he ***d*** near to the Philistine.....1Sam 17:40
arose, and came and ***d*** nigh...1Sam 17:48
armor-bearer, ***D*** thy sword....1Sam 31:4
Joab ***d*** nigh, and the.........2Sam 10:13
we will ***d*** it into the river....2Sam 17:13
he ***d*** me out of many waters...2Sam 22:17
valiant men that ***d*** the........2Sam 24:9
the days of David ***d*** nigh......1Kin 2:1
man ***d*** a bow at a venture.....1Kin 22:34
hundred men that ***d*** swords....2Kin 3:26
D thy sword and thrust.......1Chr 10:4
the Philistines, and ***d*** water....1Chr 11:18
d forth the Syrians that.......1Chr 19:16
thousand men that ***d***.........1Chr 21:5
ten thousand men that ***d***......1Chr 21:5
having a ***d*** sword in his.......1Chr 21:16
they ***d*** out the staves of.......2Chr 5:9
man ***d*** a bow at a venture.....2Chr 18:33
Esther ***d*** near, and touched....Esth 5:2
It is ***d***, and cometh out of.....Job 20:25
and every man shall ***d*** after...Job 21:33
He ***d*** also the mighty with.....Job 24:22
Canst thou ***d*** out leviathan....Job 41:1
when he ***d*** him into his net....Ps 10:9
he ***d*** me out of many waters...Ps 18:16
D me not away with the......Ps 28:3
The wicked have ***d*** out the....Ps 37:14
D nigh unto my soul, and.....Ps 69:18
is good for me to ***d*** near......Ps 73:28
thou ***d*** out thine anger........Ps 85:5
d nigh that follow after.......Ps 119:150
understanding will ***d*** it........Prov 20:5
them that are ***d*** unto death....Prov 24:11
d nigh, when thou shalt say...Eccl 12:1
D me we will run after........Song 1:4
d iniquity with cords of.......Is 5:18
with joy shall ye ***d***...........Is 12:3
swords, from the ***d*** sword.....Is 21:15
d near the time of her........Is 26:17
earth were afraid ***d*** near......Is 41:5
d near together, ye that.......Is 45:20
and ***d*** out the tongue?.......Is 57:4
d the bow, to Tubal and......Is 66:19
burial of an ass, ***d*** and cast....Jer 22:19
and I will cause him to ***d***......Jer 30:21
d up Jeremiah with cords.....Jer 38:13
d them out; surely he shall....Jer 49:20
hath ***d*** back his right hand....Lam 2:3
Thou ***d*** near in the day.......Lam 3:57
sea monsters ***d*** out the........Lam 4:3
the wind, and I will ***d*** out.....Ezek 5:2
the day ***d*** near, let not........Ezek 7:12
charge over the city to ***d***.....Ezek 9:1
and will ***d*** forth my sword.....Ezek 21:3
I the Lord have ***d*** forth my....Ezek 21:5
d their swords against the.....Ezek 28:7
d her and..her multitudes.....Ezek 32:20
I ***d*** them with cords of a......Hos 11:4
let all the men of war ***d***.......Joel 3:9
D thee waters for..siege......Nah 3:14
she ***d*** not near to her God....Zeph 3:2
pressfat for to ***d*** out fifty......Hag 2:16
This people ***d*** nigh unto me...Matt 15:8
they ***d*** to shore, and sat.......Matt 13:48
when..time of the fruit ***d***......Matt 21:34
and ***d*** his sword, and struck...Matt 26:51
Gennesaret and ***d*** to the......Mark 6:53
that stood by ***d*** a sword.......Mark 14:47
Then ***d*** near unto him all.....Luke 15:1
came and ***d*** nigh to the.......Luke 15:25
the time ***d*** near; go ye not....Luke 21:8
of unleavened bread ***d*** nigh....Luke 22:1
and the sabbath ***d*** on.........Luke 23:54
Jesus himself ***d*** near and......Luke 24:15
d nigh unto the village........Luke 24:28
saith unto them, ***D*** out now...John 2:8
servants which ***d*** the water....John 2:9
Sir, thou..nothing to ***d***........John 4:11
and ***d*** nigh unto the ship......John 6:19
which hath sent me ***d*** him.....John 6:44
they were not able to ***d***.......John 21:6
Peter went up..***d*** the net......John 21:11
d away much people after.....Acts 5:37
time of the promise ***d*** nigh....Acts 7:17
as he ***d*** near to behold it......Acts 7:31
all were ***d*** up again into.......Acts 11:10
Paul ***d*** him out of the city.....Acts 14:19
he ***d*** out his sword, and.......Acts 16:27
d Alexander out of the........Acts 19:33
to ***d*** away disciples after......Acts 20:30
d near to some country.......Acts 27:27
which we ***d*** nigh unto God....Heb 7:19
Let us ***d*** near with a true.....Heb 10:22
but if any man ***d*** back, my....Heb 10:38
we are not of them who ***d*****.....Heb 10:39
he is ***d*** away of his own.......James 1:14
men oppress you, and ***d*** you...James 2:6
D nigh to God..he will ***d***......James 4:8
coming of the Lord ***d*** nigh....James 5:8

DRAWERS OF WATER—*a lowly servant classification*
Women.................Gen 24:13
1Sam 9:11
Defeated enemies.......Josh 9:21
Young men.............Ruth 2:9
Included in covenant.....Deut 29:10-13

[*also* DRAWER]
hewer of thy wood and the ***d***..Deut 29:11
be hewers of wood and ***d***.....Josh 9:21
hewers of wood and ***d*** of......Josh 9:27

DREAD—*fear; regard with awe; awesome*

[*also* DREADFUL]
the fear of you and the ***d***.....Gen 9:2
How ***d*** is this place! this......Gen 28:17
Fear and ***d*** shall fall upon.....Ex 15:16
D not, neither be afraid.......Deut 1:29
d of you upon all the land....Deut 11:25
d not, nor be dismayed.......1Chr 22:13
and his ***d*** fall upon you?......Job 13:11
A ***d*** sound is in his ears.......Job 15:21
fear and let him be your ***d***....Is 8:13
so high that they were ***d***......Ezek 1:18
fourth beast, ***d*** and..........Dan 7:7
Lord, the great and ***d*** God....Dan 9:4
They are terrible and ***d***.......Hab 1:7
is ***d*** among the heathen.......Mal 1:14

DREAM—*thoughts and images during sleep*
Purposes of:
Restrain from evil.......Gen 20:3
Reveal God's will.......Gen 28:11-22
Encourage.............Judg 7:13-15
Reveal future...........Gen 37:5-10
Instruct................Matt 1:20

The interpretation of:
Sought anxiously ....Dan 2:1-3
Belong to God ....Gen 40:8
Revealed by God........Gen 40:8
Sought for God's will ....Num 12:6
Sometimes delusive ......Is 29:7, 8
False, by false prophets ..Deut 13:1-5

Notable examples of:
Abimelech ....Gen 20:3
Jacob..................Gen 28:10, 12
Laban ....Gen 31:24
Joseph..................Gen 37:5
Pharaoh ....Gen 41:1-13
Unnamed person ....Judg 7:13, 14
Solomon 1Kin 3:5
Job.....................Job 7:14
Nebuchadnezzar ....Dan 2:1-13
Joseph..................Matt 1:19, 20
Pilate's wife ....Matt 27:13, 19

[*also* DREAMED, DREAMETH, DREAMS]
saw in a ***d***, and, behold ....Gen 31:10
dreamed a ***d*** both of them ....Gen 40:5
each man his ***d*** in one night ...Gen 40:5
interpretation of his ***d***.........Gen 40:5
I also was in my ***d***, and ....Gen 40:16
he interpreted to us our ***d*****.....Gen 41:12
I have dreamed a ***d*** and.......Gen 41:15
thou canst understand a ***d*** .....Gen 41:15
I saw in my ***d*** and behold .....Gen 41:22
ears are seven years; the ***d*** ....Gen 41:26
the dreams which he ***d*** of .....Gen 42:9
said, Behold, I ***d*** a dream .....Judg 7:13
neither by ***d***, nor by Urim 1Sam 28:6
and, behold, it was a ***d*** 1Kin 3:15
He shall fly away as a ***d***.......Job 20:8
As a ***d*** when one awaketh .....Ps 73:20
d cometh through the ....Eccl 5:3
in the multitude of ***d*** and .....Eccl 5:7
as when an hungry man ***d***.....Is 29:8
when a thirsty man ***d*** ....Is 29:8
saying, I have ***d***, I have ***d*** .....Jer 23:25
forget my name by their ***d*** ....Jer 23:27
The prophet that hath a ***d***.....Jer 23:28
neither hearken to your ***d*** .....Jer 29:8
in all visions and ***d*** ....Dan 1:17
Nebuchadnezzar ***d*** dreams .....Dan 2:1
to make known unto me the ***d*** .Dan 2:26
This is the ***d***; and we will .....Dan 2:36
I saw a ***d*** which made me .....Dan 4:5
and I told the ***d*** before them ..Dan 4:7
tell me the visions of my ***d*** ....Dan 4:9
let not the ***d*** or the ....Dan 4:19
d be to them that hate thee ...Dan 4:19
interpreting of ***d***, and ....Dan 5:12
Daniel had a ***d*** and visions ....Dan 7:1
he wrote the ***d*** and told ....Dan 7:1
your old men shall ***d***..........Joel 2:28
a lie, and have told false ***d*** ....Zech 10:2
being warned of God in a ***d*** ...Matt 2:12
appeareth to Joseph in a ***d*** ...Matt 2:13
appeareth in a ***d*** to Joseph ....Matt 2:19
being warned of God in a ***d*** ...Matt 2:22
your old men shall ***d***..........Acts 2:17

DREAMER—*one who dreams*

[*also* DREAMERS]
Behold, this ***d*** cometh ....Gen 37:19
a prophet, or a ***d*** of dreams ...Deut 13:1
that prophet, or that ***d***........Deut 13:3
not to your ***d***, nor to ....Jer 27:9
filthy ***d*** defile the flesh ....Jude 8

DREGS—*the sediments of liquids; grounds*
Wicked shall drink down..Ps 75:8
Contains God's fury .....Is 51:17, 22

DRESS—*to prepare for use or service*
Cultivate land ....Gen 2:15
Trim lamps ....Ex 30:7
Prepare foods ....Heb 6:7
Become presentable 2Sam 19:24

[*also* DRESSED]
and he hasted to ***d*** it ....Gen 18:7
the calf which he had ***d*** ....Gen 18:8
is ***d*** in the frying pan ....Lev 7:9
plant vineyards and ***d*** ....Deut 28:39
and five sheep ready ***d*** 1Sam 25:18
d for the wayfaring man 2Sam 12:4
d it for the man that was......2Sam 12:4
Amnon's house, and ***d*** him 2Sam 13:7
that I may go in and ***d*** it......1Kin 17:12
bullock..yourselves, and ***d*** 1Kin 18:25
was given them, and they ***d*** ...1Kin 18:26

DRESSER—*one who cares for a vineyard*

[*also* DRESSERS]
vine ***d*** in the mountains 2Chr 26:10
unto the ***d*** of his vineyard .....Luke 13:7

DRINK—*to take liquid into the body*

Used literally of:
Water ....Gen 24:14
Milk...................Judg 5:25
Wine ....Gen 9:21

Used figuratively of:
Famine 2Kin 18:27
Misery..................Is 51:22, 23
Married pleasure ....Prov 5:15-19
Unholy alliances.........Jer 2:18
God's blessings ....Zech 9:15-17
Spiritual communion .....John 6:53, 54
Holy Spirit.............John 7:37-39

[*also* DRANK, DRINKETH, DRINKING, DRINKS, DRUNK]
let us make our father ***d*** ......Gen 19:32
make him ***d*** wine this night....Gen 19:34
water, and gave the lad ***d*** .....Gen 21:19
Let me, I pray thee, ***d*** ....Gen 24:17
And she said, ***D***, my lord .....Gen 24:18
her hand, and gave him ***d*** .....Gen 24:18
until they have done ***d*** ....Gen 24:19
water of thy pitcher to ***d*** .....Gen 24:43
unto her, Let me ***d***, I pray ....Gen 24:45
her shoulder, and said ***D*** ......Gen 24:46
I will give thy camels ***d*** ....Gen 24:46
And she made the camels ***d*** ...Gen 24:46
did eat and ***d*** and rose up .....Gen 25:34
and they did eat and ***d***........Gen 26:30
brought him wine, and he ***d*** ...Gen 27:25
when the flocks came to ***d*** ....Gen 30:38
when they came to ***d*** ....Gen 30:38
this it in which my lord ***d*** .....Gen 44:5
Egyptians shall lothe to ***d*** .....Ex 7:18
the river for water to ***d*** ....Ex 7:24
for they could not ***d*** of the ....Ex 7:24
saying, What shall we ***d***? ......Ex 15:24
Give..water that we may ***d*** ....Ex 17:2
saw God, and did eat, and ***d*** ..Ex 24:11
according to the ***d*** offering ....Ex 29:41
sat down to eat and to ***d*** ......Ex 32:6
neither eat bread, nor ***d***.......Ex 34:28
Do not ***d*** wine nor strong .....Lev 10:9
nor strong ***d*** thou, nor thy ....Lev 10:9
all drink that may be ***d*** on ....Lev 11:34
and the ***d*** offering thereof .....Lev 23:13
sacrifice, and ***d*** offerings ......Lev 23:37
the woman to ***d*** the bitter .....Num 5:24
he hath made her to ***d*** the ....Num 5:27
from wine and strong ***d*** ....Num 6:3
shall ***d*** no vinegar of wine .....Num 6:3
wine or vinegar of strong ***d***....Num 6:3
shall he ***d*** any liquor of ....Num 6:3
offering and his ***d*** offering.....Num 6:17
of an hin of wine for a ***d***.......Num 15:5
a ***d*** offering half an hin ......Num 15:10
is there any water to ***d***........Num 20:5
and the congregation ***d***, and ...Num 20:11
we will not ***d*** of the waters ....Num 21:22
and the ***d*** offering thereof .....Num 28:7
as the ***d*** offering thereof ......Num 28:8
burnt offering and his ***d*** ....Num 28:10
offering..his ***d*** offering ....Num 28:15
offering..his ***d*** offering ....Num 28:24
d offerings, according ....Num 29:6
meat offering and his ***d*** ....Num 29:16
and their ***d*** offerings ....Num 29:19
meat offering and his ***d*** ....Num 29:22
meat offering and his ***d*** ....Num 29:25
meat offering and his ***d*** ....Num 29:28
meat offering and his ***d*** ....Num 29:31
meat offering and his ***d*** ....Num 29:34
meat offering and his ***d*** ....Num 29:38
no water for..people to ***d*** .....Num 33:14
for money that ye may ***d***......Deut 2:6
did eat bread not ***d*** water .....Deut 9:9
for wine, or for strong ***d*** ......Deut 14:26
neither have ye ***d*** wine ....Deut 29:6
ye drunk wine or strong ***d*****.....Deut 29:6
d the wine of their drink ......Deut 32:38
wine of their ***d*** offerings? .....Deut 32:38
pray..a little water to ***d*** ....Judg 4:19
boweth..his knees to ***d*** ....Judg 7:5
eat and ***d***, and cursed ....Judg 9:27
d not wine nor strong ***d*** ....Judg 13:4
d wine or strong ***d***, nor eat ....Judg 13:14
when he had ***d***, his spirit ......Judg 15:19
did eat and ***d***, and lodged .....Judg 19:4
washed..and did eat and ***d*** ....Judg 19:21
d of that which the young ......Ruth 2:9
when Boaz had eaten and ***d*** ...Ruth 3:7
Shiloh, and after they had ***d*** ...1Sam 1:9
neither wine nor strong ***d*** 1Sam 1:15
eaten no bread, nor ***d*** any.....1Sam 30:12
eating and ***d*** and dancing......1Sam 30:16
to eat and to ***d*** and to lie 2Sam 11:11
and he made him ***d***, and at....2Sam 11:13
and ***d*** of his own cup and 2Sam 12:3
faint in the wilderness..***d*** 2Sam 16:2
one would give me ***d*** of the ...2Sam 23:15
he would not ***d*** thereof, but ...2Sam 23:16
they eat and ***d*** before him 1Kin 1:25
eating and ***d*** and making 1Kin 4:20
Eat no bread, nor ***d*** water 1Kin 13:9
eat no bread nor ***d*** water......1Kin 13:17
bread in his house, and ***d*** 1Kin 13:19
and ***d*** water in the place 1Kin 13:22
Eat no bread, and ***d*** no 1Kin 13:22
d himself ***d*** in the............1Kin 16:9
into a vessel, that I may ***d*** 1Kin 17:10
Ahab went..to eat and to ***d*** ...1Kin 18:42
eat and ***d***, and went in the 1Kin 19:8
Ben-hadad was ***d*** himself 1Kin 20:16
that ye may ***d***, both ye and....2Kin 3:17
when they had eaten and ***d***....2Kin 6:23
one tent, and did eat and ***d*** ...2Kin 7:8
and poured his ***d*** offering 2Kin 16:13
d their own piss with you? 2Kin 18:27
give me ***d*** of the water........1Chr 11:17
shall I ***d*** the blood of 1Chr 11:19
he would not ***d*** it 1Chr 11:19
three days, eating and ***d*** 1Chr 12:39
eat and ***d*** before the Lord 1Chr 29:22
all the ***d*** vessels of king 2Chr 9:20
gave them to eat and to ***d*****.....2Chr 28:15
meat and ***d*** and oil unto ......Ezra 8:7
he did eat no bread, nor ***d*** ....Ezra 10:6
eat the fat, and ***d*** the sweet ...Neh 8:10
gave them ***d*** in vessels of......Esth 1:7
the ***d*** was according to the ....Esth 1:8
eat nor ***d*** three days, night ....Esth 4:16
sisters to eat and to ***d***.........Job 1:4
daughters were eating ***d*** ....Job 1:13
poison whereof ***d*** up my ......Job 6:4
water to the weary to ***d*** ....Job 22:7
Job, who ***d*** up scorning like ...Job 34:7
d offerings of blood will.......Ps 16:4
or ***d*** the blood of goats? ......Ps 50:13
they gave me vinegar to ***d*** .....Ps 69:21
gave them ***d*** as out of the .....Ps 78:15
tears to ***d*** in great measure ....Ps 80:5
give ***d*** to every beast of ....Ps 104:11
and ***d*** the wine of violence ....Prov 4:17
eat of my bread, and ***d*** of.....Prov 9:5
Eat and ***d***, saith he to thee ....Prov 23:7
cutteth off the feet and ***d*** .....Prov 26:6
not for kings to ***d*** wine........Prov 31:4
nor for princes strong ***d*** ....Prov 31:4
Lest they ***d*** and forget ....Prov 31:5
Let him ***d***, and forget his .....Prov 31:7
that he should eat and ***d*** ......Eccl 2:24
for one to eat and to ***d*** ....Eccl 5:18
d thy wine with a merry.......Eccl 9:7
I have ***d*** my wine with my ....Song 5:1
Eat, O friends; ***d***, yea ....Song 5:1
I would cause thee to ***d*** ....Song 8:2

they may follow strong ***d*** . . . . . Is 5:11
in the watchtower, eat, ***d*** . . . . . Is 21:5
eating flesh, and ***d*** wine . . . . . Is 22:13
wine; let us eat and ***d*** . . . . . Is 22:13
They shall not ***d*** wine with . . . . Is 24:9
strong ***d*** shall be bitter . . . . . Is 24:9
be bitter to them that ***d*** . . . . . Is 24:9
strong ***d*** are out of the way . . . Is 28:7
erred through strong ***d*** . . . . . Is 28:7
the way through strong ***d*** . . . . . Is 28:7
he will cause the ***d*** of . . . . . Is 32:6
d ye every one the waters . . . . . Is 36:16
I have digged and ***d*** water . . . . . Is 37:25
d no water, and is faint . . . . . Is 44:12
shalt no more ***d*** it again . . . . . Is 51:22
hast..poured a ***d*** offering . . . . . Is 57:6
d it in the courts of my . . . . . Is 62:9
make them ***d*** in my fury . . . . . Is 63:6
shall ***d*** but ye shall be . . . . . Is 65:13
d offerings unto other gods . . . . Jer 7:18
give..water of gall to ***d*** . . . . . Jer 9:15
sit..to eat and to ***d*** . . . . . Jer 16:8
poured out ***d*** offerings . . . . . Jer 19:13
make them ***d*** the water of . . . . . Jer 23:15
to whom I send thee to ***d*** it . . . Jer 25:15
made all the nations to ***d*** . . . . . Jer 25:17
D ye, and be drunken, and . . . . Jer 25:27
the cup at thine hand to ***d*** . . . . Jer 25:28
Ye shall certainly ***d*** . . . . . Jer 25:28
and give them wine to ***d*** . . . . . Jer 35:2
We will ***d*** no wine; for . . . . . Jer 35:6
Ye shall ***d*** no wine . . . . . Jer 35:6
commanded..not to ***d*** wine . . . . Jer 35:14
unto this day they ***d*** none . . . . Jer 35:14
poured out ***d*** offerings unto . . . Jer 44:19
pour out ***d*** offerings unto . . . . . Jer 44:19
and made ***d*** with their blood . . Jer 46:10
judgment was not to ***d*** . . . . . Jer 49:12
thou shalt surely ***d*** of it . . . . . Jer 49:12
I will make ***d*** her princes . . . . . Jer 51:57
d also water by measure . . . . . Ezek 4:11
time to time shalt thou ***d*** . . . . . Ezek 4:11
d thy water with trembling . . . . Ezek 12:18
poured out there their ***d*** . . . . . Ezek 20:28
even ***d*** it and suck it out . . . . . Ezek 23:34
in their height all that ***d*** . . . . . Ezek 31:14
have ***d*** of the deep waters . . . . . Ezek 34:18
d that which ye have fouled . . . Ezek 34:19
d the blood of the princes . . . . . Ezek 39:18
Neither shall any priest ***d*** . . . . . Ezek 44:21
and of the wine which he ***d*** . . . Dan 1:5
your meat and your ***d*** . . . . . Dan 1:10
wine that they should ***d*** . . . . . Dan 1:16
d wine before the thousand . . . . Dan 5:1
They ***d*** wine and praised . . . . . Dan 5:4
have ***d*** wine in them; and . . . . . Dan 5:23
flax, mine oil and my ***d*** . . . . . Hos 2:5
the ***d*** offering is cut off . . . . . Joel 1:9
a ***d*** offering unto the Lord . . . . Joel 2:14
they ***d*** the wine of the . . . . . Amos 2:8
masters. Bring..let us ***d*** . . . . . Amos 4:1
but ye shall not ***d*** wine . . . . . Amos 5:11
vineyards, and ***d*** the wine . . . . . Amos 9:14
have ***d*** upon my holy . . . . . Obad 16
the heathen ***d*** continually . . . . . Obad 16
let them not feed, nor ***d*** . . . . . Jon 3:7
thee of wine and of strong ***d*** . . Mic 2:11
that giveth his neighbor ***d*** . . . . . Hab 2:15
but not ***d*** the wine thereof . . . . Zeph 1:13
ye ***d***, but ye are not filled . . . . . Hag 1:6
ye are not filled with ***d*** . . . . . Hag 1:6
did eat, and when ye did ***d*** . . . . Zech 7:6
eat, or what ye shall ***d*** . . . . . Matt 6:25
whosoever shall give to ***d*** . . . . . Matt 10:42
came neither eating nor ***d*** . . . . . Matt 11:18
d of the cup..I shall ***d*** . . . . . Matt 20:22
they were eating and ***d*** . . . . . Matt 24:38
eat and ***d*** with the drunken . . . . Matt 24:49
thirsty and gave thee ***d*** . . . . . Matt 25:37
saying, ***D*** ye all of it . . . . . Matt 26:27
I will not ***d*** henceforth . . . . . Matt 26:29
day when I ***d*** it new with . . . . . Matt 26:29
vinegar to ***d*** mingled with . . . . . Matt 27:34
thereof, he would not ***d*** . . . . . Matt 27:34
d with publicans and . . . . . Mark 2:16
you a cup of water to ***d*** . . . . . Mark 9:41
ye ***d*** of the cup that I ***d*** . . . . . Mark 10:38
d of the cup that I ***d*** . . . . . Mark 10:39
them and they all ***d*** of it . . . . . Mark 14:23
I will ***d*** no more of the fruit . . . Mark 14:25
until that day that I ***d*** . . . . . Mark 14:25
him to ***d*** saying, Let alone . . . . Mark 15:36
if they ***d*** any deadly thing . . . . . Mark 16:18
d neither wine nor strong ***d*** . . . Luke 1:15
eat and ***d*** with publicans . . . . . Luke 5:30
No man also having ***d*** old . . . . . Luke 5:39
neither eating bread nor ***d*** . . . . . Luke 7:33
and ***d*** such things as they . . . . . Luke 10:7
thine ease, eat, ***d***, and be . . . . . Luke 12:19
and ***d***, and to be drunken . . . . . Luke 12:45
They did eat, they ***d***, they . . . . . Luke 17:27
will not ***d*** of the fruit of . . . . . Luke 22:18
when men have well ***d***, then . . John 2:10
saith..her, Give me to ***d*** . . . . . John 4:7
Give me to ***d***; thou . . . . . John 4:10
us the well, and ***d*** thereof . . . . John 4:12
d of this water shall thirst . . . . John 4:13
d my blood, hath eternal . . . . . John 6:54
and my blood is ***d*** indeed . . . . . John 6:55
hath given me, shall I not ***d*** . . John 18:11
and neither did eat nor ***d*** . . . . . Acts 9:9
would neither eat nor ***d*** till . . . . Acts 23:12
if he thirst, give him ***d***; for . . . . Rom 12:20
of God is not meat and ***d*** . . . . . Rom 14:17
to ***d*** wine nor anything . . . . . Rom 14:21
not power to eat and to ***d***? . . . 1Cor 9:4
all ***d*** the same spiritual ***d*** 1Cor 10:4
d of that spiritual Rock 1Cor 10:4
Ye cannot ***d*** the cup of the 1Cor 10:21
houses to eat and to ***d*** in? 1Cor 11:22
do ye, as oft as ye ***d*** it 1Cor 11:25
eat this bread, and ***d*** this 1Cor 11:26
of that bread, and ***d*** of that . . . 1Cor 11:28
For he that eateth and ***d*** 1Cor 11:29
made to ***d*** into one Spirit 1Cor 12:13
eat and ***d***; for tomorrow 1Cor 15:32
judge you in meat or in ***d*** . . . . . Col 2:16
D no longer water, but use 1Tim 5:23
earth which ***d*** in the rain . . . . . Heb 6:7
stood only in meats and ***d*** . . . . . Heb 9:10
she made all nations ***d*** . . . . . Rev 14:8
same shall ***d*** of the wine . . . . . Rev 14:10
hast given them blood to ***d*** . . . . Rev 16:6

DRINK OFFERINGS—*libation for atonement*
Of wine . . . . . Hos 9:4
Of water 1Sam 7:6

DRINKERS—*drunkards*
all ye ***d*** of wine, because . . . . . Joel 1:5

DRIVE—*to chase; continue forward*

[*also* DRAVE, DRIVEN, DRIVETH, DRIVING, DROVE]

So he ***d*** out the man . . . . . Gen 3:24
thou hast ***d*** me out this day . . . Gen 4:14
Abram ***d*** them away . . . . . Gen 15:11
came and ***d*** them away . . . . . Ex 2:17
a strong hand shall he ***d*** . . . . . Ex 6:1
were ***d*** out from Pharaoh's . . . . Ex 10:11
that they ***d*** them heavily; so . . . Ex 14:25
I will not ***d*** them out from . . . . Ex 23:29
and thou shalt ***d*** them out . . . . . Ex 23:31
I ***d*** out before thee the . . . . . Ex 34:11
and ***d*** out the Amorites that . . . Num 21:32
and that I may ***d*** them out . . . . Num 22:6
he hath ***d*** out his enemies . . . . . Num 32:21
ye shall ***d*** out all the . . . . . Num 33:52
shouldest be ***d*** to worship . . . . . Deut 4:19
To ***d*** out nations from . . . . . Deut 4:38
the Lord doth ***d*** them out . . . . . Deut 9:4
Then will the Lord ***d*** out all . . . Deut 11:23
If any of thine be ***d*** out . . . . . Deut 30:4
he will without fail ***d*** out . . . . . Josh 3:10
I shall be able to ***d*** them . . . . . Josh 14:12
d thence the three sons of . . . . . Josh 15:14
of Judah could not ***d*** them . . . . Josh 15:63
d not out the Canaanites . . . . . Josh 16:10
of Manasseh could not ***d*** . . . . . Josh 17:12
and ***d*** them from out of . . . . . Josh 23:5
the Lord hath ***d*** out from . . . . . Josh 23:9
Lord ***d*** out from before us . . . . Josh 24:18
he ***d*** out the inhabitants of . . . . Judg 1:19
not ***d*** out the inhabitants . . . . . Judg 1:19
d out the inhabitants of . . . . . Judg 1:27
did Ephraim ***d*** out the . . . . . Judg 1:29
Asher ***d*** out the inhabitants . . . Judg 1:31
did Naphtali ***d*** out the . . . . . Judg 1:33
I also will not henceforth ***d*** . . . . Judg 2:21
without ***d*** them out hastily . . . . Judg 2:23
for they have ***d*** me out this . . . 1Sam 26:19
and the herds, which they ***d*** . . . 1Sam 30:20
sons of Abinadab ***d*** the 2Sam 6:3
D and go forward; slack 2Kin 4:24
the ***d*** is like the ***d*** of Jehu 2Kin 9:20
for he ***d*** furiously 2Kin 9:20
and ***d*** the Jews from Elath 2Kin 16:6
who ***d*** away the inhabitants 1Chr 8:13
Uzza and Ahio ***d*** the cart 1Chr 13:7
by ***d*** out nations from 1Chr 17:21
d out the inhabitants of this . . . 2Chr 20:7
is wisdom ***d*** quite from me? . . . Job 6:13
and shall ***d*** him to his feet . . . . Job 18:11
He shall be ***d*** from light . . . . . Job 18:18
the chaff which the wind ***d*** . . . . Ps 1:4
who ***d*** him away, and he . . . . . Ps 34: *title*
let them be ***d*** backward and . . . Ps 40:14
thou didst ***d*** out the heathen . . Ps 44:2
fled; Jordan was ***d*** back . . . . . Ps 114:3
The wicked is ***d*** away in his . . . Prov 14:32
rod of correction shall ***d*** . . . . . Prov 22:15
north wind ***d*** away rain; so . . . . Prov 25:23
they shall be ***d*** to darkness . . . . Is 8:22
I will ***d*** thee from thy . . . . . Is 22:19
and as ***d*** stubble to his bow . . . Is 41:2
the places whither I have ***d*** . . . . Jer 8:3
scattered my flock, and ***d*** . . . . . Jer 23:2
countries whither I had ***d*** . . . . . Jer 23:8
they shall be ***d*** on and fall . . . . Jer 23:12
places whither I shall ***d*** . . . . . Jer 24:9
that I might ***d*** you out, and . . . Jer 27:15
nations whither I have ***d*** . . . . . Jer 29:18
places whither they were ***d*** . . . . Jer 40:12
nations whither I have ***d*** . . . . . Jer 46:28
the lions have ***d*** him away . . . . . Jer 50:17
Gentiles, whither I will ***d*** . . . . . Ezek 4:13
d him out for..wickedness . . . . . Ezek 31:11
bring..that which was ***d*** . . . . . Ezek 34:16
they shall ***d*** thee from men . . . . Dan 4:25
he was ***d*** from men, and did . . . Dan 4:33
whither thou hast ***d*** . . . . . Dan 9:7
I will ***d*** them out of mine . . . . . Hos 9:15
that is ***d*** with the whirlwind . . . Hos 13:3
and will ***d*** him into a land . . . . . Joel 2:20
I will gather her that is ***d*** . . . . . Mic 4:6
they shall ***d*** out Ashdod at . . . . Zeph 2:4
gather her that was ***d*** out . . . . . Zeph 3:19
d him into the wilderness . . . . . Mark 1:12
d of the devil into the . . . . . Luke 8:29
he ***d*** them all out of the . . . . . John 2:15
whom God ***d*** out before the . . . Acts 7:45
into the wind, we let her ***d*** . . . . Acts 27:15
struck sail and so were ***d*** . . . . . Acts 27:17
the sea ***d*** with the wind and . . . James 1:6

DRIVER—*one who maneuvers a horse-drawn carriage*
he said unto the ***d*** of his 1Kin 22:34
he the crying of the ***d*** . . . . . Job 39:7

DROMEDARY—*a species of camel; a swift steed*
Used by Solomon 1Kin 4:28
Used by Ahasuerus . . . . . Esth 8:10
Noted for speed . . . . . Jer 2:23
Figurative of Gospel blessings . . . . . Is 60:6

DROP—*to allow to fall*

[*also* DROPPED, DROPPETH, DROPPING, DROPS]

My doctrine shall ***d*** as the . . . . . Deut 32:2
heavens ***d***, the clouds also ***d*** . . Judg 5:4
the honey ***d***; but no man 1Sam 14:26
until water ***d*** upon them 2Sam 21:10
and my speech ***d*** upon them . . Job 29:22
he maketh small the ***d*** of . . . . . Job 36:27

D

clouds do *d* and distil upon . . . .Job 36:28
and thy paths *d* fatness . . . . .Ps 65:11
also *d* at the presence of . . . . . .Ps 68:8
the clouds *d* down the dew . . . .Prov 3:20
of a wife are a continual *d* . . . .Prov 19:13
hands the house *d* through . . . .Eccl 10:18
spouse, *d* as the honeycomb . . .Song 4:11
my locks with the *d* of the . . . .Song 5:2
d sweet smelling myrrh . . . . .Song 5:13
a *d* of a bucket and are . . . . . . .Is 40:15
and *d* thy word toward the . . . .Ezek 20:46
d not thy word against the . . . .Amos 7:16
great *d* of blood falling . . . . .Luke 22:44

DROPSY—*an unnatural accumulation of fluid in parts of the body*
Healing of . . . . .Luke 14:2-4

DROSS—*impurities separated from metals*
Result of refinement . . . . .Prov 25:4
Figurative of Israel . . . . . .Is 1:22, 25

wicked of the earth like *d* . . . . .Ps 119:119
covered with silver *d* . . . . .Prov 26:23
of Israel is to me become *d* . . .Ezek 22:18
they are even the *d* of silver . . .Ezek 22:18
become *d*, behold therefore . . .Ezek 22:19

DROUGHT—*an extended dry season*
Unbearable in the day . . .Gen 31:40
Seen in the wilderness . . .Deut 8:15
Comes in summer . . . . . . .Ps 32:4
Sent as a judgment . . . . . .Hag 1:11
Only God can stop . . . . . .Jer 14:22
Descriptive of spiritual barrenness . . . . .Jer 14:1-7
The wicked dwell in . . . . .Jer 17:5, 6
The righteous endure . . . .Jer 17:8
Longest 1Kin 18:1
Luke 4:25

D and heat consume the . . . . . .Job 24:19
turned into the *d* of summer . . .Ps 32:4
and satisfy thy soul in *d* . . . . . . .Is 58:11
through a land of *d*, and of . . .Jer 2:6
A *d* is upon her waters; and . . .Jer 50:38
in the land of great *d* . . . . .Hos 13:5

DROVE—*a herd moving together*
every *d* by themselves . . . . .Gen 32:16
put a space between *d* . . . . .Gen 32:16
all that followed the *d* . . . . .Gen 33:8

DROWN—*to suffocate in water*
Of the Egyptians . . . . .Ex 14:27-30
Jonah saved from . . . . .Jon 1:15-17
Of severe judgment . . . . . .Matt 18:6
The woman saved from . .Rev 12:15, 16
Figurative of lusts 1Tim 6:9

[*also* DROWNED]
chosen captains also are *d* . . . . .Ex 15:4
neither can the floods *d* it . . . . .Song 8:7
it shall be cast out and *d* . . . . . .Amos 8:8
assaying to do were *d* . . . . .Heb 11:29

DROWSINESS—*the mental state preceding sleep*
Prelude to poverty . . . . . . .Prov 23:21
Disciples guilty of . . . . . . .Matt 26:43

DRUNKENNESS—*state of intoxication*
Evils of:
Debases . . . . .Gen 9:21, 22
Provokes anger . . . . .Prov 20:1
Poverty . . . . .Prov 23:21
Perverts justice . . . . .Is 5:22, 23
Confuses the mind . . . . . . .Is 28:7
Licentiousness . . . . .Rom 13:13
Disorderliness . . . . .Matt 24:48-51
Hinders watchfulness 1Thess 5:6, 7
Actual instances of the evil of:
Defeat in battle 1Kin 29:16-21
Degradation . . . . .Esth 1:10, 11
Debauchery . . . . .Dan 5:1-4
Weakness . . . . .Amos 4:1
Disorder 1Cor 11:21, 22
Penalties of:
Death . . . . .Deut 21:20, 21
Exclusion from fellowship . 1Cor 5:11
Exclusion from heaven . . .1Cor 6:9, 10
Figurative of:
Destruction . . . . .Is 49:26
Roaring waves . . . . .Ps 107:27
Giddiness . . . . .Is 19:14
Error . . . . .Is 28:7
Spiritual blindness . . . . . . .Is 29:9-11
International chaos . . . . . .Jer 25:15-29
Persecution . . . . .Rev 17:6

[*also* DRUNKARD, DRUNKARDS, DRUNKEN]
heart, to add *d* to thirst . . . . . . .Deut 29:19
Eli thought she had been *d* 1Sam 1:13
him, for he was very *d* 1Sam 25:36
to stagger like a *d* man . . . . . . .Job 12:25
and I was the song of the *d* . . .Ps 69:12
the *d* and the glutton shall . . . .Prov 23:21
for strength and not for *d* . . . . .Eccl 10:17
reel to and fro like a *d* . . . . .Is 24:20
hast *d* the dregs of the cup . . . .Is 51:17
inhabitants..with *d* . . . . .Jer 13:13
I am like a *d* man, and like . . .Jer 23:9
Make ye him *d*, for he . . . . .Jer 48:26
that made all the earth *d* . . . . . .Jer 51:7
and I will make them *d* . . . . . . .Jer 51:39
made me *d* with wormwood . . .Lam 3:15
d our water for money . . . . .Lam 5:4
shalt be filled with *d* and . . . . . .Ezek 23:33
drink blood till ye be *d* . . . . . . .Ezek 39:19
Awake, ye *d*, and weep and . . .Joel 1:5
and while they are *d* as *d* . . . . .Nah 1:10
to him, and makest him *d* . . . . .Hab 2:15
eat and drink, and to be *d* . . . .Luke 12:45
and *d*, and cares of this life . . .Luke 21:34
are not *d*, as ye suppose . . . . . .Acts 2:15
nor *d*, nor revilers, nor 1Cor 6:10
murders, *d*, revellings . . . . .Gal 5:21

DRUSILLA (drōō-sĭl'ä)—*"watered by dew"*
Wife of Felix, hears Paul . Acts 24:24, 25

DRY—*to free of moisture; free of moisture*

[*also* DRIED, DRIETH]
let the *d* land appear, and . . . . .Gen 1:9
of all that was in the *d* land . . .Gen 7:22
until the waters were *d* up . . . .Gen 8:7
month was the earth *d* . . . . .Gen 8:14
pour it upon the *d* land; and . . .Ex 4:9
Israel shall go on *d* ground . . . .Ex 14:16
the sea upon the *d* ground . . . .Ex 14:22
children of Israel went on *d* . . .Ex 15:19
green ears of corn *d* by the . . . .Lev 2:14
mingled with oil, and *d* . . . . . . .Lev 7:10
nor eat moist grapes or *d* . . . . .Num 6:3
d up the water of the Red . . . .Josh 2:10
stood firm on *d* ground . . . . . . .Josh 3:17
lifted up unto the *d* land . . . . . .Josh 4:18
God *d* up the waters of . . . . . . .Josh 4:23
he *d* up from before us . . . . . . .Josh 4:23
their provision was *d* and . . . . .Josh 9:5
d upon all the earth beside . . . .Judg 6:37
for it was *d* upon the fleece . . .Judg 6:40
withes that were never *d* . . . . . .Judg 16:7
put forth against him, *d* up 1Kin 13:4
two went over on *d* ground 2Kin 2:8
sole of my feet have I *d* 2Kin 19:24
midst of the sea on the *d* . . . . .Neh 9:11
the waters, and they *d* up . . . . .Job 12:15
flood decayeth and *d* up . . . . . .Job 14:11
the flame shall *d* up his . . . . . . .Job 15:30
roots shall be *d* up beneath . . . .Job 18:16
is *d* up like a potsherd . . . . .Ps 22:15
thee in a *d* and thirsty land . . . .Ps 63:1
rebellious dwell in a *d* land . . . .Ps 68:6
flood; thou *d* up mighty . . . . . . .Ps 74:15
ran in the *d* places like a . . . . . .Ps 105:41
Red Sea also, and it was *d* . . . .Ps 106:9
d ground into watersprings . . . .Ps 107:35
a *d* morsel and quietness . . . . . .Prov 17:1
but a broken spirit *d* the . . . . . .Prov 17:22
multitude *d* up with thirst . . . . .Is 5:13
shall be emptied and *d* up . . . . .Is 19:6
as the heat in a *d* place . . . . . . .Is 25:5
sole of my feet have I *d* . . . . . . .Is 37:25
and the *d* land springs of . . . . . .Is 41:18
and *d* up all their herbs . . . . . . .Is 42:15
and I will *d* up the pools . . . . . .Is 42:15
saith to the deep Be *d* . . . . .Is 44:27
and I will *d* up thy rivers . . . . . .Is 44:27
as a root out of a *d* ground . . .Is 53:2
A *d* wind of the high places . . .Jer 4:11
of the wilderness are *d* up . . . . .Jer 23:10
I will *d* up her sea, and . . . . . . .Jer 51:36
a *d* land and a wilderness . . . . .Jer 51:43
have *d* up the green tree . . . . . .Ezek 17:24
made the *d* tree to flourish . . . .Ezek 17:24
tree in thee, and every *d* . . . . . .Ezek 20:47
and lo, they were very *d* . . . . . .Ezek 37:2
they say, Our bones are *d* . . . . .Ezek 37:11
set her like a *d* land and . . . . . .Hos 2:3
root is *d* up, they shall . . . . .Hos 9:16
his spring shall become *d* . . . . . .Hos 13:15
new vine is *d* up, the oil . . . . . .Joel 1:10
rivers of waters are *d* up . . . . . .Joel 1:20
made the sea and the *d* . . . . . . .Jon 1:9
the sea and maketh it *d* . . . . . . .Nah 1:4
d, and *d* up all the rivers . . . . . .Nah 1:4
and *d* like a wilderness . . . . .Zeph 2:13
and the sea and the *d* land . . . .Hag 2:6
deeps of the river shall *d* . . . . . .Zech 10:11
his arm shall be clean *d* . . . . . . .Zech 11:17
walketh through *d* places . . . . . .Matt 12:43
fountain of her blood was *d* . . .Mark 5:29
walketh through *d* places . . . . . .Luke 11:24
the Red sea as by *d* land . . . . . .Heb 11:29
the water thereof was *d* up . . . .Rev 16:12

DRYSHOD—*with dry shoes or feet*
and make men go over *d* . . . . . .Is 11:15

DUE—*that which is owed; appropriate*

[*also* DUES]
is thy *d*, and thy sons' *d* . . . . . . .Lev 10:13
I will give thee rain in *d* . . . . . .Lev 26:4
offer unto me in their *d* . . . . . . .Num 28:2
rain of your land in his *d* . . . . .Deut 11:14
foot shall slide in *d* time . . . . . .Deut 32:35
him not after the *d* order 1Chr 15:13
for the singers, *d* for every . . . .Neh 11:23
Lord the glory *d* unto his . . . . .Ps 29:2
them their meat in *d* season . . .Ps 104:27
from them to whom it is *d* . . . .Prov 3:27
princes eat in *d* season . . . . .Eccl 10:17
pay all that was *d* unto him . . .Matt 18:34
give them meat in *d* season? . . .Matt 24:45
portion of meat in *d* season . . .Luke 12:42
receive the *d* reward of our . . .Luke 23:41
in *d* time Christ died for the . . .Rom 5:6
Render..to all their *d* . . . . .Rom 13:7
tribute to whom tribute is *d* . . .Rom 13:7
unto the wife *d* benevolence . . .1Cor 7:3
as of one born out of *d* time . .1Cor 15:8
in *d* season we shall reap . . . . . .Gal 6:9
to be testified in *d* time 1Tim 2:6
in *d* times manifested his . . . . . .Titus 1:3
he may exalt you in *d* time 1Pet 5:6

DUKE—*a nobleman*

[*also* DUKES]
These were *d* of the sons . . . . . .Gen 36:15
d Teman, *d* Omar . . . . .Gen 36:15
d Zepho, *d* Kenaz . . . . .Gen 36:15
d Nahath, *d* Zerah . . . . .Gen 36:17
d Shammah, *d* Mizzah . . . . . . .Gen 36:17
are the *d* that came of Reuel . .Gen 36:17
Edom, and these are their *d* . . .Gen 36:19
d that came of the Horites . . . .Gen 36:29
d Lotan, *d* Shobal . . . . .Gen 36:29
d Zibeon, *d* Anah . . . . .Gen 36:29
are the *d* that came of Hori . . .Gen 36:30
among their *d* in the land of . . .Gen 36:30
d Timnah, *d* Alvah *d* . . . . .Gen 36:40
D Kenaz, *d* Teman, *d* . . . . .Gen 36:42
these be the *d* of Edom . . . . . . .Gen 36:43
d of Edom shall be amazed . . .Ex 15:15
were *d* of Sihon, dwelling . . . . .Josh 13:21
and the *d* of Edom were 1Chr 1:51
d Timnah, *d* Aliah, *d* 1Chr 1:51
D Kenaz, *d* Teman, *d* 1Chr 1:53

DULCIMER—*a stringed musical instrument*
Used in Babylon ....Dan 3:5-15

DULL—*hard; slow (as of hearing)*
their ears are *d* of hearing.....Matt 13:15
their ears are *d* of hearing.....Acts 28:27
seeing ye are *d* of hearing.....Heb 5:11

DUMAH (dū'mä)—*"silence"*
1. Descendants (a tribe) of Ishmael ....Gen 25:14
2. Town in Judah ....Josh 15:52

and *D*, Massa, Hadad and.....1Chr 1:30
burden of *D*. He calleth to ....Is 21:11

DUMB—*unable to speak*

Used literally of dumbness:
Natural ....Ex 4:11
Imposed ....Ezek 3:26, 27
Demonized ....Mark 9:17, 25
Penalized ....Luke 1:20-22

Used figuratively of:
External calamity ....Ps 38:13
Submissiveness ....Is 53:7
Inefficient leaders ....Is 56:10
Helplessness 1Cor 12:2
Lamb before shearer is ..Acts 8:32
With silence ....Ps 39:2

I was *d*, I opened not my .....Ps 39:9
Open thy mouth for the *d*.....Prov 31:8
the tongue of the *d* sing.......Is 35:6
speak, and be no more *d*......Ezek 24:27
the ground, and I became *d*...Dan 10:15
trusteth therein, to make *d*....Hab 2:18
to him a *d* man possessed .....Matt 9:32
with a devil, blind, and *d* .....Matt 12:22
blind, *d* maimed, and many ...Matt 15:30
deaf to hear, and the *d* to.....Mark 7:37
out a devil, and it was *d* ......Luke 11:14
devil was gone out, the *d* .....Luke 11:14
d ass speaking with man's 2Pet 2:16

DUNG—*excrement*

Used for:
Fuel ....Ezek 4:12, 15
Food in famine 2Kin 6:25

Figurative of:
Something worthless 2Kin 9:37

and his skin, and his *d* ....Ex 29:14
and his inwards, and his *d*.....Lev 4:11
their flesh, and their *d* ....Lev 16:27
and her blood, with her *d* .....Num 19:5
as a man taketh away *d* 1Kin 14:10
they may eat their own *d* 2Kin 18:27
the *d* port, and viewed the ....Neh 2:13
But the *d* gate repaired ....Neh 3:14
perish for ever like his..*d* .....Job 20:7
became as *d* for the earth .....Ps 83:10
may eat their own *d* ....Is 36:12
shall be for *d* upon the face ...Jer 8:2
they shall be as *d* upon the ....Jer 16:4
thou shalt bake it with *d* ......Ezek 4:12
and their flesh as the *d* ....Zeph 1:17
spread *d* upon your faces......Mal 2:3
shall dig about it, and *d* it.....Luke 13:8
and do count them but *d*......Phil 3:8

DUNG GATE—*a gate of Jerusalem*
Wall dedicated near .....Neh 12:31

DUNGEON—*an underground prison*
Joseph's imprisonment ...Gen 40:8, 15
Jeremiah cast into ....Jer 37:16

brought him..out of the *d* .....Gen 41:14
captive that was in the *d* ......Ex 12:29
cast..into the *d* of Malchiah ...Jer 38:6
in the *d* there was no water ...Jer 38:6
they have cast into the *d* ......Jer 38:9
down by cords into the *d*......Jer 38:11
cut off my life in the *d*........Lam 3:53
thy name..out of the low *d*....Lam 3:55

DUNGHILL
Pile of manure ....Luke 14:35
Figurative of a wretched condition ....Ps 113:7

[*also* DUNGHILLS]
lifted..beggar from the *d* 1Sam 2:8
his house be made a *d* for.....Ezra 6:11
is trodden down for the *d* .....Is 25:10
up in scarlet embrace *d* ....Lam 4:5
houses shall be made a *d*......Dan 2:5

DURA (dū'rä)—*"fortress"*
Site of Nebuchadnezzar's golden image.........Dan 3:1

DURABLE—*lasting*
d riches and righteousness .....Prov 8:18
sufficiently and for *d*..........Is 23:18

DURETH—*endureth*
root in himself, but *d* for a ....Matt 13:21

DUST—*powdered earth*

Used literally of:
Man's body ....Gen 2:7
Dust of Egypt...........Ex 8:16, 17
Particles of soil..........Num 5:17

Used figuratively of:
Man's mortality ....Gen 3:19
Descendants ....Gen 13:16
Judgment ....Deut 28:24
Act of cursing 2Sam 16:13
Dejection ....Job 2:12
Subjection ....Is 49:23
The grave ....Is 26:19
Rejection ....Matt 10:14

and *d* shalt thou eat all ....Gen 3:14
which am but *d* and ashes .....Gen 18:27
be as the *d* of the earth ....Gen 28:14
And it shall become small *d* ...Ex 9:9
shall pour out the *d* that ......Lev 14:41
blood..and cover it with *d*.....Lev 17:13
can count the *d* of Jacob ......Num 23:10
until it was as small as *d* ......Deut 9:21
I cast the *d* thereof into ....Deut 9:21
poison of serpents of the *d* ....Deut 32:24
and put *d* upon their heads ....Josh 7:6
raiseth..poor out of the *d* 1Sam 2:8
beat them as small as the *d* ...2Sam 22:43
I exalted thee out of the *d* 1Kin 16:2
d of Samaria shall suffice......1Kin 20:10
had made them like the *d* 2Kin 13:7
people like the *d* of the 2Chr 1:9
cometh not forth of the *d* .....Job 5:6
now shall I sleep in the *d* .....Job 7:21
grow out of the *d* of the ......Job 14:19
rest together is in the *d* ....Job 17:16
lie down alike in the *d*.........Job 21:26
he heap up silver as the *d*......Job 27:16
I am become like *d* and.......Job 30:19
When the *d* groweth into.......Job 38:38
Hide..in the *d* together........Job 40:13
lay mine honor in the *d* ....Ps 7:5
brought me into the *d* of ......Ps 22:15
Shall the *d* praise thee? ....Ps 30:9
enemies shall lick the *d* ....Ps 72:9
and favor the *d* thereof ....Ps 102:14
and return to their *d*..........Ps 104:29
soul cleaveth unto the *d*.......Ps 119:25
highest part of the *d* of ....Prov 8:26
of the *d*, and all turn to *d* .....Eccl 3:20
and hide thee in the *d*, for ....Is 2:10
the ground even to the *d*......Is 25:12
bringeth it even to the *d* ......Is 26:5
shall be low out of the *d* ......Is 29:4
shall whisper out of the *d* .....Is 29:4
d made fat with fatness ....Is 34:7
comprehended the *d* of the ....Is 40:12
gave them as the *d* to his .....Is 41:2
and *d* shall be the serpent's ...Is 65:25
cast up *d* upon their heads ....Lam 2:10
ground, to cover it with *d*.....Ezek 24:7
his horses their *d* shall ....Ezek 26:10
cast up *d* upon their heads ....Ezek 27:30
them that sleep in the *d*.......Dan 12:2
pant after the *d* of.. ....Amos 2:7
Aphrah roll thyself in *d*.......Mic 1:10
clouds are the *d* of his feet ....Nah 1:3
shall heap *d* and take it ....Hab 1:10
shall be poured out as *d* ......Zeph 1:17
heaped up silver as the *d*......Zech 9:3
shake off the *d* under your ....Mark 6:11
shake off the very *d* from .....Luke 9:5
Even the very *d* of your city...Luke 10:11
shook off the *d* of..feet ....Acts 13:51
and threw *d* into the air.......Acts 22:23
they cast *d* on their heads .....Rev 18:19

DUTY—*an obligation*

Toward men:
Husband to wife.........Eph 5:25-33
Wife to husband.........Eph 5:22-24
Parents to children ......Eph 6:4
Children to parents ......Eph 6:1-3
Subject to rulers.........1Pet 2:12-20
Rulers to subjects ....Rom 13:1-7
Men to men 1Pet 3:8-16
The weak 1Cor 8:1-13

Toward God:
Love ....Deut 11:1
Obey ....Matt 12:50
Serve 1Thess 1:9
Worship ....John 4:23

and her *d* of marriage.........Ex 21:10
d of an husband's brother .....Deut 25:5
d of..husband's brother ....Deut 25:7
d of every day required 2Chr 8:14
d of every day required ....Ezra 3:4
this is the whole *d* of man.....Eccl 12:13
that which was our *d* ....Luke 17:10
d is also to minister...........Rom 15:27

DWARF—*a diminutive person*
Excluded from priesthood.Lev 21:20

DWELL—*to abide; live*

[*also* DWELLED, DWELLEST, DWELLETH, DWELLING, DWELLINGS, DWELT]
and *d* in the land of Nod......Gen 4:16
father of such as *d* in tents ....Gen 4:20
their *d* was from Mesha as ....Gen 10:30
came unto Haran and *d*.......Gen 11:31
that they might *d* together.....Gen 13:6
they could not *d* together .....Gen 13:6
the Perizzite *d* then in the.....Gen 13:7
Abram *d* in the land of ....Gen 13:12
Lot *d* in the cities of the ......Gen 13:12
that *d* in Hazezon-Tamar......Gen 14:7
he *d* in the plain of Mamre....Gen 14:13
cities in the which Lot *d* ......Gen 19:29
d in the mountain, and his ....Gen 19:30
he feared to *d* in Zoar, and ...Gen 19:30
he *d* in a cave, he and his.....Gen 19:30
he *d* in the wilderness of ......Gen 21:21
d among the children of.......Gen 23:10
Canaanites..whom I *d*.........Gen 24:3
d by the well Lahai-roi........Gen 25:11
d in the land which I shall ....Gen 26:2
And Isaac *d* in Gerar ....Gen 26:6
d shall be the fatness of.......Gen 27:39
will my husband *d* with ....Gen 30:20
ye shall *d* with us, and ....Gen 34:10
d and trade ye therein, and ...Gen 34:10
let them *d* in the land.........Gen 34:21
and they will *d* with us........Gen 34:23
when Israel *d* in that land .....Gen 35:22
than that they might *d*........Gen 36:7
And Jacob *d* in the land ......Gen 37:1
ye may *d* in the land of ....Gen 46:34
thy father and brethren to *d*...Gen 47:6
land of Goshen let them *d* ....Gen 47:6
And Israel *d* in the land of....Gen 47:27
and *d* in the land of Midian ...Ex 2:15
Moses was content to *d* with ..Ex 2:21
Israel had light in their *d*......Ex 10:23
thou hast made for thee to *d* ..Ex 15:17
that I may *d* among them .....Ex 25:8
throughout all your *d*, that ....Lev 3:17
he shall *d* alone; without ......Lev 13:46
land of Egypt, wherein ye *d*...Lev 18:3
stranger that *d* with you......Lev 19:34
of the Lord in all your *d* ......Lev 23:3
in all your *d* throughout.......Lev 23:21
Ye shall *d* in booths seven ....Lev 23:42
children of Israel to *d* in ......Lev 23:43

your fill and *d* therein in ... Lev 25:19
if a man sell a *d* house in ... Lev 25:29
thy brother that *d* by him ... Lev 25:47
your enemies which *d* ... Lev 26:32
in the midst whereof I *d* ... Num 5:3
people that *d* therein ... Num 13:18
the land is that they *d* in ... Num 13:19
they *d* in, whether in tents ... Num 13:19
The Amalekites *d* in the ... Num 13:29
Amorites *d* in the ... Num 13:29
Canaanites *d* by the sea ... Num 13:29
Canaanites *d* in the valley ... Num 14:25
we have *d* in Egypt a long ... Num 20:15
goeth down to the *d* of Ar ... Num 21:15
and Israel *d* in all the cities ... Num 21:25
which *d* at Heshbon ... Num 21:34
the people shall *d* alone ... Num 23:9
Manasseh, and he *d* therein ... Num 32:40
of the land and *d* therein ... Num 33:53
possession cities to *d* in ... Num 35:2
generations in all your *d* ... Num 35:29
come again to *d* in the land ... Num 35:32
shall inhabit, wherein I *d* ... Num 35:34
d among the children of ... Num 35:34
which *d* in Heshbon and Og ... Deut 1:4
which *d* at Astaroth in Edrei ... Deut 1:4
which *d* in that mountain ... Deut 1:44
children of Esau which *d* in ... Deut 2:4
Emim *d* therein in times ... Deut 2:10
Horim also *d* in Seir ... Deut 2:12
before them, and *d* in their ... Deut 2:12
them, and *d* in their stead ... Deut 2:21
children of Esau, which *d* ... Deut 2:22
and *d* in their stead even ... Deut 2:22
Avim which *d* in Hazerim ... Deut 2:23
them and *d* in their stead ... Deut 2:23
children of Esau which *d* in ... Deut 2:29
and the Moabites which *d* ... Deut 2:29
who *d* at Heshbon, whom ... Deut 4:46
ye shall possess it, and *d* ... Deut 11:31
and *d* in the land which the ... Deut 12:10
round about, so that ye *d* in ... Deut 12:10
them, and *d* in their land ... Deut 12:29
God hath given thee to *d* ... Deut 13:12
He shall *d* with thee, even ... Deut 23:16
and possessest, it and *d* ... Deut 26:1
thou shalt not *d* therein ... Deut 28:30
we have *d* in the land of ... Deut 29:16
Lord shall *d* in safety by ... Deut 33:12
he shall *d* between his ... Deut 33:12
he *d* as a lion and teareth ... Deut 33:20
and she *d* upon the wall ... Josh 2:15
she *d* in Israel even unto ... Josh 6:25
Peradventure ye *d* among us ... Josh 9:7
that they *d* among them ... Josh 9:16
d in the mountains are ... Josh 10:6
that *d* at Ashtaroth and at ... Josh 12:4
dukes of Sihon, *d* in the ... Josh 13:21
cities to *d* in with their ... Josh 14:4
but the Canaanites *d* among ... Josh 16:10
d in the land of the valley ... Josh 17:16
possessed it, and *d* therein ... Josh 19:47
And he shall *d* in that city ... Josh 20:6
they possessed it, and *d* ... Josh 21:43
d on the other side of the ... Josh 24:2
d on the other side Jordan ... Josh 24:8
built not, and ye *d* in them ... Josh 24:13
that *d* in the mountain ... Judg 1:9
they went and *d* among the ... Judg 1:16
Jebusites *d* with the ... Judg 1:21
the Canaanites *d* in Gezer ... Judg 1:29
Asherites *d* among the ... Judg 1:32
Amorites would *d* in mount ... Judg 1:35
Hivites that *d* in mount ... Judg 3:3
d in Harosheth of the ... Judg 4:2
way of them that *d* in tents ... Judg 8:11
went to Beer and *d* there ... Judg 9:21
they should not *d* in Shechem. . Judg 9:41
he *d* in Shamir in mount ... Judg 10:1
Israel *d* in Heshbon and her ... Judg 11:26
the Levite was content to *d* ... Judg 17:11
they *d* careless, after the ... Judg 18:7
repaired the cities, and *d* ... Judg 21:23
they *d* there..ten years ... Ruth 1:4
d with her mother in law ... Ruth 2:23

d between the cherubim ... 1Sam 4:4
made them *d* in this place ... 1Sam 12:8
on every side, and ye *d* safe ... 1Sam 12:11
and Samuel went and *d* in ... 1Sam 19:18
and *d* in strongholds at ... 1Sam 23:29
country, that I may *d* there ... 1Sam 27:5
why should thy servant *d* in ... 1Sam 27:5
d in the country of the ... 1Sam 27:7
and they *d* in the cities of ... 2Sam 2:3
d between the cherubim ... 2Sam 6:2
I *d* in a house of cedar ... 2Sam 7:2
I have not *d* in any house ... 2Sam 7:6
that they may *d* in a place ... 2Sam 7:10
Mephibosheth *d* in ... 2Sam 9:13
house in Jerusalem, and *d* ... 1Kin 2:36
Shimei *d* in Jerusalem ... 1Kin 2:38
his house where he *d* had ... 1Kin 7:8
Lord said that he would *d* ... 1Kin 8:12
God indeed *d* on the earth? ... 1Kin 8:27
hear thou in heaven thy *d* ... 1Kin 8:30
Hear thou in heaven thy *d* ... 1Kin 8:43
went to Damascus, and *d* ... 1Kin 11:24
which *d* in the cities of ... 1Kin 12:17
d an old prophet in Beth-el ... 1Kin 13:11
Syria that *d* at Damascus ... 1Kin 15:18
went and *d* by the brook ... 1Kin 17:5
in his city, *d* with Naboth ... 1Kin 21:8
I *d* among mine own people ... 2Kin 4:13
there, where we may *d* ... 2Kin 6:2
children of Israel *d* in ... 2Kin 13:5
and *d* there unto this day ... 2Kin 16:6
beginning of their *d* there ... 2Kin 17:25
came and *d* in Beth-el and ... 2Kin 17:28
d between the cherubim ... 2Kin 19:15
returned, and *d* at Nineveh ... 2Kin 19:36
d in the land, and serve ... 2Kin 25:24
of the scribes which *d* at ... 1Chr 2:55
d among plants and hedges ... 1Chr 4:23
there they *d* with the king ... 1Chr 4:23
of Ham had *d* there of old ... 1Chr 4:40
and *d* there unto this day ... 1Chr 4:43
d in their tents throughout ... 1Chr 5:10
they *d* in Gilead in Bashan ... 1Chr 5:16
tribe of Manasseh *d* in the ... 1Chr 5:23
ministered before the *d* ... 1Chr 6:32
men. These *d* in Jerusalem ... 1Chr 8:28
d with their brethren in ... 1Chr 8:32
d of the children of ... 1Chr 9:3
these *d* at Jerusalem ... 1Chr 9:34
d with their brethren ... 1Chr 9:38
And David *d* in the castle ... 1Chr 11:7
d between the cherubim ... 1Chr 13:6
I *d* in an house of cedars ... 1Chr 17:1
they shall *d* in their place ... 1Chr 17:9
build him a house to *d* ... 2Chr 2:3
a place for thy *d* for ever ... 2Chr 6:2
will God in very deed *d* with ... 2Chr 6:18
thou from heaven thy *d* place ... 2Chr 6:30
even from thy *d* place, their ... 2Chr 6:39
not *d* in the house of David ... 2Chr 8:11
d in the cities of Judah ... 2Chr 10:17
king of Syria that *d* at ... 2Chr 16:2
they *d* therein, and have ... 2Chr 20:8
d in a several house, being ... 2Chr 26:21
Israel, and that *d* in Judah ... 2Chr 30:25
d in the cities of Judah ... 2Chr 31:6
people, and on his *d* place ... 2Chr 36:15
Nethinim, *d* in their cities ... Ezra 2:70
companions that *d* in ... Ezra 4:17
Nethinim *d* in Ophel, unto ... Neh 3:26
all Israel, *d* in their cities ... Neh 7:73
children of Israel should *d* ... Neh 8:14
the people *d* at Jerusalem ... Neh 11:1
to *d* at Jerusalem ... Neh 11:2
the province that *d* in ... Neh 11:3
in the cities of Judah *d* ... Neh 11:3
sons of Perez that *d* at ... Neh 11:6
of Judah *d* at Kirjath-arba ... Neh 11:25
of Benjamin from Geba *d* at ... Neh 11:31
d in the unwalled towns ... Esth 9:19
stain it; let a cloud *d* upon ... Job 3:5
the *d* place of the wicked ... Job 8:22
wickedness *d* in thy ... Job 11:14
And he *d* in desolate cities ... Job 15:28
nor any remaining in his *d* ... Job 18:19

They that *d* in mine house ... Job 19:15
and the honorable man *d* ... Job 22:8
and the barren land his *d* ... Job 39:6
She *d* and abideth on the ... Job 39:28
only makest me *d* in safety ... Ps 4:8
neither shall evil *d* with ... Ps 5:4
to the Lord, which *d* in Zion ... Ps 9:11
shall *d* in thy holy hill? ... Ps 15:1
and they that *d* therein ... Ps 24:1
I may *d* in the house of the ... Ps 27:4
So shalt thou *d* in the land ... Ps 37:3
good; and *d* for evermore ... Ps 37:27
d places to all generations ... Ps 49:11
pluck thee out of thy *d* ... Ps 52:5
wickedness is in their *d* ... Ps 55:15
that he may *d* in thy courts ... Ps 65:4
the rebellious *d* in a dry ... Ps 68:6
congregation hath *d* ... Ps 68:10
which God desireth to *d* in ... Ps 68:16
Lord will *d* in it for ever ... Ps 68:16
let none *d* in their tents ... Ps 69:25
that love his name shall *d* ... Ps 69:36
and his *d* place in Zion ... Ps 76:2
the tribes of Israel to *d* ... Ps 78:55
d between the cherubim ... Ps 80:1
to *d* in the tents of ... Ps 84:10
Lord, thou hast been our *d* ... Ps 90:1
He that *d* in the secret ... Ps 91:1
my soul had almost *d* in ... Ps 94:17
world, and they that *d* ... Ps 98:7
that they may *d* with me ... Ps 101:6
shall not *d* within my house ... Ps 101:7
of them that *d* therein ... Ps 107:34
I *d* in the tents of Kedar! ... Ps 120:5
to *d* together in unity! ... Ps 133:1
Zion, which *d* at Jerusalem ... Ps 135:21
shall *d* in thy presence ... Ps 140:13
hearkeneth unto me shall *d* ... Prov 1:33
seeing he *d* securely by ... Prov 3:29
I wisdom *d* with prudence ... Prov 8:12
better to *d* in the wilderness ... Prov 21:19
and oil in the *d* of the wise ... Prov 21:20
Thou that *d* in the gardens ... Song 8:13
every *d* place of mount Zion ... Is 4:5
I *d* in the midst of a people ... Is 6:5
wolf also shall *d* with the ... Is 11:6
neither shall it be *d* in ... Is 13:20
Let mine outcasts *d* with ... Is 16:4
them that *d* before the Lord ... Is 23:18
down them that *d* on high ... Is 26:5
people shall *d* in Zion at ... Is 30:19
d in a peaceable habitation ... Is 32:18
and in sure *d* and in quiet ... Is 32:18
he *d* on high; he hath filled ... Is 33:5
d with the devouring fire? ... Is 33:14
shall *d* with everlasting ... Is 33:14
d on high; his place of ... Is 33:16
people that *d* therein shall ... Is 33:24
generation shall they *d* ... Is 34:17
d between the cherubim ... Is 37:16
returned, and *d* at Nineveh ... Is 37:37
place to me that I may *d* ... Is 49:20
I *d* in the high and holy ... Is 57:15
my servants shall *d* there ... Is 65:9
forsaken, and not a man *d* ... Jer 4:29
I will cause you to *d* in ... Jer 7:3
I cause you to *d* in this ... Jer 7:7
that *d* in a far country ... Jer 8:19
because our *d* have cast us ... Jer 9:19
that *d* in the wilderness ... Jer 9:26
wickedness of them that *d* ... Jer 12:4
Israel shall *d* safely and ... Jer 23:6
that *d* in the land of Egypt ... Jer 24:8
people that *d* in the desert ... Jer 25:24
Build ye houses and *d* in ... Jer 29:5
of all the people that *d* ... Jer 29:16
man to *d* among this people ... Jer 29:32
and I will cause them to *d* ... Jer 32:37
all your days ye shall *d* in ... Jer 35:7
But we have *d* in tents and ... Jer 35:10
so we *d* at Jerusalem ... Jer 35:11
and *d* with him among the ... Jer 40:5
and *d* with him among the ... Jer 40:6
behold I will *d* at Mizpah ... Jer 40:10
d in your cities that ye ... Jer 40:10

bread; and there will we *d* ....Jer 42:14
to *d* in the land of Judah......Jer 43:5
d in the land of Egypt ....Jer 44:1
which *d* at Migdol and at ......Jer 44:1
I will punish them that *d* ......Jer 44:13
people that *d* in the land of ...Jer 44:15
that *d* in the land of Egypt ....Jer 44:26
O thou daughter *d* in Egypt ...Jer 46:19
without any to *d* therein ......Jer 48:9
and *d* in the rock, and be .....Jer 48:28
Flee ye, turn back, *d* deep .....Jer 49:8
O thou that *d* in the clefts ....Jer 49:16
Flee, get you far off, *d*........Jer 49:30
nation that *d* without care .....Jer 49:31
nor any son of man *d* in it ....Jer 49:33
beasts..islands shall *d* ....Jer 50:39
the owls shall *d* therein ....Jer 50:39
against them that *d* in the .....Jer 51:1
she *d* among the heathen......Lam 1:3
Edom, that *d* in the land of ...Lam 4:21
dost *d* among scorpions ....Ezek 2:6
d by the river of Chebar ......Ezek 3:15
O thou that *d* in the land .....Ezek 7:7
daughters that *d* at thy left ....Ezek 16:46
that *d* at thy right hand is .....Ezek 16:46
and under it shall *d* all fowl ...Ezek 17:23
thee, and to make their *d* in...Ezek 25:4
they shall *d* safely therein .....Ezek 28:26
they shall *d* with confidence ....Ezek 28:26
that *d* under his shadow in ....Ezek 31:17
they shall *d* safely in the ......Ezek 34:25
ye shall *d* in the land that .....Ezek 36:28
And they shall *d* in the land...Ezek 37:25
your fathers have *d*...........Ezek 37:25
they shall *d* safely all of.......Ezek 38:8
all of them *d* without walls ....Ezek 38:11
d in the midst of the land .....Ezek 38:12
when my people of Israel *d* ...Ezek 38:14
they that *d* in the cities of.....Ezek 39:9
I will *d* in the midst of.........Ezek 43:9
gods, whose *d* is not with .....Dan 2:11
darkness, and the light *d* ......Dan 2:22
the children of men *d*.........Dan 2:38
the fowls of the heaven *d* .....Dan 4:12
d was with the wild asses......Dan 5:21
every one that *d* therein ......Hos 4:3
shall not *d* in the Lord's ......Hos 9:3
that *d* under his shadow.......Hos 14:7
the Lord your God *d* in Zion..Joel 3:17
Judah shall *d* for ever, and ....Joel 3:20
for the Lord *d* in Zion ....Joel 3:21
be taken out that *d* in ....Amos 3:12
every one mourn that *d* ....Amos 8:8
that *d* therein shall mourn.....Amos 9:5
d in the clefts of the rock .....Obad 3
thou shalt *d* in the field ....Mic 4:10
d solitarily in the wood ....Mic 7:14
and all that *d* therein ....Nah 1:5
Where is the *d* of the lions ....Nah 2:11
and of all that *d* therein.......Hab 2:8
all them that *d* in the land ....Zeph 1:18
And the sea coast shall be *d*...Zeph 2:6
rejoicing city that *d* ....Zeph 2:15
so their *d* should not be cut ...Zeph 3:7
to *d* in your ceiled houses .....Hag 1:4
d with the daughter of ....Zech 2:7
and I will *d* in the midst ......Zech 2:10
d in the midst of Jerusalem....Zech 8:3
d in the midst of Jerusalem....Zech 8:8
d in a city called Nazareth ....Matt 2:23
they enter in and *d* there ......Matt 12:45
and by him that *d* therein ......Matt 23:21
Who had his *d* among the .....Mark 5:3
all that *d* round about them ...Luke 1:65
they enter in, and *d* there .....Luke 11:26
Master, where *d* thou? ....John 1:38
my blood, *d* in me, and I in ..John 6:56
the Father that *d* in me, he ...John 14:10
he *d* with you, and shall be ...John 14:17
and let no man *d* therein ......Acts 1:20
there were *d* at Jerusalem .....Acts 2:5
them that *d* in Jerusalem .....Acts 4:16
Mesopotamia, before he *d* in ..Acts 7:2
the most High *d* not in........Acts 7:48
the Jews which *d* at Damascus .Acts 9:22
d at Lydda and Saron saw.....Acts 9:35
when they *d* as strangers in....Acts 13:17
they that *d* at Jerusalem ......Acts 13:27
to *d* on all the face of the .....Acts 17:26
all the Jews which *d* there.....Acts 22:12
Paul was suffered to *d* by .....Acts 28:16
Paul *d* two whole years in .....Acts 28:30
that do it, but sin that *d* ......Rom 7:17
that do it, but sin that *d* ......Rom 7:20
the Spirit of God *d* in you ....Rom 8:9
Jesus from the dead *d* ....Rom 8:11
by his Spirit that *d* in you .....Rom 8:11
be pleased to *d* with him 1Cor 7:12
God hath said, I will *d* in 2Cor 6:16
That Christ may *d* in your.....Eph 3:17
in him should all fulness *d* ....Col 1:19
Let the word of Christ *d* in....Col 3:16
d in the light which no man ...1Tim 6:16
d first in thy grandmother 2Tim 1:5
the Holy Ghost which *d*.......2Tim 1:14
d in tabernacles with Isaac ....Heb 11:9
spirit that *d* in us lusteth ......James 4:5
d with them according 1Pet 3:7
righteous man *d* among 2Pet 2:8
wherein *d* righteousness 2Pet 3:13
how *d* the love of God in 1John 3:17
know we that we *d* in him 1John 4:13
truth's sake, which *d* in us 2John 2
where thou *d*, even where.....Rev 2:13
among you, where Satan *d* ....Rev 2:13
them that *d* upon the earth....Rev 3:10
they that *d* upon the earth ....Rev 11:10
tormented them that *d* on .....Rev 11:10
and them that *d* in heaven ....Rev 13:6
which *d* therein to worship ....Rev 13:12
And deceiveth them that *d* ....Rev 13:14
to them that *d* on the earth ...Rev 13:14
they that *d* on the earth.......Rev 17:8
and he will *d* with them ....Rev 21:3

DWELLERS—*inhabitants*
world, and *d* before the Lord..Is 18:3
known unto all the *d* at ....Acts 1:19

DWELLING, GOD'S
In the tabernacle ....Ex 29:45, 46
In the temple 1Kin 6:12, 13
2Chr 7:1-3
In Zion ....Is 8:18
In Christ................Col 2:9
Among men ....John 1:14
In our hearts............1John 4:12-16
In the Holy Spirit 1Cor 3:16
In the New Jerusalem....Rev 7:15

DWELLINGPLACE—*a place where one lives; a home*

[*also* DWELLINGPLACES]
Strong is thy *d* and thou ......Num 24:21
and have mercy on his *d* ......Jer 30:18
shall become heaps, a *d*.......Jer 51:37
In..your *d* the cities shall......Ezek 6:6
possess the *d* that are not .....Hab 1:6
buffeted, have no certain *d*....1Cor 4:11

DYEING—*coloring*
Leather ....Ex 25:5
Clothes ....Is 63:1

[*also* DYED]
rams' skins *d* red and a ....Ex 26:14
rams' skins *d* red and a ....Ex 36:19
d garments from Bozrah? .....Is 63:1
exceeding in *d* attire upon.....Ezek 23:15

DYSENTERY—*a disease involving severe diarrhea*
Cured by Paul ....Acts 28:8

E

EACH—*every*
laid *e* piece one against ....Gen 15:10
e man his dream in one ....Gen 40:5
dreamed *e* man according .....Gen 41:11
he gave *e* man changes of .....Gen 45:22
asked *e* other of their ....Ex 18:7
e one was for the house of ....Num 1:44
offer their offering *e* prince....Num 7:11
thirty shekels, *e* bowl ....Num 7:85
Aaron, *e* of you his censer ....Num 16:17
two tenth deals to *e* ram ......Num 29:14
among you three men for *e* ...Josh 18:4
with him ten princes, of *e* .....Josh 22:14
e one was a head of the.......Josh 22:14
e one resembled..children .....Judg 8:18
return *e* to her mother's ....Ruth 1:8
e man his month in a year 1Kin 4:7
sat *e* on his throne, having 1Kin 22:10
e in his chariot, and they......2Kin 9:21
six on *e* hand, and six on *e*....1Chr 20:6
the top of *e* of them was five ..2Chr 3:15
stays on *e* side of the sitting ...2Chr 9:18
to the language of *e* ....Neh 13:24
peace have kissed *e* other .....Ps 85:10
made *e* one for himself to .....Is 2:20
of dragons, where *e* lay ....Is 35:7
have appointed thee *e* day ....Ezek 4:6
and measured *e* post of the....Ezek 40:48
doth not *e* one of you on the..Luke 13:15
and it sat upon *e* of them .....Acts 2:3
let *e* esteem other better ......Phil 2:3
toward *e* other aboundeth 2Thess 1:3
And the four beasts had *e*.....Rev 4:8

EAGLE—*a large bird of prey, often used in Scripture in a symbolic sense*
Described as:
Unclean ....Lev 11:13
A bird of prey ....Job 9:26
Large ....Ezek 17:3, 7
Swift 2Sam 1:23
Keen in vision ....Job 39:27-29
Nesting high ....Jer 49:16
Figurative of:
God's care ....Ex 19:4
Swift armies ....Jer 4:13
Spiritual renewal ....Is 40:31
Flight of riches ....Prov 23:5
False security ....Jer 49:16

[*also* EAGLE'S, EAGLES, EAGLES']
how I bare you on *e* wings ....Ex 19:4
the pelican and the gier *e* .....Lev 11:18
the *e* and the ossifrage ....Deut 14:12
earth, as swift as the *e* ....Deut 28:49
they were swifter than *e* 2Sam 1:23
Doth the *e* mount up at thy ...Job 39:27
youth is renewed like the *e*...Ps 103:5
and the young *e* shall eat it ...Prov 30:17
The way of an *e* in the air ....Prov 30:19
Behold he shall fly as an *e* ....Jer 48:40
swifter than the *e* of the ......Lam 4:19
four..had the face of an *e* .....Ezek 1:10
the fourth the face of an *e* .....Ezek 10:14
his hairs were grown like *e* ....Dan 4:33
was like a lion and had *e* ......Dan 7:4
shall come as an *e* against .....Hos 8:1
thou exalt thyself as the *e* .....Obad 4
they shall fly as the *e* that .....Hab 1:8
there will the *e* be gathered ...Matt 24:28
is, thither will the *e* be........Luke 17:37
beast was like a flying *e*.......Rev 4:7

EAR—*the organ used for hearing; the fruit of a cereal plant, such as corn*
Ceremonies respecting:
Priest's, anointed ....Ex 29:20
Leper's, anointed........Lev 14:14, 25
Servant's bored..........Ex 21:5, 6
The hearing of the unregenerate:
Deafened ....Deut 29:4
Stopped ....Ps 58:4
Dulled..................Matt 13:15
Disobedient ....Jer 7:23, 24
Uncircumcised ....Acts 7:51
Itching 2Tim 4:3, 4
Promises concerning, in:
Prophecy ....Is 64:4
Fulfillment ....Matt 13:16, 17
A miracle...............Mark 7:35

A foretaste 2Cor 12:4
Final realization 1Cor 2:9

Ears of corn:
Seen in Pharaoh's dream . Gen 41:5-7
Regulations concerning . . Lev 2:14
Ruth gleans .... Ruth 2:2
Christ's disciples pluck . . . Matt 12:1

[*also* EARS]
told..these things in their *e* .... Gen 20:8
which were in their *e* .... Gen 35:4
e came up in one stalk .... Gen 41:22
e devoured the seven good *e* . . Gen 41:24
the seven empty *e* blasted ..... Gen 41:27
I pray you, in the *e* of .... Gen 50:4
the barley was in the *e* .... Ex 9:31
mayest tell in the *e* of thy ..... Ex 10:2
give *e* to his commandments . . . Ex 15:26
rehearse it in the *e* of......... Ex 17:14
earrings..were in their *e* .... Ex 32:3
the tip of Aaron's right *e* ..... Lev 8:23
parched corn, nor green *e* ..... Lev 23:14
ye have wept in the *e* of ...... Num 11:18
voice, nor give *e* unto you .... Deut 1:45
I speak in your *e* this day ..... Deut 5:1
eyes to see, and *e* to hear ..... Deut 29:4
Moses spake in the *e* of all .... Deut 31:30
Give *e*, O ye heavens, and I . . Deut 32:1
his cause in the *e* of the .... Josh 20:4
give *e*, O ye princes; I, even . . Judg 5:3
proclaim in the *e* of the .... Judg 7:3
e of all the men of Shechem . . Judg 9:3
the *e* of every one that........ 1Sam 3:11
told Samuel in his *e* a day 1Sam 9:15
the tidings in the *e* of the 1Sam 11:4
words in the *e* of David 1Sam 18:23
spake in the *e* of Benjamin 2Sam 3:19
we have heard with our *e* 2Sam 7:22
e of corn in the husk 2Kin 4:42
tumult is come..into mine *e* . . . 2Kin 19:28
read in their *e* all..words 2Kin 23:2
we have heard with our *e* 1Chr 17:20
let thine *e* be attent unto 2Chr 6:40
but they would not give *e* 2Chr 24:19
read in their *e* all the words . . . 2Chr 34:30
Let thine *e* now be attentive . . . Neh 1:6
the *e* of all the people were . . . Neh 8:3
yet would they not give *e* ..... Neh 9:30
mine *e* received a little .... Job 4:12
mine *e* hath heard and .... Job 13:1
my declaration with your *e* .... Job 13:17
the tops of the *e* of corn ..... Job 24:24
Unto me men gave *e* and ..... Job 29:21
Then he openeth the *e* of ..... Job 33:16
give *e* unto me, ye that have . Job 34:2
openeth also their *e* to .... Job 36:10
Give *e* to my words, O Lord . . Ps 5:1
cry, give *e* unto my prayer .... Ps 17:1
before him, even into his *e* .... Ps 18:6
Bow down thine *e* to me ...... Ps 31:2
mine *e* hast thou opened ...... Ps 40:6
consider..incline thine *e* .... Ps 45:10
I will incline mine *e* to a ...... Ps 49:4
Give *e* to my prayer, O God . . Ps 55:1
incline thine *e* unto me, and . . . Ps 71:2
Give *e*, O my people, to my . . Ps 78:1
incline your *e* to the words .... Ps 78:1
give *e*, O God of Jacob .... Ps 84:8
Give *e*, O Lord, unto my ..... Ps 86:6
planted the *e*, shall he not .... Ps 94:9
have *e*, but they hear not ..... Ps 115:6
hath inclined his *e* unto me .... Ps 116:2
have *e*, but they hear not ..... Ps 135:17
O Lord, give *e* to my .... Ps 143:1
incline thine *e* unto wisdom . . . Prov 2:2
bow thine *e* to my .... Prov 5:1
e that heareth the reproof ..... Prov 15:31
e of the wise seeketh .... Prov 18:15
stoppeth his *e* at the .... Prov 21:13
Bow down thine *e* .... Prov 22:17
thine *e* to the words of........ Prov 23:12
away his *e* from hearing .... Prov 28:9
nor the *e* filled with hearing . . . Eccl 1:8
O heavens and give *e* O ...... Is 1:2
In mine *e* said the Lord of .... Is 5:9
and make their *e* heavy and . . . Is 6:10
eyes..hear with their *e* .... Is 6:10
give *e*..ye of far countries ..... Is 8:9
reapeth the *e* with his arm .... Is 17:5
be as he that gathereth *e* ...... Is 17:5
thine *e* shall hear a word ...... Is 30:21
stoppeth his *e* from hearing . . . Is 33:15
e of the people that are on . . . Is 36:11
Incline thine *e*, O Lord, and . . Is 37:17
opening the *e*, but he .... Is 42:20
among you will give *e* to ...... Is 42:23
shall say again in thine *e* ...... Is 49:20
wakeneth mine *e* to hear as . . Is 50:4
give *e* unto me, O my nation . . Is 51:4
his *e* heavy, that it cannot ..... Is 59:1
cry in the *e* of Jerusalem ...... Jer 2:2
their *e* is uncircumcised ...... Jer 6:10
nor inclined their *e* but ...... Jer 7:26
nor inclined their *e* but ...... Jer 11:8
neither inclined their *e* but .... Jer 17:23
whosoever heareth, his *e* ...... Jer 19:3
all these words in your *e* ...... Jer 26:15
word that I speak in thine *e* . . . Jer 28:7
in the *e* of all the people ...... Jer 28:7
me, neither inclined their *e* .... Jer 34:14
in the *e* of the people in ...... Jer 36:6
in the *e* of all the people ...... Jer 36:10
read in the *e* of the people .... Jer 36:14
now, and read it in our *e* ..... Jer 36:15
So Baruch read it in their *e* . . . Jer 36:15
Jehudi read it in the *e* of...... Jer 36:21
in the *e* of all the princes ..... Jer 36:21
nor inclined their *e* to turn .... Jer 44:5
hide not thine *e* at my .... Lam 3:56
heart, and hear with thine *e* .... Ezek 3:10
cried also in mine *e* with a .... Ezek 9:1
and earrings in thine *e* and .... Ezek 16:12
to hear it with thine *e*? .... Ezek 24:26
hear with thine *e* all that I .... Ezek 44:5
O my God incline thine *e* ..... Dan 9:18
give ye *e* O house of the ...... Hos 5:1
Hear this..and give *e* .... Joel 1:2
two legs or a piece of an *e* .... Amos 3:12
mouth, their *e* shall be deaf . . . Mic 7:16
stopped their *e* that they ...... Zech 7:11
what ye hear in the *e* that ..... Matt 10:27
He that hath *e* to hear, let .... Matt 11:15
Who hath *e* to hear, let him . . . Matt 13:9
come to the governor's *e* ...... Matt 28:14
went, to pluck the *e* of corn . . . Mark 2:23
If any man have *e* to hear ..... Mark 4:23
put his fingers into his *e* ...... Mark 7:33
and having *e*, hear ye not? ..... Mark 8:18
high priest, and cut off his *e* . . . Mark 14:47
salutation sounded in mine *e* . . Luke 1:44
disciples plucked the *e* of ..... Luke 6:1
sink down into your *e* .... Luke 9:44
ye have spoken in the *e* .... Luke 12:3
and cut off his right *e* .... John 18:10
unto the *e* of the church ...... Acts 11:22
their *e* are dull of hearing ..... Acts 28:27
e that they should not hear .... Rom 11:8
if the *e* shall say, Because 1Cor 12:16
turn away their *e* from the 2Tim 4:4
entered into the *e* of the ...... James 5:4
his *e* are open unto their 1Pet 3:12
He that hath an *e* let him ..... Rev 2:7
He that hath an *e* let him ..... Rev 2:11
He that hath an *e* let him ..... Rev 2:17
He that hath an *e* let him ..... Rev 2:29
any man have an *e* let him .... Rev 13:9

EARING—*plowing*

[*also* EARED]
neither be *e* nor harvest....... Gen 45:6
in *e* time and in harvest .... Ex 34:21
which is neither *e* nor sown . . . Deut 21:4

EARLY—*near the beginning*
rise up *e*, and go on your ..... Gen 19:2
Abimelech rose *e* in the .... Gen 20:8
e in the morning Laban .... Gen 31:55
Rise up *e* in the morning ...... Ex 8:20
rose up *e* in the morning ...... Ex 24:4
rose up *e* in the morning ...... Num 14:40
rose up *e* in the morning ...... Josh 7:16
the men of the city arose *e* .... Judg 6:28
Jerubbaal..rose up *e* .... Judg 7:1
rise *e* and set upon the city .... Judg 9:33
he arose *e* in the morning ..... Judg 19:8
that the people rose *e* .... Judg 21:4
they of Ashdod arose *e* on 1Sam 5:3
arose *e* and it came to pass 1Sam 9:26
rise up *e* in the morning 1Sam 29:10
as soon as ye be up *e* in 1Sam 29:10
Absalom rose up *e* and 2Sam 15:2
And they rose up *e* in the 2Kin 3:22
And they rose *e* in the 2Chr 20:20
help her, and that right *e* ..... Ps 46:5
I myself will awake *e* .... Ps 57:8
art my God; *e* will I seek ..... Ps 63:1
and inquired *e* after God ...... Ps 78:34
satisfy us *e* with thy mercy .... Ps 90:14
harp; I myself will awake *e* .... Ps 108:2
they shall seek me *e* but ...... Prov 1:28
rising *e* in the morning .... Prov 27:14
get up to the vineyards .... Song 7:12
arose *e* in the morning .... Is 37:36
rising up *e* and speaking ...... Jer 7:13
rising *e* and protesting .... Jer 11:7
rising *e* and sending them ..... Jer 25:4
rising up *e* and sending .... Jer 29:19
rising *e* and speaking; but .... Jer 35:14
rising *e* and sending them ..... Jer 44:4
arose very *e* in the morning . . . Dan 6:19
they will seek me *e* .... Hos 5:15
as the *e* dew that passeth ..... Hos 13:3
they rose *e* and corrupted ..... Zeph 3:7
went out *e* in the morning..... Matt 20:1
risen *e* the first day of .... Mark 16:9
very *e* in the morning, they . . . Luke 24:1
were *e* at the sepulcher ...... Luke 24:22
it was *e*..they themselves ...... John 18:28
cometh Mary Magdalene *e* .... John 20:1
e in the morning and .... Acts 5:21
he receive the *e* and latter .... James 5:7

EARLY, AROSE

For spiritual purposes:
Abraham—looked on Sodom and Gomorrah . Gen 19:27-28
Abraham—to offer a burnt offering .... Gen 22:2, 3
Jacob—to worship the Lord .... Gen 28:18-22
Moses—to meet God on Sinai .... Ex 34:4, 5
Elkanah and Hannah—to worship God 1Sam 1:19-28
Hezekiah—to worship God 2Chr 29:20-24
Job—to offer sacrifices . . . Job 1:5
Jesus—to pray .... Mark 1:35
Jesus—to prepare to teach .... John 8:2
The people—to hear Jesus .... Luke 21:38

For military reasons:
Joshua—to lead Israel over Jordan .... Josh 3:1-17
Joshua—to capture Jericho .... Josh 6:12-27
Joshua—to capture Ai . . . Josh 8:10
People of Jerusalem—to see dead men 2Kin 19:35

For personal reasons:
Gideon—to examine the fleece .... Judg 6:36-38
Samuel—to meet Saul . . . 1Sam 15:12
David—to obey his father. 1Sam 17:20
The ideal woman—to do her work .... Prov 31:15
Drunkards—to pursue strong drink .... Is 5:11
Certain women—to visit Christ's grave .... Mark 16:2

EARLY RISING
Hezekiah to worship God. 2Chr 29:20-24

EARNEST—*a pledge of full payment*
The Holy Spirit in the heart 2Chr 1:22
Given by God 2Cor 5:5
Guarantee of future redemption .....Eph 1:13, 14

EARNESTNESS—*a serious and intense spirit*
Warning men .....Gen 19:15-17
Ezek 18:1-32
Accepting promises .....Gen 28:12-22
Admonishing a son 1Chr 28:9, 10
Public prayer 2Chr 6:12-42
Asking forgiveness .....Ps 51:1-19
Calling to repentance .....Acts 2:38-40
Seeking salvation .....Acts 16:30-34
Preaching the Gospel .....Acts 2:18-38
Writing an epistle .....Jude 3-5

[*also* EARNEST, EARNESTLY]
Did I not *e* send unto thee .....Num 22:37
David *e* asked leave of me 1Sam 20:6
son of Zabbai *e* repaired .....Neh 3:20
As a servant *e* desireth the .....Job 7:2
For I *e* protested unto your .....Jer 11:7
I do *e* remember him still .....Jer 31:20
do evil with both hands *e* .....Mic 7:3
an agony he prayed more *e* .....Luke 22:44
and *e* looked upon him and .....Luke 22:56
why look ye so *e* on us .....Acts 3:12
e beholding the council .....Acts 23:1
the *e* expectation of the .....Rom 8:19
But covet *e* the best gifts 1Cor 12:31
e desiring to be clothed 2Cor 5:2
told us your *e* desire 2Cor 7:7
to my *e* expectation and my .....Phil 1:20
we ought to give the more *e* .....Heb 2:1
prayed *e* that it might not .....James 5:17

EARNETH—*earn*
he that *e* wages, *e* wages to .....Hag 1:6

EARRING—*ornament worn on the ear*
Sign of worldliness .....Gen 35:2-4
Made into a golden calf .....Ex 32:3-4
Spoils of war .....Judg 8:24-26
Used figuratively .....Ezek 16:12

[*also* EARRINGS]
golden *e* of half a shekel .....Gen 24:22
I put the *e* upon her face .....Gen 24:47
e and rings, and tablets .....Ex 35:22
and bracelets, rings, *e* .....Num 31:50
and every one an *e* of gold .....Job 42:11
e of gold and an ornament .....Prov 25:12
and the tablets and the *e* .....Is 3:20
with her *e* and her jewels .....Hos 2:13

EARTH—*the planet on which we live; ground*

Described as:
Inhabitable .....Is 45:18
God's footstool .....Is 66:1
A circle .....Is 40:22
Full of minerals .....Deut 8:9

Glory of God's:
Goodness .....Ps 33:5
Glory .....Is 6:3
Riches .....Ps 104:24
Mercy .....Ps 119:64

History of:
Created by God .....Gen 1:1
Given to man .....Gen 1:27-31
Affected by sin .....Rom 8:20-23
Destroyed .....Gen 7:7-24
Final destruction 2Pet 3:7-12
To be renewed .....Is 65:17

Unusual events of:
Swallows several families .Num 16:23-35
Reversed in motion 2Kin 20:8-11
Shaking .....Heb 12:26
Smiting .....Mal 4:6
Earthquake .....Matt 27:51-54

Man's relation to:
Made of 1Cor 15:47, 48
Given dominion over .....Gen 1:26
Brings curse on .....Gen 3:17
Returns to dust .....Gen 3:19

Promises respecting
Continuance of seasons .....Gen 8:21, 22
No more flood .....Gen 9:11-17
God's knowledge to fill .....Is 11:9
The meek shall inherit .....Matt 5:5
Long life upon .....Eph 6:2, 3
To be renewed .....Is 65:17

[*also* EARTHLY, EARTHY]
God looked upon the *e* and .....Gen 6:12
the *e* is filled with violence .....Gen 6:13
destroy them with the *e* .....Gen 6:13
nations of the *e* be blessed .....Gen 22:18
the *e* shook and trembled 2Sam 22:8
going to and fro in the *e* .....Job 1:7
excellent is thy name in..*e*! .....Ps 8:1
The *e* is the Lord's, and the .....Ps 24:1
the meek shall inherit the *e* .....Ps 37:11
fear before him, all the *e* .....Ps 96:9
but the *e* abideth for ever .....Eccl 1:4
e is utterly broken down .....Is 24:19
all the ends of the *e* .....Is 45:22
Ye are the salt of the *e* .....Matt 5:13
will be done in *e*, as it is .....Matt 6:10
and *e* shall pass away, but .....Matt 24:35
and *e* shall pass away .....Mark 13:31
on *e* peace, good will toward .....Luke 2:14
If I have told you *e* things .....John 3:12
first man is of the earth, *e* 1Cor 15:47
As is the *e*, such are they 1Cor 15:48
are they also that are *e* 1Cor 15:48
born the image of the *e* 1Cor 15:49
e house of this tabernacle 2Cor 5:1
into the lower parts of the *e* .....Eph 4:9
in heaven, and things in *e* .....Phil 2:10
shame, who mind *e* things .....Phil 3:19
and pilgrims on the *e* .....Heb 11:13
but is *e*, sensual, devilish .....James 3:15
he was cast out into the *e* .....Rev 12:9
a new heaven and a new *e* .....Rev 21:1

EARTHEN—*made of earth or clay*
e vessel wherein it is sodden .....Lev 6:28
birds be killed in an *e* .....Lev 14:5
take holy water in an *e* .....Num 5:17
and basins, and *e* vessels 2Sam 17:28
and get a potter's *e* bottle .....Jer 19:1
they esteemed as *e* pitchers .....Lam 4:2
this treasure in *e* vessels 2Cor 4:7

EARTHQUAKE—*earth tremors*

Expressive of God's:
Power .....Heb 12:26
Presence .....Ps 68:7, 8
Anger .....Ps 18:7
Judgments .....Is 24:18-21
Overthrowing of kingdoms ..... {Hag 2:6, 7; Rev 16:18-21}

Mentioned in the Scriptures:
Mt. Sinai .....Ex 19:18
The wilderness .....Num 16:31, 32
Saul's time 1Sam 14:15
Ahab's reign 1Kin 19:11, 12
Uzziah's reign .....Amos 1:1
Christ's death .....Matt 27:50, 51
Christ's resurrection .....Matt 28:2
Philippi .....Acts 16:26
This age .....Matt 24:7

[*also* EARTHQUAKES]
and with *e* and great noise .....Is 29:6
the *e* in the days of Uzziah .....Zech 14:5
saw the *e* and those things .....Matt 27:54
shall be *e* in divers places .....Mark 13:8
e shall be in divers places .....Luke 21:11
lo, there was a great *e* .....Rev 6:12
hour was there a great *e* .....Rev 11:13
and an *e* and great hail .....Rev 11:19

EASE—*contentment of body and mind*
Israel's .....Amos 6:1
Pagan nations' .....Zech 1:15
The rich fool's .....Luke 12:16-20

[*also* EASED]
thou wilt *e* thyself abroad .....Deut 23:13
and trode them down with *e* .....Judg 20:43
e thou somewhat the 2Chr 10:4
my couch shall *e* my .....Job 7:13
I forbear, what am I *e*? .....Job 16:6
I was at *e*, but he hath .....Job 16:12
His soul shall dwell at *e* .....Ps 25:13
e me of mine adversaries .....Is 1:24
ye women that are at *e* .....Is 32:11
and be in rest and at *e* .....Jer 46:27
of a multitude being at *e* .....Ezek 23:42
take thine *e*, eat, drink .....Luke 12:19
not that other men be *e* 2Cor 8:13

EASIER—*not as difficult*

[*also* EASILY, EASY]
so shall it be *e* for thyself .....Ex 18:22
knowledge is *e* unto him .....Prov 14:6
is *e*, to say, Thy sins be .....Matt 9:5
For my yoke is *e*, and my .....Matt 11:30
it is *e* to say to the sick .....Mark 2:9
is *e*, to say, Thy sins be .....Luke 5:23
it is *e* for a camel to go .....Luke 18:25
not *e* provoked, thinketh no 1Cor 13:5
words *e* to be understood 1Cor 14:9
sin which doth so *e* beset us .....Heb 12:1
e to be intreated, full of .....James 3:17

EAST—*direction to the right of north*

[*also* EASTWARD]
God planted a garden *e* of .....Gen 2:8
toward the *e* of Assyria .....Gen 2:14
the land of Nod on the *e* of .....Gen 4:16
they journeyed from the *e* .....Gen 11:2
a mountain on the *e* of .....Gen 12:8
tent having..Hai on the *e* .....Gen 12:8
and Lot journeyed *e* and .....Gen 13:11
e, unto the east country .....Gen 25:6
to the west, and to the *e* .....Gen 28:14
blasted with the *e* wind .....Gen 41:23
brought an *e* wind upon the .....Ex 10:13
go back by a strong *e* wind .....Ex 14:21
east side *e* shall be fifty .....Ex 27:13
the *e* side eastward fifty .....Ex 38:13
it beside the altar on the *e* .....Lev 1:16
finger upon the mercy seat *e* .....Lev 16:14
e side toward the rising of .....Num 2:3
e shall be Moses, and .....Num 3:38
the camps that lie on the *e* .....Num 10:5
coast of the Salt Sea *e* .....Num 34:3
e border from Hazar-enan .....Num 34:10
Jericho *e*, toward the .....Num 34:15
the city on the *e* side .....Num 35:5
under Ashdoth-pisgah *e* .....Deut 3:17
plain on this side Jordan *e* .....Deut 4:49
in the *e* border of Jericho .....Josh 4:19
to the Canaanite on the *e* .....Josh 11:3
unto the valley of Mizpeh *e* .....Josh 11:8
Sea of Chinneroth on the *e* .....Josh 12:3
even the Salt Sea on the *e* .....Josh 12:3
on the other side Jordan *e* .....Josh 13:27
water of Jericho on the *e* .....Josh 16:1
e unto Taanath-shiloh .....Josh 16:6
by it on the *e* to Janohah .....Josh 16:6
beyond Jordan on the *e* .....Josh 18:7
passeth on along on the *e* .....Josh 19:13
side Jordan by Jericho *e* .....Josh 20:8
children of the *e*..came up .....Judg 6:3
the children of the *e* lay .....Judg 7:12
that dwelt in tents on the *e* .....Judg 8:11
on the *e* side of the highway .....Judg 21:19
in Michmash, *e* from 1Sam 13:5
all the children of the *e* 1Kin 4:30
right side of the house *e* 1Kin 7:39
Jordan *e* all..land of Gilead 2Kin 10:33
unto the *e* side of the valley 1Chr 4:39
And *e* he inhabited unto the 1Chr 5:9
the *e* side of Jordan were 1Chr 6:78
waited in the king's gate *e* 1Chr 9:18
the *e*, and toward the west 1Chr 12:15
E were six Levites 1Chr 26:17
three looking toward the *e* 2Chr 4:4
at the *e* end of the altar 2Chr 5:12
the porter toward the *e* was 2Chr 31:14
the water gate toward the *e* .....Neh 3:26
even unto the water gate *e* .....Neh 12:37
of all the men of the *e* .....Job 1:3
e wind carrieth him away .....Job 27:21

ships of Tarshish with an *e* ....Ps 48:7
cometh neither from the *e*.....Ps 75:6
as the *e* is from the west ......Ps 103:12
be replenished from the *e* .....Is 2:6
in the day of the *e* wind ......Is 27:8
bring thy seed from the *e* .....Is 43:5
scatter them as with an *e*.....Jer 18:17
horse gate toward the *e* ....Jer 31:40
their faces toward the *e* ....Ezek 8:16
the sun toward the *e*..........Ezek 8:16
Lord's house..looketh *e* ....Ezek 11:1
mountain which is on the *e*....Ezek11:23
e wind dried up her fruit Ezek19:12
Unto the men of the *e* with ...Ezek25:10
passengers on the *e* of the.....Ezek39:11
cubits *e* and northward........Ezek40:19
gate..looketh toward the *e* Ezek40:22
inner court toward the *e* Ezek40:32
separate place toward the *e* ...Ezek41:14
of the court toward the *e* Ezek42:10
prospect is toward the *e*.......Ezek42:15
that looketh toward the *e* .....Ezek 43:1
prospect is toward the *e*.......Ezek 43:4
which looketh toward the *e*....Ezek 44:1
from the *e* side eastward ......Ezek 45:7
border unto the *e* border......Ezek 45:7
that looketh toward the *e* .....Ezek 46:1
house stood toward the *e* .....Ezek 47:1
line in his hand went forth *e* ..Ezek 47:3
e side ye shall measure........Ezek47:18
the border unto the *e* sea Ezek47:18
And this is the *e* side Ezek47:18
border of Dan, from the *e* ....Ezek 48:2
Naphtali, from the *e* side.....Ezek 48:4
of Ephraim, from the *e* side ...Ezek 48:6
of Judah from the *e* side ......Ezek 48:8
e side unto the west side ......Ezek 48:8
e side four thousand and Ezek48:16
the oblation toward the *e* Ezek48:21
the *e* side unto the west.......Ezek48:24
of Isaachar, from the *e* side ...Ezek48:26
at the *e* side four thousand Ezek48:32
the south, and toward the *e* ...Dan 8:9
followeth after the *e* wind .....Hos 12:1
with his face toward the *e*.....Joel 2:20
from the north even to the *e* ..Amos 8:12
and sat on the *e* side of ....Jon 4:5
faces shall sup up as the *e*.....Hab 1:9
save my people from the *e* ....Zech 8:7
before Jerusalem on the *e*.....Zech 14:4
midst thereof toward the *e* ....Zech 14:4
from the *e* to Jerusalem ......Matt 2:1
have seen his star in the *e*.....Matt 2:2
which they saw in the *e* ....Matt 2:9
lightning cometh out of..*e* .....Matt 24:27
they shall come from the *e* Luke13:29
angel ascending from the *e* ....Rev 7:2
way of the kings of the *e*......Rev 16:12
On the *e* three gates; on ......Rev 21:13

EAST COUNTRY—*southeastern Palestine; Arabia*
Abraham sent family there ....Gen 25:6

EAST GATE—*a gate of Jerusalem*
In Temple area..........Ezek 10:19; Ezek 11:1

EAST WIND—*a scorching desert wind, the sirocco*
Destroys vegetation ......Gen 41:6; Ezek 17:10
Destroys houses ....Job 1:19
Destroys ships...........Ps 48:7; Ezek 27:26
Brings judgment.........Is 27:8; Jer 4:11, 12
Dries springs and fountains ....Hos 13:15
Afflicts Jonah ....Jon 4:8
Called Euroclydon ....Acts 27:14

EASTER—*the Passover*
intending after *E* to bring .....Acts 12:4

EAT—*to consume*
Restrictions on:
Forbidden tree ....Gen 2:16, 17
Blood Acts15:19,20
Unclean things ....Lev 11:1-47; Deut 14:1-29
Excess, condemned ......Eccl10:16,17; Phil 3:19
Anxiety concerning, prohibited ....Matt 6:24-34
Spiritual significance of:
Covenant ....Ex 24:11
Adoption ....Jer 52:33, 34
Fellowship Luke22:15-20
Christian attitude toward:
Tradition rejected ....Mark 7:1-23
Disorderliness condemned.1Cor 11:20-22
Regard for weaker brother ....Rom 14:1-23
No work, no eating......2Thess 3:7-10

[*also* ATE, EATEN, EATEST, EATETH, EATING]
day that thou *e* thereof thou...Gen 2:17
not *e* of every tree of the .....Gen 3:1
and did *e* and gave also ....Gen 3:6
husband with her..he did *e* ....Gen 3:6
thou *e* of the tree whereof I ...Gen 3:11
hast *e* of the tree, of which I ..Gen 3:17
thee of all food that is *e* ......Gen 6:21
I have *e* of all before thou ....Gen 27:33
when they had *e* them ....Gen 41:21
they had *e* up the corn........Gen 43:2
man according to his *e* shall ...Ex 12:4
whosoever *e* leavened bread ...Ex 12:15
shall no leavened bread be *e* ..Ex 13:3
man according to his *e*.........Ex 16:18
and his flesh shall not be *e*....Ex 21:28
not be *e*, because it is holy ....Ex 29:34
unleavened bread shall..be *e*...Lev 6:16
holy place shall it be *e* ....Lev 6:26
shall be *e* in the holy place ....Lev 7:6
it shall be *e* the same day .....Lev 7:16
remainder of it shall be *e* .....Lev 7:16
soul that *e* of it shall bear .....Lev 7:18
unclean thing shall not be *e* ...Lev 7:19
For whosoever *e* the fat of ....Lev 7:25
Whatsoever soul it be that *e*...Lev 7:27
Wherefore have ye not *e* the ..Lev 10:17
if I had *e* the sin offering .....Lev 10:19
and he that *e* in the house ....Lev 14:47
that *e* any manner of blood ...Lev 17:10
against that soul that *e*........Lev 17:10
soul that *e* that which died ....Lev 17:15
e at all on the third day.......Lev 19:7
not *e* anything with the ....Lev 19:26
e up the inhabitants thereof ...Num 13:32
shall unleavened bread be *e* ...Num 28:17
when thou shalt have *e* and ...Deut 6:11
Lest when thou hast *e* and ....Deut 8:12
ye shall not *e* the blood Deut12:16
and hath not yet *e* of it? ....Deut 20:6
have not *e* bread, neither .....Deut 29:6
they had *e* of the old corn .....Josh 5:12
went on *e* and came to his ....Judg 14:9
until he shall have done *e* .....Ruth 3:3
when Boaz had *e* and drunk ...Ruth 3:7
weepest thou?..why *e* thou 1Sam 1:8
rose up after they had *e* in 1Sam 1:9
man that *e* any food until 1Sam14:24
not against the Lord in *e*......1Sam14:34
had *e* no bread all the day 1Sam28:20
when he had *e*, his spirit 1Sam30:12
had *e* no bread, nor drunk 1Sam30:12
we *e* at all of the king's 2Sam19:42
they had made an end of *e*....1Kin 1:41
e bread and drunk water 1Kin 13:22
lion had not *e* the carcase 1Kin 13:28
said unto him, Arise and *e* 1Kin 19:5
sad, that thou *e* no bread? 1Kin 21:5
they were *e* of the pottage 2Kin 4:40
when they had *e* and drunk ...2Kin 6:23
thy son, that we may *e* him ...2Kin 6:28
three days, *e* and drinking.....1Chr 12:39
for them that we may *e* and ...Neh 5:2
my brethren have not *e* the ...Neh 5:14
and his daughters were *e*......Job 1:13
hungry *e* up and taketh it .....Job 5:5
which is unsavoury be *e* ....Job 6:6
rain..upon him while he is *e* ..Job 20:23
Or have *e* my morsel myself...Job 31:17
the fatherless hath not *e* ......Job 31:17
he *e* grass as an ox ....Job 40:15
The meek shall *e* and be ......Ps 22:26
zeal of thine house hath *e*.....Ps 69:9
Man did *e* angel's food he.....Ps 78:25
I have *e* ashes like bread......Ps 102:9
similitude of an ox that *e* .....Ps 106:20
a the sacrifices of..dead ....Ps 106:28
bread *e* in secret is ....Prov 9:17
righteous *e* to the............Prov 13:25
e not the bread of idleness ....Prov 31:27
together and *e* his own........Eccl 4:5
but a stranger *e* it; this is .....Eccl 6:2
I have *e* my honeycomb with ..Song 5:1
shall *e* the good of the land ...Is 1:19
ye have *e* up the vineyard .....Is 3:14
shall return, and shall be *e* ....Is 6:13
killing sheep, *e* flesh, and .....Is 22:13
it is yet in his hand he *e* ......Is 28:4
with part thereof he *e* flesh....Is 44:16
for they have *e* up Jacob .....Jer 10:25
very evil, that cannot be *e* .....Jer 24:3
vile figs that cannot be *e* ......Jer 29:17
every man that *e* the sour .....Jer 31:30
I not *e* of that which dieth ....Ezek 4:14
and hath not *e* upon the ......Ezek 18:6
not *e* upon the mountains Ezek18:15
unleavened bread shall be *e* ...Ezek45:21
I *a* no pleasant bread ....Dan 10:3
they shall *e*, and not have .....Hos 4:10
ye have *e* the fruit of lies .....Hos 10:13
hath left hath the locust *e* .....Joel 1:4
left hath the cankerworm *e*....Joel 1:4
left hath the caterpillar *e*......Joel 1:4
they had made an end of *e*....Amos 7:2
Thou shalt *e*, but not be ......Mic 6:14
e, but ye have not enough ....Hag 1:6
what ye shall *e*, or what ye....Matt 6:25
e your Master with ....Matt 9:11
John came neither *e* nor ......Matt 11:18
they that had *e* were about....Matt 14:21
not their hands when they *e* ...Matt 15:2
to *e* with unwashen hands .....Matt 15:20
e and drinking, marrying ......Matt 24:38
Take *e*, this is my body ....Matt 26:26
as they were *e*, Jesus took ....Matt 26:26
How is it that he *e* and ......Mark 2:16
And they that had *e* were ......Mark 8:9
as they did *e*, Jesus took Mark14:22
Take, *e*, this is my body Mark14:22
the Baptist came neither *e* ....Luke 7:33
e and drinking such...........Luke 10:7
e such things as are set ....Luke 10:8
take thine ease, *e*, drink Luke12:19
We have *e* and drunk in thy...Luke13:26
receiveth sinners, and *e* ....Luke 15:2
thine house hath *e* me up ......John 2:17
Except ye *e* the flesh of.......John 6:53
e my flesh and drinketh ....John 6:54
that *e* me, even he shall.......John 6:57
He that *e* bread with me hath. .John 13:18
hungry and would have *e* .....Acts 10:10
Rise, Peter, kill, and *e*........Acts 10:13
and he was *e* of worms ....Acts 12:23
when they had *e* enough ....Acts 27:38
believeth that he may *e* all ....Rom 14:2
e of those things that are......1Cor 8:4
e not of the fruit thereof? 1Cor 9:7
e not of the milk of the 1Cor 9:7
Whether therefore ye *e*, or 1Cor 10:31
Take, *e*, this is my body 1Cor 11:24
he that *e* and drinketh 1Cor 11:29
e and drinketh damnation 1Cor 11:29
I give to *e*..tree of life ....Rev 2:7
of the angel's hand, and *a*.....Rev 10:10
as soon as I had *e* it ....Rev 10:10

EATER—*consumer of food*

[*also* EATERS]
of the *e* came forth meat......Judg 14:14

among riotous *e* of flesh ......Prov 23:20
sower, and bread to the *e* .....Is 55:10
fall into the mouth of the *e* ...Nah 3:12

EBAL (ē'băl)—*"stone; bare"*
1. Son of Shobal ....Gen 36:23
2. Same as Obal ....Gen 10:28
3. Mountain in Samaria ....Deut 27:12, 13
   Law to be written upon. .Deut 27:1-8
   Fulfilled by Joshua ......Josh 8:30-35

the curse upon mount *E* ......Deut 11:29
And *E* and Abimael, and 1Chr 1:22
and Manahath and *E* 1Chr 1:40

EBED (ē'bĕd)—*"servant"*
1. Gaal's father ....Judg 9:28, 30
2. Son of Jonathan ....Ezra 8:6

Gaal son of *E* came with ......Judg 9:26
Gaal son of *E* and his ....Judg 9:31
Gaal son of *E* went out ....Judg 9:35

EBED-MELECH (ē-bĕd-mē'lĕk)—*"the king's servant"*
Ethiopian eunuch; rescues Jeremiah ....Jer 38:7-13
Promised divine protection ....Jer 39:15-18

EBENEZER (ĕb-ĕn-ē'zer)—*"stone of help"*
Site of Israel's defeat 1Sam 4:1-10
Ark transferred from 1Sam 5:1
Site of memorial stone ...1Sam 7:10,12

EBER, HEBER (ē'ber, hē'ber)—*"the region beyond"*
1. Great-grandson of Shem .Gen 10:21-24
   Progenitor of the:
   Hebrews ....Gen 11:16-26
   Arabians and Arameans .Gen 10:25-30
2. Gadite leader 1Chr 5:13
3. Son of Elpaal...........1Chr 8:12
4. Son of Shashak 1Chr 8:22, 25
5. Postexilic priest ....Neh 12:20

See **Heber**

E were born two sons.........Gen 10:25
thirty years..begat *E* ....Gen 11:14
afflict *E*; he also shall.........Num 24:24
and Shelah began *E* 1Chr 1:18
unto *E* were born two sons....1Chr 1:19
E, Peleg, Reu 1Chr 1:25

EBIASAPH (ĕ-bī'ä-săf)—*"the father has gathered"*
Forefather of Samuel 1Chr 6:23
Same as Abiasaph ....Ex 6:16, 18, 24

son of Assir, the son of *E*.....1Chr 6:37
son of Kore, the son of *E*.....1Chr 9:19

EBONY—*black*
Black, heavy hardwood; article of trade ....Ezek 27:15

EBRONAH (ĕ'brŏn-ăh)—*"passage; opposite"*
Israelite encampment ....Num 33:34

ECCLESIASTES, BOOK OF—*a book of the Old Testament*
Vanity of earthly things . .Eccl 1:2
Material goods ....Eccl 5:10-12

ECLIPSE OF THE SUN
Foretold ....Amos 8:9

ECONOMY—*living thriftily*
The law of..............Prov 11:24
The wrong kind ....Hag 1:6, 9-11
Exemplified by Jesus ....John 6:12

ED—*witness*
The name (not in Heb.) of an altar ....Josh 22:34

EDAR (ē'der)—*"flock"*
1. Watchtower ....Gen 35:21
2. Town in Judah ....Josh 15:21
3. Benjamite 1Chr 8:15
4. Levite..................1Chr 23:23

tent beyond tower of *E* ....Gen 35:21

EDEN (ē'dĕn)—*"delight"*
1. First home ....Gen 2:8-15
   Zion becomes like ......Is 51:3
   Called the "garden of God" ....Ezek 28:13
   Terrible contrast ....Joel 2:3
2. Region in Mesopotamia .Is 37:12
3. Gershonite Levite 2Chr 29:12

from the garden of *E* ....Gen 3:23
east..garden of *E* cherubim ....Gen 3:24
And next him were *E*.........2Chr 31:15
so that all the trees of *E* ......Ezek 31:9
and all the trees of *E* ....Ezek 31:16
among the trees of *E*? ....Ezek 31:18
down with the trees of *E*......Ezek 31:18
become like the garden of *E* . .Ezek 36:35
from the house of *E* ....Amos 1:5

EDER (ē'der)—*"flock"—same as Edar*
were Kabzeel, and *E* ....Josh 15:21
Mahli and *E*, and Jeremoth ...1Chr 23:23
Mahli, and *E*, and Jerimoth ...1Chr 24:30

EDGE—*sharp intersection; boundary*

[*also* EDGES]
with the *e* of the sword ....Gen 34:26
in the *e* of the wilderness .....Ex 13:20
the *e* of the one curtain ....Ex 26:4
uttermost *e* of..curtain ....Ex 26:4
make in the *e* of the curtain ...Ex 26:5
make fifty loops on the *e* .....Ex 26:10
fifty loops in the *e*..curtain ....Ex 26:10
joined at the two *e* thereof ....Ex 28:7
on the *e* of one curtain ....Ex 36:11
uttermost *e* of the curtain .....Ex 36:17
he upon the *e* of the curtain...Ex 36:17
smote him with the *e* ....Num 21:24
in the *e* of the land of Edom . .Num 33:37
city with the *e* of the sword ...Deut 13:15
with the *e* of the sword ....Deut 13:15
with the *e* of the sword ....Deut 20:13
ass, with the *e* of the sword ...Josh 6:21
fallen on the *e* of the sword ...Josh 8:24
smote it with the *e* of sword...Josh 8:24
smote it with the *e* of..sword . .Josh 10:30
them with the *e* of..sword .....Josh 10:39
them with the *e* of..sword .....Josh 11:12
e of the Sea of Chinnereth ....Josh 13:27
smitten it..*e* of the sword .....Judg 1:8
dagger which had two *e* ....Judg 3:16
host, with the *e* of the sword . .Judg 4:15
them with the *e* of..sword .....Judg 18:27
them with the *e* of..sword .....Judg 20:48
people with the *e* of..sword ...1Sam 15:8
smote he with the *e* of..sword. .1Sam 22:19
sheep, with the *e* of..sword....1Sam 22:19
city with the *e* of..sword 2Sam 15:14
them with the *e* of..sword 2Kin 10:25
servants with the *e* of..sword . .Job 1:15
also turned the *e* of..sword ....Ps 89:43
he do not whet the *e* ....Eccl 10:10
them with the *e* of..sword .....Jer 21:7
teeth are set on *e*.............Jer 31:29
his teeth shall be set on *e* .....Jer 31:30
teeth are set on *e*? ....Ezek 18:2
fall by the *e* of the sword .....Luke 21:24
escaped the *e* of the sword ....Heb 11:34
sharp sword with two *e* ....Rev 2:12

EDIFICATION—*building up one's faith*

Objects of:
The church 1Cor 14:4-12
The body of Christ ......Eph 4:12
One another ....Rom 14:19

Accomplished by:
The ministry 2Cor 12:19
Christian gifts 1Cor 14:3-12
Word of God ....Acts 20:32
Love 1Cor 8:1
Spiritual things ....Rom 14:19
Seeking another's goods . .Rom 15:2
God's authority 2Cor 10:8

Hindrances of:
Carnal spirit 1Cor 3:1-4
Foolish questions 1Tim 1:3, 4
Spiritual luke-warmness . .Rev 3:14-22
Worldly spirit ....James 4:1-6

[*also* EDIFIED, EDIFIETH, EDIFY, EDIFYING]
churches rest..and were *e* .....Acts 9:31
for me but all things *e* not 1Cor 10:23
unknown tongue *e* himself.....1Cor 14:4
prophesieth *e* the church 1Cor 14:4
but the other is not *e* 1Cor 14:17
all things be done unto *e*......1Cor 14:26
Lord hath given me to *e* 2Cor 13:10
unto the *e* of itself in love.....Eph 4:16
which is good to..use of *e* .....Eph 4:29
and *e* one another 1Thess 5:11

EDOM (ē'dŭm)—*"red"*
1. Name given to Esau ....Gen 25:30
2. Edomites...............Num 20:18-21
3. Land of Esau; called Seir.Gen 32:3
   Called Edom and Idumea ....Mark 3:8
   Mountainous land ....Jer 49:16, 17
   People of, cursed ....Is 34:5, 6

generations of Esau..is *E*......Gen 36:1
mount Seir; Esau is *E* ....Gen 36:8
Eliphaz in the land of *E* ......Gen 36:16
Reuel in the land of *E*........Gen 36:17
of Seir in the land of *E* ....Gen 36:21
son of Beor reigned in *E*......Gen 36:32
dukes of *E* shall be amazed ...Ex 15:15
Kadesh unto the king of *E* ....Num 20:14
by the coast of the land of *E* . .Num 20:23
E shall be a possession........Num 24:18
Zin along by the coast of *E* ...Num 34:3
border of *E* the wilderness ....Josh 15:1
out of the field of *E* ....Judg 5:4
unto the king of *E*............Judg 11:17
king of *E* would not hearken . .Judg 11:17
he put garrisons in *E* 2Sam 8:14
all *E* put he garrisons 2Sam 8:14
they of *E* became..servants 2Sam 8:14
Red Sea, in the land of *E*.....1Kin 9:26
when David was in *E* 1Kin 11:15
smitten every male in *E*.......1Kin 11:15
was then no king in *E* 1Kin 22:47
through the wilderness of *E* ...2Kin 3:8
king of *E* went down to him...2Kin 3:12
even unto the king of *E*.......2Kin 3:26
E revolted from under 2Kin 8:20
E revolted from under 2Kin 8:22
Thou hast indeed smitten *E* ...2Kin 14:10
reigned in the land of *E*.......1Chr 1:43
These are the dukes of *E* 1Chr 1:54
he put garrisons in *E* 1Chr 18:13
sea side in the land of *E* 2Chr 8:17
smote of *E* in the valley.......Ps 60:*title*
Who will lead me into *E* ......Ps 60:9
over *E* will I cast out my shoe .Ps 108:9
hand upon *E* and Moab ....Is 11:14
this that cometh from *E*.......Is 63:1
Egypt, and Judah, and *E*......Jer 9:26
send them to the king of *E*....Jer 27:3
concerning *E*..saith the Lord . .Jer 49:7
he hath taken against *E* ....Jer 49:20
be glad, O daughter of *E* .....Lam 4:21
E hath dwelt against ....Ezek 25:12
lay my vengeance upon *E* .....Ezek 25:14
do in *E* according to..anger ...Ezek 25:14
out of his hand, even *E* ....Dan 11:41
E shall be a..wilderness ....Joel 3:19
to deliver them up to *E* ....Amos 1:6
three transgressions of *E* .....Amos 1:11
the Lord God concerning *E* ...Obad 1
E..We are impoverished ......Mal 1:4

EDOMITES (ē'dŭm-īts)—*descendants of Esau*

Character of:
Warlike.................Gen 27:40
Idolatrous...............2Chr 25:14,20
Superstitious ....Jer 27:3, 9
Proud ....Jer 49:16
Cruel...................Jer 49:19
Vindictive...............Ezek 25:12

Relations with Israel:
Descendants of Esau.....Gen 36:9

Refused passage to ......Num 20:18-20
Enemies of ....Ezek 35:5, 6
Wars against 1Sam 14:47
Joined enemies of 2Chr 20:10
Aided Babylon against ...Ps 137:7

Prophecies concerning:
Subjection to Israel ......Gen 27:37
Punishment for persecuting Israel ......Is 34:5-8
Utter desolation of ......Is 34:9-17
Figurative of Gentiles ....Amos 9:11,12

[*also* EDOMITE]
Esau the father of the ***E*** ......Gen 36:43
Thou shalt not abhor an ***E*** ....Deut 23:7
his name was Doeg an ***E*** 1Sam 21:7
Doeg the ***E*** turned 1Sam 22:18
E, Zidonians, and Hittites 1Kin 11:1
unto Solomon, Hadad the ***E***...1Kin 11:14
E which compassed him 2Kin 8:21
Zeruiah slew of the ***E***.........1Chr 18:12
his days the ***E*** revolted........2Chr 21:8
E revolted from under 2Chr 21:10
E had come and smitten 2Chr 28:17

EDREI (ĕd′rĕ-ī)—*"fortress"*
1. Capital of Bashan ....Deut 3:10
   Site of Og's defeat ......Num 21:33-35
2. City of Naphtali ....Josh 19:37

dwelt at Astaroth in ***E*** ....Deut 1:4
all his people..battle at ***E*** .....Deut 3:1
dwelt at Ashtaroth and at ***E***...Josh 12:4
and Ashtaroth, and ***E***.........Josh 13:31

EDUCATION—*instruction in knowledge*

Performed by:
Parents ....Eph 6:4
Tutors ....Gal 4:1-3
Teachers 2Chr 17:7-9
Learned men ....Acts 22:3

Method of:
Sharing ....Gal 6:6
Recalling God's works ...Ps 78:1-8
Learning from nature ....Prov 6:6-11
Step by step ....Is 28:10
Asking questions ....Luke 2:46

Examples of:
Moses ....Acts 7:22
Daniel..................Dan 1:17
Paul....................Acts 22:3
Timothy 2Tim 3:15, 16

EFFECT—*a result or consequence*

[*also* EFFECTED, EFFECTUAL, EFFECTUALLY]
make her vow..of none ***e***......Num 30:8
house he prosperously ***e***......2Chr 7:11
they spake to her to that ***e***....2Chr 34:22
devices of..people of none ***e***...Ps 33:10
the ***e*** of righteousness ....Is 32:17
his lies shall not so ***e*** it ....Jer 48:30
hand, and..***e*** of every vision ...Ezek 12:23
of God of none ***e***.............Matt 15:6
the faith of God without ***e***? ...Rom 3:3
the promise made of none ***e***...Rom 4:14
word of God..none ***e*** ....Rom 9:6
Christ..be made of none ***e***.....1Cor 1:17
great door and ***e*** is opened 1Cor 16:9
which is ***e*** in the enduring 2Cor 1:6
he that wrought ***e*** in Peter ....Gal 2:8
make the promise of none ***e***...Gal 3:17
Christ is..of no ***e*** unto ....Gal 5:4
the ***e*** working of his power ....Eph 3:7
e working in the measure of...Eph 4:16

EFFEMINATE—*having feminine qualities inappropriate to a man*
Curse on Egypt ....Is 19:16
The weakness of Nineveh.Nah 3:13
Rebuked by Paul 1Cor 16:13
Shall not inherit the kingdom of God 1Cor 6:9

EFFORT—*energy used to get something done*
Organized ....Neh 4:15-23
Diligence in.............Neh 6:1-4
Inspired to.............Hag 1:12-14

Ill-considered ....Luke 14:28-30
The highest ....Phil 3:11-14

EGG—*reproductive product of a hen*
Prohibition concerning that of birds ....Deut 22:6
Article of food ....Luke 11:12
White of, without taste ..Job 6:6

[*also* EGGS]
leaveth her ***e*** in the earth .....Job 39:14
gathereth ***e*** that are left ....Is 10:14
They hatch cockatrice ***e*** ....Is 59:5
eateth of their ***e*** dieth.........Is 59:5
partridge sitteth on ***e*** ....Jer 17:11

EGLAH (ĕg′lä)—*"calf"*
Wife of David...........2Sam 3:2, 5

by ***E*** his wife 1Chr 3:3

EGLAIM (ĕg′lā-ĭm)—*"pond"*
Moabite town ....Is 15:8

EGLON (ĕg′lŏn)—*"of a calf"*
1. Moabite king ....Judg 3:12-15
2. City of Judah ....Josh 15:39

unto Debir king of ***E*** ....Josh 10:3
of Lachish the king of ***E*** ......Josh 10:23
Joshua went up from ***E*** ....Josh 10:36
king of ***E***, one..king of.........Josh 12:12
brought..present unto ***E***.......Judg 3:17
E was a very fat man ....Judg 3:17

EGOTISM—*a sinful exultation of one's self*
Satan ....Is 14:13-15
Luke 4:5, 6
Goliath 1Sam 17:4-11
Haman ....Esth 6:6-12
Simon ....Acts 8:9-11
Herod ....Acts 12:20-23
Diotrephes 3John 9-10
Sign of antichrist 2Thess 2:4
Sign of the last days 2Tim 3:1-5

EGYPT (ē′jĭpt)—*"land of the soul of Ptah"—the land of the Nile in the northeast corner of Africa*

Israel's contact with:
Abram visits ....Gen 12:10
Joseph sold into ....Gen 37:28,36
Joseph becomes leader in.Gen 39:1-4
Hebrews move to.........Gen 46:5-7
Persecution by ....Ex 1:15-22
Israel leaves ....Ex 12:31-33
Army of, perishes ....Ex 14:26-28

Characteristics of:
Superstitious ....Is 19:3
Unprofitable ....Is 30:1-7
Treacherous ....Is 36:6
Ambitious ....Jer 46:8, 9

Prophecies concerning:
Israel's sojourn in ....Gen 15:13
Destruction of...........Ezek 30:24,25
Ever a lowly kingdom ...Ezek 29:14,15
Conversion of ....Is 19:18-25
Christ, called out of .....Matt 2:15

[*also* EGYPTIAN, EGYPTIAN'S, EGYPTIANS]
when the ***E*** shall see thee .....Gen 12:12
E whose name was Hagar .....Gen 16:1
saw the son of Hagar the ***E*** ...Gen 21:9
Lord blessed the ***E*** house .....Gen 39:5
Pharaoh said unto all the ***E*** ...Gen 41:55
themselves, and for the ***E***.....Gen 43:32
E might not eat bread with .....Gen 43:32
an abomination unto the ***E***....Gen 43:32
brother, whom ye sold into ***E*** .Gen 45:4
an abomination unto the ***E***....Gen 46:34
E sold every man his field.....Gen 47:20
grievous mourning to the ***E*** ...Gen 50:11
E made the children of Israel..Ex 1:13
E smiting an Hebrew ....Ex 2:11
slew the ***E***, and hid him in ....Ex 2:12
E oppress them ....Ex 3:9
children of Israel out of ***E***.....Ex 3:10
favor..sight of the ***E*** ....Ex 3:21
ye shall spoil the ***E*** ....Ex 3:22
under the burdens of the ***E***....Ex 6:6

E shall know that I am ....Ex 7:5
E could not drink of ....Ex 7:21
houses of..***E*** shall be full ......Ex 8:21
of the ***E*** to the Lord...........Ex 8:26
abomination of the ***E*** before...Ex 8:26
the houses of all the ***E***........Ex 10:6
difference between the ***E***......Ex 11:7
when he smote the ***E*** ....Ex 12:27
people favor..sight of the ***E*** ...Ex 12:36
they spoiled the ***E*** ....Ex 12:36
which ye came out from ***E*** ....Ex 13:3
E pursued after them ....Ex 14:9
that we may serve the ***E***? .....Ex 14:12
better for us to serve the ***E*** ...Ex 14:12
I will harden the hearts of..***E***..Ex 14:17
between the camp of..***E***.......Ex 14:20
looked unto the host of the ***E*** .Ex 14:24
troubled the host of the ***E***.....Ex 14:24
E said, Let us flee from ....Ex 14:25
out of the hand of the ***E*** ....Ex 14:30
I have brought upon the ***E*** ....Ex 15:26
to the ***E*** for Israel's sake ......Ex 18:8
out of..hand of the ***E*** ....Ex 18:10
from under the hand of the ***E*** .Ex 18:10
Wherefore should the ***E*** speak .Ex 32:12
whose father was an ***E*** ....Lev 24:10
Then the ***E*** shall hear it.......Num 14:13
people come out from ***E*** ......Num 22:5
hand in the sight of all..***E*** .....Num 33:3
shalt not abhor an ***E***..........Deut 23:7
E evil entreated..afflicted .....Deut 26:6
E pursued after your fathers ..Josh 24:6
out of the hand of the ***E*** ......Judg 6:9
are the Gods that smote the ***E*** .1Sam 4:8
E, and out of the hand of all ..1Sam 10:18
they found an ***E*** in the field ...1Sam 30:11
he slew an ***E***, a goodly man ...2Sam 23:21
the ***E*** had a spear in his hand .2Sam 23:21
plucked the spear out of the ***E*** .2Sam 23:21
Hittites..kings of the ***E***........2Kin 7:6
Sheshan had a servant, an ***E*** ..1Chr 2:34
E hand was a spear 1Chr 11:23
of the ***E*** hand and slew him ...1Chr 11:23
the Moabites, the ***E*** ....Ezra 9:1
hast brought a vine out of ***E*** ..Ps 80:8
the tongue of the ***E*** sea ....Is 11:15
burden of ***E***, Behold..Lord ....Is 19:1
will set the ***E*** against the ***E***....Is 19:2
E will I give over into the .....Is 19:4
lead away..***E*** prisoners ....Is 20:4
E are men, and not God ......Is 31:3
gods of the ***E*** shall he burn ....Jer 43:13
E..like a very fair heifer ....Jer 46:20
to the ***E***, and to the Assyrians .Lam 5:6
committed fornication..***E*** ......Ezek 16:26
committed whoredoms in ***E*** ...Ezek 23:3
scatter the ***E*** among ....Ezek 29:12
scatter the ***E*** among ....Ezek 30:23
flee into ***E*** and be thou there ..Matt 2:13
in all the wisdom of the ***E*** ....Acts 7:22
oppressed and smote the ***E***....Acts 7:24
he forsook ***E***, not fearing .....Heb 11:27
E assaying to do..drowned ....Heb 11:29

EGYPTIAN, THE—*an unknown insurrectionist*
Paul mistaken for........Acts 21:37, 38

EHI (ē′hī)—*"exalted brother; my brother is exalted"*
Benjamin's son ....Gen 46:21
Same as Ahiram.........Num 26:38
See AHARAH

EHUD (ē′hŭd)—*"strong"*
1. Great-grandson of Benjamin 1Chr 7:10
2. Son of Gera ....Judg 3:15
   Slays Eglon.............Judg 3:16-26

when ***E*** was dead ....Judg 4:1
these are the sons of ***E*** 1Chr 8:6

EIGHT

[*also* EIGHTH]
Seth were ***e*** hundred years ....Gen 5:4
e hundred and fifteen years ...Gen 5:10

Jared *e* hundred and thirty ....Gen 5:16
begat Enoch *e* hundred years ..Gen 5:19
son Isaac being *e* days old.....Gen 21:4
e day thou shalt give it me ....Ex 22:30
shall be *e* and twenty cubits ...Ex 26:2
curtain was twenty..*e* cubits ...Ex 36:9
it came to pass on the *e* day...Lev 9:1
e day he shall take two he ....Lev 14:10
e day he shall take..two ....Lev 15:14
the *e* day and thenceforth .....Lev 22:27
the *e* day shall be a sabbath ...Lev 23:39
e thousand and an hundred....Num 2:24
e thousand and five hundred ..Num 4:48
e day he shall bring two.......Num 6:10
on the sixth day *e* bullocks ....Num 29:29
on the *e* day ye shall have a...Num 29:35
Zered was thirty and *e* years ..Deut 2:14
forty and *e* cities with their....Josh 21:41
Chushan-rishathaim *e* years....Judg 3:8
was ninety and *e* years 1Sam 4:15
e hundred whom he slew......2Sam 23:8
Bul which is the *e* month 1Kin 6:38
ten cubits, stones of *e* cubits...1Kin 7:10
ordained a feast in the *e* 1Kin 12:32
in the thirty and *e* year of Asa .1Kin 16:29
reigned *e* years in Jerusalem...2Kin 8:17
thirty and *e* year of Azariah ...2Kin 15:8
Josiah was *e* years old when...2Kin 22:1
Johanan the *e*, Elzabad the....1Chr 12:12
six thousand and *e* hundred ...1Chr 12:24
e thousand and six hundred ...1Chr 12:35
was thirty and *e* thousand 1Chr 23:3
hundred fourscore and *e* 1Chr 25:7
e to Jeshaiah he his sons 1Chr 25:15
e captain for the *e* month 1Chr 27:11
e day they made a solemn.....2Chr 7:9
begat twenty and *e* sons.......2Chr 11:21
e years in Jerusalem 2Chr 21:5
house of the Lord in *e* days ...2Chr 29:17
Josiah was *e* years old when...2Chr 34:1
in..*e* year of his reign 2Chr 34:3
e hundred and twelve ....Ezra 2:6
a hundred twenty and *e* ....Ezra 2:23
him twenty and *e* males ....Ezra 8:11
and *e* hundred and eighteen ...Neh 7:11
six hundred forty and *e* ....Neh 7:15
of Hezekiah, ninety and *e*.....Neh 7:21
a hundred fourscore and *e* ....Neh 7:26
a hundred forty and *e*.........Neh 7:44
e day was a solemn assembly ..Neh 8:18
threescore and *e* valiant men ..Neh 11:6
e hundred twenty and two.....Neh 11:12
to seven and also to *e* ....Eccl 11:2
Jerusalem *e* hundred thirty ....Jer 52:29
porch of the gate, *e* cubits ....Ezek 40:9
e tables whereupon they slew ..Ezek 40:41
the *e* day, and so forward .....Ezek 43:27
shepherds, and *e*..men ....Mic 5:5
the *e* month, in the second ....Zech 1:1
e day..came to circumcise .....Luke 1:59
e days were accomplished .....Luke 2:21
infirmity thirty and *e* years ....John 5:5
circumcised him the *e* day .....Acts 7:8
had kept his bed *e* years ......Acts 9:33
Circumcised the *e* day ....Phil 3:5
e souls were saved by water ...1Pet 3:20
but saved Noah the *e* person ..2Pet 2:5
and is not, even he is the *e* ...Rev 17:11

EIGHTEEN

[*also* EIGHTEENTH]
house, three hundred and *e* ...Gen 14:14
the king of Moab *e* years .....Judg 3:14
Israel again *e* thousand........Judg 20:25
salt, being *e* thousand men 2Sam 8:13
brass, *e* cubits high apiece 1Kin 7:15
the *e* year of king Jeroboam ...1Kin 15:1
Israel in Samaria the *e* year ...2Kin 3:1
in the *e* year of king Josiah ...2Kin 23:23
Jehoiachin was *e* years old 2Kin 24:8
tribe of Manasseh *e* thousand ..1Chr 12:31
to Hezir the *e* Aphses 1Chr 24:15
and brethren, strong men, *e* ...1Chr 26:9
for he took *e* wives 2Chr 11:21
the *e* year of king Jeroboam ...2Chr 13:1
e year of the reign of Josiah ...2Chr 35:19
him two hundred and *e* males .Ezra 8:9
eight hundred and *e* ....Neh 7:11
the *e* year of Nebuchadrezzar ..Jer 32:1
of one pillar was *e* cubits ......Jer 52:21
about *e* thousand measures ....Ezek 48:35
or those *e*, upon whom ....Luke 13:4
lo, these *e* years, be ....Luke 13:16

EIGHTY

[*also* EIGHTIETH]
hundred *e* and seven years ....Gen 5:25
four hundred and *e* year 1Kin 6:1

EITHER—*one or the other; each*
not to Jacob *e* good or bad....Gen 31:24
took *e* of them his censer .....Lev 10:1
the garment, *e* in the warp ....Lev 13:51
garment, *e* warp, or woof .....Lev 13:58
E a bullock or a lamb ....Lev 22:23
e man or woman..separate ....Num 6:2
e good or bad of mine own ...Num 24:13
e the sun, or moon, or any of .Deut 17:3
e that all..sons of Jerubbaal ...Judg 9:2
do nothing *e* great or small....1Sam 20:2
not any *e* great or small.......1Sam 30:2
did compass *e* of them about ..1Kin 7:15
e he is talking, or he is 1Kin 18:27
E three years' famine or 1Chr 21:12
king of Judah sat *e* of them ...2Chr 18:9
knoweth *e* love or hatred .....Eccl 9:1
ask it *e* in the depth, or in ....Is 7:11
way or other, *e* on the right ...Ezek 21:16
e he will hate the one.........Matt 6:24
E how canst thou say to thy ...Luke 6:42
masters for *e* he will hate .....Luke 16:13
on *e* side one and Jesus in ....John 19:18
e to tell, or to hear some .....Acts 17:21
to you *e* by revelation 1Cor 14:6
e were already perfect ....Phil 3:12
olive berries? *e* a vine, figs? ...James 3:12
and on *e* side of the river .....Rev 22:2

EKER (ē'ker)—*"root"*
Descendant of Judah 1Chr 2:27

EKRON (ĕk'rŏn)—*"migration"*
Philistine city ....Josh 13:3
Captured by Judah ......Judg 1:18
Assigned to Dan ....Josh 19:43
Ark sent to 1Sam 5:10
Denounced by the prophets ....Jer 25:9, 20

[*also* EKRONITES]
Gittites and the *E* ....Jos 13:3
the side of *E* northward ....Jos 15:11
E even unto the sea, all.......Josh 15:46
E cried out, saying, then 1Sam 5:10
seen it, they returned to *E* 1Sam 6:16
Israel, from *E*..unto Gath 1Sam 7:14
valley and, to the gates of *E* ..1Sam 17:52
unto Gath, and unto *E*.........1Sam 17:52
Baal-zebub the god of *E* 2Kin 1:2
Baal-zebub the god of *E* 2Kin 1:16
will turn mine hand against *E* .Amos 1:8
and *E* shall be rooted up......Zeph 2:4
E for her expectation shall ....Zech 9:5
Judah, and *E* as a Jebusite ....Zech 9:7

EL—*ancient word for God; often used as a part of Hebrew names*
El-beth-el ....Gen 35:6, 7

ELADAH (ĕl'ä-dä)—*"God is ornament"*
A descendant of Ephraim.1Chr 7:20

ELAH (ē'lä)—*"oak"*
1. Duke of Edom ....Gen 36:41
2. Son of Caleb 1Chr 4:15
3. Benjamite 1Chr 9:8
4. King of Israel 1Kin 16:6, 8-10
5. Father of Hoshea 2Kin 15:30
6. Valley of 1Sam 17:2, 19
7. Father of Shimei 1Kin 4:18

in the valley of *E*, fighting 1Sam 17:19
slewest in the valley of *E* 1Sam 21:9
Baasha, and the sins of *E* 1Kin 16:13
the rest of the acts of *E*.......1Kin 16:14
began Hosea the son of *E*.....2Kin 17:1
year of Hoshea son of *E* 2Kin 18:1
year of Hoshea son of *E* 2Kin 18:9
Duke Aholibamah, duke *E* 1Chr 1:52
the sons of *E*, even Kenaz 1Chr 4:15

ELAM (ē'lăm)—*a personification of the empire of south Iran; the Elamites*
1. Son of Shem ....Gen 10:22
2. Benjamite 1Chr 8:24
3. Korahite Levite 1Chr 26:1, 3
4. Head of postexilic families ....Ezra 2:7
5. Another family head ....Ezra 2:31
6. One who signs covenant .Neh 10:1, 14
7. Priest ....Neh 12:42

Chedorlaomer the king of *E*...Gen 14:9
sons of Shem; *E* and Asshur ..1Chr 1:17
of the sons of *E*; Jeshaiah .....Ezra 8:7
Jehiel one of the sons of *E*....Ezra 10:2
sons of *E*; Mattaniah ....Ezra 10:26
children of *E* a thousand ......Neh 7:12
the children of the other *E* ....Neh 7:34
from Cush, and from *E* ....Is 11:11
E bare..quiver with chariots ...Is 22:6
and all the kings of *E*.........Jer 25:25
E and all her multitude round .Ezek 32:24
which is in the province of *E* ..Dan 8:2

ELAMITES (ē'lăm-īts)—*descendants of Elam*
A Semite (Shem) people .Gen 10:22
An ancient nation ....Gen 14:1
Connected with Media ...Is 21:2
Destruction of..........Jer 49:34-39
In Persian empire ....Ezra 4:9
Jews from, at Pentecost ..Acts 2:9

ELASAH (ĕl'ä-sä)—*"God is doer"*
1. Shaphan's son ....Jer 29:3
2. Son of Pashur ....Ezra 10:22

ELATH, ELOTH (ē'lăth, ē'lŏth)—*"terebinth tree"*
Seaport on Red Sea 1Kin 9:26
Edomite dukedom ....Gen 31:41
Conquered by David.....2Sam 8:14
Built by Azariah 2Kin 14:21, 22
Captured by Syrians 2Kin 16:6

[*also* ELOTH]
the way of the plain from *E* ...Deut 2:8
Ezion-geber..beside *E*.........1Kin 9:26
E, at the seaside in the land...2Chr 8:17
He built *E* and restored it.....2Chr 26:2

EL-BETHEL (ĕl-bĕth'ĕl)—*"God of Bethel"*
Site of Jacob's altar......Gen 35:6, 7

ELDAAH (ĕl-dā'ä)—*"God has called"*
Son of Midian...........Gen 25:4

Henoch, and Abida, and *E*....1Chr 1:33

ELDAD (ĕl'dăd)—*"God is a friend"*
Elder of Moses..........Num 11:26-29

ELDER—*older*
brother of Japheth the *e* ......Gen 10:21
Abraham said unto..*e* servant..Gen 24:2
e shall serve the younger ......Gen 25:23
goodly raiment of her *e* son ...Gen 27:15
words of Esau her *e* son ......Gen 27:42
Pharaoh the *e* of his house ....Gen 50:7
the *e* of the land of Egypt.....Gen 50:7
Reuben Israel's *e* son ....Num 1:20
the three *e* sons of Jesse 1Sam 17:13
Eliab his *e* brother heard......1Sam 17:28
Behold my *e* daughter Merab ..1Sam 18:17
for he is mine *e* brother.......1Kin 2:22
then he took his *e* son that 2Kin 3:27
and the *e* sat with him 2Kin 6:32
wine in their *e* brother's ......Job 1:13
because they were *e* than he...Job 32:4
thine *e* sister is Samaria ....Ezek 16:46
Now his *e* son was in..field ....Luke 15:25
e shall serve the younger ......Rom 9:12
e women as mothers 1Tim 5:2

ELDERLY—*older people*
Contributions of:
Counsel 1Kin 12:6-16
Job 12:12
Spiritual service ....Luke 2:36-38
Fruitfulness ....Ps 92:13, 14
Leadership ....Josh 24:2, 14, 15, 29
Attitude toward:
Minister to needs 1Kin 1:15
Respect ....Ps 71:18, 19
As cared for by God ....Is 46:4
Honor ....Lev 19:32
Prov 16:31

ELDERS IN THE CHURCH
Qualifications of, stated by:
Paul ....Titus 1:5-14
Peter 1Pet 5:1-4
Duties of:
Administer relief ....Acts 11:29, 30
Correct error ....Acts 15:4, 6, 23
Hold fast the faithful Word ....Titus 1:5, 9
Rule well 1Tim 5:17
Minister to the sick ......James 5:14, 15
Honors bestowed on:
Ordination ....Acts 14:19, 23
Obedience ....Heb 13:7, 17
Due respect 1Tim 5:1, 19
See BISHOP

ordained..*e* in every church ....Acts 14:23
unto the apostles and *e* ....Acts 15:2
pleased it..apostles and *e* ......Acts 15:22
ordained of..apostles and *e* ....Acts 16:4
called the *e* of the church .....Acts 20:17
all the *e* were present ....Acts 21:18
e that rule well be counted 1Tim 5:17
by it the *e* obtained a good ....Heb 11:2
e unto the elect lady 2John 1
e unto the well beloved 3John 1
saw four and twenty *e* ....Rev 4:4
one of the *e* saith unto me ....Rev 5:5
four and twenty *e* fell ....Rev 5:8
four and twenty *e* fell ....Rev 5:14
and one of the *e* answered ....Rev 7:13
four beasts, and the *e* ....Rev 14:3

ELDERS OF ISRAEL
Functions of, in Mosaic period:
Rule the people ....Judg 2:7
Represent the nation ....Ex 3:16, 18
Share in national guilt ...Josh 7:6
Assist in government ....Num 11:16-25
Perform religious acts ....Ex 12:21, 22
Functions of, in later periods:
Choose a king 2Sam 3:17-21
Ratify a covenant 2Sam 5:3
Assist at a dedication 1Kin 8:1-3
Counsel kings 1Kin 12:6-8, 13
Legislate reforms ....Ezra 10:8-14
Try civil cases ....Matt 26:3-68

gathered together all the *e* ....Ex 4:29
take with thee..*e* of Israel .....Ex 17:5
did so in the sight of the *e* ....Ex 17:6
Aaron came and all the *e* of ...Ex 18:12
called for the *e* of the people ..Ex 19:7
seventy of the *e* of Israel ......Ex 24:1
seventy of the *e* of Israel ......Ex 24:9
he said unto the *e*, Tarry ye ...Ex 24:14
e of the congregation shall ....Lev 4:15
his sons and the *e* of Israel ....Lev 9:1
camp, he and the *e* of Israel ...Num 11:30
e of Israel followed him ....Num 16:25
said unto the *e* of Midian .....Num 22:4
and the *e* of Moab and the ....Num 22:7
and the *e* of Midian departed ..Num 22:7
of your tribes, and your *e* .....Deut 5:23
e and thy judges shall come ...Deut 21:2
e of that city shall bring ....Deut 21:4
out unto the *e* of his city ......Deut 21:19
virginity unto..*e* of the city ....Deut 22:15
cloth before the *e* of..city .....Deut 22:17
in the presence of the *e* ....Deut 25:9
the *e* of Israel commanded ....Deut 27:1
your *e*, and your officers ......Deut 29:10
unto all the *e* of Israel ....Deut 31:9
Gather unto me all the *e* ......Deut 31:28
thy *e* and they will tell thee ...Deut 32:7
he and the *e* of Israel, before ..Josh 8:10
Israel and their *e* and ....Josh 8:33
our *e* and all the inhabitants ...Josh 9:11
their *e* and for their heads ....Josh 23:2
days of the *e* that overlived ...Josh 24:31
e thereof, even three score ....Judg 8:14
e of Gilead went to fetch .....Judg 11:5
e of Gilead..unto Jephthah ....Judg 11:8
e of Gilead..unto Jephthah ....Judg 11:10
e of the congregation said .....Judg 21:16
took ten men of the *e* ....Ruth 4:2
Boaz said unto..*e* ....Ruth 4:9
e of Israel said, Wherefore 1Sam 4:3
e of Jabesh said unto him 1Sam 11:3
the *e* of the town trembled 1Sam 16:4
the *e* of his house arose 2Sam 12:17
Absalom and the *e* of Israel ...2Sam 17:15
king of Israel called all the *e* ..1Kin 20:7
sent the letters unto the *e* 1Kin 21:8
rulers of Jezreel, to the *e* 2Kin 10:1
the *e* of the priests, covered ...2Kin 19:2
came all the *e* of Israel 1Chr 11:3
David and the *e* of Israel 1Chr 21:16
Solomon assembled the *e* 2Chr 5:2
of men..had slain all the *e* 2Chr 22:1
gathered together all the *e* 2Chr 34:29
of their God was upon the *e* ..Ezra 5:5
e of the Jews build this ....Ezra 6:7
the *e* of the Jews builded .....Ezra 6:14
with them the *e* of every city ..Ezra 10:14
in the assembly of the *e* ....Ps 107:32
when he sitteth among the *e* ...Prov 31:23
e of the priests covered ....Is 37:2
rose up certain of the *e* ....Jer 26:17
priests and mine *e* gave up ....Lam 1:19
they favored not the *e* ....Lam 4:16
e have ceased from the gate ...Lam 5:14
e of Judah sat before me ......Ezek 8:1
certain of the *e* of Israel ......Ezek 20:1
of them were Aholah the *e* ....Ezek 23:4
assembly gather the *e* and all ..Joel 1:14
transgress..tradition of the *e*? ..Matt 15:2
suffer many things of the *e* ....Matt 16:21
e of the people came unto ....Matt 21:23
the chief priests, and *e* ....Matt 26:59
to the chief priests and *e* ......Matt 27:3
chief priests..*e* persuaded ......Matt 27:20
were assembled with the *e* ....Matt 28:12
holding the tradition of the *e* ..Mark 7:3
to the tradition of the *e* ....Mark 7:5
and be rejected of the *e* ....Mark 8:31
and the scribes and the *e* ......Mark 11:27
priests and the scribes and..*e* ..Mark 14:43
with the *e* and scribes ....Mark 15:1
unto him the *e* of the Jews ....Luke 7:3
be rejected of the *e* and ....Luke 9:22
came upon him with the *e* .....Luke 20:1
e of the people and the chief ..Luke 22:66
beginning at the *e*, even unto. .John 8:9
that their rulers, and *e* ....Acts 4:5
the people, and the *e* ....Acts 6:12
to the chief priests and *e* ......Acts 23:14
chief priests and the *e* of .....Acts 25:15

ELEAD (ĕl'ĕ-ăd)—*"God is witness"*
Ephraimite 1Chr 7:21

ELEALEH (ē-lĕ-ā'lĕ)—*"God has ascended"*
Moabite town ....Is 15:1, 4
Rebuilt by Reubenites ...Num 32:37

Heshbon, and *E*..Shebam .....Num 32:3
my tears..Heshbon, and *E* .....Is 16:9
cry of Heshbon even unto *E* ...Jer 48:34

ELEASAH (ĕl-ĕ-ā'sä)—*"God has made"*
1. Descendant of Judah 1Chr 2:2-39
2. Descendant of Saul 1Chr 8:33-37

Helez, and Helez begat *E* 1Chr 2:39
E begat Sisamai..Sisamai 1Chr 2:40
Rapha was his son, *E* 1Chr 8:37
Rephaiah his son, *E* 1Chr 9:43

ELEAZAR (ĕl-ĕ-ā'zer)—*"God is helper"*
1. Son of Aaron ....Ex 6:23
Father of Phinehas ......Ex 6:25
Consecrated a priest ....Ex 28:1
Ministers in priest's position ....Lev 10:6, 7
Made chief Levite ....Num 3:32
Succeeds Aaron ....Num 20:25-28
Aids Joshua ....Josh 14:1
Buried at Ephraim ......Josh 24:33
2. Merarite Levite 1Chr 23:21, 22
3. Son of Abinadab; custodian of the ark ...1Sam 7:1
4. One of David's mighty men 2Sam 23:9
5. Priest ....Ezra 8:33
6. Son of Parosh ....Ezra 10:25
7. Musician priest ....Neh 12:27-42
8. Ancestor of Jesus ....Matt 1:15

unto Aaron, and unto *E* ......Lev 10:12
the firstborn and Abihu, *E* ....Num 3:2
office of *E* the son of Aaron ..Num 4:16
E the priest took the brazen ...Num 16:39
E the priest shall take of her ..Num 19:4
when Phinehas the son of *E* ...Num 25:7
spake unto Moses and unto *E*. .Num 26:1
born Nadab, and Abihu, *E* ....Num 26:60
before Moses, and before *E* ...Num 27:2
stand before *E* the priest ......Num 27:21
Phinehas the son of *E* ....Num 31:6
Moses, and *E* the priest ....Num 31:13
thou, and *E* the priest ....Num 31:26
Moses and *E* the priest did ....Num 31:31
Moses and *E* the priest took ...Num 31:51
commanded *E* the priest ......Num 32:28
E his son ministered in the ....Deut 10:6
are the inheritances, which *E* ..Josh 19:51
fathers of the Levites unto *E* ..Josh 21:1
son of *E* the son of Aaron ....Judg 20:28
Aaron; Nadab and Abihu, *E* ..1Chr 6:3
are the sons of Aaron, *E* 1Chr 6:50
him was *E* the son of Dodo ...1Chr 11:12
E died and had no sons 1Chr 23:22
E and Ithamar executed 1Chr 24:2
men found of the sons of *E* ...1Chr 24:4
the sons of *E* there were 1Chr 24:4
household being taken for *E* ...1Chr 24:6
son of *E* the son of Aaron ....Ezra 7:5

ELECTION—*doctrine concerning God's choice of individuals to be redeemed*
Descriptive of:
The Messiah ....Is 42:1
Israel ....Is 45:4
Good angels 1Tim 5:21
Christians ....Matt 24:22, 31
Christian ministers ....Acts 9:15
Lady or church 2John 1, 13
Characteristics of:
Eternal ....Eph 1:4
Personal ....Acts 9:15
Sovereign ....Rom 9:11-16
Unmerited ....Rom 9:11
God's foreknowledge 2Pet 1:3, 4
Of grace ....Rom 11:5, 6
Through faith 2Thess 2:13
Recorded in heaven .....Luke 10:20
Knowable 1Thess 1:4
Of high esteem 2Tim 2:4
Results in:
Adoption ....Eph 1:5
Salvation 2Thess 2:13
Conformity to Christ .....Rom 8:29
Good works ....Eph 2:10
Eternal glory ....Rom 9:23
Inheritance 1Pet 1:2, 4, 5
Proof of:
Faith 2Pet 1:10
Holiness ....Eph 1:4, 5
Divine protection ....Mark 13:20
Manifest it in life ....Col 3:12

[*also* ELECT, ELECTED, ELECT'S,]
mine *e* shall inherit ....Is 65:9
e shall long enjoy the work....Is 65:22
e sake those days shall be .....Matt 24:22
they shall deceive the very *e*...Matt 24:24
for the *e* sake, whom he hath. .Mark 13:20
if it were possible, even the *e*. .Mark 13:22
shall gather together his *e* .....Mark 13:27
shall not God avenge..own *e* . .Luke 18:7
thing to the charge of God's *e*?.Rom 8:33
e hath obtained it, and........Rom 11:7
as touching the *e* they are .....Rom 11:28
endure all things for the *e* 2Tim 2:10
to the faith of God's *e* ....Titus 1:1
E..to the foreknowledge 1Pet 1:2
e..with you, saluteth you 1Pet 5:13

EL-ELOHE-ISRAEL (ĕl-ĕl'ō-hē-ĭz'rĭ-ĕl)—*"God, the God of Israel"*
Name of Jacob's altar....Gen 33:20

ELEMENTS—*basic parts of anything*
Used literally of:
Basic forces of nature....2Pet 3:10, 12
Used figuratively of:
"Rudiments" of religion. .Gal 4:3, 9
"Rudiments" of tradition .Col 2:8, 20
"First principles" of religion ....Heb 5:12

ELEPH (ĕ'lĕph)—*"ox"*
Town of Benjamin ......Josh 18:28

ELEVEN

[*also* ELEVENTH]
took..his *e* sons and passed....Gen 32:22
e curtains shalt thou make ....Ex 26:7
e curtains he made them ......Ex 36:14
e day Pagiel..offered ....Num 7:72
on the third day *e* bullocks ....Num 29:20
e days journey from Horeb....Deut 1:2
in the fortieth year, in the *e*...Deut 1:3
e cities with their villages .....Josh 15:51
one of us *e* hundred pieces ....Judg 16:5
the *e* hundred shekels.........Judg 17:3
in the *e* year, in the month....1Kin 6:38
in the *e* year of Joram 2Kin 9:29
and he reigned *e* years 2Kin 23:36
the tenth, Machbanai the *e*.....1Chr 12:13
e to Azareel, he, his sons 1Chr 25:18
and he reigned *e* years 2Chr 36:5
of the *e* year of Zedekiah .....Jer 1:3
e years in Jerusalem ....Jer 52:1
was besieged unto the *e* year . .Jer 52:5
e year, in the first day ....Ezek 26:1
e year, in the third month .....Ezek 31:1
and the breadth *e* cubits ......Ezek 40:49
twentieth day of..*e* month .....Zech 1:7
about the *e* hour he went out. .Matt 20:6
hired about the *e* hour ....Matt 20:9
appeared unto the *e* as they ...Mark 16:14
numbered with the *e* apostles . .Acts 1:26
e, a jacinth; the twelfth ....Rev 21:20

ELEVEN, THE—*the disciples without Judas*
Were told of resurrection .Luke 24:9, 33
Met Jesus..............Matt 28:16
At Pentecost ....Acts 2:1, 14

ELHANAN (ĕl-hā'năn)—*"whom God gave; God is gracious"*
1. Son of Dodo 2Sam 23:24
 Brave man 1Chr 11:26
2. Son of Jair 1Chr 20:5
 Slays a giant...........2Sam 21:19

ELI (ē'lī)—*"my God"*
Jesus' cry on the cross ...Matt 27:46
Same as "Eloi" ....Mark 15:34

ELI (ē'lī)—*"Jehovah is high"*
Officiates in Shiloh 1Sam 1:3
Blesses Hannah 1Sam 1:12-19
Becomes Samuel's guardian 1Sam 1:20-28
Samuel ministers before . .1Sam 2:11
Sons of 1Sam 2:12-17
Rebukes sons 1Sam 2:22-25
Rebuked by a man of God..................1Sam 2:27-36
Instructs Samuel.........1Sam 3:1-18
Death of...............1Sam 4:15-18

sons of *E*, Hophni and 1Sam 1:3
now *E* the priest sat upon 1Sam 1:9
that *E* marked her mouth 1Sam 1:12
E thought she had been 1Sam 1:13
And *E* said unto her How.....1Sam 1:14
E answered and said Go 1Sam 1:17
and brought the child to *E* 1Sam 1:25
unto the Lord before *E* 1Sam 2:11
sons of *E* were sons 1Sam 2:12
and *E* blessed Elkanah 1Sam 2:20
E was very old, and heard 1Sam 2:22
a man of God unto *E*.........1Sam 2:27
unto the Lord before *E* 1Sam 3:1
when *E* was laid down in his . .1Sam 3:2
ran unto *E* and said, Here 1Sam 3:5
Samuel arose and went to *E*...1Sam 3:6
he arose and went to *E* 1Sam 3:8
E perceived that the Lord 1Sam 3:8
E said unto Samuel Go 1Sam 3:9
I will perform against *E*.......1Sam 3:12
sworn unto the house of *E* 1Sam 3:14
Samuel feared to show *E*......1Sam 3:15
Then *E* called Samuel.........1Sam 3:16
sons of *E*, Hophni 1Sam 4:4
E, Hophni and Phinehas 1Sam 4:11
E sat upon a seat............1Sam 4:13
E heard the noise 1Sam 4:14
came in hastily, and told *E*....1Sam 4:14
son of Phinehas the son of *E* . .1Sam 14:3
concerning the house of *E*.....1Kin 2:27

ELIAB (ĕ-lī'lăb)—*"God is father"*
1. Son of Helon ....Num 1:9
 Leader of Zebulun ......Num 7:24, 29
2. Father of Dathan and Abiram ....Num 16:1, 12
3. Ancestor of Samuel 1Chr 6:27, 28
 See ELIHU 1
4. Brother of David 1Sam 16:5-13
 Fights in Saul's army 1Sam 17:13
 Discounts David's worth .1Sam 17:28, 29
5. Gadite warrior 1Chr 12:1-9
6. Levite musician 1Chr 15:12-20

[*also* ELIAB'S]
E the son of Helon..captain ...Num 2:7
children of Zebulun was *E* ....Num 10:16
sons of Pallu; *E* ....Num 26:8
sons of *E*; Nemuel...........Num 26:9
sons of *E*..son of Reuben .....Deut 11:6
he looked on *E* and said 1Sam 16:6
E anger was kindled 1Sam 17:28
Jesse begat his firstborn *E*.....1Chr 2:13
Unni and *E*, and Masseiah 1Chr 15:20
Mattithiah..*E*, and Benaiah....1Chr 16:5
Abihail the daughter of *E* 2Chr 11:18

ELIADA (ĕ-lī'ä-dä)—*"God is knowing"*
1. Son of David 2Sam 5:16
 Also called Beeliada 1Chr 14:7
2. Father of Rezon 1Kin 11:23
3. Benjamite warrior.......2Chr 17:17

E, and Eliphelet, nine 1Chr 3:8

ELIAH (ĕ-lī'ä)—*"Jehovah is my God"*
1. Son of Jeroham 1Chr 8:27
2. Son of Elam ....Ezra 10:26

ELIAHBA (ĕ-lī'ä-bä)—*"God conceals"*
One of David's mighty men.................2Sam 23:32

E the Shaalbonite of the sons. .2Sam 23:32
the Baharumite, *E* the 1Chr 11:33

ELIAKIM (ē-lī'ă-kĭm)—*"God will establish"*
1. Son of Hilkiah 2Kin 18:18
 Confers with Rabshakeh .Is 36:3, 11-22
 Sent to Isaiah ....Is 37:2-5
 Becomes type of the Messiah ....Is 22:20-25
2. Son of King Josiah 2Kin 23:34
 Name changed to Jehoiakim 2Chr 36:4
3. Postexilic priest ....Neh 12:41
4. Ancestor of Christ ......Matt 1:13
 Luke 3:30

said *E* the son of Hilkiah 2Kin 18:26
came *E* the son of Hilkiah 2Kin 18:37

ELIAM (ĕ-lī'ăm)—*"my God is a kinsman; God is founder of the people"*
1. Father of Bathsheba 2Sam 11:3
 Called Ammiel 1Chr 3:5
2. Son of Ahithophel 2Sam 23:34

ELIAS—*See* ELIJAH

ELIASAPH (ĕ-lī'ä-săf)—*"God is gatherer"*
1. Gadite prince...........Num 1:4, 14
 Presents offering ....Num 7:41, 42
2. Levite.................Num 3:24

sons of Gad shall be *E*........Num 2:14
the offering of *E* the son ......Num 7:47
children of Gad was *E* ....Num 10:20

ELIASHIB (ĕ-lī'ä-shĭb)—*"God is requiter"*
1. Davidic priest 1Chr 24:1, 12
2. Divorced foreign wife ...Ezra 10:24
 Ezra 10:27
3. High priest ....Neh 12:10
 Rebuilds Sheep Gate ....Neh 3:1, 20, 21
 Allies with foreigners....Neh 13:4, 5, 28
4. Descendant of Zerubbabel..........1Chr 3:19-24

Johanan the son of *E* ....Ezra 10:6
Levites in the days of *E*.......Neh 12:22
of Johanan the son of *E* ......Neh 12:23
evil that *E* did for Tobiah .....Neh 13:7

ELIATHAH (ĕ-lī'ä-thä)—*"God is come"*
Son of Heman 1Chr 25:1-27

ELIDAD (ĕ-lī dăd)—*"God is a friend"*
Benjamite leader ....Num 34:17, 21

ELIEL (ē'lĭ-ĕl)—*"God, my God"*
1. Ancestor of Samuel 1Chr 6:33, 34
 See ELIHU 1
2. One of David's mighty men 1Chr 11:26, 46
3. Another of David's mighty men 1Chr 11:47
4. Gadite warrior 1Chr 12:1-11
5. Levite.................1Chr 15:9, 11
6. Benjamite 1Chr 8:1-21
7. Benjamite, son of Shashak 1Chr 8:22, 25
8. Manassite chief 1Chr 5:24
9. Overseer of tithes 2Chr 31:12, 13

ELIENAI (ĕl-ĭ-ē'nī)—*"unto God are my eyes"*
Benjamite chief 1Chr 8:1, 20

ELIEZER (ĕl-ĭ-ē'zer)—*"God is help"*
1. Abraham's servant ......Gen 15:2
2. Son of Moses ....Ex 18:4
3. Son of Zichri 1Chr 27:16
4. Son of Becher 1Chr 7:8
5. Priest of David 1Chr 15:24
6. Prophet 2Chr 20:37
7. Ezra's delegate ....Ezra 8:16
8, 9, 10. Three men who divorced their foreign wives ....Ezra 10:18-31
11. An ancestor of Christ . .Luke 3:29

Moses were Gershom, and *E* . .1Chr 23:15
sons of *E* were, Rehabiah 1Chr 23:17
E had none other sons 1Chr 23:17

ELIHOENAI (ĕl-ĭ-hō-ē'nī)—*"to Jehovah are my eyes"*
Son of Zerahiah ....Ezra 8:4
Korahite gatekeeper 1Chr 26:1-3

ELIHOREPH (ĕl-ĭ-hō'rĕf)—*"God of harvest grain"*
One of Solomon's scribes .1Kin 4:3

ELIHU (ĕ-lī'hū)—*"God himself"*
1. Ancestor of Samuel 1Sam 1:1
 Also called Eliab and Eliel 1Chr 6:27, 34

2. David's brother 1Chr 27:18
   Called Eliab 1Sam 16:6
3. Manassite captain 1Chr 12:20
4. Temple servant 1Chr 26:1, 7
5. One who reproved Job and his friends ....Job 32:2, 4-6

E answered and said ....Job 34:1
E spake moreover..said ....Job 35:1
E also proceeded..said ....Job 36:1

ELIJAH, ELIAS (ĕ-lī'jä, ĕ-lī'ȧs)—*"Jehovah is my God"—a great prophet of God of the ninth century B.C. in Israel*

Life of the prophet:
Denounces Ahab 1Kin 17:1
Hides by the brook Cherith 1Kin 17:3
Fed by ravens 1Kin 17:4-7
Fed by widow 1Kin 17:8-16
Restores widow's son 1Kin 17:17-24
Sends message to Ahab ..1Kin 18:1-16
Overthrows Baal prophets 1Kin 18:17-46
Flees from Jezebel 1Kin 19:1-3
Fed by angels 1Kin 19:4-8
Hears God 1Kin 19:9-14
Sent on a mission 1Kin 19:15-21
Condemns Ahab 1Kin 21:15-29
Condemns Ahaziah 2Kin 1:1-16
Taken up to heaven 2Kin 2:1-15

Miracles of:
Widow's oil 1Kin 17:14-16
Dead child raised 1Kin 17:17-24
Causes rain 1Kin 18:41-45
Causes fire to consume sacrifices 1Kin 18:24-38
Causes fire to consume soldiers 2Kin 1:10-12

Prophecies of:
Drought 1Kin 17:1
Ahab's destruction 1Kin 21:17-29
Ahaziah's death 2Kin 1:2-17
Plague 2Chr 21:12-15

Significance of:
Prophecy of his coming ..Mal 4:5, 6
Appears with Christ .....Matt 17:1-4
Type of John the Baptist .Luke 1:17

E the Tishbite who was of 1Kin 17:1
of the Lord..spake by **E** 1Kin 17:16
Lord came to **E** in the third ...1Kin 18:1
E went to show himself 1Kin 18:2
behold, **E** met him 1Kin 18:7
Art thou that my lord **E**? 1Kin 18:7
tell thy lord..**E** is here 1Kin 18:8
tell thy lord..**E** is here 1Kin 18:11
tell thy lord..**E** is here 1Kin 18:14
E said, As the Lord of hosts ..1Kin 18:15
Ahab went to meet **E** 1Kin 18:16
when Ahab saw **E** 1Kin 18:17
E came unto all the people 1Kin 18:21
Then said **E** unto the people ..1Kin 18:22
E said unto the prophets 1Kin 18:25
E mocked them and said 1Kin 18:27
E said unto all the people 1Kin 18:30
E took twelve stones 1Kin 18:31
E the prophet came near 1Kin 18:36
E said unto them, Take the ...1Kin 18:40
E brought them down to 1Kin 18:40
E said unto Ahab, Get thee up.1Kin 18:41
hand of the Lord was on **E**....1Kin 18:46
Jezebel all that **E** had done ...1Kin 19:1
Jezebel sent a messenger..**E** ...1Kin 19:2
What doest thou here, **E** 1Kin 19:9
was so..**E** heard it, that 1Kin 19:13
What doest thou here, **E**? 1Kin 19:13
he arose, and went after **E** 1Kin 19:21
Lord came to **E**..Tishbite 1Kin 21:17
E the Tishbite, Arise, go 2Kin 1:3
surely die and **E** departed 2Kin 1:4
It is **E** the Tishbite 2Kin 1:8
E..said to the captain 2Kin 1:10
E..said unto them 2Kin 1:12
fell on his knees before **E** 2Kin 1:13
angel of..Lord said unto **E** 2Kin 1:15
Lord which **E** had spoken 2Kin 1:17
Lord would take up **E** into 2Kin 2:1
E went with Elisha from 2Kin 2:1
E..unto Elisha, Tarry here 2Kin 2:2
E..unto him Elisha, tarry 2Kin 2:4
E said unto him Tarry, I pray. .2Kin 2:6
E took his mantle..wrapped ...2Kin 2:8
E said unto Elisha, Ask 2Kin 2:9
E went up by a whirlwind 2Kin 2:11
poured water on the hand of **E**.2Kin 3:11
he spake by his servant **E** 2Kin 9:36
he spake by his servant **E** 2Kin 10:10
Lord, which he spake to **E** 2Kin 10:17
Masseiah..**E**, and Shemaiah ...Ezra 10:21
E, which was for to come .....Matt 11:14
E; and others, Jeremiah ....Matt 16:14
scribes that **E** must first come?.Matt 17:10
E truly shall first come ....Matt 17:11
unto you..**E** is come already ...Matt 17:12
This man calleth for **E** ....Matt 27:47
E will come to save him ......Matt 27:49
Others said, That it is **E** ......Mark 6:15
some say, **E**; and others ......Mark 8:28
unto them **E** with Moses ......Mark 9:4
one for Moses..one for **E** .....Mark 9:5
that **E** must first come? ....Mark 9:11
E verily cometh first ....Mark 9:12
That **E** is indeed come ....Mark 9:13
Behold, he calleth **E** ....Mark 15:35
in Israel in the days of **E**......Luke 4:25
unto none of them..**E** ....Luke 4:26
that **E** had appeared ....Luke 9:8
some say, **E**; and others say ...Luke 9:19
which were Moses and **E** ......Luke 9:30
for Moses, and one for **E** .....Luke 9:33
consume them..as **E** did? ......Luke 9:54
What then? Art thou **E**? ......John 1:21
E, neither that prophet? ......John 1:25
the scripture saith of **E**........Rom 11:2
E was..man subject to like ....James 5:17

ELIJAH (ĕ-lī'jä)—*"Jehovah is my God"*
1. Priest who divorced his foreign wife ....Ezra 10:21
2. Divorced foreign wife ...Ezra 10:18, 26

ELIKA (ĕ-lī'kä)—*"God is rejector"*
David's warrior..........2Sam 23:25

ELIM (ē'lĭm)—*"oaks"*
Israel's encampment .....Ex 15:27
Place of palm trees ......Num 33:9, 10

took..journey from **E** ....Ex 16:1
Sin..is between **E** and Sinai ...Ex 16:1

ELIMELECH (ĕ-lĭm'ĕ-lĕk)—*"my God is King"*
Man of Judah ....Ruth 1:1, 2
Dies in Moab ....Ruth 1:3
Kinsman of Boaz ....Ruth 2:1, 3
Boaz buys his land ......Ruth 4:3-9

ELIOENAI (ĕ-lī-ō-ē'nī)—*"to Jehovah are my eyes"*
1. Descendant of Benjamin .1Chr 7:8
2. Simeonite head 1Chr 4:36
3. Son of Neariah 1Chr 3:23, 24
4. Postexilic priest ....Neh 12:41
   Divorced his foreign wife.Ezra 10:19, 22
5. Son of Zattu; divorced his foreign wife ....Ezra 10:27
6. Doorkeeper of the Temple 1Chr 26:1-3

Jehohanan the sixth, **E** the 1Chr 26:3
Michaiah, **E**, Zechariah ....Neh 12:41

ELIPHAL (ĕ-lī'făl)—*"God is judge"*
David's warrior..........1Chr 11:26, 35
Called Eliphelet 2Sam 23:34

ELIPHALET—*See* Eliphelet

ELIPHAZ (ĕl'ĭ-făz)—*"God is dispenser"*
1. Son of Esau ....Gen 36:2, 4
2. One of Job's friends ....Job 2:11
   Rebukes Job ....Job 4:1, 5
   Is forgiven ....Job 42:7-9

E the son of Adah the wife ...Gen 36:10
sons of **E** were Teman ....Gen 36:11
was concubine to **E** Esau's ....Gen 36:12
she bare to **E** Amalek ....Gen 36:12
sons of **E** the firstborn son ....Gen 36:15
are the dukes that came of **E** ..Gen 36:16
sons of Esau; **E**, Reuel 1Chr 1:35
the sons of **E**; Teman 1Chr 1:36
answered **E** the Temanite .....Job 15:1
E the Temanite answered .....Job 22:1

ELIPHELEH (ĕ-lĭf'ĕ-lĕ)—*"Jehovah is distinction"*
Levite singer 1Chr 15:18, 21

ELIPHELET, ELIPHALET (e-lĭf-ĕ-lĕt, ĕ-lĭf-ă-lĕt)—*"God is escape"*
1. Son of David 1Chr 3:5, 6
2. Another son of David ...2Sam 5:16
3. Descendant of Jonathan .1Chr 8:33, 39
4. David's warrior 2Sam 23:34
5. Returnee from Babylon. .Ezra 8:13
6. Son of Hashum; divorced his foreign wife ....Ezra 10:33

Elishama..Eliada, and **E** 2Sam 5:16
Elishama..Eliada, and **E** 1Chr 3:8
Elishama..Beeliada, and **E** 1Chr 14:7

ELISABETH (ĕ-lĭz'ă-bĕth)—*"God is swearer; oath of God"*
Wife of Zacharias ....Luke 1:5
Barren ....Luke 1:7, 13
Conceives a son ....Luke 1:24, 25
Cousin of Mary ....Luke 1:36
Salutation to Mary ......Luke 1:39-45
Mother of John the Baptist ....Luke 1:57-60

of Aaron and her name was **E** .Luke 1:5
because that **E** was barren ....Luke 1:7
wife **E** shall bear thee a son ...Luke 1:13
days his wife **E** conceived .....Luke 1:24
thy cousin **E**, she hath also ....Luke 1:36
of Zechariah, and saluted **E** ...Luke 1:40
E heard the salutation of......Luke 1:41
E was filled..Holy Ghost ......Luke 1:41

ELISHA, ELISEUS (ĕ-lī'shä, ĕl'ĭ-sē'ŭs)—*"God is Savior"—disciple of and successor to Elijah*

Life of:
Succeeds Elijah 1Kin 19:16
Follows Elijah 1Kin 19:19-21
Sees Elijah translated 2Kin 2:1-12
Is recognized as a prophet 2Kin 2:13-22
Mocked 2Kin 2:23-25
Deals with kings.........2Kin 3:11-20
Helps two women 2Kin 4:1-17

Miracles of:
Divides Jordan 2Kin 2:14
Purifies water 2Kin 2:19-22
Increases widow's oil ...2Kin 4:1-7
Raises Shunammite's son .2Kin 4:18-37
Neutralizes poison 2Kin 4:38-41
Multiplies bread 2Kin 4:42-44
Heals Naaman the leper. .2Kin 5:1-19
Inflicts Gehazi with leprosy 2Kin 5:26, 27
Causes iron to float......2Kin 6:6
Reveals secret counsels ..2Kin 6:8-12
Opens servant's eyes 2Kin 6:13-17
Strikes Syrian army with blindness 2Kin 6:18-23

Prophecies of:
Birth of a child..........2Kin 4:16
Abundance 2Kin 7:1
King's death 2Kin 7:2
Great famine............2Kin 8:1-3
Ben-hadad's death 2Kin 8:7-15
Joash's victories 2Kin 13:14-19

sword of Jehu shall **E** slay.....1Kin 19:17
departed thence, and found **E**. .1Kin 19:19
Elijah went with **E** from 2Kin 2:1
Elijah said unto **E**, Tarry 2Kin 2:2
E said unto him, As the Lord. .2Kin 2:2

at Beth-el came forth to *E* 2Kin 2:3
Elijah said..him, *E*, tarry......2Kin 2:4
were at Jericho came to *E* 2Kin 2:5
Elijah said unto *E*, Ask what I.2Kin 2:9
E said, I pray thee, let a......2Kin 2:9
E saw..he cried, My father 2Kin 2:12
thither; and *E* went over 2Kin 2:14
of Elijah doth rest on *E*.......2Kin 2:15
men of the city said unto *E* ...2Kin 2:19
saying of *E* which he spake....2Kin 2:22
sons of the prophets unto *E* ...2Kin 4:1
E said..What shall I do 2Kin 4:2
E passed to Shunem 2Kin 4:8
season that *E* had said unto ...2Kin 4:17
E came again to Gilgal........2Kin 4:38
of the prophets said unto *E* ...2Kin 6:1
E the prophet that is in 2Kin 6:12
E prayed..Lord, I pray........2Kin 6:17
chariots of fire..about *E*.......2Kin 6:17
E prayed unto the Lord 2Kin 6:18
according to the word of *E*....2Kin 6:18
E said unto them. This is 2Kin 6:19
E said Lord, open the eyes....2Kin 6:20
king of Israel said unto *E* 2Kin 6:21
head of *E* the son of..........2Kin 6:31
E sat in his house..elders......2Kin 6:32
great things that *E* hath done..2Kin 8:4
whom *E* restored to life 2Kin 8:5
E was fallen sick of his 2Kin 13:14
E said unto him, Take bow ...2Kin 13:15
E put his hands upon 2Kin 13:16
E said, Shoot. And he shot ...2Kin 13:17
E died, and they buried him...2Kin 13:20
man into the sepulcher of *E*...2Kin 13:21
touched the bones of *E* 2Kin 13:21
in the time of *E* the prophet ..Luke 4:27

ELISHAH (ĕ-lī'shä)—*"God is Savior"*
Son of Javan ....Gen 10:4

of Javan: *E*..Tarshish 1Chr 1:7
from the isles of *E* ....Ezek 27:7

ELISHAMA (ĕ-lĭsh'ä-mä)—*"God is hearer"*
1. Son of Ammihud ....Num 1:10
   Ancestor of Joshua 1Chr 7:26
2. Man of Judah 1Chr 2:41
3. Son of David 1Chr 3:1, 5,6
   Also called Elishua.......2Sam 5:15
4. Another son of David ...2Sam 5:16
5. Teaching priest 2Chr 17:7, 8
6. Scribe ....Jer 36:12, 20,21

the sons of Ephraim shall be *E*.Num 2:18
E the son of Ammihud ....Num 7:48
this was the offering of *E* .....Num 7:53
over his host was *E*...........Num 10:22
son of *E*, of the seed royal 2Kin 25:25
E..Beeliada, and Eliphalet 1Chr 14:7
Nethaniah the son of *E* ....Jer 41:1

ELISHAPHAT (ĕ-lĭsh'ä-făt)—*"God is judge"*
Captain 2Chr 23:1

ELISHEBA (ĕ-lĭsh'ĕ-bä)—*"God is swearer; God is an oath"*
Wife of Aaron ....Ex 6:23

ELISHUA (ĕ-ĭ-shū'ä)—*"God is hearer"*
Son of David 2Sam 5:15
Called Elishama 1Chr 3:6

And Ibhar..*E*, and Elpalet 1Chr 14:5

ELIUD (ĕ-lī'ŭd)—*"God my praise"*
Father of Eleazar ....Matt 1:14, 15

ELIZABETH—*See* Elisabeth

ELIZAPHAN (ĕl-ĭ-zā'făn)—*"God is protector"*
1. Chief of Kohathites .....Num 3:30
   Heads family 1Chr 15:5, 8
   Family consecrated 2Chr 29:12-16
2. Son of Parnach ....Num 34:25

ELIZUR (ĕ-lī'zer)—*"God is a rock"*
Reubenite warrior ....Num 1:5

children of Reuben..be *E* .....Num 2:10
fourth day *E* the son..........Num 7:30
this was the offering of *E* .....Num 7:35
was *E* the son of Shedeur .....Num 10:18

ELKANAH (ĕl-kā'nä)—*"God is possessing"*
1. Father of Samuel 1Sam 1:1-23
2. Son of Korah ....Ex 6:24
   Escapes judgment ....Num 26:11
3. Levite...................1Chr 6:23-36
4. Descendant of Korah....1Chr 6:22, 23
5. Levite...................1Chr 9:16
6. Korahite warrior 1Chr 12:1, 6
7. Officer under Ahaz 2Chr 28:7
8. Doorkeeper of the ark ..1Chr 15:23

E went to Ramah..house 1Sam 2:11
Eli blessed *E* and 1Sam 2:20

ELKOSHITE (ĕl'kŏsh-īts)—*an inhabitant of Elkosh*
Descriptive of Nahum....Nah 1:1

ELLASAR (ĕl-lā'sär)—*"oak"*
Place in Babylon ....Gen 14:1, 9

ELMODAM (ĕl-mō'dăm)—*"measure"*
Ancestor of Christ ....Luke 3:28

ELMS—*deciduous shade trees*
oaks..poplars and *E* ....Hos 4:13

ELNAAM (ĕl-nā'ăm)—*"God is pleasant"*
Father of two warriors ...1Chr 11:26, 46

ELNATHAN (ĕl-nā'thăn)—*"God is giving"*
1. Father of Nehushta 2Kin 24:8
   Goes to Egypt ....Jer 26:22
   Entreats with king ....Jer 36:25
2, 3, 4. Three Levites ......Ezra 8:16

E..Jarib, and for *E* ....Ezra 8:16
E, men of understanding ......Ezra 8:16
E the son of Achbor ....Jer 36:12

ELOI (ĕ-lō'ī)—*same as Eli (cry of Jesus)*
Jesus' cry ....Mark 15:34

ELON (ē'lŏn)—*"oak, strong"*
1. Hittite ....Gen 26:34
2. Son of Zebulun ....Gen 46:14
3. Judge in Israel..........Judg 12:11, 12
4. Town of Dan ....Josh 19:43

Adah..daughter of *E*..........Gen 36:2
E the family of..Elonites ......Num 26:26

ELON-BETH-HANAN (ē-lŏn-bĕth-hā'năn)—*"oak of the house of grace"*
Town of Dan 1Kin 4:9

ELONITES (ē'lŏn-īts)—*belonging to Elon*
Descendants of Elon.....Num 26:26

ELOQUENT—*fluent and persuasive in speech*
Moses is not ....Ex 4:10
Paul rejects 1Cor 2:1, 4, 5
Apollos is...............Acts 18:24
False prophets boast of ..2Pet 2:18

artificer..the *e* orator ....Is 3:3

ELOTH—*See* Elath

ELPAAL (ĕl-pā'ăl)—*"God is working"*
Benjamite 1Chr 8:11-18

ELPALET (ĕl-pā'lĕt)—*"God is escape"*
Son of David 1Chr 14:3, 5
Same as Eliphelet 1Chr 3:6

EL-PARAN (ĕl-pâr'ăn)—*"oak of Paran"*
Place in Canaan ....Gen 14:6

ELSE—*other; otherwise*
Give me children, or *e* I die ...Gen 30:1
e by the life of Pharaoh ....Gen 42:16
E, if thou wilt not let my .....Ex 8:21
E if thou refuse to let my .....Ex 10:4
without doing anything *e* ......Num 20:19
he is God; there is none *e* ....Deut 4:35
earth beneath..is none *e* ......Deut 4:39
E if he do in any wise go .....Josh 23:12
nothing *e* save the sword ......Judg 7:14
I taste bread, or aught *e* 2Sam 3:35
we shall not *e* escape 2Sam 15:14
that there is none *e*...........1Kin 8:60
e three days the sword of 1Chr 21:12
whosoever *e* cometh into 2Chr 23:7
is nothing *e* but sorrow ....Neh 2:2
desirest not sacrifice; *e* ....Ps 51:16
who *e* can hasten hereunto ....Eccl 2:25
Lord, and there is none *e* ....Is 45:5
Lord, and there is none *e* .....Is 45:6
there is none *e*, there is ....Is 45:14
Lord;..there is none *e*.........Is 45:18
there is no God *e* beside ......Is 45:21
I am God, and there is none *e* .Is 45:22
I am God, and there is none *e* .Is 46:9
I am, and none *e* beside me ...Is 47:8
I am and none *e* beside me ...Is 47:10
Lord your God, and none *e* ...Joel 2:27
will hate the one..or *e* ....Matt 6:24
e the bottles break and the ....Matt 9:17
Or *e* how can one enter into ..Matt 12:29
or *e* make the tree corrupt ....Matt 12:33
e the new piece that filled.....Mark 2:21
e the wine doth ....Mark 2:22
e the new wine will burst .....Luke 5:37
Or *e* while the other is yet a ..Luke 14:32
or *e* he will hold to the one ...Luke 16:13
or *e* believe me for..works ....John 14:11
spent their time in nothing *e* ..Acts 17:21
Or *e* let these same here say ..Acts 24:20
accusing or *e* excusing one ....Rom 2:15
e were your children unclean ..1Cor 7:14
E when thou shalt bless 1Cor 14:16
E what shall they do which....1Cor 15:29
come and see you, or *e* be ....Phil 1:27
or *e* I will come unto thee ....Rev 2:5
Repent; or *e* I will come unto .Rev 2:16

ELTEKEH (ĕl'tă-kē)—*"grace"*
City of Dan ....Josh 19:44
Assigned to Levites......Josh 21:23

ELTEKON (ĕl'tĕ-kŏn)—*"founded by God"*
Village in Judah ....Josh 15:59

ELTOLAD (ĕl-tō'lăd)—*"kindred of God"*
Town in Judah ....Josh 15:21, 30
Assigned to Simeonites ..Josh 19:4
Called Tolad 1Chr 4:29

ELUL (ĕ'lŭl)—*"vine"*
Sixth month of Hebrew year ....Neh 6:15

ELUZAI (ĕ-lū'zā-ī)—*"God is strong"*
Ambidextrous warrior of David 1Chr 12:1, 5

ELYMAS (ĕl'ī-măs)—*"a sorcerer"*
Arabic name of Bar-jesus, a false prophet...............Acts 13:6-12

ELZABAD (ĕl-zā'băd)—*"God is endowing"*
1. Gadite warrior 1Chr 12:8, 12
2. Korahite Levite 1Chr 26:7, 8

ELZAPHAN (ĕl'zā-făn)—*"God is protector"*
Son of Uzziel ....Ex 6:22
Given instructions by Moses ....Lev 10:4

EMANCIPATION—*a setting free from slavery*
Of Hebrew nation ....Ex 12:29-42
Of Hebrew slaves ....Ex 21:2
In the year of jubilee ....Lev 25:8-41
Proclaimed by Zedekiah. .Jer 34:8-11
By Cyrus 2Chr 36:23
Ezra 1:1-4

EMASCULATION—*castration*
Penalty of ....Deut 23:1

EMBALMING—*a method of preserving a corpse from decay*
Unknown to Abraham ...Gen 23:4
Practiced in Egypt ....Gen 50:2, 3, 26
Manner of, among Jews..2Chr 16:14
Limitation of............John 11:39, 44
Forbidden by Law ....Num 5:1-4
Num 19:11-22

EMBOLDENED—*made bold*

[*also* EMBOLDENETH]
e thee that thou answerest? ...Job 16:3
which is weak be *e* to eat? 1Cor 8:10

EMBRACE—*to hug; adopt; surround*

[*also* EMBRACED, EMBRACING]
ran to meet him and *e* him ....Gen 29:13
Esau ran to meet him and *e* ...Gen 33:4
he kissed them, and *e* them ...Gen 48:10
time of life, thou shalt *e* 2Kin 4:16
honor when thou dost *e* her ...Prov 4:8
e the bosom of a stranger? ....Prov 5:20
time to *e*, and a time to.......Eccl 3:5
a time to refrain from *e*.......Eccl 3:5
his right hand doth *e* me ......Song 2:6
his right hand should *e* me ....Song 8:3
brought up in scarlet *e* ....Lam 4:5
him the disciples, and *e* ....Acts 20:1
fell on him, and *e* him ....Acts 20:10
e them, and confessed that ....Heb 11:13

EMBROIDER—*to decorate by needlework*
In tabernacle curtains ....Ex 26:1, 36
Bezaleel and Aholiab inspired in ....Ex 35:30-35
On Sisera's garments ....Judg 5:30
Worn by women ....Ps 45:14

[*also* EMBROIDERER]
e a coat, a mitre, and a girdle..Ex 28:4
thou shalt *e* the coat ....Ex 28:39
an *e* in blue, and..purple ......Ex 38:23
clothed thee also with *e* work..Ezek 16:10
fine linen,..silk,..*e* work.......Ezek 16:13
tookest thy *e* garments ....Ezek 16:18
put off their *e* garments ....Ezek 26:16
linen with *e* work from Egypt. .Ezek 27:7

EMERALD—*a precious stone of the beryl variety*
In Tyre's trade ....Ezek 27:16
Used for ornamentation ..Ezek 28:13
Foundation stone ....Rev 21:19

second row shall be an *e* ......Ex 28:18
e, a sapphire..a diamond ......Ex 39:11
in sight like unto an *e* ....Rev 4:3

EMERODS—*hemorrhoids; boils; tumors*
Threatened as a curse....Deut 28:27
Inflicted upon Philistines .1Sam 5:6-12

Five golden *e*, and five golden .1Sam 6:4
shall make images of your *e* ...1Sam 6:5
the images of their *e*..........1Sam 6:11
these are the golden *e* 1Sam 6:17

EMIM (ē'mĭm)—*terrors*
Giant race of Anakim east of the Dead Sea ..Gen 14:5

E dwelt therein in times ......Deut 2:10
the Moabites call them *E* .....Deut 2:11

EMINENT—*prominent*
built unto thee an *e* place .....Ezek 16:24
thou buildest thine *e* place ....Ezek 16:31
throw down thine *e* place .....Ezek 16:39
upon..high mountain and *e* ....Ezek 17:22

EMMANUEL (ĕ-măn'ū-ĕl)—*a name of Jesus*
shall call his name *E*..........Matt 1:23
See IMMANUEL

EMMAUS (ĕ-mā'ŭs)—*"despised people"*
Town near Jerusalem ....Luke 24:13-18

EMMOR (ĕm'ôr)—*Greek form of Hamor*
Father of Shechem ......Acts 7:16

EMOTION—*natural feelings and reactions*

Objects of:
Self ....Job 3:1-26
Nation..................Ps 137:1-6
Family.................Gen 49:1-28
Mate 1Sam 25:24, 25
Foreigners ....Ruth 1:16-18

Kinds of:
Conviction ....Acts 2:37
Contempt 1Sam 17:42-44
Despondency...........1Kin 19:4-10
Disappointment ....Luke 18:23
Disgust ....Neh 4:1-3
Envy 1Sam 17:28
Fear...................1Kin 19:1-3
Flattery 1Sam 25:23-31
Hate ....Acts 7:54, 57
Joy ....Luke 15:22-24
Love ....Ex 32:26-29
Loyalty 2Sam 18:32, 33
Regret.................Luke 16:27-31
Revenge ....Gen 27:41-45
Sorrow 2Sam 12:13-19

Control of:
Unsuppressed 1Sam 20:30-33
Suppressed.............Is 36:21
Uncontrollable ....Mark 5:4, 5
Controlled ....Mark 5:19

EMPIRE—*domain of great extent*
published throughout..*e* ....Esth 1:20

EMPLOY—*to make use of*

[*also* EMPLOYED]
to *e* them in the siege.........Deut 20:19
they were *e* in that work 1Chr 9:33
Tikvah were *e* about this ......Ezra 10:15

EMPLOYEES—*those who work for others*

Types of:
Diligent ....Gen 30:27-31
Discontented ....Matt 20:1-15
Lazy ....Job 7:1-3
Unworthy..............Matt 21:33-41

Duties of:
Contentment ....Luke 3:14
Fulfilling terms ....Matt 20:1-15
Respect................1Tim 6:1
Diligence ....Prov 22:29

Rights of:
Equal wage ....Matt 10:10
Prompt payment.........Lev 19:13
Good treatment ....Ruth 2:4

Oppression of, by:
Arbitrary changes ....Gen 31:38-42
Unscrupulous landowners .James 5:4-6

EMPLOYERS—*those who hire others to work for them*
Must not oppress ....Deut 24:14
Must be considerate .....Job 31:31
Must be just and fair ....Col 4:1

EMPLOYMENT—*the state of one who has regular work*

Usefulness of:
Manifest graces..........Prov 31:10-31
Provided food 2Thess 3:7-12

Examples of:
Adam ....Gen 2:15
Workmen after the exile. .Neh 4:15-23
Paul....................1Thess 2:9-11

sever out men..continual *e* ....Ezek 39:14

EMPTIERS—*plunderers*
e have emptied them out ......Nah 2:2

EMPTY—*to clear out; desolate; lacking contents*

[*also* EMPTIED, EMPTINESS]
she hasted, and *e* her pitcher ..Gen 24:20
hadst sent me away now *e* ....Gen 31:42
pit was *e*..was no water ....Gen 37:24
seven *e* ears blasted with ......Gen 41:27
when ye go, ye shall not go *e* .Ex 3:21
shall appear before me *e* ......Ex 23:15
shall appear before me *e* ......Ex 34:20
command..they *e* the house ...Lev 14:36
not let him go away *e*.........Deut 15:13
not appear before the Lord *e* ..Deut 16:16
e pitchers..lamps within ....Judg 7:16
brought me home again *e* .....Ruth 1:21
Go not *e*..mother-in-law ......Ruth 3:17
send it not *e*..any wise 1Sam 6:3
because thy seat will be *e* 1Sam 20:18
and David's place was *e*.......1Sam 20:25
that David's place was *e* 1Sam 20:27
sword of Saul..not *e* 2Sam 1:22
borrow thee vessels..*e* vessels ..2Kin 4:3
officer came and *e* the chest ...2Chr 24:11
be he shaken out, and *e* ......Neh 5:13
hast sent widows away *e* ......Job 22:9
out the north over the *e* place .Job 26:7
e themselves upon the earth ...Eccl 11:3
defence shall be *e* and dried ..Is 19:6
Lord maketh the earth *e* ......Is 24:1
land shall be utterly *e*.........Is 24:3
he awaketh, and his soul is *e* ..Is 29:8
make *e*..soul of the hungry ....Is 32:6
and the stones of *e* ....Is 34:11
returned with their vessels *e* ..Jer 14:3
not been *e* from vessel to .....Jer 48:11
shall *e* his vessels, and break ..Jer 48:12
fan her, and shall *e* her ....Jer 51:2
hath made me an *e* vessel .....Jer 51:34
set it *e* upon the coals ....Ezek 24:11
Israel is an *e* vine ....Hos 10:1
She is *e*..void, and waste ......Nah 2:10
they therefore *e* their net .....Hab 1:17
the two golden pipes *e* ....Zech 4:12
he findeth it *e*, swept ....Matt 12:44
him, and sent him away *e* .....Mark 12:3
rich he hath sent *e* away ......Luke 1:53
and sent him away *e* ....Luke 20:11

EMULATION—*striving to equal or excel*

[*also* EMULATIONS]
may provoke to *e* them ....Rom 11:14
hatred, variance, *e*, wrath .....Gal 5:20

ENABLED—*made possible*
Jesus..who hath *e* me 1Tim 1:12

ENAM (ē'năm)—*"double fountains"*
Village of Judah ....Josh 15:20, 34

ENAN (ē'năn)—*"eyes; fountain"*
Father of Ahira ....Num 1:15

shall be Ahirah the son of *E* ..Num 2:29
twelfth day Ahira..son of *E* ...Num 7:78
offering of Ahira..son of *E* ....Num 7:83
Naphtali was Ahira..son of *E* ..Num 10:27

ENCAMPMENT—*a resting place on a march or journey*
Israel's, on leaving Egypt .Ex 13:20
At Sinai ....Ex 18:5
List of..................Num 33:10-46
In battle ....Josh 10:5, 31, 34

[*also* ENCAMP, ENCAMPED, ENCAMPETH, ENCAMPING]
e before Pi-hahiroth ....Ex 14:2
overtook them *e* by the sea ...Ex 14:9
they *e* there by the waters.....Ex 15:27
minister unto it..shall *e* ....Num 1:50
that *e* by him shall be.........Num 2:27
are to *e* in the wilderness .....Num 10:31
e in Gilgal, in the east ....Josh 4:19
the children of Israel *e* ....Josh 5:10
they *e* against them ....Judg 6:4
e against Thebez..took it ......Judg 9:50
together, and *e* in Gilead .....Judg 10:17
morning..*e* against Gibeah.....Judg 20:19
e against Jabesh-gilead 1Sam 11:1
lord, are *e* in the open fields ..2Sam 11:11
the people were *e* against 1Kin 16:15
Philistines *e* in the valley 1Chr 11:15
e against the fenced cities 2Chr 32:1
and *e* round about my ....Job 19:12
host should *e* against..........Ps 27:3
angel of..Lord *e* round ....Ps 34:7
bones of him that *e* against....Ps 53:5
will *e* about mine house ....Zech 9:8

ENCHANTER—*sorcerer*

[*also* ENCHANTERS]
spirits, or an *e*, or a witch.....Deut 18:10
your *e*, nor to your sorcerers ..Jer 27:9

ENCHANTMENT—*the practice of magical arts*

Practiced in:
Egypt ... Ex 7:11
Judah ... 2Kin 17:17
Babylon ... Ezek 21:21
Chaldea ... Dan 5:11
Greece ... Acts 16:16
Asia Minor ... Acts 19:13, 19

Futility of:
Vanity of ... Is 47:9-15
Inability of ... Ex 7:11, 12
Abomination of ... Deut 18:9-12

Examples of:
Simon ... Acts 8:9
Bar-jesus ... Acts 13:6-12
Slave-girl ... Acts 16:16
Vagabond Jews ... Acts 19:13
Jannes and Jambres ... 2Tim 3:8

[*also* ENCHANTMENTS]
Egypt did so with their *e* ... Ex 7:22
with their *e* to bring forth ... Ex 8:18
neither shall ye use *e* ... Lev 19:26
no *e* against Jacob ... Num 23:23
seek for *e*..set his face ... Num 24:1
observed times, and used *e* ... 2Kin 21:6
observed times, and used *e* ... 2Chr 33:6
serpent..will bite without *e* ... Eccl 10:11

ENCLOSE—*See* INCLOSE

ENCOUNTERED—*met*
and of the Stoics, *e* him ... Acts 17:18

ENCOURAGEMENT—*inspiration to hope and service*

Needed by:
Prophets ... 1Kin 19:1-19
People ... Neh 4:17-23
Servants ... 2Kin 6:15-17
Kings ... 2Kin 11:10-21
Heathen ... Dan 6:18-23

Agents of:
Angels ... Gen 32:1, 2
A dream ... Gen 28:11-22
God's promises ... Josh 1:1-9
A friend ... 1Sam 23:16-18
A relative ... Esth 4:13-16
Paul ... Acts 27:21-26

Reasons for, Christ is:
Risen ... 1Cor 15:11-58
Present ... Matt 28:19, 20
Coming ... Luke 21:25-28

[*also* ENCOURAGE, ENCOURAGED]
shall go in thither; *e* him ... Deut 1:38
men of Israel *e* themselves ... Judg 20:22
David *e* himself in..Lord ... 1Sam 30:6
overthrow it; and *e* thou ... 2Sam 11:25
might be *e* in the law of ... 2Chr 31:4
e themselves in an evil ... Ps 64:5
carpenter *e* the goldsmith ... Is 41:7

ENCUMBRANCE—*that which hinders freedom of action*
Universal ... Gen 3:16-19
Imposed ... Gen 32:31, 32
Perpetual ... Matt 27:25
Moral ... Titus 1:12, 13
Spiritual ... Heb 12:1

END—*boundary; finish; completed*

[*also* ENDED, ENDEST, ENDETH, ENDING, ENDLESS, ENDS]
on the seventh day God *e* ... Gen 2:2
e of all flesh is come ... Gen 6:13
to pass at the *e* of forty days ... Gen 8:6
had made an *e* of blessing ... Gen 27:30
year was *e*, they came ... Gen 47:18
one *e* of..borders of Egypt ... Gen 47:21
Jacob had made an *e* ... Gen 49:33
to the *e* thou mayest know ... Ex 8:22
e of the year, when thou ... Ex 23:16
two *e* of the mercy seat ... Ex 25:18
one cherub on the one *e* ... Ex 25:19
other cherub on the other *e* ... Ex 25:19
chains of pure gold at the *e* ... Ex 28:14
the two *e* of the breastplate ... Ex 28:23
other two *e* of the two ... Ex 28:25
when he had made an *e* ... Ex 31:18
boards from the one *e* to the ... Ex 36:33
the two *e* of the mercy seat ... Ex 37:7
cherub on the *e* on this side ... Ex 37:8
cherub on the other *e* ... Ex 37:8
four rings for the four *e* ... Ex 38:5
breastplate chains at..*e* ... Ex 39:15
on the *e* of the breastplate ... Ex 39:17
two *e* of the breastplate ... Ex 39:19
consecration be at an *e* ... Lev 8:33
To the *e* that the children of ... Lev 17:5
have made an *e* of covering ... Num 4:15
let my last *e* be like his! ... Num 23:10
do thee good at thy latter *e* ... Deut 8:16
even unto the *e* of the year ... Deut 11:12
the one *e* of the earth even ... Deut 13:7
even unto the *e* of the earth ... Deut 13:7
e of every seven years ... Deut 15:1
to the *e* that he may prolong ... Deut 17:20
officers have made an *e* ... Deut 20:9
e of the earth, as swift ... Deut 28:49
At the *e* of every seven years ... Deut 31:10
until they were *e* ... Deut 31:30
I will see what their *e* shall ... Deut 32:20
Moses made..*e* of speaking ... Deut 32:45
together to the *e* of the earth ... Deut 33:17
had made an *e* of slaying ... Josh 8:24
had made an *e* of slaying ... Josh 10:20
e of the valley of the giants ... Josh 15:8
to the *e* of the mountain ... Josh 18:16
had made an *e* of dividing ... Josh 19:49
he had made an *e* to offer ... Judg 3:18
pass at the *e* of two months ... Judg 11:39
the day groweth to an *e* ... Judg 19:9
they have *e* all my harvest ... Ruth 2:21
unto the *e* of barley harvest ... Ruth 2:23
more kindness at the latter *e* ... Ruth 3:10
shall judge the *e* of the earth ... 1Sam 2:10
I begin, I will also make an *e* ... 1Sam 3:12
made an *e* of prophesying ... 1Sam 10:13
he put forth the *e* of the rod ... 1Sam 14:27
had made an *e* of speaking ... 1Sam 18:1
Abner with the hinder *e* ... 2Sam 2:23
made an *e* of offering ... 2Sam 6:18
had made an *e* of speaking ... 2Sam 13:36
so they *e* the matter ... 2Sam 20:18
e of nine months and twenty ... 2Sam 24:8
had made an *e* of eating ... 1Kin 1:41
had made an *e* of building ... 1Kin 3:1
e all the work that king ... 1Kin 7:51
e of the staves were seen ... 1Kin 8:8
Solomon had made an *e* ... 1Kin 8:54
to pass at the seven years *e* ... 2Kin 8:3
had made an *e* of offering ... 2Kin 10:25
Jerusalem..one *e* to another ... 2Kin 21:16
David..made an *e* of offering ... 1Chr 16:2
right side of the east *e* ... 2Chr 4:10
e of the staves were seen ... 2Chr 5:9
made an *e* of praying ... 2Chr 7:1
them at the *e* of the brook ... 2Chr 20:16
after the *e* of two years ... 2Chr 21:19
came to pass at the *e* ... 2Chr 24:23
had made an *e* of offering ... 2Chr 29:29
till the work was *e* and until ... 2Chr 29:34
filled it from one *e* to ... Ezra 9:11
e of the house of Eliashib ... Neh 3:21
what is mine *e*..I should ... Job 6:11
Shall vain words have an *e*? ... Job 16:3
day and night come to an *e* ... Job 26:10
looketh to the *e* of the earth ... Job 28:24
The words of Job are *e* ... Job 31:40
Job may be tried unto the *e* ... Job 34:36
hold of the *e* of the earth ... Job 38:13
wicked come to an *e* ... Ps 7:9
words to the *e* of the world ... Ps 19:4
circuit unto the *e* of it ... Ps 19:6
All the *e* of the word shall ... Ps 22:27
e that my glory may sing ... Ps 30:12
e of the wicked shall be cut ... Ps 37:38
unto the *e* of the earth ... Ps 46:9
praise unto the *e* of the earth ... Ps 48:10
confidence..*e* of the earth ... Ps 65:5
e of the earth shall fear ... Ps 67:7
the river unto the *e* of ... Ps 72:8
David the son of Jesse are *e* ... Ps 72:20
then understood I their *e* ... Ps 73:17
are at their wit's *e* ... Ps 107:27
seen an *e* of all perfection ... Ps 119:96
to ascend from the *e* of ... Ps 135:7
e is bitter as wormwood ... Prov 5:4
e of..mirth is heaviness ... Prov 14:13
fool are in the *e* of ... Prov 17:24
be wise in thy latter *e* ... Prov 19:20
For surely there is an *e* ... Prov 23:18
from the beginning to the *e* ... Eccl 3:11
no *e* of all his labor ... Eccl 4:8
that is the *e* of all men ... Eccl 7:2
e..man should find nothing ... Eccl 7:14
many books there is no *e* ... Eccl 12:12
any *e* of their treasures ... Is 2:7
any *e* of their chariots ... Is 2:7
unto them from the *e* of ... Is 5:26
peace there shall be no *e* ... Is 9:7
extortioner is at an *e* ... Is 16:4
pass after the *e* of seventy ... Is 23:17
noise of them that rejoice *e* ... Is 24:8
far unto all the *e*..earth ... Is 26:15
wilt thou make an *e* of me ... Is 38:12
e of the earth were afraid ... Is 41:5
praise from the *e*..earth ... Is 42:10
daughters from the *e* of the ... Is 43:6
saved, all the *e*..earth ... Is 45:22
e from the beginning ... Is 46:10
it even to the *e* of the earth ... Is 48:20
of thy mourning shall be *e* ... Is 60:20
proclaimed unto the *e*..world ... Is 62:11
the *e* of the eleventh year ... Jer 1:3
yet will I not make a full *e* ... Jer 4:27
I..not make a full *e* with you ... Jer 5:18
summer is *e*, and we are not ... Jer 8:20
vapors to ascend from the *e* ... Jer 10:13
He shall not see our last *e* ... Jer 12:4
from the one *e* of the land ... Jer 12:12
the other *e* of the land ... Jer 12:12
even to the *e* of the earth ... Jer 25:31
from one *e* of the earth even ... Jer 25:33
made an *e* of speaking all ... Jer 26:8
make a full *e* of all nations ... Jer 30:11
not make a full *e* of thee ... Jer 30:11
e of seven years let ye go ... Jer 34:14
until there be an *e* of them ... Jer 44:27
a full *e* of all the nations ... Jer 46:28
not make a full *e* of thee ... Jer 46:28
city is taken at one *e* ... Jer 51:31
remembereth not her last *e* ... Lam 1:9
our *e* is near, our days are ... Lam 4:18
for our *e* is come ... Lam 4:18
to pass at the *e* of seven days ... Ezek 3:16
till thou hast *e* the days ... Ezek 4:8
Now is the *e* come upon thee ... Ezek 7:3
wilt thou make a full *e* of ... Ezek 11:13
fire devoureth both the *e* ... Ezek 15:4
e that they might know ... Ezek 20:26
iniquity shall have an *e* ... Ezek 21:25
e of forty years will I ... Ezek 29:13
their iniquity had an *e* ... Ezek 35:5
e toward the west was ... Ezek 41:12
made an *e* of cleansing it ... Ezek 43:23
e thereof they might stand ... Dan 1:5
e of the days that the king ... Dan 1:18
dominion to the *e* of..earth ... Dan 4:22
e of..days I Nebuchadnezzar ... Dan 4:34
to destroy it unto the *e* ... Dan 7:26
of the *e* shall be the vision ... Dan 8:17
last *e* of the indignation ... Dan 8:19
time appointed the *e* shall ... Dan 8:19
e..shall be with a flood ... Dan 9:26
e of years they shall join ... Dan 11:6
even to the time of the *e* ... Dan 11:35
yet he shall come to his *e* ... Dan 11:45
e of these wonders? ... Dan 12:6
till the time of the *e* ... Dan 12:9
go thou thy way till the *e* be ... Dan 12:13
stand in thy lot at the *e* of ... Dan 12:13
great houses shall have an *e* ... Amos 3:15
had made an *e* of eating ... Amos 7:2
e thereof as a bitter day ... Amos 7:10

e that every one of ....Obad 9
great unto the *e* of the earth ..Mic 5:4
make an utter *e* of the place ..Nah 1:8
there is none *e* of the store....Nah 2:9
at the *e* it shall speak ....Hab 2:3
river even to the *e* of the .....Zech 9:10
Jesus had *e* these sayings......Matt 7:28
endureth to the *e* shall be .....Matt 10:22
Jesus had made an *e* of ....Matt 11:1
come to pass but the *e* is not ..Matt 24:6
one *e* of heaven to the ....Matt 24:31
the servants, to see the *e*......Matt 26:58
e of the sabbath, as it began ..Matt 28:1
even unto the *e* of the world ..Matt 28:20
cannot stand, but hath an *e* ...Mark 3:26
shall endure unto the *e* ....Mark 13:13
kingdom there shall be no *e*...Luke 1:33
when they were *e*, he ....Luke 4:2
he had *e* all his sayings ....Luke 7:1
e is not by and by ....Luke 21:9
concerning me have an *e*......Luke 22:37
he loved them unto the *e* .....John 13:1
supper being *e* the devil.......John 13:2
To this *e* was I born ....John 18:37
to the *e* they might not live ...Acts 7:19
salvation unto the *e* of the ....Acts 13:47
these things were *e*, Paul......Acts 19:21
e ye may be established ....Rom 1:11
e of those things is death......Rom 6:21
the *e* everlasting life ....Rom 6:22
For Christ is the *e* of the law ..Rom 10:4
words unto the *e* of the world ..Rom 10:18
also confirm you unto the *e* ...1Cor 1:8
whom the *e* of the world are ..1Cor 10:11
cometh the *e*, when he shall ...1Cor 15:24
acknowledge even to the *e* 2Cor 1:13
e of that which is abolished ...2Cor 3:13
ages, world without *e* ....Eph 3:21
e is destruction, whose God ...Phil 3:19
the *e* he may stablish your 1Thess 3:13
to fables and *e* genealogies 1Tim 1:4
Now the *e* of..commandment ..1Tim 1:5
hope firm unto the *e*..........Heb 3:6
whose *e* is to be burned.......Heb 6:8
assurance of hope unto the *e* ..Heb 6:11
to them an *e* of all strife ......Heb 6:16
beginning of days nor *e* of ....Heb 7:3
after the power of an *e* life....Heb 7:16
e of the world hath he ....Heb 9:26
e of their conversation ....Heb 13:7
have seen the *e* of the Lord ..James 5:11
Receiving the *e* of your faith ..1Pet 1:9
hope to the *e* for the grace 1Pet 1:13
e of all things is at hand 1Pet 4:7
what shall the *e* be of them ...1Pet 4:17
latter *e* is worse with them 2Pet 2:20
the beginning and the *e* ....Rev 1:8
keepeth my works unto the *e*..Rev 2:26
beginning and the *e*, I will ....Rev 21:6
the beginning and the *e* ....Rev 22:13

END OF THE WORLD

Events connected with:
Day of salvation ended ..Matt 24:3, 14
Harvest of souls ....Matt 13:36-43
Defeat of man of sin 2Thess 2:1-12
Judgment ....Matt 25:31-46
Destruction of world.....2Thess 1:6-10

Coming of:
Denied by scoffers.......2Pet 3:3-5
Preceded by lawlessness..Matt 24:12
Preceded by apostasy ....Luke 18:8
Without warning ....Matt 24:37-42
With fire 2Thess 1:7-10

Attitude toward:
Watchfulness ....Matt 25:1-13
Industry ....Matt 25:14-30
Hopefulness............Luke 21:25-28
Holy living.............Rom 13:12-14
2Pet 3:11, 14
Seeking the lost 2Pet 3:9, 15
Waiting for eternity......2Pet 3:13
Rev 21:1

ENDAMAGE—*to cause loss or damage to*
so thou shalt *e* the revenue ....Ezra 4:13

ENDANGER—*to put into danger*

[*also* ENDANGERED]
cleaveth wood shall be *e* ......Eccl 10:9
shall ye make me *e* my head ..Dan 1:10

ENDEAVOR—*to strive to achieve or reach*

[*also* ENDEAVORED, ENDEAVORING, ENDEAVORS]
to the wickedness of the *e*.....Ps 28:4
e to go into Macedonia ....Acts 16:10
E to keep the unity of..Spirit ..Eph 4:4
e the more abundantly to see ..1Thess 2:17
will *e* that ye may be able 2Pet 1:15

EN-DOR (ĕn'dôr)—*"fountain of habitation"*
Town of Manasseh ......Josh 17:11
Site of memorable defeat .Ps 83:9, 10
Home of notorious witch .1Sam 28:1-10

ENDOW—*to furnish*
Required to wed ....Ex 22:16

[*also* ENDUED]
God hath *e* me with a good ...Gen 30:20
wise son, *e* with prudence 2Chr 2:12
e with power from on.........Luke 24:49
e with knowledge among you? .James 3:13

ENDURE—*to continue in the same state; remain firm under suffering or misfortune*

[*also* ENDURED, ENDURETH, ENDURING]
the children be able to *e* ......Gen 33:14
thou shalt be able to *e* ....Ex 18:23
he is good; for his mercy *e* 1Chr 16:34
he is good; for his mercy *e* 2Chr 5:13
Lord, because his mercy *e*.....2Chr 7:6
e for ever toward Israel ....Ezra 3:11
How can I *e* to see the evil ...Esth 8:6
I *e* to see the destruction......Esth 8:6
fast but it shall not *e* ....Job 8:15
Lord shall *e* for ever..........Ps 9:7
Lord is clean, *e* for ever ......Ps 19:9
anger *e* but a moment ....Ps 30:5
weeping may *e* for a night.....Ps 30:5
goodness of God *e* ....Ps 52:1
long as the sun and moon *e* ...Ps 72:5
peace so long as the moon *e* ..Ps 72:7
name shall *e* for ever ....Ps 72:17
should have *e* for ever ....Ps 81:15
seed also will I make to *e* .....Ps 89:29
truth *e* to all generations ......Ps 100:5
O Lord, shalt *e* for ever ......Ps 102:12
glory of the Lord shall *e* for ...Ps 104:31
he is good; for his mercy *e* ....Ps 107:1
righteousness *e* for ever ....Ps 111:3
righteousness *e* for ever ....Ps 112:3
truth of the Lord *e* for ....Ps 117:2
Israel now say..his mercy *e* ....Ps 118:2
Lord say, that his mercy *e* ....Ps 118:4
righteous judgments *e*.........Ps 119:160
O Lord, *e* for ever ....Ps 135:13
he is good; for his mercy *e* ....Ps 136:1
his mercy *e* for ever ....Ps 136:3
heavens; for his mercy *e* for ...Ps 136:5
lights; for his mercy *e* for ever .Ps 136:7
by night; for his mercy *e* for...Ps 136:9
among them; for his mercy *e* ..Ps 136:11
into parts; for his mercy *e*.....Ps 136:13
Red Sea; for his mercy *e*.......Ps 136:15
great kings; for his mercy *e* ...Ps 136:17
Amorites; for his mercy *e* .....Ps 136:19
an heritage; for his mercy *e* ...Ps 136:21
low estate; for his mercy *e* ....Ps 136:23
to all flesh; for his mercy *e*....Ps 136:25
mercy, O Lord, *e* for ever ....Ps 138:8
ever; and doth the crown *e*....Prov 27:24
for his mercy *e* for ever ....Jer 33:11
Can thine heart *e*.............Ezek 22:14
he that shall *e* unto the end ...Matt 24:13
so *e* but for a time ....Mark 4:17
e with much longsuffering .....Rom 9:22
hopeth all things, *e* all things ..1Cor 13:7
effectual in the *e* of the same ..2Cor 1:6
tribulations that ye *e*.........2Thess 1:4
what persections I *e* 2Tim 3:11
will not *e* sound doctrine 2Tim 4:3
after he had patiently *e* ....Heb 6:15
e a great fight of afflictions....Heb 10:32
a better..an *e* substance ....Heb 10:34
he *e*, as seeing him ....Heb 11:27
e the cross, despising..shame ..Heb 12:2
that *e* such contradiction ......Heb 12:3
e chastening, God dealeth .....Heb 12:7
man that *e* temptation ....James 1:12
count them happy which *e* ....James 5:11
word of the Lord *e* for ever ...1Pet 1:25
toward God *e* grief 1Pet 2:19

ENDURANCE, BLESSEDNESS OF
Commanded ....Matt 10:22
2Tim 2:3
Exemplified 2Tim 2:10
Heb 10:32, 33
Rewarded...............2Tim 3:11
James 1:12

ENDURING THINGS
God's faithfulness ......Ps 89:33
God's mercies ....Ps 103:17
God's Word ....Matt 24:35
Spiritual nourishment ....John 6:27
Spiritual rewards 1Cor 3:14
Graces 1Cor 13:13
The real things 2Cor 4:18
God's kingdom ....Heb 12:27, 28

EN-EGLAIM (ĕn-ĕg'lī-ĭm)—*"fountain of two calves"*
Place near the Dead Sea .Ezek 47:10

ENEMY—*foe; adversary; opponent*

Applied to:
Foreign nations..........Gen 14:20
Israel..................Mic 2:8
Gentiles ....Col 1:21
Unregenerate men ....Rom 5:10
The world ....Matt 22:44
Satan ....Matt 13:39
Death 1Cor 15:26

Characteristics of, hate for:
God....................Rom 1:30
The Gospel 1Thess 2:14-18
The light ....John 3:19-21

Examples of:
Amalek against Israel....Ex 17:8-16
Saul against David.......1Sam 18:29
Jezebel against Elijah 1Kin 19:1, 2
Ahab against Elijah 1Kin 21:20
Haman against the Jews. .Esth 3:10
Jews against Gentiles ....Acts 22:21, 22
Jews against Christians ...Acts 7:54-60

Christian attitude toward:
Overcome by kindness ...1Sam 26:18-21
Do not curse ....Job 31:29, 30
Feed ....Rom 12:20
Love ....Luke 6:27, 35
Forgive ....Matt 6:12-15
Pray for ....Luke 23:34

[*also* ENEMIES, ENEMIES', ENEMY'S]
shall possess the gate of..*e* ....Gen 22:17
they join also unto our *e* ......Ex 1:10
hath dashed in pieces the *e*....Ex 15:6
meet thine *e* ox or his ass .....Ex 23:4
be an *e* unto thine enemies ....Ex 23:22
all thine *e* turn their backs ....Ex 23:27
ye shall chase your *e*..........Lev 26:7
your *e* shall eat it............Lev 26:16
delivered into..hand of the *e* ..Lev 26:25
e which dwell therein ....Lev 26:32
ye be in your *e* land ....Lev 26:34
power to stand before your *e* ..Lev 26:37
into the land of their *e*........Lev 26:41
e that oppresseth you ....Num 10:9
shall be saved from your *e* ....Num 10:9
be not smitten before your *e* ..Num 14:42
eat up the nations his *e* ....Num 24:8
be a possession for his *e* ......Num 24:18
ye be smitten before your *e* ...Deut 1:42
you rest from all your *e* ....Deut 12:10
unto battle against your *e* .....Deut 20:3

shalt eat the spoil of thine *e* . . . Deut 20:14
goeth forth against thine *e* . . . . Deut 23:9
thee rest from all thine *e* . . . . . . Deut 25:19
to be smitten before thine *e* . . . Deut 28:25
shalt thou serve thine *e* . . . . Deut 28:48
thine *e* shall distress thee . . . . . . Deut 28:55
thine *e* shall distress . . . . Deut 28:57
all these curses upon thine *e* . . . Deut 30:7
render vengeance to mine *e* . . . Deut 32:41
beginning of revenges upon..*e* . Deut 32:42
e shall be found liars unto . . . . . Deut 33:29
their backs before their *e* . . . . . Josh 7:8
could not stand before their *e* . Josh 7:12
their backs before their *e* . . . . . Josh 7:12
themselves upon their *e* . . . . Josh 10:13
the Lord do to all your *e* . . . . . Josh 10:25
not a man of all their *e* . . . . Josh 21:44
delivered all their *e* into . . . . . . Josh 21:44
unto Israel from all their *e* . . . . Josh 23:1
into the hands of their *e* . . . . . . Judg 2:14
longer stand before their *e* . . . . Judg 2:14
out of the hand of their *e* . . . . . Judg 2:18
let all thine *e* perish . . . . Judg 5:31
vengeance for thee of thine *e* . . Judg 11:36
delivered Samson our *e* . . . . Judg 16:23
mouth is enlarged over..*e* 1Sam 2:1
see an *e* in my habitation 1Sam 2:32
us out of the hand of our *e* . . . 1Sam 12:10
may be avenged on mine *e* 1Sam 14:24
against all..*e* on every side 1Sam 14:47
avenged of the king's *e* 1Sam 18:25
sent away mine *e* 1Sam 19:17
at the hand of David's *e* 1Sam 20:16
if a man find his *e* 1Sam 24:19
let thine *e* and they that 1Sam 25:26
and is become thine *e*? 1Sam 28:16
fight against the *e* of my 1Sam 29:8
out of the hand of all their *e* . . 2Sam 3:18
son of Saul thine *e* which 2Sam 4:8
round about from all his *e* 2Sam 7:1
thee to rest from all thine *e* . . . 2Sam 7:11
hath avenged him of his *e* 2Sam 18:19
thine *e*..hatest thy friends 2Sam 19:6
out of the hand of all his *e* . . . 2Sam 22:1
I have pursued mine *e* 2Sam 22:38
bringeth..forth from mine *e* . . . 2Sam 22:49
asked the life of thine *e* 1Kin 3:11
smitten down before the *e* 1Kin 8:33
out to battle against their *e* 1Kin 8:44
deliver them to the *e* 1Kin 8:46
captives unto the land of..*e* 1Kin 8:46
out of the hand of all your *e* . . 2Kin 17:39
into the hand of their *e* 2Kin 21:14
prey and a spoil to all their *e* . . 2Kin 21:14
come to betray me to mine *e* . . 1Chr 12:17
have cut off all thine *e* 1Chr 17:8
that the sword of thine *e* 1Chr 21:12
nor the life of thine *e* 2Chr 1:11
to the worse before the *e* 2Chr 6:24
go out to war against their *e* . . 2Chr 6:34
them to rejoice over their *e* . . . 2Chr 20:27
into the hands of their *e* 2Chr 25:20
help the king against the *e* 2Chr 26:13
help us against..*e* in . . . . Ezra 8:22
e heard that it was known . . . . . Neh 4:15
Arabian..rest of our *e* . . . . Neh 6:1
into the hand of their *e* . . . . Neh 9:27
out of the hand of their *e* . . . . . Neh 9:27
in the hand of their *e* . . . . Neh 9:28
Agagite, the Jews' *e* . . . . Esth 3:10
e is this wicked Haman . . . . Esth 7:6
to avenge..on their *e* . . . . Esth 8:13
Jews smote all their *e* . . . . Esth 9:5
Hammedatha..*e* of the Jews . . . Esth 9:10
Jews rested from their *e* . . . . . . Esth 9:22
Deliver me from the *e* hand? . . Job 6:23
holdest me for thine *e*? . . . . Job 13:24
unto him as one of his *e* . . . . . . Job 19:11
Let mine *e* be as the wicked . . . Job 27:7
hast smitten all mine *e* . . . . Ps 3:7
old because of all mine *e* . . . . . . Ps 6:7
Let all mine *e* be ashamed . . . . Ps 6:10
without cause is mine *e* . . . . Ps 7:4
because of the rage of mine *e* . Ps 7:6
strength because of thine *e* . . . . Ps 8:2
thou mightest still the *e* . . . . Ps 8:2
mine *e* are turned back . . . . Ps 9:3
long shall mine *e* be exalted . . . Ps 13:2
from my deadly *e*, who . . . . Ps 17:9
I be saved from mine *e* . . . . Ps 18:3
delivered me from..strong *e* . . . Ps 18:17
me the necks of mine *e* . . . . Ps 18:40
delivereth me from mine *e* . . . . Ps 18:48
shall find out all thine *e* . . . . . . Ps 21:8
not mine *e* triumph over me . . . Ps 25:2
mine *e* and my foes . . . . Ps 27:2
plain path, because of mine *e* . . Ps 27:11
reproach among all mine *e* . . . . Ps 31:11
Let not them that are mine *e* . . Ps 35:19
mine *e* are lively . . . . Ps 38:19
Mine *e* speak evil of me . . . . . . Ps 41:5
e doth not triumph over me . . . Ps 41:11
oppression of the *e* . . . . Ps 43:2
will we push down our *e* . . . . . . Ps 44:5
reason of the *e* and avenger . . . Ps 44:16
in the heart of the King's *e* . . . . Ps 45:5
seen his desire upon mine *e* . . . Ps 54:7
Because of the voice of the *e* . . Ps 55:3
shall mine *e* turn back . . . . Ps 56:9
see my desire upon mine *e* . . . . Ps 59:10
a strong tower from the *e* . . . . . Ps 61:3
thine *e* submit themselves . . . . . Ps 66:3
let his *e* be scattered . . . . Ps 68:1
shall wound the head of his *e* . . Ps 68:21
e wrongfully are mighty . . . . Ps 69:4
mine *e* speak against me . . . . . . Ps 71:10
his *e* shall lick the dust . . . . Ps 72:9
the *e* hath done wickedly . . . . . . Ps 74:3
e roar in the midst of thy . . . . . Ps 74:4
that the *e* hath reproached . . . . Ps 74:18
sea overwhelmed their *e* . . . . . . Ps 78:53
his glory into the *e* hand . . . . . . Ps 78:61
e laugh among themselves . . . . . Ps 80:6
thine *e* make a tumult . . . . Ps 83:2
e shall not exact upon him . . . . Ps 89:22
made all his *e* to rejoice . . . . . . Ps 89:42
for, lo, thine *e*, O Lord . . . . Ps 92:9
for, lo, thine *e* shall perish . . . . Ps 92:9
burneth up his *e* round . . . . Ps 97:3
them stronger than their *e* . . . . . Ps 105:24
e also oppressed them . . . . Ps 106:42
redeemed from the hand of..*e* . Ps 107:2
I make thine *e* thy footstool . . . Ps 110:1
see his desire upon his *e* . . . . . . Ps 112:8
made me wiser than mine *e* . . . Ps 119:98
e have forgotten thy words . . . . Ps 119:139
shall speak with the *e* . . . . Ps 127:5
redeemed us from our *e* . . . . . . Ps 136:24
e take thy name in vain . . . . Ps 139:20
I count them mine *e* . . . . Ps 139:22
me O Lord, from mine *e* . . . . . . Ps 143:9
maketh even his *e* to be at . . . . Prov 16:7
Rejoice not when thine *e* . . . . . Prov 24:17
thine *e* be hungry, give . . . . Prov 25:21
kisses of an *e* are deceitful . . . . Prov 27:6
avenge me of mine *e* . . . . Is 1:24
e shall devour them . . . . Is 26:11
recompense to his *e* . . . . Is 59:18
e shall come in like a flood . . . . Is 59:19
recompense to his *e* . . . . Is 66:6
sword of the *e*..fear is on . . . . . Jer 6:25
soul into the hand of her *e* . . . . Jer 12:7
thee to pass with thine *e* . . . . . . Jer 15:14
cause thee to serve thine *e* . . . . Jer 17:4
an east wind before the *e* . . . . . Jer 18:17
by the sword before their *e* . . . . Jer 19:7
fall by the sword of their *e* . . . . Jer 20:4
into the hand of their *e* . . . . Jer 21:7
from the land of the *e* . . . . Jer 31:16
give into the hand of their *e* . . . Jer 34:21
e have heard a cry of . . . . Jer 48:5
they are become her *e* . . . . Lam 1:2
e hath magnified himself . . . . . . Lam 1:9
e have heard of my trouble . . . . Lam 1:21
right hand from before the *e* . . Lam 2:3
Lord was as an *e* . . . . Lam 2:5
caused thine *e* to rejoice . . . . . . Lam 2:17
our *e* have opened their . . . . Lam 3:46
e should have entered into . . . . Lam 4:12
e hath said against you . . . . Ezek 36:2
into the hand of their *e* . . . . Ezek 39:23
gathered them out of their *e* . . . Ezek 39:27
interpretation..to thine *e* . . . . . . Dan 4:19
e shall pursue him . . . . Hos 8:3
into captivity before their *e* . . . . Amos 9:4
my people is risen up as an *e* . . Mic 2:8
from the hand of thine *e* . . . . . . Mic 4:10
man's *e* are the men of his . . . . Mic 7:6
mine *e* shall see it . . . . Mic 7:10
reserveth wrath for his *e* . . . . . . Nah 1:2
seek strength because of the *e* . Nah 3:11
set wide open unto thine *e* . . . . Nah 3:13
hath cast out thine *e* . . . . Zeph 3:15
tread down their *e* . . . . Zech 10:5
neighbor, and hate thine *e* . . . . Matt 5:43
Love your *e*, bless them that . . Matt 5:44
e came and sowed tares . . . . Matt 13:25
An *e* hath done this . . . . Matt 13:28
make thine *e* thy footstool? . . . Matt 22:44
make thine *e* thy footstool . . . . Mark 12:36
should be saved from our *e* . . . Luke 1:71
love ye your *e* and do good . . . Luke 6:35
over all the power of the *e* . . . . Luke 10:19
mine *e* which would not . . . . Luke 19:27
e shall cast a trench about . . . . . Luke 19:43
make thine *e* thy footstool . . . . Luke 20:43
thou *e* of all righteousness . . . . Acts 13:10
were *e* we were reconciled . . . . Rom 5:10
they are *e* for your sakes . . . . . . Rom 11:28
hath put all *e* under his feet . . . 1Cor 15:25
Am I therefore become your *e* . Gal 4:16
are the *e* of the cross . . . . Phil 3:18
e in your mind by wicked . . . . . Col 1:21
Yet count him not as an *e* 2Thess 3:15
thine *e* thy footstool? . . . . Heb 1:13
friend of the world is the *e* . . . . James 4:4
mouth and devoureth their *e* . . Rev 11:5

ENERGY—*effective force to perform work*

God's, in nature:
Creative . . . . Job 38:4-11
Beyond natural law . . . . . . Job 26:12
Maintains matter . . . . Heb 1:3

God's, in man:
To be witnesses . . . . Acts 1:8
For abundant living . . . . . . Rom 15:13
For miracles . . . . Rom 15:14
To raise dead 1Cor 6:14
2Cor 13:4

ENFLAMING—*inflaming*
E yourselves with idols . . . . Is 57:5

ENGAGED—*committed*
that *e* his heart . . . . Jer 30:21

EN-GANNIM (ĕn-găn'ĭm)—*"fountain of gardens"*
1. Village of Judah . . . . Josh 15:34
2. Border town of Issachar . . Josh 19:21
Assigned to Levites . . . . . Josh 21:29

EN-GEDI (ĕn-gĕd'ī)—*"fountain of the goat"*
May have been originally called Hazazon-tamar . . 2Chr 20:2
Occupied by the Amorites . . . . Gen 14:7
Assigned to Judah . . . . Josh 15:62
David's hiding place 1Sam 23:29
Noted for vineyards . . . . . Song 1:14

David is in..wilderness of *E* . . . 1Sam 24:1
fishers..stand upon it from *E* . . Ezek 47:10

ENGINES—*machines designed for a distinct purpose*
Shooting arrows 2Chr 26:15

shall set *e* of war against . . . . . . Ezek 26:9

ENGRAFTED—*joined or fastened as if by grafting*
with meekness the *e* word . . . . . James 1:21

ENGRAVER—*carver of stone*
work of an *e* in stone . . . . Ex 28:11
all manner of work, of the *e* . . Ex 35:35
e and a cunning workman . . . . . Ex 38:23

ENGRAVING—*cutting or carving on some hard substance*
Stone set in priest's breastplate ....Ex 28:9-11, 21
Bezaleel, inspired in .....Ex 35:30-33
Of a seal ....Ex 28:21
Of a signet..............Ex 39:6
Of cherubim 1Kin 6:29

[*also* ENGRAVE, ENGRAVEN, ENGRAVINGS]
stone, like the *e* of a signet ...Ex 28:11
upon it, like the *e* of a signet..Ex 28:36
names, like the *e* of a signet...Ex 39:14
writing, like to the *e* ....Ex 39:30
I will *e* the graving thereof ....Zech 3:9
written and *e* in stones 2Cor 3:7

EN-HADDAH (ĕn-hăd'ä)—*"flowing strongly"*
Frontier village of Issachar ....Josh 19:17, 21

EN-HAKKORE (ĕn-hăk'ō-rē)—*"well of the one who called"*
Miraculous spring ....Judg 15:14-19

EN-HAZOR (ĕn-hā'zôr)—*"fountain of the village"*
City of Naphtali ....Josh 19:32, 37

ENJOIN—*to direct or impose; prohibit*

[*also* ENJOINED]
Esther the queen had *e* them ..Esth 9:31
Who hath *e* him his way? .....Job 36:23
bold in Christ to *e* thee ....Philem 8
God hath *e* unto you ....Heb 9:20

ENJOYMENT—*satisfaction in something*
Of material things:
Depends upon obedience .Deut 7:9-15
Withheld for disobedience.Hag 1:3-11
Must not trust in ....Luke 12:16-21
Cannot fully satisfy ......Eccl 2:1-11
Of spiritual things:
Abundant...............1Tim 6:17
Never-ending............Is 58:11
Satisfying ....Is 55:1, 2
Internal................John 7:37-39
For God's people only ...Is 65:22-24
Complete in heaven .....Ps 16:11

[*also* ENJOY, ENJOYED]
land *e* her sabbaths ....Lev 26:34
e her sabbaths................Lev 26:43
children of Israel may *e* ....Num 36:8
but thou shalt not *e* ....Deut 28:41
land of..possession and *e* ......Josh 1:15
land had *e* her sabbaths 2Chr 36:21
should make his soul *e* good...Eccl 2:24
eat and to drink and to *e* .....Eccl 5:18
Seeing that by thee we *e* ......Acts 24:2
to *e* the pleasures of sin.......Heb 11:25

ENLARGEMENT—*extension in quantity or quality*
Japheth's territory ....Gen 9:27
Israel's prosperity ....Ex 34:24
Solomon's kingdom 1Kin 4:20-25
Solomon's wisdom 1Kin 4:29-34
Pharisaical hypocrisy .....Matt 23:5
Spiritual:
Relationship 2Cor 6:11, 13
Knowledge............Eph 1:15-19
Opportunity...........Is 54:1-3

[*also* ENLARGE, ENLARGED, ENLARGETH, ENLARGING]
Lord thy God shall *e* thy ......Deut 12:20
Lord thy God *e* thy coast .....Deut 19:8
Blessed be he that *e* Gad .....Deut 33:20
is *e* over my enemies 1Sam 2:1
hast *e* my steps under me 2Sam 22:37
and *e* my coast 1Chr 4:10
shall there *e* and deliverance ..Esth 4:14
e..nations, and straiteneth .....Job 12:23
hast *e* me when I was in ....Ps 4:1
troubles of my heart are *e*.....Ps 25:17
shalt *e* my heart ....Ps 119:32
hell hath *e* herself ....Is 5:14
heart shall fear, and be *e* .....Is 60:5
there was an *e* and a winding..Ezek 41:7
might *e* their border ....Amos 1:13
e..baldness as the eagle ....Mic 1:16
who *e* his desire as hell ....Hab 2:5
we shall be *e* by you 2Cor 10:15

ENLIGHTEN—*to illuminate; furnish knowledge*

[*also* ENLIGHTENED, ENLIGHTENING]
mouth; and his eyes were *e* ...1Sam 14:27
e with the light of the living ...Job 33:30
my God will *e* my darkness ...Ps 18:28
Lord is pure, *e* the eyes.......Ps 19:8
lightnings *e* the world ....Ps 97:4
understanding being *e*.........Eph 1:18
those who were once *e*........Heb 6:4

ENLIGHTENMENT, SPIRITUAL
Source of:
From God ....Ps 18:28
Through God's Word ....Ps 19:8
By prayer..............Eph 1:18
By God's ministers ......Acts 26:18
Degrees of:
Partial now 1Cor 13:9-12
Hindered by sin 1Cor 2:14
Complete in heaven .....Is 60:19

EN-MISHPAT (ĕn-mĭsh'păt)—*"fountain of judgment"*
returned, and came to *E* ......Gen 14:7

ENMITY—*active mutual hatred*
e between thee and the woman.Gen 3:15
e smite him with his hand .....Num 35:21
thrust..suddenly without *e* .....Num 35:22
at *e* between themselves ......Luke 23:12
carnal mind is *e* against ....Rom 8:7
abolished in his flesh the *e* ....Eph 2:15
having slain the *e* thereby .....Eph 2:16
friendship of the world is *e*....James 4:4

ENOCH (ē'nŭk)—*"teacher"*
1. Son of Cain ....Gen 4:17
2. City built by Cain.......Gen 4:17
3. Father of Methuselah ...Gen 5:21
Walks with God ....Gen 5:22
Taken up to heaven.....Gen 5:24
Prophecy of, cited ......Jude 14, 15
Called Henoch..........1Chr 1:3

unto *E* was born Irad ....Gen 4:18
two years, and he begat *E* ....Gen 5:18
Jared lived after he begat *E* ...Gen 5:19
days of *E* were three hundred .Gen 5:23
which was the son of *E* ....Luke 3:37
By faith *E* was translated .....Heb 11:5
E also the seventh from........Jude 14

ENOS, ENOSH (ē'nŏs, ē'nŏsh)—*"mortal"*
Grandson of Adam ......Gen 4:25, 26
Son of Seth ....Gen 5:6-11
Ancestor of Christ.......Luke 3:38
Genealogy of 1Chr 1:1

ENOUGH—*sufficient*
straw and provender *e* ....Gen 24:25
because I have *e* ....Gen 33:11
Israel said, It is *e*.............Gen 45:28
drew water *e* for us ....Ex 2:19
more than *e* for the service ....Ex 36:5
dwelt long *e* in this mount ....Deut 1:6
The hill is not *e* for us ....Josh 17:16
is *e*: stay now thine hand......2Sam 24:16
It is *e*..Lord, take away 1Kin 19:4
is *e*, stay now thine hand 1Chr 21:15
we have had *e* to eat 2Chr 31:10
goats' milk *e* for thy food .....Prov 27:27
four things say not, It is *e* .....Prov 30:15
dogs..can never have *e*........Is 56:11
destroy till they have *e*........Jer 49:9
shall eat and not have *e*.........Hos 4:10
in pieces *e* for his whelps .....Nah 2:12
ye eat, but ye have not *e* .....Hag 1:6
shall not be room *e*............Mal 3:10
e for the disciple that he ......Matt 10:25
it is *e*, the hour is come.......Mark 14:41
have bread *e* and to spare.....Luke 15:17
they had eaten *e* ....Acts 27:38

ENQUIRE—*See* INQUIRE

ENRICH—*to make prosperous*
king will *e* him with great 1Sam 17:25
didst *e* the kings of..earth .....Ezek 27:33

EN-RIMMON (ĕn-rĭm'ŏn)—*"fount of pomegranates"*
Reinhabited after the exile ....Neh 11:29
Same as Rimmon........Zech 14:10

ENROGEL (ĕn-rō'gĕl)—*"fuller's fountain"*
Fountain outside Jerusalem.............2Sam 17:17
On Benjamin's boundary .Josh 18:11, 16
Seat of Adonijah's plot ..1Kin 1:5-9

goings out thereof..at *E* ......Josh 15:7
south..descended to *E* ....Josh 18:16
Ahimaaz stayed by *E* 2Sam 17:17
stone of Zoheleth..by *E*.......1Kin 1:9

ENSAMPLE—*See* EXAMPLE

EN-SHEMESH (ĕn-shĕm'ĭsh)—*"eye of the sun"*
spring and town near Jericho ....Josh 15:7

went forth to *E* ....Josh 18:17

ENSIGN—*a banner or standard*
Used literally of:
Hosts....................Num 1:52
Enemy ....Ps 74:4, 5
Used figuratively of:
Enemy force ....Is 5:26
God's uplifted hand .....Is 31:9
Christ ....Is 11:10, 12

e of their father's house ....Num 2:2
up an *e* on the mountains .....Is 18:3
as an *e* on an hill.............Is 30:17
lifted up as an *e* upon..land ...Zech 9:16

ENSNARED—*caught; trapped*
reign not, lest the people be *e* .Job 34:30

ENSUE—*to pursue*
let him seek peace and *e* it 1Pet 3:11

ENTANGLE—*to complicate; tangle up*

[*also* ENTANGLED, ENTANGLETH]
They are *e* in the land ....Ex 14:3
they might *e* him in..talk .....Matt 22:15
e again with..yoke of bondage..Gal 5:1
e himself with..affairs 2Tim 2:4
they are again *e* therein 2Pet 2:20

ENTAPPUAH (ĕn-tăp'ū-ă)—*"fountain of the apple tree"*
Town of Ephraim ....Josh 17:7, 8

ENTER—*to go into*

[*also* ENTERED, ENTERETH, ENTERING, ENTRANCE, ENTRANCES, ENTRIES, ENTRY]
In the selfsame day *e* Noah ...Gen 7:13
come near to *e* into Egypt ....Gen 12:11
when Lot *e* into Zoar ....Gen 19:23
he *e* into his chamber ....Gen 43:30
Moses *e* into..tabernacle ....Ex 33:9
at the *e* in of..tabernacle ......Ex 35:15
Moses was not able to *e* ......Ex 40:35
that *e* into the host, to ....Num 4:3
that *e* into the service ....Num 4:30
the curse shall *e* into her ......Num 5:24
the curse shall *e* into her ......Num 5:27
border unto the *e*............Num 34:8
cut off, shall not *e* ....Deut 23:1
A bastard shall not *e* ....Deut 23:2
generation shall he not *e* ......Deut 23:2
or Moabite shall not *e* ....Deut 23:3
shall they not *e*..............Deut 23:3
thou shouldest *e* into ....Deut 29:12
which are *e* into thine.........Josh 2:3
at the *e* of the gate of ....Josh 8:29
them not to *e* into ....Josh 10:19
of them *e* into fenced ....Josh 10:20

at the *e* of the gate of ....Josh 20:4
the *e* into the city ....Judg 1:24
unto the *e* in of Hamath ....Judg 3:3
they *e* into the land....Judg 6:5
even unto the *e* of the ....Judg 9:40
and to *e* to possess ....Judg 18:9
Dan, stood by the *e* of....Judg 18:16
in array at the *e* in of....2Sam 10:8
Abishai, and *e* into the 2Sam 10:14
and my cry did *e* into 2Sam 22:7
And for the *e* of the 1Kin 6:31
when thy feet *e* into 1Kin 14:12
before Ahab to the *e* 1Kin 18:46
and stood in the *e* in of....1Kin 19:13
leprous men at the *e* in 2Kin 7:3
If we say, We will *e* into 2Kin 7:4
and *e* into another....2Kin 7:8
king's *e* without, turned 2Kin 16:18
e into the lodgings of 2Kin 19:23
in the *e* in of the gate 2Kin 23:8
they went to the *e* 1Chr 4:39
unto the *e* in of the....1Chr 5:9
keepers of the *e* 1Chr 9:19
and *e* into the city 1Chr 19:15
e of the house, the 2Chr 4:22
priests could not *e* 2Chr 7:2
the *e* in of Hamath 2Chr 7:8
that kept the *e* of the 2Chr 12:10
king *e* into the house 2Chr 12:11
part of you *e* on the 2Chr 23:4
was come to the *e* 2Chr 23:15
howbeit he *e* not into 2Chr 27:2
e into his sanctuary 2Chr 30:8
every one that *e* into 2Chr 31:16
even to the *e* in at the 2Chr 33:14
house that I shall *e* ....Neh 2:8
and *e* by the gate of ....Neh 2:15
none might *e* into the ....Esth 4:2
he *e* with thee into ....Job 22:4
Hast thou *e* into the ....Job 38:16
sword shall *e* into their....Ps 37:15
they should not *e*....Ps 95:11
E into his gates with ....Ps 100:4
the righteous shall *e* ....Ps 118:20
The *e* of thy words ....Ps 119:130
e not into judgment ....Ps 143:2
E not into the path of ....Prov 4:14
at the *e* of the city, at ....Prov 8:3
A reproof *e* more into ....Prov 17:10
e not into the fields....Prov 23:10
E into the rock, and ....Is 2:10
there is no house, no *e* ....Is 23:1
the truth may *e* ....Is 26:2
will *e* into the height....Is 37:24
shall *e* into peace: they ....Is 57:2
and equity cannot *e*....Is 59:14
at the *e* of the gates ....Jer 1:15
when ye *e*, ye defiled ....Jer 2:7
that *e* in at these gates....Jer 7:2
if I *e* into the city ....Jer 14:18
Jerusalem, that *e* in by....Jer 17:20
which is by the *e* of the ....Jer 19:2
who shall *e* into our ....Jer 21:13
then shall there *e* in ....Jer 22:4
which had *e* into ....Jer 34:10
the *e* of the new gate ....Jer 36:10
set your faces to *e* ....Jer 42:15
is at the *e* of Pharaoh's ....Jer 43:9
the heathen *e* into ....Lam 1:10
should not *e* into thy ....Lam 1:10
the spirit *e* into me ....Ezek 2:2
for the robbers shall *e* ....Ezek 7:22
jealously in the *e* ....Ezek 8:5
and *e* into a covenant....Ezek 16:8
shall not *e* into the ....Ezek 20:38
which *e* into their....Ezek 21:14
when he shall *e* into ....Ezek 26:10
as men *e* into a city ....Ezek 26:10
the breadth of the *e* ....Ezek 40:11
of the gate of the *e*....Ezek 40:15
chambers and the *e* ....Ezek 40:38
and they *e* into....Ezek 41:6
was the *e* on the east side ....Ezek 42:9
When the priests *e* ....Ezek 42:14
and no man shall *e* in....Ezek 44:2
he shall *e* by the way ....Ezek 44:3
mark well the *e* in of ....Ezek 44:5
They shall *e* into my....Ezek 44:16
when they *e* into the....Ezek 44:21
the prince shall *e* ....Ezek 46:8
he that *e* in by the way ....Ezek 46:9
army, and shall *e* into....Dan 11:7
He shall *e* peaceably ....Dan 11:24
shall *e* also into the....Dan 11:41
and I will not *e* into ....Hos 11:9
they shall *e* in at the....Joel 2:9
seek not Bethel, nor *e* ....Amos 5:5
afflict you from the *e* in....Amos 6:14
and foreigners *e* into ....Obad 11
And Jonah began to *e* into ....Jon 3:4
of Nimrod in the *e* ....Mic 5:6
rottenness *e* into my ....Hab 3:16
and it shall *e* into the ....Zech 5:4
e into the kingdom of....Matt 5:20
thou prayest, *e* into ....Matt 6:6
E ye in at the strait gate ....Matt 7:13
Lord, shall *e* into the ....Matt 7:21
when Jesus was *e* into ....Matt 8:5
he *e* into a ship, and....Matt 9:1
of the Samaritans *e* ....Matt 10:5
one *e* into a strong ....Matt 12:29
whatsoever *e* in at the ....Matt 15:17
not *e* into the kingdom....Matt 18:3
thee to *e* into life halt ....Matt 18:8
for thee to *e* into life ....Matt 18:9
if thou wilt *e* into life ....Matt 19:17
to *e* into the kingdom....Matt 19:24
ye them that are *e*....Matt 23:13
the day that Noah *e* into ....Matt 24:38
e thou into the joy ....Matt 25:21
e thou into the joy ....Matt 25:23
that ye *e* not into....Matt 26:41
he *e* into the synagogue ....Mark 1:21
no more openly *e* into ....Mark 1:45
he *e* into Capernaum ....Mark 2:1
he *e* into a ship, and sat ....Mark 4:1
lusts of other things *e* ....Mark 4:19
that we may *e* into ....Mark 5:12
e in where the damsel ....Mark 5:40
whithersoever he *e* ....Mark 6:56
Because it *e* not into....Mark 7:19
e into an house, and....Mark 7:24
e into the ship again ....Mark 8:13
of him, and *e* no more ....Mark 9:25
for thee to *e* into life ....Mark 9:43
better for thee to *e* halt ....Mark 9:45
he shall not *e* therein ....Mark 10:15
riches to *e* into the ....Mark 10:24
as soon as ye be *e* into it ....Mark 11:2
neither *e* therein, to ....Mark 13:15
pray, lest ye *e* into ....Mark 14:38
And *e* into the house ....Luke 1:40
he *e* into one of the ....Luke 5:3
he *e* into Capernaum ....Luke 7:1
thou shouldest *e* under....Luke 7:6
many devils were *e* ....Luke 8:30
would suffer them to *e*....Luke 8:32
feared as they *e* into ....Luke 9:34
whatsoever house ye *e* ....Luke 10:5
whatsoever city ye *e* ....Luke 10:10
that he *e* into a certain....Luke 10:38
ye *e* not in yourselves....Luke 11:52
them that were *e* in ye ....Luke 11:52
Strive to *e* in at the....Luke 13:24
day that Noah *e* into the ....Luke 17:27
child shall in no wise *e*....Luke 18:17
riches *e* into the ....Luke 18:24
man to *e* into the....Luke 18:25
Then *e* Satan into Judas ....Luke 22:3
house where he *e* in ....Luke 22:10
that ye *e* not into....Luke 22:40
pray, lest ye *e* into ....Luke 22:46
they *e* in, and found ....Luke 24:3
he *e* the second time....John 3:4
cannot *e* into the ....John 3:5
and ye are *e* into ....John 4:38
disciples were *e* ....John 6:22
He that *e* not by the....John 10:1
man *e* in, he shall ....John 10:9
into the which he *e* ....John 18:1
They went forth, and *e* ....John 21:3
ask alms of them that *e* ....Acts 3:2
they *e* into the temple ....Acts 5:21
e into every house ....Acts 8:3
morrow after they *e* ....Acts 10:24
and we *e* into the ....Acts 11:12
e into the kingdom of God ....Acts 14:22
and *e* into a certain....Acts 18:7
Paul would have *e* in ....Acts 19:30
grievous wolves *e* in ....Acts 20:29
with them *e* into the ....Acts 21:26
and was *e* into the place ....Acts 25:23
sin *e* into the world....Rom 5:12
Moreover the law *e*....Rom 5:20
neither have *e* into 1Cor 2:9
what manner of *e* in we....1Thess 1:9
know our *e* in unto 1Thess 2:1
They shall not *e* into....Heb 3:11
that they could not *e* ....Heb 3:19
being left us of *e* into....Heb 4:1
which have believed do *e* ....Heb 4:3
wrath, if they shall *e*....Heb 4:3
that some must *e* therein ....Heb 4:6
e not in because of ....Heb 4:6
therefore to *e* into ....Heb 4:11
which *e* into that ....Heb 6:19
forerunner is for us *e* ....Heb 6:20
For Christ is not *e* into ....Heb 9:24
boldness to *e* into the....Heb 10:19
are *e* into the ears of ....James 5:4
e shall be ministered....2Pet 1:11
deceivers are *e* into....2John 7
spirit of life from God *e* ....Rev 11:11
was able to *e* into ....Rev 15:8
there shall in no wise *e* ....Rev 21:27
e in through the gates....Rev 22:14

ENTERPRISE—*undertaking*
perform their *e*....Job 5:12

ENTERTAINMENT—*hospitality*

Occasions of:
Child's weaning ....Gen 21:8
Ratifying covenants ....Gen 31:54
King's coronation....1Kin 1:9, 18, 19
National deliverance ....Esth 9:17-19
Marriage....Matt 22:2
Return of loved ones ....Luke 15:23-25

Features of:
Invitations sent....Luke 14:16
Preparations made....Matt 22:4
Helped by servants ....John 2:5
Under a leader....John 2:8, 9
Often with music ....Luke 15:25
Sometimes out of control 1Sam 25:36
Unusual ....Heb 13:2

ENTHUSIASM—*a spirit of intense zeal*
Caleb's ....Num 13:30-33
Phinehas' ....Num 25:7-13
David's 2Sam 6:12-22
Saul's (Paul's) ....Acts 9:1, 2
Paul's ....Phil 3:7-14

ENTICE—*to allure to evil*

[*also* ENTICE, ENTICED, ENTICETH, ENTICING]
E thy husband, that ....Judg 14:15
hath been secretly *e* ....Job 31:27
Peradventure he will be *e* ....Jer 20:10
beguile you with *e* ....Col 2:4

ENTICERS—*those who allure to evil*

Means of:
Man....Ex 22:16
Spirit....2Chr 18:20
Sinners ....Prov 1:10
Lusts ....James 1:14
Human wisdom 1Cor 2:4

Reasons proposed:
Turn from God ....Deut 13:6-8
Obtain secrets....Judg 16:5
Defeat a king 2Chr 18:4-34
Commit a sin ....James 1:14

ENTIRE—*complete*
be perfect and *e*....James 1:4

E

ENTREAT—*to plead with*

[*also* ENTREATED, ENTREATETH]
he *e* Abram well for ....Gen 12:16
e for me to Ephron ....Gen 23:8
Isaac *e* the Lord for ....Gen 25:21
Lord was *e* of him ....Gen 25:21
hast thou so evil *e* ....Ex 5:22
E the Lord, that he may ......Ex 8:8
go very far away: *e* for me ....Ex 8:28
E the Lord for it is enough....Ex 9:28
and *e* the Lord your God .....Ex 10:17
and *E* the Lord ....Ex 10:18
And the Egyptians evil *e* us ...Deut 26:6
E me not to leave thee ....Ruth 1:16
who shall *e* for him? 1Sam 2:25
after that God was *e* for 2Sam 21:14
E now the face of the Lord ...1Kin 13:6
he was *e* of them 1Chr 5:20
he was *e* of him 2Chr 33:13
and he was *e* of us ....Ezra 8:23
I *e* him with my mouth ....Job 19:16
He evil *e* the barren ....Job 24:21
people shall *e* thy favor ....Ps 45:12
I *e* favor with my.............Ps 119:58
The poor useth *e* ....Prov 18:23
e the favor of the prince ......Prov 19:6
he shall be *e* of them ....Is 19:22
cause the enemy to *e* ....Jer 15:11
e them spitefully, and ....Matt 22:6
came his father out and *e* .....Luke 15:28
and spitefully *e* ....Luke 18:32
e him shamefully, and ....Luke 20:11
and *e* them evil four ....Acts 7:6
evil *e* our fathers ....Acts 7:19
Julius courteously *e* ....Acts 27:3
Being defamed, we *e* 1Cor 4:13
Praying us with much *e* 2Cor 8:4
I *e* thee also ....Phil 4:3
were shamefully *e* 1Thess 2:2
but *e* him as a father 1Tim 5:1
e that the word should not ....Heb 12:19
easy to be *e*, full of mercy ....James 3:17

ENVIRON—*"to encircle"*
shall *e* us round ....Josh 7:9

ENVY—*resentment against another's success*
Characterized as:
Powerful ....Prov 27:4
Dominant in unregenerate nature ....Rom 1:29
Of the flesh ....Gal 5:21
Source of evil 1Tim 6:4
The evil of, among Christians:
Hinders growth..........1Pet 2:1, 2
Examples of:
Philistines ....Gen 26:14
Joseph's brothers ....Gen 37:5, 11
Aaron and Miriam ......Num 12:2
Korah ....Num 16:3
David ....Ps 73:3, 17-20
Haman ....Esth 5:13
Chief priests ....Mark 15:10
The Jews ....Acts 13:45

[*also* ENVIED, ENVIES, ENVIEST, ENVIETH, ENVIOUS, ENVYING, ENVYINGS]
and the Philistines *e* him ......Gen 26:14
Rachel *e* her sister............Gen 30:1
his brethren *e* him............Gen 37:11
unto him, *E* thou for ....Num 11:29
and *e* slayeth the silly one .....Job 5:2
be thou *e* against ....Ps 37:1
They *e* Moses also.........Ps 106:16
E thou not the oppressor.......Prov 3:31
but *e* the rottenness of.........Prov 14:30
Let not thine heart *e* ....Prov 23:17
Be not thou *e* against ....Prov 24:1
able to stand before *e*?.........Prov 27:4
this a man is *e* of his ....Eccl 4:4
their hatred, and their *e* ......Eccl 9:6
The *e* also of Ephraim ....Is 11:13
Ephraim shall not *e*...........Is 11:13
for their *e* at the people.......Is 26:11
the trees of Eden..*e* him ......Ezek 31:9
according to thine *e* ....Ezek 35:11
that for *e* they had ....Matt 27:18
moved with *e* ....Acts 7:9
not, moved with *e* ....Acts 17:5
not in strife and *e* ....Rom 13:13
e, and strife, and 1Cor 3:3
charity *e* not; charity..........1Cor 13:4
e, wraths, strifes...............2Cor 12:20
one another, *e* one ....Gal 5:26
preach Christ even of *e* ....Phil 1:15
living in malice and *e* ....Titus 3:3
But if ye have bitter *e* ....James 3:14
For where *e* and strife is ......James 3:16
in us lusteth to *e*? ....James 4:5
hypocrisies, and *e* 1Pet 2:1

EPAENETUS, EPENETUS (ĕ-pē'nē-tŭs)—*"praiseworthy"*
Addressed by Paul ......Rom 16:5

EPAPHRAS (ĕp'ä-frăs)—*"lovely"*
Leader of the Colossian church.................Col 1:7, 8
Suffers as a prisoner in Rome ....Philem 23

E, who is one of you ....Col 4:12

EPAPHRODITUS (ĕ-păf'rō-dī'tŭs)—*"lovely"*
Messenger from Philippi. .Phil 2:25-27
Brings a gift to Paul .....Phil 4:18

EPHAH (ē'fä)—*"obscurity"*
1. Son of Midian ....Gen 25:4
2. Concubine of Caleb 1Chr 2:46
3. Son of Jahdai...........1Chr 2:47

E, and Epher, and 1Chr 1:33
of Midian and *E*.............Is 60:6

EPHAH (ē'fä)—*a dry measure, equal to approximately one bushel*
Dry measure ....Ex 16:36
Used for measuring barley ....Ruth 2:17

the tenth part of an *e*.........Lev 5:11
just weights, a just *e*.........Lev 19:36
tenth part of an *e* of..........Num 5:15
unleavened cakes of an *e*......Judg 6:19
one *e* of flour, and a 1Sam 1:24
brethren an *e* of this..........1Sam 17:17
homer shall yield an *e* ....Is 5:10
and a just *e*, and a just ....Ezek 45:10
The *e* and the bath shall ......Ezek 45:11
the *e* the tenth part of ....Ezek 45:11
an *e* of an homer of wheat ....Ezek 45:13
an *e* of an homer of barley....Ezek 45:13
e for a bullock, and an *e*......Ezek 45:24
an hin of oil for an *e* ....Ezek 45:24
offering shall be an *e* for......Ezek 46:5
and an hin of oil to an *e* ......Ezek 46:5
e for a bullock, and an *e*......Ezek 46:7
an hin of oil to an *e* ....Ezek 46:7
e to a bullock, and an *e*.......Ezek 46:11
an hin of oil to an *e* ....Ezek 46:11
making the *e* small, and.......Amos 8:5
This is an *e* that goeth ....Zech 5:6
in the midst of the *e*..........Zech 5:8
do these bear the *e*? ....Zech 5:10

EPHAI (ē'fī)—*"obscuring"*
Netophathite ....Jer 40:8

EPHER (ē'fĕr)—*"calf; young deer"*
1. Son of Midian ....Gen 25:4
2. Man of Judah 1Chr 4:17
3. Chief in Manasseh 1Chr 5:23, 24

Ephah, and *E*, and Henoch ...1Chr 1:33

EPHES-DAMMIM (ē-fĕs-dăm'ĭm)—*"boundary of blood"*
Philistine encampment ...1Sam 17:1
Called Pasdammin 1Chr 11:13

EPHESIANS, THE EPISTLE TO THE—*a letter of the New Testament*
Written by Paul ....Eph 1:1
Election ....Eph 1:4-6
Salvation by grace ....Eph 1:7, 8
Eph 2:8
Headship of Christ ....Eph 4:15, 16

EPHESUS (ĕf'ĕ-sŭs)—*"desirable"—a town on the western coast of Asia Minor; an important trading center*
Site of Jewish synagogue..Acts 18:19
Paul visits................Acts 18:19-21
Miracles done here ......Acts 19:11-23
Demetrius stirs up riot in .Acts 19:24-29
Elders of, addressed by Paul at Miletus ....Acts 20:17-38
Letter sent to ....Eph 1:1
Paul sends Tychicus .....Eph 6:21
Paul leaves Timothy 1Tim 1:3
One of seven churches ...Rev 1:11

[*also* EPHESIAN, EPHESIANS, EPHESUS]
scriptures, came to *E* ....Acts 18:24
upper coasts came to *E* ....Acts 19:1
Great is Diana of the *E*.......Acts 19:28
Ye men of *E*, what man ......Acts 19:35
the city of the *E* is a..........Acts 19:35
determied to sail by *E* ....Acts 20:16
city Trophimus an *E* ....Acts 21:29
fought with beasts at *E* 1Cor 15:32
I will tarry at *E* until 1Cor 16:8
ministered unto me at *E* 2Tim 1:18
have I sent to *E*..............2Tim 4:12
angel of the church of *E* ......Rev 2:1

EPHLAL—*"judgment"*
A descendant of Judah...1Chr 2:37

EPHOD (ĕ'fŏd)—*a vest*
1. Worn by:
The high priest ....Ex 28:4-35
Samuel................1Sam 2:18
David 2Sam 6:14
Used in asking counsel of God................1Sam 23:9-12
Used in idolatry ....Judg 8:27
2. Father of Hanniel.......Num 34:23

they shall make the *e* ....Ex 28:6
of the *e*, and the *e* ....Ex 29:5
curious girdle of the *e* ....Ex 29:5
to be set for the *e* ....Ex 35:9
curious girdle of his *e*.........Ex 39:5
like the work of the *e*.........Ex 39:8
was on the side of the *e*.......Ex 39:19
the two sides of the *e* ....Ex 39:20
curious girdle of the *e* ....Ex 39:20
unto the rings of the *e* ....Ex 39:21
curious girdle of the *e* ....Ex 39:21
be loosed from the *e*...........Ex 39:21
the robe of the *e* ....Ex 39:22
put the *e* upon him, and ......Lev 8:7
curious girdle of the *e* ....Lev 8:7
these houses an *e*.............Judg 18:14
carved image, the *e* ....Judg 18:18
to wear an *e* before me? 1Sam 2:28
Shiloh, wearing an *e* 1Sam 14:3
did wear a linen *e* 1Sam 22:18
came down with an *e* in........1Sam 23:6
bring me hither the *e* 1Sam 30:7
brought thither the *e*..........1Sam 30:7
had upon him an *e* 1Chr 15:27
without an *e*, and without .....Hos 3:4

EPHPHATHA (ĕf'ä-thä)—*"be opened"*
Christ's command ....Mark 7:34

EPHRAIM (ē'frā-ĭm)—*"fruitful"*
1. Joseph's younger son ....Gen 41:52
Obtains Jacob's blessing .Gen 48:8-20
2. Tribe of Ephraim ....Josh 16:4, 10
Predictions concerning...Gen 48:20
Large number of..........Num 1:33
Joshua, an Ephraimite...Josh 19:50
Territory assigned to ....Josh 16:1-10
Make Canaanites slaves. .Judg 1:29
Assist Deborah ....Judg 5:14, 15
Assist Gideon ....Judg 7:24, 25
Quarrel with Gideon ....Judg 8:1-3
Quarrel with Jephthah...Judg 12:1-4
Attend David's coronation 1Chr 12:30

Leading tribe of kingdom of Israel.............Is 7:2-17
Provoke God by sin.....Hos 12:7-14
Many of, join Judah....2Chr 15:9
Beth-el, idolatrous city of..................1Kin 12:29
Captivity of, predicted...Hos 9:3-17
Mercy promised to......Jer 31:9, 20
Messiah promised to....Zech 9:9-13
3. Hill country in Palestine .1Sam 1:1
4. Forest where Absalom was killed 2Sam 18:6-18
5. Gate in Jerusalem.......2Kin 14:13
6. Town to which Jesus withdrew ....John 11:54
7. Ten tribes considered as a unit ....Hos 4:16, 17

[*also* EPHRAIM'S]
born Manasseh and ***E***.........Gen 46:20
sons, Manasseh and ***E***........Gen 48:1
now thy two sons, ***E*** and......Gen 48:5
and laid it upon ***E*** head.......Gen 48:14
Joseph saw ***E*** children........Gen 50:23
of ***E***; Elishama the son........Num 1:10
of the children of ***E***..........Num 1:32
of the camp of ***E***.............Num 2:18
captain of the sons of ***E***.......Num 2:18
of the camp of ***E***.............Num 2:24
prince of the children of ***E***....Num 7:48
of the children of ***E***..........Num 10:22
Of the tribe of ***E***, Oshea......Num 13:8
the sons of ***E*** after...........Num 26:35
of the children of ***E***..........Num 34:24
ten thousands of ***E***...........Deut 33:17
the children of ***E***.............Josh 17:8
Southward it was ***E***, and......Josh 17:10
if mount ***E*** be too............Josh 17:15
of Joseph, even to ***E***..........Josh 17:17
and Shechem in mount ***E***.....Josh 20:7
lot out of the tribe of ***E***.......Josh 21:20
is in mount ***E***................Josh 24:30
in the mount of ***E***, on........Judg 2:9
Bethel in mount ***E***............Judg 4:5
Shamir in mount ***E***...........Judg 10:1
Pirathon in the land of ***E*****.....Judg 12:15
man of mount ***E***.............Judg 17:1
came to mount ***E***.............Judg 18:2
the side of mount ***E***..........Judg 19:1
the side of mount ***E***..........Judg 19:18
passed through mount ***E***......1Sam 9:4
and over ***E***, and over.........2Sam 2:9
which is beside ***E***.............2Sam 13:23
of Hur, in mount ***E***...........1Kin 4:8
to me from mount ***E***.........2Kin 5:22
out of the tribe of ***E***.........1Chr 6:66
sons of ***E***; Shuthelah..........1Chr 7:20
of the children of ***E***..........1Chr 9:3
of the children of ***E***..........1Chr 27:10
Of the children of ***E***..........1Chr 27:20
which is in mount ***E***..........2Chr 13:4
and in the cities of ***E***.........2Chr 17:2
all the children of ***E***..........2Chr 25:7
from the gate of ***E*** to..........2Chr 25:23
of the children of ***E***..........2Chr 28:12
the country of ***E***.............2Chr 30:10
E also and Manasseh.........2Chr 31:1
and ***E***, and of all the.........2Chr 34:9
street of the gate of ***E***........Neh 8:16
E also is the strength of.......Ps 60:7
not the tribe of ***E***............Ps 78:67
E also is the strength.........Ps 108:8
confederate with ***E***...........Is 7:2
Manasseh, ***E***; and ***E***..........Is 9:21
The envy also of ***E***...........Is 11:13
E shall not envy Judah.......Is 11:16
shall cease from ***E***...........Is 17:3
the drunkards of ***E***...........Is 28:3
from mount ***E***................Jer 4:15
the whole seed of ***E***..........Jer 7:15
to Israel, and ***E*** is my.........Jer 31:9
Is ***E*** my dear son? is..........Jer 31:20
For Joseph, the stick of ***E***.....Ezek 37:16
side, a portion for ***E***.........Ezek 48:5
E is joined to idols: let.......Hos 4:17
I know ***E***, and Israel.........Hos 5:3
for now O ***E***, thou..........Hos 5:3
E shall be desolate..........Hos 5:9
will I be unto ***E*** as a moth....Hos 5:12
E saw his sickness............Hos 5:13
then went ***E*** to the..........Hos 5:13
O ***E***, what shall I do..........Hos 6:4
the iniquity of ***E*** was.........Hos 7:1
E, he hath mixed............Hos 7:8
E is a cake not turned........Hos 7:8
E hath hired lovers..........Hos 8:9
E shall receive shame........Hos 10:6
E is as an heifer that........Hos 10:11
I will make ***E*** to ride........Hos 10:11
I taught ***E*** also to go........Hos 11:3
not return to destroy ***E***.......Hos 11:9
E feedeth on wind...........Hos 12:1
E spake trembling...........Hos 13:1
E shall say, What have.......Hos 14:8
possess the fields of ***E***........Obad 19
filled the bow with ***E***.........Zech 9:13

EPHRAIMITE—*descendant of Ephraim*

[*also* EPHRAMITES]
dwell among the ***E***...........Josh 16:10
Jordan before the ***E***.........Judg 12:5
Art thou an ***E***...............Judg 12:5
at the time of the ***E***.........Judg 12:6

EPHRAIN (ē'frā-ĭn)—*"hamlet"*
A city of Benjamin......2Chr 13:19

EPHRATAH, EPHRATH (ĕf'rä-tä, ĕf'răth)—*"fruitfulness"—same as Bethlehem*
1. Ancient name of Bethlehem ....Ruth 4:11
Prophecy concerning....Mic 5:2
2. Land of Palestine.......Ps 132:6
3. Wife of Caleb..........1Chr 2:19, 50

little way to come to ***E***.......Gen 35:16
way to come unto ***E***..........Gen 48:7
there in the way of ***E***........Gen 48:7
Caleb took unto him ***E***.......1Chr 2:19
Hur, the firstborn of ***E***........1Chr 2:50

EPHRATHITE (ĕf'răth-īt)—*inhabitant of Bethlehem*
1. Inhabitant of Beth-lehem (Ephrath)............Ruth 1:2
2. David was the son of....1Sam 17:12
Also called Ephraimites .Judg 12:5, 6

E of Beth-lehem-judah........Ruth 1:2
son of Zuph, an ***E***............1Sam 1:1
son of Nebat, an ***E***...........1Kin 11:26

EPHRON (ē'frôn)—*"strong"*
1. Hittite who sold Machpelah to Abraham.............Gen 23:8-20
2. Landmarks of Judah....Josh 15:9

of ***E*** the son of Zohar........Gen 25:9
that is in the field of ***E***.......Gen 49:29
with the field of ***E*** the........Gen 49:30
of a burying place of ***E***.......Gen 50:13

EPICUREANS (ĕp'ĭ-kū-rē'ănz)—*followers of Epicurus*
Sect of pleasure-loving philosophers..........Acts 17:18

EPISTLE—*a letter*

[*also* EPISTLES]
they delivered the ***e***..........Acts 15:30
delivered the ***e*** to the.........Acts 23:33
Tertius, who wrote this ***e***......Rom 16:22
I wrote unto you in an ***e***......1Cor 5:9
e of commendation to you....2Cor 3:1
are our ***e*** written in...........2Cor 3:2
e of Christ ministered.........2Cor 3:3
that the same ***e***..............2Cor 7:8
when this ***e*** is read...........Col 4:16
likewise read the ***e***...........Col 4:16
this ***e*** be read unto all........1Thess 5:27
my word, or our ***e***............2Thess 2:15
our word by this ***e***, note......2Thess 3:14
the token in every ***e***..........2Thess 3:17
second ***e***, beloved, I.........2Pet 3:1
As also in all his ***e***...........2Pet 3:16

EQUAL—*impartial; the same in measure, quality, or number*

[*also* EQUALITY, EQUALLY, EQUALS]
e distant one from............Ex 36:22
the crystal cannot ***e*** it.........Job 28:17
Ethiopia shall not ***e*** it........Job 28:19
the things that are ***e***..........Ps 17:2
was thou, a man mine ***e***.......Ps 55:13
of the lame are not ***e***..........Prov 26:7
knowledge, and in ***e***...........Eccl 2:21
with ***e*** for the meek of........Is 11:4
me, or shall I be ***e***?..........Is 40:25
me, and make me ***e***...........Is 46:5
in the street, and ***e***...........Is 59:14
what shall I ***e*** to thee.........Lam 2:13
of the Lord is not ***e***..........Ezek 18:25
Is not my way ***e***?.............Ezek 18:25
of the Lord is not ***e***..........Ezek 18:29
are not my ways ***e***?...........Ezek 18:29
of the Lord is not ***e***..........Ezek 33:17
their way is not ***e***.............Ezek 33:17
of the Lord is not ***e***..........Ezek 33:20
judgment, pervert all ***e***........Mic 3:9
walked..in peace and ***e***.........Mal 2:6
thou hast made them ***e***........Matt 20:12
for they are ***e*** unto the........Luke 20:36
making himself ***e*** with.........John 5:18
But by an ***e*** that now..........2Cor 8:14
that there may be ***e***...........2Cor 8:14
many my ***e*** in mine............Gal 1:14
it not robbery to be ***e***.........Phil 2:6
which is just and ***e***...........Col 4:1
the height of it are ***e***..........Rev 21:16

EQUALITY OF MAN—*state of every person before God*

Seen in same:
Creation................Acts 17:26
Guilt...................Rom 5:12-21
Sinfulness...............Rom 3:10-19
Salvation...............John 3:16
Judgment...............2Cor 5:10

Consistent with:
God's plan..............Rom 9:6-33
Different talents.........Matt 25:14-30
Different gifts..........1Cor 12:4-31
Different functions......Eph 5:22-33
Eph 6:1-9
Rule....................Ps 9:8

EQUITY—*justice*
Jehovah judges with.....Ps 98:9

and the people with ***e***.........Ps 98:9
dost establish ***e***, thou.........Ps 99:4
and judgment, and ***e***..........Prov 1:3
and judgment, and ***e***..........Prov 2:9
to strike princes for ***e***.........Prov 17:26

ER (ûr)—*"watcher"*
1. Son of Judah...........Gen 38:1-7
Gen 46:12
2. Descendant of Judah....1Chr 4:21
3. Ancestor of Christ......Luke 3:28

sons of Judah were ***E***.........Num 26:19
and ***E*** and Onan died.........Num 26:19
The sons of Judah; ***E***..........1Chr 2:3
And ***E***, the firstborn..........1Chr 2:3

ERAN (ē'răn)—*"watcher; watchful"*
Founder of the Eranites..Num 26:36

[*also* ERANITES]
the family of the ***E***...........Num 26:36

ERASTUS (ĕ-răs'tŭs)—*"beloved"*
1. Paul's friend at Ephesus .Acts 19:22
2Tim 4:20
2. Treasurer of Corinth....Rom 16:23
May be same person as 1.

ERE—*before*
delivered ***e*** the midwives......Ex 1:19
their teeth, ***e*** it was...........Num 11:33
how long will it be ***e***..........Num 14:11

And *e* the lamp of God 1Sam 3:3
e thou bid the people 2Sam 2:26
but *e* the messenger 2Kin 6:32
How long will it be *e* ....Job 18:2
how long will it be *e* ....Jer 47:6
how long will it be *e* ....Hos 8:5
Sir, come down *e* my ....John 4:49

ERECH (ē'rĕk)—*"length"*
City of Shinar ....Gen 10:10

ERECTED—*built*
And he *e* there an altar ....Gen 33:20

ERI (ē'rī)—*"watcher"*
Son of Gad ....Gen 46:16
Founder of the Erites ....Num 26:16

ERITES (ē'rīts)—*the family of Eri*
Eri, the family of the *E* ....Num 26:16

ERRAND—*a mission; item of business*
until I have told mine *e* ....Gen 24:33
I have a secret *e* unto.........Judg 3:19
I have an *e* to thee 2Kin 9:5

ERROR—*a departure from the truth*
Deceptive 2Tim 3:13
False ....Matt 24:4, 11
Produces misunderstanding ......Matt 22:29
Against Christ...........1John 4:1-6
Sign of the end..........1Tim 4:1

[*also* ERR, ERRED, ERRETH, ERRORS]
ignorance wherein he *e* ....Lev 5:18
if ye have *e*, and not ....Num 15:22
the fool, and have *e* 1Sam 26:21
him there for his *e* 2Sam 6:7
Made Judah..to *e* 2Chr 33:9
wherein I have *e* ....Job 6:24
mine *e* remaineth ....Job 19:4
Who can understand his *e*? ....Ps 19:12
is a people that do *e* in ....Ps 95:10
I *e* not from ....Ps 119:110
down all them that *e*..........Ps 119:118
refuseth reproof *e* ....Prov 10:17
Do they not *e* that ....Prov 14:22
say thou..it was an *e*..........Eccl 5:6
thee cause thee to *e* ....Is 3:12
caused Egypt to *e* ....Is 19:14
they also have *e* ....Is 28:7
the prophet have *e* ....Is 28:7
causing them to *e*.............Is 30:28
and to utter *e* against ....Is 32:6
thou made us to *e* ....Is 63:17
and the work of *e* ....Jer 10:15
people Israel to *e*.............Jer 23:13
cause my people to *e* by ......Jer 23:32
every one that *e*, and ....Ezek 45:20
was there any *e* ....Dan 6:4
hath caused them to *e* ....Hos 4:12
lies caused them to *e* ....Amos 2:4
make my people *e*............Mic 3:5
so the last *e* shall be ....Matt 27:64
ye therefore do greatly *e* ......Mark 12:27
recompence of their *e*.........Rom 1:27
they have *e* from the 1Tim 6:10
the truth have *e* 2Tim 2:18
They do always *e* in ....Heb 3:10
himself, and for the *e*.........Heb 9:7
Do not *e*, my beloved ....James 1:16
If any of you do *e* ....James 5:19
the sinner from the *e* ....James 5:20
them who live in *e* 2Pet 2:18
ran greedily after the *e*........Jude 11

ESAIAS (ē-sā'ās)—*the Greek word for Isaiah*
See ISAIAH

ESAR-HADDON (ē-sär-hăd'ŏn)—*"Ashur has given a brother"*
Son of Sennacherib; king of Assyria (681-669 B.C.)..................2Kin 19:37

since the days of *E* king.......Ezra 4:2
E his son reigned in ....Is 37:38

ESAU (ē'sô)—*"hairy"—the eldest son of Isaac, and Jacob's twin brother*
Son of Isaac ....Rom 9:11-13
Hairy...................Gen 25:25
Hunter ....Gen 25:27
Isaac's favorite son ......Gen 25:28
Sells his birthright ....Gen 25:29-34
Unable to repent ....Heb 12:16, 17
Marries two women .....Gen 26:34
Deprived of blessing .....Gen 27:1-40
Hates his brother Jacob ..Gen 27:41-45
Reconciled to Jacob .....Gen 33:1-17
With Jacob buries his father ....Gen 35:29
Descendants of ....Gen 36:1-43
Ancestor of Edomites ....Jer 49:7, 8
Prophecy concerning .....Obad 18

[*also* ESAU'S]
they called his name *E* ....Gen 25:25
hand took hold on *E* ....Gen 25:26
E came from the field ....Gen 25:29
E said to Jacob, Feed.........Gen 25:30
E said, Behold, I am ....Gen 25:32
Then Jacob gave *E* ....Gen 25:34
Thus *E* despised his ....Gen 25:34
And *E* was forty years ....Gen 26:34
as his brother *E* ....Gen 27:23
And *E* hated Jacob ....Gen 27:41
E said in his heart ....Gen 27:41
Jacob's and *E* ....Gen 28:5
When *E* saw that Isaac........Gen 28:6
And *E* seeing that the ....Gen 28:8
Then went *E* unto ....Gen 28:9
before him to *E* ....Gen 32:3
speak unto my lord *E*.........Gen 32:4
came to thy brother *E* ....Gen 32:6
If *E* come to the one ....Gen 32:8
from the hand of *E* ....Gen 32:11
hand a present for *E*..........Gen 32:13
When *E* my brother ....Gen 32:17
sent unto my lord *E* ....Gen 32:18
shall ye speak unto *E* ....Gen 32:19
and, behold, *E* came..........Gen 33:1
And *E* ran to meet him ......Gen 33:4
E said, I have enough ....Gen 33:9
And *E* said, Let me ....Gen 33:15
from the face of *E* thy ....Gen 35:1
children of *E*, which ....Deut 2:4
Seir unto *E* for a ....Deut 2:5
children of *E*, which ....Deut 2:8
the children of *E* ....Deut 2:12
to the children of *E* ....Deut 2:22
children of *E* which..........Deut 2:29
I gave unto..and *E* ....Josh 24:4
and I gave unto *E* ....Josh 24:4
The sons of Isaac; *E* 1Chr 1:34
The sons of *E* 1Chr 1:35
the calamity of *E* ....Jer 49:8
But I have made *E* ....Jer 49:10
are the things of *E* ....Obad 6
out of the mount of *E*? ....Obad 8
of the mount of *E* ....Obad 9
and the house of *E* for........Obad 18
of the house of *E*............Obad 18
possess the mount of *E* ....Obad 19
judge the mount of *E*.........Obad 21
Was not *E* Jacob's ....Mal 1:2
I hated *E*, and laid ....Mal 1:3
loved, but *E* have I hated .....Rom 9:13
profane person, as *E*..........Heb 12:16

ESCAPE—*to flee from*

Physical things:
Flood ....Gen 7:7, 8
City of destruction ....Gen 19:15-30
Mob....................Luke 4:28-30
Insane king 1Sam 19:9-18
Wicked queen 1Kin 11:1-3
Assassination............Esth 2:21-23
Hanging ....Esth 5:14
Prison ....Acts 5:18-20
Sinking ship.............Acts 27:30-44

Spiritual things:
Sin ....Gen 39:10-12
Destruction ....Luke 21:36
Corruption 2Pet 1:4
God's wrath 1Thess 1:9, 10
The great tribulation .....Rev 7:13-17

[*also* ESCAPED, ESCAPETH, ESCAPING]
came one that had *e* ....Gen 14:13
E for thy life; look ....Gen 19:17
e to the mountain, lest ....Gen 19:17
which is left shall *e* ....Gen 32:8
of that which is *e* ....Ex 10:5
given his sons that *e* ....Num 21:29
servant which is *e* from ....Deut 23:15
of them remain or *e* ....Josh 8:22
Ehud *e* while they ....Judg 3:26
and *e* unto Seirath ....Judg 3:26
which were *e* ....Judg 12:5
taken; but the people *e* 1Sam 14:41
and David fled, and *e*.........1Sam 19:10
and *e* to the cave 1Sam 22:1
that David was *e* from 1Sam 23:13
I should speedily *e* into 1Sam 27:1
so shall I *e* out of his hand 1Sam 27:1
camp of Israel am I *e* 2Sam 1:3
we shall not else *e* from 2Sam 15:14
him fenced cities, and *e* 2Sam 20:6
let not one of them *e* 1Kin 18:40
him that *e* the sword..........1Kin 19:17
him that *e* from the...........1Kin 19:17
the king of Syria *e*...........1Kin 20:20
let none go forth nor *e*........2Kin 9:15
that is *e* of the house 2Kin 19:30
and they that *e* out of 2Kin 19:31
Amalekites that were *e* 1Chr 4:43
of the king of Syria *e* 2Chr 16:7
of you, that are *e*............2Chr 30:6
leave us a remnant to *e* ....Ezra 9:8
be no remnant nor *e*..........Ezra 9:14
we remain yet *e*, as it.........Ezra 9:15
Jews that had *e* ....Neh 1:2
thou shalt *e* in the ....Esth 4:13
I only am *e* ....Job 1:15
they shall not *e*, and ....Job 11:20
I am *e* with the skin ....Job 19:20
my *e* from the windy ....Ps 55:8
Shall they *e* by iniquity ....Ps 56:7
cause me to *e*: incline.........Ps 71:2
Our soul is *e* as a bird ....Ps 124:7
whilst that I withal *e*..........Ps 141:10
speaketh lies shall not *e*.......Prov 19:5
pleaseth God shall *e* ....Eccl 7:26
for them that are *e* ....Is 4:2
lions upon him that *e* ....Is 15:9
and how shall we *e*? ....Is 20:6
that is *e* of the house of.......Is 37:31
that are *e* of the nations ......Is 45:20
I will send those that *e*.........Is 66:19
shall not be able to *e* ....Jer 11:11
shall not *e* out of the ....Jer 32:4
shalt not *e* out of............Jer 38:18
the son of Nethaniah *e*........Jer 41:15
sojourn there, shall *e* ....Jer 44:14
a small number that *e*.........Jer 44:28
no city shall *e*; the...........Jer 48:8
fleeth, and her that *e* ....Jer 48:19
let none thereof *e* ....Jer 50:29
Lord's anger none *e* ....Lam 2:22
have some that shall *e* ....Ezek 6:8
But they that *e* of them ....Ezek 7:16
that..of them shall *e* ....Ezek 7:16
things, he shall not *e* ....Ezek 17:18
he that *e* in that day ....Ezek 24:26
to him which is *e* ....Ezek 24:27
afore he that was *e* ....Ezek 33:22
But these shall *e* out of ....Dan 11:41
and nothing shall *e* ....Joel 2:3
he that *e* of them shall........Amos 9:1
those of his that did *e* ....Obad 14
ye *e* the damnation of ....Matt 23:33
worthy to *e* all these ....Luke 21:36
but he *e* out of their ....John 10:39
should swim out, and *e* ....Acts 27:42
though he hath *e* ....Acts 28:4
shalt *e* the judgment ....Rom 2:3
also make a way to *e* 1Cor 10:13
down by the wall, and *e* 2Cor 11:33
and they shall not *e* 1Thess 5:3

How shall we *e*, if we ....Heb 2:3
of fire, *e* the edge of ....Heb 11:34
more shall not we *e* ....Heb 12:25
For if after they have *e* 2Pet 2:20

ESCHATOLOGY—*teaching dealing with final events and destiny*

In Old Testament:
Judgment ....Is 2:12-22
Messianic kingdom ......Jer 23:4-18
Jer 33:14-17

In New Testament:
Coming of Christ ....Matt 24
Luke 21:5-36
Resurrection of dead 1Cor 15:51-58
1Thess 4:13-18
Destruction of earth 2Pet 3:10-13
Reign of Christ ....Rev 20:4, 6

ESCHEW—*avoid on moral grounds*

[*also* ESCHEWED, ESCHEWETH]
that feared God, and *e* ....Job 1:1
that feareth God and *e* ....Job 1:8
Let him *e* evil, and do 1Pet 3:11

ESEK (ē'sěk)—*"strife"*
A well in Gerar ....Gen 26:20

ESH-BAAL (ěsh'bāl)—*"man or servant of Baal"*
Son of Saul 1Chr 8:33
Same as Ishbosheth 2Sam 2:12

and Abinadab, and *E* 1Chr 9:39

ESHBAN (ěsh'băn)—*"man of understanding"*
Son of Dishon ....Gen 36:26

Amram, and *E*, and 1Chr 1:41

ESHCOL (ěsh'kǒl)—*"a cluster of grapes"*
1. Brother of Aner and Mamre ....Gen 14:13, 24
2. Valley near Hebron .....Num 13:22-27
Deut 1:24

up unto the valley of *E* ....Num 32:9
unto the valley of *E* ....Deut 1:24

ESHEAN (ěsh'ĭ-ăn)—*"support"*
City of Judah ....Josh 15:52

ESHEK (ē'shěk)—*"oppressor"*
Descendant of Saul 1Chr 8:39

ESHKALONITES (ěsh'kă-lǒ-nīts)
Natives of Ashkelon .....Josh 13:3

ESHTAOL (ěsh'tā-ǒl)—*"way"*
Town of Judah ....Josh 15:20, 33
Assigned to Danites .....Josh 19:40, 41
Near Samson's home and burial site ....Judg 16:31

Zorah, and from *E* ....Judg 18:2
brethren to Zorah and *E* ......Judg 18:8
out of Zorah and out of *E* ....Judg 18:11

ESHTAULITES (ěsh'tā-o͞o-līts)
Inhabitants of Eshtaol ...1Chr 2:53

ESHTEMOA, ESHTEMOH (ěsh-tě-mō'ä, ěsh-tě-mō')—*"bosom of women"*
Town of Judah ....Josh 15:20, 50
Assigned to Levites ......Josh 21:14
David sends spoils to 1Sam 30:26, 28

[*also* ECHTEMOH]
Ishbah the father of *E* 1Chr 4:17
Garmite, and *E* the 1Chr 4:19
Jattir, and *E*, with 1Chr 6:57

ESHTON (ěsh'tǒn)—*"rest"*
Man of Judah 1Chr 4:1-12

ESLI (ěs'lī)—*"reserved"*
Ancestor of Christ ....Luke 3:25

ESPECIALLY—*of special note*
e among my neighbors ....Ps 31:11
E because I know thee ....Acts 26:3
e unto them who are ....Gal 6:10
e they who labor in 1Tim 5:17
the books, but *e* the 2Tim 4:13

ESPOUSED—*betrothed*

[*also* ESPOUSALS]
wife Michal, which I *e* 2Sam 3:14
in the day of his *e* ....Song 3:11
the love of thine *e* ....Jer 2:2
his mother Mary was *e* ....Matt 1:18
To a virgin *e* to a man ....Luke 1:27
For I have *e* you to 2Cor 11:2

ESPY—*to see*

[*also* ESPIED]
opened his sack..he *e* ....Gen 42:27
Kadesh-barnea to *e* ....Josh 14:7
stand by the way, and *e* ....Jer 48:19
into a land that I had *e* ....Ezek 20:6

ESROM—*See* HEZRON

ESTABLISH—*to make permanent*

Of earthly things:
Kingdom 2Chr 17:5
Festival ....Esth 9:21

Of spiritual things:
Messiah's kingdom 2Sam 7:13
God's Word ....Ps 119:38
Our:
Hearts 1Thess 3:13
Faith ....Col 2:7
Works 2Thess 2:17
Lives 1Pet 5:10

Accomplished by:
God 2Cor 1:21, 22

[*also* ESTABLISHED, ESTABLISHETH, ESTABLISHMENT]
with thee will I *e* my ....Gen 6:18
I will *e* my covenant ....Gen 9:11
which I have *e* ....Gen 9:17
I will *e* my covenant ....Gen 17:19
also *e* my covenant ....Ex 6:4
house..shall be *e* ....Lev 25:30
and *e* my covenant ....Lev 26:9
her husband may *e* it ....Num 30:13
then he *e* all her vows ....Num 30:14
that he may *e* his ....Deut 8:18
shall the matter be *e* ....Deut 19:15
That he may *e* thee today .....Deut 29:13
only the Lord *e* his word 1Sam 1:23
that Samuel was *e* 1Sam 3:20
shalt not be *e*, nor 1Sam 20:31
Lord had *e* him king 2Sam 5:12
and I will *e* his kingdom 2Sam 7:12
thy kingdom shall be *e* 2Sam 7:16
thy throne shall be *e* 2Sam 7:16
his kingdom was *e* 1Kin 2:12
David shall be *e* 1Kin 2:45
Then I will *e* the throne 1Kin 9:5
and I will *e* his kingdom 1Chr 17:11
his throne shall be *e* for 1Chr 17:14
Let it even be *e*, that thy 1Chr 17:24
house of David..be *e* 1Chr 17:24
Moreover I will *e* his 1Chr 28:7
David my father be *e* 2Chr 1:9
loved Israel, to *e* them 2Chr 9:8
so shall ye be *e*; believe 2Chr 20:20
So they *e* a decree to 2Chr 30:5
these things, and the *e* 2Chr 32:1
Their seed is *e* in their ....Job 21:8
he doth *e* them for ....Job 36:7
but *e* the just: for the ....Ps 7:9
and *e* it upon the floods ....Ps 24:2
For he *e* a testimony ....Ps 78:5
highest himself shall *e* ....Ps 87:5
Thy seed will I *e* for ever .....Ps 89:4
my hand shall be *e* ....Ps 89:21
and *e* thou the work of ....Ps 90:17
work of our hands *e* ....Ps 90:17
Thy throne is *e* of old ....Ps 93:2
their seed shall be *e* ....Ps 102:28
thou hast *e* the earth ....Ps 119:90
not an evil speaker be *e* ....Ps 140:11
understanding hath he *e* ....Prov 3:19
when he *e* the clouds ....Prov 8:28
lip of truth shall be *e* ....Prov 12:19
he will *e* the border of ....Prov 15:25
thy thoughts shall be *e* ....Prov 16:3
Every purpose is *e* by ....Prov 20:18
and his throne shall be *e* ......Prov 25:5
king by judgment *e* ....Prov 29:4
hath *e* all the ends of ....Prov 30:4
Lord's house shall be *e* ....Is 2:2
e it with judgment ....Is 9:7
shall the throne be *e* ....Is 16:5
shalt thou be *e* ....Is 54:14
no rest, till he *e* ....Is 62:7
hath *e* the world by ....Jer 10:12
that formed it, to *e* it ....Jer 33:2
by his power, he hath *e* ....Jer 51:15
I will *e* unto thee an ....Ezek 16:60
I was *e* in my kingdom ....Dan 4:36
together to *e* a royal ....Dan 6:7
which the king *e* ....Dan 6:15
exalt themselves to *e* ....Dan 11:14
and *e* judgment in the ....Amos 5:15
be *e* in the top of the ....Mic 4:1
thou hast *e* them for ....Hab 1:12
and it shall be *e*, and ....Zech 5:11
every word may be *e* ....Matt 18:16
were the churches *e* in ....Acts 16:5
to the end ye may be *e* ....Rom 1:11
God forbid: yea, we *e* ....Rom 3:31
about to *e* their own ....Rom 10:3
shall every word be *e* 2Cor 13:1
to *e* you, and to comfort 1Thess 3:2
was *e* upon better ....Heb 8:6
the first, that he may *e* ....Heb 10:9
be *e* in the present 2Pet 1:12

ESTATE—*state; possessions*

[*also* ESTATES]
me according to the *e* 1Chr 17:17
give her royal *e* unto ....Esth 1:19
us in our low *e* ....Ps 136:23
Lo, I am come to great *e* .....Eccl 1:16
to their former *e* ....Ezek 16:55
you after your old *e* ....Ezek 36:11
shall one stand up in his *e* ....Dan 11:7
And in his *e* shall stand ....Dan 11:21
captains, and chief *e* ....Mark 6:21
the low *e* of his ....Luke 1:48
and all the *e* of the elders .....Acts 22:5
to men of low *e* ....Rom 12:16
he might know your *e* ....Col 4:8
kept not their first *e* ....Jude 6

ESTEEM—*hold in high regard*

[*also* ESTEEMED, ESTEEMETH, ESTEEMING]
lightly *e* the Rock of ....Deut 32:15
shall be lightly *e* 1Sam 2:30
I have *e* the words of ....Job 23:12
Will he *e* thy riches? ....Job 36:19
He *e* iron as straw ....Job 41:27
I *e* all thy precepts ....Ps 119:128
shutteth his lips is *e* ....Prov 17:28
shall be *e* as the ....Is 29:16
despised, and we *e* ....Is 53:3
yet we did *e* him stricken .....Is 53:4
are they *e* as earthen ....Lam 4:2
which is highly *e* ....Luke 16:15
One man *e* one day ....Rom 14:5
but to him that *e* any ....Rom 14:14
judge who are least *e* 1Cor 6:4
e other better than ....Phil 2:3
And to *e* them very 1Thess 5:13
E the reproach of Christ ......Heb 11:26

ESTHER (ěs'ter)—*"star; (the goddess) Ishtar"*
Daughter of Abihail .....Esth 2:15
Mordecai's cousin ....Esth 2:7, 15
Selected for harem ......Esth 2:7-16
Chosen queen ....Esth 2:17, 18
Seeks to help Mordecai ..Esth 4:4-6
Told of Haman's plot ....Esth 4:7-9
Sends message to Mordecai ....Esth 4:10-12
Told to act.............Esth 4:13, 14
Seeks Mordecai's aid ....Esth 4:15-17
Appears before Ahasuerus ....Esth 5:1-5

Invites Ahasuerus to banquet .... Esth 5:4-8
Reveals Haman's plot .... Esth 7:1-7
Given Haman's house .... Esth 8:1, 2
Secures change of edict .. Esth 8:3-6
Makes further request ... Esth 9:12, 13
With Mordecai, institutes Purim .... Esth 9:29-32

[*also* ESTHER'S]
Hadassah, that is ***E*** .... Esth 2:7
E had not yet showed .... Esth 2:20
E did the commandment ...... Esth 2:20
told it unto ***E*** the queen ...... Esth 2:22
E certified the king .... Esth 2:22
E maids and her .... Esth 4:4
called ***E*** for Hatach .... Esth 4:5
E the queen did let no .... Esth 5:12
the banquet that ***E*** .... Esth 6:14
the bed whereon ***E*** .... Esth 7:8
Ahasuerus said unto ***E*** .... Esth 8:7
have given ***E*** the house .... Esth 8:7
when ***E*** came before .... Esth 9:25

ESTIMATION—*assignment of a believed or assumed value*

[*also* ESTIMATE, ESTIMATIONS]
with thy ***e*** by shekels .... Lev 5:15
thy ***e***, for a trespass .... Lev 6:6
for the Lord by thy ***e*** .... Lev 27:2
And thy ***e*** shall be of .... Lev 27:3
e shall be fifty shekels .... Lev 27:3
then thy ***e*** shall be of .... Lev 27:5
e shall be of the male .... Lev 27:6
the female thy ***e*** shall .... Lev 27:6
be poorer than thy ***e*** .... Lev 27:8
the priest shall ***e*** it .... Lev 27:14
as the priest shall ***e*** it .... Lev 27:14
the money of thy ***e*** .... Lev 27:15
according to thy ***e*** .... Lev 27:17
the money of thy ***e*** .... Lev 27:19
the worth of thy ***e*** .... Lev 27:23
he shall give thine ***e*** in .... Lev 27:23
e shall be according .... Lev 27:25
according to thine ***e*** .... Lev 27:27
according to thy ***e*** .... Lev 27:27
according to thine ***e***, for ...... Num 18:16

ESTRANGED—*removed from; at enmity with*
are verily ***e*** from me .... Job 19:13
The wicked are ***e*** from .... Ps 58:3
They were not ***e*** from .... Ps 78:30
and have ***e*** this place .... Jer 19:4
they are all ***e*** from me .... Ezek 14:5

ESTRANGEMENT FROM GOD—*being at enmity with God*

Caused by:
Natural status .... Esth 2:11, 12
Adam's sin .... Gen 3:8-11, 24
Personal sin .... Ps 51:9-12
National sin .... Jer 2:14-16

ETAM (ē'tăm)—*"wild beast's lair"*
1. Village of Simeon 1Chr 4:32
2. Rock where Samson took refuge .... Judg 15:8-19
3. Town of Judah 2Chr 11:6

the top of the rock ***E*** .... Judg 15:8
the top of the rock ***E*** .... Judg 15:11
were of the father of ***E*** 1Chr 4:3

ETERNAL—*without end*

Applied to Trinity:
God .... Ps 90:2
Christ .... Prov 8:23
Holy Spirit .... Heb 9:14

Applied to God's attributes:
Home .... Eccl 12:5
Power .... Rom 1:20
Covenant .... Is 55:3
Gospel .... Rev 14:6
Counsels .... Eph 3:10, 11
Righteousness .... Ps 119:142, 144
Kingdom .... Ps 145:13
Lovingkindness .... Ps 100:5
Love .... Jer 31:3
Father .... Is 9:6

Applied to the believer:
Comfort 2Thess 2:16
Life .... John 3:15
Redemption .... Heb 9:12
Salvation .... Heb 5:9
Inheritance .... Heb 9:15
Glory 1Pet 5:10
Kingdom 2Pet 1:11
Reward .... John 4:36
Name .... Is 56:5
Glory 2Tim 2:10
Light .... Is 60:19, 20
Joy .... Is 51:11
Dwellings .... Luke 16:9
Purpose .... Eph 3:11

Applied to the wicked:
Damnation .... Mark 3:29
Judgment .... Heb 6:2
Punishment .... Matt 25:46
Destruction 2Thess 1:9
Contempt .... Dan 12:2
Bonds .... Jude 6
Fire .... Matt 25:41
Sin .... Mark 3:29

that I may have ***e*** life? .... Matt 19:16
that I may inherit ***e*** life? ...... Mark 10:17
in the world to come ***e*** life .... Mark 10:30
shall I do to inherit ***e*** .... Luke 10:25
shall I do to inherit ***e*** .... Luke 18:18
my blood, hath ***e*** life .... John 6:54
hast the words of ***e*** life .... John 6:68
And I give unto them ***e*** life ... John 10:28
world..keep it unto life ***e*** ...... John 12:25
he should give ***e*** life to .... John 17:2
life ***e*** that they might know .... John 17:3
honor..immortality, ***e*** life ...... Rom 3:7
righteousness unto ***e*** life ...... Rom 5:21
the gift of God is ***e*** life .... Rom 6:23
e weight of glory 2Cor 4:17
the things..not seen are ***e*** 2Cor 4:18
lay hold on ***e*** life 1Tim 6:12
they may lay hold on ***e*** life 1Tim 6:19
according to..hope of ***e*** .... Titus 3:7
promise of ***e*** inheritance ...... Heb 9:15
unto you that ***e*** life 1John 1:2
promised us even ***e*** life 1John 2:25
no murderer hath ***e*** life 1John 3:15
hath given to us ***e*** life 1John 5:11
that ye have ***e*** life 1John 5:13
the true God and ***e*** life 1John 5:20
Jesus Christ unto ***e*** life .... Jude 6

ETERNITY—*time without end*
God's habitation .... Is 57:15

ETHAM (ē'tham)—*"sea-bound"*
Israel's encampment ..... Ex 13:20

pitched in ***E*** which .... Num 33:6

ETHAN (ē'thăn)—*"ancient"*
1. One noted for wisdom .. 1Kin 4:31
2. Levite 1Chr 6:44
3. Ancestor of Asaph 1Chr 6:42, 43

sons of Zerah, Zimri and ***E*** ... 1Chr 2:6
sons of ***E***, Azariah 1Chr 2:8
Merari their brethren ***E*** 1Chr 15:17
Heman, Asaph, and ***E*** 1Chr 15:19

ETHANIM (ĕth'ă-nĭm)
Seventh month in the Hebrew year, also called Tishri 1Kin 8:2

ETHBAAL (ĕth-bā'ăl)—*"Baal's man; with Baal"*
Father of Jezebel 1Kin 16:31

ETHER (ē'ther)—*"plenty"*
Town of Judah .... Josh 15:42

ETHICS—*a system setting forth standards of right conduct*
Perversion of .... Rom 1:19-32
Law of .... Rom 2:14-16
Summary of Christian .... Rom 12:1-21

ETHIOPIA (ē-thĭ-ō'pĭ'ä)—*"burnt face"*
Country south of Egypt .. Ezek 29:10
Home of the Sons of Ham .... Gen 10:6
Famous for minerals ..... Job 28:19
Merchandise of .... Is 45:14
Wealth of .... Is 43:3
Militarily strong 2Chr 12:3
Anguished people .... Ezek 30:4-9
Defeated by Asa 2Chr 14:9-15
Subdued .... Dan 11:43
Prophecies against .... Is 20:1-6
God's love for .... Amos 9:7
Hopeful promise .... Ps 68:31

the whole land of ***E*** .... Gen 2:13
Tirhakah king of ***E*** 2Kin 19:9
from India even unto ***E*** .... Esth 1:1
E shall soon stretch .... Ps 68:31
Philistia..Tyre, with ***E*** .... Ps 87:4
beyond the rivers of ***E*** .... Is 18:1
upon Egypt and upon ***E*** ...... Is 20:3
ashamed of ***E*** their .... Is 20:5
Tirhakah king of ***E*** .... Is 37:9
Persia, ***E*** and Libya .... Ezek 38:5
E and Egypt were her .... Nah 3:9
beyond the rivers of ***E*** .... Zeph 3:10

ETHIOPIANS (ē-thĭ-ō'pĭ-äns)—*"descendants of Cush"—residents of Ethiopia*
Skin of, unchangeable ... Jer 13:23
Moses' marriage to ...... Num 12:1
Ebed-melech saves Jeremiah .... Jer 38:7
Eunuch converted .... Acts 8:26-40

against..Zerah the ***E*** 2Chr 14:9
Were not the ***E*** and the 2Chr 16:8
Arabians..near the ***E*** 2Chr 21:16
Ebed-melech the ***E*** .... Jer 38:10
Ebed-melech the ***E*** .... Jer 38:12
E and the Libyans .... Jer 46:9
Ye ***E*** also, ye shall be .... Zeph 2:12
Candace queen of the ***E*** ...... Acts 8:27

ETHNAN (ĕth'năn)—*"gift"*
Judahite 1Chr 4:5-7

ETHNI (ĕth'nī)—*"my gift"*
Levite 1Chr 6:41

EUBULUS (ū-bū'lŭs)—*"of good counsel"*
Christian at Rome 2Tim 4:21

EUCHARIST—*See* LORD'S SUPPER

EUNICE (ū'nĭs)—*"conquering well"*
Mother of Timothy 2Tim 1:5

EUNUCH—*castrated man employed as a royal official*

Rules concerning:
Excluded from congregation .... Deut 23:1
Given promise .... Is 56:3-5

Duties of:
Guard .... Gen 37:36
Servant .... Gen 40:2, 7
Attendant .... Dan 1:3, 7, 10, 11
Keeper of harem .... Esth 2:3, 14
Treasurer .... Acts 8:27

[*also* EUNUCHS]
to him two or three ***e*** 2Kin 9:32
and they shall be ***e*** in 2Kin 20:18
and they shall be ***e*** .... Is 39:7
the queen and the ***e*** .... Jer 29:2
the princes..the ***e*** .... Jer 34:19
Ethiopian one of the ***e*** .... Jer 38:7
the children and the ***e*** .... Jer 41:16
e which had the charge .... Jer 52:25
of the prince of the ***e*** .... Dan 1:8
with the prince of the ***e*** .... Dan 1:9
prince of the ***e*** brought .... Dan 1:18
For there are some ***e*** .... Matt 19:12
and there are some ***e*** .... Matt 19:12

were made *e* of men ....Matt 19:12
and there be *e* which ....Matt 19:12
made themselves *e* for ....Matt 19:12
the *e* answered Philip ....Acts 8:34
the *e* said, See, here is..........Acts 8:36
both Philip and the *e* ....Acts 8:38
that the *e* saw him no..........Acts 8:39

EUODIAS (ū-ō'dĭ-ăs)—*"fragrant"*
Christian woman at Philippi ....Phil 4:2

EUPHRATES (ū-frā'tēz)—*"that which makes fruitful"*
River of Eden..........Gen 2:14
Assyria bounded by 2Kin 23:29
Babylon on ....Jer 51:13, 36
Boundary of God's promise ....Gen 15:18; 1Kin 4:21, 24
Persian boundary ....Ezek 4:10, 11
Scene of battle ....Jer 46:2, 6, 10
Exiled Jews weep there ..Ps 137:1
Angels bound there..........Rev 9:14

great river, the river *E*..........Deut 1:7
from..the river *E*, even ....Deut 11:24
great river, the river *E*..........Josh 1:4
border at the river *E* 2Sam 8:3
Egypt unto the river *E*..........2Kin 24:7
wilderness from the river *E*....1Chr 5:9
dominion by the river *E* 1Chr 18:3
fight..Carchemish by *E*..........2Chr 35:20
and arise, go to *E* ....Jer 13:4
went, and hid it by *E* ....Jer 13:5
Arise, go to *E* and ....Jer 13:6
Then I went to *E*..........Jer 13:7
upon the great river *E* ....Rev 16:12

EUROCLYDON (ū-rŏk'lĭ-dŏn)—*"east wind"*
Violent wind ....Acts 27:14

EUTYCHUS (ū'tĭ-kŭs)—*"fortunate"*
Sleeps during Paul's sermon ....Acts 20:9
Restored to life ....Acts 20:12

EVANGELISM—*proclaiming the gospel to those who have not heard or received it*

Scope:
To all nations ....Matt 28:19, 20; Mark 16:15
House to house ....Acts 5:42
Always 1Pet 3:15
As ambassadors 2Cor 5:18-20

Source:
Jesus Christ ....Gal 1:6-12
The Father..........John 6:44, 65
The Spirit..........Acts 1:8

EVANGELIST—*one who proclaims good news*
Distinct ministry..........Eph 4:11
Applied to Philip ....Acts 21:8
Timothy works as 2Tim 4:5

EVE (ēv)—*"life; life-giving"—the first woman; Adam's wife*
Made from Adam's rib...Gen 2:18-22
Named by Adam ....Gen 3:20
Deceived by Satan..........Gen 3:1-24
Leads Adam to sin 1Tim 2:13, 14

Adam knew *E* his wife..........Gen 4:1
the serpent beguiled *E* 2Cor 11:3

EVEN—*See* INTRODUCTION

EVENING—*last hours of sunlight*
Labor ceases ....Judg 19:16; Ruth 2:17
Workers paid ....Deut 24:15
Ritual impurity ends ....Lev 11:24-28; Num 19:19
Meditation ....Gen 24:63
Prayer..........Matt 14:15, 23
Eating..........Luke 24:29, 30
Sacrifice ....Ex 29:38-42; Num 28:3-8

[*also* EVENINGS, EVENINGTIDE, EVENTIDE]
e and the morning ....Gen 1:5
e and the morning ....Gen 1:8
e and the morning ....Gen 1:13
e and the morning ....Gen 1:19
e and the morning ....Gen 1:23
e and the morning ....Gen 1:31
Israel..kill it in the *e*..........Ex 12:6
shall give you in the *e* ....Ex 16:8
the morning unto the *e* ....Ex 18:13
shall order it from *e* to..........Ex 27:21
e unto the morning ....Lev 24:3
the ark..until the *e* ....Josh 7:6
upon the trees until the *e* ....Josh 10:26
day draweth toward *e* ....Judg 19:9
eateth any food until *e*..........1Sam 14:24
unto the *e* of the next day 1Sam 30:17
it came to pass in an *e*..........2Sam 11:2
bread..flesh in the *e* 1Kin 17:6
continually morning and *e*..........1Chr 16:40
offerings morning and *e*..........2Chr 2:4
every morning and every *e* 2Chr 13:11
the lamps..to burn every *e* 2Chr 13:11
offerings morning and *e*..........Ezra 3:3
at the *e* sacrifice I arose..........Ezra 9:5
e she went and on the ....Esth 2:14
destroyed..morning to *e*..........Job 4:20
E and morning and at ....Ps 55:17
at *e* let them return and..........Ps 59:14
morning and *e* to rejoice ....Ps 65:8
the *e* it is cut down, and ....Ps 90:6
unto his work..until the *e* ....Ps 104:23
hands as the *e* sacrifice..........Ps 141:2
in the *e* in the black and ....Prov 7:9
in the *e* withhold not thine ....Eccl 11:6
behold at *e* trouble ....Is 17:14
a wolf of the *e* shall ....Jer 5:6
shadows of the *e* are ....Jer 6:4
Lord was upon me in the *e*....Ezek 33:22
vision of the *e* and the ....Dan 8:26
more fierce..the *e* wolves..........Hab 1:8
shall they lie down in the *e*....Zeph 2:7
at *e* time it shall be light ....Zech 14:7
When it is *e*, ye say, it will....Matt 16:2
and now the *e* was ....Mark 11:11
in the *e* he cometh with the ...Mark 14:17
same day at *e* being the..........John 20:19
for it was now *e*..........Acts 4:3
prophets..morning till *e* ....Acts 28:23

EVENING SACRIFICE—*the daily sacrifice that was given in thanksgiving for God's provision*
Ritual described ....Ex 29:38-42
Part of continual offering .Num 28:3-8

EVENT—*occurrence; outcome*
one *e* happeneth to them all...Eccl 2:14
there is one *e* unto all ....Eccl 9:3

EVENTS, BIBLICAL CLASSIFIED

Originating, originating other events:
Creation ....Gen 1
Fall of man ....Rom 5:12

Epochal, introducing new period:
Flood ....Gen 6—8
The death of Christ..........Matt 27:50, 51; Heb 9

Typical, foreshadowing some New Testament event:
The Passover—Christ as Lamb..........Ex 12; John 1:35-37; 1Cor 5:7, 8
Jonah and great fish—Christ's death and resurrection ...Jon 1, 2; Matt 12:38-41

Prophetic, prophesying future events:
Return from exile ....2Chr 36:22, 23; Jer 29:10
Destruction of Jerusalem .Luke 19:41-44; Luke 21:20-24

Redemptive, connected with man's salvation:
Advent of Christ ....Luke 2:11; Gal 4:4, 5
Death of Christ..........Matt 20:28; Luke 24:44-47; 1Tim 1:15

Unique, those without parallel:
Creation ....Gen 1
Virgin birth ....Matt 1:18-25; Luke 1:30-37

Miraculous, those produced by supernatural means:
Plagues on Egypt..........Ex 7—12
Crossing Red Sea..........Ex 14—15
Fall of Jericho ....Josh 6
Sun's standing still..........Josh 10:12-14

Judgmental, those judging people for sins:
Flood 2Pet 2:5
Sodom and Gomorrah ...Gen 19; 2Pet 2:6
Killing of Israelites ....Ex 32:25-35; Num 25:1-9

Transforming, those producing a change:
Christ's transformation ...Matt 17:1-8
Conversion of Paul ....Acts 9; 1Tim 1:12-14
Believer's regeneration ...John 3:1-8; 2Cor 5:17

Providential, those manifesting God's providence:
Baby's cry ....Ex 2:5-10
Joseph's being sold into Egypt ....Gen 37:26-28; Gen 45:1-8
King's sleepless night ....Esth 6:1-10

Confirmatory, those confirming some promise:
Worship at Sinai ....Ex 3:12
Aaron's rod..........Num 17:1-11
Thunder and rain..........1Sam 12:16-18
Sun's shadow moved backward ....2Kin 20:8-11; Is 38:1-8

Promissory, those fulfilling some promise:
Pentecost ....Joel 2:28-32; Acts 2
Spirit's coming..........Luke 24:49; Acts 1:4, 5, 8; Acts 2:1-4
Possession of land..........Gen 15:18-21; Josh 24:3, 11-19

Eschatological, those connected with Christ's return:
Doom of antichrist 2Thess 2:1-12
Resurrection and translation 1Cor 15:35-38; 1Thess 4:13-18
Resurrection and judgment..........Matt 25:31-46; Acts 17:31; Rev 20:11-15
Destruction of the world..2Pet 3:7-15

EVER—*continually; indefinitely*

[*also* EVERMORE]
and eat, and live for *e* ....Gen 3:22
let me bear the blame for *e* ...Gen 43:9
this is my name for *e* and ....Ex 3:15
by an ordinance for *e* ....Ex 12:17
them again no more for *e* ....Ex 14:13
thee, and believe thee for *e* ...Ex 19:9
it shall be a statute for *e* ....Ex 27:21
for *e*..children of Israel ....Ex 29:28
the children of Israel for *e* ....Ex 31:17
e be burning upon the altar ...Lev 6:13
statute for *e* unto the Lord ....Lev 6:22
for *e* throughout their..........Lev 7:36
a statute for *e* as the Lord ....Lev 10:15
by a statute for *e* ....Lev 16:31
for *e* throughout your ....Lev 23:14
for *e*..your generations ....Lev 23:31
statute for *e*..generations ....Lev 24:3
be established for *e* to him ....Lev 25:30
for *e*..your generations ....Num 10:8
by an ordinance for *e* ....Num 18:8
of salt for *e* before the Lord...Num 18:19
among..for a statute for *e* ....Num 19:10
thou hast ridden *e* since ....Num 22:30
was I *e* wont to do so unto....Num 22:30

he also shall perish for *e* ......Num 24:24
Did *e* people hear the voice ...Deut 4:33
with their children for *e*! ......Deut 5:29
it shall be a heap for *e*........Deut 13:16
Lord, him and his sons for *e* ..Deut 18:5
congregation of..Lord for *e*....Deut 23:3
oppressed and spoiled *e*.......Deut 28:29
wonder and..thy seed for *e*....Deut 28:46
and say, I live for *e* ....Deut 32:40
the children of Israel for *e* ....Josh 4:7
and made it a heap for *e*......Josh 8:28
he *e* strive against Israel ......Judg 11:25
Lord and there abide for *e*....1Sam 1:22
old man in thine house for *e* ..1Sam 2:32
I will judge his house for *e*....1Sam 3:13
kingdom upon Israel for *e*.....1Sam 13:13
between thee and me for *e*....1Sam 20:23
shall be my servant for *e*......1Sam 27:12
Shall the sword devour for *e* ..2Sam 2:26
throne of his kingdom for *e* ...2Sam 7:13
established for *e* before thee...2Sam 7:16
shall be established for *e* 2Sam 7:16
his house, establish it for *e*....2Sam 7:25
continue for *e* before thee.....2Sam 7:29
thy servant be blessed for *e* ...2Sam 7:29
David and to his seed for *e* ...2Sam 22:51
lord king David live for *e* 1Kin 1:31
the head of his seed for *e* 1Kin 2:33
be peace for *e* from the Lord ..1Kin 2:33
Hiram was *e* a lover of 1Kin 5:1
to put my name there for *e* ...1Kin 9:3
the Lord loved Israel for *e* 1Kin 10:9
will be thy servants for *e*......1Kin 12:7
thee, and unto thy seed for *e* ..2Kin 5:27
ye shall observe to do for *e* ...2Kin 17:37
to minister unto him for *e* 1Chr 15:2
Lord God of Israel for *e* 1Chr 16:36
I..stablish his throne for *e*.....1Chr 17:12
throne..established for *e* 1Chr 17:14
make thine own people for *e* ..1Chr 17:22
thy name..magnified for *e* 1Chr 17:24
it may be before thee for *e*....1Chr 17:27
it shall be blessed for *e* 1Chr 17:27
and his sons for *e* to burn 1Chr 23:13
dwell in Jerusalem for *e*.......1Chr 23:25
establish his kingdom for *e* 1Chr 28:7
he will cast thee off for *e* 1Chr 28:9
of Israel our father for *e* 1Chr 29:10
an ordinance for *e* to Israel ...2Chr 2:4
place for thy dwelling for *e*....2Chr 6:2
his mercy endureth for *e* 2Chr 7:6
to establish them for *e* 2Chr 9:8
over Israel to David for *e* 2Chr 13:5
for his mercy endureth for *e*...2Chr 20:21
he hath sanctified for *e* 2Chr 30:8
will I put my name for *e* 2Chr 33:7
for his mercy endureth for *e*...Ezra 3:11
their peace or..wealth for *e*....Ezra 9:12
king, Let the king live for *e* ...Neh 2:3
congregation of God for *e*.....Neh 13:1
who *e* perished being ....Job 4:7
prevailest for *e* against ....Job 14:20
shall perish for *e* like his ......Job 20:7
doth establish them for *e*......Job 36:7
let them *e* shout for joy ......Ps 5:11
their name for *e* and *e* ....Ps 9:5
poor shall not perish for *e*.....Ps 9:18
The Lord is King for *e*........Ps 10:16
forget me, O Lord? for *e* .....Ps 13:1
there are pleasures for *e* ......Ps 16:11
length of days for *e* and *e* ....Ps 21:4
made him most blessed for *e* ..Ps 21:6
your heart shall live for *e* .....Ps 22:26
the house of the Lord for *e* ...Ps 23:6
eyes are *e* toward the Lord ....Ps 25:15
the Lord sitteth King for *e* ....Ps 29:10
counsel of the Lord..for *e* .....Ps 33:11
is *e* merciful, and lendeth .....Ps 37:26
do good; and dwell for *e*......Ps 37:27
and dwell therein for *e*........Ps 37:29
and praise thy name for *e*......Ps 44:8
God hath blessed thee for *e* ...Ps 45:2
throne, O God is for *e* and *e* ..Ps 45:6
praise thee for *e* and *e*........Ps 45:17
God will establish it for *e* .....Ps 48:8
and it ceaseth for *e* ....Ps 49:8
houses shall continue for *e* ....Ps 49:11
likewise destroy thee for *e* ....Ps 52:5
mercy of God for *e* and *e* .....Ps 52:8
abide in thy tabernacle for *e*...Ps 61:4
praise unto thy name for *e* ....Ps 61:8
He ruleth by his power for *e* ..Ps 66:7
name shall endure for *e* ....Ps 72:17
heart, and my portion for *e* ...Ps 73:26
blaspheme thy name for *e*......Ps 74:10
I will declare for *e*: I will .....Ps 75:9
his mercy clean gone for *e* ....Ps 77:8
wilt thou be angry for *e*........Ps 79:5
should have endured for *e*.....Ps 81:15
thou be angry with us for *e* ...Ps 85:5
will glorify thy name for *e*.....Ps 86:12
Mercy shall be built up for *e* ..Ps 89:2
will I make to endure for *e*....Ps 89:29
shall be established for *e* ......Ps 89:37
Blessed be the Lord for *e* .....Ps 89:52
or *e* thou hadst formed the ....Ps 90:2
they shall be destroyed for *e* ..Ps 92:7
thine house, O Lord, for *e* ....Ps 93:5
O Lord, shall endure for *e* ....Ps 102:12
will he keep his anger for *e* ...Ps 103:9
should not be removed for *e* ..Ps 104:5
the Lord shall endure for *e*....Ps 104:31
strength..seek his face *e*......Ps 105:4
his covenant for *e* ....Ps 105:8
for his mercy endureth for *e*...Ps 106:1
Thou art a priest for *e* ....Ps 110:4
e be mindful of..covenant .....Ps 111:5
They stand fast for *e* and *e*....Ps 111:8
his praise endureth for *e* ......Ps 111:10
he shall not be moved for *e* ...Ps 112:6
this time forth and for *e* ......Ps 113:2
of the Lord endureth for *e* ....Ps 117:2
his mercy endureth for *e* ......Ps 118:2
his mercy endureth for *e* ......Ps 118:3
his mercy endureth for *e* ......Ps 118:4
I keep thy law..for *e* and *e*....Ps 119:44
For *e*. O Lord thy word is ....Ps 119:89
enemies; for they are *e* ....Ps 119:98
hast founded them for *e* ......Ps 119:152
this time..and even for *e* ......Ps 121:8
removed, but abideth for *e*....Ps 125:1
from henceforth and for *e*......Ps 131:3
This is my rest for *e*: here.....Ps 132:14
blessing, even life for *e* ....Ps 133:3
mercy endureth for *e* ....Ps 136:7
bless thy name for *e* and *e* ....Ps 145:1
will praise thy name for *e* .....Ps 145:2
bless his..name for *e* and *e* ....Ps 145:21
which keepeth truth for *e* .....Ps 146:6
The Lord shall reign for *e*.....Ps 146:10
stablished them for *e* and *e*.....Ps 148:6
beginning or *e* of the earth ....Prov 8:23
for riches are not for *e*........Prov 27:24
but the earth abideth for *e* ....Eccl 1:4
God doeth, it shall be for *e* ...Eccl 3:14
e the silver cord be loosed ....Eccl 12:6
Or *e* I was aware, my soul ....Song 6:12
from henceforth even for *e*....Is 9:7
Trust ye in the Lord for *e*.....Is 26:4
he will not *e* be threshing ......Is 28:28
for the time to come for *e* ....Is 30:8
quietness..assurance for *e* .....Is 32:17
smoke..shall go up for *e* ......Is 34:10
none shall pass..it for *e* ....Is 34:10
God shall stand for *e* ....Is 40:8
my salvation shall be for *e* ....Is 51:6
righteousness shall be for *e*....Is 51:8
For I will not contend for *e* ...Is 57:16
shall inherit the land for *e*.....Is 60:21
be ye glad and rejoice for *e* ...Is 65:18
he reserve his anger for *e* .....Jer 3:5
to your fathers for *e* and *e* ....Jer 7:7
this city shall remain for *e*.....Jer 17:25
a nation before me for *e* ......Jer 31:36
that they may fear me for *e* ...Jer 32:39
neither ye, nor..sons for *e*.....Jer 35:6
dragons..desolation for *e* ......Jer 49:33
thou shalt be desolate for *e* ...Jer 51:26
Lord will not cast off for *e* ....Lam 3:31
dost thou forget us for *e* ......Lam 5:20
children's children for *e* ....Ezek 37:25
in the midst of them for *e*.....Ezek 37:26
the children of Israel for *e* ....Ezek 43:7
O king, live for *e* tell thy .....Dan 2:4
kingdoms..shall stand for *e* ....Dan 2:44
him that liveth for *e* ....Dan 4:34
him, King Darius, live for *e* ...Dan 6:6
their bones in pieces or *e* .....Dan 6:24
kingdom for *e*..*e* and *e*........Dan 7:18
as the stars for *e* and *e*........Dan 12:3
betroth thee unto me for *e* ....Hos 2:19
there hath not been *e* the .....Joel 2:2
and he kept his wrath for *e* ...Amos 1:11
thou shalt be cut off for *e*.....Obad 10
with her..about me for *e* ......Jon 2:6
taken away my glory for *e* .....Mic 2:9
of the Lord our God..and *e* ...Mic 4:5
retaineth not..anger for *e* .....Mic 7:18
prophets, do they live for *e* ...Zech 1:5
Lord hath indignation for *e*....Mal 1:4
power, and the glory, for *e*....Matt 6:13
world to this time, no, nor *e* ..Matt 24:21
fruit of thee hereafter for *e*....Mark 11:14
over the house of Jacob for *e*..Luke 1:33
Son, thou art *e* with me........Luke 15:31
told me all things that *e*.......John 4:29
Lord, *e* give us this bread .....John 6:34
bread, he shall live for *e* ......John 6:51
abideth not in..house for *e* .....John 8:35
All that *e* came before me .....John 10:8
he may abide with you for *e*...John 14:16
and we, or *e* he come near ....Acts 23:15
Creator, who is blessed for *e* ..Rom 1:25
To whom be glory for *e*.......Rom 11:36
righteousness remaineth..*e*.....2Cor 9:9
which is blessed for *e* 2Cor 11:31
whom be glory for *e* and *e* .....Gal 1:5
For no man *e* yet hated his....Eph 5:29
Father be glory for *e* and *e*....Phil 4:20
and so shall we *e* be with 1Thess 4:17
but *e* follow that which is 1Thess 5:15
Rejoice *e* 1Thess 5:16
honor and glory for *e* and *e* ...1Tim 1:17
E learning and never able 2Tim 3:7
shouldest receive him for *e* ....Philem 15
Thou art a priest for *e* after ...Heb 5:6
Thou art a priest for *e* ....Heb 7:17
he *e* liveth to make ....Heb 7:25
Son..is consecrated for *e* ......Heb 7:28
he hath perfected for *e*........Heb 10:14
whom be glory for *e* and *e* ....Heb 13:21
liveth and abideth for *e* 1Pet 1:23
and dominion for *e* and *e* 1Pet 4:11
darkness is reserved for *e* 2Pet 2:17
will of God abideth for *e*......1John 2:17
and shall be with us for *e* 2John 2
blackness of darkness for *e*....Jude 13
and dominion for *e* and *e* .....Rev 1:6
I am alive for *e* ....Rev 1:18
him that liveth for *e* and *e* ....Rev 4:10
him that liveth for *e* and *e* ....Rev 5:14
him that liveth for *e* and *e* ....Rev 10:6
ascendeth up for *e* and *e* ......Rev 14:11
smoke rose up for *e* and *e* ....Rev 19:3
shall reign for *e* and *e* ....Rev 22:5

EVERLASTING—*eternal; lasting through all time*

I may remember the *e* ....Gen 9:16
for an *e* possession ....Gen 17:8
with him for an *e* covenant ....Gen 17:19
for an *e* possession ....Gen 48:4
an *e* priesthood throughout ....Ex 40:15
this shall be an *e* statute ......Lev 16:34
covenant of an *e* priesthood ...Num 25:13
underneath are the *e* arms ....Deut 33:27
made with me an *e* covenant ..2Sam 23:5
to Israel for an *e* covenant 1Chr 16:17
be ye lift up, ye *e* doors ......Ps 24:7
Lord God of Israel from *e* ....Ps 41:13
of old; thou art from *e*........Ps 93:2
mercy of the Lord is from *e* ...Ps 103:17
Lord God of Israel from *e* ....Ps 106:48
and lead me in the way *e* .....Ps 139:24
I was set up from *e*...........Prov 8:23

the righteous is an *e* ....Prov 10:20
broken the *e* covenant ....Is 24:5
shall dwell with *e* burnings? ...Is 38:14
not heart that the *e* God ......Is 40:28
with *e* kindness will I have .....Is 54:8
an *e* sign that shall not be .....Is 55:13
e joy shall be unto them ......Is 61:7
make himself an *e* name? .....Is 68:12
living God and an *e* king ......Jer 10:10
I will bring an *e* reproach .....Jer 23:40
I will make an *e* covenant .....Jer 32:40
unto thee an *e* covenant ......Ezek 16:60
kingdom is an *e* kingdom .....Dan 4:3
dominion is an *e* dominion ....Dan 7:14
to bring in *e* righteousness ....Dan 9:24
some to *e* life and some to ....Dan 12:2
to shame and *e* contempt .....Dan 12:2
from of old, from *e* ....Mic 5:2
Art thou not from *e*, O Lord ..Hab 1:12
the *e* mountains were ....Hab 3:6
hills..bow; his ways are *e* ......Hab 3:6
feet to be cast into *e* fire ......Matt 18:8
you into *e* habitations ....Luke 16:9
not perish, but have *e* life .....John 3:16
springing up into *e* life ....John 4:14
ye think ye have *e* life ....John 5:39
meat..endureth unto *e* life .....John 6:27
believeth on me hath *e* life ....John 6:47
holiness and the end *e* life ....Rom 6:22
of the spirit reap life *e* ....Gal 6:8
punished..*e* destruction 2Thess 1:9
believe on him to life *e* 1Tim 1:16
the blood of the *e* covenant ...Heb 13:20

EVERY—*See* INTRODUCTION

EVI (ē'vī)—*"desire"*
King of Midian ....Num 31:8
Land of, assigned to Reuben ....Josh 13:15, 21

EVIDENCE—*grounds for belief*

Based upon:
Testimony of witnesses ...Matt 18:16
Personal testimony ......Acts 26:1-27
Fulfilled prophecy ....Matt 1:22, 23
Supernatural testimony ...Matt 3:17
New life 1John 3:14

Kinds of:
Circumstantial ....Gen 39:7-19
False ....Matt 26:59-61
Fabricated ....Gen 37:29-33
Confirmed ....Heb 2:3, 4
Satanic 2Thess 2:9, 10
Indisputable 1Cor 15:1-19

Need of:
Confirm weak faith ......Luke 7:19, 22
Remove doubt ....John 20:24-29
Refute mockers 2Pet 3:3-7
Attest a messenger of God ....Ex 8:18, 19
Produce faith ....John 20:30, 31

[*also* EVIDENCES, EVIDENT, EVIDENTLY]
it is *e* unto you if I lie ....Job 6:28
I subscribed the *e* and ....Jer 32:10
took the *e* of the purchase ....Jer 32:11
gave the *e* of the purchase ....Jer 32:12
this *e* of the purchase ....Jer 32:14
and this *e* which is open ......Jer 32:14
and subscribe *e* and seal ......Jer 32:44
He saw in a vision *e* about ....Acts 10:3
Jesus Christ hath been *e* set ...Gal 3:1
is to them an *e* token of ......Phil 1:28
For it is *e* that our Lord ......Heb 7:14
the *e* of things not seen ....Heb 11:1

EVIL—*that which brings distress*

Origin of:
Begins with Satan ....Is 14:12-14
Enters world ....Rom 5:12
Comes from man ....Matt 15:18, 19
Inflamed by lust ....James 1:14

Applied to:
Men ....Matt 12:35
Heart ....Jer 17:9
Imaginations ....Gen 6:5
Generation ....Matt 12:39
Age ....Gal 1:4
Our days ....Eph 5:16
Conscience ....Heb 10:22
Spirits ....Matt 12:45

Satan as "the evil one":
Unregenerate belong to ..Matt 13:38
Snatches away the good seed ....Matt 13:19
World lies in 1John 5:19
Lord safeguards against ..John 17:15
Christians can overcome. .1John 2:13

The Christian should guard against, evil:
Heart of unbelief ....Heb 3:12
Thoughts ....James 2:4
Boastings ....James 4:16
Things ....Rom 12:9
Deeds 2John 9-11
Person 1Cor 5:13
Appearance 1Thess 5:22
One (Satan) ....Eph 6:16

[*also* EVILS]
gods, knowing good and *e* .....Gen 3:5
of his heart was only *e* ....Gen 6:5
they brought up an *e* report ...Num 13:32
Lord shall separate..unto *e* ....Deut 29:21
e and troubles shall befall .....Deut 31:17
Are not these *e* come upon ...Deut 31:17
e and troubles are befallen ...Deut 31:21
it seem *e* unto you to serve ...Josh 24:15
e spirit from God troubleth 1Sam 16:15
it came to pass when the *e* 1Sam 16:23
the *e* spirit departed from 1Sam 16:23
e spirit from the Lord was 1Sam 19:9
feareth God..escheweth *e* .....Job 1:8
I will fear no *e* for thou ....Ps 23:4
Keep thy tongue from *e* ....Ps 34:13
innumerable *e* have ....Ps 40:12
There shall no *e* befall thee ...Ps 91:10
that love the Lord, hate *e* .....Ps 97:10
their feet run to *e* and ....Prov 1:16
the Lord..beholding the *e* .....Prov 15:3
call *e* good and good *e* ....Is 5:20
people..committed two *e* ....Jer 2:13
turn every man from his *e* .....Jer 26:3
the *e* which they have ....Ezek 6:9
An *e*, an only *e*, behold, is ....Ezek 7:5
Seek good and not *e* that .....Amos 5:14
they turned from their *e* way ..Jon 3:10
hate the good, and love the *e* .Mic 3:2
his sun to rise on the *e*........Matt 5:45
Sufficient unto..day is the *e* ...Matt 6:34
Why, what *e* hath he done? ...Matt 27:23
that can lightly speak *e* of .....Mark 9:39
all the *e* which Herod had .....Luke 3:19
and an *e* man out of the *e* ....Luke 6:45
because their deeds were *e* ....John 3:19
the *e* spirit answered and ......Acts 19:15
the *e* which I would not ....Rom 7:19
to no man *e* for *e* ....Rom 12:17
Be not overcome of *e* but .....Rom 12:21
but overcome *e* with good .....Rom 12:21
not then your good be *e* ......Rom 14:16
provoked, thinketh no *e* 1Cor 13:5
See that none render *e* for *e* ...1Thess 5:15
money is the root of all *e* 1Tim 6:10
speak *e* of no man, to be no ..Titus 3:2

EVIL—*that which is physically harmful: floods, earthquakes, etc.*
Part of man's curse ......Gen 3:17-19
Men cry out against .....Rev 9:18-21
Can be misinterpreted ...Luke 13:1-3
Foreseen by prudent .....Prov 22:3
Will continue to the end. .Matt 24:6-8, 14
Believers share in 2Cor 12:7-10
To be borne patiently ....Job 2:7-10 James 5:11
Prospects of relief from ..Rom 8:18-39
Relieved now by faith ...Heb 3:17-19
None in heaven ....Rev 7:14-17

EVIL COMPANIONS—*See* ASSOCIATION

EVIL DAY
Time of judgment ....Eccl 12:1

EVIL EYE
Descriptive of a man's inner being ....Mark 7:21, 22
Shown in attitudes ....Matt 20:15

EVIL SPIRITS—*demons*
Sent upon King Saul 1Sam 16:14
Ahab prompted to evil by.1Kin 22:1-23
Cast out by Jesus ....Luke 7:21
Cast out by Paul ....Acts 19:11, 12

EVILDOER—*worker of evil*
Christians wrongly called..1Pet 2:12
Christians should not be. .1Pet 4:15
Christians cry against ....Ps 119:115
Punished by magistrates ..Rom 13:1-4
End of, certain ....Ps 34:16

[*also* EVILDOERS]
not thyself because of *e* ....Ps 37:1
e shall be cut off; but ....Ps 37:9
rise up for me against the *e*? ..Ps 94:16
a seed of *e* children that ......Is 1:4
one is a hypocrite and an *e* ....Is 9:17
seed of *e* shall never be ....Is 14:20
against the house of the *e* .....Is 31:2
the poor from the hand of *e* ...Jer 20:13
strengthen..the hands of *e* .....Jer 23:14
for the punishment of *e* 1Pet 2:14
speak evil of you, as of *e* 1Pet 3:16
or as an *e* or as a busybody ...1Pet 4:15

EVILFAVOREDNESS
wherein is blemish, or any *e* ....Deut 17:1

EVIL-MERODACH (ē-vĭl-mĕ-rō'dăk)—*"the man of (the god) Marduk"*
Babylonian king (562-560 B.C.); follows Nebuchadnezzar 2Kin 25:27-30

E king of Babylon in the .....Jer 52:31

EVILSPEAKING

The evil of:
Sign of unregeneracy ....Ps 10:7
Aimed at righteous ......Ps 64:2-5
Defiles the whole body ..James 3:5-10
Disrupts fellowship 3John 9-11
Severely condemned .....James 4:11
Punished 1Cor 6:9, 10

Not to be confused with:
Denunciation of vice .....Titus 1:12, 13
Description of sinners ....Acts 13:9, 10
Defense of the faith .....Jude 4, 8-16

EWE—*mature female sheep*

[*also* EWES]
Abraham set seven *e* lambs ...Gen 21:28
seven *e* lambs shalt thou ......Gen 21:30
thy *e* and thy she goats ....Gen 31:38
and one *e* lamb of the first ....Lev 14:10
and one *e* lamb of the first ....Num 6:14
one little *e* lamb, which he 2Sam 12:3
following the *e* great with .....Ps 78:71

EXACT—*to demand from*

[*also* EXACTED, EXACTETH, EXACTION, EXACTIONS, EXACTORS]
not *e* it of his neighbor ....Deut 15:2
Menahem *e* the money of 2Kin 15:20
Ye *e* usury, every one of his ..Neh 5:7
year, and the *e* of every.......Neh 10:31
God *e* of thee less than ....Job 11:6
The enemy shall not *e* upon ...Ps 89:22
pleasure, and *e* all your ....Is 58:3
and thine *e* righteousness ......Is 60:17
take away your *e* from my ....Ezek 45:9
E no more than that which ....Luke 3:13

EXALTATION—*the state of being raised up*

Of evil man:
Originates in Satan ......Luke 4:5, 6
Defies God 2Kin 18:28-35
Perverts religion ....Dan 11:36, 37

Brings downfall ....Esth 6:6-14
Merits punishment 1Kin 16:1-4
Displayed by Herod .....Acts 12:21-23
Seen in antichrist 2Thess 2:4, 9

Of good men:
Principle of ....Matt 23:12
Follows humility.........1Pet 5:6
Restrictions upon 2Cor 10:5
Brings glory............James 1:9
False, brings sorrow 1Cor 4:6-14
Final, in heaven ....Rev 22:5

Of Christ:
Promised ....Ps 2:8, 9
Predicted by Christ ......Matt 26:64
The ascension ....Acts 2:33, 34
Seen by Stephen ....Acts 7:55, 56
Taught by the apostles ...Eph 1:20-22
Set forth as a reward ....Phil 2:9-11
Introduces priestly intercession ....Heb 1:3

[*also* EXALT, EXALTED, EXALTEST, EXALTETH]
my father's God..I will *e* ......Ex 15:2
and his kingdom shall be *e* ....Num 24:7
mine horn is *e* in the Lord 1Sam 2:1
and *e* the horn of his 1Sam 2:10
had *e* his kingdom for his 2Sam 5:12
son of Haggith *e* himself 1Kin 1:5
against whom hast thou *e* 2Kin 19:22
thou art *e* as head above 1Chr 29:11
name, which is *e* above all ....Neh 9:5
which mourn may be *e* to .....Job 5:11
therefore shalt thou not *e* .....Job 17:4
for ever, and they are *e*.......Job 36:7
when the vilest men are *e* .....Ps 12:8
God of my salvation be *e* .....Ps 18:46
and let us *e* his name ....Ps 34:3
I will be *e* among the ....Ps 46:10
I will be *e* in the earth........Ps 46:10
thou *e*, O God, above the.....Ps 57:5
let not the rebellious *e* ....Ps 66:7
of the righteous shall be *e*.....Ps 75:10
favor our horn shall be *e*......Ps 89:17
e one chosen out of the ......Ps 89:19
But my horn shalt thou *e* ....Ps 92:10
thou art *e* far above all ....Ps 97:9
E ye the Lord our God ....Ps 99:5
e..in the congregation ....Ps 107:32
his horn shall be *e* with ....Ps 112:9
thou art my God, I will *e* .....Ps 118:28
lest they *e* themselves ....Ps 140:8
E her, and she shall promote ..Prov 4:8
the upright the city is *e* ....Prov 11:11
shall be *e* above the hills......Is 2:2
Lord of hosts shall be *e* ....Is 5:16
e the voice unto them.........Is 13:2
thou art my God; I will *e* .....Is 25:1
and therefore will he be *e*.....Is 30:18
Lord is *e*, for he dwelleth .....Is 33:5
now will I be *e*; now will I ....Is 33:10
Every valley shall be *e* ....Is 40:4
he shall be *e* and extolled .....Is 52:13
have *e* the low tree, have .....Ezek 17:24
e him that is low, and ....Ezek 21:26
Therefore his height was *e* ....Ezek 31:5
e themselves for their ....Ezek 31:14
robbers of..people shall *e* .....Dan 11:14
most High, none..would *e*.....Hos 11:7
Ephraim he *e*..in Israel ....Hos 13:1
Though thou *e* thyself as ......Obad 4
which art *e* unto heaven ......Matt 11:23
seats, and *e* them of low ......Luke 1:52
humbleth himself shall be *e* ...Luke 14:11
e the people when they ....Acts 13:17
myself that ye might be *e* 2Cor 11:7
should be *e* above measure 2Cor 12:7
should be *e* above measure 2Cor 12:7
God also hath highly *e* ....Phil 2:9

EXAMINATION—*test; inspection*

[*also* EXAMINE, EXAMINED, EXAMINING]
the tenth month to *e* the ......Ezra 10:16
found him not, he *e* the.......Acts 12:19
him which should have *e* ......Acts 22:29
that, after *e* had, I might......Acts 25:26
Who, when they had *e* me ....Acts 28:18
them that do *e* me is this 1Cor 9:3

EXAMINATION OF OTHERS
Of Jesus ....Luke 23:13, 14
Of Peter ....Acts 4:8, 9
Of Paul................Acts 22:24

EXAMINATION OF SELF
Sought by David ....Ps 26:2
Must precede Lord's Supper 1Cor 11:28
Necessary for real faith ..2Cor 13:5

EXAMPLE—*a pattern to follow*

Purposes of:
Set forth sin's punishment.2Pet 2:6
Show unbelief's consequences..........Heb 4:11
Restrain from evil 1Cor 10:6, 11
Illustrate humility ....John 13:15
1Pet 3:5
Exemplify patience ......James 5:10, 11
1Pet 2:20-22
Portray Christian conduct.Phil 3:17

Of evil men:
Covetousness—Achan....Josh 7:20, 21
Immorality—Eli's sons ...1Sam 2:22-25
Rebellion—Saul 1Sam 15:17-23
Folly—Nabal 1Sam 25:25-37
Idolatry—Jeroboam 1Kin 12:26-33

Of good men:
Holy zeal—Phinehas .....Num 25:7-13
Faith—Caleb ....Josh 14:6-15
Fidelity—Joshua ....Josh 24:15-25
Courage—David.........1Sam 17:32-37
Holy life—Daniel........Ezek 14:14, 20
Patience—Job ....James 5:10, 11
Christian living—Paul ....Phil 3:17

make her a public *e* was ......Matt 1:19
happened unto them for *e*.....1Cor 10:11
ye have us for an *e* ....Phil 3:17
ye were *e* to all that believe ...1Thess 1:7
make ourselves an *e* unto 2Thess 3:9
thou an *e* of the believers 1Tim 4:12
unto the *e* and shadow ....Heb 8:5
but being *e* to the flock 1Pet 5:3
making them an *e* unto 2Pet 2:6
for an *e*, suffering the.........Jude 7

EXAMPLE OF CHRIST

Virtues illustrated by:
Meekness ....Matt 11:29
Self-denial ....Matt 16:24
Love ....John 13:34
Obedience ....John 15:10
Benevolence 2Cor 8:7, 9
Humility................Phil 2:5, 7
Forgiveness ....Col 3:13
Suffering wrongfully 1Pet 2:21-23
Purity 1John 3:3

The Christian approach to:
Progressive.............2Cor 3:18
Instructive ....Eph 4:20-24
Imitative................1Pet 2:21-23
Perfective ....Rom 8:29

EXCEED—*to be greater than; extremely*

[*also* EXCEEDED, EXCEEDEST, EXCEEDETH, EXCEEDING, EXCEEDINGLY]
prevailed *e* upon the earth ....Gen 7:19
I will multiply thy seed *e*......Gen 16:10
And I will make thee *e* ....Gen 17:6
multiply him *e* twelve ....Gen 17:20
with a great and *e* bitter ......Gen 27:34
And the man increased *e*......Gen 30:43
multiplied and waxed *e* ....Ex 1:7
the voice of the trumpet *e*.....Ex 19:16
to search it, is an *e* good......Num 14:7
he may give him, and not *e* ...Deut 25:3
Talk no more so *e* proudly 1Sam 2:3
another, until David *e* 1Sam 20:41
the fool and have erred *e* 1Sam 26:21
David took *e* much brass.......2Sam 8:8
Then Amnon hated her *e* 2Sam 13:15
wisdom and understanding *e*...1Kin 4:29
wisdom and prosperity *e* 1Kin 10:7
So king Solomon *e* all 1Kin 10:23
But they were *e* afraid 2Kin 10:4
also *e* much spoil out of.......1Chr 20:2
Lord magnified Solomon *e* 1Chr 29:25
him, and magnified him *e* 2Chr 1:1
thou *e* the fame that I 2Chr 9:6
and made them *e* strong 2Chr 11:12
his disease was *e* great 2Chr 16:12
he strengthened himself *e* 2Chr 26:8
it grieved them *e* that there ...Neh 2:10
was the queen *e* grieved ......Esth 4:4
Which rejoice *e*..are glad......Job 3:22
transgressions..have *e* ....Job 36:9
him *e* glad with thy ....Ps 21:6
yea, let them *e* rejoice ....Ps 68:3
commandment is *e* broad......Ps 119:96
testimonies..love them *e* ......Ps 119:167
soul is *e* filled with the.......Ps 123:4
earth, but they are *e* wise .....Prov 30:24
That which is far off, and *e* ...Eccl 7:24
the earth is moved *e* ....Is 24:19
of Moab, (he is *e* proud)......Jer 48:29
Israel and Judah is *e*..........Ezek 9:9
e in dyed attire upon their ....Ezek 23:15
fish of the Great Sea, *e* ....Ezek 47:10
and the furnace was *e* hot .....Dan 3:22
strong *e* and it had great ......Dan 7:7
e dreadful, whose teeth ....Dan 7:19
Then were the men *e* ....Jon 1:10
Nineveh was an *e* great ....Jon 3:3
it displeased Jonah *e* and......Jon 4:1
they rejoiced with *e* great .....Matt 2:10
him up into an *e* high.........Matt 4:8
coming out of the tombs *e* ....Matt 8:28
they were *e* amazed, saying ...Matt 19:25
And they were *e* sorrowful ....Matt 26:22
they feared *e*.................Mark 4:41
And the king was *e* sorry .....Mark 6:26
soul is *e* sorrowful unto ....Mark 14:34
Herod saw Jesus he was *e*.....Luke 23:8
was *e* fair and nourished ......Acts 7:20
being Jews do *e* trouble ....Acts 16:20
we being *e* tossed with a ......Acts 27:18
sin..might become *e* sinful.....Rom 7:13
of righteousness *e* in glory.....2Cor 3:9
a far more *e* and eternal 2Cor 4:17
e the more joyed we for the...2Cor 7:13
the *e* grace of God in you.....2Cor 9:14
more *e* zealous of the ....Gal 1:14
what is the *e* greatness of .....Eph 1:19
e abundantly above all ....Eph 3:20
Night and day praying *e* 1Thess 3:10
your faith groweth *e* and 2Thess 1:3
Lord was *e* abundant with.....1Tim 1:14
Moses said, I *e* fear and ......Heb 12:21
ye may be glad also with *e* 1Pet 4:13
us *e* great and precious 2Pet 1:4
presence of his glory with *e* ...Jude 24
plague thereof was *e* great ....Rev 16:21

EXCEL—*to be superior to; surpass in accomplishment*

[*also* EXCELLED, EXCELLEST, EXCELLETH]
as water, thou shalt not *e* .....Gen 49:4
Solomon's wisdom *e* the 1Kin 4:30
harps on the Sheminith to *e* ...1Chr 15:21
that *e* in strength, that do .....Ps 103:20
virtuously, but thou *e* them....Prov 31:29
I saw that wisdom *e* folly .....Eccl 2:13
as far as light *e* darkness ......Eccl 2:13
whose graven images did *e* ....Is 10:10
ye may *e* to the edifying of....1Cor 14:12
reason of the glory that *e* 2Cor 3:10

EXCELLENT—*eminently good*

[*also* EXCELLENCY]
e of dignity and the *e* of ......Gen 49:3
greatness of..*e* thou hast ......Ex 15:7
and in his *e* on the sky........Deut 33:26
who is the sword of thy *e*! ....Deut 33:29
Doth not their *e* which is .....Job 4:21
Though his *e* mount up to.....Job 20:6
now with majesty and *e*........Job 40:10
e is thy name in all the ....Ps 8:1, 9

e is thy loving-kindness, O ....Ps 36:7
the *e* of Jacob whom he.......Ps 47:4
his *e* is over Israel and........Ps 68:34
it shall be an *e* oil which......Ps 141:5
him according to his *e* ....Ps 150:2
I will speak of *e* things........Prov 8:6
E speech becometh not a .....Prov 17:7
not I written to thee *e* ....Prov 22:20
but the *e* of knowledge is .....Eccl 7:12
Lebanon, *e* as the cedars......Song 5:15
fruit of the earth shall be *e*....Is 4:2
beauty of the Chaldees *e*......Is 13:19
in counsel and *e* in ....Is 28:29
the *e* of Carmel and Sharon ...Is 35:2
the Lord, and the *e* of our .....Is 35:2
art come to *e* ornaments ......Ezek 16:7
the *e* of your strength the .....Ezek 24:21
whose brightness was *e*........Dan 2:31
Forasmuch as an *e* spirit ......Dan 5:12
because an *e* spirit was in .....Dan 6:3
I abhor the *e* of Jacob and ....Amos 6:8
turned away the *e* of Jacob....Nah 2:2
order, most *e* Theophilus......Luke 1:3
the most *e* governor Felix .....Acts 23:26
the things that are more *e*.....Rom 2:18
you, came not with *e* of.......1Cor 2:1
show I unto you a more *e*.....1Cor 12:31
the *e* of the power may be 2Cor 4:7
approve things that are *e*......Phil 1:10
the *e* of the knowledge of .....Phil 3:8
obtained a more *e* name ......Heb 1:4
more *e* sacrifice than Cain.....Heb 11:4
a voice to him from the *e* 2Pet 1:17

EXCEPT—*unless*

[*also* EXCEPTED]
E the God of my father, the ..Gen 31:42
e your youngest brother.......Gen 42:15
see my face, *e* your brother ...Gen 43:5
E your youngest brother ......Gen 44:23
e thou make thyself...........Num 16:13
e their Rock had sold.........Deut 32:30
e ye destroy the accursed .....Josh 7:12
e thou hadst hasted and 1Sam 25:34
God to Abner and..also *e* 2Sam 3:9
E thou take away the blind....2Sam 5:6
not thy riding for me, *e* 2Kin 4:24
e the king delighted in her ....Esth 2:14
E the Lord build the house....Ps 127:1
e the Lord keep the city, the ..Ps 127:1
sleep not, *e* they have done ...Prov 4:16
E the Lord of hosts had.......Is 1:9
e the gods whose dwelling.....Dan 2:11
Daniel, *e* we find it against....Dan 6:5
walk together, *e* they be ......Amos 3:3
e your righteousness shall .....Matt 5:20
E ye be converted and ....Matt 18:3
e those days should be ....Matt 24:22
e he will first bind the ....Mark 3:27
e they wash, they eat not .....Mark 7:4
e we should go and buy ....Luke 9:13
that thou doest, *e* God be .....John 3:2
E a man be born of water.....John 3:5
E ye see signs and wonders ...John 4:48
E ye eat the flesh of the Son. .John 6:53
E a corn of wheat fall into ....John 12:24
e it abide in the vine; no ......John 15:4
no more can ye, *e* ye abide ...John 15:4
E I shall see in his hands .....John 20:25
scattered..*e* the apostles ....Acts 8:1
E ye be circumcised after .....Acts 15:1
such as I am, *e* these bonds ...Acts 26:29
e the law had said, Thou ......Rom 7:7
e they be sent, as it is ....Rom 10:15
e it be with consent for a 1Cor 7:5
e I shall speak to you 1Cor 14:6
e ye utter by the tongue 1Cor 14:9
that he is *e*, which did put 1Cor 15:27
e it be that I myself was 2Cor 12:13
e there come a falling away ...2Thess 2:3
not crowned, *e* he strive 2Tim 2:5
of his place, *e* thou repent ....Rev 2:5

EXCESS—*undue or immoderate indulgence*
full of extortion and *e* ....Matt 23:25
drunk with wine..is *e* ....Eph 5:18
e of wine, revellings 1Pet 4:3

EXCHANGE—*trade; traders*
bread in *e* for horses..........Gen 47:17
e thereof shall be holy ....Lev 27:10
e of it shall not be...........Job 28:17
e nor alienate..first fruits ......Ezek 48:14
man give in *e* for his soul? ....Matt 16:26

EXCHANGER—*banker*
put my money to the *e*........Matt 25:27

EXCITEMENT—*something that stirs one emotionally*

Causes of:
Great sin ....Ex 32:17-20
Great victory............1Sam 17:52
God's power 1Kin 18:22-41
King's coronation........2Kin 11:12-16
Human destruction ......Esth 9:1-11
Handwriting on the wall. .Dan 5:5-9
Miracle ....Acts 19:13-29

Time of:
The giving of the Law ...Heb 12:18-21
Christ's death ....Matt 27:51-54
Pentecost ....Acts 2:1-47
Christ's return...........Luke 21:25-28

EXCLUSIVENESS—*setting boundaries against others*

Christianity's, only one:
Door ....John 10:1,7,9
Way....................John 14:6
Salvation ....Acts 4:12

The Bible's, only book:
Inspired 1Tim 3:16
Revealing God ....Heb 1:1
Written to save men .....John 20:30,31
Containing true prophecies ....John 5:45-47

[*also* EXCLUDE, EXCLUDED]
Where is boasting?..It is *e*.....Rom 3:27
they would *e* you ....Gal 4:17

EXCOMMUNICATION—*expulsion from membership in a body*

Separation from:
Kingship 1Sam 16:1
Foreigners ....Neh 13:1-3
Priesthood ....Neh 13:27, 28

Practice of:
To intimidate people.....John 9:19-23
Against true Christians...John 16:1, 2
Against false teachers 2John 10, 11

Method of:
Described..............Matt 18:15-17
Illustrated..............1Cor 5:1-13
Perverted 3John 9, 10

EXCUSE—*an explanation; to overlook*

Nature of, blaming:
Wife ....Gen 3:12
The people 1Sam 15:20, 21
God's mercy ....Jon 4:1-4
God's providence ....Num 14:1-23

Invalidity of:
Shown to Moses.........Ex 3:10-12
Proved to Gideon ....Judg 6:36-40
Made plain to Esther ....Esth 4:13-17
Illustrated by Christ .....Luke 14:16-24
Relayed to Hell's inhabitants ....Luke 16:27-31
Made evident to Thomas .John 20:24-28

[*also* EXCUSING]
they are without *e* ....Rom 1:20
or else *e* one another ....Rom 2:15
e ourselves unto you? 2Cor 12:19

EXECRATION—*the act of denouncing or cursing*
an *e*, and an astonishment.....Jer 42:18
an *e*, and an astonishment.....Jer 44:12

EXECUTE—*to carry out; put into effect*

[*also* EXECUTED, EXECUTEDST, EXECUTEST, EXECUTETH, EXECUTING, EXECUTION]
e judgment; I am the Lord ....Ex 12:12
e upon her all this law ....Num 5:30
may *e* the service of ....Num 8:11
the Lord *e* judgments ....Num 33:4
e the judgment..fatherless .....Deut 10:18
he *e* the justice of the Lord ...Deut 33:21
e his..wrath upon Amalek 1Sam 28:18
David *e* judgment..justice 2Sam 8:15
e my judgments and keep 1Kin 6:12
thou hast done well in *e* 2Kin 10:30
that *e* the priest's office 1Chr 6:10
Ithamar *e*..priest's office 1Chr 24:2
e the priest's office 2Chr 11:14
e judgment against Joash......2Chr 24:24
judgment be *e* speedily........Ezra 7:26
decree drew..to be put in *e*....Esth 9:1
the judgment which he *e* ......Ps 9:16
e judgment..righteousness .....Ps 99:4
stood up Phinehas, and *e* .....Ps 106:30
wilt thou *e* judgment on ......Ps 119:84
e judgment for..oppressed .....Ps 146:7
e upon them the judgment ....Ps 149:9
evil work is not *e* speedily.....Eccl 8:11
Take counsel, *e* judgment .....Is 16:3
man that *e* my counsel ....Is 46:11
be any that *e* judgment ....Jer 5:1
thoroughly *e* judgment ....Jer 7:5
the Lord; *E* ye judgment......Jer 22:3
until he have *e*, and till he ....Jer 23:20
he shall *e* judgment, and ......Jer 33:15
will *e* judgments in..midst .....Ezek 5:8
e judgments in thee..........Ezek 5:15
neither *e* my judgments ....Ezek 11:12
e judgments upon thee ....Ezek 16:41
hath *e* my judgments ....Ezek 18:17
e judgment upon her ....Ezek 23:10
will *e* great vengeance upon ...Ezek 25:17
when I have *e* judgments......Ezek 28:26
I *e* judgments in Egypt........Ezek 30:19
e..fierceness of mine anger ....Hos 11:9
is strong that *e* his word ......Joel 2:11
will *e* vengeance in anger .....Mic 5:15
and *e* judgment for me........Mic 7:9
E true judgment..show ....Zech 7:9
he *e* the priest's office ....Luke 1:8
authority to *e* judgment ....John 5:27
revenger to *e* wrath ....Rom 13:4
To *e* judgment upon all ....Jude 15

EXECUTIONER—*one who puts to death*
king sent an *e*..commanded....Mark 6:27

EXEMPTED—*excused*
none was *e*..took away 1Kin 15:22

EXERCISE—*to make effective in action*

[*also* EXERCISED, EXERCISETH]
I *e* myself in great matters ....Ps 131:1
sons of man to be *e* ....Eccl 1:13
Lord..*e* lovingkindness ....Jer 9:24
e robbery, and have vexed ....Ezek 22:29
Gentiles *e* dominion over .....Matt 20:25
great *e* authority upon ....Matt 20:25
Gentiles *e* lordship over ....Mark 10:42
great ones *e* authority..........Mark 10:42
kings of..earth *e* lordship ......Luke 22:25
e authority upon them ....Luke 22:25
herein do I *e* myself ....Acts 24:16
e thyself..unto godliness 1Tim 4:7
bodily *e* profiteth little 1Tim 4:8
e to discern..good and evil ....Heb 5:14
e with covetous practices 2Pet 2:14
e all the power of..first beast ..Rev 13:12

EXHORTATION—*encouraging others to commendable conduct*

Objects of:
Call to repentance ....Luke 3:17, 18
Continue in the faith ....Acts 14:22
Convict gainsayers ....Titus 1:9
Warn the unruly.........1Thess 5:14
Encourage soberness.....Titus 3:1

Strengthen godliness 1Thess 4:1-6
Stir up liberality 2Cor 9:5-7

Office of:

Commended ....Rom 12:8
Part of the ministry ......Titus 2:15
Needed in times 2Tim 4:2-5

Nature of:

Daily duty ....Heb 3:13
For holiness.............1Thess 2:3, 4
Worthy of reception .....Heb 13:22
Belongs to all ....Heb 10:25
Special need of..........Jude 3, 4

[*also* EXHORT, EXHORTED, EXHORTETH, EXHORTING]

did he testify and *e* ....Acts 2:40
e them all, that with ....Acts 11:23
word of *e* for the people ......Acts 13:15
had given them much *e* ....Acts 20:2
that *e*, on exhortation ....Rom 12:8
edification, and *e*..comfort 1Cor 14:3
he accepted the *e*............2Cor 8:17
As ye know how we *e* 1Thess 2:11
e you by..Lord Jesus..........1Thess 4:1
e by our Lord Jesus Christ 2Thess 3:12
I *e* therefore, that, first 1Tim 2:1
reading, to *e*, to doctrine......1Tim 4:13
e to be sober-minded ....Titus 2:6
but *e* one another, and so .....Heb 10:25
forgotten..*e* which speaketh ...Heb 12:5
I *e*, who am..an elder.........1Pet 5:1
written briefly, *e* 1Pet 5:12

EXILE—*banishment from one's native land*

David 1Sam 21:10-15
Jeroboam 1Kin 11:40
Jeremiah................Jer 43:4-7
Christ ....Matt 2:13-15
John ....Rev 1:9
Jehoiachin 2Kin 24:15
Judah 2Kin 25:21
Jeconiah ....Jer 27:20
Nebuchadnezzar ....Jer 29:1
Chemosh ....Jer 48:7
Syrians ....Amos 1:5
See CAPTIVITY

art a stranger..also an *e* 2Sam 15:19
The captive *e* hasteneth ....Is 51:14

EXODUS—*a departure*

Israel's, from Egypt .....Ex 12:41

EXODUS, BOOK OF—*second book of the Old Testament*

Escape from Egypt ......Ex 12:31-42
The Law................Ex 20:1-17
The tabernacle and priesthood .... Ex 24:12—31:18

EXORCISTS—*those who use oaths to drive out evil spirits*

Paul encounters ....Acts 19:13, 19

EXPANSE—*firmament; vault*

Created by God ....Gen 1:8
Stars placed in ....Gen 1:14, 17
Compared to a tent curtain ....Ps 104:2
Expressive of God's glory.Ps 19:1
Saints compared to ......Dan 12:3

EXPECTATION—*looking forward*

Conquest ....Num 14:1-24
Victory ....Josh 7:4-13
Relief 1Kin 12:4-15
Impending doom 2Kin 23:25-27
Elevation ....Esth 6:6-14
The wicked ....Prov 10:28
Righteous ....Ps 62:5
Destruction ....John 4:1-11
Death ....Acts 28:3-6

[*also* EXPECTED, EXPECTING]

e of the poor shall not ....Ps 9:18
man dieth..*e* shall perish ......Prov 11:7
e of the wicked is wrath.......Prov 11:23
thine *e* shall not be cut off ....Prov 23:18
thy *e* shall not be cut off ......Prov 24:14
Ethiopia their *e*, and..Egypt ...Is 20:5
e shall be ashamed ....Zech 9:5
as the people were in *e* ....Luke 3:15
e to receive..of them..........Acts 3:5
e of the people of the Jews....Acts 12:11
earnest *e* of the creature ......Rom 8:19
earnest *e* and my hope ....Phil 1:20
e till his enemies be made .....Heb 10:13

EXPEDIENCY—*a method of justifying an act*

To fulfill God's plan .....John 11:50
To avoid offense 1Cor 8:8-13
To save men 1Cor 9:19-23
To accomplish a task 2Cor 8:10-12
Illustrations ....Acts 16:3

[*also* EXPEDIENT]

e for you that I go away ......John 16:7
but all things are not *e*........1Cor 6:12
e of you..have begun 2Cor 8:10

EXPEL—*to force out; drive away*

[*also* EXPELLED]

e not the Geshurites ....Josh 13:13
e them from before you ....Josh 23:5
e thence..sons of Anak........Judg 1:20
not ye hate me, and *e* me .....Judg 11:7
be not *e* from him 2Sam 14:14
e them out of their coasts .....Acts 13:50

EXPENSE—*the cost involved*

Royalty, foretold 1Sam 8:11-18
Royalty, realized 1Kin 4:22, 23

[*also* EXPENSES]

let the *e* be given out ....Ezra 6:4

EXPERIENCE—*accumulated understanding*

e that the Lord hath blessed...Gen 30:27
heart had..*e* of wisdom........Eccl 1:16
patience, *e*; and *e*, hope ......Rom 5:4

EXPERIMENT—*a test designed to prove something*

Jacob...................Gen 30:37-43
Aaron's sons ....Lev 10:1-3
Philistines..............1Sam 6:1-18
Daniel..................Dan 1:11-16
God's goodness ....Mal 3:10-12

by..*e* of this ministration 2Cor 9:13

EXPERT—*experienced; having special skill or knowledge*

e in war, with..instruments 1Chr 12:33
e in war, forty thousand 1Chr 12:36
being *e* in war, every man.....Song 3:8
be as of a mighty *e* man ....Jer 50:9
e in all customs..questions .....Acts 26:3

EXPIATION—*atonement*

Under Law ....Lev 14:11-20
Lev 16:11-28
Prophecy of Isaiah ....Is 53:1-12
Fulfilled in Christ........Acts 8:27-39
1Pet 2:21-25

EXPIRED—*elapsed*

the days were not *e*..........1Sam 18:26
after the year was *e* 2Sam 11:1
when thy days be *e* 1Chr 17:11
e, king Nebuchadnezzar 2Chr 36:10
when these days were *e* ....Esth 1:5
these days are *e* ....Ezek 43:27
when forty years were *e*.......Acts 7:30
thousand years are *e* ....Rev 20:7

EXPLANATION—*that which makes plain or understandable*

Of a condition ....Luke 16:25-31
Of a phenomenon ....Acts 2:1-21
Of a decision ....Acts 15:15-31

EXPLOITS—*notable or heroic deeds*

he shall do *e*, and return ......Dan 11:28

EXPOUND—*to set forth; explain*

[*also* EXPOUNDED]

could not in three days *e*......Judg 14:14
unto them which *e*..riddle .....Judg 14:19
e all things to his disciples.....Mark 4:34
he *e* unto them in all ....Luke 24:27
e it by order unto them ....Acts 11:4
whom he *e* and testified.......Acts 28:23

EXPRESS—*to delineate; explicitly*

[*also* EXPRESSED, EXPRESSLY]

Men..*e* by their names ....Num 1:17
If I *e* say unto the lad 1Sam 20:21
which were *e* by name 1Chr 12:31
e by name rose up...........2Chr 28:15
all of them were *e* by name ...Ezra 8:20
word of the Lord came *e*......Ezek 1:3
Now the Spirit speaketh *e*.....1Tim 4:1
e image of his person ....Heb 1:3

EXPULSION—*driving out by force from*

Eden ....Gen 3:22-24
The priesthood ....Neh 13:27, 28
A city ....Luke 4:16-29
By persecution ....Acts 13:50, 51

EXTEND—*to make available*

[*also* EXTENDED, EXTENDETH]

e mercy..before the king ......Ezra 7:28
e mercy unto us in the sight ...Ezra 9:9
goodness *e* not to thee ....Ps 16:2
be none to *e* mercy ....Ps 109:12
e peace to her like a river.....Is 66:12

EXTINCT—*extinguished*

breath is corrupt..days are *e*...Job 17:1
they are *e*..quenched as ....Is 43:17

EXTOL—*to praise highly*

[*also* EXTOLLED]

I will *e* thee, O Lord ....Ps 30:1
he was *e* with my tongue......Ps 66:17
I will *e* thee my God ....Ps 145:1
shall be exalted and *e*.........Is 52:13
Nebuchadnezzar praise..*e* .....Dan 4:37

EXTORTION—*money obtained by force or threat*

Innocency from, pretended.............Matt 23:25
Fellowship with, forbidden 1Cor 5:10, 11
Sin of, proscribed ....Luke 3:13, 14
Examples of ....Gen 47:13-26

EXTORTIONER—*one who obtains by threats*

[*also* EXTORTIONERS]

e catch all that he hath ....Ps 109:11
e is at an end, the spoiler .....Is 16:4
gained of..neighbors by *e* .....Ezek 22:12
not as other men are, *e* ....Luke 18:11
nor *e*, shall inherit the 1Cor 6:10

EXTREME—*intense*

e burning, and with..sword ....Deut 28:22

EXTREMITY—*the greatest degree of something*

Human faith ....Gen 22:1-3
Grief 2Sam 18:33
Pride ....Is 14:13, 14
Pain...................Matt 27:46-50
Degradation ....Luke 15:13-16
Torments ....Luke 16:23, 24
Human endurance 2Cor 1:8-10

EYE—*an organ of sight; a small opening*

Affected by:

Age ....Gen 27:1
Wine ....Gen 49:12
Sorrow ....Job 17:7
Disease ....Lev 26:16
Grief ....Ps 6:7
Light ....Acts 22:11

Of God, figurative of:

Omniscience 2Chr 16:9
Justice.................Amos 9:8
Holiness ....Hab 1:13
Guidance ....Ps 32:8
Protection ....Ps 33:18

Of man, figurative of:

Revealed knowledge .....Num 24:3
Lawlessness ....Judg 17:6
Jealousy 1Sam 18:9

Understanding ... Ps 19:8
Agreement ... Is 52:8
Great sorrow ... Jer 9:1
Retaliation ... Matt 5:38
The essential nature ... Matt 6:22, 23
Moral state ... Matt 7:3-5
Spiritual inability ... Matt 13:15
Spiritual dullness ... Mark 8:17, 18
Future glory ... 1Cor 2:9
Illumination ... Eph 1:18
Unworthy service ... Eph 6:6
Worldliness ... 1John 2:16
Evil desires ... 2Pet 2:14

Prophecies concerning:
Shall see the Redeemer ... Job 19:25-27
Gentiles shall see ... Is 42:6, 7
Blind shall see ... Is 29:18
Will see the King ... Is 33:17
Will see Jesus ... Rev 1:7
Tears of, shall be wiped away ... Rev 7:17

[*also* EYED, EYES, EYE'S]
your *e* shall be opened ... Gen 3:5
e of them both were opened ... Gen 3:7
Lot lifted up his *e* ... Gen 13:10
mistress..despised in her *e* ... Gen 16:4
lifted up..*e* and looked ... Gen 18:2
a covering of the *e* ... Gen 20:16
Abraham lifted up his *e* ... Gen 22:4
lifted up his *e*, and saw ... Gen 24:63
Isaac was old..*e* were dim ... Gen 27:1
Leah was tender *e*; but ... Gen 29:17
rods before the *e* of..cattle ... Gen 30:41
Lift up now thine *e* ... Gen 31:12
Jacob lifted up his *e* ... Gen 33:1
find grace in your *e* ... Gen 34:11
master's wife cast her *e* ... Gen 39:7
good in the *e* of Pharaoh ... Gen 41:37
in..*e* of all his servants ... Gen 41:37
lifted..*e* and saw his brother ... Gen 43:29
your *e* see..*e* of my brother ... Gen 45:12
we die before thine *e* ... Gen 47:19
abhorred in..*e* of Pharaoh ... Ex 5:21
Egyptians before their *e* ... Ex 8:26
frontlets between thine *e* ... Ex 13:16
E for *e*, tooth for tooth ... Ex 21:24
a man smite..*e* of his servant ... Ex 21:26
e of his maid ... Ex 21:26
go free for his *e*'s sake ... Ex 21:26
e of..children of Israel ... Ex 24:17
hid from the *e* of..assembly ... Lev 4:13
hath a blemish in his *e* ... Lev 21:20
beside..manna, before our *e* ... Num 11:6
put out the *e* of these men? ... Num 16:14
sanctify me in the *e*..children ... Num 20:12
Balaam lifted up his *e* ... Num 24:2
having his *e* open ... Num 24:4
having his *e* open ... Num 24:16
Egypt before your *e* ... Deut 1:30
lift up thine *e* westward ... Deut 3:27
behold it with thine *e* ... Deut 3:27
things..thine *e* have seen ... Deut 4:9
in Egypt before your *e* ... Deut 4:34
all his household, before our *e* ... Deut 6:22
e shall have no pity upon ... Deut 7:16
brake them before your *e* ... Deut 9:17
e have seen all..acts ... Deut 11:7
as frontlets between your *e* ... Deut 11:18
is right in the *e*..Lord ... Deut 13:18
e be evil against thy poor ... Deut 15:9
gift doth blind the *e*..wise ... Deut 16:19
thine *e* shall not pity ... Deut 19:21
life shall go for life, *e* for *e* ... Deut 19:21
find no favor in his *e* ... Deut 24:1
thine *e* shall not pity her ... Deut 25:12
thine *e* shall look ... Deut 28:32
e shall be evil toward the ... Deut 28:56
trembling heart..failing of *e* ... Deut 28:65
heart to perceive..*e* to see ... Deut 29:4
his *e* was not dim, nor his ... Deut 34:7
lifted up his *e*, and looked ... Josh 5:13
e have seen what I have done ... Josh 24:7
and put out his *e* ... Judg 16:21
was right in his own *e* ... Judg 21:25
Let thine *e* be on the field ... Ruth 2:9
be to consume thine *e* ... 1Sam 2:33
e were dim..he could not ... 1Sam 4:15
thrust out all your right *e* ... 1Sam 11:2
Lord will do before your *e* ... 1Sam 12:16
e have been enlightened ... 1Sam 14:29
Saul *e* David from that day ... 1Sam 18:9
found favor in thine *e* ... 1Sam 20:29
find favor in thine *e* ... 1Sam 25:8
set by this day in mine *e* ... 1Sam 26:24
set by in the *e* of the Lord ... 1Sam 26:24
in the *e* of the handmaids ... 2Sam 6:20
kept the watch lifted up..*e* ... 2Sam 13:34
lifted up his *e* ... 2Sam 18:24
e are upon the haughty ... 2Sam 22:28
O king, the *e* of all ... 1Kin 1:20
e may be open toward this ... 1Kin 8:29
e and mine heart shall be ... 1Kin 9:3
do..is right in mine *e* ... 1Kin 11:33
which was right in mine *e* ... 1Kin 14:8
which was right in the *e* ... 1Kin 15:11
pleasant in thine *e* ... 1Kin 20:6
e upon his *e*, and his hands ... 2Kin 4:34
Lord, I pray..open his *e* ... 2Kin 6:17
opened the *e* of..young man ... 2Kin 6:17
Lord, open the *e* of..men ... 2Kin 6:20
Lord opened their *e* ... 2Kin 6:20
which is good in thine *e* ... 2Kin 10:5
open, Lord, thine *e* ... 2Kin 19:16
sons of Zedekiah before..*e* ... 2Kin 25:7
put out..*e* of Zedekiah ... 2Kin 25:7
right in the *e* of..people ... 1Chr 13:4
David lifted up his *e* ... 1Chr 21:16
e may be open upon ... 2Chr 6:20
mine *e* shall be open ... 2Chr 7:15
mine *e* had seen it ... 2Chr 9:6
e of..Lord run to and fro ... 2Chr 16:9
evil in the *e* of the Lord ... 2Chr 21:6
as ye see with your *e* ... 2Chr 29:8
laid before their *e* ... Ezra 3:12
e..God was upon the elders ... Ezra 5:5
e open..thou mayest hear ... Neh 1:6
despise their husbands in..*e* ... Esth 1:17
lifted up their *e* afar off ... Job 2:12
image..before mine *e* ... Job 4:16
e shall no more see good ... Job 7:7
Hast thou *e* of flesh? ... Job 10:4
no *e* had seen me! ... Job 10:18
e of the wicked shall fail ... Job 11:20
what do thy *e* wink at ... Job 15:12
e poureth..tears unto God ... Job 16:20
e of his children shall fail ... Job 17:5
e..dim by reason of sorrow ... Job 17:7
offspring before their *e* ... Job 21:8
e also of the adulterer ... Job 24:15
saying, No *e* shall see me ... Job 24:15
e are upon their ways ... Job 24:23
vulture's *e* hath not seen ... Job 28:7
hid from..*e* of all living ... Job 28:21
when the *e* saw me ... Job 29:11
made a covenant with..*e* ... Job 31:1
righteous in his own *e* ... Job 32:1
e from the righteous ... Job 36:7
He taketh it with his *e* ... Job 40:24
e are privily set against ... Ps 10:8
his *e* behold ... Ps 11:4
lighten..*e*, lest I sleep ... Ps 13:3
e a vile person..contemned ... Ps 15:4
e behold the things..equal ... Ps 17:2
Lord is pure, enlightening..*e* ... Ps 19:8
loving-kindness is before..*e* ... Ps 26:3
e is consumed with grief ... Ps 31:9
e of the Lord is upon them ... Ps 33:18
e of the Lord are upon ... Ps 34:15
Aha, aha, our *e* hath seen it ... Ps 35:21
no fear of God before..*e* ... Ps 36:1
flattereth himself in..own *e* ... Ps 36:2
them in order before..*e* ... Ps 50:21
e fail while I wait..God ... Ps 69:3
e stand out with fatness ... Ps 73:7
holdest mine *e* waking ... Ps 77:4
e mourneth by reason of ... Ps 88:9
thine *e* shalt thou behold ... Ps 91:8
formed the *e*, shall he not ... Ps 94:9
e shall be upon the faithful ... Ps 101:6
e have they..they see not ... Ps 115:5
mine *e* from tears ... Ps 116:8
it is marvelous in our *e* ... Ps 118:23
Open thou mine *e* ... Ps 119:18
Mine *e* fail for thy word ... Ps 119:82
Rivers of waters run down..*e* ... Ps 119:136
lift up mine *e* unto..hills ... Ps 121:1
Unto thee lift I up mine *e* ... Ps 123:1
e of servants look unto ... Ps 123:2
e of a maiden unto the hand ... Ps 123:2
e wait upon the Lord ... Ps 123:2
will not give sleep to mine *e* ... Ps 132:4
e did see my substance ... Ps 139:16
mine *e* are unto thee ... Ps 141:8
e of all wait upon thee ... Ps 145:15
The Lord openeth the *e* ... Ps 146:8
Be not wise in thine own *e* ... Prov 3:7
Let them not depart from..*e* ... Prov 4:21
are before the *e* of..Lord ... Prov 5:21
winketh with his *e* ... Prov 6:13
as the apple of thine *e* ... Prov 7:2
smoke to the *e*, so is the ... Prov 10:26
fool is right in..own *e* ... Prov 12:15
e..Lord are in every place ... Prov 15:3
light of the *e* rejoiceth ... Prov 15:30
shutteth his *e* to devise ... Prov 16:30
e of a fool are in the ends ... Prov 17:24
hearing ear..seeing *e* ... Prov 20:12
open thine *e*..and thou ... Prov 20:13
findeth no favor in his *e* ... Prov 21:10
hath a bountiful *e* shall ... Prov 22:9
e upon that which is not? ... Prov 23:5
who hath redness of *e*? ... Prov 23:29
prince whom..*e* have seen ... Prov 25:7
to be rich hath an evil *e* ... Prov 28:22
e shall have many..curse ... Prov 28:27
pure in their own *e* ... Prov 30:12
e is not satisfied..seeing ... Eccl 1:8
e desired I kept not from ... Eccl 2:10
beholding of them with..*e*? ... Eccl 5:11
night seeth sleep with his *e* ... Eccl 8:16
in the sight of thine *e* ... Eccl 11:9
fair; thou hast doves' *e* ... Song 1:15
heart with one of thine *e* ... Song 4:9
Turn away thine *e* from me ... Song 6:5
e as one that found favor ... Song 8:10
hide mine *e* from you ... Is 1:15
to provoke the *e* of his glory ... Is 3:8
e of the lofty shall be ... Is 5:15
mine *e* have seen the King ... Is 6:5
ears heavy, and shut their *e* ... Is 6:10
lest they see with their *e* ... Is 6:10
dashed to pieces before..*e* ... Is 13:16
e shall not spare children ... Is 13:18
and hath closed your *e* ... Is 29:10
e shall see thy teachers ... Is 30:20
shutteth his *e* from seeing evil ... Is 33:15
e shall see Jerusalem ... Is 33:20
open thine *e*, O Lord ... Is 37:17
e fail with looking upward ... Is 38:14
he hath shut their *e* ... Is 44:18
Lift up thine *e* round about ... Is 49:18
bare his holy arm in..*e* ... Is 52:10
Lift up thine *e* round about ... Is 60:4
neither hath the *e* seen ... Is 64:4
they are hid from mine *e* ... Is 65:16
thine *e* unto..high places ... Jer 3:2
which have *e*, and see not ... Jer 5:21
e may run down with tears ... Jer 9:18
mine *e* shall weep sore ... Jer 13:17
their *e* did fail, because ... Jer 14:6
cease out of this place in..*e* ... Jer 16:9
e are upon all their ways ... Jer 16:17
iniquity hid from mine *e* ... Jer 16:17
thine *e* and thine heart ... Jer 22:17
shall slay..before your *e* ... Jer 29:21
his *e* shall behold his *e* ... Jer 32:4
thine *e* shall behold the *e* ... Jer 34:3
put out Zedekiah's *e* ... Jer 39:7
evil in the *e* of the Lord ... Jer 52:2
put out the *e* of Zedekiah ... Jer 52:11
mine *e* runneth down ... Lam 1:16
not the apple of thine *e* ... Lam 2:18
Mine *e* trickleth down ... Lam 3:49
e as yet failed for our vain ... Lam 4:17

rings were full of *e* round .....Ezek 1:18
neither shall mine *e* spare .....Ezek 5:11
mine *e* shall not spare ....Ezek 7:9
Son of man, lift up thine *e* ....Ezek 8:5
let not your *e* spare..........Ezek 9:5
full of *e* round about ....Ezek 10:12
see not..ground with his *e* .....Ezek 12:12
None *e* pitied thee...........Ezek 16:5
lifted up his *e* to the idols .....Ezek 18:12
abominations of his *e* ....Ezek 20:7
e were after..fathers' idols .....Ezek 20:24
hid..*e* from my sabbaths ......Ezek 22:26
shalt not lift up thine *e* ....Ezek 23:27
from thee..desire of thine *e* ...Ezek 24:16
the desire of their *e* ....Ezek 24:25
sanctified in you before..*e* .....Ezek 36:23
O Gog, before their *e* ....Ezek 38:16
Son of man, behold with..*e* ....Ezek 40:4
Nebuchadnezzar lifted..*e* ......Dan 4:34
even of..horn that had *e* ......Dan 7:20
notable horn between his *e* ....Dan 8:5
e..behold our desolations ......Dan 9:18
his *e* as lamps of fire ....Dan 10:6
shall be hid from mine *e* ......Hos 13:14
meat cut off before our *e* .....Joel 1:16
mine *e* upon them for evil .....Amos 9:4
let our *e* look upon Zion ......Mic 4:11
back your captivity before..*e* ..Zeph 3:20
not in your *e* in comparison ...Hag 2:3
Then lifted I up mine *e* ....Zech 1:18
toucheth..apple of his *e* ....Zech 2:8
one stone shall be seven *e*.....Zech 3:9
turned, and lifted up mine *e* ...Zech 5:1
lifted I up mine *e*, and ....Zech 5:9
in the *e* of the remnant ....Zech 8:6
e of man, as of all..tribes .....Zech 9:1
arm, and upon his right *e* .....Zech 11:17
right *e* shall be..darkened .....Zech 11:17
e upon the house of Judah ....Zech 12:4
e shall see..ye shall say ....Mal 1:5
thy right *e* offend..pluck it ....Matt 5:29
light of the body is the *e* ......Matt 6:22
if..thine *e* be single ....Matt 6:22
But if thine *e* be evil ....Matt 6:23
mote..is in thy brother's *e* .....Matt 7:3
beam that is in thine own *e*? ..Matt 7:3
pull out the mote out of..*e* ....Matt 7:4
beam is in thine own *e*?.......Matt 7:4
beam out of thine own *e* ......Matt 7:5
mote out of thy brother's *e* ....Matt 7:5
Then touched he their *e* ......Matt 9:29
they had lifted up their *e*......Matt 17:8
e offend thee, pluck it out ....Matt 18:9
into life with one *e* ....Matt 18:9
thine *e* evil because I am......Matt 20:15
Lord..*e* may be opened ....Matt 20:33
and touched their *e*...........Matt 20:34
their *e* received sight..........Matt 20:34
it is marvelous in our *e*? ......Matt 21:42
for their *e* were heavy ....Matt 26:43
an evil *e*, blasphemy ....Mark 7:22
when he had spit on his *e* .....Mark 8:23
if..*e* offend thee, pluck it out ..Mark 9:47
kingdom of God with..*e*.......Mark 9:47
two *e* to be cast into hell......Mark 9:47
it is marvelous in our *e*? ......Mark 12:11
(for their *e* were heavy) ....Mark 14:40
mine *e* have seen..salvation....Luke 2:30
lifted..*e* on his disciples ....Luke 6:20
mote..in thy brother's *e* ....Luke 6:41
beam..in thine own *e*? ....Luke 6:41
mote that is in thine *e* ....Luke 6:42
beam..in thine own *e*? ....Luke 6:42
beam out of thine own *e* ......Luke 6:42
mote..in thy brother's *e* ....Luke 6:42
light of the body is the *e* ......Luke 11:34
when thine *e* is single ....Luke 11:34
when thine *e* is evil ....Luke 11:34
hell he lift up his *e* ....Luke 16:23
they are hid from thine *e* .....Luke 19:42
their *e* were opened, and ......Luke 24:31
Lift up your *e*, and look ......John 4:35
anointed the *e* of..blind man ..John 9:6
anointed mine *e*, and said .....John 9:11
He put clay upon mine *e*......John 9:15
who hath opened his *e* ....John 9:21
yet he hath opened mine *e* ....John 9:30
devil open the *e*..blind? ....John 10:21
Jesus lifted up his *e*..........John 11:41
He hath blinded their *e* ....John 12:40
should not see with their *e* ....John 12:40
fastening his *e* upon him ......Acts 3:4
from his *e*..had been scales ....Acts 9:18
had fastened mine *e* ....Acts 11:6
To open their *e*..turn them ....Acts 26:18
their *e* have they closed ....Acts 28:27
should see with their *e* ....Acts 28:27
no fear of God before..*e* ......Rom 3:18
Let their *e* be darkened ....Rom 11:10
Because I am not the *e* 1Cor 12:16
e cannot say unto..hand 1Cor 12:21
before whose *e* Jesus Christ ...Gal 3:1
opened unto the *e* of him .....Heb 4:13
e of the Lord are over 1Pet 3:12
we have seen with our *e* 1John 1:1
his *e* were as a flame of fire ...Rev 1:14
anoint..*e* with eyesalve ....Rev 3:18
they were full of *e* within .....Rev 4:8
e were as a flame of fire ......Rev 19:12

EYEBROW—*the ridge above the eye, often including the hair on it*
Of lepers, shaved off ....Lev 14:2, 9

e, even all his hair...........Lev 14:9

EYELIDS—*the moveable part of the eye that closes over the eyeball*
on my *e* is..shadow of death ...Job 16:16
e try the children of men......Ps 11:4
e look straight before thee ....Prov 4:25
let her take thee with her *e* ...Prov 6:25
e gush out with waters ....Jer 9:18

EYESALVE—*an ointment*
Christ mentions ....Rev 3:18

EYESERVICE—*service performed only when watched by another*
Highly obnoxious ....Eph 6:6

not with *e*, as menpleasers ....Col 3:22

EYESIGHT—*sight*
of my hands in his *e* .....Ps 18:24

EYEWITNESS—*a firsthand observer*
Consulted by Luke ......Luke 1:1, 2
Of Christ's majesty 2Pet 1:16

EZAR—*See* **Ezer**

EZBAI (ĕz'bā-ī)—*"shining; beautiful"*
Naarai's father 1Chr 11:37

EZBON (ĕz'bŏn)—*"bright"*
1. Son of Gad............Gen 46:16
2. Benjamite 1Chr 7:7

EZEKIAS (ĕz'ē-kī-äs)—*"Jehovah is strength"—an alternate spelling for Hezekiah*
Achaz..Achaz begat *E* ....Matt 1:9
E begat Manasses ....Matt 1:10

EZEKIEL (ĕ-zēk'yĕl)—*"God strengthens"*
Life of:
Hebrew prophet; son of Buzi.................Ezek 1:3
Carried captive to Babylon ....Ezek 1:1-3
Lived among exiles ......Ezek 3:15-17
His wife died ....Ezek 24:18
Persecuted ....Ezek 3:25
Often consulted ....Ezek 8:1
Prophetic minister ....Ezek 3:17-21
Visions of:
God's glory ....Ezek 1:4-28
Abominations ....Ezek 8:5-18
Valley of dry bones......Ezek 37:1-14
Messianic times ....Ezek 40:48
River of life ....Ezek 47:1-5
Methods employed by:
Threatens dumbness .....Ezek 3:26
Symbolizes siege of Jerusalem............Ezek 4:1-3
Shaves himself ....Ezek 5:1-4
Removes baggage ....Ezek 12:3-16
Uses boiling pot.........Ezek 24:1-14
Does not mourn for wife .Ezek 24:16-27
Uses parables ....Ezek 17:2-10

EZEKIEL, BOOK OF—*a book of the Old Testament*
Prophecies against Israel. . Ezek 1:1—24:27
Prophecies against the nations ....Ezek 25:1—32:32
Prophecies of restoration..Ezek 33:1—39:29
The Messianic kingdom . .Ezek 40:1—48:35

EZEL (ē'zĕl)—*"division; separation"*
David's hiding place 1Sam 20:19

EZEM (ē'zĕm)—*"bone"*
Village of Judah.........Josh 15:29
Assigned to Simeon .....Josh 19:3
See **Azem**

Bilhah and at *E* 1Chr 4:29

EZER (ē'zĕr)—*"help"*
1. Horite tribe 1Chr 1:38
Son of Seir ....Gen 36:21
2. Ephraimite 1Chr 7:21
3. Judahite.................1Chr 4:1, 4
4. Gadite warrior..........1Chr 12:9
5. Son of Jeshua ....Neh 3:19
6. Postexilic priest ....Neh 12:42

children of *E* are these ....Gen 36:27
duke *E*, duke Dishan ....Gen 36:30
sons of *E*; Bilhan..Zavan 1Chr 1:42

EZION-GEBER, EZION-GABER (ē-zĭ-ŏn-gē'ber,-gā'ber)—*"giant's backbone"*
Town on the Red Sea ...1Kin 9:26
Israelite encampment ....Num 33:35
Seaport of Israel's navy ..1Kin 22:48

And they removed from *E* ....Num 33:36
from *E*, we turned..passed ....Deut 2:8
went Solomon to *E* 2Chr 8:17
they made..ships in *E* 2Chr 20:36

EZNITE (ĕz'nīt)—*"spear; to be sharp"*
Warrior of David........2Sam 23:8
Called Tachmonite 2Sam 23:8
Called Hachmonite 1Chr 11:11

EZRA (ĕz'rä)—*"help"*
1. Postexilic priest ....Neh 12:1, 7
Called Azariah ....Neh 10:2
2. Scribe, priest and reformer of postexilic times ....Ezra 7:1-6
Commissioned by Artaxerxes ....Ezra 7:6-28
Takes exiles with him ...Ezra 8:1-20
Proclaims a fast.........Ezra 8:21-23
Commits treasures to the priests ....Ezra 8:24-30
Comes to Jerusalem .....Ezra 8:31, 32
Institutes reforms ....Ezra 9:1-15
Reads the Law ....Neh 8:1-18
Helps in dedication .....Neh 12:27-43

E were, Jether, and Mered. ...1Chr 4:17
Now when *E* had prayed ......Ezra 10:1
unto *E*, We have trespassed ...Ezra 10:2
arose *E*..made the chief ....Ezra 10:5
E rose up from before..house..Ezra 10:6
E the priest stood up ....Ezra 10:10
E the priest, with..chief ....Ezra 10:16
spake unto *E* the scribe ....Neh 8:1
E the priest brought..law......Neh 8:2
E the scribe..upon a pulpit. ...Neh 8:4
E opened the book in..sight ...Neh 8:5
E blessed the Lord..God ......Neh 8:6
E the priest the scribe ....Neh 8:9
Levites, unto *E* the scribe .....Neh 8:13
E, Meshullam; of Amariah. ...Neh 12:13
of *E* the priest..scribe ....Neh 12:26

Azariah, *E*..Meshullam........Neh 12:33
of God, and *E* the scribe......Neh 12:36

EZRA, BOOK OF—*a book of the Old Testament*
Return from exile.......Ezra 1:1—2:70
Rebuilding the Temple...Ezra 3:1—6:22
Reformation...........Ezra 9:1—10:44

EZRAHITE (ĕz'rä-hīt)—*"belonging to Ezrach"*
Family name of Ethan and Heman..........1Kin 4:31

EZRI (ĕz'rī)—*"my help"*
David's farm overseer....1Chr 27:26

F

FABLE—*a fictitious story employed for teaching purposes*

Form of allegory:
The trees..............Judg 9:7-15
The thistle.............2Kin 14:9

Form of fiction, contrary to:
Edification.............1Tim 1:4
Godliness..............1Tim 4:6, 7
Truth..................2Tim 4:4
Facts..................2Pet 1:16

[*also* FABLES]
Not..heed to Jewish *f*.........Titus 1:14

FACE—*front part of the human head; the surface*

Acts performed on:
Spitting on.............Deut 25:9
Disfiguring of..........Matt 6:16
Painting of.............2Kin 9:30
Hitting................2Cor 11:20

Acts indicated by:
Falling on—worship.....Gen 17:3
Covering of—mourning..2Sam 19:4
Hiding of—disapproval..Deut 31:17, 18
Turning away of—rejection.............2Chr 30:9
Setting of—determination.2Kin 12:17

[*also* FACES]
darkness was upon the *f*......Gen 1:2
Spirit of God moved..*f*.......Gen 1:2
watered the whole *f*..ground...Gen 2:6
driven me out..from the *f*.....Gen 4:14
and from thy *f* shall I.........Gen 4:14
multiply on the *f* of the earth..Gen 6:1
alive upon the *f* of..earth.....Gen 7:3
ark went upon the *f*..waters...Gen 7:18
upon the *f* of the ground......Gen 7:23
abated..the *f* of the ground....Gen 8:8
f of the ground was dry.......Gen 8:13
their *f* were backward.........Gen 9:23
upon the *f* of all the earth....Gen 11:8
she fled from her *f*..........Gen 16:6
his *f* toward the ground.......Gen 19:1
put the earring upon her *f*....Gen 24:27
set the *f* of the flocks.........Gen 30:40
set his *f* toward..Gilead.......Gen 31:21
have seen God *f* to *f*.........Gen 32:30
I have seen thy *f*.............Gen 33:10
I had seen the *f* of God.......Gen 33:10
fled from *f* of his brother.....Gen 35:7
f of his brother Jacob.........Gen 36:6
over all the *f* of the earth.....Gen 41:56
Ye shall not see my *f*.........Gen 43:5
ye shall see my *f* no more.....Gen 44:23
Joseph, to direct his *f*.........Gen 46:28
not thought to see thy *f*.......Gen 48:11
Joseph fell..father's *f*.........Gen 50:1
Moses fled from the *f* of.......Ex 2:15
shall cover the *f* of the earth..Ex 10:5
see my *f* no more; for in......Ex 10:28
will see thy *f* again no........Ex 10:29
flee from the *f* of Israel.......Ex 14:25
before..*f* all these words......Ex 19:7
f..look one to another........Ex 25:20
consume them from the *f*.....Ex 32:12
upon the *f* of the earth.......Ex 33:16
f shall not be seen............Ex 33:23
the skin of his *f* shone........Ex 34:30
saw the *f* of Moses...........Ex 34:35
skin of Moses' *f* shone........Ex 34:35
their *f* one to another.........Ex 37:9
and fell on their *f*............Lev 9:24
of his head toward his *f*.......Lev 13:41
will even set my *f* against.....Lev 17:10
honor the *f* of the old man....Lev 19:32
will even set my *f*............Lev 20:6
cubits high upon the *f*........Num 11:31
had but spit in her *f*..........Num 12:14
Moses..Aaron fell on their *f*...Num 14:5
he fell upon his *f*............Num 16:4
they fell upon their *f*.........Num 16:45
cover the *f* of the earth.......Num 22:5
fell flat on his *f*.............Num 22:31
not be afraid..*f* of man........Deut 1:17
from off the *f* of..earth.......Deut 6:15
that hate him to their *f*.......Deut 7:10
will repay him to his *f*........Deut 7:10
them down before thy *f*.......Deut 9:3
taken away from..thy *f*........Deut 28:31
hide my *f* from them.........Deut 32:20
the Lord knew *f* to *f*..........Deut 34:10
Joshua fell on his *f* to.........Josh 5:14
liest thou..upon thy *f*?........Josh 7:10
angel of the Lord *f* to *f*.......Judg 6:22
Then she fell on her *f*........Ruth 2:10
fallen upon his *f* to...........1Sam 5:3
fell upon his *f* to the earth....1Sam 17:49
fell on his *f* to the ground.....1Sam 20:41
before David on her *f*.........1Sam 25:23
before the *f* of the Lord.......1Sam 26:20
how..should I hold up my *f*...2Sam 2:22
Thou shalt not see my *f*.......2Sam 3:13
when..comest to see my *f*.....2Sam 3:13
fell on her *f* to the ground....2Sam 14:4
let him not see my *f*..........2Sam 14:24
saw not the king's *f*..........2Sam 14:24
let me see the king's *f*........2Sam 14:32
over..*f* of all the country......2Sam 18:8
f of all thy servants..........2Sam 19:5
king with his *f* to..ground.....1Kin 1:23
Israel set their *f* on me.......1Kin 2:15
king turned his *f* about........1Kin 8:14
destroy it from off the *f*.......1Kin 13:34
put his *f* between..knees......1Kin 18:42
with ashes upon his *f*.........1Kin 20:38
away his *f* turned............1Kin 21:4
staff upon the *f*..child........2Kin 4:29
spread it on his *f*..he died.....2Kin 8:15
he lifted up his *f* to..........2Kin 9:32
wept over his *f*..............2Kin 13:14
Judah looked..in the *f*........2Kin 14:11
turned his *f* to the wall.......2Kin 20:2
f were like the *f* of lions......1Chr 12:8
seek his *f* continually.........1Chr 16:11
and their *f* were inward.......2Chr 3:13
king turned his *f*............2Chr 6:3
pray, and seek my *f*..........2Chr 7:14
see one another in the *f*.......2Chr 25:17
turned away their *f* from......2Chr 29:6
shame of *f* to his own land....2Chr 32:21
blush to lift up my *f* to thee...Ezra 9:6
Media, which saw..king's *f*....Esth 1:14
will curse thee to thy *f*........Job 1:11
will curse thee to thy *f*........Job 2:5
spirit passed before my *f*......Job 4:15
covereth..*f* of the judges......Job 9:24
Wherefore hidest thou..*f*......Job 13:24
beareth witness to my *f*.......Job 16:8
declare his way to his *f*?......Job 21:31
covered..darkness from my *f*..Job 23:17
back the *f* of his throne.......Job 26:9
see his *f* with joy............Job 33:26
f of the world in the earth....Job 37:12
discover..*f* of his garment?....Job 41:13
way straight before my *f*......Ps 5:8
long wilt thou hide thy *f*......Ps 13:1
strings against..*f* of them......Ps 21:12
that seek thy *f*, O Jacob......Ps 24:6
Seek ye my *f*; my heart.......Ps 27:8
Thy *f*, Lord, will I seek.......Ps 27:8
Hide not thy *f* far from me....Ps 27:9
hide thy *f*..I was troubled.....Ps 30:7
their *f* were not ashamed......Ps 34:5
settest me before thy *f*.......Ps 41:12
shame of my *f* hath covered...Ps 44:15
cause thy *f* to shine upon us...Ps 67:1
not thy *f* from thy servant.....Ps 69:17
cause thy *f* to shine..........Ps 80:3
cause thy *f* to shine..........Ps 80:7
upon the *f* of thine anointed...Ps 84:9
why hidest thy *f* from me?.....Ps 88:14
truth shall go before thy *f*.....Ps 89:14
oil to make his *f* to shine.....Ps 104:15
thou renewest the *f* of........Ps 104:30
seek his *f* evermore..........Ps 105:4
Make thy *f* to shine upon.....Ps 119:135
f of thine anointed...........Ps 132:10
hide not thy *f* from me.......Ps 143:7
diligently to seek thy *f*........Prov 7:15
wicked man hardeneth his *f*...Prov 21:29
f answereth to *f*..............Prov 27:19
wisdom maketh..*f* to shine....Eccl 8:1
boldness of his *f*..changed.....Eccl 8:1
grind the *f* of the poor?.......Is 3:15
twain he covered his *f*........Is 6:2
f of the world with cities......Is 14:21
world upon..*f* of the earth.....Is 23:17
Wipe..tears from off all *f*.....Is 25:8
f of the world with fruit.......Is 27:6
his *f* now wax pale...........Is 29:22
Hezekiah turned his *f*.........Is 38:2
f from shame and spitting.....Is 50:6
f from thee for a moment.....Is 54:8
hast hid thy *f* from us.........Is 64:7
Be not afraid of their *f*.......Jer 1:8
f thereof is toward..north.....Jer 1:13
rentest..*f* with painting........Jer 4:30
made..*f* harder than a rock....Jer 5:3
discover thy skirts upon..*f*.....Jer 13:26
are not hid from my *f*.........Jer 16:17
whose *f* thou fearest.........Jer 22:25
from off the *f* of the earth....Jer 28:16
f are turned into paleness?....Jer 30:6
the back, and not the *f*.......Jer 32:33
all..men that set their *f*.......Jer 42:17
will set my *f* against you......Jer 44:11
Zion with..*f* thitherward......Jer 50:5
water before the *f* of..Lord....Lam 2:19
f..elders were not honored....Lam 5:12
And every one had four *f*.....Ezek 1:6
As for the likeness of their *f*..Ezek 1:10
f of a man..*f* of a lion........Ezek 1:10
f of an ox on the left side.....Ezek 1:10
four also had..*f* of an eagle....Ezek 1:10
f strong against their *f*........Ezek 3:8
set thy *f* against it..it shall.....Ezek 4:3
thy *f* toward the mountains....Ezek 6:2
shame shall be upon all *f*.....Ezek 7:18
fell upon my *f*, and cried......Ezek 9:8
And every one had four *f*.....Ezek 10:14
first *f* was..*f* of a cherub.....Ezek 10:14
second *f* was..*f* of a man......Ezek 10:14
third the *f* of a lion...........Ezek 10:14
fourth the *f* of an eagle.......Ezek 10:14
likeness of their *f* was.........Ezek 10:22
was the same *f* which I saw...Ezek 10:22
thou shalt cover thy *f*.........Ezek 12:6
f against the daughters........Ezek 13:17
of his iniquity before his *f*.....Ezek 14:4
will set..*f* against them.......Ezek 15:7
I plead with you *f* to *f*........Ezek 20:35
f from the south to..north.....Ezek 20:47
set thy *f* toward Jerusalem....Ezek 21:2
thy *f* against..Ammonites......Ezek 25:2
set thy *f* against Pharaoh......Ezek 29:2
set..*f* against mount Seir......Ezek 35:2
fury shall come up in..*f*.......Ezek 38:18
remain upon the *f* of..earth...Ezek 39:14
hid my *f* from them...........Ezek 39:24
from the *f* of the gate.........Ezek 40:15
breadth of the *f* of the house..Ezek 41:14
f of a man was toward..palm..Ezek 41:19

f of a young lion..palm ... Ezek 41:19
upon the *f* of the porch ... Ezek 41:25
I fell upon my *f* ... Ezek 44:4
should he see..*f* worse ... Dan 1:10
f of the whole earth ... Dan 8:5
I was in a deep sleep on..*f* ... Dan 8:18
belongeth confusion of *f* ... Dan 9:8
f..appearance of lightning ... Dan 10:6
in a deep sleep on my *f* ... Dan 10:9
f toward the ground ... Dan 10:9
He..also set his *f* to enter ... Dan 11:17
turn his *f* toward the fort ... Dan 11:19
offense, and seek my *f* ... Hos 5:15
testifieth to his *f* ... Hos 7:10
f shall gather blackness ... Joel 2:6
f toward the east sea ... Joel 2:20
upon the *f* of the earth ... Amos 9:6
hide his *f* from them ... Mic 3:4
come up before thy *f* ... Nah 2:1
f..shall gather blackness ... Nah 2:10
f..sup up as the east wind ... Hab 1:9
the *f* of the whole earth ... Zech 5:3
spread dung upon your *f* ... Mal 2:3
anoint..head..wash thy *f* ... Matt 6:17
my messenger before thy *f* ... Matt 11:10
can discern the *f* of the sky ... Matt 16:3
his *f* did shine as the sun ... Matt 17:2
f and were sore afraid ... Matt 17:6
behold the *f* of my Father ... Matt 18:10
fell on his *f*, and prayed ... Matt 26:39
send my messenger before..*f* ... Mark 1:2
cover..*f*, and to buffet him ... Mark 14:65
go before the *f* of the Lord ... Luke 1:76
prepared before the *f*..people ... Luke 2:31
seeing Jesus fell on his *f* ... Luke 5:12
my messenger before thy *f* ... Luke 7:27
his *f* to go to Jerusalem ... Luke 9:51
f was as though he ... Luke 9:53
can discern..*f* of the sky ... Luke 12:56
dwell on the *f*..whole earth ... Luke 21:35
bowed down..*f* to the earth ... Luke 24:5
f was bound..with a napkin ... John 11:44
Lord always before my *f* ... Acts 2:25
before the *f* of our fathers ... Acts 7:45
shall see my *f* no more ... Acts 20:25
have the accusers *f* to *f* ... Acts 25:16
glass, darkly..*f* to *f* ... 1Cor 13:12
stedfastly..*f* of Moses ... 2Cor 3:7
f beholding as in a glass ... 2Cor 3:18
unknown by *f* unto the ... Gal 1:22
not seen my *f* in the flesh ... Col 2:1
see your *f* with great desire ... 1Thess 2:17
beholding his natural *f* ... James 1:23
f of the Lord is against ... 1Pet 3:12
f to *f*, that our joy may ... 2John 12
we shall speak *f* to *f* ... 3John 14
third beast had a *f* as a man ... Rev 4:7
fell..throne on their *f* ... Rev 7:11
f were as the *f* of men ... Rev 9:7
f was as it were the sun ... Rev 10:1
upon..*f*, and worshiped God ... Rev 11:16
from whose *f* the earth ... Rev 20:11

FACE OF THE LORD

Toward the righteous:
Shine on ... Num 6:25
Do not hide ... Ps 102:2
Hide from our sins ... Ps 51:9
Shall see ... Rev 22:4

Toward the wicked:
Is against ... Ps 34:16
Set against ... Jer 21:10
They hide from ... Rev 6:16

FADE—*to grow dim; faint*

[*also* FADETH, FADING]
Strangers shall *f* away ... 2Sam 22:46
strangers shall *f* away ... Ps 18:45
be as an oak whose leaf *f* ... Is 1:30
earth mourneth and *f* away ... Is 24:4
world languisheth and *f* ... Is 24:4
beauty is a *f* flower ... Is 28:1
flower *f*; because ... Is 40:7
and we all do *f* as a leaf ... Is 64:6
fig tree..leaf shall *f* ... Jer 8:13
shall..rich man *f* away ... James 1:11
undefiled..*f* not away ... 1Pet 1:4

FAILURE—*unsuccessful attempt*

Causes of:
Contrary to God's will ... Gen 11:3-8
Disobedience ... Num 14:40-45
Sin ... Josh 7:3-12
Lack of prayer ... Matt 17:15-20
Mark 9:24-29
Not counting the cost ... Luke 14:28-32
Unbelief ... Heb 4:6

Examples of:
Esau ... Gen 25:29-34
Eli's sons ... 1Sam 2:12-17
King Saul ... 1Sam 16:1
Absalom ... 2Sam 18:6-17
Hananiah ... Jer 28:1-17
Haman ... Esth 7:1-10

[*also* FAIL, FAILED, FAILETH, FAILING]
heart *f* them, and they ... Gen 42:28
presence? for the money *f* ... Gen 47:15
shall look, and *f* with ... Deut 28:32
heart, and *f* of eyes ... Deut 28:65
will not *f* thee, neither ... Deut 31:8
not *f* thee nor forsake ... Josh 1:5
plain, even the Salt Sea *f* ... Josh 3:16
hath *f* of all the good things ... Josh 23:14
not one thing hath *f* ... Josh 23:14
f deliver the children ... Judg 11:30
not *f* to burn the fat ... 1Sam 2:16
no man's heart *f* because ... 1Sam 17:32
overtake..and without *f* ... 1Sam 30:8
not *f* from..house of Joab ... 2Sam 3:29
there shall not *f* thee ... 1Kin 2:4
hath not *f* one word ... 1Kin 8:56
shall not *f* thee a man ... 1Kin 9:5
neither..cruse of oil *f* ... 1Kin 17:16
not *f* thee, nor forsake ... 1Chr 28:20
shall not *f* thee a man ... 2Chr 6:16
ye *f* not to do this ... Ezra 4:22
let nothing *f* of all that ... Esth 6:10
eyes of the wicked shall *f* ... Job 11:20
eyes of..children shall *f* ... Job 17:5
My kinsfolk have *f*, and ... Job 19:14
bull gendereth, and *f* not ... Job 21:10
f from among the children ... Ps 12:1
strength *f* because ... Ps 31:10
therefore my heart *f* me ... Ps 40:12
My flesh and my heart *f* ... Ps 73:26
promise *f* for evermore? ... Ps 77:8
Mine eyes *f* for thy word ... Ps 119:82
refuge *f* me; no man cared ... Ps 142:4
O Lord; my spirit *f* ... Ps 143:7
rod of his anger shall *f* ... Prov 22:8
his wisdom *f* him ... Eccl 10:3
desire shall *f*..man ... Eccl 12:5
my soul *f* when he spake ... Song 5:6
grass *f*, there is no green ... Is 15:6
spirit of Egypt shall *f* ... Is 19:3
glory of Kedar shall *f* ... Is 21:16
they all shall *f* together ... Is 31:3
drink of the thirsty to *f* ... Is 32:6
vintage shall *f*..gathering ... Is 32:10
no one of these shall *f* ... Is 34:16
eyes *f* with looking upward ... Is 38:14
their tongue *f* for thirst ... Is 41:17
not *f* nor be discouraged ... Is 42:4
his bread should *f* ... Is 51:14
spirit should *f* before me ... Is 57:16
water, whose waters *f* ... Is 58:11
truth *f*..he that departeth ... Is 59:15
their eyes did *f*, because ... Jer 14:6
as waters that *f*? ... Jer 15:18
have caused wine to *f* from ... Jer 48:33
their might hath *f*; they ... Jer 51:30
Mine eyes do *f* with tears ... Lam 2:11
his compassions *f* not ... Lam 3:22
eyes as yet *f* for our vain ... Lam 4:17
and every vision *f*? ... Ezek 12:22
wine shall *f* in her ... Hos 9:2
poor of the land to *f* ... Amos 8:4
labor of the olive shall *f* ... Hab 3:17
judgment to light, he *f* not ... Zeph 3:5
treasure in the heavens..*f* ... Luke 12:33
ye *f*, they may receive ... Luke 16:9
hearts *f* them for fear ... Luke 21:26
that thy faith *f* not ... Luke 22:32
Charity never *f* ... 1Cor 13:8
be prophecies, they shall *f* ... 1Cor 13:8
thy years shall not *f* ... Heb 1:12
any man *f* of..grace of God ... Heb 12:15

FAIN—*rather*
f flee out of his hand ... Job 27:22
f have filled his belly ... Luke 15:16

FAINTING—*a loss of vital powers*

Causes of:
Physical fatigue ... Gen 25:29, 30
Famine ... Gen 47:13
Unbelief ... Gen 45:26
Fear ... Josh 2:24
Sin ... Lev 26:31
Sickness ... Job 4:5
Human weakness ... Is 40:29-31
Ecstasy of visions ... Dan 8:27
Disappointment ... Jon 4:8
God's reproving ... Heb 12:5

Antidotes against:
Removal of the fearful ... Deut 20:8

[*also* FAINT, FAINTED, FAINTEST, FAINTETH, FAINTHEARTED, FAINTNESS]
let not your hearts *f* ... Deut 20:3
that is fearful and *f*? ... Deut 20:8
thou wast *f* and weary ... Deut 25:18
inhabitants of the land *f* ... Josh 2:9
men that were with him, *f* ... Judg 8:4
follow me; for they be *f* ... Judg 8:5
And the people were *f* ... 1Sam 14:28
so *f* that they could not go ... 1Sam 30:10
such as be *f* in..wilderness ... 2Sam 16:2
I had *f*..I had believed ... Ps 27:13
soul longeth..even *f* for ... Ps 84:2
thou *f* in..day of adversity ... Prov 24:10
sick, and the whole heart *f* ... Is 1:5
fear not, neither be *f* ... Is 7:4
when a standard-bearer *f* ... Is 10:18
behold, he is *f* ... Is 29:8
no water, and is *f* ... Is 44:12
Thy sons have *f* ... Is 51:20
my heart is *f* in me ... Jer 8:18
I *f* in my sighing ... Jer 45:3
they are *f*; there is sorrow ... Jer 49:23
desolate and *f* all the day ... Lam 1:13
children, that *f* for hunger ... Lam 2:19
every spirit shall *f* ... Ezek 21:7
trees of the field *f* for ... Ezek 31:15
virgins and young men *f* ... Amos 8:13
When my soul *f* within ... Jon 2:7
f, and were scattered ... Matt 9:36
lest they *f* in the way ... Matt 15:32
they will *f* by the way ... Mark 8:3
to pray, and not to *f* ... Luke 18:1
received mercy, we *f* not ... 2Cor 4:1
shall reap, if we *f* not ... Gal 6:9
I desire that ye *f* not ... Eph 3:13
wearied and *f* in..minds ... Heb 12:3
labored, and hast not *f* ... Rev 2:3

FAIR—*attractive; beautiful; alluring*
Beautiful ... Gen 6:2
Song 1:15, 16
Unspotted ... Zech 3:5
Persuasive ... Prov 7:21
Gal 6:12
Good ... Matt 16:2

[*also* FAIRER, FAIREST]
thou art a *f* woman ... Gen 12:11
damsel was very *f* ... Gen 24:16
younger sister *f* than she? ... Judg 15:2
of a *f* countenance ... 1Sam 17:42
son of David had a *f* sister ... 2Sam 13:1
they sought for a *f* damsel ... 1Kin 1:3
for she was *f* to look on ... Esth 1:11
all the *f* young virgins ... Esth 2:3
F weather cometh out ... Job 37:22
f than the children of men ... Ps 45:2

a *f* woman which is without . . .Prov 11:22
O thou *f* among women . . . . . . .Song 1:8
Rise up, my love, my *f* one . . .Song 2:10
Behold, thou art *f*, my love . . .Song 4:1
behold, thou art *f*; thou . . . . . . .Song 4:1
How *f* is thy love, my sister . . .Song 4:10
O thou *f* among women? . . . . . .Song 6:1
f and..pleasant art thou . . . . . . .Song 7:6
thou make thyself *f* . . . . .Jer 4:30
f words unto thee . . . . .Jer 12:6
also taken thy *f* jewels . . . . .Ezek 16:17
take away thy *f* jewels . . . . .Ezek 23:26
f in his greatness . . . . .Ezek 31:7
f and fatter in flesh . . . . .Dan 1:15
leaves thereof were *f* . . . . .Dan 4:12
passed over upon..*f* neck . . . . . .Hos 10:11
was exceeding *f* . . . . .Acts 7:20
words and *f* speeches . . . . .Rom 16:18

FAIR HAVENS
Harbor of Crete . . . . .Acts 27:8

FAIRS—*a gathering of buyers and sellers for trade*
they traded in thy *f* . . . . .Ezek 27:12
in thy *f* with emeralds . . . . .Ezek 27:16
f with chief of all spices . . . . . . .Ezek 27:22

FAITH—*confidence in the testimony of another*

Nature of:
Fruit of the Spirit . . . . . . .Gal 5:22
Work of God . . . . .John 6:29
God's gift . . . . .Eph 2:8
Comes from the heart . . .Rom 10:9, 10
Substance of unseen things . . . . .Heb 11:1

Results from:
Scriptures . . . . .John 20:30, 31
Preaching . . . . .John 17:20
Gospel . . . . .Acts 15:7

Objects of:
God . . . . .John 14:1
Christ . . . . .John 20:31
Moses' writings . . . . .John 5:46
Writings of the prophets. .Acts 26:27
Gospel . . . . .Mark 1:15
God's promises . . . . .Rom 4:21

Kinds of:
Saving . . . . .Rom 10:9, 10
Temporary . . . . .Luke 8:13
Intellectual . . . . .James 2:19
Dead . . . . .James 2:17, 20

Described as:
Boundless . . . . .John 11:21-27
Common . . . . .Titus 1:4
Great . . . . .Matt 8:10
Holy . . . . .Jude 20
Humble . . . . .Luke 7:6, 7
Little . . . . .Matt 8:26
Mutual . . . . .Rom 1:12
Perfect . . . . .James 2:22
Precious 2Pet 1:1
Rootless . . . . .Luke 8:13
Small . . . . .Matt 17:20
Unfeigned 1Tim 1:5
United . . . . .Mark 2:5
Vain 1Cor 15:14, 17
Venturing . . . . .Matt 14:28, 29

The fruits of:
Remission of sins . . . . .Acts 10:43
Justification . . . . .Acts 13:39
Freedom from condemnation . . . . .John 3:18
Salvation . . . . .Mark 16:16
Sanctification . . . . .Acts 15:9
Freedom from spiritual death . . . . .John 11:25, 26
Spiritual light . . . . .John 12:36, 46
Spiritual life . . . . .John 20:31
Eternal life . . . . .John 3:15, 16
Adoption . . . . .John 1:12
Access to God . . . . .Eph 3:12
Edification 1Tim 1:4
Preservation . . . . .John 10:26-29
Inheritance . . . . .Acts 26:18
Peace and rest . . . . .Rom 5:1

Place of, in Christian life:
Live by . . . . .Rom 1:17
Walk by . . . . .Rom 4:12
Pray by . . . . .Matt 21:22
Resist evil by . . . . .Eph 6:16
Overcome world by 1John 2:13-17
Die in . . . . .Heb 11:13

Growth of, in Christian life:
Stand fast in 1Cor 16:13
Continue in . . . . .Acts 14:22
Be strong in . . . . .Rom 4:20-24
Abound in 2Cor 8:7
Be grounded in . . . . .Col 1:23
Hold fast 1Tim 1:19
Pray for increase of . . . . . .Luke 17:5
Have assurance of 2Tim 1:12

Examples of, in Old Testament:
Abel . . . . .Heb 11:4
Enoch . . . . .Heb 11:5
Noah . . . . .Heb 11:7
Abraham . . . . .Rom 4:16-20
Sarah . . . . .Heb 11:11
Jacob . . . . .Heb 11:21
Joseph . . . . .Heb 11:22
Moses . . . . .Heb 11:23-29
Caleb . . . . .Josh 14:6, 12
Rahab . . . . .Heb 11:31
Jonathan 1Sam 14:6
David 1Sam 17:37
Jehoshaphat 2Chr 20:5, 12
Three Hebrew captives . . .Dan 3:16, 17
Job .Job 19:25
Others . . . . .Heb 11:32-39

Examples of, in New Testament:
Centurion . . . . .Matt 8:5-10
Jairus . . . . .Mark 5:22, 23
Sick woman . . . . .Mark 5:25-34
Syrophoenician woman . . .Mark 7:24-30
Bartimaeus . . . . .Mark 10:46-52
Sinful woman . . . . .Luke 7:36-50
Ten lepers . . . . .Luke 17:11-19
Certain nobleman . . . . . . .John 4:46-54
Mary and Martha . . . . .John 11:1-32
Thomas . . . . .John 20:24-29
Multitudes . . . . .Acts 5:14
Stephen . . . . .Acts 6:8
Samaritans . . . . .Acts 8:5-12
Ethiopian eunuch . . . . .Acts 8:26-39
Barnabas . . . . .Acts 11:22-24
Lydia . . . . .Acts 16:14, 15
Philippian jailer . . . . .Acts 16:25-34
Paul . . . . .Acts 27:23-25

children in whom is no *f* . . . . . .Deut 32:20
just shall live by his *f* . . . . .Hab 2:4
O ye of little *f*? . . . . .Matt 6:30
O ye of little *f*? . . . . .Matt 8:26
f hath made thee whole . . . . . . .Matt 9:22
O thou of little *f*, wherefore . . .Matt 14:31
O ye of little *f*, why . . . . .Matt 16:8
If ye have *f*..doubt not . . . . .Matt 21:21
judgment, mercy, and *f* . . . . . . .Matt 23:23
how is it..ye have no *f*? . . . . . . .Mark 4:40
unto them, Have *f* in God . . . .Mark 11:22
when he saw their *f*, he . . . . . . .Luke 5:20
Where is your *f*? And they . . . .Luke 8:25
clothe you, O ye of little *f*? . . .Luke 12:28
f as a grain of mustard . . . . . . .Luke 17:6
he find *f* on the earth? . . . . . . .Luke 18:8
that thy *f* fail not . . . . .Luke 22:32
name through *f* in his name . . .Acts 3:16
f which is by him . . . . .Acts 3:16
turn away..deputy from the *f* . .Acts 13:8
he had *f* to be healed . . . . .Acts 14:9
had opened the door of *f* . . . . .Acts 14:27
f toward our Lord Jesus . . . . . .Acts 20:21
concerning..*f* in Christ . . . . . . .Acts 24:24
obedience to the *f* among . . . . .Rom 1:5
your *f* is spoken of . . . . .Rom 1:8
f of God without effect? . . . . . .Rom 3:3
by *f* of Jesus Christ . . . . .Rom 3:22
propitiation through *f* in . . . . . .Rom 3:25
Nay; but by the law of *f* . . . . . .Rom 3:27
man is justified by *f* . . . . .Rom 3:28
justify..circumcision by *f* . . . . . .Rom 3:30
uncircumcision through *f* . . . . . .Rom 3:30
f is counted..righteousness . . . . .Rom 4:5
f was reckoned to . . . . .Rom 4:9
righteousness of *f* . . . . .Rom 4:13
f is made void . . . . .Rom 4:14
Therefore it is of *f* . . . . .Rom 4:16
of the *f* of Abraham . . . . .Rom 4:16
being not weak in *f* . . . . .Rom 4:19
access by *f* into this grace . . . . .Rom 5:2
righteousness..is of *f* . . . . .Rom 9:30
sought it not by *f* . . . . .Rom 9:32
righteousness..is of *f* . . . . .Rom 10:6
word of *f*..we preach . . . . .Rom 10:8
f cometh by hearing . . . . .Rom 10:17
thou standest by *f* . . . . .Rom 11:20
every man..measure of *f* . . . . . .Rom 12:3
proportion of *f* . . . . .Rom 12:6
that is weak in the *f* . . . . .Rom 14:1
Hast thou *f*? . . . . .Rom 14:22
eateth not of *f* . . . . .Rom 14:23
whatsoever is not of *f* . . . . .Rom 14:23
f should not stand in 1Cor 2:5
f by the same Spirit 1Cor 12:9
though I have all *f* 1Cor 13:2
abideth *f*, hope, charity 1Cor 13:13
dominion over your *f* 2Cor 1:24
joy; for by *f* ye stand 2Cor 1:24
having the same spirit of *f* 2Cor 4:13
when your *f* is increased 2Cor 10:15
by the *f* of Jesus Christ . . . . . . .Gal 2:16
justified by the *f* of Christ . . . . .Gal 2:16
by the *f* of the Son of God . . . .Gal 2:20
the hearing of *f*? . . . . .Gal 3:2
they which are of *f* . . . . .Gal 3:7
justify..heathen through *f* . . . . .Gal 3:8
which be of *f* are blessed . . . . . .Gal 3:9
The just shall live by *f* . . . . .Gal 3:11
And the law is not of *f* . . . . . . .Gal 3:12
promise..Spirit through *f* . . . . . .Gal 3:14
promise by *f* of Jesus . . . . .Gal 3:22
might be justified by *f* . . . . .Gal 3:24
children of God by *f* . . . . .Gal 3:26
f which worketh by love . . . . . .Gal 5:6
heard of your *f* in the Lord . . .Eph 1:15
dwell in your hearts by *f* . . . . . .Eph 3:17
One Lord, one *f* . . . . .Eph 4:5
all come in..unity of the *f* . . . . .Eph 4:13
love with *f*, from God . . . . .Eph 6:23
furtherance and joy of *f* . . . . . . .Phil 1:25
sacrifice and service of..*f* . . . . . .Phil 2:17
through the *f* of Christ . . . . .Phil 3:9
righteousness..of God by *f* . . . .Phil 3:9
heard of your *f* in Christ . . . . . .Col 1:4
steadfastness of..*f* in Christ . . . .Col 2:5
through..*f* of the operation . . . .Col 2:12
your work of *f*, and labor 1Thess 1:3
comfort you concerning..*f* 1Thess 3:2
tidings of your *f*..charity 1Thess 3:6
which is lacking in..*f*? 1Thess 3:10
f groweth exceedingly 2Thess 1:3
work of *f* with power 2Thess 1:11
Timothy..son in the *f* 1Tim 1:2
f and love..is in Christ 1Tim 1:14
Gentiles in *f* and verity 1Tim 2:7
continue in *f* and charity 1Tim 2:15
great boldness in the *f* 1Tim 3:13
words of *f* and..doctrine 1Tim 4:6
cast off their first *f* 1Tim 5:12
godliness, *f*, love, patience 1Tim 6:11
Fight the good fight of *f* 1Tim 6:12
unfeigned *f* that is in thee 2Tim 1:5
overthrow the *f* of some 2Tim 2:18
f, longsuffering, charity 2Tim 3:10
sound in *f*, in charity . . . . .Titus 2:2
Hearing of thy love and *f* . . . . .Philem 5
communication of thy *f* . . . . . . .Philem 6
mixed with *f* in them . . . . .Heb 4:2
works, and of *f* toward God . . .Heb 6:1
through *f* and patience . . . . .Heb 6:12
true heart..assurance of *f* . . . . . .Heb 10:22
hold..profession of our *f* . . . . . .Heb 10:23
just shall live by *f* . . . . .Heb 10:38

Through *f* we understand .....Heb 11:3
By *f* Abraham, when..called ...Heb 11:8
By *f* he sojourned in..land ....Heb 11:9
By *f* Abraham, when..tried ....Heb 11:17
By *f* Isaac blessed Jacob ......Heb 11:20
By *f*..walls of Jericho fell .....Heb 11:30
author and finisher of..*f*.......Heb 12:2
whose *f* follow, considering ....Heb 13:7
trying..*f* worketh patience .....James 1:3
let him ask in *f*, nothing ......James 1:6
have not the *f* of our ....James 2:1
rich in *f* and heirs..kingdom ...James 2:5
a man say he hath *f* ....James 2:14
can *f* save him? ....James 2:14
f, if it hath not works.........James 2:17
Thou hast *f*..works ....James 2:18
show me thy *f* without..works .James 2:18
will show..my *f* by my works ..James 2:18
f without works is dead? ......James 2:20
how *f* wrought with his ....James 2:22
works was *f* made perfect? ....James 2:22
and not by *f* only.............James 2:24
f without works is dead ....James 2:26
prayer of *f*..save the sick ......James 5:15
through *f* unto salvation 1Pet 1:5
That the trial of your *f*........1Pet 1:7
Receiving..end of your *f* 1Pet 1:9
Whom resist steadfast in..*f* 1Pet 5:9
add to your *f* virtue 2Pet 1:5
overcometh..even our *f* 1John 5:4
f..was once delivered ....Jude 3
hast not denied my *f*...........Rev 2:13
charity..service, and *f*.........Rev 2:19
patience..*f* of the saints ....Rev 13:10
of God..the *f* of Jesus ....Rev 14:12

FAITH—*a system of beliefs*

Priest obedient to ....Acts 6:7
Churches established in ..Acts 16:5
Stand fast in 1Cor 16:13
Paul preaches ....Gal 1:23
Now revealed ....Gal 3:23
Household of ....Gal 6:10
Contending for ....Phil 1:27
Hold purely.............1Tim 3:9
Denial of 1Tim 5:8
Some erred from 1Tim 6:10, 21
Reprobate 2Tim 3:8
Paul keeps 2Tim 4:7
Chosen of God ....Titus 1:1
Common among redeemed ....Titus 1:4
To be sound in..........Titus 1:13

FAITHFULNESS—*making faith a living reality in one's life*

Manifested in:

God's service ....Matt 24:45
Declaring God's Word ...Jer 23:38
Bearing witness ....Prov 14:5
Keeping secrets ....Prov 11:13
Helping others 3John 5
Doing work 2Chr 34:12
Positions of trust ....Neh 13:13
Reproving others ....Prov 27:6
Conveying messages .....Prov 25:13
Smallest things ....Luke 16:10-12

Illustrated in lives of:

Abraham ....Gal 3:9
Abraham's servant.......Gen 24:33
Joseph.................Gen 39:22, 23
Moses ....Num 12:7
David 2Sam 22:22-25
Elijah 1Kin 19:10, 14
Josiah 2Kin 22:1, 2
Abijah 2Chr 13:4-12
Micaiah.................2Chr 18:12, 13
Jehoshaphat.............2Chr 20:1-30
Azariah.................2Chr 26:16-20
Hanani and Hananiah....Neh 7:1, 2
Isaiah ....Is 39:3-7
Jeremiah................Jer 26:1-15
Daniel..................Dan 6:10
John the Baptist.........Luke 3:7-19
Jesus ....Heb 3:2
Peter ....Acts 4:8-12
Paul ....Acts 17:16, 17

[*also* FAITHFUL, FAITHFULLY]

raise me up a *f* priest 1Sam 2:35
righteousness and his *f*........1Sam 26:23
peaceable and *f* in Israel 2Sam 20:19
for they dealt *f*...............2Kin 12:15
Lord, *f*..with a perfect 2Chr 19:9
foundest his heart *f* ....Neh 9:8
no *f* in their mouth ....Ps 5:9
f fail..among the children .....Ps 12:1
Lord preserveth the *f* ....Ps 31:23
thy *f* and thy salvation ....Ps 40:10
or thy *f* in destruction ....Ps 88:11
make known thy *f* to ....Ps 89:1
thy *f* also in..congregation .....Ps 89:5
f and my mercy..be ....Ps 89:24
f witness in heaven ....Ps 89:37
and thy *f* every night ....Ps 92:2
in *f* hast afflicted me..........Ps 119:75
All..commandments are *f* ......Ps 119:86
in thy *f* answer me ....Ps 143:1
f ambassador is health ....Prov 13:17
f man who can find? ....Prov 20:6
A *f* man shall abound..........Prov 28:20
king that *f* judgeth ....Prov 29:14
unto me *f* witnesses to ....Is 8:2
f the girdle of his reins.........Is 11:5
let him speak my word *f* ......Jer 23:28
true and *f* witness between ....Jer 42:5
forasmuch as he was *f* ....Dan 6:4
betroth thee unto me in *f* .....Hos 2:20
is *f* with the saints ....Hos 11:12
good and *f* servant ....Matt 25:21
been *f* over a few things ......Matt 25:21
good and *f* servant ....Matt 25:23
been *f* over a few things ......Matt 25:23
f and wise steward............Luke 12:42
been *f* in a very little ....Luke 19:17
judged me to be *f* to..Lord ....Acts 16:15
God is *f*, by whom ye..called ..1Cor 1:9
son, and *f* in the Lord 1Cor 4:17
God is *f*,..not suffer 1Cor 10:13
blessed with *f* Abraham ....Gal 3:9
f in Christ Jesus ....Eph 1:1
f brethren in Christ ....Col 1:2
a *f* minister..fellow servant ....Col 4:7
F is he that calleth you 1Thess 5:24
Lord is *f*..shall stablish 2Thess 3:3
for that he counted me *f* 1Tim 1:12
This is a *f* saying 1Tim 1:15
sober, *f* in all things 1Tim 3:11
f saying and worthy of all 1Tim 4:9
are *f* and beloved.............1Tim 6:2
commit thou to *f* men 2Tim 2:2
It is a *f* saying 2Tim 2:11
yet he abideth *f* 2Tim 2:13
f children not accused.........Titus 1:6
f word as..been taught ....Titus 1:9
This is a *f* saying ....Titus 3:8
merciful and *f* high priest .....Heb 2:17
for he is *f* that promised ......Heb 10:23
judged him *f* who..promised ...Heb 11:11
as unto a *f* Creator 1Pet 4:19
a *f* brother unto you 1Pet 5:12
f whatsoever thou doest 3John 5
Jesus Christ..the *f* witness .....Rev 1:5
be thou *f* unto death..........Rev 2:10
the *f* and true witness ....Rev 3:14
him was called *F* and True ....Rev 19:11
words are true and *f*..........Rev 21:5
sayings are *f* and true ....Rev 22:6

FAITHFULNESS OF GOD

Described as:

Everlasting..............Ps 119:90
Established ....Ps 89:2
Unfailing ....Ps 89:33
Infinite ....Ps 36:5
Great ....Lam 3:23
Incomparable ....Ps 89:8

Manifested in:

Counsels ....Is 25:1
Covenant-keeping ....Deut 7:9
Forgiving sins 1John 1:9
Testimonies ....Ps 119:138
Judgments ....Jer 51:29
Promises................1Kin 8:20

FAITHLESS—*lacking faith*

f and perverse generation .....Matt 17:17
f generation, how long ....Mark 9:19
f and perverse generation .....Luke 9:41
be not *f*..believing ....John 20:27

FALL—*to drop; descend; be defeated*

[*also* FALLEN, FALLEST, FALLETH, FALLING, FELL, FELLED, FELLEST]

sleep to *f* upon Adam ....Gen 2:21
his countenance *f*.............Gen 4:5
why is thy countenance *f*? .....Gen 4:6
deep sleep *f* upon Abram .....Gen 15:12
horror of great darkness *f* .....Gen 15:12
Abraham *f* upon his face ......Gen 17:17
f before him on the ground ...Gen 44:14
f upon..brother Benjamin's ....Gen 45:14
ye *f* not out by the way ....Gen 45:24
f on his neck, and wept ....Gen 46:29
brethren..went and *f* down ....Gen 50:18
there *f* out any war ....Ex 1:10
f upon us with pestilence ......Ex 5:3
ox or an ass *f* therein ....Ex 21:33
f of the people that day ....Ex 32:28
f on their faces ....Lev 9:24
they are dead, doth *f* ....Lev 11:32
whereinto any of them *f* ....Lev 11:33
any part of their carcase *f*.....Lev 11:38
man whose hair is *f* off ....Lev 13:40
on which the lot *f* to be ....Lev 16:10
and *f* in decay with thee ......Lev 25:35
shall *f* before you by..........Lev 26:7
shall *f* when none pursueth ....Lev 26:36
among them *f* a lusting ....Num 11:4
when..dew *f* upon the camp ...Num 11:9
night, the manna *f* upon it ....Num 11:9
let them *f* by the camp........Num 11:31
carcases shall *f*..wilderness ....Num 14:29
ye shall *f* by the sword ....Num 14:43
Moses heard..*f* upon his face ..Num 16:4
f upon their faces.............Num 16:45
angel of..Lord, she *f* down ....Num 22:27
f into a trance, but having ....Num 24:4
inheritance is *f* to us ....Num 32:19
the place where his lot *f* ......Num 33:54
f down before the Lord ....Deut 9:18
f down before the Lord ....Deut 9:25
as I *f* down at the first ....Deut 9:25
ass or his ox *f* down ....Deut 22:4
terror is *f* upon us ....Josh 2:9
f on his face to the earth......Josh 5:14
wall of the city shall *f*.........Josh 6:5
f to the earth upon his ....Josh 7:6
they *f* upon them ....Josh 11:7
f ten portions to Manasseh ....Josh 17:5
lord was *f* down dead ....Judg 3:25
host of Sisera *f* upon ....Judg 4:16
he *f*, he lay down ....Judg 5:27
her feet he bowed, he *f* ....Judg 5:27
smote it that it *f*.............Judg 7:13
Rise thou..*f* upon us ....Judg 8:21
f..of the Ephraimites...........Judg 12:6
thirst, and *f* into the hand.....Judg 15:18
house *f* upon the lords ....Judg 16:30
concubine was *f* down at ......Judg 19:27
f of Benjamin eighteen.........Judg 20:44
Then she *f* on her face, and ...Ruth 2:10
let *f* also some..handfuls ......Ruth 2:16
let none of his words *f*........1Sam 3:19
f of Israel thirty thousand 1Sam 4:10
f upon his face to..earth 1Sam 5:3
fear of the Lord *f*..people 1Sam 11:7
f upon his face to..earth 1Sam 17:49
Saul..to make David *f* 1Sam 18:25
f on his face to 1Sam 20:41
to *f* upon the priests 1Sam 22:17
f before David on her face 1Sam 25:23
Lord was *f* upon them 1Sam 26:12
let not my blood *f* to..earth ...1Sam 26:20
Saul *f* straightaway 1Sam 28:20

three days..I *f* sick 1Sam 30:13
Saul took a sword..*f* upon it...1Sam 31:4
f to the earth, and did 2Sam 1:2
many..people also are *f*.......2Sam 1:4
were *f* by the sword 2Sam 1:12
Go near, and *f* upon him 2Sam 1:15
How are the mighty *f*.........2Sam 1:25
f down there, and died........2Sam 2:23
Asahel *f* down and died.......2Sam 2:23
that *f* on the sword 2Sam 3:29
wicked men, so *f* thou 2Sam 3:34
prince and a great man *f*......2Sam 3:38
haste to flee, that he *f*........2Sam 4:4
f some of the people..........2Sam 11:17
king, she *f* on her face........2Sam 14:4
dew *f* on the ground............2Sam 17:12
f down to the earth............2Sam 18:28
he went forth it *f* out 2Sam 20:8
f by the hand of David 2Sam 21:22
f now into the hand of..Lord ..2Sam 24:14
shall not a hair of him *f*.......1Kin 1:52
f upon him that he died.......1Kin 2:25
as he..said, and *f* upon him ...1Kin 2:31
f upon him, and slew him 1Kin 2:34
son of Jeroboam *f* sick 1Kin 14:1
knew him..*f* on his face 1Kin 18:7
f on their faces 1Kin 18:39
f upon twenty and seven 1Kin 20:30
Ahaziah *f* down through 2Kin 1:2
mantle of Elijah that *f*........2Kin 2:13
shall *f* every good tree 2Kin 3:19
f on a day, that he came 2Kin 4:11
went in, and *f* at his feet......2Kin 4:37
Where *f* it? And he showed ...2Kin 6:6
f unto the host of 2Kin 7:4
Elisha was *f* sick of his........2Kin 13:14
shouldest *f*, even thou 2Kin 14:10
fugitives that *f* away to........2Kin 25:11
Hagarites..*f* by their hand 1Chr 5:10
f..slain in mount Gilboa 1Chr 10:1
f likewise on the sword 1Chr 10:5
Saul and his sons *f* in 1Chr 10:8
will *f* to his master Saul.......1Chr 12:19
f to him to Manasseh 1Chr 12:20
f now into the hand 1Chr 21:13
not *f* into..hand of man 1Chr 21:13
f of Israel seventy 1Chr 21:14
lot eastward *f* to Shelemiah ...1Chr 26:14
f down slain of Israel 2Chr 13:17
fear of the Lord *f* upon 2Chr 17:10
may go up and *f* at 2Chr 18:19
inhabitants of Jerusalem *f* 2Chr 20:18
dead bodies *f* to the earth 2Chr 20:24
God shall make..*f* before 2Chr 25:8
f upon the cities of Judah 2Chr 25:13
I *f* upon my knees, and ....Ezra 9:5
before whom..began to *f* ......Esth 6:13
Haman was *f* upon the bed....Esth 7:8
f down at his feet ....Esth 8:3
fear of them *f* upon ....Esth 9:2
the Sabeans *f* upon them......Job 1:15
fire of God..*f* from heaven ....Job 1:16
f upon the young men ....Job 1:19
upholden him that was *f* ......Job 4:4
when deep sleep *f* on men ....Job 4:13
his dread *f* upon you? ....Job 13:11
them *f* by..own counsels ......Ps 5:10
f into the ditch which he ......Ps 7:15
poor may *f* by his strong ones..Ps 10:10
they are *f* under my feet ......Ps 18:38
they stumbled and *f* ....Ps 27:2
workers of iniquity *f*..........Ps 36:12
Though he *f*..shall not be .....Ps 37:24
deliver my feet from *f* ....Ps 56:13
they are *f* themselves ....Ps 57:6
shall *f* by the sword ....Ps 63:10
their own tongue to *f* ....Ps 64:8
kings..*f* down before him.......Ps 72:11
f like one of the princes.......Ps 82:7
fear of them *f* upon them .....Ps 105:38
thrust sore at me..I might *f* ...Ps 118:13
wicked *f* into..own nets ....Ps 141:10
Lord upholdeth all that *f*......Ps 145:14
unless..cause some to *f*........Prov 4:16
but a prating fool shall *f* ......Prov 10:8

prating fool shall *f*...........Prov 10:10
f by his own wickedness ......Prov 11:5
no counsel..the people *f* ......Prov 11:14
messenger *f* into mischief .....Prov 13:17
haughty spirit before a *f* ......Prov 16:18
just man *f* seven times ....Prov 24:16
wicked..*f* into mischief ....Prov 24:16
righteous man *f* down ....Prov 25:26
diggeth a pit shall *f*...........Prov 26:27
f himself into..own pit ....Prov 28:10
perverse in..ways shall *f*.......Prov 28:18
if they *f* the one will lift ......Eccl 4:10
that is alone when he *f* ....Eccl 4:10
tree *f* toward the south ....Eccl 11:3
place where the tree *f* ....Eccl 11:3
is ruined, and Judah is *f* ....Is 3:8
men shall *f* by the sword ......Is 3:25
shall *f* under the slain ....Is 10:4
unto..shall *f* by the sword .....Is 13:15
art thou *f* from heaven.........Is 14:12
Babylon is *f*, is *f* ....Is 21:9
noise of the fear shall *f* ....Is 24:18
might go, and *f* backward .....Is 28:13
when the towers *f* ....Is 30:25
he that helpeth shall *f* ....Is 31:3
he that is holpen shall *f*.......Is 31:3
all their host shall *f*...........Is 34:4
as the leaf *f* off from..vine ....Is 34:4
as a *f* fig from..fig tree........Is 34:4
young men shall utterly *f*......Is 40:30
f down unto it..worshipeth ....Is 44:17
shall *f* down unto thee ....Is 45:14
mischief shall *f* upon thee .....Is 47:11
truth is *f* in the street ....Is 59:14
not cause mine anger to *f* .....Jer 3:12
sons together shall *f* upon .....Jer 6:21
f among them that *f* ....Jer 8:12
caused him to *f* upon it ....Jer 15:8
shall *f* by the sword ....Jer 20:4
f to..Chaldeans that besiege ...Jer 21:9
f grievously upon..head ....Jer 23:19
f like a pleasant vessel ....Jer 25:34
f away to..Chaldeans ....Jer 37:13
I *f* not away to..Chaldeans ....Jer 37:14
f to the Chaldeans............Jer 38:19
that *f* away, that *f* to him .....Jer 39:9
f in the land of Egypt.........Jer 44:12
made many to *f*, yea, one *f* ...Jer 46:16
spoiler is *f* upon thy summer ..Jer 48:32
moved at the noise of..*f* ......Jer 49:21
shall her young men *f*.........Jer 50:30
slain shall *f* in the land........Jer 51:4
Babylon is suddenly *f*..........Jer 51:8
slain shall *f* in the midst.......Jer 51:47
slain of Israel to *f* ....Jer 51:49
Babylon shall *f* the slain ......Jer 51:49
f away, that *f* to the king .....Jer 52:15
f into the hand of..enemy .....Lam 1:7
made my strength to *f* ....Lam 1:14
men are *f* by the sword ....Lam 2:21
I *f* upon my face ....Ezek 1:28
shall *f* by the sword ....Ezek 5:12
shall *f* by the sword ....Ezek 6:11
Lord God *f* there upon me ....Ezek 8:1
Spirit of the Lord *f* upon me ..Ezek 11:5
Ye shall *f* by the sword ....Ezek 11:10
mortar, that it shall *f* ....Ezek 13:11
hailstones, shall *f*.............Ezek 13:11
wall is *f*, shall it not be ....Ezek 13:12
with all his bands shall *f* ......Ezek 17:21
let no lot *f* upon it ....Ezek 24:6
Dedan shall *f* by the sword ....Ezek 25:13
isles tremble..day of thy *f* .....Ezek 26:18
midst of thee shall *f* ....Ezek 27:34
when the slain..*f* in Egypt .....Ezek 30:4
that uphold Egypt shall *f*......Ezek 30:6
they *f* in it by the sword ......Ezek 30:6
will cause the sword to *f* ....Ezek 30:22
shake at the sound of his *f* ....Ezek 31:16
cause thy multitude to *f*........Ezek 32:12
all..slain, *f* by the sword ......Ezek 32:22
are *f* of the uncircumcised .....Ezek 32:27
shall not *f* thereby ....Ezek 33:12
shall they *f* that are slain ......Ezek 35:8
steep places shall *f* ....Ezek 38:20

cause thine arrows to *f*........Ezek 39:3
shalt *f* upon..open field ....Ezek 39:5
so *f* they all by the sword .....Ezek 39:23
and I *f* upon my face ....Ezek 44:4
land shall *f* unto you..........Ezek 47:14
Nebuchadnezzar *f* upon..face ..Dan 2:46
f down and worship..golden ...Dan 3:5
f not down and worshipeth ....Dan 3:6
f down and worship ....Dan 3:10
f down and worship ....Dan 3:15
f down bound into the ....Dan 3:23
before whom three *f*...........Dan 7:20
quaking *f* upon them ....Dan 10:7
vision; but they shall *f* ....Dan 11:14
many shall *f* down ....Dan 11:26
Now when they shall *f* ....Dan 11:34
shalt thou *f* in the day ....Hos 4:5
prophet also shall *f* ....Hos 4:5
not understand shall *f*.........Hos 4:14
Israel and Ephraim *f*..........Hos 5:5
Judah also shall *f*.............Hos 5:5
all their kings are *f* ....Hos 7:7
to thy hills, ***F*** on us ....Hos 10:8
transgressors shall *f*..........Hos 14:9
they *f* upon the sword ....Joel 2:8
Can a bird *f* in a snare........Amos 3:5
virgin of Israel is *f*...........Amos 5:2
thy daughters shall *f* ....Amos 7:17
shall not the least grain *f*......Amos 9:9
and the lot *f* upon Jonah ......Jon 1:7
when I *f*, I shall arise ....Mic 7:8
even *f* into the mouth.........Nah 3:12
for the cedar is *f* ....Zech 11:2
f down and worshiped ....Matt 2:11
f down and worship me ....Matt 4:9
f: and great was the *f*.........Matt 7:27
not *f* on the ground ....Matt 10:29
Some *f* upon stony places .....Matt 13:5
other *f* into good ground ......Matt 13:8
both shall *f* into the ditch .....Matt 15:14
f from..masters' table ....Matt 15:27
ofttimes he *f* into the fire .....Matt 17:15
f down, and worshiped.......Matt 18:26
shall *f* on this stone...........Matt 21:44
on whomsoever it shall *f* ......Matt 21:44
f on his face, and prayed......Matt 26:39
f down before him............Mark 3:11
some *f* on stony ground ....Mark 4:5
other *f* on good ground ....Mark 4:8
and *f* down before him........Mark 5:33
he *f* on the ground ....Mark 9:20
stars of heavens shall *f*........Mark 13:25
troubled, and fear *f* upon .....Luke 1:12
child is set for the *f* ....Luke 2:34
f down at Jesus' knees ....Luke 5:8
f on his face, and besought....Luke 5:12
immediately it *f* ....Luke 6:49
some *f* by the way side ....Luke 8:5
some *f* among thorns ....Luke 8:7
time of temptation *f* away .....Luke 8:13
f among thorns are they ......Luke 8:14
f down before him.............Luke 8:28
and *f* down before him.........Luke 8:47
lightning *f* from heaven ....Luke 10:18
f among thieves, which........Luke 10:30
divided against a house *f*......Luke 11:17
whom the tower in Siloam *f*...Luke 13:4
ass or an ox *f* into a pit ....Luke 14:5
ran, and *f* on his neck ....Luke 15:20
f from the rich man's table ....Luke 16:21
Whosoever shall *f* upon ....Luke 20:18
f by the edge of the sword ....Luke 21:24
f down at his feet, saying .....John 11:32
f to the ground...............John 18:6
f headlong..burst asunder .....Acts 1:18
Judas by transgression *f*.......Acts 1:25
lot *f* upon Matthias ....Acts 1:26
f down, and gave up..ghost....Acts 5:5
had said this, he *f* asleep.....Acts 7:60
f upon none of them..........Acts 8:16
f..earth, and heard a voice ....Acts 9:4
f from his eyes as it had ......Acts 9:18
f down at his feet, and........Acts 10:25
Holy Ghost *f* on all them .....Acts 10:44
Holy Ghost *f* on them ....Acts 11:15

F

f on him a mist..darkness .....Acts 13:11
f down before Paul and ....Acts 16:29
f down from Jupiter? ....Acts 19:35
being *f* into a deep sleep ......Acts 20:9
f down from the third loft ......Acts 20:9
Paul went down..*f* on him .....Acts 20:10
I *f* unto the ground ....Acts 22:7
should *f* into..quicksands ......Acts 27:17
should have *f* upon rocks .....Acts 27:29
not a hair *f* from..head ....Acts 27:34
that they should *f*? ....Rom 11:11
through their *f* salvation is ....Rom 11:11
f of them be the riches........Rom 11:12
on them which *f*, severity .....Rom 11:22
occasion to *f* in his brother's...Rom 14:13
f in one day three 1Cor 10:8
take heed lest he *f* 1Cor 10:12
f down on his face............1Cor 14:25
but some are *f* asleep 1Cor 15:6
ye are *f* from grace ....Gal 5:4
unto me have *f* out ....Phil 1:12
except there come a *f*..........2Thess 2:3
f into the condemnation........1Tim 3:6
f into reproach and the snare ..1Tim 3:7
f into temptation and 1Tim 6:9
carcases *f* in..wilderness? ......Heb 3:17
lest any man *f* after the ....Heb 4:11
If they shall *f* away, to........Heb 6:6
f into the hands of..living .....Heb 10:31
walls of Jericho *f* down ....Heb 11:30
f into divers temptations ......James 1:2
and the flower thereof *f*.......James 1:11
f into condemnation ....James 5:12
flower thereof *f* away 1Pet 1:24
things, ye shall never *f*........2Pet 1:10
since the fathers *f* asleep 2Pet 3:4
f from your..steadfastness 2Pet 3:17
able to keep you from *f*.......Jude 24
I *f* at his feet as dead ....Rev 1:17
from whence thou art *f* ....Rev 2:5
four and twenty elders *f* ......Rev 4:10
f down and worshiped ....Rev 5:14
mountains and rocks, *F* ....Rev 6:16
f before the throne on..faces ..Rev 7:11
f a great star from heaven.....Rev 8:10
f..third part of the rivers ......Rev 8:10
I saw a star *f* from heaven ....Rev 9:1
tenth part of the city *f* ....Rev 11:13
Babylon is *f*, is *f* ....Rev 14:8
f a noisome and grievous......Rev 16:2
cities of the nations *f* ....Rev 16:19
f upon men a great hail ....Rev 16:21
five are *f*, and one is ....Rev 17:10
Babylon the great is *f*, is *f* ....Rev 18:2
f at his feet to worship........Rev 19:10

FALL OF MAN—*descent from innocence to guilt*

Occasion of:
- Satan's temptation ....Gen 3:1-5
- Eve's yielding 2Cor 11:3
- Adam's disobedience ....Rom 5:12-19

Temporal consequences of:
- Driven from Paradise ....Gen 3:24
- Condemned to hard labor.Gen 3:16, 19
- Condemned to die 1Cor 15:22

Spiritual consequences of:
- Separated from God .....Eph 4:18
- Born in sin ....John 3:6
- Evil in heart ....Matt 15:19
- Corrupt and perverse ....Rom 3:12-16
- In bondage to sin........Rom 6:19
- In bondage to Satan .....Heb 2:14, 15
- Dead in sin ....Col 2:13
- Spiritually blind ....Eph 4:18
- Utterly depraved ....Titus 1:15
- Change from, not in man .Jer 2:22
- Only God can change ....John 3:16

FALLOW DEER—*roebuck*
- Among clean animals ....Deut 14:5
- In Solomon's diet........1Kin 4:22, 23

FALLOW GROUND—*a field plowed and left for seeding*
- Used figuratively ....Jer 4:3
- To be broken ....Hos 10:12
- Used literally ("tillage"). .Prov 13:23

FALSE—*untrue*

not bear *f* witness ....Ex 20:16
not raise a *f* report ....Ex 23:1
far from a *f* matter ....Ex 23:7
shalt thou bear *f* witness ......Deut 5:20
f witness rise up against ....Deut 19:16
witness be a *f* witness ....Deut 19:18
It is *f*: tell us now 2Kin 9:12
my words shall not be *f* ....Job 36:4
f witnesses are risen up ....Ps 27:12
F witnesses did rise up ....Ps 35:11
I hate every *f* way ....Ps 119:104
I hate every *f* way ....Ps 119:128
unto thee, thou *f* tongue? .....Ps 120:3
f witness..speaketh lies ....Prov 6:19
f balance is abomination ......Prov 11:1
f witness deceit..............Prov 12:17
f witness will utter lies ....Prov 14:5
giveth heed to *f* lips ....Prov 17:4
A *f* witness shall not be ....Prov 19:5
f balance is not good ....Prov 20:23
f witness shall perish..........Prov 21:28
boasteth..of a *f* gift is ....Prov 25:14
man..beareth *f* witness ....Prov 25:18
f vision and divination ....Jer 14:14
Jeremiah, It is *f* ....Jer 37:14
seen for thee *f* burdens ....Lam 2:14
f divination in their sight ......Ezek 21:23
love no *f* oath ....Zech 8:17
have told *f* dreams ....Zech 10:2
and against *f* swearers ....Mal 3:5
thefts, *f* witness ....Matt 15:19
shalt not bear *f* witness ....Matt 19:18
many *f* prophets shall rise .....Matt 24:11
f witness against Jesus ....Matt 26:59
many *f* witnesses came ....Matt 26:60
last came two *f* witnesses......Matt 26:60
Do not bear *f* witness ....Mark 10:19
many bare *f* witness ....Mark 14:56
bare *f* witness against him .....Mark 14:57
fathers to the *f* prophets ......Luke 6:26
Do not bear *f* witness ....Luke 18:20
any man by *f* accusation ......Luke 19:8
shalt not bear *f* witness ....Rom 13:9
found *f* witnesses of God 1Cor 15:15
in perils among *f* brethren.....2Cor 11:26
f brethren unawares ....Gal 2:4
trucebreakers, *f* accusers 2Tim 3:3
not *f* accusers, not given ......Titus 2:3
many *f* prophets are gone 1John 4:1
out of the mouth..*f* prophet ...Rev 16:13
f prophet that wrought........Rev 19:20
beast and the *f* prophet ....Rev 20:10

FALSE ACCUSATIONS

Against men:
- Joseph..................Gen 39:7-20
- Moses ....Num 16:1-3, 13
- Ahimelech 1Sam 22:11-16
- David ....Ps 41:5-9
- Elijah 1Kin 18:17, 18
- Naboth 1Kin 21:1-14
- Jeremiah...............Jer 26:8-11
- Amos ....Amos 7:10, 11
- Stephen ....Acts 6:11, 13
- Paul...................Acts 21:27-29

Against Christ:
- Gluttony ....Matt 11:19
- Blasphemy ....Matt 26:64, 65
- Insanity................Mark 3:21
- Demon possession ....John 7:20
- Sabbath desecration .....John 9:16
- Treason ....John 19:12

FALSE APOSTLES
- Opposed Paul 2Cor 11:1-15

FALSE CHRISTS
- Christ foretells their coming ....Matt 24:24
- Christ warns against .....Mark 13:21-23

See ANTICHRIST

FALSE CONFIDENCE

Characteristics of:
- Self-righteous ....Rom 2:3
- Spiritually blind ....Is 28:15, 19
- Sensualist ....Gal 6:7, 8
- Worldly secure 1Thess 5:3

Causes of trusting in:
- Riches 1Tim 6:17
- Worldly success ....Luke 12:19, 20
- Men.....................Is 30:1-5
- Oneself ....Matt 26:33-35
- Ignoring God's providence.James 4:13-15

Warnings against:
- Curse on ....Jer 17:5
- Do not glory in men 1Cor 3:21
- Man's limitation 2Cor 1:9
- Mighty will fail ....Ps 33:16, 17
- Boasting 1Kin 20:11

Instances of:
- Babel's men ....Gen 11:4
- Sennacherib.............2Kin 19:20-37
- Asa 2Chr 16:7-12
- Peter ....Luke 22:33, 34

f against mine own life........2Sam 18:13
answers there remaineth *f*? ....Job 21:34
mischief..brought forth *f* ......Ps 7:14
for their deceit is *f* ....Ps 119:118
hand is a right hand of *f* ......Ps 144:8
hand is a right hand of *f* ......Ps 144:11
under *f* have we hid ....Is 28:15
transgression, a seed of *f*......Is 57:4
from the heart words of *f* .....Is 59:13
for his molten image is *f* ......Jer 10:14
and trusted in *f* ....Jer 13:25
for his molten image is *f* ......Jer 51:17
for they commit *f*.............Hos 7:1
walking in the spirit of *f* ......Mic 2:11

FALSE PROFESSIONS—*insincere promises*

Pretending to be:
- Harmless ....Josh 9:3-16
- Innocent................Matt 27:24
- Divine..................Acts 12:21-23
- Sincere ....Matt 26:48, 49
- True prophets 1Kin 22:6-12

Exposed by:
- Prophets ....Jer 28:1-17
- Christ ....John 13:21-30
- Apostles ....Acts 5:1-11

FALSE PROPHETS—*those who falsely claim inspiration*

Tests of:
- Doctrine ....Is 8:20
- Prophecies 1Kin 13:1-32
- Lives ....Matt 7:15, 16

Characteristics of:
- Prophesy peace ....Jer 23:17
- Teach a lie..............Jer 28:15
- Pretend to be true ....Matt 7:22, 23
- Teach corruption 2Pet 2:10-22

Examples of:
- Zedekiah 1Kin 22:11, 12
- Hananiah ....Jer 28:1-17
- In the last days..........Matt 24:11

FALSE TEACHERS—*those who instruct contrary to God's will*

Characteristics of:
- Grace-perverters.........Gal 1:6-8
- Money-lovers ....Luke 16:14
- Christ-deniers 2Pet 2:1
- Truth-resisters...........2Tim 3:8
- Fable-lovers.............2Tim 4:3, 4
- Destitute of the truth 1Tim 6:3-5
- Bound by traditions .....Matt 15:9
- Unstable................1Tim 1:6, 7
- Deceitful ....Eph 4:14
- Lustful 2Pet 2:12-19

Prevalence of:
- In Paul's time 2Tim 1:14, 15
- During this age..........1Tim 4:1-3
- At Christ's return 2Tim 4:3, 4

Examples of:
Balaam ... Rev 2:14
Bar-jesus ... Acts 13:6
Ephesian elders ... Acts 20:30; Rev 2:2
Epicureans ... Acts 17:18
False apostles ... 2Cor 11:5, 13; 2Cor 12:11
Herodians ... Mark 3:6; Mark 12:13
Hymenaeus ... 2Tim 2:17
Libertines ... Acts 6:9
Nicolatanes ... Rev 2:15
Pharisees ... Matt 23:26
Philetus ... 2Tim 2:17
Sadducees ... Matt 16:12
Scribes ... Matt 12:38, 39
Serpent (Satan) ... Gen 3:4
Stoic philosophers ... Acts 17:18

FALSE WEIGHTS—*deceptive measurements*
Prohibited ... Deut 25:13, 14

FALSE WITNESSES—*those who bear untrue testimony*

Features regarding:
Deceptive ... Prov 12:17
Cruel ... Prov 25:18
Utter lies ... Prov 6:19; Prov 14:5
Shall perish ... Prov 21:28
Hated by God ... Zech 8:17
Forbidden ... Ex 20:16

Sin of:
Comes from corrupt heart ... Matt 15:19
Causes suffering ... Ps 27:12
Merits punishment ... Prov 19:5, 9

Punishment of:
Specified ... Lev 6:1-5
Described ... Deut 19:16-20
Visualized ... Zech 5:3, 4

Examples of, against:
Ahimelech ... 1Sam 22:8-18
Naboth ... 1Kin 21:13
Jeremiah ... Jer 37:12-14
Jesus ... Matt 26:59-61
Stephen ... Acts 6:11, 13
Paul ... Acts 16:20, 21

FALSEHOOD—*a lie*

Manifested by false:
Witnesses ... Ps 27:12
Balances ... Prov 11:1
Tongue ... Ps 120:3
Report ... Ex 23:1
Prophets ... Jer 5:2, 31
Science ... 1Tim 6:20

God's people:
Must avoid ... Ex 23:7
Must hate ... Ps 119:104, 128
Must endure ... Acts 6:13
Are falsely charged with. . Jer 37:14; Matt 5:11

FALSELY—*deceitfully; treacherously*
wilt not deal *f* with me ... Gen 21:23
it, and sweareth *f* ... Lev 6:3
which he hath sworn *f* ... Lev 6:5
not steal, neither deal *f* ... Lev 19:11
not swear by my name *f* ... Lev 19:12
testified *f* against..brother ... Deut 19:18
have we dealt *f* in thy ... Ps 44:17
surely they swear *f* ... Jer 5:2
prophets prophesy *f* ... Jer 5:31
priest every one dealeth *f* ... Jer 6:13
commit adultery..swear *f* ... Jer 7:9
priest every one dealeth *f* ... Jer 8:10
f unto you in my name ... Jer 29:9
speakest *f* of Ishmael ... Jer 40:16
unto Jeremiah..speakest *f* ... Jer 43:2
f in making a covenant ... Hos 10:4
house of him..sweareth *f* ... Zech 5:4
manner of evil against you *f* ... Matt 5:11
neither accuse any *f* ... Luke 3:14
that *f* accuse your ... 1Pet 3:16

FALSIFY—*to misrepresent*
f the balances by deceit ... Amos 8:5

FAME—*report; renown; news*

As report or news of:
Joseph's brothers ... Gen 45:16
Israel's departure ... Num 14:15
Jesus' ministry ... Matt 4:24

As reputation or renown of:
Nation ... Ezek 16:14, 15
Joshua's exploits ... Josh 6:27
God's works ... Josh 9:9
Solomon's wisdom ... 1Kin 4:31
David's power ... 1Chr 14:17
The Temple's greatness ... 1Chr 22:5
God's glory ... Is 66:19
Mordecai's fame ... Esth 9:4
Jesus' works ... Matt 9:31

heard of the *f* of Solomon ... 1Kin 10:1
exceedeth the *f* which I ... 1Kin 10:7
heard of the *f* of Solomon ... 2Chr 9:1
exceedest the *f* that I ... 2Chr 9:6
have heard the *f* thereof ... Job 28:22
have heard the *f* thereof ... Jer 6:24
will get them praise and *f* ... Zep 3:19
f hereof went abroad ... Matt 9:26
heard of the *f* of Jesus ... Matt 14:1
immediately his *f* spread ... Mark 1:28
there went out a *f* of him ... Luke 4:14
went there a *f* abroad of him ... Luke 5:15

FAMILIAR—*those with whom one is closely acquainted*
f friends have forgotten me ... Job 19:14
Yea, mine own *f* friend ... Ps 41:9

FAMILIAR SPIRIT—*spirit or demon that prompts an individual*

Described as:
Source of defilement ... Lev 19:31
Abominable ... Deut 18:10-12
Vain ... Is 8:19

The practicers of, to be:
Cut off ... Lev 20:6
Put to death ... Lev 20:27

Consulted by:
Saul ... 1Sam 28:3-25
Manasseh ... 2Kin 21:6

[*also* FAMILIAR SPIRITS]
workers with *f s* ... 2Kin 23:24
one that had a *f s* ... 1Chr 10:13
dealt with a *f s* ... 2Chr 33:6
them that have *f s* ... Is 19:3
that hath a *f s* ... Is 29:4

FAMILY—*a household of individuals living together*

Founded on:
Divine creation ... Gen 1:27, 28
Marriage ... Matt 19:6
Monogamy ... Ex 20:14
Unity of parents ... Ex 20:12
Headship of husband ... 1Cor 11:3-7
Subordination of children ... Eph 6:1-4
Common concern ... Luke 16:27, 28

Disturbed by:
Polygamy ... Gen 4:19-24
Jealousy ... Gen 37:3, 4, 18-27
Hatred ... Gen 4:5, 8
Deceit ... Gen 37:31-35
Ambition ... 2Sam 15:1-16
Waywardness ... Luke 15:11-18
Insubordination ... Gen 34:6-31
Unbelief ... John 7:3-10
Lust ... Gen 34:1-31

Unity of:
Husband and wife ... 1Cor 7:3
Parents and children ... Jer 35:1-19
Worship ... 1Cor 16:19
Faith ... 2Tim 1:5
Baptism ... Acts 16:14, 15

Worship in:
Led by the father ... Gen 18:19
Instructed in the Scriptures ... Eph 6:4
Observing religious rites. . Acts 10:2, 47, 48
Common consecration ... Josh 24:15

[*also* FAMILIES]
their *f*, in their nations ... Gen 10:5
the *f* of the Canaanites ... Gen 10:18
are the *f* of the sons of Noah ... Gen 10:32
all *f* of the earth be blessed ... Gen 12:3
f of the earth be blessed ... Gen 28:14
Esau according to their *f* ... Gen 36:40
according to their *f* ... Gen 47:12
these be the *f* of Reuben ... Ex 6:14
lamb according to your *f* ... Ex 12:21
that man..against his *f* ... Lev 20:5
return every man unto his *f* ... Lev 25:10
shall return unto his own *f* ... Lev 25:41
their *f* that are with you ... Lev 25:45
stock of the stranger's *f* ... Lev 25:47
nigh of kin unto him of his *f* ... Lev 25:49
children of Israel, after..*f* ... Num 1:2
sons of Levi, after their *f* ... Num 4:2
people weep throughout..*f* ... Num 11:10
the *f* of the Reubenites ... Num 26:7
sons of Simeon after their *f* ... Num 26:12
children of Gad after..*f* ... Num 26:15
sons of Judah after their *f* ... Num 26:20
sons of Issachar after..*f* ... Num 26:23
sons of Zebulun after..*f* ... Num 26:26
sons of Joseph after their *f* ... Num 26:28
are the *f* of Manasseh ... Num 26:34
sons of Ephraim after..*f* ... Num 26:35
sons of Benjamin after..*f* ... Num 26:38
sons of Dan after their *f* ... Num 26:42
children of Asher after..*f* ... Num 26:44
sons of Naphtali after..*f* ... Num 26:48
done away from among his *f* ... Num 27:4
is next to him of his *f* ... Num 27:11
inheritance among your *f* ... Num 33:54
f of the children of Gilead ... Num 36:1
only to the *f* of the tribe ... Num 36:6
wife unto one of..*f* of ... Num 36:8
of the *f* of their father ... Num 36:12
f, or tribe..heart turneth ... Deut 29:18
according to the *f* thereof ... Josh 7:14
f which the Lord shall take ... Josh 7:14
took the *f* of the Zarbites ... Josh 7:17
brought the *f* of the Zarbites ... Josh 7:17
inheritance according to..*f* ... Josh 13:15
children of Judah by..*f* ... Josh 15:1
let go the man and all his *f* ... Judg 1:25
f is poor in Manasseh ... Judg 6:15
the *f* of the house of ... Judg 9:1
Zorah, of the *f* of.. ... Judg 13:2
f of Judah, who was..Levite ... Judg 17:7
sent of their *f* five men ... Judg 18:2
of the *f* of the Danites ... Judg 18:11
tribe and a *f* in Israel? ... Judg 18:19
to his tribe and to his *f* ... Judg 21:24
of the *f* of Elimelech ... Ruth 2:1
f the least of all the *f* ... 1Sam 9:21
f of Matri was taken ... 1Sam 10:21
my father's *f* in Israel ... 1Sam 18:18
sacrifice there for all the *f* ... 1Sam 20:6
f hath a sacrifice in the city ... 1Sam 20:29
f is risen against thine ... 2Sam 14:7
of the *f* of the house of Saul ... 2Sam 16:5
f of Kirjath-jearim ... 1Chr 2:53
are the *f* of the Zorathites ... 1Chr 4:2
neither did all..*f* multiply ... 1Chr 4:27
his brethren by their *f* ... 1Chr 5:7
are the *f* of the Levites ... 1Chr 6:19
left of the *f* of that tribe ... 1Chr 6:61
f of the remnant of the sons ... 1Chr 6:70
of the *f* of the half tribe ... 1Chr 6:71
among all the *f* of Issachar ... 1Chr 7:5
God remained with the *f* ... 1Chr 13:14
divisions of the *f* of ... 2Chr 35:5
division of the *f* of ... 2Chr 35:5
their *f* with their swords ... Neh 4:13
every *f*, every province ... Esth 9:28
contempt of *f* terrify me ... Job 31:34
God setteth the solitary in *f* ... Ps 68:6

maketh him *f* like a flock .....Ps 107:41
call all the *f* of..kingdoms .....Jer 1:15
one of a city, and two of a *f* ..Jer 3:14
that remain of this evil *f* ......Jer 8:3
f that call not on thy name ....Jer 10:25
God of all the *f* of Israel ......Jer 31:1
f of the countries ....Ezek 20:32
whole *f* which I brought up ...Amos 3:1
known of all the *f*..earth ......Amos 3:2
against this *f* do I devise ......Mic 2:3
f through her witchcrafts ......Nah 3:4
shall mourn, every *f* apart .....Zech 12:12
f of the house of David ....Zech 12:12
f of the house of Nathan ......Zech 12:12
f of the house of Levi apart ...Zech 12:13
f that remain, every *f* apart ...Zech 12:14
if the *f* of Egypt go not up ....Zech 14:18
f in heaven and earth ....Eph 3:15

FAMINE—*an extreme scarcity of food*

Kinds of:

Physical ....Gen 12:10
Prophetic ....Matt 24:7
Rev 6:5-8
Spiritual 2Chr 15:3
Amos 8:11

Causes of:

Hail storms ....Ex 9:23
Insects..................Joel 1:4
Enemies ....Deut 28:49-51
Siege 2Kin 6:25
Sin ....Ezek 14:12, 13
Punishment 2Kin 8:1

Characteristics of:

Often long ....Gen 41:27
Often severe ....Deut 28:49-53
Suffering intense ....Jer 14:1, 5, 6
Destructive ....Jer 14:12, 15

Instances of, in:

Abram's time ....Gen 12:10
Isaac's time ....Gen 26:1
Joseph's time ....Gen 41:53-56
Time of judges ....Ruth 1:1
David's reign............2Sam 21:1
Elisha's time 2Kin 4:38
Samaria's siege 2Kin 6:25
Reign of Claudius Caesar.Acts 11:28
Jeremiah's time ....Jer 14:1
Ahab's reign 1Kin 17:1

[*also* FAMINES]

seven years of *f* ....Gen 41:30
f shall consume the land ......Gen 41:30
land by reason of that *f* ....Gen 41:31
the seven years of *f*...........Gen 41:36
perish not through the *f*.......Gen 41:36
before the years of *f* came ....Gen 41:50
f was so sore in all lands ......Gen 41:57
f was in the land of Canaan ...Gen 42:5
for the *f* of your house........Gen 42:19
for the *f* of your households ...Gen 42:33
f was sore in the land ....Gen 43:1
years hath the *f* been in ....Gen 45:6
there are five years of *f*.......Gen 45:11
f is sore in..Canaan ....Gen 47:4
f was very sore, so that ....Gen 47:13
Canaan fainted by..*f* ....Gen 47:13
f prevailed over them ....Gen 47:20
seven years of *f* come 2Sam 24:13
If there be in the land *f*.......1Kin 8:37
sore *f* in Samaria 1Kin 18:2
then the *f* is in the city 2Kin 7:4
the *f* prevailed in the city 2Kin 25:3
Either three years *f*..........1Chr 21:12
or pestilence, or *f* 2Chr 20:9
to die by *f* and by thirst.......2Chr 32:11
f he shall redeem thee ....Job 5:20
destruction and *f* thou shalt ...Job 5:22
For want and *f* they were .....Job 30:3
keep them alive in *f* ....Ps 33:19
days of *f*..be satisfied ....Ps 37:19
called for a *f* upon the land ...Ps 105:16
I will kill thy root with *f* ......Is 14:30
and the *f* and the sword.......Is 51:19
shall we see sword nor *f* ......Jer 5:12
daughters shall die by *f* ....Jer 11:22
sword, and by the *f*..........Jer 14:12
neither shall ye have *f* ....Jer 14:13
of the *f* and the sword ....Jer 14:16
them that are sick with *f* ......Jer 14:18
are for the *f*, to the *f* ....Jer 15:2
consumed by the sword..by *f* ..Jer 16:4
deliver up..children to the *f* ...Jer 18:21
the sword, and..the *f* ....Jer 21:7
by the sword, and by..*f* ....Jer 21:9
will send the sword, the *f* .....Jer 24:10
the sword, and with the *f* .....Jer 27:8
people, by the sword, by *f* ....Jer 27:18
send upon them the sword..*f* ..Jer 29:17
of..sword, and of the *f*........Jer 32:24
Babylon by the sword, and..*f*..Jer 32:36
pestilence, and to the *f* ....Jer 34:17
die by the sword, by the *f*.....Jer 38:2
f, whereof ye were afraid .....Jer 42:16
die by the sword, by the *f*.....Jer 42:17
die by the sword, by the *f*.....Jer 42:22
by the sword and by the *f*.....Jer 44:12
Jerusalem by the sword, by..*f* .Jer 44:13
sword and by the *f* ....Jer 44:18
sword and by the *f* ....Jer 44:27
f was sore in the city ....Jer 52:6
oven because of the terrible *f*..Lam 5:10
f shall they be consumed ......Ezek 5:12
them the evil arrows of *f*......Ezek 5:16
I send upon you *f* and evil ....Ezek 5:17
fall by the sword, by the *f* ....Ezek 6:11
besieged shall die by the *f*.....Ezek 6:12
pestilence and the *f* within ....Ezek 7:15
f and pestilence..devour him...Ezek 7:15
from the sword, from the *f*....Ezek 12:16
f, and the noisome beast ......Ezek 14:21
lay no *f* upon you ....Ezek 36:29
receive no..reproach of *f*......Ezek 36:30
shall be *f* and troubles ....Mark 13:8
great *f* was throughout ....Luke 4:25
arose a mighty *f* in the land ...Luke 15:14
and *f*, and pestilences.........Luke 21:11
or *f*, or nakedness ....Rom 8:35
death, and mourning, and *f* ...Rev 18:8

FAMISH—*to starve*

[*also* FAMISHED]

all the land of Egypt *f* ....Gen 41:55
soul of the righteous to *f*......Prov 10:3
their honorable men are *f*.....Is 5:13
will *f* all the gods............Zeph 2:11

FAMOUS—*of wide renown*

f in the congregation..........Num 16:2
were *f* in the congregation ....Num 26:9
Ephratah..*f* in Beth-lehem.....Ruth 4:11
name may be *f* in Israel.......Ruth 4:14
men of valor, *f* men 1Chr 5:24
f throughout the house 1Chr 12:30
man was *f* according ....Ps 74:5
And slew *f* kings ....Ps 136:18
became *f* among women ......Ezek 23:10
daughters of the *f* nations .....Ezek 32:18

FAN—*to toss about*

Used literally of:

Fork for winnowing grain.Is 30:24

Used figuratively of judgments:

God's ....Is 30:24
Nation's ....Jer 51:2
Christ's ....Matt 3:12

Thou shalt *f* them ....Is 41:16
not to *f*, nor to cleanse ....Jer 4:11
with a *f* in the gates ....Jer 15:7
Whose *f* is in his hand ....Luke 3:17

FANATICISM—*unbridled obsession*

Kinds of:

Personal ....Acts 9:1, 2
Group 1Kin 18:22-29
Civic ....Acts 19:24-41
National ....John 19:15

Characteristics of:

Intolerance.............Acts 7:57
Persecution 1Thess 2:14-16
Inhumanity ....Rev 11:7-10
Insanity.................1Sam 18:9-12

FANNER—*one who winnows*

Babylon *f*, that shall fan ......Jer 51:2

FAR—*at a considerable distance*

That be *f* from thee to do .....Gen 18:25
wicked, that be *f* from ....Gen 18:25
not yet *f* off, Joseph said ......Gen 44:4
shall not go very *f* away.......Ex 8:28
f from a false matter..........Ex 23:7
f off about the tabernacle .....Num 2:2
name there be too *f* from .....Deut 12:21
unto thee, or *f* off from thee ..Deut 13:7
place be too *f* from thee .....Deut 14:24
cities which are very *f* ....Deut 20:15
nation against thee from *f*.....Deut 28:49
shall come from a *f* land ......Deut 29:22
neither is it *f* off ....Deut 30:11
heap very *f* from the city......Josh 3:16
go not very *f* from the city ....Josh 8:4
come from a *f* country ....Josh 9:6
f country thy servants..come ...Josh 9:9
adventured his life *f* ....Judg 9:17
they were *f* from the..........Judg 18:7
it was *f* from Zidon..........Judg 18:28
Lord saith, Be it *f* from me ...1Sam 2:30
be it *f* from me; let not the ...1Sam 22:15
in a place that was *f* off.......2Sam 15:17
he said, Be it *f* from me 2Sam 23:17
cometh out of a *f* country 1Kin 8:41
come from a *f* country 2Kin 20:14
come from a *f* country 2Chr 6:32
name spread *f* abroad.........2Chr 26:15
river, be ye *f* from thence .....Ezra 6:6
wall, one *f* from another ......Neh 4:19
Ahasuerus, both nigh and *f* ...Esth 9:20
children are *f* from safety .....Job 5:4
Withdraw thine hand *f* from ..Job 13:21
counsel of the wicked is *f* .....Job 21:16
put away iniquity *f* ....Job 22:23
f be it from God..should ......Job 34:10
f above out of his sight ....Ps 10:5
art thou so *f* from helping .....Ps 22:1
Be not *f* from me; for ....Ps 22:11
Hide not thy face *f* from ......Ps 27:9
God, be not *f* from me ....Ps 38:21
O God be not *f* from me .....Ps 71:12
f from thee shall perish ....Ps 73:27
put..mine acquaintance *f* ......Ps 88:8
exalted *f* above all gods ....Ps 97:9
f as the east is from..west .....Ps 103:12
so *f* hath he removed our .....Ps 103:12
so let it be *f* from him ....Ps 109:17
they are *f* from thy law ....Ps 119:150
perverse lips put *f* from ....Prov 4:24
Lord is *f* from the wicked .....Prov 15:29
keep his soul shall be *f* ....Prov 22:5
news from a far country ......Prov 25:25
Remove *f* from me vanity .....Prov 30:8
wise; but it was *f* from me .....Eccl 7:23
ensign to the nations from *f* ...Is 5:26
ear, all ye of *f* countries ......Is 8:9
come from a *f* country ....Is 13:5
shall turn the rivers *f* ....Is 19:6
removed it *f* unto all..ends ....Is 26:15
removed..heart *f* from ....Is 29:13
of the Lord cometh from *f* ....Is 30:27
land that is very *f* off ....Is 33:17
bring my sons from *f* ....Is 43:6
are *f* from righteousness ......Is 46:12
hearken, ye people, from *f*....Is 49:1
swallowed thee up shall be *f*...Is 49:19
send thy messengers *f* off .....Is 57:9
peace to him that is *f* off......Is 57:19
is judgment *f* from us ....Is 59:9
thy sons shall come from *f* ....Is 60:4
to bring thy sons from *f*.......Is 60:9
they are gone *f* from me ......Jer 2:5
nation upon you from *f* ....Jer 5:15
that dwell in a *f* country ......Jer 8:19
kings of the north, *f* and ......Jer 25:26
land of Moab, *f* or near.......Jer 48:24
Flee, get you *f* off, dwell......Jer 49:30
relieve my soul is *f* from .....Lam 1:16

He that is *f* off shall die ...... Ezek 6:12
have I set it *f* from .... Ezek 7:20
go *f* off from my sanctuary? ... Ezek 8:6
have cast them *f* off among ... Ezek 11:16
those that be *f* from thee ..... Ezek 22:5
carcases of their kings, *f* ...... Ezek 43:9
and that are *f* off .... Dan 9:7
will remove *f* off from you .... Joel 2:20
Sabeans, to a people *f* off .... Joel 3:8
Ye that put *f* away the evil .... Amos 6:3
was cast *f* off a strong .... Mic 4:7
horsemen shall come from *f* ... Hab 1:8
that are *f* off shall come ...... Zech 6:15
their heart is *f* from me .... Matt 15:8
went into a *f* country .... Matt 21:33
day was now *f* spent .... Mark 6:35
heart is *f* from me .... Mark 7:6
divers of them came from *f* ... Mark 8:3
went into a *f* country .... Mark 12:1
man taking a *f* journey .... Mark 13:34
not *f* from the house .... Luke 7:6
journey into a *f* country .... Luke 15:13
into a *f* country to receive .... Luke 19:12
into a *f* country for a long .... Luke 20:9
and said, Suffer ye thus *f* ..... Luke 22:51
out as *f* as to Bethany .... Luke 24:50
were not *f* from land .... John 21:8
traveled as *f* as Phoenicia ..... Acts 11:19
not *f* from every one .... Acts 17:27
us as *f* as Appii Forum .... Acts 28:15
night is *f* spent the day is ..... Rom 13:12
for us a *f* more exceeding 2Cor 4:17
F above all principality .... Eph 1:21
who sometimes were *f* off ..... Eph 2:13
up *f* above all heavens .... Eph 4:10
Christ; which is *f* better ...... Phil 1:23
is yet *f* more evident .... Heb 7:15

FARE—*to get along; succeed; cost of passage*

[*also* FARED]
look how thy brethren *f* 1Sam 17:18
he paid the *f* thereof .... Jon 1:3
f sumptuously every day ...... Luke 16:19
shall do well. *F* ye well .... Acts 15:29

FAREWELL—*expressions at departing*
Naomi's, to Orpah ...... Ruth 1:11-14
Paul's, to Ephesians ..... Acts 18:18-21
Paul's, to elders .... Acts 20:17-38
Paul's, to Tyrians .... Acts 21:3-6
Paul's, to Jews .... Acts 28:23-29

let me first go bid them *f* ..... Luke 9:61
they had against him. *F* .... Acts 23:30
Finally, brethren, *f* 2Cor 13:11

FAREWELL MESSAGE—*a final address*
Joshua's .... Josh 24:1-28
David's 1Kin 2:1-9
Christ's .... Matt 28:18-20
Paul's 2Tim 4:1-8

FARM—*land used to grow crops or raise animals*
Preferred more than a wedding .... Matt 22:1-5

FARMER—*a person who cultivates land or raises animals*
Cain, the first .... Gen 4:2
Elisha 1Kin 19:19, 20
Uzziah 2Chr 26:9, 10
Diligence required in .... Prov 24:30-34
Reward of 2Cor 9:6-11
Unwise .... Luke 12:16-21

FARMING—*the practice of agriculture*
Rechabites forbidden to engage in .... Jer 35:5-10

FARTHER—*at a greater distance*
And he went a little *f* .... Matt 26:39
he had gone a little *f* .... Mark 1:19

FARTHING—*a coin of small value*
Utmost payment .... Matt 5:26
Price of two sparrows .... Matt 10:29

[*also* FARTHINGS]
two mites which make a *f* ..... Mark 12:42
five sparrows sold for two *f* ... Luke 12:6

FASHION—*the outward form; to create*

Used physically of:
Outward form of a building .... Acts 7:44
One's appearance .... Luke 9:29

Used figuratively of:
World's life ("conformed") .... Rom 12:2
World's lusts 1Pet 1:14
World's riches .... James 1:11
World's exit 1Cor 7:31
Believer's conformity to Christ .... Phil 3:21

[*also* FASHIONED, FASHIONETH, FASHIONING, FASHIONS]
f which thou shalt make it .... Gen 6:15
according to the *f* thereof ..... Ex 26:30
f it with a graving tool .... Ex 32:4
according to all the *f* of it 1Kin 6:38
f of the altar, and..pattern 2Kin 16:10
hands..made me and *f* me ..... Job 10:8
not one *f* us in the womb? .... Job 31:15
He *f* their hearts alike .... Ps 33:15
hands have made me and *f* .... Ps 119:73
which in continuance were *f* ... Ps 139:16
respect unto him that *f* it ..... Is 22:11
coals, and *f* it with hammers .. Is 44:12
clay say to him that *f*, it ...... Is 45:9
thy breasts are *f* .... Ezek 16:7
both according to their *f* ...... Ezek 42:11
and the *f* thereof .... Ezek 43:11
We never saw it on this *f* ..... Mark 2:12
being found in *f* as a man ..... Phil 2:8
not *f* yourselves according 1Pet 1:14

FAST—*to abstain from physical nourishment*

Occasions of:
Public disasters 1Sam 31:11-13
Private emotions 1Sam 1:7
Grief 2Sam 12:16
Anxiety .... Dan 6:18-20
Approaching danger ..... Esth 4:16
National repentance 1Sam 7:5, 6
Sad news .... Neh 1:4
Sacred ordination .... Acts 13:3

Accompaniments of:
Prayer .... Luke 2:37
Confession .... Neh 9:1, 2
Mourning .... Joel 2:12
Humiliation .... Neh 9:1

Safeguards concerning:
Avoid display .... Matt 6:16-18
Remember God .... Zech 7:5-7
Chasten the soul .... Ps 69:10
Humble the soul .... Ps 35:13
Consider the true meaning of .... Is 58:1-14

Results of:
Divine guidance .... Judg 20:26
Victory over temptation .. Matt 4:1-11

Instances of:
Moses .... Ex 34:27, 28
Israelites .... Judg 20:26
Samuel 1Sam 7:5, 6
David 2Sam 12:16
Elijah 1Kin 19:8
Ninevites .... Jon 3:5-8
Nehemiah .... Neh 1:4
Darius .... Dan 6:9, 18
Daniel .... Dan 9:3
Anna .... Luke 2:36, 37
Jesus .... Matt 4:1, 2
John's disciples and the Pharisees .... Mark 2:18
Early Christians .... Acts 13:2
Apostles 2Cor 6:4, 5
Paul 2Cor 11:27

[*also* FASTED, FASTEST, FASTING, FASTINGS]
and *f* on that day, and 1Sam 7:6
tree at Jabesh, and *f* 1Sam 31:13
and *f* until even, for Saul 2Sam 1:12
didst *f* and weep for 2Sam 12:21
child was yet alive, I *f* 2Sam 12:22
Proclaim a *f*, and set 1Kin 21:9
f, and lay in sackcloth 1Kin 21:27
oak in Jabesh, and *f* 1Chr 10:12
proclaimed a *f* throughout 2Chr 20:3
So we *f* and besought .... Ezra 8:23
and *f*, and weeping .... Esth 4:3
and *f* ye for me, and .... Esth 4:16
my maidens will *f* likewise .... Esth 4:16
the matters of the *f* and .... Esth 9:31
I humbled my soul with *f* ..... Ps 35:13
are weak through *f* .... Ps 109:24
Wherefore have we *f*, say ..... Is 58:3
house upon the *f* day .... Jer 36:6
proclaimed a *f* before .... Jer 36:9
passed the night *f* .... Dan 6:18
Sanctify ye a *f*, call .... Joel 1:14
When ye *f* and mourned ...... Zech 7:5
when thou *f*, anoint .... Matt 6:17
and the Pharisees *f* .... Matt 9:14
but thy disciples *f* not? .... Matt 9:14
and then shall they *f* .... Matt 9:15
not send them away *f* .... Matt 15:32
but by prayer and *f* .... Matt 17:21
the bridechamber *f* .... Mark 2:19
bridegroom..they cannot *f* ..... Mark 2:19
shall they *f* those days .... Mark 2:20
I send them away *f* .... Mark 8:3
but by prayer and *f* .... Mark 9:29
with *f* and prayers .... Luke 2:37
the disciples of John *f* .... Luke 5:33
the bridechamber *f* .... Luke 5:34
then shall they *f* in .... Luke 5:35
I *f* twice in the week .... Luke 18:12
Four days again I was *f* .... Acts 10:30
to the Lord, and *f* .... Acts 13:2
prayed with *f*, they .... Acts 14:23
because the *f* was now .... Acts 27:9
tarried and continued *f* .... Acts 27:33
give yourselves to *f* 1Cor 7:5
in watchings, in *f* 2Cor 6:5
in *f* often, in cold and 2Cor 11:27

FASTEN—*to make secure; be faithful*

[*also* FAST, FASTENED, FASTENING]
Lord had *f* closed up .... Gen 20:18
and *f* the wreathen .... Ex 28:14
chains they *f* in the .... Ex 39:18
to *f* it on high upon .... Ex 39:31
and *f* it into the ground ...... Judg 4:21
for he was *f* asleep and ...... Judg 4:21
they bind me *f* with .... Judg 16:11
but abide here *f* by my .... Ruth 2:8
So she kept *f* by the .... Ruth 2:23
and they *f* his body to 1Sam 31:10
with a sword *f* upon 2Sam 20:8
beams should not be *f* 1Kin 6:6
hold him *f* at the door 2Kin 6:32
and *f* his head in the 1Chr 10:10
were *f* to the throne 2Chr 9:18
and this work goeth *f* on ...... Ezra 5:8
f with cords of fine .... Esth 1:6
and still he holdeth *f* .... Job 2:3
righteousness I hold *f* .... Job 27:6
foundations thereof *f*? .... Job 38:6
and it stood *f* .... Ps 33:9
say they, cleaveth *f* .... Ps 41:8
his strength setteth *f* the ...... Ps 65:6
covenant shall stand *f* .... Ps 89:28
Take *f* hold of instruction ..... Prov 4:13
f by the masters of .... Eccl 12:11
And I will *f* him as a nail ..... Is 22:23
shall the nail that is *f* .... Is 22:25
they hold *f* deceit, they .... Jer 8:5
they *f* it with nails .... Jer 10:4
affliction hasteth *f* .... Jer 48:16
a hand broad, *f* round .... Ezek 40:43
lay, and was *f* asleep .... Jon 1:5
is he: hold him *f* .... Matt 26:48
synagogue were *f* .... Luke 4:20
Peter, *f* his eyes upon .... Acts 3:4
when I had *f* mine .... Acts 11:6
made their feet *f* in .... Acts 16:24

forepart stuck *f*, and ....Acts 27:41
Watch ye, stand *f* in 1Cor 16:13
Stand *f* therefore in..........Gal 5:1
that ye stand *f* in one ....Phil 1:27
stand *f* in the Lord ....Phil 4:1
live, if ye stand *f*..........1Thess 3:8
hold *f* that which is good......1Thess 5:21
brethren, stand *f*, and..........2Thess 2:15
Hold *f* the form of 2Tim 1:13
Holding *f* the faithful ....Titus 1:9
hold *f* the confidence ....Heb 3:6
hold *f* our profession ....Heb 4:14
hold *f* the profession..........Heb 10:23
holdest *f* my name..........Rev 2:13
ye have already, hold *f* ....Rev 2:25
and hold *f*, and repent ....Rev 3:3
hold that *f* which thou ....Rev 3:11

FAT—*tissues filled with greasy, oily matter; plump; prosperous*

Figurative of best..........Gen 45:18
Of sacrifices, burned..........Ex 29:13
Lev 4:26
Figurative of pride..........Ps 119:69, 70
Sacrificed by Abel..........Gen 4:4
Offered to God ....Ex 23:18
Lev 3:14-16

[*also* FATFLESHED, FATNESS, FATTED, FATTER, FATTEST]

of heaven, and the *f*..........Gen 27:28
well favored kine and *f* ....Gen 41:2
well favored and *f*..........Gen 41:4
his bread shall be *f*..........Gen 49:20
of the ram the *f*..........Ex 29:22
the *f* that covereth..........Ex 29:22
and the *f* that is upon..........Ex 29:22
the head and the *f*, in ....Lev 1:8
with his head and his *f*..........Lev 1:12
the *f* that covereth the ....Lev 3:3
all the *f* that is upon..........Lev 3:3
and the *f* that is on them ....Lev 3:4
the *f* thereof, and the..........Lev 3:9
the *f* that covereth the ....Lev 3:9
all the *f* that is upon the ....Lev 3:9
the *f* that is upon them ....Lev 3:10
ye eat neither *f* nor ....Lev 3:17
off from it all the *f*..........Lev 4:8
the *f* that covereth the ....Lev 4:8
all the *f* that is upon ....Lev 4:8
f that is upon them ....Lev 4:9
he shall take all his *f* ....Lev 4:19
take away all the *f* ....Lev 4:31
as the *f* is taken away..........Lev 4:31
he shall burn thereon the *f*..........Lev 6:12
of it all the *f* thereof..........Lev 7:3
the *f* that covereth the ....Lev 7:3
eat no manner of *f* ....Lev 7:23
And the *f* of the beast ....Lev 7:24
and the *f* of that which ....Lev 7:24
f with the breast, it ....Lev 7:30
offerings, and the *f*..........Lev 7:33
the *f* that was upon the ....Lev 8:16
two kidneys and their *f* ....Lev 8:16
he took the *f*, and the ....Lev 8:25
the *f* that was upon..........Lev 8:25
and their *f*, and ....Lev 8:25
But the *f*, and the ....Lev 9:10
they put the *f* upon the ....Lev 9:20
and he burnt the *f* upon ....Lev 9:20
made by fire of the *f* ....Lev 10:15
and burn the *f* for a ....Lev 17:6
whether it be *f* or lean..........Num 13:20
themselves, and waxen *f* ....Deut 31:20
with *f* of lambs, and ....Deut 32:14
with the *f* of kidneys of ....Deut 32:14
Jeshurun waxed *f*, and ....Deut 32:15
art waxen *f*, thou art ....Deut 32:15
art covered with *f* ....Deut 32:15
and Eglon was a very *f* ....Judg 3:17
Should I leave my *f* ....Judg 9:9
before they burnt the *f*..........1Sam 2:15
yourselves *f* with the..........1Sam 2:29
And the woman had a *f*..........1Sam 28:24
the *f* of the mighty 2Sam 1:22
sheep and oxen and *f*..........1Kin 1:9
slain oxen and *f* cattle 1Kin 1:25
fallow deer, and *f* fowl..........1Kin 4:23
and the *f* of the peace 1Kin 8:64
they found *f* pasture 1Chr 4:40
and the *f* of the peace 2Chr 7:7
with the *f* of the peace..........2Chr 29:35
eat the *f*, and drink the ....Neh 8:10
strong cities, and a *f*..........Neh 9:25
filled, and became *f* ....Neh 9:25
his face with his *f* ....Job 15:27
maketh collops of *f* on ....Job 15:27
inclosed in their own *f*..........Ps 17:10
satisfied with the *f* of ....Ps 36:8
Lord shall be as the *f*..........Ps 37:20
thy paths drop *f*..........Ps 65:11
them, and slew the *f*..........Ps 78:31
they shall be *f* and ....Ps 92:14
and my flesh faileth of *f* ....Ps 109:24
Their heart is as *f* ....Ps 119:70
soul shall be made *f* ....Prov 11:25
maketh the bones *f*..........Prov 15:30
rams, and the *f* of fed ....Is 1:11
heart of this people *f* ....Is 6:10
send among his *f* ones ....Is 10:16
the *f* of his flesh shall..........Is 17:4
people a feast of *f*..........Is 25:6
f things full of marrow ....Is 25:6
on the head of the *f* ....Is 28:4
it is made *f* with *f* ....Is 34:6
with the *f* of the kidneys ....Is 34:6
dust made *f* with *f*..........Is 34:7
filled me with the *f* ....Is 43:24
They are waxen *f*, they ....Jer 5:28
of the priests with *f*..........Jer 31:14
the midst of her like *f* ....Jer 46:21
Ye eat the *f*, and ye ....Ezek 34:3
will destroy the *f* and ....Ezek 34:16
And ye shall eat *f* till ....Ezek 39:19
offer unto me the *f* and ....Ezek 44:15
appeared fairer and *f* ....Dan 1:15
upon the *f* places of the..........Dan 11:24
peace offerings of your *f*..........Amos 5:22
by them their portion is *f* ....Hab 1:16
eat the flesh of the *f*..........Zech 11:16
And bring hither the *f* ....Luke 15:23
the root and *f* of the..........Rom 11:17

FATHER—*male parent*

Kinds of:

Natural..........Gen 28:13
Ancestors..........Jer 35:6
Natural leaders..........Rom 9:5
Head of households ....Ex 6:14

Figuratively of:

Source..........Job 38:28
Original inventor ....Gen 4:20
Creator..........James 1:17
Spiritual likeness ....John 8:44
Counselor..........Gen 45:8
Superior 2Kin 2:12
Praise-seeking ....Matt 23:9

Powers of in Old Testament times:

Arrange son's marriage ..Gen 24:1-9
Sell children ....Ex 21:7

Duties of, toward his children:

Love ....Gen 37:4
Command ....Gen 50:16
Instruct..........Prov 1:8
Guide and warn 1Thess 2:11
Train..........Hos 11:3
Rebuke..........Gen 34:30
Restrain 1Sam 3:13
Punish..........Deut 21:18-21
Chasten ....Heb 12:7
Nourish..........Is 1:2
Supply needs..........Matt 7:8-11
Do not provoke ....Eph 6:4

Examples of devout:

Abraham ....Gen 18:18, 19
Isaac ....Gen 26:12, 13
Joshua..........Josh 24:15
Job..........Job 1:5

Christ's command about:

"Call no man your father" ....Matt 23:9

[*also* FATHER'S, FATHERS]

man leave his *f* and..........Gen 2:24
and they saw not their *f*..........Gen 9:23
to wander from my *f* ....Gen 20:13
is there room in thy *f* ....Gen 24:23
and of my *f* house ....Gen 24:40
I come again to my *f* ....Gen 28:21
that he was her *f* ....Gen 29:12
all that was our *f*..........Gen 31:1
was our *f* hath he ....Gen 31:1
for us in our *f*..........Gen 31:14
longedst after thy *f* ....Gen 31:30
sons of Zilpah, his *f* ....Gen 37:2
widow at thy *f* ....Gen 38:11
and dwelt in her *f* ....Gen 38:11
I am God, the God of thy *f*..Gen 46:3
and unto his *f*..........Gen 46:31
and all his *f*..........Gen 47:12
wentest up to thy *f* ....Gen 49:4
Joseph fell upon his *f*..........Gen 50:1
Egypt, he, and his *f* ....Gen 50:22
to water their *f*..........Ex 2:16
nor thy *f* have seen ....Ex 10:6
my *f* God, and I will ....Ex 15:2
Honor thy *f* and thy ....Ex 20:12
priest's office in his *f* ....Lev 16:32
nakedness of thy *f*..........Lev 18:8
it is thy *f* nakedness ....Lev 18:8
nakedness of thy *f*..........Lev 18:12
she is thy *f* near ....Lev 18:12
that lieth with his *f* wife..........Lev 20:11
hath uncovered his *f* ....Lev 20:11
nor of thy *f* sister..........Lev 20:19
returned unto her *f*..........Lev 22:13
she shall eat of her *f*..........Lev 22:13
the ensign of their *f* ....Num 2:2
according to their *f*..........Num 17:6
inheritance among their *f* ....Num 27:7
being in her *f* house in..........Num 30:3
ye are risen up in your *f*..........Num 32:14
unto their *f* brothers'..........Num 36:11
to the door of her *f* ....Deut 22:21
shall not take his *f* ....Deut 22:30
nor discover his *f* skirt ....Deut 22:30
that lieth with his *f* ....Deut 27:20
he uncovereth his *f*..........Deut 27:20
show kindness unto my *f*..........Josh 2:12
the harlot alive, and her *f*..........Josh 6:25
I am the least in my *f* ....Judg 6:15
because he feared his *f*..........Judg 6:27
risen up against my *f* ....Judg 9:18
expel me out of my *f* ....Judg 11:7
he went up to his *f* ....Judg 14:19
brought him into her *f*..........Judg 19:3
and the arm of thy *f*..........1Sam 2:31
to feed his *f* sheep at 1Sam 17:15
Thy servant kept his *f* 1Sam 17:34
my life, or my *f* family..........1Sam 18:18
and all his *f* house..........1Sam 22:11
the persons of thy *f*..........1Sam 22:22
gone in unto my *f*..........2Sam 3:7
Jonathan thy *f* 2Sam 9:7
as I have been thy *f* 2Sam 15:34
Go in unto thy *f* 2Sam 16:21
of my *f* house were 2Sam 19:28
it for David thy *f*..........1Kin 11:12
thicker than my *f*..........1Kin 12:10
and set him on his *f* 2Kin 10:3
made Mattaniah his *f* 2Kin 24:17
as he defiled his *f* 1Chr 5:1
heads of their *f* house..........1Chr 7:40
be on me, and on my *f* 1Chr 21:17
and I will be his *f* 1Chr 22:10
of Huram my *f*..........2Chr 2:13
slain thy brethren of thy *f*..........2Chr 21:13
not show their *f*..........Ezra 2:59
both I and my *f* house ....Neh 1:6
the place of my *f*..........Neh 2:3
and thy *f* house shall ....Esth 4:14
I was a *f* to the poor ....Job 29:16
people, and thy *f*..........Ps 45:10

A *f* of the fatherless .... Ps 68:5
Like as a *f* pitieth his .... Ps 103:13
I was my *f* son, tender .... Prov 4:3
My son, keep thy *f* .... Prov 6:20
son maketh a glad *f* .... Prov 10:1
A wise son heareth his *f* .... Prov 13:1
son is a grief to his *f* .... Prov 17:25
is the calamity of his *f* .... Prov 19:13
thy *f* friend forsake not .... Prov 27:10
people, and upon thy *f* .... Is 7:17
everlasting **F**, The .... Is 9:6
all the glory of his *f* .... Is 22:24
but obey their *f* .... Jer 35:14
that seeth all his *f* .... Ezek 18:14
were after their *f* idols .... Ezek 20:24
Have we not all one *f*? .... Mal 2:10
glorify your **F** which .... Matt 5:16
your **F** knoweth what .... Matt 6:8
F which art in heaven .... Matt 6:9
doeth the will of my **F** .... Matt 7:21
confess also before my **F** .... Matt 10:32
I also deny before my **F** .... Matt 10:33
do the will of my **F** .... Matt 12:50
Honor thy *f* and mother .... Matt 15:4
shall a man leave *f* and .... Matt 19:5
Honor thy *f* and thy .... Matt 19:19
brethren, or sisters, or *f* .... Matt 19:29
ye blessed of my **F** .... Matt 25:34
new with you in my **F** .... Matt 26:29
in the name of the **F** .... Matt 28:19
Honor thy *f* and thy .... Mark 7:10
shall a man leave his *f* .... Mark 10:7
I must be about my **F** .... Luke 2:49
to go and bury my *f* .... Luke 9:59
say, Our **F** which art in .... Luke 11:2
your **F** good pleasure .... Luke 12:32
arise and go to my *f* .... Luke 15:18
send him to my *f* .... Luke 16:27
Honor thy *f* and thy .... Luke 18:20
F, forgive them; for they .... Luke 23:34
My **F** worketh hitherto .... John 5:17
man hath seen the **F** .... John 6:46
given unto him of my **F** .... John 6:65
Where is thy **F**? .... John 8:19
know me, nor my **F** .... John 8:19
have known my **F** .... John 8:19
as my **F** hath taught me .... John 8:28
we have one **F**, even God .... John 8:41
As the **F** knoweth me .... John 10:15
that I do in my **F** name .... John 10:25
pluck them out of my **F** .... John 10:29
I and my **F** are one .... John 10:30
cometh unto the **F**, but .... John 14:6
Lord, show us the **F** .... John 14:8
that I am in my **F**, and .... John 14:20
not mine, but the **F** which .... John 14:24
and my **F** is the .... John 15:1
F the hour is come .... John 17:1
as my **F** hath sent me .... John 20:21
nourished up in his *f* .... Acts 7:20
I have made thee a *f* .... Rom 4:17
we cry, Abba, **F** .... Rom 8:15
are beloved for the *f* .... Rom 11:28
one should have his *f* 1Cor 5:1
one God, the **F**, of 1Cor 8:6
The God and **F** of our 2Cor 11:31
One God and **F** of all .... Eph 4:6
to the glory of God the **F** .... Phil 2:11
I will be to him a **F** .... Heb 1:5
of love the **F** hath 1John 3:1
F, the Word, and the 1John 5:7
set down with my **F** in .... Rev 3:21
having his **F** name .... Rev 14:1

FATHERHOOD OF GOD
Of all men .... Mal 2:10
Of Israel .... Jer 31:9
Of Gentiles .... Rom 3:29
Of Christians .... John 1:12, 13

FATHERLESS—*orphaned*
Proper attitude toward:
Share blessings with .... Deut 14:28, 29
Leave gleanings for .... Deut 24:19-22
Do not defraud .... Prov 23:10
Defend .... Ps 82:3
Visit .... James 1:27
Oppress not .... Zech 7:10
Do no violence to .... Jer 22:3
God's help toward:
Father of .... Ps 68:5
Helper of .... Ps 10:14
Hears cry of .... Ex 22:23
Executes judgment of .... Deut 10:18

not afflict any widow, or *f* .... Ex 22:22
and your children *f* .... Ex 22:24
stranger, and the *f* .... Deut 16:11
stranger, nor of the *f* .... Deut 24:17
the stranger, the *f* .... Deut 26:12
of the stranger, *f* .... Deut 27:19
overwhelm the *f*, and .... Job 6:27
the ass of the *f* .... Job 24:3
that cried, and the *f* .... Job 29:12
my hand against the *f* .... Job 31:21
to judge the *f* and the .... Ps 10:18
and murder the *f* .... Ps 94:6
Let his children be *f* .... Ps 109:9
be any to favor his *f* .... Ps 109:12
he relieveth the *f* and .... Ps 146:9
judge the *f*, plead for .... Is 1:17
they judge not the *f* .... Is 1:23
they may rob the *f* .... Is 10:2
the cause of the *f* .... Jer 5:28
the stranger, the *f* .... Jer 7:6
Leave thy *f* children, I .... Jer 49:11
We are orphans and *f* .... Lam 5:3
have they vexed the *f* .... Ezek 22:7
for in thee the *f* findeth .... Hos 14:3
the widow, and the *f* .... Mal 3:5

FATHER'S HOUSE
The family house .... Gen 12:1
1Sam 18:2
A household .... Ex 12:3
Tribal divisions .... Num 3:15, 20
Num 17:2, 3
Temple .... John 2:14-16
Heaven .... John 14:2

FATHOM—*a nautical measure; about six feet*
Mentioned in Paul's shipwreck .... Acts 27:28

FATIGUE—*physical or mental exhaustion*
From:
Marching 1Sam 30:9, 10
Fighting 2Sam 23:10, 15
Much study .... Eccl 12:12
Fasting .... Acts 27:21
In:
Sleeping .... Matt 26:45

FATLING—*a young animal fattened for slaughter*
[*also* FATLINGS]
and of the *f*, and the 1Sam 15:9
he sacrificed oxen and *f* 2Sam 6:13
burnt sacrifices of *f* .... Ps 66:15
young lion and the *f* .... Is 11:6
all of them *f* of Bashan .... Ezek 39:18
my oxen and my *f* are .... Matt 22:4

FATS—*See* VATS

FAULT—*an imperfection*
Examples of:
A promise forgotten .... Gen 41:9
Unworthy conduct 1Sam 29:3
Guilt .... John 18:38
Deficient behavior .... Matt 18:15
Human weakness .... James 5:16
Absence of:
Flawless devotion .... Rev 14:5
Ultimate sinlessness .... Jude 24

[*also* FAULTS, FAULTY]
but the *f* is in thine .... Ex 5:16
according to his *f* .... Deut 25:2
with a *f* concerning 2Sam 3:8
as one which is *f* 2Sam 14:13
me from secret *f* .... Ps 19:12
without my *f* .... Ps 59:4
none occasion nor *f* .... Dan 6:4
there any error or *f* .... Dan 6:4
now shall they be found *f* .... Hos 10:2
hands, they found *f* .... Mark 7:2
I find no *f* in this man .... Luke 23:4
have found no *f* in .... Luke 23:14
know that I find no *f* .... John 19:4
for I find no *f* in him .... John 19:6
Why doth he yet find *f*? .... Rom 9:19
there is utterly a *f* 1Cor 6:7
be overtaken in a *f* .... Gal 6:1
For finding *f* with them .... Heb 8:8
be buffeted for your *f* 1Pet 2:20
are without *f* before .... Rev 14:5

FAULTFINDERS—*carping critics*
Motives behind:
Supposed injustice .... Matt 20:9-12
Supposed defilement .... Luke 5:29, 30
Greed and avarice .... John 12:3-6
Against God's:
Choice .... Num 12:1, 2
Leading .... Num 14:1-4
Mercy .... Jon 4:1-11
Government .... Rom 9:19-23
Guilt of:
Punishable .... Num 12:2, 8-13
Productive of evil 3John 10

FAULTLESS—*without blame*
David 1Sam 29:3, 6
Daniel .... Dan 6:4
Christ .... Luke 23:4, 14

first covenant had been *f* .... Heb 8:7

FAVORITISM—*being unfairly partial*
Forbidden to:
Parents .... Deut 21:15-17
Judges .... Deut 25:1-3
Ministers 1Tim 5:21
Results in:
Family friction .... Gen 27:6-46
Jealousy .... Gen 37:3-35

FAVOR—*to be partial*
[*also* FAVORABLE, FAVORED, FAVOREST, FAVORETH]
now I have found *f* in .... Gen 18:3
beautiful and well-*f* .... Gen 29:17
him *f* in the sight of .... Gen 39:21
river seven well-*f* kine .... Gen 41:2
the ill-*f*..kine did eat .... Gen 41:4
eat up the seven well-*f* .... Gen 41:4
poor and very ill-*f* and .... Gen 41:19
were still ill-*f*, as at .... Gen 41:21
will give this people *f* .... Ex 3:21
Lord gave the people *f* .... Ex 12:36
have I not found *f* in .... Num 11:11
pass that she find no *f* .... Deut 24:1
satisfied with *f* .... Deut 33:23
they might have no *f* .... Josh 11:20
Be *f* unto them for our .... Judg 21:22
Let me find *f* in thy sight .... Ruth 2:13
and was in *f* both with 1Sam 2:26
if I have found *f* in 1Sam 20:29
the lords *f* thee not 1Sam 29:6
if I shall find *f* in the 2Sam 15:25
He that *f* Joab, and he 2Sam 20:11
Hadad found great *f* in 1Kin 11:19
servant have found *f* .... Neh 2:5
Esther obtained *f* in .... Esth 2:15
that she obtained *f* in .... Esth 5:2
If I have found *f* in thy .... Esth 7:3
granted me life and *f* .... Job 10:12
and he will be *f* unto him .... Job 33:26
with *f* wilt thou .... Ps 5:12
his *f* is life: weeping .... Ps 30:5
f thou hast made my .... Ps 30:7
that *f* my righteous .... Ps 35:27
this I know that thou *f* .... Ps 41:11
because thou hadst a *f* .... Ps 44:3
shall entreat thy *f* .... Ps 45:12

F

and will he be *f* no more? ..... Ps 77:7
thy *f* our horn shall be .... Ps 89:17
for the time to *f* her .... Ps 102:13
stones, and *f* the dust .... Ps 102:14
with the *f* that thou .... Ps 106:4
let there be any to *f* .... Ps 109:12
man showeth *f*, and .... Ps 112:5
I entreated thy *f* with .... Ps 119:58
So shalt thou find *f* .... Prov 3:4
and shall obtain *f* of .... Prov 8:35
seeketh good procureth *f* ...... Prov 11:27
good man obtaineth *f* of ...... Prov 12:2
understanding giveth *f* .... Prov 13:15
righteous there is *f* .... Prov 14:9
king's *f* is toward a wise ...... Prov 14:35
f is as a cloud of the .... Prov 16:15
obtaineth *f* of the Lord .... Prov 18:22
will entreat the *f* of the .... Prov 19:6
his *f* is as dew upon the .... Prov 19:12
neighbor findeth no *f* .... Prov 21:10
find more *f* than he that ...... Prov 28:23
F is deceitful, and beauty ..... Prov 31:30
nor yet *f* to men of skill ...... Eccl 9:11
eyes as one that found *f* ...... Song 8:10
Let *f* be showed to the .... Is 26:10
but in my *f* have I had .... Is 60:10
I will not show you *f* .... Jer 16:13
priests, they *f* not the .... Lam 4:16
no blemish, but well-*f* .... Dan 1:4
brought Daniel into *f* .... Dan 1:9
thou that art highly *f* .... Luke 1:28
for thou hast found *f* .... Luke 1:30
and having *f* with all .... Acts 2:47
Who found *f* before .... Acts 7:46
And desired *f* against .... Acts 25:3

FEAR—*anxiety caused by approaching danger*

Causes of:

Disobedience .... Gen 3:10
Impending judgment ..... Heb 11:7
Persecution .... John 20:19
Events of nature .... Acts 27:17, 29
Suspicion .... Acts 9:26
Uncertainty 2Cor 11:3
Final events .... Luke 21:26
Death .... Heb 2:15

Effects of:

Demoralization 1Sam 13:5-8
Paralysis .... Matt 28:4
Silent testimony .... John 9:22

Instances of:

Abraham .... Gen 20:11
Jacob .... Gen 32:11
Soldiers .... Matt 27:54

[*also* FEARED, FEAREST, FEARETH, FEARFUL, FEARFULLY, FEARFULNESS, FEARING, FEARS]

the *f* of you and the .... Gen 9:2
F not, Abram: I am .... Gen 15:1
for he *f* to dwell in Zoar ...... Gen 19:30
aileth thee, Hagar? *f* .... Gen 21:17
and the *f* of Isaac, had .... Gen 31:42
F not; thou shalt have .... Gen 35:17
Peace be to you, *f* .... Gen 43:23
said unto them, ***F*** .... Gen 50:19
that ye will not yet *f* .... Ex 9:30
f in praises, doing .... Ex 15:11
F and dread shall fall .... Ex 15:16
unto the people, ***F*** not: .... Ex 20:20
that his *f* may be before ...... Ex 20:20
Ye shall *f* every man .... Lev 19:3
neither *f* ye the people .... Num 14:9
the Lord is with us; *f* .... Num 14:9
said unto thee; *f* not .... Deut 1:21
Lord said unto me, ***F*** .... Deut 3:2
man is there that is *f* .... Deut 20:8
and thou shalt *f* day .... Deut 28:66
for the *f* of thine heart .... Deut 28:67
wherewith thou shalt *f* .... Deut 28:67
f not, neither be .... Deut 31:8
that I *f* the wrath of .... Deut 32:27
of all Israel; and they *f* .... Josh 4:14
they *f* greatly, because .... Josh 10:2
rather done it for *f* of .... Josh 22:24
children cease from *f* .... Josh 22:25
turn in to me; *f* not .... Judg 4:18
f not the gods of the .... Judg 6:10
Peace be unto thee; *f* not ..... Judg 6:23
because he *f* his father's ...... Judg 6:27
Whosoever is *f* and .... Judg 7:3
dwelt there, for *f* of .... Judg 9:21
my daughter, *f* not; I .... Ruth 3:11
Samuel *f* to show Eli 1Sam 3:15
F not; for thou hast 1Sam 4:20
for the people *f* the 1Sam 14:26
and fled that day for *f* 1Sam 21:10
he said unto him, ***F*** 1Sam 23:17
again, because he *f* 2Sam 3:11
said unto him, ***F*** not 2Sam 9:7
servants of David *f* to tell 2Sam 12:18
Adonijah *f* because of 1Kin 1:50
Behold, Adonijah *f* 1Kin 1:51
Elijah said unto her, ***F*** 1Kin 17:13
and had *f* other gods 2Kin 17:7
saying, Ye shall not *f* 2Kin 17:35
and ye shall not *f* other 2Kin 17:37
do it; *f* not, nor be 1Chr 28:20
Jehoshaphat *f*, and set 2Chr 20:3
f not, nor be dismayed 2Chr 20:17
f was upon them .... Ezra 3:3
who desire to *f* .... Neh 1:11
because of the *f* of .... Neh 5:15
letters to put me in *f* .... Neh 6:19
the *f* of the Jews fell .... Esth 8:17
f of Mordecai fell .... Esth 9:3
f came upon me, and .... Job 4:14
let not his *f* terrify me .... Job 9:34
steadfast, and shalt not *f* ...... Job 11:15
houses are safe from *f* .... Job 21:9
and sudden *f* troubleth .... Job 22:10
He mocketh at *f*, and is .... Job 39:22
Put them in *f*, O Lord .... Ps 9:20
were they in great *f* .... Ps 14:5
my heart shall not *f* .... Ps 27:3
f was on every side .... Ps 31:13
Therefore will not we *f* .... Ps 46:2
F took hold upon them .... Ps 48:6
also shall see, and *f* .... Ps 52:6
There were they in great *f* .... Ps 53:5
where no *f* was .... Ps 53:5
F and trembling are .... Ps 55:5
I will not *f* what flesh .... Ps 56:4
shoot at him, and *f* not .... Ps 64:4
even thou, art to be *f* .... Ps 76:7
him that ought to be *f* .... Ps 76:11
who is devoted to thy *f* .... Ps 119:38
I am *f* and wonderfully .... Ps 139:14
will mock when your *f* .... Prov 1:26
Be not afraid of sudden *f* ..... Prov 3:25
The *f* of a king is as .... Prov 20:2
The *f* of man bringeth .... Prov 29:25
as he that *f* an oath .... Eccl 9:2
and *f* shall be in the way ...... Eccl 12:5
because of *f* in the .... Song 3:8
in the dust, for *f* of the .... Is 2:10
of the earth, for *f* of the ...... Is 2:19
ragged rocks, for *f* of .... Is 2:21
and be quiet; *f* .... Is 7:4
thither the *f* of briers .... Is 7:25
neither *f* ye their *f* .... Is 8:12
let him be your *f*, and .... Is 8:13
sorrow and from thy *f* .... Is 14:3
heart panted, *f* affrighted ..... Is 21:4
hath he turned into *f* .... Is 21:4
F, and the pit, and the .... Is 24:17
from the noise of the *f* .... Is 24:18
their *f* toward me is .... Is 29:13
to his stronghold for *f* .... Is 31:9
them that are of a *f* .... Is 35:4
Be strong, *f* not .... Is 35:4
The isles saw it, and *f* .... Is 41:5
F thou not; for I am .... Is 41:10
F not; I will help thee .... Is 41:13
F not, thou worm .... Is 41:14
F not; for I have .... Is 43:1
F not; for I am with .... Is 43:5
F not, O Jacob, my .... Is 44:2
yet they shall *f*, and .... Is 44:11
f ye not the reproach .... Is 51:7
F not; for thou shalt .... Is 54:4
thou been afraid or *f* .... Is 57:11
even of old, and thou *f* .... Is 57:11
and thine heart shall *f* .... Is 60:5
and will bring their *f* .... Is 66:4
that my *f* is not in thee .... Jer 2:19
sister Judah *f* not .... Jer 3:8
of many, *f* on every side ...... Jer 20:10
them whose face thou *f* .... Jer 22:25
f thou not, O my .... Jer 30:10
for *f* of the army of the .... Jer 35:11
F not to serve the .... Jer 40:9
they *f*, nor walked in .... Jer 44:10
f was round about .... Jer 46:5
F thou not, O Jacob .... Jer 46:28
that fleeth from the *f* .... Jer 48:44
and *f* hath seized .... Jer 49:24
for *f* of the oppressing .... Jer 50:16
F and a snare is come .... Lam 3:47
f them not, neither be .... Ezek 3:9
Ye have *f* the sword .... Ezek 11:8
trembled and *f* .... Dan 5:19
said he unto me, ***F*** .... Dan 10:12
F not, O land; be glad .... Joel 2:21
roared, who will not *f*? .... Amos 3:8
and shall *f* because .... Mic 7:17
f not, but let your .... Zech 8:13
shall see it, and *f* .... Zech 9:5
master, where is my *f*? .... Mal 1:6
f wherewith he *f* me .... Mal 2:5
f not to take unto thee .... Matt 1:20
Why are ye *f*, O ye of .... Matt 8:26
F them not therefore .... Matt 10:26
f not them which kill .... Matt 10:28
f him which is able to .... Matt 10:28
F ye not therefore, ye .... Matt 10:31
he *f* the multitude .... Matt 14:5
they cried out for *f* .... Matt 14:26
we *f* the people; for all .... Matt 21:26
they *f* the multitude .... Matt 21:46
for *f* of him the keepers .... Matt 28:4
F not ye; for I know .... Matt 28:5
sepulcher with *f* and .... Matt 28:8
Why are ye so *f*? .... Mark 4:40
they *f* exceedingly .... Mark 4:41
But the woman *f* and .... Mark 5:33
For Herod *f* John .... Mark 6:20
they *f* him, because all .... Mark 11:18
lay hold on him, but *f* .... Mark 12:12
was troubled, and *f* fell .... Luke 1:12
F not, Mary; for thou .... Luke 1:30
f came on all that .... Luke 1:65
F not: for, behold, I .... Luke 2:10
were filled with *f* .... Luke 5:26
were taken with great *f* .... Luke 8:37
f as they entered into .... Luke 9:34
F not, little flock; for .... Luke 12:32
and they *f* the people .... Luke 20:19
f sights and great .... Luke 21:11
openly of him for *f* of .... John 7:13
F not, daughter of Zion ...... John 12:15
but secretly for *f* of .... John 19:38
assembled for *f* of the .... John 20:19
f came upon every soul .... Acts 2:43
great *f* came upon all .... Acts 5:11
for they *f* the people .... Acts 5:26
they *f*, when they heard .... Acts 16:38
f fell on them all, and .... Acts 19:17
the chief captain, *f* lest .... Acts 23:10
F not, Paul; thou must .... Acts 27:24
f lest we should have .... Acts 27:29
not high-minded, but *f* .... Rom 11:20
f to whom *f*; honor .... Rom 13:7
and in *f*, and in much 1Cor 2:3
fightings, within were *f* 2Cor 7:5
indignation, yea, what *f* 2Cor 7:11
with *f* and trembling 2Cor 7:15
For I *f*, lest, when I 2Cor 12:20
f them which were .... Gal 2:12
with *f* and trembling .... Eph 6:5
speak the word without *f* ...... Phil 1:14
salvation with *f* and .... Phil 2:12
all, that others also may *f* 1Tim 5:20
given us the spirit of *f* 2Tim 1:7
Let us therefore *f*, lest .... Heb 4:1

was heard in that he *f* ....Heb 5:7
certain *f* looking for ....Heb 10:27
not *f* the wrath of the.........Heb 11:27
I exceedingly *f* and ....Heb 12:21
reverence and godly *f*.........Heb 12:28
I will not *f* what man ....Heb 13:6
sojourning here in *f* 1Pet 1:17
masters with all *f*.............1Pet 2:18
coupled with *f*.................1Pet 3:2
with meekness and *f*..........1Pet 3:15
There is no *f* in love..........1John 4:18
out *f*: because *f* hath..........1John 4:18
He that *f* is not made..........1John 4:18
themselves without *f*..........Jude 12
others save with *f* ....Jude 23
saying unto me, *f* not ....Rev 1:17
F none of those things ....Rev 2:10
great *f* fell upon them ....Rev 11:11
saints, and them that *f*........Rev 11:18
afar off for the *f* of...........Rev 18:10
the *f*, and unbelieving.........Rev 21:8

FEAR, GODLY—*reverential awe*

Defined as:
Hating evil..............Prov 8:13
Satisfying ....Prov 14:27
Sanctifying ....Ps 19:9
Beginning of wisdom ....Prov 1:7

Motives to, God's
Majesty..................Jer 10:7
Holiness ....Rev 15:4
Forgiveness ....Ps 130:4
Power ....Josh 4:23, 24
Goodness 1Sam 12:24
Judgment ....Rev 14:7

Examples of:
Noah ....Heb 11:7
Abraham ....Gen 22:12
Jacob....................Gen 28:16, 17
Joseph...................Gen 42:18
David ....Ps 5:7
Obadiah 1Kin 18:12
Job......................Job 1:8
Nehemiah................Neh 5:15
Early Christians ....Acts 9:31

[*also* FEARED, FEAREST, FEARETH, FEARING]
I know that thou *f* God ....Gen 22:12
the midwives *f* God, and ......Ex 1:17
And Moses *f*, and said ....Ex 2:14
people *f* the Lord, and........Ex 14:31
of the old man, and *f*.........Lev 19:32
but *f* thy God; that ....Lev 25:36
of thee and the *f* ....Deut 2:25
that they may learn to *f*.......Deut 4:10
that they would *f* me ....Deut 5:29
That thou mightest *f*..........Deut 6:2
to *f* the Lord our God ....Deut 6:24
to *f* the Lord thy God ....Deut 10:12
f of you and the dread ....Deut 11:25
Israel shall hear, and *f*........Deut 13:11
shall hear, and *f*..............Deut 17:13
shall hear, and *f*..............Deut 19:20
shall hear, and *f*..............Deut 21:21
and he *f* not God...............Deut 25:18
they may learn, and *f*..........Deut 31:12
Lord said unto Joshua, *F* .....Josh 10:8
Only *f* the Lord, and serve 1Sam 12:24
be just, ruling in the *f* 2Sam 23:3
That they may *f* thee all 1Kin 8:40
Obadiah *f* the Lord............1Kin 18:3
that thy servant did *f* 2Kin 4:1
how they should *f* 2Kin 17:28
they *f* the Lord, and 2Kin 17:32
your God ye shall *f*...........2Kin 17:39
nations *f* the Lord 2Kin 17:41
the Lord brought the *f*.........1Chr 14:17
he also is to be *f* above 1Chr 16:25
That they may *f* thee 2Chr 6:31
the *f* of the Lord came.........2Chr 14:14
let the *f* of the Lord be 2Chr 19:7
man, and *f* God above ....Neh 7:2
and one that *f* God, and ......Job 1:1
said, Doth Job *f* God for .....Job 1:9
man, one that *f* God...........Job 2:3
the *f* of the Lord, that is ......Job 28:28
Men do therefore *f* him ....Job 37:24
Serve the Lord with *f*.........Ps 2:11
honoreth them that *f* ....Ps 15:4
Ye that *f* the Lord ....Ps 22:23
before them that *f*............Ps 22:25
What man is he that *f* ....Ps 25:12
is with them that *f*............Ps 25:14
up for them that *f*............Ps 31:19
Let all the earth *f* the.........Ps 33:8
is upon them that *f*...........Ps 33:18
round about them that *f* ......Ps 34:7
O *f* the Lord, ye his saints ....Ps 34:9
is no want to them that *f* .....Ps 34:9
I will teach you the *f* of.......Ps 34:11
is no *f* of God before his......Ps 36:1
heritage of those that *f*........Ps 61:5
hear, all ye that *f*.............Ps 66:16
shall *f* thee as long ....Ps 72:5
unite my heart to *f* thy........Ps 86:11
God is greatly to be *f* in ......Ps 89:7
f before him, all the earth.....Ps 96:9
toward them that *f* ....Ps 103:11
pitieth them that *f*............Ps 103:13
upon them that *f* ....Ps 103:17
unto them that *f*..............Ps 111:5
The *f* of the Lord is the........Ps 111:10
Ye that *f* the Lord, trust ......Ps 115:11
Let them now that *f*...........Ps 118:4
on my side; I will not *f* ....Ps 118:6
of all them that *f*.............Ps 119:63
those that *f* thee turn ....Ps 119:79
is every one that *f* the ....Ps 128:1
ye that *f* the Lord, bless ......Ps 135:20
in them that *f* ....Ps 147:11
did not choose the *f* of........Prov 1:29
thou understand the *f* of ......Prov 2:5
f the Lord, and depart ....Prov 3:7
The *f* of the Lord is the.......Prov 9:10
f of the Lord prolongeth ......Prov 10:27
but he that *f* the ....Prov 13:13
A wise man *f*, and ....Prov 14:16
In the *f* of the Lord is ....Prov 14:26
Better is little with the *f* ......Prov 15:16
by the *f* of the Lord ....Prov 16:6
be thou in the *f* of the ....Prov 23:17
f thou the Lord and the ....Prov 24:21
but a woman that *f* ....Prov 31:30
that men should *f* ....Eccl 3:14
divers vanities: but *f* ....Eccl 5:7
he that *f* God shall ....Eccl 7:18
with them that *f* God ....Eccl 8:12
which *f* before him ....Eccl 8:12
F God, and keep his ....Eccl 12:13
knowledge and of the *f* ....Is 11:2
is among you that *f*............Is 50:10
shall they *f* the name of.......Is 59:19
Let us now *f*, the Lord ....Jer 5:24
did he not *f* the Lord, and ....Jer 26:19
I will put my *f* in their ....Jer 32:40
f my lord the king, who ....Dan 1:10
shall *f* the Lord and his ....Hos 3:5
we *f* not the Lord ....Hos 10:3
I *f* the Lord, the God of ......Jon 1:9
the men *f* the Lord ....Jon 1:16
Surely thou wilt *f*.............Zeph 3:7
the people did *f* before ....Hag 1:12
and *f* not me, saith the ....Mal 3:5
they that *f* the Lord ....Mal 3:16
before him for them that *f* ....Mal 3:16
whom ye shall *f*: *F* him ....Luke 12:5
I say unto you, *F* him ....Luke 12:5
judge, which *f* not God ....Luke 18:2
For I *f* thee, because thou ....Luke 19:21
Dost not thou *f* God..........Luke 23:40
and walking in the *f* of........Acts 9:31
just man, and one that *f* ......Acts 10:22
and ye that *f* God, give ....Acts 13:16
whosoever among you *f* ....Acts 13:26
there is no *f* of God ....Rom 3:18
perfecting holiness in the *f* 2Cor 7:1
one to another in the *f*.........Eph 5:21
singleness of heart, *f*..........Col 3:22
F God. Honor the king 1Pet 2:17
that *f* him, both small.........Rev 19:5

FEARLESSNESS—*without fear*

Source of:
Believing God's promise. .Num 13:30
Challenge of duty ....Ex 32:26-29
Regard for God's holiness................Num 25:1-9
Believing God...........Acts 27:22-26

Exemplified by:
Abram ....Gen 14:14-16
Jonathan................1Sam 14:6-14
David 1Sam 17:34-37
Nehemiah...............Neh 4:1-23
Hebrew men ....Dan 3:16-30
Peter and John ....Acts 4:13
Paul....................Acts 21:10-14

FEAST—*a periodic religious observance commemorating an important moment from the past; an elaborate meal*

[*also* FEASTING, FEASTS]
Abraham made a great *f*......Gen 21:8
place, and made a *f* ....Gen 29:22
we must hold a *f* unto ....Ex 10:9
ye shall keep it a *f* to ....Ex 12:14
shall keep it a *f* by an ....Ex 12:14
day shall be a *f* ....Ex 13:6
Tomorrow is a *f* to the.........Ex 32:5
thou shalt observe the *f*.......Ex 34:22
f of ingathering at the ....Ex 34:22
Concerning the *f* of the ....Lev 23:2
even these are my *f* ....Lev 23:2
in your solemn *f*, to ....Num 15:3
of this month is the *f* ....Num 28:17
thou shalt keep the *f* of ....Deut 16:10
shalt rejoice in thy *f* ....Deut 16:14
in the *f* of unleavened ....Deut 16:16
f of weeks, and in the *f*.......Deut 16:16
Samson made there a *f* ....Judg 14:10
seven days, while their *f* ......Judg 14:17
that were with him a *f*.........2Sam 3:20
and made a *f* to all his........1Kin 3:15
and on the set *f*, by 1Chr 23:31
and on the solemn *f* of.........2Chr 2:4
the king in the *f*..............2Chr 5:3
Solomon kept the *f* seven 2Chr 7:8
f of unleavened bread.........2Chr 8:13
and in the *f* of weeks 2Chr 8:13
in the *f* of tabernacles 2Chr 8:13
kept the *f* of unleavened 2Chr 30:21
and for the set *f*..............2Chr 31:3
f of unleavened bread.........2Chr 35:17
and of all the set *f* of ....Ezra 3:5
kept the *f* of unleavened ......Ezra 6:22
in booths in the *f*.............Neh 8:14
the set *f*, and for the ....Neh 10:33
the queen made a *f*............Esth 1:9
king made a great *f*...........Esth 2:18
even Esther's *f* ....Esth 2:18
made it a day of *f* ....Esth 9:17
made it a day of *f* ....Esth 9:18
make them days of *f*...........Esth 9:22
when the days of their *f*.......Job 1:5
mockers in *f* ....Ps 35:16
on our solemn *f* day ....Ps 81:3
hath a continual *f* ....Prov 15:15
to go to the house of *f*.........Eccl 7:2
A *f* is made for laughter ......Eccl 10:19
your appointed *f* my soul .....Is 1:14
unto all people a *f* of fat ......Is 25:6
f of wines on the lees ....Is 25:6
go into the house of *f*.........Jer 16:8
I will make their *f*............Jer 51:39
none come to the solemn *f*.....Lam 1:4
as in the day of a solemn *f*....Lam 2:7
in her solemn *f*...............Ezek 36:38
the passover, a *f* of seven .....Ezek 45:21
in the solemn *f*...............Ezek 46:9
the king made a great *f* ....Dan 5:1
her *f* days, her new ....Hos 2:11
all her solemn *f* ....Hos 2:11
days of the solemn *f* ....Hos 12:9
I hate, I despise your *f* ....Amos 5:21
I will turn your *f* into ....Amos 8:10
keep thy solemn *f* ....Nah 1:15

and cheerful *f* . . . . .Zech 8:19
and to keep the *f* of . . . . .Zech 14:16
of your solemn *f* . . . . .Mal 2:3
uppermost rooms at *f* . . . . .Matt 23:6
two days is the *f* of the . . . . . . .Matt 26:2
day of the *f* of unleavened . . . .Matt 26:17
uppermost rooms at *f* . . . . .Mark 12:39
two days was the *f* of . . . . .Mark 14:1
at that *f* he released . . . . .Mark 15:6
every year at the *f* of . . . . .Luke 2:41
made him a great *f* . . . . .Luke 5:29
and the chief rooms at *f* . . . . . .Luke 20:46
the *f* of unleavened bread . . . . .Luke 22:1
governor of the *f* . . . . .John 2:8
When the ruler of the *f* . . . . . . .John 2:9
the governor of the *f* . . . . .John 2:9
at Jerusalem at the *f* . . . . .John 4:45
also went unto the *f* . . . . .John 4:45
a *f* of the Jews, was nigh . . . . . .John 6:4
Go ye up unto this *f* . . . . .John 7:8
I go not up yet unto this *f* . . . .John 7:8
sought him at the *f* . . . . .John 7:11
Jerusalem the *f* of the . . . . .John 10:22
were come to the *f* . . . . .John 12:12
need of against the *f* . . . . .John 13:29
means keep this *f* . . . . .Acts 18:21
deceivings while they *f* 2Pet 2:13
are spots in your *f* of . . . . .Jude 12
of charity, when they *f* . . . . .Jude 12

FEASTS, HEBREW—*festivals that commemorated the great events of Israel's history*

Three annual:
Passover . . . . .Lev 23:5-8
Weeks (Pentecost) . . . . . . .Ex 23:16
Tabernacle . . . . .Lev 23:34-44

Purposes of:
Unify the nation . . . . .Deut 12:5-14
Worship God . . . . .Ex 5:1
Illustrate spiritual truths . .John 7:37-39
Foretell the Messiah 1Cor 11:23-26

Brief history of:
Pre-Sinaitic observance . . .Ex 12:1-27
Three instituted at Sinai. .Ex 23:14-17
Celebrated in the wilderness . . . . .Num 9:3-5
Again at beginning of conquest . . . . .Josh 5:10, 11
At dedication of Temple. .1Kin 8:2, 65
"Dedication" introduced by Solomon 2Chr 7:9-11
Idolatrous counterfeits introduced by Jeroboam 1Kin 12:27-33
Observed in Hezekiah's reign 2Chr 30:1
Perversion of, by Jews . . .Is 1:13, 14
Restored in Josiah's reformation 2Kin 23:22, 23
Failure in, cause of exile. .2Chr 36:20, 21
Restored after the exile . .Ezra 3:4
Purim instituted by Mordecai . . . . .Esth 9:17-32
Christ attends . . . . .John 2:23
John 13:1
Christ fulfills the Passover.1Cor 5:8
Christianity begins with Pentecost . . . . .Acts 2:1-41
All fulfilled in Christ 2Cor 3:3-18

FEASTS, SOCIAL—*secular celebrations*

Worldly, occasions of:
Idolatry . . . . .Ex 32:6
Drunkenness 1Sam 25:36
Proud display . . . . .Esth 1:1-8
Profane carousals . . . . .Dan 5:1-16
Licentiousness . . . . .Mark 6:21, 22

Proper, occasions of:
Refreshment . . . . .Gen 19:1-3
Reconciliation . . . . .Gen 31:54, 55
Reunion . . . . .Gen 43:16-34
Restoration . . . . .Luke 15:22-24
See ENTERTAINMENT

FEATHERS—*the outer covering, or plumage, of birds*

[*also* FEATHERED]
his crop with his *f* . . . . .Lev 1:16
wings and *f* unto the . . . . .Job 39:13
her *f* with yellow gold . . . . .Ps 68:13
f fowls like as the sand . . . . . .Ps 78:27
cover thee with his *f* . . . . .Ps 91:4
longwinged, full of *f* . . . . .Ezek 17:3
Speak unto every *f* fowl . . . . . .Ezek 39:17
grown like eagles' *f* . . . . .Dan 4:33

FEEBLE—*weak*

[*also* FEEBLEMINDED, FEEBLENESS, FEEBLER]
when the cattle were *f* . . . . . . .Gen 30:42
so the *f* were Laban's . . . . .Gen 30:42
even all that were *f* . . . . .Deut 25:18
children is waxed *f* 1Sam 2:5
his hands were *f*, and 2Sam 4:1
and carried all the *f* of 2Chr 28:15
What do these *f* Jews? . . . . .Neh 4:2
hast strengthened the *f* . . . . . . .Job 4:4
I am *f* and sore broken . . . . . . .Ps 38:8
conies are but a *f* folk . . . . .Prov 30:26
shall be very small and *f* . . . . . .Is 16:14
our hands wax *f* . . . . .Jer 6:24
to their children for *f* . . . . .Jer 47:3
and his hands waxed *f* . . . . .Jer 50:43
All hands shall be *f*, and . . . . . .Ezek 7:17
and he that is *f* among . . . . .Zech 12:8
which seem to be more *f* 1Cor 12:22
comfort the *f*, support 1Thess 5:14
hang down, and the *f* . . . . .Heb 12:12

FEED—*food; to eat*

Used naturally of:
Food for men 2Sam 19:33
Food for animals . . . . .Gen 30:36
God's provision . . . . .Matt 6:26

Used figuratively of:
Instruction and care 2Sam 5:2
Messiah . . . . .Ezek 34:23
Good deeds . . . . .Matt 25:37
Supernatural supply . . . . . .Rev 12:6
Elemental teaching 1Cor 3:2
Change of nature . . . . .Is 11:7
Corruption . . . . .Ps 49:14
Vanity . . . . .Hos 12:1

[*also* FED, FEEDEST, FEEDETH, FEEDING]
F me, I pray thee, with . . . . . . .Gen 25:30
I will again *f* and keep . . . . .Gen 30:31
as he *f* the asses of . . . . .Gen 36:24
was *f* the flock with his . . . . . . .Gen 37:2
favored; and they *f* in a . . . . . . .Gen 41:18
trade hath been to *f* . . . . .Gen 46:32
the God who *f* me all . . . . .Gen 48:15
I have *f* you in the . . . . .Ex 16:32
shall *f* in another man's . . . . . . .Ex 22:5
to hunger, and *f* thee . . . . .Deut 8:3
Saul to *f* his father's 1Sam 17:15
to *f* my people Israel 2Sam 7:7
put them in ward and *f* 2Sam 20:3
the ravens to *f* thee 1Kin 17:4
and *f* them with bread 1Kin 18:4
Thou shalt *f* my people 1Chr 11:2
over the herds that *f* in 1Chr 27:29
and *f* him with bread 2Chr 18:26
plowing, and the asses *f* . . . . . . .Job 1:14
take away flocks, and *f* . . . . . . .Job 24:2
f them also, and lift . . . . .Ps 28:9
verily thou shalt be *f* . . . . .Ps 37:3
brought him to *f* Jacob . . . . .Ps 78:71
f them with the bread . . . . .Ps 80:5
He should have *f* them . . . . .Ps 81:16
of the righteous *f* . . . . .Prov 10:21
mouth of fools *f* on . . . . .Prov 15:14
loveth, where thou *f* . . . . .Song 1:7
f thy kids beside the . . . . .Song 1:8
I am his: he *f* among . . . . .Song 2:16
beds of spices, to *f* in the . . . . .Song 6:2
rams and the fat of *f* . . . . .Is 1:11
the lambs *f* after their . . . . .Is 5:17
of the poor shall *f* . . . . .Is 14:30
shall thy cattle *f* in large . . . . . .Is 30:23

He *f* on ashes: a deceived . . . . .Is 44:20
They shall *f* in the ways . . . . . . .Is 49:9
f thee with the heritage . . . . . . .Is 58:14
wolf and the lamb shall *f* . . . . . .Is 65:25
which shall *f* you with . . . . .Jer 3:15
when I had *f* them to . . . . .Jer 5:7
I will *f* them, even this . . . . .Jer 9:15
over them which shall *f* . . . . . . .Jer 23:4
he shall *f* on Carmel . . . . .Jer 50:19
that did *f* delicately . . . . .Lam 4:5
honey, wherewith I *f* . . . . .Ezek 16:19
Israel that do *f* . . . . .Ezek 34:2
but ye *f* not the flock . . . . .Ezek 34:3
but the shepherds *f* . . . . .Ezek 34:8
and *f* not my flock . . . . .Ezek 34:8
them to cease from *f* . . . . .Ezek 34:10
and *f* them upon the . . . . .Ezek 34:13
I will *f* them in a good . . . . .Ezek 34:14
pasture they shall *f* . . . . .Ezek 34:14
I will *f* them with . . . . .Ezek 34:16
and all flesh was *f* of it . . . . . . .Dan 4:12
that *f* of the portion of . . . . .Dan 11:26
the Lord will *f* them as . . . . . . .Hos 4:16
Ephraim *f* on wind, and . . . . . .Hos 12:1
let them not *f*, nor . . . . .Jon 3:7
and *f* in the strength of . . . . . . .Mic 5:4
F thy people with thy . . . . .Mic 7:14
let them *f* in Bashan . . . . .Mic 7:14
they shall *f* thereupon . . . . .Zeph 2:7
F the flock of the . . . . .Zech 11:4
and I *f* the flock . . . . .Zech 11:7
Then said I, I will not *f* . . . . . . .Zech 11:9
herd of many swine *f* . . . . .Matt 8:30
great herd of swine *f* . . . . .Mark 5:11
they that *f* the swine fled . . . . .Mark 5:14
many swine *f* on the . . . . .Luke 8:32
they that *f* them saw . . . . .Luke 8:34
and God *f* them: how . . . . .Luke 12:24
him into his fields to *f* . . . . .Luke 15:15
desiring to be *f* with the . . . . . .Luke 16:21
He saith unto him, *F* my . . . . . .John 21:15
Jesus saith unto him, *F* . . . . . . .John 21:17
to *f* the church of God . . . . .Acts 20:28
enemy hunger, *f* him . . . . .Rom 12:20
who *f* a flock, and eateth 1Cor 9:7
bestow all my goods to *f* 1Cor 13:3
f themselves without . . . . .Jude 12
the throne shall *f* . . . . .Rev 7:17

FEEDING PLACE—*pasture*
and the *f* of the young . . . . .Nah 2:11

FEEL—*to touch; perceive*

[*also* FEELING, FELT]
will *f* me and I shall . . . . .Gen 27:12
and he *f* him, and said . . . . .Gen 27:22
darkness which may be *f* . . . . . .Ex 10:21
Suffer me that I may *f* . . . . .Judg 16:26
shall not *f* quietness in . . . . .Job 20:20
Before your pots can *f* . . . . .Ps 58:9
I *f* it not: when shall I . . . . .Prov 23:35
commandment shall *f* . . . . .Eccl 8:5
f in her body that she . . . . .Mark 5:29
if haply they might *f* after . . . . .Acts 17:27
beast into the fire, and *f* . . . . . . .Acts 28:5

FEET—*See* FEET

FEIGN—*to give a false appearance of*

[*also* FEIGNED, FEIGNEDLY, FEIGNEST]
and *f* himself mad in 1Sam 21:13
thee, *f* thyself to be a 2Sam 14:2
f herself to be another 1Kin 14:5
why *f* thou thyself to 1Kin 14:6
thou *f* them out of thine . . . . . . .Neh 6:8
goeth not out of *f* lips . . . . .Ps 17:1
her whole heart, but *f* . . . . .Jer 3:10
spies which should *f* . . . . .Luke 20:20
with *f* words make 2Pet 2:3

FELIX (fē'lĭks)—*"happy"*
Governor of Judaea . . . . .Acts 23:24, 26
Letter addressed to . . . . . .Acts 23:25-30
Paul's defense before . . . .Acts 24:1-21
Convicted, but unchanged.Acts 24:22-25
Subject to bribery . . . . . . .Acts 24:26, 27

[*also* FELIX'S]
Festus came into *F* room ...... Acts 24:27
man left in bonds by *F* .... Acts 25:14

FELL—*to cut; knock down*

[*also* FELLED, FELLEST, FELLING]
wicked men, so *f* thou 2Sam 3:34
f all the good trees 2Kin 3:25
one was *f* a beam 2Kin 6:5

FELLER—*one who cuts down trees*
no *f* is come up against .... Is 14:8

FELLOES—*obsolete word meaning rims*
Of wheels 1Kin 7:33

FELLOW—*one's peer; companion*

[*also* FELLOW'S, FELLOWS]
smitest thou thy *f*? .... Ex 2:13
told a dream unto his *f* .... Judg 7:13
sword against his *f* .... Judg 7:22
virginity, I and my *f* .... Judg 11:37
was against his *f* 1Sam 14:20
have brought this *f* to 1Sam 21:15
shall this *f* come into 1Sam 21:15
Make this *f* return, that 1Sam 29:4
caught every one his *f* by 2Sam 2:16
thrust his sword in his *f* 2Sam 2:16
as one of the vain *f* 2Sam 6:20
Put this *f* in the prison 1Kin 22:27
came this mad *f* 2Kin 9:11
Put this *f* in the prison 2Chr 18:26
gladness above thy *f* .... Ps 45:7
the one will lift up his *f* ...... Eccl 4:10
satyr shall cry to his *f* .... Is 34:14
Behold, all his *f* shall be ...... Is 44:11
tribes of Israel his *f* .... Ezek 37:19
sought Daniel and his *f* .... Dan 2:13
more stout than his *f* .... Dan 7:20
every one to his *f* .... Jon 1:7
thou, and thy *f* .... Zech 3:8
man that is my *f* .... Zech 13:7
calling unto their *f* .... Matt 11:16
This *f* doth not cast out .... Matt 12:24
This *f* said, I am able to ...... Matt 26:61
This *f* was also with .... Matt 26:71
a truth this *f* also .... Luke 22:59
We found this *f* .... Luke 23:2
as for this *f*, we know .... John 9:29
certain lewd *f* of the .... Acts 17:5
Saying, This *f* persuadeth ..... Acts 18:13
Away with such a *f* from ...... Acts 22:22
this man a pestilent *f* .... Acts 24:5
gladness above thy *f* .... Heb 1:9

FELLOW CITIZENS
With the saints .... Eph 2:19

FELLOW COUNTRYMAN
Shall not hate .... Lev 19:17
Becomes poor .... Lev 25:25
Judge righteously .... Deut 1:16
Lord gives rest .... Deut 3:20
Save some .... Rom 11:14

FELLOW DISCIPLES
Didymus, unto his *f d*, Let .... John 11:16

FELLOW HEIRS
Gentiles should be *f h* .... Eph 3:6

FELLOW HELPER

[*also* FELLOW HELPERS]
partner and *f h* concerning 2Cor 8:23
that we might be *f h* to the ... 3John 8

FELLOW LABORER

[*also* FELLOW LABORERS]
also, and with other my *f l* .... Phil 4:3
our *f l* in the gospel of 1Thess 3:2
our dearly beloved, and *f l* .... Philem 1
Demas, Lucas, my *f l* .... Philem 24

FELLOW PRISONER

[*also* FELLOW PRISONERS]
my kinsmen, and my *f f* .... Rom 16:7
Aristarchus my *f f* saluteth .... Col 4:10
my *f f* in Christ Jesus .... Philem 23

FELLOW SERVANT
Were to be killed .... Rev 6:11
Who hold fast the testimony of Jesus ..... Rev 19:10
Who heed the words ..... Rev 22:9

[*also* FELLOW SERVANTS]
found one of his *f s* .... Matt 18:28
And his *f s* fell down at .... Matt 18:29
Epaphras our dear *f s*, who ... Col 1:7

FELLOW SLAVE
Who owed a hundred denarii .... Matt 18:28-33
Evil slave beats .... Matt 24:48, 49

FELLOW SOLDIER
in labor, and *f s* .... Phil 2:25
Archippus our *f s*, and .... Philem 2

FELLOW WORKERS
In the truth 3John 8
In the kingdom .... Col 4:11
Prisca and Aquila described as .... Rom 16:3
Urbanas .... Rom 16:9
Timothy .... Rom 16:21
Paul 1Cor 3:1-9
Titus 2Cor 8:23
Epaphroditus .... Phil 2:25
Philemon .... Philem 1
Marcus. Aristarchus, Demas, Lucas .... Philem 24

FELLOWSHIP—*sharing together*

Based upon common:
Purpose .... Ps 133:1-3
Belief .... Acts 2:42
Conviction 2Pet 3:8
Work .... Neh 4:1-23
Hope .... Heb 11:39, 40
Faith 1Sam 20:30-42
Suffering .... Dan 3:16-30
Need 2Cor 8:1-15

Persons sharing together:
Father, the Son, and Christians 1John 1:3
Christ and Christians 1Cor 1:9
Holy Spirit and Christians. Phil 2:1
Apostles .... Acts 2:42
Believers 1John 1:7

Things shared together:
Material things 2Cor 8:4
Suffering .... Phil 3:10
The Gospel ministry ..... Gal 2:9
Gospel privileges .... Phil 1:5
Gospel mystery .... Eph 3:9

in *f*, or in a thing taken .... Lev 6:2
of iniquity have *f* with .... Ps 94:20
that ye should have *f* with 1Cor 10:20
f hath righteousness 2Cor 6:14
And have no *f* with the .... Eph 5:11
If we say that we have *f* 1John 1:6

FEMALE—*a girl or woman; the sex that bears the young*
male and *f* created he them ... Gen 1:27
Male and *f* created he them ... Gen 5:2
they shall be male and *f* ...... Gen 6:19
sevens, the male and his *f* .... Gen 7:2
two, the male and his *f* .... Gen 7:2
sevens, the male and the *f* .... Gen 7:3
ark, the male and the *f* .... Gen 7:9
went in male and *f* of all ...... Gen 7:16
whether it be a male or *f* ..... Lev 3:1
of the goats, a *f* without ...... Lev 4:28
f from the flock, a lamb ...... Lev 5:6
if it be a *f*, then thy .... Lev 27:4
the *f* thy estimation .... Lev 27:6
Both male and *f* shall ye ...... Num 5:3
the likeness of male or *f* ...... Deut 4:16
made them male and *f* .... Matt 19:4
made them male and *f* .... Mark 10:6
there is neither male nor *f* .... Gal 3:28

FENCE—*means of protection; barrier preventing escape or intrusion*

[*also* FENCED]
ones shall dwell in the *f* .... Num 32:17
thy high and *f* walls .... Deut 28:52
of them entered into *f* .... Josh 10:20
touch them must be *f* 2Sam 23:7
shall smite every *f* 2Kin 3:19
of the watchmen to the *f* 2Kin 17:9
come up against all the *f* 2Kin 18:13
the king put in the *f* 2Chr 17:19
f me with bones and .... Job 10:11
f up my way that I .... Job 19:8
and as a tottering *f* .... Ps 62:3
tower, and upon every *f* ...... Is 2:15
And he *f* it, and gathered ..... Is 5:2
shall impoverish thy *f* .... Jer 5:17
cities are become *f* .... Ezek 36:35
alarm against the *f* .... Zeph 1:16

FENCED CITIES—*walled cities*
Means of protection 2Sam 20:6
Mighty and strong .... Deut 9:1
Conquerable .... Deut 3:5
Utterly destroyed 2Kin 3:19, 25
No substitute for God ... Hos 8:14

the *f c* are Ziddim .... Josh 19:35
f c, and of country 1Sam 6:18
f c, with walls, gates 2Chr 8:5
unto every *f c*: and he 2Chr 11:23
And he built *f c* in 2Chr 14:6
things, with *f c* in 2Chr 21:3
war in all the *f c* 2Chr 33:14
take the most *f c* .... Dan 11:15

FENS—*low lands covered partly or wholly with water*
covert of the reed, and *f* ...... Job 40:21

FERRET—*an unclean animal*
Either the gecho (wall lizard) or the field mouse .... Lev 11:30

FERRYBOATS—*a boat used to carry people or objects across a body of water*
David's use of 2Sam 19:16-18

FERVENT—*earnest*

[*also* FERVENTLY]
being *f* in the spirit, he .... Acts 18:25
f in spirit; serving the .... Rom 12:11
your *f* mind toward me 2Cor 7:7
laboring *f* for you in .... Col 4:12
f prayer of a righteous .... James 5:16
with a pure heart *f* 1Pet 1:22
have *f* charity among 1Pet 4:8
shall melt with *f* 2Pet 3:10
shall melt with *f* 2Pet 3:12

FESTUS (fĕs'tŭs)—*"swine-like"—successor of Felix*
Governor of Judaea ...... Acts 24:27
Paul's defense made to ... Acts 25:1-22

[*also* FESTUS']
and *F* said, King Agrippa ..... Acts 25:24
F said with a loud voice ..... Acts 26:24
not mad, most noble *F* .... Acts 26:25
said Agrippa unto *F* .... Acts 26:32

FETCH—*to bring or take back*

[*also* FETCHED, FETCHETH, FETCHT]
Let a little water..be *f* .... Gen 18:4
And I will *f* a morsel of .... Gen 18:5
and *f* a calf tender and .... Gen 18:7
obey my voice, and go *f* .... Gen 27:13
let him *f* your brother .... Gen 42:16
she sent her maid to *f* it ...... Ex 2:5
we *f* you water out of this ..... Num 20:10
his hand *f* a stroke with .... Deut 19:5
city shall send and *f* .... Deut 19:12
into his house to *f* his .... Deut 24:10
not go again to *f* .... Deut 24:19
and *f* a compass to .... Josh 15:3
elders of Gilead went to *f* ..... Judg 11:5
f the carved image, the .... Judg 18:18
Let us *f* the ark of the 1Sam 4:3
and *f* up the ark of the 1Sam 7:1
Send and *f* him; for we 1Sam 16:11

come over and *f* 1Sam 26:22
though they would have *f* 2Sam 4:6
but *f* a compass behind 2Sam 5:23
sent and *f* her to his 2Sam 11:27
To *f* about this form of 2Sam 14:20
king Solomon sent and *f* 1Kin 7:13
F me, I pray thee, a little 1Kin 17:10
they *f* a compass of 2Kin 3:9
I may send and *f* him 2Kin 6:13
And they *f* up, and 2Chr 1:17
F quickly Micaiah the 2Chr 18:8
and *f* olive branches .... Neh 8:15
I will *f* my knowledge .... Job 36:3
I will *f* wine, and we .... Is 56:12
they *f* forth Urijah out .... Jer 26:23
king sent Jehudi to *f* .... Jer 36:21
come themselves and *f* .... Acts 16:37
from thence we *f* a compass .... Acts 28:13

FETTERS—*shackle for binding the feet*

Used literally of:
Imprisonment .... Ps 105:18
Bondage .... Luke 8:29

Used figuratively of:
Trouble .... Job 36:8
Subjection .... Ps 149:8

and bound him with *f* .... Judg 16:21
nor thy feet put into *f* 2Sam 3:34
and bound him with *f* 2Kin 25:7
and bound him with *f* 2Chr 33:11
often bound with *f* and .... Mark 5:4
the *f* broken in pieces .... Mark 5:4

FETUS—*unborn child*
Protected by law .... Ex 21:22
Possesses sin nature .... Ps 51:5
Fashioned by God .... Ps 139:13-16
Called by God .... Is 49:1
Jer 1:5
Active .... Luke 1:41

FEVER—*abnormally high body temperature*
Sent as a judgment .... Deut 28:22
Rebuked by Christ .... Luke 4:38, 39
Healed by Paul .... Acts 28:8

laid, and sick of a *f* .... Matt 8:14
mother lay sick of a *f* .... Mark 1:30
at the seventh hour the *f* .... John 4:52

FEW—*not many*
Days .... Gen 47:9
Do not determine God's power 1Sam 14:6
Words in prayer .... Eccl 5:2
The saved .... Matt 7:14
Gospel messengers .... Matt 9:37
The chosen .... Matt 22:14

[*also* FEWER, FEWEST, FEWNESS]
abide with us a *f* days .... Gen 24:55
unto him but a *f* days .... Gen 29:20
I being *f* in number, they .... Gen 34:30
according to the *f* of years .... Lev 25:16
if there remain but *f* .... Lev 25:52
when the cloud was a *f* .... Num 9:20
and to *f* thou shalt give .... Num 26:54
and to the *f* ye shall give .... Num 33:54
from them that have *f* .... Num 35:8
and ye shall be left *f* in .... Deut 4:27
ye were the *f* of all people .... Deut 7:7
And ye shall be left *f* in .... Deut 28:62
for they are but *f* .... Josh 7:3
hast thou left those *f* 1Sam 17:28
borrow not a *f* 2Kin 4:3
When ye were but *f*, even 1Chr 16:19
even a *f*, and strangers 1Chr 16:19
the priests were too *f* 2Chr 29:34
I and some *f* men with me .... Neh 2:12
but the people were *f* .... Neh 7:4
Are not my days *f*? Cease .... Job 10:20
When a *f* years are come .... Job 16:22
When they were but a *f* .... Ps 105:12
very *f*, and strangers .... Ps 105:12

Let his days be *f*: and .... Ps 109:8
let thy words be *f* .... Eccl 5:2
because they are *f* .... Eccl 12:3
cut off nations not a *f* .... Is 10:7
earth are burned, and *f* .... Is 24:6
they shall not be *f* .... Jer 30:19
always take thereof a *f* in .... Ezek 5:3
f days he shall be .... Dan 11:20
Seven, and a *f* little fishes .... Matt 15:34
many be called but *f* .... Matt 20:16
faithful over a *f* .... Matt 25:21
he laid hands upon a *f* .... Mark 6:5
they had a *f* small .... Mark 8:7
but the laborers are *f* .... Luke 10:2
shall be beaten with *f* .... Luke 12:48
Lord, are there *f* that be .... Luke 13:23
chief women not a *f* .... Acts 17:4
us of thy clemency a *f* .... Acts 24:4
as I wrote afore in *f* .... Eph 3:3
verily for a *f* days .... Heb 12:10
wherein *f*, that is, eight 1Pet 3:20
But I have a *f* things .... Rev 2:14
I have a *f* things against .... Rev 2:20
Thou hast a *f* names even .... Rev 3:4

FIDELITY—*faithfulness in the performance of duty*
In finances 2Kin 12:15
In industry 2Chr 34:11, 12
Seen in Joseph .... Gen 39:6
Seen in Daniel .... Dan 6:1-3, 28

but showing all good *f* .... Titus 2:10

FIELD—*open or cleared land*

Used literally of:
Cultivated land .... Gen 47:20
A city .... Ps 78:12, 43

Laws regarding:
Fires .... Ex 22:6
Mixed seed .... Lev 19:19
Coveting others' .... Deut 5:21
Destruction of trees .... Deut 20:19, 20
Total harvest of .... Deut 24:19-22
Sabbath rest .... Lev 25:3-12
Redemption of .... Lev 27:16-24
Title of .... Ruth 4:5-11

Figurative of:
World .... Matt 13:38, 44
Harvest of souls .... John 4:35

[*also* FIELDS]
every plant of the *f* before .... Gen 2:5
every herb of the *f* .... Gen 2:5
to every beast of the *f* .... Gen 2:20
every beast of the *f* .... Gen 3:14
when they were in the *f* .... Gen 4:8
the *f* give I thee, and the .... Gen 23:11
And the *f* of Ephron .... Gen 23:17
the *f*, and the cave .... Gen 23:17
that were in the *f* .... Gen 23:17
the *f*, and the cave that .... Gen 23:20
that walketh in the *f* .... Gen 24:65
The *f* which Abraham .... Gen 25:10
Esau came from the *f* .... Gen 25:29
And Esau went to the *f* .... Gen 27:5
son is as the smell of a *f* .... Gen 27:27
and behold a well in the *f* .... Gen 29:2
Jacob came out of the *f* .... Gen 30:16
he bought a parcel of a *f* .... Gen 33:19
sons..came out of the *f* .... Gen 34:7
smote Midian in the *f* .... Gen 36:35
wandering in the *f* .... Gen 37:15
the food of the *f*, which .... Gen 41:48
seed of the *f*, and for .... Gen 47:24
cave that is in the *f* .... Gen 49:30
with the *f* of Ephron .... Gen 49:30
the cave of the *f* of .... Gen 50:13
bought with the *f* .... Gen 50:13
villages, and out of the *f* .... Ex 8:13
cattle which is in the *f* .... Ex 9:3
all that thou hast in the *f* .... Ex 9:19
shall be found in the *f* .... Ex 9:19
all that was in the *f*, both .... Ex 9:25
every herb of the *f* .... Ex 9:25

brake every tree of the *f* .... Ex 9:25
or in the herbs of the *f* .... Ex 10:15
If a man shall cause a *f* .... Ex 22:5
feed in another man's *f* .... Ex 22:5
of the best of his own *f* .... Ex 22:5
of beasts in the *f* .... Ex 22:31
hast sown in the *f* .... Ex 23:16
in thy labors out of the *f* .... Ex 23:16
loose into the open *f* .... Lev 14:7
the city into the open *f* .... Lev 14:53
the corners of thy *f* .... Lev 19:9
the corners of thy *f* .... Lev 23:22
neither sow thy *f* .... Lev 25:4
the *f* of the suburbs of .... Lev 25:34
is not of the *f* of his .... Lev 27:22
us inheritance of *f* .... Num 16:14
not pass through the *f* .... Num 20:17
the grass of the *f* .... Num 22:4
brought him into the *f* .... Num 23:14
house, his *f*, or his .... Deut 5:21
I will send grass in thy *f* .... Deut 11:15
the *f* bringeth forth year .... Deut 14:22
lying in the *f*, and it be .... Deut 21:1
For he found her in the *f* .... Deut 22:27
thine harvest in thy *f* .... Deut 24:19
forgot a sheaf in the *f* .... Deut 24:19
shalt thou be in the *f* .... Deut 28:16
of the *f* of Gomorrah .... Deut 32:32
of Ai in the *f* .... Josh 8:24
to ask of her father a *f* .... Josh 15:18
the *f* of the city, and the .... Josh 21:12
to ask of her father a *f* .... Judg 1:14
in the high places of the *f* .... Judg 5:18
went out into the *f* .... Judg 9:27
went out into the *f* .... Judg 9:42
as she sat in the *f* .... Judg 13:9
other to Gibeah in the *f* .... Judg 20:31
Let me now go to the *f* .... Ruth 2:2
gleaned in the *f* after .... Ruth 2:3
part of the *f* belonging .... Ruth 2:3
on the *f* that they do .... Ruth 2:9
not in any other *f* .... Ruth 2:22
of the army in the *f* 1Sam 4:2
this day in the *f* 1Sam 6:18
take your *f*, and your 1Sam 8:14
trembling..in the *f* 1Sam 14:15
my father in the *f* 1Sam 19:3
us go out into the *f* 1Sam 20:11
went out..into the *f* 1Sam 20:11
went out into the *f* 1Sam 20:35
every one of you give *f* 1Sam 22:7
when we were in the *f* 1Sam 25:15
rain, upon you, nor *f* of 2Sam 1:21
by themselves in the *f* 2Sam 10:8
strove together in the *f* 2Sam 14:6
See, Joab's *f* is near mine 2Sam 14:30
set the *f* on fire 2Sam 14:30
thy servants set my *f* 2Sam 14:31
of her whelps in the *f* 2Sam 17:8
highway into the *f* 2Sam 20:12
unto thine own *f* 1Kin 2:26
were alone in the *f* 1Kin 11:29
dieth of his in the *f* 1Kin 16:4
him that dieth in the *f* 1Kin 21:24
went out into the *f* to 2Kin 4:39
all the fruits of the *f* 2Kin 8:6
the *f* in the portion of 2Kin 9:37
as the grass of the *f* 2Kin 19:26
Jerusalem in the *f* of 2Kin 23:4
smote Midian in the *f* of 1Chr 1:46
the *f* of the city, and the 1Chr 6:56
storehouses in the *f*, in 1Chr 27:25
did the work of the *f* 1Chr 27:26
the *f* of the burial which 2Chr 26:23
which were in the *f* of 2Chr 31:19
the villages, with their *f* .... Neh 11:25
of the *f* of Geba and .... Neh 12:29
fled every one to his *f* .... Neh 13:10
waters upon the *f* .... Job 5:10
with the stones of the *f* .... Job 5:23
reap..corn in the *f* .... Job 24:6
the beasts of the *f* .... Ps 8:7
the wild beast of the *f* .... Ps 80:13
flower of the *f*, so he .... Ps 103:15
sow the *f*, and plant .... Ps 107:37

had not made..the f ....Prov 8:26
for thyself in the f ....Prov 24:27
I went by the f of the........Prov 24:30
are the price of the f ....Prov 27:26
She considereth a f, and ......Prov 31:16
is served by the f........Eccl 5:9
by the hinds of the f........Song 2:7
go forth into the f........Song 7:11
that lay f to f........Is 5:8
and of his fruitful f........Is 10:18
For the f of Heshbon........Is 16:8
turned into a fruitful f........Is 29:17
be a fruitful f........Is 32:15
the fruitful f be counted......Is 32:15
remain in the fruitful f........Is 32:16
the grass of the f........Is 37:27
The beast of the f shall......Is 43:20
ye beasts of the f, come......Is 56:9
As keepers of a f, are......Jer 4:17
with their f and wives........Jer 6:12
upon the trees of the f........Jer 7:20
and the herbs of every f......Jer 12:4
abominations..in the f........Jer 13:27
hind also calved in the f......Jer 14:5
O my mountain in the f........Jer 17:3
shall be plowed like a f........Jer 26:18
the beasts of the f have........Jer 27:6
Buy thee my f that is in........Jer 32:7
And I bought the f of........Jer 32:9
Houses and f and........Jer 32:15
Buy thee the f for money......Jer 32:25
Men shall buy f for........Jer 32:44
have we vineyard, nor f........Jer 35:9
which were in the f........Jer 40:7
taken from the plentiful f......Jer 48:33
of the fruits of the f........Lam 4:9
he that is in the f shall die......Ezek 7:15
the bud of the f........Ezek 16:7
planted it in a fruitful f........Ezek 17:5
all the trees of the f shall......Ezek 17:24
which are in the f........Ezek 26:6
beasts of the f and to........Ezek 29:5
fall upon the open f........Ezek 29:5
all the trees of the f........Ezek 31:5
beasts of the f shall be........Ezek 31:13
forth upon the open f........Ezek 32:4
to all the beasts of the f......Ezek 34:5
tree of the f shall yield........Ezek 34:27
the beasts of the f........Ezek 38:20
fall upon the open f........Ezek 39:5
and to every beast of the f......Ezek 39:17
the beasts of the f and........Dan 2:38
the tender grass of the f......Dan 4:15
the tender grass of the f......Dan 4:23
with the beasts of the f......Dan 4:23
with the beasts of the f......Dan 4:32
beasts of the f shall eat......Hos 2:12
with the beasts of the f......Hos 4:3
furrows of the f........Hos 12:11
f is wasted, the land........Joel 1:10
all the trees of the f........Joel 1:12
beasts of the f cry also........Joel 1:20
f..and the f of Samaria........Obad 19
as a heap of the f........Mic 1:6
covet f, and take them........Mic 2:2
thou shalt dwell in the f........Mic 4:10
f shall yield no meat........Hab 3:17
every one grass in the f........Zech 10:1
the time in the f........Mal 3:11
Consider the lilies of the f......Matt 6:28
good seed in his f........Matt 13:24
and sowed in his f........Matt 13:31
him which is in the f........Matt 24:18
them the potter's f........Matt 27:7
through the corn f........Mark 2:23
him that is in the f not........Mark 13:16
shepherds abiding in the f......Luke 2:8
through the corn f........Luke 6:1
elder son was in the f........Luke 15:25
he that is in the f, let him......Luke 17:31
look on the f; for they are......John 4:35
purchased a f with the........Acts 1:18
f is called in their proper......Acts 1:19
is to say, The f of blood......Acts 1:19
reaped down your f........James 5:4

FIELD OF BLOOD

A field, predicted in the Old Testament, bought as a cemetery for Judas' burial........Zech 11:12, 13; Matt 27:1-10

FIERCE—*zeal or vehemence; furiously active or determined*

[*also* FIERCER, FIERCENESS]

their anger, for it was f........Gen 49:7
Turn from thy f wrath........Ex 32:12
f anger of the Lord may......Num 25:4
turn from the f of his........Deut 13:17
nation of f countenance......Deut 28:50
turned from the f of his........Josh 7:26
arose from the table in f......1Sam 20:34
words of the men..were f......2Sam 19:43
not from the f of his great......2Kin 23:26
f wrath of the Lord is........2Chr 28:11
that his f wrath may........2Chr 29:10
the f of his wrath may........2Chr 30:8
until the f wrath of our........Ezra 10:14
voice of the f lion, and........Job 4:10
nor the f lion passed by it......Job 28:8
the ground with f........Job 39:24
cast upon them the f of........Ps 78:49
thyself from the f of thine......Ps 85:3
Thy f wrath goeth over........Ps 88:16
the f anger of Rezin with......Is 7:4
and in the day of his f........Is 13:13
Thou shalt not see a f........Is 33:19
f anger of the Lord is not......Jer 4:8
revenues because of the f......Jer 12:13
because of his f anger........Jer 25:38
because of the f of the........Jer 25:38
evil upon them, even my f......Jer 49:37
me in the day of his f........Lam 1:12
he hath poured out his f........Lam 4:11
a king of f countenance........Dan 8:23
not execute the f of mine......Hos 11:9
turn away from his f........Jon 3:9
can abide in the f of his........Nah 1:6
more f than the evening........Hab 1:8
the f anger of the Lord........Zeph 2:2
exceeding f, so that no........Matt 8:28
they were the more f........Luke 23:5
accusers, incontinent f........2Tim 3:3
driven of f winds, yet........James 3:4
of the wine of the f of his......Rev 16:19

FIERY—*burning; blazing*

f serpent, and set it........Num 21:8
make them as a f........Ps 21:9
fruit shall be a f flying........Is 14:29
midst of a burning f........Dan 3:6
midst of a burning f........Dan 3:11
us from the burning f........Dan 3:17
of the burning f........Dan 3:21
of the burning f........Dan 3:23
his throne was like the f......Dan 7:9
all the f darts of the........Eph 6:16
and f indignation, which......Heb 10:27
the f trial which is to........1Pet 4:12

FIERY SERPENTS—*(Exact meaning uncertain)*

Attack Israelites........Num 21:6, 8

were f s, and scorpions......Deut 8:15

FIFTEEN

[*also* FIFTEENTH]

eight hundred and f........Gen 5:10
threescore and f........Gen 25:7
f day of the second month......Ex 16:1
of the gate shall be f........Ex 27:14
side of the gate were f........Ex 38:14
threescore and f shekels........Ex 38:25
f day of the same........Lev 23:6
the f day of the seventh........Lev 23:39
shall be f shekels........Lev 27:7
in the f day of this month......Num 28:17
and threescore and f........Num 31:37
the f day of the first........Num 33:3
about f thousand men, all......Judg 8:10
Ziba had f sons and........2Sam 9:10
forty five pillars, f in a........1Kin 7:3
eighth month, on the f........1Kin 12:32
king of Israel f........2Kin 14:17
In the f year of Amaziah......2Kin 14:23
The f to Bilgah, the........1Chr 24:14
the f year of the reign........2Chr 15:10
Jehoahaz king of Israel f......2Chr 25:25
f day of the same they........Esth 9:18
will add unto thy days f........Is 38:5
in the f day of the month......Ezek 32:17
f shekels, shall be your......Ezek 45:12
to me for f pieces of silver......Hos 3:2
Now in the f year of the......Luke 3:1
unto Jerusalem, about f........John 11:18

FIFTH—*See* FIVE

FIFTY

[*also* FIFTIES, FIFTIETH]

the breadth of it f cubits......Gen 6:15
of the hundred and f........Gen 8:3
nine hundred and f........Gen 9:29
Peradventure there be f........Gen 18:24
spare the place for the f......Gen 18:24
shall lack five of the f........Gen 18:28
rulers of f, and rulers of......Ex 18:21
F loops shalt thou make......Ex 26:5
one curtain, and f loops........Ex 26:5
thou shalt make f taches......Ex 26:6
shalt make f loops on the......Ex 26:10
and f loops in the edge........Ex 26:10
shall be hangings of f........Ex 27:12
and the breadth f every........Ex 27:18
two hundred and f........Ex 30:23
two hundred and f........Ex 30:23
F loops made he in one........Ex 36:12
and f loops made he in........Ex 36:12
f loops upon the........Ex 36:17
and f loops made he........Ex 36:17
were hangings of f........Ex 38:12
and five hundred and f........Ex 38:26
shall ye number f days........Lev 23:16
And ye shall hallow the f......Lev 25:10
be valued at f shekels of......Lev 27:16
f and nine thousand and......Num 1:23
f and four thousand........Num 1:29
f and three thousand........Num 1:43
f and four thousand........Num 2:6
f and nine thousand........Num 2:13
thousand and f........Num 2:16
f and three thousand........Num 2:30
five hundred and f........Num 2:32
until f years old shalt........Num 4:23
even unto f years........Num 4:35
upward even unto f........Num 4:39
two hundred and f........Num 16:2
two hundred and f........Num 16:35
f and two thousand........Num 26:34
f and three thousand........Num 26:47
take one portion of f........Num 31:30
seven hundred and f........Num 31:52
captains over f, and........Deut 1:15
the damsel's father f........Deut 22:29
a wedge of gold of f........Josh 7:21
smote of the people f........1Sam 6:19
captains over f; and will......1Sam 8:12
f men to run before........2Sam 15:1
and f men to run before......1Kin 1:5
length thereof was f........1Kin 7:6
for a hundred and f........1Kin 10:29
Lord's prophets by f........1Kin 18:13
four hundred and f........1Kin 18:22
captain of f with his f........2Kin 1:9
to the captain of f........2Kin 1:10
consume thee and thy f........2Kin 1:10
consumed him and his f........2Kin 1:10
consume thee and thy f........2Kin 1:12
consumed him and his f........2Kin 1:12
the third f with his f........2Kin 1:13
third captain of f........2Kin 1:13
the life of these f thy........2Kin 1:13
captains of the former f........2Kin 1:14
be with thy servants f........2Kin 2:16
people to Jehoahaz but f........2Kin 13:7
of each man f shekels........2Kin 15:20
In the f year of Azariah........2Kin 15:23

F

and reigned *f* and five 2Kin 21:1
of their camels *f*..............1Chr 5:21
two hundred and *f*............1Chr 5:21
nine hundred and *f*............1Chr 9:9
for a hundred and *f* 2Chr 1:17
of the nails was *f* shekels......2Chr 3:9
four hundred and *f* 2Chr 8:18
and he reigned *f* and five 2Chr 33:1
thousand two hundred *f*.......Ezra 2:7
of Adin, four hundred *f*.......Ezra 2:15
The children of Nebo, *f*.......Ezra 2:29
thousand two hundred *f*.......Ezra 2:31
of Nekoda, six hundred *f* .....Ezra 2:60
Jonathan, and with him *f* .....Ezra 8:6
an hundred and *f* of the.......Neh 5:17
of Arah, six hundred *f*........Neh 7:10
of Adin, six hundred *f*........Neh 7:20
thousand two hundred *f*.......Neh 7:34
f basins, five hundred ....Neh 7:70
gallows be made of *f* ....Esth 5:14
captain of *f*, and the ....Is 3:3
of the inner gate were *f*.......Ezek 40:15
the length was *f* cubits ....Ezek 40:25
the length was *f* cubits ....Ezek 40:36
the length thereof was *f*.......Ezek 42:7
and *f* cubits round about ......Ezek 45:2
north two hundred and *f*......Ezek 48:17
south two hundred and *f*......Ezek 48:17
east two hundred and *f* ....Ezek 48:17
west two hundred and *f*.......Ezek 48:17
draw out *f* vessels out..........Hag 2:16
by hundreds, and by *f* ....Mark 6:40
pence, and the other *f* ....Luke 7:41
them sit down by *f* in a ....Luke 9:14
Thou art not yet *f* years.......John 8:57
of four hundred and *f*.........Acts 13:20

FIG—*pear-shaped fruit of fig tree*

[*also* FIGS]
and of the *f*.................Num 13:23
barley, and vines, and *f*.......Deut 8:8
the trees said to the *f*.........Judg 9:10
two hundred cakes of *f* 1Sam 25:18
every one of his *f* tree 2Kin 18:31
said, Take a lump of *f* 2Kin 20:7
meat, meal, cakes of *f* 1Chr 12:40
also wine, grapes, and *f*.......Neh 13:15
vines also and their *f* ....Ps 105:33
Whoso keepeth the *f* tree .....Prov 27:18
f tree putteth forth her.........Song 2:13
putteth forth her green *f* ......Song 2:13
falling *f* from the *f* ....Is 34:4
Let them take a lump of *f* .....Is 38:21
eat up thy vines and thy *f* .....Jer 5:17
nor *f* on the *f* tree, and ....Jer 8:13
had very good *f* ....Jer 24:2
even like the *f* that are ....Jer 24:2
had very naughty *f* ....Jer 24:2
Like these good *f*, so ....Jer 24:5
make them like vile *f* ....Jer 29:17
barked my *f* tree ....Joel 1:7
vineyards and your *f*...........Amos 4:9
under his *f* tree; and..........Mic 4:4
holds shall be like *f*...........Nah 3:12
with the firstripe *f*............Nah 3:12
the *f* tree shall not ....Hab 3:17
the vine, and the *f* ....Hag 2:19
the vine and under the *f* ......Zech 3:10
grapes of thorns, or *f* of ......Matt 7:16
soon is the *f* tree ....Matt 21:20
a *f* tree afar off having........Mark 11:13
for the time of *f* was..........Mark 11:13
the *f* tree which thou ....Mark 11:21
men do not gather *f* ....Luke 6:44
seeking fruit on this *f* tree .....Luke 13:7
Can the *f* tree, my ....James 3:12
either a vine, *f*? so can ....James 3:12
casteth her untimely *f*.........Rev 6:13

FIG CAKES—*a poultice*
Prescribed for boils ......Is 38:21

FIG TREE—*one of the favorite trees of the East*

The leaves of, used for:
Covering nakedness......Gen 3:7
Shade ....John 1:48, 50

Fruit of:
Used for food 1Sam 30:12
Sent as present 1Sam 25:18
Sold in markets ....Neh 13:15
Used for healing ....Is 38:21
Sometimes fails..........Hab 3:17

Figuratively of:
Prosperity and peace 1Kin 4:25
Righteous and the wicked.Jer 24:1-10
Fathers of Israel.........Hos 9:10
Barren religion ....Matt 21:19
Jewish nation ....Luke 13:6-9
Christ's return...........Matt 24:32, 33
Final judgment ....Rev 6:13

FIGHT—*a conflict*

Used literally of:
War.....................Ex 17:8, 10
Individual combat 1Sam 17:10, 32

Used figuratively of:
Determined resolve 1Cor 9:26
Opposition of evil men...1Cor 15:32
Christian life 1Tim 6:12
Dissension ....James 4:1, 2
Spiritual conflict ....Rev 12:7

[*also* FIGHTETH, FIGHTING, FIGHTINGS, FOUGHT]
our enemies, and *f* ....Ex 1:10
The Lord shall *f* for you ......Ex 14:14
The Lord *f* for them ....Ex 14:25
came Amalek and *f* with ......Ex 17:8
go out, *f* with Amalek ....Ex 17:9
then he *f* against Israel........Num 21:1
who had *f* against the ....Num 21:26
he shall *f* for you ....Deut 1:30
Go not up, neither *f*..........Deut 1:42
your God he shall *f* for ....Deut 3:22
nigh unto a city to *f* ....Deut 20:10
to *f* with Joshua and ....Josh 9:2
the Lord *f* for Israel ....Josh 10:14
encamped against it, and *f* ....Josh 10:31
to Debir; and *f* against it......Josh 10:38
the Lord God of Israel *f* ......Josh 10:42
of Merom, to *f* against ....Josh 11:5
your God is he that hath *f* ....Josh 23:3
he it is that *f* for you ....Josh 23:10
the men of Jericho *f*..........Josh 24:11
Canaanites first, to *f*..........Judg 1:1
they *f* against him, and ....Judg 1:5
down to *f* against the ....Judg 1:9
kings came and *f*, then *f* .....Judg 5:19
They *f* from heaven ....Judg 5:20
stars in their courses *f* ....Judg 5:20
out, I pray now, and *f* ....Judg 9:38
Shechem, and *f* with ....Judg 9:39
and *f* against it, and ....Judg 9:52
is he that will begin to *f* .....Judg 10:18
f against the children ....Judg 11:8
come against me to *f* in.......Judg 11:12
children of Ammon to *f*.......Judg 11:32
unto me this day, to *f* ....Judg 12:3
and *f* with Ephraim: and ......Judg 12:4
like men, and *f*...............1Sam 4:9
And the Philistines *f*..........1Sam 4:10
together to *f* with Israel.......1Sam 13:5
and *f* against all his 1Sam 14:47
If he be able to *f* with me.....1Sam 17:9
of Elah, *f* with the 1Sam 17:19
was going forth to the *f*.......1Sam 17:20
this Philistine to *f* 1Sam 17:33
the Philistines *f* against........1Sam 23:1
Keilah, and *f* with the 1Sam 23:5
my lord *f* the battles of 1Sam 25:28
may not go *f* against the 1Sam 29:8
David, and *f* with him 2Sam 10:17
the city when ye did *f*? 2Sam 11:20
And Joab *f* against 2Sam 12:26
and *f* against it, and took 2Sam 12:29
to *f* against the house 1Kin 12:21
us *f* against them in 1Kin 20:23
up to Aphek, to *f* against 1Kin 20:26
turned aside to *f* against 1Kin 22:32
kings were come up to *f* 2Kin 3:21
he *f* against Hazael king 2Kin 8:29
Syria went up, and *f*..........2Kin 12:17
he *f* with Amaziah king 2Kin 14:15
he is come out to *f* 2Kin 19:9
the Philistines *f* against........1Chr 10:1
the Syrians, they *f* with 1Chr 19:17
to *f* against Israel, that........2Chr 11:1
f ye not against the Lord......2Chr 13:12
about him to *f* 2Chr 18:31
the Lord *f* against the.........2Chr 20:29
host of *f* men, that went 2Chr 26:11
He *f* also with the king 2Chr 27:5
purposed to *f* against 2Chr 32:2
Egypt came up to *f*............2Chr 35:20
might *f* with him, and.........2Chr 35:22
came to *f* in the valley of 2Chr 35:22
to *f* against Jerusalem..........Neh 4:8
our God shall *f* for us ....Neh 4:20
f against them that *f*..........Ps 35:1
he *f* daily oppresseth me ......Ps 56:1
and *f* against me without ......Ps 109:3
and my fingers to *f* ....Ps 144:1
and they shall *f* every ....Is 19:2
and *f* against Ashdod ....Is 20:1
the nations that *f* against ......Is 29:7
even all that *f* against..........Is 29:7
to *f* for mount Zion, and......Is 31:4
they shall *f* against thee ....Jer 1:19
ye *f* against the king of ....Jer 21:4
though ye *f* with the ....Jer 32:5
They come to *f* with the ......Jer 33:5
the people *f* against...........Jer 34:1
and *f* against this city ....Jer 37:8
to *f* with Ishmael the son .....Jer 41:12
will I return to *f* with ....Dan 10:20
and they shall *f*, because ......Zech 10:5
as when he *f* in the day ....Zech 14:3
Judah also shall *f* at ....Zech 14:14
then would my servants *f* .....John 18:36
without were *f*, within 2Cor 7:5
I have *f* a good *f*, I have 2Tim 4:7
endured a great *f* of ....Heb 10:32
waxed valiant in *f*, turned .....Heb 11:34
come wars and *f* among ....James 4:1
f against them with the ....Rev 2:16

FIGHTING AGAINST GOD—*an expression used to convey intense resistance to God*

Manifested by:
Pharaoh ....Ex 5:1, 2
Rabshakeh 2Kin 18:28-36
Jeroboam 2Chr 13:8-19

Futility of:
Seen by Gamaliel........Acts 5:34, 39
Admitted by Pharisees ...Acts 23:9
Experienced by Satan....Rev 12:7-17
Blasphemy of unregenerate ....Rev 16:9-21

FIGURE—*form; symbol*

[*also* FIGURES]
similitude of any *f*............Deut 4:16
carved *f* of cherubim..........1Kin 6:29
maketh it after the *f* of ....Is 44:13
f which ye made to ....Acts 7:43
is the *f* of him that was ....Rom 5:14
I have in a *f* transferred.......1Cor 4:6
was a *f* for the time then......Heb 9:9
which are the *f* of the.........Heb 9:24
he received him in a *f* ....Heb 11:19
like *f* whereunto even..........1Pet 3:21

FIGURE OF SPEECH—*symbolic form of communication*

Allegory ....Gal 4:24
Fable ....Judg 9:8-15; 1Tim 4:7
Hyperbole ....1Sam 13:5; John 21:25
Interrogation 1Cor 12:29, 30
Irony ....Luke 15:7-10
Metaphor ....Luke 13:32
Parable ....Matt 13:10
Parallelism ....Gen 4:23, 24
Personification ....Is 55:12

Proverb 1Kin 4:32
Sarcasm . . . . Matt 27:29
Simile . . . . Is 1:8, 9
Similitude . . . . Ps 90:4-6

FIGUREHEAD—*symbol on a ship's prow*
Twin Brothers . . . . Acts 28:11

FILE—*a tool used to sharpen other tools*
had a *f* for the mattocks 1Sam 13:21

FILIAL DEVOTION—*showing love and respect for one's parents*

Duty of:
Commanded . . . . Ex 20:12
Corrupted . . . . Matt 15:4-6
Confirmed . . . . Eph 6:1-3

Examples of:
Joseph . . . . Gen 47:12
David 1Sam 22:3
Solomon 1Kin 2:19
Elisha 1Kin 19:19, 20
Young man . . . . Matt 19:16-20

Obedience:
Continual . . . . Prov 6:20-22
Total . . . . Col 3:20
Lack of, severely punished . . . . Deut 21:18-21
Lack of, cursed . . . . Prov 20:20

FILL—*to put into something as much as it can hold*

[*also* FILLED, FILLEDST, FILLEST, FILLETH, FILLING]
and *f* the waters in the seas . . . Gen 1:22
earth was *f* with violence . . . . . . Gen 6:11
f the bottle with water . . . . Gen 21:19
and *f* them with earth . . . . Gen 26:15
F the men's sacks with food . . . Gen 44:1
the land was *f* with them . . . . . . Ex 1:7
And they shall *f* thy houses . . . Ex 10:6
morning ye shall be *f* with . . . . Ex 16:12
And I have *f* him with the . . . . Ex 31:3
he *f* with wisdom of heart . . . . . Ex 35:35
eat your *f*, and dwell . . . . Lev 25:19
earth shall be *f* with..glory . . . . Num 14:21
good things, which thou *f* . . . . . Deut 6:11
mayest eat grapes thy *f* at . . . . . Deut 23:24
eat within thy gates..be *f* . . . . . . Deut 26:12
bottles of wine, which we *f* . . . . Josh 9:13
f thine horn with oil, and 1Sam 16:1
and he was *f* with wisdom 1Kin 7:14
glory of the Lord had *f* the 1Kin 8:11
F four barrels with water 1Kin 18:33
the Syrians *f* the country 1Kin 20:27
that valley shall be *f* with 2Kin 3:17
every man his stone, and *f* 2Kin 3:25
and *f* their places with the 2Kin 23:14
house was *f* with a cloud 2Chr 5:13
the glory of the Lord *f* the 2Chr 7:1
was *f* with sweet odors 2Chr 16:14
have *f* it from one end to . . . . . . Ezra 9:11
so they did eat, and were *f* . . . . Neh 9:25
f their houses with silver . . . . . . Job 3:15
Till he *f* thy mouth with . . . . . . Job 8:21
but *f* me with bitterness . . . . Job 9:18
When he is about to *f* his . . . . . Job 20:23
f their houses with good . . . . . . Job 22:18
f the appetite of the young . . . . Job 38:39
belly thou *f* with thy hid . . . . . . Ps 17:14
f with a loathsome disease . . . . Ps 38:7
whole earth be *f* with his . . . . . . Ps 72:19
take deep root, and it *f* the . . . Ps 80:9
mouth wide and I will *f* . . . . Ps 81:10
the rain also *f* the pools . . . . Ps 84:6
he shall *f* the places with . . . . . . Ps 110:6
are exceedingly *f* with . . . . Ps 123:3
our mouth *f* with laughter . . . . . Ps 126:2
Wherewith the mower *f* not . . . Ps 129:7
fruit of their own way. *f* . . . . . . Prov 1:31
strangers be *f* with thy . . . . Prov 5:10
let us take our *f* of love . . . . Prov 7:18
backslider in heart..be *f* . . . . Prov 14:14
his mouth shall be *f* with . . . . . . Prov 20:17
be *f* therewith, and vomit . . . . . Prov 25:16
fool when he is *f* with . . . . Prov 30:22
nor the ear *f* with hearing . . . . . Eccl 1:8
and yet the appetite is not *f* . . . Eccl 6:7
head is *f* with dew, and my . . . Song 5:2
and his train *f* the temple . . . . . Is 6:1
f the breadth of thy land . . . . . . Is 8:8
Therefore are my loins *f* . . . . . . Is 21:3
f the face of the world with . . . Is 27:6
sword of the Lord is *f* with . . . . Is 34:6
old man that hath not *f* his . . . . Is 65:20
Every bottle shall be *f* with . . . Jer 13:12
bottle shall be *f* with wine? . . . . Jer 13:12
I will *f* all the inhabitants . . . . . Jer 13:13
have *f* mine inheritance . . . . Jer 16:18
f them with the dead bodies . . . Jer 33:5
the son of Nethaniah *f* it . . . . . . Jer 41:9
their land was *f* with sin . . . . . . Jer 51:5
hath *f* me with bitterness . . . . . . Lam 3:15
f thy bowels with this roll . . . . . Ezek 3:3
f the land with violence . . . . Ezek 8:17
f the courts with the slain . . . . . Ezek 9:7
house was *f* with the cloud . . . . Ezek 10:4
Thou shalt be *f* with . . . . Ezek 23:33
f it with the choice bones . . . . . Ezek 24:4
thou *f* many people: thou . . . . . Ezek 27:33
f the beasts of the whole . . . . . . Ezek 32:4
and I will *f* his mountains . . . . . Ezek 35:8
the waste cities be *f* with . . . . . . Ezek 36:38
the glory of the Lord *f* the . . . . Ezek 43:5
mountain, and *f* the whole . . . . . Dan 2:35
pasture, so were they *f* . . . . Hos 13:6
and *f* his holes with prey . . . . . . Nah 2:12
be *f* with the knowledge . . . . . . Hab 2:14
f their masters' houses . . . . Zeph 1:9
but ye are not *f* with drink . . . . Hag 1:6
and I will *f* this house with . . . . Hag 2:7
f the bow with Ephraim . . . . Zech 9:13
for they shall be *f* . . . . Matt 5:6
which is put in to *f* it up . . . . . . Matt 9:16
they did all eat, and were *f* . . . Matt 15:37
F ye up then the measure . . . . . Matt 23:32
and *f* it with vinegar . . . . Matt 27:48
the new piece that *f* it up . . . . . Mark 2:21
Let the children first be *f* . . . . . Mark 7:27
f a sponge full of vinegar . . . . . Mark 15:36
he shall be *f* with the Holy . . . . Luke 1:15
He hath *f* the hungry with . . . . Luke 1:53
in spirit, *f* with wisdom . . . . Luke 2:40
valley shall be *f*, and . . . . Luke 3:5
things were *f* with wrath . . . . . . Luke 4:28
were *f* with fear, saying . . . . Luke 5:26
hunger now for ye shall be *f* . . Luke 6:21
they did eat, and were all *f* . . . Luke 9:17
And he would fain have *f* . . . . . Luke 15:16
F the water pots with . . . . John 2:7
they *f* them up to the brim . . . . John 2:7
and *f* twelve baskets with . . . . . John 6:13
eat the loaves, and were *f* . . . . . John 6:26
house was *f* with the odor . . . . . John 12:3
sorrow hath *f* your heart . . . . . . John 16:6
and they *f* a sponge with . . . . . . John 19:29
f all the house where they . . . . . Acts 2:2
all *f* with the Holy Ghost . . . . . . Acts 2:4
they were *f* with wonder . . . . . . Acts 3:10
Then Peter, *f* with the Holy . . . Acts 4:8
all *f* with the Holy Ghost . . . . . . Acts 4:31
hath Satan *f* thine heart to . . . . Acts 5:3
were *f* with indignation . . . . Acts 5:17
be *f* with the Holy Ghost . . . . . . Acts 9:17
they were *f* with envy, and . . . . Acts 13:45
And the disciples were *f* . . . . . . Acts 13:52
f our hearts with food and . . . . Acts 14:17
city was *f* with confusion . . . . . . Acts 19:29
f with all unrighteousness . . . . . Rom 1:29
f you with all joy and peace . . . Rom 15:13
f with all knowledge, able . . . . . Rom 15:14
f with your company . . . . Rom 15:24
f with comfort, I am 2Cor 7:4
fulness of him that *f* all . . . . Eph 1:23
be *f* with all the fulness . . . . Eph 3:19
that he might *f* all things . . . . . . Eph 4:10
but be *f* with the Spirit . . . . Eph 5:18
f with the fruits of . . . . Phil 1:11
be *f* with the knowledge . . . . Col 1:9
f up that which is behind . . . . . . Col 1:24
to *f* up their sins alway 1Thess 2:16
that I may be *f* with joy 2Tim 1:4
peace, be ye warmed and *f* . . . . James 2:16
f it with fire of the altar . . . . . . Rev 8:5
is *f* up the wrath of God . . . . . . Rev 15:1
temple was *f* with smoke . . . . . . Rev 15:8
hath *f f* to her double . . . . Rev 18:6
the fowls were *f* with their . . . . Rev 19:21

FILLET—*ribbon used as a headband*

[*also* FILLETED, FILLETS]
their *f* shall be of silver . . . . Ex 27:10
about the court shall be *f* . . . . . Ex 27:17
chapiters and their *f* with . . . . . Ex 36:38
and their *f* were of silver . . . . . . Ex 38:10
pillars and their *f* of silver . . . . . Ex 38:12
their chapiters and their *f* . . . . . Ex 38:19
their chapiters, and *f* . . . . Ex 38:28
f of twelve cubits did . . . . Jer 52:21

F

FILTH—*uncleanliness; defilement; corruption*
Men . . . . Job 15:16; Ps 14:2, 3
Garments and furniture . . Is 4:1-4; Is 28:8
Ceremonial uncleanness . . Ezek 22:15
Unrighteousness . . . . Is 64:6; Ezek 16:6

[*also* FILTHINESS, FILTHY]
the *f* out of the holy place 2Chr 29:5
from the *f* of the heathen . . . . . Ezra 6:21
are altogether become *f* . . . . Ps 53:3
is not washed from their *f* . . . . . Prov 30:12
Her *f* is in her skirts; she . . . . . Lam 1:9
Because thy *f* was poured . . . . . Ezek 16:36
the *f* of it may be molten . . . . . Ezek 24:11
In thy *f* is lewdness . . . . Ezek 24:13
not be purged from thy *f* . . . . . . Ezek 24:13
be clean: from all your *f* . . . . . . Ezek 36:25
will cast abominable *f* upon . . . Nah 3:6
Woe to her that is *f* and . . . . . . Zeph 3:1
clothed with *f* garments . . . . Zech 3:3
made as the *f* of the world 1Cor 4:13
f of the flesh and spirit 2Cor 7:1
Neither *f*, nor foolish . . . . Eph 5:4
f communication out of . . . . Col 3:8
much wine, not greedy of *f* 1Tim 3:8
lay apart all *f* and . . . . James 1:21
putting away of the *f* of the . . . 1Pet 3:21
with the *f* conversation of 2Pet 2:7
these *f* dreamers defile . . . . Jude 8
full of abominations and *f* . . . . . Rev 17:4
he which is *f*, let him be *f* . . . . . Rev 22:11

FILTHY LUCRE—*money*
Bishop (elders) forbidden to seek 1Tim 3:3
no striker, not..to *f l* . . . . Titus 1:7
not for *f l*, but of a 1Pet 5:2

FINALLY—*lastly*
F, brethren, farewell 2Cor 13:11
F, my brethren, be strong . . . . . Eph 6:10
F, my brethren, rejoice in . . . . . Phil 3:1
F, brethren, pray for us 2Thess 3:1
F, be ye all of one mind 1Pet 3:8

FIND—*to discover; detect*

[*also* FINDEST, FINDETH, FINDING, FOUND]
there was not *f* an help . . . . Gen 2:20
one that *f* me shall slay me . . . . Gen 4:14
lest any *f* him should kill . . . . . . Gen 4:15
f no rest for the sole of her . . . Gen 8:9
And the angel of the Lord *f* . . . Gen 16:7
now I have *f* favor in thy . . . . . Gen 18:3
f in Sodom fifty righteous . . . . . Gen 18:26
Peradventure..thirty be *f* . . . . . . Gen 18:30
I will not do it, if I *f* thirty . . . . Gen 18:30
Peradventure ten shall be *f* . . . . Gen 18:32
f there a well of springing . . . . . Gen 26:19
How is it that thou hast *f* . . . . . Gen 27:20
have *f* favor in thine eyes . . . . . Gen 30:27
with whomsoever thou *f* thy . . . Gen 31:32
all the tent, but *f* them not . . . . Gen 31:34
thou *f* of all thy household . . . . Gen 31:37

to *f* grace in the sight of my ... Gen 33:8
Let me *f* grace in your eyes ... Gen 34:11
that *f* the mules in the ... Gen 36:24
and *f* them in Dothan ... Gen 37:17
woman's hand: but he *f* ... Gen 38:20
And Joseph *f* grace in his ... Gen 39:4
Can we *f* such a one as this ... Gen 41:38
of thy servants it be *f*, both ... Gen 44:9
cup was *f* in Benjamin's ... Gen 44:12
God hath *f* out the iniquity ... Gen 44:16
with whom the cup is *f* ... Gen 44:16
the money that was *f* in the ... Gen 47:14
now I have *f* grace in your ... Gen 50:4
beast which shall be *f* in ... Ex 9:19
in the wilderness, and *f* no ... Ex 15:22
or if he be *f* in his hand, he ... Ex 21:16
If the theft be certainly *f* in ... Ex 22:4
If the thief be not *f*, then ... Ex 22:8
I have *f* grace in thy sight ... Ex 33:13
I may *f* grace in thy sight ... Ex 33:13
hast *f* grace in my sight ... Ex 33:17
with whom was *f* blue, and ... Ex 35:23
have *f* that which was lost ... Lev 6:3
I not *f* favor in thy sight ... Num 11:11
they *f* a man that gathered ... Num 15:32
have *f* grace in thy sight ... Num 32:5
be sure your sin will *f* you ... Num 32:23
If there be *f* among you ... Deut 17:2
the people that is *f* therein ... Deut 20:11
he hath lost, and thou hast *f* ... Deut 22:3
I *f* not thy daughter a maid ... Deut 22:17
If a man be *f* lying with a ... Deut 22:22
a man *f* a betrothed damsel ... Deut 22:25
lie with her, and they be *f* ... Deut 22:28
she *f* no favor in his eyes ... Deut 24:1
If a man be *f* stealing any ... Deut 24:7
enemies shall be *f* liars ... Deut 33:29
all the way, but *f* them not ... Josh 2:22
And they *f* Adoni-bezek in ... Judg 1:5
as thou shalt *f* occasion ... Judg 9:33
ye had not *f* out my riddle ... Judg 14:18
sojourn where he could *f* a ... Judg 17:8
And they *f* among the ... Judg 21:12
ye may *f* rest, each of you ... Ruth 1:9
Why have I *f* grace in thine ... Ruth 2:10
Let me *f* favor in thy sight ... Ruth 2:13
handmaid *f* grace in thy ... 1Sam 1:18
Shalisha, but they *f* them ... 1Sam 9:4
Benjamites, but they *f* ... 1Sam 9:4
f young maidens going ... 1Sam 9:11
ye shall straightway *f* him ... 1Sam 9:13
about this time ye shall *f* ... 1Sam 9:13
thou wentest to seek are *f* ... 1Sam 10:2
him, he could not be *f* ... 1Sam 10:21
smith *f* throughout all the ... 1Sam 13:19
neither sword nor spear *f* in ... 1Sam 13:22
Jonathan..was there *f* ... 1Sam 13:22
he hath *f* favor in my sight ... 1Sam 16:22
saying, Go *f* out the arrows ... 1Sam 20:21
have *f* favor in thine eyes ... 1Sam 20:29
my father shall not *f* thee ... 1Sam 23:17
let the young men *f* favor ... 1Sam 25:8
If I have now *f* grace in ... 1Sam 27:5
for I have not *f* evil in thee ... 1Sam 29:6
they *f* an Egyptian in the ... 1Sam 30:11
thy servant *f* in his heart ... 2Sam 7:27
I shall *f* favor in the eyes ... 2Sam 15:25
place where he shall be *f* ... 2Sam 17:12
had sought and could not *f* ... 2Sam 17:20
f Abishag a Shunammite ... 1Kin 1:3
weight of the brass *f* out ... 1Kin 7:47
the Shilonite *f* him in the ... 1Kin 11:29
he went and *f* his carcase ... 1Kin 13:28
peradventure we may *f* ... 1Kin 18:5
and nation, that they *f* thee ... 1Kin 18:10
a lion *f* him, and slew him ... 1Kin 20:36
thou *f* me, O mine enemy? ... 1Kin 21:20
three days, but *f* him not ... 2Kin 2:17
f no more of her than the ... 2Kin 9:35
the money that was *f* in the ... 2Kin 12:10
vessels that were *f* in the ... 2Kin 14:14
the king of Assyria *f* ... 2Kin 17:4
and *f* the king of Assyria ... 2Kin 19:8
I have *f* the book of the law ... 2Kin 22:8
words of this book that is *f* ... 2Kin 22:13
that Hilkiah the priest *f* ... 2Kin 23:24
which were *f* in the city ... 2Kin 25:19
land that were *f* in the city ... 2Kin 25:19
And they *f* fat pasture and ... 1Chr 4:40
they *f* Saul and his sons ... 1Chr 10:8
and *f* it to weigh a talent of ... 1Chr 20:2
were *f* among them mighty ... 1Chr 26:31
precious stones were *f* ... 1Chr 29:8
and to *f* out every device ... 2Chr 2:14
and they were *f* an hundred ... 2Chr 2:17
ye seek him, he will be *f* of ... 2Chr 15:2
and he was *f* of them ... 2Chr 15:15
they *f* among them in ... 2Chr 20:25
and *f* the princes of Judah ... 2Chr 22:8
vessels that were *f* in the ... 2Chr 25:24
your children shall *f* ... 2Chr 30:9
Hilkiah the priest *f* a book ... 2Chr 34:14
the money that was *f* in the ... 2Chr 34:17
the covenant that was *f* in ... 2Chr 34:30
genealogy..were not *f* ... Ezra 2:62
thou *f* in the book of the ... Ezra 4:15
there was *f* at Achmetha ... Ezra 6:2
priests there were *f* that ... Ezra 10:18
and if thy servant have *f* ... Neh 2:5
And I *f* a register of the ... Neh 7:5
genealogy, but it was not *f* ... Neh 7:64
and therein was *f* written ... Neh 13:1
of the matter, it was *f* out ... Esth 2:23
f written, that Mordecai ... Esth 6:2
if I have *f* favor in his ... Esth 8:5
when they can *f* the grave? ... Job 3:22
doeth great things past *f* ... Job 9:10
Canst thou by searching *f* ... Job 11:7
thou *f* out the Almighty ... Job 11:7
the root of the matter is *f* ... Job 19:28
I knew where I might *f* him! ... Job 23:3
where shall wisdom be *f*? ... Job 28:12
lifted up myself when evil *f* ... Job 31:29
say, We have *f* out wisdom ... Job 32:13
Behold, he *f* occasions ... Job 33:10
Almighty we cannot *f* him ... Job 37:23
were no women *f* so fair ... Job 42:15
wickedness till thou *f* none ... Ps 10:15
Thine hand shall *f* out all ... Ps 21:8
thy right hand shall *f* out ... Ps 21:8
time when thou mayest be *f* ... Ps 32:6
iniquity be *f* to be hateful ... Ps 36:2
sought him..could not be *f* ... Ps 37:36
and for comforters, but I *f* ... Ps 69:20
men of might have *f* their ... Ps 76:5
yea, the sparrow hath *f* an ... Ps 84:3
I have *f* David my servant ... Ps 89:20
they *f* no city to dwell in ... Ps 107:4
me: I *f* trouble and sorrow ... Ps 116:3
thy word as one that *f* ... Ps 119:162
Until I *f* out a place for the ... Ps 132:5
We shall *f* all precious ... Prov 1:13
Lord, and *f* the knowledge ... Prov 2:5
Happy is the man that *f* ... Prov 3:13
are life unto those that *f* ... Prov 4:22
But if he be *f*, he shall ... Prov 6:31
and *f* out knowledge of ... Prov 8:12
understanding wisdom is *f* ... Prov 10:13
matter wisely shall *f* good ... Prov 16:20
hath a froward heart *f* no ... Prov 17:20
Whoso *f* a wife *f* a good ... Prov 18:22
neighbor *f* no favor in ... Prov 21:10
when thou hast *f* it, then ... Prov 24:14
reprove thee, and thou be *f* ... Prov 30:6
thee, and thou be *f* ... Prov 30:10
Who can *f* a virtuous ... Prov 31:10
no man can *f* out the work ... Eccl 3:11
exceeding deep, who can *f* ... Eccl 7:24
have I *f*, saith the preacher ... Eccl 7:27
one by one, to *f* out the ... Eccl 7:27
among a thousand have I *f* ... Eccl 7:28
all those have I not *f* ... Eccl 7:28
man cannot *f* out the work ... Eccl 8:17
yet he shall not *f* it ... Eccl 8:17
shall he not be able to *f* it ... Eccl 8:17
Whatsoever thy hand *f* to ... Eccl 9:10
Now there was *f* in it a poor ... Eccl 9:15
sought to *f* out acceptable ... Eccl 12:10
I sought him, but I *f* him ... Song 3:1
but I *f* him whom my soul ... Song 3:4
but I could not *f* him; I ... Song 5:6
should *f* thee without, I ... Song 8:1
I in his eyes as one that *f* ... Song 8:10
As my hand hath *f* the ... Is 10:10
Every one that is *f* shall be ... Is 13:15
there shall not be *f* in the ... Is 30:14
and *f* for herself a place of ... Is 34:14
and *f* the king of Assyria ... Is 37:8
joy and gladness shall be *f* ... Is 51:3
thou hast *f* the life of thine ... Is 57:10
of your fast ye *f* pleasure ... Is 58:3
nor *f* thine own pleasure ... Is 58:13
As the new wine is *f* in the ... Is 65:8
What iniquity..fathers *f* ... Jer 2:5
in her month they shall *f* ... Jer 2:24
in thy skirts is *f* the blood ... Jer 2:34
among my people are *f* ... Jer 5:26
and ye shall *f* rest for your ... Jer 6:16
came to the pits, and *f* no ... Jer 14:3
have I *f* their wickedness ... Jer 23:11
And ye shall seek me, and *f* ... Jer 29:13
left of the sword *f* grace in ... Jer 31:2
But ten men were *f* among ... Jer 41:8
was he *f* among thieves? ... Jer 48:27
shall not be *f*: for I will ... Jer 50:20
which were *f* in the city ... Jer 52:25
she *f* no rest: all her ... Lam 1:3
like harts that *f* no pasture ... Lam 1:6
we have *f*, we have seen it ... Lam 2:16
Son of man, eat that thou *f* ... Ezek 3:1
not destroy it: but I *f* none ... Ezek 22:30
till iniquity was *f* in thee ... Ezek 28:15
all was *f* none like Daniel ... Dan 1:19
I have *f* a man of the ... Dan 2:25
wisdom of the gods, was *f* ... Dan 5:11
and excellent wisdom is *f* ... Dan 5:14
to *f* occasion against Daniel ... Dan 6:4
they could *f* none occasion ... Dan 6:4
there any error or fault *f* in ... Dan 6:4
not *f* occasion against this ... Dan 6:5
Daniel, except we *f* it ... Dan 6:5
him innocency was *f* in me ... Dan 6:22
stumble and fall and not be *f* ... Dan 11:19
that she shall not *f* her ... Hos 2:6
they shall not *f* him: he ... Hos 5:6
I *f* Israel like grapes in the ... Hos 9:10
he *f* him in Beth-el, and ... Hos 12:4
From me is thy fruit *f* ... Hos 14:8
of the Lord, and shall not *f* ... Amos 8:12
and he *f* a ship going to ... Jon 1:3
of Israel were *f* in thee ... Mic 1:13
shall a deceitful tongue be *f* ... Zeph 3:13
and iniquity was not *f* in ... Mal 2:6
seek, and ye shall *f*; knock ... Matt 7:7
he that seeketh *f*; and to ... Matt 7:8
I have not *f* so great faith ... Matt 8:10
He that *f* his life shall lose ... Matt 10:39
his life for my sake shall *f* ... Matt 10:39
places, seeking rest, and *f* ... Matt 12:43
he had *f* one pearl of great ... Matt 13:46
lose his life..shall *f* it ... Matt 16:25
if so be that he *f* it, verily I ... Matt 18:13
and *f* others standing idle ... Matt 20:6
ye shall *f* an ass tied, and a ... Matt 21:2
f nothing thereon, but ... Matt 21:19
as many as ye shall *f*, bid ... Matt 22:9
all as many as they *f*, both ... Matt 22:10
when he cometh shall *f* so ... Matt 24:46
f them asleep, and saith ... Matt 26:40
But *f* none: yea, though ... Matt 26:60
witnesses came, yet *f* they ... Matt 26:60
unwashen, hands, they *f* ... Mark 7:2
she *f* the devil gone out ... Mark 7:30
ye shall *f* a colt tied ... Mark 11:2
he *f* nothing but leaves ... Mark 11:13
coming suddenly he *f* you ... Mark 13:36
he cometh, and *f* them ... Mark 14:37
returned, he *f* them asleep ... Mark 14:40
Mary: for thou hast *f* ... Luke 1:30
Ye shall *f* the babe wrapped ... Luke 2:12
came with haste, and *f* ... Luke 2:16
And when they *f* him not ... Luke 2:45
they *f* him in the temple ... Luke 2:46
f the place where it was ... Luke 4:17
might *f* an accusation ... Luke 6:7

f the servant whole that.......Luke 7:10
and *f* the man, out of whom ..Luke 8:35
voice was past, Jesus was *f*....Luke 9:36
you; seek, and ye shall *f*......Luke 11:9
and he that seeketh *f*.........Luke 11:10
and *f* none, he saith, I will ....Luke 11:24
when he cometh shall *f*.......Luke 12:37
when he cometh shall *f* so.....Luke 12:43
that which is lost, until he *f*...Luke 15:4
when he hath *f* it, he layeth ...Luke 15:5
I have *f* my sheep which ......Luke 15:6
and seek diligently till she *f*...Luke 15:8
when she hath *f* it, she........Luke 15:9
I have *f* the piece which I.....Luke 15:9
and was lost, and is *f*.........Luke 15:32
shall he *f* faith on the earth? ..Luke 18:8
and *f* even as he had said .....Luke 19:32
could not *f* what they might ...Luke 19:48
he *f* them sleeping for ....Luke 22:45
I *f* no fault in this man ....Luke 23:4
you, have *f* no fault in this ....Luke 23:14
And they *f* the stone rolled ...Luke 24:2
when they *f* not his body......Luke 24:23
and *f* the eleven gathered .....Luke 24:33
He first *f* his own brother .....John 1:41
We have *f* the Messiah........John 1:41
Philip *f* Nathanael, and ....John 1:45
And *f* in the temple those .....John 2:14
seek me, and shall not *f* me ...John 7:34
and shall not *f* me: and ....John 7:36
and when he had *f* him, he ....John 9:35
shall go in and out, and *f*.....John 10:9
he had *f* a young ass, sat......John 12:14
may know that I *f* no fault ....John 19:4
of the ship, and ye shall *f*.....John 21:6
f nothing how they might .....Acts 4:21
young men came in, and *f* ....Acts 5:10
prison truly *f* we shut in all ...Acts 5:23
had opened, we *f* no man .....Acts 5:23
and our fathers *f* no ....Acts 7:11
But Philip was *f* at Azotus ....Acts 8:40
And there he *f* a certain man..Acts 9:33
when he had *f* him, he ....Acts 11:26
f a certain sorcerer, a false ....Acts 13:6
they *f* no cause of death ......Acts 13:28
I *f* an altar with this ....Acts 17:23
f it fifty thousand pieces of ....Acts 19:19
And *f* a ship sailing over ......Acts 21:2
We *f* no evil in this man ......Acts 23:9
they neither *f* me in the.......Acts 24:12
if they have *f* any evil doing ...Acts 24:20
And there the centurion *f* a ...Acts 27:6
and *f* it twenty fathoms ....Acts 27:28
and *f* it fifteen fathoms ....Acts 27:28
as..to the flesh, hath *f*? ....Rom 4:1
that which is good I *f* not .....Rom 7:18
Why doth he yet *f* fault? ......Rom 9:19
was *f* of them that sought .....Rom 10:20
and his ways past *f* out! ....Rom 11:33
stewards, that a man be *f*.....1Cor 4:2
I *f* not Titus my brother 2Cor 2:13
before Titus, is *f* a truth 2Cor 7:14
me, and *f* you unprepared.....2Cor 9:4
that I shall be *f* unto you 2Cor 12:20
ourselves also are *f* sinners ....Gal 2:17
being *f* in fashion as a man....Phil 2:8
deacon, being *f* blameless 1Tim 3:10
very diligently, and *f* me 2Tim 1:17
he may *f* mercy of the Lord ...2Tim 1:18
obtain mercy, and *f* grace .....Heb 4:16
For *f* fault with them, he .....Heb 8:8
and was not *f*, because God ...Heb 11:5
might be *f* unto praise and 1Pet 1:7
ye may be *f* of him in peace...2Pet 3:14
f of thy children walking in....2John 4
not, and hast *f* them liars .....Rev 2:2
for I have not *f* thy works.....Rev 3:2
no man was *f* worthy to.......Rev 5:4
seek death, and shall not *f* ....Rev 9:6
neither was their place *f* ....Rev 12:8
And in their mouth was *f* .....Rev 14:5
the mountains were not *f* .....Rev 16:20
shall be *f* no more at all ......Rev 18:21
f the blood of prophets ....Rev 18:24
And whosoever was not *f* .....Rev 20:15

FINE—*penalty or payment*
Paid by guilty ....Ex 21:23-30
Deut 22:19
Restitution ....Ex 22:5-15

FINE—*superior in quality or appearance*

[*also* FINEST]
arrayed him in vestures of *f* ...Gen 41:42
scarlet, and *f* linen, and ....Ex 25:4
and *f* twined linen of ....Ex 26:31
for the court of *f* twined ......Ex 27:9
the height five cubits of *f* .....Ex 27:18
purple, of scarlet, and *f*.......Ex 28:6
f twined linen, shalt thou .....Ex 28:15
shalt make the mitre of *f*......Ex 28:39
and of scarlet, and of *f* ....Ex 35:25
ten curtains of *f* twined ....Ex 36:8
and *f* twined linen, of.........Ex 36:37
were of *f* twined linen ....Ex 38:16
purple, and in scarlet and *f*....Ex 38:23
purple, and scarlet, and *f* .....Ex 39:2
in the scarlet, and in the *f* ....Ex 39:3
and scarlet, and *f* twined ......Ex 39:5
And a mitre of *f* linen, and ...Ex 39:28
goodly bonnets of *f* linen......Ex 39:28
linen breeches of *f* twined .....Ex 39:28
offering shall be of *f* flour .....Lev 2:1
be of *f* flour unleavened ......Lev 2:5
tenth part of an ephah of *f*....Lev 5:11
cakes mingled with oil, of *f* ...Lev 7:12
and one tenth deal of *f* flour ..Lev 14:21
tenth deals..shall be of *f* ......Lev 23:17
And thou shalt take *f* flour....Lev 24:5
cakes of *f* flour mingled ....Num 6:15
both of them full of *f* flour ....Num 7:79
was thirty measures of *f*.......1Kin 4:22
measure of *f* flour be sold 2Kin 7:1
a measure of *f* flour for a 2Kin 7:18
of them that wrought *f*........1Chr 4:21
clothed with a robe of *f*.......1Chr 15:27
in blue, and in *f* linen, and 2Chr 2:14
he overlaid it with *f* gold 2Chr 3:8
two vessels of *f* copper........Ezra 8:27
fastened with cords of *f*.......Esth 1:6
place for gold where they *f*....Job 28:1
or have said to the *f* gold .....Job 31:24
yea, than much *f* gold ....Ps 19:10
them also with the *f* of the ....Ps 81:16
filleth thee with the *f* of the ...Ps 147:14
and the gain thereof than *f*....Prov 3:14
is better than gold..than *f* .....Prov 8:19
She maketh *f* linen, and ......Prov 31:24
head is as the most *f* gold .....Song 5:11
The glasses, and the *f* linen ...Is 3:23
is the most *f* gold changed! ....Lam 4:1
I girded thee about with *f* .....Ezek 16:10
thy raiment was of *f* linen .....Ezek 16:13
thou didst eat *f* flour, and .....Ezek 16:13
F linen with embroidered work.Ezek 27:7
to temper with the *f* flour .....Ezek 46:14
image's head was of *f* gold ....Dan 2:32
and *f* gold as the mire of the ..Zech 9:3
And he bought *f* linen, and ...Mark 15:46
was clothed in purple and *f* ...Luke 16:19
his feet like unto *f* brass ......Rev 1:15
and of pearls, and *f* linen .....Rev 18:12
city, that was clothed in *f* .....Rev 18:16
she should be arrayed in *f*.....Rev 19:8
f linen is the righteousness ....Rev 19:8

FINER—*refiner*

[*also* FINING]
The *f* pot is for silver, and ....Prov 17:3
come forth a vessel for the *f* ..Prov 25:4
As the *f* pot for silver, and....Prov 27:21

FINGER—*a digit of the hand*

Used literally of:
Man's fingers ....John 20:25, 27
Deformity 2Sam 21:20
Measurement ....Jer 52:21
Mysterious hand........Dan 5:5

Used figuratively of:
God's power ....Ex 8:19
Inspiration ....Ex 31:18
Suggestiveness ....Prov 6:13
Contrast of burdens 1Kin 12:10
Lord's authority ....Luke 11:20

[*also* FINGERS]
the altar with thy *f* ....Ex 29:12
priest shall dip his *f* in the ....Lev 4:6
of the sin offering with his *f*...Lev 4:25
of the sin offering with his *f*...Lev 4:34
he dipped his *f* in the blood ..Lev 9:9
priest shall dip his right *f* ....Lev 14:16
sprinkle of the oil with his *f* ...Lev 14:16
sprinkle it with his *f* upon .....Lev 16:14
the blood with his *f* seven .....Lev 16:14
take of her blood with his *f* ..Num 19:4
written with the *f* of God .....Deut 9:10
f and toes were four and 1Chr 20:6
My little *f* shall be thicker.....2Chr 10:10
heavens, the work of thy *f* ....Ps 8:3
my hands to war, and my *f*....Ps 144:1
Bind them upon thy *f*, write ...Prov 7:3
my *f* with sweet smelling ......Song 5:5
that which their own *f* have ...Is 2:8
the putting forth of the *f*......Is 58:9
and your *f* with iniquity ....Is 59:3
them with one of their *f* ......Matt 23:4
put his *f* into his ears, and ....Mark 7:33
burdens with one of your *f*....Luke 11:46
may dip the tip of his *f* in.....Luke 16:24
with his *f* wrote on the........John 8:6

FINISH—*to complete; establish*

[*also* FINISHED]
heavens and the earth were *f*..Gen 2:1
cubit shalt thou *f* it above .....Gen 6:16
tent of the congregation *f* .....Ex 39:32
in a book until they were *f*....Deut 31:24
until every thing was *f* that ....Josh 4:10
until he have *f* the thing ......Ruth 3:18
he built the house, and *f* it 1Kin 6:9
until he had *f* all the house....1Kin 6:22
and he *f* all his house 1Kin 7:1
when Solomon had *f* the 1Kin 9:1
began to number, but he *f* not .1Chr 27:24
Huram *f* the work that he 2Chr 4:11
Solomon *f* the house of the ...2Chr 7:11
when they had *f* it, they 2Chr 24:14
when all this was *f*, all 2Chr 31:1
building, and yet it is not *f*....Ezra 5:16
house was *f* on the third ......Ezra 6:15
wall was *f* in the twenty.......Neh 6:15
thy kingdom, and *f* it ....Dan 5:26
to *f* the transgression, and.....Dan 9:24
his hands shall also *f* it........Zech 4:9
when Jesus had *f* these........Matt 13:53
when Jesus had *f* all these.....Matt 26:1
he have sufficient to *f* it.......Luke 14:28
build, and was not able to *f*...Luke 14:30
sent me, and to *f* his work ....John 4:34
Father hath given me to *f*.....John 5:36
I have *f* the work which.......John 17:4
said, It is *f*: and he bowed ....John 19:30
I might *f* my course with ......Acts 20:24
when we had *f* our course .....Acts 21:7
will *f* the work, and cut it .....Rom 9:28
he would also *f* in you the 2Cor 8:6
I have *f* my course, I have 2Tim 4:7
works were *f* from the ....Heb 4:3
sin, when it is *f*, bringeth .....James 1:15
mystery of God should be *f* ...Rev 10:7
they shall have *f* their.........Rev 11:7
the thousand years were *f*.....Rev 20:5

FINISHER—*perfecter*
Jesus the author and *f* ....Heb 12:2

FINS—*appendages used by fish to guide or propel*
Signs of a clean fish .....Lev 11:9

Whatsoever hath no *f* nor .....Lev 11:12
f and scales shall ye eat ....Deut 14:9

FIR—*a tree of the pine family*
Tree of Lebanon 1Kin 5:8, 10
Used in Solomon's temple 1Kin 6:15, 34

Used in ships ....Ezek 27:5
Used for musical instruments 2Sam 6:5

cedar trees and *f* trees 1Kin 9:11
the choice *f* trees thereof......2Kin 19:23
also cedar trees, *f* trees 2Chr 2:8
stork, the *f* trees are her ......Ps 104:17
cedar, and our rafters of *f*.....Song 1:17
the *f* trees rejoice at thee .....Is 14:8
I will set in the desert the *f* ...Is 41:19
f tree, the pine tree, and ......Is 60:13
f trees were not like his ....Ezek 31:8
I am like a green *f* tree ....Hos 14:8
f trees shall be terribly ....Nah 2:3
f tree; for the cedar is ....Zech 11:2

FIRE—*combustion*

Physical uses of:
Warmth ....John 18:18
Cooking ....Ex 16:23
Signs ....Judg 20:38, 40
Sacrifices ....Gen 8:20, 21
Refining ....Ps 12:6
Torture ....Dan 3:6
Sacrifice of children 2Kin 16:3

Supernatural uses of:
Manifest God ....Ex 3:2
Indicate God's power ....Ex 9:24
Express God's approval ..Lev 9:24
Vindicate God's wrath ...2Kin 1:9-12
Guide Israel ....Ex 13:21, 22
Transport a saint to heaven 2Kin 2:11

Used figuratively of:
God's protection ....Zech 2:5
God's vengeance ....Heb 12:29
God's Word ....Jer 5:14
Christ ....Mal 3:2
Holy Spirit ....Acts 2:3
Angels ....Heb 1:7
Tongue ....James 3:6
Persecution ....Luke 12:49-53
Affliction ....Is 43:2
Purification ....Is 6:5-7
Love ....Song 8:6
Lust ....Prov 6:27, 28

Final uses of:
Destroy world..........2Pet 3:10-12
Punish wicked..........Matt 25:41

[*also* FIRES]
brimstone and *f* from the .....Gen 19:24
Behold, the *f* and the wood ...Gen 22:7
the bush burned with *f*........Ex 3:2
the *f* ran along upon the ......Ex 9:23
f, and unleavened bread ......Ex 12:8
morning..burn with *f*..........Ex 12:10
the pillar of *f* and of the ......Ex 14:24
If *f* break out, and catch in ...Ex 22:6
that kindled the *f* shall ....Ex 22:6
like devouring *f* on the top ....Ex 24:17
offering made by *f* unto ....Ex 29:18
offering made by *f* unto ....Ex 29:25
an offering made by *f* unto ....Ex 29:41
burnt it in the *f*, and ....Ex 32:20
then I cast it into the *f*........Ex 32:24
kindle no *f* throughout ....Ex 35:3
the priest shall put *f* upon .....Lev 1:7
the wood in order upon the *f*..Lev 1:7
an offering made by *f*.........Lev 1:9
offering made by *f*, of a........Lev 1:13
the wood that is upon the *f* ...Lev 1:17
offering made by *f*, of a.......Lev 1:17
offerings of the Lord..by *f* ....Lev 2:3
offerings of the Lord..by *f* ....Lev 2:10
ears of corn dried by the *f* ....Lev 2:14
an offering made by *f* unto ....Lev 3:3
the wood that is on the *f*......Lev 3:5
offering made by *f*, of a........Lev 3:5
the offering made by *f* unto ...Lev 3:11
made by *f* for a sweet ....Lev 3:16
offerings made by *f* unto ......Lev 4:35
the *f* of the altar shall be .....Lev 6:9
f..altar shall be burning ....Lev 6:12
of my offerings made by *f*.....Lev 6:17
it shall be burnt in the *f* ......Lev 6:30
third day..be burnt with *f* .....Lev 7:17
offering made by *f* unto ....Lev 7:25
offerings of the Lord..by *f* ....Lev 7:35
an offering made by *f* unto ....Lev 8:21
bread shall ye burn with *f*.....Lev 8:32
them his censer, and put *f* ....Lev 10:1
strange *f* before the Lord ......Lev 10:1
offerings of the Lord..by *f* ....Lev 10:12
the offerings made by *f* of.....Lev 10:15
thou shalt burn it in the *f* .....Lev 13:55
full of burning coals of *f* ......Lev 16:12
they shall burn in the *f* ....Lev 16:27
it shall be burnt in the *f* ......Lev 19:6
offerings of the Lord..by *f* ....Lev 21:6
offerings of the Lord..by *f* ....Lev 21:21
an offering made by *f* unto ....Lev 22:27
an offering made by *f*.........Lev 23:18
offer an offering made by *f*....Lev 23:25
offer an offering made by *f*....Lev 23:36
offer an offering made by *f*....Lev 23:37
offerings of the Lord..by *f* ....Lev 24:9
offered strange *f* before the ...Num 3:4
were the appearance of *f*......Num 9:15
f of the Lord burnt among ....Num 11:1
unto the Lord, the *f* was ......Num 11:2
in a pillar of *f* by night ....Num 14:14
for an offering made by *f* ......Num 15:10
offering..by *f*, of a sweet ......Num 15:14
f therein, and put incense .....Num 16:7
there came out a *f* from the ...Num 16:35
put *f* therein from off the .....Num 16:46
offering made by *f*, for a ......Num 18:17
time the *f* devoured two ......Num 26:10
my sacrifices made by *f* ....Num 28:2
sacrifice made by *f* unto ......Num 28:6
made by *f* unto the Lord ......Num 28:13
of the sacrifice made by *f* .....Num 28:24
a sacrifice made by *f*, of ......Num 29:13
thing that may abide the *f* .....Num 31:23
make it go through the *f* ......Num 31:23
abideth not the *f* ye shall ......Num 31:25
the mountain burned with *f*....Deut 4:11
out of the midst of the *f*......Deut 4:12
out of the midst of the *f*......Deut 4:15
speaking out..midst of the *f*....Deut 4:33
words out..midst of the *f* ......Deut 4:36
afraid by reason of the *f*.......Deut 5:5
mountain did burn with *f* ......Deut 5:23
this great *f* will consume ....Deut 5:25
their graven images with *f* ......Deut 7:5
as a consuming *f* he shall ......Deut 9:3
the mount burned with *f* ......Deut 9:15
mount out..midst of the *f*......Deut 10:4
burnt in the *f* to their gods ....Deut 12:31
offerings..Lord made by *f*.....Deut 18:1
neither..see this great *f* ....Deut 18:16
For a *f* is kindled in mine .....Deut 32:22
set on *f* the foundations of.....Deut 32:22
thing shall be burnt with *f*.....Josh 7:15
ye shall set the city on *f* ......Josh 8:8
burn their chariots with *f*......Josh 11:6
he burnt Hazor with *f* ....Josh 11:11
of the sword..the city on *f* ....Judg 1:8
rose up *f* out of the rock ......Judg 6:21
f come out of the bramble ....Judg 9:15
f come out from Abimelech ...Judg 9:20
let *f* come out from the men ..Judg 9:20
set the hold on *f* upon ....Judg 9:49
the tower to burn it with *f* ....Judg 9:52
thy father's house with *f* ......Judg 14:15
he had set the brands on *f* ....Judg 15:5
her and her father with *f*......Judg 15:6
broken when it toucheth the *f* .Judg 16:9
they set on *f* all the cities .....Judg 20:48
offerings made by *f* of the 1Sam 2:28
behold, it was burned with *f*...1Sam 30:3
hath barley there..set it on *f*...2Sam 14:30
servants set my field on *f*? 2Sam 14:31
and *f* out of his mouth 2Sam 22:9
before him were coals of *f* 2Sam 22:13
Gezer, and burned it with *f* ...1Kin 9:16
lay it on wood, and put no *f* ..1Kin 18:23
the God that answereth by *f*...1Kin 18:24
Then the *f* of the Lord fell 1Kin 18:38
after the *f* a still small 1Kin 19:12
there came *f* down from 2Kin 1:14
of horses and chariots of *f* 2Kin 6:17
strong holds..thou set on *f* 2Kin 8:12
daughters to pass..the *f* 2Kin 17:17
cast their gods into the *f* 2Kin 19:18
to pass through the *f* to 2Kin 23:10
man's house burnt he with *f*...2Kin 25:9
they were burned with *f* 1Chr 14:12
f came down from heaven 2Chr 7:1
burnt his children in the *f*.....2Chr 28:3
roasted the passover with *f*....2Chr 35:13
the gates..are burned with *f*...Neh 1:3
gates..were consumed with *f*...Neh 2:13
in the night by a pillar of *f*...Neh 9:12
The *f* of God is fallen from ...Job 1:16
the spark of his *f* shall not ....Job 18:5
remnant of them the *f* ....Job 22:20
For it is a *f* that consumeth ...Job 31:12
f and brimstone, and ....Ps 11:6
and *f* out of his mouth ....Ps 18:8
hail stones and coals of *f*......Ps 18:12
the *f* shall devour them ....Ps 21:9
I was musing the *f* burned ....Ps 39:3
burneth the chariot in the *f* ...Ps 46:9
among them that are set on *f*..Ps 57:4
f and through water ....Ps 66:12
as wax melteth before the *f* ...Ps 68:2
They have cast *f* into thy......Ps 74:7
the night with a light of *f* .....Ps 78:14
f consumed their young ....Ps 78:63
It is burned with *f*, it is cut ...Ps 80:16
As the *f* burneth a wood ......Ps 83:14
setteth the mountains on *f* ....Ps 83:14
A *f* goeth before him, and ....Ps 97:3
his ministers a flaming *f*......Ps 104:4
and flaming *f* in their land ......Ps 105:32
a *f* was kindled in their ....Ps 106:18
let them be cast into the *f*.....Ps 140:10
F, and hail; snow, and ....Ps 148:8
lips there is as a burning *f* ....Prov 16:27
shalt heap coals of *f* upon .....Prov 25:22
no wood is, there the *f* ....Prov 26:20
and the *f* that saith not ....Prov 30:16
cities are burned with *f* ....Is 1:7
the shining of a flaming *f* .....Is 4:5
f devoureth the stubble ....Is 5:24
For wickedness burneth..*f*.....Is 9:18
people..as the fuel of the *f* ....Is 9:19
like the burning of a *f* ....Is 10:16
glorify ye the Lord in the *f*....Is 24:15
the *f* of thine enemies shall....Is 26:11
and the flame of devouring *f* ..Is 29:6
tongue as a devouring *f*.......Is 30:27
pile thereof is *f* and much .....Is 30:33
saith the Lord, whose *f* is .....Is 31:9
your breath, as *f*, shall ....Is 33:11
dwell with the devouring *f*? ...Is 33:14
it hath set him on *f* round .....Is 42:25
thou walkest through the *f* ....Is 43:2
He burneth part..in the *f*......Is 44:16
burned part of it in the *f*......Is 44:19
the *f* shall burn them ....Is 47:14
to warm at, nor *f* to sit ....Is 47:14
walk in the light of your *f*.....Is 50:11
when the melting *f* burneth....Is 64:2
the *f* causeth the waters to ....Is 64:2
thee, is burned up with *f*......Is 64:11
the Lord will come with *f* .....Is 66:15
his rebuke with flames of *f*....Is 66:15
For by *f* and by his sword.....Is 66:16
neither shall their *f* be ....Is 66:24
lest my fury come..like *f* ......Jer 4:4
sign of *f* in Beth-haccerem ....Jer 6:1
the fathers kindle the *f*........Jer 7:18
he hath kindled *f* upon it .....Jer 11:16
have kindled a *f* in mine ......Jer 17:4
to burn their sons with *f* ......Jer 19:5
as a burning *f* shut up in ......Jer 20:9
and he shall burn it with *f* ....Jer 21:10
and I will kindle a *f* in the ....Jer 21:14
Is not my word like as a *f*?....Jer 23:29
shall come and set *f* on ....Jer 32:29
and he shall burn it with *f* ....Jer 34:2
and there was a *f* on the ......Jer 36:22

f that was on the hearth ......Jer 36:23
roll was consumed in the f ....Jer 36:23
take it, and burn it with f .....Jer 37:8
city..not be burned with f .....Jer 38:17
this city to be burned with f ...Jer 38:23
houses of the people with f ....Jer 39:8
Egyptians..he burn with f .....Jer 43:13
daughters..burned with f ......Jer 49:2
and I will kindle a f in his ....Jer 50:32
high gates..burned with f ......Jer 51:58
men, burned he with f ....Jer 52:13
above hath he sent f into .....Lam 1:13
poured out his fury like f .....Lam 2:4
f infolding itself, and a ....Ezek 1:4
out of the midst of the f ......Ezek 1:4
was like burning coals of f ....Ezek 1:13
f was bright..out of the f ......Ezek 1:13
the appearance of f round .....Ezek 1:27
were the appearance of f ......Ezek 1:27
them into the midst of the f ...Ezek 5:4
and burn them in the f ....Ezek 5:4
thereof..a f come forth ....Ezek 5:4
likeness..appearance of f ......Ezek 8:2
downward f; and from his .....Ezek 8:2
Take f from between the ......Ezek 10:6
into the f for fuel; the f ......Ezek 15:4
which I have given to the f ....Ezek 15:6
they shall go out from one f ..Ezek 15:7
and another f shall devour ....Ezek 15:7
burn thine houses with f ......Ezek 16:41
And f is gone out of a rod ....Ezek 19:14
sons to pass through the f .....Ezek 20:31
against thee in the f of my ....Ezek 21:31
blow the f upon it, to melt ....Ezek 22:20
with the f of my wrath ....Ezek 22:31
pass for them through the f ....Ezek 23:37
make the pile for f great ......Ezek 24:9
her scum shall be in the f .....Ezek 24:12
the midst of the stones of f ....Ezek 28:16
I have set a f in Egypt ....Ezek 30:8
And I will set f in Egypt ......Ezek 30:16
in the f of my wrath have I ...Ezek 38:19
I will send a f on Magog ......Ezek 39:6
and shall set on f and burn ....Ezek 39:9
burn them with f seven ....Ezek 39:9
the flame of the f slew those ..Dan 3:22
walking in..midst of the f .....Dan 3:25
whose bodies the f had no ....Dan 3:27
smell of f had passed on ......Dan 3:27
and his eyes as lamps of f .....Dan 10:6
it burneth as a flaming f ......Hos 7:6
for the f hath devoured the ...Joel 1:19
A f devoureth before them ....Joel 2:3
and f, and pillars of smoke ....Joel 2:30
will send a f into the house ...Amos 1:4
I will send a f on the wall .....Amos 1:10
will kindle a f in the wall .....Amos 1:14
I will send a f upon Judah ....Amos 2:5
called to contend by f ....Amos 7:4
house of Jacob shall be a f ....Obad 18
wax before the f, and as the...Mic 1:4
fury is poured out like f.......Nah 1:6
There shall the f devour ....Nah 3:15
people..labor in the very f ....Hab 2:13
shall be devoured by the f ....Zeph 1:18
shall be devoured with f ......Zech 9:4
like a hearth of f among ......Zech 12:6
the third part through the f ...Zech 13:9
neither do ye kindle f on......Mal 1:10
hewn down, and..into the f....Matt 3:10
chaff with unquenchable f .....Matt 3:12
hewn down, and..into the f....Matt 7:19
them into a furnace of f.......Matt 13:42
he falleth into the f..........Matt 17:15
to be cast into hell f ....Matt 18:9
it hath cast him into the f .....Mark 9:22
and the f is not quenched .....Mark 9:44
and the f is not quenched .....Mark 9:46
and the f is not quenched .....Mark 9:48
warmed himself at the f.........Mark 14:54
hewn down, and..into the f....Luke 3:9
the Holy Ghost and with f ....Luke 3:16
burn with f unquenchable .....Luke 3:17
it rained f and brimstone ......Luke 17:29
when they had kindled a f ....Luke 22:55
beheld..as he sat by the f .....Luke 22:56
and cast them into the f........John 15:6
they saw a f of coals there ....John 21:9
blood, and f, and vapor of ....Acts 2:19
kindled a f, and received ......Acts 28:2
shook..beast into the f ....Acts 28:5
shalt heap coals of f on his ....Rom 12:20
be revealed by f; and the f 1Cor 3:13
be saved; yet so as by f 1Cor 3:15
In flaming f..vengeance 2Thess 1:8
Quenched the violence of f....Heb 11:34
great a matter a little f........James 3:5
eat your flesh as it were f .....James 5:3
though it be tried with f 1Pet 1:7
reserved unto f against the 2Pet 3:7
the vengeance of eternal f.....Jude 7
pulling them out of the f.......Jude 23
eyes were as a flame of f .....Rev 1:14
hath his eyes..a flame of f.....Rev 2:18
buy..gold tried in the f........Rev 3:18
seven lamps of f burning ......Rev 4:5
hail and f mingled with ....Rev 8:7
having breastplates of f ....Rev 9:17
of their mouths issued f ....Rev 9:17
and his feet as pillars of f .....Rev 10:1
maketh f come down from ....Rev 13:13
which had power over f ....Rev 14:18
him to scorch men with f .....Rev 16:8
be utterly burned with f.......Rev 18:8
and f came down from God ...Rev 20:9

FIRE, LAKE OF—*place of eternal punishment*
The beast ....Rev 19:20
The false prophet........Rev 19:20
The devil ....Rev 20:10
Death and evil ....Rev 20:14
Sinners ....Rev 21:8

FIREBRAND—*torch*
Figurative of enemies ....Is 7:4
Thrown by a madman ...Prov 26:18
Have no fear of ....Is 7:4
All who encircle.........Is 50:11
Snatched from a blaze ...Amos 4:11

[*also* FIREBRANDS]
tail to tail, and put a f........Judg 15:4
ye were as a f plucked out ....Amos 4:11

FIREPAN—*a shovel used for carrying fire*
Part of the altar worship. .Ex 27:3

[*also* FIREPANS]
the fleshhooks, and the f......Ex 38:3
And the f, and the bowls 2Kin 25:15
the basins, and the f, and .....Jer 52:19

FIRKINS—*a measure of about ten gallons*
containing two or three f......John 2:6

FIRM—*secure or solid*
covenant of the Lord..f ....Josh 3:17
they are f in themselves.......Job 41:23
is as f as a stone ....Job 41:24
but their strength is f ....Ps 73:4
and to make a f decree ....Dan 6:7
rejoicing of the hope f unto ...Heb 3:6

FIRMAMENT—*expanse of the sky*
Created by God ....Gen 1:8
Stars placed in ....Gen 1:14, 17
Compared to a tent......Ps 104:2
Expressive of God's glory.Ps 19:1
Saints compared to ......Dan 12:3

Let there be a f in the midst ..Gen 1:6
God made the f, and divided ..Gen 1:7
which were under the f from ..Gen 1:7
the waters..were above the f ..Gen 1:7
for lights in the f of heaven ...Gen 1:15
earth in the open f of heaven..Gen 1:20
praise him in the f of his ......Ps 150:1
the likeness of the f upon the. .Ezek 1:22
under the f were their wings...Ezek 1:23
there was a voice from the f...Ezek 1:25
And above the f that was over.Ezek 1:26
the f that was above the head. .Ezek 10:1

FIRST—*preceding all others*
Came out red ....Gen 25:25
This came out ....Gen 38:28
These should set forth ...Num 2:9
Amalek, of nations ......Num 24:20
Hands of witness shall be.Deut 17:7
Altar Solomon built 1Sam 14:35
Case pleaded............Prov 18:17
Seek ....Matt 6:33
Cast out beam ....Matt 7:5
Luke 6:42
Last state worse than ....Luke 11:26
The blade, then the head.Mark 4:28
Let the children ....Mark 7:27
Desire to be ....Mark 9:35
Commandment ....Mark 12:28
Gospel must be published.Mark 13:10
Appeared to Mary Magdalene ....Mark 16:9
Not sit down ....Luke 14:28
Stepped in, made whole. .John 5:4
Gave themselves 2Cor 8:5
Trusted in Christ ....Eph 1:12
A falling away 2Thess 2:3
Let these also 1Tim 3:10
Dwelt, in 2Tim 1:5
He takes away ....Heb 10:9

and the morning were the f ...Gen 1:5
on the f day of the month.....Gen 8:5
in the six hundredth and f.....Gen 8:13
the f month, the f day ....Gen 8:13
the f famine that was in the ...Gen 26:1
saying, This came out f ....Gen 38:28
did eat up the f seven fat .....Gen 41:20
came indeed down at the f ....Gen 43:20
hearken to the voice of the f ..Ex 4:8
be the f month of the year ....Ex 12:2
a male of the f year ....Ex 12:5
the f day ye shall put away....Ex 12:15
the f day until the seventh ....Ex 12:15
f month, on the fourteenth ....Ex 12:18
offer the f of thy ripe fruits ...Ex 22:29
The f of the first fruits of thy..Ex 23:19
the f row shall be a sardius....Ex 28:17
this shall be the f row ....Ex 28:17
of stone like unto the f ....Ex 34:1
the words that were in the f...Ex 34:1
f of the first fruits of thy......Ex 34:26
carbuncle: this was the f ......Ex 39:10
On the f day of the f month...Ex 40:2
the f month in the second .....Ex 40:17
on the f day of the month.....Ex 40:17
burn him as he burned the f...Lev 4:21
a lamb, both of the f year....Lev 9:3
shall bring a lamb of the f ....Lev 12:6
the fourteenth day of the f ....Lev 23:5
without blemish of the f ......Lev 23:12
two lambs of the f year for....Lev 23:19
the f day shall be a holy ......Lev 23:35
take you on the f day the .....Lev 23:40
the f day of the second ....Num 1:1
the f day of the second ....Num 1:18
shall bring a lamb of the f ....Num 6:12
one ram, one lamb of the f ...Num 7:15
goats, five lambs of the f......Num 7:29
one ram, one lamb of the f ...Num 7:69
lambs of the f year sixty .....Num 7:88
the f month of the second .....Num 9:1
they f took their journey ......Num 10:13
up a cake of the f of your.....Num 15:20
bring a she goat of the f .....Num 15:27
the desert of Zin in the f .....Num 20:1
lambs of the f year without....Num 28:3
fourteenth day of the f month. .Num 28:16
and seven lambs of the f year. .Num 28:19
seventh month, on the f day...Num 29:1
and seven lambs of the f year .Num 29:8
fourteen lambs of the f ....Num 29:17
fourteen lambs of the f ....Num 29:20
ram, seven lambs of the f .....Num 29:36
from Rameses in the f month. .Num 33:3
on the fifteenth day of the f...Num 33:3
the f day of the month, that...Deut 1:3
as I fell down at the f ....Deut 9:25
tables of stone like unto the f. .Deut 10:1
the words that were in the f...Deut 10:2

according to the *f* writing .....Deut 10:4
the *f* rain and the latter rain...Deut 11:14
thou sacrificedst the *f* day at ..Deut 16:4
f of the fleece of thy..........Deut 18:4
thou shalt take of the *f* of all ..Deut 26:2
he provided the *f* part for .....Deut 33:21
out against us, as at the *f* .....Josh 8:5
Levi had: for..was the *f* lot ....Josh 21:10
us against the Canaanites *f* ....Judg 1:1
Which of us shall go up *f* .....Judg 20:18
themselves in array the *f*......Judg 20:22
down before us, as in the *f*....Judg 20:39
f bring Michal Saul's..........2Sam 3:13
I am come the *f* this day of ...2Sam 19:20
the days of harvest in the *f*....2Sam 21:9
he attained not to the *f*.......2Sam 23:23
the thirty and *f* year of Asa ...1Kin 16:23
for yourselves, and dress it *f* ..1Kin 18:25
of the provinces went out *f*....1Kin 20:17
f inhabitants that dwelt in 1Chr 9:2
smiteth the Jebusites *f* 1Chr 11:6
the son of Zeruiah went *f* up ..1Chr 11:6
attained not to the *f* three 1Chr 11:25
went over Jordan in the *f* 1Chr 12:15
David delivered *f* this psalm ...1Chr 16:7
Micah the *f*, and Jesiah the 1Chr 23:20
Rehabiah, the *f* was Isshiah ...1Chr 24:21
f lot came forth for Asaph 1Chr 25:9
captains of the host for the *f* ..1Chr 27:3
f measure was threescore......2Chr 3:3
the acts of Rehoboam, *f* 2Chr 12:15
f ways of his father David 2Chr 17:3
the acts of Amaziah, *f* and 2Chr 25:26
acts and of all his ways, *f* 2Chr 28:26
He in the *f* year of his reign...2Chr 29:3
in the *f* month, opened the 2Chr 29:3
on the *f* day of the *f*..........2Chr 29:17
in the sixteenth day of the *f*...2Chr 29:17
And his deeds, *f* and last 2Chr 35:27
the *f* year of Cyrus king of ....Ezra 1:1
that had seen the *f* house .....Ezra 3:12
f year of Cyrus the king.......Ezra 6:3
upon the *f* day of the *f* month .Ezra 7:9
and on the *f* day of the fifth...Ezra 7:9
in the *f* day of the tenth ......Ezra 10:16
by the *f* day of the *f* month ...Ezra 10:17
of them..came up at the *f* .....Neh 7:5
the *f* day unto the last day ....Neh 8:18
sat the *f* in the kingdom ......Esth 1:14
the thirteenth day of the *f*.....Esth 3:12
Art thou the *f* man that was...Job 15:7
restore thy judges as at the *f* ..Is 1:26
the Lord, the *f*, and with .....Is 41:4
Thy *f* father hath sinned ......Is 43:27
am the *f*, and I am the last.....Is 44:6
he: I am the *f*, I also am......Is 48:12
bringeth forth her *f* child ......Jer 4:31
f I will recompense their ......Jer 16:18
f year of Nebuchadrezzar .....Jer 25:1
will build them, as at the *f* ....Jer 33:7
of the land, as at the *f*........Jer 33:11
away: *f* the king of Assyria ....Jer 50:17
the *f* face was the face of a ...Ezek 10:14
in the *f* month, in the *f* day ...Ezek 29:17
in the *f* day of the month .....Ezek 29:17
in the *f* day of the month .....Ezek 31:1
after the measure of the *f*.....Ezek 40:21
unto the priest the *f* of your...Ezek 44:30
the *f* month, in the *f* day......Ezek 45:18
lamb of the *f* year without ....Ezek 46:13
even unto the *f* year of king...Dan 1:21
In the *f* year of Belshazzar ....Dan 7:1
three..*f* horns plucked up ......Dan 7:8
appeared unto me at the *f* ....Dan 8:1
In the *f* year of Darius the ....Dan 9:1
and twentieth day of the *f*.....Dan 10:4
I in the *f* year of Darius ......Dan 11:1
return to my *f* husband ....Hos 2:7
and the latter rain in the *f* ....Joel 2:23
captive with the *f* that go .....Amos 6:7
f dominion; the kingdom ......Mic 4:8
in the *f* day of the month .....Hag 1:1
f chariot were red horses......Zech 6:2
unto the place of the *f* gate ...Zech 14:10
f be reconciled to thy ....Matt 5:24
suffer me *f* to go and bury ....Matt 8:21
except he *f* bind the strong ....Matt 12:20
that man is worse than the *f*...Matt 12:45
Gather ye together *f* the ......Matt 13:30
Elijah truly shall *f* come ......Matt 17:11
But many that are *f* shall .....Matt 19:30
last; and the last shall be *f*....Matt 19:30
the *f* came, they supposed......Matt 20:10
the last shall be *f*, and the *f*...Matt 20:16
and he came to the *f*, and.....Matt 21:28
servants more than the *f* ....Matt 21:36
f and great commandment.....Matt 22:38
Now the *f* day of the feast ....Matt 26:17
last error..worse than the *f*....Matt 27:64
will *f* bind the strong man.....Mark 3:27
the scribes that Elijah must *f* .Mark 9:11
man desire to be *f*, the same ..Mark 9:35
But many that are *f* shall be...Mark 10:31
shall be last: and the last *f* ....Mark 10:31
f of all the commandments ....Mark 12:29
this is the *f* commandment ....Mark 12:30
f day of unleavened bread.....Mark 14:12
of all things from the very *f* ..Luke 1:3
second sabbath after the *f*.....Luke 6:1
suffer me *f* to go and bury ....Luke 9:59
f say, Peace be to this house ..Luke 10:5
not *f* washed before dinner ....Luke 11:38
shall be *f*, and there are *f* .....Luke 13:30
sitteth not down *f*, and........Luke 14:31
But *f* must he suffer many ....Luke 17:25
and the *f* took a wife, and ....Luke 20:29
these things must *f* come to ...Luke 21:9
Now upon the *f* day of the ....Luke 24:1
f findeth his own brother......John 1:41
let him *f* cast a stone at her ...John 8:7
not his disciples at the *f*.......John 12:16
and brake the legs of the *f* ...John 19:32
Peter, and came *f* to the ......John 20:4
Unto you *f* God, having ......Acts 3:26
were called Christians *f* in .....Acts 11:26
When John had *f* preached ....Acts 13:24
should *f* have been spoken ....Acts 13:46
from the *f* day that I came ....Acts 20:18
showed *f* unto them of........Acts 26:20
should be the *f* that should ....Acts 26:23
cast themselves *f* into the .....Acts 27:43
F, I thank my God through ...Rom 1:8
to the Jew *f*, and also to the ..Rom 1:16
the Jew *f*, and also of the .....Rom 2:9
the Jew *f*, and also to the .....Rom 2:10
F Moses saith, I will..........Rom 10:19
Or who hath *f* given to him ...Rom 11:35
if *f* I be somewhat filled with ..Rom 15:24
For *f* of all, when ye come 1Cor 11:18
by, let the *f* hold his peace 1Cor 14:30
f man Adam was made a 1Cor 15:45
The *f* man is of the earth 1Cor 15:47
if there be *f* a willing mind 2Cor 8:12
the gospel unto you at the *f*...Gal 4:13
descended *f* into the lower ....Eph 4:9
gospel from the *f* day until ....Phil 1:5
dead in Christ shall rise *f* 1Thess 4:16
in me *f* Jesus Christ might 1Tim 1:16
Adam was *f* formed, then 1Tim 2:13
them learn *f* to show piety 1Tim 5:4
they have cast off their *f* 1Tim 5:12
must be *f* partaker of the 2Tim 2:6
f and second admonition ......Titus 3:10
bringeth in the *f* begotten .....Heb 1:6
which at the *f* began to be ....Heb 2:3
to whom it was *f* preached ....Heb 4:6
f principles of the oracles .....Heb 5:12
f for his own sins, and then ...Heb 7:27
that *f* covenant had been......Heb 8:7
he hath made the *f* old ....Heb 8:13
Then verily the *f* covenant ....Heb 9:1
the *f*, wherein was the ....Heb 9:2
while as the *f* tabernacle ......Heb 9:8
f testament was dedicated .....Heb 9:18
is *f* pure, then peaceable ......James 3:17
and if it *f* begin at us, what ...1Pet 4:17
this *f*, that no prophecy 2Pet 1:20
him, because he *f* loved us 1John 4:19
which kept not their *f*.........Jude 6
the *f* begotten of the dead ....Rev 1:5
Alpha and Omega, the *f* ......Rev 1:11
Fear not: I am the *f* and ......Rev 1:17
because thou hast left thy *f*....Rev 2:4
and do the *f* works: or else....Rev 2:5
last to be more than the *f*.....Rev 2:19
the *f* beast was like a lion .....Rev 4:7
all the power of the *f* beast ...Rev 13:12
to worship the *f* beast........Rev 13:12
the *f* went, and poured out....Rev 16:2
This is the *f* resurrection ......Rev 20:5
part in the *f* resurrection ......Rev 20:6
the *f* foundation was jasper....Rev 21:19
the end, the *f* and the last ....Rev 22:13

FIRST (THINGS MENTIONED)

Altar ....Gen 8:20
Archer ....Gen 21:20
Artificer ....Gen 4:22
Bigamist ....Gen 4:19
Birthday celebration .....Gen 40:20
Book ....Gen 5:1
Bottle ....Gen 21:14
Bridal veil ....Gen 24:64-67
Cave dwellers ....Gen 19:30
Christian martyr ....Acts 22:19, 20
City builder ....Gen 4:17
Coffin ....Gen 50:26
Command ....Gen 1:3
Commanded by Christ ...Matt 6:33
Commissioners ....Dan 6:2
Cremation 1Sam 31:12
Curse ....Gen 3:14
Death ....Gen 4:8
Diet....................Jer 52:31-34
Doubt ....Gen 3:1
Dream ....Gen 20:3
Drunkenness ....Gen 9:21
Emancipator ....Ex 3:7-22
Embalming ....Gen 50:2, 3
European convert ....Acts 16:14, 15
Execution ....Gen 40:20-22
Family..................Gen 4:1, 2
Famine ....Gen 12:10
Farewell address.........Josh 23:1-16
Farmer ....Gen 4:2
Female government......Judg 4:4, 5
Ferry boat 2Sam 19:18
Food control ....Gen 41:25-27
Frying pan ....Lev 2:7
Gardener ....Gen 2:15
Gold ....Gen 2:11
Harp ....Gen 4:21
Hebrew (Jew) ....Gen 14:13
High priest..............Ex 28:1
Hunter ....Gen 10:8, 9
Idolatry.................Josh 24:2
"In-law" trouble..........Gen 26:34, 35
Iron bedstead ....Deut 3:11
Judge 1Sam 7:15
Kiss ....Gen 27:26, 27
Left-handed man ....Judg 3:15
Letter 2Sam 11:14
Liar ....Gen 3:1-5
Man to hang himself.....2Sam 17:23
Man to shave ....Gen 41:14
Man to wear a ring ......Gen 41:42
Miracles of Christ ....John 2:1-11
Mother of twins ....Gen 25:21-28
Murderer ....Gen 4:8
Musician................Gen 4:21
Navy 1Kin 9:26
Oath ....Gen 21:24
Orchestra 2Sam 6:5
Organ ....Gen 4:21
Pilgrim ....Gen 12:1-8
Prayer ....Gen 4:26
Prison ....Gen 39:20
Prophecy ....Gen 3:15
Prophetess ....Ex 15:20
Proposal of adultery .....Gen 39:7-12
Pulpit ....Neh 8:4
Purchase of land ....Gen 23:3-20
Question ....Gen 3:1
Rainbow................Gen 9:13, 14
Rape ....Judg 19:24, 25

Riddle .... Judg 14:12-18
Sabbath .... Gen 2:2, 3
Sacrifice .... Gen 8:20
Saddle .... Gen 22:3
Scribe .... Ex 24:4
Selective Service .... Num 31:3-6
Shepherd .... Gen 4:2
Shepherdess .... Gen 29:9
Sheriffs .... Dan 3:2
Shipbuilder .... Gen 6:14
Sin .... Gen 3:1-24
Singing school 1Chr 25:5-7
Sunstroke 2Kin 4:18-20
Surveying of land .... Josh 18:8, 9
Temptation .... Gen 3:1-6
Theater .... Acts 19:29-31
To be named before birth. Gen 16:11
To confess Christ .... John 1:49
Tombstone .... Gen 35:20
Tower .... Gen 11:4, 5
Vagabond .... Gen 4:9-12
Voluntary fasting .... Judg 20:26
Wage contract .... Gen 29:15-20
War .... Gen 14:2-12
Warships .... Num 24:24
Well .... Gen 16:14
Whirlwind 2Kin 2:1
Wife .... Gen 3:20
Winding stairs 1Kin 6:8
Woman thief .... Gen 31:19
Woman to curse .... Judg 17:1, 2
Woman to use cosmetics. . 2Kin 9:30
Words spoken to man ... Gen 1:28
Worship .... Gen 4:3-5

FIRST DAY OF THE WEEK—*Sunday*
Day of Christ's resurrection .... Mark 16:9; John 20:1, 19
Day after the Sabbath ... Matt 28:1; Mark 16:1, 2
Day of Christian worship . Acts 20:7; 1Cor 16:1, 2
Called "the Lord's day". . Rev 1:10

FIRST FRUIT—*the earliest crops*
Regulations concerning:
Law specified .... Lev 23:9-14
Brought to God's house . . Ex 34:26
Ritual of, described ...... Deut 26:3-10
Considered holy .... Ezek 48:14
God honored by .... Prov 3:9
Figurative of:
Israel's position .... Rom 11:16
Christ's place in resurrection 1Cor 15:20, 23
Christians .... James 1:18
First converts .... Rom 16:5

[*also* FIRST FRUITS]
the *f f* of thy labors, which .... Ex 23:16
The first of the *f f* of thy land . Ex 23:19
f f of wheat harvest, and the . . Ex 34:22
oblation of the *f f*, ye shall .... Lev 2:12
offer a meat offering of thy *f f*. Lev 2:14
for the meat offering of thy *f f*. Lev 2:14
are the *f f* unto the Lord ...... Lev 23:17
with the bread of the *f f* ...... Lev 23:20
f f of them which they shall ... Num 18:12
Also in the day of the *f f* ..... Num 28:26
f f also of thy corn, of thy .... Deut 18:4
bread of the *f f*, twenty 2Kin 4:42
the *f f* of corn, wine, and oil . . 2Chr 31:5
bring the *f f* of our ground .... Neh 10:35
and the *f f* of all fruit trees .... Neh 10:35
should bring the *f f* of our .... Neh 10:37
for the *f f*, and for the tithes . . Neh 12:44
at times appointed..the *f f*..... Neh 13:31
the Lord, and the *f f* of his ... Jer 2:3
and the *f f* of your oblations . . Ezek 20:40
have the *f f* of the Spirit ...... Rom 8:23
if the *f f* be holy .... Rom 11:16
Stephanas, that it is the *f f* 1Cor 16:15
f f unto God and to the Lamb . Rev 14:4

FIRST RIPE—*earliest ripe*
the time of the *f r* grapes ..... Num 13:20
I saw your fathers as the *f r* . . Hos 9:10
soul desired the *f r* fruit .... Mic 7:1
like fig trees with the *f r* ...... Nah 3:12

FIRSTBEGOTTEN—*See* FIRST; BEGOTTEN

FIRST-BORN—*the eldest*
Said to the younger ...... Gen 19:31; Gen 19:34
Bore a son .... Gen 19:37
Give younger before ..... Gen 29:26
According to birthright . . . Gen 43:33
Israel is My .... Ex 4:22
Will slay your .... Ex 4:23
All in the land of Egypt. . Ex 11:5
Will smite all .... Ex 12:12
Killed all the .... Ex 13:15; Ps 105:36
Sanctify to me all .... Ex 13:2
Of Israel are Mine ...... Num 3:13
Lay foundation in .... Josh 6:26
Of death shall .... Job 18:13
Give birth .... Luke 2:7
Of all creation .... Col 1:15
So that he who destroyed. Heb 11:28
Privileges of:
First in family .... Gen 48:13, 14
Delegated authority of . . . Gen 27:1-29
Received father's special blessing .... Gen 27:4, 35
Bears father's title 2Chr 21:1, 3
Given double portion of inheritance .... Deut 21:17
Object of special love .... Jer 31:9, 20
Precious and valuable .... Mic 6:7
Laws concerning:
Dedicated to God .... Ex 22:29-31
To be redeemed .... Ex 34:20
Redemption price of ..... Num 3:46-51
Tribe of Levi substituted for .... Num 3:11-45
Death of, next brother substituted .... Matt 22:24-28
Change of, forbidden .... Deut 21:15-17
Forfeited by evil deeds . . . Gen 49:3, 4, 8
Forfeited by sale .... Heb 12:16, 17
Changed sovereignty 1Sam 16:6-12
Christ subject to .... Luke 2:22-24
Figurative of, Christ in:
Authority .... Ps 89:27
Honor .... Heb 1:6
Resurrection .... Col 1:18
Church .... Rom 8:29
Glory .... Heb 12:22, 23

Canaan begat Sidon his *f* ...... Gen 10:15
f went in, and lay with her .... Gen 19:33
Huz his *f*, and Buz his .... Gen 22:21
he said, I am thy son, thy *f* . . . Gen 27:32
Reuben, Jacob's *f*, and .... Gen 35:23
Judah..a wife for Er his *f* ..... Gen 38:6
the name of the *f* Manasseh . . . Gen 41:51
sons; Reuben, Jacob's *f* .... Gen 46:8
my father: for this is the *f*..... Gen 48:18
the *f* of Israel: Hanoch and . . . Ex 6:14
will smite all the *f* in the ...... Ex 12:12
Lord smote all the *f* in the .... Ex 12:29
from the *f* of Pharaoh that .... Ex 12:29
unto the *f* of the captive ...... Ex 12:29
dungeon; and all the *f* of ...... Ex 12:29
the *f* of man among thy .... Ex 13:13
the Lord slew all the *f* in ..... Ex 13:15
of Egypt, both the *f* of man . . . Ex 13:15
of man, and the *f* of beast .... Ex 13:15
all the *f* of my children I ...... Ex 13:15
Nadab the *f*, and Abihu ...... Num 3:2
even instead the *f* of all the . . . Num 8:16
For all the *f* of the children . . . Num 8:17
day that I smote every *f* in .... Num 8:17
f of man shalt thou surely ..... Num 18:15
f which she beareth shall ...... Deut 25:6
for he was the *f* of Joseph .... Josh 17:1
Machir the *f* of Manasseh .... Josh 17:1
he said unto Jether his *f* ..... Judg 8:20
the name of his *f* was Joel 1Sam 8:2
Eliab the *f*, and next unto 1Sam 17:13
and his *f* was Amnon, of 2Sam 3:2
foundation..in Abiram his *f* . . . 1Kin 16:34
Canaan begat Zidon his *f* 1Chr 1:13
Er, the *f* of Judah, was evil . . . 1Chr 2:3
f of Hezron..Ram the *f* 1Chr 2:25
of Jerahmeel..Mesha his *f* 1Chr 2:42
the *f* Amnon of Ahinoam 1Chr 3:1
the sons of Hur, the *f* of 1Chr 4:4
the sons of Reuben the *f* 1Chr 5:1
for he was the *f*; but 1Chr 5:1
the sons of Samuel: the *f* 1Chr 6:28
his *f* son Abdon and Zur 1Chr 8:30
Asaiah the *f*, and his sons 1Chr 9:5
his *f* son Abdon, then Zur 1Chr 9:36
Shemiah the *f*, Jehozabad 1Chr 26:4
to Jehoram..was the *f* 2Chr 21:3
Also the *f* of our sons, and .... Neh 10:36
smote all the *f* in Egypt .... Ps 78:51
Who smote the *f* of Egypt .... Ps 135:8
that smote Egypt in their *f* .... Ps 136:10
And the *f* of the poor shall .... Is 14:30
that is in bitterness for his *f* . . . Zech 12:10
she had brought forth her *f* . . . Matt 1:25

FIRSTLING—*first produce; first of any group of things*
Abel brought .... Gen 4:4
Set apart every .... Ex 13:12; Ex 34:19
Of an ass thou shall redeem .... Ex 13:13; Ex 34:20
Lords, no man shall sanctify .... Lev 27:26
Of unclean beasts .... Num 18:15
Ye shall bring, of your herd .... Deut 12:6
Males sanctify .... Deut 15:19
Glory is like .... Deut 33:17

[*also* FIRSTLINGS]
every *f* that cometh of a ...... Ex 13:12
instead of all the *f* among ..... Num 3:41
But the *f* of a cow, or the *f* . . . Num 18:17
a sheep or the *f* of a goat ..... Num 18:17
the *f* of thy herds or of thy .... Deut 12:17
the *f* of thy herds and of ...... Deut 14:23
f of our herds and of our ..... Neh 10:36

FISH—*an aquatic animal*
Features regarding:
Created by God .... Gen 1:20, 21
Worship of forbidden .... Deut 4:15-18
Caught by net .... Matt 4:18
Worshiped by pagans 1Sam 5:4
Some disciples called as fishermen .... Matt 4:18-21
Miracles concerning:
Jonah's life in .... Jon 1:17
Multiplied by Christ ..... Matt 14:17-21
Bearing a coin .... Matt 17:27
Figurative of:
Men in the sea of life .... Ezek 47:9, 10
Ministers as fishermen . . . Matt 4:19
Ignorant men .... Eccl 9:12

[*also* FISHES, FISHING, FISH'S]
dominion over the *f* of .... Gen 1:26
upon all the *f* of the sea ...... Gen 9:2
f that is in the river .... Ex 7:18
f..in the river died .... Ex 7:21
the *f*, which we did eat .... Num 11:5
shall all the *f* of the sea .... Num 11:22
creeping things, and of *f* 1Kin 4:33
brought *f*, and all manner ..... Neh 13:16
f of the sea shall declare ...... Job 12:8
or his head with *f* spears? ..... Job 41:7
f of the sea, and whatsoever . . . Ps 8:8
blood, and slew their *f* .... Ps 105:29
they shall *f* them .... Jer 16:16
cause the *f* of thy rivers .... Ezek 29:4
all the *f* of thy rivers shall ..... Ezek 29:4
and all the *f* of thy rivers ..... Ezek 29:5
So that the *f* of the sea .... Ezek 38:20
f of the sea also shall be ...... Hos 4:3
Lord..prepared a great *f* ...... Jon 1:17
Jonah..the belly of the *f* ...... Jon 1:17
Lord his God out of the *f* ..... Jon 2:1

Lord spake unto the *f* ....Jon 2:10
men as the *f* of the sea ....Hab 1:14
and the *f* of the sea and ......Zeph 1:3
Or if he ask a *f* ....Matt 7:10
but five loaves, and two *f* .....Matt 14:17
five loaves, and two *f*.........Matt 14:19
Seven, and a few little *f*.......Matt 15:34
seven loaves and the *f* ....Matt 15:36
take up the *f* that first ....Matt 17:27
they say, Five, and two *f*......Mark 6:38
five loaves and the two *f*......Mark 6:41
two *f* divided he among ....Mark 6:41
fragments, and of the *f* ....Mark 6:43
they had a few small *f* ....Mark 8:7
a great multitude of *f*.........Luke 5:6
draught of the *f* which ....Luke 5:9
but five loaves and two *f*.......Luke 9:13
five loaves and the two *f*......Luke 9:16
ask a *f* will he for a *f* give ....Luke 11:11
a piece of a broiled *f* ....Luke 24:42
loaves, and two small *f* ....John 6:9
likewise of the *f* as much......John 6:11
Peter saith..I go a *f*...........John 21:3
for the multitude of *f*.........John 21:6
dragging the net with *f*........John 21:8
f laid thereon, and bread......John 21:9
f..ye have now caught ....John 21:10
the net to land full of..*f*.......John 21:11
giveth them, and *f* likewise ....John 21:13
of *f*, and another of birds 1Cor 15:39

FISH GATE—*a gate of Jerusalem*
Manasseh built wall there.2Chr 33:13, 14
Built by sons of Hassenaah ....Neh 3:3
Two choirs took their stand ....Neh 12:38-40
A cry there prophesied ..Zeph 1:10

FISHERMEN—*ones who fish*

[*also* FISHER'S, FISHERS]
The *f* also shall mourn ....Is 19:8
I will send for many *f*.........Jer 16:16
the *f* shall stand upon it.......Ezek 47:10
the sea: for they were *f* ....Matt 4:18
I will make you *f* of men .....Matt 4:19
the sea; for they were *f* ....Mark 1:16
make you to become *f* of .....Mark 1:17
f were gone out of them ......Luke 5:2
girt his *f* coat unto him ....John 21:7

FISHHOOK—*a barbed hook for catching fish*
Cannot catch Leviathan ..Job 41:1
Fishing in the brooks ....Is 19:8

[*also* FISHHOOKS]
and your posterity with *f*......Amos 4:2

FISHPOOL—*water in which fish swim (used figuratively)*
eyes like the *f* in Heshbon ....Song 7:4

FIST—*a clenched hand*

[*also* FISTS]
gathered the wind in his *f*.....Prov 30:4
with the *f* of wickedness ......Is 58:4

FIST FIGHTING—*brawling*
Punishment of..........Ex 21:18, 19

FIT—*prepared; suitable; acceptable*

[*also* FITTED, FITTETH, FITLY]
by the hand of a *f* man ....Lev 16:21
gold *f* upon the carved work ..1Kin 6:35
soldiers, *f* to go out for war ...1Chr 7:11
of war *f* for the battle 1Chr 12:8
Is it *f* to say to a king ....Job 34:18
withal be *f* in thy lips ....Prov 22:18
f for thyself in the field ....Prov 24:27
word *f* spoken is like ....Prov 25:11
washed with milk, and *f* ......Song 5:12
he *f* it with planes, and he ....Is 44:13
f for the kingdom of God .....Luke 9:62
neither *f* for the land ....Luke 14:35
not *f* that he should live ......Acts 22:22
of wrath *f* to destruction ......Rom 9:22
building *f* framed together.....Eph 2:21
the whole body *f* joined.......Eph 4:16
as it is *f* in the Lord ....Col 3:18

FITCHES—*vetches; tares*
Annual plant for forage ..Is 28:25, 27
Same as rye in ....Ezek 4:9

FIVE

[*also* FIFTH]
morning were the *f* day ....Gen 1:23
lived an hundred and *f*........Gen 5:6
nine hundred and *f* years......Gen 5:11
Enoch lived sixty and *f* ....Gen 5:21
Noah was *f* hundred years.....Gen 5:32
f hundred years, and begat ....Gen 11:11
Abram was seventy and *f* .....Gen 12:4
Peradventure..shall lack *f* .....Gen 18:28
destroy..city for lack of *f*......Gen 18:28
the *f* part of the land ....Gen 41:34
and yet there are *f* years ......Gen 45:6
are *f* years of famine ....Gen 45:11
Pharaoh should have the *f* ....Gen 47:26
restore *f* oxen for an ox........Ex 22:1
and shall add the *f* part ....Lev 5:16
in the *f* year shall ye eat ......Lev 19:25
he shall add a *f* part ....Lev 27:13
and shall add a *f* part of ......Lev 27:27
six thousand..*f* hundred ....Num 1:21
add unto it the *f* part ....Num 5:7
on the *f* day nine bullocks.....Num 29:26
f kings of Midian; Balaam.....Num 31:8
about *f* thousand men.........Josh 8:12
f kings of the Amorites ....Josh 10:5
f lords of the Philistines.......Josh 13:3
forty and *f* years, even ....Josh 14:10
day fourscore and *f* years .....Josh 14:10
f lot came out for the tribe ....Josh 19:24
f lords of the Philistines ....Judg 3:3
on the *f* day to depart ....Judg 19:8
smote him under the *f* rib 2Sam 2:23
there under the *f* rib 2Sam 3:27
smote him..in the *f* rib 2Sam 20:10
songs..a thousand and *f*.......1Kin 4:32
f cubits was the one wing 1Kin 6:24
side posts were a *f* part 1Kin 6:31
Solomon's work, *f* hundred 1Kin 9:23
f year of Joram the son of 2Kin 8:16
the fourth, Raddai the *f* 1Chr 2:14
fourth, and Rapha the *f*........1Chr 8:2
f to Malchijah, the sixth 1Chr 24:9
Elam the *f*, Jehohanan the 1Chr 26:3
f captain for the *f* month......1Chr 27:8
wing of..cherub was *f*.........2Chr 3:11
wing was likewise *f* cubits 2Chr 3:11
and *f* cubits the height 2Chr 4:2
scaffold, of *f* cubits long 2Chr 6:13
f year of king Rehoboam 2Chr 12:2
Jerusalem in the *f* month......Ezra 7:8
f time with an open letter .....Neh 6:5
captive in the *f* month ....Jer 1:3
in the *f* year of Jehoiakim.....Jer 36:9
f day of the month ....Ezek 1:1
in the *f* day of the month .....Ezek 1:2
f year of king Jehoiachin's ....Ezek 1:2
seventh year, in the *f*.........Ezek 20:1
hundred and *f* and thirty ......Dan 12:12
I weep in the *f* month ....Zech 7:3
f and the fast of the seventh...Zech 8:19
f loaves and two fishes ....Matt 14:17
f loaves, and the two fishes ...Matt 14:19
And *f* of them were wise......Matt 25:2
wise, and *f* were foolish........Matt 25:2
unto one he gave *f* talents.....Matt 25:15
had received the *f* talents .....Matt 25:16
made them other *f* talents .....Matt 25:16
that had received *f* talents.....Matt 25:20
brought other *f* talents ....Matt 25:20
deliveredst unto me *f* ....Matt 25:20
gained beside them *f*..........Matt 25:20
say, *F*, and two fishes ....Mark 6:38
he had taken the *f* loaves .....Mark 6:41
were about *f* thousand men ....Mark 6:44
When I brake the *f* loaves ....Mark 8:19
among the *f* thousand ....Mark 8:19
hid herself *f* months ....Luke 1:24
one owed *f* hundred pence ....Luke 7:41
f loaves and two fishes........Luke 9:13
were about *f* thousand ....Luke 9:14
f loaves and the two fishes ....Luke 9:16
f sparrows sold for two ....Luke 12:6
shall be *f* in one house........Luke 12:52
bought *f* yoke of oxen ....Luke 14:19
thou hast had *f* husbands......John 4:18
Bethesda, having *f* porches ....John 5:2
number about *f* thousand .....John 6:10
men was about *f* thousand ....Acts 4:4
I had rather speak *f* words 1Cor 14:19
seen..*f* hundred brethren 1Cor 15:6
f times received I forty........2Cor 11:24
he had opened the *f* seal ......Rev 6:9
be tormented *f* months ....Rev 9:5
to hurt men *f* months ....Rev 9:10
f angel poured out his vial ....Rev 16:10
f are fallen, and one is........Rev 17:10

FIXED—*stable; made secure*
O God, my heart is *f*: I will ..Ps 57:7
O God, my heart is *f*; I will ..Ps 108:1
heart is *f*, trusting in..........Ps 112:7
you there is a great gulf *f* .....Luke 16:26

FLAG—*"fluttering"—water plant; weed*
Name of many water plants ....Ex 2:3-5
Rendered as "weeds" in .Jon 2:5

[*also* FLAGS]
the *f* grow without water? .....Job 8:11
reeds and *f* shall wither ....Is 19:6

FLAGELLATION—*punishment by whipping, flogging*
For immorality ....Lev 19:20
For defamation ....Deut 22:16-18
Forty blows ....Deut 25:3
Of Christ ....Matt 27:26
Mark 15:15
Thirty-nine lashes 2Cor 11:24
Of apostles ....Acts 5:40

FLAGON—*flask*
Small vessels for liquids ..Is 22:24

[*also* FLAGONS]
of flesh, and a *f* of wine 2Sam 6:19
of flesh, and a *f* of wine 1Chr 16:3
Stay me with *f*, comfort ....Song 2:5
gods, and love *f* of wine ......Hos 3:1

FLAKES—*folds*
the *f* of his flesh are joined ...Job 41:23

FLAME—*blazing combustion; to shine*

[*also* FLAMES, FLAMING]
f sword which turned ....Gen 3:24
Lord appeared..in a *f*.........Ex 3:2
a *f* from the city of Sihon .....Num 21:28
f went up toward heaven......Judg 13:20
Lord ascended in the *f* of .....Judg 13:20
make a great *f* with smoke ....Judg 20:38
when the *f* began to arise .....Judg 20:40
f of the city ascended up ......Judg 20:40
f shall dry up his branches ....Job 15:30
f goeth out of his mouth ......Job 41:21
Lord divideth the *f* ....Ps 29:7
f setteth the mountains........Ps 83:14
and his ministers a *f* fire ......Ps 104:4
and *f* fire in their land ....Ps 105:32
f burned up the wicked ....Ps 106:18
hath a most vehement *f*........Song 8:6
shining of a *f* fire by night ....Is 4:5
f consumeth the chaff..........Is 5:24
and his Holy One for a *f*......Is 10:17
their faces shall be as *f* ....Is 13:8
and the *f* of devouring fire ....Is 29:6
f of a devouring fire ....Is 30:30
neither shall the *f* kindle ......Is 43:2
from the power of the *f*.......Is 47:14
his rebuke with *f* of fire.......Is 66:15
f from the midst of Sihon .....Jer 48:45
against Jacob like a *f* fire .....Lam 2:3
the *f f* shall not be quenched ..Ezek 20:47
f of the fire slew those men ...Dan 3:22

throne was like the fiery *f* ..... Dan 7:9
and given to the burning *f* .... Dan 7:11
by the sword, and by the *f* .... Dan 11:33
it burneth as a *f* fire .... Hos 7:6
behind them a *f* burneth ...... Joel 2:3
the noise of a *f* of fire .... Joel 2:5
house of Joseph a *f* .... Obad 18
be with *f* torches in the day ... Nah 2:3
I am tormented in this *f* ...... Luke 16:24
in a *f* of fire in a bush .... Acts 7:30
In *f* fire taking vengeance 2Thess 1:8
his ministers a *f* of fire .... Heb 1:7
eyes were as a *f* of fire .... Rev 1:14
eyes like unto a *f* of fire ...... Rev 2:18
His eyes were as a *f* of fire .... Rev 19:12

FLANKS—*sides of something*
on them, which is by the *f* .... Lev 3:4
which is by the *f* .... Lev 3:10
which is by the *f* .... Lev 4:9
on them, which is by the *f* .... Lev 7:4
collops of fat on his *f* .... Job 15:27

FLASH—*sudden burst of light*
of a *f* of lightning .... Ezek 1:14

FLAT—*horizontal*
bowed..head, and fell *f* .... Num 22:31
wall of..shall fall down *f* ...... Josh 6:5
wall fell down *f*, so that .... Josh 6:20

FLAT NOSE—*a disfigurement*
Disqualifies for service ... Lev 21:18

FLATTERY—*unjustified praise*
Used by:
False prophets .... Rom 16:18
Hypocrites .... Ps 78:36
Wicked .... Ps 36:1-4
Prostitutes .... Prov 2:16
Attitude of saints toward:
Should avoid users of .... Prov 20:19
Pray against .... Ps 5:8, 9
Should not use 1Thess 2:5
Dangers of:
Leads to ruin .... Prov 26:28
Brings deception .... Prov 29:5
Corrupts .... Dan 11:21, 25, 27
Brings death .... Acts 12:21-23

[*also* FLATTERETH, FLATTERIES, FLATTERING]
speaketh *f* to his friends ...... Job 17:5
give *f* titles unto man .... Job 32:21
I know not to give *f* titles ..... Job 32:22
f lips and with a double heart .. Ps 12:2
Lord shall cut off all *f* lips .... Ps 12:3
from the *f* of the tongue of .... Prov 6:24
which *f* with her words .... Prov 7:5
the *f* of her lips she forced .... Prov 7:21
he that *f* with the tongue ...... Prov 28:23
vain vision nor *f* divination .... Ezek 12:24
shall he corrupt by *f* .... Dan 11:32
cleave to them with *f* .... Dan 11:34
used we *f* words, as ye 1Thess 2:5

FLAX—*the flax plant*
Grown in Egypt and Palestine .... Ex 9:31
Used for:
Cords .... Judg 15:14
Spinning .... Is 19:9
Garments ("linen") ...... Deut 22:1

hid them with..stalks of *f* ..... Josh 2:6
seeketh wool, and *f*, and ...... Prov 31:13
with a line of *f* in his hand .... Ezek 40:3
wool and my *f*, mine oil .... Hos 2:5
smoking *f* shall he not .... Matt 12:20

FLAY—*to strip off the skin*

[*also* FLAYED]
shall *f* the burnt offering ...... Lev 1:6
f all the burnt offering 2Chr 29:34
and the Levites *f* them 2Chr 35:11
f their skin from off them ..... Mic 3:3

FLEA—*a parasitic, blood-sucking insect*
Figurative of insignificance 1Sam 24:14

is come out to seek a *f* 1Sam 26:20

FLEE—*to run away from danger or evil*

[*also* FLED, FLEEDEST, FLEEING, FLEETH]
of Sodom and Gomorrah *f* .... Gen 14:10
remained *f* to the mountain ... Gen 14:10
she *f* from her face .... Gen 16:6
I *f* from the face of .... Gen 16:8
f thou to Laban my brother ... Gen 27:43
he *f* with all that he had ...... Gen 31:21
f from the face of Esau .... Gen 35:1
f from..his brother .... Gen 35:7
garment in her hand..*f* .... Gen 39:13
garment with me, and *f* .... Gen 39:18
f from the face Pharaoh .... Ex 2:15
servants and his cattle *f* ...... Ex 9:20
Egypt that the people *f* .... Ex 14:5
a place whither he shall *f* ..... Ex 21:13
f when none pursueth .... Lev 26:17
f, as *f* from a sword .... Lev 26:36
let them that hate thee *f* ...... Num 10:35
were round about them *f* ...... Num 16:34
that he may *f* thither .... Num 35:6
person unawares may *f* .... Num 35:15
refuge, whither he was *f* ...... Num 35:26
the slayer might *f* thither ...... Deut 4:42
f unto one of these cities ...... Deut 4:42
slayer, which shall *f* .... Deut 19:4
f into one of these cities ...... Deut 19:11
f before thee seven ways ...... Deut 28:7
f before the men of Ai .... Josh 7:4
that we will *f* before them ..... Josh 8:5
f before us, as at the first .... Josh 8:6
we will *f* before them .... Josh 8:6
people..*f* to the wilderness .... Josh 8:20
But these five kings *f*, and .... Josh 10:16
and unwittingly may *f* .... Josh 20:3
any person..might *f* .... Josh 20:9
But Adoni-bezek *f* .... Judg 1:6
Sisera *f* away on his feet ...... Judg 4:17
host *f* to Beth-shittah .... Judg 7:22
Jotham ran away, and *f* .... Judg 9:21
f all the men and women ...... Judg 9:51
Let us *f*, and draw them ...... Judg 20:32
f toward the wilderness .... Judg 20:45
f every man into his tent 1Sam 4:10
Israel is *f* before 1Sam 4:17
f from him, and were sore 1Sam 17:24
slaughter; and they *f* from 1Sam 19:8
he went, and *f*, and escaped ... 1Sam 19:12
they knew when he *f* 1Sam 22:17
the son of Ahimelech *f* 1Sam 23:6
rode upon camels, and *f* 1Sam 30:17
that the men of Israel *f* 1Sam 31:7
forsook the cities, and *f* 1Sam 31:7
are *f* from the battle 2Sam 1:4
nurse took him up, and *f* 2Sam 4:4
she made haste to *f* 2Sam 4:4
that the Syrians were *f* 2Sam 10:14
f they also before Abishai 2Sam 10:14
up upon his mule, and *f* 2Sam 13:29
Absalom *f*..went to Talmai 2Sam 13:37
people..with him shall *f* 2Sam 17:2
all Israel *f* every one to 2Sam 18:17
when they *f* into battle 2Sam 19:3
now he if *f* out of the land 2Sam 19:9
f because of Absalom thy 1Kin 2:7
Joab was *f* unto the 1Kin 2:29
f from his lord Hadadezer 1Kin 11:23
f from the presence of king ... 1Kin 12:2
chariot, to *f* to Jerusalem 1Kin 12:18
Syrians *f*; and Israel 1Kin 20:20
f to Aphek, into the city 1Kin 20:30
Ben-hadad *f*, and came 1Kin 20:30
so that they *f* before them 2Kin 3:24
arose and *f* in the twilight 2Kin 7:7
and *f* for their life 2Kin 7:7
open the door, and *f* and 2Kin 9:3
opened the door, and *f* 2Kin 9:10
f by the way of the garden 2Kin 9:27
he *f* to Megiddo, and died 2Kin 9:27
he *f* to Lachish, but 2Kin 14:19
the men of Israel *f* from 1Chr 10:1
the valley saw that they *f* 1Chr 10:7
forsook their cities, and *f* 1Chr 10:7
battle; and they *f* before 1Chr 19:14
saw that the Syrians were *f* 1Chr 19:15
likewise *f* before Abishai 1Chr 19:15
f from..Solomon 2Chr 10:2
to his chariot, to *f* to 2Chr 10:18
and the Ethiopians *f* 2Chr 14:12
f to Lachish; but 2Chr 25:27
Should such a man as I *f* ...... Neh 6:11
that did the work, were *f* ..... Neh 13:10
f away, they see no good ..... Job 9:25
he *f* also as a shadow, and .... Job 14:2
fain *f* out of his hand .... Job 27:22
f into the wilderness in .... Job 30:3
abhor me, they *f* far from ..... Job 30:10
arrow cannot make him *f* ..... Job 41:28
he *f* from Absalom his .... Ps 3: *title*
F as a bird to your .... Ps 11:1
f from Saul in the .... Ps 57: *title*
the sea saw it, and *f* .... Ps 114:3
O thou sea, that thou *f* .... Ps 114:5
I *f* from thy presence? .... Ps 139:7
wicked *f* when no man .... Prov 28:1
and the shadows *f* away .... Song 2:17
whom will ye *f* for help? ...... Is 10:3
afraid; Gibeah of Saul is *f* ..... Is 10:29
f every one into his own ...... Is 13:14
and they shall *f* far off .... Is 17:13
they *f* from the swords .... Is 21:15
thy rulers are *f* together .... Is 22:3
which have *f* from far .... Is 22:3
who *f* from the noise of the ... Is 24:18
f upon horses..shall ye *f* ...... Is 30:16
thousand shall *f* at the .... Is 30:17
rebuke of five shall ye *f* .... Is 30:17
sorrow and sighing shall *f* ..... Is 35:10
and mourning shall *f* .... Is 51:11
birds of the heavens were *f* .... Jer 4:25
city shall *f* for the noise .... Jer 4:29
shepherds..have no way to *f* ... Jer 25:35
afraid and *f*..into Egypt .... Jer 26:21
beaten down, and are *f* .... Jer 46:5
swift *f* away, nor the .... Jer 46:6
F, save your lives, and be ..... Jer 48:6
F ye, turn back, dwell .... Jer 49:8
F, get you far off, dwell ...... Jer 49:30
voice of them that *f* and ...... Jer 50:28
f away and wandered .... Lam 4:15
they *f* to hide themselves ...... Dan 10:7
for they have *f* from me ...... Hos 7:13
mighty shall *f* away naked ..... Amos 2:16
f thee away into the land ..... Amos 7:12
f of them shall not *f* .... Amos 9:1
Jonah..*f* unto Tarshish .... Jon 1:3
he *f* from the presence .... Jon 1:10
look upon thee shall *f* .... Nah 3:7
cankerworm spoileth, and *f* .... Nah 3:16
f from..the north .... Zech 2:6
f to the valley of the .... Zech 14:5
f from..the earthquake .... Zech 14:5
f, like as ye fled from .... Zech 14:5
f into Egypt, and be thou ..... Matt 2:13
f from the wrath to come? .... Matt 3:7
And they that kept them *f* .... Matt 8:33
f ye into another; for .... Matt 10:23
disciples forsook him and *f* .... Matt 26:56
that fed the swine *f* .... Mark 5:14
them that be in Judea *f* to .... Mark 13:14
all forsook him, and *f* .... Mark 14:50
and *f* from the sepulcher ...... Mark 16:8
f from the wrath to come? .... Luke 3:7
them which are in Judea *f* ..... Luke 21:21
f from him: for they know .... John 10:5
leaveth the sheep, and *f* ...... John 10:12
f Moses at this saying .... Acts 7:29
and *f* unto Lystra and Derbe .. Acts 14:6
the prisoners had been *f* ...... Acts 16:27
about to *f* out of the ship ..... Acts 27:30
F fornication 1Cor 6:18
beloved, *f* from idolatry 1Cor 10:14
man of God, *f* these things 1Tim 6:11
F also youthful lusts: but 2Tim 2:22

f for refuge to lay hold ....Heb 6:18
and he will *f* from you ....James 4:7
death shall *f* from them ....Rev 9:6
woman *f* into..wilderness ......Rev 12:6
earth and the heaven *f*........Rev 20:11

FLEECE—*freshly sheared wool*
Given to priests ....Deut 18:3, 4
Sign to Gideon ....Judg 6:36-40
Warm ....Job 31:20

were not warmed with the *f*...Job 31:20

FLESH—*soft part of an animal; human nature*
Used to designate:
All created life ....Gen 6:13, 17, 19
Kinsmen (of same nature).Rom 9:3, 5, 8
The body ....Job 33:25
Marriage................Matt 19:5
Human nature ....John 1:14
Christ's mystical nature ..John 6:51, 53-63
Human weakness ....Matt 16:17
Outward appearance 2Cor 5:16
The evil principle in man .Rom 7:18
Food ....Ex 16:12
In a bad sense, described as:
Having passions ....Gal 5:24
Producing evil works.....Gal 5:19-21
Dominating the mind ....Eph 2:3
Absorbing the affections..Rom 13:14
Seeking outward display..Gal 6:12, 13
Antagonizing the Spirit ..Gal 5:17
Fighting against God's Law ....Rom 8:7
Reaping corruption ......Gal 6:8
Producing death ....Rom 7:5
Christian's attitude toward:
Still confronts ....Rom 7:18-23
Source of opposition .....Gal 5:17
Make no provision for ...Rom 13:14
Do not love.............1John 2:15-17
Do not walk in..........Rom 8:1, 4
Do not live in..........Rom 8:12, 13
Crucified ....Gal 5:24

[*also* FLESHLY]
closed up the *f* instead ....Gen 2:21
and they shall be one *f* ....Gen 2:24
man for that he also is *f* ......Gen 6:3
all *f* had corrupted his way ....Gen 6:12
two of all *f*, wherein is the ....Gen 7:15
all *f* died that moved upon ....Gen 7:21
But *f* with the life thereof .....Gen 9:4
living creature of all *f*.........Gen 9:15
a flood to destroy all *f*........Gen 9:15
between me and all *f* ....Gen 9:17
covenant shall be in your *f*....Gen 17:13
circumcised the *f*..foreskin.....Gen 17:25
art my bone and my *f* ....Gen 29:14
birds shall eat thy *f* from ......Gen 40:19
turned again as his other *f* ....Ex 4:7
carry forth aught of the *f* .....Ex 12:46
give you *f* to eat ....Ex 16:8
his *f* shall not be eaten........Ex 21:28
f of the bullock..his skin ......Ex 29:14
shall eat the *f* of the ram .....Ex 29:32
f shall it not be poured ....Ex 30:32
all his *f*, with his head ....Lev 4:11
shall touch the *f*.............Lev 6:27
of the *f* of the sacrifice........Lev 7:17
f that toucheth any unclean ...Lev 7:19
for the *f*, all that be clean .....Lev 7:19
soul that eateth of the *f*.......Lev 7:20
bullock and his hide, his *f*.....Lev 8:17
f shall ye not eat, and ....Lev 11:3
eighth day the *f* of his ....Lev 12:3
have in the skin of his *f*.......Lev 13:2
plague in the skin of the *f*.....Lev 13:3
deeper than..skin of his *f* .....Lev 13:3
quick raw *f* in the rising.......Lev 13:10
leprosy..covered all his *f* .....Lev 13:13
priest shall see the raw *f* .....Lev 13:15
raw *f* is unclean; it is a ....Lev 13:15
The *f* also, in which, even.....Lev 13:18
any *f*, in the skin whereof .....Lev 13:24
quick *f* that burneth have .....Lev 13:24
spots in the skin of their *f*.....Lev 13:39
shall wash his *f* in water ......Lev 14:9
his *f* run with his issue ....Lev 15:3
f be stopped from his issue ....Lev 15:3
bathe his *f* in..water ....Lev 15:13
issue in her *f* be blood ....Lev 15:19
linen breeches upon his *f*......Lev 16:4
shall he wash his *f* in water ...Lev 16:4
bathe his *f* in water, and ......Lev 16:26
and bathe his *f* in water.......Lev 16:28
For it is the life of all *f*.......Lev 17:14
blood of no manner of *f* ......Lev 17:14
life of all *f* is the blood ....Lev 17:14
any cuttings in your *f* ....Lev 19:28
he wash his *f* with water ......Lev 22:6
shall eat the *f* of your sons ....Lev 26:29
f of your daughters shall ......Lev 26:29
Who shall give us *f* to eat .....Num 11:4
Give us *f*, that we may eat ....Num 11:13
and ye shall eat *f*............Num 11:18
Who shall give us *f* to eat? ....Num 11:18
the Lord will give you *f*.......Num 11:18
And while the *f* was yet.......Num 11:33
God of the spirits of all *f* .....Num 16:22
f of them shall be thine ....Num 18:18
shall bathe his *f* in water ......Num 19:7
God of the spirits of all *f* .....Num 27:16
For who is there of all *f* ......Deut 5:26
thou shalt say, I will eat *f*.....Deut 12:20
thy soul longeth to eat *f* ......Deut 12:20
thou mayest eat *f*............Deut 12:20
f and the blood, upon ....Deut 12:27
and thou shalt eat the *f*.......Deut 12:27
there any thing of the *f*.......Deut 16:4
f of his children whom he .....Deut 28:55
the *f* he put in a basket ....Judg 6:19
touched the *f* and the ....Judg 6:21
consumed the *f* and the ....Judg 6:21
I am your bone and your *f*....Judg 9:2
the *f* was in seething.........1Sam 2:13
f to roast for the priest 1Sam 2:15
will not have sodden *f* 1Sam 2:15
f that I have killed for my 1Sam 25:11
we are thy bone and thy *f*.....2Sam 5:1
ye are my bones and my *f* 2Sam 19:12
bread and *f* in the 1Kin 17:6
boiled their *f* with the 1Kin 19:21
f of the child waxed warmed ..2Kin 4:34
f came..like unto the *f*........2Kin 5:14
dogs eat the *f* of Jezebel 2Kin 9:36
are thy bone and thy *f*........1Chr 11:1
With him is an arm of *f*.......2Chr 32:8
Yet now our *f* is as the *f* of ...Neh 5:5
touch his bone and his *f* ......Job 2:5
stones? or is my *f* of brass ....Job 6:12
Hast thou eyes of *f*? or ....Job 10:4
Wherefore do I take my *f*.....Job 13:14
to my skin and to my *f*.......Job 19:20
yet in my *f* shall I see God....Job 19:26
Oh that we had of his *f*.......Job 31:31
flakes of his *f* are joined ......Job 41:23
f also shall rest in hope ....Ps 16:9
is no soundness in my *f*.......Ps 38:3
eat the *f* of bulls, or drink ....Ps 50:13
f longeth for thee in a dry ....Ps 63:1
My *f* and my heart faileth .....Ps 73:26
rained *f* also upon them.......Ps 78:27
f of thy saints unto the........Ps 79:2
and my *f* faileth of fatness ....Ps 109:24
Who giveth food to all *f* ......Ps 136:25
and health to all their *f* ....Prov 4:22
is cruel troubleth his own *f*....Prov 11:17
among riotous eaters of *f* .....Prov 23:20
and eateth his own *f*..........Eccl 4:5
put away evil from thy *f* ......Eccl 11:10
every man the *f* of his own ....Is 9:20
eating *f* and drinking wine ....Is 22:13
f shall see it together ....Is 40:5
part thereof he eateth *f* ....Is 44:16
oppress thee with their own *f*..Is 49:26
the Lord plead with all *f*......Is 66:16
f come to worship before .....Is 66:23
your sacrifices and eat *f*.......Jer 7:21
no *f* shall have peace ....Jer 12:12
cause them to eat the *f* of.....Jer 19:9
the *f* of their daughters ....Jer 19:9
eat every one the *f* of his .....Jer 19:9
the Lord, the God of all *f*.....Jer 32:27
violence done..to my *f* ....Jer 51:35
My *f* and my skin hath he.....Lam 3:4
abominable *f* into my mouth ..Ezek 4:14
they are the *f*, and this city ...Ezek 11:7
stony heart out of their *f*......Ezek 11:19
give them a heart of *f* ....Ezek 11:19
f shall see that I the Lord .....Ezek 20:48
f may know that I the Lord ...Ezek 21:5
consume the *f*, and spice it ....Ezek 24:10
stony heart out of your *f*......Ezek 36:26
will bring up *f* upon you ......Ezek 37:6
may eat *f*, and drink blood ....Ezek 39:17
upon the tables was the *f* .....Ezek 40:43
nor uncircumcised in *f* ....Ezek 44:9
and all *f* was fed of it.........Dan 4:12
f nor wine in my mouth.......Dan 10:3
f for the sacrifices ....Hos 8:13
my spirit upon all *f*...........Joel 2:28
f from off their bones.........Mic 3:2
eat the *f* of my people ....Mic 3:3
as *f* within the caldron ....Mic 3:3
as dust, and their *f* as the .....Zeph 1:17
if one bear holy *f* in the ......Hag 2:12
O all *f* before the Lord ....Zech 2:13
shall eat the *f* of the fat.......Zech 11:16
no more twain, but one *f* .....Matt 19:6
there should no *f* be saved ....Matt 24:22
but the *f* is weak ....Matt 26:41
the twain shall be one *f*.......Mark 10:8
no more twain, but one *f* .....Mark 10:8
no *f* should be saved..........Mark 13:20
is ready, but the *f* is weak ....Mark 14:38
f shall see the salvation ....Luke 3:6
spirit hath not *f* and bones ....Luke 24:39
nor of the will of the *f*........John 1:13
which is born of the *f* is *f*.....John 3:6
man give us his *f* to eat?......John 6:52
the *f*; I judge no man.........John 8:15
my Spirit upon all *f*...........Acts 2:17
also my *f* shall rest in hope....Acts 2:26
his loins according to the *f* ....Acts 2:30
his *f* did see corruption ....Acts 2:31
David according to the *f* ......Rom 1:3
which is outward in the *f*......Rom 2:28
f be justified in his sight ......Rom 3:20
the infirmity of your *f* ....Rom 6:19
with the *f* the law of sin ....Rom 7:25
it was weak through the *f* ......Rom 8:3
in the likeness of sinful *f*......Rom 8:3
condemned sin in the *f*........Rom 8:3
they that are after *f* ....Rom 8:5
do mind the things of the *f*....Rom 8:5
the *f* cannot please God ......Rom 8:8
But ye are not in the *f*, but ...Rom 8:9
emulation them..my *f*.........Rom 11:14
It is good neither to eat *f* .....Rom 14:21
wise men after the *f* 1Cor 1:26
destruction of the *f* 1Cor 5:5
saith he, shall be one *f*........1Cor 6:16
have trouble in the *f*..........1Cor 7:28
Behold Israel after the *f* 1Cor 10:18
All *f* is not the same *f* 1Cor 15:39
is one kind of *f* of men 1Cor 15:39
another *f* of beasts 1Cor 15:39
not with *f* wisdom, but by 2Cor 1:12
purpose according to the *f* 2Cor 1:17
in *f* tables of the heart 2Cor 3:3
manifest in our mortal *f*.......2Cor 4:11
all filthiness of the *f* and 2Cor 7:1
walked according to the *f* 2Cor 10:2
many glory after the *f* 2Cor 11:18
not with *f* and blood..........Gal 1:16
shall no *f* be justified ....Gal 2:16
which I now live in the *f*.......Gal 2:20
made perfect by the *f*? ....Gal 3:3
infirmity of the *f* I............Gal 4:13
born after the *f* ....Gal 4:23
for an occasion to the *f* ....Gal 5:13
not fulfil the lust of the *f* .....Gal 5:16
past Gentiles in the *f* ....Eph 2:11

the circumcision in the *f* .....Eph 2:11
no man even hated his own *f*. .Eph 5:29
of his *f*, and of his bones .....Eph 5:30
and they two shall be one *f* ...Eph 5:31
masters according to the *f*.....Eph 6:5
wrestle not against *f* and ......Eph 6:12
if I live in the *f*, this is........Phil 1:22
no confidence in the *f* ....Phil 3:3
have confidence in the *f* ......Phil 3:4
he might trust in the *f* ....Phil 3:4
body of his *f* through ....Col 1:22
not seen my face in the *f* .....Col 2:1
body of the sins of the *f* ......Col 2:11
puffed up by his *f* mind ....Col 2:18
the satisfying of the *f* ....Col 2:23
God was manifest in the *f*.....1Tim 3:16
in the *f* and in the Lord? .....Philem 16
children are partakers of *f*.....Heb 2:14
Who in the days of his *f* ......Heb 5:7
to the purifying the *f* ....Heb 9:13
veil, that is to say, his *f*.......Heb 10:20
have had fathers of our *f*......Heb 12:9
eat your *f* as it were fire ......James 5:3
f is grass, and all the glory 1Pet 1:24
abstain from *f* lusts 1Pet 2:11
to death in the *f*, but 1Pet 3:18
away of the filth of the *f*......1Pet 3:21
suffered for us in the *f*........1Pet 4:1
hath suffered in the *f* 1Pet 4:1
rest of his time in the *f* 1Pet 4:2
according to men in the *f* 1Pet 4:6
walk after the *f* in the lust 2Pet 2:10
Christ is come in the *f*........1John 4:2
Christ is come in the *f*........2John 7
going after strange *f*, are ......Jude 7
filthy dreamers defile the *f* ....Jude 8
garment spotted by the *f*......Jude 23
shall eat her *f*, and burn ......Rev 17:16
f of kings, and the *f* of........Rev 19:18

FLESHHOOK—*a large pronged fork used in sacrificial services*
In tabernacle ....Ex 27:3
Num 4:14
By priests..............1Sam 2:12-14
In Temple 1Chr 28:11, 17
2Chr 4:16

[*also* FLESHHOOKS]
and the *f*, and the firepans ....Ex 38:3

FLEW—*See* FLY

FLIES—*small winged insects*
Cause of evil odor ....Eccl 10:1
Figurative of Egypt ......Is 7:18
Plague upon the Egyptians .... Ex 8:21-31; Ps 78:45

FLIGHT—*See* FLY

FLINT—*a very hard stone*
Water from ....Deut 8:15
Oil from ....Deut 32:13
Turning into fountain of water................Ps 114:8
Hoofs shall seem like ....Is 5:28
Figurative of a fixed course .... Is 50:7; Ezek 3:9

FLOATS—*barges*

[*also* FLOTES]
convey them by sea in *f*.......1Kin 5:9
will bring it to thee in *f*.......2Chr 2:16

FLOCK—*a group of domesticated animals; a group under the guidance of a leader*
Sheep and goats ....Gen 27:9
Nations ....Jer 51:23
National leaders ....Jer 25:34, 35
Jewish people ....Jer 13:17, 20
True church............Is 40:11
Acts 20:28

[*also* FLOCKS]
firstlings of his *f* and ....Gen 4:4
Abram, had *f* and herds ......Gen 13:5
possession of *f*, and..........Gen 26:14
three *f* of sheep lying by ......Gen 29:2
well they watered the *f* ......Gen 29:2
until all the *f* be gathered .....Gen 29:8
watered the *f* of Laban ....Gen 29:10
pass through all thy *f* ....Gen 30:32
he had pilled before the *f* .....Gen 30:38
when the *f* came to drink .....Gen 30:38
f toward the ringstreaked .....Gen 30:40
his own *f* by themselves ....Gen 30:40
Leah to the field unto his *f*....Gen 31:4
f, and herds, and the ....Gen 32:7
one day, all the *f* will die .....Gen 33:13
to feed their father's *f* ....Gen 37:12
and well with the *f* ....Gen 37:14
send thee a kid from the *f* ....Gen 38:17
and thy *f*, and thy herds ......Gen 45:10
my brethren, and their *f* ......Gen 47:1
exchange for..the *f* ....Gen 47:17
water their father's *f*..........Ex 2:16
for us, and watered the *f*......Ex 2:19
kept the *f* of..his father ....Ex 3:1
f to the..desert ....Ex 3:1
our *f* and with our herds ......Ex 10:9
your *f* and your herds.........Ex 12:32
neither let the *f* nor herds .....Ex 34:3
of the herd, and of the *f*......Lev 1:2
his offering be of the *f*........Lev 1:10
female from the *f*, a lamb .....Lev 5:6
ram..out of the *f* ....Lev 6:6
f and the herds be slain ....Num 11:22
Lord..herd, or of the *f*........Num 15:3
of the asses, and of the *f*......Num 31:30
and the *f* of thy sheep, in .....Deut 7:13
herds and thy *f* multiply ......Deut 8:13
your herds and of your *f* ......Deut 12:6
thy herds or of thy *f*..........Deut 12:17
of thy herds and of thy *f*......Deut 14:23
thy *f*, and out of thy floor.....Deut 15:14
of the *f* and the herd in.......Deut 16:2
thy kine, or *f* of thy sheep ....Deut 28:51
hear the bleatings of the *f*? ....Judg 5:16
and took a lamb out of the *f* ..1Sam 17:34
David took..*f* and the herd 1Sam 30:20
many *f* and herds............2Sam 12:2
like two little *f* of kids 1Kin 20:27
to seek pasture for their *f*.....1Chr 4:39
f was Jaziz the Hagerite.......1Chr 27:31
Arabians brought him *f* 2Chr 17:11
possessions of *f* and herds 2Chr 32:29
to the people, of the *f* 2Chr 35:7
they offered a ram of the *f*....Ezra 10:19
of our herds and of our *f* .....Neh 10:36
their little ones like a *f* ....Job 21:11
they violently take away *f*.....Job 24:2
pastures are clothed with *f* ....Ps 65:13
leddest thy people like a *f*.....Ps 77:20
leadest Joseph like a *f* ....Ps 80:1
to know the state to thy *f*.....Prov 27:23
makest thy *f* to rest at noon ..Song 1:7
turneth aside by the *f*.........Song 1:7
thy hair is as a *f* of goats .....Song 4:1
teeth are like a *f* of sheep.....Song 4:2
teeth are as a *f* of sheep ......Song 6:6
they shall be for *f*, which .....Is 17:2
f of Kedar..be gathered ....Is 60:7
with the shepherd of his *f*? ....Is 63:11
Sharon shall be a fold of *f* ....Is 65:10
their *f* and their herds ....Jer 3:24
shepherds with their *f*.........Jer 6:3
scattered my *f*, and driven ....Jer 23:2
gather the remnant of my *f*....Jer 23:3
of the principal of the *f*.......Jer 25:36
as a shepherd doth his *f*.......Jer 31:10
young of the *f* and..herd ......Jer 31:12
cities of Judah, shall the *f*.....Jer 33:13
least at the *f* shall draw ....Jer 49:20
the he goats before the *f*......Jer 50:8
least of the *f* shall draw ....Jer 50:45
Take the choice of the *f* ......Ezek 24:5
a couching place for *f*.........Ezek 25:5
my *f* was scattered upon ......Ezek 34:6
my *f* became a prey ....Ezek 34:8
my *f* became meat to every ...Ezek 34:8
shepherds search for my *f*.....Ezek 34:8
fed themselves..not my *f*......Ezek 34:8
require my *f* at their hand.....Ezek 34:10
I will feed my *f*, and I will ....Ezek 34:15
And as for my *f*, they eat .....Ezek 34:19
my *f*, the *f* of my pasture .....Ezek 34:31
f, as the *f* of Jerusalem ....Ezek 36:38
cities be filled with *f* of ....Ezek 36:38
one lamb out of the *f*, out ....Ezek 45:15
f and with their herds.........Hos 5:6
f of sheep are..desolate ....Joel 1:18
eat the lambs out of the *f*.....Amos 6:4
beast, herd nor *f*, taste.......Jon 3:7
f in the midst of their fold .....Mic 2:12
lion among the *f* of sheep .....Mic 5:8
the *f* of thine heritage ....Mic 7:14
f..cut off from the fold........Hab 3:17
shepherds, and folds for *f*.....Zeph 2:6
day as the *f* of his people .....Zech 9:16
Lord..hath visited his *f*........Zech 10:3
feed the *f* of slaughter ....Zech 11:7
even you, O poor of the *f*.....Zech 11:7
Bands; and I fed the *f*........Zech 11:7
shepherd..leaveth the *f*.......Zech 11:17
which hath in his *f* a male.....Mal 1:14
sheep of the *f*..be scattered....Matt 26:31
watch over their *f* by night ....Luke 2:8
Fear not, little *f*; for it ....Luke 12:32
yourselves and to all the *f*.....Acts 20:28
who feedeth a *f*, and eateth ...1Cor 9:7
not of the milk of the *f*? 1Cor 9:7
f of God which is among......1Pet 5:2

FLOOD—*overflowing of water*
Used literally of:
Earth's flood ....Gen 6:17
Used figuratively of:
Great trouble ....Ps 32:6
Hostile world powers ....Ps 93:3
An invading army ....Jer 46:7, 8
Great destruction........Dan 9:26
Testing ....Matt 7:25, 27
Persecution ....Rev 12:15, 16

[*also* FLOODS]
f of waters..upon the earth ....Gen 7:6
waters of the *f* were upon .....Gen 7:10
more by the waters of a *f*.....Gen 9:11
shall there any more be a *f*....Gen 9:11
Noah lived after the *f*.........Gen 9:28
divided..after the *f* ....Gen 10:32
f stood upright as an heap ....Ex 15:8
the other side of the *f* ....Josh 24:2
the other side of the *f* ....Josh 24:14
f of ungodly men made me....2Sam 22:5
f decayeth and drieth up .....Job 14:11
not see the rivers, the *f*.......Job 20:17
The *f* breaketh out from ......Job 28:4
the *f* from overflowing ....Job 28:11
f of ungodly men made me....Ps 18:4
established it upon the *f* ......Ps 24:2
Lord sitteth upon the *f*........Ps 29:10
where the *f* overflow me ......Ps 69:2
the fountain and the *f* ....Ps 74:15
f clap their hands: let the .....Ps 98:8
neither can the *f* drown it .....Song 8:7
f of mighty waters ....Is 28:2
f upon the dry ground ....Is 44:3
shall be an overflowing *f*......Jer 47:2
f..and the great waters ....Ezek 31:15
with the arms of a *f* shall .....Dan 11:22
shall rise up wholly as a *f* .....Amos 8:8
as by the *f* of Egypt ....Amos 8:8
rise up wholly like a *f* ....Amos 9:5
as by the *f* of Egypt ....Amos 9:5
But with an overrunning *f*.....Nah 1:8
f they were eating and ....Matt 24:38
f arose, the stream beat.......Luke 6:48
bringing in the *f* upon the 2Pet 2:5
of his mouth water as a *f* .....Rev 12:15
be carried away of the *f*.......Rev 12:15

FLOODGATES—*gates for controlling the flow of water*
Descriptive of judgment..Gen 7:11

FLOOR—*bottom surface*
For threshing wheat .....Judg 6:37
1Kin 22:10
Of a building 1Kin 6:15

[*also* FLOORS]
mourning in the *f* of Atad.....Gen 50:11
of the dust that is in the *f*.....Num 5:17
thy flock, and out of thy *f*....Deut 15:14
and get thee down to the *f*....Ruth 3:3
a woman came into the *f*....Ruth 3:14
f and the walls with boards....1Kin 6:16
f of the house he overlaid.....1Kin 6:30
one side of the *f* to the.......1Kin 7:7
to *f* the houses which the.....2Chr 34:11
and the corn of my *f*.........Is 21:10
The *f* and the winepress......Hos 9:2
f shall be full of wheat........Joel 2:24
the sheaves into the *f*.........Mic 4:12
will thoroughly purge his *f*....Matt 3:12
will thoroughly purge his *f*....Luke 3:17

FLOUR—*finely ground wheat*
Offered in sacrifices.....Lev 5:11, 13

wheaten *f* shalt thou make....Ex 29:2
offering shall be of fine *f*......Lev 2:1
unleavened cakes of fine *f*.....Lev 2:4
be made of fine *f* with oil.....Lev 2:7
part of an ephah of fine *f*.....Lev 5:11
his handful, of the *f*..........Lev 6:15
cakes..of fine *f*..............Lev 7:12
and one tenth deal of fine *f*...Lev 14:21
they shall be of fine *f*.........Lev 23:17
cakes of fine *f* mingled........Num 6:15
fine *f* mingled with oil........Num 7:19
fine *f* mingled with oil........Num 8:8
two tenth deals of *f*...........Num 15:6
of *f* for a meat offering.......Num 28:5
three tenth deals of *f* for a....Num 28:12
two tenths deals of *f* for a.....Num 28:12
be of *f* mingled with oil.......Num 28:20
be of *f* mingled with oil.......Num 29:3
be of *f* mingled with oil.......Num 29:14
cakes of an ephah of *f*........Judg 6:19
and one ephah of *f*............1Sam 1:24
she took *f*, and kneaded.......2Sam 13:8
thirty measures of fine *f*......1Kin 4:22
a measure of fine *f* be sold....2Kin 7:1
a measure of fine *f* for a......2Kin 7:18
the fine *f*, and the wine.......1Chr 9:29
eat fine *f*, and honey........Ezek 16:13
to temper with the fine *f*......Ezek 46:14
fine *f*, and wheat, and........Rev 18:13

FLOURISH—*to thrive; prosper*

[*also* FLOURISHED, FLOURISHETH, FLOURISHING]
days shall the righteous *f*......Ps 72:7
and they of the city shall *f*....Ps 72:16
morning it *f*, and groweth.....Ps 90:6
workers of iniquity do *f*.......Ps 92:7
The righteous shall *f* like......Ps 92:12
f in the courts of our God....Ps 92:13
they shall be fat and *f*........Ps 92:14
flower of the field, so he *f*....Ps 103:15
himself shall his crown *f*......Ps 132:18
righteous shall *f* as a.........Prov 11:28
of the upright shall *f*..........Prov 14:11
the almond tree shall *f*........Eccl 12:5
see whether the vine *f*........Song 6:11
let us see if the vine *f*........Song 7:12
thou make thy seed to *f*.......Is 17:11
bones shall *f* like an herb.....Is 66:14
made the dry tree to *f*........Ezek 17:24
your care of me hath *f*........Phil 4:10

FLOW—*to move in a stream; smooth; uninterrupted*

[*also* FLOWED, FLOWETH, FLOWING]
f with milk and honey........Ex 3:8
land *f* with milk and honey....Ex 13:5
that *f* with milk and honey....Lev 20:24
it *f* with milk and honey......Num 13:27
f with milk and honey........Num 16:13
f with milk and honey........Deut 6:3
f with milk and honey........Deut 26:9
f with milk and honey........Deut 31:20
and *f* over all his banks, as....Josh 4:18
f with milk and honey........Josh 5:6
shall *f* away in the day........Job 20:28
to blow, and the waters *f*.....Ps 147:18
of wisdom as a *f* brook.......Prov 18:4
spices thereof may *f* out......Song 4:16
all nations shall *f* unto it......Is 2:2
waters to *f* out of the rock....Is 48:21
shalt see, and *f* together......Is 60:5
f down at thy presence........Is 64:3
of the Gentiles like a *f*........Is 66:12
a land *f* with milk...........Jer 11:5
f together to the goodness.....Jer 31:12
f with milk and honey........Jer 32:22
Waters *f* over mine head.......Lam 3:54
f with milk and honey........Ezek 20:6
the hills shall *f* with milk......Joel 3:18
and people shall *f* unto it.....Mic 4:1
shall *f* rivers of living water...John 7:38

FLOWER—*a plant known for its blossoms*
Described as:
Wild..................Ps 103:15, 16
Beautiful..............Matt 6:28, 29
Sweet.................Song 5:13
Fading.................Is 40:7, 8
Figurative of:
Shortness of life.........Job 14:2
Israel...................Is 28:1
Man's glory.............James 1:10, 11

[*also* FLOWERS]
bowls, his knobs, and his *f*....Ex 25:31
knob and a *f* in one branch...Ex 25:33
his *f* were of the same........Ex 37:17
branch, a knob and a *f*.......Ex 37:19
branch, a knob and a *f*.......Ex 37:19
her *f* be upon him, he shall...Lev 15:24
f thereof, was beaten work....Num 8:4
die in the *f* of their age......1Sam 2:33
knobs and open *f*: all was.....1Kin 6:18
palm trees and open *f*, and....1Kin 6:32
brim of a cup, with *f* of.......1Kin 7:26
of a cup, with *f* of lilies.......2Chr 4:5
cast off his *f* as the olive......Job 15:33
The *f* appear on the earth.....Song 2:12
grape is ripening in the *f*......Is 18:5
shall be a fading *f*, and as.....Is 28:4
as the *f* of the field..........Is 40:6
f fadeth: but the word of our..Is 40:8
f of Lebanon languisheth......Nah 1:4
if she pass the *f* of her age....1Cor 7:36
glory of man as the *f* of.......1Pet 1:24
f thereof falleth away.........1Pet 1:24

FLUTE—*a hollow musical instrument*
In Babylon..............Dan 3:5
Used in God's worship...Ps 150:4

the sound of the cornet, *f*.....Dan 3:10

FLUTTERETH—*flap wings rapidly*
her nest, *f* over her young....Deut 32:11

FLUX—*discharge*
sick of..a bloody *f*...........Acts 28:8

FLY—*to move or pass through the air, usually with wings*

[*also* FLEW, FLIETH, FLIGHT, FLYING]
fowl that may *f* above the.....Gen 1:20
ye eat of every *f* creeping.....Lev 11:21
put ten thousand to *f*.........Lev 26:8
winged fowl that *f*...........Deut 4:17
as swift as the eagle *f*........Deut 28:49
put ten thousand to *f*.........Deut 32:30
people *f* upon the spoil.......1Sam 14:32
but didst *f* upon the spoil.....1Sam 15:19
upon a cherub, and did *f*......2Sam 22:11
and they put to *f* all them.....1Chr 12:15
as the sparks *f* upward.......Job 5:7
hawk *f* by thy wisdom........Job 39:26
upon a cherub, and did *f*......Ps 18:10
he did *f* upon the wings.......Ps 18:10
soon cut off, and we *f* away...Ps 90:10
creeping things, and *f* fowl...Ps 148:10
f away as an eagle toward.....Prov 23:5
as the swallow by *f*, so the....Prov 26:2
and with twain he did *f*.......Is 6:2
f one of the seraphims........Is 6:6
shall *f* upon the shoulders.....Is 11:14
his fruit..a fiery *f* serpent.....Is 14:29
birds *f*, so will the Lord of....Is 31:5
with haste, nor go by *f*........Is 52:12
he shall *f* as an eagle........Jer 48:40
souls to make them *f*.........Ezek 13:20
being caused to *f* swiftly......Dan 9:21
glory shall *f* away like a......Hos 9:11
f shall perish from the........Amos 2:14
f as the eagle that hasteth.....Hab 1:8
looked, and behold a *f* roll....Zech 5:1
that your *f* be not in.........Matt 24:20
that your *f* be not in.........Mark 13:18
turned to *f* the armies of......Heb 11:34
beast was like a *f* eagle.......Rev 4:7
f into the wilderness.........Rev 12:14
fowls that *f* in the midst......Rev 19:17

FOAL—*a colt; young donkey*
Given to Esau..........Gen 32:13-15
Ridden by Christ........Zech 9:9
Matt 21:5

Binding his *f* unto..vine.......Gen 49:11
upon a colt the *f* of an ass....Zech 9:9
and a colt the *f* of an ass.....Matt 21:5

FOAM—*to froth*

[*also* FOAMETH, FOAMING]
as the *f* upon the water.......Hos 10:7
f, and gnasheth with..........Mark 9:18
ground, and wallowed *f*.......Mark 9:20
it teareth him that he *f*.......Luke 9:39
sea, *f* out their own shame....Jude 13

FODDER—*food for domestic animals*
Given to oxen and wild ass.......Job 6:5; Is 30:24

FOES—*enemies*
be destroyed before thy *f*.....1Chr 21:12
f seventy and five thousand...Esth 9:16
mine enemies and my *f*.......Ps 27:2
beat down his *f* before his.....Ps 89:23
a man's *f* shall be they........Matt 10:36
I make thy *f* thy footstool.....Acts 2:35

FOLD—*to entwine; a shelter*

[*also* FOLDEN, FOLDETH, FOLDING, FOLDS]
f for your sheep; and........Num 32:24
of the one door were *f*.......1Kin 6:34
of the other door were *f*......1Kin 6:34
nor he goats out of thy *f*......Ps 50:9
f of the hands to sleep........Prov 6:10
fool *f* his hands together......Eccl 4:5
shepherds make their *f*........Is 13:20
bring them again to their *f*....Jer 23:3
of Israel shall their *f*.........Ezek 34:14
flock in..their *f*..............Mic 2:12
be *f* together as thorns........Nah 1:10
flock..cut off from the *f*.......Hab 3:17
shepherds, and *f* for flocks....Zeph 2:6
which are not of this *f*........John 10:16
a vesture shalt thou *f* them....Heb 1:12

FOLK—*people*

[*also* FOLKS]
leave..some of the *f*..........Gen 33:15
conies are but a feeble *f*......Prov 30:26
f in the fire, and they.........Jer 51:58
laid his hands upon..sick *f*.....Mark 6:5
a great multitude of impotent *f*.John 5:3
bringing sick *f*, and them......Acts 5:16

FOLLOW—*to proceed behind*
In Old Testament:
Commanded...........Deut 8:6
Brought reward.........Deut 19:9
Covenant..............2Kin 23:3
In New Testament:
Multitudes.............Matt 4:25
Matt 12:15
Disciples...............Matt 8:19
Luke 5:11-27
Left all................Matt 4:18-22
In light................John 8:12
After Christ's example...John 13:15
1John 2:6

Example of Godly men { Phil 3:17 / Heb 6:12 / James 5:10

[*also* FOLLOWED, FOLLOWEDST, FOLLOWETH, FOLLOWING]

will not be willing to *f* me ..... Gen 24:5
the woman will not *f* me ...... Gen 24:39
f the man: and the servant .... Gen 24:61
by reason of that famine *f* ..... Gen 41:31
all the people that *f* thee ...... Ex 11:8
and they shall *f* them .... Ex 14:17
And if any mischief *f*, then .... Ex 21:23
f me fully, him will I .... Num 14:24
they have not wholly *f* me .... Num 32:11
he hath wholly *f* the Lord ..... Deut 1:36
turn away thy son from *f* ...... Deut 7:4
just shalt thou *f* .... Deut 16:20
the covenant of the Lord *f* .... Josh 6:8
hast wholly *f* the Lord .... Josh 14:9
turn away this day from *f* ..... Josh 22:16
to turn from *f* the Lord .... Josh 22:23
f other gods, of the gods ...... Judg 2:12
f other gods to serve them .... Judg 2:19
said unto them, *F* after me .... Judg 3:28
inclined to *f* Abimelech .... Judg 9:3
bough, and *f* Abimelech ...... Judg 9:49
return from *f* after thee .... Ruth 1:16
as thou *f* not young men ...... Ruth 3:10
f the Lord your God 1Sam 12:14
people *f* him trembling 1Sam 13:7
from *f* the Philistines 1Sam 14:46
and *f* Saul to the battle 1Sam 17:13
from *f* the Philistines 1Sam 24:1
young men that *f* my lord 1Sam 25:27
the Philistines *f* hard upon 1Sam 31:2
chariots and horsemen *f* 2Sam 1:6
to the left from *f* Abner 2Sam 2:19
Turn thee aside from *f* 2Sam 2:22
from *f* his brother 2Sam 2:27
And king David himself *f* 2Sam 3:31
f the sheep, to be ruler 2Sam 7:8
the people that *f* Absalom 2Sam 17:9
that his counsel was not *f* 2Sam 17:23
f Adonijah helped him 1Kin 1:7
that *f* the house of David 1Kin 12:20
half of the people *f* Tibni 1Kin 16:21
make him king; and half *f* 1Kin 16:21
that *f* Omri prevailed 1Kin 16:22
the people that *f* Tibni 1Kin 16:22
God, *f* him: but if Baal 1Kin 18:21
all the people that *f* me 1Kin 20:10
the army which *f* them 1Kin 20:19
very abominably in *f* idols 1Kin 21:26
for the cattle that *f* them 2Kin 3:9
So Gehazi *f* after Naaman 2Kin 5:21
f me, and I will bring you 2Kin 6:19
And Jehu *f* after him, and 2Kin 9:27
f her kill with the sword 2Kin 11:15
and *f* the sins of Jeroboam 2Kin 13:2
Israel from *f* the Lord 2Kin 17:21
the Philistines *f* hard after 1Chr 10:2
even from *f* the sheep 1Chr 17:7
men of the guard which *f* ..... Neh 4:23
and mercy shall *f* me .... Ps 23:6
her companions that *f* .... Ps 45:14
tell it to the generation *f* ...... Ps 48:13
My soul *f* hard after thee ..... Ps 63:8
players on instruments *f* .... Ps 68:25
generation *f* let their name .... Ps 109:13
that *f* after mischief .... Ps 119:150
that *f* vain persons is void ..... Prov 12:11
that *f* after righteousness ...... Prov 21:21
loveth gifts, and *f* after .... Is 1:23
they may *f* strong drink .... Is 5:11
being a pastor to *f* thee .... Jer 17:16
the head looked they *f* it ...... Ezek 10:11
foolish prophets, that *f* .... Ezek 13:3
none *f* thee to commit .... Ezek 16:34
she shall *f* after her lovers ..... Hos 2:7
and *f* after the east wind ...... Hos 12:1
left their nets, and *f* .... Matt 4:20
great multitudes *f* him .... Matt 8:1
I will *f* thee whithersoever .... Matt 8:19
Jesus said unto him, *F* .... Matt 8:22
into a ship, his disciples *f* ..... Matt 8:23
he saith unto him, *F* me ...... Matt 9:9
he arose, and *f* him .... Matt 9:9
Jesus arose, and *f* .... Matt 9:19
f after me, is not worthy ...... Matt 10:38
f him on foot out of the ...... Matt 14:13
take up his cross, and *f* .... Matt 16:24
heaven: and come and *f* me ... Matt 19:21
we have forsaken all, and *f* .... Matt 19:27
Jericho..multitude *f* him .... Matt 20:29
went before, and that *f* .... Matt 21:9
f Jesus from Galilee .... Matt 27:55
forsook their nets, and *f* ...... Mark 1:18
said unto him, *F* me .... Mark 2:14
he arose and *f* him .... Mark 2:14
multitude from Galilee *f* ...... Mark 3:7
suffered no man to *f* him ..... Mark 5:37
and his disciples *f* him .... Mark 6:1
take up his cross, and *f* .... Mark 8:34
in thy name, and he *f* not ..... Mark 9:38
take up the cross, and *f* .... Mark 10:21
left all, and have *f* thee ...... Mark 10:28
received his sight..*f* .... Mark 10:52
bearing..water: *f* him .... Mark 14:13
f him a..young man .... Mark 14:51
Peter *f* him afar off, even ..... Mark 14:54
when he was in Galilee, *f* ..... Mark 15:41
these signs shall *f* them ...... Mark 16:17
confirming..with signs *f* ...... Mark 16:20
he said unto him, *F* me .... Luke 5:27
he left all, rose up, and *f* ..... Luke 5:28
when they knew it, *f* .... Luke 9:11
take up his cross..*f* me .... Luke 9:23
forbade him, because he *f* ..... Luke 9:49
f thee whithersoever thou ...... Luke 9:57
said unto another, *F* me ...... Luke 9:59
said, Lord, I will *f* thee ...... Luke 9:61
tomorrow, and the day *f* .... Luke 13:33
treasure in heaven..*f* me ...... Luke 18:22
received his sight, and *f* ...... Luke 18:43
saw what would *f* .... Luke 22:49
house. And Peter *f* afar .... Luke 22:54
and the women that *f* him ..... Luke 23:49
him speak, and they *f* Jesus ... John 1:37
Jesus..saw them *f* .... John 1:38
saith unto him, *F* me .... John 1:43
a great multitude *f* him .... John 6:2
day *f*, when the people .... John 6:22
he that *f* me shall not walk .... John 8:12
stranger will they not *f* .... John 10:5
know them, and they *f* me .... John 10:27
man serve me, let him *f* .... John 12:26
not *f*..but thou shalt *f* me .... John 13:36
why cannot I *f* thee now? ..... John 13:37
And Simon Peter *f* Jesus ...... John 18:15
whom Jesus loved *f* .... John 21:20
what is that to thee? *f* .... John 21:22
Samuel and those that *f* .... Acts 3:24
he went out, and *f* him .... Acts 12:9
proselytes *f* Paul and .... Acts 13:43
and the day *f* unto Rhodes .... Acts 21:1
multitude of the people *f* ...... Acts 21:36
the night *f* the Lord stood .... Acts 23:11
f not after righteousness ...... Rom 9:30
therefore *f* after the things .... Rom 14:19
that spiritual Rock that *f* 1Cor 10:4
F after charity, and desire 1Cor 14:1
f after..I may apprehend ...... Phil 3:12
f that which is good 1Thess 5:15
know how ye ought to *f* us 2Thess 3:7
example unto you to *f* us 2Thess 3:9
diligently *f*..good work 1Tim 5:10
and some men they *f* after 1Tim 5:24
f righteousness, faith 2Tim 2:22
F peace with all men, and .... Heb 12:14
whose faith *f*, considering ..... Heb 13:7
and the glory that should *f* 1Pet 1:11
not *f* cunningly devised 2Pet 1:16
shall *f* their pernicious 2Pet 2:2
f the way of Balaam the 2Pet 2:15
f not that which is evil 3John 11
and Hell *f* with him .... Rev 6:8
they which *f* the Lamb .... Rev 14:4
f another angel, saying .... Rev 14:8
armies..in heaven *f* .... Rev 19:14

FOLLOWERS—*adherents; disciples*

beseech you, be ye *f* of me 1Cor 4:16
Be ye therefore *f* of God ..... Eph 5:1
f together with me, and mark. . Phil 3:17
f of us, and of the Lord 1Thess 1:6
f of the churches of God 1Thess 2:14
f of them..through faith .... Heb 6:12
f of that which is good 1Pet 3:13

FOLLY—*contemptuous disregard of holy things; foolishness*

Described as:
Unnatural sin .... Judg 19:22-24

Associated with:
Deception .... Prov 14:8
Hasty spirit .... Prov 14:29
Gullibility .... Prov 13:16
Ferociousness .... Prov 17:12
Disgust .... Prov 26:11

Warnings against:
Saints not to return to ... Ps 85:8
Prophets guilty of .... Jer 23:13
Angels charged with ..... Job 4:18
Apostles subject to 2Cor 11:1

he had wrought *f* in Israel ..... Gen 34:7
hath wrought *f* in Israel .... Deut 22:21
because he hath wrought *f* .... Josh 7:15
committed lewdness and *f* ..... Judg 20:6
Nabal is his name, and *f* is 1Sam 25:25
Israel: do not thou this *f* 2Sam 13:12
God layeth not *f* to them ..... Job 24:12
This their way is their *f* .... Ps 49:13
in the greatness of his *f* he .... Prov 5:23
The simple inherit *f*: but ...... Prov 14:18
F is joy to him that is .... Prov 15:21
rather than a fool in his *f* ..... Prov 17:12
a fool according to his *f* .... Prov 26:4
to know madness and *f* .... Eccl 1:17
hold on *f*, till I might see ..... Eccl 2:3
and madness, and *f* .... Eccl 2:12
The simple inherit *f*: but ...... Prov 14:18
F is joy to him that is .... Prov 15:21
rather than a fool in his *f* ..... Prov 17:12
a fool according to his *f* .... Prov 26:4
to know madness and *f* .... Eccl 1:17
hold on *f*, till I might see ..... Eccl 2:3
and madness, and *f* .... Eccl 2:12
that wisdom excelleth *f* .... Eccl 2:13
the wickedness of *f* .... Eccl 7:25
F is set in great dignity .... Eccl 10:6
every mouth speaketh *f* .... Is 9:17
seen *f* in the prophets .... Jer 23:13
bear with me..in my *f* 2Cor 11:1
f shall be manifest unto all ... 2Tim 3:9

FOOD—*something that nourishes*

Features regarding:
Given by God .... Ps 104:21, 27
Necessary for man .... Gen 1:29, 30
Gives physical strength ... Acts 9:19
Revives the spirit 1Sam 30:12
Object of daily prayer ... Matt 6:11
Object of thanksgiving ... 1Sam 9:13
Sanctified by prayer 1Tim 4:4, 5
Scruples recognized ...... Rom 14:2-23

Lack of:
Testing of faith .... Hab 3:17

Provided by:
God .... Ps 145:15
Christ .... John 21:5, 6

Prohibitions concerning:
Dead animals .... Ex 22:31
Eating blood .... Deut 12:16
Clean and unclean .... Deut 14:4-20
Wine .... Prov 23:29-35
Strangled animals .... Acts 21:25
Not in itself commendable 1Cor 8:8
Not to be a stumbling block 1Cor 8:13
Life more important than. Matt 6:25

Miracles connected with:
Destruction of .... Ps 105:29-35

Provision for ....Ps 105:40, 41
Supply of 1Kin 17:4-6
Multiplication of.........John 6:5-13
Refused ....Matt 4:1-4

Figurative of:

God's will ....John 4:32, 34
Christ ....John 6:27, 55
Strong doctrines 1Cor 3:2

Specific kinds:

Almonds................Gen 43:11
Barley ....Judg 7:13
Beans ....Ezek 4:9
Beef...................1Kin 4:22, 23
Beef stew 1Kin 19:21
Bread 1Sam 17:17
Broth ....Judg 6:19
Cakes 2Sam 13:8
Cheese ....Job 10:10
Cucumbers..............Num 11:5
Curds of cows...........Deut 32:14
Eggs ....Deut 22:6
Figs ....Num 13:23
Fish ....Matt 7:10
Fowl 1Kin 4:23
Fruit 2Sam 16:2
Garlic ....Num 11:5
Goat's milk ....Prov 27:27
Grain ....Ruth 2:14
Grapes ....Deut 23:24
Grasshoppers ....Lev 11:22
Herbs ....Ex 12:8
Honey..................Is 7:15
Leeks ....Num 11:5
Lentils..................Gen 25:34
Locusts ....Matt 3:4
Meal ....Matt 13:33
Melons ....Num 11:5
Nuts....................Gen 43:11
Oil ....Prov 21:17
Olives ....Deut 28:40
Onions ....Num 11:5
Pomegranates ....Num 13:23
Pottage ....Gen 25:30
Pulse 2Sam 17:28
Quail ....Num 11:32, 33
Raisins 2Sam 16:1
Salt ....Job 6:6
Sheep ....Deut 14:4
Sheep's milk ....Deut 32:14
Spices ....Gen 43:11
Veal ....Gen 18:7, 8
Vegetables ....Prov 15:17
Vinegar.................Num 6:3
Venison ....Gen 25:28
Wild honey ....Ps 19:10
Wine ....John 2:3, 10

to the sight, and good for *f* ...Gen 2:9
the tree was good for *f* ....Gen 3:6
let them gather all the *f*.......Gen 41:35
them keep *f* in the cities ......Gen 41:35
he gathered up all the *f*.......Gen 41:48
laid up the *f* in the cities ......Gen 41:48
to buy *f* are thy servants ......Gen 42:10
Go again, buy us a little *f*.....Gen 43:2
at the first time to buy *f* .....Gen 43:20
Fill the men's sacks with *f*.....Gen 44:1
seed of..and for your *f*........Gen 47:24
her *f*, her raiment, and her ....Ex 21:10
it is the *f* of the offering ......Lev 3:11
it is the *f* of the offering ......Lev 3:16
things; because it is his *f*......Lev 22:7
giving him *f* and raiment ......Deut 10:18
the man that eateth any *f* 1Sam 14:24
the man that eateth any *f* 1Sam 14:28
son may have *f* to eat.........2Sam 9:10
in giving *f* for my household...1Kin 5:9
more than my necessary *f* .....Job 23:12
for the raven his *f*? ....Job 38:41
Man did eat angels' *f* ....Ps 78:25
bring..*f* out of the earth.......Ps 104:14
Who giveth *f* to all flesh ......Ps 136:25
giveth *f* to the hungry.........Ps 146:7
giveth to the beast his *f*.......Ps 147:9
gathereth..*f* in the harvest .....Prov 6:8
f is in the tillage..poor ....Prov 13:23
goats' milk enough for thy *f*...Prov 27:27
for the *f* of thy household .....Prov 27:27
feed me with *f* convenient .....Prov 30:8
diminished..ordinary *f*.........Ezek 16:27
f unto them that serve the ....Ezek 48:18
hearts with *f* and gladness .....Acts 14:17
minister bread for your *f*......2Cor 9:10
having *f* and raiment let 1Tim 6:8
and destitute of daily *f*........James 2:15

FOOD RATIONING

First.....................Gen 41:25-27
Final ....Rev 13:11-17

FOOD, SPIRITUAL

Elements of:

The Word ....Ps 19:10
Christ ....John 6:48-51

Need of, by:

The naive...............Prov 9:1-5
The immature 1Cor 3:1, 2
The mature ....Heb 5:14
All ....Matt 22:4

Characteristics of:

Abundant...............Is 55:1-3
Satisfying ....Ps 22:26
Enduring ....John 6:48-51
Life-giving ....John 6:53-63

FOOL—*those who misuse true wisdom*

Described as:

Atheistic................Ps 14:1
Blasphemous ....Ps 74:18
Contentious ....Prov 18:6
Hypocritical.............Luke 11:39, 40
Idle ....Eccl 4:5
Vexation................Prov 12:16
Materialistic.............Luke 12:16-21
Meddling ....Prov 20:3
Mischievous ....Prov 10:23
Mocking ....Prov 14:9
Raging ....Prov 14:16
Self-confident ....Prov 28:26
Self-righteous ....Prov 12:15
Self-sufficient ....Rom 1:22
Slandering ....Prov 10:18
Wasteful................Prov 21:20
Wordy..................Eccl 10:12-14

Further characteristics of:

Hate knowledge ....Prov 1:22
Come to shame ....Prov 3:35
Mock at sin ....Prov 14:9
Cannot attain to wisdom..Prov 24:7
Trust in their hearts .....Prov 28:26
Walk in darkness ....Eccl 2:14

Examples of:

Nabal 1Sam 25:3, 25
Rehoboam 1Kin 12:8
Pharisees ....Matt 23:17, 19
The rich man ....Luke 12:16-21

[*also* FOOL'S, FOOLS]

behold, I have played the *f*....1Sam 26:21
Died Abner as a *f* dieth? 2Sam 3:33
as one of the *f* in Israel 2Sam 13:13
and maketh the judges *f* ......Job 12:17
They were children of *f* ....Job 30:8
f and the brutish person ....Ps 49:10
f hath said in his heart ....Ps 53:1
I said unto the *f*, Deal not ....Ps 75:4
doth a *f* understand...........Ps 92:6
f, when will ye be wise? ......Ps 94:8
F, because of..transgression ...Ps 107:17
f despise wisdom and ....Prov 1:7
prosperity of *f* shall ....Prov 1:32
f to the correction of the ......Prov 7:22
ye *f*, be..an understanding.....Prov 8:5
but a prating *f* shall fall ....Prov 10:10
f shall be servant to..wise .....Prov 11:29
f wrath is presently known ....Prov 12:16
the heart of *f* proclaimeth .....Prov 12:23
a *f* layeth open his folly ....Prov 13:16
companion of *f*..destroyed .....Prov 13:20
F make a mock at sin ....Prov 14:9
is in the midst of *f* ....Prov 14:33
f despiseth..instruction ....Prov 15:5
f feedeth on foolishness ....Prov 15:14
hundred stripes into a *f* ....Prov 17:10
hand of a *f* to get wisdom .....Prov 17:16
begetteth a *f* doeth ....Prov 17:21
father of a *f* hath no joy ......Prov 17:21
f..holdeth his peace ....Prov 17:28
f mouth is his destruction .....Prov 18:7
perverse in his lips..a *f*........Prov 19:1
stripes for the back of *f* ....Prov 19:29
every *f* will be meddling ......Prov 20:3
Wisdom is too high for a *f* ....Prov 24:7
Answer not a *f* according .....Prov 26:4
message by the hand of a *f*....Prov 26:6
rewardeth the *f*, and ....Prov 26:10
is more hope of a *f* than of ...Prov 26:12
f wrath is heavier than ....Prov 27:3
trusteth..own heart is a *f*......Prov 28:26
is more hope of a *f* than of ...Prov 29:20
f walketh in darkness ....Eccl 2:14
wise more than of the *f*.......Eccl 2:16
dieth..wise man? as the *f*......Eccl 2:16
f foldeth his hands............Eccl 4:5
to give the sacrifice of *f*.......Eccl 5:1
a *f* voice is known by ....Eccl 5:3
heart of *f* is in the house ......Eccl 7:4
so is the laughter of the *f* .....Eccl 7:6
anger..in the bosom of *f* ....Eccl 7:9
every one that he is a *f* ....Eccl 10:3
A *f* also is full of words........Eccl 10:14
the princes of Zoan are *f* .....Is 19:11
wayfaring men, though *f* ......Is 35:8
and at his end shall be a *f* ....Jer 17:11
the prophet is a *f*, the ....Hos 9:7
whosoever shall say..*f*.........Matt 5:22
Thou *f*, this night thy soul ....Luke 12:20
O *f*, and slow of heart to .....Luke 24:25
become a *f*, that he may be ...1Cor 3:18
We are *f* for Christ's sake 1Cor 4:10
Let no man think me a *f*.......2Cor 11:16
ye suffer *f* gladly, seeing 2Cor 11:19
(I speak as a *f*) I am more 2Cor 11:23
become a *f* in glorying 2Cor 12:11
not as *f*, but as..............Eph 5:15

FOOLISH—*those who misuse widsom; misuse of wisdom*

Those described as:

Clamorous woman ....Prov 9:13
Builder on sand ....Matt 7:26
Five virgins ....Matt 25:1-13
Galatians ....Gal 3:1, 3
Gentiles ....Titus 3:3

Things described as:

The Heart ....Rom 1:21
Things..................1Cor 1:27
Lusts 1Tim 6:9
Questions 2Tim 2:23

Characteristics of:

Destructive ....Prov 10:14
Despicable ....Prov 15:20
Disappointing ....Prov 19:13

[*also* FOOLISHLY]

thou hast now done *f* in so ....Gen 31:28
wherein we have done *f*.......Num 12:11
f people and unwise? ....Deut 32:6
Thou hast done *f*: thou 1Sam 13:13
for I have done very *f* 2Sam 24:10
for I have done very *f* 1Chr 21:8
Herein thou hast done *f* 2Chr 16:9
nor charged God *f*............Job 1:22
speakest as one of the *f*.......Job 2:10
seen the *f* taking root ....Job 5:3
f shall not stand in thy ....Ps 5:5
not the reproach of the *f*.......Ps 39:8
For I was envious at the *f*.....Ps 73:3
f man reproacheth thee ....Ps 74:22
Deal not *f*: and to the ....Ps 75:4
Forsake the *f*, and live ....Prov 9:6
a *f* son is the heaviness of.....Prov 10:1
but the *f* plucketh it down ....Prov 14:1
Go from the presence of a *f*...Prov 14:7
is soon angry dealeth *f*........Prov 14:17
heart of the *f* doeth not so ....Prov 15:7

f son is a grief to his father ... Prov 17:25
but a f man spendeth it up ... Prov 21:20
thou hast done f in lifting ... Prov 30:32
an old and f king, who will ... Eccl 4:13
labor of the f wearieth ... Eccl 10:15
maketh their knowledge f ... Is 44:25
people is f, they have not ... Jer 4:22
Hear now this, O f people ... Jer 5:21
seen vain and f things for ... Lam 2:14
Woe unto the f prophets ... Ezek 13:3
instruments of a f shepherd ... Zech 11:15
an instructor of the f, a ... Rom 2:20
hath not God made f the ... 1Cor 1:20
but as it were f, in this ... 2Cor 11:17
I speak f, I am bold also ... 2Cor 11:21
nor f talking, nor jesting ... Eph 5:4
f questions, and genealogies ... Titus 3:9
silence the ignorance of f ... 1Pet 2:15

FOOLISHNESS—*disregard of final issues; wicked or imprudent behavior*

Characteristics of:
Form of sin ... Prov 24:9
Originates in the heart ... Mark 7:21-23
Sign of wickedness ... Eccl 7:25
Known by God ... Ps 69:5

Consequences of:
Brings sorrow ... Ps 38:4-10
Perverts man's way ... Prov 19:3
Spiritual blindness ... 1Cor 1:18

counsel of Ahithopel into f ... 2Sam 15:31
fools proclaim f ... Prov 12:23
mouth of fools poureth..f ... Prov 15:2
F is..the heart of a child ... Prov 22:15
not his f depart from him ... Prov 27:22
words of his mouth is f ... Eccl 10:13
eye, blasphemy, pride, f ... Mark 7:22
the f of preaching to save ... 1Cor 1:21
f of God is wiser than men ... 1Cor 1:25
this world is f with God ... 1Cor 3:19

FOOT—*the part of the leg used for walking*

To sit at, figurative of:
Teachableness ... Luke 10:39

To be under, figurative of:
God's sovereignty ... Ps 8:6
Christ's victory ... Ps 110:1
Conquest ... Josh 10:24

Examples, figurative of:
Prosperity ... Deut 33:24
Possession ... Josh 1:3
Reverence ... Josh 5:15
Whole person ... Prov 1:15

Acts performed by or on, indicating:
Subjection ... Josh 10:24
Conquest ... 2Sam 22:39
Humiliation ... Judg 5:27
Submission and entreaty ... 1Sam 25:24, 41
Great love ... Luke 7:38, 44-46
Worship ... Rev 19:10
Learner's position ... Luke 10:39
Humility ... John 13:5-14
Changed nature ... Luke 8:35
Rejection ... Matt 10:14

Figurative of:
God's holiness ... Ex 3:5
God's nature ... Ex 24:10
Clouds ... Nah 1:3
God's messengers ... Rom 10:15
Final conquest ... Rom 16:20

Unusual features concerning:
No swelling ... Neh 9:21
Lameness ... 2Sam 9:3, 13
Neglected ... 2Sam 19:24
Impotent ... Acts 14:8-10
Binding ... Acts 21:11

[*also* FEET]
for the sole of her f ... Gen 8:9
and wash your f ... Gen 19:2
and water to wash his f ... Gen 24:32
and the men's f that were ... Gen 24:32
from between his f ... Gen 49:10
your shoes on your f ... Ex 12:11
hundred thousand on f ... Ex 12:37
that are on the four f ... Ex 25:26
of their right f ... Ex 29:20
shall wash..their f ... Ex 30:21
the laver and his f ... Ex 30:28
the laver and his f ... Ex 35:16
the laver and his f ... Ex 39:39
washed..their f ... Ex 40:31
and his f, to sanctify ... Lev 8:11
of their right f ... Lev 8:24
which have four f ... Lev 11:23
his head even to his f ... Lev 13:12
toe of his right f ... Lev 14:17
toe of his right f ... Lev 14:28
go through on my f ... Num 20:19
crushed Balaam's f ... Num 22:25
no, not so much as a f ... Deut 2:5
pass through on my f ... Deut 2:28
wateredst it with thy f ... Deut 11:10
from off his f ... Deut 25:9
the sole of her f upon ... Deut 28:56
from between her f ... Deut 28:57
not waxen old upon thy f ... Deut 29:5
and let him dip his f in oil ... Deut 33:24
the sole of your f shall ... Josh 1:3
of the f of the priests ... Josh 3:13
where the priests' f stood ... Josh 4:3
soles of the priests' f ... Josh 4:18
land whereon thy f have ... Josh 14:9
he covereth his f in his ... Judg 3:24
fled away on his f ... Judg 4:15
he was sent on f into ... Judg 5:15
they washed their f ... Judg 19:21
uncover his f, and lay ... Ruth 3:4
woman lay at his f ... Ruth 3:8
He will keep the f of his ... 1Sam 2:9
went in to cover his f ... 1Sam 24:3
was as light of f as a wild ... 2Sam 2:18
nor thy f put into fetters ... 2Sam 3:34
cut off..their f ... 2Sam 4:12
house, and wash thy f ... 2Sam 11:8
and on every f six toes ... 2Sam 21:20
was under his f ... 2Sam 22:10
so that my f did not slip ... 2Sam 22:37
that were on his f ... 1Kin 2:5
the sound of her f ... 1Kin 14:6
was diseased in his f ... 1Kin 15:23
she caught him by the f ... 2Kin 4:27
sound of his master's f ... 2Kin 6:32
and stood up on his f ... 2Kin 13:21
Neither will I make the f ... 2Kin 21:8
and six on each f ... 1Chr 20:6
stood up upon his f ... 1Chr 28:2
they stood on their f ... 2Chr 3:13
any more remove the f ... 2Chr 33:8
fell down at his f, and ... Esth 8:3
the sole of his f unto ... Job 2:7
ready to slip with his f ... Job 12:5
puttest my f also in the ... Job 13:27
the heels of my f ... Job 13:27
shall drive him to his f ... Job 18:11
forgotten of the f ... Job 28:4
they push away my f ... Job 30:12
forgetteth that the f ... Job 39:15
all things under his f ... Ps 8:6
they hid is their own f ... Ps 9:15
my f like hinds' f ... Ps 18:33
under me, that my f did ... Ps 18:36
are fallen under my f ... Ps 18:38
pierced my hands and my f ... Ps 22:16
he shall pluck my f out ... Ps 25:15
thou hast set my f in a ... Ps 31:8
Let not the f of pride ... Ps 36:11
and set my f upon a rock ... Ps 40:2
not thou deliver my f ... Ps 56:13
through the flood on f ... Ps 66:6
suffereth not our f to be ... Ps 66:9
thy f may be dipped in ... Ps 68:23
for me, my f were almost ... Ps 73:2
f unto the perpetual ... Ps 74:3
I said, My f slippeth ... Ps 94:18
whose f they hurt with ... Ps 105:18
f have they, but they ... Ps 115:7
from tears, and my f from ... Ps 116:8
turned my f unto thy ... Ps 119:59
refrained my f from every ... Ps 119:101
is a lamp unto my f ... Ps 119:105
Our f shall stand within ... Ps 122:2
refrain thy f from their ... Prov 1:15
their f run to evil, and ... Prov 1:16
shall keep thy f from ... Prov 3:26
Ponder the path of thy f ... Prov 4:26
Her f go down to death ... Prov 5:5
speaketh with his f, he ... Prov 6:13
f that be swift in running ... Prov 6:18
his f not be burned? ... Prov 6:28
her f abide not in her ... Prov 7:11
that hasteth with his f ... Prov 19:2
f from thy neighbor's ... Prov 25:17
a fool cutteth off the f ... Prov 26:6
spreadeth a net for his f ... Prov 29:5
Keep thy f when thou ... Eccl 5:1
I have washed my f ... Song 5:3
From the sole of the f ... Is 1:6
tinkling with their f ... Is 3:16
he covered his f ... Is 6:2
trodden under f ... Is 14:19
and trodden under f ... Is 18:7
thy shoe from thy f ... Is 20:2
even the f of the poor ... Is 26:6
The f shall tread it down ... Is 26:6
be trodden under f ... Is 28:3
thither the f of the ox ... Is 32:20
called him to his f ... Is 41:2
not gone with his f ... Is 41:3
lick up the dust of thy f ... Is 49:23
the f of him that bringeth ... Is 52:7
turn away thy f from the ... Is 58:13
Their f run to evil, and ... Is 59:7
make the place of my f ... Is 60:13
down at the soles of thy f ... Is 60:14
Withhold thy f from ... Jer 2:25
your f stumble upon ... Jer 13:16
and hid snares for my f ... Jer 18:22
spread a net for my f ... Lam 1:13
hath trodden under f ... Lam 1:15
their f were straight f ... Ezek 1:7
and the sole of their f ... Ezek 1:7
the sole of a calf's f ... Ezek 1:7
man, stand upon thy f ... Ezek 2:1
and set me upon my f ... Ezek 3:24
thy shoes upon thy f ... Ezek 24:17
stamped with the f ... Ezek 25:6
No f of man shall pass ... Ezek 29:11
shall the f of man ... Ezek 32:13
down with your f the ... Ezek 34:18
the residue with your f? ... Ezek 34:18
have trodden with your f ... Ezek 34:19
ye have fouled with your f ... Ezek 34:19
place of the soles of my f ... Ezek 43:7
his f part of iron and ... Dan 2:33
f and toes, part of potters' ... Dan 2:41
made stand upon the f ... Dan 7:4
residue with his f ... Dan 7:19
to be trodden under f? ... Dan 8:13
that is swift of f shall ... Amos 2:15
went forth at his f ... Hab 3:5
And his f shall stand in ... Zech 14:4
the soles of your f ... Mal 4:3
time thou dash thy f ... Matt 4:6
them under their f ... Matt 7:6
followed him on f out of ... Matt 14:13
down at Jesus' f ... Matt 15:30
having two hands or two f ... Matt 18:8
fell down at his f ... Matt 18:29
Bind him hand and f, and ... Matt 22:13
held him by the f ... Matt 28:9
he fell at his f ... Mark 5:22
dust under your f for a ... Mark 6:11
and came and fell at his f ... Mark 7:25
And if thy f offend thee ... Mark 9:45
having two f to be cast ... Mark 9:45
guide our f into the way ... Luke 1:79
thou dash thy f against a ... Luke 4:11
fell down at Jesus' f ... Luke 8:41
the very dust from your f ... Luke 9:5
and shoes on his f ... Luke 15:22
my hands and my f ... Luke 24:39
and wiped his f with her ... John 11:2

hand and *f* with ....John 11:44
anointed the *f* of Jesus ....John 12:3
wiped his *f* with her ....John 12:3
and the other at the *f*.........John 20:12
his *f* and ankle bones ....Acts 3:7
down at the apostles' *f*........Acts 4:35
it at the apostles' *f* ....Acts 4:37
it at the apostles' *f* ....Acts 5:2
the *f* of them which have .....Acts 5:9
so much as to set his *f*........Acts 7:5
thy shoes from thy *f* ....Acts 7:33
fell down at his *f*.............Acts 10:25
the dust of their *f* ....Acts 13:51
made their *f* fast in the ....Acts 16:24
in this city at the *f* of ....Acts 22:3
stand upon thy *f*...............Acts 26:16
Their *f* are swift to shed ......Rom 3:15
If the *f* shall say, Because 1Cor 12:15
the head to the *f* 1Cor 12:21
enemies under his *f*............1Cor 15:25
things under his *f*..............1Cor 15:27
things under his *f*..............Eph 1:22
your *f* shod with the ....Eph 6:15
subjection under his *f*.........Heb 2:8
trodden under *f* the Son ....Heb 10:29
paths for your *f* ....Heb 12:13
garment down to the *f*........Rev 1:13
And his *f* like unto fine ....Rev 1:15
and his *f* are like fine ....Rev 2:18
his *f* as pillars of fire ....Rev 10:1
he set his right *f*..............Rev 10:2
his left *f* on the earth ....Rev 10:2
the moon under her *f*..........Rev 12:1
and his *f* were as the *f*........Rev 13:2
before the *f* of the angel ......Rev 22:8

FOOTMAN—*member of the infantry*
10,000 in Samaria 2Kin 13:6, 7

[*also* FOOTMEN]
six hundred thousand *f*........Num 11:21
thousand *f*..drew sword ....Judg 20:2
of Israel thirty thousand *f* 1Sam 4:10
king said unto the *f* that 1Sam 22:17
and twenty thousand *f* 2Sam 8:4
hundred thousand *f* in one 1Kin 20:29
and twenty thousand *f* 1Chr 18:4
If thou hast run with the *f* ....Jer 12:5

FOOTSTEPS—*way of life or conduct*
paths, that my *f* slip not ......Ps 17:5
the *f* of thine anointed ....Ps 89:51
forth by the *f* of the flock .....Song 1:8

FOOTSTOOL—*a low stool that supports the foot*

Used literally of:
In the Temple...........2Chr 9:18
Prominent seat ....James 2:3

Used figuratively of:
Earth...................Matt 5:35
Ark 1Chr 28:2
Temple worship ....Ps 99:5
Subjector ....Acts 2:35

make thine enemies thy *f* .....Ps 110:1
and the earth is my *f* ....Is 66:1
I remembered not his *f* ....Lam 2:1
thine enemies thy *f*? ....Matt 22:44
thine enemies thy *f* ....Mark 12:36
thine enemies thy *f* ....Luke 20:43
and earth is my *f*.............Acts 7:49
thine enemies thy *f* ....Heb 1:13
enemies be made his *f* ....Heb 10:13

FOOTWASHING—*a practice that showed respect and honor*
Performed on guests .....Gen 18:4
Proffered by Abigail 1Sam 25:40, 41
On Jesus, with tears .....Luke 7:44
Performed by Jesus ......John 13:5
Duty of saints 1Tim 5:10

FOR—*See* INTRODUCTION

FORASMUCH—*in view of the fact that; since*
F as God hath showed thee ...Gen 41:39
f as thou knowest how ....Num 10:31
f as he hath no part nor ......Deut 12:12
f as the Lord hath blessed.....Josh 17:14
f as the Lord hath taken ......Judg 11:36
f as we have sworn both of....1Sam 20:42
f as my lord the king is 2Sam 19:30
unto Solomon, *F* as this is 1Kin 11:11
F as I exalted thee from 1Kin 14:7
F as thou..sent messengers 2Kin 1:16
f as he defiled his father's.....1Chr 5:1
F as it was in thine heart 2Chr 6:8
F as thou art sent of..........Ezra 7:14
F as this people refuseth ......Is 8:6
F as there is none like unto ...Jer 10:6
f as iron breaketh in ....Dan 2:40
F as thou sawest that ....Dan 2:45
F as an excellent spirit ....Dan 5:12
f as before him..was ....Dan 6:22
But *f* as he had not to pay ....Matt 18:25
And *f* as Lydda was nigh to ...Acts 9:38
F as we have heard, that......Acts 15:24
F as I know that thou hast ....Acts 24:10
f as ye are..spiritual 1Cor 14:12
F as ye are..declared 2Cor 3:3
F then as the children are .....Heb 2:14
F as ye know that ye were 1Pet 1:18

FORBID—*prohibit*

[*also* FORBADE, FORBIDDEN, FORBIDDETH, FORBIDDING]
God *f* that thy servants ....Gen 44:7
which are *f* to be done by .....Lev 5:17
My lord Moses, *f* them ....Num 11:28
the Lord our God *f* us ....Deut 2:37
Lord thy God hath *f* thee .....Deut 4:23
God *f* that we should rebel....Josh 22:29
God *f* that I should sin 1Sam 12:23
he said unto him, God *f* 1Sam 20:2
Lord *f*..I should stretch 1Sam 26:11
Lord *f* it me, that I should 1Kin 21:3
And said, My God *f* it me 1Chr 11:19
God *f* that I should justify ....Job 27:5
John *f* him, saying, I have ....Matt 3:14
f them not, to come unto .....Matt 19:14
we *f* him..he followeth ....Mark 9:38
But Jesus said, *F* him not .....Mark 9:39
f not to take thy coat also.....Luke 6:29
we *f* him..he followeth ....Luke 9:49
and *f* them not: for of such ...Luke 18:16
f to give tribute to Caesar.....Luke 23:2
Can any man *f* water, that ....Acts 10:47
f..Holy Ghost to preach.......Acts 16:6
confidence, no man *f* him .....Acts 28:31
God *f*: let God be true ....Rom 3:4
God *f*: yea, we establish ......Rom 3:31
but under grace? God *f* ....Rom 6:15
death unto me? God *f* ....Rom 7:13
of an harlot? God *f*...........1Cor 6:15
F us to speak to..Gentiles 1Thess 2:16
F to marry, and 1Tim 4:3
f..madness of the prophet 2Pet 2:16
f them that would, and 3John 10

FORCE—*to compel; rape*

[*also* FORCED, FORCING]
take by *f* thy daughters ....Gen 31:31
the trees thereof by *f* an axe ..Deut 20:19
man *f* her, and lie with her....Deut 22:25
Amorites *f* the children of.....Judg 1:34
if not, I will take it by *f* 1Sam 2:16
I *f* myself therefore, and 1Sam 13:12
my brother, do not *f* me 2Sam 13:12
f her, and lay with her 2Sam 13:14
the day that he *f* his sister 2Sam 13:32
to cease by *f* and power.......Ezra 4:23
f the queen also before me ....Esth 7:8
the great *f* of my disease ......Job 30:18
flattering of her lips she *f* .....Prov 7:21
f of wrath bringeth..strife .....Prov 30:33
blood by the *f* of the sword ...Jer 18:21
Heshbon because of the *f* ......Jer 48:45
but with *f* and with cruelty ....Ezek 34:4
shall not strengthen his *f*......Amos 2:14
and the violent take it by *f*....Matt 11:12
by *f*, to make him a king .....John 6:15
take him by *f* from among ....Acts 23:10
testament is of *f* after men ....Heb 9:17

FORCED LABOR—*conscripted workers or slaves*
Prisoners of war ....Deut 20:10, 11
As slaves ....Ex 13:3
By Solomon 1Kin 9:20, 21

FORCES—*military power*
False worship of.........Dan 11:10, 38
Weakness of ....Zech 4:6
Destruction of great .....Rev 20:7-10

f in all the fenced cities 2Chr 17:2
nor all the *f* of strength ....Job 36:19
f of the Gentiles shall come ...Is 60:5
all the captains of the *f* ....Jer 40:7
the *f* that were with him ......Jer 41:11
the *f* which were with him ....Jer 42:8
the captains of the *f*, took.....Jer 43:5
carried away captive his *f* .....Obad 11

FORCIBLE—*powerful*
Power of right words ....Job 6:25

FORD—*a shallow crossing of a body of water*
Of the Jabbok ....Gen 32:22
Of the Jordan ....Judg 3:28

[*also* FORDS]
way to Jordan unto the *f*.....Josh 2:7
Moab..at the *f* of Arnon ......Is 16:2

FOREBEARANCE—*restraint; patience*

God's forbearance:
1. *God's withholding of judgment, upon:*
The Amorites ....Gen 15:16
Sodom ....Gen 18:23-32
Israel...................Neh 9:30, 31
Nineveh ....Jon 4:10, 11
The world ....Rom 3:25

2. *Attitudes toward:*
Not to be despised ......Rom 2:4
To be remembered 2Pet 3:8-10
Means of preparation ....Mal 3:1-6

FOREBEARANCE TOWARD OTHERS
Expression of love 1Cor 13:7
Christian grace ....Eph 4:2

[*also* FORBARE, FORBEAR, FORBEARETH, FORBEARING, FORBORN]
wouldest *f* to help him ....Ex 23:5
and *f* to keep the passover ....Num 9:13
But if thou shalt *f* to vow .....Deut 23:22
and he *f* to go forth 1Sam 23:13
battle, or shall I *f*? And........1Kin 22:6
or shall I *f*? And they said 2Chr 18:5
f; why shouldest thou be 2Chr 25:16
the prophet *f*, and said.........2Chr 25:16
and though I *f*, what am I ....Job 16:6
If thou *f* to deliver them ......Prov 24:11
f is a prince persuaded ....Prov 25:15
I was weary with *f*, and I .....Jer 20:9
with me into Babylon, *f*.......Jer 40:4
he *f*, and slew them not.......Jer 41:8
men..have *f* to fight ....Jer 51:30
or whether they will *f*.........Ezek 2:5
or whether they will *f*.........Ezek 3:11
he that *f*, let him *f* ....Ezek 3:27
F to cry..no mourning ....Ezek 24:17
not, *f*. So they weighed ....Zech 11:12
we power to *f* working 1Cor 9:6
I *f*, lest any man should.......2Cor 12:6
ministers of sin? God *f*........Gal 2:17
God *f* that I should glory .....Gal 6:14
F one another, and ....Col 3:13
when we could no longer *f* 1Thess 3:1

FORECAST—*to see the consequences in advance*
f his devices against the ....Dan 11:24
f devices against him ....Dan 11:25

FOREFATHERS—*ancestors*
to the iniquities of their *f* .....Jer 11:10
serve from my *f* with pure 2Tim 1:3

FOREFRONT—*front*
in the *f* of the tabernacle......Ex 26:9
upon his *f*, did he put the.....Lev 8:9
f of the one was situate 1Sam 14:5

the *f* of the hottest battle 2Sam 11:15
f of the house, from 2Kin 16:14
Jehoshaphat in the *f* of 2Chr 20:27
f of the lower gate unto ....Ezek 40:19
f of the house stood ....Ezek 47:1

FOREHEAD—*upper part of the face*

Used literally of:
Aaron's.................Ex 28:38
Philistines'..............1Sam 17:49
Uzziah's 2Chr 26:19, 20

Used figuratively of:
Shamelessness ....Rev 17:5
Stronger power ....Ezek 3:8, 9
Devotion to God ....Ezek 9:4
Christ's true servants ....Rev 7:3

[*also* FOREHEADS]
is *f* bald: yet is he clean.......Lev 13:41
f, a white reddish sore ....Lev 13:42
bald head, or his bald *f* ....Lev 13:42
thou hadst a whore's *f* ....Jer 3:3
And I put a jewel on thy *f* ....Ezek 16:12
the seal of God in their *f* .....Rev 9:4
Father's name..in their *f* .....Rev 14:1
receive his mark in his *f* ......Rev 14:9
name shall be in their *f* ....Rev 22:4

FOREIGN AFFAIRS—*dealings with other countries*
War ....Gen 14:1-16
Josh 8:1-29
Treaties ....Josh 9:1-27
Trade agreement 1Kin 5:1-18
Alliances 1Kin 15:16-22
1Kin 22:1-6
Conquest 2Kin 25:1-11

FOREIGN MISSIONARIES
Jonah as ....Jon 1:1 2
Came from Antioch church ....Acts 13:1-3
Report of ....Acts 15:7-12

FOREIGNERS—*sojourners in Israel; those not native to a specific country*
Kept from feast ....Ex 1:43-45
Taxable.................Deut 15:2, 3
Figurative of Gentiles ....Eph 2:19
See STRANGERS

FOREKNOW—*to know ahead of time*

[*also* FOREKNEW, FOREKNOWLEDGE]
and *f* of God, ye have taken ..Acts 2:23
For whom he did *f*, he also ...Rom 8:29
cast away his people..he *f* .....Rom 11:2
Elect according to the *f* 1Pet 1:2

FOREKNOWLEDGE OF CHRIST—*Jesus' ability to know beforehand*

Concerning:
Men's nature ....John 1:47, 48
Men's acts ....John 6:64
His death and resurrection .... Matt 20:18, 19; John 13:1
Jerusalem's destruction ...Luke 19:41-44
Prophetic events ....Matt 24:1-51

FOREKNOWLEDGE OF GOD—*God's knowledge projected into the future*

Manifested in:
Naming a place 1Kin 13:2, 3
Matt 2:5, 6
Setting a time ....Mark 1:15
Determining the boundaries of nations ..Acts 17:26
Indicating successive nations ....Dan 2:26-47
Announcing Israel's captivity ....Dan 9:2, 24
Foretelling Christ's death .Acts 2:23

Based upon God's:
Infinite knowledge ....Is 41:22, 23
Eternal being ....Is 43:9-13
Foredetermination of events ....Rom 8:29

Plan of Salvation:
Planned in eternity ......Eph 1:3-12
Announces from beginning ....Gen 3:15
Expanded to include Gentiles ....Gal 3:8
Elaborated in details .....Is 53:1-12
Visualized in prophecy ...Zech 3:1-10
Consummated in Christ's death ....John 19:30

FOREMOST—*first; preeminent*
And he commanded the *f* .....Gen 32:17
the running of the *f* is like 2Sam 18:27

FOREORDAINED—*predestined*
Who verily was *f* before 1Pet 1:20

FOREPART—*in front; before*
the *f* thereof, over against .....Ex 28:27
oracle in the *f* was twenty 1Kin 6:20
on the *f* of the chambers ......Ezek 42:7
f stuck fast, and remained .....Acts 27:41

FORERUNNER—*one who goes before others*
the *f* is for us entered.........Heb 6:20

FORESEE—*to see something before it takes place*
Approaching evil ....Prov 22:3
Resurrection of Christ ...Acts 2:31
Salvation of Gentiles.....Gal 3:8

[*also* FORSEEING, FORESEETH, FORESAW]
A prudent man *f* the evil .....Prov 27:12
I *f* the Lord always before ....Acts 2:25

FORESHIP—*the bow area of a boat or ship*
have cast anchors out of the *f*. .Acts 27:30

FORESKIN—*fold of skin that covers the penis*

Used literally of:
Circumcision ....Gen 17:9-17
Death 1Sam 18:25

Figuratively of:
Regeneration............Jer 4:4
See CIRCUMCISION

[*also* FORESKINS]
circumcised..their *f* ....Gen 17:23
cut off the *f* of her son ....Ex 4:25
flesh of his *f*..be circumcised ..Lev 12:3
Circumcise therefore the *f*.....Deut 10:16
of Israel at the hill of the *f*....Josh 5:3
f of the Philistines 2Sam 3:14
let thy *f* be uncovered ....Hab 2:16

FOREST—*wooded land*

Descriptive of wooded areas in:
Hareth 1Sam 22:5
Lebanon 1Kin 7:2
Beth-el 2Kin 2:23, 24
Arabia ....Is 21:13

Used figuratively of:
Army ....Is 10:18, 19
Kingdom ....Jer 21:14
Unfruitfulness ....Jer 26:18
Hos 2:12

[*also* FORESTS]
house of the *f* of Lebanon 1Kin 10:17
into the *f* of his Carmel 2Kin 19:23
house of the *f* of Lebanon 2Chr 9:16
in the *f* he built castles........2Chr 27:4
the keeper of the king's *f* .....Neh 2:8
and discovereth the *f* ....Ps 29:9
every beast of the *f* is mine ...Ps 50:10
in the thickets of the *f* ....Is 9:18
cut..thickets of the *f* ....Is 10:34
of the house of the *f*..........Is 22:8
field be counted for a *f* ....Is 32:15
and the *f* of his Carmel ....Is 37:24
O *f* and every tree therein ....Is 44:23
lion out of the *f* shall slay .....Jer 5:6
unto me as a lion in the *f* .....Jer 12:8
They shall cut down her *f* .....Jer 46:23
among the trees of the *f* ......Ezek 15:2
prophesy against the *f* of ......Ezek 20:46
cut down any out of the *f* .....Ezek 39:10
Will a lion roar in the *f* ....Amos 3:4
house..high places of the *f* ....Mic 3:12
f of the vintage is come ....Zech 11:2

FORETHOUGHT—*thinking ahead*
In meeting a danger .....Gen 32:3-23
In anticipating evil.......Prov 22:3
Concerning physical needs.................Phil 4:10-19
Neglect of, dangerous ....Matt 25:8-13
Examples of ant, in......Prov 6:6-8
For eternal riches........Luke 12:23-34

FORETOLD—*predicted*
Destruction of Jerusalem .Mark 13:1, 2
Gospel blessings ....Acts 3:24
Paul's trip to Corinth 2Cor 13:2

[*also* FORETELL]
I have *f* you all things ....Mark 13:23
f you as if I were present 2Cor 13:2

FOREVER—*See* EVER

FOREWARN—*to warn beforehand*
God's judgment ....Luke 12:5
God's vengeance 1Thess 4:6

[*also* FOREWARNED]
f you whom ye shall fear ......Luke 12:5
as we also have *f* you and 1Thess 4:6

FORFEIT—*loss incurred by one's failure*
Leadership 1Sam 15:16-28
Possessions.............Ezra 10:8
Salvation ....Matt 16:26

FORFEITING SPIRITUAL RIGHTS
Birthright ....Gen 25:34
Headship ....Gen 49:3, 4
Apostleship ....Matt 26:14-16
Spiritual heritage ....Acts 13:45-48

FORGER—*a counterfeiter*
Applied to David's enemies ....Ps 119:69

[*also* FORGERS]
ye are *f* of lies, ye are all .....Job 13:4

FORGET—*to lose one's memory of; disregard*
God does not ....Is 49:15
Our sinful past ....Phil 3:13

[*also* FORGAT, FORGETTEST, FORGETTETH, FORGOT, FORGOTTEN]
and he *f* that which thou ......Gen 27:45
remember Joseph, but *f*.......Gen 40:23
all the plenty shall be *f* in .....Gen 41:30
f the things which thine ....Deut 4:9
nor *f* the covenant of thy .....Deut 4:31
Beware..*f* not the Lord ....Deut 8:11
thou *f* the Lord thy God ......Deut 8:14
if thou..*f* the Lord thy God ...Deut 8:19
hast *f* a sheaf in the field .....Deut 24:19
heaven; thou shalt not *f* it.....Deut 25:19
neither have I *f* them ....Deut 26:13
f God that formed thee ....Deut 32:18
and *f* the Lord their God .....Judg 3:7
they *f* the Lord their God 1Sam 12:9
I will *f* my complaint ....Job 9:27
thou shalt *f* thy misery ....Job 11:16
familiar friends have *f* me .....Job 19:14
f that the foot may crush......Job 39:15
he *f* not the cry of the ....Ps 9:12
all the nations that *f* God .....Ps 9:17
needy shall not always be *f*....Ps 9:18
hand; *f* not the humble ....Ps 10:12
How long wilt thou *f* me ......Ps 13:1
I am *f* as a dead man out .....Ps 31:12
yet have we not *f* thee ....Ps 44:17
and *f* our affliction and our ...Ps 44:24
f also thine own people ....Ps 45:10
f God, lest I tear you in ......Ps 50:22
f not the congregation of......Ps 74:19
Hath God *f* to be gracious ....Ps 77:9
And *f* his works..wonders .....Ps 78:11
so that I *f* to eat my bread ....Ps 102:4
They *f* God their savior ....Ps 106:21
thy statutes; I will not *f*.......Ps 119:16
I will never *f* thy precepts .....Ps 119:93
yet do I not *f* thy law.........Ps 119:109
mine enemies have *f*..........Ps 119:139
yet do not I *f* thy precepts ....Ps 119:141
If I *f* thee, O Jerusalem.......Ps 137:5

let my right hand *f* her........Ps 137:5
f the covenant of her God ....Prov 2:17
My son, *f* not my law, but ....Prov 3:1
they drink and *f* the law ......Prov 31:5
to come shall all be *f* ....Eccl 2:16
the memory of them is *f* ......Eccl 9:5
thou hast *f* the God of thy ....Is 17:10
harlot that hast been *f* ....Is 23:16
and my Lord hath *f* me ....Is 49:14
And *f* the Lord thy maker ....Is 51:13
f the shame of thy youth ......Is 54:4
yet my people have *f* me ......Jer 2:32
because thou hast *f* me ....Jer 13:25
confusion shall never be *f* .....Jer 20:11
I, even I, will utterly *f* you ....Jer 23:39
shame, which shall not be *f* ...Jer 23:40
f the wickedness..fathers ......Jer 44:9
have *f* their restingplace........Jer 50:6
feasts and sabbaths to be *f* ....Lam 2:6
far off from peace; I *f* ....Lam 3:17
Wherefore dost thou *f* us ....Lam 5:20
f me, saith the Lord God .....Ezek 22:12
after her lovers and *f* me ......Hos 2:13
hast *f* the law of thy God .....Hos 4:6
therefore have they *f* me ......Hos 13:6
never *f* any of their works.....Amos 8:7
they had *f* to take bread ......Matt 16:5
had *f* to take bread ....Mark 8:14
one of them is *f* before God...Luke 12:6
to *f* your work and labor ......Heb 6:10
ye have *f* the exhortation ......Heb 12:5
and to communicate *f* not .....Heb 13:16
f what manner of man ....James 1:24
hath *f* that he was purged 2Pet 1:9

FORGETFUL—*unable to remember*
Concerning our hearing ..James 1:25

[*also* FORGETFULNESS]
righteousness..land of *f*? ......Ps 88:12
Be not *f* to entertain...........Heb 13:2

FORGETTING GOD—*neglecting to remember God's proper place in life*

Seen in forgetting God's:
Covenant ....Deut 4:23
Works ....Ps 78:7, 11
Blessings................Ps 103:2
Law ....Ps 119:153, 176
Word ....James 1:25

Characteristics of:
Wicked ....Is 65:11
Form of backsliding .....Jer 3:21, 22
Instigated by false teachers ....Jer 23:26, 27

FORGIVENESS—*the act of pardoning*

Synonyms of:
"Blotteth out" ....Is 43:25
"Remission" ....Matt 26:28
"Pardon" ....Is 55:7
"Remember no more" ...Jer 31:34
"Healed" 2Chr 30:18-20

Basis of:
God's nature ....Ps 86:5
God's grace ....Luke 7:42
Shedding of blood ....Heb 9:22
Christ's death ....Col 1:14
Son's power.............Luke 5:21-24
Man's repentance........Acts 2:38
Our forgiveness ....Matt 6:12-14
Faith in Christ ....Acts 10:43

Significance of:
Shows God's righteousness..........Rom 3:25
Makes salvation real .....Luke 1:77
Must be preached ....Luke 24:47

[*also* FORGAVE, FORGAVEST, FORGIVE, FORGIVEN, FORGIVENESSES, FORGIVETH, FORGIVING]
F I pray thee now the ....Gen 50:17
f the trespass of the ....Gen 50:17
Now therefore *f*, I pray ....Ex 10:17
for thousands *f* iniquity ....Ex 34:7
for them, and it shall be *f*.....Lev 4:20
for him, and it shall be *f*......Lev 4:31
and it shall be *f* him ....Lev 5:10
and it shall be *f* him ....Lev 5:16
f him for any thing of all......Lev 6:7
of great mercy *f* iniquity ......Num 14:18
and as thou hast *f* this ....Num 14:19
be *f* all the congregation ......Num 15:26
the Lord shall *f* her...........Num 30:5
void; and the Lord shall *f*.....Num 30:12
And the blood shall be *f*......Deut 21:8
not *f* your transgressions ......Josh 24:19
I pray thee, *f* the trespass 1Sam 25:28
and when thou hearest *f* 1Kin 8:30
f the sin of thy servants 1Kin 8:36
And *f* thy people that have....1Kin 8:50
and when thou hearest *f* 2Chr 6:21
thou from heaven and *f*........2Chr 6:27
and *f* thy people which........2Chr 6:39
my pain; and *f* all my sins.....Ps 25:18
whose transgression is *f* ....Ps 32:1
f the iniquity of my sin ....Ps 32:5
f..iniquity, and destroyed......Ps 78:38
Who *f* all thine iniquities ......Ps 103:3
But there is *f* with thee ....Ps 130:4
himself; therefore *f* them......Is 2:9
that dwell..be *f* their..........Is 33:24
f not their iniquity............Jer 18:23
that I may *f* their iniquity .....Jer 36:3
God belong mercies and *f*.....Dan 9:9
O Lord hear; O Lord, *f*.......Dan 9:19
O Lord God, *f*, I beseech .....Amos 7:2
If ye *f* not men their..........Matt 6:15
will your Father *f* your........Matt 6:15
good cheer; thy sins be *f*......Matt 9:2
hath power on earth to *f*......Matt 9:6
and blasphemy shall be *f*......Matt 12:31
the Son of man..be *f* him .....Matt 12:32
Holy Ghost..not be *f* him .....Matt 12:32
sin against me and I *f*.........Matt 18:21
loosed him, and *f* him the.....Matt 18:27
f not every one his brother ....Matt 18:35
Son, thy sins be *f* thee ....Mark 2:5
who can *f* sins but God ....Mark 2:7
power on earth to *f* sins.......Mark 2:10
All sins shall be *f* unto........Mark 3:28
Holy Ghost hath never *f*......Mark 3:29
Man, thy sins are *f* thee......Luke 5:20
f, and ye shall be *f* ....Luke 6:37
to pay, he frankly *f* them .....Luke 7:42
which are many, are *f* ....Luke 7:47
to whom little is *f*, the ....Luke 7:47
unto her, Thy sins are *f*.......Luke 7:48
Who is this that *f* sins ....Luke 7:49
f us our sins; for we also *f* ...Luke 11:4
the Son..it shall be *f* him......Luke 12:10
the Holy Ghost..not be *f*.......Luke 12:10
and if he repent, *f* him.........Luke 17:3
I repent; thou shalt *f* him ......Luke 17:4
repentance to Israel and *f* .....Acts 5:31
of thine heart may be *f* ....Acts 8:22
preached unto you the *f* of ....Acts 13:38
that they may receive *f* of .....Acts 26:18
whose iniquities are *f* ....Rom 4:7
if I *f*..to whom I *f* it 2Cor 2:10
to you? *f* me this wrong.......2Cor 12:13
the *f* of sins, according to .....Eph 1:7
Christ's sake hath *f*...........Eph 4:32
him, having *f* you all ....Col 2:13
and *f* one another, if any .....Col 3:13
even as Christ *f* you, so ....Col 3:13
faithful and just to *f* us our ...1John 1:9
your sins are *f* you for 1John 2:12

FORGIVING ONE ANOTHER

The measure of:
Seventy times seven .....Matt 18:21, 22
Unlimited...............Luke 17:3, 4
As God forgave us ......Eph 4:32

Benefits of:
Means of our forgiveness .Mark 11:25, 26
Restored Christian fellowship.............2Cor 2:7-10
Spiritual cleansing ....James 5:15, 16

Examples of:
Esau and Jacob ....Gen 33:4-15
Joseph..................Gen 45:8-15
Moses ....Num 12:1-13
David 2Sam 19:18-23
Solomon 1Kin 1:53
Jesus ....Luke 23:34
Stephen ....Acts 7:60
Paul....................2Tim 4:16

FORK—*a tool for eating*

Rendered:
"Three-pronged fork"....1Sam 2:13, 14
"Fork" ....Is 30:24

[*also* FORKS]
the coulters, and for the *f*.....1Sam 13:21

FORM—*the outward appearance*

Of physical things:
Earth without ....Gen 1:2
Man in the womb ....Is 44:24
Sexes...................1Tim 2:13
Idols ....Is 44:10

Of spiritual realities:
Incarnate Christ ....Is 53:2
Rom 9:20
Molder ....Rom 9:20
Christian truth ....Rom 6:17
New birth...............Gal 4:19

[*also* FORMED, FORMETH, FORMS]
And the Lord God *f* man .....Gen 2:7
the Lord God *f* every beast ...Gen 2:19
hast forgotten God that *f* .....Deut 32:18
said unto her, What *f* is he 1Sam 28:14
To fetch about this *f* of 2Sam 14:20
of ancient times..have *f* it 2Kin 19:25
gold according to their *f* 2Chr 4:7
I could not discern the *f* ......Job 4:16
Dead things are *f* from........Job 26:5
I also am *f* out of the clay ....Job 33:6
or ever thou hadst *f* the.......Ps 90:2
and his hands *f* the dry ....Ps 95:5
The great God that *f* all ......Prov 26:10
he that *f* them will show ......Is 27:11
he that *f* thee, O Israel ....Is 43:1
me there was no God *f* ....Is 43:10
and *f* thee from the womb ....Is 44:2
have *f* thee; thou art my ......Is 44:21
I *f* the light, and create ....Is 45:7
God himself that *f* the ....Is 45:18
he *f* it to be inhabited ....Is 45:18
No weapon that is *f*..thee .....Is 54:17
and, lo, it was without *f* ......Jer 4:23
put forth the *f* of an hand.....Ezek 8:3
the *f* of a man's hand ....Ezek 10:8
show them the *f* of the........Ezek 43:11
f..and all the ordinances ......Ezek 43:11
all the *f*..and all the laws......Ezek 43:11
may keep the whole *f*.........Ezek 43:11
the *f* thereof was terrible ......Dan 2:31
f of the fourth is like the......Dan 3:25
he that *f* the mountains ....Amos 4:13
he appeared in another *f*......Mark 16:12
hast the *f* of knowledge ....Rom 2:20
Who, being in the *f* of God ..Phil 2:6
took upon him the *f* of a......Phil 2:7
Hold fast the *f* of sound 2Tim 1:13
having a *f* of godliness 2Tim 3:5

FORMALISM—*following established form or rule to a fault*

Characterized by:
Outward forms of religion ....Is 1:10-15
Lifelessness ....Is 58:1-14
Coldness................Rev 3:14-18

Sign of:
Hypocrisy...............Luke 18:10-12
Deadness ....Phil 3:4-8
Last days 2Tim 3:1, 5

FORMER—*preceding; previous*
after the *f* manner when ......Gen 40:13
against the *f* king of Moab ....Num 21:26
Her *f* husband, which sent ....Deut 24:4

this was the manner in *f* ......Ruth 4:7
answered him again..the *f* 1Sam 17:30
two captains of the *f* fifties 2Kin 1:14
but they did after their *f* 2Kin 17:40
the *f* governors that had ......Neh 5:15
inquire..of the *f* age ....Job 8:8
not against us *f* iniquities ......Ps 79:8
remembrance of *f* things ......Eccl 1:11
let them show the *f* things .....Is 41:22
declare this, and show us *f* ....Is 43:9
Remember the *f* things of .....Is 46:9
raise up the *f* desolations ......Is 61:4
f troubles are forgotten ....Is 65:16
both the *f* and the latter ......Jer 5:24
f kings which were before .....Jer 34:5
he is the *f* of all things ....Jer 51:19
shall return to their *f* ....Ezek 16:55
return to your *f* estate ....Ezek 16:55
a multitude greater..*f* ....Dan 11:13
latter and *f* rain unto ....Hos 6:3
given you the *f* rain ....Joel 2:23
be greater than of the *f* ....Hag 2:9
unto whom the *f* prophets .....Zech 1:4
his spirit by the *f* prophets ....Zech 7:12
half of them toward the *f* .....Zech 14:8
the days of old and as in *f* ....Mal 3:4
The *f* treatise have I made ....Acts 1:1
the *f* conversation ....Eph 4:22
call to remembrance the *f* .....Heb 10:32
according to the *f* lusts 1Pet 1:14
for the *f* things are passed .....Rev 21:4

FORMULA—*a prescribed method*
Success ....Prov 22:29
Prosperity ....Matt 6:32, 33
Peace ....Is 26:3
Making friends ....Prov 18:24

FORNICATION—*sex relations between the unmarried*

Evil of:
Comes from evil heart ...Matt 15:19
Sins against the body 1Cor 6:18
Excludes from God's kingdom 1Cor 6:9
Disrupts Christian fellowship 1Cor 5:9-11

[*also* FORNICATIONS]
of Jerusalem to commit *f* 2Chr 21:11
and shall commit *f* with ....Is 23:17
pouredst out thy *f* on every ...Ezek 16:15
also committed *f* with ....Ezek 16:26
saving for the cause of *f* ......Matt 5:32
his wife, except it be for *f* .....Matt 19:9
evil thoughts, adulteries, *f* .....Mark 7:21
We be not born of *f*, we ......John 8:41
from *f*, and from things ....Acts 15:20
strangled and from *f* ....Acts 15:29
strangled, and from *f* ....Acts 21:25
f, wickedness ....Rom 1:29
that there is *f* among you 1Cor 5:1
such *f* as is not so much as 1Cor 5:1
Now the body is not for *f* 1Cor 6:13
to avoid *f*, let every man 1Cor 7:2
Neither let us commit *f* 1Cor 10:8
and *f* and lasciviousness 2Cor 12:21
Adultery, *f*, uncleanness ....Gal 5:19
But *f* and all uncleanness .....Eph 5:3
f, uncleanness, inordinate .....Col 3:5
ye should abstain from *f* 1Thess 4:3
giving themselves over to *f* ....Jude 7
unto idols, and to commit *f* ...Rev 2:14
space to repent of her *f* ....Rev 2:21
wine of the wrath of her *f* .....Rev 14:8
earth have committed *f* ....Rev 17:2
drunk..the wine of her *f* ....Rev 17:2
wine of the wrath of her *f* .....Rev 18:3
have committed *f* with her ....Rev 18:3
did corrupt..with her *f* ....Rev 19:2

FORNICATOR—*indulger in sexual excesses*

[*also* FORNICATORS]
altogether with the *f* of 1Cor 5:10
Lest there be any *f* ....Heb 12:16

FORSAKE—*to abandon; turn away from*

[*also* FORSAKETH, FORSAKING, FORSOOK, FORSOOKEST]
not *f* thee neither destroy .....Deut 4:31
thou shalt not *f* him; for ......Deut 14:27
not fail thee, neither *f* ....Deut 31:8
will *f* them, and I will hide ....Deut 31:17
then he *f* God which made ....Deut 32:15
I will not fail thee, nor *f* ......Josh 1:5
If ye *f* the Lord, and serve ....Josh 24:20
f the Lord God of their ....Judg 2:12
Should I *f* my sweetness ......Judg 9:11
f the Lord and served not .....Judg 10:6
the Lord will not *f* his 1Sam 12:22
they *f* the cities and fled 1Sam 31:7
And I will not *f* my people 1Kin 6:13
they *f* the Lord their God 1Kin 9:9
and *f* the old men's counsel ...1Kin 12:13
And I will *f* the remnant 2Kin 21:14
he *f* the Lord God of his 2Kin 21:22
then they *f* their cities 1Chr 10:7
if thou *f* him, he will cast 1Chr 28:9
if ye turn away, and *f* my 2Chr 7:19
they *f* the Lord God of their ..2Chr 7:22
Rehoboam *f* the counsel of 2Chr 10:13
is against all them that *f* ......Ezra 8:22
kindness, and *f* them not ......Neh 9:17
consume them, nor *f* them ....Neh 9:31
f the fear of the Almighty .....Job 6:14
Though he spare it, and *f* .....Job 20:13
leave me not, neither *f* me ....Ps 27:9
from anger, and *f* wrath ......Ps 37:8
and *f* not his saints ....Ps 37:28
f me not when my strength ....Ps 71:9
he *f* the tabernacle ....Ps 78:60
if his children *f* my law ....Ps 89:30
will keep thy statutes: O *f* .....Ps 119:8
f not the works of thine ....Ps 138:8
and *f* not the law..mother .....Prov 1:8
f the guide of her youth ....Prov 2:17
doctrine, *f* ye not my law .....Prov 4:2
and *f* not the law..mother .....Prov 6:20
father's friend, *f* not ....Prov 27:10
confesseth and *f* them ....Prov 28:13
that *f* the Lord shall be ....Is 1:28
there be a great *f* in the ......Is 6:12
I do unto them and not *f* .....Is 42:16
f not the ordinance..God ......Is 58:2
But ye..that *f* the Lord ....Is 65:11
calved in the field and *f* it .....Jer 14:5
even *f* you, saith the Lord ....Jer 23:33
she is not healed: *f* her ....Jer 51:9
forget us for ever, and *f* ....Lam 5:20
they *f* the idols of Egypt ......Ezek 20:8
that *f* the holy covenant ....Dan 11:30
lying vanities *f* their own ......Jon 2:8
all the disciples *f* him ....Matt 26:56
f their nets, and followed .....Mark 1:18
they all *f* him and fled ....Mark 14:50
f all, and followed him ....Luke 5:11
that *f* not all that he hath .....Luke 14:33
the Gentiles to *f* Moses ....Acts 21:21
with me, but all men *f* me 2Tim 4:16
Not *f* the assembling of ....Heb 10:25
By faith he *f* Egypt, not ......Heb 11:27
never leave thee nor *f* thee ....Heb 13:5

FORSAKEN—*abandoned*
God's house ....Neh 13:11
God's children ....Ps 37:25
Messiah ....Is 53:3
God's Son ....Matt 27:46

whereby thou hast *f* me ....Deut 28:20
now the Lord hath *f* us ....Judg 6:13
have *f* me..other gods ....Judg 10:13
have *f* me..other gods 1Sam 8:8
have *f* thy covenant 1Kin 19:10
they have *f* me and have 2Kin 22:17
the Lord, Ye have *f* me 2Chr 12:5
God, but ye have *f* him 2Chr 13:11
have *f* the Lord..also *f* you ...2Chr 24:20
because they had *f* the Lord ...2Chr 28:6
f me and have burned 2Chr 34:25
yet our God hath not *f* us .....Ezra 9:9
the earth be *f* for thee? ....Job 18:4
hast not *f* them that seek .....Ps 9:10
God hath *f* him: persecute ....Ps 71:11
they have *f* the Lord, they ....Is 1:4
abhorrest shall be *f* of ....Is 7:16
his strong cities be as a *f* ......Is 17:9
palaces shall be *f*; the ....Is 32:14
thee as a woman *f* and ....Is 54:6
thou hast been *f* and hated ....Is 60:15
Sought out, A city not *f* ......Is 62:12
who have *f* me, and have .....Jer 1:16
thou hast *f* the Lord thy ......Jer 2:17
every city shall be *f*, and ......Jer 4:29
as ye have *f* me, and ....Jer 5:19
they have *f* my law which I ...Jer 9:13
f mine house, I have left ......Jer 12:7
have *f* me, saith the Lord .....Jer 16:11
f me, and have not kept ......Jer 16:11
from another place be *f*? ......Jer 18:14
f the covenant of the Lord ....Jer 22:9
Israel hath not been *f*, nor ....Jer 51:5
the Lord hath *f* the earth ......Ezek 8:12
The Lord hath *f* the earth .....Ezek 9:9
the cities that are *f* which .....Ezek 36:4
she is *f* upon her land ....Amos 5:2
Gaza shall be *f* and ....Zeph 2:4
we have *f* all, and followed ....Matt 19:27
God, my God..thou *f* me? ....Mark 15:34
Persecuted, but not *f*, cast 2Cor 4:9
Demas hath *f* me, having 2Tim 4:10
Which have *f* the right way 2Pet 2:15

FORSAKING CHRIST
Disciples left ....Matt 26:56
Cause of separation ......John 6:66-70

FORSAKING GOD

Manifested in:
Going after idols 1Kin 11:33
Going backward ....Jer 15:6
Following human forms ..Jer 2:13

Evil of:
Manifests ingratitude .....Jer 2:5-12
Brings confusion ....Jer 17:13
Merits God's wrath ......Ezra 8:22

Examples of:
Israel 2Kin 17:7-18
Judah 2Chr 12:1, 5

FORSOMUCH—*inasmuch as*
f..also is a son of Abraham ...Luke 19:9

FORSWEAR—*reject or renounce*
Thou shalt not *f* thyself ....Matt 5:33

FORT—*military stronghold*
In Jerusalem 2Sam 5:9

[*also* FORTS]
they built *f* against it round ...2Kin 25:1
fortress of the high *f* of thy ...Is 25:12
and I will raise *f* against ......Is 29:3
and built *f* against it round ....Jer 52:4
and build a *f* against it ....Ezek 4:2
mounts and building *f* ....Ezek 17:17
he shall make a *f* against ......Ezek 26:8
turn his face toward the *f* .....Dan 11:19

FORTH—*See* INTRODUCTION

FORTHWITH—*immediately*
f expenses be given unto ......Ezra 6:8
f they sprung up, because .....Matt 13:5
f, when they were come ......Mark 1:29
f Jesus gave them leave ....Mark 5:13
f came..blood and water ......John 19:34

FORTIETH—*See* FORTY

FORTIFICATIONS—*walls or towers for protection*
Cities 1Kin 9:15; 2Chr 11:5-11
City of David 2Sam 5:7-9

[*also* FORTIFIED, FORTIFY]
they *f* the city against thee ....Judg 9:31
turning of the wall, and *f* 2Chr 26:9
f Jeruslaem..broad wall ....Neh 3:8

F

Jews?..*f* themselves? .... Neh 4:2
ye broken down to *f* the ...... Is 22:10
should *f* the height of her ..... Jer 51:53
Assyria, and from the *f* .... Mic 7:12
loins strong, *f* thy power ...... Nah 2:1
f thy strong holds; go into ..... Nah 3:14

FORTIFIED CITIES—*cities with strengthened defenses*
Means of protecting 2Sam 20:6
Mighty and strong .... Deut 9:1
Conquerable .... Deut 3:5
Utterly destroyed 2Kin 3:19, 25
No substitute for God ... Hos 8:14

FORTRESS—*center of military strength*
Nation's security 2Chr 26:9
Illustrative of God's protection .... Ps 18:2
Typical of Christ .... Is 33:16, 17
Applied to God's prophets .... Jer 6:27

[*also* FORTRESSES]
Lord is my rock, and my *f* 2Sam 22:2
art my rock and my *f* .... Ps 31:3
art my rock and my *f* .... Ps 71:3
He is my refuge and my *f* ..... Ps 91:2
My goodness and my *f* .... Ps 144:2
f also shall cease from .... Is 17:3
and brambles in the *f* .... Is 34:13
O inhabitant of the *f* .... Jer 10:17
enter into the *f* of the king .... Dan 11:7
all thy *f* shall be spoiled .... Hos 10:14
shall come against the *f* .... Amos 5:9
and from the *f* even to the .... Mic 7:12

FORTUNATUS (fôr-tū-nā'tŭs)—*"fortunate"*
Christian at Corinth 1Cor 16:17

FORTY

[*also* FORTIETH, FORTY'S]
Mahalaleel..hundred and *f* .... Gen 5:13
pass at the end of *f* days ...... Gen 8:6
shall be *f* found there .... Gen 18:29
I will not do it for *f* sake ..... Gen 18:29
Esau was *f* years old when .... Gen 26:34
Jacob was a hundred *f* .... Gen 47:28
make *f* sockets of silver .... Ex 26:19
with the Lord *f* days and *f* .... Ex 34:28
their *f* sockets of silver .... Ex 36:26
shall be unto thee *f* and .... Lev 25:8
f and six thousand and five .... Num 1:21
were *f* thousand and five ..... Num 1:33
f and six thousand and five .... Num 2:11
were *f* thousand and five ...... Num 2:19
wander in the wilderness *f* .... Num 14:33
searched the land, even *f* ..... Num 14:34
bear your iniquities even *f* .... Num 14:34
them, *f* thousand and five ..... Num 26:18
were *f* and five thousand ...... Num 26:50
and died there, in the *f* .... Num 33:38
shall add *f* and two cities ...... Num 35:6
f years the Lord thy God ..... Deut 2:7
did thy foot swell, these *f* ..... Deut 8:4
at the end of *f* days and *f* ..... Deut 9:11
before the Lord *f* days and *f* .. Deut 9:25
F stripes he may give him ..... Deut 25:3
About *f* thousand prepared .... Josh 4:13
F years..when Moses the ...... Josh 14:7
were *f* and eight cities .... Josh 21:41
land had rest *f* years .... Judg 3:11
land had rest *f* years .... Judg 5:31
country was in quietness *f* ..... Judg 8:28
Ephraimites *f* and two .... Judg 12:6
of the Philistines *f* years ...... Judg 13:1
had judged Israel *f* years 1Sam 4:18
Saul's son was *f* years 2Sam 2:10
and *f* thousand horsemen 2Sam 10:18
temple..was *f* cubits long 1Kin 6:17
over all Israel was *f* years 1Kin 11:42
Rehoboam was *f* and one 1Kin 14:21
tare *f* and two children of 2Kin 2:24
and *f* men; neither left 2Kin 10:14
reigned *f* and one years 2Kin 14:23
were four and *f* thousand 1Chr 5:18
chariots and *f* thousand 1Chr 19:18
f year of the reign of David ... 1Chr 26:31
Jerusalem over all Israel *f* 2Chr 9:30
and died in the one and *f* 2Chr 16:13
F and two..was Ahaziah 2Chr 22:2
of Zattu, nine hundred *f* ...... Ezra 2:8
children of Azmaveth, *f* .... Ezra 2:24
of Jericho, three hundred *f* .... Ezra 2:34
together was *f* and two .... Ezra 2:64
beside *f* shekels of silver ...... Neh 5:15
of Binnui, six hundred *f* ...... Neh 7:15
seven hundred *f* and .... Neh 7:29
thousand two hundred *f* .... Neh 7:41
of Nekoda, six hundred *f* ..... Neh 7:62
two hundred *f* and five .... Neh 7:67
f years didst thou sustain ...... Neh 9:21
lived Job a hundred and *f* ..... Job 42:16
F years long was I grieved .... Ps 95:10
seven hundred *f* and five ...... Jer 52:30
house of Judah *f* days .... Ezek 4:6
shall it be inhabited *f* .... Ezek 29:11
the length thereof, *f* cubits .... Ezek 41:2
you *f* years through the .... Amos 2:10
he had fasted *f* days and *f* ..... Matt 4:2
in the wilderness *f* days .... Mark 1:13
F and six years was this .... John 2:20
For the man was above *f* ...... Acts 4:22
And when *f* years were .... Acts 7:30
f years in the wilderness? ..... Acts 7:42
Benjamin, by the space of *f* ... Acts 13:21
of them more than *f* men ..... Acts 23:21
saw my works *f* years .... Heb 3:9
sealed a hundred and *f* .... Rev 7:4
him to continue *f* and two ..... Rev 13:5
but the hundred and *f* and .... Rev 14:3

FORTY DAYS
Length of flood .... Gen 7:17
Israel's embalming .... Gen 50:2, 3
Moses on Mt. Sinai ...... Ex 24:18
Spies in Canaan .... Num 13:25
Moses' prayer .... Deut 9:25-29
The Philistine's arrogance. 1Sam 17:16
Elijah's fast 1Kin 19:2, 8
Nineveh's probation ..... Jon 3:4
Christ's temptation ...... Luke 4:1, 2
Christ's ministry after His resurrection .... Acts 1:3

FORTY STRIPES
Limit for scourging ...... Deut 25:3
Paul's, one less 2Cor 11:24

FORTY YEARS
Isaac's age at marriage ... Gen 25:20
Israel's diet .... Ex 16:35
Israel's wanderings ...... Num 32:13
Same shoes for .... Deut 29:5
Period of rest .... Judg 3:11
Egypt's desolation .... Ezek 19:11-13
Saul's reign .... Acts 13:21
David's reign 1Kin 2:11
Solomon's reign 1Kin 11:42

FORUM—*marketplace; public place*
to meet us as far as Appii *F* .. Acts 28:15

FORWARD—*moving ahead*
waxed great and went *f* .... Gen 26:13
of Israel, that they go *f* .... Ex 14:15
the tabernacle setteth *f* .... Num 1:51
congregation shall set *f* .... Num 2:17
so shall they set *f*, every ...... Num 2:17
and so they set *f*, every .... Num 2:34
as the camp is to set *f* .... Num 4:15
the sons of Merari set *f* .... Num 10:17
And the Kohathites set *f* ...... Num 10:21
the children of Dan set *f* ...... Num 10:25
when the ark set *f* .... Num 10:35
children of Israel set *f* .... Num 22:1
with him, rushed *f* and .... Judg 9:44
Then shalt thou go on *f* 1Sam 10:3
David from that day and *f* 1Sam 18:9
f smiting the Moabites 2Kin 3:24
shall the shadow go *f* ten 2Kin 20:9
to set *f* the work of the 1Chr 23:4
to set it *f* and other of the 2Chr 34:12
to set *f* the work of the .... Ezra 3:8
I go *f* but he is not there ..... Job 23:8
went backward and not *f* ...... Jer 7:24
went every one straight *f* ...... Ezek 1:9
went every one straight *f* ...... Ezek 10:22
and so *f*, the priests shall ..... Ezek 43:27
helped *f* the affliction .... Zech 1:15
And he went *f* a little and .... Mark 14:35
the Jews putting him *f* .... Acts 19:33
but also to be *f* a year ago 2Cor 8:10
being more *f* of his own 2Cor 8:17
which I also was *f* to do ...... Gal 2:10
bring *f* on their journey 3John 6

FORWARDNESS—*haste; overboldness*
Peter's faltering .... Matt 14:28, 29
Paul's desire for the Corinthians 2Cor 8:8, 10

I know the *f* of your mind 2Cor 9:2

FOUL—*offensive*

[*also* FOULED, FOULEDST]
My face is *f* with weeping ..... Job 16:16
ye must *f* the residue with ..... Ezek 34:18
It will be *f* weather today ..... Matt 16:3
he rebuked the *f* spirit .... Mark 9:25
hold of every *f* spirit .... Rev 18:2

FOUND—*See* FIND

FOUNDATION—*the base or support*

Used literally of:
Cities .... Josh 6:26
Walls .... Ezra 4:12
Houses .... Luke 6:48
Prison house .... Acts 16:26
House of the Lord 1Kin 6:37
Towers .... Luke 14:28, 29

Used figuratively of:
Christ .... Is 28:16
Matt 16:18
Christian truth .... Eph 2:20
God decrees 2Tim 2:19
Security of parents 1Tim 6:19
Eternal city .... Heb 11:10

Importance of:
Must be on a rock .... Matt 7:24
Matt 16:18
Must be firm .... Luke 6:48
Must be Christ 1Cor 3:11
Without, hopeless .... Ps 11:3

[*also* FOUNDATIONS]
the *f* thereof even until .... Ex 9:18
the *f* of the mountains .... Deut 32:22
the *f* of heaven moved and 2Sam 22:8
stones, to lay the *f* of the 1Kin 5:17
even from the *f* unto the 1Kin 7:9
he laid the *f* thereof in 1Kin 16:34
day of the *f* of the house 2Chr 8:16
began to lay the *f* of the 2Chr 31:7
f of the temple of the Lord ... Ezra 3:6
let the *f* thereof be strongly ... Ezra 6:3
whose *f* is in the dust .... Job 4:19
thou when I laid the *f* of ...... Job 38:4
f also of the hills moved ...... Ps 18:7
all of the *f* of the earth .... Ps 82:5
His *f* is in the holy .... Ps 87:1
rase it, even to the *f* .... Ps 137:7
he appointed the *f* of the ..... Prov 8:29
righteous..everlasting *f* .... Prov 10:25
f of Kir-hareseth shall ye ...... Is 16:7
from the *f* of the earth? .... Is 40:21
to the temple, Thy *f* shall ..... Is 44:28
Mine hand..laid the *f* of .... Is 48:13
and lay the *f* of the earth ..... Is 51:16
f of many generations .... Is 58:12
f of the earth searched .... Jer 31:37
a corner, nor a stone for *f* .... Jer 51:26
and it hath devoured the *f* .... Lam 4:11
the *f*..shall be discovered ...... Ezek 13:14
and her *f* shall be broken ..... Ezek 30:4
and I will discover the *f* ...... Mic 1:6
discovering the *f* unto the ..... Hab 3:13
f of the Lord's temple was .... Hag 2:18
have laid the *f* of this .... Zech 4:9

and layeth the *f* of the ....Zech 12:1
secret from the *f* of the ....Matt 13:35
for you from the *f* of the......Matt 25:34
shed from the *f* of the ....Luke 11:50
after he hath laid the *f*........Luke 14:29
lovedst me before the *f* of.....John 17:24
build upon another man's *f*....Rom 15:20
I have laid the *f*, and 1Cor 3:10
upon this *f* gold, silver 1Cor 3:12
in him before the *f* of the .....Eph 1:4
hast laid the *f* of the earth ....Heb 1:10
finished from the *f* of the .....Heb 4:3
again the *f* of repentance......Heb 6:1
suffered since the *f* of the .....Heb 9:26
before the *f* of the world......1Pet 1:20
Lamb slain from the *f* of......Rev 13:8
of life from the *f* of the ....Rev 17:8
the wall..city had twelve *f*.....Rev 21:14
The first *f* was jasper ....Rev 21:19

FOUNDATION, GATE OF THE—*a gate of Jerusalem*
Levites stationed there ...2Chr 23:2-5
Possibly the Horse Gate. .2Kin 11:16
2Chr 23:15

FOUNDED—*established*

[*also* FOUNDEST]
f his heart faithful before.....Neh 9:8
he hath *f* it upon the seas .....Ps 24:2
which thou hast *f* for them ....Ps 104:8
Lord by wisdom hath *f*........Prov 3:19
the Lord hath *f* Zion, and.....Is 14:32
and hath *f* his troop in the ....Amos 9:6
for it was *f* upon a rock.......Matt 7:25
for it was *f* upon a rock.......Luke 6:48

FOUNDER—*a refiner of metals*
and gave them to the *f*........Judg 17:4
f melteth in vain; for the......Jer 6:29
every *f* is confounded by ......Jer 10:14

FOUNTAIN—*a flow of water from the earth*

Figurative of:
Mouth of the righteous ..Prov 10:11
Understanding ....Prov 16:22
Rich blessings ....Jer 2:13

[*also* FOUNTAINS]
were all the *f* of the great.....Gen 7:11
found her by a *f* of water .....Gen 16:7
by the *f* in the way to Shur ...Gen 16:7
Nevertheless a *f* or pit ....Lev 11:36
he hath discovered her *f*......Lev 20:18
she hath uncovered the *f*......Lev 20:18
in Elim were twelve *f* of ......Num 33:9
of *f* and depths that spring ....Deut 8:7
f of Jacob shall be upon a.....Deut 33:28
the *f* of the water of..........Josh 15:9
Israelites pitched by a *f*.......1Sam 29:1
unto all *f* of water, and 1Kin 18:5
to stop the waters of the *f* 2Chr 32:3
And at the *f* gate, which ......Neh 12:37
with thee is the *f* of life.......Ps 36:9
Lord, from the *f* of Israel .....Ps 68:26
Thou didst cleave the *f* ....Ps 74:15
thy *f* be dispersed abroad .....Prov 5:16
Let thy *f* be blessed; and......Prov 5:18
he strengtheneth the *f* of ......Prov 8:28
The law of the wise is a *f*.....Prov 13:14
The fear of the Lord is a *f*....Prov 14:27
troubled *f*, and a corrupt......Prov 25:26
pitcher be broken at the *f*.....Eccl 12:6
a spring shut up, a *f* sealed....Song 4:12
a *f* of gardens, a well of ......Song 4:15
and *f* in the midst of the ......Is 41:18
and mine eyes a *f* of tears.....Jer 9:1
and his *f* shall be dried up ....Hos 13:15
a *f* shall come forth of the ....Joel 3:18
that day there shall be a *f*.....Zech 13:1
straightway the *f* of her ....Mark 5:29
lead them unto living *f* of .....Rev 7:17
sea, and the *f* of waters.......Rev 14:7
that is athirst of the *f* of ......Rev 21:6

FOUNTAIN GATE—*a gate of Jerusalem*
Viewed by Nehemiah ....Neh 2:13, 14
Repaired ....Neh 3:15

FOUR

[*also* FOURTH]
the morning were the *f* ....Gen 1:19
parted, and became into *f*.....Gen 2:10
he begat Eber *f* hundred .....Gen 11:15
he begat Peleg *f* hundred .....Gen 11:17
afflict them *f* hundred.........Gen 15:13
the *f* generation they shall.....Gen 15:16
Heth, *f* hundred shekels of ....Gen 23:16
and with him *f* hundred ....Gen 33:1
was *f* hundred and thirty ......Ex 12:40
the third and *f* generation .....Ex 20:5
an ox, and *f* sheep for a ......Ex 22:1
thou shalt cast *f* rings of ......Ex 25:12
put them in the *f* corners .....Ex 25:12
shalt make for it *f* rings of ....Ex 25:26
and put the rings in the *f* ....Ex 25:26
are on the *f* feet thereof ......Ex 25:26
breadth of one curtain *f*.......Ex 26:2
breadth of one curtain *f*.......Ex 26:8
f pillars of shittim wood.......Ex 26:32
gold, upon the *f* sockets of....Ex 26:32
net shalt thou make *f*.........Ex 27:4
rings in the *f* corners ....Ex 27:4
and their pillars shall be *f*.....Ex 27:16
and their sockets *f*............Ex 27:16
f part of a hin of beaten ......Ex 29:40
the third and to the *f*.........Ex 34:7
breadth of one curtain *f*.......Ex 36:9
f pillars of shittim wood.......Ex 36:36
he cast for them *f* sockets .....Ex 36:36
And he cast for it *f* rings......Ex 37:3
to be set by the *f* corners .....Ex 37:3
And he cast for it *f* rings......Ex 37:13
put the rings upon the *f*.......Ex 37:13
that were in the *f* feet ....Ex 37:13
were *f* bowls made like ....Ex 37:20
he cast *f* rings for the *f* ....Ex 38:5
And their pillars were *f*.......Ex 38:19
And their sockets of brass *f* ...Ex 38:19
set in it *f* rows of stones ......Ex 39:10
creep, going upon all *f*........Lev 11:20
things, which have *f* feet ......Lev 11:23
goeth upon all *f*..............Lev 11:42
in the *f* year all the fruit ......Lev 19:24
fifty and *f* thousand and *f*.....Num 1:29
and five thousand and *f*.......Num 1:37
fifty and *f* thousand and *f* .....Num 2:6
and six thousand and *f*........Num 2:9
and five thousand and *f*........Num 2:23
Two wagons and *f* oxen he ....Num 7:7
f wagons and eight oxen ......Num 7:8
On the *f* day Elizur the ....Num 7:30
were twenty and *f* bullocks ....Num 7:88
with the *f* part of a hin ....Num 15:4
the number of the *f* part of ...Num 23:10
plague were twenty and *f* .....Num 25:9
threescore and *f* thousand .....Num 26:25
and three thousand and *f* .....Num 26:47
the *f* part of a hin for the .....Num 28:7
on the *f* day ten bullocks......Num 29:23
and *f* cubits the breadth of ....Deut 3:11
the third and *f* generation .....Deut 5:9
Ashan; *f* cities and their ......Josh 19:7
f lot came out to Issachar .....Josh 19:17
Nahalal..suburbs; *f* cities ......Josh 21:35
with her suburbs; *f* cities ......Josh 21:39
Shechem in *f* companies ......Judg 9:34
and was there *f* whole ....Judg 19:2
it came to pass on the *f*.......Judg 19:5
f hundred thousand men ....Judg 20:17
f hundred young virgins ....Judg 21:12
the field about *f* thousand.....1Sam 4:2
f part of a shekel of silver.....1Sam 9:8
David about *f* hundred........1Sam 25:13
David pursued, he and *f* 1Sam 30:10
And the *f*, Adonijah the 2Sam 3:4
six toes, *f* and twenty in 2Sam 21:20
f hundred and eightieth 1Kin 6:1
in the *f* year of Solomon's.....1Kin 6:1
f year was the foundation 1Kin 6:37
lily work in the porch, *f*.......1Kin 7:19
f cubits was the length of 1Kin 7:27
and *f* cubits the breadth.......1Kin 7:27

every base had *f* brazen.......1Kin 7:30
f corners thereof had 1Kin 7:30
f undersetters to the *f*.........1Kin 7:34
f hundred pomegranates 1Kin 7:42
thousand and *f* hundred........1Kin 10:26
the prophets of Baal *f* 1Kin 18:19
Baal's prophets are *f*..........1Kin 18:22
together, about *f* hundred 1Kin 22:6
f part of a cab of dove's 2Kin 6:25
And there were *f* leprous 2Kin 7:3
of Israel..*f* generation 2Kin 15:12
the *f* month the famine 2Kin 25:3
Nethaneel the *f*, Raddai 1Chr 2:14
Nathan, and Solomon, *f* 1Chr 3:5
the third Zedekiah, the *f*......1Chr 3:15
Puah, Jashub..Shimrom, *f*.....1Chr 7:1
In *f* quarters were the 1Chr 9:24
Mishmannah the *f* 1Chr 12:10
Levi *f* thousand and six 1Chr 12:26
f hundred threescore and......1Chr 21:5
twenty and *f* thousand 1Chr 23:4
Moreover *f* thousand were 1Chr 23:5
and *f* thousand praised the 1Chr 23:5
Izhar, Hebron..Uzziel, *f* 1Chr 23:12
third to Harim, the *f* to 1Chr 24:8
The *f* to Izri, he, his sons 1Chr 25:11
The *f* and twentieth to 1Chr 25:31
the third, and Sacar the *f* 1Chr 26:4
f at the causeway, and 1Chr 26:18
in his course were..*f* 1Chr 27:2
The *f* captain for the *f* 1Chr 27:7
a thousand and *f* hundred 2Chr 1:14
month, in the *f* year of his 2Chr 3:2
f hundred and fifty talents....2Chr 8:18
even *f* hundred thousand 2Chr 13:3
the corner gate, *f* hundred 2Chr 25:23
were five thousand and *f*......Ezra 1:11
Adin, *f* hundred fifty and *f*....Ezra 2:15
of Hodaviah, seventy and *f*....Ezra 2:40
hundred rams, *f* hundred ......Ezra 6:17
Now on the *f* day was the.....Ezra 8:33
Yet they sent unto me *f*.......Neh 6:4
Bezai, three hundred..*f* ....Neh 7:23
of Hodevah, seventy and *f* ....Neh 7:43
Now in the twenty and *f* ......Neh 9:1
their God one *f* part of the....Neh 9:3
and another *f* part they ....Neh 9:3
f hundred three score and.....Neh 11:6
two hundred fourscore..*f*......Neh 11:18
smote the *f* corners of the .....Job 1:19
f things say not, It is ....Prov 30:15
yea, *f* which I know not.......Prov 30:18
f things which are little ....Prov 30:24
from the *f* corners of the ......Is 11:12
I will appoint over them *f*.....Jer 15:3
Judah in the *f* year of.........Jer 25:1
pass in the *f* year of ....Jer 36:1
the *f* year of Jehoiakim the....Jer 45:1
smote in the *f* year of.........Jer 46:2
the *f* winds from the *f* ....Jer 49:36
And in the *f* month, in the ....Jer 52:6
persons were *f* thousand ......Jer 52:30
in the *f* month, in the fifth ....Ezek 1:1
the likeness of *f* living ....Ezek 1:5
And every one had *f* faces ....Ezek 1:6
and every one had *f* wings ....Ezek 1:6
they *f* had the face of a.......Ezek 1:10
f also had the face of an ......Ezek 1:10
living creatures, with his *f*.....Ezek 1:15
they *f* had one likeness ....Ezek 1:16
they went upon their *f*........Ezek 1:17
eyes round about them *f*......Ezek 1:18
f wheels by the cherubim .....Ezek 10:9
they *f* had one likeness ....Ezek 10:10
they went upon their *f*........Ezek 10:11
And every one had *f* faces ....Ezek 10:14
Every one had *f* faces.........Ezek 10:21
and every one *f* wings ....Ezek 10:21
Come from the *f* winds, O ....Ezek 37:9
F tables were on this side .....Ezek 40:41
and *f* tables on that side ......Ezek 40:41
of every side chamber, *f* ......Ezek 41:5
greater settle shall be *f*........Ezek 43:14
altar shall be *f* cubits ....Ezek 43:15
altar and upward shall be *f*....Ezek 43:15

fourteen broad in the *f*........Ezek 43:17
upon the *f* corners of the.....Ezek 45:19
in the *f* corners of the........Ezek 46:22
f corners were of one.........Ezek 46:22
the north side *f* thousand.....Ezek 48:16
the south side *f* thousand.....Ezek 48:16
the east side *f* thousand.......Ezek 48:16
the west side *f* thousand.......Ezek 48:16
at the east side, *f* thousand....Ezek 48:32
At the west side *f* thousand...Ezek 48:34
these *f* children, God gave....Dan 1:17
And the *f* kingdom shall be...Dan 2:40
the *f* winds of the heaven.....Dan 7:2
And *f* great beasts came......Dan 7:3
upon the back of it *f* wings....Dan 7:6
the beast had also *f* heads.....Dan 7:6
behold a *f* beast, dreadful.....Dan 7:7
The *f* beast shall be the *f*.....Dan 7:23
and for it came up *f*..........Dan 8:8
toward the *f* winds of.........Dan 8:8
f stood up for it, *f*............Dan 8:22
in the *f* and twentieth day.....Dan 10:4
of Damascus, and for *f*, I.....Amos 1:3
transgressions of Tyrus..*f*......Amos 1:9
Ammon, and for *f*, I will.....Amos 1:13
of Judah, and for *f*, I will.....Amos 2:4
In the *f* and twentieth day....Hag 1:15
from the *f* and twentieth......Hag 2:18
Upon the *f* and twentieth.....Zech 1:7
the Lord showed me *f*........Zech 1:20
there came *f* chariots out......Zech 6:1
the *f* chariot grizzled and......Zech 6:3
pass..*f* year of king Darius....Zech 7:1
in the *f* day..ninth month.....Zech 7:1
And in the *f* watch of the.....Matt 14:25
f thousand men, beside.......Matt 15:38
together his elect from..*f*......Matt 24:31
palsy, which was borne of *f*...Mark 2:3
and about the *f* watch........Mark 6:48
seven among *f* thousand......Mark 8:20
his elect from the *f* winds.....Mark 13:27
of about fourscore and *f*......Luke 2:37
not ye, There are yet *f*........John 4:35
for he hath been dead *f*........John 11:39
number of men, about *f*......Acts 5:36
great sheet knit at the *f*.......Acts 10:11
down from heaven by *f*.......Acts 11:5
and delivered him to *f*........Acts 12:4
the same man had *f*..........Acts 21:9
wilderness *f* thousand men....Acts 21:38
f hundred and thirty years.....Gal 3:17
throne were *f* and twenty.....Rev 4:4
I saw *f* and twenty elders.....Rev 4:4
f beast was like a flying.......Rev 4:7
And the *f* beasts had each....Rev 4:8
of the throne and of the *f*.....Rev 5:6
And the *f* beasts said.........Rev 5:14
f and twenty elders fell.......Rev 5:14
in the midst of the *f* beasts....Rev 6:6
when he had opened the *f*....Rev 6:7
I heard the voice of the *f*.....Rev 6:7
after these things I saw *f*......Rev 7:1
on the *f* corners of the........Rev 7:1
holding the *f* winds...........Rev 7:1
hundred and forty and *f*......Rev 7:4
And the *f* angel sounded......Rev 8:12
I heard a voice from the *f*.....Rev 9:13
And the *f* angels were........Rev 9:15
a hundred forty and *f*.........Rev 14:1
and before the *f* beasts........Rev 14:3
hundred and forty and *f*......Rev 14:3
the *f* and twenty elders.......Rev 19:4
a hundred and forty and *f*.....Rev 21:17
a chalcedony; the *f*, an........Rev 21:19

FOURFOLD—*four times*
shall restore the lamb *f*.......2Sam 12:6
accusation, I restore him *f*....Luke 19:8

FOURFOOTED—*having four feet, rather than two*
manner of *f* beasts of the.....Acts 10:12
f beasts, and creeping.........Rom 1:23

FOURSCORE—*eighty*
Abram was *f* and six years....Gen 16:16
And Moses was *f* years old....Ex 7:7
and Aaron *f* and three........Ex 7:7
hundred thousand and *f*.......Num 2:9
I am this day *f* and five.......Josh 14:10
And the land had rest *f*.......Judg 3:30
slew on that day *f* and five....1Sam 22:18
a very aged man, even *f*......2Sam 19:32
and *f* thousand hewers in.....1Kin 5:15
an ass's head was sold for *f*...2Kin 6:25
a hundred *f* and five..........2Kin 19:35
genealogies *f* and seven.......1Chr 7:5
was two hundred *f* and........1Chr 25:7
and *f* thousand to hew in.....2Chr 2:2
hundred and *f* thousand.......2Chr 11:1
him two hundred and *f*.......2Chr 17:15
with him *f* priests..Lord.......2Chr 26:17
Michael, and with him *f*......Ezra 8:8
Netophah, a hundred *f*........Neh 7:26
days..hundred and *f* days.......Esth 1:4
if by reason of strength..*f*.....Ps 90:10
queens, and *f* concubines......Song 6:8
a hundred and *f* and five......Is 37:36
and from Samaria, even *f*.....Jer 41:5
widow of about *f* and four....Luke 2:37

FOURSQUARE—*square*
Altar...................Ex 27:1
Breastplate.............Ex 39:8, 9
City of God............Rev 21:16

F it shall be being doubled....Ex 28:16
it was *f*; and two cubits.......Ex 37:25
with their borders, *f*, not......1Kin 7:31
a hundred cubits broad, *f*.....Ezek 40:47
offer the holy oblation *f*......Ezek 48:20

FOURTEEN

[*also* FOURTEENTH]
f year came Chedorlaomer....Gen 14:5
I served thee *f* years for......Gen 31:41
shall keep it up until the *f*....Ex 12:6
In the *f* day of the first.......Lev 23:5
f thousand..six hundred.......Num 1:27
In the *f* day of this month.....Num 9:3
f day of the second month....Num 9:11
were *f* thousand and seven....Num 16:49
to each lamb..*f* lambs.........Num 29:15
and *f* lambs of the............Num 29:23
the passover on the *f* day.....Josh 5:10
f cities with their villages......Josh 15:36
and seven days, even *f*........1Kin 8:65
f year of king Hezekiah.......2Kin 18:13
Huppah..*f* to Jeshebeab.......1Chr 24:13
And God gave to Heman *f*....1Chr 25:5
mighty, and married *f*.........2Chr 13:21
the passover on the *f* day.....2Chr 30:15
the passover upon the *f*.......Ezra 6:19
on the *f* day also of the.......Esth 9:15
and on the *f* thereof..........Esth 9:18
they should keep the *f* day....Esth 9:21
he had *f* thousand sheep......Job 42:12
f year of king Hezekiah.......Is 36:1
f year after that the city.......Ezek 40:1
settle shall be *f* cubits long....Ezek 43:17
f broad in the four squares....Ezek 43:17
Abraham to David are *f*......Matt 1:17
Babylon are *f* generations.....Matt 1:17
Christ are *f* generations.......Matt 1:17
But when the *f* night was.....Acts 27:27
a man in Christ above *f*.......2Cor 12:2
f years after I went up........Gal 2:1

FOWL—*winged, feathered creatures*
Bird...................Gen 1:20, 21
Clean, edible...........Deut 14:20
Solomon's knowledge of. .1Kin 4:33

[*also* FOWLS]
let *f* multiply in the earth.....Gen 1:22
of the earth, and to every *f*...Gen 1:30
and to the *f* of the air, and....Gen 2:20
thing, and the *f* of the air.....Gen 6:7
f also of the air by sevens.....Gen 7:3
both of *f*, and of cattle........Gen 7:21
both of *f*, and of cattle........Gen 8:17
and of every clean *f*..........Gen 8:20
that is with you, of the *f*......Gen 9:10
f came down upon the........Gen 15:11
his offering..Lord be of *f*......Lev 1:14
manner of blood..it be of *f*....Lev 7:26
All *f* that creep, going........Lev 11:20
and catcheth any beast or *f*....Lev 17:13
likeness of any winged *f*......Deut 4:17
But of all clean *f* ye may......Deut 14:20
I will give thy flesh..*f*.........1Sam 17:44
fallow deer, and fatted *f*......1Kin 4:23
the field shall the *f* of the.....1Kin 14:11
the field shall the *f* of the.....1Kin 21:24
also *f* were prepared for......Neh 5:18
and the *f* of the air, and.....Job 12:7
is a path which no *f*..........Job 28:7
us wiser than the *f* of.........Job 35:11
The *f* of the air, and the......Ps 8:8
I know all the *f* of the........Ps 50:11
and feathered *f* like as the....Ps 78:27
meat unto the *f* of the........Ps 79:2
By them shall the *f* of the.....Ps 104:12
creeping things..flying *f*.......Ps 148:10
the *f* of the mountains........Is 18:6
people shall be meat..*f*........Jer 7:33
both the *f* of the heavens.....Jer 9:10
meat for the *f* of heaven......Jer 16:4
shall be for meat unto the *f*...Jer 34:20
shall dwell all *f* of every......Ezek 17:23
to the *f* of the heaven........Ezek 29:5
all the *f* of the heaven........Ezek 31:13
the sea and the *f* of the.......Ezek 38:20
feathered *f*, and to every......Ezek 39:17
or torn, whether it be *f* or....Ezek 44:31
f of the heaven hath he.......Dan 2:38
it..*f* from his branches........Dan 4:14
back of it four wings of a *f*....Dan 7:6
with the *f* of heaven, and.....Hos 2:18
down as the *f* of heaven; I....Hos 7:12
I will consume the *f* of the....Zeph 1:3
Behold, the *f* of the air.......Matt 6:26
and the *f* of the air came.....Mark 4:4
the *f* of the air may lodge.....Mark 4:32
f of the air devoured it.......Luke 8:5
are ye better than the *f*?......Luke 12:24
and the *f* of the air lodged....Luke 13:19
creeping things, and *f*..air.....Acts 10:12
creeping things, and *f*..air.....Acts 11:6
saying to all the *f* that fly.....Rev 19:17
f were filled with..flesh.......Rev 19:21

FOWLER—*one who catches birds*
Law restricting..........Deut 22:6, 7
Figurative of false prophets..............Hos 9:8
Figurative of temptations .Ps 91:3
Ps 124:7

FOX—*a dog-like animal*
Described as:
Plentiful................Judg 15:4
Destructive.............Neh 4:3
Crafty..................Luke 13:32
Carnivorous.............Ps 63:10
Living in holes..........Matt 8:20
Loves grapes............Song 2:15
Figurative of:
False prophets..........Ezek 13:4
Enemies................Song 2:15
Deceivers..............Luke 13:32

[*also* FOXES]
desolate, the *f* walk upon.....Lam 5:18
F have holes, and birds..air...Luke 9:58

FRAGMENT—*a part of a larger whole*
Of food...............Mark 6:43

[*also* FRAGMENTS]
took up of the *f* that.........Matt 14:20
baskets full of *f* took.........Mark 8:19
taken up of *f* that remained...Luke 9:17
Gather up the *f* that.........John 6:12

FRAGRANCE—*a sweet odor*
Of perfume.............John 12:3
Figurative of restoration. .Hos 14:6

FRAIL—*weak*
that I may know how *f* I......Ps 39:4

FRAME—*to form; physical makeup*

[*also* FRAMED, FRAMETH]
could not *f* to pronounce it ....Judg 12:6
evil, and thy tongue *f*........Ps 50:19
For he knoweth our *f*; he .....Ps 103:14
or shall the thing *f* say of .....Is 29:16
I *f* evil against you, and.......Jer 18:11
by which was as the *f* of a ....Ezek 40:2
They will not *f* their doings ...Hos 5:4
In whom..building fitly *f*......Eph 2:21
the worlds were *f* by the ......Heb 11:3

FRANKINCENSE—*a fragrant gum of a tree*
Used in holy oil ....Ex 30:34-38
Used in meal offerings ...Lev 2:1, 2, 15
Excluded from certain offerings ....Lev 5:11
Used in the showbread...Lev 24:7
Product of Arabia ....Is 60:6
Presented to Jesus ....Matt 2:11
Figurative of worship ....Ps 141:2

with all the *f* thereof..........Lev 2:16
all the *f* which is upon the ....Lev 6:15
put *f* thereon; for it is an .....Num 5:15
the oil, and the *f*..spices 1Chr 9:29
the *f*, and the vessels ....Neh 13:5
perfumed with myrrh..*f* ....Song 3:6
myrrh..to the hill of *f*.........Song 4:6
with all trees of *f*; myrrh ......Song 4:14
f, and wine, and oil ....Rev 18:13

FRANKLY—*openly; honestly*
to pay, he *f* forgave them .....Luke 7:42

FRATRICIDE—*murder of a brother*
Abel, by Cain...........Gen 4:8
70, by Abimelech........Judg 9:1, 5
Amnon, by Absalom 2Sam 13:28
Adonijah, by Solomon ...1Kin 2:23-25
Six, by Jehoram 2Chr 21:4
Predicted ....Matt 10:21

FRAUD—*something designed to deceive*

Examples of:
Rebekah's, on Isaac .....Gen 27:5-36
Laban's, on Jacob ....Gen 29:21-25
Gibeonites', on Israelites .Josh 9:3-9
Jonathan's, on Saul 1Sam 20:11-17

Discovery of, by:
A miracle...............Ex 7:9-12
Events..................Matt 28:11-15
Character ....Matt 26:47-50

of cursing and deceit and *f* ....Ps 10:7
is of you kept back by *f*.......James 5:4

FRAY—*frighten*
no man shall *f* them away .....Deut 28:26
none shall *f* them away ....Jer 7:33
these are come to *f* them .....Zech 1:21

FRECKLED—*spotted*
it is a *f* spot that groweth .....Lev 13:39

FREE MORAL AGENCY OF MAN—*one's ability to choose*
Resulted in sin ....Gen 2:16, 17
Recognized by God......Gen 4:6-10
John 7:17
Appealed to ....Is 1:18-20
Jer 36:3, 7

FREEDOM—*unrestricted action; lack of restraints; not a slave*

Of the unregenerate, limited by:
Sin.....................John 8:34
Inability ....John 8:43
Satan...................John 8:41, 44
Bondage ....Rom 6:20
Deadness ....Eph 2:1

Of the regenerate:
Made free by Christ .....John 8:36
Freed from bondage .....Rom 6:18, 22
Not of license 1Pet 2:16
Not of bondage again ....Gal 5:1
Not of the flesh ....Gal 5:13

[*also* FREE, FREED, FREELY]
tree..garden thou mayest *f* ....Gen 2:16
seventh he shall go out *f* ......Ex 21:2
she go out *f* without money ...Ex 21:11
let him go *f* for his tooth's ....Ex 21:27
brought yet unto him *f*........Ex 36:3
at all redeemed, nor *f* ....Lev 19:20
to death, because..not *f*.......Lev 19:20
be thou *f* from this bitter .....Num 5:19
we did eat in Egypt *f* ....Num 11:5
thou shalt let him go *f* ....Deut 15:12
sendest him away *f* from ......Deut 15:18
he shall be *f* at home one .....Deut 24:5
there shall none of you be *f*...Josh 9:23
the people had eaten *f*........1Sam 14:30
father's house *f* in Israel 1Sam 17:25
in the chambers were *f*........1Chr 9:33
and as many as were of a *f*....2Chr 29:31
f for the house of God to .....Ezra 2:68
the servant is *f* from his.......Job 3:19
Who hath sent..wild ass *f*? ....Job 39:5
and uphold me with thy *f* .....Ps 51:12
I will *f* sacrifice unto thee .....Ps 54:6
people, and let him go *f* ......Ps 105:20
to let the oppressed go *f* ......Is 58:6
a Hebrew..Hebrewess, go *f*....Jer 34:9
whom they had let go *f*, to ....Jer 34:11
I will love them *f*: for.........Hos 14:4
f ye have received, *f* give .....Matt 10:8
or his mother, he shall be *f* ...Matt 15:6
Then are the children *f* ....Matt 17:26
be profited by me; he..*f* ......Mark 7:11
truth shall make you *f* ....John 8:32
Son therefore..make you *f* ....John 8:36
ye shall be *f* indeed...........John 8:36
let me *f* speak unto you of ....Acts 2:29
great sum obtained I this *f* ....Acts 22:28
And Paul said, But I was *f*....Acts 22:28
Being justified *f* by his ....Rom 3:24
the offence, so also is..*f*.......Rom 5:15
the *f* gift came upon all ....Rom 5:18
For he that is dead is *f* ....Rom 6:7
Being then made *f* from sin ...Rom 6:18
f from righteousness ....Rom 6:20
she is *f* from that law, so .....Rom 7:3
hath made me *f* from the .....Rom 8:2
shall he not with him also *f* ...Rom 8:32
know the things that are *f*.....1Cor 2:12
if thou mayest be made *f* 1Cor 7:21
a servant, is the Lord's *f*......1Cor 7:22
not an apostle? am I not *f*? ...1Cor 9:1
For though I be *f* from all 1Cor 9:19
whether we be bond or *f*......1Cor 12:13
to you the gospel of God *f*? ..2Cor 11:7
Greek..neither bond nor *f*.....Gal 3:28
bondmaid, the other by a *f*....Gal 4:22
But Jerusalem..above is *f* .....Gal 4:26
heir with the son of the *f* .....Gal 4:30
bondwoman, but of the *f*......Gal 4:31
wherewith Christ hath..*f* ......Gal 5:1
whether he be bond or *f* ......Eph 6:8
Barbarian, Scythian..*f*.........Col 3:11
of the Lord may have *f* 2Thess 3:1
As *f*, and not using your 1Pet 2:16
every bondman, and every *f*...Rev 6:15
rich and poor, *f* and bond .....Rev 13:16
all men, both *f* and bond .....Rev 19:18
fountain..water of life *f* ....Rev 21:6
him take the water of life *f*....Rev 22:17

FREEMAN—*a man that has been set free from slavery*
a servant, is the Lord's *f*.......1Cor 7:22

FREEWILL OFFERING—*an offering given by one's free choice*
Obligatory ....Deut 12:6
Must be perfect ....Lev 22:17-25
Eaten in tabernacle by the priests ....Lev 7:16, 17
First fruits ....Prov 3:9
According to one's ability.Deut 16:17
Willing mind 2Cor 8:10-12
Cheerful heart 2Cor 9:6, 7

[*also* FREEWILL OFFERINGS]
all your *f o*, which ....Lev 23:38
a vow, or in a *f o* ....Num 15:3
thy *f o*, or heave offerings.....Deut 12:17
a *f o*, according as thou ....Deut 23:23
the *f o* of God, to distribute...2Chr 31:14
the *f o* for the house of God ..Ezra 1:4
are minded of their own *f o* ...Ezra 7:13
a *f o* unto the Lord God of ...Ezra 8:28
the *f o* of my mouth ....Ps 119:108

FREEWOMAN—*a woman who is not a slave*
bondmaid, the other by a *f*....Gal 4:22
of the *f* was by promise ....Gal 4:23
heir with..the *f*...............Gal 4:30

FREQUENT—*often*
in prisons more *f*, in 2Cor 11:23

FRESH—*new; unspoiled*

[*also* FRESHER]
taste..was as the taste of *f*.....Num 11:8
My glory was *f* in me, and ....Job 29:20
His flesh shall be *f* than a .....Job 33:25
I shall be anointed with *f* .....Ps 92:10
both yield salt water and *f* ....James 3:12

FRETTING—*a peevish state of mind; spreading*
Of the saints, forbidden ..Ps 37:1, 7, 8

[*also* FRET, FRETTED, FRETTETH]
the plague is a *f* leprosy.......Lev 13:51
burn it in the fire; it is *f* ......Lev 13:55
a *f* leprosy in the house ....Lev 14:44
sore, for to make her *f* 1Sam 1:6
heart *f* against the Lord ....Prov 19:3
F not thyself because of ......Prov 24:19
hungry, they shall *f*...........Is 8:21
hast *f* me..these things ....Ezek 16:43

FRIED—*cooked in a pan*
with oil, of fine flour, *f* ....Lev 7:12
and for that which is *f* 1Chr 23:29

FRIEND—*acquaintance; one highly esteemed*

Nature of, common:
Interest.................1Sam 18:1
Love 1Sam 20:17
Sympathy ....Job 2:11
Sacrifice ....John 15:13

Value of:
Constructive criticism ....Prov 27:6
Helpful advice ....Prov 27:7
Valuable in time of need .Prov 27:10
Always faithful ....Prov 17:17

Dangers of:
May entice to sin ....Deut 13:6
Some are necessary ......Prov 14:20
Some are untrustworthy ..Ps 41:9

Examples of:
God and Abraham ......Is 41:8
David and Jonathan 1Sam 18:1
David and Hushai 2Sam 15:37
Elijah and Elisha 2Kin 2:1-14
Christ and His disciples ..John 15:13-15
Paul and Timothy 2Tim 1:2

[*also* FRIENDS]
and Ahuzzath one of his *f*.....Gen 26:26
f Hirah the Adullamite........Gen 38:12
face, as a man speaketh..*f*.....Ex 33:11
whom he had used as his *f* ....Judg 14:20
to his *f*, saying, Behold a 1Sam 30:26
his brethren, and to his *f*......2Sam 3:8
Amnon had a *f*, whose........2Sam 13:3
principal officer..king's *f* 1Kin 4:5
his kinsfolks, nor of his *f*......1Kin 16:11
seed of Abraham thy *f*........2Chr 20:7
sent and called for his *f*.......Esth 5:10
told Zeresh his wife..his *f* .....Esth 6:13
pity should be showed..*f* ......Job 6:14
My *f* scorn me: but mine......Job 16:20
pity upon me, O ye my *f* .....Job 19:21
thee, and against thy two *f*....Job 42:7
as though..been my *f* or ......Ps 35:14
My lovers and my *f* stand .....Ps 38:11
Lover and *f* hast thou put .....Ps 88:18
son..be surety for thy *f* ....Prov 6:1
art..the hand of thy *f* ....Prov 6:3

F

thyself..sure thy *f* ... Prov 6:3
but the rich hath many *f* ... Prov 14:20
whisperer separateth chief *f* ... Prov 16:28
a matter separateth very *f* ... Prov 17:9
in the presence of his *f* ... Prov 17:18
A man that hath *f* must ... Prov 18:24
Wealth maketh many *f* ... Prov 19:4
man is a *f* to him that ... Prov 19:6
sweetness of a man's *f* by ... Prov 27:9
blesseth his *f* with a loud ... Prov 27:14
eat, O *f*; drink, yea, drink ... Song 5:1
my *f*, O daughters of ... Song 5:16
neighbor and his *f* shall ... Jer 6:21
terror to thyself..thy *f* ... Jer 20:4
say, Thy *f* have set thee ... Jer 38:22
f have dealt treacherously ... Lam 1:2
yet, love a woman beloved..*f* ... Hos 3:1
Trust ye not in a *f*, put ye ... Mic 7:5
wounded..house of my *f* ... Zech 13:6
f of publicans and sinners ... Matt 11:19
F, I do thee no wrong ... Matt 20:13
F, how camest thou in ... Matt 22:12
when his *f* heard of it, they ... Mark 3:21
Go home to thy *f*, and tell ... Mark 5:19
centurion sent *f* to him ... Luke 7:6
f of publicans and sinners! ... Luke 7:34
Which of you shall have a *f* ... Luke 11:5
unto him, *F*, lend me three ... Luke 11:5
him, because he is his *f* ... Luke 11:8
And I say unto you my *f* ... Luke 12:4
call not thy *f*, nor thy ... Luke 14:12
he calleth together his *f* ... Luke 15:6
her *f* and her neighbors ... Luke 15:9
yourselves *f* of the mammon ... Luke 16:9
brethren, and kinsfolks..*f* ... Luke 21:16
day Pilate and Herod..*f* ... Luke 23:12
the *f* of the bridegroom ... John 3:29
thou art not Caesar's *f* ... John 19:12
his kinsmen and near *f* ... Acts 10:24
made Blastus..their *f* ... Acts 12:20
to go unto his *f* to refresh ... Acts 27:3
he was called the *F* of God ... James 2:23
Our *f* salute thee ... 3John 14
Greet the *f* by name ... 3John 14

FRIENDLESS—*not having a friend*
David's plight ... Ps 142:4
Prodigal son ... Luke 15:16

FRIENDSHIP—*the condition of being friends*

Kinds of:
True ... 1Sam 18:1-3
Close ... Prov 18:24
Ardent ... 2Cor 2:12, 13
Treacherous ... Matt 26:48-50
Dangerous ... Deut 13:6-9
Unfaithful ... Job 19:14-19
False ... 2Sam 16:16-23
Worldly ... James 4:4

Tests of:
Continued loyalty ... 2Sam 1:23
Willingness to sacrifice ... John 15:13
Obedient spirit ... John 15:14, 15
Likemindedness ... Phil 2:19-23

[*also* FRIENDLY]
to speak *f* unto her, and to ... Judg 19:3
f unto thine handmaid ... Ruth 2:13
friends must show himself *f* ... Prov 18:24
Make no *f* with an angry ... Prov 22:24
f..world is enmity with God? ... James 4:4

FRINGE—*ornamental border*

[*also* FRINGES]
the *f* of the borders a ... Num 15:38
may make them *f* in the ... Num 15:38
thee *f*..four quarters ... Deut 22:12

FRO—*from*
in the house to and *f* ... 2Kin 4:35
eyes of the Lord run..*f* ... 2Chr 16:9
going to and *f* in the earth ... Job 1:7
full of tossings to and *f* ... Job 7:4
They reel to and *f*, and ... Ps 107:27
a vanity tossed to and *f* ... Prov 21:6
reel..*f* like a drunkard ... Is 24:20
and removing to and *f*? ... Is 49:21
ye to and *f* through the ... Jer 5:1
Dan also and Javan going..*f* ... Ezek 27:19
many shall run to and *f* ... Dan 12:4
shall run to and *f* in the ... Joel 2:9
they shall run to and *f* to ... Amos 8:12
to walk to and *f* through ... Zech 1:10
of the Lord, which run..*f* ... Zech 4:10
might walk to and *f* through ... Zech 6:7
Get you hence, walk..*f* ... Zech 6:7
So they walked to and *f* ... Zech 6:7
tossed to and *f*, and carried ... Eph 4:14

FROG—*a small, leaping creature*
Plague on Egypt ... Ps 78:45
Of unclean spirits ... Rev 16:13

[*also* FROGS]
all thy borders with *f* ... Ex 8:2
he may take away the *f* ... Ex 8:8
the *f* shall depart from ... Ex 8:11
f died out of the houses ... Ex 8:13

FROM—*See* INTRODUCTION

FRONT—*forward part*
Joab saw..*f* of the battle ... 2Sam 10:9
that was..*f* of the house ... 2Chr 3:4

FRONTIERS—*far edges of a country*
cities which are on his *f* ... Ezek 25:9

FRONTLETS—*ornaments worn on the forehead*
Of God's Word ... Deut 6:6-9
for *f* between thine eyes ... Ex 13:16
they may be as *f* between ... Deut 11:18

FROST—*a covering of small ice crystals*
Figurative of God's power ... Job 37:10
Figurative of God's creative ability ... Job 38:29
consumed me, and the *f* by ... Gen 31:40
small as the hoar *f* on the ... Ex 16:14
sycamore trees with *f* ... Ps 78:47
the heat..the night to the *f* ... Jer 36:30

FROWARDNESS—*perverseness*
Comes from the heart ... Prov 6:14
Issues from the mouth ... Prov 2:12
Causes strife ... Prov 16:28
Abomination to God ... Prov 11:20
Hard way ... Prov 22:5
Shall be cut off ... Prov 10:31

[*also* FROWARD, FROWARDLY]
with the *f* thou wilt show ... Ps 18:26
a *f* heart shall depart from ... Ps 101:4
the man that speaketh *f* ... Prov 2:12
delight in the *f*..wicked ... Prov 2:14
and they *f* in their paths ... Prov 2:15
the *f* is abomination to the ... Prov 3:32
away from thee a *f* mouth ... Prov 4:24
walketh with a *f* mouth ... Prov 6:12
nothing *f* or perverse in ... Prov 8:8
and the *f* mouth, do I hate ... Prov 8:13
mouth..wicked speaketh *f* ... Prov 10:32
A *f* man soweth strife; and ... Prov 16:28
his eyes to devise *f* things ... Prov 16:30
a *f* heart findeth no good ... Prov 17:20
of man is *f* and strange ... Prov 21:8
he went on *f* in the way of ... Is 57:17
gentle, but also to the *f* ... 1Pet 2:18

FROZEN—*hard as a stone*
the face of the deep is *f* ... Job 38:30

FRUGALITY—*thrift*
Manifested by Jesus ... John 6:11-13
Wrong kind ... Prov 11:24, 25

FRUIT—*a reward of one's efforts; a juicy, seedbearing growth of plants*

Used literally of:
Produce of trees ... Gen 1:29
Produce of the earth ... Gen 4:3
Progeny of livestock ... Deut 28:51

Factors destructive of:
Blight ... Joel 1:12
Locusts ... Joel 1:4
Enemies ... Ezek 25:4
Drought ... Hag 1:10
God's anger ... Jer 7:20

Used figuratively of:
Repentance ... Matt 3:8
Industry ... Prov 31:16, 31
Christian graces ... Gal 5:22, 23
Holy life ... Prov 11:30
Christian converts ... John 4:36
Christ ... Ps 132:11
Sinful life ... Matt 7:16
Reward of righteousness ... Phil 1:11

[*also* FRUITS]
f tree yielding *f* after his ... Gen 1:11
the *f* of the trees of the ... Gen 3:2
took of the *f* thereof, and ... Gen 3:6
thee the *f* of the womb? ... Gen 30:2
take of the best *f* in the ... Gen 43:11
f of the trees which the ... Ex 10:15
the first of thy ripe *f*, and ... Ex 22:29
gathered in the *f* of the land ... Lev 23:39
and gather in the *f* thereof ... Lev 25:3
the *f* he shall sell unto thee ... Lev 25:15
the land shall yield her *f* ... Lev 25:19
yet of old *f* until the ninth ... Lev 25:22
until her *f* come in ye shall ... Lev 25:22
trees..land yield their *f* ... Lev 26:20
f of the tree, is the Lord's ... Lev 27:30
bring of the *f* of the land ... Num 13:20
honey; and this is the *f* ... Num 13:27
took of the *f* of the land ... Deut 1:25
f of thy womb, and the *f* of ... Deut 7:13
the land yield not her *f* ... Deut 11:17
lest the *f* of thy seed ... Deut 22:9
f..vineyard, be defiled ... Deut 22:9
the *f* of thy body, and the *f* ... Deut 28:4
f of thy body, and in the *f* ... Deut 28:11
and in the *f* of thy ground ... Deut 28:11
f of thy land, and all thy ... Deut 28:33
All thy trees and *f* of thy ... Deut 28:42
eat the *f* of thine own body ... Deut 28:53
f of thy body, and in the *f* ... Deut 30:9
thy cattle, and in the *f* of ... Deut 30:9
they did eat of the *f* of the ... Josh 5:12
sweetness and my good *f* ... Judg 9:11
bring in the *f*, that thy ... 2Sam 9:10
bread and summer *f* for ... 2Sam 16:2
all the *f* of the field since ... 2Kin 8:6
downward and bear *f* ... 2Kin 19:30
and *f* trees in abundance ... Neh 9:25
first fruits of all *f* of all ... Neh 10:35
I have eaten the *f* thereof ... Job 31:39
bringeth forth his *f* in his ... Ps 1:3
f..shall shake like Lebanon ... Ps 72:16
satisfied with the *f* of thy ... Ps 104:13
may yield *f* of increase ... Ps 107:37
f of the womb is his reward ... Ps 127:3
they eat of the *f* of their ... Prov 1:31
My *f* is better than gold ... Prov 8:19
the *f* of the wicked to sin ... Prov 10:16
of the righteous yieldeth *f* ... Prov 12:12
shall eat good by the *f* of his ... Prov 13:2
that love it shall eat the *f* ... Prov 18:21
in them of all kind of *f* ... Eccl 2:5
and his *f* was sweet to my ... Song 2:3
with pleasant *f*; camphire ... Song 4:13
to see the *f* of the valley ... Song 6:11
those that keep the *f* thereof ... Song 8:12
they shall eat the *f* of their ... Is 3:10
the *f* of the stout heart of ... Is 10:12
his *f* shall be a fiery flying ... Is 14:29
shouting for thy summer *f* ... Is 16:9
is all the *f* to take away his ... Is 27:9
vineyards, and eat the *f* ... Is 37:30
I create the *f* of the lips ... Is 57:19
eat the *f* thereof and the ... Jer 2:7
tree, fair, and of goodly *f* ... Jer 11:16
grow, yea, they bring forth *f* ... Jer 12:2
according to the *f* of his ... Jer 17:10
gardens, and eat the *f* of ... Jer 29:5
wine, and summer *f*, and ... Jer 40:10
is fallen upon thy summer *f* ... Jer 48:32
Shall the women eat their *f* ... Lam 2:20
want of the *f* of the field ... Lam 4:9
that it might bear *f*, that it ... Ezek 17:8

forth boughs and bear *f* .... Ezek 17:23
which hath devoured her *f* .... Ezek 19:14
of the field shall yield her *f* ... Ezek 34:27
shall increase and bring *f* ...... Ezek 36:11
the *f* thereof be consumed .... Ezek 47:12
it shall bring forth new *f* ...... Ezek 47:12
f thereof shall be for meat .... Ezek 47:12
f..much, and in it was meat ... Dan 4:12
f..much, and in it was meat ... Dan 4:21
they shall bear no *f*; yea ...... Hos 9:16
bringeth forth *f* unto .... Hos 10:1
to the multitude of his *f* .... Hos 10:1
From me is thy *f* found .... Hos 14:8
the tree beareth her *f*, the .... Joel 2:22
destroyed his *f* from above .... Amos 2:9
a gatherer of sycamore *f* ...... Amos 7:14
said, A basket of summer *f* ... Amos 8:2
f of my body for the sin of .... Mic 6:7
gathered the summer *f* .... Mic 7:1
therein, for the *f* of their ...... Mic 7:13
neither shall *f* be..vines .... Hab 3:17
vine shall give her *f* and ...... Zech 8:12
f thereof, even his meat .... Mal 1:12
not destroy the *f* of your ...... Mal 3:11
bringeth not forth good *f* ...... Matt 3:10
tree bringeth forth good *f* ..... Matt 7:17
tree bringeth forth evil *f* ...... Matt 7:17
tree cannot bring..evil *f* .... Matt 7:18
a corrupt tree..good *f* .... Matt 7:18
by their *f* ye shall know .... Matt 7:20
tree good, and his *f* good ..... Matt 12:33
tree corrupt..*f* corrupt .... Matt 12:33
the tree is known by his *f* ..... Matt 12:33
up, and brought forth *f* .... Matt 13:26
the time of the *f* drew .... Matt 21:34
render him the *f* in their ...... Matt 21:41
and choked it..yielded no *f* .... Mark 4:7
and bring forth *f*, some .... Mark 4:20
But when the *f* is brought ..... Mark 4:29
the husbandmen of the *f* of ... Mark 12:2
blessed is the *f* of thy womb .. Luke 1:42
f worthy of repentance .... Luke 3:8
bringeth not..corrupt *f* .... Luke 6:43
tree is known by his own *f* .... Luke 6:44
bring no *f* to perfection .... Luke 8:14
room where to bestow my *f*? .. Luke 12:17
bestow all my *f* and my .... Luke 12:18
he came and sought *f* .... Luke 13:6
And if it bear *f*, well; and ..... Luke 13:9
will not drink of the *f* .... Luke 22:18
go and bring forth *f* .... John 15:16
and that your *f* should .... John 15:16
that of the *f* of his loins..he ... Acts 2:30
I might have some *f* among ... Rom 1:13
to bring forth *f* unto death .... Rom 7:5
have sealed to them this *f* ..... Rom 15:28
and eateth not of the *f* 1Cor 9:7
the *f* of your righteousness 2Cor 9:10
f of the Spirit is in all .... Eph 5:9
this is the *f* of my labor .... Phil 1:22
but I desire *f* that may .... Phil 4:17
be first partaker of the *f* 2Tim 2:6
it yieldeth the peaceable *f* ..... Heb 12:11
f of our lips giving thanks ..... Heb 13:15
full of mercy and good *f* ...... James 3:17
And the *f* of righteousness .... James 3:18
for the precious *f* of the .... James 5:7
tree whose *f* withereth .... Jude 12
without *f*, twice dead .... Jude 12
the *f* that thy soul lusted ...... Rev 18:14
and yielded her *f* every .... Rev 22:2
See First Fruits

FRUIT TREES
Protected by law .... Lev 19:23-25

FRUIT-BEARING—*producing*
Old age .... Ps 92:14
Good hearers .... Matt 13:23
Christian converts .... Col 1:6, 10
Abiding .... John 15:2-8

FRUITFULNESS—*abundantly productive*
Literally, dependent upon:
Right soil .... Matt 13:8
Rain .... James 5:18
Sunshine .... Deut 33:14
Seasons .... Matt 21:34
Cultivation .... Luke 13:8
God's blessing .... Acts 14:17
Spiritually, dependent upon:
Death .... John 12:24
New life .... Rom 7:4
Abiding in Christ .... John 15:2-8
Yielding to God .... Rom 6:13-23
Christian effort 2Pet 1:5-11
Absence of, reprobated .. Matt 21:19

[*also* FRUITFUL]
Be *f*, and multiply, and fill .... Gen 1:22
be *f*, and multiply upon .... Gen 8:17
be ye *f*, and multiply .... Gen 9:7
will make him *f*, and will ..... Gen 17:20
bless thee and make thee *f* .... Gen 28:3
God hath caused me to be *f* ... Gen 41:52
Joseph is a *f* bough..a *f* .... Gen 49:22
children of Israel were *f* ...... Ex 1:7
unto you, and make you *f* ..... Lev 26:9
A *f* land into barrenness ...... Ps 107:34
all hills, *f* trees and all .... Ps 148:9
a vineyard in a very *f* hill ..... Is 5:1
the outmost *f* branches .... Is 17:6
Lebanon..turned into a *f* ...... Is 29:17
and the *f* field shall .... Is 29:17
wilderness be a *f* field .... Is 32:15
f field be counted for a .... Is 32:15
f place was a wilderness .... Jer 4:26
and planted it in a *f* field ..... Ezek 17:5
f among his brethren .... Hos 13:15
being *f* in every good work .... Col 1:10

FRUITLESS DISCUSSION—*self-conceited talk against God*
Characteristic of false teachers 1Tim 1:6, 7

FRUSTRATE—*to thwart*

[*also* FRUSTRATETH]
to *f* their purpose, all the ..... Ezra 4:5
f the tokens of the liars .... Is 44:25
I do not *f* the grace of God ... Gal 2:21

FRYING PAN—*a pot in which the cereal offering was prepared*
Mentioned in .... Lev 2:7
all that is dressed in the *f p* ... Lev 7:9

FUEL—*material used to produce heat by burning*
be with burning and *f* of ...... Is 9:5
it is cast into the fire for *f* .... Ezek 15:4
Thou shalt be for *f* to the ..... Ezek 21:32

FUGITIVE—*one who flees or tries to escape*

[*also* FUGITIVES]
f and a vagabond shalt .... Gen 4:12
Ye Gileadites are *f* of .... Judg 12:4
the *f* that fell away to the 2Kin 25:11
his *f* shall flee unto Zoar ...... Is 15:5
his *f* with all his bands .... Ezek 17:21

FULFILL—*to bring something to its intended end; to satisfy*
Spoken of God's:
Word .... Ps 148:8
Prophecy 1Kin 2:27
Threat 2Chr 36:20, 21
Promise .... Acts 13:32, 33
Righteousness .... Matt 3:15
Good pleasure 2Thess 1:11
Will .... Acts 13:22
Spoken of the believer's:
Love .... Rom 13:8
Righteousness .... Rom 8:4
Burden-bearing .... Gal 6:2
Mission .... Col 1:25
Ministry .... Col 4:17

[*also* FULFILLED, FULFILLING]
days..delivered were *f* .... Gen 25:24
F her week and we will .... Gen 29:27
Jacob did so and *f* her .... Gen 29:28
And forty days were *f* for ..... Gen 50:3
for so are *f* the days of .... Gen 50:3
F your works, your daily ...... Ex 5:13
Wherefore have ye not *f* ...... Ex 5:14
the number..days I will *f* ...... Ex 23:26
days of her purifying be *f* ..... Lev 12:4
until the days be *f*, in the ..... Num 6:5
when thy days be *f*, and 2Sam 7:12
hath with his hand *f* it 1Kin 8:15
heed to *f* the statutes 1Chr 22:13
who hath with his hands *f* 2Chr 6:4
of Jeremiah might be *f* .... Ezra 1:1
f the judgment of the .... Job 36:17
the months that they *f*? .... Job 39:2
and *f* all thy counsel .... Ps 20:4
the Lord *f* all thy petitions .... Ps 20:5
with your mouths and *f* .... Jer 44:25
he hath *f* his word that he .... Lam 2:17
the days of the siege are *f* ..... Ezek 5:2
same hour was the thing *f* ..... Dan 4:33
done, that it might be *f* .... Matt 1:22
Then was *f* that which was .... Matt 2:17
it might be *f* which was .... Matt 4:14
come to destroy, but to *f* ..... Matt 5:17
it might be *f* which was .... Matt 8:17
And in them is *f* the .... Matt 13:14
it might be *f* which was .... Matt 21:4
shall the scriptures be *f* .... Matt 26:54
was *f* that which was .... Matt 27:9
The time is *f*, and the .... Mark 1:15
the scriptures must be *f* .... Mark 14:49
shall be *f* in their season ...... Luke 1:20
day is this scripture *f* in .... Luke 4:21
times of the Gentiles be *f* ..... Luke 21:24
until it be *f* in the kingdom ... Luke 22:16
this my joy therefore is *f* ...... John 3:29
the scripture may be *f* .... John 13:18
the scripture might be *f* .... John 17:12
saying might be *f*, which ...... John 18:9
scripture might be *f*, which .... John 19:24
the scripture should be *f* ...... John 19:36
must needs have been *f* .... Acts 1:16
that many days were *f* .... Acts 9:23
as John *f* his course, he .... Acts 13:25
f all that was written of .... Acts 13:29
for the work which they *f* ..... Acts 14:26
if it *f* the law, judge thee ..... Rom 2:27
of the law might be *f* in us .... Rom 8:4
love is the *f* of the law .... Rom 13:10
when your obedience is *f* 2Cor 10:6
all the law is *f* in one word .... Gal 5:14
shall not *f* the lust of the ..... Gal 5:16
f the desires of the flesh ...... Eph 2:3
F ye my joy, that ye be .... Phil 2:2
you, to *f* the word of God .... Col 1:25
If ye *f* the royal law .... James 2:8
the scripture was *f* which ...... James 2:23
killed as they were..be *f* ...... Rev 6:11
to *f* his will, and to agree ..... Rev 17:17
the words of God shall be *f* ... Rev 17:17

FULL—*complete*
Of natural things:
Years .... Gen 25:8
Breasts .... Job 21:24
Children .... Ps 127:5
Wagon .... Amos 2:13
Leprosy .... Luke 5:12
Of miraculous things:
Guidance .... Judg 6:38
Supply 2Kin 4:4, 6
Protection 2Kin 6:17
Of evil emotions:
Evil .... Eccl 9:3
Fury .... Dan 3:19
Wrath .... Acts 19:28
Envy .... Rom 1:29
Cursing .... Rom 3:14
Deadly poison .... James 3:8
Adultery 2Pet 2:14
Of good things:
Power .... Mic 3:8
Grace, truth .... John 1:14
Joy .... John 15:11
Faith .... Acts 6:5, 8

Good works ....Acts 9:36
Holy Spirit..............Acts 11:24

of the Amorites is not yet *f* ...Gen 15:16
old and *f* of days; and his .....Gen 35:29
the seven rank and *f* ears .....Gen 41:7
money in *f* weight and we .....Gen 43:21
of the Egyptians shall be *f* ....Ex 8:21
morning bread to the *f*.........Ex 16:8
should make *f* restitution ....Ex 22:3
corn beaten out of *f* ears ......Lev 2:14
take a censer *f* of burning .....Lev 16:12
f of sweet incense beaten .....Lev 16:12
become *f* of wickedness ....Lev 19:29
a *f* year may he redeem it.....Lev 25:29
eat your bread to the *f*.........Lev 26:5
of them were *f* of fine flour ...Num 7:13
f of fine flour mingled with....Num 7:19
f of fine flour mingled with....Num 7:25
both of them *f* of fine flour ...Num 7:31
f of fine flour mingled with....Num 7:37
both of them *f* of fine flour ...Num 7:43
both of them *f* of fine flour ...Num 7:49
f of fine flour mingled with....Num 7:55
f of fine flour mingled with....Num 7:61
f of fine flour mingled with....Num 7:67
f of fine flour mingled with....Num 7:73
f of fine flour mingled with....Num 7:79
were twelve, *f* of incense .....Num 7:86
me his house *f* of silver ....Num 22:18
me his house *f* of silver ....Num 24:13
houses *f* of all good things ....Deut 6:11
thou hast eaten and art *f*......Deut 8:10
thou mayest eat and be *f*......Deut 11:15
f with the blessing..Lord ......Deut 33:23
of the fleece, a bowl *f* of......Judg 6:38
went out *f*, and the Lord......Ruth 1:21
They that were *f* have 1Sam 2:5
of the Philistines was a *f* 1Sam 27:7
and with one *f* line to keep ...2Sam 8:2
Absalom dwelt two *f* years 2Sam 14:28
Lord, Make this valley *f* of....2Kin 3:16
and *f* ears of corn in the 2Kin 4:42
was *f* of garments and 2Kin 7:15
of Baal was *f* from one end ...2Kin 10:21
a parcel of ground *f* 1Chr 11:13
will verily buy it for the *f* 1Chr 21:24
f of days, riches and 1Chr 29:28
and was *f* of days when he 2Chr 24:15
possessed houses *f* of all ......Neh 9:25
was Haman *f* of wrath ....Esth 3:5
come to thy grave in a *f* age ..Job 5:26
I am *f* of confusion..see ....Job 10:15
is of few days and *f* of ....Job 14:1
One dieth in his *f* strength ....Job 21:23
I am *f* of matter, the spirit ....Job 32:18
Job died, being old and *f* .....Job 42:17
His mouth is *f* of cursing ......Ps 10:7
their right hand is *f* of ....Ps 26:10
of the Lord is *f* of majesty ....Ps 29:4
earth is *f* of the goodness .....Ps 33:5
river of God, which is *f* of ....Ps 65:9
of a *f* cup are wrung out ......Ps 73:10
the earth are *f* of the ....Ps 74:20
it is *f* of mixture; and he ......Ps 75:8
he, being *f* of compassion .....Ps 78:38
For my soul is *f* of troubles ...Ps 88:3
trees of the Lord are *f* of .....Ps 104:16
the earth is *f* of thy riches.....Ps 104:24
he is gracious and *f* of ....Ps 112:4
That our garners may be *f* ....Ps 144:13
Lord is gracious and *f* of ......Ps 145:8
a house *f* of sacrifices ....Prov 17:1
and destruction are never *f*....Prov 27:20
yet the sea is not *f*; unto .....Eccl 1:7
the hands *f* with travail ....Eccl 4:6
A fool also is *f* of words ......Eccl 10:14
f of the burnt offerings of .....Is 1:11
it was *f* of judgment ....Is 1:21
land also is *f* of silver and.....Is 2:7
land is also *f* of horses ....Is 2:7
the whole earth is *f* of his .....Is 6:3
be *f* of doleful creatures ....Is 13:21
art *f* of stirs, a tumultuous ....Is 22:2
fat things *f* of marrow, of .....Is 25:6
his lips are *f* of indignation ....Is 30:27
a *f* wind from those places ....Jer 4:12
I had fed them to the *f* ....Jer 5:7
I will not make a *f* end ....Jer 5:18
As a cage is *f* of birds ....Jer 5:27
their houses *f* of deceit........Jer 5:27
f of the fury of the Lord ......Jer 6:11
aged with him that is *f* of .....Jer 6:11
two *f* years will I bring........Jer 28:3
make a *f* end of all nations....Jer 30:11
yet will I not make a *f* end....Jer 30:11
make a *f* end of all the ....Jer 46:28
that was *f* of people!..........Lam 1:1
their rings were *f* of eyes ......Ezek 1:18
land is *f* of bloody crimes .....Ezek 7:23
and the city is *f* of violence ...Ezek 7:23
and the land is *f* of blood ....Ezek 9:9
the city *f* of perverseness ......Ezek 9:9
f of eyes round about ....Ezek 10:12
longwinged, *f* of feathers ......Ezek 17:3
f of wisdom and perfect in ....Ezek 28:12
destitute of that..it was *f* .....Ezek 32:15
shall eat fat till ye be *f*........Ezek 39:19
mourning three *f* weeks ....Dan 10:2
floors shall be *f* of wheat......Joel 2:24
is all *f* of lies and robbery.....Nah 3:1
earth was *f* of his praise.......Hab 3:3
the city shall be *f* of boys .....Zech 8:5
body shall be *f* of light........Matt 6:22
when it was *f*, they drew ......Matt 13:48
was left seven baskets *f* ......Matt 15:37
f of dead men's bones ....Matt 23:27
after that the *f* corn in the ....Mark 4:28
baskets *f* of the fragments .....Mark 6:43
baskets *f* of fragments ....Mark 8:19
ran and filled a sponge *f* ......Mark 15:36
Elisabeth's *f* time came ....Luke 1:57
the whole body also is *f* of .....Luke 11:34
body also is *f* of darkness ......Luke 11:34
body therefore be *f* of light ...Luke 11:36
whole shall be *f* of light.......Luke 11:36
laid at his gate *f* of sores ......Luke 16:20
my time is not yet *f* come .....John 7:8
that your joy may be *f*.........John 16:24
f of great fishes, an hundred ..John 21:11
men are *f* of new wine ....Acts 2:13
f of the Holy Ghost and ......Acts 6:3
when he was *f* forty years .....Acts 7:23
O *f* of all subtilty and all......Acts 13:10
ye are also *f* of goodness ......Rom 15:14
and was *f* of heaviness ....Phil 2:26
I am *f*, having received of.....Phil 4:18
the *f* assurance of ....Col 2:2
of an evangelist, make *f* 2Tim 4:5
to them that are of *f*..........Heb 5:14
in *f* assurance of faith.........Heb 10:22
f of mercy and good fruits ....James 3:17
joy unspeakable and *f* of 1Pet 1:8
you, that your joy may be *f* ...1John 1:4
that we receive a *f* reward 2John 8
f of eyes before and behind ...Rev 4:6
and golden vials *f* of odors ....Rev 5:8
his kingdom was *f* of ....Rev 16:10
cup in her hand *f* of ....Rev 17:4

FULLER—*one who treats or dyes cloth*
Outside city 2Kin 18:17
Is 7:3
God is like..............Mal 3:2
Makes white ....Mark 9:3

[*also* FULLER'S, FULLERS']
the highway of the *f* field .....Is 36:2
refiner's fire and like *f* soap ...Mal 3:2

FULLNESS—*completion*
Of time:
Christ's advent ....Gal 4:4
Gentile age ....Rom 11:25
Age of grace ....Eph 1:10
Of Christ:
Eternal Christ ....Col 2:9
Incarnate Christ ....John 1:16
Glorified Christ ....Eph 1:22, 23

[*also* FULLY]
had *f* set up the tabernacle ....Num 7:1
as the *f* of the winepress ......Num 18:27
things of the earth and *f* ......Deut 33:16
It hath *f* been showed me .....Ruth 2:11
went not *f* after the Lord 1Kin 11:6
Let the sea roar, and the *f* 1Chr 16:32
In the *f* of his sufficiency......Job 20:22
in thy presence is *f* of joy .....Ps 16:11
world is mine, and the *f* ......Ps 50:12
let the sea roar, and the *f*.....Ps 96:11
of the sons of men is *f* set ....Eccl 8:11
f of bread and abundance of ..Ezek 16:49
be devoured as stubble *f* ....Nah 1:10
the day of Pentecost was *f* ....Acts 2:1
being *f* persuaded that ....Rom 4:21
how much more their *f*? ......Rom 11:12
every man be *f* persuaded .....Rom 14:5
f preached the gospel of ......Rom 15:19
in the *f* of the blessing ....Rom 15:29
is the Lord's and the *f* 1Cor 10:26
is the Lord's and the *f* 1Cor 10:28
filled with all the *f* of God ....Eph 3:19
stature of the *f* of Christ ......Eph 4:13
that in him should all *f* ......Col 1:19
thou hast *f* known my 2Tim 3:10
the preaching might be *f* 2Tim 4:17
for her grapes are *f* ripe ......Rev 14:18

FUNERAL—*burial rites*
Sad 1Kin 13:29, 30
Joyful ....Luke 7:11-17

FURBISH—*to polish*

[*also* FURBISHED]
f the spears, and put on.......Jer 46:4
is sharpened and also *f*.........Ezek 21:9
he hath given it to be *f* ....Ezek 21:11
and it is *f* to give it into ......Ezek 21:11
the slaughter it is *f* to.........Ezek 21:28

FURIOUS—*angry; noisy or excited*

[*also* FURIOUSLY]
Nimshi; for he driveth *f*........2Kin 9:20
with a *f* man thou shalt not ...Prov 22:24
in fury and in *f* rebukes ....Ezek 5:15
and they shall deal *f* with .....Ezek 23:25
was angry and very *f* ....Dan 2:12
Lord revengeth, and is *f* ......Nah 1:2

FURLONG—*a Greek measure of length (660 linear feet)*
Measure on land or sea ..Luke 24:13

[*also* FURLONGS]
five and twenty or thirty *f*.....John 6:19
a thousand..six hundred *f* .....Rev 14:20

FURNACE—*enclosed structure containing a hot fire*
Used literally of:
Smelting ovens ....Gen 19:28
Baker's oven ....Hos 7:4
Used figuratively of:
Egyptian bondage ....Deut 4:20
Spiritual refinement......Ps 12:6
Lust ....Hos 7:4
Hell ....Matt 13:42, 50
Punishment ....Ezek 22:18-22

[*also* FURNACES]
behold a smoking *f* and a .....Gen 15:17
handfuls of ashes of the *f* .....Ex 9:8
ascended as the smoke of a *f*..Ex 19:18
and the tower of the *f* ....Neh 3:11
and the *f* pot is for silver .....Prov 17:3
and his *f* in Jerusalem ....Is 31:9
from the iron *f*, saying ....Jer 11:4
of a burning fiery *f* ....Dan 3:6
as if they burned in a *f* ....Rev 1:15

FURNACE, FIERY
Deliverance from ....Dan 3:8-26

FURNISH—*to supply*

[*also* FURNISHED]
f him liberally out of thy ......Deut 15:14
Hiram the King of Tyre had *f* .1Kin 9:11
God *f* a table..wilderness?.....Ps 78:19
she hath also *f* her table ......Prov 9:2

f the drink offering unto ......Is 65:11
f thyself to go into captivity ...Jer 46:19
the wedding was *f* with ....Matt 22:10
large upper room *f* and ....Mark 14:15
you a large upper room *f* .....Luke 22:12
thoroughly *f* unto all good 2Tim 3:17

FURNITURE—*objects that make a room more useful, for example: tables, chairs, or couches*
Tabernacle ....Ex 31:7
Room 2Kin 4:8-10

the camel's *f* and sat upon ....Gen 31:34
the table and his *f* and the ....Ex 31:8
candlestick with all his *f* ......Ex 31:8
for the light and his *f*.........Ex 35:14
out of all the pleasant *f*.......Nah 2:9

FURROW—*the track of a plow; a deep wrinkle*

[*also* FURROWS]
f likewise thereof complain ....Job 31:38
with his band in the *f*? ....Job 39:10
settlest the *f* thereof; thou .....Ps 65:10
by the *f* of her plantation .....Ezek 17:7
as hemlock in the *f* of the .....Hos 10:4
are as heaps in the *f* of the....Hos 12:11

FURTHER—*going beyond; in addition to*

[*also* FURTHERMORE]
And the Lord said *f* unto .....Ex 4:6
angel of the Lord went *f*......Num 22:26
F the Lord was angry with ....Deut 4:21
speak *f* unto the people ....Deut 20:8
inquired of the Lord *f* 1Sam 10:22
David said *f*. As the Lord 1Sam 26:10
F I tell thee that the Lord 1Chr 17:10
F David the king said unto....1Chr 29:1
F he made the court of the 2Chr 4:9
is thy request *f*? and it ....Esth 9:12
F Elihu answered and said ....Job 34:1
shalt thou come but no *f*......Job 38:11
And *f*, by these, my son ......Eccl 12:12
He said *f* unto me, Son of ....Ezek 8:6
what *f* need have we of ....Matt 26:65
troublest..Master any *f*? ....Mark 5:35
need we any *f* witness? ....Luke 22:71
spread no *f* among the ....Acts 4:17
proceeded *f* to take Peter .....Acts 12:3
I be not *f* tedious unto........Acts 24:4
F when I came to Troas 2Cor 2:12
F then we beseech you 1Thess 4:1
proceed no *f* for their.........2Tim 3:9
f need was there that ....Heb 7:11
F we have had fathers of .....Heb 12:9

FURTHER—*to advance*

[*also* FURTHERANCE, FURTHERED]
they *f* the people and the .....Ezra 8:36
f not his wicked device........Ps 140:8
unto the *f* of the gospel ....Phil 1:12

FURY—*anger; wrath*
until thy brother's *f* turn ......Gen 27:44
contrary unto you also in *f*....Lev 26:28
God shall cast the *f* of his.....Job 20:23
F is not in me; who would ....Is 27:4
and his *f* upon all their ....Is 34:2
upon him the *f* of his anger ...Is 42:25
of the *f* of the oppressor ......Is 51:13
is the *f* of the oppressor? .....Is 51:13
of the Lord the cup of his *f*...Is 51:17
they are full of the *f* of the....Is 51:20
dregs of the cup of my *f*......Is 51:22
f to his adversaries ....Is 59:18
and trample them in my *f*.....Is 63:3
and my *f*, it upheld me ....Is 63:5
render his anger with *f*.........Is 66:15
my *f* come forth like fire ......Jer 4:4
full of the *f* of the Lord.......Jer 6:11
mine anger and my *f* shall.....Jer 7:20
Pour out thy *f* upon the.......Jer 10:25
in *f* and in great wrath........Jer 21:5
my *f* go out like fire, and .....Jer 21:12
the Lord is gone forth in *f*....Jer 23:19
Take the wine cup of this *f*....Jer 25:15
the Lord goeth forth with *f*....Jer 30:23
of mine anger and of my *f*....Jer 32:31
and in my *f* and in great .....Jer 32:37
in mine anger and in my *f* ....Jer 33:5
f that the Lord hath ....Jer 36:7
and my *f* hath been poured ...Jer 42:18
my *f* be poured forth upon ....Jer 42:18
f and mine anger was ....Jer 44:6
poured out his *f* like fire ......Lam 2:4
hath accomplished his *f* ....Lam 4:11
cause my *f* to rest upon ....Ezek 5:13
have accomplished my *f* in ....Ezek 5:13
in *f* and in furious rebukes ....Ezek 5:15
I accomplish my *f* upon ....Ezek 6:12
Now will I..pour out my *f*.....Ezek 7:8
will I also deal in *f* ....Ezek 8:18
in thy pouring out of thy *f* ....Ezek 9:8
with a stormy wind in my *f*....Ezek 13:13
hailstones in my *f* to ....Ezek 13:13
pour out my *f* upon it in ......Ezek 14:19
I will give thee blood in *f* .....Ezek 16:38
I make my *f* toward thee......Ezek 16:42
plucked up in *f* she was ....Ezek 19:12
I will pour out my *f* upon .....Ezek 20:8
I would pour out my *f*........Ezek 20:13
would pour out my *f* upon ....Ezek 20:21
and with *f* poured out, will ....Ezek 20:33
stretched out arm..with *f*......Ezek 20:34
I will cause my *f* to rest.......Ezek 21:17
in mine anger and in my *f* ....Ezek 22:20
poured out my *f* upon ....Ezek 22:22
That it might cause *f* to ....Ezek 24:8
caused my *f* to rest upon ......Ezek 24:13
and according to my *f* ....Ezek 25:14
I will pour my *f* upon Sin .....Ezek 30:15
in my jealousy and in my *f*....Ezek 36:6
f upon them for the blood ....Ezek 36:18
my *f* shall come up in my .....Ezek 38:18
rage and *f* commanded to .....Dan 3:13
Nebuchadnezzar full of *f*......Dan 3:19
him in the *f* of his power .....Dan 8:6
thine anger and thy *f* be ......Dan 9:16
go forth with great *f* to ....Dan 11:44
in anger and *f* upon the ....Mic 5:15
f is poured out like fire ....Nah 1:6
jealous for her with great *f*....Zech 8:2

FUTURE—*that which is beyond the present*
Only God knows ....Is 41:21-23

Revealed by:
Christ ....John 13:19
The Spirit...............John 16:13

G

GAAL (gā'ăl)—*"rejection"*
Son of Ebed; vilifies
Abimelech ....Judg 9:26-41

GAASH (gā'ăsh)—*"earthquake"*
Hill of Ephraim ....Judg 2:9
Joshua's burial near .....Josh 24:30

Hiddai of the brooks of *G*.....2Sam 23:30
Hurai of the brooks of *G* 1Chr 11:32

GABA—*"hill"*
City of Benjamin ....Josh 18:21, 24

children of Ramah and *G* .....Ezra 2:26
The men of Ramah and *G* ....Neh 7:30

GABBAI (găb'ā-ī)—*"collector"*
Postexilic Benjamite .....Neh 11:8

GABBATHA (găb'ä-thä)—*"pavement"*
Place of Pilate's court....John 19:13

GABRIEL (gā'brĭ-ĕl)—*"man of God"—an angel*
Interprets Daniel's vision .Dan 8:16-27
Reveals the prophecy of
70 weeks ....Dan 9:21-27
Announces John's birth ..Luke 1:11-22
Announces Christ's birth .Luke 1:26-38
Stands in God's presence .Luke 1:19

GAD (găd)—*"fortune"*
1. Son of Jacob by Zilpah ..Gen 30:10, 11
Father of seven sons who
founded tribal families .Gen 46:16
2. Descendants of the tribe
of Gad ....Deut 27:13
Census of ....Num 1:24, 25
Territory of ....Num 32:20-36
Captivity of 1Chr 5:26
Later references to ......Rev 7:5
3. Seer of David 1Sam 22:5
Message of, to David ...2Sam 24:10-16

Leah's handmaid, *G* and ......Gen 35:26
G a troop shall overcome .....Gen 49:19
Dan, and Naphtali, *G* and.....Ex 1:4
Of *G*, Eliasaph the son of.....Num 1:14
Then the tribe of *G* and.......Num 2:14
captain of the sons of *G*.......Num 2:14
of the children of *G* was ......Num 10:20
The children of *G* after ....Num 26:15
and the children of *G* had .....Num 32:1
said unto the children of *G*....Num 32:6
tribe of the children of *G* .....Num 34:14
And of *G* he said, Blessed ....Deut 33:20
and the children of *G* and .....Josh 4:12
children of *G* after their.......Josh 13:28
the tribe of *G* and Golan......Josh 20:8
of the tribe of *G*, Ramoth.....Josh 21:38
Reuben and children of *G*.....Josh 22:25
children of *G* and to the ......Josh 22:31
children of Reuben and *G*....Josh 22:33
Jordan to the land of *G*.......1Sam 13:7
prophet *G* said unto David ...1Sam 22:5
the river of *G* and toward 2Sam 24:5
G came that day to David 2Sam 24:18
Benjamin, Naphtali, *G* 1Chr 2:2
the children of *G* dwelt 1Chr 5:11
out of the tribe of *G* and......1Chr 6:63
And out of the tribe of *G* 1Chr 6:80
sons of *G*, captains of the 1Chr 12:14
And the Lord spake unto *G*...1Chr 21:9
So *G* came to David and said..1Chr 21:11
David said unto *G*, I am in....1Chr 21:13
Lord commanded *G* to say 1Chr 21:18
went up at the saying of *G* 1Chr 21:19
the book of *G* the Seer 1Chr 29:29
David and of *G* the king's.....2Chr 29:25
why..their king inherit *G* ......Jer 49:1
unto the west side *G* a ....Ezek 48:27
And by the border of *G*.......Ezek 48:28
one gate of *G*, one gate of ....Ezek 48:34

GADARENES (găd-ä-rēnz')—*people from the area of Gadara*
People east of the Sea of
Galilee ....Mark 5:1
Healing of
demon-possessed here. .Matt 8:28-34

arrived..country of the *G*......Luke 8:26
of the country of the *G* ....Luke 8:37
See GERGESENES

GADDEST—*go with little purpose*
Why *g* thou about so much....Jer 2:36

GADDI (găd'ī)—*"my fortune"*
Manassite spy ....Num 13:11

GADDIEL (găd'ĭ-ĕl)—*"fortune of God"*
Zebulunite spy ....Num 13:10

GADI (gā'dī)—*"fortunate"*
Father of King Menahem .2Kin 15:14

Menahem the son of *G* to 2Kin 15:17

GADITE—*an inhabitant of Gad*

[*also* GADITES]
Reubenites and to the *G* ......Deut 3:12
the *G* I gave from Gilead .....Deut 3:16
Gilead, of the *G* and ....Deut 4:43
and to the *G* and to the.......Deut 29:8
and to the *G* and to half ......Josh 1:12
the Reubenites and the *G* .....Josh 12:6
the Reubenites and the *G* .....Josh 13:8
and the *G* and the half.......Josh 22:1
land of Gilead the *G* and 2Kin 10:33

G and half the tribe of........1Chr 5:18
G and the half tribe of........1Chr 5:26
of the *G* there separated......1Chr 12:8
and the *G* and of the half.....1Chr 12:37
the *G* and the half tribe of....1Chr 26:32

GAHAM (gā'hăm)—*"blackness"*
Son of Nahor...........Gen 22:23, 24

GAHAR (gā'här)—*"prostration; concealment"*
Head of a family of
Temple servants.......Ezra 2:47

of Giddel, the children of *G*...Neh 7:49

GAIN—*resources or earnings; to acquire*

[*also* GAINED]
they took no *g* of money......Judg 5:19
or is it *g* to him, that thou....Job 22:3
he hath *g*, when God.........Job 27:8
g thereof than fine gold.......Prov 3:14
He that is greedy of *g*........Prov 15:27
despiseth the *g* of............Is 33:15
one for his *g* from his.........Is 56:11
thou hast greedily *g* of........Ezek 22:12
hand at thy dishonest *g*.......Ezek 22:13
souls to get dishonest *g*.......Ezek 22:27
certainty that ye would *g*......Dan 2:8
shall divide the land for *g*.....Dan 11:39
consecrate their *g* unto the....Mic 4:13
he shall *g* the whole world....Matt 16:26
thou hast *g* thy brother.......Matt 18:15
received two, he also *g*.......Matt 25:17
I have *g* beside them five.....Matt 25:20
g two other talents beside.....Matt 25:22
he shall *g* the whole world....Mark 8:36
he *g* the whole world and.....Luke 9:25
Man had *g* by trading.........Luke 19:15
pound hath *g* ten pounds......Luke 19:16
pound hath *g* five pounds.....Luke 19:18
her masters much *g* by........Acts 16:16
brought no small *g* unto......Acts 19:24
have *g* this harm and loss.....Acts 27:21
all, that I might *g* the more...1Cor 9:19
that I might *g* the Jews.......1Cor 9:20
that I might *g* them that.......1Cor 9:20
g them that are without.......1Cor 9:21
that I might *g* the weak.......1Cor 9:22
Did I make a *g* of you by.....2Cor 12:17
Did Titus make a *g* of you?...2Cor 12:18
Christ, and to die is *g*........Phil 1:21
But what things were *g* to.....Phil 3:7
supposing..*g* is godliness......1Tim 6:5
with contentment is great *g*....1Tim 6:6
and buy and sell, and get *g*...James 4:13

GAIN THROUGH LOSS
Elements of:
Death first..............John 12:24
Servant status...........Mark 9:35
Discount all temporal
gains.................Matt 19:29
Loss of "life"...........Mark 8:35
Examples of:
Abraham................Heb 11:8-19
Moses..................Heb 11:24-27
Ruth...................Ruth 1:16-18
Abigail.................1Sam 25:18-42
Esther..................Esth 2:1-17
Christ..................Phil 2:5-11

GAINS UNJUSTLY GOTTEN
By:
Deceit..................Josh 7:15-26
Violence................Prov 1:19
Oppression..............Prov 22:16
Divination..............Acts 16:16, 19
Unjust wages...........James 5:4

GAINSAY—*to deny; dispute; oppose*

[*also* GAINSAYING]
not be able to *g* nor resist.....Luke 21:15
came I unto you without *g*....Acts 10:29
a disobedient and *g* people....Rom 10:21
perished in the *g* of Korah....Jude 11

GAINSAYERS—*those in opposition*
exhort and to convince the *g*..Titus 1:9

GAIUS (gā'yŭs)—*"lord"*
1. Companion of Paul.....Acts 19:29
2. Convert at Derbe.......Acts 20:4
3. Paul's host at Corinth...Rom 16:23
Corinthian convert......1Cor 1:14
4. One addressed by John..3John 1-5

GALAL (gā'lăl)—*"great; rolling"*
1. Levite..................1Chr 9:15
2. Another Levite.........1Chr 9:16

Shammua, the son of *G*.......Neh 11:17

GALATIA (gă-lā'shĭ-ä)—*"land of Galli"—a province of central Asia Minor*
Paul's first visit to.......Acts 16:6
Paul's second visit to....Acts 18:23
Churches of.............1Cor 16:1
Peter writes to Christians
in...................1Pet 1:1

unto the churches of *G*........Gal 1:2
Crescens to *G*, Titus unto.....2Tim 4:10

GALATIANS (gă-lā'shĭ-ănz)—*people of Galatia*
Paul's:
Rebuke of their instability.Gal 1:6, 7
Defense of the Gospel
among them..........Gal 1:8-24
Concern for them.......Gal 4:9-31
Confidence in them......Gal 5:7-13

O foolish *G* who hath.........Gal 3:1

GALATIANS, THE EPISTLE TO—*a book of the New Testament*
True gospel............Gal 1:6-12
Freedom from the Law..Gal 2:15—4:31
Fruits of the Holy Spirit..Gal 5:22, 23

GALBANUM—*a yellowish brown aromatic resin*
Used in the holy oil.....Ex 30:34

GALEED (găl'ĕ-ĕd)—*"heap of witness"*
Memorial site...........Gen 31:48

but Jacob called it *G*.........Gen 31:47

GALILEAN (găl-ĭ-lē'ăn)—*an inhabitant of Galilee*
Speech of...............Mark 14:70
Slaughter of............Luke 13:1
Faith of................John 4:45
Pilate's cruelty toward...Luke 13:1, 2

[*also* GALILEANS]
with him, for he is a *G*.......Luke 22:59
whether the man were a *G*....Luke 23:6
all these which speak *G*?......Acts 2:7

GALILEE (găl'ĭ-lē)—*"circle"—large Roman district of Palestine and primary region of Jesus' ministry*
History of:
Moses' prophecy
concerning...........Deut 33:18-23
Conquered by Syrians....1Kin 15:18, 20
Conquered by Assyrians.2Kin 15:29
Dialect of, distinctive....Matt 26:73
Herod's jurisdiction over.Luke 3:1
Christian churches in....Acts 9:31
Christ's contacts with:
Resided in..............Matt 2:22
Chooses disciples from...Matt 4:18, 21
Fulfills prophecy
concerning...........Matt 4:14, 15
Performs many miracles
in...................Matt 4:23
People of, receive Him..Matt 4:25
Seeks refuge in..........John 4:1, 3
Women of, minister to
Him..................Matt 27:55
Seen in, after His
resurrection..........Matt 26:32

Kedesh in *G* in mount........Josh 20:7
Kedesh in *G* with her.........Josh 21:32
cities in the land of *G*.........1Kin 9:11
Kedesh in *G* with her.........1Chr 6:76
beyond Jordan, in *G* of the....Is 9:1
Jesus from *G* to Jordan.......Matt 3:13
prison, he departed into *G*....Matt 4:12
nigh unto the sea of *G*........Matt 15:29
he departed from *G*, and......Matt 19:1
also wast with Jesus of *G*.....Matt 26:69
he goeth before you into *G*....Matt 28:7
disciples went away into *G*....Matt 28:16
Jesus..Nazareth of *G*..........Mark 1:9
he walked by the sea of *G*....Mark 1:16
synagogues throughout all *G*...Mark 1:39
and chief estates of *G*.........Mark 6:21
and passed through *G*.........Mark 9:30
he was in *G*, followed.........Mark 15:41
of *G*, named Nazareth........Luke 1:26
they returned into *G*..........Luke 2:39
power of the Spirit into *G*.....Luke 4:14
in the synagogues of *G*........Luke 4:44
which is over against *G*.......Luke 8:26
beginning from *G* to this......Luke 23:5
that followed him from *G*.....Luke 23:49
you when he was yet in *G*.....Luke 24:6
Jesus would go..into *G*........John 1:43
did Jesus in Cana of *G*........John 2:11
departed..and went into *G*....John 4:43
came again into Cana of *G*....John 4:46
come out of Judea into *G*.....John 4:54
things Jesus walked in *G*......John 7:1
Shall Christ come out of *G*?...John 7:41
Art thou also of *G*? Search....John 7:52
for out of *G* ariseth no........John 7:52
Nathanael of Cana in *G*.......John 21:2
men of *G*, why stand ye.......Acts 1:11
from *G* after the baptism......Acts 10:37

GALILEE, SEA OF—*large lake in northern Palestine*
Scene of many events in
Christ's life...........Mark 7:31
Called Chinnereth.......Num 34:11
Later called Gennesaret..Luke 5:1

GALL—*bile*
Used literally of:
Liver secretion..........Job 16:13
Poisonous herb..........Matt 27:34
Used figuratively of:
State of sin.............Acts 8:23

beareth *g* and wormwood.....Deut 29:18
sword cometh out of his *g*.....Job 20:25
gave me also *g* for my meat...Ps 69:21
given us water of *g* to drink...Jer 8:14
them water of *g* to drink......Jer 9:15
them drink the water of *g*.....Jer 23:15
compassed me with *g* and.....Lam 3:5
turned judgment into *g*.......Amos 6:12

GALLANT—*brave; full of spirit*
neither shall *g* ship pass.......Is 33:21

GALLANTRY—*a chivalrous act of bravery*
Example of.............Ex 2:16-21

GALLERY—*corridor; porch*

[*also* GALLERIES]
the king is held in the *g*.......Song 7:5
g thereof on the one side.....Ezek 41:15
g against *g* in..stories.........Ezek 42:3
for the *g* were higher than....Ezek 42:5

GALLEY—*a large ship*
wherein shall go no *g* with....Is 33:21

GALLIM (gă'ĭm)—*"heaps"*
Village north of
Jerusalem.............Is 10:29, 30
Home of Phalti..........1Sam 25:44

GALLIO (găl'ĭ-ō)—*"who lives on milk"*
Roman proconsul of
Achaia; dismisses
charges against Paul...Acts 18:12-17

G said unto the Jews, If it....Acts 18:14
And *G* cared for none of......Acts 18:17

GALLOWS—*a structure used for hanging people*
Haman had made ....Esth 5:14
Haman hanged on ....Esth 7:9, 10
Haman's sons hanged on .Esth 9:13, 25

to hang Mordecai on the *g* ....Esth 6:4
have hanged upon the *g* ......Esth 8:7

GAMALIEL (gä-mā'lĭ-ĕl)—*"reward or recompense of God"*
1. Leader of Manasseh .....Num 2:20
2. Famous Jewish teacher ..Acts 22:3
Respected by people ....Acts 5:34-39

G the son of Pedahzur ....Num 7:54
this was the offering of *G* .....Num 7:59
children of Manasseh was *G* ...Num 10:23

GAME—*the flesh of wild animals*
Isaac's favorite dish ......Gen 27:1-33

GAMES—*various kinds of contests*
Figurative examples of, (as of a race):
Requiring discipline 1Cor 9:25-27
Requiring obedience to rules 2Tim 2:5
Testing the course ....Gal 2:2
Press on to the goal .....Phil 3:13, 14

GAMMADIM (găm'ä-dĭm)—*"warriors"*
Manned Tyre's towers ...Ezek 27:11

GAMUL (gā'mŭl)—*"weaned"*
Descendant of Aaron 1Chr 24:17

GAP—*a pass*

[*also* GAPS]
have not gone up into the *g* ...Ezek 13:5
and stand in the *g* before .....Ezek 22:30

GAPED—*to gaze stupidly*
g upon me with their mouth ...Job 16:10
g upon me with their mouths ..Ps 22:13

GARDEN—*a protected and cultivated place*
Notable examples of:
In Eden ....Gen 2:15
In Egypt ....Deut 11:10
In Shushan ....Esth 1:5
In Gethsemane ....Mark 14:32
A royal 2Kin 25:4

Used for:
Festivities ....Esth 1:5
Idolatry ....Is 65:3
Meditations ....Matt 26:36
Burial ....John 19:41

Figurative of:
Desolation ....Amos 4:9
Fruitfulness ....Is 51:3
Prosperity ....Is 58:11
Righteousness ....Is 61:11

[*also* GARDENS]
the Lord God planted a *g* .....Gen 2:8
out of Eden to water the *g* ....Gen 2:10
g thou mayest freely eat ......Gen 2:16
fruit of the trees of the *g* .....Gen 3:2
Lord God walking in the *g* ....Gen 3:8
I heard thy voice in the *g* .....Gen 3:10
the east of the *g* of Eden .....Gen 3:24
as *g* by the river's side ....Num 24:6
may have it for a *g* of herbs ...1Kin 21:2
he fled by the way of the *g* ...2Kin 9:27
buried in the *g* of his own 2Kin 21:18
g of Uzza; and Amon his 2Kin 21:18
of Siloah by the king's *g* ......Neh 3:15
went into the palace *g* ....Esth 7:7
shooteth forth in his *g* ....Job 8:16
I made me *g* and orchards ....Eccl 2:5
A *g* inclosed is my sister ......Song 4:12
g, a well of living waters ......Song 4:15
south; blow upon my *g* ....Song 4:16
beloved come into his *g* ....Song 4:16
is gone down into his *g* ....Song 6:2
Thou that dwellest in the *g* ....Song 8:13
lodge in a *g* of cucumbers .....Is 1:8
the *g* that ye have chosen .....Is 1:29
a *g* that hath no water ....Is 1:30
the *g* behind one tree in ......Is 66:17
plant *g* and eat the fruit ....Jer 29:5
their soul..as a watered *g* .....Jer 31:12
which was by the king's *g* .....Jer 52:7
as if it were of a *g* ....Lam 2:6
been in Eden the *g* of God ....Ezek 28:13
The cedars in the *g* of God ...Ezek 31:8
any tree in the *g* of God .....Ezek 31:8
is become like the *g* of Eden ..Ezek 36:35
the land is as the *g* of Eden ..Joel 2:3
make *g* and eat the fruit of ....Amos 9:14
took and cast into his *g* ....Luke 13:19
where was a *g* into the ....John 18:1

GARDENER—*one whose work is gardening*
Adam, the first ....Gen 2:15
Christ, mistaken for .....John 20:15, 16

GAREB (gā'rĕb)—*"reviler; despiser"*
1. One of David's warriors .2Sam 23:38
2. Hill near Jerusalem .....Jer 31:39

Ira the Ithrite, *G* the 1Chr 11:40

GARLAND—*ceremonial headdress or wreath*
Brought by priests of Jupiter ....Acts 14:13
Of grace ....Prov 4:9
Granted to those who mourn ....Is 61:3
Worn by bridegrooms ....Is 61:10

GARLIC—*an onion-like plant*
Egyptian food ....Num 11:5

GARMENT—*a piece of clothing*

[*also* GARMENTS]
and Japheth took a *g* ....Gen 9:23
change your *g* ....Gen 35:2
the *g* of her widowhood ....Gen 38:19
she caught him by his *g* ....Gen 39:12
he left his *g* in her hand ......Gen 39:12
that he left his *g* with me .....Gen 39:15
left his *g* with me and ....Gen 39:18
make holy *g* for Aaron ....Ex 28:2
these are the *g* which they ....Ex 28:4
make holy *g* for Aaron ....Ex 28:4
thou shalt take the *g*, and .....Ex 29:5
his *g* and upon his sons ....Ex 29:21
upon the *g* of his sons ....Ex 29:21
be hallowed, and his *g* ....Ex 29:21
his sons, and his sons' *g* ....Ex 29:21
holy *g* for Aaron the priest ....Ex 31:10
g of his sons, to minister ......Ex 31:10
holy *g* for Aaron the priest ....Ex 35:19
g of his sons, to minister ......Ex 35:19
made the holy *g* for Aaron ....Ex 39:1
holy *g* for Aaron the priest ....Ex 39:41
his sons, *g*, to minister ....Ex 39:41
shall put on his linen *g* ....Lev 6:10
his *g*, and put on other *g* .....Lev 6:11
upon Aaron, and upon his *g* ..Lev 8:30
and upon his sons' *g* with .....Lev 8:30
Aaron and his *g*, and his ......Lev 8:30
and his sons' *g* with him ......Lev 8:30
g..the plague of leprosy ....Lev 13:47
woollen *g* or a linen *g* ....Lev 13:47
plague be spread in the *g* .....Lev 13:51
be not spread in the *g* ....Lev 13:53
if it appear still in the *g* ......Lev 13:57
in a *g* of woollen or linen .....Lev 13:59
every *g* and every skin ....Lev 15:17
shall put off the linen *g* ....Lev 16:23
clothes, even the holy *g* ....Lev 16:32
in the borders of their *g* ......Num 15:38
stripped Aaron of his *g* ....Num 20:28
a man put on a woman's *g* ....Deut 22:5
Babylonish *g* and two ....Josh 7:21
and old *g* upon them; and .....Josh 9:5
they spread a *g* and did ....Judg 8:25
and thirty changes of *g* ....Judg 14:12
gave change of *g* unto them ...Judg 14:19
his *g* even to his sword 1Sam 18:4
off their *g* in the middle 2Sam 10:4
had a *g* of divers colors 2Sam 13:18
Joab's *g* that he had put on ...2Sam 20:8
vessels of gold, and *g*, and 1Kin 10:25
clad himself with a new *g* 1Kin 11:29
and two changes of *g* 2Kin 5:22
with two changes of *g* 2Kin 5:23
all the way was full of *g* 2Kin 7:15
and took every man his *g* 2Kin 9:13
and cut off their *g* in the 1Chr 19:4
and one hundred priests' *g* ....Ezra 2:69
I rent my *g* and my mantle ....Ezra 9:3
five..and thirty priests' *g* ......Neh 7:70
and with a *g* of fine linen .....Esth 8:15
as a *g* that is moth-eaten ......Job 13:28
How thy *g* are warm ....Job 37:17
I made the cloud the *g* ....Job 38:9
discover the face of his *g*? .....Job 41:13
They part my *g* among ....Ps 22:18
I made sackcloth also my *g* ....Ps 69:11
violence covereth..as a *g* ....Ps 73:6
them shall wax old like a *g* ....Ps 102:26
with light as with a *g* ....Ps 104:2
with the deep as with a *g* .....Ps 104:6
cursing like as with his *g* ......Ps 109:18
Let it be unto him as the *g* ....Ps 109:19
down to the skirts of his *g* ....Ps 133:2
his *g* that is surety for a ....Prov 20:16
As he that taketh away a *g* ....Prov 25:20
Take his *g* that is surety ......Prov 27:13
bound the waters in a *g*? ......Prov 30:4
Let thy *g* be always white .....Eccl 9:8
the smell of thy *g* is like the ...Song 4:11
and *g* rolled in blood ....Is 9:5
they all shall wax old as a *g* ...Is 50:9
shall wax old like a *g* ....Is 51:6
shall eat them up like a *g* .....Is 51:8
webs shall not become *g* ......Is 59:6
the *g* of praise..spirit of ....Is 61:3
clothed me with the *g* of ......Is 61:10
g like him that treadeth ....Is 63:2
afraid, nor rent their *g* ....Jer 36:24
shepherd putteth on his *g* .....Jer 43:12
that men..touch their *g* ....Lam 4:14
And of thy *g* thou didst ....Ezek 16:16
covered the naked with a *g* ....Ezek 18:7
put off their embroidered *g* ...Ezek 26:16
they shall lay their *g* ....Ezek 42:14
and shall put on other *g* ......Ezek 42:14
they shall put off their *g* ......Ezek 44:19
they shall put on other *g* ......Ezek 44:19
the people with their *g* ....Ezek 44:19
their other *g* and were cast ....Dan 3:21
whose *g* was white as snow ....Dan 7:9
your heart, and not your *g* ....Joel 2:13
off the robe with the *g* ....Mic 2:8
flesh in the skirt of his *g* ......Hag 2:12
was clothed with filthy *g* ......Zech 3:3
and clothed him with *g* ....Zech 3:5
wear a rough *g* to deceive .....Zech 13:4
covereth violence with his *g* ...Mal 2:16
new cloth unto an old *g* ....Matt 9:16
touched the hem of his *g* ......Matt 9:20
only touch the hem of his *g* ...Matt 14:36
spread their *g* in the way ......Matt 21:8
not having a wedding *g*? ......Matt 22:12
and parted his *g*, casting ......Matt 27:35
They parted my *g* among .....Matt 27:35
of new cloth on an old *g* ......Mark 2:21
but the border of his *g* ....Mark 6:56
and cast their *g* on him ....Mark 11:7
again for to take up his *g* .....Mark 13:16
they parted his *g*, casting ......Mark 15:24
a piece of a new *g* upon an ...Luke 5:36
they cast their *g* upon the .....Luke 19:35
let him sell his *g*, and buy .....Luke 22:36
showing the coats and *g* ....Acts 9:39
Cast thy *g* about thee ....Acts 12:8
shall wax old as doth a *g* ......Heb 1:11
and your *g* are moth-eaten ....James 5:2
hating even the *g* spotted .....Jude 23
clothed with a *g* down to ......Rev 1:13
have not defiled their *g* ....Rev 3:4

GARMITE (gär'mīt)—*"bony"*
Gentile name applied to Keilah 1Chr 4:19

GARNER—*a place for storing grain*
Full, prayed for ....Ps 144:13
Desolate, lamented ......Joel 1:17

Figurative of heaven .....Matt 3:12
Translated "barn" ....Matt 6:26

gather the wheat into his *g* ....Luke 3:17

GARNISH—*to adorn; decorate*
Literally, of buildings ....Luke 11:24, 25
Figuratively, of the heavens..............Job 26:13
Of the new Jerusalem....Rev 21:19

[*also* GARNISHED]
g the house with precious 2Chr 3:6
it empty, swept, and *g* ....Matt 12:44
and *g* the sepulchers of the....Matt 23:29

GARRISON—*a military post*
Smitten by Jonathan 1Sam 13:3, 4
Attacked by Jonathan....1Sam 14:1-15

[*also* GARRISONS]
is the *g* of the Philistines 1Sam 10:5
the *g* of the Philistines 1Sam 13:23
Then David put *g* in Syria 2Sam 8:6
And he put *g* in Edom........2Sam 8:14
all Edom put he *g*............2Sam 8:14
and the *g* of the Philistines 2Sam 23:14
the Philistines' *g* was then 1Chr 11:16
put *g* in Syria-damascus 1Chr 18:6
and set *g* in..land of Judah 2Chr 17:2
and thy strong *g* shall go ......Ezek 26:11
kept the city of..with a *g*......2Cor 11:32

GASHMU (găsh′mū)—*"rain storm; corporealness"—an enemy of the Jews who opposed them upon their return from the Exile*
Opposes Nehemiah ......Neh 6:6

GAT—*See* GET

GATAM (gā′tăm)—*"burnt valley"*
Esau's grandson; chief of Edomite clan..........Gen 36:11-16

Zephi, and *G*, Kenaz 1Chr 1:36

GATE—*an entrance*

Made of:
Wood ....Neh 2:3, 17
Iron ....Acts 12:10
Brass ....Ps 107:16
Stones ....Rev 21:12

Opening for:
Camps...................Ex 32:26, 27
Cities....................Judg 16:3
Palaces ....Neh 2:8
Sanctuary ....Ezek 44:1, 2
Tombs...................Matt 27:60
Prisons ....Acts 12:5, 10

Used for:
Business transactions.....1Kin 22:10
Legal business...........Ruth 4:1-11
Criminal cases...........Deut 25:7-9
Proclamations ....Jer 17:19, 20
Festivities ....Ps 24:7
Protection 2Sam 18:24, 33

Figurative of:
Satanic power ....Matt 16:18
Death ....Is 38:10
Righteousness ....Ps 118:19, 20
Salvation ....Matt 7:13
Heaven ....Rev 21:25

[*also* GATES]
Lot sat in the *g* of............Gen 19:1
possess the *g* of his ....Gen 22:17
all that went in at the *g*.......Gen 23:10
let thy seed possess the *g* .....Gen 24:60
unto the *g* of their city........Gen 34:20
out of the *g* of his city ....Gen 34:24
that went out of the *g* ....Gen 34:24
stranger..is within thy *g* ....Ex 20:10
of one side of the *g* ....Ex 27:14
of the one side of the *g*........Ex 38:14
the hanging for the *g* of.......Ex 38:18
hanging for the court *g* ....Ex 39:40
hanging of the court *g* ....Ex 40:33
for the door of the *g* ....Num 4:26
with high walls, *g* and ....Deut 3:5
of thy house, and on thy *g* ....Deut 6:9
thine house and upon thy *g* ...Deut 11:20
Levite that is within your *g*....Deut 12:12
not eat within thy *g* ....Deut 12:17
thou shalt eat in thy *g* ....Deut 12:21
Levite that is within thy *g*.....Deut 14:27
within thy *g*, shall come.......Deut 14:29
shalt eat it within thy *g* ....Deut 15:22
Levite that is within thy *g*.....Deut 16:11
make thee in all thy *g* ....Deut 16:18
wicked thing, unto thy *g* ......Deut 17:5
Levite come from..thy *g* ......Deut 18:6
unto the *g* of his place ....Deut 21:19
elders of the city in the *g* .....Deut 22:15
them both out unto the *g* .....Deut 22:24
are in thy land within thy *g* ...Deut 24:14
besiege thee in all thy *g*.......Deut 28:52
shall distress thee in thy *g*.....Deut 28:57
time of shutting of the *g* ......Josh 2:5
shall he set up the *g* of it .....Josh 6:26
them from before the *g* ....Josh 7:5
at the entering of the *g* ....Josh 20:4
then was war in the *g*.........Judg 5:8
in the entering of the *g* ....Judg 9:35
in the entering of the *g* ....Judg 9:44
by the entering of the *g*.......Judg 18:16
by the side of the *g*..........1Sam 4:18
the valley, and to the *g* of 1Sam 17:52
on the doors of the *g* 1Sam 21:13
took him aside in the *g* 2Sam 3:27
unto the entering of the *g*.....2Sam 11:23
king stood by the *g* side.......2Sam 18:4
sat between the two *g* 2Sam 18:24
king arose and sat in the *g* 2Sam 19:8
the king doth sit in the *g*......2Sam 19:8
Beth-lehem..by the *g*!.........2Sam 23:15
that was by the *g* and took 2Sam 23:16
up the *g* thereof in his 1Kin 16:34
when he came to the *g* of 1Kin 17:10
shekel, in the *g* of Samaria 2Kin 7:1
to have the charge of the *g*....2Kin 7:17
trode upon him in the *g*.......2Kin 7:17
trode upon him in the *g*.......2Kin 7:20
entering in of the *g* until 2Kin 10:8
at the *g* behind the guard 2Kin 11:6
g of Ephraim unto..corner *g*...2Kin 14:13
the high places of the *g* 2Kin 23:8
g of Joshua the governor 2Kin 23:8
left hand at the *g* of the 2Kin 23:8
waited in the king's *g* 1Chr 9:18
of the *g* of the tabernacle 1Chr 9:19
oversight of the *g* of the 1Chr 9:23
was by the *g*, and took it 1Chr 11:18
of their fathers, for every *g* ...1Chr 26:13
with walls, *g*, and bars 2Chr 8:5
their courses at every *g* 2Chr 8:14
at the *g* of the foundation 2Chr 23:5
set the porters at the *g*........2Chr 23:19
came through the high *g* 2Chr 23:20
g of Ephraim to the corner *g* ..2Chr 25:23
He built the high *g* of the 2Chr 27:3
the entering in at the fish *g* ...2Chr 33:14
g..are burned with fire ....Neh 1:3
I went on to the *g* of the .....Neh 2:14
fish *g* did the sons of ....Neh 3:3
valley *g* repaired Hanun ......Neh 3:13
the wall unto the dung *g* ......Neh 3:13
g of the fountain repaired .....Neh 3:15
horse *g* repaired the ....Neh 3:28
against the *g* Miphkad ....Neh 3:31
set up the doors upon the *g* ...Neh 6:1
that was before the water *g* ...Neh 8:1
brethren that kept the *g* ......Neh 11:19
and the *g* and the wall ....Neh 12:30
when the *g* of Jerusalem ......Neh 13:19
that the *g* should be shut......Neh 13:19
my servants set I at the *g* .....Neh 13:19
sat in the king's *g* ....Esth 2:19
that were in the king's *g* ......Esth 3:2
even before the king's *g* ......Esth 4:2
enter into the king's *g* ....Esth 4:2
against the *g* of the house .....Esth 5:1
Jew sitting at the king's *g* .....Esth 5:13
came again to the king's *g* ....Esth 6:12
they are crushed in the *g*......Job 5:4
I saw my help in the *g*........Job 31:21
g of death been opened ....Job 38:17
liftest me up from the *g* of ....Ps 9:13
O ye *g*; even lift them up .....Ps 24:9
They that sit in the *g* ....Ps 69:12
Enter into his *g* with..........Ps 100:4
draw near unto the *g* ....Ps 107:18
Open to me the *g* of...........Ps 118:19
shall stand within thy *g* ....Ps 122:2
with the enemies in the *g* .....Ps 127:5
in the openings of the *g*.......Prov 1:21
watching daily at my *g* ....Prov 8:34
he that exalteth his *g* ....Prov 17:19
not his mouth in the *g* ....Prov 24:7
husband is known in the *g* ....Prov 31:23
by the *g* of Bath-rabbim ......Song 7:4
our *g* are all manner of ....Song 7:13
her *g* shall lament and ....Is 3:26
O *g*; cry, O city; thou ....Is 14:31
the *g* is smitten with ....Is 24:12
Open ye the *g*, that the ....Is 26:2
that reproveth in the *g*........Is 29:21
him the two leaved *g* ....Is 45:1
the *g* shall not be shut ....Is 45:1
break in pieces the *g* ....Is 45:2
thy *g* shall be open ....Is 60:11
walls Salvation, and thy *g* .....Is 60:18
through the *g*; prepare ye .....Is 62:10
the entering of the *g* of ....Jer 1:15
in the *g* of the Lord's house ...Jer 7:2
that enter in at these *g* to .....Jer 7:2
Judah mourneth, and the *g*....Jer 14:2
bring it in by the *g* of.........Jer 17:21
shall there enter into the *g* ....Jer 17:25
entering in at the *g* of ....Jer 17:27
I kindle a fire in the *g* ....Jer 17:27
is by the entry of the east *g* ...Jer 19:2
enter in by the *g* of this.......Jer 22:4
in the entry of the new *g* .....Jer 26:10
at the entry of the new *g* .....Jer 36:10
king then sitting in the *g* ......Jer 38:7
by the *g* betwixt the two ......Jer 39:4
have neither *g* nor bars ....Jer 49:31
g are desolate; her priests .....Lam 1:4
entered into the *g* of...........Lam 4:12
elders..ceased from the *g*......Lam 5:14
to the door of the inner *g*.....Ezek 8:3
me to the door of the *g* of ....Ezek 8:14
at the door of the east *g* ......Ezek 10:19
the east *g* of the Lord's ....Ezek 11:1
behold at the door of the *g* ...Ezek 11:1
sword against all their *g*.......Ezek 21:15
was the *g* of the people ....Ezek 26:2
having neither bars nor *g* .....Ezek 38:11
Then came he unto the *g* .....Ezek 40:6
the threshold of the *g*.........Ezek 40:6
other threshold of the *g*.......Ezek 40:6
threshold of the *g* by the ......Ezek 40:7
porch of the *g* within was .....Ezek 40:7
he the porch of the *g* ....Ezek 40:9
porch of the *g* was inward.....Ezek 40:9
little chambers of the *g* ....Ezek 40:10
of the entry of the *g*, ten .....Ezek 40:11
length of the *g*, thirteen.......Ezek 40:11
the court round about the *g* ...Ezek 40:14
of the *g* of the entrance ....Ezek 40:15
of the inner *g* were fifty.......Ezek 40:15
by the side of the *g* over ......Ezek 40:18
against the length of the *g* ....Ezek 40:18
forefront of the lower *g* ....Ezek 40:19
the measure of the first *g* .....Ezek 40:21
the *g* of the inner court ....Ezek 40:23
against the *g* toward the ......Ezek 40:23
g to *g* an hundred cubits ......Ezek 40:23
was a *g* in the inner court .....Ezek 40:27
inner court by the south *g*.....Ezek 40:28
he measured the south *g* ....Ezek 40:28
brought me to the north *g* ....Ezek 40:35
the entry of the north *g* ....Ezek 40:40
at the porch of the *g*, were ....Ezek 40:40
without the inner *g* were the ..Ezek 40:44
at the side of the north *g* .....Ezek 40:44
at the side of the east *g*.......Ezek 40:44
forth toward the *g* whose .....Ezek 42:15

house by the way of the *g* . . . . . Ezek 43:4
way of the porch of that *g* . . . . Ezek 44:3
charge at the *g* of the . . . . Ezek 44:11
in at the *g* of the inner . . . . Ezek 44:17
they minister in the *g* of . . . . . . Ezek 44:17
posts of the *g* of the inner . . . . Ezek 45:19
way of the porch of that *g* . . . . Ezek 46:2
stand by the post of the *g* . . . . . Ezek 46:2
the threshold of the *g* . . . . Ezek 46:2
but the *g* shall not be shut . . . . Ezek 46:2
way of the porch of that *g* . . . . Ezek 46:8
the way of the north *g* to . . . . . Ezek 46:9
by the way of the south *g* . . . . . Ezek 46:9
by the way of the north *g* . . . . . Ezek 46:9
return by the way of the *g* . . . . Ezek 46:9
the *g* that looketh toward . . . . . Ezek 46:12
forth one shall shut the *g* . . . . . Ezek 46:12
out of the way of the *g* . . . . Ezek 47:2
without unto the outer *g* . . . . . . Ezek 47:2
And the *g* of the city shall . . . . Ezek 48:31
three *g* northward; one *g* of . . . Ezek 48:31
one *g* of Judah, one *g* of . . . . . Ezek 48:31
three *g*; one *g* of Joseph . . . . . . Ezek 48:32
one *g* of Benjamin, one *g* . . . . . Ezek 48:32
three *g*; one *g* of Simeon . . . . . . Ezek 48:33
g of Issachar, one *g* of . . . . Ezek 48:33
their three *g*; one *g* of Gad . . . Ezek 48:34
g of Asher, one *g* of . . . . Ezek 48:34
Daniel sat in the *g* of the . . . . . . Dan 2:49
that rebuketh in the *g* . . . . Amos 5:10
judgment in the *g* . . . . Amos 5:15
entered into his *g* . . . . Obad 11
not..entered into the *g* of . . . . . Obad 13
he is come unto the *g* of . . . . . . Mic 1:9
have passed through the *g* . . . . . Mic 2:13
g of the rivers shall be . . . . Nah 2:6
truth and peace in your *g* . . . . . Zech 8:16
first *g*, unto the corner *g* . . . . . . Zech 14:10
wide is the *g*, and broad . . . . . . Matt 7:13
he came nigh to the *g* of . . . . . . Luke 7:12
to enter in at the strait *g* . . . . . . Luke 13:24
which was laid at his *g* . . . . Luke 16:20
the *g* of the temple which . . . . . Acts 3:2
they watched the *g* day and . . . Acts 9:24
and stood before the *g* . . . . Acts 10:17
at the door of the *g* . . . . Acts 12:13
she opened not the *g* for . . . . . . Acts 12:14
Peter stood before the *g* . . . . . . Acts 12:14
suffered without the *g* . . . . Heb 13:12
On the east three *g* . . . . Rev 21:13
on the north three *g* . . . . Rev 21:13
on the south three *g* . . . . Rev 21:13
and on the west three *g* . . . . Rev 21:13
the twelve *g* were twelve . . . . . . Rev 21:21
enter in through the *g* into . . . . Rev 22:14

GATEKEEPER—*one who tends or guards a gate*

Duty of:
Zechariah 1Chr 9:21
Shallum 1Chr 9:17
Akkub 1Chr 9:17
Talmon 1Chr 9:17
Ahiman 1Chr 9:17
Ben 1Chr 15:18
Jaaziel 1Chr 15:18
Shemiramoth 1Chr 15:18
Jehiel 1Chr 15:18
Unni 1Chr 15:18
Eliab 1Chr 15:18
Benaiah 1Chr 15:18
Maaseiah 1Chr 15:18
Mattithiah 1Chr 15:18
Eliphelehu 1Chr 15:18
Mikneiah 1Chr 15:18
Obed-edom 1Chr 15:18
Jeiel 1Chr 15:18
Heman 1Chr 15:17
Asaph 1Chr 15:17
Ethan 1Chr 15:17
Berechiah 1Chr 15:23
Elkanah 1Chr 15:23
Jehiah 1Chr 15:24
Jeduthun 1Chr 16:38
Hosah 1Chr 16:38

GATES OF JERUSALEM—*the entries into the holy city*

1. Corner Gate 2Chr 26:9
2. Dung Gate . . . . Neh 12:31
3. Of Ephraim . . . . Neh 8:16
4. Fish Gate . . . . Zeph 1:10
5. Fountain Gate . . . . Neh 12:37
6. Horse Gate . . . . Jer 31:40
7. Benjamin's Gate . . . . Zech 14:10
8. Prison gate . . . . Neh 12:39
9. Sheep Gate . . . . Neh 3:1
10. Upper Benjamin Gate . . Jer 20:2
11. Valley Gate . . . . Neh 2:13
12. Water Gate . . . . Neh 8:16

GATH (găth)—*"wine press"*

Philistine city 1Sam 6:17
Last of Anakim here . . . . Josh 11:22
Ark carried to 1Sam 5:8
Home of Goliath 1Sam 17:4
David takes refuge in 1Sam 21:10-15
David's second flight to . . 1Sam 27:3-12
Captured by David 1Chr 18:1
Captured by Hazael 2Kin 12:17
Rebuilt by Rehoboam . . . 2Chr 11:5, 8
Uzziah broke down walls of 2Chr 26:6
Destruction of, prophetic . Amos 6:1-3
Name becomes proverbial. Mic 1:10

from Ekron even unto *G* 1Sam 7:14
Philistine of *G*, Goliath 1Sam 17:23
Shaaraim, even unto *G* 1Sam 17:52
son of Maoch, king of *G* 1Sam 27:2
Tell it not in *G*, publish 2Sam 1:20
a battle in *G*, where was a 2Sam 21:20
of Maachah king of *G* 1Kin 2:39
saddled his ass..went to *G* 1Kin 2:40
brought..servants from *G* 1Kin 2:40
Elead, whom the men of *G* . . . 1Chr 7:21
at *G*, where was a man 1Chr 20:6
Philistines took him in *G* . . . . . . Ps 56:*title*

GATHER—*to bring together; collect*

[*also* GATHERED, GATHEREST, GATHERETH, GATHERING, GATHERINGS]

g together unto one place . . . . . Gen 1:9
g together of the waters . . . . Gen 1:10
and thou shalt *g* it to the . . . . . Gen 6:21
and was *g* to his people . . . . Gen 25:8
were all the flocks *g* . . . . Gen 29:3
until all the flocks be *g* . . . . Gen 29:8
g themselves together . . . . Gen 34:30
was *g* unto his people . . . . Gen 35:29
Joseph *g* corn as the sand . . . . . Gen 41:49
G yourselves together . . . . Gen 49:1
G yourselves together . . . . Gen 49:2
shall the *g* of the people . . . . . . Gen 49:10
to be *g* unto my people . . . . Gen 49:29
he *g* up his feet into the . . . . . . Gen 49:33
and was *g* unto his people . . . . . Gen 49:33
and *g* the elders of Israel . . . . . Ex 3:16
g together all the elders . . . . Ex 4:29
g straw for themselves . . . . Ex 5:7
to *g* stubble instead . . . . Ex 5:12
waters were *g* together . . . . Ex 15:8
people shall go out and *g* . . . . . Ex 16:4
G of it every man . . . . Ex 16:16
he that *g* much had . . . . Ex 16:18
that *g* little had no lack . . . . Ex 16:18
g every man according to . . . . . Ex 16:18
the sixth day they *g* twice . . . . . Ex 16:22
Six days ye shall *g* it; but . . . . . Ex 16:26
g in the fruits thereof . . . . Ex 23:10
g themselves together unto . . . . Ex 32:1
g all the congregation . . . . Ex 35:1
g..all the congregation . . . . Lev 8:3
assembly was *g* together . . . . . . Lev 8:4
neither shall thou *g* every . . . . . Lev 19:10
prune thy vineyard, and *g* . . . . . Lev 25:3
g the grapes in it of thy . . . . Lev 25:11
when ye are *g* together . . . . Lev 26:25
shalt *g* the whole assembly . . . . Num 8:9
congregation is to be *g* . . . . Num 10:7
G unto me seventy men of . . . . Num 11:16
all the fish of the sea be *g* . . . . Num 11:22
they *g* the quails . . . . Num 11:32
that *g* least *g* ten homers . . . . . . Num 11:32
they found a man that *g* . . . . . . Num 15:32
they that found him *g* . . . . Num 15:33
are *g* together against the . . . . . Num 16:11
g all the congregation . . . . Num 16:19
he that *g* ashes of the . . . . Num 19:10
g themselves together . . . . Num 20:2
g thou the assembly . . . . Num 20:8
Aaron shall be *g* unto his . . . . . Num 20:24
but Sihon *g* all his people . . . . . Num 21:28
shalt be *g* unto thy people . . . . Num 27:13
Aaron thy brother was *g* . . . . . . Num 27:13
G me the people together . . . . . Deut 4:10
thou shalt *g* all the spoil . . . . . . Deut 13:16
after that thou hast *g* in . . . . Deut 16:13
When thou *g* the grapes of . . . . Deut 24:21
shalt *g* but little in; for . . . . Deut 28:38
and *g* thee from all the . . . . Deut 30:3
G the people together . . . . Deut 31:12
and be *g* unto thy people . . . . . Deut 32:50
and was *g* unto his people . . . . . Deut 32:50
That they *g* themselves . . . . Josh 9:2
in the mountains are *g* . . . . Josh 10:6
Joshua *g* all the tribes of . . . . . . Josh 24:1
g their meat under my . . . . Judg 1:7
And he *g* unto him the . . . . Judg 3:13
were *g* together, and went . . . . Judg 6:33
who also was *g* after . . . . Judg 6:35
of Ephraim *g* themselves . . . . . . Judg 7:24
and *g* their vineyards and . . . . . Judg 9:27
children of Ammon were *g* . . . . Judg 10:17
Sihon *g* all his people . . . . Judg 11:20
Jephthah *g* together all . . . . Judg 12:4
to Micah's house were *g* . . . . . . Judg 18:22
the men of Israel were *g* . . . . . . Judg 20:11
me glean and *g* after the . . . . . . Ruth 2:7
sent..and *g* all the lords 1Sam 5:8
G all Israel to Mizpeh 1Sam 7:5
g together to Mizpeh 1Sam 7:6
of Israel *g* themselves 1Sam 8:4
Philistines *g* themselves 1Sam 13:11
And Saul *g* the people 1Sam 15:4
g together their armies 1Sam 17:1
g together at Shochoh 1Sam 17:1
Jonathan's lad *g* up the 1Sam 20:38
all the Israelites were *g* 1Sam 25:1
Philistines *g* themselves 1Sam 28:4
g all Israel together and 1Sam 28:4
children of Benjamin *g* 2Sam 2:25
and will *g* all Israel unto 2Sam 3:21
David *g* together all the 2Sam 6:1
told David, he *g* all Israel 2Sam 10:17
which cannot be *g* up 2Sam 14:14
and they were *g* together 2Sam 20:14
that were there *g* together 2Sam 23:9
And Solomon *g* together 1Kin 10:26
widow woman was there *g* 1Kin 17:10
g to me all Israel unto 1Kin 18:19
g the prophets together 1Kin 18:20
of Israel *g* the prophets 1Kin 22:6
they *g* all that were able to 2Kin 3:21
into the field to *g* herbs 2Kin 4:39
Ben-hadad king of Syria *g* 2Kin 6:24
of the door have *g* of the 2Kin 22:4
shalt be *g* into thy grave 2Kin 22:20
all Israel *g* themselves to 1Chr 11:1
they may *g* themselves 1Chr 13:2
So David *g* all Israel 1Chr 13:5
of Ammon *g* themselves 1Chr 19:7
David commanded to *g* 1Chr 22:2
And he *g* together all the 1Chr 23:2
And Solomon *g* chariots 2Chr 1:14
that were *g* together to 2Chr 12:5
And he *g* all Judah and 2Chr 15:9
the king of Israel *g* 2Chr 18:5
were three days in *g* of the 2Chr 20:25
g the Levites out of all the 2Chr 23:2
g of all Israel money to 2Chr 24:5
g money in abundance 2Chr 24:11
g together the vessels 2Chr 28:24
And they *g* their brethren 2Chr 29:15
the people *g* themselves 2Chr 30:3
g much people together 2Chr 32:4

G

g of the hand of Manasseh 2Chr 34:9
shalt be *g* to thy grave 2Chr 34:28
the people *g* themselves . . . . . . .Ezra 3:1
And I *g* them together to . . . . .Ezra 8:15
they should *g* themselves . . . . . .Ezra 10:7
yet will I *g* them from . . . . .Neh 1:9
all my servants were *g* . . . . .Neh 5:16
on the second day were *g* . . . . .Neh 8:13
to *g* into them out of the . . . . .Neh 12:44
I *g* them together, and set . . . .Neh 13:11
may *g* together all the fair . . . .Esth 2:3
many maidens were *g* . . . . .Esth 2:8
to *g* themselves together . . . . . .Esth 8:11
The Jews *g* themselves . . . . .Esth 9:2
g themselves together . . . . .Esth 9:16
and shut up or *g* together . . . . .Job 11:10
they have *g* themselves . . . . .Job 16:10
the nettles they were *g* . . . . .Job 30:7
if he *g* unto himself . . . . .Job 34:14
G not my soul with . . . . .Ps 26:9
he *g* the waters of the sea . . . . .Ps 33:7
and *g* themselves together . . . . .Ps 35:15
not who shall *g* them . . . . .Ps 39:6
princes of the people are *g* . . . .Ps 47:9
G my saints together unto . . . . .Ps 50:5
g themselves together . . . . .Ps 56:6
g themselves together . . . . .Ps 94:21
When the people are *g* . . . . .Ps 102:22
thou givest them they *g* . . . . . . .Ps 104:28
And *g* them out of the . . . . .Ps 107:3
are they *g* together for . . . . .Ps 140:2
g together the outcasts of . . . . .Ps 147:2
g her food in the harvest . . . . . .Prov 6:8
He that *g* in summer is a . . . . .Prov 10:5
he that *g* by labor shall . . . . . . .Prov 13:11
of the mountains are *g* . . . . .Prov 27:25
g it for him that will pity . . . . . .Prov 28:8
I *g* me also silver and gold . . . .Eccl 2:8
g and to heap up, that he . . . . .Eccl 2:26
I have *g* my myrrh with . . . . . . .Song 5:1
in the gardens, and to *g* . . . . . . .Song 6:2
it, and *g* out the stones . . . . . . .Is 5:2
one *g* eggs that are left . . . . . . .Is 10:14
inhabitants of Gebim *g* . . . . .Is 10:31
kingdoms of nations *g* . . . . .Is 13:4
when the harvestman *g* . . . . . . .Is 17:5
that *g* ears in the valley . . . . . . .Is 17:5
they shall be *g* together . . . . . . .Is 24:22
ye shall be *g* one by one . . . . . .Is 27:12
shall fail, the *g* shall not . . . . . .Is 32:10
and *g* under her shadow . . . . . . .Is 34:15
shall the vultures also be *g* . . . .Is 34:15
and *g* thee from the west . . . . .Is 43:5
Let all the nations be *g* . . . . . . .Is 43:9
Though Israel be not *g* . . . . .Is 49:5
with great mercies will I *g* . . . . .Is 54:7
shall surely *g* together . . . . .Is 54:15
whosoever shall *g* together . . . .Is 54:15
which *g* the outcasts of . . . . .Is 56:8
Yet will I *g* others to him . . . . .Is 56:8
beside those that are *g* . . . . .Is 56:8
all they *g* themselves . . . . .Is 60:4
flocks of Kedar shall be *g* . . . . .Is 60:7
I will *g* all nations and . . . . .Is 66:18
all the nations shall be *g* . . . . . .Jer 3:17
trumpet in the land; cry, *g* . . . . .Jer 4:5
children *g* wood, and the . . . . . .Jer 7:18
G up thy wares out of the . . . . .Jer 10:17
I will *g* the remnant of my . . . .Jer 23:3
not be lamented, neither *g* . . . .Jer 25:33
I will *g* you from all the . . . . . .Jer 29:14
scattered Israel will *g* him . . . . .Jer 31:10
g ye wine, and summer . . . . . . .Jer 40:10
and *g* wine and summer . . . . . . .Jer 40:12
G ye together and come . . . . . .Jer 49:14
the arrows, *g* the shields . . . . . .Jer 51:11
I will even *g* you from . . . . .Ezek 11:17
therefore I will *g* all thy . . . . . . .Ezek 16:37
will even *g* them round . . . . . . .Ezek 16:37
and *g* you out of the . . . . .Ezek 20:41
they *g* silver, and brass . . . . . . .Ezek 22:20
so will I *g* you in mine . . . . .Ezek 22:20
G the pieces thereof into . . . . . .Ezek 24:4
I shall have *g* the house of . . . .Ezek 28:25
and *g* them from the . . . . .Ezek 34:13

and will *g* them on every . . . . . .Ezek 37:21
is *g* out of many people . . . . . . .Ezek 38:8
g thy company to take a . . . . . .Ezek 38:13
have *g* them unto their . . . . .Ezek 39:28
to *g* together the princes . . . . . .Dan 3:2
g together unto the . . . . .Dan 3:3
children of Israel be *g* . . . . .Hos 1:11
now will I *g* them and . . . . .Hos 8:10
g the elders and all the . . . . . . .Joel 1:14
G the people sanctify the . . . . . .Joel 2:16
assemble the elders, *g* the . . . . .Joel 2:16
g yourselves together . . . . .Joel 3:11
she *g* it of the hire of an . . . . . .Mic 1:7
surely *g* the remnant of . . . . . . .Mic 2:12
for he shall *g* them as the . . . . .Mic 4:12
they have *g* the summer . . . . . .Mic 7:1
the faces of them all *g* . . . . .Nah 2:10
mountains and no man *g* . . . . . .Nah 3:18
shall *g* the captivity as . . . . .Hab 1:9
g unto him all nations . . . . .Hab 2:5
G yourselves together . . . . .Zeph 2:1
g together, O nation not . . . . . .Zeph 2:1
I will *g* them that are . . . . .Zeph 3:18
in the time that I *g* you . . . . . . .Zeph 3:20
and *g* them; for I have . . . . .Zech 10:8
people of the earth be *g* . . . . . .Zech 12:3
g all nations against . . . . .Zech 14:2
he had *g* all the chief . . . . .Matt 2:4
and *g* his wheat into the . . . . . .Matt 3:12
do they reap, nor *g* into . . . . . .Matt 6:26
Do men *g* grapes of thorns . . . .Matt 7:16
he that *g* not with me . . . . .Matt 12:30
Nay, lest while ye *g* up . . . . . . .Matt 13:29
G ye together first the . . . . .Matt 13:30
but *g* the wheat into my . . . . . . .Matt 13:30
therefore the tares are *g* . . . . . .Matt 13:40
into the sea, and *g* of every . . .Matt 13:47
g the good into vessels . . . . .Matt 13:48
three are *g* together in my . . . .Matt 18:20
and *g* together all as many . . . .Matt 22:10
the Pharisees were *g* . . . . .Matt 22:41
often would I have *g* thy . . . . . .Matt 23:37
the eagles be *g* together . . . . . . .Matt 24:28
they shall *g* together his . . . . . . .Matt 24:31
g where thou hast not . . . . .Matt 25:24
and *g* where I have not . . . . . . .Matt 25:26
before him shall be *g* all . . . . . .Matt 25:32
were *g* together, Pilate . . . . .Matt 27:17
city was *g* together at the . . . . .Mark 1:33
was *g* unto him a great . . . . . . .Mark 4:1
the apostles *g* themselves . . . . . .Mark 6:30
and shall *g* together his . . . . . . .Mark 13:27
will *g* the wheat into his . . . . . .Luke 3:17
thorns men do not *g* figs . . . . . .Luke 6:44
of a bramble bush *g* they . . . . .Luke 6:44
much people were *g* . . . . .Luke 8:4
he that *g* not with me . . . . .Luke 11:23
people were *g* thick . . . . .Luke 11:29
there were *g* together an . . . . . .Luke 12:1
how often would I have *g* . . . . .Luke 13:34
as a hen doth *g* her brood . . . .Luke 13:34
the younger son *g* all . . . . .Luke 15:13
will the eagles be *g* . . . . .Luke 17:37
and found the eleven *g* . . . . .Luke 24:33
and *g* fruit unto life . . . . .John 4:36
G up the fragments that . . . . . . .John 6:12
they *g* them together . . . . .John 6:13
also he should *g* together . . . . .John 11:52
and men *g* them, and cast . . . . .John 15:6
g together at Jerusalem . . . . . . .Acts 4:6
rulers were *g* together . . . . .Acts 4:26
people of Israel, were *g* . . . . . . .Acts 4:27
were *g* together praying . . . . . . .Acts 12:12
g the church together . . . . .Acts 14:27
assuredly *g* that the Lord . . . . . .Acts 16:10
g a company and set all . . . . . .Acts 17:5
And when Paul had *g* . . . . .Acts 28:3
when ye are *g* together 1Cor 5:4
that there be no *g* when I 1Cor 16:2
He that had *g* much had 2Cor 8:15
he might *g* together in . . . . .Eph 1:10
our *g* together unto him 2Thess 2:1
g the clusters of the vine . . . . . .Rev 14:18
g the vine of the earth . . . . .Rev 14:19
he *g* them together into a . . . . .Rev 16:16

Come and *g* yourselves . . . . . . .Rev 19:17
their armies, *g* together to . . . .Rev 19:19

GATHERER—*tree dresser*
and a *g* of sycamore fruit . . . . .Amos 7:14

GATH-HEPHER (găth-hē′fer)—*"wine press of digging"*
Birthplace of Jonah 2Kin 14:25
Boundary of Zebulun . . . .Josh 19:13

GATH-RIMMON (găth-rĭm′ŭn)—*"pomegranate press"*
1. City of Dan . . . . .Josh 19:40-45
Assigned to Levites . . . . .Josh 21:24
2. Town in Manasseh . . . . . .Josh 21:25

and *G* with her suburbs 1Chr 6:69

GAVE, GAVEST—See GIVE

GAY—*brilliant in color*
g clothing and say unto . . . . . . .James 2:3

GAZA (gā′zä)—*"strong"*
1. Philistine city . . . . .Josh 13:3
Conquered by Joshua . . .Josh 10:41
Refuge of Anakim . . . . . .Josh 11:22
Assigned to Judah . . . . . .Josh 15:47
Gates of, removed by Samson . . . . .Judg 16:1-3
Samson deceived by Delilah here . . . . .Judg 16:4-20
Samson blinded here . . . .Judg 16:21
Ruled by Solomon 1Kin 4:22, 24
Sin of, condemned . . . . . .Amos 1:6, 7
Judgment pronounced upon . . . . .Jer 25:20
Philip journeys to . . . . . . .Acts 8:26
See AZZAH
2. Ephraimite town 1Chr 7:28

comest to Gerar, unto *G* . . . . . .Gen 10:19
Also Judah took *G* with . . . . . . .Judg 1:18
come unto *G*; and left no . . . . .Judg 6:4
for Ashdod one, for *G* one 1Sam 6:17
Philistines, even unto *G* 2Kin 18:8
that Pharaoh smote *G* . . . . .Jer 47:1
upon *G*; Ashkelon . . . . .Jer 47:5
For *G* shall be forsaken . . . . . . .Zeph 2:4
G also shall see it, and be . . . . .Zech 9:5
king shall perish from *G* . . . . . .Zech 9:5

GAZATHITES, GAZITES (gā′zä-thīts, gā′zīts)
Inhabitants of Gaza . . . . . .Judg 16:2

GAZE—*to stare at intently*
[*also* GAZING]
unto the Lord to *g* . . . . .Ex 19:21
why stand ye *g* up into . . . . .Acts 1:11

GAZELLE—*medium-sized antelope; translated "roe" or "roebuck"*
Used for food . . . . .Deut 12:15
Figurative of speed . . . . . .Prov 6:5

GAZER (gā′zĕr)—*"dividing"*—*Canaanite town beside the Mediterranean Sea*
until thou come to *G* 2Sam 5:25
from Gibeon even to *G* 1Chr 14:16

GAZEZ (gā′zĕz)—*"shearer"*
1. Son of Caleb 1Chr 2:46
2. Grandson of Caleb 1Chr 2:46

GAZINGSTOCK—*an object of contempt*
Ignominy of . . . . .Nah 3:6
Lot of Christians . . . . .Heb 10:33

GAZITES (gā′zīts) *See* GAZATHITES

GAZZAM (găz′ăm)—*"devourer; swaggerer"*
Head of family of Temple servants . . . . .Ezra 2:48

The children of *G*, the . . . . .Neh 7:51

GEBA (gē′bä)—*"hill"*
City of Benjamin . . . . .Josh 18:24
Assigned to Levites . . . . . .Josh 21:17
Crag rose opposite 1Sam 14:4, 5
Rebuilt by Asa 1Kin 15:22
Repossessed after the exile . . . . .Neh 11:31

Philistines that was in *G* 1Sam 13:3
Philistines from *G* until 2Sam 5:25
from *G* to Beer-sheba 2Kin 23:8
G with her suburbs 1Chr 6:60
of the inhabitants of *G* 1Chr 8:6
he built..*G* and Mizpah 2Chr 16:6
out of the fields of *G* ....Neh 12:29
their lodging at *G* ....Is 10:29
turned as a plain from *G* ......Zech 14:10

GEBAL (gē'băl)—*"mountain"*
1. Phoenician maritime town ....Ezek 27:9
Translated "stonesquarers" 1Kin 5:18
Inhabitants called Giblites ....Josh 13:5
2. Mountainous region in Edom ....Ps 83:7

GEBER (gē'ber)—*"man; strong one"*
Solomon's purveyors 1Kin 4:13, 19

GEBIM (gē'bĭm)—*"ditches"*
Place north of Jerusalem .Is 10:31

GEDALIAH (gĕd-ä-lī'ä)—*"Jehovah is great"*
1. Jeduthun's son 1Chr 25:3, 9
2. Pashur's son ....Jer 38:1
3. Grandfather of Zephaniah ....Zeph 1:1
4. Ahikam's son ....Jer 39:14
Made governor of Judea .2Kin 25:22-26
Befriends Jeremiah ......Jer 40:5, 6
Murdered by Ishmael ...Jer 41:2, 18
Postexilic priest ....Ezra 10:18

sons of Jeduthun; *G*, and 1Chr 25:3
the second to *G* who with 1Chr 25:9
G the son of Ahikam ....Jer 40:7
And *G* the son of Ahikam ....Jer 40:9
Judah, to *G*, unto Mizpah .....Jer 40:12
But *G* the son of Ahikam .....Jer 40:14
G the son of Ahikam said .....Jer 40:16
even with *G* at Mizpah ....Jer 41:3
unto them, Come to *G* ....Jer 41:6
committed to *G* the son of ....Jer 41:10
guard had left with *G* the .....Jer 43:6

GEDEON—*See* GIDEON

GEDER (gē'dĕr)—*"wall"*
Town of Judah ....Josh 12:13

GEDERAH (gĕ-dĕ'rä)—*"sheepfold"*
Town in Judah ....Josh 15:36

GEDERATHITE (gĕ-dē'rä-thīt)
Native of Gederah 1Chr 12:4

GEDERITE (gē'dĕr-īt)
Native of Geder 1Chr 27:28

GEDEROTH (gĕ-dĕ'rŏth)—*"sheepfolds"*
Town of Judah ....Josh 15:41
Captured by Philistines ...2Chr 28:18

GEDEROTHAIM (gĕd-ĕ-rō-thā'ĭm)—*"two sheepfolds"*
Town of Judah ....Josh 15:36

GEDOR (gē'dôr)—*"wall"*
1. Town of Judah ....Josh 15:58
2. Simeonite town 1Chr 4:39
3. Town of Benjamin 1Chr 12:7
4. Family in Judah 1Chr 4:4, 18

G, and Ahio, and Zacher 1Chr 8:31
G, and Ahio, and Zechariah ...1Chr 9:37

GEHAZI (gĕ-hā'zī)—*"valley of vision; diminisher"*
Elisha's servant 2Kin 5:25
Seeks reward from Naaman 2Kin 5:20-24
Afflicted with leprosy 2Kin 5:25-27
Relates Elisha's deeds to Jehoram 2Kin 8:4-6

said to *G* his servant, Call 2Kin 4:12
to *G* his servant, Behold 2Kin 4:25
G, Gird up thy loins, and 2Kin 4:29
And he called *G*, and said 2Kin 4:36

GEHENNA (gĕ-hĕn'ä)—*See* HELL

GELILOTH (gĕ-lī'lŏth)—*"circles"*
Probably Gilgal, in the land of Benjamin ......Josh 18:17

GEMALLI (gĕ-măl'ī)—*"camel owner"*
Father of Ammiel ....Num 13:12

GEMARIAH (gĕm-ä-rī'ä)—*"Jehovah has accomplished"*
1. Hilkiah's son ....Jer 29:3
2. Shaphan's son ....Jer 36:10-25

GEMS—*precious stones*
On breastplate ....Ex 28:15-21
Figurative of value ......Prov 3:15; Prov 31:10
In commerce ....Ezek 27:16
In New Jerusalem ....Rev 21:19-21

GENDER—*to beget*

[*also* GENDERED, GENDERETH]
shalt not let thy cattle *g* ....Lev 19:19
Their bull *g*, and faileth ....Job 21:10
heaven, who hath *g* it? ....Job 38:29
g to bondage, which is ....Gal 4:24
knowing that they do *g* 2Tim 2:23

GENEALOGY—*ancestral lineage*

Importance:
Chronology ....Matt 1:17
Priesthood claims ....Ezra 2:61, 62; Neh 7:63, 64
Messiahship ....Matt 1:1-17

Lists of:
Patriarchs' ....Gen 5:1-32
Noah's ....Gen 10:1-32
Shem's ....Gen 10:21-32
Abraham's 1Chr 1:28-34
Jacob's ....Gen 46:8-27
Esau's ....Gen 36:1-43
Israel's 1Chr 9:1-44
David's 1Chr 3:1-16
Levites' 1Chr 6:1-81

[*also* GENEALOGIES]
habitations, and their *g* 1Chr 4:33
and the *g* is not to be 1Chr 5:1
when the *g* of their 1Chr 5:7
were reckoned by *g* in 1Chr 5:17
reckoned in all by their *g* 1Chr 7:5
were reckoned by their *g* 1Chr 7:7
after their *g* by their 1Chr 7:9
throughout the *g* of them 1Chr 7:40
Iddo the seer concerning *g* 2Chr 12:15
Beside their *g* of males 2Chr 31:16
the *g* of the priests by the 2Chr 31:17
g of all their little ones 2Chr 31:18
that were reckoned by *g* 2Chr 31:19
the *g* of them that went ....Ezra 8:1
were reckoned by *g* of the ....Ezra 8:3
might be reckoned by *g* ....Neh 7:5
found a register of the *g* ......Neh 7:5
to fables and endless *g* 1Tim 1:4
foolish questions, and *g* ....Titus 3:9

GENEALOGY OF JESUS
Seed of Abraham ....Gal 3:16
Through Joseph ....Matt 1:2-17
Through Mary ....Luke 3:23-38

GENERAL—*chief military authority*
Commander ....1Chr 27:34; Rev 6:15
Also rendered "princes". .Gen 12:15

GENERAL—*pertaining to the whole*

[*also* GENERALLY]
all Israel be *g* gathered 2Sam 17:11
shall be lamentation *g* ....Jer 48:38
To the *g* assembly and ....Heb 12:23

GENERATION—*group of individuals born and living contemporaneously; a group forming a step in the line of descent from a single ancestor*

Descriptive of:
Period of time ....Gen 9:12
Living people or race ....Matt 24:34
Descendants ....Matt 12:34
Eternity ....Eph 3:21

[*also* GENERATIONS]
the book of the *g* of Adam ....Gen 5:1
These are the *g* of Noah ......Gen 6:9
just man and perfect in his *g* ..Gen 6:9
These are the *g* of the ....Gen 10:1
their *g*, in their nations ....Gen 10:32
These are the *g* of Shem ......Gen 11:10
these are the *g* of Terah ......Gen 11:27
his brethren, and all that *g* ....Ex 1:6
my memorial unto all *g* ....Ex 3:15
of Levi according to their *g* ...Ex 6:19
your *g*; ye shall keep ....Ex 12:14
observe this day in your *g* .....Ex 12:17
be kept for your *g*; that ....Ex 16:32
Amalek from *g* to *g* ....Ex 17:16
the third and fourth *g* of ......Ex 20:5
for ever unto their *g* ....Ex 27:21
the Lord throughout your *g* ...Ex 30:8
seed throughout their *g* ....Ex 30:21
you throughout your *g* ....Ex 31:13
third and to the fourth *g* ....Ex 34:7
throughout their *g* ....Ex 40:15
perpetual statute for your *g* ...Lev 3:17
ever throughout their *g* ....Lev 7:36
them throughout their *g* ....Lev 17:7
your seed among your *g* ......Lev 22:3
throughout your *g* ....Lev 23:21
statute for ever in your *g* .....Lev 23:41
statute for ever in your *g* .....Lev 24:3
eldest son, by their *g* ....Num 1:20
children of Gad, by their *g* ....Num 1:24
of Issachar, by their *g* ....Num 1:28
of Joseph, by their *g*, by ......Num 1:32
of Benjamin, by their *g* ....Num 1:36
of Asher, by their *g*, after .....Num 1:40
These also are the *g* ....Num 3:1
be among you in your *g* ....Num 15:14
heave offering in your *g* ......Num 15:21
throughout their *g* ....Num 15:38
until all the *g* that had ....Num 32:13
throughout your *g* in all ....Num 35:29
these men of this evil *g* ....Deut 1:35
all the *g* of the men of war ....Deut 2:14
the third and fourth *g* of ......Deut 5:9
to a thousand *g* ....Deut 7:9
even to his tenth *g* shall ....Deut 23:2
even to their tenth *g* shall .....Deut 23:3
the Lord in their third *g* ......Deut 23:8
So that the *g* to come of ......Deut 29:22
a perverse and crooked *g* .....Deut 32:5
they are a very froward *g* .....Deut 32:20
and our *g* after us ....Josh 22:27
that *g* were gathered unto .....Judg 2:10
arose another *g* after ....Judg 2:10
Only that the *g* of the ....Judg 3:2
children of the fourth *g* 2Kin 10:30
of Israel unto the fourth *g* 2Kin 15:12
These are their *g*: The 1Chr 1:29
genealogy of their *g* was 1Chr 5:7
men of might in their *g* 1Chr 7:2
them, by their *g*, after 1Chr 7:4
by their *g*, chief men 1Chr 8:28
chief throughout their *g* 1Chr 9:34
according to the *g* of his 1Chr 26:31
kept throughout every *g* ......Esth 9:28
sons' sons, even four *g* ....Job 42:16
preserve them from this *g* .....Ps 12:7
in the *g* of the righteous ......Ps 14:5
to the Lord for a *g* ....Ps 22:30
is the *g* of them that seek .....Ps 24:6
of his heart to all *g* ....Ps 33:11
be remembered in all *g* ....Ps 45:17
ye may tell it to the *g* ....Ps 48:13
dwelling places to all *g* ....Ps 49:11
he shall go to the *g* of his .....Ps 49:19

G

and his years as many *g*.......Ps 61:6
thy strength unto this *g*.......Ps 71:18
endure, throughout all *g*.......Ps 72:5
against the *g* of thy...........Ps 73:15
showing to the *g* to come.....Ps 78:4
That the *g* to come might.....Ps 78:6
stubborn and rebellious *g*.....Ps 78:8
g that set not their heart......Ps 78:8
show..thy praise to all *g*.......Ps 79:13
thine anger to all *g*?..........Ps 85:5
thy faithfulness to all *g*........Ps 89:1
build..thy throne to all *g*......Ps 89:4
dwelling place in all *g*.........Ps 90:1
was I grieved with this *g*......Ps 95:10
truth endureth to all *g*........Ps 100:5
written for the *g* to come.....Ps 102:18
are throughout all *g*.........Ps 102:24
to a thousand *g*.............Ps 105:8
righteousness unto all *g*.......Ps 106:31
in the *g* following let.........Ps 109:13
g of the upright shall be......Ps 112:2
O Lord, throughout all *g*......Ps 135:13
One *g* shall praise thy........Ps 145:4
endureth throughout all *g*.....Ps 145:13
thy God, O Zion, unto all *g*...Ps 146:10
crown endure to every *g*?.....Prov 27:24
is a *g* that curseth their.....Prov 30:11
a *g* that are pure in their......Prov 30:12
is a *g*, O how lofty are........Prov 30:13
is a *g*, whose teeth are as.....Prov 30:14
g passeth away..another *g*....Eccl 1:4
be dwelt in from *g* to *g*.......Is 13:20
from *g* to *g* it shall lie.......Is 34:10
g to *g* shall they dwell........Is 34:17
calling the *g* from the.........Is 41:4
my salvation from *g* to *g*.......Is 51:8
who shall declare his *g*?.......Is 53:8
foundations of many *g*........Is 58:12
a joy of many *g*..............Is 60:15
the desolations of many *g*.....Is 61:4
g, see ye the word of the.....Jer 2:31
and forsaken the *g* of his......Jer 7:29
it be dwelt in from *g* to *g*.....Jer 50:39
thy throne from *g* to *g*........Lam 5:19
dominion is from *g* to *g*.......Dan 4:3
kingdom is from *g* to *g*........Dan 4:34
their children another *g*.......Joel 1:3
to the years of many *g*........Joel 2:2
Jerusalem from *g* to *g*........Joel 3:20
the book of the *g* of Jesus....Matt 1:1
all the *g* from Abraham.......Matt 1:17
to David are fourteen *g*.......Matt 1:17
Babylon are fourteen *g*.......Matt 1:17
unto Christ are fourteen *g*.....Matt 1:17
O *g* of vipers, who hath.......Matt 3:7
shall I liken this *g*?...........Matt 11:16
An evil and adulterous *g*.......Matt 12:39
in judgment with this *g*.......Matt 12:41
the judgment with this *g*......Matt 12:42
also unto this wicked *g*........Matt 12:45
wicked and adulterous *g*.......Matt 16:4
O faithless and perverse *g*.....Matt 17:17
Ye serpents, ye *g* of vipers....Matt 23:33
shall come upon this *g*........Matt 23:36
This *g* shall not pass, till......Matt 24:34
why doth this *g* seek after.....Mark 8:12
sign be given unto this *g*......Mark 8:12
adulterous and sinful *g*........Mark 8:38
g, how long shall I be........Mark 9:19
that this *g* shall not pass......Mark 13:30
all *g* shall call me blessed.....Luke 1:48
that fear him from *g* to *g*.....Luke 1:50
O *g* of vipers, who hath.......Luke 3:7
I liken the men of this *g*......Luke 7:31
O faithless and perverse *g*.....Luke 9:41
to say, This is an evil *g*.......Luke 11:29
Son of man be to this *g*.......Luke 11:30
the men of this *g*, and........Luke 11:31
with this *g*, and shall.........Luke 11:32
may be required of this *g*.....Luke 11:50
shall be required of this *g*.....Luke 11:51
in their *g* wiser than the.....Luke 16:8
and be rejected of this *g*......Luke 17:25
This *g* shall not pass away.....Luke 21:32
from this untoward *g*.........Acts 2:40
who shall declare his *g*?.......Acts 8:33
he had served his own *g*......Acts 13:36
hid from ages and from *g*.....Col 1:26
I was grieved with that *g*......Heb 3:10
g, a royal priesthood..........1Pet 2:9

GENESIS, BOOK OF—*the first book of the Old Testament*

Creation................Gen 1:1—2:25
The fall................Gen 3:1-24
The flood..............Gen 6:8—7:24
Abraham...............Gen 12:1—25:18
Isaac..................Gen 25:19—26:35
Jacob..................Gen 27:1—36:43
Joseph.................Gen 37:1—50:26

GENIUS—*unusual mental ability; above the norm*

Applicable to Solomon...1Kin 4:29-34

GENNESARET (gě-nĕs'ä-rět)—*"garden of the prince"—another name for the Sea of Galilee*

came into the land of *G*.......Matt 14:34
into the land of *G*, and.......Mark 6:53
he stood by the lake of *G*.....Luke 5:1

GENTILES—*non-Jews*

Described as:

Superstitious............Deut 18:14
Ignorant of God.........Rom 1:21
Without the Law........Rom 2:14
Wicked.................Rom 1:23-32
Idolatrous..............1Cor 12:2
Uncircumcised..........Eph 2:11
Without Christ..........Eph 2:12
Dead in sins............Eph 2:1

Blessings promised to:

Included in God's covenant............{Gen 12:3; Gal 3:8}
Given to Christ.........Ps 2:8
Conversion predicted....Is 11:10; Rom 15:9-16
Christ their light........Is 49:6
Included in "all flesh"...Joel 2:28-32
Called "other sheep"....John 10:16

Conversion of:

Predicted...............Is 60:1-14
Proclaimed.............Matt 4:12-17
Anticipated............John 10:16
Questioned............Acts 10:9-29
Realized...............Acts 10:34-48
Explained..............Acts 11:1-18
Hindered..............Acts 13:45-51
Debated...............Acts 15:1-22
Confirmed.............Acts 15:23-31
Vindicated.............Acts 28:25-29

Present position:

Barrier removed.........Eph 2:11-12
Brought near............Eph 2:13
Fellow citizens..........Eph 2:19
Fellow heirs............Eph 3:6
In body................Eph 3:6

[*also* GENTILE]

were the isles of the *G*........Gen 10:5
in Harosheth of the *G*........Judg 4:2
unto Harosheth of the *G*......Judg 4:16
bring..judgment to the *G*......Is 42:1
for a light of the *G*..........Is 42:6
lift up mine hand to the *G*.....Is 49:22
seed shall inherit the *G*.......Is 54:3
the forces of the *G* shall......Is 60:5
also suck the milk of the *G*....Is 60:16
eat the riches of the *G*........Is 61:6
be known among the *G*.......Is 61:9
G shall see thy..............Is 62:2
G like a flowing stream........Is 66:12
my glory among the *G*........Is 66:19
destroyer of the *G* is on.......Jer 4:7
the *G* shall come unto........Jer 16:19
princes are among the *G*......Lam 2:9
defiled bread among the *G*....Ezek 4:13
shall they be among the *G*....Hos 8:8
Proclaim..this among the *G*....Joel 3:9
shall be among the *G*.........Mic 5:8
cast out the horns of the *G*....Zech 1:21
be great among the *G*.........Mal 1:11
Jordan, Galilee of the *G*......Matt 4:15
all these things do the *G*......Matt 6:32
not into the way of the *G*.....Matt 10:5
against them and the *G*.......Matt 10:18
show judgment to the *G*.......Matt 12:18
in his name shall the *G*.......Matt 12:21
princes of the *G* exercise......Matt 20:25
shall deliver him to the *G*.....Mark 10:33
to rule over the *G*...........Mark 10:42
A light to lighten the *G*.......Luke 2:32
be delivered unto the *G*.......Luke 18:32
be trodden down of the *G*.....Luke 21:24
the times of the *G* be........Luke 21:24
kings of the *G* exercise........Luke 22:25
dispersed among the *G*........John 7:35
and teach the *G*?.............John 7:35
the *G*, and the people of......Acts 4:27
the possession of the *G*.......Acts 7:45
my name before the *G*........Acts 9:15
the *G* besought that these.....Acts 13:42
lo, we turn to the *G*..........Acts 13:46
Jews stirred up the *G*.........Acts 14:2
door of faith unto the *G*......Acts 14:27
the conversion of the *G*.......Acts 15:3
I will go unto the *G*..........Acts 18:6
wrought among the *G*.........Acts 21:19
As touching the *G* which......Acts 21:25
thee far hence unto the *G*.....Acts 22:21
people, and from the *G*.......Acts 26:17
the people, and to the *G*......Acts 26:23
Jew first, and also to the *G*...Rom 2:9
Jew first, and also to the *G*...Rom 2:10
blasphemed among the *G*.....Rom 2:24
proved both Jews and *G*......Rom 3:9
of the *G*? Yes, of the *G*.......Rom 3:29
Jews only, but also of the *G*...Rom 9:24
the *G*, which followed not.....Rom 9:30
is come unto the *G*...........Rom 11:11
them the riches of the *G*......Rom 11:12
For I speak to you *G*.........Rom 11:13
I am the apostle of the *G*.....Rom 11:13
to make the *G* obedient.......Rom 15:18
all the churches of the *G*......Rom 16:4
as named among the *G*.......1Cor 5:1
to the Jews, nor to the *G*.....1Cor 10:32
whether we be Jews or *G*.....1Cor 12:13
I preach among the *G*........Gal 2:2
he did eat with the *G*: but....Gal 2:12
after the manner of *G*........Gal 2:14
the *G* to live as do the........Gal 2:14
come on the *G* through Jesus..Gal 3:14
of Jesus Christ for you *G*.....Eph 3:1
preach among the *G*..........Eph 3:8
mystery among the *G*.........Col 1:27
us to speak to the *G*..........1Thess 2:16
a teacher of the *G* in faith....1Tim 2:7
and a teacher of the *G*........2Tim 1:11
honest among the *G*..........1Pet 2:12
taking nothing of the *G*.......3John 7
for it is given unto the *G*......Rev 11:2

GENTLENESS—*mildness combined with tenderness*

Examples of:

God's..................2Sam 22:36
Christ's................Matt 11:29
Paul's.................1Thess 2:7
Holy Spirit............Gal 5:22

A Christian essential in:

Living in the world......Titus 3:1, 2
Instruction.............2Tim 2:24, 25
Restoring a brother......Gal 6:1
Calling.................Eph 4:1, 2
Marriage...............1Pet 3:1-4

Commandments concerning:

Put it on...............Col 3:12
Follow after............1Tim 6:11

[*also* GENTLE, GENTLY]

Deal *g* for my sake with......2Sam 18:5

g hath made me great 2Sam 22:36
G hath made me great ....Ps 18:35
g lead those that are with .....Is 40:11
meekness and *g* of Christ 2Cor 10:1
longsuffering, *g*, goodness .....Gal 5:22
but be *g* unto all men.........2Tim 2:24
g, and easy to be entreated ...James 3:17
not only to the good and *g*....1Pet 2:18

GENUBATH (gĕn'ū-băth)—*"theft"*
Edomite 1Kin 11:20

GERA (gē'rä)—*"enmity"; "grain"*
1. Son of Bela ....Gen 46:21
2. A descendant of Bela ...1Chr 8:3-9
3. Father of Ehud ....Judg 3:15
4. Father of Shimei 2Sam 16:5

Shimei the son of *G*, a 2Sam 19:16
Shimei the son of *G* fell........2Sam 19:18
thee Shimei the son of *G*......1Kin 2:8
G and Shephuphan, and 1Chr 8:5
and *G*, he removed them......1Chr 8:7

GERAH (gē'rä)—*smallest coin and weight among the Jews*
Twentieth part of a shekel .... {Ex 30:13 / Lev 27:25}

[*also* GERAHS]
the shekel is twenty *g*.........Num 3:47
which is twenty *g*.............Num 18:16
shekel shall be twenty *g*.......Ezek 45:12

GERAR (gē'rär)—*"halting place"*
Town of Philistia ....Gen 10:19
Visited by Abraham .....Gen 20:1-18
Visited by Isaac ....Gen 26:1-17
Abimelech, king of ......Gen 26:1, 26

herdmen of *G* did strive.......Gen 26:20
him pursued them unto *G*.....2Chr 14:13
the cities round about *G* 2Chr 14:14

GERGESENES (gŭr-gĕ-sēns)—*people from the village of Gergesa*
into the country of the *G* .....Matt 8:28
See GADARENES

GERIZIM (gĕ-rī'zĭm)—*"cutters; wasteland"*
Mountain of blessing in Ephraim ....Deut 11:29
Jotham's parable ....Judg 9:7
Samaritans' sacred mountain ....John 4:20, 21

upon mount *G* to bless the ....Deut 27:12
against mount *G*, and half.....Josh 8:33

GERSHOM (gŭr'shŏm)—*"exile"*
1. Son of Levi 1Chr 6:16-20
   Called Gershon ....Gen 46:11
   Founder of Gershonites. .Num 3:17-26
2. Son of Moses ....Ex 2:21, 22
   Circumcised ....Ex 4:25
   Founder of Levite family.1Chr 23:14-16
3. Descendant of Phinehas. .Ezra 8:2
4. Father of Jonathan ......Judg 18:30

the name of the one was *G*....Ex 18:3
son of Jahath, the son of *G* ...1Chr 6:43
of *G* throughout their 1Chr 6:62
sons of *G* were given out......1Chr 6:71
Of the sons of *G*; Joel the 1Chr 15:7
And Shebuel the son of *G* 1Chr 26:24

GERSHON (gûr'shŏn)—*"exile"*
Eldest son of Levi ....Ex 6:16
Father of Libni and Shimei................Ex 6:17
See GERSHOM

sum of the sons of *G* ....Num 4:22
the sons of *G* in the ....Num 4:28
numbered of the sons of *G*....Num 4:38
families of the sons of *G* ......Num 4:41
gave unto the sons of *G*.......Num 7:7
sons of *G* and the sons of .....Num 10:17
G, the family of the ....Num 26:57
G had by lot out of the ....Josh 21:6
unto the children of *G* ....Josh 21:27
sons of Levi; *G*, Kohath 1Chr 6:1
sons of Levi, namely *G* 1Chr 23:6

GERSHONITES (gûr'shŏn-īts)—*the inhabitants of Gershon*
Descendants of Gershon (Gershom) ....Num 3:21, 22
Tabernacle servants ......Num 3:25, 26
Achievements of 1Chr 15:7-19

[*also* GERSHONITE]
families of the *G* shall ....Num 3:23
father of the *G* shall be ....Num 3:24
of the families of the *G* ....Num 4:24
of the sons of the *G* ....Num 4:27
the family of the *G* ....Num 26:57
cities of the *G* according ......Josh 21:33
Of the *G* were, Laadan 1Chr 23:7
the sons of the *G* Laadan 1Chr 26:21
even of Laadan the *G*.........1Chr 26:21
the hand of Jehiel the *G* 1Chr 29:8
the *G*; Joah the son of 2Chr 29:12

GESHAN, GESHAM (gē'shăn, gē'shăm)—*"firm"—the third son of Jahdai*
Descendant of Caleb.....1Chr 2:47

GESHEM (gē'shĕm)—*"rain storm; corporealness"—an enemy of the Jews on their return from the Exile*
G the Arabian, heard it ....Neh 2:19
Tobiah, and *G* the Arabian....Neh 6:1
Sanballat and *G* sent ....Neh 6:2

GESHUR (gē'sher)—*"bridge"*
Not expelled ....Josh 13:13
Taimai, king of..........2Sam 3:3
Absalom flees to 2Sam 13:37, 38

Joab arose and went to *G* 2Sam 14:23
am I come from *G*? 2Sam 14:32
vow while I abode at *G* in 2Sam 15:8
And he took *G*, and Aram 1Chr 2:23
daughter of..king of *G* 1Chr 3:2

GESHURITES, GESHURI (gē'sher-īts, gē'sher-ē)
1. People of Geshur ....Deut 3:14
2. People living south of Philistia 1Sam 27:8

G and the Maachathites ....Josh 12:5
the Philistines, and all *G* ......Josh 13:2
border of the *G* and ....Josh 13:11
the *G* and the Maachathites ...Josh 13:13

GET—*to gain; possess; receive*

[*also* GAT, GETTETH, GETTING, GOT, GOTTEN]
I have *g* a man from the ......Gen 4:1
G thee out of thy country .....Gen 12:1
And Abraham *g* up early in ...Gen 19:27
g thee into the land of ....Gen 22:2
our father's hath he *g* all......Gen 31:1
his goods which he had *g* .....Gen 31:18
cattle of his *g*, which he *g*.....Gen 31:18
G me this damsel to wife......Gen 34:4
which he had *g* in the land ....Gen 36:6
with me, and fled, and *g* .....Gen 39:15
g you down thither, and ......Gen 42:2
g you unto the land of ....Gen 45:17
so *g* them up out of the.......Ex 1:10
g you straw where ye can .....Ex 5:11
G thee from me, take heed....Ex 10:28
g you forth from among ......Ex 12:31
when I have *g* me honor ......Ex 14:18
Away, *g* thee down, and ......Ex 19:24
he hath deceitfully *g* ....Lev 6:4
he be poor, and cannot *g* .....Lev 14:21
pigeons, such as he can *g* .....Lev 14:30
hand is not able to *g* that .....Lev 14:32
that that his hand shall *g*......Num 6:21
And Moses *g* him into the ....Num 11:30
g you into the wilderness......Num 14:25
g up from the tabernacle ......Num 16:27
I will *g* me back again ....Num 22:34
what every man hath *g*, of ....Num 31:50
and *g* you over the brook .....Deut 2:13
G you into your tents ....Deut 5:30
mine hand hath *g* me this .....Deut 8:17
g thee down quickly from .....Deut 9:12
is within thee shall *g* up.......Deut 28:43
G you to the mountain........Josh 2:16
g thee up to the wood ....Josh 17:15
g thee down unto the host ....Judg 7:9
Abimelech *g* him up to ....Judg 9:48
G her for me; for she ....Judg 14:3
man rose up, and *g* him.......Judg 19:28
g thee down to the floor ......Ruth 3:3
Now therefore *g* you up 1Sam 9:13
Samuel arose, and *g* him 1Sam 13:15
let me *g* away, I pray thee 1Sam 20:29
David made haste to *g*........1Sam 23:26
they *g* them away, and no.....1Sam 26:12
g them away through the 2Sam 4:7
Whosoever *g* up to the........2Sam 5:8
every man *g* him up upon 2Sam 13:29
Moreover, if he be *g* into 2Sam 17:13
And the people *g* them 2Sam 19:3
lest he *g* him fenced cities.....2Sam 20:6
clothes, but he *g* no heat......1Kin 1:1
my lord the king may *g* heat ..1Kin 1:2
G thee to Anathoth, unto 1Kin 2:26
g thee to Shiloh: behold 1Kin 14:2
G thee hence, and turn 1Kin 17:3
G thee up, eat and drink......1Kin 18:41
It cannot be *g* for gold........Job 28:15
they *g* not the land in.........Ps 44:3
arm, hath *g* him the ....Ps 98:1
the pains of hell *g* hold ....Ps 116:3
man that *g* understanding .....Prov 3:13
G wisdom, *g* ....Prov 4:5
therefore *g* wisdom: and ......Prov 4:7
with all thy *g* *g* understanding .Prov 4:7
a scorner *g* to himself.........Prov 9:7
rebuketh a wicked man *g* .....Prov 9:7
Wealth *g* by vanity shall ......Prov 13:11
better is it to *g* wisdom ....Prov 16:16
to *g* understanding rather .....Prov 16:16
the prudent *g* knowledge ......Prov 18:15
g of treasures by a lying ......Prov 21:6
learn his ways, and *g* a ....Prov 22:25
and have *g* more wisdom.....Eccl 1:16
I *g* me servants and ....Eccl 2:7
I *g* me men singers and ....Eccl 2:8
A time to *g*, and a time to ....Eccl 3:6
will *g* me to the mountain.....Song 4:6
abundance they have *g*........Is 15:7
Go, *g* thee unto this ....Is 22:15
shalt say unto it, *G* thee ......Is 30:22
g thee into darkness, O ....Is 47:5
I will *g* me unto the great .....Jer 5:5
So I *g* a girdle according ......Jer 13:2
he that *g* riches, and not ......Jer 17:11
and *g* a potter's earthen.......Jer 19:1
it may flee and *g* away.........Jer 48:9
riches that he hath *g*..........Jer 48:36
Arise, *g* you up unto the ......Jer 49:31
me about, that I cannot *g* .....Lam 3:7
We *g* our bread with the ......Lam 5:9
g thee unto the house of ......Ezek 3:4
G you far from the Lord ......Ezek 11:15
thou hast *g* thee riches ....Ezek 28:4
and hast *g* gold and silver .....Ezek 28:4
let the beasts *g* away from ....Dan 4:14
hast *g* thee renown, as at .....Dan 9:15
come, *g* you down: for the ....Joel 3:13
and I will *g* them praise.......Zeph 3:19
G you hence, walk to and .....Zech 6:7
G thee hence, Satan: for it ....Matt 4:10
unto Peter, *G* thee behind.....Matt 16:23
disciples to *g* into the ship ....Mark 6:45
G thee behind me, Satan ......Luke 4:8
G thee out, and depart........Luke 13:31
G thee out of thy country .....Acts 7:3
after we were *g* from them ....Acts 21:1
g thee quickly out of ....Acts 22:18
Lest Satan should *g* an........2Cor 2:11
and buy and sell, and *g* ....James 4:13
that had *g* the victory ....Rev 15:2

GETHER (gē'ther)—*a personification of an unknown people*
Son of Aram ....Gen 10:23

and Uz, and Hul, and *G* 1Chr 1:17

GETHSEMANE (gĕth-sĕm'ä-nē)—*"oil press"*
Garden near Jerusalem ..Matt 26:30, 36

Scene of Christ's agony and betrayal .... Matt 26:36-56; John 18:1-12
Often visited by Christ . . . Luke 22:39

place which was named *G* . . . . . Mark 14:32

GEUEL (gě-ū'ěl)—*"salvation of God"*
Gadite spy . . . . Num 13:15, 16

GEZER (gē'zer)—*"dividing"*
Canaanite city . . . . Josh 10:33
Not expelled . . . . Josh 16:10
Assigned to Kohathites . . Josh 21:21
Scene of warfare 1Chr 14:16
Burned by Egyptian king . 1Kin 9:16
Rebuilt by Solomon 1Kin 9:17

Eglon, one; the king of *G* . . . . . Josh 12:12
the nether, and to *G* . . . . Josh 16:3
G..Canaanites dwelt in *G* . . . . . Judg 1:29
and Megiddo, and *G* 1Kin 9:15
they gave also *G* with her 1Chr 6:67
at *G* with the Philistines 1Chr 20:4

GEZERITES (gē'zer-īts)—*inhabitants of Gezer*
Geshurites, and the *G* 1Sam 27:8

GHOST—*spirit*
Christ thought to be . . . . . Matt 14:26; Mark 6:49
Worshiped by Egyptians. . Is 19:3

Abraham gave up the *g* . . . . Gen 25:8
And Isaac gave up the *g* . . . . . . Gen 35:29
why did I not give up the *g* . . . Job 3:11
that I had given up the *g* . . . . . Job 10:18
be as the giving up of the *g* . . . Job 11:20
yea, man giveth up the *g* . . . . . . Job 14:10
she hath given up the *g* . . . . Jer 15:9
mine elders gave up the *g* . . . . . Lam 1:19
with child of the Holy *G* . . . . . . Matt 1:18
with the Holy *G*, and with . . . . Matt 3:11
against the Holy *G* . . . . Matt 12:32
yielded up the *g* . . . . Matt 27:50
the Son, and of the Holy *G* . . . Matt 28:19
baptize you with the Holy *G* . . Mark 1:8
said by the Holy *G* . . . . Mark 12:36
voice, and gave up the *g* . . . . . . Mark 15:37
be filled with the Holy *G* . . . . . Luke 1:15
was filled with the Holy *G* . . . . Luke 1:41
the Holy *G* was upon him . . . . . Luke 2:25
baptize you with the Holy *G* . . Luke 3:16
being full of the Holy *G* . . . . . . Luke 4:1
For the Holy *G* shall teach . . . . Luke 12:12
thus, he gave up the *g* . . . . Luke 23:46
baptizeth with the Holy *G* . . . . . John 1:33
Holy *G*, whom the Father . . . . . John 14:26
head, and gave up the *g* . . . . . . John 19:30
Receive ye the Holy *G* . . . . John 20:22
through the Holy *G* . . . . Acts 1:2
after that the Holy *G* . . . . Acts 1:8
the Holy *G* by the mouth . . . . . Acts 1:16
all filled with the Holy *G* . . . . . Acts 2:4
the gift of the Holy *G* . . . . Acts 2:38
all filled with the Holy *G* . . . . . Acts 4:31
fell down and gave up the *g* . . . Acts 5:5
and so is also the Holy *G* . . . . . Acts 5:32
of faith and of the Holy *G* . . . . Acts 6:5
being full of the Holy *G* . . . . . . Acts 7:55
they received the Holy *G* . . . . . Acts 8:17
he may receive the Holy *G* . . . . Acts 8:19
the comfort of the Holy *G* . . . . Acts 9:31
Holy *G* fell on all them . . . . Acts 10:44
have received the Holy *G* . . . . . Acts 10:47
baptized with the Holy *G* . . . . . Acts 11:16
worms and gave up the *g* . . . . . Acts 12:23
sent forth by the Holy *G* . . . . . . Acts 13:4
joy, and with the Holy *G* . . . . . Acts 13:52
seemed good to the Holy *G* . . . Acts 15:28
ye received the Holy *G* . . . . Acts 19:2
the Holy *G* came on them . . . . . Acts 19:6
Holy *G* hath made you . . . . Acts 20:28
the Holy *G* by Isaiah . . . . Acts 28:25
by the Holy *G* which is . . . . Rom 5:5
and joy in the Holy *G* . . . . Rom 14:17
sanctified by the Holy *G* . . . . . . Rom 15:16
the Holy *G* teacheth 1Cor 2:13
Lord, but by the Holy *G* 1Cor 12:3
the Holy *G*, by love 2Cor 6:6
power, and in the Holy *G* 1Thess 1:5
by the Holy *G* which 2Tim 1:14
renewing of the Holy *G* . . . . Titus 3:5
gifts of the Holy *G* . . . . Heb 2:4
partakers of the Holy *G* . . . . Heb 6:4
Holy *G* also is a witness . . . . Heb 10:15
Holy *G* sent down from 1Pet 1:12
moved by the Holy *G* 2Pet 1:21
Holy *G*: and these three 1John 5:7
praying in the Holy *G* . . . . Jude 20

GIAH (gī'ä)—*"waterfall"*
Place near Ammah 2Sam 2:24

GIANT—*man of unusually large size*

Names of:
Nephilim . . . . Gen 6:4
Rephaim . . . . Gen 14:5
Anakim . . . . Num 13:28-33
Emim . . . . Gen 14:5
Zamzummim . . . . Deut 2:20
Goliath 1Sam 17:4-7
Og . . . . Deut 3:11, 13
Others 2Sam 21:16-22

Destroyed by:
Moses . . . . Deut 3:3-11
Joshua . . . . Josh 11:21
David 1Sam 17:48-51
David and his men 2Sam 21:16-22

[*also* GIANTS]
accounted *g*, as the . . . . Deut 2:11
of the remnant of the *g* . . . . . . Josh 12:4
of the remnant of the *g* . . . . . . Josh 13:12
end of the valley of the *g* . . . . . Josh 15:8
the Perizzites and of the *g* . . . . Josh 17:15
is in the valley of the *g* . . . . Josh 18:16
of the children of the *g* 1Chr 20:4
also was the son of the *g* 1Cor 20:6
born unto the *g* in Gath 1Chr 20:8
runneth upon me like a *g* . . . . . Job 16:14

GIBBAR (gĭb'är)—*"high; mighty"*
Family head . . . . Ezra 2:20

GIBBETHON (gĭb'ĕ-thŏn)—*"high house"*
Town of Dan . . . . Josh 19:44
Assigned to Levites . . . . . . Josh 21:20-23
Nadab's assassination at . . 1Kin 15:27, 28
Besieged by Omri 1Kin 16:17

encamped against *G* 1Kin 16:15
Omri went up from *G* 1Kin 16:17

GIBEA (gĭb'ĕ-ä)—*"highlander"*
Caleb's grandson 1Chr 2:49

GIBEAH (gĭb'ĕ-ä)—*"hill"*
1. Village of Judah . . . . Josh 15:57
2. Town of Benjamin . . . . . . Judg 19:14-16
   Known for wickedness . . . Judg 19:12-30
   Destruction . . . . Judg 20:1-48
   Saul's birthplace 1Sam 10:26
   Saul's political capital . . . 1Sam 15:34
   Saul's sons executed 2Sam 21:6-10
   Wickedness of, long remembered . . . . Hos 9:9
   Also called Gibeath . . . . . Josh 18:28
3. Hill or town where Eleazar was buried . . . . Josh 24:33

we will pass over to *G* . . . . Judg 19:12
judge all night, in *G*, or in . . . . Judg 19:13
came the messengers to *G* 1Sam 11:4
were with Jonathan in *G* 1Sam 13:2
him up from Gilgal unto *G* 1Sam 13:15
abode in *G* of Benjamin 1Sam 13:16
the uttermost part of *G* 1Sam 14:2
southward over against *G* 1Sam 14:5
of Saul in *G* of Benjamin 1Sam 14:16
G under a tree in Ramah 1Sam 22:6
the Ziphites to Saul to *G* 1Sam 23:19
came unto Saul to *G* 1Sam 26:1
of Abinadab that was in *G* 2Sam 6:3
Abinadab which was at *G* 2Sam 6:4
of *G* of the children of 2Sam 23:29
Ithai the son of Ribai of *G* 1Chr 11:31
the daughter of Uriel of *G* 2Chr 13:2
Ramah is afraid; *G* of . . . . Is 10:29
Blow ye the cornet in *G* . . . . . . Hos 5:8
sinned from the days of *G* . . . . . Hos 10:9
battle in *G* against the . . . . Hos 10:9

GIBEATHITES (gĭb'ĕ-ä-thīt)
Inhabitants of Gibeah 1Chr 12:3

GIBEON (gĭb'ĕ-ŭn)—*"hill height"*
Hivite town . . . . Josh 9:3, 7
Mighty, royal city . . . . Josh 10:2
Sun stands still at . . . . Josh 10:12
Assigned to Benjamin . . . Josh 18:25
Given to Levites . . . . Josh 21:17
Location of tabernacle . . . 1Chr 16:39
Joab struck Amasa 2Sam 20:8-10
Joab killed here 1Kin 2:28-34
Site of Solomon's sacrifice and dream 1Kin 3:5-15
Natives of, return from exile . . . . Neh 3:7

inhabitants of *G* had . . . . Josh 10:1
of Goshen, even unto *G* . . . . . . Josh 10:41
the inhabitants of *G* . . . . Josh 11:19
went..from Mahanaim to *G* 2Sam 2:12
together by the pool of *G* 2Sam 2:13
Helkath-hazzurim..is in *G* 2Sam 2:16
way of the wilderness of *G* 2Sam 2:24
brother Asahel at *G* in 2Sam 3:30
king went to *G* to sacrifice 1Kin 3:4
appeared unto him at *G* 1Kin 9:2
at *G* dwelt the father of *G* 1Chr 8:29
in *G* dwelt the father of *G* 1Chr 9:35
Philistines from *G* even to 1Chr 14:16
in the high place at *G* 1Chr 21:29
high place that was at *G* 2Chr 1:3
high place that was at *G* 2Chr 1:13
The children of *G*, ninety . . . . . Neh 7:25
wroth as in the valley of *G* . . . . Is 28:21
which was of *G* . . . . Jer 28:1
great waters that are in *G* . . . . . Jer 41:12
brought again from *G* . . . . Jer 41:16

GIBEONITES (gĭb'ĕ-ŭn-īts)—*inhabitants of Gibeon*
Deceive Joshua . . . . Josh 9:3-15
Deception discovered . . . . Josh 9:16-20
made hewers of wood . . . . Josh 9:21-27
Rescued by Joshua . . . . . . Josh 10:1-43
Massacred by Saul 2Sam 21:1
Avenged by David 2Sam 21:2-9

[*also* GIBEONITE]
Ismaiah the *G*, a mighty 1Chr 12:4
Melatiah the *G*, and Jadon . . . . Neh 3:7

GIBLITES (gĭb'līts)—*inhabitants of Gebal*
And the land of the *G* . . . . Josh 13:5

GIDDALTI (gĭ-dăl'tī)—*"I have magnified"*
Son of Heman 1Chr 25:4

GIDDEL (gĭd'ĕl)—*"very great"*
1. Head of family of Temple servants . . . . . . Ezra 2:47
2. Children of Solomon's servants . . . . Ezra 2:56; Neh 7:58

GIDEON, GEDEON (gĭd'ĕ-ŭn, gĕd'ĭ-ŭn)—*"great warrior; feller of trees"*
Son of Joash . . . . Judg 6:11
Called by an angel . . . . . . Judg 6:11-24
Destroys Baal's altar . . . . . Judg 6:25-32
Fleece confirms call from God . . . . Judg 6:36-40
His army reduced . . . . Judg 7:2-8
Encouraged by a dream . . Judg 7:9-15
Employs successful strategy . . . . Judg 7:16-25
Soothes angry Ephraimites . . . . Judg 8:1-3
Takes revenge on Succoth and Penuel . . . . Judg 8:4-22
Refuses kingship . . . . Judg 8:22, 23
Unwisely makes an ephod Judg 8:24-27
Judgeship of forty years . . Judg 8:28, 29
Father of 71 sons . . . . Judg 8:30, 31
His death brings apostasy . Judg 8:32-35

Called Jerebbaal.........Judg 8:35
Man of faith............Heb 11:32

his son *G* threshed wheat .....Judg 6:11
of the Lord came upon *G* .....Judg 6:34
who is *G*, and all the people ..Judg 7:1
G, By the three hundred ......Judg 7:7
sword of the Lord, and of *G* ..Judg 7:18
So *G*, and the hundred men ...Judg 7:19
Israel said unto *G*, Rule ......Judg 8:22

GIDEONI (gĭd-ĕ-ō'nī)—*"feller"*
Benjamite ....Num 1:11
Father of Abidan........Num 1:11
Brought offering for the tribe of Benjamin .....Num 7:60–65
Over tribal army of Benjamin ....Num 10:24

be Abidan the son of *G*.......Num 2:22

GIDOM (gī'dŏm)—*"desolation"*
Village of Benjamin .....Judg 20:45

GIER-EAGLE—*most likely the Egyptian vulture*
Unclean bird............Lev 11:18

pelican, and the *g* ....Deut 14:17

GIFT—*something freely given and received*

Of God:

1. ***Material:***
Food ....Matt 6:25, 26
Rain ....Matt 5:45
Health..................Phil 2:25-30
Sleep ....Prov 3:24
Rest....................Deut 12:10
All things 1Tim 6:17
All needs ....Phil 4:19

2. ***Spiritual:***
Christ ....John 3:16
Holy Spirit..............Luke 11:13
Grace ....James 4:6
Wisdom ....James 1:5
Repentance ....Acts 11:18
Faith ....Eph 2:8
New heart ....Ezek 11:19
Peace ....Phil 4:7
Rest....................Heb 4:1, 9
Glory 1Pet 5:10
Eternal life ....John 10:28

Of man:

1. ***Purposes of:***
Confirm covenants.......Gen 21:27-32
Appease anger 1Sam 25:27-35
Show respect............Judg 6:18-21
Manifest friendship 1Sam 30:26-31
Reward 2Sam 18:11, 12
Memorialize an event ....Esth 9:20-22
Render worship ....Matt 2:11
Give help...............Phil 4:10-18
Seal friendship 1Sam 18:3, 4

2. ***Times given:***
Betrothals ....Gen 24:50-53
Weddings...............Ps 45:12
Departures..............Gen 45:21-24
Returns home ....Luke 15:22, 23
Times of recovery ......Job 42:10, 11
Trials, forbidden ....Ex 23:8

Spiritual:
Listed and explained.....Rom 12:6-8
1Cor 12:4-30
Came from God.........James 1:17
Assigned sovereignty.....1Cor 12:28
Cannot be bought ....Acts 8:18-20
Always for edification....Rom 1:11
Counterfeited by Satan...2Cor 11:13-15
Spiritually discerned 1Cor 12:2, 3
Love, the supreme 1Cor 13:1-13

[*also* GIFTS]
Abraham gave *g*, and sent ....Gen 25:6
never so much dowry and *g* ...Gen 34:12
hallow all their holy *g* ....Ex 28:38
beside your *g*, and beside .....Lev 23:38
given the Levites as a *g* ....Num 8:19
given as a *g* for the Lord .....Num 18:6
unto you as a service of *g* .....Num 18:7
heave offering of their *g* ......Num 18:11
Out of all your *g* ye shall .....Num 18:29
neither take a *g*: for a *g* ......Deut 16:19
servants, and brought *g* 2Sam 8:2
or hath he given us any *g* 2Sam 19:42
servants, and brought *g* 1Chr 18:2
of persons, nor taking of *g* 2Chr 19:7
Ammonites gave *g* to 2Chr 26:8
many brought *g* unto the 2Chr 32:23
the provinces, and gave *g* .....Esth 2:18
thou hast received *g* for ....Ps 68:18
and Seba shall offer *g*.........Ps 72:10
though thou givest many *g* ....Prov 6:35
but he that hateth *g* shall .....Prov 15:27
A *g* is as a precious stone .....Prov 17:8
A wicked man taketh a *g* .....Prov 17:23
A man's *g* maketh room ......Prov 18:16
friend to him that giveth *g* ....Prov 19:6
A *g* in secret pacifieth ....Prov 21:14
himself of a false *g* ....Prov 25:14
receiveth *g* overthroweth ......Prov 29:4
of all his labor; it is the *g* .....Eccl 3:13
in his labor; this is the *g* ......Eccl 5:19
a *g* destroyeth the heart.......Eccl 7:7
loveth *g*, and followeth ....Is 1:23
They give *g* to all whores .....Ezek 16:33
I polluted them in their..*g*.....Ezek 20:26
name no more with your *g* ....Ezek 20:39
prince give a *g* unto any of....Ezek 46:16
give a *g* of his inheritance .....Ezek 46:17
shall receive of me *g* and .....Dan 2:6
Let thy *g* be to thyself ....Dan 5:17
if thou bring thy *g* to the .....Matt 5:23
Leave there thy *g* before ......Matt 5:24
then come and offer thy *g*.....Matt 5:24
give good *g* unto your ....Matt 7:11
g that Moses commanded .....Matt 8:4
It is a *g*, by whatsoever ....Matt 15:5
sweareth by the *g* that is ......Matt 23:18
whether is greater the *g*.......Matt 23:19
altar that sanctifieth the *g*? ....Matt 23:19
Corban, that is to say, a *g* ....Mark 7:11
good *g* unto your children.....Luke 11:13
casting their *g* into the ....Luke 21:1
with goodly stones and *g* ......Luke 21:5
thou knewest the *g* of God ....John 4:10
the *g* of the Holy Ghost ......Acts 2:38
the *g* of the Holy Ghost ......Acts 10:45
God gave them the like *g* .....Acts 11:17
so also is the free *g*..........Rom 5:15
grace of God, and the *g* ......Rom 5:15
that sinned, so is the *g*........Rom 5:16
the free *g* is of many ....Rom 5:16
g of righteousness shall ....Rom 5:17
the free *g* came upon all ......Rom 5:18
the *g* of God is eternal........Rom 6:23
For the *g* and calling of ....Rom 11:29
ye come behind in no *g* 1Cor 1:7
man hath his proper *g* of......1Cor 7:7
concerning spiritual *g* 1Cor 12:1
covet earnestly the best *g* 1Cor 12:31
spiritual *g*, but rather 1Cor 14:1
are zealous of spiritual *g* 1Cor 14:12
for the *g* bestowed upon 2Cor 1:11
we would receive the *g* 2Cor 8:4
God for his unspeakable *g* 2Cor 9:15
according to the *g* of the ......Eph 3:7
the measure of the *g* of ....Eph 4:7
and gave *g* unto men ....Eph 4:8
Neglect not the *g* that is 1Tim 4:14
stir up the *g* of God 2Tim 1:6
and *g* of the Holy Ghost ......Heb 2:4
may offer both *g* and ....Heb 5:1
tasted of the heavenly *g*.......Heb 6:4
ordained to offer *g* and ....Heb 8:3
are priests that offer *g* ....Heb 8:4
were offered both *g* and ......Heb 9:9
God testifying of his *g* ....Heb 11:4
man hath received the *g* 1Pet 4:10
send *g* one to another ....Rev 11:10

GIHON (gī'hŏn)—*"gush forth"*
1. River of Eden ....Gen 2:13
2. Spring outside Jerusalem .1Kin 1:33-45
3. Source of water supply ..2Chr 32:30

on the west side of *G* 2Chr 33:14

GILALAI (gĭl'ă-lī)—*"rolling; weighty"*
Levite musician ....Neh 12:36

GILBOA (gĭl-bō'ä)—*"hill country"*
Range of limestone hills in Issachar 1Sam 28:4
Scene of Saul's death 1Sam 31:1-7
Philistines desecrate Saul's body 1Sam 31:8, 9
Under David's curse 2Sam 1:21

by chance upon mount *G* 2Sam 1:6
had slain Saul in *G* 2Sam 21:12
fell down slain in mount *G* 1Chr 10:1
sons fallen in mount *G* 1Chr 10:8

GILEAD (gĭl'ĕ-ăd)—*"strong; rocky; rough"*
1. Grandson of Manasseh ..Num 26:29, 30
2. Father of Jephthah......Judg 11:1
3. Gadite 1Chr 5:14
4. Condemned city ....Hos 6:8
5. Mountain ....Judg 7:3
6. Tableland east of the Jordan between the Arnon and Jabbok rivers ....Judg 20:1
Possessed by Israel......Num 21:21-31
Assigned to Reuben, Gad, and Manasseh ...Deut 3:12-17
Rebuked by Deborah ...Judg 5:17
Hebrews flee to.........1Sam 13:7
Ish-bosheth's rule over ..2Sam 2:8, 9
David takes refuge in ...2Sam 17:26, 27
2Sam 19:31
In David's census 2Sam 24:1, 6
Elijah's birthplace.......1Kin 17:1
Smitten by Hazael 2Kin 10:32, 33
Mentioned by Amos ....Amos 1:3, 13

[*also* GILEAD'S]
face toward the mount *G*......Gen 31:21
him in the mount *G* ....Gen 31:23
Ishmaelites came from *G* ......Gen 37:25
These are the sons of *G*.......Num 26:30
and the land of *G*, that ....Num 32:1
give them the land of *G*.......Num 32:29
Moses gave *G* unto Machir ....Num 32:40
by the river, even unto *G* .....Deut 2:36
of the plain, and all *G*, and ...Deut 3:10
and Ramoth in *G*, of the......Deut 4:43
him all the land of *G* ....Deut 34:1
and from half *G*, even ....Josh 12:2
and *G*, and the border of .....Josh 13:11
half *G*, and Ashtaroth ....Josh 13:31
the father of *G*: because ......Josh 17:1
therefore he had *G* and ....Josh 17:1
besides the land of *G* and .....Josh 17:5
Ramoth in *G* out of the ....Josh 20:8
go into the country of *G* .....Josh 22:9
unto the land of *G*, and ....Josh 22:15
which are in the land of *G* ....Judg 10:4
together and encamped in *G*...Judg 10:17
princes of *G* said to one.......Judg 10:18
all the inhabitants of *G* ....Judg 10:18
And *G* wife bare him sons ....Judg 11:2
elders of *G* went to fetch......Judg 11:5
of *G* said unto Jephthah ......Judg 11:8
all the inhabitants of *G* ....Judg 11:8
the elders of *G* said unto......Judg 11:10
he passed over *G*, and ....Judg 11:29
passed over Mizpeh of *G*......Judg 11:29
and from Mizpeh of *G* he .....Judg 11:29
gathered..all the men of *G* ....Judg 12:4
and the men of *G* smote ......Judg 12:4
men of *G* said unto him.......Judg 12:5
buried in..the cities of *G* ......Judg 12:7
they came to *G*, and to 2Sam 24:6
was in the country of *G* 1Kin 4:19
Know ye that Ramoth in *G* 1Kin 22:3
and Hazor, and *G*, and 2Kin 15:29
the father of *G*, whom he 1Chr 2:21
of Machir the father of *G* 1Chr 2:23
all the east land of *G* 1Chr 5:10

and they dwelt in *G*, in 1Chr 5:16
Machir the father of *G*........1Chr 7:14
of valor at Jazer of *G*........1Chr 26:31
G is mine, and Manasseh .....Ps 60:7
appear from mount *G*.........Song 4:1
Go up into *G*, and take ....Jer 46:11
mount Ephraim and *G*........Jer 50:19
Damascus, and from *G*.......Ezek 47:18
Is there iniquity in *G*? ....Hos 12:11
Benjamin shall possess *G*......Obad 19
Bashan and *G*, as in the ......Mic 7:14
into the land of *G* and ....Zech 10:10

GILEAD, BALM OF—*an aromatic gum for medicinal purposes*

Figurative of:
National healing.........Jer 8:22
Jer 51:8

GILEADITE—*descendant of Gilead*

[*also* GILEADITES]
after him arose Jair, a *G*......Judg 10:3
daughter of Jephthah the *G*...Judg 11:40
Ye *G* are fugitives of ....Judg 12:4
the *G* took the passages of ....Judg 12:5
Then died Jephthah the *G*.....Judg 12:7
of Barzillai the *G*, and let 1Kin 2:7
him fifty men of the *G*........2Kin 15:25
daughters of Barzillai the *G*...Ezra 2:61
daughters of Barzillai the *G*...Neh 7:63

GILGAL (gĭl'găl)—*"rolling"*
1. Memorial site between Jordan and Jericho....Josh 4:19-24
Israel circumcised ....Josh 5:2-9
Passover observed.......Josh 5:10
Site of Gibeonite covenant.............Josh 9:3-15
On Samuel's circuit 1Sam 7:16
Saul made king 1Sam 11:15
Saul rejected 1Sam 13:4-15
Denounced for idolatry..Hos 9:15
2. Town near Bethel.......2Kin 2:1
Home of Elisha..........2Kin 4:38

champaign over against *G*.....Deut 11:30
to the camp to *G*, saying......Josh 10:6
Joshua ascended from *G*......Josh 10:7
went up from *G* all night......Josh 10:9
unto the camp to *G*...........Josh 10:15
unto the camp to *G*...........Josh 10:43
king of the nations of *G*.......Josh 12:23
came unto Joshua in *G*........Josh 14:6
looking toward *G*, that is......Josh 15:7
Lord came up from *G* to ......Judg 2:1
quarries that were by *G*.......Judg 3:19
circuit to Beth-el, and *G*......1Sam 7:16
go down before me to *G*.......1Sam 10:8
Come, and let us go to *G*.....1Sam 11:14
on, and gone down to *G*.......1Sam 15:12
the Lord thy God in *G*........1Sam 15:21
before the Lord in *G*..........1Sam 15:33
Judah came to *G*, to go........2Sam 19:15
king went on to *G*, and........2Sam 19:40
Also from the house of *G*.....Neh 12:29
and come not ye unto *G*......Hos 4:15
sacrifice bullocks in *G*.........Hos 12:11
G multiply transgression.......Amos 4:4
nor enter into *G*, and pass ....Amos 5:5
G shall surely go into ....Amos 5:5
him, from Shittim unto *G*.....Mic 6:5

GILOH (gī'lō)—*"he that overturns"*
Town of Judah ....Josh 15:51

city, even from *G*, while he ...2Sam 15:12

GILONITE (gī'lō-nīt)—*native of Giloh*
Ahitophel called.........2Sam 15:12

the son of Ahithophel the *G*...2Sam 23:34

GIMEL (gĭm'ĕl)
Third letter in Hebrew alphabet..............Ps 119:17-24

GIMZO (gĭm'zō)—*"sycamore"*
Village of Judah.........2Chr 28:18

GIN—*a trap*
Used for catching beasts or birds.................Amos 3:5
Used figuratively ....Ps 141:9

[*also* GINS]
g shall take him by the ....Job 18:9
wayside; they have set *g*......Ps 140:5
for a *g* and for a snare to .....Is 8:14

GINATH (gī'năth)—*"protection"*
Father of Tibni..........1Kin 16:21, 22

GINNETHO (gĭn-ĕ-thō)—*"great protection"*
Postexilic priest ....Neh 12:4

GINNETHON (gĭn'ĕ-thŏn)—*"great protection"*
Family head and signer of document.............Neh 10:6
Probably same as Ginnethoi

Iddo, Zechariah; of *G*........Neh 12:16

GIRD—*to put on, as a belt*

Purposes of:
Strengthening ....Prov 31:17
Supporting clothing......2Kin 4:29

Figurative of:
Gladness................Ps 30:11
Truth...................Eph 6:14
Readiness...............1Pet 1:13

Those girding:
Priests..................Ex 28:4, 39
Warriors................1Sam 18:4
Jesus...................John 13:3, 4

[*also* GIRDED, GIRDEDST, GIRDETH, GIRDING, GIRT]
eat it; with your loins *g*.......Ex 12:11
and *g* him with the curious ....Ex 29:5
shalt *g* them with girdles ......Ex 29:9
and *g* him with the girdle .....Lev 8:7
he *g* him with the curious .....Lev 8:7
be *g* with a linen girdle ....Lev 16:4
ye had *g* on every man ....Deut 1:41
did *g* it under his raiment .....Judg 3:16
stumbled are *g* with 1Sam 2:4
g with a linen ephod.........1Sam 2:18
David *g* his sword upon.......1Sam 17:39
g on every man his sword......1Sam 25:13
David also *g* on his sword.....1Sam 25:13
G ye on every man his........1Sam 25:13
g you with sackcloth, and 2Sam 3:31
David was *g* with a linen......2Sam 6:14
that he had put on was *g*......2Sam 20:8
being *g* with a new sword 2Sam 21:16
For thou hast *g* me with 2Sam 22:40
and he *g* up his loins, and ran .1Kin 18:46
Let not him that *g* on his 1Kin 20:11
g with a girdle of leather......2Kin 1:8
G up thy loins, and take 2Kin 4:29
G up thy loins, and take 2Kin 9:1
had his sword *g* by his ....Neh 4:18
g their loins with a girdle .....Job 12:18
G up now thy loins like a .....Job 38:3
G up thy loins now like ....Job 40:7
It is God that *g* me with ......Ps 18:32
For thou hast *g* me with ......Ps 18:39
G thy sword upon thy.........Ps 45:3
mountains: being *g* with.......Ps 65:6
he is *g* continually ....Ps 109:19
stomacher a *g* of sackcloth ....Is 3:24
g yourselves, and ye ....Is 8:9
g themselves with.............Is 15:3
and *g* sackcloth upon your ....Is 32:11
I *g* thee, though thou hast ....Is 45:5
therefore *g* up thy loins ....Jer 1:17
this *g* you with sackcloth ......Jer 4:8
g thee with sackcloth, and.....Jer 6:26
g you with sackcloth ....Jer 49:3
they have *g* themselves........Lam 2:10
shall also *g* themselves ....Ezek 7:18
I *g* thee about with fine ....Ezek 16:10
G with girdles upon their......Ezek 23:15
and *g* them with sackcloth.....Ezek 27:31
shall not *g* themselves.........Ezek 44:18
loins were *g* with fine ....Dan 10:5

a virgin *g* with sackcloth ......Joel 1:8
G yourselves, and lament .....Joel 1:13
Let your loins be *g* about .....Luke 12:35
shall *g* himself, and make .....Luke 12:37
g thyself, and serve me ....Luke 17:8
towel wherewith he was *g*.....John 13:5
he *g* his fisher's coat unto .....John 21:7
thou wast young, thou *g* ......John 21:18
another shall *g* thee, and .....John 21:18
G thyself, and bind on thy ....Acts 12:8
your loins *g* about with ....Eph 6:14
g up the loins of your.........1Pet 1:13
and *g* about the paps with.....Rev 1:13
breasts *g* with golden ....Rev 15:6

GIRDLE—*waistcloth; sash; belt*
Priestly garment.........Ex 28:4, 39
Worn by warriors........1Sam 18:4

[*also* GIRDLES]
shalt make for them *g*, and....Ex 28:40
the curious *g* of the ephod ....Ex 29:5
curious *g* of his ephod ....Ex 39:5
and girded him with the *g*.....Lev 8:7
the curious *g* of the ephod ....Lev 8:7
girded them with *g*, and ......Lev 8:13
ten shekels of silver and a *g*...2Sam 18:11
blood of war upon his *g*.......1Kin 2:5
girt with a *g* of leather........2Kin 1:8
their loins with a *g* ....Job 12:18
g wherewith he is girded ......Ps 109:19
delivereth *g* unto the ....Prov 31:24
and instead of a *g* a rent......Is 3:24
shall the *g* of their loins be....Is 5:27
shall be the *g* of his ....Is 11:5
and faithfulness the *g*.........Is 11:5
Go and get thee a linen *g*.....Jer 13:1
Take the *g* that thou hast .....Jer 13:4
took the *g* from the place .....Jer 13:7
g was marred, it was..........Jer 13:7
For as the *g* cleaveth to ....Jer 13:11
with *g* upon their loins........Ezek 23:15
and a leathern *g* about his ....Matt 3:4
with a *g* of a skin about.......Mark 1:6
he took Paul's *g*, and ....Acts 21:11
man that owneth this *g* ....Acts 21:11
the paps with a golden *g*......Rev 1:13
girded with golden *g*..........Rev 15:6

GIRGASHITES (gûr'gä-shīts)
Descendants of Canaan ..Gen 10:15, 16
Land of, given to Abraham's descendants.Gen 15:18, 21
Delivered to Israel ......Josh 24:11

the Canaanites, and the *G*.....Gen 15:21
the Hittites, and the *G*.........Deut 7:1
the Perizzites, and the *G*......Josh 3:10
the Amorite, and the *G*.......1Chr 1:14
Jebusites, and the *G*, to.......Neh 9:8

GIRL—*a young, unmarried woman*
Sold for wine ....Joel 3:3
Prophecy concerning.....Zech 8:4, 5

GIRZITES (gûr'zīts)—*inhabitants of Gezer*
Raided by David 1Sam 27:8

GISPA (gĭs'pä)—*"listening; attentive"*
Overseer................Neh 11:21

GITTAH-HEPHER (gĭt'ä-hē'fĕr)—*"winepress of digging"*
east to *G*, to Ittah-kazin ......Josh 19:13

GITTAIM (gĭt'ā-ĭm)—*"two winepresses"*
Village of Benjamin .....Neh 11:31, 33
Refuge of the Beerothites.2Sam 4:2, 3

GITTITES (gĭt'īts)—*natives of Gath*
600 follow David 2Sam 15:18-23

[*also* GITTITE]
the *G*, and the Ekronites......Josh 13:3
house of Obed-edom the *G*....2Sam 6:10
house of Obed-edom the *G*....2Sam 6:11
the hand of Ittai the *G*........2Sam 18:2
brother of Goliath the *G*.......2Sam 21:19
house of Obed-edom the *G*....1Chr 13:13
brother of Goliath the *G*......1Chr 20:5

GITTITH (gĭt'ĭth)—*belonging to Gath*
Musical instrument or tune .... Ps 8; 81; 84 *titles*

GIVE—*to make a present of; yield; offer; bestow*

[*also* GAVE, GAVEST, GIVEST, GIVETH, GIVING]
Adam *g* names to all cattle .... Gen 2:20
woman whom thou *g* to be .... Gen 3:12
she *g* me of the tree .... Gen 3:12
he *g* him tithes of all .... Gen 14:20
g her to her husband Abram .. Gen 16:3
g them unto Abraham .... Gen 20:14
and *g* the lad drink .... Gen 21:19
her hand, and *g* him drink .... Gen 24:18
had done *g* him drink .... Gen 24:19
g them to Rebekah; he *g* ..... Gen 24:53
Abraham *g* gifts, and sent ..... Gen 25:6
g up the ghost and died .... Gen 25:17
g the savory meat .... Gen 27:17
g him a charge, saying .... Gen 28:6
surely *g* the tenth unto thee ... Gen 28:22
g him Rachel his daughter .... Gen 29:28
g him Bilhah her handmaid ... Gen 30:4
and *g* them into the hand ..... Gen 30:35
he *g* it her, and came in ...... Gen 38:18
g him favor in the sight .... Gen 39:21
g the cup into Pharaoh's ...... Gen 40:21
g them water..washed .... Gen 43:24
Joseph *g* them wagons .... Gen 45:21
g each man changes of raiment. Gen 45:22
to Benjamin he *g* three .... Gen 45:22
Bilhah..Laban *g* unto .... Gen 46:25
Joseph *g*..bread in exchange ... Gen 47:17
he *g* goodly words .... Gen 49:21
he *g* Moses Zipporah his ...... Ex 2:21
Lord *g* the people favor .... Ex 11:3
g light by night to these .... Ex 14:20
he *g* you on the sixth .... Ex 16:29
every man..*g* it willingly ...... Ex 25:2
So they *g* it me..I cast it ...... Ex 32:24
Moses *g* commandment .... Ex 36:6
g any of his seed unto Molech . Lev 20:2
all that any man *g* .... Lev 27:9
Moses *g* the money of them ... Num 3:51
any man *g* the priest .... Num 5:10
four oxen he *g*..the sons ...... Num 7:7
sons of Kohath he *g* none ..... Num 7:9
every one of their princes *g* ... Num 17:6
Moses *g* the tribute, which .... Num 31:41
Moses *g* unto them, even ..... Num 32:33
Moses *g* Gilead unto Machir .. Num 32:40
which the Lord *g* .... Deut 2:12
which the Lord our God *g* .... Deut 2:29
kingdom of Og *g* I unto the ... Deut 3:13
g from Gilead even unto the .. Deut 3:16
Lord thy God *g* thee .... Deut 4:21
land which the Lord thy God *g*. Deut 5:16
Lord thy God *g* thee not ...... Deut 9:6
Lord *g* me the two tables ..... Deut 9:11
Lord *g* them unto me .... Deut 10:4
g him food and raiment .... Deut 10:18
land which the Lord..*g* .... Deut 11:31
Lord your God *g* you .... Deut 12:9
God *g* you to inherit .... Deut 12:10
when he *g* you rest from ...... Deut 12:10
Lord thy God *g* thee .... Deut 15:4
thou *g* him nought; and he .... Deut 15:9
Lord thy God *g* thee .... Deut 16:5
Everyman shall *g* as he is ..... Deut 16:17
which the Lord thy God *g* .... Deut 16:20
Lord thy God *g* thee .... Deut 17:14
land the Lord thy God *g* ...... Deut 19:1
God *g* thee to inherit .... Deut 19:3
God *g* thee to possess .... Deut 19:14
Lord thy God *g* thee .... Deut 21:23
Lord thy God *g* thee .... Deut 24:4
which the Lord thy God *g* .... Deut 25:19
Lord thy God *g* thee .... Deut 26:2
God *g* thee, a land..floweth ... Deut 27:3
g it for an inheritance .... Deut 29:8
Lord your God *g* you .... Josh 1:11
land which Moses *g* .... Josh 1:14
g it for an inheritance .... Josh 11:23
Joshua *g* unto the tribes ...... Josh 12:7
inheritance, which Moses *g* .... Josh 13:8
Moses the servant of..Lord *g* .. Josh 13:8
Moses *g* unto the tribe .... Josh 13:15
g inheritance unto the half .... Josh 13:29
unto the Levites he *g* none .... Josh 14:3
g unto Caleb the son .... Josh 14:13
g him Achsah his daughter .... Josh 15:17
g her the upper springs .... Josh 15:19
he *g* them an inheritance ...... Josh 17:4
of Israel *g* an inheritance ...... Josh 19:49
of Israel *g* unto the Levites .... Josh 21:3
g out of the tribe of the .... Josh 21:9
villages..*g* they to Caleb ...... Josh 21:12
they *g* them Shechem with .... Josh 21:21
Lord *g* unto Israel all .... Josh 21:43
servant of the Lord *g* you ..... Josh 22:4
his seed and *g* him Isaac ..... Josh 24:3
I *g* unto Isaac Jacob and Esau . Josh 24:4
g unto Esau mount Seir .... Josh 24:4
g him Achsah his daughter .... Judg 1:13
Caleb *g* her the upper springs . Judg 1:15
g Hebron unto Caleb .... Judg 1:20
g..daughters to their sons ..... Judg 3:6
and she *g* him milk .... Judg 5:25
g him threescore..ten pieces .. Judg 9:4
Chemosh thy god *g* thee ...... Judg 11:24
g change of garments .... Judg 14:19
g them to the founder .... Judg 17:4
men of Israel *g* place to .... Judg 20:36
visited his people in *g* them ... Ruth 1:6
g to her..she had reserved ..... Ruth 2:18
and *g* it to his neighbor .... Ruth 4:7
neighbors *g* it a name .... Ruth 4:17
he *g* to Peninnah his wife 1Sam 1:4
g her son suck until..weaned .. 1Sam 1:23
God *g* him another heart 2Sam 10:9
g them in full tale to 1Sam 18:27
Saul *g* him Michal his 1Sam 18:27
priest *g* him hallowed bread ... 1Sam 21:6
Achish *g* him Ziklag that 1Sam 27:6
g him a piece of a cake of 1Sam 30:12
g thee thy master's house 2Sam 12:8
king *g* all the captains 2Sam 18:5
God *g* Solomon wisdom 1Kin 4:29
g food for my household 1Kin 5:9
Solomon *g* Hiram twenty 1Kin 5:11
g Solomon to Hiram year 1Kin 5:11
unto the land which thou *g* 1Kin 8:34
land which thou *g* unto 1Kin 8:40
g Hiram twenty cities 1Kin 9:11
g the king an hundred 1Kin 10:10
queen of Sheba *g* to king 1Kin 10:10
Solomon *g* unto the queen 1Kin 10:13
Solomon *g* her of his royal 1Kin 10:13
which *g* him an house 1Kin 11:18
victuals, and *g* him land 1Kin 11:18
counsel that they *g* him 1Kin 12:13
house of David, and *g* it 1Kin 14:8
g unto the people, and 1Kin 19:21
And he *g* him his hand 2Kin 10:15
they *g* the money, being 2Kin 12:11
Lord *g* Israel a savior 2Kin 13:5
and *g* him presents 2Kin 17:3
g it to the king of Assyria 2Kin 18:16
Hilkiah *g*..book to Shaphan ... 2Kin 22:8
g judgment upon him 2Kin 25:6
g his daughter to Jarha 1Chr 2:35
they *g* to Caleb the son 1Chr 6:56
Israel *g* to the Levites 1Chr 6:64
g unto them, of the cities 1Chr 6:67
g also Gezer with..suburbs 1Chr 6:67
O *g* thanks unto the Lord 1Chr 16:34
Joab *g* the sum of..number 1Chr 21:5
g to Heman fourteen sons 1Chr 25:5
g of gold by weight for 1Chr 28:14
gold basins he *g* gold 1Chr 28:17
precious stones were found *g* .. 1Chr 29:8
by *g* him according to his 2Chr 6:23
land which thou *g* to them 2Chr 6:25
in the land which thou *g* 2Chr 6:31
their land, which thou *g* 2Chr 6:38
g the king a hundred 2Chr 9:9
queen of Sheba *g* King 2Chr 9:9
counsel which the old men *g* .. 2Chr 10:8
God of Israel *g* the kingdom .. 2Chr 13:5
Lord *g* them rest round 2Chr 15:15
g it to the seed of Abraham ... 2Chr 20:7
father *g* them great gifts 2Chr 21:3
g him the testimony 2Chr 23:11
Ammonites *g* gifts to Uzziah .. 2Chr 26:8
g them to eat and to drink 2Chr 28:15
g them up to desolation 2Chr 30:7
and he *g* him a sign 2Chr 32:24
artificers and builders *g* 2Chr 34:11
g willingly unto the people 2Chr 35:8
g..priests for the passover 2Chr 35:8
g them all into his hand 2Chr 36:17
They *g* after their ability ...... Ezra 2:69
g thanks unto the Lord .... Ezra 3:11
he *g* them into the hand ...... Ezra 5:12
they *g* their hands that .... Ezra 10:19
I took up the wine, and *g* ..... Neh 2:1
I *g* my brother Hanani .... Neh 7:2
fathers *g* unto the work .... Neh 7:70
Tirshatha *g* to the treasure .... Neh 7:70
rest of the people *g* .... Neh 7:72
g him the name of Abraham .. Neh 9:7
g them right judgments .... Neh 9:13
g them bread from heaven .... Neh 9:15
g also thy good spirit to .... Neh 9:20
g them water for their thirst .. Neh 9:20
g..kingdoms and nations ...... Neh 9:22
g them into their hands .... Neh 9:24
g them saviors, who saved .... Neh 9:27
g thou them into the hand .... Neh 9:30
goodness that thou *g* them .... Neh 9:35
land..thou *g* unto our fathers . Neh 9:36
of them that *g* thanks .... Neh 12:31
of them that *g* thanks .... Neh 12:40
g them drink in vessels .... Esth 1:7
speedily *g* her things .... Esth 2:9
and *g* it unto Haman .... Esth 3:10
g him..copy of the writing ..... Esth 4:8
and *g* it unto Mordecai .... Esth 8:2
Lord *g*, and the Lord hath .... Job 1:21
Who *g* rain upon the earth .... Job 5:10
as the *g* up of the ghost .... Job 11:20
eye saw me, it *g* witness ..... Job 29:11
Almighty *g*..understanding .... Job 32:8
I *g* ear to your reasons .... Job 32:11
When he *g* quietness, who .... Job 34:29
what *g* thou him? or what ..... Job 35:7
cry, but none *g* answer .... Job 35:12
he *g* meat in abundance .... Job 36:31
G thou the goodly wings ...... Job 39:13
man also *g* him a piece of ..... Job 42:11
shall *g* thee the heathen for.... Ps 2:8
Highest *g* his voice .... Ps 18:13
deliverance *g* he to..king ...... Ps 18:50
of thee, and thou *g* it him ..... Ps 21:4
Thou *g* thy mouth to evil ..... Ps 50:19
that *g* strength and power ..... Ps 68:35
g me also gall for my meat .... Ps 69:21
my thirst they *g* me vinegar ... Ps 69:21
g him to be meat to..people ... Ps 74:14
Unto thee..do we *g* thanks .... Ps 75:1
unto thee do we *g* thanks ..... Ps 75:1
g them drink as out .... Ps 78:15
g also their increase .... Ps 78:46
g their life over..pestilence .... Ps 78:50
g them up unto their own ..... Ps 81:12
thou *g* them they gather ...... Ps 104:28
g them hail for rain, and ...... Ps 105:32
he *g* them their request .... Ps 106:15
it *g* understanding unto .... Ps 119:130
g their land for a heritage ..... Ps 135:12
who *g* food to all flesh .... Ps 136:25
g food to the hungry .... Ps 146:7
g snow like wool .... Ps 147:16
Lord *g* wisdom; out of .... Prov 2:6
g grace unto the lowly .... Prov 3:34
content, though thou *g* .... Prov 6:35
g to the sea his decree .... Prov 8:29
understanding *g* favor .... Prov 13:15
wicked doer *g* heed to .... Prov 17:4
liar *g* ear to a naughty .... Prov 17:4
righteous *g*, and spareth not ... Prov 21:26
he that *g* to the rich .... Prov 22:16
My son *g* me thine heart ...... Prov 23:26
kiss his lips that *g*..answer ..... Prov 24:26

G

g unto the poor..not lack .....Prov 28:27
g my heart to seek..search ....Eccl 1:13
g my heart to know wisdom ...Eccl 1:17
God *g* to a man that is ....Eccl 2:26
of his life, which God *g*.......Eccl 5:18
wisdom *g* life to them.........Eccl 7:12
return unto God who *g* ....Eccl 12:7
yea, he *g* good heed, and .....Eccl 12:9
but he *g* me no answer ....Song 5:6
He *g* power to the faint ....Is 40:29
g the nations before him ......Is 41:2
g them as the dust............Is 41:2
Who *g* Jacob for a spoil.......Is 42:24
I *g* Egypt for thy ransom......Is 43:3
Lord our God, that *g* rain.....Jer 5:24
land that I *g* to your fathers ...Jer 7:7
land..I *g* unto their fathers ....Jer 16:15
heritage that I *g* thee ....Jer 17:4
I *g* you and your fathers ....Jer 23:39
land..I *g* to their fathers ......Jer 30:3
g the sun for a light ....Jer 31:35
I *g* the evidence of..purchase . .Jer 32:12
g it to Baruch the scribe ......Jer 36:32
g them vineyards and fields ...Jer 39:10
captain of the guard *g* ....Jer 40:5
he *g* judgment upon him ......Jer 52:9
mine elders *g* up the ghost .....Lam 1:19
g his cheek to him..smiteth ....Lam 3:30
thou *g* him not warning ....Ezek 3:18
meat also which I *g* thee ......Ezek 16:19
in that thou *g* a reward ....Ezek 16:34
I *g* them my statutes..........Ezek 20:11
also I *g* them my sabbaths ....Ezek 20:12
the land that I *g* to your ......Ezek 36:28
as he shall be able to *g* ....Ezek 46:5
Lord *g* Jehoiakim king ....Dan 1:2
prince of the eunuchs *g* ....Dan 1:7
g unto Daniel the name ....Dan 1:7
g them knowledge and skill ...Dan 1:17
g wisdom unto the wise ....Dan 2:21
g it to whomsoever he will ....Dan 4:25
God *g* Nebuchadnezzar ....Dan 5:18
g thanks before his God ......Dan 6:10
I *g* her corn, and wine ....Hos 2:8
g..Nazarites wine to drink .....Amos 2:12
that *g* his neighbor drink ......Hab 2:15
g them to him for the fear ....Mal 2:5
shall *g* his angels charge ......Matt 4:6
g light unto all that ....Matt 5:15
G us this day our daily........Matt 6:11
g commandment to depart ....Matt 8:18
g the loaves to his disciples....Matt 14:19
g thanks, and brake them .....Matt 15:36
g to his disciples...............Matt 15:36
g in exchange for his soul? ....Matt 16:26
who *g* thee this authority?.....Matt 21:23
and *g* in marriage ....Matt 24:38
unto one he *g* five talents .....Matt 25:15
and ye *g* me meat ....Matt 25:35
thirsty and ye *g* me drink .....Matt 25:35
and ye *g* me no meat ....Matt 25:42
thirsty, and ye *g* me no drink..Matt 25:42
g thanks, and *g* it to them ....Matt 26:27
g them for..potter's field ......Matt 27:10
g him vinegar to drink ....Matt 27:34
and *g* him to drink ....Matt 27:48
g also to them which were ....Mark 2:26
g them power over unclean....Mark 6:7
damsel *g* it to her mother .....Mark 6:28
g them to his disciples ....Mark 6:41
loaves and *g* thanks...........Mark 8:6
g to his disciples to set........Mark 8:6
shall a man *g* in exchange .....Mark 8:37
g thee this authority to........Mark 11:28
brake it, and *g* to them ....Mark 14:22
they *g* him to drink wine ......Mark 15:23
g him to drink, saying ....Mark 15:36
loud voice, and *g* up the ......Mark 15:37
g the body to Joseph ....Mark 15:45
g thanks likewise unto..Lord . .Luke 2:38
g also to them that were with .Luke 6:4
G, and it shall be given ....Luke 6:38
g me no water for my feet ....Luke 7:44
g me no kiss: but this woman .Luke 7:45
g them power and authority ...Luke 9:1
g to the disciples to set ....Luke 9:16
and *g* them to the host........Luke 10:35
G us day by day our daily.....Luke 11:3
yet thou never *g* me a kid.....Luke 15:29
at his feet, *g* him thanks ......Luke 17:16
saw it, *g* praise unto God .....Luke 18:43
then *g* thou not my ....Luke 19:23
he that *g* thee this authority ...Luke 20:2
g thanks, and said, Take ......Luke 22:17
g thanks, and brake it ....Luke 22:19
g unto them, saying. This .....Luke 22:19
and the paps which never *g* ...Luke 23:29
and brake and *g* to them ......Luke 24:30
g he power to become the sons.John 1:12
g his only begotten Son ....John 3:16
g not the Spirit by measure ...John 3:34
Jacob *g* to his son Joseph .....John 4:5
water that I shall *g* him ....John 4:14
Son of man..*g* unto you ....John 6:27
bread from heaven *g* them .....John 6:31
Father *g* you the true bread ...John 6:32
g life unto the world..........John 6:33
All that the Father *g* me ....John 6:37
g unto you circumcision ....John 7:22
good shepherd *g* his life.......John 10:11
he *g* me a commandment .....John 12:49
my peace I *g* unto you: not ...John 14:27
not as the world *g*, *g* I.......John 14:27
Father *g* me commandment ....John 14:31
work which thou *g* me to .....John 17:4
g me out of the world ....John 17:6
and thou *g* them me ....John 17:6
words which thou *g* me ....John 17:8
thou *g* me I have kept ....John 17:12
glory which thou *g* me I ......John 17:22
g me have I lost none ....John 18:9
Jesus *g* him no answer ....John 19:9
and Pilate *g* him leave ....John 19:38
taketh bread, and *g* them .....John 21:13
they *g* forth their lots ....Acts 1:26
as the Spirit *g*..utterance ......Acts 2:4
g heed unto them ....Acts 3:5
such as I have *g* I thee........Acts 3:6
and *g* up the ghost ....Acts 5:5
g him the covenant of ....Acts 7:8
g them up to worship the .....Acts 7:42
g out that himself was ....Acts 8:9
To whom they all *g* heed .....Acts 8:10
g much alms to the people ....Acts 10:2
people *g* a shout, saying ......Acts 12:22
g not God the glory ....Acts 12:23
eaten of worms, and *g* up .....Acts 12:23
God *g* unto them Saul ....Acts 13:21
g testimony unto the word ....Acts 14:3
g audience to Barnabas ....Acts 15:12
seeing he *g* to all life ....Acts 17:25
blessed to *g* than to receive ...Acts 20:35
g him audience unto this ......Acts 22:22
I *g* my voice against them .....Acts 26:10
g thanks to God in presence...Acts 27:35
g them over to a reprobate ....Rom 1:28
in faith, *g* glory to God ....Rom 4:20
freely *g* us all things ....Rom 8:32
he that *g*, let him do ....Rom 12:8
for he *g* God thanks; and .....Rom 14:6
and *g* God thanks ....Rom 14:6
g account of himself to God ...Rom 14:12
as the Lord *g* to every man? . .1Cor 3:5
God that *g* the increase 1Cor 3:7
g her in marriage doeth 1Cor 7:38
g her not in marriage 1Cor 7:38
without life *g* sound 1Cor 14:7
verily *g* thanks well 1Cor 14:17
God which *g* us the victory 1Cor 15:57
but the Spirit *g* life 2Cor 3:6
G no offense in any thing 2Cor 6:3
g their own selves to the 2Cor 8:5
g himself for our sins ....Gal 1:4
we *g* place by subjection ......Gal 2:5
g to me and Barnabas ....Gal 2:9
and *g* himself for me ....Gal 2:20
God *g* it to Abraham by ......Gal 3:18
g him to be the head over ....Eph 1:22
and *g* gifts unto men..........Eph 4:8
he *g* some, apostles ....Eph 4:11
but rather *g* of thanks ....Eph 5:4
concerning *g* and receiving ....Phil 4:15
G thanks unto the Father .....Col 1:12
intercessions, and *g* of thanks. .1Tim 2:1
g us richly all..to enjoy 1Tim 6:17
g heed to Jewish fables ....Titus 1:14
g attendance at the altar ......Heb 7:13
g thanks to his name ....Heb 13:15
of God that *g* to all men ......James 1:5
But he *g* more grace ....James 4:6
the heaven *g* rain, and the ....James 5:18
the dead, and *g* him glory 1Pet 1:21
g honor unto the wife.........1Pet 3:7
ability which God *g*...........1Pet 4:11
g all diligence, add to your 2Pet 1:5
as he *g* us commandment 1John 3:23
I *g* all diligence to write.......Jude 3
g themselves..to fornication ...Jude 7
which God *g* unto him ....Rev 1:1
g thee a crown of life ....Rev 2:10
g her space to repent of.......Rev 2:21
and *g* glory to the God of.....Rev 11:13
dragon *g* him his power ....Rev 13:2
g power unto the beast ....Rev 13:4
g unto the seven ....Rev 15:7
sea *g* up the dead ....Rev 20:13
Lord God *g* them light........Rev 22:5
g every man according as .....Rev 22:12

GIVEN—*See* INTRODUCTION

GIVER—*one who gives*
with the *g* of usury to him ....Is 24:2
God loveth a cheerful *g*.......2Cor 9:7

GIVING TO GOD—*offerings of resources and abilities*

Manner of:
Without show ....Matt 6:1-4
According to ability 1Cor 16:1, 2
Willingly.................1Chr 29:3-9
Liberally.................2Cor 9:6-15
Cheerfully 2Cor 9:7
Proportionately..........Mal 3:10

Examples of:
Israelites................Ex 35:21-29
Princes of Israel.........Num 7:2-28
Poor widow ....Luke 21:2-4
Macedonian churches 2Cor 8:1-5

GIZONITE (gī'zō-nīt)—*an inhabitant of Gizon*
Hashem thus described...1Chr 11:34

GLADNESS—*feeling of pleasure, joy, or delight*

Causes of:
Forgiveness ....Ps 51:8
Salvation ....Is 51:3, 11
John 8:56
Recovery of a son ....Luke 15:32
Restoration of hope .....John 20:20
Temporal blessings ......Acts 14:17
Christ's coming..........1Pet 4:13

Wrong kinds of:
At an enemy's downfall . .Prov 24:17
At wickedness...........Hos 7:3

[*also* GLAD, GLADLY]
he will be *g* in his heart.......Ex 4:14
Also in the day of your *g* .....Num 10:10
and with *g* of heart ....Deut 28:47
priest's heart was *g* ....Judg 18:20
men of Jabesh..were *g* 1Sam 11:9
the city of David with *g*.......2Sam 6:12
joyful and *g* of heart..........1Kin 8:66
strength and *g* are in his 1Chr 16:27
Let the heavens be *g* 1Chr 16:31
on that day with great *g* 1Chr 29:22
g and merry in heart..........2Chr 7:10
sang praises with *g* 2Chr 29:30
seven days with great *g* 2Chr 30:21
And there was very great *g* ...Neh 8:17
keep the dedication with *g* ....Neh 12:27
joyful and with a *g* heart......Esth 5:9
Jews had light, and *g* ....Esth 8:16
Jews had joy and *g*, a feast ...Esth 8:17

it a day of feasting and *g* .....Esth 9:17
month Adar a day of *g* ....Esth 9:19
rejoice..and are *g*.............Job 3:22
hast put *g* in my heart ....Ps 4:7
g and rejoice in thee..........Ps 9:2
and Israel shall be *g* ....Ps 14:7
heart is *g*, and my glory.......Ps 16:9
made him exceeding *g* ....Ps 21:6
and girded me with *g* ....Ps 30:11
be *g* and rejoice in..mercy ....Ps 31:7
Be *g* in the Lord, and ....Ps 32:11
hear thereof, and be *g* ....Ps 34:2
shout for joy, and be *g* ....Ps 35:27
anointed..with the oil of *g*.....Ps 45:7
they have made thee *g*.........Ps 45:8
make *g* the city of God ....Ps 46:4
daughters of Judah be *g* ......Ps 48:11
and Israel shall be *g* ....Ps 53:6
righteous shall be *g* in the .....Ps 64:10
let the nations be *g* and sing ..Ps 67:4
let the righteous be *g* ....Ps 68:3
shall see this, and be *g*........Ps 69:32
rejoice and be *g* in thee.......Ps 70:4
make us *g* according to ....Ps 90:15
made me *g* through thy work ..Ps 92:4
let the earth be *g*; let the .....Ps 96:11
Zion heard, and was *g* ....Ps 97:8
g for the upright in heart .....Ps 97:11
Serve the Lord with *g* ....Ps 100:2
wine..maketh *g* the heart......Ps 104:15
and his chosen with *g*.........Ps 105:43
are they *g* because they ....Ps 107:30
rejoice and be *g* in it ....Ps 118:24
fear thee will be *g*............Ps 119:74
g when they said unto me .....Ps 122:1
for us; whereof we are *g* ......Ps 126:3
son maketh a *g* father ....Prov 10:1
hope of the righteous..be *g*....Prov 10:28
good word maketh it *g*.........Prov 12:25
son maketh a *g* father ....Prov 15:20
father and thy mother..be *g* ...Prov 23:25
and make my heart *g* ....Prov 27:11
be *g* and rejoice in thee.......Song 1:4
day of the *g* of his heart ......Song 3:11
g is taken away, and joy ......Is 16:10
will be *g* and rejoice in his ....Is 25:9
solitary place shall be *g* ....Is 35:1
shall obtain joy and *g*.........Is 35:10
be ye *g* and rejoice for ever ...Is 65:18
g with her, all ye that love ....Is 66:10
mirth, and the voice of *g*......Jer 7:34
thee: making him very *g* ......Jer 20:15
Sing with *g* for Jacob ....Jer 31:7
joy and *g* is taken from ....Jer 48:33
Because ye were *g*, because ...Jer 50:11
g that thou hast done it ....Lam 1:21
Rejoice and be *g* ....Lam 4:21
king exceeding *g* for him ......Dan 6:23
g from the house of our God ..Joel 1:16
O land; be *g* and rejoice ......Joel 2:21
Jonah was exceeding *g* ....Jon 4:6
they rejoice and are *g* ....Hab 1:15
be *g* and rejoice with all ......Zeph 3:14
shall see it and be *g* ....Zech 10:7
Rejoice and be exceeding *g* ...Matt 5:12
receive it with *g*.............Mark 4:16
things, and heard him *g*.......Mark 6:20
common people heard him *g* ..Mark 12:37
they heard it, they were *g*.....Mark 14:11
shalt have joy and *g* ....Luke 1:14
to shew thee these *g* tidings ...Luke 1:19
g tidings of the kingdom ......Luke 8:1
people *g* received him ....Luke 8:40
they were *g*..covenanted ......Luke 22:5
saw Jesus, he was..*g* ....Luke 23:8
I am *g* for your sakes ....John 11:15
and my tongue was *g* ....Acts 2:26
that *g* received his word ......Acts 2:41
g and singleness of heart ......Acts 2:46
was *g*, and exhorted them .....Acts 11:23
opened not the gate for *g* .....Acts 12:14
declare unto you *g* tidings .....Acts 13:32
heard this, they were *g* ....Acts 13:48
and bring *g* tidings ....Rom 10:15
I am *g* therefore on your.....Rom 16:19
g of the coming of Stephanas ..1Cor 16:17
he then that maketh me *g*.....2Cor 2:2
For ye suffer fools *g* 2Cor 11:19
g therefore will I rather 2Cor 12:9
very *g* spend and be spent 2Cor 12:15
are *g*, when we are weak 2Cor 13:9
in the Lord with all *g*.........Phil 2:29
anointed..with the oil of *g*.....Heb 1:9
Let us be *g* and rejoice ....Rev 19:7

GLASS—*a transparent or translucent substance*

Used literally of:
Crystal ....Job 28:17, 18

Used figuratively of:
Christ's glory............2Cor 3:18
God's nature ....Rev 4:6
New Jerusalem ....Rev 21:18, 21

[*also* GLASSES]
The *g* and the fine linen ......Is 3:23
see through a *g* darkly 1Cor 13:12
his natural face in a *g*.........James 1:23
sea of *g* mingled with fire .....Rev 15:2
sea of *g*, having the harps .....Rev 15:2

GLEAN—*to gather grain left by reapers*
Laws providing for ......Lev 19:9, 10
Illustrated by Ruth ......Ruth 2:2-23
Gideon's reference to ....Judg 8:2

[*also* GLEANED, GLEANING]
shalt thou gather any *g* ....Lev 23:22
shalt not *g* it afterward........Deut 24:21
g of them in the highways .....Judg 20:45
g grapes shall be left in it .....Is 17:6
g grapes when the vintage .....Is 24:13
thoroughtly *g* the remnant.....Jer 6:9
not leave some *g* grapes? .....Jer 49:9

GLEDE—*a bird listed as unclean*
A bird of prey ....Deut 14:12, 13

GLITTER—*sparkling brilliancy*

[*also* GLISTERING, GLITTERING]
if I whet my *g* sword ....Deut 32:41
g stones, and of divers 1Chr 29:2
g sword cometh out of ....Job 20:25
furbished that it may *g*........Ezek 21:10
consume because of the *g* .....Ezek 21:28
sword and the *g* spear ....Nah 3:3
shining of thy *g* spear ....Hab 3:11
raiment was white and *g* ......Luke 9:29

GLOOMINESS—*despondency*
day of darkness and of *g*......Joel 2:2
day of darkness and *g* ....Zeph 1:15

GLORIFICATION OF CHRIST—*visible revelation and fulfillment of his perfection and position as the Son*

Nature of:
Predicted ....Is 55:5
Prayed for ....John 12:28
Not of Himself ....Heb 5:5
Predetermined ....John 17:1

Accomplished by:
Father ....John 13:31, 32
Holy Spirit..............John 16:13, 14
Miracles ....John 11:4
His resurrection ....Acts 3:13
Believers ....Acts 21:20

[*also* GLORIFIED]
synagogues, being *g* of all .....Luke 4:15
Jesus was not yet *g* ....John 7:39
but when Jesus was *g* ....John 12:16
Son of man should be *g*........John 12:23
come to be *g* in his saints 2Thess 1:10

GLORIFY GOD—*to exalt and honor God*

By means of:
Praise ....Ps 50:23
Fruitfulness ....John 15:8
Service 1Pet 4:11
Suffering................1Pet 4:14, 16

Reason for:
Deliverance ....Ps 50:15
Mercy shown............Rom 15:9
Subjection 2Cor 9:13

Extent of:
Universal ....Ps 86:9
In body and soul 1Cor 6:20

[*also* GLORIFIED, GLORIFY]
all the people will be *g* ....Lev 10:3
seed of Jacob, *g* him..........Ps 22:23
g thy name for evermore ......Ps 86:12
Wherefore *g* ye the Lord ......Is 24:15
Jacob..*g* himself in Israel ......Is 44:23
Israel in whom I will be *g*.....Is 49:3
g the house of my glory.......Is 60:7
because he hath *g* thee.......Is 60:9
that he might be *g*...........Is 61:3
Let the Lord be *g*; but he .....Is 66:5
also *g* them, and they shall ....Jer 30:19
I will be *g* in the midst of ....Ezek 28:22
thy ways, hast thou not *g* .....Dan 5:23
I will be *g*, saith the Lord .....Hag 1:8
see your good works, and *g* ...Matt 5:16
marveled, and *g* God ....Matt 9:8
all amazed and *g* God ....Mark 2:12
g and praising God for all .....Luke 2:20
departed to..house, *g* God ....Luke 5:25
all amazed, and they *g* God ...Luke 5:26
g God, saying, That a ....Luke 7:16
followed him, *g* God..........Luke 18:43
Father may be *g* in the Son ...John 14:13
have *g* thee on the earth ......John 17:4
men *g* God for that which.....Acts 4:21
g the word of the Lord ....Acts 13:48
g him not as God ....Rom 1:21
And they *g* God in me........Gal 1:24
have free course and be *g* 2Thess 3:1
g God in..day of visitation 1Pet 2:12
O Lord, and *g* thy name? .....Rev 15:4

GLORY—*splendor; honor; renown; fullness of perfection*

Of temporal things:
Granted by God.........Dan 2:37
Used to entrap ....Matt 4:8
Not to be sought 1Thess 2:6
Quickly passes 1Pet 1:24

Of believers:
Given by God...........John 17:22
Transformed by the Spirit.2Cor 3:18
Through Christ's death ...Heb 2:9, 10
Follows salvation 2Tim 2:10
In suffering ....Rom 5:3
In the cross ....Gal 6:14
Greater than present suffering ....Rom 8:18
Hope of ....Col 1:27
At Christ's advent ....Col 3:4

[*also* GLORIEST, GLORIETH, GLORIFIED, GLORIOUS, GLORIOUSLY, GLORYING]
hath he gotten all this *g*.......Gen 31:1
Lord..hath triumphed *g* ....Ex 15:1
like thee, *g* in holiness ....Ex 15:11
shall see the *g* of the Lord ....Ex 16:7
g of the Lord appeared ....Ex 16:10
brother for *g* and for beauty...Ex 28:2
be sanctified by my *g* ....Ex 29:43
while my *g* passeth by ....Ex 33:22
g of the Lord shall appear ....Lev 9:6
g of the Lord appeared ....Num 14:10
men which have seen my *g*....Num 14:22
g of the Lord appeared ....Num 16:42
God hath showed us his *g*.....Deut 5:24
this *g* and fearful name ....Deut 28:58
g to the Lord God of Israel ...Josh 7:19
them inherit the throne of *g*...1Sam 2:8
g is departed from Israel 1Sam 4:21
g is departed from Israel 1Sam 4:22
give *g* unto the God of Israel..1Sam 6:5
How *g* was the king of Israel ..2Sam 6:20
Declare..*g* among the heathen .1Chr 16:24
G and honor are in his 1Chr 16:27
Lord the *g* due unto..name 1Chr 16:29
g throughout all countries 1Chr 22:5
the power, and the *g* 1Chr 29:11
and praise thy *g* name 1Chr 29:13

G

g of the Lord had filled 2Chr 5:14
g of the Lord had filled 2Chr 7:2
blessed be thy *g* name ....Neh 9:5
the riches of his *g* kingdom....Esth 1:4
Haman told them of the *g* ....Esth 5:11
hath stripped me of my *g* .....Job 19:9
My *g* was fresh in me.........Job 29:20
g of his nostrils is terrible .....Job 39:20
array thyself with *g* and ....Job 40:10
my *g* lifter up of mine ....Ps 3:8
set thy *g* above the heavens ...Ps 8:1
crowned him with *g* and ......Ps 8:5
heavens declare the *g* of God..Ps 19:1
g is great in thy salvation .....Ps 21:5
Who is this king of *g*? ....Ps 24:8
Who is this king of *g*? ....Ps 24:10
he is the King of *g* ....Ps 24:10
the *g* due unto his name ......Ps 29:2
every one speak of his *g* ......Ps 29:9
with thy *g* and thy majesty ....Ps 45:3
daughter is all *g* within........Ps 45:13
g of his house is increased ....Ps 49:16
Awake up, my *g*; awake ......Ps 57:8
In God is my salvation..*g* .....Ps 62:7
To see thy power and..*g* ......Ps 63:2
make his praise *g*.............Ps 66:2
blessed be his *g* name for .....Ps 72:19
earth be filled with his *g* ......Ps 72:19
afterward receive me to *g* .....Ps 73:24
more *g* and excellent ....Ps 76:4
g into the enemy's hand ......Ps 78:61
Lord will give grace and *g* .....Ps 84:11
g may dwell in our land.......Ps 85:9
G things are spoken of thee ...Ps 87:3
the *g* of their strength ....Ps 89:17
hast made his *g* to cease ......Ps 89:44
g unto their children ....Ps 90:16
unto the Lord *g* and strength ..Ps 96:7
the people see his *g* ....Ps 97:6
he shall appear in his *g* ....Ps 102:16
G ye in his holy name ....Ps 105:3
they changed their *g* ....Ps 106:20
give praise, even with my *g* ...Ps 108:1
g above all the earth..........Ps 108:5
work is honorable and *g* ......Ps 111:3
unto thy name give *g* ....Ps 115:1
will speak of the *g* honor .....Ps 145:5
speak of the *g* of..kingdom ....Ps 145:11
g majesty of his kingdom .....Ps 145:12
Let the saints be joyful in *g* ...Ps 149:5
wise shall inherit *g* ....Prov 3:35
hoary head is a crown of *g* ....Prov 16:31
g of children are..fathers ......Prov 17:6
g..pass over a transgression....Prov 19:11
g of young men is..strength ...Prov 20:29
g of God to conceal a thing ...Prov 25:2
search their own *g* is not *g* ....Prov 25:27
rejoice, there is great *g* ....Prov 28:12
for the *g* of his majesty ....Is 2:10
provoke the eyes of his *g* .....Is 3:8
g, and their multitude.........Is 5:14
whole earth is full of his *g* ....Is 6:3
of Assyria, and all his *g*.......Is 8:7
where will ye leave your *g*? ...Is 10:3
and the *g* of his high looks ....Is 10:12
consume the *g* of his forest....Is 10:18
his rest shall be *g*.............Is 11:10
Babylon the *g* of kingdoms ....Is 13:19
nations..all of them, lie in *g* ...Is 14:18
be as the *g* of the children ....Is 17:3
and of Egypt their *g* ....Is 20:5
chariots of thy *g* shall be ......Is 22:18
stain the pride of all *g* ....Is 23:9
even *g* to the righteous ....Is 24:16
before his ancients *g* ....Is 24:23
the nation; thou art *g* ....Is 26:1
g beauty is a fading...........Is 28:1
Lord..be for a crown of *g* .....Is 28:5
But there the *g* Lord ....Is 33:21
g of Lebanon shall be given ...Is 35:2
shall see the *g* of the Lord ....Is 35:2
g of Lord..be revealed ....Is 40:5
g in the Holy One of Israel ...Is 41:16
g will I not give to another ....Is 42:8
them give *g* unto the Lord ....Is 42:12

I have created him for my *g*...Is 43:7
be justified, and shall *g* ....Is 45:25
not give my *g* unto another *g*..Is 48:11
g in the eyes of the Lord .....Is 49:5
g from the rising of the sun ...Is 59:19
g shall be seen upon thee .....Is 60:2
g of Lebanon shall come ......Is 60:13
make the place of my feet *g*...Is 60:13
in their *g* shall ye boast ....Is 61:6
shalt also be a crown of *g*.....Is 62:3
g in his apparel, traveling .....Is 63:1
the abundance of her *g* ....Is 66:11
shall come, and see my *g* .....Is 66:18
neither have seen my *g* ....Is 66:19
declare my *g* among..Gentiles .Is 66:19
people have changed their *g*...Jer 2:11
Let not the wise man *g* ....Jer 9:23
let not the mighty man *g*.......Jer 9:23
let not the rich man *g* ....Jer 9:23
let him that *g* *g* in ....Jer 9:24
for a praise, and for a *g* ......Jer 13:11
Give *g* to the Lord your God..Jer 13:16
even the crown of your *g* .....Jer 13:18
A *g* high throne from ....Jer 17:12
Ah Lord! or, Ah his *g*! ....Jer 22:18
g thou in the valleys ....Jer 49:4
likeness of the *g* of the ....Ezek 1:28
g of the Lord stood there .....Ezek 3:23
g which I saw by the river ....Ezek 3:23
g of the God of Israel was ....Ezek 9:3
g of the Lord went up from ...Ezek 10:4
brightness of the Lord's *g* .....Ezek 10:4
g of the God of Israel was ....Ezek 10:19
g of the Lord went up from ...Ezek 11:23
which is the *g* of all lands .....Ezek 20:15
the *g* of the country ....Ezek 25:9
replenished, and made very *g*..Ezek 27:25
art thou thus like in *g* ....Ezek 31:18
g of the God of Israel ....Ezek 43:2
g of the Lord came into.......Ezek 43:4
g of the Lord filled the ....Ezek 44:4
and majesty, and *g* ....Dan 5:18
given him dominion, and *g* ....Dan 7:14
shall stand in the *g* land.......Dan 11:16
and increase with *g* ....Dan 11:39
enter also into the *g* land .....Dan 11:41
seas in the *g* holy mountain ...Dan 11:45
will I change their *g* ....Hos 4:7
rejoiced on it, for the *g* ....Hos 10:5
Adullam the *g* of Israel ....Mic 1:15
none end of the store and *g*...Nah 2:9
the knowledge of the *g* ....Hab 2:14
art filled with shame for *g*.....Hab 2:16
shameful spewing..on thy *g*.....Hab 2:16
g covered the heavens ....Hab 3:3
saw this house in her first *g*...Hag 2:3
I will fill this house with *g* ....Hag 2:7
g of this latter house..........Hag 2:9
will be the *g* in the midst of...Zech 2:5
he shall bear the *g* ....Zech 6:13
g of the house of David.......Zech 12:7
g of the inhabitants of ....Zech 12:7
give *g* unto my name ....Mal 2:2
world, and the *g* of them .....Matt 4:8
power and the *g*, for ever .....Matt 6:13
come in the *g* of his Father ...Matt 16:27
with power and great *g* ....Matt 24:30
sit upon the throne of his *g* ...Matt 25:31
cometh in the *g* of his Father..Mark 8:38
clouds with..power and *g*......Mark 13:26
g of the Lord shone around ...Luke 2:9
g of thy people Israel ....Luke 2:32
shall come in his own *g* ....Luke 9:26
saw his *g*, and the two men ...Luke 9:32
g things that were done ....Luke 13:17
returned to give *g* to God .....Luke 17:18
cloud with power and great *g*..Luke 21:27
himself seeketh his own *g* .....John 7:18
seeketh his *g* that sent him ....John 7:18
shouldest see the *g* of God? ...John 11:40
they may behold my *g* ....John 17:24
God of *g* appeared unto ......Acts 7:2
see for the *g* of that light .....Acts 22:11
seek for *g* and honor ....Rom 2:7
g, honor, and peace ....Rom 2:10

through my lie unto his *g* .....Rom 3:7
he hath whereof to *g* ....Rom 4:2
strong in faith..*g* to God ......Rom 4:20
rejoice in hope of the *g* of ....Rom 5:2
dead by the *g* of the father....Rom 6:4
may be also *g* together........Rom 8:17
g liberty of the children of ....Rom 8:21
justified, them he also *g* ......Rom 8:30
adoption, and the *g*...........Rom 9:4
known the riches of his *g* .....Rom 9:23
afore prepared unto *g*.........Rom 9:23
to whom be *g* for ever. Amen .Rom 11:36
received us to the *g* of God ..Rom 15:7
To God only wise be *g* ....Rom 16:27
no flesh..*g* in his presence.....1Cor 1:29
g, let him *g* in the Lord 1Cor 1:31
before the world unto our *g*...1Cor 2:7
have crucified the Lord of *g*...1Cor 2:8
let no man *g* in men 1Cor 3:21
Your *g* is not good. Know 1Cor 5:6
man should make my *g* void...1Cor 9:15
I have nothing to *g* of 1Cor 9:16
long hair..is a *g* to her 1Cor 11:15
g of the celestial is one 1Cor 15:40
g of the terrestial is another...1Cor 15:40
one *g* of the sun.............1Cor 15:41
another *g* of the moon 1Cor 15:41
another *g* of the stars 1Cor 15:41
differeth from..star in *g* 1Cor 15:41
it is raised in *g* 1Cor 15:43
unto the *g* of God by us 2Cor 1:20
engraven in stones, was *g* 2Cor 3:7
g of..countenance; which *g* 2Cor 3:7
of condemnation be *g*.........2Cor 3:9
righteousness exceed in *g* 2Cor 3:9
made *g* had no *g* 2Cor 3:10
reason of..*g* that excelleth 2Cor 3:10
which is done away was *g* 2Cor 3:11
that which remaineth is *g* 2Cor 3:11
of the *g* gospel of Christ 2Cor 4:4
eternal weight of *g* 2Cor 4:17
occasion to *g* on our behalf ...2Cor 5:12
which *g* in appearance 2Cor 5:12
great is my *g* of you 2Cor 7:4
and the *g* of Christ 2Cor 8:23
let him *g* in the Lord 2Cor 10:17
g after the flesh, I will *g* 2Cor 11:18
for me doubtless to *g* 2Cor 12:1
Of such an one will I *g* 2Cor 12:5
yet of myself I will not *g*......2Cor 12:5
rather *g* in my infirmities......2Cor 12:9
I am become a fool in *g* 2Cor 12:11
To whom be *g* for ever ....Gal 1:5
may *g* in your flesh...........Gal 6:13
praise of the *g* of his grace ....Eph 1:6
be to the praise of his *g*.......Eph 1:12
unto the praise of his *g* ....Eph 1:14
Father of *g*..give unto you ....Eph 1:17
tribulations for you..*g*.........Eph 3:13
present it to himself a *g*.......Eph 5:27
the *g* and praise of God.......Phil 1:11
to the *g* of God the Father....Phil 2:11
g is in their shame...........Phil 3:19
fashioned like unto his *g* ......Phil 3:21
his riches in *g* by Christ.......Phil 4:19
our Father be *g* for ever ......Phil 4:20
according to his *g* power ......Col 1:11
Nor of men sought we *g* 1Thess 2:16
For ye are our *g* and joy......1Thess 2:20
g gospel of the blessed God ...1Tim 1:11
be honor and *g* for ever.......1Tim 1:17
to whom be *g* for ever 2Tim 4:18
g appearing of the great God ..Titus 2:13
brightness of his *g* ....Heb 1:3
of more *g* than Moses ....Heb 3:3
Christ, the Lord of *g* ....James 2:1
g not, and lie not against .....James 3:14
g at the appearing of 1Pet 1:7
unspeakable and full of *g* 1Pet 1:8
g that should follow 1Pet 1:11
For what *g* is it, if when ye ...1Pet 2:20
be *g* through Jesus Christ 1Pet 4:11
when his *g* shall be revealed...1Pet 4:13
partaker of the *g* that 1Pet 5:1
receive a crown of *g* 1Pet 5:4

called us unto his eternal *g* 1Pet 5:10
g and dominion for ever 1Pet 5:11
called us to *g* and virtue 2Pet 1:3
from..Father honor and *g* 2Pet 1:17
to him from the excellent *g* ...2Pet 1:17
Savior, be *g* and majesty ......Jude 25
to him be *g* and dominion.....Rev 1:6
g and honor and power ....Rev 4:11
Amen: Blessing, and *g*........Rev 7:12
Fear God, and give *g*.........Rev 14:7
earth was lightened with..*g*....Rev 18:1
How much she hath *g* herself..Rev 18:7
g of God did lighten it........Rev 21:23

GLORY OF CHRIST—*his exaltation*

Aspects of:
Manifested to men ......John 2:11
Not selfish ....John 8:50
Given by God...........John 17:22
Crowned with ....Heb 2:9
Ascribed to forever ......Heb 13:21

Stages of:
Before creation..........John 17:5
Revealed in Old Testament ....John 12:41
In His incarnation ....John 1:14
In His transfiguration ....Luke 9:28-36
In His resurrection ......Luke 24:26
In His exaltation 1Tim 3:16
At His return ....Matt 25:31
In heaven...............Rev 5:12

GLORY OF GOD—*manifestation of his nature*

Manifested to:
Moses ....Ex 24:9-17
Stephen ....Acts 7:55

Reflected in:
Christ ....John 1:14
Man....................1Cor 11:7

Appearances of:
The tabernacle ....Ex 40:34
The Temple.............1Kin 8:11
At Jesus' birth ....Luke 2:8-11

The believer's relation to:
Does all for.............1Cor 10:31
Illuminated by 2Cor 4:6
Will stand in presence of .Jude 24

Man's relation to:
Corrupts................Rom 1:23
Falls short of...........Rom 3:23
Refuse to give to God ...Acts 12:23

GLORY OF MAN—*man's dignity and place in the creation*
Prefigured in creation ....Heb 2:6-8
Lost by sin..............Rom 3:23
Soon passes away........1Pet 1:24
Removed by death ......Ps 49:17
Restored by Christ 2Cor 5:17

GLUTTONY—*excessive appetite and eating*
Sternly forbidden ....Prov 23:1-3
Characteristic of the wicked ....Phil 3:19
Leads to poverty ....Prov 23:21
Christ accused of ....Matt 11:19

[*also* GLUTTON, GLUTTONOUS]
he is a *g*, and a drunkard .....Deut 21:20
g man, and a winebibber......Luke 7:34

GNASH—*to grind together*

[*also* GNASHED, GNASHETH, GNASHING]
g upon me with his teeth......Job 16:9
g upon me with their teeth ....Ps 35:16
g upon him with his teeth .....Ps 37:12
he shall *g* with his teeth.......Ps 112:10
hiss and *g* the teeth...........Lam 2:16
be weeping and *g* of teeth.....Matt 8:12
be wailing and *g* of teeth......Matt 13:42
be weeping and *g* of teeth.....Matt 22:13
be weeping and *g* of teeth.....Matt 24:51
be weeping and *g* of teeth.....Matt 25:30
and *g* with his teeth ....Mark 9:18
be weeping and *g* of teeth.....Luke 13:28
g on him with their teeth .....Acts 7:54

GNAT—*small flying insect*
Third plague on Egypt, produced from dust....Ex 8:16-18
Used as illustration ......Matt 23:24

GNAW—*to chew on*

[*also* GNAWED]
g not the bones till ....Zeph 3:3
g their tongues for pain ....Rev 16:10

GNOSTICISM—*a heresy confronted by the church in the first two centuries in which the key to salvation was believed to be the possession of secret knowledge that would unite the soul with God*
Warned against..........Col 2:8, 18
Arrogant 1Cor 8:1
False 1Tim 6:20
Surpassed by Christ......Eph 3:19

GO—See INTRODUCTION

GOAD—*a pointed rod*
Used as a weapon ....Judg 3:31
Figurative of pointed morals...............Eccl 12:11
Figurative of conscience ..Acts 26:14
Sharpened by files 1Sam 13:21

GOALS, SPIRITUAL—*the ends toward which Christians strive*
Provide motivation ......Phil 3:12-14
Promise reward 1Cor 9:24, 25

GOAT—*a domesticated animal*

Literal uses of:
Clothing ....Num 31:20
Heb 11:37
Milk of, food ....Prov 27:27
Curtains ....Ex 26:7
Bottles ....Josh 9:4
Sacrifices ....Ex 12:5

Figurative uses of:
Great leaders ....Jer 50:8
Kingdom of Greece......Dan 8:5, 21
Wicked ....Matt 25:32, 33

[*also* GOATS, GOATS']
she *g* of three years old.......Gen 15:9
two good kids of the *g*........Gen 27:9
speckled among the *g*.........Gen 30:32
removed that day the he *g* ....Gen 30:35
she *g* that were speckled ......Gen 30:35
Two hundred she *g*, and ......Gen 32:14
and twenty he *g*, two ....Gen 32:14
fine linen, and *g* hair ....Ex 35:6
made curtains of *g* hair ....Ex 36:14
of the sheep, or of the *g*......Lev 1:10
if his offering be a *g*..........Lev 3:12
a lamb or a kid of the *g*.......Lev 5:6
of ox, or of sheep, or of *g* ....Lev 7:23
Moses diligently sought..*g*.....Lev 10:16
g for a sin offering ....Lev 16:5
cast lots upon the two *g*........Lev 16:8
g on which the lot fell ....Lev 16:10
of the blood of the *g* ....Lev 16:18
the head of the live *g*.........Lev 16:21
upon the head of the *g*........Lev 16:21
g shall bear upon him all......Lev 16:22
go the *g* in the wilderness .....Lev 16:22
g for the sin offering..........Lev 16:27
bullock, or a sheep, or a *g* ....Lev 22:27
kid of the *g*..a sin offering ....Lev 23:19
g for a sin offering ....Num 7:16
five rams, five he *g*, five ......Num 7:17
five he *g*, five lambs ....Num 7:23
g for a sin offering ....Num 7:82
the *g* for sin offering..........Num 7:87
g for a sin offering ....Num 15:24
he shall bring a she *g*.........Num 15:27
one *g* for a sin offering ....Num 28:22
one kid of the *g*, to make .....Num 28:30
the *g* for a sin offering........Num 29:11
ox, the sheep and the *g*.......Deut 14:4
breed of Bashan and *g*.........Deut 32:14
pillow of *g* hair for his bolster .1Sam 19:13
upon the rocks of the wild *g* ..1Sam 24:2
and seven hundred he *g*.......2Chr 17:11
brought forth the he *g* 2Chr 29:23
all Israel, twelve he *g*.........Ezra 6:17
wild *g* of the rock bring.......Job 39:1
nor he *g* out of thy folds ......Ps 50:9
I will offer bullocks with *g* ....Ps 66:15
g are the price of the field ....Prov 27:26
greyhound; a he *g* also........Prov 30:31
thy hair is as a flock of *g* .....Song 4:1
blood of bullocks..of he *g*......Is 1:11
slaughter like rams with he *g*..Jer 51:40
lambs and rams, and *g*........Ezek 27:21
of rams, of lambs, and of *g* ...Ezek 39:18
day a *g* for a sin offering......Ezek 43:25
a kid of the *g* daily for a sin ..Ezek 45:23
he *g* came from the west ......Dan 8:5
g had a notable horn ....Dan 8:5
rough *g* is the king of Grecia ..Dan 8:21
I punished the *g*; for the ......Zech 10:3
Neither by the blood of *g* .....Heb 9:12
blood of calves and of *g* ......Heb 9:19

GOATH (gō'ăth)—*"constancy"*
Place near Jerusalem ....Jer 31:39

GOATSKINS—*the skins of goats*
about in sheepskins and *g*.....Heb 11:37

GOB (gŏb)—*"cistern"*
Plain where Hebrews and Philistines fought 2Sam 21:18, 19
Also called Gezer 1Chr 20:4

GOBLET—*a bowl or basin*
Used as a comparison....Song 7:2
Same word translated "basins" and "cups" . { Ex 24:6; Is 22:24 }

GOD—*the Being perfect in power, wisdom, and goodness; the Creator and Ruler of the universe*

Names of:
God....................Gen 1:1
Lord God...............Gen 2:4
Most high God..........Gen 14:18-22
Lord God...............Gen 15:2, 8
Almighty God...........Gen 17:1
Everlasting God ....Gen 21:33
God Almighty...........Gen 28:3
I Am...................Ex 3:14
Jehovah ....Ex 6:3
Jealous ....Ex 34:14
Eternal God ....Deut 33:27
Living God ....Josh 3:10
God of hosts ....Ps 80:7
Lord of hosts ....Is 1:24
Holy One of Israel ......Is 43:3, 14, 15
Mighty God.............Jer 32:18
God of heaven ....Jon 1:9
Heavenly Father.........Matt 6:26
King eternal 1Tim 1:17
Only Potentate 1Tim 6:15
Father of lights..........James 1:17

Manifestations of:
Face of ....Gen 32:30
Voice of ....Deut 5:22-26
Glory of ....Ex 40:34, 35
Angel of................Gen 16:7-13
Name of................Ex 34:5-7
Form of ....Num 12:6-8
Comes from Teman .....Hab 3:3

Nature of:
Spirit...................John 4:24
One....................Deut 6:4
Personal................John 17:1-3
Trinitarian 2Cor 13:14
Omnipotent ....Rev 19:6

Natural attributes of:
Incomparable 2Sam 7:22
Invisible ....John 1:18
Inscrutable.............Is 40:28
Unchangeable...........Num 23:19
Unequaled..............Is 40:13-25
Unsearchable ....Rom 11:33, 34
Infinite 1Kin 8:27
Eternal ....Is 57:15
Omnipotence............Jer 32:17, 27
(All-powerful)

Omnipresence ....Ps 139:7-12
(Ever-present)
Omniscience 1John 3:20
(All-knowing)
Foreknowledge ....Is 48:3, 5
Wise ....Acts 15:18

Moral attributes of:

Hatred ....Ps 5:5, 6
Holiness ....Rev 4:8
Impartiality 1Pet 1:17
Justice ....Ps 89:14
Long-suffering...........Ex 34:6, 7
Love 1John 4:8, 16
Mercy ....Lam 3:22, 23
Truth....................Ps 117:2
Vengeance ....Deut 32:34-41
Wrath ....Deut 32:22

Human expressions applied to:

Fear....................Deut 32:26, 27
Grief ....Gen 6:6
Repentance ....Gen 6:7
Jealousy ....Ex 34:14
Swearing................Jer 44:26
Laughing ....Ps 2:4
Sleeping ....Ps 78:65
Human parts ....Ex 33:21-23

Titles given to:

Creator ....Is 40:12, 22, 26
Judge ....Ps 96:10, 13
King ....Ps 47:2, 7, 8
Defender ....Ps 18:35
Preserver ....Ps 121:3-8
Shepherd ....Gen 49:24

Works of, described as:

Terrible ....Ps 66:3
Incomparable ....Ps 86:8
Great ....Ps 92:5
Manifold................Ps 104:24
Marvelous ....Ps 139:14

Ways of, described as:

Perfect ....Ps 18:30
Knowledgeable ....Ps 86:11
Made known ....Ps 103:7
Righteous...............Ps 145:17
Not like man's ....Is 55:8, 9
Everlasting.............Hab 3:6
Inscrutable ....Rom 11:33
Just and true ....Rev 15:3

See GOODNESS OF GOD; LOVE OF GOD; POWER OF GOD

[*also* GOD'S, GODS]

G created the heaven ....Gen 1:1
G called the dry land Earth ...Gen 1:10
G saw that it was good........Gen 1:18
G created great whales, and ...Gen 1:21
G said, Behold, I have given ..Gen 1:29
Lord *G* took the man, and put .Gen 2:15
the voice of the Lord *G*.......Gen 3:8
day that *G* created man ....Gen 5:1
Enoch walked with *G*.........Gen 5:24
he was not; for *G* took him ...Gen 5:24
G looked upon the earth ......Gen 6:12
G spake unto Noah, and to ...Gen 9:8
Abram said, Lord *G*, what ....Gen 15:2
G said, Sarah thy wife shall ...Gen 17:19
which *G* had spoken to him ...Gen 21:2
swear unto me here by *G* .....Gen 21:23
the Lord *G* of my master .....Gen 24:27
I am the Lord *G* of Abraham. .Gen 28:13
G hath taken away my ....Gen 30:23
G hath seen mine affliction ....Gen 31:42
This is *G* host: and he ....Gen 32:2
I had seen the face of *G* ......Gen 33:10
I am *G* Almighty ....Gen 35:11
in whom the spirit of *G* is? ....Gen 41:38
G hath found out the iniquity..Gen 44:16
G Almighty appeared unto me .Gen 48:3
am I in the place of *G*? ....Gen 50:19
G looked upon the children ....Ex 2:25
Moses said unto *G*, Behold ....Ex 3:13
sacrifice to the Lord our *G* ....Ex 3:18
Egyptians to the Lord our *G* ..Ex 8:26
sacrifice unto the Lord our *G*..Ex 10:25
Would to *G* we had died by ...Ex 16:3
G shall be with thee ....Ex 18:19
a jealous *G*, visiting the ....Ex 20:5
house of the Lord thy *G* ......Ex 23:19
besought the Lord his *G* ......Ex 32:11
house of the Lord thy *G* ......Ex 34:26
I am the Lord your *G* ....Lev 18:30
your *G*, which brought you ....Lev 19:36
anointing oil of his *G* is ....Lev 21:12
Egypt: I am the Lord your *G*..Lev 23:43
and will be your *G* ....Lev 26:12
Heal her now, O *G*, I beseech .Num 12:13
Would *G* that we had died ....Num 20:3
G anger was kindled ....Num 22:22
G is not a man, that he ....Num 23:19
was zealous for his *G* ....Num 25:13
Lord your *G* which goeth ......Deut 1:30
Lord our *G* delivered all ......Deut 2:36
Lord thy *G* hath destroyed ....Deut 4:3
thy *G* is a consuming fire .....Deut 4:24
hath *G* assayed to go and .....Deut 4:34
thy *G* hath commanded ....Deut 5:12
all that the Lord our *G* ....Deut 5:27
shalt love the Lord thy *G* .....Deut 6:5
thy *G* shall deliver them ......Deut 7:2
Lord thy *G* will send the ......Deut 7:20
bless the Lord thy *G* for ......Deut 8:10
provokedst the Lord thy *G* ....Deut 9:7
your *G* is *G* of *g*.............Deut 10:17
your *G* shall lay the fear ......Deut 11:25
the Lord your *G* giveth ....Deut 12:10
the altar of the Lord thy *G*....Deut 12:27
the Lord thy *G* hath given ....Deut 13:12
Lord thy *G* hath blessed ......Deut 14:24
Lord thy *G* redeemed thee ....Deut 15:15
Lord thy *G* shall choose.......Deut 16:7
blessing of the Lord thy *G* ....Deut 16:17
the Lord thy *G* giveth.........Deut 17:14
desiredst of the Lord thy *G* ...Deut 18:16
Lord thy *G* is with thee ....Deut 20:1
hanged is accursed of *G*.......Deut 21:23
vow unto the Lord thy *G* .....Deut 23:21
thy *G* hath given thee rest.....Deut 25:19
worship..the Lord thy *G* ......Deut 26:10
altar unto the Lord thy *G* .....Deut 27:5
the Lord thy *G* giveth.........Deut 28:8
Would *G* it were even! ....Deut 28:67
belong unto the Lord our *G* ...Deut 29:29
voice of the Lord thy *G*.......Deut 30:10
to fear the Lord your *G*.......Deut 31:13
Moses the man of *G* ....Deut 33:1
words of the Lord your *G*.....Josh 3:9
Lord *G* of Israel fought ....Josh 10:42
Lord your *G* hath given ....Josh 22:4
Lord your *G* hath done ....Josh 23:3
Lord your *G* promised you ....Josh 23:15
unto the Lord *G* of Israel .....Josh 24:23
sing praise to the Lord *G* .....Judg 5:3
G did so that night: for it .....Judg 6:40
would to *G* this people were...Judg 9:29
A man of *G* came unto me....Judg 13:6
O Lord *G*, remember me, I ...Judg 16:28
came unto the house of *G*......Judg 20:26
Lord is a *G* of knowledge 1Sam 2:3
trembled for the ark of *G* 1Sam 4:13
Let the ark of the *G* of 1Sam 5:8
cry unto the Lord our *G* 1Sam 7:8
G gave him another heart 1Sam 10:9
G forbid that I should sin 1Sam 12:23
wrought with *G* this day 1Sam 14:45
there is a *G* in Israel..........1Sam 17:46
Then said David, O Lord *G* ...1Sam 23:10
as an angel of *G*.............1Sam 29:9
his hand to the ark of *G* 2Sam 6:6
thou art great, O Lord *G* 2Sam 7:22
show the kindness of *G* unto ..2Sam 9:3
wisdom of an angel of *G*......2Sam 14:20
G do so to me, and more also .2Sam 19:13
who is *G*, save the Lord? 2Sam 22:32
offerings unto the Lord my *G*. .2Sam 24:24
G do so to me, and more also .1Kin 2:23
Blessed be the Lord *G* of 1Kin 8:15
unto the Lord our *G* day 1Kin 8:59
the Lord, the *G* of Israel 1Kin 11:31
the man of *G* besought the 1Kin 13:6
carcase of the man of *G*.......1Kin 13:29
As the Lord thy *G* liveth......1Kin 17:12
if the Lord be *G*, follow him ..1Kin 18:21
he is not *G* of the valleys 1Kin 20:28
man of *G*, then let fire........2Kin 1:10
on the bed of the man of *G* ...2Kin 4:21
Am I *G*, to kill and to make ..2Kin 5:7
servant of the man of *G*.......2Kin 6:15
and the man of *G* wept 2Kin 8:11
manner of the *G* of the land...2Kin 17:26
thou art the *G*, even thou 2Kin 19:15
Lord, the *G* of David thy 2Kin 20:5
for they cried to *G* in the 1Chr 5:20
about the house of *G* 1Chr 9:27
carried the ark of *G* in a new..1Chr 13:7
did as *G* commanded 1Chr 14:16
they brought the ark of *G*.....1Chr 16:1
Who am I, O Lord *G*.........1Chr 17:16
for the cities of our *G* 1Chr 19:13
name of the Lord my *G*.......1Chr 22:7
governors of the house of *G*...1Chr 24:5
the Lord *G* of Israel chose 1Chr 28:4
might for the house of my *G* ..1Chr 29:2
blessed the Lord *G* of their....1Chr 29:20
for great is our *G* above all ...2Chr 2:5
O Lord *G* of Israel 2Chr 6:16
David the man of *G* 2Chr 8:14
charge of the Lord our *G* 2Chr 13:11
O Lord our *G*; for we rest 2Chr 14:11
relied on the Lord thy *G*......2Chr 16:7
O Lord *G* of our fathers 2Chr 20:6
battle is not yours, but *G* 2Chr 20:15
was hid in the house of *G*.....2Chr 22:12
spirit of *G* came upon.........2Chr 24:20
not hear; for it came of *G*.....2Chr 25:20
forsaken the Lord *G* of their ..2Chr 28:6
G had prepared the people 2Chr 29:36
Lord *G* of his fathers 2Chr 30:19
G should be able to deliver....2Chr 32:14
the house of *G*, of which *G* ...2Chr 33:7
the house of the Lord his *G*...2Chr 34:8
the sight of the Lord his *G* 2Chr 36:12
freely for the house of *G*......Ezra 2:68
servants of the *G* of heaven ...Ezra 5:11
unto the *G* of heaven ....Ezra 6:10
for the house of their *G*.......Ezra 7:16
by the good hand of our *G*....Ezra 8:18
my face to thee, my *G* ....Ezra 9:6
fierce wrath of our *G* for......Ezra 10:14
because of the fear of *G* ......Neh 5:15
worshiped the Lord their *G* ...Neh 9:3
to walk in *G* law, which.......Neh 10:29
bring to the house of our *G* ...Neh 10:36
our *G* turned the curse........Neh 13:2
feared *G*, and eschewed evil...Job 1:1
I would seek unto *G*..........Job 5:8
by searching find out *G*? ......Job 11:7
him that knoweth not *G* ......Job 18:21
sayest, How doth *G* know? ....Job 22:13
G understandeth the way......Job 28:23
to thy wish in *G* stead ....Job 33:6
G hath taken away my ....Job 34:5
G will not do wickedly ....Job 34:12
yet to speak on *G* behalf......Job 36:2
know when *G* disposed them ..Job 37:15
O Lord my *G*, if I have done..Ps 7:3
in his heart, There is no *G* ....Ps 14:1
who is *G* save the Lord? ......Ps 18:31
who is a rock save our *G* .....Ps 18:31
G of Jacob defend thee ....Ps 20:1
My *G*, my *G*, why hast thou...Ps 22:1
I said, Thou art my *G* ....Ps 31:14
My soul thirsteth for *G* ....Ps 42:2
for the living *G*: when shall ...Ps 42:2
unto *G* my exceeding joy......Ps 43:4
G is in the midst of her ....Ps 46:5
know that I am *G*: I will be ...Ps 46:10
in the city of our *G*...........Ps 48:8
show the salvation of *G* ....Ps 50:23
in his heart, There is no *G* ....Ps 53:1
have not called upon *G* ....Ps 53:4
In *G* I will praise his word ....Ps 56:4
in *G* I have put my trust ......Ps 56:4
he is a *G* that judgeth in ......Ps 58:11
Hear my cry, O *G*; attend.....Ps 61:1

shall declare the work of G....Ps 64:9
G shall bless us; and all.......Ps 67:7
G might dwell among them....Ps 68:18
Save me, O G; for the waters..Ps 69:1
G hath forsaken him..........Ps 71:11
put my trust in the Lord G....Ps 73:28
Hath G forgotten to be ....Ps 77:9
inquired early after G.........Ps 78:34
joyful noise unto the G of.....Ps 81:1
doorkeeper..house of my G ...Ps 84:10
to everlasting, thou art G .....Ps 90:2
For the Lord is a great G .....Ps 95:3
Know..that the Lord he is G ..Ps 100:3
Hold not thy peace, O G .....Ps 109:1
unto the G of g: for his ....Ps 136:2
people, whose G is the Lord ..Ps 144:15
Happy is he that hath the G...Ps 146:5
hope is in the Lord his G .....Ps 146:5
Every word of G is pure ......Prov 30:5
G giveth to a man that is .....Eccl 2:26
utter any thing before G ......Eccl 5:2
G hath made man upright .....Eccl 7:29
poor? saith the Lord G ....Is 3:15
Behold, G is my salvation .....Is 12:2
day, Lo, this our G...........Is 25:9
sent to reproach the living G ..Is 37:4
G will come with strong.......Is 40:10
beside me there is no G.......Is 44:6
there is no G else beside me ..Is 45:21
the Lord G will help me ......Is 50:7
Lord G which gathereth.......Is 56:8
spirit of the Lord G is upon ...Is 61:1
forsaken the Lord thy G ......Jer 2:19
now fear the Lord our G......Jer 5:24
thou he, O Lord our G? ......Jer 14:22
of hosts, the G of Israel.......Jer 25:27
Zion unto the Lord our G.....Jer 31:6
G of Israel; Behold, I will.....Jer 35:17
the voice of the Lord our G...Jer 42:6
the G of Israel; Wherefore ....Jer 44:7
As G overthrew Sodom ....Jer 50:40
the word of the Lord G ....Ezek 6:3
and said, Ah Lord G!.........Ezek 11:13
you, saith the Lord G.........Ezek 13:8
Lord G; How much more .....Ezek 14:21
Lord G; A great eagle ....Ezek 17:3
I am the Lord your G; walk...Ezek 20:19
saith the Lord G; Remove ....Ezek 21:26
saith the Lord G; Behold .....Ezek 24:21
saith the Lord G to Tyrus .....Ezek 26:15
Eden the garden of G.........Ezek 28:13
Lord G; I will also make ......Ezek 30:10
As I live, saith the Lord G ....Ezek 33:11
saith the Lord G; Behold .....Ezek 35:3
and I will be your G..........Ezek 36:28
saith the Lord G; Art thou ....Ezek 38:17
glory of the G of Israel came ..Ezek 43:2
saith the Lord G; If the ....Ezek 46:16
G of heaven set up a ....Dan 2:44
the most high G ruled ....Dan 5:21
prayed unto the Lord my G ...Dan 9:4
against the G of g ....Dan 11:36
knowledge of G more than ....Hos 6:6
for I am G, and not man......Hos 11:9
turn unto the Lord your G ....Joel 2:13
as G overthrew Sodom and....Amos 4:11
Lord G called to contend by...Amos 7:4
upon thy G, if so be that G ...Jon 1:6
for there is no answer of G....Mic 3:7
walk humbly with thy G? .....Mic 6:8
G, thou hast established.......Hab 1:12
we have heard that G is with ..Zech 8:23
Will a man rob G? Yet ye ....Mal 3:8
interpreted is, G with us ......Matt 1:23
heaven; for it is G throne .....Matt 5:34
Jesus, thou Son of G? art .....Matt 8:29
but one, that is, G............Matt 19:17
shalt love the Lord thy G .....Matt 22:37
glorified G, saying, We ....Mark 2:12
G made them male and female.Mark 10:6
G the things that are G ....Mark 12:17
for there is one G ....Mark 12:32
G nothing..shall be impossible..Luke 1:37
G is able of these stones .....Luke 3:8
all night in prayer to G ....Luke 6:12
said, The Christ of G ....Luke 9:20
shalt love the Lord thy G .....Luke 10:27
what is the kingdom of G .....Luke 13:18
feared not G, neither ....Luke 18:2
kingdom of G sake ....Luke 18:29
they said, G forbid ....Luke 20:16
Art thou then the Son of G? ..Luke 22:70
G, and the Word was G.......John 1:1
G so loved the world, that ....John 3:16
for him hath G the Father.....John 6:27
have one Father, even G......John 8:41
of G heareth G words.........John 8:47
works of G should be made ...John 9:3
thou wilt ask of G, G will .....John 11:22
ye believe in G, believe ....John 14:1
and to my G, and your G .....John 20:17
the Lord our G shall call......Acts 2:39
all men glorified G for that....Acts 4:21
ought to obey G rather ....Acts 5:29
I am the G of thy fathers .....Acts 7:32
saw the glory of G, and ....Acts 7:55
on the right hand of G........Acts 7:55
feared G with all his house ....Acts 10:2
Him G raised up the third.....Acts 10:40
preached the word of G.......Acts 13:5
into the kingdom of G ....Acts 14:22
To The Unknown G ....Acts 17:23
G wrought special miracles ....Acts 19:11
Revilest thou G high priest? ...Acts 23:4
have hope toward G, which ...Acts 24:15
he thanked G, and took.......Acts 28:15
G hath showed it unto ....Rom 1:19
respect of persons with G .....Rom 2:11
truth of G hath more ....Rom 3:7
even G, who quickeneth ......Rom 4:17
love of G is shed abroad ......Rom 5:5
G forbid. How shall we ....Rom 6:2
G sending his own Son in .....Rom 8:3
are led by the Spirit of G .....Rom 8:14
they are the sons of G ....Rom 8:14
G elect? It is G that ....Rom 8:33
G according to election ....Rom 9:11
maketh intercession to G......Rom 11:2
there is no power but of G ....Rom 13:1
they are G ministers ....Rom 13:6
give account of himself to G..Rom 14:12
your prayers to G for me .....Rom 15:30
that in the wisdom of G.......1Cor 1:21
But G hath revealed them 1Cor 2:10
ye are G husbandry...........1Cor 3:9
ye are G building.............1Cor 3:9
for the temple of G is holy 1Cor 3:17
therefore glorify G in your 1Cor 6:20
in your spirit, which are G 1Cor 6:20
there is but one G, the........1Cor 8:6
speaking by the Spirit of G 1Cor 12:3
found false witnesses of G.....1Cor 15:15
Blessed be G, even the 2Cor 1:3
the G of all comfort 2Cor 1:3
our sufficiency is of G 2Cor 3:5
we have a building of G.......2Cor 5:1
G did beseech you by us 2Cor 5:20
G loveth a cheerful giver 2Cor 9:7
I cannot tell: G knoweth 2Cor 12:3
before G, I lie not...........Gal 1:20
are all the children of G .....Gal 3:26
G is not mocked.............Gal 6:7
gift of the grace of G given....Eph 3:7
another in the fear of G.......Eph 5:21
G which worketh in you ......Phil 2:13
peace, from G our Father .....Col 1:2
let the peace of G rule in .....Col 3:15
not as pleasing men, but G 1Thess 2:4
in holiness before G, even.....1Thess 3:13
We are bound to thank G.....2Thess 1:3
into the love of G, and 2Thess 3:5
one mediator between G 1Tim 2:5
but in the living G, who.......1Tim 6:17
I pray G that it may not 2Tim 4:16
faith of G elect..............Titus 1:1
appearing of the great G ......Titus 2:13
G, even thy G, hath ....Heb 1:9
the word of G is quick ....Heb 4:12
priest of the most high G .....Heb 7:1
the hands of the living G......Heb 10:31
ashamed to be called their G ..Heb 11:16
our G is a consuming fire .....Heb 12:29
believest that there is one G...James 2:19
by the word of G, which 1Pet 1:23
long-suffering of G waited 1Pet 3:20
lords over G heritage 1Pet 5:3
the mighty hand of G.........1Pet 5:6
that G is light, and in 1John 1:5
born of G..not commit sin.....1John 3:9
because he is born of G......1John 3:9
children of G are manifest.....1John 3:10
righteousness is not of G 1John 3:10
G sent his only begotten 1John 4:9
Jesus is the Christ..of G.......1John 5:1
G hath given to us eternal.....1John 5:11
denying the only Lord G ......Jude 4
beginning of the creation of G .Rev 3:14
G shall wipe away all tears ....Rev 7:17
hath a place prepared of G....Rev 12:6
full of the wrath of G.........Rev 15:7
worshiped G that sat on the ...Rev 19:4
G shall wipe away all tears ....Rev 21:4
G shall take away his part.....Rev 22:19

GODDESS—*a female deity*
g of the Zidonians............1Kin 11:33
temple of the great g Diana ...Acts 19:27
blasphemers of your g ....Acts 19:37

GODHEAD—*the Trinity; emphasizes the unity of the three persons*
Revealed to mankind ....Rom 1:20
Corrupted by mankind ...Acts 17:29
Incarnated in Jesus Christ.Col 2:9

eternal power and G..........Rom 1:20

GODLINESS—*holy living*
Profitable 1Tim 4:7, 8
Perverted 1Tim 6:5
Pursuit 1Tim 6:11
Duty ....Titus 2:12
See HOLINESS OF CHRISTIANS

[*also* GODLY]
him that is g for himself ......Ps 4:3
every one that is g pray.......Ps 32:6
might seek a g seed ....Mal 2:15
simplicity and g sincerity 2Cor 1:12
g sorrow worketh repentance ..2Cor 7:10
over you with g jealousy 2Cor 11:2
rather than g edifying 1Tim 1:4
life in all g and honesty 1Tim 2:2
women professing g...........1Tim 2:10
great is the mystery of g 1Tim 3:16
doctrine..according to g 1Tim 6:3
g with contentment is..gain 1Tim 6:6
Having a form of g 2Tim 3:5
will live g in Christ Jesus......2Tim 3:12
truth which is after g ....Titus 1:1
soberly, righteously, and g ....Titus 2:12
with reverence and g fear .....Heb 12:28
pertain unto life and g 2Pet 1:3
patience; and to patience g....2Pet 1:6
g brotherly kindness 2Pet 1:7
how to deliver the g out 2Pet 2:9
journey after a g sort 3John 6

GODS, FALSE—*the gods of the people around Israel; gods which are not the one true God*
Names of:
Adrammelech (Syria) 2Kin 17:31
Anammelech (Babylon) ..2Kin 17:31
Ashtoreth (Canaan) 1Kin 11:5
Baal (Canaan) 1Kin 18:19
Baal-peor (Moab) ....Num 25:1-9
Beelzebub (Philistine)....Luke 11:19-23
Bel (Babylon)...........Jer 51:44
Calf worship (Egypt) ....Ex 32:1-6
Chemosh (Moab).........1Kin 11:7
Dagon (Philistine) 1Sam 5:1-7
Diana (Greek) ....Acts 19:35
Jupiter (Roman).........Acts 14:12, 13
Milcom (Ammon) 1Kin 11:5
Molech (Ammon) 1Kin 11:7
Nebo (Babylon) ....Is 46:1
Nisroch (Assyria)........2Kin 19:37

Rimmon (Syria) 2Kin 5:18
Tammuz (Babylon) ......Ezek 8:14

Evils connected with:
Immorality ....Num 25:1-9
Prostitution 2Kin 23:7
Divination ....Lev 20:1-6
Sacrilege ....Dan 5:4
Pride 2Kin 18:28-35
Persecution 1Kin 19:1-3
Child sacrifice ....Jer 7:29-34

be as *g* knowing good.........Gen 3:5
whomsoever..findest thy *g*.....Gen 31:32
unto Jacob all the strange *g*...Gen 35:4
the *g* of Egypt I will execute ..Ex 12:12
Lord is greater than all *g* .....Ex 18:11
make with me *g* of silver ......Ex 20:23
make unto you *g* of gold ......Ex 20:23
the name of other *g* ....Ex 23:13
with them, nor with their *g*....Ex 23:32
be thy *g*, O Israel ....Ex 32:8
have made them *g* of gold ....Ex 32:31
go a whoring after their *g* .....Ex 34:15
sacrifice unto their *g* ....Ex 34:15
go a whoring after their *g* .....Ex 34:16
make to yourselves molten *g* ..Lev 19:4
there ye shall serve *g* ....Deut 4:28
shall not go after other *g*......Deut 6:14
g of the people..are round ....Deut 6:14
neither shalt thou serve..*g*.....Deut 7:16
walk after other *g* ....Deut 8:19
is God of *g*, and Lord of......Deut 10:17
serve other *g*, and worship ....Deut 11:16
to go after other *g*, which .....Deut 11:28
down the graven images of..*g*..Deut 12:3
inquire not after their *g* ....Deut 12:30
these nations serve their *g*?....Deut 12:30
have they done unto their *g*...Deut 12:31
burnt in the fire to their *g* ....Deut 12:31
go and serve other *g*..........Deut 13:6
go and serve other *g*..........Deut 13:13
gone and served other *g* ......Deut 17:3
speak in the name of other *g*..Deut 18:20
go after other *g* to serve ......Deut 28:14
thou shalt serve other *g*.......Deut 28:64
went and served other *g* ......Deut 29:26
away, and worship other *g* ....Deut 30:17
turned unto other *g*...........Deut 31:18
jealousy with strange *g*........Deut 32:16
to *g* whom they know not .....Deut 32:17
to new *g* that came newly up ..Deut 32:17
God of *g*, the Lord God of *g*..Josh 22:22
gone and served other *g* ......Josh 23:16
put away the *g* which your ....Josh 24:14
whether the *g* which your .....Josh 24:15
the *g* of the Amorites.........Josh 24:15
the Lord, to serve other *g*.....Josh 24:16
serve strange *g*, then he.......Josh 24:20
g shall be a snare unto you....Judg 2:3
went a whoring after other *g* ..Judg 2:17
sons, and served their *g*.......Judg 3:6
fear not the *g* of the Amorites .Judg 6:10
g of Syria and..*g* of Zidon ....Judg 10:6
g of Moab and the *g*..........Judg 10:6
the *g* of the Philistines ....Judg 10:6
g which ye have chosen ....Judg 10:14
Micah had an house of *g*......Judg 17:5
her people, and unto her *g*....Ruth 1:15
off you, and from off your *g* ..1Sam 6:5
forsaken me, and served..*g*....1Sam 8:8
Go, serve other *g* 1Sam 26:19
from the nations and their *g*...2Sam 7:23
go and serve other *g*..........1Kin 9:6
away your heart after..*g* 1Kin 11:2
sacrificed unto their *g*.........1Kin 11:8
behold thy *g*, O Israel 1Kin 12:28
call ye on the name of your *g* .1Kin 18:24
Their *g* are *g* of the hills 1Kin 20:23
sacrifice unto other *g* 2Kin 5:17
every nation made *g* of their ..2Kin 17:29
served their own *g*, after 2Kin 17:33
Ye shall not fear other *g*.......2Kin 17:35
ye shall not fear other *g* 2Kin 17:37
g of the nations delivered 2Kin 19:12
cast their *g* into the fire 2Kin 19:18
for they were no *g* 2Kin 19:18
whoring after the *g* 1Chr 5:25
when they had left their *g*.....1Chr 14:12
g of the people are idols 1Chr 16:26
great is our God above all *g*...2Chr 2:5
laid hold on other *g* 2Chr 7:22
priest of them that are no *g* ...2Chr 13:9
brought..*g* of the children 2Chr 25:14
set them up to be his *g* 2Chr 25:14
sought after the *g* of Edom....2Chr 25:20
unto the *g* of Damascus 2Chr 28:23
g of the kings of Syria 2Chr 28:23
were the *g* of the nations 2Chr 32:13
g of the nations of other 2Chr 32:17
took away the strange *g*.......2Chr 33:15
them in the house of his *g* ....Ezra 1:7
he judgeth among the *g*.......Ps 82:1
is to be feared above all *g* ....Ps 96:4
worship him, all ye *g* ....Ps 97:7
that our Lord is above all *g* ...Ps 135:5
before the *g* will I sing praise..Ps 138:1
images of her *g*..hath broken ..Is 21:9
Where are the *g* of Hamath ...Is 36:19
are the *g* of Sepharvaim? .....Is 36:19
g of the nations delivered .....Is 37:12
cast their *g* into the fire ....Is 37:19
for they were no *g* ....Is 37:19
molten images, Ye are our *g* ..Is 42:17
burned incense unto other *g*...Jer 1:16
their *g* which are yet no *g*.....Jer 2:11
are thy *g* that thou hast ....Jer 2:28
number of thy cities are..*g* ....Jer 2:28
served strange *g* in..land ......Jer 5:19
other *g* whom ye know not ....Jer 7:9
g that have not made..heavens .Jer 10:11
go, and cry unto the *g* ....Jer 11:12
walk after other *g* ....Jer 13:10
walked after other *g* ....Jer 16:11
ye serve other *g* day ....Jer 16:13
Shall a man make *g* unto .....Jer 16:20
and they are no *g*? ....Jer 16:20
drink offerings unto other *g* ...Jer 19:13
And go not after other *g*......Jer 25:6
and go not after other *g* ......Jer 35:15
houses of..*g* of the Egyptians ..Jer 43:13
burn no incense unto other *g* ..Jer 44:5
burned incense unto other *g*...Jer 44:15
burneth incense to his *g*.......Jer 48:35
g whose dwelling is not ....Dan 2:11
they serve not thy *g* ....Dan 3:12
we will not serve thy *g*........Dan 3:18
spirit of the holy *g* ....Dan 4:9
spirit of the holy *g* ....Dan 5:11
like the wisdom of the *g* ......Dan 5:11
hast praised the *g* of silver ....Dan 5:23
of women, nor regard any *g* ...Dan 11:37
look to other *g*, and love .....Hos 3:1
out of the house of thy *g* .....Nah 1:14
famish all the *g* of the earth ...Zeph 2:11
I said, Ye are *g*? ....John 10:34
Make us *g* to go before us ....Acts 7:40
g are come down to us.........Acts 14:11
setter forth of strange *g* ....Acts 17:18
that they be no *g*, which are ..Acts 19:26
there be that are called *g* 1Cor 8:5
as there be *g* many, and 1Cor 8:5
which by nature are no *g* .....Gal 4:8

GOD-WARD—*toward God*
Be thou for the people to *G*...Ex 18:19
we through Christ to *G* 2Cor 3:4
your faith to *G* is spread 1Thess 1:8

GOEST, GOETH—*See* INTRODUCTION

GOG (gŏg)—*"high mountain"*
1. Reubenite 1Chr 5:4
2. Prince of Rosh, Meshech and Tubal ....Ezek 38:2, 3
3. Leader of the final battle.Rev 20:8-15

prophesy and say unto *G*......Ezek 38:14
G shall come against the land..Ezek 38:18
prophesy against *G* and ....Ezek 39:1
am against thee, O *G*, the .....Ezek 39:1
I will give unto *G* a place .....Ezek 39:11
there shall they bury *G* ....Ezek 39:11

GOING, GOINGS—*See* INTRODUCTION

GOLAN (gō'lăn)—*"passage"*
City of Bashan ....Deut 4:43
Assigned to Levites ......Josh 21:27
City of refuge ....Josh 20:8

Manasseh, *G* in Bashan 1Chr 6:71

GOLD—*precious mineral used in coinage*

Found in:
Havilah.................Gen 2:11, 12
Ophir 1Kin 9:28
Sheba 1Kin 10:2, 10
Arabia 2Chr 9:14

Used for:
Money ....Matt 10:9
Offerings ....Ex 35:22
Presents ....Matt 2:11
Holy adornment ....Ex 28:4-6
Jewelry ....Gen 24:22
Physical adornment ......Ex 36:34, 38
Idols ....Ex 32:31

Figurative of:
Saints refined ....Job 23:10
Babylonian empire ......Dan 2:38
Redeemed 2Tim 2:20
Faith purified 1Pet 1:7
Christ's doctrine ....Rev 3:18

[*also* GOLDEN]

cattle, in silver, and in *g* ......Gen 13:2
man took a *g* earring of.......Gen 24:22
and herds, and silver and *g*....Gen 24:35
a *g* chain about his neck ......Gen 41:42
of silver, and jewels of *g*......Ex 3:22
of silver, and jewels of *g*......Ex 12:35
make unto you gods of *g*......Ex 20:23
take of them, *g*, and silver ....Ex 25:3
overlay it with pure *g*.........Ex 25:11
upon it a crown of *g*...........Ex 25:11
and overlay them with *g* ......Ex 25:13
a mercy seat of pure *g*........Ex 25:17
cherubim of *g* of beaten ......Ex 25:18
overlay it with pure *g*.........Ex 25:24
make thereto a crown of *g* ....Ex 25:24
thou shalt make a *g* crown ....Ex 25:25
them with *g* that ....Ex 25:28
a candlestick of pure *g*........Ex 25:31
thereof, shall be of pure *g* ....Ex 25:38
make fifty taches of *g*.........Ex 26:6
overlay the boards with *g* .....Ex 26:29
and make their rings of *g* .....Ex 26:29
overlay the bars with *g*........Ex 26:29
wood overlaid with *g* ....Ex 26:32
and overlay them with *g* ......Ex 26:37
their hooks shall be of *g* ......Ex 26:37
to be set in ouches of *g*.......Ex 28:11
two chains of pure *g* at ....Ex 28:14
they shall be set in *g* in ....Ex 28:20
breastplate two rings of *g* .....Ex 28:23
shalt make two rings of *g* .....Ex 28:26
bells of *g* between them.......Ex 28:33
overlay it with pure *g*.........Ex 30:3
make unto it a crown of *g* ....Ex 30:3
And two *g* rings shalt thou ....Ex 30:4
to work in *g*, and in silver ....Ex 31:4
brake off the *g* earrings ....Ex 32:3
offering of the Lord, *g* and....Ex 35:5
to work in *g* and in silver .....Ex 35:32
and overlaid them with *g*.......Ex 36:36
their hooks were of *g* and .....Ex 36:36
he overlaid it with pure *g* .....Ex 37:2
and made a crown of *g* to it...Ex 37:2
and overlaid them with *g*......Ex 37:4
made two cherubim of *g* ......Ex 37:7
he overlaid it with pure *g* .....Ex 37:11
made thereunto crown of *g*....Ex 37:11
cast for it four rings of *g*......Ex 37:13
to cover withal, of pure *g* .....Ex 37:16
one beaten work of pure *g* ....Ex 37:22
talent of pure *g* made he ......Ex 37:24
he overlaid it with pure *g* .....Ex 37:26
made unto it a crown of *g* ....Ex 37:26
And he made two rings of *g*...Ex 37:27
and overlaid them with *g*.....Ex 37:28

g that was occupied for ....Ex 38:24
the g of the offering, was .....Ex 38:24
beat the g into thin plates .....Ex 39:3
g, blue, and purple and ....Ex 39:5
the ephod, of g, blue, and ....Ex 39:8
wreathen work of pure g ......Ex 39:15
two wreathen chains of g......Ex 39:17
they made bells of pure g .....Ex 39:25
g altar and..anointing oil ......Ex 39:38
shalt set the altar of g ....Ex 40:5
did he put the g plate, the ....Lev 8:9
upon the g altar they shall ....Num 4:11
spoon of ten shekels of g .....Num 7:14
g spoon of ten shekels ....Num 7:26
bowls, twelve spoons of g .....Num 7:84
The g spoons were twelve .....Num 7:86
candlestick was of beaten g....Num 8:4
house full of silver and g......Num 24:13
gotten of jewels of g..........Num 31:50
all the g of the offering ....Num 31:52
not desire the silver or g ......Deut 7:25
multiply..silver and g ....Deut 17:17
all the silver, and g and ....Josh 6:19
wedge of g of fifty shekels ....Josh 7:21
silver, and with g, and ....Josh 22:8
for they had g earrings........Judg 8:24
hundred shekels of g..........Judg 8:26
Five g emerods and five g.....1Sam 6:4
jewels of g, which ye return ...1Sam 6:8
the jewels of g were 1Sam 6:15
ornaments of g upon your 2Sam 1:24
vessels of g and..of brass 2Sam 8:10
weight..was a talent of g 2Sam 12:30
overlaid it with pure g 1Kin 6:20
house within with pure g 1Kin 6:21
chains of g before the..........1Kin 6:21
and he overlaid it with g 1Kin 6:21
he overlaid with g until he 1Kin 6:22
oracle he overlaid with g 1Kin 6:22
house he overlaid with g 1Kin 6:30
and overlaid them with g......1Kin 6:32
g upon the cherubim..........1Kin 6:32
altar of g..table of g 1Kin 7:48
the candlesticks of pure g 1Kin 7:49
lamps and the tongs of g 1Kin 7:49
and the censers of pure g 1Kin 7:50
and the hinges of g, both 1Kin 7:50
and fir trees, and with g 1Kin 9:11
of g that came to Solomon 1Kin 10:14
and six talents of g 1Kin 10:14
targets of beaten g 1Kin 10:16
six hundred shekels of g 1Kin 10:16
shields of beaten g 1Kin 10:17
three pound of g went to one .1Kin 10:17
overlaid it with the best g 1Kin 10:18
drinking vessels were of g 1Kin 10:21
of Lebanon were of pure g 1Kin 10:21
of silver, and vessels of g 1Kin 10:25
away all the shields of g 1Kin 14:26
all the silver and the g 1Kin 15:18
silver and thy g is mine 1Kin 20:3
my silver, and for my g 1Kin 20:7
six thousand pieces of g.......2Kin 5:5
g calves..in Beth-el 2Kin 10:29
vessels of g, or vessels 2Kin 12:13
he took all the g and silver....2Kin 14:14
and thirty talents of g.........2Kin 18:14
and the g and the spices 2Kin 20:13
silver, and the g to Pharaoh ...2Kin 23:35
exacted the silver and..g 2Kin 23:35
things as were of g, in g 2Kin 25:15
of vessels of g and silver 1Chr 18:10
to weigh a talent of g.........1Chr 20:2
shekels of g by weight 1Chr 21:25
g, the silver, and the brass 1Chr 22:16
g by weight for things of g 1Chr 28:14
of g, and for their lamps of g..1Chr 28:15
pure g for the fleshhooks 1Chr 28:17
basins he gave g..............1Chr 28:17
altar of incense refined g......1Chr 28:18
g for the pattern of the 1Chr 28:18
good, of g and silver..........1Chr 29:3
thousand talents of g 1Chr 29:4
the g of Ophir, and seven 1Chr 29:4
g five thousand talents and 1Chr 29:7
silver and g at Jerusalem 2Chr 1:15
skillful to work in g and in 2Chr 2:14
he overlaid with fine g 2Chr 3:5
the doors thereof, with g......2Chr 3:7
nails was fifty shekels of g 2Chr 3:9
the upper chambers with g 2Chr 3:9
ten candlesticks of g 2Chr 4:7
g altar also, and the tables 2Chr 4:19
the oracle, of pure g..........2Chr 4:20
and the censers of pure g 2Chr 4:22
the silver and the g and 2Chr 5:1
spices and g in abundance 2Chr 9:1
brought g from Ophir.........2Chr 9:10
Now the weight of g that 2Chr 9:13
and six talents of g 2Chr 9:13
targets of beaten g 2Chr 9:15
shekels of beaten g 2Chr 9:15
shields he made of beaten g ...2Chr 9:16
three hundred shekels of g 2Chr 9:16
footstool of g which were 2Chr 9:18
of king Solomon were of g 2Chr 9:20
of Lebanon were of pure g 2Chr 9:20
silver and vessels of g.........2Chr 9:24
candlestick of g with the 2Chr 13:11
brought out silver and g 2Chr 16:2
gifts of silver and of g 2Chr 21:3
took all the g and and silver...2Chr 25:24
silver and a talent of g........2Chr 36:3
with silver, and with g ....Ezra 1:4
thirty chargers of g a ....Ezra 1:9
vessels of g and of silver ......Ezra 1:11
vessels also of g and ....Ezra 5:14
the g and silver vessels........Ezra 6:5
silver and g that thou ....Ezra 7:16
the silver and the g ....Ezra 8:25
Also twenty basins of g ....Ezra 8:27
fine copper, precious as g .....Ezra 8:27
silver, and the g, and the .....Ezra 8:30
thousand drams of g, fifty .....Neh 7:70
thousand drams of g ....Neh 7:72
beds were of g and silver .....Esth 1:6
shall hold out the g scepter....Esth 4:11
g scepter toward Esther ....Esth 8:4
with a great crown of g ....Esth 8:15
Or with princes that had g ....Job 3:15
shalt thou lay up g as dust ....Job 22:24
g of Ophir as the stones ......Job 22:24
place for g where they fine ....Job 28:1
it cannot be gotten for g ......Job 28:15
g and the crystal cannot.......Job 28:17
be for jewels of fine g ....Job 28:17
If I have made g my hope ....Job 31:24
or have said to the fine g .....Job 31:24
every one an earring of g .....Job 42:11
be desired are they than g ....Ps 19:10
yea, than much fine g.........Ps 19:10
the queen in g of Ophir.......Ps 45:9
her feathers with yellow g.....Ps 68:13
also with silver and g ....Ps 105:37
me than thousands of g ....Ps 119:72
commandments above g.......Ps 119:127
above fine g ....Ps 119:127
gain thereof than fine g ....Prov 3:14
My fruit is better than g ......Prov 8:19
yea, than fine g; and my ......Prov 8:19
better..wisdom than g! ....Prov 16:16
is g and a multitude ....Prov 20:15
apples of g in pictures of......Prov 25:11
As an earring of g and........Prov 25:12
an ornament of fine g so ......Prov 25:12
I gathered..silver and g ....Eccl 2:8
or the g bowl be broken ......Eccl 12:6
thy neck with chains of g .....Song 1:10
bottom thereof of g, the ......Song 3:10
g rings set with the beryl......Song 5:14
is full of silver and g.........Is 2:7
more precious than fine g .....Is 13:12
of thy molten images of g .....Is 30:22
and the g, and the spices......Is 39:2
lavish g out of the bag ....Is 46:6
silver and their g with ....Is 60:9
thee with ornaments of g......Jer 4:30
g from Uphaz, the work ....Jer 10:9
Babylon hath been a g cup ....Jer 51:7
How is the g become dim! ....Lam 4:1
the most fine g changed! ......Lam 4:1
their g shall be removed ......Ezek 7:19
decked with g and silver ......Ezek 16:13
precious stones and g ....Ezek 27:22
and the carbuncle and g ......Ezek 28:13
image's head was of fine g ....Dan 2:32
Thou art this head of g ....Dan 2:38
king made an image of g......Dan 3:1
worship the g image ....Dan 3:5
and worship the g image ....Dan 3:10
nor worship the g image ......Dan 3:14
worship the g image which ....Dan 3:18
commanded to bring the g ....Dan 5:2
a chain of g about his neck....Dan 5:7
the gods of silver, and g ......Dan 5:23
girded with fine g of Uphaz ...Dan 10:5
honor with g, and silver.......Dan 11:38
multiplied her silver and g ....Hos 2:8
taken my silver and my g .....Joel 3:5
take the spoil of g for ....Nah 2:9
laid over with g and silver.....Hab 2:19
their silver nor their g ....Zeph 1:18
silver is mine and the g ....Hag 2:8
a candlestick all of g with a ...Zech 4:2
through the two g pipes ....Zech 4:12
fine g as the mire of the ......Zech 9:3
gathered together g ....Zech 14:14
purge them as g and silver ....Mal 3:3
swear by the g of the temple ..Matt 23:16
whether is greater, the g ......Matt 23:17
that sanctifieth the g? ....Matt 23:17
Silver and g have I none ......Acts 3:6
the Godhead is like unto g ....Acts 17:29
coveted no man's g ....Acts 20:33
upon this foundation g 1Cor 3:12
not with braided hair, or g 1Tim 2:9
Which had the g censer ....Heb 9:4
round about with g ....Heb 9:4
wherein was the g pot that ....Heb 9:4
a g ring in goodly apparel.....James 2:2
g and silver is cankered ....James 5:3
things, as silver and g.........1Pet 1:18
hair, and of wearing of g......1Pet 3:3
saw seven g candlesticks ......Rev 1:12
the seven g candlesticks ....Rev 1:20
their heads crowns of g ....Rev 4:4
g vials full of odors ....Rev 5:8
having a g censer; and ....Rev 8:3
upon the g altar which was ....Rev 8:3
devils, and idols of g and .....Rev 9:20
on his head a g crown ....Rev 14:14
seven g vials full of the ....Rev 15:7
decked with g and precious....Rev 17:4
The merchandise of g and......Rev 18:12
g reed to measure the city ....Rev 21:15
and the city was pure g ....Rev 21:18
street..was pure g ....Rev 21:21

GOLDEN APPLES—*probably refers to skilled art work in gold and silver*
Appropriate word ....Prov 25:11

GOLDEN CITY—*an expression for Babylon*
Babylon called ....Is 14:4

GOLDEN RULE—*"do unto others as you would have them do unto you"*
For Christian conduct ....Matt 7:12
Luke 6:31

GOLDEN WEDGE—*an item of uncertain identity, possibly serving as a means of identification in commerce*
Figurative term..........Is 13:12
Stolen by Achan ....Josh 7:21

GOLDSMITH—*one who works with gold*
In the tabernacle ....Ex 31:1-4
Refiners ....Mal 3:3
Shapers of objects ....Ex 25:11, 18
Makers of idols ....Num 33:52
Guilds..................Neh 3:8, 32

[*also* GOLDSMITH'S, GOLDSMITHS]
repaired Malchiah the g son ...Neh 3:31
and the g spreadeth it over....Is 40:19
carpenter encouraged the g....Is 41:7
hire a g; and he maketh ......Is 46:6

GOLGOTHA (gŏl'gŏ-thä)—*"skull"—hill just outside Jerusalem*
Where Jesus died . . . . .Matt 27:33-35

bring him unto the place *G* . . . .Mark 15:22
called in the Hebrew *G* . . . . . . .John 19:17

GOLIATH (gō-lī'ăth)—*"an exile or soothsayer"*
1. Giant of Gath 1Sam 17:4
Killed by David 1Sam 17:50
2. Another giant; killed by Elhanan 2Sam 21:19
See GIANT

G by name, out of the 1Sam 17:23
sword of *G* the Philistine 1Sam 21:9
gave him the sword of *G* 1Sam 22:10
slew...the brother of *G* 1Chr 20:5

GOMER (gō'mer)—*"completion; heat"*
1. Son of Japheth . . . . .Gen 10:2, 3
1Chr 1:5, 6
Northern nation . . . . .Ezek 38:6
2. Wife of Hosea . . . . .Hos 1:2, 3

GOMORRAH, GOMORRHA (gŏ-mŏr'ä)—*"submersion"—one of the five Cities of the Plain destroyed along with Sodom*
In a fruitful valley . . . . . . .Gen 13:10
Defeated by Chedorlaomer . . . . .Gen 14:8-11
Destroyed by God . . . . . . .Gen 19:23-29
Symbol of evil . . . . .Is 1:10
Symbol of destruction . . . .Amos 4:11
Punishment of . . . . .Matt 10:15

unto Sodom, and *G* . . . . .Gen 10:19
Lord destroyed Sodom and *G* .Gen 13:10
with Birsha king of *G* . . . . .Gen 14:2
the cry of Sodom and *G* . . . . . .Gen 18:20
overthrow of Sodom, and *G* . . .Deut 29:23
have been like unto *G* . . . . .Is 1:9
God overthrew Sodom and *G*. .Is 13:19
inhabitants thereof as *G* . . . . . . .Jer 23:14
God overthrew Sodom and *G*. .Jer 50:40
children of Ammon as *G* . . . . . .Zeph 2:9
tolerable for Sodom and *G* . . . .Mark 6:11
and been made like unto *G* . . .Rom 9:29
turning the cities..and *G* 2Pet 2:6
Even as Sodom and *G*, and . . .Jude 7

GONE—*See* INTRODUCTION

GOOD—*See* INTRODUCTION

GOOD FOR EVIL—*a response that is commanded of Christians*
Illustrated by Joseph . . . . .Gen 45:5-15
Christian duty . . . . .Luke 6:27, 35

GOODLINESS—*pleasantly attractive*

[*also* GOODLIER, GOODLIEST, GOODLY]
Rebekah took *g* raiment of . . . .Gen 27:15
loose; he giveth *g* words . . . . . .Gen 49:21
that he was a *g* child . . . . .Ex 2:2
the boughs of *g* trees . . . . .Lev 23:40
How *g* are thy tents, O . . . . . . .Num 24:5
that *g* mountain, and . . . . .Deut 3:25
and hast built *g* houses . . . . .Deut 8:12
among the spoils a *g* . . . . .Josh 7:21
your *g* young men, and 1Sam 8:16
choice young man, and a *g* 1Sam 9:2
of Israel a *g* person than 1Sam 9:2
he slew an Egyptian, a *g* 2Sam 23:21
he also was a very *g* man 1Kin 1:6
thy children, even the *g* 1Kin 20:3
the *g* vessels of the house 2Chr 36:10
g wings unto the peacocks . . . . .Job 39:13
yea, I have a *g* heritage . . . . . . .Ps 16:6
g heritage of the hosts of . . . . .Jer 3:19
that it might be a *g* vine . . . . . .Ezek 17:8
land they have made *g* . . . . .Hos 10:1
temples my *g* pleasant . . . . .Joel 3:5
his *g* horse in the battle . . . . . . .Zech 10:3
man, seeking *g* pearls . . . . .Matt 13:45
adorned with *g* stones and . . . .Luke 21:5
in *g* apparel, and there . . . . .James 2:2
dainty and *g* are departed . . . . .Rev 18:14

GOODMAN—*householder; master; husband*
For the *g* is not at home . . . . . .Prov 7:19
against the *g* of the house . . . . .Matt 20:11
say ye to the *g* of the house . . .Mark 14:14
g of the house had known . . . . .Luke 12:39

GOODNESS—*what is beneficial*
all my *g* pass before thee . . . . .Ex 33:19
g the Lord shall do unto . . . . . .Num 10:32
g which he had showed . . . . . . .Judg 8:35
promised this *g* unto thy 2Sam 7:28
glad of heart for all the *g* 1Kin 8:66
promised this *g* unto thy 1Chr 17:26
let thy saints rejoice in *g* 2Chr 6:41
acts of Hezekiah..his *g* 2Chr 32:32
themselves in thy great *g* . . . . . .Neh 9:25
my *g* extendeth not to thee . . . .Ps 16:2
him with the blessings of *g* . . . .Ps 21:3
Surely *g* and mercy shall . . . . . .Ps 23:6
remember..me for thy *g* . . . . . . .Ps 25:7
g of the Lord in the land . . . . .Ps 27:13
full of the *g* of the Lord . . . . . .Ps 33:5
crownest the year with..*g* . . . . .Ps 65:11
of thy *g* for the poor . . . . .Ps 68:10
praise the Lord for his *g* . . . . . .Ps 107:8
filleth..hungry soul with *g* . . . . .Ps 107:9
My *g*, and my fortress; my . . . .Ps 144:2
every one his own *g* . . . . .Prov 20:6
g toward the house of Israel . . .Is 63:7
the fruit thereof and the *g* . . . .Jer 2:7
to the *g* of the Lord . . . . .Jer 31:12
and tremble for all the *g* . . . . . .Jer 33:9
fear the Lord and his *g* in . . . . .Hos 3:5
to the *g* of his . . . . .Hos 10:1
For how great is his *g*, and . . . .Zech 9:17
despisest..riches of his *g* . . . . . .Rom 2:4
the *g* and severity of God . . . . .Rom 11:22
but toward thee, *g*, if thou . . . .Rom 11:22
if thou continue in his *g* . . . . . . .Rom 11:22
gentleness, *g*, faith . . . . .Gal 5:22
fruit of the Spirit..all *g* . . . . .Eph 5:9
good pleasure of his *g* 2Thess 1:11

GOODNESS OF GOD—*one of God's essential attributes*

Described as:
Abundant . . . . .Ex 34:6
Great . . . . .Ps 31:19
Enduring . . . . .Ps 52:1
Satisfying . . . . .Ps 65:4
Universal . . . . .Ps 145:9

Manifested in:
Material blessings . . . . . . .Matt 5:45
Acts 14:17
Spiritual blessings . . . . . . .Ps 31:19
Forgiving sin . . . . .Ps 86:5

Saints' attitude toward:
Rejoice in . . . . .Ex 18:9
Remember . . . . .Ps 145:7
Be satisfied with . . . . .Jer 31:14

GOODS—*possessions; wealth*
took all the *g* of Sodom . . . . . . .Gen 14:11
he brought back all the *g* . . . . .Gen 14:16
his brother Lot, and his *g* . . . . .Gen 14:16
g of his master were in his . . . .Gen 24:10
his *g* which he had gotten . . . . .Gen 31:18
took their cattle, and..*g* . . . . . . .Gen 46:6
unto his neighbor's *g* . . . . .Ex 22:8
Korah, and all their *g* . . . . .Num 16:32
cattle, and for their *g* . . . . .Num 35:3
plenteous in *g*, in the fruit . . . .Deut 28:11
thy wives, and all thy *g* 2Chr 21:14
with gold, and with *g* . . . . .Ezra 1:4
king's *g*, even of the tribute . . .Ezra 6:8
houses full of all *g*, wells . . . . . .Neh 9:25
hands shall restore their *g* . . . . .Job 20:10
and his *g* shall flow away . . . . .Job 20:28
g increase, they are . . . . .Eccl 5:11
have gotten cattle and *g* . . . . . .Ezek 38:12
g shall become a booty . . . . .Zeph 1:13
spoil his *g*, except he first . . . . .Matt 12:29
him ruler over all his *g* . . . . . . .Matt 24:47
delivered unto them his *g* . . . . . .Matt 25:14
and spoil his *g*, except he . . . . .Mark 3:27
away thy *g* ask them not . . . . . .Luke 6:30
bestow..my fruits and my *g* . . . .Luke 12:18
thou hast much *g* laid up . . . . .Luke 12:19
me the portion of *g* that . . . . . .Luke 15:12
that he had wasted his *g* . . . . . .Luke 16:1
Lord..half of my *g* I give . . . . . .Luke 19:8
sold..possessions and *g* . . . . .Acts 2:45
though I bestow all my *g* 1Cor 13:3
the spoiling of your *g* . . . . .Heb 10:34
rich, and increased with *g* . . . . .Rev 3:7

GOPHER WOOD—*the wood used in the ark, probably of the conifer family*
Used in Noah's ark . . . . . .Gen 6:14

GORE—*to push or thrust*
By an ox . . . . .Ex 21:28-32
Rendered "push" . . . . .Deut 33:17
Rendered "thrust" . . . . . . .Ezek 34:21

GORGEOUS—*splendidly brilliant; beautiful*

[*also* GORGEOUSLY]
and rulers clothed most *g* . . . . .Ezek 23:12
which are *g* appareled . . . . .Luke 7:25
arrayed him in a *g* robe . . . . . . .Luke 23:11

GOSHEN (gō'shĕn)—*"drawing near"*
1. District of Egypt where Israel lived . . . . .Gen 45:10
Land of pastures . . . . .Gen 47:1-6
Called the land of Rameses . . . . .Gen 47:6-11
2. Region in south Judah . .Josh 10:41
3. City of Judah . . . . .Josh 15:51

to direct his face unto *G* . . . . . .Gen 46:28
came into the land of *G* . . . . . . .Gen 46:28
may dwell in the land of *G* . . . .Gen 46:34
in the country of *G* . . . . .Gen 47:27
in that day the land of *G* . . . . . .Ex 8:22
and all the country of *G* . . . . . .Josh 10:41

GOSPEL—*"good news"*

Described as, of:
God .Rom 1:1
Christ 2Cor 2:12
The kingdom . . . . .Matt 24:14
Grace of God . . . . .Acts 20:24
Peace . . . . .Eph 6:15
Salvation . . . . .Eph 1:13
Glory of Christ 2Cor 4:4

Defined as:
Of supernatural origin . . .Gal 1:10-12
God's power . . . . .Rom 1:16
Mystery . . . . .Eph 6:19
Revelation . . . . .Eph 3:1-6
Deposit of truth 1Cor 15:1-4

Source of:
Hope . . . . .Col 1:23
Salvation 2Thess 2:13, 14
Faith . . . . .Acts 15:7
Life .1Cor 4:15
Immortality 2Tim 1:10
Afflictions . . . . .Phil 1:16
Peace . . . . .Eph 6:15

Proclaimed by or in:
Old Testament . . . . .Gal 3:8
Prophets . . . . .Rom 1:1, 2
John . . . . .Mark 1:1-4
Jesus Christ . . . . .Mark 1:14, 15
Chosen men 1Pet 1:12

Should be proclaimed:
To all people . . . . .Mark 16:15, 16
Everywhere . . . . .Rom 15:19, 20
At all times . . . . .Rev 14:6
With great urgency 1Cor 9:16
With boldness . . . . .Eph 6:19
As a testimony . . . . .Matt 24:14

Proclaimers of, are:
Separated . . . . .Rom 1:1
Called . . . . .Acts 16:10
Entrusted with it 1Thess 3:2
Set apart for its defense . .Phil 1:7, 16, 27
Under divine orders 1Cor 9:16

Negative reactions to, some:
Disobey 2Thess 1:8
Are blinded to 2Cor 4:3, 4
Hinder 1Cor 9:12
Pervert .... Gal 1:7

Believer's reaction to:
Believing .... Eph 1:13
Submitting to 2Cor 9:13
Being established by .... Rom 16:25
Living by .... Phil 1:27
Defending .... Phil 1:7, 16, 27

[*also* GOSPEL'S]
preaching..*g* of the kingdom .... Matt 4:23
the *g* preached to them .... Matt 11:5
g of the kingdom shall .... Matt 24:14
Wheresoever this *g* shall .... Matt 26:13
life for my sake and the *g* .... Mark 8:35
lands, for my sake, and..*g* .... Mark 10:29
g must first be published .... Mark 13:10
this *g* shall be preached .... Mark 14:9
preach the *g* to the poor .... Luke 4:18
the poor the *g* is preached .... Luke 7:22
preaching the *g*, and .... Luke 9:6
temple, and preached the *g* .... Luke 20:1
preached the *g* in many .... Acts 8:25
there they preached the *g* .... Acts 14:7
they had preached the *g* .... Acts 14:21
spirit in the *g* of his Son .... Rom 1:9
to preach the *g* to you that .... Rom 1:15
Christ according to my *g* .... Rom 2:16
that preach the *g* of peace .... Rom 10:15
have not all obeyed the *g* .... Rom 10:16
As concerning the *g*, they .... Rom 11:28
ministering the *g* of God .... Rom 15:16
blessing of the *g* of Christ .... Rom 15:29
but to preach the *g*: not 1Cor 1:17
they which preach the *g* 1Cor 9:14
should live of the *g* 1Cor 9:14
a dispensation of the *g* is 1Cor 9:17
when I preach the *g*, I may 1Cor 9:18
I may make the *g* of Christ 1Cor 9:18
abuse not..power in the *g* 1Cor 9:18
this I do for the *g* sake 1Cor 9:23
whose praise is in the *g* 2Cor 8:18
preaching the *g* of Christ 2Cor 10:14
preach the *g* in the regions 2Cor 10:16
or another *g*, which ye 2Cor 11:4
to you the *g* of God 2Cor 11:7
preach any other *g* unto .... Gal 1:8
man preach any other *g* .... Gal 1:9
communicated..that *g* .... Gal 2:2
the truth of the *g* might .... Gal 2:5
the *g* of the uncircumcision .... Gal 2:7
as the *g* of the circumcision .... Gal 2:7
to the truth of the *g* .... Gal 2:14
your fellowship in the *g* .... Phil 1:5
the furtherance of the *g* .... Phil 1:12
set for the defense of the *g* .... Phil 1:17
served with me in the *g* .... Phil 2:22
labored with me in the *g* .... Phil 4:3
in the beginning of the *g* .... Phil 4:15
word of the truth of the *g* .... Col 1:5
our *g* came not unto you 1Thess 1:5
speak unto you..*g* of God 1Thess 2:2
be put in trust with the *g* 1Thess 2:4
not the *g* of God only, but 1Thess 2:8
preached..the *g* of God 1Thess 2:9
According to the glorious *g* 1Tim 1:11
afflictions of the *g* 2Tim 1:8
dead according to my *g* 2Tim 2:8
in the bonds of the *g* .... Philem 13
unto us was the *g* preached .... Heb 4:2
that have preached the *g* 1Pet 1:12
by the *g* is preached unto 1Pet 1:25
g preached also to them 1Pet 4:6
obey not the *g* of God? 1Pet 4:17

GOSSIP—*idle talk or rumors about others*
Forbidden .... Lev 19:16
Cause of friction .... Prov 16:28
Warns against associating with .... Prov 20:19
Called "talebearer" .... Prov 11:13
Prov 20:19
Called "infamy" .... Ezek 36:3
Called "whisperers" .... Rom 1:29
Caled "whisperings" 2Cor 12:20
Called "tattlers" 1Tim 5:13

GOTTEN—*See* INTRODUCTION

GOURD—*a running plant with large leaves*
shade variety .... Jon 4:6-10
poison variety 2Kin 4:39-41

GOVERN—*to exercise authority over*
thou now *g* the kingdom 1Kin 21:7
even he that hateth right *g*? .... Job 34:17
g the nations upon earth .... Ps 67:4

GOVERNMENT—*recognized rulership*

Types of:
Patriarchal, in families .... Gen 27:29-39
Theocratic, under God .... Ex 18:13-26
Monarchial, under kings. 1Sam 8:5-22
Antichristian, under antichrist 2Thess 2:3-12
Absolute and final, under Christ .... Is 9:6, 7

Characteristics of:
Ruled by God .... Is 45:1-13
Successions of, determined by God .... Dan 2:28-45
Ignorant of spiritual things 1Cor 2:8
Providentially used .... Acts 26:32

Christian attitude toward:
Occupy positions in .... Gen 42:6
Pay taxes to .... Matt 22:18-21
Pray for 1Tim 2:1-3
Obey rules of .... Rom 13:1-7
But obey God first .... Acts 5:29

[*also* GOVERNMENTS]
I will commit thy *g* into .... Is 22:21
g, diversities of tongues 1Cor 12:28
uncleanness, and despise *g* 2Pet 2:10

GOVERNOR—*a ruler*
Title used of Zerubbabel .... Ezra 2:63
Applied to Nehemiah .... Neh 8:9
Prime minister .... Gen 42:6
Provincial ruler .... Acts 23:24, 26
Chief of ceremonies .... John 2:8, 9
Household teachers .... Gal 4:2
Magistrates .... Matt 10:18
Christ .... Matt 2:6

[*also* GOVERNOR'S, GOVERNORS]
he is *g* over all the land .... Gen 45:26
heart is toward..*g* of Israel .... Judg 5:9
of the *g* of the country 1Kin 10:15
Obadiah, which was *g* of 1Kin 18:3
gate of Joshua the *g* of the 2Kin 23:8
g of the sanctuary, and *g* 1Chr 24:5
the Lord to be the chief *g* 1Chr 29:22
every *g* in all Israel, the 2Chr 1:2
g of the country brought 2Chr 9:14
Azrikam the *g* of the house 2Chr 28:7
them Tatnai, *g* on this side .... Ezra 5:3
whom he had made *g* .... Ezra 5:14
the *g* of the Jews and the .... Ezra 6:7
the *g* on this side the river .... Ezra 8:36
given me to the *g* beyond .... Neh 2:7
throne of the *g* on this side .... Neh 3:7
appointed to be their *g* .... Neh 5:14
not eaten..bread of the *g* .... Neh 5:14
But the former *g* that had .... Neh 5:15
days of Nehemiah the *g* .... Neh 12:26
g among the nations .... Ps 22:28
g in the house of the Lord .... Jer 20:1
g over the cities of Judah .... Jer 40:5
Babylon had made *g* over .... Jer 41:2
Then the princes, the *g* .... Dan 3:3
the *g* and the princes .... Dan 6:7
son of Shealtiel, *g* of .... Hag 1:1
son of Shealtiel, *g* of .... Hag 1:14
he shall be as a *g* in Judah .... Zech 9:7
g of Judah shall say in .... Zech 12:5
offer it now unto thy *g* .... Mal 1:8
Jesus stood before the *g* .... Matt 27:11
the *g* asked him, saying .... Matt 27:11
the *g* was wont to release .... Matt 27:15
g said, Why, what evil .... Matt 27:23
if this come to the *g* ears .... Matt 28:14
Cyrenius was *g* of Syria .... Luke 2:2
power and authority of..*g* .... Luke 20:20
he made him *g* over Egypt .... Acts 7:10
delivered..epistle to the *g* .... Acts 23:33
informed the *g* against Paul .... Acts 24:1
the king rose up, and the *g* .... Acts 26:30
g under Aretas the king 2Cor 11:32
whithersoever the *g* listeth .... James 3:4
Or unto *g*, as unto them 1Pet 2:14

GOZAN (gō'zăn)—*"food"*
Town and district in Mesopotamia 2Kin 17:6
Israelites deported to 2Kin 18:11

fathers..destroyed as *G* 2Kin 19:12
Hara, and to the river *G* 1Chr 5:26
fathers..destroyed; as *G* .... Is 37:12

G

GRACE—*unmerited favor; mercy; compassion*

Descriptive of:
God's favor .... Gen 6:8
God's forgiving mercy .... Rom 11:6
Gospel .... John 1:17
Gifts (miracles, etc.) 1Pet 4:10
Eternal life 1Pet 1:13

Is the source of:
Salvation .... Acts 15:11
Call of God .... Gal 1:15
Faith .... Acts 18:27
Justification .... Rom 3:24
Forgiveness .... Eph 1:7
Consolation 2Thess 2:16

Described as:
All-abundant .... Rom 5:15-20
All-sufficient 2Cor 12:9
Glorious .... Eph 1:6
Great .... Acts 4:33
Manifold 1Pet 4:10
Rich .... Eph 2:4, 5
Undeserved 1Tim 1:12-16

Believers:
Are under .... Rom 6:14
Receive .... John 1:16
Stand in .... Rom 5:2
Abound in 2Cor 9:8
Be strong in 2Tim 2:1
Grow in 2Pet 3:18
Speak with .... Eph 4:29
Inherit 1Pet 3:7

Dangers of, can:
Be abused .... Jude 4
Be frustrated .... Gal 2:21
Be turned from .... Gal 5:3, 4

[*also* GRACIOUS, GRACIOUSLY]
thy servant hath found *g* .... Gen 19:19
I may find *g* in thy sight .... Gen 32:5
God..*g* given thy servant .... Gen 33:5
have found *g* in thy sight .... Gen 33:10
Let me find *g* in your eyes .... Gen 34:11
God be *g* unto thee, my .... Gen 43:29
g in the sight of my lord .... Gen 47:25
have found *g* in your eyes .... Gen 50:4
that I will hear; for I am *g* .... Ex 22:27
also found *g* in my sight .... Ex 33:12
have found *g* in thy sight .... Ex 33:13
I may find *g* in thy sight .... Ex 33:13
have found *g* in thy sight? .... Ex 33:16
hast found *g* in my sight .... Ex 33:17
Lord God, merciful and *g* .... Ex 34:6
thee, and be *g* unto thee .... Num 6:25
have found *g* in thy sight .... Num 32:5
have found *g* in thy sight .... Judg 6:17
whose sight I shall find *g* .... Ruth 2:2
handmaid find *g* in thy 1Sam 1:18
now found *g* in thine eyes 1Sam 27:5
God will be *g* to me, that 2Sam 12:22
that I have found *g* in 2Sam 14:22
the Lord was *g* unto them 2Kin 13:23
Lord your God is *g* and 2Chr 30:9
a little space *g* hath been .... Ezra 9:8

to pardon, *g* and merciful .....Neh 9:17
he is *g* unto him, and ....Job 33:24
g is poured into thy lips ....Ps 45:2
Hath God forgotten to be *g* ...Ps 77:9
the Lord is merciful and *g* ....Ps 103:8
g, and full of compassion .....Ps 112:4
and grant me thy law *g* ....Ps 119:29
Lord is *g*, and full of ....Ps 145:8
an ornament of *g* unto thy ....Prov 1:9
giveth *g* unto the lowly ....Prov 3:34
g woman retaineth honor .....Prov 11:16
g of his lips the king shall .....Prov 22:11
wise man's mouth are *g* ....Eccl 10:12
that he may be *g* unto you ....Is 30:18
O Lord, be *g* unto us; we .....Is 33:2
g shall thou be when pangs....Jer 22:23
found *g* in the wilderness .....Jer 31:2
receive us *g*: so will we ....Hos 14:2
is *g* and merciful, slow to .....Joel 2:13
God of hosts will be *g* ....Amos 5:15
that thou art a *g* God ....Jon 4:2
crying, *G*, *g* unto it ....Zech 4:7
God that he will be *g* unto ....Mal 1:9
and the *g* of God was upon ...Luke 2:40
wondered at the *g* words ......Luke 4:22
Father,) full of *g* and truth ....John 1:14
continue in the *g* of God ......Acts 13:43
unto the word of his *g* ....Acts 14:3
recommended..*g* of God ......Acts 14:26
brethren unto the *g* of God ...Acts 15:40
gospel of the *g* of God ....Acts 20:24
and to the word of his *g* ......Acts 20:32
By whom..have received *g* ....Rom 1:5
G to you..peace from God ....Rom 1:7
not reckoned of *g*, but of .....Rom 4:4
that it might be by *g* ....Rom 4:16
even so might *g* reign ....Rom 5:21
the law, but under *g*? ....Rom 6:15
to the election of *g* ....Rom 11:5
through the *g* given unto ......Rom 12:3
according to the *g* that is ......Rom 12:6
because of the *g* that is ....Rom 15:15
g of our Lord Jesus Christ ....Rom 16:20
g of our Lord Jesus Christ ....Rom 16:24
G be unto you, and peace 1Cor 1:3
g of God which is given you ...1Cor 1:4
According to the *g* of God 1Cor 3:10
For if I by *g* be a partaker 1Cor 10:30
by the *g* of God I am what....1Cor 15:10
his *g* which was bestowed 1Cor 15:10
g of God which was with 1Cor 15:10
g of our Lord Jesus Christ 1Cor 16:23
G be to you and peace 2Cor 1:2
by the *g* of God, we have 2Cor 1:12
abundant *g* might through 2Cor 4:15
ye receive not the *g* of God ...2Cor 6:1
you to wit of the *g* of God 2Cor 8:1
finish in you the same *g* 2Cor 8:6
that ye abound in this *g* 2Cor 8:7
ye know the *g* of our Lord 2Cor 8:9
travel with us with this *g* 2Cor 8:19
for the exceeding *g* of God....2Cor 9:14
The *g* of the Lord Jesus 2Cor 13:14
G be to you and peace ....Gal 1:3
called..into the *g* of Christ ....Gal 1:6
perceived the *g* that was ......Gal 2:9
g of our Lord Jesus Christ ....Gal 6:18
G be to you, and peace ....Eph 1:2
exceeding riches of his *g* ......Eph 2:7
by *g* are ye saved through .....Eph 2:8
dispensation..*g* of God ....Eph 3:2
the gift of the *g* of God ....Eph 3:7
this *g* given, that I should .....Eph 3:8
every one of us is given *g* .....Eph 4:7
it may minister *g* unto the .....Eph 4:29
G be with all them that ....Eph 6:24
G be unto you, and peace .....Phil 1:2
all are partakers of my *g* ......Phil 1:7
The *g* of our Lord Jesus ......Phil 4:23
G be unto you, and peace .....Col 1:2
the *g* of God in truth ....Col 1:6
g in your hearts to ....Col 3:16
speech be alway with *g* ....Col 4:6
G be with you. Amen ....Col 4:18
G be unto you, and peace 1Thess 1:1
The *g* of our Lord Jesus 1Thess5:28
G unto you, and peace 2Thess 1:2
according to the *g* of our 2Thess1:12
The *g* of our Lord Jesus 2Thess3:18
G be with thee. Amen 1Tim 6:21
G, mercy, and peace, from 2Tim 1:2
to his own purpose and *g* 2Tim 1:9
G be with you. Amen 2Tim 4:22
G, mercy, and peace, from ....Titus 1:4
the *g* of God that bringeth ....Titus 2:11
being justified by his *g* ....Titus 3:7
G be with you all. Amen ......Titus 3:15
G to you, and peace, from ....Philem 3
g of our Lord Jesus Christ ....Philem 25
he by the *g* of God should ....Heb 2:9
come..unto the throne of *g* ....Heb 4:16
g to help in time of need .....Heb 4:16
unto the Spirit of *g*? ....Heb 10:29
man fail of the *g* of God ......Heb 12:15
let us have *g*, whereby we .....Heb 12:28
be established with *g* ....Heb 13:9
G be with you all. Amen ......Heb 13:25
g of the fashion of it ....James 1:11
But he giveth more *g* ....James 4:6
giveth *g* unto the humble .....James 4:6
G unto you, and peace, be 1Pet 1:2
g that should come unto 1Pet 1:10
the *g* that it is to be brought ..1Pet 1:13
tasted that the Lord is *g* 1Pet 2:3
giveth *g* to the humble 1Pet 5:5
But the God of all *g*, who 1Pet 5:10
g of God wherein ye stand 1Pet 5:12
G and peace be multiplied 2Pet 1:2
G be with you, mercy, and 2John 3
G be unto you, and peace .....Rev 1:4
The *g* of our Lord Jesus ......Rev 22:21

GRACES, CHRISTIAN—*qualities that are intended to be a part of the Christian's life*
Growth in, commanded ..2Pet 1:5-8

GRAFT—*to unite a portion of one thing to another*
Gentiles, on Israel's stock.Rom11:17-24

GRAIN—*the generic term for cereal grasses*
Features regarding:
Grown in Palestine 2Kin 18:32
Article of food Gen42:1, 2, 19
Offered mixed with oil ...Lev 2:14, 15
Roasted ....Ruth 2:14
Figurative of:
Blessings...............Ezek 36:29
Christ ....John 12:24
Life's maturity ....Job 5:26

shall not the least *g* fall ....Amos 9:9
like to a *g* of mustard seed ....Matt 13:31
like a *g* of mustard seed ....Mark 4:31
like a *g* of mustard seed ......Luke 13:19
that shall be, but bare *g* 1Cor 15:37

GRANDCHILDREN—*the child of one's son or daughter*
Lot becomes father of,
through incest ....Gen 19:30-38
Abdon's ....Judg 12:13, 14
Widow's 1Tim 5:4
Iniquity visited on ....Ex 34:7
Served idols 2Kin 17:41
Crown of old men ....Prov 17:6
Practice piety toward
family 1Tim 5:4

GRANDMOTHER—*the mother of one's father or mother*
Lois thus called 2Tim 1:5

GRANT—*to bestow; permit; allow fulfillment of*

[*also* GRANTED]
g a redemption for..land ......Lev 25:24
Lord *g* you that ye may ....Ruth 1:9
God of Israel *g* thee thy 1Sam 1:17
God *g* him that which he 1Chr 4:10
G me the place of this 1Chr 21:22
knowledge is *g* unto thee 2Chr 1:12
g them some deliverance 2Chr 12:7
according to the *g* that ....Ezra 3:7
king *g* him all his request .....Ezra 7:6
g him mercy in the sight ......Neh 1:11
king *g* me, according to ....Neh 2:8
and it shall be *g* thee ....Esth 5:6
it please the king to *g* my .....Esth 5:8
the king *g* the Jews which .....Esth 8:11
let it be *g* to the Jews ....Esth 9:13
God would *g* me the thing ....Job 6:8
Thou hast *g* me life and.......Job 10:12
G thee according to thine .....Ps 20:4
g me thy law graciously ....Ps 119:29
the righteous shall be *g* ....Prov 10:24
G that these my two sons .....Matt 20:21
G unto us that we may sit .....Mark 10:37
That he would *g* unto us ......Luke 1:74
murderer to be *g* unto you ....Acts 3:14
g unto thy servants, that ......Acts 4:29
g signs and wonders to be .....Acts 14:3
g you to be likeminded one ...Rom 15:5
That he would *g* you ....Eph 3:16
Lord *g* unto him that he 2Tim 1:18
overcometh will I *g* to sit .....Rev 3:21

GRAPE—*a berry often used to make wine*
Grown in Palestine ......Num 13:23
Used for wine ....Num 6:3
"Sour grapes" ....Ezek 18:2
Figurative of judgment ...Rev 14:18
See VINE, VINEYARD

[*also* GRAPES]
brought forth ripe *g* ....Gen 40:10
clothes in the blood of *g* ......Gen 49:11
shalt thou gather every *g* ......Lev 19:10
gather the *g* of thy vine ....Lev 25:5
time of the firstripe *g* ....Num 13:20
because of the cluster of *g* ....Num 13:24
thou mayest eat *g* thy fill .....Deut 23:24
shalt not gather the *g* ....Deut 28:30
the pure blood of the *g* ....Deut 32:14
their *g* are *g* of gall, their .....Deut 32:32
the gleaning of the *g* of ....Judg 8:2
also wine, *g*, and figs, and ....Neh 13:15
shake off his unripe *g* ....Job 15:33
the vines with the tender *g* ....Song 2:13
for our vines have tender *g*....Song 2:15
that it should bring forth *g* ....Is 5:2
it should bring forth *g* ....Is 5:4
brought it forth wild *g*? ....Is 5:4
and the sour *g* is ripening .....Is 18:5
gleaning *g* when the vintage ...Is 24:13
shall be no *g* on the vine......Jer 8:13
fathers..eaten a sour *g* ....Jer 31:29
leave some gleaning *g*? ....Jer 49:9
like *g* in the wilderness ....Hos 9:10
the treader of *g* him that ......Amos 9:13
they not leave some *g*? ....Obad 5
Do men gather *g* of thorns ....Matt 7:16
bramble bush gather they *g* ...Luke 6:44

GRAPE GATHERER—*one who harvests grapes*

[*also* GRAPE GATHERERS]
turn back thine hand as a *g g* .Jer 6:9
If *g g* come to thee, would ....Jer 49:9
if the *g g* came to thee ....Obad 5

GRAPE GLEANINGS—*the grapes left over following the harvest*
as the *g g* of the vintage ......Mic 7:1

GRASS—*herbage fit for grazing animals*
Features:
Created by God ....Gen 1:11, 12
Produced by rain ....Deut 32:2
Adorns earth ....Matt 6:30
Failure of, a calamity ....Jer 14:5, 6
Nebuchadnezzar eats.....Dan 4:1, 33
Disappears ....Prov 27:25
Withered away ....Is 15:6
Figurative of:
Life's shortness ....Ps 90:5, 6
Prosperous wicked ....Ps 92:7
God's grace ....Ps 72:6

licketh up the *g* of the field ...Num 22:4
I will send *g* in thy fields ......Deut 11:15

nor any *g* groweth therein . . . . .Deut 29:23
g springing out of..earth 2Sam 23:4
peradventure we may find *g* . . .1Kin 18:5
were as the *g* of the field 2Kin 19:26
as the *g* of the earth . . . . .Job 5:25
he eateth *g* as an ox . . . . .Job 40:15
be cut down like the *g* . . . . .Ps 37:2
upon the mown *g*: as . . . . .Ps 72:6
city shall flourish like *g* . . . . . . .Ps 72:16
and withered like *g* . . . . .Ps 102:4
man, his days are as *g* . . . . .Ps 103:15
an ox that eateth *g* . . . . .Ps 106:20
who maketh *g* to grow . . . . .Ps 147:8
favor is as dew upon the *g* . . . .Prov 19:12
g with reeds and rushes . . . . . . .Is 35:7
were as the *g* of the field . . . . .Is 37:27
as the *g* on the housetops . . . . .Is 37:27
I cry? All flesh is *g* . . . . .Is 40:6
The *g* withereth, the flower . . .Is 40:7
surely the people is *g* . . . . .Is 40:7
The *g* withereth, the flower . . .Is 40:8
spring up as among the *g* . . . . .Is 44:4
heifer at *g*, and bellow . . . . .Jer 50:11
in the tender *g* of the field . . . .Dan 4:15
beasts in the *g* of the earth . . . .Dan 4:15
shall make thee to eat *g* . . . . . .Dan 4:25
fed him with *g* like oxen . . . . . .Dan 5:21
an end of eating the *g* . . . . .Amos 7:2
as the showers upon the *g* . . . . .Mic 5:7
to every one *g* in the field . . . .Zech 10:1
to sit down on the *g*, and . . . . .Matt 14:19
upon the green *g* . . . . .Mark 6:39
If then God so clothe the *g* . . .Luke 12:28
was much *g* in the place . . . . . .John 6:10
flower of the *g* he shall pass . . .James 1:10
For all flesh is as *g*, and 1Pet 1:24
of man as the flower of *g* 1Pet 1:24
g withereth, and the flower 1Pet 1:24
not hurt the *g* of the earth . . . .Rev 9:4

GRASSHOPPER—*a locust-like insect*

Used as food . . . . .Lev 11:22
Inferiority . . . . .Num 13:33
Insignificance . . . . .Is 40:22
Burden . . . . .Eccl 12:5
Destroys crops . . . . .Ps 78:46
See LOCUST

[*also* GRASSHOPPERS]
make him afraid as a *g*? . . . . . .Job 39:20
they are more than the *g* . . . . . .Jer 46:23
formed *g* in the beginning . . . . .Amos 7:1
as the great *g*, which camp . . . .Nah 3:17

GRATE—*frame to hold a fire*
make for it a *g* of network . . . .Ex 27:4
for the altar a brazen *g* . . . . . . .Ex 38:4
the brazen *g* for it, and . . . . . . .Ex 38:30

GRATITUDE—*the state of being thankful*

Reasons for:
Deliverance from an enemy . . . . .Judg 8:22, 23
Deliverance from death . .1Sam 26:21-25
Interpretation of a dream .Dan 2:46-48
Rescue from murderers . .Esth 6:1-6

Examples of:
Ruth to Boaz . . . . .Ruth 2:8-17
Israelites to Jonathan 1Sam 14:45
Abigail to David 1Sam 25:40-42
David to Jonathan 2Sam 9:1
David to Hanum 2Sam 10:1, 2
Pagans to Paul . . . . .Acts 28:1-10
See THANKFULNESS

GRAVE—*earnest disposition; serious*
must the deacons be *g* 1Tim 3:8
must their wives be *g* 1Tim 3:11
aged men be sober, *g* . . . . .Titus 2:2

GRAVE—*a place of burial*

Features regarding:
Dug in ground . . . . .Gen 50:5
Some in caves . . . . .Gen 23:9
Marker set on . . . . .Gen 35:20
Touching of, makes unclean . . . . .Num 19:16, 18

Resurrection from:
Symbolized . . . . .Ezek 37:1-14

[*also* GRAVE'S, GRAVES]
into the *g* unto my son . . . . .Gen 37:35
hairs with sorrow to the *g* . . . . .Gen 42:38
hairs with sorrow to the *g* . . . . .Gen 44:29
father with sorrow to the *g* . . . . .Gen 44:31
there were no *g* in Egypt . . . . .Ex 14:11
g on them the names of . . . . . . .Ex 28:9
he bringeth down to the *g* 1Sam 2:6
and wept at the *g* of Abner . . .2Sam 3:32
go down to the *g* in peace 1Kin 2:6
his carcase in his own *g* 1Kin 13:30
be gathered into thy *g* 2Kin 22:20
powder thereof upon the *g* 2Kin 23:6
to *g* with the cunning men 2Chr 2:7
strewed it upon the *g* of 2Chr 34:4
gathered to thy *g* in peace 2Chr 34:28
when they can find the *g*? . . . . .Job 3:22
goeth down to the *g* shall . . . . .Job 7:9
wouldest hide me in the *g* . . . . .Job 14:13
extinct, the *g* are ready . . . . . . .Job 17:1
moment go down to the *g* . . . . .Job 21:13
so doth the *g* those which . . . . .Job 24:19
draweth near unto the *g* . . . . . .Job 33:22
the *g* who shall give thee . . . . . .Ps 6:5
up my soul from the *g* . . . . .Ps 30:8
let them be silent in the *g* . . . . .Ps 31:17
sheep they are laid in the *g* . . .Ps 49:14
beauty shall consume in the *g* .Ps 49:14
draweth nigh unto the *g* . . . . . .Ps 88:3
be declared in the *g*? or . . . . . . .Ps 88:11
scattered at the *g* mouth . . . . . .Ps 141:7
them up alive as the *g* . . . . .Prov 1:12
nor wisdom, in the *g* . . . . .Eccl 9:10
jealousy is cruel as the *g* . . . . . .Song 8:6
is brought down to the *g* . . . . . .Is 14:11
go to the gates of the *g* . . . . . . .Is 38:10
made his *g* with the wicked . . .Is 53:9
Which remain among the *g* . . . .Is 65:4
Jerusalem, out of their *g* . . . . . .Jer 8:1
mother..have been my *g* . . . . . .Jer 20:17
he went down to the *g* . . . . .Ezek 31:15
company: his *g* are about . . . . .Ezek 32:22
is round about her *g* . . . . .Ezek 32:23
round about her *g* . . . . .Ezek 32:24
her *g* are round about . . . . .Ezek 32:25
her *g* are round about . . . . .Ezek 32:26
from the power of the *g* . . . . . .Hos 13:14
g, I will be thy destruction . . . .Hos 13:14
thy *g*; for thou art vile . . . . .Nah 1:14
g were opened; and many . . . . .Matt 27:52
are as *g* which appear not . . . . .Luke 11:44
that are in the *g* shall hear . . . .John 5:28
had lain in the *g* four days . . . .John 11:17
goeth into the *g* to weep . . . . . .John 11:31
in himself cometh to the *g* . . . .John 11:38
O *g*, where is thy victory? 1Cor 15:55
dead bodies to be put in *g* . . . .Rev 11:9

GRAVE CLOTHES—*strips of cloth used to bind a corpse*
Lazarus attired in . . . . .John 11:43, 44
Jesus lays His aside . . . . . .Luke 24:12

GRAVEL—*small pebbles*

Figurative of:
Distress . . . . .Prov 20:17
Numerous offspring; rendered "grains" . . . . .Is 48:19
Suffering . . . . .Lam 3:16

GRAVEN IMAGE—*an idol*
Of Canaanites, to be destroyed . . . . {Deut 7:1-5, 25; Deut 12:2, 3}
Cause of God's anger . . . .Ps 78:58; Jer 8:19

See IDOLS, IDOLATRY

[*also* GRAVEN IMAGES]
unto thee any *g i* . . . . .Ex 20:4
you no idols nor *g i* . . . . .Lev 26:1
and make you a *g i* . . . . .Deut 4:16
and make a *g i* . . . . .Deut 4:25
any *g* or molten *i* . . . . .Deut 27:15
to make a *g i* and a . . . . .Judg 17:3
teraphim, and a *g i* . . . . .Judg 18:14
teraphim, and the *g i* . . . . .Judg 18:20
them up Micah's *g i* . . . . .Judg 18:31
and served their *g i* 2Kin 17:41
up groves and *g i* 2Chr 33:19
to jealousy with their *g i* . . . . . .Ps 78:58
whose *g i* did excel . . . . .Is 10:10
covering of thy *g i* . . . . .Is 30:22
to prepare a *g i*, that . . . . .Is 40:20
that trust in *g i*, that . . . . .Is 42:17
or molten a *g i* that is . . . . .Is 44:10
maketh a god, even his *g i* . . . .Is 44:17
them, and my *g i* . . . . .Is 48:5
confounded by the *g i* . . . . .Jer 51:17
do judgment upon her *g i* . . . . .Jer 51:52
burned incense to *g i* . . . . .Hos 11:2
all the *g i* thereof . . . . .Mic 1:7
will I cut off the *g i* . . . . .Nah 1:14
profiteth the *g i* . . . . .Hab 2:18

GRAVING—*carving; engraving*

[*also* GRAVED, GRAVEN, GRAVETH, GRAVINGS]
fashioned it with a *g* tool . . . . .Ex 32:4
g, as signets are *g*, with . . . . . . .Ex 39:6
the mouth of it were *g* 1Kin 7:31
he *g* cherubim, lions, and 1Kin 7:36
grave any manner of *g* 2Chr 2:14
g cherubim on the walls 2Chr 3:7
were *g* with an iron pen . . . . . . .Job 19:24
and that *g* an habitation . . . . . .Is 22:16
g upon the table of their . . . . . .Jer 17:1
will engrave the *g* thereof . . . . .Zech 3:9
g by art and man's device . . . . .Acts 17:29

GRAVITY—*sobriety; dignity*
in subjection with all *g* 1Tim 3:4
uncorruptness, *g*, sincerity . . . . .Titus 2:7

GRAY—*a mixture of black and white; dreary*

[*also* GRAYHEADED, GREY, GREYHEADED]
my *g* hairs with sorrow . . . . .Gen 42:38
g hairs of thy servant our . . . . .Gen 44:31
with the man of *g* hairs . . . . . . .Deut 32:25
old and *g*; and, behold, my . . .1Sam 12:2
g and very aged men, much . . .Job 15:10
also when I am old and *g* . . . . .Ps 71:18
beauty of old men is the *g* . . . .Prov 20:29
g hairs are here and there . . . . .Hos 7:9

GREASE—*oily matter, often animal fat*
Their heart is as fat as *g* . . . . . .Ps 119:70

GREAT—*notable; large; ample*

Descriptive of:
Sun and moon . . . . .Gen 1:16
Euphrates . . . . .Gen 15:18
Mediterranean . . . . .Josh 1:4
Nineveh . . . . .Jon 3:2, 3
Babylon . . . . .Rev 14:8

Applied to God's:
Nature . . . . .Deut 10:17
Signs and miracles . . . . . . .Deut 29:3
Works . . . . .Judg 2:7
Victory 2Sam 23:10, 12
Mercy 2Chr 1:8
Wrath 2Chr 34:21
Glory . . . . .Ps 21:5
Power . . . . .Ps 147:5

Descriptive of Christ as:
God .Titus 2:13
Prophet . . . . .Luke 7:16
Priest . . . . .Heb 4:14
King . . . . .Luke 1:32, 33; Rev 11:17
Shepherd . . . . .Heb 13:20

Applied to the believer's:
Reward . . . . .Matt 5:12
Faith . . . . .Matt 15:28
Joy . . . . .Acts 8:8
Zeal .Col 4:13
Affliction 2Cor 8:2
Boldness 1Tim 3:13
Promises 2Pet 1:4

Applied to final things:
Gulf fixed . . . . .Luke 16:26
Wrath . . . . .Rev 6:17

Tribulation..............Rev 7:14
White throne judgment ..Rev 20:11

[*also* GREATER, GREATEST, GREATLY, GREATNESS]
will *g* multiply thy sorrow .....Gen 3:16
punishment..*g* than I can......Gen 4:13
pressed upon them *g*; and .....Gen 19:3
Jacob was *g* afraid and........Gen 32:7
throne will I be *g* than thou ...Gen 41:40
the *g* of thine excellency ......Ex 15:7
by the *g* of thine arm they ....Ex 15:16
the Lord is *g* than all gods ....Ex 18:11
whole mount quaked *g*.........Ex 19:18
of the Lord was kindled *g*.....Num 11:10
make of thee a *g* nation.......Num 14:12
unto the *g* of thy mercy.......Num 14:19
people is *g* and taller ....Deut 1:28
show thy servant thy *g*........Deut 3:24
his glory and his *g*, and we ....Deut 5:24
nations *g* and mightier ....Deut 7:1
nation mightier and *g* than ....Deut 9:14
redeemed through thy *g*.......Deut 9:26
his *g*, his mighty hand ....Deut 11:2
for the Lord shall *g* bless ....Deut 15:4
ascribe ye *g* unto our God ....Deut 32:3
feared *g*, because Gibeon .....Josh 10:2
because it was *g* than Ai ......Josh 10:2
they were *g* distressed ....Judg 2:15
his anger was kindled *g* 1Sam 11:6
people *g* feared the Lord......1Sam 12:18
not..a much *g* slaughter 1Sam 14:30
dismayed, and *g* afraid........1Sam 17:11
and his heart *g* trembled 1Sam 28:5
David was *g* distressed 1Sam 30:6
the men were *g* ashamed......2Sam 10:5
g than the love wherewith 2Sam 13:15
sinned *g* in that I have 2Sam 24:10
make his throne *g* than 1Kin 1:37
kingdom was established *g* 1Kin 2:12
Obadiah feared the Lord *g* 1Kin 18:3
house..fathers increased *g* 1Chr 4:38
So David waxed *g* and 1Chr 11:9
a hundred, and the *g* over 1Chr 12:14
hast thou done all this *g* 1Chr 17:19
the men were *g* ashamed......1Chr 19:5
Thine, O Lord, is the *g*.......1Chr 29:11
the *g* house he ceiled with 2Chr 3:5
g of thy wisdom was not 2Chr 9:6
g kindled against Judah 2Chr 25:10
according to the *g* of..mercy...Neh 13:22
this man Mordecai waxed *g* ...Esth 9:4
the *g* of Mordecai, whereunto .Esth 10:2
was the *g* of all the men of....Job 1:3
which I *g* feared is come ......Job 3:25
that God is *g* than man ....Job 33:12
how *g* shall he rejoice! ....Ps 21:1
my heart *g* rejoiceth ....Ps 28:7
I am bowed down *g*; I go .....Ps 38:6
unto God: he is *g* exalted .....Ps 47:9
g to be praised in the city .....Ps 48:1
I shall not be *g* moved........Ps 62:2
through the *g* of thy power....Ps 66:3
Thou shalt increase my *g*......Ps 71:21
lips shall *g* rejoice when ......Ps 71:23
according to the *g* of..power...Ps 79:11
God is *g* to be feared in the...Ps 89:7
and *g* to be praised: he is .....Ps 96:4
he increased his people *g* ......Ps 105:24
g praise the Lord with my.....Ps 109:30
spoken: I was *g* afflicted ......Ps 116:10
Lord, and *g* to be praised .....Ps 145:3
and his *g* is unsearchable......Ps 145:3
and I will declare thy *g* ....Ps 145:6
according to his excellent *g*....Ps 150:2
in the *g* of his folly he ....Prov 5:23
righteous shall *g* rejoice ....Prov 23:24
by the *g* of his might, for .....Is 40:26
they shall be *g* ashamed.......Is 42:17
wearied in..*g* of thy way ......Is 57:10
in the *g* of his strength?.......Is 63:1
not that land be *g* polluted ....Jer 3:1
least even unto the *g* of.......Jer 6:13
we are *g* confounded ....Jer 9:19
For the *g* of thine iniquity.....Jer 13:22
least of them unto the *g* of....Jer 31:34
the least even to the *g* ....Jer 42:1
people is *g* than..punishment ..Lam 4:6
shalt see *g* abominations ......Ezek 8:6
shalt see *g* abominations ......Ezek 8:15
sabbaths they *g* polluted ......Ezek 20:13
art thou like in thy *g*? ....Ezek 31:2
Thus was he fair in his *g*......Ezek 31:7
and in *g* among the trees......Ezek 31:18
for thy *g* is grown, and ....Dan 4:22
king Belshazzar *g* troubled ....Dan 5:9
and the *g* of the kingdom .....Dan 7:27
man *g* beloved, understand ....Dan 10:11
multitude *g* than..former ......Dan 11:13
border *g* than your border? ...Amos 6:2
thou art *g* despised ....Obad 2
g of them even to the least....Jon 3:5
it is near, and hasteth *g*.......Zeph 1:14
house shall be *g* than the .....Hag 2:9
Rejoice *g*, O daughter of .....Zech 9:9
not risen a *g* than John ....Matt 11:11
is one *g* than the temple ......Matt 12:6
a *g* than Solomon is here .....Matt 12:42
g among herbs..becometh .....Matt 13:32
same is *g* in the kingdom .....Matt 18:4
for whether is *g*, the gold .....Matt 23:17
the governor marveled *g* ......Matt 27:14
feared *g*, saying, Truly ....Matt 27:54
becometh *g* than all herbs .....Mark 4:32
besought him *g*, saying........Mark 5:23
g amazed, and running........Mark 9:15
who should be the *g* ....Mark 9:34
ye therefore do *g* err ....Mark 12:27
shall receive *g* damnation .....Mark 12:40
is not a *g* prophet than ....Luke 7:28
which of them should be *g* ....Luke 9:46
a *g* than Solomon is here .....Luke 11:31
down my barns..build *g* ....Luke 12:18
but he that is *g* among you....Luke 22:26
whether is *g*..that sitteth .....Luke 22:27
shalt see *g* things than ....John 1:50
rejoiceth *g* because of the .....John 3:29
g than our father Jacob ....John 4:12
g works than these, that ......John 5:20
But I have *g* witness than .....John 5:36
g than..father Abraham ....John 8:53
gave them me, is *g* than ......John 10:29
The servant is not *g* than .....John 13:16
neither he that is sent *g*.......John 13:16
g works than these shall ......John 14:12
for my Father is *g* than I......John 14:28
G love hath no man than .....John 15:13
unto thee hath the *g* sin.......John 19:11
Solomon's, *g* wondering........Acts 3:11
from the least to the *g*........Acts 8:10
lay upon you no *g* burden.....Acts 15:28
the *g* of these is charity 1Cor 13:13
g is he that prophesieth 1Cor 14:5
g part remain unto this 1Cor 15:6
g desired him to come 1Cor 16:12
g of his power to us-ward .....Eph 1:19
how *g* I long after you all .....Phil 1:8
desiring *g* to see us, as we 1Thess 3:6
G desiring to see thee.........2Tim 1:4
swear by no *g*, he sware ......Heb 6:13
g..more perfect tabernacle.....Heb 9:11
receive the *g* condemnation ...James 3:1
Wherein ye *g* rejoice 1Pet 1:6
are *g* in power and might 2Pet 2:11
God is *g* than our heart.......1John 3:20
g is he that is in you.........1John 4:4
the witness of God is *g* 1John 5:9
I rejoiced *g* that I found of....2John 4
I rejoiced *g*, when..brethren ...3John 3
have no *g* joy than to hear 3John 4

GREAT FISH—*unknown, thought by some to be a whale*
Swallows Jonah ....Jon 1:17

GREAT SEA—*See* MEDITERRANEAN SEA

GREATNESS, TRUE—*genuine greatness*
Hinges on:
God's gentleness ....Ps 18:35
Great work ....Neh 6:3
Unselfishness...........Jer 45:5
Servanthood ....Matt 23:11
God's estimate ....Matt 5:19

GREAVES—*armor for the leg*
g of brass upon his legs 1Sam 17:6

GRECIANS—*the inhabitants of Greece*
1. The people of Greece ...Joel 3:6
2. Greek-speaking Jews ....Acts 6:1
Hostile to Paul ....Acts 9:29
Gospel preached unto ...Acts 11:20

GREECE—*the southern extremity of the Balkan peninsula*
Prophecy concerning .....Dan 8:21
Paul preaches in.........Acts 17:16-31
Called Javan ....Is 66:19

[*also* GRECIA]
rough goat is the king of *G*....Dan 8:21
forth, lo, the prince of *G*......Dan 10:20
all against the realm of *G* .....Dan 11:2
against thy sons, O *G*.........Zech 9:13
exhortation, he came into *G*...Acts 20:2

GREED—*excessive or reprehensible desire for things*
Productive of:
Defeat..................Josh 7:11-26
Murder 1Kin 21:1-16
Betrayal ....Luke 22:1-6
Examples of:
Samuel's sons 1Sam 8:1, 3
False prophets ....Is 56:10, 11
False teachers 2Pet 2:14, 15
See AVARICE; COVETOUSNESS

[*also* GREEDILY, GREEDINESS, GREEDY]
as a lion that is *g* of his.......Ps 17:12
every one that is *g* of gain ....Prov 1:19
He coveteth *g* all the day .....Prov 21:26
they are *g* dogs which can.....Is 56:11
and thou hast *g* gained of .....Ezek 22:12
all uncleanness with *g*.........Eph 4:19
no striker, not *g* of filthy......1Tim 3:3
ran *g*..error of Balaam ....Jude 11

GREEK—*related to Greece; a native or inhabitant of Greece*
1. Native of Greece ....Acts 16:1
Spiritual state of ....Rom 10:12
Some believe ....Acts 14:1
2. Foreigners speaking Greek ....John 12:20
3. Language of Greece.....Acts 21:37

[*also* GREEKS]
woman was a *G*, a...........Mark 7:26
of *G*, and Latin, and..........Luke 23:38
there were certain *G*..........John 12:20
in Hebrew, and *G*, and ....John 19:20
that his father was a *G*........Acts 16:3
the devout *G* a great..........Acts 17:4
persuaded the Jews and the *G* .Acts 18:4
the *G* took Sosthenes, the.....Acts 18:17
Lord Jesus, both Jews..*G* .....Acts 19:10
Jews, and also to the *G* ....Acts 20:21
Canst thou speak *G*?..........Acts 21:37
I am debtor both to the *G* ....Rom 1:14
the Jew first..to the *G* ....Rom 1:16
the *G* seek after wisdom 1Cor 1:22
unto the *G* foolishness 1Cor 1:23
in the *G* tongue hath his ......Rev 9:11

GREEN—*a color; not yet ripe*

[*also* GREENISH, GREENNESS]
have given every *g* herb.......Gen 1:30
Jacob took him rods of *g* .....Gen 30:37
there remained not any *g* .....Ex 10:15
of thy first fruits *g* ears ....Lev 2:14
the plague be *g* or reddish ....Lev 13:49
hollow strakes, *g* or reddish ...Lev 14:37
hills, and under every *g* ....Deut 12:2
seven *g* withes that were ......Judg 16:7
hill, and under every *g*........1Kin 14:23
hills, and under every *g* 2Kin 16:4
hills, and under every *g* 2Chr 28:4
white, *g*, and blue, hangings...Esth 1:6

Whilst it is yet in his *g* . . . . .Job 8:12
He is *g* before the sun . . . . .Job 8:16
he searcheth after every *g* . . . . .Job 39:8
lie down in *g* pastures . . . . .Ps 23:2
himself like a *g* bay tree . . . . . .Ps 37:35
yea, pleasant..bed is *g* . . . . .Song 1:16
grass faileth, there is no *g* . . . . .Is 15:6
very *g* tree, slaying . . . . .Is 57:5
under every *g* tree thou . . . . . . .Jer 2:20
under every *g* tree, and ye . . . .Jer 3:13
the *g* trees upon the high . . . . .Jer 17:2
under every *g* tree, and . . . . . . .Ezek 6:13
shall devour every *g* tree . . . . . .Ezek 20:47
him; I am like a *g* fir tree . . . . .Hos 14:8
by companies upon the *g* . . . . . .Mark 6:39
do these things in a *g* . . . . .Luke 23:31
and all *g* grass was burnt . . . . . .Rev 8:7

GREET—*to address with good wishes; meet*

[*also* GREETETH, GREETING, GREETINGS]
go to Nabal, and *g* him in 1Sam 25:5
And *g* in the markets, and . . . .Matt 23:7
synagogues and *g*..markets . . . .Luke 11:43
send *g* unto the brethren . . . . . .Acts 15:28
G Priscilla and Aquila my . . . . .Rom 16:3
G Mary; who bestowed much . .Rom 16:6
G them that be..household . . . .Rom 16:11
All the brethren *g* you. *G* 1Cor 16:20
G one another..holy kiss 2Cor 13:12
which are with me *g* you . . . . . .Phil 4:21
physician, and Demas, *g* . . . . . .Col 4:14
G all the brethren with an 1Thess 5:26
Eubulus *g* thee, and Pudens . . .2Tim 4:21
G them that love us in . . . . .Titus 3:15
are scattered abroad, *g* . . . . .James 1:1
G ye one another with a 1Pet 5:14
of thy elect sister *g* thee 2John 13
G the friends by 3John 14

GREW—*See* GROW

GREY—*See* GRAY

GREYHOUND—*a tall, slender dog*
Poetically described . . . . . .Prov 30:29, 31

GRIEF—*deep distress caused by bereavement*

Causes of:
Son's marriage . . . . .Gen 26:34, 35
Barrenness 1Sam 1:11, 16
Death 2Sam 19:1, 2
Disease . . . . .Job 2:11-13
Sinners . . . . .Ps 119:158
Foolish son . . . . .Prov 17:25

Descriptive of:
Messiah . . . . .Is 53:3, 4, 10
God . . . . .Ps 95:10
Holy Spirit . . . . .Eph 4:30
God's saints . . . . .Ps 139:21

See SORROW

[*also* GRIEFS, GRIEVANCE, GRIEVE, GRIEVED, GRIEVETH, GRIEVING, GRIEVOUS, GRIEVOUSLY, GRIEVOUSNESS]
and it *g* him at his heart . . . . . .Gen 6:6
the famine was *g*..land . . . . .Gen 12:10
because their sin is very *g* . . . . .Gen 18:20
the thing..*g* in Abraham . . . . . .Gen 21:11
Let it not be *g* in thy sight . . . .Gen 21:12
following; for it..very *g* . . . . . . .Gen 41:31
be not *g*, nor angry with . . . . . .Gen 45:5
a *g* mourning to the Egyptians .Gen 50:11
And they were *g* because . . . . .Ex 1:12
there came a *g* swarm of . . . . . .Ex 8:24
there shall be a very *g* . . . . .Ex 9:3
it to rain a very *g* hail . . . . .Ex 9:18
coasts of Egypt; very *g* . . . . .Ex 10:14
thine heart shall not be *g* . . . . .Deut 15:10
soul was *g* for the misery . . . . .Judg 10:16
for it *g* me much for . . . . .Ruth 1:13
and why is thy heart *g*? 1Sam 1:8
thine eyes, and to *g* thine 1Sam 2:33
know this, lest he be *g* 1Sam 20:3
soul of all the people was *g* . . .1Sam 30:6
the king was *g* for his son 2Sam 19:2
cursed me with a *g* curse 1Kin 2:8
father made our yoke *g* 1Kin 12:4
thou the *g* service of thy 1Kin 12:4
from evil, that may it not *g* . . .1Chr 4:10
own sore and his own *g* 2Chr 6:29
father made our yoke *g* 2Chr 10:4
it *g* them exceedingly . . . . .Neh 2:10
it *g* me sore; therefore . . . . . . .Neh 13:8
queen exceedingly *g* . . . . .Esth 4:4
with thee, wilt thou be *g*? . . . . .Job 4:2
my *g* were thoroughly . . . . .Job 6:2
I speak, my *g* is not . . . . .Job 16:6
is consumed because of *g* . . . . .Ps 6:7
His ways are always *g* . . . . .Ps 10:5
For my life is spent with *g* . . . .Ps 31:10
Thus my heart was *g*, and I . . .Ps 73:21
wilderness, and *g* him in . . . . . .Ps 78:40
wicked shall see it and be *g* . . .Ps 112:10
wrath; but *g* words stir . . . . . . .Prov 15:1
A foolish son is a *g* to his . . . . .Prov 17:25
it *g* him to bring it again . . . . . .Prov 26:15
in much wisdom is much *g* . . . .Eccl 1:18
under the sun is *g* unto . . . . . . .Eccl 2:17
afterward did more *g* . . . . .Is 9:1
that write *g* which . . . . .Is 10:1
out; his life shall be *g* . . . . .Is 15:4
a heap in the day of *g* . . . . .Is 17:11
hath borne our *g* and . . . . .Is 53:4
he hath put him to *g* . . . . .Is 53:10
a woman forsaken and *g* . . . . . .Is 54:6
have not *g*; thou hast . . . . .Jer 5:3
before me continually is *g* . . . . .Jer 6:7
They are all *g* revolters . . . . . . .Jer 6:28
hurt! my wound is *g* . . . . .Jer 10:19
great breach, with a very *g* . . . .Jer 14:17
They shall die of *g* death . . . . . .Jer 16:4
even a *g* whirlwind . . . . .Jer 23:9
whirlwind; it shall fall *g* . . . . . . .Jer 23:19
Lord hath added *g* to my . . . . .Jer 45:3
Jerusalem hath *g* sinned . . . . . . .Lam 1:8
though he cause *g*, yet . . . . .Lam 3:32
nor *g* the children of . . . . .Lam 3:33
me by trespassing *g* . . . . .Ezek 14:13
nor any *g* thorn of all that . . . .Ezek 28:24
I Daniel was *g* in my . . . . .Dan 7:15
they are not *g* for the . . . . .Amos 6:6
to deliver him from his *g* . . . . . .Jon 4:6
thy wound is *g*: all that . . . . . . .Nah 3:19
cause me to behold *g*? . . . . .Hab 1:3
sick of the palsy, *g* . . . . .Matt 8:6
heavy burdens and *g* to . . . . . . .Matt 23:4
g for the hardness of their . . . .Mark 3:5
burdens *g* to be borne . . . . .Luke 11:46
Peter was *g* because he . . . . . . .John 21:17
g that they taught the people . .Acts 4:2
shall *g* wolves enter in . . . . .Acts 20:29
g complaints against Paul . . . . .Acts 25:7
if thy brother by *g* with . . . . . . .Rom 14:15
not that ye should be *g* 2Cor 2:4
if any have caused *g*, he 2Cor 2:5
to me indeed is not *g*, but . . . .Phil 3:1
I was *g* with that generation . . .Heb 3:10
seemeth to be joyous, but *g* . . .Heb 12:11
with joy, and not with *g* . . . . . .Heb 13:17
conscience toward God..*g* 1Pet 2:19
commandments are not *g* 1John 5:3
noisome and *g* sore upon . . . . .Rev 16:2

GRIND—*to reduce to small fragments by friction*

[*also* GRINDING]
and he did *g* in the prison . . . . .Judg 16:21
Then let my wife *g* unto . . . . . .Job 31:10
when the sound of the *g* . . . . . .Eccl 12:4
pieces, and *g* the faces of . . . . .Is 3:15
took the young men to *g* . . . . . .Lam 5:13
shall fall, it will *g* him . . . . .Matt 21:44
two women shall be *g* at . . . . . .Matt 24:41
Two women shall be *g* . . . . .Luke 17:35
shall fall, it will *g* him to . . . . . .Luke 20:18

GRINDERS—*teeth*
the *g* cease because they . . . . . .Eccl 12:3

GRISLED—*See* GRIZZLED

GRIZZLED—*gray or roan colored*
ringstreaked, speckled..*g* . . . . . .Gen 31:10
fourth chariot *g* and bay . . . . . .Zech 6:3

GROAN—*to moan*

[*also* GROANED, GROANETH, GROANING, GROANINGS]
God heard their *g* . . . . .Ex 2:24
because of their *g* by . . . . .Judg 2:18
stroke is heavier than my *g* . . . .Job 23:2
Men *g* from out of the city . . . .Job 24:12
I am weary with my *g* . . . . .Ps 6:6
the voice of my *g* . . . . .Ps 102:5
land the wounded shall *g* . . . . . .Jer 51:52
he shall *g* before him . . . . .Ezek 30:24
g of a deadly wounded . . . . .Ezek 30:24
How do the beasts *g*! . . . . .Joel 1:18
g in the spirit, and was . . . . . . .John 11:33
therefore again *g* in . . . . .John 11:38
and I have heard their *g* . . . . . .Acts 7:34
g and travaileth in pain . . . . . . .Rom 8:22
we ourselves *g* within . . . . .Rom 8:23
with *g* which cannot be . . . . . . .Rom 8:26
in this we *g*, earnestly 2Cor 5:2
are in this tabernacle do *g* 2Cor 5:4

GROPE—*to feel blindly for something*

[*also* GROPETH]
thou shalt *g* at noonday . . . . . . .Deut 28:29
as the blind *g* in darkness . . . . .Deut 28:29
g in the noonday . . . . .Job 5:14
g in the dark without . . . . .Job 12:25
We *g* for the wall like the . . . . .Is 59:10

GROSS—*great; dull*
earth, and *g* darkness the . . . . .Is 60:2
of death, and make it *g* . . . . . . .Jer 13:16
people's heart is waxed *g* . . . . .Matt 13:15
heart of this people is waxed *g* .Acts 28:27

GROUND—*earth, soil; planted*

[*also* GROUNDED]
was not a man to till the *g* . . . .Gen 2:5
man of the dust of the *g* . . . . . .Gen 2:7
out of the *g* the Lord God . . . .Gen 2:19
cursed is the *g* for thy sake . . . .Gen 3:17
till thou return unto the *g* . . . . .Gen 3:19
Cain was a tiller of the *g* . . . . . .Gen 4:2
crieth unto me from the *g* . . . . .Gen 4:10
the *g* which the Lord hath . . . .Gen 5:29
from off the face of the *g* . . . . .Gen 8:8
I will not again curse the *g* . . . .Gen 8:21
with his face toward the *g* . . . . .Gen 19:1
himself to the *g* seven . . . . .Gen 33:3
down every man his sack..*g* . . .Gen 44:11
thou standest is holy *g* . . . . .Ex 3:5
he said, Cast it on the *g* . . . . . .Ex 4:3
And he cast it on the *g* . . . . . . .Ex 4:3
fire ran along upon the *g* . . . . .Ex 9:23
midst..sea upon the dry *g* . . . . .Ex 14:22
the fire, and *g* it to powder . . .Ex 32:20
that creepeth on the *g* . . . . .Lev 20:25
gathered it, and *g* it in . . . . .Num 11:8
that creepeth on the *g* . . . . .Deut 4:18
shalt pour it upon the *g* . . . . . . .Deut 15:23
the fruit of thy *g*, and the . . . . .Deut 28:4
sole of her foot upon the *g* . . . .Deut 28:56
stood firm on dry *g* in the . . . . .Josh 3:17
passed over on dry *g* . . . . .Josh 3:17
fastened it into the *g*: for . . . . .Judg 4:21
there was dew on all the *g* . . . .Judg 6:40
fell on their faces to the *g* . . . . .Judg 13:20
destroyed down to the *g* . . . . . .Judg 20:21
bowed herself to the *g* . . . . .Ruth 2:10
of his words fall to the *g* 1Sam 3:19
will set them to ear his *g* 1Sam 8:12
and slew them on the *g* 1Sam 14:32
Jesse liveth upon the *g* 1Sam 20:31
and bowed herself to the *g* 1Sam 25:23
with his face to the *g* 1Sam 28:14
should I smite thee to the *g*? . .2Sam 2:22
fell on her face to the *g* 2Sam 14:4
Joab fell to the *g* on his 2Sam 14:22
the dew falleth on the *g* 2Sam 17:12
smite him there to the *g*? 2Sam 18:11
a piece of *g* full of lentils 2Sam 23:11
stood in the midst of the *g* 2Sam 23:12
king on his face upon the *g* . . .2Sam 24:20

G

king with his face to..*g* 1Kin 1:23
they two went over on dry *g* ..2Kin 2:8
naught, and the *g* barren 2Kin 2:19
cast him into the plat of *g* 2Kin 9:26
was a parcel of *g* full of 1Chr 11:13
the field for tillage of the *g* ...1Chr 27:26
in the clay *g* between 2Chr 4:17
with his face to the *g* 2Chr 20:18
Lord with their faces to the *g* .Neh 8:6
the tithes of our *g* unto ....Neh 10:37
down upon the *g*, and ....Job 1:20
trouble spring out of the *g* ....Job 5:6
out my gall upon the *g* ....Job 16:13
the desolate and waste *g* ....Job 38:27
place of thy name to the *g* ....Ps 74:7
his throne down to the *g* ....Ps 89:44
watersprings into dry *g* ....Ps 107:33
smitten my life down to the *g* .Ps 143:3
desolate shall sit upon the *g* ...Is 3:26
he hath broken unto the *g* ....Is 21:9
layeth it low, even to the *g* ....Is 26:5
shalt speak out of the *g* ....Is 29:4
spirit, out of the *g* ....Is 29:4
thou shalt sow the *g* ....Is 30:23
every place where the *g* ....Is 30:32
parched *g* shall become a .....Is 35:7
sit on the *g*: there is no ....Is 47:1
hast laid thy body as the *g* ....Is 51:23
Break up your fallow *g* ....Jer 4:3
they are black unto the *g* .....Jer 14:2
shall be dung upon the *g* ......Jer 25:33
them down to the *g* ....Lam 2:2
sit upon the *g*, and keep ......Lam 2:10
down their heads to the *g* .....Lam 2:10
that thou see not the *g* ....Ezek 12:6
bring it down to the *g*, so .....Ezek 13:14
in a dry and thirsty *g* ....Ezek 19:13
shall go down to the *g* ....Ezek 26:11
I will cast thee to the *g* ....Ezek 28:17
and from the *g* up to the ......Ezek 41:16
middlemost from the *g* ....Ezek 42:6
touched not the *g* ....Dan 8:5
of the stars to the *g* ....Dan 8:10
on my face toward the *g* ......Dan 8:18
I set my face toward the *g* ....Dan 10:15
creeping things of the *g* ....Hos 2:18
break up your fallow *g* ....Hos 10:12
be cut off, and fall to the *g* ...Amos 3:14
bring me down to the *g*? ......Obad 3
upon that which the *g* ....Hag 1:11
and the *g* shall give her ....Zech 8:12
not destroy the fruits of..*g* ....Mal 3:11
shall not fall on the *g* ....Matt 10:29
But other fell into good *g* .....Matt 13:8
received seed into the good *g* ..Matt 13:23
And some fell on stony *g* .....Mark 4:5
other fell on good *g*, and .....Mark 4:8
which are sown on stony *g* ....Mark 4:16
which are sown on good *g* ....Mark 4:20
cast seed into the *g* ....Mark 4:26
he fell on the *g* and ....Mark 9:20
other fell on good *g* and ......Luke 8:8
g of a certain rich man........Luke 12:16
why cumbereth it the *g*? ......Luke 13:7
I have bought a piece of *g* ....Luke 14:18
lay thee even with the *g* ......Luke 19:44
blood falling down to the *g*....Luke 22:44
near to the parcel of *g* ....John 4:5
his finger wrote on the *g* ......John 8:6
down, and wrote on the *g* .....John 8:8
wheat fall into the *g* ....John 12:24
thou standest is holy *g* ....Acts 7:33
I fell unto the *g*, and heard ...Acts 22:7
ye, being rooted and *g* ....Eph 3:17
continue in the faith *g* ....Col 1:23
the pillar and *g* of the 1Tim 3:15

GROVE—*a cluster of trees; shrine of the idol Asherah*
1. Tamarisk tree ....Gen 21:33
   1Sam 22:6
2. Idolatrous shrine (Asherah) .... Deut 12:3; 2Kin 21:7
   Destruction of, commanded ....Ex 34:13
   Israel's fondness for .....Jer 17:2
   Punishment ....Is 27:9

[*also* GROVES]
images, and cut down their *g* ..Deut 7:5
shalt not plant thee a *g* ....Deut 16:21
served Baalim and the *g* ......Judg 3:7
cut down the *g* that is by .....Judg 6:25
the *g* was cut down that.......Judg 6:28
they have made their *g* 1Kin 14:15
had made an idol in a *g*.......1Kin 15:13
prophets of the *g* four 1Kin 18:19
remained the *g* also in 2Kin 13:6
and *g* in every high hill 2Kin 17:10
made a *g*, as did Ahab........2Kin 21:3
for Baal, and for the *g*........2Kin 23:4
wove hangings for the *g*........2Kin 23:7
images, and cut down the *g* ...2Kin 23:14
images, and cut down the *g* ...2Chr 14:3
had made an idol in a *g*.......2Chr 15:16
hast taken away the *g*.........2Chr 19:3
pieces, and cut down the *g* ...2Chr 31:1
and set up *g* and graven 2Chr 33:19
altars and the *g*, and had 2Chr 34:7
either the *g*, or the images ....Is 17:8
I will pluck up thy *g* out ......Mic 5:14

GROW—*to develop to or toward maturity*

Of material things:
Power 2Sam 3:1
Age ....Josh 23:1
Sound ....Ex 19:19

Of immaterial things:
Spirituality ....Luke 2:40
God's hand ....Num 11:23
Old covenant ....Heb 8:13
God's kingdom ....Luke 13:18, 19

[*also* GREW, GROWETH, GROWN, GROWTH]
of the field before it *g* ....Gen 2:5
the Lord God to *g* every ......Gen 2:9
the child *g*, and was ....Gen 21:8
And the boys *g*: and Esau ....Gen 25:27
till Shelah my son be *g* ....Gen 38:11
possessions therein and *g*......Gen 47:27
more they multiplied and *g*....Ex 1:12
when Moses was *g*, that he....Ex 2:11
every tree which *g* for you ....Ex 10:5
there is black hair *g* up ....Lev 13:37
freckled spot that *g* in the .....Lev 13:39
of the hair of his head *g* ......Num 6:5
beareth, nor any grass *g* ......Deut 29:23
art waxen fat, thou art *g* ......Deut 32:15
and his wife's sons *g* up.......Judg 11:2
hair of his head began to *g*....Judg 16:22
the day *g* to an end, lodge ....Judg 19:9
for them till they were *g*? .....Ruth 1:13
child Samuel *g* before the 1Sam 2:21
Samuel *g*, and the Lord 1Sam 3:19
And David went on and *g* 2Sam 5:10
until your beards be *g* 2Sam 10:5
he make it not to *g*...........2Sam 23:5
that were *g* up with him 1Kin 12:8
And when the child was *g*.....2Kin 4:18
things as *g* of themselves 2Kin 19:29
until your beards be *g* 1Chr 9:5
why should damage *g* to ......Ezra 4:22
our trespass is *g* up unto ......Ezra 9:6
Can the rush *g* up without .....Job 8:11
washest away..things which *g* ..Job 14:19
When the dust *g* into ....Job 38:38
good liking, they *g* up ....Job 39:4
they are like grass which *g* ....Ps 90:5
g like a cedar in Lebanon .....Ps 92:12
which withereth afore it *g* .....Ps 129:6
as plants *g* up in their ....Ps 144:12
who maketh grass to *g* ....Ps 147:8
it was all *g* over with ....Prov 24:31
how the bones do *g* in the ....Eccl 11:5
Branch shall *g* out of his ......Is 11:1
thou make thy plant to *g*......Is 17:11
corn blasted before it be *g* ....Is 37:27
eat this year such as *g* of......Is 37:30
For he shall *g* up before ......Is 53:2
have taken root: they *g* ....Jer 12:2
are *g* fat as the heifer at ......Jer 50:11
fashioned..thine hair is *g* ......Ezek 16:7
g and became a spreading .....Ezek 17:6
nor suffer their locks to *g* .....Ezek 44:20
tree *g*, and was strong ....Dan 4:11
that are *g* and become ....Dan 4:22
till his hairs were *g* like ....Dan 4:33
he shall *g* as the lily, and ......Hos 14:5
shooting up of the latter *g* ....Amos 7:1
was the latter *g* after ....Amos 7:1
neither madest it *g* ....Jon 4:10
he shall *g* up out of his ....Zech 6:12
and *g* up as calves of the......Mal 4:2
lilies..field, how they *g*........Matt 6:28
both *g* together until the ......Matt 13:30
when it is *g*, it is the ....Matt 13:32
no fruit *g* on thee ....Matt 21:19
thorns *g* up, and choked ......Mark 4:7
seed should spring and *g* ......Mark 4:27
when it is sown, it *g* up ....Mark 4:32
And the child *g* and ....Luke 1:80
Consider the lilies how..*g* .....Luke 12:27
whereunto this would *g* ....Acts 5:24
people *g* and multiplied in ....Acts 7:17
So mightily *g* the word of .....Acts 19:20
g unto a holy temple in ....Eph 2:21
your faith *g* exceedingly.......2Thess 1:3
g in grace, and in the 2Pet 3:18

GROWTH, SPIRITUAL—*the process of moving toward maturity in one's relationship with God and with other people*

Expressed by words indicating:
Fruitfulness ....John 15:2, 5
Increase 2Cor 9:10
Addition 2Pet 1:5-10
Growth 1Pet 2:2
Building up ....Jude 20

Hindrances to:
Lack of knowledge ......Acts 18:24-28
Carnality 1Cor 3:1-3
Instability ....Eph 4:14, 15
Dullness ....Heb 5:11-14

GRUDGE—*to harbor resentment*
Forbidden ....Lev 19:18

[*also* GRUDGING, GRUDGINGLY]
bear any *g* against the ....Lev 19:18
and *g* if they be not ....Ps 59:15
not *g* or of necessity 2Cor 9:7
G not one against ....James 5:9
one to another without *g* 1Pet 4:9

GUARD—*one who watches or protects*

Aspects of:
Called mighty 2Sam 23:8-23
Often foreigners 2Sam 20:7
Respected ....Jer 40:1-5

Duties of:
Run before chariots 2Sam 15:1
Form a military guard ...1Sam 22:17
Keep watch 2Kin 11:6
Carry out commandments.Jer 39:11-14
Execute criminals........Dan 2:14

[*also* GUARD'S]
and captain of the *g* ....Gen 37:36
house of the captain of the *g* ..Gen 40:3
in the captain of the *g* ....Gen 41:10
servant to the captain..*g* ......Gen 41:12
hands of the chief of the *g* 1Kin 14:27
that the *g* bare them, and 1Kin 14:28
them back into the *g* 1Kin 14:28
that Jehu said to the *g* 2Kin 10:25
the captains and the *g* 2Kin 11:4
And the *g* stood every 2Kin 11:11
the captains, and the *g*........2Kin 11:19
gate of the *g* to the king's 2Kin 11:19
with the captain of the *g* 2Kin 25:10
the captain of the *g* left 2Kin 25:12
the captain of the *g* took 2Kin 25:18
David set him over his *g* 1Chr 11:25
the chief of the *g*, that 2Chr 12:10
the *g* came and fetched 2Chr 12:11
them again into the *g* 2Chr 12:11
the night they may be a *g* .....Neh 4:22

captain of the *g* carried ....Jer 39:9
the captain of the *g* had.......Jer 40:1
the captain of the *g* had.......Jer 43:6
captain of the *g* brake ....Jer 52:14
the captain of the *g* left ....Jer 52:16
the captain of the *g* took ......Jer 52:24
the captain of the *g*..........Jer 52:30
thee and be thou a *g* ....Ezek 38:7
prisoners to the captain..*g*.....Acts 28:16

GUARDIAN—*a custodian*
Christ, of our souls 2Tim 1:12

GUARDIAN ANGELS—*angels that protect and help*
Helpers................Gen 24:7
Heb 1:1-14
Protectors..............Ps 91:11
Matt 18:10
Aided apostles ....Acts 5:17-19
Acts 8:26

GUDGODAH (gŭd-gō'dä)—*"incision"*
Israelite encampment ....Deut 10:7
Also called Hor-hagidgad .Num 33:32

GUEST—*a person entertained in one's residence and toward whom hospitality is extended*

Kinds of:
Terrified...............1Kin 1:41, 49
Dead..................Prov 9:18
Unwelcomed...........Prov 25:17
Unprepared............Matt 22:11
Criticized ....Luke 7:39-50
Congenial...............Acts 18:1-3
Courteous 1Cor 10:27
Angelic................Heb 13:2

[*also* GUESTS]
he hath bid his *g* ....Zeph 1:7
wedding was furnished with *g*..Matt 22:10
gone to be *g* with a man ......Luke 19:7

GUEST CHAMBER—*room for guests' use*
Master saith, Where is the *g c* .Mark 14:14
unto thee, Where is the *g c* ...Luke 22:11

GUIDANCE, DIVINE—*God's leading His people in the way they are to go or live*
To the meek ....Ps 25:9
To the wise ....Prov 23:19
To a good man..........Ps 112:5
In God's strength........Ex 15:13
On every side 2Chr 32:22
With God's eye ....Ps 32:8
With counsel............Ps 73:24
Like a flock.............Ps 78:52
By skillfulness...........Ps 78:72
Continually ....Is 58:11

GUIDE—*one who leads or directs; to lead or direct*

Kinds of:
Human ....Num 10:29-32
Supernatural ....Ex 13:20-22
Blind..................Matt 23:16, 24

Goals of:
Peace ....Luke 1:79
Truth..................John 16:13
God's word ....Acts 8:30, 31

[*also* GUIDED, GUIDES, GUIDING]
Manasseh's head, *g* his........Gen 48:14
a father, and I have *g* ....Job 31:18
canst thou *g* Arcturus ....Job 38:32
name's sake lead me, and *g* ...Ps 31:3
will *g* thee with mine eye .....Ps 32:8
he will be our *g* even unto ....Ps 48:14
g, and mine acquaintance .....Ps 55:13
Thou shalt *g* me with thy .....Ps 73:24
forsaketh the *g* of her........Prov 2:17
having no *g*, overseer, or .....Prov 6:7
of the upright shall *g* ....Prov 11:3
springs of water shall he *g* ....Is 49:10
There is none to *g* her ....Is 51:18
art the *g* of my youth?........Jer 3:4
ye not confidence in a *g* ......Mic 7:5
g to them that took Jesus .....Acts 1:16

art a *g* of the blind, a light ....Rom 2:19
g the house, give none 1Tim 5:14

GUILE—*duplicity; deceitful cunning*
to slay him with *g*; thou.......Ex 21:14
whose spirit there is no *g* .....Ps 32:2
deceit and *g* depart not ....Ps 55:11
indeed, in whom is no *g*!.......John 1:47
crafty, I caught you with *g* 2Cor 12:16
uncleanness, nor in *g* 1Thess 2:3
laying aside all malice..*g* 1Pet 2:1
neither was *g* found in 1Pet 2:22
lips that they speak no *g* 1Pet 3:10
their mouth was found no *g* ...Rev 14:5

GUILT—*the fact of having committed a wrong*

[*also* GUILTINESS, GUILTY]
shouldest have brought *g*......Gen 26:10
verily *g* concerning our........Gen 42:21
by no means clear the *g*.......Ex 34:7
not be done, and are *g* ....Lev 4:13
not to be done, and be *g* .....Lev 4:27
of it, then he shall be *g*.......Lev 5:3
he shall be *g* in one of........Lev 5:5
he hath sinned and is *g* ....Lev 6:4
Lord, and that person be *g*....Num 5:6
he shall not be *g* of blood.....Num 35:27
shalt put away the *g* of ....Deut 19:13
put away the *g* of innocent ....Deut 21:9
time, that ye should be *g* .....Judg 21:22
wives; and being *g*, they ......Ezra 10:19
and thou be found *g* ....Prov 30:10
Thou art become *g* in thy .....Ezek 22:4
hold themselves not *g*.........Zech 11:5
gift that is upon it, he is *g* ....Matt 23:18
condemned him to be *g*........Mark 14:64
may become *g* before God ....Rom 3:19
shall be *g* of the body and 1Cor 11:27
offend in one point, he is *g* ...James 2:10

GUILT, UNIVERSALITY OF—*man's status before God*

Described as:
Filthy rags ....Is 64:6
Fall short ....Rom 3:23
All declared ....Rom 5:12-14
Gal 3:22

GUILTLESS—*without guilt*
Lord will not hold him *g* ......Ex 20:7
man be *g* from iniquity ....Num 5:31
Lord will not hold him *g* ......Deut 5:11
head, and we will be *g*........Josh 2:19
Lord's anointed, and be *g*? 1Sam 26:9
I and my kingdom are *g* 2Sam 3:28
hold him not *g*: for thou 1Kin 2:9
not have condemned the *g* ....Matt 12:7

GULF—*deep chasm*
and you there is a great *g* .....Luke 16:26

GUNI (gū'nī)—*"protected"*
1. One of Naphtali's sons ..Gen 46:24
1Chr 7:13
Descendants called
Gunites ....Num 26:48
2. Gadite 1Chr 5:15
G, the family of the Gunites...Num 26:48

GUNITES (gū'nīts)—*the descendants of Guni*
Of Guni, the family of the *G* ..Num 26:48

GUR (gûr)—*"whelp"*
Site of Ahaziah's death ..2Kin 9:27

GUR-BAAL (gûr-bā'ăl)—*"dwelling place of Baal"*
Place in Arabia 2Chr 26:7

GUSH—*to outpour suddenly*

[*also* GUSHED]
till the blood *g* out upon 1Kin 18:28
that the waters *g* out ....Ps 78:20
and the waters *g* out ....Ps 105:41
rock also, and the waters *g*....Is 48:21
our eyelids *g* out with.........Jer 9:18
midst, and all his bowels *g* ....Acts 1:18

GUTTER—*a trough for catching and redirecting surface liquids*

[*also* GUTTERS]
before the flocks in the *g* .....Gen 30:38
eyes of the cattle in the *g* .....Gen 30:41
Whosoever getteth up to the *g* .2Sam 5:8

H

HA—*an exclamation*
H, *h*; and he smelleth........Job 39:25

HAAHASHTARI (hā-ä-hăsh'tä-rī)—*"the courier"*
Son of Ashur 1Chr 4:5, 6

HABAIAH (hä-bā'yä)—*"Jehovah is protection"*
Father of excommunicated
Jewish priests ....Ezra 2:61, 62
Also spelled Hobaiah ....Neh 7:63, 64

HABAKKUK (hä-băk'ŭk)—*"love's embrace"—a prophet in Judah during the reigns of Jehoiakim and Josiah*

Complaints of:
God's silence............Hab 1:2-4
God's response ....Hab 1:5-11
Chaldean cruelty ....Hab 1:12-17
God's response ....Hab 2:1-20

Prayer of:
Praise of God ....Hab 3:1-19

HABAKKUK—*a book of the Old Testament*
Author ....Hab 1:1
Setting ....Hab 1:2-4
Historical reference ......Hab 1:6
The life of the just ......Hab 2:4
Warning ....Hab 2:1-20

HABAZINIAH (hăb-ä-zī-nī'ä)—*"Jehovah's light"*
Grandfather of Jaazaniah .Jer 35:3

HABERGEON—*a coat of mail*
Worn by priests ....Ex 28:32
Ex 39:23

[*also* HABERGEONS]
helmets, and *h*, and bows 2Chr 26:14
shields..bows, and the *h* ......Neh 4:16
spear, the dart nor the *h* ......Job 41:26

HABIT—*custom; mode of behavior*

Kinds of:
Doing evil ....Jer 13:23
Doing good ....Acts 10:38
Of animals, instinctive ...2Pet 2:22

HABITABLE—*capable of being lived in*
in the *h* part of his earth......Prov 8:31

HABITATION—*a place of residence*

Used literally of:
Canaan ....Num 15:2
A tree..................Dan 4:20, 21
Nation..................Acts 17:26

Used figuratively of:
Eternity ....Is 57:15
God's throne ....Is 63:15
Sky ....Hab 3:11
Heaven ....Luke 16:9
New Jerusalem ....Is 33:20

[*also* HABITATIONS]
according to their *h* in the ....Gen 36:43
of cruelty are in their *h* ....Gen 49:5
in all your *h* shall ye eat ......Ex 12:20
I will prepare him a *h* ....Ex 15:2
no fire throughout your *h* .....Ex 35:3
the camp shall his *h* ....Lev 13:46
shall bring out of your *h* ......Lev 23:17
even unto his *h* shall ye ....Deut 12:5
down from thy holy *h*.........Deut 26:15
I have commanded in my *h* ...1Sam 2:29
shalt see an enemy in my *h* ...1Sam 2:32
me both it, and his *h* 2Sam 15:25

These were their *h*, and 1Chr 4:33
the *h* that were found 1Chr 4:41
possessions and *h* were 1Chr 7:28
have built a house of *h* 2Chr 6:2
faces from the *h* of the Lord ..2Chr 29:6
Israel, whose *h* is in ....Ezra 7:15
suddenly I cursed his *h* ....Job 5:3
thou shalt visit thy *h*, and .....Job 5:24
h of thy righteousness ....Job 8:6
I have loved the *h* of thy .....Ps 26:8
From the place of his *h* he ....Ps 33:14
is God in his holy *h* ....Ps 68:5
Let their *h* be desolate ....Ps 69:25
Be thou my strong *h* ....Ps 71:3
are full of the *h* of cruelty ....Ps 74:20
camp, round about their *h* ....Ps 78:28
the *h* of thy throne ....Ps 89:14
even the Most High, thy *h* ....Ps 91:9
judgment are the *h* of his .....Ps 97:2
fowls..heaven have their *h* ....Ps 104:12
might go to a city of *h* ....Ps 107:7
may prepare a city for *h* ......Ps 107:36
h for the mighty God ....Ps 132:5
hath desired it for his *h* ....Ps 132:13
but he blesseth the *h* of ....Prov 3:33
graveth a *h* for himself in .....Is 22:16
and the *h* forsaken ....Is 27:10
dwell in a peaceable *h* ....Is 32:18
and it shall be a *h* of ....Is 34:13
the *h* of dragons, where ....Is 35:7
the curtains of thine *h* ....Is 54:2
Thine *h* is in the midst of .....Jer 9:6
the *h* of the wilderness ....Jer 9:10
made his *h* desolate ....Jer 10:25
who shall enter into our *h*? ....Jer 21:13
his voice from his holy *h* ......Jer 25:30
mightily roar upon his *h* ......Jer 25:30
the peaceable *h* are cut ....Jer 25:37
O *h* of justice ....Jer 31:23
a *h* of shepherds causing ......Jer 33:12
dwelt in the *h* of ....Jer 41:17
against the *h* of the strong ....Jer 49:19
he shall make their *h* ....Jer 49:20
he shall make their *h* ....Jer 50:45
swallowed up all the *h* of .....Lam 2:2
Diblath, in all their *h* ....Ezek 6:14
Pathros..land of their *h* ....Ezek 29:14
h of the shepherds shall ....Amos 1:2
whose *h* is high; that saith ....Obad 3
raised up out of his holy *h* ....Zech 2:13
Let his *h* be desolate, and .....Acts 1:20
for a *h* of God through ....Eph 2:22
but left their own *h*, he ....Jude 6
become the *h* of devils ....Rev 18:2

HABOR (hā-'bôr)—*"fertile"—a tributary of the Euphrates River*
On the river of Gozan ...2Kin 17:6

in Halah and in *H* by 2Kin 18:11
them unto Halah, and *H* 1Chr 5:26

HACHALIAH (hăk-ä-lī'ä)—*"Jehovah is hidden"*
Father of Nehemiah .....Neh 1:1

Tirshatha, the son of *H* ....Neh 10:1

HACHILAH (hä-kī'lä)—*"gloomy"*
Hill in the wilderness of Ziph where David hid .1Sam 23:19-26

David hide himself..hill of *H* ..1Sam 26:1
Saul pitched in the hill of *H* ...1Sam 26:3

HACHMONI (hăk'mō-nī)—*"the wise"*
Tutor to king's son 1Chr 27:32

HACHMONITE—*descendant of Hachmoni*
Jashobeam, a *H*, the 1Chr 11:11

HAD—*See* INTRODUCTION

HADAD (hā'dăd)—*"the god"*
1. Ishmael's son ....Gen 25:13, 15; 1Chr 1:30
2. King of Edom ....Gen 36:35, 36
3. Another king of Edom ..1Chr 1:50
Called Hadar ....Gen 36:39
4. Edomite leader 1Kin 11:14-25

[*also* HADAR]
H, and Tema, Jetur ....Gen 25:15
and *H* reigned in his ....Gen 36:39
H the son of Bedad 1Chr 1:46
H was dead, Samlah 1Chr 1:47
H died also. And the 1Chr 1:51

HADADEZER, HADAREZER (hăd-ăd-ē'zer, hăd-ă-rē'zer)—*"(the god) Hadad is my help"*
King of Zobah 2Sam 8:3-13
Defeated by David 2Sam 10:6-19

fled from his lord *H* 1Kin 11:23
David smote *H* king of 1Chr 18:3
came to help *H* king of 1Chr 18:5
on the servants of *H* 1Chr 18:7
from Chun, cities of *H* 1Chr 18:8
smitten all the host of *H* 1Chr 18:9
he had fought against *H* 1Chr 18:10
for *H* had war with Tou 1Chr 18:10
captain of the host of *H* 1Chr 19:16
when the servants of *H* 1Chr 19:19

HADADRIMMON (hā-dăd-rĭm'ŏn)—*"Hadad and Rimmon"*
Name of the two Aramean deities; a place in Jezreel ....Zech 12:11

HADAR—*See* HADAD 2

HADAREZER—*See* HADADEZER

HADASHAH (hä-dăsh'ä)—*"new"*
Village of Judah ....Josh 15:37

HADASSAH (hä-dăs'ä)—*"myrtle"*
Esther's Jewish name ....Esth 2:7

HADATTAH (hä-dăt'ä)—*"new"*
Town in south Judah; probably should be read as Hazorhadattah .Josh 15:25

HADES—*See* HELL

HADID (hā'dĭd)—*"point"*
Town of Benjamin ......Neh 11:31, 34

The children of Lod, *H* ....Ezra 2:33
of Lod, *H*, and Ono, seven ...Neh 7:37

HADLAI (hăd'lī)—*"resting"*
Ephraimite 2Chr 28:12

HADORAM (hä-dō'răm)—*"Hadad is high"*
1. Son of Joktan ....Gen 10:26, 27
2. Son of Tou 1Chr 18:9, 10
3. Rehoboam's tribute officer 2Chr 10:18
Called Adoram 1Kin 12:18
Probably same as Adoniram 1Kin 4:6

H also, and Uzal, and 1Chr 1:21

HADRACH (hā'drăk)—*"dwelling"*
Place in Syria ....Zech 9:1

HADST—*See* INTRODUCTION

HAFT—*handle of a weapon*
the *h* also went in after ....Judg 3:22

HAGAB (hā'găb)—*"locust"*
Head of a family of Temple servants ....Ezra 2:46

HAGABA (hăg'ä-bä)—*"locust"*
Head of a family of Temple servants ....Neh 7:46, 48

HAGABAH (hăg'ä-bä)—*"locust"*
Head of a family of Temple servants ....Ezra 2:43, 45

HAGAR, AGAR (hā'gär, ā'gär)—*"wandering"*
Sarah's Egyptian handmaid ....Gen 16:1
Flees from Sarah ....Gen 16:5-8
Returns; becomes mother of Ishmael ....Gen 16:3-16
Abraham sends her away .Gen 21:14
Paul's allegory of ....Gal 4:22-26

angel of God called to *H* ......Gen 21:17
What aileth thee, *H*? ....Gen 21:17
Abraham's son, whom *H* ......Gen 25:12

HAGARITES (hā'gär-īts)—*a nation to the east of the Promised Land and which was dispossessed by the Tribe of Reuben*
Nomad people east of Gilead 1Chr 5:10-22
Called Hagarenes ....Ps 83:6

HAGERITE (hā'gĕr-īt)—*a descendant of Hagar*
Jaziz, keeper of David's flocks 1Chr 27:31

HAGGAI (hăg'ā-ī)—*"festive"*
Postexilic prophet ....Ezra 5:1, 2
Contemporary of Zechariah ....Ezra 6:14
Prophecies of, dated in reign of Darius Hystaspes (520 B.C.) . Hag 1:1, 15; Hag 2:1, 10, 20

HAGGAI, THE BOOK OF—*a book of the Old Testament*
Purpose ....Hag 1:1-15
The coming glory ....Hag 2:4-9
On Levitical cleanliness ..Hag 2:10-14

HAGGEDOLIM (hăg-gĕ-dō'lĭm)—*"a great one"*
Father of Zabdiel ....Neh 11:14

HAGGERI (hăg'ĕ-rī)—*"wanderer"*
A mighty man of David's guard 1Chr 11:38
Called "Bani the Gadite" in 2Sam 23:36

HAGGI (hăg'ī)—*"festive"*
Son of Gad ....Gen 46:16
Head of tribal family ....Num 26:15

HAGGIAH (hă-gī'ä)—*"feast of Jehovah"*
Merarite Levite 1Chr 6:30

HAGGITES—*See* HAGGI

HAGGITH (hăg'ĭth)—*"festal"*
One of David's wives 2Sam 3:4
Mother of Adonijah 1Kin 1:5

HAI (hā'ī)—*"same as Ai; near Bethel, where Abraham pitched his tent*
Beth-el on the west, and *H* ....Gen 12:8
Between Beth-el and *H* ....Gen 13:3

HAIL—*frozen rain*
Illustrative of God's:
Wonders ....Job 38:22
Glory ....Ps 18:12
Chastening ....Is 28:2, 17
Wrath ....Rev 8:7

[*also* HAILSTONES]
to rain a very grievous *h* ......Ex 9:18
the *h* shall come down ....Ex 9:19
Lord sent thunder and *h* ......Ex 9:23
h upon the land of Egypt .....Ex 9:23
the *h* smote throughout ....Ex 9:25
the *h* smote every herb of .....Ex 9:25
mighty thunderings and *h* .....Ex 9:28
the thunders and *h* ceased .....Ex 9:33
remaineth unto you from the *h*.Ex 10:5
of the trees which the *h* ....Ex 10:15
more which died with *h* ....Josh 10:11
his voice; *h* stones and ....Ps 18:13
destroyed their vines with *h* ...Ps 78:47
He gave them *h* for rain ......Ps 105:32
scattering, and tempest, and *h* .Is 30:30
When it shall *h*, coming ......Is 32:19
ye, O great *h*, shall fall ....Ezek 13:11
and great *h*, fire, and ....Ezek 38:22
with mildew and with *h* ....Hag 2:17
fell upon men a great *h* ....Rev 16:21
because of the plague of the *h* .Rev 16:21

HAIL—*a salutation ("hale be thou")*
Gabriel to Mary ....Luke 1:26-28

Judas to Christ ....Matt 26:47-49
Soldiers to Christ ....Matt 27:27-29

Jesus met them..All *h* ....Matt 28:9
him, *H*, King of the Jews! .....Mark 15:18
And said, *H*, King of the Jews!.John 19:3

HAIR—*a slender, thread-like growth in the skin of a mammal*

Of women:
Covering................1Cor 11:15
Uses of................Luke 7:38
Prohibitions concerning ..1Tim 2:9
1Pet 3:3

Of men:
Not to be worn long 1Cor 11:14
Rules for cutting ....Lev 19:27
Long, during Nazarite vow ....Num 6:5
Gray, sign of age 1Sam 12:2
Absalom's beautiful......2Sam 14:25, 26
Numbered ....Matt 10:30

Figurative of:
Minuteness..............Judg 20:16
Complete safety 1Sam 14:45
Fear....................Job 4:14, 15
Great numbers ....Ps 40:12
Grief ....Ezra 9:3
Respect.................Prov 16:31
Attractiveness ....Song 5:2, 11
Affliction ....Is 3:17, 24
Entire destruction ....Is 7:20
Decline and fall ....Hos 7:9

[*also* HAIRS, HAIRY]
red, all over like an *h* ....Gen 25:25
because his hands were *h* .....Gen 27:23
bring down my gray *h* ....Gen 42:38
the gray *h* of thy servant ......Gen 44:31
fine linen, and goats' *h* ....Ex 25:4
scarlet, and fine linen..*h* ....Ex 35:6
up in wisdom spun goats' *h* ...Ex 35:26
and when the *h* in the ....Lev 13:3
it have turned the *h* white.....Lev 13:10
no white *h* therein, and ....Lev 13:21
the *h* in the bright spot ....Lev 13:25
in it a yellow thin *h* ....Lev 13:30
there be in it no yellow *h* .....Lev 13:32
and that there is black *h* ......Lev 13:37
he that hath his *h* fallen.......Lev 13:41
shave off all his *h*, and........Lev 14:8
he shall shave all his *h*........Lev 14:9
eyebrows, even all his *h* ......Lev 14:9
shall take the *h* of the ....Num 6:18
of goats' *h*, and all things .....Num 31:20
with the man of gray *h* ....Deut 32:25
the *h* of his head began ....Judg 16:22
there shall not one *h* of 1Sam 14:45
a pillow of goats' *h* for........1Sam 19:16
there shall not one *h* of 2Sam 14:11
there shall not a *h* of 1Kin 1:52
answered him, He was..*h* 2Kin 1:8
and plucked off their *h* ......Neh 13:25
the *h* scalp of such a one .....Ps 68:21
cause are more than the *h* ....Ps 69:4
thy *h* is as a flock of goats ....Song 4:1
thy *h* is as a flock of goats ....Song 6:5
and the *h* of thine head ....Song 7:5
even to hoar *h* will I..........Is 46:4
that plucked off the *h*..........Is 50:6
off thine *h*, O Jerusalem ......Jer 7:29
to weigh, and divide the *h* ....Ezek 5:1
nor was a *h* of their head .....Dan 3:27
his *h* were grown like ....Dan 4:33
his raiment of camel's *h*.......Matt 3:4
John was clothed..camel's *h* ...Mark 1:6
wiped them with the *h* of .....Luke 7:44
But even the very *h* of........Luke 12:7
But there shall not a *h*........Luke 21:18
wiped his feet with her *h*......John 11:2
wiped his feet with her *h*......John 12:3
a *h* fall from the head ....Acts 27:34
if a woman have long *h* 1Cor 11:15
His head and his *h* were ......Rev 1:14
black as sackcloth of *h* ....Rev 6:12
And they had *h* as the *h* ......Rev 9:8

HAKKATAN (hăk'ä-tăn)—*"the little one"*
Johanan's father ....Ezra 8:12

HAKKOZ (hăk'ŏz)—*"the nimble"*
Descendant of Aaron 1Chr 24:1, 10
Descendants of, kept from priesthood ....Ezra 2:61, 62

HAKUPHA (hä-kū'fä)—*"incitement"*
Ancestors of certain Temple servants ....Ezra 2:43, 51
the children of *H*, the.........Neh 7:53

HALAH (hā'lä)—*"moist table"*
Israelite captives carried to 2Kin 17:6

and put them in *H* and in 2Kin 18:11
and brought them unto *H* 1Chr 5:26

HALAK (hā'lăk)—*"smooth"*
Mountain near Seir ......Josh 11:17

mount *H*, that goeth..Seir .....Josh 12:7

HALF—*one of two equal parts of a whole*
a golden earring of *h* a ....Gen 24:22
Moses took *h* of the blood ....Ex 24:6
and *h* of the blood he ....Ex 24:6
two cubits and a *h* shall ....Ex 25:10
and a cubit and a *h* the ....Ex 25:10
cubit and a *h* the height........Ex 25:10
two cubits and a *h* shall ....Ex 25:17
and a cubit and a *h*...........Ex 25:17
h curtain that remaineth ......Ex 26:12
give less than *h* a shekel ......Ex 30:15
a board one cubit and a *h*.....Ex 36:21
two cubits and a *h* was the ....Ex 37:1
and a cubit and a *h* the ....Ex 37:1
and a cubit and a *h* the ....Ex 37:1
two cubits and a *h* was the ....Ex 37:6
one cubit and a *h* the ....Ex 37:6
h a shekel, after the ....Ex 38:26
h of..morning, and *h* ....Lev 6:20
of whom the flesh is *h* ....Num 12:12
for a drink offering *h* a ....Num 15:10
Take it of their *h*, and give ...Num 31:29
h, which was the portion ......Num 31:36
the *h* that pertained unto ......Num 31:43
nine tribes, and to the *h* ......Num 34:13
The two tribes and the *h*......Num 34:15
h mount Gilead, and the ......Deut 3:12
unto the river Arnon *h* ....Deut 3:16
h the tribe of Manasseh ....Josh 1:12
h of them over against ....Josh 8:33
and from *h* Gilead, even ......Josh 12:2
Gadites, and the *h* tribe ......Josh 12:6
and *h* the land of the ....Josh 13:25
h tribe of Manasseh ....Josh 13:29
possession of the *h* ....Josh 13:29
h Gilead, and Ashtaroth ......Josh 13:31
one *h* of the children ....Josh 13:31
two tribes and a *h* tribe ....Josh 14:3
And out of the *h* tribe of .....Josh 21:25
the Gadites, and the *h* ....Josh 22:1
Now to the one *h* of the ......Josh 22:7
but unto the other *h* ....Josh 22:7
Gad and the *h* tribe of.........Josh 22:10
and to the *h* tribe of..........Josh 22:13
within as it were a *h*..........1Sam 14:14
shaved off the one *h* of 2Sam 10:4
and also *h* the people of 2Sam 19:40
give *h* to the one, and *h* 1Kin 3:25
a wheel was a cubit and *h*.....1Kin 7:32
the *h* was not told me 1Kin 10:7
Zimri, captain of *h* his 1Kin 16:9
h of the people followed 1Kin 16:21
and *h* followed Omri 1Kin 16:21
Haroeh, and *h* of the 1Chr 2:52
the one *h* of the greatness.....2Chr 9:6
ruler..*h* part of Jerusalem .....Neh 3:9
ruler of the *h* part of Beth-zur.Neh 3:16
the ruler of the *h* part of......Neh 3:18
the *h* of my servants ....Neh 4:16
h of them held the spears .....Neh 4:21
and the *h* of the people ....Neh 12:38
their children spake *h* in ......Neh 13:24
to the *h* of the kingdom.......Esth 5:3
to the *h* of the kingdom.......Esth 7:2
shall not live out *h* their ......Ps 55:23
hath Samaria committed *h* of ..Ezek 16:51
cubit and a *h* long ....Ezek 40:42
cubit and a *h* broad ....Ezek 40:42
for a time, times, and a *h*.....Dan 12:7
of barley, and a *h* homer .....Hos 3:2
h of the city shall go forth ....Zech 14:2
h of the mountain shall ....Zech 14:4
and *h* of it toward the ....Zech 14:4
h of them toward the ....Zech 14:8
h of them toward the ....Zech 14:8
it thee, unto the *h* of my......Mark 6:23
departed, leaving, him *h* ......Luke 10:30
the *h* of my goods I give ......Luke 19:8
about the space of *h* an ....Rev 8:1
three days and a *h* the ....Rev 11:11

HALFHEARTEDNESS—*lack of enthusiasm*

Causes of:
Sin.....................2Sam 11:25-27
Indecision..............Hos 10:1, 2
Selfishness ....Hag 1:4-11
Unconcern 2Cor 8:10-12

Examples of:
Jehu....................2Ki 10:31
Joash...................2Ki 13:18, 19
Judah ....Jer 3:10

HALF-SHEKEL TAX—*a temple tax*
Commanded ....Ex 30:13, 14
Also called "two-drachma tax" ....Matt 17:24-27

HALF-TRIBE OF MANASSEH—*the part of Manasseh east of the Jordan*

Clans of:
Machir ....Josh 17:1
Hezron 1Chr 2:21-23

h the tribe of Manasseh.......1Chr 5:18
the *h* tribe of Manasseh.......1Chr 5:26
out of the *h* tribe, namely.....1Chr 6:61
the *h* tribe of Manasseh.......1Chr 6:61
the *h* tribe of Manasseh.......1Chr 6:71
the *h* tribe of Manasseh.......1Chr 12:37
h tribe of Manasseh, Joel 1Chr 27:20

HALHUL (hăl'hŭl)—*"tremble"*
A city in Judah ....Josh 15:20, 21, 58

HALI (hā'lī)—*"sickness"*
Town of Asher ....Josh 19:25

HALING—*hauling*

[*also* HALE]
he *h* thee to the judge ....Luke 12:58
h men and women............Acts 8:3

HALL—*a large building; an auditorium*
Jesus into the common *h*......Matt 27:27
a fire in the midst of the *h*....Luke 22:55
unto the *h* of judgment ....John 18:28
not into the judgment *h*.......John 18:28
entered into the judgment *h*...John 18:33
into the judgment *h* ....John 19:9
kept in Herod's judgment *h* ...Acts 23:35

HALLELUJAH—*See* ALLELUIA

HALLOHESH (hă-lō'hĕsh)—*"the whisperer; the slanderer"—the father of one who repaired the walls of Jerusalem*
Repairs walls and signs covenant ....Neh 3:12; Neh 10:24

HALLOW—*to make holy; set apart for holy use*

[*also* HALLOWED]
the sabbath day, and *h* it .....Ex 20:11
children of Israel shall *h* ......Ex 28:38
to *h* them, to minister ....Ex 29:1
and he shall be *h*, and his .....Ex 29:21
and shalt *h* it, and all the .....Ex 40:9
she shall touch no *h* thing .....Lev 12:4
cleanse it, and *h* it from ......Lev 16:19
profaned the *h* thing..........Lev 19:8
those things which they *h* .....Lev 22:2
the children of Israel *h*........Lev 22:3

I will be *h* among the . . . . Lev 22:32
I am the Lord which *h* . . . . Lev 22:32
And ye shall *h* the fiftieth . . . . . Lev 25:10
I *h* unto me all the first . . . . Num 3:13
every man's *h* things shall . . . . . Num 5:10
and shall *h* his head that . . . . . . Num 6:11
fire yonder; for they are *h* . . . . Num 16:37
therefore they are *h* . . . . Num 16:38
all the *h* things of the . . . . Num 18:8
even the *h* part thereof . . . . Num 18:29
I have brought away the *h* . . . . Deut 26:13
there is *h* bread; if the 1Sam 21:4
the priest gave him *h* 1Sam 21:6
same day did the king *h* 1Kin 8:64
I have *h* his house 1Kin 9:3
which I have *h* for my 1Kin 9:7
h things that Jehoshaphat 2Kin 12:18
and his own *h* things, and 2Kin 12:18
Moreover Solomon *h* the 2Chr 7:7
the Lord which he had *h* 2Chr 36:14
but *h* ye the sabbath day . . . . . . Jer 17:22
but *h* the sabbath day, to . . . . . Jer 17:24
to *h* the sabbath day, and . . . . . Jer 17:27
h my sabbaths; and they . . . . . . Ezek 20:20
they shall *h* my sabbaths . . . . . . Ezek 44:24
in heaven, *H* be thy name . . . . . Matt 6:9
in heaven, *H* be thy name . . . . . Luke 11:2

HALT—*to stop; lame*

[*also* HALTED, HALTETH, HALTING]
him, and he *h* upon his . . . . Gen 32:31
How long *h* ye between 1Kin 18:21
I am ready to *h*, and my . . . . . . Ps 38:17
familiars watched for my *h* . . . . Jer 20:10
will I assemble her that *h* . . . . . Mic 4:6
I will make her that *h* a . . . . Mic 4:7
I will save her that *h*, and . . . . . Zeph 3:19
to enter into life *h* or . . . . Matt 18:8
better for thee to enter *h* . . . . . Mark 9:45
the maimed, and the *h* . . . . Luke 14:21
of blind, *h*, withered . . . . John 5:3

HAM (hăm)—*"hot"*
1. Noah's youngest son . . . . Gen 5:32
   Enters ark . . . . Gen 7:7
   His immoral behavior merits Noah's curse . . . Gen 9:22-25
   Father of descendants of repopulated earth . . . . Gen 10:6-20
2. Poetical name of Egypt . . Ps 105:23, 27
3. Hamites at Gedor 1Chr 4:39, 40
4. Place where Chedorlaomer defeated the Zuzim . . . . Gen 14:5

begat three sons, Shem, *H* . . . . Gen 6:10
Noah, and Shem, and *H* . . . . . Gen 7:13
were Shem, and *H*, and . . . . Gen 9:18
and *H* is the father of . . . . Gen 9:18
Shem, *H*, and Japheth . . . . Gen 10:1
Noah, Shem, *H*, and 1Chr 1:4
The sons of *H*; Cush 1Chr 1:8
in the tabernacles of *H* . . . . Ps 78:51
works in the land of *H* . . . . Ps 106:22

HAMAN (hā'măn)—*"celebrated Human (Humban)"—the prime minister of Ahasuerus who plotted against the Jews*
   Plots to destroy Jews . . . . Esth 3:3-15
   Invited to Esther's banquet . . . . Esth 5:1-14
   forced to honor Mordecai. Esth 6:5-14
   Hanged on his own gallows . . . . Esth 7:1-10

[*also* HAMAN'S]
H..son of Hammedatha . . . . Esth 3:1
bowed, and reverenced *H* . . . . . Esth 3:2
of the money that *H* had . . . . . . Esth 4:7
Now *H* was come into the . . . . . Esth 6:4
the house of *H* the Jews' . . . . . . Esth 8:1
which he had taken from *H* . . . Esth 8:2
Mordecai over the house of *H* . Esth 8:2
put away the mischief of *H* . . . Esth 8:3
the letters devised by *H* . . . . . . Esth 8:5
given Esther the house of *H* . . . Esth 8:7
The ten sons of *H* the son . . . . Esth 9:10
and the ten sons of *H* . . . . Esth 9:12
and let *H* ten sons be . . . . Esth 9:13
and they hanged *H* ten . . . . Esth 9:14
Because *H* the son of . . . . Esth 9:24

HAMATH (hā'măth)—*"anger"*
   Hittite city north of Damascus . . . . Josh 13:5
   Spies visit . . . . Num 13:21
   Israel's northern limit . . . . Num 34:8
   Solomon's boundary 1Kin 8:65
   Storage cities built 2Chr 8:3, 4
   Captured by the Assyrians 2Kin 18:34
   People of, deported to Samaria 2Kin 17:24, 30
   Israelites exiled . . . . Is 11:11
   Mentioned by Jeremiah . . Jer 49:23
   Limit of Ezekiel's prophecy . . . . Ezek 47:16-20
   Called Hemeth . . . . Amos 6:14

unto the entering in of *H* . . . . . Judg 3:3
When Toi king of *H* 2Sam 8:9
from the entering of *H* 2Kin 14:25
and *H*, which belonged 2Kin 14:28
Where is the king of *H* 2Kin 19:13
at Riblah in the land of *H* 2Kin 23:33
Riblah in the land of *H* 2Kin 25:21
king of Zobah unto *H* 1Chr 18:3
when Tou king of *H* heard 1Chr 18:9
of *H* unto the river of 2Chr 7:8
is not *H* as Arpad? is not . . . . . Is 10:9
Where are the gods of *H* . . . . . . Is 36:19
Where is the king of *H* . . . . Is 37:13
Riblah in the land of *H* . . . . Jer 52:9
in Riblah in the land of *H* . . . . Jer 52:27
Hethlon, as one goeth to *H* . . . Ezek 48:1
Damascus northward..*H* . . . . . . Ezek 48:1
from thence go ye to *H* . . . . Amos 6:2
H also shall border thereby . . . . Zech 9:2

HAMATHITES (hā'măth-īts)
   People of Hamath . . . . Gen 10:18

[*also* HAMATHITE]
the Zemarite, and the *H* 1Chr 1:16

HAMATH-ZOBAH (hā-măth-zō'bä)—*"fortress of Zobah"*
   Captured by Solomon 2Chr 8:3

HAMMATH (hăm'ăth)—*"hot spring"*
1. City of Naphtali . . . . Josh 19:35
   Probably the same as Hammon and Hammothdor . 1Chr 6:76
2. Founder of the Rechabites 1Chr 2:55

HAMMEDATHA (hăm-ĕ-dā'thä)—*"given by the moon"*
   Father of Haman . . . . Esth 3:1

Haman the son of *H* the . . . . . . Esth 3:10
by Haman the son of *H* . . . . Esth 8:5
of Haman the son of *H* . . . . Esth 9:10
son of *H*, the Agagite, the . . . . Esth 9:24

HAMMELECH (hăm'ĕ-lĕk)—*general title meaning "king"*
   Father of Jerahmeel . . . . . Jer 36:26

Malchiah the son of *H* . . . . Jer 38:6

HAMMER—*a workman's tool*

Literal uses of:
   Drive tent pegs . . . . Judg 4:21
   Not used in Temple 1Kin 6:7
   Straighten metal . . . . Is 41:7

Figurative uses of:
   God's Word . . . . Jer 23:29
   Babylon . . . . Jer 50:23

[*also* HAMMERS]
right hand..workmen's *h* . . . . . . Judg 5:26
and with the *h* she smote . . . . . Judg 5:26
work at once with axes and *h* . Ps 74:6
and fashioneth it with *h* . . . . Is 44:12
fasten it with nails..*h* . . . . Jer 10:4

HAMMOLEKETH (hă-mŏl'ĕ-kĕth)—*"the queen"*
   Sister of Gilead 1Chr 7:17, 18

HAMMON (hăm'ŏn)—*"hot waters"*
1. Village of Asher . . . . Josh 19:28
2. Town of Naphtali 1Chr 6:76
See HAMMATH

HAMMOTH-DOR (hăm'ŏth-dôr)—*"hot spring"*
   City of refuge . . . . Josh 21:32
   See HAMMATH

HAMONAH (hă-mō'nä)—*"multitude"*
   Site of Gog's defeat . . . . . Ezek 39:11-16

HAMON-GOG (hā'mŏn-gŏg)—*"multitude of Gog"*
   Memorial name of Gog's burial . . . . Ezek 39:11

buried it in the valley of *H* . . . . Ezek 39:15

HAMOR, EMMOR (hā'môr, ē'môr)—*"ass"*
   Sells land to Jacob . . . . . . Gen 33:18-20
   Killed by Jacob's sons . . . Gen 34:1-31

bought of the sons of *H* . . . . Josh 24:32
serve the men of *H*, the . . . . Judg 9:28

HAMUEL (hăm'ū-ĕl)—*"wrath of God"*
   Son of Mishma 1Chr 4:26

HAMUL (hā'mŭl)—*"pity"*
   Son of Pharez . . . . Gen 46:12
   Founder of tribal family . . Num 26:21

of Pharez; Hezron, and *H* 1Chr 2:5

HAMUTAL (hă-mū'tăl)—*"kinsman of the dew"*
   Wife of King Josiah 2Kin 23:30, 31
   Mother of Jehoahaz and Zedekiah 2Kin 24:18
   Daughter of Jeremiah of Libnah . . . . Jer 52:1

HANAMEEL (hăn'ă-mēl)—*"gift of grace of God"*
   Cousin of Jeremiah the prophet . . . . Jer 32:7

so *H* mine uncle's son . . . . Jer 32:8
I bought the field of *H* . . . . Jer 32:9
the sight of *H* mine . . . . Jer 32:12

HANAN (hā'năn)—*"merciful"*
1. One of David's mighty men 1Chr 11:26, 43
2. Benjamite 1Chr 8:23, 25
3. Descendant of Jonathan . 1Chr 8:38
4. Prophet . . . . Jer 35:4
5. Head of Temple servants. Ezra 2:46
6. Explained Law . . . . Neh 8:7
7. Nehemiah's assistant treasurer . . . . Neh 13:13
8. Signers of the covenant . . Neh 10:22, 26

Obadiah, and *H*: these 1Chr 9:44
The children of *H*, the . . . . Neh 7:49
Kelita, Pelaiah, *H* . . . . Neh 10:10

HANANEEL (hă-năn'ĕ-ĕl)—*"God is gracious"*
   Tower at Jerusalem . . . . . . Jer 31:38

unto the tower of *H* . . . . Neh 3:1
the tower of *H*, and the . . . . Neh 12:39
the tower of *H* unto the . . . . Zech 14:10

HANANI (hă-nā'nī)—*"gracious"*
1. Father of Jehu the prophet 1Kin 16:1, 7
   Rebukes Asa; confined to prison 2Chr 16:7-10
2. Son of Heman; head of Levitical course 1Chr 25:4, 25
3. Priest who divorced his foreign wife . . . . Ezra 10:20
4. Nehemiah's brother; brings news concerning the Jews . . . . Neh 1:2
   Becomes a governor of Jerusalem . . . . Neh 7:2
5. Levite musician . . . . Neh 12:35, 36

Jehu the son of *H* the seer 2Chr 19:2
book of Jehu the son of *H* 2Chr 20:34

like Daniel, ***H***, Mishael .... Dan 1:19
the thing known to ***H*** .... Dan 2:17

HANANIAH (hăn-ä-nī'ä)—*"Jehovah is gracious"*

1. Benjamite chief 1Chr 8:24, 25
2. Son of Heman; head of Levitical division 1Chr 25:4, 23
3. One of King Uzziah's captains 2Chr 26:11
4. Father of Zedekiah .... Jer 36:12
5. False prophet who contradicts Jeremiah . Jer 28:1-17
6. Ancestor of Irijah ...... Jer 37:13-15
7. Hebrew name of Shadrach .... Dan 1:6, 7, 11
8. Son of Zerubbabel ..... 1Chr 3:19-21 Probably same as Joanna .... Luke 3:27
9. Son of Bebai; divorced his foreign wife ...... Ezra 10:28
10. Postexilic workman .... Neh 3:8, 30
11. Postexilic priest .... Neh 12:41
12. Postexilic chief; signs document .... Neh 10:23
13. Postexilic ruler .... Neh 7:2
14. Priest of Joiakim's time . Neh 12:12

none like Daniel, ***H***, Mishael .. Dan 1:19
made the thing known to ***H*** ... Dan 2:17

HAND—*the extremity of the arm*

Unusual incidents:
Mysterious .... Dan 5:1-6
Healing withered .... Mark 3:1-3
Offending, to be cut off .. Matt 18:8

Uses of hands:
Clapping—in joy 2Kin 11:12
Washing—in innocency ... Matt 27:24
Joining—in agreement ... 2Kin 10:15
Striking—in suretyship ... Prov 17:16-18
Striking—in anger ...... Num 24:10
Under thigh—in oaths ... Gen 47:29, 31

Right hand, expressive of:
Honor .... Ps 45:9
Power .... Ps 110:1
Love .... Song 2:6
Oath .... Is 62:8
Accusation .... Zech 3:1
Self-denial .... Matt 5:30
Fellowship .... Gal 2:9

[*also* HANDS]
our work and toil of our ***h*** .... Gen 5:29
submit thyself under her ***h*** .... Gen 16:9
innocency of my ***h*** have I ..... Gen 20:5
two bracelets for her ***h*** .... Gen 24:22
bracelets upon his sister's ***h*** ... Gen 24:30
bracelets upon her ***h*** .... Gen 24:47
of the goats upon his ***h*** .... Gen 27:16
the ***h*** are the ***h*** of Esau .... Gen 27:22
him not, because his ***h*** .... Gen 27:23
as his brother Esau's ***h*** .... Gen 27:23
the labor of my ***h*** and .... Gen 31:42
delivered him out of their ***h*** ... Gen 37:21
rid him out of their ***h*** to ...... Gen 37:22
bought him out of the ***h*** .... Gen 39:1
we brought down in our ***h*** .... Gen 43:22
guiding his ***h*** wittingly .... Gen 48:14
the arms of his ***h*** were .... Gen 49:24
by the ***h*** of the mighty God ... Gen 49:24
I will spread abroad my ***h*** ..... Ex 9:29
spread abroad his ***h*** unto ...... Ex 9:33
O Lord, which thy ***h*** .... Ex 15:17
But Moses' ***h*** were heavy ..... Ex 17:12
Hur stayed up his ***h***, the ...... Ex 17:12
his ***h*** were steady until .... Ex 17:12
h upon the head of the .... Ex 29:10
h upon the head of the .... Ex 29:15
the ***h*** of Aaron, and in the ***h*** .. Ex 29:24
receive them of their ***h*** .... Ex 29:25
sons shall wash their ***h*** .... Ex 30:19
they shall wash their ***h*** .... Ex 30:21
cast the tables out of his ***h*** .... Ex 32:19
did spin with their ***h*** and ...... Ex 35:25
washed their ***h*** and their ...... Ex 40:31
His own ***h*** shall bring the ...... Lev 7:30
their ***h*** upon the head of ...... Lev 8:14
and hath not rinsed his ***h*** ..... Lev 15:11
his ***h*** full of sweet incense ..... Lev 16:12
offering of memorial in her ***h*** .. Num 5:18
upon the ***h*** of the Nazarite .... Num 6:19
Levites shall lay their ***h*** .... Num 8:12
fruit of the land in their ***h*** ..... Deut 1:25
God delivered into our ***h*** ...... Deut 3:3
work of men's ***h***, wood .... Deut 4:28
covenant were in my two ***h*** .... Deut 9:15
cast them out of my two ***h*** .... Deut 9:17
thou puttest thine ***h*** .... Deut 12:18
all the works of thine ***h*** .... Deut 16:15
The ***h*** of the witnesses .... Deut 17:7
afterward the ***h*** of all the ..... Deut 17:7
delivered it into thine ***h*** .... Deut 20:13
shall wash their ***h*** over .... Deut 21:6
in all the work of thine ***h*** ..... Deut 24:19
the ***h*** of the craftsman .... Deut 27:15
through the work of your ***h*** ... Deut 31:29
let his ***h*** be sufficient for ...... Deut 33:7
hath delivered into our ***h*** ...... Josh 2:24
delivered them into the ***h*** ..... Judg 2:14
sold them into the ***h*** of .... Judg 2:14
into the ***h*** of the Midianites ... Judg 6:13
the Midianites into their ***h*** .... Judg 7:2
delivered into your ***h*** .... Judg 8:3
to those deserving of his ***h*** .... Judg 9:16
the ***h*** of the Philistines .... Judg 10:7
into the ***h*** of the children ..... Judg 10:7
of Ammon into mine ***h*** .... Judg 11:30
delivered them into his ***h*** ...... Judg 11:32
me not out of their ***h*** .... Judg 12:2
meat offering at our ***h*** .... Judg 13:23
he took thereof in his ***h*** ...... Judg 14:9
bands loosed from off his ***h*** ... Judg 15:14
hath delivered into our ***h*** ...... Judg 16:24
hath given it into your ***h*** ..... Judg 18:10
her ***h*** were upon the .... Judg 19:27
both the palms of his ***h*** 1Sam 5:4
of the ***h*** of the Philistines 1Sam 7:14
shalt receive of their ***h*** 1Sam 10:4
by the ***h*** of messengers 1Sam 11:7
climbed up upon his ***h*** 1Sam 14:13
he will give you into our ***h*** 1Sam 17:47
himself mad in their ***h*** 1Sam 21:13
deliver me into the ***h*** of my ... 1Sam 30:15
now let your ***h*** be 2Sam 2:7
Thy ***h*** were not bound, nor ... 2Sam 3:34
his ***h*** were feeble and all 2Sam 4:1
the ***h*** of all that are with 2Sam 16:21
he delivered them into the ***h*** .. 2Sam 21:9
the cleanness of my ***h*** 2Sam 22:21
cannot be taken with ***h*** 2Sam 23:6
spread forth his ***h*** toward 1Kin 8:22
the ***h*** of the chief of the 1Kin 14:27
the work of his ***h***, in being 1Kin 16:7
poured water on the ***h*** of 2Kin 3:11
and his ***h*** upon his ***h*** 2Kin 4:34
in not receiving at his ***h*** 2Kin 5:20
Joram turned his ***h***, and 2Kin 9:23
I have brought into your ***h*** 2Kin 10:24
the ***h*** of them that did the 2Kin 12:11
his ***h*** upon the king's ***h*** 2Kin 13:16
the work of men's ***h***, wood 2Kin 19:18
the works of their ***h*** 2Kin 22:17
is no wrong in mine ***h*** 1Chr 12:17
under the ***h*** of Asaph 1Chr 25:2
to be made by the ***h*** of 1Chr 29:5
who hath with his ***h*** 2Chr 6:4
by the ***h*** of his servants 2Chr 8:18
the ***h*** of the chief of the 2Chr 12:10
let not your ***h*** be weak 2Chr 15:7
were the work of the ***h*** 2Chr 32:19
the works of their ***h*** 2Chr 34:25
the blood from their ***h*** 2Chr 35:11
them strengthened their ***h*** ..... Ezra 1:6
weakened the ***h*** of the .... Ezra 4:4
and prospereth in their ***h*** ...... Ezra 5:8
to strengthen their ***h*** in .... Ezra 6:22
and spread out my ***h*** unto ..... Ezra 9:5
gave their ***h*** that they .... Ezra 10:19
they strengthened their ***h*** ...... Neh 2:18
one of his ***h*** wrought in ...... Neh 4:17
Their ***h*** shall be weakened .... Neh 6:9
O God, strengthen my ***h*** ...... Neh 6:9
with lifting up their ***h*** .... Neh 8:6
gavest them into their ***h*** .... Neh 9:24
hast blessed the work..***h*** ...... Job 1:10
strengthened the weak ***h*** ...... Job 4:3
their ***h*** cannot perform .... Job 5:12
and make my ***h*** never so ...... Job 9:30
desire to the work of thine ***h*** .. Job 14:15
any injustice in mine ***h*** .... Job 16:17
he that hath clean ***h*** shall ..... Job 17:9
by the pureness of thine ***h*** .... Job 22:30
the strength of their ***h*** .... Job 30:2
all are the work of his ***h*** ...... Job 34:19
there be iniquity in my ***h*** ...... Ps 7:3
work of his own ***h*** .... Ps 9:16
the cleanness of my ***h*** in ...... Ps 18:24
they pierced my ***h*** and my .... Ps 22:16
He that hath clean ***h***, and ..... Ps 24:4
I will wash mine ***h*** in .... Ps 26:6
when I lift up my ***h*** toward .... Ps 28:2
the operation of his ***h***, he ..... Ps 28:5
o clap your ***h***, all ye .... Ps 47:1
the violence of your ***h*** in ...... Ps 58:2
shall..stretch out her ***h*** .... Ps 68:31
might have found their ***h*** ...... Ps 76:5
his ***h*** were delivered from ..... Ps 81:6
the work of our ***h*** upon us .... Ps 90:17
work of our ***h*** establish .... Ps 90:17
bear thee up in their ***h*** .... Ps 91:12
in the works of thy ***h*** .... Ps 92:4
Let the floods clap their ***h*** .... Ps 98:8
They have ***h***, but they .... Ps 115:7
Thy ***h*** have made me and ..... Ps 119:73
eat the labor of thine ***h*** .... Ps 128:2
your ***h*** in the sanctuary .... Ps 134:2
gold, the work of men's ***h*** ..... Ps 135:15
from the ***h*** of the wicked ...... Ps 140:4
I muse on the work of thy ***h*** .. Ps 143:5
teacheth my ***h*** to war .... Ps 144:1
a little folding of the ***h*** .... Prov 6:10
and ***h*** that shed innocent ...... Prov 6:17
recompense of a man's ***h*** ...... Prov 12:14
h refuse to labor .... Prov 21:25
one of them that strike ***h*** ..... Prov 22:26
a little folding of the ***h*** .... Prov 24:33
willingly with her ***h*** .... Prov 31:13
layeth her ***h*** to the spindle .... Prov 31:19
and her ***h*** hold the distaff ..... Prov 31:19
reacheth forth her ***h*** .... Prov 31:20
Give her the fruit of her ***h*** .... Prov 31:31
the works that my ***h*** had ...... Eccl 2:11
than both the ***h*** full with ...... Eccl 4:6
her ***h*** as bands: whoso .... Eccl 7:26
and my ***h*** dropped with .... Song 5:5
the work of the ***h*** of a .... Song 7:1
ye spread forth your ***h*** .... Is 1:15
your ***h*** are full of blood .... Is 1:15
the work of their own ***h*** .... Is 2:8
the operation of his ***h*** .... Is 5:12
the work of his ***h***, neither ..... Is 17:8
shall spread forth his ***h*** .... Is 25:11
spreadeth forth his ***h*** .... Is 25:11
together..spoils of their ***h*** ..... Is 25:11
the work of mine ***h***, in the .... Is 29:23
your own ***h*** have made .... Is 31:7
shaketh his ***h*** from .... Is 33:15
Strengthen ye the weak ***h*** ..... Is 35:3
the work of men's ***h*** .... Is 37:19
the work of my ***h*** .... Is 45:11
I, even my ***h***, have .... Is 45:12
upon the palms of my ***h*** .... Is 49:16
your ***h*** are defiled with blood .. Is 59:3
the work of my ***h***, that I ...... Is 60:21
enjoy the work of their ***h*** ..... Is 65:22
the works of their own ***h*** ...... Jer 1:16
that spreadeth her ***h*** .... Jer 4:31
the work of the ***h*** of the ...... Jer 10:3
and by the ***h*** of them that ..... Jer 19:7
they strengthen also the ***h*** ..... Jer 23:14
works of your ***h*** to your .... Jer 25:7
his ***h*** on his loins, as a .... Jer 30:6
the ***h*** of him that telleth ..... Jer 33:13
he weakeneth the ***h*** of .... Jer 38:4
the ***h*** of all the people .... Jer 38:4

children for feebleness of ***h*** ... Jer 47:3
his ***h*** waxed feeble ... Jer 50:43
delivered me into their ***h*** ... Lam 1:14
that pass by clap their ***h*** ... Lam 2:15
up our heart with our ***h*** ... Lam 3:41
the work of the ***h*** of the ... Lam 4:2
The ***h*** of the pitiful ... Lam 4:10
And they had the ***h*** of a ... Ezek 1:8
into the ***h*** of the strangers ... Ezek 7:21
and put it into the ***h*** of ... Ezek 10:7
h of a man was under ... Ezek 10:21
strengthened the ***h*** of the ... Ezek 13:22
I put bracelets upon thy ***h*** ... Ezek 16:11
smite thine ***h*** together ... Ezek 21:14
can thine ***h*** be strong ... Ezek 22:14
bracelets upon their ***h*** ... Ezek 23:42
thou hast clapped thine ***h*** ... Ezek 25:6
stone was cut out without ***h*** ... Dan 2:34
deliver you out of my ***h***? ... Dan 3:15
more to the work of our ***h*** ... Hos 14:3
laid ***h*** on their substance ... Obad 1:13
the violence..in their ***h*** ... Jon 3:8
worship the work of thine ***h*** ... Mic 5:13
thee shall clap the ***h*** over ... Nah 3:19
and lifted up his ***h*** on ... Hab 3:10
Zion, Let not thine ***h*** ... Zeph 3:16
all the labor of the ***h*** ... Hag 1:11
all the labors of your ***h*** ... Hag 2:17
The ***h*** of Zerubbabel have ... Zech 4:9
his ***h*** shall also finish it ... Zech 4:9
Let your ***h*** be strong, ye ... Zech 8:9
fear not, but let your ***h*** be ... Zech 8:13
in their ***h*** they shall bear ... Matt 4:6
if thy right ***h*** offend thee ... Matt 5:30
left ***h*** know what thy right ***h*** ... Matt 6:3
but to eat with unwashen ***h*** ... Matt 15:20
rather than having two ***h*** ... Matt 18:8
right ***h***, other on left ***h*** ... Matt 20:21
sit on right ***h*** and on my ... Matt 20:23
Bind him ***h*** and foot ... Matt 22:13
but the goats on the left ***h*** ... Matt 25:33
left ***h***, Depart from me ... Matt 25:41
is betrayed into the ***h*** of ... Matt 26:45
crucified on right ***h*** ... Matt 27:38
there which had a withered ***h*** ... Mark 3:1
his ***h*** was restored whole ... Mark 3:5
except they wash their ***h*** ... Mark 7:3
his eyes, and put his ***h*** ... Mark 8:23
is delivered into the ***h*** ... Mark 9:31
than having two ***h*** to go ... Mark 9:43
is betrayed into the ***h*** ... Mark 14:41
temple that is made with ***h*** ... Mark 14:58
build another..without ***h*** ... Mark 14:58
with the palms of their ***h*** ... Mark 14:65
And in their ***h*** they shall ... Luke 4:11
rubbing them in their ***h*** ... Luke 6:1
whose right ***h*** was withered ... Luke 6:6
put his ***h*** to the plough ... Luke 9:62
into thy ***h*** I commend my ... Luke 23:46
Behold my ***h*** and my feet ... Luke 24:39
he lifted up his ***h***, and ... Luke 24:50
forth, bound ***h*** and foot ... John 11:44
but also my ***h*** and my ... John 13:9
showed unto them his ***h*** ... John 20:20
finger, and behold my ***h*** ... John 20:27
wicked ***h*** have crucified ... Acts 2:23
He is on my right ***h*** that ... Acts 2:25
Stretching forth thy ***h*** to ... Acts 4:30
by the ***h*** of the apostles ... Acts 5:12
in temples made with ***h*** ... Acts 7:48
and putting his ***h*** on him ... Acts 9:17
king stretched forth his ***h*** ... Acts 12:1
in temples made with ***h*** ... Acts 17:24
which are made with ***h*** ... Acts 19:26
bound his own ***h*** and feet ... Acts 21:11
deliver him into the ***h*** ... Acts 21:11
him away out of our ***h*** ... Acts 24:7
have stretched forth my ***h*** ... Rom 10:21
working with our own ***h*** ... 1Cor 4:12
Because I am not the ***h*** ... 1Cor 12:15
say unto the ***h***, I have no ... 1Cor 12:21
righteousness on right ***h*** ... 2Cor 6:7
in the flesh made by ***h*** ... Eph 2:11
circumcision made without ***h*** ... Col 2:11
work with your own ***h*** ... 1Thess 4:11
lifting up holy ***h***, without ... 1Tim 2:8
by the putting on of my ***h*** ... 2Tim 1:6
heavens..works of thine ***h*** ... Heb 1:10
holy places made with ***h*** ... Heb 9:24
lift up the ***h*** which hang ... Heb 12:12
Cleanse your ***h***, ye ... James 4:8
and our ***h*** have handled ... 1John 1:1
pair of balances in his ***h*** ... Rev 6:5
in his ***h*** a little book ... Rev 10:2
book which is open in the ***h*** ... Rev 10:8
mark in their right ***h*** ... Rev 13:16
in forehead or in his ***h*** ... Rev 14:9
a golden cup in her ***h*** ... Rev 17:4
and a great chain in his ***h*** ... Rev 20:1
foreheads, or in their ***h*** ... Rev 20:4

HAND, AT—*close, proximate*
kingdom of heaven is at ***h*** ... Matt 3:2
My time is at ***h*** ... Matt 26:18
hour is at ***h***, and the Son ... Matt 26:45
the kingdom of God is at ***h*** ... Mark 1:15
far spent, the day is at ***h*** ... Rom 13:12
end of all things is at ***h*** ... 1Pet 4:7
for the time is at ***h*** ... Rev 1:3

HAND OF GOD—*a metaphor for God's power*

Expressive of:
Judgment ... Ex 9:3
Chastening ... Job 19:21
Security ... John 10:29
Miracles ... Ex 3:20
Providence ... Ps 31:15
Provision ... Ps 145:16
Protection ... Ps 139:10
Punishment ... Ps 75:8
Pleading ... Is 65:2

[*also* HANDS]
by the ***h*** of the mighty God ... Gen 49:24
O Lord, which thou ***h*** ... Ex 15:17
Thine ***h*** have made me ... Job 10:8
The works of his ***h*** are ... Ps 111:7

HANDBREADTH—*measurement based on the width of a hand*
Border of ... Ex 37:12
Figurative of human life. . Ps 39:5

thickness of it was a ***h*** ... 2Chr 4:5

HANDFUL—*as much as the hand can grasp*
Of fine flour ... Lev 2:2—5:12
Of grain offering ... Num 5:26
Of barley ... Ezek 13:19

[*also* HANDFULS]
earth brought forth by ***h*** ... Gen 41:47
Take to you ***h*** of ashes of ... Ex 9:8
take of it his ***h*** ... Lev 6:15
took a ***h*** thereof, and burnt ... Lev 9:17
let fall also some of the ***h*** ... Ruth 2:16
a ***h*** of meal in a barrel ... 1Kin 17:12
Samaria shall suffice for ***h*** ... 1Kin 20:10
There shall be a ***h*** of ... Ps 72:16
Better is a ***h*** with quietness ... Eccl 4:6

HANDIWORK—*work done personally*
firmament showeth his ***h*** ... Ps 19:1

HANDKERCHIEF—*a piece of cloth used for an article of dress, to carry articles, or to wipe clean*
Touch of, brings healing. . Acts 19:12
Rendered "napkin" ... John 11:44
John 20:7

HANDLE—*to manage with the hands*

Used literally for:
Hold ... 2Chr 25:5
Touch ... Luke 24:39
Feel ... Ps 115:7

Used figuratively for:
Give attention ... Prov 16:20
Treat ... Mark 12:4

[*also* HANDLED, HANDLES, HANDLETH, HANDLING]
father of all such as ***h*** ... Gen 4:21
they that ***h*** the pen of the ... Judg 5:14
that could ***h*** shield and ... 1Chr 12:8
He that ***h*** a matter wisely ... Prov 16:20
upon the ***h*** of the lock ... Song 5:5
and they that ***h*** the law ... Jer 2:8
the Libyans, that ***h*** the ... Jer 46:9
the Lydians, that ***h*** and ... Jer 46:9
and him that ***h*** the sickle ... Jer 50:16
furbished that it may be ***h*** ... Ezek 21:11
all that ***h*** the oar, the ... Ezek 27:29
shields, all of them ***h*** ... Ezek 38:4
shall he stand that ***h*** the ... Amos 2:15
h the word of God ... 2Cor 4:2
touch not; taste not; ***h*** ... Col 2:21
and our hands have ***h*** ... 1John 1:1

HANDMAID—*female servant*

Examples of:
Hagar ... Gen 16:1
Zilpah ... Gen 29:24
Bilhah ... Gen 30:4

Expressive of humility:
Ruth ... Ruth 2:13
Woman of Endor ... 1Sam 28:7, 21, 22
Mary ... Luke 1:38

[*also* HANDMAIDEN, HANDMAIDENS, HANDMAIDS]
the Egyptian, Sarah's ***h*** ... Gen 25:12
Bilhah his ***h*** to be her ... Gen 29:29
Rachel and unto the two ***h*** ... Gen 33:1
he put the ***h*** and their ... Gen 33:2
Then the ***h*** came near ... Gen 33:6
sons of Bilhah, Rachel's ***h*** ... Gen 35:25
sons of Zilpah, Leah's ***h*** ... Gen 35:26
the son of thy ***h*** and the ... Ex 23:12
also for me, and for thy ***h*** ... Judg 19:19
like unto one of thine ***h*** ... Ruth 2:13
I am Ruth thine ***h*** ... Ruth 3:9
thy skirt over thine ***h*** ... Ruth 3:9
the affliction of thine ***h*** ... 1Sam 1:11
me, and not forget thine ***h*** ... 1Sam 1:11
but wilt give unto thine ***h*** ... 1Sam 1:11
Count not thine ***h*** for a ... 1Sam 1:16
Let thine ***h*** find grace in ... 1Sam 1:18
let thine ***h***, I pray thee ... 1Sam 25:24
hear the words of thine ***h*** ... 1Sam 25:24
but I thine ***h*** saw not the ... 1Sam 25:25
which thine ***h*** hath ... 1Sam 25:27
forgive the trespass of thine ***h***. . 1Sam 25:28
then remember thine ***h*** ... 1Sam 25:31
let thine ***h*** be a servant ... 1Sam 25:41
And thy ***h*** had two sons ... 2Sam 14:6
family is risen against..***h*** ... 2Sam 14:7
woman said, Let thine ***h*** ... 2Sam 14:12
and thy ***h*** said, I will now ... 2Sam 14:15
perform the request of his ***h*** ... 2Sam 14:15
to deliver his ***h*** out of the ... 2Sam 14:16
Then thine ***h*** said, The ... 2Sam 14:17
in the mouth of thine ***h*** ... 2Sam 14:19
Hear the words of thine ***h*** ... 2Sam 20:17
king, swear unto thine ***h*** ... 1Kin 1:13
Lord thy God unto thine ***h*** ... 1Kin 1:17
while thine ***h*** slept, and ... 1Kin 3:20
Thine ***h*** hath not any thing ... 2Kin 4:2
do not lie unto thine ***h*** ... 2Kin 4:16
save the son of thine ***h*** ... Ps 86:16
and the son of thine ***h*** ... Ps 116:16
and a ***h*** that is heir to ... Prov 30:23
for servants and for ***h*** ... Jer 34:11
every man his ***h***, whom ... Jer 34:16
you for servants and for ***h*** ... Jer 34:16
upon the ***h*** in those days ... Joel 2:29
the low estate of his ***h*** ... Luke 1:48
my servants and on my ***h*** ... Acts 2:18

HANDS, LAYING ON OF—*an action symbolizing God's anointing or power*

In the Old Testament:
Blessing a person ... Gen 48:14, 20
Transferring one's guilt . . Lev 4:14, 15
Setting apart for service . . Num 8:10, 11
Inaugurating a successor. . Num 27:18-23

In the New Testament:
Blessing ... Matt 19:13-15
Healing ... Matt 9:18

Ordaining deacons ....Acts 6:6
Sending out missionaries. .Acts 13:2, 3
Ordaining officers 1Tim 4:14
In bestowing the Holy Spirit ....Acts 8:17, 18

Aaron shall lay both his ***h***.....Lev 16:21
lay their ***h*** upon his head .....Lev 24:14
Moses had laid his ***h*** upon ....Deut 34:9
they laid ***h*** on her; and 2Chr 23:15
they laid their ***h*** upon.........2Chr 29:23
ye do so again, I will lay ***h***....Neh 13:21
he thought scorn to lay ***h*** .....Esth 3:6
but they laid not their ***h*** ......Esth 9:16
laid his ***h*** upon a few sick .....Mark 6:5
they shall lay ***h*** on the ....Mark 16:18
And he laid his ***h*** on her ......Luke 13:13
they shall lay their ***h*** on ....Luke 21:12
but no man laid ***h*** on him .....John 7:30
and no man laid ***h*** on him ....John 8:20
laying on of the apostles' ***h***....Acts 8:18
prayed, and laid their ***h*** ....Acts 13:3
when Paul had laid his ***h*** ......Acts 19:6
laid his ***h*** on him, and ....Acts 28:8
Lay ***h*** suddenly on no.........1Tim 5:22
and of laying on of ***h*** ....Heb 6:2

HANDSTAVES—*a long, pointed wooden staff that foot soldiers used as a weapon*
the arrows, and the ***h*** ....Ezek 39:9

HANDWRITING—*writing done by hand, as in a manuscript*
Of a king, changeable ...Dan 6:8-27
Of God, unchangeable ...Dan 5:5-31

Blotting out the ***h*** of..........Col 2:14

HANES (hā'nēz)—*"mercury"*
Probably an Egyptian city.Is 30:4

HANG—*to suspend*

[*also* HANGED, HANGETH, HANGING, HANGINGS]
shall ***h*** over the backside ......Ex 26:12
thou shalt ***h*** it upon four ......Ex 26:32
shalt make a ***h*** for the ....Ex 26:36
thou shalt make for the ***h*** .....Ex 26:37
southward there shall be ***h*** ....Ex 27:9
west side shall be ***h*** of ....Ex 27:12
other side shall be ***h*** ....Ex 27:15
gate of the court shall be a ***h*** ..Ex 27:16
and the ***h*** for the door at .....Ex 35:15
h for the door of the court ....Ex 35:17
he made a ***h*** for the ....Ex 36:37
the ***h*** of the court were of.....Ex 38:9
for the west side were ***h*** ......Ex 38:12
that hand, were ***h*** of fifteen ...Ex 38:15
h for the gate of the court ....Ex 38:18
answerable to the ***h*** of the ....Ex 38:18
h for the tabernacle door .....Ex 39:38
the ***h*** for the court gate ....Ex 39:40
put the ***h*** of the door ....Ex 40:5
h up the ***h*** at the court ....Ex 40:8
he set up the ***h*** at the door....Ex 40:28
set up the ***h*** of the court ......Ex 40:33
and the ***h*** for the door ....Num 3:25
And the ***h*** of the court.........Num 3:26
h, and all the service ....Num 3:31
and the ***h*** for the door ....Num 4:25
h for the door of the gate .....Num 4:26
h them up before the Lord ....Num 25:4
thy life shall ***h*** in doubt ....Deut 28:66
where the women wove ***h*** 2Kin 23:7
white, green, and blue, ***h*** .....Esth 1:6
and ***h*** the earth upon ....Job 26:7
We ***h*** our harps upon the .....Ps 137:2
there ***h*** a thousand ....Song 4:4
And they shall ***h*** upon ....Is 22:24
the virgins of Jerusalem ***h*** .....Lam 2:10
Princes are ***h*** up by their ......Lam 5:12
men take a pin of it to ***h*** ......Ezek 15:3
they ***h*** the shield and ....Ezek 27:10
they ***h*** their shields upon ......Ezek 27:11
that a millstone were ***h*** ....Matt 18:6
h all the law and the prophets .Matt 22:40
that a millstone were ***h*** ....Mark 9:42
that a millstone were ***h*** ....Luke 17:2
venomous beast ***h*** on his ......Acts 28:4
lift up the hands which ***h***......Heb 12:12

HANGING—*a form of punishment*
Absalom................2Sam 18:9-17
Ahithophel.............2Sam 17:23
Judas..................Matt 27:5
Chief baker ....Gen 40:19, 22
King of Ai ....Josh 8:29
Five Canaanite kings.....Josh 10:26, 27
Ish-bosheth's murderers ..2Sam 4:12
Bodies of Saul and Jonathan 2Sam 21:12
Law of ....Ezra 6:11
Haman ....Esth 7:10
Haman's sons ....Esth 9:14
Curse of ....Gal 3:13
Saul's descendants 2Sam 21:9
Jesus Christ ....John 19:31

[*also* HANGED]
But he ***h*** the chief baker ......Gen 40:22
mine office, and him he ***h***.....Gen 41:13
and thou ***h*** him on a tree .....Deut 21:22
h is accursed of God..........Deut 21:23
and ***h*** himself, and died 2Sam 17:23
I saw Absalom ***h*** in an........2Sam 18:10
and we will ***h*** them up 2Sam 21:6
bones of them that were ***h*** 2Sam 21:13
therefore they were both ***h*** ....Esth 2:23
king that Mordecai may be ***h*** ..Esth 5:14
to ***h*** Mordecai on the ....Esth 6:4
Then the king said, ***H*** ....Esth 7:9
him they have ***h*** upon the .....Esth 8:7
let Haman's ten sons be ***h***.....Esth 9:13
he and his sons should be ***h*** ...Esth 9:25
malefactors which were ***h*** .....Luke 23:39
ye slew and ***h*** on a tree ....Acts 5:30

HANNAH (hăn'ä)—*"grace"*
Favored wife of Elkanah .1Sam 1:5
Childless................1Sam 1:5, 6
Provoked by Peninnah ...1Sam 1:6, 7
Wrongly accused by Eli ..1Sam 1:14
Prayerful 1Sam 1:10
Attentive to her child 1Sam 1:22
Fulfills her vows.........1Sam 1:11-28
Magnifies God 1Sam 2:1-10
Recognizes the Messiah ("his anointed").......1Sam 2:10
Model of Mary's song....Luke 1:46-54

name of the one was ***H*** 1Sam 1:2
but ***H*** had no children 1Sam 1:2
H, why weepest thou? 1Sam 1:8
So ***H*** rose up after they 1Sam 1:9
the Lord visited ***H***, so 1Sam 2:21

HANNATHON (hăn'ä-thŏn)—*"dedicated to grace"*
Town of Zebulun........Josh 19:14

HANNIEL, HANIEL (hăn'ĭ-ĕl, hăn'ĭ-ĕl)—*"God is gracious"*
1. Manassite prince ....Num 34:23
2. Asherite 1Chr 7:30, 39

HANOCH (hā'nŏk)—*"dedicated"*
1. Descendant of Abraham .Gen 25:4; 1Chr 1:33
2. Son of Reuben ....Gen 46:9
3. Head of tribal family ....Num 26:5

[*also* HANOCHITES]
H and Pallu, Hezron, and .....Ex 6:14
cometh the family..***H*** ....Num 26:5
H, and Pallu, Hezron 1Chr 5:3

HANUN (hā'nŭn)—*"favored"*
1. King of Ammon 2Sam 10:1
Disgraces David's ambassadors 2Sam 10:2-5
Is defeated by David 2Sam 10:6-14
2, 3. Postexilic workmen ...Neh 3:13, 30

I will show kindness unto ***H***...1Chr 19:2
children of Ammon to ***H***......1Chr 19:2
H took David's servants.......1Chr 19:4

HAP—*by chance*

[*also* HAPLY]
her ***h*** was to light on a........Ruth 2:3
if ***h*** the people had eaten 1Sam 14:30
if ***h*** he might find any ....Mark 11:13
Lest ***h***, after he hath laid .....Luke 14:29
lest ***h*** ye be found even to ....Acts 5:39
Lest ***h*** if they of Macedonia ...2Cor 9:4

HAPHARAIM (hăf-ä-rā'ĭm)—*"two pits"*
Town of Issachar ....Josh 19:19

HAPPEN—*to occur*

[*also* HAPPENED, HAPPENETH]
it was a chance that ***h*** to 1Sam 6:9
shall no punishment ***h*** 1Sam 28:10
As I ***h*** by chance upon........2Sam 1:6
all that had ***h*** unto him ....Esth 4:7
There shall no evil ***h*** to ....Prov 12:21
that one event ***h*** to them......Eccl 2:14
As it ***h*** to the fool............Eccl 2:15
so it ***h*** even to me ....Eccl 2:15
men, unto whom it ***h*** ....Eccl 8:14
wicked men, to whom it ***h*** ....Eccl 8:14
time and chance ***h*** to ....Eccl 9:11
show us what shall ***h***..........Is 41:22
therefore this evil is ***h*** ....Jer 44:23
what things should ***h***...........Mark 10:32
these things which had ***h*** ......Luke 24:14
at that which had ***h*** unto ......Acts 3:10
blindness in part is ***h*** to ....Rom 11:25
all these things ***h*** unto 1Cor 10:11
that the things which ***h***........Phil 1:12
some strange thing ***h***..........1Pet 4:12
But it is ***h*** unto them 2Pet 2:22

HAPPINESS OF THE SAINTS
Is derived from:
Fear of God ....Ps 128:1, 2
Trust in God............Prov 16:20
Obedience to God.......John 13:15, 17
Wisdom's ways ....Prov 3:13-18
Examples of:
Israel...................Deut 33:29
Job.....................James 5:11
Mary ....Luke 1:46-55
Paul....................Acts 26:2
In spite of:
Discipline ....Job 5:17
Suffering...............1Pet 4:12-14
Persecution ....Matt 5:10-12
Lack ....Phil 4:6, 7
Trouble 2Cor 4:7-18
Described as:
Blessed ....Matt 5:3-12
Filled...................Ps 36:8
In God alone ....Ps 73:25, 26
See GLADNESS; JOY

HAPPINESS OF THE WICKED
Described as:
Short ....Job 20:5
Uncertain ....Luke 12:20
Vain ....Eccl 2:1, 2
Limited to this life ......Luke 16:24, 25
Under God's judgment...Job 15:21; Ps 73:18-20
Derived from:
Prominence ....Job 21:7; Ps 37:35
Prosperity...............Ps 17:14; Ps 37:7
Sensuality...............Is 22:13
Saints:
Sometimes stumble at ....Ps 73:2, 3
Should not envy ....Ps 37:1, 7
Will see end ....Ps 73:17-20

HAPPY—*joyousness; sense of well-being*

[*also* HAPPIER]
Leah said, ***H*** am I, for........Gen 30:13
H are thy men, ***h*** are 1Kin 10:8
H are thy men, and ***h*** are 2Chr 9:7
H is the man that hath........Ps 127:5
h..he be, that rewardeth ......Ps 137:8

H is that people, that is ....Ps 144:15
h is that people, whose God ...Ps 144:15
hath mercy on the poor, *h* ....Prov 14:21
H is the man that feareth .....Prov 28:14
are all they *h* that deal........Jer 12:1
now we call the proud *h* ......Mal 3:15
H is he that condemneth ......Rom 14:22
she is *h* if she so abide........1Cor 7:40
for righteousness' sake, *h* 1Pet 3:14

HARA (hā'rä)—*"hill"*
Place in Assyria where captive Israelites settled.1Chr 5:26

HARADAH (hä-rā'dä)—*"fear"*
Israelite encampment ....Num 33:24

And they removed from *H* ....Num 33:25

HARAN, CHARRAN (hā'răn, chăr-răn')—*"mountains; strong; enlightened"*
1. Abraham's younger brother ....Gen 11:26-31
2. Gershonite Levite 1Chr 23:9
3. Son of Caleb 1Chr 2:46
4. City of Mesopotamia ....Gen 11:31
   Abraham lives in ....Acts 7:2, 4
   Abraham leaves ....Gen 12:4, 5
   Jacob flees to...........Gen 27:43
   Jacob dwells at ....Gen 29:4-35
   Center of idolatry ....Gen 35:2
   2Kin 19:12

years; and Terah died in *H*....Gen 11:32
and went toward *H* ....Gen 28:10
H, and Rezeph, and the ......Is 37:12
H, and Canneh, and Eden ....Ezek 27:23

HARANITE (hā'răn-īt)—*"mountaineer"*
Applied to David's mighty men 2Sam 23:11, 33; 1Chr 11:34, 35

HARBONA (här-bō'nä)—*"ass-driver"*
Chamberlain of Ahasuerus ....Esth 1:10
Same as Harbonah ......Esth 7:9

HARD—*not easy; unfeeling; callous; opposite of soft*

[*also* HARDEN, HARDENED, HARDENETH, HARDER]
any thing too *h* for the Lord?. .Gen 18:14
when she was in *h* labor ......Gen 35:17
sinned yet more, and *h* ....Ex 9:34
the *h* causes they brought .....Ex 18:26
he take off *h* by the ....Lev 3:9
the cause that is too *h* for .....Deut 1:17
the Lord thy God *h* his ....Deut 2:30
there arise a matter too *h* .....Deut 17:8
and went *h* unto the door .....Judg 9:52
Wherefore then do ye *h* 1Sam 6:6
and Pharaoh *h* their 1Sam 6:6
even they also followed *h* 1Sam 14:22
and horsemen followed *h* 2Sam 1:6
and Amnon thought it *h* 2Sam 13:2
to prove him with *h* 1Kin 10:1
Thou hast asked a *h* 2Kin 2:10
would not hear, but *h* 2Kin 17:14
the Philistines followed *h*......1Chr 10:2
prove Solomon with *h* 2Chr 9:1
h their necks..hearkened ......Neh 9:16
h their neck, and would ....Neh 9:29
yea, I would *h* myself in ......Job 6:10
who hath *h* himself ....Job 9:4
h as a piece of the nether .....Job 41:24
hast showed thy people *h* .....Ps 60:3
Thy wrath lieth *h* upon ....Ps 88:7
way of transgressors is *h* ......Prov 13:15
A brother offended is *h* to ....Prov 18:19
A wicked man *h* his face ......Prov 21:29
being often reproved *h*........Prov 29:1
the *h* bondage wherein.........Is 14:3
from thy ways, and *h* our .....Is 63:17
made their faces *h* than a .....Jer 5:3
but *h* their neck; they.........Jer 7:26
and there is nothing too *h*.....Jer 32:17
is there any thing too *h* ....Jer 32:27
and of a *h* language, but ......Ezek 3:5
As an adamant *h* than flint ....Ezek 3:9
showing of *h* sentences ....Dan 5:12
up, and his mind *h* in.........Dan 5:20
men rowed *h* to bring it.......Jon 1:13
that thou art a *h* man ....Matt 25:24
how *h* is it for them that ......Mark 10:24
This is a *h* saying; who ....John 6:60
h for thee to kick against .....Acts 9:5
But when divers were *h*.......Acts 19:9
it is *h* for thee to kick ....Acts 26:14
and whom he will he *h* ....Rom 9:18
h through the deceitfulness ....Heb 3:13
things to say, and *h* to be .....Heb 5:11
some things *h* to be 2Pet 3:16

HARD LABOR—*strenuous labor*

Spiritual:
Subduing flesh 1Cor 9:24-27
Striving against sin ......Heb 12:4
Reaching goal ....Phil 3:11-14

Physical:
Jacob....................Gen 31:40-42
Israelites.................Ex 1:11-14
Gibeonites ....Josh 9:3-27
Samson ....Judg 16:20, 21

HARDLY—*harshly; barely*
And when Sarai dealt *h*.......Gen 16:6
Pharaoh would *h* let us ....Ex 13:15
through it, *h* bestead and .....Is 8:21
a rich man shall *h* enter ....Matt 19:23
How *h* shall they that have ....Mark 10:23
bruising him *h* departeth ......Luke 9:39
How *h* shall they that.........Luke 18:24
And, *h* passing it, came ....Acts 27:8

HARDNESS OF HEART—*stubborn impenitence*

Causes of:
God ....Rom 9:18
Man.....................Job 9:4
Unbelief ....John 12:40
Sin ....Heb 3:13

Examples of:
Pharaoh ....Ex 4:21
Zedekiah 2Chr 36:11-13
Israel...................Ezek 3:7
Nebuchadnezzar ....Dan 5:20
Jews....................Mark 3:5
Believers ....Mark 6:52

Warnings against:
Recognized by Egyptians .1Sam 6:6
Unheeded by Israel.......Jer 5:3
Lamented by the prophets ....Is 63:17
Addressed to Christians . .Heb 3:8-15
Heb 4:7

[*also* HARDEN, HARDENED, HARDHEARTED]
but I will *h* his heart..........Ex 4:21
I will *h* Pharaoh's heart ....Ex 7:3
And he *h* Pharaoh's heart .....Ex 7:13
Pharaoh's heart was *h* ....Ex 7:22
Pharaoh's heart was *h* ....Ex 8:19
heart of Pharaoh was *h* ....Ex 9:7
the Lord *h* the heart of ....Ex 9:12
I have *h* the heart, and the....Ex 10:1
the Lord *h* Pharaoh's ....Ex 10:20
the Lord *h* Pharaoh's ....Ex 10:27
the Lord *h* Pharaoh's ....Ex 11:10
I will *h* Pharaoh's heart ....Ex 14:4
the Lord *h* the heart of ....Ex 14:8
will *h* the hearts of the........Ex 14:17
thou shalt not *h* thine ....Deut 15:7
and *h* his heart from 2Chr 36:13
the dust groweth into *h* ....Job 38:38
h not your heart, as in the ....Ps 95:8
Israel are impudent and *h* .....Ezek 3:7
for their heart was *h*..........Mark 6:52
have ye your heart yet *h*? .....Mark 8:17
blinded their eyes, and *h*......John 12:40
thy *h* and impenitent ....Rom 2:5
H not your hearts, as in.......Heb 3:8
voice, *h* not your hearts ....Heb 3:15
his voice, *h* not your..........Heb 4:7

HARE—*an unclean animal*
the *h*, because he cheweth ....Lev 11:6
the camel, and the *h*, and .....Deut 14:7

HAREM—*a group of women married to one man*
Esther a member of King Ahasuerus'............Esth 2:8-14

HAREPH (hā'rĕf)—*"early born"*
Son of Caleb 1Chr 2:50, 51

HARETH (hā'rĕth)—*a forest in which David hid*
Forest in Judah 1Sam 22:5

HARHAIAH (här-hā'yä)—*"Jehovah is protecting"*
Father of Uzziel ....Neh 3:8

HARHAS (här'hăs)—*"glitter"*
Grandfather of Shallum . .2Kin 22:14

HARHUR (här'hûr)—*"nobility; distinction"*
Ancestor of returning Temple servants ....Ezra 2:43, 51

Hakupha, the children of *H* . . .Neh 7:53

HARIM (hā'rĭm)—*"snub-nosed"*
1. Descendant of Aaron . . .1Chr 24:1, 6, 8
2. Postexilic leader ....Ezra 2:32, 39
3. Father of Malchijah .....Neh 3:11
4. Signer of the covenant . .Neh 10:1, 5
5. Signer of the covenant . .Neh 10:1, 27
6. Family house of priests . .Neh 12:12, 15
7. Descendants of, divorced foreign wives ....Ezra 10:19, 21

of the sons of *H*; Eliezer ......Ezra 10:31
The children of *H*, three ......Neh 7:35
The children of *H*, a ....Neh 7:42

HARIPH (hā'rĭf)—*"early born"*
Family of returnees ......Neh 7:24
Signers of covenant ......Neh 10:19
Same as Jorah ....Ezra 2:18

HARLOT—*a prostitute*

Characteristics of:
Shameless...............Jer 3:3
Painted ....Ezra 23:40
Enticing ....Prov 9:14-18
Roaming streets ....Prov 7:12
Expensive...............Prov 29:3

Evils of:
Profanes God's name ....Amos 2:7
Connected with idolatry . .Ex 34:15, 16
Brings spiritual error .....Hos 4:10-19
Cause of divorce ....Jer 3:8, 14

Prohibitions concerning:
Forbidden in Israel ......Lev 19:29
Priests not to marry .....Lev 21:1, 7, 14
To be shamed ....Prov 5:3-20
Punishment ....Lev 21:9

Examples of:
Tamar ....Gen 38:13-20
Rahab ....Josh 2:1-21
Jephthah's mother ....Judg 11:1
Samson's ....Judg 16:1
Hosea's wife ....Hos 1:2
The great ....Rev 17:1-18

Figurative of:
Tyre....................Is 23:15, 17
Israel...................Is 1:21
Spiritual adultery ....Is 57:7-9
Rev 17:1-18

See ADULTERY

[*also* HARLOT'S, HARLOTS, HARLOTS']
our sister as with a *h*? ....Gen 34:31
Where is the *h*, that was ......Gen 38:21
There was no *h* in this ....Gen 38:21
there was no *h* in this.........Gen 38:22
daughter-in-law hath played..*h* .Gen 38:24
only Rahab the *h* shall ....Josh 6:17
Go into the *h* house, and .....Josh 6:22
Joshua saved Rahab the *h*......Josh 6:25
two women, that were *h* 1Kin 3:16
woman with the attire of a *h* . .Prov 7:10
keepeth company with *h* ......Prov 29:3

thou wanderest, playing the *h* .Jer 2:20
played the *h* with many ....Jer 3:1
and there hath played the *h* ...Jer 3:6
by troops in the *h* houses .....Jer 5:7
playedst the *h* because ....Ezek 16:15
playedst the *h* thereupon ......Ezek 16:16
hast not been as a *h*, in ....Ezek 16:31
cease from playing the *h* ......Ezek 16:41
she had played the *h* in ....Ezek 23:19
mother hath played the *h* .....Hos 2:5
thou shalt not play the *h* ......Hos 3:3
they sacrifice with *h* ....Hos 4:14
have given a boy for a *h* ......Joel 3:3
Thy wife shall be a *h* in ....Amos 7:17
of the hire of a *h*.............Mic 1:7
return to the hire of a *h* ......Mic 1:7
of the well-favored *h*, the .....Nah 3:4
h go into the kingdom ....Matt 21:31
and the *h* believed him ....Matt 21:32
devoured thy living with *h* ....Luke 15:30
them the members of a *h*? 1Cor 6:15
is joined to a *h* is one 1Cor 6:16
By faith the *h* Rahab ....Heb 11:31
was not Rahab the *h* ....James 2:25

HARM—*injury; hurt; mischief*
pillar unto me, for *h*..........Gen 31:52
h that he hath done in ....Lev 5:16
neither sought his *h* ....Num 35:23
I will no more do thee *h* 1Sam 26:21
son of Bichri do us more *h* ...2Sam 20:6
there was no *h* in the pot 2Kin 4:41
and do my prophets no *h* 1Chr 16:22
and do my prophets no *h* .....Ps 105:15
if he have done thee no *h* .....Prov 3:30
and do him no *h* ....Jer 39:12
Do thyself no *h*; for we ....Acts 16:28
to have gained this *h* and .....Acts 27:21
the fire, and felt no *h*.........Acts 28:5
saw no *h* come to him ....Acts 28:6
showed or spake any *h* of .....Acts 28:21
who is he that will *h* you......1Pet 3:13

HARMLESS—*free from injury; innocuous*
wise as serpents, and *h* as .....Matt 10:16
may be blameless and *h*.......Phil 2:15
who is holy, *h*, undefiled ......Heb 7:26

HARMONY—*agreement; co-operation*
Husband and wife..... 1Cor 7:3-6; Eph 5:22-23; Col 3:18, 19
Christians ....John 13:34, 35; Rom 15:5-7
Christians and unbelievers Rom 12:16-18; Heb 12:14

HARNEPHER (här'nĕ-fer)—*"panting"*
Asherite 1Chr 7:36

HARNESS—*military equipment of a man or horse; to put a harness on*
Horses ....Jer 46:4

[*also* HARNESSED]
children of Israel went up *h* ...Ex 13:18
him that girdeth on his *h*......1Kin 20:11
raiment, *h*, and spices 2Chr 9:24

HAROD (hā'rŏd)—*"trembling"*
Well near Gideon's camp .Judg 7:1

HARODITE (hā'rŏ-dīt)—*the home of two of David's mighty men*
Inhabitant of Harod 2Sam 23:25
Same as Harorite 1Chr 11:27

HAROEH (här'ō-ĕ)—*"the seer"*
Judahite 1Chr 2:50, 52
Called Reaiah 1Chr 4:2

HARORITE—*See* HARODITE

HAROSHETH (hä-rō'shĕth)—*"carving"*
Residence of Sisera ......Judg 4:2, 13, 16

HARP—*a stringed musical instrument*
Used by:
The wicked ....Is 5:11, 12
David 1Sam 16:16, 23
Prophets 1Sam 10:5
Temple orchestra 1Chr 16:5
Temple worshipers ......Ps 33:2
Celebrators 2Chr 20:27, 28
Jewish captives ....Ps 137:2
Worshipers in heaven ....Rev 5:8

[*also* HARPED, HARPING, HARPS]
such as handle the *h* and ......Gen 4:21
with tabret, and with *h*? ......Gen 31:27
on *h*, and on psalteries........2Sam 6:5
h also and psalteries for.......1Kin 10:12
h, and with psalteries 1Chr 13:8
with *h* on the Sheminith 1Chr 15:21
should prophesy with *h* 1Chr 25:1
who prophesied with a *h* 1Chr 25:3
cymbals..psalteries and *h* 2Chr 5:12
psalteries, and with *h* 2Chr 29:25
take the timbrel and *h* ....Job 21:12
My *h* also is turned to ....Job 30:31
upon the *h* will I praise ....Ps 43:4
my dark saying upon the *h* ....Ps 49:4
awake, psaltery and *h*: I ......Ps 57:8
will I sing with the *h* ....Ps 71:22
the pleasant *h*..psaltery ....Ps 81:2
upon the *h* with a solemn .....Ps 92:3
unto the Lord with the *h*......Ps 98:5
with the *h*, and the voice .....Ps 98:5
Awake, psaltery and *h*: I......Ps 108:2
sing praise upon the *h* ....Ps 147:7
with the timbrel and *h* ....Ps 149:3
with the psaltery and *h* ....Ps 150:3
bowels shall sound like a *h* ....Is 16:11
Take a *h*, go about the ....Is 23:16
endeth, the joy of the *h*.......Is 24:8
shall be with tabrets and *h* ....Is 30:32
sound of thy *h* shall be no ....Ezek 26:13
flute, *h*, sackbut ....Dan 3:5
sound, whether pipe or *h* 1Cor 14:7
known what is piped or *h*? 1Cor 14:7
voice of harpers *h* with..*h* .....Rev 14:2
sea of glass..the *h* of God .....Rev 15:2

HARPERS—*harp players*
voice of *h* harping with ....Rev 14:2
And the voice of *h*, and ......Rev 18:22

HARPOON—*a barbed spear for hunting large fish*
Used against Leviathan ..Job 41:7

HARROW—*an agricultural machine, possibly even a threshing machine*
Instrument for breaking clods ....Job 39:10
Figurative of affliction ...Is 28:24

[*also* HARROWS]
saws, and under *h* of iron 2Sam 12:31
and with *h* of iron, and 1Chr 20:3

HARSHA (här'shä)—*"artificer"*
Head of Temple servants .Ezra 2:43, 52; Neh 7:46, 54

HART—*a male deer*
Described as:
Clean animal...........Deut 12:15
Hunted animal ....Lam 1:6
Figurative of:
Christ ....Song 2:9, 17
Afflicted saints ....Ps 42:1-3
Converted sinners ....Is 35:6

[*also* HARTS]
as the roebuck and the *h*......Deut 12:22
The *h*, and the roebuck ....Deut 14:5
the roebuck, and as the *h* .....Deut 15:22
hundred sheep, beside *h* 1Kin 4:23
to a young *h*..mountains ......Song 8:14

HARUM (hā'rŭm)—*"elevated"*
Judahite 1Chr 4:8

HARUMAPH (hä-ro͞o'măf)—*"slit-nosed"*
Father of Jedaiah........Neh 3:10

HARUPHITE (hä-ro͞o'fīt)—*a native of Hariph*
Designation of Shephatiah 1Chr 12:5
Member of Hariph's family ....Neh 7:24

HARUZ (hā'rŭz)—*"industrious"*
Father-in-law of King Manasseh 2Kin 21:19

HARVEST—*gathering in of ripe crops*
Occasion of:
Great joy ....Is 9:3
Bringing the first fruits ...Lev 23:10
Remembering the poor ..Lev 19:9, 10
Figuratively of:
Seasons of grace.........Jer 8:20
Judgment ....Jer 51:33
God's wrath ....Rev 14:15
Gospel opportunities.....Matt 9:37, 38
World's end.............Matt 13:30, 39
Measure of fruitfulness ...2Cor 9:6
Promises concerning:
To continue............Gen 8:22
Rain ....Jer 5:24
Patience ....James 5:7
Failure caused by:
Drought ....Amos 4:7
Locusts ....Joel 1:4
Sin ....Is 17:4-12

in the days of wheat *h* ....Gen 30:14
feast of *h*, the first fruits ......Ex 23:16
in earing time and in *h* ....Ex 34:21
the first fruits of wheat *h* .....Ex 34:22
when ye reap the *h* of ....Lev 23:22
gather any gleaning of thy *h*...Lev 23:22
its own accord of thy *h* ....Lev 25:5
thou cuttest down thine *h* .....Deut 24:19
his banks all the time of *h* ....Josh 3:15
in the time of wheat *h* ....Judg 15:1
the beginning of barley *h* .....Ruth 1:22
barley *h* and of wheat *h*.......Ruth 2:23
their wheat *h* in the valley 1Sam 6:13
Is it not wheat *h* today?.......1Sam 12:17
to death in the days of *h*......2Sam 21:9
beginning of barley *h* 2Sam 21:9
came to David in the *h* 2Sam 23:13
Whose *h* the hungry eateth....Job 5:5
gathereth her food in the *h*....Prov 6:8
he that sleepeth in *h* is a ......Prov 10:5
therefore shall he beg in *h* ....Prov 20:4
cold of snow in the time of *h*..Prov 25:13
as rain in *h*, so honor is.......Prov 26:1
summer fruits and for thy *h* ...Is 16:9
dew in the heat of *h* ....Is 18:4
For afore the *h*, when the .....Is 18:5
the *h* of the river, is her ......Is 23:3
they shall eat up thine *h* ......Jer 5:17
the sickle in the time of *h*.....Jer 50:16
he hath set a *h* for thee ....Hos 6:11
h of the field is perished ......Joel 1:11
sickle, for the *h* is ripe ....Joel 3:13
the sickle, because the *h* ......Mark 4:29
The *h* truly is great ....Luke 10:2
therefore the Lord of the *h* ...Luke 10:2
forth laborers into his *h* ....Luke 10:2
four months..cometh *h*? ....John 4:35
are white already to *h* ....John 4:35

HARVESTMAN—*those who gather in crops*
when the *h* gathereth the .....Is 17:5
the handful after the *h*........Jer 9:22

HASADIAH (hăs-ä-dī'ä)—*"Jehovah is kind"*
Son of Zerubbabel 1Chr 3:20

HASENUAH (hăs'e-no͞o'ä)—*"the violated"*
Benjamite family ....1Chr 9:7; Neh 11:7-9

HASHABIAH (hăsh-ä-bī'ä)—*"Jehovah is associated"*
1. Merarite Levite 1Chr 6:44, 45
   Perhaps the same as in ..1Chr 9:14
2. Levite musician 1Chr 25:3, 19
3. Kohathite Levite 1Chr 26:30
4. Levite ruler 1Chr 27:17
5. Chief Levite during Josiah's reign 2Chr 35:9
6. Postexilic Levite ....Ezra 8:19, 24
   Probably the same in ....Neh 10:11
7. Postexilic ruler..........Neh 3:17

8. Descendant of Asaph . . .Neh 11:22
9. Priest in the time of Joiakim . . . . .Neh 12:21

Next unto him repaired *H* . . . . .Neh 3:17
the son of *H*, the son of . . . . . .Neh 11:15
chief of the Levites; *H* . . . . .Neh 12:24

HASHABNAH (hä-shăb'nä)—*"Jehovah is a friend"*
Signed covenant . . . . .Neh 10:25

HASHABNIAH (häsh-ăb-nī'a)—*"Jehovah is a friend"*
1. Father of Hattush . . . . . . .Neh 3:10
2. Postexilic Levite . . . . .Neh 9:5
Probably the same as Hashabiah 6.

HASHBADANA (hăsh-băd'ä-nä)—*"judge"*
Assistant to Ezra . . . . .Neh 8:4

HASHEM (hā'shĕm)—*"shining"*
Father of David's warriors 1Chr 11:34
Also called Jashen 2Sam 23:32

HASHMONAH (hăsh-mō'nä)—*"fruitfulness"*
Israelite encampment . . . .Num 33:29

And they departed from *H* . . . .Num 33:30

HASHUB (hā'shŭb)—*"associate"*
1. Postexilic workman . . . . .Neh 3:11
2. Signer of the covenant . .Neh 10:23
3. Levite chief . . . . .Neh 11:15

Hoshea, Hananiah, *H* . . . . .Neh 10:23

HASHUBAH (hä-shōō'bä)—*"association"*
Son of Zerubbabel 1Chr 3:19, 20

HASHUM (hā'shŭm)—*"shining"*
Founder of postexilic family . . . . .Ezra 2:19
Assists Ezra and signs document . . . . {Neh 8:4 / Neh 10:18}

sons of *H*; Mattenai . . . . .Ezra 10:33
The children of *H*, three . . . . . .Neh 7:22

HASHUPHA (hă shū'fä)—*See* HASUPHA

HASRAH (hăz'rä)—*"glitter"*
Grandfather of Shallum . .2Chr 34:22
Called Harhas 2Kin 22:14

HASSENAAH (hăs'ĕ-nā'ä)—*"the thorn hedge"*
Father of postexilic workmen . . . . .Neh 3:3
Same as Senaah . . . . .Ezra 2:35
Neh 7:38

HASSHUB (hăsh'ŭb)—*See* HASHUB

HASTE—*swiftness; to do something quickly; to urge on*
Prompted by good 2Chr 35:21
Luke 19:5, 6
Prompted by evil . . . . .Prov 14:29
Prov 28:20

[*also* HASTED, HASTEN, HASTENED, HASTENETH, HASTETH, HASTILY, HASTING, HASTY]

And Abraham *h* into the . . . . . .Gen 18:6
young man; and he *h* to . . . . . .Gen 18:7
H thee, escape thither . . . . .Gen 19:22
And she *h*, and emptied . . . . . .Gen 24:20
And she made *h*, and let . . . . . .Gen 24:46
and they brought him *h* . . . . .Gen 41:14
And Joseph made *h*; for . . . . . .Gen 43:30
H ye, and go up to my . . . . . . .Gen 45:9
and ye shall *h* and bring . . . . . .Gen 45:13
the taskmasters *h* them . . . . . .Ex 5:13
for Moses and Aaron in *h* . . . . .Ex 10:16
ye shall eat it in *h*; it is . . . . . . .Ex 12:11
them out of the land in *h* . . . . .Ex 12:33
And Moses made *h*, and . . . . . .Ex 34:8
the land of Egypt in *h* . . . . .Deut 16:3
people *h* and passed over . . . . .Josh 4:10
and *h* and set the city on . . . . .Josh 8:19
without driving them..*h* . . . . . . .Judg 2:23
make *h*, and do as I have . . . . . .Judg 9:48
the liers in wait *h*, and . . . . .Judg 20:37
And the man came in *h* 1Sam 4:14
make *h* now for he came 1Sam 9:12
that David *h*, and ran 1Sam 17:48
king's business required *h* 1Sam 21:8
H thee, and come; for 1Sam 23:27
Then Abigail made *h*, and 1Sam 25:18
except thou hadst *h* and 1Sam 25:34
and she *h*, and killed it 1Sam 28:24
she made *h* to flee, that 2Sam 4:4
was of Bahurim, *h* and 2Sam 19:16
and did *h* catch it; and 1Kin 20:33
And he *h*, and took the 1Kin 20:41
H hither Micaiah the son 1Kin 22:9
had cast away in their *h* 2Kin 7:15
Then they *h*, and took 2Kin 9:13
and see that ye *h* the 2Chr 24:5
Howbeit the Levites *h* it 2Chr 24:5
himself *h* also to go out 2Chr 26:20
up in *h* to Jerusalem . . . . .Ezra 4:23
posts went out, being *h* . . . . . . .Esth 3:15
Cause Haman to make *h* . . . . . .Esth 5:5
h to his house mourning . . . . . .Esth 6:12
as the eagle that *h* to the . . . . .Job 9:26
and for this I make *h* . . . . .Job 20:2
or if my foot hath *h* to . . . . .Job 31:5
be multiplied that *h* after . . . . .Ps 16:4
my strength, *h* thee to . . . . .Ps 22:19
For I said in my *h*, I am . . . . . .Ps 31:22
h to help me, O Lord . . . . .Ps 38:22
O Lord, make *h* to help . . . . . .Ps 40:13
they were troubled, and *h* . . . . .Ps 48:5
I would *h* my escape from . . . .Ps 55:8
Make *h*, O God, to deliver . . . .Ps 70:1
h to help me, O Lord . . . . .Ps 70:1
my God, make *h* for my . . . . . . .Ps 71:12
I said in my *h*, All men . . . . . . .Ps 116:11
I made *h*, and delayed not . . . .Ps 119:60
I cry unto thee; make *h* . . . . . . .Ps 141:1
evil, and make *h* to shed . . . . . .Prov 1:16
as a bird *h* to the snare . . . . . . .Prov 7:23
but he that is *h* of spirit . . . . . . .Prov 14:29
inheritance may be gotten *h* . . .Prov 20:21
every one that is *h* only to . . . .Prov 21:5
Go not forth *h* to strive . . . . . . .Prov 25:8
He that *h* to be rich hath . . . . .Prov 28:22
Seest thou a man that is *h* . . . .Prov 29:20
the sun goeth down, and *h* . . . .Eccl 1:5
or who else can *h* . . . . .Eccl 2:25
let not thine heart be *h* to . . . .Eccl 5:2
Be not *h* in thy spirit to . . . . . . .Eccl 7:9
Be not *h* to go out of his . . . . .Eccl 8:3
Make *h*, my beloved, and . . . . .Song 8:14
him make speed, and *h* . . . . . . .Is 5:19
judgment, and *h* . . . . .Is 16:5
the *h* fruit before the . . . . .Is 28:4
believeth shall not make *h* . . . .Is 28:16
The captive exile *h* that . . . . . . .Is 51:14
ye shall not go out with *h* . . . . .Is 52:12
Lord will *h* it in his time . . . . . .Is 60:22
I will *h* my word to . . . . .Jer 1:12
And let them make *h*, and . . . .Jer 9:18
I have not *h* from being . . . . . . .Jer 17:16
come, and his affliction *h* . . . . .Jer 48:16
Why is the decree so *h* . . . . . . .Dan 2:15
Daniel before the king in *h* . . .Dan 2:25
went in *h* unto the den of . . . . .Dan 6:19
they shall make *h* to the . . . . . .Nah 2:5
that bitter and *h* nation . . . . . .Hab 1:6
is near, it is near, and *h* . . . . . .Zeph 1:14
came in straightway with *h* . . . .Mark 6:25
the hill country with *h* . . . . .Luke 1:39
that she rose up *h* and . . . . .John 11:31
he *h*, if it were possible . . . . . . .Acts 20:16
Make *h*, and get thee . . . . .Acts 22:18
h unto the coming of the 2Pet 3:12

HASUPHA (hä-sū'fä)—*"stripped"*
Head of Temple servants .Ezra 2:43
Same as Hashupha . . . . . .Neh 7:46

HATACH (hā'tăk)—*"chamberlain"*
Esther's attendant . . . . . . .Esth 4:5-10

HATCH—*to produce young by incubation*

[*also* HATCHETH]

her nest, and lay, and *h* . . . . . . .Is 34:15
They *h* cockatrice eggs . . . . .Is 59:5
sitteth on eggs, and *h* . . . . .Jer 17:11

HATE—*to feel extreme enmity toward*

Meanings of:
React as God does . . . . . .Rev 2:6
Twist moral judgments . . .Prov 8:36
Esteem of less value . . . . .John 12:25
Make a vital distinction . .Luke 14:26
Despise . . . . .Is 1:14

Causes of:
Parental favoritism . . . . . .Gen 37:4, 5
Rape 2Sam 13:15, 22
Failure to please 1Kin 22:8
God's purpose . . . . .Ps 105:25
Belonging to Christ . . . . . .Matt 24:9, 10
Evil nature . . . . .John 3:20

Objects of:
God's people . . . . .Gen 26:27
God .Ex 20:5
Christ . . . . .John 15:25
Light . . . . .John 3:20
Evil men . . . . .Ps 26:5
Wickedness . . . . .Ps 45:7

Toward Christians, sign of their:
Discipleship . . . . .Matt 24:9
Election . . . . .John 15:19
Regeneration 1John 3:13-15

[*also* HATED, HATEST, HATETH, HATING, HATRED]

the gate of those which *h* . . . . .Gen 24:60
Esau *h* Jacob because . . . . .Gen 27:41
Lord saw that Leah was *h* . . . . .Gen 29:31
Lord hath heard that I was *h* . .Gen 29:33
they *h* him yet the more . . . . . .Gen 37:8
and shot at him, and *h* . . . . .Gen 49:23
Joseph will peradverture *h* . . . .Gen 50:15
of truth, *h* covetousness . . . . . . .Ex 18:21
see the ass of him that *h* . . . . . .Ex 23:5
Thou shalt not *h* thy . . . . .Lev 19:17
let them that *h* thee flee . . . . . .Num 10:35
But if he thrust him of *h* . . . . . .Num 35:20
Because the Lord *h* us . . . . .Deut 1:27
fourth generation..that *h* . . . . . .Deut 5:9
not be slack to him that *h* . . . . .Deut 7:10
upon all them that *h* . . . . .Deut 7:15
and because he *h* them . . . . .Deut 9:28
which the Lord thy God *h* . . . . .Deut 16:22
as he *h* him not in time . . . . . . .Deut 19:6
any man *h* his neighbor . . . . . . .Deut 19:11
beloved, and another *h* . . . . . . .Deut 21:15
the beloved and the *h* . . . . .Deut 21:15
son be hers that was *h* . . . . .Deut 21:15
acknowledge the son of the *h* . .Deut 21:17
go in unto her, and *h* her . . . . .Deut 22:13
them that *h* thee, which . . . . . . .Deut 30:7
and of them that *h* him . . . . . . .Deut 33:11
neighbor unwittingly, and *h* . . .Josh 20:5
Did not ye *h* me, and expel . . .Judg 11:7
that thou hadst utterly *h* . . . . . .Judg 15:2
that are *h* of David's soul 2Sam 5:8
that the *h* wherewith he 2Sam 13:15
thine enemies, and *h* thy 2Sam 19:6
and from them that *h* me 2Sam 22:18
I might destroy them that *h* . . .2Sam 22:41
but I *h* him; for he never 2Chr 18:7
had rule over them that *h* . . . . .Esth 9:1
They that *h* thee shall be . . . . .Job 8:22
in his wrath, who *h* me . . . . . . .Job 16:9
destruction of him that *h* . . . . . .Job 31:29
he that *h* right govern? . . . . . . .Job 34:17
thou *h* all workers of . . . . .Ps 5:5
of them that *h* me, thou . . . . . . .Ps 9:13
loveth violence his soul *h* . . . . .Ps 11:5
and from them which *h* me . . . .Ps 18:17
shall find out those that *h* . . . . .Ps 21:8
they *h* me with cruel *h* . . . . .Ps 25:19
I have *h* them that regard . . . . .Ps 31:6
and they that *h* the . . . . .Ps 34:21
eye that *h* me without . . . . .Ps 35:19
they that *h* me wrongfully . . . . .Ps 38:19
and they which *h* us spoil . . . . .Ps 44:10
Seeing thou *h* instruction . . . . . .Ps 50:17

neither was it he that *h* ....Ps 55:12
let them also that *h* him ......Ps 68:1
delivered from them that *h* ....Ps 69:14
that they which *h* me may .....Ps 86:17
Ye that love the Lord, *h* ......Ps 97:10
good, and *h* for my love ......Ps 109:5
therefore I *h* every false ......Ps 119:104
right; and I *h* every false ......Ps 119:128
turned back that *h* Zion ......Ps 129:5
h them with perfect...........Ps 139:22
scorning, and fools *h* ....Prov 1:22
For that they *h* knowledge ....Prov 1:29
fear of the Lord is to *h* ....Prov 8:13
froward mouth, do I *h* ....Prov 8:13
H stirreth up strifes ....Prov 10:12
and he that *h* suretyship ......Prov 11:15
A righteous man *h* lying ......Prov 13:5
He that spareth his rod *h* .....Prov 13:24
man of wicked devices is *h* ....Prov 14:17
The poor is *h* even of his .....Prov 14:20
he that *h* reproof shall ....Prov 15:10
than a stalled ox and *h* ....Prov 15:17
brethren of the poor do *h* .....Prov 19:7
He that *h* dissembleth ....Prov 26:24
he that *h* covetousness ....Prov 28:16
The bloodthirsty *h* the ....Prov 29:10
Therefore I *h* life..............Eccl 2:17
time to love and a time to *h* ..Eccl 3:8
man knoweth either love or *h* .Eccl 9:1
hast been forsaken and *h* .....Is 60:15
I *h* robbery for burnt ....Is 61:8
therefore have I *h* it ....Jer 12:8
abominable thing that I *h* .....Jer 44:4
the will of them that *h* ....Ezek 16:27
all them that thou hast *h* ......Ezek 16:37
hand of them whom thou *h* ...Ezek 23:28
they shall deal with thee *h* ....Ezek 23:29
destroy it for the old *h* ....Ezek 25:15
thou hast not *h* blood ....Ezek 35:6
dream be to them that *h* ......Dan 4:19
iniquity, and the great *h* ......Hos 9:7
for there I *h* them; for ....Hos 9:15
They *h* him that rebuketh .....Amos 5:10
I *h*, I despise your feast ....Amos 5:21
h his palaces; therefore ....Amos 6:8
Who *h* the good, and love ....Mic 3:2
these are things that I *h* ....Zech 8:17
I *h* Esau, and laid his ....Mal 1:3
saith that he *h* putting ....Mal 2:16
love thy neighbor, and *h* ......Matt 5:43
do good to them that *h* ....Matt 5:44
for either he will *h* the ....Matt 6:24
ye shall be *h* of all men ....Matt 10:22
And ye shall be *h* of all ....Mark 13:13
from the hand of all that *h* ....Luke 1:71
when men shall *h* you ....Luke 6:22
do good to them which *h* .....Luke 6:27
and *h* not his father, and ......Luke 14:26
either he will *h* the one ....Luke 16:13
But his citizens *h* him, and ...Luke 19:14
cannot *h* you; but me it *h* .....John 7:7
If the world *h* you, ye ....John 15:18
ye know that it *h* me ....John 15:18
me before it *h* you ....John 15:18
He that *h* me *h* my Father ....John 15:23
they both seen and *h* ....John 15:24
the world hath *h* them ....John 17:14
do I not; but what I *h* ....Rom 7:15
I loved, but Esau have I *h* ....Rom 9:13
h, variance, emulations ....Gal 5:20
no man ever yet *h* his ....Eph 5:29
envy, hateful, and *h* one ......Titus 3:3
loved righteousness, and *h* ....Heb 1:9
light, and *h* his brother 1John 2:9
But he that *h* his brother 1John 2:11
Whosoever *h* his brother 1John 3:15
and *h* his brother, he is a 1John 4:20
h even the garment ....Jude 23
thou *h* the deeds of...........Rev 2:6
Nicolatanes which thing I *h* ...Rev 2:15
these shall *h* the whore ....Rev 17:16

HATEFUL—*to be hated*

[*also* HATEFULLY]
iniquity be found to be *h* .....Ps 36:2
they shall deal with thee *h* ....Ezek 23:29
envy, *h*, and hating one ....Titus 3:3
of every unclean and *h*........Rev 18:2

HATERS—*dispisers*
h of the Lord should ....Ps 81:15
h of God, despiteful, proud ...Rom 1:30

HATH—*See* INTRODUCTION

HATHATH (hă'thăth)—*"terror"*
Son of Othniel 1Chr 4:13

HATIPHA (hä-tī'fä)—*"taken; captive"*
Head of Temple servants .Ezra 2:43, 54

Neziah, the children of *H* .....Neh 7:56

HATITA (hä-tī'tä)—*"exploration"*
Father of porters ....Ezra 2:42
Neh 7:45

HATS—*coverings for the head*
their hosen, and their *h* ....Dan 3:21

HATTIL (hăt'ĭl)—*"decaying"*
Ancestor of Solomon's servants .... {Ezra 2:55, 57; Neh 7:57-59}

HATTUSH (hăt'ŭsh)—*"contender"*
1. Descendant of David ....Ezra 8:2
2. Man of Judah 1Chr 3:22
Probably the same as 1
3. Priest returning with Zerubbabel..........Neh 12:1, 2
4. Postexilic workman .....Neh 3:10
5. Priest who signs covenant Neh 10:1, 4

HAUGHTINESS—*an arrogant spirit*
Precedes a fall ....Prov 16:18
To be brought low ......Is 2:11, 17
Guilt of Jerusalem for ...Ezek 16:50
Zeph 3:11

[*also* HAUGHTILY, HAUGHTY]
thine eyes are upon the *h* 2Sam 22:28
my heart is not *h*, nor ....Ps 131:1
the heart of man is *h* ....Prov 18:12
Proud and *h* scorner is his ....Prov 21:24
daughters of Zion are *h* ....Is 3:16
h people..earth do languish ....Is 24:4
and the *h* of his heart.........Jer 48:29
neither shall ye go *h* ....Mic 2:3

HAUNT—*to frequent a place*
Place of abode 1Sam 23:22

his men were wont to *h* 1Sam 30:31
terror to be on all that *h* ......Ezek 26:17

HAURAN (hä-oo-rän')—*"black land"*
District southeast of Mt. Hermon ....Ezek 47:16

ye shall measure from *H* ......Ezek 47:18

HAVE—*See* INTRODUCTION

HAVEN—*a sheltered area*
Zebulun's assets ....Gen 49:13
Desired ....Ps 107:30
Near Lasea ....Acts 27:8

[*also* HAVENS]
h was not commodious ....Acts 27:12
which is a *h* at Crete ....Acts 27:12

HAVILAH (hăv'ĭ-lä)—*"circle; a desert tribe"*
1. Son of Cush ....Gen 10:7
2. Son of Joktan ....Gen 10:29
3. District of Arabia ....Gen 2:11
Limit of Ishmaelite territory.............Gen 25:18
Saul defeated Amalekites.1Sam 15:7

Cush; Seba, and *H*, and Sabta .1Chr 1:9
Ophir, and *H*, and Jobab 1Chr 1:23

HAVING—*See* INTRODUCTION

HAVOC—*devastation*
he made *h* of the church ......Acts 8:3

HAVOTH-JAIR (hăv-ōth-jā'ĭr)—*"tent villages of Jair"*
Villages of Jordan in Gilead ....Num 32:40, 41
Or in Bashan ....Deut 3:13, 14
Taken by Jair ....Num 32:41

which are called *H* unto ....Judg 10:4

HAWK—*a bird of prey*
Ceremonially unclean ....Lev 11:16
Migratory ....Job 39:26

the owl, and the night *h* ......Deut 14:15
cuckow, and the *h* after ....Deut 14:15

HAY—*grass; food for cattle*
Build with 1Cor 3:12
Rendered "leeks" ....Num 11:5

The *h* appeareth, and the .....Prov 27:25
for the *h* is withered away ....Is 15:6

HAZAEL (hăz'ā-ĕl)—*"God sees"*
King over Syria 1Kin 19:15-17
Defeats Joram of Israel ..2Kin 8:25-29
Defeats Jehu 2Kin 10:31, 32
Oppresses Israel 2Kin 13:3-7, 22
His son defeated 2Kin 13:24, 25

the king said unto *H*..........2Kin 8:8
So *H* went to meet him 2Kin 8:9
H said, Why weepeth 2Kin 8:12
And *H* said, But what, is 2Kin 8:13
H reigned in his stead 2Kin 8:15
all Israel, because of *H* 2Kin 9:14
when he fought with *H* 2Kin 9:15
Then *H* king of Syria 2Kin 12:17
and *H* set his face to go.......2Kin 12:17
sent it to *H* king of Syria 2Kin 12:18
to war against *H* king of 2Chr 22:5
Ramah, when he fought..*H*....2Chr 22:6
a fire into the house of *H* .....Amos 1:4

HAZAIAH (hä-zā'yä)—*"Jehovah is seeing"*
Man of Judah ....Neh 11:5

HAZAR-ADDAR (hā'zär-ăd'är)—*"village of Addar"*
Place in Canaan ....Num 34:4
See HEZRON

HAZARDED—*risked*
Men that have *h* their ...Acts 15:26

HAZAR-ENAN (hā'zär-ē'năn)—*"village of fountains"*
Village of north Palestine.Num 34:9, 10

from the sea shall be *H* ....Ezek 47:17
one goeth to Hamath, *H* ......Ezek 48:1

HAZAR-GADDAH (hā-zär-găd'ä)—*"town of Gadah"*
Town on the border of Judah ....Josh 15:21, 27

HAZAR-HATTICON (hā-zär-hăt'ă-kŏn)—*"enclosure"*
Town on the border of Hauran ....Ezek 47:16

HAZAR-MAVETH (hā'zär-mā'vĕth)—*"court of death"*
Descendants of Joktan ...Gen 10:26

Sheleph, and *H*, and 1Chr 1:20

HAZAR-SHUAL (hā-zär-shōō'ăl)—*"fox village"*
Town in south Judah ....Josh 15:21, 28
Assigned to Simeon .....Josh 19:1, 3
Reoccupied after exile ...Neh 11:27

Beer-sheba, and Moladah..*H* ..1Chr 4:28

HAZAR-SUSAH (hā-zär-sū'sä)—*"captive mares"*
Simeonite village ....Josh 19:5

HAZAR-SUSIM (hā-zär-sū'sĭm)—*same as Hazar-susah*
Beth-marcaboth, and *H* 1Chr 4:31

HAZAZON-TAMAR—*See* HAZEZON-TAMAR

HAZEL—*almond*
Jacob peeled ....Gen 30:37

HAZELELPONI (hăz-ĕ-lĕl-pō'nī)—*"protection of the face of"*
Female descendant of Judah 1Chr 4:3

HAZERIM (hä-zē'rĭm)—*"villages"*
Habitations of the Avim. .Deut 2:23

HAZEROTH (hä-zē'rŏth)—*"enclosures"*
Israelite camp ....Num 33:17
Scene of sedition of Miriam and Aaron ....Num 12:1-16

Kibroth-hattaavah unto *H* .....Num 11:35
and abode at *H* ....Num 11:35
And they departed from *H* ....Num 33:18
Laban, and *H*, and Dizahab ...Deut 1:1

HAZEZON-TAMAR (hăz-'ē-zŏn-tā'mär)—*"sandy surface of the palm tree"*
Dwelling of Amorites ....Gen 14:7
Also called Engedi 2Chr 20:2

HAZIEL (hā'zĭ-ĕl)—*"God is seeing"*
Gershonite Levite 1Chr 23:9

HAZO (hā'zō)—*"vision; seer"*
Son of Nabor ....Gen 22:22, 23

HAZOR (hā'zôr)—*"enclosure"*
1. Royal Canaanite city destroyed by Joshua...Josh 11:1-13
Rebuilt and assigned to Naphtali ....Josh 19:32, 36
Army of, defeated by Deborah and Barak ...Judg 4:1-24
Fortified by Solomon 1Kin 9:15
Captured by Tiglathpileser 2Kin 15:29
2. Town in south Judah ....Josh 15:21, 25
3. Another town of south Judah ....Josh 15:21, 23
4. Town of Benjamin ......Neh 11:31, 33
5. Region in the Arabian desert ....Jer 49:28-33

Madon, one; the king of *H* ....Josh 12:19
captain of the host of *H*.......1Sam 12:9

HAZOR-HADATTAH (hā-zôr-hä-dăt'ä)—*"new Hazor"*
Town in south Judah ....Josh 15:25

HE (hā)
Fifth letter of Hebrew alphabet ....Ps 119:33-40

HE—*See* INTRODUCTION

HEAD—*the uppermost portion of the body; the leader; first*

Attitudes expressed by:
Covered, in grief 2Sam 15:30
Covered, in subjection ...1Cor 11:5
Hand upon, in sorrow ...2Sam 13:19
Ashes upon, in dismay ...Josh 7:6
Uncovered, in leprosy ...Lev 13:45
Wagging, in derision .....Matt 27:39
Anointed, in dedication ..Matt 6:17

Figurative of:
God 1Cor 11:3
Christ ....Eph 1:22
Husband 1Cor 11:3, 7
Protection ....Ps 140:7
Judgment ....Is 15:2
Confidence...............Luke 21:28
Pride ....Ps 83:2
Exaltation ....Ps 27:6
Joy and prosperity ....Ps 23:5

[*also* HEADS]
and became into four *h* ....Gen 2:10
it shall bruise thy *h*, and ......Gen 3:15
And I bowed down my *h* .....Gen 24:48
three white baskets on my *h*...Gen 40:16
Pharaoh lift up thy *h* ....Gen 40:19
himself upon the bed's *h* ......Gen 47:31
laid it upon Ephraim's *h* ......Gen 48:14
left hand upon Manasseh's *h* ..Gen 48:14
hand upon the *h* of Ephraim ..Gen 48:17
Ephraim's *h* unto Manasseh's *h*.Gen 48:17
shall be on the *h* of Joseph....Gen 49:26
and on the crown of the *h* ....Gen 49:26
then they bowed their *h* ......Ex 4:31
h of the fathers of the ....Ex 6:25
his *h* with his legs, and ....Ex 12:9
together above the *h* of ....Ex 26:24
oil, and pour it upon his *h* ....Ex 29:7
upon the *h* of the bullock .....Ex 29:10
hands upon the *h* of the ram ..Ex 29:15
hands upon the *h* of the ram ..Ex 29:19
coupled together at the *h* .....Ex 36:29
upon the *h* of the burnt ....Lev 1:4
pieces, with his *h* and his .....Lev 1:12
hand upon the *h* of his........Lev 3:2
hand upon the bullock's *h*.....Lev 4:4
upon the *h* of the bullock .....Lev 4:15
upon the *h* of the sin ....Lev 4:29
put the mitre upon his *h* ......Lev 8:9
upon the *h* of the bullock ......Lev 8:14
burnt the *h*, and the pieces....Lev 8:20
pieces thereof, and the *h*......Lev 9:13
Uncover not your *h* ....Lev 10:6
a plague upon the *h* or the ....Lev 13:29
hair is fallen off his *h*.........Lev 13:40
if there be in the bald *h* ......Lev 13:42
sprung up in his bald *h* ....Lev 13:42
his plague is in his *h*..........Lev 13:44
shave all his hair off his *h*.....Lev 14:9
the *h* of him that is to be .....Lev 14:29
hands upon the *h* of the ......Lev 16:21
them upon the *h* of the ....Lev 16:21
baldness upon their *h* ....Lev 21:5
whose *h* the anointing ....Lev 21:10
shall not uncover his *h*........Lev 21:10
lay their hands upon his *h*.....Lev 24:14
one *h* of the house of his .....Num 1:4
fathers, *h* of thousands........Num 1:16
no razor come upon his *h* .....Num 6:5
of his God is upon his *h* ......Num 6:7
defiled the *h* of his ....Num 6:9
shall shave his *h* in the........Num 6:9
Nazarite shall shave the *h* .....Num 6:18
the hair of the *h* of his........Num 6:18
upon the *h* of the bullocks ....Num 8:12
were *h* of the children ....Num 13:3
and he bowed down his *h* .....Num 22:31
he was *h* over a people ....Num 25:15
unto the *h* of the tribes ....Num 30:1
made them *h* over you ....Deut 1:15
the *h* slippeth from the ....Deut 19:5
Lord shall make thee the *h*....Deut 28:13
foot unto the top of thy *h*.....Deut 28:35
when the *h* of the people .....Deut 33:5
upon the *h* of Joseph ....Deut 33:16
and upon the top of the *h*.....Deut 33:16
blood shall be upon his *h* .....Josh 2:19
blood shall be on our *h* ....Josh 2:19
the *h* of the fathers of the.....Josh 14:1
h of the fathers of the Levites .Josh 21:1
h of the fathers of the tribes ..Josh 21:1
each one was a *h* of the.......Josh 22:14
h of the thousands of Israel ...Josh 22:30
and for their *h* ....Josh 24:1
Sisera, she smote off his *h* ....Judg 5:26
brought the *h* of Oreb and ....Judg 7:25
God render upon their *h* ......Judg 9:57
h over all the inhabitants......Judg 10:18
me, shall I be your *h*? ....Judg 11:9
razor shall come on his *h* .....Judg 13:5
come a razor upon mine *h* ....Judg 16:17
the hair of his *h* began to .....Judg 16:22
no razor come upon his *h* 1Sam 1:11
and the *h* of Dagon and 1Sam 5:4
one hair of his *h* fall to the ...1Sam 14:45
helmet of brass upon his *h* 1Sam 17:5
helmet of brass upon his *h* 1Sam 17:38
him, and cut off his *h*.........1Sam 17:51
with the *h* of the Philistine 1Sam 17:57
thee keeper of mine *h* for 1Sam 28:2
it not be with the *h* of 1Sam 29:4
rent, and earth upon his *h* 2Sam 1:2
Thy blood be upon thy *h* 2Sam 1:16
Am I a dog's *h*, which 2Sam 3:8
beheaded him, and took his *h* .2Sam 4:7
the *h* of Ish-bosheth 2Sam 4:8
Behold the *h* of Ish-bosheth ...2Sam 4:8
king's crown from off his *h*....2Sam 12:30
and it was set on David's *h* ...2Sam 12:30
laid her hand on her *h*........2Sam 13:19
And when he polled his *h*.....2Sam 14:26
weighed the hair of his *h*......2Sam 14:26
and take off his *h* 2Sam 16:9
his *h* shall be thrown to 2Sam 20:21
kept me to be *h* of the........2Sam 22:44
let not his hoar *h* go down 1Kin 2:6
his blood upon his own *h* 1Kin 2:32
return upon the *h* of Joab 1Kin 2:33
and upon the *h* of his seed 1Kin 2:33
wickedness upon thine own *h*..1Kin 2:44
all the *h* of the tribes, the.....1Kin 8:1
cruse of water at his *h* 1Kin 19:6
and put ropes on their *h* 1Kin 20:32
thy master from thy *h* 2Kin 2:3
his father, My *h*, my *h*........2Kin 4:19
the axe *h* fell into the.........2Kin 6:5
an ass's *h* was sold for 2Kin 6:25
sent to take away mine *h*? 2Kin 6:32
he poured the oil on his *h* 2Kin 9:6
take ye the *h* of the men......2Kin 10:6
have brought the *h* of the 2Kin 10:8
Jerusalem hath shaken her *h* ..2Kin 19:21
h of the house of their........1Chr 5:24
h of the house of their........1Chr 7:7
h of their father's house 1Chr 7:40
were his sons, *h* of the........1Chr 8:10
These were *h* of the 1Chr 8:28
they took his *h*, and his.......1Chr 10:9
fastened his *h* in the 1Chr 10:10
to the jeopardy of our *h* 1Chr 12:19
crown..king from off his *h* 1Chr 20:2
thou art exalted as *h*..........1Chr 29:11
and bowed down their *h* 1Chr 29:20
put them on the *h* of the 2Chr 3:16
his way upon his own *h* 2Chr 6:23
h of the children of Ephraim ..2Chr 28:12
plucked off..hair of my *h* .....Ezra 9:3
reproach upon their own *h* ....Neh 4:4
bowed their *h*, and ....Neh 8:6
the royal crown upon her *h* ...Esth 2:17
and having his *h* covered......Esth 6:12
return upon his own *h* ....Esth 9:25
mantle, and shaved his *h*......Job 1:20
sprinkled dust upon their *h*....Job 2:12
you, and shake mine *h*........Job 16:4
and his *h* reach unto the ......Job 20:6
candle shined upon my *h*......Job 29:3
irons? or his *h* with fish ....Job 41:7
and the lifter up of mine *h* ....Ps 3:3
return upon his own *h* ....Ps 7:16
made me the *h* of the..........Ps 18:43
the lip, they shake the *h* ......Ps 22:7
Lift up your *h*, O ye gates ....Ps 24:7
are gone over mine *h* ....Ps 38:4
shaking of the *h* among ....Ps 44:14
men to ride over our *h* ....Ps 66:12
shall wound the *h* of his ......Ps 68:21
Thou brakest the *h* ....Ps 74:14
strength of mine *h*............Ps 108:8
wound the *h* over many.......Ps 110:6
shall he lift up the *h* ....Ps 110:7
become the *h* stone of the ....Ps 118:22
the *h* of those that ....Ps 140:9
which shall not break my *h*....Ps 141:5
ornament of grace upon thy *h* .Prov 1:9
Blessings are upon the *h* ......Prov 10:6
The hoary *h* is a crown of.....Prov 16:31
beauty of old men..gray *h* .....Prov 20:29
heap coals of fire upon his *h* ..Prov 25:22
wise man's eyes are in his *h* ...Eccl 2:14
left hand is under my *h* ....Song 2:6
His *h* is as the most fine ......Song 5:11
Thine *h* upon thee is like .....Song 7:5
and the hair of thine *h*........Song 7:5
the whole *h* is sick, and.......Is 1:5
scab the crown of the *h* ....Is 3:17
the *h* of Syria is Damascus ....Is 7:8
h of Damascus is Rezin ....Is 7:8
h of Samaria is Remaliah's ....Is 7:9
will cut off from Israel *h* ......Is 9:14
the *h* or tail, branch or ....Is 19:15
which is on the *h* of the.......Is 28:4

everlasting joy upon their *h* ...Is 35:10
hath shaken her *h* at thee .....Is 37:22
joy shall be upon their *h* ......Is 51:11
to bow down his *h* as a ....Is 58:5
salvation upon his *h* ....Is 59:17
broken the crown of thy *h* ....Jer 2:16
Oh that my *h* were waters ....Jer 9:1
and covered their *h* ....Jer 14:3
me, and the *h* of Lebanon ....Jer 22:6
with pain upon the *h* ....Jer 30:23
of the *h* of the tumultuous ....Jer 48:45
cast up dust upon their *h* .....Lam 2:10
they hiss and wag their *h* .....Lam 2:15
crown is fallen from our *h* ....Lam 5:16
upon the *h* of the living ....Ezek 1:22
stretched forth over their *h*....Ezek 1:22
firmament..over their *h* ....Ezek 1:26
upon thine *h* and upon........Ezek 5:1
their way upon their *h* ....Ezek 9:10
whither the *h* looked they .....Ezek 10:11
way upon their own *h* ....Ezek 11:21
beautiful crown upon thine *h* ..Ezek 16:12
eminent place..the *h* of ....Ezek 16:31
recompense upon his own *h* ...Ezek 17:19
at the *h* of the two ways ......Ezek 21:21
in dyed attire upon their *h* ....Ezek 23:15
tires shall be upon your *h* .....Ezek 24:23
every *h* was made bald.........Ezek 29:18
their swords under their *h*.....Ezek 32:27
blood shall be upon his own *h* .Ezek 33:4
was a door in the *h* of the ....Ezek 42:12
Neither shall they shave..*h* ....Ezek 44:20
they shall only poll their *h* ....Ezek 44:20
me endanger my *h* to the .....Dan 1:10
This image's *h* was of fine.....Dan 2:32
Thou art this *h* of gold........Dan 2:38
nor was a hair of their *h* ......Dan 3:27
and visions of his *h* upon .....Dan 7:1
the beast had also four *h*......Dan 7:6
visions of my *h* troubled ......Dan 7:15
ten horns that were in his *h* ...Dan 7:20
appoint themselves one *h* .....Hos 1:11
recompense upon your own *h*. .Joel 3:4
of the earth on the *h* of.......Amos 2:7
cut them in the *h*, all of ......Amos 9:1
return upon thine own *h* ......Obad 15
were wrapped about my *h*.....Jon 2:5
the sun beat upon the *h*.......Jon 4:8
and the Lord on the *h* ....Mic 2:13
Hear, I pray you, O *h* ....Mic 3:1
The *h* thereof judge for ....Mic 3:11
woundedst the *h* out ....Hab 3:13
no man did lift up his *h*.......Zech 1:21
set a fair mitre upon his *h* ....Zech 3:5
shalt thou swear by thy *h* .....Matt 5:36
hath not where to lay his *h*....Matt 8:20
hairs of your *h* are all ....Matt 10:30
me here John Baptist's *h*......Matt 14:8
is become the *h* of the ....Matt 21:42
they put it upon his *h*.........Matt 27:29
set up over his *h* his ....Matt 27:37
The *h* of John the Baptist .....Mark 6:24
commanded his *h* to be ....Mark 6:27
and wounded him in the *h* ....Mark 12:4
and poured it on his *h* ....Mark 14:3
they smote him on the *h* ......Mark 15:19
on him, wagging their *h*.......Mark 15:29
with the hairs of her *h* ....Luke 7:38
My *h* with oil thou didst ......Luke 7:46
hairs of your *h* are all ....Luke 12:7
shall not a hair of your *h* .....Luke 21:18
also my hands and my *h* ....John 13:9
and he bowed his *h*, and ......John 19:30
blood be upon your own *h* ....Acts 18:6
not a hair fall from the *h* .....Acts 27:34
heap coals of fire on his *h* ....Rom 12:20
prophesying, having his *h* 1Cor 11:4
covered, dishonoreth his *h* 1Cor 11:4
woman to have power on her *h* 1Cor 11:10
again the *h* to the feet 1Cor 12:21
the *h* of all principality........Col 2:10
And not holding the *H*........Col 2:19
His *h* and his hairs were ......Rev 1:14
had on their *h* crowns ....Rev 4:4
and the *h* of the horses ....Rev 9:17
horses were as the *h* of ....Rev 9:17
her *h* a crown of twelve.......Rev 12:1
having seven *h* and ten ....Rev 12:3
seven crowns upon his *h* ......Rev 12:3
having seven *h* and ten ....Rev 13:1
upon his *h* the name of ....Rev 13:1
having seven *h* and ten ....Rev 17:3
The seven *h* are seven ....Rev 17:9
and on his *h* were many ....Rev 19:12

HEAD OF THE CHURCH—*position of preeminence in the Church*
Christ................ Eph 1:22; Eph 5:23; Col 1:18
Prophesied ....Dan 7:13, 14

HEADBAND—*probably a girdle*
Part of feminine attire ...Is 3:20

HEADLONG—*plunging head foremost; lacking in counsel or restraint*
the froward is carried *h* ....Job 5:13
might cast him down *h*........Luke 4:29
of iniquity; and falling *h* ......Acts 1:18

HEADSHIP—*office of authority, responsibility*
Of Christ:
Over all things ....Eph 4:15
Over man................1Cor 11:3
Of Church ....Eph 5:23
Col 1:18
Of the Corner Stone .....Acts 4:11
1Pet 2:7, 8
Of the Father:
Over Christ 1Cor 11:3
Gives authority..........John 5:26, 27
1Cor 15:25-28
Of Man:
Of human race ....Rom 5:12
Over woman 1Cor 11:3
Eph 5:23

HEADSTONE—*the cornerstone*
Christ promised as.......Zech 4:7
Christ fulfills ....Acts 4:11
1Pet 2:7

HEADY—*conceited*
Traitors, *h*, high-minded 2Tim 3:4

HEALER—*one who heals*
saying, I will not be a *h*.......Is 3:7

HEALING—*restoration of health*
Resulting from:
Intercession ....Num 12:10-15
Repentance 1Kin 13:1-6
Prayer ....James 5:14, 15
Faith ....Num 21:8, 9
John 4:46-53
God's Word ....Ps 107:20
Power of:
Belongs to God ....Gen 20:17, 18
Possessed by Jesus.......Matt 4:24
Matt 8:16
Given to apostles ....Matt 10:1-8
Given as a gift 1Cor 12:9
Eternal in heaven ....Rev 22:2
See DISEASES; SICKNESS

[*also* HEAL, HEALED, HEALETH, HEALINGS]
for I am the Lord that *h* ......Ex 15:26
him to be thoroughly *h* ....Ex 21:19
thereof, was a boil and is *h* ...Lev 13:18
if the plague of leprosy be *h* ..Lev 14:3
whereof thou canst not be *h*...Deut 28:27
I make alive; I wound, and I *h*.Deut 32:39
then ye shall be *h*, and it 1Sam 6:3
the Lord, I have *h* these 2Kin 2:21
Joram went back to be *h*......2Kin 8:29
I will *h* thee: on the third 2Kin 20:5
he returned to be *h* in 2Chr 22:6
O Lord, *h* me, for my ....Ps 6:2
and thou hast *h* me...........Ps 30:2
be merciful unto me, *h* ....Ps 41:4
iniquities who *h* all thy.......Ps 103:3
to kill, and a time to *h* ....Eccl 3:3
and *h* the stroke of their ......Is 30:26
seen his ways, and will *h* him. .Is 57:18
saith the Lord, and I will *h* ...Is 57:19
They have *h* also the ....Jer 6:14
us, and there is no *h* for ......Jer 14:19
and for the time of *h*, and ....Jer 14:19
which refuseth to be *h*? ....Jer 15:18
up: thou hast no *h* ....Jer 30:13
I will *h* thee of thy wounds....Jer 30:17
pain, if so be she may be *h* ...Jer 51:8
We would have *h* Babylon ....Jer 51:9
Babylon, but she is not *h* .....Jer 51:9
like the sea: who can *h* ....Lam 2:13
not be bound up to be *h*......Ezek 30:21
yet could he not *h* you........Hos 5:13
When I would have *h*.........Hos 7:1
I will *h* their backsliding ......Hos 14:4
There is no *h* of thy ....Nah 3:19
nor *h* that that is broken ......Zech 11:16
h all manner of sickness ......Matt 4:23
I will come and *h* him ....Matt 8:7
my servant shall be *h* ....Matt 8:8
and to *h* all manner ....Matt 10:1
H the sick, cleanse the........Matt 10:8
followed him, and he *h* ....Matt 12:15
converted, and I should *h* .....Matt 13:15
toward them, and he *h*........Matt 14:14
followed him; and he *h* ....Matt 19:2
he *h* many that were sick .....Mark 1:34
he would *h*..on the sabbath ...Mark 3:2
to have power to *h* ....Mark 3:15
that she may be *h* ....Mark 5:23
upon a few sick folk, and *h* ...Mark 6:5
sent me to *h* the ....Luke 4:18
proverb, Physician, *h* ....Luke 4:23
every one of them, and *h* .....Luke 4:40
the Lord was present to *h*.....Luke 5:17
would *h* on the sabbath ....Luke 6:7
h of their diseases ....Luke 6:17
virtue out of him, and *h* ......Luke 6:19
would come and *h* his ....Luke 7:3
women, which had been *h* ....Luke 8:2
neither could be *h* of any .....Luke 8:43
the gospel, and *h* every ....Luke 9:6
h them that had need of ......Luke 9:11
h the sick that are therein.....Luke 10:9
Jesus had *h* on the sabbath....Luke 13:14
lawful to *h* on the ....Luke 14:3
him, and *h* him, and let.......Luke 14:4
he touched his ear, and *h* .....Luke 22:51
And he that was *h* wist ....John 5:13
converted, and I should *h* .....John 12:40
man which was *h* held ....Acts 3:11
the man which was *h* ....Acts 4:14
this miracle of *h* was..........Acts 4:22
stretching..thine hand to *h* ....Acts 4:30
they were *h* every one ....Acts 5:16
that were lame, were *h* ....Acts 8:7
and *h* all that were ....Acts 10:38
that he had faith to be *h* ......Acts 14:9
his hands on him and *h* ....Acts 28:8
miracles, then gifts of *h* 1Cor 12:28
Have all the gifts of *h*? 1Cor 12:30
but let it rather be *h*..........Heb 12:13
another, that ye may be *h*.....James 5:16
whose stripes ye were *h* 1Pet 2:24
his deadly wound was *h* ....Rev 13:3

HEALING, SPIRITUAL
Source of:
Only in God ....Jer 17:14
Through Christ ....Is 53:5
Through the Gospel .....Ezek 47:8-11
Provided for:
Heartbroken ....Ps 147:3
Repentant 2Chr 7:14
Egyptians ....Is 19:22-25
Faithful ....Mal 4:2
Necessary because of man's:
Sin ....Ps 41:4
Backsliding ....Jer 3:22
Spiritual sickness ....Is 6:10

HEALTH—*freedom from disease*
Factors conducive to:
Exercise 1Tim 4:8

H

Food ....Acts 27:34
Temperance ....Jer 35:5-8
Obedience ....Prov 4:20-22
Cheerfulness ....Prov 17:22
God's will ....John 9:1-3

Factors destructive of:

Moral looseness ....Prov 7:22-27
Wickedness ....Ps 55:23
Disease 1Sam 5:6-12
Injury ....Luke 10:30
Debauchery ....Titus 1:12

our father is in good ***h*** ....Gen 43:28
thou in ***h***, my brother? 2Sam 20:9
the ***h*** of my countenance ......Ps 42:11
the ***h*** of my countenance ......Ps 43:5
thy..***h*** among all nations ......Ps 67:2
It shall be ***h*** to thy navel ......Prov 3:8
tongue of the wise is ***h*** ....Prov 12:18
faithful ambassador is ***h*** ....Prov 13:17
the soul, and ***h*** to the bones...Prov 16:24
and thine ***h*** shall spring ....Is 58:8
and for a time of ***h***, and ......Jer 8:15
the ***h*** of the daughter of ......Jer 8:22
For I will restore ***h*** unto ......Jer 30:17
thou mayest prosper..***h*** 3John 2

HEAP—*to pile; a pile*

[*also* HEAPED, HEAPETH, HEAPS]
gathered them together upon ***h***.Ex 8:14
floods stood upright as a ***h*** ....Ex 15:8
and it shall be a ***h*** for ....Deut 13:16
they shall stand upon a ***h*** .....Josh 3:13
over him a great ***h*** ....Josh 7:26
raise thereon a great ***h*** ....Josh 8:29
jawbone of an ass, ***h*** upon ***h*** ..Judg 15:16
down at the end of the ***h*** .....Ruth 3:7
very great ***h*** of stones 2Sam 18:17
Lay ye them in two ***h*** 2Kin 10:8
God, and laid them by ***h*** 2Chr 31:6
princes came and saw the ***h*** ...2Chr 31:8
stones out of the ***h*** of the .....Neh 4:2
roots are wrapped about the ***h*** .Job 8:17
are ready to become ***h*** ....Job 15:28
Though he ***h*** up silver as ......Job 27:16
the sea together as a ***h*** ....Ps 33:7
he ***h*** up riches, and ....Ps 39:6
have laid Jerusalem on ***h*** ....Ps 79:1
shalt ***h*** coals of fire upon ......Prov 25:22
gather and to ***h*** up, that ......Eccl 2:26
thy belly is like a ***h*** of ....Song 7:2
and it shall be a ruinous ***h*** ....Is 17:1
hast made of a city a ***h*** ....Is 25:2
defenced cities into ruinous ***h***..Is 37:26
Jerusalem shall become ***h*** .....Jer 26:18
be builded upon her own ***h*** ....Jer 30:18
cast her up as ***h***, and ....Jer 50:26
H on wood, kindle the fire ....Ezek 24:10
their altars are as ***h*** in ....Hos 12:11
make Samaria as a ***h*** of ....Mic 1:6
Jerusalem shall become ***h*** .....Mic 3:12
for they shall ***h*** dust, and .....Hab 1:10
h unto him all people ....Hab 2:5
came to a ***h*** of twenty ....Hag 2:16
and ***h*** up silver as the ....Zech 9:3
shalt ***h*** coals of fire on his .....Rom 12:20
they ***h*** to themselves 2Tim 4:3
Ye have ***h*** treasure ....James 5:3

HEAP OF STONES—*a monument of stones*

Symbolic of:

Shameful acts ....Josh 7:26
Covenant ....Gen 31:46-52
Judgment ....Jer 9:11

HEAR—*to apprehend by means of the ear*

[*also* HEARD, HEARDEST, HEAREST, HEARETH, HEARING]
they ***h*** the voice of the Lord ..Gen 3:8
And God ***h*** their groaning ....Ex 2:24
he ***h*** your murmurings ....Ex 16:7
and the Lord ***h*** it; and his .....Num 11:1
in the day that he ***h*** ....Num 30:5
and I will make them ***h*** ....Deut 4:10
thou ***h*** his words out of ....Deut 4:36
h the voice of the living God ..Deut 5:26
when he ***h*** the words of ....Deut 29:19
before all Israel in their ***h*** .....Deut 31:11
ye ***h*** the sound of the ....Josh 6:5
thou ***h*** in that day how the ....Josh 14:12
Boaz unto Ruth, ***H*** thou ......Ruth 2:8
I ***h*** of your evil dealings 1Sam 2:23
Lord; for thy servant ***h*** 1Sam 3:9
of every one that ***h*** it 1Sam 3:11
Wherefore ***h*** thou men's 1Sam 24:9
when thou ***h*** the sound of 2Sam 5:24
first, that whosoever ***h*** it 2Sam 17:9
for in our ***h*** the king 2Sam 18:12
and when thou ***h***, forgive 1Kin 8:30
was neither voice, nor ***h*** 2Kin 4:31
that whosoever ***h*** of it 2Kin 21:12
h what I spake against 2Kin 22:19
and when thou ***h***, forgive 2Chr 6:21
then will I ***h*** from heaven 2Chr 7:14
thou ***h*** his words against 2Chr 34:27
and ***h*** their cry by the ....Neh 9:9
thou hast spoken in my ***h*** .....Job 33:8
H my words, O ye wise ....Job 34:2
and he ***h*** the cry of the ....Job 34:28
h thee in the day of ....Ps 20:1
in the daytime, but thou ***h*** ....Ps 22:2
H, O Lord, when I cry ....Ps 27:7
thou ***h*** the voice of my ....Ps 31:22
I sought the Lord, and he ***h*** ..Ps 34:4
and the Lord ***h*** and ....Ps 34:17
for who, say they, doth ***h***? ....Ps 59:7
for the Lord ***h*** the poor ....Ps 69:33
h what God the Lord will .....Ps 85:8
Zion ***h***, and was glad; and ....Ps 97:8
wise man will ***h***, and will ......Prov 1:5
Blessed is the man that ***h*** .....Prov 8:34
wise son ***h*** his father's ....Prov 13:1
scorner ***h*** not rebuke ....Prov 13:1
The ear that ***h*** the reproof ....Prov 15:31
a matter before he ***h*** ....Prov 18:13
The ***h*** ear, and the seeing eye .Prov 20:12
Lest he that ***h*** it put thee .....Prov 25:10
nor the ear filled with ***h*** ....Eccl 1:8
us ***h*** the conclusion of the .....Eccl 12:13
voice of the turtle is ***h*** in ......Song 2:12
H ye indeed, but ....Is 6:9
reprove after the ***h*** of his .....Is 11:3
I was bowed down at the ***h*** ...Is 21:3
stoppeth his ears from ***h*** ......Is 33:15
not known? have ye not ***h***? ...Is 40:21
there is none that ***h*** your ......Is 41:26
the day when thou ***h*** them ....Is 48:7
h and your soul shall live .....Is 55:3
whosoever ***h***, his ears ....Jer 19:3
He that ***h***, let him hear ....Ezek 3:27
others he said in mine ***h*** ......Ezek 9:5
h the prayer of thy servant ....Dan 9:17
of ***h*** the words of the Lord ....Amos 8:11
unto the Lord, and he ***h*** ......Jon 2:2
hell cried I, and thou ***h*** my ....Jon 2:2
Ye have ***h*** that it was ....Matt 5:21
whosoever ***h*** these sayings .....Matt 7:24
He that hath ears to ***h*** ....Matt 11:15
seeing see not: and ***h*** ....Matt 13:13
their ears are dull of ***h*** ....Matt 13:15
any one ***h*** the word of the ....Matt 13:19
the thorns is he that ***h*** the ....Matt 13:22
I am well pleased; ***h*** ye him ...Matt 17:5
unto him, ***H*** thou what ....Matt 21:16
ye shall ***h*** of wars and ....Matt 24:6
they may ***h***, and not ....Mark 4:12
maketh both the deaf to ***h*** ....Mark 7:37
for thy prayer is ***h***; and ....Luke 1:13
both ***h*** them, and asking ......Luke 2:46
cometh to me, and ***h*** my .....Luke 6:47
He that ***h*** you ***h*** me; and .....Luke 10:16
h the multitude pass by ......Luke 18:36
ye shall ***h*** of wars ....Luke 21:9
and thou ***h*** the sound ....John 3:8
which standeth and ***h*** him .....John 3:29
hath seen and ***h*** that he ....John 3:32
shall ***h*** the voice of the Son ...John 5:25
He that is of God ***h*** God's .....John 8:47
we know that God ***h*** not ......John 9:31
doeth his will, him he ***h*** ....John 9:31
and the sheep ***h*** his voice .....John 10:3
My sheep ***h*** my voice, and ....John 10:27
any man ***h*** my words, and .....John 12:47
every man ***h*** them speak ......Acts 2:6
h we every man in our ....Acts 2:8
Ananias ***h*** these words fell ....Acts 5:5
he fell to the earth, and ***h*** .....Acts 9:4
h a voice, but seeing no ....Acts 9:7
city together, to ***h*** the ....Acts 13:44
to tell, or to ***h*** some new .....Acts 17:21
h not the voice of him ....Acts 22:9
reserved unto the ***h*** of ....Acts 25:21
they ***h*** without a preacher? ....Rom 10:14
So then faith cometh by ***h*** .....Rom 10:17
h by the word of God ....Rom 10:17
Eye hath not seen nor ear ***h***...1Cor 2:9
an eye, where were the ***h***? 1Cor 12:17
whole were ***h***, where were 1Cor 12:17
me to be, or that he ***h*** 2Cor 12:6
of the law, or by the ***h*** ....Gal 3:2
If so be that ye have ***h*** ....Eph 4:21
H of thy love and faith ....Philem 5
with faith in them that ***h*** ......Heb 4:2
seeing ye are dull of ***h*** ....Heb 5:11
let every man be swift to ***h*** ....James 1:19
Ye have ***h*** of the patience .....James 5:11
them, in seeing and ***h*** 2Pet 2:8
we have ***h***, which we have 1John 1:1
world, and the world ***h*** 1John 4:5
he that knoweth God ***h*** us 1John 4:6
he that is not of God ***h*** not ...1John 4:6
hast thou received and ***h*** ......Rev 3:3
if any man ***h*** my voice ....Rev 3:20
John saw these things, and ***h*** ..Rev 22:8
And when I had ***h*** and seen ...Rev 22:8
And let him that ***h*** say ....Rev 22:17

HEARER—*one who gains knowledge of by hearing*

Element necessary in:

Attentiveness ....Neh 8:1-3
Belief ....Rom 10:14
Conviction ....Acts 2:37
Discrimination ....Luke 8:18

Reactions of:

Responsiveness 2Sam 7:17-29
Repentance 2Sam 12:12,13
Rebellion ....Ezek 33:30-33
Retreat ....John 6:60-66
Resistance ....Acts 7:51-54
Rejoicing ....Acts 13:48
Rejection ....Acts 28:23-29
Research ....Acts 17:11

[*also* HEARERS]
For not the ***h*** of the law ......Rom 2:13
minister grace unto the ***h*** .....Eph 4:29
to the subverting of the ***h*** 2Tim 2:14
doers of the word, and not ***h*** ..James 1:22
if any be a ***h*** of the word .....James 1:23

HEARKEN—*to give respectful attention to*

[*also* HEARKENED, HEARKENEDST, HEARKENETH, HEARKENING]
hast ***h*** unto the voice of ....Gen 3:17
wives of Lamech, ***h*** unto ......Gen 4:23
My lord, ***h*** unto me: the ......Gen 23:15
And Abraham ***h*** unto ....Gen 23:16
And God ***h*** to her, and ....Gen 30:22
that he ***h*** not unto her ....Gen 39:10
and ***h*** unto Israel your ....Gen 49:2
And they shall ***h*** to thy ....Ex 3:18
neither ***h*** to the voice of ......Ex 4:8
they ***h*** not unto Moses ....Ex 6:9
and how shall Pharaoh ***h*** ......Ex 6:30
Pharaoh's heart, that he ***h*** .....Ex 7:13
neither did he ***h*** unto ....Ex 7:22
was hardened and he ***h*** not ....Ex 8:19
If thou wilt diligently ***h*** ....Ex 15:26
they ***h*** not unto Moses ....Ex 16:20
But if ye will not ***h*** unto ......Lev 26:14
will not ***h*** unto me; I will .....Lev 26:21
have not ***h*** to my voice ....Num 14:22
h..thou son of Zippor ....Num 23:18
Lord would not ***h*** to your .....Deut 1:45
if ye ***h*** to these judgments .....Deut 7:12
Lord ***h*** unto me at that ....Deut 9:19

Lord ***h*** unto me at that ....Deut 10:10
Thou shalt not ***h*** unto the .....Deut 13:3
h to the voice of the Lord ....Deut 13:18
h unto the priest that ....Deut 17:12
whosoever will not ***h*** unto .....Deut 18:19
thy God would not ***h*** unto ....Deut 23:5
I have ***h*** to the voice..Lord....Deut 26:14
Take heed, and ***h***, O Israel ...Deut 27:9
if thou shalt ***h*** unto the ....Deut 28:2
if thou wilt not ***h*** unto the ....Deut 28:15
because thou ***h*** not unto ......Deut 28:45
in all things, so will we ***h*** .....Josh 1:17
as we ***h*** unto Moses in all .....Josh 1:17
But I would not ***h*** unto ....Josh 24:10
would not ***h*** unto their ....Judg 2:17
and have not ***h*** unto my ......Judg 2:20
H unto me, ye men of ....Judg 9:7
Shechem, that God may ***h*** ....Judg 9:7
king of Edom would not ***h*** ....Judg 11:17
And God ***h*** to the voice of....Judg 13:9
Benjamin would not ***h*** to .....Judg 20:13
h not unto the voice 1Sam 2:25
H unto the voice of the 1Sam 8:7
H unto their voice, and 1Sam 8:22
to ***h*** than the fat of............1Sam 15:22
Saul ***h*** unto the voice of 1Sam 19:6
and have ***h*** unto thy 1Sam 28:21
For who will ***h*** unto you 1Sam 30:24
he would not ***h*** unto our 2Sam 12:18
But he would not ***h*** unto 2Sam 13:16
to ***h*** unto the cry and to 1Kin 8:28
And ***h*** thou to the.............1Kin 8:30
thou wilt ***h*** unto all that I 1Kin 11:38
the king ***h*** not unto the 1Kin 12:15
They ***h*** therefore to the 1Kin 12:24
H, O people, every one 1Kin 22:28
if ye will ***h*** unto my voice 2Kin 10:6
and the Lord ***h*** unto him......2Kin 13:4
H not to Hezekiah: for 2Kin 18:31
And Hezekiah ***h*** unto 2Kin 20:13
our fathers have not ***h*** 2Kin 22:13
to ***h*** unto the cry and the 2Chr 6:19
H therefore unto the..........2Chr 6:21
So the king ***h*** not unto the 2Chr 10:15
And he said, ***H***, all ye 2Chr 18:27
Then the king ***h*** unto 2Chr 24:17
Lord ***h*** to Hezekiah, and 2Chr 30:20
but they would not ***h*** 2Chr 33:10
h not to thy commandments ...Neh 9:16
h not..thy commandments .....Neh 9:29
Shall we then ***h*** unto you .....Neh 13:27
unto him, he ***h*** not unto ......Esth 3:4
and ***h*** to the pleadings of .....Job 13:6
speeches, and ***h*** to all my .....Job 33:1
If not, ***h*** unto me: hold ....Job 33:33
this: ***h*** to the voice of my .....Job 34:16
H unto this, O Job: stand .....Job 37:14
H unto the voice of my ....Ps 5:2
H, O daughter, and ....Ps 45:10
O Israel, if thou wilt ***h***........Ps 81:8
Oh that my people had ***h*** .....Ps 81:13
h unto the voice of his ....Ps 103:20
But whoso ***h*** unto me..........Prov 1:33
H unto me now therefore .....Prov 7:24
H unto thy father that ....Prov 23:22
the companions ***h*** to thy ......Song 8:13
he ***h*** diligently with much .....Is 21:7
my voice; ***h***, and hear my .....Is 28:23
h ye people: let the earth .....Is 34:1
who will ***h*** and hear for ....Is 42:23
H unto me, ye stouthearted ...Is 46:12
and ***h***, ye people, from far ....Is 49:1
H unto me, my people ....Is 51:4
h diligently unto me, and .....Is 55:2
and they cannot ***h*** ....Jer 6:10
H to the sound of the.........Jer 6:17
they have not ***h*** unto my ......Jer 6:19
Yet they ***h*** not unto me ....Jer 7:26
cry unto me, I will not ***h***......Jer 11:11
to pass, if ye diligently ***h***......Jer 17:24
h to the voice of them that....Jer 18:19
but ye have not ***h*** ....Jer 25:3
Yet ye have not ***h*** unto me....Jer 25:7
If so be they will ***h***, and ......Jer 26:3
To ***h*** to the words of my ......Jer 26:5
h not unto the words of........Jer 27:14
H not unto them; serve the ...Jer 27:17
pray unto me, and I will ***h*** ....Jer 29:12
they have not ***h*** to my ....Jer 29:19
but your fathers ***h*** not ....Jer 34:14
speaking; but ye ***h*** not ....Jer 35:14
but this people hath not ***h***.....Jer 35:16
h unto the words of the Lord..Jer 37:2
But he ***h*** not to him ....Jer 37:14
of the Lord, we will not ***h*** ....Jer 44:16
them, they would have ***h***......Ezek 3:6
house of Israel will not ***h*** .....Ezek 3:7
thee; for they will not ***h***.......Ezek 3:7
also, if ye will not ***h*** unto .....Ezek 20:39
we ***h*** unto thy servants ....Dan 9:6
O Lord ***h*** and do; defer........Dan 9:19
h, ye house of Israel; and .....Hos 5:1
h, O earth, and all that ....Mic 1:2
did not hear, nor ***h*** unto ......Zech 1:4
the Lord ***h***, and heard ....Mal 3:16
H; Behold, there went ....Mark 4:3
unto you, and ***h*** to my........Acts 2:14
in the sight of God to ***h***.......Acts 4:19
Men, brethren, and fathers, ***h*** .Acts 7:2
damsel came to ***h***, named .....Acts 12:13
Men and brethren, ***h*** unto.....Acts 15:13
Sirs, ye should have ***h*** unto ...Acts 27:21
H, my beloved brethren.......James 2:5

HEART—*symbolic of intellectual, moral, and emotional functions of individuals; one's inner being*

Seat of:
Adultery.................Matt 5:28
Desire...................Rom 10:1
Doubt...................Mark 11:23
Fear....................Is 35:4
Hatred ....Lev 19:17
Gladness................Acts 2:26
Love ....Mark 12:30, 33
Lust....................Rom 1:24
Meditation ....Ps 19:14
Mischief ....Ps 28:3
Obedience ....Rom 6:17
Pride ....Prov 16:5
Purpose 2Cor 9:7
Reason ....Mark 2:8
Rebellion ....Jer 5:23
Sorrow ....John 14:1
Thought ....Matt 9:4

Of the wicked, described as:
Blind..................Eph 4:18
Darkened..............Rom 1:21
Covetous 2Pet 2:14
Full of evil............Gen 6:5
Unrepentant ....Rom 2:5
Lustful ....Prov 6:25
Proud ....Jer 49:16
Rebellious ....Jer 5:23
Uncircumcised ....Acts 7:51

God's action upon:
Knows.................Ps 44:21
Searches 1Chr 28:9
Enlightens 2Cor 4:6
Opens ....Acts 16:14
Recreates ....Ezek 11:19
Examines ....Jer 12:3
Strengthens ....Ps 27:14
Establishes 1Thess 3:13

Regenerate's, described as:
Circumcised............Rom 2:29
Clean ....Ps 73:1
Contrite ....Ps 51:17
Enlarged...............Ps 119:32
Enlightened 2Cor 4:6
Fixed..................Ps 57:7
Joyful in God 1Sam 2:1
Meditative ....Ps 4:4
Perfect ....Ps 101:2
Prayerful 1Sam 1:12, 13
Pure...................Matt 5:8
Glad and sincere ....Acts 2:46
Tender 2Kin 22:19
Treasury of good ....Matt 12:35
Wise ....Prov 10:8

Regenerate's, responses of:
Believe with ....Rom 10:10
Keep with diligence......Prov 4:23
Love God with all.......Matt 22:37
Sanctify God in 1Pet 3:15
Serve God with all ....Deut 26:16
Walk before God with all.1Kin 2:4
Trust the Lord with all...Prov 3:5
Regard not iniquity in ...Ps 66:18
Do God's will from......Eph 6:6

[*also* HEARTED, HEART'S, HEARTS, HEARTS']
thoughts of his ***h*** was only ....Gen 6:5
and comfort ye your ***h*** ....Gen 18:5
harden the ***h*** of the Egyptians .Ex 14:17
speak unto all..are wise ***h***......Ex 28:3
And every wise ***h*** among.......Ex 35:10
the women that were wise ***h***...Ex 35:25
he filled with wisdom of ***h*** ....Ex 35:35
and every wise ***h*** man.........Ex 36:2
a faintness into their ***h*** ....Lev 26:36
serve him with all your ***h*** .....Deut 11:13
let nor your ***h*** faint, fear ......Deut 20:3
Set your ***h*** unto all the........Deut 32:46
our ***h*** did melt, neither did ....Josh 2:11
Lord to harden their ***h***........Josh 11:20
to serve him with all your ***h***...Josh 22:5
h inclined to follow ....Judg 9:3
they were making their ***h*** .....Judg 19:22
My ***h*** rejoiceth in the Lord....1Sam 2:1
then do ye harden your ***h*** 1Sam 6:6
Pharaoh hardened their ***h***? 1Sam 6:6
Lord with all your ***h*** 1Sam 7:3
prepare your ***h*** unto the Lord. .1Sam 7:3
the Lord with all your ***h*** 1Sam 12:20
Absalom stole the ***h*** of the 2Sam 15:6
thou only, knowest the ***h***......1Kin 8:39
followed me with all his ***h***.....1Kin 14:8
h right, as my ***h*** is with thy ***h***? .2Kin 10:15
they were not of double ***h***.....1Chr 12:33
triest the ***h***, and hast 1Chr 29:17
before thee with all their ***h*** 2Chr 6:14
such as set their ***h*** to seek.....2Chr 11:16
all their ***h*** and with all 2Chr 15:12
nothing else but sorrow of ***h***..Neh 2:2
and cursed God in their ***h***.....Job 1:5
He is wise in ***h***, and mighty ...Job 9:4
understanding to the ***h***? ....Job 38:36
righteous God trieth the ***h*** ....Ps 7:9
wicked boasteth of his ***h*** ......Ps 10:3
The fool hath said in his ***h*** ....Ps 14:1
clean hands and a pure ***h*** .....Ps 24:4
against me, my ***h*** shall not ....Ps 27:3
He fashioneth their ***h*** ....Ps 33:15
them that are of a broken ***h***...Ps 34:18
knoweth the secrets of the ***h*** ..Ps 44:21
Create in me a clean ***h***, O ....Ps 51:10
one of them, and the ***h*** ....Ps 64:6
they have more than ***h***........Ps 73:7
said in their ***h***, Let us.........Ps 74:8
their ***h*** was not right with .....Ps 78:37
them up unto their own ***h*** .....Ps 81:12
may apply our ***h*** unto..........Ps 90:12
that are upright in their ***h*** .....Ps 125:4
Search me..know my ***h***.........Ps 139:23
Keep thy ***h*** with all ....Prov 4:23
then the ***h*** of the children .....Prov 15:11
the Lord pondereth the ***h*** .....Prov 21:2
as he thinketh in his ***h***, so.....Prov 23:7
My son, give me thine ***h*** ......Prov 23:26
wise man's ***h*** discerneth ....Eccl 8:5
gladness of ***h***, as when ....Is 30:29
see; and their ***h*** that they .....Is 44:18
revive the ***h*** of the contrite ....Is 57:15
my ***h*** maketh a noise in ....Jer 4:19
triest the reins and the ***h***......Jer 11:20
the ***h*** is deceitful above ....Jer 17:9
I will give them a ***h*** to ....Jer 24:7
unto me with their whole ***h*** ...Jer 24:7
and write it in their ***h***.........Jer 31:33
ye dissembled in your ***h***.......Jer 42:20
Give them sorrow of ***h***.......Lam 3:65
I will give them one ***h*** ....Ezek 11:19
prophesy out of their own ***h***...Ezek 13:2
A new ***h*** also will I give ......Ezek 36:26

both these kings' *h* shall ......Dan 11:27
they consider not in their *h* ...Hos 7:2
And rend your *h*, and not.....Joel 2:13
they made their *h* as an.......Zech 7:12
he shall turn the *h* of the .....Mal 4:6
Blessed are the pure in *h* .....Matt 5:8
treasure is, there will your *h* ..Matt 6:21
I am meek and lowly in *h*.....Matt 11:29
out of the *h* proceed evil.....Matt 15:19
from your *h* forgive not ....Matt 18:35
and reasoning in their *h*.......Mark 2:6
for the hardness of their *h* ....Mark 3:5
out of the *h* of men ....Mark 7:21
the hardness of your *h* ....Mark 10:5
to turn the *h* of the fathers....Luke 1:17
laid them up in their *h*........Luke 1:66
all men mused in their *h* ......Luke 3:15
the good treasure of his *h*.....Luke 6:45
away the word out of their *h* ..Luke 8:12
treasure is there will your *h* ...Luke 12:34
Settle it therefore in your *h* ...Luke 21:14
any time your *h* be ....Luke 21:34
and slow of *h* to believe all ...Luke 24:25
Let not your *h* be troubled ....John 14:1
which knowest the *h* of ....Acts 1:24
and uncircumcised in *h*........Acts 7:51
filling our *h* with food and ....Acts 14:17
them, purifying their *h* by .....Acts 15:9
the law written in their *h* .....Rom 2:15
God is shed abroad in our *h* ..Rom 5:5
he that searcheth the *h* ....Rom 8:27
my *h* desire and prayer to God.Rom 10:1
believe in thine *h* that God....Rom 10:9
with the *h* man believeth......Rom 10:10
deceive the *h* of the simple....Rom 16:18
have entered into the *h* 1Cor 2:9
the counsels of the *h* 1Cor 4:5
earnest of the Spirit in our *h* ..2Cor 1:22
that ye are in our *h* to die 2Cor 7:3
Spirit of his Son into your *h*...Gal 4:6
Christ may dwell in your *h* ....Eph 3:17
shall keep your *h* and.........Phil 4:7
That their *h* might be ....Col 2:2
singing with grace in your *h* ...Col 3:16
singleness of *h*, fearing God ...Col 3:22
God, which trieth our *h*.......1Thess 2:4
Comfort your *h*, and..........2Thess 2:17
is charity out of a pure *h* 1Tim 1:5
Harden not your *h*, as ....Heb 3:8
harden not your *h* ....Heb 4:7
thoughts and intents of the *h* ..Heb 4:12
put my laws into their *h* ......Heb 10:16
draw near with a true *h*.......Heb 10:22
having our *h* sprinkled ....Heb 10:22
envying and strife in your *h* ...James 3:14
ye have nourished your *h* .....James 5:5
the Lord God in your *h*.......1Pet 3:15
day star arise in your *h* 2Pet 1:19
and shall assure our *h* 1John 3:19
For if our *h* condemn us 1John 3:20
God is greater than our *h* 1John 3:20
searcheth the reins and *h* .....Rev 2:23

HEARTH—*the floor of a fireplace*
Bed of live coals ....Is 30:14
Ps 102:3

and make cakes upon the *h* ...Gen 18:6
fire on the *h* burning ....Jer 36:22
the fire that was on the *h* .....Jer 36:23
the fire that was on the *h* .....Jer 36:23

HEARTLESSNESS—*without moral feeling; cruelty*

Among unbelievers:
Philistines, toward Samson ....Judg 16:21
Saul, toward David 1Sam 18:25
Nabal, toward David 1Sam 25:4-12
Haman, toward Jews ....Esth 3:8, 9
Priest, toward a certain man ....Luke 10:30-32

Among professing believers:
Laban, toward Jacob ....Gen 31:7, 36-42
Jacob's sons, toward Joseph................Gen 37:18-35
David, toward Uriah.....2Sam 11:9-27

HEARTY—*enthusiastically; merry*

[*also* HEARTILY]
of a man's friend by *h* ....Prov 27:9
whatsoever ye do, do it *h* .....Col 3:23

HEAT—*high temperature; to make hot*
Figurative of:
God's wrath ....Deut 9:19
Man's anger ....Deut 19:6
Determination...........Gen 31:36
Zeal....................Ps 39:3
Persecution ....Matt 13:6, 21
Heavy toil ....Matt 20:12
Real faith...............Rev 3:15

[*also* HEATED]
and cold and *h*, and ....Gen 8:22
meaneth the *h* of this great....Deut 29:24
Ammonites until the *h* of 1Sam 11:11
came about the *h* of the 2Sam 4:5
clothes, but he gat no *h*.......1Kin 1:1
Drought and *h* consume ......Job 24:19
nothing hid from the *h*........Ps 19:6
together, then they have *h* ....Eccl 4:11
in the daytime from the *h*.....Is 4:6
like a clear *h* upon herbs......Is 18:4
a cloud of dew in the *h* ....Is 18:4
strangers, as the *h* in a........Is 25:5
the *h* with the shadow ....Is 25:5
and shall not see when *h*......Jer 17:8
their *h* I will make their ......Jer 51:39
bitterness, in the *h* of my .....Ezek 3:14
that they should *h* the ....Dan 3:19
than it was wont to be *h* ......Dan 3:19
as an oven *h* by the baker ....Hos 7:4
ye say, There will be *h* ....Luke 12:55
came a viper out of the *h* .....Acts 28:3
risen with a burning *h* ....James 1:11
shall melt with fervent *h* 2Pet 3:10
shall melt with fervent *h* 2Pet 3:12
sun light on them nor any *h* ...Rev 7:16

HEATH—*a desert plant*
Figurative of:
Self-sufficient man ....Jer 17:6
Devastation ....Jer 48:6

HEATHEN—*Gentiles; people or nation that does not acknowledge God*
the *h* that are round about ....Lev 25:44
scatter you among the *h* ......Lev 26:33
shall perish among the *h* ......Lev 26:38
few in number among the *h* ...Deut 4:27
kept me to be head of the *h* ..2Sam 22:44
to the abominations of the *h* ..2Kin 16:3
did the *h* whom the Lord 2Kin 17:11
went after the *h* that were 2Kin 17:15
the abominations of the *h* 2Kin 21:2
his glory among the *h*.........1Chr 16:24
all the kingdoms of the *h*? 2Chr 20:6
abominations of the *h*.........2Chr 28:3
to do worse than the *h*.........2Chr 33:9
the abominations of the *h* 2Chr 36:14
the filthiness of the *h* of ......Ezra 6:21
which were sold unto the *h*....Neh 5:8
unto us from among the *h* ....Neh 5:17
all the *h* that were about ......Neh 6:16
Why do the *h* rage, and.......Ps 2:1
Thou hast rebuked the *h* ......Ps 9:5
let the *h* be judged in thy .....Ps 9:19
made me the head of the *h* ...Ps 18:43
the counsel of the *h* to........Ps 33:10
scattered us among the *h*......Ps 44:11
us a byword among the *h* .....Ps 44:14
h raged, the kingdoms ....Ps 46:6
will be exalted among the *h* ...Ps 46:10
God reigneth over the *h* ......Ps 47:8
shalt have all the *h* in.........Ps 59:8
h are come into thine ....Ps 79:1
Wherefore should the *h* ....Ps 79:10
be known among the *h* in .....Ps 79:10
He that chastiseth the *h*.......Ps 94:10
Say among the *h* that the Lord.Ps 96:10
So the *h* shall fear the ....Ps 102:15
were mingled among the *h* ....Ps 106:35
gather us from among the *h* ...Ps 106:47
them the heritage of the *h* ....Ps 111:6
said they among the *h* ....Ps 126:2
execute vengeance upon the *h* .Ps 149:7
lords of the *h* have broken ....Is 16:8
scatter them also among the *h* .Jer 9:16
Learn not the way of the *h*...Jer 10:2
for the *h* are dismayed at .....Jer 10:2
Ask ye now among the *h* .....Jer 18:13
thee small among the *h* ....Jer 49:15
they said among the *h* ....Lam 4:15
we shall live among the *h* .....Lam 4:20
will bring the worst of the *h*...Ezek 7:24
them far off among the *h* .....Ezek 11:16
went forth among the *h*........Ezek 16:14
be polluted before the *h* ......Ezek 20:14
scatter them among the *h* .....Ezek 20:23
sanctified in you before the *h*..Ezek 20:41
scatter thee among the *h*......Ezek 22:15
gone a whoring after the *h* ....Ezek 23:30
Judah is like unto all the *h*....Ezek 25:8
shall be the time of the *h* .....Ezek 30:3
shadow in the midst of the *h* ..Ezek 31:17
bear the shame of the *h*.......Ezek 34:29
to the residue of the *h*........Ezek 36:4
borne the shame of the *h* .....Ezek 36:6
the shame of the *h* any ....Ezek 36:15
they entered unto the *h* ....Ezek 36:20
ye have profaned among..*h*....Ezek 36:22
was profaned among the *h* ....Ezek 36:23
h shall know that I am the ....Ezek 36:23
you from among the *h* ....Ezek 36:24
of famine among the *h*........Ezek 36:30
Israel from among the *h* ......Ezek 37:21
that the *h* may know me ....Ezek 38:16
h shall know that I..Lord .....Ezek 39:7
set my glory among the *h* .....Ezek 39:21
all the *h* shall see my ....Ezek 39:21
captivity among the *h*.........Ezek 39:28
that the *h* should rule over ....Joel 2:17
and come, all ye *h* ....Joel 3:11
Let the *h* be wakened ....Joel 3:12
to judge all the *h* round.......Joel 3:12
of all the *h*, which are ....Amos 9:12
ambassador..among the *h* .....Obad 1
Lord is near upon all the *h*....Obad 15
anger and fury upon the *h* ....Mic 5:15
Behold ye among the *h* ....Hab 1:5
even all the isles of the *h* .....Zeph 2:11
of the kingdoms of the *h*......Hag 2:22
sore displeased with the *h*.....Zech 1:15
speak peace unto the *h* ....Zech 9:10
smite the *h* that come..........Zech 14:18
shall be great among the *h* ....Mal 1:11
is dreadful among the *h*.......Mal 1:14
vain repetitions as the *h* ......Matt 6:7
let him be unto thee as a *h* ...Matt 18:17
Why did the *h* rage, and ......Acts 4:25
in perils by the *h*, in perils 2Cor 11:26
preach him among the *h* ......Gal 1:16
we should go unto the *h* ......Gal 2:9
God would justify the *h*.......Gal 3:8

HEAVE OFFERING—*an offering in which the items presented to the Lord were lifted up to Him as gifts before they were given to the priests*

Consisted of:
First fruits ....Num 5:19-21
Tenth of all tithes ....Num 18:21-28

Part of:
All gifts ....Num 18:29
Spoils ....Num 31:26-47
Offerings ....Ex 29:27
Lev 7:14, 32

Requirements concerning:
To be the best ....Num 18:29
Brought to God's house..Deut 12:6
Given to priests ....Ex 29:27, 28
Sanctified the whole offering................Num 18:27-32
Eaten in a clean place ...Lev 10:12-15

[*also* HEAVE]
and the *h* shoulder have I .....Lev 7:34
the wave breast and *h* ....Num 6:20
shall offer up a *h o* ....Num 15:19
the charge of mine *h* ....Num 18:8
the *h o* of their gift with ......Num 18:11
the *h o* of the holy ....Num 18:19
and the *h o* of your hand .....Deut 12:11
h o of thine hand............Deut 12:17

HEAVEN—*the place of everlasting bliss*

Inhabitants of:
God 1Kin 8:30
Christ ....Heb 9:12, 24
Holy Spirit..............Ps 139:7, 8
Angels ....Matt 18:10
Just men................Heb 12:22, 23

Things lacking in:
Marriage................Matt 22:30
Death ....Luke 20:36
Flesh and blood 1Cor 15:50
Corruption..............1Cor 15:42, 50
Sorrow ....Rev 7:17
Pain....................Rev 21:4
Curse ....Rev 22:3
Night...................Rev 22:5
Wicked people ....Rev 22:15
End ....Matt 25:46
Rev 22:5

Positive characteristics of:
Joy.....................Luke 15:7, 10
Rest....................Rev 14:13
Peace ....Luke 16:25
Righteousness 2Pet 3:13
Service ....Rev 7:15
Reward..................Matt 5:11, 12
Inheritance..............1Pet 1:4
Glory ....Rom 8:17, 18

Entrance into, for:
Righteous...............Matt 23:34, 37
Changed................1Cor 15:51
Saved ....John 3:5, 18, 21
Called 2Pet 1:10, 11
Overcomers..............Rev 2:7, 10, 11
Those recorded..........Luke 10:20
Obedient ....Rev 22:14
Holy ....Rev 19:8

Believer's present attitude toward:
Given foretaste of ....Acts 7:55, 56
Earnestly desires 2Cor 5:2, 8
Looks for 2Pet 3:12
Considers "far better" than now ....Phil 1:23
Puts treasure there ......Luke 12:33

Described as:
House ....John 14:2
Kingdom ....Matt 25:34
Abraham's bosom ....Luke 16:22, 23
Paradise 2Cor 12:2, 4
Better country ....Heb 11:10, 16
Holy city..............Rev 21:2, 10-27; Rev 22:1-5

[*also* HEAVENLY, HEAVENS]
and this is the gate of *h*.......Gen 28:17
I have talked with you from *h* .Ex 20:22
the *h* and the *h* of *h*.........Deut 10:14
He bowed the *h* also, and......2Sam 22:10
walketh in the circuit of *h*.....Job 22:14
He that sitteth in the *h* ....Ps 2:4
exalted, O God above the *h*...Ps 57:5
exalted, O God above the *h*...Ps 57:11
their mouth against the *h* .....Ps 73:9
thou establish in the very *h* ...Ps 89:2
prepared his throne in the *h*...Ps 103:19
mercy is great above the *h* ....Ps 108:4
and his glory above the *h* .....Ps 113:4
even the *h* are the Lord.......Ps 115:16
I will shake the *h*, and........Is 13:13
The *h* is my throne, and ......Is 66:1
our hands unto God in the *h* ..Lam 3:41
that the *h* were opened ....Ezek 1:1
the four spirits of the *h* ....Zech 6:5
Our Father which art in *h*.....Matt 6:9
your *h* Father will also ....Matt 6:14
yet your *h* Father feedeth .....Matt 6:26
h Father knoweth that ye .....Matt 6:32
shall my *h* Father do also .....Matt 18:35
he saw the *h* opened..........Mark 1:10
your *h* Father give the ....Luke 11:13
not ascended into the *h* ....Acts 2:34
whom the *h* must receive .....Acts 3:21
H is my throne, and earth.....Acts 7:49
God is revealed from *h* ....Rom 1:18
and as is the *h*, such are 1Cor 15:48
are they also that are *h* 1Cor 15:48
spiritual blessings in *h* ....Eph 1:3
own right hand in the *h*........Eph 1:20
in *h* places in Christ Jesus.....Eph 2:6
powers in *h* places might ......Eph 3:10
ascended up far above all *h* ...Eph 4:10
preserve me unto his *h*........2Tim 4:18
brethren, partakers of the *h* ...Heb 3:1
tasted of the *h* gift, and ....Heb 6:4
throne of the Majesty in the *h* .Heb 8:1
example and shadow of *h* .....Heb 8:5
h things themselves ....Heb 9:23
better country that is a *h*.......Heb 11:16
of the living God, the *h*.......Heb 12:22
three that bear record in *h* 1John 5:7
a door was opened in *h* ....Rev 4:1
was silence in *h* about the .....Rev 8:1
God was opened in *h* ....Rev 11:19
a great wonder in *h* ....Rev 12:1

HEAVENS, NATURAL—*the sky and its stars*

Facts regarding:
Created by God ....Gen 1:1
Stretched out ....Is 42:5; Jer 10:12
Will be destroyed........Heb 1:10-12; 2Pet 3:10
New heavens to follow ...Is 65:17; 2Pet 3:13

Purposes of:
To declare God's glory...Ps 19:1
To declare God's righteousness..........Ps 50:6
To manifest God's wisdom ....Prov 8:27

[*also* HEAVEN, HEAVEN'S]
God called the firmament *H*...Gen 1:8
the *h* and the earth were......Gen 2:1
the generations of the *h*.......Gen 2:4
made the earth and the *h* .....Gen 2:4
precious things of *h*, for ......Deut 33:13
also his *h* shall drop down ....Deut 33:28
and the *h* dropped, the ....Judg 5:4
would make windows in *h*.....2Kin 7:2
like to the stars of the *h* 1Chr 27:23
the *h* and *h* of *h* cannot.......2Chr 2:6
hear thou from the *h* 2Chr 6:25
then will I hear from *h* 2Chr 7:14
is grown up unto the *h*........Ezra 9:6
thou hast made *h*, the *h* of *h* ..Neh 9:6
alone spreadeth out the *h* .....Job 9:8
h are not clean in his ....Job 15:15
he hath garnished the *h* ....Job 26:13
When I consider thy *h* ....Ps 8:3
also thundered in the *h* ....Ps 18:13
word of the Lord were the *h* ..Ps 33:6
He shall call to the *h* from ....Ps 50:4
h also dropped at the ....Ps 68:8
Whom have I in *h* but ....Ps 73:25
who in the *h* can be ....Ps 89:6
but the Lord made the *h*......Ps 96:5
The *h* declare his ....Ps 97:6
and the *h* are the work of.....Ps 102:25
as the *h* is high above the .....Ps 103:11
stretchest out the *h* like a .....Ps 104:2
To him that by wisdom..*h*.....Ps 136:5
Praise ye the Lord, from the *h*.Ps 148:1
Praise him, ye *h* of *h*, and ....Ps 148:4
waters that be above the *h* ....Ps 148:4
hath he established the *h*......Prov 3:19
every purpose under the *h* ....Eccl 3:1
Hear, O *h*, and give ear ......Is 1:2
and meted out *h* with the .....Is 40:12
stretcheth out the *h* as a ......Is 40:22
Sing, O ye *h*; for the Lord ....Is 44:23
Drop down, ye *h*, from ....Is 45:8
Lord that created the *h* ....Is 45:18
Sing, O *h*; and be joyful ......Is 49:13
Lift up your eyes to the *h*.....Is 51:6
hath stretched forth the *h* .....Is 51:13
as the *h* are higher than.......Is 55:9
that thou wouldest rend the *h*. .Is 64:1
as the new *h* and the new .....Is 66:22
Be astonished, O ye *h*, at .....Jer 2:12
and all the birds of the *h* .....Jer 4:25
the fowl of the *h* and ....Jer 9:10
that have not made the *h* .....Jer 10:11
and from under these *h* ....Jer 10:11
multitude of waters in the *h* ...Jer 10:13
Do not I fill *h* and earth ......Jer 23:24
If *h* above can be measured ...Jer 31:37
hath stretched out the *h* ......Jer 51:15
multitude of waters in the *h* ...Jer 51:16
I will cover the *h*, and ....Ezek 32:7
have known that the *h* do .....Dan 4:26
his will in the army of *h* ......Dan 4:35
man came with the clouds of *h*.Dan 7:13
I will hear the *h*, and they ....Hos 2:21
the *h* shall tremble: the sun ...Joel 2:10
the *h* and the earth shall ......Joel 3:16
His glory covered the *h* ....Hab 3:3
the *h* over you is stayed.......Hag 1:10
I will shake the *h*, and........Hag 2:6
stretcheth forth the *h* ....Zech 12:1
open you the windows of *h*....Mal 3:10
for the kingdom of *h* is at.....Matt 3:2
lo, the *h* were opened ....Matt 3:16
Till *h* and earth pass..........Matt 5:18
Swear not..neither by *h* ....Matt 5:34
kingdom of *h* sake ....Matt 19:12
powers of the *h* shall be ......Matt 24:29
sign of the Son of man in *h* ...Matt 24:30
coming in the clouds of *h* .....Matt 26:64
to the uttermost part of *h* .....Mark 13:27
a multitude of the *h* host......Luke 2:13
and praying, the *h* was........Luke 3:21
Hereafter ye shall see *h* ....John 1:51
believe, if I tell you of *h* ......John 3:12
disobedient unto the *h* ....Acts 26:19
gods, whether in *h* or in 1Cor 8:5
bear the image of the *h* 1Cor 15:49
with hands, eternal in the *h* ...2Cor 5:1
family in *h* and earth is ....Eph 3:15
of things in *h*, and things .....Phil 2:10
that are in *h*, and that are ....Col 1:16
the word of God the *h*.........2Pet 3:5
But the *h*, and the earth 2Pet 3:7
Therefore rejoice, ye *h*, and...Rev 12:12
I saw a new *h* and a new .....Rev 21:1

HEAVINESS—*a spirit of grief or anxiety*
Unrelieved by mirth .....Prov 14:13
God's children experience.Phil 2:26
Needed exchange ....James 4:9
Experienced by Christ ...Ps 69:20, 21
Remedy for ....Prov 12:25

I arose up from my *h*.........Ezra 9:5
I will leave off my *h*, and .....Job 9:27
My soul melteth for *h* ....Ps 119:28
foolish son is the *h* of his .....Prov 10:1
end of that mirth is *h*.........Prov 14:13
and there shall be *h* and ......Is 29:2
great *h* and continual ....Rom 9:2
come again to you in *h* 2Cor 2:1
ye are in *h* through 1Pet 1:6

HEAVY—*oppressive; having great weight*

Used literally of:
Eli's weight 1Sam 4:18
Absalom's hair 2Sam 14:26
Stone..................Prov 27:3

Used figuratively of:
Fatigue ....Matt 26:43
Burdens 2Chr 10:11, 14
Sins ....Is 24:20

Sullenness 1Kin 21:4
God's judgments 1Sam 5:6, 11

[*also* HEAVIER, HEAVILY]
that they drove them **h** ....Ex 14:25
Moses' hands were **h**; and .....Ex 17:12
alone, because it is too **h** .....Num 11:14
his **h** yoke which he put.......1Kin 12:4
did lade you with a **h** yoke 1Kin 12:11
went to his house **h** and.......1Kin 20:43
his **h** yoke that he put 2Chr 10:4
bondage was **h** upon this ......Neh 5:18
now it would be **h** than ......Job 6:3
my stroke is **h** than my ....Job 23:2
shall my hand be **h** ....Job 33:7
night thy hand was **h** ....Ps 32:4
I bowed down **h**, as one ......Ps 35:14
over mine head: as a **h** ....Ps 38:4
burden they are too **h** for .....Ps 38:4
that singeth songs to a **h** ......Prov 25:20
stone is **h**, and the sand.......Prov 27:3
unto those that be of **h** ....Prov 31:6
make their ears **h**, and ....Is 6:10
the burden thereof is **h** ....Is 30:27
hast thou very **h** laid thy ......Is 47:6
to undo the **h** burdens ....Is 58:6
he hath made my chain **h** .....Lam 3:7
ye that labor and are **h** ....Matt 11:28
be sorrowful and very **h**.......Matt 26:37
sore amazed, and to be very **h** .Mark 14:33
were with him were **h**.........Luke 9:32

HEBER, EBER (hē'ber, ē'ber)—*"companion"*
1. Son of Beriah ....Gen 46:17
Descendants called
Heberites ....Num 26:45
2. Husband of Jael, the
slayer of Sisera ....Judg 4:11-24
3. Descendants of Ezra 1Chr 4:17, 18
4. Gadite chief 1Chr 5:11, 13
5. Benjamite 1Chr 8:17
6. Benjamite chief 1Chr 8:22
7. In Christ's genealogy ....Luke 3:35
Same as Eber in ....Gen 10:24
1Chr 1:25

Jael the wife of **H** the ....Judg 5:24
And the sons of Beriah; **H** 1Chr 7:31
And **H** begat Japhlet 1Chr 7:32

HEBREW—*"one from the other side"*

Applied to:
Abram ....Gen 14:13
Israelites 1Sam 4:6, 9
Jews...................Acts 6:1
Paul, a sincere ....Phil 3:5

[*also* HEBREWS, HEBREWESS]
he hath brought in a **H** ....Gen 39:14
out of the land of the **H** ......Gen 40:15
us a young man, a **H** ....Gen 41:12
Egypt spake to the **H** ....Ex 1:15
Because the **H** women ....Ex 1:19
an Egyptian smiting a **H** ......Ex 2:11
two men of the **H** strove ......Ex 2:13
God of the **H** hath met ....Ex 5:3
the Lord God of the **H** ....Ex 9:1
the Lord God of the **H** ....Ex 9:13
a **H** man, or a **H** woman ......Deut 15:12
the land, saying, Let the **H** 1Sam 13:3
the **H** make them swords......1Sam 13:19
H that were with the Philistines 1Sam 14:21
being a **H** or a **H**, go free .....Jer 34:9
said unto them, I am a **H** .....Jon 1:9
Are they **H**? so am I 2Cor 11:22

HEBREW—*the Semitic language of the ancient Hebrews*
Called "the Jews'
language"............2Kin 18:26, 28
Alphabet of, in divisions .Ps 119
Language of Christ's time.John 19;13, 20
Acts 21:40
See ARAMAIC

Greek, and Latin, and **H**.....Luke 23:38
called in the **H** tongue ....John 5:2
which is called in the **H** ....John 19:17
that he spake in the **H** ....Acts 22:2
saying in the **H** tongue ....Acts 26:14
name in the **H** tongue is ......Rev 9:11
H tongue Armageddon........Rev 16:16

HEBREWS, EPISTLE TO THE—*a book of the New Testament*
Christ greater than the
angels ....Heb 1:3, 4
Christ of the order of Melchizedek ....Heb 4:14—5:10
The new covenant ....Heb 8:1—10:18
The life of faith ....Heb 10:19—13:17

HEBRON (hē'brŏn)—*"friendship"*
1. Ancient town in Judah ..Num 13:22
Originally called
Kirjatharba...........Gen 23:2
Abram dwells here ......Gen 13:18
Abraham buys cave here .Gen 23:2-20
Isaac and Jacob sojourn
here ....Gen 35:27
Visited by spies ....Num 13:22
Defeated by Joshua .....Josh 10:1-37
Caleb expels Anakim
from ....Josh 14:12-15
Assigned to Levites .....Josh 21:10-13
City of refuge ....Josh 20:7
David's original capital ..2Sam 2:1-3, 11
Birthplace of David's
sons 2Sam 3:2
Abner's death here 2Sam 4:1
Absalom's rebellion here .2Sam 15:7-10
Fortified by Rehoboam ..2Chr 11:10
2. Town of Asher ....Josh 19:28
3. Son of Kohath ....Ex 6:18
Descendants called
Hebronites ....Num 3:19, 27
4. Descendant of Caleb 1Chr 2:42, 43

[*also* HEBRONITES]
sent him out of the vale of **H**. .Gen 37:14
and the family of the **H** ....Num 3:27
Now **H** was built seven years ..Num 13:22
as he had done to **H**, so .....Josh 10:39
the mountains, from **H**........Josh 11:21
the king of **H**, one ....Josh 12:10
Anak, which city is **H**.........Josh 15:13
Kirjath-arba, which is **H** ......Josh 15:54
Canaanites that dwelt in **H** ....Judg 1:10
now the name of **H**..........Judg 1:10
gave **H** unto Caleb, as ....Judg 1:20
an hill that is before **H**........Judg 16:3
to them which were in **H**......1Sam 30:31
they came to **H** at break 2Sam 2:32
were born to David in **H**......2Sam 3:5
Abner came to David to **H**....2Sam 3:20
Abner was returned to **H** 2Sam 3:27
unto David to **H** 2Sam 4:8
up over the pool in **H** 2Sam 4:12
sepulcher of Abner in **H** 2Sam 4:12
came to the king to **H** 2Sam 5:3
a league with them in **H** 2Sam 5:3
after he was come from **H** 2Sam 5:13
seven years reigned he in **H** ...1Kin 2:11
were born unto him in **H** 1Chr 3:1
six were born unto him in **H** ..1Chr 3:4
Amram, Izhar, and **H**.........1Chr 6:2
Amram, and Izhar, and **H** 1Chr 6:18
gave them **H** in the land of....1Chr 6:55
themselves to David unto **H** ..1Chr 11:1
Israel to the king to **H** 1Chr 11:3
covenant with them in **H** 1Chr 11:3
with a perfect heart to **H**.......1Chr 12:38
Amram, Izhar, **H**, and 1Chr 23:12
And the sons of **H** 1Chr 24:23
and the Izharites, the **H**.......1Chr 26:23
Among the **H** was Jerijah 1Chr 26:31
among the **H**, according.......1Chr 26:31
years reigned he in **H**.........1Chr 29:27

HEDGE—*a fence or barrier; to encircle or hem in*

Illustrative of:
God's protection ....Job 1:10
Afflictions ....Job 19:8
Slothfulness ....Prov 15:19
Removal of protection ...Ps 80:12

[*also* HEDGED, HEDGES]
dwelt among plants and **h** 1Chr 4:23
hid, and whom God hath **h** ...Job 3:23
hast broken down all his **h** ....Ps 89:40
and whoso breaketh a **h** ......Eccl 10:8
I will take away the **h** ....Is 5:5
run to and fro by the **h** ....Jer 49:3
He hath **h** me about, that I ...Lam 3:7
h for the house of Israel ......Ezek 13:5
I will **h** up thy way with ......Hos 2:6
is sharper than a thorn **h**......Mic 7:4
which camp in the **h** in ....Nah 3:17
a vineyard, and **h** it round ....Matt 21:33
and set an **h** about it, and.....Mark 12:1
out into the highways and **h** ...Luke 14:23

HEDGEHOG—*a porcupine*
Rendered "bittern" ......Is 14:23
Zeph 2:14

HEEDFULNESS—*giving proper attention to something important*

Objects of:
God's commandments....Josh 22:5
Our ways ....Ps 39:1
False teachers ....Matt 16:6
God's Word 2Pet 1:19

Admonitions to Christians, concerning:
Deception ....Matt 24:4
Outward display ....Matt 6:1
Worldliness ....Luke 21:34
Duty ....Acts 20:28-31
Foundation 1Cor 3:10
Liberty 1Cor 8:9
Security 1Cor 10:12
Effectiveness ....Gal 5:15
Ministry ....Col 4:17
Fables 1Tim 1:4
Unbelief ....Heb 3:12
See CAUTION

[*also* HEED]
Take **h** that thou speak ....Gen 31:24
Get thee from me, take **h**.....Ex 10:28
Take **h** to thyself, lest ....Ex 34:12
Must I not take **h** to speak ....Num 23:12
good **h** unto yourselves ....Deut 2:4
Take ye therefore good **h** .....Deut 4:15
Take **h** to yourselves, that.....Deut 11:16
h to thyself that thou ....Deut 12:19
Take **h** in the plague of ....Deut 24:8
take **h** to thyself until the 1Sam 19:2
Amasa took no **h** to the 2Sam 20:10
If thy children take **h** to 1Kin 2:4
Jehu took no **h** to walk in.....2Kin 10:31
prosper if thou takest **h** 1Chr 22:13
thy children take **h** to.........2Chr 6:16
take **h** and do it: for there 2Chr 19:7
Take **h** now that ye fail ....Ezra 4:22
h, regard not iniquity ....Job 36:21
wicked doer giveth **h** to ....Prov 17:4
Also take no **h** unto all ....Eccl 7:21
Take **h**, and be quiet ....Is 7:4
Take ye **h** every one of his ....Jer 9:4
us not give **h** to any of his ....Jer 18:18
have left off to take **h** ....Hos 4:10
Therefore take **h** to your ......Mal 2:15
Take **h** that ye despise not ....Matt 18:10
Take **h** what ye hear: with ....Mark 4:24
Take **h** lest any man ....Mark 13:5
take ye **h**: behold, I have .....Mark 13:23
Take **h** therefore how ye ......Luke 8:18
Take **h**, and beware of........Luke 12:15
Take **h** that ye be not ....Luke 21:8
he gave **h** unto them..........Acts 3:5
accord gave **h** unto those......Acts 8:6
Take **h** what thou doest.......Acts 22:26
take **h** lest he also spare ......Rom 11:21
giving **h** to seducing 1Tim 4:1
Not giving **h** to Jewish fables ..Titus 1:14
the more earnest **h** to the ....Heb 2:1

HEEL—*the back part of the human foot*
Used literally of:
Esau's ....Gen 25:26
Used figuratively of:
Seed of the woman ......Gen 3:15
Enemy of Dan ....Gen 49:17
The wicked ....Job 18:5, 9
Friend of David ....Ps 41:9

[*also* HEELS]
thou shalt bruise his *h* ....Gen 3:15
settest a print upon the *h* .....Job 13:27
iniquity of my *h* shall ....Ps 49:5
discovered, and thy *h* ....Jer 13:22
He took his brother by the *h* . .Hos 12:3
hath lifted up his *h* ....John 13:18

HEGAI, HEGE (hĕg'ā-ī, hĕg'ī)
Eunuch under King
Ahasuerus ....Esth 2:3, 8, 15
unto the custody of *H* the .....Esth 2:3

HEIFER—*a young cow*
Ceremonial uses of:
In a covenant ....Gen 15:9
In purification ....Num 19:1-22
Red heifer, ceremony concerning:
Without spot ....Num 19:2
Never yoked ....Num 19:2
Slaughtered and burned
outside the camp ......Num 19:3-8
Ashes kept..............Num 19:9, 10
Ashes, with water, used
to purify ....Num 19:11-22
Significance of ....Heb 9, 13, 14
Figurative of:
Improper advantage .....Judg 14:18
Contentment ....Jer 50:11
Stubborn ....Hos 4:16

[*also* HEIFER'S]
that city shall take a *h* ....Deut 21:3
down the *h* unto a rough......Deut 21:4
shall strike off the *h* neck .....Deut 21:4
wash their hands over the *h* . . .Deut 21:6
Take a *h* with thee, and 1Sam 16:2
unto Zoar, a *h* of three ....Is 15:5
Egypt is like a very fair *h* .....Jer 46:20
Ephraim is as a *h* that is ......Hos 10:11

HEIGHT—*the distance from the bottom to the top of something*

[*also* HEIGHTS]
and the *h* of it thirty..........Gen 6:15
cubit and a half the *h*.........Ex 25:10
the *h* five cubits of fine ....Ex 27:18
a cubit and a half the *h* ....Ex 37:1
and two cubits was the *h* ......Ex 37:25
the *h* in the breadth was ......Ex 38:18
or on the *h* of his stature 1Sam 16:7
and the *h* thereof thirty 1Kin 6:2
The *h* of the one cherub 1Kin 6:26
the *h* of the one chapiter.......1Kin 7:16
the *h* of the other chapiter 1Kin 7:16
all about, and his *h* was five. . .1Kin 7:23
the *h* of a wheel was a........1Kin 7:32
come up to the *h* of the.......2Kin 19:23
h of the one pillar was........2Kin 25:17
the *h* of the chapiter three 2Kin 25:17
the *h* was a hundred and......2Chr 3:4
and five cubits the *h*..........2Chr 4:2
the *h* thereof threescore.......Ezra 6:3
Is not God in the *h* of ....Job 22:12
behold the *h* of the stars ......Job 22:12
down from the *h* of his ....Ps 102:19
praise him in the *h* ....Ps 148:1
The heaven for *h*, and the ....Prov 25:3
in the depth; or in the *h* ......Is 7:11
ascend above the *h* of the......Is 14:14
come up to the *h* of the.......Is 37:24
will enter into the *h* of his ....Is 37:24
come and sing in the *h* of .....Jer 31:12
should fortify the *h* of her.....Jer 51:53
and the *h* of one chapiter .....Jer 52:22
mountain of the *h* of Israel....Ezek 17:23
in the mountain of the *h* ......Ezek 20:40
lifted up thyself in *h* ....Ezek 31:10
heart is lifted up in his *h* ......Ezek 31:10
themselves for their *h* ....Ezek 31:14
trees stand up in their *h* ......Ezek 31:14
one reed: and the *h*, one ......Ezek 40:5
whose *h* was threescore ....Dan 3:1
the *h* thereof reached ....Dan 4:11
whose *h* was like the *h*........Amos 2:9
Nor *h*, nor depth, nor any ....Rom 8:39
length, and depth, and *h* ......Eph 3:18
breadth and the *h* of it........Rev 21:16

HEINOUS—*abominable; shockingly evil*
For this is a *h* crime; yea .....Job 31:11

HEIRS—*persons who inherit*

[*also* HEIR]
born in my house is mine *h* . . .Gen 15:3
This shall not be thine *h* ......Gen 15:4
own bowels shall be thine *h* . . .Gen 15:4
and we will destroy the *h* 2Sam 14:7
handmaid that is *h* to her .....Prov 30:23
unto them that were his *h*.....Jer 49:2
Yet will I bring an *h* unto .....Mic 1:15
This is the *h*; come, let us ....Mark 12:7
This is the *h*; come, let us ....Luke 30:14
he should be the *h* of the .....Rom 4:13
children, then *h*; *h* of God ....Rom 8:17
That the *h*, as long as he .....Gal 4:1
to show unto the *h* of promise .Heb 6:17

HEIRS, NATURAL—*those who inherit*
Persons and property involved:
First-born ....Deut 21:15-17
Sons of concubines ......Gen 21:10
Daughters ....Num 27:1-11
Widows.................Ruth 3:12, 13
Order of succession......Num 27:8-11
Exceptions:
Father could make
concubines' sons heirs. .Gen 49:12-27
Daughters receive
marriage portion ......Gen 29:24, 29
Daughters sometimes
share with sons........Job 42:15
Daughters receive, if no
sons ....Num 27:8
Examples of heirship changes by divine election:
Ishmael to Isaac.........Gen 21:10, 11
Esau to Jacob ....Gen 27:37
Rom 9:13
Reuben to Joseph ....Gen 49:24-26
Adonijah to Solomon 1Kin 1:11-14
See BIRTHRIGHT; INHERITANCE, EARTHLY

HEIRS, SPIRITUAL—*those who inherit God's blessings*
Of Christ:
Recognized ....Matt 21:38
Appointed ....Heb 1:2
Of Christians, means of:
By promise ....Gal 3:29
Through Christ ....Gal 4:7
Through faith ....Rom 4:13, 14
By grace................Gal 4:28-31
Of Christians, receiving:
Grace 1Pet 3:7
Promise ....Heb 11:9
Kingdom ....James 2:5
Salvation ....Heb 1:14
Righteousness ....Heb 11:7
Eternal life ....Titus 3:7
See INHERITANCE, SPIRITUAL

HELAH (hē'lä)—*"tenderness"*
One of Asher's wives 1Chr 4:5, 7

HELAM (hē'lăm)—*"fortress"*
Place between Damascus
and Hamath where
David defeated Syrians .2Sam 10:16-19

HELBAH (hĕl'bä)—*"fertile"*
City of Asher ....Judg 1:31

HELBON (hĕl'bŏn)—*"fat"*
City north of Damascus . .Ezek 27:18

HELD—*See* HOLD

HELDAI (hĕl'dā-ī)—*"enduring"*
1. One of David's captains .1Chr 27:15
Probably same as Heled
and Heleb.............1Chr 11:30
2. Exile from Babylon
bearing gifts ....Zech 6:10, 11
Called Helem ....Zech 6:14

HELEB (hē'lĕb)—*"fat"*
H the son of Baanah, a 2Sam 23:29

HELED (hē'lĕd)
H the son of Baanah 1Chr 11:30
See HELDAI

HELEK (hē'lĕk)—*"portion"*
Son of Gilead ....Num 26:30
Founder of a family .....Josh 17:2

HELEM (hē'lĕm)—*"strength"*
1. Asherite 1Chr 7:34, 35
2. Same as Heldai ....Zech 6:11
Called Hotham 1Chr 7:32

HELEPH (hē'lĕf)—*"passing over"*
Frontier town of Naphtali.Josh 19:32, 33

HELEZ (hē'lĕz)—*"vigor"*
1. One of David's captains .2Sam 23:26
2. Judahite................1Chr 2:39
the Harorite, *H* the 1Chr 11:27
seventh month was *H* the 1Chr 27:10

HELI (hē'lī)—*"climbing"*
Father of Joseph,
husband of Mary ......Luke 3:23

HELKAI (hĕl'kā-ī)—*"Jehovah is my portion"*
Postexilic priest ....Neh 12:15

HELKATH (hĕl'kăth)—*"part"*
Frontier town of Asher . .Josh 19:24, 25
Assigned to Levites .....Josh 21:31
Same as Hukok 1Chr 6:75

HELKATH-HAZZURIM (hĕl-kăth-hăz-ū-rĭm)—*"field of rock"*
Scene of bloody combat . .2Sam 2:16

HELL—*the grave; place of eternal torment*
Described as:
Everlasting fire..........Matt 25:41
Everlasting punishment . .Matt 25:46
Outer darkness..........Matt 8:12
Everlasting destruction . . .2Thess 1:9
Lake of fire.............Rev 19:20
Prepared for:
Devil and his angels .....Matt 25:41
Wicked ....Rev 21:8
Disobedient ....Rom 2:8, 9
Fallen angels............2Pet 2:4
Beast and the false
prophet...............Rev 19:20
Worshipers of the beast . .Rev 14:11
Rejectors of the Gospel . .Matt 10:15
Punishment of, described as:
Bodily ....Matt 5:29, 30
In the soul..............Matt 10:28
With degrees............Matt 23:14
burn unto the lowest *h*........Deut 32:22
The sorrows of *h* 2Sam 22:6
deeper than *h*; what ....Job 11:8
H is naked before him ....Job 26:6
wicked shall be turned into *h* . .Ps 9:17
not leave my soul in *h* ....Ps 16:10
The sorrows of *h* ....Ps 18:5
go down quick into *h* ....Ps 55:15
my soul from the lowest *h* ....Ps 86:13
the pains of *h* gat hold........Ps 116:3
if I make my bed in *h* ....Ps 139:8
her steps take hold on *h* ......Prov 5:5
Her house is the way to *h*.....Prov 7:27
guests are in the depths of *h* . .Prov 9:18
H and destruction are ....Prov 15:11
he may depart from *h* ....Prov 15:24
deliver his soul from *h* ....Prov 23:14

H and destruction are . . . . .Prov 27:20
Therefore *h* hath enlarged . . . . .Is 5:14
H from beneath is moved . . . . .Is 14:9
shalt be brought down to *h* . . . .Is 14:15
and with *h* are we at . . . . .Is 28:15
agreement with *h* shall . . . . .Is 28:18
debase thyself even unto *h* . . . .Is 57:9
I cast him down to *h* with . . . . .Ezek 31:16
out of the midst of *h* . . . . .Ezek 32:21
Though they dig into *h* . . . . . . .Amos 9:2
out of the belly of *h* cried . . . . .Jon 2:2
enlargeth his desire as *h* . . . . . .Hab 2:5
shall be in danger of *h* . . . . .Matt 5:22
be brought down to *h* . . . . .Matt 11:23
and the gates of *h* shall . . . . . . .Matt 16:18
two eyes to be cast into *h* . . . . . .Matt 18:9
more the child of *h* than . . . . . .Matt 23:15
escape the damnation of *h*? . . .Matt 23:33
two hands to go into *h* . . . . .Mark 9:43
two feet to be cast into *h* . . . . .Mark 9:45
two eyes to be cast into *h* . . . . .Mark 9:47
shalt be thrust down to *h* . . . . .Luke 10:15
hath power to cast into *h* . . . . .Luke 12:5
in *h* he lift up his eyes . . . . . . .Luke 16:23
not leave my soul in *h* . . . . .Acts 2:27
and it is set on fire of *h* . . . . .James 3:6
have the keys of *h* and of . . . . .Rev 1:18
death and *h* delivered up . . . . . .Rev 20:13

HELM—*apparatus for steering a ship*
with a very small *h* . . . . .James 3:4

HELMET—*armor for the head*
Used figuratively of salvation:
Prepared . . . . .Is 59:17
Provided . . . . .Eph 6:17
Promised 1Thess 5:8

[*also* HELMETS]
had a *h* of brass upon 1Sam 17:5
spears and *h* and 2Chr 26:14
stand forth with your *h* . . . . . . .Jer 46:4
buckler and shield and *h* . . . . . .Ezek 23:24
with shield and *h* . . . . .Ezek 38:5

HELON (hē'lŏn)—*"valorous"*
Father of Eliab . . . . .Num 1:9

Eliab the son of *H* shall . . . . . . .Num 2:7
of Eliab the son of *H* . . . . .Num 7:29

HELP—*to give assistance or support*
[*also* HELPED, HELPETH, HELPING, HOLPEN]
of thy father, who shall *h* . . . . .Gen 49:25
Moses stood up and *h* . . . . .Ex 2:17
father, said he, was mine *h* . . . .Ex 18:4
and wouldest forbear to *h* . . . . .Ex 23:5
thou shalt surely *h* with . . . . . . .Ex 23:5
shalt surely *h* him to lift . . . . . .Deut 22:4
a *h* to him from his . . . . .Deut 33:7
Lord, the shield of thy *h* . . . . . .Deut 33:29
men of valor, and *h* them . . . . .Josh 1:14
quickly, and save us and *h* . . . .Josh 10:6
not to the *h* of the Lord . . . . . .Judg 5:23
Hitherto hath the Lord *h* 1Sam 7:12
for me, then thou shalt *h* 2Sam 10:11
Syrians feared to *h* the 2Sam 10:19
they following Adonijah *h* 1Kin 1:7
him saying, *H*, my lord 2Kin 6:26
And they were *h* against 1Chr 5:20
peaceably unto me to *h* 1Chr 12:17
helpers; for thy God *h* 1Chr 12:18
And they *h* David against 1Chr 12:21
of Damascus came to *h* 1Chr 18:5
for me, then thou shalt *h* 1Chr 19:12
for thee, then I will *h* 1Chr 19:12
princes of Israel to *h* 1Chr 22:17
it is nothing with thee to *h* 2Chr 14:11
no power: *h* us, O Lord 2Chr 14:11
cried out and the Lord *h* 2Chr 18:31
to ask *h* of the Lord 2Chr 20:4
God hath power to *h* 2Chr 25:8
God *h* him against the 2Chr 26:7
kings of Assyria to *h* 2Chr 28:16
king of Assyria, but he *h* 2Chr 28:21
kings of Syria *h* them 2Chr 28:23
I sacrifice to them that *h* 2Chr 28:23
brethren the Levites did *h* 2Chr 29:34
city; and they did *h* 2Chr 32:3
place *h* him with silver . . . . .Ezra 1:4
were the prophets of God *h* . . .Ezra 5:2
Shabbethai the Levite *h* . . . . . . .Ezra 10:15
officers of the king *h* the . . . . . .Esth 9:3
Is not my *h* in me? and is . . . . .Job 6:13
thou *h* him that is without . . . .Job 26:2
him that had none to *h* . . . . . . .Job 29:12
There is no *h* for him in God .Ps 3:2
h Lord, for the godly . . . . .Ps 12:1
Send thee *h* from the . . . . .Ps 20:2
why art thou so far from *h* . . . .Ps 22:1
strength, hast thee to *h* . . . . . . .Ps 22:19
thou hast been my *h* . . . . .Ps 27:9
trusted in him, and I am *h* . . . .Ps 28:7
Lord: he is our *h* and our . . . . .Ps 33:20
And the Lord shalt *h* . . . . .Ps 37:40
O Lord, make haste to *h* . . . . .Ps 40:13
thou art my *h* and my . . . . .Ps 40:17
h of his countenance . . . . .Ps 42:5
very present *h* in trouble . . . . . .Ps 46:1
God shall *h* her and that . . . . . .Ps 46:5
fault, awake to *h* me and . . . . .Ps 59:4
Give us *h* from trouble . . . . . . .Ps 60:11
trouble: for vain is the *h* . . . . . .Ps 60:11
thou hast been my *h* . . . . .Ps 63:7
me; make haste to *h* me . . . . . .Ps 70:1
God, make haste for my *h* . . . .Ps 71:12
H us O God of our . . . . .Ps 79:9
they have *h* the children . . . . . .Ps 83:8
I have laid *h* upon one . . . . .Ps 89:19
the Lord had been my *h* . . . . . . .Ps 94:17
and there was none to *h* . . . . . .Ps 107:12
Give us *h* from trouble . . . . . . .Ps 108:12
trouble; for vain is the *h* . . . . . .Ps 108:12
is their *h* and their . . . . .Ps 115:9
I might fall but the Lord *h* . . . .Ps 118:13
wrongfully; *h* thou me . . . . .Ps 119:86
and let thy judgments *h* . . . . . . .Ps 119:175
h cometh from the Lord . . . . . .Ps 121:2
in whom there is no *h* . . . . .Ps 146:3
God of Jacob for his *h* . . . . .Ps 146:5
he hath not another to *h* . . . . . .Eccl 4:10
to whom will ye flee for *h*? . . .Is 10:3
be a *h* nor profit but a . . . . .Is 30:5
go down to Egypt for *h* . . . . . . .Is 31:1
both he that *h* shall fall . . . . . . .Is 31:3
he that is *h* shall fall down . . . .Is 31:3
They *h* every one his . . . . .Is 41:6
I will *h* thee, yea, I will . . . . . . .Is 41:10
I will *h* thee, saith the . . . . .Is 41:14
the Lord God will *h* me . . . . .Is 50:7
the Lord God will *h* me . . . . .Is 50:9
and there was none to *h* . . . . . .Is 63:5
which is come forth to *h* . . . . . .Jer 37:7
the enemy and none did *h* . . . .Lam 1:7
all that are about him to *h* . . . .Ezek 12:14
shall be *h* with a little *h* . . . . . . .Dan 11:34
but in me is thine *h* . . . . .Hos 13:9
and they *h* forward the . . . . . . .Zech 1:15
worshiped him, saying, Lord, *h*.Matt 15:25
compassion on us and *h* . . . . . . .Mark 9:22
I believe; *h* thou mine . . . . .Mark 9:24
He hath *h* his servant . . . . .Luke 1:54
that they should come and *h* . .Luke 5:7
h them much which had . . . . . .Acts 18:27
Crying out Men of Israel *h* . . . .Acts 21:28
therefore obtained *h* of God . . .Acts 26:22
and to every one that *h* 1Cor 16:16
Ye also *h* together by prayer . .2Cor 1:11
h those women which . . . . .Phil 4:3
the earth *h* the woman . . . . .Rev 12:16

HELPER—*one who assists another*
Used of:
God .Heb 13:6
Christ . . . . .Heb 4:15, 16
Holy Spirit . . . . .Rom 8:26
Angels . . . . .Dan 10:13
Woman . . . . .Gen 2:18, 20
Levites 2Chr 29:3, 4
Christians . . . . .Acts 16:9
2Cor 1:24
As the Holy Spirit:
With believers forever . . .John 14:16
Teaches . . . . .John 14:26
Testifies of Christ . . . . . . .John 15:26
Convicts . . . . .John 16:7-11

[*also* HELPERS]
nor any left, nor any *h* 2Kin 14:26
the mighty men, *h* of the 1Chr 12:1
the proud *h* do stoop . . . . .Job 9:13
calamity, they have no *h* . . . . . .Job 30:13
thou art the *h* of the . . . . .Ps 10:14
Lord be thou my *h* . . . . .Ps 30:10
Behold, God is mine *h* . . . . .Ps 54:4
and him that hath no *h* . . . . . . .Ps 72:12
and Zidon every *h* that . . . . . . .Jer 47:4
when all her *h* shall be . . . . .Ezek 30:8
Put and Lubim were thy *h* . . . .Nah 3:9
And Aquila my *h* in Christ . . . .Rom 16:3
Urbane, our *h* in Christ . . . . . . .Rom 16:9

HELPS—*the acts of bearing one another's burdens*
A gift to the Church 1Chr 12:28
Christians admonished to .1Thess 5:14
Elders admonished to . . . .Acts 20:28, 35

they used *h* undergirding . . . . . .Acts 27:17

HELVE—*handle of a tool or weapon*
head slippeth from the *h* . . . . . .Deut 19:5

HEM—*edge or border of a garment*
upon the *h* of it thou shalt . . . .Ex 28:33
upon the *h* of the robe . . . . .Ex 28:34
round about the *h* of the . . . . . .Ex 39:26
touched the *h* of his . . . . .Matt 9:20

HEMAM (hē'măm)—*"raging"*
Son of Lotan . . . . .Gen 36:22
Same as Homam 1Chr 1:39

HEMAN (hē'măn)—*"faithful"*
1. Famous wise man 1Kin 4:31
Judahite 1Chr 2:6
Composer of a Psalm . . .Ps 88:*title*
2. Musician under David; grandson of Samuel . . .1Chr 6:33
Appointed as chief singer.1Chr 15:16, 17
Man of spiritual insight . .1Chr 25:5

the singers, *H* Asaph 1Chr 15:19
H and Jeduthun with 1Chr 16:42
Of *H*, the son of *H* 1Chr 25:4
Asaph, Jeduthun, and *H* 1Chr 25:6
Asaph, of *H*, of Jeduthun 2Chr 5:12
and Asaph, and *H*, and 2Chr 35:15

HEMATH (hē'măth)—*"warm"*
Kenites that came of *H* 1Chr 2:55
the entering in of *H* unto . . . . .Amos 6:14

HEMDAN (hĕm'dăn)—*"pleasant"*
Descendant of Seir . . . . . .Gen 36:26
Same as Amram 1Chr 1:41

HEMLOCK—*a bitter poisonous substance*
Properly means "gall" . . .Amos 6:12

h in the furrows of the . . . . .Hos 10:4

HEMORRHAGE—*a flow of blood*
Healed . . . . .Luke 8:43, 44
Woman suffered from, for 12 years . . . . Matt 9:20; Mark 5:25

HEMS—*edges or borders of garments*
made upon the *h* . . . . .Ex 39:24

HEN (hĕn)—*"favor"*
1. Son of Zephaniah . . . . . . .Zech 6:14
2. Domestic fowl . . . . .Matt 23:37

as a *h* doth gather her . . . . .Luke 13:34

HENA (hē'nä)—*"troubling"*
City captured by the Assyrians 2Kin 18:34

city of Sepharvaim, of *H* 2Kin 9:13
city of Sepharvaim, *H* . . . . .Is 37:13

HENADAD (hĕn'ä-dăd)—*"Hadad is gracious"*
Postexilic Levite . . . . .Ezra 3:9
Sons of, help Nehemiah . .Neh 3:18, 24

Binnui of the sons of *H* . . . . . . .Neh 10:9

HENCE—*from this place; from this time; from this point on*

[*also* HENCEFORTH, HENCEFORWARD]
it shall not *h* yield unto ....Gen 4:12
They are departed *h*, for ......Gen 37:17
carry up my bones from *h* .....Gen 50:25
he will let you go *h*...........Ex 11:1
surely thrust you out *h* ....Ex 11:1
and go up *h* thou and the .....Ex 33:1
and *h* among your ....Num 15:23
Israel *h* come nigh the ....Num 18:22
get thee down quickly from *h*. .Deut 9:12
Ye shall *h* return no more ....Deut 17:16
you *h* out of the midst of .....Josh 4:3
will not *h* drive out any ....Judg 2:21
Depart not *h*, I pray thee .....Judg 6:18
neither go from *h* but ....Ruth 2:8
Get thee *h* and turn thee 1Kin 17:3
for thy servant will *h* offer 2Kin 5:17
from *h* thou shalt have 2Chr 16:9
before I go *h* and be no ......Ps 39:13
his people from *h* even ....Ps 125:2
with justice from *h* even ......Is 9:7
say unto it, Get thee *h*........Is 30:22
saith the Lord, from *h* and ....Is 59:21
Take from *h* thirty men ....Jer 38:10
shalt no more *h* bereave ......Ezek 36:12
Get you *h* walk to and fro ....Zech 6:7
Get thee *h* Satan; for it is.....Matt 4:10
no fruit grow on thee *h* ....Matt 21:19
Ye shall not see me *h* till .....Matt 23:39
from *h* all generations ....Luke 1:48
cast thyself down from *h* ......Luke 4:9
h there shall be five in ....Luke 12:52
would pass from *h* to you .....Luke 16:26
Take these things *h* ....John 2:16
from *h* ye know him, and .....John 14:7
Arise, let us go *h*.............John 14:31
if thou have borne him *h* .....John 20:15
Holy Ghost not many days *h* . .Acts 1:5
speak *h* to no man in this .....Acts 4:17
h we should not serve ....Rom 6:6
should not *h* live unto 2Cor 5:15
h know we no man after.......2Cor 5:16
yet now *h* know we him 2Cor 5:16
From *h* let no man ....Gal 6:17
That we *h* be no more ....Eph 4:14
ye *h* walk not as other ....Eph 4:17
H there is laid up for me 2Tim 4:8
come they not *h* even of ......James 4:1
die in the Lord from *h*........Rev 14:13

HENOCH (hē′nŏk)—*"dedicated"*
1. Same as Enoch 1Chr 1:3
2. Same as Hanoch 1 ......1Chr 1:33

HEPHER (hē′fer)—*"pit"*
1. Town west of the Jordan.Josh 12:17
   Name applied to a district 1Kin 4:10
2. Founder of Hepherites . .Num 26:30, 32
3. Son of Ashur 1Chr 4:5, 6
4. One of David's guards . .1Chr 11:26, 36

Zelophehad the son of *H* .....Num 26:33
the son of *H*, the son of ......Num 27:1
for the children of *H* ....Josh 17:2
Zelophehad, the son of *H*.....Josh 17:3

HEPHZIBAH (hĕf′zĭ-bä)—*"my delight is in her"*
Mother of King Manasseh.2Kin 21:1

but thou shalt be called *H*.....Is 62:4

HER—*See* INTRODUCTION

HERALD—*a representative of a government official*
Of Nebuchadnezzar......Dan 3:3, 4
Of Pharaoh ....Gen 41:42, 43
Zion ....Is 40:9

HERB—*plant valued for its medicinal, savory, or aromatic qualities; grass or leafy vegetable*
Bitter, used at Passover . .Ex 12:8
Poisonous, not fit........2Kin 4:39, 40

[*also* HERBS]
the *h* yielding seed and ....Gen 1:11
I have given you every *h*......Gen 1:29
every *h* of the field before ....Gen 2:5
even as the green *h* have......Gen 9:3
every *h* of the field ....Ex 9:22
and eat every *h* of the land ...Ex 10:12
the trees or in the *h* of ....Ex 10:15
unleavened bread and bitter *h* .Num 9:11
rain upon the tender *h* ....Deut 32:2
have it for a garden of *h*.......1Kin 21:2
and as the green *h*, as the.....2Kin 19:26
and wither as the green *h* .....Ps 37:2
did eat up all the *h* in ....Ps 105:35
Better is a dinner of *h* ....Prov 15:17
like a clear heat upon *h*.......Is 18:4
field, and as the green *h* ......Is 37:27
hills, and dry up all their *h*....Is 42:15
h of every field wither for.....Jer 12:4
it is the greatest among *h* .....Matt 13:32
becometh greater than all *h* ...Mark 4:32
rue and all manner of *h*.......Luke 11:42
who is weak, eateth *h* ....Rom 14:2
and bringeth forth *h* meet .....Heb 6:7

HERD—*a group of animals; a crowd*

[*also* HERDS]
Abram had flocks and *h* ......Gen 13:5
Abraham ran unto the *h* ......Gen 18:7
and possession of *h* and.......Gen 26:14
and the flocks and *h* with .....Gen 33:13
and their *h* and all that ....Gen 46:32
for the cattle of the *h*.........Gen 47:17
their flocks, and their *h* ....Gen 50:8
flocks and with our *h* will .....Ex 10:9
take your flocks and your *h* . . .Ex 12:32
flocks nor *h* feed before ......Ex 34:3
even of the *h* and of the ......Lev 1:2
if he offer it of the *h* ....Lev 3:1
Shall the flocks and the *h* .....Num 11:22
the Lord of the *h* or of the....Num 15:3
when thy *h* and thy flocks.....Deut 8:13
firstlings of thy *h* or of thy ....Deut 12:17
shalt kill of thy *h* and of ......Deut 12:21
of the flock and the *h*, in .....Deut 16:2
came after the *h* out of the....1Sam 11:5
all the flocks and the *h* 1Sam 30:20
exceeding many flocks and *h* . .2Sam 12:2
flock and of his own *h* 2Sam 12:4
the *h* that fed in Sharon 1Chr 27:29
h that were in the valleys 1Chr 27:29
possessions of flocks and *h* 2Chr 32:29
firstlings of our *h* and of ......Neh 10:36
flocks and look well to thy *h* . .Prov 27:23
a place for the *h* to lie ....Is 65:10
their flocks and their *h*........Jer 3:24
of the flock and of the *h* ....Jer 31:12
their *h* to seek the Lord ......Hos 5:6
the *h* of cattle are ....Joel 1:18
man nor beast, *h* nor ....Jon 3:7
and there shall be no *h* in.....Hab 3:17
them a *h* of many swine ......Matt 8:30
they went into the *h* of ....Matt 8:32
the whole *h* of swine ran ......Matt 8:32
mountains a great *h* of........Mark 5:11
a *h* of many swine ....Luke 8:32

HERDMAN—*one who tends cattle*
Conflict among ....Gen 13:7, 8

[*also* HERDMEN]
the *h* of Gerar did strive ......Gen 26:20
did strive with Isaac's *h* ....Gen 26:20
the chiefest of the *h* that 1Sam 21:7
among the *h* of Tekoa ....Amos 1:1
I was a *h*, and a gatherer .....Amos 7:14

HERE—*at this place*
Have I also *h* looked after ....Gen 16:13
daughters, which are *h* ....Gen 19:15
he said, Behold, *h* I am.......Gen 22:1
he said, *H* am I, my son ......Gen 22:7
I stand *h* by the well of........Gen 24:13
H am I; who art thou ....Gen 27:18
set it *h* before my brethren....Gen 31:37
h also have I done nothing ....Gen 40:15
Jacob..he said, *H* am I........Gen 46:2
Moses..he said, *H* am I ....Ex 3:4
shall it be known *h* that I .....Ex 33:16
Lo we be *h*, and will go up ...Num 14:40
pray you, tarry ye also *h* ......Num 22:19
Build me *h* seven altars ....Num 23:1
prepare me *h* seven oxen .....Num 23:1
Build me *h* seven altars ....Num 23:29
prepare me *h* seven bullocks . .Num 23:29
will build sheepfolds *h* for.....Num 32:16
who are all of us *h* alive ......Deut 5:3
the things that we do *h* ....Deut 12:8
him that standeth *h* with us . . .Deut 29:15
him that is not *h* with us ......Deut 29:15
cast lots for you *h* before .....Josh 18:6
cities which are *h*.............Josh 21:9
say, Is there any man *h*? ......Judg 4:20
lodge *h*, that thine heart ......Judg 19:9
give *h* your advice ....Judg 20:7
Sit ye down *h*, And they ......Ruth 4:2
woman that stood by thee *h* . . .1Sam 1:26
he answered, *H* am I 1Sam 3:4
H am I; for thou calledst......1Sam 3:5
he answered, *H* am I 1Sam 3:16
Is the seer *h* 1Sam 9:11
sheep, and slay them *h* 1Sam 14:34
not *h* under thine hand 1Sam 21:8
it is *h* wrapped in a cloth 1Sam 21:9
no other save that *h* 1Sam 21:9
we be afraid *h* in Judah 1Sam 23:3
I answered, *H* am I............2Sam 1:7
h am I, let him do to me 2Sam 15:26
be thou *h* present 2Sam 20:4
Nay; but I will die *h*..........1Kin 2:30
Behold, Elijah is *h* 1Kin 18:14
thy servant was busy *h* 1Kin 20:40
Tarry *h*, I pray thee; 2Kin 2:2
Tarry, I pray thee, *h*; 2Kin 2:6
Is there not *h* a prophet 2Kin 3:11
H is Elisha, the son of 2Kin 3:11
if we sit still *h*, we die 2Kin 7:4
people, which are present *h* ...1Chr 29:17
h shall thy proud waves be ....Job 38:11
h will I dwell; for I have ......Ps 132:14
said I, *H* am I; send me ......Is 6:8
What hast thou *h*? ....Is 22:16
whom hast thou *h* ....Is 22:16
hewed thee out a sepulcher *h*. .Is 22:16
h a little, and there a ....Is 28:13
and he shall say, *H* I am ......Is 58:9
Israel committeth *h* ....Ezek 8:6
which they commit *h*? ....Ezek 8:17
gray hairs are *h* and there .....Hos 7:9
a greater than Jonas is *h* ......Matt 12:41
Give me *h* John Baptist's .....Matt 14:8
standing *h*, which shall not ....Matt 16:28
it is good for us to be *h*.......Matt 17:4
make *h* three tabernacles......Matt 17:4
not be left *h* one stone........Matt 24:2
Sit ye *h*, while I go and ....Matt 26:36
He is not *h*: for he is risen ....Matt 28:6
some of them that stand *h* ....Mark 9:1
what buildings are *h* ....Mark 13:1
Sit ye *h*, while I shall pray ....Mark 14:32
he is risen; he is not *h* ....Mark 16:6
Capernaum, do also *h* in thy . .Luke 4:23
standing *h*, which shall ....Luke 9:27
greater than Solomon is *h* .....Luke 11:31
Lo *h*! or, lo there! ....Luke 17:21
behold, *h* is thy pound ....Luke 19:20
He is not *h*, but is risen.......Luke 24:6
There is a lad *h*, which ....John 6:9
doth this man stand *h*.........Acts 4:10
h he hath authority ....Acts 9:14
for we are all *h* ....Acts 16:28
let these same *h* say ....Acts 24:20
at Jerusalem, and also *h* ......Acts 25:24
things which are done *h*.......Col 4:9
h men that die receive ....Heb 7:8
Sit thou *h* in a good place.....James 2:3
your sojourning *h* 1Pet 1:17
H is the patience and the .....Rev 13:10
H is the patience of the ....Rev 14:12
h is the mind which hath ......Rev 17:9

HEREAFTER—*in the future; from now on*
things that are to come ***h*** .....Is 41:23
and ***h*** also, if ye will not ......Ezek 20:39
what should come to pass ***h*** ...Dan 2:29
H shall ye see the Son of .....Matt 26:64
man eat fruit of thee ***h***........Mark 11:14
H shall the Son of man sit ....Luke 22:69
H ye shall see heaven open ...John 1:51
H I will not talk much with ...John 14:30
should ***h*** believe on him 1Tim 1:16
the things which shall be ***h*** ....Rev 1:19
come two woes more ***h*** ....Rev 9:12

HEREBY—*by this means*
H ye shall be proved ....Gen 42:15
Moses said, ***H*** ye shall ....Num 16:28
Joshua said, ***H*** ye shall........Josh 3:10
yet am I not ***h*** justified 1Cor 4:4
h we do know that we do 1John 2:3
H perceive we the love of 1John 3:16
h we know that he abideth 1John 3:24
H know we the spirit of.......1John 4:6

HEREDITY—*transmission of physical and mental traits*
Factors involved:
Likeness of nature ....Gen 5:3
Common transgression ...Rom 5:12
Sinful nature ....John 3:6, 7
Family and national traits.Titus 1:12
Physical traits ....Jer 13:26
God's purpose or plan ...Gen 9:22-27
Consistent with:
Individual responsibility ..Jer 31:29, 30
God's sovereign plan ....Rom 9:6-16
Need of a new nature....Matt 3:9
John 3:1-12
Family differences 1John 3:12
Child different from his parents 1Sam 8:1-5

HEREIN—*in this*
h will the men consent........Gen 34:22
H thou hast done foolishly 2Chr 16:9
h is that saying true ....John 4:37
H is my Father glorified ......John 15:8
h do I exercise myself ....Acts 24:16
h I give my advice............2Cor 8:10
H is love, not that we loved ...1John 4:10

HEREOF—*of this*
the fame ***h*** went abroad.......Matt 9:26
by reason ***h*** he ought ....Heb 5:3

HERES (hĭr'ĭz)—*"sun"*
1. Mountain in Dan ....Judg 1:35, 36
Probably connected with Beth-shemesh or Irshemesh .... { 1Kin 4:9; Josh 19:40, 41 }
2. Egyptian city; probably is the "city of destruction" referred to.........Is 19:18

HERESH (hē'rĕsh)—*"work; silence"*
Levite 1Chr 9:15

HERESY—*a teaching contrary to the truth*
Applied to:
Religious sect ....Acts 5:17
Pharisees ....Acts 26:5
Christians (derisively) ....Acts 24:5, 14
Characteristics of:
Damnable 2Pet 2:1
Contagious..............2Pet 2:2
Subversive ....Gal 1:7
Attitude toward:
Recognize purpose 1John 2:18, 19
Withdraw 1Tim 6:4, 5, 11
Do not receive 2John 9-11

[*also* HERESIES]
must be also ***h*** among you 1Cor 11:19
wrath, strife, seditions, ***h***......Gal 5:20

HERETIC—*one who has disbelieved or departed from the truth*
A man that is an ***h*** after ......Titus 3:10

HERETOFORE—*up to this time*
not eloquent, neither ***h*** ....Ex 4:10
which they did make ***h***........Ex 5:8
have not passed this way ***h*** ....Josh 3:4
which thou knewest not ***h*** .....Ruth 2:11
not been such a thing ***h***.......1Sam 4:7
write to them which ***h*** have ...2Cor 13:2

HEREUNTO—*to this*
who else can hasten ***h*** ....Eccl 2:25
For even ***h*** were ye called.....1Pet 2:21

HEREWITH—*with this*
thou wast not satisfied ***h*** ......Ezek 16:29
prove me now ***h***, saith the ....Mal 3:10

HERITAGE, EARTHLY—*birthright while on earth*
Of believers:
Children ....Ps 127:3
Long life ....Ps 91:16
Of Israel:
Promised land...........Ex 6:8
Forsaken of God ....Jer 12:7-9
Discontinue ....Jer 17:4
Return to ....Jer 12:15

[*also* HERITAGES]
I will give it you for a ***h*** ......Ex 6:8
the ***h*** appointed unto him .....Job 20:29
the ***h*** of oppressors ....Job 27:13
I have a goodly ***h*** ....Ps 16:6
O Lord, and afflict thine ***h***....Ps 94:5
have I taken as a ***h***...........Ps 119:111
gave their land for a ***h***........Ps 135:12
gave their land for a ***h***........Ps 136:21
to inherit the desolate ***h*** ......Is 49:8
mine ***h*** an abomination ....Jer 2:7
a goodly ***h*** of the hosts of .....Jer 3:19
I have left mine ***h***; I have .....Jer 12:7
Mine ***h*** is unto me as a lion ....Jer 12:8
Mine ***h*** is unto me as a ....Jer 12:9
every man to his ***h*** ....Jer 12:15
discontinue from thine ***h*** ......Jer 17:4
O ye destroyers of mine ***h*** ....Jer 50:11
give not thine ***h*** to reproach ...Joel 2:17
people and for my ***h*** Israel ....Joel 3:2
even a man and his ***h***.........Mic 2:2
the flock of thine ***h***..........Mic 7:14
the remnant of his ***h***?.........Mic 7:18
laid his..***h*** waste ....Mal 1:3

HERITAGE, SPIRITUAL—*birthright in God's kingdom*
Described as:
Laid up.................Ps 31:19
Col 1:5
Reserved 1Pet 1:4
Prepared................1Cor 2:9
Consists of:
Protection ....Is 54:17
Provision ....Is 58:14
Unseen things ....Matt 25:34
Kingdom 1Cor 2:9-12
All things ....Rom 8:32
as being lords over God's ***h*** ...1Pet 5:3

HERMAS (hûr'măs)—*"Mercury; interpreter"*
Christian at Rome ....Rom 16:14

HERMES (hûr'mēz)—*"Mercury (the god); interpreter"*
Christian at Rome ....Rom 16:14

HERMOGENES (hûr-mŏj'ĕ-nēz)—*"born of Hermes"*
Turns from Paul.........2Tim 1:15

HERMON (hûr'mŏn)—*"devoted to destruction"*
Hightest mountain (9,166 ft.) in Syria; also called Sirion, Shenir ....Deut 3:8, 9
Northern limit of conquest ....Josh 11:3, 17
Joined with Tabor, Zion and Lebanon in Hebrew poetry ....Ps 89:12
mount Zion, which is ***H***.......Deut 4:48
reigned in mount ***H***...........Josh 12:5
Baal-gad under mount ***H*** ......Josh 13:5
all mount ***H***, and all ....Josh 13:11
Senir, and unto mount ***H*** 1Chr 5:23
As the dew of ***H*** ....Ps 133:3
top of Shenir and ***H*** ....Song 4:8

HERMONITES—*inhabitants of Hermon*
of Jordan, and of the ***H***.......Ps 42:6

HERO—*a person acclaimed for unusual deeds*
Caleb, a rejected ....Num 13:30-33
Phinehas, a rewarded ....Num 25:7-13
Deborah, a militant......Judg 4:4-16
Jonathan, a rescued 1Sam 14:6-17, 38-45
David, a popular 1Sam 18:5-8
Esther, a hesitant........Esth 4:10-17

HEROD (hĕr'ŭd)—*"heroic"*
1. Herod the Great, procurator of Judea (37—4 B.C.) ....Luke 1:5
Inquires of Jesus' birth ..Matt 2:3-8
Slays Bethlehem infants .Matt 2:12-18
2. Archelaus (4 B.C.—A.D. 6) succeeds Herod the Great ....Matt 2:22
3. Herod Antipas, the tetrarch, ruler of Galilee and Peraea (4 B.C.—A.D. 39) .....Luke 3:1
Imprisons John the Baptist ....Luke 3:18-21
Has John the Baptist beheaded............Matt 14:1-12
Disturbed about Jesus ...Luke 9:7-9
Jesus sent to him ....Luke 23:7-11
Becomes Pilate's friend ..Luke 23:12
Opposes Jesus ....Acts 4:27
4. Philip, tetrarch of Ituraea and Trachonitis (4 B.C.—A.D. 34) ... { Luke 3:1; Acts 13:1 }
5. Herod Philip, disinherited son of Herod the Great......Matt 14:3
6. Herod Agrippa I (A.D. 37-44) ....Acts 12:1, 19
Kills James ....Acts 12:1, 2
Imprisons Peter ....Acts 12:3-11, 19
Slain by an angel ....Acts 12:20-23
7. Herod Agrippa II (A.D. 53-70), called Agrippa and King Agrippa ... { Acts 25:22, 23; Acts 25:24, 26 }
Festus tells him about Paul ....Acts 25:13-27
Paul makes a defense before ....Acts 26:1-23
Rejects the Gospel ......Acts 26:24-30
Recognizes Paul's innocency ....Acts 26:31, 32
8. Aristobulus; identified by some as son of Herod the Great ....Rom 16:10

[*also* HEROD'S]
But when ***H*** was dead ....Matt 2:19
when ***H*** birthday was kept ....Matt 14:6
king ***H*** heard of him ....Mark 6:14
But when ***H*** heard thereof ....Mark 6:16
H himself had sent forth ......Mark 6:17
For John had said unto ***H*****.....Mark 6:18
For ***H*** feared John...........Mark 6:20
H on his birthday made ....Mark 6:21
danced and pleased ***H*** ....Mark 6:22
wife of Chuza ***H*** steward ......Luke 8:3
for ***H*** will kill thee ....Luke 13:31
he belonged unto ***H*** ....Luke 23:7
nor yet ***H***; for I sent you......Luke 23:15
kept in ***H*** judgment hall ......Acts 23:35

HERODIANS (hĕ-rō'dĭ-ănz)—*an influential Jewish party*
Join Pharisees against Jesus ....Mark 3:6

Seek to trap Jesus ....Matt 22:15-22
Jesus warns against ......Mark 8:15

Pharisees and of the *H* ....Mark 12:13

HERODIAS (hĕ-rō'dĭ-ăs)—*"heroic"*
Granddaughter of Herod the Great; plots John's death ....Matt 14:3-12
Married her uncle ....Mark 6:17

[*also* HERODIAS']
put him in prison for *H* ....Matt 14:3
H had a quarrel against ....Mark 6:19
daughter of the said *H* ....Mark 6:22
reproved by him for *H* ....Luke 3:19

HERODION (hĕ-rō'dĭ-ŏn)—*"heroic"*
Christian at Rome ....Rom 16:11

HERON—*a long-necked wading bird*
Unclean bird ....Lev 11:19
Deut 14:18

HER, HERS—*See* INTRODUCTION

HERSELF—*her normal self; her own person*
Sarah laughed within *h* ....Gen 18:12
a veil, and covered *h* ....Gen 24:65
came down to wash *h* at the ...Ex 2:5
she shall number to *h* seven ...Lev 15:28
she thrust *h* unto the wall .....Num 22:25
she returned answer to *h* ......Judg 5:29
and bowed *h* to the ....Ruth 2:10
were dead, she bowed *h* 1Sam 4:19
and bowed *h* on her 1Sam 25:41
he saw a woman washing *h* 2Sam 11:2
she shall feign *h* to be 1Kin 14:5
bowed *h* to the ground........2Kin 4:37
the swallow a nest for *h*.......Ps 84:3
She maketh *h* coverings of ....Prov 31:22
hell hath enlarged *h* ....Is 5:14
as a bride adorneth *h* with ....Is 61:10
Israel hath justified *h* ....Jer 3:11
turneth *h* to flee, and fear ....Jer 49:24
maketh idols against *h* ....Ezek 22:3
their idols she defiled *h* ....Ezek 23:7
she decked *h* with her earrings .Hos 2:13
Tyrus did build *h* a strong.....Zech 9:3
For she said within *h* ....Matt 9:21
bringeth forth fruit of *h* ....Mark 4:28
hid *h* five months.............Luke 1:24
she turned *h* back, and saw ...John 20:14
Through faith also Sara *h* .....Heb 11:11
Jezebel, which calleth *h* ....Rev 2:20
wife hath made *h* ready ....Rev 19:7

HESED (hē'sĕd)—*"kindness"*
Father of one of Solomon's officers 1Kin 4:7, 10

HESHBON (hĕsh'bŏn)—*"stronghold"*
Ancient Moabite city; taken by Sihon, king of the Amorites ....Num 21:25-34
Taken by Moses ....Num 21:23-26
Assigned to Reubenites ..Num 32:1-37
Built by Reuben.........Num 32:37
On Gad's southern boundary ....Josh 13:26
Levitical city ....Josh 21:39
Later held by Moabites ..Is 15:1-4
Judgment of, announced. .Is 16:8-14
Fall of, predicted ....Jer 48:2, 34, 35
Fishpools in ....Song 7:4

Amorites, which dwelt in *H* ...Deut 1:4
unto Sihon king of *H* ....Deut 2:26
Amorites, which dwelt at *H* ...Deut 3:2
Amorites who dwelt at *H* .....Deut 4:46
to Sihon king of *H* ....Josh 9:10
border of Sihon king of *H*.....Josh 12:5
H, and all her cities that ......Josh 13:17
kingdom of Sihon king of *H* ...Josh 13:27
Amorites, the king of *H* ......Judg 11:19
H with her suburbs 1Chr 6:81
the land of the king of *H* .....Neh 9:22
the cry of *H*, even unto ....Jer 48:34
under the shadow of *H* ....Jer 48:45
shall come forth out of *H* .....Jer 48:45
O *H*, for Ai is spoiled ....Jer 49:3

HESHMON (hĕsh'mŏn)—*"rich soil"*
Town of Judah ....Josh 15:21, 27

HESITATION—*delay prompted by indecision*
Causes of:
Uncertain about God's will 1Sam 23:1-13
Fear of man ....John 9:18-23
Selfish unconcern 2Cor 8:10-14
Unbelief ....John 20:24-28

HETH (hĕth)—*a personification of the Hittites*
Son of Canaan ....Gen 10:15
Ancestor of the Hittites ..Gen 23:10
Abraham buys field from sons of ....Gen 23:3-20
Esau marries daughters of Gen 27:46
See HITTITES

purchased of the sons of *H* ....Gen 25:10
was from the children of *H* ....Gen 49:32
Zidon his firstborn, and *H* 1Chr 1:13

HETHLON (hĕth'lŏn)—*"fearful dwelling"*
Place indicating Israel's ideal northern boundary ....Ezek 47:15

to the coast of the way of *H* ..Ezek 48:1

HEW—*to cut with heavy cutting instrument*

[*also* HEWED, HEWETH, HEWN]
shalt not build it of *h* ....Ex 20:25
he *h* two tables of stone ......Ex 34:4
H thee two tables of stone ....Deut 10:1
h two tables of stone like .....Deut 10:3
shall *h* down the graven.......Deut 12:3
his neighbor to *h* wood ....Deut 19:5
and *h* them in pieces 1Sam 11:7
Samuel *h* Agag in pieces 1Sam 15:33
they *h* me cedar trees.........1Kin 5:6
to *h* timber like unto the......1Kin 5:6
costly stones, and *h* stones 1Kin 5:17
Hiram's builders did *h* 1Kin 5:18
with three rows of *h* stone 1Kin 6:36
to the measures of *h* stone 1Kin 7:9
measures of *h* stones..........1Kin 7:11
with three rows of *h* stones....1Kin 7:12
buy timber and *h* stone 2Kin 12:12
h stone to repair the..........2Kin 22:6
to *h* in the mountain..........2Chr 2:2
buy *h* stone, and timber 2Chr 34:11
she hath *h* out her seven ......Prov 9:1
we will build with *h* stones ....Is 9:10
itself against him that *h* ....Is 10:15
stature shall be *h* down ....Is 10:33
thou hast *h* thee out a ....Is 22:16
he that *h* him out a...........Is 22:16
Lebanon is..*h* down ....Is 33:9
He *h* him down cedars ....Is 44:14
the rock whence ye are *h* .....Is 51:1
h them out cisterns ....Jer 2:13
H ye down trees, and cast.....Jer 6:6
my ways with *h* stone ....Lam 3:9
four tables were of *h* stone ....Ezek 40:42
H down the tree, and cut .....Dan 4:14
I *h* them by the prophets .....Hos 6:5
built houses of *h* stone ....Amos 5:11
is *h* down, and cast into.......Matt 3:10
is *h* down, and cast into.......Matt 7:19
he had *h* out in the rock ......Matt 27:60
a sepulcher which was *h* out ...Mark 15:46
is *h* down, and cast into.......Luke 3:9
a sepulcher that was *h* ....Luke 23:53

HEWERS—*woodcutters*
A slave classification:
Gibeonites ....Josh 9:17-27
Classed with "drawers of water" ....Josh 9:21, 23

the *h* of thy wood unto ....Deut 29:11
thousand *h* in..mountains 1Kin 5:15
h and workers of stone 1Chr 22:15
servants, the *h* that cut 2Chr 2:10
to be *h* in the mountain.......2Chr 2:18

HEZEKI (hĕz'ĕ-kī)—*"Jehovah is strength"*
Benjamite 1Chr 8:17

HEZEKIAH, EZEKIAS (hĕz-ĕ-kī'ä, ĕ-zē-kī'ăs)—*"Jehovah is strength"*
1. King of Judah 2Chr 29:1-3
   Reforms Temple services.2Chr 29:3-36
   Restores pure worship ...2Chr 31:1-19
   Military exploits of 2Kin 18:7-12
   Defeated by Sennacherib.2Kin 18:13
   Sends messengers to Isaiah 2Kin 19:1-5
   Rabshakeh's further taunts 2Kin 19:8-13
   Prays earnestly 2Kin 19:14-19
   Encouraged by Isaiah ...2Kin 19:20-37
   Healed; his life prolonged 15 years 2Kin 20:1-11
   His thanks ....Is 38:9-22
   Rebuked for his pride ...2Kin 20:12-19
   Death of 2Kin 20:20, 21
   Ancestor of Christ ......Matt 1:9
2. Ancestor of returning exiles ....Ezra 2:1, 16
3. Ancestor of Zephaniah, spelled Hizkiah ....Zeph 1:1
4. Postexilic workman who returned with Zerubbabel...........Ezra 2:16

H his son reigned in his 2Kin 16:20
H the son of Ahaz 2Kin 18:1
H king of Judah sent to 2Kin 18:14
Assyria appointed unto *H* 2Kin 18:14
H gave him all the silver 2Kin 18:15
H cut off the gold 2Kin 18:16
H king of Judah had..........2Kin 18:16
from Lachish to king *H* 2Kin 18:17
Speak ye now to *H*, Thus 2Kin 18:19
whose altars *H* hath taken.....2Kin 18:22
Let not *H* deceive 2Kin 18:29
Neither let *H* make you 2Kin 18:30
Hearken not to *H* 2Kin 18:31
hearken not unto *H* 2Kin 18:32
H with their clothes rent 2Kin 18:37
son of Amoz sent to *H* 2Kin 19:20
high places which *H* 2Kin 21:3
Ahaz his son, *H* his son.......1Chr 3:13
came in the days of *H* 1Chr 4:41
H his son reigned in his 2Chr 28:27
H sent to all Israel 2Chr 30:1
But *H* prayed for them 2Chr 30:18
Lord hearkened to *H* 2Chr 30:20
H spake comfortably unto 2Chr 30:22
H king of Judah did give 2Chr 30:24
thus did *H* throughout all 2Chr 31:20
H saw that Sennacherib 2Chr 32:2
unto *H* king of Judah 2Chr 32:9
Hath not the same *H* 2Chr 32:12
against his servant *H*..........2Chr 32:16
for this cause *H* the king 2Chr 32:20
to *H* king of Judah 2Chr 32:23
H rendered not again 2Chr 32:25
H humbled himself 2Chr 32:26
them in the days of *H* 2Chr 32:26
same *H* also stopped the 2Chr 32:30
the rest of the acts of *H* 2Chr 32:32
which *H* his father had........2Chr 33:3
The children of Ater of *H*.....Neh 7:21
men of *H* king of Judah.......Prov 25:1
Ahaz, and *H*, kings of ....Is 1:1
fourteenth year of king *H* .....Is 36:1
unto king *H* with a great ......Is 36:2
altars *H* hath taken ....Is 36:7
Neither let *H* make you ....Is 36:15
Beware lest *H* persuade ....Is 36:18
when king *H* heard it ....Is 37:1
servants of king *H* came ......Is 37:5
Thus shall ye speak to *H*......Is 37:10
H received the letter..........Is 37:14
H went up unto the ....Is 37:14
Isaiah..sent unto *H* ....Is 37:21
Then *H* turned his face ....Is 38:2
H was glad of them...........Is 39:2
that *H* showed them ....Is 39:2
unto king *H*..................Is 39:3

H

H said, They are come ....Is 39:3
said Isaiah to ***H***, Hear ....Is 39:5
Manasseh the son of ***H*** ....Jer 15:4
Did ***H*** king of Judah..........Jer 26:19
Ahaz, and ***H*** kings ....Hos 1:1
Jotham, Ahaz, and ***H*** ....Mic 1:1

HEZION (hē'zĭ-ŏn)—*"vision"*
Grandfather of
Ben-hadad 1Kin 15:18

HEZIR (hē'zer)—*"returning home"*
1. Descendant of Aaron ...1Chr 24:1, 15
2. One who signs document.Neh 10:1, 20

HEZRAI (hĕz'rī)—*"blooming; beautiful"—one of David's warriors*
H the Carmelite 2Sam 23:35

HEZRO (hĕz'rō)—*"blooming"*
One of David's mighty
men 1Chr 11:37

HEZRON, ESROM (hĕz'rŏn, es'rŏm)—*"blooming"*
1. Place in south Judah ....Josh 15:1, 3
Same as Hazaraddar ....Num 34:4
2. Son of Reuben ....Gen 46:9
Founder of the
Hezronites ....Num 26:6
3. Son of Pharez ....Gen 46:12
Head of tribal family ....Num 26:21
Ancestor of David ......Ruth 4:18-22
Ancestor of Christ ......Matt 1:3

[*also* HEZRON'S]

Hanoch, and Pallu, ***H***.........Ex 6:14
H, which is Hazor ....Josh 15:25
sons of Pharez; ***H***, and........1Chr 2:5
sons also of ***H***, that............1Chr 2:9
Caleb the son of ***H***, begat 1Chr 2:18
H went in to the daughter.....1Chr 2:21
after that ***H*** was dead 1Chr 2:24
Abiah ***H*** wife bare him 1Chr 2:24
the firstborn of ***H*** 1Chr 2:25
sons of Judah; Pharez ***H*** 1Chr 4:1
Hanoch, and Pallu, ***H***.........1Chr 5:3

HIDDAI (hĭd'ā-ī)—*"mighty; chief"*
One of David's warriors. .2Sam 23:30
Same as Hurai 1Chr 11:32

HIDDEKEL (hĭd'ĕ-kĕl)—*"sound"*
Hebrew name of the
river Tigris..............Gen 2:14

HIDE—*skin of an animal*
the bullock, and his ***h***.........Lev 8:17

HIDE—*to conceal*

Used literally of:
Man in Eden............Gen 3:10
Baby Moses.............Ex 2:2, 3
Spies ....Josh 6:17, 25

Used figuratively of:
God's face ....Deut 31:17, 18
Protection ....Is 49:2
Darkness ....Ps 139:12
The Gospel 2Cor 4:3
Believer's life ....Col 3:3

[*also* HID, HIDDEN, HIDEST, HIDETH, HIDING]

Adam and his wife ***h*** ....Gen 3:8
from thy face shall I be ***h*** .....Gen 4:14
Shall I ***h*** from Abraham that . .Gen 18:17
Jacob ***h*** them under ....Gen 35:4
will not ***h*** it from my Lord ....Gen 47:18
h him in the sand ....Ex 2:12
thing be ***h*** from the eyes ......Lev 4:13
if it be ***h*** from him ....Lev 5:2
it be ***h*** from him ....Lev 5:4
h their eyes from the man .....Lev 20:4
be ***h*** from the eyes of her .....Num 5:13
h themselves from thee ....Deut 7:20
thou mayest not ***h*** thyself .....Deut 22:3
It is not ***h*** from thee..........Deut 30:11
I will ***h*** my face from ....Deut 32:20
of treasures ***h*** in the sand .....Deut 33:19
took the two men, and ***h***.....Josh 2:4
h them with the stalks ....Josh 2:6
h yourselves there three days . .Josh 2:16
are ***h*** in the earth ....Josh 7:21
five kings fled, and ***h***.........Josh 10:16
wherein they had been ***h***......Josh 10:27
to ***h*** it from the Midianites ....Judg 6:11
Jerubbaal was left; for he ***h*** . . .Judg 9:5
h it not from me 1Sam 3:17
if thou ***h*** any thing 1Sam 3:17
and ***h*** nothing from him.......1Sam 3:18
holes where they had ***h***.......1Sam 14:11
in a secret place, and ***h***.......1Sam 19:2
that I may ***h*** myself...........1Sam 20:5
David ***h***..in the field 1Sam 20:24
Doth not David ***h*** himself 1Sam 23:19
places where he ***h*** himself 1Sam 23:23
H not from me 2Sam 14:18
was not any thing ***h*** from 1Kin 10:3
h thyself by the brook 1Kin 17:3
how I ***h*** a hundred men.......1Kin 18:13
Lord hath ***h*** it from me 2Kin 4:27
and went and ***h*** it 2Kin 7:8
out of the camp to ***h*** 2Kin 7:12
they ***h*** him, even him 2Kin 11:2
four sons with him ***h***..........1Chr 21:20
nothing ***h*** from Solomon 2Chr 9:2
an inner chamber to ***h*** 2Chr 18:24
h him from Athaliah...........2Chr 22:11
h sorrow from mine eyes......Job 3:10
Or as a ***h*** untimely birth .....Job 3:16
to a man whose way is ***h***......Job 3:23
wherein the snow is ***h***.........Job 6:16
then will I not ***h*** myself ....Job 13:20
Wherefore ***h*** thou thy face ....Job 13:24
and have not ***h*** it.............Job 15:18
he ***h*** it under his tongue ......Job 20:12
darkness shall be ***h*** ....Job 20:26
he ***h*** himself on the right......Job 23:9
not ***h*** from the Almightly ......Job 24:1
Seeing it is ***h*** from the eyes . . .Job 28:21
by ***h*** mine iniquity in my......Job 31:33
h pride from man ....Job 33:17
The waters are ***h*** as with ......Job 38:30
H them in the dust ....Job 40:13
Who is he that ***h*** counsel......Job 42:3
net which they ***h*** is their ......Ps 9:15
why ***h*** thou thyself............Ps 10:1
he ***h*** his face; he will ....Ps 10:11
wilt thou ***h*** thy face...........Ps 13:1
there is nothing ***h*** from the ....Ps 19:6
of trouble he shall ***h*** me ......Ps 27:5
tabernacle shall he ***h*** me ....Ps 27:5
thou didst ***h*** thy face...........Ps 30:7
iniquity have I not ***h***...........Ps 32:5
Thou art my ***h*** place ....Ps 32:7
net that he hath ***h*** catch.......Ps 35:8
not ***h*** thy righteousness ....Ps 40:10
in the ***h*** part thou shalt ....Ps 51:6
H thy face from my sins ......Ps 51:9
O God, and ***h*** not thyself .....Ps 55:1
I would have ***h*** myself ....Ps 55:12
H me from the secret ....Ps 64:2
not ***h*** them from their ....Ps 78:4
why ***h*** thou thy face ....Ps 88:14
H not thy face from me ....Ps 102:2
Thy word have I ***h*** in mine ....Ps 119:11
The proud have ***h*** a snare .....Ps 140:5
h not thy face from me ....Ps 143:7
for her as for ***h*** treasures......Prov 2:4
He that ***h*** hatred with lying . . .Prov 10:18
foreseeth the evil, and ***h*** ......Prov 22:3
foreseeth the evil, and ***h*** ......Prov 27:12
wicked rise, a man is ***h*** ....Prov 28:12
that ***h*** his eyes shall have .....Prov 28:27
I will ***h*** mine eyes ....Is 1:15
their sin..they ***h*** it not ....Is 3:9
that ***h*** his face from the ....Is 8:17
h thyself as it were for ....Is 26:20
falsehood have we ***h***...........Is 28:15
waters shall overflow the ***h*** ....Is 28:17
My way is ***h*** from the Lord . . .Is 40:27
h riches of secret places ....Is 45:3
thou art a God that ***h***..........Is 45:15
shadow..hath he ***h*** me ....Is 49:2
we ***h*** as it were our faces .....Is 53:3
I ***h*** me, and was wroth........Is 57:17
h not thyself from thine ....Is 58:7
for thou hast ***h*** thy face ....Is 64:7
h it there is a hole ....Jer 13:4
h it by Euphrates..............Jer 13:5
are not ***h*** from my face ....Jer 16:17
iniquity ***h*** from mine eyes .....Jer 16:17
Can any ***h*** himself in secret . . .Jer 23:24
I have ***h*** my face from this ....Jer 33:5
h nothing from me ....Jer 38:14
h them in the clay ....Jer 43:9
stones that I have ***h*** ....Jer 43:10
h not thine ear at my ....Lam 3:56
h their eyes from my ....Ezek 22:26
no secret that they can ***h***......Ezek 28:3
h my face from them ....Ezek 39:24
Neither will I ***h*** my face.......Ezek 39:29
so that they fled to ***h*** ....Dan 10:7
Israel is not ***h*** from me ....Hos 5:3
repentance shall be ***h*** ....Hos 13:14
they ***h*** themselves in the ......Amos 9:3
be ***h*** from my sight ....Amos 9:3
how are his ***h*** things sought . . .Obad 6
he will even ***h*** his face from . . .Mic 3:4
thou shalt be ***h***, thou also .....Nah 3:11
the ***h*** of his power............Hab 3:4
it may be ye shall be ***h*** ....Zeph 2:3
on an hill cannot be ***h*** ....Matt 5:14
thou hast ***h*** these things.......Matt 11:25
is like unto treasure ***h*** ....Matt 13:44
man hath found, he ***h***.........Matt 13:44
h thy talent in the earth.......Matt 25:25
For there is nothing ***h*** ....Mark 4:22
h herself five months ....Luke 1:24
saw that she was not ***h***........Luke 8:47
thou hast ***h*** these things.......Luke 10:21
h in three measures...........Luke 13:21
they are ***h*** from thine ....Luke 19:42
Jesus ***h*** himself, and went .....John 8:59
did ***h*** himself from them ......John 12:36
none of these things are ***h***.....Acts 26:26
the ***h*** wisdom, which God 1Cor 2:7
the ***h*** things of dishonesty 2Cor 4:2
hath been ***h*** in God, who .....Eph 3:9
hath been ***h*** from ages ....Col 1:26
In whom are ***h*** all the ....Col 2:3
otherwise cannot be ***h*** 1Tim 5:25
was ***h*** three months...........Heb 11:23
h a multitude of sins..........James 5:20
the ***h*** man of the heart........1Pet 3:4
I give to eat of the ***h*** manna . .Rev 2:17
h themselves in the dens ......Rev 6:15
h us from the face of him .....Rev 6:16

HIEL (hī'ĕl)—*"God is living"*
Native of Beth-el;
rebuilds Jericho 1Kin 16:34
Fulfills Joshua's curse ....Josh 6:26

HIERAPOLIS (hī-er-ăp'ō-lĭs)—*"holy city"*
City of Asia Minor;
center of Christian
activity ....Col 4:13

HIGGAION (hĭ-gā'yŏn)—*"a deep sound"*
Used as a musical term . .Ps 9:16
Translated "meditation"
in ....Ps 19:14
Translated "solemn
sound" in.............Ps 92:3

HIGH—*exalted; lofty; elevated*

Descriptive of:
Rich....................Ps 49:2
Eminent people 1Chr 17:17
God's mercy ....Ps 103:11

[*also* HIGHER, HIGHEST, HIGHLY, HIGHNESS]

king shall be ***h*** than Agag .....Num 24:7
he was ***h*** than any of the......1Sam 9:2
He built the ***h*** gate 2Kin 15:35
and on the ***h*** places............Neh 4:13
by reason of his ***h*** I could .....Job 31:23
clouds which are ***h*** than.......Job 35:5
the ***H*** gave his voice ....Ps 18:13
to the rock that is ***h*** than I ....Ps 61:2
h than the kings...............Ps 89:27
h part of the dust of the ......Prov 8:26

for he that is *h* than the *h* ....Eccl 5:8
them that rejoice in my *h* .....Is 13:3
heavens are *h* than the........Is 55:9
in the *h* court, at the entry ....Jer 36:10
the way of the *h* gate ....Ezek 9:2
the *h* branch of the cedar .....Ezek 17:3
lowest chamber to the *h* ......Ezek 41:7
the *h* place of the altar ....Ezek 43:13
one was *h* than the other ......Dan 8:3
Hosanna in the *h*.............Matt 21:9
Hosanna in the *h*.............Mark 11:10
thou that art *h* favored........Luke 1:28
be called the Son of the *H* ....Luke 1:32
power of the *H* shall..........Luke 1:35
the prophet of the *H* ....Luke 1:76
Glory to God in the *h* ....Luke 2:14
the children of the *H* ....Luke 6:35
sit not down in the *h* room....Luke 14:8
Friend, go up *h* ....Luke 14:10
and glory in the *h* ....Luke 19:38
h seats in the synagogues .....Luke 20:46
Herod was *h* displeased ....Acts 12:20
think of himself more *h* ....Rom 12:3
subject unto the *h* powers .....Rom 13:1
God..hath *h* exalted him ......Phil 2:9
esteem them very *h* in love....1Thess 5:13
made *h* than the heavens......Heb 7:26

HIGH PLACES—*places of idolatrous worship*

Evils of:
Contrary to one sanctuary.Deut 12:1-14
Source of idolatry 2Kin 12:3
Place of child sacrifices ..Jer 7:31
Cause of God's wrath....1Kin 14:22, 23
Ps 78:58
Denounced by the prophets .... Ezek 6:1-6; Hos 4:11-14
Cause of exile ....Lev 26:29-34

Built by:
Solomon 1Kin 11:7-11
Jeroboam 1Kin 12:26-31
Jehoram 2Chr 21:9, 11
Ahaz 2Chr 28:24, 25
Manasseh 2Kin 21:1, 3
People of Judah 1Kin 14:22, 23
People of Israel 2Kin 17:9
Sepharvites 2Kin 17:32

Destroyed by:
Asa 2Chr 14:3, 5
Jehoshaphat............2Chr 17:6
Hezekiah 2Kin 18:4, 22
Josiah 2Kin 23:5, 8, 13

HIGH PRIEST—*chief, head priest*

Duties of:
Offer gifts and sacrifices .Heb 5:1
Make atonement ....Lev 16:1-34
Inquire of God..........1Sam 23:9-12
Consecrate Levites ......Num 8:11-21
Anoint kings 1Kin 1:34
Bless the people........Num 6:22-27
Preside over courts ......Matt 26:3, 57-62

Typical of Christ's priesthood:
Called of God..........Heb 5:4, 5
Making atonement.......Lev 16:33
Subject to temptation ....Heb 2:18
Exercise of compassion ..Heb 4:15, 16
Holiness of position .....Lev 21:15
Marrying a virgin........2Cor 11:2
Alone entering Holy of Holies ....Heb 9:7, 12, 24
Ministry of intercession ..Num 16:43-48
Heb 7:25
Blessing people..........Acts 3:26

HIGH-MINDEDNESS—*a self-righteous spirit*
Christians warned against .Rom 11:20
Rich tempted to 1Tim 6:17
To prevail in last days ...2Tim 3:1-5

HIGHWAY—*a main thoroughfare*

Characteristics of:
Roads for public use .....Num 20:19
Straight and broad.......Is 40:3
Made to cities of refuge..Deut 19:2, 3
Robbers use ....Luke 10:30-33
Animals infest..........Is 35:8, 9
Beggars sit by..........Matt 20:30
Byways sometimes better .Judg 5:6

Figurative of:
Holy way ....Prov 16:17
Israel's restoration ....Is 11:16
Gospel's call ....Is 40:3
Way of salvation ....Is 35:8-10
Two destinies ....Matt 7:13, 14
Christ ....John 14:6

[*also* HIGHWAYS]
in the *h*, of which one goeth ..Judg 20:31
gleaned of them in the *h*.......Judg 20:45
on the east side of the *h* ......Judg 21:19
went along the *h*, lowing 1Sam 6:12
blood in the midst of the *h*....2Sam 20:12
Amasa out of the *h*...........2Sam 20:12
the *h* of the fuller's field 2Kin 18:17
pool in the *h* of the fuller's....Is 7:3
there be a *h* out of Egypt .....Is 19:23
The *h* lie waste..............Is 33:8
in the *h* of the fuller's ....Is 36:2
cast up, cast up the *h*.........Is 62:10
set thine heart toward the *h* ...Jer 31:21
they shall say in all the *h* .....Amos 5:16
Go ye therefore into the *h* ....Matt 22:9
Timeas, sat by the *h* side .....Mark 10:46
Go out into the *h* ....Luke 14:23

HILEN (hī'lĕn)—*"grief"*
Town of Judah 1Chr 6:57, 58
Also called Holon ....Josh 15:51

HILKIAH (hĭl-kī'ä)—*"Jehovah is protection; my portion"*
1. Levite, son of Amzi.....1Chr 6:45, 46
2. Levite, son of Hosah 1Chr 26:11
3. Father of Eliakim ....Is 22:20
4. Priest, father of Jeremiah.Jer 1:1
5. Father of Gemariah .....Jer 29:3
6. Shallum's son...........1Chr 6:13
High priest in Josiah's reign.................2Chr 34:9-22
Oversees Temple work ..2Kin 22:4-7
Finds the book of the Law 2Kin 22:8-14
Aids in reformation 2Kin 23:4
7. Chief of postexilic priest .Neh 12:1, 7
Later descendants of ....Neh 12:12, 21
8. One of Ezra's assistants. .Neh 8:4

[*also* HILKIAH'S]
Eliakim the son of *H* 2Kin 18:18
Eliakim the son of *H* 2Kin 18:37
the book that *H* the priest 2Kin 23:24
Azariah the son of *H* 1Chr 9:11
H and Zechariah and 2Chr 35:8
Azariah, the son of *H* ....Ezra 7:1
Seraiah the son of *H*..........Neh 11:11
Eliakim, the son of *H*.........Is 22:20
H son, which was over.........Is 36:3

HILL—*an elevated mound of land lower than a mountain*
Rendered "Gibeah" 1Sam 11:4
Rendered "hills" ....Luke 23:30

[*also* HILL'S, HILLS]
all the high *h*, that were ......Gen 7:19
stand on the top of the *h* .....Ex 17:9
an altar under the *h* ....Ex 24:4
to go up unto the *h* top.......Num 14:44
from the *h* I behold him ....Num 23:9
in the *h*, and in the vale ......Deut 1:7
ready to go up into the *h* .....Deut 1:41
of whose *h* thou mayest.......Deut 8:9
a land of *h* and valleys........Deut 11:11
upon the *h*, and under ....Deut 12:2
at the *h* of the foreskins ......Josh 5:3
this side Jordan, in the *h*......Josh 9:1
the *h*, and all the south ....Josh 11:16
drawn from the top of the *h*...Josh 15:9
hear the *h* that lieth on the ...Josh 18:13
Hebron, in the *h* country of ...Josh 21:11
buried him in a *h*............Josh 24:33
on the north side of the *h*.....Judg 2:9
up to the top of a *h* ....Judg 16:3
Abinadab in the *h*............1Sam 7:1
thou shalt come to the *h* 1Sam 10:5
in the *h* of Hachilah 1Sam 23:19
David hide himself in the *h* ...1Sam 26:1
stood on the top of a *h* 1Sam 26:13
they were come to the *h* 2Sam 2:24
the way of the *h* side 2Sam 13:34
Shimei went along on the *h* ...2Sam 16:13
they hanged them in the *h* 2Sam 21:9
in the *h* that is before 1Kin 11:7
bought the *h* Samaria 1Kin 16:24
built on the *h* 1Kin 16:24
of Shemer, owner of the *h* 1Kin 16:24
gods are gods of the *h*........1Kin 20:23
Israel scattered upon the *h* 1Kin 22:17
he sat on the top of a *h*.......2Kin 1:9
on the *h*, and under every 2Kin 16:4
groves in every high *h* 2Kin 17:10
on the *h*, and under every 2Chr 28:4
thou made before the *h*? ......Job 15:7
my king upon my holy *h* ......Ps 2:6
shall dwell in thy holy *h*? .....Ps 15:1
foundations also of the *h*......Ps 18:7
Who shall ascend into the *h* ...Ps 24:3
from the *h* Mizar ....Ps 42:6
bring me unto thy holy *h* .....Ps 43:3
cattle upon a thousand *h*......Ps 50:10
little *h* rejoice on every ....Ps 65:12
h of God is as the *h* ....Ps 68:15
a high *h* as the *h* of ....Ps 68:15
Why leap ye, ye high *h*? ......Ps 68:16
This is the *h* which God ......Ps 68:16
little *h*, by righteousness ......Ps 72:3
strength of the *h* is his ....Ps 95:4
h melted like wax at the ......Ps 97:5
let the *h* be joyful ....Ps 98:8
high *h* are a refuge for........Ps 104:18
he toucheth the *h*, and they ...Ps 104:32
ye little *h*, like lambs? ....Ps 114:6
lift up mine eyes unto the *h* ...Ps 121:1
mountains, and all *h*..........Ps 148:9
before the *h* was I brought....Prov 8:25
skipping upon the *h* ....Song 2:8
to the *h* of frankincense.......Song 4:6
be exalted above the *h*........Is 2:2
in a very fruitful *h*............Is 5:1
the *h* did tremble.............Is 5:25
as an ensign on a *h*...........Is 30:17
and for the *h* thereof ....Is 31:4
and the *h* in a balance ....Is 40:12
waste mountains and *h*........Is 42:15
the *h* shall break ....Is 55:12
when upon every high *h* ......Jer 2:20
hoped for from the *h* ....Jer 3:23
abominations on the *h* ....Jer 13:27
over against it upon the *h*.....Jer 31:39
gone from mountain to *h* .....Jer 50:6
to the *h*, to the rivers.........Ezek 6:3
altars, upon every high *h*......Ezek 6:13
upon every high *h* ....Ezek 34:6
to the *h*, to the rivers.........Ezek 36:4
burn incense upon the *h* ......Hos 4:13
the *h* shall flow with milk .....Joel 3:18
and all the *h* shall melt ....Amos 9:13
be exalted above the *h*........Mic 4:1
the *h* melt, and the earth .....Nah 1:5
the perpetual *h* did bow ......Hab 3:6
great crashing from the *h* .....Zeph 1:10
A city that is set on a *h*.......Matt 5:14
went into the *h* country ....Luke 1:39
all the *h* country ....Luke 1:65
unto the brow of the *h*........Luke 4:29
Fall on us; and to the *h*.......Luke 23:30
Paul stood in..Mars' *h* ....Acts 17:22

HILLEL (hĭl'ĕl)—*"praised greatly"*
Father of Abdon the judge.................Judg 12:13, 15

HIM—*See* INTRODUCTION

HIMSELF—*See* INTRODUCTION

HIN—*unit of measurement, equal to about one and a half gallons*

sixth part of an *h* . . . . .Ezek 4:11
h of oil to an ephah . . . . .Ezek 46:5
h of oil to an ephah . . . . .Ezek 46:11

HIND—*a doe; female deer*

Figurative of:
Spiritual vivacity 2Sam 22:34
Buoyancy of faith . . . . . . .Hab 3:19
Peaceful quietude . . . . . . .Song 2:7

[*also* HINDS, HINDS']
Naphtali is a *h* let loose . . . . . . .Gen 49:21
mark when the *h* do calve? . . . .Job 39:1
maketh my feet like *h* feet . . . .Ps 18:33
maketh the *h* to calve . . . . .Ps 29:9
Let her be as the loving *h* . . . . .Prov 5:19
h of the field that ye stir . . . . . .Song 3:5
h also calved in the field . . . . . .Jer 14:5

HINDER—*to hamper; to hold back*

[*also* HINDERED, HINDERETH]
said unto them, *H* me not . . . . .Gen 24:56
h thee from coming unto me . .Num 22:16
h end of the spear smote him. .2Sam 2:23
that they be not *h* . . . . .Ezra 6:8
against Jerusalem and to *h* . . . .Neh 4:8
taketh away, who can *h* him? . .Job 9:12
is persecuted, and none *h* . . . . .Is 14:6
h part toward the utmost sea . .Joel 2:20
half of them toward the *h* sea .Zech 14:8
that were entering in ye *h* . . . . .Luke 11:52
doth *h* me to be baptized? . . . .Acts 8:36
been much *h* from coming . . . .Rom 15:22
we should *h* the gospel 1Cor 9:12
h you that ye should not . . . . . .Gal 5:7
but Satan *h* us 1Thess 2:18
that your prayers be not *h* 1Pet 3:7

HINDER PARTS—*rear (as of an army)*
God smites enemies in . . .Ps 78:66

their *h p* were inward 1Kin 7:25
their *h p* were inward 2Chr 4:4

HINDERMOST—*farthest to the rear*

[*also* HINDMOST]
Rachel and Joseph *h* . . . . .Gen 33:2
go *h* with their standards . . . . . .Num 2:31
smote the *h* of thee . . . . .Deut 25:18
enemies, and smite the *h* . . . . . .Josh 10:19
h of the nations shall be . . . . . .Jer 50:12

HINDRANCES—*things which obstruct one's way*

Physical:
Heavy armor 1Sam 17:38, 39
Ship's cargo . . . . .Acts 27:18-38

Spiritual:
Satanic temptations . . . . . .Matt 4:8-10
Riches . . . . .Matt 19:24
Unbelief . . . . .Matt 11:21-24
Ceremonialism . . . . .Matt 15:1-9
Love of world 2Tim 4:10
Sin .Heb 12:1

Removal of, by:
Faith . . . . .Matt 17:20, 21
God's armor . . . . .Eph 6:11-18
Walking in the Spirit . . . .Gal 5:16, 17
Self-control 1Cor 9:25-27

HINGE—*a pivot of a door*
Of gold 1Kin 7:50

[*also* HINGES]
door turneth upon its *h* . . . . . . .Prov 26:14

HINNOM (hĭn'ŏm)—*"their riches"—a narrow valley southwest of Jerusalem*

Location of:
Near Jerusalem . . . . .Jer 19:2
Boundary line . . . . .Josh 15:8
Topheth . . . . .Jer 19:6, 11-14

Uses of:
For idol worship 1Kin 11:7
For sacrificing children . . .2Chr 28:3
Defiled by Josiah 2Kin 23:10-14
Jeremiah addresses people here . . . . .Jer 19:1-5
Will become "valley of the slaughter" . . . . .Jer 7:31, 32
Make holy . . . . .Jer 31:40

the valley of the son of *H* . . . . .Josh 18:16
descended to the valley of *H* . .Josh 18:16
fire in the valley of..son of *H*. .2Chr 33:6
Beer-sheba unto..valley of *H* . .Neh 11:30
the valley of the son of *H* . . . . .Jer 32:35

HIP—*the area where the leg and pelvis are joined*
smote their *h* and thigh with . .Judg 15:8

HIRAH (hī'rä)—*"distinction"*
Adullamite, a friend of Judah . . . . .Gen 38:1, 12

HIRAM (hī'răm)—*"my brother is the exalted"—abbreviated form of Ahiram*
1. King of Tyre 2Sam 5:11
Provides men and material for David's palace 1Chr 14:1
David's friend 1Kin 5:1
Provides men and material for Solomon's Temple 1Kin 5:1-12
Refuses gifts of cities from Solomon 1Kin 9:10-13
Helps Solomon with money and seamen . . 1Kin 9:14, 26-28; 1Kin 10:11
Called Huram 2Chr 2:11
2. Craftsman; a son of a Tyrian and a widow of Naphtali 1Kin 7:13, 14
Sent by King Solomon to work on Temple . . 1Kin 7:14-40, 45
Called Huram 2Chr 2:11

[*also* HIRAM'S]
Solomon's..and *H* builders 1Kin 5:18
with the navy of *H* 1Kin 10:22

HIRE—*wages; employment*

Used literally of payments to:
Prostitute . . . . .Deut 23:18
Priests . . . . .Judg 18:4
Pay the poor . . . . .James 5:4
Mercenary soldiers 2Sam 10:6
Mercenary prophets . . . . .Deut 23:4
Gospel messengers . . . . . .Luke 10:7

Used figuratively of:
Spiritual adultery . . . . .Ezek 16:33
Sexual relations . . . . .Gen 30:16
Reward ("wages") . . . . . . .John 4:36

See WAGES

[*also* HIRED, HIRES]
God hath given me my *h* . . . . .Gen 30:18
of such shall be my *h* . . . . .Gen 30:32
shall come for my *h* before . . . .Gen 30:33
ringstreaked shall be thy *h* . . . .Gen 31:8
h servant shall not eat . . . . .Ex 12:45
it came for his *h* . . . . .Ex 22:15
wages of him that is *h* . . . . .Lev 19:13
thy *h* servant and for thy . . . . . .Lev 25:6
as a *h* servant..sojourner . . . . . .Lev 25:40
to the time of a *h* servant . . . . .Lev 25:50
worth a double *h* servant . . . . . .Deut 15:18
oppress a *h* servant . . . . .Deut 24:14
thou shalt give him his *h* . . . . . .Deut 24:15
Abimelech *h* vain and . . . . .Judg 9:4
h out themselves for bread 1Sam 2:5
will I give *h* for thy servants . . .1Kin 5:6
Israel hath *h* against us 2Kin 7:6
h..chariots and horsemen 1Chr 19:6
h thirty and two thousand 1Chr 19:7
h masons and carpenters 2Chr 24:12
h counselors against them . . . . .Ezra 4:5
Tobiah and Sanballat..*h* him . . .Neh 6:12
h Balaam against them . . . . .Neh 13:2
shave with a razor that is *h* . . .Is 7:20
she shall turn to her *h* . . . . .Is 23:17
and *h* a goldsmith . . . . .Is 46:6
h men are in the midst of her. .Jer 46:21
in that thou scornest *h* . . . . .Ezek 16:31
Ephraim hath *h* lovers . . . . .Hos 8:9
h thereof shall be burned . . . . .Mic 1:7
gathered it of..*h* of a harlot . . .Mic 1:7
return to the *h* of a harlot . . . .Mic 1:7
priests thereof teach for *h* . . . . .Mic 3:11
h for man, nor..*h* for beast . . . .Zech 8:10
h laborers into..vineyard . . . . . .Matt 20:1
Because no man hath *h* us . . . .Matt 20:7
give them their *h* . . . . .Matt 20:8
ship with the *h* servants . . . . . . .Mark 1:20
h servants of my father's . . . . . .Luke 15:17
years in his own *h* house . . . . . .Acts 28:30

HIRELING—*a common laborer*
Anxious for the day to close . . . . .Job 7:1, 2
Figurative of man's life . .Job 14:6
Subject to oppression . . . .Mal 3:5
Guilty of neglect . . . . .John 10:12, 13

as the years of a *h* . . . . .Is 16:14
according to..years of a *h* . . . . .Is 21:16

HIS—*See* INTRODUCTION

HISS—*a sibilant sound of warning, enticement, or disapproval*

Applied to:
Nations . . . . .Is 5:26
Egypt and Assyria . . . . . . .Is 7:18
Israel . . . . .Zech 10:8

[*also* HISSING]
be astonished and shall *h* 1Kin 9:8
to astonishment and to *h* 2Chr 29:8
h him out of his place . . . . .Job 27:23
desolate and a perpetual *h* . . . .Jer 18:16
astonished and *h* because . . . . .Jer 19:8
an astonishment, and a *h* . . . . .Jer 25:9
astonishment, a *h* . . . . .Jer 25:18
an astonishment, and a *h* . . . . .Jer 29:18
astonished and *h* at..plagues . . .Jer 50:13
h and wag their head . . . . .Lam 2:15
merchants..people shall *h* . . . . .Ezek 27:36
inhabitants thereof a *h* . . . . .Mic 6:16
that passeth by her shall *h* . . . .Zeph 2:15

HISTORY, BIBLICAL—*the events of the Bible and their meaning*

Characteristics of:
Dated with human events. Hag 1:1, 15; Luke 3:1
Inspired 2Tim 3:16
Free of myths 2Pet 1:16

Valuable for:
Outline of ancient history. Acts 7:1-53
Spiritual lessons 1Cor 10:1-11
Prophecy and fulfillment. .Acts 4:24-28

HIT—*to strike*
Saul and the archers *h* him 1Sam 31:3
Saul and the archers *h* him 1Chr 10:3

HITHER—*to this place; near or adjacent side*
they shall come *h* again . . . . . . .Gen 15:16
that ye sold me *h* . . . . .Gen 45:5
you that sent me *h* . . . . .Gen 45:8
Draw not nigh *h* . . . . .Ex 3:5
came men in *h* tonight . . . . .Josh 2:2
bring the description *h* to me . .Josh 18:6
Samson is come *h* . . . . .Judg 16:2
We will not turn aside *h* . . . . . . .Judg 19:12
At mealtime come thou *h* . . . . . .Ruth 2:14
Bring *h* a burnt offering 1Sam 13:9
Bring me *h* every man his ox . .1Sam 14:34
Draw ye near *h* 1Sam 14:38
not sit down till he come *h* 1Sam 16:11
Bring *h* the ephod 1Sam 23:9
Have brought them *h* 2Sam 1:10
shalt not come in *h* 2Sam 5:6
David cannot come in *h* 2Sam 5:6
Come near *h* 2Sam 20:16
h Micaiah the son of Imlah 1Kin 22:9
and they were divided *h* 2Kin 2:8
man of God is come *h* 2Kin 8:7
Thou shalt not come *h* 1Chr 11:5
not bring in the captives *h* 2Chr 28:13
which brought us up *h* . . . . .Ezra 4:2
his people return *h* . . . . .Ps 73:10
let him turn in *h* . . . . .Prov 9:4
let him turn in *h* . . . . .Prov 9:16

draw near *h* ye sons ....Is 57:3
unto thee art thou brought *h* ..Ezek 40:4
come forth, and come *h* ......Dan 3:26
thou come *h* to torment us ....Matt 8:29
bring him *h* to me ....Matt 17:17
straightway he will send..*h* ....Mark 11:3
Bring thy son *h* ....Luke 9:41
bring *h* the fatted calf........Luke 15:23
loose him and bring him *h* ....Luke 19:30
thirst not, neither come *h* .....John 4:15
Rabbi, when camest thou *h*? ..John 6:25
Reach *h* thy finger ....John 20:27
reach *h* thy hand ....John 20:27
came *h* for that intent ....Acts 9:21
upside down are come *h* ......Acts 17:6
when they were come *h*.......Acts 25:17
Come up *h* and I will show ...Rev 4:1
Come *h* I will show...........Rev 17:1

HITHERTO—*up to this time*
h thou wouldest not hear .....Ex 7:16
Lord hath blessed me *h*? ......Josh 17:14
H thou hast mocked me ......Judg 16:13
grief have I spoken *h* 1Sam 1:16
thou hast brought me *h*? 2Sam 7:18
Who *h* waited in 1Chr 9:18
thou hast brought me *h*? 1Chr 17:16
H shalt thou come ....Job 38:11
h..I declared thy wondrous ....Ps 71:17
terrible from..beginning *h* .....Is 18:2
H is the end of the matter ....Dan 7:28
My father worketh *h*.........John 5:17
H have ye asked nothing .....John 16:24
unto you, but was let *h* ....Rom 1:13
h..were not able to bear it 1Cor 3:2

HITTITES (hĭt'īts)—*an ancient nation*

Facts concerning:
Descendants of Canaan ..Gen 10:15
One of seven Canaanite nations ....Deut 7:1
Original inhabitants of Palestine.............Ezek 16:3, 45
Ruled by kings 1Kin 10:29
Great nation 2Kin 7:6
Their land promised to Israel.................Gen 15:18, 20
Destruction of commanded..........Deut 7:1, 2, 24
Destruction of, incomplete ....Judg 3:5

Intermarriage with:
By Esau ....Gen 36:2
By Israelites after the conquest.............Judg 3:5, 6
By Solomon 1Kin 11:1
By Israelites after the exile ....Ezra 9:1, 2

Notable persons of:
Ephron ....Gen 49:30
Ahimelech 1Sam 26:6
Uriah 2Sam 11:6, 21

[*also* HITTITE]
Ephron the *H* answered ....Gen 23:10
daughter of Beeri, the *H* ......Gen 26:34
daughter of Elon the *H* ....Gen 26:34
daughter of Elon the *H* ....Gen 36:2
field of Ephron the *H*.........Gen 49:29
burying place of Ephron the *H*.Gen 50:13
place of the Canaanites..*H* ....Ex 3:8
land of the Canaanites..*H* .....Ex 13:5
and the *H* ....Ex 23:23
Canaanite, and the *H* ....Ex 34:11
the *H*, and the Jebusites ......Num 13:29
destroy them namely, the *H* ...Deut 20:17
all the land of the *H*.........Josh 1:4
against Lebanon, the *H* ....Josh 9:1
in the south country; the *H* ...Josh 12:8
man went into the land of..*H*..Judg 1:26
to Ahimelech the *H* 1Sam 26:6
wife of Uriah the *H*? 2Sam 11:3
Send me Uriah the *H*.........2Sam 11:6
Uriah the *H* is dead 2Sam 11:21
the *H* to be thy wife 2Sam 12:10
left of the Amorites, *H* 1Kin 9:20
matter of Uriah the *H* 1Kin 15:5
Uriah the *H*, Zabad 1Chr 11:41
horses for..kings of the *H* 2Chr 1:17
land of the Canaanites..*H* .....Neh 9:8
and thy mother a *H* ....Ezek 16:3

HIVITES (hī'vīts)—*one of the nations displaced when Israel entered Canaan*
Descendants of Canaan ..Gen 10:15, 17
One of seven Canaanite nations ....Deut 7:1
Esau intermarries with ...Gen 36:2
Gibeonites belong to.....Josh 9:3, 7
Land of, promised to Israel.............. Ex 3:8; Ex 23:23

Destruction of:
Commanded ....Deut 7:1, 2, 24
Incomplete ....Judg 3:3

[*also* HIVITE]
son of Hamor the *H* ....Gen 34:2
the *H* and the Jebusites ....Ex 3:17
drive out the *H* ....Ex 23:28
Perizzite, and the *H* ....Ex 34:11
the *H* and the Jebusites ....Deut 20:17
H, and the Perizzites ....Josh 3:10
Perizzite, the *H* ....Josh 9:1
save the *H* the inhabitants.....Josh 11:19
and the Girgashites, the *H* ....Josh 24:11
Perizzites and *H* ....Judg 3:5
to all the cities of the *H* 2Sam 24:7
H, and Jebusites.............1Kin 9:20
And the *H*, and the Arkite 1Chr 1:15
the *H* and the Jebusites 2Chr 8:7

HIZKIAH (hĭz-kī'ä)—*"Jehovah is strength"*
Son of Neariah 1Chr 3:23

son of *H*, in..days of Josiah ...Zeph 1:1

HIZKIJAH (hĭz-kī'jä)—*"Jehovah is strength"*
Ancestor of returning exiles................Neh 10:17

HO—*used to call attention to*
H, every one that thirsteth ....Is 55:1
H, *h* come forth ....Zech 2:6

HOAR—*white*
Applied to frost ....Ex 16:14
Applied to gray hair .....Lev 19:32

[*also* HOARY]
rise up before the *h* head .....Lev 19:32
let not his *h* head go down 1Kin 2:6
h frost of heaven ....Job 38:29
h head is a crown of glory ....Prov 16:31
even to *h* hairs will I carry ....Is 46:4

HOARFROST—*frost*
scattereth the *h* like ashes .....Ps 147:16

HOBAB (hō'băb)—*"beloved"—the father-in-law or brother-in-law of Moses*
Town north of Damascus .Gen 14:15

Moses said unto *H* ....Num 10:29
children of *H* ....Judg 4:11
See JETHRO

HOBAH (hō'bä)—*"hiding place"*
Town north of Damascus .Gen 14:15

HOD (hŏd)—*"majesty"*
Asherite 1Chr 7:30, 37

HODAVIAH, HODAIAH (hō-dä-vī'ä, hō-dī'ä)—*"honorer of Jehovah"*
1. Son of Elioenai 1Chr 3:24
2. Chief of Manasseh 1Chr 5:23, 24
3. Benjamite 1Chr 9:7
4. Levite, founder of a family...............Ezra 2:40
   Called Judah ....Ezra 3:9
   Called Hodevah ....Neh 7:43

HODESH (hō'dĕsh)—*"new moon"*
Wife of Shaharaim 1Chr 8:8, 9

HODEVAH (hō-dē'vä)—*"honorer of Jehovah"*
children of *H* ....Neh 7:43
See HODAVIAH 4

HODIAH, HODIJAH (hō-dī'ä, hō-dī'jä)—*"splendor (or honor) of Jehovah"*
1. Judahite................1Chr 4:1, 19
2. Levite interpreter ....Neh 8:7
   Leads in prayer ....Neh 9:5
   Probably the same as one of the signers of the covenant ....Neh 10:10, 13
3. Signer of the covenant ..Neh 10:18

HOGLAH (hŏg'lä)—*"partridge"*
Daughter of Zelophehad..Num 26:33

Mahlah, Noah and *H* ....Num 27:1
Mahlah, and Noah, *H* ....Josh 17:3

HOHAM (hō'hăm)—*"whom Jehovah impels; Jehovah protects the multitude"*
Amorite king defeated by Joshua................Josh 10:3-27

HOISTED—*lift*
and *h* up the mainsail.........Acts 27:40

HOLD—*to possess; bear; carry*

[*also* HELD, HOLDEN, HOLDEST, HOLDETH, HOLDING, HOLDS]
men laid *h* upon his hand .....Gen 19:16
wondering at her *h* his peace ..Gen 24:21
hand took *h* on Esau's heel ...Gen 25:26
h up his father's hand.........Gen 48:17
that they may *h* a feast ....Ex 5:1
must *h* a feast unto the Lord ..Ex 10:9
sorrow shall take *h* on the ....Ex 15:14
Moses *h* up his hand..........Ex 17:11
Lord will not *h* him guiltless...Ex 20:7
And Aaron *h* his peace ....Lev 10:3
father shall *h* his peace ....Num 30:4
h his peace at her in the day ..Num 30:7
h his peace at her in the day ..Num 30:14
Lord will not *h* him guiltless...Deut 5:11
lay *h* on her ....Deut 22:28
h the lamps in..left hands .....Judg 7:20
into a *h* of the house ....Judg 9:46
put them to the *h* ....Judg 9:49
set the *h* on fire upon them ...Judg 9:49
H thy peace.................Judg 18:19
hast upon thee and *h* it ....Ruth 3:15
she *h* it he measured ....Ruth 3:15
But he *h* his peace 1Sam 10:27
laid *h* upon the skirt of his 1Sam 15:27
Abide not in the *h* 1Sam 22:5
David took *h* on his clothes ...2Sam 1:11
h up my face to Joab 2Sam 2:22
ark of God and took *h* of it ...2Sam 6:6
h now thy peace, my sister 2Sam 13:20
for Joab *h* back the people 2Sam 18:16
David was then in an *h* 2Sam 23:14
caught *h* on the horns of 1Kin 1:50
h him not guiltless...........1Kin 2:9
Solomon *h* a feast 1Kin 8:65
taken *h* upon other gods 1Kin 9:9
h ye your peace 2Kin 2:3
h him fast at the door 2Kin 6:32
people *h* their peace 2Kin 18:36
was not *h* such a passover 2Kin 23:22
passover was *h* to the Lord....2Kin 23:23
David was then in the *h* 1Chr 11:16
Judah to the *h* unto David 1Chr 12:16
h three thousand 2Chr 4:5
laid *h* on other gods 2Chr 7:22
half of them *h* both..spears....Neh 4:16
half of them *h* the spears .....Neh 4:21
H your peace for the day .....Neh 8:11
king shall *h* out the golden ....Esth 4:11
altogether *h* thy peace at......Esth 4:14
king *h* out to Esther ....Esth 5:2
king *h* out..golden scepter .....Esth 8:4
he *h* fast his integrity ....Job 2:3
I will *h* my tongue...........Job 6:24
wilt not *h* me innocent ....Job 9:28
altogether *h* your peace! ......Job 13:5
if I *h* my tongue.............Job 13:19
h me for thine enemy?........Job 13:24
righteous..also *h* on his way ..Job 17:9
and trembling taketh *h*........Job 21:6
My foot hath *h* his steps ......Job 23:11

My righteousness I *h* fast .....Job 27:6
Terrors take *h* on him ....Job 27:20
h thy peace, and I will speak ..Job 33:31
h thy peace, and I shall teach .Job 33:33
be *h* in cords of affliction .....Job 36:8
judgment and justice take *h* ...Job 36:17
that layeth at him cannot *h*....Job 41:26
H up my goings in thy paths ..Ps 17:5
right hand hath *h* me up ....Ps 18:35
whose mouth must be *h* in ....Ps 32:9
h not thy peace at my tears ...Ps 39:12
Fear took *h* upon them ....Ps 48:6
Which *h* our soul in life.......Ps 66:9
h me be my right hand ....Ps 73:23
h mine eyes waking...........Ps 77:4
h not thy peace and be not....Ps 83:1
thy mercy, O Lord, *h* me up ..Ps 94:18
H not thy peace ....Ps 109:1
Horror hath taken *h* ....Ps 119:53
anguish have taken *h* ....Ps 119:143
neither take..*h* of the paths ..Prov 2:19
Take fast *h* of instruction .....Prov 4:13
h with the cords of his sins ....Prov 5:22
man of understanding *h* ....Prov 11:12
spider taketh *h* with..hands....Prov 30:28
lay *h* on folly ....Eccl 2:3
I *h* him and..not let him go ...Song 3:4
They all *h* swords ....Song 3:8
man..take *h* of his brother ....Is 3:6
lay *h* of the prey ....Is 5:29
pangs have taken *h* upon me ..Is 21:3
hands from *h* of bribes........Is 33:15
they *h* their peace ....Is 36:21
h thine hand, and will keep ...Is 42:6
long time *h* my peace ....Is 42:14
take *h* of my covenant ....Is 56:4
will I not *h* my peace ....Is 62:1
stirreth himself up to take *h*...Is 64:7
can *h* no water ....Jer 2:13
I am weary with *h* in ....Jer 6:11
lay *h* on bow and spear ....Jer 6:23
h fast deceit, they refuse ......Jer 8:5
h the height of the hill ....Jer 49:16
took them captives *h* them ....Jer 50:33
h the bow and the lance ......Jer 50:42
remained in their *h* ....Jer 51:30
h of thee by thy hand.........Ezek 29:7
that they might have *h* ....Ezek 41:6
that *h* with me in these ....Dan 10:21
when he *h* up his right hand...Dan 12:7
h the scepter from..house .....Amos 1:5
shall he say, *H* thy tongue ....Amos 6:10
h thy tongue when..wicked ....Hab 1:13
H thy peace at the presence ...Zeph 1:7
not take *h* of your fathers? ....Zech 1:6
shall take *h* out of all ....Zech 8:23
shall take *h* of the skirt ....Zech 8:23
h every one on the hand ....Zech 14:13
or else he will *h* to the one ...Matt 6:24
h a council against him ....Matt 12:14
Herod..laid *h* on John ....Matt 14:3
for all *h* John as a prophet ....Matt 21:26
ye laid no *h* on me ....Matt 26:55
came and *h* him by the feet ...Matt 28:9
H thy peace and come out ....Mark 1:25
But they *h* their peace ....Mark 3:4
laid *h* upon John ....Mark 6:17
h the tradition of..elders ......Mark 7:3
ye *h* the tradition of men .....Mark 7:8
sought to lay *h* on him........Mark 12:12
But he *h* his peace ....Mark 14:61
H thy peace and come out ....Luke 4:35
And they *h* their peace ....Luke 14:4
he should *h* his peace ....Luke 18:39
might take *h* of his words .....Luke 20:20
that *h* Jesus mocked him ......Luke 22:63
laid *h* upon one Simon........Luke 23:26
But their eyes were *h*.........Luke 24:16
he should be *h* of it ....Acts 2:24
man which was healed *h* Peter .Acts 3:11
put them in *h* unto the........Acts 4:3
and part *h* with the Jews ......Acts 14:4
speak, and *h* not thy peace....Acts 18:9
h the truth in unrighteousness .Rom 1:18
being dead..we were *h* ....Rom 7:6
Yea, he shall be *h* up.........Rom 14:4
let the first *h* his peace 1Cor 14:30
H forth the word of life ....Phil 2:16
h such in reputation ....Phil 2:29
not *h* the Head...............Col 2:19
h the traditions...............2Thess 2:15
H faith and a..conscience 1Tim 1:19
H the mystery of the faith.....1Tim 3:9
lay *h* on eternal life 1Tim 6:12
H fast the form of..words 2Tim 1:13
if we *h* the beginning ....Heb 3:14
Let us *h* fast the profession ...Heb 10:23
that *h* the seven stars in.......Rev 2:1
thou *h* fast my name..........Rev 2:13
h the doctrine of Balaam......Rev 2:14
and heard and *h* fast..........Rev 3:3
testimony which they *h* ....Rev 6:9
h the four winds of the earth ..Rev 7:1
h of every foul spirit and......Rev 18:2

HOLD FAST—*keep securely in one's possession*
Good thing 1Thess 5:21
Faithful word ....Titus 1:9
Our confidence..........Heb 3:6
Our profession ....Heb 4:14
What we have...........Rev 2:25
Rev 3:11

HOLE—*a hollow place; an empty place*

[*also* HOLE'S, HOLES]
be a *h* in the top of it ....Ex 28:32
work round about the *h* of it ..Ex 28:32
the *h* of a habergeon ....Ex 28:32
was a *h* in the midst of ....Ex 39:23
as the *h* of a habergeon.......Ex 39:23
a band round about the *h* .....Ex 39:23
Hebrews come..out of the *h*...1Sam 14:11
bored a *h* in the lid of it 2Kin 12:9
hand by..*h* of the door........Song 5:4
go into the *h* of the rocks .....Is 2:19
play on the *h* of the asp .....Is 11:8
all of them snared in *h*........Is 42:22
hide it..in a *h* of the rock .....Jer 13:4
out of the *h* of the rocks ......Jer 16:16
sides of the *h* mouth..........Jer 48:28
behold a *h* in the wall ....Ezek 8:7
move out of their *h*...........Mic 7:17
filled his *h* with prey..........Nah 2:12
into a bag with *h* ....Hag 1:6
consume away in their *h* ......Zech 14:12
The foxes have *h* ....Matt 8:20
Foxes have *h*, and the birds ...Luke 9:58

HOLINESS—*a unique quality of divinity; consecration to God; spiritual purity*
like thee, glorious in *h* ....Ex 15:11
of a signet, *H* to the Lord.....Ex 28:36
of a signet, *H* to the Lord.....Ex 39:30
the Lord in the beauty of *h* ...1Chr 16:29
praise the beauty of *h* 2Chr 20:21
the Lord in the beauty of *h* ...Ps 29:2
sitteth..throne of his *h* ....Ps 47:8
God hath spoken in his *h* .....Ps 60:6
h becometh thine house ....Ps 93:5
remembrance of his *h*..........Ps 97:12
in the beauties of *h*...........Ps 110:3
hire shall be *h* to the Lord ....Is 23:18
drink it in..courts of my *h*.....Is 62:9
people of thy *h*..possessed it...Is 63:18
Israel was *h* unto the Lord ....Jer 2:3
justice and, mountain of *h* ....Jer 31:23
God hath sworn by his *h*......Amos 4:2
there shall be *h* ....Obad 17
H unto the Lord ....Zech 14:20
Judah hath profaned the *h* ....Mal 2:11

HOLINESS OF CHRIST

Announced in:
Psalms..................Ps 16:10
Prophets ....Is 11:4, 5

Proclaimed by:
Gabriel ....Luke 1:35
Demons ....Mark 1:24
Centurion...............Luke 23:47
Peter ....Acts 4:27, 30
Paul 2Cor 5:21
John 1John 2:1, 29

Manifested negatively in freedom from:
Sin 1John 3:5
Guilt ....John 8:46
Defilement.............Heb 7:26, 27

Manifested as "the Holy One" applied by:
Demons ....Mark 1:24
Peter ....Acts 2:27
Paul...................Acts 13:35
John 1John 2:20
Christ Himself ....Rev 3:7

HOLINESS OF CHRISTIANS

In their calling:
Elected to ....Rom 8:29
Called to 1Thess 4:7
Created in ....Eph 4:24
Possessed by 1Cor 3:16, 17

In their lives:
Bodies..................Rom 6:13, 19
Manner of life 1Pet 1:15
Fruitfulness ....John 15:8

Reasons for:
God's holiness 1Pet 1:15, 16
God's mercies ....Rom 12:1, 2
Christ's love 2Cor 5:14, 15
World's end............2Pet 3:11
Inheritance in kingdom ..Eph 5:5

God's means of:
Word...................John 17:17
Chastisement...........Heb 12:10
Grace ....Titus 2:3, 11, 12

See GODLINESS; SANCTIFICATION

in *h* and righteousness ....Luke 1:75
by our own power or *h* ....Acts 3:12
according to the spirit of *h* ....Rom 1:4
have your fruit unto *h* ....Rom 6:22
a living sacrifice, *h* ....Rom 12:1
perfecting *h* in..fear of God ...2Cor 7:1
be *h* and without blame ....Eph 1:4
h and unblameable ....Col 1:22
h before God 1Thess 3:13
lifting up *h* hands, without 1Tim 2:8
called us with a *h* calling 2Tim 1:9
is *h*, harmless, undefiled ....Heb 7:26
peace with all men and *h* .....Heb 12:14
called you is *h*, so be ye *h* 1Pet 1:15
a *h* priesthood 1Pet 2:5
h conversation and godliness ..2Pet 3:11
saith he that is *h* ....Rev 3:7
and that is *h*, let him be ......Rev 22:11

HOLINESS TO THE LORD
Breastplate insignia ......Ex 28:36

HOLLOW—*an indentation; indented*
touched the *h* of his thigh .....Gen 32:25
h of Jacob's thigh ....Gen 32:25
h of the thigh ....Gen 32:32
touched the *h* of Jacob's ......Gen 32:32
H with boards..thou make.....Ex 27:8
house with *h* strakes ....Lev 14:37
God clave a *h* place ....Judg 15:19
waters in the *h* of his hand ....Is 40:12
four fingers; it was *h* ....Jer 52:21

HOLON (hō'lŏn)—*"grief"*
1. City of Judah ....Josh 15:51
See HILEN
2. City of Moab ....Jer 48:21

And *H* with her suburbs ......Josh 21:15

HOLPEN—*See* HELP

HOLY—*uniquely divine; separated from sin; morally perfect; consecrated to God*

[*also* HOLIER, HOLIEST, HOLILY]
thou standest is *h* ground .....Ex 3:5
sabbath therefore for it is *h* ...Ex 31:14
between *h* and unholy ....Lev 10:10
be ye *h* for I am the Lord ....Lev 20:7
place..thou standest is *h* ......Josh 5:15
none *h* as the Lord 1Sam 2:2
perceive..this is an *h* man 2Kin 4:9

hear..from his *h* heaven ....Ps 20:6
H, *h*, *h* is the Lord of hosts ...Is 6:3
Lord..made bare his *h* arm ....Is 52:10
for I am *h* than thou ....Is 65:5
between the *h* and profane ....Ezek 22:26
h thing which shall be born ...Luke 1:35
Father's, and of the *h* angels ..Luke 9:26
h..justly and unblameably 1Thess 2:10
is called the *H* of all ....Heb 9:3
h by the blood of Jesus ....Heb 10:19

HOLY DAY—*the Jewish high holidays*
Sabbath ....Ex 35:2
"Holyday" ....Col 2:16
Rendered "Feast" ....Luke 2:41

HOLY GHOST—*an English variation for "Holy Spirit"*

in her is of the *H G* ....Matt 1:20
baptize you with the *H G*......Mark 1:8
shall be filled with the *H G* ...Luke 1:15
The *H G* shall come upon .....Luke 1:35
Jesus being full of the *H G* ....Luke 4:1
which baptizeth with the *H G*..John 1:33
them, Receive ye the *H G* ....John 20:22
were all filled with the *H G* ...Acts 2:4
receive the gift of the *H G* ....Acts 2:38
heart to lie to the *H G*........Acts 5:3
do always resist the *H G* ......Acts 7:51
with the *H G* and with power..Acts 10:38
it seemed good to the *H G*....Acts 15:28
Have ye received the *H G*.....Acts 19:2
peace and joy in the *H G*. ....Rom 14:17
See GHOST; HOLY SPIRIT

HOLY LAND—*See* CANAAN, LAND OF

HOLY OF HOLIES—*the innermost sanctuary of the tabernacle*

Described as:
Sanctuary ....Lev 4:6
Holy sanctuary ....Lev 16:33
Holy place ....Ex 28:29
Holy of Holies ....Ex 26:33
Heb 9:3
Inner sanctuary..........1Kin 6:5-20

Contents of:
Ark of the testimony ....Ex 26:33
Mercy seat ....Ex 26:34
Cherubim ....Ex 25:18-22
Altar of incense ....Heb 9:4
Pot of manna ....Ex 16:33
Aaron's rod ....Num 17:10
Written copy of the Law..Deut 31:26
2Kin 22:8

Entrance to, by the high priest:
Not at all times ....Lev 16:2
Alone, once a year ......Heb 9:7
With blood ....Lev 16:14, 15
To make atonement .....Lev 16:15-17, 33, 34

Significance of:
Abolished by Christ's death.................Matt 27:51
Typical of heaven ....Ps 102:19
Believers now enter boldly ....Heb 10:19
See TABERNACLE

HOLY SPIRIT—*the Third Person of the triune God*

Titles applied to:
Spirit of:
God ....Gen 1:2
The Lord God ....Is 61:1
The Father ....Matt 10:20
Grace ....Zech 12:10
Truth................John 14:17
Holiness ....Rom 1:4
Life ....Rom 8:2
Christ ....Rom 8:9
Adoption ....Rom 8:15
The Son ....Gal 4:6
Glory 1Pet 4:14
Prophecy ....Rev 19:10
My Spirit ....Gen 6:3
Holy Spirit.............Ps 51:11
The Comforter ....John 14:16, 26
Eternal Spirit ....Heb 9:14

Deity of:
Called God ....Acts 5:3, 4
Joined with the Father and Son ....Matt 28:19; 2Cor 13:14
Eternal ....Heb 9:14
Omnipotent ....Luke 1:35
Omniscient.............1Cor 2:10, 11
Omnipresent ....Ps 139:7-13
Creator ....Gen 1:2
Sovereign 1Cor 12:6, 11
New creation...........John 3:3, 8
Sin against, eternal ......Matt 12:31, 32

Personality of:
Speaks ....Acts 28:25
Teaches ....John 14:26
Strives with sinners ......Gen 6:3
Comforts ....Acts 9:31
Helps our infirmities .....Rom 8:26
Is grieved ....Eph 4:30
Is resisted..............Acts 7:51

Work in the world:
Creates ....Job 33:4
Renews ....Is 32:15
Convicts men ....John 16:8-11
Stirs up pagan king 2Chr 36:22

Work of, in Christ's ministry:
Christ conceived by ......Luke 1:35
Miracles performed by ...Matt 12:28
Anointed by ....Matt 3:16
Supported by ....Luke 4:1, 17
Filled by..............Luke 4:1
Offered to God by ......Heb 9:14
Raised by..............Rom 1:4
Justified by 1Tim 3:16

Work of, in the Scriptures:
Speaks in:
Prophets ....Acts 28:25
Psalms...............Acts 1:16
All Scripture 2Tim 3:16
His sword ....Eph 6:17

Ministry of, among believers:
Regenerates............John 3:3, 5
Indwells ....Rom 8:11
Anoints................1John 2:20, 27
Baptizes ....Acts 2:17-41
Guides ....John 16:13
Empowers ....Mic 3:8
Sanctifies ....Rom 15:16
2Thess 2:13
Bears witness ....Rom 8:16
Heb 10:15
Comforts ....John 14:16-26
Gives joy ....Rom 14:17
Gives discernment 1Cor 2:10-16
1John 4:1-6
Bears fruit ....Gal 5:22, 23
Give gifts 1Cor 12:3-11

Ministry of, in the Church:
Fills ....Acts 2:4
Baptizes 1Cor 12:13
Appoints officers ....Acts 20:17, 18
Sends out missionaries ...Acts 13:2, 4
Directs missionaries......Acts 8:29
Comforts the Church ....Acts 9:31
Sanctifies the Church ....Rom 15:16

Reception of:
Promised ....Joel 2:28-32
Awaits Christ's glorification ....John 7:38, 39
Realized at Pentecost ....Acts 2:1-21
Realized by Gentiles .....Acts 10:45
Contingent ....Acts 2:38
Acts 5:32
Can be sinned against....Matt 12:31, 32

Filling of:
Bezaleel ....Ex 31:2
Jesus ....Luke 4:1
John the Baptist........Luke 1:15, 60
Elizabeth ....Luke 1:41
Zechariah ....Luke 1:67
Pentecost Christians .....Acts 2:1-4
Peter ....Acts 4:8
Seven men ....Acts 6:3-5
Stephen ....Acts 7:55
Barnabas ....Acts 11:22, 24
Paul ....Acts 13:9
Certain disciples ....Acts 13:52

As teacher:
Illuminates the mind 1Cor 2:12, 13
Eph 1:16, 17
Reveals things of God ...Is 40:13, 14
1Cor 2:10, 13

HOMAM (hō'măm)
A Horite in Edom.......1Chr 1:39
See HEMAM

HOME—*the dwelling place of a family; center of a family's life*

Things associated with:
Eating 1Cor 11:34
Keeping house ....Titus 2:5
Religious training........1Tim 5:4
Entertainment ....Luke 15:6

Domestic:
Counsel 1Cor 14:35
Discord 2Sam 14:13-24
Land ....Ruth 1:22
Friends ....Mark 5:19
Present life 2Cor 5:6
See HOUSE

until his lord came *h*.........Gen 39:16
Bring these men *h*...........Gen 43:16
And when Joseph came *h* .....Gen 43:26
shall not be brought *h* ....Ex 9:19
she be born at *h*, or born .....Lev 18:9
bring her *h* to thine house ....Deut 21:12
household, *h* unto thee ....Josh 2:18
bring me *h* again to fight......Judg 11:9
brought me *h* again empty ....Ruth 1:21
went unto their own *h* 1Sam 2:20
shut up their calves at *h* 1Sam 6:10
go no more *h* to his father's...1Sam 18:2
David sent *h* to Tamar........2Sam 13:7
got him *h* to his house 2Sam 17:23
two months at *h*..............1Kin 5:14
Come *h* with me, and eat 1Kin 13:15
glory of this, and tarry at *h* ...2Kin 14:10
I bring the ark of God *h* 1Chr 13:12
out of Ephraim, to go *h* 2Chr 25:10
returned *h* in great anger 2Chr 25:10
when he came *h*, he sent......Esth 5:10
will bring *h* thy seed ....Job 39:12
tarried at *h* divided..spoil .....Ps 68:12
For the goodman is not at *h*..Prov 7:19
man goeth to his long *h*.......Eccl 12:5
he should carry him *h* ....Jer 39:14
at *h* there is as death ....Lam 1:20
neither keepeth at *h* ....Hab 2:5
when ye brought it *h* ....Hag 1:9
my servant lieth at *h*..........Matt 8:6
Go *h* to thy friends ....Mark 5:19
bid them farewell..*h* ....Luke 9:61
disciple took her unto..*h* .....John 19:27
they returned *h* again ....Acts 21:6

HOMEBORN—*native born*
One law..be to him that is *h* ..Ex 12:49
is he a *h* slave? ....Jer 2:14

HOMELESS—*having no home*
Christ's condition ....Luke 9:58
True of apostles also.....1Cor 4:11

HOMER—*"a heap"*
Measure; equal to about 11 bushels ....Ezek 45:11, 14

[*also* HOMERS]
h of barley seed..be valued ....Lev 27:16
least gathered ten *h* ....Num 11:32
seed of a *h* shall yield ....Is 5:10
part of an ephah of a *h* ....Ezek 45:13
a *h* of ten baths ....Ezek 45:14
ten baths are a *h* ....Ezek 45:14
for a *h* of barley ....Hos 3:2
a half *h* of barley ....Hos 3:2

HOMESICKNESS—*a longing for home and family while absent*
Jacob . . . . . Gen 30:25
Edomite Hadad 1Kin 11:21, 22
Exiles . . . . . Ps 137:1-6
Prodigal son . . . . . Luke 15:11-19
Epaphroditus . . . . . Phil 2:25, 26

HOMESTEAD—*family dwelling*
Redeemable . . . . . Lev 25:25-30

HOMICIDE—*killing of a human being*
Provisions provided:
Distinction between guilty and innocent . . Ex 21:12-14; Num 35:16-23
Determination of guilt . . . Num 35:24, 30
Detention in cities of refuge . . . . . Num 35:11, 15, 25-29
Defilement of land by slack justice . . . . . Num 35:31-34
See MURDER

HOMOSEXUALITY—*sexual desire toward a member of one's own sex*
Forbidden . . . . . Lev 18:22
Considered an abomination 1Kin 14:24
Punishment . . . . . Lev 20:13
Unclean . . . . . Rom 1:24, 26, 27

HONEST—*free from fraud or deception; truthful; reputable; praiseworthy*
Necessity of:
Signs of a righteous man . Ps 1:1-3; Luke 8:15
Means of testimony 1Pet 2:12
Obligatory upon Christians 2Cor 13:7
Blessings of:
Brings advancement . . . . . Is 33:15-17
Makes acceptable with God . . . . . Ps 15:1, 2
Examples of:
Samuel 1Sam 12:1-5
David 1Sam 25:7, 15
Workmen 2Kin 12:15
Zacchaeus . . . . . Luke 19:8
Paul 2Cor 8:20, 21

[*also* HONESTLY, HONESTY]
in an ***h*** and good heart . . . . . Luke 8:15
you seven men of ***h*** report . . . . Acts 6:3
h in the sight of all men . . . . . Rom 12:17
Let us walk ***h***, as in the day . . . Rom 13:13
whatsoever things are ***h*** . . . . . Phil 4:8
That ye may walk ***h*** 1Thess 4:12
life in all godliness and ***h*** 1Tim 2:2
all things willing to live ***h*** . . . . . Heb 13:18

HONEY—*a sweet fluid produced by bees*
Characteristics of:
Product of bees . . . . . Judg 14:8, 9
Not acceptable in offerings Lev 2:11
Offered as part of first fruits 2Chr 31:5
Figurative of:
God's Word . . . . . Ps 19:10
God's blessings . . . . . Ex 3:8, 17
Wisdom . . . . . Prov 24:13, 14
Pleasant words . . . . . Prov 16:24
Prostitute's enticements . . . Prov 5:3
Immanuel's diet . . . . . Is 7:14, 15

a little ***h***, spices . . . . . Gen 43:11
flowing with milk and ***h*** . . . . . Ex 3:17
flowing with milk and ***h*** . . . . . Ex 13:5
like wafers made with ***h*** . . . . . Ex 16:31
flowing with milk and ***h*** . . . . . Ex 33:3
floweth with milk and ***h*** . . . . . Lev 20:24
floweth with milk and ***h*** . . . . . Num 13:27
floweth with milk and ***h*** . . . . . Num 16:13
floweth with milk and ***h*** . . . . . Deut 6:3
floweth with milk and ***h*** . . . . . Deut 11:9
floweth with milk and ***h*** . . . . . Deut 27:3
made him to suck ***h*** out of . . . . Deut 32:13
floweth with milk and ***h*** . . . . . Josh 5:6
a swarm of bees and ***h*** . . . . . Judg 14:8
What is sweeter than ***h***? . . . . . Judg 14:18
was ***h*** upon the ground 1Sam 14:25
tasted a little of this ***h*** 1Sam 14:29
h, and butter, and sheep 2Sam 17:29
a cruse of ***h*** 1Kin 14:3
land of oil olive and of ***h*** 2Kin 18:32
wine, and oil, and ***h*** 2Chr 31:5
brooks of ***h*** and butter . . . . . Job 20:17
h out of the rock . . . . . Ps 81:16
Hast thou found ***h***? . . . . . Prov 25:16
not good to eat much ***h*** . . . . . Prov 25:27
h and milk are under..tongue . . Song 4:11
butter and ***h***..every one eat . . . . Is 7:22
flowing with milk and ***h*** . . . . . Jer 11:5
barley, and of, oil, and of ***h*** . . . Jer 41:8
in my mouth as ***h*** . . . . . Ezek 3:3
gave..flour and oil, and ***h*** . . . . . Ezek 16:19
h, and oil, and balm . . . . . Ezek 27:17
meat was locusts and..***h*** . . . . . Matt 3:4
did eat locusts and wild ***h*** . . . . . Mark 1:6
in thy mouth sweet as ***h*** . . . . . Rev 10:9

HONEYCOMB—*mass of wax built by bees*
dipped it in a ***h*** 1Sam 14:27
than honey and the ***h*** . . . . . Ps 19:10
woman drop as a ***h*** . . . . . Prov 5:3
the ***h***..sweet to thy taste . . . . . Prov 24:13
O my spouse, drop as the ***h*** . . . Song 4:11
broiled fish, and of a ***h*** . . . . . Luke 24:42

HONOR—*to esteem or regard highly; merited respect*
Those worthy of:
God 1Tim 1:17
Christ . . . . . John 5:23
Parents . . . . . Eph 6:2
Aged 1Tim 5:1, 3
Church officers . . . . . Phil 2:25, 29
Obtainable by:
Wisdom . . . . . Prov 3:16
Graciousness . . . . . Prov 11:16
Discipline . . . . . Prov 13:18
Humility . . . . . Prov 15:33
Peaceableness . . . . . Prov 20:3
Righteousness and mercy . . Prov 21:21
Honoring God 1Sam 2:30
Serving Christ . . . . . John 12:26
Those advanced to:
Joseph . . . . . Gen 41:41-43
Phinehas . . . . . Num 25:7-13
Joshua . . . . . Num 27:18-20
Solomon 1Kin 3:13
Abishai 1Chr 11:20, 21
Daniel . . . . . Dan 2:48
Mordecai . . . . . Esth 8:15
Apostles . . . . . Matt 19:27-29

[*also* HONORABLE, HONORED, HONOREST, HONORETH, HONORS]
more ***h*** than all the house . . . . Gen 34:19
mine ***h***, be not thou united . . . . Gen 49:6
I will be ***h*** upon Pharaoh . . . . . Ex 14:4
get me ***h*** upon Pharaoh . . . . . Ex 14:17
H thy father and..mother . . . . . Ex 20:12
h the person of the mighty . . . . Lev 19:15
h the face of the old man . . . . . Lev 19:32
more ***h*** than they . . . . . Num 22:15
promote thee unto..great ***h*** . . . . Num 22:17
promote thee unto great ***h*** . . . . Num 24:11
H thy father and..mother . . . . . Deut 5:16
shall not be for thine ***h*** . . . . . Judg 4:9
we may do thee ***h***? . . . . . Judg 13:17
h thy sons above me 1Sam 2:29
he is an ***h*** man 1Sam 9:6
shall I be had in ***h*** 2Sam 6:22
was he not most ***h*** of three? . . . 2Sam 23:19
man with his master and ***h*** . . . 2Kin 5:1
more ***h*** than his brethren 1Chr 4:9
he was ***h*** among the thirty 1Chr 11:25
Glory and ***h*** are in..presence . . 1Chr 16:27
David doth ***h*** thy father 1Chr 19:3
Both riches and ***h*** come of 1Chr 29:12
full of days, riches, and ***h*** 1Chr 29:28
asked riches, wealth, or ***h*** 2Chr 1:11
riches and ***h*** in abundance 2Chr 17:5
neither shall it be for thine ***h*** . . 2Chr 26:18
Jerusalem did him ***h*** 2Chr 32:33
h of his excellent majesty . . . . . Esth 1:4
h and dignity..been done . . . . . Esth 6:3
the king delighteth to ***h***? . . . . . Esth 6:6
the king delight to do ***h*** . . . . . Esth 6:6
the king delighteth to ***h*** . . . . . Esth 6:9
sons come to ***h*** . . . . . Job 14:21
and the ***h*** man dwelt in it . . . . . Job 22:8
lay mine ***h*** in the dust . . . . . Ps 7:5
crowned..with glory and ***h*** . . . . . Ps 8:5
h them that fear the Lord . . . . . Ps 15:4
h and majesty..thou laid . . . . . Ps 21:5
where thine ***h*** dwelleth . . . . . Ps 26:8
were among thy ***h*** women . . . . . Ps 45:9
being in ***h*** abideth not . . . . . Ps 49:12
in ***h***, and understandeth not . . . Ps 49:20
Sing forth the ***h*** of his name . . . Ps 66:2
with thy ***h*** all the day . . . . . Ps 71:8
deliver him, and ***h*** him . . . . . Ps 91:15
H and majesty are before . . . . . Ps 96:6
clothed with ***h*** and majesty . . . . Ps 104:1
glorious ***h*** of thy majesty . . . . . Ps 145:5
H the Lord with thy substance . Prov 3:9
she shall bring thee to ***h*** . . . . . Prov 4:8
Riches and ***h*** are with me . . . . . Prov 8:18
than he that ***h*** himself . . . . . Prov 12:9
regardeth reproof shall be ***h*** . . . Prov 13:18
multitude..is the king's ***h*** . . . . . Prov 14:28
before ***h*** is humility . . . . . Prov 18:12
Lord are riches, and ***h*** . . . . . Prov 22:4
h of kings is to search . . . . . Prov 25:2
h is not seemly for a fool . . . . . Prov 26:1
h..uphold the humble in spirit . . Prov 29:23
riches, wealth, and ***h*** . . . . . Eccl 6:2
of fifty, and the ***h*** man . . . . . Is 3:3
their ***h*** men are famished . . . . . Is 5:13
traffickers are the ***h*** of the . . . . Is 23:8
with their lips do ***h*** me . . . . . Is 29:13
magnify the law, and make it ***h*** Is 42:21
h me with thy sacrifices . . . . . Is 43:23
holy of the Lord, ***h*** . . . . . Is 58:13
shalt ***h*** him, not doing . . . . . Is 58:13
praise and an ***h*** before . . . . . Jer 33:9
all that ***h*** her despise her . . . . . Lam 1:8
rewards and great ***h*** . . . . . Dan 2:6
power, for the ***h*** of my . . . . . Dan 4:30
h him that liveth for ever . . . . . Dan 4:34
mine ***h*** and brightness . . . . . Dan 4:36
h the King of heaven . . . . . Dan 4:37
majesty and glory and ***h*** . . . . . Dan 5:18
h the God of forces . . . . . Dan 11:38
fathers knew not shall he ***h*** . . . . . Dan 11:38
cast lots for her ***h*** men . . . . . Nah 3:10
A son ***h*** his father . . . . . Mal 1:6
I be a father, where is..***h***? . . . . Mal 1:6
h not..father or his mother . . . . Matt 15:6
h me with their lips . . . . . Matt 15:8
A prophet is not without ***h*** . . . . Mark 6:4
h me with their lips . . . . . Mark 7:6
H thy father and mother . . . . . Mark 10:19
Arimathea..***h*** counselor . . . . . Mark 15:43
more ***h*** man than thou be . . . . . Luke 14:8
h thy father and..mother . . . . . Luke 18:20
h in his own country . . . . . John 4:44
that ***h*** not the Son ***h*** . . . . . John 5:23
I receive not ***h*** from men . . . . . John 5:41
receive ***h*** one of another . . . . . John 5:44
h..cometh from God only? . . . . John 5:44
h my Father, and ye do . . . . . John 8:49
If I ***h*** myself . . . . . John 8:54
my ***h*** is nothing . . . . . John 8:54
devout and ***h*** women . . . . . Acts 13:50
h us with many ***h*** . . . . . Acts 28:10
for glory and ***h*** . . . . . Rom 2:7
glory, ***h***, and peace . . . . . Rom 2:10
to make one vessel unto ***h*** . . . . Rom 9:21
in ***h*** preferring..another . . . . . Rom 12:10
fear to..fear; ***h*** to whom ***h*** . . . . Rom 13:7
ye are ***h***, but we are 1Cor 4:10
bestow more abundant ***h*** 1Cor 12:23
one member be ***h***, all the 1Cor 12:26
h and dishonor, by evil 2Cor 6:8
H thy father and mother . . . . . Eph 6:2
not in any ***h*** to..satisfying . . . . Col 2:23

sanctification and *h* 1Thess 4:4
H widows that are widows 1Tim 5:3
worthy of double *h* 1Tim 5:17
masters worthy of all *h* 1Tim 6:1
h and power everlasting 1Tim 6:16
h, and some to dishonor 2Tim 2:20
be a vessel unto *h* 2Tim 2:21
crownedst..with glory and *h* ...Heb 2:7
builded..house hath more *h* ...Heb 3:3
Marriage is *h* in all ....Heb 13:4
found unto praise and *h* 1Pet 1:7
H all men. Love the 1Pet 2:17
Fear God. *H* the king 1Pet 2:17
from God the Father *h* 2Pet 1:17
beasts give glory and *h* ....Rev 4:9
h and glory and blessing ......Rev 5:12
h and power, and might ......Rev 7:12
rejoice and give *h* to him .....Rev 19:7
the glory and *h* of..nations ....Rev 21:26

HOODS—*coverings for the head*
h, and the veils ....Is 3:23

HOOF—*the horny covering of the feet of certain animals*
Test of clean animals ....Lev 11:3-8
All must leave with Israel.Ex 10:26
Break because of prancings ....Judg 5:22
Like flint ....Is 5:28
Cause noise ....Jer 47:3

[*also* HOOFS]
beast which divideth the *h* ....Lev 11:26
beast that parteth the *h* ....Deut 14:6
that divide the cloven *h* ....Deut 14:7
divide not the *h* ....Deut 14:7
it divideth the *h* ....Deut 14:8
hath horns and *h* ....Ps 69:31
h of his horses..he tread ......Ezek 26:11
I will make thy *h* brass ....Mic 4:13

HOOK—*a curved or bent device for holding, catching, or pulling something*
Used:
For curtains ....Ex 26:32, 37
In fishing ....Job 41:1, 2
For pruning ....Is 2:4
Expressive of God's sovereignty 2Kin 19:28

[*also* HOOKS]
h shall be of gold ....Ex 26:37
h shall be of silver ....Ex 27:17
pillars of it with their *h* .....Ex 36:38
h of silver and..overlaying ......Ex 38:19
cut..sprigs with pruning *h* .....Is 18:5
put my *h* in thy nose ....Is 37:29
will put *h* in thy jaws ....Ezek 29:4
And within were *h* ....Ezek 40:43
will take you away with *h* .....Amos 4:2
to the sea, and cast a *h* ....Matt 17:27

HOPE—*reliance on God's blessing and provision; the expectation of future good*
Kinds of:
Natural expectation ......Acts 27:20
Sinful expectation ....Acts 24:26
Impossible ....Rom 4:18
Spiritual assurance 2Cor 1:7
Described as:
Living 1Pet 1:3
Blessed ....Titus 2:13
Good 2Thess 2:16
Better ....Heb 7:19
Sure and steadfast ....Heb 6:19
One of the great virtues .1Cor 13:13
Productive of:
Purity 1John 3:3
Patience ....Rom 8:25
Courage ....Rom 5:4, 5
Joy ....Rom 12:12
Salvation ....Rom 8:23
Assurance ....Heb 6:18, 19
Stability ....Col 1:23
Grounds of:
God's Word ....Ps 119:42-81
Rom 15:4
God's promises ....Acts 26:6, 7
Titus 1:2
Objects of:
God ....Ps 39:7
Christ 1Cor 15:19
Salvation ....Rom 5:1-5
Resurrection ....Acts 23:6
Eternal life ....Titus 1:2
Glory ....Rom 5:2
Christ's return ....Rom 8:22-25

[*also* HOPED, HOPE'S, HOPETH, HOPING]
If I should say, I have *h* ......Ruth 1:12
there is *h* in Israel ....Ezra 10:2
enemies of the Jews *h* ....Esth 9:1
fear thy confidence, thy *h* .....Job 4:6
So the poor hath *h* ....Job 5:16
strength, that I should *h*? .....Job 6:11
because they had *h* ....Job 6:20
are spent without *h* ....Job 7:6
hypocrite's *h* shall perish .....Job 8:13
Whose *h* shall be cut off ......Job 8:14
because there is *h* ....Job 11:18
h shall be as the giving up ....Job 11:20
there is *h* of a tree ....Job 14:7
destroyest the *h* of man ....Job 14:19
And where is now my *h*? ......Job 17:15
for my *h*, who shall see it? ....Job 17:15
h hath he removed like a tree .Job 19:10
what is the *h* of..hypocrite ....Job 27:8
If I have made gold my *h* .....Job 31:24
h of him is in vain ....Job 41:9
my flesh also shall rest in *h* ...Ps 16:9
didst make me *h* when I was ..Ps 22:9
all ye that *h* in the Lord ......Ps 31:24
them that *h* in his mercy ......Ps 33:18
according as we *h* in thee .....Ps 33:22
in thee, O Lord, do I *h* ....Ps 38:15
my *h* is in thee ....Ps 39:7
in me? *h* thou in God ....Ps 42:5
within me? *h* thou in God .....Ps 42:11
h in God: for I shall ....Ps 43:5
art my *h*, O Lord God ....Ps 71:5
But I will *h* continually ....Ps 71:14
might set their *h* in God ......Ps 78:7
have *h* in thy judgments ......Ps 119:43
my shield: I *h* in thy word ....Ps 119:114
not be ashamed of my *h* ......Ps 119:116
and cried: I *h* in thy word .....Ps 119:147
in his word do I *h* ....Ps 130:5
Let Israel *h* in the Lord ....Ps 130:7
Let Israel *h* in the Lord ....Ps 131:3
h is in the Lord his God ......Ps 146:5
those that *h* in..mercy ....Ps 147:11
h of the righteous shall be ....Prov 10:28
h of unjust men perisheth .....Prov 11:7
H deferred maketh..heart .....Prov 13:12
righteous hath *h* in..death .....Prov 14:32
son while there is *h* ....Prov 19:18
h of a fool than of him ....Prov 26:12
h of a fool than of him ....Prov 29:20
joined to all the living..*h* ......Eccl 9:4
into..pit cannot *h* for ....Is 38:18
There is no *h* ....Is 57:10
There is no *h* ....Jer 2:25
Truly in vain is salvation *h* ....Jer 3:23
O the *h* of Israel ....Jer 14:8
whose *h* the Lord is ....Jer 17:7
O Lord, the *h* of Israel ....Jer 17:13
art my *h* in..day of evil ....Jer 17:17
they said, There is no *h* ....Jer 18:12
h of their fathers ....Jer 50:7
strength and my *h* ....Lam 3:18
therefore have I *h* ....Lam 3:21
therefore will I *h* in him ......Lam 3:24
if so be there may be *h* ....Lam 3:29
have made others to *h* ....Ezek 13:6
waited, and her *h* was lost ....Ezek 19:5
are dried, and our *h* is lost ....Ezek 37:11
of Achor for a door of *h* ......Hos 2:15
Lord..the *h* of his people .....Joel 3:16
ye prisoners of *h* ....Zech 9:12
whom ye *h* to receive ....Luke 6:34
h for nothing again ....Luke 6:35
he *h* to..seen some miracle ....Luke 23:8
flesh shall rest in *h* ....Acts 2:26
h of their gains was gone .....Acts 16:19
h sake, King Agrippa ....Acts 26:7
h of Israel I am bound ....Acts 28:20
against *h* believed in *h* ....Rom 4:18
subjected the same in *h* ....Rom 8:20
God of *h* fill you with..joy ....Rom 15:13
ye may abound in *h* ....Rom 15:13
that ploweth..plow in *h* 1Cor 9:10
he that thresheth in *h* 1Cor 9:10
be partaker of his *h* 1Cor 9:10
all things, *h* all things 1Cor 13:7
that we have such *h* 2Cor 3:12
they did, not as we *h* 2Cor 8:5
having *h*, when your faith is ...2Cor 10:15
wait for..*h* of righteousness ....Gal 5:5
know what is the *h* of his .....Eph 1:18
are called in one *h* ....Eph 4:4
expectation and my *h* ....Phil 1:20
Him therefore I *h* to send .....Phil 2:23
h which is laid up for you .....Col 1:5
Christ in you the *h* of glory ...Col 1:27
patience of *h* in our Lord 1Thess 1:3
as others which have no *h* 1Thess 4:13
Christ, which is our *h* 1Tim 1:1
thee *h* to come unto thee 1Tim 3:14
h of eternal life ....Titus 3:7
rejoicing of the *h* ....Heb 3:6
assurance of *h* unto the end ...Heb 6:11
substance of things *h* for ......Heb 11:1
h to the end for the grace 1Pet 1:13
faith and *h* might be in God ...1Pet 1:21
reason of the *h* that is in 1Pet 3:15

HOPELESSNESS—*without hope*
Conditions of the wicked .Eph 2:12
Their unchangeable condition ....Luke 16:23-31

HOPHNI (hŏf'nī)—*"strong"*
Son of Eli; brother of Phinehas 1Sam 1:3
Called "sons of Belial"...1Sam 2:12
Guilty of unlawful practices 1Sam 2:13-17
Immoral 1Sam 2:22
Eli's warning rejected by .1Sam 2:23-25
Cursed by a man of God .1Sam 2:27-36
Warned by Samuel 1Sam 3:11-18
Ark taken to battle by ...1Sam 4:1-8
Slain in battle 1Sam 4:11
News of, causes Eli's death 1Sam 4:12-18

HOPHRA—*See* PHARAOH-HOPHRA; PHARAOH

HOR (hôr)—*"hill"*
Mountain of Edom ......Num 20:23
Scene of Aaron's death ..Num 20:22-29
Num 33:37-39
Prominent peak of the Lebanon range ....Num 34:7, 8
come unto mount *H* ....Num 20:22
bring..up unto mount *H* ....Num 20:25
journeyed from mount *H* ......Num 21:4
went up into mount *H* ....Num 33:38
departed from mount *H* ....Num 33:41
From mount *H* ye..point out ..Num 34:8
brother died in mount *H* ......Deut 32:50

HORAM (hō'răm)—*"height"*
King of Gezer ....Josh 10:33

HOREB (hō'rĕb)—*"desert"*
God appears to Moses ...Ex 3:1-22
Water flows from ....Ex 17:6
Law given here ....Mal 4:4
Site of Israel's great sin ..Deut 9:8, 9
Ps 106:19
Covenant made ....Deut 29:1
Elijah lodged here 40 days 1Kin 19:8, 9
See SINAI
mountain of God even to *H* ...Ex 3:1
ornaments by..mount *H* ....Ex 33:6
eleven days' journey from *H* ..Deut 1:2
when we departed from *H* ....Deut 1:19

Lord spake unto you in *H* .....Deut 4:15
in *H* ye provoked the Lord ....Deut 9:8
made with them in *H* ....Deut 29:1
Moses put there at *H* 1Kin 8:9
Moses put therein at *H* 2Chr 5:10
made a calf in *H* ....Ps 106:19
I commanded unto him in *H* ..Mal 4:4

HOREM (hō'rĕm)—*"dedicated to God"*
City of Naphtali ....Josh 19:32, 38

HOR-HAGIDGAD (hôr'hä-gĭd-găd)—*"cleft mountain"*
Israelite encampment ....Num 33:32
Called Gudgodah ....Deut 10:7

HORI (hō'rī)—*"free; noble"*
1. Son of Lotan ....Gen 36:22
1Chr 1:39
2. Horites ....Gen 36:21-30
3. Father of Shaphat the spy ....Num 13:5

HORIM, HORITES (hō'rĭm, hō'rīts)—*"cave dwellers"*
Inhabitants of Mt. Seir ...Gen 36:20
Defeated by Chedorlaomer ....Gen 14:5, 6
Ruled by chieftains ......Gen 36:29, 30
Driven out by Esau's descendants ....Gen 36:20-29; Deut 2:12, 22

HORMAH (hôr'mä)—*"dedicated to God"*
Originally called Zephath .Judg 1:17
Scene of Israel's defeat ..Num 14:45
Destroyed by Israel ......Num 21:1-3
Assigned to Judah ....Josh 15:30
Transferred to Simeon ...Josh 19:4
David sends spoils to 1Sam 30:26, 30

even unto *H* ....Deut 1:44
The king of *H*, one ....Josh 12:14
And at Bethuel, and at *H* 1Chr 4:30

HORN—*bone-like protrusion from an animal's head*

Descriptive of:
Ram's ....Gen 22:13
Ox's ....Ex 21:29
Unicorn's ....Ps 92:10
Goat's ....Dan 8:5
Altar's 1Kin 1:50

Uses of:
For trumpets ....Josh 6:4, 13
For vessels 1Sam 16:1-13

Figurative of:
God's power ....Hab 3:4
Christ's power...........Rev 5:6
Power of the wicked .....Ps 22:21
Power of earthly kingdoms ....Dan 7:7, 8, 24
Power of the antichrist ...Rev 13:1
Arrogance 1Kin 22:11
Conquests ....Deut 33:17
Exaltation 1Sam 2:1, 10
Degradation ....Job 16:15
Destruction ....Jer 48:25
Salvation ....Luke 1:69

As musical instrument:
Heard at Sinai ....Ex 19:16
Sounded in jubilee year ..Lev 25:9
Used on occasions 1Chr 15:28
A part of worship 2Chr 15:14
Used in Babylon ....Dan 3:7, 10

[*also* HORNS]
h are like..*h* of unicorns ......Deut 33:17
long blast with the ram's *h* ....Josh 6:5
seven trumpets of rams' *h* ....Josh 6:6
h of my salvation 2Sam 22:3
priest took a *h* of oil 1Kin 1:39
words of God, to lift up..*h* 1Chr 25:5
made him *h* of iron 2Chr 18:10
h of my salvation ....Ps 18:2
bullock..hath *h* and hoofs .....Ps 69:31
Lift not up the *h* ....Ps 75:4
Lift not up your *h* on high ....Ps 75:5
h of the wicked..will I cut .....Ps 75:10
h of the righteous ....Ps 75:10
favor our *h* shall be exalted ...Ps 89:17
name shall his *h* be exalted ....Ps 89:24
h shalt be exalted with honor ..Ps 112:9
make the *h* of David to bud ...Ps 132:17
exalteth the *h* of his people ...Ps 148:14
upon the *h* of your altars .....Jer 17:1
fierce anger all..*h* of Israel ....Lam 2:3
set up the *h* of..adversaries ....Lam 2:17
present *h* of ivory and ebony ..Ezek 27:15
h of the house of Israel ....Ezek 29:21
diseased with your *h* ....Ezek 34:21
upward shall be four *h* ....Ezek 43:15
on the four *h* of it ....Ezek 43:20
among them another little *h* ...Dan 7:8
h were eyes like ....Dan 7:8
words which the *h* spake ......Dan 7:11
even of that *h* that had eyes ...Dan 7:20
ten *h* that were in his head ....Dan 7:20
same *h* made war with..saints ..Dan 7:21
ram which had two *h* ....Dan 8:3
two *h* were high ....Dan 8:3
ram that had two *h* ....Dan 8:6
brake his two *h* ....Dan 8:7
great *h* was broken ....Dan 8:8
came forth a little *h* ....Dan 8:9
h that is between his eyes .....Dan 8:21
not taken to us *h* ....Amos 6:13
I will make thine *h* iron ....Mic 4:13
and behold four *h* ....Zech 1:18
h..have scattered Judah ....Zech 1:19
which lifted up their *h* ....Zech 1:21
to cast..*h* of the Gentiles ......Zech 1:21
four *h* of the golden altar .....Rev 9:13
seven heads and ten *h* ....Rev 12:3
two *h* like a lamb ....Rev 13:11
seven heads and ten *h* ....Rev 17:3
seven heads and ten *h* ....Rev 17:7
ten *h* which thou sawest are ...Rev 17:12
ten *h* which thou sawest upon .Rev 17:16

HORNETS—*large, strong wasps*
God's agents ....Ex 23:28
Deut 7:20
Kings driven out by .....Josh 24:12

HORNS OF THE ALTAR—*the protruding points at the four corners of an altar*
Description ....Ex 27:2
Provides sanctuary 1Kin 1:50

it upon the *h* of the altar .....Ex 29:12
h..shall be of the same ....Ex 30:2
and the *h* thereof..............Ex 30:3
an atonement upon the *h* ......Ex 30:10
h thereof were of the same ....Ex 37:25
and the *h* of it ....Ex 37:26
made the *h*..on the four ....Ex 38:2
h thereof were of the same ....Ex 38:2
blood upon the *h* of the altar ..Lev 4:7
blood upon the *h* of the altar ..Lev 4:18
upon the *h* of the altar.........Lev 4:25
put it upon the *h* of..altar .....Lev 8:15
put it upon the *h* of..altar .....Lev 9:9
put it upon the *h* of..altar .....Lev 16:18

HORONAIM (hôr-ō-nā'ĭm)—*"double caves"*
Moabite city ....Is 15:5

crying shall be from *H* ....Jer 48:3
going down of *H* ....Jer 48:5
Zoar even unto *H* ....Jer 48:34

HORONITE (hôr'ō-nīt)
Native of Horonaim .....Neh 2:10, 19

Sanballat the *H* ....Neh 13:28

HOROSCOPE—*fortune-telling by astrology*
Forbidden ....Jer 10:2
Unprofitable ....Deut 17:2-5
Punishment ....Is 47:13, 14

HORRIBLE—*extremely unpleasant*

[*also* HORRIBLY]
a *h* tempest ....Ps 11:6
me up also out of a *h* pit .....Ps 40:2
and be *h* afraid ....Jer 2:12
wonderful and *h* thing ....Jer 5:30
Israel hath done a..*h* thing ....Jer 18:13
prophets of Jerusalem a *h* .....Jer 23:14
their kings..be *h* afraid ....Ezek 32:10
I have seen a *h* thing ....Hos 6:10

HORROR—*painful intense fear*
h of great darkness fell ....Gen 15:12
h hath overwhelmed me ......Ps 55:5
H hath taken hold upon me ...Ps 119:53
h shall cover them ....Ezek 7:18

HORSE—*a large herbivorous mammal used as a beast of burden and for transportation*

Used for:
Travel ....Deut 17:16
War ....Ex 14:9
Bearing burdens ....Neh 7:68
Sending messages ....Esth 8:10
Idolatry.................2Kin 23:11

Figurative of:
Human trust ....Hos 14:3
Obstinacy ....Ps 32:9
James 3:3
Impetuosity in sin ....Jer 8:6
God's protection 2Kin 2:11

[*also* HORSES, HORSES']
bread in exchange for *h* ....Gen 47:17
biteth the *h* heels ....Gen 49:17
field, upon the *h* ....Ex 9:3
even all Pharaoh's *h* ....Ex 14:23
h and his rider hath he ....Ex 15:1
h and his rider hath he ....Ex 15:21
unto their *h* ....Deut 11:4
and seest *h*, and chariots ......Deut 20:1
h and chariots very many .....Josh 11:4
he houghed their *h* ....Josh 11:9
prepared him chariots and *h* ...2Sam 15:1
forty thousand stalls of *h* 1Kin 4:26
armor, and spices, *h* 1Kin 10:25
h for a hundred and fifty......1Kin 10:29
save the *h* and mules alive 1Kin 18:5
smote the *h* and chariots 1Kin 20:21
h for *h*..chariot for chariot 1Kin 20:25
my *h* as thy *h* 2Kin 3:7
sent he thither *h* 2Kin 6:14
full of *h* and chariots 2Kin 6:17
left their tents, and their *h* 2Kin 7:7
five of the *h* that remain 2Kin 7:13
on the wall and on the *h* 2Kin 9:33
way by the which the *h* 2Kin 11:16
deliver thee two thousand *h* ...2Kin 18:23
houghed all the chariot *h* 1Chr 18:4
h brought out of Egypt 2Chr 1:16
h for a hundred and fifty......2Chr 1:17
harness, and spices, *h*.........2Chr 9:24
Solomon *h* out of Egypt 2Chr 9:28
h were seven hundred thirty ...Ezra 2:66
h that the king rideth ....Esth 6:8
take the apparel and the *h* ....Esth 6:10
scorneth the *h* and his rider ...Job 39:18
given the *h* strength? ....Job 39:19
chariots, and some in *h* ....Ps 20:7
h is a vain thing ....Ps 33:17
both the chariot and *h* ....Ps 76:6
not in the strength of the *h* ...Ps 147:10
h is prepared against..day .....Prov 21:31
seen servants upon *h* ....Eccl 10:7
company of *h* in Pharaoh's ....Song 1:9
land is also full of *h* ....Is 2:7
h hoofs shall be counted ......Is 5:28
for we will flee upon *h*........Is 30:16
stay on *h*..trust in chariots ....Is 31:1
give thee two thousand *h* .....Is 36:8
forth the chariot and *h*........Is 43:17
h are swifter than eagles ......Jer 4:13
They were as fed *h* ....Jer 5:8
they ride upon *h* ....Jer 6:23
thou contend with *h*? ....Jer 12:5
in chariots and on *h* ....Jer 22:4
corner of the *h* gate toward ...Jer 31:40
Come up, ye *h*; and rage .....Jer 46:9
A sword is upon their *h*.......Jer 50:37
cause the *h* to come up as ....Jer 51:27
they might give him *h* ....Ezek 17:15

horsemen riding upon *h* ....Ezek 23:12
all of them riding upon *h* .....Ezek 23:23
abundance of his *h* ....Ezek 26:10
h and horsemen and mules ....Ezek 27:14
all of them riding upon *h* .....Ezek 38:15
by battle, by *h* ....Hos 1:7
as the appearance of *h* ....Joel 2:4
he that rideth the *h*...........Amos 2:15
have taken away your *h*.......Amos 4:10
that I will cut off thy *h* ....Mic 5:10
of the prancing *h* ....Nah 3:2
h also are swifter ....Hab 1:8
through the sea with thine *h*...Hab 3:15
h and their riders.............Hag 2:22
man riding upon a red *h* ......Zech 1:8
behind him were there..*h* .....Zech 1:8
first chariot were red *h* ....Zech 6:2
second chariot black *h* ....Zech 6:2
third chariot white *h* ....Zech 6:3
grizzled and bay *h* ....Zech 6:3
black *h* which are therein .....Zech 6:6
them as his goodly *h*..........Zech 10:3
riders on *h*..be confounded ....Zech 10:5
smite every *h* with ....Zech 12:4
smite every *h* of the people ...Zech 12:4
bits in the *h* mouths ....James 3:3
I saw, and behold a white *h*...Rev 6:2
beheld, and lo a black *h* ......Rev 6:5
looked, and behold a pale *h*...Rev 6:8
locusts were like unto *h*.......Rev 9:7
I saw the *h* in the vision ......Rev 9:17
heads of the *h* ....Rev 9:17
behold a white *h* ....Rev 19:11
followed him upon white *h* ....Rev 19:14
him that sat upon the *h* ....Rev 19:21

HORSE GATE—*a gate of Jerusalem*
Restored by Nehemiah...Neh 3:28

HORSE TRADERS—*buyers and sellers of horses*
Tyre famous for ....Ezek 27:2, 14

HORSEBACK—*riding on a horse*
there went one on *h* 2Kin 9:18
on *h* through the street ....Esth 6:9

HORSEHOOFS—*hard growth which surrounds horses' feet*
Then were the *h* broken by ...Judg 5:22

HORSELEECH—*a large leech*
Figurative of insatiable appetite ....Prov 30:15, 16

HORSEMAN—*man on horseback; plural, cavalry*

[*also* HORSEMEN]
both chariots and *h* ....Gen 50:9
Pharaoh and his *h* ....Ex 14:9
horses, his chariots, and..*h* ....Ex 14:23
covered..chariots and the *h*....Ex 14:28
with chariots and *h* ....Josh 24:6
and to be his *h*...............1Sam 8:11
h followed hard after him 2Sam 1:6
and forty thousand *h* 2Sam 10:18
prepared..chariots and *h* 1Kin 1:5
and cities for his *h* 1Kin 9:19
gathered..chariots and *h* 1Kin 10:26
on a horse with the *h*.........1Kin 20:20
chariot of Israel, and the *h*....2Kin 2:12
Joram said, Take a *h* 2Kin 9:17
chariot of Israel, and the *h*....2Kin 13:14
and seven thousand *h* 1Chr 18:4
gathered chariots and *h* 2Chr 1:14
and the cities of the *h* 2Chr 8:6
and twelve thousand *h* 2Chr 9:25
very many chariots and *h*? 2Chr 16:8
band of soldiers and *h* ....Ezra 8:22
captains of the army and *h* ....Neh 2:9
saw a chariot with..*h* ....Is 21:7
chariots of men and *h* ....Is 22:6
nor bruise it with his *h*........Is 28:28
for chariots and for *h*? ....Is 36:9
for the noise of the *h* ....Jer 4:29
h riding upon horses ....Ezek 23:6
with chariots, and with *h*......Ezek 26:7
fairs with horses and *h* ....Ezek 27:14
with chariots, and with *h*......Dan 11:40
battle, by horses, nor by *h* ....Hos 1:7
as *h*, so shall they run ....Joel 2:4
h lifteth up both the bright ....Nah 3:3
h shall spread themselves .....Hab 1:8
h shall come from far ....Hab 1:8
and *h* threescore and ten ......Acts 23:23
number of the army of the *h* ..Rev 9:16

HOSAH (hō'sä)—*"refuge"*
1. Village of Asher ....Josh 19:29
2. Temple porter 1Chr 16:38

H of the children of Merari ...1Chr 26:10
brethren of *H* were thirteen ...1Chr 26:11
To Shuppim and *H* 1Chr 26:16

HOSANNA—*"save, now, we beseech thee"*
Triumphal acclaim ....Matt 21:9, 15
Mark 11:9

H in the highest ....Mark 11:10
H: Blessed is the King ....John 12:13

HOSEA, OSEE (hō-zā'ä, ō-sē')—*"help; Jehovah is help"*
Son of Beeri, prophet of the northern kingdom..Hos 1:1
Reproved idolatory ......Hos 1—2
Threatens God's judgment; calls to repentance ....Hos 3—6
Foretells impending judgment ....Hos 7—10
Calls an ungrateful people to repentance; promises God's blessings ....Hos 11—14

HOSEN—*trousers*
Bound in ....Dan 3:21

HOSHAIAH (ho-sha'ya)—*"whom Jehovah helps"*
1. Father of Jezaniah and Azariah ....Jer 42:1
2. Participant in a dedication ....Neh 12:31, 32

Azariah the son of *H* ....Jer 43:2

HOSHAMA (hŏsh'ä-mä)—*"whom Jehovah heareth"*
Son of King Jeconiah 1Chr 3:17, 18

HOSHEA, OSHEA (hō-shē'ä, ō-shē'ä)—*"Jehovah is help or salvation"*
1. Original name of Joshua, the son of Nun ....Deut 32:44
See JOSHUA, JEHOSHUA
2. Ephraimite chieftain.....1Chr 27:20
3. One who signs covenant .Neh 10:1, 23
4. Israel's last king; usurps throne 2Kin 15:30
5. Reigns wickedly; Israel taken to Assyria during reign.................2Kin 17:1-23

year of *H* son of Elah 2Kin 18:1
seventh year of *H* 2Kin 18:9
ninth year of *H* 2Kin 18:10

HOSPITALITY—*reception and entertainment of strangers and guests*

Kinds of:
Treacherous............Judg 4:17-21
Rewarded..............Josh 6:17-25
Unwise 2Kin 20:12-19
Critical ....Luke 7:36-50
Unwelcomed ....Luke 9:51-53
Joyful ....Luke 19:5, 6
Turbulent ....Acts 17:5-9
Forbidden 3John 1, 9, 10

Acts of:
Commanded ....Rom 12:13
Required of church leaders 1Tim 3:2
Discipleship ....Matt 25:35

Courtesies of:
Protection provided......Gen 19:6-8
Shelter and food ....Luke 11:5-8
Washing of feet ....Luke 7:44
Kissing ....Luke 7:45
Denied with indignities...Judg 19:15-28
Luke 10:10-16

Examples of:
Abraham to angels ......Gen 18:1-8
Lot to an angel ....Gen 19:1-11
Laban to Abraham's servant ....Gen 24:31-33
Joseph to his brothers ...Gen 43:31-34
Pharaoh to Jacob ....Gen 45:16-20
Rahab to the spies ....Josh 2:1-16
David to Mephibosheth ..2Sam 9:6-13
Martha to Jesus ....Luke 10:38-42
Lydia to Paul and Silas ..Acts 16:14, 15
Barbarians to Paul.......Acts 28:2, 7

But a lover of *h* ....Titus 1:8
Use *h* one to another 1Pet 4:9

HOST—*one who entertains; a large army; a multitude*

[*also* HOSTS]
and all the *h* of them ....Gen 2:1
the chief captain of his *h*......Gen 21:32
h of the Lord went out ....Ex 12:41
Pharaoh, and upon all his *h*...Ex 14:4
unto the *h* of the Egyptians ...Ex 14:24
troubled the *h* of the Egyptians.Ex 14:24
Pharaoh's chariots and his *h*...Ex 15:4
throughout their *h* ....Num 1:52
h and those that were.........Num 2:4
all that enter into the *h* ....Num 4:3
over the *h* of the tribe ....Num 10:15
over the *h* of the tribe ....Num 10:19
over the *h* of the tribe ....Num 10:23
camps throughout their *h* .....Num 10:25
over the *h* of the tribe ....Num 10:26
over thousands of the *h* ....Num 31:48
wasted out from among the *h*. .Deut 2:14
or any of the *h* of heaven .....Deut 17:3
When the *h* goeth forth ....Deut 23:9
Pass through the *h* ....Josh 1:11
captain of the *h* of the Lord...Josh 5:14
all the *h*..on the north of .....Josh 8:13
they and all their *h* ....Josh 10:5
captain of..*h* was Sisera ....Judg 4:2
chariots, and after the *h* ......Judg 4:16
the *h* of Sisera fell upon ......Judg 4:16
h of Midian was beneath ......Judg 7:8
thy servant down to the *h*.....Judg 7:10
to go down unto the *h* ....Judg 7:11
men that were in the *h* ....Judg 7:11
delivered Midian, and..*h* ....Judg 7:14
returned into..*h* of Israel ......Judg 7:15
into..hand the *h* of Midian ....Judg 7:15
even throughout all the *h* .....Judg 7:22
h fled to Beth-shittah ....Judg 7:22
and their *h* with them.........Judg 8:10
discomfited all the *h* ....Judg 8:12
the Lord of *h* in Shiloh 1Sam 1:3
covenant of the Lord of *h*.....1Sam 4:4
into the midst of the *h* 1Sam 11:11
was trembling in the *h* 1Sam 14:15
he gathered a *h*, and smote ...1Sam 14:48
as the *h* was going forth 1Sam 17:20
the captain of the *h* 1Sam 17:55
h of the Philistines 1Sam 28:5
coming in with me in the *h*....1Sam 29:6
captain of Saul's *h*............2Sam 2:8
smite the *h* of..Philistines 2Sam 5:24
name of the Lord of *h* 2Sam 6:18
David had smitten all the *h* ...2Sam 8:9
h of the mighty men 2Sam 10:7
Shobach..captain of their *h*....2Sam 10:18
be not captain of the *h* 2Sam 19:13
the *h* of the Philistines 2Sam 23:16
against..captains of the *h*......2Sam 24:4
captains of the *h* went 2Sam 24:4
Joab the captain of the *h* 1Kin 1:19
two captains of the *h* 1Kin 2:5
captain of the *h* of Israel......1Kin 2:32
Jehoiada in his room over..*h* ..1Kin 2:35
Joab the captain of the *h* 1Kin 11:15
the captain of the *h* 1Kin 16:16
carry me out of the *h*.........1Kin 22:34

H

was no water for the **h** 2Kin 3:9
Naaman, captain of the **h** 2Kin 5:1
a **h** compassed the city 2Kin 6:15
let us fall unto the **h** 2Kin 7:4
made the **h** of the Syrians 2Kin 7:6
even the noise of a great **h** 2Kin 7:6
captains of..**h** were sitting 2Kin 9:5
Hezekiah with a great **h** 2Kin 18:17
worshiped all..**h** of heaven 2Kin 21:3
he, and all his **h** 2Kin 25:1
being over the **h** of the Lord ..1Chr 9:19
brake through the **h** 1Chr 11:18
were captains in the **h** 1Chr 12:21
smite the **h** of..Philistines 1Chr 14:15
smitten all..**h** of Hadarezer 1Chr 18:9
h of the mighty men 1Chr 19:8
Shophach..captain of the **h** 1Chr 19:18
captains of the **h** 1Chr 26:26
The third captain of the **h** 1Chr 27:5
h of a thousand 2Chr 14:9
h of the king of Syria 2Chr 16:7
h of heaven standing..........2Chr 18:18
hundreds..set over the **h** 2Chr 23:14
Lord delivered a..great **h** 2Chr 24:24
throughout all the **h** 2Chr 26:14
captains of the **h** of..king 2Chr 33:11
h should encamp ....Ps 27:3
saved by the multitude of a **h**. .Ps 33:16
mustereth the **h** of..battle .....Is 13:4
punish the **h** of the high ones. .Is 24:21
destroy ye utterly all her **h** ....Jer 51:3
principal scribe of the **h** ....Jer 52:25
as the noise of an **h** ....Ezek 1:24
even to the prince of the **h** ....Dan 8:11
both the sanctuary and the **h** ..Dan 8:13
captivity of this **h** ....Obad 20
gave them to the **h** ....Luke 10:35

HOST OF HEAVEN

Used of stars as objects of worship:
Objects of idolatry ......Deut 4:19
Practiced in Israel 2Kin 17:16
Introduced by Manasseh .2Kin 21:5
Abolished by Josiah 2Kin 23:4-12
Worship of, on roofs ....Jer 19:13

Used of stars as created things:
Created by God ....Is 45:12
Cannot be numbered ....Jer 33:22
Named by God..........Is 40:26
To be dissolved ....Is 34:4

Used of angels:
Created by God ....Neh 9:6
Around the throne 1Kin 22:19

HOSTAGE—*a person held for security*
Captive for pledge 2Kin 14:14
2Chr 25:24

HOSTS, LORD OF—*a title of God*

Commander of:
Israel's armies 1Sam 17:45
Is 31:4
Armies (angels) of heaven .... { Gen 28:12, 13; Hos 12:4, 5; Ps 89:6-8
Same as Sabaoth ....Rom 9:29

God of **h** was with him 2Sam 5:10
The Lord of **h** is the God 2Sam 7:26
As the Lord of **h** liveth 1Kin 18:15
As the Lord of **h** liveth 2Kin 3:14
for the Lord of **h** 1Chr 11:9
The Lord of **h** is the God 1Chr 17:24
Lord of **h**, he is the King .....Ps 24:10
city of the Lord of **h** ....Ps 48:8
O Lord God of **h** ....Ps 69:6
Turn us again, O God of **h** ....Ps 80:7
O Lord God of **h** ....Ps 80:19
O Lord of **h**! ....Ps 84:1
O Lord of **h**, my King ....Ps 84:3
O Lord of **h**, blessed is..man . .Ps 84:12
ye the Lord, all ye his **h** ......Ps 103:21
praise ye him, all his **h** ....Ps 148:2
Except the Lord of **h** ....Is 1:9
day of the Lord of **h** ....Is 2:12
saith the Lord God of **h** ......Is 3:15
ears said the Lord of **h** ....Is 5:9
the law of the Lord of **h** ......Is 5:24
seen the King, the Lord of **h** . .Is 6:5
Israel from the Lord of **h** .....Is 8:18
they seek the Lord of **h** ....Is 9:13
the Lord, the Lord of **h** ....Is 10:16
saith the Lord God of **h** ......Is 10:24
the Lord of **h** ....Is 10:33
wrath of the Lord of **h** ....Is 13:13
saith the Lord of **h** ....Is 14:23
Lord of **h** hath purposed ......Is 14:27
brought unto the Lord of **h** ...Is 18:7
name of the Lord of **h** ....Is 18:7
Lord of **h** hath purposed ......Is 19:12
counsel of the Lord of **h** ......Is 19:17
witness unto the Lord of **h** ....Is 19:20
heard of the Lord of **h** ....Is 21:10
perplexity by..Lord God of **h** . .Is 22:5
did the Lord God of **h** ....Is 22:12
mine ears by the Lord of **h** ....Is 22:14
saith the Lord God of **h** ....Is 22:14
saith the Lord of **h** ....Is 22:25
Lord of **h** shall reign..........Is 24:23
Lord of **h** be for a crown .....Is 28:5
cometh..from the Lord of **h** ...Is 28:29
the Lord of **h** ....Is 31:5
O Lord of **h**, God of Israel ...Is 37:16
word of the Lord of **h** ....Is 39:5
saith the Lord of **h** ....Is 45:13
the Lord of **h** is his name .....Is 48:2
Lord of **h** is his name ....Is 54:5
saith the Lord God of **h** ......Jer 2:19
saith the Lord God of **h** ......Jer 5:14
saith the Lord of **h** ....Jer 6:9
Lord of **h** the God of Israel ...Jer 7:3
saith the Lord of **h** ....Jer 8:3
Lord of **h** the God of Israel ...Jer 9:15
Lord of **h** is his name ....Jer 10:16
Lord of **h** that judgest ....Jer 11:20
O Lord God of **h** ....Jer 15:16
Lord of **h**, the God of Israel ..Jer 19:3
Lord of **h**, the God of Israel ..Jer 19:15
thus saith the Lord of **h** ....Jer 23:15
of the Lord of **h** our God .....Jer 23:36
Lord of **h**, the God of Israel ..Jer 25:27
saith the Lord of **h** ....Jer 25:29
Thus saith the Lord of **h** ....Jer 26:18
intercession to..Lord of **h** .....Jer 27:18
Lord of **h**, the God of Israel ..Jer 27:21
Lord of **h**, the God of Israel ..Jer 28:14
Lord of **h**, the God of Israel ..Jer 29:8
Lord of **h**, the God of Israel ..Jer 29:21
Lord of **h**, the God of Israel ..Jer 31:23
Lord of **h**, the God of Israel ..Jer 32:14
Praise the Lord of **h** ....Jer 33:11
Lord of **h**, the God of Israel ..Jer 35:13
Lord of **h**, the God of Israel ..Jer 39:16
Lord of **h**, the God of Israel ..Jer 43:10
saith..Lord, the God of **h** .....Jer 44:7
Lord of **h**, the God of Israel ..Jer 44:25
day of the Lord God of **h** .....Jer 46:10
God of **h** hath a sacrifice......Jer 46:10
Lord of **h**, the God of Israel ..Jer 46:25
Lord of **h**, the God of Israel ..Jer 48:1
saith the Lord God of **h** ......Jer 49:5
saith the Lord of **h** ....Jer 49:26
Lord of **h**, the God of Israel ..Jer 50:18
saith the Lord God of **h** ......Jer 50:31
Lord of **h** is his name ....Jer 50:34
Judah of his God..Lord of **h** ..Jer 51:5
Lord of **h** is his name ....Jer 51:19
name is the Lord of **h** ....Jer 51:57
saith..God, the God of **h** ......Amos 3:13
the Lord, the God of **h** ....Amos 5:14
the Lord, the God of **h** ....Amos 5:16
saith the Lord..God of **h** ....Amos 6:8
Lord God of **h** is he ....Amos 9:5
Lord of **h** hath spoken it ......Mic 4:4
saith the Lord of **h** ....Nah 2:13
not of the Lord of **h** ....Hab 2:13
worship the **h** of heaven ......Zeph 1:5
Lord of **h**, the God of Israel ..Zeph 2:9
the people of the Lord of **h** ...Zeph 2:10
Thus speaketh the Lord of **h** ..Hag 1:2
saith the Lord of **h** ....Hag 1:7
the house of the Lord of **h** ....Hag 1:14
saith the Lord of **h** ....Hag 2:6
saith the Lord of **h** ....Hag 2:8
saith the Lord of **h** ....Hag 2:9
saith the Lord of **h** ....Hag 2:23
Thus saith the Lord of **h** ......Zech 1:3
saith the Lord of **h** ....Zech 1:3
saith the Lord of **h** ....Zech 1:3
Like as the Lord of **h** ....Zech 1:6
Thus saith the Lord of **h** ......Zech 1:14
Thus saith the Lord of **h** ......Zech 1:17
Lord of **h** hath sent me ....Zech 2:9
Thus saith the Lord of **h** ......Zech 3:7
day, saith the Lord of **h** ....Zech 3:10
Lord of **h** hath sent me unto ..Zech 4:9
speaketh the Lord of **h** ....Zech 6:12
the house of the Lord of **h** ....Zech 7:3
speaketh the Lord of **h** ....Zech 7:9
which the Lord of **h**..sent .....Zech 7:12
wrath from the Lord of **h** ......Zech 7:12
the word of the Lord of **h** .....Zech 8:1
mountain of the Lord of **h** ....Zech 8:3
Thus saith the Lord of **h** ......Zech 8:6
saith the Lord of **h** ....Zech 8:6
Thus saith the Lord of **h** ......Zech 8:9
house of the Lord of **h** ....Zech 8:9
saith the Lord of **h** ....Zech 8:14
saith the Lord of **h** ....Zech 8:14
saith the Lord of **h** ....Zech 8:19
seek the Lord of **h** ....Zech 8:21
Thus saith the Lord of **h** ......Zech 8:23
Lord of **h** hath visited ....Zech 10:3
saith the Lord of **h** ....Zech 13:2
King, the Lord of **h** ....Zech 14:16
holiness unto the Lord of **h** ...Zech 14:21
house of the Lord of **h** ....Zech 14:21
thus saith the Lord of **h** ....Mal 1:4
saith the Lord of **h** ....Mal 1:8
pleasure in you..Lord of **h** ....Mal 1:10
snuffed at it..Lord of **h** ....Mal 1:13
unto my name..Lord of **h** .....Mal 2:2
messenger of the Lord of **h** ...Mal 2:7
offering unto the Lord of **h** ...Mal 2:12
he shall come..Lord of **h** ......Mal 3:1
saith the Lord of **h** ....Mal 3:7
saith the Lord of **h** ....Mal 3:11
before the Lord of **h**? ....Mal 3:14
saith the Lord of **h** ....Mal 4:1

HOT—*a high temperature; fiery; raging*
[*also* HOTLY, HOTTEST]
hast so **h** pursued after me? ...Gen 31:36
the sun waxed **h**, it melted ....Ex 16:21
And my wrath shall wax **h** ....Ex 22:24
wrath may wax **h** against ......Ex 32:10
and Moses' anger waxed **h** ....Ex 32:19
skin..there is a **h** burning .....Lev 13:24
anger and **h** displeasure ....Deut 9:19
our bread we took **h** for our ..Josh 9:12
the anger of..Lord was **h** ......Judg 2:14
Let not thine anger be **h** ....Judg 6:39
by that time the sun be **h** 1Sam 11:9
forefront of the **h** battle 2Sam 11:15
opened until the sun be **h** .....Neh 7:3
when it is **h**..are consumed ....Job 6:17
chasten me..**h** displeasure .....Ps 6:1
chasten me..**h** displeasure .....Ps 38:1
My heart was **h** within me ....Ps 39:3
Can one go upon **h** coals ......Prov 6:28
brass of it may be **h**, and .....Ezek 24:11
furnace exceeding **h**, the ......Dan 3:22
They are all **h** as an oven .....Hos 7:7
seared with a **h** iron 1Tim 4:2
art neither cold nor **h** ....Rev 3:15
I would thou wert cold or **h** ...Rev 3:15
and neither cold nor **h** ....Rev 3:16

HOTHAM, HOTHAN (hō'thăm, hō'thăn)—*"determination"*
1. Asherite 1Chr 7:30, 32
See HELEM 2
2. Father of two of David's valiant men 1Chr 11:26, 44

HOTHIR (hō'ther)—*"abundance"*
Son of Heman; a musician 1Chr 25:4, 28

HOUGH—*to cut the tendons of a leg*
To render captured animals useless ...... Josh 11:6, 9; 2Sam 8:4

[*also* HOUGHED]
he *h* their horses .... Josh 11:9
David also *h* all the..horses ... 1Chr 18:4

HOUR—*one twenty-fourth of a day; a particular time*

Used literally of:
One-twelfth of daylight .. Matt 20:1-12
One-twelfth of night ..... Luke 12:39

Reckoned from 6 P.M. and from 6 A.M.:
Third (9 A.M.) .... Matt 20:3
Sixth and ninth (12 noon; 3 P.M.) .... Matt 20:5
Ninth (3 P.M.) .... Acts 3:1
Eleventh (5 P.M.) .... Matt 20:6, 9, 12
Third (9 P.M.) .... Acts 23:23

Used literally and descriptively of Christ's:
Death .... Mark 14:35
Betrayal .... Matt 26:45
Glorification .... John 13:1
Set time .... John 7:30
Predestined time .... John 12:27

Used prophetically of:
Gospel age .... John 4:21
Great tribulation .... Rev 3:10
God's judgment .... Rev 14:7, 15
Christ's return .... Matt 24:42, 44, 50

[*also* HOURS]
h be cast into the midst .... Dan 3:6
was astonished for one *h* ...... Dan 4:19
same *h* came forth fingers ..... Dan 5:5
healed in the selfsame *h* ...... Matt 8:13
h what ye shall speak .... Matt 10:19
cured from that very *h* .... Matt 17:18
day and *h* knoweth no man ... Matt 24:36
neither the day nor the *h* ..... Matt 25:13
not watch with me one *h*? ..... Matt 26:40
In that same *h* said Jesus ..... Matt 26:55
sixth *h* there was darkness .... Matt 27:45
the land unto the ninth *h* ..... Matt 27:45
given you in that *h* .... Mark 13:11
that *h* knoweth no man .... Mark 14:35
couldest not..watch one *h*? .... Mark 14:37
it is enough, the *h* is come .... Mark 14:41
third *h*, and they crucified .... Mark 15:25
the sixth *h* was come .... Mark 15:33
land until the ninth *h* .... Mark 15:33
same *h* he cured many .... Luke 7:21
the same *h* what..to say .... Luke 12:12
a *h* when ye think not .... Luke 12:40
same *h* sought to lay hands .... Luke 20:19
but this is your *h* .... Luke 22:53
it was about the sixth *h* .... Luke 23:44
earth until the ninth *h* .... Luke 23:44
it was about the tenth *h* .... John 1:39
mine *h* is not yet come .... John 2:4
it was about the sixth *h* .... John 4:6
the *h* cometh and now is ...... John 4:23
inquired he of them the *h* ..... John 4:52
Yesterday at the seventh *h* .... John 4:52
The *h* is coming, and now is .. John 5:25
the *h* is coming, in the which .. John 5:28
his *h* was not yet come .... John 8:20
Are there not twelve *h* in ..... John 11:9
The *h* is come, that the Son ... John 12:23
because her *h* is come .... John 16:21
Father the *h* is come .... John 17:1
that *h*..disciple took her .... John 19:27
the space of three *h* after ..... Acts 5:7
ninth *h* of the day an angel ... Acts 10:3
I was fasting until this *h* ...... Acts 10:30
the ninth *h* I prayed .... Acts 10:30
he came out the same *h* .... Acts 16:18
the same *h* I looked up .... Acts 22:13
present *h* we both hunger 1Cor 4:11
in jeopardy every *h*? 1Cor 15:30
subjection, no, not for an *h* ... Gal 2:5
know what *h* I will come ...... Rev 3:3
the space of half an *h* .... Rev 8:1
same *h* was there a great ...... Rev 11:13
power as kings one *h* .... Rev 17:12
in one *h* so great riches .... Rev 18:17

HOURS OF PRAYER—*specific times set aside for prayer*

Characteristics of:
Jewish custom .... Luke 1:10
Centered in the Temple .. Luke 18:10
Directed toward Jerusalem 1Kin 8:48

Times of:
Three times daily .... Dan 6:10
First, at third hour (9 A.M.) .... Acts 2:15
Second, at sixth hour (12 noon) .... Acts 10:9
Third, at ninth hour (3 P.M.) .... Acts 3:1

HOUSE—*a building in which a family lives; a household*

Descriptive of:
Family dwelling .... Judg 11:34; Acts 16:34
Family .... Gen 14:14; Acts 16:31
Descendants .... Gen 18:19; Luke 2:4
Racial or religious group . Is 7:13; Jer 31:31
Tabernacle or Temple ... Ex 34:26; 1Kin 6:1

Figuratively of:
Grave .... Job 30:23
Body 2Cor 5:1
Visible Church .... Gal 6:10
True Church .... Heb 10:21
Earthly life .... Ps 119:54
Heaven .... John 14:2
Security and insecurity ... Matt 7:24-27
Division .... Mark 3:25

See HOME

[*also* HOUSES]
and from thy father's *h* .... Gen 12:1
corn for the famine of your *h* . Gen 42:19
God that he made them *h* ..... Ex 1:21
frogs from thee and thy *h* ..... Ex 8:9
the frogs died out of the *h* .... Ex 8:13
people and into thy *h* .... Ex 8:21
h of the Egyptians shall .... Ex 8:21
his cattle flee into the *h* .... Ex 9:20
And they shall fill thy *h* .... Ex 10:6
the *h* of all thy servants .... Ex 10:6
the *h* of all the Egyptians ..... Ex 10:6
for a token upon the *h* .... Ex 12:13
no leaven found in your *h* ..... Ex 12:19
over the *h* of..Israel .... Ex 12:27
and delivered our *h* .... Ex 12:27
But the *h* of the villages ...... Lev 25:31
the *h* of the..Levites .... Lev 25:33
the *h* of their fathers .... Num 4:22
according to their fathers' *h* ... Num 17:6
h full of all good things .... Deut 6:11
cities, and in their *h* .... Deut 19:1
our provision out of our *h* .... Josh 9:12
is in these *h* an ephod .... Judg 18:14
Solomon had built the two *h* .. 1Kin 9:10
and the *h* of thy servants 1Kin 20:6
in the *h* of the high places 2Kin 17:29
the *h* of the sodomites 2Kin 23:7
and all the *h* of Jerusalem 2Kin 25:9
David made..*h* in the city 1Chr 15:1
the *h* of their fathers 2Chr 25:5
the *h* of your fathers 2Chr 35:4
your wives, and your *h* .... Neh 4:14
oliveyards, and their *h* .... Neh 5:11
after the *h* of our fathers ...... Neh 10:34
sons..feasted in their *h* .... Job 1:4
that dwell in *h* of clay .... Job 4:19
Their *h* are safe from fear ..... Job 21:9
he filled their *h* with good .... Job 22:18
in the dark..dig through *h* ..... Job 24:16
dwell in the *h* of the Lord .... Ps 23:6
zeal of thine *h* hath eaten ...... Ps 69:9
sparrow hath found a *h* .... Ps 84:3
go into the *h* of the Lord ..... Ps 122:1
Wisdom hath builded her *h* ... Prov 9:1
The *h* of the wicked shall ..... Prov 14:11
go to the *h* of mourning ...... Eccl 7:2
unto them that join *h* to *h* .... Is 5:8
and the *h* without man .... Is 6:11
their *h* shall be spoiled .... Is 13:16
cry in their desolate *h* .... Is 13:22
on the tops of their *h* .... Is 15:3
the *h* of Jerusalem .... Is 22:10
h have ye broken down .... Is 22:10
are hid in prison *h* .... Is 42:22
by troops in the harlots' *h* ..... Jer 5:7
their *h* shall be turned .... Jer 6:12
cry be heard from their *h* ..... Jer 18:22
h of Jerusalem and the *h* ...... Jer 19:13
because of all the *h* .... Jer 19:13
build ye *h* and dwell in .... Jer 29:28
and burn it with the *h* .... Jer 32:29
concerning the *h* of..city ...... Jer 33:4
h of the kings of Judah .... Jer 33:4
h of the people with fire ...... Jer 39:8
the *h* of the gods .... Jer 43:13
and all the *h* of Jerusalem ..... Jer 52:13
the *h* of the great men .... Jer 52:13
our *h* to aliens .... Lam 5:2
they shall possess their *h* ...... Ezek 7:24
they shall burn thine *h* .... Ezek 16:41
destroy thy pleasant *h* .... Ezek 26:12
in the doors of the *h* .... Ezek 33:30
h shall be made a dunghill .... Dan 2:5
I will place them in their *h* .... Hos 11:11
shall climb up upon the *h* ..... Joel 2:9
the *h* of ivory shall perish ..... Amos 3:15
have built *h* of hewn stone .... Amos 5:11
h of Achzib shall be a lie ..... Mic 1:14
out from their pleasant *h* ...... Mic 2:9
fill..master's *h* with violence ... Zeph 1:9
and their *h* a desolation .... Zeph 1:13
they shall also build *h* .... Zeph 1:13
to dwell in your ceiled *h* ...... Hag 1:4
be taken, and the *h* rifled ..... Zech 14:2
light unto all..in the *h* .... Matt 5:15
when ye come into a *h* .... Matt 10:12
city or *h* divided against ...... Matt 12:25
enter into a strong man's *h* .... Matt 12:29
h is left unto you desolate ..... Matt 23:38
like a man which built a *h* .... Luke 6:48
a *h* divided against a *h* .... Luke 11:17
sweep the *h* and seek .... Luke 15:8
down to his *h* justified .... Luke 18:14
Father's *h* a *h* of .... John 2:16
zeal of thine *h* hath eaten me . John 2:17
h was filled with the odor ..... John 12:3
Father's *h* are..mansions ...... John 14:2
all the *h* where they were ..... Acts 2:2
wandering about from *h* to *h* .. 1Tim 5:13
in a great *h* there are not 2Tim 2:20
must begin at the *h* of God ... 1Pet 4:17

HOUSE OF GOD—*any place where God is worshiped*
Tabernacle called .... Luke 6:4
Temple described .... Ezra 5:2, 8
Church named 1Tim 3:15
Center of God's worship . Ps 42:4

HOUSE OF PRAYER—*the Temple*
Corrupted into a den of thieves .... Matt 21:13; Mark 11:17

HOUSEHOLD—*a family; those dwelling together in a single unit*

[*also* HOUSEHOLDS]
found of all thy *h* stuff? .... Gen 31:37
food for the famine of your *h* . Gen 42:33
lest thou, and thy *h* .... Gen 45:11
his father's *h* with bread ...... Gen 47:12
food, and for them of your *h* .. Gen 47:24
his *h* came with Jacob .... Ex 1:1
for himself, and for his *h* ..... Lev 16:17
every place ye and your *h* ..... Num 18:31
Pharaoh, and upon all his *h* ... Deut 6:22
swallowed them..their *h* .... Deut 11:6
Lord shall choose..thy *h* ...... Deut 15:20

H

father's *h* home unto thee .....Josh 2:18
shall come by *h* ....Josh 7:14
h which the Lord shall take ...Josh 7:14
he feared his father's *h* ....Judg 6:27
and against all his *h* 1Sam 25:17
every man with his *h* 2Sam 2:3
David returned to bless..*h*......2Sam 6:20
for the king's *h* to ride on.....2Sam 16:2
boat to carry..the king's *h*.....2Sam 19:18
Ahishar was over the *h* 1Kin 4:6
giving food for my *h*..........1Kin 5:9
Genubath..in Pharaoh's *h* 1Kin 11:20
go and tell the king's *h* 2Kin 7:9
she went with her *h* 2Kin 8:2
which was over the *h* 2Kin 19:2
principal *h* being taken.......1Chr 24:6
all the *h* stuff of Tobiah.......Neh 13:8
and a very great *h*............Job 1:3
for the food of thy *h* ....Prov 27:27
Hilkiah, that was over the *h*...Is 36:22
they call them of his *h*? ....Matt 10:25
hath made ruler over his *h* ....Matt 24:45
shall make ruler over his *h* ....Luke 12:42
called two of his *h* servants....Acts 10:7
which are of Aristobulus' *h*....Rom 16:10
baptized..*h* of Stephanas 1Cor 1:16
saints, and of the *h* of God ...Eph 2:19
that are of Caesar's *h*.........Phil 4:22
and the *h* of Onesiphorus 2Tim 4:19

HOUSEHOLD IDOLS—*the family "gods" that were commonly viewed as protecting the home*
- Laban's stolen by Rachel .Gen 31:19-35
- Used in idolatry ....Hos 3:4

HOUSEHOLDER—*master of the house*
- Parable of ....Matt 13:27, Matt 21:33

like unto a man that is a *h* ....Matt 13:52
like unto a man that is a *h* ....Matt 20:1
certain *h* which planted ....Matt 21:33

HOUSEKEEPER—*one who takes care of the home*
- Sarah...................Gen 18:6
- Rebekah................Gen 27:6-9
- Abigail 1Sam 25:41, 42
- Happy..................Ps 113:9
- Ideal woman ....Prov 31:10-31
- Martha ....Luke 10:40, 41

HOUSETOP—*roof of a house*

[*also* HOUSETOPS]
be as the grass upon the *h* ....Ps 129:6
dwell in a corner of the *h* .....Prov 21:9
dwell in the corner of the *h* ...Prov 25:24
wholly gone up to the *h*? .....Is 22:1
upon all the *h* of Moab ....Jer 48:38
host of heaven upon the *h* ....Zeph 1:5
that preach ye upon the *h*.....Matt 10:27
Let him which is on the *h*.....Matt 24:17
let him that is on the *h* not ...Mark 13:15
they went upon the *h* ....Luke 5:19
be proclaimed upon the *h* .....Luke 12:3
which shall be upon the *h*.....Luke 17:31
Peter..upon the *h* to pray .....Acts 10:9

HOW—*See* INTRODUCTION

HOWBEIT—*nevertheless; although*
H Sisera fled away ....Judg 4:17
H the hair of his head ....Judg 16:22
H we may not give them ......Judg 21:18
h there is a kinsman nearer ...Ruth 3:12
h yet protest solemnly 1Sam 8:9
H he refused to turn aside 2Sam 2:23
H he would not hearken 2Sam 13:14
h he attained not 2Sam 23:19
h the kingdom is turned 1Kin 2:15
H I will not rend away........1Kin 11:13
H I will not take the whole ...1Kin 11:34
h the slingers went about 2Kin 3:25
H from the sins of Jeroboam ..2Kin 10:29
H the high places.............2Kin 14:4
H every nation made gods 2Kin 17:29
H there was no reckoning 2Kin 22:7
h he attained not to 1Chr 11:21
H I believed not..words 2Chr 9:6
H the high places.............2Chr 20:33
H they buried him 2Chr 21:20
h he entered not..temple 2Chr 27:2
H thou art just in all ....Neh 9:33
H he will not stretch out ......Job 30:24
H he meaneth not so ....Is 10:7
H I sent unto you all ....Jer 44:4
H this kind goeth not out .....Matt 17:21
H Jesus suffered him not ......Mark 5:19
H there came other boats .....John 6:23
H we know this man..........John 7:27
H when he, the Spirit.........John 16:13
H many of them, which heard .Acts 4:4
H as the disciples stood ....Acts 14:20
H we must be cast............Acts 27:26
H we speak wisdom 1Cor 2:6
h in the spirit he speaketh 1Cor 14:2
H that was not first which.....1Cor 15:46
H whereinsoever any is bold...2Cor 11:21
H..when ye know not God ....Gal 4:8
H for this..I obtained mercy ...1Tim 1:16
h not all that came out ....Heb 3:16

HOWL—*to make a loud, doleful sound*

[*also* HOWLED, HOWLING, HOWLINGS]
in the waste *h* wilderness......Deut 32:10
H ye, for the day of..Lord ....Is 13:6
Moab shall *h* over Nebo ......Is 15:2
the *h* thereof unto Eglaim.....Is 15:8
h thereof unto Beer-elim ......Is 15:8
h for Moab, every one..*h* .....Is 16:7
h, ye inhabitants of the isle ...Is 23:6
make them to *h* ....Is 52:5
sackcloth, lament and *h*.......Jer 4:8
a *h* of the principal ....Jer 25:36
the inhabitants..shall *h* ....Jer 47:2
h and cry; tell ye it in Arnon ..Jer 48:20
Therefore will I *h* for Moab ...Jer 48:31
H, O Heshbon for Ai..........Jer 49:3
Cry and *h*, son of man........Ezek 21:12
they *h* upon their beds ....Hos 7:14
and *h*, all ye drinkers ....Joel 1:5
h, ye ministers of the altar ....Joel 1:13
songs of the temple shall be *h* .Amos 8:3
I will wail and *h*, I will go ....Mic 1:8
H, ye inhabitants ....Zeph 1:11
H fir tree; for the cedar.......Zech 11:2
h, O ye oaks of Bashan.......Zech 11:2
the *h* of the shepherds ....Zech 11:3
weep and *h* for your miseries ..James 5:1

HOWSOEVER—*in whatever manner*
h let all thy wants lie upon me .Judg 19:20
h let me, I pray thee, also 2Sam 18:22
cut off *h* I punished them .....Zeph 3:7

HUGE—*very large*
and the Lubim a *h* host 2Chr 16:8

HUKKOK (hĭk'ŏk)—*"hewn"*
- Border town of Naphtali .Josh 19:32, 34

HUKOK (hū'kŏk)—*"ditch"*
- Land given as place of refuge 1Chr 6:75
- *See* HELKATH

HUL (hŭl)—*"circle"*
- Aram's second son ......Gen 10:23

Uz and *H* and Gether ....Gen 10:23
Aram, and Uz, and *H*..Gether .1Chr 1:17

HULDAH (hŭl'dä)—*"weasel"*
- Wife of Shallum.........2Kin 22:14
- Foretells Jerusalem's ruin .2Kin 22:15-17, 2Chr 34:22-25
- Exempts Josiah from trouble 2Kin 22:18-20

HUMAN DIGNITY

Based on:
- God's image ....Gen 1:26
- Elevated by God ....Ps 8:3-8
- Loved ....John 3:16
- Chosen ....John 15:16

HUMAN NATURE OF CHRIST

Predicted as seed of:
- Woman..................Gen 3:15
- Abraham ....Gal 3:8, 16
- David ....Luke 1:31, 32

Proved by:
- Virgin's conception ......Matt 1:18
- Birth ....Matt 1:16, 25
- Incarnation ....John 1:14
- Circumcision ....Luke 2:21
- Growth ....Luke 2:52
- Genealogy ....Matt 1:1-17

Manifested in:
- Hunger ....Matt 4:2
- Thirst ....John 19:28
- Weariness...............John 4:6
- Sleep ....Matt 8:24
- Suffering...............Luke 22:44
- Death ....John 19:30
- Burial ....Matt 27:59, 60
- Resurrection ....Luke 24:39, 1John 1:1, 2

Importance of, necessary for:
- Sinlessness ....John 8:46
- His death ....Heb 2:14, 17
- His resurrection 2Tim 2:8
- His exaltation ....Phil 2:9-11
- His priestly intercession ..Heb 7:26, 28
- His return ....Heb 9:24-28
- Faith 2John 7-11

See INCARNATION OF CHRIST

HUMAN SACRIFICE—*the practice of killing a human being in order to placate false gods*

Practiced by:
- Canaanites ....Deut 12:31
- Ammonites ....Lev 20:2, 3
- Moabites 2Kin 3:26, 27
- Phoenicians ....Jer 19:5
- Israel..................2Kin 16:3, 4
- Judah 2Chr 28:3

Sin of:
- Condemned ....Lev 18:21
- Source of defilement .....Ezek 20:31
- Source of demonism .....Ps 106:37, 38
- Cause of captivity 2Kin 17:17, 18

HUMANENESS—*compassion; sympathy; kindness*
- Toward animals ....Ex 23:5
- Not shown by Balaam ...Num 22:27-30

HUMANITARIANISM—*promoting the welfare of humanity*
- Illustrated by Jesus ......Luke 10:30-37
- Enjoined on Christians ...1Thess 5:15

HUMBLE—*modest; meek; having a proper sense of one's worth; not proud or arrogant*

[*also* HUMBLED, HUMBLEDST, HUMBLENESS, HUMBLETH, HUMBLY]
thou refuse to *h* thyself ....Ex 10:3
uncircumcised hearts be *h* .....Lev 26:41
to *h* thee, and to prove thee ..Deut 8:2
h thee, and suffered thee .....Deut 8:3
he..*h* his neighbor's wife .....Deut 22:24
h ye them, and do ....Judg 19:24
I *h* beseech thee that 2Sam 16:4
how Ahab *h* himself 1Kin 21:29
he *h* himself before me 1Kin 21:29
thou hast *h* thyself before 2Kin 22:19
of Zebulun *h* themselves 2Chr 30:11
h himself greatly before 2Chr 33:12
h not himself before the Lord .2Chr 33:23
his father had *h* himself 2Chr 33:23
thou didst *h* thyself before 2Chr 34:27
and *h* thyself before me 2Chr 34:27
and he shall save the *h* ....Job 22:29
not the cry of the *h* ....Ps 9:12
croucheth and *h* himself.......Ps 10:10
hand: forget not the *h* ....Ps 10:12
heard the desire of the *h*......Ps 10:17
the *h* shall hear thereof ....Ps 34:2
I *h* my soul with fasting ....Ps 35:13
The *h* shall see this ....Ps 69:32

Who ***h*** himself to behold ...... Ps 113:6
h thyself, and make sure ...... Prov 6:3
Better..to be of a ***h*** spirit ..... Prov 16:19
honor shall uphold the ***h*** ...... Prov 29:23
the great man ***h*** himself .... Is 2:9
The lofty looks..shall be ***h*** .... Is 2:11
the mighty man shall be ***h***..... Is 5:15
eyes of the lofty shall be ***h*** ..... Is 5:15
They are not ***h*** even unto this . Jer 44:10
remembrance, and is ***h*** in me .. Lam 3:20
they ***h*** her that was set .... Ezek 22:10
hast not ***h*** thine heart .... Dan 5:22
love mercy and to walk ***h*** ..... Mic 6:8
he that shall ***h*** himself .... Matt 23:12
he ***h*** himself, and became ..... Phil 2:8
kindness, ***h*** of mind .... Col 3:12
and giveth grace to the ***h*** 1Pet 5:5
H yourselves therefore 1Pet 5:6

HUMILIATION—*reduction to a lower state; a state of deflated pride*

Causes of:
Pride .... Esth 6:6-13
Arrogance .... Dan 4:29-33
Boastfulness 1Sam 17:42-50
National sins .... Dan 9:1-21
Self-will .... Luke 15:11-19

Remedies against:
Be humble .... Luke 14:8-11
Avoid sinners .... Judg 16:16-21
Obey God .... Josh 7:11-16
Avoid self-sufficiency .... Luke 22:31-34
Rely upon God's grace ... 2Cor 12:6-10

In his ***h*** his judgment was ..... Acts 8:33

HUMILIATION OF CHRIST—*the state that He took while on earth*

Exhibited in His:
Taking our nature .... Phil 2:7
Birth .... Matt 1:18-25
Obedience .... Luke 2:51
Submission to ordinances . Matt 3:13-15
Becoming a servant ...... Matt 20:28
Menial acts .... John 13:4-15
Suffering .... Matt 26:67, 68
Death .... John 10:15-18

Rewards of:
Exalted by God .... Acts 2:22-36
Crowned king .... Heb 1:1, 2
Perfected forever .... Heb 2:10
Acceptable high priest ... Heb 2:17

HUMILITY—*recognition of one's true position before God*

Factors involved in sense of:
One's sinfulness .... Luke 18:13, 14
One's unworthiness ..... Luke 15:17-21
One's limitations 1Kin 3:6-14
God's holiness .... Is 6:1-8
God's righteousness ...... Phil 3:4-7

Factors producing:
Affliction .... Deut 8:3
Impending doom 2Chr 12:5-12
Submissiveness .... Luke 10:39
Christ's example .... Matt 11:29

Rewards of:
Road to honor 1Kin 3:11-14
Leads to riches .... Prov 22:4
Brings blessings 2Chr 7:14, 15
Guarantees exaltation .... James 4:10
Insures God's presence ... Is 57:15
Makes truly great .... Matt 18:4
Unlocks more grace ..... Prov 3:34
James 4:6

Christians exhorted to:
Put on .... Col 3:12
Be clothed with 1Pet 5:5
Walk with .... Eph 4:1, 2
Avoid false .... Col 2:18-23

Examples of:
Abraham .... Gen 18:27, 32
Jacob .... Gen 32:16
Moses .... Ex 3:11
Joshua .... Josh 7:6
David 1Sam 18:18-23
Job .... Job 42:2-6
Jeremiah .... Jer 1:6
Daniel .... Dan 2:30
Elizabeth .... Luke 1:43
John the Baptist .... John 3:29, 30
Jesus .... Matt 11:29
Paul .... Acts 20:19

and before honor is ***h*** .... Prov 15:33
and before honor is ***h*** .... Prov 18:12

HUMTAH (hŭm'tä)—*"place of lizards"*
Town of Judah .... Josh 15:54

HUNDRED

[*also* HUNDREDFOLD, HUNDREDS, HUNDREDTH]

Cainan were nine ***h*** and ten ... Gen 5:14
Noah five ***h*** ninety and five ... Gen 5:30
ark shall be three ***h*** cubits ..... Gen 6:15
six ***h*** year of Noah's life .... Gen 7:11
afflict them four ***h*** years ...... Gen 15:13
Abraham was a ***h*** years old ... Gen 21:5
in the same year a ***h*** .... Gen 26:12
for a ***h*** pieces of money .... Gen 33:19
took six ***h*** chosen chariots ..... Ex 14:7
rulers of ***h***, rulers of fifties .... Ex 18:21
seven ***h*** and thirty shekels ..... Ex 38:24
five of you shall chase a ***h*** .... Lev 26:8
Reuben were a ***h*** thousand .... Num 2:16
Ephraim were a ***h*** thousand ... Num 2:24
camp of Dan were a ***h*** .... Num 2:31
a ***h*** and thirty shekels .... Num 7:13
fire devoured two ***h*** and fifty .. Num 26:10
children of Israel, six ***h*** .... Num 26:51
and captains over ***h*** .... Num 31:14
thousand and five ***h*** sheep ..... Num 31:43
and of the captains of ***h*** .... Num 31:52
Aaron was a ***h*** and twenty .... Num 33:39
captains over ***h*** .... Deut 1:15
slew of the Philistines six ***h*** .... Judg 3:31
and caught three ***h*** foxes ...... Judg 15:4
four ***h*** thousand footmen ...... Judg 20:2
four ***h*** young virgins, that .... Judg 21:12
and captains of ***h*** 1Sam 22:7
after David about four ***h*** men. . 1Sam 25:13
David came to the two ***h*** men . 1Sam 30:21
and a ***h*** bunches of raisins 2Sam 16:1
and captains of ***h*** over 2Sam 18:1
many soever they be, a ***h*** 2Sam 24:3
pomegranates were two ***h*** in ... 1Kin 7:20
for six ***h*** shekels of silver 1Kin 10:29
he had seven ***h*** wives 1Kin 11:3
Israel an ***h*** thousand lambs 2Kin 3:4
fetched the rulers over ***h*** 2Kin 11:4
the captains over ***h*** did 2Kin 11:10
he took the rulers over ***h*** 2Kin 11:19
of sheep two ***h*** and fifty 1Chr 5:21
spear against three ***h*** slain 1Chr 11:11
captains of thousands and ***h*** ... 1Chr 13:1
captains of thousands and ***h*** ... 1Chr 27:1
captains of thousands and of ***h*** . 1Chr 29:6
captains of thousands and of ***h*** . 2Chr 1:2
six ***h*** overseers to set 2Chr 2:18
Solomon made two ***h*** targets .. 2Chr 9:15
and three ***h*** chariots 2Chr 14:9
to the captains of ***h*** spears 2Chr 23:9
he took the captains of ***h*** 2Chr 23:20
h and thirty years old was 2Chr 24:15
brethren two ***h*** thousand 2Chr 28:8
Shephatiah, three ***h*** seventy ... Ezra 2:4
Adin, four ***h*** fifty and four .... Ezra 2:15
Harim, three ***h*** and twenty .... Ezra 2:32
Jericho, three ***h*** forty and ..... Ezra 2:34
two ***h*** singing men and .... Ezra 2:65
and to a ***h*** baths of wine ...... Ezra 7:22
silver vessels a ***h*** talents ...... Ezra 8:26
the ***h*** part of the money .... Neh 5:11
Bebai, six ***h*** twenty and .... Neh 7:16
Gaba, six ***h*** twenty and one ... Neh 7:30
Asaph, a ***h*** forty and eight .... Neh 7:44
seven ***h*** and twenty asses ..... Neh 7:69
even a ***h*** and fourscore days ... Esth 1:4
slew and destroyed five ***h*** men . Esth 9:6
Job a ***h*** and forty years ...... Job 42:16
a man beget a ***h*** children ...... Eccl 6:3
h cubits eastward and .... Ezek 40:19
measuring reed, five ***h*** reeds ... Ezek 42:16
a ***h*** and twenty princes .... Dan 6:1
some a ***h***, some sixtyfold ...... Matt 13:8
bringeth forth, some a ***h*** ...... Matt 13:23
shall receive a ***h*** .... Matt 19:29
two ***h*** pennyworth of bread .... Mark 6:37
ranks, by ***h***, and by fifties ..... Mark 6:40
receive a ***h*** now in this .... Mark 10:30
up, and bare fruit a ***h*** .... Luke 8:8
great fishes, a ***h*** and fifty ..... John 21:11
four ***h*** and thirty years after ... Gal 3:17

HUNGER, PHYSICAL

Causes of:
Fasting .... Matt 4:1-3
Fatigue .... Gen 25:30
Famine .... Luke 15:14-17
God's judgment .... Is 9:19-21

Some results of:
Selling birthright .... Gen 25:30-34
Murmuring .... Ex 16:2, 3
Breaking God's Law 1Sam 14:31-34
Cannibalism 2Kin 6:28, 29
Cursing God .... Is 8:21

Satisfaction of:
Supplied:
By friends 1Sam 17:27-29
Supernaturally .... Ex 16:4-21
Sent as a judgment ...... Ps 106:14, 15
Provided by God .... Matt 6:11
Christian duty 1Sam 30:11, 12
Complete in heaven ..... Rev 7:14-17

Examples of:
David 1Sam 21:3-6
Elijah 1Kin 17:11-13
Jeremiah .... Jer 38:9
Peter .... Acts 10:10
Paul 1Cor 4:11

Strike:
By forty men .... Acts 23:11-16

[*also* AHUNGERED, HUNGERBITTEN, HUNGRY]

in ***h***, and in thirst, and in ..... Deut 28:48
They shall be burnt with ***h*** .... Deut 32:24
they that were ***h*** ceased 1Sam 2:5
The people is ***h***, and weary ... 2Sam 17:29
They know that we be ***h*** 2Kin 7:12
from heaven for their ***h*** .... Neh 9:15
harvest the ***h*** eateth up .... Job 5:5
His strength shall be ***h*** .... Job 18:12
withholden bread from..***h*** ...... Job 22:7
take..the sheaf from the ***h***..... Job 24:10
lions do lack, and suffer ***h*** .... Ps 34:10
If I were ***h***, I would not ...... Ps 50:12
H and thirsty, their soul ...... Ps 107:5
filleth the ***h*** soul .... Ps 107:9
he maketh the ***h*** to dwell ..... Ps 107:36
which giveth food to the ***h*** .... Ps 146:7
to satisfy..when he is ***h*** .... Prov 6:30
an idle soul shall suffer ***h*** ..... Prov 19:15
If thine enemy be ***h*** .... Prov 25:21
to the ***h*** soul every bitter ...... Prov 27:7
when a ***h*** man dreameth ...... Is 29:8
make empty..soul of the ***h*** .... Is 32:6
he is ***h***, and his strength ...... Is 44:12
They shall not ***h*** nor thirst .... Is 49:10
to deal thy bread to the ***h***..... Is 58:7
draw out thy soul to the ***h*** .... Is 58:10
eat, but ye shall be ***h*** .... Is 65:13
given his bread to the ***h*** .... Ezek 18:7
no more consumed with ***h***..... Ezek 34:29
his disciples were a ***h*** .... Matt 12:1
returned into the city, he ***h***.... Matt 21:18
I was ***a*** and ye gave me .... Matt 25:35
For I was a ***h***, and ye gave .... Matt 25:42
he had need, and was a ***h***..... Mark 2:25
hath filled the ***h*** with good .... Luke 1:53
were ended, he afterward ***h*** .. Luke 4:2
David did, when..a ***h*** .... Luke 6:3
Blessed are ye that ***h*** now ..... Luke 6:21
are full! for ye shall ***h*** .... Luke 6:25
to spare..I perish with ***h*** ...... Luke 15:17
if thine enemy ***h***, feed .... Rom 12:20

H

one is *h*, and another is 1Cor 11:21
if any man *h*, let him eat 1Cor 11:34
often, in *h* and thirst 2Cor 11:27
both to be full and to be *h*....Phil 4:12
kill with sword, and with *h*....Rev 6:8

HUNGER, SPIRITUAL—*desire to know God*
More important than physical...............Deut 8:3
Sent as a judgment ......Amos 4:11-13
Will be satisfied ....Is 55:1, 2
Blessing of ....Matt 5:6
Satisfied by Christ ....John 6:33-35

HUNT—*to pursue with intent to capture*

[*also* HUNTED, HUNTEST, HUNTETH, HUNTING]
h and catcheth any beast ......Lev 17:13
thou *h* my soul to take it 1Sam 24:11
h a partridge 1Sam 26:20
Thou *h* me as a fierce lion ....Job 10:16
Wilt thou *h* the prey ....Job 38:39
evil shall *h* the violent ....Ps 140:11
will *h* for the precious ....Prov 6:26
roasteth not..took in *h* ....Prov 12:27
will I send for many *h* ....Jer 16:16
h them from every mountain ..Jer 16:16
They *h* our steps, that we .....Lam 4:18
every stature to *h* souls ....Ezek 13:18
ye there *h* the souls to ....Ezek 13:20
souls that ye *h* to make ....Ezek 13:20
in your hand to be *h* ....Ezek 13:21
h every man his brother ......Mic 7:2

HUNTER—*one who hunts game*

Purposes of:
Kill harmful beasts 1Sam 17:34-36

Methods of:
Decoys ....Job 18:10
Nets ....Amos 3:5
Pits 2Sam 23:20
Bows and quiver ....Gen 27:3
Sword, etc. ....Job 41:26-30

Examples of:
Nimrod ....Gen 10:8, 9
Ishmael ....Gen 21:20
Esau ....Gen 27:3, 5, 30

[*also* HUNTERS]
Esau was a cunning *h*........Gen 25:27
roe from the hand of the *h*....Prov 6:5

HUPHAM (hū'făm)—*"coast-inhabitant; protected"*
Son of Benjamin; founder of Huphamites ....Num 26:39
Called Huppim ....Gen 46:21

HUPPAH (hŭp'ä)—*"protection"*
Descendant of Aaron 1Chr 24:1, 13

HUPPIM (hŭp'ĭm)—*"coast-inhabitant; protection"*
1. Son of Benjamin ....Gen 46:21
2. Son of Ir 1Chr 7:12

See Hupham

took to wife the sister of *H* ...1Chr 7:12

HUR (hûr)—*"free; noble"*
1. Man of Judah; of Caleb's house 1Chr 2:18-20
   Grandfather of Bezaleel .Ex 31:1, 2
   Supports Moses' hands ..Ex 17:10-12
   Aids Aaron ....Ex 24:14
2. King of Midian ....Josh 13:21
3. Father of Rephaiah .....Neh 3:9

son of Uri, the son of *H* ......Ex 35:30
son of Uri, the son of *H* ......Ex 38:22
H, and Reba, five kings.......Num 31:8
Zur, and *H*, and Reba ....Josh 13:21
The son of *H*, in..Ephraim 1Kin 4:8
sons of Caleb the son of *H*....1Chr 2:50
Carmi, and *H*, and Shobal 1Chr 4:1
sons of *H*, the firstborn of 1Chr 4:4
son of Uri, the son of *H* 2Chr 1:5

HURAI (hū'rā-ī)—*"mighty; chief"*
One of David's mighty men 1Chr 11:32

See Hiddai

HURAM (hū'răm)—*same as Hiram*
1. Son of Bela 1Chr 8:5
2. King of Tyre 2Chr 2:11

See Hiram 1

Solomon sent to *H* the king ...2Chr 2:3
H said moreover, Blessed 2Chr 2:12
understanding, of *H* 2Chr 2:13
H made the pots, and the 2Chr 4:11
H finished the work that 2Chr 4:11
cities which *H* had restored....2Chr 8:2
And the servants also of *H*....2Chr 9:10

HURI (hū'rī)—*"linen weaver"*
Gadite 1Chr 5:14

HURL—*to throw forcefully*

[*also* HURLETH, HURLING]
h at him by laying of wait.....Num 35:20
in *h* stones and shooting 1Chr 12:2
as a storm *h* him out ....Job 27:21

HURT—*to inflict pain; suffer pain*

[*also* HURTFUL, HURTING]
suffered him not to *h* me .....Gen 31:7
and *h* a woman with child.....Ex 21:22
or be *h*, or driven away ....Ex 22:10
he will turn and do you *h*.....Josh 24:20
peace to thee, and no *h*.......1Sam 20:21
were with us, we *h* them not ..1Sam 25:7
kept me back from *h* thee.....1Sam 25:34
against thee to do thee *h*......2Sam 18:32
shouldest..meddle to thy *h* 2Kin 14:10
shouldest..meddle to thine *h*...2Chr 25:19
rebellious city, and *h* unto ....Ezra 4:15
grow to the *h* of the kings? ...Ezra 4:22
on such as sought their *h* .....Esth 9:2
wickedness may *h* a man......Job 35:8
sweareth to his own *h* ....Ps 15:4
that rejoice at mine *h*.........Ps 35:26
against me do..devise my *h*....Ps 41:7
confusion, that desire my *h*....Ps 70:2
dishonor that seek my *h* ......Ps 71:13
feet they *h* with fetters........Ps 105:18
servant from the *h* sword .....Ps 144:10
owners thereof to their *h*......Eccl 5:13
another to his own *h* ....Eccl 8:9
removeth stones shall be *h* ....Eccl 10:9
shall not *h* nor destroy in .....Is 11:9
lest any *h* it, I will keep ......Is 27:3
shall not *h* nor destroy in .....Is 65:25
healed..*h* of the daughter .....Jer 6:14
healed..*h* of the daughter .....Jer 8:11
the *h* of the daughter of ......Jer 8:21
of my people am I *h*..........Jer 8:21
Woe is me for my *h* ....Jer 10:19
kingdoms..for their *h* ....Jer 24:9
and I will do you no *h*........Jer 25:6
your hands to your own *h*.....Jer 25:7
of this people, but the *h* ......Jer 38:4
fire, and they have no *h* ......Dan 3:25
that they have not *h* me ......Dan 6:22
O king, have I done no *h*.....Dan 6:22
deadly..shall not *h* them ......Mark 16:18
out of him, and *h* him not ....Luke 4:35
nothing shall..*h* you ....Luke 10:19
no man shall..to *h* thee ....Acts 18:10
with *h* and much damage .....Acts 27:10
many foolish and *h* lusts 1Tim 6:9
not be *h* of the second death ..Rev 2:11
see thou *h* not the oil and.....Rev 6:6
it was given to *h* the earth ....Rev 7:2
not *h* the grass of the earth ...Rev 9:4
and with them they do *h*......Rev 9:19
any man will *h* them, fire .....Rev 11:5
if any man will *h* them........Rev 11:5

HUSBAND—*a married man*

Regulations concerning:
One flesh ....Matt 19:5, 6
Until death ....Rom 7:2, 3
Rights of 1Cor 7:1-5
Sanctified by wife 1Cor 7:14-16

Duties of, toward wife:
Love ....Eph 5:25-33
Live with for life ....Matt 19:3-9
Be faithful to ....Mal 2:14, 15
Be satisfied with........Prov 5:18, 19
Instruct 1Cor 14:34, 35
Honor 1Pet 3:7
Confer with ....Gen 31:4-16
Provide for 1Tim 5:8
Rule over ....Gen 3:16

Kinds of:
Adam, blaming..........Gen 3:9-12
Isaac, loving ....Gen 24:67
Elkanah, sympathetic 1Sam 1:8-23
Nabal, evil 1Sam 25:3
Ahab, weak.............1Kin 21:5-16
David, ridiculed 2Sam 6:20
Job, strong..............Job 2:7-10

[*also* HUSBAND'S, HUSBANDS]
gave her to her *h* Abram .....Gen 16:3
therefore my *h* will love me ...Gen 29:32
my *h* be joined unto me ......Gen 29:34
given my maiden to my *h* .....Gen 30:18
Surely a bloody *h* art thou ....Ex 4:25
as the woman's *h* will lay .....Ex 21:22
betrothed to a *h*..............Lev 19:20
which hath had no *h*..........Lev 21:3
woman put away from her *h* ..Lev 21:7
hid from the eyes of her *h* ....Num 5:13
another instead of thy *h* ......Num 5:19
another, instead of thy *h* ......Num 5:20
with thee beside thine *h* ......Num 5:20
trespass against her *h* ....Num 5:27
to another instead of her *h*....Num 5:29
a *h*, when she vowed ....Num 30:6
her *h* heard it, and held.......Num 30:7
if her *h* disallowed her ....Num 30:8
vowed in her *h* house ....Num 30:10
her *h* heard it, and held.......Num 30:11
if her *h* hath utterly made.....Num 30:12
her *h* hath made them void ...Num 30:12
her *h* may establish ....Num 30:13
her *h* may make it void ....Num 30:13
h altogether hold his peace ....Num 30:14
be her *h*, and she shall be.....Deut 21:13
a woman married to a *h* ......Deut 22:22
be betrothed unto a *h* ....Deut 22:23
if the latter *h* hate her ....Deut 24:3
if the latter *h* die, which .....Deut 24:3
former *h*..sent her away.......Deut 24:4
her *h* brother shall go in ......Deut 25:5
the duty of a *h* brother ....Deut 25:5
My *h* brother refuseth to......Deut 25:7
the duty of my *h* brother......Deut 25:7
to deliver her *h* out of the ....Deut 25:11
be evil toward the *h* of her....Deut 28:56
came and told her *h* ....Judg 13:6
but Manoah her *h* was not ....Judg 13:9
ran, and showed her *h* ....Judg 13:10
Entice thy *h*, that he may .....Judg 14:15
And her *h* arose, and went....Judg 19:3
Levite, the *h* of the woman ...Judg 20:4
Elimelech Naomi's *h* died .....Ruth 1:3
of her two sons and her *h*.....Ruth 1:5
each..in the house of her *h*....Ruth 1:9
that they may be your *h*? .....Ruth 1:11
I am too old to have a *h*......Ruth 1:12
I should have a *h* also ....Ruth 1:12
stay..them from having *h*?.....Ruth 1:13
kinsman of her *h*, a mighty....Ruth 2:1
since the death of thine *h* .....Ruth 2:11
she came up with her *h* 1Sam 2:19
father-in-law and her *h*........1Sam 4:19
father-in-law and her *h*........1Sam 4:21
she told not her *h* Nabal 1Sam 25:19
and took her from her *h* 2Sam 3:15
her *h* went with her along 2Sam 3:16
Uriah her *h* was dead 2Sam 11:26
she mourned for her *h* 2Sam 11:26
and mine *h* is dead 2Sam 14:5
shall not leave to my *h* 2Sam 14:7

Thy servant my *h* is dead 2Kin 4:1
she said unto her *h*, Behold ...2Kin 4:9
no child, and her *h* is old 2Kin 4:14
And she called unto her *h* 2Kin 4:22
is it well with thy *h*? 2Kin 4:26
they shall despise their *h* ......Esth 1:17
wives..to their *h* honor ....Esth 1:20
woman is a crown to her *h* .....Prov 12:4
heart of her *h* doth..trust .....Prov 31:11
Her *h* is known in the gates ...Prov 31:23
her *h* also..praiseth her ....Prov 31:28
For thy Maker is thine *h* ......Is 54:5
departeth from her *h* ....Jer 3:20
h with the wife shall be ....Jer 6:11
give your daughters to *h* ......Jer 29:6
I was a *h* unto them ....Jer 31:32
strangers instead of her *h* .....Ezek 16:32
that loathed her *h* and her ....Ezek 16:45
loathed their *h* and..children ..Ezek 16:45
sister that hath had no *h* ......Ezek 44:25
neither am I her *h*............Hos 2:2
I will..return to my first *h* .....Hos 2:7
sackcloth for the *h* of her .....Joel 1:8
Joseph the *h* of Mary, of......Matt 1:16
Then Joseph her *h*, being a ...Matt 1:19
shall put away her *h* ....Mark 10:12
lived with a *h* seven years .....Luke 2:36
is put away from her *h*........Luke 16:18
Go, call thy *h*, and come .....John 4:16
said, I have no *h* ....John 4:17
hast well said, I have no *h* ....John 4:17
For thou hast had five *h* ......John 4:18
thou now hast is not thy *h* ....John 4:18
which have buried thy *h* are ...Acts 5:9
buried her by her *h*..........Acts 5:10
the wife depart from her *h* 1Cor 7:10
or be reconciled to her *h*.....1Cor 7:11
not the *h* put away his wife ...1Cor 7:11
a *h* that believeth not 1Cor 7:13
how she may please her *h* 1Cor 7:34
as long as her *h* liveth 1Cor 7:39
if her *h* be dead, she is 1Cor 7:39
espoused you to one *h* 2Cor 11:2
than she which hath a *h*.......Gal 4:27
submit..unto your own *h* ......Eph 5:22
For the *h* is the head ....Eph 5:23
own *h* in every thing..........Eph 5:24
H, love your wives, even .....Eph 5:25
submit..unto your own *h* ......Col 3:18
H, love your wives, and be ....Col 3:19
the *h* of one wife, vigilant 1Tim 3:2
deacons be the *h* of one wife ..1Tim 3:12
the *h* of one wife, having .....Titus 1:6
love their *h*, to love their .....Titus 2:4
obedient to their own *h* ....Titus 2:5
wives, in subjection to..*h*......1Pet 3:1
subjection unto their own *h* ...1Pet 3:5
a bride adorned for her *h* .....Rev 21:2

HUSBANDMAN—*a tiller of the soil*
Farmer ....Gen 9:20; 2Kin 25:12
Tenant farmer...........Matt 21:33-42
Takes share of crops 2Tim 2:6

[*also* HUSBANDMEN]
Noah began to be a *h* ....Gen 9:20
to be vine dressers and *h* 2Kin 25:12
h also, and vine dressers 2Chr 26:10
h, and they..with flocks ....Jer 31:24
I break in pieces the *h*........Jer 51:23
for vinedressers and for *h* .....Jer 52:16
Be ye ashamed, O ye *h* ....Joel 1:11
call the *h* to mourning ....Amos 5:16
I am no prophet, I am a *h* ...Zech 13:5
let it out to *h*, and went ......Mark 12:1
he sent to the *h* a servant .....Mark 12:2
receive from the *h* of the .....Mark 12:2
h said among themselves ......Mark 12:7
will come and destroy the *h* ...Mark 12:9
and let it forth to *h*..........Luke 20:9
sent a servant to the *h* ....Luke 20:10
h beat him, and sent him .....Luke 20:10
when the *h* saw him, they .....Luke 20:14
come and destroy these *h* .....Luke 20:16
the *h* waiteth for..fruit ....James 5:7

HUSBANDRY—*the control or use of resources*
in Carmel: for he loved *h* 2Chr 26:10
with God: ye are God's *h* 1Cor 3:9

HUSHAH (hū'shä)—*"haste"*
Judahite 1Chr 4:4

HUSHAI (hū'shī)—*"quick"*
Archite; David's friend...2Sam 15:32-37
Feigns sympathy with Absalom...............2Sam 16:16-19
Defeats Ahithophel's advice 2Sam 17:5-23

the son of *H* was in Asher 1Kin 4:16
H the Archite was the king's ..1Chr 27:33

HUSHAM (hū'shăm)—*"hasting; alert"*
Temanite king of Edom ..Gen 36:34,35

H..of the Temanites 1Chr 1:45
when *H* was dead, Hadad 1Chr 1:46

HUSHATHITE (hū'shăth-īt)
Inhabitant of Hushah 2Sam 21:18

Mebunnai the *H*..............2Sam 23:27
Sibbecai the *H*, Ilai the 1Chr 11:29
time Sibbechai the *H* slew 1Chr 20:4
month was Sibbecai the *H*.....1Chr 27:11

HUSHIM (hū'shĭm)—*"hasting; hasters"*
1. Head of a Danite family .Gen 46:23
   Called Shuham ....Num 26:42
2. Sons of Aher 1Chr 7:12
3. Wife of Shaharaim 1Chr 8:8, 11

HUSKS—*outer coverings of seeds or fruits; the pods of the carob or locust tree*
Fed to swine ....Luke 15:15,16

[*also* HUSK]
kernels even to the *h* ....Num 6:4
ears of corn in the *h*..........2Kin 4:42

HUZ (hŭz)—*"firm"*
H his firstborn, and Buz ......Gen 22:21

HUZZAB (hŭz'ăb)—*meaning uncertain*
May refer to Assyrian queen or to Nineveh; or may be rendered "it is decreed" ....Nah 2:7

HYMENAEUS (hī-mĕ-nē'ŭs)—*"nuptial"*
False teacher excommunicated by Paul 1Tim 1:19, 20
Teaches error 2Tim 2:17, 18

HYMN—*a spiritual song*

Occasions producing:
Great deliverance ....Ex 15:1-19
Great victory............Judg 5:1-31
Prayer answered.........1Sam 2:1-10
Mary's "Magnificat" .....Luke 1:46-55
Father's ecstasy ....Luke 1:68-79
Angel's delight ....Luke 2:14
Old man's faith ....Luke 2:29-32
Heaven's eternal praise ..Rev 5:9-14

Purposes of:
Worship God 2Chr 23:18
Express joy ....Matt 26:30
Edify 1Cor 14:15
Testify to others.........Acts 16:25

[*also* HYMNS]
sung a *h*, they went out ....Mark 14:26
psalms and *h* and spiritual.....Eph 5:19
psalms and *h* and spiritual.....Col 3:16

HYPOCRISY—*empty display of religion; pretending to be what one is not or believe what one does not*

Kinds of:
Worldly ....Matt 23:5-7
Legalistic ....Rom 10:3
Evangelical 2Pet 2:10-22
Satanic 2Cor 11:13-15

Described as:
Self-righteous ....Luke 18:11,12
"Holier than thou" ......Is 65:5
Blind ....Matt 23:17-26
Covetous 2Pet 2:3
Showy ....Matt 6:2,5,16
Highly critical ....Matt 7:3-5
Indignant ....Luke 13:14-16
Bound by traditions .....Matt 15:1-9
Neglectful of major duties ....Matt 23:23,24
Pretended but unpracticed ....Ezek 33:31,32
Interested in the externals..............Luke 20:46,47
Fond of titles ....Matt 23:6, 7
Inwardly unregenerate ...Luke 11:39

Examples of:
Jacob..................Gen 27:6-35
Jacob's sins ....Gen 37:29-35
Delilah ....Judg 16:4-20
Ishmael................Jer 41:6, 7
Herod ....Matt 2:7, 8
Pharisees ....John 8:4-9
Judas..................Matt 26:25-49
Ananias ....Acts 5:1-10
Peter ....Gal 2:11-14

[*also* HYPOCRISIES, HYPOCRITICAL]
With *h* mockers in feasts ......Ps 35:16
him against a *h* nation ....Is 10:6
iniquity, to practice *h*, ...Is 32:6
within ye are full of *h* and ....Matt 23:28
leaven..which is *h* ....Luke 12:1
Speaking lies in *h* 1Tim 4:2
partiality, and without *h* ......James 3:17
guile, and *h*, and envies........1Pet 2:1

HYPOCRITE—*one who affects virtues or qualities he does not have*

[*also* HYPOCRITE'S, HYPOCRITES]
the *h* hope shall perish........Job 8:13
a *h* shall not come before .....Job 13:16
the congregation of *h* shall ....Job 15:34
stir up himself against the *h* ...Job 17:8
the joy of the *h* but for a .....Job 20:5
what is the hope of the *h* .....Job 27:8
That the *h* reign not ....Job 34:30
But the *h* in heart heap up ....Job 36:13
A *h* with this mouth ....Prov 11:9
for every one is a *h* ....Is 9:17
hath surprised the *h* ....Is 33:14
O ye *h*, ye can discern ....Matt 16:3
Why tempt ye me, ye *h*? ......Matt 22:18
scribes and Pharisees, *h*! ......Matt 23:13
scribes and Pharisees, *h*! ......Matt 23:14
scribes and Pharisees, *h*! ......Matt 23:29
Isaiah prophesied of you *h* ....Mark 7:6
Thou *h*, cast out..beam ....Luke 6:42
scribes and Pharisees, *h*! ......Luke 11:44
Ye *h*, ye can discern..........Luke 12:56

HYSSOP—*plant used for purification by the Hebrews*
Grows from walls........1Kin 4:33
Used in sprinking blood ..Ex 12:22
Used to offer Jesus vinegar ....John 19:28,29
Typical of spiritual cleansing..............Ps 51:7

wood, and scarlet, and *h* ......Lev 14:4
and the scarlet, and the *h* .....Lev 14:6
wood, and scarlet, and *h* ......Lev 14:49
the cedar wood, and the *h* ....Lev 14:51
cedar wood, and with the *h* ...Lev 14:52
cedar wood, and *h* ....Num 19:6
a clean person shall take *h* ....Num 19:18
scarlet wool, and *h*, and ......Heb 9:19

I

I—*See* INTRODUCTION

I AM—*a title indicating self-existence; applied to God*
Revealed to Moses ......Ex 3:14
Said by Christ...........John 8:57, 58

Christ expressing, refers to:
Bread of Life ....John 6:35,41, 48,51

Light of the world ....John 8:12
John 9:5
Door of the sheep ....John 10:7, 9
Good Shepherd ....John 10:11, 14
Resurrection and the Life. John 11:25
True and living Way .....John 14:6
True Vine ....John 15:1, 5

IBHAR (ĭb'här)—*"chooser; Jehovah chooses"—one of David's sons*
I also, and Elishua 2Sam 5:15
I also, and Elishama 1Chr 3:6
And *I*, and Elishua 1Chr 14:5

IBLEAM (ĭb'lē-ăm)—*"ancient people"*
City assigned to Manasseh ....Josh 17:11, 12
Canaanites remain in ....Judg 1:27
Called Bileam 1Chr 6:70
Ahaziah slain near 2Kin 9:27

IBNEIAH (ĭb-nē'yä)—*"Jehovah builds up"*
Head of a Benjamite family 1Chr 9:8

IBNIJAH (ĭb-nī'jä)—*"Jehovah builds up"*
Father of Reuel 1Chr 9:8

IBRI (ib'rī)—*"one who passes over; a Hebrew"*
Son of Jaaziah 1Chr 24:27

IBSAM—*See* JIBSAM

IBZAN (ĭb'zăn)—*"famous; splendid"*
Judge of Israel ....Judg 12:8
Father of 60 children ....Judg 12:8, 9

died *I*, and was buried ....Judg 12:10

ICE—*frozen water*

Figurative of:
God casts forth..........Ps 147:17
By reason of ....Job 6:16

whose womb came the *i* ? .....Job 38:29

ICHABOD (ĭk'ä-bŏd)—*"inglorious"*
Son of Phinehas 1Sam 4:19-22

[*also* ICHABOD'S]
Ahitub, *I* brother.............1Sam 14:3

ICONIUM (ī-cō'nĭ-ŭm)—*"coming"*
City of Asia Minor; visited by Paul ....Acts 13:51
Many converts in ....Acts 14:1-6
Paul visits again ....Acts 14:21
Timothy's ministry ....Acts 16:1, 2
Paul persecuted 2Tim 3:11

Jews from Antioch and *I* ......Acts 14:19

ICONOCLAST—*a breaker of images*
Moses, an angry ....Ex 32:19, 20
Gideon, an inspired .....Judg 6:25-32
Jehu, a subtle 2Kin 10:18-31
Josiah, a reforming 2Kin 23:12-25

IDALAH (ĭd'ä-lä)—*"land of slander"*
Border town of Zebulun. .Josh 19:15

IDBASH (ĭd'băsh)—*"honey-sweet"*
Man of Judah 1Chr 4:3

IDDO (ĭd'ō)—*"beloved"*
1. Chief officer under David 1Chr 27:21
2. Father of Abinadab 1Kin 4:14
3. Leader of Jews at Casiphia ....Ezra 8:17-20
4. Gershonite Levite 1Chr 6:20, 21
Called Adaiah 1Chr 6:41
5. Seer whose writings are cited 2Chr 9:29
6. Grandfather of Zechariah the prophet ....Zech 1:1, 7
7. Postexilic priest ....Neh 12:4, 16

and of *I* the seer 2Chr 12:15
the story of the prophet *I* 2Chr 13:22
and Zechariah the son of *I* ....Ezra 5:1
and Zechariah the son of *I* ....Ezra 6:14
the son of *I* the prophet ....Zech 1:7

IDENTIFICATION—*something used to prove who a person is*

Among men:
At birth ....Gen 25:22-26
By the life ....Luke 6:43-45
By speech ....Judg 12:6
By a search 2Kin 10:23
By a kiss ....Matt 26:48, 49

Of Christ the Messiah, by:
A divine sign ....John 1:31-34
A divine voice ....Matt 17:5
Divine works............Matt 11:2-6
Human testimony ....John 3:26-36
Scriptures ....John 5:39-47

Of spiritual things:
New birth...............2Cor 5:17
Apostates ....Matt 7:22, 23
Antichrist 2Thess 2:1-12
Believers and unbelievers .Matt 25:31-46

IDENTIFYING WITH CHRIST

Proper time, when tempted:
To harm ....Prov 1:10-19
To violate convictions ....Dan 1:8
To conform to world ....Rom 12:2
To rebellion ....Rom 13:1-5
To learn evil ....Rom 16:19
Prov 19:27
With improper associations 2Cor 6:14-17

Results:
Hatred ....John 17:14
Separation ....Luke 6:22, 23
Suffering................1Pet 2:20, 21
Witness 1Pet 3:15
Good conscience 1Pet 3:16

Basis:
Future glory ....Rom 8:18
Life of Christ ....Gal 2:20
Reward 2Tim 2:12

IDLENESS—*inactivity; slothfulness*

Consequences of:
Poverty ....Prov 20:13
Begging ....Prov 20:4
Hunger ....Prov 19:15
Bondage ....Prov 12:24
Ruin ....Prov 24:30-34

Admonitions against, consider:
Ant ....Prov 6:6-11
Ideal woman ....Prov 31:10-31
Lord ....John 9:4
Apostles 2Thess 3:7-9
Judgment 1Cor 3:8-15

See LAZINESS; SLOTHFULNESS

[*also* IDLE]
for they be *i* ....Ex 5:8
Ye are *i*, ye are *i*..............Ex 5:17
through *i* of the hands ....Eccl 10:18
abundance of *i* was in..........Ezek 16:49
That every *i* word that men ...Matt 12:36
and saw others standing *i* .....Matt 20:3
found others standing *i*........Matt 20:6
Why stand ye..all the day *i*?...Matt 20:6
words seemed..as *i* tales ......Luke 24:11
withal they learn to be *i* 1Tim 5:13
not only *i*, but tattlers 1Tim 5:13

IDOL—*symbol or object of worship; false god*

Described as:
Irrational ....Acts 17:29
Degrading ....Rom 1:22, 23
Demonical 1Cor 10:20, 21
Defiling 2Cor 6:15-18
Enslaving ....Gal 4:8, 9
Abominable.............1Pet 4:3

Brief history of:
Begins in man's apostasy .Rom 1:21-25
Prevails in Ur ....Josh 24:2, 14
In Laban's household ....Gen 31:19-35
Judgments on Egyptian ..Num 33:4
Brought from Egypt by Israel..................Josh 24:14
Forbidden in Law at Sinai ....Ex 20:1-5
Warnings against, at Sinai. Ex 34:13-16
Israel yields to, at Sinai ..Ex 32:1-8
Moabites entice Israel to..Num 25:1-18
Early zeal against........Josh 22:10-34
Gideon destroys ....Judg 6:25-32
Gideon becomes an occasion of ....Judg 8:24-27
Enticements to Baalism ..Judg 10:6-16
Levite corrupted by......Judg 17:1-13
Danites establish, at Shiloh ....Judg 18:30, 31
Overthrow of Philistines. .1Sam 5:1-12
Revival against, under Samuel 1Sam 7:3-6
Solomon yields to 1Kin 11:1-8
Jeroboam establishes in Jerusalem 1Kin 12:26-33; 2Chr 11:15
Rehoboam tolerates in Judah 1Kin 14:22-24
Conflict—Elijah and Ahab 1Kin 18:1-46
Wicked kings of Israel ...1Kin 21:25, 26
2Kin 16:3
Prophet denounces in Israel..................Hos 4:12-19
Cause of Israel's exile....2Kin 17:5-23
Judah follows Israel's example 2Chr 28:1-4
Manasseh climaxes Judah's apostasy in ..2Kin 21:1-18; 2Chr 33:1-11
Reformation against, under Asa 2Chr 14:3-5
Under Hezekiah.........2Chr 29:15-19
Under Josiah 2Kin 23:1-20
Prophets denounce in Judah ....Jer 16:11-21
Cause of Judah's exile ...2Kin 23:26, 27

Christians warned against:
No company with........1Cor 5:11
Flee from 1Cor 10:14
No fellowship with 1Cor 10:19, 20
Keep from 1John 5:21
Testify against ....Acts 14:15
Turn from 1Thess 1:9

Enticements to, due to:
Heathen background .....Josh 24:2
Ezek 16:44, 45
Contact with idolaters....Num 25:1-6
Intermarriage 1Kin 11:1-13
Imagined good ....Jer 44:15-19
Corrupt heart ....Rom 1:21-23

Removed through:
Punishment ....Deut 17:2-5
Display of powerlessness .1Sam 5:1-5
1Kin 18:25-29
Logic ....Is 44:6-20
Display of God's power ..2Kin 19:10-37
Denunciation............Mic 1:5-7
Exile ....Zeph 1:4-6
Hos 8:5-14
New birth...............Amos 5:26, 27
Hos 14:1-9

[*also* IDOL'S, IDOLS]
turn ye not unto *i* ....Lev 19:4
Ye shall make you no *i* ....Lev 26:1
their *i*, wood and stone ....Deut 29:17
stubbornness is as..*i* 1Sam 15:23
in the house of their *i* 1Sam 31:9
removed all the *i* that his 1Kin 15:12
she had made an *i*............1Kin 15:13
Asa destroyed her *i*...........1Kin 15:13
For they served *i* 2Kin 17:12
served the *i* that his father 2Kin 21:21
carry tidings unto their *i* 1Chr 10:9
put away the abominable *i* 2Chr 15:8
because she had made an *i* 2Chr 15:16
Asa cut down her *i* 2Chr 15:16
the *i* which he had made 2Chr 33:7
i out of the house of the Lord .2Chr 33:15
cut down all the *i* 2Chr 34:7

gods of the nations are *i* ...... Ps 96:5
And they served their *i* .... Ps 106:36
Their *i* are silver and gold ..... Ps 115:4
The *i* of the heathen .... Ps 135:15
Their land also is full of *i* ..... Is 2:8
unto Samaria and her *i* .... Is 10:11
do to Jerusalem and her *i*? .... Is 10:11
they shall seek to the *i* .... Is 19:3
man shall cast away his *i* ...... Is 31:7
and his *i* of gold .... Is 31:7
i were upon the beasts .... Is 46:1
Mine *i* hath done them .... Is 48:5
as if he blessed an *i* .... Is 66:3
a despised broken *i*? .... Jer 22:28
her *i* are confounded .... Jer 50:2
slain men before your *i* .... Ezek 6:4
your *i* may be broken .... Ezek 6:6
shall be among their *i* .... Ezek 6:13
sweet savor to all their *i* ...... Ezek 6:13
men have set up their *i* .... Ezek 14:3
setteth up his *i* in his heart .... Ezek 14:4
to the multitude of his *i* .... Ezek 14:4
turn yourselves from your *i* .... Ezek 14:6
with all the *i* of thy .... Ezek 16:36
lifted up his eyes to the *i* ..... Ezek 18:12
not yourselves with the *i* of ... Ezek 20:7
heart went after their *i* .... Ezek 20:16
were after their fathers' *i* ...... Ezek 20:24
serve ye every one his *i* .... Ezek 20:39
and with your *i* .... Ezek 20:39
defiled thyself in thine *i* .... Ezek 22:4
polluted with their *i* .... Ezek 23:30
slain..children to their *i* .... Ezek 23:39
I will also destroy the *i* .... Ezek 30:13
and for their *i* .... Ezek 36:18
any more with their *i* .... Ezek 37:23
unto them before their *i* ...... Ezek 44:12
Ephraim is joined to *i* .... Hos 4:17
i according to their own .... Hos 13:2
to make dumb *i*? .... Hab 2:18
the *i* have spoken vanity ...... Zech 10:2
Woe to the *i* shepherd that .... Zech 11:17
offered sacrifice unto the *i* .... Acts 7:41
abstain from pollutions of *i* .... Acts 15:20
abstain from meats offered to *i* . Acts 15:29
the city wholly given to *i* ...... Acts 17:16
from things offered to *i* .... Acts 21:25
thou that abhorrest *i* .... Rom 2:22
things offered to *i* 1Cor 8:1
offered in sacrifice unto *i* 1Cor 8:4
we know that an *i* is 1Cor 8:4
with conscience of the *i* 1Cor 8:7
as a thing offered unto an *i* ... 1Cor 8:7
sit at meat in the *i* temple 1Cor 8:10
things..are offered to *i* 1Cor 8:10
that the *i* is anything 1Cor 10:19
offered in sacrifice unto *i* 1Cor 10:28
i witchcraft, hatred .... Gal 5:20
covetousness, which is *i* .... Col 3:5
eat things sacrificed unto *i* .... Rev 2:14
eat things sacrificed unto *i* .... Rev 2:20
i of gold, and silver .... Rev 9:20

IDOL MAKERS—*those who make idols*
Maacah 1Kin 15:13
Foreign peoples .... Is 45:16
Men of Judah .... Is 2:20
People of Jerusalem ..... Ezek 22:3

IDOL MAKING—*creating idols*
Described by Isaiah ...... Is 44:9-18

IDOLATER—*one who worships idols*

[*also* IDOLATERS]
or extortioners, or with *i* 1Cor 5:10
neither fornicators, nor *i* 1Cor 6:9
Neither be *i*, as were some 1Cor 10:7
covetous man, who is an *i* .... Eph 5:5
i and all liars, shall have ...... Rev 21:8
and murderers, and *i*, and ..... Rev 22:15

IDOLATRY—*the worship of idols*

[*also* IDOLATROUS]
he put down the *i* priests 2Kin 23:5
beloved, flee from *i* 1Cor 10:14

IDUMEA (ĭd-ū-mē'ä)—*"red"*
Name used by Greek and Romans to designate Edom .... Mark 3:8
See EDOM

it shall come down upon *I* .... Is 34:5
O Mount Seir, and all *I* .... Ezek 35:15

IF—*See* INTRODUCTION

IGAL (ī'găl)—*"Jehovah redeems"*
1. Issachar's spy .... Num 13:2, 7
2. One of David's mighty men 2Sam 23:36
3. Shemaiah's son 1Chr 3:22

IGDALIAH (ĭg-dä-lī'ä)—*"Jehovah is great"*
Father of Hanan the prophet .... Jer 35:4

IGEAL (ī'gĕ-ăl)—*"Jehovah redeems"—same as Igal*
Hattush, and *I* and Bariah 1Chr 3:22

IGNOMINY—*humiliation and disgrace*
and with *i* reproach .... Prov 18:3

IGNORANCE—*lack of knowledge*

Kinds of:
Pardonable .... Luke 23:34
Pretended .... Luke 22:57-60
Innocent .... Acts 19:2-5
Excusable .... Acts 17:30
Judicial .... Rom 1:28
Guilty .... Rom 1:19-25
Partial 1Cor 13:12
Confident .... Heb 11:8

Causes of:
Unregeneracy .... Eph 4:18
Unbelief 1Tim 1:13
Spiritual:
Darkness 1John 2:11
Immaturity 1Cor 8:7-13

Productive of:
Unbelief .... John 8:19-43
Error .... Matt 22:29

Objects of:
God .... John 8:55
Scriptures .... Matt 22:29
Christ's return 1Thess 4:13, 14

[*also* IGNORANT, IGNORANTLY]
soul shall sin through *i* .... Lev 4:2
of Israel sin through *i* .... Lev 4:13
done somewhat through *i* ..... Lev 4:22
and sin through *i* .... Lev 5:15
if aught be committed by *i* .... Num 15:24
forgiven them; for it is *i* ...... Num 15:25
before the Lord, for their *i* .... Num 15:25
if any soul sin through *i* .... Num 15:27
for the soul that sinneth *i* ..... Num 15:28
that sinneth through *i* .... Num 15:29
Whoso killeth..neighbor *i* ..... Deut 19:4
So foolish was I, and *i*: .... Ps 73:22
they are all *i*, they are all ..... Is 56:10
though Abraham be *i* of us .... Is 63:16
they were unlearned and *i* ..... Acts 4:13
Whom therefore ye *i* worship .. Acts 17:23
Now I would not have you *i* .. Rom 1:13
For they being *i* of God's ..... Rom 10:3
that ye should be *i* of this .... Rom 11:25
I would not that ye..be *i* 1Cor 10:1
I would not have you *i* 1Cor 12:1
any man be *i*, let him be *i* 1Cor 14:38
not, brethren, have you *i* 2Cor 1:8
for we are not *i* of his 2Cor 2:11
can have compassion on..*i* ..... Heb 5:2
the former lusts in your *i* 1Pet 1:14
silence the *i* of foolish men 1Pet 2:15
For this they willingly are *i* 2Pet 3:5
be not *i* of this one thing 2Pet 3:8

IIM (ī'ĭm)—*"heaps"*
Town of Judah .... Josh 15:29

And they departed from *I* .... Num 33:45

IJE-ABARIM (ī-jĕ-ăb'ä-rĭm)—*"ruins of Abraham"*
Wilderness camp .... Num 21:11
Same as Iim .... Num 33:44, 45

IJON (ī-jŏn)—*"heap; ruin"*
Town of Naphtali;
captured by Benhadad .. 1Kin 15:20
Captured by Tiglath-pileser 2Kin 15:29

and they smote *I*, and Dan 2Chr 16:4

IKKESH (ĭk'ĕsh)—*"subtle; crooked"*
Father of Ira 2Sam 23:26
Commander of 24,000 ... 1Chr 27:9

the son of *I* the Tekoite 1Chr 11:28

ILAI (ī'lā-ī)—*"supreme"*
One of David's mighty men 1Chr 11:26, 29
Called Zalmon 2Sam 23:28

ILL—*sick; evil*
out of the river, *i*-favored ..... Gen 41:3
poor and very *i* .... Gen 41:19
they were still *i*-favored .... Gen 41:21
dealt so *i* with me, as to tell ... Gen 43:6
blind, or have any *i* blemish ... Deut 15:21
it shall go *i* with him that ..... Job 20:26
that it went *i* with Moses ...... Ps 106:32
it shall be *i* with him .... Is 3:11
it seem *i* unto thee to come ... Jer 40:4
his *i* savor shall come .... Joel 2:20
they have behaved..*i* .... Mic 3:4
Love worketh no *i* to his ...... Rom 13:10

ILLUMINATION—*enlightenment; understanding*
Of Daniel .... Dan 5:11, 14
By the Gospel .... John 1:9
At conversion .... Heb 6:4
In Christian truth .... Eph 1:18
By Holy Spirit .... John 16:13-16
By God 1Cor 4:5

[*also* ILLUMINATED]
after ye were *i*, ye .... Heb 10:32

ILLUSTRATION—*something used to explain something else*

From:
Ancient history 1Cor 10:1-14
Current history .... Mark 12:1-11
Nature .... Prov 6:6-11

ILLYRICUM (ĭ-lĭr'ĭ-kŭm)—*"joy"—a Roman province of Europe*
Paul preaches .... Rom 15:19

IMAGE—*exact likeness; idol*

[*also* IMAGERY, IMAGE'S, IMAGES]
own likeness, after his *i* .... Gen 5:3
Rachel had stolen the *i* that ... Gen 31:19
but found not the *i* .... Gen 31:35
not make..any graven *i* .... Ex 20:4
break down their *i* .... Ex 23:24
make you no..graven *i* .... Lev 26:1
neither rear you up a..*i* .... Lev 26:1
neither shall ye set up any *i* ... Lev 26:1
cut down your *i* .... Lev 26:30
destroy all their molten *i* ...... Num 33:52
and make you a graven *i* ...... Deut 4:16
and make a graven *i* .... Deut 4:25
and break down their *i* .... Deut 7:5
burn..graven *i* with fire .... Deut 7:5
they..made them a molten *i* ... Deut 9:12
ye shall hew down the..*i* ...... Deut 12:3
maketh any..molten *i* .... Deut 27:15
to make a graven *i* .... Judg 17:3
and a molten *i* .... Judg 17:3
a graven *i* and a molten *i*? .... Judg 18:14
and took the graven *i* .... Judg 18:17
teraphim, and the molten *i* .... Judg 18:17
and fetched the carved *i* ...... Judg 18:18
and the molten *i* .... Judg 18:18
children of Dan set..graven *i* .. Judg 18:30

ye shall make *i* of your 1Sam 6:5
i of your mice that mar 1Sam 6:5
Michal took an *i* 1Sam 19:13
there they left their *i* 2Sam 5:21
other gods, and molten *i* 1Kin 14:9
he put away the *i* of Baal 2Kin 3:2
i out of the house of Baal.....2Kin 10:26
they set them up *i* and groves .2Kin 17:10
and served their graven *i*......2Kin 17:41
he set a graven *i* of the 2Kin 21:7
he brake in pieces the *i* 2Kin 23:14
he made two cherubim of *i*....2Chr 3:10
brake down the *i* 2Chr 14:3
altars and his *i* in pieces 2Chr 23:17
and brake the *i* in pieces 2Chr 31:1
sacrificed unto all the carved *i* .2Chr 33:22
and the carved *i*.............2Chr 34:3
groves..and the molten *i* 2Chr 34:3
the *i*, that were on high 2Chr 34:4
groves and the carved *i* 2Chr 34:4
and the molten *i* 2Chr 34:4
an *i* was before mine eyes .....Job 4:16
thou shalt despise their *i* ......Ps 73:20
jealousy with their graven *i*....Ps 78:58
whose graven *i* did excel ......Is 10:10
all the graven *i* of her gods....Is 21:9
covering of thy graven *i*.......Is 30:22
ornament of thy molten *i* .....Is 30:22
melteth a graven *i*............Is 40:19
my praise to graven *i* ....Is 42:8
that trust in graven *i*..........Is 42:17
say to the molten *i*, Ye are....Is 42:17
They that make a graven *i* ....Is 44:9
he maketh it a graven *i* ....Is 44:15
the wood of their graven *i* ....Is 45:20
and my graven *i*..............Is 48:5
molten *i*, hath commanded ....Is 48:5
anger with their graven *i*......Jer 8:19
confounded by the graven *i* ...Jer 10:14
his molten *i* is falsehood ......Jer 10:14
her *i* are broken in ....Jer 50:2
confounded by the graven *i* ...Jer 51:17
his molten *i* is falsehood ......Jer 51:17
the graven *i* of Babylon.......Jer 51:47
your *i* shall be broken ....Ezek 6:4
i of their abominations.........Ezek 7:20
seat of the *i* of jealousy ....Ezek 8:3
he consulted with *i* ....Ezek 21:21
cause their *i* to cease out......Ezek 30:13
and behold a great *i* ....Dan 2:31
This *i* head was of..gold ......Dan 2:32
smote the *i* upon his feet......Dan 2:34
the king made an *i* of gold ....Dan 3:1
the dedication of the *i* ....Dan 3:3
they stood before the *i*........Dan 3:3
worshiped the golden *i*........Dan 3:7
nor worship the golden *i* ....Dan 3:12
fall down and worship the *i* ...Dan 3:15
and without an *i*..............Hos 3:4
they have made goodly *i* ......Hos 10:1
he shall spoil their *i* ....Hos 10:2
burned incense to graven *i* ....Hos 11:2
Moloch and Chiun your *i* .....Amos 5:26
graven *i* thereof shall be ......Mic 1:7
Thy graven *i* also will I cut....Mic 5:13
thy standing *i* out of the ......Mic 5:13
graven *i* and the molten *i* .....Nah 1:14
What profiteth the graven *i* ...Hab 2:18
the molten *i*, and a teacher....Hab 2:18
Whose is this *i* and ....Matt 22:20
Whose is this *i* and ....Mark 12:16
Whose *i* and superscription....Luke 20:24
i..fell down from Jupiter? .....Acts 19:35
i made like to corruptible .....Rom 1:23
we have borne the *i* of the 1Cor 15:49
bear the *i* of the heavenly 1Cor 15:49
Christ, who is the *i* of God....2Cor 4:4
the express *i* of his person ....Heb 1:3
make an *i* to the beast ....Rev 13:14
life unto the *i* of the beast ....Rev 13:15
i of the beast should both .....Rev 13:15
worship the *i* of the beast .....Rev 13:15
worship the beast and his *i*....Rev 14:11
the beast, neither his *i* ....Rev 20:4
See IDOL

IMAGE OF GOD—*that which resembles God in man*

In man:
Created in ....Gen 1:26, 27
Reason for sanctity of life.Gen 9:6
Reason for man's headship..............1Cor 11:7
Restored by grace ....Col 3:10
Transformed of..........2Cor 3:18

In Christ:
In essential nature ....Col 1:15
Manifested on earth .....John 1:14, 18
Believers conformed .....Rom 8:29

IMAGINATION—*creating a mental picture of*

Described as:
Evil ....Gen 6:5
Willful..................Jer 18:12
Deceitful ....Prov 12:20
Vain ....Rom 1:21

Cleansing of:
Promised ....Jer 3:17
By the power of God 2Cor 10:5

[*also* IMAGINATIONS, IMAGINE, IMAGINED, IMAGINETH]

the *i* of man's heart is evil ....Gen 8:21
which they have *i* to do ....Gen 11:6
I walk in the *i* of mine........Deut 29:19
all the *i* of the thoughts 1Chr 28:9
keep this for ever in the *i* 1Chr 29:18
Do ye *i* to reprove words .....Job 6:26
the people *i* a vain thing? .....Ps 2:1
devices that they have *i* ....Ps 10:2
ye *i* mischief against a man? ..Ps 62:3
Which *i* mischiefs in their .....Ps 140:2
heart..deviseth wicked *i* ....Prov 6:18
heart of them that *i* evil.......Prov 12:20
and all their *i* against me......Lam 3:60
the *i* of their evil heart........Jer 3:17
the *i* of their own heart ....Jer 9:14
walk in the *i* of their heart.....Jer 13:10
the *i* of his evil heart ....Jer 16:12
after the *i* of his own heart....Jer 23:17
yet do they *i* mischief ....Hos 7:15
ye *i* against the Lord? ....Nah 1:9
that *i* evil against the Lord ....Nah 1:11
you *i* evil against his ....Zech 7:10
none of you *i* evil against .....Zech 8:17
proud in the *i* of their hearts ..Luke 1:51
and the people *i* vain things? ..Acts 4:25

IMITATION—*attempting to duplicate*

Of the good:
God ....Eph 5:1
Paul's conduct...........2Thess 3:7, 9
Apostles 1Thess 1:6
Heroes of the faith ......Heb 6:12
Good...................3John 11
Other churches 1Thess 2:14

See EXAMPLE OF CHRIST

IMLA (ĭm'lä)—*"fullness"*
Father of Micaiah the prophet...............2Chr 18:7, 8
As Imiah 1Kin 22:8, 9

IMMANUEL (ĭ-măn'ū-ĕl)—*"God (is) with us"*
Name given to the child born of the virgin ... Is 7:14; Matt 1:23
Emmanuel in ....Matt 1:23

the breadth of thy land, O *I*...Is 8:8

IMMEDIATELY—*without interval of time*

And they *i* left the ship ....Matt 4:22
And *i* Jesus stretched forth ....Matt 14:31
i after the tribulation ....Matt 24:29
i the spirit driveth him into....Mark 1:12
i the fever left her ....Mark 1:31
i when Jesus perceived ....Mark 2:8
and *i* it sprang up ....Mark 4:5
word, *i* receive it with ....Mark 4:16
i he putteth in the sickle ......Mark 4:29
Jesus *i* knowing in himself.....Mark 5:30
i he talked with them ....Mark 6:50
And *i* while he yet spake .....Mark 14:43
his mouth was opened *i* ....Luke 1:64
i the leprosy departed.........Luke 5:13
beat vehemently, and *i* it fell ..Luke 6:49
how she was healed *i* ....Luke 8:47
i she was made straight ....Luke 13:13
kingdom of God should *i* .....Luke 19:11
And *i*, while he yet spake .....Luke 22:60
received the sop went *i* out....John 13:30
entered into a ship *i* ....John 21:3
i his feet and ankle bones .....Acts 3:7
make thy bed. And he arose *i* .Acts 9:34
i there were three men........Acts 11:11
i there fell on him a mist .....Acts 13:11
i all the doors were opened ...Acts 16:26
i the brethren sent away ......Acts 17:14
i I conferred not with flesh ....Gal 1:16
And *i* I was in the spirit ......Rev 4:2

IMMER (ĭm'er)—*"loquacious; prominent"*
1. Descendant of Aaron ...1Chr 24:1-14
2. Father of Pashur........Jer 20:1
3. Founder of a postexilic family...............Ezra 2:37
   The same as the father of Meshillemith 1Chr 9:12
   Also the ancestor of priests marrying foreigners ....Ezra 10:19, 20
4. Person or place in Babylonia ....Neh 7:61
5. Zadok's father ....Neh 3:29

Cherub, Addan, and *I* ....Ezra 2:59
the children of *I*.............Neh 7:40
the son of *I*..................Neh 11:13

IMMORALITY—*state of a wrongful act or relationship*

Attitude toward:
Consider sanctity of the body 1Cor 6:13-20
Flee from it 1Cor 6:18
Get married 1Cor 7:2
Abstain from it..........1Thess 4:3
Mention it not ....Eph 5:3
Corrupts the earth.......Rev 19:2

IMMORTALITY—*external existence*

Proof of, based upon:
God's image in man .....Gen 1:26, 27
Translation of Enoch and Elijah .... Gen 5:24; 2Kin 2:11, 12
Promises of Christ.......John 11:25, 26; John 14:2, 3
Appearance of Moses and Elijah ....Matt 17:2-9
Eternal rewards and punishments .... Matt 25:31-46; Luke 16:19-31
Resurrection of Christ ...Rom 8:11; 1Cor 15:12-58
Resurrection of men .....Dan 12:2, 3; John 5:28, 29

Expression indicative of:
"I am" ....Matt 22:32
"Today" ....Luke 23:43
"Shall never die" ....John 11:25, 26
"The redemption of our body" ....Rom 8:22, 23
"Neither death" ....Rom 8:38, 39
"We know" 2Cor 5:1-10
"A lively hope" 1Pet 1:3-8
"We shall be like him" ..1John 3:2

See ETERNAL; EVERLASTING; LIFE, ETERNAL

[*also* IMMORTAL, IMMORTALITY]

glory and honor and *i*.........Rom 2:7
this mortal must put on *i*......1Cor 15:53
the King eternal *i* 1Tim 1:17
Who only hath *i*.............1Tim 6:16
brought life and *i* to light 2Tim 1:10

IMMUNITY—*exemption from something*

From:
Egyptian plagues ....Ex 8:22, 23
Disease ....Deut 7:15
Corruption ....Ps 16:10, 11

Harm .... Luke 10:19
Second death .... Rev 20:6

IMMUTABILITY—*unchangeableness*

Of God, expressed by:
"I AM" .... Ex 3:14
"Thou art the same" .... Ps 102:25-27
"I change not" .... Mal 3:6
"Are without repentance". Rom 11:29
"Who cannot lie" .... Titus 1:2
"The immutability" ...... Heb 6:17, 18
"No variableness" .... James 1:17

Of Christ, expressed by:
"I am" .... John 8:58
"Thou art the same" .... Heb 1:12
"Unchangeable" .... Heb 7:22-24
"The same" .... Heb 13:8
"I am Alpha and Omega" .... Rev 1:8-18

Of God, characteristics of:
Unique .... Is 43:10
Purposive .... Ps 138:8
Active .... Phil 1:6

IMNA (ĭm'nä)—*"lugging"*
Asherite chief 1Chr 7:35

IMNAH (ĭm'nä)—*"lugging"*
1. Eldest son of Asher 1Chr 7:30
Called Jimna and Jimnah. Num 26:44
Gen 46:17
2. Levite in Hezekiah's reign 2Chr 31:14

IMPART—*to convey or grant*

[*also* IMPARTED]
he *i* to her understanding ..... Job 39:17
i to him that hath none .... Luke 3:11
i unto you..spiritual gift .... Rom 1:11
willing to have *i* unto you 1Thess 2:8

IMPARTIALITY—*that which is equitable, just, and fair*

In God's:
Material blessings .... Matt 5:45
Spiritual blessings .... Acts 10:34, 35
Judgments .... Rom 2:3-12

IMPATIENCE—*inability to control one's desire for action*

Causes of:
Lust .... Gen 19:4-9
Revenge .... Gen 34:25-27
Irritability .... Num 20:10

Consequences of:
Kept from promised land . Num 20:10-12
Great sin .... Ex 32:1, 21, 30
Foolish statements .... Job 2:7-9
Loss of birthright .... Gen 25:29-34
Shipwreck .... Acts 27:29-34

IMPECCABILITY—*See* HOLINESS OF CHRIST

IMPEDIMENT—*something that hinders one's activity*
In speech, cured .... Mark 7:32-35
Avoided by obedience ... Prov 4:10, 12

IMPENITENCE—*without a change of mind*

Expressed by:
Willful disobedience ..... Jer 44:15-19
Hardness of heart .... John 12:37-40
Refusing to hear .... Luke 16:31
Rebellion against the truth 1Thess 2:15, 16

Consequences of:
Spiritual bondage .... John 8:33-44
Judicial blindness .... John 9:39-41
Eternal destruction 2Thess 1:8, 9

[*also* IMPENITENT]
thy hardness and *i* heart ...... Rom 2:5

IMPERFECTION OF MAN

Manifested in:
Falling short of God's glory .... Rom 3:23
Total corruption .... Is 1:5, 6

Remedy for:
New creature 2Cor 5:17
Conformity to Christ 1John 3:2, 3

IMPERIOUS—*arrogant; proud*
work of an *i* whorish woman .. Ezek 16:30

IMPERISHABLE—*enduring, lasting forever*
Resurrected body 1Cor 15:42, 52, 53
Christian's inheritance ... 1Pet 1:4
Seed of Christian life 1Pet 1:23

IMPERTINENCE—*an action or remark inappropriate for the occasion*
Christ rebukes Peter's .... Mark 8:31-33

IMPETUOUSNESS—*acting with little thought*

Characterized by:
Ill-considered judgment .. Esth 1:10-22
Enraged disposition ...... Gen 34:25-31
Hasty action .... Josh 22:10-34

IMPLACABLE—*ruthless*
without natural affection, *i* .... Rom 1:31

IMPLEAD—*bring charges against*
let them *i* one another .... Acts 19:38

IMPORT—*receive from other countries*

Things imported:
Horses 1Kin 10:28
Chariots 2Chr 1:17
Fish .... Neh 13:16

IMPORTUNITY IN PRAYER—*urgency in prayer*
Need involved .... Luke 11:5-13
Christ's example .... Luke 22:44
Great intensity of .... Acts 12:5
Results of .... Mark 7:24-30
See PRAYER

IMPOSE—*to levy; take advantage of; force*

[*also* IMPOSED]
shall not be lawful to *i* toll .... Ezra 7:24
i on them until the time of .... Heb 9:10

IMPOSSIBILITIES—*powerlessness; weakness*

Natural:
Change one's color ...... Jer 13:23
Hide from God .... Ps 139:7-12
Change one's size .... Matt 6:27
Control the tongue ...... James 3:7, 8

Spiritual:
God to sin .... Hab 1:13
God to fail His promises . Titus 1:2
Believers to be lost ...... John 10:27-29

[*also* IMPOSSIBLE]
nothing shall be *i* unto you .... Matt 17:20
with men this is *i*; but with .... Matt 19:26
With men it is *i*, but not ...... Mark 10:27
with God nothing shall be *i* ... Luke 1:37
is *i* but that offenses will ...... Luke 17:1
which are *i* with men .... Luke 18:27
it is *i* for those who were ..... Heb 6:4
it was *i* for God to lie .... Heb 6:18
without faith it is *i* to .... Heb 11:6

IMPOSTER—*a pretender*

Characteristics of:
Not believed as .... Jer 40:14-16
Speaks falsely .... Josh 9:3-14
Poses as real 2Cor 11:13-15
Much like the real .... Matt 7:21-23
Deception of, revealed to prophets .... Acts 13:8-12

Examples of:
Jannes and Jambres 2Tim 3:8
Judas .... John 13:18-30
Antichrist 2Thess 2:1-4

IMPOTENT—*powerless*
Moab .... Is 16:14

a great multitude of *i* folk ..... John 5:3
The *i* man answered him .... John 5:7
good deed done to the *i* man .. Acts 4:9
certain man..*i* in his feet ...... Acts 14:8

IMPOVERISH—*to make poor*

[*also* IMPOVERISHED]
And Israel was greatly *i* ...... Judg 6:6
so *i* that he hath no oblation .. Is 40:20
shall *i* thy fenced cities .... Jer 5:17
Edom saith, We are *i* .... Mal 1:4

IMPRECATION—*pronouncing a curse*
God's enemies .... Ps 55:5-15
One's enemies .... Ps 35:4-8, 26
Heretics .... Gal 1:9
Persecutors .... Jer 11:18-20
Forbidden .... Luke 9:54-56
See CURSE, CURSING

IMPRISONMENT—*physical confinement in jail*

Of Old Testament persons:
Joseph .... Gen 39:20
Simeon .... Gen 42:19, 24
Samson .... Judg 16:21, 25
Jehoiachin 2Kin 25:27-29
Micaiah 2Chr 18:26
Jeremiah .... Jer 32:2, 8, 12

Of New Testament persons:
John the Baptist .... Mark 6:17-27
Apostles .... Acts 5:18
Peter .... Acts 12:4
Paul and Silas .... Acts 16:24
Paul .... Acts 23:10, 18
John .... Rev 1:9
See PRISONERS

[*also* IMPRISONED, IMPRISONMENTS]
confiscation of goods, or to *i* .. Ezra 7:26
know that I *i* and beat in ..... Acts 22:19
In stripes, in *i*, in tumults 2Cor 6:5
moreover of bonds and *i* ...... Heb 11:36

IMPROVEMENT—*a betterment*

Expressed by:
Growth 1Pet 2:2
Addition 2Pet 1:5-11
Press on .... Phil 3:13-15

IMPROVIDENCE—*wasting one's possessions; not preparing properly for the future*
Material things .... Luke 15:11-13
Spiritual things .... Luke 12:16-23
Eternal things .... Luke 16:19-31

IMPUDENT—*contemptuous boldness; disregard for others*
and with an *i* face .... Prov 7:13
i children and stiffhearted ..... Ezek 2:4
all the house of Israel are *i* .... Ezek 3:7

IMPURE—*ritually unclean; mixed with foreign elements*

Things impure:
Discharge .... Lev 15:30
Hands .... Mark 7:2
Person .... Eph 5:5
Sons of Israel .... Lev 16:16
Nations .... Ezra 6:21

IMPURITY—*See* UNCLEAN

IMPUTATION—*counting or crediting something to another*

Described as charging:
Evil to an innocent person .... Philem 18
Evil to an evil person .... Lev 17:4
Good to a good person .. Ps 106:30, 31

Of Adam's sin to the race:
Based on the fall .... Gen 3:1-19
Explained fully .... Rom 5:12-21
The wider implications of . Rom 8:20-23

Of the believer's sin to Christ:
Our iniquity laid on Him . Is 53:5, 6
Made to be sin for us 2Cor 5:21
Became a curse for us ... Gal 3:13
Takes away our sins ..... John 1:29
Heb 9:28

Of Christ's righteousness to the believer:
Negatively stated .... Rom 4:6-8
Positively affirmed .... Rom 10:4-10

Explained graphically ....Luke 15:22-24
God justifies the ungodly .Rom 5:18, 19
Christ becomes our righteousness..........1Cor 1:30
We become the righteousness of God in Him..................2Cor 5:21
Illustrated by Abraham's faith..................Rom 4:3
See JUSTIFICATION

[*also* IMPUTE, IMPUTED, IMPUTETH, IMPUTING]
it be *i* unto him..............Lev 7:18
shall be *i* unto that man.......Lev 17:4
king *i* anything unto his.......1Sam 22:15
Let not my lord *i* iniquity.....2Sam 19:19
the Lord *i* not inquity.........Ps 32:2
i this his power unto his......Hab 1:11
God *i* righteousness...........Rom 4:6
the Lord will not *i* sin........Rom 4:8
might be *i* unto them also.....Rom 4:11
it was *i* to him for............Rom 4:22
that it was *i* to him...........Rom 4:23
to whom it shall be *i*..........Rom 4:24
sin is not *i* when there is......Rom 5:13
not *i* their trespasses unto.....2Cor 5:19
it was *i* unto him for..........James 2:23

IMRAH (ĭm'rä)—*"height of Jehovah; stubborn"*
Son of Zophah..........1Chr 7:36

IMRI (ĭm'rī)—*"talkative; projecting"*
1. Son of Bani............1Chr 9:4
2. Father of Zaccur........Neh 3:2
3. May be Amariah in.....Neh 11:4

IN—*See* INTRODUCTION

INASMUCH—*in view of the fact that*
of death, *i* as he hated him....Deut 19:6
i as thou followedst not.......Ruth 3:10
I as ye have done it unto.....Matt 25:40
I as ye did it not.............Matt 25:45
i as I am the apostle of the...Rom 11:13
i as both in my bonds.........Phil 1:7
i as he who hath builded......Heb 3:3
i as ye are partakers of.......1Pet 4:13

INCARNATION OF CHRIST
Foreshadowed by:
Angel..................Josh 5:13-15
Prophecies..............Is 7:14
Described as:
Becoming flesh..........John 1:14
Born of woman.........Gal 4:4
Coming in flesh.........1John 4:2
Appearing in flesh.......1Tim 3:16
Our likeness...........Rom 8:3
Heb 2:14
Body..................Heb 10:5, 10
1John 1:1-3
Dying in flesh...........1Pet 3:18
1Pet 4:1
Purposes of:
Reveal the Father.......John 14:8-11
Do God's will..........Heb 10:5-9
Fulfill prophecy.........Luke 4:17-21
Die for our sins.........1Pet 3:18
Fulfill all righteousness...Matt 3:15
Reconcile the world.....2Cor 5:18-21
Become our high priest..Heb 7:24-28
Become our example....1Pet 2:21-23
Importance of:
Evidence Christ's deity...Rom 9:3-5
Confirm Christ's resurrection...........Acts 2:24-32
Mark of believers........1John 4:1-6
See HUMAN NATURE OF CHRIST

INCENSE—*sweet perfume which exudes from certain spices and gums when burned*
Offered:
By priests...............Lev 16:12, 13
On the altar............Ex 30:1-8
On day of atonement....Lev 16:12, 13
According to strict formula...............Ex 30:34-36
Illegal offering of:
Forbidden..............Ex 30:37, 38
Excluded from certain offerings...............Lev 5:11
Punished severely.......Lev 10:1, 2
2Chr 26:16-21
Among idolaters.........Is 65:3
Typical of:
Worship................Ps 141:2
Prayer.................Rev 5:8
Rev 8:3, 4
Praise.................Mal 1:11
Approved service........Eph 5:2
Purposes of:
Used in holy oil.........Ex 30:34-38
Used in meal offerngs...Lev 2:1, 2, 15
Excluded from certain offerings..............Lev 5:11
Used in the showbread...Lev 24:7
Product of Arabia.......Is 60:6
Presented to Jesus.......Matt 2:11
Figurative of worship....Ps 141:2

Ye shall offer no strange *i*....Ex 30:9
and the altar of *i*.............Ex 31:8
and for the sweet *i*...........Ex 35:8
the *i* altar, and his staves.....Ex 35:15
oil, and the sweet *i*...........Ex 35:15
made the *i* altar of..wood.....Ex 37:25
oil, and the sweet *i*...........Ex 39:38
And he burnt sweet *i*.........Ex 40:27
of the altar of sweet *i*........Lev 4:7
light, and the sweet *i*........Num 4:16
of ten shekels, full of *i*........Num 7:20
golden spoons..full of *i*........Num 7:86
and put *i* in them.............Num 16:17
men that offered *i*............Num 16:35
off the altar, and put on *i*.....Num 16:46
they shall put *i* before thee....Deut 33:10
to burn *i*, to wear an ephod...1Sam 2:28
he sacrificed and burnt *i*......1Kin 3:3
wives, which burnt *i*..........1Kin 11:8
stood by the altar to burn *i*...1Kin 13:1
people offered and burnt *i*....1Kin 22:43
sacrificed and burnt *i*.........2Kin 12:3
sacrificed and burnt *i*.........2Kin 15:4
burnt *i* in the high places.....2Kin 16:4
children of Israel did burn *i*...2Kin 18:4
had ordained to burned *i*......2Kin 23:5
them also that burn *i*.........2Kin 23:5
and on the altar of *i*..........1Chr 6:49
for the altar of *i* refined.......1Chr 28:18
burn before him sweet *i*.......2Chr 2:4
and burned *i* unto them.......2Chr 25:14
he burnt *i* in the valley.......2Chr 28:3
to burn *i* unto other gods.....2Chr 28:25
minister unto him..burn *i*.....2Chr 29:11
and burn *i* upon it?...........2Chr 32:12
with the *i* of rams.............Ps 66:15
i is an abomination...........Is 1:13
burned *i* unto other gods......Jer 1:16
burn *i* unto Baal..............Jer 7:9
altars to burn *i* unto Baal.....Jer 11:13
me to anger in offering *i*......Jer 11:17
they have burned *i* to vanity...Jer 18:15
i unto all the host of heaven...Jer 19:13
offerings and *i* in..hand.......Jer 41:5
burn no *i* unto other gods.....Jer 44:5
had burned *i* unto..gods.......Jer 44:15
to burn *i* to the queen........Jer 44:18
i that ye burned in..cities.....Jer 44:21
to burn *i* to the queen........Jer 44:25
a thick cloud of *i* went up.....Ezek 8:11
thou hast set mine *i*..........Ezek 23:41
she burned *i* to them.........Hos 2:13
burned *i* to graven images.....Hos 11:2
and burn *i* unto their drag....Hab 1:16
his lot was to burn *i*..........Luke 1:9
right side of the altar of *i*.....Luke 1:11
was given unto him much *i*....Rev 8:3

INCENSED—*angered*
they that were *i* against thee..Is 41:11
all that are *i* against him......Is 45:24

INCENTIVES TO GOOD WORKS
Reap kindness..........Hos 10:12
Remain.................John 15:16
Reap...................Gal 6:7-10

INCEST—*sexual intercourse between closely related individuals*
Relations prohibited:
Same family............Lev 18:6-12
Grandchildren...........Lev 18:10
Aunts and uncles........Lev 18:12-14
In-laws................Lev 18:15, 16
Near kin................Lev 18:17, 18
Punishment for:
Death..................Lev 20:11-17
Childlessness...........Lev 20:19-21
A curse.................Deut 27:20-23
Examples of:
Lot—with his daughters..Gen 19:30-38
Reuben—with his father's concubine.............Gen 35:22

INCLINE—*become drawn to a course of conduct*

[*also* INCLINED, INCLINETH]
i your heart unto the Lord....Josh 24:23
and their hearts *i* to follow....Judg 9:3
That he may *i* our hearts......1Kin 8:58
i thine ear unto me...........Ps 17:6
and he *i* unto me.............Ps 40:1
I will *i* mine ear..............Ps 49:4
i your ears to the words.......Ps 78:1
i thine ear unto me...........Ps 102:2
I have *i* mine heart...........Ps 119:112
I not my heart to any evil.....Ps 141:4
i thine ear unto wisdom.......Prov 2:2
her house *i* unto death........Prov 2:18
i mine ear to them that.......Prov 5:13
I thine ear, O Lord...........Is 37:17
nor *i* their ear................Jer 7:24
not unto me, nor *i* their ear...Jer 7:26
they obeyed not, nor *i* their...Jer 11:8
neither *i* their ear............Jer 17:23
nor *i* your ear to hear........Jer 25:4
neither *i* their ear............Jer 34:14
not *i* your ear................Jer 35:15
O my God, *i* thine ear........Dan 9:18

INCLOSE—*variant of enclose*

[*also* INCLOSED, INCLOSING]
be set in gold in their *i*.......Ex 28:20
onyx stones *i* in ouches.......Ex 39:6
of gold in their *i*.............Ex 39:13
they *i* the Benjamites.........Judg 20:43
They are *i* in their own fat....Ps 17:10
A garden *i* is my sister........Song 4:12
we will *i* her with boards......Song 8:9
He hath *i* my ways...........Lam 3:9
they *i* a great multitude.......Luke 5:6

INCONSISTENCY—*incompatibility between two facts or claims*
Between:
Criticism of ourselves and others................Matt 7:3
Legalism and human mercy................John 7:23
Profession and reality....Luke 22:31-62
Preaching and practice...Rom 2:21-23
Private and public convictions............Gal 2:11-14
Faith and works.........James 2:14-26
Profession and works....Titus 1:16

INCONSTANCY—*inability to stand firm in crisis*
Causes of:
Little faith..............Matt 13:19-22
Satan...................Luke 22:31-34
False teachers...........Gal 1:6-10
Doubt..................James 1:6-8
Immaturity.............2Pet 1:5-10

Remedies against:
Firm foundation ....Matt 7:24-27
Strong faith ....Hab 3:16-19
Full armor ....Eph 6:10-20

INCONTINENCY—*uncontrolled indulgence of the passions*

Expressed in:
Unbridled sexual morals. .Ex 32:6, 18, 25
Abnormal sexual desires. .2Sam 13:1-15
Unnatural sexual appetities .... Gen 19:5-9; Rom 1:26, 27

Sources of:
Lust 1Pet 4:2, 3
Satan 1Cor 7:5
Apostasy 2Tim 3:3

[*also* INCONTINENT]
false accusers *i*, fierce 2Tim 3:3

INCORRUPTIBLE—*not subject to decay or dissolution*

[*also* INCORRUPTION]
crown; but we an *i* 1Cor 9:25
corruption; it is raised in *i* 1Cor 15:42
corruption inherit *i* 1Cor 15:50
dead shall be raised *i* 1Cor 15:52
must put on *i*, and this........1Cor 15:53
corruptible shall..put on *i* 1Cor 15:54
To an inheritance *i* 1Pet 1:4
corruptible seed, but of *i*......1Pet 1:23

INCREASE—*to become more abundant*

Used literally of:
Descendants 1Sam 2:33
Knowledge..............Dan 12:4

Used spiritually of:
Messiah's kingdom ......Is 9:7
Wisdom ....Luke 2:52
Faith ....Luke 17:5
Esteem ....John 3:30
God's Word ....Acts 6:7
Spiritual fruit 2Cor 9:10
Knowledge of God ......Col 1:10
Love 1Thess 4:9, 10
Ungodliness 2Tim 2:16

[*also* INCREASED, INCREASEST, INCREASETH]
waters *i* and bare up.........Gen 7:17
i unto a multitude ....Gen 30:30
come to pass in the *i*, that ....Gen 47:24
fruitful, and *i* abundantly......Ex 1:7
yield unto you the *i* ....Lev 19:25
ye shall eat the *i* thereof ......Lev 25:12
shalt *i* the price thereof ....Lev 25:16
nor gather in our *i* ....Lev 25:30
Take..no usury of him, or *i* ..Lev 25:36
lend him thy victuals for *i*.....Lev 25:37
land shall not yield..*i* ....Lev 26:20
i of the threshing floor ....Num 18:30
i of sinful men, to augment ...Num 32:14
that ye may *i* mightily ....Deut 6:3
lest..beast of the field *i* ....Deut 7:22
tithe all the *i* of thy seed ......Deut 14:22
all the tithe of thine *i*.........Deut 14:28
all the tithes of thine *i* ....Deut 26:12
the *i* of thy kine, and ....Deut 28:18
might eat the *i* of..fields ......Deut 32:13
destroyed the *i* of..earth ......Judg 6:4
Philistines went on and *i* 1Sam 14:19
people *i* continually...........2Sam 15:12
battle *i* that day 1Kin 22:35
house of their fathers *i*........1Chr 4:38
battle *i* that day 2Chr 18:34
of all the *i* of the field 2Chr 31:5
iniquities are *i* over our ....Ezra 9:6
to *i* the trespass of Israel......Ezra 10:10
much *i* unto the kings.........Neh 9:37
substance is *i* in the land......Job 1:10
latter end should greatly *i* .....Job 8:7
i thine indignation ....Job 10:17
would root out all mine *i* .....Job 31:12
Lord, how are they *i* ....Ps 3:1
corn and their wine *i* ....Ps 4:7
i thy wealth by their price .....Ps 44:12
the earth yield her *i* ....Ps 67:6
they *i* in riches ....Ps 73:12
rise up against thee *i* ....Ps 74:23
land shall yield her *i* ....Ps 85:12
i his people greatly ....Ps 105:24
Lord shall *i* you more.........Ps 115:14
man will hear..*i* learning ......Prov 1:5
first fruits of all thine *i*........Prov 3:9
will *i* in learning ....Prov 9:9
years of my life shall be *i* .....Prov 9:11
is that scattereth, and yet *i* ....Prov 11:24
gathereth by labor shall *i*.......Prov 13:11
i is by the strength of ....Prov 14:4
the poor to *i* his riches ....Prov 22:16
i the transgressors among .....Prov 23:28
usury and unjust gain *i*.........Prov 28:8
i knowledge, *i* sorrow ....Eccl 1:18
was great, and *i* more ....Eccl 2:9
loveth abundance with *i*.......Eccl 5:10
they are *i* that eat them ....Eccl 5:11
many things that *i* vanity ......Eccl 6:11
and not *i* the joy ....Is 9:3
i of his government ....Is 9:7
Thou hast *i* the nation ....Is 26:15
thou hast *i* the nation ....Is 26:15
bread of the *i* of the earth ....Is 30:23
no might he *i* strength ....Is 40:29
first fruits of his *i*............Jer 2:3
multiplied and *i* in the land ...Jer 3:16
widows are *i* to me above .....Jer 15:8
because thy sins were *i*.........Jer 30:14
i in the daughter of Judah .....Lam 2:5
i the famine upon you ....Ezek 5:16
hast *i* and waxen great ....Ezek 16:7
and hath taken *i*..............Ezek 18:13
hast taken usury and *i* ....Ezek 22:12
she *i* her whoredoms..........Ezek 23:14
shall *i* and bring fruit ....Ezek 36:11
and the *i* of the field ....Ezek 36:30
i them with men like a flock ..Ezek 36:37
i from the lowest chamber ....Ezek 41:7
i thereof shall be for food .....Ezek 48:18
acknowledge and *i*............Dan 11:39
As they were *i* ....Hos 4:7
and shall not *i* ....Hos 4:10
daily *i* lies and desolation .....Hos 12:1
i that which is not his.........Hab 2:6
ground shall give her *i* ....Zech 8:12
fruit that sprang up and *i* .....Mark 4:8
and *i* in number daily ....Acts 16:5
but God gave the *i* 1Cor 3:6
i the fruits of your............2Cor 9:10
when your faith is *i*...........2Cor 10:15
i of the body unto the ....Eph 4:16
i with the *i* of God ....Col 2:19
Lord make you to *i* and.......1Thess 3:12
I am rich and *i* with goods ....Rev 3:17

INCREDIBLE—*unbelievable*
thought a thing *i* with you.....Acts 26:8

INCREDULITY—*an unwillingness to believe*

Characterized by:
Exaggerated demand for evidence ....John 20:24, 25
Desire for more signs ....Judg 6:37-40
Attempts to nullify plain evidence ....John 9:13-41
Blindness of mind ....Acts 28:22-29

INCURABLE—*not capable of being healed*
bowels with an *i* disease 2Chr 21:18
wound is *i* without............Job 34:6
wound *i*..refuseth to be ....Jer 15:18
i for the multitude ....Jer 30:15
For her wound is *i* ....Mic 1:9

INDEBTED—*owing something to someone*
forgive every one that is *i* .....Luke 11:4

INDECENCY—*unseemliness; offensiveness to morality*
Noah guilty of ....Gen 9:21-23
Israelites sin in ....Ex 32:25
Forbidden, to priests.....Ex 20:26
Michal rebukes David for.2Sam 6:20-23
Men committing ....Rom 1:27

INDECISION—*inability to decide between issues considered*

Manifested in, mixing:
Truth and idolatry 1Kin 18:21
Duty and compromise ...John 19:12-16
Holiness and sin.........Gal 5:1-7
Faith and works ....Gal 3:1-5

Results in:
Spiritual unfitness ....Luke 9:59-62
Instability ....James 1:6-8
Sinful compromise 2Cor 6:14-18
Spiritual defeat ....Rom 6:16-22
Spiritual deadness ....Rev 3:15-17

Examples of:
Israel at Kadesh ....Num 13:26-33
Joshua at Ai ....Josh 7:6-10
David at Keilah 1Sam 23:1-5
Pilate ....Matt 27:11-24
Felix ....Acts 24:25, 26

See INCONSTANCY

INDEED—*without any question*
wife shall bear thee a son *i*....Gen 17:19
Shalt thou *i* reign over us? ....Gen 37:8
i have dominion over ....Gen 37:8
For *i* I was stolen away ....Gen 40:15
whereby *i* he divineth? ....Gen 44:5
if ye will obey my voice *i* .....Ex 19:5
should *i* have eaten it ....Lev 10:18
Hath the Lord *i* spoken ....Num 12:2
I not able *i* to promote ....Num 22:37
i the hand of the Lord ....Deut 2:15
I I have sinned against ....Josh 7:20
wilt *i* look on..affliction 1Sam 1:11
I am *i* a widow woman 2Sam 14:5
God *i* dwell on the earth? 1Kin 8:27
Thou hast *i* smitten Edom.....2Kin 14:10
wouldest bless me *i* 1Chr 4:10
be it *i* that I have erred ....Job 19:4
ye *i* speak righteousness.......Ps 58:1
Hear ye *i*, but understand .....Is 6:9
see ye *i* but perceive not ......Is 6:9
For if ye do this thing *i* ....Jer 22:4
I *i* baptize you with water .....Matt 3:11
Ye shall drink *i* of my cup ....Matt 20:23
spirit *i* is willing ....Matt 26:41
I *i* have baptized you ....Mark 1:8
Ye shall *i* drink of the cup ....Mark 10:39
Son of man *i* goeth ....Mark 14:21
i baptize you with water ......Luke 3:16
i justly; for we receive ....Luke 23:41
Behold an Israelite *i* ....John 1:47
For my flesh is meat *i* ....John 6:55
and my blood is drink *i* ....John 6:55
are ye my disciples *i* ....John 8:31
i a noble miracle hath ....Acts 4:16
with me saw *i* the light........Acts 22:9
to be dead *i* unto sin ....Rom 6:11
All things *i* are pure ....Rom 14:20
i ought not to cover his 1Cor 11:7
i he accepted the exhortation ..2Cor 8:17
i preach Christ even of envy...Phil 1:15
to me *i* is not grievous ....Phil 3:1
things have *i* a show ....Col 2:23
i ye do it toward all 1Thess 4:10
widows that are widows *i* 1Tim 5:3
disallowed *i* of men...........1Pet 2:4

INDEPENDENCE—*control of one's affairs apart from outside influences*

Virtues of:
Freedom of action ....Gen 14:22-24
Responsibility ....John 9:21, 23

Evils of:
Arbitrary use of authority.1Sam 14:24-45
Selfishness 1Sam 25:1-11
Mismanagement ....Luke 15:12-16
Arrogance 3John 9, 10

INDIA (ĭn'dĭ-ä)
Eastern limit of Persian Empire ....Esth 1:1

from *I* unto Ethiopia ....Esth 8:9

INDICTMENT—*formal accusation for a crime*
For real crimes:
Korah's company ....Num 16:1-50
Achan ....Josh 7:1-26
Baal worshipers 1Kin 18:10-42
David 2Sam 12:1-14
Ananias ....Acts 5:1-10
For supposed crimes:
Certain tribes ....Josh 22:10-34
Naboth 1Kin 21:1-16
Three Hebrew men ......Dan 3:1-28
Jews.....................Ezra 5:3-17
Esth 3:8, 9
Christ ....Matt 26:61-65
Stephen ....Acts 6:11, 13
Paul.....................Acts 17:7
Acts 16:20, 21

INDIFFERENCE—*lack of interest or concern*
Characteristic of:
Unbelievers ....Luke 17:26-30
Backsliders..............Rev 3:15, 16
As a good feature concerning, worldly:
Comforts ....Phil 4:11-13
Applause ....Gal 1:10
Traditions...............Col 2:16-23
As a bad feature:
Inhumanitarianism ....Luke 10:30-32
In the use of one's talents ....Luke 19:20-26
Moral callousness........Matt 27:3, 4
Religious unconcern .....Acts 18:12-16

INDIGNATION—*extreme wrath against something sinful*
God's:
Irresistible ....Nah 1:6
Victorious ....Hab 3:12
Poured out..............Zeph 3:8
Toward His enemies .....Is 66:14
On Israel ....Deut 29:28
Against Edom forever ...Mal 1:4
Angels, instruments of ...Ps 78:49
On believers ....Job 10:17
Will hide His own from . .Is 26:20
Entreated, on the wicked .Ps 69:24
As punishment ....Rom 2:8
Man's against:
Others..................Esth 5:9
Jews....................Neh 4:1
Christ ....Luke 13:14
Christians ....Acts 5:17

great *i* against Israel 2Kin 3:27
wroth, and took great *i* ....Neh 4:1
thine *i* and thy wrath ....Ps 102:10
in their hand is mine *i* ....Is 10:5
weapons of his *i* to destroy ....Is 13:5
his lips are full of *i* ....Is 30:27
i of the Lord is upon ....Is 34:2
not be able to abide his *i* .....Jer 10:10
the weapons of his *i* ....Jer 50:25
the *i* of his anger ....Lam 2:6
pour out mine *i* upon them....Ezek 21:31
poured out..*i* upon them ......Ezek 22:31
the last end of the *i* ....Dan 8:19
till the *i* be accomplished......Dan 11:36
had *i* these threescore.........Zech 1:12
were moved with *i* against.....Matt 20:24
had *i* saying, To what.........Matt 26:8
had *i* within themselves ....Mark 14:4
what *i*, yea, what fear 2Cor 7:11
of judgment and fiery *i* ....Heb 10:27
into the cup of his *i* ....Rev 14:10

INDIGNITIES SUFFERED BY CHRIST
Against His body:
Spit on ....Matt 26:67
Struck ....John 18:22, 23
Crowned with thorns ....Matt 27:29
Crucified ....Matt 27:31-35
Against His person:
Called guilty without a trial ....John 18:30, 31
Mocked and derided .....Matt 27:29, 31, 39-44
Rejected in favor of a murderer ....Matt 27:16-21
Crucified between two men ....John 19:18

INDISCRIMINATION—*showing lack of distinction in*
Devastation ....Is 24:1-4
Judgment ....Ezek 18:1-32
God's providences ....Matt 5:45

INDITING—*overflowing*
heart is *i* a good matter ....Ps 45:1

INDULGE—*to yield to desires*
Fleshly desires ....Eph 2:3
Corrupt desires..........2Pet 2:10
Gross immorality ....Jude 7

INDULGENCE—*lenience; granting a favor or wish*
Parental 1Sam 3:11-14
Kingly 2Sam 13:21-39
Priestly ....Judg 17:1-13

INDUSTRY—*diligence in one's work*
Characteristics of:
Established ....Gen 2:15
Commanded 1Thess 4:11
Commendable...........Prov 27:23-27
Done willingly ....Prov 31:13
Mark of wisdom.........Prov 10:5
Suspended on Sabbath ...Ex 20:10
Neglect of, rebuked 2Thess 3:10-12
Necessity of:
Our needs 1Thess 2:9
Needs of others ....Acts 20:35
Faithful witness 1Tim 5:8
Blessings of:
Wealth ....Prov 10:4, 5
Praise ....Prov 31:28, 31
Food sufficient ....Prov 12:11
Will rule ....Prov 12:24

[*also* INDUSTRIOUS]
young man that he was *i* 1Kin 11:28

INDWELLING OF BELIEVERS
By Christ:
Through faith ....Eph 3:14-19
Mystery ....Col 1:27
Spirit:
Every believer ....Rom 8:9-11
Body, a temple of God . .1Cor 3:16

INEXCUSABLE—*without excuse*
thou art *i*, O man ....Rom 2:1

INFALLIBLE—*incontrovertible; undeniably true*
by many *i* proofs ....Acts 1:3

INFAMOUS—*having an evil reputation*

[*also* INFAMY]
thine *i* turn not away ....Prov 25:10
mock thee, which art *i* ....Ezek 22:5
are an *i* of the people..........Ezek 36:3

INFANT—*a very young child; in the first period of life*
Acts performed upon:
Naming.................Ruth 4:17
Blessing ....Luke 1:67, 76-79
Circumcision ....Luke 2:21
Capacity to:
Believe ....Matt 18:6
Know the Scriptures 2Tim 3:15
Receive training ....Eph 6:4
Worship in God's house. .1Sam 1:24, 28
Murder of:
By Pharaoh ....Ex 1:16
By Herod the Great .....Matt 2:16-18
In war ....Num 31:17

[*also* INFANTS]
i which never saw light........Job 3:16
more thence an *i* of days ......Is 65:20
i shall be dashed in pieces.....Hos 13:16
brought unto him also *i* ....Luke 18:15

INFERIOR—*of lower degree or quality*
I am not *i* to you ....Job 12:3
I am not *i* unto you ....Job 13:2
another kingdom *i* to thee.....Dan 2:39
were *i* to other churches 2Cor 12:13

INFIDELITY—*unbelief of God's revelation*
Causes of:
Unregenerate heart ......Rom 2:5
Hatred of the light ......John 3:19-21
Spiritual blindness 1Cor 2:8, 14
Self-trust................Is 47:10, 11
Unbelief ....Acts 6:10-15
Inveterate prejudice .....Acts 7:54, 57
Worldly wisdom 1Cor 1:18-22
Manifested in:
Rejecting God's Word ...2Pet 3:3-5
Scoffing at God's servants.2Chr 30:6, 10
Hiding under lies ....Is 28:15
Living without God ......Job 22:13-17
Using derisive words .....Matt 12:24
Doubting God's righteousness ....Ps 10:11, 13
Calling religion worthless .Mal 3:14
Punishment of:
Eternal separation from God 2Thess 1:8, 9
God's wrath 1Thess 2:14-16
Hell ....Luke 16:23-31
Severe punishment ......Heb 10:28, 29
Remedies against:
Remember the end ......Ps 73:16-28
Trust when you can't explain ....Job 2:9, 10
Stand upon the Word ....Matt 4:3-11
Use God's armor ....Eph 6:10-19
Grow spiritually 2Pet 1:4-11

[*also* INFIDEL]
he that believeth with an *i*? ...2Cor 6:15
is worse than an *i* 1Tim 5:8

INFINITE—*subject to no limitation*
God's understanding .....Ps 147:5

and thine iniquities *i*? ....Job 22:5
strength, and it was *i* ....Nah 3:9

INFIRMITIES—*weaknesses of our human nature*
Kinds of:
Sickness or disease ......Matt 8:17
Imperfections of the body.2Cor 11:30
Moral defects ....Rom 8:26
Our duties with reference to:
Rejoice in 2Cor 12:10
Help those afflicted with .Rom 15:1
Gal 6:1
Not to despise in others . .Gal 4:13, 14
Be sympathetic concerning .... Heb 5:2, 3; Heb 7:27, 28
Make us humble ....Rom 6:19
Come to Jesus with ......Heb 4:15, 16
Serve God more, if without ....Josh 14:10-14

[*also* INFIRMITY]
days of..separation for her *i* ...Lev 12:2
This is my *i* ....Ps 77:10
a man will sustain his *i*........Prov 18:14
healed by him of their *i*.......Luke 5:15
healed of evil spirits and *i*.....Luke 8:2
which had a spirit of *i* ....Luke 13:11
i thirty and eight years ....John 5:5
not glory, but in mine *i* 2Cor 12:5
rather glory in my *i*...........2Cor 12:9
and thine often *i* 1Tim 5:23

INFLAME—*to excite to unnatural behavior; local reaction to disease or injury*

[*also* INFLAMMATION]
it is an *i* of the burning ......Lev 13:28

with a fever and with an *i* ..... Deut 28:22
until night, till wine *i* them! ... Is 5:11

INFLICTED—*imposed; afflicted*
punishment, which was *i* 2Cor 2:6

INFLUENCE—*the ability to affect or determine events or decisions to act*

Christians should be:
As salt .... Matt 5:13
As light .... Matt 5:14-16
Phil 2:15
As examples 1Thess 1:7, 8
Beneficial to spouse 1Pet 3:1, 2
1Cor 7:14, 16
Above criticism 1Cor 8:10-13
Honorable 1Tim 6:1
Permanent .... Heb 11:4
Beneficial to others 1Pet 2:11, 12
Without reproach .... Phil 2:15, 16

INFOLDING—*folding inward*
fire *i* itself, and a brightness ... Ezek 1:4

INFORM—*to communicate knowledge to*

[*also* INFORMED]
according to all that they *i* .... Deut 17:10
i me and talked with me ...... Dan 9:22
i of thee that thou teachest .... Acts 21:21
i the governor against Paul .... Acts 24:1
Jews *i* him against Paul .... Acts 25:2

INGATHERING—*bringing in*
And the feast of *i* .... Ex 23:16
feast of *i* at..year's end .... Ex 34:22

INGENUITY—*skill or cleverness*
Of God .... Job 38:4-41
Ps 139:13-16
Of man .... { Ex 35:30-33
Ex 2:1-9
Gen 27:7-29 }

INGRATITUDE—*unthankfulness for blessings received*

Characteristics of:
Inconsiderate .... Deut 32:6, 7
Unreasonable .... Jer 2:5-7
Unnatural .... Is 1:2, 3
Ungrateful .... Jer 5:7-9, 24

Causes of:
Prosperity .... Deut 6:10-12
Self-sufficiency .... Deut 8:12-18
Forgetfulness .... Luke 17:12-18
Fear 1Sam 23:5, 12
Greed 1Sam 25:4-11
Pride .... Dan 5:18-20

Attitudes toward:
Acknowledged 1Sam 24:17-19
Abused 2Chr 24:22
Revealed 1Sam 23:5-12
Forgiven by kindness 1Sam 25:14-35
Long remembered .... Deut 25:17-19
Overcome by faithfulness . Gen 31:38-42

Examples of:
Moses by Israel .... Ex 17:1-3
Gideon by Israel .... Judg 8:33-35
God by Saul 1Sam 15:16-23
God by David 2Sam 12:7-14
Jeremiah by Judah ...... Jer 18:19, 20
God by the world .... Rom 1:21

INHABIT—*to dwell*

[*also* INHABITED, INHABITEST, INHABITETH, INHABITING]
Horite, who *i* the land .... Gen 36:20
until they came to a land *i* .... Ex 16:35
iniquities unto a land not *i* .... Lev 16:22
land which ye shall *i* .... Num 35:34
Canaanites that *i* Zephath ..... Judg 1:17
i unto the entering in 1Chr 5:9
houses which no man *i* .... Job 15:28
flood breaketh out from the *i*. Job 28:4
thou that *i* the praises of ...... Ps 22:3
to the people *i* the wilderness. . Ps 74:14
the wicked shall not *i* .... Prov 10:30
It shall never be *i* .... Is 13:20
villages that Kedar doth *i* ..... Is 42:11
he formed it to be *i* .... Is 45:18
One that *i* eternity .... Is 57:15
not build and another *i* .... Is 65:22
desolate, a land not *i* .... Jer 6:8
shall *i* the parched places ..... Jer 17:6
cities which are not *i* .... Jer 22:6
it shall not be *i* .... Jer 50:13
that are *i* shall be laid .... Ezek 12:20
like the cities that are not *i* ... Ezek 26:19
shall it be *i* forty years .... Ezek 29:11
i those wastes of the land ..... Ezek 33:24
cities shall be *i* .... Ezek 36:10
desolate places that are now *i* . Ezek 38:12
build the waste cities, and *i* ... Amos 9:14
build houses, but not *i* .... Zeph 1:13
Jerusalem..be *i* as towns ...... Zech 2:4
when Jerusalem was *i* .... Zech 7:7
men *i* the south and the .... Zech 7:7
Jerusalem shall be *i* again ..... Zech 12:6
Jerusalem shall be safely *i* ..... Zech 14:11

INHABITANT—*dweller; native*

[*also* INHABITANTS, INHABITERS]
all the *i* of the cities .... Gen 19:25
i of the land the Canaanites ... Gen 50:11
hold on the *i* of Palestina ...... Ex 15:14
i of Canaan shall melt away ... Ex 15:15
deliver the *i* of the land .... Ex 23:31
covenant with the *i* of the land. Ex 34:15
land..vomiteth out her *i* .... Lev 18:25
land that eateth up the *i* ...... Num 13:32
cities because of the *i* .... Num 32:17
ye shall dispossess the *i* .... Num 33:53
withdrawn the *i* of their city ... Deut 13:13
i of the land faint .... Josh 2:9
i of the land shall hear .... Josh 7:9
destroyed all the *i* of Ai ...... Josh 8:26
i of our country spake .... Josh 9:11
i of Gibeon had made peace .. Josh 10:1
All the *i* of the hill country ... Josh 13:6
Jebusites the *i* of Jerusalem ... Josh 15:63
i of Dor and her towns .... Josh 17:11
i of En-dor and her towns ..... Josh 17:11
i of Taanach and her towns .... Josh 17:11
i of Megiddo and her towns ... Josh 17:11
against the *i* of Debir .... Judg 1:11
he drove out the *i* of the ...... Judg 1:19
drive out the *i* of..valley ...... Judg 1:19
i of Beth-shean and her towns . Judg 1:27
i of Dor and her towns .... Judg 1:27
i of Ibleam and her towns ..... Judg 1:27
i of Megiddo and her towns ... Judg 1:27
drive out the *i* of Kitron ...... Judg 1:30
nor the *i* of Nahalol .... Judg 1:30
drive out the *i* of Accho ...... Judg 1:31
i of Zidon, nor of Ahlab ...... Judg 1:31
Canaanites, the *i* of..land ..... Judg 1:32
out the *i* of Beth-shemesh ..... Judg 1:33
nor the *i* of Beth-anath .... Judg 1:33
Canaanites, the *i* of..land ..... Judg 1:33
i of Beth-shemesh .... Judg 1:33
league with the *i* of this ...... Judg 2:2
i of the villages ceased .... Judg 5:7
curse ye bitterly..*i* thereof .... Judg 5:23
over all the *i* of Gilead .... Judg 11:8
i of Gibeah..were numbered .. Judg 20:15
smite the *i* of Jabesh-gilead ... Judg 21:10
But it before the *i* .... Ruth 4:4
i of Kirjath-jearim 1Sam 6:21
nations were of old the *i* 1Sam 27:8
Jebusites, the *i* of..land 2Sam 5:6
who was of the *i* of Gilead 1Kin 17:1
nobles who were the *i* in 1Kin 21:11
i were of small power 2Kin 19:26
against the *i* thereof 2Kin 22:19
fathers of the *i* of Geba 1Chr 8:6
fathers of the *i* of Aijalon 1Chr 8:13
drove away the *i* of Gath 1Chr 8:13
the *i* of the land 1Chr 11:4
i of the land into mine 1Chr 22:18
were upon all the *i* of 2Chr 15:5
and ye *i* of Jerusalem 2Chr 20:15
ye *i* of Jerusalem 2Chr 20:20
against the *i* of mount Seir 2Chr 20:23
had made an end of the *i* 2Chr 20:23
i of Jerusalem to go a whoring . 2Chr 21:13
i of Jerusalem from..hand 2Chr 32:22
i of Jerusalem did him honor .. 2Chr 32:33
and upon the *i* thereof 2Chr 34:24
upon the *i* of the same 2Chr 34:28
i of Jerusalem did according ... 2Chr 34:32
i of Judah and Jersualem ...... Ezra 4:6
i of Zanoah..built it .... Neh 3:13
the *i* of the land .... Neh 9:24
waters, and the *i* thereof ...... Job 26:5
i of the world stand in awe .... Ps 33:8
all ye *i* of the world .... Ps 49:1
i thereof are dissolved .... Ps 75:3
the Philistines with the *i* ...... Ps 83:7
i of Jerusalem, and men ...... Is 5:3
great and fair, without *i* .... Is 5:9
i of Samaria that say in .... Is 9:9
put down..*i* like a valiant ..... Is 10:13
All ye *i* of the world .... Is 18:3
i of this isle shall say in .... Is 20:6
be a father to the *i* .... Is 22:21
howl, ye *i* of the isle .... Is 23:6
defiled under the *i* thereof .... Is 24:5
i of the world will learn .... Is 26:9
punish the *i* of the earth ...... Is 26:21
i shall not say, I am sick ...... Is 33:24
with the *i* of the world .... Is 38:11
i..are as grasshoppers .... Is 40:22
the isles, and the *i* .... Is 42:10
let the *i* of the rock sing ...... Is 42:11
narrow by reason of the *i* ..... Is 49:19
upon all the *i* of the land ...... Jer 1:14
cities are burned without *i* .... Jer 2:15
hand upon the *i* of the land ... Jer 6:12
Judah desolate, without an *i* .. Jer 9:11
sling out the *i* of the land ..... Jer 10:18
among the *i* of Jerusalem ..... Jer 11:9
will fill all the *i* of this .... Jer 13:13
all the *i* of Jerusalem .... Jer 17:20
to the *i* of Jerusalem .... Jer 18:11
and to the *i* thereof .... Jer 19:12
O *i* of the valley .... Jer 21:13
i thereof as Gomorrah .... Jer 23:14
against the *i* thereof .... Jer 25:9
against all the *i* of the earth .. Jer 25:30
be desolate without an *i* ...... Jer 26:9
and the *i* of Jerusalem .... Jer 32:32
a desolation without an *i* ...... Jer 34:22
all the *i* of Jerusalem .... Jer 35:17
upon the *i* of Jerusalem .... Jer 42:18
desolate without an *i* .... Jer 46:19
all the *i* of the land shall ...... Jer 47:2
O *i* of Moab, saith the Lord .. Jer 48:43
against the *i* of Teman .... Jer 49:20
against the *i* of Pekod .... Jer 50:21
upon the *i* of Babylon .... Jer 50:35
to all the *i* of Chaldea .... Jer 51:24
all the *i* of the world .... Lam 4:12
whom the *i* of Jerusalem ...... Ezek 11:15
I give the *i* of Jerusalem ...... Ezek 15:6
i of Zidon and Arvad .... Ezek 27:8
all the *i* of Egypt shall know .. Ezek 29:6
i of the earth are reputed ..... Dan 4:35
to the *i* of Jerusalem .... Dan 9:7
controversy with the *i* of ...... Hos 4:1
all ye *i* of the land .... Joel 1:2
all the *i* of the land tremble ... Joel 2:1
cut off the *i* from the plain .... Amos 1:5
Pass ye away, thou *i* of .... Mic 1:11
i of Zaanan came not forth .... Mic 1:11
O thou *i* of Lachish .... Mic 1:13
O *i* of Mareshah .... Mic 1:15
i thereof have spoken lies ..... Mic 6:12
all the *i* of Jerusalem .... Zeph 1:4
Woe unto the *i* of..sea coast .. Zeph 2:5
i of many cities .... Zech 8:20
i of one city shall go to .... Zech 8:21
no more pity the *i* of the land . Zech 11:6
i of Jerusalem do not .... Zech 12:7
upon the *i* of Jerusalem .... Zech 12:10
woe, to the *i* of the earth ..... Rev 8:13
Woe to the *i* of the earth ..... Rev 12:12
i of the earth have been ...... Rev 17:2

INHERITANCE—*something received as a right or divine portion*

[*also* INHERIT, INHERITANCES, INHERITED, INHERITETH]
thou mayest *i* the land ....Gen 28:4
any portion or *i* for us ....Gen 31:14
in the mountain of thine *i*.....Ex 15:17
they shall *i* it for ever.........Ex 32:13
Ye shall *i* their land ....Lev 20:24
i them for a possession........Lev 25:46
as an *i* for your children ......Lev 25:46
i of fields and vineyards.......Num 16:14
thou shalt have no *i* in ....Num 18:20
thy part and thine *i* among ....Num 18:20
children of Israel..have no *i* ...Num 18:23
given to the Levites to *i*.......Num 18:24
from them for your *i* ....Num 18:26
shalt give the more *i*..........Num 26:54
thou shalt give the less *i* ......Num 26:54
their fathers they shall *i*.......Num 26:55
there was no *i* given ....Num 26:62
have *i* every man his *i* ....Num 32:18
will not *i* with them ....Num 32:19
the possession of our *i* on .....Num 32:32
divide the land by lot for an *i* .Num 33:54
ye shall give the more *i* ....Num 33:54
fewer ye shall give the less *i*...Num 33:54
i shall be in the place ....Num 33:54
land..ye shall *i* by lot ....Num 34:13
have received their *i*..........Num 34:14
of Manasseh have received..*i* ..Num 34:14
to divide the land by *i* ....Num 34:18
the *i* of their possession ....Num 35:2
his inheritance which he *i* .....Num 35:8
give the land for an *i* by lot ...Num 36:2
i of Zelophehad..brother ......Num 36:2
their *i* be taken from the *i* ....Num 36:3
be put to the *i* of the tribe ....Num 36:3
taken from the lot of our *i* ....Num 36:3
i be put unto the *i*............Num 36:4
i be taken away from the *i* ....Num 36:4
i remained in the tribe ....Num 36:12
shall cause Israel to *i* it ....Deut 1:38
cause them to *i* the land ....Deut 3:28
unto him a people of *i* ....Deut 4:20
give thee their land for an *i* ...Deut 4:38
no part nor *i* with his ....Deut 10:9
Lord is his *i*, according ....Deut 10:9
God giveth you to *i* ....Deut 12:10
hath no part nor *i* with you ...Deut 12:12
no part nor *i* with thee........Deut 14:29
mayest live, and *i* the land ....Deut 16:20
part nor *i* with Israel ....Deut 18:1
made by fire, and his *i*........Deut 18:1
shall they have no *i*...........Deut 18:2
Lord is their *i*, as he hath .....Deut 18:2
old time have set in thine *i*....Deut 19:14
shalt *i* in the land that ....Deut 19:14
God giveth thee for an *i* ......Deut 21:23
giveth thee for an *i* ....Deut 25:19
i unto the Reubenites ....Deut 29:8
shalt cause them to *i* it.........Deut 31:7
Jacob is the lot of his *i* ....Deut 32:9
divide for an *i* the land ....Josh 1:6
unto the Israelites for an *i* ....Josh 13:6
Israel *i* in the land of ....Josh 14:1
distributed for *i* to them ......Josh 14:1
Moses had given the *i* of two ..Josh 14:3
the Levites he gave none *i* ....Josh 14:3
son of..Hebron for an *i* ....Josh 14:13
i of the tribe of ....Josh 15:20
border of their *i* on the east ...Josh 16:5
i of..children of Manasseh .....Josh 16:9
to give us an *i* among.........Josh 17:4
an *i* among the brethren ......Josh 17:4
lot and one portion to *i*.......Josh 17:14
i of..children of Benjamin .....Josh 18:28
had in their *i* Beer-sheba ......Josh 19:2
i of..children of Simeon ....Josh 19:9
children of Simeon had..*i* .....Josh 19:9
within the *i* of them ....Josh 19:9
i of..children of Zebulun ......Josh 19:16
coast of their *i* was Zorah .....Josh 19:41
dividing the land for *i*.........Josh 19:49
are the *i*, which Eleazar.......Josh 19:51
divided for an *i* by lot ....Josh 19:51
to be an *i* for your tribes......Josh 23:4
him in the border of his *i* .....Josh 24:30
man unto his *i* to possess .....Judg 2:6
not *i* in our father's house.....Judg 11:2
Danites sought them an *i* .....Judg 18:1
i had not fallen unto ....Judg 18:1
must be an *i* for them ....Judg 21:17
every man to his *i* ....Judg 21:24
lest I mar mine own *i*.........Ruth 4:6
them *i* the throne of glory.....1Sam 2:8
to be captain over his *i*? 1Sam 10:1
together out of the *i* of God...2Sam 14:16
swallow up the *i* of the Lord? .2Sam 20:19
given to thy people for an *i* ...1Kin 8:36
of the earth to be thine *i* 1Kin 8:53
Canaan the lot of your *i* 1Chr 16:18
given unto thy people for..*i* ...2Chr 6:27
hast given us to *i* 2Chr 20:11
for an *i* to your children ......Ezra 9:12
Judah everyone in his *i* ....Neh 11:20
i of the Almighty from on.....Job 31:2
i among their brethren ....Job 42:15
Lord is the portion of..*i*........Ps 16:5
hath chosen for his own *i* .....Ps 33:12
Lord, they shall *i*..earth ....Ps 37:9
meek shall *i* the earth.........Ps 37:11
i shall be for ever ....Ps 37:18
blessed of him..*i* the earth ....Ps 37:22
righteous shall *i* the land ......Ps 37:29
exalt thee to *i* the land........Ps 37:34
shall choose our *i* for us ......Ps 47:4
rod of thine *i*, which thou .....Ps 74:2
was wroth with his *i* ....Ps 78:62
and Israel his *i* ....Ps 78:71
thou shalt *i* all nations ....Ps 82:8
neither will he forsake his *i* ...Ps 94:14
Canaan the lot of your *i* ......Ps 105:11
i the labor of the people ......Ps 105:44
I may glory with thine *i*.......Ps 106:5
love me to *i* substance ....Prov 8:21
good man leaveth an *i* ....Prov 13:22
simple *i* folly: but the prudent .Prov 14:18
the *i* among the brethren......Prov 17:2
i may be gotten hastily.........Prov 20:21
Wisdom is good with an *i* .....Eccl 7:11
and Israel mine *i* ....Is 19:25
to *i* the desolate heritages .....Is 49:8
shall *i* my holy mountain ......Is 57:13
the tribes of thine *i* ....Is 63:17
for an *i* unto your fathers .....Jer 3:18
fields to them that shall *i* .....Jer 8:10
our fathers have *i* lies.........Jer 16:19
for the right of *i* is thine ......Jer 32:8
why then doth their king *i* ....Jer 49:1
i is turned to strangers ....Lam 5:2
shalt take thine *i* in..........Ezek 22:16
i the land: but we are.........Ezek 33:24
the *i* of the house of Israel ....Ezek 35:15
thou shalt be their *i* ....Ezek 36:12
divide by lot the land for *i* ....Ezek 45:1
i thereof shall be his sons .....Ezek 46:16
shall be their possession by *i* ..Ezek 46:16
gift of his *i* to one of his ......Ezek 46:17
his *i* shall be his sons'.........Ezek 46:17
not take of the people's *i* .....Ezek 46:18
give his sons *i* out of ....Ezek 46:18
ye shall *i* the land ....Ezek 47:13
divide it by lot for an *i* unto...Ezek 47:22
have *i* with you among........Ezek 47:22
ye give him his *i* ....Ezek 47:23
tribes of Israel for *i*..........Ezek 48:29
Lord shall *i* Judah ....Zech 2:12
meek for they shall *i*..........Matt 5:5
do that I may *i* eternal life? ...Mark 10:17
and the *i* shall be ours ....Mark 12:7
shall I do to *i* eternal life? ....Luke 10:25
divide the *i* with me ....Luke 12:13
that the *i* may be ours ....Luke 20:14
gave him none *i* in it ....Acts 7:5
i among them which are ....Acts 26:18
corruption *i* incorruption 1Cor 15:50
i the kingdom of God.........Gal 5:21
we have obtained an *i* ....Eph 1:11
the glory of his *i* in the saints. .Eph 1:18
be partakers of the *i* of ....Col 1:12
hath by *i* obtained a more.....Heb 1:4
after receive for an *i*..........Heb 11:8
would have *i* the blessing .....Heb 12:17

INHERITANCE, EARTHLY

Among Israelites:
God the owner ....Lev 25:23, 28
Possessed by families ....Num 27:4, 7
Law of transmission .....Num 27:8-11
If sold, restored in year of jubilee ....Lev 25:25-34
Must remain in tribe.....Num 36:6-10
Repossessed by kinsman. .Ruth 4:3-5, 10

General characteristics of:
From fathers ....Prov 19:14
Uncertain use ....Eccl 2:18, 19
Object of seizure ....1Kin 21:3, 4; Matt 21:38
Squandered ....Luke 15:11-13
Foolish not blessed ......Prov 11:29
Descendants blessed .....Ps 25:12, 13

See HEIRS, NATURAL

INHERITANCE OF ISRAEL—*the land God promised to Israel*

Basic features of:
Lord, Israel's ....Deut 9:26, 29
Land promised to Abraham's seed ....Gen 15:7-18
Limits defined...........Gen 15:18-21
Limits fulfilled 1Kin 4:21, 24
Possession of, based on obedience.............2Kin 21:12-15
Blessed by the Lord .....Deut 15:4
Tribes destroyed from ...Deut 20:16-18
Possessed by degrees ....Ex 23:29-31
Apportioned ....Josh 13:7-33
Tribes encouraged to possess ....Josh 18:1-10
Levites excluded from ...Num 18:20-24
Lost by sin..............Ps 79:1
Restored after the captivity ....Neh 11:20

Figurative of:
Messianic blessings ......Ps 2:8
Call of the Gentiles......Is 54:3
Elect remnant ....Is 65:8, 9
Eternal possessions ......Is 60:21

INHERITANCE, SPIRITUAL—*benefits God promises for faithfulness*

Objects of:
Kingdom ....Matt 25:34
Eternal life ....Matt 19:29
Promises................Heb 6:12
Blessing 1Pet 3:9
All things ....Rev 21:7
Glory ....Prov 3:35

Nature of:
Sealed by the Spirit......Eph 1:13, 14
Received from the Lord. .Col 3:24
Results from Christ's death ....Heb 9:15
Depends on belief ....Gal 3:18, 22
Incorruptible 1Pet 1:4
Final, in heaven 1Pet 1:4

Restrictions upon, only:
For the righteous 1Cor 6:9, 10
For the sanctified........Acts 20:32
In Christ................Eph 1:11, 12
For the transformed 1Cor 15:50-53

See HEIRS, SPIRITUAL

INHERITOR—*one who inherits*
Judah an *i* of my mountains ...Is 65:9

INHOSPITALITY—*unwillingness to entertain strangers*
Edomites ....Num 20:17-21
Sihon...................Num 21:22, 23
Gibeah ....Judg 19:15
Nabal 1Sam 25:10-17
Samaritans ....Luke 9:53

Diotrephes ... 3John 10
Penalty for ... Deut 23:3, 4
Luke 10:10-16

INIQUITY—*gross injustice; wickedness*

Sources of:
Heart ... Ps 41:6
Matt 23:28

Effects upon man:
Insatiable appetite for ... Ezek 7:16, 19
Perversion ... Ezek 9:9

God's attitude toward:
Cannot look on ... Hab 1:13
Does not do ... Zeph 3:5
Remembers and punishes ... Jer 14:10
Visits on children ... Ex 34:7
Pardons and subdues ... Mic 7:18, 19
Takes away from us ... Zech 3:4
Lays upon the Messiah ... Is 53:5, 6, 11
Remembers no more ... Heb 8:12

Christ's relation to:
Bears our ... Is 53:5, 6, 11
Makes reconciliation for. ... Dan 9:24
Redeems us ... Titus 2:14

Believer's relation to:
Will declare it ... Ps 38:18
Confesses ... Neh 9:2
Prays for pardon of ... Ps 25:11
Forgiven of ... Ps 32:5
Must depart from ... 2Tim 2:19
Protection from ... Ps 125:3
Separation from God ... Is 59:2
Prays for freedom from ... Ps 119:133
Hindrance to prayer ... Ps 66:18

Punishment for:
Wanderings ... Num 14:34
Loss of strength ... Ps 31:10
Destruction ... Gen 19:15
Captivity ... Ezra 9:7
Death ... Ezek 18:24, 26
Less than deserved ... Ezra 9:13
Remembered forever ... 1Sam 3:13, 14
In hell ... Ezek 32:27

[*also* INIQUITIES]
i of the Amorites is not yet ... Gen 15:16
found out..*i* of thy servants ... Gen 44:16
visiting the *i* of the fathers ... Ex 20:5
that they bear not *i* ... Ex 28:43
pardon our *i* and our sin ... Ex 34:9
then he shall bear his *i* ... Lev 5:1
eateth of it shall bear his *i* ... Lev 7:18
i of the children of Israel ... Lev 16:21
then he shall bear his *i* ... Lev 17:16
eateth it shall bear his *i* ... Lev 19:8
they shall bear their *i* ... Lev 20:19
pine away in their *i* in ... Lev 26:39
i of their fathers shall they ... Lev 26:39
punishment of their *i* ... Lev 26:41
i to remembrance ... Num 5:15
man be guiltless from *i* ... Num 5:31
woman shall bear her *i* ... Num 5:31
forgiving *i* and ... Num 14:18
visiting the *i* of the fathers ... Num 14:18
his *i* shall be upon him ... Num 15:31
bear the *i* of the sanctuary ... Num 18:1
bear the *i* of..priesthood ... Num 18:1
not beheld *i* in Jacob ... Num 23:21
visiting the *i* of..fathers ... Deut 5:9
God of truth and without *i* ... Deut 32:4
perished not alone in his *i* ... Josh 22:20
stubbornness is as *i* ... 1Sam 15:23
if there be in me *i* ... 1Sam 20:8
he commit *i* I will chasten ... 2Sam 7:14
if there be any *i* in me ... 2Sam 14:32
kept myself from mine *i* ... 2Sam 22:24
do away the *i* of thy servant ... 1Chr 21:8
no *i* with the Lord our God ... 2Chr 19:7
i are increased over..head ... Ezra 9:6
cover not their *i* ... Neh 4:5
plow *i* and sow wickedness ... Job 4:8
pray you, let it not be *i* ... Job 6:29
Is there *i* in my tongue? ... Job 6:30
and take away mine *i*? ... Job 7:21
acquit me from mine *i* ... Job 10:14
If *i* be in thine hand ... Job 11:14
many are mine *i* and sins? ... Job 13:23
mouth uttereth thine *i* ... Job 15:5
drinketh *i* like water? ... Job 15:16
heaven shall reveal his *i* ... Job 20:27
and thine *i* infinite? ... Job 22:5
i far from thy tabernacles ... Job 22:23
i to be punished by the judges ... Job 31:11
hiding mine *i* in my bosom ... Job 31:33
neither is there *i* in me ... Job 33:9
company with the workers of *i* ... Job 34:8
the workers of *i* may hide ... Job 34:22
done *i*, I will do no more ... Job 34:32
that they return from *i* ... Job 36:10
Thou hast wrought *i*? ... Job 36:23
hatest all workers of *i* ... Ps 5:5
all ye workers of *i* ... Ps 6:8
if there be *i* in my hands ... Ps 7:3
he travaileth with *i* ... Ps 7:14
workers of *i* no knowledge? ... Ps 14:4
with the workers of *i* ... Ps 28:3
Lord imputeth not *i* ... Ps 32:2
i be found to be hateful ... Ps 36:2
are the workers of *i* fallen ... Ps 36:12
envious against..workers of *i* ... Ps 37:1
i are gone over mine head ... Ps 38:4
dost correct man for *i* ... Ps 39:11
i of my heels shall compass ... Ps 49:5
me thoroughly from mine *i* ... Ps 51:2
I was shapen in *i* ... Ps 51:5
blot out all mine *i* ... Ps 51:9
workers of *i* no ... Ps 53:4
Shall they escape by *i*? ... Ps 56:7
insurrection of..workers of *i* ... Ps 64:2
I prevail against me ... Ps 65:3
Add *i* unto their *i* ... Ps 69:27
remember not..former *i* ... Ps 79:8
forgiven the *i* of thy people ... Ps 85:2
hast set our *i* before ... Ps 90:8
workers of *i* do flourish ... Ps 92:7
workers of *i* boast ... Ps 94:4
throne of *i* have fellowship ... Ps 94:20
Who forgiveth all thine *i* ... Ps 103:3
rewarded us according to..*i* ... Ps 103:10
we have commited *i* ... Ps 106:6
all *i* shall stop her mouth ... Ps 107:42
They also do no *i* ... Ps 119:3
with the workers of *i* ... Ps 125:5
If..Lord, shouldest mark *i* ... Ps 130:3
gins of the workers of *i* ... Ps 141:9
own *i* shall take the wicked ... Prov 5:22
be to the workers of *i* ... Prov 10:29
of the wicked devoureth *i* ... Prov 19:28
soweth *i* shall reap vanity ... Prov 22:8
that *i* was there ... Eccl 3:16
a people laden with *i* ... Is 1:4
that draw *i* with cords ... Is 5:18
wicked for their *i* ... Is 13:11
this *i* shall not be purged ... Is 22:14
i of Jacob be purged ... Is 27:9
watch for *i* are cut of ... Is 29:20
help of them that work *i* ... Is 31:2
shall be forgiven their *i* ... Is 33:24
for your *i* have ye sold ... Is 50:1
i of his covetousness ... Is 57:17
mischief, and bring forth *i* ... Is 59:4
thoughts are thoughts of *i* ... Is 59:7
as for our *i*, we know them ... Is 59:12
consumed us, because of..*i* ... Is 64:7
i have your fathers found ... Jer 2:5
Only acknowledge thine *i* ... Jer 3:13
Your *i* have turned away ... Jer 5:25
greatness of thine *i* ... Jer 13:22
i testify against us ... Jer 14:7
the *i* of our fathers ... Jer 14:20
i hid from mine ... Jer 16:17
forgive not their *i* ... Jer 18:23
multitude of thine *i* ... Jer 30:14
one shall die for his own *i* ... Jer 31:30
recompensest the *i* of the ... Jer 32:18
will pardon all their *i* ... Jer 33:8
I may forgive their *i* ... Jer 36:3
i of Israel shall be sought ... Jer 50:20
have not discovered thine *i* ... Lam 2:14
i of her priests ... Lam 4:13
punishment of thine *i* ... Lam 4:22
he will visit thine *i* ... Lam 4:22
wicked man..die in his *i* ... Ezek 3:18
righteousness..commit *i* ... Ezek 3:20
i of the house of Israel ... Ezek 4:4
it thou shalt bear their *i* ... Ezek 4:4
years of their *i* ... Ezek 4:5
thou bear the *i* of the house ... Ezek 4:5
consume away for their *i* ... Ezek 4:17
i of the house of Israel ... Ezek 9:9
stumbling block of his *i* ... Ezek 14:4
i of thy sister Sodom ... Ezek 16:49
die for the *i* of his father ... Ezek 18:17
son bear the *i* of the father? ... Ezek 18:19
not bear the *i* of the father ... Ezek 18:20
father bear the *i* of the son ... Ezek 18:20
i shall not be your ruin ... Ezek 18:30
call to remembrance the *i* ... Ezek 21:23
when *i* shall have an end ... Ezek 21:25
shall pine away for your *i* ... Ezek 24:23
till *i* was found in thee ... Ezek 28:15
bringeth..*i* to remembrance ... Ezek 29:16
wicked man shall die in..*i* ... Ezek 33:8
righteousness, and commit *i* ... Ezek 33:13
i that he hath committed ... Ezek 33:13
and committeth *i*, he shall ... Ezek 33:18
cleansed you from all your *i* ... Ezek 36:33
went into captivity for their *i* ... Ezek 39:23
house of Israel to fall into *i* ... Ezek 44:12
they shall bear their *i* ... Ezek 44:12
thine *i* by showing mercy to ... Dan 4:27
and have committed *i* ... Dan 9:5
for the *i* of our fathers ... Dan 9:16
set their heart on their *i* ... Hos 4:8
city of them that work *i* ... Hos 6:8
will he remember their *i* ... Hos 8:13
he will remember their *i* ... Hos 9:9
ye have reaped *i* ... Hos 10:13
Is there *i* in Gilead? ... Hos 12:11
hast fallen by thine *i* ... Hos 14:1
Take away all *i* ... Hos 14:2
punish you for all your *i* ... Amos 3:2
Woe to them that devise *i* ... Mic 2:1
he will subdue our *i* ... Mic 7:19
Why dost thou show me *i* ... Hab 1:3
stablisheth a city by *i*! ... Hab 2:12
remnant of Israel..not do *i* ... Zeph 3:13
remove the *i* of that land ... Zech 3:9
i was not found in his lips ... Mal 2:6
turn many away from *i* ... Mal 2:6
from me, ye that work *i* ... Matt 7:23
i shall abound, the love of ... Matt 24:12
all ye workers of *i* ... Luke 13:27
a field with the reward of *i* ... Acts 1:18
every one of you from his *i* ... Acts 3:26
they whose *i* are forgiven ... Rom 4:7
uncleanness and to *i* unto *i* ... Rom 6:19
Rejoiceth not in *i* ... 1Cor 13:6
mystery of *i*..already work ... 2Thess 2:7
righteousness and hated *i* ... Heb 1:9
sins and *i*..remember no more ... Heb 10:17
tongue is a fire, a world of *i* ... James 3:6
But was rebuked for his *i* ... 2Pet 2:16
God hath remembered her *i* ... Rev 18:5

INJOIN—*See* ENJOIN

INJURIOUS—*harm; harmful*

[*also* INJURED]
ye have not *i* me at all ... Gal 4:12
a persecutor, and *i*: but I ... 1Tim 1:13

INJUSTICE—*that which violates another's rights*

Examples of, among men:
Laban's treatment of
Jacob ... Gen 31:36-42
Saul's treatment of:
Priests ... 1Sam 22:15-23
David ... 1Sam 24:8-22
1Sam 26:14-25
David's treatment of
Uriah ... 2Sam 12:1-12
Irijah's treatment of
Jeremiah ... Jer 37:11-21

Charges made against God for His:
Choice ....Num 16:1-14
Inequality ....Ezek 18:25
Partiality ....Rom 9:14
Delay ....Rev 6:10

Punishment on executed:
Severely 1Sam 15:32, 33
Swiftly ....Esth 7:9, 10
According to prophecy . . .1Kin 22:34-38

See JUST; JUSTICE

INK—*a colored liquid used for writing*
Used for writing a book. .Jer 36:18
Used in letter writing 2John 12
3John 13

written not with *i* 2Cor 3:3

INKHORN—*a case for pens and ink*
Writer's tool ....Ezek 9:2, 3

had the *i* by his side ....Ezek 9:11

INN—*a shelter providing lodging for travelers*
Lodging place ....Jer 9:2
Place for rest ....Luke 2:7

give his ass provender in the *i* .Gen 42:27
when we came to the *i* ....Gen 43:21
came to pass by..way in the *i*. .Ex 4:24
brought him to an *i* ....Luke 10:34

INNER—*situated further within*

[*also* INNERMOST]
cherubim within the *i* house . . .1Kin 6:27
i court of the house 1Kin 7:12
city, into an *i* chamber 1Kin 20:30
carry him to an *i* chamber 2Kin 9:2
i parlors thereof 1Chr 28:11
i doors thereof for the 2Chr 4:22
shalt go into an *i* chamber 2Chr 18:24
the king into the *i* court.......Esth 4:11
down into the *i* parts of.......Prov 18:8
down into the *i* parts of.......Prov 26:22
door of the *i* gate ....Ezek 8:3
cloud filled the *i* court ....Ezek 10:3
forefront of the *i* court ....Ezek 40:19
gate in the *i* court toward .....Ezek 40:27
brought me into the *i* court . . .Ezek 40:32
i gate were the chambers ......Ezek 40:44
singers in the *i* court ....Ezek 40:44
door, even unto the *i* house . . .Ezek 41:17
an end of measuring the *i* .....Ezek 42:15
in at the gates of the *i* court . . .Ezek 44:17
minister in the gates of the *i* . .Ezek 44:17
sanctuary, unto the *i* ....Ezek 44:27
the gate of the *i* court that ....Ezek 46:1
thrust them into the *i* prison . . .Acts 16:24
by his Spirit in the *i* man .....Eph 3:16

INNER GROUP—*a small, close circle*
At girl's bedside ....Mark 5:35-40
At Christ's transfiguration. Mark 9:2
In Gethsemane ....Matt 26:36, 37

INNER MAN—*man's genuine identity*
Often hidden ....Matt 23:27, 28
Seen by God 1Sam 16:7
Strengthened ....Eph 3:16

INNER NATURES, CONFLICT OF—*spiritual warfare*

Sin nature:
Called flesh ....Rom 8:5
Called old self ....Col 3:9
Corrupt and deceitful ....Eph 4:22
Works of ....Gal 5:19-21
Cannot please God ......Rom 8:8
To be mortified ....Col 3:5

New nature:
By Spirit's indwelling 1Cor 3:16
Strengthened by Spirit . . .Eph 3:16
Called inward man 2Cor 4:16
Called new man ....Col 3:10
Fruits of ....Gal 5:22, 23

Conflict:
Called warfare ....Rom 7:19-23
Gal 5:17

Victory:
Recognize source ....James 1:14-16
Realize former condition. .Eph 2:1-7
Put off former conversation ....Eph 4:22
Make no provision ......Rom 13:14
Complete surrender to God ....Rom 12:1, 2
Spiritual food 1Pet 2:1, 2

INNOCENCE—*freedom from guilt or sin*

Loss of, by:
Disobedience ....Rom 5:12
Idolatry ....Ps 106:34-39

Kinds of:
Absolute 2Cor 5:21
Legal ....Luke 23:4
Moral ....Josh 22:10-34
Spiritual 2Pet 3:14

Of Christ:
In prophecy ....Is 53:7-9
In type 1Pet 1:19
In reality 1Pet 3:18
By examination ....Luke 23:13-22
By testimony ....Acts 13:28

[*also* INNOCENCY, INNOCENT, INNOCENTS]
i of my hands have I done ....Gen 20:5
i and righteous slay thou ......Ex 23:7
i blood be not shed ....Deut 19:10
lay not *i* blood unto thy.......Deut 21:8
reward to slay an *i* person.....Deut 27:25
wilt thou sin against *i* 1Sam 19:5
mayest take away the *i* 1Kin 2:31
Manasseh shed *i* blood 2Kin 21:16
i blood that he shed 2Kin 24:4
Jerusalem with *i* blood 2Kin 24:4
who ever perished, being *i*? . . .Job 4:7
thou wilt not hold me *i* ....Job 9:28
i laugh them to scorn ....Job 22:19
i shall divide the silver ....Job 27:17
doth he murder the *i* ....Ps 10:8
taketh reward against the *i* ....Ps 15:5
i from..great transgression .....Ps 19:13
wash mine hands in *i* ....Ps 26:6
washed my hands in *i* ....Ps 73:13
lurk privily for the *i* ....Prov 1:11
hands that shed *i* blood ....Prov 6:17
toucheth her shall not be *i* ....Prov 6:29
haste to be rich..not be *i* ......Prov 28:20
haste to shed *i* blood ....Is 59:7
blood of the souls of..poor *i* . . .Jer 2:34
Because I am *i* ....Jer 2:35
place with the blood of *i* ......Jer 19:4
shed *i* blood in this place .....Jer 22:3
shall surely bring *i* blood ......Jer 26:15
as before him *i* was found .....Dan 6:22
ere they attain to *i*? ....Hos 8:5
have shed *i* blood in their .....Joel 3:19
lay not upon us *i* blood: for . . .Jon 1:14
I have betrayed the *i* blood . . .Matt 27:4
I am *i* of the blood of ....Matt 27:24

INNOCENTS, MASSACRE OF—*the slaughter of the children of Bethlehem by Herod following the birth of Jesus*
Mourning foretold ....Jer 31:15
After Jesus' birth ....Matt 2:16-18

INNUMERABLE—*uncounted multitude*
Evils ....Ps 40:12
Animal life ....Ps 104:25
Descendants ....Heb 11:12
People ....Luke 12:1
Angels ....Heb 12:22

as there are *i* before him ......Job 21:33
grasshoppers, and are *i* ....Jer 46:23

INORDINATE—*immoderate; excessive*
more corrupt in her *i* love.....Ezek 23:11
uncleanness, *i* affection ....Col 3:5

INQUIRY—*a consulting or seeking for counsel*
By Israel ....Ex 18:15
With ephod 1Sam 23:9, 11
Unlawful method 1Sam 28:6, 7
Through prayer ....James 1:5
2Cor 12:7-9

INQUISITION—*an inquiry or examination*
judges shall make diligent *i*. . . .Deut 19:18
i was made of the matter .....Esth 2:23
he maketh *i* for blood ....Ps 9:12

INSANITY—*mental derangement*

Characteristics of:
Abnormal behavior ......Dan 4:32-34
Self-destruction ....Matt 17:14-18
Distinct from demon possession ....Matt 4:24

Figurative of:
Moral instability ....Jer 25:15-17
Jer 51:7
God's judgment ....Zech 12:4

INSCRIPTION—*a statement written or engraved*
On Christ's cross ....John 19:19-22
On an altar ....Acts 17:23
Roman coin ....Mark 12:16

INSECTS

Characteristics of:
Created by God ....Gen 1:24, 25
Some clean ....Lev 11:21, 22
Some unclean ....Lev 11:23, 24
Fed by God ....Ps 104:25, 27

List of:
Ant ....Prov 6:6
Bee ....Judg 14:8
Beetle ....Lev 11:22
Cankerworm ....Joel 1:4
Caterpillar ....Ps 78:46
Flea 1Sam 24:14
Fly ....Eccl 10:1
Gnat ....Matt 23:24
Grasshopper ....Lev 11:22
Hornet ....Deut 7:20
Horseleech ....Prov 30:15
Locust ....Ex 10:4
Moth ....Is 50:9
Spider ....Prov 30:28
Worms ....Ex 16:20

Illustrative of:
Design in nature ....Prov 30:24-28
Troubles ....Ps 118:12
Insignificance 1Sam 24:14
Desolation ....Joel 1:4
Appetite ....Prov 30:15
Transitoriness ....Is 51:8
Matt 6:20
Vast numbers ....Judg 6:5

INSECURITY—*a state of anxiety about earthly needs*

Descriptive of:
Wicked ....Ps 37:1, 2, 10
Riches 1Tim 6:17
Those trusting in themselves ....Luke 12:16-21

Cure of:
Steadfast of mind ....Is 26:3
Rely upon God's promises ....Ps 37:1-26
Remember God's provision ....Phil 4:9-19
Put God first ....Matt 6:25-34

INSENSIBILITY—*deadness of spiritual life*

Kinds of:
Physical ....Judg 19:26-29
Spiritual ....Jer 5:3, 21
Judicial ....Acts 28:25-28

Causes of:
Seared conscience 1Tim 4:2
Spiritual ignorance ....Eph 4:18, 19
Wanton pleasure 1Tim 5:6

INSIDE—*inner side*
covered..on the *i* with wood . . .1Kin 6:15

INSINCERITY—*hypocritical; not genuine*

Manifested in:
Mock ceremonies........Is 58:3-6
Unwilling preaching .....Jon 4:1-11
Trumped-up questions ...Matt 22:15-22
Boastful pretentions .....Luke 22:33

Those guilty of:
Hypocrites..............Luke 11:42-47
False teachers ....Gal 6:12, 13
Immature Christians 1Cor 4:17-21
See HYPOCRISY

INSOMNIA—*inability to sleep*

Causes of:
Excessive work ....Gen 31:40
Worry ....Esth 6:1
Dreams.................Dan 2:1
Conscience..............Dan 6:9, 18

Cure of:
Trust ....Ps 3:5, 6
Peacefulness ....Ps 4:8
Confidence..............Ps 127:1, 2
Obedience ....Prov 6:20-22

INSOMUCH—*inasmuch*
i that he regardeth not the ....Mal 2:13
i that ship was covered........Matt 8:24
i that they were astonished ....Matt 13:54
i that, if it were possible ......Matt 24:24
i that they questioned among ..Mark 1:27
i that there was no room......Mark 2:2
i that they pressed upon him ..Mark 3:10
i that they trode one upon ....Luke 12:1
i as that field is called ....Acts 1:19
i that we despaired even of....2Cor 1:8
i that Barnabas also was ......Gal 2:13

INSPIRATION—*divine influence*
i of the Almighty giveth them. .Job 32:8
scripture is given by *i* of God. .2Tim 3:16

INSPIRATION OF THE SCRIPTURES—*the activity of the Spirit of God through which prophets and apostles wrote the authoritative Word of God*

Expressed by:
"Thus saith the Lord" ...Jer 13:1
"The word of the Lord came"...............1Kin 16:1
"It is written"..........Rom 10:15
"As the Holy Spirit saith"................Heb 3:7
"According to the Scripture"...........James 2:8
"My words in thy mouth".Jer 1:9

Described as:
Inspired by God.........2Tim 3:16
Moved by the Holy Spirit.2Pet 1:21
Christ-centered ....Luke 24:27
2Cor 13:3

Modes of:
Various.................Heb 1:1
Inner impulse ....Judg 13:25
Jer 20:9
A voice.................Rev 1:10
Dreams.................Dan 7:1
Visions ....Ezek 11:24, 25

Proofs of:
Fulfilled prophecy ....Jer 28:15-17
Luke 24:27-45
Miracles attesting........Ex 4:1-9
2Kin 1:10-14
Teachings supporting ....Deut 4:8
Ps 19:7-11

Design of:
Reveal God's mysteries ..Amos 3:7
1Cor 2:10
Reveal the future........Acts 1:16
1Pet 1:10-12
Instruct and edify........Mic 3:8
Acts 1:8
Counteract distortion 2Cor 13:1-3
Gal 1:6-11

Results of Scriptures:
Unbreakable ....John 10:34-36
Eternal ....Matt 24:35
Authoritative...........Matt 4:4, 7, 10
Trustworthy............Ps 119:160
Verbally accurate......Matt 22:32, 43-46; Gal 3:16
Sanctifying 2Tim 3:16, 17
Effective ....Jer 23:29
2Tim 2:15
See WORD OF GOD

INSTABILITY—*lack of firmness of convictions*

Causes of:
Deception ....Gal 3:1
Col 2:4-8
Immaturity.............1Tim 3:6
False teaching ....Gal 1:6-11
2Cor 11:3, 4
Lack of depth ....Heb 5:11-14
Unsettled mind ....Eph 4:14
James 1:6-8

Examples of:
Pharaoh ....Ex 10:8-20
Israel..................Judg 2:17
Solomon 1Kin 11:1-8
Disciples...............John 6:66
John Mark ....Acts 15:38
Galatians ....Gal 1:6

INSTANT—*at that moment; immediately*

[*also* INSTANTLY]
yea, it shall be at an *i* ....Is 29:5
At what *i* I shall speak........Jer 18:7
in that *i* gave thanks ....Luke 2:38
besought him *i* ....Luke 7:4
i serving God day and night ...Acts 26:7
continuing *i* in prayer ....Rom 12:12
be *i* in season 2Tim 4:2

INSTEAD—*as an alternative to; rather*
and closed up the flesh *i* ......Gen 2:21
let thy servant abide *i*.........Gen 44:33
even he shall be to thee *i* of...Ex 4:16
Egypt to gather stubble *i*......Ex 5:12
Israel *i* of all the first-born ....Num 3:12
i of all the first-born among ...Num 3:41
i of all the firstlings among ....Num 3:41
Levites *i* of all the first-born...Num 3:45
Levites *i* of their cattle........Num 3:45
to another *i* of thy husband ...Num 5:20
i..as open every womb ....Num 8:16
be to us *i* of eyes............Num 10:31
I pray thee, *i* of her ....Judg 15:2
captain of the host *i* of Joab ...2Sam 17:25
servant king *i* of David 1Kin 3:7
king *i* of..father Amaziah 2Kin 14:21
king *i* of David his father 1Chr 29:23
I of which king Rehoboam 2Chr 12:10
king be queen *i* of Vashti .....Esth 2:4
i of wheat, and cockle *i* of ....Job 31:40
I of thy fathers shall be ....Ps 45:16
i of sweet smell there shall ....Is 3:24
and *i* of a girdle a rent........Is 3:24
i of well set hair baldness .....Is 3:24
i of a stomacher a girding .....Is 3:24
and burning *i* of beauty ....Is 3:24
I of the thorn shall come up...Is 55:13
i of the brier shall come up ...Is 55:13
reigned *i* of Josiah his father ..Jer 22:11
strangers *i* of her husband! ....Ezek 16:32

INSTINCT—*inbred characteristics of*
Animals ....Is 1:3
Birds ....Jer 8:7

INSTRUCTION—*imparting knowledge to others*

Given by:
Parents ....Deut 6:6-25
Priests ....Deut 24:8
God....................Jer 32:33
Pastors ....Eph 4:11
Pedagogues ....Neh 8:7, 8
Paraclete (the Holy Spirit) ....John 14:26

Means of:
Nature ....Prov 6:6-11
Human nature ....Prov 24:30-34
Law ....Rom 2:18
Proverbs ....Prov 1:1-30
Songs ....Deut 32:1-44
History 1Cor 10:1-11
God's Word 2Tim 3:15, 16
See EDUCATION; TEACHING, TEACHERS

[*also* INSTRUCT, INSTRUCTED, INSTRUCTING]
that he might *i* thee ....Deut 4:36
he *i* him, he kept him as ......Deut 32:10
Jehoiada the priest *i* him 2Kin 12:2
he *i* about the song 1Chr 15:22
Solomon was *i* for the building.2Chr 3:3
good spirit to *i* them..........Neh 9:20
Behold thou hast *i* many ......Job 4:3
ears of men, and sealeth..*i* ....Job 33:16
Almighty *i* him?..............Job 40:2
be *i*, ye judges of the earth ...Ps 2:10
reins also *i* me in the night ....Ps 16:7
will *i* thee and teach thee .....Ps 32:8
Seeing thou hatest *i* ....Ps 50:17
children the *i* of a father ......Prov 4:1
Take fast hold of *i* ....Prov 4:13
How have I hated *i*...........Prov 5:12
ear to them that *i* me! ....Prov 5:13
reproofs of *i* are the way of ...Prov 6:23
Receive my *i* and not silver ...Prov 8:10
Hear *i*, and be wise ....Prov 8:33
Give *i* to a wise man ....Prov 9:9
way of life that keepeth *i* .....Prov 10:17
loveth *i* loveth knowledge .....Prov 12:1
son heareth his father's *i* ......Prov 13:1
to him that refuseth *i* ....Prov 13:18
A fool despiseth..father's *i* ....Prov 15:5
refuseth *i* despiseth his ....Prov 15:32
the Lord is the *i* of wisdom ...Prov 15:33
Hear counsel and receive *i* ....Prov 19:20
Apply thine heart unto *i* ......Prov 23:12
who would *i* me ....Song 8:2
i me that I should not ....Is 8:11
doth *i* him to discretion ....Is 28:26
Be thou *i*, O Jerusalem ....Jer 6:8
not hear, nor receive *i* ....Jer 17:23
not hearkened to receive *i* .....Jer 32:33
not receive *i* to hearken.......Jer 35:13
i and an astonishment.........Ezek 5:15
among the people shall *i* ......Dan 11:33
thou wilt receive *i* ....Zeph 3:7
i unto the kingdom of heaven. .Matt 13:52
before *i* of her mother ....Matt 14:8
wherein thou hast been *i*......Luke 1:4
man was *i* in..way of the Lord .Acts 18:25
being *i* out of the law.........Rom 2:18
he may *i* him? 1Cor 2:16
I am *i* both to be full ....Phil 4:12
In meekness *i* those..oppose ...2Tim 2:25

INSTRUCTOR—*a teacher*

[*also* INSTRUCTORS]
i of every artificer in brass ....Gen 4:22
i of the foolish ....Rom 2:20
ten thousand *i* in Christ 1Cor 4:15

INSTRUMENT—*a tool or implement*
Tabernacle furniture .....Num 3:8
For threshing 2Sam 24:22
For sacrifices............Ezek 40:42
Of iron 2Sam 12:31
Figurative of Jesus.......Acts 9:15
Body members, used as ..Rom 6:13

[*also* INSTRUMENTS]
i of cruelty are in their........Gen 49:5
pattern of all the *i* thereof ....Ex 25:9
all the *i* of the tabernacle .....Num 3:8
all the *i* of their service ....Num 4:26
with all their *i*...............Num 4:32
reckon the *i* of the charge.....Num 4:32
the holy *i*, and the trumpets ...Num 31:6
smite him with an *i* of iron ....Num 35:16
i of war, and *i* of his 1Sam 8:12
manner of *i* made of fir 2Sam 6:5
flesh with the *i* of the oxen....1Kin 19:21

all the *i* of the sanctuary 1Chr 9:29
all manner of *i* of war 1Chr 12:37
with musical *i* of God 1Chr 16:42
Lord with the *i* which I made. . 1Chr 23:5
i of all manner of service 1Chr 28:14
for all *i* of silver by 1Chr 28:14
i of every kind of service 1Chr 28:14
and all their *i* 2Chr 4:16
cymbals and *i* of music 2Chr 5:13
singers with *i* of music 2Chr 23:13
i ordained by David king 2Chr 29:27
could skill of *i* of music 2Chr 34:12
with the musical *i* of David .... Neh 12:36
for him the *i* of death .... Ps 7:13
psaltery and an *i* of ten .... Ps 33:2
players on *i* shall be there ..... Ps 87:7
upon a psaltery and an *i* .... Ps 144:9
musical *i*, and that of all ...... Eccl 2:8
with a threshing *i* .... Is 28:27
i also of the churl are evil ..... Is 32:7
thee a new sharp threshing *i* .. Is 41:15
bringeth..an *i* for his work .... Is 54:16
can play well on an *i* .... Ezek 33:32
neither were *i* of music .... Dan 6:18
Gilead with threshing *i* of ..... Amos 1:3
invent..*i* of music .... Amos 6:5
singer on my stringed *i* .... Hab 3:19
i of a foolish shepherd .... Zech 11:15

INSULT—*to treat insolently*
Ignored by King Saul 1Sam 10:26, 27
Job treated with .... Job 30:1, 9, 10
Children slain because of . 2Kin 2:23, 24
Pharisees treat Jesus with . Matt 12:24, 25
Paul's reaction to .... Acts 23:1-5
Forbidden 1Pet 3:8, 9

INSURRECTION—*rebellion against constituted authority*
In Jerusalem .... Ezra 4:19
Absalom's miserable 2Sam 18:33
Attempted by Jews ...... Mark 15:7
Acts 18:12

i of..workers of iniquity .... Ps 64:2

INTEGRITY—*moral uprightness*

Manifested in:
Moral uprightness .... Gen 20:3-10
Unselfish service .... Num 16:15
Performing vows .... Jer 35:12-19
Rejecting bribes .... Acts 8:18-23
Honest behavior 2Cor 7:2

Illustrated in:
Job's life .... Job 2:3, 9, 10
David's kingship .... Ps 7:8
Nehemiah's service ...... Neh 5:14-19
Daniel's rule .... Dan 6:1-4
Paul's ministry 2Cor 4:2

father walked, in *i* of heart 1Kin 9:4
I will not remove mine *i* ...... Job 27:5
God may know mine *i* .... Job 31:6
i and uprightness .... Ps 25:21
I have walked in mine *i* .... Ps 26:1
I will walk in mine *i* .... Ps 26:11
upholdest me in mine *i* .... Ps 41:12
according to..*i* of his heart .... Ps 78:72
i of the upright shall guide .... Prov 11:3
poor that walketh in his *i* ..... Prov 19:1
just man walketh in his *i* ...... Prov 20:7

INTELLIGENCE—*the ability to learn or understand*
i with them that forsake ...... Dan 11:30

INTEMPERANCE—*not restraining the appetites*

Manifested in:
Drunkenness .... Prov 23:19-35
Gluttony .... Titus 1:12
Immorality .... Rom 1:26, 27

Evils of:
Puts the flesh first .... Phil 3:19
Brings about death 1Sam 25:36-38

See DRUNKENNESS

INTENTION—*a fixed determination to do a specified thing*

Good:
Commended but not allowed 1Kin 8:17-19
Planned but delayed ..... Rom 15:24-28

Evil:
Restrained by God ...... Gen 31:22-31
Turned to good by God . . Gen 45:4-8
Overruled by God's providence .... Esth 9:23-25

Of Christ:
Predicted .... Ps 40:6-8
Announced .... Matt 20:18-28
Misunderstood .... Matt 16:21-23
Fulfilled .... John 19:28-30
Explained .... Luke 24:25-47

[*also* INTEND, INTENDED, INTENDEST, INTENDING, INTENT, INTENTS]

i thou to kill me .... Ex 2:14
not *i* to go up against .... Josh 22:33
i that the Lord might bring 2Sam 17:14
i that he might destroy 2Kin 10:19
i that he might let none go 2Chr 16:1
i to add more to our sins 2Chr 28:13
they *i* evil against thee .... Ps 21:11
performed..*i* of his heart ..... Jer 30:24
i that I might show them ...... Ezek 40:4
i that the living may know .... Dan 4:17
i to build a tower .... Luke 14:28
to the *i* ye may believe .... John 11:15
i to bring this man's blood .... Acts 5:28
came hither for that *i* .... Acts 9:21
i after Easter to bring him .... Acts 12:4
i we should not lust after 1Cor 10:6
To the *i* that now unto .... Eph 3:10
thoughts and *i* of the heart .... Heb 4:12

INTERBREEDING—*crossbreeding*
Forbidden:
In animals, vegetables, cloth .... Lev 19:19

INTERCESSION—*prayer offered in behalf of others*

Purposes of:
Secure healing .... James 5:14-16
Avert judgment .... Num 14:11-21
Insure deliverance 1Sam 7:5-9
Give blessings .... Num 6:23-27
Obtain restoration .... Job 42:8-10
Encourage repentance ... Rom 10:1-4

Characteristics of:
Pleading .... Gen 18:23-33
Specific .... Gen 24:12-15
Victorious .... Ex 17:9-12
Very intense .... Ex 32:31, 32
Quickly answered .... Num 27:15-23
Confessing 2Sam 24:17
Personal 1Chr 29:19
Covenant pleading .... Neh 1:4-11
Unselfish .... Acts 7:60

Examples of:
Moses .... Ex 32:11-13
Joshua .... Josh 7:6-9
Jehoshaphat 2Chr 20:5-13
Isaiah 2Chr 32:20
Daniel .... Dan 9:3-19
Christ .... John 17:1-26
Paul .... Col 1:9-12

[*also* INTERCESSIONS]

made *i* for..transgressors ...... Is 53:12
neither make *i* to me .... Jer 7:16
had made *i* to the king .... Jer 36:25
Spirit itself maketh *i* .... Rom 8:26
who also maketh *i* for us ...... Rom 8:34
i to God against Israel .... Rom 11:2
i, and giving of thanks 1Tim 2:1
liveth to make *i* for them ..... Heb 7:25

INTERCESSOR—*an advocate*
wondered..there was no *i* ..... Is 59:16

INTEREST—*amount charged on borrowed money*
From poor man, forbidden .... Ex 22:25
From a stranger, permitted .... Deut 23:19, 20
Exaction of, unprofitable . Prov 28:8
Condemned as a sin ..... Ezek 18:8-17
Exaction of, rebuked .... Neh 5:1-13
Reward for non-exaction of .... Ps 15:5
Used to illustrate .... Luke 19:23

INTERMEDDLE—*to meddle impertinently*

[*also* INTERMEDDLETH]

doth not *i* with his joy .... Prov 14:10
seeketh and *i* with all wisdom. . Prov 18:1

INTERMEDIATE STATE—*the state of the believer between death and the resurrection*

Described as:
Like sleep .... John 11:11-14
"Far better" .... Phil 1:21, 23
"Present with the Lord" . 2Cor 5:6, 8

Characteristics of:
Persons identifiable ...... Matt 17:3
Conscious and enjoyable . Ps 17:15
Luke 16:25
Unchangeable .... Luke 16:26
Without the body 2Cor 5:1-4
Rev 6:9
Awaiting the resurrection . Phil 3:20, 21
1Thess 4:13-18

See IMMORTALITY

INTERMISSION—*ceasing*
ceaseth not, without any *i* ..... Lam 3:49

INTERPRETATION—*making known or understandable the unknown or incomprehensible*

Things in need of:
Dreams .... Gen 41:15-36
Languages .... Gen 42:23
Writings .... Dan 5:7-31
Scripture .... Acts 8:30-35
Tongues 1Cor 12:10

Agents of:
Jesus Christ .... Luke 24:25-47
Holy Spirit 1Cor 2:11-16
Angels .... Luke 1:26-37
Prophets and apostles .... Eph 3:2-11

[*also* INTERPRET, INTERPRETATIONS, INTERPRETED]

according to..*i* of his dream ... Gen 40:5
Do not *i* belong to God? ...... Gen 40:8
baker saw..the *i* was good ..... Gen 40:16
as Joseph had *i* to them .... Gen 40:22
none that could *i* them .... Gen 41:8
according to..*i* of his dream ... Gen 41:11
as he *i* to us, so it was .... Gen 41:13
is none that can *i* it .... Gen 41:15
the dream, and the *i* thereof .. Judg 7:15
i in the Syrian tongue .... Ezra 4:7
proverb, and the *i* .... Prov 1:6
knoweth the *i* of a thing? ..... Eccl 8:1
and we will show the *i* .... Dan 2:4
the dream and the *i* thereof ... Dan 2:6
dream, and the *i* thereof ...... Dan 2:6
can show me the *i* thereof ..... Dan 2:9
show unto the king the *i* ...... Dan 2:24
have seen, and the *i* thereof? . . Dan 2:26
we will tell the *i* thereof ...... Dan 2:36
unto me the *i* of the dream ... Dan 4:6
I have seen, and..*i* thereof .... Dan 4:9
declare the *i* thereof .... Dan 4:18
known unto me the *i* .... Dan 4:18
dream, or the *i* thereof .... Dan 4:19
i thereof to thine enemies ..... Dan 4:19
show me the *i* thereof .... Dan 5:7
he will show the *i* .... Dan 5:12
not show the *i* of the thing .... Dan 5:15
make known to him the *i* ..... Dan 5:17
This is the *i* of the thing ...... Dan 5:26
made me know the *i* of .... Dan 7:16
being *i* is, God with us .... Matt 1:23

which is, being *i*, Damsel .....Mark 5:41
being *i*, My God, my God ....Mark 15:34
to say, being *i*, Master ....John 1:38
Cephas, which is by *i* ....John 1:42
by *i* is called Dorcas ....Acts 9:36
with tongues? do all *i*? 1Cor 12:30
with tongues except he *i* 1Cor 14:5
tongue pray that he may *i*.....1Cor 14:13
hath a revelation, hath an *i* ...1Cor 14:26
by course; and let one *i*.......1Cor 14:27
i King of righteousness........Heb 7:2
scripture is of..private *i* 2Pet 1:20

INTERPRETER—*a translator*
there is no *i* of it ....Gen 40:8
an *i*, one among a thousand ...Job 33:23
be no *i*, let him keep 1Cor 14:28

INTIMIDATION—*suggesting possible harm if one acts contrary to another's wishes*
Attitudes toward:
Discovers its deceit ......Neh 6:5-13
Do not yield ....Jer 26:8-16
Go steadfastly on........Dan 6:6-10
Answer boldly ....Amos 7:12-17

INTO—*See* INTRODUCTION

INTOLERANCE—*active opposition to the views of others*
Of the state against:
Jews.....................Esth 3:12, 13
Rival religions...........Dan 3:13-15
Christian faith...........Rev 13:1-18
Of the Jews against:
Their prophets ....Matt 23:31-35
Christ ....Luke 4:28-30
Christians...............Acts 5:40, 41
Christianity ....Acts 17:1-8
Of the Church against:
Evil 2Cor 6:14-18
False teaching 2John 10, 11
False religions ....Gal 1:6-9
Manifestations of:
Prejudice ....Acts 21:27-32
Persecution ....Acts 13:50
Passion ....Acts 9:1, 2, 21

INTREAT—*See* ENTREAT

INTRIGUE—*stealthy, secretive plotting*
Characteristics of:
Deceit...................Gen 27:6-23
Plausible arguments......Judg 9:1-6
Subtle maneuvers........2Sam 15:1-13
False front 2Kin 10:18-28
Political trickery ....Esth 3:5-10
Against Christ by:
Herod ....Matt 2:8, 12-16
Satan....................Matt 4:3-11
Jews.....................Luke 11:53, 54

INTRUDING—*thrusting oneself where he is not welcome*
i into those things which ......Col 2:18

INVADE—*to enter for conquest or plunder*
[*also* INVADED, INVASION]
Philistines have *i*..land 1Sam 23:27
Amalekites had *i* the south 1Sam 30:1
We made an *i* upon 1Sam 30:14
bands of the Moabites *i* 2Kin 13:20
wouldest not let Israel *i* 2Chr 20:10
Philistines also had *i* 2Chr 28:18
he will *i* them with ....Hab 3:16

INVENTION—*something new made by man*
Product of wisdom ......Prov 8:12
Products made by ....Gen 4:21, 22
Skill required in 2Chr 26:15
Many made ....Eccl 7:29
Of evil things ....Ps 106:39
God provoked by........Ps 106:29
God takes vengeance on..Ps 99:8
[*also* INVENT, INVENTED]
engines, *i* by cunning men.....2Chr 26:15
i to themselves instruments ....Amos 6:5

INVENTORS—*those who invent*
i of evil things ....Rom 1:30

INVESTIGATION—*close examination*
Characteristics of:
Involves research ....Ezra 6:1-13
Causes sought out ....Eccl 1:13, 17
Claims checked..........Num 13:1-25
Suspicions followed through..............Josh 22:10-30
Historic parallels cited ..Jer 26:17-24
Lack of:
Cause of later trouble....Josh 9:3-23
Productive of evil........Dan 5:22

INVESTMENTS, SPIRITUAL
In heavenly riches ....Matt 6:20
Dividends later paid 1Tim 6:19

INVISIBLE—*the unseeable*
God is..................1Tim 1:17
Faith sees...............Heb 11:17
i things of him from ....Rom 1:20
the image of the *i* God ....Col 1:15
are in earth, visible and *i* .....Col 1:16

INVITATIONS OF THE BIBLE
Come:
And reason ....Is 1:18
My people ....Is 26:20
Buy wine and milk ......Is 55:1
"Unto Me" ....Is 55:3
And see ....John 1:46
And rest................Matt 11:28
After Me ....Mark 1:17
Take up the cross ....Mark 10:21
To the marriage ....Matt 22:4
Everything is ready ......Luke 14:17
The blessed ....Matt 25:34
Threefold ....Rev 22:17
[*also* INVITED]
I have *i* the people 1Sam 9:24
Absalom *i* all..king's sons 2Sam 13:23
I *i* unto her also with ....Esth 5:12

INWARD—*towards the inner side; towards the inner being*
[*also* INWARDLY, INWARDS]
in the side of the ephod *i* .....Ex 28:26
fat that covereth the *i*.........Ex 29:13
wash the *i* of him.............Ex 29:17
fat that covereth the *i*.........Ex 29:22
side of the ephod *i* ....Ex 39:19
his *i* and his legs shall he .....Lev 1:9
shall wash the *i* ....Lev 1:13
fat that covereth the *i*.........Lev 3:3
fat that is upon the *i*..........Lev 3:3
fat that covereth the *i*.........Lev 3:9
fat that is upon the *i*..........Lev 3:9
fat that covereth the *i*.........Lev 3:14
fat that is upon the *i*..........Lev 3:14
fat that covereth the *i*.........Lev 4:8
fat that is upon the *i*..........Lev 4:8
with his legs, and his *i* ....Lev 4:11
fat that covereth the *i*.........Lev 7:3
fat that was upon the *i*........Lev 8:16
washed the *i* and the legs .....Lev 8:21
fat that was upon the *i*........Lev 8:25
wash the *i* and the legs ....Lev 9:14
which covereth the *i* ....Lev 9:19
it is fret *i* ....Lev 13:55
about from Millo and *i*........2Sam 5:9
all their hinder parts were *i* ...1Kin 7:25
their faces were *i* 2Chr 3:13
their hinder parts were *i* 2Chr 4:4
i friends abhorred me ....Job 19:19
put wisdom in the *i* parts? ....Job 38:36
i part is very wickedness ......Ps 5:9
i thought is ....Ps 49:11
desirest truth in..*i* parts ....Ps 51:6
but they curse *i* ....Ps 62:4
i thought of every one ....Ps 64:6
i parts of the belly............Prov 20:27
do stripes the *i* parts of ....Prov 20:30
i parts for Kir-haresh ....Is 16:11

put my law in their *i* parts ....Jer 31:33
porch of the gate was *i* ....Ezek 40:9
windows..round about *i* ....Ezek 40:16
went he *i*, and measured ......Ezek 41:3
walk of ten cubits breadth *i* ...Ezek 42:4
i..are ravening wolves.........Matt 7:15
i part is full of ravening.......Luke 11:39
he is a Jew, which is one *i* ....Rom 2:29
law of God after the *i* man....Rom 7:22
i man is renewed day by 2Cor 4:16
i affection..more abundant 2Cor 7:15

IPHEDEIAH (ĭ'ĕ-dē'yä)—*"Jehovah redeems"*
A descendant of Benjamin 1Chr 8:1, 25

IR (ĭr)—*"watcher"; "city"*
Huppim..children of *I*.........1Chr 7:12

IRA (ī'rä)—*"watchful"*
1. Priest to David 2Sam 20:26
2. One of David's mighty men 2Sam 23:26; 1Chr 11:28
3. Ithrite..................2Sam 23:38; 1Chr 11:40

IRAD (ī'răd)—*"fleet"*
Son of Enoch; grandson of Cain ....Gen 4:18

IRAM (ī'răm)—*"citizen"*
Edomite chief ....Gen 36:43; 1Chr 1:54

IRI (ī'rī)—*"watchful"*
Benjamite 1Chr 7:7

IRIJAH (ī-rī'jä)—*"seen of Jehovah"*
Accuses Jeremiah of desertion ....Jer 37:13, 14

IRNAHASH (ĭr-nā'hăsh)—*"serpent city"*
City of Judah 1Chr 4:1, 12

IRON—*a heavy, malleable magnetic metal*
Features concerning:
Used very early ....Gen 4:22
Used in weapons ....Job 20:24
Items made of:
Armor..................2Sam 23:7
Axe 2Kin 6:5
Bedstead ....Deut 3:11
Chariot ....Josh 17:16, 18
Gate ....Acts 12:10
Gods ....Dan 5:4, 23
Tools 1Kin 6:7; 2Sam 12:31
Vessels ....Josh 6:24
Weapons ....Job 20:24
Yokes ....Deut 28:48
Implements ....Gen 4:22
Stylus ....Job 19:24
Figurative of:
Affliction ....Deut 4:20
Barrenness..............Deut 28:23
Authority ....Ps 2:9
Stubbornness............Is 48:4
Slavery ....Jer 28:13, 14
Strength ....Dan 2:33-41
Insensibility 1Tim 4:2
[*also* IRONS]
make your heaven as *i*........Lev 26:19
silver, the brass, the *i*.........Num 31:22
with an instrument of *i*........Num 35:16
land whose stones are *i* ....Deut 8:9
shalt not lift up any *i* tool.....Deut 27:5
shoes shall be *i* and brass .....Deut 33:25
vessels of brass and *i* ....Josh 6:19
no man hath lift up any *i* .....Josh 8:31
with brass, and with *i*.........Josh 22:8
they had chariots of *i* ....Judg 1:19
nine hundred chariots of *i*.....Judg 4:3
nine hundred chariots of *i*.....Judg 4:13
six hundred shekels of *i*.......1Sam 17:7
midst of the furnace of *i* 1Kin 8:51
made him horns of *i* 1Kin 22:11
the *i* did swim.................2Kin 6:6
harrows of *i* and with axes 1Chr 20:3

prepared *i* in abundance 1Chr 22:3
brass and *i* without weight 1Chr 22:14
brass, and the *i* 1Chr 22:16
the *i* for things of *i* 1Chr 29:2
thousand talents of *i* 1Chr 29:7
in brass, and in *i* 2Chr 2:7
in silver, in brass, in *i* 2Chr 2:14
had made him horns of *i* 2Chr 18:10
I is taken out of the earth ...... Job 28:2
bones are like bars of *i* ...... Job 40:18
fill his skin with barbed *i*? ...... Job 41:7
He esteemeth *i* as straw ...... Job 41:27
he was laid in *i* ...... Ps 105:18
cut the bars of *i* in sunder ...... Ps 107:16
nobles wih fetters of *i* ...... Ps 149:8
I sharpeneth *i* ...... Prov 27:17
If the *i* be blunt ...... Eccl 10:10
thickets of..forest with *i* ...... Is 10:34
cut in sunder the bars of *i* ...... Is 45:2
gold, and for *i* ...... Is 60:17
wood brass..for stones *i* ...... Is 60:17
i pillar and brazen ...... Jer 1:18
they are brass and *i* ...... Jer 6:28
from the *i* furnace ...... Jer 11:4
i break the northern *i* ...... Jer 15:12
written with a pen of *i* ...... Jer 17:1
take..unto thee an *i* pan ...... Ezek 4:3
set it for a wall of *i* ...... Ezek 4:3
are brass, and tin, and *i* ...... Ezek 22:18
silver, and brass, and *i* ...... Ezek 22:20
silver, *i*, tin, and lead ...... Ezek 27:12
bright *i*, cassia, and ...... Ezek 27:19
toes of the feet..part of *i* ...... Dan 2:42
i mixed with miry clay ...... Dan 2:43
i is not mixed with clay ...... Dan 2:43
it brake in pieces the *i* ...... Dan 2:45
even with a band of *i* ...... Dan 4:15
it had great *i* teeth ...... Dan 7:7
threshing instruments of *i* ...... Amos 1:3
will make thine horn *i* ...... Mic 4:13
came unto the *i* gate ...... Acts 12:10
rule them with a rod of *i* ...... Rev 2:27
were breastplates of *i* ...... Rev 9:9
nations with a rod of *i* ...... Rev 12:5
and of brass, and *i* ...... Rev 18:12
rule them with a rod of *i* ...... Rev 19:15

IRON (ī'rŏn)—*"pious; place of terror"*
City of Naphtali ...... Josh 19:38

IRONY—*a device whereby one conveys meaning through words that have the opposite meaning*
Show contempt 2Sam 6:20
Mockery 1Kin 18:27
Rebuke distrust 1Kin 22:15
Multiply transgression ...... Amos 4:4
Mocked honor ...... Matt 27:29
Deflate the wise 2Cor 11:19, 20

IRPEEL (ĭr'pē-ĕl)—*"God heals"*
Town of Benjamin ...... Josh 18:21, 27

IRRECONCILABLE—*impossible to reconcile or compromise*
Characteristic of the last days 2Tim 3:1, 3

IRRIGATION—*the supplying of water through artificial means*
Not usually needed ...... Deut 11:11, 14
Source of ...... Eccl 2:5, 6
Figurative of spiritual life ...... Is 43:19, 20; Is 58:11

IRRITABILITY—*the quality of being easily provoked to anger*

Characteristics of:
Quick temper 1Sam 20:30-33
Morose disposition 1Sam 25:3, 36-39
Hotheaded ...... Gen 49:6
Complaining ...... Ex 14:10-14

Cure by God's:
Love 1Cor 13:4-7
Peace ...... Phil 4:7, 8
Spirit ...... Gal 5:22-26

IRRITATE—*to excite impatience, displeasure, or anger*
Of Hannah 1Sam 1:6

IR-SHEMESH (ĭr-shĕm'ĭsh)—*"city of the sun"*
Danite city ...... Josh 19:41
Same as Beth-shemesh 1Kin 4:9

IRU (ī'rōō)—*"watch"*
Son of Caleb 1Chr 4:15

IS—*See* INTRODUCTION

ISAAC (ī'zăk)—*"laughter"—the son of Abraham and Sarah, born to them in their old age, and the father of Jacob and Esau*

Life of:
Son of Abraham and Sarah ...... Gen 21:1-3
His birth promised ...... Gen 17:16-18
Heir of the covenant ...... Gen 17:19, 21
Born and circumcised ...... Gen 21:1-8
Offered up as a sacrifice ...... Gen 22:1-19
Secures Rebekah as wife ...... Gen 24:1-67
Covenant confirmed to ...... Gen 26:2-5
Buries his father ...... Gen 25:8, 9
Father of Esau and Jacob ...... Gen 25:19-26
Prefers Esau ...... Gen 25:27, 28
Lives in Gerar ...... Gen 26:1, 6
Covenant reaffirmed with ...... Gen 26:2-5
Calls Rebekah his sister ...... Gen 26:7-11
Becomes prosperous ...... Gen 26:12-14
Trouble over wells ...... Gen 26:14-22
Covenant with Abimelech ...... Gen 26:23-33
Grieves over Esau ...... Gen 26:34, 35
Deceived by Jacob ...... Gen 27:1-25
Blesses his sons ...... Gen 27:26-40
Dies in his old age ...... Gen 35:28, 29

Character of:
Obedient ...... Gen 22:9
Peaceable ...... Gen 26:14-22
Thoughtful ...... Gen 24:63
Prayerful ...... Gen 25:21; Gen 26:25

Significance of:
Child of promise ...... Gal 4:22, 23
Man of faith ...... Heb 11:9, 20
Type of believers ...... Gal 4:28-31
Ancestor of Christ ...... Luke 3:34
Patriarch of Israel ...... Ex 32:13

heir with my son..with *I* ...... Gen 21:10
I shall thy seed be called ...... Gen 21:12
gave all that he had unto *I* ...... Gen 25:5
away from *I* his son ...... Gen 25:6
God blessed his son *I* ...... Gen 25:11
I dwelt by..well Lahai-roi ...... Gen 25:11
I loved Esau ...... Gen 25:28
Rebekah said to *I* ...... Gen 27:46
I called Jacob and blessed ...... Gen 28:1
I sent away Jacob ...... Gen 28:5
I had blessed Jacob ...... Gen 28:6
daughters..pleased not *I* ...... Gen 28:8
and the God of *I* ...... Gen 28:13
go to *I* his father in ...... Gen 31:18
Abraham, and the fear of *I* ...... Gen 31:42
fear of his father *I* ...... Gen 31:53
God of my father *I* ...... Gen 32:9
I gave Abraham and *I* ...... Gen 35:12
Jacob came unto *I* ...... Gen 35:27
Abraham and *I* sojourned ...... Gen 35:27
God of his father *I* ...... Gen 46:1
Abraham and *I* did walk ...... Gen 48:15
fathers Abraham and *I* ...... Gen 48:16
I and Rebekah his wife ...... Gen 49:31
to Abraham, to *I* ...... Gen 50:24
Abraham, with *I* ...... Ex 2:24
Abraham, the God of *I* ...... Ex 3:6
God of *I*..God of Jacob ...... Ex 3:15
God of Abraham, of *I* ...... Ex 3:16
God of *I*..God of Jacob ...... Ex 4:5
unto Abraham, unto *I* ...... Ex 6:3
give it to Abraham, to *I* ...... Ex 6:8
swear unto Abraham, to *I* ...... Ex 33:1
also my covenant with *I* ...... Lev 26:42
unto Abraham, unto *I* ...... Num 32:11
your fathers, Abraham, *I* ...... Deut 1:8
to Abraham, to *I* ...... Deut 6:10
fathers, Abraham, *I* ...... Deut 9:5
servants, Abraham, *I* ...... Deut 9:27
to Abraham, to *I* ...... Deut 29:13
to Abraham, to *I* ...... Deut 30:20
unto Abraham, unto *I* ...... Deut 34:4
his seed, and gave him *I* ...... Josh 24:3
I gave..*I* Jacob and Esau ...... Josh 24:4
God of Abraham, *I* 1Kin 18:36
covenant with Abraham, *I* 2Kin 13:23
sons of Abraham; *I* 1Chr 1:28
And Abraham begat *I* 1Chr 1:34
sons of *I*; Esau and Israel 1Chr 1:34
and his oath unto *I* 1Chr 16:16
God of Abraham, *I* 1Chr 29:18
God of Abraham, *I* 2Chr 30:6
and his oath unto *I* ...... Ps 105:9
seed of Abraham, *I* ...... Jer 33:26
places of *I* shall be desolate ...... Amos 7:9
word against the house of *I* ...... Amos 7:16
begat *I*; and *I* begat Jacob ...... Matt 1:2
with Abraham, and *I* ...... Matt 8:11
God of *I*..God of Jacob? ...... Matt 22:32
God of Abraham..God of *I* ...... Mark 12:26
see Abraham, and *I* ...... Luke 13:28
God of *I*..God of ...... Luke 20:37
God of Abraham and of *I* ...... Acts 3:13
Abraham begat *I* ...... Acts 7:8
I begat Jacob; and Jacob ...... Acts 7:8
In *I* shall thy seed be called ...... Rom 9:7
was tried, offered up *I* ...... Heb 11:17
in *I* shall thy seed be called ...... Heb 11:18
I his son upon the altar? ...... James 2:21

ISAIAH, ESAIAS (ī-zā'yä, ē-zā'ăs)—*"salvation of Jehovah"—a prophet in Israel*

Life of:
Son of Amoz ...... Is 1:1
Prophesies during reigns of Uzziah, Jotham, Ahza and Hezekiah ...... Is 1:1
Contemporary of Amos and Hosea ...... Amos 1:1; Hos 1:1
Responds to prophetic call ...... Is 6:1-13
Protests against policy of Ahaz ...... Is 7:1-25; Is 8:1-22
Gives symbolic names to his sons ...... Is 8:1-4, 18
Walks naked and barefoot ...... Is 20:2, 3
Encourages Hezekiah 2Kin 19:1-34
Warns Hezekiah of death 2Kin 20:1
Instructs Hezekiah concerning his recovery 2Kin 20:4-11
Upbraids Hezekiah for his acts 2Kin 20:12-19
Writes Uzziah's biography 2Chr 26:22
Writes Hezekiah's biography 2Chr 32:32

Messianic prophecies of:
Christ's birth ...... Is 7:14; Is 11:1-9; Matt 1:22, 23
John's coming ...... Is 40:3; Matt 3:3
Christ's mission ...... Is 61:1, 2; Luke 4:17-19
Christ's death ...... Is 53:1-12; Matt 8:17; 1Pet 2:21-25
Christ as Servant ...... Is 42:1-4; Matt 12:17-21
Gospel invitation ...... Is 55:1-13; Acts 13:34
Conversion of Gentiles ...... Is 11:10; Rom 15:8-12

Other prophecies of:
Assyrian invasion ...... Is 8:1-4
Babylon's fall ...... Is 13:1-22
Devastation of Moab ...... Is 16:1-14
Tyre and Sidon condemned ...... Is 23:1-18

Destruction of Sennacherib .... Is 37:14-38
Babylonian captivity ..... Is 39:3-7

Other features concerning:
Calls Christ Immanuel ... Is 7:14
Names Cyrus .... Is 45:1-3
Eunuch reads from ...... Acts 8:27, 28, 30
Quoted in New Testament .... Rom 9:27, 29; Rom 10:16, 20, 21; Rom 11:26, 27

I the son of Amoz 2Chr 32:20
I the son of Amoz .... Is 2:1
spoken of by the prophet *I* .... Matt 3:3
fulfilled..spoken by *I* .... Matt 8:17
Well hath *I* prophesied .... Mark 7:6
book of the words of *I* .... Luke 3:4
as said the prophet *I* .... John 1:23
not believe, because..*I* .... John 12:39
in his chariot read *I* .... Acts 8:28
spake the Holy Ghost by *I* .... Acts 28:25
I also crieth concerning .... Rom 9:27

ISAIAH, THE BOOK OF—*a book of the Old Testament*
Call of Isaiah .... Is 6
Promise of Immanuel .... Is 7:10-25
Prophecies against nations .... Is 13—23
Historical section .... Is 36—39
Songs of the servant .... Is 42, 49—53
Future hope of Zion ..... Is 66

ISCAH (ĭs'kä)—*"Jehovah is looking; who looks"*
Daughter of Haran ...... Gen 11:29

ISCARIOT, JUDAS (ĭs-kăr'ĭ-ŏt, jōō'däs)—*the disciple who betrayed Jesus*

Life of:
Listed among the Twelve . Mark 3:14, 19
Called Iscariot and a traitor .... Luke 6:16
Criticizes Mary .... John 12:3-5
Treasurer .... John 13:29
Identified as betrayer .... John 13:21-26
Sells out Christ .... Matt 26:14-16
Betrays Christ with a kiss . Mark 14:10, 11, 43-45
Returns betrayal money .. Matt 27:3-10
Commits suicide .... Matt 27:5
Goes to his own place ... Acts 1:16-20, 25
Better not to have been born .... Matt 26:24

Described as:
Thief .... John 12:6
Callous .... John 12:4-6
Deceitful .... Matt 26:14-16
Possessed by Satan ...... John 13:27
Son of perdition .... John 17:12
Devil .... John 6:70, 71

J I who also betrayed him .... Matt 10:4
J I, one of the twelve .... Mark 14:10
J surnamed *I* being of the ..... Luke 22:3
J I the son of Simon: for he .. John 6:71
it into the heart of *J I* .... John 13:2
he gave it to *J I*, the son of .. John 13:26
Judas saith unto him not *I* .... John 14:22

ISHBAH (ĭsh'bä)—*"praising; appeaser"*
Man of Judah 1Chr 4:17

ISHBAK (ĭsh'băk)—*"leaning; free"*
Son of Abraham and Keturah .... Gen 25:2

ISHBI-BENOB (ĭsh-bī-bē'nŏb)—*"dweller at Nob"*
Philistine giant 2Sam 21:16, 17

ISH-BOSHETH (ĭsh-bō'shĕth)—*"man of shame"*
One of Saul's sons 2Sam 2:8
Made king 2Sam 2:8-10
Offends Abner 2Sam 3:7-11
Slain; but assassins executed 2Sam 4:1-12
Same as Esh-baal 1Chr 8:33

servants of *I*..son of Saul 2Sam 2:12
pertained to *I*..son of Saul 2Sam 2:15
sent messengers to *I* Saul's 2Sam 3:14
I sent and took her from 2Sam 3:15

ISHHOD (ĭsh'hŏd)—*"man of majesty"*
Manassite 1Chr 7:18

ISHI (ĭsh'ī)—*"salutary"*
1. Son of Appaim 1Chr 2:31
2. Descendant of Judah 1Chr 4:20
3. Simeonite whose sons destroyed Amalekites . 1Chr 4:42
4. Manassite leader 1Chr 5:23, 24

ISHI (ĭsh'ī)—*"my husband"*
Symbolic name of God... Hos 2:16, 17

ISHIAH (ī-shī'ä)—*"Jehovah exists"*
Son of Izrahiah 1Chr 7:3

ISHIJAH (ī-shī'jä)—*"Jehovah exists"*
Son of Harim .... Ezra 10:31

ISHMA (ĭsh'mä)—*"high; desolate"*
Man of Judah 1Chr 4:1, 3

ISHMAEL (ĭsh'mā-ĕl)—*"God hears"*
1. Abram's son by Hagar .. Gen 16:3, 4, 15
   Angel foretells his name and character .... Gen 16:11-16
   Circumcised at 13 .... Gen 17:25
   Mocks at Isaac's feast ... Gen 21:8, 9
   Evidence of fleshly origin .... Gal 4:22-31
   Becomes an archer ...... Gen 21:20
   Dwells in wilderness .... Gen 21:21
   Marries an Egyptian .... Gen 21:21
   Buries his father .... Gen 25:9
   Dies at age 137 .... Gen 25:17
   His generations .... Gen 25:12-19
   His descendants 1Chr 1:29-31
2. Descendant of Jonathan . 1Chr 8:38
3. Father of Zebadiah 2Chr 19:11
4. Military officer under Joash 2Chr 23:1-3, 11
5. Son of Nethaniah; instigates murder of Gedaliah 2Kin 25:22-25
6. Priest who divorced his foreign wife .... Ezra 10:22

[*also* ISHAMEL'S]
I might live before thee! ...... Gen 17:18
as for *I*, I have heard .... Gen 17:20
Abraham took *I* his son .... Gen 17:23
circumcised, and *I* his son ..... Gen 17:26
Then went Esau unto *I* .... Gen 28:9
Mahalath..daughter of *I* .... Gen 28:9
Bashemath *I* daughter .... Gen 36:3
of Abraham; Isaac, and *I* 1Chr 1:28
I..Sheariah, and Obadiah 1Chr 9:44
even *I*..son of Nethaniah ..... Jer 40:8
slay *I*..son of Nethaniah .... Jer 40:15
speakest falsely of *I* .... Jer 40:16
I the son of Nethaniah .... Jer 41:1
arose *I*..son of Nethaniah ..... Jer 41:2
I also slew all the Jews .... Jer 41:3
I the son of Nethaniah .... Jer 41:6
I the son of Nethaniah .... Jer 41:7
them that said unto *I* .... Jer 41:8
I had cast all..dead bodies .... Jer 41:9
I the son of Nethaniah .... Jer 41:9
I carried away captive all ..... Jer 41:10
I the son of Nethaniah .... Jer 41:10
I..son of Nethaniah had done . Jer 41:11
fight with *I* .... Jer 41:12
with *I* saw Johanan .... Jer 41:13
people that *I* had carried ...... Jer 41:14
I..son of Nethaniah escaped .. Jer 41:15
he had recovered from *I* ...... Jer 41:16
I..son of Nethaniah had slain . Jer 41:18

ISHMAELITES (ĭsh'mā-ĕl-īts)—*descendants of Ishmael*
Settle at Havilah .... Gen 25:17, 18
Joseph sold to .... Gen 37:25-28
Sell Joseph to Potiphar .. Gen 39:1
Wear golden earrings .... Judg 8:22, 24
Become known as Arabians 2Chr 17:11

[*also* ISHAMELITE, ISHMEELITE, ISHMEELITES]
Amasa was Jether the *I* 1Chr 2:17
camels also was Obil the *I* 1Chr 27:30
tabernacles of Edom, and..*I* ... Ps 83:6

ISHMAIAH (ĭs-mā'yä)—*"Jehovah hears"*
1. Gibeonite 1Chr 12:4
2. Tribal chief in Zebulun .. 1Chr 27:19

ISHMERAI (ĭsh'mĕ-rī)—*"Jehovah is keeper"*
Benjamite 1Chr 8:18

ISHOD (ī'shŏd)—*"man of majesty"*
Manassite 1Chr 7:18

ISHPAN (ĭsh'păn)—*"he will hide"*
Son of Shashak 1Chr 8:22, 25

ISH-TOB (ĭsh'tŏb)—*"good man"*
Small kingdom of Aram. . 2Sam 10:6, 8
Jephthah seeks asylum in . Judg 11:3, 5

ISHUAH, ISUAH (ĭsh'ū-ä, ĭs'ū-ă)—*"he will level"*
Son of Asher .... Gen 46:17; 1Chr 7:30

ISHUAI (ĭsh'ū-ī)—*"equal"*
1. Son of Asher and chief .. 1Chr 7:30
   Called Isui .... Gen 46:17
   Called Jesui .... Num 26:44
2. Son of Saul 1Sam 14:49

ISLAND—*a body of land surrounded by water*

Descriptive of:
Coastal land of Palestine . Is 20:6
Land surrounded by water .... Is 23:2
Remote regions .... Is 42:10

List of:
Caphtor (Crete?) .... Jer 47:4
Clauda .... Acts 27:16
Chios .... Acts 20:15
Coos .... Acts 21:1
Crete .... Acts 27:12
Cyprus .... Acts 11:19
Elishah .... Ezek 27:7
Kittim (Cyprus) .... Jer 2:10
Melita .... Acts 28:1, 7, 9
Patmos .... Rev 1:9
Rhodes .... Acts 21:1
Samos .... Acts 20:15
Samothrace .... Acts 16:11
Syracuse .... Acts 28:12
Tyre .... Is 23:1, 2

[*also* ISLANDS, ISLE, ISLES]
i of the Gentiles divided ...... Gen 10:5
and upon the *i* of the sea ..... Esth 10:1
shall deliver the *i* .... Job 22:30
i shall bring presents .... Ps 72:10
multitude of *i* be glad .... Ps 97:1
Hamath, and from the *i* .... Is 11:11
wild beasts of the *i*..cry .... Is 13:22
inhabitants of this *i* .... Is 20:6
ye inhabitant of the *i* .... Is 23:6
in the *i* of the sea .... Is 24:15
with the wild beasts of the *i* .. Is 34:14
taketh up the *i* as a .... Is 40:15
silence before me, O *i* .... Is 41:1
The *i* saw it, and feared .... Is 41:5
i shall wait for his law .... Is 42:4
declare his praise in the *i* ..... Is 42:12
I will make the rivers *i* .... Is 42:15
Listen, O *i*, unto me .... Is 49:1
i shall wait upon me .... Is 51:5
i he will repay recompense .... Is 59:18
Surely the *i* shall wait for ..... Is 60:9
to Tubal, and Javan to the *i* ... Is 66:19
i which are beyond the sea .... Jer 25:22
declare it in the *i* afar off .... Jer 31:10
beasts of the *i* shall dwell ..... Jer 50:39
i shake at the sound of .... Ezek 26:15

i tremble in the day of ....Ezek 26:18
i that are in the sea shall ......Ezek 26:18
people for many *i* ....Ezek 27:3
out of the *i* of Chittim ....Ezek 27:6
i were the merchandise ....Ezek 27:15
All the inhabitants of the *i* ....Ezek 27:35
dwell carelessly in the *i* ....Ezek 39:6
turn his face unto the *i* ....Dan 11:18
all the *i* of the heathen ....Zeph 2:11
through the *i* unto Paphos .....Acts 13:6
be cast upon a certain *i* ....Acts 27:26
which had wintered in the *i* ...Acts 28:11
mountain and *i* were moved ...Rev 6:14
And every *i* fled away ....Rev 16:20

ISMACHIAH (ĭs-mä-kī'ä)—*"Jehovah will sustain"*
Temple overseer.........2Chr 31:13

ISMAIAH (ĭs-mā'yä)—*"Jehovah hears"*
I the Gibeonite, a mighty.1Chr 12:4

ISPAH (ĭs'pä)—*"to lay bare"*
Benjamite 1Chr 8:16

ISRAEL (ĭs'rā-ĕl)—*"God strives"*

Used literally of:
Jacob...................Gen 32:28
Descendants of Jacob ....Gen 49:16, 28
Ten northern tribes (in contrast to Judah) 1Sam 11:8
Restored nation after exile ....Ezra 9:1

Used spiritually of:
Messiah ....Is 49:3
God's redeemed ones ....Rom 9:6-13
True church.............Gal 6:16

See JACOB

[*also* ISRAEL'S]
called no more Jacob, but *I* ...Gen 32:28
Jacob, but *I* shall be thy ......Gen 35:10
I said unto them, If it must ...Gen 43:11
children of *I* to serve with.....Ex 1:13
saith the Lord, *I* is my son ....Ex 4:22
obey his voice to let *I* go? ....Ex 5:2
neither will I let *I* go ....Ex 5:2
of the children of *I* ....Ex 5:14
bring out the children of *I* ....Ex 7:5
let the children of *I* go ....Ex 10:20
called for all..elders of *I* ......Ex 12:21
did all the children of *I* ....Ex 12:50
say of the children of *I* ....Ex 14:3
after the children of *I*.........Ex 14:8
of *I* went into the midst of ....Ex 14:22
Lord saved *I* that day out of ...Ex 14:30
I saw that great work which ...Ex 14:31
Moses brought *I* from the Red .Ex 15:22
I journeyed from the ....Ex 17:1
say unto the children of *I* .....Ex 20:22
names of the children of *I*.....Ex 28:21
Abraham, Isaac, and *I* ....Ex 32:13
with thee and with *I* ....Ex 34:27
unto the children of *I*.........Ex 35:30
iniquities of..children of *I* .....Lev 16:21
things of the children of *I* .....Lev 22:2
unto the children of *I*.........Lev 24:15
to go forth to war in *I* ....Num 1:45
children of *I* did.............Num 1:54
males of the children of *I* .....Num 3:40
bless the children of *I*.........Num 6:23
name upon the children of *I*...Num 6:27
among the children of *I* ....Num 8:19
I took their journeys..........Num 10:12
before all the children of *I* ....Num 14:10
children of *I* murmured ....Num 16:41
things of the children of *I* .....Num 18:32
I vowed a vow unto the Lord .Num 21:2
the children of *I* set ....Num 21:10
thy tabernacles, O *I*! ....Num 24:5
I joined himself unto ....Num 25:3
Lord was kindled against *I* ....Num 25:3
numbered of..children of *I* ....Num 26:51
before the congregation of *I* ...Num 32:4
unto the children of *I*, and ....Num 35:10
before the children of *I* ....Deut 4:44
Hear, O *I*: The Lord our God .Deut 6:4
Lord, unto thy people *I* ....Deut 21:8
name shall be called in *I* ......Deut 25:10
unto all the elders of *I*........Deut 31:9
Happy art thou, O *I*: who.....Deut 33:29
children of *I* hearkened ....Deut 34:9
again the children of *I* ....Josh 5:2
hath wrought folly in *I* ....Josh 7:15
altar unto the Lord God of *I* ..Josh 8:30
all *I*, and their elders ....Josh 8:33
before the children of *I* ....Josh 10:12
come against *I* in battle ....Josh 11:20
unto the children of *I*.........Josh 18:10
the Lord gave unto *I* all ......Josh 21:43
whole congregation of *I*.......Josh 22:18
unto the Lord God of *I*........Josh 24:23
deliverer to..children of *I* .....Judg 3:9
I again did evil in the sight....Judg 4:1
of his villages in *I* ....Judg 5:11
God, If thou wilt save *I*.......Judg 6:36
before the children of *I* ....Judg 8:28
children of *I* said unto ....Judg 10:15
so *I* possessed all the ....Judg 11:21
he judged *I* seven years ....Judg 12:9
said the children of *I* ....Judg 20:3
are all children of *I*...........Judg 20:7
Then all the children of *I* .....Judg 20:26
I turned again upon the.......Judg 20:48
thee of the Lord God of *I* ....Ruth 2:12
his sons did unto all *I*.........1Sam 2:22
glory is departed from *I*.......1Sam 4:21
taken from *I* were restored 1Sam 7:14
wrought salvation in *I*.........1Sam 11:13
So the Lord saved *I* that 1Sam 14:23
to all the children of *I* 1Sam 15:6
I returned from chasing 1Sam 17:53
warfare, to fight with *I*........1Sam 28:1
the throne of David over *I* 2Sam 3:10
out and broughtest in *I* 2Sam 5:2
Thou shalt feed my people *I* ..2Sam 5:2
established him king over *I*....2Sam 5:12
to be over my people *I* 2Sam 7:11
ought to be done in *I*.........2Sam 13:12
Absalom and the elders of *I*...2Sam 17:15
man to his tents, O *I* 2Sam 20:1
Lord was kindled against *I* 2Sam 24:1
Judah and *I* dwelt safely 1Kin 4:25
among the children of *I* 1Kin 6:13
not forsake my people *I* 1Kin 6:13
Lord God of *I*, there is no 1Kin 8:23
and of thy people *I*...........1Kin 8:36
set thee on the throne of *I* 1Kin 10:9
made him king over all *I*.......1Kin 12:20
had against the cities of *I* 1Kin 15:20
Chronicles of the Kings of *I*? ..1Kin 16:20
even all the children of *I*......1Kin 20:15
king of *I* said unto his 1Kin 22:3
anger the Lord God of *I*........1Kin 22:53
God in all..earth, but in *I* 2Kin 5:15
anointed thee king over *I* 2Kin 9:12
Nebat, who made *I* sin........2Kin 13:11
nor any helper for *I* 2Kin 14:26
walked in the statutes of *I* 2Kin 17:19
saith the Lord God of *I*........2Kin 22:15
came all the elders of *I* 1Chr 11:3
O ye seed of *I* his servant.....1Chr 16:13
fell of *I* seventy thousand 1Chr 21:14
would increase *I* like to the ...1Chr 27:23
an ordinance for ever to *I*.....2Chr 2:4
servant, and..thy people *I* 2Chr 6:21
in Jerusalem over all *I* 2Chr 9:30
children of *I* fled before 2Chr 13:16
So the king of *I* and 2Chr 18:28
let not..army of *I* go with 2Chr 25:7
for the Lord is not with *I* 2Chr 25:7
I that were present at.........2Chr 30:21
to the children of *I* 2Chr 34:33
house of God, the God of *I* ...Ezra 6:22
sins of the children of *I* ....Neh 1:6
for my sake, O God of *I*.......Ps 69:6
to *I* for an everlasting.........Ps 105:10
O *I*, trust thou in the Lord....Ps 115:9
keepeth *I* shall neither ....Ps 121:4
hosts is the house of *I* ....Is 5:7
Lord God of *I* in the isles .....Is 24:15
One, the creator of *I*, your....Is 43:15
Thou art my servant, O *I* .....Is 49:3
glean the remnant of *I* as .....Jer 6:9
Lord God of *I* against ....Jer 23:2
spoken unto thee against *I* ....Jer 36:2
children of *I* shall come ....Jer 50:4
toward the mountains of *I*.....Ezek 6:2
prophets..*I* which prophesy....Ezek 13:16
of the elders of *I* came to .....Ezek 20:1
reed to the house of *I* ....Ezek 29:6
are the whole house of *I* ......Ezek 37:11
spirit upon the house of *I* .....Ezek 39:29
to the twelve tribes of *I*.......Ezek 47:13
I shall cry unto me, My God ..Hos 8:2
against you, O children of *I* ...Amos 3:1
unto me, O children of *I*? .....Amos 9:7
Jacob, as..excellency of *I*......Nah 2:2
Lord of hosts, the God of *I* ...Zeph 2:9
scattered Judah, *I*, and.......Zech 1:19
word of the Lord to *I*..........Mal 1:1
shall rule my people *I* ....Matt 2:6
lost sheep of the house of *I* ...Matt 10:6
lost sheep of the house of *I* ...Matt 15:24
children of *I* shall he turn .....Luke 1:16
for the consolation of *I* ....Luke 2:25
thou art the King of *I* ....John 1:49
King of *I* that cometh in the ..John 12:13
brethren the children of *I* .....Acts 7:23
promise raised unto *I* ....Acts 13:23
hope of *I* I am bound.........Acts 28:20
also crieth concerning *I* ....Rom 9:27
I hath not obtained that ......Rom 11:7
And so all *I* shall be saved ....Rom 11:26
Behold *I* after the flesh 1Cor 10:18
mercy, and upon the *I* of .....Gal 6:16
from the commonwealth of *I* ..Eph 2:12
of the stock of *I*, of the ....Phil 3:5
covenant with the house of *I* ..Heb 8:8
departing of..children of *I*.....Heb 11:22
tribes of the children of *I* .....Rev 21:12

ISRAEL, THE RELIGION OF

History of:
Call of Abraham ....Gen 12:1-3
Canaan promised ....Gen 15:18-21
Covenant at Sinai ....Ex 20
Covenant at Shechem ....Josh 24:1-28
Ark brought to Jerusalem.2Sam 6
Dedication of the Temple.1Kin 8:1-66
Reform movements 2Kin 23:4-14
2Chr 29:3-36
Destruction of Jerusalem .Jer 6
Restoration of the Law ..Neh 8, 9

Beliefs about God:
Creator.................Gen 1:1
Ps 104:24
Sustainer of creation .....Ps 104:27-30
Active in human affairs ..Deut 26:5-15
Omniscient..............Ps 139:1-6
Omnipresent ....Jer 23:23, 24
Everlasting..............Ps 90:2
Moral ....Ex 34:6, 7

ISRAELITES (ĭs'rā-ĕl-īts)—*descendants of Israel*

Brief history of:
Begin as a nation in Egypt ....Ex 1:12, 20
Afflicted in Egypt ....Ex 1:12-22
Moses becomes their leader ....Ex 3:1-22
Saved from plagues ......Ex 9:4, 6, 26
Expelled from Egypt.....Ex 12:29-36
Pass through Red Sea....Ex 14:1-31
Receive Law at Sinai ....Ex 19:1-25
Sin at Sinai ....Ex 32:1-35
Rebel at Kadesh ....Num 13:1-33
Wander 40 years ....Num 14:26-39
Cross Jordan ....Josh 4:1-24
Conquer Canaan ....Josh 12:1-24
Ruled by judges ....Judg 2:1-23
Samuel becomes leader ..1Sam 7:1-17
Seek to have a king 1Sam 8:1-22
Saul chosen king 1Sam 10:18-27
David becomes king 2Sam 2:1-4
Solomon becomes king...1Kin 1:28-40

Kingdom divided 1Kin 12:1-33
Israel (northern kingdom)
carried captive 2Kin 17:5-23
Judah (southern kingdom)
carried captive 2Kin 24:1-20
70 years in exile 2Chr36:20, 21
Return after exile . . . . . . .Ezra 1:1-5
Nation rejects Christ . . . . .Matt 27:20-27
Nation destroyed Luke21:20-24
1Thess2:14-16

Blessed with:
Great leaders . . . . .Heb 11:8-40
Inspired prophets 1Pet 1:10-12
God's oracles . . . . .Rom 3:2
Priesthood . . . . .Rom 9:3-5
The Law . . . . .Gal 3:16-25
Messianic promises . . . . . .Acts 3:18-26
Temple . . . . .Heb 9:1-10
Messiah . . . . .Dan 9:24-27
God's covenant . . . . .Jer 31:31-33
Regathering . . . . .Is 27:12
Jer 16:15, 16

Sins of:
Idolatry . . . . .Hos 13:1-4
Hypocrisy . . . . .Is 1:11-14
Disobedience . . . . .Jer 7:22-28
Externalism . . . . .Matt 23:1-33
Unbelief . . . . .Rom 11:1-31
Works—righteousness . . . .Phil 3:4-9

Punishments upon:
Defeat . . . . .Lev 26:36-38
Curses upon . . . . .Deut 28:15-46
Captivity . . . . .Judg 2:13-23
Destruction Luke19:42-44
Dispersion . . . . .Deut 4:26-28
Blindness . . . . .Rom 11:25
Forfeiture of blessings . . .Acts 13:42-49
Replaced by Gentiles . . . .Rom 11:11-20
See Jews

[*also* ISRAELITE, ISRAELITISH]
not one of the cattle of the *I* . .Ex 9:7
I born..dwell in booths . . . . .Lev 23:42
the son of an *I* woman . . . . .Lev 24:10
son of the *I* woman . . . . .Lev 24:10
I woman's son blasphemed . . . .Lev 24:11
name of the *I* that was slain . . .Num 25:14
I passed over on dry . . . . .Josh 3:17
I returned unto Ai . . . . .Josh 8:24
lot unto the *I* for an . . . . .Josh 13:6
dwell among the *I* until . . . . . . .Josh 13:13
to the ground of the *I* . . . . .Judg 20:21
in Shiloh unto all the *I* 1Sam 2:14
I went down to..Philistines 1Sam13:20
be with the *I* that were 1Sam14:21
I were gathered together 1Sam 25:1
I pitched by a fountain 1Sam 29:1
all the *I* were troubled 2Sam 4:1
name was Ithra an *I* 2Sam17:25
I rose up and smote 2Kin 3:24
all the multitude of the *I* 2Kin 7:13
the *I*, the priests, Levites 1Chr 9:2
Behold an *I* indeed . . . . .John 1:47
Are they *I*? so am I 2Cor 11:22

ISSACHAR (ĭs'ä-kär)—*"reward"*
1. Jacob's fifth son Gen30:17, 18
2. Tribe of, descendants of
Jacob's fifth son Num26:23, 24
Prophecy concerning Gen49:14, 15
Census at Sinai . . . . .Num 1:28, 29
On Gerizim . . . . .Deut 27:12
Inheritance of . . . . .Josh 19:17-23
Assists Deborah . . . . .Judg 5:15
At David's coronation . . .1Chr 12:32
Census in David's time . .1Chr 7:1-5
Attended Hezekiah's
Passover 2Chr 30:18
Prominent person of . . . .Judg 10:1
3. Doorkeeper 1Chr 26:1, 5

Judah, and *I*, and Zebulun . . . .Gen 35:23
I, Zebulun, and Benjamin . . . . .Ex 1:3
Of *I*; Nethaneel..son of Zuar . .Num 1:8
shall be the tribe of *I* . . . . .Num 2:5
captain of the children of *I* . . . .Num 2:5
tribe of the children of *I* . . . . . .Num 10:15
These are the families of *I* . . . .Num 26:25
thy going out; and, *I* Deut33:18
on the north, and in *I* . . . . .Josh 17:10
families of the tribe of *I* . . . . . .Josh 21:6
son of Paruah, in *I* 1Kin 4:17
Simeon, Levi, and Judah, *I* . . .1Chr 2:1
out of the tribe of *I* 1Chr 6:72
of *I*, Omri..son of Michael 1Chr 27:18
west side, *I* a portion Ezek48:25
one gate of *I*; one gate of Ezek48:33
tribe of *I* were sealed . . . . .Rev 7:7

ISSHIAH (ĭs-shī'ä)—*"Jehovah exists"*
1. Descendant of Issachar . .1Chr 7:1, 3
Son of Izrahiah 1Chr 7:3
2. Mighty man of David . . .1Chr 12:1, 6
3. Kohathite Levite 1Chr 23:20
1Chr 24:25
4. Levite and family head . .1Chr 24:21

ISSUE—*offspring; discharge; to flow out of*

[*also* ISSUED, ISSUES]
i, which thou begettest . . . . .Gen 48:6
cleansed from the *i* of . . . . .Lev 12:7
man hath a running *i* . . . . .Lev 15:2
because of..*i* he is unclean . . . .Lev 15:2
be his uncleanness in his *i* . . . . .Lev 15:3
flesh run with his *i* . . . . .Lev 15:3
flesh be stopped from his *i* . . . .Lev 15:3
he sat that hath the *i* . . . . .Lev 15:6
he that hath the *i* spit . . . . .Lev 15:8
toucheth that hath the *i* . . . . . . .Lev 15:11
when he that hath an *i* . . . . .Lev 15:13
is cleansed of his *i* . . . . .Lev 15:13
And if a woman have an *i* . . . .Lev 15:19
her *i* in her flesh be blood . . . .Lev 15:19
if a woman have..*i* of..blood . .Lev 15:25
i of her uncleanness . . . . .Lev 15:25
if she be cleansed of her *i* . . . . .Lev 15:28
law of him that hath an *i* . . . . .Lev 15:32
leper, or hath a running *i* . . . . .Lev 22:4
every one that hath an *i* . . . . . .Num 5:2
i out of the city against . . . . . .Josh 8:22
one that hath an *i* 2Sam 3:29
that shall *i* from thee 2Kin 20:18
if it had *i* out of the womb? . . .Job 38:8
Lord belong..*i* from death . . . . .Ps 68:20
for out of it are the *i* of life . . .Prov 4:23
offspring and the *i* . . . . .Is 22:24
i is like the *i* of horses Ezek23:20
waters *i* out from under . . . . . . .Ezek 47:1
stream *i* and came forth . . . . . .Dan 7:10
i of blood twelve years . . . . .Matt 9:20
i of blood twelve years . . . . .Mark 5:25
i of blood twelve years . . . . .Luke 8:43
out of their mouths *i* fire . . . . . .Rev 9:17

ISUAH—*See* Ishuah

ISUI—*See* Ishuai

IT—*See* Introduction

ITALY—*a peninsula of southern Europe*
Soldiers of, in Caesarea . .Acts 10:1
Jews expelled from . . . . . .Acts 18:2
Paul sails for . . . . .Acts 27:1, 6
Christians in . . . . .Acts 28:14

They of *I* salute you . . . . .Heb 13:24

ITCH—*an irritation of the skin*
scab, and with the *i* Deut28:27

ITCHING EARS—*descriptive of desire to hear something exciting or new*
Characteristic of the last
days 2Tim 4:2, 3

ITHAI (ĭth'ā-ī)—*"being"*
Son of Ribai 1Chr 11:31
Also called Ittai 2Sam 23:29

ITHAMAR (ĭth'ä-mär)—*"land; island of palms"*
Youngest son of Aaron . .Ex 6:23
Consecrated as priest . . . .Ex 28:1
Duty entrusted to . . . . . . .Ex 38:21
Jurisdiction over Gershonites
and Merarites . . . . .Num 4:21-33
Founder of Levitical
family 1Chr 24:4-6

unto Eleazar and unto *I* . . . . . .Lev 10:6
unto Eleazar and unto *I* . . . . . .Lev 10:12
Abihu, Eleazar, and *I* . . . . .Num 3:2
under the hand of *I* . . . . .Num 4:28
under the hand of *I* . . . . .Num 7:8
Abihu, Eleazar, and *I* 1Chr 6:3
Eleazar and *I* executed 1Chr 24:2
Gershom; of the sons of *I* . . . . .Ezra 8:2

ITHIEL (ĭth'ĭ-ĕl)—*"God is"*
1. Man addressed by Agur. .Prov 30:1
2. Benjamite . . . . .Neh 11:7

ITHMAH (ĭth'mä)—*"bereavement"*
Moabite of David's
mighty men 1Chr 11:46

ITHNAN (ĭth'năn)—*"given"*
Town in southern Judah. .Josh 15:23

ITHRA (ĭth'rä)—*"abundance"*
Israelite for Ishmaelite
father of Amasa 2Sam 17:25
Called Jether 1Kin 2:5, 32

ITHRAN (ĭth'răn)—*"excellent"*
1. Son of Dishon . . . . .Gen 36:26
2. Son of Zophah 1Chr 7:37
Same as Jether 1Chr 7:38

Amram, and Eshban, and *I* . . .1Chr 1:41

ITHREAM (ĭth'rĕ-ăm)—*"residue of the people"*
Son of David 2Sam 3:2-5

sixth, *I* by Eglah his wife 1Chr 3:3

ITHRITE (ĭth'rīt)—*"pre-eminence"*
Family dwelling at
Kirjath-jearim 1Chr 2:53
One of David's guard 2Sam 23:38

Ira the *I*, Gareb the *I* 1Chr 11:40

ITSELF—*it's true self*
seed is in *i*, upon the earth . . . .Gen 1:11
the beast that dieth of *i* . . . . . . .Lev 7:24
land *i* vomiteth out her . . . . . . .Lev 18:25
reap..which groweth of *i* . . . . . .Lev 25:11
any thing that dieth of *i* Deut14:21
were of the very base *i* 1Kin 7:34
of darkness, as darkness *i* . . . . .Job 10:22
gathereth iniquity to *i* . . . . .Ps 41:6
heart may discover *i* . . . . .Prov 18:2
which bewrayeth *i* . . . . .Prov 27:16
Shall..axe boast *i* against . . . . . .Is 10:15
shall the saw magnify *i* . . . . .Is 10:15
rod should shake *i* against . . . . .Is 10:15
staff should lift up *i* . . . . .Is 10:15
your soul delight *i* in fatness . . .Is 55:2
shall dwell in Judah *i* . . . . .Jer 31:24
a fire infolding *i* . . . . .Ezek 1:4
might not lift *i* up Ezek17:14
any thing that is dead of *i* Ezek44:31
bear, and it raised up *i* . . . . . . .Dan 7:5
take thought for the things..*i* . .Matt 6:34
kingdom divided against *i* . . . . .Matt 12:25
house divided against *i* . . . . .Matt 12:25
kingdom be divided against *i* . .Mark 3:24
kingdom divided against *i* Luke11:17
cannot bear fruit of *i* . . . . .John 15:4
world *i* could not contain . . . . .John 21:25
Spirit *i* beareth witness . . . . .Rom 8:16
Spirit *i* maketh intercession . . . .Rom 8:26
even nature *i* teach you 1Cor 11:14
not behave *i* unseemly 1Cor 13:5
high thing that exalteth *i* 2Cor 10:5
unto the edifying of *i* . . . . .Eph 4:16
into heaven *i* now to appear . . .Heb 9:24
of all men, and..truth *i* 3John 12

ITTAH-KAZIN (ĭt-ä-kā'zĭn)—*"gather"*
On border of Zebulun . . .Josh19:13, 16

ITTAI (ĭt'ā-ī)—*"timely"*
1. One of David's guard . . .2Sam 23:23-29
See Ithai

2. Native of Gath; one of David's commanders . .2Sam 15:18-22

under the hand of *I* 2Sam 18:2
Joab and Abishai and *I* 2Sam 18:5
charged..Abishai and *I* 2Sam 18:12

ITUREA (ĭt-ū-rē'ä)—*"mountains"—a small province on the northwest boundary of Palestine at the base of Mount Hermon*
Ruled by Philip ....Luke 3:1

IVAH (ī'vä)—*"hamlet"*
City conquered by the Assyrians ....Is 37:13

of Sepharvaim, Hena, and *I*? . .2Kin 18:34
Sepharvaim, of Hena, and *I*? . .2Kin 19:13

IVORY—*the tusks of certain mammals*
Imported from Tharshish .1Kin 10:22
Imported from Chittim . . .Ezek 27:6, 15
Ahab's palace made of . . .1Kin 22:39
Thrones made of 1Kin 10:18
Beds made of ....Amos 6:4
Sign of luxury ....Amos 3:15
Figuratively used ....Song 5:14
Descriptive of wealth ....Ps 45:8
Among Babylon's trade . .Rev 18:12

made a great throne of *i* 2Chr 9:17
silver, *i*, and apes 2Chr 9:21
neck is as a tower of *i* ....Song 7:4

IZHAR, IZEHAR (ĭz'här, ĭz'ĕ-här)—*"shining"*
Son of Kohath ....Ex 6:18, 21
Num 3:19
Ancestor of the Izharites .Num 3:27
1Chr 6:38

son of *I* the son of Kohath ....Num 16:1
sons of Kohath; Amram, *I* 1Chr 6:2
Kohath were, Amram, and *I* . .1Chr 6:18
of Kohath; Amram, *I* 1Chr 23:12
I, Shelomith 1Chr 23:18

IZHARITES, IZEHARITES (ĭz-här'īts, ĭz-ĕ-här'its)—*See* IZHAR

IZLIAH (ĭz-lī'ä)—*"Jehovah delivers"*
Son of Elpaal 1Chr 8:18

IZRAHIAH (ĭz-rä-hī'ä)—*"Jehovah shines"*
Chief of Issachar 1Chr 7:1, 3

IZRAHITE (ĭz-rä-hīt)
Applied to Shamhuth 1Chr 27:8

[*also* IZRAHITES]
Of the *I*; Shelomoth 1Chr 24:22
Amramites, and the *I* 1Chr 26:23
Of the *I*, Chenaniah 1Chr 26:29

IZRI (ĭz'rī)—*"fashioner"*
Leader of Levitical choir .1Chr 25:11
Also called Zeri 1Chr 25:3

J

JAAKAN, JAKAN (jā'ä-kăn; jā'kăn)—*"intelligent"*
Son of Ezer 1Chr 1:42
Also called Akan ....Gen 36:27
Of Horite origin ....Gen 36:20-27
Tribe of at Beeroth ......Deut 10:6
Dispossessed by Edomites.Deut 2:12
Same as Benejaakan .....Num 33:31, 32

JAAKOBAH (jā-ä-kō'bä)—*"to Jacob"*
Simeonite 1Chr 4:36

JAALA, JAALAH (jā-ä-lä)—*"elevation"*
Family head of exile returnees ....Ezra 2:56
Descendants of Solomon's servants ....Neh 7:57, 58

JAALAM (jā'ä-lăm)—*"hidden"*
Son of Esau ....Gen 36:5, 18

to Esau Jeush and *J* ....Gen 36:14
and Jeush, and *J* 1Chr 1:35

JAANAI (jā-ä-nī)—*"answerer"*
Gadite chief 1Chr 5:12

JAARE-OREGIM (jā-ä-rĕ-ôr'ĕ-jĭm)—*"foresters"*
Father of Elhanan 2Sam 21:19
Also called Jair 1Chr 20:5

JAASAU (jā-ä'sô)—*"Jehovah makes"*
Son of Bani; divorced foreign wife ....Ezra 10:37

JAASIEL (jā-ā'sĭ-ĕl)—*"God is maker"*
1. One of David's mighty men 1Chr 11:47
2. Son of Abner...........1Chr 27:21

JAAZANIAH (jā-ăz-ä-nī'ä)—*"Jehovah is hearing"*
1. Military commander supporting Gedaliah . . .2Kin 25:23
See JEZANIAH
2. Rechabite leader ....Jer 35:3
3. Idolatrous Israelite elder .Ezek 8:11
4. Son of Azur; seen in Ezekiel's vision ....Ezek 11:1

J..son of Maachathite 2Kin 25:23

JAAZER—*See* JAZER

JAAZIAH (jā-ä-zī'ä)—*"Jehovah is determining"*
Merarite Levite 1Chr 24:26, 27

Mushi; the sons of *J* 1Chr 24:25

JAAZIEL (jā-ā'zĭ-ĕl)—*"God is determining"*
Levite musician 1Chr 15:18, 20
See AZIEL

JABAL (jā'băl)—*"moving"*
Son of Lamech; father of herdsmen ....Gen 4:20

JABBOK (jăb'ŏk)—*"flowing"*
River entering the Jordan about 20 miles north of the Dead Sea ....Num 21:24
Scene of Jacob's conflict. .Gen 32:22-32
Boundary marker........Deut 3:16

any place of the river *J* ....Deut 2:37
even unto the river *J* ....Josh 12:2
from Arnon even unto *J* ......Judg 11:13
from Arnon even unto *J* ......Judg 11:22

JABESH (jā'bĕsh)—*"dry place"*
1. Father of Shallum 2Kin 15:10, 13, 14
2. Abbreviated name of Jabesh-gilead 1Sam 11:1-10

came to *J*, and burnt 1Sam 31:12
buried..under a tree at *J* 1Sam 31:13
brought them to *J* 1Chr 10:12
bones under the oak in *J* 1Chr 10:12

JABESH-GILEAD (jā-bĕsh-gĭl'ĕ-ăd)—*"dry"*
Consigned to destruction .Judg 21:8-15
Saul struck the Ammonites here 1Sam 11:1-11
Citizens of, rescue Saul's body 1Sam 31:11-13
David thanks citizens of. .2Sam 2:4-7
See JABESH 2

his son from the men of *J* 2Sam 21:12
J heard all..the Philistines 1Chr 10:11

JABEZ (jā'bĕz)—*"height"*
1. City of Judah 1Chr 2:55
2. Man of Judah noted for his prayer 1Chr 4:9, 10

JABIN (jā'bĭn)—*"intelligent; observed"*
1. Canaanite king of Hazor; leads confederacy against Joshua ....Josh 11:1-14
2. Another king of Hazor; oppresses Israelites . . . .Judg 4:2
Defeated by Deborah and Barak ....Judg 4:3-24
Immortalized in poetry . .Judg 5:1-31

[*also* JABIN'S]
God subdued on that day *J* . . .Judg 4:23
J at the brook of Kison ....Ps 83:9

JABNEEL (jăb'nĕ-ĕl)—*"building of God"*
1. Town in northern Judah .Josh 15:11
Probably same as Jabneh.2Chr 26:6
2. Town of Naphtali ....Josh 19:33

JACHAN (jā'kăn)—*"afflicting"*
Gadite chief 1Chr 5:13

JACHIN (jā'kĭn)—*"founding; he will establish"*
1. Son of Simeon ....Gen 46:10
Family head ....Num 26:12
Called Jarib 1Chr 4:24
2. Descendant of Aaron . . .1Chr 24:1, 17
Representatives of ......Neh 11:10
3. One of two pillars in front of Solomon's Temple 1Kin 7:21, 22

Jamin, and Ohad, and *J* ......Ex 6:15
Jehoiarib, and *J* 1Chr 9:10
on the right hand *J* 2Chr 3:17

JACINTH (jā'sĭnth)—*a sapphire stone*
In high priest's breastplate ....Ex 28:19
Foundation stone ....Rev 21:20
Breastplates the color of. .Rev 9:17

JACKAL—*a wild dog*
Probably referred to as:
"Wild beasts" ....Is 13:22
"Dragons" ....Is 34:13
"Doleful creatures" ......Is 13:21
Dwells in ruins ....Is 35:7
Goes in packs ....Judg 15:4
Loves grapes ....Song 2:15

JACOB (jā'kŭb)—*"supplanter; following after"—the son of Isaac and Rebekah and twin brother of Esau; became the father of the Jewish nation*
Son of Isaac and Rebekah............Gen 25:20-26; Hos 12:3
Born in answer to prayer .Gen 25:21
Rebekah's favorite.......Gen 25:27, 28
Obtains Esau's birthright .Gen 25:29-34
Heb 12:16
Obtains Isaac's blessing . .Gen 27:1-38
Hated by Esau ....Gen 27:41-46
Departs for Haran ....Gen 28:1-5
Sees heavenly ladder.....Gen 28:10-19
Makes a vow............Gen 28:20-22
Meets Rachel and Laban .Gen 29:1-14
Serves for Laban's daughters ....Gen 29:15-30
His children.............Gen 29:31-35
Requests departure from Laban ....Gen 30:25-43
Flees from Laban.........Gen 31:1-21
Overtaken by Laban .....Gen 31:22-43
Covenant with Laban ....Gen 31:44-55
Meets angels ....Gen 32:1, 2
Sends message to Esau . . .Gen 32:3-8
Prays earnestly ....Gen 32:9-12
Sends gifts to Esau ......Gen 32:13-21
Wrestles with an angel . . .Gen 32:22-32
Hos 12:3, 4
Name becomes Israel ....Gen 32:32
Reconciled to Esau ......Gen 33:1-16
Erects altar at Shechem . .Gen 33:17-20
Trouble over Dinah .....Gen 34:1-31
Renewal at Bethel ....Gen 35:1-15
Buries Rachel ....Gen 35:16-20
List of 12 sons ....Gen 35:22-26
Buries Isaac.............Gen 35:27-29
His favoritism toward Joseph.............Gen 37:1-31
Mourns over Joseph .....Gen 37:32-35
Sends sons to Egypt for food...................Gen 42:1-5
Allows Benjamin to go . .Gen 43:1-15
Revived by good news . . .Gen 45:25-28

Goes with family to
Egypt .... Gen 46:1-27
Meets Joseph .... Gen 46:28-34
Meets Pharaoh .... Gen 47:7-12
Makes Joseph swear .... Gen 47:28-31
Blesses Joseph's sons .... Gen 48:1-22
Blesses his own sons .... Gen 49:1-28
Dies in Egypt .... Gen 49:29-33
Burial in Canaan .... Gen 50:1-14
See ISRAEL

[*also* JACOB'S]
his name was called *J* .... Gen 25:26
J was a plain man .... Gen 25:27
And *J* sod pottage .... Gen 25:29
Rebekah spake unto *J* .... Gen 27:6
Isaac said unto *J*, Come .... Gen 27:21
J went near unto Isaac .... Gen 27:22
made an end of blessing *J* .... Gen 27:30
Esau hated *J* because of .... Gen 27:41
will I slay my brother *J* .... Gen 27:41
J awaked out of his sleep .... Gen 28:16
J rose up early .... Gen 28:18
J vowed a vow, saying .... Gen 28:20
when *J* saw Rachel .... Gen 29:10
J went near, and rolled .... Gen 29:10
she bare *J* no children .... Gen 30:1
said unto *J*, Give me .... Gen 30:1
J anger was kindled .... Gen 30:2
J went in unto her .... Gen 30:4
bare *J* a son .... Gen 30:5
bare *J* a second son .... Gen 30:7
and gave her *J* to wife .... Gen 30:9
Leah's maid bare *J* a son .... Gen 30:10
bare *J* a second son .... Gen 30:12
And *J* came out of the field .... Gen 30:16
bare *J* the fifth son .... Gen 30:17
bare *J* the sixth son .... Gen 30:19
J said unto Laban, Send .... Gen 30:25
J said, Thou shalt not give .... Gen 30:31
betwixt himself and *J* .... Gen 30:36
J fed..Laban's flocks .... Gen 30:36
J took him..green poplar .... Gen 30:37
J did separate the lambs .... Gen 30:40
that *J* laid the rods before .... Gen 30:41
And *J* was left alone .... Gen 32:24
What is thy name..he said *J* .... Gen 32:27
be called no more *J* .... Gen 32:28
J asked him, and said .... Gen 32:29
J called the name of the .... Gen 32:30
J lifted up his eyes .... Gen 33:1
J said, Nay, I pray thee .... Gen 33:10
God said unto *J*, Arise, go .... Gen 35:1
J said unto his household .... Gen 35:2
gave unto *J*..strange gods .... Gen 35:4
J hid them under the oak .... Gen 35:4
pursue after the sons of *J* .... Gen 35:5
J came to Luz, which is in .... Gen 35:6
God appeared unto *J* .... Gen 35:9
Thy name is *J* .... Gen 35:10
not be called any more *J* .... Gen 35:10
J set..a pillar in the place .... Gen 35:14
J called..the place .... Gen 35:15
came unto *J* their father .... Gen 42:29
J their father said unto .... Gen 42:36
the sons of Israel carried *J* .... Gen 46:5
came into Egypt, *J*, and all .... Gen 46:6
came into Egypt, *J* and his .... Gen 46:8
to Abraham, to Isaac..to *J* .... Gen 50:24
his household came with *J* .... Ex 1:1
with Isaac, and with *J* .... Ex 2:24
of Isaac, and of *J* .... Ex 3:16
unto Isaac, and unto *J* .... Ex 6:3
thou say to the house of *J* .... Ex 19:3
remember..covenant with *J* .... Lev 26:42
Come, curse me *J* .... Num 23:7
not beheld iniquity in *J* .... Num 23:21
no enchantment against *J* .... Num 23:23
it shall be said of *J* .... Num 23:23
shall come a Star out of *J* .... Num 24:17
unto Isaac, and unto *J* .... Num 32:11
Abraham, Isaac, and *J* .... Deut 1:8
Abraham, Isaac, and *J* .... Deut 9:5
Abraham, to Isaac, and to *J* .... Deut 29:13
J is..lot of his inheritance .... Deut 32:9
teach *J* thy judgments .... Deut 33:10
unto Isaac, and unto *J* .... Deut 34:4
I gave unto Isaac *J* .... Josh 24:4
J and his children went .... Josh 24:4
J was come into Egypt 1Sam 12:8
anointed of the God of *J* 2Sam 23:1
tribes of the sons of *J* 1Kin 18:31
Abraham, Isaac, and *J* 2Kin 13:23
children of *J*, his chosen 1Chr 16:13
J shall rejoice, and Israel .... Ps 14:7
the seed of *J*, glorify .... Ps 22:23
command deliverances for *J* .... Ps 44:4
of *J* whom he loved .... Ps 47:4
know that God ruleth in *J* .... Ps 59:13
At thy rebuke, O God of *J* .... Ps 76:6
established..testimony in *J* .... Ps 78:5
brought him to feed *J* his .... Ps 78:71
joyful noise unto..God of *J* .... Ps 81:1
give ear, O God of *J* .... Ps 84:8
all the dwellings of *J* .... Ps 87:2
righteousness in *J* .... Ps 99:4
confirmed the same unto *J* .... Ps 105:10
house of *J* from a people of .... Ps 114:1
unto the mighty God of *J* .... Ps 132:2
Lord hath chosen *J* unto .... Ps 135:4
He showeth his word unto *J* .... Ps 147:19
the house of the God of *J* .... Is 2:3
forsaken..the house of *J* .... Is 2:6
Lord sent a word into *J* .... Is 9:8
even the remnant of *J* .... Is 10:21
Lord will have mercy on *J* .... Is 14:1
cleave to the house of *J* .... Is 14:1
come of *J* to take root .... Is 27:6
concerning the house of *J* .... Is 29:22
J shall not now be ashamed .... Is 29:22
sanctify the Holy One of *J* .... Is 29:23
J whom I have chosen .... Is 41:8
reasons, saith the King of *J* .... Is 41:21
Lord that created thee, O *J* .... Is 43:1
have given *J* to the curse .... Is 43:28
Fear not, O *J* my servant .... Is 44:2
Remember these, O *J* .... Is 44:21
for *J* my servant's sake .... Is 45:4
Hearken..O house of *J* .... Is 46:3
Hearken unto me, O *J* .... Is 48:12
to bring *J* again to him .... Is 49:5
Redeemer..mighty One of *J* .... Is 49:26
with the heritage of *J* .... Is 58:14
Redeemer..mighty One of *J* .... Is 60:16
word of..Lord, O house of *J* .... Jer 2:4
The portion of *J* is not like .... Jer 10:16
even the time of *J* trouble .... Jer 30:7
fear thou not, O my servant *J* .... Jer 30:10
J shall return, and shall .... Jer 30:10
the captivity of *J* tents .... Jer 30:18
the Lord hath redeemed *J* .... Jer 31:11
I cast away the seed of *J* .... Jer 33:26
seed of Abraham, Isaac..*J* .... Jer 33:26
fear not thou O my servant *J* .... Jer 46:27
J shall return..be in rest .... Jer 46:27
The portion of *J* is not like .... Jer 51:19
burned against *J* like a .... Lam 2:3
the seed of the house of *J* .... Ezek 20:5
that I have given unto *J* .... Ezek 37:25
plow, and *J* shall break .... Hos 10:11
J fled into the country .... Hos 12:12
testify in the house of *J* .... Amos 3:13
by whom shall *J* arise? .... Amos 7:2
destroy the house of *J* .... Amos 9:8
against thy brother *J* .... Obad 10
house of *J* shall be a fire .... Obad 18
the transgression of *J* is .... Mic 1:5
the transgression of *J*? .... Mic 1:5
art named the house of *J* .... Mic 2:7
I pray you, O heads of *J* .... Mic 3:1
ye heads of the house of *J* .... Mic 3:9
remnant of *J* shall be in .... Mic 5:7
wilt perform the truth to *J* .... Mic 7:20
away the excellency of *J* .... Nah 2:2
Was not Esau *J* brother? .... Mal 1:2
saith the Lord: yet I loved *J* .... Mal 1:2
ye sons of *J* are not .... Mal 3:6
and *J* begat Judas .... Matt 1:2
God of Isaac..the God of *J* .... Matt 22:32
God of Isaac..the God of *J*? .... Mark 12:26
reign over the house of *J* .... Luke 1:33
Abraham and Isaac and *J* .... Luke 13:28
Now *J* well was there .... John 4:6
Abraham..of Isaac and of *J* .... Acts 3:13
when *J* heard that there .... Acts 7:12
J went down into Egypt .... Acts 7:15
tabernacle for the God of *J* .... Acts 7:46
J have I loved, but Esau .... Rom 9:13
tabernacles with Isaac and *J* .... Heb 11:9
By faith *J* when he was .... Heb 11:21

JACOB (jā'kŭb)—*"supplanter; following after"*
Father of Joseph, Mary's
husband .... Matt 1:15, 16

JACOB'S ORACLES—*blessings and curses on the twelve tribes*
Recorded .... Gen 49:1-27

JACOB'S WELL—*the well Jacob dug*
Christ teaches a
Samaritan woman .... John 4:5-26

JADA (jā'dä)—*"knowing"*
Grandson of Jerahmeel 1Chr 2:26, 28, 32

JADAU (jā'dô)—*"friend"*
Son of Nebo .... Ezra 10:43

JADDUA (jă-dū'ä)—*"very knowing; known"*
1. Chief layman who signs
the document .... Neh 10:21
2. Levite who returns with
Zerubbabel .... Neh 12:8, 11

Joiada, and Johanan and *J* .... Neh 12:22

JADON (jā'dŏn)—*"judging"*
Meronothite worker .... Neh 3:7

JAEL (jē'ĕl)—*"a wild goat"*
Wife of Heber the Kenite .... Judg 4:17
Slays Sisera .... Judg 4:17-22
Praised by Deborah .... Judg 5:24-27

days of *J* the highways .... Judg 5:6

JAGUR (jā'ger)—*"husbandman"*
Town in southern Judah .... Josh 15:21

JAH (jä)—*poetic form of Jehovah*
Found only in poetry and
in proper names .... Ps 68:4

JAHATH (jā'hăth)—*"comfort; revival"*
1. Grandson of Judah 1Chr 4:2
2. Great-grandson of Levi 1Chr 6:20, 43
3. Son of Shimei 1Chr 23:10
4. Son of Shelemoth 1Chr 24:22
5. Merarite Levite 2Chr 34:12

And *J* was the chief 1Chr 23:11

JAHAZ (jā'hăz)—*"a place trodden under foot"*
Town in Moab at which
Sihon was defeated .... Num 21:23
Assigned to Reubenites .... Josh 13:18
Levitical city .... Josh 21:36
Regained by Moabites .... Is 15:4
Same as Jahzah 1Chr 6:78

[*also* JAHAZAH]
his people, to fight at *J* .... Deut 2:32
pitched in *J*, and fought .... Judg 11:20
upon *J*, and upon Mephaath .... Jer 48:21
unto *J*, have they uttered .... Jer 48:34

JAHAZIAH (jä-hä-zī'ä)—*"Jehovah reveals"*
Postexilic returnee .... Ezra 10:15

JAHAZIEL (jä-hā'zĭ-ĕl)—*"God reveals"*
1. Kohathite Levite 1Chr 23:19
2. Benjamite warrior 1Chr 12:4
3. Priest 1Chr 16:6
4. Inspired Levite 2Chr 20:14

J the third, Jekameam the 1Chr 24:23
son of *J* and with him .... Ezra 8:5

JAHDAI (jä'dā-ī)—*"Jehovah leads"*
Judahite 1Chr 2:47

JAHDIEL (jä'dĭ-ĕl)—*"union of God; God gives joy"*
Manassite chief 1Chr 5:24

JAHDO (jä'dō)—*"union"*
Gadite 1Chr 5:14

JAHLEEL (jä'lĕ-ĕl)—*"God waits; wait for God"*
Son of Zebulun . . . . Gen 46:14
Family head . . . . Num 26:26

JAHLEELITES (jä'lĕ-ĕl-īts)
Descendants of Jahleel . . . Num 26:26

JAHMAI (jä'mă-ī)—*"Jehovah protects"*
Descendant of Issachar . . . 1Chr 7:1, 2

JAHZAH—*See* JAHAZ

JAHZEEL (jä'zĕ-ĕl)—*"God apportions"*
Son of Naphtali . . . . Gen 46:24
Same as Jahziel 1Chr 7:13

JAHZEELITES (jä'zĕ-ĕl-īts)
Descendants of Jahzeel . . Num 26:48

JAHZERAH (jä'zĕ-rä)—*"Jehovah protects"*
Priest 1Chr 9:12
Called Ahasai . . . . Neh 11:13

JAHZIEL (jä'zĭ-ĕl)—*"God apportions"*
Son of Naphtali 1Chr 7:13
See JAHZEEL

JAILER—*one who guards a prison*
Converted by Paul at Philippi . . . . Acts 16:19-34

JAIR (jä'er)—*"Jehovah enlightens"*
1. Manassite warrior . . . . Num 32:41; Deut 3:14
Conquers towns in Gilead . . . . Num 32:41
2. Eighth judge of Israel . . . Judg 10:3-5
3. Father of Mordecai, Esther's uncle . . . . Esth 2:5
4. Father of Elhanan 1Chr 20:5
Called Jaare-oregim 2Sam 21:19

towns of *J*, which are in . . . . . . Josh 13:30
pertained the towns of *J* 1Kin 4:13
Segub begat *J*, who had 1Chr 2:22
Aram, with the towns of *J* 1Chr 2:23

JAIRITE (jā'er-īt)
Descendant of Jair, the Manassite 2Sam 20:26

JAIRUS (jā'ī-rŭs)—*"enlightened"—Greek form of "jair"*
Ruler of the synagogue;
Jesus raises his daughter . . . . Mark 5:22-24, 35-43

came a man named *J* . . . . Luke 8:41

JAKAN—*See* JAAKAN

JAKEH (jā'kĕ)—*"hearkening"*
Father of Agur . . . . Prov 30:1

JAKIM (jā'kĭm)—*"a setter up"*
1. Descendant of Aaron . . . 1Chr 24:1, 12
2. Benjamite 1Chr 8:19

JALON (jā'lŏn)—*"Jehovah abides"*
Calebite, son of Ezra 1Chr 4:17

JAMBRES (jăm'brēz)—*"opposer"*
Egyptian magician 2Tim 3:8
See JANNES AND JAMBRES

JAMES (jāmz)—*Greek form of Jacob*
1. Son of Zebedee . . . . Matt 4:21
Fisherman . . . . Matt 4:21
One of the Twelve . . . . . . Matt 10:2
In business with Peter . . . Luke 5:10
Called Boanerges . . . . Mark 3:17
Of fiery disposition . . . . . Luke 9:52-55
Makes a contention . . . . . Mark 10:35-45
One of inner circle . . . . . . Matt 17:1
Sees the risen Lord . . . . . John 21:1, 2
Awaits the Holy Spirit . . Acts 1:13
Slain by Herod Agrippa . Acts 12:2
2. Son of Alphaeus; one of the Twelve . . . . Matt 10:3, 4
Identified usually as "the less" . . . . Mark 15:40
Brother of Joses . . . . Matt 27:56
3. Son of Joseph and Mary . Matt 13:55, 56
Lord's brother . . . . Gal 1:19
Rejects Christ's claim . . . Mark 3:21
Becomes a believer . . . . . Acts 1:13, 14
Sees the risen Lord 1Cor 15:7
Becomes moderator of Jerusalem Council . . . . Acts 15:13-23
Paul confers with him . . . Gal 2:9, 12
Wrote an epistle . . . . James 1:1
Brother of Jude . . . . Jude 1

J the son of Alpheus . . . . Matt 10:3
brethren, *J*, and Joses . . . . Matt 13:55
Mary the mother of *J* . . . . Matt 27:56
J the son of Zebedee . . . . Mark 1:19
Andrew with *J* and John . . . . . . Mark 1:29
and *J* the son of Alpheus . . . . . Mark 3:18
the brother of *J* and Joses . . . . Mark 6:3
with him Peter, and *J* . . . . Mark 9:2
displeased with *J* and . . . . Mark 10:41
Peter and *J* and John . . . . Mark 13:3
with him Peter and *J* . . . . Mark 14:33
Mary the mother of *J* . . . . Mark 15:40
Mary the mother of *J* . . . . Mark 16:1
Andrew his brother *J* . . . . Luke 6:14
J the son of Alpheus . . . . Luke 6:15
Judas the brother of *J* . . . . Luke 6:16
save Peter and *J* and . . . . Luke 8:51
Peter and John and *J* . . . . Luke 9:28
Mary the mother of *J* . . . . Luke 24:10
he killed *J* the brother of . . . . . Acts 12:2
show these things unto *J* . . . . . . Acts 12:17
Paul went..with us unto *J* . . . . . Acts 21:18
save *J* the Lord's brother . . . . . Gal 1:19

JAMES, THE EPISTLE OF—*a book of the New Testament*
Trials . . . . James 1:2-8
Temptation . . . . James 1:12-18
Doing the word . . . . James 1:19-25
Faith and works . . . . James 2:14-26
Patience . . . . James 5:7-11
Converting the sinner . . . . James 5:19, 20

JAMIN (jā'mĭn)—*"right hand; favor"*
1. Son of Simeon . . . . Gen 46:10
Family head . . . . Ex 6:14, 15
2. Man of Judah 1Chr 2:27
3. Postexilic Levite; interprets the law . . . . . Neh 8:7, 8

of *J* the family of the . . . . Num 26:12
were Nemuel and *J* 1Chr 4:24

JAMINITES (jā'mĭn-īts)
Descendants of Jamin . . . . Num 26:12

JAMLECH (jăm'lĕk)—*"Jehovah rules"*
Simeonite chief 1Chr 4:34

JANAI (jā'nā-ī)—*"answer"*
Gadite chief 1Chr 5:12

JANGLING—*self-conceited talk against God*
Characteristic of false teachers 1Tim 1:6, 7
Translated also "babblings" 1Tim 6:20

JANNA (jăn-nä)—*an ancestor of Joseph, the husband of Mary*
Melchi, which was the son of *J*. Luke 3:24

JANNAI (jă'nā-ī)—*a form of John*
Ancestor of Christ . . . . Luke 3:23, 24

JANNES AND JAMBRES (jăn'ēz; jăm'brēz)—*Egyptian magicians at the time of the Exodus*
Two Egyptian magicians; oppose Moses 2Tim 3:8
Compare account . . . . Ex 7:11-22

JANOAH, JANOHAH (jä-nō'ä, jä-nō'hä)—*"resting"*
1. Town of Naphtali 2Kin 15:29
2. Border town of Ephraim . Josh 16:6, 7

JANUM (jā'nŭm)—*"sleeping"*
Town near Hebron . . . . . . Josh 15:53

JAPHETH (jā'fĕth)—*"the extender; fair; enlarged"*
One of Noah's three sons . Gen 5:32
Saved in the ark 1Pet 3:20
Receives Messianic blessing . . . . Gen 9:20-27
His descendants occupy Asia Minor and Europe . Gen 10:2-5

three sons, Shem, Ham.. *J* . . . . . Gen 6:10
and Shem, and Ham, and *J* . . . Gen 7:13
were Shem, and Ham, and *J* . . Gen 9:18
of Noah, Shem, Ham and *J* . . . Gen 10:1
of Eber, the brother of *J* . . . . . Gen 10:21
Noah, Shem, Ham and *J* 1Chr 1:4
sons of *J*: Gomer 1Chr 1:5

JAPHIA (jä-fī'ä)—*"enlarging"*
1. King of Lachish; slain by Joshua . . . . Josh 10:3-27
2. One of David's sons 2Sam 5:13-15
3. Border town of Zebulun . Josh 19:10, 12

and goeth up to *J* . . . . Josh 19:12
and Nepheg and *J* 1Chr 3:7
and Nepheg and *J* 1Chr 14:6

JAPHLET (jăf'lĕt)—*"Jehovah causes to escape"*
Asherite family 1Chr 7:32, 33

JAPHLETI (jăf'lĕt-ī)—*"to shine"*
Unidentified tribe on Joseph's boundary . . . . . Josh 16:1, 3

JAPHO (jā'fō)—*"beauty"*
Hebrew form of Joppa . . . Josh 19:46

JARAH (jā'rä)—*"unveiler; honey"*
Descendant of King Saul . 1Chr 9:42
Called Jehoaddah 1Chr 8:36

JAREB (jā'rĕb)—*"contender; avenger"*
Figurative description of Assyrian king . . . . Hos 5:13

for a present to king *J* . . . . Hos 10:6

JARED, JERED (jā'rĕd, jĕ'rĕd)—*"descending"*
Father of Enoch . . . . Gen 5:15-20
Ancestor of Noah 1Chr 1:2
Ancestor of Christ . . . . Luke 3:37

JARESIAH (jăr-ĕ-sī'ä)—*"Jehovah gives a couch"*
Benjamite head 1Chr 8:27

JARHA (jär'hä)—*"the Lord nourishes"*
Egyptian slave; marries master's daughter 1Chr 2:34-41

JARIB (jā'rĭb)—*"striving"*
1. Head of a Simeonite family 1Chr 4:24
Called Jachin . . . . Gen 46:10
2. Man sent to search for Levites . . . . Ezra 8:16, 17
3. Priest who divorced his foreign wife . . . . Ezra 10:18

JARMUTH (jär'mŭth)—*"height"*
1. Royal city of Canaan . . . . Josh 10:3
King of, slain by Joshua . Josh 10:3-27
Assigned to Judah . . . . . . Josh 15:20, 35
Inhabited after exile . . . . . Neh 11:29
2. Town in Issachar assigned to the Levites . Josh 21:28, 29
Called Ramoth 1Chr 6:73
Called Remeth . . . . Josh 19:21

king of *J* one, the king . . . . . . Josh 12:11

JAROAH (jä-rō'ä)—*"new moon"*
Gadite chief 1Chr 5:14

JASHEN (jā'shĕn)—*"shining"*
Sons of, in David's bodyguard 2Sam 23:32
Called Hashem 1Chr 11:34

JASHER (jā'shĕr)—*"upright"*
Book of, quoted . . . . Josh 10:13

written in the book of *J* 2Sam 1:18

JASHOBEAM (jä-shō'bĕ-ăm)—*"the people return"*
1. Chief of David's mighty men 1Chr 11:11
Becomes military captain . 1Chr 27:2, 3
Called Adino 2Sam 23:8
2. Benjamite warrior 1Chr 12:1, 2, 6

JASHUB (jā'shŭb)—*"turning back"*
1. Issachar's son 1Chr 7:1
Head of family . . . . Num 26:24
Called Job . . . . Gen 46:13
2. Son of Bani; divorced his foreign wife . . . . Ezra 10:29

JASHUBI-LEHEM (jä-sho͞o-bĭ-lē'hĕm)—*"turning back to Bethlehem"*
A man of Judah 1Chr 4:22

JASHUBITES (jā'sho͞o-bīts)
Descendants of Jashub . . . Num 26:24

JASIEL (jā'sĭ-ĕl)—*"God is Maker"—same as Jaasiel*

and *J* the Mesobaite 1Chr 11:47

JASON (jā'sŭn)—*"healing"*
Welcomes Paul at Thessalonica . . . . Acts 17:5-9
Described as Paul's kinsman . . . . Rom 16:21

JASPER—*a precious stone (quartz)*
Set in high priest's breastplate . . . . Ex 28:20
Descriptive of:
Tyre's adornments . . . . . . Ezek 28:12, 13
Heavenly vision . . . . Rev 4:3

a beryl, an onyx and a *j* . . . . . . Ex 39:13
j stone, clear as crystal . . . . Rev 21:11
the wall of it was of *j* . . . . Rev 21:18
first foundation was *j* . . . . Rev 21:19

JATHNIEL (jăth'nĭ-ĕl)—*"God is giving"*
Korahite porters 1Chr 26:1, 2

JATTIR (jăt'er)—*"preeminence"*
Town of Judah . . . . Josh 15:48
Assigned to Aaron's children . . . . Josh 21:13, 14
David sends spoil to 1Sam 30:26, 27

with her suburbs and *J* 1Chr 6:57

JAVAN (jā'văn)—*the son of Japheth, as well as his descendants*
Son of Japheth . . . . Gen 10:2, 4
Descendants of, to receive good news . . . . . Is 66:19, 20
Trade with Tyre . . . . Ezek 27:13, 19
King of, in Daniel's visions . . . . Dan 8:21
Conflict with . . . . Zech 9:13

J and Tubal 1Chr 1:5
sons of *J*: Elishah 1Chr 1:7

JAVELIN—*a light, short spear*
Used by Saul 1Sam 18:10

and took a *j* in his hand . . . . . . Num 25:7
Saul cast the *j* 1Sam 18:11
with his *j* in his hand 1Sam 19:9
to the wall with the *j* 1Sam 19:10
smote the *j* into the wall 1Sam 19:10
Saul cast a *j* at him 1Sam 20:33

JAW—*the bony, framing part of the mouth*
Used figuratively of:
Power over the wicked . . . Job 29:17
Prov 30:14
God's sovereignty . . . . Is 30:28
Human trial . . . . Hos 11:4

[*also* JAWS]
with the *j* of an ass have I . . . . Judg 15:16
hollow place that was in the *j* . Judg 15:19
or bore his *j* through with . . . . . Job 41:2
tongue cleaveth to my *j* . . . . Ps 22:15
I will put hooks in thy *j* . . . . . . Ezek 29:4
and put books into thy *j* . . . . . . Ezek 38:4

JAWBONE—*cheekbone*
Weapon used by Samson . Judg 15:15-19

JAZER, JAAZER (jā'zer, jā-ā'zĕr)—*"helpful"*
Town east of Jordan near Gilead 2Sam 24:5
Amorites driven from . . . . Num 21:32
Assigned to Gad . . . . Josh 13:24, 25
Becomes Levitical city . . . Josh 21:34, 39
Taken by Moabites . . . . . . Is 16:8, 9
Desired by sons of Reuben and Gad . . . . . . Num 32:1-5

Atroth, Shophan, and *J* . . . . Num 32:35
J with her suburbs 1Chr 6:81
men of valor at *J* 1Chr 26:31
with the weeping of *J* . . . . Jer 48:32
reach even to the sea of *J* . . . . . Jer 48:32

JAZIZ (jā-zĭz)—*"shining"*
Shepherd over David's flocks 1Chr 27:31

JEALOUSY—*envy*
Kinds of:
Divine . . . . Ex 20:5
Marital . . . . Num 5:12-31
Motherly . . . . Gen 30:1
Brotherly . . . . Gen 37:4-28
Sectional 2Sam 19:41-43
National . . . . Judg 8:1-3
Good causes of:
Zeal for the Lord . . . . Num 25:11
Concern over Christians . . 2Cor 11:2
Evil causes of:
Favoritism . . . . Gen 37:3-11
Regard for names 1Cor 3:3-5
Carnality 2Cor 12:20
Amos 3:14-16
Described as:
Implacable . . . . Prov 6:34, 35
Cruel . . . . Song 8:6
Burning . . . . Deut 29:20
Godly 2Cor 11:2

[*also* JEALOUS]
name is *J* is a *j* God . . . . Ex 34:14
spirit of *j* come upon him . . . . . Num 5:14
consuming fire, even a *j* God . . Deut 4:24
Lord thy God am a *j* God . . . . Deut 5:9
Lord thy God is a *j* God . . . . . . Deut 6:15
provoked him to *j* . . . . Deut 32:16
They have moved me to *j* . . . . . Deut 32:21
I will move them to *j* . . . . Deut 32:21
a holy God; he is a *j* God . . . . . Josh 24:19
provoked him to *j* 1Kin 14:22
I have been very *j* for the 1Kin 19:10
moved him to *j* with their . . . . . Ps 78:58
shall thy *j* burn like fire? . . . . . . Ps 79:5
shall stir up *j* like a man . . . . . . Is 42:13
the seat of the image of *j* . . . . . Ezek 8:3
which provoketh to *j* . . . . Ezek 8:3
altar this image of *j* . . . . Ezek 8:5
give thee blood in fury and *j* . . Ezek 16:38
j shall depart from thee . . . . Ezek 16:42
will set my *j* against thee . . . . . Ezek 23:25
fire of my *j* have I spoken . . . . Ezek 36:5
have spoken in my *j* and in . . . Ezek 36:6
in my *j* and in the fire of . . . . . Ezek 38:19
will be *j* for my holy name . . . . Ezek 39:25
the Lord be *j* for his land . . . . . Joel 2:18
God is *j* and the Lord . . . . Nah 1:2
devoured by..fire of his *j* . . . . . . Zeph 1:18
devoured with..fire of my *j* . . . . Zeph 3:8
I am *j* for Jerusalem . . . . Zech 1:14
for Zion with a great *j* . . . . Zech 1:14
I was *j* for Zion with great *j* . . . Zech 8:2
and I was *j* for her with great . Zech 8:2
I will provoke you to *j* . . . . Rom 10:19
provoke the Lord to *j* 1Cor 10:22

JEARIM (jē'ä-rĭm)—*"woods"*
Mountain 10 miles west of Jerusalem . . . . Josh 15:10

JEATERAI (jĕ-ăt'ĕ-rī)—*"steadfast"*
Descendant of Levi 1Chr 6:21
Also called Ethni 1Chr 6:41

JEBERECHIAH (jĕ-bĕr-e-kī'ä)—*"Jehovah is blessing"*
Father of Zechariah (not the prophet) . . . . Is 8:2

JEBUS (jē'bŭs)—*"manager"*
Same as Jerusalem 1Chr 11:4
Entry denied to David . . . 1Chr 11:5
Levite came near . . . . Judg 19:1, 11
See ZION; SION

came over against *J* . . . . Judg 19:10

JEBUSI (jĕ'bŭs-ī)—*"trodden underfoot"*
Assigned to Benjamin . . . Josh 18:28
Same as Jerusalem . . . . . Josh 18:28
On the border of Judah . . Josh 15:8

JEBUSITES (jĕ'bŭs-ītes)
Descendants of Canaan . . Gen 10:15, 16
Mountain tribe . . . . Num 13:29
Land of, promised to Israel . . . . Gen 15:18-21
Adoni-zedek, their king, raises confederacy . . . . . Josh 10:1-5
Their king killed by Joshua . . . . Josh 10:23-26
Join fight against Joshua . Josh 11:1-5
Assigned to Benjamin . . . Josh 18:28
Royal city not taken . . . . . Judg 1:21
Taken by David 2Sam 5:6-8
Old inhabitants remain . . . 2Sam 24:16-25
Become slaves 1Kin 9:20, 21

[*also* JEBUSITE]
and the Hivites, and the *J* . . . . Ex 3:8
and the Hivites, and the *J* . . . . Ex 3:17
and the Hivites, and the *J* . . . . Ex 13:5
the Hivites, and the *J* . . . . Ex 23:23
and the Hivites, and the *J* . . . . Deut 7:1
the Hivites, and the *J* . . . . Deut 20:17
the Amorites, and the *J* . . . . . . Josh 3:10
Hivite, and the *J*, heard . . . . . . Josh 9:1
the *J* in the mountains . . . . Josh 11:3
the Hivites, and the *J* . . . . Josh 12:8
J..inhabitants of Jerusalem . . . . Josh 15:63
J dwell with the children . . . . . . Josh 15:63
the Hivites, and the *J* . . . . Josh 24:11
and Hivites, and *J* . . . . Judg 3:5
turn into this city of the *J* . . . . . Judg 19:11
of Araunah the *J* 2Sam 24:16
of Araunah the *J* 2Sam 24:18
J also and the Amorite 1Chr 1:14
where the *J* were 1Chr 11:4
Whosoever smiteth the *J* 1Chr 11:6
of Ornan the *J* 2Chr 3:1
the Perizzites, the *J* . . . . Ezra 9:1
the *J*, and the Girgashites . . . . . Neh 9:8
and Ekron as a *J* . . . . Zech 9:7

JECAMIAH (jĕk-ä-mī'ä)—*"may Jehovah establish"—a son of King Jeconiah*
Shenaar, *J*, Hoshama 1Chr 3:18

JECHONIAH—*See* JECONIAH

JECHONIAS—*See* JECONIAH

JECOLIAH (Jĕk-ō-lī'ä)—*"Jehovah is able"*
Mother of King Azariah. . 2Kin 15:2
Called Jechiliah 2Chr 26:3

JECONIAH (jĕk-ō-nī'ä)—*"Jehovah establishes"*
Variant form of Jehoiachin 1Chr 3:16, 17
Abbreviated to Coniah . . . Jer 22:24, 28
Son of Josiah . . . . Matt 1:11
See JEHOIACHIN

carried away with *J* . . . . Esth 2:6
had carried away captive *J* . . . . Jer 24:1
he carried away captive *J* . . . . . Jer 27:20
I will bring..to this place *J* . . . . Jer 28:4
(After that *J* the king . . . . Jer 29:2

JEDAIAH (jĕ-dā'yä)—*"Jehovah is praise"*
1. Priestly family 1Chr 24:7

J

2. Head of the priests .....Neh 12:6
3. Another head priest .....Neh 12:7, 21
4. Simeonite 1Chr 4:37
5. Postexilic worker........Neh 3:10
6. One who brings gifts for the Temple...........Zech 6:10, 14

of the priests; *J*, and 1Chr 9:10
the children of *J*, of the.......Ezra 2:36
the children of *J*, of ....Neh 7:39
Of the priests: *J* the son of....Neh 11:10
of Joiarib, Mattenai; of *J* .....Neh 12:19

JEDIAEL (jĕ-dī'ā-ĕl)—*"God knows"*
1. Son of Benjamin and family head 1Chr 7:6, 10, 11
2. Manassite; joins David ..1Chr 12:20
3. One of David's mighty men 1Chr 11:45
4. Korahite porter..........1Chr 26:1, 2

JEDIDAH (jĕ-dī'dä)—*"beloved"*
mother's name was *J* 2Kin 22:1

JEDIDIAH (jĕd-ĭ-dī'ä)—*"beloved of Jehovah"*
Name given to Solomon by Nathan 2Sam 12:24, 25

JEDUTHUN (jĕ-dū'thŭn)—*"a choir of praise"*
1. Levite musician appointed by David ...1Chr 16:41, 42
Heads a family of musicians.............2Chr 5:12
Name appears in Psalm titles..................Ps 39; 62; 77
Family officiates after Exile ....Neh 11:17
Possibly same as Ethan ..1Chr 15:17, 19
2. Father of Obed-edom ...1Chr 16:38

son of Galal, the son of *J*.....1Chr 9:16
and of Heman, and of *J* 1Chr 25:1
Of *J*; the sons of *J* 1Chr 25:3
hands of their father *J* 1Chr 25:3
order to Asaph, *J*, and 1Chr 25:6
and of the sons of *J* 2Chr 29:14
and *J* the king's seer..........2Chr 35:15

JEEZER (jĕ-ē'zer)—*"father of help"—contracted form of Abiezer*

[*also* JEEZERITES]
J, the family of the Jeezerites. .Num 26:30

JEEZERITES—*See* JEZER

JEGAR-SAHADUTHA (jē-gär-sā-hä-dū'thä)—*"heap of witness"*
Name given to Laban to memorial stones.......Gen 31:46, 47

JEHALELEEL (jē-hä-lē'lĕ-ĕl)—*"God is praised"*
1. Man of Judah and family head 1Chr 4:16
2. Merarite Levite 2Chr 29:12

JEHDEIAH (jĕ-dē'yä)—*"union of Jehovah"*
1. Kohathite Levite 1Chr 24:20
2. Meronothite in charge of David's asses 1Chr 27:30

JEHEZEKEL (jĕ-hĕz'ĕ-kĕl)—*"God is strong"*
Descendant of Aaron 1Chr 24:1, 16

JEHIAH (jĕ-hī'ä)—*"Jehovah is living"*
Doorkeeper 1Chr 15:24
See JEIEL 4

JEHIEL (jĕ-hī'ĕl)—*"God is living"*
1. Levite musician 1Chr 15:18, 20
2. Gershonite and family head 1Chr 23:8
3. Son of Hachmoni 1Chr 27:32
4. Son of King Jehoshaphat 2Chr 21:2, 4
5. Hemanite Levite 2Chr 29:14
6. Overseer in Hezekiah's reign..................2Chr 31:13
7. Official of the Temple ..2Chr 35:8
8. Father of Obadiah, a returned exile ....Ezra 8:9
9. Father of Shechaniah ...Ezra 10:2
10. Postexilic priest ....Ezra 10:21
11. Postexilic priest ....Ezra 10:26

JEHIELI (jĕ-hī'ĕ-lī)
A Levite family 1Chr 26:21, 22

JEHIZKIAH (jē-hĭz-kī'ä)—*"Jehovah is strong; Jehovah strengthens"*
Ephraimite chief.........2Chr 28:12

JEHOADAH (jē-hō-ăd'ä)—*"unveiler; honey"*
Descendant of Saul 1Chr 8:36
Also called Jarah 1Chr 9:42

JEHOADDAN (jē-hō-ăd'ăn)—*"Jehovah gives delight"*
Mother of Amaziah......2Kin 14:2

his mother's name was *J* 2Chr 25:1

JEHOAHAZ (jĕ-hō'ä-hăz)—*"Jehovah upholds"*
1. Son and successor of Jehu, king of Israel ...2Kin 10:35
Seeks the Lord in defeat .2Kin 13:2-9
2. Son and successor of Josiah, king of Judah..2Kin 23:30-34
Called Shallum 1Chr 3:15
3. Another form of Ahaziah, youngest son of King Joram 2Chr 21:17

J the son of Jehu began.......2Kin 13:1
year of Joash son of *J* 2Kin 14:1
Jehoash, the son of *J* 2Kin 14:8
death of Jehoash son of *J* 2Kin 14:17
to Joash, the son of *J*.........2Chr 25:17
son of Joash, the son of *J*.....2Chr 25:23
death of Joash son of *J* 2Chr 25:25
the land took *J* the son of 2Chr 36:1
J was twenty and three 2Chr 36:2
Necho took *J* his brother 2Chr 36:4

JEHOASH—*See* JOASH

JEHOHANAN, JOHANAN (jē-hō-hā'năn, jō'hā-năn)—*"Jehovah is gracious"*
1. Korahite Levite 1Chr 26:3
2. Captain under Jehoshaphat 2Chr 17:10, 15
3. Father of Ishmael, Jehoiada's supporter ..2Chr 23:1
4. Priestly family head .....Neh 12:13
5. Priest who divorced his wife ....Ezra 10:28
6. Son of Tobiah the Ammonite.............Neh 6:17, 18
7. Postexilic singer.........Neh 12:42

JEHOIACHIN (jĕ-hoi'ä-kĭn)—*"Jehovah establishes"*
Son of Jehoiakim; next to the last king of Judah..2Kin 24:8
Deported to Babylon 2Kin 24:8-16
Liberated by Evil-merodach.........Jer 52:31-34
See JECONIAH

[*also* JEHOIACHIN'S]
year of the captivity of *J*......2Kin 25:27
lift up the head of *J* king 2Kin 25:27
J his son reigned in his 2Chr 36:8
J was eight years old when 2Chr 36:9
fifth year of king *J* ....Ezek 1:2

JEHOIADA (jĕ-hoi'ä-dä)—*"Jehovah knows"*
1. Aaronite supporter of David.................1Chr 12:27
2. Father of Benaiah, one of David's officers 2Sam 8:18
3. Son of Benaiah; one of David's counselors 1Chr 27:34
4. High priest 2Kin 11:9
Proclaims Joash king 2Kin 11:4-16
Institutes a covenant 2Kin 11:17-21
Instructs Joash 2Kin 12:2
Commanded to repair the Temple...........2Kin 12:3-16
Receives honorable burial 2Chr 24:15, 16
5. Deposed priest ....Jer 29:26
6. Postexilic returnee ......Neh 3:6

Benaiah the son of *J* was 2Sam 20:23
Benaiah the son of *J*, the 2Sam 23:20
did Benaiah the son of *J*......2Sam 23:22
Benaiah the son of *J*, and.....1Kin 1:8
Benaiah the son of *J*, and.....1Kin 1:26
Benaiah the son of *J* 1Kin 1:32
Benaiah the son of *J* 1Kin 1:36
Benaiah the son of *J* 1Kin 1:38
Benaiah the son of *J* 1Kin 2:25
Benaiah the son of *J* 1Kin 2:29
Benaiah the son of *J* went 1Kin 2:34
Benaiah the son of *J* in his....1Kin 2:35
Benaiah the son of *J* 1Kin 2:46
Benaiah the son of *J* was 1Kin 4:4
Benaiah the son of *J* 1Chr 11:22
did Benaiah the son of *J*......1Chr 11:24
Benaiah the son of *J* was 1Chr 18:17
Benaiah the son of *J* 1Chr 27:5
Jehoshabeath..wife of *J* 2Chr 22:11
year *J* strengthened 2Chr 23:1
J the priest had commanded...2Chr 23:8
for *J*..dismissed not the 2Chr 23:8
J..delivered to the 2Chr 23:9
J and his sons anointed 2Chr 23:11
J..brought out the captains 2Chr 23:14
J made a covenant 2Chr 23:16
J appointed the offices 2Chr 23:18
the Lord all the days of *J* 2Chr 24:2
J took for him two wives 2Chr 24:3
king called for *J* the chief 2Chr 24:6
J gave it to such as did 2Chr 24:12
before the king and *J* 2Chr 24:14
continually all the days of *J* ...2Chr 24:14
the death of *J* came the.......2Chr 24:17
Zechariah the son of *J*........2Chr 24:20
kindness which *J* his father 2Chr 24:22
the blood of the sons of *J*.....2Chr 24:25

JEHOIAKIM (jĕ-hoi'ä-kĭm)—*"Jehovah sets up; Jehovah has established"*
Son of King Josiah 2Kin 23:34, 35
Made Pharaoh's official ..2Kin 23:34, 36
Wicked king 2Chr 36:5, 8
Burns Jeremiah's roll ....Jer 36:1-32
Becomes Nebuchadnezzar's servant 2Kin 24:1
Punished by the Lord....2Kin 24:2-4
Taken by Nebuchadnezzar 2Chr 36:5, 6
Returns to idolatry 2Chr 36:5, 8
Treats Jeremiah with contempt ....Jer 36:21-28
Kills a true prophet......Jer 26:20-23
Bound in fetters 2Chr 36:6
Buried as an ass.........Jer 22:18, 19
Curse on ....Jer 36:30, 31
See ELIAKIM 2

the rest of the acts of *J* 2Kin 24:5
J slept with his fathers 2Kin 24:6
according to all that *J* had 2Kin 24:19
Johanan, the second *J* 1Chr 3:15
sons of *J*: Jeconiah 1Chr 3:16
and turned his name to *J* 2Chr 36:4
It came also in the days of *J* ..Jer 1:3
the Lord concerning *J* ....Jer 22:18
Coniah the son of *J* king......Jer 22:24
Jeconiah the son of *J* ....Jer 24:1
fourth year of *J* the son of ....Jer 25:1
beginning of the reign of *J* ....Jer 26:1
beginning of the reign of *J* ....Jer 27:1
Jeconiah the son of *J* ....Jer 27:20
place Jeconiah the son of *J*....Jer 28:4
days of *J* the son of Josiah ....Jer 35:1
of Coniah the son of *J* ....Jer 37:1
of *J* the son of Josiah ....Jer 45:1
in the fourth year of *J* ....Jer 46:2
according to all that *J* had ....Jer 52:2

third year of the reign of *J* ....Dan 1:1
Lord gave *J* king of Judah ....Dan 1:2

JEHOIARIB (jĕ-hoi'ä-rĭb)—*"Jehovah contends"*
Descendant of Aaron 1Chr 24:1, 6, 7
Founder of an order of priests 1Chr 9:10, 13

JEHONADAB (jĕ-hŏn'ä-dăb)—*"Jehovah is liberal"*
A Rechabite 2Kin 10:15
See JONADAB

JEHONATHAN (jĕ-hŏn'ä-thăn)—*"Jehovah gives"*
1. Levite teacher 2Chr 17:8
2. Postexilic priest ....Neh 12:1, 18
3. Son of Uzzah 1Chr 27:25

JEHORAM, JORAM (jĕ-hō'răm, jō'răm)—*"Jehovah is high"*
1. King of Judah; son and successor of Jehoshaphat 1Kin 22:50
   Called Joram 2Kin 8:21, 23, 24
   Reigns eight years 2Kin 8:16, 17
   Marries Athaliah, who leads him astray 2Kin 8:18, 19
   Killed his brothers 2Chr 21:2, 4, 13
   Edom revolts from 2Kin 8:20-22
   Elijah predicts his terrible end 2Chr 21:12-15
   Nations fight against 2Chr 21:16, 17
   Smitten by the Lord; dies in disgrace 2Chr 21:18-20
2. King of Israel; son of Ahab 2Kin 1:17
   Called Joram 2Kin 8:16, 25, 28
   Reigns 12 years 2Kin 3:1
   Puts away Baal 2Kin 3:2
   Joins Jehoshaphat against Moabites 2Kin 3:1-27
   Naaman sent to, for cure.2Kin 5:1-27
   Informed by Elijah of Syria's plans 2Kin 6:8-23
   Wounded in war with Syria.................2Kin 8:28, 29
3. Levite teacher 2Chr 17:8

J and Ahaziah, his fathers 2Kin 12:18
J his son reigned in his 2Chr 21:1
the kingdom gave he to *J* 2Chr 21:3
J was thirty and two years 2Chr 21:5
J went forth with his 2Chr 21:9
Ahaziah the son of *J* king 2Chr 22:1
J the Son of Ahab king of 2Chr 22:5
Azariah the son of *J* king 2Chr 22:6
went down to see *J* the son ...2Chr 22:6
he went out with *J* against 2Chr 22:7
the daughter of king *J* 2Chr 22:11

JEHOSHABEATH (jē-hō-shăb'ĕ-ăth)—*"Jehovah makes oath"*
Safeguards Joash from Athaliah 2Chr 22:11

JEHOSHAPHAT, JOSAPHAT (jĕ-hŏsh'ä-făt, jō'să-făt)—*"Jehovah is judge"*
1. King of Judah; son and successor of Asa 1Kin 15:24
   Reigns 25 years 1Kin 22:42
   Fortifies his kingdom 2Chr 17:2
   Institutes reforms 2Chr 17:3
   Inaugurates public instruction 2Chr 17:7-9
   Honored and respected ..2Chr 17:10-19
   Joins Ahab against Ramoth-gilead 1Kin 22:1-36
   Rebuked by a prophet ..2Chr 19:2, 3
   Develops legal system ...2Chr 19:4-11
   By faith defeats invading forces 2Chr 20:1-30
   Navy of, destroyed 2Chr 20:35-37
   Provision for his children.2Chr 21:2, 3
   Death of 2Chr 21:1
   Ancestor of Christ ......Matt 1:8
2. Son of Ahilud 2Sam 8:16
   Recorder under David and Solomon 2Sam 20:24
3. Father of King Jehu 2Kin 9:2
4. A priest under David ...1Chr 15:24

J the son of Ahilud..........2Sam 8:16
J the son of Ahilud..........2Sam 20:24
J the son of Ahilud..........1Kin 4:3
J the son of Paruah 1Kin 4:17
J made peace with the 1Kin 22:44
the rest of the acts of *J* 1Kin 22:45
J made ships of Tarshish 1Kin 22:48
the son of Ahab unto *J* 1Kin 22:49
But *J* would not..............1Kin 22:49
J slept with his fathers 1Kin 22:50
seventeenth year of *J* 1Kin 22:51
Jehoram the son of *J* 2Kin 1:17
the eighteenth year of *J* 2Kin 3:1
to *J* the king of Judah 2Kin 3:7
J said, Is there not here 2Kin 3:11
J said, The word of the 2Kin 3:12
J and the king of Edom........2Kin 3:12
I regard the presence of *J* 2Kin 3:14
J being then king of Judah 2Kin 8:16
Jehoram the son of *J* king 2Kin 8:16
Jehu the son of *J*............2Kin 9:14
took all the..things that *J* 2Kin 12:18
Asa his son, *J* his son 1Chr 3:10
J the son of Alilud 1Chr 18:15
J his son reigned in his 2Chr 17:1
Judah brought to *J* presents ...2Chr 17:5
Now *J* had riches.............2Chr 18:1
king of Israel said unto *J* 2Chr 18:3
J said unto the king of Israel ..2Chr 18:4
J said, Is there not here a.....2Chr 18:6
king of Israel said unto *J* 2Chr 18:7
J said, Let not the king say ...2Chr 18:7
J king of Judah sat 2Chr 18:9
king of Israel said to *J* 2Chr 18:17
J the king of Judah went......2Chr 18:28
king of Israel said unto *J* 2Chr 18:29
captains of the chariot saw *J* ..2Chr 18:31
J cried out, and the Lord 2Chr 18:31
J the king of Judah returned ..2Chr 19:1
And *J* reigned over Judah.....2Chr 20:31
the rest of the acts of *J* 2Chr 20:34
walked in the ways of *J* 2Chr 21:12
they, he is the son of *J* 2Chr 22:9

JEHOSHAPHAT, VALLEY OF—*the valley situated between Jerusalem and the Mount of Olives*
Described as a place of judgment ....Joel 3:2, 12

JEHOSHEBA (jĕ-hŏsh'ĕ-bä)—*"Jehovah makes oath"*
King Joram's daughter ...2Kin 11:2

JEHOSHUA—*See* JOSHUA

JEHOSHUAH—*See* JOSHUA

JEHOVAH (jĕ-hō'vä)—*the personal, revealed name of God translated from the Hebrew consonants YHWH*
Defined ....Ex 6:3-5
Early known ....Gen 4:26
Usually rendered LORD in Old Testament ....Ex 17:14
Used in certain combinations ....Gen 22:14
Often found in names (e.g., Jehoshaphat, Elijah) 1Kin 15:24
Applied to Christ as Lord .... Is 40:3; Matt 3:3

whose name alone is *J* ....Ps 83:18
J is my strength ....Is 12:2
the Lord *J* is everlasting ......Is 26:4

JEHOVAH-JIREH (jĕ-hō'vä-jī-'rĕ)—*"the Lord will provide"*
Name used by Abraham Gen 22:14

JEHOVAH-NISSI (jĕ-hō'vä-nĭs'ī)—*"the Lord is my banner"*
Name used by Moses for memorial ....Ex 17:15, 16

JEHOVAH-SHALOM (jĕ-hō'vä-shä'lŏm)—*"the Lord send peace"*
Name used by Gideon for significant visit ....Judg 6:23, 24

JEHOZABAD (jĕ-hŏz'ä-băd)—*"Jehovah endows"*
1. Son of Obed-edom 1Chr 26:4
2. Son of a Moabitess; assassinates Joash 2Kin 12:20, 21
   Put to death............2Chr 25:3
3. Military captain under King Jehoshaphat 2Chr 17:18

J the son of Shimrith 2Chr 24:26

JEHOZADAK (jĕ-hŏz'ä-dăk)—*"Jehovah is righteous"*
Son of Seriah, the high priest.................1Chr 6:14
His father killed 2Kin 25:18-21
Carried captive to Babylon 1Chr 6:15
Father of Joshua the high priest.................Hag 1:1, 12, 14

JEHU (jē'hū)—*"Jehovah is he"*
1. Benjamite warrior.......1Chr 12:3
2. Prophet and son of Hanani...............1Kin 16:1
   Denounces Baasha 1Kin 16:2-4, 7
   Rebukes Jehoshaphat ...2Chr 19:2, 3
   Writes Jehoshaphat's biography 2Chr 20:34
3. Descendant of Judah 1Chr 2:38
4. Simeonite 1Chr 4:35
5. Grandson of Nimshi.....2Kin 9:2
   Commander under Ahab .2Kin 9:25
   Divinely commissioned to destroy Ahab's house .1Kin 19:16, 17
   Carries out orders with zeal..................2Kin 9:11-37
   Killed Ahab's sons 2Kin 10:1-17
   Destroys worshipers of Baal 2Kin 10:18-28
   Serves the Lord outwardly 2Kin 10:29-31

J said, Unto which of all......2Kin 9:5
the rest of the acts of *J* 2Kin 10:34
J slept with his fathers 2Kin 10:35
J reigned over Israel..........2Kin 10:36
seventh year of *J* Jehoash 2Kin 12:1
Jehoahaz the son of *J*.........2Kin 13:1
son of Jehoahaz son of *J* 2Kin 14:8
which he spake unto *J* 2Kin 15:12
with Jehoram against *J*........2Chr 22:7
J was executing judgment 2Chr 22:8
and brought him to *J* 2Chr 22:9
Jehoahaz, the son of *J* 2Chr 25:17
upon the house of *J* ....Hos 1:4

JEHUBBAH (jĕ-hŭb'ä)—*"hidden"*
Asherite 1Chr 7:34

JEHUCAL (jĕ-hū'kăl)—*"Jehovah is able"*
Son of Shelemiah; sent by Zedekiah to Jeremiah . .Jer 37:3
Also called Jucal ....Jer 38:1

JEHUD (jē'hŭd)—*"praising"*
Town of Dan ....Josh 19:40, 45

JEHUDI (jĕ-hū'dī)—*"a Jew"*
Reads Jeremiah's roll ....Jer 36:14, 21, 23

JEHUDIJAH (jĕ-hū-dī'jä)—*"the Jewess"*
One of Mered's two wives; should be rendered "the Jewess" .1Chr 4:18

JEHUSH—*See* JEUSH

JEIEL (jĕ-ī'ĕl)—*"God snatches away"*
1. Ancestor of Saul 1Chr 9:35-39

2. One of David's mighty men 1Chr 11:44
Reubenite prince 1Chr 5:6, 7
3. Levite musician 1Chr 16:5
4. Porter..................1Chr 15:18, 21
May be the same as 3 ...1Chr 16:5
Called Jehiah 1Chr 15:24
5. Inspired Levite 2Chr 20:14
6. Levite chief 2Chr 35:9
7. Scribe...................2Chr 26:11
8. Temple Levite 2Chr 29:13
9. One who divorced his foreign wife ....Ezra 10:19, 43

JEKABZEEL (jĕ-kăb'zĕ-ĕl)—*"congregation of God"*
Town in Judah ....Neh 11:25
Called Kabzeel ....Josh 15:21
Home of Benaiah, David's friend 2Sam 23:20

JEKAMEAM (jĕk-ä-mē'ăm)—*"standing of the people"*
Kohathite Levite 1Chr 23:19

J the fourth 1Chr 24:23

JEKAMIAH (jĕk-ä-mī'ä)—*"may Jehovah establish"*
1. Son of Shallum 1Chr 2:41
2. Son of Jeconiah..........1Chr 3:17, 18

JEKUTHIEL (jĕ-kū'thĭ-ĕl)—*"God is mighty"*
Man of Judah 1Chr 4:18

JEMIMA (jĕ-mī'mä)—*"little dove"*
Job's daughter ....Job 42:14

JEMUEL (jĕ-mū'ĕl)—*"God is speaking"*
Son of Simeon ....Gen 46:10
Called Nemuel ....Num 26:12

J, and Jamin ....Ex 6:15

JEOPARDY—*exposure to danger*

[*also* JEOPARDED]
a people that *j* their lives .....Judg 5:18
the men that went in *j* of 2Sam 23:17
have put their lives in *j*? 1Chr 11:19
for with the *j* of their lives 1Chr 11:19
Saul to the *j* of our heads 1Chr 12:19
and were in *j* ....Luke 8:23
why stand we in *j* 1Cor 15:30

JEPHTHAH, JEPHTHAE (jĕf'thä)—*"an opposer"*
Gilead's son by a harlot..Judg 11:1
Flees to Tob; becomes a leader ....Judg 11:2-11
Cites historical precedents against invading Ammonites ....Judg 11:12-27
Makes a vow before battle.................Judg 11:28-31
Smites Ammonites.......Judg 11:32, 33
Fulfills vow ....Judg 11:34-40
Defeats quarrelsome Ephraimites ....Judg 12:1-7
Cited by Samuel.........1Sam 12:11
In faith's chapter ....Heb 11:32

J the Gileadite was a ....Judg 11:1
J judged Israel six years .....Judg 12:7
Then died *J* the Gileadite .....Judg 12:7
and Bedan, and *J* 1Sam 12:11

JEPHUNNEH (jĕ-fŭn'ĕ)—*"appearing"*
1. Caleb's father ....Num 13:6
2. Asherite 1Chr 7:38

Caleb the son of *J*............Num 14:6
save Caleb the son of *J* ....Num 14:30
Caleb the son of *J*............Num 14:38
save Caleb the son of *J* ....Num 26:65
Save Caleb the son of *J*.......Num 32:12
Caleb the son of *J*............Num 34:19
Save Caleb the son of *J*.......Deut 1:36
Caleb the son of *J*............Josh 14:6
unto Caleb the son of *J* ....Josh 14:13
of Caleb the sons of *J* ....Josh 14:14
unto Caleb the son of *J*.......Josh 15:13
gave..to Caleb the son of *J*....Josh 21:12
sons of Caleb the son of *J* 1Chr 4:15
gave to Caleb the son of *J* 1Chr 6:56
the sons of Jether; *J*, and 1Chr 7:38

JERAH (jē'rä)—*"moon"*
Son of Joktan; probably an Arabian tribe .... {Gen 10:26, 1Chr 1:20}

JERAHMEEL (jĕ-rä'mĕ-ĕl)—*"God is merciful"*
1. Great-grandson of Judah .1Chr 2:9, 25-41
2. Son of Kish, not Saul's father 1Chr 24:29
3. King Jehoiakim's officer .Jer 36:26

Caleb the brother of *J* 1Chr 2:42

JERAHMEELITES (jĕ-rä'mĕ-ĕl-īts)—*descendants of Jerahmeel, the great-grandson of Judah*
Raided by David 1Sam 27:10

in the cities of the *J* 1Sam 30:29

JERED (jē'rĕd)—*"low; flowing"*
A descendant of Judah...1Chr 4:18
See JARED

JEREMAI (jĕr'ĕ-mī)—*"Jehovah is high"*
One who divorced his foreign wife ....Ezra 10:19, 33

JEREMIAH, JEREMIAS, JEREMY (jĕr-ĕ-mī'ä, jĕr-ĕ-mī'ăs, jĕr'ĕ-mē)—*"Jehovah is high"—the second of the major prophets of the Old Testament*

Life of:
Son of Hilkiah; a Benjamite ....Jer 1:1
Native of Anathoth ......Jer 1:1
Called before birth ......Jer 1:4-10
Prophet under kings Josiah, Jehoiakim, and Zedekiah ....Jer 1:2, 3
Imprisoned by Pashur ....Jer 20:1-6
Writes his prophecy; Jehoiakim burns it .....Jer 36:1-26
Prophecy rewritten ......Jer 36:27-32
Accused of desertion ....Jer 37:1-16
Released by Zedekiah ...Jer 37:17-21
Cast into a dungeon .....Jer 38:1-6
Saved by an Ethiopian ...Jer 38:7-28
Set free by Nebuchadnezzar ....Jer 39:11-14
Given liberty of choice by Nebuzaradan ....Jer 40:1-6
Forced to flee to Egypt ..Jer 43:5-7
Last prophecies at Tahpanhes, Egypt .....Jer 43:8-13

Characteristics of:
Forbidden to marry ......Jer 16:1-13
Has internal conflicts ....Jer 20:7-18
Has incurable pain ......Jer 15:18
Motives misunderstood ...Jer 37:12-14
Tells captives to build in Babylon ....Jer 29:4-9
Denounces false prophets in Babylon ....Jer 29:20-32
Rebukes idolatry ....Jer 7:9-21

Prophecies of, foretell:
Egypt's fall ....Jer 43:8-13
70 years of captivity 2Chr 36:21
Restoration to land ......Jer 16:14-18
New covenant ....Jer 31:31-34
Herod's massacre ....Jer 31:15

Teachings of:
God's sovereignty ....Jer 18:5-10
God's knowledge ....Jer 17:5-10
Shame of idolatry ....Jer 10:14, 15
Spirituality of worship, etc. ....Jer 3:16, 17
Need of regeneration ....Jer 9:26
Man's sinful nature .....Jer 2:22
Gospel salvation.........Jer 23:5, 6
Call of the Gentiles......Jer 3:17-19

[*also* JEREMIAH'S]
the daughter of *J* 2Kin 24:18
J lamented for Josiah 2Chr 35:25
humbled not..before *J* 2Chr 36:12
spoken by the mouth of *J*......2Chr 36:22
by the mouth of *J* ....Ezra 1:1
J the son of Hilkiah ....Jer 1:1
J, what seest thou? ....Jer 1:11
word that came to *J* ....Jer 7:1
word that came to *J* ....Jer 11:1
came to *J* concerning ....Jer 14:1
word which came to *J* ....Jer 18:1
devise devices against *J* ....Jer 18:18
Then came *J* from Tophet ....Jer 19:14
heard that *J* prophesied ....Jer 20:1
which came unto *J* from ......Jer 21:1
Then said *J* unto them ....Jer 21:3
What seest thou, *J*? ....Jer 24:3
word that came to *J* ....Jer 25:1
J the prophet spake ....Jer 25:2
J hath prophesied against .....Jer 25:13
people heard *J* speaking ......Jer 26:7
J had made an end of ....Jer 26:8
people..gathered against *J*.....Jer 26:9
spake *J* unto all the princes ...Jer 26:12
to all the words of *J*..........Jer 26:20
Shaphan was with *J* ....Jer 26:24
unto *J* from the Lord ....Jer 27:1
J said unto the prophet ....Jer 28:5
prophet *J* said, Amen.........Jer 28:6
yoke from off the prophet *J* ...Jer 28:10
prophet *J* went his way ....Jer 28:11
word..came unto *J* ....Jer 28:12
the neck of the prophet *J* .....Jer 28:12
said the prophet *J* unto ....Jer 28:15
words of the letter that *J* .....Jer 29:1
word that came to *J* ....Jer 30:1
The word that came to *J*......Jer 32:1
J the prophet was shut up.....Jer 32:2
J said, The word of the ....Jer 32:6
word of the Lord unto *J* ......Jer 32:26
Lord came unto *J* the.........Jer 33:1
word of..Lord came unto *J*....Jer 33:19
word of the Lord came to *J* ...Jer 33:23
unto *J* from the Lord ....Jer 34:1
Then *J*..spake all these ....Jer 34:6
came unto *J* from the ....Jer 34:8
word of the Lord came to *J* ...Jer 34:12
unto *J* from the Lord ....Jer 35:1
word of the Lord unto *J* ......Jer 35:12
And *J* said unto ....Jer 35:18
J abode in the court ....Jer 38:28
gave charge concerning *J*......Jer 39:11
took *J* out of the court ....Jer 39:14
word of..Lord came unto *J*....Jer 39:15
came to *J* from the Lord......Jer 40:1
captain of the guard took *J* ...Jer 40:2
went *J* unto Gedaliah ....Jer 40:6
said unto *J* the prophet ....Jer 42:2
J the prophet said unto ....Jer 42:4
They said to *J*, The Lord .....Jer 42:5
word..came unto *J* ....Jer 42:7
J had made an end of ....Jer 43:1
proud men, saying unto *J* .....Jer 43:2
word that came to *J* ....Jer 44:1
in Pathros, answered *J*........Jer 44:15
J said unto all the people .....Jer 44:20
J said unto all the people .....Jer 44:24
word that *J* the prophet.......Jer 45:1
at the mouth of *J* ....Jer 45:1
word of the Lord..to *J*........Jer 46:1
word..the Lord spake to *J* ....Jer 46:13
word of the Lord..to *J*........Jer 47:1
word of the Lord..to *J*........Jer 49:34
land of the Chaldeans by *J*....Jer 50:1
J the prophet commanded.....Jer 51:59
J wrote in a book all the.....Jer 51:60
J said Seraiah, When ....Jer 51:61
Thus far are the words of *J* ...Jer 51:64
the daughter of *J*.............Jer 52:1
word of the Lord came to *J* ...Dan 9:2
that which was spoken by *J* ...Matt 2:17
J, or one of the prophets .....Matt 16:14
that which was spoken by *J* ...Matt 27:9

JEREMIAH—*(Others bearing this name)*
1. Benjamite warrior.......1Chr 12:4

2. Gadite warrior 1Chr 12:10
3. Another Gadite warrior .1Chr 12:13
4. Manassite head 1Chr 5:23, 24
5. Father of Hamutal, a
   wife of Josiah 2Kin 23:31
6. Father of Jaazaniah .....Jer 35:3
7. Postexilic priest ....Neh 12:1, 7
   Head of a priestly line ..Neh 12:12
8. Priest who signs the
   covenant ....Neh 10:2

JEREMIAH, THE BOOK OF—*a book of the Old Testament*
Jeremiah's call ....Jer 1:1-19
Jeremiah's life...........Jer 26:1—45:5
Israel's sin against God ..Jer 2:1—10:25
Against false prophets ..Jer 23:9-40
Against foreign nations ..Jer 46:1—51:64
The Messianic king ......Jer 23:1-8

JEREMIAS—*See* JEREMIAH

JEREMOTH (jĕr'ĕ-mŏth)—*"elevation"*
1. Son of Becher ....1Chr 7:8°
2. Benjamite 1Chr 8:14
3. Merarite Levite 1Chr 23:23
4. Musician of David 1Chr 25:22
5. Ruler of Napthali 1Chr 27:19
6. One who divorced his
   foreign wife ....Ezra 10:26
7. Another who divorced
   his foreign wife ....Ezra 10:27
8. Spelled Jerimoth 1Chr 24:30

JEREMY—*See* JEREMIAH

JERIAH, JERIJAH (jĕ-rī'ä, jĕ-rī'jä)—*"Jehovah is foundation"*
Kohathite Levite 1Chr 23:19, 23
Hebronite chief 1Chr 26:31

J the first, Amariah the 1Chr 24:23
Hebronites was *J*..chief 1Chr 26:31

JERIBAI (jĕr'ĭ-bī)—*"Jehovah contends"*
One of David's warriors. .1Chr 11:46

JERICHO (jĕr'ĭ-kō)—*"his sweet smell"—a fortified city of Canaan conquered by the Israelites*
City near the Jordan .....Num 22:1
Viewed by Moses........Deut 34:1-3
Called the city of palm
   trees ....Deut 34:3
Viewed by spies ....Josh 2:1
Home of Rahab the
   harlot ....Heb 11:31
Scene of Joshua's vision..Josh 5:13-15
Destroyed by Joshua .....Heb 11:30
Curse of rebuilding of ...Josh 6:26
Assigned to Benjamin ...Josh 16:1, 7
Moabites retake ....Judg 3:12, 13
David's envoys tarry here.2Sam 10:4, 5
Rebuilt by Hiel 1Kin 16:34
Visited by Elijah and
   Elisha 2Kin 2:4-22
Zedekiah captured here ..2Kin 25:5
Reinhabited after exile ...Ezra 2:34
People of, help rebuild
   Jerusalem.............Neh 3:2
Blind men of, healed by
   Jesus ....Matt 20:29-34
Home of Zacchaeus .....Luke 19:1-10

Moab on this..Jordan by *J* ....Num 22:1
Moab by Jordan near *J* ....Num 26:3
Moab by Jordan near *J* ....Num 26:63
are by Jordan near *J* ....Num 31:12
Moab by Jordan near *J* ....Num 33:48
Moab by Jordan near *J* ....Num 33:50
this side Jordan near *J*........Num 34:15
Moab by Jordan near *J* ....Num 35:1
Moab by Jordan near *J* ....Num 36:13
that is over against *J* ....Deut 32:49
Go view the land, even *J* .....Josh 2:1
it was told the king of *J* ......Josh 2:2
king of *J* sent unto Rahab ....Josh 2:3
over right against *J* ....Josh 3:16
battle, to the plains of *J* .....Josh 4:13
in the east border of *J* ....Josh 4:19
even in the plains of *J* ....Josh 5:10
J was straitly shut up ....Josh 6:1
given into thine hand *J* ....Josh 6:2
Joshua sent to spy out *J* ......Josh 6:25
Joshua sent men from *J*.......Josh 7:2
as thou didst unto *J* and ......Josh 8:2
Joshua had done unto *J*.......Josh 9:3
as he had done to *J* and ......Josh 10:1
he did unto the king of *J* .....Josh 10:28
he did unto the king of *J* .....Josh 10:30
The king of *J*, one; the ....Josh 12:9
the other side Jordan, by *J*....Josh 13:32
went up to the side of *J* ......Josh 18:12
to their families were *J* ....Josh 18:21
the other side Jordan by *J* ....Josh 20:8
Jordan, and came unto *J*......Josh 24:11
men of *J* fought against ....Josh 24:11
other side Jordan by *J* 1Chr 6:78
Tarry at *J* until your 1Chr 19:5
and brought them to *J* 2Chr 28:15
the children of *J*, three ....Neh 7:36
Zedekiah in the plains of *J*....Jer 39:5
Zedekiah in the plains of *J*....Jer 52:8
as they departed from *J*.......Matt 20:29
came to *J*..went out of *J* ......Mark 10:46
from Jerusalem to *J* ....Luke 10:30
he was come nigh unto *J*......Luke 18:35

JERIEL (jē'rĭ-ĕl)—*"foundation of God"*
Son of Tola 1Chr 7:2

JERIJAH—*See* JERIAH

JERIMOTH (jĕr'ĭ-mŏth)—*"elevation"*
1. Son of Bela 1Chr 7:7
2. Warrior of David 1Chr 12:5
3. Musician of David 1Chr 25:4
4. Son of David 2Chr 11:18
5. Levite overseer 2Chr 31:13
6. Spelled Jeremoth 1Chr 23:23
See JEREMOTH

Mahli, and Eder, and *J* 1Chr 24:30

JERIOTH (jĕr'ĭ-ŏth)—*"tremulousness"*
One of Caleb's wives 1Chr 2:18

JEROBOAM (jĕr-ō-bō'ăm)—*"enlarger; he pleads the people's cause"*
1. Son of Nebat 1Kin 11:26
   Rebels against Solomon. .1Kin 11:26-28
   Ahijah's prophecy
      concerning 1Kin 11:29-39
   Flees to Egypt 1Kin 11:40
   Recalled, made king 1Kin 12:1-3, 12, 20
   Perverts the true religion.1Kin 12:25-33
   Casts Levites out 2Chr 11:14
   Rebuked by a man of
      God 1Kin 13:1-10
   Leads people astray 1Kin 13:33, 34
   His wife consults Ahijah .1Kin 14:1-18
   War with Abijam 1Kin 15:7
   Reigns 22 years 1Kin 14:20
   Struck by the Lord......2Chr 13:20
2. Jeroboam II; king of
      Israel 2Kin 13:13
   Successor of Joash
      (Jehoash) 2Kin 14:16, 23
   Conquers Hamath and
      Damascus 2Kin 14:25-28
   Reigns wickedly 41 years.2Kin 14:23, 24
   Denounced by Amos ....Amos 7:7-13
   Death of 2Kin 14:29

[*also* JEROBOAM'S]
J the son of Nebat, an 1Kin 11:26
the Shilonite unto *J* 1Kin 12:15
all Israel heard that *J* 1Kin 12:20
J wife did so and arose 1Kin 14:4
because of the sins of *J* 1Kin 14:16
J wife arose, and departed 1Kin 14:17
J reigned were two and 1Kin 14:20
between Rehoboam and *J* 1Kin 14:30
eighteenth year of king *J* 1Kin 15:1
between Rehoboam and *J*.....1Kin 15:6
between Abijam and *J*........1Kin 15:7
twentieth year of *J* king.......1Kin 15:9
Nadab the son of *J* began 1Kin 15:25
smote all the house of *J* 1Kin 15:29
he left not to *J* any that 1Kin 15:29
of the sins of *J* which he 1Kin 15:30
walked in the way of *J*........1Kin 15:34
walked in the way of *J*........1Kin 16:2
house like the house of *J* 1Kin 16:3
being like the house of *J*......1Kin 16:7
in walking in the way of *J* 1Kin 16:19
walked in all the way of *J*.....1Kin 16:26
to walk in the sins of *J* 1Kin 16:31
house like the house of *J* 1Kin 21:22
and in the way of *J*...........1Kin 22:52
cleaved unto the sins of *J* 2Kin 3:3
Ahab like the house of *J*......2Kin 9:9
from the sins of *J* the son 2Kin 10:29
not from the sins of *J*.........2Kin 10:31
and followed the sins of *J*.....2Kin 13:2
sins of the house of *J* 2Kin 13:6
from all the sins of *J* 2Kin 13:11
J his son reigned in...........2Kin 14:16
J the son of Joash king 2Kin 14:23
from all the sins of *J* 2Kin 14:24
J slept with his fathers 2Kin 14:29
and seventh year of *J* king 2Kin 15:1
Zachariah the son of *J*.........2Kin 15:8
not from the sins of *J*.........2Kin 15:9
days from the sins of *J*.......2Kin 15:18
from the sins of *J* 2Kin 15:24
J the son of Nebat king 2Kin 17:21
J drove Israel from 2Kin 17:21
walked in all the sins of *J*.....2Kin 17:22
the high place which *J* 2Kin 23:15
days of *J* king of Israel 1Chr 5:17
Iddo the seer against *J*........2Chr 9:29
to pass, when *J*..heard it 2Chr 10:2
J returned out of Egypt 2Chr 10:2
J and all Israel came and 2Chr 10:3
J and all the people came 2Chr 10:12
Ahijah the Shilonite to *J*......2Chr 10:15
from going against *J* 2Chr 11:4
between Rehoboam and *J*.....2Chr 12:15
eighteenth year of king *J*......2Chr 13:1
between Abijah and *J* 2Chr 13:2
J also set the battle in 2Chr 13:3
Hear me, thou *J*, and all.......2Chr 13:4
J the son of Nebat, the 2Chr 13:6
calves, which *J* made you 2Chr 13:8
J caused an ambushment.......2Chr 13:13
God smote *J* and all Israel 2Chr 13:15
Abijah pursued after *J*........2Chr 13:19
days of *J* the son of Joash ....Hos 1:1
days of *J* the son of Joash ....Amos 1:1
priest..sent to *J* king..........Amos 7:10

JEROHAM (jĕ-rō'hăm)—*"loved"*
1. Grandfather of Samuel ..1Sam 1:1
2. Benjamite 1Chr 9:8
3. Father of several
   Benjamite chief men ..1Chr 8:27
4. Benjamite of Gedor 1Chr 12:7
5. Father of Adaiah 1Chr 9:12
6. Danite chief's father 1Chr 27:22
7. Military captain 2Chr 23:1

J his son, Elkanah his son 1Chr 6:27
of Elkanah, the son of *J* 1Chr 6:34
and Adaiah the son of *J* ......Neh 11:12

JERUBBAAL (jĕr-ŭb-bā'ăl)—*"contender with Baal"*
Name given to Gideon for
   destroying Baal's altar .Judg 6:32

J who is Gideon, and all ......Judg 7:1
J the son of Joash went.......Judg 8:29
kindness to the house of *J* ....Judg 8:35
Abimelech the son of *J* .....Judg 9:1
that all the sons of *J*..........Judg 9:2
brethren the sons of *J* ....Judg 9:5
the youngest son of *J* was .....Judg 9:5
have dealt well with *J* ....Judg 9:16
dealt..sincerely with *J*.........Judg 9:19
ten sons of *J* might come .....Judg 9:24
is not he the son of *J*? ....Judg 9:28
of Jotham the son of *J*.........Judg 9:57
And the Lord sent *J*, and 1Sam 12:11

J

JERUBBESHETH (jĕr-ŭb-bē'shĕth)—*"contender with the idol"*
Father of Abimelech.....2Sam 11:21

JERUEL (jĕ-rōō'ĕl)—*"vision of God"*
Wilderness west of the Dead Sea.............2Chr 20:16

JERUSALEM (jĕ-rōō'sä-lĕm)—*"possession of peace"—the capital of Judah and city of David*

Names applied to:
City of God.............Ps 46:4
City of David...........2Sam 5:6, 7
City of Judah...........2Chr 25:28
Zion...................Ps 48:12
Jebusi..................Josh 18:28
Holy city...............Matt 4:5
Faithful city............Is 1:21, 26
City of righteousness.....Is 1:26
City of truth............Zech 8:3
City of the great King ...Ps 48:2
Salem...................Gen 14:18

History of:
Originally Salem.........Gen 14:18
Occupied by Jebusite ....Josh 15:8
King of, defeated by Joshua................Josh 10:5-23
Assigned to Benjamin ...Josh 18:28
Attacked by Judah ......Judg 1:8
Jebusites remain in .....Judg 1:21
David brings Goliath's head to...............1Sam 17:54
Conquered by David.....2Sam 5:6-8
Name changed 2Sam 5:7-9
Ark brought to..........2Sam 6:12-17
Saved from destruction...2Sam 24:16
Solomon builds Temple here...................1Kin 5:5-8
Suffers in war...........1Kin 14:25-27
Plundered by Israel......2Kin 14:13, 14
Besieged by Syrians .....Is 7:1
Earthquake damages.....Amos 1:1
Miraculously saved 2Kin 19:31-36
Ruled by Egypt 2Kin 23:33-35
Beseiged by Babylon 2Kin 24:10, 11
Captured by Babylon ....Jer 39:1-8
Desolate 70 years........Jer 25:11, 12
Temple rebuilt in........Ezra 1:1-4
Exiles return to ....Ezra 2:1-70
Work on, hindered ......Ezra 5:1-17
Walls of, dedicated ......Neh 12:27-47
Christ:
Enters as King ....Matt 21:9, 10
Laments for...........Matt 23:37
Crucified at ....Luke 9:31
Weeps over ....Luke 19:41, 42
Predicts its destruction .Luke 19:43, 44
Gospel preached at ......Luke 24:47
Many miracles performed in..........John 4:45
Church begins here ......Acts 2:1-47
Christians of, persecuted............Acts 4:1-30
Stephen martyred at .....Acts 7:1-60
First Christian council held here............Acts 15:1-29
Paul:
Visits.................Acts 20:16
Arrested in ....Acts 21:30-36
Taken from ....Acts 23:12-33

Prophecies concerning:
Destruction by Babylon ..Jer 20:5
Utter ruin ....Jer 26:18
Rebuilding by Cyrus .....Is 44:26-28
Christ's entry into ....Zech 9:9
Gospel proclaimed from ..Is 2:3
Perilous times ....Matt 24:1-22
Being under Gentiles ....Luke 21:24

Described:
Physically—strong ....Ps 48:12, 13
Ps 125:2
Morally—corrupt ....Is 1:1-16
Jer 5:1-5
Spiritually—the redeemed.Gal 4:26-30
Prophetically—New Jerusalem.............Rev 21:1-27
See Zion; Sion

[*also* JERUSALEM'S]
the ark of God again to *J*.....2Sam 15:29
for *J* sake which I have 1Kin 11:13
David's sake, and for *J* sake ..1Kin 11:32
Lord said, In *J* will I put 2Kin 21:4
in *J*, which I have chosen 2Kin 21:7
he carried away all *J*, and.....2Kin 24:14
house of the Lord in *J*........1Chr 6:32
may dwell in *J* for ever 1Chr 23:25
So I came to *J*, and was ......Neh 2:11
Zion, which dwelleth at *J*.....Ps 135:21
J is ruined..Judah is fallen ....Is 3:8
beautiful garments, O *J*.......Is 52:1
for *J* sake I will not rest ......Is 62:1
wilderness, *J* a desolation .....Is 64:10
O *J*, wash thine heart from ...Jer 4:14
and *J* shall dwell safely ....Jer 33:16
brake down the walls of *J*.....Jer 39:8
away captive from *J*..........Jer 52:29
J remembered in the days.....Lam 1:7
J hath grievously sinned ......Lam 1:8
men from the east to *J*.......Matt 2:1
was troubled, and all *J*........Matt 2:3
brought him to *J*, to present ..Luke 2:22
went up to *J* after the ....Luke 2:42
Jesus tarried behind in *J*......Luke 2:43
O *J*, *J*..killest the prophets ....Luke 13:34
tarry ye in the city of *J*.......Luke 24:49
witnesses unto me both in *J*...Acts 1:8
were dwelling at *J* Jews.......Acts 2:5
the church which was at *J*.....Acts 8:1
and elders which were at *J*....Acts 16:4
I go unto *J* to minister........Rom 15:25
J which is above is free ....Gal 4:26
living God, the heavenly *J*....Heb 12:22
the city of my God..new *J*....Rev 3:12
saw the holy city, new *J*......Rev 21:2
great city, the holy *J*.........Rev 21:10

JERUSHA (jĕ-rōō'shä)—*"possession"*
Wife of King Uzziah.....2Kin 15:33
Called Jerushah 2Chr 27:1

JESHAIAH (jĕ-shā'yä)—*"Jehovah is helper"*
1. Musician of David 1Chr 25:3
2. Grandson of Zerubbabel .1Chr 3:21
3. Levite in David's reign ..1Chr 26:25
4. Son of Athaliah; returns from Babylon.........Ezra 8:7
5. Levite who returns with Ezra................Ezra 8:19
6. Benjamite ....Neh 11:7

eighth to *J*, he, his sons.......1Chr 25:15

JESHANAH (jĕsh'ä-nä)—*"old"*
City of Ephraim taken by Abijah 2Chr 13:19

JESHARELAH (jĕsh-ä-rē'lä)—*"Jehovah is joined; whom God has bound"*
Levite musician 1Chr 25:14
Called Asarelah 1Chr 25:2

JESHEBEAB (jĕ-shĕb'ē-ăb)—*"seat of the father"*
Descendant of Aaron 1Chr 24:13

JESHER (jē'sher)—*"rightness"*
Caleb's son 1Chr 2:18

JESHIMON (jĕ-shī'mŏn)—*"solitude"*
Wilderness west of the Dead Sea............1Sam 23:19, 24

that looketh toward *J*.........Num 23:28
which is before *J*?...........1Sam 26:1
Hachilah, which is before *J* ...1Sam 26:3

JESHISHAI (jĕ-shĭsh'ā-ī)—*"Jehovah is ancient; aged"*
Gadite..................1Chr 5:14

JESHOHAIAH (jĕsh-ō-hā'yä)—*"humbled by Jehovah"*
Leader in Simeon 1Chr 4:36

JESHUA (jĕsh'ū-ä)—*"Jehovah is deliverance"*
1. Joshua, the military leader after Moses ....Neh 8:17
2. Descendant of Aaron ...Ezra 2:36
3. Levite treasurer.........2Chr 31:14, 15
4. Postexilic high priest ....Zech 3:8
Returns with Zerubbabel.Ezra 2:2
Aids in Temple rebuilding ....Ezra 3:2-8
Withstands opponents ...Ezra 4:1-3
Figurative act performed on..................Zech 3:1-10
See Joshua
5. Levite assistant ....Ezra 2:40
Explains the Law ....Neh 8:7
Leads in worship........Neh 9:4, 5
Seals the covenant ......Neh 10:1, 9
6. Repairer of the wall.....Neh 3:19
7. Man of the house of Pahath-moab ....Ezra 2:6
8. Village in southern Judah Neh 11:26

then stood *J* with his sons.....Ezra 3:9
and *J* the son of Jozadak .....Ezra 5:2
Jozabad the son of *J*..........Ezra 8:33
sons of *J* the son of Jozadak ..Ezra 10:18
Zerubbabel, *J*, Nehemiah .....Neh 7:7
children of *J* and Joab ....Neh 7:11
Jedaiah, of the house of *J*.....Neh 7:39
children of *J*, of Kadmiel .....Neh 7:43
the son of Shealtiel and *J*.....Neh 12:1
brethren in the days of *J*......Neh 12:7
the Levites: *J*, Binnui.........Neh 12:8
J begat Joiakim, Joiakim......Neh 12:10
and *J* the son of Kadmiel .....Neh 12:24
of Joiakim the son of *J*.......Neh 12:26

JESHUAH (jĕsh'ū-ä)—*"Jehovah is deliverance"—same as Jeshua*
The ninth to *J* the tenth 1Chr 24:11

JESHURUN (jĕsh'ū-rŭn)—*"blessed"*
Poetic name of endearment for Israel ..Deut 32:15

king in *J* when the heads .....Deut 33:5
none like unto the God of *J*...Deut 33:26

JESIAH—*See* Isshiah

JESIMIEL (jĕ-sĭm'ĭ-ĕl)—*"God sets"*
Simeonite leader 1Chr 4:36

JESSE (jĕs'ē)—*"Jehovah exists; wealthy"*
Grandson of Ruth and Boaz................Ruth 4:17-22
Father of:
David 1Sam 16:18, 19
Eight sons 1Sam 16:10, 11
Two daughters 1Chr 2:15, 16
Citizen of Bethlehem 1Sam 16:1, 18
Protected by David 1Sam 22:1-4
Of humble origin 1Sam 18:18, 23
Mentioned in prophecy ..Is 11:1, 10
Ancestor of Christ.......Matt 1:5, 6

call *J* to the sacrifice..........1Sam 16:3
sanctified *J* and his sons 1Sam 16:5
J called Abinadab, and 1Sam 16:8
Then *J* made Shammah 1Sam 16:9
J took an ass laden with 1Sam 16:20
Saul sent to *J*, saying 1Sam 16:22
whose name was *J*; and 1Sam 17:12
three eldest sons of *J*.........1Sam 17:13
J said unto David his son 1Sam 17:17
went, as *J* had commanded....1Sam 17:20
the son of thy servant *J*.......1Sam 17:58
cometh not the son of *J* to 1Sam 20:27
chosen the son of *J* to 1Sam 20:30
long as the son of *J* liveth.....1Sam 20:31
son of *J* give every one 1Sam 22:7
league with the son of *J*......1Sam 22:8
I saw the son of *J* coming.....1Sam 22:9
thou and the son of *J*.........1Sam 22:13
and who is the son of *J*?......1Sam 25:10
inheritance in the son of *J* 2Sam 20:1
David the son of *J* said 2Sam 23:1
inheritance in the son of *J* 1Kin 12:16

and Obed begat *J* 1Chr 2:12
J begat his firstborn Eliab 1Chr 2:13
unto David the son of *J* 1Chr 10:14
on thy side, thou son of *J* 1Chr 12:18
David the son of *J* reigned 1Chr 29:26
inheritance in the son of *J* 2Chr 10:16
of Eliab the son of *J* 2Chr 11:18
of David the son of *J* .... Ps 72:20
Which was the son of *J* .... Luke 3:32
found David the son of *J* ..... Acts 13:22
There shall be a root of *J* ..... Rom 15:12

JESTING—*giving a humorous twist to something spoken*
Condemned .... Eph 5:4
Lot appeared to be ...... Gen 19:14
Of godless men .... Ps 35:16

JESUI (jĕs'ū-ī)—*"equal"—the third son of Asher*
[*also* JESUITES]
J, the family of the *J* .... Num 26:44
See ISHUAI

JESURUN (jĕs'ū-rŭn)—*"blessed"—a symbolic name for Israel*
J, whom I have chosen .... Is 44:2

JESUS (jē'zŭs)—*"Jehovah is salvation"—the son of the Virgin Mary; came to earth as the Messiah and died for the salvation of His people*
[*also* JESUS']
the generation of *J* Christ ..... Matt 1:1
thou shalt call his name *J* ..... Matt 1:21
and he called his name *J* ...... Matt 1:25
J was born in Bethlehem of ... Matt 2:1
J, when he was baptized ...... Matt 3:16
saith *J* unto him, Get thee .... Matt 4:10
J said unto him, Follow me ... Matt 8:22
thee, *J*, thou son of God? ..... Matt 8:29
J seeing their faith said .... Matt 9:2
J said..A prophet is .... Matt 13:57
J constrained his disciples ..... Matt 14:22
tell no man that he was *J* ..... Matt 16:20
time forth began *J* to show .... Matt 16:21
and *J* rebuked the devil .... Matt 17:18
J called a little child unto ..... Matt 18:2
J said, Suffer little children .... Matt 19:14
J said unto him, If thou .... Matt 19:21
J had compassion on them .... Matt 20:34
J the prophet of Nazareth ..... Matt 21:11
might take *J* by subtlety ...... Matt 26:4
J took bread, and blessed it ... Matt 26:26
they that had laid hold on *J* ... Matt 26:57
false witness against *J* .... Matt 26:59
J held his peace. And the ..... Matt 26:63
Thou also wast with *J* of ...... Matt 26:69
remembered the word of *J* .... Matt 26:75
took counsel against *J* to ...... Matt 27:1
J stood before the governor ... Matt 27:11
J said unto him, Thou .... Matt 27:11
Barabbas, and destroy *J* ...... Matt 27:20
J which is called Christ? ...... Matt 27:22
scourged *J*, he delivered ...... Matt 27:26
of the governor took *J* .... Matt 27:27
J The King Of The Jews .... Matt 27:37
ninth hour *J* cried with a ...... Matt 27:46
J, when he had cried again .... Matt 27:50
himself was *J* disciple .... Matt 27:57
and begged the body of *J* ..... Matt 27:58
I know that ye seek *J* .... Matt 28:5
J met them, saying, All hail ... Matt 28:9
J came and spake unto .... Matt 28:18
When *J* saw their faith, he .... Mark 2:5
I to do with thee *J* .... Mark 5:7
J said..A prophet is not .... Mark 6:4
J called his disciples unto ..... Mark 8:1
J said, Forbid him not: for .... Mark 9:39
say, *J*, thou son of David ..... Mark 10:47
they brought the colt to *J* ..... Mark 11:7
J entered into Jerusalem ...... Mark 11:11
J went into the temple, and ... Mark 11:15
J said, Let her alone: why .... Mark 14:6
J took bread, and blessed ..... Mark 14:22
they led *J* away to the high ... Mark 14:53
delivered *J*, when he had ..... Mark 15:15
ninth hour *J* cried with a ...... Mark 15:34
and *J* cried with a loud voice .. Mark 15:37
when *J* was risen early .... Mark 16:9
shalt call his name *J* .... Luke 1:31
brought in the child *J* .... Luke 2:27
the child *J* tarried behind ..... Luke 2:43
J increased in wisdom and .... Luke 2:52
that *J* also being baptized ..... Luke 3:21
J of Nazareth? art thou .... Luke 4:34
he fell down at *J* knees .... Luke 5:8
have I to do with thee, *J* ..... Luke 8:28
sitting at the feet of *J* .... Luke 8:35
fell down at *J* feet, and .... Luke 8:41
J said, Who touched me? ..... Luke 8:45
J perceiving the thought ...... Luke 9:47
Then said *J* unto him, Go ..... Luke 10:37
Mary..sat at *J* feet .... Luke 10:39
J, Master, have mercy on ..... Luke 17:13
J said unto him, Receive ...... Luke 18:42
J said unto him, Judas .... Luke 22:48
when Herod saw *J*, he was .... Luke 23:8
willing to release *J*, spake ..... Luke 23:20
he delivered *J* to their will .... Luke 23:25
said *J*, Father, forgive them ... Luke 23:34
he said unto *J*, Lord .... Luke 23:42
not the body of the Lord *J* .... Luke 24:3
J himself drew near, and ...... Luke 24:15
J himself stood in the midst ... Luke 24:36
truth came by *J* Christ .... John 1:17
John seeth *J* coming unto him . John 1:29
speak, and they followed *J* .... John 1:37
the mother of *J* was there ..... John 2:1
beginning of miracles did *J* .... John 2:11
J said unto them, My meat .... John 4:34
Then said *J* unto him .... John 4:48
J took the loaves; and when .. John 6:11
seen the miracle that *J* did .... John 6:14
see *J* walking on the sea ...... John 6:19
J answered and said unto ..... John 6:29
J said..I am the bread .... John 6:35
J answered, Ye neither .... John 8:19
day when *J* made the clay ..... John 9:14
J spake of his death: but ...... John 11:13
J said..I am the resurrection .. John 11:25
J therefore saw her weeping .. John 11:33
J wept .... John 11:35
they came not for *J* sake ...... John 12:9
Sir, we would see *J* .... John 12:21
J cried and said, He that ...... John 12:44
J knew that his hour was ..... John 13:1
J knowing that the Father ..... John 13:3
was leaning on *J* bosom .... John 13:23
He then lying on *J* breast ..... John 13:25
J said, Now is the Son of ..... John 13:31
J saith..I am the way .... John 14:6
J answered, I have told .... John 18:8
officers of the Jews took *J* .... John 18:12
Simon Peter followed *J*, and .. John 18:15
high priest then asked *J* of .... John 18:19
J answered, My kingdom ..... John 18:36
J answered, Thou sayest ...... John 18:37
Pilate therefore took *J* .... John 19:1
But *J* gave him no answer .... John 19:9
when they had crucified *J* ..... John 19:23
take away the body of *J* ...... John 19:38
back, and saw *J* standing ...... John 20:14
and knew not that it was *J* .... John 20:14
J saith unto him, Thomas ..... John 20:29
believe that *J* is the Christ .... John 20:31
this same *J*, which is taken .... Acts 1:11
This *J* hath God raised up .... Acts 2:32
having raised up his Son *J* .... Acts 3:26
and preached unto him *J* ...... Acts 8:35
J Christ is the Son of God .... Acts 8:37
J whom thou persecutest ...... Acts 9:5
God anointed *J* of Nazareth ... Acts 10:38
unto Israel a Savior, *J* .... Acts 13:23
scriptures that *J* was Christ .... Acts 18:28
said..I am *J* of Nazareth ...... Acts 22:8
confess..the Lord *J* .... Rom 10:9
your servants for *J* sake 2Cor 4:5
the dying of the Lord *J* 2Cor 4:10
the life also of *J* might 2Cor 4:10
unto death for *J* sake 2Cor 4:11
which raised up the Lord *J* 2Cor 4:14
shall raise up us also by *J* 2Cor 4:14
body the marks of the Lord *J* . Gal 6:17
as the truth is in *J* .... Eph 4:21
That at the name of *J* every ... Phil 2:10
confess..*J* Christ is Lord ...... Phil 2:11
trust in the Lord *J* to send .... Phil 2:19
believe that *J* died and rose ... 1Thess 4:14
sleep in *J* will God bring 1Thess 4:14
J came into the world to 1Tim 1:15
the holiest by the blood of *J* .. Heb 10:19
from the dead our Lord *J* ..... Heb 13:20
confess that *J* is the Son 1John 4:15
that *J* is the Christ is 1John 5:1
that *J* is the Son of God? 1John 5:5
J Christ is come in the flesh ... 2John 7
blood of the martyrs of *J* ..... Rev 17:6
Even so, come, Lord *J* .... Rev 22:20
See CHRIST

JESUS—*Greek form of Joshua, son of Nun*
Found in .... Heb 4:8

JETHER (jē'ther)—*"preeminent"*
1. Gideon's oldest son ..... Judg 8:20, 21
2. Descendant of Judah 1Chr 2:32
3. Son of Ezra 1Chr 4:17
4. Asherite; probably same as Ithran 1Chr 7:30-38
5. Amasa's father 1Kin 2:5, 32
Called Ithra 2Sam 17:25

unto Amasa the son of *J* 1Kin 2:5
Amasa the son of *J* 1Kin 2:32
father of Amasa was *J* 1Chr 2:17

JETHETH (jē'thĕth)—*"subjection"*
Chief of Edom .... Gen 36:40

duke Aliah, duke *J* 1Chr 1:51

JETHLAH (jĕth'lä)—*"an overhanging place"*
Danite town .... Josh 19:42

JETHRO (jĕth'rō)—*"preeminence"*
Priest of Midian; Moses' father-in-law .... Num 10:29
Called Reuel .... Ex 2:18
Called Raguel .... Num 10:29
Moses marries his daughter Zipporah ..... Ex 2:16-22
Moses departs from ...... Ex 4:18-26
Visits and counsels Moses. Ex 18:1-27
See JETHER

Moses kept the flock of *J* ..... Ex 3:1

JETUR (jē'ter)—*meaning uncertain*
Son of Ishmael .... Gen 25:15
Conflict with Israel 1Chr 5:18, 19
Tribal descendants of the Ituraeans .... Luke 3:1

J, Naphish, and Kedemah 1Chr 1:31

JEUEL (jĕ-ū'ĕl)—*"snatching away"*
Son of Zorah 1Chr 9:6

JEUSH, JEHUSH (jē'-ŭsh, jē'hŭsh)—*"collector"*
1. Son of Esau and Edomite chief .... Gen 36:5, 18
2. Benjamite head 1Chr 7:10
3. Gershonite Levite 1Chr 23:10, 11
4. Descendant of Jonathan . 1Chr 8:39
5. Rehoboam's son 2Chr 11:19

she bare to Esau *J*, and .... Gen 36:14
Reuel, and *J*, and Jaalam 1Chr 1:35

JEUZ (jē'ŭz)—*"counselor"*
Benjamite 1Chr 8:8, 10

JEW—*post-exilic term for an Israelite*

Descriptive of:
Hebrew race .... Esth 3:6, 13
Postexilic Hebrew nation . Ezra 5:1, 5
Believers .... Rom 2:28, 29

Kinds of:
Hypocritical .... Matt 23:1-31
Persecuting 1Thess 2:14, 15

Prejudiced .... John 4:9
Penitent .... John 12:10, 11

Their sins:

Self-righteousness .... Rom 10:1-3
Hypocrisy .... Rom 2:17-25
Persecution 1Thess 2:14, 15
Rejection of Christ .... Matt 27:21-25
Rejection of the Gospel .. Acts 13:42-46
Embitter Gentiles .... Acts 14:2-6
Spiritual blindness .... John 3:1-4
Ignorance .... Luke 19:41, 42

Their punishment:

Blinded .... Rom 11:25
Cast out .... Matt 8:11, 12
Desolation as a nation .... Luke 21:20-24
Scattered .... Deut 28:48-64

[*also* JEW, JEWISH, JEWRY, JEWS']

drove the J from Elath 2Kin 16:6
talk not..in the J language 2Kin 18:26
voice in the J language 2Kin 18:28
the J and the Chaldees 2Kin 25:25
the J which came up from .... Ezra 4:12
to Jerusalem unto the J .... Ezra 4:23
let the governor of the J .... Ezra 6:7
elders of the J built .... Ezra 6:7
to the elders of these J .... Ezra 6:8
elders of the J builded .... Ezra 6:14
had I as yet told it to the J .... Neh 2:16
and mocked the J .... Neh 4:1
What do these feeble J? .... Neh 4:2
the J which dwelt by them .... Neh 4:12
wives against..the J .... Neh 5:1
have redeemed..the J .... Neh 5:8
at my table..J and rulers .... Neh 5:17
the J think to rebel .... Neh 6:6
in those days also saw I J .... Neh 13:23
speak in the J language .... Neh 13:24
palace there was a certain J .... Esth 2:5
told them that he was a J .... Esth 3:4
the Agagite, the J enemy .... Esth 3:10
to cause to perish all J .... Esth 3:13
mourning among the J .... Esth 4:3
king's treasuries for the J .... Esth 4:7
more than all the J .... Esth 4:13
deliverance arise to the J .... Esth 4:14
gather together all the J .... Esth 4:16
Mordecai the J sitting at .... Esth 5:13
do even so to Mordecai the J. .. Esth 6:10
be of the seed of the J .... Esth 6:13
the house of Haman the J .... Esth 8:1
devised against the J .... Esth 8:3
he wrote to destroy the J .... Esth 8:5
and to Mordecai the J .... Esth 8:7
laid his hand upon the J .... Esth 8:7
Write ye also for the J as .... Esth 8:8
commanded unto the J .... Esth 8:9
J according to..writing .... Esth 8:9
the king granted the J .... Esth 8:11
J should be ready against .... Esth 8:13
J had light and gladness .... Esth 8:16
J had joy and gladness .... Esth 8:17
people of the land became J .... Esth 8:17
the fear of the J fell upon .... Esth 8:17
J hoped to have power .... Esth 9:1
the J had rule over them .... Esth 9:1
J gathered themselves .... Esth 9:2
officers..helped the J .... Esth 9:3
J smote all their enemies .... Esth 9:5
the palace the J slew .... Esth 9:6
the enemy of the J slew .... Esth 9:10
J have slain and destroyed .... Esth 9:12
let it be granted to the J .... Esth 9:13
J that were in Shushan .... Esth 9:15
J..in the king's provinces .... Esth 9:16
J..at Shushan assembled .... Esth 9:18
the J of the villages .... Esth 9:19
sent letters unto all the J .... Esth 9:20
J rested from their enemies .... Esth 9:22
the J undertook to do as .... Esth 9:23
the enemy of all the J .... Esth 9:24
devised against the J to .... Esth 9:24
devised against the J .... Esth 9:25
J ordained, and took upon .... Esth 9:27
fail from among the J .... Esth 9:28
and Mordecai the J .... Esth 9:29
the letters unto all the J .... Esth 9:30
Mordecai the J and Esther .... Esth 9:31
great among the J .... Esth 10:3
Mordecai the J was next .... Esth 10:3
speak not to us in the J .... Is 36:11
voice in the J language .... Is 36:13
J that sat in the court of .... Jer 32:12
to wit, of a J his brother .... Jer 34:9
afraid of the J that are .... Jer 38:19
the J that were in Moab .... Jer 40:11
J returned out of all places .... Jer 40:12
J which are gathered .... Jer 40:15
Ishmael also slew all the J .... Jer 41:3
concerning all the J which .... Jer 44:1
year three thousand J .... Jer 52:28
away captive of the J .... Jer 52:30
and accused the J .... Dan 3:8
certain J whom thou hast .... Dan 3:12
father brought out of J? .... Dan 5:13
skirt of him that is a J .... Zech 8:23
is born King of the J? .... Matt 2:2
thou the King of the J? .... Matt 27:11
Hail, King of the J! .... Matt 27:29
Jesus The King Of The J .... Matt 27:37
reported among the J .... Matt 28:15
Pharisees, and all the J .... Mark 7:3
thou the King of the J? .... Mark 15:2
release..King of the J? .... Mark 15:9
call the King of the J? .... Mark 15:12
Hail, King of the J! .... Mark 15:18
The King Of The J .... Mark 15:26
the elders of the J .... Luke 7:3
the King of the J? .... Luke 23:3
teaching throughout all J .... Luke 23:5
thou be the king of the J .... Luke 23:37
Is The King Of The J .... Luke 23:38
Arimathea, a city of the J .... Luke 23:51
when the J sent priests .... John 1:19
purifying of the J .... John 2:6
J passover was at hand .... John 2:13
Then answered the J and .... John 2:18
Then said the J, Forty .... John 2:20
John's disciples and the J .... John 3:25
being a J askest drink of .... John 4:9
was a feast of the J .... John 5:1
J therefore said unto him .... John 5:10
the J that it was Jesus .... John 5:15
did the J persecute Jesus .... John 5:16
J sought the more to kill .... John 5:18
passover, a feast of the J .... John 6:4
J then murmured at him .... John 6:41
J therefore strove among .... John 6:52
he would not walk in J .... John 7:1
J sought to kill him .... John 7:1
J feast of tabernacles .... John 7:2
J sought him at the feast .... John 7:11
of him for fear of the J .... John 7:13
J marveled saying .... John 7:15
J among themselves .... John 7:35
J, Will he kill himself? .... John 8:22
Jesus to those J which .... John 8:31
Then answered the J and .... John 8:48
Then said the J unto him .... John 8:52
Then said the J unto him .... John 8:57
the J did not believe .... John 9:18
they feared the J .... John 9:22
the J had agreed already .... John 9:22
division..among the J .... John 10:19
the J round about him .... John 10:24
J took up stones again .... John 10:31
J answered him, saying .... John 10:33
J of late sought to stone .... John 11:8
the J came to Martha .... John 11:19
J then which were with .... John 11:31
and the J also weeping .... John 11:33
Then said the J, Behold .... John 11:36
J which came to Mary .... John 11:45
openly among the J .... John 11:54
J passover was nigh .... John 11:55
people of the J therefore .... John 12:9
many of the J went away .... John 12:11
as I said unto the J .... John 13:33
officers of the J took Jesus .... John 18:12
gave counsel to the J .... John 18:14
the J always resort .... John 18:20
J therefore said unto .... John 18:31
thou the King of the J? .... John 18:33
Pilate answered, Am I a J? .... John 18:35
not be delivered to the J .... John 18:36
went out again unto the J .... John 18:38
release..King of the J? .... John 18:39
Hail, King of the J .... John 19:3
J answered him, We have .... John 19:7
the J cried out, saying .... John 19:12
saith unto the J, Behold .... John 19:14
The King Of The J .... John 19:19
then read many of the J .... John 19:20
chief priests of the J .... John 19:21
The King of the J .... John 19:21
said I am King of the J .... John 19:21
The J..besought Pilate .... John 19:31
secretly for fear of the J .... John 19:38
manner of the J is to bury .... John 19:40
the J preparation day .... John 19:42
assembled for fear of the J .... John 20:19
dwelling at Jerusalem J .... Acts 2:5
of Rome J and proselytes .... Acts 2:10
J which dwelt at Damascus .... Acts 9:22
J took counsel to kill him .... Acts 9:23
all the nation of the J .... Acts 10:22
man that is a J to keep .... Acts 10:28
in the land of the J .... Acts 10:39
to none but unto the J .... Acts 11:19
he saw it pleased the J .... Acts 12:3
expectation..of the J .... Acts 12:11
in the synagogues of the J .... Acts 13:5
J, whose name was Bar-jesus .. Acts 13:6
J stirred up the devout .... Acts 13:50
the synagogue of the J .... Acts 14:1
multitude both of the J .... Acts 14:1
certain J from Antioch .... Acts 14:19
him because of the J .... Acts 16:3
J do exceedingly trouble .... Acts 16:20
a synagogue of the J .... Acts 17:1
J which believed not .... Acts 17:5
the synagogue of the J .... Acts 17:10
the J of Thessalonica .... Acts 17:13
the synagogue with the J .... Acts 17:17
certain J named Aquila .... Acts 18:2
J to depart from Rome .... Acts 18:2
persuaded the J and the .... Acts 18:4
testified to the J that .... Acts 18:5
J made insurrection with .... Acts 18:12
Gallio said unto the J .... Acts 18:14
O ye J, reason would that .... Acts 18:14
and reasoned with the J .... Acts 18:19
certain J named Apollos .... Acts 18:24
mightily convinced the J .... Acts 18:28
Lord Jesus, both J and Greeks .. Acts 19:10
certain of the vagabond J .... Acts 19:13
Sceva, a J and chief of .... Acts 19:14
was known to all the J .... Acts 19:17
J putting him forward .... Acts 19:33
knew that he was a J .... Acts 19:34
the J laid wait for him .... Acts 20:3
the lying in wait of the J .... Acts 20:19
Testifying both to the J .... Acts 20:21
shall the J at Jerusalem .... Acts 21:11
how many thousands of J .... Acts 21:20
thou teacheth all the J .... Acts 21:21
the J which were of Asia .... Acts 21:27
which am a J of Tarsus .... Acts 21:39
am a J born in Tarsus .... Acts 22:3
a good report of all the J .... Acts 22:12
he was accused of the J .... Acts 22:30
certain of the J banded .... Acts 23:12
J have agreed to desire .... Acts 23:20
man was taken of the J .... Acts 23:27
J laid wait for the man .... Acts 23:30
sedition among all the J .... Acts 24:5
J also assented, saying .... Acts 24:9
J from Asia found me .... Acts 24:18
show the J a pleasure .... Acts 24:27
chief of the J informed him .... Acts 25:2
J which came down from .... Acts 25:7
against the law of the J .... Acts 25:8
to do the J a pleasure .... Acts 25:9
J have I done no wrong .... Acts 25:10

elders of the *J* informed ......Acts 25:15
multitude of the *J* have ......Acts 25:24
I am accused of the *J*........Acts 26:2
questions..among the *J*........Acts 26:3
Jerusalem, know all the *J* .....Acts 26:4
I am accused of the *J*.........Acts 26:7
J caught me in the temple ....Acts 26:21
called the chief of the *J*.......Acts 28:17
the *J* spake against it ....Acts 28:19
words, the *J* departed.........Acts 28:29
J first..to the Greek ....Rom 1:16
J first..of the Gentile ....Rom 2:9
J first..to the Gentile ....Rom 2:10
advantage then hath the *J*?....Rom 3:1
proved both *J* and Gentiles ...Rom 3:9
he the God of the *J* only? ....Rom 3:29
called, not of the *J* only ......Rom 9:24
the *J* and the Greek ....Rom 10:12
For the *J* require a sign.......1Cor 1:22
J a stumbling block...........1Cor 1:23
called both *J* and Greeks 1Cor 1:24
J I became as a Jew..........1Cor 9:20
Jews I became as a *J* 1Cor 9:20
that I might gain the *J*........1Cor 9:20
offense neither to the *J* 1Cor 10:32
we be *J* or Gentiles 1Cor 12:13
J five times received I 2Cor 11:24
past in the *J* religion..........Gal 1:13
profited in the *J* religion ......Gal 1:14
the other *J* dissembled ....Gal 2:13
If thou being a *J* livest........Gal 2:14
and not as do the *J*...........Gal 2:14
to live as do the *J*? ....Gal 2:14
We who are *J* by nature ......Gal 2:15
neither *J* nor Greek ....Gal 3:28
is neither Greek nor *J* ....Col 3:11
giving heed to *J* fables........Titus 1:14
which say they are *J* and......Rev 2:9
which say they are *J* and......Rev 3:9

JEWEL—*a precious stone used as an ornament*

Used for:
Ornaments..............Is 3:18-24
Evil offering ....Ex 32:1-5
Good offering...........Ex 35:22
Spoils of war............2Chr 20:25
Farewell gifts ....Ex 11:2

Significance of:
Betrothal present........Gen 24:22, 53
Sign of wealth...........James 2:2
Standard of value.........Prov 3:15
Tokens of repentance ....Gen 35:4
Tokens of love ....Ezek 16:11-13
Indications of worldliness .1Tim :9
Figurative of God's own .Matt 13:45, 46

[*also* JEWELS]
in her house, *j* of silver ....Ex 3:22
and *j* of gold, and raiment ....Ex 3:22
of the Egyptians *j* of silver ....Ex 12:35
and *j* of gold, and raiment ....Ex 12:35
of *j* of gold, chains, and.......Num 31:50
gold..even all wrought *j* ....Num 31:51
put the *j* of gold, which ye 1Sam 6:8
wherein the *j* of gold 1Sam 6:15
all manner of pleasant *j*.......2Chr 32:27
not be for *j* of fine gold.......Job 28:17
j of gold in a swine's snout ....Prov 11:22
knowledge are a precious *j* ....Prov 20:15
cheeks..with rows of *j*.........Song 1:10
thy thighs are like *j*...........Song 7:1
bride adorneth..her *j*..........Is 61:10
I put a *j* on thy forehead......Ezek 16:12
hast also taken thy fair *j* ......Ezek 16:17
take thy fair *j*, and leave ......Ezek 16:39
and take away thy fair *j*.......Ezek 23:26
her earrings and her *j*.........Hos 2:13
day when I make up my *j*.....Mal 3:17

JEWESS—*a female Jew*
Woman of the Hebrew
race ....Acts 24:24

JEWISH CALENDAR—*the months and feasts of the Jewish year*

List of months of:
Abib, or Nisan
(March—April) ....Ex 13:4
Zif or Iyyar (April—May) 1Kin 6:1, 37
Sivan (May—June) ......Esth 8:9
Tammuz (June—July) ...Jer 39:2
Ab (July—August) ......Num 33:38
Elul
(August—September)..Neh 6:15
Ethanim or Tishri
(September—October) .1Kin 8:2
Bul or Heshvan
(October—November) .1Kin 6:38
Chisleu or Kislev (November—
December)............Neh 1:1
Tebeth
(December—January)..Esth 2:16
Shebat or Sebat
(January—February)...Zech 1:7
Adar (February—March) .Esth 3:7

Feasts of:
Abib (14)—Passover.....Ex 12:18
Abib (15-21)—
Unleavened Bread.....Lev 23:5, 6
Abib (16)—First fruits ...Lev 23:10, 11
Zif (14)—Later Passover .Num 9:10, 11
Sivan (6)—Pentecost,
Feast of Weeks,
Harvest...............Lev 23:15-21
Ethanim (1)—Trumpets ..Lev 23:24
Ethanim (10)—Day of
Atonement ....Lev 16:29-34
Ethanim
(15-21)—Tabernacles...Lev 23:34, 35
Ethanim (22)—Holy
Convocation ....Lev 23:36
Chisleu (25)—Dedication .John 10:22

JEWISH MEASURES

Long Measures:
Finger (¾ inch) ....Jer 52:21
Handbreadth (3 to 4
inches) ....Ex 25:25
Span (about 9 inches)....Ex 28:16
Cubit of man (about 18
inches) ....Gen 6:15
Pace (about 3 feet) 2Sam 6:13
Fathom (about 6 feet) ...Acts 27:28
Reed (about 11 feet) ....Ezek 40:5
Line (146 feet) ....Ezek 40:3

Land measures:
Cubit (1¾ feet) ....Josh 3:4
Mile (1760 yds.).........Matt 5:41
Sabbath day's journey (3/5
mile) ....Acts 1:12
Day's journey (24 miles) .Gen 30:36
Furlong (660 feet) ....Luke 24:13

Weights and dry measures:
Cab (about 2 quarts) 2Kin 6:25
Omer (about 7 pints) ....Ex 16:16-18, 36
Ephah (about 4½ pecks) .Ex 16:36
Homer (about 11 bushels) Num 11:32
Hos 3:2
Talent (about 93 pounds) .Ex 25:39

Liquid measures:
Log (about 1 pint).......Lev 14:10, 15
Hin (about 1½ gallons) ..Num 15:4-10
Bath (about 9 gallons) ...Is 5:10
Homer or Cor (c. 85
gallons)..............Ezek 45:11, 14

JEZANIAH (jĕz-ä-nī'ä)—*"Jehovah is hearing"*
Judahite military officer ..Jer 40:7, 8
Seeks advice from
Jeremiah.............Jer 42:1-3
Called Jaazaniah 2Kin 25:23

JEZEBEL (jĕz-ĕ'bĕl)—*"unexalted; unhusbanded"*
1. Daughter of Ethbaal;
Ahab's wife 1Kin 16:31
Follows her idolatry.....1Kin 16:32, 33
Destroyed Jehovah's
prophets 1Kin 18:4-13
Plans Elijah's death 1Kin 19:1, 2
Secures Naboth's death ..1Kin 21:1-15
Sentence:
Pronounced upon 1Kin 21:23
Fulfilled by Jehu 2Kin 9:7, 30-37
2. Type of paganism in the
church ....Rev 2:20

[*also* JEZEBEL'S]
he took to wife *J* the 1Kin 16:31
which eat at *J* table 1Kin 18:19
Lord, whom *J* his wife 1Kin 21:25
Lord, at the hand of *J* 2Kin 9:7
the dogs shall eat *J* in the.....2Kin 9:10
whoredoms of thy mother *J* ...2Kin 9:22

JEZER (jē'zer)—*"formation"*
Son of Naphtali ....Gen 46:24
Family head of the
Jezerites ....Num 26:49

JEZIAH (jĕ-zī'ä)—*"Jehovah unites"*
One who divorced his
foreign wife ....Ezra 10:25

JEZIEL (jē'zī-ĕl)—*"God unites"*
Benjamite warrior 1Chr 12:2, 3

JEZLIAH (jĕz-lī'ä)—*"Jehovah delivers"*
Son of Elpaal 1Chr 8:18

JEZOAR (jĕ-zō'er)—*"he will shine"*
Descendant of Judah 1Chr 4:7

JEZRAHIAH (jĕz-rä hī'ä)—*"Jehovah is shining"*
Leads singing at
dedication service .....Neh 12:42

JEZREEL (jĕz-rē'ĕl)—*"God sows"*
1. Fortified city of Issachar .Josh 19:17, 18
Gideon fights Midianites
in valley of ....Judg 6:33
Israelites camp here 1Sam 29:1, 11
Center of Ish-bosheths'
rule.................2Sam 2:8, 9
Capital city 1Kin 18:45
Home of Naboth........1Kin 21:1, 13
Site of Jezebel's tragic
end 1Kin 21:23
Heads of Ahab's sons
piled here 2Kin 10:1-10
City of bloodshed.......Hos 1:4
Judgment in valley of ...Hos 1:5
2. Town of Judah ....Josh 15:56
David's wife from 1Sam 25:43
3. Judahite 1Chr 4:3
4. Symbolic name of
Hosea's son ....Hos 1:4
5. Symbolic name of the
new Israel...........Hos 2:22, 23

who are of the valley of *J*.....Josh 17:16
Saul and Jonathan out of *J*....2Sam 4:4
by Zartanah beneath *J*........1Kin 4:12
Ahab to the entrance of *J*.....1Kin 18:46
back to be healed in *J* 2Kin 8:29
the son of Ahab in *J* 2Kin 8:29
Jezebel in the portion of *J* 2Kin 9:10
returned to be healed in *J* 2Kin 9:15
city to go to tell it in *J* 2Kin 9:15
a chariot and went to *J* 2Kin 9:16
on the tower in *J*............2Kin 9:17
Jehu was come to *J* 2Kin 9:30
in the portion of *J* shall.......2Kin 9:36
field in the portion of *J* 2Kin 9:37
the house of Ahab in *J* 2Kin 10:11
returned to be healed in *J* 2Chr 22:6
the son of Ahab at *J* 2Chr 22:6
great shall be the day of *J* ....Hos 1:11

JEZREELITE (jĕz'rē-ĕl-īt)—*a person from Jezreel*
Naboth 1Kin 21:1

Naboth the *J* had spoken 1Kin 21:4
I spake unto Naboth the *J* 1Kin 21:6
vineyard of Naboth the *J* 1Kin 21:7

vineyard of Naboth the *J* 1Kin 21:15
vineyard of Naboth the *J* 1Kin 21:16
the portion of Naboth the *J*...2Kin 9:21
the field of Naboth the *J*......2Kin 9:25

JEZREELITESS (jĕz'rē-ĕl-īt'ĕs)—*a female from Jezreel*
Ahinoam 1Sam 30:5

two wives, Ahinoam the *J* 1Sam 27:3
wives also, Ahinoam the *J* 2Sam 2:2
Amnon of Ahinoam the *J*.....2Sam 3:2
Amnon, of Ahinoam the *J* 1Chr 3:1

JIBSAM (jĭb'săm)—*"lovely scent"*
Descendant of Issachar...1Chr 7:2

JIDLAPH (jĭd'lăf)—*"melting away"*
Son of Nahor ....Gen 22:22

JIMNA, JIMNAH (jĭm'nä)—*"lugging"*
Son of Asher ....Gen 46:17

J..the family of the Jimnites...Num 26:44
See **Imnah**

JIMNITES—*descendants of Jimna*
Jimna..the family of the *J*.....Num 26:44

JIPHTAH (jĭft'tä)—*"breaking through"*
City of Judah ....Josh 15:43

JIPHTHAH-EL (jĭf'thä-ĕl)—*"God opens"*
Valley between Asher and Naphtali ....Josh 19:10-27

JOAB (jō'ăb)—*"Jehovah is father"*
1. Son of Zeruiah, David's half-sister 2Sam 8:16
Leads David's army to victory over Ishbosheth 2Sam 2:10-32
Assassinates Abner deceptively 2Sam 3:26, 27
David rebukes him 2Sam 3:28-39
Commands David's army against Edomites......1Kin 11:14-17
Defeats Syrians and Ammonites...........2Sam 10:1-14
Obeys David's orders concerning Uriah 2Sam 11:6-27
Allows David to beseige Rabbah 2Sam 11:1
Makes David favorable toward Absalom 2Sam 14:1-33
Remains loyal to David .2Sam 18:1-5
Killed Absalom 2Sam 18:9-17
Rebukes David's grief ...2Sam 19:1-8
Demoted by David 2Sam 19:13
Puts down Sheba's revolt.2Sam 20:1-22
Killed Amasa 2Sam 20:8-10
Regains command.......2Sam 20:23
Opposes David's numbering of the people .... {2Sam 24:1-9; 1Chr 21:1-6}
Supports Adonijah 1Kin 1:7
David's dying words against 1Kin 2:1-6
His crimes punished by Solomon 1Kin 2:28-34
2. Son of Seraiah 1Chr 4:13, 14
3. Family head of exiles....Ezra 2:6

[*also* **joab's**]
of Zeruiah, brother of *J* 1Sam 26:6
servants of David and *J*.......2Sam 3:22
When *J* and all the host 2Sam 3:23
they told *J*, saying, Abner 2Sam 3:23
Then *J* came to the king 2Sam 3:24
David sent to *J*, saying 2Sam 11:6
J sent Uriah to David 2Sam 11:6
J fought against Rabbah 2Sam 12:26
J sent messengers to 2Sam 12:27
J came to the king and 2Sam 14:33
of the host instead of *J* 2Sam 17:25
sister to Zeruiah *J* mother 2Sam 17:25
J said unto him, Thou 2Sam 18:20
Then said *J* to Cushi, Go 2Sam 18:21
bowed himself unto *J* 2Sam 18:21
son of Zadok yet again to *J*...2Sam 18:22
J said, Wherefore wilt 2Sam 18:22
J sent the king's servant 2Sam 18:29
Abishai, the brother of *J*......2Sam 23:18
brother of *J* was one of 2Sam 23:24
armor-bearer to *J* the son 2Sam 23:37
J the captain of the host 1Kin 1:19
J heard the sound of the 1Kin 1:41
J the son of Zeruiah 1Kin 2:22
Then tidings came to *J*........1Kin 2:28
J..turned after Adonijah 1Kin 2:28
J fled unto the tabernacle 1Kin 2:28
J the captain of the host 1Kin 11:21
Zeruiah; Abishai and *J* 1Chr 2:16
Ataroth the house of *J*........1Chr 2:54
So *J* the son of Zeruiah........1Chr 11:6
J repaired the rest of the 1Chr 11:8
brother of *J* he was chief 1Chr 11:20
Asahel the brother of *J* 1Chr 11:26
the armor-bearer of *J* the 1Chr 11:39
J the son of Zeruiah was......1Chr 18:15
heard of it, he sent *J* 1Chr 19:8
J saw that the battle 1Chr 19:10
So *J* and the people that 1Chr 19:14
Then *J* came to Jerusalem 1Chr 19:15
J led forth the power of 1Chr 20:1
J smote Rabbah and..........1Chr 20:1
and *J* the son of Zeruiah......1Chr 26:28
Asahel the brother of *J* 1Chr 27:7
J the son of Zeruiah began....1Chr 27:24
general of..army was *J*........1Chr 27:34
Of the sons of *J*, Obadiah ....Ezra 8:9
children of Jeshua and *J* ......Neh 7:11
J returned and smote ....Ps 60:*title*

JOAH (jō'ä)—*"Jehovah is brother"*
1. Son of Obed-edom 1Chr 26:4
2. Gershonite Levite 1Chr 6:21
Hezekiah's assistant 2Chr 29:12
3. Son of Aspha; a recorder under Hezekiah.......Is 36:3, 11, 22
4. Son of Joahaz 2Chr 34:8

J the son of Asaph the 2Kin 18:18
Shebna and *J*, unto 2Kin 18:26
J the son of Asaph the 2Kin 18:37

JOAHAZ (jō'ä-hăz)—*"Jehovah helps"*
Father of Joah, a recorder 2Chr 34:8

JOANNA (jō-ăn'ä)—*"God-given"*
1. Ancestor of Christ ......Luke 3:27
See **Hananiah** 8
2. Wife of Chuza, Herod's steward ....Luke 8:1-3
With others, heralds Christ's resurrection...Luke 23:55, 56

JOASH, JEHOASH (jō'ăsh, jĕ-hō'ă-hăz)—*"Jehovah has given; Jehovah supports"*
1. Father of Gideon ....Judg 6:11-32
2. Judahite................1Chr 4:21, 22
3. Benjamite warrior.......1Chr 12:3
4. Son of Ahab 1Kin 22:26
5. Son and successor of Ahaziah, king of Judah 2Kin 11:1-20
Rescued and hid by Jehosheba 2Kin 11:1-3
Proclaimed king by Jehoiada 2Kin 11:4-12
Instructed by Jehoiada ..2Kin 12:1, 2
Repairs the Temple 2Kin 12:4-16
Turns to idols after Jehoiada's death 2Chr 24:17-19
Murdered Zechariah, Jehoiada's son ....Matt 23:35
Killed, not buried with kings.................2Chr 25:23-28
6. Son and successor of Jehoahaz, king of Israel 2Kin 13:10-13
Follows idolatry.........2Kin 13:11
Laments Elijah's sickness.2Kin 13:14-19
Defeats:
Syria 2Kin 13:24, 25
Amaziah 2Kin 13:12
of Gideon the son of *J*........Judg 7:14
son of *J* returned from........Judg 8:13
son of *J* went and dwelt ......Judg 8:29
Gideon the son of *J* died .....Judg 8:32
sepulcher of *J* his father ......Judg 8:32
the rest of the acts of *J* 2Kin 12:19
slew *J* in the house 2Kin 12:20
and twentieth year of *J* 2Kin 13:1
J his son reigned in...........2Kin 13:9
second year of *J* son of 2Kin 14:1
son of *J* king of Judah 2Kin 14:1
all things as *J* his father.......2Kin 14:3
son of *J* king of Judah 2Kin 14:17
Amaziah the son of *J*..........2Kin 14:23
Jeroboam the son of *J* 2Kin 14:23
Jeroboam the son of *J* 2Kin 14:27
to *J* the king's son............2Chr 18:25
took *J* the son of Ahaziah 2Chr 22:11
J was seven years old.........2Chr 24:1
J did that which was right.....2Chr 24:2
J was minded to repair 2Chr 24:4
J the king remembered 2Chr 24:22
judgment against *J* 2Chr 24:24
took advice and sent to *J* 2Chr 25:17
J king of Israel sent to........2Chr 25:18
J the king of Israel went 2Chr 25:21
J the king of Israel took 2Chr 25:23
king of Judah, the son of *J*....2Chr 25:23
Amaziah the son of *J* king 2Chr 25:25
death of *J* son of Jehoahaz 2Chr 25:25
Jeroboam the son of *J* ....Hos 1:1
Jeroboam the son of *J* ....Amos 1:1

JOASH (jō'ăsh)—*"Jehovah has given"*
1. Benjamite 1Chr 7:8
2. Officer of David 1Chr 27:28

JOATHAM—*See* **Jotham**

JOB (jōb)—*"hated; persecuted"—a pious man of Uz whose endurance in fierce trial resulted in marvelous blessing*

Life of:
Lives in Uz ....Job 1:1
Afflicted by Satan ....Job 1:6-19
Debate between Job and his three friends ....Job 3—33
Elihu intervenes ....Job 34—37
Lord answers Job........Job 38—41
His final reply...........Job 42:1-6
The Lord rebukes Job's three friends ....Job 42:7-9
Restored to prosperity ...Job 42:10-15
Dies "old and full of days"................Job 42:16, 17

Strength of his:
Faith ....Job 19:23-27
Patience ....James 5:11
Integrity ....Job 31:1-40

Sufferings of:
Lost property ....Job 1:13-17
Lost children............Job 1:18, 19
Lost health ....Job 2:4-8
Misunderstood by friends............. {Job 4:1-8; Job 8:1-6; Job 11:1-20}

Restoration of:
After repentance ....Job 42:1-6
After prayer ....Job 42:8-10
To greater prosperity ....Job 42:11-17

[*also* **job's**]
that *J* sent and sanctified......Job 1:5
J said, It may be that my .....Job 1:5
Thus did *J* continually ....Job 1:5
Then *J* arose, and rent his ....Job 1:20
In all this *J* sinned not ....Job 1:22
considered my servant *J* ......Job 2:3
smote *J* with sore boils ....Job 2:7
In all this did not *J* sin ....Job 2:10
J three friends heard ....Job 2:11
against *J* was his wrath ....Job 32:2
J hath said, I am righteous ....Job 34:5
J hath spoken without ....Job 34:35
J open his mouth in vain......Job 35:16
Hearken unto this O *J*........Job 37:14

spoken these words unto *J* . . . .Job 42:7
right, as my servant *J* hath . . . .Job 42:7
the Lord also accepted *J* . . . . . .Job 42:9
Lord turned..captivity of *J* . . . .Job 42:10
gave *J* twice as much as . . . . . . .Job 42:10
blessed the latter end of *J* . . . . .Job 42:12
J died being old and . . . . .Job 42:17

JOB—*See* **Jashub 1**

JOB, THE BOOK OF—*a book of the Old Testament*
Wisdom described . . . . . . .Job 1:1-5
Wisdom tested . . . . .Job 1:6—2:10
Wisdom sought . . . . .Job 3—37
God challenges Job . . . . . .Job 38—41
Wisdom in humility . . . . . .Job 42:1-6

JOBAB (jō'băb)—*"to call shrilly"*
1. Son of Joktan . . . . .Gen 10:29
Tribal head 1Chr 1:23
2. King of Edom . . . . .Gen 36:31, 33
3. Canaanite king defeated by Joshua . . . . .Josh 11:1, 7-12
4. Benjamite 1Chr 8:9
5. Another Benjamite 1Chr 8:18

And *J* died, and Husham . . . . .Gen 36:34
J the son of Zerah of 1Chr 1:44
when *J* was dead, Husham 1Chr 1:45

JOCHEBED (jŏk'ĕ-bĕd)—*"Jehovah is honor or glory"*
Daughter of Levi; mother of Miriam, Aaron, and Moses . . . . .Ex 6:20

of Amram's wife was *J* . . . . . . .Num 26:59

JOD (jŏd)
Tenth letter of the Hebrew alphabet . . . . . .Ps 119:73-80

JODA—*See* **Judah**

JOED (jo'ed)—*"Jehovah is witness"*
Benjamite . . . . .Neh 11:7

JOEL (jō'ĕl)—*"Jehovah is God"*
1. Son of Samuel 1Sam 8:1, 2
1Chr 6:28, 33
Father of Heman the singer 1Chr 15:17
2. Kohathite Levite 1Chr 6:36
3. Leader of Simeon 1Chr 4:35
4. Reubenite chief 1Chr 5:4, 8, 9
5. Gadite chief 1Chr 5:12
6. Chief man of Issachar . .1Chr 7:3
7. One of David's mighty men 1Chr 11:38
8. Gershonite Levite 1Chr 15:7, 11, 17
Probably the same as in 1Chr 23:8
9. Manassite chief officer . .1Chr 27:20
10. Kohathite Levite during Hezekiah's reign 2Chr 29:12
11. Son of Nebo; divorced his foreign wife . . . . . . .Ezra 10:43
12. Benjamite overseer under Nehemiah . . . . . .Neh 11:9
13. Prophet . . . . .Joel 1:1

Zetham, and *J* his brother 1Chr 26:22
spoken by the prophet *J* . . . . . .Acts 2:16

JOEL, BOOK OF—*a book of the Old Testament*
Prophecies of:
Predict Pentecost . . . . .Joel 2:28-32
Proclaim salvation in Christ . . . . .Joel 2:32
Portray the universal judgment . . . . .Joel 3:1-16
Picture the eternal age . . .Joe 3:17-21

JOELAH (jō-ē'lä)—*"God is snatching; may he avail!"*
David's recruit at Ziklag. .1Chr 12:7

JOEZER (jō-ē'zer)—*"Jehovah is help"*
One of David's supporters at Ziklag . . .1Chr 12:6

JOGBEHAH (jŏg'bĕ-hä)—*"high"*
Town in Gilead . . . . .Judg 8:11

and Jaazer and *J* . . . . .Num 32:35

JOGLI (jŏg'lī)—*"exiled"*
Father of Bukki, a Danite prince . . . . .Num 34:22

JOHA (jō'hä)—*"Jehovah is living"*
1. Benjamite 1Chr 8:16
2. One of David's mighty men 1Chr 11:45

JOHANAN (jō-hā'năn)—*"Jehovah is gracious"*
1. One of David's mighty men 1Chr 12:2, 4
2. Gadite captain of David.1Chr 12:12, 14
3. Father of Azariah the priest 1Chr 6:10
4. Ephraimite leader 2Chr 28:12
5. Son of King Josiah 1Chr 3:15
6. Son of Kareah 2Kin 25:22, 23
Supports Gedaliah . . . . .Jer 40:8, 9
Warns Gedaliah of assassination plot . . . .Jer 40:13, 14
Avenges Gedaliah's murder . . . . .Jer 41:11-15
Removes Jewish remnant to Egypt against Jeremiah's warning . . .Jer 41:16-18
7. Elioenai's son 1Chr 3:24
8. Returned exile . . . . .Ezra 8:12
9. Son of Tobiah . . . . .Neh 6:17, 18
10. Postexilic high priest . . .Neh 12:22
11. A priest . . . . .Ezra 10:6

and Azariah begat *J* 1Chr 6:9
even until the days of *J* . . . . . . .Neh 12:23
Then *J* the son of Kareah . . . . .Jer 40:15
son of Ahikam said unto *J* . . . .Jer 40:16
the captains..and *J* . . . . .Jer 42:1
J the son of Kareah . . . . .Jer 42:8
J the son of Kareah . . . . .Jer 43:2
So *J* the son of Kareah . . . . . . .Jer 43:4
But *J* the son of Kareah . . . . . .Jer 43:5

JOHN (jŏn)—*"gift of God"*
1. Father of Simon Peter . . .John 1:42
Called Barjona . . . . .Matt 16:17
2. Jewish official . . . . .Acts 4:6
3. Also called Mark . . . . . . .Acts 12:12, 25
4. John the Apostle . . . . . . .Matt 4:21
See separate article
5. John the Baptist . . . . .Matt 3:1
See separate article

Galilee to Jordan unto *J* . . . . . .Matt 3:13
J forbade him, saying, I . . . . . .Matt 3:14
to him the disciples of *J* . . . . . .Matt 9:14
J had heard in the prison . . . . .Matt 11:2
Go and show *J* again . . . . .Matt 11:4
multitudes concerning *J* . . . . . . .Matt 11:7
This is *J* the Baptist . . . . .Matt 14:2
thou art *J* the Baptist . . . . .Matt 16:14
Peter, James, and *J* his . . . . . . .Matt 17:1
unto them of *J* the Baptist . . . .Matt 17:13
The baptism of *J* whence . . . . .Matt 21:25
for all hold *J* as a prophet . . . .Matt 21:26
J came unto you in the . . . . . . .Matt 21:32
J did baptize in the . . . . .Mark 1:4
J was clothed with camel's . . . .Mark 1:6
baptized of *J* in Jordan . . . . . . .Mark 1:9
that *J* was put in prison . . . . . . .Mark 1:14
Zebedee and *J* his brother . . . .Mark 1:19
with James and *J* . . . . .Mark 1:29
the disciples of *J* and of . . . . . . .Mark 2:18
Why do the disciples of *J* . . . . .Mark 2:18
J the brother of James . . . . . . .Mark 3:17
J the Baptist was risen . . . . .Mark 6:14
It is *J* whom I beheaded . . . . . .Mark 6:16
The head of *J* the Baptist . . . . .Mark 6:24
head of *J* the Baptist . . . . .Mark 6:25
answered *J* the Baptist . . . . .Mark 8:28
Peter and James and *J* . . . . .Mark 9:2
with James and *J* . . . . .Mark 10:41
baptism of *J* was it from . . . . . .Mark 11:30
all men counted *J* that he . . . . .Mark 11:32
Peter and James and *J* . . . . .Mark 14:33
but he shall be called *J* . . . . . . .Luke 1:60
saying, His name is *J* . . . . .Luke 1:63
in their hearts of *J* . . . . .Luke 3:15
J answered, saying unto . . . . . . .Luke 3:16
he shut up *J* in prison . . . . .Luke 3:20
disciples of *J* fast often . . . . . . .Luke 5:33
and *J*, Philip and . . . . .Luke 6:14
disciples of *J* showed him . . . . .Luke 7:18
J calling unto him two of . . . . . .Luke 7:19
J the Baptist hath sent us . . . . .Luke 7:20
tell *J* what things ye have . . . . .Luke 7:22
messengers of *J* were . . . . .Luke 7:24
the people concerning *J* . . . . . . .Luke 7:24
prophet than *J* the Baptist . . . .Luke 7:28
with the baptism of *J* . . . . .Luke 7:29
J the Baptist came neither . . . .Luke 7:33
Peter and James and *J* . . . . .Luke 8:51
that *J* was risen from the . . . . .Luke 9:7
J have I beheaded . . . . .Luke 9:9
said *J* the Baptist . . . . .Luke 9:19
he took Peter and *J* and . . . . . .Luke 9:28
J answered..Master . . . . .Luke 9:49
J also taught his disciples . . . . .Luke 11:1
prophets were until *J* . . . . .Luke 16:16
baptism of *J* was it from . . . . . .Luke 20:4
that *J* was a prophet . . . . .Luke 20:6
from God whose name was *J* . .John 1:6
J bare witness of him and . . . . .John 1:15
And this is the record of *J* . . . .John 1:19
J answered them, saying . . . . . .John 1:26
where *J* was baptizing . . . . .John 1:28
two which heard *J* speak . . . . . .John 1:40
And *J* also was baptizing . . . . . .John 3:23
For *J* was not yet cast . . . . .John 3:24
baptized more..than *J* . . . . .John 4:1
witness than that of *J* . . . . .John 5:36
where *J* at first baptized . . . . . .John 10:40
said, *J* did no miracle . . . . .John 10:41
that *J* spake of this man . . . . . .John 10:41
J truly baptized with water . . . .Acts 1:5
from the baptism of *J* . . . . .Acts 1:22
baptism which *J* preached . . . . .Acts 10:37
J indeed baptized with . . . . .Acts 11:16
killed James..brother of *J* . . . . .Acts 12:2
also *J* to their minister . . . . .Acts 13:5
J departing from them . . . . .Acts 13:13
J, whose surname was Mark . . .Acts 15:37
only the baptism of *J* . . . . .Acts 18:25
J verily baptized with the . . . . .Acts 19:4
And I *J* saw the holy city . . . . .Rev 21:2
And I *J* saw these things . . . . . .Rev 22:8

JOHN THE APOSTLE—*the son of Zebedee and one of the twelve apostles*
Life of:
Son of Zebedee . . . . .Matt 4:21
Fisherman . . . . .Luke 5:1-11
Leaves his business for Christ . . . . .Matt 4:21, 22
Called to be an apostle . .Matt 10:2
Rebuked by Christ . . . . . .Luke 9:54, 55
Mark 13:3
Sent to prepare a Passover . . . . .Luke 22:8-13
Close to Jesus at Last Supper . . . . .John 13:23-25
Christ commits His mother to . . . . .John 19:26, 27
Witnesses Christ's ascension . . . . .Acts 1:9-13
With Peter, heals a man. .Acts 3:1-11
Imprisoned with Peter . . .Acts 4:1-21
With Peter, becomes a missionary . . . . .Acts 8:14-25
Encourages Paul . . . . .Gal 2:9
Exiled on Patmos . . . . .Rev 1:9
Wrote a Gospel . . . . .John 21:23-25
Wrote three epistles . . . . { 1John, 2John, 3John }
Wrote the Revelation . . . .Rev 1:1, 4, 9
Described as:
Uneducated . . . . .Acts 4:13
Intolerant . . . . .Mark 9:38

Ambitious .... Mark 10:35-37
Trustworthy .... John 19:26, 27
Humble .... Rev 19:10
Beloved by Jesus .... John 21:20

JOHN THE BAPTIST—*the son of Zechariah and Elisabeth who came to prepare the way for the Messiah*

Life of:
Prophecies:
Concerning .... Is 40:3-5
Fulfilled by .... Matt 3:3
Angel announces birth of .... Luke 1:11-20
Set apart as Nazarite .... Num 6:2, 3
Luke 1:15
Lives in deserts .... Luke 1:63, 80
Ministry of, dated .... Luke 3:1-3
Public confusion .... Luke 3:15
Identifies Jesus as the Messiah .... John 1:29-36
Bears witness to Christ .... John 5:33
Exalts Christ .... John 3:25-36
Baptizes Christ .... Matt 3:13-16
Doubts .... Matt 11:2-6
Identified with Elijah .... Matt 11:13, 14
Public reaction to .... Matt 11:16-18
Christ's testimony concerning .... Matt 11:9-13
Reproves Herod for adultery .... Mark 6:17, 18
Imprisoned by Herod .... Matt 4:12
Beheaded by Herod .... Matt 14:3-12

Described as:
Fearless .... Matt 14:3, 4
Righteous .... Mark 6:20
Humble .... John 3:25-31
Faithful .... Acts 13:24, 25
Resourceful .... Matt 3:4
Baptism of, insufficient .... Acts 18:24-26
Acts 19:1-5
Preaching a baptism of repentance .... Luke 3:2-18

JOHN, THE EPISTLES OF—*books of the New Testament*

1 John:
God is light 1John 1:5-7
True knowledge 1John 2:3, 4
Love one another 1John 3:11-24
God is love 1John 4:7-21
Eternal life 1John 5:13-21

2 John:
Commandment to love 2John 4-6
Warning against deceit 2John 7-11

3 John:
Walking in truth 3John 3, 4
Service to the brethren 3John 5-8
Rebuke to Diotrephes 3John 9, 10
Do good 3John 11, 12

JOHN, THE GOSPEL OF—*a book of the New Testament*
Deity of Christ .... John 1:1-18
Testimony of the Baptist .... John 1:19-34
Wedding at Cana .... John 2:1-11
Samaritan mission .... John 4:1-42
Feast of Tabernacles .... John 7:1-53
The Good Shepherd .... John 10:1-42
Lazarus raised .... John 11:1-57
Priestly prayer .... John 17:1-26
Sufferings and glory .... John 18:1—20:31
Purpose of .... John 20:30, 31

JOIADA (joi'ä-dä)—*"Jehovah knows"*
1. Son of Meshullam .... Neh 3:6
2. Postexilic high priest .... Neh 12:10, 11, 22
Son banished from priesthood .... Neh 13:28

JOIAKIM (joi'ä-kĭm)—*"Jehovah sets up"*
Postexilic high priest; son of Jeshua .... Neh 12:10-26

JOIARIB (joi'ä-rĭb)—*"Jehovah contends"*
1. Teacher sent by Ezra .... Ezra 8:16, 17
2. Postexilic Judahite chief .... Neh 11:5
3. Founder of an order of priests .... Neh 11:10
4. Postexilic priest .... Neh 12:6
Father of Joiakim .... Neh 12:19

JOIN—*to bring together*

[*also* JOINED, JOINING, JOININGS]
were *j* together in the vale .... Gen 14:3
they *j* battle with them in .... Gen 14:8
my husband be *j* unto me .... Gen 29:34
j also unto our enemies .... Ex 1:10
shoulderpieces thereof *j* at .... Ex 28:7
so it shall be *j* together .... Ex 28:7
they may be *j* unto thee .... Num 18:2
they shall be *j* unto thee .... Num 18:4
Israel *j* himself unto .... Num 25:3
that were *j* unto Baal-peor .... Num 25:5
they *j* battle, Israel was 1Sam 4:2
wheels were *j* to the base 1Kin 7:32
day the battle was *j* 1Kin 20:29
the gates and for the *j* 1Chr 22:3
j to the wing of the other 2Chr 3:12
and *j* affinity with Ahab 2Chr 18:1
king of Judah *j* himself 2Chr 20:35
j himself..to make ships 2Chr 20:36
j thyself with Ahaziah 2Chr 20:37
and *j* the foundations .... Ezra 4:12
j in affinity with the people .... Ezra 9:14
all the wall was *j* together .... Neh 4:6
such as *j* themselves unto .... Esth 9:27
j unto the days of the year .... Job 3:6
They are *j* one to another .... Job 41:17
flakes of his flesh are *j* .... Job 41:23
Assur also is *j* with them .... Ps 83:8
j themselves also unto .... Ps 106:28
hand *j* in hand the wicked .... Prov 11:21
though hand *j* in hand, he .... Prov 16:5
that is *j* to all the living .... Eccl 9:4
them that *j* house to house .... Is 5:8
him, and *j* his enemies .... Is 9:11
every one that is *j* unto .... Is 13:15
strangers shall be *j* with .... Is 14:1
not be *j* with them in burial .... Is 14:20
hath *j* himself to the Lord .... Is 56:3
j themselves to the Lord .... Is 56:6
j ourselves to the Lord .... Jer 50:5
wings were *j* one to .... Ezek 1:9
wings of every one were *j* .... Ezek 1:11
j them one to another into .... Ezek 37:17
courts *j* of forty cubits .... Ezek 46:22
they shall *j* themselves .... Dan 11:6
Ephraim is *j* to idols; let .... Hos 4:17
shall be *j* to the Lord .... Zech 2:11
therefore God hath *j* .... Matt 19:6
therefore God hath *j* .... Mark 10:9
and *j* himself to a citizen of .... Luke 15:15
durst no man *j* himself to .... Acts 5:13
about four hundred *j* .... Acts 5:36
j thyself to this chariot .... Acts 8:29
j himself to the disciples .... Acts 9:26
j hard to the synagogue .... Acts 18:7
that ye be perfectly *j* 1Cor 1:10
he which is *j* to a harlot 1Cor 6:16
he that is *j* unto the Lord 1Cor 6:17
the whole body fitly *j* .... Eph 4:16
shall be *j* unto his wife .... Eph 5:31

JOINT—*where two objects are connected*

[*also* JOINTS]
Jacob's thigh was out of *j* .... Gen 32:25
the *j* of the harness 1Kin 22:34
the *j* of the harness 2Chr 18:33
my bones are out of *j* .... Ps 22:14
tooth and a foot out of *j* .... Prov 25:19
the *j* of thy thighs are like .... Song 7:1
j of his loins were loosed .... Dan 5:6
which every *j* supplieth .... Eph 4:16
all the body by *j* and bands .... Col 2:19
and of the *j* and marrow .... Heb 4:12

JOINT HEIRS—*heirs together*
of God and *j h* with Christ .... Rom 8:17

JOKDEAM (jŏk'dĕ-ăm)—*"anger of the people"*
City of Judah .... Josh 15:56

JOKIM (jō'kĭm)—*"Jehovah sets up"*
Judahite 1Chr 4:22

JOKMEAM (jŏk'mĕ-ăm)—*"revenge of the people"*
Town of Ephraim 1Chr 6:68
Home of Kohathite Levites 1Chr 6:66, 68
Same as Kibzaim in .... Josh 21:22
Called Jokneam 1Kin 4:12

JOKNEAM (jŏk'nĕ-ăm)—*"building up of the people"*
1. Town near Mt. Carmel .... John 12:22
In tribe of Zebulun .... Josh 19:11
Assigned to Levites .... Josh 21:34
2. Town of Ephraim 1Kin 4:12
See JOKMEAM

JOKSHAN (jŏk'shăn)—*"fowler"*
Son of Abraham and Keturah .... Gen 25:1, 2

And *J* begat Sheba .... Gen 25:3
she bare Zimran and *J* 1Chr 1:32
the sons of *J*; Sheba 1Chr 1:32

JOKTAN (jŏk'tăn)—*"he will be made small"*
A descendant of Shem .... Gen 10:21, 25

J begat Almodad .... Gen 10:26
these were the sons of *J* .... Gen 10:29
his brother's name was *J* 1Chr 1:19
J begat Almodad 1Chr 1:20
these were the sons of *J* 1Chr 1:23

JOKTHEEL (jŏk'thĕ-ĕl)
1. Village of Judah .... Josh 15:20, 38
2. Name given by King Amaziah to Selah 2Kin 14:7

JONA, JONAS (jō'nä, jō'näs)—*"a dove"*
Father of Peter .... John 1:42
See JOHN 1

JONADAB (jŏn'ä-dăb)—*"Jehovah is liberal"*
1. Son of Shimeah; David's nephew 2Sam 13:3
Very subtle man 2Sam 13:3-6, 32-36
2. Son of Rechab .... Jer 35:6
Makes Rechabites primitive and temperate .... Jer 35:5-17
Blessing upon .... Jer 35:18, 19
Opposes idolatry 2Kin 10:15, 16, 23
Called Jehonadab 2Kin 10:15, 23

JONAH, JONAS (jō'nä, jō'näs)—*"a dove"*
Son of Amittai .... Jon 1:1
Ordered to go to Nineveh .... Jon 1:2
Flees to Tarshish .... Jon 1:3
Cause of storm; cast into sea .... Jon 1:4-16
Swallowed by a great fish .... Jon 1:17
Prays in fish's belly .... Jon 2:1-9
Vomited upon land .... Jon 2:10
Obeys second order to go to Nineveh .... Jon 3:1-10
Grieved at Nineveh's repentance .... Jon 4:1-3
Taught God's mercy .... Jon 4:4-11
Type of Christ's resurrection .... Matt 12:39, 40

hand of his servant *J* 2Kin 14:25
J rose up to flee .... Jon 1:3
took up *J*, and cast him .... Jon 1:15
fish to swallow up *J* .... Jon 1:17
J was in the belly of the .... Jon 1:17
vomited out *J* upon the .... Jon 2:10
J went out of the city .... Jon 4:5
to come up over *J* .... Jon 4:6
J was exceeding glad of .... Jon 4:6
the sign of the prophet *J* .... Matt 16:4

the sign of *J* the prophet ...... Luke 11:29
J was a sign unto the .... Luke 11:30
at the preaching of *J* .... Luke 11:32
a greater than *J* is here .... Luke 11:32

JONAN (jō'năn)—*"grace"*
Ancestor of Christ .... Luke 3:30

JONAS—*See* **JONAH; JONA**

JONATHAN (jŏn'ä-thăn)—*"Jehovah is given"*
1. Levite; becomes Micah's priest .... Judg 17:1-13
Follows Danites to idolatrous Dan .... Judg 18:3-31
Grandson of Moses (Manasseh) .... Judg 18:30
2. King Saul's eldest son .. 1Sam 14:49
Smites Philistine garrison 1Sam 13:2, 3
Attacks Michmash 1Sam 14:1-14
Saved from his father's vow 1Sam 14:24-45
Makes covenant with David 1Sam 18:1-4
Pleads for David's life .. 1Sam 19:1-7
Warns David of Saul's wrath 1Sam 20:1-42
Makes second covenant with David 1Sam 23:15-18
Killed by Philistines 1Sam 31:2, 8
Mourned by David 2Sam 1:17-27
David provides for his son 2Sam 9:1-8
3. Uncle of King David ... 1Chr 27:32
4. Son of the high priest Abiathar 2Sam 15:27
Remains faithful to David 2Sam 15:26-36
Brings David Absalom's plans 2Sam 17:15-22
Informs Adonijah of David's choice 1Kin 1:41-49
5. Son of Shimeah 2Sam 21:21, 22
6. One of David's mighty men 2Sam 23:32
7. Judahite 1Chr 2:32, 33
8. Son of Kareah .... Jer 40:8, 9
9. Scribe .... Jer 37:15, 20
10. Opponents of Ezra's reforms .... Ezra 10:15
11. Descendant of Adin .... Ezra 8:6
12. Levite of Asaph's line .. Neh 12:35
13. Head of a priestly house .... Neh 12:14
14. Postexilic high priest ... Neh 12:11

[*also* **JONATHAN'S**]
thousand were with *J* 1Sam 13:2
Saul, and *J* his son 1Sam 13:16
that were with Saul and *J* 1Sam 13:22
with *J* his son was there 1Sam 13:22
J the son of Saul said unto 1Sam 14:1
J and his armor-bearer 1Sam 14:17
that were with Saul and *J* 1Sam 14:21
soul of *J* was knit with the 1Sam 18:1
J loved him as his own 1Sam 18:1
Philistines slew *J* 1Sam 31:2
Saul and *J* his son are 2Sam 1:4
that Saul and *J* his son 2Sam 1:5
Saul, and for *J* his son 2Sam 1:12
J, Saul's son, had a son 2Sam 4:4
tidings came of Saul and *J* 2Sam 4:4
and *J* the son of Abiathar 2Sam 15:27
J and Ahimaaz stayed 2Sam 17:17
spared..the son of *J* 2Sam 21:7
between David and *J* 2Sam 21:7
Saul and the bones of *J* 2Sam 21:12
Saul and the bones of *J* 2Sam 21:13
the bones of Saul and *J* 2Sam 21:14
Saul begat *J*, and 1Chr 8:33
son of *J* was Merib-baal 1Chr 8:34
Saul begat *J*, and 1Chr 9:39
son of *J* was Merib-baal 1Chr 9:40
and the Philistines slew *J* 1Chr 10:2
J the son of Shage the 1Chr 11:34
J the son of Shimea 1Chr 20:7
to return to *J* house .... Jer 38:26

JONATH-ELEM-RECHOKIM (jō'năth-ē'lĕm-rĕ-kō'kĭm)—*"the silent dove of the far ones"*
Musical tune .... Ps 56:*title*

JOPPA, JAPHO (jŏp'pä, jā'fō)—*"beauty"*
Allotted to Dan .... Josh 19:40, 46
Seaport city 2Chr 2:16
Center of commerce ..... Ezra 3:7
Scene of Peter's vision ... Acts 10:5-23, 32

in floats by sea to *J* 2Chr 2:16
and went down to *J* .... Jon 1:3
there was at *J* a certain .... Acts 9:36
as Lydda was nigh to *J* .... Acts 9:38
known throughout all *J* .... Acts 9:42
he tarried many days in *J* ..... Acts 9:43
now send men to *J* .... Acts 10:5
I was in the city of *J* .... Acts 11:5
Send men to *J*, and call .... Acts 11:13

JORAH (jō'rä)—*"early born"*
Family of returnees ...... Ezra 2:18
Called Hariph .... Neh 7:24

JORAI (jō'rā-ī)—*"rainy"*
Gadite chief 1Chr 5:13

JORAM, JEHORAM (jō'răm, jĕ-hō'răm)—*"Jehovah is high"*
1. Son of Toi, king of Hamath 2Sam 8:10
Called Hadoram 1Chr 18:10
2. Levite 1Chr 26:25
3. Son of Ahab, king of Israel 2Kin 3:1
Institutes some reforms .. 2Kin 3:2, 3
Joins Judah against Moab 2Kin 3:1-27
Slain by Jehu 2Kin 9:14-26
Called Jehoram 2Kin 1:17
4. Priest sent to teach the people 2Chr 17:8
5. Son and successor of Jehoshaphat, king of Judah 2Kin 8:16
Murders his brothers 2Chr 21:1-4
His wife, Ahab's daughter, leads him astray 2Kin 8:17, 18
Edomites revolt against .. 2Chr 21:8-10
Unable to withstand invaders 2Chr 21:16, 17
Elijah's prophecy against . 2Chr 21:12-15
Dies horribly without mourners 2Chr 21:18-20
Called Jehoram 2Chr 21:1, 5

So *J* went over to Zair 2Kin 8:21
the rest of the acts of *J* 2Kin 8:23
J slept with his fathers 2Kin 8:24
twelfth year of *J* the son 2Kin 8:25
he went with *J* the son of 2Kin 8:28
the Syrians wounded *J* 2Kin 8:28
king *J* went back to be 2Kin 8:29
to see *J* the son of Ahab 2Kin 8:29
eleventh year of *J* the son of .. 2Kin 9:29
the daughter of king *J* 2Kin 11:2
J his son, Ahaziah his son 1Chr 3:11
and the Syrians smote *J* 2Chr 22:5
was of God by coming to *J* ... 2Chr 22:7
Jehoshaphat begat *J*, and *J* .... Matt 1:8

JORDAN (jôr'dăn)—*"the descender"*—*a river in Palestine*
Canaan's eastern boundary .... Num 34:12
Despised by foreigners ... 2Kin 5:10, 12
Lot dwells near .... Gen 13:8-13
Jacob crosses .... Gen 32:10
Moses forbidden to cross . Deut 3:27
Israel crosses miraculously. Josh 3:1-17
Stones commemorate crossing of .... Josh 4:1-24
David crosses in flight ... 2Sam 17:22, 24
Divided by Elijah 2Kin 2:5-8
Divided by Elisha 2Kin 2:13, 14
Naama healed in 2Kin 5:10, 14
John's baptism in .... Matt 3:6
Christ baptized in .... Matt 3:13-17

all the plain of *J* .... Gen 13:11
staff I passed over this *J* ...... Gen 32:10
which is beyond *J* .... Gen 50:10
which is beyond *J* .... Gen 50:11
by the coast of *J* .... Num 13:29
Moab on this side *J* .... Num 22:1
in the plains of Moab by *J* .... Num 26:3
in the plains of Moab by *J* .... Num 26:63
of Moab, which are by *J* ...... Num 31:12
and bring us not over *J* .... Num 32:5
them on yonder side *J* .... Num 32:19
fallen to us on this side *J* ..... Num 32:19
go all of you armed over *J* .... Num 32:21
Reuben will pass..over *J* ...... Num 32:29
on this side *J* may be ours .... Num 32:32
the plains of Moab by *J* .... Num 33:48
pitched by *J*, from .... Num 33:49
the plains of Moab by *J* .... Num 33:50
over *J* into the land .... Num 33:51
inheritance on this side *J* ...... Num 34:15
the plains of Moab by *J* .... Num 35:1
ye be come over *J* into the .... Num 35:10
three cities on this side *J* ...... Num 35:14
the plains of Moab by *J* .... Num 36:13
on this side *J* in the .... Deut 1:1
On this side *J*, in the land .... Deut 1:5
until I shall pass over *J* .... Deut 2:29
that was on this side *J* .... Deut 3:8
plain also, and *J*, and the ..... Deut 3:17
given them beyond *J* .... Deut 3:20
good land that is beyond *J* .... Deut 3:25
I should not go over *J* .... Deut 4:21
I must not go over *J* .... Deut 4:22
ye go over *J* to possess .... Deut 4:26
three cities on this side *J* ..... Deut 4:41
On this side *J*, in the .... Deut 4:46
this side *J* toward the .... Deut 4:47
the plain on this side *J* .... Deut 4:49
Thou art to pass over *J* .... Deut 9:1
not on the other side *J* .... Deut 11:30
For ye shall pass over *J* .... Deut 11:31
But when ye go over *J* .... Deut 12:10
when ye shall pass over *J* ..... Deut 27:2
when ye be gone over *J* .... Deut 27:4
when ye are come over *J* ..... Deut 27:12
passest over *J* to go to .... Deut 30:18
shalt not go over this *J* .... Deut 31:2
land whither ye go over *J* ..... Deut 31:13
whither ye go over *J* to .... Deut 32:47
go over this *J*, thou .... Josh 1:2
ye shall pass over this *J* .... Josh 1:11
gave you on this side *J* .... Josh 1:14
J toward the sunrising .... Josh 1:15
them the way to *J* unto .... Josh 2:7
were on the other side *J* ...... Josh 2:10
ground in the midst of *J* ...... Josh 3:17
were passed clean over *J* ...... Josh 3:17
were on the side of *J* .... Josh 5:1
dried up the waters of *J* ...... Josh 5:1
brought this people over *J* .... Josh 7:7
dwelt on the other side *J*! ..... Josh 7:7
which were on this side *J* ..... Josh 9:1
that were beyond *J* .... Josh 9:10
land on the other side *J* .... Josh 12:1
smote on this side *J* on .... Josh 12:7
beyond *J* eastward .... Josh 13:8
border..of Reuben was *J* ...... Josh 13:23
of Heshbon, *J* and his .... Josh 13:27
on the other side *J* .... Josh 13:32
tribe on the other side *J* ...... Josh 14:3
even unto the end of *J* .... Josh 15:5
at the uttermost part of *J* ..... Josh 15:5
of Joseph fell from *J* by .... Josh 16:1
Jericho, and went out at *J* .... Josh 16:7
were on the other side *J* ...... Josh 17:5
their inheritance beyond *J* ..... Josh 18:7
the north side was from *J* ..... Josh 18:12
at the south end of *J* .... Josh 18:19
J was the border of it .... Josh 18:20

their border were at *J* ....Josh 19:22
the outgoings..were at *J* ......Josh 19:33
to Judah upon *J* toward.......Josh 19:34
other side *J* by Jericho........Josh 20:8
gave you on the other side *J* ..Josh 22:4
on this side *J* westward ....Josh 22:7
unto the borders of *J* ....Josh 22:10
built there an altar by *J*.........Josh 22:10
in the borders of *J*, at the.....Josh 22:11
the Lord hath made *J* ....Josh 22:25
for your tribes, from *J* ....Josh 23:4
dwelt on the other side *J* .....Josh 24:8
ye went over *J*, and came .....Josh 24:11
took the fords of *J* toward ....Judg 3:28
Gilead abode beyond *J* ....Judg 5:17
waters unto..*J*..................Judg 7:24
on the other side *J* ....Judg 7:25
Gideon came to *J* ....Judg 8:4
were on the other side *J* ......Judg 10:8
of Ammon passed over *J* .....Judg 10:9
unto Jabbok, and unto *J* ......Judg 11:13
wilderness even unto *J*........Judg 11:22
took the passages of *J* ....Judg 12:5
at the passages of *J*............Judg 12:6
the Hebrews went over *J* 1Sam 13:7
on the other side *J* 1Sam 31:7
passed over *J*, and went 2Sam 2:29
and passed over *J* 2Sam 10:17
returned, and came to *J* 2Sam 19:15
conduct the king over *J* 2Sam 19:15
they went over *J* before.........2Sam 19:17
as he was come over *J*...........2Sam 19:18
and went over *J*..................2Sam 19:31
to conduct him over *J* 2Sam 19:31
servant will go..over *J* 2Sam 19:36
the people went over *J* 2Sam 19:39
men with him, over *J*? 2Sam 19:41
from *J* even to Jerusalem 2Sam 20:2
they passed over *J*..............2Sam 24:5
down to meet me at *J* 1Kin 2:8
In the plain of *J* did the 1Kin 7:46
Cherith, that is before *J* 1Kin 17:3
go, we pray thee, unto *J* 2Kin 6:2
when they came to *J* 2Kin 6:4
they went after them unto *J* ...2Kin 7:15
From *J* eastward, all 2Kin 10:33
on the other side *J* 1Chr 6:78
on the east side of *J*...........1Chr 6:78
they that went over *J* 1Chr 12:15
on the other side of *J*..........1Chr 12:37
Israel, and passed over *J*......1Chr 19:17
of Israel on this side *J* 1Chr 26:30
In the plain of *J* did the 2Chr 4:17
he can draw up *J* into his .....Job 40:23
thee from the land of *J* ....Ps 42:6
fled: *J* was driven back ....Ps 114:3
thou *J*, that thou wast ....Ps 114:5
way of the sea, beyond *J* .....Is 9:1
do in the swelling of *J*? ....Jer 12:5
from the swelling of *J* ....Jer 49:19
from the swelling of *J* ....Jer 50:44
the land of Israel by *J* ....Ezek 47:18
the pride of *J* is spoiled ....Zech 11:3
the region round about *J*.......Matt 3:5
baptized of him in *J* ....Matt 3:6
Jesus from Galilee to *J* ....Matt 3:13
of the sea, beyond *J*...........Matt 4:15
and from beyond *J* ....Matt 4:25
coasts of Judea beyond *J*......Matt 19:1
of him in the river of *J* ....Mark 1:5
was baptized of John in *J* .....Mark 1:9
and from beyond *J* ....Mark 3:8
by the farther side of *J* ....Mark 10:1
all the country about *J*.........Luke 3:3
Holy Ghost returned from *J* ...Luke 4:1
in Bethabara beyond *J* ....John 1:28
he that was..beyond *J* ....John 3:26
went away again beyond *J* ....John 10:40

JORIM (jō'rĭm)—*"Jehovah is high"*
Ancestor of Christ.......Luke 3:29

JORKOAM (jôr'kō-ăm)—*"spreading the people"*
Judahite family name 1Chr 2:44

May be same as Jokdeam
in ....Josh 15:56

JOSABAD (jŏs'ă-băd)—*"Jehovah endows"*
One of David's mighty
men 1Chr 12:4

JOSAPHAT—*See* JEHOSHAPHAT

JOSE (jō'sē)
Ancestor of Christ.......Luke 3:29

JOSEDECH (jŏs'ĕ-dĕk)—*"Jehovah is righteous"*
Father of the high priest
Joshua................Hag 1:1, 12, 14

to Joshua the son of *J* ....Hag 2:2
Joshua, son of *J*, the high .....Hag 2:4
of Joshua the son of *J* ....Zech 6:11

JOSEPH (jō'zĕf)—*"may he increase"*
1. Son of Jacob by Rachel.Gen 30:22-24
See separate article
2. Father of one of the
spies ....Num 13:7
3. Son of Asaph..........1Chr 25:2, 9
4. One who divorced his
foreign wife ....Ezra 10:32, 42
5. Pre-exilic ancestor of
Christ.................Luke 3:30
6. Priest in the days of
Joiakim ....Neh 12:14
7. Postexilic ancestor of
Christ.................Luke 3:26
8. Son of Mattathias, in
Christ's ancestry ......Luke 3:24, 25
9. Husband of Mary,
Jesus' mother.........Matt 1:16
Of Davidic lineage .....Matt 1:20
Angel explains Mary's
condition to ....Matt 1:19-25
With Mary at Jesus'
birth ....Luke 2:16
Obeys Old Testament
ordinances ....Luke 2:21-24
Takes Jesus and Mary
to Egypt ....Matt 2:13-15
Returns to Nazareth
with family ....Matt 2:19-23
Jesus subject to ....Luke 2:51
10. Man of Arimathea .....John 19:38
Devout man ....Luke 23:50, 51
Secret disciple ....John 19:38
Obtains Christ's body;
prepares it ....Mark 15:43, 46
Receives Nicodemus'
help ....John 19:39, 40
Puts Christ's body in his
new tomb ....Luke 23:53
11. Called Barsabas; one of
two chosen to occupy
Judas' place ....Acts 1:22-26
12. Also called Barnabas ...Acts 4:36

Mary was espoused to *J* ......Matt 1:18
man of Arimathea, named *J*...Matt 27:57
J had taken the body ....Matt 27:59
he gave the body to *J* ....Mark 15:45
a man whose name was *J* .....Luke 1:27
J also went up from ....Luke 2:4
J and his mother ....Luke 2:33
J and his mother knew.........Luke 2:43
supposed the son of *J*..........Luke 3:23
Jesus..the son of *J*............John 1:45
this Jesus..son of *J* ....John 6:42

JOSEPH (jō'zĕf)—*"may he increase"—the son of Jacob and Rachel; he was sold into slavery but became the prime minister of Egypt*

Life of:
Jacob's son by Rachel ...Gen 30:22-25
Jacob's favorite..........Gen 37:3
Aroused his brothers'
hatred ....Gen 37:4
Sold into Egypt ....Gen 37:25-30
Wins esteem in Egypt....Gen 39:1-23
Interprets Pharaoh's
dream ....Gen 41:1-37
Made Pharaoh's Prime
Minister ....Gen 41:38-46
Recognizes his brothers ..Gen 42:1-8
Reveals his identity ......Gen 45:1-16
Invites Jacob to Egypt ...Gen 45:17-28
Enslaves Egypt ....Gen 47:13-26
Put under oath by Jacob .Gen 47:28-31
His sons blessed by Jacob.Gen 48:1-22
Blessed by Jacob ....Gen 49:22-26
Mourns his father's death.Gen 50:1-14
Deals kindly with his
brothers ....Gen 50:15-21
His death at 110.........Gen 50:22-26
Descendants of ....Num 26:28-37

Character of:
Spiritually sensitive ......Gen 37:2
Wise and prudent ....Gen 41:38-49
Of strong emotions ......Gen 43:29-31
Sees God's hand in
human events ....Gen 45:7, 8
Forgiving ....Gen 50:19-21
Man of faith ....Heb 11:22

[*also* JOSEPH'S]
and Rachel and *J*.............Gen 33:2
after came *J* near.............Gen 33:7
sons of Rachel; *J*, and ....Gen 35:24
J dreamed a dream ....Gen 37:5
Israel said unto *J*, Do not .....Gen 37:13
J went after his brethren ......Gen 37:17
when *J* was come unto his ....Gen 37:23
that they stripped *J* out of ....Gen 37:23
drew and lifted up *J* out of....Gen 37:28
sold *J* to the Ishmaelites ......Gen 37:28
they brought *J* into Egypt .....Gen 37:28
they took *J* coat ....Gen 37:31
J is without doubt rent in .....Gen 37:33
J was brought down to........Gen 39:1
the Lord was with *J* ....Gen 39:2
J found grace in his sight .....Gen 39:4
J was a goodly person ....Gen 39:6
wife cast her eyes upon *J* .....Gen 39:7
as she spake to *J* day by ......Gen 39:10
that *J* went into the house ....Gen 39:11
place where *J* was bound .....Gen 40:3
of the guard charged *J*.........Gen 40:4
J came in unto them..........Gen 40:6
J said unto them, Do not .....Gen 40:8
butler told his dream to *J* .....Gen 40:9
J said unto him, This ....Gen 40:12
he said unto *J*, I also was .....Gen 40:16
J answered and said, This.....Gen 40:18
as *J* had interpreted to........Gen 40:22
chief butler remember *J* ....Gen 40:23
Pharaoh sent and called *J* .....Gen 41:14
Pharaoh said unto *J* ....Gen 41:15
J answered Pharaoh ....Gen 41:16
Pharaoh said unto *J* ....Gen 41:17
J said unto Pharaoh ....Gen 41:25
unto *J* were born two sons ....Gen 41:50
J called the name of the ......Gen 41:51
according as *J* had said ....Gen 41:54
the Egyptians, Go unto *J* .....Gen 41:55
J opened all the ....Gen 41:56
came into Egypt to *J* for to ...Gen 41:57
J remembered the dreams.....Gen 42:9
J said unto them, That is .....Gen 42:14
J said unto them the third ....Gen 42:18
not that *J* understood ....Gen 42:23
J commanded to fill their .....Gen 42:25
J is not, and Simeon is not....Gen 42:36
Egypt, and stood before *J*.....Gen 43:15
J saw Benjamin with ....Gen 43:16
the man did as *J* bade ....Gen 43:17
the men into *J* house ....Gen 43:17
they were brought into *J* ......Gen 43:18
near to the steward of *J* ......Gen 43:19
the men into *J* house ....Gen 43:24
present against *J* came at .....Gen 43:25
when *J* came home, they......Gen 43:26
word that *J* had spoken ....Gen 44:2
J said unto his steward........Gen 44:4
his brethren came to *J* ....Gen 44:14

J said unto them, What . . . . Gen 44:15
J shall put his hand upon . . . . . Gen 46:4
Rachel Jacob's wife; *J* . . . . Gen 46:19
J in the land of Egypt . . . . Gen 46:20
sons of *J*, which were born . . . . Gen 46:27
Judah before him unto *J* . . . . . . Gen 46:28
J made ready his chariot . . . . . . Gen 46:29
Israel said unto *J*, Now . . . . Gen 46:30
J said unto his brethren . . . . Gen 46:31
J came and told Pharaoh . . . . . . Gen 47:1
Pharaoh spake unto *J* . . . . Gen 47:5
J brought in Jacob his . . . . Gen 47:7
J placed his father . . . . Gen 47:11
J nourished his father . . . . Gen 47:12
And *J* dwelt in Egypt, he . . . . . Gen 50:22
J lived a hundred and ten . . . . . Gen 50:22
J saw Ephraim's children . . . . . . Gen 50:23
J said unto his brethren . . . . Gen 50:24
J took an oath of the . . . . Gen 50:25
J died, being a hundred . . . . Gen 50:26
for *J* was in Egypt already . . . . Ex 1:5
J died, and all his brethren . . . . Ex 1:6
Egypt, which knew not *J* . . . . . . Ex 1:8
Moses took the bones of *J* . . . . Ex 13:19
Jacob gave to his son *J* . . . . John 4:5
sold *J* into Egypt . . . . Acts 7:9
J was made known to his . . . . . Acts 7:13
sent *J*, and called his . . . . Acts 7:14
which knew not *J* . . . . Acts 7:18
blessed both the sons of *J* . . . . . Heb 11:21

JOSEPH, TRIBE OF—*the descendants of Joseph, the son of Jacob; one of the twelve tribes of Israel*

Of the children of *J* . . . . Num 1:10
Of the children of *J* . . . . Num 1:32
Of the tribe of *J*, namely . . . . . Num 13:11
of Manasseh the son of *J* . . . . . Num 27:1
of Manesseh the son of *J* . . . . . Num 32:33
prince of the children of *J* . . . . Num 34:23
families of the sons of *J* . . . . Num 36:1
The tribe of the sons of *J* . . . . . Num 36:5
of Manesseh the son of *J* . . . . . Num 36:12
Issachar, and *J*, and . . . . Deut 27:12
of *J* he said, Blessed . . . . Deut 33:13
come upon the head of *J* . . . . . Deut 33:16
the children of *J* were two . . . . Josh 14:4
the children of *J* fell from . . . . . Josh 16:1
So the chldren of *J* . . . . Josh 16:4
he was the first-born of *J* . . . . . Josh 17:1
of Manasseh the son of *J* . . . . . Josh 17:2
children of *J* spake unto . . . . . . Josh 17:14
the children of *J* said . . . . Josh 17:16
unto the house of *J* . . . . Josh 17:17
the house of *J* shall abide . . . . . Josh 18:5
and the children of *J* . . . . Josh 18:11
of the children of *J* . . . . Josh 24:32
the house of *J*, they also . . . . . . Judg 1:22
house of *J* sent to descry . . . . . . Judg 1:23
hand of the house of *J* . . . . Judg 1:35
of all the house of *J* 2Sam 19:20
charge of the house of *J* 1Kin 11:28
Dan, *J*, and Benjamin 1Chr 2:2
given unto the sons of *J* 1Chr 5:1
the birthright was *J* 1Chr 5:2
dwelt the children of *J* 1Chr 7:29
the sons of Jacob and *J* . . . . Ps 77:15
the tabernacle of *J* . . . . Ps 78:67
thou that leadest *J* like a . . . . . Ps 80:1
he ordained in *J* for a . . . . Ps 81:5
man before them, even *J* . . . . . Ps 105:17
For *J*, the stick of . . . . Ezek 37:16
I will take the stick of *J* . . . . . . Ezek 37:19
Israel: *J* shall have two . . . . Ezek 47:13
one gate of *J*, one gate . . . . Ezek 48:32
like fire in the house of *J* . . . . . Amos 5:6
unto the remnant of *J* . . . . Amos 5:15
for the affliction of *J* . . . . Amos 6:6
the house of *J* a flame . . . . Obad 18
I will save the house of *J* . . . . . Zech 10:6
the tribe of *J* were sealed . . . . . Rev 7:8

JOSES (jō'sēz)—*"helped"—one of Jesus' brothers*

James, and *J*, and Simon . . . . . Matt 13:55
the mother of James and *J* . . . . Matt 27:56
brother of James and *J* . . . . Mark 6:3
James the less and of *J* . . . . Mark 15:40
Mary the mother of *J* . . . . Mark 15:47

JOSHAH (jō'shä)—*"Jehovah is a gift"*

Simeonite leader 1Chr 4:34, 38

JOSHAPHAT (jŏsh'ä-făt)—*"Jehovah judges"*

1. Mighty man of David . . . 1Chr 11:43
2. Priestly trumpeter 1Chr 15:24

JOSHAVIAH (jŏsh-ä-vī'ä)—*"Jehovah is equality"*

One of David's mighty men 1Chr 11:46

JOSHBEKASHAH (jŏsh-bĕ-kā'shä)—*"seated in hardness"*

Head of musical order . . . 1Chr 25:4, 24

JOSHUA, JESHUA, JESHUAH (jŏsh'ū-ä, jĕ-shū'ä, jĕ-shū'ä)—*"Jehovah is salvation"*

1. Native of Beth-shemesh. . 1Sam 6:14, 18
2. Governor of Jerusalem during Josiah's reign . . 2Kin 23:8
3. High priest during Zerubbabel's time . . . . . Hag 1:1, 12, 14
   Called Jeshua in Ezra and Nehemiah . . . . Ezra 2:2
   Type of Christ . . . . Zech 6:11-13
4. Son of Nun . . . . Num 13:8, 16
   See separate entry

to *J* the son of Josedech . . . . . . Hag 2:2
O *J*, son of Josedech . . . . Hag 2:4
he showed me *J* the high . . . . . Zech 3:1
J was clothed with filthy . . . . . . Zech 3:3
the Lord protested unto *J* . . . . . Zech 3:6
Hear now, O *J* the high . . . . . . Zech 3:8
that I have laid before *J* . . . . . . Zech 3:9

JOSHUA, JEHOSHUA (jŏsh'ū-ä, jĕ-hŏsh'ū-ä)—*"Jehovah saves"—the successor to Moses and the leader who led Israel's conquest of the Promised Land*

Life of:

Son of Nun; an Ephraimite . . . . Num 13:8, 16
Defeats Amalek . . . . Ex 17:8-16
Minister under Moses . . . . Ex 24:13
One of the spies . . . . Num 13:1-3, 8, 16
Reports favorably . . . . Num 14:6-10
Moses' successor . . . . Num 27:18-23
Inspired by God . . . . Num 27:18
Unifies the people . . . . . . Josh 1:10-18
Sends spies out . . . . Josh 2:1-24
Crosses Jordan . . . . Josh 3:1-17
Destroys Jericho . . . . Josh 6:1-27
Conquers Canaan . . . . Josh 10—12
Divides the land . . . . Josh 13—19
Orders Israel's leaders . . . Josh 23:1-16
Final address to the nation . . . . Josh 24:1-28
Dies at 110 . . . . Josh 24:29, 30
Called:
  Oshea . . . . Num 13:8, 16
  Hoshea . . . . Deut 32:44
  Jehoshuah 1Chr 7:27
  Jeshua . . . . Neh 8:17

Character of:

Courageous . . . . Num 14:6-10
Emotional . . . . Josh 7:6-10
Wise military man . . . . . . Josh 8:3-29
Easily beguiled . . . . Josh 9:3-27
Prophetic . . . . Josh 6:26, 27
Strong religious leader . . . Judg 2:7

when *J* heard the noise . . . . Ex 32:17
but his servant *J*, the son of . . . Ex 33:11
J the son of Nun . . . . Num 11:28
Jephunneh, and *J* the son . . . . . Num 14:30
J the son of Nun, and . . . . Num 14:38
Jephunneh, and *J* the son . . . . . Num 26:65
he took *J*, and set him . . . . Num 27:22
the Kenezite, and *J* the son . . . Num 32:12
J the son of Nun, and the . . . . . Num 32:28
and *J* the son of Nun . . . . Num 34:17
J the son of Nun, which . . . . . . Deut 1:38
I commanded *J* . . . . Deut 3:21
charge *J*, and encourage . . . . . . Deut 3:28
and *J*, he shall go over . . . . Deut 31:3
Moses called unto *J*, and . . . . . . Deut 31:7
call *J*, and present . . . . Deut 31:14
Moses and *J* went, and . . . . Deut 31:14
he gave *J* the son of Nun a . . . Deut 31:28
J the son of Nun was full . . . . . Deut 34:9
Lord spake unto *J* the son . . . . Josh 1:1
And *J* the son of Nun sent . . . . Josh 2:1
J rose early in the . . . . Josh 3:1
the Lord spake unto *J*, saying . Josh 4:1
J called the twelve men . . . . Josh 4:4
J said unto them, Pass over . . . Josh 4:5
did so as *J* commanded . . . . Josh 4:8
as the Lord spake unto *J* . . . . . Josh 4:8
J set up twelve stones . . . . Josh 4:9
Lord commanded *J* to . . . . Josh 4:10
that Moses commanded *J* . . . . . Josh 4:10
the Lord magnified *J* . . . . Josh 4:14
the Lord spake unto *J* . . . . Josh 4:15
J therefore commanded the . . . Josh 4:17
did *J* pitch in Gilgal . . . . Josh 4:20
the Lord said unto *J* . . . . Josh 5:2
J made him sharp knives . . . . . . Josh 5:3
why *J* did circumcise . . . . Josh 5:4
them *J* circumcised . . . . Josh 5:7
Lord said unto *J*, This day . . . . Josh 5:9
when *J* was by Jericho . . . . Josh 5:13
J went unto him, and said . . . . Josh 5:13
J fell on his face to the . . . . Josh 5:14
the Lord's host said unto *J* . . . . Josh 5:15
And *J* did so . . . . Josh 5:15
Lord said unto *J*, See . . . . Josh 6:2
J sent men from Jericho . . . . . . Josh 7:2
they returned to *J*, and . . . . Josh 7:3
So *J* rose up early in the . . . . . . Josh 7:16
J said unto Achan, My son . . . . Josh 7:19
Achan answered *J*, and said . . . Josh 7:20
So *J* sent messengers, and . . . . . Josh 7:22
brought them unto *J*, and . . . . . Josh 7:23
J, and all Israel with him . . . . . Josh 7:24
J said, Why hast thou . . . . Josh 7:25
Lord said unto *J*, Fear not . . . . Josh 8:1
J burnt Ai, and made it . . . . Josh 8:28
J commanded that they . . . . Josh 8:29
J built an altar unto the . . . . Josh 8:30
J read not before all the . . . . . . Josh 8:35
to fight with *J* and with . . . . Josh 9:2
how *J* had taken Ai . . . . Josh 10:1
Lord said unto *J*, Be not . . . . . . Josh 11:6
of the country which *J* . . . . Josh 12:7
J gave unto the tribes . . . . Josh 12:7
J was old and stricken . . . . Josh 13:1
The Lord also spake unto *J* . . . Josh 20:1
unto *J* the son of Nun . . . . Josh 21:1
J called the Reubenites . . . . Josh 22:1
J blessed them, and sent . . . . . . Josh 22:6
the other half..gave *J* . . . . Josh 22:7
when *J* sent them away . . . . Josh 22:7
the Lord all the days of *J* . . . . . Josh 24:31
elders that overlived *J* . . . . Josh 24:31
after the death of *J* it came . . . Judg 1:1
when *J* had let the people . . . . . Judg 2:6
J the son of Nun, the . . . . Judg 2:8
nations which *J* left when . . . . . Judg 2:21
he them in the hand of *J* . . . . . Judg 2:23
he spake by *J* the son of 1Kin 16:34

JOSHUA, THE BOOK OF—*a book of the Old Testament*

Entering promised land . . Josh 1:1—5:12
The divine captain . . . . Josh 5:13—6:5
Capture of Jericho . . . . Josh 6:6-27
Capture of Ai . . . . Josh 8:1-29
Apportionment of the land . . . . Josh 13:1—22:34
Covenant at Shechem . . . . Josh 24:1-28
Death of Joshua . . . . Josh 24:29-33

JOSIAH, JOSIAS (jō-sī'ä, jō-sī'äs)—*"Jehovah supports"*

1. Son and successor of Amon, king of Judah . 2Kin 21:25, 26

J

Crowned at 8; reigns righteously 31 years ...2Kin 22:1
Named before birth 1Kin 13:1, 2
Repairs the Temple 2Kin 22:3-9
Receives the Book of Law 2Kin 22:10-17
Saved from predicted doom 2Kin 22:18-20
Reads the Law 2Kin 23:1, 2
Makes a covenant 2Kin 23:3
Destroys idolatry........2Kin 23:4, 20, 24
Observes the Passover...2Kin 23:21-23
Exceptional king 2Kin 23:25
Slain in battle 2Chr 35:20-24
Lamented by Jeremiah ..2Chr 35:25-27
Commended by Jeremiah.Jer 22:15-18
Ancestor (Josias) of Christ................Matt 1:10, 11
2. Son of Zephaniah ....Zech 6:10

of the land made *J* his son 2Kin 21:24
as *J* turned himself, he........2Kin 23:16
J took away, and did to.......2Kin 23:19
the rest of the acts of *J* 2Kin 23:28
king *J* went against him.......2Kin 23:29
Jehoahaz the son of *J*.........2Kin 23:30
of *J* king in the room of *J* 2Kin 23:34
Amon his son, *J* his son 1Chr 3:14
the sons of *J* were 1Chr 3:15
of the land made *J* his son 2Chr 33:25
J was eight years old 2Chr 34:1
J took away all the 2Chr 34:33
J kept a passover unto the 2Chr 35:1
J gave to the people 2Chr 35:7
commandment of king *J* 2Chr 35:16
keep such a passover as *J* 2Chr 35:18
reign of *J* was this 2Chr 35:19
Jehoahaz the son of *J*.........2Chr 36:1
days of *J* the son of Amon ....Jer 1:2
Jehoiakim the son of *J*........Jer 1:3
Zedekiah the son of *J* ....Jer 1:3
unto me in the days of *J* ......Jer 3:6
of Jehoiakim the son of *J* .....Jer 25:1
year of *J* the son of Amon ....Jer 25:3
Jehoiakim the son of *J*........Jer 26:1
Jehoiakim the son of *J*........Jer 27:1
of Jehoiakim the son of *J* .....Jer 35:1
of Jehoiakim the son of *J* .....Jer 36:1
from the days of *J*, even ......Jer 36:2
of Jehoiakim the son of *J* .....Jer 36:9
Zedekiah the son of *J* ....Jer 37:1
Jehoiakim the son of *J*........Jer 45:1
Jehoiakim the son of *J*........Jer 46:2
days of *J* the son of Amon ....Zeph 1:1
of *J* the son of Zephaniah.....Zech 6:10

JOSIBIAH (jŏs-ĭ-bī'ä)—*"Jehovah causes to dwell"*
Simeonite 1Chr 4:35

JOSIPHIAH (jŏs-ĭ-fī'ä)—*"Jehovah abides"*
Father of a postexilic Jew.Ezra 8:10

JOT (jŏt)—*Greek iota (i); Hebrew yodh (y)*
Figurative of the smallest detail................Matt 5:18

JOTBAH (jŏt'bä)—*"goodness"*
City of Haruz, the father of Meshullemeth 2Kin 21:19

JOTBATH, JOTBATHAH (jŏt'băth, jŏt'bä-thä)—*"goodness"*
Israelite encampment ....Num 33:33
Called Jotbath ....Deut 10:7

Hor-hagidgad, and pitched in *J*.Num 33:33
removed from *J*, and ....Num 33:34

JOTHAM, JOATHAM (jō'thăm, jō-ā'thăm)—*"Jehovah is perfect"*
1. Gideon's youngest son...Judg 9:5
Escapes Abimelech's massacre ....Judg 9:5, 21
Utters a prophetic parable ....Judg 9:7-21
Sees his prophecy fulfilled ....Judg 9:22-57
2. Son and successor of Azariah (Uzziah), king of Judah 2Kin 15:5, 7
Reign of, partly good ...2Kin 15:32-38
Conquers Ammonites ...2Chr 27:5-9
Contemporary of Isaiah and Hosea ....Is 1:1
Ancestor (Joatham) of Christ...............Matt 1:9
3. Son of Jahdai 1Chr 2:47

year of *J* the son of Uzziah ...2Kin 15:30
Ahaz the son of *J* king 2Kin 16:1
Azariah his son, *J* his son 1Chr 3:12
J his son reigned in his 2Chr 26:23
J was twenty and five 2Chr 27:1
days of Ahaz the son of *J*.....Is 7:1
the days of *J*, Ahaz, and ......Mic 1:1

JOURNEY—*an extended trip*
Preparation for, by:
Prayer ....Rom 1:10
God's providence acknowledged ....James 4:13-17

[*also* JOURNEYED, JOURNEYING, JOURNEYINGS, JOURNEYS]
as they *j* from the east ....Gen 11:2
Abram *j*, going on still........Gen 12:9
he went on his *j* from the .....Gen 13:3
Lot *j* east; and they ....Gen 13:11
Abraham *j* from thence ....Gen 20:1
had made his *j* prosperous ....Gen 24:21
Jacob went on his *j*...........Gen 29:1
set three days *j* betwixt ....Gen 30:36
after him seven days *j* ....Gen 31:23
Let us take our *j*, and let .....Gen 33:12
Jacob *j* to Succoth ....Gen 33:17
they *j*; and the terror ....Gen 35:5
Israel took his *j* with all.......Gen 46:1
three days *j* into the ....Ex 3:18
three days *j* into the desert ....Ex 5:3
three days *j* into the ....Ex 8:27
children of Israel *j* from ....Ex 12:37
they took their *j* from.........Ex 13:20
they took their *j* from.........Ex 16:1
Israel *j* from the wilderness....Ex 17:1
after their *j*, according to .....Ex 17:1
went onward in all their *j* .....Ex 40:36
they *j* not till the day that.....Ex 40:37
or be in a *j* afar off..........Num 9:10
the children of Israel *j* ....Num 9:17
and for the *j* of the camps ....Num 10:2
side shall take their *j* ....Num 10:6
blow an alarm for their *j*......Num 10:6
j of the children of Israel .....Num 10:28
as it were a day's *j* on this ....Num 11:31
And the people *j* from ....Num 11:35
j not till Miriam was ....Num 12:15
whole congregation, *j* from ....Num 20:22
they *j* from mount Hor ....Num 21:4
are the *j* of the children of ....Num 33:1
went three days *j* in the ....Num 33:8
they *j* from Rissah, and ....Num 33:22
eleven days *j* from Horeb .....Deut 1:2
took our *j* into the ....Deut 2:1
of Israel took their *j* from .....Deut 10:6
they *j* unto Gudgodah ....Deut 10:7
victuals with you for the *j*.....Josh 9:11
the *j* that thou takest shall ....Judg 4:9
went a day's *j* into the 1Kin 19:4
a compass of seven days *j* 2Kin 3:9
Nor scrip for your *j*..........Matt 10:10
straightway took his *j* ....Matt 25:15
take nothing for their *j*.........Mark 6:8
is as a man taking a far *j* .....Mark 13:34
went a day's *j* ....Luke 2:44
take nothing for your *j*........Luke 9:3
a friend of mine in his *j*.......Luke 11:6
and *j* toward Jerusalem ....Luke 13:22
took his *j* into a far..........Luke 15:13
being wearied with his *j*.......John 4:6
a sabbath day's *j* ....Acts 1:12
the men which *j* with him .....Acts 9:7
as they went on their *j*.........Acts 10:9
as I made my *j*, and was ......Acts 22:6
them which *j* with me.........Acts 26:13
I take my *j* into Spain ....Rom 15:24
I trust to see you in my *j* .....Rom 15:24
in *j* often, in perils of 2Cor 11:26
bring forward on their *j* 3John 6

JOY—*great delight; gladness of heart*
Kinds of:
Foolish ....Prov 15:21
Temporary...............Matt 13:20
Motherly ....Ps 113:9
Figurative ....Is 52:9
Future..................Matt 25:21, 23
Described as:
Everlasting..............Is 51:11
Great ....Acts 8:8
Full 1John 1:4
Abundant................2Cor 8:2
Unspeakable 1Pet 1:8
Causes of:
Victory 1Sam 18:6
Christ's birth ....Luke 2:10, 11
Christ's resurrection .....Matt 28:7, 8
Sinner's repentance ......Luke 15:5, 10
Miracles among the Gentiles ....Acts 8:7, 8
Forgiveness ....Ps 51:8, 12
God's Word ....Jer 15:16
Spiritual discovery ....Matt 13:44
Names written in heaven .Luke 10:17, 20
True faith...............1Pet 1:8
Place of, in:
Prayer ....Is 56:7
Christian:
Fellowship ....Phil 1:25
Tribulation............2Cor 7:4-7
Giving 2Cor 8:2
Contrasted with:
Weeping ....Ezra 3:12, 13; Ps 30:5
Tears ....Ps 126:5
Sorrow ....Is 35:10
Mourning ....Jer 31:13
Pain ....John 16:20, 21
Loss....................Heb 13:17; Heb 10:34
Adversity ....Eccl 7:14
Discipline ....Ps 51:8; Heb 12:11
Persecution ....Luke 6:22, 23
Of angels:
At creation ....Job 38:4, 7
At Christ's birth.........Luke 2:10, 13, 14
At sinner's conversion ...Luke 15:10
Expressed by:
Songs ....Gen 31:27
Musical instruments......1Sam 18:6
Sounds 1Chr 15:16
Praises 2Chr 29:30
Shouting ....Ezra 3:12, 13
Heart 1Kin 21:7
See GLADNESS; HAPPINESS OF THE SAINTS

[*also* JOYED, JOYING, JOYOUS]
with tabrets, with *j* 1Sam 18:6
rejoiced with great *j* 1Kin 1:40
for there was *j* in Israel 1Chr 12:40
lifting up the voice with *j* 1Chr 15:16
also rejoiced with great *j*......1Chr 29:9
again to Jerusalem with *j*......2Chr 20:27
great *j* in Jerusalem..........2Chr 30:26
many shouted aloud for *j* .....Ezra 3:12
of this house of God with *j*....Ezra 6:16
the *j* of the Lord is your ......Neh 8:10
rejoice with great *j* ....Neh 12:43
that the *j* of Jerusalem ....Neh 12:43
and gladness, and *j* ....Esth 8:16
turned..sorrow to *j* ....Esth 9:22
days of feasting and *j* ....Esth 9:22
the *j* of the hypocrite ....Job 20:5
widow's heart to sing for *j* ....Job 29:13
shall see his face with *j* ....Job 33:26
sons of God shouted for *j*? ....Job 38:7

sorrow is turned into *j* ....Job 41:22
let them ever shout for *j* ......Ps 5:11
presence is fullness of *j* ....Ps 16:11
king shall *j* in thy strength ....Ps 21:1
tabernacle sacrifices of *j*.......Ps 27:6
j cometh in the morning ......Ps 30:5
shout for *j*, all ye that are .....Ps 32:11
Let them shout for *j* ....Ps 35:27
voice of *j* and praise ....Ps 42:4
God my exceeding *j* ....Ps 43:4
the *j* of the whole earth.......Ps 48:2
Make me to hear *j* and ....Ps 51:8
be glad and sing for *j*.........Ps 67:4
forth his people with *j* ....Ps 105:43
sow in tears shall reap in *j* ....Ps 126:5
let thy saints shout for *j*.......Ps 132:9
above my chief *j* ....Ps 137:6
counselors of peace is *j* ....Prov 12:20
intermeddle with his *j*.........Prov 14:10
Folly is *j* to him that is ....Prov 15:21
father of a fool hath no *j* .....Prov 17:21
It is *j* to the just to do ....Prov 21:15
a wise child shall have *j*.......Prov 23:24
not my heart from any *j* ......Eccl 2:10
in the *j* of his heart...........Eccl 5:20
eat thy bread with *j* ....Eccl 9:7
not increased the *j*...........Is 9:3
they *j* before thee ....Is 9:3
to the *j* in harvest ....Is 9:3
with *j* shall ye draw water .....Is 12:3
j out of the plentiful field .....Is 16:10
tumultuous city, a *j* city ....Is 22:2
j and gladness, slaying ....Is 22:13
Is this your *j* city, whose ......Is 23:7
the *j* of the harp ceaseth ......Is 24:8
also shall increase their *j* ......Is 29:19
houses of *j* in the *j* city ....Is 32:13
rejoice even with *j*............Is 35:2
songs and everlasting *j* ....Is 35:10
they shall obtain *j* and ....Is 35:10
j and gladness shall be ....Is 51:3
For ye shall go out with *j* .....Is 55:12
a *j* of many generations ....Is 60:15
the oil of *j* for mourning ......Is 61:3
servants shall sing for *j*........Is 65:14
he shall appear to your *j* ......Is 66:5
the *j* and rejoicing of mine ....Jer 15:16
turn their mourning into *j* .....Jer 31:13
shall be to me a name of *j* ....Jer 33:9
thou skippedst for *j* ....Jer 48:27
the city of my *j* ....Jer 49:25
The *j* of the whole earth? .....Lam 2:15
the *j* of their glory............Ezek 34:25
Rejoice not, O Israel, for *j*....Hos 9:1
j is withered away from ....Joel 1:12
I will *j* in the God of my......Hab 3:18
rejoice over thee with *j* ....Zeph 3:17
j over thee with singing ....Zeph 3:17
Judah *j* and gladness..........Zech 8:19
rejoiced..exceeding great *j*.....Matt 2:10
shalt have *j* and gladness ......Luke 1:14
babe leaped in my womb for *j* .Luke 1:44
good tidings of great *j* ....Luke 2:10
that day, and leap for *j* ....Luke 6:23
receive the word with *j* ....Luke 8:13
seventy returned..with *j* ....Luke 10:17
j..in heaven over one sinner ...Luke 15:7
they yet believed not for *j*.....Luke 24:41
my *j* therefore is fulfilled......John 3:29
that my *j*..remain in you ......John 15:11
that your *j* might be full ......John 15:11
sorrow shall be turned into *j* ..John 16:20
your *j* no man taketh from ....John 16:22
have my *j* fulfilled in ....John 17:13
shalt make me full of *j*........Acts 2:28
disciples were filled with *j*.....Acts 13:52
caused great *j* unto all the.....Acts 15:3
j in God through our Lord ....Rom 5:11
j in the Holy Ghost...........Rom 14:17
fill you with all *j* and peace ...Rom 15:13
may come unto you with *j* ....Rom 15:32
but are helpers of your *j* 2Cor 1:24
in you all, that my *j* is 2Cor 2:3
j we for the *j* of Titus.........2Cor 7:13
fruit of the Spirit is love, *j* ....Gal 5:22
making request with *j* ....Phil 1:4
Fulfill ye my *j*, that ye be .....Phil 2:2
longed for, my *j* and crown ...Phil 4:1
spirit, *j* and beholding ....Col 2:5
with *j* of the Holy Ghost 1Thess 1:6
what is our hope, or *j*, or 1Thess 2:19
For ye are our glory and *j* 1Thess 2:20
wherewith we *j* for your 1Thess 3:9
that I may be filled with *j*.....2Tim 1:4
we have great *j* and ....Philem 7
who for the *j*..set before ......Heb 12:2
that they may do it with *j* .....Heb 13:17
count it all *j* when ye fall .....James 1:2
and your *j* to heaviness ....James 4:9
rejoice with *j* unspeakable 1Pet 1:8
be glad also with exceeding *j* ..1Pet 4:13
face, that our *j* may be full 2John 12
I have no greater *j* than to 3John 4
his glory with exceeding *j* .....Jude 24

JOYFUL—*full of joy*

[*also* JOYFULLY, JOYFULNESS]
the Lord thy God with *j* ......Deut 28:47
my soul shall be *j* in the ......Ps 35:9
Make a *j* noise unto God ......Ps 66:1
make a *j* noise unto the God ..Ps 81:1
the people that know the *j* ....Ps 89:15
let us make a *j* noise to the ....Ps 95:1
Let the field be *j*, and all .....Ps 96:12
Make a *j* noise unto the.......Ps 98:4
make a *j* noise before the .....Ps 98:6
let the hills be *j* together ......Ps 98:8
Make a *j* noise unto the.......Ps 100:1
be a *j* mother of children .....Ps 113:9
children of Zion be *j* in their ..Ps 149:2
Let the saints be *j* in glory ....Ps 149:5
the day of prosperity be *j* .....Eccl 7:14
Live *j* with the wife whom ....Eccl 9:9
Sing, O heavens; and be *j*.....Is 49:13
j in my house of prayer ....Is 56:7
my soul shall be *j* in ....Is 61:10
down, and received him *j* .....Luke 19:6
I am exceeding *j* in all 2Cor 7:4
and long-suffering with *j* ......Col 1:11
took *j* the spoiling of your ....Heb 10:34

JOZABAD (jŏz'ä-băd)—*"Jehovah endows"*
1, 2, 3. Three of David's
mighty men 1Chr 12:4, 20
4. Levite overseer in
Hezekiah's reign 2Chr 31:13
5. Chief Levite in Josiah's
reign.................2Chr 35:9
6. Levite, son of Jeshua....Ezra 8:33
Probably the same as in .Ezra 10:23
7. Expounder of the Law ..Neh 8:7
8. Levitical chief ....Neh 11:16
Some consider 6, 7, 8
the same person
9. Priest who divorced his
foreign wife ....Ezra 10:22

JOZACHAR (jŏz'ä-kär)—*"Jehovah remembers"*
Assassin of Joash 2Kin 12:19-21
Called Zabad 2Chr 24:26

JOZADAK (jŏz'ä-dăk)—*"Jehovah is righteous"*
Postexilic priest ....Ezra 3:2

and Jeshua the son of *J* ....Ezra 5:2
sons of Jeshua the son of *J*....Ezra 10:18
son of Jeshua, the son of *J* ....Neh 12:26

JUBAL (jo͞o'băl)—*"playing; nomad"*
Son of Lamech ....Gen 4:21

JUBILEE, YEAR OF—*the year in which slaves were set free, property was returned to its original owner, debts were to be forgiven, and the land was allowed to rest, all of which were reminders of the refreshing the Lord provides His people*

Regulations concerning:
Introduced by trumpet ...Lev 25:9
After 49 years...........Lev 25:8
Rules for fixing prices ...Lev 25:15, 16, 25-28

Purposes of:
Restore liberty (to the enslaved) ....Lev 25:38-43
Restore property (to the original owner)........Lev 25:23-28
Remit debt (to the indebted) ....Lev 25:47-55
Restore rest (to the land).Lev 25:11, 12, 18-22

Figurative of:
Christ's mission ....Is 61:1-3
Earth's jubilee ....Rom 8:19-24

sold..unto the year of *j* ....Lev 25:50
his field from the year of *j* ....Lev 27:17

JUCAL (jo͞o'kăl)—*"Jehovah is able"*
J the son of Shelemiah........Jer 38:1
See JEHUCAL

JUDAEA—*See* JUDEA

JUDAH, JUDA (jo͞o'dä, jo͞o'dä)—*"praise"*
1. Son of Jacob and Leah ..Gen 29:15-35
Intercedes for Joseph....Gen 37:26, 27
Marries a Canaanite.....Gen 38:1-10
Fathers Perez and Zerah by Tamar ....Gen 38:11-30
Through Tamar, an ancestor of David .....Ruth 4:18-22
Ancestor of Christ ......Matt 1:3-16
Offers himself as Benjamin's ransom ....Gen 44:33, 34
Leads Jacob to Goshen..Gen 46:28
Jacob bestows birthright on ....Gen 49:3-10
Messiah promised through ....Gen 49:10
2. Judah, Tribe of:
See separate article
3. Postexilic Levite ....Ezra 3:9
4. Levite returning with
Zerubbabel...........Neh 12:8
5. Levite divorced his
foreign wife ....Ezra 10:23
6. Postexilic overseer ......Neh 11:9
7. Priest and musician .....Neh 12:36
Probably same as 4 and 5
8. Postexilic prince ....Neh 12:32-34
9. An ancestor of Jesus ....Luke 3:26

JUDAH (jo͞o'dä)—*"praise"—son of Jacob and Leah*
she called his name *J* ....Gen 29:35
And Er, *J* firstborn, was ......Gen 38:7
J said unto Israel.............Gen 43:8
J, thou art he whom..........Gen 49:8
this is the blessing of *J*........Deut 33:7

JUDAH, THE LAND OF
Israel that dwelt in..*J* 2Chr 10:17
wrath..Lord was upon *J* 2Chr 29:8
In *J* is God known ....Ps 76:1
Jerusalem is ruined, and *J* ....Is 3:8
word of..Lord, all ye of *J* .....Jer 7:2
concerning Israel and..*J* ......Jer 30:4
Beth-lehem, in the land of *J* ..Matt 2:6

JUDAH, TRIBE OF—*the Israelite tribe that descended from the patriarch Judah and from which Christ came*
Descendants of Judah....Gen 29:35
Prophecy concerning .....Gen 49:8-12
Five families of..........Num 26:19-22
Leads in wilderness journey...............Num 2:3, 9
Numbering of, at Sinai...Num 1:26, 27
Numbering of, in Moab ..Num 26:22
Leads in conquest of Canaan ....Judg 1:1-19
Territory assigned to .....Josh 15:1-63
Fights against Gibeah ....Judg 20:18
Makes David king 2Sam 2:1-11
Elders of, upbraided by David 2Sam 19:11, 15
Conflict with other tribes .2Sam 19:41-43

Loyal to David during
Sheba's rebellion 2Sam 20:1, 2
Loyal to Davidic house at
Jeroboam's rebellion ...1Kin 12:20
Becomes leader of southern
kingdom (Judah) 1Kin 14:21, 22
Taken to Babylon 2Kin 24:1-16
Returns after exile.......2Chr 36:20-23
Christ comes of ....Luke 3:23-33

[*also* JUDAH'S]
even of the tribe of *J*.........Num 1:27
Of the tribe of *J*, Caleb.......Num 34:19
tribe of *J* was taken ....Josh 7:16
tribe of the children of *J*......Josh 15:1
tribe of the children of *J*......Josh 15:20
children of *J* could not........Josh 15:63
thousand men of *J* went to ....Judg 15:11
king over the house of *J*......2Sam 2:4
J have anointed me king 2Sam 2:7
but the tribe of *J* only 1Kin 12:20
all the house of *J* and 1Kin 12:23
fathers, kings of *J*, had 2Kin 12:18
son of Ahaziah king of *J*.......2Kin 13:1
J was put to the worse........2Kin 14:12
Joash king of *J* lived..........2Kin 14:17
began to send against *J*.......2Kin 15:37
Also *J* kept not the...........2Kin 17:19
Chronicles of..Kings of *J*? 2Kin 20:20
for all *J*, concerning the 2Kin 22:13
horses that the kings of *J* 2Kin 23:11
will remove *J* also out..my 2Kin 23:27
J was carried away out of 2Kin 25:21
prince of the children of *J* 1Chr 2:10
of Solomon, king of *J* 2Chr 11:3
of Israel fled before *J*.........2Chr 13:16
And all *J* rejoiced at the 2Chr 15:15
the congregation of *J* and 2Chr 20:5
J that were at Jerusalem 2Chr 32:9
wrath upon him, and upon *J* ..2Chr 32:25
all *J* and the inhabitants 2Chr 32:33
children of *J* dwelt at ....Neh 11:25
half of the princes of *J*........Neh 12:32
chose the tribe of *J*...........Ps 78:68
and to the house of *J*.........Is 22:21
escaped of the house of *J* .....Is 37:31
house of *J* with the seed ......Jer 31:27
was in the king of *J* house ....Jer 32:2
those days shall *J* be saved ....Jer 33:16
left in the king of *J* house.....Jer 38:22
left a remnant of *J* ....Jer 40:11
took all the remnant of *J* .....Jer 43:5
sight of the men of *J* ....Jer 43:9
all the men of *J* that are ......Jer 44:27
sins of *J*, and they shall.......Jer 50:20
children of *J* were oppressed ..Jer 50:33
J was carried away captive ....Jer 52:27
J is gone into captivity........Lam 1:3
against the house of *J* ....Ezek 25:3
J is like unto all..heathen .....Ezek 25:8
were of the children of *J*......Dan 1:6
man of the captives of *J* ......Dan 2:25
princes of *J* were like ....Hos 5:10
house of *J* as rottenness ......Hos 5:12
hand of the children of *J*......Joel 3:8
against..children of *J* ....Joel 3:19
three transgressions of *J* ......Amos 2:4
over the children of *J*.........Obad 12
among the thousands of *J*.....Mic 5:2
remnant of the house of *J*.....Zeph 2:7
house of *J* joy and ....Zech 8:19
upon the house of *J* ....Zech 12:4
governors of *J* shall say ....Zech 12:5
shall the offering of *J*.........Mal 3:4
and with the house of *J*.......Heb 8:8
the Lion of the tribe of *J* .....Rev 5:5
Of the tribe of *J* were ....Rev 7:5

JUDAS (jōō'dăs)—*"praise"*
1. Judah, Jacob's son ......Matt 1:2, 3
See JUDAH
2. Judas Lebbaeus,
surnamed Thaddaeus ..Matt 10:3
One of Christ's apostles. .Luke 6:13, 16
Offers a question ....John 14:22
3. Betrayer of Christ.......Luke 6:13, 16
See ISCARIOT, JUDAS
4. Brother of Christ (see
Brethren of Christ) ...Matt 13:55
See JUDE
5. Leader of an insurrection.Acts 5:37
6. Jew of Damascus ....Acts 9:11
7. Judas Barsabbas, a chief
deputy ....Acts 15:22-32
Probably related to the
disciple Joseph........Acts 1:23

Jacob begat *J* and his ....Matt 1:2
J Iscariot, who..betrayed ......Matt 10:4
twelve, called *J* Iscariot ....Matt 26:14
J, which had betrayed ....Matt 27:3
J Iscariot, one of the twelve ...Mark 14:10
cometh *J*, one of the twelve ...Mark 14:43
J the brother of James........Luke 6:16
J Iscariot, which also was .....Luke 6:16
Satan into *J* surnamed ....Luke 22:3
and he that was called *J* ......Luke 22:47
He spake of *J* Iscariot the.....John 6:71
J Iscariot, Simon's son ....John 12:4
the heart of *J* Iscariot.........John 13:2
because *J* had the bag ....John 13:29
J also, which betrayed him ....John 18:2
J also, which betrayed him ....John 18:5
J the brother of James........Acts 1:13
J by transgression fell.........Acts 1:25
of *J* for one called Saul ....Acts 9:11
have sent..*J* and Silas ....Acts 15:27

JUDE, JUDAS (jōōd, (jōō'dăs)—*"praise"*
Brother of Christ ....Matt 13:55
Does not believe in
Christ ....John 7:5
Becomes Christ's disciple .Acts 1:14
Writes an Epistle ....Jude 1
See JUDAS

JUDE, THE EPISTLE OF—*a book of the New Testament*
Author ....Jude 1
Against false teachers ....Jude 3-5
Against the ungodly .....Jude 6-16
Exhortation ....Jude 17-23
Acts 9:31

JUDEA (jōō-dē'ä)—*"the praise of the Lord"*
District under a governor .Luke 3:1
All Palestine ....Luke 23:5
All the land of the Jews. .Acts 10:37
Rural people outside
Jerusalem.............Matt 4:25
Wilderness country near
Dead Sea ....Matt 3:1
Christ born in ....Matt 2:1, 5, 6
Hostile toward Christ ....John 7:1
Gospel preached in ......Acts 8:1, 4
Churches established in ..Acts 9:31

into the province of *J*.........Ezra 5:8
in Bethehem of *J*.............Matt 2:6
least among the princes of *J*...Matt 2:6
coasts of *J* beyond Jordan .....Matt 19:1
be in *J* flee into ....Matt 24:16
unto him all the land of *J* .....Mark 1:5
followed him, and from *J* .....Mark 3:7
into the coasts of *J* ....Mark 10:1
in *J* flee to the mountains .....Mark 13:14
Herod, the king of *J*..........Luke 1:5
out of..Nazareth, into *J* ....Luke 2:4
every town of Galilee, and *J* ..Luke 5:17
multitude..out of all *J* ....Luke 6:17
went forth throughout all *J*....Luke 7:17
are in *J* flee to the ....Luke 21:21
his disciples into..*J* ....John 3:22
He left *J*, and departed ....John 4:3
Depart hence, and go into *J*...John 7:3
disciples, Let us go into *J* .....John 11:7
in all *J*, and in Samaria ....Acts 1:8
in Mesopotamia, and in *J* .....Acts 2:9
brethren that were in *J* ....Acts 11:1
down from *J* to Caesarea .....Acts 12:19
men which came down from *J* .Acts 15:1
there came down from *J* ......Acts 21:10
all the coasts of *J* ....Acts 26:20
received letters out of *J*.......Acts 28:21
that do not believe in *J* ....Rom 15:31
on my way toward *J*..........2Cor 1:16
unto the churches of *J* ....Gal 1:22
which in *J* are in Christ 1Thess 2:14

JUDGE—*one authorized to hear and decide cases of law; to try, govern, rule; form an opinion*

History of, in scripture:
Family head ....Gen 38:24
Established by Moses ....Ex 18:13-26
Deut 1:9-17
Rules for ....Deut 16:18-20
Deut 17:2-13
Circuit..................1Sam 7:6, 15-17
King acts as............2Sam 15:2
1Kin 3:9, 28
Levites assigned 1Chr 23:1-4
Jehoshaphat established
court 2Chr 19:5-11
Restored after exile......Ezra 7:25

Procedure before:
Public trial.............Ex 18:13
Case presented ....Deut 1:16
Deut 25:1
Position of parties ....Zech 3:1
Accused heard ....John 7:51
Witness ....Deut 19:15-19
Priests ....Deut 17:8-13
Oath ....Ex 22:11
Heb 6:16
Casting of lots sometimes
used..................Prov 18:18
Divine will sought ....Lev 24:12-14

Office of:
Divinely instituted 2Sam 7:11
Limits to human affairs ..1Sam 2:25
Restricted by
righteousness..........Deut 16:18-20
Needful of great wisdom .1Kin 3:9
Easily corrupted ....Mic 7:3
Unjustly used ....Acts 23:3
Acts 25:9-11
Fulfilled perfectly in the
Messiah............. { Is 2:4; Is 11:3, 4; Acts 17:31 }

[*also* JUDGES]
J of all the earth ....Gen 18:25
a prince and a *j* over us?......Ex 2:14
shall bring him unto the *j* .....Ex 21:6
be brought unto the *j* ....Ex 22:8
shall come before the *j*.........Ex 22:9
whom the *j* shall condemn ....Ex 22:9
Moses said unto the *j* of ......Num 25:5
And I charged your *j* at.......Deut 1:16
the *j*..in those days ....Deut 17:9
before the priests and *j* ....Deut 19:17
elders and thy *j* shall ....Deut 21:2
that the *j* may judge them.....Deut 25:1
our enemies..being *j* ....Deut 32:31
their *j*, stood on this side .....Josh 8:33
for their *j*..their officers ....Josh 24:1
the Lord raised up *j* ....Judg 2:16
Lord raised them up *j* ....Judg 2:18
Lord was with the *j*, and ......Judg 2:18
all the days of the *j*...........Judg 2:18
the *j* was dead, that they......Judg 2:19
the days when the *j* ruled .....Ruth 1:1
Oh that I were made *j* in 2Sam 15:4
days of the *j* that judged 2Kin 23:22
to any of the *j* of Israel 1Chr 17:6
six thousand were..*j* 1Chr 23:4
to the *j*, and to..governor 2Chr 1:2
said to the *j*, Take heed.......2Chr 19:6
set magistrates and *j* ....Ezra 7:25
of every city, and the *j*........Ezra 10:14
make supplication to my *j*.....Job 9:15
covereth the faces of the *j*.....Job 9:24
I be delivered..from my *j* .....Job 23:7
to be punished by the *j* ....Job 31:11
ye *j* of the earth..............Ps 2:10

j of the widows, is God ....Ps 68:5
God is the *j*; he putteth ....Ps 75:7
thyself, thou *j* of the earth ....Ps 94:2
even all the *j* of the earth ....Prov 8:16
I will restore thy *j* ....Is 1:26
the *j*, and the prophet ....Is 3:2
the Lord is our *j*, the Lord ....Is 33:22
and the captains, the *j* ....Dan 3:2
and against our *j* that judge ....Dan 9:12
have devoured their *j* ....Hos 7:7
cut off the *j* from..midst ....Amos 2:3
shall smite the *j* of Israel ....Mic 5:1
her *j* are evening wolves ....Zeph 3:3
deliver thee to the *j* ....Matt 5:25
j deliver thee to ....Matt 5:25
they shall be your *j* ....Matt 12:27
shall they be your *j* ....Luke 11:19
a *j* or a divider over you? ....Luke 12:14
lest he hale thee to the *j* ....Luke 12:58
j deliver thee to ....Luke 12:58
There was in a city a *j* ....Luke 18:2
Hear what the unjust *j* ....Luke 18:6
thee a ruler and *j* over us? ....Acts 7:27
the *J* of quick and dead ....Acts 10:42
after that he gave..them *j* ....Acts 13:20
for I will be no *j* of such ....Acts 18:15
been of many years a *j* ....Acts 24:10
be *j* of these things before ....Acts 25:9
the Lord, the righteous *j* 2Tim 4:8
to God the *J* of all ....Heb 12:23
And are become *j* of evil ....James 2:4
a doer of the law, but a *j* ....James 4:11
j standeth before the door ....James 5:9

JUDGE—*to decide matters; discriminate*

[*also* JUDGED, JUDGEST, JUDGETH, JUDGING]

shall serve, will I *j* ....Gen 15:14
Rachel said, God hath *j* me ....Gen 30:6
they may *j* betwixt us ....Gen 31:37
Dan shall *j* his people ....Gen 49:16
Moses sat to *j* the people ....Ex 18:13
let them *j* the people at all ....Ex 18:22
they *j* the people ....Ex 18:26
shalt thou *j* thy neighbor ....Lev 19:15
the congregation shall *j* ....Num 35:24
j righteously between ....Deut 1:16
that the judge may *j* them ....Deut 25:1
Lord shall *j* his people ....Deut 32:36
he *j* Israel, and went out ....Judg 3:10
he *j* Israel twenty and ....Judg 10:2
And Jephthah *j* Israel six ....Judg 12:7
he *j* Israel seven years ....Judg 12:9
Elon, a Zebulonite *j* Israel ....Judg 12:11
and he *j* Israel ten years ....Judg 12:11
colts: and he *j* Israel ....Judg 12:14
he *j* Israel twenty years ....Judg 16:31
Lord shall *j* the ends of 1Sam 2:10
I will *j* his house for ever 1Sam 3:13
And he *j* Israel forty years 1Sam 4:18
Samuel *j* Israel all the 1Sam 7:15
there he *j* Israel 1Sam 7:17
make us a king to *j* us 1Sam 8:5
that our king may *j* us 1Sam 8:20
The Lord therefore be *j* 1Sam 24:15
time that I commanded *j* 2Sam 7:11
which the king had *j* 1Kin 3:28
throne where he might *j* 1Kin 7:7
and *j* thy servants 1Kin 8:32
j the people of the land 2Kin 15:5
days of the judges that *j* Israel 2Kin 23:22
he cometh to *j* the earth 1Chr 16:33
who can *j* this thy people 2Chr 1:10
and *j* thy servants 2Chr 6:23
God, wilt thou not *j* them? 2Chr 20:12
j the people of the land 2Chr 26:21
which may *j* all the people ....Ezra 7:25
he *j* those that are high ....Job 21:22
by them *j* he the people ....Job 36:31
Lord shall *j* the people ....Ps 7:8
j me, O Lord, according to ....Ps 7:8
God *j* the righteous, and ....Ps 7:11
satest in the throne *j* right ....Ps 9:4
shall *j* the world ....Ps 9:8
heathen be *j* in thy sight ....Ps 9:19
j the fatherless..oppressed ....Ps 10:18
J me, O Lord; for I have ....Ps 26:1
J me, O Lord my God ....Ps 35:24
nor condemn him when he is *j* ....Ps 37:33
J me, O God, and plead ....Ps 43:1
for God is *j* himself ....Ps 50:6
and be clear when thou *j* ....Ps 51:4
do ye *j* uprightly, O ye ....Ps 58:1
God that *j* in the earth ....Ps 58:11
thou shalt *j* the people ....Ps 67:4
j thy people with ....Ps 72:2
j the poor of the people ....Ps 72:4
he *j* among the gods ....Ps 82:1
Arise, O God, *j* the earth ....Ps 82:8
he shall *j* the people ....Ps 96:10
he cometh to *j* the earth ....Ps 96:13
j the world with ....Ps 96:13
he cometh to *j* the earth ....Ps 98:9
shall he *j* the world ....Ps 98:9
he shall be *j*..be condemned ....Ps 109:7
He shall *j* among the heathen. ....Ps 110:6
Lord will *j* his people, and ....Ps 135:14
all *j* of the earth ....Ps 148:11
The king that faithfully *j* ....Prov 29:14
thy mouth, *j* righteously ....Prov 31:9
God shall *j* the righteous ....Eccl 3:17
j the fatherless, plead for ....Is 1:17
standeth to *j* the people ....Is 3:13
j, I pray you, betwixt me ....Is 5:3
of David, *j*, and seeking ....Is 16:5
they *j* not the cause ....Jer 5:28
O Lord of hosts, that *j* ....Jer 11:20
He *j* the cause of the poor ....Jer 22:16
my wrong: *j* thou my cause ....Lam 3:59
will *j* thee according to ....Ezek 7:8
I will *j* you in the border ....Ezek 11:10
I will *j* thee, as women ....Ezek 16:38
wedlock and shed blood are *j*. ....Ezek 16:38
j them, son of man ....Ezek 20:4
I will *j* thee in the place ....Ezek 21:30
son of man, wilt thou *j* ....Ezek 22:2
wilt thou *j* the bloody city ....Ezek 22:2
Son of man, wilt thou *j* ....Ezek 23:36
shall they *j* thee ....Ezek 24:14
the wounded shall be *j* in ....Ezek 28:23
j between cattle and cattle ....Ezek 34:17
j between cattle and cattle ....Ezek 34:22
according to their doings I *j* ....Ezek 36:19
and against our judges that *j* us ....Dan 9:12
Zion to *j* the mount of Esau ....Obad 21
heads thereof *j* for reward ....Mic 3:11
thou shalt also *j* my house ....Zech 3:7
J not, that ye be not *j* ....Matt 7:1
with what *j* ye *j*, ye shall be *j*. ....Matt 7:2
j the twelve tribes of Israel ....Matt 19:28
J not, and ye shall not be *j* ....Luke 6:37
Thou hast rightly *j* ....Luke 7:43
thrones *j* the twelve tribes ....Luke 22:30
the Father *j* no man ....John 5:22
J not..the appearance ....John 7:24
but *j* righteous judgment ....John 7:24
Ye *j* after the flesh; I *j* no ....John 8:15
to say and to *j* of you ....John 8:26
believe not, I *j* him not ....John 12:47
I came not to *j* the world ....John 12:47
hath one that *j* him ....John 12:48
prince of this world is *j* ....John 16:11
j him according to..law ....John 18:31
more than unto God, *j* ye ....Acts 4:19
If ye have *j* me to be ....Acts 16:15
and there be *j* of these ....Acts 25:20
now I stand and am *j* for ....Acts 26:6
whosoever thou art that *j* ....Rom 2:1
wherein thou *j* another ....Rom 2:1
thou that *j* doest the same ....Rom 2:1
in the law shall be *j* ....Rom 2:12
if it fulfill the law, *j* thee ....Rom 2:27
how shall God *j* the world? ....Rom 3:6
am I also *j* as a sinner? ....Rom 3:7
which eateth not *j* him that ....Rom 14:3
Who art thou that *j* ....Rom 14:4
Let us not..*j* one another ....Rom 14:13
but *j* this rather, that no ....Rom 14:13
he that is spiritual *j* all 1Cor 2:15
he himself is *j* of no man 1Cor 2:15
that I should be *j* of you 1Cor 4:3
he that *j* me is the Lord 1Cor 4:4
in spirit, have *j* already 1Cor 5:3
to *j* them..that are without 1Cor 5:12
do not ye *j* them that are 1Cor 5:12
that are without God *j* 1Cor 5:13
saints shall *j* the world? 1Cor 6:2
If the world shall be *j* by 1Cor 6:2
unworthy to *j* the smallest 1Cor 6:2
we shall *j* angels? 1Cor 6:3
j who are least esteemed 1Cor 6:4
to *j* between his brethren? 1Cor 6:5
wise men; *j* ye what I say 1Cor 10:15
is my liberty *j* of another 1Cor 10:29
J in yourselves: is it comely 1Cor 11:13
we would *j* ourselves 1Cor 11:31
when we are *j*, we are 1Cor 11:32
three, and let the others *j* 1Cor 14:29
we thus *j*, that if one 2Cor 5:14
Let no man therefore *j* you ....Col 2:16
j the quick and the dead 2Tim 4:1
The Lord shall *j* his people ....Heb 10:30
she *j* him faithful who had ....Heb 11:11
and adulterers God will *j* ....Heb 13:4
that shall be *j* by the law ....James 2:12
and *j* his brother ....James 4:11
j the law: but if thou *j* ....James 4:11
who..thou that *j* another? ....James 4:12
j according to every man's 1Pet 1:17
j the quick and the dead 1Pet 4:5
they might be *j* according 1Pet 4:6
j and avenge our blood ....Rev 6:10
dead, that they should be *j* ....Rev 11:18
the Lord God who *j* her ....Rev 18:8
he hath *j* the great whore ....Rev 19:2
the dead were *j* out of ....Rev 20:12
they were *j* every man ....Rev 20:13

JUDGE, GOD AS

Manner of:

According to righteousness 1Pet 2:23
According to one's works 1Pet 1:17
Openly ....Rom 2:16
By Christ ....John 5:22, 30
In a final way ....Joel 3:12-14

JUDGES OF ISRAEL—*those leaders who ruled Israel prior to the monarchy*

Characteristics of era:

No central authority ....Judg 17:6; Judg 21:25
Spiritual decline ....Judg 2:18; Judg 18:1-31

List of:

Othniel ....Judg 3:9-11
Ehud ....Judg 3:15-30
Shamgar ....Judg 3:31
Deborah and Barak ....Judg 4:4-9
Gideon ....Judg 6:11-40
Abimelech ....Judg 9:1-54
Tola ....Judg 10:1-2
Jair ....Judg 10:3-5
Jephthah ....Judg 12:1-7
Ibzan ....Judg 12:8-10
Elon ....Judg 12:11, 12
Abdon ....Judg 12:13-15
Samson ....Judg 15:20
Eli 1Sam 4:15, 18
Samuel 1Sam 7:15
Samuel's sons 1Sam 8:1-3

JUDGES, THE BOOK OF—*a book of the Old Testament*

The death of Joshua ....Judg 2:6-10
Deborah and Barak ....Judg 4:1—5:31
Gideon ....Judg 6:1—8:32
Jephthah ....Judg 10:6—11:40
Samson ....Judg 13:1—16:31
Micah and the Danites ....Judg 18
The war against Benjamin ....Judg 19:1—21:25

JUDGMENT—*an authoritative opinion, decision, or sentence; justice*

[*also* JUDGMENTS]
Lord, to do justice and *j* ... Gen 18:19
out arm, and with great *j* ... Ex 6:6
Egypt I will execute *j* ... Ex 12:12
j which thou shalt set ... Ex 21:1
after many to wrest *j* ... Ex 23:2
make the breastplate of *j* ... Ex 28:15
put in the breastplate of *j* ... Ex 28:30
Aaron shall bear the *j* of ... Ex 28:30
Ye shall do my *j*, and keep ... Lev 18:4
keep my statutes and my *j* ... Lev 18:26
no unrighteousness in *j* ... Lev 19:15
statutes and all my *j* ... Lev 20:22
or if your soul abhor my *j* ... Lev 26:15
statutes and *j* and laws ... Lev 26:46
Israel a statute of *j* ... Num 27:11
the Lord executed *j* ... Num 33:4
before the congregation in *j* ... Num 35:12
commandments and the *j* ... Num 36:13
not respect persons in *j* ... Deut 1:17
for the *j* is God's ... Deut 1:17
statutes and unto the *j* ... Deut 4:1
statutes and *j* so righteous ... Deut 4:8
the statutes, and the *j* ... Deut 4:45
j which thou shalt teach ... Deut 5:31
j which the Lord our God ... Deut 6:20
if ye hearken to these *j* ... Deut 7:12
and his statutes, and his *j* ... Deut 11:1
These are the statutes and *j* ... Deut 12:1
judge..people with just *j* ... Deut 16:18
too hard for thee in *j* ... Deut 17:8
according to the *j* which ... Deut 17:11
they come unto *j* ... Deut 25:1
commandments, and his *j* ... Deut 26:17
all his ways are *j*: a God ... Deut 32:4
Lord and his *j* with Israel ... Deut 33:21
the congregation for *j* ... Josh 20:6
Israel came up to her for *j* ... Judg 4:5
took bribes..perverted *j* ... 1Sam 8:3
David executed *j* and justice ... 2Sam 8:15
came to the king for *j* ... 2Sam 15:6
all his *j* were before me ... 2Sam 22:23
his *j* and his testimonies ... 1Kin 2:3
understanding to discern *j* ... 1Kin 3:11
Israel heard of the *j* which ... 1Kin 3:28
wisdom of God..to do *j* ... 1Kin 3:28
j, which he commanded ... 1Kin 8:58
king, to do *j* and justice ... 1Kin 10:9
my statutes and my *j* ... 1Kin 11:33
Riblah; and they gave *j* ... 2Kin 25:6
and the *j* of his mouth ... 1Chr 16:12
executed *j* and justice ... 1Chr 18:14
to fulfill the statutes and *j* ... 1Chr 22:13
my statutes and my *j* ... 2Chr 7:17
king over them to do *j* ... 2Chr 9:8
who is with you in the *j* ... 2Chr 19:6
for the *j* of the Lord, and ... 2Chr 19:8
j, or pestilence, or famine ... 2Chr 20:9
executed *j* against Joash ... 2Chr 24:24
in Israel statutes and *j* ... Ezra 7:10
let *j* be executed speedily ... Ezra 7:26
nor the statutes, nor the *j* ... Neh 1:7
but sinned against thy *j* ... Neh 9:29
all that knew law and *j* ... Esth 1:13
Doth God pervert *j*? ... Job 8:3
we..come together in *j* ... Job 9:32
I cry aloud, but there is no *j* ... Job 19:7
he enter with thee into *j*? ... Job 22:4
my *j* was as a robe ... Job 29:14
Let us choose to us *j* ... Job 34:4
will the Almighty pervert *j* ... Job 34:12
yet *j* is before him ... Job 35:14
fulfill the *j* of the wicked ... Job 36:17
j and justice take hold ... Job 36:17
Wilt thou also disannul my *j*? ... Job 40:8
shall not stand in the *j* ... Ps 1:5
j that thou hast commanded ... Ps 7:6
prepared his throne for *j* ... Ps 9:7
by the *j* which he executeth ... Ps 9:16
thy *j* are far above out of ... Ps 10:5
the *j* of the Lord are true ... Ps 19:9
meek will he guide in *j* ... Ps 25:9
righteousness and *j* ... Ps 33:5
thy *j* are a great deep ... Ps 36:6
thy *j* as the noonday ... Ps 37:6
Lord loveth *j* ... Ps 37:28
be glad because of thy *j* ... Ps 48:11
didst cause *j* to be heard ... Ps 76:8
God arose to *j*, to save all ... Ps 76:9
Justice and *j* are the ... Ps 89:14
law and walk not in my *j* ... Ps 89:30
righteousness and *j* are ... Ps 97:2
rejoiced because of thy *j* ... Ps 97:8
strength also loveth *j* ... Ps 99:4
executest *j* and righteousness ... Ps 99:4
I will sing of mercy and *j* ... Ps 101:1
j for all that are oppressed ... Ps 103:6
and the *j* of his mouth ... Ps 105:5
Blessed are they that keep *j* ... Ps 106:3
Phinehas, and executed *j* ... Ps 106:30
hands are verity and *j* ... Ps 111:7
learned thy righteous *j* ... Ps 119:7
unto thy *j* at all times ... Ps 119:20
I fear; for thy *j* are good ... Ps 119:39
for I have hoped in thy *j* ... Ps 119:43
I remembered thy *j* of old ... Ps 119:52
Teach me good *j* ... Ps 119:66
that thy *j* are right ... Ps 119:75
I will keep thy righteous *j* ... Ps 119:106
Lord, and teach me thy *j* ... Ps 119:108
I am afraid of thy *j* ... Ps 119:120
I have done *j* and justice ... Ps 119:121
me according to thy *j* ... Ps 119:149
me according to thy *j* ... Ps 119:156
because of thy righteous *j* ... Ps 119:164
are set thrones of *j* ... Ps 122:5
enter not into *j* with thy ... Ps 143:2
executeth *j* for..oppressed ... Ps 146:7
his statutes and his *j* ... Ps 147:19
wisdom, justice, and *j* ... Prov 1:3
He keepeth the paths of *j* ... Prov 2:8
righteousness, and *j* ... Prov 2:9
is destroyed for want of *j* ... Prov 13:23
to pervert the ways of *j* ... Prov 17:23
witness scorneth *j* ... Prov 19:28
J are prepared for scorners ... Prov 19:29
To do justice and *j* ... Prov 21:3
It is joy to the just to do *j* ... Prov 21:15
Evil men understand not *j* ... Prov 28:5
every man's *j* cometh ... Prov 29:26
I saw..the place of *j* ... Eccl 3:16
discerneth both time and *j* ... Eccl 8:5
every purpose..time and *j* ... Eccl 8:6
God will bring thee into *j* ... Eccl 11:9
bring every work into *j* ... Eccl 12:14
seek *j*, relieve..oppressed ... Is 1:17
it was full of *j* ... Is 1:21
Zion..redeemed with *j* ... Is 1:27
The Lord will enter into *j* ... Is 3:14
by the spirit of *j* ... Is 4:4
and he looked for *j*, but ... Is 5:7
Lord..be exalted in *j* ... Is 5:16
to establish it with *j* ... Is 9:7
turn aside the needy from *j* ... Is 10:2
Take counsel, execute *j* ... Is 16:3
and seeking *j*, and hasting ... Is 16:5
Yea, in the way of thy *j* ... Is 26:8
j to him that sitteth in *j* ... Is 28:6
they stumble in *j* ... Is 28:7
the Lord is a God of *j* ... Is 30:18
j shall dwell..wilderness ... Is 32:16
people of my curse, to *j* ... Is 34:5
taught him..the path of *j* ... Is 40:14
my *j* is passed over ... Is 40:27
bring..*j* to the Gentiles ... Is 42:1
he shall bring forth *j* ... Is 42:3
my *j* is with the Lord ... Is 49:4
from prison and from *j* ... Is 53:8
Keep ye *j*, and do justice ... Is 56:1
Therefore is *j* far from us ... Is 59:9
j is turned away backward ... Ps 59:14
I the Lord love *j*, I hate ... Is 61:8
I will utter my *j* against ... Jer 1:16
in truth, in *j*, and in ... Jer 4:2
nor the *j* of their God ... Jer 5:4
if ye thoroughly execute *j* ... Jer 7:5
j, and righteousness, in the ... Jer 9:24
Execute *j* in the morning ... Jer 21:12
drink and do *j* and justice ... Jer 22:15
execute *j* and righteousness ... Jer 33:15
j is come upon the plain ... Jer 48:21
whose *j* was not to drink ... Jer 49:12
j upon the graven images ... Jer 51:47
where he gave *j* upon him ... Jer 52:9
she hath changed my *j* into ... Ezek 5:6
for they have refused my *j* ... Ezek 5:6
neither have kept my *j* ... Ezek 5:7
done according to the *j* of ... Ezek 5:7
will execute *j* in the midst ... Ezek 5:8
I will execute *j* in thee ... Ezek 5:10
I shall execute *j* in thee ... Ezek 5:15
will execute *j* among you ... Ezek 11:9
sore *j* upon Jerusalem ... Ezek 14:21
executed true *j* between man ... Ezek 18:8
my statutes..kept my *j* ... Ezek 18:9
and showed them my *j* ... Ezek 20:11
they despised my *j*, and ... Ezek 20:16
my statutes and keep my *j* ... Ezek 20:19
had not executed my *j* ... Ezek 20:24
I will set *j* before them ... Ezek 23:24
judge..according to their *j* ... Ezek 23:24
I shall have executed *j* in her ... Ezek 28:22
in Zoan, and will execute *j* ... Ezek 30:14
ye shall keep my *j*, and do ... Ezek 36:27
heathen shall see my *j* ... Ezek 39:21
judge it according to my *j* ... Ezek 44:24
and execute *j* and justice ... Ezek 45:9
are truth, and his ways *j* ... Dan 4:37
j was given to the saints ... Dan 7:22
precepts and from thy *j* ... Dan 9:5
j, and in loving-kindness ... Hos 2:19
oppressed and broken in *j* ... Hos 5:11
thy *j* are as the light that ... Hos 6:5
keep mercy and *j*, and ... Hos 12:6
Ye..turn *j* to wormwood ... Amos 5:7
let *j* run down as waters ... Amos 5:24
Is it not for you to know *j*? ... Mic 3:1
that abhor *j*, and pervert ... Mic 3:9
and *j* doth never go forth ... Hab 1:4
j and their dignity shall ... Hab 1:7
which have wrought his *j* ... Zeph 2:3
Lord hath taken..thy *j* ... Zeph 3:15
Execute..*j* and show mercy ... Zech 7:9
Where is the God of *j*? ... Mal 2:17
with the statutes and *j* ... Mal 4:4
shall be in danger of the *j* ... Matt 5:21
Gomorrha in the day of *j* ... Matt 10:15
of Sodom in the day of *j* ... Matt 11:24
show *j* to the Gentiles ... Matt 12:18
till he send forth *j* ... Matt 12:20
give account..in the day of *j* ... Matt 12:36
Nineveh shall rise in *j* ... Matt 12:41
j, mercy, and faith ... Matt 23:23
Gomorrah in the day of *j* ... Mark 6:11
for Tyre and Sidon at the *j* ... Luke 10:14
of Nineveh..rise up in the *j* ... Luke 11:32
hath committed all *j* unto ... John 5:22
I judge; and my *j* is just ... John 5:30
but judge righteous *j* ... John 7:24
if I judge, my *j* is true ... John 8:16
For *j* I am come..world ... John 9:39
Now is the *j* of this world ... John 12:31
righteousness, and of *j* ... John 16:8
Of *j*, because the prince of ... John 16:11
Caiaphas unto the hall of *j* ... John 18:28
went not into the *j* hall ... John 18:28
went again into the *j* hall ... John 19:9
and sat down in the *j* seat ... John 19:13
his *j* was taken away ... Acts 8:33
drove them from the *j* seat ... Acts 18:16
beat him before the *j* seat ... Acts 18:17
be kept in Herod's *j* hall ... Acts 23:35
temperance, and *j* to come ... Acts 24:25
I stand at Caesar's *j* seat ... Acts 25:10
morrow I sat on the *j* seat ... Acts 25:17
the *j* of God is..truth ... Rom 2:2
shalt escape the *j* of God? ... Rom 2:3
j was..to condemnation ... Rom 5:16
by the offense of one *j* ... Rom 5:18
how unsearchable are his *j* ... Rom 11:33
same mind and in the same *j* ... 1Cor 1:10
ye have *j* of things ... 1Cor 6:4

yet I give my *j*, as one 1Cor 7:25
if she so abide, after my *j* 1Cor 7:40
troubleth you shall bear his *j* .. Gal 5:10
the righteous *j* of God 2Thess 1:5
going before to *j* 1Tim 5:24
the dead, and of eternal *j* ..... Heb 6:2
for of *j* and .... Heb 10:27
draw you before the *j* seats? ... James 2:6
For he shall have *j* without .... James 2:13
mercy rejoiceth against *j* ...... James 2:13
time is come that *j* must 1Pet 4:17
j now of a long time 2Pet 2:3
reserve the unjust unto..*j* 2Pet 2:9
boldness in the day of *j* 1John 4:17
unto the *j* of the great day .... Jude 6
To execute *j* upon all, and .... Jude 15
the hour of his *j* is come ...... Rev 14:7
for thy *j* are made manifest ... Rev 15:4
true and righteous are thy *j* ... Rev 16:7
the *j* of the great whore .... Rev 17:1
in one hour is thy *j* come ..... Rev 18:10
true and righteous are his *j* .... Rev 19:2
j was given unto them .... Rev 20:4

JUDGMENT, DIVINE—*God's judgment on man's activities*

Design of:
Punish evil .... Ex 20:5
Chasten 2Sam 7:14, 15
Manifest God's righteousness .... Ex 9:14-16
Correct .... Hab 1:12
Warn others .... Luke 13:3, 5

Causes of:
Disobedience 2Chr 7:19-22
Rejecting God's warnings . 2Chr 36:16, 17
Idolatry .... Jer 7:30-34
Sins of rulers 2Chr 21:1-17
Loving evil .... Rom 1:18-32

Kinds of:
Physical destruction ...... Deut 28:15-68
Material loss .... Mal 3:11
Spiritual blindness .... Is 6:9, 10
Eternal destruction ...... Luke 12:16-21
Luke 16:19-31

Avoidance of, by:
Turning to God .... Deut 30:1-3
Turning from sin .... Jer 7:3-7
Humiliation .... Jon 1:1-17
Prayer 2Kin 19:14-36
2Chr 20:5-30

JUDGMENT HALL—*the palace of the ruler, in which public judgments were made*
Of Solomon 1Kin 7:1, 7
Pilate's .... John 18:28
Herod's .... Acts 23:35

JUDGMENT, HUMAN

Weaknesses of:
Often circumstantial ..... Josh 22:10-34
Sometimes wrong .... Gen 39:10-20
Hasty and revengeful 1Sam 25:20-35
Full of conceit .... Esth 5:11-14
Prejudicial .... Luke 7:38-50

Rules regarding:
Begin with self-judgment . Matt 7:1-5
Become spiritually minded 1Cor 2:12-15
Abound in love .... Phil 1:9, 10
Await the final judgment . Rom 14:10

Basis of:
Circumstance .... Gen 39:10-20
Opinion .... Acts 28:22
Moral Law .... Rom 2:14-16
Conscience 1Cor 10:27-29
Nature 1Cor 11:13, 14
Apostolic authority 1Cor 5:3, 4
Law of Christ .... Gal 6:2-4
Divine illumination ...... Josh 7:10-15

JUDGMENT, THE LAST—*the judgment of all unbelievers of the ages*

Described as:
Day of wrath .... Rom 2:5
Day of judgment 2Pet 3:7
Judgment seat of Christ . Matt 25:31

Time of:
After death .... Heb 9:27
At Christ's return .... Matt 25:31
Appointed day .... Acts 17:31
After the world's destruction 2Pet 3:7-15

Grounds of:
One's works 1Cor 3:11-15
One's faith .... Matt 7:22, 23
Conscience .... Rom 2:12, 14-16
Law .... Rom 2:12
Gospel .... James 2:12
Christ's Word .... John 12:48
Book of Life .... Rev 20:12, 15

Results of:
Separation of righteous from the wicked .... Matt 13:36-43
Retribution for disobedience 2Thess 1:6-10
Crown of righteousness .. 2Tim 4:8

Attitudes toward:
Be prepared for 1Thess 5:1-9
Beware of deception ..... Matt 7:21-27
Warn the wicked concerning 2Cor 5:10, 11

JUDITH (jōō'dĭth)—*"Jewess"*
Hittite wife of Esau ..... Gen 26:34
Called Aholibamah ...... Gen 36:2

JUICE—*liquid derived from fruit*
of the *j* of my pomegranate ... Song 8:2

JULIA (jōōl'yă)—*"soft-haired"*
Christian woman at Rome Rom 16:15

JULIUS (jōōl'yŭs)—*"soft-haired"—the family name of the Caesars*
Roman centurion assigned to guard Paul .... Acts 27:1, 3
Disregards Paul's warning. Acts 27:11
Accepts Paul's warning... Acts 27:31
Saves Paul's life .... Acts 27:42-44

JUMPING—*bouncing; jolting*
and of the *j* chariots .... Nah 3:2

JUNIA (jōō'nĭ-ă)—*"youth"—a kinsman of Paul*
Jewish Christian at Rome. Rom 16:7

JUNIPER—*a shrub of the broom family*
Roots produce charcoal .. Ps 120:4
Leaves provide little shade 1Kin 19:4, 5
Roots eaten in desperation .... Job 30:3, 4

JUPITER (jōō'pĭ-ter)—*chief god of Roman mythology*
Barnabas called .... Acts 14:12
Then the priest of *J* .... Acts 14:13
image which fell down from *J*? . Acts 19:35

JURISDICTION—*territory over which one has authority*
belonged unto Herod's *j* ...... Luke 23:7

JUSHAB-HESED (jōō-shăb-hē'sĕd)—*"kindness is returned"*
Son of Zerubbabel 1Chr 3:20

JUST—*proper; right*

[*also* JUSTLY]
J balances, *j* weights, a *j* ...... Lev 19:36
judge..with *j* judgment .... Deut 16:18
a perfect and *j* weight .... Deut 25:15
ruleth over men must be *j* 2Sam 23:3
thou art *j* in all that is .... Neh 9:33
man be more *j* than God? ..... Job 4:17
j upright man is laughed ...... Job 12:4
in this thou art not *j* .... Job 33:12
establish the *j*: for the .... Ps 7:9
the habitation of the *j* .... Prov 3:33
teach a *j* man, and he will .... Prov 9:9
memory of the *j* is blessed .... Prov 10:7
mouth of the *j* bringeth .... Prov 10:31
a *j* weight is his delight .... Prov 11:1
But the *j* shall come out of .... Prov 12:13
sinner is laid up for the *j* ...... Prov 13:22
he that condemneth the *j* ..... Prov 17:15
in his own cause seemeth *j* .... Prov 18:17
It is joy to the *j* to do .... Prov 21:15
but the *j* seek his soul .... Prov 29:10
j man that perisheth in .... Eccl 7:15
there be *j* men, unto .... Eccl 8:14
way of the *j* is uprightness .... Is 26:7
dost weigh the path of the *j* ... Is 26:7
a *j* God and a Savior .... Is 45:21
shed the blood of the *j* .... Lam 4:13
if a man be *j*, and do that ...... Ezek 18:5
Ye shall have *j* balances ...... Ezek 45:10
and a *j* ephah and a *j* bath .... Ezek 45:10
the *j* shall walk in them .... Hos 14:9
they afflict the *j*, they take .... Amos 5:12
to do *j*, and to love mercy .... Mic 6:8
j shall live by his faith .... Hab 2:4
The *j* Lord is in the midst ..... Zeph 3:5
husband, being a *j* man .... Matt 1:19
rain on the *j* and..unjust ...... Matt 5:45
wicked from among the *j* ...... Matt 13:49
nothing to do with that *j* man . Matt 27:19
the blood of this *j* person ..... Matt 27:24
that he was a *j* man and ...... Mark 6:20
to the wisdom of the *j* .... Luke 1:17
at the resurrection of the *j* .... Luke 14:14
ninety and nine *j* persons ..... Luke 15:7
should feign themselves *j* ...... Luke 20:20
And we indeed *j*; for we ...... Luke 23:41
was a good man, and a *j* ...... Luke 23:50
my judgment is *j* .... John 5:30
the coming of the *J* One ...... Acts 7:52
will, and see that *J* One ...... Acts 22:14
The *j* shall live by faith .... Rom 1:17
law are *j* before God .... Rom 2:13
whose damnation is *j* .... Rom 3:8
commandment holy, and *j* ..... Rom 7:12
The *j* shall live by faith .... Gal 3:11
whatsoever things are *j* .... Phil 4:8
that which is *j* and equal ...... Col 4:1
how holily and *j* and 1Thess 2:10
good men, sober, *j*, holy ...... Titus 1:8
a *j* recompense of reward ..... Heb 2:2
condemned and killed the *j* .... James 5:6
for sins, the *j* for the unjust ... 1Pet 3:18
delivered *j* Lot, vexed 2Pet 2:7
j to forgive us our sins 1John 1:9
j and true are thy ways .... Rev 15:3

JUSTICE—*righteousness; administration of what is right*

Descriptive of:
Righteous man .... Gen 6:9
Upright Gentile .... Acts 10:22
God's nature .... Deut 32:4
Promised Messiah .... Zech 9:9
Christ .... Acts 3:14
Saved .... Heb 12:23

Produced by:
True wisdom .... Prov 8:15
Parental instruction ...... Gen 18:19
True faith .... Heb 10:38

See INJUSTICE

executed the *j* of the Lord .... Deut 33:21
David executed..*j* 2Sam 8:15
to do judgment and *j* 1Kin 10:9
executed judgment and *j* 1Chr 18:14
to do judgment and *j* 2Chr 9:8
doth the Almighty pervert *j* ... Job 8:3
judgment, and in plenty of *j* .. Job 37:23
do *j* to the afflicted .... Ps 82:3
J and judgment are the .... Ps 89:14
of wisdom, *j* and judgment .... Prov 1:3
and princes decree *j* .... Prov 8:15
To do *j* and judgment is ...... Prov 21:3
perverting of judgment and *j* .. Eccl 5:8
with judgment and with *j* ..... Is 9:7
ask of me the ordinances of *j* .. Is 58:2
neither doth *j* overtake us ..... Is 59:9
O habitation of *j*, and .... Jer 31:23
execute judgment and *j* .... Ezek 45:9

JUSTIFICATION—*God's accounting the guilty to be righteous and acceptable because of Christ's death*

Negatively considered, not by:
The Law ....Rom 3:20, 28
Men's righteousness .....Rom 10:1-5
Human works ....Rom 4:1-5
Faith mixed with works ..Acts 15:1-29
Gal 2:16
A dead faith ....James 2:14-26

Positively considered, by:
Grace ....Rom 5:17-21
Christ:
Blood ....Rom 5:9
Resurrection ....Rom 4:25
Righteousness ....Rom 10:4
Faith ....Rom 3:26, 27

Fruits of:
Forgiveness of sins ......Acts 13:38, 39
Peace ....Rom 5:1
Holiness ....Rom 6:22
Imputed righteousness ...2Cor 5:21
Outward righteousness ...Rom 8:4
Eternal life ....Titus 3:7

Evidence of:
Works (by faith) ....James 2:18
Wisdom ....James 3:17
Patience ....James 5:7, 8
Suffering................James 5:10, 11

See IMPUTATION

[*also* JUSTIFIED, JUSTIFIETH, JUSTIFY, JUSTIFYING]
I will not *j* the wicked ....Ex 23:7
they shall *j* the righteous ......Deut 25:1
and *j* the righteous, to give 1Kin 8:32
by *j* the righteous.............2Chr 6:23
I *j* myself, mine own..........Job 9:20
a man full of talk be *j*? ....Job 11:2
I know that I shall be *j* ....Job 13:18
can man be *j* with God? ......Job 25:4
he *j* himself rather than ....Job 32:2
speak, for I desire to *j* ....Job 33:32
be *j* when thou speakest ......Ps 51:4
shall no man living *j* ....Ps 143:2
He that *j* the wicked, and .....Prov 17:15
Which *j* the wicked for........Is 5:23
witnesses, that they..be *j* ......Is 43:9
shall all..Israel be *j* ....Is 45:25
He is near that *j* me; who .....Is 50:8
backsliding Israel hath *j* ....Jer 3:11
and hast *j* thy sisters in ....Ezek 16:51
wisdom is *j* of..children ....Matt 11:19
words thou shalt be *j* ....Matt 12:37
and the publicans, *j* God ......Luke 7:29
wisdom is *j*..her children ......Luke 7:35
he, willing to *j* himself ....Luke 10:29
went down to his house *j* .....Luke 18:14
that believe are *j* from all .....Acts 13:39
doers of the law shall be *j*.....Rom 2:13
be *j* in thy sayings ....Rom 3:4
shall no flesh be *j* in his.......Rom 3:20
Being *j* freely by his grace ....Rom 3:24
man is *j* by faith without ......Rom 3:28
j the circumcision by..........Rom 3:30
Abraham were *j* by works.....Rom 4:2
being *j* by faith, we have ......Rom 5:1
on him that *j* the ungodly .....Rom 4:5
was raised again for our *j* .....Rom 4:25
being *j* by faith, we have ......Rom 5:1
being now *j* by his blood ......Rom 5:9
of many offenses unto *j* ......Rom 5:16
he called, them he also *j* ......Rom 8:30
elect? It is God that *j*.........Rom 8:33
yet am I not hereby *j* 1Cor 4:4
j in the name of the Lord 1Cor 6:11
is not *j* by the works of ....Gal 2:16
j by the faith of Christ ....Gal 2:16
shall no flesh be *j* ....Gal 2:16
j the heathen through faith ....Gal 3:8
no man is *j* by the law in .....Gal 3:11
we might be *j* by faith ....Gal 3:24
whosoever of you are *j* by.....Gal 5:4
in the flesh, *j* in the Spirit.....1Tim 3:16
being *j* by his grace, we ....Titus 3:7
not Abraham our father *j* .....James 2:21
by works a man is *j* ....James 2:24
not Rahab..*j* by works ....James 2:25

JUSTIFIER—*one who makes right*
j of him which believeth in ....Rom 3:26

JUSTLE—*jostle*
they shall *j* one against........Nah 2:4

JUSTUS (jŭś-tŭs)—*"just"*
1. Surname of Joseph ......Acts 1:23
2. Man of Corinth; befriends Paul ....Acts 18:7
3. Converted Jew ....Col 4:11

JUTTAH (jŭt'ä)—*"turning away"*
Town of Judah ....Josh 15:55
Assigned to the priests ...Josh 21:13, 16

JUVENILE DELINQUENTS—*juveniles who violate the law or show antisocial behavior*

Examples of:
Eli's sons 1Sam 2:12-17
Samuel's sons 1Sam 8:1-5
Elisha's mockers.........2Kin 2:22-24

Safeguards against:
Praying mother..........1Sam 1:9-28
Strict discipline ....Prov 13:24
Early training ....Prov 22:6

K

KABZEEL (kăb'zĕ-ĕl)—*"the congregation of God"*
Town in southern Judah .Josh 15:21
Benaiah's home town 2Sam 23:20
Called Jekabzeel ....Neh 11:25

son of a valiant man of *K* 1Chr 11:22

KADESH (kā'dĕsh)—*"holy"*
Location of ....Num 27:14
Captured by Chedorlaomer ....Gen 14:5-7
Hagar flees near.........Gen 16:7, 14
Abraham dwells here ....Gen 20:1
Spies sent from..........Num 13:3, 26
Miriam buried here ......Num 20:1
Moses strikes rock there .Num 20:1-13
Request passage through Edom here ....Num 20:14-22
Figurative of God's power.Ps 29:8
Boundary in the new Israel................Ezek 47:19

See KADESH-BARNEA

the people abode in *K* ....Num 20:1
wilderness of Zin..is *K* ....Num 33:36
they removed from *K* ....Num 33:37
abode in *K* many days ....Deut 1:46
Red Sea, and came to *K* ......Judg 11:16
and Israel abode in *K* ....Judg 11:17

KADESH-BARNEA (kā-dĕsh-bär'nĕ-ä)—*"holy"*
Boundary of promised land.................Num 34:1-4
Extent of Joshua's military campaign .....Josh 10:41
Same as Kadesh ....Num 27:14
Same as Meribah-Kadesh .Deut 32:51

sent them from *K* to see ......Num 32:8
mount Seir unto *K*...........Deut 1:2
and we came to *K* ....Deut 1:19
in which we came from *K* .....Deut 2:14
Lord sent you from *K*.........Deut 9:23
me and thee in *K*............Josh 14:6
servant..sent me from *K* ......Josh 14:7
on the south side unto *K*......Josh 15:3

KADMIEL (kăd'mĭ-ĕl)—*"God the primeval; before God"*
1. Levite family head; returns from Babylon .Ezra 2:40
2. Takes part in rebuilding .Ezra 3:9
Participates in national repentance ....Neh 9:4, 5

children of Jeshua, of *K*.......Neh 7:43
the sons of Henadad, *K* ....Neh 10:9
Binnui, *K*, Shereblah ....Neh 12:8
Jeshua the son of *K* ....Neh 12:24

KADMONITES (kăd'mō-nīts)—*"easterners"*
Tribe whose land Abraham is to inherit ..Gen 15:18, 19

KALLAI (kăl'ā-ī)—*"Jehovah is light; swift"*
Postexilic priest ....Neh 12:1, 20

KANAH (kā'nä)—*"of reeds"*
1. Brook between Ephraim and Manasseh ....Josh 16:8
2. Border town of Asher ...Josh 19:28

descended unto the river *K* ....Josh 17:9

KAREAH (kä-rē'ä)—*"bald head"*
Johanan the son of *K* ....Jer 40:13
the son of *K* spake to ....Jer 40:15
Johanan the son of *K* ....Jer 40:16
Johanan the son of *K* ....Jer 41:11
Johanan the son of *K* ....Jer 41:14
and Johanan the son of *K* .....Jer 42:1
Johanan the son of *K* ....Jer 43:2
But Johanan the son of *K* .....Jer 43:5

See CAREAH

KARKA (kär'kä)—*"floor; deep ground"*
Place in southern Judah ..Josh 15:3

KARKOR (kär'kôr)—*"they rested; even or deep ground"*
Place in eastern Jordan ..Judg 8:10

KARNAIM (kär-nā'ĭm)—*a city in northern Transjordan; also translated "horns"*
Conquered ....Amos 6:13

Rephaim in Ashteroth *K* ......Gen 14:5

KARTAH (kär'tä)—*"city"*
Levitical town in Zebulun.Josh 21:34

KARTAN (kär'tăn)—*"town; city"*
Town in Naphtali assigned to Levites ....Josh 21:32
Called Kirjathaim 1Chr 6:76

KATTATH (kăt'ăth)—*"small"*
Town of Zebulun........Josh 19:15, 16
Same as Kitron..........Judg 1:30

KEDAR (kē'der)—*"powerful; dark"*
Son of Ishmael ....Gen 25:12, 13
Skilled archers ....Is 21:17
Prophecy against ....Jer 49:28, 29
Inhabit villages ....Is 42:11
Famous for flocks ....Is 60:7
Tents of, called black ....Song 1:5
Type of barbarous people.Ps 120:5

Nebaioth; then *K* 1Chr 1:29
the glory of *K* shall fail ....Is 21:16
and send unto *K*, and ....Jer 2:10
all the princes of *K* ....Ezek 27:21

KEDEMAH (kĕd'ĕ-mä)—*"eastward"*
Ishmaelite tribe ....Gen 25:15

KEDEMOTH (kĕd'ĕ-mŏth)—*"antiquity; old age"*
City east of the Jordan assigned to the tribe of Reuben...............Josh 13:15, 18
Assigned to Merarite Levites ....Josh 21:34, 37
Messengers sent from ....Deut 2:26

KEDESH (kĕ'dĕsh)—*"holy"*
1. Town in southern Judah .Josh 15:23
2. City of Issachar assigned to Gershonite Levites .1Chr 6:72
Called Kishion..........Josh 19:20
3. Canaanite town taken by Joshua and assigned to Naphtali ....Josh 12:22
Called Kedesh in Galilee.Josh 20:7
Called Kedesh–naphtali ..Judg 4:6

City of refuge ... Josh 21:27,32
Home of Barak ... Judg 4:6
People of, carried captive 2Kin 15:29

The king of **K**, one ... Josh 12:22
And **K**, and Edrei, and ... Josh 19:37
appointed **K** in Galilee ... Josh 20:7
went with Barak to **K** ... Judg 4:9
Zebulun and Naphtali to **K** ... Judg 4:10
Zaanaim, which is by **K** ... Judg 4:11
K in Galilee with her ... 1Chr 6:76

KEDESH-NAPHTALI—*See* Kedesh

KEEP—*to hold or observe something firmly*

Christian objects of:
Christ's commandments ... John 14:15-23
God's commandments ... 1John 5:2
God's Word ... Rev 22:7, 9
Unity of the Spirit ... Eph 4:3
Faith ... 2Tim 4:7
Purity ... 1Tim 5:22
Oneself ... 1John 5:18
In God's love ... Jude 21

Manner of, by God's:
Power ... John 10:28,29
Name ... John 17:11,12

Promises respecting:
Provision ... Ps 121:3-8
Preservation ... John 17:11,12
Power ... Rev 2:26
Purity ... Rev 16:15

See Heart

[*also* keepest, keepeth, keeping, kept]

Eden to dress it and to **k** ... Gen 2:15
the ark, to **k** them alive ... Gen 6:19
to **k** seed alive upon the ... Gen 7:3
covenant which ye shall **k** ... Gen 17:10
k my charge, my ... Gen 26:5
will **k** thee in all places ... Gen 28:15
feed and **k** thy flock ... Gen 30:31
neither hath he **k** back ... Gen 39:9
them **k** food in the cities ... Gen 41:35
ye shall be **k** in prison ... Gen 42:16
Egyptians **k** in bondage ... Ex 6:5
Moses **k** the flock of ... Ex 8:1
ye shall **k** it a feast to the ... Ex 12:14
shall **k** it a feast by an ... Ex 12:14
Israel shall **k** it ... Ex 12:47
let him come near and **k** it ... Ex 12:48
k this ordinance ... Ex 13:10
to **k** my commandments ... Ex 16:28
k for your generations ... Ex 16:32
the Testimony, to be **k** ... Ex 16:34
and **k** my commandments ... Ex 20:6
he die not, but **k** his bed ... Ex 21:18
owner hath not **k** him in ... Ex 21:36
money or stuff to **k** ... Ex 22:7
or any beast, to **k** ... Ex 22:10
K thee far from a false ... Ex 23:7
k the feast of..bread ... Ex 23:15
my sabbaths ye shall **k** ... Ex 31:13
Israel shall **k** the sabbath ... Ex 31:16
K mercy for thousands ... Ex 34:7
was delivered him to **k** ... Lev 6:2
k the charge of the Lord ... Lev 8:35
Ye shall..**k** my statutes ... Lev 18:5
shall ye **k** mine ordinance ... Lev 18:30
Ye shall **k** my statutes ... Lev 19:19
ye shall **k** my statutes ... Lev 20:8
shall..**k** mine ordinance ... Lev 22:9
k a feast unto the Lord ... Lev 23:39
k a sabbath unto the Lord ... Lev 25:2
Ye shall **k** my sabbaths ... Lev 26:2
k..charge of the tabernacle ... Num 1:53
shall **k** all the instruments ... Num 3:8
k the charge of..sanctuary ... Num 3:28
husband, and be **k** close ... Num 5:13
Lord bless thee and **k** ... Num 6:24
Israel also **k** the passover ... Num 9:2
shall **k** it in his appointed ... Num 9:3
ceremonies..shall ye **k** it ... Num 9:3
not **k** the passover on that ... Num 9:6
wherefore are we **k** back ... Num 9:7
at even they shall **k** it ... Num 9:11
to **k** the passover ... Num 9:13
they **k** the charge of the ... Num 9:23
they shall **k** thy charge ... Num 18:3
k the charge of the ... Num 18:5
be **k** for the congregation ... Num 19:9
k a feast unto the Lord ... Num 29:12
k the charge of the ... Num 31:30
k the charge of the ... Num 31:47
k..to his own inheritance ... Num 36:9
k the commandments of ... Deut 4:2
K therefore and do them ... Deut 4:6
and **k** thy soul diligently ... Deut 4:9
learn them, and **k**, and do ... Deut 5:1
K the sabbath day to ... Deut 5:12
k all my commandments ... Deut 5:29
k the commandments ... Deut 6:17
k covenant and mercy ... Deut 7:9
k his commandments to a ... Deut 7:9
judgments, and **k**, and do ... Deut 7:12
k his commandments ... Deut 8:2
God, in not **k** his ... Deut 8:11
To **k** the commandments ... Deut 10:13
k all the commandments ... Deut 11:8
k his commandments ... Deut 13:4
k the passover unto ... Deut 16:1
shalt..**k** a solemn feast ... Deut 16:15
k all the words of this law ... Deut 17:19
k all these commandments ... Deut 19:9
k thee from every wicked ... Deut 23:9
of thy lips thou shalt **k** ... Deut 23:23
ways and to **k** his statutes ... Deut 26:17
K all the commandments ... Deut 27:1
to **k** his commandments ... Deut 28:45
k his commandments ... Deut 30:10
to **k** his commandments ... Deut 30:16
he **k** him as the apple of ... Deut 32:10
k the passover on the ... Josh 5:10
set men by it for to **k** ... Josh 10:18
have **k** all that Moses ... Josh 22:2
to **k** and to do all that is ... Josh 23:6
will **k** the way of the Lord ... Judg 2:22
king: who said, **K** ... Judg 3:19
shalt **k** fast by my young ... Ruth 2:21
she **k** fast by the maidens ... Ruth 2:23
will **k** the feet of his saints ... 1Sam 2:9
hath it been **k** for thee ... 1Sam 9:24
not **k** that which the Lord ... 1Sam 13:14
behold, he **k** the sheep ... 1Sam 16:11
have **k**..from women ... 1Sam 21:4
with them **k** the sheep ... 1Sam 25:16
vain have I **k** all that this ... 1Sam 25:21
k me back from hurting ... 1Sam 25:34
not **k** thy lord the king? ... 1Sam 26:15
one full line to **k** alive ... 2Sam 8:2
And the young man that **k** ... 2Sam 13:34
which he hath left to **k** ... 2Sam 16:21
had left to **k** the house ... 2Sam 20:3
k myself from mine iniquity ... 2Sam 22:24
k the charge of the Lord ... 1Kin 2:3
ways, to **k** his statutues ... 1Kin 2:3
hast thou not **k** the oath ... 1Kin 2:43
k all my commandments ... 1Kin 6:12
who **k** covenant and mercy ... 1Kin 8:23
k with thy servant David ... 1Kin 8:24
k his commandments ... 1Kin 8:58
k my statutes, and my ... 1Kin 9:4
not **k** my covenant ... 1Kin 11:11
to **k** my statutes and my ... 1Kin 11:33
not **k** the commandment ... 1Kin 13:21
k the door of the..house ... 1Kin 14:27
said, **K** this man ... 1Kin 20:39
Now Joram had **k** ... 2Kin 9:14
shall ye **k** the watch ... 2Kin 11:6
k my commandments ... 2Kin 17:13
k not the commandments ... 2Kin 17:19
K the passover unto the ... 2Kin 23:21
wouldest **k** me from evil ... 1Chr 4:10
word of..which he **k** not ... 1Chr 10:13
part of them had **k** ... 1Chr 12:29
men..that could **k** rank ... 1Chr 12:38
k the charge ... 1Chr 23:32
k this for ever ... 1Chr 29:18
k covenant, and showest ... 2Chr 6:14
k with thy servant David ... 2Chr 6:15
k with thy servant David ... 2Chr 6:16
k the dedication ... 2Chr 7:9
no power to **k**..kingdom ... 2Chr 22:9
to **k** under the children ... 2Chr 28:10
to **k** the passover ... 2Chr 30:2
to **k** the passover ... 2Chr 30:5
present at Jerusalem **k** the ... 2Chr 30:21
took counsel to **k** other ... 2Chr 30:23
Levites that **k** the doors ... 2Chr 34:9
and to **k** his commandments ... 2Chr 34:31
Josiah **k** a passover ... 2Chr 35:1
no passover like to that **k** ... 2Chr 35:18
kings..**k** such a passover ... 2Chr 35:18
Josiah was this passover **k** ... 2Chr 35:19
captivity **k** the passover ... Ezra 6:19
and **k** them, until ye ... Ezra 8:29
k covenant and mercy ... Neh 1:5
not **k** the commandments ... Neh 1:7
and **k** my commandments ... Neh 1:9
k covenant and mercy ... Neh 9:32
nor our fathers, **k** thy law ... Neh 9:34
porters **k** the ward ... Neh 12:25
the porters **k** the ward ... Neh 12:45
come and **k** the gates ... Neh 13:22
which **k** the concubines ... Esth 2:14
neither **k** they the king's ... Esth 3:8
would **k** these two days ... Esth 9:27
days..be remembered and **k** ... Esth 9:28
k me secret, until thy ... Job 14:13
his way have I **k**, and not ... Job 23:11
k silence at my counsel ... Job 29:21
He **k** back his soul ... Job 33:18
Thou shalt **k** them ... Ps 12:7
I have **k** me from the paths ... Ps 17:4
K me as the apple of the ... Ps 17:8
I **k** myself from mine ... Ps 18:23
k of them there is great ... Ps 19:11
K back thy servant also ... Ps 19:13
such as **k** his covenant ... Ps 25:10
shalt **k** them secretly in ... Ps 31:20
When I **k** silence, my bones ... Ps 32:3
K thy tongue from evil ... Ps 34:13
He **k** all his bones ... Ps 34:20
Lord, and **k** his way ... Ps 37:34
k him alive ... Ps 41:2
done, and I **k** silence ... Ps 50:21
k his commandments ... Ps 78:7
k not his testimonies ... Ps 78:56
My mercy will I **k** ... Ps 89:28
k thee in all thy ways ... Ps 91:11
To such as **k** his covenant ... Ps 103:18
they that **k** judgment ... Ps 106:3
k his testimonies ... Ps 119:2
k thy statutes ... Ps 119:5
live, and **k** thy word ... Ps 119:17
I have **k** thy testimonies ... Ps 119:22
and I shall **k** thy law ... Ps 119:34
I **k** thy precepts ... Ps 119:56
would **k** thy words ... Ps 119:57
them that **k** thy precepts ... Ps 119:63
I **k** the testimony ... Ps 119:88
that I might **k** thy word ... Ps 119:101
k the commandments ... Ps 119:115
so will I **k** thy precepts ... Ps 119:134
I will **k** thy statutes ... Ps 119:145
they **k** not thy word ... Ps 119:158
I have **k** thy precepts ... Ps 119:168
he that **k** thee ... Ps 121:3
he that **k** Israel ... Ps 121:4
the Lord **k** the city ... Ps 127:1
K me, O Lord ... Ps 140:4
k the door of my lips ... Ps 141:3
K me from the snares ... Ps 141:9
He **k** the paths of judgment ... Prov 2:8
understanding shall **k** ... Prov 2:11
k my commandments ... Prov 3:1
k thy foot from being taken ... Prov 3:26
k my commandments ... Prov 4:4
she shall **k** thee ... Prov 4:6
k them in..thine heart ... Prov 4:21
K thy heart ... Prov 4:23
thy lips may **k** knowledge ... Prov 5:2
sleepest, it shall **k** thee ... Prov 6:22
My son, **k** my words ... Prov 7:1
k thee from the strange ... Prov 7:5
they that **k** my ways ... Prov 8:32

He that *k* his mouth .... Prov 13:3
k him that is upright .... Prov 13:6
he that *k* understanding .... Prov 19:8
Whoso *k* his mouth and his ... Prov 21:23
he that doth *k* his soul .... Prov 22:5
he that *k* thy soul .... Prov 24:12
Whoso *k* the law .... Prov 28:7
wise man *k* it in .... Prov 29:11
he that *k* the law, happy ...... Prov 29:18
eyes desired I *k* not .... Eccl 2:10
time to *k*, and a time to ...... Eccl 3:6
K thy foot .... Eccl 5:1
Whoso *k* the commandment ... Eccl 8:5
k his commandments .... Eccl 12:13
vineyard have I not *k* .... Song 1:6
those that *k* the fruit .... Song 8:12
nation which *k* the truth ...... Is 26:2
k him in perfect peace .... Is 26:3
I the Lord do *k* it .... Is 27:3
I will *k* it night and day .... Is 27:3
a holy solemnity is *k* .... Is 30:29
hand, and will *k* thee .... Is 42:6
K not back .... Is 43:6
K ye judgment .... Is 56:1
of the Lord, *k* not silence ..... Is 62:6
will he *k* it to the end? .... Jer 3:5
and I will not *k* anger .... Jer 3:12
have not *k* my law .... Jer 16:11
k him, as a shepherd .... Jer 21:10
I will *k* nothing back .... Jer 42:4
k back his sword .... Jer 48:10
He sitteth..and *k* silence ...... Lam 3:28
k my judgments .... Ezek 5:7
k mine ordinances .... Ezek 11:20
by *k* of his covenant .... Ezek 17:14
hath *k* all my statutes .... Ezek 18:19
k my judgments .... Ezek 20:19
k the whole form .... Ezek 43:11
ye have not *k* the charge ...... Ezek 44:8
k my laws and my .... Ezek 44:24
which have *k* my charge ...... Ezek 48:11
whom he would he *k* alive .... Dan 5:19
k the covenant and mercy ..... Dan 9:4
k his commandments .... Dan 9:4
k mercy and judgment .... Hos 12:6
for a wife he *k* sheep .... Hos 12:12
he *k* his wrath for ever .... Amos 1:11
the prudent shall *k* silence ..... Amos 5:13
the statutes of Omri are *k* ..... Mic 6:16
k the doors of thy mouth ..... Mic 7:5
proud man, neither *k* at .... Hab 2:5
let all the earth *k* silence ..... Hab 2:20
if thou wilt *k* my charge .... Zech 3:7
also *k* my courts .... Zech 3:7
man taught me to *k* cattle ..... Zech 13:5
k the feast of tabernacles ...... Zech 14:18
lips should *k* knowledge .... Mal 2:7
ye have not *k* my ways .... Mal 2:9
we have *k* his ordinance ...... Mal 2:14
they that *k* them fled .... Matt 8:33
things..*k* secret .... Matt 13:35
Herod's birthday was *k* .... Matt 14:6
k the commandments .... Matt 19:17
I *k* from my youth up .... Matt 19:20
any thing *k* secret .... Mark 4:22
k your own tradition .... Mark 7:9
k watch over their flock .... Luke 2:8
Mary *k* all these things .... Luke 2:19
charge over thee, to *k* thee .... Luke 4:10
heard the word, *k* it .... Luke 8:15
was *k* bound with chains ...... Luke 8:29
man armed *k* his palace .... Luke 11:21
hear the word..and *k* it .... Luke 11:28
I *k* from my youth up .... Luke 18:21
k the good wine until now .... John 2:10
none of you *k* the law? .... John 7:19
If a man *k* my saying .... John 8:51
If a man *k* my saying .... John 8:52
k it unto life eternal .... John 12:25
k my commandments .... John 14:15
commandments, and *k* them ... John 14:21
he will *k* my words .... John 14:23
I have *k* my Father's .... John 15:10
If ye *k* my commandments .... John 15:10
they will *k* yours also .... John 15:20
they have *k* thy word .... John 17:6
I *k* them in thy name .... John 17:12
gavest me I have *k* .... John 17:12
k them from the evil .... John 17:15
the damsel that *k* the door .... John 18:17
k back part of the price .... Acts 5:2
k back part of the price .... Acts 5:3
which had *k* his bed .... Acts 9:33
soldiers to *k* him .... Acts 12:4
the door *k* the prison .... Acts 12:6
circumcised, and *k* the law .... Acts 15:24
the decrees for to *k* .... Acts 16:4
I must..*k* this feast .... Acts 18:21
how I *k* back nothing .... Acts 20:20
and *k* the law .... Acts 21:24
that they *k* themselves .... Acts 21:25
k the raiment of them .... Acts 22:20
a centurion to *k* Paul .... Acts 24:23
Paul should be *k* .... Acts 25:4
Paul, *k* them .... Acts 27:43
if thou *k* the law .... Rom 2:25
k secret since the world .... Rom 16:25
let us *k* the feast 1Cor 5:8
k of the commandments 1Cor 7:19
that he will *k* his virgin 1Cor 7:37
I *k* under my body 1Cor 9:27
k the ordinances 1Cor 11:2
women *k* silence 1Cor 14:34
k..from being burdensome 2Cor 11:9
so will I *k* myself 2Cor 11:9
we were *k* under the law ...... Gal 3:23
circumcised *k* the law .... Gal 6:13
k you from evil 2Thess 3:3
k this commandment 1Tim 6:14
k that which I have 2Tim 1:12
I have *k* the faith 2Tim 4:7
he *k* the passover .... Heb 11:28
to *k* himself unspotted .... James 1:27
shall *k* the whole law .... James 2:10
of you *k* back by fraud .... James 5:4
k by the power of God 1Pet 1:5
the *k* of their souls 1Pet 4:19
same word are *k* in store 2Pet 3:7
if we *k* his commandments 1John 2:3
k not his commandments 1John 2:4
k his commandments 1John 3:24
we *k* his commandments 1John 5:3
k not their first estate .... Jude 6
able to *k* you from falling ..... Jude 24
k those things..written .... Rev 1:3
k my works unto the end ..... Rev 2:26
hast *k* my word .... Rev 3:8
k the word of my patience .... Rev 3:10
k the commandments .... Rev 12:17
he that *k* the sayings of .... Rev 22:7

KEEPER—*one who watches over or guards*

Guardian of:

Sheep .... Gen 4:2
Brother .... Gen 4:9
Wardrobe 2Kin 22:14
Gate .... Neh 3:29
1Chr 9:21
Women .... Esth 2:3, 8
Prison .... Acts 16:27

[*also* KEEPERS]

sight of the *k* of the prison .... Gen 39:21
k of the prison looked not .... Gen 39:23
and left the sheep with a *k* 1Sam 17:20
make thee *k* of mine head 1Sam 28:2
even be *k* of the watch of 2Kin 11:5
the *k* of the door, to bring 2Kin 23:4
k of the gates of..tabernacle ... 1Chr 9:19
Hasrah, *k* of the wardrobe 2Chr 34:22
Asaph..*k* of the king's forest .. Neh 2:8
the *k* of the women .... Esth 2:15
the *k* of the door .... Esth 6:2
a booth that the *k* maketh .... Job 27:18
The Lord is thy *k*: the Lord ... Ps 121:5
the *k* of the house shall .... Eccl 12:3
made me *k* of the vineyards ... Song 1:6
k of the walls took away ...... Song 5:7
As *k* of a field, are they ...... Jer 4:17
Maaseiah..the *k* of the door ... Jer 35:4
the *k* of the charge of the ..... Ezek 40:45
ye have set *k* of my charge .... Ezek 44:8
for fear of him the *k* did ...... Matt 28:4
k standing without before ..... Acts 5:23
he examined the *k* .... Acts 12:19
the *k* of the prison told .... Acts 16:36
discreet, chaste, *k* at home .... Titus 2:5

KEHELATHAH (kē-hē-lā'thä)—*"a whole; a congregation"*

Israelite camp .... Num 33:22, 23

KEILAH (kĕ-ī'lä)—*"fortress"*

Town of Judah .... Josh 15:21, 44
Rescued from Philistines by David 1Sam 23:1-5
Betrays David 1Sam 23:6-12
David escapes from 1Sam 23:13
Reoccupied after the exile Neh 3:17

KELAIAH (kĕ-lā'yă)—*"Jehovah is light; swift for Jehovah"*

Levite who divorced foreign wife .... Ezra 10:18, 19, 23
See KELITA

father of *K* the Garmite 1Chr 4:19
ruler of the half part of *K* ..... Neh 5:18

KELITA (kĕl'ĭ-tä)—*"littleness"*

Levite who divorced foreign wife .... Ezra 10:23
Explains the Law .... Neh 8:7
Called Kelaiah .... Ezra 10:23

Hodijah, *K*, Pelaiah .... Neh 10:10

KEMUEL (kĕm'ū-ĕl)—*"God stands; God's mound"*

1. Son of Nahor; father of six sons .... Gen 22:20, 21
2. Ephraimite prince .... Num 34:24
3. Levite in David's time ... 1Chr 27:17

KENAN (kē'năn)—*"acquired"*

Descendant of Adam 1Chr 1:2
See CAINAN

KENATH (kē'năth)—*"possession"*

City of Gilead near Bozrah taken by Nobah Num 32:40, 42
Reconquered by Geshur and Aram 1Chr 2:23

KENAZ (kē'năz)—*"side; hunting"*

1. Descendant of Esau ..... Gen 36:10, 11
2. Edomite duke .... Gen 36:42
3. Caleb's brother; father of Othniel .... Josh 15:17
Family called Kenezites .. Num 32:12
4. Grandson of Caleb 1Chr 4:15

duke Zepho, duke *K* .... Gen 36:15
And Othniel the son of *K* ..... Judg 1:13
even Othniel the son of *K* ..... Judg 3:9
And Othniel the son of *K* ..... Judg 3:11
Zephi, and Gatam, *K* 1Chr 1:36
Duke *K*, duke Teman 1Chr 1:53
the sons of *K*; Othniel 1Chr 4:13

KENEZITE, KENIZZITE (kĕn'ĕ-zīt)

1. Canaanite tribe whose land is promised to Abraham's seed .... Gen 15:19
2. Title applied to Caleb ... Num 32:12
Probably related to Kenaz, the Edomite ... Gen 36:11-42

KENITE (kĕn'īt)—*"pertaining to coppersmiths"*

Canaanite tribe whose land is promised to Abraham's seed .... Gen 15:19
Subjects of Balaam's prophecy .... Num 24:20-22
Mix with Midianites ..... Num 10:29
Member of, becomes Israel's guide .... Num 10:29-32
Settle with Judahites ..... Judg 1:16
Heber separates from Kenites .... Judg 4:11
Heber's wife (Jael) slays Sisera .... Judg 4:17-22

Spared by Saul in war with Amalekites 1Sam 15:6
David shows friendship to. 1Sam 30:29
Recorded among Judahites; ancestors of Rechabites 1Chr 2:55

Jael the wife of Heber the ***K*** .. Judg 5:24
against the south of the ***K*** 1Sam 27:10

KENIZZITE—*See* KENEZITE

KEPT—*See* KEEP

KERCHIEF—*a covering for the head*
Worn by idolatrous women of Israel .... Ezek 13:18, 21

KEREN-HAPPUCH (kĕr-ĕn-hăp'ŭk)—*"horn of antimony"*
Daughter of Job .... Job 42:14

KERIOTH (kĕr'ĭ-ŏth)—*"the cities"*
1. Town in southern Judah . Josh 15:25
2. City of Moab .... Amos 2:2

upon ***K***, and upon Bozrah ..... Jer 48:24
K is taken .... Jer 48:41

KERNELS—*inner soft part of seeds or nuts*
from the ***k*** even to the husk ... Num 6:4

KEROS (kē'rŏs)—*"fortress; crooked"*
Head of a Nethinim family returning from exile .... Ezra 2:44

The children of ***K*** .... Neh 7:47

KETTLE—*pot*
Large cooking vessel 1Sam 2:14
Same word rendered "pots" .... Ps 81:6

KETURAH (kĕ-tū'rä)—*"incense"*
Abraham's second wife .. Gen 25:1

Sons of:
Listed .... Gen 25:1, 2
Given gifts and sent away. Gen 25:6

the children of ***K*** .... Gen 25:4
the sons of ***K***, Abraham's 1Chr 1:32
All these are the sons of ***K*** 1Chr 1:33

KEY—*a small instrument for unlocking doors*

Used literally for:
Doors .... Judg 3:25

Used figuratively of:
Prophetic authority of Christ .... Is 22:22
Present authority of Christ .... Rev 1:18
Plenary authority of Christ's apostles .... Matt 16:19
Teachers .... Luke 11:52

[*also* KEYS]
they took a ***k***, and opened .... Judg 3:25
the ***k*** of knowledge .... Luke 11:52
hath the ***k*** of David .... Rev 3:7
k of the bottomless pit .... Rev 9:1
k of the bottomless pit .... Rev 20:1

KEZIA (kĕ-zī'ä)—*"cassia"*
Daughter of Job .... Job 42:14

KEZIZ (kē'zĭz)—*"the angle; border; cassia tree"*
City of Benjamin .... Josh 18:21

KIBROTH-HATTAAVAH (kĭb-rŏth-hă-tā'-ä-vä)—*"the graves of lust"*
Burial site of Israelites slain by God .... Num 11:33-35

Sinai, and pitched at ***K*** .... Num 33:16
And they departed from ***K*** .... Num 33:17
at ***K***, ye provoked the Lord ... Deut 9:22

KIBZAIM (kĭb-zā'ĭm)—*"double gathering"*
Ephramite city assigned to Kohathite Levites ... Josh 21:22
Called Jokmeam 1Chr 6:68
See JOKMEAM

KICK—*to make a blow with the foot; resist*

[*also* KICKED]
Jeshurun waxed fat, and ***k*** .... Deut 32:15
k ye at my sacrifice 1Sam 2:29
k against the pricks .... Acts 9:5
k against the pricks .... Acts 26:14

KID—*a young goat*

Used for:
Food .... Gen 27:9
Payment .... Gen 38:17-23
Sacrifices .... Lev 4:23
Offerings .... Judg 13:15, 19
Festive occasions .... Luke 15:29

Figurative of:
Weakness .... Judg 14:6
Peacefulness .... Is 11:6
See GOAT

[*also* KIDS]
killed a ***k*** of the goats .... Gen 37:31
a ***k*** in his mother's milk .... Ex 23:19
a ***k*** in his mother's milk .... Ex 34:26
offering, a ***k*** of the goats ..... Lev 4:28
a ***k*** of the goats for a sin ..... Lev 5:6
a ***k*** of the goats for a sin ...... Lev 9:3
two ***k*** of the goats .... Lev 16:5
sacrifice one ***k*** of the goats .... Lev 23:19
the ***k*** of the goats for sin ...... Num 7:87
or for a lamb, or a ***k*** .... Num 15:11
k of the goats for a sin .... Num 28:15
k of the goats for a sin .... Num 29:5
k in his mother's milk .... Deut 14:21
made ready a ***k*** .... Judg 6:19
one carrying three ***k*** 1Sam 10:3
a bottle of wine, and a ***k*** 1Sam 16:20
of the flock, lambs and ***k*** 2Chr 35:7
offer a ***k*** of the goats .... Ezek 43:22
a ***k*** of the goats daily .... Ezek 45:23

KIDNAPPING—*taking a person away against his will*

Punishment for:
Death .... Ex 21:26

Examples of:
Joseph .... Gen 37:23-28
Daughters of Shiloh ..... Judg 21:20-23
Joash 2Kin 11:1-12
Jeremiah .... Jer 43:1-8

KIDNEYS—*organs that produce urine in the body*
the two ***k***, and the fat .... Ex 29:13
the two ***k***, and the fat .... Ex 29:22
the two ***k***, and the fat .... Lev 3:4
the two ***k***, and the fat .... Lev 4:9
the two ***k***, and the fat .... Lev 7:4
liver, and the two ***k*** .... Lev 8:16
liver, and the two ***k*** .... Lev 8:25
the fat, and the ***k*** .... Lev 9:10
with the fat of ***k*** of wheat ..... Deut 32:14
goats, with the fat of the ***k*** .... Is 34:6

KIDRON (kĭd'rŏn)—*"obscure; making black or sad"*
Valley (dry except for winter torrents) near Jerusalem .... John 18:1
East boundary of Jerusalem .... Jer 31:40
Crossed by David and Christ .... John 18:1
Used for burials .... Jer 26:23
Site of dumping of idols . 2Chr 29:16
See CEDRON

passed over the brook ***K*** 2Sam 15:23
passest over the brook ***K*** 1Kin 2:37
Jerusalem in the fields of ***K*** .. 2Kin 23:4
burnt it at the brook ***K*** 2Chr 15:16

KILL—*to cause life to cease*

Reasons for:
Take another's wife ...... Gen 12:12
Take another's property .. 1Kin 21:19
Take revenge .... Gen 27:42
Satisfy anger .... Num 22:29
Hate .... John 5:18
Execute God's wrath .... Num 31:2, 16-19
Destroy people .... Ex 1:16
Seize a throne 2Kin 15:25
Put down rebellion 1Kin 12:27
Fulfill prophecy 1Kin 16:1-11
Fear of punishment ...... Acts 16:27
Get rid of an unwanted person .... Matt 21:38

Reasons against:
God's Law .... Ex 20:13
Regard for:
Life .... Gen 37:21
One's position 1Sam 24:10

Of Christians:
In God's hand .... Luke 12:4, 5
Result of persecution .... Matt 24:9
Time will come .... John 16:2
Under antichrist .... Rev 11:7
Rev 13:5

[*also* KILLED, KILLEDST, KILLEST, KILLETH, KILLING]
any finding him should ***k*** ...... Gen 4:15
k me for Rebekah .... Gen 26:7
k a kid of the goats .... Gen 37:31
intendest thou to ***k*** me .... Ex 2:14
as thou ***k*** the Egyptian? .... Ex 2:14
k it in the evening .... Ex 12:6
k this whole assembly .... Ex 16:3
but that he hath ***k*** a man ..... Ex 21:29
ox, or a sheep, and ***k*** it .... Ex 22:1
thou shalt ***k*** the bullock .... Ex 29:11
k the bullock before .... Lev 1:5
k it at the door .... Lev 3:2
and ***k*** the bullock before ...... Lev 4:4
the bullock shall be ***k*** .... Lev 4:15
k the burnt offering .... Lev 4:24
the burnt offering is ***k*** .... Lev 6:25
sin offering be ***k*** .... Lev 6:25
k the burnt offering .... Lev 7:2
k the trespass offering .... Lev 7:2
one of the birds be ***k*** .... Lev 14:5
k the burnt offering .... Lev 14:19
k the one of the birds .... Lev 14:50
he ***k*** the goat of the sin .... Lev 16:15
k an ox, or lamb .... Lev 17:3
k it out of the camp .... Lev 17:3
thou shalt ***k*** the woman .... Lev 20:16
k a beast shall make it good .. Lev 24:18
he that ***k*** a beast he shall ..... Lev 24:21
he that ***k*** a man he shall be ... Lev 24:21
k me, I pray thee .... Num 11:15
k us in the wilderness .... Num 16:13
k the people of the Lord ...... Num 16:41
k any person at unawares ..... Num 35:11
revenger of blood ***k*** the .... Num 35:27
Whoso ***k*** any person .... Num 35:30
k his neighbor unawares ...... Deut 4:42
k and eat flesh .... Deut 12:15
thou shalt surely ***k*** him .... Deut 13:9
Whoso ***k*** his neighbor .... Deut 19:4
I ***k***, and I make alive .... Deut 32:39
slayer that ***k*** any person ...... Josh 20:3
in the ***k*** of his brethren .... Judg 9:24
the Lord were pleased to ***k*** .... Judg 13:23
day, we shall ***k*** him .... Judg 16:2
smite and ***k*** of..Israel .... Judg 20:39
Lord ***k***, and maketh alive 1Sam 2:6
Saul hear it, he will ***k*** me 1Sam 16:2
fight with me, and to ***k*** me 1Sam 17:9
prevail against him and ***k*** 1Sam 17:9
man that ***k*** this Philistine 1Sam 17:26
Saul my father seeketh to ***k*** ... 1Sam 19:2
k it, and took flour 1Sam 28:24
that thou wilt neither ***k*** me 1Sam 30:15
k Uriah the Hittite 2Sam 12:9
Amnon; then ***k*** him 2Sam 13:28
let him ***k*** me 2Sam 14:32
sought..to ***k*** Jeroboam 1Kin 11:40
Am I God, to ***k*** 2Kin 5:7
if they ***k*** us, we shall but 2Kin 7:4

K

followeth her *k* 2Kin 11:15
k Shophach the captain 1Chr 19:18
Ahab *k* sheep and oxen 2Chr 18:2
So they *k* the bullocks 2Chr 29:22
when they had *k* the rams 2Chr 29:22
k also the lambs 2Chr 29:22
k the passover 2Chr 30:15
the *k* of the passovers 2Chr 30:17
So *k* the passover 2Chr 35:6
they *k* the passover 2Chr 35:11
k the passover ....Ezra 6:20
to *k*, and to cause to ....Esth 3:13
wrath *k* the foolish man ....Job 5:2
for thy sake are we *k* ....Ps 44:22
watched the house to *k* him ...Ps 59:*title*
She hath *k* her beasts ....Prov 9:2
desire of the slothful *k* ....Prov 21:25
time to *k*, and a time to ......Eccl 3:3
I will *k* thy root ....Is 14:30
slaying oxen, and *k* sheep .....Is 22:13
He that *k* an ox is as if ....Is 66:3
thou hast *k*, and not pitied ....Lam 2:21
ye *k* them that are fed ....Ezek 34:3
swearing, and lying, and *k* ....Hos 4:2
Thou shalt not *k* ....Matt 5:21
k shall be in danger of ....Matt 5:21
fear not them which *k* ....Matt 10:28
not able to *k* the soul ....Matt 10:28
be *k*, and be raised again .....Matt 16:21
they shall *k* him ....Matt 17:23
let us *k* him ....Matt 21:38
my fatlings are *k* ....Matt 22:4
ye shall *k* and crucify ....Matt 23:34
thou that *k* the prophets ......Matt 23:37
afflicted, and shall *k* you ......Matt 24:9
to save life, or to *k*? ....Mark 3:4
would have *k* him ....Mark 6:19
he is *k*, he shall rise ....Mark 9:31
Do not *k*, Do not steal ....Mark 10:19
beating some, and *k* some .....Mark 12:5
let us *k* him ....Mark 12:7
they took him, and *k* him .....Mark 12:8
your fathers *k* them ....Luke 11:47
for they indeed *k* them ....Luke 11:48
Jerusalem..*k* the prophets .....Luke 13:34
thy father hath *k* the fatted ....Luke 15:27
Do not *k* ....Luke 18:20
out of the vineyard, and *k* ....Luke 20:15
how they might *k* him ....Luke 22:2
the Jews sought to *k* him ......John 7:1
who goeth about to *k* thee? ...John 7:20
Will he *k* himself? ....John 8:22
now ye seek to *k* me ....John 8:40
And *k* the Prince of life ....Acts 3:15
Wilt thou *k* me, as thou ....Acts 7:28
day and night to *k* him ....Acts 9:24
Rise, Peter: *k*, and eat ....Acts 10:13
he *k* James the brother of .....Acts 12:2
they went about to *k* him .....Acts 21:31
till they had *k* Paul ....Acts 23:12
are ready to *k* him ....Acts 23:15
and should have been *k* ....Acts 23:27
laying wait in the way to *k* ....Acts 25:3
went about to *k* me ....Acts 26:21
to *k* the prisoners ....Acts 27:42
For thy sake we are *k* ....Rom 8:36
Thou shalt not *k* ....Rom 13:9
letter *k*, but the spirit 2Cor 3:6
chastened, and not *k* 2Cor 6:9
Who both *k* the Lord 1Thess 2:15
also, Do not *k* ....James 2:11
ye *k* and desire to have ....James 4:2
condemned and *k* the just .....James 5:6
I will *k* her children ....Rev 2:23
to *k* with sword ....Rev 6:8
should be *k* as they were ......Rev 6:11
k by these plagues ....Rev 9:20
be *k* with the sword ....Rev 13:10
he that *k* with the sword ......Rev 13:10

KIN—*See* KINDRED

KINAH (kē'nä)—*"buying; dirge; lamentation"*
Village in southern Judah.Josh 15:22

KIND—*type; category*

[*also* KINDS]
fruit after his *k* ....Gen 1:11
seed after his *k* ....Gen 1:12
seed was in itself, after his *k* ..Gen 1:12
abundantly, after their *k* ......Gen 1:21
every winged fowl after his *k* ..Gen 1:21
creature after his *k* ....Gen 1:24
beast of the earth after his *k* ..Gen 1:24
beast of the earth after his *k* ..Gen 1:25
cattle after their *k* ....Gen 1:25
creepeth..after his *k* ....Gen 1:25
Of fowls after their *k* ....Gen 6:20
and of cattle after their *k* .....Gen 6:20
thing of the earth after his *k* ..Gen 6:20
every beast after his *k* ....Gen 7:14
all the cattle after their *k* .....Gen 7:14
creepeth..after his *k* ....Gen 7:14
every fowl after his *k* ....Gen 7:14
earth, after their *k* ....Gen 8:19
the kite after his *k* ....Lev 11:14
the hawk after his *k* ....Lev 11:16
the locust after his *k* ....Lev 11:22
bald locust after his *k* ....Lev 11:22
beetle after his *k* ....Lev 11:22
grasshopper after his *k* ....Lev 11:22
thy cattle..with a diverse *k* ....Lev 19:19
the vulture after his *k* ....Deut 14:13
the hawk after his *k* ....Deut 14:15
instruments of every *k* 1Chr 28:14
divers *k* of spices 2Chr 16:14
sellers of all *k* ....Neh 13:20
trees in them of all *k* of ....Eccl 2:5
will appoint over them four *k*. .Jer 15:3
of all *k* of riches ....Ezek 27:12
shall be according to their *k* ...Ezek 47:10
all *k* of music ....Dan 3:5
and all *k* of music ....Dan 3:10
gathered of every *k* ....Matt 13:47
this *k* goeth not out ....Matt 17:21
This *k* can come forth ....Mark 9:29
divers *k* of tongues 1Cor 12:10
a *k* of firstfruits ....James 1:18
See KINDNESS

KINDLE—*to start a fire; stir up*

[*also* KINDLED, KINDLETH]
Jacob's anger was *k* ....Gen 30:2
Lord was *k* against Moses .....Ex 4:14
shall *k* no fire ....Ex 35:3
which the Lord hath *k* ....Lev 10:6
his anger was *k* ....Num 11:1
wrath of the Lord was *k* ......Num 11:33
God's anger was *k* ....Num 22:22
Balak's anger was *k* ....Num 24:10
Lord's anger was *k* ....Num 32:10
anger of the Lord..be *k* ....Deut 6:15
Lord's wrath be *k* ....Deut 11:17
my anger shall be *k* ....Deut 31:17
anger of the Lord was *k* ......Josh 7:1
Ebed, his anger was *k* ....Judg 9:30
and his anger was *k* 1Sam 11:6
Saul's anger was *k* 1Sam 20:30
anger of the Lord was *k* 2Sam 6:7
coals were *k* by it 2Sam 22:9
anger of the Lord was *k* 2Sam 24:1
anger of the Lord was *k* 2Kin 13:3
my wrath shall be *k* 2Kin 22:17
anger of the Lord was *k* 1Chr 13:10
their anger was greatly *k* 2Chr 25:10
k his wrath against me ....Job 19:11
k the wrath of Elihu ....Job 32:2
against Job was his wrath *k* ...Job 32:2
his wrath was *k* ....Job 32:5
His breath *k* coals ....Job 41:21
when his wrath is *k* ....Ps 2:12
fire was *k* against Jacob ....Ps 78:21
the wrath of the Lord *k* ....Ps 106:40
contentious man to *k* strife ....Prov 26:21
the anger of the Lord *k* ....Is 5:25
k in the thickets ....Is 9:18
brimstone doth *k* it ....Is 30:33
he *k* it, and baketh bread .....Is 44:15
all ye that *k* a fire ....Is 50:11
the fathers *k* the fire ....Jer 7:18
tumult he hath *k* fire ....Jer 11:16
ye have *k* a fire ....Jer 17:4
I will *k* a fire in the forest ....Jer 21:14
k a fire in the houses ....Jer 43:12
and I will *k* a fire ....Jer 50:32
hath *k* a fire in Zion ....Lam 4:11
behold, I will *k* a fire ....Ezek 20:47
I the Lord have *k* it ....Ezek 20:48
mine anger is *k* ....Hos 8:5
k a fire in the wall ....Amos 1:14
they shall *k* in them ....Obad 18
k against the shepherds ....Zech 10:3
neither do ye *k* fire ....Mal 1:10
what will I, if it be already *k*? .Luke 12:49
they had *k* a fire ....Luke 22:55
for they *k* a fire ....Acts 28:2
a little fire *k*! ....James 3:5

KINDNESS—*quality or state of being kind*

Kinds of:
Extraordinary ....Acts 28:2
Acquired ....Col 3:12
Developed ....Prov 31:26
Commended 2Cor 6:6
Divine ....Neh 9:17

Of God, described as:
Great ....Neh 9:17
Everlasting ....Is 54:8
Not removable ....Is 54:10
Manifested ....Ps 31:21
Through Christ ....Eph 2:7
Cause of man's salvation .Titus 3:4-7

Manifestation of:
Rewarded 1Sam 15:6
Recalled 2Sam 2:5, 6
Rebuffed 2Sam 3:8
Remembered 2Sam 9:1-7
Refused 2Sam 10:1-6

[*also* KIND, KINDLY]
thy *k* which thou shalt show ...Gen 20:13
show *k* unto my master ....Gen 24:12
if ye will deal *k* ....Gen 24:49
well with thee, and show *k* ....Gen 40:14
and deal *k* and truly ....Gen 47:29
I have showed you *k* ....Josh 2:12
will deal *k* and truly ....Josh 2:14
showed they *k* to the house ...Judg 8:35
Lord deal *k* with you ....Ruth 1:8
not left off his *k* ....Ruth 2:20
ye showed *k* to all 1Sam 15:6
shalt deal *k* with thy 1Sam 20:8
show me the *k* of the Lord 1Sam 20:14
not cut off thy *k* 1Sam 20:15
have showed this *k* unto 2Sam 2:5
the Lord show *k* and truth 2Sam 2:6
will requite you this *k* 2Sam 2:6
k for Jonathan's sake? 2Sam 9:1
show thee *k* for Jonathan 2Sam 9:7
will show *k* unto Hanun 2Sam 10:2
as his father showed *k* 2Sam 10:2
show *k* unto the sons 1Kin 2:7
he spake *k* to him 2Kin 25:28
show *k* unto Hanun 1Chr 19:2
remembered not the *k* 2Chr 24:22
she obtained *k* of him ....Esth 2:9
his merciful *k* is great ....Ps 117:2
merciful *k* be for my comfort ..Ps 119:76
smite me: it shall be a *k* ......Ps 141:5
desire of a man is his *k* ....Prov 19:22
with everlasting *k* ....Is 54:8
the *k* of thy youth ....Jer 2:2
spake *k* unto him ....Jer 52:32
slow to anger, and of great *k*. .Joel 2:13
slow to anger, and of great *k*. .Jon 4:2
k unto the unthankful ....Luke 6:35
Be *k* affectioned ....Rom 12:10
Charity..is *k* 1Cor 13:4
be ye *k* one to another ....Eph 4:32
godliness brotherly *k* 2Pet 1:7
to brotherly *k* charity 2Pet 1:7

KINDRED—*one's relatives*

Manifestation of:
Felt with great emotion ..Esth 8:6

Through faith ....Josh 6:23
By gospel ....Acts 3:25
Rev 14:6

[*also* KIN, KINDREDS, KINSFOLK, KINSFOLKS, KINSMAN, KINSMAN'S, KINSMEN, KINSWOMAN, KINSWOMEN)]

unto my country, and to my ***k*** .Gen 24:4
father's house, and to my ***k*** ...Gen 24:38
when thou comest to my ***k*** ....Gen 24:41
unto the land of thy ***k*** ....Gen 31:13
that is near of ***k*** to him ....Lev 18:6
she is thy father's near ***k*** ......Lev 18:12
for they are her near ***k*** ....Lev 18:17
for his ***k***, that is near ....Lev 21:2
the man have no ***k*** ....Num 5:8
they brought out all her ***k*** .....Josh 6:23
Naomi had a ***k*** of her ....Ruth 2:1
the ***k*** of Elimelech ....Ruth 2:3
man is near of ***k*** unto us ......Ruth 2:20
one of our next ***k*** ....Ruth 2:20
it is true that I am thy near ***k*** .Ruth 3:12
there is a ***k*** nearer than I .....Ruth 3:12
let him do the ***k*** part ....Ruth 3:13
will not do the part of a ***k*** ....Ruth 3:13
the part of a ***k*** to thee ....Ruth 3:13
part of a ***k*** to thee ....Ruth 3:13
the ***k*** whom Boaz spake ....Ruth 4:1
the ***k*** said, I cannot redeem ...Ruth 4:6
left thee this day without a ***k*** ..Ruth 4:14
the king is near of ***k*** to 2Sam 19:42
neither of his ***k***, nor of his 1Kin 16:11
his great men, and his ***k*** 2Kin 10:11
Benjamin, the ***k*** of Saul 1Chr 12:29
unto the Lord, ye ***k*** 1Chr 16:28
Esther..showed her ***k*** ....Esth 2:20
My ***k*** have failed ....Job 19:14
the Buzite, of the ***k*** of Ram ...Job 32:2
all the ***k*** of the nations ....Ps 22:27
my ***k*** stand afar off ....Ps 38:11
call understanding thy ***k***........Prov 7:4
brethren, the men of thy ***k*** ....Ezek 11:15
among his own ***k*** ....Mark 6:4
thy ***k*** that is called ....Luke 1:61
sought him among their ***k*** .....Luke 2:44
neither thy ***k***, nor thy rich .....Luke 14:12
and brethren, and ***k*** ....Luke 21:16
being his ***k*** whose ear ....John 18:26
all the ***k*** of the earth ....Acts 3:25
the ***k*** of the high priest ....Acts 4:6
all his ***k***, threescore ....Acts 7:14
together his ***k*** ....Acts 10:24
my ***k*** according to the flesh ....Rom 9:3
Salute Herodion my ***k*** ....Rom 16:11
and Sosipater, my ***k*** ....Rom 16:21
all ***k*** of the earth ....Rev 1:7
blood out of every ***k*** ....Rev 5:9
k and tongues and nations .....Rev 11:9

KINE—*archaic for cow, ox, steer*

Used for:
Ox ....Deut 7:13
Cattle ....Deut 32:14
Cow ....Gen 32:15
1Sam 6:7

river seven well-favored ***k*** .....Gen 41:2
seven other ***k*** came up ....Gen 41:3
the other ***k*** upon the brink ....Gen 41:3
lean-fleshed ***k*** ....Gen 41:4
seven well-favored..***k*** ....Gen 41:4
seven other ***k*** came up ....Gen 41:19
lean and ill-favored ***k*** ....Gen 41:20
eat up the first seven fat ***k*** ....Gen 41:20
seven thin and ill-favored ***k***....Gen 41:27
increase of thy ***k*** ....Deut 7:13
increase of thy ***k*** ....Deut 28:51
and took two milch ***k*** 1Sam 6:10
and offered the ***k***.............1Sam 6:14
sheep, and cheese of ***k*** 2Sam 17:29
Hear this word, ye ***k***..........Amos 4:1

KING—*supreme ruler*

Some characteristics of:
Arose over Egypt ....Ex 1:8
Desired by people 1Sam 8:5, 6
Under God's control .....Dan 4:25, 37
Rule by God's permission.Dan 2:20, 21
Subject to temptations ...2Sam 11:1-5
Prov 31:5
Good 2Kin 22:1, 2
Evil 2Kin 21:1-9

Position of before God, by God:
Chosen 1Chr 28:4-6
Anointed 1Sam 16:12
Removed and established .Dan 2:21
Rejected 1Sam 15:10-26

Duties of:
Make covenants ....Gen 21:22-32
Read Scriptures ....Deut 17:19
Make war...............1Sam 11:5-11
Pardon 2Sam 14:1-11
2Sam 19:18-23
Judge 2Sam 15:2
Govern righteously 2Sam 23:3, 4
Keep Law 1Kin 2:3
Make decrees ....Dan 3:1-6, 29

[*also* KINGLY, KING'S, KINGS, KINGS']

the ***k*** that were with him ......Gen 14:5
the ***k*** of Sodom..fled ....Gen 14:10
which is in the ***k*** dale ....Gen 14:17
k shall come out...............Gen 17:6
k shall come out...............Gen 35:11
k that reigned in the land .....Gen 36:31
go by the ***k*** high way ....Num 20:17
the shout of a ***k*** ....Num 23:21
they slew the ***k*** of Midian .....Num 31:8
Hur, and Reba, five ***k*** ....Num 31:8
hand of the two ***k*** ....Deut 3:8
two ***k*** of the Amorites ....Deut 4:47
Og, ***k*** of the Amorites ....Deut 31:4
two ***k*** of the Amorites ....Josh 2:10
all the ***k*** of the Amorites ......Josh 5:1
all the ***k*** of the Canaanites ....Josh 5:1
two ***k*** of the Amorites ....Josh 9:10
all the ***k*** of the Amorites ......Josh 10:6
five ***k*** fled, and hid ....Josh 10:16
The five ***k*** are found hid ......Josh 10:17
brought forth those five ***k*** .....Josh 10:23
brought out those ***k***............Josh 10:24
the necks of these ***k*** ....Josh 10:24
all these ***k*** and their land .....Josh 10:42
all these ***k*** were met ....Josh 11:5
all the cities of those ***k***........Josh 11:12
all the ***k*** of them ....Josh 11:12
long time with all those ***k*** .....Josh 11:18
k of the country ....Josh 12:7
two ***k*** of the Amorites ....Josh 24:12
Threescore and ten ***k*** ....Judg 1:7
The ***k*** came and fought ....Judg 5:19
fought the ***k*** of Canaan ....Judg 5:19
took the two ***k*** of Midian .....Judg 8:12
make us a ***k*** to judge us 1Sam 8:5
shouted..God save the ***k*** 1Sam 10:24
against the ***k*** of Zobah 1Sam 14:47
be the ***k*** son-in-law 1Sam 18:22
avenged of the ***k*** enemies 1Sam 18:25
be the ***k*** son-in-law 1Sam 18:27
the ***k*** business required........1Sam 21:8
deliver him into the ***k*** hand ...1Sam 23:20
Behold the ***k*** spear!...........1Sam 26:22
David ***k*** over..Judah 2Sam 2:4
as one of the ***k*** sons 2Sam 9:11
k that were servants 2Sam 10:19
the roof of the ***k*** house 2Sam 11:2
at the door of the ***k*** house 2Sam 11:9
some of the ***k*** servants 2Sam 11:24
thou, being the ***k*** son 2Sam 13:4
Absalom invited..***k*** sons 2Sam 13:23
Then all the ***k*** sons arose 2Sam 13:29
slain all..the ***k*** sons 2Sam 13:32
Behold, the ***k*** sons come 2Sam 13:35
k heart was toward 2Sam 14:1
shekels after the ***k*** weight 2Sam 14:26
let me see the ***k*** face 2Sam 14:32
hear out of the ***k*** house 2Sam 15:35
hand against the ***k*** son 2Sam 18:12
because the ***k*** son is dead 2Sam 18:20
carry over the ***k*** household 2Sam 19:18
the ***k*** word prevailed..........2Sam 24:4
all his brethren the ***k*** sons 1Kin 1:9
hath called all the ***k*** sons 1Kin 1:25
God save ***k*** Solomon...........1Kin 1:34
ride upon the ***k*** mule 1Kin 1:44
a seat..for the ***k*** mother 1Kin 2:19
not be any among the ***k***........1Kin 3:13
from all ***k*** of the earth 1Kin 4:34
Lord, and the ***k*** house 1Kin 9:1
Solomon exceeded all the ***k*** ...1Kin 10:23
the ***k*** merchants received 1Kin 10:28
all the ***k*** of the Hittites 1Kin 10:29
for the ***k*** of Syria 1Kin 10:29
k hand was restored him 1Kin 13:6
the door of the ***k*** house 1Kin 14:27
chronicles of the ***k*** of Judah? ..1Kin 14:29
chronicles of the ***k*** of Israel? ..1Kin 15:31
the palace of the ***k*** house 1Kin 16:18
all the ***k*** of Israel 1Kin 16:33
the ***k*** in the pavilions 1Kin 20:12
pavilions, he and the ***k***.........1Kin 20:16
thirty and two ***k*** that helped ...1Kin 20:16
the ***k*** of the house 1Kin 20:31
Israel are merciful ***k*** 1Kin 20:31
deliver it into the ***k*** hand......1Kin 22:12
chronicles..***k*** of Judah? 1Kin 22:45
chronicles..***k*** of Israel? 2Kin 1:18
k were come up to fight.......2Kin 3:21
the ***k*** of the Hittites 2Kin 7:6
the ***k*** of the Egyptians 2Kin 7:6
tell the ***k*** household 2Kin 7:9
chronicles..***k*** of Judah? 2Kin 8:23
she is a ***k*** daughter 2Kin 9:34
they took the ***k*** sons 2Kin 10:7
chronicles..***k*** of Israel? 2Kin 10:34
from among the ***k*** sons.........2Kin 11:2
watch of the ***k*** house 2Kin 11:5
and they made him ***k*** 2Kin 11:12
horses..into the ***k*** house 2Kin 11:16
sword beside the ***k*** house 2Kin 11:20
k of Judah, had dedicated 2Kin 12:18
and in the ***k*** house 2Kin 12:18
chronicles..***k*** of Israel? 2Kin 13:8
treasures of the ***k*** house 2Kin 14:14
chronicles..***k*** of Israel? 2Kin 14:15
chronicles..***k*** of Judah? 2Kin 14:18
fathers..the ***k*** of Israel 2Kin 14:29
chronicles..***k*** of Israel 2Kin 15:11
palace of the ***k*** house 2Kin 15:25
chronicles..***k*** of Israel 2Kin 15:26
the way of the ***k*** of Israel 2Kin 16:3
the ***k*** burnt sacrifice 2Kin 16:15
not as the ***k*** of Israel 2Kin 17:2
among all the ***k*** of Judah 2Kin 18:5
treasures of the ***k*** house 2Kin 18:15
k of Assyria have destroyed ...2Kin 19:17
chronicles..***k*** of Judah? 2Kin 21:17
Asahiah a servant of the ***k*** 2Kin 22:12
k of Judah had given 2Kin 23:11
k of Israel had made 2Kin 23:19
nor of the ***k*** of Judah 2Kin 23:22
chronicles..***k*** of Judah? 2Kin 24:5
k mother, and the ***k*** wives 2Kin 24:15
Nebuchadnezzar ***k*** of 2Kin 25:1
which is by the ***k*** garden 2Kin 25:4
in the ***k*** presence 2Kin 25:19
k that reigned in..Edom 1Chr 1:43
waited in the ***k*** gate 1Chr 9:18
Israel, to make him ***k*** 1Chr 11:10
yea, he reproved ***k*** 1Chr 16:21
k go out to battle.............1Chr 20:1
k word was abominable 1Chr 21:6
the ***k*** order to Asaph 1Chr 25:6
with the ***k*** sons 1Chr 27:32
Ahithophel..***k*** counselor 1Chr 27:33
Archite was the ***k*** companion ..1Chr 27:33
rulers of the ***k*** work 1Chr 29:6
made me ***k*** over a people 2Chr 1:9
the ***k*** merchants received 2Chr 1:16
the ***k*** of the Hittites 2Chr 1:17
for the ***k*** of Syria 2Chr 1:17
to the ***k*** palace 2Chr 9:11
all the ***k*** of the earth 2Chr 9:22
he reigned over all the ***k*** 2Chr 9:26
come to make him ***k***............2Chr 10:1
treasures of the ***k*** house 2Chr 12:9
of the ***k*** house 2Chr 16:2

K

Joash the ***k*** son ... 2Chr 18:25
the book of the ***k*** of Israel ... 2Chr 20:34
found in the ***k*** house ... 2Chr 21:17
the sepulchers of the ***k*** ... 2Chr 21:20
the ***k*** son shall reign ... 2Chr 23:3
brought out the ***k*** son ... 2Chr 23:11
gate into the ***k*** house ... 2Chr 23:20
unto the ***k*** office ... 2Chr 24:11
the ***k*** scribe ... 2Chr 24:11
city of David among the ***k*** ... 2Chr 24:16
story of the book of the ***k*** ... 2Chr 24:27
treasures of the ***k*** house ... 2Chr 25:24
over the ***k*** house ... 2Chr 26:21
burial..belonged to the ***k*** ... 2Chr 26:23
ways of the ***k*** of Israel ... 2Chr 28:2
gods of the ***k*** of Syria ... 2Chr 28:23
the sepulchers of the ***k*** ... 2Chr 28:27
of Gad the ***k*** seer ... 2Chr 29:25
should the ***k*** of Assyria ... 2Chr 32:4
book of the ***k*** of Israel ... 2Chr 33:18
Asaiah a servant of the ***k*** ... 2Chr 34:20
the ***k*** commandment ... 2Chr 35:10
k of Israel keep ... 2Chr 35:18
book of the ***k*** of Israel ... 2Chr 36:8
the revenue of the ***k*** ... Ezra 4:13
from the ***k*** palace ... Ezra 4:14
to see the ***k*** dishonor ... Ezra 4:14
insurrection against ***k*** ... Ezra 4:19
damage..the hurt of the ***k***? ... Ezra 4:22
the ***k*** treasure house ... Ezra 5:17
of the ***k*** goods, even of ... Ezra 6:8
Artaxerxes, king of ***k*** ... Ezra 7:12
this in the ***k*** heart ... Ezra 7:27
the ***k*** commissions ... Ezra 8:36
unto the ***k*** lieutenants ... Ezra 8:36
our ***k***, and our priests ... Ezra 9:7
into the hand of the ***k*** ... Ezra 9:7
I was the ***k*** cupbearer ... Neh 1:11
gave them the ***k*** letters ... Neh 2:9
the ***k*** words..spoken ... Neh 2:18
from the ***k*** high house ... Neh 3:25
their ***k***, and the people ... Neh 9:24
on our ***k***, on our princes ... Neh 9:32
the ***k*** of Assyria ... Neh 9:32
the ***k*** whom thou hast set ... Neh 9:37
it was the ***k*** commandment ... Neh 11:23
garden of the ***k*** palace ... Esth 1:5
k manner toward all ... Esth 1:13
all the ***k*** princes ... Esth 1:18
the ***k*** decree ... Esth 1:20
all the ***k*** provinces ... Esth 1:22
Hege the ***k*** chamberlain ... Esth 2:3
the ***k*** commandment ... Esth 2:8
brought..unto the ***k*** house ... Esth 2:8
women unto the ***k*** house ... Esth 2:13
Hegai the ***k*** chamberlain ... Esth 2:15
Mordecai sat in the ***k*** gate ... Esth 2:21
two of the ***k*** chamberlains ... Esth 2:21
k servants..in the ***k*** gate ... Esth 3:3
the ***k*** commandment? ... Esth 3:3
keep they the ***k*** laws ... Esth 3:8
not for the ***k*** profit ... Esth 3:8
were the ***k*** scribes called ... Esth 3:12
unto the ***k*** lieutenants ... Esth 3:12
sealed with the ***k*** ring ... Esth 3:12
by the ***k*** commandment ... Esth 3:15
even before the ***k*** gate ... Esth 4:2
enter into the ***k*** gate ... Esth 4:2
one of the ***k*** chamberlains ... Esth 4:5
pay to the ***k*** treasuries ... Esth 4:7
All the ***k*** servants ... Esth 4:11
people of the ***k*** provinces ... Esth 4:11
court of the ***k*** house ... Esth 5:1
against the ***k*** house ... Esth 5:1
Mordecai..at the ***k*** gate ... Esth 5:13
k servants that ministered ... Esth 6:3
k servants said unto him ... Esth 6:5
sitteth at the ***k*** gate ... Esth 6:10
came the ***k*** chamberlains ... Esth 6:14
out of the ***k*** mouth ... Esth 7:8
all the ***k*** provinces ... Esth 8:5
in the ***k*** name ... Esth 8:8
seal it with the ***k*** ring ... Esth 8:8
written in the ***k*** name ... Esth 8:8
sealed with the ***k*** ring ... Esth 8:8

sealed it with the ***k*** ring ... Esth 8:10
the ***k*** commandment ... Esth 8:17
Mordecai..in the ***k*** house ... Esth 9:4
Jews..in the ***k*** provinces ... Esth 9:16
chronicles of the ***k*** of Media ... Esth 10:2
With ***k*** and counselors ... Job 3:14
to the ***k*** of terrors ... Job 18:14
k are they on the throne ... Job 36:7
k of the earth ... Ps 2:2
Yet have I set my ***k*** ... Ps 2:6
The Lord is ***K*** for ever ... Ps 10:16
the ***K*** of glory shall come ... Ps 24:7
Who is this ***K*** of glory? ... Ps 24:8
he is the ***K*** of glory ... Ps 24:10
the heart of the ***k*** enemies ... Ps 45:5
k daughters were among ... Ps 45:9
enter into the ***k*** palace ... Ps 45:15
lo, the ***k*** were assembled ... Ps 48:4
Almighty scattered ***k*** in it ... Ps 68:14
righteousness..***k*** son ... Ps 72:1
k of Tarshish and of the isles ... Ps 72:10
k of Sheba and Seba ... Ps 72:10
For God is my ***K*** of old ... Ps 74:12
terrible to the ***k*** of the earth ... Ps 76:12
all the ***k*** of the earth ... Ps 102:15
in the chambers of their ***k*** ... Ps 105:30
testimonies also before ***k*** ... Ps 119:46
To him which smote great ***k*** ... Ps 136:17
the ***k*** of the earth ... Ps 138:4
k of the earth, and all people ... Ps 148:11
Zion be joyful in their ***K*** ... Ps 149:2
By me ***k*** reign, and princes ... Prov 8:15
of people is the ***k*** honor ... Prov 14:28
lips are the delight of ***k*** ... Prov 16:13
light of the ***k*** countenance ... Prov 16:15
The ***k*** heart is in the hand ... Prov 21:1
he shall stand before ***k*** ... Prov 22:29
fear thou the Lord and the ***k*** ... Prov 24:21
the honor of ***k*** is to search ... Prov 25:2
and is in ***k*** palaces ... Prov 30:28
that which destroyeth ***k*** ... Prov 31:3
It is not for ***k***, O Lemuel ... Prov 31:4
It is not for ***k*** to drink wine ... Prov 31:4
peculiar treasure of ***k*** ... Eccl 2:8
that cometh after the ***k***? ... Eccl 2:12
keep the ***k*** commandment ... Eccl 8:2
when thy ***k*** is a child ... Eccl 10:16
Curse not the ***k*** ... Eccl 10:20
Hezekiah, ***k*** of Judah ... Is 1:1
eyes have seen the ***K*** ... Is 6:5
princes altogether ***k***? ... Is 10:8
All the ***k*** of the nations ... Is 14:18
k of the earth ... Is 24:21
for the ***k*** commandment ... Is 36:21
k of Assyria ... Is 37:18
will loose the loins of ***k*** ... Is 45:1
k..be thy nursing fathers ... Is 49:23
k to the brightness of ... Is 60:3
k may be brought ... Is 60:11
all ***k*** thy glory ... Is 62:2
against the ***k*** of Judah ... Jer 1:18
bones of the ***k*** of Judah ... Jer 8:1
and an everlasting ***k*** ... Jer 10:10
k of Judah come in ... Jer 17:19
k and princes sitting ... Jer 17:25
nor the ***k*** of Judah ... Jer 19:4
treasures of the ***k*** of Judah ... Jer 20:5
unto the ***k*** house of Judah ... Jer 22:6
great ***k*** shall serve themselves ... Jer 25:14
cities of Judah, and the ***k*** ... Jer 25:18
k of the land of Uz ... Jer 25:20
k of the land..Philistines ... Jer 25:20
all the ***k*** of Zidon ... Jer 25:22
k of the isles ... Jer 25:22
all the ***k*** of Arabia ... Jer 25:24
k of the mingled people ... Jer 25:24
k of Zimri, and..***k*** of Elam ... Jer 25:25
all the ***k*** of the Medes ... Jer 25:25
great ***k*** shall serve ... Jer 27:7
houses of the ***k*** of Judah ... Jer 33:4
down into the ***k*** house ... Jer 36:12
out of the ***k*** house ... Jer 38:8
Chaldeans burned the ***k*** ... Jer 39:8
and the ***k*** daughters ... Jer 43:6
wickedness of the ***k*** ... Jer 44:9

your ***k***, and your princes ... Jer 44:21
k shall be raised up from ... Jer 50:41
nations with..***k*** of the Medes ... Jer 51:28
and the ***k*** house ... Jer 52:13
the ***k*** of the earth ... Lam 4:12
hath taken of the ***k*** seed ... Ezek 17:13
Babylon, a king of ***k*** ... Ezek 26:7
k shall be sore afraid ... Ezek 27:35
k shall be horribly afraid ... Ezek 32:10
neither they, nor their ***k*** ... Ezek 43:7
carcases of their ***k*** ... Ezek 43:7
and of the ***k*** seed ... Dan 1:3
stand in the ***k*** palace ... Dan 1:4
portion of the ***k*** meat ... Dan 1:8
eat the portion of..***k*** meat ... Dan 1:15
the captain of the ***k*** guard ... Dan 2:14
removeth ***k***..setteth up ***k*** ... Dan 2:21
known unto us the ***k*** matter ... Dan 2:23
O ***k***, art a ***k*** of ***k*** ... Dan 2:37
days of these ***k***..the God ... Dan 2:44
and a Lord of ***k*** ... Dan 2:47
and the ***k*** counselors ... Dan 3:27
word was in the ***k*** mouth ... Dan 4:31
k countenance was changed ... Dan 5:6
deposed from his ***k*** throne ... Dan 5:20
k concerning the ***k*** decree ... Dan 6:12
are four, are four ***k*** ... Dan 7:17
kingdom are ten ***k*** ... Dan 7:24
he shall subdue three ***k*** ... Dan 7:24
spake in thy name to our ***k*** ... Dan 9:6
with the ***k*** of Persia ... Dan 10:13
k daughter of the south ... Dan 11:6
both these ***k*** hearts shall ... Dan 11:27
Hezekiah, ***k*** of Judah ... Hos 1:1
They have set up ***k*** ... Hos 8:4
growth after the ***k*** mowings ... Amos 7:1
it is the ***k*** chapel ... Amos 7:13
it is the ***k*** court ... Amos 7:13
Hezekiah, ***k*** of Judah ... Mic 1:1
they shall scoff at the ***k*** ... Hab 1:10
and the ***k*** children ... Zeph 1:8
Lord shall be ***k*** over all ... Zech 14:9
Hananeel unto the ***k*** ... Zech 14:10
born ***K*** of the Jews? ... Matt 2:2
city of the great ***K*** ... Matt 5:35
k for my sake ... Matt 10:18
soft clothing are in ***k*** houses ... Matt 11:8
the ***K*** of the Jews? ... Matt 27:11
before rulers and ***k*** ... Mark 13:9
are in ***k*** courts ... Luke 7:25
prophets and ***k*** have desired ... Luke 10:24
k, going to make war ... Luke 14:31
Blessed be the ***K*** ... Luke 19:38
k of the Gentiles ... Luke 22:25
himself is Christ a ***K*** ... Luke 23:2
by force, to make him a ***k*** ... John 6:15
Art thou a ***k*** then? ... John 18:37
Thou sayest that I am a ***k*** ... John 18:37
Behold your ***K***! ... John 19:14
k of the earth stood up ... Acts 4:26
Blastus the ***k*** chamberlain ... Acts 12:20
another ***k***, one Jesus ... Acts 17:7
reigned as ***k*** without us ... 1Cor 4:8
unto the ***K*** eternal, immortal ... 1Tim 1:17
For ***k***, and for all ... 1Tim 2:2
K of ***k***..Lord of lords ... 1Tim 6:15
the slaughter of the ***k*** ... Heb 7:1
the ***k*** commandment ... Heb 11:23
prince of..***k*** of the earth ... Rev 1:5
us unto our God ***k*** ... Rev 5:10
nations, and tongues, and ***k*** ... Rev 10:11
go forth unto the ***k*** ... Rev 16:14
there are seven ***k*** ... Rev 17:10
horns..sawest are ten ***k*** ... Rev 17:12
receive power as ***k*** ... Rev 17:12
Lord of lords, and ***K*** of ***k*** ... Rev 17:14
over the ***k*** of the earth ... Rev 17:18
k of the earth ... Rev 18:9
K of ***K*** and Lord of Lords ... Rev 19:16
eat the flesh of ***k*** ... Rev 19:18
k of the earth do bring ... Rev 21:24

KING, CHRIST AS—*one of His offices*

In Old Testament prophecy:

Judah's tribe ... Gen 49:10

With a scepter ... Num 24:15-17
David's lineage ... 2Sam 7:1-29
Divine origin ... Is 9:6, 7
In righteousness ... Is 11:1-5
At God's appointed time . Ezek 21:27
Will endure forever ... Dan 2:44
Born in Bethlehem ... Mic 5:2, 3
As Priest-king ... Zech 6:9-15
Having salvation ... Zech 9:9
He is coming ... Mal 3:1-5

Christ's right to rule, determined by:
Divine decree ... Ps 2:6, 7
Prophecy ... Ps 45:6, 7
Birth ... Is 9:6, 7
Being seated at God's right hand ... Ps 16:8-11; Ps 110:1, 2; Acts 2:34-36
Crowning ... Zech 6:11-15

Described as:
Eternal ... Rev 11:15
Spiritual ... John 18:36, 37
Not for immoral or impure person ... Eph 5:5
For redeemed ... Col 1:13

KINGDOM—*domain of a king*

[*also* KINGDOMS]

beginning of his *k* ... Gen 10:10
be unto me a *k* of priests ... Ex 19:6
Agag..*k* shall be exalted ... Num 24:7
k of Sihon king ... Num 32:33
k of Og king of Bashan ... Num 32:33
the *k* of Og in Bashan ... Deut 3:4
being the *k* of Og ... Deut 3:13
all the *k*..thou passest ... Deut 3:21
prolong his days in his *k* ... Deut 17:20
head of all those *k* ... Josh 11:10
All the *k* of Og in Bashan ... Josh 13:12
k of Sihon ... Josh 13:27
k of Og in Bashan ... Josh 13:31
matter of the *k* ... 1Sam 10:16
out of the hand of all *k* ... 1Sam 10:18
renew the *k* there ... 1Sam 11:14
k shall not continue ... 1Sam 13:14
rent the *k* of Israel ... 1Sam 15:28
established, nor thy *k* ... 1Sam 20:31
rent the *k* out of..hand ... 1Sam 28:17
k from the house of Saul ... 2Sam 3:10
exalted his *k* for his people ... 2Sam 5:12
stablish the throne of his *k* ... 2Sam 7:13
restore me the *k* of my father . 2Sam 16:3
on the throne of the *k* ... 1Kin 1:46
knowest that the *k* was mine ... 1Kin 2:15
howbeit the *k* is turned ... 1Kin 2:15
ask for him the *k* also ... 1Kin 2:22
Solomon reigned over all *k* ... 1Kin 4:21
throne of thy *k* upon Israel ... 1Kin 9:5
I will surely rend the *k* ... 1Kin 11:11
I will rend the *k* ... 1Kin 11:31
I will take the *k* ... 1Kin 11:35
k return to..house of David ... 1Kin 12:26
there is no nation or *k* ... 1Kin 18:10
he took an oath of the *k* ... 1Kin 18:10
k was confirmed in his hand ... 2Kin 14:5
of all the *k* of the earth ... 2Kin 19:15
turned the *k* unto David ... 1Chr 10:14
to turn the *k* of Saul ... 1Chr 12:23
k to another people ... 1Chr 16:20
in my *k* for ever ... 1Chr 17:14
throne of the *k* of the Lord ... 1Chr 28:5
thine is the *k* ... 1Chr 29:11
all the *k* of the countries ... 1Chr 29:30
David was strengthened..*k* ... 2Chr 1:1
a house for his *k* ... 2Chr 2:12
not the like made in any *k* ... 2Chr 9:19
strengthened the *k* of Judah ... 2Chr 11:17
k of the countries ... 2Chr 12:8
gave the *k* over Israel ... 2Chr 13:5
k was quiet before him ... 2Chr 14:5
all the *k* of the heathen? ... 2Chr 20:6
k gave he to Jehoram ... 2Chr 21:3
no power to keep still..*k* ... 2Chr 22:9
when the *k* was established ... 2Chr 25:3
no god of any nation or *k* ... 2Chr 32:15
the reign of the *k* of Persia ... 2Chr 36:20
throughout all his *k* ... 2Chr 36:22
All the *k* of the earth ... 2Chr 36:23
throughout all his *k* ... Ezra 1:1
given me..*k* of the earth ... Ezra 1:2
gavest them *k* and nations ... Neh 9:22
not served thee in their *k* ... Neh 9:35
sat on the throne of his *k* ... Esth 1:2
sat the first in the *k* ... Esth 1:14
whole *k* of Ahasuerus ... Esth 3:6
art come to the *k* ... Esth 4:14
even to the half of the *k* ... Esth 5:6
provinces of the *k* ... Esth 9:30
For the *k* is the Lord's ... Ps 22:28
thy *k* is a right scepter ... Ps 45:6
the *k* were moved ... Ps 46:6
the *k* that have not called ... Ps 79:6
his *k* ruleth over all ... Ps 103:19
all the *k* of Canaan ... Ps 135:11
speak of the glory of thy *k* ... Ps 145:11
glorious majesty of his *k* ... Ps 145:12
Thy *k* is an everlasting *k* ... Ps 145:13
in his *k* becometh poor ... Eccl 4:14
upon his *k*, to order it ... Is 9:7
found the *k* of the idols ... Is 10:10
Babylon, the glory of *k* ... Is 13:19
and *k* against *k* ... Is 19:2
he shook the *k* ... Is 23:11
all the *k* of the ... Is 27:17
The lady of *k* ... Is 47:5
k that will not serve thee ... Is 60:12
over the nations and..*k* ... Jer 1:10
nations, and in all their *k* ... Jer 10:7
a *k*, to pluck up ... Jer 18:7
removed into all the *k* ... Jer 24:9
nation and *k*..will not serve ... Jer 27:8
and against great *k* ... Jer 28:8
all the *k* of the earth ... Jer 34:1
concerning the *k* of Hazor ... Jer 49:28
against her the *k* of Ararat ... Jer 51:27
polluted the *k* and princes ... Lam 2:2
didst prosper into a *k* ... Ezek 16:13
be there a base *k* ... Ezek 29:14
be the basest of the *k* ... Ezek 29:15
heaven hath given thee a *k* ... Dan 2:37
arise another *k* inferior ... Dan 2:39
third *k* of brass ... Dan 2:39
k shall be divided ... Dan 2:41
God of heaven set up a *k* ... Dan 2:44
k shall not be left ... Dan 2:44
consume all these *k* ... Dan 2:44
ruleth in the *k* of men ... Dan 4:17
ruleth in the *k* of men ... Dan 4:25
palace of the *k* of Babylon ... Dan 4:29
k is departed from thee ... Dan 4:31
his *k* is from generation ... Dan 4:34
established in my *k* ... Dan 4:36
There is a man in thy *k* ... Dan 5:11
thy father a *k* ... Dan 5:18
God hath numbered thy *k* ... Dan 5:26
third ruler in the *k* ... Dan 5:29
Darius to set over the *k* ... Dan 6:1
be over the whole *k* ... Dan 6:1
All the presidents of the *k* ... Dan 6:7
every dominion of my *k* ... Dan 6:26
his *k* that which shall not ... Dan 6:26
and glory, and a *k* ... Dan 7:14
his *k* that which shall not ... Dan 7:14
most High shall take the *k* ... Dan 7:18
possess the *k* for ever ... Dan 7:18
fourth *k* upon earth ... Dan 7:23
And the *k* and dominion ... Dan 7:27
greatness of the *k* ... Dan 7:27
k is an everlasting *k* ... Dan 7:27
four *k* shall stand up ... Dan 8:22
prince of the *k* of Persia ... Dan 10:13
his *k* shall be broken ... Dan 11:4
k shall be plucked up ... Dan 11:4
strength of his whole *k* ... Dan 11:17
give the honor of the *k* ... Dan 11:21
obtain the *k* by flatteries ... Dan 11:21
cease the *k*..house of Israel ... Hos 1:4
better than these *k*? ... Amos 6:2
God are upon the sinful *k* ... Amos 9:8
k shall be the Lord's ... Obad 21
k shall come to the daughter ... Mic 4:8
and the *k* thy shame ... Nah 3:5
may assemble the *k* ... Zeph 3:8
overthrow the throne of *k* ... Hag 2:22
destroy..strength of the *k* ... Hag 2:22
showeth him..*k* of the world ... Matt 4:8
k divided against itself ... Matt 12:25
how shall..his *k* stand? ... Matt 12:26
keys of the *k* of heaven ... Matt 16:19
Son of man coming in..*k* ... Matt 16:28
greatest in..*k* of heaven? ... Matt 18:1
shall not enter into the *k* ... Matt 18:3
same is greatest in the *k* ... Matt 18:4
eunuchs for the *k* ... Matt 19:12
such is the *k* of heaven ... Matt 19:14
hardly enter..*k* of heaven ... Matt 19:23
k of heaven is like..a man ... Matt 20:1
harlots go into..*k* of God ... Matt 21:31
k of God..taken from you ... Matt 21:43
k of heaven is like ... Matt 22:2
and *k* against *k* ... Matt 24:7
k of heaven be likened ... Matt 25:1
k prepared for you ... Matt 25:34
gospel of the *k* of God ... Mark 1:14
if a *k* be divided ... Mark 3:24
So is the *k* of God ... Mark 4:26
unto the half of my *k* ... Mark 6:23
enter into the *k* of God ... Mark 9:47
such is the *k* of God ... Mark 10:14
shall not receive the *k* ... Mark 10:15
enter into the *k* of God! ... Mark 10:23
Blessed be..*k* of our father ... Mark 11:10
art not far from..*k* of God ... Mark 12:34
and *k* against *k* ... Mark 13:8
drink it new in..*k* of God ... Mark 14:25
waited for the *k* of God ... Mark 15:43
k there shall be no end ... Luke 1:33
all the *k* of the world ... Luke 4:5
preach the *k* of God ... Luke 4:43
yours is the *k* of God ... Luke 6:20
least in the *k* of God ... Luke 7:28
mysteries of the *k* of God ... Luke 8:10
spake unto them of the *k* ... Luke 9:11
preach the *k* of God ... Luke 9:60
is fit for the *k* of God ... Luke 9:62
k of God is come nigh ... Luke 10:9
Thy *k* come. Thy will be ... Luke 11:2
k divided against itself ... Luke 11:17
how shall his *k* stand? ... Luke 11:18
k of God is come upon ... Luke 11:20
seek ye the *k* of God ... Luke 12:31
pleasure to give you the *k* ... Luke 12:32
what is the *k* of God like? ... Luke 13:18
prophets, in the *k* of God ... Luke 13:28
sit down in the *k* of God ... Luke 13:29
eat bread in the *k* ... Luke 14:15
k of God is preached ... Luke 16:16
k of God should come ... Luke 17:20
k of God cometh not ... Luke 17:20
k of God is within you ... Luke 17:21
such is the *k* of God ... Luke 18:16
riches enter into the *k* ... Luke 18:24
for the *k* of God's sake ... Luke 18:29
to receive for himself a *k* ... Luke 19:12
and *k* against *k* ... Luke 21:10
k of God is nigh at ... Luke 21:31
fulfilled in the *k* of God ... Luke 22:16
k of God shall come ... Luke 22:18
at my table in my *k* ... Luke 22:30
comest into thy *k* ... Luke 23:42
waited for the *k* of God ... Luke 23:51
My *k* is not of this world ... John 18:36
my *k* were of this world ... John 18:36
k not from hence ... John 18:36
pertaining to..*k* of God ... Acts 1:3
restore..the *k* to Israel? ... Acts 1:6
concerning the *k* of God ... Acts 19:8
testified the *k* of God ... Acts 28:23
k of God is not in word ... 1Cor 4:20
not inherit the *k* of God? ... 1Cor 6:9
shall inherit the *k* of God ... 1Cor 6:10
delivered up the *k* to God ... 1Cor 15:24
inherit the *k* of God ... 1Cor 15:50
not inherit the *k* of God ... Gal 5:21
worthy of the *k* of God ... 2Thess 1:5

dead..appearing and his *k* 2Tim 4:1
scepter of thy *k* ....Heb 1:8
through faith subdued *k* ....Heb 11:33
a *k* which cannot be ....Heb 12:28
heirs of the *k*..he hath ....James 2:5
k and patience of Jesus ....Rev 1:9
k of this world are ....Rev 11:15
k of our Lord ....Rev 11:15
the *k* of our God ....Rev 12:10
his *k* was full of darkness .....Rev 16:10
give their *k* unto the beast ....Rev 17:17

KINGDOM OF GOD—*God's kingly rule; wherever God rules*

Described as, of:
God ....Mark 1:15
Heaven ....Matt 3:2
Christ and God ....Eph 5:5
Their Father ....Matt 13:43
My Father's ....Matt 26:29
His dear Son ....Col 1:13

Special features of:
Gospel of ....Matt 24:14
Word of ....Matt 13:19
Mysteries of ....Mark 4:10-13
Key of David ....Rev 3:7

Entrance into, by:
New birth ....John 3:1-8
Granted ....Luke 22:29
Divine call 1Thess 2:12
Repentance ....Matt 3:2

Members of:
Seek it first ....Matt 6:33
Suffer tribulation ....Acts 14:22
Preach it ....Acts 8:12
Pray for it ....Matt 6:10
Work in ....Col 4:11

Nature of:
Spiritual ....Rom 14:17
Eternal 2Pet 1:11

KING'S GARDEN—*a garden of Jerusalem*
Near a gate 2Kin 25:4
By the pool of Siloah ....Neh 3:15

KING'S HIGHWAY—*an important passageway connecting Damascus and Egypt*
Use of, requested ....Num 20:17

KINGS OF ANCIENT ISRAEL

Over the United Kingdom:
Saul ....1Sam 11:15—31:13
David ....2Sam 2:4—1Kin 2:11
Solomon ....1Kin 1:39—11:43

Over Israel (the northern kingdom):
Jeroboam (22 yrs.) ......1Kin 12:20—14:20
Nadab (2 yrs.) 1Kin 15:25-27, 31
Baasha (24 yrs.) 1Kin 15:28-34
1Kin 16:1-7
Elah (2 yrs.) 1Kin 16:8-14
Zimri (7 days) 1Kin 16:15
Omri (12 yrs.) 1Kin 16:23-28
Ahab (22 yrs.) ....1Kin 16:29—22:40
Ahaziah (2 yrs.) 1Kin 22:51-53
Jehoram (Joram)(12 yrs.) .2Kin 3:1—9:26
Jehu (28 yrs.) ....2Kin 9:2—10:36
Jehoahaz (17 yrs.) 2Kin 13:1-9
Jehoash (Joash)(16 yrs.) .2Kin 13:10-25
Jeroboam II (41 yrs.) 2Kin 14:23-29
Zechariah (6 mos.) 2Kin 15:8-12
Shallum (1 mo.) 2Kin 15:13-15
Menahem (10 yrs.) 2Kin 15:16-22
Pekahiah (2 yrs.) 2Kin 15:23-26
Pekah (20 yrs.) 2Kin 15:27-31
Hoshea (9 yrs.) 2Kin 17:1-6

Over Judah (the southern kingdom):
Rehoboam (17 yrs.) 1Kin 12:21-24
Abijam (Abijah) (3 yrs.) .1Kin 15:1-8
Asa (41 yrs.) 1Kin 15:9-24
Jehoshaphat (25 yrs.) 1Kin 22:41-50
Jehoram (Joram) (8 yrs.) .2Kin 8:16-24
Ahaziah (1 yr.) 2Kin 8:25-29
Athaliah (Queen) (usurper) (6 yrs.) 2Kin 11:1-3
Joash (Jehoash) (40 yrs.) .2Kin 12:1, 21
Amaziah (29 yrs.) 2Kin 14:1-20
Azariah (Uzziah) (52 yrs.) 2Kin 15:1, 2
Jotham (16 yrs.) 2Kin 15:32-38
Ahaz (16 yrs.) 2Kin 16:1-20
Hezekiah (29 yrs.) ....2Kin 18:1—20:21
Manasseh (55 yrs.) 2Kin 21:1-18
Amon (2 yrs.) 2Kin 21:19-26
Josiah (31 yrs.) ....2Kin 22:1—23:30
Jehoahaz (Shallum) (3 mos.) 2Kin 23:31-33
Jehoiakim (11 yrs.) ......2Kin 23:34—24:6
Jehoiachin (Jeconiah) (3 mos.) 2Kin 24:8-16
Zedekiah (Mattaniah) (11 yrs.) ....2Kin 24:17—25:7

KINGS, THE BOOKS OF—*books of the Old Testament*

1 Kings
Solomon ascends to the throne ....1Kin 1:1—2:46
The kingdom of Solomon .1Kin 3:1—10:13
The fall of Solomon 1Kin 11:1-40
Rehoboam against Jeroboam 1Kin 12:1-33
Ahab and Jezebel 1Kin 16:29-34
Ministry of Elijah ....1Kin 17:1—19:21
Syria against Samaria 1Kin 20:1-34
Ahab and Naboth 1Kin 21:1-29

2 Kings
Ministry of Elijah and Elisha ....2Kin 1:1—9:1
Reign of Jehu ....2Kin 9:11—10:36
Fall of Israel 2Kin 17:1-41
Reign of Hezekiah ......2Kin 18:1—20:21
Reform of Judah ....2Kin 22:1—23:30
Fall of Jerusalem 2Kin 25:1-21

KINGSHIP OF GOD—*the position of God as sovereign ruler of the universe*
Over Jerusalem ....Matt 5:35
Over all ....Ps 103:19
Of all kingdoms 2Kin 19:15

KINSFOLK—*See* **Kindred**

KINSMAN, KINSWOMAN—*See* **Kindred**

KIR (kĭr)—*"a city; wall; meeting"*
1. Place mentioned by Amos to which Syrians were taken ....Amos 1:5
   Tiglath-pileser carries people of Damascus here 2Kin 16:9
   Inhabitants of, against Judah ....Is 22:6
2. Fortified city of Moab ...Is 15:1
   Same as Kir-hareseth ....Is 16:7, 11
   Strong place 2Kin 3:25

KIR-HARASETH (kĭr-hăr'ä-sĕth)—*"city of the sun; wall of burnt brick"—a fortified city*
in *K* left they the stones 2Kin 3:25

KIR-HARESETH (kĭr-hăr'ĕ-sĕth)—*same as Kir-haraseth*
foundations of *K* shall ye ......Is 16:7

KIR-HARESH (kĭr-hăr'ĕsh)—*same as Kir-haraseth*
mine inward parts for *K* ....Is 16:11

KIR-HERES (kĭr-hē'rĕs)—*"city of the sun; wall of burnt brick"—probably the same as Kir-haraseth*
mourn for the men of *K* ....Jer 48:31
like pipes for the men of *K* ....Jer 48:36

KIRIATHAIM, KIRJATHAIM (kĭr-ĭ-ä-thā'ĭm, kĭr-jä-thā'ĭm)—*"double city"*
1. Assigned to Reuben .....Num 32:37
   Repossessed by Moabites .Jer 48:1-23
2. Town in Naphtali 1Chr 6:76
   Same as Kartan ....Josh 21:32

KIRIOTH (kĭr'ĭ-ŏth)—*same as Kerioth*
devour the palaces of *K* ....Amos 2:2

KIRJATH (kĭr'jăth)—*"city; vocation; meeting"*
Town of Benjamin ......Josh 18:21, 28

KIRJATHAIM—*See* **Kiriathaim**

KIRJATH-ARBA (kĭr-jăth-är'bä)—*"fourth city"*
Ancient name of Hebron .Gen 23:2
Named after Arba the Anakite ....Josh 15:54
City of refuge ....Josh 20:7
Possessed by Judah ......Judg 1:10
name of Hebron before was *K* .Josh 14:15

KIRJATH-ARIM (kĭr-jăth-ā'rĭm)—*same as Kirjath-jearim*
The children of *K* ....Ezra 2:25

KIRJATH-BAAL (kĭr-jăth-bā'ăl)—*same as Kirjath-jearim*
K..is Kirjath-jearim ....Josh 15:60
goings out..were at *K* ....Josh 18:14

KIRJATH-HUZOTH (kĭr-jăth-hŭ'zŏth)
and they came to *K* ....Num 22:39

KIRJATH-JEARIM (kĭr-jăth-kē'ä-rĭm)—*"city of woods"—a city of the Gibeonites*
Gibeonite town ....Josh 9:17
Assigned to Judah ....Josh 15:60
Reassigned to Benjamin .Josh 18:28
Ark taken from 1Chr 13:5
Home of Urijah ....Jer 26:20
Called:
  Baalah ....Josh 15:9, 10
  Kirjath-baal ....Josh 15:60
  Baale of Judah 2Sam 6:2
Shortened to Kirjath-arim .Ezra 2:25

K, a city of the children ....Josh 18:14
and pitched in *K* ....Judg 18:12
to the inhabitants of *K* 1Sam 6:21
the men of *K* came 1Sam 7:1
Shobal the father of *K* 1Chr 2:50
Shobal the father of *K* 1Chr 2:52
to Baalah, that is, to *K* 1Chr 13:6
David brought up from *K* 2Chr 1:4
men of *K*, Chephirah ....Neh 7:29

KIRJATH-SANNAH (kĭr-jăth-săn'ä)—*"city of destruction"*
City of Judah; also called Debir ....Josh 15:49

KIRJATH-SEPHER (kĭr-jăth-sē'fer)—*"city of books"*
Same as Debir ....Judg 1:11-13
Taken by Othniel ....Josh 15:15-17
See **Kirjath-sannah**

KISH (kĭsh)—*"bow; power"*
1. Benjamite of Gibeah; father of King Saul ..1Sam 9:1-3; Acts 13:21
2. Benjamite of Jerusalem ..1Chr 8:30
3. Merarite Levite in David's time 1Chr 23:21, 22
4. Another Merarite Levite in Hezekiah's time 2Chr 29:12
5. Benjamite and great-grandfather of Mordecai ....Esth 2:5

come unto the son of *K*? 1Sam 10:11
K was the father of Saul 1Sam 14:51
Ner begat *K*, and *K*..........1Chr 8:33
Ner begat *K*; and *K*..........1Chr 9:39
Saul the son of *K*.............1Chr 12:1
Concerning *K*; the son of *K* ...1Chr 24:29
Saul the son of *K*.............1Chr 26:28

KISHI (kĭsh'ī)—*"snarer; fowler"*
One of David's singers ...1Chr 6:31, 44
Called Kushaiah 1Chr 15:17

KISHION (kĭsh'ĭ-ŏn)—*"hardness"*
Border town of Issachar. .Josh 19:17, 20
Called Kishon ....Josh 21:28
See KEDESH

KISHON, KISON (kī'-shŏn, kī'sŏn)—*"bending; crooked"—river of northern Palestine*
Sisera's army swept away by....................Judg 4:7, 13
Elijah slew Baal prophets here .... 1Kin 18:40; Ps 83:9
See KISHION

unto thee to the river *K*.......Judg 4:7
river of *K* swept them away ...Judg 5:21
river, the river *K* ....Judg 5:21
down to the brook *K* 1Kin 18:40

KISS—*a physical sign of affection; to show such affection*
Times employed, at:
Departure ....Gen 31:28, 55
Separation ....Acts 20:37
Reunions ....Luke 15:20
Great joy ....Luke 7:38, 45
Blessing ....Gen 48:10-16
Anointings 1Sam 10:1
Reconciliation ....Gen 33:4
Death ....Gen 50:1
Figurative of:
Complete:
Submission to evil .....Hos 13:2
Submission to God ....Ps 2:12
Reconciliation ....Ps 85:10
Utmost affection ....Song 1:2
Kinds of:
Deceitful ....2Sam 20:9, 10; Luke 22:48
Insincere...............2Sam 15:5
Fatherly ....Gen 27:26, 27
Friendship ....Ex 18:7; 1Sam 20:41
Esteem 2Sam 19:32, 39
Sexual love ....Gen 29:11; Song 1:2
Illicit love..............Prov 7:13
False religion ....1Kin 19:18; Hos 13:2
Holy love ....Rom 16:16; 1Cor 16:20

[*also* KISSED, KISSES]
and *k* me, my son ....Gen 27:26
came near, and *k* him.........Gen 27:27
embraced him, and *k* him .....Gen 29:13
he *k* all his brethren ....Gen 45:15
mount of God, and *k* him .....Ex 4:27
Then she *k* them ....Ruth 1:9
they *k* one another,...........1Sam 20:41
king *k* Absalom 2Sam 14:33
king *k* Barzillai 2Sam 19:39
right hand to *k* him 2Sam 20:9
mouth which hath not *k* him ..1Kin 19:18
k my father and my mother ...1Kin 19:20
mouth hath *k* my hand.........Job 31:27
caught him, and *k* him ....Prov 7:13
k his lips that giveth ....Prov 24:26
k of..enemy are deceitful......Prov 27:6
I would *k* thee ....Song 8:1
Whomsoever I shall *k*.........Matt 26:48
Hail, master; and *k* him ....Matt 26:49
Whomsoever I shall *k*.........Mark 14:44
master; and *k* him ....Mark 14:45
unto Jesus to *k* him...........Luke 22:47
with a holy *k*.................Rom 16:16
one another with a holy *k* 1Cor 16:20
Greet..with a holy *k* 2Cor 13:12
brethren with a holy *k* 1Thess 5:26
another with a *k* of charity 1Pet 5:14

KITE—*a bird of the falcon family*
Ceremonially unclean ....Lev 11:14

k, and the vulture after his ....Deut 14:13

KITHLISH (kĭth'lĭsh)—*"it is a wall"*
Town of Judah ....Josh 15:1, 40

KITRON (kĭt'rŏn)—*"making sweet"*
Town in Zebulun ....Judg 1:30
See KATTATH

KITTIM (kĭt'ĭm)
Sons of Javan ....Gen 10:4
See CHITTIM

KNEAD—*to mix elements together*
Part of food process .....Gen 18:6
Done by women ....Jer 7:18

[*also* KNEADED]
took flour, and *k* it 1Sam 28:24
she took flour, and *k* it 2Sam 13:8
hath *k* the dough ....Hos 7:4

KNEADING TROUGH—*a bowl for kneading dough*
Overcome by frogs ......Ex 8:3
Carried out of Egypt ....Ex 12:33-34

KNEE—*the joint of the middle leg*
Place of weakness, due to:
Terror ....Dan 5:6
Fasting ....Ps 109:24
Disease ....Deut 28:35
Lack of faith ....Is 35:3
Lying upon:
Sign of true parentage or adoption ....Gen 30:3
Place of fondling ....Is 66:12
Place of sheep ....Judg 16:19
Bowing of, act of:
Respect.................2Kin 1:13
False worship 1Kin 19:18
True worship............Rom 14:11
Bowing of, in prayer:
Solomon 2Chr 6:13, 14
Daniel..................Dan 6:10
Christ ....Luke 22:41
Stephen ....Acts 7:59, 60
Peter ....Acts 9:40
Paul ....Acts 20:36
Christians ....Acts 21:5

[*also* KNEES]
Bow the *k* ....Gen 41:43
out from between his *k* ....Gen 48:12
up upon Joseph's *k* ....Gen 50:23
kneeling on his *k* 1Kin 8:54
put his face between his *k*.....1Kin 18:42
he sat on her *k* till noon 2Kin 4:20
kneeled down upon his *k*......2Chr 6:13
I fell upon my *k*.............Ezra 9:5
Why did the *k* prevent me? ...Job 3:12
strengthened the feeble *k* .....Job 4:4
unto me every *k* shall bow ....Is 45:23
all *k*..be weak as water ....Ezek 7:17
all *k*..be weak as water ....Ezek 21:7
waters were to the *k*..........Ezek 47:4
kneeled upon his *k* ....Dan 6:10
which set me upon my *k* ......Dan 10:10
k smite together ....Nah 2:10
bowed the *k* before him.......Matt 27:29
bowing..*k* worshiped him......Mark 15:19
he fell down at Jesus *k*........Luke 5:8
bowed the *k* to the image .....Rom 11:4
bow my *k* unto the Father ....Eph 3:14
name of Jesus every *k* ....Phil 2:10
and the feeble *k*.............Heb 12:12

KNEEL—*to rest on one's knee*

[*also* KNEELED, KNEELING]
made his camels to *k* down....Gen 24:11
from *k* on his knees 1Kin 8:54
k down upon his knees........2Chr 6:13
let us *k* before the Lord.......Ps 95:6
k upon his knees ....Dan 6:10
k down to him ....Matt 17:14
and *k* down to him ....Mark 1:40
came one running, and *k*......Mark 10:17
k down, and prayed ....Luke 22:41
he *k* down and cried ....Acts 7:60
k down, and prayed ....Acts 9:40
he *k* down, and prayed ....Acts 20:36
we *k* down on the shore ......Acts 21:5

KNEW—*See* KNOW

KNIFE—*a sharp-cutting instrument*
Used for:
Slaying animals.........Gen 22:6-10
Circumcision ....Josh 5:2, 3
Dismembering a body....Judg 19:29
Sharpening pens ....Jer 36:23
Figurative of:
Inordinate appetite ......Prov 23:2
Cruel oppressors ....Prov 30:14

[*also* KNIVES]
fire in his hand, and a *k* ......Gen 22:6
he took a *k*, and laid hold ....Judg 19:29
nine and twenty *k* ....Ezra 1:9
put a *k* to thy throat..........Prov 23:2
take thee a sharp *k* ....Ezek 5:1

KNIT—*to link firmly (closely)*
k together as one man ....Judg 20:11
Jonathan was *k* with the soul.. 1Sam 18:1
mine heart shall be *k* unto 1Chr 12:17
sheet *k* at the four corners ....Acts 10:11
being *k* together in love ....Col 2:2
k together, increaseth with ....Col 2:19

KNOB—*an ornament*
Round protrusions on lampstand ....Ex 25:31-34
Ornaments carved on the walls of the temple .. 1Kin 6:18; 1Kin 7:24

[*also* KNOBS]
k and their branches..........Ex 25:36
a *k* and a flower.............Ex 37:19
a *k* and a flower.............Ex 37:19
his *k*, and his flowers ....Ex 37:20
k and their branches..........Ex 37:22

KNOCK—*to rap on a door*
Rewarded..............Luke 11:9, 10
Expectant ....Luke 12:36
Disappointed...........Luke 13:25-27
Unexpected ....Acts 12:13, 16
Invitation ....Rev 3:20

[*also* KNOCKED, KNOCKETH]
voice of my beloved that *k* ....Song 5:2
k, and it shall be opened......Matt 7:7
as Peter *k* at the door ....Acts 12:13

KNOP—*See* KNOB

KNOW—*to understand; have sexual relations*

[*also* KNEW, KNEWEST, KNOWEST, KNOWETH, KNOWING, KNOWN]
k good and evil ....Gen 3:5
k that they were naked ......Gen 3:7
k good and evil ....Gen 3:22
Adam *k* Eve his wife ....Gen 4:1
Cain *k* his wife ....Gen 4:17
Noah *k*..waters were abated ...Gen 8:11
daughters which have not *k* ...Gen 19:8
and I *k* it not ....Gen 28:16
thou *k* my service ....Gen 30:26
k that the children are ....Gen 33:13
he *k* it and said ....Gen 37:33
k not that she was his.........Gen 38:16
k not aught he had ....Gen 39:6
k that they had eaten ....Gen 41:21
k his brethren, but they *k* .....Gen 42:8
Joseph made himself *k* ....Gen 45:1
k any men of activity ....Gen 47:6
which *k* not Joseph ....Ex 1:8
Surely this thing is *k* ....Ex 2:14
k thou not ....Ex 10:7
k that the ox hath used ....Ex 21:36

sinned against it, is **k** .... Lev 4:14
when he **k** of it .... Lev 5:3
k how we are to encamp .... Num 10:31
Lord will make myself **k** .... Num 12:6
k all the travail .... Num 20:14
I **k** not that thou stoodest .... Num 22:34
k the knowledge .... Num 24:16
that have not **k** a man .... Num 31:18
k among your tribes .... Deut 1:13
he **k** thy walking through .... Deut 2:7
mightest **k** that the Lord .... Deut 4:35
diseases of Egypt..thou **k** .... Deut 7:15
with manna which thou **k** .... Deut 8:3
which thy fathers **k** not .... Deut 8:16
from the day..I **k** you .... Deut 9:24
children which have not **k** .... Deut 11:2
which thou hast not **k** .... Deut 13:2
Only the trees..thou **k** .... Deut 20:20
be not **k** who..slain him .... Deut 21:1
thou nor thy fathers have **k** .... Deut 28:64
which have not **k** any .... Deut 31:13
to gods whom they **k** not .... Deut 32:17
Lord **k** face to face .... Deut 34:10
k the thing that the Lord .... Josh 14:6
Lord God of gods, he **k** .... Josh 22:22
k all..works of the Lord .... Josh 24:31
which **k** not the Lord .... Judg 2:10
k all the wars of Canaan .... Judg 3:1
and she **k** no man .... Judg 11:39
K..not that the Philistines .... Judg 15:11
k the voice of the young man .... Judg 18:3
k not that evil was near .... Judg 20:34
people which thou **k** .... Ruth 2:11
make not thyself **k** unto..man .... Ruth 3:3
Elkanah **k** Hannah his wife 1Sam 1:19
did not yet **k** the Lord 1Sam 3:7
iniquity which he **k** 1Sam 3:13
k that Samuel was established 1Sam 3:20
be **k** to you why his hand 1Sam 6:3
k not that Jonathan was 1Sam 14:3
k certainly that evil 1Sam 20:9
lad **k** not any thing 1Sam 20:39
Jonathan and David **k** 1Sam 20:39
they **k** when he fled 1Sam 22:17
David **k** that Saul..practised 1Sam 23:9
Saul my father **k** 1Sam 23:17
Saul **k** David's voice 1Sam 26:17
k what Saul hath done 1Sam 28:9
k Abner the son of Ner 2Sam 3:25
but David **k** it not 2Sam 3:26
k ye not..they would shoot 2Sam 11:20
thy servant **k**..I have found 2Sam 14:22
k thy father and his men 2Sam 17:8
the thing was not **k** 2Sam 17:19
I **k** not what it was 2Sam 18:29
but the king **k** her not 1Kin 1:4
David our lord **k** it not? 1Kin 1:11
my lord the king..**k** it not 1Kin 1:18
k what thou oughtest to do 1Kin 2:9
my father David not **k** 1Kin 2:32
k all the wickedness 1Kin 2:44
k that there is not among 1Kin 5:6
whose heart thou **k** 1Kin 8:39
k the hearts of all..children 1Kin 8:39
may **k** that the Lord is God 1Kin 8:60
be not **k** to be the wife 1Kin 14:2
be it **k** this day 1Kin 18:36
k thou that the Lord 2Kin 2:3, 5
for they **k** them not 2Kin 4:39
make **k** his deeds among 1Chr 16:8
for thou **k** thy servant 1Chr 17:18
k that the Lord he was God 2Chr 33:13
it **k** unto the king .... Ezra 4:12
Be it **k** now unto the king .... Ezra 4:13
it **k** unto the king .... Ezra 5:8
rulers **k** not whither .... Neh 2:16
enemies heard that it was **k** .... Neh 4:15
k that they dealt proudly .... Neh 9:10
which **k** the times .... Esth 1:13
k law and judgment .... Esth 1:13
thing was **k** to Mordecai .... Esth 2:22
who **k** whether thou art come .... Esth 4:14
k him not, they lifted up .... Job 2:12
k that I am not wicked .... Job 10:7
he **k** vain men; he seeth .... Job 11:11

Who **k** not in all these .... Job 12:9
k that the day of darkness .... Job 15:23
k that my redeemer liveth .... Job 19:25
K thou not this of old .... Job 20:4
How doth God **k**? .... Job 22:13
I **k** where I might find him .... Job 23:3
he **k** the way that I take .... Job 23:10
Man **k** not the price .... Job 28:13
I **k** not I searched out .... Job 29:16
he **k** their works .... Job 34:25
measures thereof if thou **k**? .... Job 38:5
K thou it because thou wast .... Job 38:21
K thou the time when .... Job 39:1
k the way of the righteous .... Ps 1:6
Lord is **k** by the judgment .... Ps 9:16
k my soul in adversities .... Ps 31:7
charge things that I **k** not .... Ps 35:11
k not who shall gather them .... Ps 39:6
O Lord, thou **k** .... Ps 40:9
k the secrets of the heart .... Ps 44:21
Be still, and **k** .... Ps 46:10
way may be **k** upon earth .... Ps 67:2
How doth God **k**? .... Ps 73:11
any that **k** how long .... Ps 74:9
in Judah is God **k** .... Ps 76:1
we have heard and **k** .... Ps 78:3
heathen..have not **k** thee .... Ps 79:6
thy wonders be **k** in..dark? .... Ps 88:12
he hath **k** my name .... Ps 91:14
A brutish man **k** not .... Ps 92:6
Lord..made **k** his salvation .... Ps 98:2
K ye that the Lord..is God .... Ps 100:3
he **k** our frame; he .... Ps 103:14
make **k** his deeds among .... Ps 105:1
that have **k** thy testimonies .... Ps 119:79
proud he **k** afar off .... Ps 138:6
searched me, and **k** me .... Ps 139:1
Thou **k** my downsitting .... Ps 139:2
O God, and **k** my heart .... Ps 139:23
then thou **k** my path .... Ps 142:3
they have not **k** them .... Ps 147:20
I will make **k** my words .... Prov 1:23
k not that it is for his life .... Prov 7:23
k not that the dead are there .... Prov 9:18
fool's wrath is presently **k** .... Prov 12:16
child is **k** by his doings .... Prov 20:11
Behold, we **k** it not .... Prov 24:12
who **k** ruin of them .... Prov 24:22
k not what a day may bring .... Prov 27:1
husband is **k** in the gates .... Prov 31:23
k whether he..be a wise .... Eccl 2:19
fool's voice is **k** by .... Eccl 5:3
k to walk before the living? .... Eccl 6:8
it is **k** that it is man .... Eccl 6:10
thine own heart **k** that .... Eccl 7:22
k not that which shall be .... Eccl 8:7
man also **k** not his time .... Eccl 9:12
k not what is the way of .... Eccl 11:5
k not the works of God .... Eccl 11:5
The ox **k** his owner .... Is 1:3
this is **k** in all the earth .... Is 12:5
But I **k** thy abode .... Is 37:28
children..make **k** thy truth .... Is 38:19
Hast thou not **k**? .... Is 40:28
not **k** nor understood .... Is 44:18
thou hast not **k** me .... Is 45:5
I **k** that thou art obstinate .... Is 48:4
yea, thou **k** not .... Is 48:8
I **k** that thou wouldest deal .... Is 48:8
my people shall **k** my name .... Is 52:6
shall **k** in that day .... Is 52:6
nation that thou **k** not .... Is 55:5
thy name **k** to..adversaries .... Is 64:2
formed thee in the belly I **k** .... Jer 1:5
they have not **k** me .... Jer 4:22
whose language thou **k** not .... Jer 5:15
heaven **k** her..times .... Jer 8:7
nor their fathers have **k** .... Jer 9:16
understandeth and **k** me .... Jer 9:24
I **k** not that they had devised .... Jer 11:19
into a land which thou **k** not .... Jer 15:14
in the land which thou **k** not .... Jer 17:4
thou **k** all their counsel .... Jer 18:23
the prophet be **k** .... Jer 28:9
and no man **k** it .... Jer 41:4

which **k** that their wives .... Jer 44:15
are not **k** in the streets .... Lam 4:8
shall **k** that I am the Lord .... Ezek 6:7
I **k** that they were the .... Ezek 10:20
made myself **k** unto them .... Ezek 20:5
countries..thou hast not **k** .... Ezek 32:9
be it **k** unto you .... Ezek 36:32
O Lord God, thou **k** .... Ezek 37:3
make my holy name **k** in .... Ezek 39:7
not make **k** unto me the dream .... Dan 2:5
made the thing **k** to .... Dan 2:17
he **k** what is in..darkness .... Dan 2:22
made **k** unto me now what .... Dan 2:23
hast now made **k** unto us .... Dan 2:23
made **k** unto me the dream .... Dan 2:26
k to thee what shall come .... Dan 2:29
God..made **k** to the king .... Dan 2:45
k unto me..interpretation .... Dan 4:6, 7
k that the heavens do rule .... Dan 4:26
make **k**..the interpretation .... Dan 5:15
make **k**..the interpretation .... Dan 5:17
k..the most high God ruled .... Dan 5:21
though thou **k** all this .... Dan 5:22
K thou wherefore I come .... Dan 10:20
fathers **k** not..he honor .... Dan 11:38
thou shalt **k** the Lord .... Hos 2:20
they have not **k** the Lord .... Hos 5:4
and he **k** it not .... Hos 7:9
upon him, yet he **k** not .... Hos 7:9
made princes and I **k** it not .... Hos 8:4
Who **k** if he will return .... Joel 2:14
You only have I **k** .... Amos 3:2
unjust **k** no shame .... Zeph 3:5
K thou not what these be? .... Zech 4:5
nations whom they **k** not .... Zech 7:14
day..shall be **k** to the Lord .... Zech 14:7
priest's lips should keep **k** .... Mal 2:7
k her not till she..brought .... Matt 1:25
left hand **k** what..right hand .... Matt 6:3
k what things ye have need .... Matt 6:8
k them by their fruits .... Matt 7:16
by..fruits ye shall **k** them .... Matt 7:20
I never **k** you .... Matt 7:23
Jesus **k** their thoughts .... Matt 9:4
that shall not be **k** .... Matt 10:26
no man **k** the Son .... Matt 11:27
Jesus **k** it, he withdrew .... Matt 12:15
should not make him **k** .... Matt 12:16
Jesus **k** their thoughts .... Matt 12:25
tree is **k** by his fruit .... Matt 12:33
K thou that the Pharisees .... Matt 15:12
and they **k** him not .... Matt 17:12
k not what hour your Lord .... Matt 24:42
k..the day nor the hour .... Matt 25:13
I **k** thee that thou art .... Matt 25:24
k..I reap where I sowed .... Matt 25:26
k that for envy they had .... Matt 27:18
because they **k** him .... Mark 1:34
should not make him **k** .... Mark 3:12
he **k** not how .... Mark 4:27
k in himself that virtue .... Mark 5:30
k that he was a just man .... Mark 6:20
they **k**, they say, Five .... Mark 6:38
when Jesus **k** it .... Mark 8:17
k the commandments .... Mark 10:19
he **k** that the chief priests .... Mark 15:10
k it of the centurion .... Mark 15:45
Lord hath made **k** unto us .... Luke 2:15
they made **k** abroad .... Luke 2:17
Joseph and his mother **k** not .... Luke 2:43
k that he was Christ .... Luke 4:41
But he **k** their thoughts .... Luke 6:8
tree is **k** by his own fruit .... Luke 6:44
k who and what manner of .... Luke 7:39
k that she was dead .... Luke 8:53
they **k** it, followed him .... Luke 9:11
no man **k** who the Son is .... Luke 10:22
k their thoughts, said unto .... Luke 11:17
that shall not be **k** .... Luke 12:2
k his lord's will .... Luke 12:47
k not, and did commit .... Luke 12:48
God **k** your hearts .... Luke 16:15
k the commandments .... Luke 18:20
k that I was an austere .... Luke 19:22
If thou hadst **k** .... Luke 19:42

Woman I ***k*** him not ... Luke 22:57
k that he belonged ... Luke 23:7
k of them in breaking of ... Luke 24:35
the world ***k*** him not ... John 1:10
I ***k*** him not but he that sent ... John 1:33
k not whence it was ... John 2:9
drew the water ***k*** ... John 2:9
k what was in man ... John 2:25
If thou ***k*** the gift of God ... John 4:10
k that this indeed..Christ ... John 4:42
k that it was at the same ... John 4:53
himself ***k*** what he would do ... John 6:6
Jesus ***k*** from..beginning ... John 6:64
seeketh to be ***k*** openly ... John 7:4
How ***k*** this man letters ... John 7:15
no man ***k*** whence he is ... John 7:27
k not the law are cursed ... John 7:49
if ye had ***k*** me ... John 8:19
should have ***k*** my Father ... John 8:19
am ***k*** of mine ... John 10:14
As the Father ***k*** me ... John 10:15
any man ***k*** where he were ... John 11:57
k not whither he goeth ... John 12:35
k that his hour was come ... John 13:1
k that the Father had given ... John 13:3
him, What I do thou ***k*** not ... John 13:7
k who should betray him ... John 13:11
K..what I have done to you? ... John 13:12
And whither I go ye ***k*** ... John 14:4
and the way ye ***k*** ... John 14:4
yet hast thou not ***k*** me ... John 14:9
seeth him not, neither ***k*** ... John 14:17
k not what his lord doeth ... John 15:15
have not ***k*** the Father ... John 16:3
k that they were desirous ... John 16:19
sure that thou ***k*** all things ... John 16:30
k surely that I came out ... John 17:8
world hath not ***k*** thee ... John 17:25
but I have ***k*** thee ... John 17:25
k that thou hast sent me ... John 17:25
k unto the high priest ... John 18:16
k..not that I have power ... John 19:10
Jesus ***k***..all things were now ... John 19:28
as yet they ***k*** not..scripture ... John 20:9
k not that it was Jesus ... John 21:4
Lord, thou ***k*** all things ... John 21:17
thou ***k*** that I love thee ... John 21:17
not for you to ***k*** the times ... Acts 1:7
k unto all the dwellers ... Acts 1:19
k the hearts of all men ... Acts 1:24
made ***k*** to me the ways ... Acts 2:28
k that God had sworn with ... Acts 2:30
k..he which sat for alms ... Acts 3:10
not ***k*** what was done ... Acts 5:7
Joseph was made ***k*** ... Acts 7:13
kindred was made ***k*** ... Acts 7:13
laying await was ***k*** of Saul ... Acts 9:24
when the brethren ***k*** ... Acts 9:30
they ***k*** him not ... Acts 13:27
Be it ***k*** unto you therefore ... Acts 13:38
God, which ***k*** the hearts ... Acts 15:8
K unto God are all..works ... Acts 15:18
k only the baptism of John ... Acts 18:25
was ***k*** to all the Jews ... Acts 19:17
k not wherefore they were ... Acts 19:32
k that he was a Roman ... Acts 22:29
I would have ***k*** the cause ... Acts 23:28
king ***k*** of these things ... Acts 26:26
they ***k*** not the land ... Acts 27:39
may be ***k*** of God ... Rom 1:19
when they ***k*** God ... Rom 1:21
k the judgment of God ... Rom 1:32
k his will, and approvest ... Rom 2:18
k that tribulation worketh ... Rom 5:3
K that Christ being raised ... Rom 6:9
I had not ***k*** sin ... Rom 7:7
k..mind of the Spirit ... Rom 8:27
k..all things work together ... Rom 8:28
to make his power ***k*** ... Rom 9:22
k the mind of the Lord? ... Rom 11:34
world by wisdom ***k*** not God ... 1Cor 1:21
for had they ***k*** it ... 1Cor 2:8
k the things of a man ... 1Cor 2:11
things of God ***k*** no man ... 1Cor 2:11
neither can he ***k*** them ... 1Cor 2:14
k the thoughts of the wise ... 1Cor 3:20
For what ***k*** thou, O wife ... 1Cor 7:16
man think..he ***k*** any thing ... 1Cor 8:2
he ***k*** nothing yet as he ... 1Cor 8:2
the same is ***k*** of him ... 1Cor 8:3
I would have you ***k*** ... 1Cor 11:3
k in part, and we prophesy ... 1Cor 13:9
k what is piped or harped? ... 1Cor 14:7
ye ***k*** that your labor ... 1Cor 15:58
k that as ye are partakers ... 2Cor 1:7
k and read of all men ... 2Cor 3:2
we ***k*** that if our earthly ... 2Cor 5:1
k we no man after ... 2Cor 5:16
k we him no more ... 2Cor 5:16
be sin for us, who ***k*** no sin ... 2Cor 5:21
pureness, by ***k*** ... 2Cor 6:6
unknown, and yet well ***k*** ... 2Cor 6:9
I ***k*** the forwardness of ... 2Cor 9:2
I love you not? God ***k*** ... 2Cor 11:11
I cannot tell; God ***k*** ... 2Cor 12:2
I ***k*** such a man, (whether in ... 2Cor 12:3
K..a man is not justified ... Gal 2:16
when ye ***k*** not God, ye did ... Gal 4:8
after ye have ***k*** God ... Gal 4:9
rather are ***k*** of God ... Gal 4:9
k what is the hope ... Eph 1:18
not made ***k*** unto the sons ... Eph 3:5
to ***k*** the love of Christ ... Eph 3:19
this ye ***k***, that no ... Eph 5:5
K..whatsoever good thing ... Eph 6:8
k the mystery of the gospel ... Eph 6:19
also may ***k*** my affairs ... Eph 6:21
k..I am set for the defense ... Phil 1:17
I ***k*** that I shall abide ... Phil 1:25
moderation be ***k*** unto God ... Phil 4:5
be made ***k*** unto God ... Phil 4:6
k the grace of God in truth ... Col 1:6
make ***k*** what is the riches ... Col 1:27
that ye ***k*** what great ... Col 2:1
K that..ye shall receive ... Col 3:24
k that ye also have ... Col 4:1
that ye may ***k*** how ... Col 4:6
he might ***k*** your estate ... Col 4:8
K, brethren beloved, your ... 1Thess 1:4
K this..law is not made ... 1Tim 1:9
a man ***k*** not how to ... 1Tim 3:5
k whom I have believed ... 2Tim 1:12
This thou ***k***, that all they ... 2Tim 1:15
Lord ***k*** them that are his ... 2Tim 2:19
k..they do gender strifes ... 2Tim 2:23
this ***k*** also, that in ... 2Tim 3:1
have not ***k*** my doctrine ... 2Tim 3:10
preaching might be fully ***k*** ... 2Tim 4:17
K that he that is such ... Titus 3:11
K that thou wilt also do more. ... Philem 21
have not ***k*** my ways ... Heb 3:10
k him that hath said ... Heb 10:30
k in yourselves that ye ... Heb 10:34
K..the trying of your ... James 1:3
wilt thou ***k***, O vain ... James 3:13
k not what shall be on ... James 4:14
to him that ***k*** to do good ... James 4:17
ye ***k*** that ye were ... 1Pet 1:18
k..ye are thereunto called ... 1Pet 3:9
K..shortly I must put off ... 2Pet 1:14
made ***k*** unto you the power ... 2Pet 1:16
k how to deliver the godly ... 2Pet 2:9
not to have ***k*** the way ... 2Pet 2:21
after they have ***k***..to turn ... 2Pet 2:21
k this..there shall come ... 2Pet 3:3
we do ***k*** that we ***k*** him ... 1John 2:3
k we that we are in him ... 1John 2:5
k not whither he goeth ... 1John 2:11
k him..from the beginning ... 1John 2:13
ye have ***k*** the Father ... 1John 2:13
we ***k*** that this is the last ... 1John 2:18
and ye ***k*** all things ... 1John 2:20
because ye ***k*** not the truth ... 1John 2:21
ye ***k*** that he is righteous ... 1John 2:29
ye ***k*** that every one that ... 1John 2:29
world ***k*** us not, because ... 1John 3:1
because it ***k*** him not ... 1John 3:1
seen him, neither ***k*** him ... 1John 3:6
and ***k*** all things ... 1John 3:20
born of God, and ***k*** God ... 1John 4:7
k..ye have eternal life ... 1John 5:13
they that have ***k*** the truth ... 2John 1
though ye once ***k*** this ... Jude 5
no man ***k*** saving he that ... Rev 2:17
not ***k*** the depths of Satan ... Rev 2:24
k not..thou art wretched ... Rev 3:17
written, that no man ***k*** ... Rev 19:12

KNOWLEDGE—*content of the mind; sexual intimacy*

Kinds of:
Natural ... Matt 24:32
Deceptive ... Gen 3:5
Sinful ... Gen 3:7
Personal ... Josh 24:31
Practical ... Ex 36:1
Experimental ... Ex 14:4, 18
Friendly ... Ex 1:8
Intuitive ... 1Sam 22:22
Intellectual ... John 7:15, 28
Saving ... John 17:3
Spiritual ... 1Cor 2:14
Revealed ... Luke 10:22

Sources of:
God ... Ps 94:10
Nature ... Ps 19:2
Scriptures ... 2Tim 3:15
Doing God's will ... John 7:17

Believer's attitude toward:
Not to be pulled up ... 1Cor 8:1
Should grow in ... 2Pet 3:18
Should add to ... 2Pet 1:5
Not to be forgetful of ... 2Pet 3:17
Accept our limitations of ... 1Cor 13:8-12
Be filled with ... Phil 1:9

Christ's, of:
God ... Luke 10:22
Man's nature ... John 2:24, 25
Man's thoughts ... Matt 9:4
Believers ... John 10:14, 27
Things future ... 2Pet 1:14
All things ... Col 2:3

Attitude of sinful men toward:
Turn from ... Rom 1:21
Ignorant of ... 1Cor 1:21
Raised up against ... 2Cor 10:5
Did not acknowledge God ... Rom 1:28
Never able to come to ... 2Tim 3:7

Value of:
Superior to gold ... Prov 8:10
Increases strength ... Prov 24:5
Keeps from destruction ... Is 5:13
Insures stability ... Is 33:6

tree of ***k*** of good and evil ... Gen 2:9
understanding, and in ***k*** ... Ex 31:3
he hath sinned, come to his ***k*** ... Lev 4:23
the ***k*** of the congregation ... Num 15:24
k between good and evil ... Deut 1:39
shouldest take ***k*** of me ... Ruth 2:10
Lord is a God of ***k*** ... 1Sam 2:3
shipmen that had ***k*** of the sea ... 1Kin 9:27
Give me now wisdom and ***k*** ... 2Chr 1:10
Wisdom and ***k*** is granted ... 2Chr 1:12
the good ***k*** of the Lord ... 2Chr 30:22
every one having ***k*** ... Neh 10:28
wise man utter vain ***k*** ... Job 15:2
Shall any teach God ***k***? ... Job 21:22
ear unto me ye that have ***k*** ... Job 34:2
words without ***k*** ... Job 35:16
perfect in ***k*** is with thee ... Job 36:4
which is perfect in ***k***? ... Job 37:16
hideth counsel without ***k***? ... Job 42:3
workers of iniquity no ***k***? ... Ps 14:4
workers of iniquity no ***k***? ... Ps 53:4
k in the Most High? ... Ps 73:11
good judgment and ***k*** ... Ps 119:66
Such ***k*** is too wonderful ... Ps 139:6
thou takest ***k*** of him ... Ps 144:3
man ***k*** and discretion ... Prov 1:4
and fools hate ***k***? ... Prov 1:22
Yea, if thou criest after ***k*** ... Prov 2:3

out of his mouth cometh ***k*** ....Prov 2:6
k the depths are broken up....Prov 3:20
right to them that find ***k*** ......Prov 8:9
k of witty inventions ....Prov 8:12
k of..holy is understanding ....Prov 9:10
Wise men lay up ***k*** ....Prov 10:14
loveth instruction loveth ***k*****.....Prov 12:1
man dealeth with ***k*** ....Prov 13:16
perceivest not..lips of ***k*** ....Prov 14:7
tongue of the wise useth ***k*** ....Prov 15:2
understanding seeketh ***k*******.......Prov 15:14
hath ***k*** spareth his words ......Prov 17:27
prudent getteth ***k*** ....Prov 18:15
ear of the wise seeketh ***k*******......Prov 18:15
he will understand ***k*** ....Prov 19:25
lips of ***k*** are a..jewel ....Prov 20:15
eyes of the Lord preserve ***k*** ...Prov 22:12
apply thine heart unto my ***k*** ...Prov 22:17
things in counsels and ***k*******.......Prov 22:20
by ***k***..the chambers be filled ...Prov 24:4
k increased strength ....Prov 24:5
k of wisdom be unto ....Prov 24:14
nor have the ***k*** of the holy ....Prov 30:3
experience of wisdom and ***k*** ...Eccl 1:16
k increaseth sorrow ....Eccl 1:18
labor is in wisdom, and in ***k*** ...Eccl 2:21
excellency of ***k*** is ....Eccl 7:12
taught the people ***k*** ....Eccl 12:9
they have no ***k*** ....Is 5:13
spirit of ***k*** and of the fear .....Is 11:2
Whom shall he teach ***k***? ......Is 28:9
wisdom and ***k*** shall be ....Is 33:6
taught him ***k***, and showed .....Is 40:14
k nor understanding ....Is 44:19
have no ***k*** that set up ....Is 45:20
k shall my righteous servant ...Is 53:11
which shall feed you with ***k*** ...Jer 3:15
Every man is brutish in his ***k*** ..Jer 10:14
Every man is brutish by his ***k***. .Jer 51:17
and cunning in ***k*** ....Dan 1:4
God gave them ***k*** ....Dan 1:17
k to them that know ....Dan 2:21
k shall be increased ....Dan 12:4
nor mercy, nor ***k*** of God ......Hos 4:1
destroyed for lack of ***k*** ....Hos 4:6
thou hast rejected ***k*** ....Hos 4:6
k of God more than burnt ....Hos 6:6
of that place had ***k*** of him ....Matt 14:35
and they took ***k*** of them ......Acts 4:13
take ***k*** of all these things ......Acts 24:8
retain God in their ***k*** ....Rom 1:28
by the law is the ***k*** of sin......Rom 3:20
wisdom and ***k*** of God ....Rom 11:33
all utterance, and in all ***k*** 1Cor 1:5
see thee which hast ***k*** 1Cor 8:10
word of ***k*** by..Spirit 1Cor 12:8
all mysteries, and all ***k*** 1Cor 13:2
some have not the ***k*** of God...1Cor 15:34
manifest the savor of his ***k*** 2Cor 2:14
light of the ***k*** of the glory 2Cor 4:6
pureness, by ***k*** 2Cor 6:6
against the ***k*** of God 2Cor 10:5
revelation in the ***k*** of him .....Eph 1:17
k in the mystery of Christ .....Eph 3:4
love of Christ..passeth ***k*** ......Eph 3:19
k of the Son of God ....Eph 4:13
excellency of the ***k***..Christ .....Phil 3:8
be filled with..***k*** of his will ....Col 1:9
increasing in the ***k*** of God ....Col 1:10
treasures of wisdom and ***k*** .....Col 2:3
renewed in ***k*** after the image ..Col 3:10
come unto the ***k*** of the truth ..1Tim 2:4
come to the ***k*** of the truth 2Tim 3:7
received the ***k*** of the truth ....Heb 10:26
endued with ***k*** among you? ....James 3:13
dwell..them according to ***k*** 1Pet 3:7
through the ***k*** of God 2Pet 1:2
k of him that hath called us ...2Pet 1:3
And to ***k***, temperance 2Pet 1:6
k of our Lord Jesus Christ 2Pet 1:8
k of the Lord and Savior 2Pet 2:20

KOA (kō'ä)—*"male camel"*
People described as
enemies of Jerusalem ..Ezek 23:23

KOHATH (kō'hăth)—*"assembly"*
Second son of Levi ......Gen 46:8, 11
Goes with Levi to Egypt .Gen 46:11
Brother of Jochebed,
mother of Aaron and
Moses ....Ex 6:16-20
Dies at age 133 ....Ex 6:18

their names, Gershon, and ***K*** ..Num 3:17
of ***K*** was the family of the ....Num 3:27
sum of the sons of ***K*** ....Num 4:2
sons of ***K***..come to bear it .....Num 4:15
burden of the sons of ***K*** ....Num 4:15
Izhar, the son of ***K***, the son ...Num 16:1
And ***K*** begat Amram ....Num 26:58
rest of the children of ***K*** ......Josh 21:5
families of..children of ***K*** ......Josh 21:20
remained of the children of ***K*** .Josh 21:20
sons of Levi, Gershon, ***K*** 1Chr 6:1
sons of Levi; Gershon, ***K*** 1Chr 6:16
unto the sons of ***K***, which 1Chr 6:61
remnant of the sons of ***K*** 1Chr 6:70
of Levi, namely, Gershon, ***K*** ..1Chr 23:6

KOHATHITES (kō'hăth-īts)—*descendants of Kohath*

History of:
Originate in Levi's son
(Kohath) ....Gen 46:11
Divided into 4 groups
(Amram, Izhar,
Hebron, Uzziel) ....Num 3:19, 27
Numbering of ....Num 3:27, 28
Duties assigned to ....Num 4:15-20
Cities assigned to ....Josh 21:4-11

Privileges of:
Aaron and Moses ....Ex 6:20
Special charge of sacred
instruments ....Num 4:15-20
Temple music by Heman
the Kohathite 1Chr 6:31-38
Under Jehoshaphat, lead
in praise 2Chr 20:19
Under Hezekiah, help to
cleanse Temple 2Chr 29:12, 15

Sins of:
Korah (of Izhar) leads
rebellion .... {Num 16:1-35; Jude 11}

father of..families of the ***K*** ....Num 3:30
numbered the sons of the ***K*** ...Num 4:34
K set forward, bearing the ....Num 10:21
families of the ***K*** 1Chr 6:54
of the sons of the ***K*** 1Chr 9:32
of the sons of the ***K*** 2Chr 34:12

KOLAIAH (kō-lā'yä)—*"voice of Jehovah"*
1. Father of the false
prophet Ahab ....Jer 29:21-23
2. Postexilic Benjamite
family................Neh 11:7

KOPH (kōf)
Letter of the Hebrew
alphabet ....Ps 119:145-152

KORAH, CORE (kō'rä, kōr)—*"baldness"*
1. Son of Esau ....Gen 36:5, 14, 18
2. Son of Eliphaz and
grandson of Esau .....Gen 36:16
3. Calebite.................1Chr 2:42, 43
4. Son of Izhar the
Kohathite ....Ex 6:21, 24
Leads a rebellion against
Moses and Aaron .....Num 16:1-3
Warned by Moses.......Num 16:4-27
Supernaturally destroyed .Num 16:28-35
Sons of, not destroyed ..Num 26:9-11
Sons of, porters..........1Chr 26:19

he be not as ***K***, and as his ....Num 16:40
about the matter of ***K*** ....Num 16:49
Lord in the company of ***K***.....Num 27:3
Jeush and Jaalam, and ***K*** 1Chr 1:35
Musician for the sons of ***K*** ....Ps 44: *title*
Shoshannim, for..sons of ***K***....Ps 45: *title*
A Psalm for the sons of ***K*** ....Ps 47: *title*
for the sons of ***K*** ....Ps 87: *title*
for the sons of ***K*** ....Ps 88: *title*

KORAHITES (kō'rä-īts)—*the Levites who were descendants of Korah*
Descendants of Korah ...Ex 6:24
Some become:
David's warriors.......1Chr 12:6
Servants 1Chr 9:19-31
Musicians 1Chr 6:22-32
A maschil for ....Ps 42 *title*
Called Korathites........1Chr 9:19

KORE (kō'rĕ)—*"one who proclaims"*
1. Korahite Levite 1Chr 9:19
2. Porter of the eastern
gate 2Chr 31:14

[*also* KORHITES]
K was Meshelemiah...........1Chr 26:1
Meshelemiah the son of ***K***.....1Chr 26:1
children of the ***K*** stood 2Chr 20:19

KOZ (kŏz)—*"thorn"*
Father of Anub 1Chr 4:8

the children of ***K*** ....Neh 7:63

KUSHAIAH (kū-shā'yä)—*"snarer; fowler"*
Merarite Levite musician .1Chr 15:17
Called Kishi 1Chr 6:44

L

LAADAH (lā'ä-dä)—*"order; festival"*
Judahite 1Chr 4:21

LAADAN (lā'ä-dăn)—*"festive-born; ordered"*
1. Son of Gershon, the son
of Levi...............1Chr 23:7-9
Called Libni 1Chr 6:17
2. Ephraimite 1Chr 7:26

concerning the sons of ***L*** 1Chr 26:21
sons of the Gershonite ***L*** 1Chr 26:21
L the Gershonite, were 1Chr 26:21

LABAN (lā'băn)—*"white, glorious"*
1. Son of Bethuel ....Gen 24:24, 29
Brother of Rebekah.....Gen 24:15, 29
Father of Leah and
Rachel ....Gen 29:16
Chooses Rebekah for
Isaac.................Gen 24:29-60
Entertains Jacob ....Gen 29:1-14
Deceives Jacob in
marriage arrangement .Gen 29:15-30
Agrees to Jacob's
business arrangement ..Gen 30:25-43
Changes attitude toward
Jacob ....Gen 31:1-9
Pursues after fleeing
Jacob ....Gen 31:21-25
Rebukes Jacob ....Gen 31:26-30
Rebuked by Jacob ......Gen 31:31-42
Makes covenant with
Jacob ....Gen 31:43-55
2. City in the wilderness ...Deut 1:1

sister to ***L*** the Syrian ....Gen 25:20
flee thou to ***L*** my brother .....Gen 27:43
thence of the daughters of ***L*** ..Gen 28:2
went to Padan-aram unto ***L*** ...Gen 28:5
seen all..***L*** doeth unto thee ....Gen 31:12
L went to shear his sheep .....Gen 31:19
stole away unawares to ***L*** .....Gen 31:20
have sojourned with ***L*** ....Gen 32:4
L gave to Leah his daughter...Gen 46:18
L gave unto Rachel his ....Gen 46:25

LABOR—*physical or mental effort*

Physical:

Nature of:
As old as creation ....Gen 2:5, 15
Ordained by God........Gen 3:17-19
One of the
commandments........Ex 20:9

From morning until night . Ps 104:23
With the hands . 1Thess 4:11
To life's end . Ps 90:10
Without God, vanity . Eccl 2:11
Shrinking from, denounced . 2Thess 3:10

Benefits of:
Profit . Prov 14:23
Happiness . Ps 128:2
Proclaim gospel . 1Thess 2:9
Supply of other's needs . Acts 20:35; Eph 4:28
Restful sleep . Eccl 5:12
Double honor . 1Tim 5:17
Eternal life . John 6:27
Not in vain . 1Cor 15:58; Phil 2:16

Spiritual:
Characteristics of:
Commissioned by Christ . John 4:38
Accepted by few . Matt 9:37, 38
Working with God . 1Cor 3:9
By God's grace . 1Cor 15:10
Result of faith . 1Tim 4:10
Characterized by love . 1Thess 1:3
Done in prayer . Col 4:12
Subject to discouragement . Is 49:4; Gal 4:11
Interrupted by Satan . 1Thess 3:5

Problems:
Inspired by opposition . Ezra 4:1-6
Complaint over wages . Matt 20:1-16
Mistreatment of employees . Matt 21:33-35
Characteristics of last days . James 5:1-6

[*also* LABORED, LABORETH, LABORING, LABORS]
l of my hands . Gen 31:42
she had hard *l* . Gen 35:16
when she was in hard *l* . Gen 35:17
they may *l* therein . Ex 5:9
firstfruits of thy *l* . Ex 23:16
gathered in thy *l* out of the . Ex 23:16
Six days thou shalt *l* . Deut 5:13
l, and our oppression . Deut 26:7
fruit of thy land..thy *l* . Deut 28:33
not all the people to *l* . Josh 7:3
which ye did not *l*? . Josh 24:13
So we *l* in the work . Neh 4:21
guard to us, and *l* on the . Neh 4:22
his house, and from his *l* . Neh 5:13
why then *l* I in vain? . Job 9:29
l for shall he restore . Job 20:18
thou leave thy *l* to him? . Job 39:11
l is in vain without fear? . Job 39:16
their *l* unto the locust . Ps 78:46
inherited the *l* of the people . Ps 105:44
brought down..heart with *l* . Ps 107:12
strangers spoil his *l* . Ps 109:11
l in vain that build it . Ps 127:1
eat the *l* of thine hands . Ps 128:2
oxen may be strong to *l* . Ps 144:14
l be in..house of a stranger . Prov 5:10
l of the righteous . Prov 10:16
gathereth by *l* shall increase . Prov 13:11
In all *l* there is profit . Prov 14:23
He that *l*..for himself . Prov 16:26
his hands refuse to *l* . Prov 21:25
L not to be rich . Prov 23:4
hath a man of all his *l* . Eccl 1:3
All things are full of *l* . Eccl 1:8
heart rejoiced in all my *l* . Eccl 2:10
my portion of all my *l* . Eccl 2:10
on the *l* that I had *l* to do . Eccl 2:11
I hated all my *l* . Eccl 2:18
all my *l* wherein I have *l* . Eccl 2:19
l which I took under the sun . Eccl 2:20
man whose *l* is in wisdom . Eccl 2:21
man that hath not *l* therein . Eccl 2:21
hath man of all his *l* . Eccl 2:22
he hath *l* under the sun? . Eccl 2:22
soul enjoy good in his *l* . Eccl 2:24
worketh wherein he *l*? . Eccl 3:9
enjoy the good of all his *l* . Eccl 3:13
no end of all his *l* . Eccl 4:8
For whom do I *l* . Eccl 4:8
good reward for their *l* . Eccl 4:9
sleep of a *l* man is sweet . Eccl 5:12
shall take nothing of his *l* . Eccl 5:15
hath *l* for the wind? . Eccl 5:16
enjoy the good of all his *l* . Eccl 5:18
to rejoice in his *l* . Eccl 5:19
the *l* of man is for..mouth . Eccl 6:7
abide with him of his *l* . Eccl 8:15
man *l* to seek it out . Eccl 8:17
l which thou takest . Eccl 9:9
l of the foolish wearieth . Eccl 10:15
l not to comfort me . Is 22:4
The *l* of Egypt, and . Is 45:14
hast *l* from thy youth . Is 47:12
with whom thou hast *l* . Is 47:15
l for..which satisfied not? . Is 55:2
exact all your *l* . Is 58:3
which thou hast *l* . Is 62:8
They shall not *l* in vain . Is 65:23
shame hath devoured the *l* . Jer 3:24
all the *l* thereof . Jer 20:5
out of the womb to see *l* . Jer 20:18
people shall *l* in vain . Jer 51:58
we *l*, and have no rest . Lam 5:5
his *l*..he served against . Ezek 29:20
l till the going down of..sun . Dan 6:14
l they..find none iniquity . Hos 12:8
which thou hast not *l* . Jon 4:10
shall *l* in the very fire . Hab 2:13
l of the olive shall fail . Hab 3:17
all the *l* of the hands . Hag 1:11
in all the *l* of your hands . Hag 2:17
Come unto me, all ye that *l* . Matt 11:28
L not for the meat which . John 6:27
so *l* ye ought to support . Acts 20:35
bestowed much *l* on us . Rom 16:6
who *l* in the Lord . Rom 16:12
which *l* much in the Lord . Rom 16:12
reward according to his..*l* . 1Cor 3:8
l, working with our..hands . 1Cor 4:12
your *l* is not in vain . 1Cor 15:58
helpeth with us, and *l* . 1Cor 16:16
Wherefore we *l*, that . 2Cor 5:9
in tumults, in *l* . 2Cor 6:5
that is, of other men's *l* . 2Cor 10:15
in *l* more abundant . 2Cor 11:23
rather let him *l* . Eph 4:28
this is the fruit of my *l* . Phil 1:22
neither *l* in vain . Phil 2:16
companion in *l* . Phil 2:25
l with me in the gospel . Phil 4:3
Whereunto I also *l* . Col 1:29
our *l* and travail . 1Thess 2:9
for *l* night and day . 1Thess 2:9
which *l* among you . 1Thess 5:12
wrought with *l* and travail . 2Thess 3:8
we both *l* and suffer . 1Tim 4:10
l in the word and doctrine . 1Tim 5:17
husbandman that *l* . 2Tim 2:6
l..to enter into that rest . Heb 4:11
your work and *l* of love . Heb 6:10
know thy works, and thy *l* . Rev 2:2
for my name's sake hast *l* . Rev 2:3
they may rest from their *l* . Rev 14:13

LABOR—*the process of giving birth*
***Of a woman's*, described as:**
Fearful . Ps 48:6
Painful . Is 13:8
Hazardous . Gen 35:16-19
Joyful afterwards . John 16:21

Figurative of:
New Israel . Is 66:7, 8
Messiah's birth . Mic 4:9, 10
Redemption . Mic 5:3
New birth . Gal 4:19
Creation's rebirth . Rom 8:22

LABORER—*a worker*

[*also* LABORERS]
Call the *l*, and give them . Matt 20:8
but the *l* are few . Luke 10:2
would send forth *l* into his . Luke 10:2
l is worthy of his reward . 1Tim 5:18

LACE—*a cord or heavy thread*
Of priest's garments . Ex 28:28; Ex 39:21

put it on a blue *l* . Ex 28:37
tied unto it a *l* of blue . Ex 39:31

LACHISH (lā'kĭsh)—*"who exists of himself"*
Town in southern Judah . Josh 15:1, 39
Joins coalition against Gibeonites . Josh 10:3-5
Defeated by Joshua . Josh 10:6-33
Fortified by Rehoboam . 2Chr 11:5, 9
City of sin . Mic 1:13
Amaziah murdered here . 2Kin 14:19; 2Chr 25:27
Taken by Sennacherib . 2Kin 18:13-17
Military headquarters . Is 36:1, 2; Is 37:8
Flights against Nebuchadnezzar . Jer 34:1, 7
Reoccupied after exile . Neh 11:30

from *L* Joshua passed . Josh 10:34
all that he had done to *L* . Josh 10:35
Jarmuth, one; the king of *L* . Josh 12:11
that he was departed from *L* . 2Kin 19:8
himself laid siege against *L* . 2Chr 32:9

LACK—*something still needed; to need*
How to avoid:
Remember God's promises . Deut 2:7
Work diligently . 1Thess 4:11, 12
Live chastely . Prov 6:32
Share in common . Acts 4:34

Things subject to:
Food . 2Sam 3:29
Physical needs . 2Cor 11:9
Possessions . 1Sam 30:19
Service to others . Phil 2:30
Entire commitment . Luke 18:22
Wisdom . James 1:5
Graces . 2Pet 1:9

[*also* LACKED, LACKEST, LACKETH, LACKING]
l five of the fifty . Gen 18:28
all the city for *l* of five . Gen 18:28
gathered little had no *l* . Ex 16:18
l from thy meat offering . Lev 2:13
superfluous or *l* in his parts . Lev 22:23
l not one man of us . Num 31:49
shalt not *l* any thing in it . Deut 8:9
l of David's servants . 2Sam 2:30
morning light there *l* not . 2Sam 17:22
in his month: they *l* nothing . 1Kin 4:27
what hast thou *l* with me . 1Kin 11:22
they *l* nothing . Neh 9:21
they wander for *l* of meat . Job 38:41
himself, and *l* bread . Prov 12:9
thy head *l* no ointment . Eccl 9:8
neither shall they be *l* . Jer 23:4
destroyed for *l* of knowledge . Hos 4:6
youth up; what *l* I yet? . Matt 19:20
unto him, One thing thou *l* . Mark 10:21
because it *l* moisture . Luke 8:6
scrip, and shoes, *l* ye any . Luke 22:35
honor to that part which *l* . 1Cor 12:24
that which was *l* on your . 1Cor 16:17
which is *l* in your faith? . 1Thess 3:10

LAD—*a young boy*
Heard by God . Gen 21:17-20
Saved by God . Gen 22:12
Loved by his father . Gen 44:22-34
Slain with Samson . Judg 16:26-30
Unsuspecting . 1Sam 20:21-41
Tattling . 2Sam 17:18
Providing . John 6:9

[*also* LAD'S, LADS]
I and the *l* will go yonder . Gen 22:5
the *l* was with the sons of . Gen 37:2
Send the *l* with me, and we . Gen 43:8
his life is bound up in the *l* . Gen 44:30

all evil, bless the *l* ....Gen 48:16
And he said to a *l*, Carry him .2Kin 4:19

LADDER—*a steep set of steps, usually connected by two long sidepieces*
Jacob's ....Gen 28:10-12
Christ's ....John 1:51

LADE—*to load*

[*also* LADED, LADEN, LADETH, LADING, LOADEN, LOADETH]
they *l* their asses with the .....Gen 42:26
l your beasts, and go ....Gen 45:17
ten asses *l* with the good ......Gen 45:23
Jesse took an ass *l* with 1Sam 16:20
l you with a heavy yoke.......1Kin 12:11
burdens, with those that *l* .....Neh 4:17
bringing in sheaves, and *l* .....Neh 13:15
who daily *l* us with benefits ...Ps 68:19
people *l* with iniquity ....Is 1:4
carriages were heavy *l* ....Is 46:1
l himself with thick clay.......Hab 2:6
that labor and are heavy *l*.....Matt 11:28
l men with burdens ....Luke 11:46
not only of the *l* and ship .....Acts 27:10
l us with such things as ....Acts 28:10
silly women *l* with sins 2Tim 3:6

LADY—*a woman of superior social position; a woman*
Applied to females of high rank ....Judg 5:29
Among royalty ....Esth 1:18
Elect 2John 1, 5
Figurative of Babylon ....Is 47:5-7

[*also* LADIES]
Her wise *l* answered her ......Judg 5:29
l of Persia and Media say .....Esth 1:18

LAEL (lā'ĕl)—*"belonging to God"*
Gershonite Levite ....Num 3:24

LAHAD (lā-hăd)—*"oppression; dark-colored"*
Judahite 1Chr 4:2

LAHAI-ROI (lā-hī'roi)—*"of the living one who sees me"*
Name of a well..........Gen 24:62
Same as Beer-lahairoi ....Gen 6:7, 14

Isaac dwelt by the well *L* .....Gen 25:11

LAHMAM (lä'măm)—*"their bread"*
City of Judah ....Josh 15:1, 40

LAHMI (lä'mī)—*"Beth-lehemite"*
Brother of Goliath slain by Elhanan 1Chr 20:5

LAID—*See* LAY

LAIN—*See* LIE

LAISH (lā'ĭsh)—*"lion"*
1. Benjamite 1Sam 25:44
2. City in northern Palestine at the head of the Jordan ....Judg 18:7, 14
Called Leshem..........Josh 19:47
3. Village in Benjamin between Anathoth and Gallim ....Is 10:30

he had, and came unto *L* .....Judg 18:27
the name of the city was *L* ....Judg 18:29
from Phaltiel the son of *L*.....2Sam 3:15

LAKE—*a large body of standing inland water; a pool*
Sea of Galilee is called...Luke 5:1, 2
Luke 8:22-33
Bottomless pit described as ....Rev 19:20

LAKE OF FIRE—*the place of final punishment*
Those consigned to:
The beast and false prophet ....Rev 19:20
The devil ....Rev 20:10
Death and hell ....Rev 20:14
Those whose names are not in book of life .....Rev 20:15
Described as:
Burning brimstone ....Rev 19:20
Second death ....Rev 20:14

was cast into the *l* of fire .....Rev 20:10
hell were cast into the *l* ......Rev 20:14
of life was cast into the *l* ......Rev 20:15
their part in the *l* which ....Rev 21:8

LAKUM (lā'kŭm)—*obstruction*
Town of Naphtali........Josh 19:32, 33

LAMA (lä'mä)—*the Aramaic word for "Why?"*
Spoken by Christ on the cross ....Matt 27:46

saying, Eloi, Eloi, *l* ....Mark 15:34

LAMB—*a young sheep*
Used for:
Food 2Sam 12:4
Clothing ....Prov 27:26
Trade ....Ezra 7:17
Tribute 2Kin 3:4
Covenants ....Gen 21:28-32
Sacrifices ....Ex 12:5
Figurative of:
God's people............Is 5:17
Weak believers..........Is 40:11
God's ministers..........Luke 10:3
God's dealing with the wicked ....Ps 37:20
Messiah's reign ....Is 11:6

[*also* LAMB'S, LAMBS]
the *l* for a burnt offering? .....Gen 22:7
God will provide himself a *l*...Gen 22:8
Jacob did separate the *l*........Gen 30:40
take to them every man a *l* ...Ex 12:3
of their fathers, a *l* for an .....Ex 12:3
be too little for the *l*..........Ex 12:4
make your count for the *l*.....Ex 12:4
Draw out and take you a *l* ....Ex 12:21
two *l* of the first year ....Ex 29:38
The one *l* thou shalt offer .....Ex 29:39
the other *l* thou shalt offer ....Ex 29:39
the other *l* thou shalt offer ....Ex 29:41
he offer a *l* for his offering ....Lev 3:7
if he bring a *l* for a sin ....Lev 4:32
he be not able to bring a *l* ....Lev 5:7
she shall bring a *l* of the ......Lev 12:6
shall take two he *l* without ....Lev 14:10
one ewe *l* of the first year.....Lev 14:10
shall slay the *l* in the place ....Lev 14:13
take the *l* of the trespass ......Lev 14:24
kill the *l* of the trespass ....Lev 14:25
l that hath any thing ....Lev 22:23
he *l* without blemish of the ....Lev 23:12
two *l* of the first year for .....Lev 23:19
shall bring a *l* of the first .....Num 6:12
one he *l* of the first year ......Num 6:14
one ewe *l* of the first year.....Num 6:14
he goats, five *l* of the first ....Num 7:17
the *l* of the first year ....Num 7:87
sixty, the *l* of the first year ....Num 7:88
sacrifice, for one *l* ....Num 15:5
two *l* of the first year ....Num 28:3
The one *l* shalt thou offer .....Num 28:4
the other *l* shalt thou offer ....Num 28:4
the other *l* shalt thou offer ....Num 28:8
seven *l* of the first year ....Num 28:11
fourth part of a hin unto a *l*...Num 28:14
throughout the seven *l* ....Num 28:21
one *l*, throughout the seven *l* ..Num 28:29
throughout the seven *l* ....Num 29:4
one *l*, throughout the seven *l* ..Num 29:10
each lamb of the fourteen *l* ...Num 29:15
for the rams, and for the *l* ....Num 29:18
for the rams, and for the *l* ....Num 29:21
fourteen *l* of the first year.....Num 29:26
fourteen *l* of the first year.....Num 29:32
seven *l* of the first year ....Num 29:36
with fat of *l*, and rams of .....Deut 32:14
Samuel took a sucking *l*.......1Sam 7:9
and the *l*, and all that was 1Sam 15:9
save one little ewe *l* 2Sam 12:3
he shall restore the *l*..........2Sam 12:6
rams, and a thousand *l*........1Chr 29:21
seven *l*, and seven he goats ...2Chr 29:21
rams, and two hundred *l* 2Chr 29:32
bullocks, and rams, and *l* .....Ezra 6:9
rams, seventy and seven *l* .....Ezra 8:35
and the little hills like *l* ....Ps 114:4
and ye little hills, like *l*? ......Ps 114:6
The *l* are for thy clothing .....Prov 27:26
Send ye the *l* to the ruler .....Is 16:1
and with the blood of *l* ....Is 34:6
wolf and the *l* shall feed ......Is 65:25
But I was like a *l* or an ox....Jer 11:19
like *l* to the slaughter ....Jer 51:40
occupied with thee in *l*........Ezek 27:21
one *l* out of the flock, out ....Ezek 45:15
six *l* without blemish, and .....Ezek 46:4
blemish and six *l*, and a ram ..Ezek 46:6
and to the *l* as he is able......Ezek 46:11
shall they prepare the *l* ....Ezek 46:15
feed them as a *l* in a large ....Hos 4:16
eat the *l* out of the flock ......Amos 6:4
He saith unto him, Feed my *l* .John 21:15
he had two horns like a *l* .....Rev 13:11

LAMB OF GOD, THE—*a figure of speech used to describe the sacrificial nature of Jesus' life*
Descriptive of Christ as:
Predicted ....Is 53:7
Presented to Israel ......John 1:29
Preached to world ....Acts 8:32-35
Praised throughout eternity...............Rev 5:6, 13
Descriptive of Christ as:
Sacrifice 1Pet 1:19
Rev 7:13, 14
Redeemer ....Rev 5:9
King ....Rev 15:3

[*also* LAMB, LAMB'S]
Behold the *L* of *G* ....John 1:36
L opened one of the seals .....Rev 6:1
throne, and before the *L* ......Rev 7:9
white in the blood of the *L*....Rev 7:14
him by the blood of the *L*.....Rev 12:11
in the book of life of the *L*....Rev 13:8
lo, a *L* stood on the mount ....Rev 14:1
they which follow the *L* ....Rev 14:4
first fruits unto God..to the *L*. .Rev 14:4
shall make war with the *L*.....Rev 17:14
the *L* shall overcome them ....Rev 17:14
marriage supper of the *L*......Rev 19:9
thee the bride, the *L* wife ......Rev 21:9
Lord God..and the *L* are......Rev 21:22
and the *L* is the light ....Rev 21:23
are written in the *L* book .....Rev 21:27
throne of God and of the *L* ...Rev 22:1

LAME—*inability to walk properly*
Healing of, by:
Christ ....Matt 11:5
Peter ....Acts 3:2-7
Philip ....Acts 8:5-7
Figurative of:
Extreme weakness 2Sam 5:6, 8
Inconsistency ....Prov 26:7
Weak believers ....Jer 31:8
Healed ....Is 35:6
Causes of:
Birth defect ....Acts 3:2
Accident................2Sam 4:4
Renders unfit for:
Priesthood ....Lev 21:17, 18
Sacrifice ....Deut 15:21
Active life 2Sam 9:13
2Sam 19:24-26

a blind man, or a *l*, or he .....Lev 21:18
as if it be *l*, or blind ....Deut 15:21
son that was *l* of his feet 2Sam 4:4
that he fell, and became *l* 2Sam 4:4
son, which is *l* on his feet 2Sam 9:3
because thy servant is *l* 2Sam 19:26
and feet was I to the *l* ....Job 29:15

the *l* take the prey .... Is 33:23
offer the *l* and sick, is it ...... Mal 1:8
and the *l*, and the sick .... Mal 1:13
those that were *l*, blind .... Matt 15:30
the *l* came to him in the ...... Matt 21:14
l walk, the lepers are .... Luke 7:22
the *l* man which was .... Acts 3:11
which is *l* be turned out of .... Heb 12:13

LAMECH (lā′mĕk)—*"strong youth; overthrower"*

1. Son of Methusael, of Cain's race .... Gen 4:17, 18
   Had two wives .... Gen 4:19
2. Son of Methuselah; father of Noah .... Gen 5:25-31
   Man of faith .... Gen 5:29
   In Christ's ancestry ..... Luke 3:36

And *L* said unto his wives ..... Gen 4:23
ye wives of *L*, hearken unto ... Gen 4:23
truly *L* seventy and .... Gen 4:24
Henoch, Methuselah, *L* 1Chr 1:3

LAMED (lä′mĕd)
Letter of the Hebrew alphabet .... Ps 119:89-96

LAMENTATION—*mournful speech; elegy; dirge*

Historical of:
Jeremiah over Josiah 2Chr 35:25
David over Saul 2Sam 1:17-27
David over Abner 2Sam 3:33, 34
Jeremiah over Jerusalem. . Lam 1:1

Prophetic of:
Isaiah over Babylon ..... Is 14:1-32
Jeremiah over Jerusalem . Jer 7:28-34
Ezekiel over Tyre .... Ezek 27:2-36
Christ over Jerusalem .... Luke 19:41-44
John over Babylon ...... Rev 18:1-24

[*also* LAMENT, LAMENTABLE, LAMENTATIONS, LAMENTED]
great and very sore *l* .... Gen 50:10
to *l* the daughter of .... Judg 11:40
the people *l*, because the 1Sam 6:19
and *l* him, and buried him 1Sam 25:1
And David *l* with this 2Sam 1:17
And Jeremiah *l* for Josiah 2Chr 35:25
their widows made no *l* .... Ps 78:64
her gates shall *l* and mourn ... Is 3:26
into the brooks shall *l* .... Is 19:8
They shall *l* for the teats ...... Is 32:12
you with sackcloth, *l* .... Jer 4:8
an only son, most bitter *l* ..... Jer 6:26
of the wilderness a *l* .... Jer 9:10
they shall not be *l*; neither .... Jer 16:4
neither shall men *l* for them .. Jer 16:6
They shall not *l* for him .... Jer 22:18
in Ramah, *l*, and bitter .... Jer 31:15
There shall be *l* generally ..... Jer 48:38
l, and run to and fro by .... Jer 49:3
of Judah mourning and *l* ...... Lam 2:5
rampart and the wall to *l* ..... Lam 2:8
there was written therein *l* .... Ezek 2:10
up a *l* for the princes of .... Ezek 19:1
they shall take up a *l* for ...... Ezek 26:17
for thee, and *l* over thee ...... Ezek 27:32
take up a *l* upon the king ..... Ezek 28:12
l wherewith they shall *l* ...... Ezek 32:16
of the nations shall *l* her ...... Ezek 32:16
l for her, even for Egypt ...... Ezek 32:16
cried with a *l* voice unto ...... Dan 6:20
L like a virgin girded with ..... Joel 1:8
Gird yourselves, and *l*, ye ..... Joel 1:13
you, even a *l*, O house of ..... Amos 5:1
and all your songs into *l* ...... Amos 8:10
and *l* with a doleful *l* .... Mic 2:4
a voice heard, *l* and weeping .. Matt 2:18
unto you, and ye have not *l* ... Matt 11:17
which also bewailed and *l* ..... Luke 23:27
That ye shall weep and *l* ...... John 16:20
and made great *l* over him .... Acts 8:2
shall bewail her, and *l* for ..... Rev 18:9

LAMENTATIONS, THE BOOK OF—*a book of the Old Testament*
The suffering of Zion .... Lam 1:1—2:22
Individual prayer .... Lam 3:1—66
Collective prayer .... Lam 5:1—22

LAMP—*a vessel with a wick for burning a flammable liquid to create light*

Used in:
Tabernacle .... Ex 37:23
Temple 1Chr 28:15
Processions .... Matt 25:1-8

Figurative of:
God 2Sam 22:29
God's Word .... Prov 6:23; Ps 119:105
God's justice .... Zeph 1:12
Conscience .... Prov 20:27
Prosperity .... Job 29:3
Industry .... Prov 31:18
Death .... Job 18:6
Churches .... Rev 1:20
Christ .... Dan 10:6; Rev 1:14

[*also* LAMPS]
burning *l* that passed .... Gen 15:17
shalt make the seven *l* .... Ex 25:37
they shall light the *l* .... Ex 25:37
to cause the *l* to burn .... Ex 27:20
when Aaron lighteth the *l* ..... Ex 30:8
and his *l*, with the oil for ..... Ex 35:14
candlestick, with the *l* .... Ex 39:37
even with the *l* to be set ...... Ex 39:37
he lighted the *l* before the .... Ex 40:25
to cause the *l* to burn .... Lev 24:2
the light, and his *l*, and his .... Num 4:9
When thou lightest the *l* ...... Num 8:2
the seven *l* shall give light ..... Num 8:2
l of God went out in the 1Sam 3:3
and the *l*, and the tongs of 1Kin 7:49
his God give him a *l* in 1Kin 15:4
candlesticks with their *l* 2Chr 4:20
of gold with the *l* thereof 2Chr 13:11
as a *l* despised in the .... Job 12:5
of his mouth go burning *l* ..... Job 41:19
ordained a *l* for mine .... Ps 132:17
the *l* of the wicked shall be ... Prov 13:9
the salvation thereof as a *l* .... Is 62:1
like the appearance of *l* .... Ezek 1:13
and his eyes as *l* of fire .... Dan 10:6
top of it, and his seven *l* ...... Zech 4:2
seven pipes to the seven *l* ..... Zech 4:2
for our *l* are gone out .... Matt 25:8
seven *l* of fire burning .... Rev 4:5
burning as it were a *l* .... Rev 8:10

LANCE—*a spear*
Used in war .... Jer 50:42

LANCET—*a javelin or light spear*
Used by Baal's priests ... 1Kin 18:28

LAND—*earth; a region*

[*also* LANDS]
and let the dry *l* appear .... Gen 1:9
Gentiles divided in their *l* ..... Gen 10:5
unto a *l* that I will .... Gen 12:1
seed will I give this *l* .... Gen 12:7
bring thee again into this *l* .... Gen 28:15
the dearth was in all *l* .... Gen 41:54
but our bodies and our *l* ...... Gen 47:18
unto a good *l* and a large ..... Ex 3:8
bring you in unto the *l* .... Ex 6:8
made the sea dry *l* .... Ex 14:21
sabbath of rest unto the *l* ..... Lev 25:4
for your *l* shall not yield ...... Lev 26:20
the *l* enjoy her sabbaths ...... Lev 26:34
hearts in the *l* of their .... Lev 26:36
Moses sent to spy out the *l* .... Num 13:16
the *l* shall be divided for ...... Num 26:53
given you the *l* to possess ..... Num 33:53
blood it defileth the *l* .... Num 35:33
l that floweth with milk .... Deut 6:3
l which he sware unto .... Deut 6:10
shall bring thee into the *l* ..... Deut 7:1
thy God for the good *l* which . Deut 8:10
plucked from off the *l* whither . Deut 28:63
be merciful unto his *l* .... Deut 32:43
l which I sware unto .... Deut 34:4
to go in to possess the *l* .... Josh 1:11
over this Jordan on dry *l* ...... Josh 4:22
restore those *l* again .... Judg 11:13
Assyria have done to all *l* 2Kin 19:11
David went out into all *l* 1Chr 14:17
sin, and will heal their *l* 2Chr 7:14
Egypt, and out of all *l* 2Chr 9:28
all the kingdoms of the *l* 2Chr 17:10
all the people of other *l*? 2Chr 32:13
of the nations of those *l* 2Chr 32:13
ways able to deliver their *l* 2Chr 32:13
from the people of the *l* ...... Ezra 9:1
hand of the kings of the *l* ..... Ezra 9:7
We have mortgaged our *l* ..... Neh 5:3
men have our *l* and .... Neh 5:5
hand of the people of the *l* ... Neh 9:30
fat *l* which thou gavest .... Neh 9:35
l of darkness and the shadow . . Job 10:21
righteous shall inherit the *l* .... Ps 37:29
call their *l* after their .... Ps 49:11
noise unto God, all ye *l* .... Ps 66:1
his hands formed the dry *l* .... Ps 95:5
unto the Lord, all ye *l* .... Ps 100:1
to scatter them in the *l* .... Ps 106:27
Lord in the *l* of the living ..... Ps 116:9
me into the *l* of uprightness ... Ps 143:10
upright shall dwell in the *l* .... Prov 2:21
woe to thee, O *l* .... Eccl 10:16
if one look unto the *l* .... Is 5:30
all the gods of these *l* .... Is 36:20
they shall inherit the *l* .... Is 60:21
thy *l* any more be termed ..... Is 62:4
I cast you out of this *l* .... Jer 16:13
the *l* whither he had driven ... Jer 16:15
plant them in this *l* .... Jer 32:41
I will make the *l* desolate ..... Ezek 15:8
which is the glory of all *l* ..... Ezek 20:6
desolate *l* shall be tilled .... Ezek 36:34
a holy portion of the *l* .... Ezek 45:1
not dwell in the Lord's *l* ...... Hos 9:3
l is as the garden of Eden ..... Joel 2:3
ye shall be a delightsome *l* .... Mal 3:12
children, or *l*, for my..sake .... Matt 19:29
darkness over all the *l* unto ... Matt 27:45
wife, or children, or *l*, for ..... Mark 10:29
as were possessors of *l* or ..... Acts 4:34
having *l*, sold it, and .... Acts 4:37
part of the price of the *l*? ..... Acts 5:3
sojourned in the *l* of promise . . Heb 11:9

LAND OF PROMISE—*the land which God promised to Abraham and the descendants of his son Isaac; Canaan*

Described as:
The land of promise ..... Heb 11:9
The land of Canaan ..... Ezek 16:3, 29
The land of the Jews .... Acts 10:39
The holy land .... Zech 2:12
"Beulah" .... Is 62:4

Conquest of, by:
Divine command .... Ex 23:24
God's angel .... Ex 23:20, 23
Hornets .... Ex 23:28
Degrees .... Ex 23:29, 30

Inheritance of:
Promised to Abraham's seed .... Gen 12:1-7
Awaits God's time .... Gen 15:7-16
Boundaries of, specified . . Gen 15:18-21
Some kept from .... Deut 1:34-40
For the obedient .... Deut 5:16
Sin separates from .... Deut 28:49-68

Laws concerning:
Land allotted to 12 tribes . Num 26:52-55
None for priests .... Num 18:20, 24
Sale and redemption of . . Lev 25:15-33
Transfer of title .... Ruth 4:3-8
Witness of sale .... Ruth 4:9-11
Relieved of debt on ..... Neh 5:3-13
Leased to others .... Matt 21:33-41
Widow's right in .... Ruth 4:3-9
Rights of unmarried women in .... Num 27:1-11

Rest of, on the seventh years . . . . .Ex 23:11

Original inhabitants of:

Seven Gentile nations . . . .Deut 7:1; Josh 24:11
Mighty . . . . .Deut 4:38
Tall . . . . .Deut 9:1, 2
Idolatrous . . . . .Ex 23:23, 24; Deut 12:29-31
Corrupt . . . . .Lev 18:1-30; Ezek 16:47
Mingled with Israel . . . . . .Ps 106:34-38

LANDED—*went ashore from a boat; disembarked*

[*also* LANDING]

when he had *l* at Caesarea . . . .Acts 18:22
into Syria, and *l* at Tyre . . . . . .Acts 21:3
l at Syracuse, we tarried . . . . . .Acts 28:12

LANDMARK—*a boundary marker*

Removal of, forbidden . . .Deut 19:14

[*also* LANDMARKS]

removeth his neighbor's *l* . . . . .Deut 27:17
Some removed the *l*; they . . . . .Job 24:2
Remove not the ancient *l* . . . . .Prov 22:28
Remove not the old *l* . . . . .Prov 23:10

LANES—*narrow passageways or routes*

into the streets and *l* of the . . .Luke 14:21

LANGUAGE—*a system of communicating ideas and feelings*

Kinds of:

Jews .2Kin 18:28
Chaldean . . . . .Dan 1:4
Syrian 2Kin 18:26
Egyptian . . . . .Ps 114:1
Arabic . . . . .Acts 2:11
Greek . . . . .Acts 21:37
Latin . . . . .John 19:19, 20
Lycaonian . . . . .Acts 14:11
Medes and Persians . . . . . .Esth 3:12

Varieties of:

Result of confusion (Babel) . . . . .Gen 11:1-9
Result of division of Noah's three sons . . . .Gen 10:5, 20, 31
Seen in one empire . . . . . .Esth 1:22; Dan 3:4, 7, 29
Seen in Christ's inscription . . . . .John 19:19, 20
Witnessed at Pentecost . . .Acts 2:6-12
Evident in heaven . . . . . . .Rev 5:9

See TONGUE

[*also* LANGUAGES]

not speak in the Jews' *l* . . . . . . .Neh 13:24
the *l* of each people . . . . .Neh 13:24
every people after their *l* . . . . . .Esth 8:9
according to their *l* . . . . .Esth 8:9
There is no speech nor *l* . . . . . .Ps 19:3
hear a *l* that I understood . . . . .Ps 81:5
speak the *l* of Canaan . . . . .Is 19:18
servants in the Syrian *l* . . . . .Is 36:11
not to us in the Jews' *l* . . . . .Is 36:11
loud voice in the Jews' *l* . . . . . .Is 36:13
nation whose *l* thou . . . . .Jer 5:15
speech and of a hard *l* . . . . .Ezek 3:5
all people, nations, and *l* . . . . . .Dan 4:1
people, nations, and *l* . . . . .Dan 5:19
all people, nations, and *l* . . . . . .Dan 6:25
all people, nations, and *l* . . . . . .Dan 7:14
turn to the people a pure *l* . . . .Zeph 3:9
hold out of all *l* of the . . . . .Zech 8:23

LANGUISH—*to become weak*

[*also* LANGUISHED, LANGUISHETH, LANGUISHING]

him upon the bed of *l* . . . . .Ps 41:3
For the fields of Heshbon *l* . . . .Is 16:8
upon the waters shall *l* . . . . .Is 19:8
people of the earth do *l* . . . . . . .Is 24:4
the world *l* and fadeth . . . . .Is 24:4
wine mourneth, the vine *l* . . . . .Is 24:7
earth mourneth and *l* . . . . .Is 33:9
and the gates thereof *l* . . . . .Jer 14:2
She that hath borne seven *l* . . .Jer 15:9
wall to lament; they *l* . . . . .Lam 2:8
dwelleth therein shall *l* . . . . .Hos 4:3
wine is dried up, the oil *l* . . . . .Joel 1:10
dried up and the fig tree *l* . . . . .Joel 1:12
Bashan *l* and Carmel . . . . .Nah 1:4
flower of Lebanon *l* . . . . .Nah 1:4

LANTERN—*an enclosed lamp*

Used by soldiers arresting Jesus . . . . .John 18:3

LAODICEA (lā-ŏd-ĭ-sē'ä)—*a chief city of Asia Minor*

Church of, sharply rebuked . . . . .Rev 1:11
Epaphras labors here . . . .Col 4:12, 13
Paul writes letter to . . . . .Col 4:16
Not visited by Paul . . . . . .Col 2:1; Col 4:15

LAP—*the front part of the trunk and lower thighs of a seated person; to drink by licking*

As a loose skirt of a garment

For carrying objects 2Kin 4:39
Lots cast into . . . . .Prov 16:33

As an act of dogs:

For selecting Gideon's army . . . . .Judg 7:5, 6, 7

LAPIDOTH (lăp'ĭ-dŏth)—*"flames; torches"*

Husband of Deborah the prophetess . . . . .Judg 4:4

LAPWING—*a bird of the plover family (hoopoe)*

Unclean bird . . . . .Lev 11:19

after her kind and the *l* . . . . . . .Deut 14:18

LARGE—*ample; having more than usual; big*

[*also* LARGENESS]

it is *l* enough for them . . . . .Gen 34:21
unto a good land and a *l* . . . . . .Ex 3:8
secure and to a *l* land . . . . .Judg 18:10
me forth also into a *l* place 2Sam 22:20
much, and *l* of heart 1Kin 4:29
The work is great and *l* . . . . . . .Neh 4:19
the city was *l* and great . . . . . . .Neh 7:4
in the *l* and fat land which . . . .Neh 9:35
forth also into a *l* place . . . . . . .Ps 18:19
set my feet in a *l* room . . . . .Ps 31:8
and set me in a *l* place . . . . .Ps 118:5
like a ball into a *l* country . . . .Is 22:18
cattle feed in *l* pastures . . . . . . .Is 30:23
he hath made it deep and *l* . . . .Is 30:33
wide house and *l* chambers . . . .Jer 22:14
sister's cup deep and *l* . . . . .Ezek 23:32
them as a lamb in a *l* place . . .Hos 4:16
gave *l* money unto the . . . . .Matt 28:12
he will show you a *l* upper . . . .Mark 14:15
he shall show you a *l* . . . . .Luke 22:12
the length is as *l* as the . . . . . . .Rev 21:16

LASCIVIOUSNESS—*unbridled lust*

Flows from the heart . . . .Mark 7:20-23
Seen in the flesh . . . . .Gal 5:19
Characterizes the old life .1Pet 4:3
Found among Gentiles . . .Eph 4:19, 20
Sign of apostasy . . . . .Jude 4
Among Christians, lamentable 2Cor 12:21
To be cast away ("wantonness") . . . . . . .Rom 13:13

LASEA (lä-sē'ä)—*"wise"*

Seaport of Crete . . . . .Acts 27:8

LASH—*a punishment imposed with a whip or scourge*

Rendered "stripes" . . . . . .Deut 25:3
Imposed on Paul 2Cor 11:24

LASHA (lā'shä)—*"to anoint"*

Boundary town of southeast Palestine . . . .Gen 10:19

LASHARON (lä-shā'rŏn)—*"of or to Sharon"*

Town possessed by Joshua . . . . .Josh 12:1, 18

LAST—*the terminal point; to endure; continue*

Senses of:

Final consequence . . . . . . .Prov 23:32
God .Is 44:6

Of events last:

Day (resurrection) . . . . . . .John 6:39, 40
Day (judgment) . . . . .John 12:48
Days (present age) . . . . . .Acts 2:17
Time (present age) 1John 2:18
Times (present age) 1Pet 1:20
Days (time before Christ's return) 2Tim 3:1; 2Pet 3:3
Enemy (death) 1Cor 15:26
Time (Christ's return) 1Pet 1:5
Trump (Christ's return) . .1Cor 15:52

[*also* LASTED, LASTING]

befall you in the *l* days . . . . . . .Gen 49:1
he shall overcome at the *l* . . . . .Gen 49:19
let my *l* end be like his . . . . . . .Num 23:10
precious things of the *l* . . . . .Deut 33:15
days, while their feast *l* . . . . . . .Judg 14:17
ye the *l* to bring the king 2Sam 19:11
are ye the *l* to bring back 2Sam 19:12
the *l* words of David 2Sam 23:1
For by the *l* words of David . . .1Chr 23:27
David the king, first and *l* 1Chr 29:29
acts of Solomon, first and *l* 2Chr 9:29
of Rehoboam, first and *l* 2Chr 12:15
acts of Asa, first and *l* 2Chr 16:11
acts of Amaziah, first and *l* . . .2Chr 25:26
of all his ways, first and *l* 2Chr 28:26
of the *l* sons of Adonikam . . . .Ezra 8:13
first day unto the *l* day . . . . . . .Neh 8:18
At the *l* it biteth like a . . . . . . .Prov 23:32
come to pass in the *l* days . . . . .Is 2:2
the first, and with the *l* . . . . . . .Is 41:1
the first, I also am the *l* . . . . . . .Is 48:12
He shall not see our *l* end . . . .Jer 12:4
she remembereth not her *l* . . . .Lam 1:9
at the *l* Daniel came in . . . . . . .Dan 4:8
what shall be in the *l* . . . . .Dan 8:19
slay the *l* of them with the . . . .Amos 9:1
in the *l* days it shall come . . . . .Mic 4:1
l state of that man is worse . . .Matt 12:45
that are first shall be *l* . . . . .Matt 19:30
and the *l* shall be first . . . . .Matt 19:30
These *l* have wrought but . . . . .Matt 20:12
l..be first and the first *l* . . . . . . .Matt 20:16
l of all the woman died . . . . . . .Matt 22:27
At the *l* came two false . . . . . . .Matt 26:60
the same shall be *l* of all . . . . . .Mark 9:35
he sent him also *l* unto . . . . . . .Mark 12:6
l state of that man is worse . . .Luke 11:26
are *l* which shall be first . . . . . .Luke 13:30
are first which shall be *l* . . . . . .Luke 13:30
In the *l* day, that great day . . . .John 7:37
eldest, even unto the *l* . . . . .John 8:9
resurrection at the *l* day . . . . . .John 11:24
set forth us the apostles *l* 1Cor 4:9
l Adam was made a 1Cor 15:45
at the *l* your care of me . . . . . . .Phil 4:10
Hath in the *l* days spoken . . . . .Heb 1:2
treasure together for the *l* . . . . .James 5:3
should be mockers in the *l* . . . .Jude 18
the first and the *l* . . . . .Rev 1:11
saith the first and the *l* . . . . .Rev 2:8
having the seven *l* plagues . . . . .Rev 15:1
vials full of the seven *l* . . . . .Rev 21:9
the first and the *l* . . . . .Rev 22:13

LAST SUPPER—*the meal eaten by Jesus and his disciples on the night He was betrayed*

At Feast of Unleavened Bread . . . . .Matt 26:17; Mark 14:12
Fulfills Passover . . . . .Luke 22:15-18

LATCHET—*the thong binding the sandal to the foot*

Descriptive of:

Something insignificant . . .Gen 14:23
Menial task . . . . .Luke 3:16

not the *l* of their shoes be . . . . .Is 5:27
l of whose shoes I am not . . . . .Mark 1:7
shoe's *l* I am not worthy to . . .John 1:27

LATE—*near the end; in recent times*

[*also* LATELY]
to rise up early to sit up *l* ... Ps 127:2
of *l* my people is risen up ... Mic 2:8
Jews of *l* sought to stone ... John 11:8
l come from Italy with his ... Acts 18:2

LATIN—*the language of Rome*
Used in writing Christ's inscription ... John 19:19, 20; Luke 23:38

LATTER—*of or pertaining to the end*
the voice of the *l* sign ... Ex 4:8
to thy people in the *l* days ... Num 24:14
even in the *l* days, if thou ... Deut 4:30
do thee good at thy *l* end ... Deut 8:16
the first rain and the *l* rain ... Deut 11:14
if the *l* husband hate her ... Deut 24:3
or if the *l* husband die ... Deut 24:3
evil will befall you in the *l* ... Deut 31:29
they would consider their *l* ... Deut 31:29
more kindness in the *l* end ... Ruth 3:10
will be bitterness in the *l* ... 2Sam 2:26
thy *l* end should greatly ... Job 8:7
mouth wide as for the *l* rain ... Job 29:23
favor is as a cloud of the *l* ... Prov 16:15
and know the *l* end of them ... Is 41:22
there hath been no *l* rain ... Jer 3:3
in the *l* days ye shall ... Jer 23:20
of Moab in the *l* days ... Jer 48:47
in the *l* years thou shalt ... Ezek 38:8
what shall be in the *l* days ... Dan 2:28
befall thy people in the *l* ... Dan 10:14
his goodness in the *l* days ... Hos 3:5
l rain in the first month ... Joel 2:23
l growth after the king's ... Amos 7:1
shooting up of the *l* growth ... Amos 7:1
glory of this *l* house shall ... Hag 2:9
in the time of the *l* rain ... Zech 10:1
l times some shall depart ... 1Tim 4:1
he receive the early and *l* ... James 5:7
l end is worse with them ... 2Pet 2:20

LATTICE—*a framework of crossed wood or metal strips*
Window of Sisera's mother ... Judg 5:28
Ahaziah fell through ... 2Kin 1:2

himself through the *l* ... Song 2:9

LAUD—*to acclaim; praise*
and *l* him, all ye people ... Rom 15:11

LAUGH—*to express joy vocally*

[*also* LAUGHED, LAUGHETH]
fell upon his face and *l* ... Gen 17:17
Sarah *l* within herself ... Gen 18:12
Sarah denied saying I *l* not ... Gen 18:15
God hath made me to *l* ... Gen 21:6
all that hear will *l* with me ... Gen 21:6
despised thee, and *l* thee ... 2Kin 19:21
l at the trial of the innocent ... Job 9:23
the just upright man is *l* to ... Job 12:4
innocent *l* them to scorn ... Job 22:19
I *l* on them, they believed ... Job 29:24
he *l* at the shaking of a ... Job 41:29
The Lord shall *l* at him ... Ps 37:13
fear, and shall *l* at him ... Ps 52:6
our enemies *l* among ... Ps 80:6
I also will *l* at your ... Prov 1:26
despised thee, and *l* thee to ... Is 37:22
be *l* to scorn and had in ... Ezek 23:32
they *l* him to scorn ... Mark 5:40
weep now; for ye shall *l* ... Luke 6:21
Woe unto you that *l* now! ... Luke 6:25
they *l* him to scorn ... Luke 8:53

LAUGHTER—*an expression of joy, mirth or ridicule*

Kinds of:
Divine ... Ps 59:8
Natural ... Job 8:21
Derisive ... Neh 2:19
Fake ... Prov 14:13
Scornful ... 2Cor 30:10
Confident ... Job 5:22
Joyful ... Ps 126:2

Causes of:
Man's folly ... Ps 2:4
Something unusual ... Gen 18:12-15
Something untrue ... Matt 9:24
Ridicule ... 2Chr 30:10
Highly contradictory ... Ps 22:7, 8

I said of *l*, It is mad ... Eccl 2:2
to weep, and a time to *l* ... Eccl 3:4
Sorrow is better than *l* ... Eccl 7:3
so is the *l* of the fool ... Eccl 7:6
A feast is made for *l* ... Eccl 10:19
let your *l* be turned to ... James 4:9

LAUNCH—*to set afloat*

[*also* LAUNCHED]
L out into the deep ... Luke 5:4
of the lake. And they *l* ... Luke 8:22
from them, and had *l* ... Acts 21:1
we *l*, meaning to sail by ... Acts 27:2
when we had *l* from thence ... Acts 27:4

LAVER—*a basin for washing*
Made for the tabernacle. . Ex 30:18

[*also* LAVERS]
and the *l* and his foot ... Ex 30:28
the *l* and his foot ... Ex 35:16
the *l* and his foot ... Ex 39:39
he set the *l* between the ... Ex 40:30
the *l* and his foot ... Lev 8:11
under the *l* were ... 1Kin 7:30
Then made he ten *l* of brass ... 1Kin 7:38
one *l* contained forty baths ... 1Kin 7:38
every *l* was four cubits ... 1Kin 7:38
one of the ten bases one *l* ... 1Kin 7:38
and ten *l* on the bases ... 1Kin 7:43
He made also ten *l* and put ... 2Chr 4:6

LAVISH—*to bestow profusely*
They *l* gold out of the bag ... Is 46:6

LAW—*an authoritative rule of conduct*
Law of man ... Luke 20:22
Natural law written upon the heart ... Rom 2:14, 15
Law of Moses ... Gal 3:17-21
Entire Old Testament ... John 10:34
Expression of God's will. . Rom 7:2-9
Operating principle ... Rom 3:27

[*also* LAWS]
my statutes, and my *l* ... Gen 26:5
Joseph made it a *l* over the ... Gen 47:26
One *l* shall be to him that ... Ex 12:49
they will walk in my *l* ... Ex 16:4
commandments and my *l*? ... Ex 16:28
them ordinances and *l* ... Ex 18:20
tables of stone, and a *l* ... Ex 24:12
the *l* of the burnt offering ... Lev 6:9
the *l* of the sin offering ... Lev 6:25
there is one *l* for them ... Lev 7:7
the *l* of the burnt offering ... Lev 7:37
the *l* for her that hath born ... Lev 12:7
shall be the *l* of the leper ... Lev 14:2
This is the *l* for all manner ... Lev 14:54
the *l* of him that hath an ... Lev 15:32
and judgments and *l* ... Lev 26:46
This is the *l* of jealousies ... Num 5:29
is the *l* of the Nazarite ... Num 6:13
is the *l* of the Nazarite ... Num 6:21
the *l* of his separation ... Num 6:21
One *l* and one manner ... Num 15:16
is the ordinance of the *l* ... Num 19:2
the ordinance of the *l* ... Num 31:21
Moses to declare this *l* ... Deut 1:5
so righteous as all this *l* ... Deut 4:8
this is the *l* which Moses ... Deut 4:44
to the sentence of the *l* ... Deut 17:11
write him a copy of this *l* ... Deut 17:18
do all the words of this *l* ... Deut 28:58
written..this book of the *l* ... Deut 29:21
do all the words of this *l* ... Deut 32:46
Moses commanded us a *l* ... Deut 33:4
and Israel thy *l* ... Deut 33:10
commandment and the *l* ... Josh 22:5
words..book of the *l* of God ... Josh 24:26
written in the *l* of ... 1Kin 2:3
to walk in the *l* of the ... 2Kin 10:31
book of the *l* of Moses ... 2Kin 14:6
all the *l* that my servant ... 2Kin 21:8
words of the book of the *l* ... 2Kin 22:11
to all the *l* of Moses ... 2Kin 23:25
is written in the *l* of the ... 1Chr 16:40
their way to walk in my *l* ... 2Chr 6:16
to do the *l* and the ... 2Chr 14:4
book of the *l* of the Lord ... 2Chr 17:9
written in the *l* of Moses ... 2Chr 23:18
to the *l* of Moses the ... 2Chr 30:16
in the *l* of the Lord ... 2Chr 31:4
to the whole *l* and the ... 2Chr 33:8
was written in the *l* of the ... 2Chr 35:26
written in the *l* of Moses ... Ezra 3:2
to seek the *l* of the Lord ... Ezra 7:10
according to the *l* of thy ... Ezra 7:14
as know the *l* of thy God ... Ezra 7:25
will not do the *l* of thy God ... Ezra 7:26
be done according to the *l* ... Ezra 10:3
read in the book of the *l* ... Neh 9:3
judgments, and true *l* ... Neh 9:13
them again unto thy *l* ... Neh 9:29
of the lands unto the *l* of ... Neh 10:28
to walk in God's *l* ... Neh 10:29
as it is written in the *l* ... Neh 10:34
portions of the *l* for the ... Neh 12:44
was according to the *l* ... Esth 1:8
Vashti according to *l* ... Esth 1:15
l of the Persians and the ... Esth 1:19
their *l* are diverse from all ... Esth 3:8
keep they the king's *l* ... Esth 3:8
is not according to the *l* ... Esth 4:16
I pray thee, the *l* from his ... Job 22:22
his delight is in the *l* of ... Ps 1:2
in his *l* doth he meditate ... Ps 1:2
l of the Lord is perfect ... Ps 19:7
l of his God is in his heart ... Ps 37:31
thy *l* is within my heart ... Ps 40:8
appointed a *l* in Israel ... Ps 78:5
a *l* of the God of Jacob ... Ps 81:4
teachest him out of thy *l* ... Ps 94:12
same unto Jacob for a *l* ... Ps 105:10
his statutes and keep his *l* ... Ps 105:45
walk in the *l* of the Lord ... Ps 119:1
things out of thy *l* ... Ps 119:18
I shall keep thy *l*; yea ... Ps 119:34
I not declined from thy *l* ... Ps 119:51
and have kept thy *l* ... Ps 119:55
but I delight in thy *l* ... Ps 119:70
The *l* of thy mouth is better ... Ps 119:72
for thy *l* is my delight ... Ps 119:77
l had been my delights ... Ps 119:92
O how love I thy *l*! it is my ... Ps 119:97
yet do I not forget thy *l* ... Ps 119:109
they have made void thy *l* ... Ps 119:126
and thy *l* is the truth ... Ps 119:142
for I do not forget thy *l* ... Ps 119:153
they which love thy *l* ... Ps 119:165
forsake not the *l* of thy ... Prov 1:8
forsake ye not my *l* ... Prov 4:2
not the *l* of thy mother ... Prov 6:20
is a lamp; and the *l* is light ... Prov 6:23
l of the wise is a fountain ... Prov 13:14
they that forsake the *l* ... Prov 28:4
as keep the *l* contend with ... Prov 28:4
Whoso keepeth the *l* is a ... Prov 28:7
his ear from hearing the *l* ... Prov 28:9
he that keepeth the *l* ... Prov 29:18
drink, and forget the *l* ... Prov 31:5
Zion shall go forth the *l* ... Is 2:3
have cast away the *l* of the ... Is 5:24
the *l* among my disciples ... Is 8:16
To the *l* and to the ... Is 8:20
have transgressed the *l* ... Is 24:5
isles shall wait for his *l* ... Is 42:4
he will magnify the *l*, and ... Is 42:21
they obedient unto his *l* ... Is 42:24
in whose heart is my *l* ... Is 51:7
that handle the *l* knew me ... Jer 2:8
l of the Lord is with us? ... Jer 8:8
and have not kept my *l* ... Jer 16:11
to me, to walk in my *l* ... Jer 26:4
will put my *l* in their ... Jer 31:33
according to the *l* and ... Jer 32:11

L

nor walked in my *l* .... Jer 44:10
the *l* is no more; her .... Lam 2:9
the *l* shall perish from the ..... Ezek 7:26
priests have violated my *l* ..... Ezek 22:26
and all the *l* thereof .... Ezek 43:11
This is the *l* of the house ..... Ezek 43:12
this is the *l* of the house ...... Ezek 43:12
they shall keep my *l* and ...... Ezek 44:24
concerning the *l* of his God ... Dan 6:5
l of the Medes and .... Dan 6:8
to change times and *l* .... Dan 7:25
have transgressed thy *l* .... Dan 9:11
that is written in the *l* of ...... Dan 9:11
forgotten the *l* of thy God .... Hos 4:6
the great things of my *l* .... Hos 8:12
despised the *l* of the Lord ..... Amos 2:4
for the *l* shall go forth of ..... Mic 4:2
Therefore the *l* is slacked ..... Hab 1:4
done violence to the *l* .... Zeph 3:4
priests concerning the *l* .... Hag 2:11
they should hear the *l* .... Zech 7:12
The *l* of truth was in his ...... Mal 2:6
many to stumble at the *l* ...... Mal 2:8
is the *l* and the prophets ...... Matt 7:12
have ye not read in the *l* ...... Matt 12:5
hang all the *l* and .... Matt 22:40
according to the *l* of Moses ... Luke 2:22
said in the *l* of the Lord ...... Luke 2:24
to the *l* of the Lord .... Luke 2:39
What is written in the *l*? ...... Luke 10:26
one tittle of the *l* to fall ...... Luke 16:17
the *l* was given by Moses ..... John 1:17
of whom Moses in the *l* .... John 1:45
not Moses give you the *l* ...... John 7:19
none of you keepeth the *l*? .... John 7:19
who knoweth not the *l* are .... John 7:49
Doth our *l* judge any man .... John 7:51
Moses in the *l* commanded .... John 8:5
out of the *l* that Christ .... John 12:34
that is written in their *l* .... John 15:25
him according to your *l* .... John 18:31
a *l* and by our *l* he ought ..... John 19:7
Gamaliel, a doctor of the *l* .... Acts 5:34
received the *l* by the .... Acts 7:53
after the reading of the *l* ...... Acts 13:15
not be justified by the *l* .... Acts 13:39
and keep the *l* .... Acts 15:24
God contrary to the *l* .... Acts 18:13
l is open and there are .... Acts 19:38
are all zealous of the *l* .... Acts 21:20
and keepest the *l* .... Acts 21:24
perfect manner of the *l* .... Acts 22:3
man according to the *l* .... Acts 22:12
to judge me after the *l* .... Acts 23:3
of questions of their *l* .... Acts 23:29
which are written in the *l* ..... Acts 24:14
both out of the *l* of .... Acts 28:23
as have sinned without *l* ...... Rom 2:12
shall also perish without *l* ..... Rom 2:12
as have sinned in the *l* .... Rom 2:12
shall be judged by the *l* .... Rom 2:12
not the hearers of the *l* are .... Rom 2:13
the doers of the *l* shall be ..... Rom 2:13
and restest in the *l* .... Rom 2:17
of the truth in the *l* .... Rom 2:20
makest thy boast of the *l* ...... Rom 2:23
through breaking the *l* .... Rom 2:23
if thou keep the *l* .... Rom 2:25
thou be a breaker of the *l* ..... Rom 2:25
nature, if it fulfill the *l* .... Rom 2:27
dost transgress the *l*? .... Rom 2:27
of God without the *l* is .... Rom 3:21
being witnessed by the *l* ...... Rom 3:21
without the deeds of the *l* ..... Rom 3:28
make void the *l* through ...... Rom 3:31
yea, we establish the *l* .... Rom 3:31
to his seed, through the *l* ..... Rom 4:13
if they which are of the *l* ..... Rom 4:14
the *l* worketh wrath .... Rom 4:15
no *l* is, there is no .... Rom 4:15
until the *l* sin was in the ...... Rom 5:13
where there is no *l* .... Rom 5:13
ye are not under the *l* .... Rom 6:14
to them that know the *l* .... Rom 7:1
the *l* hath dominion over a .... Rom 7:1
that the *l* is spiritual .... Rom 7:14
I consent unto the *l* that it .... Rom 7:16
I find then a *l* that, when ..... Rom 7:21
I delight in the *l* of God .... Rom 7:22
I see another *l* in my .... Rom 7:23
warring against the *l* of .... Rom 7:23
captivity to the *l* of sin .... Rom 7:23
the flesh the *l* of sin .... Rom 7:25
the *l* of the Spirit of life ...... Rom 8:2
me free from the *l* of sin ...... Rom 8:2
What the *l* could not do ...... Rom 8:3
the righteousness of the *l* ..... Rom 8:4
and the giving of the *l* .... Rom 9:4
after the *l* of righteousness .... Rom 9:31
to the *l* of righteousness ...... Rom 9:31
Christ is the end of the *l* ...... Rom 10:4
is the fulfilling of the *l* .... Rom 13:10
go to *l* before the unjust 1Cor 6:1
brother goeth to *l* with 1Cor 6:6
ye go to *l* one with another ... 1Cor 6:7
or saith not the *l* the same 1Cor 9:8
under the *l*, as under the *l* 1Cor 9:20
them that are under the *l* 1Cor 9:20
without *l*, as without *l* 1Cor 9:21
not without *l* to God 1Cor 9:21
but under the *l* to Christ 1Cor 9:21
them that are without *l* 1Cor 9:21
as also saith the *l* 1Cor 14:34
strength of sin is the *l* 1Cor 15:56
by the works of the *l* .... Gal 2:16
not by the works of the *l* ..... Gal 2:16
by the works of the *l* shall .... Gal 2:16
I through the *l* am dead to .... Gal 2:19
righteousness come by the *l* ... Gal 2:21
by the works of the *l* .... Gal 3:5
are of the works of the *l* ...... Gal 3:10
written in the book of the *l* ... Gal 3:10
the *l* is not of faith: but ...... Gal 3:12
from the curse of the *l* .... Gal 3:13
we were kept under the *l* ..... Gal 3:23
woman, made under the *l* ...... Gal 4:4
that were under the *l* .... Gal 4:5
a debtor to do the whole *l* .... Gal 5:3
you are justified by the *l* ...... Gal 5:4
l is fulfilled in one word ...... Gal 5:14
against such there is no *l* ...... Gal 5:23
so fulfill the *l* of Christ .... Gal 6:2
circumcised keep the *l* .... Gal 6:13
l of commandments .... Eph 2:15
as touching the *l*, a Pharisee ... Phil 3:5
which is in the *l* .... Phil 3:6
which is of the *l* .... Phil 3:9
to be teachers of the *l* 1Tim 1:7
we know that the *l* is good 1Tim 1:8
l is not made for a 1Tim 1:9
and strivings about the *l* ...... Titus 3:9
people according to the *l* ...... Heb 7:5
a change also of the *l* .... Heb 7:12
the *l* made nothing perfect .... Heb 7:19
For the *l* maketh men high .... Heb 7:28
oath, which was since the *l* .... Heb 7:28
I will put my *l* into their ...... Heb 8:10
l having a shadow of good .... Heb 10:1
He that despised Moses' *l* ..... Heb 10:28
the perfect *l* of liberty .... James 1:25
If ye fulfill the royal *l* .... James 2:8
are convinced of the *l* .... James 2:9
shall keep the whole *l* .... James 2:10
a transgressor of the *l* .... James 2:11
judged by the *l* of liberty ..... James 2:12
the *l*, and judgeth the *l* .... James 4:11
but if thou judge the *l* .... James 4:11
not a doer of the *l*, but a ..... James 4:11
transgresseth also the *l* 1John 3:4
is the transgression of the *l* 1John 3:4
See Law of Moses

LAW OF MOSES—*the Pentateuch, the first five books of the Old Testament*

History of:
Given at Sinai .... Ex 20:1-26
Called a covenant .... Deut 4:13, 23
Dedicated with blood .... Heb 9:18-22
Called the Law of Moses . Josh 8:30-35
Restated in Deuteronomy. Deut 4:44-46
Written on stone .... Deut 4:4:13
Plaster-coated stone ..... Deut 27:3-8
Placed with the ark ...... Deut 31:9, 26
Given to Joshua .... Josh 1:1-9
Repeated by Joshua ..... Josh 23:6-16
Disobeyed by:
Israel .... Judg 2:10-20
Israel's kings 2Kin 10:31
The Jews .... Is 1:10-18
Finding of book of 2Chr 34:14-33
Disobedience to, cause of exile 2Kin 17:3-41
Read to postexilic assembly .... Neh 8:1-18
Recalled at close of Old Testament .... Mal 4:4
Meaning of, fulfilled by Christ .... Matt 5:17-48
Pharisees insist on observance of .... Acts 15:1-29

Purposes of:
Knowledge of sin .... Rom 3:20
Manifest God's righteousness .... Rom 7:12
Lead to Christ .... Gal 3:24, 25

Christ's relation to:
Born under .... Gal 4:4
Explains proper meaning to .... Matt 5:17-48; Matt 12:1-14
Redeems sinners from curse of .... Gal 3:13
Shows fulfillment of, in Himself .... Luke 24:27, 44

Christian's relation to:
Freed from .... Acts 15:1-29
Spirit of, fulfilled in love . Rom 13:8-10
Now written on the heart . 2Cor 3:3-1

Inadequacies of, cannot:
Make worshiper perfect . . Heb 9:9-15
Justify .... Acts 13:38, 39

LAWFUL—*according to the law*

[*also* lawfully]
it shall not be *l* to impose ..... Ezra 7:24
and do that which is *l* and .... Ezek 18:5
and do that which is *l* and .... Ezek 18:21
and do that which is *l* and .... Ezek 33:14
and do that which is *l* and .... Ezek 33:19
It is not *l* for thee to have .... Matt 14:4
It is not *l* for to put them ..... Matt 27:6
day that which is not *l*? .... Mark 2:24
Is it *l* to do good on the ...... Mark 3:4
It is not *l*..to have thy .... Mark 6:18
l for a man to put away his ... Mark 10:2
Is it *l* to give tribute to .... Mark 12:14
which is not *l* to do on .... Luke 6:2
it *l* on the sabbath days to .... Luke 6:9
Is it *l* to heal on the .... Luke 14:3
l for us to put any man to .... John 18:31
which are not *l* for us to ...... Acts 16:21
be determined in a *l* .... Acts 19:39
All things are *l* unto me 1Cor 6:12
all things are *l* for me 1Cor 6:12
All things are *l* for me, but ... 1Cor 10:23
is good, if a man use it *l* 1Tim 1:8
except he strive *l* 2Tim 2:5

LAWGIVER—*a lawmaker*
Only one .... James 4:12
The Lord is .... Is 33:22

nor a *l* from between his ...... Gen 49:10
by the direction of the *l* .... Num 21:18
a portion of the *l* was he ...... Deut 33:21
of mine head; Judah is my *l* .. Ps 60:7
of mine head; Judah is my *l* .. Ps 108:8

LAWLESSNESS—*living outside or contrary to law*

Described as:
Wickedness .... Acts 2:23
Iniquity .... Matt 13:41
Unrighteousness 2Cor 6:14

Features concerning:
Called sin 1John 3:4

Incompatible with
righteousness 2Cor 6:14
Torments the righteous .. Matt 24:12
2Pet 2:8
Led to crucifixion .... Acts 2:22, 23
Descriptive of antichrist .. 2Thess 2:7, 8
Scribes and Pharisees full
of .... Matt 23:27, 28
Basis for condemnation .. Matt 7:23
Law made for 1Tim 1:9
Forgiven .... Rom 4:7
Titus 2:14
Forgotten .... Heb 8:12
Heb 10:17

LAWSUITS—*suing another for damages*
Between Christians, forbidden .... Matt 5:25, 40; 1Cor 6:1-8

LAWYER—*interpreters of the law*
Test Jesus .... Matt 22:34-40
Jesus answers one .... Luke 10:25-37
Condemned by Jesus .... Luke 11:45-52
Zenas, a Christian .... Titus 3:13

[*also* LAWYERS]
a *l* asked him a question ...... Matt 22:35
l rejected the counsel of ...... Luke 7:30
a certain *l* stood up and .... Luke 10:25
Woe unto you, *l*! for ye .... Luke 11:52
spake unto the *l* and .... Luke 14:3
Bring Zenas the *l* and .... Titus 3:13

LAY—*to put; place*

[*also* LAID, LAIDST, LAYEDST, LAYEST, LAYETH, LAYING]
l it upon both their .... Gen 9:23
the men *l* hold upon his .... Gen 19:16
l it upon Isaac .... Gen 22:6
and *l* the wood in order .... Gen 22:9
l him on the altar .... Gen 22:9
Jacob *l* the rods before the .... Gen 30:41
l no hand upon him; that ..... Gen 37:22
she *l* up his garment by her ... Gen 39:16
city, *l* he up in the same ...... Gen 41:48
l his right hand upon the ...... Gen 48:17
she *l* it in the flags by .... Ex 2:3
work be *l* upon the men ...... Ex 5:9
l it up before the Lord .... Ex 16:33
l before their faces all .... Ex 19:7
If..be *l* on him a sum of ...... Ex 21:30
his life whatsoever is *l* .... Ex 21:30
l the wood in order upon ..... Lev 1:7
the priest shall *l* them in ...... Lev 1:12
he shall *l* his hand .... Lev 3:2
shall *l* his hand upon the ...... Lev 4:4
he shall *l* his hand .... Lev 4:24
l the burnt offering in .... Lev 6:12
his sons *l* their hands .... Lev 8:14
his sons *l* their hands .... Lev 8:18
Aaron shall *l* both his .... Lev 16:21
Levites shall *l* their hands ..... Num 8:12
l the burden of all this .... Num 11:11
thee, *l* not the sin upon us .... Num 12:11
l incense thereon and stood ... Num 16:18
shalt *l* them up in the .... Num 17:4
l them waste even unto .... Num 21:30
l thine hand upon him .... Num 27:18
or hurl at him by *l* of wait .... Num 35:20
will *l* them upon all them ..... Deut 7:15
l up these my words .... Deut 11:18
your God shall *l* the fear ...... Deut 11:25
shalt *l* it up within .... Deut 14:28
l not innocent blood unto ..... Deut 21:8
and *l* hold on her, and *l* ...... Deut 22:28
l upon us hard bondage .... Deut 26:6
the Lord hath *l* upon it .... Deut 29:22
Is not this *l* up in store .... Deut 32:34
Moses had *l* his hands .... Deut 34:9
she had *l* in order upon the ... Josh 2:6
l them down there .... Josh 4:8
he shall *l* the foundation ...... Josh 6:26
l them out before the Lord .... Josh 7:23
l great stones in the .... Josh 10:27
l them upon this rock .... Judg 6:20
it, that the tent *l* along .... Judg 7:13
blood be *l* upon Abimelech ... Judg 9:24
l hold on his concubine .... Judg 19:29
uncover his feet, and *l* .... Ruth 3:4
uncovered his feet, and *l* her .. Ruth 3:7
the child and *l* it in her .... Ruth 4:16
the Lord and *l* it upon the 1Sam 6:8
l the ark of the Lord upon 1Sam 6:11
l hold upon the skirt of his 1Sam 15:27
David *l* up these words in 1Sam 21:12
l thou a snare for my life 1Sam 28:9
l thee hold on one of the 2Sam 2:21
and *l* a very great heap of 2Sam 18:17
slept and *l* it in her bosom 1Kin 3:20
to *l* the foundation of the 1Kin 5:17
of the house of the Lord *l* 1Kin 6:37
saying, *L* hold on him 1Kin 13:4
man of God, and *l* it upon 1Kin 13:29
Israel *l* siege to Gibbethon 1Kin 15:27
cut it in pieces, and *l* it 1Kin 18:23
l him on the bed of the 2Kin 4:21
the Lord *l* this burden upon ... 2Kin 9:25
L ye them in two heaps at 2Kin 10:8
l it out to the carpenters 2Kin 12:11
took and *l* it on the boil 2Kin 20:7
an oath be *l* upon him to 2Chr 6:22
l him in the bed which was 2Chr 16:14
their God and *l* them by 2Chr 31:6
l the foundation of the 2Chr 31:7
of the temple..was not yet *l* ... Ezra 3:6
house of Lord was *l* .... Ezra 3:11
sepulchers *l* waste .... Neh 2:3
who also *l* the beams .... Neh 3:3
they *l* the meat offerings ...... Neh 13:5
I will *l* hands on you .... Neh 13:21
to *l* hand on the king .... Esth 2:21
l his hand upon the Jews ...... Esth 8:7
to *l* hand on such as .... Esth 9:2
on the prey they *l* not their ... Esth 9:15
Ahasuerus *l* a tribute .... Esth 10:1
l your hand upon your .... Job 21:5
God *l* up his iniquity for ...... Job 21:19
Then shalt thou *l* up gold ..... Job 22:24
and *l* their hand on .... Job 29:9
he will not *l* upon man .... Job 34:23
l the foundations of the .... Job 38:4
or who *l* the corner stone ..... Job 38:6
L thine hand upon him .... Job 41:8
sword of him that *l* at him .... Job 41:26
l me down and slept; I .... Ps 3:5
I will both *l* me down .... Ps 4:8
net that they have *l* privily .... Ps 31:4
he *l* up the depth in .... Ps 33:7
l to my charge things that ..... Ps 35:11
they commune of *l* snares ..... Ps 64:5
thou *l* affliction upon our ..... Ps 66:11
Jacob, and *l* waste .... Ps 79:7
she may *l* her young .... Ps 84:3
Thou hast *l* me in the .... Ps 88:6
l help upon one that is .... Ps 89:19
Who *l* the foundations of ...... Ps 104:5
judgments have I *l* before ..... Ps 119:30
and *l* thine hand upon me ..... Ps 139:5
they privily *l* a snare for ...... Ps 142:3
He *l* up sound wisdom for .... Prov 2:7
life to them that *l* hold .... Prov 3:18
Wise men *l* up knowledge ..... Prov 10:14
of the sinner is *l* up for .... Prov 13:22
and *l* up deceit within him .... Prov 26:24
evil, *l* thine hand upon thy .... Prov 30:32
to *l* hold on folly, till I .... Eccl 2:3
which I have *l* up for thee .... Song 7:13
And I will *l* it waste; it .... Is 5:6
roar, and *l* hold of the prey ... Is 5:29
he *l* it upon my mouth .... Is 6:7
they shall *l* their hand upon ... Is 11:14
will *l* low the haughtiness ..... Is 13:11
Since thou art *l* down, no ..... Is 14:8
the night Ar of Moab is *l* ..... Is 15:1
the night Kir of Moab is *l* ..... Is 15:1
for it is *l* waste, so that .... Is 23:1
not be treasured nor *l* up ..... Is 23:18
the lofty city, he *l* it low ...... Is 26:5
l in Zion for a foundation ..... Is 28:16
Judgment also will I *l* to .... Is 28:17
l a snare for him that .... Is 29:21
generation it shall *l* waste ..... Is 34:10
Assyria have *l* waste .... Is 37:18
l waste defensed cities .... Is 37:26
yet he *l* it not to heart .... Is 42:25
hast thou very heavily *l* .... Is 47:6
didst not *l*..things to thy ...... Is 47:7
and *l* the foundations of ...... Is 51:13
Lord hath *l* on him the .... Is 53:6
will *l* thy stones with fair ...... Is 54:11
l thy foundations with .... Is 54:11
the son of man that *l* hold .... Is 56:2
our pleasant things are *l* ...... Is 64:11
thy cities shall be *l* waste ..... Jer 4:7
l hold on bow and spear ...... Jer 6:23
but in heart he *l* his wait ...... Jer 9:8
they *l* up the roll in the .... Jer 36:20
they *l* wait for us in the .... Lam 4:19
I *l* a stumbling block before ... Ezek 3:20
l siege against it, and build .... Ezek 4:2
I have *l* upon thee the .... Ezek 4:5
I will *l* the dead carcases ...... Ezek 6:5
the cities shall be *l* waste ...... Ezek 6:6
your altars may be *l* waste .... Ezek 6:6
are inhabited shall be *l* .... Ezek 12:20
I shall *l* my vengeance .... Ezek 25:17
now she is *l* waste .... Ezek 26:2
l away their robes and put .... Ezek 26:16
will *l* thy flesh upon the .... Ezek 32:5
be thou *l* with the .... Ezek 32:19
are *l* by them that were .... Ezek 32:29
I have *l* the land most .... Ezek 33:29
I will *l* thy cities waste .... Ezek 35:4
whereas it *l* desolate in .... Ezek 36:34
my hand that I have *l* upon ... Ezek 39:21
shall they *l* the most holy ..... Ezek 42:13
l them in the holy .... Ezek 44:19
l upon the mouth of the ...... Dan 6:17
and I *l* meat unto them .... Hos 11:4
He hath *l* my vine waste ...... Joel 1:7
they *l* themselves down upon .. Amos 2:8
clothes *l* to pledge by every ... Amos 2:8
thy bread have *l* a wound ..... Obad 7
he *l* his robe from him .... Jon 3:6
thereof will I *l* desolate .... Mic 1:7
he hath *l* siege against us ..... Mic 5:1
say, Nineveh is *l* waste .... Nah 3:7
l over with gold and silver .... Hab 2:19
a stone was *l* upon a stone .... Hag 2:15
the stone that I have *l* .... Zech 3:9
they *l* the pleasant land .... Zech 7:14
l the foundation of the .... Zech 12:1
they shall *l* hold every one .... Zech 14:13
l his mountains and his .... Mal 1:3
if ye will not *l* it to heart ..... Mal 2:2
axe is *l* unto the root of .... Matt 3:10
L not up for yourselves .... Matt 6:19
l up for yourselves .... Matt 6:20
man hath not where to *l* ...... Matt 8:20
will he not *l* hold on it .... Matt 12:11
Herod had *l* hold on John ..... Matt 14:3
he *l* his hands on them .... Matt 19:15
l them on men's shoulders .... Matt 23:4
and ye *l* no hold on me .... Matt 26:55
l it in his own new tomb ...... Matt 27:60
they went out to *l* hold on .... Mark 3:21
he *l* his hands upon a few .... Mark 6:5
up his corpse and *l* it in a .... Mark 6:29
l aside the commandment of ... Mark 7:8
they sought to *l* hold on him .. Mark 12:12
the young men *l* hold on him .. Mark 14:51
named Barabbas, which *l* ..... Mark 15:7
l them up in their hearts ..... Luke 1:66
axe is *l* unto the root of ...... Luke 3:9
and to *l* him before him .... Luke 5:18
l the foundation on a rock .... Luke 6:48
man hath not where to *l* ...... Luke 9:58
L wait for him and seeking .... Luke 11:54
he that *l* up treasure for ...... Luke 12:21
he *l* his hands on her .... Luke 13:13
Lazarus which was *l* at his .... Luke 16:20
takest up that thou *l* not ...... Luke 19:21
taking up that I *l* not down .. Luke 19:22
shall *l* thee even with the ..... Luke 19:44
they shall *l* their hands on ..... Luke 21:12
they *l* hold upon one Simon ... Luke 23:26
on him they *l* the cross .... Luke 23:26

l it in a sepulcher that was ....Luke 23:53
never man before was *l* ....Luke 23:53
l a great multitude of ....John 5:3
no man *l* hands on him ....John 7:30
and no man *l* hands on ....John 8:20
I *l* down my life for the ....John 10:15
because I *l* down my life ....John 10:17
but I *l* it down of myself ......John 10:18
I have power to *l* it down .....John 10:18
Where have ye *l* him? ....John 11:34
place where the dead was *l*....John 11:41
and *l* aside his garments ......John 13:4
I will *l* down my life ....John 13:37
man *l* down his life for his ....John 15:13
wherein was never man yet *l* ..John 19:41
know not where they have *l* ...John 20:2
not *l* with the linen clothes ....John 20:7
l them down at the ....Acts 4:35
l it at the apostles' feet ....Acts 5:2
l their hands on the apostles...Acts 5:18
l not this sin to their charge ...Acts 7:60
Then *l* they their hands on ....Acts 8:17
through *l* on of the apostles'...Acts 8:18
and *l* their hands on them .....Acts 13:3
was *l* unto his fathers ....Acts 13:36
to *l* upon you no greater ......Acts 15:28
Paul had *l* his hands upon .....Acts 19:6
people and *l* hands on him ....Acts 21:27
the crime *l* against him........Acts 25:16
l them on the fire ....Acts 28:3
father of Publius *l* sick ....Acts 28:8
Who shall *l* anything to the ...Rom 8:33
my life *l* down their own ......Rom 16:4
I have *l* the foundation 1Cor 3:10
foundation can no man *l* 1Cor 3:11
no man *l* than that is *l*........1Cor 3:11
for necessity is *l* upon me 1Cor 9:16
not to *l* up for the parents 2Cor 12:14
hope which is *l* up for you ....Col 1:5
with the *l* on of the hands.....1Tim 4:14
L hands suddenly on no.......1Tim 5:22
they may *l* hold on eternal 1Tim 6:19
there is *l* up for me a crown...2Tim 4:8
hast *l* the foundation of the ...Heb 1:10
not *l* again the foundation.....Heb 6:1
to *l* hold upon the hope set ...Heb 6:18
l apart all filthiness ....James 1:21
l aside all malice and all 1Pet 2:1
l in Zion a chief corner 1Pet 2:6
because he *l* down his life 1John 3:16
we ought to *l* down our 1John 3:16
he *l* his right hand upon ......Rev 1:17

LAZARUS (lăz'ä-rŭs)—*"God has helped"—Latin form of the Hebrew name "Eleazar"*
1. Beggar described in a parable ....Luke 16:20-25
2. Brother of Mary and Martha; raised from the dead ....John 11:1-44
   Attends a supper ....John 12:1, 2
   Jews seek to kill ....John 12:9-11

LAZINESS—*unwillingness to work; indolence*

Leads to:
Poverty ....Prov 6:9-11
Waste ....Prov 18:9
Loss of all ....Matt 25:26-30

Admonitions against:
Make the most of time...Eph 5:16
Have a great work ......Neh 6:3
Work day and night 1Thess 2:9
Consider the ant ....Prov 6:6-8
No work, no eat 2Thess 3:10-12

LEAD—*a heavy metal*
Purified by fire ....Num 31:22, 23
Engraved with ....Job 19:23, 24
Very heavy ....Ex 15:10
Object of trade..........Ezek 27:12

lifted up a talent of *l* ....Zech 5:7

LEAD—*to guide on a way*

[*also* LEADEST, LEADETH, LED, LEDDEST]
l the flock to the backside.....Ex 3:1
God *l* the people about ....Ex 13:18
a cloud to *l* them.............Ex 13:21
l the people ....Ex 32:34
which may *l* them out.........Num 27:17
the Lord shall *l* you ....Deut 4:27
l thee these forty years........Deut 8:2
armies to *l* the people ....Deut 20:9
the Lord shall *l* thee ....Deut 28:37
l you forty years..............Deut 29:5
l him throughout all ....Josh 24:3
l thy captivity captive ....Judg 5:12
the way to *l* to Ophrah 1Sam 16:17
they may *l* them away 1Sam 30:22
he that *l* out 2Sam 5:2
l them away captive 1Kin 8:48
But he *l* them to Samaria 2Kin 6:19
he that *l* out 1Chr 11:2
l forth the power 1Chr 20:1
l forth his people 2Chr 25:11
them that *l* them captive 2Chr 30:9
l them in the day ....Neh 9:12
to *l* them in the way ....Neh 9:19
He *l* counselors away ....Job 12:17
L me, O Lord................Ps 5:8
l me beside the still waters ....Ps 23:2
L me in thy truth............Ps 25:5
l me in a plain path ....Ps 27:11
name's sake, *l* me ....Ps 31:3
let them *l* me; let them ....Ps 43:3
l me to the rock..............Ps 61:2
thou hast *l* captivity ....Ps 68:18
Thou *l* thy people ....Ps 77:20
he *l* them on safely ....Ps 78:53
thou that *l* Joseph ....Ps 80:1
he *l* them forth...............Ps 107:7
Lord shall *l* them forth........Ps 125:5
l me in the way ....Ps 139:24
I have *l* thee in right ....Prov 4:11
goest, it shall *l* thee ....Prov 6:22
I *l* in the way ....Prov 8:20
l him into the way that is not..Prov 16:29
I would *l* thee ....Song 8:2
they which *l* thee cause thee...Is 3:12
l of them are destroyed ....Is 9:16
l away the Egyptians..........Is 20:4
gently *l* those that are ....Is 40:11
l them in paths ....Is 42:16
l thee by the way that thou ...Is 48:17
mercy on them shall *l*.........Is 49:10
be *l* forth with peace ....Is 55:12
I will *l* him also and restore ...Is 57:18
l them through the deep ......Is 63:13
so didst thou *l* thy people .....Is 63:14
l us through the wilderness ....Jer 2:6
l is consumed of the fire ......Jer 6:29
whither they have *l* him.......Jer 22:12
he shall *l* Zedekiah ....Jer 32:5
He hath *l* me and brought .....Lam 3:2
l them with him to Babylon ...Ezek 17:12
tin and iron, and *l*............Ezek 22:18
l me about the way ....Ezek 47:2
l you forty years.............Amos 2:10
Huzzab shall be *l* away ....Nah 2:7
maids shall *l* her.............Nah 2:7
Jesus *l* up of the spirit ....Matt 4:1
l us not into temptation ....Matt 6:13
way, that *l* to destruction .....Matt 7:13
they *l* him away ....Matt 27:2
l him away to crucify him .....Matt 27:31
l him out of the town ....Mark 8:23
l them up into a high ....Mark 9:2
when they shall *l* you ....Mark 13:11
the soldiers *l* him away ....Mark 15:16
l him out to crucify him.......Mark 15:20
l by the spirit ....Luke 4:1
Can the blind *l* the blind? .....Luke 6:39
l him away to watering? ......Luke 13:15
be *l* away captive ....Luke 21:24
l him into their council........Luke 22:66
as they *l* him away ....Luke 23:26
he *l* them out as far as to .....Luke 24:50
sheep by name and *l*..........John 10:3
And *l* him away to Annas......John 18:13
they took Jesus and *l* him .....John 19:16
l as a sheep to the............Acts 8:32
l him by the hand ....Acts 9:8
the iron gate that *l* ....Acts 12:10
some to *l* him by the hand ....Acts 13:11
Paul was to be *l*..............Acts 21:37
l out into the wilderness ......Acts 21:38
l by the hand of them ....Acts 22:11
God *l* thee to repentance? ....Rom 2:4
l by the Spirit of God.........Rom 8:14
power to *l* about a sister 1Cor 9:5
even as ye were *l*.............1Cor 12:2
But if ye be *l* of the Spirit ....Gal 5:18
he *l* captivity captive ....Eph 4:8
l a quiet and peaceable life....1Tim 2:2
l captive silly women 2Tim 3:6
l away with divers lusts 2Tim 3:6
to *l* them out of the land......Heb 8:9
l away with the error 2Pet 3:17
l them unto living fountains ...Rev 7:17
He that *l* into captivity........Rev 13:10

LEADER—*a guide*

Kinds of:
False ....Is 3:12
Blind..................Luke 6:39
Young..................Is 11:6
Safe ....Ps 78:53
Gentle.................Is 40:11
Faithful................Deut 8:2, 15

Names of:
The LORD ....Ex 13:21
Christ ....John 10:3
The Lamb ....Rev 7:17
The Spirit..............Luke 4:1
Gal 5:18

Course of, in:
God's truth ....Ps 25:5
Righteousness ....Ps 5:8
Way you should go ......Is 48:17
Unknown ways..........Is 42:16
Plain path ....Ps 27:11
Everlasting way ....Ps 139:24

[*also* LEADERS]
l of the Aaronites 1Chr 12:27
with every *l*..................1Chr 13:1
l and captains in the camp 2Chr 32:21
the *l* of this people ....Is 9:16
a *l* and commander to the.....Is 55:4
they be blind *l* of the blind....Matt 15:14

LEAF—*the flat, thin end of a plant's stem*
Trees..................Matt 21:19
Doors 1Kin 6:34
Book ....Jer 36:23

[*also* LEAVED, LEAVES]
they sewed fig *l* together ......Gen 3:7
in her mouth was an olive *l* ...Gen 8:11
the sound of a shaken *l*........Lev 26:36
two *l* of the one 1Kin 6:34
a *l* driven to and fro?.........Job 13:25
his *l* also shall not wither .....Ps 1:3
an oak whose *l* fadeth ....Is 1:30
when they cast their *l*..........Is 6:13
as the *l* falleth off ....Is 34:4
we all do fade as a *l*..........Is 64:6
fig tree, and the *l* shall fade ..Jer 8:13
wither in all the *l* of her ......Ezek 17:9
two *l* apiece, two turning *l* ....Ezek 41:24
two *l* for the one door ....Ezek 41:24
two *l* for the other door.......Ezek 41:24
whose *l* shall not fade.........Ezek 47:12
shake off his *l*................Dan 4:14
tender, and putteth forth *l* ....Matt 24:32
a fig tree afar off having *l*.....Mark 11:13
he found nothing but *l*........Mark 11:13
putteth forth *l*...............Mark 13:28
l of the trees were for ....Rev 22:2

LEAGUE—*an agreement between two or more parties*
Fraudulent ....Josh 9:3-6
Forbidden ....Judg 2:2
Secret 1Sam 22:8
Conditional 1Sam 3:12,13
Acceptable.............2Sam 3:21
Unifying 2Sam 5:1-3

International 1Kin 5:12
Purchased..............1Kin 15:18-21
Deceitful ....Dan 11:23

how shall we make a *l* ....Josh 9:7
made a *l* with them..........Josh 9:15
a *l* between me and thee 2Chr 16:3
be in *l* with the stones ....Job 5:23
the land that is in *l* ....Ezek 30:5
after the *l* made with him .....Dan 11:23

LEAH (lē'ä)—*"weary"*
Laban's eldest daughter ..Gen 29:16,17
By Laban's deceit, becomes Jacob's wife ..Gen 29:19-27
Hated by Jacob ....Gen 29:30-33
Mother of seven children .Gen 30:19-21
Buried in Machpelah's cave ....Gen 49:31
Builder of house of Israel.Ruth 4:11

[*also* LEAH'S]
L saw that she had left........Gen 30:9
Zilpah *L* maid bare ....Gen 30:10
L said, Happy am I...........Gen 30:13
unto his mother *L* ....Gen 30:14
Rachel said to *L*, Give me ....Gen 30:14
sent and called Rachel and *L* ..Gen 31:4
Jacob's tent and into *L*........Gen 31:33
divided the children unto *L*....Gen 33:1
and *L* also with her children...Gen 33:7
The sons of *L*; Reuben ....Gen 35:23
Zilpah, *L* handmaid ....Gen 35:26
Laban gave to *L*.............Gen 46:18

LEAN—*lacking fatness*

[*also* LEANFLESHED, LEANNESS]
river, ill-favored and *l* ....Gen 41:3
ill-favored and *l* kine ....Gen 41:4
very ill-favored and *l* ....Gen 41:19
l and the ill-favored kine ......Gen 41:20
whether it be fat or *l* ....Num 13:20
and my *l* rising up in me ......Job 16:8
sent *l* into their soul ....Ps 106:15
send among his fat ones *l* .....Is 10:16
his flesh shall wax *l*...........Is 17:4
My *l*, my *l*, woe unto me .....Is 24:16
fat cattle and between the *l* ...Ezek 34:20

LEAN—*to bend; cast one's weight to the side*

[*also* LEANED, LEANETH, LEANING]
that I may *l* upon them ....Judg 16:26
Saul *l* upon his spear 2Sam 1:6
or that *l* on a staff...........2Sam 3:29
and he *l* on my hand 2Kin 5:18
on whose hand the king *l* 2Kin 7:2
on which if a man *l*...........2Kin 18:21
he shall *l* upon his house ......Job 8:15
l not unto thine ....Prov 3:5
l upon her beloved? ....Song 8:5
if a man *l*, it will go into ......Is 36:6
when they *l* upon thee ....Ezek 29:7
l his hand on the wall.........Amos 5:19
they *l* upon the Lord ....Mic 3:11
l on Jesus' bosom one ....John 13:23
also *l* on his breast ....John 21:20
worshiped, *l* upon the top .....Heb 11:21

LEANNOTH (lē-än'ōth)—*a musical term, possibly suggesting a responsive reading or singing*
Musician upon Mahalath *L* ....Ps 88:*title*

LEAP—*to spring or bound forward suddenly*
Used physically of:
Insects..................Joel 2:5
Men....................1Kin 18:26
Unborn child...........Luke 1:41, 44
Lame man ....Acts 3:8
Expressive of:
Great joy 2Sam 6:16
Renewed life ....Is 35:6
Victory in persecution ...Luke 6:22, 23

[*also* LEAPED, LEAPING]
the rams which *l* ....Gen 31:12
l withal upon the earth........Lev 11:21
he shall *l* from Bashan ....Deut 33:22
by my God have I *l* over a 2Sam 22:30
sparks of fire *l* out ....Job 41:19
by my God have I *l* over a ....Ps 18:29
Why *l* ye, ye high hills? ....Ps 68:16
l upon the mountains ....Song 2:8
Then shall the lame man *l* ....Is 35:6
mountains shall they *l*.........Joel 2:5
all those that *l* on the ....Zeph 1:9
ye in that day, and *l* for joy ...Luke 6:23
And he *l* up stood, and ....Acts 3:8
l, and praising God ....Acts 3:8
And he *l* and walked ....Acts 14:10
evil spirit was *l* on them ......Acts 19:16

LEARN—*to acquire knowledge through experience or instruction; acts of acquiring knowledge*
Aspects of:
God's statutes ....Ps 119:71, 73
Righteousness ....Is 26:9, 10
Good works ....Titus 3:14
Obedience ....Heb 5:8
Objects of:
Abominable things ......Deut 18:9
Heathen ways ....Ps 106:35; Deut 18:9
Fear of the LORD .....Deut 14:23; Deut 17:19; Deut 31:13
Sources of:
Experience.............Gen 30:27
Worldly knowledge ......John 7:15
Christian experience .....Phil 4:11
Scriptures ....Rom 15:4

[*also* LEARNED, LEARNING]
that they may *l* to fear me ....Deut 4:10
that ye may *l* them ....Deut 5:1
that they may *l*, and fear......Deut 31:12
l thy righteous judgments .....Ps 119:7
I might *l* thy statutes ....Ps 119:71
hear, and will increase *l*.......Prov 1:5
he will increase in *l* ....Prov 9:9
the lips increaseth *l* ....Prov 16:21
addeth *l* to his lips ....Prov 16:23
Lest thou *l* his ways ....Prov 22:25
I neither *l* wisdom nor ....Prov 30:3
L to do well, seek ....Is 1:17
neither shall they *l* war ....Is 2:4
world will *l* righteousness .....Is 26:9
deliver to one that is *l* ....Is 29:11
to him that is not *l* ....Is 29:12
he saith, I am not *l*...........Is 29:12
that murmured shall *l*.........Is 29:24
the tongue of the *l* ....Is 50:4
mine ear to hear as the *l*......Is 50:4
Lord, *L* not the way ....Jer 10:2
diligently *l* the ways ....Jer 12:16
it *l* to catch the prey ....Ezek 19:3
l to catch the prey ....Ezek 19:6
they might teach the *l* ....Dan 1:4
neither shall they *l* war ....Mic 4:3
go ye and *l* what that ....Matt 9:13
my yoke..and *l* of me ....Matt 11:29
l a parable of the fig tree .....Matt 24:32
l a parable of the fig tree .....Mark 13:28
hath *l* of the Father ....John 6:45
Moses was *l* in all the wisdom .Acts 7:22
l doth make thee mad ....Acts 26:24
doctrine which ye have *l* ......Rom 16:17
might *l* in us not to think 1Cor 4:6
one by one, that all may *l*.....1Cor 14:31
if they will *l* any thing 1Cor 14:35
This only would I *l* of you ....Gal 3:2
But ye have not so *l* Christ....Eph 4:20
which ye have both *l* ....Phil 4:9
As ye also *l* of Epaphras ......Col 1:7
may *l* not to blaspheme 1Tim 1:20
Let the woman *l* in silence 1Tim 2:11
l first to show piety 1Tim 5:4
withal they *l* to be idle........1Tim 5:13
Ever *l*, and never able to 2Tim 3:7
things which thou hast *l*.......2Tim 3:14
of whom thou has *l*...........2Tim 3:14
l to maintain good works......Titus 3:14
l he obedience by the things...Heb 5:8
no man could *l* that song......Rev 14:3

LEASING—*an old word for "lie" or sin*
Translated "leasing" in...Ps 4:2
Same Hebrew word elsewhere translated "lies" ....Ps 40:4
Illustrated by Joab's conduct...............2Sam 3:27

LEAST—*See* LESS

LEATHER—*an animal's dried skin*
Worn by John the Baptist.Matt 3:4

LEAVE—*to depart from; abandon*

[*also* LEAVETH, LEAVING, LEFT, LEFTEST]
man *l* his father and his ....Gen 2:24
and they *l* off to build ....Gen 11:8
he *l* of talking with him ....Gen 17:22
l destitute my master ....Gen 24:27
Judah, and *l* bearing ....Gen 29:35
company which is *l* ....Gen 32:8
now *l* with thee some ....Gen 33:15
l all that he had in Joseph's ...Gen 39:6
he had *l* his garment..........Gen 39:13
l his garment with me.........Gen 39:18
he is *l* alone ....Gen 42:38
is dead, and he alone is *l* .....Gen 44:20
lad cannot *l* his father ....Gen 44:22
is not ought *l* in the sight .....Gen 47:18
l in the land of Goshen ....Gen 50:8
is it that ye have *l* the man?...Ex 2:20
all that the hail hath *l* ....Ex 10:12
Let no man *l* of it ....Ex 16:19
l of it until the morning.......Ex 16:20
l of the meat offering ....Lev 2:10
not *l* any of it ....Lev 7:15
sons of Aaron which were *l* ...Lev 10:16
l them for the poor ....Lev 19:10
thou shalt *l* them unto the ....Lev 23:22
them that are *l* alive ....Lev 26:36
The land also shall be *l* ....Lev 26:43
l none of it unto the ....Num 9:12
refuseth to give me *l*..........Num 22:13
until none was *l* to him ....Deut 3:3
shall not *l* thee either corn ....Deut 28:51
And ye shall be *l* few in ......Deut 28:62
l them in the lodging place ....Josh 4:3
there was not a man *l* in Ai ...Josh 8:17
l the city open, and pursued...Josh 8:17
he *l* none remaining ....Josh 10:37
he *l* none remaining ....Josh 10:40
neither *l* they any ....Josh 11:14
none of the Anakims *l*.........Josh 11:22
not *l* your brethren these.......Josh 22:3
nations which Joshua *l*........Judg 2:21
nations which the Lord *l* ......Judg 3:1
there was not a man *l* ....Judg 4:16
son of Jerubbaal was *l* ....Judg 9:5
Should I *l* my fatness ....Judg 9:9
she was *l* and her two sons ....Ruth 1:3
Intreat me not to *l* thee ....Ruth 1:16
she *l* speaking unto her ....Ruth 1:18
was sufficed, and *l*............Ruth 2:14
hath not *l* thee this day ....Ruth 4:14
every one that is *l* 1Sam 2:36
l caring for the asses 1Sam 9:5
l the care of the asses.........1Sam 10:2
l the sheep with a keeper 1Sam 17:20
hast thou *l* those few sheep ...1Sam 17:28
asked *l* of me that he 1Sam 20:6
l of all that pertain 1Sam 25:22
l neither man nor woman 1Sam 27:9
there they *l* their images 2Sam 5:21
not *l* to my husband 2Sam 14:7
shall not be *l* so much as......2Sam 17:12
he set up the *l* pillar 1Kin 7:21
Solomon *l* all the vessels 1Kin 7:47
let him not *l* us, nor 1Kin 8:57
all the people that were *l* 1Kin 9:20
him that is..*l* in Israel........1Kin 14:10
he *l* off building of Ramah 1Kin 15:21
he *l* him not one that 1Kin 16:11
Judah, and *l* his servant.......1Kin 19:3

L

have *l* me seven thousand 1Kin 19:18
thousand..men that were *l*.....1Kin 20:30
I will not *l* thee 2Kin 2:2
in Kir-haraseth *l* they the 2Kin 3:25
They shall eat, and shall *l*.....2Kin 4:43
l their tents 2Kin 7:7
which are *l* in the city 2Kin 7:13
multitude..that are *l* in it......2Kin 7:13
him that is shut up and *l*......2Kin 9:8
neither *l* he any of them 2Kin 10:14
l all the commandments........2Kin 17:16
the people that were *l* 2Kin 25:11
king of Babylon had *l*.........2Kin 25:22
when they had *l* their gods 1Chr 14:12
l it for an inheritance 1Chr 28:8
people..*l* of the Hittites 2Chr 8:7
Levites *l* their suburbs 2Chr 11:14
he *l* off building of Ramah 2Chr 16:5
was never a son *l* him 2Chr 21:17
they *l* the house of..God 2Chr 24:18
ten thousand *l* alive...........2Chr 25:12
eat and have *l* plenty 2Chr 31:10
is *l* is this great store 2Chr 31:10
l us a remnant to escape ......Ezra 9:8
l it for an inheritance ....Ezra 9:12
l of the captivity..............Neh 1:2
I pray you, let us *l* off ....Neh 5:10
there was no breach *l*...........Neh 6:1
l thou them in the hand........Neh 9:28
l the seventh year ....Neh 10:31
I will *l* off my heaviness.......Job 9:27
none of his meat be *l*..........Job 20:21
or wilt thou *l* thy labor ....Job 39:11
l her eggs in the earth ....Job 39:14
thou wilt not *l* my soul.........Ps 16:10
l me not, neither forsake ....Ps 27:9
he hath *l* off to be wise ....Ps 36:3
perish and *l* their wealth ....Ps 49:10
l not my soul destitute ....Ps 141:8
Who *l*..paths of uprightness ...Prov 2:13
good man *l* an inheritance.....Prov 13:22
a child *l* to himself ....Prov 29:15
l it unto the man ....Eccl 2:18
l not thy place ....Eccl 10:4
daughter of Zion is *l*..........Is 1:8
the Lord of hosts had *l* ....Is 1:9
every one eat that is *l* ....Is 7:22
where will ye *l* your glory? ....Is 10:3
eggs that are *l*.................Is 10:14
gleaning grapes shall be *l* .....Is 17:6
They shall be *l* together.......Is 18:6
In the city is *l* desolation......Is 24:12
be *l* as a beacon...............Is 30:17
multitude..shall be *l* ....Is 32:14
nothing shall be *l*..............Is 39:6
that I might *l* my people ......Jer 9:2
I have *l* mine heritage ....Jer 12:7
shall *l* them in the midst ......Jer 17:11
vessels which are *l*............Jer 27:18
not *l* thee..unpunished ....Jer 30:11
all the cities..that were *l* ......Jer 34:7
they *l* off speaking............Jer 38:27
the people that were *l* ....Jer 40:6
for we are *l* but a few ....Jer 42:2
l off to burn incense ....Jer 44:18
I not *l* thee..unpunished ......Jer 46:28
not *l* some gleaning grapes? ...Jer 49:9
let nothing of her be *l* ....Jer 50:26
face of an ox on the *l* side ....Ezek 1:10
Yet will I *l* a remnant ....Ezek 6:8
slaying them, and I was *l* .....Ezek 9:8
l thee naked and bare ....Ezek 16:39
l she her whoredoms..........Ezek 23:8
shall *l* thee naked and bare....Ezek 23:29
cut him off, and have *l* him ...Ezek 31:12
shadow, and have *l* him.......Ezek 31:12
l thee upon the land ....Ezek 32:4
that which was *l* was...........Ezek 41:9
the place that was *l*...........Ezek 41:11
l was five cubits ....Ezek 41:11
kingdom shall not be *l* ....Dan 2:44
l the stump of his roots ....Dan 4:15
l the stump of the..roots ......Dan 4:26
neither is there breath *l*.......Dan 10:17
l off to take heed.............Hos 4:10
shall he *l* his blood ....Hos 12:14
the palmerworm hath *l*........Joel 1:4
the locust hath *l* hath ....Joel 1:4
the cankerworm hath *l* ....Joel 1:4
l a blessing behind him ....Joel 2:14
by a thousand shall *l*..........Amos 5:3
an hundred shall *l* ten ....Amos 5:3
would they not *l*...............Obad 5
l in the midst..an afflicted .....Zeph 3:12
Who is *l* among you ....Hag 2:3
shepherd that *l* the flock ......Zech 11:17
one..*l* of all the nations ....Zech 14:16
l them neither root nor ....Mal 4:1
Then the devil *l* him ....Matt 4:11
l Nazareth, he came ....Matt 4:13
straightway *l* their nets........Matt 4:20
L there thy gift before the ....Matt 5:24
the fever *l* her ....Matt 8:15
And he *l* them ....Matt 16:4
l the ninety and nine ....Matt 18:12
shall a man *l* father and.......Matt 19:5
he *l* them and went out ....Matt 21:17
l him, and went their way .....Matt 22:22
not to *l* the other undone .....Matt 23:23
shall not be *l* here one ....Matt 24:2
he *l* them, and went away .....Matt 26:44
and they *l* their father ....Mark 1:20
forthwith Jesus gave them *l* ...Mark 5:13
meat..*l* seven baskets ....Mark 8:8
a man *l* his father and ....Mark 10:7
we have *l* all, and have ....Mark 10:28
they *l* him, and went their ....Mark 12:12
die, and *l* his wife behind him .Mark 12:19
and *l* no children ....Mark 12:19
neither *l* he any seed ....Mark 12:21
not be *l* one stone upon.......Mark 13:2
he *l* the linen cloth ....Mark 14:52
fever; and it *l* her ....Luke 4:39
And he *l* all, rose up ....Luke 5:28
departed, *l* him half dead .....Luke 10:30
not to *l* the other undone .....Luke 11:42
your house is *l*..desolate ......Luke 13:35
not *l* the ninety and nine ......Luke 15:4
taken and the other *l* ....Luke 17:35
Peter said, Lo, we..*l* all ....Luke 18:28
shall not *l*..one stone ....Luke 19:44
they *l* no children ....Luke 20:31
He *l* Judea, and departed .....John 4:3
the fever *l* him ....John 4:52
the Father hath not *l* me ......John 8:29
l the sheep, and fleeth ....John 10:12
will not *l* you comfortless .....John 14:18
I *l* the world, and go ....John 16:28
shall *l* me alone ....John 16:32
Pilate gave him *l* ....John 19:38
thou wilt not *l* my soul.........Acts 2:27
his soul was not *l* in hell ......Acts 2:31
took his *l* of the brethren .....Acts 18:18
to Ephesus and *l* them ....Acts 18:19
l the horsemen to go with .....Acts 23:32
certain man *l* in bonds ....Acts 25:14
l the natural use of the ....Rom 1:27
Lord of Sabaoth had *l* us .....Rom 9:29
let her not *l* him 1Cor 7:13
taking my *l* of them 2Cor 2:13
a man *l* his father ....Eph 5:31
thought it good to be *l*........1Thess 3:1
cloak that I *l* at Troas 2Tim 4:13
l I thee in Crete...............Titus 1:5
l nothing that is not put.......Heb 2:8
l the principles of the ....Heb 6:1
I will never *l* thee ....Heb 13:5
suffered..*l* us an example......1Pet 2:21
but *l* their own habitation .....Jude 6
thou hast *l* thy first love ......Rev 2:4
without the temple *l* out ......Rev 11:2

LEAVED, LEAVES—*See* LEAF

LEAVEN—*the agent causing fermentation*

Forbidden in:
Passover ....Ex 12:8-20
Meat offerings ....Lev 2:11

Permitted in:
Peace offerings ....Lev 7:13
First fruits of grain ......Lev 23:17; Num 15:20, 21

Figurative of:
Kingdom of heaven ......Matt 13:33
Corrupt teaching ....Matt 16:6, 12
Infectious sin............1Cor 5:5-7
False doctrine ....Gal 5:1-9

[*also* LEAVENED]
dough before it was *l* ....Ex 12:34
Egypt for it was not *l*.........Ex 12:39
no *l* bread be eaten...........Ex 13:3
no *l* bread be seen ....Ex 13:7
be *l* seen with thee in.........Ex 13:7
sacrifice with *l* bread..........Ex 23:18
blood of my sacrifice with *l* ...Ex 34:25
shall not be baked with *l*......Lev 6:17
eat it without *l* beside the .....Lev 10:12
Thou shalt eat no *l* bread .....Deut 16:3
shall be no *l* bread seen.......Deut 16:4
dough, until it be *l* ....Hos 7:4
thanksgiving with *l* ....Amos 4:5
the *l* of the Pharisees ....Mark 8:15
and of the *l* of Herod ....Mark 8:15
Beware..*l* of the Pharisees.....Luke 12:1
like *l*, which a woman took ...Luke 13:21
meal, till the whole was *l* .....Luke 13:21
feast, not with old *l* 1Cor 5:8
neither with the *l* of malice....1Cor 5:8

LEBANAH, LEBANA (lĕ-bā'nä)—*"white"*
Founder of a family of returning exiles......Ezra 2:43, 45; Neh 7:48
Called Lebana ....Neh 7:48

LEBANON (lĕb'ä-nŏn)—*"white"—one of two mountain ranges in northern Palestine*

Source of:
Wood for Solomon's temple................1Kin 5:5, 6
Stones for Solomon's temple................1Kin 5:14, 18
Wood for the second temple................Ezra 3:7

Significant as:
A sight desired by Moses .Deut 3:25
Israel's northern boundary ....Deut 1:7
Captured by Joshua .....Josh 11:16, 17; Josh 12:7
Assigned to Israelites ....Josh 13:5-7
Not completely conquered Judg 3:1-3
Possessed by Assyria.....Is 37:24

Figurative of:
Great kingdoms ....Is 10:24, 34
Spiritual transformation ..Is 29:17
Jerusalem and the Temple ....Ezek 17:3
Spiritual growth ....Hos 14:5-7
Messiah's glory ....Is 35:2

Noted for:
Blossoms ....Nah 1:4
Wine ....Hos 14:6, 7
Wild beast 2Kin 14:9
Snow ....Jer 5:15
Cedars ....Song 5:15; Is 14:8

from the wilderness and *L*.....Deut 11:24
the wilderness and this *L*......Josh 1:4
Great Sea over against *L*......Josh 9:1
devour the cedars of *L*........Judg 9:15
the cedar tree that is in *L* 1Kin 4:33
bring them down from *L* 1Kin 5:9
house of the forest of *L*.......1Kin 7:2
house of the forest of *L*.......1Kin 10:17
thistle that was in *L* 2Kin 14:9
the cedar that was in *L* 2Kin 14:9
wild beast that was in *L*.......2Kin 14:9
algum trees, out of *L* 2Chr 2:8
skill to cut timber in *L*........2Chr 2:8
in Jerusalem, and in *L* 2Chr 8:6
house of the forest of *L*.......2Chr 9:20
The thistle that was in *L* 2Chr 25:18
the cedar that was in *L* 2Chr 25:18
a wild beast that was in *L*.....2Chr 25:18

breaketh the cedars of *L* ....Ps 29:5
fruit..shall shake like *L* ....Ps 72:16
grow like a cedar in *L* ....Ps 92:12
cedars of *L*, which he hath ....Ps 104:16
chariot of the wood of *L* ......Song 3:9
Come with me from *L*........Song 4:8
from *L*; took from the top ....Song 4:8
streams from *L*..............Song 4:15
nose is as the tower of *L*......Song 7:4
upon all the cedars of *L*.......Is 2:13
thee and the cedars of *L* ......Is 14:8
L is ashamed and hewn ....Is 33:9
L is not sufficient to burn .....Is 40:16
leave the snow of *L* ....Jer 18:14
Go up to *L*; and cry ....Jer 22:20
cedars from *L* to make ....Ezek 27:5
and I caused *L* to mourn......Ezek 31:15
flower of *L* languisheth ....Nah 1:4
the land of Gilead and *L*......Zech 10:10
Open thy doors, O *L* ....Zech 11:1

LEBAOTH (lĕ-bā'ŏth)—*"lioness"*
Town of southern Judah. .Josh 15:32
Also called Beth-labaoth. .Josh 19:6

LEBBEUS (lĕ-bē'ŭs)
Surname of Judas (Jude) .Matt 10:3
See **Jude 3**

LEBONAH (lĕ-bō'nä)—*"incense"*
Town north of Shiloh ....Judg 21:19

LECAH (lē'kä)—*"walking; addition"*
Descendant of Judah 1Chr 4:21

LED—*See* **Lead**

LEDGE—*a protrusion around an altar*
Part of altars rendered "compass" ....Ex 27:5

[*also* **ledges**]
borders were between the *l*....1Kin 7:28
the borders..between the *l* 1Kin 7:29
upon the *l* there was a base ...1Kin 7:29

LEECH—*See* **Horseleech**

LEEK—*an onion-like plant*
Desired by Israelites .....Num 11:5

LEES—*sediment in wine jars*
Figurative of:
Negligence and ease .....Jer 48:11
Spiritual riches ....Is 25:6

that are settled on their *l* .....Zeph 1:12

LEFT—*the direction opposite of right*
Of direction:
Location ....Gen 14:15
Making a choice ....Gen 13:9
Position ....Matt 20:21-23
Of the hand:
Unusual capacity of 700 men ....Judg 20:15,16
Lesser importance of ....Gen 48:13-20
Figurative of:
Weakness ....Eccl 10:2
Shame ....Matt 25:33,41
Bride's choice ....Song 2:6
Singleness of purpose ....Matt 6:3
Riches ....Prov 3:16
Ministry of God 2Cor 6:7

right hand, and on their *l* .....Ex 14:22
oil that is in his *l* hand.......Lev 14:16
oil that is in his *l* hand.......Lev 14:27
the right hand nor to the *l* ....Num 20:17
to the right hand or to the *l*...Num 22:26
the right hand nor to the *l* .....Deut 2:27
the right hand or to the *l* .....Deut 5:32
the right hand nor to the *l* ....Deut 17:11
the right hand, or to the *l*.....Deut 28:14
the right hand or to the *l* .....Josh 1:7
the lamps in their *l* hands .....Judg 7:20
the right hand or to the *l* 1Sam 6:12
nor to the *l* from following 2Sam 2:19
the right hand nor to the *l* 2Sam 14:19
his right hand and on his *l* 2Sam 16:6
his right hand and on his *l* 1Kin 22:19
l corner of the temple 2Kin 11:11
the right hand or to the *l* 2Kin 22:2
sons of Merari stood on the *l*. .1Chr 6:44
the *l* in hurling stones.........1Chr 12:2
the other on the *l* 2Chr 3:17
name of that on the *l* Boaz....2Chr 3:17
five on the *l* 2Chr 4:7
the right hand, nor to the *l*....2Chr 34:2
On the *l* hand, where he ......Job 23:9
the right hand nor to the *l* ....Prov 4:27
His *l* hand should be under ...Song 8:3
the right hand and on the *l*....Is 54:3
daughters that dwell at thy *l*...Ezek 16:46
thy bow out of thy *l* hand .....Ezek 39:3
their right hand and their *l* ....Jon 4:11
the other upon the *l* side ......Zech 4:3
the right hand and on the *l*....Zech 12:6
let not thy *l* hand know ....Matt 6:3
the other on thy *l* hand ....Mark 10:37
the other on the *l* ....Luke 23:33
on the *l* hand, and sailed......Acts 21:3
the right hand and on the *l*....2Cor 6:7

LEFT—*that which remains*
Descriptive of:
Aloneness ....Gen 32:24
Entire destruction ....Josh 11:11,12
Entire separation ....Ex 10:26
Survival ....Num 26:65
Remnant ....Is 11:11, 16
Heir...................2Sam 14:7
Blessings upon:
Equal booty 1Sam 30:9-25
Greater heritage ....Is 49:21-23
Holiness ....Is 4:3
Lord's protection ....Rom 11:3-5
Not wasted ....Matt 15:37

LEFT—*See* **Leave**

LEFTHANDED—*the quality of using the left hand more easily than the right*
a Benjamite, a man *l* ....Judg 3:15

LEG—*lower part of human or animal bodies*
Used literally of:
Animal's ....Ex 12:9
Man's 1Sam 17:6
Christ's ....John 19:31,33
Used figuratively of:
Fool...................Prov 26:7
Man's weakness ....Ps 147:10
Children of Israel........Amos 3:12
Strength ....Dan 2:33, 40
Christ's appearance ......Song 5:15

[*also* **legs**]
wash the inwards..his *l*........Ex 29:17
his *l* shall he wash in ....Lev 1:9
his head, and with his *l* ....Lev 4:11
he did wash..the *l* ....Lev 9:14
in the knees, and in the *l* .....Deut 28:35
make bare the *l* ....Is 47:2
brake the *l* of the first ....John 19:32

LEGACY—*that which is bequeathed to heirs*
Left by:
Abraham ....Gen 25:5, 6
David 1Kin 2:1-7
Christ ....John 14:15-27

LEGAL—*lawful*
Kingship, determined by David 1Kin 1:5-48
Priests' rights, divinely enforced 2Chr 26:16-21
priesthood, rejected .....Neh 7:63-65
Right to rebuild, confirmed............Ezra 5:3-17
Mixed marriages, condemned ....Ezra 10:1-44
David's act, justified .....Matt 12:3-8
Christ's trial, exposed ....Matt 27:4-31
Paul's right of appeal, recognized ....Acts 26:31,32

LEGION—*a great number or multitude*
Demons ....Mark 5:9, 15
Christ's angels..........Matt 26:53

thy name? And he said, *L* ....Luke 8:30

LEHABIM (lĕ-hā'bĭm)—*"flame; red"*
Nation (probably the Libyans) related to the Egyptians ....Gen 10:13

Ludim, and Anamim, and *L*...1Chr 1:11

LEHI (lē'hī)—*"jawbone"*
Place in Judah; Samson kills Philistines ....Judg 15:9-19

LEISURE—*spare time*
None found ....Mark 6:31

LEMUEL (lĕm'ū-ĕl)—*"Godward; dedicated"*
King taught by his mother ....Prov 31:1-31

LEND—*give to another for temporary use*
As a gift:
Expecting no return .....Luke 6:34, 35
To the Lord 1Sam 1:28
1Sam 2:20
As a blessing:
Recognized by God......Deut 28:12,44
Remembered by God ....Ps 112:5, 6
Rewarded by God ....Ps 37:25, 26
See **Borrow**

[*also* **lendeth, lent, loan**]
l unto them such things ....Ex 12:36
thou *l* money to..my people ...Ex 22:25
l him thy victuals ....Lev 25:37
Every creditor that *l* ....Deut 15:2
thou shalt *l* unto many ....Deut 15:6
shalt surely *l* him sufficient ....Deut 15:8
Thou shalt not *l* upon.........Deut 23:19
any..that is *l* upon usury ......Deut 23:19
thou mayest *l* upon usury .....Deut 23:20
thou shalt not *l* upon ....Deut 23:20
When thou dost *l* thy ....Deut 24:10
man to whom thou dost *l* .....Deut 24:11
thou shalt *l* unto many ....Deut 28:12
I have *l* him to the Lord 1Sam 1:28
he shall be *l* to the Lord 1Sam 1:28
the *l* which is *l* to the Lord....1Sam 2:20
pity upon the poor *l* ....Prov 19:17
I have neither *l* on usury......Jer 15:10
nor men have *l* to me on .....Jer 15:10
Friend, *l* me three loaves .....Luke 11:5

LENDER—*one who loans to others*
borrower is servant to the *l* ...Prov 22:7
with the *l*, so..borrower ....Is 24:2

LENGTH—*the distance from one point to another*

[*also* **lengthen, lengthened**]
l of the ark..three hundred ....Gen 6:15
cubits and a half..the *l*........Ex 25:10
l of one curtain shall be.......Ex 26:2
the *l* of the curtains ....Ex 26:13
side in *l* there shall be ....Ex 27:11
a span shall be the *l* ....Ex 28:16
l of one curtain was twenty....Ex 36:9
l of a board was ten cubits ....Ex 36:21
cubits and a half was the *l* ....Ex 37:6
the *l* of it was a cubit ....Ex 37:25
twenty cubits was the *l*........Ex 38:18
nine cubits was the *l*..........Deut 3:11
that thy days may be *l* ....Deut 25:15
and the *l* of thy days ....Deut 30:20
two edges, of a cubit *l* ....Judg 3:16
the *l* whereof..threescore 1Kin 6:2
twenty cubits in *l* 1Kin 6:20
the *l* thereof was fifty 1Kin 7:6
l by cubits after the first 2Chr 3:3
the *l* whereof was according ...2Chr 3:8
l of days understanding ....Job 12:12
even *l* of days for ever ....Ps 21:4
for *l* of days, and long life ....Prov 3:2
L of days is in her right.......Prov 3:16
become his son at the *l* ....Prov 29:21

in the *l* of his branches ....Ezek 31:7
against the *l* of the gates ......Ezek 40:18
l thereof was fifty cubits ......Ezek 40:21
the *l* was fifty cubits and ......Ezek 40:36
measured the *l* thereof ....Ezek 41:2
and the *l*..ninety cubits........Ezek 41:12
and the *l*..two cubits ....Ezek 41:22
the *l* thereof, and the walls ....Ezek 41:22
l thereof was fifty cubits ......Ezek 42:7
the *l* shall be the *l* of five .....Ezek 45:1
thou measure the *l* ....Ezek 45:3
the *l* shall be over against .....Ezek 45:7
and in *l* as one of the ....Ezek 48:8
and twenty thousand in *l*......Ezek 48:10
and twenty thousand in *l*......Ezek 48:10
and twenty thousand in *l*......Ezek 48:13
l shall be five and twenty .....Ezek 48:13
and what is the *l* thereof ......Zech 2:2
at *l* I might have a ....Rom 1:10
what is the breadth and *l* .....Eph 3:18
l is as large as..breadth ....Rev 21:16
l and the breadth..height ......Rev 21:16

LENGTH OF LIFE—*the age one lives, or may expect to live*

Factors prolonging:
Keeping commandments .1Kin 3:14
Wisdom ....Prov 3:13, 16
Prayer 2Kin 20:1-11
Honor to parents ....Eph 6:3
Fear of the LORD ....Prov 10:27

Factors decreasing:
Killing..................2Sam 3:27
God's judgment ....Job 22:15, 16
Suicide ....Matt 27:5

LENT—*See* LEND

LENTIL—*plant of the legume family*
Prepared as Esau's pottage ....Gen 25:29-34
Bread made of ....Ezek 4:9

[*also* LENTILS]
corn, and beans, and *l* 2Sam 17:28
piece of ground full of *l*.......2Sam 23:11

LEOPARD—*a spotted feline*

Characteristics of:
Swift ....Hab 1:8
Watches ....Jer 5:6
Lies in wait ....Hos 13:7
Lives in mountains ......Song 4:8

Figurative of:
Man's inability to change .Jer 13:23
Transformation ....Is 11:6
Greek empire ....Dan 7:6
Antichrist ....Rev 13:2

LEPROSY—*disease causing loss of sensation, muscle paralysis, and deformities; common in ancient times*

Characteristics of:
Many diseased with ......Luke 4:27
Unclean ....Lev 13:44, 45
Outcast 2Kin 15:5
Considered incurable 2Kin 5:7
Often hereditary.........2Sam 3:29
Excluded from the priesthood ....Lev 22:2-4

Kinds of, in:
Man....................Luke 17:12
House ....Lev 14:33-57
Clothing ....Lev 13:47-59

Treatment of:
Symptoms described .....Lev 13:1-46
Cleansing prescribed ....Lev 14:1-32
Healing by a miracle.....Ex 4:6, 7

Used as a sign:
Miriam ....Num 12:1-10
Gehazi 2Kin 5:25, 27
Uzziah 2Chr 26:16-21
Moses ....Ex 4:6, 7

[*also* LEPER, LEPERS, LEPROUS]
l in whom the plague is ....Lev 13:45
this shall be the law of the *l*...Lev 14:2
l be healed in the *l* ....Lev 14:3
I put the plague of *l* in a......Lev 14:34
seed of Aaron is a *l* ....Lev 22:4
put out of the camp every *l* ...Num 5:2
Take heed in the plague of *l* ..Deut 24:8
an issue, or that is a *l* 2Sam 3:29
in valor, but he was a *l* 2Kin 5:1
recover him of his *l*...........2Kin 5:3
recover him of his *l*...........2Kin 5:6
and recover the *l* 2Kin 5:11
The *l*..of Naaman shall........2Kin 5:27
a *l* as white as snow 2Kin 5:27
were four *l* men at the 2Kin 7:3
l came to the uttermost 2Kin 7:8
was a *l* unto the day of his 2Kin 15:5
Uzziah the king was a *l* 2Chr 26:21
several house, being a *l* 2Chr 26:21
for they said, He is a *l*........2Chr 26:23
came a *l* and worshiped ....Matt 8:2
his *l* was cleansed ....Matt 8:3
sick, cleanse the *l*, raise ....Matt 10:8
l are cleansed..the deaf ....Matt 11:5
house of Simon the *l* ....Matt 26:6
there came a *l* to him.........Mark 1:40
the *l* departed from ....Mark 1:42
house of Simon the *l* ....Mark 14:3
many *l* were in Israel ....Luke 4:27
behold a man full of *l* ....Luke 5:12
the *l* departed from ....Luke 5:13
l are cleansed..deaf hear ......Luke 7:22
ten men that were *l* ....Luke 17:12

LESHEM (lē'shĕm)—*"a lion"—same as "Laish"*
up to fight against *L* ....Josh 19:47
and called *L*, Dan ....Josh 19:47

LESS—*fewer; smaller; of lower rank*

[*also* LEAST, LESSER]
l light to rule the night........Gen 1:16
with us a few days at the *l* ....Gen 24:55
some more, some *l* ....Ex 16:17
l gathered ten homers.........Num 11:32
God, to do *l* or more ....Num 22:18
give the *l* inheritance ....Num 33:54
l such as before knew.........Judg 3:2
my family the *l* of all the 1Sam 9:21
nothing..*l* or more 1Sam 22:15
how much *l* this house 1Kin 8:27
l of my master's servants 2Kin 18:24
one of the *l* was over a 1Chr 12:14
how much *l* this house 2Chr 6:18
how much *l* shall your God ...2Chr 32:15
punished us *l* than our ....Ezra 9:13
How much *l* in them that .....Job 4:19
exacteth of thee *l* than ....Job 11:6
much *l* do lying lips a.........Prov 17:7
the treading of *l* cattle ....Is 7:25
l of my master's servants ......Is 36:9
counted to him *l* than nothing .Is 40:17
l of them even unto the ....Jer 6:13
l of them unto the greatest ....Jer 31:34
l even unto the greatest ....Jer 42:1
l even unto the greatest ....Jer 44:12
the *l* of the flock shall ....Jer 50:45
from the *l* settle even to ......Ezek 43:14
not the *l* grain fall upon.......Amos 9:9
even to the *l* of them ....Jon 3:5
the *l* among the princes ....Matt 2:6
one of..*l* commandments ......Matt 5:19
the *l* in the kingdom of ....Matt 5:19
l in the kingdom of heaven ....Matt 11:11
indeed is the *l* of all seeds ....Matt 13:32
l of these my brethren ....Matt 25:40
did it not to one of the *l* ......Matt 25:45
l than all the seeds that ......Mark 4:31
that is *l* in the kingdom ....Luke 7:28
for he that is *l* among you ....Luke 9:48
do that thing which is *l* ....Luke 12:26
faithful in that which is *l* ......Luke 16:10
he that is unjust in the *l* ......Luke 16:10
that at the *l* the shadow........Acts 5:15
to judge who are *l*............1Cor 6:4
think to be *l* honorable 1Cor 12:23
I am the *l* of the apostles 1Cor 15:9
I love you, the *l* I be 2Cor 12:15
am *l* than the least of all ......Eph 3:8
I may be the *l* sorrowful ......Phil 2:28
l is blessed of the better ......Heb 7:7
from the *l* to the greatest .....Heb 8:11

LEST—*for fear that*
neither shall ye touch it, *l*.....Gen 3:3
l any finding him should ......Gen 4:15
l thou shouldest say, I ....Gen 14:23
l thou be consumed...........Gen 19:17
l..the men of the place........Gen 26:7
l he will come and smite ......Gen 32:11
l that he should give seed .....Gen 38:9
to her, *l* we be shamed ....Gen 38:23
l..I see the evil that ....Gen 44:34
l they multiply, and it.........Ex 1:10
L..the people repent ....Ex 13:17
l the Lord break forth ....Ex 19:22
God speak with us *l* we die ...Ex 20:19
l they make thee sin ....Ex 23:33
l thou make a covenant ....Ex 34:12
l it be for a snare in the ......Ex 34:12
rend your clothes; *l* ye ....Lev 10:6
l wrath come upon all ....Lev 10:6
congregation, *l* ye die ....Lev 10:9
l they bear sin for it ....Lev 22:9
any holy thing, *l* they ....Num 4:15
l ye be consumed in all ....Num 16:26
l they bear sin ....Num 18:22
l thou forget the things ....Deut 4:9
l they depart from thy ....Deut 4:9
l thou lift up thine eyes ....Deut 4:19
l thou forget the Lord ....Deut 6:12
l the beasts of the field ....Deut 7:22
l thou be a cursed thing.......Deut 7:26
L the land whence thou ....Deut 9:28
L the avenger of the blood ....Deut 19:6
l he die in the battle, and .....Deut 20:5
l his brethren's heart faint.....Deut 20:8
l he cry against thee unto .....Deut 24:15
L there should be among......Deut 29:18
l their adversaries ....Deut 32:27
and *l* they should say ....Deut 32:27
l the pursuers meet you ....Josh 2:16
let them live, *l* wrath be ......Josh 9:20
l Israel vaunt themselves ......Judg 7:2
l angry fellows run upon ......Judg 18:25
l I mar mine own.............Ruth 4:6
l my father leave caring 1Sam 9:5
l I destroy you with them 1Sam 15:6
L they should tell on us 1Sam 27:11
l these uncircumcised 1Sam 31:4
l the daughters of the..........2Sam 1:20
l I take the city, and it.........2Sam 12:28
l they destroy my son 2Sam 14:11
l the king be swallowed 2Sam 17:16
l..the spirit of the 2Kin 2:16
l these uncircumcised 1Chr 10:4
l ye should say, We ....Job 32:13
l he take thee away with ......Job 36:18
Kiss the Son, *l* he be angry ...Ps 2:12
l I sleep the sleep of death ....Ps 13:3
l, if thou be silent to me ......Ps 28:1
l otherwise they..rejoice.......Ps 38:16
l my people forget............Ps 59:11
l the righteous put forth ......Ps 125:3
l I be like unto them that .....Ps 143:7
L thou shouldest ponder ......Prov 5:6
l thou give thine honor ....Prov 5:9
not a scorner, *l* he hate ....Prov 9:8
l thou learn his ways..........Prov 22:25
l thou know not what to ....Prov 25:8
l thou be filled therewith......Prov 25:16
l thou also be like ....Prov 26:4
l he reprove thee, and ....Prov 30:6
l he curse thee, and thou .....Prov 30:10
l thou hear thy servant........Eccl 7:21
l they see with their eyes......Is 6:10
l your bands be made strong ..Is 28:22
l thou shouldest say, Mine ....Is 48:5
l I confound thee before ......Jer 1:17
l my soul depart from thee ....Jer 6:8
l thou bring me to nothing ....Jer 10:24
Jonathan the scribe, *l* I die....Jer 37:20

And *l* your heart faint ....Jer 51:46
L I strip her naked, and ......Hos 2:3
l he break out like fire........Amos 5:6
l I come out and smite the ....Mal 4:6
l..thou dash thy foot..........Matt 4:6
l they trample them ....Matt 7:6
l while ye gather..tares.......Matt 13:29
l we should offend them ......Matt 17:27
l there be an uproar ....Matt 26:5
l his disciples come by ....Matt 27:64
l they should throng him ......Mark 3:9
l any man deceive you ....Mark 13:5
l there be an uproar of ....Mark 14:2
l..thou dash thy foot..........Luke 4:11
l he hale thee to the judge ....Luke 12:58
l they also bid thee again .....Luke 14:12
l they also come into this .....Luke 16:28
l at any time your hearts ......Luke 21:34
l his deeds should be reproved .John 3:20
l darkness come upon you.....John 12:35
l they should be defiled ....John 18:28
l they should..been stoned ....Acts 5:26
l that come upon you ....Acts 13:40
fearing *l* they should fall ......Acts 27:17
l any of them should swim ....Acts 27:42
heed *l* he also spare not.......Rom 11:21
l I..build upon another.........Rom 15:20
L any should say that I 1Cor 1:15
l by any means this liberty 1Cor 8:9
l we..hinder the gospel........1Cor 9:12
take heed *l* he fall 1Cor 10:12
l, when I came, I should 2Cor 2:3
L Satan should get an.........2Cor 2:11
l our boasting of you 2Cor 9:3
l by any means, as the 2Cor 11:3
l I should be exalted above....2Cor 12:7
For I fear, *l*, when I come 2Cor 12:20
l there be debates 2Cor 12:20
l being present I should use ...2Cor 13:10
l by any means I should run...Gal 2:2
l thou also be tempted ....Gal 6:1
l I should have sorrow upon...Phil 2:27
l any man should beguile......Col 2:4
l they be discouraged ....Col 3:21
l..the tempter have 1Thess 3:5
l being lifted up with pride 1Tim 3:6
l..we should let them ....Heb 2:1
l any of you be hardened .....Heb 3:13
l any man fall after the ....Heb 4:11
l ye be wearied and faint......Heb 12:3
l any man fail of the grace ....Heb 12:15
l any root of bitterness........Heb 12:15
l ye be condemned ....James 5:9
beware *l* ye also, being led 2Pet 3:17
l he walk naked, and they.....Rev 16:15

LET—*See* INTRODUCTION

"LET US"—*an imperative, indicating either a request or a proposal*
"Arise, go hence" ....John 14:31
"Cast off the works of darkness" ....Rom 13:12
"Walk honestly" ....Rom 13:13
"Be sober" 1Thess 5:8
"Fear" ....Heb 4:1
"Labor to enter into that rest" ....Heb 4:11
"Come boldly" ....Heb 4:16
"Go on unto perfection" .Heb 6:1
"Draw near" ....Heb 10:22
"Hold fast" ....Heb 10:23
"Consider one another"..Heb 10:24
"Run with patience".....Heb 12:1
"Go forth" ....Heb 13:13
"Offer sacrifice".........Heb 13:15

LETTER—*written communication*

Kinds of:
Forged 1Kin 21:7, 8
Rebellious ....Jer 29:24-32
Authoritative...........Acts 22:5
Instructive ....Acts 15:23-29
Weighty 2Cor 10:10
Causing sorrow..........2Cor 7:8

Descriptive of:
One's writing ....Gal 6:11
Learning................John 7:15
External ....Rom 2:27, 29
Legalism................Rom 7:6
Christians 2Cor 3:1, 2

[*also* LETTERS]
David wrote a *l* to Joab 2Sam 11:14
And he wrote in the *l* 2Sam 11:15
And she wrote in the *l*........1Kin 21:9
and I will send a *l* unto 2Kin 5:5
And he brought the *l* to 2Kin 5:6
Now when this *l* is come 2Kin 5:6
Jehu wrote *l* and sent to 2Kin 10:1
as soon as this *l* cometh.......2Kin 10:2
to pass, when the *l* came 2Kin 10:7
wrote *l* also to Ephraim 2Chr 30:1
l to rail on the Lord 2Chr 32:17
writing of the *l* was written....Ezra 4:7
copy of the *l* that they sent....Ezra 4:11
copy of king Artaxerxes' *l*.....Ezra 4:23
copy of the *l* that Tatnai ......Ezra 5:6
copy of the *l* that the king ....Ezra 7:11
let *l* be given me to the ....Neh 2:7
l unto Asaph the keeper ......Neh 2:8
sent many *l*..Tobiah ....Neh 6:17
the *l* of Tobiah came unto ....Neh 6:17
And Tobiah sent *l* to put .....Neh 6:19
written to reverse the *l*........Esth 8:5
sent *l* unto all the Jews ....Esth 9:20
all the words of this *l* ....Esth 9:26
And he sent the *l* unto all......Esth 9:30
Hezekiah received the *l* ....Is 37:14
sent *l* and a present ....Is 39:1
words of the *l* that Jeremiah...Jer 29:1
over him in *l* of Greek ....Luke 23:38
desired..*l* to Damascus ....Acts 9:2
he wrote a *l* after this..........Acts 23:25
received *l* out of Judea........Acts 28:21
spirit, and not in the *l* ....Rom 2:29
approve by your *l* 1Cor 16:3
not of the *l*, but of the spirit ..2Cor 3:6
l killeth, but the spirit 2Cor 3:6
I would terrify you by *l*.......2Cor 10:9
by *l* when we are absent 2Cor 10:11
nor by word, nor by *l* as 2Thess 2:2
I have written a *l* unto ....Heb 13:22

LETTEST—*See* INTRODUCTION

LETTING

[*also* LETTEST, LETTETH]
in not *l* the people go to ......Ex 8:29
he that *l* him go, his life 2Kin 10:24
l such words go out of ....Job 15:13
a cord which thou *l* down? ....Job 41:1
strife is as when one *l* out .....Prov 17:14
l thou thy servant depart ......Luke 2:29
he who now *l* will let 2Thess 2:7

LETUSHIM (lĕ-tū'shĭm)—*"sharpened"*
Tribe descending from Dedan...............Gen 25:3

LEUMMIM (lĕ-ŭm'ĭm)—*"peoples"*
Tribe descending from Dedan...............Gen 25:3

LEVI (lē'vī)—*"joined"*
1. Third son of Jacob and Leah................Gen 29:34
   Participates in revenge ..Gen 34:25-31
   Father of Gershon, Kohath, Merari ....Gen 46:11
   Descendants of, to be scattered ....Gen 49:5-7
   Dies in Egypt at age 137.Ex 6:16
2. Ancestor of Christ ......Luke 3:24
3. Another ancestor of Christ..............Luke 3:29
4. Apostle called Matthew. .Luke 5:27, 29
5. Tribe descending from Levi ....Ex 32:26, 28

and Simeon, and *L* ....Gen 35:23
Simeon and *L* are brethren ....Gen 49:5
Reuben, Simeon, *L*, and ......Ex 1:2
a man of the house of *L* ......Ex 2:1
to wife a daughter of *L* ....Ex 2:1
life of *L* were a hundred ......Ex 6:16
these are the families of *L* ....Ex 6:19
not number the tribe of *L*.....Num 1:49
Number the children of *L* .....Num 3:15
among the sons of *L*..........Num 4:2
upon you, ye sons of *L* ....Num 16:7
brethren the sons of *L* ....Num 16:10
for the house of *L* was ....Num 17:8
given the children of *L*........Num 18:21
Jochebed, the daughter of *L*...Num 26:59
bare to *L* in Egypt ....Num 26:59
separated the tribe of *L*.......Deut 10:8
L hath no part nor ....Deut 10:9
the sons of *L* shall come ......Deut 21:5
the priests the sons of *L* ......Deut 31:9
L he gave none inheritance....Josh 13:14
of the children of *L*...........Josh 21:10
were not of the sons of *L* 1Kin 12:31
Reuben, Simeon, *L*, and 1Chr 2:1
son of *L* the son of Israel 1Chr 6:38
of Merari, the son of *L* 1Chr 6:47
children of *L* four thousand ...1Chr 12:26
among the sons of *L*..........1Chr 23:6
These were the sons of *L* 1Chr 23:24
none of the sons of *L*.........Ezra 8:15
children of *L* shall bring ......Neh 10:39
bless the Lord, O house of *L*. .Ps 135:20
among the sons of *L*..........Ezek 40:46
family..of *L* apart.............Zech 12:13
covenant might be with *L* .....Mal 2:4
shall purify the sons of *L*......Mal 3:3
they that are of the sons of *L*. .Heb 7:5
L were sealed twelve ....Rev 7:7

LEVIATHAN (lē-vī'ā-thăn)—*"twisted; coiled"*
Great beast created by God..................Ps 104:26
Habit of, graphically described (crocodile)...Job 41:1-34
God's power over ....Ps 74:14

shall punish *l* the piercing .....Is 27:1
l that crooked serpent ....Is 27:1

LEVITES (lē'vīts)—*descendants of Levi*

History of:
Descendants of Levi, Jacob's son ....Gen 29:34
Jacob's prophecy concerning ....Gen 49:5-7
Divided into three families..............Ex 6:16-24
Aaron, great-grandson of Levi, chosen for priesthood ....Ex 28:1
Tribe of Levi rewarded for dedication ....Ex 32:26-29
Chosen by God for holy service...............Deut 10:8
Not numbered among Israel.................Num 1:47-49
Substituted for Israel's first-born ....Num 3:12-45
Given as gifts to Aaron's sons.................Num 8:6-21
Rebellion among, led by Korah ....Num 16:1-50
Choice of, confirmed by the Lord.............Num 17:1-13
Bear ark of the covenant across the Jordan......Josh 3:2-17
Hear Law read.........Josh 8:31-35
Cities (48) assigned to ...Num 35:2-8; Josh 14:3, 4
One of, becomes Micah's idolatrous priest .....Judg 17:5-13; Judg 18:18-31
Perform priestly functions.1Sam 6:15
Appointed over service of song..................1Chr 6:31-48
Service of heads of households............1Chr 9:26-34
Excluded by Jeroboam ...2Chr 11:13-17
Help repair the Temple ..1Chr 23:2-4

Carried to Babylon 2Chr 36:19, 20
Return from exile .... Ezra 2:40-63
Tithes withheld from ..... Neh 13:10-13
Intermarry with foreigners .... Ezra 10:2-24
Seal the covenant .... Neh 10:1, 9-28
Present defiled offerings will be purified ..... { Mal 1:6-14, Mal 3:1-4 }

Duties of:
Serve the Lord .... Deut 10:8
Serve the priesthood ..... Num 3:5-9
Attend to sanctuary duties .... Num 18:3
Distribute the tithe 2Chr 31:11-19
Prepare sacrifices for priests 2Chr 35:10-14
Teach the people 2Chr 17:9-11
Declare verdicts of Law .. Deut 17:9-11
Protect the king 2Chr 23:2-10
Perform music 1Chr 25:1-7
Precede the army 2Chr 20:20, 21, 28

Spiritual truths illustrated by:
Representation—duties of the congregation ...... Num 3:6-9
Substitution—place of the first-born .... { Num 3:12, 13, 41, 45 }
Subordination—service to the Temple .... Num 3:5-10
Consecration—separated for God's work .... Num 8:9-14
Holiness—cleansed ...... Num 8:6, 7, 21
Election—God's choice .. Num 17:7-13
Inheritance—in the Lord .. Num 18:20
See PRIEST

[also LEVITE, LEVITICAL]
Aaron the ***L*** thy brother? ..... Ex 4:14
of the fathers of the ***L*** .... Ex 6:25
the cities of the ***L*** .... Lev 25:32
may the ***L*** redeem at any ..... Lev 25:32
a man purchase of the ***L*** ..... Lev 25:33
of the cities of the ***L*** .... Lev 25:33
appoint the ***L*** over the .... Num 1:50
the ***L*** shall take it down .... Num 1:51
the ***L*** shall set it up .... Num 1:51
the ***L*** shall pitch round .... Num 1:53
L shall keep the charge .... Num 1:53
L were not numbered .... Num 2:33
give the ***L*** unto Aaron .... Num 3:9
and the ***L*** shall be mine .... Num 3:45
are more than the ***L*** .... Num 3:46
Kohathites from..the ***L*** .... Num 4:18
give them unto the ***L*** .... Num 7:5
separate the ***L*** from among .... Num 8:14
and the ***L*** shall be mine .... Num 8:14
went the ***L*** in to do their ...... Num 8:22
Moses concerning the ***L*** .... Num 8:22
shalt thou do unto the ***L*** ...... Num 8:26
the ***L*** shall do the service ..... Num 18:23
Thus speak unto the ***L*** .... Num 18:26
numbered of the ***L*** .... Num 26:57
the families of the ***L*** .... Num 26:58
that they give unto the ***L***...... Num 35:2
L that is within your gates .... Deut 12:12
forsake not the ***L*** as long ..... Deut 12:19
the ***L***, because he hath .... Deut 14:29
and the ***L***, the stranger .... Deut 16:14
before the priests the ***L*** .... Deut 17:18
The priests the ***L***, and all ...... Deut 18:1
as all his brethren the ***L*** .... Deut 18:7
the ***L***, and the stranger .... Deut 26:11
given them unto the ***L*** .... Deut 26:13
L spake unto all Israel .... Deut 27:9
Moses commanded the ***L*** ...... Deut 31:25
L have no part among .... Josh 18:7
Israel gave unto the ***L*** .... Josh 21:3
gave by lot unto the ***L*** .... Josh 21:8
of the families of the ***L*** .... Josh 21:27
of the families of the ***L*** .... Josh 21:40
of the young man the ***L*** .... Judg 18:3
a certain ***L*** sojourning .... Judg 19:1
all the ***L*** were with him 2Sam 15:24
did the priests and the ***L*** 1Kin 8:4
the families of the ***L*** 1Chr 6:19
Israel gave to the ***L*** 1Chr 6:64
the priests ***L***, and the 1Chr 9:2
And of the ***L***; Shemaiah 1Chr 9:14
also to the priests and ***L*** 1Chr 13:2
of Aaron, and the ***L*** 1Chr 15:4
chief of the fathers of the ***L*** ... 1Chr 15:12
children of the ***L*** bare the ark .. 1Chr 15:15
the ***L*** appointed Heman 1Chr 15:17
when God helped the ***L*** 1Chr 15:26
appointed certain of the ***L*** 1Chr 16:4
Nethaneel..one of the ***L*** 1Chr 24:6
fathers of the priests and ***L*** 1Chr 24:6
fathers of the priests and ***L*** 1Chr 24:31
And of the ***L***, Ahijah was 1Chr 26:20
courses of..the ***L*** 1Chr 28:13
the ***L*** took up the ark 2Chr 5:4
L which were the singers 2Chr 5:12
the ***L*** to their charges 2Chr 8:14
the ***L*** left their suburbs 2Chr 11:14
sons of Aaron, and the ***L*** 2Chr 13:9
And with them he sent ***L*** 2Chr 17:8
and Tob-adonijah, ***L*** 2Chr 17:8
L shall be officers before 2Chr 19:11
a ***L*** of the sons of Asaph 2Chr 20:14
hand of the priests the ***L*** 2Chr 23:18
the priests and the ***L*** 2Chr 24:5
Howbeit the ***L*** hastened 2Chr 24:5
by the hand of the ***L*** 2Chr 24:11
them, hear me, ye ***L*** 2Chr 29:5
L took it, to carry it 2Chr 29:16
L stood with the instruments .. 2Chr 29:26
the ***L*** did help them 2Chr 29:34
L were more upright in heart .. 2Chr 29:34
received..of the ***L*** 2Chr 30:16
L and the priests praised 2Chr 30:21
the priests and the ***L*** 2Chr 30:25
the ***L*** after their courses 2Chr 31:2
L for burnt offerings and 2Chr 31:2
with the priests and the ***L*** 2Chr 31:9
L that kept the doors 2Chr 34:9
Jahath and Obadiah, the ***L*** 2Chr 34:12
other of the ***L***, all that 2Chr 34:12
the priests, and the ***L***, and 2Chr 34:30
L that taught all Israel 2Chr 35:3
the priests, and to the ***L*** 2Chr 35:8
Jozabad, chief of the ***L*** 2Chr 35:9
gave unto the ***L*** for 2Chr 35:9
brethren the ***L*** prepared 2Chr 35:15
and the priests, and the ***L*** 2Chr 35:18
and the priests, and the ***L*** ..... Ezra 1:5
and the ***L***, and some of the ... Ezra 2:70
priests and the ***L*** .... Ezra 3:8
appointed the ***L***, from .... Ezra 3:8
L the sons of Asaph with ..... Ezra 3:10
the priests and the ***L*** .... Ezra 6:16
L were purified together ...... Ezra 6:20
and of his priests and ***L*** .... Ezra 7:13
the service of the ***L*** .... Ezra 8:20
the priests and the ***L*** .... Ezra 8:30
the priests, and the ***L*** .... Ezra 9:1
After him repaired the ***L*** ...... Neh 3:17
L: the children of Jeshua ...... Neh 7:43
L, caused the people .... Neh 8:7
L stilled all the people .... Neh 8:11
upon the stairs, of the ***L*** ...... Neh 9:4
princes, ***L***, and priests .... Neh 9:38
among the priests, the ***L*** ...... Neh 10:34
tithes..unto the ***L*** .... Neh 10:37
L might have the tithes in ..... Neh 10:37
L, when the ***L*** take tithes ..... Neh 10:38
L shall bring up the tithe ...... Neh 10:38
Also of the ***L***: Shemaiah ...... Neh 11:15
All the ***L*** in the holy city ..... Neh 11:18
overseer also of the ***L*** at ...... Neh 11:22
priests and the ***L*** that .... Neh 12:1
L in the days of Eliashib ...... Neh 12:22
sought the ***L*** out of all .... Neh 12:27
for the priests and ***L*** .... Neh 12:44
sancitified..unto the ***L*** .... Neh 12:47
L sanctified them unto .... Neh 12:47
to be given to the ***L*** .... Neh 13:5
And I commanded the ***L*** ...... Neh 13:22
wards of the priests and the ***L***.. Neh 13:30
take of them..for ***L*** .... Is 66:21
shall the priests the ***L*** want .... Jer 33:18
and the ***L*** that minister .... Jer 33:22
give to the priests the ***L*** .... Ezek 43:19
priests the ***L***, the sons of ...... Ezek 44:15
as the ***L*** went astray .... Ezek 48:11
L..have five and twenty .... Ezek 48:13
likewise a ***L***, when he .... Luke 10:32
Jews sent priests and ***L*** .... John 1:19
son of consolation, a ***L*** .... Acts 4:36
were by the ***L*** priesthood ..... Heb 7:11

LEVITICUS, THE BOOK OF—*a book of the Old Testament*
Laws of sacrifice .... Lev 1:1—7:38
Laws of purity .... Lev 11:1—15:33
Day of atonement .... Lev 16:1-34
Laws of holiness .... Lev 17:1—25:55
Blessings and curses ..... Lev 26:1-46

LEVY—*to force labor upon a people*
Israelites 1Kin 5:13-15
Canaanites 1Kin 9:15, 21

And ***l*** a tribute unto the Lord. . Num 31:28

LEWD—*wicked; salacious; licentious*

Characteristics of:
Shameful .... Ezek 16:27
Sexual .... Ezek 22:11
Youthful .... Ezek 23:21
Adulterous .... Jer 13:27
Filthiness .... Ezek 24:13
Folly .... Judg 20:6

Committed by:
Men of Gibeah .... Judg 20:5
Israel .... Hos 2:10
Jerusalem .... Ezek 16:27, 43

[*also* LEWDNESS]
she hath wrought ***l*** with .... Jer 11:15
Thou hast borne thy ***l*** .... Ezek 16:58
midst of thee they commit ***l*** ... Ezek 22:9
will I make thy ***l*** to cease ..... Ezek 23:27
thy ***l*** and thy whoredoms ...... Ezek 23:29
bear thou also thy ***l*** and .... Ezek 23:35
unto Aholibah, the ***l*** women ... Ezek 23:44
will I cause ***l*** to cease .... Ezek 23:48
not to do after your ***l*** .... Ezek 23:48
shall recompense your ***l*** .... Ezek 23:49
matter of wrong or wicked ***l*** .. Acts 18:14

LIAR—*one who tells untruths*

Defined as:
Nature of the devil ...... John 8:44
Denial that Jesus is Christ 1John 2:22
Not keeping Christ's commandments 1John 2:4
Hating one's brother 1John 4:20
All that is not of the truth 1John 2:21, 27

Those who speak:
Wicked .... Ps 58:3
False witnesses .... Prov 14:5, 25
Astrologers .... Dan 2:9
Israel .... Hos 7:3, 13
Judah .... Jer 9:1-5

Attitude of the wicked toward:
Are always .... Titus 1:12
Forge against the righteous .... Ps 119:69
Change God's truth into. . Rom 1:25

Attitude of the righteous toward:
Keep far from .... Prov 30:8
Shall not speak .... Zeph 3:13
Pray for deliverance from. Ps 120:2
"Put away" .... Eph 4:25

Attitude of God toward:
Will not .... Num 23:19
Is an abomination .... Prov 6:16-19
Will discover man's ...... Is 28:15, 17
Is against .... Ezek 13:8

Punishment of, shall:
Not escape ....Prov 19:5
Be stopped ....Ps 63:11
Be silenced ....Ps 31:18
Be short-lived ....Prov 12:19
End in lake of fire ......Rev 21:8, 27

The evils of:
Produces error ....Amos 2:4
Increases wickedness .....Prov 29:12
Destruction ....Hos 10:13-15
Death ....Prov 21:6
Zech 13:3

[*also* LIARS]
shall be found *l* unto thee .....Deut 33:29
who will make me a *l*.........Job 24:25
I said..All men are *l*..........Ps 116:11
l giveth ear to a naughty ......Prov 17:4
speaketh *l* shall perish ....Prov 19:9
and thou be found a *l* ....Prov 30:6
the tokens of the *l*............Is 44:25
altogether unto me as a *l* .....Jer 15:18
A sword is upon the *l* ....Jer 50:36
God be true..every man a *l* ...Rom 3:4
for *l* for perjured persons 1Tim 1:10
sinned, we make him a *l*......1John 1:10
not God hath made him a *l* ...1John 5:10
and hast found them *l* ....Rev 2:2
and idolaters, and all *l*........Rev 21:8

LIBERALITY—*a generous spirit in helping the needy*

Object of:
Poor ....Deut 15:11
Strangers ....Lev 25:35
Afflicted ....Luke 10:30-35
Servants (slaves).........Deut 15:12-18
All men ....Gal 6:10
God's children 2Cor 8:1-9, 12

Reasons for:
Make our faith real......James 2:14-16
Secure true riches ....Luke 12:33
1Tim 6:17-19
Follow Christ's example ..2Cor 8:9
Help God's kingdom.....Phil 4:14-18
Relieve distress..........2Cor 9:12

Blessings of:
God remembers ....Prov 3:9, 10
Will return abundantly ...Prov 11:24-27
Brings deliverance in time
of need ....Is 58:10, 11
Insures sufficiency ....Ps 37:25, 26
Brings reward ....Ps 112:5-9
Matt 25:40
Provokes others to 2Cor 9:2

[*also* LIBERAL, LIBERALLY]
furnish him *l* out of thy flock ..Deut 15:14
l soul shall be made fat ....Prov 11:25
shall be no more called *l*......Is 32:5
the *l* deviseth *l* things ....Is 32:8
and by *l* things shall he ....Is 32:8
bring your *l* unto Jerusalem ...1Cor 16:3
unto the riches of their *l* 2Cor 8:2
for your *l* distribution 2Cor 9:13
God, that giveth to all men *l* ..James 1:5

LIBERTINES—*"freedmen"—Jews who had been set free from Roman slavery*
Jews opposing Stephen ...Acts 6:9

LIBERTY—*freedom*
proclaim *l* throughout all ......Lev 25:10
And I will walk at *l* for I .....Ps 119:45
to proclaim *l* to the captives ...Is 61:1
in proclaiming *l* every.........Jer 34:15
ye had set at *l* at their ....Jer 34:16
in proclaiming *l* every.........Jer 34:17
I proclaim a *l* for you.........Jer 34:17
be his to the year of *l* ....Ezek 46:17
to set at *l* them that are.......Luke 4:18
Paul, and to let him have *l*....Acts 24:23
might have been set at *l* ......Acts 26:32
gave him *l* to go unto his .....Acts 27:3
glorious *l* of the children ......Rom 8:21
she is at *l* to be married 1Cor 7:39
any means this *l* of yours 1Cor 8:9
for why is my *l* judged of 1Cor 10:29
the Spirit..is, there is *l*........2Cor 3:17
to spy out our *l* which we .....Gal 2:4
the *l* wherewith Christ ....Gal 5:1
have been called unto *l* ....Gal 5:13
use not *l* for an occasion ......Gal 5:13
Timothy is set at *l* ....Heb 13:23
the perfect law of *l* ....James 1:25
judged by the law of *l* ....James 2:12
not using your *l* for a cloak ...1Pet 2:16
While they promise them *l* 2Pet 2:19

LIBERTY, CIVIL—*freedom originating from a government*

Obtained by:
Purchase ....Acts 22:28
Birth ....Acts 22:28
Release ....Deut 15:12-15
Victory ....Ex 14:30, 31

LIBERTY, SPIRITUAL—*freedom which originates through one's relationship to Christ*

Described as:
Predicted ....Is 61:1
Where the spirit is.......2Cor 3:17

Relation of Christians toward, they:
Are called to............Gal 5:13
Abide by ....James 1:25
Should walk at ....Ps 119:45
Have in Jesus Christ .....Gal 2:4, 5
See FREEDOM

LIBNAH (lĭb'nä)—*"white"*
1. Israelite camp ....Num 33:20, 21
2. Canaanite city near
Lachish ....Josh 10:29-32
Captured by Joshua .....Josh 10:30, 39
In Judah's territory .....Josh 15:42
Given to Aaron's
descendants ....Josh 21:13
Fought against by
Assyria 2Kin 19:8, 9
Home of Hamutal 2Kin 23:31

The king of *L*, one; the ....Josh 12:15
Then *L* revolted at the 2Kin 8:22
of Jeremiah of *L* 2Kin 24:18
and *L* with her suburbs 1Chr 6:57
did *L* revolt from under.......2Chr 21:10
Assyria warring against *L* .....Is 37:8
of Jeremiah of *L* ....Jer 52:1

LIBNI (lĭb'nī)—*"whiteness; distinguished"*
1. Son of Gershon..........Num 3:18, 21
Family of, called
Libnites ....Num 3:21
Called Laadan 1Chr 23:7
2. Descendant of Merari ...1Chr 6:29

[*also* LIBNITES]
sons of Gershon: *L*, and ....Ex 6:17
the family of the *L*, the ....Num 26:58
sons of Gershom; *L*, and 1Chr 6:17
Of Gershom; *L* his son 1Chr 6:20

LIBYA (lĭb'ĭ-ä)—*"heart of the sea"—the land and people west of Egypt*
Called Lubim ....Nah 3:9
Will fall by the sword....Ezek 30:5
Will be controlled ....Dan 11:43
Some from, at Pentecost .Acts 2:1-10
See PHUT

[*also* LIBYANS]
the Ethiopians and the *L*......Jer 46:9
Ethiopia, and *L* with them ....Ezek 38:5

LICE—*small insects known for their irritating bites*
Third plague upon Egypt,
produced from dust....Ex 8:16-18

flies, and *l* in all their.........Ps 105:31

LICENSE—*authority to do something*
Granted to Paul ....Acts 21:40

[*also* LICENCE]
l to answer for himself ....Acts 25:16

LICK—*to lap up*

[*also* LICKED, LICKETH]
as the ox *l* up the grass ....Num 22:4
Now shall this company *l* .....Num 22:4
l up the water that was in 1Kin 18:38
of Naboth shall dogs *l* thy.....1Kin 21:19
dogs *l* the blood of 1Kin 21:19
the dogs *l* up his blood 1Kin 22:38
enemies shall *l* the dust ....Ps 72:9
l up the dust of thy feet.......Is 49:23
l the dust like a serpent.......Mic 7:17
dog's came and *l* his sores.....Luke 16:21

LID—*a cover*
and bored a hole in the *l* 2Kin 12:9

LIE—*to intentionally tell an untruth*

[*also* LIED, LIES, LYING]
lost, and *l* concerning it ....Lev 6:3
not a man, that he should *l* ...Num 23:19
mocked me and told me *l* .....Judg 16:10
But he *l* unto him 1Kin 13:18
be a *l* spirit in the mouth 1Kin 22:22
Lord hath put a *l* spirit in 1Kin 22:23
not *l* unto thine handmaid.....2Kin 4:16
be a *l* spirit in the mouth 2Chr 18:21
Lord hath put a *l* spirit in 2Chr 18:22
is evident unto you if I *l* ......Job 6:28
thy *l* make men hold their ....Job 11:3
Should I *l* against my ....Job 34:6
that regard *l* vanities ....Ps 31:6
and *l* rather than ....Ps 52:3
l unto him with their tongues ..Ps 78:36
against me with a *l* tongue ....Ps 109:2
proud have forged a *l*.........Ps 119:69
I hate and abhor *l*: but ....Ps 119:163
proud look, a *l* tongue ....Prov 6:17
l tongue is but a moment .....Prov 12:19
A righteous man hateth *l* .....Prov 13:5
faithful witness will not *l*......Prov 14:5
treasures by a *l* tongue........Prov 21:6
If a ruler hearken to *l*, all.....Prov 29:12
prophet that teacheth *l*........Is 9:15
is a rebellious people, *l* ....Is 30:9
Is there not a *l* in my ....Is 44:20
feared, that thou hast *l* ....Is 57:11
your lips have spoken *l* ....Is 59:3
Trust ye not in *l* words ....Jer 7:4
prophesy *l* in my name........Jer 14:14
thou hast prophesied *l* ....Jer 20:6
people to err by their *l* ....Jer 23:32
they prophesy a *l* unto ....Jer 27:14
they prophesy a *l* unto ....Jer 27:16
prophesy a *l* unto you in ......Jer 29:21
have spoken *l* words in ....Jer 29:23
have seen vanity and *l* ....Ezek 13:6
vanity, and that divine *l*.......Ezek 13:9
by your *l* to my people ....Ezek 13:19
with *l* ye have made the ......Ezek 13:22
wearied herself with *l* ....Ezek 24:12
prepared *l* and corrupt words ..Dan 2:9
they shall speak *l* at one ......Dan 11:27
By swearing, and *l*, and ....Hos 4:2
ye have eaten the fruit of *l*....Hos 10:13
daily increaseth *l* and ....Hos 12:1
l caused them to err ....Amos 2:4
that observe *l* vanities.........Jon 2:8
shall be a *l* to the kings ....Mic 1:14
inhabitants..have spoken *l*.....Mic 6:12
it is all full of *l* and...........Nah 3:1
it shall speak, and not *l*.......Hab 2:3
and a teacher of *l* ....Hab 2:18
diviners have seen a *l*.........Zech 10:2
Satan filled thine heart to *l*....Acts 5:3
thou hast not *l* unto men......Acts 5:4
truth of God into a *l* ....Rom 1:25
truth in Christ, I *l* not ....Rom 9:1
knoweth that I *l* not 2Cor 11:31
before God, I *l* not ....Gal 1:20
Wherefore putting away *l* .....Eph 4:25
L not one to another ....Col 3:9
all power and signs and *l*......2Thess 2:9
that they should believe a *l*....2Thess 2:11
truth in Christ, and *l* not......1Tim 2:7
Speaking *l* in hypocrisy 1Tim 4:2

L

impossible for God to *l* ....Heb 6:18
l not against the truth.........James 3:14
we *l*, and do not the truth 1John 1:6
that no *l* is of the truth 1John 2:21
and is truth, and is no *l*........1John 2:27
and are not, but do *l* ....Rev 3:9
abomination or maketh a *l* ....Rev 21:27
loveth and maketh a *l* ....Rev 22:15

LIE—*to recline; hide; have sexual relations*

[*also* LAIN, LAY, LIEST, LIETH, LYING]
doest not well, sin *l* at ....Gen 4:7
they *l* down, the men ....Gen 19:4
we will *l* with him, that we ....Gen 19:32
and *l* with her father...........Gen 19:33
younger arose and *l* with ....Gen 19:35
he perceived not when she *l*...Gen 19:35
and *l* down in that place to....Gen 28:11
three flocks of sheep *l* ....Gen 29:2
shall *l* with thee to night ......Gen 30:15
And he *l* with her that.........Gen 30:16
he took her, and *l* with her ...Gen 34:2
to *l* by her or to be with ......Gen 39:10
he came in unto me to *l* ......Gen 39:14
I will *l* with my fathers.........Gen 47:30
the dew *l* round about the ....Ex 16:13
dew that *l* was gone up ....Ex 16:14
there *l* a small round ....Ex 16:14
if a man *l* not in wait ....Ex 21:13
Whosoever *l* with a beast ......Ex 22:19
hateth thee *l* under his ....Ex 23:5
thou shall let it rest and *l* .....Ex 23:11
he *l* that hath the issue ....Lev 15:4
if any man *l* with her ....Lev 15:24
bed whereon he *l* shall be .....Lev 15:24
Thou shalt not *l* with ....Lev 18:22
Neither shalt thou *l* with ......Lev 18:23
before a beast to *l* down ......Lev 18:23
if a man *l* with his daughter ...Lev 20:12
if a man *l* with a beast, he ....Lev 20:15
if a man shall *l* with a ....Lev 20:18
ye shall *l* down, and none .....Lev 26:6
a man *l* with her carnally .....Num 5:13
If no man have *l* with thee .....Num 5:19
camps that *l* on the south .....Num 10:6
l down until he eat of the .....Num 23:24
known man by *l* with him .....Num 31:17
not known a man by *l* with....Num 31:35
and *l* in wait for him ....Deut 19:11
l in the field, and it be not ....Deut 21:1
the man force her, and *l* ......Deut 22:25
judge shall cause him to *l* .....Deut 25:2
written in this book shall *l* ....Deut 29:20
before they were *l* down, she ..Josh 2:8
l thou thus upon thy face? ....Josh 7:10
ye shall *l* in wait against ......Josh 8:4
went to *l* in ambush ....Josh 8:9
l in ambush between...........Josh 8:12
mountain that *l* before the ....Josh 15:8
sea, all that *l* near Ashdod ....Josh 15:46
that *l* before Shechem ....Josh 17:7
the hill that *l* before ....Josh 18:14
Judah which *l* in the south ....Judg 1:16
Sisera *l* dead, and the nail ....Judg 4:22
he fell, he *l* down ....Judg 5:27
and *l* in wait in the field ....Judg 9:32
with him, from *l* in wait........Judg 9:35
l wait in the field, and ....Judg 9:43
l wait for him all night in .....Judg 16:2
Samson *l* till midnight..........Judg 16:3
in the valley that *l* by ....Judg 18:28
set *l* in wait round about ......Judg 20:29
woman that hath *l* by man ....Judg 21:11
known no man by *l* with any ..Judg 21:12
Go and *l* in wait in the ....Judg 21:20
when he *l* down, that thou ....Ruth 3:4
went to *l* down at the...........Ruth 3:7
a woman *l* at his feet ....Ruth 3:8
she *l* at his feet until the .....Ruth 3:14
how they *l* with the women ...1Sam 2:22
when Eli was *l* down in his....1Sam 3:2
Samuel was *l* down to 1Sam 3:3
I called not; *l* down again 1Sam 3:5
And he went and *l* down.......1Sam 3:5
my son; *l* down again 1Sam 3:6
Eli said unto Samuel, Go, *l* ...1Sam 3:9
Samuel went and *l* down in ...1Sam 3:9
how he *l* wait for him in the ..1Sam 15:2
l down naked all that day 1Sam 19:24
me, to *l* in wait, as at.........1Sam 22:8
the place where Saul *l* 1Sam 26:5
Saul *l* in the trench and the ...1Sam 26:5
Saul *l* sleeping within the 1Sam 26:7
the people *l* round about......1Sam 26:7
that *l* before Giah by the 2Sam 2:24
l on his bed in his 2Sam 4:7
to drink and to *l* with my 2Sam 11:11
his own cup and *l* in his.......2Sam 12:3
he shall *l* with thy wives in 2Sam 12:11
went in unto her, and *l* with...2Sam 12:24
Amnon *l* down and made 2Sam 13:6
Amnon's house..he was *l*......2Sam 13:8
his garments and *l* on the 2Sam 13:31
and let her *l* in thy bosom 1Kin 1:2
l him upon his own bed 1Kin 17:19
l and slept under a juniper 1Kin 19:5
drink, and *l* him down 1Kin 19:6
into the chamber, and *l* 2Kin 4:11
and *l* upon his bed 2Kin 4:32
he went up and *l* upon the 2Kin 4:34
the servant of God *l* upon.....2Chr 24:9
timber is *l* in the wall ....Ezra 5:8
treasures were *l* up in..........Ezra 6:1
of such as *l* in wait by the.....Ezra 8:31
tower which *l* out from the ....Neh 3:25
the great tower that *l* out .....Neh 3:27
many *l* in sackcloth and ....Esth 4:3
I have *l* still and been ....Job 3:13
and my calamity *l* in the ......Job 6:2
might *l* his hand upon us ......Job 9:33
Also thou shalt *l* down..........Job 11:19
So man *l* down and riseth .....Job 14:12
They shall *l* down alike in.....Job 21:26
l in wait secretly as a lion .....Ps 10:9
he *l* in wait to catch the........Ps 10:9
me to *l* down in green ....Ps 23:2
that seek after my life *l* ....Ps 38:12
Like sheep they are *l* in.......Ps 49:14
they *l* in wait for my soul .....Ps 59:3
be *l* in the balance, they ....Ps 62:9
slain that *l* in the grave ....Ps 88:5
Thou compassest..my *l* down ..Ps 139:3
let us *l* wait for blood.........Prov 1:11
When thou *l* down, thou ......Prov 3:24
l in wait at every corner ......Prov 7:12
thou shall be as he that *l*......Prov 23:34
as he that *l* upon the top......Prov 23:34
if two *l* together then they ....Eccl 4:11
l all night betwixt my ....Song 1:13
leopard shall *l* down with .....Is 11:6
beasts of the desert shall *l*.....Is 13:21
the needy shall *l* down in .....Is 14:30
not be treasured nor *l* up .....Is 23:18
and there shall he *l* down .....Is 27:10
owl make her nest and *l* ....Is 34:15
they *l* at the head of all........Is 51:20
l down, loving to slumber .....Is 56:10
a place for the herds to *l*......Is 65:10
We *l* down in our shame ....Jer 3:25
l wait as he that setteth ....Jer 5:26
causing their flocks to *l* ....Jer 33:12
young and the old *l* on the ....Lam 2:21
He was unto me as a bear *l* ...Lam 3:10
they *l* wait for us in the ....Lam 4:19
L thou also upon thy left......Ezek 4:4
that thou shalt *l* upon it.......Ezek 4:4
l again on thy right side.......Ezek 4:6
days that thou shalt *l* upon ....Ezek 4:9
which *l* toward the north .....Ezek 9:2
are inhabited shall be *l*........Ezek 12:20
for in her youth they *l* ....Ezek 23:8
l in the midst of...............Ezek 31:18
they *l* uncircumcised, slain ....Ezek 32:21
they shall not *l* with ....Ezek 32:27
shalt *l* with them that are .....Ezek 32:28
I will cause them to *l* down ....Ezek 34:15
will make them to *l* down ....Hos 2:18
l all night in sackcloth ....Joel 1:13
That *l* upon beds of ivory .....Amos 6:4
he *l* and was fast asleep ....Jon 1:5
they all *l* in wait for blood ....Mic 7:2
her that *l* in thy bosom ....Mic 7:5
they *l* down in the evening ....Zeph 2:7
place for beasts to *l* down .....Zeph 2:15
and this house *l* waste? ....Hag 1:4
the place where the Lord *l* ....Matt 28:6
Simon's wife's mother *l* ....Mark 1:30
daughter *l* at the point of .....Mark 5:23
in where..damsel was *l*.........Mark 5:40
her daughter *l* upon ....Mark 7:30
beheld where he was *l* ....Mark 15:47
clothes *l* in a manger ....Luke 2:12
of age, and she *l* a dying......Luke 8:42
the linen clothes *l* by ....Luke 24:12
When Jesus saw him *l* ....John 5:6
l in the grave four days ....John 11:17
He then *l* on Jesus' breast......John 13:25
l daily at the gate of the ......Acts 3:2
l in the sepulcher that ....Acts 7:16
the Jews *l* wait for him ....Acts 20:3
the *l* in wait of the Jews ....Acts 20:19
the Jews *l* wait for the man ...Acts 23:30
l wait in the way to kill ....Acts 25:3
as much as *l* in you, live ......Rom 12:18
they *l* in wait to deceive ......Eph 4:14
world *l* in wickedness 1John 5:19
the city *l* foursquare ....Rev 21:16

LIER—*one who reclines or hides*

[*also* LIERS]
l in wait on the west of ....Josh 8:13
of Shechem set *l* in wait for ..Judg 9:25
set *l* in wait round about ......Judg 20:29
they trusted unto the *l* in .....Judg 20:36
the *l* in wait hasted and ....Judg 20:37
the *l* in wait drew ....Judg 20:37

LIEUTENANTS—*military officers*
unto the king's *l* and...........Ezra 8:36
unto the king's *l*...............Esth 3:12
the provinces, and the *l* ....Esth 9:3

LIFE—*the duration of existence; that which distinguishes a functioning being from a dead object; spiritual existence*

[*also* LIFETIME, LIVE, LIVED, LIVES, LIVEST, LIVETH, LIVING]
creature that hath *l* ....Gen 1:20
and every *l* creature that ......Gen 1:21
wherein there is *l*.............Gen 1:30
the breath of *l* ....Gen 2:7
and man became a *l* soul.......Gen 2:7
tree of *l* also in the midst .....Gen 2:9
all the days of thy *l*...........Gen 3:17
she was the mother of all *l* ....Gen 3:20
tree of life, and eat, and *l*.....Gen 3:22
the way of the tree of *l* ....Gen 3:24
Adam *l* a hundred and.........Gen 5:3
Seth *l* after he begat ....Gen 5:7
Enos *l* after he begat ....Gen 5:10
Cainan *l* after he begat ....Gen 5:13
Mahalaleel *l* after he begat ....Gen 5:16
Jared *l* after he begat ....Gen 5:19
And Methuselah *l* after he ....Gen 5:26
Lamech *l* after he begat........Gen 5:30
and every *l* substance that.....Gen 7:4
the..year of Noah's *l*...........Gen 7:11
was the breath of *l* ....Gen 7:22
Noah, and every *l* thing ....Gen 8:1
smite any more every thing *l* ..Gen 8:21
Every moving thing that *l* shall.Gen 9:3
require the *l* of man ....Gen 9:5
of your *l* will I require ....Gen 9:5
and every *l* creature that is ....Gen 9:12
l creature of all flesh ....Gen 9:16
And Noah *l* after the flood....Gen 9:28
Shem *l* after he begat.........Gen 11:11
Arphaxad *l* after he begat .....Gen 11:13
Salah *l* after he begat ....Gen 11:15
Eber *l* after he begat ....Gen 11:17
Peleg *l* after he begat ....Gen 11:19
Reu *l* after he begat ....Gen 11:21
Serug *l* after he begat.........Gen 11:23
Nahor *l* after he begat ....Gen 11:25
my soul shall *l* because........Gen 12:13
that Ishmael might *l* ....Gen 17:18

to the time of *l*............... Gen 18:14
in saving my *l*............... Gen 19:19
for thee and thou shalt *l*...... Gen 20:7
his son, while he yet *l*........ Gen 25:6
years of Abraham's *l*......... Gen 25:7
I am weary of my *l*........... Gen 27:46
what good shall my *l* do ...... Gen 27:46
thy gods, let him not *l*........ Gen 31:32
and my *l* is preserved......... Gen 32:30
by the *l* of Pharaoh surely..... Gen 42:16
third day, This do, and *l*...... Gen 42:18
his *l*..in the lad's *l*............ Gen 44:30
doth my father yet *l*.......... Gen 45:3
before you to preserve *l*...... Gen 45:5
the years of my *l* been........ Gen 47:9
years of the *l* of my fathers ... Gen 47:9
Thou hast saved our *l*......... Gen 47:25
Jacob *l* in the land of.......... Gen 47:28
l bitter with hard bondage..... Ex 1:14
daughter, then she shall *l*..... Ex 1:16
for they are *l*, and are........ Ex 1:19
dead which sought thy *l*....... Ex 4:19
years of the *l* of Kohath ...... Ex 6:18
thou shalt give *l* for *l*......... Ex 21:23
they shall sell the *l* ox........ Ex 21:35
no man see me, and *l*......... Ex 33:20
any *l* thing..in the waters...... Lev 11:10
the *l* bird he shall take it...... Lev 14:6
the *l* bird in the blood........ Lev 14:6
the *l* bird loose into..field..... Lev 14:7
and with the *l* bird........... Lev 14:52
shall bring the *l* goat.......... Lev 16:20
the *l* of the flesh............ Lev 17:11
it is the *l* of all flesh.......... Lev 17:14
blood of it is for the *l*........ Lev 17:14
l of all flesh is the blood...... Lev 17:14
he shall *l* in them............ Lev 18:5
any manner of *l* thing......... Lev 20:25
thy brother may *l* with thee ... Lev 25:36
unto them, that they may *l*.... Num 4:19
As truly as I *l*, saith the ...... Num 14:28
to search the land, *l* still...... Num 14:38
who shall *l* when God doeth... Num 24:23
for the *l* of a murderer........ Num 35:31
ye may *l*, and go in and....... Deut 4:1
all the days of thy *l*........... Deut 4:9
as thou hast heard, and *l*?..... Deut 4:33
doth talk with man, and he *l*.. Deut 5:24
voice of the *l* God............ Deut 5:26
fire, as we have, and *l*?....... Deut 5:26
that ye may *l* and that it...... Deut 5:33
man doth not *l* by bread...... Deut 8:3
of the Lord doth man *l*....... Deut 8:3
as long as thou *l*............. Deut 12:19
for the blood is the *l*......... Deut 12:23
mayest not eat the *l*.......... Deut 12:23
that thou mayest *l*............ Deut 16:20
all the days of his *l*........... Deut 17:19
unto one of those cities, and *l*. Deut 19:5
of the field is man's *l*......... Deut 20:19
thy *l* shall hang in doubt...... Deut 28:66
have none assurance of..*l*..... Deut 28:66
that thou mayest *l*............ Deut 30:16
I have set before you *l*........ Deut 30:19
therefore choose *l*............ Deut 30:19
for he is thy *l*, and the length.. Deut 30:20
as long as ye *l* in the land..... Deut 31:13
Let Reuben *l*, and not die .... Deut 33:6
because it is your *l*........... Deut 32:47
all the days of thy *l*.......... Josh 1:5
deliver our *l* from death ...... Josh 2:13
Our *l* for yours, if ye utter.... Josh 2:14
the *l* God is among you....... Josh 3:10
the harlot shall *l*............. Josh 6:17
we will even let them *l*........ Josh 9:20
people that jeoparded their *l*.. Judg 5:18
the Lord *l*, if ye had saved.... Judg 8:19
and adventured his *l* far....... Judg 9:17
which he slew in his *l*......... Judg 16:30
his kindness to the *l*.......... Ruth 2:20
to thee, as the Lord *l*......... Ruth 3:13
a restorer of thy *l*........... Ruth 4:15
all the days of his *l*.......... 1Sam 1:11
my Lord, as thy soul *l*........ 1Sam 1:26
as the Lord *l*, which saveth.... 1Sam 14:39
the armies of the *l* God....... 1Sam 17:26
As thy soul *l*, O king......... 1Sam 17:55
and what is my *l*............. 1Sam 18:18
If thou save not thy *l*......... 1Sam 19:11
Lord *l*, and as thy soul *l*...... 1Sam 20:3
not only while yet I *l*......... 1Sam 20:14
long as the son of Jesse *l*..... 1Sam 20:31
seeketh my *l* seeketh thy *l*.... 1Sam 22:23
Lord *l*, and as thy soul *l*...... 1Sam 25:26
bound in the bundle of *l*...... 1Sam 25:29
As the Lord *l*, the Lord shall.. 1Sam 26:10
as thy *l* was much set......... 1Sam 26:24
my *l* be much set by.......... 1Sam 26:24
saying, As the Lord *l*......... 1Sam 28:10
I..put my *l* in my hand........ 1Sam 28:21
because my *l* is yet whole..... 2Sam 1:9
not *l* after..he was fallen...... 2Sam 1:10
pleasant in their *l*............ 2Sam 1:23
Joab said, As God *l*.......... 2Sam 2:27
thy soul *l*, I will not do this... 2Sam 11:11
the *l* of his brother.......... 2Sam 14:7
As the Lord *l*, there shall..... 2Sam 14:11
king..said, As the Lord *l*...... 2Sam 15:21
as my lord the king *l*......... 2Sam 15:21
seeketh my *l*................. 2Sam 16:11
Absalom in his *l* had taken.... 2Sam 18:18
this day have saved thy *l*...... 2Sam 19:5
and the *l* of thy sons.......... 2Sam 19:5
l of thy wives, and the *l*...... 2Sam 19:5
that if Absalom had *l*......... 2Sam 19:6
How long have I to *l*......... 2Sam 19:34
l in widowhood............... 2Sam 20:3
mayest save thine own *l*....... 1Kin 1:12
the *l* of thy son Solomon...... 1Kin 1:12
and said, As the Lord *l*....... 1Kin 1:29
Let my lord king David *l*..... 1Kin 1:31
for thyself long *l*............ 1Kin 3:11
asked the *l* of thine enemies... 1Kin 3:11
but the *l* is my son........... 1Kin 3:22
and the *l* is my son........... 1Kin 3:22
and my son is the *l*.......... 1Kin 3:23
This is my son that *l*......... 1Kin 3:23
whose the *l* child was......... 1Kin 3:26
give her the *l* child........... 1Kin 3:26
all the days of his *l*.......... 1Kin 11:34
father while he yet *l*......... 1Kin 12:6
all the days of his *l*.......... 1Kin 15:6
As the Lord thy God *l*........ 1Kin 17:12
As the Lord thy God *l*........ 1Kin 18:10
he arose and went for his *l*.... 1Kin 19:3
they seek my *l*, to take....... 1Kin 19:10
they seek my *l*, to take....... 1Kin 19:14
saith, I pray thee, let me *l*.... 1Kin 20:32
shall thy *l* be for his *l*........ 1Kin 20:39
Micaiah said, As the Lord *l*... 1Kin 22:14
my *l*, and the *l* of these....... 2Kin 1:13
the Lord *l*, and as thy soul *l*.. 2Kin 2:2
l thou and thy children........ 2Kin 4:7
according to the time of *l*..... 2Kin 4:16
the Lord *l*, and as thy soul *l*.. 2Kin 4:30
As the Lord *l*, I will run...... 2Kin 5:20
and fled for their *l*........... 2Kin 7:7
restored a dead body to *l*..... 2Kin 8:5
he had restored to *l*.......... 2Kin 8:5
her son..restored to *l*........ 2Kin 8:5
be wanting, he shall not *l*..... 2Kin 10:19
the son of Joash..*l*............ 2Kin 14:17
to reproach the *l* God........ 2Kin 19:4
for thou shalt die, and not *l*... 2Kin 20:1
all the days of his *l*.......... 2Kin 25:29
their *l* in jeopardy............ 1Chr 11:19
jeopardy of their *l*........... 1Chr 11:19
nor the *l* of thine enemies..... 2Chr 1:11
yet has asked long *l*.......... 2Chr 1:11
long as they *l* in the land..... 2Chr 6:31
pray for the *l* of the king..... Ezra 6:10
go..temple to save his *l*....... Neh 6:11
do, he shall *l* in them........ Neh 9:29
scepter, that he may *l*........ Esth 4:11
let my *l* be given me.......... Esth 7:3
and to stand for their *l*........ Esth 8:11
and stood for their *l*.......... Esth 9:16
l unto the bitter in soul....... Job 3:20
my *l* is wind................. Job 7:7
I loathe it; I would not *l*...... Job 7:16
I would despise my *l*......... Job 9:21
hast granted me *l*............ Job 10:12
the soul of every *l* thing....... Job 12:10
know that my Redeemer *l*..... Job 19:25
Wherefore do the wicked *l*.... Job 21:7
no man is sure of *l*........... Job 24:22
hid from the eyes of all *l*...... Job 28:21
house appointed for all *l*...... Job 30:23
hath given me *l*.............. Job 33:4
his *l* abhorreth bread......... Job 33:20
his *l* shall see the light........ Job 33:28
with the light of the *l*......... Job 33:30
their *l* is among..unclean...... Job 36:14
After this *l* Job............... Job 42:16
my *l* upon the earth.......... Ps 7:5
their portion in this *l*......... Ps 17:14
The Lord *l*; and blessed be.... Ps 18:46
your heart shall *l*............ Ps 22:26
all the days of my *l*.......... Ps 23:6
nor my *l* with bloody men..... Ps 26:9
the strength of my *l*.......... Ps 27:1
in the land of the *l*.......... Ps 27:13
in his favor is *l*.............. Ps 30:5
devised to take away my *l*..... Ps 31:13
that seek after my *l*.......... Ps 38:12
thirsteth for..the *l* God........ Ps 42:2
prayer unto the God of my *l*.. Ps 42:8
while he *l* he blessed his...... Ps 49:18
out of the land of the *l*....... Ps 52:5
men shall not *l*..their days..... Ps 55:23
in the light of the *l*?.......... Ps 56:13
both *l*, and in his wrath....... Ps 58:9
wilt prolong the king's *l*....... Ps 61:6
holdeth our soul in *l*.......... Ps 66:9
your heart shall *l*............ Ps 69:32
crieth out for the *l* God....... Ps 84:2
my *l* draweth nigh unto my.... Ps 88:3
redeemeth thy *l* from......... Ps 103:4
unto the Lord as long as I *l*.. Ps 104:33
in the land of the *l*.......... Ps 116:9
I shall not die, but *l*.......... Ps 118:17
I may *l*, and keep thy word... Ps 119:17
come unto me that I may *l*.... Ps 119:77
understanding and I shall *l*.... Ps 119:144
Let my soul *l*, and it shall.... Ps 119:175
all the days of thy *l*.......... Ps 128:5
portion in the land of the *l*.... Ps 142:5
no man *l* be justified......... Ps 143:2
he hath smitten my *l*.......... Ps 143:3
the desire of every *l* thing..... Ps 145:16
While I *l* will I praise the..... Ps 146:2
they lurk..for their own *l*...... Prov 1:18
the *l* of the owners.......... Prov 1:19
length of days, and long *l*..... Prov 3:2
So shall they be *l* unto........ Prov 3:22
my commandments and *l*...... Prov 4:4
for she is thy *l*.............. Prov 4:13
of it are the issues of *l*........ Prov 4:23
instruction are the way of *l*.... Prov 6:23
not that it is for his *l*......... Prov 7:23
Forsake the foolish, and *l*..... Prov 9:6
thy *l* shall be increased........ Prov 9:11
righteous tendeth to *l*......... Prov 10:16
righteousness tendeth to *l*..... Prov 11:19
man regardeth the *l*.......... Prov 12:10
his mouth keepeth his *l*....... Prov 13:3
it is a tree of *l*.............. Prov 13:12
the Lord is a fountain of *l*.... Prov 14:27
A..tongue is a tree of *l*....... Prov 15:4
heareth the reproof of *l*....... Prov 15:31
a wellspring of *l*............. Prov 16:22
the Lord tendeth to *l*......... Prov 19:23
riches, and honor and *l*....... Prov 22:4
all the days of their *l*........ Eccl 2:3
to do good in his *l*........... Eccl 3:12
the *l* which are yet alive...... Eccl 4:2
the days of his *l*.............. Eccl 5:20
children, and *l* many years.... Eccl 6:3
to walk before the *l*?......... Eccl 6:8
good for man in this *l*........ Eccl 6:12
days of his vain *l* which he.... Eccl 6:12
l will lay it to his heart....... Eccl 7:2
prolongeth his *l* in his........ Eccl 7:15
in their heart while they *l*..... Eccl 9:3
that is joined to all the *l*...... Eccl 9:4

L

a *l* dog is better than a dead . . Eccl 9:4
l know that they shall die . . . . . Eccl 9:5
all the days of the *l* of . . . . Eccl 9:9
thy portion in this *l* . . . . Eccl 9:9
But if a man *l* many years . . . . Eccl 11:8
a well of *l* waters . . . . Song 4:15
among the *l* in Jerusalem . . . . . Is 4:3
having a *l* coal in his hand . . . . Is 6:6
for the *l* to the dead? . . . . Is 8:19
his *l* shall be grievous . . . . Is 15:4
Thy dead men shall *l* . . . . Is 26:19
sent to reproach the *l* God . . . . Is 37:17
things is the *l* of my spirit . . . . . Is 38:16
by these things men *l* . . . . Is 38:16
recover me..make me to *l* . . . . . Is 38:16
The *l*, the *l*, he shall praise . . . . Is 38:19
and people for thy *l* . . . . Is 43:4
hear, and your soul shall *l* . . . . Is 55:3
the fountain of *l* waters . . . . Jer 2:13
The Lord *l*, in truth . . . . Jer 4:2
they will seek thy *l* . . . . Jer 4:30
from the land of the *l* . . . . Jer 11:19
men..that seek thy *l* . . . . Jer 11:21
by my name, The Lord *l* . . . . . . Jer 12:16
The Lord *l*, that brought . . . . . . Jer 16:15
them that seek their *l* . . . . Jer 19:7
I set before..the way of *l* . . . . . . Jer 21:8
besiege you, he shall *l* . . . . Jer 21:9
hand of them that seek thy *l* . . Jer 22:25
But, The Lord *l* which . . . . Jer 23:8
the words of the *l* God . . . . Jer 23:36
serve..his people, and *l* . . . . . . Jer 27:12
of them that seek their *l* . . . . . . Jer 34:21
that ye may *l* many days . . . . . . Jer 35:7
to the Chaldeans shall *l* . . . . Jer 38:2
his life for..and shall *l* . . . . Jer 38:2
men that seek thy *l* . . . . Jer 38:16
then thy soul shall *l* . . . . Jer 38:17
and thou shalt *l*, and thine . . . . Jer 38:17
saying, The Lord God *l* . . . . Jer 44:26
them that seek his *l* . . . . Jer 44:30
thy *l*, will I give unto thee . . . . Jer 45:5
As I *l*, saith the King . . . . Jer 46:18
those that seek their *l* . . . . Jer 46:26
all the days of his *l* . . . . Jer 52:33
for the *l* of thy young . . . . Lam 2:19
doth a *l* man complain . . . . Lam 3:39
thou hast redeemed my *l* . . . . . . Lam 3:58
Under his shadow we shall *l* . . . Lam 4:20
with the peril of our *l* . . . . Lam 5:9
of four *l* creatures . . . . Ezek 1:5
Likeness of the *l* creatures . . . . . Ezek 1:13
down among the *l* creatures . . . Ezek 1:13
as I beheld the *l* creatures . . . . . Ezek 1:15
earth by the *l* creatures . . . . Ezek 1:15
the *l* creatures went . . . . Ezek 1:19
l creatures were lifted up . . . . . . Ezek 1:19
the heads of the *l* creature . . . . Ezek 1:22
wicked way, to save his *l* . . . . . . Ezek 3:18
not sin, he shalt surely *l* . . . . . . Ezek 3:21
This is the *l* creature that . . . . . Ezek 10:15
This is the *l* creature that . . . . . Ezek 10:20
souls..that should not *l* . . . . Ezek 13:19
by promising him *l* . . . . Ezek 13:22
as I *l*, saith the Lord . . . . Ezek 14:18
as I *l*, saith the Lord . . . . Ezek 14:20
thou wast in thy blood, *L* . . . . . Ezek 16:6
As I *l*, saith the Lord God . . . . Ezek 17:16
As I *l*, saith the Lord God . . . . Ezek 18:3
is just, he shall surely *l* . . . . Ezek 18:9
shall he then *l* . . . . Ezek 18:13
he shall not *l* . . . . Ezek 18:13
he shall surely *l* . . . . Ezek 18:19
he hath done he shall *l* . . . . Ezek 18:22
the wicked..shall he *l* . . . . Ezek 18:24
turn yourselves, and *l* ye . . . . . . Ezek 18:32
he shall even *l* in them . . . . Ezek 20:11
whereby they should not *l* . . . . . Ezek 20:25
As I *l*, saith the Lord God . . . . Ezek 20:33
terror in the land of the *l* . . . . . Ezek 32:23
caused in the land of the *l* . . . . Ezek 32:25
mighty in the land of the *l* . . . . Ezek 32:27
As I *l*, saith the Lord God . . . . Ezek 33:11
turn from his way and *l* . . . . Ezek 33:11
that he shall surely *l* . . . . Ezek 33:13

walk in the statutes of *l* . . . . Ezek 33:15
right; he shall surely *l* . . . . Ezek 33:16
As I *l*, surely they that are . . . . Ezek 33:27
as I *l*, saith the Lord God . . . . . Ezek 35:6
enter into you..ye shall *l* . . . . . . Ezek 37:5
these slain, that they may *l* . . . . Ezek 37:9
breath came..and they *l* . . . . Ezek 37:10
that every thing that *l* . . . . Ezek 47:9
rivers shall come, shall *l* . . . . . . Ezek 47:9
shall, *l* whither the river . . . . . . Ezek 47:9
Syriac, O king, *l* for ever . . . . . Dan 2:4
that I have more than any *l* . . . Dan 2:30
and honored him that *l* for . . . . Dan 4:34
and said, O king, *l* for ever . . . Dan 5:10
Daniel, servant of the *l* God . . Dan 6:20
the king, O king, *l* forever . . . . Dan 6:21
some to everlasting *l* . . . . Dan 12:2
Ye are the sons of the *l* God . . Hos 1:10
nor swear, The Lord *l* . . . . Hos 4:15
and we shall *l* in his sight . . . . . Hos 6:2
Seek ye me, and ye shall *l* . . . . Amos 5:4
and not evil, that ye may *l* . . . . Amos 5:14
and say, Thy god, O Dan, *l* . . . Amos 8:14
The manner of Beer-sheba *l* . . . Amos 8:14
not perish for this man's *l* . . . . . Jon 1:14
better..me to die than to *l* . . . . Jon 4:3
I beseech thee, my *l* from me. . Jon 4:3
the just shall *l* by his faith . . . . Hab 2:4
as I *l*, saith the Lord of . . . . Zeph 2:9
prophets, do they *l* forever . . . . Zech 1:5
unto him, Thou shalt not *l* . . . . Zech 13:3
that *l* waters shall go out . . . . . . Zech 14:8
covenant was with him of *l* . . . . Mal 2:5
sought the young child's *l* . . . . . Matt 2:20
Man shall not *l* by bread . . . . . . Matt 4:4
way, which leadeth unto *l* . . . . . Matt 7:14
upon her and she shall *l* . . . . . . Matt 9:18
Christ, the Son of the *l* God . . Matt 16:16
save his *l* shall lose it . . . . Matt 16:25
will lose his *l* for my sake . . . . . Matt 16:25
for thee to enter into *l* halt . . . . Matt 18:8
to enter into *l* with one eye . . . Matt 18:9
that I may have eternal *l* . . . . . . Matt 19:16
if thou wilt enter into *l* . . . . Matt 19:17
to give his *l* a ransom for . . . . . Matt 20:28
God of the dead, but of the *l*. . Matt 22:32
I adjure thee by the *l* God . . . . Matt 26:63
do evil? to save *l*, or to . . . . Mark 3:4
be healed; and she shall *l* . . . . . Mark 5:23
will save his *l* shall lose it . . . . . Mark 8:35
shall lose his *l* for my sake . . . . Mark 8:35
for thee to enter halt into *l* . . . . Mark 9:45
the world to come eternal *l* . . . Mark 10:30
dead, but the God of the *l* . . . . Mark 12:27
him, all the days of our *l* . . . . . Luke 1:75
and had *l* with a husband . . . . . Luke 2:36
man shall not *l* by bread . . . . . . Luke 4:4
to save *l*, or to destroy it . . . . . Luke 6:9
and pleasures of this *l* . . . . Luke 8:14
had spent all her *l* upon . . . . Luke 8:43
will save his *l* shall lose . . . . Luke 9:24
will lose his *l* for my sake . . . . . Luke 9:24
this do, and thou shalt *l* . . . . Luke 10:28
for a man's *l* consisteth not . . . . Luke 12:15
Take no thought for your *l* . . . . Luke 12:22
The *l* is more than meat . . . . . . Luke 12:23
sisters, yea, and his own *l* . . . . . Luke 14:26
substance with riotous *l* . . . . Luke 15:13
thou in thy *l* receivedst thy . . . . Luke 16:25
seek to save his *l* shall lose . . . . Luke 17:33
lose his *l* shall preserve it . . . . . Luke 17:33
God of the dead, but of the *l*. . Luke 20:38
of the living; for all *l* unto . . . . Luke 20:38
hath cast in all the *l* that . . . . . . Luke 21:4
and cares of this *l* . . . . Luke 21:34
seek ye the *l* among the dead. . Luke 24:5
In him was *l*, and the *l* . . . . John 1:4
he would have given thee *l* . . . . John 4:10
him, Go thy way; thy son *l* . . . . John 4:50
told him, saying, Thy son *l* . . . . John 4:51
and they that hear shall *l* . . . . . John 5:25
For as the Father hath *l* . . . . John 5:26
to the Son to have *l* in . . . . John 5:26
unto the resurrection of *l* . . . . . John 5:29
me, that ye might have *l* . . . . . . John 5:40

endureth unto everlasting *l* . . . . John 6:27
and giveth *l* unto the world . . . John 6:33
them, I am the bread of *l* . . . . . John 6:35
may have everlasting *l* . . . . John 6:40
on me hath everlasting *l* . . . . . . John 6:47
I am that bread of *l* . . . . John 6:48
I am the *l* bread which . . . . John 6:51
As the *l* Father hath sent . . . . . . John 6:57
hath sent me, and I *l* by the . . . John 6:57
eateth me, even he shall *l* . . . . . John 6:57
are spirit, and they are *l* . . . . . . John 6:63
Christ, the Son of the *l* . . . . John 6:69
belly shall flow rivers of *l* . . . . . John 7:38
shall have the light of *l* . . . . John 8:12
that they might have *l* . . . . John 10:10
giveth his *l* for the sheep . . . . . . John 10:11
and I lay down my *l* for the . . . John 10:15
because I lay down my *l* . . . . . . John 10:17
I will lay down my *l* for thy . . . John 13:37
thou lay down thy *l* for my . . . . John 13:38
man lay down his *l* for his . . . . John 15:13
known to me the ways of *l* . . . . Acts 2:28
all the words of this *l* . . . . Acts 5:20
to the end they might not *l* . . . . Acts 7:19
granted repentance unto *l* . . . . . Acts 11:18
were ordained to eternal *l* . . . . . Acts 13:48
vanities unto the *l* God . . . . Acts 14:15
not yourselves; for his *l* is . . . . . Acts 20:10
is not fit that he should *l* . . . . . . Acts 22:22
I have *l* in all good . . . . Acts 23:1
My manner of *l* from my . . . . . . Acts 26:4
vengeance suffereth not to *l* . . . Acts 28:4
and immortality, eternal *l* . . . . . Rom 2:7
we shall be saved by his *l* . . . . . Rom 5:10
in *l* by one, Jesus Christ . . . . . . Rom 5:17
her husband so long as he *l* . . . Rom 7:2
which was ordained to *l*, I . . . . Rom 7:10
the law of the Spirit of *l* . . . . . Rom 8:2
neither death, nor *l*, nor . . . . . . Rom 8:38
the children of the *l* God . . . . . Rom 9:26
doeth those things shall *l* . . . . . . Rom 10:5
of them be, but *l* from the . . . . Rom 11:15
your bodies a *l* sacrifice . . . . Rom 12:1
in you, *l* peaceably with all . . . . Rom 12:18
both of the dead and *l* . . . . Rom 14:9
As I *l*, saith the Lord, every . . Rom 14:11
or *l*, or death, or things 1Cor 3:22
pertaining to this *l*, set 1Cor 6:4
as long as her husband *l* 1Cor 7:39
holy things *l* of the things 1Cor 9:13
the gospel should *l* of the 1Cor 9:14
If in this *l* only we have 1Cor 15:19
man Adam was made a *l* soul. . 1Cor 15:45
that we despaired even of *l* 2Cor 1:8
the savor of *l* unto *l* 2Cor 2:16
but with the Spirit of the *l* 2Cor 3:3
but the spirit giveth *l* 2Cor 3:6
For we which *l* are always 2Cor 4:11
might be swallowed up of *l* 2Cor 5:4
as dying, and, behold, we *l* 2Cor 6:9
our hearts to die and *l* with . . . 2Cor 7:3
yet he *l* by the power of God. . 2Cor 13:4
we shall *l* with him by the 2Cor 13:4
be of one mind, *l* in 2Cor 13:11
the Gentiles to *l* as do the . . . . Gal 2:14
l after the manner of . . . . Gal 2:14
the law, that I might *l* unto . . . Gal 2:19
The just shall *l* by faith . . . . Gal 3:11
that doeth them shall *l* in . . . . . Gal 3:12
which could have given *l* . . . . . . Gal 3:21
being alienated from the *l* . . . . . Eph 4:18
mayest *l* long on the earth . . . . Eph 6:3
body, whether it be by *l*, or . . . Phil 1:20
For to me to *l* is Christ, and . . Phil 1:21
But if I *l* in the flesh, this . . . . . Phil 1:22
Holding forth the word of *l* . . . Phil 2:16
not regarding his *l*, to . . . . Phil 2:30
as though *l* in the world . . . . Col 2:20
to serve the *l* and true God . . . 1Thess 1:9
For now we *l*, if ye stand fast. . 1Thess 3:8
believe on him to *l* 1Tim 1:16
lead a quiet and peaceable *l* . . . 1Tim 2:2
which is the church of the *l* . . . 1Tim 3:15
promise of the *l* that now is . . . 1Tim 4:8
l in pleasure is dead while 1Tim 5:6

riches, but in the *l* God 1Tim 6:17
with the affairs of this *l* 2Tim 2:4
we shall also *l* with him 2Tim 2:11
my doctrine, manner of *l*......2Tim 3:10
pleasures, *l* in malice and .....Titus 3:3
their *l* subject to bondage .....Heb 2:15
in departing from the *l* God ...Heb 3:12
of days, nor end of *l*..........Heb 7:3
it is witnessed that he *l* ....Heb 7:8
the power of an endless *l* .....Heb 7:16
at all while the testator *l* ......Heb 9:17
By a new and *l* way, which....Heb 10:20
into the hands of the *l* God ...Heb 10:31
Now the just shall *l* by faith...Heb 10:38
their dead raised to *l* ....Heb 11:35
the Father of spirits, and *l* ....Heb 12:9
unto the city of the *l* God.....Heb 12:22
in all things willing to *l* ....Heb 13:18
shall receive the crown of *l*....James 1:12
have *l* in pleasure on the ......James 5:5
by the word of God, which *l* ..1Pet 1:23
whom coming, as unto a *l*.....1Pet 2:4
should *l* unto righteousness....1Pet 2:24
together of the grace of *l* 1Pet 3:7
For he that will love *l*, and....1Pet 3:10
l according to God in the 1Pet 4:6
that pertain unto *l* and 2Pet 1:3
those that after should *l*.......2Pet 2:6
escaped from them who *l* in ...2Pet 2:18
promised us, even eternal *l*....1John 2:25
hath eternal *l* abiding in 1John 3:15
he laid down his *l* for us 1John 3:16
that we might *l* through 1John 4:9
that ye have eternal *l* 1John 5:13
shall give him *l* for them 1John 5:16
the true God, and eternal *l*....1John 5:20
Jesus Christ unto eternal *l*.....Jude 21
I am he that *l*, and was dead ..Rev 1:18
give to eat of the tree of *l* ....Rev 2:7
name that thou *l*, and art .....Rev 3:1
name out of the book of *l*.....Rev 3:5
him that *l* for ever and ever ...Rev 4:10
having the seal of the *l* God...Rev 7:2
them unto *l* fountains of ......Rev 7:17
by him that *l* for ever and.....Rev 10:6
Spirit of *l* from God entered ..Rev 11:11
wound by a sword, and did *l* ..Rev 13:14
power to give *l* unto the ......Rev 13:15
and every *l* soul died in the ...Rev 16:3
glorified herself, and *l* ....Rev 18:7
l and reigned with Christ a ....Rev 20:4
which is the book of *l* ....Rev 20:12
fountain of the water of *l* .....Rev 21:6
pure river of water of *l* ....Rev 22:1
was there the tree of *l* ....Rev 22:2
let him take the water of *l* ....Rev 22:17

LIFE, ETERNAL—*everlasting life; life with God*

Defined as:
Knowing the true God ...John 17:3
God's commandment ....John 12:50
Jesus Christ 1John 1:2
He gives ....John 10:28, 29
God's gift ....Rom 6:23

Christ's relation to:
It is in Him 2Tim 1:1
Manifested through Him. .2Tim 1:10
He has the words of .....John 6:68
It comes through Him ...Rom 5:21

Means of securing, by:
God's gift ....Rom 6:22, 23
Having the Son 1John 5:11, 12
Knowing the true God ...John 17:3
Knowing the Scriptures ..John 20:31
Believing the Son........John 3:15-36
Drinking the water of life.John 4:14
Eating the bread of life ..John 6:50-58
Reaping ....John 4:36
Fight the good fight of faith.................1Tim 6:12, 19

Present aspect of, for Christians, they:
Believe in the Son ....John 3:36
Have assurance of ....John 5:24
Have promise of ....Titus 1:2
Have hope of ....Titus 3:7
Take hold of 1Tim 6:12, 19
Hates his life in this world................John 12:25

Future aspect of, for Christians, they shall:
Inherit..................Matt 19:29
In the world to come ....Luke 18:30
In them you think you have ....John 5:39
Reap ....Gal 6:8

LIFE, NATURAL—*that which distinguishes animate beings from dead ones*

Origin of, by:
God's creation ....Acts 17:28, 29
Natural birth ....Gen 4:1, 2
Supernatural conception ..Luke 1:31-35

Shortness of, described as:
Dream ....Job 20:8
Shadow 1Chr 29:15
Cloud ....Job 7:9
Flower ....Job 14:1, 2
Vapor ....James 4:14
Sleep ....Ps 90:5
Tale told ....Ps 90:9
Pilgrimage ....Gen 47:9
Grass...................1Pet 1:24

God's concern for, its:
Preservation ....Gen 7:1-3
Protection ....Ps 34:7, 17, 19
Perpetuity (continuance). .Gen 1:28
Provisions...............Ps 104:27, 28
Punishment ....Gen 3:14-19
Perfection in glory ....Col 3:4

Believer's attitude toward:
Seeks to preserve it......Acts 27:10-31
Attends to needs of .....Acts 27:34
Accepts suffering of .....Job 2:4-10
Makes God's kingdom first in...............Matt 6:25-33
Gives it up for Christ ....Matt 10:39
Lays it down for others ..Acts 15:26
Prizes it not too highly...Acts 20:24
Puts Jesus first in........2Cor 4:10-12
Regards God's will in ....James 4:13-15
Puts away the evil of ....Col 3:5-9
Does not run with 1Pet 4:1-4
Praises God all the days of ....Ps 63:3, 4
Doesn't fear enemies of ..Luke 12:4

Cares of:
Stunt spiritual growth ....Luke 8:14
Divide loyalty ....Luke 16:13
Delay preparedness ......Luke 17:26-30; Luke 21:34
Hinder service 2Tim 2:4

LIFE, SPIRITUAL—*life lived in relationship with God*

Source of:
God ....Ps. 36:9
Christ ....John 14:6
Holy Spirit..............Ezek 37:14
God's Word ....James 1:18

Described as:
New birth...............John 3:3-8
Resurrection ....John 5:24
Translation..............Acts 26:18
New creation............2 Cor 5:17
Seed 1John 3:9
Crucifixion ....Gal 2:20

Evidences of:
Growth 1Pet 2:2
Love 1John 3:14
Obedience ....Rom 6:16-22
Victory ....Rom 6:1-15
Spiritual-mindedness .....Rom 8:6
Possession of the Spirit ..Rom 8:9-13
Spirit's testimony ....Rom 8:15-17
Walking in the Spirit ....Gal 5:16, 25
Bearing the fruit of the Spirit..................Gal 5:22
Name in the book of life..Phil 4:3; Rev. 17:8

Growth of:
Begins in birth ....John 3:3-8
Feeds on milk in infancy .1Pet 2:2
Must not remain in infancy ....Heb 5:11-14
Comes to adulthood 1John 2:13, 14
Arrives at maturity ......Eph 4:14-16

Characteristics of:
Imperishable ....John 11:25, 26
Transforming............Rom 12:1, 2
Invisible ....Col 3:3, 4
Abides forever ....1 John 2:17

Enemies of:
Devil...................Eph 6:11-17
World 1John 2:15-17
Flesh ....Gal 5:16-21

LIFE, TRIUMPHANT CHRISTIAN—*the life God wants for His people*

Over:
Sorrow ....John 16:22-24; 1Thess 4:13-18
The world ....John 16:33; 1John 5:4, 5
Transgressions.........Rom 6:6, 7, 11-18; 1John 5:4, 5; Rom 8:1-4; Eph 2:5, 6
Circumstances ....Rom 8:37; Phil 4:11-13
Death ....1Cor 15:54-57; Rom 6:6-9

Through:
Prayer ....John 16:22-24
Christ's death ....Rom 6:6, 7
Doctrine ....Rom 6:17
Holy Spirit.............Rom 8:1, 2
Christ ....Phil 4:13
Grace ....Eph 2:7; Rom 6:14
Exaltation with Christ....Eph 2:5, 6
God's will ....Phil 2:13
Hope of resurrection.....1Thess 4:16
Return of Christ.........1Thess 4:16, 17
Faith 1John 5:4, 5

When?
Forever 1Cor 15:54
Always 2Cor 2:14

By whom? Those who:
Are in Christ ....Rom 8:1
Were dead in transgressions ....Eph 2:5
Are born of God 1John 5:4
Believe 1John 5:5

Goal:
To demonstrate God's grace ....Eph 3:7-10
To glorify Christ ....1Pet 4:11; Rom 8:16-18

LIFT—*to raise; rise; elevate; transport*

[LIFTED, LIFTEST, LIFTETH, LIFTING]

it was *l* up above the earth....Gen 7:17
Lot *l* up his eyes, and ....Gen 13:10
I have *l* up mine hand unto ...Gen 14:22
he *l* up his eyes and looked ...Gen 18:2
Abraham *l* up his eyes, and ...Gen 22:13
Rebekah *l* up her eyes, and ...Gen 24:64
Rachel, and *l* up his voice.....Gen 29:11
L up now thine eyes, and .....Gen 31:12
Jacob *l* up his eyes, and.......Gen 33:1
they *l* up their eyes and ....Gen 37:25
I *l* up my voice and cried .....Gen 39:15
three days shall Pharaoh *l*.....Gen 40:19
l up the head of the chief .....Gen 40:20
l up the rod, and smote the ...Ex 7:20
l thou up thy rod, and ....Ex 14:16
Aaron *l* up his hand toward ...Lev 9:22

Lord *l* up his countenance.....Num 6:26
the congregation *l* up their ....Num 14:1
and *l* up himself as a young ..Num 23:24
Balaam *l* up his eyes, and .....Num 24:2
l up thine eyes westward ......Deut 3:27
Then thine heart be *l* up ......Deut 8:14
help him to *l* them up again ..Deut 22:4
I *l* up my hand to heaven ....Deut 32:40
the priests' feet were *l* up .....Josh 4:18
which no man hath *l* up any...Josh 8:31
people *l* up their voice, and ..Judg 2:4
l up his voice, and cried ......Judg 9:7
l up their voices, and wept ....Judg 21:2
and they *l* up their voice ......Ruth 1:9
he bringeth low, and *l* up 1Sam 2:7
l up their eyes, and saw the ...1Sam 6:13
And Saul *l* up his voice 1Sam 24:16
the king *l* up his voice 2Sam 3:32
came, and *l* up their voice 2Sam 13:36
men that *l* up their hand 2Sam 18:28
thou also hast *l* me up on 2Sam 22:49
l up his spear against eight 2Sam 23:8
he *l* up his hand against the ...1Kin 11:26
l up his face to the window ...2Kin 9:32
l up thy prayer for the 2Kin 19:4
and *l* up thine eyes on high? ..2Kin 19:22
l up his spear against three ...1Chr 11:11
for *l* up his spear against 1Chr 11:20
David *l* up his eyes, and saw ..1Chr 21:16
the words of God, to *l* up the .1Chr 25:5
when they *l* up their voice 2Chr 5:13
heart was *l* up in the ways 2Chr 17:6
heart *l* thee up to boast 2Chr 25:19
was *l* up to his destruction 2Chr 26:16
and blush to *l* up my face to ..Ezra 9:6
Amen, with *l* up their heads...Neh 8:6
when they *l* up their eyes .....Job 2:12
yet will I not *l* up my head....Job 10:15
shalt *l* up thy face unto God ..Job 22:26
thou shalt say, There is *l* up...Job 22:29
Thou *l* me up to the wind .....Job 30:22
have *l* up my hand against ....Job 31:21
time she *l* up herself on ....Job 39:18
Lord, *l* thou up the light of ...Ps 4:6
l up thyself because of the ....Ps 7:6
thou that *l* me up from the ....Ps 9:13
O Lord; O God, *l* up thine ...Ps 10:12
hath not *l* up his soul unto ....Ps 24:4
L up your heads, O ye gates ..Ps 24:7
be ye *l* up, ye everlasting .....Ps 24:7
L up your heads, O ye gates ..Ps 24:9
l them up, ye everlasting ......Ps 24:9
I *l* up my hands toward thy ...Ps 28:2
thou hast *l* me up, and hast ...Ps 30:1
I will *l* up my hands in thy ...Ps 63:4
had *l* up axes upon the ....Ps 74:5
wicked, *L* not up the horn ....Ps 75:4
L not up your horn on high ...Ps 75:5
O Lord, do I *l* up my soul ....Ps 86:4
floods have *l* up, O Lord ......Ps 93:3
floods have *l* up their voice ...Ps 93:3
the floods *l* up their waves ....Ps 93:3
L up thyself, thou judge of ....Ps 94:2
for thou hast *l* me up, and ....Ps 102:10
l up the waves thereof ....Ps 107:25
My hands also will I *l* up .....Ps 119:48
I will *l* up mine eyes unto .....Ps 121:1
Unto thee *l* I up mine eyes....Ps 123:1
l up of my hands as the ....Ps 141:2
walk; for I *l* up my soul.......Ps 143:8
The Lord *l* up the meek ......Ps 147:6
l up thy voice for............Prov 2:3
and their eyelids are *l* up .....Prov 30:13
hast done foolishly in *l* up.....Prov 30:32
the one will *l* up his fellow ....Eccl 4:10
nation shall not *l* up sword ....Is 2:4
and upon every one that is *l*...Is 2:12
all the hills that are *l* up ......Is 2:14
mount up like the *l* up of .....Is 9:18
itself against them that *l* it ....Is 10:15
the staff should *l* up itself .....Is 10:15
so shall he *l* it up after the ....Is 10:26
L ye up a banner upon the ....Is 13:2
when he *l* up an ensign on ....Is 18:3
when thy hand is *l* up, they ...Is 26:11
now will I *l* up myself ....Is 33:10
wherefore *l* up thy prayer .....Is 37:4
l up thy voice with ....Is 40:9
l it up, be not afraid; say .....Is 40:9
He shall not cry, nor *l* up .....Is 42:2
L up thine eyes round ....Is 49:18
L up your eyes to the.........Is 51:6
spare not, *l* up thy voice ......Is 58:1
the Lord shall *l* up a..........Is 59:19
L up thine eyes round ....Is 60:4
L up thine eyes unto the ......Jer 3:2
neither *l* up cry nor prayer ....Jer 7:16
neither *l* up a cry or prayer ...Jer 11:14
l up thy voice in Bashan ......Jer 22:20
l himself up in his ....Jer 51:3
heaven, and is *l* up even to ...Jer 51:9
l up thy hands toward him ....Lam 2:19
Let us *l* up our heart with.....Lam 3:41
living creatures were *l* up .....Ezek 1:19
the wheels were *l* up over .....Ezek 1:20
those were *l* up from the ......Ezek 1:21
the wheels were *l* up over .....Ezek 1:21
spirit *l* me up between the ....Ezek 8:3
l up thine eyes now the ....Ezek 8:5
And the cherubim were *l* .....Ezek 10:15
and when they were *l* up......Ezek 10:17
these *l* up themselves also .....Ezek 10:17
spirit *l* me up, and brought.....Ezek 11:1
that it might not *l* itself ....Ezek 17:14
hath *l* up his eyes to the ......Ezek 18:12
l up mine hand unto the ......Ezek 20:5
when I *l* up mine hand unto...Ezek 20:5
also I *l* up my hand unto......Ezek 20:15
I *l* up mine hand to give it ....Ezek 20:28
thou shalt not *l* up thine ......Ezek 23:27
Because thine heart is *l* up ....Ezek 28:2
l up because of thy beauty ....Ezek 28:17
hast *l* up thyself in height .....Ezek 31:10
heart is *l* up in his height .....Ezek 31:10
l up your eyes toward your....Ezek 33:25
I *l* up mine hand against ......Ezek 44:12
I Nebuchadnezzar *l* up mine...Dan 4:34
l up thyself against the Lord...Dan 5:23
Then I *l* up mine eyes, and ...Dan 8:3
his heart shall be *l* up.........Dan 11:12
nation shall not *l* up a ....Mic 4:3
Thine hand shall be *l* up ......Mic 5:9
horseman *l* up both the ....Nah 3:3
soul which is *l* up is not.......Hab 2:4
Then *l* I up mine eyes, and ...Zech 1:18
so that no man did *l* up his ...Zech 1:21
I *l* up mine eyes again, and ...Zech 2:1
was *l* up a talent of lead ......Zech 5:7
l I up mine eyes, and looked ..Zech 5:9
l up the ephah between the ...Zech 5:9
And I turned, and *l* up mine ..Zech 6:1
shall be *l* up, and inhabited ...Zech 14:10
he not lay hold on it, and *l* ...Matt 12:11
they had *l* up their eyes.......Matt 17:8
by the hand, and *l* her up .....Mark 1:31
by the hand, and *l* him up ....Mark 9:27
he *l* up his eyes on his ....Luke 6:20
and could in no wise *l* up .....Luke 13:11
they *l* up their voices, and ....Luke 17:13
would not *l* up so much as ....Luke 18:13
then look up, and *l* up your ....Luke 21:28
as Moses *l* up the serpent .....John 3:14
L up your eyes, and look on ..John 4:35
Jesus then *l* up his eyes ....John 6:5
Jesus had *l* up himself ....John 8:10
ye have *l* up the Son of man ..John 8:28
And Jesus *l* up his eyes ....John 11:41
if I be *l* up from the earth ....John 12:32
l up his heel against me ....John 13:18
But Peter..*l* up his voice ....Acts 2:14
l up their voice to God ....Acts 4:24
they *l* up their voices ....Acts 14:11
l up holy hands, without 1Tim 2:8
lest being *l* up with pride 1Tim 3:6
l up the hands which hang ....Heb 12:12
the Lord, and he shall *l*.......James 4:10
the earth *l* up his hand to .....Rev 10:5

LIFTER—*one who raises or lifts something*
glory, and the *l* up of mine....Ps 3:3

LIGHT—*that which makes vision possible; brightness; not heavy; unimportant*

Kinds of:
Cosmic ....Gen 1:3-5
Natural ....Judg 19:26
Miraculous ....Acts 12:7
Artificial................Acts 16:29

Descriptive of God's:
Nature 1John 1:5
Word....................Ps 119:105
Wisdom ....Dan 2:21, 22
Guidance ....Ps 78:14
Ps 89:15
Favor ....Ps 4:6

Descriptive of Christ's:
Preincarnation ....John 1:4-9
Person...................2Cor 4:6
Prediction...............Is 42:6
Presentation to the world.Luke 2:32
Proclamation ....John 8:12
Perfection in glory ....Rev 21:23, 24

Descriptive of Christians as:
Forerunners ....John 5:35
Examples ....Matt 5:14, 16
Missionaries.............Matt 10:27
Transformed people .....Eph 5:8-14
Heirs of glory ....Rev 21:23

[*also* LIGHTED, LIGHTEN, LIGHTENED, LIGHTENETH, LIGHTER, LIGHTEST, LIGHTETH, LIGHTS]
be *l* in the firmament of ......Gen 1:14
give *l* upon the earth ....Gen 1:15
God made two great *l* ....Gen 1:16
greater *l* to rule the day.......Gen 1:16
lesser *l* to rule the night.......Gen 1:16
divide the *l* from..darkness ....Gen 1:18
had *l* in their dwellings........Ex 10:23
pillar of fire, to give them *l* ...Ex 13:21
gave *l* by night to these ....Ex 14:20
they shall *l* the lamps ....Ex 25:37
may give *l* over against ....Ex 25:37
Aaron *l* the lamps at even ....Ex 30:8
oil for the *l*, and spices ....Ex 35:8
candlestick also for the *l* ......Ex 35:14
with the oil for the *l* ....Ex 35:14
vessels thereof..oil for *l* ....Ex 39:37
l the lamps before the Lord ...Ex 40:25
oil olive beaten for the *l* ......Lev 24:2
cover the candlestick of the *l* ..Num 4:9
When thou *l* the lamps........Num 8:2
seven lamps shall give *l* ....Num 8:2
he *l* the lamps thereof over....Num 8:3
l upon his neighbor ....Deut 19:5
that setteth *l* by his father.....Deut 27:16
hired vain and *l* persons ......Judg 9:4
to *l* on a part of the field .....Ruth 2:3
will *l* his hand from off you ...1Sam 6:5
spoil..until the morning *l*......1Sam 14:36
Seemeth it to you a *l* thing....1Sam 18:23
to him by the morning *l*.......1Sam 25:22
until the morning *l* 1Sam 25:36
Asahel was as *l* of foot as 2Sam 2:18
l upon him as the dew falleth..2Sam 17:12
quench not the *l* of Israel 2Sam 21:17
Lord will *l* my darkness 2Sam 22:29
windows of narrow *l* 1Kin 6:4
l was against *l* in three ranks ..1Kin 7:4
which he put upon us, *l*.......1Kin 12:4
make thou it *l* unto us 1Kin 12:10
l thing for him to walk 1Kin 16:31
a *l* thing in the sight 2Kin 3:18
to give him always a *l* 2Kin 8:19
make thou it somewhat *l*.......2Chr 10:10
promised to give a *l* to........2Chr 21:7
our God may *l* our eyes.......Ezra 9:8
l in the way wherein they .....Neh 9:12
Jews had *l* and gladness ....Esth 8:16
neither let the *l* shine upon....Job 3:4
infants which never saw *l* .....Job 3:16
Why is *l* given to a man ......Job 3:23
out to *l* the shadow of death ..Job 12:22
l is short because of ....Job 17:12
l..be dark in his tabernacle ....Job 18:6
l shall shine upon thy ways ....Job 22:28

murderer rising with the *l* .....Job 24:14
doth not his *l* arise? ....Job 25:3
by his *l* I walked through .....Job 29:3
when I waited for *l*, there .....Job 30:26
enlightened with the *l* of ......Job 33:30
clouds he covereth the *l*.......Job 36:32
men see not the bright *l* ......Job 37:21
Where is the way where *l* ....Job 38:19
his sneezings a *l* doth shine ....Job 41:18
l mine eyes, lest I sleep ....Ps 13:3
Lord is my *l*..my salvation ....Ps 27:1
looked unto him..were *l* ......Ps 34:5
in thy *l* shall we see *l* ....Ps 36:9
righteousness as the *l* ....Ps 37:6
as for the *l* of mine eyes ......Ps 38:10
they shall never see *l* ....Ps 49:19
altogether *l* than vanity ....Ps 62:9
prepared the *l* and the sun ....Ps 74:16
the *l* of thy countenance ....Ps 89:15
L is sown for the righteous ....Ps 97:11
coverest thyself with *l*.........Ps 104:2
fire to give *l* in the night ......Ps 105:39
which hath showed us *l* ....Ps 118:27
and a *l* unto my path ....Ps 119:105
thy words giveth *l* ....Ps 119:130
To him that made great *l* ......Ps 136:7
night shall be *l* about me ......Ps 139:11
darkness and the *l* are both ...Ps 139:12
the just is as the shining *l* .....Prov 4:18
is a lamp; and the law is *l*.....Prov 6:23
l of the righteous rejoiceth ....Prov 13:9
l of the king's countenance ....Prov 16:15
the Lord *l* both their eyes .....Prov 29:13
far as *l* excelleth darkness .....Eccl 2:13
While the sun or the *l*, or .....Eccl 12:2
us walk in the *l* of the Lord ...Is 2:5
darkness for *l*, and *l* for ....Is 5:20
l is darkened in the heavens ...Is 5:30
darkness have seen a great *l*...Is 9:2
upon them hath the *l* shined...Is 9:2
shall not give their *l* ....Is 13:10
l of the moon shall ....Is 30:26
be as the *l* of the sun ....Is 30:26
l of the sun..be sevenfold .....Is 30:26
l of seven days, in the day ....Is 30:26
darkness *l* before them........Is 42:16
l think that thou shouldest ....Is 49:6
thee for a *l* to the Gentiles ....Is 49:6
walk in the *l* of your fire ......Is 50:11
Then shall thy *l* break ....Is 58:8
wait for *l*, but behold ....Is 59:9
Gentiles shall come to thy *l* ...Is 60:3
sun shall be no more thy *l* ....Is 60:19
moon give *l* unto thee ....Is 60:19
unto thee an everlasting *l* .....Is 60:19
heavens, and they had no *l*....Jer 4:23
and the *l* of the candle ....Jer 25:10
the sun for a *l* by day.........Jer 31:35
stars for a *l* by night ....Jer 31:35
into darkness, but not into *l*...Lam 3:2
l thing to the house of Judah ..Ezek 8:17
In thee have they set *l* by .....Ezek 22:7
bright *l* of heaven will I.......Ezek 32:8
of thy father *l* and............Dan 5:11
judgments are as the *l* ....Hos 6:5
Lord is darkness and not *l* ....Amos 5:18
ship into the sea, to *l* it ....Jon 1:5
when the morning is *l*.........Mic 2:1
Lord shall be a *l* unto me .....Mic 7:8
bring me forth to the *l*........Mic 7:9
brightness was as the *l* ....Hab 3:4
are *l* and treacherous ....Zeph 3:4
l shall not be clear, nor ....Zech 14:6
sat in darkness saw great *l* ....Matt 4:16
death *l* is sprung up ....Matt 4:16
Neither do men *l* a candle ....Matt 5:15
giveth *l* unto all that are ......Matt 5:15
l of the body is the eye ....Matt 6:22
whole body shall be full of *l*...Matt 6:22
yoke is easy..burden is *l* ......Matt 11:30
they made *l* of it, and went ...Matt 22:5
moon shall not give her *l* .....Mark 13:24
l to them..sit in darkness......Luke 1:79
A light to *l* the Gentiles ......Luke 2:32
when he hath *l* a candle.......Luke 8:16
enter in may see the *l* ....Luke 8:16
when he hath *l* a candle.......Luke 11:33
which come in may see..*l* .....Luke 11:33
l of the body is the eye ....Luke 11:34
whole body..is full of *l*........Luke 11:34
whole body..be full of *l* ....Luke 11:36
whole shall be full of *l*........Luke 11:36
candle doth give thee *l*........Luke 11:36
and your *l* burning ....Luke 12:35
doth not *l* a candle ....Luke 15:8
l out of the one part under ....Luke 17:24
l every man that cometh ......John 1:9
l is come into the world.......John 3:19
darkness rather than *l*.........John 3:19
doeth evil hateth the *l* ....John 3:20
neither cometh to the *l* ....John 3:20
I am the *l* of the world ....John 9:5
there is no *l* in him ....John 11:10
little while is the *l* with ....John 12:35
walk while ye have the *l* ......John 12:35
ye have *l*, believe in the *l* .....John 12:36
may be the children of *l* ....John 12:36
I am come a *l* into..world .....John 12:46
about him a *l* from heaven ....Acts 9:3
thee to be a *l* of the Gentiles ..Acts 13:47
were many *l* in the upper .....Acts 20:8
from heaven a great *l* round ...Acts 22:6
for the glory of that *l* ....Acts 22:11
saw in..way a *l* from heaven ...Acts 26:13
them from darkness to *l* ......Acts 26:18
next day they *l* the ship ....Acts 27:18
l of them which are in ....Rom 2:19
bring to *l* the hidden things ...1Cor 4:5
l of the glorious gospel of 2Cor 4:4
our *l* affliction, which is 2Cor 4:17
transformed into..angel of *l* ...2Cor 11:14
inheritance of..saints in *l* .....Col 1:12
are all the children of *l* 1Thess 5:5
dwelling in..*l* which no man ...1Tim 6:16
life and immortality to *l*.......2Tim 1:10
down from the Father of *l* ....James 1:17
into his marvelous *l*...........1Pet 2:9
walk in the *l*, as he is in..*l* 1John 1:7
true *l* now shineth 1John 2:8
that saith he is in the *l*.........1John 2:9
shall the sun *l* on them ....Rev 7:16
earth was *l* with his glory .....Rev 18:1
l was like unto a stone ....Rev 21:11
neither *l* of the sun ....Rev 22:5
Lord God giveth them *l*.......Rev 22:5

LIGHTED—*to dismount; descend; land upon*
[*also* LIGHTING]
she *l* off the camel ....Gen 24:64
she *l* off her ass ....Josh 15:18
she *l* from off her ass ....Judg 1:14
l off the ass and fell before....1Sam 25:23
l down from the chariot 2Kin 5:21
it hath *l* upon Israel ....Is 9:8
show the *l* down of his arm ...Is 30:30
like a dove, and *l* upon him ...Matt 3:16

LIGHTLY—*unconcernedly; with little regard for*
[*also* LIGHTNESS]
l have lain with thy wife ......Gen 26:10
l esteemed the Rock ....Deut 32:15
shall be *l* esteemed 1Sam 2:30
l afflicted the land of Zebulun .Is 9:1
through the *l* of her whoredom.Jer 3:9
all the hills moved *l* ....Jer 4:24
can *l* speak evil of me ....Mark 9:39
was thus minded, did I use *l*?. .2Cor 1:17

LIGHTNING—*electrical discharges between the clouds and the earth*

Used literally of God's:
Visitation at Sinai ....Ex 19:16
A power in storms ......Job 38:35

Descriptive of:
Swiftness ....Nah 2:4
Brightness ....Matt 28:3
God's judgments ....Rev 11:19
Christ's coming..........Luke 17:24
Satan's fall.............Luke 10:18

[*also* LIGHTNINGS]
thunderings, and the *l* ....Ex 20:18
l, and discomfited them 2Sam 22:15
way for the *l* of the thunder ...Job 28:26
l unto the ends of the earth ...Job 37:3
way for the *l* of thunder ......Job 38:25
he shot out *l*, and discomfited .Ps 18:14
l lightened the world..........Ps 77:18
he maketh *l* for the rain ......Ps 135:7
Cast forth *l*, and scatter ....Ps 144:6
he maketh *l* with rain ....Jer 10:13
out of the fire went forth *l* ....Ezek 1:13
face as the appearance of *l* ....Dan 10:6
arrow shall go forth as the *l* ...Zech 9:14
l cometh out of the east.......Matt 24:27
of the throne proceeded *l* .....Rev 4:5
and thunderings, and *l* ....Rev 8:5
and thunders, and *l*...........Rev 16:18

LIGN—*a type of wood*
trees of *l* aloes ....Num 24:6

LIGURE—*a gem*
Worn by the high priest. .Ex 28:19
See JACINTH

third row, a *l*, an agate ....Ex 39:12

LIKE, LIKED, LIKEN—*See* INTRODUCTION

LIKEMINDED—*having same disposition or purpose*
to be *l* one toward another ...Rom 15:5
Fulfill ye my joy, that ye be *l*. .Phil 2:2

LIKENESS—*similarity; image; one's features or characteristics*

Between:
Spiritual and the moral . .2Cor 3:6
Spiritual and the physical .Jer 23:29
Two events 2Chr 35:18
God and idols...........Is 46:5, 6, 9
Believers and unbelievers .Ps 73:5
Now and the future......1John 3:2

in our image, after our *l* ......Gen 1:26
begat a son in his own *l*.......Gen 5:3
or any *l* of any thing..........Ex 20:4
l of male or female ....Deut 4:16
l of any beast that is on.......Deut 4:17
l of any winged fowl that flieth.Deut 4:17
l of..thing that creepeth ....Deut 4:18
l of any fish that is in.........Deut 4:18
graven image, or the *l* of......Deut 4:25
l of any thing..in heaven ......Deut 5:8
when I awake, with thy *l*......Ps 17:15
what *l* will ye compare ....Is 40:18
came the *l* of four living ......Ezek 1:5
had the *l* of a man ....Ezek 1:5
As for the *l* of their faces .....Ezek 1:10
and they four had one *l*.......Ezek 1:16
heads was the *l* of a throne ...Ezek 1:26
upon the *l* of the throne ......Ezek 1:26
l as the appearance of ....Ezek 1:26
lo a *l* as the appearance of ....Ezek 8:2
they four had one *l*...........Ezek 10:10
l of their faces was the ....Ezek 10:22
come down to us in the *l* of ...Acts 14:11
in the *l* of his death ....Rom 6:5
in the *l* of his resurrection.....Rom 6:5
Son in the *l* of sinful flesh .....Rom 8:3

LIKEWISE—*similarly; in addition*
L shalt thou do with thine.....Ex 22:30
l for the north side in.........Ex 27:11
L this is the law of the........Lev 7:1
L when the Lord sent you.....Deut 9:23
maidservant thou shalt do *l*....Deut 15:17
l will go with thee into........Judg 1:3
Look on me, and do *l* ....Judg 7:17
l cut down every man.........Judg 9:49
L all the men of Israel.........1Sam 14:22
he fell *l* upon his sword 1Sam 31:5
l all the men that were.........2Sam 1:11
l did he for all his strange 1Kin 11:8
he fell *l* on the sword 1Chr 10:5
l fled before Abishai..........1Chr 19:15
l cast lots over against 1Chr 24:31
l silver for the tables of 1Chr 28:16

L

all the sons l of king..........1Chr 29:24
other wing was l five........2Chr 3:11
L at the same time said I.....Neh 4:22
L shall the ladies of Persia....Esth 1:18
furrows l thereof complain....Job 31:38
l the fool and the brutish.....Ps 49:10
thyself l hast cursed..........Eccl 7:22
oxen l and the young asses....Is 30:24
L when all the Jews that......Jer 40:11
L, thou son of man...........Ezek 13:17
L the people of the land.......Ezek 46:3
they be quiet, and l many.....Nah 1:12
L shall also the Son of........Matt 17:12
ninth hour, and did l.........Matt 20:5
to the second and said l.......Matt 21:30
L the second also, and the....Matt 22:26
l he that had received two....Matt 25:17
L also the chief priests........Matt 27:41
are they l which are sown.....Mark 4:16
L also said they all...........Mark 14:31
gave thanks l unto..Lord......Luke 2:38
soldiers l demanded of him....Luke 3:14
do ye also to them l..........Luke 6:31
Go, and do thou l............Luke 10:37
ye shall all l perish...........Luke 13:5
l joy shall be in heaven.......Luke 15:7
l Lazarus evil things..........Luke 16:25
L also as it was in the days....Luke 17:28
said l to him, Be thou also....Luke 19:19
L also the cup after...........Luke 22:20
also doeth the Son l..........John 5:19
giveth them, and fish l........John 21:13
have l foretold of these.......Acts 3:24
l also the men................Rom 1:27
L the Spirit also helpeth......Rom 8:26
l also the wife unto the.......1Cor 7:3
l also he that is called, being..1Cor 7:22
Jews dissembled l with him....Gal 2:13
that ye l read the epistle......Col 4:16
L must the deacons be grave..1Tim 3:8
aged women l; that they be...Titus 2:3
l took part of the same.......Heb 2:14
L also was not Rahab the.....James 2:25
L ye husbands, dwell with.....1Pet 3:7
L ye younger, submit.........1Pet 5:5
L also these filthy............Jude 8
part of it and the night l......Rev 8:12

LIKHI (lĭk'hī)—*"learned"*
Manassite...............1Chr 7:19

LILITH (lĭl'ĭth)—*an evil female demon in Babylonian mythology*
Rendered "screech owl,"
suggesting desolation...Is 34:14

LILY—*a bulbous flowering plant*
Descriptive of:
Beauty.................Song 5:13
Spiritual growth.........Hos 14:4, 5
Christ...................Song 2:1

[*also* LILIES]
of a cup, with flowers of l.....1Kin 7:26
of a cup, with flowers of l.....2Chr 4:5
the l of the valleys...........Song 2:1
he feedeth among the l.......Song 2:16
lips like l, dropping sweet.....Song 5:13
he feedeth among the l.......Song 6:3
Consider the l of the field.....Matt 6:28
Consider..l how they grow....Luke 12:27

LILY WORK—*decorations upon the capitals of columns*
In Solomon's Temple....1Kin 7:19, 22

pillars were of l in............1Kin 7:19

LIME—*powdered limestone*
Descriptive of:
Cruel treatment.........Amos 2:1
Devastating judgment....Is 33:12

LIMIT—*boundary; extent*

[*also* LIMITED, LIMITETH]
l the Holy One of Israel......Ps 78:41
whole l thereof round about...Ezek 43:12
l a certain day, saying........Heb 4:7

LINE—*a device for measuring; a sound*
Literal uses of:
As a measurement.......Jer 31:39
Rahab's cord............Josh 2:18, 21
Figurative uses of:
God's providences.......Ps 16:6
God's judgments........Is 28:17

[*also* LINEAGE, LINES]
measured them with a l.......2Sam 8:2
with two l measured.........2Sam 8:2
l of twelve cubits............1Kin 7:15
over Jerusalem the l of......2Kin 21:13
l of thirty cubits did.........2Chr 4:2
stretched the l upon it?.......Job 38:5
l is gone out through all......Ps 19:4
upon it the l of confusion.....Is 34:11
marketh it out with a l........Is 44:13
he hath stretched out a l......Lam 2:8
with a l of flax in his hand....Ezek 40:3
land shall be divided by l.....Amos 7:17
l..be stretched forth.........Zech 1:16
of..house and l of David.....Luke 2:4
boast in another man's l......2Cor 10:16

LINEN—*cloth made from flax*
Used for:
Priestly garments........Ex 28:1, 39
Tabernacle curtains......Ex 26:1
Sacred veil..............Ex 26:31, 36
Garments for royalty....Esth 8:15
Levitical singers.........2Chr 5:12
Gifts to a woman........Ezek 16:10, 13
Clothing of the rich......Luke 16:19
Embalming.............Matt 27:59
Figurative of:
Righteousness..........Rev 19:8
Purity..................Rev 19:14
Babylon's pride.........Rev 18:2, 16

him in vestures of fine l.......Gen 41:42
scarlet and fine l............Ex 25:4
court of fine twined l.........Ex 27:9
five cubits of fine twined l....Ex 27:18
of scarlet, and fine twined l...Ex 28:6
and of fine twined l..........Ex 28:15
embroider the coat of fine l...Ex 28:39
make the mitre of fine l.......Ex 28:39
scarlet, and fine l............Ex 35:6
scarlet and in fine l...........Ex 35:35
scarlet, and fine twined l......Ex 36:35
court were of fine twined l....Ex 38:9
scarlet, and fine twined l......Ex 38:18
scarlet, and fine twined l......Ex 39:2
scarlet, and fine twined l......Ex 39:5
purple and scarlet, and..l......Ex 39:24
and goodly bonnets of fine l...Ex 39:28
l breeches of fine twined......Ex 39:28
priest shall put on his l.......Lev 6:10
l breeches shall he put........Lev 6:10
warp, or woof; of l...........Lev 13:48
a garment of woollen or l.....Lev 13:59
put on the holy l coat.........Lev 16:4
l breeches upon his flesh......Lev 16:4
be girded with a l girdle......Lev 16:4
l mitre shall he be attired.....Lev 16:4
put on the l clothes...........Lev 16:32
as of woollen and l...........Deut 22:11
girded with a l ephod.........1Sam 2:18
David was girded with a l.....2Sam 6:14
out of Egypt, and l yarn......1Kin 10:28
the l yard at a price..........1Kin 10:28
them that wrought fine l......1Chr 4:21
clothed with a robe of fine l...1Chr 15:27
upon him an ephod of l.......1Chr 15:27
out of Egypt, and l yarn......2Chr 1:16
the l yard at a price..........2Chr 1:16
and crimson and fine l........2Chr 3:14
hangings..cords of fine l.......Esth 1:6
works, with fine l of..........Prov 7:16
glasses, and the fine l.........Is 3:23
Go and get thee a l girdle.....Jer 13:1
them was clothed with l.......Ezek 9:2
man clothed with l...........Ezek 9:11
man clothed with l...........Ezek 10:6
l with embroidered work......Ezek 27:7
clothed with l garments.......Ezek 44:17
l bonnets upon their heads....Ezek 44:18
l breeches upon their loins....Ezek 44:18
a certain man clothed in l.....Dan 10:5
heard the man clothed in l....Dan 12:7
l cloth cast about..body.......Mark 14:51
And he bought fine l.........Mark 15:46
wrapped him in the l.........Mark 15:46
and wrapped it in l...........Luke 23:53
l clothes laid by..............Luke 24:12
wound it in l clothes..........John 19:40
seeth the l clothes lie.........John 20:6
clothed in pure and white l....Rev 15:6
clothed in fine l.............Rev 18:16
be arrayed in fine l...........Rev 19:8
for the fine l is..............Rev 19:8

LINGERED—*tarried*

[*also* LINGERETH]
while he l the men laid.......Gen 19:16
For except we had l..........Gen 43:10
now of a long time l not......2Pet 2:3

LINTEL—*a beam of wood overhanging the door*
Sprinkled with blood.....Ex 12:22, 23
Command to smite......Amos 9:1
Descriptive of Nineveh's
fall...................Zeph 2:14

l and side posts were a fifth...1Kin 6:31

LINUS (lī'nŭs)—*"net"*
Christian at Rome.......2Tim 4:21

LION—*a large, catlike animal*
Described as:
Strongest among beasts..Prov 30:30
Destructive.............Amos 3:12
Strong..................Judg 14:18
Fierce..................Job 10:16
Stealthy................Ps 10:9
Majestic................Prov 30:29, 30
Provoking fear..........Amos 3:8
God's use of:
Slay the disobedient.....1Kin 13:24, 26
Punish idolaters.........2Kin 17:25, 26
Show His power over....Dan 6:16-24
Figurative of:
Tribe of Judah..........Gen 49:9
Christ..................Rev 5:5
Devil...................1Pet 5:8
Transformation..........Is 11:6-8
Victory.................Ps 91:13
Boldness................Prov 28:1
Persecutors.............Ps 22:13
World empire...........Dan 7:1-4
Antichrist..............Rev 13:2

[*also* LIONESS, LIONESSES, LIONLIKE, LION'S, LIONS, LIONS']
shall rise up as a great l.......Num 23:24
up himself as a young l.......Num 23:24
he lay down as a l............Num 24:9
and as a great l..............Num 24:9
he dwelleth as a l............Deut 33:20
l roared against him..........Judg 14:5
to see the carcase of the l.....Judg 14:8
in the carcase of the l.........Judg 14:8
there came a l...............1Sam 17:34
out of the paw of the l........1Sam 17:37
were stronger than l..........2Sam 1:23
heart is as the heart of a l....2Sam 17:10
slew two l men of Moab......2Sam 23:20
between the ledges were l.....1Kin 7:29
beneath the l and oxen.......1Kin 7:29
two l stood beside the stays...1Kin 10:19
l standing by the carcase......1Kin 13:25
l standing by the carcase......1Kin 13:28
a l shall slay thee............1Kin 20:36
l found him and slew him.....1Kin 20:36
slew two l men of Moab......1Chr 11:22
a l in a pit in a snowy day....1Chr 11:22
faces were like the faces of l..1Chr 12:8
two l standing by the stays....2 Chr 9:18
roaring of the l...............Job 4:10
the voice of the fierce l.......Job 4:10

teeth of the young *l* ....Job 4:10
stout *l* whelps are scattered....Job 4:11
the fierce *l* passed by it ....Job 28:8
thou hunt the prey for the *l*? ..Job 38:39
he tear my soul like a *l* ....Ps 7:2
Like as a *l* that is greedy of ...Ps 17:12
a young *l* lurking in ....Ps 17:12
ravening and a roaring *l* ......Ps 22:13
Save me from the *l* mouth ....Ps 22:21
The young *l* do lack ....Ps 34:10
My soul is among *l* ....Ps 57:4
young *l* roar after ....Ps 104:21
is as the roaring of a *l* ....Prov 19:12
is as the roaring of a *l* ....Prov 20:2
There is a *l* in the way........Prov 26:13
As a roaring *l*..................Prov 28:15
dog is better than a dead *l* ....Eccl 9:4
Hermon, from the *l* dens......Song 4:8
roaring shall be like a *l* ....Is 5:29
roar like young *l* ....Is 5:29
And he cried, A *l*: My lord ...Is 21:8
as the *l* and the young ....Is 31:4
young *l* roaring on his prey....Is 31:4
l so will he break.............Is 38:13
young *l* roared upon him......Jer 2:15
like a destroying *l* ....Jer 2:30
l out of the forest shall slay ..Jer 5:6
his covert, as the *l*...........Jer 25:38
he shall come up like a *l*......Jer 50:44
roar together like *l* ....Jer 51:38
yell as *l* whelps ....Jer 51:38
as a *l* in secret places ....Lam 3:10
face of a *l*, on the right side ...Ezek 1:10
third the face of a *l*...........Ezek 10:14
What is thy mother? A *l* ......Ezek 19:2
she lay down among *l*.........Ezek 19:2
her whelps among young *l* ....Ezek 19:2
it became a young *l* ....Ezek 19:3
went up and down among..*l* ...Ezek 19:6
became a young *l*.............Ezek 19:6
a young *l* of the nations.......Ezek 32:2
be cast into the den of *l* ......Dan 6:7
be cast into the den of *l*? .....Dan 6:12
from the power of the *l* ....Dan 6:27
be unto Ephraim as a *l* ....Hos 5:14
young *l* to the house of ....Hos 5:14
teeth are the teeth of a *l*......Joel 1:6
Will a *l* roar in the forest .....Amos 3:4
will a young *l* cry out of ......Amos 3:4
man did flee from a *l* ....Amos 5:19
l among the beasts of ....Mic 5:8
young *l* among the flocks .....Mic 5:8
is the dwelling of the *l*........Nah 2:11
feeding place of the young *l* ...Nah 2:11
where the *l*, even the old *l* ...Nah 2:11
within her are roaring *l* ....Zeph 3:3
of the roaring of young *l*......Zech 11:3
out of the mouth of the *l* 2Tim 4:17
stopped the mouths of *l*.......Heb 11:33
first beast was like a *l* ....Rev 4:7
teeth were as the teeth of *l*....Rev 9:8
as when a *l* roareth ....Rev 10:3

LIP—*either of the fleshy folds that appear at the top and the bottom of the mouth*

Described as:
Uncircumcised ....Ex 6:12, 30
Unclean ....Is 6:5, 7
Stammering ....Is 28:11
Flattering ....Ps 12:2, 3
Perverse ....Prov 4:24
Righteous ....Prov 16:13
False ....Prov 17:4
Burning ....Prov 26:23

Of the righteous, used for:
Knowledge ....Job 33:3
Prayer ....Ps 17:1
Silent prayer 1Sam 1:13
Righteousness ....Ps 40:9
Grace ....Ps 45:2
Praise ....Ps 51:15
Vows ....Ps 66:13, 14
Singing ....Ps 71:23
God's judgments ....Ps 119:13
Feeding many ....Prov 10:21
Spiritual fruitfulness .....Hos 14:2
Heb 13:15

Of the wicked, used for:
Flattery ....Prov 7:21
Mocking ....Ps 22:7
Defiance ....Ps 12:4
Lying ....Is 59:3
Poison ....Ps 140:3, 9
Mischief ....Prov 24:2
Evil ....Prov 16:27, 30
Deception ....Prov 24:28

Warnings:
Put away perverse ....Prov 4:24
Refrain use ....Prov 17:28
1Pet 3:10
Of an adulteress, avoid ..Prov 5:3-13
Hypocrites ....Mark 7:6

[*also* LIPS]
pronouncing with his *l* ....Lev 5:4
covering upon his upper *l* .....Lev 13:45
uttered aught out of her *l* .....Num 30:6
proceeded out of her *l* ....Num 30:12
which is gone out of thy *l* .....Deut 23:23
only her *l* moved 1Sam 1:13
and my bridle in thy *l* 2Kin 19:28
did not Job sin with his *l*......Job 2:10
open his *l* against thee ....Job 11:5
own *l* testify against thee ......Job 15:6
commandment of his *l* ....Job 23:12
will open my *l* and answer ....Job 32:20
up their names into my *l*......Ps 16:4
word of thy *l* I have kept .....Ps 17:4
lying *l* be put to silence ....Ps 31:18
l from speaking guile ....Ps 34:13
O Lord, open thou my *l* ......Ps 51:15
words of their *l* ....Ps 59:12
praise thee with joyful *l*.......Ps 63:5
that is gone out of my *l* ....Ps 89:34
unadvisedly with his *l* ....Ps 106:33
My *l* shall utter praise ....Ps 119:171
O Lord, from lying *l*..........Ps 120:2
l may keep knowledge ....Prov 5:2
l of a strange woman drop ....Prov 5:3
of my *l* shall be right ....Prov 8:6
is an abomination to my *l* .....Prov 8:7
hideth hatred with lying *l* .....Prov 10:18
l of the righteous know ....Prov 10:32
l of truth shall be.............Prov 12:19
Lying *l* are abomination.......Prov 12:22
he that openeth wide his *l*.....Prov 13:3
l of the wise shall ....Prov 14:3
in him the *l* of knowledge .....Prov 14:7
l tendeth only to penury ......Prov 14:23
l of the wise disperse ....Prov 15:7
divine sentence is in the *l* .....Prov 16:10
Righteous *l* are the delight ....Prov 16:13
sweetness of the *l* ....Prov 16:21
do lying *l* a prince ....Prov 17:7
l enter into contention ....Prov 18:6
l are the snare of his soul .....Prov 18:7
increase of his *l* shall he ......Prov 18:20
l of knowledge are ....Prov 20:15
grace of his *l* the king ....Prov 22:11
when thy *l* speak right ....Prov 23:16
Every man shall kiss his *l* .....Prov 24:26
and not thine own *l* ....Prov 27:2
l of a fool shall swallow ....Eccl 10:12
l are like a thread of ....Song 4:3
l like lilies, dropping sweet ....Song 5:13
l of those that are asleep......Song 7:9
with the breath of his *l* ....Is 11:4
with their *l* do honor me ....Is 29:13
and my bridle in thy *l* ....Is 37:29
came out of my *l* was right ....Jer 17:16
l of those that rose up ....Lam 3:62
cover not thy *l* ....Ezek 24:17
taken up in the *l* of talkers ....Ezek 36:3
sons of men touched my *l*.....Dan 10:16
shall all cover their *l*..........Mic 3:7
my *l* quivered at the voice ....Hab 3:16
iniquity..not found in his *l* ....Mal 2:6
honoreth me with their *l* .....Matt 15:8
honoreth me with their *l* ......Mark 7:6
of asps is under their *l* ....Rom 3:13
other tongues and other *l* 1Cor 14:21
l that they speak no guile 1Pet 3:10

LIQUOR—*beverage, usually fermented*

[*also* LIQUORS]
ripe fruits, and of thy *l* ....Ex 22:29
he drink any *l* of grapes.......Num 6:3
goblet, which wanteth not *l* ...Song 7:2

LISTED—*willed; pleased*

[*also* LISTETH]
him whatsoever they *l* ....Matt 17:12
him whatsoever they *l* ....Mark 9:13
wind bloweth where it *l*.......John 3:8
whithersoever..governor *l* .....James 3:4

LISTEN—*to pay heed; hear attentively*
L, O isles, unto me ....Is 49:1

LITIGATION—*a lawsuit*
Christ's warning concerning ....Matt 5:25, 40
Paul's warning concerning.1 Cor. 6:1, 2

LITTER—*a covered framework for carrying a single passenger*
Of nations ....Is 66:20

[*also* LITTERS]
in chariots, and in *l*...........Is 66:20

LITTLE—*not much; small; trivial*
a *l* water, I pray you ....Gen 18:4
and it is a *l* one ....Gen 19:20
(is it not a *l* one?) ....Gen 19:20
l water of thy pitcher ....Gen 24:43
all their *l* ones, and.........Gen 34:29
Go again buy us a *l* food .....Gen 43:2
a *l* balm, and a *l* honey ....Gen 43:11
child of his old age, a *l* one ...Gen 44:20
land of Egypt for your *l*.......Gen 45:19
for food for your *l* ones ....Gen 47:24
only their *l* ones..............Gen 50:8
will let you go, and your *l* ....Ex 10:10
household be too *l* for ....Ex 12:4
By *l* and *l* I will drive.........Ex 23:30
l owl, and the cormorant......Lev 11:17
l ones, which ye said ....Num 14:31
and their *l* ones ....Num 31:9
cities for our *l* ones...........Num 32:16
Build you cities for your *l*.....Num 32:24
your *l* ones which ye said .....Deut 1:39
your wives, and you *l* ones ....Deut 3:19
before thee by *l* and *l*.........Deut 7:22
l owl, and the great owl.......Deut 14:16
shalt gather but *l* in ....Deut 28:38
Your wives, your *l* ones.......Josh 1:14
went out too *l* for them ....Josh 19:47
l pray thee, a *l* water ....Judg 4:19
she tarried a *l* in the house ....Ruth 2:7
mother made him a *l* coat 1Sam 2:19
I did but taste a *l* honey 1Sam 14:43
wast *l* in thine own sight 1Sam 15:17
and a *l* lad with him 1Sam 20:35
save one *l* ewe lamb 2Sam 12:3
l ones that were with him 2Sam 15:22
l past the top of the hill.......2Sam 16:1
I am but a *l* child 1Kin 3:7
Hadad being yet a *l* child 1Kin 11:17
I pray thee, a *l* water 1Kin 17:10
make me..a *l* cake first 1Kin 17:13
like two *l* flocks of kids 1Kin 20:27
l children out of the city 2Kin 2:23
out of the land of Israel a *l* ...2Kin 5:2
departed from him a *l* way 2Kin 5:19
My *l* finger shall be thicker....2Chr 10:10
genealogy of all their *l*........2Chr 31:18
for us, and for our *l* ones .....Ezra 8:21
l space grace hath been ....Ezra 9:8
l reviving in our bondage .....Ezra 9:8
trouble seem *l* before thee ....Neh 9:32
l children and women.........Esth 3:13
mine ear received a *l* ....Job 4:12
forth their *l* ones like a ....Job 21:11
how *l* a portion is heard ......Job 26:14
wrath is kindled but a *l* ....Ps 2:12
made him a *l* lower than ......Ps 8:5
For yet a *l* while ....Ps 37:10

L

l hills rejoice on every side ....Ps 65:12
l hills, by righteousness ....Ps 72:3
ye *l* hills, like lambs? ....Ps 114:6
a *l* sleep, a *l* slumber ....Prov 6:10
l folding of the hands to ....Prov 6:10
heart of the wicked is *l* ....Prov 10:20
l with the fear of the Lord ....Prov 15:16
l with righteousness ....Prov 16:8
a *l* sleep, a *l* slumber ....Prov 24:33
l folding of the hands ....Prov 24:33
four things which are *l* ....Prov 30:24
whether he eat *l* or much .....Eccl 5:12
so doth a *l* folly him ....Eccl 10:1
us the foxes the *l* foxes ....Song 2:15
We have a *l* sister ....Song 8:8
For yet a very *l* while ....Is 10:25
as it were for a *l* moment .....Is 26:20
here a *l* and there a *l* ....Is 28:10
here a *l*, and there a *l* ....Is 28:13
isles as a very *l* thing ....Is 40:15
A *l* one shall become a ....Is 60:22
their *l* ones to the waters .....Jer 14:3
yet a *l* while, and the time ....Jer 51:33
maids, and *l* children ....Ezek 9:6
to them as a *l* sanctuary.......Ezek 11:16
if that were a very *l* thing .....Ezek 16:47
l chamber was one reed ....Ezek 40:7
between the *l* chambers ....Ezek 40:7
before the *l* chambers ....Ezek 40:12
l chambers were six cubits .....Ezek 40:12
windows to the *l* chambers ....Ezek 40:16
l chambers thereof............Ezek 40:29
them another *l* horn ....Dan 7:8
be holpen with a *l* help ....Dan 11:34
for yet a *l* while ....Hos 1:4
l house with clefts ....Amos 6:11
l among the thousands ....Mic 5:2
sown much, and bring in *l* ....Hag 1:6
lo, it came to *l* ....Hag 1:9
Yet once, it is a *l* while ....Hag 2:6
I was but a *l* displeased ....Zech 1:15
O ye of *l* faith? ....Matt 6:30
O ye of *l* faith? ....Matt 8:26
unto one of these *l* ones ......Matt 10:42
O thou of *l* faith ....Matt 14:31
and a few *l* fishes.............Matt 15:34
O ye of *l* faith ....Matt 16:8
Jesus called a *l* child unto .....Matt 18:2
humble himself as this *l* ....Matt 18:4
offend one of these *l* ones.....Matt 18:6
one of these *l* ones should .....Matt 18:14
brought unto him *l* ....Matt 19:13
went a *l* farther ....Matt 26:39
had gone a *l* farther ....Mark 1:19
l daughter lieth at ....Mark 5:23
offend one of these *l* ones.....Mark 9:42
Suffer the *l* children to ....Mark 10:14
And he went forward a *l*......Mark 14:35
thrust out a *l* from the land ...Luke 5:3
O ye of *l* faith? ....Luke 12:28
offend one of these *l* ones.....Luke 17:2
kingdom of God as a *l*.........Luke 18:17
been faithful in a very *l* ....Luke 19:17
one of them may take a *l* .....John 6:7
l while is the light with ....John 12:35
yet a *l* while I am with........John 13:33
Yet a *l* while and the world ...John 14:19
A *l* while and ye shall not.....John 16:16
a *l* while and ye shall see .....John 16:16
A *l* while and ye shall not see .John 16:17
a *l* while and ye shall see .....John 16:17
A *l* while and ye shall not.....John 16:19
a *l* while and ye shall see .....John 16:19
put the apostles forth a *l*......Acts 5:34
had gone a *l* further ....Acts 27:28
that a *l* leaven leaveneth 1Cor 5:6
gathered *l* had no lack 2Cor 8:15
I may boast myself a *l* 2Cor 11:16
My *l* children of whom I ......Gal 4:19
exercise profiteth *l*............1Tim 4:8
him a *l* lower than.............Heb 2:7
made a *l* lower than ....Heb 2:9
For yet a *l* while ....Heb 10:37
tongue is a *l* member ....James 3:5
matter a *l* fire kindleth........James 3:5
My *l* children these things 1John 2:1
I write unto you, *l* children....1John 2:13
l children, abide in him 1John 2:28
My *l* children let us not 1John 3:18
L children, keep..............1John 5:21
thou hast a *l* strength ....Rev 3:8
had in his hand a *l* book ......Rev. 10:2
Give me the *l* book...........Rev 10:9
must be loosed a *l* season .....Rev 20:3

LIVE, LIVING—*See* LIFE

LIVELY—*active*

But mine enemies are *l* ....Ps 38:19
the *l* oracles to give unto us ...Acts 7:38
begotten us again unto a *l*.....1Pet 1:3

LIVER—*body organ that secretes bile*

Used literally of:

Animals:

In sacrifice ....Ex 29:13, 22
For divination ....Ezek 21:21

Used figuratively of:

Extreme pain or death ...Prov 7:23

caul above the *l* ....Lev 3:4
caul that is above the *l*........Lev 7:4
caul above the *l* of the sin ....Lev 9:10
l is poured upon the earth ....Lam 2:11

LIVING, CHRISTIAN—*a phrase referring to the Christian's life*

Source—Christ ....John 14:19
Length—forever ....John 11:25, 26
Means—faith in Christ ...Rom 1:17
Kind—resurrected 2Cor 5:15
End—to God ....Rom 14:7, 8
Purpose—for Christ......1Thess 5:10
Motivation—Christ ......Gal 2:20
Atmosphere—in the Spirit Gal 5:25
Manner—righteously .....Titus 2:12
Enemies—flesh and sin ..Rom 8:12, 13
Price—persecution 2Tim 3:12

LIVING CREATURES—*a phrase referring to animals or living beings*

Aquatic animals ....Gen 1:21
Land animals ....Gen 1:24
Angelic beings ....Ezek 1:5

LIZARD—*a small, swift legged reptile*

Ceremonially unclean ....Lev 11:29, 30

LO—*used to call attention to, or express wonder or surprise*

l in her mouth was an olive ...Gen 8:11
l, a horror of great darkness...Gen 15:12
l, Sarah thy wife shall.........Gen 18:10
l, there were three flocks .....Gen 29:2
l, my sheaf arose ....Gen 37:7
l, here is seed for you ....Gen 47:23
swear, saying, *L*, I die ....Gen 50:5
l, he cometh forth ....Ex 8:20
L, I come unto thee in a thick .Ex 19:9
L, we be here ....Num 14:40
l, he stood by his burnt ....Num 23:6
l, the Lord kept thee back ....Num 24:11
l, he hath given occasions .....Deut 22:17
l, I am this day fourscore .....Josh 14:10
l, a cake of barley bread ......Judg 7:13
l, Eli sat upon a seat 1Sam 4:13
l, I must die 1Sam 14:43
l, the chariots and horsemen ..2Sam 1:6
l, while she yet talked 1Kin 1:22
l, I have given thee a wise 1Kin 3:12
l, I give thee the oxen 1Chr 21:23
l, they are written in..book 2Chr 16:11
l, they are written in..book 2Chr 27:7
l, we bring into bondage ......Neh 5:5
L, let that night be solitary ....Job 3:7
L, he goeth by me.............Job 9:11
L, mine eye hath seen all this .Job 13:1
L, these are parts of ....Job 26:14
L now, his strength is ....Job 40:16
l, the wicked bend their bow ..Ps 11:2
Then said I, *L*, I come ....Ps 40:7
l, the kings were assembled ...Ps 48:4
L, then would I wander ....Ps 55:7
l, he doth send out ....Ps 68:33
l, thine enemies make ....Ps 83:2
l, thine enemies, O Lord......Ps 92:9
l, thine enemies shall perish ...Ps 92:9
L, we heard of it at Ephratah .Ps 132:6
l, it was all grown over ....Prov 24:31
L, I am come to great estate ..Eccl 1:16
l the winter is past ....Song 2:11
L, this hath touched thy lips...Is 6:7
L, thou trustest...............Is 36:6
l, they all shall wax old ....Is 50:9
l, I will call all the families ....Jer 1:15
l, they trembled ....Jer 4:24
l, the fruitful place ....Jer 4:26
L..in vain made he it ....Jer 8:8
l, I begin to bring evil ....Jer 25:29
l, I will save thee from........Jer 30:10
l, I will make thee small ......Jer 49:15
l, a roll of a book ....Ezek 2:9
l a likeness as..appearance ....Ezek 8:2
l, others daubed it with ....Ezek 13:10
l, he had given his hand ......Ezek 17:18
l, even he shall die ....Ezek 18:18
and *l*, they came ....Ezek 23:40
l, it shall not be bound up ....Ezek 30:21
l, they were very dry ....Ezek 37:2
l, there were chambers........Ezek 40:17
L, I see four men loose ....Dan 3:25
l, Michael, one of the chief ...Dan 10:13
l, they are gone because of....Hos 9:6
l, the days shall come upon ...Amos 4:2
l, it was the latter growth .....Amos 7:1
l, I raise up the Chaldeans ....Hab 1:6
l, it came to little............Hag 1:9
l, I come and I will dwell .....Zech 2:10
l, I will raise up ....Zech 11:16
l, the star, which they saw ....Matt 2:9
l a voice from heaven ....Matt 3:17
l, there thou hast that ....Matt 25:25
l, I have told you.............Matt 28:7
L, we have left all ....Mark 10:28
l, he that betrayeth me ....Mark 14:42
l, as soon as the voice ....Luke 1:44
l, a spirit taketh him..........Luke 9:39
L, these many years do I serve.Luke 15:29
L, here! or *l* there! ....Luke 17:21
l, nothing worthy of death ....Luke 23:15
l, he speaketh boldly ....John 7:26
l, we turn to the Gentiles .....Acts 13:46
L, I come (in the volume .....Heb 10:7
l, in the midst of the throne ...Rev 5:6
l..was a great earthquake .....Rev 6:12
l, a Lamb stood on the mount .Rev 14:1

LOAD, LOADEN—*See* LADE

LOAF—*a shaped piece of bread*

[*also* LOAVES]

And one *l* of bread ....Ex 29:23
l of two tenth deals ....Lev 23:17
l of bread unto the people ....Judg 8:5
carrying three *l* of bread 1Sam 10:3
corn, and these ten *l*..........1Sam 17:17
took two hundred *l* 1Sam 25:18
upon them two hundred *l* 2Sam 16:1
take with thee ten *l*...........1Kin 14:3
twenty *l* of barley 2Kin 4:42
to every one a *l* of bread 1Chr 16:3
We have here but five *l*.......Matt 14:17
five *l* and the two fishes.......Matt 14:19
gave the *l* to his disciples .....Matt 14:19
How many *l* have ye?.........Matt 15:34
seven *l* and the fishes ....Matt 15:36
Neither the seven *l* ....Matt 16:10
How many *l* have ye?.........Mark 6:38
had taken the five *l*...........Mark 6:41
blessed, and brake the *l*.......Mark 6:41
not the miracle of the *l* ....Mark 6:52
How many *l* have ye?.........Mark 8:5
seven *l* and gave thanks ....Mark 8:6
with them more than one *l* ....Mark 8:14
have no more but five *l* ....Luke 9:13
Friend, lend me three *l* ....Luke 11:5
which hath five barley *l* ....John 6:9
of the five barley *l* ....John 6:13
ye did eat of the *l* ....John 6:26

LO-AMMI (lō-ăm'ī)—*"not my people"*
Symbolic name of
Hosea's son ....Hos 1:8, 9

LOAN—*See* **Borrow; Lending**

LOATHE—*to despise*

[*also* **loatheth, loathsome, lothe, lothed, lotheth, lothing**]
Egyptians shall *l* to drink .....Ex 7:18
and it be *l* unto you ....Num 11:20
soul *l* this light bread ....Num 21:5
broken, and become *l*.........Job 7:5
I *l* it; I would not live ....Job 7:16
filled with a *l* disease ....Ps 38:7
a wicked man is *l*.............Prov 13:5
full soul *l* an honeycomb ......Prov 27:7
hath thy soul *l* Zion? ....Jer 14:19
l themselves for the evils ......Ezek 6:9
to the *l* of thy person ....Ezek 16:5
l her husband and her ....Ezek 16:45
l their husbands ....Ezek 16:45
l yourselves in your own ......Ezek 20:43
l yourselves in your own ......Ezek 36:31
my soul *l* them ....Zech 11:8

LOCK—*a curl of hair; a device for securing doors, gates, or drawers, for example*
Doors ....Judg 3:23, 24
Hair ....Judg 16:13, 19
City gates ....Neh 3:6, 13, 14

[*also* **locks**]
l of the hair of his head ....Num 6:5
doves' eyes within thy *l* ....Song 4:1
pomegranate within thy *l*......Song 4:3
upon the handles of the *l* .....Song 5:5
l are bushy, and black ....Song 5:11
uncover thy *l*, make bare .....Is 47:2
took me by a *l* of mine head ..Ezek 8:8
nor suffer their *l* to grow......Ezek 44:20

LOCUST—*a devastating, migratory insect*

Types, or stages, of:
Eating ....Joel 1:4
Devastating ....Lev 11:22

Using literally of insects:
Miraculously brought forth ....Ex 10:12-19
Sent as a judgment ......Deut 28:38
1Kin 8:37
Used for food ....Matt 3:4

Used figuratively of:
Weakness ....Ps 109:23, 24
Running men ....Is 33:4
Nineveh's departing glory .Nah. 3:15, 17
Final plagues ....Rev 9:3, 7

See **Grasshopper**

[*also* **locusts**]
bring the *l* into thy coast ......Ex 10:4
the *l* after his kind ....Lev 11:22
bald *l* after his kind ....Lev 11:22
be blasting, or mildew, *l* 2Chr 6:28
command the *l* to devour 2Chr 7:13
their labor unto the *l* ....Ps 78:46
spake, and the *l* came ....Ps 105:34
the *l* have no king ....Prov 30:27
hath the *l* eaten ....Joel 1:4
that which the *l* hath left ......Joel 1:4
years that the *l* hath eaten ....Joel 2:25
eat *l* and wild honey ....Mark 1:6

LOD (lŏd)—*"nativity"*
Benjamite town 1Chr 8:1, 12
Mentioned in postexilic books ....Ezra 2:33
Aeneas healed here, called Lydda ....Acts 9:32-35

of *L*, Hadid, and Ono ....Neh 7:37
L, and Ono ....Neh 11:35

LO-DEBAR (lō-dē'ber)
City in Manasseh (in Gilead) 2Sam 9:4, 5
David flees to 2Sam 17:27

LODGE—*to pass the night; place to stay*
Travelers—in a house ....Judg 19:4-20
Spies—in a house ....Josh 2:1
Animals—in ruins ....Zeph 2:14
Birds—in trees ....Matt 13:32
Righteousness—in a city. .Is 1:21
Thought—in Jerusalem . .Jer. 4:14

[*also* **lodged, lodgest, lodgeth, lodging, lodgings**]
father's house..to *l* in? ....Gen 24:23
l there that same night ....Gen 32:13
l that night in the company ....Gen 32:21
L here this night ....Num 22:8
l there before they passed .....Josh 3:1
leave them in the *l* place ......Josh 4:3
where ye..*l* this night ....Josh 4:3
and *l* in the camp ....Josh 6:11
house of Micah, they *l* there ..Judg 18:2
and my concubine, to *l* ....Judg 20:4
and where thou *l*, I will *l* .....Ruth 1:16
will not *l* with the people 2Sam 17:8
unto a cave, and *l* 1Kin 19:9
enter into the *l* of his borders .2Kin 19:23
l round about the house 1Chr 9:27
one with his servant *l* ....Neh 4:22
sellers of all kind of ware *l* ....Neh 13:20
naked to *l* without clothing ....Job 24:7
let us *l* in the villages ....Song 7:11
as a *l* in a garden.............Is 1:8
taken up their *l* at Geba ......Is 10:29
l in the monuments ....Is 65:4
had in the wilderness a *l* ......Jer 9:2
into Bethany; and he *l* ....Matt 21:17
air may *l* under the shadow ...Mark 4:32
round about, and *l* ....Luke 9:12
fowls of the air *l* ....Luke 13:19
l with one Simon a tanner.....Acts 10:6
Peter, were *l* there ....Acts 10:18
l in the house of one Simon ...Acts 10:32
with whom we should *l* ....Acts 21:16
l us three days courteously ....Acts 28:7
came many to him into his *l*...Acts 28:23
if she have *l* strangers.........1Tim 5:10
withal prepare me also a *l*.....Philem 22

LOFT—*an upstairs room*
Dead child taken to 1Kin 17:19-24
Young man falls from....Acts 20:9

carried him up into a *l*........1Kin 17:19

LOFTY—*haughty, overbearing character; elevated*

[*also* **loftily, loftiness**]
oppression: they speak *l* ......Ps 73:8
nor mine eyes *l* ....Ps 131:1
O how *l* are their eyes ....Prov 30:13
l looks of man shall be........Is 2:11
every one that is proud and *l*. .Is 2:12
l of man shall be bowed down .Is 2:17
eyes of the *l* shall be humbled .Is 5:15
l and high mountain ....Is 57:7
high and *l* one that inhabiteth. .Is 57:15
l, and his arrogancy ....Jer 48:29

LOG—*a unit of volume (liquid)*
and one *l* of oil ....Lev 14:10
take some of the *l* of oil ......Lev 14:15
offering, and the *l* of oil ......Lev 14:24

LOINS—*abdominal region; also generative organs*

Used literally of:
Hips...................Gen. 37:34
Ex 28:42
Waist...................2Sam 20:8

Used figuratively of:
Physical strength ....Ps 66:11
Source of knowledge.....Eph. 6:14
Source of hope 1Pet 1:13

shall come out of thy *l*........Gen 35:11
which came out of his *l* ....Gen 46:26
souls that came out of the *l* ...Ex 1:5
l even unto the thighs.........Ex 28:42
smite through the *l* ....Deut 33:11
sword fastened upon his *l* 2Sam 20:8
girdle that was about his *l* 1Kin 2:5
thicker than my father's *l* 1Kin 12:10
put sackcloth on our *l* 1Kin 20:31
of leather about his *l* 2Kin 1:8
Gird up thy *l* 2Kin 9:1
come forth out of thy *l* 2Chr 6:9
their *l* with a girdle ....Job 12:18
Gird up now thy *l* ....Job 38:3
strength is in his *l* ....Job 40:16
l are filled with a loathsome ...Ps 38:7
l continually to shake ....Ps 69:23
girdeth her *l* with strength.....Prov 31:17
girdle of their *l* be loosed .....Is 5:27
sackcloth from off thy *l* ....Is 20:2
gird sackcloth upon your *l*.....Is 32:11
therefore gird up thy *l* ....Jer 1:17
Lord, and put it on my *l*.......Jer 13:2
the girdle cleaveth to the *l* ....Jer 13:11
and upon the *l* sackcloth ......Jer 48:37
appearance of his *l* even ......Ezek 1:27
of his *l* even upward ....Ezek 8:2
from his *l* even upward ....Ezek 8:2
with girdles upon their *l* ......Ezek 23:15
breeches upon their *l* ....Ezek 44:18
joints of his *l* were loosed .....Dan 5:6
up sackcloth upon all *l*........Amos 8:10
way, make thy *l* strong.........Nah 2:1
leathern girdle about his *l* .....Matt 3:4
with a girdle..about his *l* ......Mark 1:6
Let your *l* be girded about ....Luke 12:35
that of the fruit of his *l* ....Acts 2:30
l girt about with truth.........Eph 6:14
out of the *l* of Abraham ......Heb 7:5
gird up the *l* of your mind 1Pet 1:13

LOIS (lō'ĭs)—*"pleasing; better"*
Timothy's grandmother ..2Tim 1:5

LONELINESS—*sadness due to being separated from someone or something*
Jacob—in prayer ....Gen 32:23-30
Joseph—in weeping......Gen 43:30, 31
Elijah in discouragement .1Kin 19:3-14
Jeremiah—in witnessing ..Jer 15:17
Nehemiah—in a vigil ....Neh 2:12-16
Christ—in agony ....Matt 26:36-45
Paul—in prison 2Tim 4:16

LONG—*a considerable period of time; a great distance from one end to another; to have strong desire*

[*also* **longed, longedst, longer, longeth, longing**]
had been there a *l* time ....Gen 26:8
l after thy father's house ......Gen 31:30
soul of my son Shechem *l* .....Gen 34:8
she could not *l* hide him ......Ex 2:3
How *l* wilt thou refuse to .....Ex 10:3
How *l* shall this man be a .....Ex 10:7
the trumpet soundeth *l*........Ex 19:13
days may be *l* upon the ....Ex 20:12
of a hundred cubits *l* for ......Ex 27:9
as *l* as she is put apart ....Lev 18:19
As *l* as it lieth desolate ....Lev 26:35
as *l* as the cloud abode ....Num 9:18
l will this people provoke .....Num 14:11
l will it be ere they believe ....Num 14:11
dwelt in Egypt a *l* time ....Num 20:15
have dwelt *l* enough in........Deut 1:6
remained *l* in the land ....Deut 4:25
thy soul *l* to eat flesh ....Deut 12:20
if the way be too *l* for thee ...Deut 14:24
besiege a city a *l* time ....Deut 20:19
l for them all the day ....Deut 28:32
plagues, and of *l* continuance ..Deut 28:59
and of *l* continuance ....Deut 28:59
cover him all the day *l*........Deut 33:12
l blast with the ram's horn ....Josh 6:5
made war a *l* time with all ....Josh 11:18
l time after that the Lord .....Josh 23:1
l stand before..enemies ....Judg 2:14
his chariot so *l* in coming? ....Judg 5:28
as *l* as he liveth he shall 1Sam 1:28
How *l* wilt thou mourn for 1Sam 16:1
l as we were conversant.......1Sam 25:15
how *l* shall it be then, ere 2Sam 2:26

David *l* to go forth unto 2Sam 13:39
woman that had a *l* time 2Sam 14:2
tarried *l* than the set time 2Sam 20:5
not asked for thyself *l* life 1Kin 3:11
How *l* halt ye between two 1Kin 18:21
wait for the Lord any *l*? 2Kin 6:33
l as the whoredoms of 2Kin 9:22
And David *l*, and said 1Chr 11:17
yet has asked *l* life 2Chr 1:11
scaffold, of five cubits *l* 2Chr 6:13
for a *l* season Israel hath 2Chr 15:3
had not done it of a *l* time 2Chr 30:5
l as I see Mordecai the Jew ...Esth 5:13
Which *l* for death, but it ......Job 3:21
How *l* wilt thou not depart ....Job 7:19
How *l* wilt thou speak ....Job 8:2
how *l* shall the words ....Job 8:2
thereof is *l* than the earth .....Job 11:9
How *l* will it be ere ye.........Job 18:2
How *l* will ye vex my soul ....Job 19:2
l will ye turn my glory ....Ps 4:2
how *l* will ye love vanity ....Ps 4:2
but thou, O Lord, how *l*? ......Ps 6:3
How *l* wilt thou forget me ....Ps 13:1
l wilt thou hide thy face........Ps 13:1
How *l* shall I take counsel ....Ps 13:2
how *l* shall mine enemy be ....Ps 13:2
Lord, how *l* wilt thou look ....Ps 35:17
go mourning all the day *l* .....Ps 38:6
God we boast all the day *l* .....Ps 44:8
l will ye imagine mischief .....Ps 62:3
my flesh *l* for thee in a dry....Ps 63:1
as *l* as the sun and moon .....Ps 72:5
continued as *l* as the sun ......Ps 72:17
any that knoweth how *l*........Ps 74:9
l wilt thou be angry against ...Ps 80:4
l, Lord? Wilt thou hide ....Ps 89:46
l life will I satisfy him ....Ps 91:16
how *l* shall the wicked ....Ps 94:3
l shall the wicked triumph .....Ps 94:3
sing unto the Lord as *l* as .....Ps 104:33
satisfieth the *l* soul, and........Ps 107:9
call upon him as *l* as I live ....Ps 116:2
I have *l* after thy precepts .....Ps 119:40
I have *l* for thy salvation ......Ps 119:174
they made *l* their furrows .....Ps 129:3
How *l* ye simple ones, will ....Prov 1:22
How *l* wilt thou sleep, O ....Prov 6:9
He coveteth..all the day *l* .....Prov 21:26
that tarry *l* at the wine ....Prov 23:30
man goeth to his *l* home ......Eccl 12:5
Then said I, Lord, how *l*? .....Is 6:11
Hast thou not heard *l* ago .....Is 37:26
elect shall *l* enjoy the work.....Is 65:22
How *l* shall thy vain thoughts..Jer 4:14
l shall the land mourn ....Jer 12:4
This captivity is *l*: build ye ....Jer 29:28
the Lord could no *l* bear ....Jer 44:22
how *l* wilt thou cut thyself ....Jer 47:5
and children of a span *l*? ......Lam 2:20
his branches became *l*.........Ezek 31:5
chamber was one reed *l*........Ezek 40:7
five and twenty cubits *l* ....Ezek 40:30
of a cubit and an half *l* ....Ezek 40:42
house a hundred cubits *l* ......Ezek 41:13
a hundred cubits *l* ....Ezek 41:13
as *l* as they, and as broad .....Ezek 42:11
altar..be twelve cubits *l* ....Ezek 43:16
suffer their locks to grow *l* ....Ezek 44:20
joined of forty cubits *l* ....Ezek 46:22
l shall be the vision ....Dan 8:13
How *l* shall it be to the end ..Dan 12:6
l will it be ere they attain .....Hos 8:5
O Lord, how *l* shall I cry ......Hab 1:2
l wilt thou not have mercy .....Zech 1:12
as *l* as the bridegroom is ......Matt 9:15
how *l* shall I be with you? ....Matt 17:17
how *l* shall I suffer you? ......Matt 17:17
After a *l* time the lord of .....Matt 25:19
as *l* as they have the..........Mark 2:19
how *l* shall I be with you? ....Mark 9:19
how *l* shall I suffer you? ......Mark 9:19
love to go in *l* clothing.........Mark 12:38
in a *l* white garment ....Mark 16:5
tarried so *l* in the temple......Luke 1:21
how *l* shall I be with you .....Luke 9:41
mayest be no *l* steward ....Luke 16:2
a far country for a *l* time .....Luke 20:9
a show make *l* prayers ....Luke 20:47
now a *l* time in that case ......John 5:6
How *l* dost thou make us .....John 10:24
of *l* time he had bewitched ....Acts 8:11
they abode *l* time with the ....Acts 14:28
desired him to tarry *l* time ....Acts 18:20
talked a *l* while, even till......Acts 20:11
l abstinence Paul stood........Acts 27:21
l to see you, that I may ....Rom 1:11
dead to sin, live any *l*.........Rom 6:2
law to her husband so *l* as ....Rom 7:2
All day *l* I have stretched .....Rom 10:21
as *l* as her husband liveth 1Cor 7:39
If a man have *l* hair, it is 1Cor 11:14
Charity suffereth *l*, and is 1Cor 13:4
l after you for the..grace 2Cor 9:14
no *l* under a schoolmaster .....Gal 3:25
heir, as *l* as he is a child ......Gal 4:1
mayest live *l* on the earth ......Eph 6:3
how greatly I *l* after you ......Phil 1:8
For he *l* after you all, and ....Phil 2:26
we could no *l* forbear, we 1Thess 3;1
But if I tarry *l*, that thou 1Tim 3:15
Drink no *l* water, but use 1Tim 5:23
Today, after so *l* a time........Heb 4:7
and hath *l* patience for it......James 5:7
ye are, as *l* as ye do well 1Pet 3:6
he no *l* should live the rest 1Pet 4:2
l as I am in this tabernacle 2Pet 1:13
How *l*, O Lord, holy and .....Rev 6:10
there should be time no *l* .....Rev 10:6

LONGEVITY—*a great span of life*
Allotted years, 70 ....Ps 90:10
See LENGTH OF LIFE

LONG-SUFFERING—*forebearance*

Manifested in God's:
Description of His nature.Ex 34:6
Delay in executing wrath .Rom 9:22
Dealing with sinful men ..Rom 2:4
Desire for man's salvation.2Pet 3:9, 15

As a Christian grace:
Exemplified by the prophets ("patience")..James 5:10
Manifested by Old Testament saints ("patience") ....Heb 6:12
Produced by the Spirit ...Gal. 5:22
Witnessed in Paul's life ..2Cor 6:6
Taught as a virtue ....Eph 4:1
Given power for.........Col 1:11
Set for imitation.........2Tim 3:10
Needed by preachers 2Tim 4:2

Lord is *l*, and of great mercy ..Num 14:18
l, and plenteous in mercy .....Ps 86:15
take me not away in thy *l*.....Jer 15:15
humbleness..meekness, *l* ......Col 3:12
l of God waited in the days ...1Pet 3:20

LONGWINGED—*having lengthy wings*
eagle with great wings, *l* ......Ezek 17:3

LOOK—*to direct one's gaze; search; stare at; appear to be*
Promise ....Gen 15:5
Warning ....Gen 19:17, 26
Astonishment ....Ex 3:2-6
Disdain 1Sam 17:42
Lust 2Sam 11:2-4
Encouragement.........Ps 34:5
Disappointment ....Is 5:2, 4
Salvation ....Is 45:22
Glory ....Acts 7:55

[*also* LOOKED, LOOKEST, LOOKETH, LOOKING, LOOKS]

And God *l* upon the earth ....Gen 6:12
and I will *l* upon it, that ......Gen 9:16
l from the place where ....Gen 13:14
l after him that seeth me? .....Gen 16:13
and *l* toward Sodom ....Gen 18:16
damsel was very fair to *l* ......Gen 24:16
Philistines *l* out..window ......Gen 26:8
Lord..*l* upon my affliction .....Gen 29:32
lifted up their eyes and *l* ......Gen 37:25
in the morning, and *l* upon....Gen 40:6
Wherefore *l* ye so sadly ....Gen 40:7
do ye *l* one upon another? ....Gen 42:1
and *l* on their burdens ....Ex 2:11
God *l* upon the children of....Ex 2:25
l upon their affliction ....Ex 4:31
The Lord *l* upon you, and ....Ex 5:21
morning watch the Lord *l* .....Ex 14:24
l toward the wilderness ....Ex 16:10
faces shall *l* one to another....Ex 25:20
Moses did *l* upon..the work ...Ex 39:43
priest shall *l* on the plague ....Lev 13:3
the priest shall *l* on him........Lev 13:3
priest shall *l* on him again .....Lev 13:6
wheresoever the priest *l*.......Lev 13:12
the priest shall *l* upon it.......Lev 13:25
the priest shall *l* upon him ....Lev 13:27
priest shall *l* on the plague ....Lev 13:32
the priest shall *l* on him.......Lev 13:36
the priest shall *l* upon it.......Lev 13:43
he shall *l* on the plague ....Lev 13:51
priest shall *l*, and, behold .....Lev 13:53
priest shall *l* on the plague ....Lev 13:55
priest shall *l*, and, behold .....Lev 14:3
l: and, behold, if the plague ..Lev 14:39
priest shall come and *l*........Lev 14:44
and Aaron *l* upon Miriam .....Num 12:10
that ye may *l* upon it ....Num 15:39
they *l*, and took every man....Num 17:9
he *l* upon it, shall live ....Num 21:8
that *l* toward Jeshimon........Num 23:28
l on the Kenites, and took ....Num 24:21
And I *l*, and..ye had sinned ..Deut 9:16
l not unto the stubbornness.....Deut 9:27
thine eyes shall *l*, and fail .....Deut 28:32
lifted up his eyes and *l*........Josh 5:13
the bay that *l* southward ....Josh 15:2
northward, *l* toward Gilgal ....Josh 15:7
Sisera *l* out at a window ......Judg 5:28
L on me, and do likewise .....Judg 7:17
laid wait in the field, and *l* ....Judg 9:43
Manoah and his wife *l* on .....Judg 13:20
l on the affliction of thine 1Sam 1:11
l into the ark of the Lord 1Sam 6:19
I have *l* upon my people 1Sam 9:16
border that *l* to the valley 1Sam 13:18
in Gibeah of Benjamin *l* 1Sam 14:16
man *l* on the outward 1Sam 16:7
the Lord *l* on the heart 1Sam 16:7
and goodly to *l* to 1Sam 16:12
And when the Philistine *l* 1Sam 17:42
when he *l* behind him.........2Sam 1:7
daughter *l* through a 2Sam 6:16
l upon such a dead dog as I ...2Sam 9:8
Lord..*l* on mine affliction 2Sam 16:12
lifted up his eyes, and *l* 2Sam 18:24
Araunah *l*, and saw the king ..2Sam 24:20
oxen, three *l* toward the north .1Kin 7:25
and three *l* toward the west ...1Kin 7:25
and three *l* toward the south ..1Kin 7:25
and three *l* toward the east....1Kin 7:25
Go up now, *l* toward the sea ..1Kin 18:43
And he went up, and *l*, and ..1Kin 18:43
he turned back, and *l* on 2Kin 2:24
I would not *l* toward thee 2Kin 3:14
l out there Jehu the son of 2Kin 9:2
and *l* out at a window 2Kin 9:30
l that there be here with 2Kin 10:23
she *l*, behold, the king 2Kin 11:14
the God of our fathers *l* 1Chr 12:17
l out at a window saw king....1Chr 15:29
Ornan *l* and saw David 1Chr 21:21
oxen three *l* toward the north .2Chr 4:4
and three *l* toward the west ...2Chr 4:4
and three *l* toward the south ..2Chr 4:4
and three *l* toward the east....2Chr 4:4
Judah *l* back, behold 2Chr 13:14
l, and, behold, the king 2Chr 23:13
The Lord *l* upon it, and.......2Chr 24:22
I *l*, and rose up, and said .....Neh 4:14
for she was fair to *l* on ....Esth 1:11
all them that *l* upon her.......Esth 2:15
l for light, but have..........Job 3:9

troops of Tema *l*, the ....Job 6:19
hireling *l* for the reward of ....Job 7:2
l narrowly unto all my paths...Job 13:27
no man *l* for his goods........Job 20:21
He *l* upon men, and if any ....Job 33:27
L on every one that is ....Job 40:12
prayer unto thee and will *l* ....Ps 5:3
Lord *l* down from heaven ......Ps 14:2
but wilt bring down high *l*......Ps 18:27
L upon mine affliction and ....Ps 25:18
The Lord *l* from heaven ......Ps 33:13
They *l* unto him, and were ....Ps 34:5
that I am not able to *l* up .....Ps 40:12
God *l* down from heaven .....Ps 53:2
I *l* for some to take pity ......Ps 69:20
l upon the face..anointed......Ps 84:9
high *l* and a proud heart ......Ps 101:5
l down from the height of .....Ps 102:19
l on the earth..it trembleth ....Ps 104:32
eyes of servants *l* unto the ....Ps 123:2
I *l* on my right hand, and .....Ps 142:4
Let thine eyes *l* right on ......Prov 4:25
A proud *l*, a lying tongue .....Prov 6:17
I *l* through my casement ....Prov 7:6
prudent man *l* well to his .....Prov 14:15
L not thou upon the wine .....Prov 23:31
I *l* upon it, and received ......Prov 24:32
She *l* well to the ways of......Prov 31:27
I *l* on all the works that.......Eccl 2:11
l out of the windows..........Eccl 12:3
L not upon me, because I .....Song 1:6
the sun hath *l* upon me ....Song 1:6
he *l* forth at the windows .....Song 2:9
that we may *l* upon thee ......Song 6:13
which *l* toward Damascus .....Song 7:4
l of man shall be humbled ....Is 2:11
he *l* for judgment, but ....Is 5:7
and if one *l* unto the land .....Is 5:30
their God, and *l* upward ......Is 8:21
they shall *l* unto the earth.....Is 8:22
shall narrowly *l* upon thee.....Is 14:16
shall a man *l* to his Maker ....Is 17:7
shall not *l* to the altars........Is 17:8
l in that day to the armor .....Is 22:8
he that *l* upon it seeth ....Is 28:4
L upon Zion, the city of ......Is 33:20
eyes fail with *l* upward........Is 38:14
l, ye blind, that ye may see ...Is 42:18
L unto me, and be ye saved...Is 45:22
l unto the rock whence ye.....Is 51:1
L unto Abraham your ....Is 51:2
l upon the earth beneath ......Is 51:6
they all *l* to their own way ....Is 56:11
I *l* and there was none to .....Is 63:5
L down from heaven, and .....Is 63:15
l upon the carcases of..men ...Is 66:24
l for peace, but no good ......Jer 8:15
while ye *l* for light, he turn ...Jer 13:16
Take him, and *l* well to ....Jer 39:12
and I will *l* well unto thee.....Jer 40:4
fled apace, and *l* not back.....Jer 46:5
the fathers shall not *l* back ....Jer 47:3
this is the day that we *l*.......Lam 2:16
Till the Lord *l* down, and .....Lam 3:50
l and behold, a whirlwind .....Ezek 1:4
nor be dismayed at their *l*.....Ezek 2:6
l, behold, a hand ....Ezek 2:9
that *l* toward the north........Ezek 8:3
I *l*, and..in the firmament .....Ezek 10:1
the head *l* they followed it ....Ezek 10:11
images, he *l* in the liver ....Ezek 21:21
all of them princes to *l*........Ezek 23:15
which *l* toward the east ....Ezek 40:6
that *l* toward the east ....Ezek 43:1
shall *l* toward the east ....Ezek 43:17
I *l*, and, behold, the glory.....Ezek 44:4
that *l* toward the east ....Ezek 46:1
the way that *l* eastward ....Ezek 47:2
our countenances be *l* upon ...Dan 1:13
l was more stout than his .....Dan 7:20
I Daniel *l*, and, behold ....Dan 12:5
who *l* to other gods............Hos 3:1
shouldest not have *l* on ....Obad 12
l again toward thy holy ......Jon 2:4
let our eye *l* upon Zion ....Mic 4:11
I will *l* unto the Lord ....Mic 7:7
cry; but none shall *l* back .....Nah 2:8
canst not *l* on iniquity ....Hab 1:13
l thou upon them that ....Hab 1:13
Ye *l* for much, and, lo, it .....Hag 1:9
lifted..eyes again, and *l*.......Zech 2:1
lifted up mine eyes, and *l* .....Zech 5:1
lifted up mine eyes, and *l* .....Zech 6:1
shall *l* upon me whom they....Zech 12:10
l on a woman to lust after ....Matt 5:28
or do we *l* for another? ....Matt 11:3
l up to heaven, he blessed ....Matt 14:19
day when he *l* not for him ....Matt 24:50
when he had *l* round ....Mark 3:5
l round about to see her ......Mark 5:32
l up to heaven, he sighed .....Mark 7:34
he *l* up, and said, I see men...Mark 8:24
eyes, and made him *l* up ......Mark 8:25
they had *l* round about ....Mark 9:8
when he had *l* round about....Mark 11:11
were also women *l* on afar ....Mark 15:40
And when they *l*, they saw ....Mark 16:4
in the days wherein he *l* on ...Luke 1:25
l round about upon them .....Luke 6:10
or *l* we for another? ....Luke 7:19
l up to heaven, he blessed ....Luke 9:16
I beseech thee, *l* upon my son .Luke 9:38
l on him, and passed ....Luke 10:32
day when he *l* not for him ....Luke 12:46
l up, and saw the rich men ....Luke 21:1
and for *l* after those things ....Luke 21:26
l up, and lift up your heads ...Luke 21:28
Lord..*l* upon Peter ....Luke 22:61
l upon Jesus as he walked.....John 1:36
eyes, and *l* on the fields.......John 4:35
disciples *l* one on another .....John 13:22
l on him whom they pierced....John 19:37
l steadfastly toward heaven ....Acts 1:10
with John, said, *L* on us ......Acts 3:4
why *l* ye so earnestly on us....Acts 3:12
l ye out among you seven .....Acts 6:3
l steadfastly on him, saw ......Acts 6:15
he *l* on him, he was afraid ....Acts 10:4
of your law, *l* ye to it.........Acts 18:15
they *l* when he should have ...Acts 28:6
after they had *l* a great ....Acts 28:6
l for him with the brethren 1Cor 16:11
not steadfastly *l* to the end 2Cor 3:13
l not at the things which 2Cor 4:18
l on things after the outward ..2Cor 10:7
L not every man on his ....Phil 2:4
also we *l* for the Savior ....Phil 3:20
L for that blessed hope ....Titus 2:13
unto them that *l* for him ......Heb 9:28
fearful *l* for of judgment ......Heb 10:27
l for a city which hath ....Heb 11:10
L unto Jesus the author ....Heb 12:2
L diligently lest any man ......Heb 12:15
l into perfect law of ....James 1:25
the angels desire to *l* into 1Pet 1:12
L for and hasting unto the 2Pet 3:12
l for new heavens and a.......2Pet 3:13
which we have *l* upon, and....1John 1:1
L to yourselves, that we ......2 John 8
l for the mercy of our Lord ...Jude 21
After this I *l*, and, behold .....Rev 4:1
was to *l* upon like a jasper ....Rev 4:3
read the book, neither to *l* ....Rev 5:4
I *l*, and, lo, a Lamb stood ....Rev 14:1
I *l* and behold a white cloud ..Rev 14:14
And after that I *l*, and........Rev 15:5

LOOKING GLASSES—*mirrors*

l g of the women assembling ..Ex 38:8

LOOPS—*devices for tying down the covering of the Tabernacle*

l of blue upon the edge ....Ex 26:4
Fifty *l* shalt thou make in .....Ex 26:5
l may take hold one of another.Ex 26:5
fifty *l*..edge of the curtain .....Ex 26:10
made *l* of blue on the edge....Ex 36:11
Fifty *l* made he in one ....Ex 36:12
fifty *l* made he in the edge ....Ex 36:12
the *l* held one curtain to ......Ex 36:12
fifty *l* made he upon the edge. .Ex 36:17

LOOSE—*to unfasten; relieve; not tight; not confined; not fastened*

[*also* LOOSED, LOOSETH, LOOSING]

Naphtali is a hind let *l*........Gen 49:21
breastplate be not *l* from......Ex 28:28
living bird *l* into the open .....Lev 14:7
l his shoe from off his foot ....Deut 25:9
him that hath his shoe *l*........Deut 25:10
L thy shoe from off thy foot...Josh 5:15
bands *l* from off his hands ....Judg 15:14
he would let *l* his hand ....Job 6:9
He *l* the bond of kings........Job 12:18
Because he hath *l* my cord ....Job 30:11
let *l* the bridle before me .....Job 30:11
l the bands of Orion..........Job 38:31
l those that are appointed .....Ps 102:20
The king sent and *l* him.......Ps 105:20
thou hast *l* my bonds ....Ps 116:16
The Lord *l* the prisoners ......Ps 146:7
Or ever the silver cord be *l* ...Eccl 12:6
girdle of their loins be *l*.......Is 5:27
l the sackcloth from off thy ...Is 20:2
hasteneth that he may be *l* ....Is 51:14
l thyself from the bands of ....Is 52:2
l the bands of wickedness .....Is 58:6
I *l* thee..from the chains ......Jer 40:4
Lo, I see four men *l*..........Dan 3:25
joints of his loins were *l* ......Dan 5:6
thou shalt *l* on earth ....Matt 16:19
earth shall be *l* in heaven .....Matt 16:19
ye shall *l* on earth shall ....Matt 18:18
earth shall be *l* in heaven .....Matt 18:18
compassion, and *l* him ....Matt 18:27
l them, and bring them ....Matt 21:2
string of his tongue was *l* .....Mark 7:35
man sat; *l* him, and bring .....Mark 11:2
What do ye, *l* the colt ....Mark 11:5
tongue *l*, and he spake........Luke 1:64
on the sabbath *l* his ox or .....Luke 13:15
l..this bond on the sabbath ....Luke 13:16
ask you, Why do ye *l* him?....Luke 19:31
as they were *l* the colt ....Luke 19:33
L him, and let him go ....John 11:44
l the pains of death...........Acts 2:24
I am not worthy to *l*..........Acts 13:25
l from Troas, we came ....Acts 16:11
every one's bands were *l* ......Acts 16:26
not have *l* from Crete..........Acts 27:21
l from the law of her husband .Rom 7:2
a wife? seek not to be *l*.......1Cor 7:27
Art thou *l* from a wife? 1Cor 7:27
and to *l* the seals ....Rev 5:2
L the four angels which ....Rev 9:14
And the four angels were *l*....Rev 9:15
must be *l* a little season ....Rev 20:3
Satan..*l* out of his prison ......Rev 20:7

LOP—*to chop off*

l the bough with terror........Is 10:33

LORD—*a title of majesty and kingship, including Christ as Lord*

Applied to:

God ....Gen 3:1-23
Christ ....Luke 6:46
Masters ....Gen 24:14, 27
Men ("sir") ....Matt 21:29
Husbands ....Gen 18:12
1Pet 3:6

As applied to Christ, "kyrios" indicates:

Identity with Jehovah ....Joel 2:32
Confession of Christ's Lordship ("Jesus as Lord") ....Rom 10:9
Absolute Lordship ....Phil 2:11

[*also* LORD'S, LORDS]

L had said unto Abram ....Gen 12:1
thing too hard for the *L*?.....Gen 18:14
he said, Behold now, my *l* ....Gen 19:2
shall the *L* be my God ....Gen 28:21
in the ward of his *l* house .....Gen 40:7
we steal out of thy *l* house ....Gen 44:8
also will be my *l* bondmen ....Gen 44:9
we are my *l* servants..........Gen 44:16
speak a word in my *l* ears.....Gen 44:18

ordinance of man for the *L*....1Pet 2:13
being *l* over God's heritage....1Pet 5:3
one day is with the *L* as a.....2Pet 3:8
L is not slack concerning......2Pet 3:9
day of the *L* will come as a ...2Pet 3:10
the *L* cometh with ten ....Jude 14
was in the Spirit on the *L*.....Rev 1:10
Holy, holy, holy, *L* God ......Rev 4:8
L of *l*, and King of kings......Rev 17:14
the *L* God omnipotent ....Rev 19:6
King of Kings, And *L* of *L*....Rev 19:16
Even so, come *L* Jesus........Rev 22:20

LORDLY—*grand*
brought..butter in a *l* dish.....Judg 5:25

LORD'S DAY—*See* FIRST DAY OF WEEK

LORD'S PRAYER—*Jesus' model prayer*
Taught by Jesus to His disciples .... Matt 6:9-13; Luke 11:1-4

LORD'S SUPPER—*communion; the eucharist; Jesus' final meal with his disciples before he was taken away to be crucified*

Described as:
Sharing of communion ...1Cor 10:16
Breaking of bread ....Acts 2:42, 46
Lord's supper 1Cor 11:20
Eucharist "Giving of thanks" ....Luke 22:17,19

Features concerning:
Instituted by Christ ......Matt 26:26-29
Commemorative of Christ's death ....Luke 22:19,20
Introductory to the new covenant..............Matt 26:28
Means of Christian fellowship..............Acts 2:42, 46
Memorial feast 1Cor 11:23-26
Inconsistent with demon fellowship............1Cor 10:19-22
Preparation for, required .1Cor 11:27-34
Spiritually explained .....John 6:26-58

LORDSHIP—*supreme authority*
Human kings............Mark 10:42
Divine King.............Phil 2:9-11

Gentiles exercise *l* over ....Luke 22:25

LO-RUHAMAH (lō-rōō-hä'mä)—*"receiving no compassion"*
Symbolic name of Hosea's daughter ......Hos 1:6

when she had weaned *L* ......Hos 1:8

LOSE—*to fail to keep; misplace*

[*also* LOSETH, LOSS, LOST]
not unto thee; I bare the *l*....Gen 31:39
pay for the *l* of his time.......Ex 21:19
for any manner of *l* thing .....Ex 22:9
found that which was *l*........Lev 6:3
days..before shall be *l* ....Num 6:12
all *l* things of thy brother's ....Deut 22:3
he hath *l*, and thou hast ......Deut 22:3
and thou *l* thy life, with.......Judg 18:25
asses of..father were *l*.........1Sam 9:3
we *l* not all the beasts 1Kin 18:5
army that thou hast *l* 1Kin 20:25
owners..to *l* their life ....Job 31:39
gone astray like a *l* sheep .....Ps 119:176
and *l* thy sweet words.........Prov 23:8
to get, and a time to *l* ....Eccl 3:6
I know the *l* of children.......Is 47:8
after thou hast *l* the other .....Is 49:20
people hath been *l* sheep......Jer 50:6
and her hope was *l* ....Ezek 19:5
seek that which was *l* ....Ezek 34:16
salt have *l* his savor ....Matt 5:13
findeth his life shall *l* it ....Matt 10:39
l his life for my sake shall .....Matt 10:39
will save his life shall *l*........Matt 16:25
will *l* his life for my sake ......Matt 16:25
will save his life shall *l*........Mark 8:35
world, and *l* his own soul? ....Mark 8:36
salt have *l* his saltness ....Mark 9:50
gain the whole world, and *l* ...Luke 9:25
the salt have *l* his savor ....Luke 14:34
if she *l* one piece, doth not....Luke 15:8
found the piece which I had *l* .Luke 15:9
save that which was *l* ....Luke 19:10
remain, that nothing be *l*.......John 6:12
hath given me I should *l* ......John 6:39
thou gavest me have I *l* ....John 18:9
gained this harm and *l* ....Acts 27:21
I counted *l* for Christ ....Phil 3:7
I count all things but *l* for.....Phil 3:8
I have suffered the *l* of all ....Phil 3:8
l not those things which.......2John 8

LOSS, SPIRITUAL—*losses that can be experienced in the realm of one's spirit*

Kinds of:
One's soul ....Luke 9:24, 25
Reward 1Cor 3:13-15
Heaven ....Luke 16:19-31

Causes of:
Love of this life ....Luke 17:33
Sin ....Ps 107:17, 34

LOST—*unable to find the way; helpless*

Descriptive of men as:
Separated from God .....Luke 15:24,32
Unregenerated ....Matt 15:24
Objects of Christ's mission ....Luke 15:4-6
Blinded by Satan 2Cor 4:3, 4
Defiled ....Titus 1:15, 16

LOT—(lŏt)—*"veiled"—Abraham's nephew who escaped from wicked Sodom*

Life of:
Abraham's nephew ......Gen 11:27-31
Goes with Abraham to Canaan ....Gen 12:5
Accompanies Abraham to Egypt ....Gen 13:1
Settles in Sodom ....Gen 13:5-13
Rescued by Abraham ....Gen 14:12-16
Befriends angels ....Gen 19:1-14
Saved from Sodom's destruction............Gen 19:15,26
His wife, disobedient, becomes pillar of salt ..Gen 19:15,26
His daughters commit incest with ....Gen 19:30-38
Unwilling father of Moabites and Ammonites ....Gen 19:37,38

Character of:
Makes selfish choice .....Gen 13:5-13
Lacks moral stability.....Gen 19:6-10
Loses moral influence....Gen 19:14,20
Still "vexed" by Sodomites 2Pet 2:7, 8

and *L* went with him: and.....Gen 12:4
L was separated from him.....Gen 13:14
when *L* entered into Zoar.....Gen 19:23
sent *L* out of the midst ....Gen 19:29
cities in the which *L* dwelt ....Gen 19:29
unto the children of *L* ....Deut 2:9
unto the children of *L* ....Deut 2:19
helped the children of *L* ......Ps 83:8
it was in the days of *L*........Luke 17:28
that *L* went out of Sodom.....Luke 17:29

LOT—*a portion given*

[*also* LOTS]
Come up with me into my *l*...Judg 1:3
will go with thee into thy *l*....Judg 1:3
Give a perfect *l* 1Sam 14:41
for theirs was the *l* 1Chr 6:54
of Merari were given by *l*.....1Chr 6:63
the *l* of your inheritance 1Chr 16:18
l came forth to Jehoiarib 1Chr 24:7
l eastward fell to Shelemiah ...1Chr 26:14
Hosah the *l* came forth 1Chr 26:16
thou maintainest my *l*.........Ps 16:5
upon the *l* of the righteous ....Ps 125:3
Cast in thy *l* among us ....Prov 1:14
The *l* causeth contentions .....Prov 18:18
the *l* of them that rob us......Is 17:14
thy portion..they are thy *l*.....Is 57:6
This is thy *l*, the portion of ...Jer 13:25
piece by piece; let no *l* fall....Ezek 24:6
stand in thy *l* at the end ......Dan 12:13
and the *l* fell upon Jonah .....Jon 1:7
neither part nor *l* in this ......Acts 8:21
divided their land..by *l*........Acts 13:19

LOTAN (lō'tăn)—*"hidden"*
Tribe of Horites in Mt. Seir .... Gen 36:20, 29; 1Chr 1:38, 39

L, and Shobal, and Zibeon....1Chr 1:38

LOTHE—*See* LOATHE

LOTS—*small tokens used to decide matters*

Characteristic of:
Preceded by prayer ......Acts 1:23-26
With divine sanction .....Num 26:55
Considered final.........Num 26:56
Used also by the ungodly.Matt 27:35

Used for:
Selection of scapegoat ...Lev 16:8
Detection of a criminal ..Josh 7:14-18
Selection of warriors .....Judg 20:9, 10
Choice of a king 1Sam 10:19-21
Deciding priestly rotation.Luke 1:9

l fell to be the scapegoat ......Lev 16:10
shall divide the land by *l*......Num 33:54
place where his *l* falleth ....Num 33:54
land for an inheritance by *l* ...Num 36:2
Jacob is the *l* of his...........Deut 32:9
divide thou it by *l* unto the....Josh 13:6
l of the tribe of..Judah........Josh 15:1
l for the tribe of Manasseh ....Josh 17:1
thou given me but one *l* ......Josh 17:14
cast *l* for you here before .....Josh 18:6
Joshua cast *l* for them in......Josh 18:10
l of the tribe of the children....Josh 18:11
the second *l* came forth to ....Josh 19:1
l came out to Issachar ....Josh 19:17
l came out to the children.....Josh 19:32
inheritance by *l* in Shiloh .....Josh 19:51
l came out for the families ....Josh 21:4
l out of the tribe of Judah ....Josh 21:4
Israel gave by *l* unto the ......Josh 21:8
had the cities of their *l* out ....Josh 21:20
divided unto you by *l* these ...Josh 23:4
Cast *l* between me and........1Sam 14:42
cast *l* over against their 1Chr 24:31
cast *l*, as well the small 1Chr 26:13
cast the *l* among the priests ...Neh 10:34
cast Pur, that is, the *l*.........Esth 3:7
cast *l* upon my vesture ....Ps 22:18
shall divide it by *l* for an......Ezek 47:22
have cast *l* for my people .....Joel 3:3
cast *l* upon Jerusalem ....Obad 11
Come, and let us cast *l* ....Jon 1:7
So they cast *l*, and the ....Jon 1:7
that shall cast a cord by *l* .....Mic 2:5
cast *l* for her honorable ....Nah 3:10
parted..garments, casting *l* ....Matt 27:35
my vesture did they cast *l*.....Matt 27:35
casting *l* upon them...........Mark 15:24
his raiment, and cast *l* ....Luke 23:34
not rend it, but cast *l* for .....John 19:24
my vesture they did cast *l*.....John 19:24
they gave forth their *l*; and....Acts 1:26

LOT'S WIFE—*the wife of Abraham's nephew who was turned into a pillar of salt when she fled Sodom*
Disobedient, becomes pillar of salt...........Gen 19:26
Event to be remembered .Luke 17:32

LOUD—*intense volume of sound; noisy*

[*also* LOUDER]
I cried with a *l* voice ....Gen 39:14
of the trumpet exceeding *l* ....Ex 19:16
men of Israel with a *l* voice ...Deut 27:14
she cried with a *l* voice 1Sam 28:12
country wept with a *l* voice....2Sam 15:23
congregation..with a *l* voice ...1Kin 8:55
with a *l* voice in the Jews'.....2Kin 18:28

L

therefore *l* is the fulfilling .....Rom 13:10
for them that *l* him 1Cor 2:9
if any man *l* God, the same ...1Cor 8:3
man *l* not the Lord Jesus 1Cor 16:22
l be with you all in Christ 1Cor 16:24
might know the *l* which 2Cor 2:4
Holy Ghost, by *l* unfeigned ...2Cor 6:6
diligence and in your *l* 2Cor 8:7
prove..sincerity of your *l* 2Cor 8:8
the proof of your *l* 2Cor 8:24
I *l* you, the less I be *l* 2Cor 12:15
l of God, and the communion..2Cor 13:14
faith which worketh by *l* ......Gal 5:6
but by *l* serve one another ....Gal 5:13
l thy neighbor as thyself ......Gal 5:14
fruit of the Spirit is *l*, joy .....Gal 5:22
without blame before him in *l*. .Eph 1:4
and *l* unto all the saints ....Eph 1:15
rooted and grounded in *l*......Eph 3:17
forbearing one another in *l* ....Eph 4:2
speaking the truth in *l* ....Eph 4:15
edifying of itself in *l* ....Eph 4:16
And walk in *l*, as Christ ......Eph 5:2
Husbands, *l* your wives ....Eph 5:25
He that *l* his wife *l* himself ....Eph 5:28
l his wife even as himself .....Eph 5:33
all them that *l* our Lord.......Eph 6:24
l may abound yet more ....Phil 1:9
other of *l*, knowing that.......Phil 1:17
Christ, if any comfort of *l*.....Phil 2:1
having the same *l*..............Phil 2:2
of the *l* which ye have to .....Col 1:4
being knit together in *l* ....Col 2:2
of faith, and labor of *l* 1Thess 1:3
abound in *l* one toward 1Thess 3:12
touching brotherly *l* ye need...1Thess 4:9
are taught of God to *l* one 1Thess 4:9
highly in *l* for their work's 1Thess 5:13
received not the *l* of the 2Thess 2:10
Father, which hath *l* us 2Thess 2:16
l which is in Christ Jesus 1Tim 1:14
l of money is the root of all...1Tim 6:10
l, patience, meekness 1Tim 6:11
l, and of a sound mind........2Tim 1:7
also that *l* his appearing.......2Tim 4:8
having *l* this present world 2Tim 4:10
to *l* their husbands ....Titus 2:4
to *l* their children............Titus 2:4
kindness and *l* of God ....Titus 3:4
them that *l* us in the faith .....Titus 3:15
Hearing of thy *l* and faith .....Philem 5
for *l* sake I rather beseech ....Philem 9
hast *l* righteousness, and ......Heb 1:9
your work and labor of *l* ......Heb 6:10
provoke unto *l* and to good ...Heb 10:24
For whom the Lord *l* he ......Heb 12:6
Let brotherly *l* continue ....Heb 13:1
promised to them that *l*.......James 1:12
l thy neighbor as thyself .....James 2:8
having not seen, ye *l* 1Pet 1:8
unfeigned *l* of the brethren 1Pet 1:22
ye *l* one another with a 1Pet 1:22
of another, *l* as brethren 1Pet 3:8
who *l* the wages of 2Pet 2:15
l his brother abideth in 1John 2:10
L not the world, neither 1John 2:15
If any man *l* the world 1John 2:15
l of the Father is not in 1John 2:15
he that *l* not his brother 1John 3:10
we should *l* one another 1John 3:11
because we *l* the brethren 1John 3:14
l not his brother abideth in....1John 3:14
the *l* of God in him? 1John 3:17
children, let us not *l* in word ..1John 3:18
Son Jesus Christ, and *l* one ...1John 3:23
every one that *l* him that......1John 5:1
l him also that is begotten.....1John 5:1
we *l* the children of God 1John 5:2
when we *l* God, and keep 1John 5:2
her children, whom I *l* in 2John 1
that we *l* one another 2John 5
whom I *l* in the truth 3John 1
l to have the preeminence 3John 9
Mercy..and peace, and *l* ......Jude 2
Unto him that *l* us, and ....Rev 1:5
hast left thy first *l* ....Rev 2:4
know that I have *l* thee ....Rev 3:9
they *l* not their lives unto .....Rev 12:11
l and maketh a lie ....Rev 22:15

LOVE, CHRISTIAN—*the love that a Christian is to exhibit*

Toward God:
First commandment......Matt 22:37,38
With all the heart ....Matt 22:37
More important than ritual ....Mark 12:31-33
Gives boldness 1John 4:17-19

Toward Christ:
Sign of true faith ....John 8:42
Manifested in obedience. .John 14:15, 21, 23
Leads to service 2Cor 5:14

Toward others:
Second command ....Matt 22:37-39
Commanded by Christ ...John 13:34
Described in detail 1Cor 13:1-13

LOVE OF CHRIST, THE—*the love Christ exhibited when He was on earth*

Objects of:
Father ....John 14:31
Believers ....Gal 2:20
Church ....Eph 5:2, 25

Described as:
Knowing................Eph 3:19
Personal ....Gal 2:20
Conquering ....Rom 8:37
Unbreakable ....Rom 8:35
Intimate ....John 14:21
Imitative...............1John 3:16
Like the Father's ....John 15:9
Sacrificial ....Gal 2:20

Expressions of:
In taking our nature .....Heb 2:16-18
In dying for us ....John 15:13

LOVE OF GOD, THE—*God's absolute, unqualified good will*

Objects of:
Christ ....John 3:35
Christians 2Thess 2:16
Mankind ....Titus 3:4
Cheerful giver 2Cor 9:7

Described as:
Great ....Eph 2:4
Everlasting..............Jer 31:3
Sacrificial ....Rom 5:8

As seen in believers':
Hearts..................Rom 5:5
Regeneration............Eph 2:4, 5
Love 1John 4:7-12
Faith 1John 4:16
Security 2Thess 3:5
Daily life 1John 2:15-17
Obedience 1John 2:5
Without fear 1John 4:18-21
Glorification 1John 3:1, 2

LOVE, PHYSICAL—*sexual desire*
Isaac and Rebekah ......Gen 24:67
Jacob and Rachel........Gen 29:11-30
Boaz and Ruth ....Ruth 2:4-15
Samson and Delilah .....Judg 16:4, 15

LOVELY—*beautiful*
Jonathan were *l* and pleasant ..2Sam 1:23
yea, he is altogether *l*.........Song 5:16
as a very *l* song of...........Ezek 33:32
whatsoever things are *l*........Phil 4:8

LOVER—*one who loves*

[*also* LOVERS]
Hiram was ever a *l* of David ..1Kin 5:1
My *l* and my friends stand ....Ps 38:11
l and friend hast thou put .....Ps 88:18
the harlot with many *l* ....Jer 3:1
thy *l* will despise thee ....Jer 4:30
for all thy *l* are destroyed .....Jer 22:20
l shall go into captivity........Jer 22:22
thy *l* have forgotten thee ......Jer 30:14
among all her *l* she hath ......Lam 1:2
I called for my *l*, but they.....Lam 1:19
givest thy gifts to all thy *l* .....Ezek 16:33
thy whoredoms with thy *l* .....Ezek 16:36
all them that thou hast *l* ......Ezek 16:37
doted on her *l*, on the ....Ezek 23:5
into the hand of her *l*.........Ezek 23:9
raise up thy *l* against thee .....Ezek 23:22
I will go after my *l*, that ......Hos 2:5
she shall follow after her *l* ....Hos 2:7
lewdness in..sight of her *l* .....Hos 2:10
rewards that my *l* have........Hos 2:12
she went after her *l* and.......Hos 2:13
Ephraim hath hired *l* ....Hos 8:9
men shall be *l* of their own....2Tim 3:2
highminded, *l* of pleasures 2Tim 3:4
more than *l* of God...........2Tim 3:4
l of hospitality, a *l* of good ....Titus 1:8

LOVING-KINDNESS—*gentle and steadfast mercy*

Attitude of believers, to:
Expect ....Ps 17:7
Ps 36:10
Rejoice in ....Ps 63:3
Ps 69:16

[*also* LOVING-KINDNESSES]
tender mercies and thy *l* ......Ps 25:6
thy *l* is before mine eyes ......Ps 26:3
excellent is thy *l*, O God! .....Ps 36:7
I have not concealed thy *l*.....Ps 40:10
l and thy truth continually.....Ps 40:11
Lord will command his *l* ......Ps 42:8
thought of thy *l*, O God ......Ps 48:9
O God, according to thy *l*.....Ps 51:1
l be declared in the grave? ....Ps 88:10
my *l* will I not utterly take ....Ps 89:33
where are thy former *l*........Ps 89:49
forth thy *l* in the morning .....Ps 92:2
crowneth thee with *l* and......Ps 103:4
understand the *l* of the Lord ..Ps 107:43
Quicken me after thy *l*; so ....Ps 119:88
voice according unto thy *l*....Ps 119:149
Lord, according to thy *l*.......Ps 119:159
for thy *l* and for thy truth .....Ps 138:2
hear thy *l* in the morning .....Ps 143:8
mention the *l* of the Lord .....Is 63:7
the multitude of his *l* ....Is 63:7
the Lord which exercise *l* .....Jer 9:24
saith the Lord, even *l* and.....Jer 16:5
with *l* have I drawn thee .....Jer 31:3
showest *l* unto thousands ......Jer 32:18
and in *l*, and in mercies ....Hos 2:19

LOW—*the furthest down; deep; depressed; common; level; soft; humble*

[*also* LOWER, LOWEST, LOWLINESS, LOWLY]
l, second, and third stories ....Gen 6:16
be in sight *l* than the skin .....Lev 13:20
be no *l* than the other skin ....Lev 13:26
shalt come down very *l* ....Deut 28:43
shall burn unto the *l* hell ......Deut 32:22
hast brought me very *l*........Judg 11:35
bringeth *l*, and lifteth up 1Sam 2:7
priests of the *l* of the people ..1Kin 12:31
l of them priests of..high 2Kin 17:32
that were in the *l* plains.......1Chr 27:28
that are in the *l* plains 2Chr 9:27
the cities of the *l* country 2Chr 28:18
set I in the *l* places behind ....Neh 4:13
on high those that be *l*........Job 5:11
but are gone and brought *l* ....Job 24:24
a little *l* than the angels ....Ps 8:5
l and high, rich and poor .....Ps 49:2
for we are brought very *l* .....Ps 79:8
my soul from the *l* hell ....Ps 86:13
are minished and brought *l*....Ps 107:39
us in our *l* estate ....Ps 136:23
he respect unto the *l*..........Ps 138:6
wrought in the *l* parts.........Ps 139:15
giveth grace unto the *l*........Prov 16:19
l in the presence of...........Prov 25:7
pride shall bring him *l* ....Prov 29:23
and the rich sit in *l*...........Eccl 10:6
sound of the grinding is *l* .....Eccl 12:4

L

music shall be brought *l* . . . . . . .Eccl 12:4
he shall be brought *l* . . . . .Is 2:12
will lay *l* the haughtiness . . . . . .Is 13:11
the waters of the *l* pool . . . . . . .Is 22:9
lay *l*, and bring to the ground. .Is 25:12
lofty city, he layeth it *l* . . . . . . .Is 26:5
layeth it *l*, even to the . . . . .Is 26:5
and the city shall be *l* . . . . .Is 32:19
and hill shall be made *l* . . . . . . .Is 40:4
out of the *l* dungeon . . . . .Lam 3:55
spreading vine of *l* stature . . . . .Ezek 17:6
exalt him that is *l* . . . . .Ezek 21:26
gates was the *l* pavement . . . . . .Ezek 40:18
forefront of the *l* gate . . . . .Ezek 40:19
from the *l* chamber to . . . . .Ezek 41:7
ground even to the *l* settle . . . .Ezek 48:14
l and riding upon an ass . . . . . .Zech 9:9
I am meek and *l* in heart . . . . .Matt 11:29
hath regarded the *l* estate . . . . .Luke 1:48
and hill shall be brought *l* . . . . .Luke 3:5
shame to take the *l* room . . . . .Luke 14:9
but condescend to men of *l* . . .Rom 12:16
With all *l* and meekness . . . . . .Eph 4:2
first into the *l* parts . . . . .Eph 4:9
l of mind let each esteem . . . . .Phil 2:3
a little *l* than the angels . . . . . . .Heb 2:7
brother of *l* degree rejoice . . . .James 1:9

LOWING—*a sound made by cattle*

[*also* LOWETH]
l as they went, and turned 1Sam 6:12
or *l* the ox over his fodder? . . .Job 6:5

LOWRING—*gloomy*
for the sky is red and *l* . . . . . . .Matt 16:3

LOYALTY—*fidelity to a person or cause*
Kinds of:
People . . . . .Acts 25:7-11
Relatives . . . . .Esth 2:21-23
King 1Sam 24:6-10
Cause 2Sam 11:9-11
Oath 2Sam 21:7
Signs of:
General obedience . . . . . . .Rom 13:1, 2
Prayer for rulers . . . . .Ezra 6:10
Hatred of disloyalty . . . . . .Josh 22:9-20

LUBIM (lū'bĭm)—*"dwellers in a thirsty land"—the people who lived in the North African continent west of Egypt, now Libya*
the *L*, the Sukkiim, and 2Chr 12:3
and *L* were thy helpers . . . . . . .Nah 3:9

LUCAS (lū'kăs)—*same as Luke*
L, my fellow laborers . . . . .Philem 24

LUCIFER (lū'sĭ-fer)—*"light-bearer"*
Name applied to Satan . . .Is 14:12
Allusion to elsewhere . . . .Luke 10:18

LUCIUS (lū'shĭ-ŭs)—*"morning-born; of light"*
1. Prophet and teacher at Antioch . . . . .Acts 13:1
2. Paul's companion in Corinth . . . . .Rom 16:21

and *L* of Cyrene and Manasen .Acts 13:1
my workfellow, and *L* . . . . .Rom 16:21

LUCRE—*gain; money*
Priests guilty of 1Sam 8:3
Elders must avoid 1Tim 3:2, 3
Deacons must shun 1Tim 3:8
Sign of false teachers . . . .Titus 1:11

[*also* LUCRE'S]
not greedy of filthy *l* 1Tim 3:3
striker, not given to filthy *l* . . . .Titus 1:7
not, for filthy *l* sake . . . . .Titus 1:11
not for filthy *l* 1Pet 5:2

LUD, LUDIM (lŭd, lū'dĭm)—*a personification of the Lydians*
1. Lud, a people descending from Shem 1Chr 1:17
2. Ludim, a people descending from Mizraim (Egypt) . . . . . .Gen 10:13

Mentioned as men of war .Ezek 27:10

and Arphaxad, and *L* . . . . .Gen 10:22
Mizraim begat *L*, and 1Chr 1:11
and *L*, that draw the bow . . . . .Is 66:19

LUHITH (lū'hĭth)—*"made of boards"*
Moabite town . . . . .Is 15:5

going up of *L* continual . . . . . . .Jer 48:5

LUKE (lūk)—*"light-giving"—evangelist, physician, and author of the Gospel of Luke and the Book of Acts*
"The beloved physician". .Col 4:14
Paul's last companion 2Tim 4:11

LUKE, THE GOSPEL OF—*a book of the New Testament*
The anunciation . . . . .Luke 1:26-56
John the Baptist . . . . .Luke 3:1-22
The temptation . . . . .Luke 4:1-13
Public ministry begins . . . .Luke 4:15
The disciples chosen . . . . .Luke 6:12-19
The disciple's instructions .Luke 10:25—13:21
The Jerusalem ministry . .Luke 19:28—21:38
The Last Supper . . . . .Luke 22:1-38
The Crucifixion . . . . .Luke 22:39—23:56
The Resurrection . . . . .Luke 24:1-53

LUKEWARM—*neither hot nor cold*
Descriptive of Laodicea . .Rev. 3:14-16

LUMP—*a shapeless mass; a pile*
Isaiah said, Take a *l* of figs . . .2Kin 20:7
Let them take a *l* of figs . . . . . .Is 38:21
same *l* to make one vessel . . . .Rom 9:21
firstfruit be holy, the *l* is . . . . . .Rom 11:16
leaveneth the whole *l*? 1Cor 5:6
that ye may be a new *l* 1Cor 5:7
leaveneth the whole *l* . . . . .Gal 5:9

LUNATIC—*an insane person*
David acts as 1Sam 21:13-15
Nebuchadnezzar afflicted as . . . . .Dan 4:31-36
Christ heals . . . . .Matt 4:24
Christ declared . . . . .John 10:20
Paul called . . . . .Acts 26:24

LURK—*to hide; move furtively*

[*also* LURKING]
knowledge of all the *l* places . .1Sam 23:23
l places of the villages . . . . .Ps 10:8
lion *l* in secret places . . . . .Ps 17:12
l privily for the innocent . . . . . .Prov 1:11
l privily for their own lives . . . .Prov 1:18

LUST—*evil desire*
Origin of, in:
Satan 1John 3:8-12
Heart . . . . .Matt 15:19
Flesh . . . . .James 1:14,15
World 2Pet 1:4
Described as:
Deceitful . . . . .Eph 4:22
Enticing . . . . .James 1:14, 15
Hurtful 1Tim 6:9
Numerous 2Tim 3:6
Among the unregenerate, they:
Live and walk in . . . . .Eph 2:3
Are punished with . . . . . . .Rom 1:24-32
Among false teachers, they:
Walk after . . . . .2 Pet 2:10-22
Will prevail in the last days 2Pet 3:3
Are received because of. .2Tim 4:3, 4
Among Christians:
Once lived in . . . . .Eph 2:3
Consider it dead . . . . .Col 3:5
Deny . . . . .Titus 2:12
Flee from 2Tim 2:22
Not carry out . . . . .Gal 5:16

[*also* LUSTED, LUSTETH, LUSTING, LUSTS, LUSTY]
my *l* shall be satisfied upon . . .Ex 15:9
was among them fell a *l* . . . . . . .Num 11:4
buried the people that *l* . . . . . . .Num 11:34
eat..whatsoever thy soul *l* . . . . .Deut 12:15
flesh, whatsoever thy soul *l* . . . .Deut 12:20
gates whatsoever thy soul *l* . . . .Deut 12:21
whatsoever thy soul *l* after . . . .Deut 14:26
l, and all men of valor . . . . .Judg 3:29
by asking meat for their *l* . . . . .Ps 78:18
not estranged from their *l* . . . . .Ps 78:30
unto their own hearts' *l* . . . . . . .Ps 81:12
But *l*..in the wilderness . . . . . . .Ps 106:14
L not after her beauty in . . . . . .Prov 6:25
looketh on a woman to *l* . . . . . .Matt 5:28
l of other things entering . . . . . .Mark 4:19
l of your father ye will do . . . . .John 8:44
ye should obey it in the *l* . . . . .Rom 6:12
for I had not known *l* . . . . .Rom 7:7
the flesh, to fulfill the *l* . . . . . . .Rom 13:14
should not *l* after evil 1Cor 10:6
evil things, as they also *l* 1Cor 10:6
not fulfill the *l* of the flesh . . . .Gal 5:16
flesh *l* against the Spirit . . . . . . .Gal 5:17
flesh with..affections and *l* . . . .Gal 5:24
in the *l* of concupiscence 1Thess 4:5
Flee also youthful *l*: but 2Tim 2:22
denying..worldly *l* . . . . .Titus 2:12
divers *l* and pleasures . . . . .Titus 3:3
l that war in your members . . .James 4:1
Ye *l*, and have not: ye kill . . . .James 4:2
consume it upon your *l* . . . . . . .James 4:3
dwelleth in us *l* to envy? . . . . . .James 4:5
former *l* in your ignorance 1Pet 1:14
abstain from fleshly *l* 1Pet 2:11
time in the flesh to the *l* 1Pet 4:2
walked in lasciviousness, *l* 1Pet 4:3
l of the flesh, and the *l* 1John 2:16
passeth away, and the *l* 1John 2:17
walking after their own *l* . . . . . .Jude 16
after their own ungodly *l* . . . . . .Jude 18
fruits that thy soul *l* after . . . . .Rev 18:14

LUXURIES—*rich or sumptuous surroundings*
Characteristic of:
Egypt . . . . .Heb 11:24-27
Tyre . . . . .Ezek 27:1-27
Ancient Babylon . . . . .Dan 4:30
Israel . . . . .Amos 6:1-7
Persia . . . . .Esth 1:3-11
Harlot Babylon . . . . .Rev 18:10-13
Productive of:
Temptations . . . . .Josh 7:20, 21
Physical weakness . . . . . . .Dan 1:8, 10-16
Moral decay . . . . .Nah 3:1-19
Spiritual decay . . . . .Rev 3:14-17

LUZ (lŭz)—*"separation"*
1. Ancient Canaanite town .Gen 28:19
Called Bethel . . . . .Gen 35:6
2. Hittite town . . . . .Judg 1:23-26

Almighty appeared..at *L* . . . . . .Gen 48:3
out from Beth-el to *L* . . . . .Josh 16:2
toward *L*, to the side of *L* . . . . .Josh 18:13

LYCAONIA (lĭk-ā-ō'nĭ-ä)—*"she-wolf"—a rugged, inland district of Asia Minor*
Paul preaches in three of its cities . . . . .Acts 14:6, 11

LYCIA (lĭsh'ĭ-ä)—*"land of Lycus"—a province of Asia Minor*
Paul:
Visits Patara, a city of . . .Acts 21:1, 2
Lands at Myra, a city of .Acts 27:5, 6

came to Myra, a city of *L* . . . . .Acts 27:5

LYDDA—*See* LOD

LYDIA (lĭd'ĭ-ä)—*"Lydus land; native of Lydia"*
1. Woman of Thyatira;
Paul's first European convert . . . . .Acts 16:14, 15, 40

2. District of Asia Minor containing Ephesus, Smyrna, Thyatira, and Sardis ....Rev 1:11

[*also* LYDIANS]

L..handle and bend the bow . . .Jer 46:9
Ethiopia, and Libya, and *L* . . . .Ezek 30:5

LYING—*See* LIAR; LIE

LYSANIAS (lī-sā'nĭ-ăs)—*"that drives away sorrow"*
Tetrarch of Abilene .....Luke 3:1

LYSIAS, CLAUDIUS (lĭs'ĭ-ăs, klô'dĭ-ŭs)—*"lame dissolution"*
Roman captain who rescues Paul ....Acts 23:10
Listens to Paul's nephew .Acts 23:16-22
Sends Paul to Felix ......Acts 23:23-31
Felix awaits arrival of . . . .Acts 24:22

LYSTRA (lĭs'trä)—*"that dissolves"—a city of Lycaonia*
Visited by Paul ....Acts 14:6, 21
Lame man healed here . . .Acts 14:8-10
People of, attempt to worship Paul and Barnabas ....Acts 14:11-18
Paul stoned here 2Tim 3:11
Home of Timothy ....Acts 16:1, 2

came he to Derbe and *L* ......Acts 16:1
brethren that were at *L* ....Acts 16:2

M

MAACAH, MAACHAH (mā'ä-kä)—*"depression"*
1. Daughter of Nahor .....Gen 22:24
2. Small Syrian kingdom near Mt. Hermon . . . .Deut 3:14
   Not possessed by Israel..Josh 13:13
   Called Syria-maachah . .1Chr 19:6, 7
3. Machir's wife 1Chr 7:15, 16
4. One of Caleb's concubines 1Chr 2:48
5. Father of Shephatiah . . .1Chr 27:16
6. Ancestress of King Saul.1Chr 8:29
   1Chr 9:35
7. One of David's warriors.1Chr 11:43
8. Father of Achish, king of Gath 1Kin 2:39
9. David's wife and mother of Absalom . .2Sam 3:3
10. Wife of Rehoboam; mother of King Abijah 2Chr 11:18-21
    Makes idol, is deposed as queenmother 1Kin 15:13

of king *M* a thousand men 2Sam 10:6
M, were by themselves in 2Sam 10:8
his mother's name was *M* 1Kin 15:2
son of *M* the daughter of 1Chr 3:2
and the king of *M* and his.....1Chr 19:7
Abijah the son of *M* the 2Chr 11:22
concerning *M* the mother of . . .2Chr 15:16

MAACHATHITES (mā'ä-kä-thīts)—*inhabitants of Maachah*
Not conquered by Israel. .Josh 13:13
Among Israel's warriors . .2Sam 23:34
See MAACAH

of the Geshurites and the *M* . . .Josh 12:5
of the Geshurites and *M* ......Josh 13:11
Jaazaniah the son of a *M* 2Kin 25:23
and Eshtemoa the *M* 1Chr 4:19
and Jezaniah the son of a *M*. . .Jer 40:8

MAADAI (mā-ä-dā'ī)—*"Jehovah is ornament"*
Postexilic Jew; divorced his foreign wife ....Ezra 10:34

MAADIAH (mā-ä-dī'ä)—*"Jehovah is ornament"*
Priest who returns from Babylon with Zerubbabel ....Neh 12:5, 7
Same as Moadiah in .....Neh 12:17

MAAI (mā-ā'ī)—*"Jehovah is compassionate"*
Postexilic trumpeter .....Neh 12:35, 36

MAALEH-ACRABBIM (mā-ä-lĕ-ä-krăb'ĭm)—*"ascent of scorpions"*
Ascent south of the Dead Sea...................Josh 15:3

MAARATH (mā'ä-răth)—*"den"*
Town of Judah ....Josh 15:1, 59

MAASEIAH (mā-ä-sē'yä)—*"Jehovah is a refuge"*
1. Levite musician during David's reign 1Chr15:16, 18
2. Levite captain under Jehoiada 2Chr 23:1
3. Official during King Uzziah's reign 2Chr 26:11
4. Son of Ahaz, slain by Zichri 2Chr 28:7
5. Governor of Jerusalem during King Josiah's reign................2Chr 34:1, 8
6. Ancestor of Baruch . . . .Jer. 32:12
7. Father of the false prophet Zedekiah . . . .Jer 29:21
8. Father of Zephaniah the priest ....Jer 21:1
9. Temple doorkeeper . . . .Jer 35:4
10. Judahite postexilic Jew. .Neh 11:5
    See ASAIAH 4
11. Benjamite ancestor of a postexilic Jew........Neh 11:7
12, 13, 14. Three priests who divorced their foreign wives Ezra10:18, 21, 22
15. Layman who divorced his foreign wife ....Ezra 10:30
16. Representative who signs the covenant . . . .Neh 10:1, 25
17. One who stood by Ezra.Neh 8:4
18. Levite who explains the Law ....Neh 8:7
19. Priest who takes part in dedication services . . . .Neh 12:41
20. Another participating priest ....Neh 12:42
21. Father or ancestor of Azariah ....Neh 3:23

M, and Benaiah, with 1Chr 15:20
to Zephaniah the son of *M* . . . .Jer 29:25
Zephaniah the son of *M* ......Jer 37:3
the son of *M*, when he went . . .Jer 51:59

MAASIAI (mā-ăs'ĭ-ī)—*"work of Jehovah"*
Priest of Immer's family. .1Chr 9:12

MAATH (mā'ăth)—*"small"*
Ancestor of Christ ....Luke 3:26

MAAZ (mā'ăz)—*"counselor"*
Judahite 1Chr 2:27

MAAZIAH (mā-ä-zī'ä)—*"strength of Jehovah"*
1. Descendant of Aaron; heads a course of priests 1Chr 24:1-18
2. One who signs the covenant ....Neh 10:1, 8

MACEDONIA (măs-ĕ-dō'nĭ-ä)—*a nation lying to the north of Greece proper*

In Old Testament prophecy:
Called the kingdom of Grecia ....Dan 11:2
Brazen part of Nebuchadnezzar's image ....Dan 2:32, 39
Described as a leopard with four heads ....Dan 7:6, 17
Described as a "he" goat .Dan 8:5, 21
Dan 11:4

In New Testament missions:
Man of, appeals to ......Acts 16:9, 10
Paul preaches in, at Philippi, etc. ....Acts 16:10—17:14
Paul's troubles in 2Cor 7:5
Churches of, very generous ....Rom 15:26; 2Cor 8:1-5

[*also* MACEDONIANS]

Timothy were come from *M*. . .Acts 18:5
he had passed through *M* .....Acts 19:21
he sent into *M* two of them . . .Acts 19:22
of *M*, Paul's companions ....Acts 19:29
departed for to go into *M* .....Acts 20:1
purposed to return..*M* ....Acts 20:3
Aristarchus a *M* being with . . . .Acts 27:2
I shall pass through *M* 1Cor 16:5
for I do pass through *M*.......1Cor 16:5
to pass by you into *M* 2Cor 1:16
come again out of *M* unto.....2Cor 1:16
I went from thence into *M* 2Cor 2:13
I boast of you to them of *M*. . .2Cor 9:2
lest haply if they of *M* 2Cor 9:4
brethren which came from *M* . .2Cor 11:9
when I departed from *M* ......Phil 4:15
to all that believe in *M* 1Thess 1:7
of the Lord not only in *M*.....1Thess 1:8
brethren which are in all *M* . . .1Thess 4:10
Ephesus, when I went into *M*. .1Tim 1:3

MACHBANAI (măk'bä-nī)—*"thick"*
One of David's mighty men 1Chr 12:13

MACHBENAH (măk-bē'nä)—*"knob; lump"*
Son of Sheva 1Chr 2:49

MACHI (mā'kī)—*"decrease"*
Father of the Gadite spy. .Num 13:15

MACHIR (mā'kĭr)—*"salesman; sold"*
1. Manasseh's only son ....Gen 50:23
   Founder of the family of Machirites ....Num 26:29
   Conqueror of Gilead Num32:39, 40
   Name used of Manasseh tribe ....Judg 5:14
2. Son of Ammiel 2Sam 9:4, 5
   Provides food for David .2Sam17:27-29

son of *M*, the son of Manasseh.Num 27:1
of Gilead, the son of *M*.......Num 36:1
And I gave Gilead unto *M* . . . .Deut 3:15
unto the children of *M* ....Josh 13:31
one half of the children of *M* . .Josh 13:31
M the firstborn of Manasseh . . .Josh 17:1
son of *M*, the son of Manasseh.Josh 17:3
M the son of Ammiel 2Sam 17:27
went in to the daughter of *M* . .1Chr 2:21
belonged to the sons of *M* 1Chr 2:23
concubine..Aramitess bare *M* . .1Chr 7:14
And *M* took to wife the.......1Chr 7:15
the wife of *M* bare a son 1Chr 7:16
son of *M*, the son of Manasseh.1Chr 7:17

MACHNADEBAI (măk-năd'ĕ-bī)—*"liberal; gift of the noble one"*
Son of Bani; divorced foreign wife ....Ezra 10:34, 40

MACHPELAH (măk-pē'lä)—*"double"*
Field containing a cave; bought by Abraham . . .Gen 23:9-18
Sarah and Abraham buried here ....Gen 23:19
Isaac, Rebekah, Leah, and Jacob buried here. .Gen 49:29-31

buried him in the cave of *M* . . .Gen 25:9
in the cave of the field of *M* . .Gen 50:13

MAD—*emotionally or mentally deranged; angry*

Kinds of:
Extreme jealousy 1Sam 18:8-10
Extreme rage ....Luke 6:11

Causes of:
Disobedience to God's Laws . . . . . Deut 28:28
Judgment sent by God . . . Dan 4:31-33

Manifestations of:
Irrational behavior 1Sam 21:12-15
Uncontrollable emotions. . Mark 5:1-5
Moral decay . . . . . Jer 50:38

be ***m*** for the sight of thine . . . . Deut 28:34
feigned himself ***m*** in their 1Sam 21:13
Lo, ye see the man is ***m*** 1Sam 21:14
Have I need of ***m*** men, that . . . 1Sam 21:15
the ***m*** man in my presence? . . . 1Sam 21:15
came this ***m*** fellow to thee? . . . 2Kin 9:11
m against me are sworn . . . . . Ps 102:8
a ***m*** man who casteth . . . . . Prov 26:18
I said of laughter, It is ***m*** . . . . . Eccl 2:2
maketh a wise man ***m*** . . . . . Eccl 7:7
and maketh diviners ***m*** . . . . . Is 44:25
and be moved, and be ***m*** . . . . . Jer 25:16
every man that is ***m***, and . . . . . Jer 29:26
and they are ***m*** upon their . . . . Jer 50:38
therefore the nations are ***m*** . . . Jer 51:7
fool, the spiritual man is ***m*** . . . . Hos 9:7
He hath a devil, and is ***m*** . . . . John 10:20
said unto her, Thou art ***m*** . . . . . Acts 12:15
exceedingly ***m*** against . . . . . Acts 26:11
learning doth make thee ***m*** . . . . Acts 26:24
not ***m***, most noble Festus . . . . . Acts 26:25
they not say that ye are ***m***? . . . 1Cor 14:23

MADAI (măd'ā-ī)—*a personification of the Medes*
Third son of Japheth; ancestor of the Medes. . Gen 10:2

MADE—*See* **MAKE**

MADMANNAH (măd-măn'ä)—*"measure of a gift"*
Town in south Judah . . . . Josh 15:20, 31
Son of Shaaph 1Chr 2:49

MADMEN—*"dunghill"*
Moabite town . . . . . Jer 48:2

MADMENAH (măd-mē'nä)—*"dung heap"*
Town near Jerusalem . . . . Is 10:31

MADON (mā'dŏn)—*"strife"*
Canaanite town . . . . . Josh 12:19
Joins confederacy against Joshua . . . . . Josh 11:1-12

MAGBISH (măg'bĭsh)—*"strong"*
Town of Judah . . . . . Ezra 2:30

MAGDALA (măg'dä-lä)—*"tower"*
City of Galilee . . . . . Matt 15:39

MAGDALENE (măg'dä-lēn, măg-dä-lē'nĕ)—*"of Magdala"*
Descriptive of one of the Marys . . . . . Matt 27:56
See **MARY**

Among which was Mary ***M*** . . . . Matt 27:56
there was Mary ***M***, and the . . . Matt 27:61
came Mary ***M*** and the other . . . Matt 28:1
among whom was Mary ***M*** . . . . Mark 15:40
Mary ***M*** and Mary the . . . . . Mark 15:47
Mary ***M***, and Mary the . . . . . Mark 16:1
appeared first to Mary ***M*** . . . . . Mark 16:9
Mary called ***M***, out of whom . . Luke 8:2
it was Mary ***M***, and Joanna . . . Luke 24:10
of Cleophas, and Mary ***M*** . . . . . John 19:25
the week cometh Mary ***M*** . . . . . John 20:1
Mary ***M*** came and told . . . . . John 20:18

MAGDIEL (măg'dĭ-ĕl)—*"God is renowned"*
Edomite duke . . . . . Gen 36:43

MAGI (mā'jī)—*a priestly sect in Persia*
Brings gifts to the infant Jesus . . . . . Matt 2:1, 2

MAGIC—*the art of doing superhuman things by "supernatural" means, especially through the use of illusions or sleight of hand*

Special manifestations of:
At the exodus . . . . . Ex 7:11
During apostolic Christianity . . . . . Acts 8:9, 18-24

Modified power of:
Acknowledged in history . Ex 7:11, 22
Recognized in prophecy . . 2Thess 2:9-12
Fulfilled in antichrist . . . . . Rev 13:13-18

Failure of, to:
Perform miracles . . . . . Ex 8:18, 19
Overcome demons . . . . . Acts 19:13-19

Condemnation of, by:
Explicit Law . . . . . Lev 20:27
Their inability . . . . . Ex 8:18
Final judgment . . . . . Rev 21:8
See **DIVINATION**

[*also* **MAGICIAN, MAGICIANS**]
and called for all the ***m*** of . . . . Gen 41:8
I told this unto the ***m***; but . . . . Gen 41:24
m did so with their . . . . . Ex 8:7
m could not stand before . . . . . Ex 9:11
the boil was upon the ***m*** . . . . . Ex 9:11
times better than all the ***m*** . . . . Dan 1:20
commanded to call the ***m*** . . . . . Dan 2:2
asked such things at any ***m*** . . . . Dan 2:10
the astrologers, the ***m*** . . . . . Dan 2:27
in the ***m***, the astrologers . . . . . Dan 4:7
Belteshazzar master of the ***m*** . . Dan 4:9
father, made master of the ***m*** . . Dan 5:11

MAGISTRATE—*civil authority or ruler*

Descriptive of:
Ruler . . . . . Judg 18:7
Authorities . . . . . Luke 12:11

Office of:
Ordained by God . . . . . Rom 13:1, 2
Due proper respect . . . . . Acts 23:5

Duties of:
To judge:
Impartially . . . . . Deut 1:17
Righteously . . . . . Deut 25:1

Christian's attitude toward:
Pray for 1Tim 2:1, 2
Honor . . . . . Ex 22:28
Submit to 1Pet 2:13, 14

[*also* **MAGISTRATES**]
m and judges, which may . . . . . Ezra 7:25
thine adversary to the ***m*** . . . . . Luke 12:58
brought them to the ***m*** . . . . . Acts 16:20
the ***m*** rent off their clothes . . . . Acts 16:22
the ***m*** sent the sergeants . . . . . Acts 16:35
m have sent to let you go . . . . . Acts 16:36
told these words unto the ***m*** . . . Acts 16:38
to obey ***m***, to be ready to . . . . . Titus 3:1

MAGNANIMITY—*loftiness of spirit*

Expressions of, toward men:
Abram's offer to Lot . . . . Gen 13:7-12
Jacob's offer to Esau . . . . Gen 33:8-11

Expression of, toward God:
Moses' plea for Israel . . . . Ex 32:31-33
Paul's prayer for Israel . . . Rom 9:1-3

MAGNIFICAL—*See* **MAGNIFICENT**

MAGNIFICAT—*"he magnifies"*
Poem of the Virgin Mary . Luke 1:46-55

MAGNIFICENT—*splendid; opulent; grandiose*

[*also* **MAGNIFICENCE**]
Lord must be exceeding ***m*** 1Chr 22:5
her ***m*** should be destroyed . . . . Acts 19:27

MAGNIFY—*to make or declare great*

Concerning God's:
Name 2Sam 7:26
Word . . . . . Ps 138:2
Law . . . . . Is 42:21
Christ's name . . . . . Acts 19:17

Duty of, toward God:
With others . . . . . Ps 34:3
With thanksgiving . . . . . Ps 69:30
In the body . . . . . Phil 1:20

[*also* **MAGNIFIED**]
and thou hast ***m*** thy mercy . . . . Gen 19:19
begin to ***m*** thee in the sight . . . Josh 3:7
m Joshua in the sight of all . . . . Josh 4:14
that thy name may be ***m*** for . . . 1Chr 17:24
the Lord ***m*** Solomon 1Chr 29:25
with him, and ***m*** him 2Chr 1:1
was ***m*** in the sight of all 2Chr 32:23
man, that thou shouldest ***m*** . . . Job 7:17
ye will ***m*** yourselves against . . . Job 19:5
Remember that thou ***m*** his . . . . Job 36:24
that ***m*** themselves against . . . . . Ps 35:26
Let the Lord be ***m***, which . . . . . Ps 35:27
they ***m*** themselves against . . . . . Ps 38:16
The Lord be ***m*** . . . . . Ps 40:16
me that did ***m*** himself . . . . . Ps 55:12
Let God be ***m*** . . . . . Ps 70:4
the saw ***m*** itself against him . . . Is 10:15
for he ***m*** himself against . . . . . Jer 48:26
hath ***m*** himself against the . . . . Jer 48:42
the enemy hath ***m*** himself . . . . . Lam 1:9
Thus will I ***m*** myself, and . . . . . Ezek 38:23
he ***m*** himself even to the . . . . . Dan 8:11
he shall ***m*** himself in his . . . . . Dan 8:25
and ***m*** himself above every . . . . Dan 11:36
for he shall ***m*** himself above . . . Dan 11:37
m themselves against their . . . . . Zeph 2:8
m themselves against the . . . . . Zeph 2:10
not ***m*** themselves against . . . . . Zech 12:7
Lord will be ***m*** from the . . . . . Mal 1:5
said, My soul doth ***m*** the . . . . . Luke 1:46
to them: but the people ***m*** . . . . Acts 5:13
speak with tongues, and ***m*** . . . . Acts 10:46
of the Gentiles, I ***m*** mine . . . . . Rom 11:13

MAGOG (mā'gŏg)—*"covering; roof"*
People among Japheth's descendants . . . . . Gen 10:2
Associated with Gog . . . . Ezek 38:2
Representatives of final enemies . . . . . Rev. 20:8

of Japheth; Gomer, and ***M*** 1Chr 1:5
I will send a fire on ***M*** . . . . . Ezek 39:6

MAGOR-MISSABIB (mā-gŏr-mĭs'ä-bĭb)—*"terror is about"*
Name indicating Pashur's end . . . . . Jer 20:3

MAGPIASH (măg'pĭ-ăsh)—*"collector of a cluster of stars; moth-killer"*
Signer of the covenant . . . Neh 10:20

MAHALAH (mä-hā'lä)—*"tenderness"*
Manassite 1Chr 7:14, 18

MAHALALEEL, MALELEEL (mä-hā'lä-lē-ĕl, mä-lē'ĕl)—*"God is splendor"*
1. Descendant of Seth . . . . . Gen 5:12
2. Postexilic Judahite . . . . . Neh 11:4

Cainan lived after he begat ***M*** . Gen 5:13
And ***M*** lived sixty and five . . . . Gen 5:15
M lived after he begat Jared . . . Gen 5:16
And all the days of ***M*** were . . . Gen 5:17
Kenan, ***M***, Jered 1Chr 1:2

MAHALATH (mā'hä-lăth)—*"mild"*
1. One of Esau's wives . . . . Gen 28:9
Called Bashemath . . . . . Gen 36:3, 4, 13
2. One of Rehoboam's wives 2Chr 11:18
3. Musical term . . . . . Ps 53:*title*

MAHALI—*See* **MAHLIL**

MAHANAIM (mā-hä-nā'ĭm)—*"tents"*
Name given by Jacob to a sacred site . . . . . Gen 32:2
On boundary between Gad and Manasseh . . . . Josh 13:26, 30
Assigned to Merarite Levites . . . . . Josh 21:38
Becomes Ish-bosheth's capital 2Sam 2:8-29
David flees to, during Absalom's rebellion . . . 2Sam 17:24, 27
Solomon places Ahinadab over 1Kin 4:14

sustenance while he lay at ***M*** . .2Sam 19:32
in the day when I went to ***M*** . .1Kin 2:8
and ***M*** with her suburbs 1Chr 6:80

MAHANEH-DAN (mā'hä-nĕ-dăn)—*"tents of judgment"*
Place between Zorah and Eshtaol . . . . .Judg 13:25

they called that place ***M*** . . . . . .Judg 18:12

MAHARAI (mä-hăr'ā-ī)—*"hasty"*
One of David's mighty men 2Sam 23:28
Becomes an army captain.1Chr 27:13

MAHATH (mā'hăth)—*"dissolution; snatching"*
1. Kohathite Levite 1Chr 6:35
2. Levite in Hezekiah's reign 2Chr 29:12
Appointed an overseer of tithes 2Chr 31:13

MAHAVITE (mā'hä-vīt)—*probably a term used for any resident of Mahanaim*
Applied to Eliel 1Chr 11:46

MAHAZIOTH (mä-hā'zĭ-ŏth)—*"visions"*
Levite musician 1Chr 25:4, 30

MAHER-SHALAL-HASH-BAZ (mā-her-shăl-ăl-hăsh-băz)—*"the spoil hastens, the prey speeds"*
Symbolic name of Isaiah's second son; prophetic of the fall of Damascus and Samaria . . . . .Is 8:1-4

MAHLAH (mä'lä)—*"mildness; sick"*
1. Zelophehad's daughter . .Num 26:33
2. Child of Hammoleketh . .1Chr 7:18

M, Noah, and Hoglah, and . . . .Num 27:1
For ***M***, Tirzah, and Hoglah . . . .Num 36:11
names of his daughters, ***M*** . . . .Josh 17:3

MAHLI (mä'lī)—*"mild; sickly"*
1. Eldest son of Merari . . . .Num 3:20
Father of three sons 1Chr 6:29
Father of tribal family . . .Num 3:33
Called Mahali . . . . .Ex 6:19
2. Another Merarite Levite; nephew of 1 . . . 1Chr 6:47; 1Chr 23:23; 1Chr 24:30

Sons of Merari; ***M***, and 1Chr 6:19
sons of Merari; ***M***, and 1Chr 23:21
of the sons of ***M*** . . . . .Ezra 8:18

MAHLON (mä'lŏn)—*"mild; sickly"*
Husband of Ruth; without child . . . . .Ruth 1:2-5

MAHOL (mā'hŏl)—*"dancer"*
Father of certain wise men 1Kin 4:31

MAID—*a young woman*

Descriptive of:
Young girl 1Sam 9:11
Virgin . . . . .Ex 22:16

Characteristics of:
Fond of ornaments . . . . . .Jer 2:32
Beautiful . . . . .Esth 2:7
Obedient . . . . .Ps 123:2
Sexually attractive . . . . . . .Prov 30:19-20

Provision for:
Physical needs of . . . . .Prov 27:27
Spiritual blessings upon . .Deut 5:14
Accepted as wives . . . . . . .Gen 30:3

[*also* MAIDEN, MAIDENS, MAID'S, MAIDS]
I pray thee, go in unto my ***m***. .Gen 16:2
Hagar her ***m*** the Egyptian . . . . .Gen 16:3
given my ***m*** into thy bosom . . .Gen 16:5
Behold, thy ***m*** is in thy hand . .Gen 16:6
Sarai's ***m***, Whence camest . . . . .Gen 16:8
Zilpah his ***m*** for a handmaid . .Gen 29:24
his handmaid to be her ***m*** . . . . .Gen 29:29
Rachel's ***m*** conceived again . . . .Gen 30:7
she took Zilpah her ***m***, and . . .Gen 30:9
Zilpah Leah's ***m*** bare Jacob . . .Gen 30:10
Leah's ***m*** bare Jacob a . . . . .Gen 30:12
given my ***m*** to my husband . . . .Gen 30:18
her ***m*** walked along by the . . . .Ex 2:5
flags, she sent her ***m*** to . . . . . . .Ex 2:5
the ***m*** went and called the . . . . .Ex 2:8
his servant or his ***m*** . . . . .Ex 21:20
or the eye of his ***m*** . . . . .Ex 21:26
if she bear a ***m*** child, then . . . .Lev 12:5
thy servant, and for thy ***m*** . . . .Lev 25:6
her, I found her not a ***m*** . . . . . .Deut 22:14
found not thy daughter a ***m*** . . .Deut 22:17
here is my daughter a ***m*** . . . . . .Judg 19:24
but abide here fast by my ***m***. . .Ruth 2:8
that thou go out with his ***m*** . . .Ruth 2:22
So she kept fast by the ***m*** of . .Ruth 2:23
kindred, with whose ***m*** thou . . .Ruth 3:2
land of Israel a little ***m*** 2Kin 5:2
Thus and thus said the ***m*** 2Kin 5:4
upon young man or ***m*** 2Chr 36:17
their servants and their ***m*** . . . . .Ezra 2:65
m pleased him, and she . . . . . . .Esth 2:9
he preferred her and her ***m*** . . .Esth 2:9
every ***m*** turn was come to . . . . .Esth 2:12
came every ***m*** unto the . . . . .Esth 2:13
So Esther's ***m*** and . . . . .Esth 4:4
and my ***m*** will fast likewise . . . .Esth 4:16
my ***m***, count me for a . . . . .Job 19:15
should I think upon a ***m***? . . . . .Job 31:1
thou bind him for thy ***m***? . . . . .Job 41:5
m were not given to marriage. .Ps 78:63
both young men, and ***m***; old . .Ps 148:12
She hath sent forth her ***m*** . . . . .Prov 9:3
and a portion to her ***m*** . . . . .Prov 31:15
I got me servants and ***m*** . . . . . .Eccl 2:7
the young man and the ***m*** . . . . .Jer 51:22
and the ***m*** in the cities of . . . . .Lam 5:11
old and young, both ***m***, and . . .Ezek 9:6
shall take ***m*** of the seed . . . . . . .Ezek 44:22
will go in unto the same ***m*** . . . .Amos 2:7
her ***m*** shall lead her as with . . .Nah 2:7
and new wine the ***m*** . . . . .Zech 9:17
the ***m*** is not dead, but . . . . .Matt 9:24
her by the hand, and the ***m*** . . .Matt 9:25
into the porch, another ***m*** . . . . .Matt 26:71
of the ***m*** of the high priest . . . .Mark 14:66
a ***m*** saw him again, and . . . . . . .Mark 14:69
and the mother of the ***m*** . . . . . .Luke 8:51
hand, and called, saying, ***M*** . . .Luke 8:54
beat the menservants and ***m*** . . .Luke 12:45
a certain ***m*** beheld him as . . . . .Luke 22:56

MAIDSERVANT—*a female servant*

[*also* MAIDSERVANT'S, MAIDSERVANTS]
and menservants, and ***m*** . . . . . .Gen 12:16
Abimelech,..wife and his ***m*** . . .Gen 20:17
menservants, and ***m***, and . . . . . .Gen 24:35
and ***m***, and menservants . . . . . .Gen 30:43
and into the two ***m*** tents . . . . . .Gen 31:33
unto the firstborn of the ***m*** . . . .Ex 11:5
thy manservant, nor thy ***m*** . . . .Ex 20:10
his manservant, nor his ***m*** . . . . .Ex 20:17
his daughter to be a ***m*** . . . . .Ex 21:7
push a manservant or a ***m*** . . . . .Ex 21:32
manservant's tooth, or his ***m*** . .Ex 21:27
thy menservant, nor thy ***m*** . . . .Deut 5:14
thy ***m*** may rest as well . . . . . . .Deut 5:14
or his manservant, or his ***m*** . . .Deut 5:21
thy manservant, and thy ***m*** . . . .Deut 12:18
unto thy ***m*** thou shalt do . . . . . .Deut 15:17
manservant, and thy ***m*** . . . . .Deut 16:11
Abimelech, the son of his ***m*** . . .Judg 9:18
menservants, and your ***m*** 1Sam 8:16
of the ***m*** which thou hast 2Sam 6:22
and menservants, and ***m***? 2Kin 5:26
manservants and their ***m***, of . . .Neh 7:67
my manservant or of my ***m*** . . . .Job 31:13
and every man his ***m*** . . . . .Jer 34:9

MAIL—*matter posted from one person to another; armor*
Letters were sent . . . . .Esth 3:13
Applied to armor 1Sam 17:5

MAIMED—*crippled; wounded*
Blind, or broken, or ***m*** . . . . .Lev 22:22
were lame, blind, dumb, ***m*** . . . .Matt 15:30
dumb to speak, the ***m*** to be . . .Matt 15:31
to enter into life halt or ***m*** . . . .Matt 18:8
thee to enter into life ***m*** . . . . . . .Mark 9:43
feast, call the poor, the ***m*** . . . . .Luke 14:13
hither the poor, and the ***m*** . . . .Luke 14:21

MAINSAIL—*the lowest sail on the foremast, providing directional control*
Hoisted . . . . .Acts 27:40

MAINTENANCE—*provision for support; sustenance*
Household supply . . . . . . .Prov 27:27
King's service . . . . .Ezra 4:14
Solomon's supply 1Kin 4:22, 23

[*also* MAINTAIN, MAINTAINED, MAINTAINEST]
supplication, and ***m*** their 1Kin 8:45
dwelling place, and ***m*** their 1Kin 8:49
that he ***m*** the cause of his 1Kin 8:59
to ***m*** the house of the Lord . . .1Chr 26:27
supplication, and ***m*** their 2Chr 6:35
supplications, and ***m*** their 2Chr 6:39
I will ***m*** mine own ways . . . . . . .Job 13:15
m my right and my cause . . . . .Ps 9:4
and of my cup: thou ***m*** my . . . .Ps 16:5
will ***m*** the cause of the . . . . .Ps 140:12
might be careful to ***m*** good . . . .Titus 3:8
ours also learn to ***m*** good . . . . .Titus 3:14

MAJESTY—*the dignity and power of a ruler*

Of God:
Splendor of . . . . .Is 2:2, 19, 21
Voice of . . . . .Ps 29:4
Clothed with . . . . .Ps 93:1

Of Christ:
Promised to . . . . .Mic 5:2-4
Laid upon . . . . .Ps 21:5
Eyewitness 2Pet 1:16

Of kings:
Solomon 1Chr 29:25
Nebuchadnezzar . . . . .Dan 4:28, 30, 36; Dan 5:18-21

and the victory, and the ***m*** 1Chr 29:11
upon him such royal ***m*** 1Chr 29:25
honor of his excellent ***m*** . . . . . .Esth 1:4
with God is terrible ***m*** . . . . .Job 37:22
Deck thyself now with ***m*** . . . . . .Job 40:10
with thy glory and thy ***m*** . . . . . .Ps 45:3
thy ***m*** ride prosperously . . . . . . .Ps 45:4
Honor and ***m*** are before . . . . . .Ps 96:6
clothed with honor and ***m*** . . . . .Ps 104:1
the glorious honor of thy ***m*** . . .Ps 145:5
glorious ***m*** of his kingdom . . . . .Ps 145:12
and for the glory of his ***m*** . . . . .Is 2:10
sing for the ***m*** of the Lord . . . .Is 24:14
will not behold the ***m*** of . . . . . .Is 26:10
ornament, he set it in ***m*** . . . . . .Ezek 7:20
and for the honor of my ***m***? . . .Dan 4:30
excellent ***m*** was added unto . . .Dan 4:36
m, and glory, and honor . . . . . .Dan 5:18
And for the ***m*** that he gave . . .Dan 5:19
the right hand of the ***M*** on . . . .Heb 1:3
throne of the ***M*** in the . . . . .Heb 8:1
be glory and ***m***, dominion . . . . .Jude 25

MAKAZ (mā'kăz)—*"an end"*
Town in Judah 1Kin 4:9

MAKE—*to construct; to force*

[*also* MADE, MADEST, MAKER, MAKEST, MAKETH, MAKING]
Let us ***m*** man in our image . . .Gen 1:26
I will ***m*** him a help meet . . . . . .Gen 2:18
to be desired to ***m*** one wise . . .Gen 3:6
I will ***m*** of thee a great . . . . . . .Gen 12:2
I will ***m*** him a great nation . . . .Gen 21:18
who ***m*** the dumb, or deaf . . . . .Ex 4:11
not fulfilled your task in ***m*** . . . .Ex 5:14
the priest that ***m*** atonement . . .Lev 7:7
blood that ***m*** an atonement . . . .Lev 17:11
I will ***m*** your cities waste . . . . . .Lev 26:31
m his son or his daughter . . . . .Deut 18:10
time, in ***m*** war against it to . . .Deut 20:19
m his sons to inherit that . . . . . .Deut 21:16

M

man that *m* any graven or .....Deut 27:15
Lord thy God *m* with thee ....Deut 29:12
shall come upon them *m* haste .Deut 32:35
what *m* thou in this place? ....Judg 18:3
they were *m* their hearts ......Judg 19:22
The Lord killeth, and *m* 1Sam 2:6
he will *m* thee a house 2Sam 7:11
m speed to depart 2Sam 15:14
power; and he *m* my way 2Sam 22:33
and drinking, and *m* merry 1Kin 4:20
m a noise with psalteries 1Chr 15:28
m confession to the Lord......2Chr 30:22
commanded me to *m* haste 2Chr 35:21
m a covenant with him to .....Neh 9:8
And *m* known unto them .....Neh 9:14
Cause Haman to *m* haste .....Esth 5:5
be more pure than his *M*?.....Job 4:17
For he *m* sore, and bindeth ..Job 5:18
spoiled, and *m* the judges .....Job 12:17
m me to possess the ....Job 13:26
m collops of fat on his ....Job 15:27
and for this I *m* haste.........Job 20:2
him, that thou *m* thy ways ....Job 22:3
m peace in his high places.....Job 25:2
my *M* would soon take me ....Job 32:22
Where is God my *m*, who ....Job 35:10
and *m* us wiser than the.......Job 35:11
righteousness to my *M* ....Job 36:3
He *m* the deep to boil like a ..Job 41:31
m the sea like a pot of........Job 41:31
Lord, only *m* me dwell in .....Ps 4:8
m him to have dominion ......Ps 8:6
he *m* inquisition for blood.....Ps 9:12
they *m* ready their arrow......Ps 11:2
He *m* my feet like hinds' ......Ps 18:33
Lord is sure, *m* wise the ......Ps 19:7
shalt thou *m* them turn ....Ps 21:12
He *m* them also to skip like ...Ps 29:6
m the devices of the people ..Ps 33:10
M haste to help me...........Ps 38:22
Lord, *m* me to know mind end.Ps 39:4
m his beauty to consume......Ps 39:11
m haste to help me ....Ps 40:13
Thou *m* us to turn back ....Ps 44:10
Thou *m* us a reproach to ......Ps 44:13
Thou *m* us a byword among ...Ps 44:14
He *m* wars to cease unto ......Ps 46:9
thou *m* the outgoings of.......Ps 65:8
thou *m* it soft with showers....Ps 65:10
M haste, O God, to deliver ...Ps 70:1
m haste for my help ....Ps 71:12
Thou *m* us a strife unto our ...Ps 80:6
thou *m* strong for thyself......Ps 80:15
thou *m* strong for thyself......Ps 80:17
M us glad according to the ....Ps 90:15
kneel before the Lord our *M* ..Ps 95:6
who *m* his angels spirits ....Ps 104:4
Thou *m* darkness, and it is ....Ps 104:20
He *m* the storm a calm, so ....Ps 107:29
and *m* him families like a .....Ps 107:41
he *m* lightnings for the rain ...Ps 135:7
m haste unto me ....Ps 141:1
man, that thou *m* account .....Ps 144:3
He *m* peace in thy borders ....Ps 147:14
and *m* haste to shed blood ....Prov 1:16
A wise son *m* a glad father....Prov 10:1
blessing of the Lord, it *m* .....Prov 10:22
in the heart of man *m* it ......Prov 12:25
there is that *m* himself rich ....Prov 13:7
there is that *m* himself poor ...Prov 13:7
the poor reproacheth his *M* ...Prov 14:31
A merry heart *m* a cheerful ...Prov 15:13
a good report *m* the bones ....Prov 15:30
the poor reproacheth his *M* ...Prov 17:5
A man's gift *m* room for ......Prov 18:16
Lord is the *m* of them all .....Prov 22:2
he that *m* haste to be rich.....Prov 28:20
She *m* fine linen, and ....Prov 31:24
out the work that God *m* ......Eccl 3:11
man's wisdom *m* his face to ...Eccl 8:1
not the works of God who *m*..Eccl 11:5
thou *m* thy flock to rest at ....Song 1:7
M haste, my beloved, and .....Song 8:14
and *m* a tinkling with their ....Is 3:16
Let him *m* speed, and ....Is 5:19

shall a man look to his *M* .....Is 17:7
every one that *m* mention .....Is 19:17
looked unto the *m* thereof ....Is 22:11
the Lord *m* the earth empty ...Is 24:1
and *m* it waste, and turneth ...Is 24:1
believeth shall not *m* haste ....Is 28:16
he *m* the judges of the earth ..Is 40:23
I will *m* waste mountains ......Is 42:15
m it after the figure of ....Is 44:13
m a god, and worshipeth ......Is 44:15
he *m* it a graven image, ...Is 44:15
the Lord that *m* all things .....Is 44:24
liars, and *m* diviners mad .....Is 44:25
m their knowledge foolish .....Is 44:25
him that striveth with his *M*! ..Is 45:9
that fashioneth it, What *m* ....Is 45:9
Holy One of Israel, and his *M* .Is 45:11
together that are *m* of idols ...Is 45:16
liken me, and *m* me equal ....Is 46:5
Thy children shall *m* haste ....Is 49:17
forgettest the Lord thy *m* .....Is 51:13
For thy *M* is thine husband....Is 54:5
m it bring forth and bud ......Is 55:10
m haste to shed innocent ......Is 59:7
my heart *m* a noise in me .....Jer 4:19
And let them *m* haste.........Jer 9:18
trusteth in man, and *m* flesh...Jer 17:5
m thy nest in the cedars.......Jer 22:23
thou *m* this people to trust ....Jer 28:15
that is mad, and *m* himself ....Jer 29:26
Thus saith the Lord the *m* ....Jer 33:2
dove that *m* her nest in the ...Jer 48:28
I will *m* thee waste, and ......Ezek 5:14
even to *m* all ready ....Ezek 7:14
m to thyself images of men....Ezek 16:17
and *m* thine high place in .....Ezek 16:31
m idols against herself to......Ezek 22:3
of the wares of thy *m*.........Ezek 27:16
m all their loins to be at a ....Ezek 29:7
will *m* the land of Egypt ......Ezek 29:10
I will *m* the rivers dry ....Ezek 30:12
and *m* known to the king .....Dan 2:28
and *m* supplication before .....Dan 6:11
m his petition three times .....Dan 6:13
the abomination that *m* ....Dan 12:11
Israel hath forgotten his *M* ....Hos 8:14
swearing falsely in *m* a ....Hos 10:4
that *m* the morning ....Amos 4:13
that *m* the seven stars and ....Amos 5:8
and *m* the day dark with ......Amos 5:8
m the ephah small, and the ...Amos 8:5
not labored, neither *m* it ......Jon 4:10
in *m* thee desolate because .....Mic 6:13
He rebuketh the sea, and *m* ...Nah 1:4
shall *m* haste to the wall ......Nah 2:5
And *m* men as the fishes of ...Hab 1:14
the *m* thereof hath graven it...Hab 2:18
the *m* of his work trusteth.....Hab 2:18
Behold, I will *m* Jerusalem ....Zech 12:2
And did not he *m* one? ....Mal 2:15
for he *m* his sun to rise on ....Matt 5:45
and the people *m* a noise .....Matt 9:23
m it as sure as ye can ....Matt 27:65
Why *m* ye this ado, and.......Mark 5:39
M the word of God of none ...Mark 7:13
he *m* both the deaf to hear....Mark 7:37
there *m* ready for us ....Mark 14:15
to *m* ready a people ....Luke 1:17
then both the new *m* a rent ...Luke 5:36
When thou *m* a dinner or .....Luke 14:12
M ready wherewith I may sup .Luke 17:8
furnished: there *m* ready ......Luke 22:12
Father, *m* himself equal ....John 5:18
are dead: whom *m* thou ....John 8:53
dost thou *m* us to doubt? .....John 10:24
whosoever *m* himself a king ...John 19:12
Jesus Christ *m* thee whole .....Acts 9:34
before these days *m* an ....Acts 21:38
M haste, and get thee.........Acts 22:18
M request, if by any means ...Rom 1:10
law, and *m* thy boast of God ..Rom 2:17
hope *m* not ashamed...........Rom 5:5
Spirit itself *m* intercession .....Rom 8:26
also *m* intercession for us .....Rom 8:34
m manifest the counsels of 1Cor 4:5

For who *m* thee to differ......1Cor 4:7
who is he then that *m* me 2Cor 2:2
as poor, yet *m* many rich 2Cor 6:10
they were, it *m* no matter .....Gal 2:6
m in himself of twain one .....Eph 2:15
m increase of the body unto...Eph 4:16
doth *m* manifest is light ....Eph 5:13
and *m* melody in your heart ...Eph 5:19
for you all *m* request with.....Phil 1:4
That I may *m* it manifest......Col 4:4
m mention of you in our 1Thess 1:2
m mention of thee always .....Philem 4
Who *m* his angels spirits ......Heb 1:7
m him a little lower than......Heb 2:7
law *m* men high priests ....Heb 7:28
m the Son, who is ....Heb 7:28
whose builder and *m* is God...Heb 11:10
m them an example unto......2Pet 2:6
compassion, *m* a difference....Jude 22
he *m* fire come down from ....Rev 13:13
Behold, I *m* all things new ....Rev 21:5
and whosoever loveth and *m* ..Rev 22:15

MAKHELOTH (măk-hē'lŏth)—*"congregations"*
Israelite camp ....Num 33:25, 26

MAKKEDAH (mă-kē'dä)—*"worshiping"*
Canaanite town assigned to Judah ....Josh 15:20, 41

to Azekah, and unto *M* ....Josh 10:10
are found hid in a cave at *M* ..Josh 10:17
And that day Joshua took *M* ..Josh 10:28
Then Joshua passed from *M* ...Josh 10:29
and Naamah, and *M* ....Josh 15:41

MAKTESH (măk'tĕsh)—*"mortar"*
Valley in Jerusalem......Zeph 1:11

MALACHI (măl'ä-kī)—*"messenger of Jehovah; my messenger"*
Prophet and writer ......Mal 1:1

MALACHI, THE BOOK OF—*a book of the Old Testament*
God's love for Jacob.....Mal 1:1-5
The priesthood rebuked. .Mal 1:6—2:17
The messenger of the Lord ....Mal 3:1-5
The Day of the Lord ....Mal 4:1-6

MALCHAM (măl'kăm)—*"their king"*
Benjamite leader 1Chr 8:9

MALCHIEL (măl'kĭ-ĕl)—*"God is a king"*
Grandson of Asher; founder of Malchielites .Gen 46:17

of Beriah; Heber, and *M*......1Chr 7:31

MALCHIELITES—*descendants of Malchiel*
Malchiel, the family of the *M*. .Num 26:45

MALCHIJAH, MALCHIAH, MELCHIAH (măl-kī'jä, măl-kī'ä, mĕl-kī'ä)—*"Jehovah is king"*

1. Gershonite Levite......1Chr 6:40
2. The father of Pashur ...1Chr 9:12; Jer 21:1
3. Head of priestly division 1Chr 24:1, 6, 9
4. Royal prince ....Jer 38:6
5, 6. Two sons of Parosh; divorced their foreign wives ....Ezra 10:25
7. Son of Harim; divorced his foreign wife ......Ezra 10:31
   Helps rebuild walls.....Neh 3:11
8. Son of Rechab; repairs gates................Neh 3:14
9. Postexilic goldsmith ....Neh 3:31
10. Ezra's assistant ....Neh 8:4
11. Signer of the covenant .Neh 10:1, 3
12. Choir member ....Neh 12:42
13. Father of Pashur ....Jer 21:1

MALCHIRAM (măl-kī'răm)—*"my king is exalted"*
Son of King Jeconiah 1Chr 3:17, 18

MALCHI-SHUA, MELCHI-SHUA (măl-kī-shōō'ä, mĕl-kī–shōō'ä)—*"the king is salvation"*
Son of King Saul 1Sam 14:49
Killed at Gilboa 1Sam 31:2

Saul begat Jonathan, and *M* ...1Chr 8:33
and Abinadab, and *M*, the 1Chr 10:2

MALCHUS (măl'kŭs)—*"counselor; ruler"*
Servant of the high priest.John 18:10

MALE—*the sex that begets the young*

[*also* MALES]
m and female created he ......Gen 1:27
thee; they shall be *m* and .....Gen 6:19
by sevens, the *m* and his ......Gen 7:2
clean by two, the *m* and his ...Gen 7:2
into the ark, the *m* and the ...Gen 7:9
every *m* among the men of ....Gen 17:23
m among us be circumcised ...Gen 34:22
boldly, and slew all the *m* .....Gen 34:25
a *m* of the first year ....Ex 12:5
let all his *m* be circumcised....Ex 12:48
openeth the matrix, being *m*...Ex 13:15
offer a *m* without blemish .....Lev 1:3
whether it be a *m* or..........Lev 3:1
goats, a *m* without blemish ....Lev 4:23
the *m* among the children .....Lev 6:18
her that hath born a *m* or a ...Lev 12:7
of the *m* from twenty years....Lev 27:3
be of the *m* five shekels of ....Lev 27:6
names, every *m* by their ......Num 1:2
every *m* from a month old ....Num 3:15
to the number of all the *m* ....Num 3:22
to the number of all the *m* ....Num 3:34
all the firstborn of the *m* ......Num 3:40
every *m* shall eat it: it shall ...Num 18:10
m from a month old and ......Num 26:62
figure, the likeness of *m* or....Deut 4:16
firstling *m* that come of thy ...Deut 15:19
shalt smite every *m* thereof....Deut 20:13
out of Egypt, that were *m*.....Josh 5:4
m children of Manasseh the ...Josh 17:2
utterly destroy every *m* ....Judg 21:11
he had smitten every *m* in.....1Kin 11:15
Beside their genealogy of *m* ...2Chr 31:16
by genealogy of the *m* a ......Ezra 8:3
with him three hundred *m*.....Ezra 8:5
and with him seventy *m*.......Ezra 8:7
two hundred and eighteen *m* ..Ezra 8:9
hundred and threescore *m*.....Ezra 8:10
him twenty and eight *m* ....Ezra 8:11
an hundred and ten *m* ....Ezra 8:12
and with them threescore *m* ...Ezra 8:13
and with them seventy *m*......Ezra 8:14
made them *m* and female .....Matt 19:4
God made them *m* and ....Mark 10:6
Every *m* that openeth the .....Luke 2:23
free, there is neither *m* nor....Gal 3:28

MALEFACTOR—*rebel; criminal*
Christ accused of ....John 18:30
Christ crucified between .Luke 23:32, 33
One unrepentant; one repentant ....Luke 23:39-43

MALELEEL (mä-lē'lĕ-ĕl)—*Greek form of Mahalaleel*
Ancestor of Christ ....Luke 3:37

MALFORMATION—*irregular features*
Of a giant 2Sam 21:20

MALICE—*active intent to harm others*
Causes of:
Unregenerate heart ......Prov 6:14-16, 18, 19
Satanic hatred..........1John 3:12
Jealousy 1Sam 18:8-29
Racial prejudice ....Esth 3:5-15
Christian's attitude toward:
Pray for those guilty of ..Matt 5:44
Clean out...............1Cor 5:7, 8
Put away ....Eph 4:31
Put aside ....Col 3:8
Putting aside 1Pet 2:1
Avoid manifestations 1Pet 2:16

Characteristics:
Unregenerate ....Rom 1:29; Titus 3:3
God's wrath ....Rom 1:18, 29
Brings own punishment ..Ps 7:15, 16

[*also* MALICIOUS, MALICIOUSNESS]
wickedness, covetousness, *m*...Rom 1:29
howbeit in *m* be ye children ...1Cor 14:20
in *m* and envy, hateful, and ...Titus 3:3
prating against us with *m*......3John 10

MALIGNITY—*malicious behavior*
Full of envy.............Rom 1:29

MALLOTHI (măl'ō-thī)—*"Jehovah is speaking"*
Son of Heman 1Chr 25:4, 26

MALLOWS—*"saltiness"*
Perennial shrub that grows in salty marshes. .Job 30:4

MALLUCH (măl'ŭk)—*"counselor; ruling"*
1. Merarite Levite 1Chr 6:44
2. Chief of postexilic priests.Neh 12:2, 7
3. Son of Bani; divorced his foreign wife ....Ezra 10:29
4. Son of Harim; divorced his foreign wife ....Ezra 10:32
5, 6. Two who sign the covenant ....Neh 10:4, 27

MAMMON—*wealth or possessions*
Served as a master other than God ....Matt 6:24

faithful in the unrighteous *m* ..Luke 16:11
Ye cannot serve God and *m*...Luke 16:13

MAMRE (măm'rĕ)—*"firmness; vigor"*
1. Town or district near Hebron ....Gen 23:19
West of Machpelah ....Gen 23:17, 19
Abraham dwelt by the oaks of ....Gen 13:18
2. Amorite, brother of Eschol ....Gen 14:13

me, Aner, Eshcol, and *M* .....Gen 14:24
unto him in the plains of *M* ...Gen 18:1
Hittite, which is before *M* .....Gen 25:9
Isaac his father unto *M* ....Gen 35:27
Machpelah, which is before *M* .Gen 49:30
Ephron the Hittite, before *M* ..Gen 50:13

MAN—*human being, male or female; the male human*
Original state of:
Created for God's pleasure and glory ...Is 43:7; Rev 4:11
Created by God ....Gen 1:26, 27
Made in God's image ....Gen 9:6
Formed of dust..........Gen 2:7
Made upright ....Eccl 7:29
Endowed with intelligence Gen 2:19, 20; Col 3:10
Wonderfully made ....Ps 139:14-16
Given wide dominion ....Gen 1:28
From one ....Acts 17:26-28
Male and female ....Gen 1:27
Superior to animals ......Matt 10:31
Living being (soul) ......Gen 2:7
Sinful state of:
Result of Adam's disobedience ....Gen 2:16, 17; Gen 3:1-6
Makes all sinners ....Rom 5:12
Brings physical death...Gen 2:16, 17, 19; Rom 5:12-14
Makes spiritually dead ...Eph 2:1
Redeemed state of:
Originates in God's love. .John 3:16
Provides salvation for ....Titus 2:11
Accomplished by Christ's death...................1Pet 1:18-21
Fulfills the new covenant .Heb 8:8-13
Entered by new birth ....John 3:1-12
Final state of:
Continues eternally ......Matt 25:46

Cannot be changed ....Luke 16:26
Determined by faith or by unbelief ....John 3:36; 2Thess 1:6-10
Christ's relation to:
Gives light to ....John 1:9
Knows nature of ....John 2:25
Took nature of..........Heb 2:14-16
In the likeness ....Rom 8:3
Only Mediator for 1Tim 2:5
Died for ....Heb 9:26, 28; 1Pet 1:18-21
Certain aspects of:
First—Adam 1Cor 15:45, 47
Last—Christ 1Cor 15:45
Natural—unregenerate ...1Cor 2:14
Outward—physical.......2Cor 4:16
Inner—spiritual..........Rom 7:22
New—regenerate ....Eph 2:15

[*also* MAN'S, MEN, MEN'S]
the ground any more for *m*....Gen 8:21
Whoso sheddeth *m* blood .....Gen 9:6
the children of *m* builded .....Gen 11:5
commanded his *m* ....Gen 12:20
the *m* feet that were with .....Gen 24:32
he and the *m* that were ....Gen 24:54
the *m* of the place asked ....Gen 26:7
We are all one *m* sons; we ....Gen 42:11
every *m* bundle of money was .Gen 42:35
Fill the *m* sacks with food .....Gen 44:1
every *m* money in his sack's ...Gen 44:1
him, Who hath made *m*.......Ex 4:11
work be laid upon *m* ....Ex 5:9
We are all dead *m*............Ex 12:33
Joshua, Choose us out *m*......Ex 17:9
m, such as fear God ....Ex 18:21
if one *m* ox hurt another's ....Ex 21:35
and it be stolen out of the *m* ..Ex 22:7
sent young *m* of the ....Ex 24:5
that offereth any *m* burnt .....Lev 7:8
adultery with another *m*.......Lev 20:10
every *m* hallowed things ......Num 5:10
write..every *m* name upon.....Num 17:2
every *m* inheritance shall be ...Num 33:54
serve gods, the work of *m*.....Deut 4:28
as a *m* chasteneth his ....Deut 8:5
shall no *m* be able ....Deut 11:25
every *m* whatsoever is ....Deut 12:8
among you a poor *m* ....Deut 15:7
for the tree of the field is *m*...Deut 20:19
for he taketh a *m* life to ......Deut 24:6
he put a trumpet in every *m*...Judg 7:16
down at the door of the *m* ....Judg 19:26
The *m* name with whom I .....Ruth 2:19
Go ye every *m* to 1Sam 8:22
thou taken aught of any *m* 1Sam 12:4
Let no *m* heart fail because ...1Sam 17:32
Wherefore hearest thou *m*.....1Sam 24:9
took the poor *m* lamb, and 2Sam 12:4
which Amasa was a *m* son 2Sam 17:25
forsook the old *m* counsel 1Kin 12:13
m bones shall be burnt........1Kin 13:2
out of the sea, like a *m* 1Kin 18:44
What manner of *m* was 2Kin 1:7
that cometh into any *m* 2Kin 12:4
no gods, but the work of *m* ...2Kin 19:18
and burned *m* bones upon.....2Kin 23:20
great *m* house burnt he with...2Kin 25:9
Should such a *m* as I flee .....Neh 6:11
do according to every *m* ......Esth 1:8
despise the cause of my *m* ....Job 31:13
and gold, the work of *m* ......Ps 115:4
and gold, the work of *m* ......Ps 135:15
The rich *m* wealth is his.......Prov 10:15
ransom of a *m* life are his .....Prov 13:8
A *m* heart deviseth his way ...Prov 16:9
The rich *m* wealth is his.......Prov 18:11
A *m* belly shall be satisfied....Prov 18:20
are many devices in a *m* ......Prov 19:21
so doth the sweetness of a *m* ..Prov 27:9
m judgment cometh from .....Prov 29:26
The wise *m* eyes are in his ....Eccl 2:14
m heart discerneth both ....Eccl 8:5
wise *m* heart is at his right ....Eccl 10:2
roll, and write in it with a *m* ..Is 8:1

M

no gods, but the work of *m* . . .Is 37:19
him, and become another *m* . . .Jer 3:1
m is brutish in his . . . . .Jer 10:14
way of *m* is not in himself . . . . .Jer 10:23
mighty *m* hearts in Moab . . . . .Jer 48:41
given thee cow's dung for *m* . . .Ezek 4:15
m sword shall be against . . . . . .Ezek 38:21
in the *m* hand a measuring . . . .Ezek 40:5
came forth fingers of a *m* . . . . .Dan 5:5
heard a *m* voice between the . .Dan 8:16
a *m* uncle shall take him . . . . . .Amos 6:10
let us not perish for this *m* . . . .Jon 1:14
a *m* enemies are the men of . . .Mic 7:6
because of *m* blood, and . . . . . .Hab 2:8
M shall not live by bread . . . . .Matt 4:4
your light shine before *m* . . . . .Matt 5:16
do not your alms before *m* . . . .Matt 6:1
No *m* can serve two masters . . .Matt 6:24
liken him unto a wise *m* . . . . . .Matt 7:24
shall confess me before *m* . . . . .Matt 10:32
shall deny me before *m* . . . . . . .Matt 10:33
a *m* foes shall be they of . . . . . .Matt 10:36
one enter into a strong *m* . . . . .Matt 12:29
Whom do *m* say that I..am? . . .Matt 16:13
If any *m* will come after me . . .Matt 16:24
together, let not *m* put . . . . . . .Matt 19:6
call no *m*..father upon the . . . . .Matt 23:9
are within full of dead *m* . . . . . .Matt 23:27
sabbath was made for *m* . . . . . .Mark 2:27
not *m* for the sabbath . . . . .Mark 2:27
can enter into a strong *m* . . . . .Mark 3:27
If any *m* hath ears to hear . . . .Mark 4:23
With *m* it is impossible . . . . .Mark 10:27
seeing I know not a *m*? . . . . . . .Luke 1:34
peace, good will toward *m* . . . .Luke 2:14
for I am a sinful *m* . . . . .Luke 5:8
thou shalt catch *m* . . . . .Luke 5:10
as evil, for the Son of *m* . . . . . .Luke 6:22
not come to destroy *m* lives . . .Luke 9:56
that denieth me before *m* . . . . .Luke 12:9
in that which is another *m* . . . .Luke 16:12
any *m* brother die, having . . . . .Luke 20:28
M hearts failing them for . . . . . .Luke 21:26
I find no fault in this *m* . . . . . .Luke 23:4
Except a *m* be born again . . . . .John 3:3
If any *m* thirst, let him . . . . . . .John 7:37
will draw all *m* unto me . . . . . . .John 12:32
if any *m* hear my words . . . . . . .John 12:47
no *m* cometh unto the Father . .John 14:6
Greater love hath no *m* . . . . . . .John 15:13
thou also one of this *m* . . . . . . .John 18:17
Behold the *m*! . . . . .John 19:5
how hear we every *m* . . . . .Acts 2:8
to bring this *m* blood upon . . . .Acts 5:28
to obey God rather than *m* . . . .Acts 5:29
and we entered into the *m* . . . .Acts 11:12
Neither is worshiped with *m* . . .Acts 17:25
stone, graven by art and *m* . . . .Acts 17:29
I have coveted no *m* silver . . . .Acts 20:33
so death passed upon all *m* . . . .Rom 5:12
if by one *m* offense death . . . . .Rom 5:17
O wretched *m* that I am! . . . . . .Rom 7:24
condescend to *m* of low . . . . . . .Rom 12:16
that judgest another *m* . . . . .Rom 14:4
with enticing words of *m* 1Cor 2:4
Every *m* work shall be made . . .1Cor 3:13
fire shall try every *m* work 1Cor 3:13
If any *m* work shall be 1Cor 3:15
made all things to all *m* 1Cor 9:22
judged of another *m* 1Cor 10:29
m without the woman 1Cor 11:11
neither the woman without..*m* .1Cor 11:11
if *m* have long hair 1Cor 11:14
With *m* of other tongues and . .1Cor 14:21
we are of all *m* most 1Cor 15:19
by *m* came death 1Cor 15:21
by *m* came also..resurrection . .1Cor 15:21
every *m* conscience in the 2Cor 4:2
if any *m* be in Christ 2Cor 5:17
that is, of other *m* labors 2Cor 10:15
me: God accepteth no *m* . . . . . .Gal 2:6
works, lest any *m*..boast . . . . . .Eph 2:9
and gave gifts unto *m* . . . . .Eph 4:8
put on the new *m*..after God . .Eph 4:24
not as pleasing *m*, but God 1Thess 2:4
we eat any *m* bread for 2Thess 3:8
will have all *m* to be saved 1Tim 2:4
I will therefore that *m* pray . . .1Tim 2:8
Lay hands suddenly on no *m* . .1Tim 5:22
be partaker of other *m* sins 1Tim 5:22
Some *m* sins are open 1Tim 5:24
Follow peace with all *m* . . . . . . .Heb 12:14
double-minded *m* is unstable . .James 1:8
his own heart, this *m* . . . . .James 1:26
according to every *m* work 1Pet 1:17
as a busybody in other *m* 1Pet 4:15
holy *m* of God spake as they . .2Pet 1:21
dumb ass speaking with *m* 2Pet 2:16
any *m* sin, we have..advocate . .1John 2:1
having *m* persons in . . . . .Jude 16
if any *m* hear my voice . . . . . . .Rev 3:20
every..*m*, hid themselves . . . . . .Rev 6:15
tabernacle of God is with *m* . . .Rev 21:3

MAN OF SIN—*See* ANTICHRIST

MANAEN (măn'ä-ĕn)—*"comforter"*
Prophet and teacher in church at Antioch . . . . .Acts 13:1

MANAHATH (măn'ä-hăth)—*"resting place; rest"*
1. Son of Shobal . . . . .Gen 36:23
2. City of exile for sons of Ehud 1Chr 8:6
Citizens of, called Manahethites 1Chr 2:54

MANASSEH, MANASSES (mä-năs´ĕ, mä-năs'sĕs)—*"causing forgetfulness"*
1. Joseph's first-born son . . .Gen 41:50, 51
Adopted by Jacob . . . . . .Gen 48:5, 6
Loses his birthright to Ephraim . . . . .Gen 48:13-20
Ancestor of a tribe . . . . . .Num 1:34, 35
2. Sons of . . . . .Num 26:28-34
Census of . . . . .Num 1:34, 35
One half of, desire region in east Jordan . .Num 32:33-42
Help Joshua against Canaanites . . . . .Josh 1:12-18
Division of, into eastern and western . . . . .Josh 22:7
Region assigned to eastern half . . . . .Deut 3:12-15
Land assigned to western half . . . . .Josh 17:1-13
Zelophehad's daughters included in . . . . .Josh 17:3, 4
Question concerning altar.Josh 22:9-34
Joshua's challenge to . . . .Josh 17:14-18
City (Golan) of refuge in.Josh 20:8
Did not drive out Canaanites . . . . .Judg 1:27, 28
Gideon, a member of . . .Judg 6:15
Some of, help David 1Chr 12:19-31
Many support Asa 2Chr 15:9
Attend Passovers 2Chr 30:1-18
Idols destroyed in 2Chr 31:1
3. Intentional change of Moses' name to . . . . . . .Judg 18:30
4. Son and successor of Hezekiah, king of Judah 2Kin 21:1
Reigns wickedly; restores idolatry . . . . {2Kin 21:1-16; 2Chr 33:1-9}
Captured and taken to Babylon 2Chr 33:10, 1
Repents and is restored .2Chr 33:12, 13
Removes idols and altars.2Chr 33:14-20
5, 6. Two men who divorce their foreign wives . . . .Ezra 10:30, 33

[*also* MANASSEH'S]
Egypt were born *M* and . . . . . . .Gen 46:20
him his two sons, *M* and . . . . . .Gen 48:1
also of Machir the son of *M* . . .Gen 50:23
the son of Ammihud: of *M* . . . .Num 1:10
him shall be the tribe of *M* . . . .Num 2:20
captain of the children of *M* . . .Num 2:20
prince of the children of *M* . . . .Num 7:54
tribe of the children of *M* . . . . .Num 10:23
namely, of the tribe of *M* . . . . .Num 13:11
of *M* of the families of *M* . . . . .Num 27:1
tribe of the children of *M* . . . . .Num 34:23
son of *M*, of the families . . . . . .Num 36:1
families of the sons of *M* . . . . . .Num 36:12
and to the half tribe of *M* . . . . .Deut 29:8
are the thousands of *M* . . . . . . .Deut 33:17
land of Ephraim, and *M* . . . . . .Deut 34:2
half the tribe of *M*, passed . . . .Josh 4:12
and the half tribe of *M* . . . . . . .Josh 12:6
and the half tribe of *M* . . . . . . .Josh 13:7
unto the half tribe of *M* . . . . . . .Josh 13:29
tribe of the children of *M* . . . . .Josh 13:29
of Machir the son of *M* . . . . . . .Josh 13:31
of Joseph were two tribes, *M* . .Josh 14:4
M and Ephraim, took their . . . .Josh 16:4
inheritance..children of *M* . . . . .Josh 16:9
half the tribe of *M*, have . . . . . .Josh 18:7
out of the half tribe of *M* . . . . .Josh 21:5
of the half tribe of *M* in . . . . . .Josh 21:6
out of the half tribe of *M* . . . . .Josh 21:25
of the other half tribe of *M* . . .Josh 21:27
and the half tribe of *M* . . . . . . .Josh 22:1
messengers throughout all *M* . .Judg 6:35
of Asher, and out of all *M* . . . .Judg 7:23
passed over Gilead, and *M* . . . .Judg 11:29
towns of Jair the son of *M* 1Kin 4:13
M his son reigned in his 2Kin 20:21
the rest of the acts of *M* 2Kin 21:17
M slept with his fathers 2Kin 21:18
of the Lord, as his father *M* . . .2Kin 21:20
altars which *M* had made 2Kin 23:12
provocations that *M* had 2Kin 23:26
for the sins of *M*, according . . .2Kin 24:3
son, Hezekiah his son, *M* 1Chr 3:13
and half the tribe of *M* 1Chr 5:18
of the half tribe of *M* 1Chr 5:23
and the half tribe of *M* 1Chr 5:26
out of the half tribe of *M* 1Chr 6:61
of the tribe of *M* in Bashan . . .1Chr 6:62
out of the half tribe of *M* 1Chr 6:70
family of the half tribe of *M* . . .1Chr 6:71
The sons of *M*; Ashriel 1Chr 7:14
son of Machir, the son of *M* . . .1Chr 7:17
borders of the children of *M* . .1Chr 7:29
children of Ephraim, and *M* . . .1Chr 9:3
and of the half tribe of *M* 1Chr 12:37
and the half tribe of *M* 1Chr 26:32
the half tribe of *M*, Joel 1Chr 27:20
Of the half tribe of *M* 1Chr 27:21
M his son reigned in his 2Chr 32:33
of the Lord, as did *M* his 2Chr 33:22
images which *M* his father 2Chr 33:22
as *M* his father had humbled . .2Chr 33:23
so did he in the cities of *M* 2Chr 34:6
gathered of the hand of *M* 2Chr 34:9
Gilead is mine, and *M* is . . . . . .Ps 60:7
and *M* stir up thy strength . . . .Ps 80:2
Gilead is mine; *M* is mine . . . . .Ps 108:8
M, Ephraim..Ephraim, *M* . . . . .Is 9:21
of *M* the son of Hezekiah . . . . .Jer 15:4
west side, a portion for *M* . . . . .Ezek 48:4
by the border of *M*, from . . . . .Ezek 48:5

MANASSES (mä-năs'ēz)—*same as Manasseh; those of the tribe of Manasseh*

[*also* MANASSITES]
And Hezekiah begat *M* . . . . . . .Matt 1:10
M begat Amon; and Amon . . . .Matt 1:10
the tribe of *M* were sealed . . . .Rev 7:6

MANASSITES—*descendants of Manasses*
Golan in Bashan, of the *M* . . . .Deut 4:43
Ephraimites, and among the *M*.Judg 12:4
the Reubenites, and the *M* 2Kin 10:33

MANDRAKE—*a rhubarb-like herb having narcotic qualities*
Supposed to induce human fertility . . . . . . {Gen 30:14-16; Song 7:13}

MANEH (mā'nĕ)—*a weight; consists of 50 shekels*
fifteen shekels..be your *m* . . . . .Ezek 45:12

MANGER—*a feeding place for cattle*
Place of Jesus' birth . . . . .Luke 2:7, 12

Called "crib" ....Is 1:3
Same as "stall" in ....Luke 13:15

MANIFEST—*to make something clear or abundant*

Applied to God's:
Nature ....Rom 1:19
Revelation ....Col 1:26
Knowledge 2Cor 2:14
Love 1John 4:9

Applied to Christ's:
Nature 1Tim 3:16
Presence ....John 1:31
Life 1John 1:2

Applied to evil:
Works of the flesh ....Gal 5:19
Man's:
Deeds ....John 3:21
Folly 2Tim 3:9

[*also* MANIFESTATION, MANIFESTED, MANIFESTLY]
that God might *m* them ....Eccl 3:18
hid, which shall not be *m* .....Mark 4:22
that shall not be made *m* ......Luke 8:17
of Galilee, and *m* forth his ....John 2:11
of God should be made *m* ....John 9:3
him, and will *m* myself to .....John 14:21
that thou wilt *m* thyself ....John 14:22
I have *m* thy name unto the ...John 17:6
is *m* to all them that dwell ....Acts 4:16
of God without the law is *m*...Rom 3:21
for the *m* of the sons of God ..Rom 8:19
I was made *m* unto them......Rom 10:20
But now is made *m*, and by ...Rom 16:26
man's work shall be made *m* ..1Cor 3:13
make *m* the counsels of the ...1Cor 4:5
may be made *m* among you ...1Cor 11:19
But the *m* of the Spirit is 1Cor 12:7
secrets of his heart made *m* ...1Cor 14:25
it is *m* that he is excepted 1Cor 15:27
m declared to be the epistle ...2Cor 3:3
m of the truth commending ...2Cor 4:2
Jesus might be made *m* in 2Cor 4:10
of Jesus might be made *m*.....2Cor 4:11
we are made *m* unto God 2Cor 5:11
I trust also are made *m* in.....2Cor 5:11
been thoroughly made *m* 2Cor 11:6
reproved are made *m* by the ..Eph 5:13
whatsoever doth make *m* is....Eph 5:13
my bonds in Christ are *m* in...Phil 1:13
I may make it *m*, as I ought...Col 4:4
a *m* token of the righteous 2Thess 1:5
good works of some are *m* 1Tim 5:25
made *m* by the appearing 2Tim 1:10
But hath in due times *m* his ...Titus 1:3
creature that is not *m* in his ...Heb 4:13
all was not yet made *m* ....Heb 9:8
was *m* in these last times 1Pet 1:20
they might be made *m* that 1John 2:19
that he was *m* to take away ...1John 3:5
the Son of God was *m* 1John 3:8
the children of God are *m* 1John 3:10
thy judgments are made *m* ....Rev 15:4

MANIFOLD—*bountiful; various*
thou in thy *m* mercies........Neh 9:19
according to thy *m* mercies ....Neh 9:27
O Lord, how *m* are thy ....Ps 104:24
your *m* transgressions ....Amos 5:12
Who shall not receive *m* ......Luke 18:30
the church the *m* wisdom of ...Eph 3:10
through *m* temptations 1Pet 1:6
stewards of the *m* grace of 1Pet 4:10

MANKIND—*human beings, male and female; also refers to males only*
Thou shalt not lie with *m* .....Lev 18:22
If a man also lie with *m*.......Lev 20:13
and the breath of all *m* ....Job 12:10
of themselves with *m* 1Cor 6:9
defile themselves with *m* 1Tim 1:10

MANLINESS—*masculine characteristics*

Qualities of:
Self-control 1Cor 9:25-27
Mature understanding....1Cor 14:20
Courage in danger.......2Sam 10:11, 12
Endure hardship.........2Tim 2:3-5

Examples of:
Caleb ....Num 13:30
Joshua..................Josh 1:1-11
Jonathan 1Sam 14:1, 6-14
Daniel..................Dan 6:1-28

MANNA—*the name the Israelites gave to the food miraculously provided them during their wilderness wandering*

Features regarding:
Description of..........Num 11:7-9
Bread given by God .....Ex 16:4, 15
John 6:30-32
Previously unknown .....Deut 8:3, 16
Fell at evening ....Num 11:9
Despised by people ......Num 11:4-6
Ceased at conquest ......Josh 5:12

Illustrative of:
God's glory ....Ex 16:7
Christ as the true bread ..John 6:32-35

called the name thereof *M* ....Ex 16:31
and put an omer full of *m*.....Ex 16:33
children of Israel did eat *m*....Ex 16:35
they did eat *m*, until they .....Ex 16:35
And the *m* was as coriander ...Num 11:7
withheldest not thy *m* from ....Neh 9:20
rained down *m* upon them ....Ps 78:24
Your fathers did eat *m* in .....John 6:49
not as your fathers did eat *m* ..John 6:58
the golden pot that had *m*.....Heb 9:4
give to eat of the hidden *m* ...Rev 2:17

MANNER—*way of behavior; type or kind; custom*

Evil kinds:
Sexual immorality ....Gen 19:31-36
Customs of other nations .Lev 20:23
Careless living..........Judg 18:7

Good kinds:
Prayer ....Matt 6:9
Faithfulness ....Acts 20:18

[*also* MANNERS]
with Sarah after the *m* of .....Gen 18:11
from thee to do after this *m* ...Gen 18:25
two *m* of people shall be ......Gen 25:23
this *m* shall ye speak unto .....Gen 32:19
After this *m* did thy servant ...Gen 39:19
the former *m* when thou ......Gen 40:13
father he sent after this *m* ....Gen 45:23
in all *m* of service in the ......Ex 1:14
no *m* of work shall be done ...Ex 12:16
For all *m* of trespass ....Ex 22:9
or for any *m* of lost thing .....Ex 22:9
in all *m* of workmanship ......Ex 31:3
willing to bring for all *m* of ...Ex 35:29
to make any *m* of cunning ....Ex 35:33
all *m* of work for the service ..Ex 36:1
offering, according to the *m* ...Lev 5:10
ye shall eat no *m* of blood ....Lev 7:26
offered it according to the *m* ..Lev 9:16
any *m* of creeping thing ....Lev 11:44
you, that eateth any *m*........Lev 17:10
have planted all *m* of trees ....Lev 19:23
Ye shall do no *m* of work .....Lev 23:31
she be taken with the *m* ......Num 5:13
do these things after this *m*....Num 15:13
offering, according to the *m* ...Num 15:24
After this *m* ye shall offer .....Num 28:24
according unto their *m* ....Num 29:6
and of the flocks, of all *m*.....Num 31:30
ye saw no *m* of similitude .....Deut 4:15
like *m* shalt thou do with .....Deut 22:3
the same *m* seven times ....Josh 6:15
m of men were they whom ....Judg 8:18
this was the *m* in former ......Ruth 4:7
m of the king that shall 1Sam 8:9
the people the *m* of the 1Sam 10:25
answered him after this *m* 1Sam 17:27
and spake after the same *m* ...1Sam 17:30
again after the former *m* 1Sam 17:30
before Samuel in like *m*.......1Sam 19:24
will be his *m* all the while 1Sam 27:11
m of instruments made of 2Sam 6:5
And is this the *m* of man 2Sam 7:19
and speak on this *m* unto 2Sam 14:3
hath spoken after this *m* 2Sam 17:6
of the bases was on this *m* 1Kin 7:28
cut themselves after their *m* ...1Kin 18:28
And one said on this *m*, and ..1Kin 22:20
and another said on that *m*....1Kin 22:20
What *m* of man was he 2Kin 1:7
not the *m* of the God of the...2Kin 17:26
them the *m* of the God of.....2Kin 17:27
they do after the former *m* 2Kin 17:34
did after their former *m*.......2Kin 17:40
appointed unto all *m* of 1Chr 6:48
all *m* of vessels of gold and ...1Chr 18:10
and timber, and all *m* of 1Chr 22:15
cunning men for every *m*.......1Chr 22:15
Lord, according to their *m* 1Chr 24:19
for all *m* of workmanship 1Chr 28:21
all *m* of precious stones 1Chr 29:2
to grave any *m* of graving 2Chr 2:14
priests after the *m* of the 2Chr 13:9
spake saying after this *m* 2Chr 18:19
another saying after that *m*....2Chr 18:19
for all *m* of pleasant jewels....2Chr 32:27
the work in any *m* of service ..2Chr 34:13
we unto them after this *m*.....Ezra 5:4
them after the same *m* ....Neh 6:4
according unto the *m* ....Neh 8:18
figs, and all *m* of burdens .....Neh 13:15
king's *m* toward all that ....Esth 1:13
Their soul abhorreth all *m* ....Ps 107:18
our gates are all *m* of.........Song 7:13
the lambs feed after their *m* ...Is 5:17
he lift it up after the *m* of.....Is 10:26
After this *m* will I mar the ....Jer 13:9
shall remain after the *m*.......Jer 30:18
after the *m* of the heathen ....Ezek 11:12
after the *m* of your fathers? ...Ezek 20:30
them after the *m* of..........Ezek 23:45
no *m* of hurt was found ....Dan 6:23
pestilence after the *m* of ......Amos 4:10
healing all *m* of sickness ......Matt 4:23
say all *m* of evil against ......Matt 5:11
What *m* of man is this, that ...Matt 8:27
to heal all *m* of sickness.......Matt 10:1
of sickness and all *m* of ....Matt 10:1
What *m* of man is this, that ...Mark 4:41
So ye in like *m*, when ye......Mark 13:29
what *m* of salutation this ......Luke 1:29
in the like *m* did their ....Luke 6:23
What *m* of man is this! for ....Luke 8:25
mint and rue and all *m* of ....Luke 11:42
What *m* of communications....Luke 24:17
m of the purifying of the ......John 2:6
as the *m* of the Jews is........John 19:40
like *m* as ye have seen him....Acts 1:11
their *m* in the wilderness ......Acts 13:18
circumcised after the *m* of.....Acts 15:1
And Paul, as his *m* was, went .Acts 17:2
to the perfect *m* of the law ....Acts 22:3
is not the *m* of the Romans ...Acts 25:16
My *m* of life from my youth ...Acts 26:4
I speak after the *m* of men ....Rom 6:19
after this *m*, and another 1Cor 7:7
If after the *m* of men I have ..1Cor 15:32
corrupt good *m*..............1Cor 15:33
made sorry after a godly *m*....2Cor 7:9
after the *m* of Gentiles........Gal 2:14
ye know what *m* of men we ...1Thess 1:5
In like *m* also, that women 1Tim 2:9
my doctrine, *m* of life 2Tim 3:10
in divers *m* spake in time .....Heb 1:1
together, as the *m* of some ....Heb 10:25
forgetteth what *m* of man .....James 1:24
what *m* of time the Spirit 1Pet 1:11
ye holy in all *m* of...........1Pet 1:15
For after this *m* in the old 1Pet 3:5
what *m* of persons ought ye ...2Pet 3:11
what *m* of love the Father.....1John 3:1
cities about them in like *m* ....Jude 7
them, he must in this *m* be ....Rev 11:5
wood, and all *m* vessels of ....Rev 18:12

m vessels of most precious ....Rev 18:12
which bare twelve *m* of ....Rev 22:2

MANOAH (mä-nō'ä)—*"rest"*
Danite; father of Samson .Judg 13:1-25

MANSERVANT—*a male servant*
[*also* MANSERVANT'S, MANSERVANTS, MENSERVANTS]
oxen, and he asses, and *m* ....Gen 12:16
and silver, and gold, and *m* ...Gen 24:35
and asses, flocks, and *m* ......Gen 32:5
son, nor thy daughter, thy *m* ..Ex 20:10
she shall not go out as the *m* ..Ex 21:7
if he smite out his *m* tooth ....Ex 21:27
If the ox shall push a *m* or a ..Ex 21:32
nor thy daughter, nor thy *m* ...Deut 5:14
house, his field, or his *m*......Deut 5:21
m, and your maidservants .....Deut 12:12
thy daughter, and thy *m* ......Deut 16:11
he will take your *m*, and 1Sam 8:16
and sheep, and oxen, and *m*...2Kin 5:26
Besides their *m* and their .....Neh 7:67
despise the cause of my *m* ....Job 31:13
every man should let his *m*....Jer 34:9
every one should let his *m* ....Jer 34:10
shall begin to beat the *m*......Luke 12:45

MANSIONS—*dwelling places*
Father's house are many *m*....John 14:2

MANSLAYER—*one who accidentally kills another by striking*
[*also* MANSLAYERS]
ye shall appoint for the *m*.....Num 35:6
that the *m* shall not die ....Num 35:12
murderers of mothers, for *m* ..1Tim 1:9

MANTLE—*a garment*
Sheet or rug ....Judg 4:18
Female garment ....Is 3:22
Upper garment (coat)....1Sam 15:27
Outer garment (robe).. 1Kin 19:13, 19; 2Kin 2:8, 13, 14
and he is covered with a *m*....1Sam 28:14
rent my garment and my *m* ...Ezra 9:3
rent my garment and my *m* ...Ezra 9:5
Job arose, and rent his *m* .....Job 1:20
they rent every one his *m* .....Job 2:12
own confusion, as with a *m* ...Ps 109:29

MANY—*See* INTRODUCTION

MAOCH (mā'ŏk)—*"poor"*
Father of Achish, king of Gath 1Sam 27:2

MAON (mā'ŏn)—*"place of sin"*
1. Village in Judah ....Josh 15:55
David stayed at 1Sam 23:24, 25
House of Nabal 1Sam 25:2
2. Shammai's son..........1Chr 2:45
3. People called Maonites among Israel's oppressors............Judg 10:12
Called Mehunim 2Chr 26:7
Listed among returnees . .Ezra 2:50; Neh 7:52

MAR—*to injure; spoil; destroy*
[*also* MARRED]
thou *m* the corners of thy .....Lev 19:27
I *m* mine own inheritance .....Ruth 4:6
your mice that *m* the land 1Sam 6:5
and *m* every good piece of 2Kin 3:19
They *m* my path, they set .....Job 30:13
his visage was so *m* more .....Is 52:14
the girdle was *m*, it was ....Jer 13:7
will I *m* the pride of Judah ....Jer 13:9
out, and *m* their vine ....Nah 2:2
and the bottles will be *m*......Mark 2:22

MARA (mä'rä)—*"bitter"*
Name chosen by Naomi . .Ruth 1:20

MARAH (mā'rä)—*"bitter"*
First Israelite camp after passing through the Red Sea ....Num 33:8, 9
when they came to *M*, they ...Ex 15:23
not drink of the waters of *M* ..Ex 15:23
the name of it was called *M* ...Ex 15:23

MARALAH (măr'ä-lä)—*"sleep"*
Village in Zebulun ......Josh 19:11

MARANATHA (măr-ä-năth'ä)—*"our Lord, come"*
Aramaic phrase expressive of Christ's return 1Cor 16:22
Compare the same thought in ....Phil 4:5

MARBLE—*crystalline limestone*
In columns ....Esth 1:6
In Babylon's trade ....Rev 18:12

MARCH—*walk with measured steps to a cadence*
[*also* MARCHED, MARCHEDST]
Egyptians *m* after them ....Ex 14:10
thou *m* out of the field of .....Judg 5:4
didst *m* through the ....Ps 68:7
for they shall *m* with an........Jer 46:22
they shall *m* every one on .....Joel 2:7
m through the breadth ....Hab 1:6
Thou didst *m* through the .....Hab 3:12

MARCUS—*See* MARK

MARDUK (măr'dūk)—*"bold"*
Supreme deity of the Babylonians...........Jer 50:2
Otherwise called Bel .....Is 46:1

MARESHAH (mä-rē'shä)—*"possession"*
1. Father of Hebron 1Chr 2:42
2. Judahite 1Chr 4:21
3. Town of Judah ....Josh 15:44
City built for defense by Rehoboam 2Chr 11:5, 8
Great battle here between Asa and Zerah 2Chr 14:9-12
the son of Dodavah of *M* 2Chr 20:37
unto thee. O inhabitant of *M*. .Mic 1:15

MARINERS—*sailors*
Skilled..................1Kin 9:27
Fearful ....Jon 1:5
Weeping ....Ezek 27:8-36
Storm-tossed ....Acts 27:27-31

MARISHES—*marsh*
m thereof shall not be healed . .Ezek 47:11

MARK—*a visible sign or symbol; goal; to observe; designate*
As object, thing:
Sign for preservation.....Ezek 9:4-6
Sign of those following antichrist............ Rev 13:16, 17; Rev 14:9, 11; Rev 20:4
[*also* MARKED, MARKEST, MARKETH, MARKS]
dead, nor print any *m* upon ...Lev 19:28
m the place where he shall ....Ruth 3:4
the Lord, and Eli *m* her 1Sam 1:12
as though I shot at a *m* 1Sam 20:20
M ye now when Amnon's 2Sam 13:28
M, I pray you, and see how ...1Kin 20:7
thou set me as a *m* against ....Job 7:20
If I sin, then thou *m* me, and .Job 10:14
m, and afterward we will ......Job 18:2
Hast thou *m* the old way ......Job 22:15
in the stocks, he *m* all my .....Job 33:11
M well, O Job, hearken ....Job 33:31
M the perfect man, and ....Ps 37:37
M ye well her bulwarks ....Ps 48:13
they *m* my steps, when they ...Ps 56:6
thou, Lord, shouldest *m* ....Ps 130:3
m it out with a line; he ....Is 44:13
m it out with the compass .....Is 44:13
thine iniquity is *m* before .....Jer 2:22
and set me as a *m* for the .....Lam 3:12
m upon the foreheads of ......Ezek 9:4
Son of man, *m* well, and ......Ezek 44:5
m well the entering in of ......Ezek 44:5
when he *m* how they chose ....Luke 14:7
m them which cause ....Rom 16:17
my body the *m* of the Lord ...Gal 6:17
press toward the *m* for the ....Phil 3:14
m them which walk so as .....Phil 3:17
to receive a *m* in their right ...Rev 13:16
and receive his *m* in his ....Rev 14:9
his image, and over his *m* .....Rev 15:2
had received the *m* of the .....Rev 19:20

MARK (JOHN)—*"a large hammer"—a Christian convert and missionary companion of Paul, as well as the writer of The Gospel of Mark*
Son of Mary, a believer . .Acts 12:12
Cousin of Barnabas ......Col 4:10
Returns with Barnabas to Antioch ....Acts 12:25
Leaves Paul and Barnabas at Perga .....Acts 13:13
Paul refuses to take him again ....Acts 15:37-39
Paul's approval of 2Tim 4:11
Peter's companion 1Pet 5:13

MARK, THE GOSPEL OF—*a book of the New Testament*
John the Baptist.........Mark 1:1-11
Choosing of the disciples .Mark 3:13-19
Parables ....Mark 4:1-34
Galilean tours ....Mark 1:21-45; Mark 6:1-44
Peter's confession ....Mark 8:27-30
The transfiguration ......Mark 9:1-13
Foretelling of Jesus' death Mark 10:32-34
Entry into Jerusalem.....Mark 11:1-11
Controversy with Jews ...Mark 11:27—12:40
Events of the crucifixion. .Mark 14:43—15:47
The resurrection ....Mark 16:1-20

MARKET—*a public place where trade and assembly are conducted*
Greetings in the ....Mark 11:16
[*also* MARKETS]
children sitting in the *m*.......Matt 11:16
they come from the *m* ....Mark 7:4
and greetings in the *m* ....Luke 11:43
love greetings in the *m*........Luke 20:46
Jerusalem by the sheep *m* .....John 5:2

MARKET OF APPIUS—*the marketplace of Appius, a town about forty miles southeast of Rome*
Called Forum ....Acts 28:15

MARKETPLACE—*same as market*
Place of:
Greetings ....Matt 23:7
Public trial ....Acts 16:19, 20
Evangelism ....Acts 17:17
[*also* MARKETPLACES]
standing idle in the *m*.........Matt 20:3
and love salutations in the *m* . .Mark 12:38
children sitting in the *m*.......Luke 7:32

MAROTH (mā'rŏth)—*"bitterness"*
Town of Judah ....Mic 1:12

MARRIAGE—*wedlock; the institution by which men and women are joined together and form a family*
Described as:
Instituted by God ....Gen 2:18-24
Honorable in all.........Heb 13:4
Permanent bond ....Matt 19:6
Intimate bond ....Matt 19:5
Blessed of God for having children ....Gen 1:27, 28
Dissolved by death ......Rom 7:2, 3
Means of sexual love ....Prov 5:15-19
Centered in love and obedience ....Eph 5:21-33
Worthy of Jesus' presence John 2:1-11
Prohibitions concerning:
Near of kin ....Lev 18:6-18

Fornication excludes remarriage ....Matt 5:32
Polygamy forbidden .....Lev 18:18
Idol worshipers ....Ex 34:16

Arrangements for (among Hebrews):
Arranged by parents .....Gen 21:21
Parties consenting ....Gen 24:8
Parental concern in ......Gen 26:34, 35
Romance involved in ....Gen 29:10, 11
Commitment considered binding ....Gen 24:58, 60
Unfaithfulness in, brings God's judgment ....Heb 13:4

Ceremonies of (among Hebrews):
Time of joy ....Jer 7:34
Bride richly attired ......Ps 45:13-15
Bride veiled ....Gen 24:65
Bridegroom decks himself. Is 61:10
Wedding feast in bridegroom's house ....Matt 22:1-10
Distinctive clothing of guests ....Matt 22:11, 12
Christ attends ....John 2:1-11
Festivities following ......John 2:8-10
Gifts bestowed at ....Ps 45:12
Parental blessing on .....Gen 24:60
Change of name ....Ps 45:10, 16
Consummation of ....Gen 29:23
Proof of virginity ....Deut 22:13-21

Purposes of:
Man's happiness ....Gen 2:18
Continuance of the race ..Gen 1:28
Godly seed ....Mal 2:14, 15
Prevention of fornication .1Cor 7:2, 9
Complete satisfaction ....Prov 5:19
1Tim 5:14

Denial of:
As a prophetic sign ......Jer 16:2
For a specific purpose ...Matt 19:10-12
As a sign of apostasy 1Tim 4:1-3
To those in heaven ......Matt 22:30

Figurative of:
God's union with Israel ..Is 54:5
Christ's union with His Church ....Eph 5:23-32

[*also* MARRIAGES]
make ye *m* with us, and give ..Gen 34:9
raiment, and her duty of *m*....Ex 21:10
Neither shalt thou make *m* ....Deut 7:3
shall make *m* with them ....Josh 23:12
our God in *m* strange wives ...Neh 13:27
maidens were not given to *m* ..Ps 78:63
marrying and giving in *m*......Matt 24:38
marry, nor are given in *m*.....Mark 12:25
they were given in *m*, until ....Luke 17:27
marry, and are given in *m*.....Luke 20:34
marry, nor are given in *m*.....Luke 20:35
that giveth her in *m* doeth 1Cor 7:38
giveth her not in *m* doeth 1Cor 7:38
the *m* of the Lamb is come....Rev 19:7
the *m* supper of the Lamb ....Rev 19:9

MARROW—*the vascular tissue which occupies the cavities of bones*

Used literally of:
Healthy man ....Job 21:23, 24
Inner being ....Heb 4:12

Used figuratively of:
Spiritual sustenance ......Ps 63:5

to thy navel, and *m* to thy ....Prov 3:8
of fat things full of *m*, of......Is 25:6

MARRY—*to take a spouse*

[*also* MARRIED, MARRIETH, MARRYING]
sons-in-law, which *m* his ......Gen 19:14
thy brother's wife, and *m* .....Gen 38:8
if he were *m*, then his wife ....Ex 21:3
priest's daughter also be *m* ....Lev 22:12
woman whom he had *m*.......Num 12:1
he had *m* an Ethiopian.........Num 12:1
And if they be *m* to any of....Num 36:3
them *m* to whom they think ...Num 36:6
of their father shall they *m* ....Num 36:6
m unto their father's ....Num 36:11
were *m* into the families ......Num 36:12
with a woman *m* to ....Deut 22:22
hath taken a wife, and *m* .....Deut 24:1
not *m* without unto a ....Deut 25:5
m when he was threescore 1Chr 2:21
mighty, and *m* fourteen 2Chr 13:21
that had *m* wives of Ashdod ...Neh 13:23
our God in *m* strange wives ...Neh 13:27
odious woman when she is *m* ..Prov 30:23
than the children of the *m* ....Is 54:1
thee, and thy land shall be *m* ..Is 62:4
as a young man *m* a virgin ....Is 62:5
virgin, so shall thy sons *m*.....Is 62:5
Lord; for I am *m* unto you ....Jer 3:14
m the daughter of a strange ...Mal 2:11
m another, committeth ....Matt 19:9
whoso *m* her which is put .....Matt 19:9
his brother shall *m* his wife ....Matt 22:24
the first, when he had *m* a ....Matt 22:25
m and giving in marriage ......Matt 24:38
Philip's wife: for he had *m* ....Mark 6:17
put away his wife, and *m* .....Mark 10:11
husband, and be *m* to.........Mark 10:12
they neither *m*, nor are ....Mark 12:25
another said, I have *m* a ......Luke 14:20
his wife, and *m* another ....Luke 16:18
whosoever *m* her that is put ...Luke 16:18
did eat, they drank, they *m* ...Luke 17:27
The children of this world *m* ..Luke 20:34
the dead, neither *m*, nor ......Luke 20:35
liveth, she be *m* to another....Rom 7:3
though she be *m* to another ...Rom 7:3
that ye should be *m* to........Rom 7:4
unto the *m* I command, yet ...1Cor 7:10
if thou *m*, thou hast not.......1Cor 7:28
if a virgin *m*, she hath not ...1Cor 7:28
he that is *m* careth for the 1Cor 7:33
she that is *m* careth for the....1Cor 7:34
liberty to be *m* to whom she ..1Cor 7:39
against Christ, they will *m*.....1Tim 5:11

MARS HILL—*hill west of the Acropolis in Athens*
Paul stood in the midst of *M H*. Acts 17:22
See AREOPAGUS

MARSENA (mär-sē'nä)—*"worthy"*
Persian prince ....Esth 1:14

MARSH—*an area of grassy, soft, wet land*
Spelled "marish" ....Ezek 47:11

MART—*market*
Tyre, to all nations ......Is 23:1-4

MARTHA (mär'thä)—*"lady"*
Sister of Mary and Lazarus ....John 11:1, 2
Welcomes Jesus into her home ....Luke 10:38
Rebuked by Christ ......Luke 10:38-42
Affirms her faith ....John 11:21-32
Serves supper ....John 12:1-3

Jesus loved *M*, and her ....John 11:5
the Jews came to *M* and ......John 11:19
Then *M*, as soon as she ....John 11:20
M, the sister of him that ......John 11:39

MARTYRDOM—*death for the sake of one's faith*

Causes of:
Evil deeds 1John 3:12
Antichrist's persecution ..Rev 13:15
Harlot Babylon's hatred ..Rev 17:5, 6
Our Christian faith ......Rev 6:9

Believer's attitude toward:
Remember Christ's warning..............Matt 10:21, 22
Do not fear ....Matt 10:28
Be prepared ....Matt 16:24, 25
Be ready to, if necessary .Acts 21:13

Examples of:
Prophets and apostles ....Luke 11:50, 51
John the Baptist ....Mark 6:18-29
Stephen ....Acts 7:58-60
Early disciples of the Lord ....Acts 9:1, 2

MARVEL—*to express astonishment; something that causes wonder*

Expressed by Christ because of:
Centurion's faith ....Matt 8:10

Expressed by men because of Christ's:
Power ....Matt 8:27
Knowledge ....John 7:15

[*also* MARVELED, MARVELOUS, MARVELOUSLY, MARVELS]
men *m* one at another ....Gen 43:33
thy people I will do *m* ....Ex 34:10
Remember his *m* works 1Chr 16:12
m works among all nations 1Chr 16:24
for he was *m* helped 2Chr 26:15
m things without number ......Job 5:9
showest thyself *m* upon me ....Job 10:16
God thundereth *m* with ....Job 37:5
show forth all thy *m* works ....Ps 9:1
Show thy *m* loving-kindness ...Ps 17:7
showed me his *m* kindness ....Ps 31:21
They saw it, and so they *m*....Ps 48:5
M things did he ....Ps 78:12
he hath done *m* things ....Ps 98:1
Remember his *m* works ....Ps 105:5
Lord's doing; it is *m* ....Ps 118:23
m not at the matter...........Eccl 5:8
I will proceed to do a *m* ......Is 29:14
a *m* work and a wonder.......Is 29:14
speak *m* things against..God ...Dan 11:36
I show unto him *m* things .....Mic 7:15
and regard, and wonder *m* ....Hab 1:5
m in the eyes of the remnant ..Zech 8:6
it..be *m* in mine eyes? ....Zech 8:6
multitudes saw it, they *m* .....Matt 9:8
the multitudes *m*, saying ......Matt 9:33
disciples saw it, they *m* ....Matt 21:20
and it is *m* in our eyes? ....Matt 21:42
heard these words, they *m* ....Matt 22:22
and all men did *m* ....Mark 5:20
and it is *m* in our eyes? ....Mark 12:11
God's. And they *m* at him .....Mark 12:17
answered nothing..Pilate *m* ....Mark 15:5
Pilate *m* if he were..dead .....Mark 15:44
m that he tarried so long......Luke 1:21
name is John. And they *m* all .Luke 1:63
Joseph and his mother *m*......Luke 2:33
heard these things, he *m* ......Luke 7:9
m that he had not first........Luke 11:38
and they *m* at his answer......Luke 20:26
M not that I said unto ....John 3:7
m that he talked with the .....John 4:27
that ye may *m* ....John 5:20
M not at this: for the hour ....John 5:28
one work, and ye all *m* ....John 7:21
Why herein is a *m* thing ......John 9:30
they were all amazed and *m* ...Acts 2:7
men of Israel, why *m* ye ......Acts 3:12
and ignorant men, they *m* .....Acts 4:13
And no *m*; for Satan 2Cor 11:14
I *m* that ye are so soon ....Gal 1:6
darkness into his *m* light 1Pet 2:9
M not my brethren, if 1John 3:13
in heaven, great and *m* ....Rev 15:1
m are thy works, Lord ....Rev 15:3
Wherefore didst thou *m*? ......Rev 17:7

MARY (mâr'ĭ)—*Greek form of Miriam; "strong"*
1. Jesus' mother ....Matt 1:16
Prophecies concerning ...Is 7:14
Engaged to Joseph ......Luke 1:26, 27
Told of virginal conception ....Luke 1:28-38
Visits Elizabeth ....Luke 1:39-41
Offers praise ....Luke 1:46-55
Gives birth to Jesus .....Luke 2:6-20
Flees with Joseph to Egypt ....Matt 2:13-18
Mother of other children. Mark 6:3
Visits Jerusalem with Jesus ....Luke 2:41-52

Intrusted to John's care .John 19:25-27
2. Wife of Cleophas ....John 19:25
Mother of James and Joses.................Matt 27:56
Looking on the crucified Savior ....Matt 27:55, 56
Follows Jesus' body to the tomb ....Matt 27:61
Sees the risen Lord .....Matt 28:1, 9, 10
Tells His disciples of resurrection .... Matt 28:7-9; Luke 24:9-11
3. Mary Magdalene ....Matt 27:56, 61
Delivered from seven demons ....Luke 8:2
Contributes to support of Christ ....Luke 8:2, 3
Looks on the crucified Savior ....Matt 27:55, 56
Follows Jesus' body to the tomb ....Matt 27:61
Visits Jesus' tomb with Mary, mother of James Mark 16:1-8
Tells the disciples ....John 20:2
First to see the risen Lord .... Mark 16:9; John 20:11-18
4. Mary, the sister of Martha and Lazarus . . .John 11:1, 2
Commended by Jesus . . .Luke 10:38-42
Grieves for Lazarus .....John 11:19, 20, 28-33
Anoints Jesus..........John 12:1-3, 7
Jesus commends again . . .Matt 26:7-13
5. Mark's mother..........Acts 12:12-17
6. Christian disciple at Rome ....Rom 16:6

mother *M* was espoused.......Matt 1:18
to take unto thee *M* ....Matt 1:20
child with *M* his mother.......Matt 2:11
is not his mother called *M*? . . .Matt 13:55
was *M* Magdalene ....Mark 15:40
M the mother of James ....Mark 15:40
M Magdalene and ....Mark 15:47
M the mother of Joses ....Mark 15:47
And *M* said, Behold the ......Luke 1:38
And *M* abode with her........Luke 1:56
taxed with *M* his espoused ....Luke 2:5
that *M* which anointed ....John 11:2
Jews which came to *M* ....John 11:45
M the mother of Jesus ....Acts 1:14

MASCHIL (mäs'kēl)—*"attentive"—a Hebrew term that indicates a type of psalm*
A Psalm of David, *M* ....Ps 32:*title*
To the chief Musician, *M* .....Ps 42:*title*
for the sons of Korah, *M* .....Ps 44:*title*
sons of Korah, a *M*...........Ps 45:*title*
the chief Musician, a *M* ....Ps 52:*title*
Musician upon Mahalath, a *M* .Ps 53:*title*
Musician on Neginoth, a *M* . . .Ps 54:*title*
Musician on Neginoth, *M* .....Ps 55:*title*
M of Asaph ....Ps 74:*title*
M of Asaph ....Ps 78:*title*
M of Heman ....Ps 88:*title*
M of Ethan ....Ps 89:*title*
M of David. A prayer ....Ps 142:*title*

MASH (măsh)—*one of the sons of Aram*
Division of the Arameans. Gen 10:23
Called Meshech 1Chr 1:17

MASHAL (mā'shăl)—*"parable"*
Refuge city given to the Levites 1Chr 6:74
Called Mishal ....Josh 19:26; Josh 21:30

MASON—*one who lays stones or bricks*
Sent by Hiram to help:
David 2Sam 5:11
Solomon 1Kin 5:18
Used in Temple:
Repairs 2Chr 24:12
Rebuilding ....Ezra 3:7

[*also* MASONS]
And to *m*, and hewers 2Kin 12:12
and builders, and *m* 2Kin 22:6
with *m* and carpenters, to 1Chr 14:1
he set *m* to hew..stones 1Chr 22:2

MASREKAH (măs'rĕ-kä)—*"whistling"*
City of Edom ....Gen 36:36

MASSA (măs'ä)—*"burden; oracle"*
Son of Ishmael ....Gen 25:12, 14

MASSAH AND MERIBAH (măs'ä, mĕr'ĭ-bä)—*"temptation; quarrel"*
Named together ....Ex 17:7
Named separately ....Deut 33:8
First, at Rephidim, Israel just out of Egypt ......Ex 17:1-7
Levites proved ....Deut 33:8
Second, at Kadesh-barnea, 40 years later . .Num 20:1-13
Moses and Aaron rebel here ....Num 20:24
Tragic events recalled by Moses ....Deut 6:16
Events later recalled .....Ps 81:7
Used as a boundary of the land ....Ezek 47:17, 19
Used for spiritual lesson. .Heb 3:7-12

MAST—*a vertical support for sails and rigging on a sailing ship*
Used literally of:
Cedars of Lebanon ......Ezek 27:5
Used figuratively of:
Strength of enemies .....Is 33:23

[*also* MASTS]
cedars..to make *m* ....Ezek 27:5

MASTER—*one who has authority over another*
Descriptive of:
Owner of slaves ....Ex 21:4-6
King 1Chr 12:19
Prophet.................2Kin 2:3, 5
Teacher ....Matt 23:8
Kinds of:
Unmerciful..............1Sam 30:13-15
Angry ....Luke 14:21
Good...................Gen 24:9-35
Believing 1Tim 6:2
Heavenly ....Col 4:1

[*also* MASTER'S, MASTERS, MASTERS']
And Sarah my *m* wife bare . . . .Gen 24:36
bare a son to my *m* when .....Gen 24:36
my *m* made me swear.........Gen 24:37
I said unto my *m* ....Gen 24:39
God of my *m* Abraham ....Gen 24:42
appointed..for my *m* son ....Gen 24:44
God of my *m* Abraham ....Gen 24:48
my *m* brother's daughter ......Gen 24:48
deal kindly..with my *m*........Gen 24:49
Send me away unto my *m*.....Gen 24:54
that I may go to my *m*........Gen 24:56
It is my *m* ....Gen 24:65
his *m* the Egyptian ....Gen 39:2
his *m* saw that the Lord.......Gen 39:3
m wife cast her eyes upon .....Gen 39:7
my *m* wotteth not what is .....Gen 39:8
his *m* heard the words ....Gen 39:19
And Joseph's *m* took him .....Gen 39:20
If she please not her *m* ....Ex 21:8
give unto their *m* thirty ....Ex 21:32
m of the house shall be ....Ex 22:8
not deliver unto his *m* the .....Deut 23:15
is escaped from his *m*..........Deut 23:15
servant said unto his *m* ....Judg 19:11
And his *m* said unto him.......Judg 19:12
to the *m* of the house ....Judg 19:22
the *m* of the house, went .....Judg 19:23
and came to his *m*............1Sam 20:38
do this thing unto my *m* 1Sam 24:6
every man from his *m* 1Sam 25:10
is determined against our *m* . . .1Sam 25:17
ye have not kept your *m* 1Sam 26:16
reconcile himself unto his *m*? . .1Sam 29:4
thy *m* servants that are........1Sam 29:10
my *m* left me, because 1Sam 30:13
your *m* Saul is dead 2Sam 2:7
have given unto thy *m* son 2Sam 9:9
m son may have food to 2Sam 9:10
thy *m* son shall eat bread 2Sam 9:10
I gave thee thy *m* house 2Sam 12:8
m wives into thy bosom 2Sam 12:8
And where is thy *m* son? 2Sam 16:3
These have no *m* 1Kin 22:17
pray thee, and seek thy *m*......2Kin 2:16
was a great man with his *m* . . .2Kin 5:1
when my *m* goeth into 2Kin 5:18
my *m* hath spared Naaman 2Kin 5:20
My *m* hath sent me 2Kin 5:22
and stood before his *m*........2Kin 5:25
said, Alas, *m*! for it was 2Kin 6:5
him, Alas, my *m*! how shall . . .2Kin 6:15
drink, and go to their *m* 2Kin 6:22
they went to their *m* 2Kin 6:23
the sound of his *m* feet 2Kin 6:32
Elisha, and came to his *m*.....2Kin 8:14
the house of Ahab thy *m* 2Kin 9:7
who slew his *m*?..............2Kin 9:31
meetest of your *m* sons 2Kin 10:3
and fight for your *m* 2Kin 10:3
I conspired against my *m*......2Kin 10:9
least of my *m* servants 2Kin 18:24
my *m* sent me to thy *m* 2Kin 18:27
the king of Assyria his *m* 2Kin 19:4
shall ye say to your *m* 2Kin 19:6
and Chenaniah the *m* of 1Chr 15:27
These have no *m* 2Chr 18:16
servant is free from his *m* .....Job 3:19
unto the hand of their *m*......Ps 123:2
refresheth..his *m* ....Prov 25:13
he that waiteth on his *m* ......Prov 27:18
not a servant unto his *m* ......Prov 30:10
by the *m* of assemblies ....Eccl 12:11
and the ass his *m* crib ....Is 1:3
the servant, so with his *m* .....Is 24:2
my *m* sent me to thy ....Is 36:12
shall ye say unto your *m* ......Is 37:6
to say unto their *m* ....Jer 27:4
shall ye say unto your *m* ......Jer 27:4
Ashpenaz the *m* of his ....Dan 1:3
made *m* of the magicians......Dan 5:11
say to their *m*, Bring ....Amos 4:1
m houses with violence........Zeph 1:9
and a servant his *m*...........Mal 1:6
and if I be a *m*, where is......Mal 1:6
the *m* and the scholar ....Mal 2:12
No man can serve two *m*......Matt 6:24
M, I will follow thee..........Matt 8:19
disciple is not above his *m* ....Matt 10:24
that he be as his *m* ....Matt 10:25
they have called the *m*........Matt 10:25
fall from their *m* table ....Matt 15:27
Doth not your *m* pay ....Matt 17:24
M, we know that thou art .....Matt 22:16
M, which is the great ....Matt 22:36
is your *M*, even Christ ....Matt 23:8
is your *M*, even Christ ....Matt 23:10
The *M* saith, My time is ......Matt 26:18
answered and said, *M*, is it I? .Matt 26:25
M, carest thou not that ....Mark 4:38
troublest thou the *M* any......Mark 5:35
M, it is good for us to be .....Mark 9:5
M, we saw one casting ....Mark 9:38
M, all these have I ....Mark 10:20
M, behold, the fig tree........Mark 11:21
M, Moses wrote unto us ......Mark 12:19
M, see what manner of ....Mark 13:1
when the *m* of the house......Mark 13:35
The *M* saith, Where is the ....Mark 14:14
M, what shall we do? ....Luke 3:12
is not above his *m* ....Luke 6:40
perfect shall be as his *m* ......Luke 6:40
M, *M*, we perish ....Luke 8:24
is dead; trouble not the *M* ....Luke 8:49
M, I beseech thee, look ....Luke 9:38
M, what shall I do............Luke 10:25
M, speak to my brother ....Luke 12:13
the *m* of the house is ....Luke 13:25
Jesus, *M*, have mercy ....Luke 17:13
M, rebuke thy disciples ....Luke 19:39
M, Moses wrote unto us ......Luke 20:28

M, but when shall these.......Luke 21:7
being interpreted, *M*..........John 1:38
him, saying, *M*, eat...........John 4:31
M, who did sin, this man.....John 9:2
The *M* is come, and calleth...John 11:28
Ye call me *M* and Lord.......John 13:13
If I then, your Lord and *M*...John 13:14
brought her *m* much gain.....Acts 16:16
the *m* and the owner.........Acts 27:11
to his own *m* he standeth.....Rom 14:4
obedient to..your *m*..........Eph 6:5
your *M* also is in heaven......Eph 6:9
obey in all things your *m*......Col 3:22
their own *m* worthy of all.....1Tim 6:1
and meet for the *m* use........2Tim 2:21
obedient unto their own *m*....Titus 2:9
be not many *m*...............James 3:1
subject to your *m*.............1Pet 2:18

MASTER BUILDER—*chief builder*
Paul describes himself as .1Cor 3:10

MASTER WORKMEN—*craftsmen*
Bezaleel ....Ex 31:1-5
Hiram of Tyre 1Kin 7:13-50
Aquila and Priscilla......Acts 18:2, 3
Demetrius ....Acts 19:24

MASTERY—*dominion; ascendancy; skill or knowledge*

[*also* MASTERIES]
of them that shout for *m*......Ex 32:18
lions had the *m* of them.......Dan 6:24
man that striveth for the *m*....1Cor 9:25
if a man also strive for *m*.....2Tim 2:5

MATE—*either member of a pair*
God provides for ....Is 34:15, 16

MATERIALISTIC—*overly concerned for worldly goods*
Christ condemns.........Luke 12:16-21
Sadducees described .....Acts 23:8
Christians forbidden to live as 1Cor 15:30-34

"MATHEMATICS," SPIRITUAL

General:
Addition:
God's Word ....Deut 4:2
Knowledge will increase..Dan 12:4
Increased riches ....Ps 62:10
Subtraction:
God's commandments....Deut 12:32
Multiplication:
Human family..........Gen 1:28

Unrighteous:
Addition:
Wealth ....Ps 73:12
Guilt 2Chr 28:13
Sin ....Is 30:1
Subtraction:
Wealth obtained by fraud.Prov 13:11
Life shortened ....Ps 55:23; Prov 10:27
Multiplication:
Sorrow by idolatry.......Ps 16:4
Transgression ....Prov 29:16

Righteous:
Addition:
Years ....Prov 3:1, 2; Prov 4:10
Blessing without sorrow..Prov 10:22
By putting God first.....Matt 6:33
Graces 2Pet 1:5-7
In latter years..........Job 42:12
Subtraction:
Disease ....Ex 15:26
Taken from evil ....Is 57:1
Multiplication:
Prosperity..............Deut 8:1, 11-13
Length of days ....Deut 11:18-21; Prov 9:11
Mercy, peace, love ......Jude 2
Church ....Acts 9:31

MATHUSALA—*See* METHUSELAH

MATRED (mā'trĕd)—*"God is pursuer; expulsion"*
Mother-in-law of Hadar (Hadad), an Edomite king.................Gen 36:39

MATRI (mā'trī)—*"Jehovah is watching; rainy"*
Saul's Benjamite family..1Sam 10:21

MATRIX—*the womb*
all that openeth the *m*........Ex 13:12
all that openeth the *m*........Ex 13:15
All that openeth the *m* is.....Ex 34:19
first-born that openeth..*m*.....Num 3:12
that openeth the *m*...........Num 18:15

MATTAN (măt'ăn)—*"gift"*
1. Priest of Baal..........2Kin 11:18
Killed by the people....2Chr 23:16, 17
2. Father of Shephatiah....Jer 38:1

MATTANAH (măt'ä-nä)—*"gift of Jehovah"*
Israelite camp...........Num 21:18, 19

MATTANIAH (măt-ä-nī'ä)—*"gift of Jehovah"*
1. King Zedekiah's original name 2Kin 24:17
2. Son of Mica, a Levite and Asaphite 1Chr 9:15
3. Musician, son of Heman 1Chr 25:4, 16
4. Spirit of the LORD came upon.........2Chr 20:14
5. Levite under King Hezekiah............2Chr 29:13
6. Postexilic Levite and singer...............Neh 11:17
7. Levite gatekeeper ......Neh 12:25
8. Postexilic Levite ....Neh 12:35
9. Levite in charge of treasuries ....Neh 13:13
10, 11, 12, 13. Four postexilic Jews who divorced foreign wives ....Ezra 10:26-37

MATTATHA (măt'ä-thä)—*"gift"*
Son of Nathan; ancestor of Christ.............Luke 3:31

MATTATHAH (măt-ä-thä)—*"gift"*
Jew who put away his foreign wife ....Ezra 10:33

MATTATHIAS (măt-ä-thī'ăs)—*"God's gift"*
1. Postexilic ancestor of Christ.................Luke 3:25
2. Another postexilic ancestor of Christ.....Luke 3:26

MATTENAI (măt-ĕ-nā'ī)—*"gift of Jehovah"*
1. Priest in the time of Joiakim ....Neh 12:19
2, 3. Two postexilic Jews who put away their foreign wives ....Ezra 10:33, 37

MATTER—*subject under consideration*
Descriptive of:
Lawsuit................1Cor 6:1
Sum of something ....Eccl 12:13
Love affair.............Ruth 3:18
News ....Mark 1:45
Speech 1Sam 16:18
Kinds of:
Good ....Ps 45:1
Evil ....Ps 64:5
Unknown ....Dan 2:5, 10
Revealed ....Dan 2:23

[*also* MATTERS]
sware..concerning that *m*......Gen 24:9
When they have a *m*.........Ex 24:16
every great *m* they shall.......Ex 18:22
but every small *m* they........Ex 18:26
If any man have any *m*........Ex 24:14
about the *m* of Korah.........Num 16:49
the Lord in the *m* of Peor.....Num 31:16
speak no more..of this *m*......Deut 3:26
m of controversy within.......Deut 17:8
shall the *m* be established.....Deut 19:15
how the *m* will fall ....Ruth 3:18
of the *m* of the kingdom......1Sam 10:16
David knew the *m*............1Sam 20:39
unto you in this *m*?...........1Sam 30:24
How went the *m*?.............2Sam 1:4
telling the *m* of the war.......2Sam 11:19
speakest thou..of thy *m*?......2Sam 19:29
be ye angry for this *m*?.......2Sam 19:42
as the *m* shall require.........1Kin 8:59
every *m* pertaining to God....1Chr 26:32
Levites concerning any *m*.....2Chr 8:15
in all *m* of the Lord..........2Chr 19:11
for all the king's *m*..........2Chr 19:11
m belongeth unto thee........Ezra 10:4
wrath of..God for this *m*......Ezra 10:14
month to examine the *m*......Ezra 10:16
might have *m* for an evil......Neh 6:13
m concerning the people......Neh 11:24
was made of the *m*...........Esth 2:23
Mordecai's *m* would stand.....Esth 3:4
the root of the *m* is found.....Job 19:28
account of any of his *m*......Job 33:13
devise deceitful *m* against.....Ps 35:20
spirit concealeth the *m*........Prov 11:13
that handleth a *m* wisely......Prov 16:20
he that repeateth a *m*.........Prov 17:9
answereth a *m* before he......Prov 18:13
kings is to search out a *m*.....Prov 25:2
marvel not at the *m*..........Eccl 5:8
the *m* was not perceived......Jer 38:27
by his side, reported the *m*....Ezek 9:11
he consented..in this *m*.......Dan 1:14
m of wisdom................Dan 1:20
This *m* is by the decree of....Dan 4:17
is the end of the *m*...........Dan 7:28
but I kept the *m* in my.......Dan 7:28
weightier *m* of the law........Matt 23:23
part nor lot in this *m*.........Acts 8:21
to consider of this *m*..........Acts 15:6
a *m* of wrong or wicked.......Acts 18:14
no judge of such *m*...........Acts 18:15
know the uttermost of your *m*.Acts 24:22
be judged of these *m*.........Acts 25:20
to judge the smallest *m*?......1Cor 6:2
to be clear in this *m*..........2Cor 7:11
be ready, as a *m* of bounty....2Cor 9:5
it maketh no *m* to me ....Gal 2:6
defraud his brother in any *m*..1Thess 4:6
a *m* a little fire kindleth.......James 3:5
busybody in other men's *m*....1Pet 4:15

MATTHAN (măt'thăn)—*"gift"*
Ancestor of Joseph ......Matt 1:15, 16

MATTHAT (măt'thăt)—*"gift"*
1. Ancestor of Christ ....Luke 3:24
2. Another ancestor of Christ................Luke 3:29

MATTHEW (măth'ū)—*"gift of God"—one of the twelve apostles and the writer of the Gospel of Matthew*
Tax gatherer ....Matt 9:9
Becomes Christ's follower.Matt 9:9
Appointed an apostle ....Matt 10:2, 3
Called Levi, the son of Alphaeus ....Mark 2:14
Entertains Jesus with a great feast ....Mark 2:14, 15
In the upper room.......Acts 1:13

Bartholomew, and *M*.........Mark 3:18
M and Thomas, James ....Luke 6:15

MATTHEW, THE GOSPEL OF—*a book of the New Testament*
Events of Jesus' birth ....Matt 1:18—2:23
John the Baptist.........Matt 3:1-17
The temptation..........Matt 4:1-11
Jesus begins His ministry .Matt 4:12-17
The Great Sermon ......Matt 5:1—7:29
Christ, about John the Baptist ....Matt 11:1-19

Conflict with the Pharisees and Sadducees .... Matt 15:39—16:6
Peter's confession .... Matt 16:13-20
Prophecy of death and resurrection .... Matt 20:17-19
Jerusalem entry .... Matt 21:1-11
Authority of Jesus .... Matt 21:23—22:14
Woes to the Pharisees ... Matt 23:1-36
Garden of Gethsemane .. Matt 26:36-56
Crucifixion and burial .... Matt 27:27-66
Resurrection of Christ ... Matt 28:1-20

MATTHIAS (mă-thī'ăs)—*"God's gift"*
Chosen by lot to replace Judas .... Acts 1:15-26

MATTITHIAH (măt-ĭ-thī'ä)—*"gift of Jehovah"*
1. Korahite Levite 1Chr 9:31
2. Levite, son of Jeduthun, and Temple musician .. 1Chr 15:18, 21
3. Jew who put away his foreign wife .... Ezra 10:43
4. Levite attendant to Ezra . Neh 8:4

Jehiel, and *M* 1Chr 16:5
Hashabiah, and *M* 1Chr 25:3
fourteenth to *M* 1Chr 25:21

MATTOCK—*an agricultural instrument for digging and hoeing*
Sharpened for battle 1Sam 13:20-22

MATURITY, SPIRITUAL—*living wisely before God*
Do away with childish things 1Cor 13:11
Be mature in your thinking 1Cor 14:20
Solid food is for .... Heb 5:11-14
Overcoming the evil one . 1John 2:14

MAUL—*a stick or a club*
Used against neighbor ... Prov 25:18

MAW—*the fourth stomach of ruminants (divided-hoof animals such as cows)*
Given to the priests ..... Deut 18:3

MAY, MAYEST—*See* INTRODUCTION

MAZZAROTH (măz'ä-rŏth)—*the signs of the Zodiac or a constellation*
Descriptive of God's power .... Job 38:32
Objects of idolatrous worship 2Kin 23:5

ME—*See* INTRODUCTION

MEADOW—*a grassland*
1. Reed grass or papyrus thickets .... Is 19:6, 7
Translated "flag" in ..... Job 8:11
2. Place near Gibeah ...... Judg 20:33

and they fed in a *m* .... Gen 41:2
and they fed in a *m* .... Gen 41:18

MEAH (mē'ä)—*a tower*
Restored by Eliashib ..... Neh 3:1

MEAL—*ground grain used for food*
tenth part of an ephah ... Num 5:15
Used in offerings 1Kin 4:22
"Then bring" 2Kin 4:41
Millstones and grind ..... Is 47:2
Three pecks of .... Matt 13:33

three measures of fine *m* ...... Gen 18:6
handful of *m* in a barrel 1Kin 17:12
barrel of *m* shall not waste 1Kin 17:14
barrel of *m* wasted not 1Kin 17:16
in three measures of *m* .... Luke 13:21

MEALS—*times of eating*

Times of:
Early morning .... John 21:4-12
At noon (for laborers) ... Ruth 2:14
In the evening .... Gen 19:1-3

Extraordinary and festive:
Guests invited .... Matt 22:3, 4
Received with a kiss ..... Luke 7:45
Feet washed .... Luke 7:44
Anointed with ointment .. Luke 7:38
Proper dress .... Matt 22:11, 12
Seated according to rank . Matt 23:6
Special guest honored 1Sam 9:22-24
Entertainment provided .. Luke 15:25
Temperate habits taught . Prov 23:1-3
Intemperance condemned . Amos 6:4-6
See ENTERTAINMENT; FEASTS

MEAN—*to intend; to have in mind*
[*also* MEANEST, MEANETH, MEANING, MEANT]
What *m* thou by all this .... Gen 33:8
God *m* it unto good .... Gen 50:20
What *m* ye by this .... Ex 12:26
no *m* clearing the guilty .... Num 14:18
What *m* the testimonies .... Deut 6:20
what *m* the heat of this .... Deut 29:24
What *m* ye by these stones? .. Josh 4:6
What *m* the noise of this 1Sam 4:6
m then this bleating 1Sam 15:14
unto Ziba, What *m* thou 2Sam 16:2
m ye that ye beat my people .. Is 3:15
Howbeit he *m* not so .... Is 10:7
what these things *m*? .... Ezek 17:12
not show us what thou *m* ..... Ezek 37:18
vision, and sought for the *m* .. Dan 8:15
What *m* thou, O sleeper? ..... Jon 1:6
learn what that *m* .... Matt 9:13
ye had known what this *m* .... Matt 12:7
rising from the dead should *m* . Mark 9:10
asked what these things *m* .... Luke 15:26
one to another, What *m* ...... Acts 2:12
vision..should *m* .... Acts 10:17
know..what these things *m* .... Acts 17:20
what *m* ye to weep .... Acts 21:13
m to sail by the coasts of ..... Acts 27:2
the *m* of the voice 1Cor 14:11
upon us by the *m* of many 2Cor 1:11
I *m* not that other men 2Cor 8:13
lest by any *m* I should run .... Gal 2:2
by any *m* I might attain .... Phil 3:11
that by *m* of death .... Heb 9:15
m of those miracles .... Rev 13:14

MEAN—*concurrent*
in the *m* time, when there ..... Luke 12:1
the *m* while accusing .... Rom 2:15

MEAN—*ordinary; humble*
he shall not stand before *m* ... Prov 22:29
the *m* man shall be brought ... Is 5:15
a citizen of no *m* city .... Acts 21:39

MEAN—*that which serves a purpose; personal resources*
[*also* MEANS]
what *m* ye by this service ..... Ex 12:26
by the *m* of the prancings ..... Judg 5:22
yet doth he devise *m*, that 2Sam 14:14
bring them out by their *m* 1Kin 10:29
kings of Syria, by their *m* 2Chr 1:17
by this *m* thou shalt have ..... Ezra 4:16
can by any *m* redeem his ...... Ps 49:7
by *m* of a whorish woman ..... Prov 6:26
priests..rule by their *m* .... Jer 5:31
this hath been by your *m* ..... Mal 1:9
Thou shalt by no *m* come ..... Matt 5:26
sought *m* to bring him .... Luke 5:18
shall by any *m* hurt you .... Luke 10:19
by what *m* he now seeth ...... John 9:21
by what *m* he is made .... Acts 4:9
if by any *m* they might .... Acts 27:12
if by any *m*..I might .... Rom 1:10
lest by any *m* this liberty 1Cor 8:9
lest by any *m*, when I 1Cor 9:27

MEANS OF GRACE—*ways by which God's grace is received or offered*

Agents of:
Holy Spirit .... Gal 5:16-26
God's Word 1Thess 2:13
Prayer .... Rom 8:15-27
Christian fellowship ...... Mal 3:16-18
Public worship 1Thess 5:6
Christian witnessing ...... Acts 8:4

Words expressive of:
Stir up the gift 1Tim 1:6
Neglect not the spiritual gift 1Tim 4:14
Take heed to the ministry. Col 4:17
Grow in grace 2Pet 3:18

Use of, brings:
Assurance 2Pet 1:5-12
Stability .... Eph 4:11-16

Enemies of:
Devil 1Thess 3:5
World 1John 2:15-17
Coldness .... Rev 3:14-18

MEANWHILE—*during the intervening time*
came to pass in the *m* 1Kin 18:45
the *m* his disciples prayed ..... John 4:31

MEARAH (mē-ā'rä)—*"den"*
Unconquered by Joshua .. Josh 13:1, 4

MEASURE—*a standard of size, quantity, or values; to take measurements*

Objectionable:
Differing (different) ..... Deut 25:14, 15
Scant .... Mic 6:10
Using themselves as a gauge 2Cor 10:12

As indicative of:
Earth's weight .... Is 40:12
Punishment inflicted ..... Matt 7:2

Figurative of:
Great size .... Hos 1:10
Sin's ripeness .... Matt 23:32
The Spirit's infilling ...... John 3:34
Man's ability 2Cor 10:13
Perfection of faith .... Eph 4:13, 16

[*also* MEASURED, MEASURES, MEASURING]
three *m* of fine meal .... Gen 18:6
curtains shall have one *m* ..... Ex 26:2
in weight, or in *m* .... Lev 19:35
m from without the city .... Num 35:5
shall *m* unto the cities .... Deut 21:2
in thine house divers *m* .... Deut 25:14
two thousand cubits by *m* ..... Josh 3:4
measured six *m* of barley ..... Ruth 3:15
it, he *m* six measures .... Ruth 3:15
five *m* of parched corn 1Sam 25:18
Moab, and *m* them with a 2Sam 8:2
even with two lines *m* he 2Sam 8:2
thirty *m* of fine flour 1Kin 4:22
threescore *m* of meal 1Kin 4:22
twenty thousand *m* of wheat ... 1Kin 5:11
and twenty *m* of pure oil 1Kin 5:11
of one *m* and one 1Kin 6:25
to the *m* of hewed stones 1Kin 7:9
the *m* of hewed stones 1Kin 7:11
and two *m* of barley for 2Kin 7:1
m of fine flour be sold for 2Kin 7:1
m of fine flour for a shekel 2Kin 7:18
all manner of *m* and size 1Chr 23:29
m of beaten wheat 2Chr 2:10
m of barley 2Chr 2:10
m was threescore cubits 2Chr 3:3
a hundred *m* of wheat .... Ezra 7:22
The *m* thereof is longer .... Job 11:9
weigheth the waters by *m* ..... Job 28:25
hath laid the *m* thereof .... Job 38:5
and the *m* of my days .... Ps 39:4
weights, and divers *m* .... Prov 20:10
her mouth without *m* .... Is 5:14
In *m*, when it shooteth .... Is 27:8
I *m* their former work .... Is 65:7
portion of thy *m* from me ..... Jer 13:25
I will correct thee in *m* .... Jer 30:11
If heaven above can be *m* ..... Jer 31:37
m line shall yet go forth .... Jer 31:39
the sand of the sea *m* .... Jer 33:22
the *m* of thy covetousness ..... Jer 51:13
drink also water by *m* .... Ezek 4:11
in his hand, and a *m* reed ..... Ezek 40:3
in the man's hand a *m* reed ... Ezek 40:5
he *m*..the building .... Ezek 40:5

m also the porch of the ....Ezek 40:8
they three were of one *m* .....Ezek 40:10
the posts had one *m* on ....Ezek 40:10
And he *m*..the entry ....Ezek 40:11
Then he *m* the breadth ....Ezek 40:19
after the *m* of the gate ....Ezek 40:22
m from gate to gate ....Ezek 40:23
according to these *m* ....Ezek 40:24
and he *m* from gate to gate ...Ezek 40:27
according to these *m* ....Ezek 40:29
he *m* the gate according ....Ezek 40:32
were according to these *m* .....Ezek 40:33
m the court, a hundred ....Ezek 40:47
and *m* the posts, six cubits ....Ezek 41:1
inward, and *m*..the door ......Ezek 41:3
m the wall of the house ....Ezek 41:5
he *m*..the building ....Ezek 41:15
within and without, by *m* .....Ezek 41:17
an end of *m* the inner ....Ezek 42:15
He *m* the east side with ....Ezek 42:16
east side with the *m* reed .....Ezek 42:16
m reed round about ....Ezek 42:16
reeds with the *m* reed..........Ezek 42:19
are the *m* of the altar ....Ezek 43:13
of this *m* shalt thou ....Ezek 45:3
the bath shall be of one *m* ....Ezek 45:11
the *m* thereof shall be ....Ezek 45:11
Again he *m* a thousand ....Ezek 47:4
east side ye shall *m* from ......Ezek 47:18
and five hundred *m* ....Ezek 48:30
eighteen thousand *m* ....Ezek 48:35
he stood, and *m* the earth .....Hab 3:6
to a heap of twenty *m* ....Hag 2:16
with a *m* line in his hand ......Zech 2:1
To *m* Jerusalem, to see ....Zech 2:2
hid in three *m* of meal ....Matt 13:33
With what *m* ye mete ....Mark 4:24
mete, it shall be *m* to you .....Mark 4:24
in themselves beyond *m* ....Mark 6:51
beyond *m* astonished ....Mark 7:37
good *m*, pressed down ....Luke 6:38
with the same *m* that ye ......Luke 6:38
withal it shall be *m* to you ....Luke 6:38
hid in three *m* of meal ....Luke 13:21
An hundred *m* of wheat ......Luke 16:7
every man the *m* of faith ......Rom 12:3
ourselves beyond our *m* 2Cor 10:14
boasting without our *m* 2Cor 10:15
stripes above *m*, in prisons 2Cor 11:23
lest I..be exalted above *m* 2Cor 12:7
lest I..be exalted above *m* 2Cor 12:7
beyond *m* I persecuted ....Gal 1:13
the *m* of the gift of Christ ....Eph 4:7
A *m* of wheat for a penny ....Rev 6:6
three *m* of barley for a ....Rev 6:6
temple leave out, and *m* ......Rev 11:2
m the city with the reed.......Rev 21:16
the *m* of a man ....Rev 21:17
he *m* the wall thereof, an .....Rev 21:17

MEASURING LINE—*a cord of specified length for measuring*
Signifies hope ....Jer 31:38-40
Zech 2:1

MEAT—*solid food; meal; substance; animal flesh*

Characteristics of:
Given by God ....Ps 104:21, 27
Necessary for man ....Gen 1:29, 30

Lack of:
Testing of faith ....Hab 3:17
Provided by:
God ....Ps 145:15
Christ ....John 21:5, 6

Prohibitions concerning:
Not in itself commendable 1Cor 8:8
Not to be a stumbling block 1Cor 8:13
Life more important than .Matt 6:25

Figurative of:
God's will ....John 4:32, 34
Christ ....John 6:27, 55
Strong doctrines 1Cor 3:2

[*also* MEATS]
liveth shall be *m* for you ......Gen 9:3
make me savory *m* ....Gen 27:4
make me savory *m*, that ....Gen 27:7
mother made savory *m* ....Gen 27:14
he also had made savory *m*....Gen 27:31
m offering of the morning .....Ex 29:41
and the *m* offering............Ex 40:29
will offer a *m* offering ....Lev 2:1
oblation of a *m* offering.......Lev 2:4
it is a *m* offering ....Lev 2:6
bring the *m* offering ....Lev 2:8
which is left of the *m* offering. .Lev 2:10
oblation of thy *m* offering .....Lev 2:13
from thy *m* offering...........Lev 2:13
m offering of thy first fruits ...Lev 2:14
offer for the *m* offering ....Lev 2:14
priest's, as a *m* offering ....Lev 5:13
the flour of the *m* offering ....Lev 6:15
is upon the *m* offering ....Lev 6:15
pieces of the *m* offering ....Lev 6:21
And all the *m* offering ....Lev 7:9
of the *m* offering ....Lev 7:37
he brought the *m* offering .....Lev 9:17
all *m* which may be eaten .....Lev 11:34
m offering upon the altar .....Lev 14:20
with the *m* offering ....Lev 14:31
shall eat of her father's *m* .....Lev 22:13
a new *m* offering unto ....Lev 23:16
and a *m* offering ....Lev 23:37
the increase thereof be *m* .....Lev 25:7
and the daily *m* offering ......Num 4:16
offer also his *m* offering.......Num 6:17
oil for a *m* offering ....Num 7:79
with their *m* offering..........Num 7:87
m offering of a tenth deal .....Num 15:4
m offering of three tenth ......Num 15:9
every *m* offering of theirs .....Num 18:9
m offering of the morning .....Num 28:8
of flour for a *m* offering ......Num 28:9
m offering shall be of flour ....Num 28:20
bring a new *m* offering........Num 28:26
and his *m* offering ....Num 28:31
m offering shall be of flour ....Num 29:3
his *m* offering, and the ....Num 29:6
and his *m* offering, and ....Num 29:6
and the *m* offering of it ....Num 29:11
m offering, and his drink ......Num 29:16
the *m* offering thereof ....Num 29:19
and his *m* offering ....Num 29:22
offering, his *m* offering........Num 29:25
and his *m* offering, and ....Num 29:28
m offering, and his drink ......Num 29:31
m offering, and his drink ......Num 29:34
and his *m* offering, and his ....Num 29:38
Ye shall buy *m* of them ....Deut 2:6
they be not trees for *m* ....Deut 20:20
offering or *m* offering ....Josh 22:23
gathered their *m* under........Judg 1:7
m offering at our hands ....Judg 13:23
Out of the eater came..*m* .....Judg 14:14
to sit with the king at *m* 1Sam 20:5
the son of Jesse to *m* 1Sam 20:27
eat *m* while it was yet day 2Sam 3:35
it did eat of his own *m*........2Sam 12:3
Tamar come, and give me *m* ..2Sam 13:5
dress the *m* in my sight 2Sam 13:5
offerings, and *m* offerings 1Kin 8:64
of that *m* forty days 1Kin 19:8
m offering was offered 2Kin 3:20
evening *m* offering............2Kin 16:15
and his *m* offering, with.......2Kin 16:15
their *m* offering, and..........2Kin 16:15
on oxen, and *m*, meal 1Chr 12:40
fine flour for *m* offering.......1Chr 23:29
m offerings, and the fat 2Chr 7:7
and *m*, and drink, and oil .....Ezra 3:7
the continual *m* offering.......Neh 10:33
m offering and the...........Neh 13:9
are as my sorrowful *m* ....Job 6:7
m in his bowels is turned.....Job 20:14
juniper roots for their *m* ......Job 30:4
and his soul dainty *m* ....Job 33:20
as the mouth tasteth *m*........Job 34:3
they wander for lack of *m* .....Job 38:41

My tears have been my *m* .....Ps 42:3
wander up and down for *m*....Ps 59:15
gave me also gall for my *m*....Ps 69:21
asking *m* for their lust ....Ps 78:18
food; he sent them *m* ....Ps 78:25
have they given to be *m* ......Ps 79:2
give them their *m* in due ......Ps 104:27
hath given *m* unto them ....Ps 111:5
Provideth her *m* in the ....Prov 6:8
desire thou his dainty *m* ......Prov 23:6
fool when he is filled with *m* ..Prov 30:22
giveth *m* to her household.....Prov 31:15
hast offered a *m* offering ......Is 57:6
dust shall be the serpent's *m* ..Is 65:25
cascases..people shall be *m* ...Jer 7:33
m offerings, and incense .....Jer 17:26
to kindle *m* offerings..........Jer 33:18
pleasant things for *m* ....Lam 1:11
their *m* in the destruction .....Lam 4:10
m which thou shalt eat ....Ezek 4:10
for *m* to the beasts of.........Ezek 29:5
became *m* to every beast ......Ezek 34:8
and the *m* offering ....Ezek 42:13
for a *m* offering, and for a ....Ezek 45:15
offerings, and *m* offerings .....Ezek 45:17
and the *m* offering, and ....Ezek 45:17
according to the *m* offering....Ezek 45:25
m offering shall be an ephah ..Ezek 46:5
m offering for the lambs ......Ezek 46:5
shalt prepare a *m* offering .....Ezek 46:14
a *m* offering continually ....Ezek 46:14
the *m* offering, and the oil ....Ezek 46:15
shall grow all trees for *m*.......Ezek 47:12
fruit thereof shall be for *m* ....Ezek 47:12
provision of the king's *m* ......Dan 1:5
hath appointed your *m* ....Dan 1:10
portion of the king's *m*........Dan 1:15
and in it was *m* for all ....Dan 4:12
feed of the portion of his *m* ...Dan 11:26
and I laid *m* unto them ....Hos 11:4
The *m* offering and the drink ..Joel 1:9
Is not the *m* cut off before ....Joel 1:16
and your *m* offerings..........Amos 5:22
fat, and their *m* plenteous .....Hab 1:16
wine, or oil, or any *m* ....Hag 2:12
his *m*, is contemptible ....Mal 1:12
m was locusts and wild honey. .Matt 3:4
is not the life more than *m* ....Matt 6:25
as Jesus sat at *m* in the ....Matt 9:10
which sat with him at *m*.......Matt 14:9
them *m* in due season.........Matt 24:45
ahungered, and ye gave me *m* .Matt 25:35
and ye gave me no *m* ....Matt 25:42
as Jesus sat at *m* in his........Mark 2:15
draught, purging all *m*? ....Mark 7:19
as he sat at *m*, there came ....Mark 14:3
the eleven as they sat at *m* ....Mark 16:14
he that hath *m*, let him ....Luke 3:11
sat at *m* in the Pharisee's .....Luke 7:37
commanded to give her *m*.....Luke 8:55
buy *m* for all this people ......Luke 9:13
went in, and sat down to *m* ...Luke 11:37
them to sit down to *m* ....Luke 12:37
that sit at *m* with thee ....Luke 14:10
Go and sit down to *m*? ....Luke 17:7
greater, he that sitteth at *m* ...Luke 22:27
is not he that sitteth at *m*? ....Luke 22:27
Have ye here any *m*? ....Luke 24:41
unto the city to buy *m* ....John 4:8
Children, have ye any *m*? .....John 21:5
eat their *m* with gladness......Acts 2:46
abstain from *m* offered to .....Acts 15:29
set *m* before them, and ....Acts 16:34
besought them all to take *m* ...Acts 27:33
I pray you to take some *m* ....Acts 27:34
be grieved with thy *m*.........Rom 14:15
Destroy not him with thy *m* ...Rom 14:15
kingdom of God is not *m* ......Rom 14:17
m destroy not the work ....Rom 14:20
M for the belly, and the 1Cor 6:13
and the belly for *m*: but.......1Cor 6:13
sit at *m* in the idol's temple ...1Cor 8:10
eat the same spiritual *m*.......1Cor 10:3
no man..judge you in *m* ......Col 2:16
to abstain from *m* 1Tim 4:3

M

milk, and not of strong *m* .....Heb 5:12
strong *m* belongeth to.........Heb 5:14
Which stood only in *m*........Heb 9:10
m sold his birthright.........Heb 12:16
not with *m*, which have ....Heb 13:9

MEBUNNAI (mĕ-bŭn'ī)—*"Jehovah is intervening"*
One of David's mighty men..................2Sam 23:27
Called Sibbecai..........1Chr 11:29

MECHERATHITE (mē-kĕr'ă-thīt)—*a dweller in Mecharah*
Descriptive of Hepher, one of David's mighty men..................1Chr 11:36

MEDAD (mē'dăd)—*"love"*
One of the seventy elders receiving the Spirit ....Num 11:26-29

MEDAN (mē'dăn)—*"judgment"*
Son of Abraham by Keturah ....Gen 25:1, 2

MEDDLE—*interfere with the affairs of others*
Brings a king's death 2Chr 35:21-24
Christians..............1Pet 4:15
Such called "busybodies" .2Thess 3:11

[*also* MEDDLED, MEDDLETH, MEDDLING]
why shouldest thou *m*.........2Kin 14:10
shouldest thou *m* to thine 2Chr 25:19
before it be *m* with ....Prov 17:14
but every fool will be *m*.......Prov 20:3
m not with him that ....Prov 20:19
m not with them that ....Prov 24:21
m with strife belonging........Prov 26:17

MEDEBA (mĕd'ĕ-bä)—*"waters of grief"*
Old Moabite town.......Num 21:29, 30
Assigned to Reuben .....Josh 13:9, 16
Syrians defeated here 1Chr 19:6, 7
Reverts to Moab ....Is 15:2

MEDES, MEDIA (mēds, mē'dĭ-ä)—*"middle land"—the people and country of the Medes*

Characteristics of:
Descendants of Japheth ..Gen 10:2
Part of Medo-Persian empire ....Esth 1:19
Inflexible laws of ....Dan 6:8, 12, 15
Among those at Pentecost Acts 2:9

Kings of, mentioned in the Bible:
Cyrus ....Ezra 1:1
Ahasuerus ....Ezra 4:6
Artaxerxes I ....Ezra 4:7
Darius..................Ezra 6:1
Xerxes ....Dan 11:2
Artaxerxes..............Ezra 6:14

Place of, in Bible history:
Israel deported to 2Kin 17:6
Babylon falls to ....Dan 5:30, 31
"Darius the Mede," new ruler of Babylon ......Dan 5:31
Daniel rises high in the kingdom of ....Dan 6:1-28
Cyrus, king of Persia, allows Jews to return ..2Chr 36:22, 23
Esther and Mordecai live under Ahasuerus, king of..................Esth 1:3, 19

Prophecies concerning:
Agents in Babylon's fall..Is 13:17-19
Cyrus, king of, God's servant ....Is 44:28
"Inferior" kingdom ......Dan 2:39
Compared to a bear .....Dan 7:5
Kings of ....Dan 11:2
War with Greece ....Dan 11:2

and in the cities of the *M* 2Kin 18:11
in the province of the *M* ......Ezra 6:2
princes of Persia and *M* ....Esth 1:14
the ladies of Persia and *M* ....Esth 1:18
chronicles of the kings of *M* ...Esth 10:2
O Elam: besiege, O *M*........Is 21:2
all the kings of the *M*.........Jer 25:25
spirit of the kings of the *M*....Jer 51:11
with the kings of the *M*.......Jer 51:28
divided, and given to the *M*....Dan 5:28
horns are the kings of *M*......Dan 8:20
Ahasuerus, of..the *M* ....Dan 9:1

MEDIAN (mē'dĭ-ăn)—*one from Media*
Darius the *M* took...........Dan 5:31

MEDIATION—*intervention designed to render assistance; the reconciliation of differences*

Purposes of:
Save a life ....Gen 37:21, 22
Save a people ....Ex 32:11-13
Obtain a wife 1Kin 2:13-25
Obtain justice ....Job 9:33

Motives prompting:
People's fear ....Deut 5:5
Regard for human life ...Jer 38:7-13
Sympathy for a sick man .2Kin 5:6-8; Matt 17:15

Methods used:
Intense prayer...........Deut 9:20-29
Flattery.................1Sam 25:23-25
Appeal to self-preservation ....Esth 4:12-17

[*also* MEDIATOR]
in the hand of a *m* ....Gal 3:19
m is not a *m* of one, but God. .Gal 3:20

MEDIATOR, CHRIST OUR—*Christ as the One who reconciles us to God*

His qualifications:
Bears God's image, man's likeness....... Phil 2:6-8; Heb 2:14-17
Is both sinless and sin-bearer........... Is 53:6-10; Eph 2:13-18
Endures God's wrath, brings Gods righteousness..........Rom 5:6-19
Is sacrifice and the priest .Heb 7:27; Heb 10:5-22

How He performs the function:
Took our nature.........1John 1:1-3
Died as our substitute ...1Pet 1:18, 19
Reconciled us to God....Eph 2:16

[*also* MEDIATOR]
one *m* between God 1Tim 2:5
m of a better covenant ....Heb 8:6
m of the new testament ....Heb 9:15
m of the new covenant........Heb 12:24

MEDICINE—*something prescribed to cure an illness*

General prescriptions:
Merry heart.............Prov 15:13
Rest....................Ps 37:7-11
Sleep...................John 11:12, 13
Quarantine..............Lev 12:1-4
Sanitation..............Deut 23:10-14

Specific prescriptions:
Figs ....Is 38:21
Roots and leaves ....Ezek 47:12
Wine 1Tim 5:23

Used figuratively of:
Salvation ....Jer 8:22
Incurableness ....Jer 46:11
Spiritual stubbornness....Jer 51:8, 9

See DISEASES

MEDITATION—*contemplation of spiritual truths*

Objects of, God's:
Word...................Ps 119:148
Law....................Josh 1:8
Instruction 1Tim 4:15

Value of, for:
Understanding ....Ps 49:3
Spiritual satisfaction .....Ps 63:5, 6
Superior knowledge......Ps 119:99

Extent of:
All the day ....Ps 119:97
At evening..............Gen 24:63
In night watches.........Ps 119:148

[*also* MEDITATE]
doth he *m* day and night ......Ps 1:2
O Lord, consider my *m* ....Ps 5:1
the *m* of my heart, be ....Ps 19:14
I will *m* also of all thy work ...Ps 77:12
m of him shall be sweet ....Ps 104:34
I will *m* in thy precepts ....Ps 119:15
did *m* in thy statutes ....Ps 119:23
I will *m* in thy statutes ....Ps 119:48
I will *m* in thy precepts ....Ps 119:78
It is my *m* all the day ....Ps 119:97
I *m* on all thy works ....Ps 143:5
Thine heart shall *m* terror .....Is 33:18
not to *m* before what ye ......Luke 21:14

MEDITERRANEAN SEA—*the sea on Israel's western border*

Described as:
Sea.....................Gen 49:13
Great Sea...............Josh 1:4; Josh 9:1
Sea of the Philistines ....Ex 23:31
Uttermost Sea.......... Deut 11:24; Joel 2:20; Zech 14:8

MEDIUM—*a communicator between humans and the spirit world*

Described as:
Source of defilement.....Lev 19:31
Abomination ....Deut 18:10-12
Whisperers..............Is 8:19

The practicers, to be:
Cut off ....Lev 20:6
Put to death ....Lev 20:27

Consulted by:
Saul 1Sam 28:3-25
Manasseh 2Kin 21:6

Condemned by:
Josiah 2Kin 23:24

MEEK—*patient; steadfast; not harboring resentment*

Blessings upon:
Gospel ....Is 61:1
Spiritual satisfaction .....Ps 22:26
Guidance and instruction .Ps 25:9
Salvation ....Ps 76:9

A Christian essential in:
Living in the Spirit ......Gal 5:22, 23
Receving the Word ......James 1:21
Stating our assurance ....James 3:13

[*also* MEEKNESS]
man Moses was very *m* ....Num 12:3
m shall inherit the earth ......Ps 37:11
truth and *m* and ....Ps 45:4
The Lord lifteth up the *m*.....Ps 147:6
will beautify the *m* with ....Ps 149:4
equity for the *m* of the earth ..Is 11:4
The *m* also shall increase......Is 29:19
turn aside the way of the *m* ...Amos 2:7
Lord, all ye *m* of the earth ....Zeph 2:3
seek righteousness, seek *m* ....Zeph 2:3
Blessed are the *m*: for ....Matt 5:5
for I am *m* and lowly in.......Matt 11:29
m, and sitting upon an ass ....Matt 21:5
love, and in the spirit of *m*? ...1Cor 4:21
m and gentleness of Christ 2Cor 10:1
such a one in the spirit of *m* ..Gal 6:1
With all lowliness and *m* ......Eph 4:2
of mind, *m*, long-suffering.....Col 3:12
faith, love, patience, *m* 1Tim 6:11
in *m* instructing those 2Tim 2:25
gentle, showing all *m* ....Titus 3:2
a *m* and quiet spirit...........1Pet 3:4
that is in you with *m* and 1Pet 3:15

MEET—*to approach; appropriate or suitable; helper; useful*

[*also* MEETEST, MEETETH, MEETING, MET]
will make him a help *m* ....Gen 2:18

king of Sodom went out to *m* .Gen 14:17
rose up to *m* them...........Gen 19:1
walketh in the field to *m* us? . .Gen 24:65
Leah went out to *m* him ......Gen 30:16
the angels of God *m* him......Gen 32:1
he cometh to *m* thee..........Gen 32:6
Esau ran to *m* him, and.......Gen 33:4
all this drove which I *m*? ......Gen 33:8
went up to *m* Israel his ....Gen 46:29
Hebrews hath *m* with us ....Ex 3:18
he cometh forth to *m* thee ....Ex 4:14
that the Lord *m* him, and .....Ex 4:24
and *m* him in the mount ......Ex 4:27
Hebrews hath *m* with us ......Ex 5:3
they *m* Moses and Aaron .....Ex 5:20
Moses said, It is not *m* so .....Ex 8:26
of the camp to *m* with God ...Ex 19:17
there I will *m* with thee ....Ex 25:22
I will *m* with the children .....Ex 29:43
where I will *m* with thee ....Ex 30:36
testimony, where I will *m* .....Num 17:4
Lord will come to *m* me ....Num 23:3
And God *m* Balaam ....Num 23:4
Lord *m* Balaam, and put ......Num 23:16
to *m* them without the ....Num 31:13
all that are *m* for the war .....Deut 3:18
they *m* you not with bread ....Deut 23:4
How he *m* thee by the way....Deut 25:18
lest the pursuers *m* you ....Josh 2:16
all these kings were *m* ....Josh 11:5
m together in Asher ....Josh 17:10
Jael went out to *m* Sisera .....Judg 4:18
m for the necks of them ......Judg 5:30
of my house to *m* me ....Judg 11:31
to *m* him with timbrels........Judg 11:34
he rejoiced to *m* him ....Judg 19:3
that they *m* thee not in ....Ruth 2:22
shall *m* thee three men........1Sam 10:3
thou shalt *m* a company.......1Sam 10:5
a company of prophets *m* 1Sam 10:10
Saul went out to *m* him 1Sam 13:10
Samuel rose early to *m* Saul ...1Sam 15:12
drew nigh to *m* David 1Sam 17:48
army to *m* the Philistine 1Sam 17:48
m king Saul, with tabrets......1Sam 18:6
against her and she *m* them ...1Sam 25:20
sent thee this day to *m* me 1Sam 25:32
they went forth to *m* David ...1Sam 30:21
m the people that were with ...1Sam 30:21
m together by the pool........2Sam 2:13
of Saul came out to *m* David ..2Sam 6:20
Archite came to *m* him 2Sam 15:32
Mephibosheth *m* him 2Sam 16:1
Absalom *m* the servants of 2Sam 18:9
Gilgal, to go to *m* the king 2Sam 19:15
of Judah to *m* king David 2Sam 19:16
of Saul came down to *m* 2Sam 19:24
he came down to *m* me at 1Kin 2:8
the king rose up to *m* her 1Kin 2:19
a lion *m* him by the way 1Kin 13:24
behold, Elijah *m* him 1Kin 18:7
Obadiah went to *m* Ahab 1Kin 18:16
Ahab went to *m* Elijah 1Kin 18:16
go down to *m* Ahab king 1Kin 21:18
go up to *m* the messengers 2Kin 1:3
which came up to *m* you 2Kin 1:7
they came to *m* him 2Kin 2:15
Run now, I pray thee to *m*....2Kin 4:26
he went again to *m* him.......2Kin 4:31
from the chariot to *m* him.....2Kin 5:21
go, *m* the man of God 2Kin 8:8
send to *m* them, and let.......2Kin 9:17
m him in the portion of 2Kin 9:21
m with the brethren of 2Kin 10:13
And David went out to *m*.....1Chr 12:17
he sent to *m* them: for the 1Chr 19:5
he went out to *m* Asa, and....2Chr 15:2
Hanani the seer went out to *m*.2Chr 19:2
m for us to see the king's .....Ezra 4:14
let us *m* together in some .....Neh 6:2
m not the children of ....Neh 13:2
were *m* to be given her ....Esth 2:9
They *m* with darkness in ......Job 5:14
it is *m* to be said unto God ...Job 34:31
to *m* the armed men ....Job 39:21

Mercy and truth are *m*........Ps 85:10
m him a woman with the......Prov 7:10
came I forth to *m* thee........Prov 7:15
withholdeth more than is *m* ...Prov 11:24
robbed of her whelps *m* a .....Prov 17:12
The rich and poor *m*..........Prov 22:2
and the deceitful man *m* ......Prov 29:13
Go forth now to *m* Ahaz......Is 7:3
is moved for thee to *m*........Is 14:9
beasts..shall also *m* ....Is 34:14
I will not *m* thee as a man ....Is 47:3
m him that rejoiceth ....Is 64:5
as seemeth good and *m* ....Jer 26:14
unto whom it seemed *m* ....Jer 27:5
from Mizpah to *m* them.......Jer 41:6
as he *m* them, he said ....Jer 41:6
One post shall run to *m*.......Jer 51:31
messenger to *m* another.......Jer 51:31
Is it *m* for any work? ....Ezek 15:4
I will *m* them as a bear ....Hos 13:8
prepare to *m* thy God ....Amos 4:12
a lion, and a bear *m* him......Amos 5:19
angel went out to *m* him ......Zech 2:3
fruits *m* for repentance........Matt 3:8
m him two possessed with .....Matt 8:28
city came out to *m* Jesus ......Matt 8:34
not *m* to take the children's ...Matt 15:26
forth to *m* the bridegroom ....Matt 25:1
Jesus *m* them, saying ....Matt 28:9
m him out of the tombs a .....Mark 5:2
not *m* to take the children's ...Mark 7:27
a place where two ways *m* ....Mark 11:4
m you a man bearing a ....Mark 14:13
m him out of the city a ....Luke 8:27
hill, much people *m* him ......Luke 9:37
to *m* him that cometh.........Luke 14:31
m that we should make ....Luke 15:32
m him ten men that were .....Luke 17:12
a man *m* you, bearing a.......Luke 22:10
his servants *m* him, and ....John 4:51
coming, went and *m* him ......John 11:20
place where Martha *m* him ....John 11:30
and went forth to *m* him ......John 12:13
the people also *m* him ....John 12:18
was coming in, Cornelius *m* ...Acts 10:25
with a spirit of divination *m* ...Acts 16:16
daily with them that *m*........Acts 17:17
he *m* with us at Assos ....Acts 20:14
works *m* for repentance ....Acts 26:20
place where two seas *m* ....Acts 27:41
m us as far as Appii Forum ...Acts 28:15
of their error which was *m*. ...Rom 1:27
m to be called an apostle 1Cor 15:9
it if be *m* that I go also 1Cor 16:4
m for me to think this of......Phil 1:7
made us *m* to be partakers ....Col 1:12
to *m* the Lord in the air 1Thess 4:17
for you brethren as it is *m* 2Thess 1:3
m for the master's use 2Tim 2:21
forth herbs *m* for them by.....Heb 6:7
m Abraham returning from....Heb 7:1
when Melchizedek *m* him .....Heb 7:10
I think it *m*, as long as I 2Pet 1:13

MEGIDDO, MEGIDDON (mĕ-gĭd'ō, mĕ-gĭd'dŏn)—*"declaring a message"*
City conquered by Joshua.Josh 12:21
Assigned to Manasseh ...Josh 17:11
Inhabitants of, made slaves ....Judg 1:27, 28
Canaanites defeated here .Judg 5:19-21
Site of Baana's headquarters 1Kin 4:12
Fortified by Solomon 1Kin 9:15-19
King Ahaziah dies here ..2Kin 9:27
King Josiah killed here...2Kin 23:29, 30
Mentioned in prophecy ..Zech 12:11
Site of Armageddon .....Rev 16:16

M and her towns, Dor 1Chr 7:29
to fight in the valley of *M*.....2Chr 35:22

MEHETABEL, MEHETABEEL (mĕ-hĕt'ä-bĕl, mĕ-hĕt'ä-bēl)—*"God is doing good"*
1. King Hadar's wife.......Gen 36:39
2. Father of Delaiah ....Neh 6:10

MEHIDA (mĕ-hī'dä)—*"famous"*
Ancestor of a family of returning Temple servants ....Ezra 2:52

MEHIR (mē'her)—*"dexterity"*
Judahite 1Chr 4:11

MEHOLATHITE (mē-hō'lă-thīt)—*a native of Meholah*
Descriptive of Adriel 1Sam 18:19

MEHUJAEL (mĕ-hū'jā-ĕl)—*"God is combating"*
Cainite; father of Methusael ....Gen 4:18

MEHUMAN, MEUNIM (mĕ-hū'măn, mĕ-ū'nĭm)—*"true"*
Eunuch under King Ahasuerus ....Esth 1:10

MEHUNIM (mĕ-hū'nĭm)—*one whose descendants returned*
Arabian tribe near Mt. Seir 2Chr 26:7
Smitten by Simeonites ...1Chr 4:39-42
Descendants of, serve as Nethinim ....Ezra 2:50

ME-JARKON (mē-jär'kŏn)—*"the waters of Jordan"*
Territory of Dan near Joppa ....Josh 19:40, 46

MEKONAH (mĕ-kō'nä)—*"provision"*
Town of Judah ....Neh 11:25, 28

MELATIAH (mĕl-ä-tī'ä)—*"Jehovah delivers"*
Postexilic workman ......Neh 3:7

MELCHI (mĕl'kī)—*"my king"*
Two ancestors of Jesus...Luke 3:24, 28

MELCHIAH—*See* MALCHIAH

MELCHIZEDEK, MELCHISEDEC (mĕl-kĭz'ĕ-dĕk)—*"king of righteousness"*

Described as:
King of Salem...........Gen 14:18
Priest of God ....Gen 14:18
Receiver of a tenth of Abram's goods ....Gen 14:18-20
King of righteousness ....Heb 7:2
Without parentage ....Heb 7:3
Great man ....Heb 7:4

Typical of Christ's:
Eternity ....Heb 7:3
Priesthood ....Ps 110:4
Kingship ....Heb 8:1

after the order of *M* ....Heb 5:6
priest after the order of *M* ....Heb 5:10
ever after the order of *M* .....Heb 6:20
For this *M*, king of Salem .....Heb 7:1
of his father, when *M* met ....Heb 7:10
rise after the order of *M* ......Heb 7:11
after the similitude of *M* ......Heb 7:15
ever after the order of *M* .....Heb 7:17
ever after the order of *M* .....Heb 7:21

MELEA (mē'lĕ-ä)—*"full"*
Ancestor of Jesus........Luke 3:31

MELECH (mē'lĕk)—*"king"*
Son of Micah, grandson of Jonathan 1Chr 8:35

MELICU (mĕl'ĭ-kū)—*"counselor; ruling"*
Head of a household ....Neh 12:14

MELITA (mĕl'ĭ-tä)—*"affording honey"—the island of Malta, in the Mediterranean Sea*
Paul's shipwreck ....Acts 28:1-8

MELODY—*song*
make sweet *m*, sing many .....Is 23:16
and the voice of *m* ....Is 51:3
hear the *m* of thy viols........Amos 5:23
making *m* in your heart ....Eph 5:19

MELON—*either the watermelon or the cantaloupe*
Desired by Israelites in wilderness ....Num 11:5

M

MELT—*to soften; dissolving; blending; subduing*

Used figuratively of:

Complete destruction . . . . Ex 15:15
Discouragement . . . . Josh 7:5
Defeatism . . . . Josh 5:1
National discouragement. . Is 19:1
Destruction of the wicked. Ps 68:2
God's presence . . . . Mic 1:4
Testings . . . . Jer 9:7
Troubled sea . . . . Ps 107:26
Christ's pain on the cross . Ps 22:14

[*also* MELTED, MELTETH, MELTING]

the sun waxed hot, it *m* . . . . Ex 16:21
things, our hearts did *m* . . . . Josh 2:11
the heart of the people *m* . . . . . Josh 14:8
The mountains *m* from . . . . Judg 5:5
the multitude *m* away 1Sam 14:16
heart of a lion..utterly *m* 2Sam 17:10
his voice, the earth *m* . . . . Ps 46:6
m away as waters which . . . . Ps 58:7
As a snail which *m*, let . . . . Ps 58:8
hills *m* like wax at the . . . . Ps 97:5
with his teeth, and *m* away . . . . Ps 112:10
my soul *m* for heaviness . . . . . . Ps 119:28
his word, and *m* them . . . . Ps 147:18
man's heart shall *m* . . . . Is 13:7
mountains..*m* with their . . . . Is 34:3
m a graven image . . . . Is 40:19
when the *m* fire burneth . . . . . . Is 64:2
the founder *m* in vain . . . . Jer 6:29
every heart shall *m*, and . . . . . . Ezek 21:7
the fire upon it, to *m* it . . . . Ezek 22:20
leave you there, and *m* you . . . Ezek 22:20
and ye shall be *m* in the . . . . . . Ezek 22:21
As silver is *m* in the midst . . . . Ezek 22:22
so shall ye be *m* in the . . . . Ezek 22:22
land, and it shall *m* . . . . Amos 9:5
all the hills shall *m* . . . . Amos 9:13
the hills *m*, and the earth . . . . . Nah 1:5
the heart *m*, and the knees . . . . Nah 2:10
elements shall *m* 2Pet 3:10
elements shall *m* 2Pet 3:12

MELZAR (měl'zär)—*"the overseer"*

Steward placed over Daniel . . . . Dan 1:11, 16

MEM (měm)

Letter of the Hebrew alphabet . . . . Ps 119:97-104

MEMBER—*a part of a larger whole*

Descriptive of:

Parts of the body . . . . Matt 5:29, 30
Union with Christ 1Cor 6:15
True Church 1Cor 12:27

Of the body:

Effect of sin in . . . . Rom 7:5
Struggle in . . . . Rom 7:23

Illustrative of:

Variety of Christian gifts. . Rom 12:4, 5
God's design in 1Cor 12:18, 24

[*also* MEMBERS]

or hath his privy *m* cut . . . . Deut 23:1
all my *m* are as a shadow . . . . . Job 17:7
in thy book all my *m* . . . . Ps 139:16
Neither yield ye your *m* as . . . . . Rom 6:13
and your *m* as instruments . . . . Rom 6:13
yielded your *m* servants . . . . Rom 6:19
now yield your *m* servants . . . . . Rom 6:19
body is one, and hath many *m* . 1Cor 12:12
all the *m* of that one body 1Cor 12:12
For the body is not one *m* 1Cor 12:14
And if they were all one *m* 1Cor 12:19
And now are they many *m* 1Cor 12:20
more those *m* of the body 1Cor 12:22
And those *m* of the body 1Cor 12:23
the *m* should have the same . . . 1Cor 12:25
And whether one *m* suffer 1Cor 12:26
suffer, all the *m* suffer 1Cor 12:26
or one *m* be honored 1Cor 12:26
honored, all the *m* rejoice 1Cor 12:26
for we are *m* one of another . . Eph 4:25
For we are *m* of his body . . . . . Eph 5:30
Mortify therefore your *m* . . . . . . Col 3:5
the tongue is a little *m* . . . . James 3:5
the tongue among our *m* . . . . . . James 3:6
lusts that war in your *m*? . . . . . . James 4:1

MEMORIALS—*things established to commemorate an event or a truth*

Established by men:

Jacob's stone . . . . Gen 28:18-22
Altar at Jordan . . . . Josh 22:9-16
Feast of Purim . . . . Esth 9:28

Established by God:

Passover . . . . Ex 12:14
Pot of manna . . . . Ex 16:32-34
Lord's Supper . . . . Luke 22:19

[*also* MEMORIAL]

m unto all generations . . . . Ex 3:15
a *m* between thine eyes . . . . . . Ex 13:9
Write this for a *m* in a book . . Ex 17:14
ephod for stones of *m* . . . . Ex 28:12
for a *m* before the Lord . . . . Ex 28:29
a *m* unto the children . . . . Ex 30:16
stones for a *m* . . . . Ex 39:7
the priest shall burn the *m* . . . . Lev 2:2
a *m* thereof, and burn it . . . . . . Lev 5:12
the *m* of it, unto the Lord . . . . Lev 6:15
a *m* of blowing of trumpets . . . . Lev 23:24
on the bread for a *m* . . . . Lev 24:7
an offering of *m* . . . . Num 5:15
they may be to you for a *m* . . . Num 10:10
a *m* unto the children of . . . . . . Num 16:40
a *m* for the children of . . . . Num 31:54
stones shall be for a *m* . . . . Josh 4:7
nor *m*, in Jerusalem . . . . Neh 2:20
and thy *m*, O Lord . . . . Ps 135:13
the Lord is his *m* . . . . Hos 12:5
for a *m* in the temple . . . . Zech 6:14
be told for a *m* of her . . . . Matt 26:13
spoken of for a *m* of her . . . . . . Mark 14:9
alms are come up for a *m* . . . . . Acts 10:4

MEMORY—*mental recall of past events or experiences*

Uses of, to recall:

Past blessings . . . . Ezra 9:5-15
Past sins . . . . Josh 22:12-20
God's blessings . . . . Neh 9:1-38
God's promises . . . . Neh 1:8-11
Christian truths 2Pet 1:15-21
Prophecies . . . . John 2:19-22
Lost opportunities . . . . Ps 37:1-3

Aids to:

Reminder 2Sam 12:1-13
Prick of conscience . . . . . . Gen 41:9
Holy Spirit . . . . John 14:26

[*also* MEMORIES]

cut off the *m* of them from . . . . Ps 109:15
m of thy great goodness . . . . . . Ps 145:7
The *m* of the just is blessed . . . Prov 10:7
m of them is forgotten . . . . Eccl 9:5
all their *m* to perish . . . . Is 26:14
if ye keep in *m* 1Cor 15:2

MEMPHIS (měm'fĭs)—*"abode of the good"*

Ancient capital of Egypt. . Hos 9:6
Prophesied against by Isaiah . . . . Is 19:13
Jews flee to . . . . Jer 44:1
Denounced by the prophets . . . . Jer 46:19

MEMUCAN (mĕ-mū'kăn)

Persian prince . . . . Esth 1:14-21

MEN—*See* MAN

MENAHEM (mĕn-ä'hĕm)—*"comforter"*

Cruel king of Israel 2Kin 15:14-18

M gave Pul a thousand 2Kin 15:19
M exacted the money 2Kin 15:20
the rest of the acts of *M* 2Kin 15:21
M slept with his fathers 2Kin 15:22
son of *M* began to reign 2Kin 15:23

MENAN (mē'năn)

Ancestor of Jesus . . . . Luke 3:31

MENCHILDREN—*male children*

shall all your *m* appear . . . . Ex 34:23

MENDING—*restoring or repairing something*

Of nets . . . . Matt 4:21
Used figuratively . . . . Luke 5:36

[*also* MEND]

brass to *m* the house 2Chr 24:12

MENE (mē'nĕ)—*"numbered"*

Sentence of doom . . . . Dan 5:25, 26

MENE, TEKEL, UPHARSIN (mē'nĕ; tĕ'kĕl'-ū-fär'sĭn)—*words written on the wall of Balshazzar's palace meaning "numbered, weighed, and divided"*

Written by God . . . . Dan 5:5, 25
Interpreted by Daniel . . . . Dan 5:24-29

MENPLEASERS—*those who seek the favor of men*

Not with eyeservice, as *m* . . . . . Eph 6:6
not with eyeservice, as *m* . . . . . Col 3:22

MENSTEALERS—*those who seize another by force*

Condemned by law 1Tim 1:10

MENSTRUATION—*a woman's monthly flow*

Intercourse during, prohibited . . . . Lev 18:19
End of, in old age . . . . Gen 18:11

Called:

"Sickness" . . . . Lev 20:18
"The custom of women". . Gen 31:35

[*also* MENSTROUS]

cast them away as a *m* cloth . . . Is 30:22
Jerusalem is as a *m* woman . . . . Lam 1:17
near to a *m* woman . . . . Ezek 18:6

MENTION—*to allude; cite; call attention to*

[*also* MENTIONED]

m of me unto Pharaoh . . . . Gen 40:14
make no *m* of the name . . . . Ex 23:13
cities which are here *m* . . . . Josh 21:9
m of the names of their gods . . Josh 23:7
he made *m* of the ark 1Sam 4:18
m by their names were 1Chr 4:38
m in the book of the kings 2Chr 20:34
m shall be made of coral . . . . . . Job 28:18
m of thy righteousness . . . . Ps 71:16
m of Rahab and Babylon . . . . . Ps 87:4
make *m* that his name is . . . . . . Is 12:4
every one that maketh *m* . . . . . . Is 19:17
we make *m* of thy name . . . . . . Is 26:13
m of the God of Israel . . . . Is 48:1
he made *m* of my name . . . . Is 49:1
make *m* of the Lord . . . . Is 62:6
m the loving kindnesses . . . . Is 63:7
Make ye *m* to the nations . . . . . Jer 4:16
I said, I will not make *m* . . . . . . Jer 20:9
burden..shall ye *m* . . . . Jer 23:36
Sodom was not *m* . . . . Ezek 16:56
they shall not be *m* . . . . Ezek 18:22
shall not be *m* . . . . Ezek 18:24
hath committed shall be *m* . . . . Ezek 33:16
make *m* of the name of . . . . Amos 6:10
m of you..in my prayers . . . . . . Rom 1:9
m of you in my prayers . . . . Eph 1:16
m of you in our prayers 1Thess 1:2
m of thee..in my prayers . . . . . . Philem 4
made *m* of the departing . . . . . . Heb 11:22

MEONENIM (mĕ-ŏ'nĕ-nĭm)—*"regardless of time"*

Tree or place where soothsayers performed. . Judg 9:37

MEONENIM, PLAIN OF—*"regardless of time"*

Abimelech's route . . . . Judg 9:35, 37

MEONOTHAI (mĕ-ŏn'ō'thī)—*"Jehovah is dwelling; my dwelling"*

Judahite 1Chr 4:14

MEPHAATH (mĕf'ā-ăth)—*"force of waters"*

Reubenite town . . . . Josh 13:18

Assigned to Merarite Levites .... Josh 21:34, 37
Repossessed by Moabites.. Jer 48:21

MEPHIBOSHETH (mĕ-fĭb'ō-shĕth)—*"idol breaker"*
1. Son of King Saul 2Sam 21:8
2. Grandson of King Saul; crippled son of Jonathan 2Sam 4:4-6
Reared by Machir 2Sam 9:6
Sought out and honored by David 2Sam 9:1-13
Accused by Ziba 2Sam 16:1-4
Later explains his side to David 2Sam 19:24-30
Spared by David 2Sam 21:7
Father of Micah 2Sam 9:12
Called Merib-baal 1Chr 8:34

MERAB (mē'răb)—*"increase"*
King Saul's eldest daughter 1Sam 14:49
Saul promises her to David, but gives her to Adriel 1Sam 18:17-19
Five sons of, hanged 2Sam 21:8, 9

MERAIAH (mĕ-rā'yä)—*"revelation of Jehovah"*
Postexilic priest .... Neh 12:12

MERAIOTH (mĕ-rā'yŏth)—*"revelations"*
1. Levite 1Chr 6:6, 7
2. Son of Ahitub and father of Zadok 1Chr 9:11
3. Priestly household in Joiakim's time .... Neh 12:15
Called Meremoth .... Neh 12:3

Azariah, the son of ***M*** .... Ezra 7:3
Zadok, the son of ***M*** .... Neh 11:11

MERARI (mĕ-rā'rī)—*"bitter; excited"*
1. Third son of Levi; brother of Gershon and Kohath .... Gen 46:11
Goes with Jacob to Egypt .... Gen 46:8, 11
2. Descendants of Merari; called Merarites .... Num 26:57
Divided into two groups . Ex 6:19
Duties assigned to ...... Num 3:35-37
Follow Judah in march .. Num 10:14, 17
Twelve cities assigned to . Josh 21:7, 34-40
Superintend Temple music 1Chr 6:31-47
Help David bring up the ark 1Chr 15:1-6
Divided into courses 1Chr 23:6-23
Their duties described ... 1Chr 26:10-19
Participate in cleansing the house of the Lord 2Chr 29:12-19
After exile, help Ezra ... Ezra 8:18, 19

Gershon, Kohath, and ***M*** ..... Gen 46:11
Kohath, and ***M*** .... Ex 6:16
Kohath, and ***M*** .... Num 3:17
the sons of ***M*** .... Num 3:20
M was the family of the .... Num 3:33
these are the families of ***M*** .... Num 3:33
the sons of ***M***, thou shalt ..... Num 4:29
he gave unto the sons of ***M*** ... Num 4:33
of unto the sons of ***M*** .... Num 7:8
Gershon, Kohath, and ***M*** 1Chr 6:1
Gershom, Kohath, and ***M*** 1Chr 6:16
sons of ***M***; Mahli, and 1Chr 6:19
Unto the sons of ***M*** 1Chr 6:63
rest of the children of ***M*** 1Chr 6:77
sons of ***M*** their brethren 1Chr 15:17
sons of ***M*** were Mahli and 1Chr 24:26
sons of ***M*** by Jaaziah 1Chr 24:27
Levites, of the sons of ***M*** 2Chr 34:12

MERARITES (mĕ-rā'rīts)—*See* **MERARI**

MERATHAIM (mĕr-ä-thā'ĭm)—*"double rebellion"*
Name applies to Babylon . Jer 50:21

MERCHANDISE—*goods offered for sale or trade*

Characteristics of:
Countries employed in ... Is 45:14
Men occupied with ...... Matt 22:5
Not mixed with spiritual things .... John 2:16
To be abolished .... Rev 18:11, 12

Figurative of:
Wisdom's profit .... Prov 3:13, 14
Gospel transformation ... Is 23:18

shalt not make ***m*** of her ...... Deut 21:14
maketh ***m*** of him .... Deut 24:7
perceiveth that her ***m*** is .... Prov 31:18
make a prey of thy ***m*** .... Ezek 26:12
to occupy thy ***m*** .... Ezek 27:9
isles were the ***m*** .... Ezek 27:15
cedar, among thy ***m*** .... Ezek 27:24
and thy fairs, thy ***m*** .... Ezek 27:27
the occupiers of thy ***m*** .... Ezek 27:27
of thy riches and of thy ***m*** ..... Ezek 27:33
thy ***m*** and all thy company .... Ezek 27:34
By the multitude of thy ***m*** ..... Ezek 28:16
with feigned words make ***m*** ... 2Pet 2:3

MERCHANTS—*traders or sellers*

Characteristics of:
Crossed the sea .... Is 23:2
Lamentation over .... Ezek 27:2-36
Some do not observe the Sabbath .... Neh 3:19-21
Burden people with debts. Neh 5:1-13
Peddle goods .... Neh 13:16
Trade with farmers ...... Prov 31:24
Form guilds .... Neh 3:8-32
Destroyed with Babylon. . Rev 18:3-19
Sailors, in Solomon's service 1Kin 9:27, 28
Bring Solomon 2Chr 9:14
Bring Solomon 2Chr 9:28

[*also* MERCHANTMEN, MERCHANT'S, MERCHANTS']
current money with the ***m***..... Gen 23:16
passed by Midianites ***m*** .... Gen 37:28
he had of the ***m*** 1Kin 10:15
of the spice ***m*** 1Kin 10:15
king's ***m*** received the linen 1Kin 10:28
which chapmen and ***m*** brought . 2Chr 9:14
part him among the ***m***? .... Job 41:6
She is like the ***m*** ships .... Prov 31:14
all powders of the ***m***? .... Song 3:6
city, whose ***m*** are princes ..... Is 23:8
against the ***m*** city .... Is 23:11
labored, even thy ***m*** .... Is 47:15
he set it in a city of ***m*** .... Ezek 17:4
and the ***m*** of Tarshish .... Ezek 38:13
a ***m***, the balances of deceit .... Hos 12:7
multiplied thy ***m*** .... Nah 3:16
the ***m*** people are cut down .... Zeph 1:11
heaven is like unto a ***m*** man .. Matt 13:45

MERCURIUS (mûr-kū'rĭ-ŭs)—*a Roman god*
Paul acclaimed as .... Acts 14:12

MERCY—*compassion or forbearance shown to an offender*

Described as:
Great .... Is 54:7
Sure .... Is 55:3
Abundant 1Pet 1:3
Tender .... Ps 25:6
New every morning ...... Lam 3:22, 23

Of God, seen in:
Regeneration 1Pet 1:3
Salvation .... Titus 3:5
Christ's mission .... Luke 1:72, 78
Forgiveness .... Ps 51:1

In the Christian life:
Received in salvation 1Cor 7:25
Taught as a principle of life .... Matt 5:7
Practiced as a gift .... Rom 12:8
Evidenced in God's provinces .... Phil 2:27
Obtained in prayer ...... Heb 4:16
Reason of consecration . . Rom 12:1
Reason for hope .... Jude 21

Special injunctions concerning:
Put on .... Col 3:12

Examples of:
David to Saul 1Sam 24:10-17
Christ to sinners .... Matt 9:13

Attitude of believers, to:
Cast themselves on 2Sam 24:14
Look for .... Jude 21

[*also* MERCIES, MERCIES', MERCIFUL]
the Lord being ***m*** unto him.... Gen 19:16
magnified thy ***m*** .... Gen 19:19
least of all the ***m*** .... Gen 32:10
Joseph, and showed him ***m***.... Gen 39:21
Thou in thy ***m*** hast led .... Ex 15:13
show ***m*** on whom I will .... Ex 33:19
The Lord God, ***m*** .... Ex 34:6
the greatness of thy ***m*** .... Num 14:19
God is a ***m*** God .... Deut 4:31
showing ***m*** unto thousands .... Deut 5:10
covenant and ***m*** .... Deut 7:9
anger, and show thee ***m*** .... Deut 13:17
will be ***m*** unto his land .... Deut 32:43
we will show thee ***m*** .... Judg 1:24
my ***m*** shall not depart 2Sam 7:15
With the ***m*** thou wilt show 2Sam 22:26
showeth ***m*** to his anointed 2Sam 22:51
Lord, for his ***m*** are great 2Sam 24:14
David my father great ***m*** 1Kin 3:6
Israel are ***m*** kings 1Kin 20:31
his ***m*** endureth for ever 1Chr 16:34
not take my ***m*** away 1Chr 17:13
very great are his ***m*** 1Chr 21:13
showed great ***m*** unto David ... 2Chr 1:8
m unto thy servants 2Chr 6:14
remember the ***m*** of David 2Chr 6:42
his ***m*** endureth for ever 2Chr 7:6
God is gracious and ***m*** 2Chr 30:9
his ***m*** endureth for ever .... Ezra 3:11
hath extended ***m*** unto us ...... Ezra 9:9
keepeth covenant and ***m*** ...... Neh 1:5
gracious and ***m*** .... Neh 9:17
thou in thy manifold ***m*** .... Neh 9:19
according to thy manifold ***m***... Neh 9:27
them according to thy ***m*** ...... Neh 9:28
for thy great ***m*** sake .... Neh 9:31
keepest covenant and ***m*** .... Neh 9:32
or for his land, or for ***m*** ...... Job 37:13
have ***m*** upon me, and hear .... Ps 4:1
Have ***m*** upon me, O Lord .... Ps 6:2
save me for thy ***m*** sake .... Ps 6:4
I have trusted in thy ***m*** .... Ps 13:5
With the ***m*** thou wilt show .... Ps 18:25
the ***m*** of the most High .... Ps 21:7
according to thy ***m*** .... Ps 25:7
have ***m*** upon me .... Ps 25:16
redeem me, and be ***m*** .... Ps 26:11
Lord, and have ***m*** upon me ... Ps 30:10
Have ***m*** upon me, O Lord .... Ps 31:9
save me for thy ***m*** sake .... Ps 31:16
them that hope in his ***m*** .... Ps 33:18
Thy ***m***, O Lord, is in the ..... Ps 36:5
not thou thy tender ***m*** .... Ps 40:11
Lord, be ***m*** unto me .... Ps 41:4
redeem us for thy ***m*** sake ..... Ps 44:26
I trust in the ***m*** of God .... Ps 52:6
Be ***m*** unto me, O God .... Ps 56:1
God shall send forth his ***m*** .... Ps 57:3
not ***m*** to..transgressors .... Ps 59:5
The God of my ***m*** .... Ps 59:10
the God of my ***m*** .... Ps 59:17
O Lord, belongeth ***m*** .... Ps 62:12
in the multitude of thy ***m*** ..... Ps 69:13
multitude of thy tender ***m***..... Ps 69:16
shut up his tender ***m***? .... Ps 77:9
let thy tender ***m*** .... Ps 79:8
Show us thy ***m***, O Lord .... Ps 85:7
Be ***m*** unto me, O Lord .... Ps 86:3

M

plenteous in *m* unto all .... Ps 86:5
and plenteous in *m* .... Ps 86:15
sing of the *m* of the Lord ..... Ps 89:1
M shall be built up .... Ps 89:2
my *m* shall be with him .... Ps 89:24
satisfy us early with thy *m* ..... Ps 90:14
He hath remembered his *m* ... Ps 98:3
will sing of *m* .... Ps 101:1
lovingkindness and tender *m* ... Ps 103:4
plenteous in *m* .... Ps 103:8
the *m* of the Lord is from ..... Ps 103:17
not the multitude of thy *m* .... Ps 106:7
the multitude of his *m* .... Ps 106:45
his *m* endureth for ever .... Ps 107:1
to extend *m* unto him .... Ps 109:12
thy *m* is good, deliver .... Ps 109:21
thy *m*, and for thy truth's ..... Ps 115:1
yea, our God is *m* .... Ps 116:5
his *m* endureth for ever .... Ps 118:2
thy *m* come also unto me ..... Ps 119:41
be *m* unto me, according to ... Ps 119:58
The earth..is full of thy *m* ..... Ps 119:64
Let thy tender *m* come......... Ps 119:77
be *m* unto me, as thou usest .. Ps 119:132
Great are thy tender *m* .... Ps 119:156
God, until that he have *m* ..... Ps 123:2
with the Lord there is *m* ...... Ps 130:7
his *m* endureth for ever .... Ps 136:1
thy *m*, O Lord, endureth ...... Ps 138:8
anger, and of great *m* .... Ps 145:8
his tender *m* are over all ...... Ps 145:9
Let not *m* and truth forsake ... Prov 3:3
The *m* man doeth good .... Prov 11:17
tender *m* of the wicked .... Prov 12:10
m and truth shall be to them .. Prov 14:22
m and truth iniquity is purged . Prov 16:6
throne is upholden by *m* ...... Prov 20:28
them shall have have *m* .... Prov 28:13
m on their fatherless .... Is 9:17
in *m* shall the throne be .... Is 16:5
he may have *m* upon you ..... Is 30:18
he that hath *m* on them .... Is 49:10
kindness will I have *m* .... Is 54:8
he will have *m* upon him ...... Is 55:7
m men are taken away .... Is 57:1
on them according to his *m* ... Is 63:7
of thy bowels and of thy *m* .... Is 63:15
I am *m*, saith the Lord .... Jer 3:12
cruel, and have no *m* .... Jer 6:23
nor spare, nor have *m* .... Jer 13:14
loving-kindness and *m* .... Jer 16:5
have pity, nor have *m* .... Jer 21:7
I will surely have *m* .... Jer 31:20
to return and have *m* .... Jer 33:26
I will show *m* unto you .... Jer 42:12
cruel, and will not show *m* .... Jer 50:42
the multitude of his *m* .... Lam 3:32
have *m* upon the whole house .. Ezek 39:25
they would desire *m* .... Dan 2:18
by showing *m* to the poor ..... Dan 4:27
Lord our God belong *m* .... Dan 9:9
righteousnesses..great *m* .... Dan 9:16
have *m* upon the house .... Hos 1:6
have *m* upon her children ..... Hos 2:4
loving-kindness, and in *m* ..... Hos 2:19
I will have *m* upon her .... Hos 2:23
had not obtained *m* .... Hos 2:23
I desired *m*, and not sacrifice .. Hos 6:6
the fatherless findeth *m* .... Hos 14:3
he is gracious and *m* .... Joel 2:13
forsake their own *m* .... Jon 2:8
art a gracious God, and *m* .... Jon 4:2
he delighteth in *m* .... Mic 7:18
in wrath remember *m* .... Hab 3:2
not have *m* on Jerusalem ...... Zech 1:12
returned to Jerusalem with *m* .. Zech 1:16
I have *m* upon them .... Zech 10:6
m, and not sacrifice .... Matt 12:7
Have *m* on me, O Lord .... Matt 15:22
Lord, have *m* on my son ...... Matt 17:15
Have *m* on us, O Lord .... Matt 20:30
the law, judgment, *m* .... Matt 23:23
son of David, have *m* .... Mark 10:47
his *m* is on them that fear ..... Luke 1:50
in remembrance of his *m* ...... Luke 1:54
Lord had showed great *m* ..... Luke 1:58
m, as your Father also is *m* ... Luke 6:36
He that showed *m* on him ..... Luke 10:37
Father Abraham, have *m* ..... Luke 16:24
Jesus, Master, have *m* on us .. Luke 17:13
son of David, have *m* .... Luke 18:38
the sure *m* of David .... Acts 13:34
yet have now obtained *m* ..... Rom 11:30
through your *m* they also ..... Rom 11:31
also may obtain *m* .... Rom 11:31
he might have *m* upon all ..... Rom 11:32
glorify God for his *m* .... Rom 15:9
Father of *m* and the God of ... 2Cor 1:3
as we have received *m* 2Cor 4:1
peace be on them, and *m* ..... Gal 6:16
God, who is rich in *m* .... Eph 2:4
if any bowels and *m* .... Phil 2:1
Grace, *m*, and peace 1Tim 1:2
I obtained *m* 1Tim 1:13
for this cause I obtained *m* 1Tim 1:16
Grace, *m*, and peace 2Tim 1:2
Lord give *m* unto the house ... 2Tim 1:16
he may find *m* of the Lord 2Tim 1:18
Grace, *m*, and peace .... Titus 1:4
m and faithful high priest ..... Heb 2:17
Moses' law died without *m* .... Heb 10:28
judgment without *m* .... James 2:13
that hath showed no *m* .... James 2:13
m rejoiceth against .... James 2:13
full of *m* and good fruits ..... James 3:17
pitiful, and of tender *m* .... James 5:11
which had not obtained *m* 1Pet 2:10
but now have obtained *m* 1Pet 2:10
Grace be with you, *m* 2John 3
M unto you, and peace .... Jude 2

MERCY SEAT—*the covering, a lid, of the ark of the covenant*
Made of pure gold ...... Ex 25:17
Blood sprinkled upon .... Lev 16:14, 15
God manifested over .... Lev 16:2
Figurative of Christ ...... Heb 9:5-12

make a *m s* of pure gold ...... Ex 25:17
even of the *m s* shall ye make . Ex 25:19
the *m s* with their wings .... Ex 25:20
toward the *m s* shall the ...... Ex 25:20
with thee from above the *m s* . Ex 25:22
before the *m s* that is over .... Ex 30:6
staves thereof, with the *m s* ... Ex 35:12
on the two ends of the *m s* .... Ex 37:7
their wings over the *m s* ...... Ex 37:9
even to the *m s* were the ...... Ex 37:9
and put the *m s* above .... Ex 40:20
the veil before the *m s* .... Lev 16:2
incense may cover the *m s* .... Lev 16:13
his finger upon the *m s* .... Lev 16:14
before the *m s* shall he .... Lev 16:14
and before the *m s* .... Lev 16:15
unto him from off the *m s* .... Num 7:89

MERED (mē'rĕd)—*"rebellious"*
Judahite 1Chr 4:17
Had two wives 1Chr 4:17, 18

MEREMOTH (mĕr'ĕ-mŏth)—*"strong; firm"*
1. Signer of the covenant .. Neh 10:5
Called Meraioth .... Neh 12:15
2. One who divorced his foreign wife .... Ezra 10:34, 36
3. Priest, son of Uriah; weighs silver and gold . Ezra 8:33
Repairs wall of Jerusalem Neh 3:4, 21

MERES (mē'rēz)—*"worthy"*
Persian prince .... Esth 1:13, 14

MERIBAH—*See* MASSAH AND MERIBAH

MERIBAH-KADESH—*See* KADESH-BARNEA

MERIB-BAAL (mĕr-ĭb-bā'ă)—*"idol breaker"*
Another name for Mephibosheth 1Chr 8:34

the son of Jonathan was *M* 1Chr 9:40
and *M* begat Micah 1Chr 9:40

MERIT—*reward given for praiseworthy actions*

Of human beings:
None is good .... Rom 3:12
None is righteous .... Rom 3:10
We are all sinful .... Is 6:5
Our good comes from God 1Cor 15:9, 10
Our righteousness:
Is unavailing .... Matt 5:20
Is Christ's 2Cor 5:21
Cannot save .... Rom 10:1-4

Of Christ:
Secured by obedience .... Rom 5:17-21
Secured by his death ..... Is 53:10-12
Obtained by faith .... Phil 3:8, 9

MERODACH (mĕ-rō'dăk)—*"bold"*
Supreme deity of the Babylonians .... Jer 50:2
Otherwise called Bel ..... Is 46:1

MERODACH-BALADAN (mĕ-rō'dăk-băl'ă-dăn)—*"(the god) Marduk has given a son"*
Sends ambassadors to Hezekiah .... Is 39:1-8
Also called Berodach-baladan 2Kin 20:12

MEROM (mē'rŏm)—*"elevations"*
Lake on Jordan north of the Sea of Galilee ..... Josh 11:5, 7

MERONOTHITE (mĭ-rŏn'ŏ-thīt)
Citizen of Meronoth 1Chr 27:30

MEROZ (mē'rŏz)—*"secret"*
Town cursed for failing to help the Lord .... Judg 5:23

MERRY—*full of gaiety*

Good, comes from:
Heart .... Prov 15:13, 15
Restoration .... Jer 30:18, 19
Christian joy .... James 5:13

Evil, results from:
Careless unconcern ...... Judg 9:27
Gluttony 1Sam 25:36
False optimism 1Kin 21:7
Sinful glee .... Rev 11:10

[*also* MERRILY, MERRYHEARTED]

they drank, and were *m* .... Gen 43:34
grapes, and made *m* .... Judg 9:27
their hearts were *m* .... Judg 16:25
let thine heart be *m* .... Judg 19:6
thine heart may be *m* .... Judg 19:9
making their hearts *m* .... Judg 19:22
drunk, and his heart was *m* ... Ruth 3:7
Nabal's heart was *m* 1Sam 25:36
Amnon's heart is *m* 2Sam 13:28
drinking, and making *m* 1Kin 4:20
let thine heart be *m* 1Kin 21:7
glad and *m* in heart 2Chr 7:10
heart of the king was *m* .... Esth 1:10
A *m* heart maketh a .... Prov 15:13
he that is of a *m* heart .... Prov 15:15
A *m* heart doeth good .... Prov 17:22
to drink, and to be *m* .... Eccl 8:15
drink thy wine with a *m* .... Eccl 9:7
wine maketh *m* .... Eccl 10:19
all the *m* do sigh .... Is 24:7
voice of them that make *m* .... Jer 30:19
dances of them that make *m* .. Jer 31:4
eat, drink, and be *m* .... Luke 12:19
let us eat, and be *m* .... Luke 15:23
they began to be *m* .... Luke 15:24
make *m* with my friends ...... Luke 15:29
we should make *m* .... Luke 15:32
Is any *m*? let him sing .... James 5:13
over them, and make *m* .... Rev 11:10

MESECH—*See* MESHECH

MESHA (mē'shă)—*"salvation"*
1. Border of Joktan's descendants .... Gen 10:30
2. Benjamite 1Chr 8:8, 9
3. Son of Caleb 1Chr 2:42
4. King of Moab 2Kin 3:4

MESHACH (mē'shăk)—*"the shadow of the prince; who is this?"*
Name given to Mishael . . Dan 1:7
Advanced to high position . . . . Dan 2:49
Remains faithful in testing . . . . Dan 3:13-30

MESHECH, MESECH (mē'shĕk, mē'sĕk)—*"tall"*
1. Son of Japheth . . . . Gen 10:2
Called Mesech . . . . Ps 120:5
Famous traders . . . . Ezek 27:13
Confederates with Gog . . Ezek 38:2, 3
Inhabitants of the nether world . . . . Ezek 32:18, 26
2. Son of Shem 1Chr 1:17
Same as Mash . . . . Gen 10:23

MESHELEMIAH (mĕ-shĕl-ĕ-mī'ä)—*"Jehovah repays"*
Father of Zechariah 1Chr 9:21
Porter in the Temple 1Chr 26:1
Called Shelemiah 1Chr 26:14

sons of *M* were Zechariah 1Chr 26:2
M had sons and brethren 1Chr 26:9

MESHEZABEEL (mĕ-shĕz'ä-bēl)—*"God delivers"*
1. Postexilic wall repairer . . Neh 3:4
2. One who signs covenant . Neh 10:21
3. Judahite . . . . Neh 11:24

MESHILLEMITH (mĕ-shĭl'ĕ-mĭth)—*"recompense"*
Postexilic priest 1Chr 9:10-12
Called Meshillemoth . . . . . Neh 11:13

MESHILLEMOTH (mĕ-shĭl'ĕ-mŏth)—*"recompense"*
Ephraimite leader 2Chr 28:12

MESHOBAB (mĕ-shō'băb)—*"restored"*
Descendant of Simeon . . . 1Chr 4:34-38

MESHULLAM (mĕ-shŭl'ăm)—*"associate; friend"*
1,2,3. Three Benjamites . . . 1Chr 8:17
4. Gadite leader 1Chr 5:11, 13
5. Shaphan's grandfather . . 2Kin 22:3
6. Hilkiah's father 1Chr 9:11
7. Son of Zerubbabel 1Chr 3:19
8. Priest 1Chr 9:10-12
9. Kohathite overseer 2Chr 34:12
10. Man commissioned to secure Levites . . . . Ezra 8:16
11. Levite who supports Ezra's reforms . . . . Ezra 10:15
12. One who divorced his foreign wife . . . . Ezra 10:29
13. Postexilic workman . . . . Neh 3:4, 30
His daughter married Tobiah's son . . . . Neh 6:18
14. Postexilic workman . . . . Neh 3:6
15. One of Ezra's attendants . . . . Neh 8:4
16, 17. Two priests who sign covenant . . . . Neh 10:7, 20
18, 19. Two priests in Joiakim's time . . . . Neh 12:13, 16
20. Porter . . . . Neh 12:25
21. Participant in dedication services . . . . Neh 12:33

Sallu the son of *M* 1Chr 9:7
M the son of Shephatiah 1Chr 9:8
Sallu the son of *M* . . . . Neh 11:7
Hilkiah, the son of *M* . . . . Neh 11:11

MESHULLEMETH (mĕ-shŭl'ĕ-mĕth)—*"friend"*
Wife of King Manasseh . . 2Kin 21:18, 19

MESOBAITE (mĕ-sō'bä-īt)—*"found of Jehovah"*
Title given Jasiel 1Chr 11:47

MESOPOTAMIA (mĕs-ō-pō-tā'mĭ-ä)—*"the country between two rivers"*
Abraham's native home . . Acts 7:2
Place of Laban's household . . . . Gen 24:4, 10, 29
Called:
Padan-aram . . . . Gen 25:20
Syria . . . . Gen 31:20, 24
Balaam came from . . . . . . Deut 23:4
Israel enslaved to . . . . Judg 3:8, 10
Chariots and horsemen hired from 1Chr 19:6
Called Haran; conquered by Sennacherib 2Kin 19:12, 16
People from, at Pentecost. Acts 2:9

he arose, and went to *M* . . . . . . Gen 24:10
Abraham, when he was in *M* . . Acts 7:2

MESS—*a portion of food*
Set before Joseph's brothers . . . . Gen 43:30, 34
Provided for Uriah 2Sam 11:8

MESSAGE—*communication*
I have a *m* from God . . . . Judg 3:20
Ben-hadad heard this *m* 1Kin 20:12
He that sendeth a *m* . . . . Prov 26:6
sent a *m* after him . . . . Luke 19:14
m which we have heard 1John 1:5
the *m* that ye heard 1John 3:11

MESSENGER—*one sent on a mission*

Mission of, to:
Appease wrath . . . . Gen 32:3-6
Ask for favors . . . . Num 20:14-17
Spy out . . . . Josh. 6:17, 25
Assemble a nation . . . . Judg. 6:35
Secure provisions 1Sam 25:4-14
Relay news 1Sam 11:3-9
Stir up war . . . . Judg 11:12-28
Sue for peace 2Sam 3:12, 13
Offer sympathy 1Chr 19:2
Call for help 2Kin 17:4
Issue an ultimatum 1Kin 20:2-9
Deliver the Lord's message . . . . Hag 1:13

Reception of:
Rejected . . . . Deut 2:26-30
Humiliated 1Chr 19:2-4
Rebuked 2Kin 1:2-5, 16

Significant examples of:
John the Baptist . . . . Mal 3:1
Paul's thorn 2Cor 12:7
Gospel workers 2Cor 8:23
Phil 2:25

[*also* MESSENGERS]
they sent a *m* unto Joseph . . . . Gen 50:16
Israel sent *m* unto Sihon . . . . . . Num 21:21
He sent *m* therefore unto . . . . . Num 22:5
Spake I not also to thy *m* . . . . . Num 24:12
Joshua sent *m* . . . . Josh 7:22
Gideon sent *m* . . . . Judg 7:24
he sent *m* unto Abimelech . . . . Judg 9:31
the *m* answered and said 1Sam 4:17
sent *m* to the inhabitants 1Sam 6:21
Saul sent *m* unto Jesse 1Sam 16:19
m unto David's house 1Sam 19:11
Saul sent *m* to take David 1Sam 19:14
Saul sent the *m* again to 1Sam 19:15
when the *m* were come in 1Sam 19:16
Saul sent *m* to take David 1Sam 19:20
spirit of God was upon the *m* . 1Sam 19:20
Saul, he sent other *m* 1Sam 19:21
Saul sent *m* again 1Sam 19:21
there came a *m* unto Saul 1Sam 23:27
she went after the *m* 1Sam 25:42
David sent *m* unto the men . . . 2Sam 2:5
David sent *m* to 2Sam 3:14
he sent *m* after Abner 2Sam 3:26
Tyre sent *m* to David 2Sam 5:11
David sent *m* and took her 2Sam 11:4
charged the *m*, saying 2Sam 11:19
the *m* went, and came 2Sam 11:22
the *m* said unto David 2Sam 11:23
David said unto the *m* 2Sam 11:25
Joab sent *m* to David 2Sam 12:27
there came a *m* to David 2Sam 15:13
Jezebel sent a *m* 1Kin 19:2
the *m* that was gone 1Kin 22:13
meet the *m* of the king 2Kin 1:3
Elisha sent a *m* unto him 2Kin 5:10
ere the *m* came to him 2Kin 6:32
when the *m* cometh 2Kin 6:32
the *m* came down unto him . . . 2Kin 6:33
the *m* returned, and told 2Kin 7:15
The *m* came to them 2Kin 9:18
And there came a *m* 2Kin 10:8
Amaziah sent *m* to Jehoash . . . 2Kin 14:8
So Ahaz sent *m* 2Kin 16:7
he sent *m* again 2Kin 19:9
letter of the hand of the *m* . . . 2Kin 19:14
thy *m* thou hast reproached . . . 2Kin 19:23
king of Tyre sent *m* to David . . 1Chr 14:1
Israel, they sent *m* 1Chr 19:16
m that went to call Micaiah . . . 2Chr 18:12
fathers sent to them by his *m* . . 2Chr 36:15
they mocked the *m* of God 2Chr 36:16
I sent *m* unto them . . . . Neh 6:3
there came a *m* unto Job . . . . . . Job 1:14
If there be a *m* with him . . . . . . Job 33:23
a wicked *m* falleth . . . . Prov 13:17
wrath of a king is as *m* . . . . Prov 16:14
a cruel *m* shall be sent . . . . Prov 17:11
is a faithful *m* to them . . . . Prov 25:13
the *m* of the nation? . . . . Is 14:32
Go, ye swift *m*, to a nation . . . Is 18:2
he sent *m* to Hezekiah . . . . Is 37:9
letter from the hand of the *m*. . Is 37:14
or deaf, as my *m* . . . . Is 42:19
the counsel of his *m* . . . . Is 44:26
didst send thy *m* far off . . . . Is 57:9
by the hand of the *m* . . . . Jer 27:3
one *m* to meet another . . . . Jer 51:31
and sent *m* unto them . . . . Ezek 23:16
unto whom a *m* was sent . . . . . . Ezek 23:40
that day shall *m* go forth . . . . . . Ezek 30:9
the voice of thy *m* . . . . Nah 2:13
he is the *m* of the Lord . . . . Mal 2:7
I send my *m* before thy face . . . Matt 11:10
the *m* of John were departed . . Luke 7:24
I send my *m* before thy face . . . Luke 7:27
sent *m* before his face . . . . Luke 9:52
she had received the *m* . . . . James 2:25

MESSIAH, MESSIAS, THE (mĕ-sī'ä, mĕ-sī'äs)—*"anointed one"—the One promised by God to be the great Deliverer of Israel*

Described as:
Seed of woman . . . . Gen 3:15
Promised seed . . . . Gen 12:1-3
Gal 3:16
Star out of Jacob . . . . Num 24:17
Luke 3:34
Of Judah's tribe . . . . Gen 49:10
Heb 7:14
Son of David . . . . Is 11:1-10
Matt 1:1
Prophet . . . . Deut 18:15-19
Acts 3:22, 23
Priest after Melchizedek's order . . . . Ps 110:4; Heb 6:20
King of David's line . . . . . Jer 23:5
Luke 1:32, 33
Son of God . . . . Ps 2:7, 8
Acts 13:33
Son of Man . . . . Dan 7:13
Mark 8:38
Immanuel . . . . Is 7:14
Matt 1:22, 23
Branch . . . . Jer 23:5
Zech 3:8
Headstone . . . . Ps 118:22
1Pet 2:4, 7
Servant . . . . Is 42:1-4
Matt 12:18, 21

Mission of, to:
Introduce the new covenant . . . . Jer 31:31-34; Matt 26:26-30
Preach the Gospel . . . . Is 61:1-3
Luke 4:17-19

Bring peace .... Is 9:6, 7
Heb 2:14-16
Die for man's sin .... Is 53:4-6
1Pet 1:18-20
Unite God's people ...... Is 19:23-25
Eph 2:11-22
Call the Gentiles .... Is 11:10
Rom 15:9-12
Be a priest .... Zech 6:12, 13
Heb 1:3
Heb 8:1
Rule from David's throne . Ps 45:5-7
Acts 2:30-36
Destroy Satan .... Rom 16:20
1John 3:8
Bring in everlasting righteousness .... Dan 9:24
Matt 3:15
2Cor 5:21

Christ the true Messiah, proved by:
Birth at Bethlehem ...... Mic 5:2
Luke 2:4-7
Born of a virgin .... Is 7:14
Matt 1:18-25
Appearing in the second Temple .... Hag 2:7, 9
John 18:20
Working miracles .... Is 35:5, 6
Matt 11:4, 5
Rejection by the Jews ... John 1:11
Vicarious death .... Is 53:1-12
1Pet 3:18
Coming at the appointed time .... Dan 9:24-27
Mark 1:15

Other prophecies concerning:
Worship .... Ps 72:10-15
Matt 2:1-11
Flight to Egypt .... Hos 11:1
Matt 2:13-15
Forerunner .... Mal 3:1
Mark 1:1-8
Zeal .... Ps 69:9
John 2:17
Triumphal entry .... Zech 9:9, 10
Matt 21:1-11
Betrayal .... Ps 41:9
Mark 14:10
Being sold .... Zech 11:12
Matt 26:15
Silent defense .... Is 53:7
Matt 26:62, 63
Being spit on .... Is 50:6
Mark 14:65
Being crucified with sinners .... Is 53:12
Matt 27:38
Piercing of hands and feet .... Ps 22:16
John 19:36, 37
Being mocked .... Ps 22:6-8
Matt 27:39-44
Dying drink .... Ps 69:21
John 19:29
Prayer for the enemies ... Ps 109:4
Luke 23:34
Side pierced .... Zech 12:10
John 19:34
Garments gambled for ... Ps 22:18
Mark 15:24
Death without broken bones .... Ps 34:20
John 19:33
Separation from God .... Ps 22:1
Matt 27:46
Burial with the rich ...... Is 53:9
Matt 27:57-60
Preservation from decay. . Ps 16:8-10
Acts 2:31
Ascension .... Ps 68:18
Eph 4:8-10
Exaltation .... Ps 2:6-12
Phil 2:9, 10

See CHRIST

METALLURGY—*mining and processing of metal*
Mining and refining ...... Job 28:1, 2
Heat needed .... Jer 6:29

METAPHORS—*figure of speech in which a striking comparison is made between two things*

Concerning God, as:
Rock .... Deut 32:4
Sun and shield .... Ps 84:11
Consuming fire .... Heb 12:29
Husbandman .... John 15:1

Concerning Christ, as:
Bread of Life .... John 6:35
Light of the World ...... John 8:12
Door .... John 10:9
Good Shepherd .... John 10:14
Way, Truth, Life .... John 14:6
True Vine .... John 15:1

Concerning Christians, as:
Light .... Matt 5:14
Salt .... Matt 5:13
Epistles 2Cor 3:3
Living stones 1Pet 2:5

Concerning the Bible, as:
Fire .... Jer 5:14
Hammer .... Jer 23:29
Light; lamp .... Ps 119:105
Sword .... Eph 6:17

METE—*to measure out*
Dry measure .... Ex 16:18
Linear measure .... Is 40:12
Figurative measure ...... Matt 7:2

[*also* METED]
and *m* out the valley .... Ps 60:6
a nation *m* out and trodden ... Is 18:2
with what measure ye *m* ...... Mark 4:24
the same measure that ye *m* ... Luke 6:38

METEYARD—*an archaic word for a measuring stick*
in *m*, in weight .... Lev 19:35

METHEG-AMMAH (mē-thĕg-ăm'ä)—*"bridle of bondage"*
Probably a figurative name for Gath 2Sam 8:1

METHUSAEL (mĕ-thū'sā-ĕl)—*"man of God"*
Cainite, father of Lamech. .... Gen 4:18
See MAON

METHUSELAH, MATHUSALA (mĕ-thū'zĕ-lä, mä-thū'sä-lä)—*"man of a javelin"*
Son of Enoch .... Gen 5:21
Oldest man on record .... Gen 5:27
Ancestor of Christ .... Luke 3:37

after he begat *M* .... Gen 5:22
M lived a hundred .... Gen 5:25
M lived after he begat .... Gen 5:26
Henoch, *M*, Lamech 1Chr 1:3

MEUNIM—*See* MEHUNIM

MEZAHAB (mĕz'ā-hăb)—*"offspring of the shining one"*
Grandfather of Mehetabel, wife of King Hadar .... Gen 36:39

MIAMIN—*See* MIJAMIN

MIBHAR (mĭb'här)—*"choice; youth"*
One of David's mighty men 1Chr 11:38

MIBSAM (mĭb'săm)—*"sweet odor"*
1. Son of Ishmael .... Gen 25:13
2. Simeonite 1Chr 4:25

MIBZAR (mĭb'zär)—*fortified"*
Edomite duke .... Gen 36:42

MICAH, MICHA (mī'kä)—*"who is like Jehovah?"*
1. Ephraimite who hires a traveling Levite .... Judg 17:1-13
2. Reubenite 1Chr 5:1, 5
3. Son of Mephibosheth 2Sam 9:12
4. Descendant of Asaph ... 1Chr 9:15
Called Michaiah .... Neh 12:35
5. Kohathite Levite 1Chr 23:20
6. Father of Abdon 2Chr 34:20
7. Prophet, contemporary of Isaiah .... Is 1:1; Mic 1:1
8. One who signs the covenant .... Neh 10:11

[*also* MICAH'S]
Ephraim, to the house of *M* ... Judg 18:2
they were by the house of *M* .. Judg 18:3
Thus and thus dealeth *M* ...... Judg 18:4
came unto the house of *M* .... Judg 18:13
even unto the house of *M* ..... Judg 18:15
these went into *M* house ...... Judg 18:18
from the house of *M* .... Judg 18:22
houses near to *M* house .... Judg 18:22
said unto *M*, What aileth ...... Judg 18:23
when *M* saw that they .... Judg 18:26
M graven image .... Judg 18:31
and Merib-baal begat *M* 1Chr 8:34
the sons of *M* were Pithon 1Chr 8:35
and Merib-baal begat *M* 1Chr 9:40
the sons of *M* were Pithon 1Chr 9:41
Mattaniah the son of *M* .... Neh 11:17
Mattaniah, the son of *M* ...... Neh 11:22
M the Morasthite .... Jer 26:18

MICAH, THE BOOK OF—*a book of the Old Testament*
Judgment of Israel and Judah .... Mic 1:2-16
Promise to the remnant .. Mic 2:12, 13
Judgment on those in authority .... Mic 3:1-12
The coming peace .... Mic 4:1-8
The Redeemer from Bethlehem .... Mic 5:1-4
Hope in God .... Mic 7:8-20

MICAIAH, MICHAIAH (mī-kā'yä)—*"who is like Jehovah?"*
1. Wife of King Rehoboam . 2Chr 13:2
2. Prophet who predicts Ahab's death 1Kin 22:8-28
3. Teaching official 2Chr 17:7
4. Father of Achbor 2Kin 22:12
Called Micah 2Chr 34:20
5. Contemporary of Jeremiah .... Jer 36:11-13
6. Descendant of Asaph ... Neh 12:35
7. Priest in dedication service .... Neh 12:41

M the son of Imlah 1Kin 22:8
Hasten hither *M* 1Kin 22:9
M the son of Imla 2Chr 18:7
Fetch quickly *M* the son 2Chr 18:8
that went to call *M* 2Chr 18:12
M said, As the Lord liveth 2Chr 18:13
king said unto him, *M* 2Chr 18:14
smote *M* upon the cheek 2Chr 18:23
M said, Behold 2Chr 18:24
Take ye *M*, and carry him 2Chr 18:25
M said, If thou certainly 2Chr 18:27

MICHAEL (mī'kā-ĕl)—*"who is like God?"*
1. Father of an Asherite spy .... Num 13:13
2, 3. Two Gadites 1Chr 5:13, 14
4. Levite ancestor of Asaph 1Chr 6:40
5. Issacharian chief 1Chr 7:3
6. Benjamite 1Chr 8:16
7. Manassite chief under David 1Chr 12:20
8. Father of Omri 1Chr 27:18
9. Son of King Jehoshaphat 2Chr 21:2
10. Father of Zebadiah .... Ezra 8:8
11. Chief prince, archangel . Dan 10:13, 21
Stands against forces ... Dan 10:21
Disputes with Satan .... Jude 9
Fights the dragon ...... Rev 12:7-9

M, one of the chief princes .... Dan 10:13
things, but *M* your prince ..... Dan 10:21
at that time shall *M* stand ..... Dan 12:1
Yet *M* the archangel .... Jude 9
M and his angels fought .... Rev 12:7

MICHAH (mī'kä)—*"who is like Jehovah?"*
Of the sons of Uzziel; *M* 1Chr 24:24
of the sons of *M*; Shamir 1Chr 24:24
brother of *M* was Isshiah 1Chr 24:25

MICHAL (mī'kăl)—*"who is like God?"*
Daughter of King Saul ...1Sam 14:49
Loves and marries David .1Sam 18:20-28
Saves David from Saul ...1Sam 19:9-17
Given to Phalti 1Sam 25:44
David demands her from Abner 2Sam 3:13-16
Ridicules David; becomes barren 2Sam 6:16-23

M Saul's daughter loved 1Sam 18:20
Saul gave him *M* 1Sam 18:27
bring *M* Saul's daughter 2Sam 3:13
Deliver me my wife *M* 2Sam 3:14
M Saul's daughter looked 2Sam 6:16
M the daughter of Saul 2Sam 6:20
David said unto *M* 2Sam 6:21
M the daughter of Saul 2Sam 6:23

MICHMASH, MICHMAS (mĭk'măsh, mĭk'măs)—*"he that strikes"*
Town occupied by Saul's army 1Sam 13:2
Site of battle with Philistines 1Sam 13:5, 11, 16, 23
Scene of Jonathan's victory 1Sam 14:1-18
Mentioned in prophecy ..Is 10:28
Exiles return ....Ezra 2:1, 27

Philistines that day from *M* 1Sam 14:31
The men of *M*, a hundred .....Neh 7:31
from Geba dwelt at *M* ....Neh 11:31

MICHMETHAH (mĭk'mĕ-thä)—*"the gift of a striker"*
Place on the border of Ephraim and Manasseh.Josh 16:5, 6

MICHRI (mĭk'rī)—*"Jehovah possesses"*
Benjamite 1Chr 9:8

MICHTAM (mĭk'tăm)—*a writing, especially a psalm*
Word of unknown meaning used in titles of ....Ps 16; 56—60

MIDDAY—*noon*
when *m* was past 1Kin 18:29
from the morning until *m* .....Neh 8:3
At *m*, O king, I saw in the ....Acts 26:13

MIDDIN (mĭd'ĭn)—*"judgment"*
In the wilderness ....Josh 15:61

MIDDLE—*between the ends; amongst*

[*also* MIDDLEMOST, MIDST]
firmament in the *m* ....Gen 1:6
land in the *m* of the sea ....Ex 14:29
m bar in the *m* of the ....Ex 26:28
made the *m* bar to shoot ......Ex 36:33
from the *m* of the river ....Josh 12:2
beginning of the *m* watch .....Judg 7:19
down by the *m* of the land ....Judg 9:37
hold of the two *m* pillars ......Judg 16:29
out of the *m* of a sling 1Sam 25:29
off their garments in the *m* 2Sam 10:4
the *m* was six cubits 1Kin 6:6
door for the *m* chamber 1Kin 6:8
winding stairs into the *m* 1Kin 6:8
out of the *m* into the third 1Kin 6:8
the king hallow the *m* 1Kin 8:64
gone out into the *m* court 2Kin 20:4
hallowed the *m* of the court ...2Chr 7:7
God is in the *m* of her ....Ps 46:5
in the *m* of the sea ....Prov 23:34
Holy One of Israel in the *m* ...Is 12:6
in, and sat in the *m* gate ......Jer 39:3
a wheel in the *m* of a wheel ...Ezek 1:16
the *m* of the building ....Ezek 42:5
the *m* from the ground ....Ezek 42:6
walking in the *m* of the fire ...Dan 3:25
the Holy One in the *m* ....Hos 11:9
sheep in the *m* of wolves ......Matt 10:16
child, and set him in the *m* ....Mark 9:36
Jesus..stood in the *m* ....Luke 24:36
Jesus and stood in the *m* ......John 20:19
broken down the *m* wall ......Eph 2:14

MIDIAN (mĭd'ĭ-ăn)—*"contention"*
1. Son of Abraham by Keturah ....Gen 25:1-4
2. Region in the Abrabian desert occupied by the Midianites ....Gen 25:6

smote *M* in the field ....Gen 36:35
dwelt in the land of *M* ....Ex 2:15
priest of *M* had seven ....Ex 2:16
the priest of *M* ....Ex 3:1
said unto Moses in *M*, Go .....Ex 4:19
Jethro, the priest of *M* ....Ex 18:1
Smote with the princes of *M* ..Josh 13:21
host of *M* was beneath him ....Judg 7:8
tumbled into the host of *M* ....Judg 7:13
hath God delivered *M* ....Judg 7:14
your hand the host of *M* ......Judg 7:15
and pursued *M* ....Judg 7:25
hands the princes of *M* ....Judg 8:3
and Zalmunna, kings of *M* ....Judg 8:5
took the two kings of *M* ......Judg 8:12
from the hand of *M* ....Judg 8:22
that was on the kings of *M* ....Judg 8:26
M subdued before ....Judg 8:28
you out of the hand of *M* .....Judg 9:17
they arose out of *M* 1Kin 11:18
and Medan, and *M* 1Chr 1:32
the sons of *M*; Ephah 1Chr 1:33
smote *M* in the field 1Chr 1:46
as in the day of *M* ....Is 9:4
slaughter of *M* at the rock ....Is 10:26
the dromedaries of *M* ....Is 60:6
curtains of the land of *M* ......Hab 3:7

MIDIANITES (mĭd'ĭ-ăn-īts)—*descendants of Midian*

Characteristics of:
Descendants of Abraham by Keturah ....Gen 25:1, 2
Moses fled to ....Ex 2:15
Retain worship of Jehovah ....Ex 2:16
Ruled by kings ....Num 31:8
Immoral people ....Num 25:18

Contacts with Israel:
Joining Moab in cursing ..Num 22:4-7
Seduction of ....Num 25:1-18
Defeat because of ....Num 31:1-18
Being sent as punishment .Judg 6:1-10

[*also* MIDIANITISH]
passed by *M* merchantmen ....Gen 37:28
M sold him into Egypt unto ...Gen 37:36
son of Raguel the *M* ....Num 10:29
a *M* woman in the sight ....Num 25:6
slain with the *M* woman ......Num 25:14
name of the *M* woman ....Num 25:15
Vex the *M*, and smite ....Num 25:17
hide it from the *M* ....Judg 6:11
into the hands of the *M* ....Judg 6:13
Israel from the hand of the *M* .Judg 6:14
thou shalt smite the *M* ....Judg 6:16
the *M* and the Amalekites .....Judg 6:33
host of the *M* were ....Judg 7:1
the *M* into their hands ....Judg 7:2
deliver the *M* into thine ....Judg 7:7
M and the Amalekites ....Judg 7:12
pursued after the *M* ....Judg 7:23
Come down against the *M* ....Judg 7:24
two princes of the *M* ....Judg 7:25
to fight with the *M*? ....Judg 8:1
Do unto them as unto the *M* ..Ps 83:9

MIDNIGHT—*twelve o'clock at night*

Significant happenings at:
Death in Egypt..........Ex 11:4
Prayer meeting ....Acts 16:25
Possible time of Christ's return ....Matt 25:6

Other happenings at:
Quick departure ....Judg 16:2, 3
Friend's need ....Luke 11:5
Greater fear ....Job 34:20

at *m* the Lord smote ....Ex 12:29
it came to pass at *m* ....Ruth 3:8
she arose at *m* 1Kin 3:20
At *m* I will rise to give ....Ps 119:62
at *m* or at the cockcrowing ....Mark 13:35
his speech until *m* ....Acts 20:7
m the shipmen deemed ....Acts 27:27

MIDST—*See* MIDDLE

MIDWIFE—*one who assists at childbirth*
Helps in the birth of a child ....Gen 35:17

[*also* MIDWIVES]
m took and bound ....Gen 38:28
spake to the Hebrew *m* ....Ex 1:15
do the office of a *m* ....Ex 1:16
the *m* feared God, and did ....Ex 1:17
the *m* said unto Pharaoh ......Ex 1:19
ere the *m* come in ....Ex 1:19
the *m* feared God ....Ex 1:21

MIGDAL-EL (mĭg'dăl-ĕl)—*"tower of God"*
City of Naphtali ....Josh 19:38

MIGDAL-GAD (mĭg'dăl-găd)
Town of Judah ....Josh 15:37

MIGDOL (mĭg'dŏl)—*"tower"*
1. Israelite encampment ....Ex 14:2
2. Place in Egypt to which Jews flee ....Jer 44:1

and they pitched before *M* ....Num 33:7
Egypt, and publish in *M* ......Jer 46:14

MIGHT—*effective power*

God's:
Irresistible 2Chr 20:6
God's hand is 1Chr 29:12
Unutterable ....Ps 106:2

Man's physical:
Boasted in, brings destruction ....Dan 4:30-33
Not to be gloried in .....Deut 8:17
Will fail ....Jer 51:30
Exhortation concerning ..Eccl 9:10

Man's intellectual and moral:
Invites self-glory ....Jer 9:23
Makes salvation difficult. .1Cor 1:26

Man's spiritual, comes from:
God ....Eph 1:19
Christ ....Col 1:28, 29
The Spirit...............Mic 3:8

according to thy *m*? ....Deut 3:24
soul, and with all thy *m* ....Deut 6:5
the *m* of thy terrible acts ......Ps 145:6
Not by *m*, nor by power ......Zech 4:6
to be strengthened with *m* .....Eph 3:16
Strengthened with all *m* ....Col 1:11
m, be unto our God ....Rev 7:12

MIGHT (MAY)—*See* INTRODUCTION

MIGHTEST—*See* INTRODUCTION

MIGHTY—*powerful*

Literally of:
Hunter ....Gen 10:9
Nation..................Gen 18:18
Prince ....Gen 23:6
Waters ....Ex 15:10
Hand ....Ex 32:11
Acts....................Deut 3:24
Deeds 2Sam 23:20
Men of valor 1Chr 7:9-11
Warrior.................2Chr 32:21
Kings...................Ezra 4:20
Wind ....Job 8:2
Strength ....Job 9:4
Thunder ....Job 26:14
Fear....................Job 41:25

[*also* MIGHTIER, MIGHTIES, MIGHTIEST, MIGHTILY]
the same became *m* men ......Gen 6:4

a *m* hunter before the Lord . . .Gen 10:9
m hunter before the Lord . . . . .Gen 10:9
a *m* prince among us . . . . .Gen 23:6
for thou art much *m* . . . . .Gen 26:16
and waxed exceeding *m* . . . . . . .Ex 1:7
of Israel are more and *m* . . . . . .Ex 1:9
no, not by a *m* hand . . . . .Ex 3:19
a *m* strong west wind . . . . .Ex 10:19
the *m* men of Moab . . . . .Ex 15:15
a greater nation and *m* . . . . .Num 14:12
they are too *m* for me . . . . .Num 22:6
greatness and thy *m* hand . . . . .Deut 3:24
with his *m* power out . . . . .Deut 4:37
greater and *m* than thou . . . . . .Deut 4:38
that ye may increase *m* . . . . . . .Deut 6:3
Egypt with a *m* hand . . . . .Deut 6:21
nations greater and *m* . . . . .Deut 7:1
m hand, and the stretched . . . . .Deut 7:19
destroy them with a *m* . . . . .Deut 7:23
greater and *m* than thyself . . . .Deut 9:1
a nation *m* and greater . . . . .Deut 9:14
by thy *m* power . . . . .Deut 9:29
God, his greatness, his *m* hand.Deut 11:2
m than yourselves . . . . .Deut 11:23
out of Egypt with a *m* hand . . .Deut 26:8
all the *m* men of valor . . . . .Josh 1:14
the *m* men of valor . . . . .Josh 6:2
thirty thousand *m* men . . . . .Josh 8:3
all the *m* men of valor . . . . .Josh 10:7
years he *m* oppressed . . . . .Judg 4:3
dominion over the *m* . . . . .Judg 5:13
the Lord against the *m* . . . . .Judg 5:23
Gileadite was a *m* man . . . . .Judg 11:1
spirit of the Lord came *m* . . . . .Judg 14:6
a *m* man of wealth . . . . .Ruth 2:1
bows of the *m* men 1Sam 2:4
a Benjamite, a *m* man 1Sam 9:1
how are the *m* fallen! 2Sam 1:19
from the fat of the *m* 2Sam 1:22
How are the *m* fallen 2Sam 1:27
m men were on his right hand .2Sam 16:6
thy father is a *m* man 2Sam 17:10
names of the *m* men whom 2Sam 23:8
the three *m* men brake 2Sam 23:16
among three *m* men 2Sam 23:22
m men which belonged 1Kin 1:8
Jeroboam was a *m* man 1Kin 11:28
he was also a *m* man 2Kin 5:1
all the *m* men of valor 2Kin 24:14
he began to be *m* 1Chr 1:10
fathers, *m* men of valor 1Chr 7:7
m men of valor, chief 1Chr 7:40
m men whom David had 1Chr 11:10
one of the three *m* 1Chr 11:12
things did these three *m* 1Chr 11:19
name among the three *m* 1Chr 11:24
among the *m* men, helpers 1Chr 12:1
all *m* men of valor 1Chr 12:21
a young man *m* of valor 1Chr 12:28
all the host of the *m* men 1Chr 19:8
m men of valor at Jazer 1Chr 26:31
officers, and with the *m* men . .1Chr 28:1
thy *m* hand and thy stretched . .2Chr 6:32
But Abijah waxed *m* 2Chr 13:21
m men of valor 2Chr 17:13
hundred thousand *m* men 2Chr 17:16
m men of valor out of Israel . .2Chr 25:6
made war with *m* power 2Chr 26:13
Zichri, a *m* man 2Chr 28:7
all the king's *m* princes . . . . . . .Ezra 7:28
unto the house of the *m* . . . . . .Neh 3:16
a stone into the *m* waters . . . . .Neh 9:11
their brethren, *m* men . . . . .Neh 11:14
from the hand of the *m* . . . . . . .Job 5:15
the strength of the *m* . . . . .Job 12:21
old, yea, are *m* in power? . . . . .Job 21:7
But as for the *m* man . . . . .Job 22:8
the *m* shall be taken away . . . . .Job 34:20
the arm of the *m* . . . . .Job 35:9
God is *m*, and despiseth . . . . . .Job 36:5
he is *m* in strength . . . . .Job 36:5
strong and *m*, the Lord *m* . . . . .Ps 24:8
a *m* man is not delivered . . . . . .Ps 33:16
The *m* God, even the Lord . . . .Ps 50:1
the *m* are gathered . . . . .Ps 59:3
enemies wrongfully are *m* . . . . .Ps 69:4
m man that shouteth . . . . .Ps 78:65
the sons of the *m* . . . . .Ps 89:6
Thou hast a *m* arm . . . . .Ps 89:13
all the *m* people . . . . .Ps 89:50
Lord on high is *m* than . . . . . . .Ps 93:4
the *m* waves of the sea . . . . .Ps 93:4
his *m* power to be known . . . . .Ps 106:8
Sharp arrows of the *m* . . . . .Ps 120:4
vowed unto the *m* God . . . . . . .Ps 132:2
nations, and slew *m* kings . . . . .Ps 135:10
shall declare thy *m* acts . . . . . . .Ps 145:4
sons of men his *m* acts . . . . .Ps 145:12
better than the *m* . . . . .Prov 16:32
scaleth the city of the *m* . . . . . .Prov 21:22
For their redeemer is *m* . . . . . . .Prov 23:11
with him that is *m* than he . . . .Eccl 6:10
more than ten *m* men . . . . .Eccl 7:19
all shields of *m* men . . . . .Song 4:4
Lord of hosts, the *m* One . . . . .Is 1:24
thy *m* in the war . . . . .Is 3:25
m to drink wine . . . . .Is 5:22
Counselor, The *m* God . . . . . . .Is 9:6
Jacob, unto the *m* God . . . . . . .Is 10:21
with his *m* wind shall be . . . . . .Is 11:15
the rushing of *m* waters! . . . . . .Is 17:12
away with a *m* captivity . . . . . . .Is 22:17
Lord hath a *m* and strong . . . . .Is 28:2
as a flood of *m* waters . . . . .Is 28:2
the sword, not of a *m* man . . . .Is 31:8
a path in the *m* waters . . . . .Is 43:16
the captives of the *m* . . . . .Is 49:25
the *m* One of Jacob . . . . .Is 60:16
it is a *m* nation . . . . .Jer 5:15
let the *m* man glory . . . . .Jer 9:23
Lord is with me as a *m* terrible.Jer 20:11
he shall *m* roar upon his . . . . . .Jer 25:30
the Great, the *M* God . . . . .Jer 32:18
show thee great and *m* things . .Jer 33:3
their *m* ones are beaten . . . . . . .Jer 46:5
and let the *m* men come . . . . . .Jer 46:9
are *m* and strong men for the .Jer 48:14
the *m* men of Edom . . . . .Jer 49:22
a sword is upon her *m* men . . .Jer 50:36
Babylon, and her *m* men . . . . . .Jer 51:56
trodden under foot all my *m* . .Lam 1:15
taken the *m* of the land . . . . . . .Ezek 17:13
surely with a *m* hand . . . . .Ezek 20:33
By the swords of the *m* . . . . . . .Ezek 32:12
not lie with the *m* . . . . .Ezek 32:27
terror of the *m* in the land . . . .Ezek 32:27
eat the flesh of the *m* . . . . .Ezek 39:18
he commanded the most *m* . . . .Dan 3:20
And his power shall be *m* . . . . .Dan 8:24
Egypt with a *m* hand . . . . .Dan 9:15
And a *m* king shall stand . . . . .Dan 11:3
a very great and *m* army . . . . . .Dan 11:25
multitude of thy *m* men . . . . . . .Hos 10:13
They shall run like *m* men . . . .Joel 2:7
thy *m* ones to come down . . . . .Joel 3:11
neither shall the *m* deliver . . . . .Amos 2:14
your *m* sins: they afflict . . . . . . .Amos 5:12
thy *m* men, O Teman . . . . .Obad 9
a *m* tempest in the sea . . . . .Jon 1:4
cry *m* unto God . . . . .Jon 3:8
fortify thy power *m* . . . . .Nah 2:1
shield of his *m* men . . . . .Nah 2:3
m God, thou hast established . .Hab 1:12
m man shall cry . . . . .Zeph 1:14
the sword of a *m* man . . . . .Zech 9:13
shall be like a *m* man . . . . .Zech 10:7
the *m* are spoiled . . . . .Zech 11:2
cometh after me is *m* . . . . .Matt 3:11
his *m* works were done . . . . . . .Matt 11:20
if the *m* works, which . . . . .Matt 11:23
he did not many *m* works . . . . .Matt 13:58
cometh one *m* than I . . . . .Mark 1:7
such *m* works are wrought . . . . .Mark 6:2
he could there do no *m* work . .Mark 6:5
m works do show forth . . . . . . .Mark 6:14
he that is *m* hath done . . . . .Luke 1:49
one *m* than I cometh . . . . .Luke 3:16
m power of God . . . . .Luke 9:43
m famine in that land . . . . .Luke 15:14
a prophet *m* in deed . . . . .Luke 24:19
a rushing *m* wind . . . . .Acts 2:2
m in words and in deeds . . . . . .Acts 7:22
m in the scriptures . . . . .Acts 18:24
m grew the word of God . . . . . .Acts 19:20
m signs and wonders . . . . .Rom 15:19
the things which are *m* 1Cor 1:27
but *m* through God 2Cor 10:4
is not weak, but is *m* 2Cor 13:3
m in me toward the Gentiles . .Gal 2:8
which worketh in me *m* . . . . . . .Col 1:29
heaven with his *m* angels 2Thess 1:7
under the *m* hand of God 1Pet 5:6
she is shaken of a *m* wind . . . . .Rev 6:13
another *m* angel come down . . .Rev 10:1
cried *m* with a strong voice . . . .Rev 18:2
Babylon, that *m* city! . . . . .Rev 18:10
voice of *m* thunderings . . . . .Rev 19:6

MIGRON (mĭg'rŏn)—*"fear"*
1. Place where Saul stayed .1Sam 14:2
2. Village north of
   Michmash . . . . .Is 10:28

MIJAMIN, MIAMIN (mĭj'ä-mĭn, mī'ä-mĭn)—*"fortunate"*
1. Descendant of Aaron . . .1Chr 24:1, 6, 9
2. Chief priest; returns with
   Zerubbabel . . . . .Neh 12:5, 7
   Probably same as 1
3. Divorced his foreign wife.Ezra 10:25
4. Priest who signs the
   covenant . . . . .Neh 10:7
   Same as Miniamin in . . . .Neh 12:17, 41

MIKLOTH (mĭk'lŏth)—*"twigs; sticks"*
1. Ruler under David 1Chr 27:4
2. Benjamite 1Chr 8:32

Zechariah, and *M* 1Chr 9:37
and *M* begat Shimeam 1Chr 9:38

MIKNEIAH (mĭk-nē'yä)—*"Jehovah is jealous"*
Porter and musician in
David's time 1Chr 15:18, 21

MILALAI (mĭl-ä-lā'ī)—*"Jehovah is elevated"*
Levite musician in
dedication service . . . . .Neh 12:36

MILCAH (mĭl'kä)—*"counsel"*
1. Wife of Nahor . . . . .Gen 11:29
   Mother of eight children .Gen 22:20-22
   Grandmother of
   Rebekah . . . . .Gen 22:23
2. Daughter of Zelophehad .Num 26:33

Bethuel, son of *M* . . . . .Gen 24:15
Bethuel the son of *M* . . . . .Gen 24:24
son, whom *M* bare . . . . .Gen 24:47
and Hoglah, and *M* . . . . .Num 27:1
Hoglah, and *M* . . . . .Num 36:11
and Noah, Hoglah, *M* . . . . .Josh 17:3

MILCH—*cows; milk giving*
Thirty *m* camels . . . . .Gen 32:15
take two *m* kine 1Sam 6:7
took two *m* kine 1Sam 6:10

MILCOM (mĭl'cŏm)—*an Ammonite god*
Solomon went after 1Kin 11:5
Altar destroyed by Josiah.2Kin 23:12, 13
Same as Molech 1Kin 11:7

after *M* the abomination 1Kin 11:5
M the abomination of the 2Kin 23:13

MILDEW—*a grain disease incurred through prolonged dampness*
Threatened as a
punishment . . . . .Deut 28:22
Sent upon Israel . . . . .Amos 4:9
Removed by repentance .1Kin 8:37-39

if there be blasting, or *m* 2Chr 6:28
with blasting and with *m* . . . . . .Hag 2:17

MILE—*a thousand paces (about 12/13 of an English mile)*
Used illustratively . . . . . . .Matt 5:41
See Jewish measures

MILETUS, MILETUM (mī-lē-tŭs, mī-lē'tŭm)—*"scarlet"—a coastal city of Asia Minor*
Paul meets Ephesian elders here ... Acts 20:15-38
Paul leaves Trophimus here ... 2 Tim 4:20

MILK—*a white liquid produced by mammary glands*

Produced by:
Goats ... Prov 27:27
Sheep ... Deut 32:14
Camels ... Gen 32:15
Cows ... 1Sam 6:7, 10
Humans ... Is 28:9

Figurative of:
Abundance ... Deut 32:14
Egypt's supposed blessing ... Num 16:13
Elementary teaching ... 1Cor 3:2
Pure doctrine ... 1Pet 2:2

he took butter, and **m**, and ... Gen 18:8
a land flowing with **m** and ... Ex 3:8
floweth with **m** and honey ... Num 13:27
which floweth with **m** and ... Num 14:8
that floweth with **m** and ... Deut 6:3
a kid in his mother's **m** ... Deut 14:21
that floweth with **m** and ... Deut 27:3
that floweth with **m** and ... Josh 5:6
she opened a bottle of **m** ... Judg 4:19
water, and she gave him **m** ... Judg 5:25
not poured me out as **m** ... Job 10:10
honey and **m** are under thy ... Song 4:11
of waters, washed with **m** ... Song 5:12
abundance of **m** that they ... Is 7:22
buy wine and **m** without ... Is 55:1
suck the **m** of the Gentiles ... Is 60:16
that ye may **m** out, and be ... Is 66:11
a land flowing with **m** and ... Jer 11:5
they were whiter than **m** ... Lam 4:7
flowing with **m** and honey ... Ezek 20:6
flowing with **m** and honey ... Ezek 20:15
and they shall drink thy **m** ... Ezek 25:4
hills shall flow with **m** ... Joel 3:18
eateth not of the **m** of the ... 1Cor 9:7
such as have need of **m** ... Heb 5:12
every one that useth **m** is ... Heb 5:13

MILL—*a machine used for grinding grain, usually round and between eighteen inches to two feet in diameter*

Uses of:
Grinding grain ... Num 11:8
Weapon ... Judg 9:53
Pledge, forbidden ... Deut 24:6
Weight ... Matt 18:6

Operated by:
Women ... Matt 24:41
Maidservant ... Ex 11:5
Prisoners ... Judg 16:21

Figurative of:
Courage ... Job 41:24
Old age ... Eccl 12:4
Desolation ... Jer 25:10

[*also* MILLSTONE, MILLSTONES]
maidservant..behind the **m** ... Ex 11:5
woman cast a piece of a **m** ... 2Sam 11:21
take the **m**, and grind meal ... Is 47:2
shall be grinding at the **m** ... Matt 24:41
a **m** were hanged about his ... Mark 9:42
a **m** were hanged about his ... Luke 17:2
up a stone like a great **m** ... Rev 18:21
the sound of a **m** shall be ... Rev 18:22

MILLENNIUM—*a time in which Christ will reign and holiness will fill the earth*
Latin for a thousand years ... Rev 10:1-10

MILLET—*a cereal*
Ezekiel makes bread of ... Ezek 4:9

MILLIONS
mother of thousands of **m** ... Gen 24:60

MILLO (mĭl'ō)—*"fullness"*
1. House or stronghold at Shechem, called Bethmillo ... Judg 9:6, 20
2. Fort at Jerusalem ... 2Sam 5:9
Prepared by Solomon ... 1Kin 9:15
Strengthened by Hezekiah ... 2Chr 32:5
Scene of Joash's death ... 2Kin 12:20, 21

then did he build **M** ... 1Kin 9:24
Solomon built **M**, and ... 1Kin 11:27
about, even from **M** around ... 1Chr 11:8

MINCING—*affected elegance in walking*
Denounced ... Is 3:16

MIND—*the reasoning facility of an individual; memory; intention*

Faculties of:
Perception ... Luke 9:47
Remembrance ... Titus 3:1
Reasoning ... Rom 7:23, 25
Feelings ... 2Sam 17:8
Desire ... Neh 4:6
Imagination ... Gen 6:5
Purpose ... 2Cor 1:15, 17

Of the unregenerate, described as:
Alienated ... Ezek 23:17-22
Despiteful ... Ezek 36:5
Reprobate ... Rom 1:28
Blinded ... 2Cor 3:14
Hostile ... Col 1:21
Defiled ... Titus 1:15

Of the regenerate, described as:
Willing ... 1Chr 28:9
In peace ... Rom 8:6
Right ... Luke 8:35
Renewed ... Rom 12:2
Having Christ's ... 1Cor 2:16
Obedient ... Heb 8:10

Dangers of, to the Christian:
Worry ... Luke 12:29
Doubt ... Rom 14:5
Disunity ... Rom 12:16; Phil 4:2
Mental disturbance ... 2Thess 2:2
Spiritual disturbance ... Rom 7:23, 25
Grow weary ... Heb 12:3

Exhortations concerning, to Christians:
Love God with all ... Matt 22:37

[*also* MINDED, MINDFUL, MINDING, MINDS]
it be your **m** that I should ... Gen 23:8
grief of **m** unto Isaac and ... Gen 26:35
m of the Lord might be ... Lev 24:12
done them of mine own **m** ... Num 16:28
good or bad of mine own **m** ... Num 24:13
all the desire of his **m** ... Deut 18:6
of eyes, and sorrow of **m** ... Deut 28:65
thou shalt call them to **m** ... Deut 30:1
she was steadfastly **m** to go ... Ruth 1:18
mine heart and in my **m** ... 1Sam 2:35
days ago, set not thy **m** on ... 1Sam 9:20
they be chafed in their **m** ... 2Sam 17:8
If it be your **m**, then let ... 2Kin 9:15
was in my **m** to build an ... 1Chr 22:7
was **m** to repair the house ... 2Chr 24:4
are **m** of their own freewill ... Ezra 7:13
neither were **m** of thy ... Neh 9:17
he is one **m**, and who can ... Job 23:13
it be according to thy **m**? ... Job 34:33
is man, that thou art **m** ... Ps 8:4
as a dead man out of **m** ... Ps 31:12
Lord hath been **m** to us ... Ps 115:12
bringeth it with a wicked **m**? ... Prov 21:27
a fool uttereth all his **m** ... Prov 29:11
not been **m** of the rock ... Is 17:10
peace, whose **m** is stayed ... Is 26:3
men: bring it again to **m** ... Is 46:8
remembered, nor come into **m** ... Is 65:17
neither shall it come to **m** ... Jer 3:16
yet my **m** could not be ... Jer 15:1
neither came it into my **m** ... Jer 19:5
neither came it into my **m** ... Jer 32:35
and came it not into his **m**? ... Jer 44:21
Jerusalem..into your **m** ... Jer 51:50
This I recall to my **m** ... Lam 3:21
that come into your **m** ... Ezek 11:5
her **m** was alienated from ... Ezek 23:17
then my **m** was alienated ... Ezek 23:18
m was alienated from her ... Ezek 23:18
whereupon they set their **m** ... Ezek 24:25
came into thy **m** upon thy ... Dan 2:29
Then shall his **m** change ... Hab 1:11
was **m** to put her away ... Matt 1:19
clothed, and in his right **m** ... Mark 5:15
Peter called to **m** the word ... Mark 14:72
and cast in her **m** what ... Luke 1:29
strength, and with all thy **m** ... Luke 10:27
made their **m** evil affected ... Acts 14:2
appointed, **m** himself to go ... Acts 20:13
Lord with all humility of **m** ... Acts 20:19
into the which they were **m** ... Acts 27:39
them over to a reprobate **m** ... Rom 1:28
flesh do **m** the things of the ... Rom 8:5
to be carnally **m** is death ... Rom 8:6
spiritually **m** is life and ... Rom 8:6
carnal **m** is enmity against ... Rom 8:7
what is the **m** of the Spirit ... Rom 8:27
known the **m** the Lord ... Rom 11:34
the same **m** one toward ... Rom 12:16
may with one **m** and one ... Rom 15:6
as putting you in **m** ... Rom 15:15
together in the same **m** ... 1Cor 1:10
I was **m** to come unto you ... 2Cor 1:15
when I..was thus **m**, did ... 2Cor 1:17
But their **m** were blinded ... 2Cor 3:14
mourning, your fervent **m** ... 2Cor 7:7
there be first a willing **m** ... 2Cor 8:12
the forwardness of your **m** ... 2Cor 9:2
m should be corrupted ... 2Cor 11:3
be of one **m**, live in peace ... 2Cor 13:11
will be none otherwise **m** ... Gal 5:10
desires of the flesh and..**m** ... Eph 2:3
in the spirit of your **m** ... Eph 4:23
one **m** striving together ... Phil 1:27
of one accord, of one **m** ... Phil 2:2
in lowliness of **m** let each ... Phil 2:3
Let this **m** be in you, which ... Phil 2:5
as be perfect, be thus **m** ... Phil 3:15
thing ye be otherwise **m** ... Phil 3:15
let us **m** the same thing ... Phil 3:16
shame, who **m** earthly things ... Phil 3:19
keep your hearts and **m** ... Phil 4:7
puffed up by his fleshly **m** ... Col 2:18
humbleness of **m**, meekness ... Col 3:12
of men of corrupt **m** ... 1Tim 6:5
being **m** of thy tears, that I ... 2Tim 1:4
and of love, and of sound **m** ... 2Tim 1:7
of corrupt **m**, reprobate ... 2Tim 3:8
likewise exhort..sober-**m** ... Titus 2:6
But without thy **m** would I ... Philem 14
is man, that thou art **m** of ... Heb 2:6
and in their **m** will I write ... Heb 10:16
double-**m** man is unstable ... James 1:8
your hearts, ye double-**m** ... James 4:8
gird up the loins of your **m** ... 1Pet 1:13
I stir up your pure **m** by ... 2Pet 3:1
be ye all of one **m**, having ... 2Pet 3:8
here is the **m** which hath ... Rev 17:9
These have one **m**, and ... Rev 17:13

MINE—*See* INTRODUCTION

MINERALS—*inorganic deposits within the earth*

Features concerning:
Mined ... Job 28:1-11
Plentiful in Canaan ... Deut 8:9
Refined by fire ... Ezek 22:18, 20
Trade in ... Ezek 27:12

List of:
Asphalt (bitumen) ... Gen 11:3
Brass ... Num 21:9
Brimstone (sulphur) ... Deut 29:23
Chalk ... Is 27:9
Clay ... Is 41:25
Copper (brass) ... Deut 8:9
Coral ... Job 28:18
Flint ... Deut 32:13

Gold ....Gen 2:11, 12
Iron ....Gen 4:22
Lead ....Job 19:24
Lime ....Amos 2:1
Nitre ....Jer 2:22
Salt ....Gen 14:3
Sand ....Prov 27:3
Silver ....Gen 44:2
Slime (asphalt) ....Gen 6:14
Tin ....Num 31:22

MINGLE—*to put different elements together*

Instances of:
Offerings ....Lev 2:4, 5
Garment ....Lev 19:19
Judgments ....Rev 8:7
Human sacrifice ....Luke 13:1
Intermarriage ....Ezra 9:2

Figurative of:
Sorrow ....Ps 102:9
Wisdom ....Prov 9:2, 5
Instability ....Is 19:14
Severity ....Ps 75:8
Impurity ....Is 1:22
Intoxication ....Is 5:22
Worldliness ....Hos 7:8

[*also* MINGLED]
was hail, and fire ***m*** with ......Ex 9:24
of flour ***m*** with the fourth .....Ex 29:40
every meat offering, ***m*** with ...Lev 7:10
unleavened cakes ***m*** with ....Lev 7:12
cakes ***m*** with oil, of fine ......Lev 7:12
flour for a meat offering ***m*** ....Lev 14:10
tenth deals of fine flour ***m*** ....Lev 23:13
cakes of fine flour ***m*** with .....Num 6:15
of fine flour ***m*** with oil........Num 7:13
m with the fourth part of .....Num 15:4
of flour ***m*** with half a hin .....Num 15:9
m with the fourth part of .....Num 28:5
tenth deal of flour ***m*** with .....Num 28:13
meat offering of flour ***m*** ......Num 28:28
shall be of flour ***m*** with oil ....Num 29:9
were ***m*** among the heathen ....Ps 106:35
of strength to ***m*** strong........Is 5:22
And all the ***m*** people, and ....Jer 25:20
upon all the ***m*** people that ....Jer 50:37
all the ***m*** people, and Chub ...Ezek 30:5
m themselves with the ....Dan 2:43
vinegar to drink ***m*** with ....Matt 27:34
him to drink wine ***m*** with .....Mark 15:23
were a sea of glass ***m*** with ....Rev 15:2

MINIAMIN (mĭn'yä-mĭn)—*"fortunate"*
1. Levite assistant 2Chr 31:14, 15
2. Postexilic priest ....Neh 12:17
3. Priestly participant in dedication ....Neh 12:41

MINISH—*obsolete for diminish*
To make something less . .Ex 5:19

MINISTER—*one who serves*

Descriptive of:
Proclaiming the Word....Acts 13:5
Court attendants 1Kin 10:5
Angels ....Ps 103:20
Priests and Levites ......Joel 1:9, 13
Servant ....Matt 20:22-27
Ruler...................Rom 13:4, 6
Christ ....Rom 15:8
Christ's messengers 1Cor 3:5
False teachers 2Cor 11:15

Christian, qualifications of:
Able to teach 1Tim 3:2
Courageous ....Acts 20:22-24
Diligent 1Cor 15:10
Faithful................Rom 15:17-19
Impartial 1Tim 5:21
Industrious..............2Cor 10:12-16
Meek..................2Tim 2:25
Obedient ....Acts 16:9, 10
Persevering 2Cor 11:23-33
Prayerful ....Acts 6:4
Sincere 2Cor 4:1, 2
Spirit-filled..............Acts 1:8
Studious 1Tim 4:13, 15
Sympathetic ....Heb 5:2
Temperate 1Cor 9:25-27
Willing 1Pet 5:2
Worthy of imitation 1Tim 4:12

Sins to avoid:
Arrogance 1Pet 5:3
Contentiousness ....Titus 1:7
Discouragement 2Cor 4:8, 9
Insincerity ....Phil 1:15, 16
Perverting the truth......2Cor 11:3-15
Unfaithfulness ....Matt 24:48-51

Duties of:
Preach:
Gospel: 1Cor 1:17
Christ crucified 1Cor 1:23
Christ's riches ....Eph 3:8-12
Feed the Church ....John 21:15-17
Edify the Church ....Eph 4:12
Pray for people ....Col 1:9
Teach 2Tim 2:2
Exhort ....Titus 1:9
Rebuke ....Titus 2:15
Warn of apostasy 2Tim 4:2-5
Comfort 2Cor 1:4-6
Win souls 1Cor 9:19-23

Attitude of believers toward:
Pray for ....Eph 6:18-20
Follow the example of ...1Cor 11:1
Obey 1Cor 4:1, 2
Esteem highly 1Thess 5:12, 13
Provide for 1Cor 9:6-18

[*also* MINISTERS]
attendance of his ***m***..........2Chr 9:4
his ***m*** a flaming fire ....Ps 104:4
call you the ***m*** of our God ....Is 61:6
Levites the priests, my ***m*** .....Jer 33:21
where the ***m*** of the house .....Ezek 46:24
the priests, ***m*** of the Lord .....Joel 2:17
among you, shall be your ***m*** ...Mark 10:43
to make thee a ***m*** ....Acts 26:16
hath made us able ***m*** 2Cor 3:6
is..Christ the ***m*** of sin? ....Gal 2:17
you a faithful ***m*** of Christ .....Col 1:7
a good ***m*** of Jesus Christ 1Tim 4:6
A ***m*** of the sanctuary ....Heb 8:2

MINISTER—*to serve*

[*also* MINISTERED, MINISTERETH, MINISTERING]
m unto me in the priest's .....Ex 28:3
m unto me in the priest's .....Ex 28:41
m unto me in the priest's .....Ex 29:1
to ***m*** to me in the priest's .....Ex 29:44
m unto me in the priest's .....Ex 30:30
sons, to ***m*** in the priest's ......Ex 35:19
to ***m*** in the priest's office .....Ex 39:41
m unto me in the priest's .....Ex 40:15
to ***m*** unto the Lord in the .....Lev 7:35
and they shall ***m*** unto it ....Num 1:50
Ithamar ***m*** in the priest's ......Num 3:4
priest, that they may ***m*** ....Num 3:6
wherewith they ***m*** unto it .....Num 4:9
wherewith they ***m*** about it ....Num 4:14
the congregation to ***m*** unto ....Num 16:9
joined unto thee, and ***m*** ......Num 18:2
sons with thee shall ***m*** ....Num 18:2
his son ***m*** in the priest's ....Deut 10:6
before the Lord to ***m*** ....Deut 10:8
m in the name of the Lord ....Deut 18:5
God hath chosen to ***m*** unto ...Deut 21:5
Joshua..of Nun, Moses ***m*** .....Josh 1:1
And the child did ***m*** unto 1Sam 2:11
Samuel ***m*** before the Lord 1Sam 2:18
Samuel ***m*** unto the Lord 1Sam 3:1
called his servant that ***m*** 2Sam 13:17
cherished the king, and ***m*** 1Kin 1:4
could not stand to ***m***..........1Kin 8:11
went after Elijah, and ***m*** 1Kin 19:21
vessels of brass..they ***m*** 2Kin 25:14
m before the dwelling 1Chr 6:32
charge of the ***m*** vessels 1Chr 9:28
of God, and to ***m*** unto him ...1Chr 15:2
m before ark continually 1Chr 16:37
to ***m*** in the house..Lord 1Chr 26:12
could not stand to ***m*** by.......2Chr 5:14
David praised by their ***m*** 2Chr 7:6
the priests, which ***m*** unto 2Chr 13:10
of Ahaziah..***m*** to Ahaziah 2Chr 22:8
even vessels to ***m***, and to 2Chr 24:14
to ***m***, and to give thanks 2Chr 31:2
should bring unto us ***m*** ....Ezra 8:17
m in the house of our God ....Neh 10:36
king's servants that ***m*** ....Esth 2:2
shall ***m*** judgment to the ....Ps 9:8
rams of Nebaioth..***m*** unto .....Is 60:7
and the Levites that ***m*** ....Jer 33:22
vessels of brass..they ***m*** ....Jer 52:18
near to the Lord to ***m*** ....Ezek 40:46
approach unto me, to ***m*** ......Ezek 43:19
of the house, and ***m*** to the ....Ezek 44:11
be ***m*** in my sanctuary ....Ezek 44:11
they ***m*** unto them before ......Ezek 44:12
come near to me to ***m*** ....Ezek 44:15
m in the gates of the inner ....Ezek 44:17
thousand thousands ***m*** ....Dan 7:10
angels came and ***m*** unto ......Matt 4:11
and she arose, and ***m*** unto ....Matt 8:15
not to be ***m*** unto, but to ***m***....Matt 20:28
prison, and did not ***m*** unto ....Matt 25:44
Jesus from Galilee, ***m*** unto ....Matt 27:55
beasts; and the angels ***m*** ......Mark 1:13
not to be ***m*** unto, but to ***m***....Mark 10:45
she arose and ***m*** unto them....Luke 4:39
m to the Lord, and fasted .....Acts 13:2
hands have ***m*** unto my ....Acts 20:34
none..to ***m*** or come unto......Acts 24:23
the Gentiles, ***m*** the gospel ....Rom 15:16
Jerusalem to ***m*** unto ....Rom 15:25
to ***m*** unto them in carnal......Rom 15:27
sower both ***m*** bread for 2Cor 9:10
Now he that ***m*** seed to the 2Cor 9:10
that ***m*** to you the Spirit ....Gal 3:5
m grace unto the hearers......Eph 4:29
and he that ***m*** to my wants ....Phil 2:25
having nourishment ***m*** ....Col 2:19
m questions, rather than 1Tim 1:4
he ***m*** unto me at Ephesus 2Tim 1:18
might have ***m*** unto me in .....Philem 13
sent forth to ***m*** for them ......Heb 1:14
Are they not all ***m*** spirits .....Heb 1:14
m to the saints, and do ***m*** .....Heb 6:10
priest standeth daily ***m*** and ....Heb 10:11
but unto us they did ***m*** the 1Pet 1:12
even so ***m*** the same one to 1Pet 4:10
if any man ***m***, let him do it ...1Pet 4:11
an entrance shall be ***m***........2Pet 1:11

MINISTRY—*service*

[*also* MINISTRATION]
all the instruments of ***m***.......Num 4:12
by the ***m*** of the prophets......Hos 12:10
obtained part of this ***m***........Acts 1:17
were neglected in the daily ***m***. .Acts 6:1
Or ***m***, let us wait on our ***m***....Rom 12:7
addicted..to the ***m*** of the saints.1Cor 16:15
given..***m*** of reconciliation 2Cor 5:18
for the work of the ***m***.........Eph 4:12
putting me into the ***m***.........1Tim 1:12
obtained a more excellent ***m***. . .Heb 8:6

MINNI (mĭn'ī)—*a people of Armenia; Manneans*
Summoned to destroy Babylon ....Jer 51:27

MINNITH (mĭn'ĭth)—*"prepared"*
Wheat-growing Ammonite town ....Ezek 27:17

MINORITY—*less than half of any group*
On God's side ....Num 14:1-10
To be preferred ....Ex 23:2
Saved are ....Matt 7:13-23

MINSTREL—*a player of a stringed instrument*
Used by Elisha 2Kin 3:15
Among funeral attendants.Matt 9:23

MINT—*a fragrant herb*
Tithed by Pharisees .....Matt 23:23

MIPHKAD (mĭf'kăd)—*"appointed place"*
Gate of Jerusalem rebuilt by Nehemiah ... Neh 3:31

MIRACLE—*an intervention in the natural universe by God*

Described:
Signs ... Acts 4:30
Wonders ... Acts 6:8
Works ... John 10:25-38

Kinds of, over:
Nature ... Josh 10:12-14
Animals ... Num 22:28
Human beings ... Gen 19:26
Nations ... Ex 10:1, 2
Sickness and disease ... 2Kin 5:10-14
Natural laws ... 2Kin 6:5-7
Future events ... 2Kin 6:8-13
Death ... John 11:41-44

Produced by:
God's power ... Acts 15:12
Christ's power ... Matt 10:1
Spirit's power ... Matt 12:28

Design of:
Manifest:
God's glory ... John 11:40-42
Christ's glory ... John 2:11
God's presence ... Judg 6:11-24
Proof of God's messengers ... Ex 4:2-9
Produce obedience ... Ex 16:4
Vindicate God ... Ex 17:4-7
Produce faith ... John 20:30, 31
Proof of Jesus as the Messiah ... Matt 11:2-5
Signs of a true apostle ... 2Cor 12:12
Authenticate the Gospel. . Rom 15:18, 19
Fulfill prophecy ... John 12:37-41

Effect of, upon people:
Forced acknowledgment ... John 11:47; Acts 4:16
Amazement ... Mark 6:49-51
Faith ... John 2:23; John 11:42
God glorified ... Matt 9:1-8

False:
Not to be followed ... Deut 13:1-3
Sign of antichrist ... 2Thess 2:3, 9; Rev 13:13
Predicted by Christ ... Matt 24:24

Evidence of:
Logic ... John 9:16
Sufficient to convince ... John 3:2; John 6:14
Insufficient to convince ... Luke 16:31; John 12:37
Sought by Jews ... John 2:18
Demanded unreasonably ... Matt 27:42, 43
Incurs guilt ... Matt 11:20-24; John 15:24

[*also* MIRACLES]
his ***m***, and his acts, which ... Deut 11:3
signs, and those great ***m*** ... Deut 29:3
considered not the ***m*** ... Mark 6:52
which shall do a ***m*** in my ... Mark 9:39
hoped to have seen some ***m*** ... Luke 23:8
second ***m*** that Jesus did ... John 4:54
because they saw his ***m*** ... John 6:2
seen the ***m*** that Jesus did ... John 6:14
not because ye saw the ***m*** ... John 6:26
will he do more ***m*** than ... John 7:31
that is a sinner do such ***m***? ... John 9:16
and said, John did no ***m*** ... John 10:41
heard..he had done his ***m*** ... John 12:18
he had done so many ***m*** ... John 12:37
approved of God..by ***m*** ... Acts 2:22
notable ***m*** hath been done ... Acts 4:16
m of healing was showed ... Acts 4:22
and seeing the ***m*** which he ... Acts 8:6
m and signs which were ... Acts 8:13
m by the hands of Paul ... Acts 19:11
another the working of ***m*** ... 1Cor 12:10
m, then gifts of healings ... 1Cor 12:28
are all workers of ***m***? ... 1Cor 12:29
worketh ***m*** among you ... Gal 3:5
and wonders..divers ***m*** ... Heb 2:4
m which he had power to do ... Rev 13:14
spirits of devils, working ***m*** ... Rev 16:14
the false prophet that..***m*** ... Rev 19:20

MIRACLES OF THE NEW TESTAMENT

The Miracles of Jesus:
Water made wine (Cana) ... John 2:1-11
Son of nobleman healed (Cana) ... John 4:46-54
Passed unseen through crowd (Nazareth) ... Luke 4:28-30
Man with unclean spirit in synagogue cured (Capernaum) ... Mark 1:13-26; Luke 4:33-35
Peter's mother-in-law healed (Capernaum) ... Matt 8:14-17; Mark 1:29-31; Luke 4:38-39
Net full of fishes (Lower Galilee) ... Luke 5:1-11
Leper cleansed (Capernaum) ... Matt 8:1-4; Mark 1:40-45; Luke 5:12-15
Paralytic cured (Capernaum) ... Matt 9:1-8; Mark 2:3-12; Luke 5:18-26
Man healed (Jerusalem) ... John 5:1-9
Withered hand restored (Galilee) ... Matt 12:10-13; Mark 3:1-5; Luke 6:6-11
Centurion's servant cured of palsy (Capernaum) ... Matt 8:5-13; Luke 7:1-10
Widow's son raised from dead (Nain) ... Luke 7:11-17
Demon-possessed man healed (Galilee) ... Matt 12:22, 23; Luke 11:14
Tempest stilled (Lower Galilee) ... Matt 8:23-27; Mark 4:37-41; Luke 8:22-25
Two demon-possessed men cured (Gadara) ... Matt 8:28-34; Mark 5:1-20; Luke 8:26-39
Raised Jairus' daughter (Capernaum) ... Matt 9:23; Mark 5:23; Luke 8:41
Woman with issue of blood healed (Capernaum) ... Matt 9:20-22; Mark 5:25-34; Luke 8:43-48
Blind men cured (Capernaum) ... Matt 9:27-31
Dumb spirit cast out (Capernaum) ... Matt 9:32, 33
Five thousand fed (Lower Galilee) ... Matt 14:15-21; Mark 6:35-44; Luke 9:10-17; John 6:1-14
Walking on the sea (Lower Galilee) ... Matt 14:25-33; Mark 6:48-52; John 6:15-21
Syrophoenician's daughter healed (District of Tyre) ... Matt 15:21-28; Mark 7:24-30
Four thousand fed (Lower Galilee) ... Matt 15:32-39; Mark 8:1-9
Deaf and dumb man cured (Lower Galilee) ... Mark 7:31-37
Blind man healed (Bethsaida) ... Mark 8:22-26
Demon cast out of boy (near Caesarea) ... Matt 17:14-18; Mark 9:14-29; Luke 9:37-43
Tribute money provided (Capernaum) ... Matt 17:24-27
Passed unseen through crowd (in Temple) ... John 8:59
Ten lepers cleansed (Samaria) ... Luke 17:11-19
Man born blind, healed (Jerusalem) ... John 9:1-7
Lazarus raised from dead (Bethany) ... John 11:38-44
Woman with sickness cured (Peraea) ... Luke 13:11-17
Man with dropsy cured (Peraea) ... Luke 14:1-6
Two blind men cured (Jericho) ... Matt 20:29-34; Mark 10:46-52; Luke 18:35-43
Fig tree withered (Mt. Olivet) ... Matt 21:18-22; Mark 11:12-14
Malchus' ear healed (Gethsemane) ... Luke 22:50, 51
Second net full of fishes (Lower Galilee) ... John 21:1-14
Resurrection of Christ ... Luke 24:6; John 10:18

Appearances of Christ after his resurrection, to:
Mary Magdalene (Jerusalem) ... Mark 16:9
Other women (Jerusalem) ... Matt 28:9
Two disciples (Emmaus) ... Luke 24:15-31
Peter (Jerusalem) ... 1Cor 15:5
Ten apostles, Thomas absent (Jerusalem) ... John 20:19, 24
Eleven apostles, Thomas present (Jerusalem) ... John 20:26-28
Seven disciples fishing (Lower Galilee) ... John 21:1-24
Eleven apostles (Galilee) ... Matt 28:16, 17
Five hundred brethren ... 1Cor 15:6
James ... 1Cor 15:7
Eleven apostles on day of His ascension (Bethany) ... Acts 1:2-9
Paul at his conversion ... Acts 9:1-5; 1Cor 15:8

Those associated with Peter:
Lame man cured ... Acts 3:6
Death of Ananias and Sapphira ... Acts 5:5, 10
Sick healed ... Acts 5:15
Aeneas healed of palsy ... Acts 9:34
Dorcas restored to life ... Acts 9:40
His release from prison ... Acts 12:7-11

Those associated with Paul:
His sight restored ... Acts 9:17-18; Acts 22:12-13
Elymas blinded ... Acts 13:11
Lame man cured ... Acts 14:10
Damsel freed of evil spirits ... Acts 16:18; Acts 19:11, 12
Earthquake at Philippi ... Acts 16:25, 26
Evil spirits overcame Sceva's seven sons ... Acts 19:13-16
Eutychus restored to life ... Acts 20:10
Unharmed by viper's bite ... Acts 28:5
Publius' father healed ... Acts 28:8

Other miracles of the New Testament:
Outpouring of the Holy Spirit ... Acts 2:1-14
Gift of tongues ... Acts 2:3, 4, 11; Acts 10:46; Acts 19:6
Apostles freed from prison ... Acts 5:19; Acts 12:7-11
Agabus' prophesies ... Acts 11:28; Acts 21:11
Three apostles' visions ... Matt 17:2; Luke 9:32
Stephen ... Acts 7:55, 56
Ananias' ... Acts 9:10
Peter's ... Acts 10:1-48; Acts 11:1-30
Cornelius' ... Acts 10:3, 4, 30-32
Paul's ... Acts 16:9; 2Cor 12:1-5
John's on Patmos ... Rev 1:10; Rev 4—22
Miracles by the seventy ... Luke 10:17
Stephen performed great miracles ... Acts 6:8
Philip cast out unclean spirits ... Acts 8:6-13

M

MIRACLES OF THE OLD TESTAMENT
Creation ....Gen 1:1-27
Enoch's translation ......Gen 5:24
The Flood ....Gen 7:17-24
Confusion of tongues at Babel ....Gen 11:3-9
Sodom and Gomorrah destroyed ....Gen 19:24
Lot's wife turned to a pillar of salt...........Gen 19:26
Ass speaking ....Num 22:21-35

Those associated with Moses and Aaron:
Burning bush ....Ex 3:3
Moses' rod changed into a serpent ....Ex 4:3, 4, 30
Moses' hand made leprous ....Ex 4:6, 7, 30
Aaron's rod changed into a serpent ....Ex 7:8-10
Ten plagues:
River turned to blood . .Ex 7:20-25
Frogs ....Ex 8:1-15
Lice ....Ex 8:16-19
Flies ....Ex 8:20-24
Murrain ....Ex 9:1-7
Boils ....Ex 9:8-12
Hail ....Ex 9:18-24
Locusts ....Ex 10:1-20
Darkness ....Ex 10:21-23
First-born destroyed . . .Ex 12:29-30
Pillar of cloud and fire .Ex 13:21-22; Ex 14:19-20
Crossing the sea ....Ex 14:21, 23
Bitter waters sweetened . .Ex 15:25
Manna sent ....Ex 16:13-36
Water from the rock at Rephidim ....Ex 17:5-8
Amalek defeated ....Ex 17:9-13
Fire on Aaron's sacrifice .Lev 9:24
Nadab and Abihu devoured ....Lev 10:1, 2
Israel's judgment by fire .Num 11:1-3
Miriam's leprosy.........Num 12:10-15
Destruction of Korah ....Num 16:31-35
Aaron's rod blossoms ....Num 17:8
Water from the rock in Kadesh ....Num 20:8-11
Brass serpent ....Num 21:9

Those associated with Joshua:
Jordan divided ....Josh 3:14-17
Fall of Jericho ....Josh 6:6-20
Sun and moon stand still .Josh 10:12-14

Those associated with Samson:
Lion killed ....Judg 14:5, 6
Thirty Philistines killed . . .Judg 14:19
Water from the hollow place in Lehi ....Judg 15:19
Gates of the city carried away ....Judg 16:3
Dagon's house pulled down ....Judg 16:29, 30

Those associated with Elijah:
Drought ....1Kin 17:1; James 5:17
Fed by ravens 1Kin 17:4-6
Widow's oil and meal increased 1Kin 17:12-16
Widow's son raised from dead 1Kin 17:17-23
Sacrifice consumed by fire 1Kin 18:38
Rain in answer to prayer .1Kin 18:41
Captains consumed by fire 2Kin 1:9-12
Jordan divided 2Kin 2:8
Translated to heaven in a chariot of fire 2Kin 2:11

Those associated with Elisha:
Jordan divided 2Kin 2:14
Waters of Jericho healed .2Kin 2:20-22
Mocking young men destroyed by bears 2Kin 2:24
Water supplied for Jehoshaphat...........2Kin 3:16-20
Widow's oil multiplied . . .2Kin 4:1-7
Shunammite's child raised from dead 2Kin 4:19-37
Poisoned pottage made harmless 2Kin 4:38-41
Hundred fed with twenty loaves 2Kin 4:42-44
Naaman cured of leprosy .2Kin 5:10-14
Gehazi struck with leprosy 2Kin 5:27
Axe head caused to float .2Kin 6:5-7
Ben-hadad's plans revealed 2Kin 6:8-13
Syrian army defeated 2Kin 6:18-20
Revival of a man by touch with Elisha's bones 2Kin 13:21

Those associated with Isaiah:
Hezekiah healed.........2Kin 20:7
Shadow turns backward on sun dial 2Kin 20:11

Other miracles of the Old Testament:
Dew on Gideon's fleece . .Judg 6:37-40
Dagon's fall before the ark 1Sam 5:1-12
Men of Beth-shemesh destroyed 1Sam 6:19, 20
Thunder and rain in harvest 1Sam 12:18
Uzzah's death 2Sam 6:6, 7
Jeroboam's hand withered and restored 1Kin 13:4-6
Rending of the altar 1Kin 13:5
Sennacherib's army destroyed 2Kin 19:35
Uzziah afflicted with leprosy 2Chr 26:16-21
Three men protected from the fiery furnace. .Dan 3:19-27
Daniel delivered from the lion's den ....Dan 6:16-23
Preservation of Jonah in stomach of fish three days ....Jon 2:1-10

MIRACLES PRETENDED, OR FALSE
Egyptian magicians ......Ex 7:11-22; Ex 8:18, 19
In support of false religions ....Deut 13:1-3
Witch of Endor 1Sam 28:9-12
False prophets ....Matt 7:22, 23; Matt 24:24
False christs.............Matt 24:24
Deceive the ungodly .....Rev. 13:13; Rev. 19:20
Sign of apostasy ....2Thess 2:3, 9; Rev 13:13

MIRE—*deep mud*
Places of:
Dungeon ....Jer 38:22
Streets..................Is 10:6
Figurative of:
Affliction ....Job 30:19
External prosperity ......Job 8:11
Insecurity ....Is 57:20
Subjection 2Sam 22:43
Plentifulness ....Zech 9:3

[*also* MIRY]
pointed things upon the ***m*** ....Job 41:30
horrible pit, out of the ***m*** .....Ps 40:2
I sink in deep ***m***, where ....Ps 69:2
Deliver me out of the ***m*** ......Ps 69:14
there was no water, but ***m*** ....Jer 38:6
so Jeremiah sunk in the ***m*** ....Jer 38:6
But the ***m*** places thereof ......Ezek 47:11
the iron mixed with ***m*** clay ....Dan 2:41
sawest iron mixed with ***m*** .....Dan 2:43
as the ***m*** of the streets ....Mic 7:10
enemies in the ***m*** of the streets.Zech 10:5
to her wallowing in the ***m*** 2Pet 2:22

MIRIAM (mĭr'ĭ-ăm)—*"fat; thick; strong"*
1. Sister of Aaron and Moses ....Num 26:59
Chosen by God; called a prophetess ....Ex 15:20
Leads in victory song....Ex 15:20, 21
Punished for rebellion . . .Num 12:1-16
Buried at Kadesh ....Num 20:1
2. Judahite.................1Chr 4:17

Lord thy God did unto ***M*** .....Deut 24:9
Aaron, and Moses, and ***M*** 1Chr 6:3
thee Moses, Aaron, and ***M*** ....Mic 6:4

MIRMA (mûr'mä)—*"height"*
Benjamite 1Chr 8:10

MIRROR—*a polished, smooth surface that allows for images to be seen by reflection*
In the tabernacle ....Ex 38:8
Of molten brass ....Job 37:18
Used figuratively.......1Cor 13:12; 2Cor 3:18; James 1:23, 25

MIRTH—*a spirit of gaiety*
Occasions of ....Gen 31:27; Neh 8:10-12
Absence of ....Jer 25:10, 11; Hos 2:11
Inadequacy of ....Prov 14:13; Eccl 2:1, 2

portions and to make great ***m***. .Neh 8:12
wasted us required of us ***m*** ....Ps 137:3
fools is in the house of ***m*** .....Eccl 7:4
Then I commended ***m*** ....Eccl 8:15
The ***m*** of tabrets ceaseth ......Is 24:8
the ***m*** of the land is gone .....Is 24:11
voice of ***m***, and the voice .....Jer 7:34
your days, the voice of ***m*** .....Jer 16:9
from them the voice of ***m*** .....Jer 25:10
should we then make ***m***? ......Ezek 21:10
will also cause all her ***m*** to ....Hos 2:11

MISCARRIAGE—*early loss of a fetus during pregnancy*
Wished for.............Job 3:16; Eccl 6:3
Against the wicked ......Ps 58:8

[*also* MISCARRYING]
give them a ***m*** womb and .....Hos 9:14

MISCHIEF—*injury; damage; evil*
Descriptive of:
Moral evil ....Ps 36:4
Physical harm ....Ex 21:22, 23
Trouble.................1Kin 11:25
Of the wicked, they:
Boast...................Ps 52:1
Devise..................Ps 62:3; Prov 6:14
Practice.................1Sam 23:9; Prov 10:23
Run to ....Prov 6:18
Think to do ....Neh 6:2
Seek 1Kin 20:7

[*also* MISCHIEFS, MISCHIEVOUS]
Lest peradventure ***m*** befall ....Gen 42:4
if ***m*** befall him by the way ....Gen 42:38
this also from me, and ***m*** .....Gen 44:29
for ***m*** did he bring them ......Ex 32:12
that they are set on ***m*** ....Ex 32:22
I will heap ***m*** upon them .....Deut 32:23
thou art taken in thy ***m*** 2Sam 16:8
light, some ***m*** will come 2Kin 7:9
tears to put away the ***m*** of ....Esth 8:3
They conceive ***m***, and.........Job 15:35
and hath conceived ***m***.........Ps 7:14
under his tongue is ***m*** and .....Ps 10:7
they imagined a ***m*** device .....Ps 21:11
in whose hands is ***m***, and .....Ps 26:10
but ***m*** is in their hearts........Ps 28:3
Thy tongue deviseth ***m***........Ps 52:2
m also and sorrow are in ......Ps 55:10
which frameth ***m*** by a law? ....Ps 94:20
imagine ***m*** in their hearts.......Ps 140:2
m of their own lips cover .....Ps 140:9
except they have done ***m***......Prov 4:16
he that seeketh ***m***, it shall .....Prov 11:27

wicked..be filled with ***m*** ......Prov 12:21
wicked messenger..into ***m*** .....Prov 13:17
a perverse tongue..into ***m*** .....Prov 17:20
and their lips talk of ***m*** ....Prov 24:2
evil shall be called a ***m***.......Prov 24:8
wicked shall fall into ***m*** ....Prov 24:16
his heart shall fall into ***m***......Prov 28:14
the end of his talk is ***m*** ....Eccl 10:13
m shall fall upon thee..........Is 47:11
they conceive ***m***, and bring ....Is 59:4
M shall come upon ***m***........Ezek 7:26
are the men that devise ***m***.....Ezek 11:2
king's hearts shall be..***m*** ......Dan 11:27
do they imagine ***m*** against.....Hos 7:15
he uttereth his ***m*** desire ....Mic 7:3
of all subtilty and all ***m*** ....Acts 13:10

MISER—*one who hoards his possessions*
Characteristics of:
Selfish ....Eccl 4:8
Covetous ....Luke 12:15
Divided loyalty ....Matt 6:24
Punishment of:
Dissatisfaction ....Eccl 5:10
Loss....................Matt 6:19
Sorrows 1Tim 6:10
Destruction ....Ps 52:5, 7
Examples of:
Rich fool ....Luke 12:16-21
Rich ruler ....Luke 18:18-23
Ananias and Sapphira....Acts 5:1-11

MISERABLE—*the wretched; state of suffering brought about by affliction*
State of:
Wicked ....Rom 3:12-16
Trapped ....Rom 7:24
Lost....................Luke 13:25-28
Caused by:
Forgetfulness of God ....Is 22:12-14
Ignorance ....Luke 19:42-44

[*also* MISERABLY]
m comforters are ye all ....Job 16:2
m destroy those wicked ....Matt 21:41
we are of all men most ***m*** 1Cor 15:19
thou art wretched, and ***m*** .....Rev 3:17

MISERY—*suffering*

[*also* MISERIES]
grieved for the ***m*** of Israel ....Judg 10:16
remember his ***m*** no more .....Prov 31:7
and ***m*** are in their ways ....Rom 3:16
weep and howl for your ***m*** ....James 5:1

MISFORTUNE—*an unexpected adversity*
Explained by the nations .Deut 29:24-28
Misunderstood by Gideon.Judg 6:13
Understood by David 2Sam 16:5-13
Caused by sin ....Is 59:1, 2

MISGAB (mĭs'găb)—*"light"*
Moabite city ....Jer 48:1
Capital of Moab ....Is 15:1
Translated "high fort" ...Is 25:12

MISHAEL (mĭsh'ā-ĕl)—*"who is what God is?"*
1. Kohathite Levite ....Ex 6:22
Removes dead bodies ...Lev 10:4, 5
2. Hebrew name of Meshach ....Dan 1:6-19
3. One of Ezra's assistants. .Neh 8:4

MISHAL, MISHEAL (mī'shăl, mī'shē'ăl)—*"requiring"*
Town in Asher ....Josh 19:24, 26
Assigned to Levites......Josh 21:30
Called Mashal...........1Chr 6:74

MISHAM (mī'shăm)—*"impetuous; fame"*
Son of Elpaal 1Chr 8:12

MISHEAL—*See* MISHAL

MISHMA (mĭsh'mä)—*"fame"*
1. Son of Ishmael ....Gen 25:13, 14
1Chr 1:30
2. Descendant of Simeon...1Chr 4:25

MISHMANNAH (mĭsh-măn'ä)—*"fatness"*
One of David's Gadite warriors 1Chr 12:10

MISHRAITES (mĭsh'rä-īts)
Family living in Kirjath-jearim 1Chr 2:53

MISPAR (mĭs'pär)—*"writing"*
Exile returnee ....Ezra 2:2
Called Mispereth ....Neh 7:7

MISREPHOTH-MAIM (mĭs-rĕ-fŏth-mā'ĭm)—*"hot waters"*
Haven of fleeing Canaanites ....Josh 11:8
Near the Sidonians ......Josh 13:6

MISS—*to fail to touch, attain, or hit*

[*also* MISSED, MISSING]
hair breadth, and not ***m***.......Judg 20:16
if thy father at all ***m*** me 1Sam 20:6
and thou shalt be ***m*** 1Sam 20:18
neither was there ought ***m*****.....1Sam 25:7
not hurt, neither ***m*** we any 1Sam 25:15
nothing was ***m*** of all 1Sam 25:21
if by any means he be ***m*** 1Kin 20:39

MISSION OF CHRIST—*the assignment Christ took upon Himself in coming to earth*
Do God's will ....John 6:38
Save sinners ....Luke 19:10
Bring in everlasting righteousness...........Dan 9:24
Destroy Satan's works ...Heb 2:14
1John 3:8
Fulfill the Old Testament .Matt 5:17
Give life ....John 10:10, 28
Stop sacrifices ....Dan 9:27
Complete revelation .....Heb 1:3

MISSIONARIES—*those sent out to spread the Gospel*
Jonah ....Jon 3:2, 3
The early church ....Acts 8:4
Philip ....Acts 8:5
Some from Cyrene become missionaries ...Acts 11:20
Paul and Barnabas ......Acts 13:1-4
Peter ....Acts 15:7
Apollos ....Acts 18:24
Noah 2Pet 2:5

MISSIONS—*the carrying out of the Great Commission to "teach all nations, baptizing them in the name of the Father, and of the Son, and of the Holy Ghost" (Matt 28:19)*
Commands concerning:
"Shall be" ....Matt 24:14
"Go" ....Matt 28:18-20
"Tarry" ....Luke 24:49
"Come" ....Acts 16:9
Motives prompting:
God's love ....John 3:16
Christ's love 2Cor 5:14, 15
Mankind's need ....Rom 3:9-31
Equipment for:
Word ....Rom 10:14, 15
Spirit ....Acts 1:8
Prayer ....Acts 13:1-4

MIST—*a vapor*
Physical (vapor) ....Gen 2:6
Spiritual (blindness) .....Acts 13:11
Eternal (darkness) 2Pet 2:17

MISTAKE—*an error arising from human weakness*
Causes of:
Motives misunderstood ...Josh 22:9-29
Appearance misjudged ...1Sam 1:13-15
Trust misplaced ....Josh 9:3-27

MISTRESS—*a married woman; a woman with authority*
Over a maid ....Gen 16:4, 8, 9
Figurative of Nineveh ....Nah 3:4
m of the house, fell sick 1Kin 17:17
And she said unto her ***m***......2Kin 5:3
unto the hand of her ***m*** ....Ps 123:2
that is heir to her ***m*** ....Prov 30:23
the maid, so with her ***m***.......Is 24:2
the ***m*** of witchcrafts, that .....Nah 3:4

MISUNDERSTANDINGS—*disagreements*
Israelites ....Josh 22:9-29
Christ's disciples ....Matt 20:20-27
Apostles ....Gal 2:11-15
Christians ....Acts 6:1

MISUSED—*put to a wrong use*
Guilt of, brings wrath 2Chr 36:16

MITE—*the Jews' smallest coin*
Widow's ....Mark 12:42

[*also* MITES]
hast paid the very last ***m*** ......Luke 12:59
casting in thither two ***m*** ....Luke 21:2

MITHCAH (mĭth'kä)—*"sweetness"*
Israelite encampment ....Num 33:28, 29

MITHNITE (mĭth'nīt)
Descriptive of Joshaphat, David's officer 1Chr 11:43

MITHREDATH (mĭth'rĕ-dăth)—*"given by the god Mithra"*
1. Treasurer of Cyrus ......Ezra 1:8
2. Persian official..........Ezra 4:7

MITRE—*a headdress or turban*
Worn by the high priest . .Ex 28:36-39
Inscription "Holiness to the Lord" worn on .....Ex 39:28-31
Worn by Aaron for anointing and on Day of Atonement .... Lev 8:9; Lev 16:4
Uncovering of upper lip a sign of uncleanness and mourning ....Lev 13:45
Uncovering of, forbidden .Lev 21:10-12
Removal of, because of sin ....Ezek 21:26
Symbolic restoration of . .Zech 3:5
embroidered coat, a ***m***, and ...Ex 28:4
put the ***m*** upon his head ......Ex 29:6
the holy crown upon the ***m***....Ex 29:6

MITYLENE (mĭt-ĭ-lē'nē)—*"purity"—the principal city of the island of Lesbos*
Visited by Paul ....Acts 20:13-15

MIXED, MIXT—*See* MIXTURE

MIXTURE—*a combination or blending into one*

[*also* MIXED, MIXT]
m multitude went up also .....Ex 12:38
the ***m*** multitude that was......Num 11:4
Israel all the ***m*** multitude .....Neh 13:3
wine is red; it is full of ***m***.....Ps 75:8
they that go to seek ***m*** wine ...Prov 23:30
thy wine ***m*** with water ....Is 1:22
the iron ***m*** with miry clay .....Dan 2:41
iron ***m*** with miry clay ....Dan 2:43
even as iron is not ***m*** with.....Dan 2:43
he hath ***m*** himself among .....Hos 7:8
brought a ***m*** of myrrh and.....John 19:39
not being ***m*** with faith in......Heb 4:2
is poured out without ***m*** ......Rev 14:10

MIZAR (mī'zär)—*"little"*
Hill east of Jordan ......Ps 42:6

MIZPAH, MIZPEH (mĭz'pä, mĭz'pē)—*"watchtower"*
1. Site of covenant between Jacob and Laban......Gen 31:44-53
2. Town in Gilead; probably same as 1 ...Judg 10:17
Jephthah's home ....Judg 11:11, 29, 34
Probably same as Ramathmizpeh........Josh 13:26
3. Region near Mt. Hermon Josh 11:3, 8
4. Town in Judah ....Josh 15:1, 38
5. Place in Moab; David brings his parents to . .1Sam 22:3, 4

6. Town of Benjamin ......Josh 18:21, 26
   Outraged Israelites
   gather here ....Judg 20:1, 3
   Samuel gathers Israel....1Sam 7:5-16
   1Sam 10:17-25
   Built by Asa............1Sam 15:22
   Residence of Gedaliah ..2Kin 25:23, 25
   Home of exile returnees .Neh 3:7, 15, 19

and encamped in *M* ....Judg 10:17
words before the Lord in *M*...Judg 11:11
passed over *M* of Gilead ......Judg 11:29
M of Gilead he passed ....Judg 11:29
came to *M* unto his house .....Judg 11:34
of Israel had sworn in *M*......Judg 21:1
not up to the Lord to *M* ......Judg 21:5
that came not up to *M* to .....Judg 21:8
Geba of Benjamin and *M* 1Kin 15:22
he built..Geba and *M*.........2Chr 16:6
Gedaliah..of Ahikam to *M* .....Jer 40:6
they came to Gedaliah to *M*...Jer 40:8
behold, I will dwell at *M*......Jer 40:10
Judah, to Gedaliah, unto *M*...Jer 40:12
came to Gedaliah to *M* ....Jer 40:13
spake to Gedaliah in *M* ....Jer 40:15
the son of Ahikam to *M* ......Jer 41:1
eat bread together in *M*.......Jer 41:1
at *M* and the Chaldeans.......Jer 41:3
went forth from *M* to meet....Jer 41:6
people that were in *M* ....Jer 41:10
people that remained in *M*....Jer 41:10
carried away captive from *M* ..Jer 41:14
from *M* after that he had .....Jer 41:16
ye have been a snare on *M*....Hos 5:1

MIZPAR—*See* Mispar

MIZRAIM (mĭz'rā-ĭm)—*the personification of Egypt*
1. Son of Ham; ancestor of
   Ludim, Anamim, etc. .1Chr 1:8, 11
2. Hebrew name for Egypt .Gen 50:11
   Called the land of Ham .Ps 105:23, 27

sons of Ham, Cush, and *M*....Gen 10:6
and *M* begat Ludim and ....Gen 10:13

MIZZAH (mĭz'ä)—*"terror; joy"*
Grandson of Esau; a
duke of Edom ....Gen 36:13, 17

MNASON (nā'sŏn)—*"remembering"*
Christian of Cyprus and
Paul's host............Acts 21:16

MOAB (mō'ăb)—*"from my father"*
1. Son of Lot ....Gen 19:33-37
2. Country of the Moabites .Deut 1:5

Midian in the field of *M* ......Gen 36:35
the mighty men of *M* ....Ex 15:15
wilderness which is before *M* ..Num 21:11
Arnon is the border of *M* .....Num 21:13
M and the Amorites ....Num 21:13
upon the border of *M*.........Num 21:15
in the country of *M*, to the ....Num 21:20
Woe to thee, *M*! thou art .....Num 21:29
pitched in the plains of *M*.....Num 22:1
M was sore afraid of the......Num 22:3
M was distressed because .....Num 22:3
the elders of *M* and the ....Num 22:7
princes of *M* abode with ......Num 22:8
king of *M* hath sent unto......Num 22:10
the princes of *M* rose up ......Num 22:14
with the princes of *M*.........Num 22:21
meet him unto a city of *M* ....Num 22:36
he, and all the princes of *M*...Num 23:6
and the princes of *M* with .....Num 23:17
smite the corners of *M*........Num 24:17
with the daughters of *M* ......Num 25:1
with them in the plains of *M* ..Num 26:3
of Israel in the plains of *M*....Num 26:63
camp at the plains of *M*.......Num 31:13
in the border of *M* ....Num 33:44
pitched in the plains of *M*.....Num 33:48
in the plains of *M* ....Num 33:49
unto Moses in the plains of *M* .Num 33:50
unto Moses in the plains of *M* .Num 35:1
of Israel in the plains of *M*....Num 36:12
way of the wilderness of *M*....Deut 2:8
through Ar, the coast of *M*....Deut 2:18
of Israel in the land of *M* .....Deut 29:1
which is in the land of *M* .....Deut 32:49
up from the plains of *M*.......Deut 34:1
Lord died..the land of *M*......Deut 34:5
a valley in the land of *M*......Deut 34:6
for Moses in the plains of *M* ..Deut 34:8
inheritance in the plains of *M* .Josh 13:32
Eglon the king of *M*..........Judg 3:12
served Eglon the king of *M* ...Judg 3:14
unto Eglon the king of *M*.....Judg 3:15
unto Eglon king of *M*.........Judg 3:17
fords of Jordan toward *M* .....Judg 3:28
slew of *M* at that time ....Judg 3:29
M was subdued that day ......Judg 3:30
Zidon and the gods of *M* ......Judg 10:6
took not away the land of *M* ..Judg 11:15
the son of Zippor, king of *M*? .Judg 11:25
the hand of the king of *M*.....1Sam 12:9
slew two lionlike men of *M* ...2Sam 23:20
M rebelled against Israel 2Kin 1:1
Midian in the field of *M* 1Chr 1:46
who had the dominion in *M*...1Chr 4:22
children in the country of *M*..1Chr 8:8
slew two lionlike men of *M* ...1Chr 11:22
smote *M* and the Moabites 1Chr 18:2
from *M*, and from the 1Chr 18:11
that the children of *M* and 2Chr 20:1
children of Ammon and *M*....2Chr 20:10
the children of Ammon, *M*....2Chr 20:22
children of Ammon and *M*....2Chr 20:23
M is my washpot over ....Ps 60:8
of *M*, and the Hagarenes......Ps 83:6
M is my washpot; over........Ps 108:9
the daughters of *M* shall ......Is 16:2
outcasts dwell with thee, *M* ...Is 16:4
heard of the pride of *M*.......Is 16:6
shall *M* howl for *M* ....Is 16:7
sound like an harp for *M* .....Is 16:11
M is weary on the high ....Is 16:12
hath spoken concerning *M* ....Is 16:13
the glory of *M* shall be.......Is 16:14
M shall be trodden down......Is 25:10
M, and all that are in the .....Jer 9:26
and *M* and the children of ....Jer 25:21
the Jews that were in *M* ......Jer 40:11
be no more praise of *M*.......Jer 48:2
M is destroyed; her little .....Jer 48:4
Give wings unto *M* that it.....Jer 48:9
M shall be ashamed of ....Jer 48:13
M is spoiled, and gone up.....Jer 48:15
The calamity of *M* is near......Jer 48:16
spoiler of *M* shall come ....Jer 48:18
M is confounded; for it is .....Jer 48:20
Arnon, that *M* is spoiled ......Jer 48:20
all the cities of the land of *M*. .Jer 48:24
The horn of *M* is cut off ......Jer 48:25
M also shall wallow in his .....Jer 48:26
O ye that dwell in *M*, leave ...Jer 48:28
Therefore will I howl for *M* ...Jer 48:31
I will cry out for all *M*........Jer 48:31
and from the land of *M* ....Jer 48:33
I will cause to cease in *M* .....Jer 48:35
heart shall sound for *M* ....Jer 48:36
upon all the housetops of *M*...Jer 48:38
for I have broken *M* like a ....Jer 48:38
M turned the back with ....Jer 48:39
M be a derision and a ....Jer 48:39
spread his wings over *M* ......Jer 48:40
mighty men's hearts in *M* .....Jer 48:41
M shall be destroyed from ....Jer 48:42
thee, O inhabitant of *M*.......Jer 48:43
bring upon it, even upon *M* ...Jer 48:44
devour the corner of *M* ....Jer 48:45
Woe be unto thee O *M*! ....Jer 48:46
again the captivity of *M*.......Jer 48:47
far is the judgment of *M* ......Jer 48:47
Because that *M* and Seir ......Ezek 25:8
open the side of *M* from ......Ezek 25:9
execute judgments upon *M* ....Ezek 25:11
even Edom, and *M* and ....Dan 11:41
what Balak king of *M*.........Mic 6:5
heard the reproach of *M* ......Zeph 2:8
M shall be as Sodom ....Zeph 2:9

MOABITES (mō'ă-bīts)—*inhabitants of Moab*

History of:
Descendants of Lot ......Gen 19:36, 37
Became a great nation ...Num 21:28, 30
Governed by kings ......Num 23:7
Josh 24:9
Driven out of their
territory by Amorites ..Num 21:26
Refused to let Israel pass .Judg 11:17, 18
Joined Midian to curse
Israel.................Num 22:4
Excluded from Israel ....Deut 23:3-6
Friendly relation with
Israel.................Ruth 1:1, 4, 16
Defeated by Saul 1Sam 14:47
Refuge for David's
parents 1Sam 22:3, 4
Defeated by David 2Sam 8:2, 12
Solomon married women
of....................1Kin 11:1, 3
Paid tribute to Israel.....2Kin 3:4
Fought Israel and Judah. .2Kin 3:5-7
Conquered by Israel and
Judah 2Kin 3:8-27
Intermarried with Jews...Ezra 9:1, 2
Neh 13:23

Characteristics of:
Idolatrous...............1Kin 11:7
Wealthy ....Jer 48:1, 7
Superstitious ....Jer 27:3, 9
Satisfied ....Jer 48:11
Proud ....Jer 48:29

Prophecies concerning their:
Desolation ....Is 15:1-9
Ruin and destruction ....Jer 27:3, 8
Punishment ....Amos 2:1-3
Subjection ....Is 11:14

[*also* moabite, moabitess, moabitish]
of Zippor was king of the *M* ..Num 22:4
Distress not the *M*...........Deut 2:9
the *M* call them Emims ....Deut 2:11
M which dwell in Ar, did .....Deut 2:29
Ammonite or *M* shall not .....Deut 23:3
delivered your enemies the *M*. .Judg 3:28
and Ruth the *M*, her ....Ruth 1:22
And Ruth the *M* said unto ....Ruth 2:2
It is the *M* damsel that........Ruth 2:6
Ruth the *M* said, He said .....Ruth 2:21
buy it also of Ruth the *M*.....Ruth 4:5
Moreover Ruth the *M*, the ...Ruth 4:10
Chemosh the god of the *M*....1Kin 11:33
bands of the *M* invaded 2Kin 13:20
the abomination of..*M* 2Kin 23:13
Syrians and bands of the *M* ...2Kin 24:2
Elnaam, and Ithmah the *M*....1Chr 11:46
The *M* became David's 1Chr 18:2
the son of Shimrith a *M*.......2Chr 24:26
and the *M* should not come ...Neh 13:1

MOADIAH (mō-ä-dī'ä)—*"Jehovah is ornament"—same as Maadiah*
Zichri, of Miniamin, of *M*.....Neh 12:17

MOB—*a lawless crowd*
Caused Pilate to pervert
justice ....Matt 27:20-25
Made unjust charges .....Acts 17:5-9
Paul saved from ....Acts 21:27-40

MOCKER—*one who ridicules*

[*also* mockers]
Are there not *m* with me? ....Job 17:2
hypocritical *m* in feasts........Ps 35:16
Wine is a *m*, strong drink .....Prov 20:1
be ye not *m*, lest your ....Is 28:22
not in the assembly of the *m* ..Jer 15:17

MOCKING—*imitating in fun or derision*

Evil agents of:
Children 2Kin 2:23
Men of Israel 2Chr 30:10
Men of Judah 2Chr 36:16
Fools ....Prov 14:9
Wine ....Prov 20:1

Jews .Matt 20:19
Roman soldiers . . . . .Luke 23:36
False teachers . . . . .Jude 18

Good agents of:
Ass . . . . .Num 22:29
Samson . . . . .Judg 16:10-15
Elijah 1Kin 18:27
Wisdom (God) . . . . .Prov 1:20, 26
The Lord . . . . .Ps 2:4

Reasons for, to:
Show unbelief 2Chr 36:16
Portray scorn 2Chr 30:10
Ridicule . . . . .Acts 2:13
Insult . . . . .Gen 39:14, 17

Objects of:
Christ . . . . .Luke 23:11, 36
Believers . . . . .Heb 11:36

[*also* MOCK, MOCKED, MOCKEST, MOCKETH]
that ***m*** unto his sons-in-law . . . .Gen 19:14
born unto Abraham, ***m*** . . . . . . .Gen 21:9
in a Hebrew unto us to ***m*** . . . . .Gen 39:14
came in unto me to ***m*** me . . . . .Gen 39:17
indignation and ***m*** the Jews . . . .Neh 4:1
when thou ***m***, shall no man . . .Job 11:3
one ***m*** of his neighbor . . . . .Job 12:4
mocketh another, do ye so ***m*** . .Job 13:9
or as one man ***m*** another . . . . .Job 13:9
after that I have spoken, ***m*** . . .Job 21:3
He ***m*** at fear, and is not . . . . . .Job 39:22
m when your fear cometh . . . . .Prov 1:26
m the poor reproacheth . . . . . . .Prov 17:5
eye that ***m*** at his father . . . . . . .Prov 30:17
derision daily, every one ***m*** . . . .Jer 20:7
into their hand, and they ***m*** . . .Jer 38:19
did ***m*** at her sabbaths . . . . .Lam 1:7
and a ***m*** to all countries . . . . . . .Ezek 22:4
be far from thee, shall ***m*** . . . . . .Ezek 22:5
he was ***m*** of the wise men . . . . .Matt 2:16
the knee before him, and ***m*** . . .Matt 27:29
after that they had ***m*** him . . . . .Matt 27:31
also the chief priests ***m*** . . . . .Matt 27:41
they shall ***m*** him, and shall . . . .Mark 10:34
And when they had ***m*** him . . . .Mark 15:20
also the chief priests ***m*** . . . . .Mark 15:31
that behold it begin to ***m*** . . . . . .Luke 14:29
shall be ***m*** and spitefully . . . . . .Luke 18:32
men that held Jesus ***m*** him . . . .Luke 22:63
set him at nought and ***m*** . . . . . .Luke 23:11
the soldiers also ***m*** him . . . . . . .Luke 23:36
resurrection..dead, some ***m*** . . . .Acts 17:32
Be not deceived; God is not ***m*** .Gal 6:7

MODERATION—*not abundant; forbearance*

[*also* MODERATELY]
you the former rain ***m*** . . . . .Joel 2:23
Let your ***m*** be known unto . . . .Phil 4:5

MODESTY IN DRESS—*discreet attire*

Of women:
Instructed 1Tim 2:9
Illustrated in Israel 1Pet 3:3-5
Lack of, an enticement . .2Sam 11:2-5

Of men:
Lack of, condemned . . . . .Gen 9:21-27
Illustrated . . . . .John 21:7
Manifested in conversion .Mark 5:15

MOISTURE—*liquid condensed in relatively small quantity*

[*also* MOIST, MOISTENED]
nor eat ***m*** grapes, or dried . . . .Num 6:3
bones are ***m*** with marrow . . . . .Job 21:24
my ***m*** is turned into the . . . . . . .Ps 32:4
it withered..it lacked ***m*** . . . . . . .Luke 8:6

MOLADAH (mŏl'ä-dä)—*"generation"*
Town of Judah . . . . .Josh 15:1, 26
Inheritance of Simeon . . .Josh 19:1, 2
Returning Levites inhabit .Neh 11:26

MOLDING—*a decorative ledge of gold*

Around:
Ark .Ex 25:11
Incense altar . . . . .Ex 30:3, 4

MOLE—*a small, burrowing animal*
Among unclean animals . .Is 2:20

MOLECH, MOLOCH (mō'lĕk, mō'lŏk)—*"king"—an Ammonite deity*

Worship of:
By Ammonites 1Kin 11:7
By human sacrifice 2Kin 23:10
Strongly condemned . . . . . .Lev 18:21
Introduced by Solomon . .1Kin 11:7

Prevalence of, among Jews:
Favored by Solomon 1Kin 11:7

See HUMAN SACRIFICE

[*also* MOLOCH]
any of his seed unto ***M*** . . . . . . .Lev 20:2
given of his seed unto ***M*** . . . . . .Lev 20:3
giveth of his seed unto ***M*** . . . . .Lev 20:4
commit whoredom with ***M*** . . . .Lev 20:5
through the fire unto ***M*** . . . . . . .Jer 32:35
the tabernacle of your ***M*** . . . . . .Amos 5:26
took up the tabernacle of ***M*** . . .Acts 7:43

MOLID (mō'lĭd)—*"begetter"*
Judahite 1Chr 2:29

MOLLIFIED—*soothed*
neither ***m*** with ointment . . . . . .Is 1:6

MOLOCH—*See* MOLECH

MOLTEN—*melted metal*

Applied to:
Great basin in the Temple 1Kin 7:16-33
Mirror . . . . .Job 37:18
Images . . . . .Ex 32:4, 8

Of images:
Making of forbidden . . . . .Ex 34:17
Made by Israel 2Kin 17:16
Worshiped by Israel . . . . .Ps 106:19
Destroyed by Josiah 2Chr 34:3, 4
Folly of . . . . .Is 42:17
Vanity . . . . .Is 41:29

See GODS, FALSE

he had made it a ***m*** calf . . . . . . .Ex 32:4
made them a ***m*** calf and . . . . . .Ex 32:8
nor make to yourselves ***m*** . . . . .Lev 19:4
destroy all their ***m*** images . . . . .Num 33:52
have made them a ***m*** image . . .Deut 9:12
any graven or ***m*** image . . . . . . .Deut 27:15
a graven image and a ***m*** . . . . . . .Judg 17:3
the teraphim and the ***m*** . . . . . . .Judg 18:17
other gods, and ***m*** images 1Kin 14:9
made a ***m*** sea of ten cubits 2Chr 4:2
carved images, and the ***m*** 2Chr 34:3
brass is ***m*** out of the stone . . . .Job 28:2
ornament of thy ***m*** images . . . . .Is 30:22
god or ***m*** a graven image . . . . . .Is 44:10
my ***m*** image, hath . . . . .Is 48:5
his ***m*** image is falsehood . . . . . .Jer 10:14
his ***m*** image is falsehood . . . . . .Jer 51:17
filthiness of it may be ***m*** . . . . . .Ezek 24:11
m images of their silver . . . . . . .Hos 13:2
mountains shall be ***m*** . . . . .Mic 1:4
graven image and the ***m*** . . . . . .Nah 1:14
m image and a teacher . . . . .Hab 2:18

MOMENT—*a minute portion of time*

Descriptive of:
Man's life . . . . .Job 34:20
Lying tongues . . . . .Prov 12:19
Satan's temptation . . . . . . .Luke 4:5

Descriptive of God's:
Anger . . . . .Num 16:21, 45
Punishment . . . . .Is 47:9
Destruction . . . . .Jer 4:20

Descriptive of the believer's:
Problems . . . . .Job 7:18
Protection . . . . .Is 26:20, 21
Perfection in glory 1Cor 15:52

the midst of thee in a ***m*** . . . . . .Ex 33:5
of the hypocrite but for a ***m***? . .Job 20:5
a ***m*** go down to the grave . . . . .Job 21:13
his anger endureth but a ***m*** . . . .Ps 30:5
into desolation, as in a ***m***! . . . . .Ps 73:19
I will water it every ***m*** . . . . .Is 27:3
small ***m*** have I forsaken . . . . . . .Is 54:7
my face from thee for a ***m*** . . . .Is 54:8
was overthrown as in a ***m*** . . . . .Lam 4:6
shall tremble at every ***m*** . . . . . .Ezek 26:16
shall tremble at every ***m*** . . . . . .Ezek 32:10
affliction..is but for a ***m*** 2Cor 4:17

MONARCHY—*the rule of a king*
Described by Samuel 1Sam 8:11-18

MONEY—*something accepted or traded as a medium of exchange; currency*

Wrong uses of:
Misuse . . . . .Gen 31:15
Forced tribute 2Kin 15:20
Make interest on . . . . .Ps 15:5
Bribe . . . . .Ps 15:5
Miser . . . . .Matt 25:18
Buy spiritual gifts . . . . .Acts 8:18, 20

Good uses of:
Buy property . . . . .Gen 23:9, 13
Buy food . . . . .Deut 2:6, 28
Give as an offering . . . . . .Deut 14:22-26
Repair God's house 2Kin 12:4-15
Pay taxes . . . . .Matt 17:27
Matt 22:19-21
Use for the Lord . . . . .Matt 25:27

Evils connected with:
Greed 2Kin 5:20-27
Debts . . . . .Neh 5:2-11

or bought with ***m*** of any . . . . . .Gen 17:12
that is bought with thy ***m*** . . . . .Gen 17:13
that were bought with his ***m*** . . .Gen 17:23
and bought with ***m*** of the . . . .Gen 17:27
m with the merchant . . . . .Gen 23:16
for a hundred pieces of ***m*** . . . . .Gen 33:19
espied his ***m***; for, behold . . . . . .Gen 42:27
man's bundle of ***m*** was in . . . . .Gen 42:35
father saw the bundles of ***m*** . . .Gen 42:35
And take double ***m*** in your . . .Gen 43:12
m that was brought again . . . . .Gen 43:12
m that was returned in our . . . .Gen 43:18
m was in the mouth of his . . . .Gen 43:21
of his sack, our ***m*** in full . . . . . .Gen 43:21
other ***m*** have we brought . . . . .Gen 43:22
who put our ***m*** in our sacks . . .Gen 43:22
every man's ***m*** in his sack's . . . .Gen 44:1
the ***m*** which we found in . . . . . .Gen 44:8
Joseph gathered..the ***m*** . . . . . . .Gen 47:14
Joseph brought..***m*** into . . . . .Gen 47:14
m failed in the land of Egypt . .Gen 47:15
in thy presence? for the ***m*** . . . .Gen 47:15
my lord, how that our ***m*** is . . . .Gen 47:18
servant that is bought for ***m*** . . .Ex 12:44
punished: for he is his ***m*** . . . . . .Ex 21:21
give ***m*** unto the owner of . . . . .Ex 21:34
unto his neighbor ***m*** or . . . . .Ex 22:7
If thou lend ***m*** to any of . . . . . .Ex 22:25
buy any soul with his ***m*** . . . . . . .Lev 22:11
out of the ***m*** that he has . . . . . .Lev 25:51
shall reckon unto him the ***m*** . . .Lev 27:18
thou shalt give the ***m*** . . . . .Num 3:48
of Israel took he the ***m*** . . . . . . .Num 3:50
for the ***m*** of five shekels . . . . . .Num 18:16
not sell her at all for ***m*** . . . . . . .Deut 21:14
they took no gain of ***m*** . . . . . . .Judg 5:19
he restored the ***m*** unto his . . . .Judg 17:4
thee the worth of it in ***m*** 1Kin 21:2
refused to give thee for ***m*** 1Kin 21:15
The trespass ***m*** and sin ***m*** 2Kin 12:16
made with them of the ***m*** 2Kin 22:7
servants have gathered the ***m*** . .2Kin 22:9
taxed the land to give the ***m*** . . .2Kin 23:35
all Israel ***m*** to repair the 2Chr 24:5
saw that there was much ***m*** 2Chr 24:11
gathered ***m*** in abundance 2Chr 24:11
delivered the ***m*** that was 2Chr 34:9
they gathered together the ***m*** . .2Chr 34:17
They gave ***m*** also unto the . . . .Ezra 3:7
buy speedily with this ***m*** . . . . . .Ezra 7:17
the ***m*** that Haman had . . . . .Esth 4:7
the fruits thereof without ***m*** . . .Job 31:39
gave him a piece of ***m*** . . . . .Job 42:11
hath taken a bag of ***m*** with . . . .Prov 7:20

M

is a defense and ***m*** is a........Eccl 7:12
m answereth all things........Eccl 10:19
me no sweet cane with ***m***.....Is 43:24
be redeemed without ***m***.......Is 52:3
and he that hath no ***m***........Is 55:1
milk without ***m*** and without ...Is 55:1
weighed him the ***m*** even ......Jer 32:9
Buy thee the field for ***m***......Jer 32:25
drunken our water for ***m***......Lam 5:4
prophets thereof divine for ***m***..Mic 3:11
that received tribute ***m***.......Matt 17:24
large ***m*** unto the soldiers......Matt 28:12
So they took the ***m***, and did...Matt 28:15
bread, no ***m*** in their purse ....Mark 6:8
the people cast ***m*** into the.....Mark 12:41
promised to give him ***m***.......Mark 14:11
neither bread, neither ***m***......Luke 9:3
thou my ***m*** into the bank......Luke 19:23
changers of ***m*** sitting..........John 2:14
poured out the changers' ***m***...John 2:15
sold it, and brought the ***m***....Acts 4:37
bought for a sum of ***m***........Acts 7:16
hoped also that ***m*** should .....Acts 24:26
the love of ***m*** is the root of ...1Tim 6:10

MONEY CHANGERS—*those who converted money from one country's currency to another*
Christ drives them out ...Matt 21:12

MONOGAMY—*marriage to one person only*
Commanded ....Matt 19:3-9
1Cor 7:1-16
Example of Christ and the Church ....Eph 5:25-33
Demanded of bishop.....1Tim 3:2

MONOTHEISM—*a belief in one God*
Statements of:
The great commandment .Deut 6:4, 5
Song of Moses ....Deut 32:36-39
About eternal life ....John 17:3, 22

MONSTERS—*possibly referring to a sea serpent or some other large marine animal*
sea ***m*** draw out the breast.....Lam 4:3

MONTH—*a measure of time of approximately thirty days*

[*also* MONTHLY, MONTHS]
of Noah's life, in the second ***m***.Gen 7:11
the seventeenth day of the ***m***..Gen 7:11
ark rested in the seventh ***m***...Gen 8:4
seventeenth day of the ***m***.....Gen 8:4
continually until the tenth ***m***...Gen 8:5
in the tenth ***m***, on the first ....Gen 8:5
on the first day of the ***m***......Gen 8:5
first year, in the first ***m***.......Gen 8:13
the first day of the ***m***.........Gen 8:13
And in the second ***m***, on.......Gen 8:14
and twentieth day of the ***m***....Gen 8:14
came to pass about three ***m***...Gen 38:24
child, she hid him three ***m***....Ex 2:2
This ***m*** shall be unto you.......Ex 12:2
be the first ***m*** of the year .....Ex 12:2
fourteenth day of the same ***m***.Ex 12:6
first ***m***, on the fourteenth .....Ex 12:18
fourteenth day of the ***m*** at ....Ex 12:18
and twentieth day of the ***m***....Ex 12:18
keep this service in this ***m***.....Ex 13:5
In the third ***m***, when the ......Ex 19:1
in the time of the ***m*** Abib.....Ex 34:18
the ***m*** Abib thou camest ......Ex 34:18
in the first ***m*** of the second....Ex 40:17
on the first day of the ***m***......Ex 40:17
m, on the tenth day of the ***m***..Lev 16:29
fifteenth day of the same ***m***...Lev 23:6
tenth day of this seventh ***m***....Lev 23:27
in the ninth day of the ***m***.....Lev 23:32
fifteenth day of the seventh ***m***.Lev 23:39
tenth day of the seventh ***m***....Lev 25:9
first day of the second ***m***......Num 1:1
from a ***m*** old and upward .....Num 3:22
names, from a ***m*** old and .....Num 3:43
fourteenth day of this ***m***......Num 9:3
fourteenth day of the second ***m***.Num 9:11
the beginnings of your ***m***......Num 10:10
twentieth day of the second ***m***.Num 10:11
they may eat a whole ***m***........Num 11:21
desert of Zin in the first ***m***....Num 20:1
males from a ***m*** old and.......Num 26:62
throughout the ***m*** of the ......Num 28:14
fourteenth day of the first ***m***..Num 28:16
And in the seventh ***m***, on.....Num 29:1
first day of the ***m***, ye shall ....Num 29:1
tenth day of this seventh ***m***....Num 29:7
from Rameses in the first ***m***...Num 33:3
the first day of the ***m***.........Deut 1:3
Observe the ***m*** of Abib, and...Deut 16:1
in the ***m*** of Abib the Lord ....Deut 16:1
tenth day of the first ***m***.......Josh 4:19
let me alone two ***m***, that I ....Judg 11:37
to pass at the end of two ***m***...Judg 11:39
in the rock Rimmon four ***m***...Judg 20:47
of the Philistines seven ***m***.....1Sam 6:1
the second day of the ***m***......1Sam 20:27
of Obed-edom..three ***m***.......2Sam 6:11
flee three ***m*** before thine......2Sam 24:13
each man his ***m*** in a year 1Kin 4:7
ten thousand a ***m*** by..........1Kin 5:14
Lebanon, and two ***m*** at home .1Kin 5:14
m Zif which is the second ***m***...1Kin 6:1
eleventh year, in the ***m*** Bul ...1Kin 6:38
Bul, which is the eighth ***m***....1Kin 6:38
feast of the ***m*** Ethanim 1Kin 8:2
which is the seventh ***m***........1Kin 8:2
a feast in the eighth ***m***........1Kin 12:32
the fifteenth day of the ***m***.....1Kin 12:32
fifteenth day of the eighth ***m***..1Kin 12:33
even in the ***m*** which he had ...1Kin 12:33
reign..in Samaria six ***m***........2Kin 15:8
ninth day of the fourth ***m***.....2Kin 25:3
to pass in the seventh ***m***......2Kin 25:25
of Judah in the twelfth ***m***.....2Kin 25:27
twentieth day of the ***m***.........2Kin 25:27
seven years and six ***m***.........1Chr 3:4
over Jordan in the first ***m***.....1Chr 12:15
three ***m*** to be destroyed.......1Chr 21:12
first ***m*** was Jashobeam 1Chr 27:2
course of the second ***m*** was ...1Chr 27:4
the fourth ***m*** was Asahel 1Chr 27:7
for the sixth ***m*** was Ira........1Chr 27:9
eighth ***m*** was Sibbecai the 1Chr 27:11
the tenth ***m*** was Maharai......1Chr 27:13
the twelfth ***m*** was Haldai......1Chr 27:15
second day of the second ***m***....2Chr 3:2
day of the seventh ***m***.........2Chr 7:10
of his reign in the first ***m***.....2Chr 29:3
first day of the first ***m*** to......2Chr 29:17
on the eighth day of the ***m***....2Chr 29:17
sixteenth day of the first ***m***....2Chr 20:17
bread in the second ***m***.........2Chr 30:13
the third ***m*** they began to 2Chr 31:7
them in the seventh ***m***.........2Chr 31:7
he reigned three ***m*** in.........2Chr 36:2
the seventh ***m*** was come ....Ezra 3:1
m, began Zerubbabel the .....Ezra 3:6
fourteenth day of the first ***m***..Ezra 6:19
first day of the first ***m***........Ezra 7:9
twelfth day of the first ***m***......Ezra 8:31
ninth ***m*** on the twentieth ......Ezra 10:9
twentieth day of the ***m***........Ezra 10:9
by the first day of the first ***m***..Ezra 10:17
to pass in the ***m*** Chisleu .....Neh 1:1
and fifth day of the ***m*** Elul....Neh 6:15
first day of the seventh ***m***.....Neh 8:2
and fourth day of this ***m***......Neh 9:1
she had been twelve ***m***........Esth 2:12
to wit, six ***m*** with oil of ....Esth 2:12
m with sweet odors ....Esth 2:12
which is the ***m*** Tebeth ....Esth 2:16
the first ***m***..the ***m*** Nisan ....Esth 3:7
to day, and from ***m*** to ***m***......Esth 3:7
twelfth ***m*** that is, the ***m*** Adar..Esth 3:7
twelfth ***m***..the ***m*** Adar ....Esth 3:13
twelfth ***m***..the ***m*** Adar ....Esth 8:12
fourteenth day..***m*** Adar ....Esth 9:15
fourteenth day..***m*** Adar ....Esth 9:19
the ***m*** which was turned........Esth 9:22
into the number of the ***m*** .....Job 3:6
number of his ***m*** are with .....Job 14:5
that I were as in ***m*** past.......Job 29:2
m prognosticators, stand ......Is 47:13
captive in the fifth ***m***.........Jer 1:3
year and in the fifth ***m***........Jer 28:1
the ninth ***m*** that they ....Jer 36:9
m came Nebuchadrezzar ....Jer 39:1
to pass in the seventh ***m***......Jer 41:1
the ninth day of the ***m***........Jer 52:6
twelfth ***m*** in the five ....Jer 52:31
thirtieth year, the fourth ***m***....Ezek 1:1
in the fifth day of the ***m*** as....Ezek 1:1
sixth year, in the sixth ***m***......Ezek 8:1
In the fifth day of the ***m***......Ezek 8:1
seventh year, in the fifth ***m***....Ezek 20:1
tenth day of the ***m***, that.......Ezek 20:1
ninth year, in the tenth ***m***.....Ezek 24:1
in the tenth day of the ***m***.....Ezek 24:1
tenth year, in the tenth ***m***.....Ezek 29:1
in the twelfth day of the ***m***....Ezek 29:1
twentieth year in the first ***m***...Ezek 29:17
in the first day of the ***m***.......Ezek 29:17
eleventh year in the first ***m***....Ezek 30:20
in the seventh day of the ***m***...Ezek 30:20
eleventh year in the third ***m***...Ezek 31:1
in the first day of the ***m***.......Ezek 31:1
the twelfth year..twelfth ***m***....Ezek 32:1
in the first day of the ***m***.......Ezek 32:1
captivity, in the tenth ***m***......Ezek 33:21
seven ***m*** shall the house of ....Ezek 39:12
in the tenth day of the ***m***.....Ezek 40:1
Lord God, in the first ***m***......Ezek 45:18
in the first day of the ***m***.......Ezek 45:18
first ***m*** in the fourteenth ......Ezek 45:21
fourteenth day of the ***m***.......Ezek 45:21
In the seventh ***m*** in the ....Ezek 45:25
the fifteenth day of the ***m***.....Ezek 45:25
fruit according to his ***m***.......Ezek 47:12
At the end of the twelve ***m***...Dan 4:29
twentieth day of the first ***m***...Dan 10:4
now shall a ***m*** devour them....Hos 5:7
latter rain in the first ***m***......Joel 2:23
were yet three ***m*** to the ....Amos 4:7
m, in the first day of the ***m***...Hag 1:1
In the seventh ***m***, in the ......Hag 2:1
twentieth day of the ***m***.........Hag 2:1
and twentieth day of the ***m***....Hag 2:20
eighth ***m*** in the second........Zech 1:1
day of the eleventh ***m***.........Zech 1:7
the ***m*** Sebat, in the second ....Zech 1:7
Should I weep in the fifth ***m***..Zech 7:3
The fast of the fourth ***m***......Zech 8:19
conceived and hid..five ***m***.....Luke 1:24
sixth ***m*** the angel Gabriel .....Luke 1:26
shut..three years and six ***m***....Luke 4:25
There are yet four ***m***.........John 4:35
his father's house three ***m***.....Acts 7:20
for the space of three ***m***......Acts 19:8
after three ***m*** we departed.....Acts 28:11
Ye observe days, and ***m***......Gal 4:10
was hid three ***m*** of his ....Heb 11:23
of three years and six ***m***......James 5:17
tormented five ***m***.............Rev 9:5
and a day, and a ***m***, and a ....Rev 9:15
under foot forty and two ***m***...Rev 11:2

MONUMENTS—*burial vaults*
graves and lodge in the ***m***.....Is 65:4

MOON—*the earth's natural satellite*
Miraculous use of:
Standing still ....Hab 3:11
Darkened ....Is 13:10
Turned to blood ....Acts 2:20
Worship of:
Among Jews ....Jer 7:18
Forbidden ....Deut 4:19
Punishable ....Jer 8:1-3
Illustrative of:
Eternity ....Ps 72:5, 7
Universal praise ....Is 66:23
God's faithfulness ....Jer 31:35-37
Greater light of Gospel age.................Is 30:26
Purpose of:
Rule the night ....Gen 1:16
Marking time ....Gen 1:14

Designating seasons......Ps 104:19
Signaling prophetic events. Matt 24:29
Luke 21:25

[*also* MOONS]
sun..the **m** and eleven ....Gen 37:9
either the sun, or **m**, or any ...Deut 17:3
thou, **M**, in the valley of ......Josh 10:12
sun stood still and the **m** ......Josh 10:13
tomorrow is the new **m** 1Sam 20:5
and when the new **m** was 1Sam 20:24
neither new **m**, nor sabbath ...2Kin 4:23
the new **m**, and on the set 1Chr 23:31
on the new **m**, and on the.....2Chr 2:4
the new **m**, and for the set 2Chr 31:3
both of the new **m**, and of ....Ezra 3:5
sabbaths, of the new **m**, for ...Neh 10:33
the **m**, and it shineth not ......Job 25:5
m and the stars, which ....Ps 8:3
the trumpet in the new **m** .....Ps 81:3
established for ever as the **m** ..Ps 89:37
by day, nor the **m** by night ....Ps 121:6
Praise ye him, sun and **m** .....Ps 148:3
m, or the stars, be not ....Eccl 12:2
fair as the **m**, clear ....Song 6:10
the new **m** and sabbaths ......Is 1:13
new **m** and your appointed .....Is 1:14
round tires like the **m**.........Is 3:18
the **m** shall be confounded ....Is 24:23
light of the **m** shall be as ......Is 30:26
shall the **m** give light unto.....Is 60:19
the **m** shall not give her ....Ezek 32:7
feasts, and in the new **m** ......Ezek 45:17
sabbaths and in the new **m** ....Ezek 46:3
her feast days, her new **m** .....Hos 2:11
the sun and the **m** shall be .....Joel 2:10
sun and the **m** shall be ....Joel 3:15
When will the new **m** be ....Amos 8:5
m shall not give her light......Mark 13:24
and another glory of the **m** 1Cor 15:41
or of the new **m**, or of the ....Col 2:16
the **m** became as blood ....Rev 6:12
the sun, and the **m** under .....Rev 12:1
the sun, neither of the **m**......Rev 21:23

MORALITY—*principles of right conduct*

Of the unregenerate:
Based upon conscience...Rom 2:14, 15
Commanded by law .....John 8:3-5
Limited to outward
appearance ....Is 1:14, 15
Object of boasting.......Mark 10:17-20

Of the regenerated:
Based upon the new birth. 2Cor 5:17
Prompted by the Spirit...Gal 5:22, 23
Comes from the heart ...Heb 8:10
No boasting except in Christ .... 1Cor 15:10; Phil 3:7-10

MORASTHITE (mô-răs'thīt)—*a native of Moresheth*
Descriptive of Micah.....Jer 26:18

MORDECAI (môr'dĕ-kī)—*"dedicated to Mars"*
1. Jew exiled in Persia .....Esth 2:5, 6
Brings up Esther........Esth 2:7
Directs Esther's
movements ....Esth 2:10-20
Reveals plot to kill the
king ....Esth 2:22, 23
Refuses homage to
Haman...............Esth 3:1-6
Gallows made for ....Esth 5:14
Honored by the king ....Esth 6:1-12
Becomes a third ruler ...Esth 8:7, 15
Becomes famous ....Esth 9:4
Writes to Jews about
Feast of Purim........Esth 9:20-31
2. Postexilic returnee ......Ezra 2:2

Nahamaini, **M**, Bilshan........Neh 7:7
while **M** sat in the king's ......Esth 2:21
M perceived all that was ......Esth 4:1
M rent his clothes and ....Esth 4:1
sent raiment to clothe **M** ......Esth 4:4
Hatach went forth to **M**.......Esth 4:6
Esther the words of **M**........Esth 4:9
told to **M** Esther's words ....Esth 4:12
bade them return **M** this ......Esth 4:15
Haman saw **M** in the kings' ...Esth 5:9
of indignation against **M** ......Esth 5:9
so long as I see **M** the Jew ....Esth 5:13
If **M** be of the seed of the ....Esth 6:13
which Haman had made for **M**.Esth 7:9
M came before the king........Esth 8:1
Haman, and gave in unto **M**...Esth 8:2
Esther set **M** over the.........Esth 8:2
Esther..and to **M** the Jew .....Esth 8:7
that **M** commanded unto ....Esth 8:9
the fear of **M** fell upon ....Esth 9:3
of the greatness of **M** ....Esth 10:2
For **M** the Jew was next ......Esth 10:3

MORE—*See* INTRODUCTION

MOREH (mō'rĕ)—*"stretching"*
1. Place (oak tree or grove)
near Shechem ....Gen 12:6
Probably place of:
Idol-burying ....Gen 35:4
Covenant-stone ....Josh 24:26
2. Hill in the valley of
Jezreel ....Judg 7:1

MOREOVER—*besides*
ye **m**, Behold, thy servant.....Gen 32:20
They said **m** unto Pharaoh ....Gen 47:4
God said **m** unto Moses.......Ex 3:15
M thou shalt make the ....Ex 26:1
M the soul that shall..........Lev 7:21
M he that goeth into the ......Lev 14:46
M of the children of the ......Lev 25:45
and **m** we saw the children ....Num 13:28
M it shall come to pass ....Num 33:56
m we have seen the sons of ...Deut 1:28
M the Lord thy God will ......Deut 7:20
M he will bring upon thee......Deut 28:60
M the children of Ammon ....Judg 10:8
M Ruth the Moabitess the ....Ruth 4:10
M his mother made him 1Sam 2:19
M as for me, God forbid 1Sam 12:23
M the Hebrews that were 1Sam 14:21
And David sware **m**, and said .1Sam 20:3
M the Lord will also 1Sam 28:19
M I will appoint a place.......2Sam 7:10
Absalom said **m**, Oh that 2Sam 15:4
M, if he be gotten into a.......2Sam 17:13
M thou knowest also what 1Kin 2:5
The king said **m** to Shimei 1Kin 2:44
M the king made a great 1Kin 10:18
M they reckoned not with 2Kin 12:15
M the altar that was at........2Kin 23:15
m in time past, even when 1Chr 11:2
M I will subdue all thine 1Chr 17:10
M there are workmen with 1Chr 22:15
M David and the captains 1Chr 25:1
M I will establish his..........1Chr 28:7
M the brazen altar, that.......2Chr 1:5
M he made an altar of 2Chr 4:1
M concerning the stranger 2Chr 6:32
M the king made a great 2Chr 9:17
M in Jerusalem did 2Chr 19:8
M the Lord stirred up 2Chr 21:16
M Amaziah gathered 2Chr 25:5
M Uzziah had a host of 2Chr 26:11
M he burnt incense in the 2Chr 28:3
M Hezekiah the king and 2Chr 29:30
M he provided him cities 2Chr 32:29
M all the chief of the 2Chr 36:14
M I make a decree what ye ...Ezra 6:8
M of Israel, of the sons of ....Ezra 10:25
M I said unto the king, If .....Neh 2:7
M the old gate repaired ....Neh 3:6
M from the time that I was ...Neh 5:14
M there were at my table .....Neh 5:17
M in those days the nobles ....Neh 6:17
M thou gavest them ....Neh 9:22
Haman said **m**, Yea, Esther ...Esth 5:12
M Job continued his ....Job 27:1
Elihu spake **m**, and said ......Job 35:1
M by them is..servant........Ps 19:11
M he called for a famine ......Ps 105:16
m I saw under the sun the ....Eccl 3:16
M he hath not seen the sun ...Eccl 6:5
M the Lord saith, Because ....Is 3:16
M they that work in fine ......Is 19:9
M the light of the moon ....Is 30:26
M the word of the Lord.......Jer 1:11
M thou shalt say unto.........Jer 8:4
M the word of the Lord.......Jer 33:23
M he put out Zedekiah's ......Jer 39:7
M Jeremiah said unto all ......Jer 44:24
M he said unto me, Son ......Ezek 3:1
M take thou unto thee an .....Ezek 4:3
M I will make thee waste .....Ezek 5:14
M the spirit lifted me up .....Ezek 11:1
M thou hast taken thy ....Ezek 16:20
M the word of the Lord.......Ezek 17:11
M also I gave them my ....Ezek 20:12
M the word of the Lord.......Ezek 22:1
M this they have done unto ...Ezek 23:38
M the word of the Lord.......Ezek 36:16
M I will make a covenant .....Ezek 37:26
M the prince shall not take....Ezek 46:18
M the word of the Lord.......Zech 4:8
M when ye fast, be not, as ....Matt 6:16
m the dogs came and licked ...Luke 16:21
m also my flesh shall rest .....Acts 2:26
M ye see and hear, that not ...Acts 19:26
M the law entered, that ....Rom 5:20
M it is required in stewards ...1Cor 4:2
M brethren, I declare 1Cor 15:1
M I call God for a record 2Cor 1:23
M he must have a good 1Tim 3:7
M he sprinkled with blood ....Heb 9:21
M I will endeavor that ye 2Pet 1:15

MORESHETH-GATH—*possession of Gath*
Birthplace of Micah the
prophet ....Mic 1:14

MORIAH (mō-rī'ä)—*"bitterness of the Lord"*
God commands Abraham
to sacrifice Isaac here ..Gen 22:1-13
Site of Solomon's Temple. 2Chr 3:1

MORNING—*the first part of the day*

Early risers in:
Do the Lord's will.......Gen 22:3
Worship ....Ex 24:4
Do the Lord's work .....Josh 6:12
Fight the Lord's battles ..Josh 8:10
Depart on a journey .....Judg 19:5, 8
Correct an evil ....Dan 6:19
Pray....................Mark 1:35
Visit the tomb ....Mark 16:2
Preach..................Acts 5:21

For the righteous, a time for:
Joy.....................Ps 30:5
God's loving-kindness ....Ps 92:2
God's mercies ....Lam 3:23

For the unrighteous, a time of:
Dread ....Deut 28:67
Destruction ....Is 17:14

Figurative of:
Man's unrighteousness ...Hos 6:4
Judgment ....Zeph 3:5
God's light ....Amos 5:8
Christ's return...........Rev 2:28

evening and the **m** were.......Gen 1:5
evening and the **m** were.......Gen 1:13
evening and the **m** were.......Gen 1:23
And when the **m** arose ....Gen 19:15
rose up early in the **m** ....Gen 21:14
they rose up in the **m**, and ....Gen 24:54
Jacob rose up early in the **m** ..Gen 28:18
early in the **m** Laban rose .....Gen 31:55
it came to pass in the **m** ....Gen 41:8
in the **m** he shall devour ......Gen 49:27
thee unto Pharaoh in the **m** ...Ex 7:15
Rise up early in the **m**, and ...Ex 9:13
of it remain until the **m** ....Ex 12:10
remaineth of it until the **m** ....Ex 12:10
m watch the Lord looked .....Ex 14:24
And in the **m** then ye shall ....Ex 16:7
and in the **m** ye shall be ....Ex 16:12
no man leave of it till the **m**..Ex 16:19

they gathered it every *m* ......Ex 16:21
they laid it up till the *m*.......Ex 16:24
stand by thee from *m* unto ....Ex 18:14
sacrifice remain until the *m*....Ex 23:18
evening to *m* before the.......Ex 27:21
sweet incense every *m* ....Ex 30:7
ready in the *m* and come......Ex 34:2
and come up in the *m* unto ...Ex 34:2
passover be left unto the *m* ...Ex 34:25
altar all night unto the *m* .....Lev 6:9
perpetual half of it in the *m* ...Lev 6:20
the burnt sacrifice of the *m*...Lev 9:17
the evening unto the *m* ....Lev 24:3
leave none of it unto the *m* ...Num 9:12
abode from even unto the *m* ..Num 9:21
the cloud was taken up..*m* ....Num 9:21
Balaam rose up in the *m*......Num 22:13
the burnt offering in the *m* ....Num 28:23
remain all night until the *m* ...Deut 16:4
Joshua rose early in the *m* ....Josh 3:1
In the *m* therefore ye shall ....Josh 7:14
city arose early in the *m* ......Judg 6:28
it shall be, that in the *m* ......Judg 9:33
her all..night until the *m* ......Judg 19:25
her lord rose up in the *m* .....Judg 19:27
even from the *m* until now ....Ruth 2:7
it shall be in the *m*, that if ....Ruth 3:13
liveth, lie down until the *m*....Ruth 3:13
they rose up in the *m* early....1Sam 1:19
arose early on the morrow *m* ..1Sam 5:4
and spoil them until the *m* 1Sam 14:36
drew near *m* and evening 1Sam 17:16
heed to thyself until the *m* 1Sam 19:2
it came to pass in the *m* 1Sam 20:35
unto Nabal by the *m* light 1Sam 25:34
it came to pass in the *m* 1Sam 25:37
now rise up early in the *m* 1Sam 29:10
as ye be up early in the *m* 1Sam 29:10
then in the *m* the people 2Sam 2:27
by the *m* light there lacked 2Sam 17:22
be as the light of the *m* 2Sam 23:4
riseth, even a *m* without 2Sam 23:4
upon Israel from the *m* 2Sam 24:15
I rose in the *m* to give my 1Kin 3:21
had considered it in the *m* 1Kin 3:21
bread and flesh in the *m* 1Kin 17:6
it came to pass in the *m* 2Kin 3:20
if we tarry till the *m* light 2Kin 7:9
it came to pass in the *m* 2Kin 10:9
they arose early in the *m*......2Kin 19:35
opening thereof every *m* 1Chr 9:27
every *m* to thank and 1Chr 23:30
the burnt offerings *m* and 2Chr 2:4
they rose early in the *m*........2Chr 20:20
burnt offerings *m* and ....Ezra 3:3
the rising of the *m* till the .....Neh 4:21
and rose up early in the *m* ....Job 1:5
shouldest visit him every *m*....Job 7:18
forth thou shalt be as the *m* ..Job 11:17
When the *m* stars sang ....Job 38:7
like the eyelids of the *m* ......Job 41:18
shalt thou hear in the *m* ......Ps 5:3
in the *m* will I direct my ....Ps 5:3
dominion over them in the *m*..Ps 49:14
aloud of thy mercy in the *m*...Ps 59:16
and chastened every *m* ....Ps 73:14
m they are like grass..........Ps 90:5
from the womb of the *m* ......Ps 110:3
the dawning of the *m* ....Ps 119:147
they that watch for the *m* .....Ps 130:6
If I take the wings of the *m* ...Ps 139:9
thy loving-kindness in the *m*...Ps 143:8
our fill of love until the *m* ....Prov 7:18
thy princes eat in the *m*! .....Eccl 10:16
that looketh forth as the *m* ....Song 6:10
that rise up early in the *m* ....Is 5:11
in the *m* shalt thou make .....Is 17:11
m cometh and also the ....Is 21:12
be thou their arm every *m* ....Is 33:2
reckoned till *m* that as a ......Is 38:13
light break forth as the *m* .....Is 58:8
as fed horses in the *m* ....Jer 5:8
Execute judgment in the *m* ....Jer 21:12
The *m* is come unto thee......Ezek 7:7
the *m* came the word of the ...Ezek 12:8
unto the people in the *m* ......Ezek 24:18
I did in the *m* was I as........Ezek 24:18
shalt prepare it every *m*.......Ezek 46:13
every *m* for a..offering ....Ezek 46:15
of the evening and the *m* .....Dan 8:26
forth is prepared as the *m*.....Hos 6:3
m it burneth as a flaming .....Hos 7:6
shall be as the *m* cloud ....Hos 13:3
m spread upon the ....Joel 2:2
bring your sacrifices..*m* ....Amos 4:4
maketh the *m* darkness ....Amos 4:13
when the *m* rose the next day .Jon 4:7
when the *m* is light they ......Mic 2:1
m, It will be foul weather .....Matt 16:3
in the *m* as he returned ....Matt 21:18
in the *m* as they passed ....Mark 11:20
in the *m* the chief priests......Mark 15:1
people came early in the *m*....Luke 21:38
early in the *m* he came ....John 8:2
the prophets from *m* till.......Acts 28:23

MORNING SACRIFICE—*a part of Israelite worship*
Ritual described ....Ex 29:38-42
Part of continual offering .Num 28:3-8
Under Ahaz 2Kin 16:15

MORNING STAR—*the planet Venus as it appears at dawn*
Figurative of Christ:
To church at Thyatira....Rev 2:24, 28
Christ, of Himself ....Rev 22:16
Applied to Christ........2Pet 1:19
Name of Lucifer.........Is 14:12

MORROW—*the next day*
it came to pass on the *m*......Gen 19:34
Lord did that thing on the *m* ..Ex 9:6
rose up early on the *m*........Ex 32:6
the *m* also the remainder......Lev 7:16
leave none of it until the *m* ...Lev 22:30
you from the *m* after the......Lev 23:15
that on the *m* Moses went.....Num 17:8
on the *m* after the passover ...Num 33:3
the manna ceased on the *m* ...Josh 5:12
he rose up early on the *m*.....Judg 6:38
to pass on the *m* that the .....Judg 21:4
arose early on the *m*..........1Sam 5:3
was so on the *m*, that Saul 1Sam 11:11
came to pass on the *m* 1Sam 20:27
m, when the Philistines 1Sam 31:8
Jerusalem that day and the *m*. .2Sam 11:12
m when the Philistines 1Chr 10:8
on the *m* she returned into ....Esth 2:14
on the *m* that Pashur ....Jer 20:3
gnaw not the bones till the *m*. .Zeph 3:3
no thought for the *m* ....Matt 6:34
the *m* shall take thought ......Matt 6:34
on the *m*, when they were ....Mark 11:12
the *m* when he departed ......Luke 10:35
to pass on the *m*, that their ...Acts 4:5
And on the *m* Peter went .....Acts 10:23
ready to depart on the *m* .....Acts 20:7
m they left the horsemen......Acts 23:32
See TOMORROW

MORSEL—*a small piece of food*
Offered to angels........Gen 18:5
Rejected by a doomed
man.................1Sam 28:22
Asked of a dying woman .1Kin 17:11, 12
Better than strife ....Prov 17:1
Exchanged for a
birthright ....Heb 12:16

[*also* MORSELS]
heart with a *m* of bread ....Judg 19:5
bread, and dip thy *m* in the ...Ruth 2:14
piece of silver and a *m* of 1Sam 2:36
have eaten my *m* myself ....Job 31:17
casteth forth his ice like *m* ....Ps 147:17
The *m* which thou hast........Prov 23:8

MORTAL—*subject to death*

[*also* MORTALLY]
smite him *m* that he die.......Deut 19:11
m man be more just than .....Job 4:17
reign in your *m* body ....Rom 6:12
m must put on immortality 1Cor 15:53
m shall have put on 1Cor 15:54
be made manifest in our *m* 2Cor 4:11

MORTALITY—*state of being which results in death*
m might be swallowed up 2Cor 5:4

MORTAR—*a vessel*
Vessel used for beating
grains ....Num 11:8
Used figuratively ....Prov 27:22

MORTAR—*a building material*
Made of:
Clay....................Is 41:25
Slime (bitumen) ....Gen 11:3
Plaster..................Lev 14:42, 45

[*also* MORTER]
hard bondage, in *m* and in ....Ex 1:14
upon princes as upon *m*.......Is 41:25
daubed it with untempered *m*. .Ezek 13:10
daub it with untempered *m*....Ezek 13:11
daubed with untempered *m*....Ezek 13:14
daubed with untempered *m*....Ezek 22:28
into clay, and tread the *m*.....Nah 3:14

MORTGAGE—*something given in security for a debt*
Postexilic Jews burdened
with..................Neh 5:3

MORTIFY—*to put to death*
Objects of:
Law....................Rom 7:4
Sin.....................Rom 6:6, 11
Flesh ....Rom 13:14
Members of earthly body .Col 3:5
Agents of:
Holy Spirit..............Rom 8:13
Our obedience ....Rom 6:17-19

MOSERA, MOSEROTH (mōs-sē'rä, mō-sē'rŏth)—*"bonds; discipline"*
Place of Aaron's death
and burial ....Deut 10:6
Israelite encampment ....Num 33:30, 41

MOSES (mō'zĕz)—*"drawer out; one born"—the great lawgiver and prophet of Israel who led his people out of bondage in Egypt*
***Early life of* (first 40 years):**
Descendant of Levi......Ex 2:1
Son of Amram and
Jochebed ....Ex 6:16-20
Brother of Aaron and
Miriam ....Ex 15:20
Born under slavery ......Ex 2:1-10
Hid by mother ....Ex 2:2, 3
Educated in Egyptian
wisdom ....Acts 7:22
Refused Egyptian sonship.Heb 11:23-27
Defended his people .....Ex 2:11-14
Rejected, flees to Midian .Ex 2:15
***In Midian* (second 40 years):**
Married Zipporah ....Ex 2:16-21
Father of two sons ......Ex 2:22
Acts 7:29
Became Jethro's shepherd.Ex 3:1
***Leader of Israel* (last 40 years; to the end of his life):**
Heard God's voice ......Ex 3:2-6
God's plan revealed to
him ....Ex 3:7-10
Argued with God........Ex 4:1-17
Met Aaron..............Ex 4:14-28
Assembled elders of
Israelites.............Ex 4:29-31
Rejected by Pharaoh and
Israel ....Ex 5:1-23
Conflict with Pharaoh;
ten plagues sent ....Ex 7—12
Commanded to institute the Passover .... Ex 12:1-29; Heb 11:28
From Egypt to Sinai:
Led people from Egypt ..Ex 12:30-38

Observed the Passover . . .Ex 12:39-51
Healed bitter waters . . . . .Ex 15:22-27
People hunger; flesh and manna supplied . . . . . Ex 16:1-36; John 6:31, 32
Came to Sinai . . . . .Ex 19:1, 2

At Sinai:
Called to God's presence .Acts 7:38
Prepared Israel for the Law . . . . .Ex 19:7-25
Received the Law . . . . . . .Ex 20—23
Confirmed the covenant with Israel . . . . .Ex 24:1-11
Stayed 40 days on Sinai . .Ex 24:12-16
Shown the pattern of the tabernacle . . . . .Ex 25—31
Israel sins; Moses interceded . . . . .Ex 32:1-35
Recommissioned and encouraged . . . . .Ex 33:1-23
Instructions received; tabernacle erected . . . . .Ex 36—40
Consecrated Aaron . . . . . .Lev 8:1-36
Numbered the men . . . . . .Num 1:1-54
Observed the Passover . . .Num 9:1-5

From Sinai to Kadesh-barnea:
Resumed journey to Canaan . . . . .Num 10:11-36
Complained; 70 elders appointed . . . . .Num 11:1-35
Spoke against by Miriam and Aaron . . . . .Num 12:1-6

At Kadesh-barnea:
Sent spies to Canaan . . . .Num 13:1-33
Pleaded with rebellious Israel . . . . .Num 14:1-19
Announced God's judgment . . . . .Num 14:20-45

Wanderings:
Instructions received . . . . .Num 15:1-41
Sinned in anger . . . . .Num 20:1-13
Sent messengers to Edom.Num 20:14-21
Made a brass serpent . . . .Num 21:4-9; John 3:14
Traveled toward Canaan .Num 21:10-20
Ordered destruction . . . . .Num 25:1-18
Numbered the people . . . .Num 26:1-65
Gave instruction concerning inheritance .Num 27:1-11
Commissioned Joshua as his successor . . . . .Num 27:12-23
Received further laws . . . .Num 28—30
Conquered Midianites . . . .Num 31:1-54
Final instruction and records . . . . .Num 32—36
Enough . . . . .Deut 3:24-27
Reinterpreted the Law . . .Deut 1—31
Gave farewell messages . .Deut 32—33
Committed written Law to the priests . . . . .Deut 31:9, 26
Saw the promised land . . .Deut 34:1-4
Died, in full strength, at 120 . . . . .Deut 34:5-7
Israel wept over . . . . .Deut 34:8

Character of:
Believer . . . . .Heb 11:23-28
Faithful . . . . .Num 12:7; Heb 3:2-5
Meek . . . . .Num 12:3
Respected . . . . .Ex 33:8-10
Logical . . . . .Num 14:12-20
Impatient . . . . .Ex 5:22, 23
Given to anger . . . . .Ex 32:19

[*also* MOSES']

God said unto ***M***, I am . . . . . . .Ex 3:14
M and Aaron went in unto . . . .Ex 7:10
M took the bones of . . . . .Ex 13:19
M stretched out his hand . . . . . .Ex 14:21
unto ***M***, Stretch out thine . . . . .Ex 14:26
M hands were heavy . . . . .Ex 17:12
Then Jethro, ***M*** father-in . . . . . .Ex 18:2
took Zipporah, ***M*** wife . . . . . . .Ex 18:2
M father-in-law, took a . . . . . . .Ex 18:12
to eat bread with ***M*** . . . . .Ex 18:12
And ***M*** father-in-law said . . . . . .Ex 18:17
And ***M*** went up unto God . . . .Ex 19:3
the Lord said unto ***M*** . . . . .Ex 20:22
M was in the mount forty . . . . .Ex 24:18
Lord said unto ***M***, Hew . . . . . . .Ex 34:1
the Lord said unto ***M*** . . . . .Ex 34:27
of testimony in ***M*** hand . . . . . . .Ex 34:29
ram of consecration it was ***M*** . .Lev 8:29
Lord spake unto ***M*** in . . . . .Lev 25:1
the Lord said unto ***M*** . . . . .Num 3:40
the Midianite, ***M*** father . . . . . . .Num 10:29
M lifted up his hand . . . . .Num 20:11
the Lord spake unto ***M*** . . . . . . .Num 20:12
M called unto Joshua . . . . .Deut 31:7
after the death of ***M*** the . . . . . .Josh 1:1
the son of Nun, ***M*** . . . . .Josh 1:1
we hearkened unto ***M*** in . . . . . .Josh 1:17
thee, as he was with ***M*** . . . . . . .Josh 1:17
the Kenite, ***M*** father-in-law . . . .Judg 1:16
appeared unto them ***M*** . . . . .Matt 17:3
Pharisees sit in ***M*** seat . . . . .Matt 23:2
them Elijah with ***M*** . . . . .Mark 9:4
two men, which were ***M*** . . . . . .Luke 9:30
but we are ***M*** disciples . . . . .John 9:28
In which time ***M*** was . . . . .Acts 7:20
behold the face of ***M*** 2Cor 3:7
as also ***M*** was faithful . . . . .Heb 3:2
M said, I exceedingly . . . . .Heb 12:21
about the body of ***M*** . . . . .Jude 9
sing the song of ***M*** the . . . . .Rev 15:3

MOSES, ORACLES OF—*blessings on the tribes of Israel*
Pronounced . . . . .Deut 33:6-25
Song introduces . . . . .Deut 33:2-5
Song concludes . . . . .Deut 33:26-29

MOST—*greatest; highest*
was the priest of the ***m*** . . . . . . .Gen 14:18
the holy place and the ***m*** . . . . . .Ex 26:33
it shall be an altar ***m*** . . . . .Ex 29:37
that they may be ***m*** holy . . . . . .Ex 30:29
it shall be an altar ***m*** . . . . .Ex 40:10
a thing ***m*** holy of the . . . . .Lev 2:3
the Lord: it is ***m*** holy . . . . .Lev 6:25
offering: it is ***m*** holy . . . . .Lev 7:1
the altar: for it is ***m*** . . . . .Lev 10:12
trespass offering: it is ***m*** . . . . . .Lev 14:13
is ***m*** holy unto him of the . . . . .Lev 24:9
about the ***m*** holy things . . . . . . .Num 4:4
shall be thine of the ***m*** . . . . .Num 18:9
be ***m*** holy for thee and . . . . . . .Num 18:9
the knowledge of the ***m*** . . . . . . .Num 24:16
oracle, even for the ***m*** 1Kin 6:16
of the house, to the ***m*** 1Kin 8:6
work of the place ***m*** 1Chr 6:49
he made the ***m*** holy house 2Chr 3:8
doors thereof for the ***m*** 2Chr 4:22
the Lord, and the ***m*** holy 2Chr 31:14
should not eat of the ***m*** . . . . . . .Neh 7:65
one of the king's ***m*** noble . . . . .Esth 6:9
condemn him that is ***m*** . . . . . . .Job 34:17
name of the Lord ***m*** . . . . .Ps 7:17
hast made him ***m*** blessed . . . . . .Ps 21:6
upon thy thigh, O ***m*** . . . . .Ps 45:3
against me, O thou ***m*** . . . . .Ps 56:2
there knowledge in the ***m*** . . . . .Ps 73:11
M men will proclaim . . . . .Prov 20:6
His mouth is ***m*** sweet . . . . .Song 5:16
an only son, ***m*** bitter . . . . .Jer 6:16
the ***m*** proud shall stumble . . . . .Jer 50:32
how is the ***m*** fine gold . . . . .Lam 4:1
for they are ***m*** rebellious . . . . . .Ezek 2:7
For I will lay the land ***m*** . . . . . .Ezek 33:28
and I will make thee ***m*** . . . . . . .Ezek 35:3
unto me, This is the ***m*** . . . . .Ezek 41:4
Lord shall eat the ***m*** holy . . . . .Ezek 42:13
shall they lay the ***m*** holy . . . . . .Ezek 42:13
holy things, in the ***m*** holy . . . . .Ezek 44:13
be unto them a thing ***m*** . . . . . . .Ezek 48:12
commanded the ***m*** mighty . . . . .Dan 3:20
may know that the ***m*** . . . . .Dan 4:17
great words against the ***m*** . . . . .Dan 7:25
the saints of the ***m*** . . . . .Dan 7:25
and to anoint the ***m*** Holy . . . . .Dan 9:24
he do in the ***m*** strong . . . . .Dan 11:39
return, but not to the ***m*** . . . . . .Hos 7:16
provoked him to anger ***m*** . . . . .Hos 12:14
the ***m*** upright is sharper . . . . . . .Mic 7:4
m of his mighty works . . . . .Matt 11:20
are ***m*** surely believed . . . . .Luke 1:1
them will love him ***m***? . . . . .Luke 7:42
Jesus, thou Son of God ***m*** . . . . .Luke 8:28
Sorrowing ***m*** of all for the . . . . .Acts 20:38
unto the ***m*** excellent . . . . .Acts 23:26
and in all places, ***m*** noble . . . . .Acts 24:3
that after the ***m*** straitest . . . . . .Acts 26:5
it be by two, or at the ***m*** 1Cor 14:27
M gladly therefore will I 2Cor 12:9
yourselves on your ***m*** . . . . .Jude 20
was like unto a stone ***m*** . . . . . . .Rev 12:11

MOST HIGH—*a name of God signifying His greatness*
Melchizedek, priest of . . .Heb 7:1
Applied to Jesus by demons . . . . .Mark 5:7, 8
Paul and Silas called servants of . . . . .Acts 16:17

blessed be the ***M H*** . . . . .Gen 14:20
When the ***M H*** divided . . . . . .Deut 32:8
and the ***M H*** uttered 2Sam 22:14
For the Lord ***M H*** is . . . . .Ps 47:2
by provoking the ***M H*** . . . . .Ps 78:17
art the ***M H*** over all . . . . .Ps 83:18
even the ***M H***, thy . . . . .Ps 91:9
thou, Lord, art ***M H*** for . . . . . .Ps 92:8
I will be like the ***M H*** . . . . .Is 14:14
know that the ***M H*** . . . . .Dan 4:25
M H God gave . . . . .Dan 5:18
saints of the ***M H*** shall . . . . . . .Dan 7:18
M H dwelleth not in . . . . .Acts 7:48

MOTE—*a small particle*
Used in contrast to a beam . . . . .Matt 7:3, 5

me pull out the ***m*** out of . . . . . .Matt 7:4
the ***m*** that is in thy . . . . .Luke 6:41
pull out the ***m*** that is in . . . . . . .Luke 6:42
the ***m*** that is in thy . . . . .Luke 6:42

MOTH—*a garment-destroying insect*

Used figuratively of:
Inner corruption . . . . .Is 50:9
God's judgments . . . . .Hos 5:12
Man's insecurity . . . . .Job 4:19
Man's fading glory . . . . . . .Job 13:28

buildeth his house as a ***m*** . . . . .Job 27:18
consume away like a ***m*** . . . . . . .Ps 39:11
For the ***m*** shall eat them . . . . . .Is 51:8
where ***m*** and rust doth . . . . .Matt 6:19
where neither ***m*** nor rust . . . . . .Matt 6:20
approacheth, neither ***m*** . . . . . . .Luke 12:33

MOTH-EATEN—*eaten into by moth larvae; delapidated*
your garments are ***m*** . . . . .James 5:2

MOTHER—*a female parent*

Described as:
Loving . . . . .Ex 2:1-25
Appreciative 2Kin 4:19-37
Weeping . . . . .Luke 7:12-15
Remembering . . . . .Luke 2:51

Kinds of:
Idolatrous . . . . .Judg 17:1-4
Troubled 1Kin 17:17-24
Cruel 2Kin 11:1, 2
Joyful . . . . .Ps 113:9
Good . . . . .Prov 31:1
Scheming . . . . .Matt 20:20-23
Prayerful . . . . .Acts 12:12

Duties toward:
Honor . . . . .Eph 6:2
Obedience . . . . .Deut 21:18, 19
Protection . . . . .Gen 32:11
Provision . . . . .John 19:25-27

Figurative of:
Israel . . . . .Hos 2:2, 5
Judah . . . . .Ezek 19:2, 10
Heavenly Jerusalem . . . . .Gal 4:26

Duties performed by:
Selecting son's wife ...... Gen 21:21
Hospitality .... Gen 24:55
Nourishment .... Ex 2:8, 9
Provision 1Kin 1:11-21
Comfort .... Is 66:12, 13

Dishonor of, punished by:
Death .... Lev 20:9
Shame .... Prov 19:26
Darkness .... Prov 20:20
Destruction .... Prov 28:24

[*also* MOTHER'S, MOTHERS, MOTHERS']
his father and his ***m*** .... Gen 2:24
because she was the ***m*** of ..... Gen 3:20
and she shall be a ***m*** of .... Gen 17:16
the daughter of my ***m*** .... Gen 20:12
told them of her ***m*** house ..... Gen 24:28
and to her ***m*** precious .... Gen 24:53
be thou the ***m*** of thousands ... Gen 24:60
to Rebekah his ***m*** .... Gen 27:11
brought them to his ***m*** .... Gen 27:14
let thy ***m*** sons bow down ...... Gen 27:29
house of Bethuel thy ***m*** .... Gen 28:2
daughters of Laban thy ***m*** ..... Gen 28:2
Jacob's and Esau's ***m*** .... Gen 28:5
daughter of Laban his ***m*** ...... Gen 29:10
sheep of Laban his ***m*** .... Gen 29:10
flock of Laban his ***m*** .... Gen 29:10
them unto his ***m*** .... Gen 30:14
I and thy ***m*** and thy .... Gen 37:10
he alone is left of his ***m*** .... Gen 44:20
thy father and thy ***m*** .... Ex 20:12
he that curseth..his ***m*** .... Ex 21:17
seethe a kid in his ***m*** .... Ex 23:19
nakedness of thy ***m*** .... Lev 18:7
she is thy ***m***, thou shalt .... Lev 18:7
daughter of thy ***m*** .... Lev 18:9
the nakedness of thy ***m*** .... Lev 18:13
for she is thy ***m***, near .... Lev 18:13
fear every man his ***m*** .... Lev 19:3
take a wife and her ***m*** .... Lev 20:14
or his ***m*** daughter, and .... Lev 20:17
the nakedness of thy ***m*** .... Lev 20:19
father, or for his ***m*** .... Lev 21:11
father, or for his ***m*** .... Num 6:7
he cometh out of his ***m*** .... Num 12:12
whom her ***m*** bare to Levi ...... Num 26:59
Honor thy father and thy ***m*** ... Deut 5:16
seethe a kid in his ***m*** .... Deut 14:21
her father and her ***m*** .... Deut 21:13
damsel, and her ***m*** .... Deut 22:15
daughter of his ***m*** .... Deut 27:22
father and to his ***m*** .... Deut 33:9
my father, and my ***m*** .... Josh 2:13
and her father, and her ***m*** ..... Josh 6:23
arose, that I arose a ***m*** .... Judg 5:7
even the sons of my ***m*** .... Judg 8:19
to Shechem unto his ***m*** .... Judg 9:1
of the house of his ***m*** .... Judg 9:1
Then his father and his ***m*** ..... Judg 14:3
his father and his ***m***, to .... Judg 14:5
came to his father and ***m*** ...... Judg 14:9
told it to my father nor my ***m*** . Judg 14:16
unto God from my ***m*** womb .. Judg 16:17
Go, return each to her ***m*** ..... Ruth 1:8
and Orpah kissed her ***m*** ...... Ruth 1:14
hast left thy father and thy ***m***.. Ruth 2:11
when she came to her ***m*** ...... Ruth 3:16
his ***m*** made him a little 1Sam 2:19
the confusion of thy ***m*** 1Sam 20:30
Let my father and my ***m*** 1Sam 22:3
sister to Zeruiah Joab's ***m*** 2Sam 17:25
to destroy a city and a ***m*** 2Sam 20:19
and his ***m*** bare him after 1Kin 1:6
to Bath-sheba the ***m*** 1Kin 2:13
her, Ask on, my ***m*** 1Kin 2:20
slay it; she is the ***m*** 1Kin 3:27
whose ***m*** name was Zeruah ... 1Kin 11:26
And his ***m*** name was 1Kin 15:2
also Maachah his ***m*** 1Kin 15:13
Kiss my father and my ***m*** 1Kin 19:20
in the way of his ***m*** 1Kin 22:52
father, and like his ***m*** 2Kin 3:2
the prophets of thy ***m*** 2Kin 3:13
And his ***m*** name was 2Kin 8:26
thy ***m*** Jezebel and her 2Kin 9:22
And his ***m*** name was 2Kin 14:2
And his ***m*** name was 2Kin 15:33
And his ***m*** name was 2Kin 21:1
And his ***m*** name was 2Kin 22:1
And his ***m*** name was 2Kin 23:36
his ***m***, and his servants 2Kin 24:12
and the king's ***m***, and 2Kin 24:15
And his ***m*** name was 2Kin 24:18
Atarah, she was the ***m*** 1Chr 2:26
And his ***m*** name was 2Chr 12:13
Maachah the ***m*** of Asa 2Chr 15:16
And his ***m*** name was 2Chr 20:31
Athaliah the ***m*** of 2Chr 22:10
His ***m*** name also was 2Chr 24:1
His ***m*** name also was 2Chr 26:3
And his ***m*** name was 2Chr 29:1
neither father nor ***m*** .... Esth 2:7
when her father and ***m*** .... Esth 2:7
came I out of my ***m*** .... Job 1:21
Thou art my ***m***, and my .... Job 17:14
guided her from my ***m*** .... Job 31:18
when I was upon my ***m*** .... Ps 22:9
my father and my ***m*** .... Ps 27:10
slanderest thine own ***m*** .... Ps 50:20
and in sin did my ***m*** .... Ps 51:5
that took me out of my ***m*** ..... Ps 71:6
is weaned of his ***m*** .... Ps 131:2
forsake not the law of thy ***m*** .. Prov 1:8
the law of thy ***m*** .... Prov 6:20
heaviness of his ***m*** .... Prov 10:1
foolish man despiseth his ***m*** ... Prov 15:20
despise not thy ***m*** when .... Prov 23:22
despise not thy ***m*** when .... Prov 23:22
Thy father and thy ***m*** .... Prov 23:25
to himself bringeth his ***m*** ...... Prov 29:15
despiseth to obey his ***m*** .... Prov 30:17
As he came forth of his ***m*** .... Eccl 5:15
my ***m*** children were .... Song 1:6
wherewith his ***m*** crowned ..... Song 3:11
the breasts of my ***m*** .... Song 8:1
bring thee into my ***m*** .... Song 8:2
My father, and my ***m*** .... Is 8:4
queens thy nursing ***m*** .... Is 49:23
is the bill of your ***m*** .... Is 50:1
transgressions is your ***m*** .... Is 50:1
against the ***m*** of the .... Jer 15:8
concerning their ***m*** that .... Jer 16:3
father or for their ***m*** .... Jer 16:7
my ***m*** might have been .... Jer 20:17
Your ***m*** shall be sore .... Jer 50:12
And his ***m*** name was .... Jer 52:1
poured out into their ***m*** .... Lam 2:12
They say to their ***m*** .... Lam 2:12
fatherless, our ***m*** are as .... Lam 5:3
an Amorite, and thy ***m*** .... Ezek 16:3
As is the ***m***, so is her .... Ezek 16:44
Thou art thy ***m*** daughter ...... Ezek 16:45
your ***m*** was an Hittite .... Ezek 16:45
light by father and ***m*** .... Ezek 22:7
but for father, or for ***m*** .... Ezek 44:25
I will destroy thy ***m*** .... Hos 4:5
m was dashed in pieces .... Hos 10:14
riseth up against her ***m*** .... Mic 7:6
father and his ***m*** that .... Zech 13:3
his ***m*** Mary was espoused to ... Matt 1:18
child with Mary his ***m*** .... Matt 2:11
young child and his ***m*** .... Matt 2:13
young child and his ***m*** .... Matt 2:14
young child and his ***m*** .... Matt 2:20
young child and his ***m*** .... Matt 2:21
he saw his wife's ***m*** laid .... Matt 8:14
daughter against her ***m*** .... Matt 10:35
that loveth father or ***m*** .... Matt 10:37
his ***m*** and his brethren .... Matt 12:46
Who is my ***m***? and who .... Matt 12:48
and sister, and ***m*** .... Matt 12:50
instructed of her ***m*** .... Matt 14:8
Honor thy father and ***m*** .... Matt 15:4
that curseth father or ***m*** .... Matt 15:4
his father or his ***m*** .... Matt 15:6
leave father and ***m*** .... Matt 19:5
born from their ***m*** womb ...... Matt 19:12
father, or ***m***, or wife, or ...... Matt 19:29
Mary the ***m*** of James .... Matt 27:56
But Simon's wife's ***m*** lay ...... Mark 1:30
thy ***m*** and thy brethren .... Mark 3:32
Who is my ***m***, or my .... Mark 3:33
Behold my ***m*** and my .... Mark 3:34
father and the ***m*** of .... Mark 5:40
damsel gave it to her ***m*** .... Mark 6:28
father and thy ***m*** .... Mark 7:10
curseth father or ***m*** .... Mark 7:10
his father or his ***m*** .... Mark 7:12
Honor thy father and ***m*** .... Mark 10:19
and sisters, and ***m***, and .... Mark 10:30
Mary the ***m*** of James the ..... Mark 15:40
Mary the ***m*** of James, and .... Mark 16:1
Ghost, even from his ***m*** .... Luke 1:15
the ***m*** of my Lord should ..... Luke 1:43
Joseph and his ***m*** marveled .... Luke 2:33
Joseph and his ***m*** knew .... Luke 2:43
and his ***m*** said unto him ...... Luke 2:48
Simon's wife's ***m*** was .... Luke 4:38
Then came to him his ***m*** ...... Luke 8:19
My ***m*** and my brethren .... Luke 8:21
the ***m*** against the daughter .... Luke 12:53
daughter against the ***m*** .... Luke 12:53
Honor thy father and thy ***m*** .. Luke 18:20
and the ***m*** of Jesus was .... John 2:1
His ***m*** saith unto the .... John 2:5
second time into his ***m*** .... John 3:4
and Mary the ***m*** of Jesus ...... Acts 1:14
man lame from his ***m*** .... Acts 3:2
in the Lord, and his ***m*** .... Rom 16:13
separated me from my ***m*** ...... Gal 1:15
leave his father and ***m*** .... Eph 5:31
Lois, and thy ***m*** Eunice 2Tim 1:5
Without father, without ***m*** ..... Heb 7:3
Great, The ***M*** of Harlots ...... Rev 17:5

MOTHERHOOD—*the state of being a mother*

Described as:
Painful .... Gen 3:16
Sometimes dangerous .... Gen 35:16-20
Yet joyful .... John 16:21
Object of prayer .... Gen 25:21

Blessings of:
Fulfills divine Law ...... Gen 1:28
Makes joyful .... Ps 113:9
Woman's "preserved" 1Tim 2:15

MOTHER-IN-LAW—*the mother of one's spouse*
Judith's—grief .... Gen 26:34, 35
Ruth's—loved .... Ruth 1:14-17
Peter's—healed by Christ . Matt 8:14, 15

against her ***m-in-l*** .... Matt 10:35
m-in-l against her daughter .... Luke 12:53
against her ***m-in-l*** .... Luke 12:53

MOTIONS—*actions*
the ***m*** of sin, which were ...... Rom 7:5

MOTIVE—*impulse or desire from within which causes a person to act*

Good:
Questioned 2Kin 5:5-8
Misapplied .... Esth 6:6-11
Misrepresented .... Job 1:9-11
Misunderstood .... Acts 21:26-31

Evil:
Prompted by Satan ...... Matt 16:22, 23
Designed to deceive ..... Acts 5:1-10

MOULDY—*musty or stale*
Applied to bread .... Josh 9:5, 12

MOUNT—*to climb*
excellency ***m*** up to the .... Job 20:6
They ***m*** up to the heaven ..... Ps 107:26
m up like the lifting up .... Is 9:18
shall ***m*** up with wings .... Is 40:31
Babylon should ***m*** up .... Jer 51:53
wings to ***m*** up from .... Ezek 10:16

MOUNT BAALAH (bā'ăl-ä)—*"mistress"—a mountain located between Exron and Jabneel*
Part of the territory of
Judah .... Josh 15:11

MOUNT BAAL-HERMON (bā'ăl-hûr' mŏn)—*"lord of Hermon"—a mount on the eastern slope of Mount Hermon*
Lived on by nations that tested Israel .... Judg 3:3, 4

MOUNT CARMEL (kär'mĕl)—*"orchard"—a range of mountains about 15 miles (24 km.) in length in northwestern Palestine*
Prophets gathered together here 1Kin 18:19, 20
Elisha journeyed to 2Kin 2:25
Shunammite woman comes to Elisha 2Kin 4:25

MOUNT EBAL (ē'băl)—*"stone"—a mountain alongside Mount Gerizim*
Cursed by God .... Deut 11:29
Joshua built an altar here . Josh 8:30

MOUNT GAASH (gā'ăsh)—*"earthquake"—a hill in the territory of Ephraim, just south of Timnath-serah*
Place of Joshua's burial . . Josh 24:30

MOUNT GERIZIM (gĕ'rĭ-zĭm)—*"cutters; wasteland"—a high mountain in central Palestine facing Mount Ebal*
Place the blessed stood . . Deut 27:12
Jotham spoke to people of Shechem here ...... Judg 9:7

MOUNT GILBOA (gĭl-bō'ä)—*"hill country"—a mountain overlooking the Plain of Jezreel*
Men of Israel slain 1Sam 31:1
Saul and his sons slain here 1Sam 31:8

MOUNT GILEAD (gĭl'ĕ-ăd)—*"strong; rocky; rough"—a mountain jutting onto the Plain of Jezreel*
Gideon divides the people for battle .... Judg 7:3

MOUNT HOR (hôr)—*"hill"—a mountain on the boundary of Edom*
Lord spoke to Moses and Aaron .... Num 20:23
Aaron died there .... Num 20:25-28

MOUNT HOREB (hō'rĕb)—*"desert"—the range of mountains of which Mount Sinai is the chief*
Sons of Israel stripped of ornaments .... Ex 33:6

MOUNT OF OLIVES—*a hill on the eastern border of Jerusaelm opposite the Temple*
Prophecy concerning ..... Zech 14:4
Jesus sent disciples for donkey .... Matt 21:1, 2; Mark 11:1, 2
Jesus speaks of the signs of His coming .... Matt 24:3; Mark 13:3, 4
After the Lord's supper went out to .... Matt 26:30; Mark 14:26
Called Mount Olivet ..... Luke 19:29; Luke 21:37

MOUNT SEIR (sē'ĭr)—*"tempest"—a mountain range through Edom from the Dead Sea south to the Elanitic Gulf*
Horites defeated by Chedorlaomer .... Gen 14:5, 6

MOUNT SHAPHER (shā'fer)—*"beauty"—a mountain encampment during Israel's wanderings*
Israelites camped at ..... Num 33:23, 24

MOUNT SINAI (sī'nī)—*"a bush"—the mountain on which Moses received the Ten Commandments*
Lord descended upon, in fire .... Ex 19:18
Lord called Moses to the top .... Ex 19:20
The glory of the Lord rested on, for six days .... Ex 24:16

MOUNT TABOR (tā'ber)—*"purity"—a mountain located in the northern part of the Valley of Jezreel some 5.5 miles (8.8 km.) southeast of Nazareth*
Deborah sent Barak there to defeat Canaanites . . . Judg 4:6-14

MOUNT ZION—*"monument; fortress"—a hill of Jerusalem*
Survivors shall go out from 2Kin 19:31
See Zion

MOUNTAIN—*a high elevation of the earth*

Mentioned in the Bible:
Abarim .... Num 33:47, 48
Ararat .... Gen 8:4
Bashan .... Ps 68:15
Carmel 1Kin 18:19
Ebal .... Deut 27:13
Gaash .... Judg 2:9
Gerizim .... Deut 11:29
Gilboa 2Sam 1:6, 21
Hachilah 1Sam 23:19
Hermon .... Josh 13:11
Hor .... Num 34:7, 8
Horeb (same as Sinai) . . . Ex 3:1
Lebanon .... Deut 3:25
Mizar .... Ps 42:6
Moreh .... Judg 7:1
Moriah .... Gen 22:2
Nebo .... Deut 34:1
Olives or Olivet .... Matt 24:3
Pisgah .... Num 21:20
Sinai .... Ex 19:2-20
Sion or Zion 2Sam 5:7
Tabor .... Judg 4:6-14

In Christ's life, place of:
Temptation .... Matt 4:8
Sermon .... Matt 5:1
Prayer .... Matt 14:23
Transfiguration .... Matt 17:1
Prophecy .... Matt 24:3
Agony .... Matt 26:30, 31
Ascension .... Luke 24:50

Uses of:
Boundaries .... Num 34:7, 8
Distant vision .... Deut 3:27
Hunting 1Sam 26:20
Warfare 1Sam 17:3
Protection .... Amos 6:1
Refuge .... Matt 24:16
Idolatrous worship .... Is 65:7
Assembly sites .... Josh 8:30-33

Significant Old Testament events on:
Ark rested upon (Ararat) . Gen 8:4
Abraham's testing (Moriah) .... Gen 22:1-19
Giving of the Law (Sinai) . Ex 19:2-25
Moses view of Canaan (Pisgah) .... Deut 34:1
Combat with Baalism (Carmel) 1Kin 18:19-42
David's city (Zion) 2Sam 5:7

Figurative of:
God's:
Protection .... Is 31:4
Dwelling .... Is 8:18
Judgments .... Jer 13:16
Gospel age .... Is 27:13
Messiah's advent .... Is 40:9
Great joy .... Is 44:23
Great difficulties .... Matt 21:21
Pride of man .... Luke 3:5
Supposed faith 1Cor 13:2

[*also* mount, mountains]
prevail; and the ***m*** were .... Gen 7:20
were the tops of the ***m*** .... Gen 8:5
unto Sephar a ***m*** of the ...... Gen 10:30
unto a ***m*** on the east of .... Gen 12:8
escape to the ***m***, lest thou ..... Gen 19:17
and dwelt in the ***m***, and .... Gen 19:30
in the ***m*** of the Lord it .... Gen 22:14
overtook him in the ***m*** Gilead . Gen 31:23
pitched his tent in the ***m*** ...... Gen 31:25
pitched in the ***m*** of Gilead .... Gen 31:25
sacrifice upon the ***m*** .... Gen 31:54
tarried all night in the ***m*** ...... Gen 31:54
the Edomites in ***m*** Seir .... Gen 36:9
serve God upon this ***m*** .... Ex 3:12
met him in the ***m*** of God ..... Ex 4:27
in the ***m*** of thine .... Lev 15:17
encamped at the ***m*** of God .... Ex 18:5
Israel camped before the ***m*** . . . Ex 19:2
go not up into the ***m*** .... Ex 19:12
whosoever toucheth the ***m*** ..... Ex 19:12
went down from the ***m*** .... Ex 19:14
nether part of the ***m*** .... Ex 19:17
cannot come up to ***m*** Sinai .... Ex 19:23
Set bounds about the ***m*** .... Ex 19:23
trumpet, and the ***m*** .... Ex 20:18
up to me into the ***m*** .... Ex 24:12
Moses went up into the ***m*** ..... Ex 24:15
a cloud covered the ***m*** .... Ex 24:15
the Lord abode upon ***m*** Sinai . . Ex 24:16
fire on the top of the ***m*** .... Ex 24:17
gat him up into the ***m*** .... Ex 24:18
showed thee in the ***m*** .... Ex 25:40
showed thee in the ***m*** .... Ex 27:8
come down out of the ***m*** ...... Ex 32:1
to slay them in the ***m*** .... Ex 32:12
brake them beneath the ***m*** .... Ex 32:19
in the morning unto ***m*** Sinai . . . Ex 34:2
me in the top of the ***m*** .... Ex 34:2
throughout all the ***m*** .... Ex 34:3
herds feed before that ***m*** ...... Ex 34:3
came down from ***m*** Sinai ...... Ex 34:29
came down from the ***m*** .... Ex 34:29
commanded Moses in ***m*** Sinai. . Lev 7:38
in ***m*** Sinai by the hand .... Lev 26:46
spake with Moses in ***m*** Sinai . . Num 3:1
go up into the ***m*** .... Num 13:17
Amorites, dwell in the ***m*** ..... Num 13:29
into the top of the ***m*** .... Num 14:40
Kadesh, and came unto ***m*** Hor . Num 20:22
they journeyed from ***m*** Hor . . . Num 21:4
Aram, out of the ***m*** of the .... Num 23:7
Get thee up into this ***m*** .... Num 27:12
ordained in ***m*** Sinai .... Num 28:6
Kadesh, and pitched in ***m*** Hor . Num 33:37
priest went up into ***m*** Hor .... Num 33:38
they departed from ***m*** Hor .... Num 33:41
From ***m*** Hor ye shall .... Num 34:8
Horeb by the way of ***m*** Seir . . . Deut 1:2
to the ***m*** of the Amorites ..... Deut 1:7
the way of the ***m*** of the ...... Deut 1:19
went up into the ***m*** .... Deut 1:24
have compassed this ***m*** .... Deut 2:3
I have given ***m*** Seir unto ...... Deut 2:5
unto the cities in the ***m*** ...... Deut 2:37
Arnon, and half ***m*** Gilead ..... Deut 3:12
stood under the ***m*** .... Deut 4:11
and the ***m*** burned with .... Deut 4:11
face to face in the ***m*** .... Deut 5:4
your assembly in the ***m*** .... Deut 5:22
gone up into the ***m*** .... Deut 9:9
I abode in the ***m*** forty .... Deut 9:9
came down from the ***m*** .... Deut 9:15
and the ***m*** burned with .... Deut 9;15
unto me into the ***m*** .... Deut 10:1
Lord spake unto you in the ***m*** . Deut 10:4
the blessing upon ***m*** Gerizim . . Deut 11:29
in ***m*** Ebal, and thou shalt ..... Deut 27:4
foundations of the ***m*** .... Deut 32:22
Get thee up into this ***m*** .... Deut 32:49
unto ***m*** Nebo, which is in ..... Deut 32:49
die in the ***m*** whither thou ..... Deut 32:50
thy brother died in ***m*** Hor .... Deut 32:50
call the people unto the ***m*** .... Deut 33:19
Get you to the ***m***, lest .... Josh 2:16
descended from the ***m*** .... Josh 2:23
them over against ***m*** Gerizim . . Josh 8:33
them over against ***m*** Ebel ..... Josh 8:33
that dwell in the ***m*** .... Josh 10:6
the Jebusite in the ***m*** .... Josh 11:3
from the ***m*** Halak, that .... Josh 11:17
of Lebanon under ***m*** Hermon . . Josh 11:17
the Anakim from the ***m*** .... Josh 11:21
and from all the ***m*** of .... Josh 11:21

and from all the *m* of . . . . .Josh 11:21
reigned in *m* Hermon . . . . .Josh 12:5
Baal-gad under *m* Hermon . . . . .Josh 13:5
m of the valley . . . . .Josh 13:19
therefore give me this *m* . . . . . .Josh 14:12
Baalah westward unto *m* Seir . .Josh 15:10
unto the side of *m* Jearim . . . . .Josh 15:10
And passed along to *m* Baalah .Josh 15:11
And in the *m*, Shamir . . . . .Josh 15:48
Jericho throughout *m* Bethel . .Josh 16:1
But the *m* shall be thine . . . . . .Josh 17:18
Timnath-serah in *m* Ephraim . .Josh 19:50
Kedesh in Galilee in *m* . . . . . . .Josh 20:7
and Shechem in *m* Ephraim . . .Josh 20:7
which is Hebron, in the *m* . . . .Josh 20:7
I gave unto Esau *m* Seir . . . . . .Josh 24:4
was given him in *m* Ephraim . .Josh 24:33
that dwelt in the *m* . . . . .Judg 1:9
children of Dan into the *m* . . . .Judg 1:34
would dwell in *m* Heres . . . . . .Judg 1:35
in the *m* of Ephraim, on . . . . . .Judg 2:9
with him from the *m* . . . . .Judg 3:27
and Beth-el in *m* Ephraim . . . . .Judg 4:5
m melted from before the . . . . .Judg 5:5
him in the top of the *m* . . . . . . .Judg 9:25
from the top of the *m* . . . . . . .Judg 9:36
the shadow of the *m* . . . . .Judg 9:36
gat him up to *m* Zalmon . . . . . .Judg 9:48
virginity upon the *m* . . . . .Judg 11:38
in the *m* of the Amalekites . . . .Judg 12:15
he came to *m* Ephraim . . . . .Judg 17:8
passed thence unto *m* Ephraim .Judg 18:13
which was also of *m* Ephraim . .Judg 19:16
of *m* Ephraim, and his 1Sam 1:1
Michmash and in *m* Bethel 1Sam 13:2
hid themselves in *m* Ephraim . .1Sam 14:22
remained in a *m* in the 1Sam 23:14
on this side of the *m* 1Sam 23:26
men on that side of the *m* 1Sam 23:26
a partridge in the *m* 1Sam 26:20
chance upon *m* Gilboa 2Sam 1:6
to the top of the *m* 2Sam 15:32
son of Hur, in *m* Ephraim 1Kin 4:8
thousand hewers in the *m* 1Kin 5:15
nights unto Horeb the *m* 1Kin 19:8
strong wind rent the *m* 1Kin 19:11
cast him upon some *m* 2Kin 2:16
the height of the *m* 2Kin 19:23
right hand of the *m* of 2Kin 23:13
men, went to *m* Seir 1Chr 4:42
Shechem in *m* Ephraim 1Chr 6:67
his sons fallen in *m* Gilboa 1Chr 10:8
the roes upon the *m* 1Chr 12:8
thousand to hew in the *m* 2Chr 2:2
Lord at Jerusalem in *m* Moriah.2Chr 3:1
stood up upon *m* Zemaraim . . .2Chr 13:4
which is in *m* Ephraim 2Chr 13:4
scattered upon the *m* 2Chr 18:16
Beer-sheba to *m* Ephraim 2Chr 19:4
Amnon Moab, and *m* Seir 2Chr 20:22
vine dressers in the *m* 2Chr 26:10
he had built in the *m* of 2Chr 33:15
Go forth unto the *m*, and . . . . .Neh 8:15
Which removeth the *m* . . . . .Job 9:5
the *m* falling cometh to . . . . . . .Job 14:18
excellency *m* up to the . . . . .Job 20:6
he overturneth the *m* by . . . . . .Job 28:9
Surely the *m* bring him . . . . . . .Job 40:20
Flee as a bird to your *m*? . . . . .Ps 11:1
hast made my *m* to stand . . . . .Ps 30:7
is like the great *m* . . . . .Ps 36:6
m shake with the swelling . . . . .Ps 46:3
our God, in the *m* of his . . . . . .Ps 48:1
whole earth, is *m* Zion . . . . .Ps 48:2
I know all the fowls of the *m* . .Ps 50:11
strength setteth fast the *m* . . . . .Ps 65:6
The *m* shall bring peace . . . . . . .Ps 72:3
m Zion, wherein thou . . . . .Ps 74:2
and excellent than the *m* . . . . . .Ps 76:4
foundation is in the holy *m* . . . .Ps 87:1
Before the *m* were brought . . . .Ps 90:2
waters stood above the *m* . . . . .Ps 104:6
The *m* skipped like rams . . . . . .Ps 114:4
the *m* are round about . . . . .Ps 125:2
touch the *m*, and they . . . . .Ps 144:5
m, and all hills; fruitful . . . . . . .Ps 148:9
Before the *m* were settled . . . . .Prov 8:25
he cometh leaping upon the *m* .Song 2:8
goats that appear from *m* . . . . .Song 4:1
I will get me to the *m* of . . . . . .Song 4:6
dens, from the *m* of the . . . . . . .Song 4:8
the *m* of the Lord's house . . . . .Is 2:2
in the top of the *m* . . . . .Is 2:2
dwelling place of *m* Zion . . . . . .Is 4:5
the *m* of the daughter of . . . . . .Is 10:32
destroy in all my holy *m* . . . . . .Is 11:9
a multitude in the *m* . . . . .Is 13:4
the *m* of the daughter . . . . .Is 16:1
as the chaff of the *m* . . . . .Is 17:13
unto the fowls of the *m* . . . . . . .Is 18:6
shall reign in *m* Zion . . . . .Is 24:23
in this *m* shall the Lord . . . . . . .Is 25:6
For in this *m* shall the . . . . .Is 25:10
rise up as in *m* Perazim . . . . . . .Is 28:21
fight against *m* Zion . . . . .Is 29:8
be upon every high *m* . . . . .Is 30:25
the *m* shall be melted . . . . .Is 34:3
that escape out of *m* Zion . . . . .Is 37:32
and every *m* and hill shall . . . . .Is 40:4
weighed the *m* in scales . . . . . . .Is 40:12
from the top of the *m* . . . . .Is 42:11
I will make waste *m* and . . . . . .Is 42:15
break forth into singing, O *m* . .Is 49:13
beautiful upon the *m* . . . . .Is 52:7
For the *m* shall depart . . . . .Is 54:10
the *m* and the hills shall . . . . . . .Is 55:12
I bring to my holy *m* . . . . .Is 56:7
shall inherit my holy *m* . . . . . . .Is 57:13
that the *m* might flow . . . . .Is 64:1
the *m* flowed down at . . . . .Is 64:3
destroy in all my holy *m* . . . . . .Is 65:25
gone up upon every high *m* . . .Jer 3:6
from the multitude of *m* . . . . . .Jer 3:23
affliction from *m* Ephraim . . . . .Jer 4:15
I beheld the *m*, and, lo . . . . . . .Jer 4:24
For the *m* will I take up . . . . . .Jer 9:10
O my *m* in the field, I will . . . .Jer 17:3
and from the *m*, and from . . . .Jer 17:26
upon the *m* Ephraim shall . . . . .Jer 31:6
of justice, and *m* of holiness . . .Jer 31:23
in the cities of the *m* . . . . .Jer 32:44
Tabor is among the *m* . . . . .Jer 46:18
thee, O destroying *m* . . . . .Jer 51:25
make thee a burnt *m* . . . . .Jer 51:25
pursued us upon the *m* . . . . .Lam 4:19
Because of the *m* of Zion . . . . .Lam 5:18
against it, and cast a *m* . . . . . . .Ezek 4:2
thy face toward the *m* of . . . . . .Ezek 6:2
Ye *m* of Israel, hear the . . . . . .Ezek 6:3
the Lord God to the *m* . . . . . . .Ezek 6:3
sounding again of the *m* . . . . . .Ezek 7:7
stood upon the *m* which . . . . . .Ezek 11:23
In the *m* of the height of . . . . . .Ezek 17:23
not eaten upon the *m* . . . . .Ezek 18:6
not eaten upon the *m* . . . . .Ezek 18:15
For in mine holy *m* in the . . . . .Ezek 20:40
in the *m* of the height of . . . . . .Ezek 20:40
to cast a *m*, and to build . . . . . .Ezek 21:22
in thee they eat upon the *m* . . .Ezek 22:9
as profane out of the *m* . . . . . . .Ezek 28:16
lay thy flesh upon the *m* . . . . . .Ezek 32:5
the *m* of Israel shall be . . . . . . .Ezek 33:28
feed them upon the *m* of . . . . . .Ezek 34:13
upon the high *m* of Israel . . . . .Ezek 34:14
they feed upon the *m* of . . . . . .Ezek 34:14
set thy face against *m* Seir . . . .Ezek 35:2
will I make *m* Seir most . . . . . . .Ezek 35:7
will fill his *m* with his . . . . .Ezek 35:8
spoken against the *m* . . . . .Ezek 35:12
prophesy unto the *m* . . . . .Ezek 36:1
Ye *m* of Israel, hear the . . . . . .Ezek 36:1
say unto the *m*,and to . . . . .Ezek 36:6
in the land upon the *m* of . . . . .Ezek 37:22
the *m* shall be thrown . . . . .Ezek 38:20
bring thee upon the *m* of . . . . .Ezek 39:2
sacrifice upon the *m* of . . . . .Ezek 39:17
Upon the top of the *m* the . . . .Ezek 43:12
image became a great *m* . . . . . .Dan 2:35
Jerusalem, thy holy *m* . . . . .Dan 9:16
come, and cast up a *m* . . . . .Dan 11:15
in the glorious holy *m* . . . . .Dan 11:45
upon the tops of the *m* . . . . . . .Hos 4:13
an alarm in my holy *m* . . . . .Joel 2:1
morning spread upon the *m* . . .Joel 2:2
m Zion and in Jerusalem . . . . . .Joel 2:32
the *m* shall drop down . . . . .Joel 3:18
yourselves upon the *m* . . . . .Amos 3:9
that are in the *m* of Samaria . .Amos 4:1
and the *m* shall drop . . . . .Amos 9:13
understanding out of the *m* . . . .Obad 8
every one of the *m* of Esau . . .Obad 9
drunk upon my holy *m* . . . . .Obad 16
upon *m* Zion shall be . . . . .Obad 17
shall come up on *m* Zion . . . . .Obad 21
to judge the *m* of Esau . . . . . . .Obad 21
to the bottoms of the *m* . . . . . . .Jon 2:6
the *m* shall be molten . . . . .Mic 1:4
and the *m* of the house . . . . . . .Mic 3:12
in the top of the *m* . . . . .Mic 4:1
let us go up to the *m* of . . . . . . .Mic 4:2
reign over them in *m* Zion . . . .Mic 4:7
contend thou before the *m* . . . .Mic 6:1
The *m* quake at him, and . . . . .Nah 1:5
is scattered upon the *m* . . . . . . .Nah 3:18
the everlasting *m* were . . . . .Hab 3:6
because of my holy *m* . . . . .Zeph 3:11
Go up to the *m* and bring . . . . .Hag 1:8
upon the land, and upon the *m*.Hag 1:11
Who art thou, O great *m*? . . . .Zech 4:7
from between two *m* . . . . .Zech 6:1
and the *m* were *m* of . . . . .Zech 6:1
half of the *m* shall remove . . . .Zech 14:4
to the valley of the *m* . . . . .Zech 14:5
for the valley of the *m* . . . . .Zech 14:5
laid his *m* and his . . . . .Mal 1:3
come down from the *m* . . . . .Matt 8:1
went up into a *m*, and sat . . . . .Matt 15:29
came down from the *m* . . . . .Matt 17:9
ye shall say unto this *m* . . . . . . .Matt 17:20
goeth into the *m*, and . . . . .Matt 18:12
Galilee, into a *m* where . . . . . . .Matt 28:16
And he goeth up into a *m* . . . .Mark 3:13
night and day, he was in the *m*.Mark 5:5
up into an high *m* . . . . .Mark 9:2
shall say unto this *m* . . . . .Mark 11:23
Judea flee to the *m* . . . . .Mark 13:14
him up into an high *m* . . . . .Luke 4:5
swine feeding on the *m* . . . . . . .Luke 8:32
at the descent of the *m* of . . . . .Luke 19:37
Judea flee to the *m* . . . . .Luke 21:21
out, and abode in..the *m* . . . . . .Luke 21:37
begin to say to the *m*, Fall . . . .Luke 23:30
worshiped in this *m* . . . . .John 4:20
Jesus went up into a *m* . . . . . . .John 6:3
Jesus went unto the *m* of . . . . .John 8:1
from the *m* called Olivet . . . . . .Acts 1:12
spake to him in the *m* . . . . .Acts 7:38
the one from the *m* Sinai . . . . .Gal 4:24
showed to thee in the *m* . . . . . .Heb 8:5
in deserts and in *m* . . . . .Heb 11:38
a beast touch the *m* . . . . .Heb 12:20
ye are come unto *m* Zion . . . . .Heb 12:22
with him in the holy *m* 2Pet 1:18
every *m* and island were . . . . . .Rev 6:14
dens and in the rocks of the *m*.Rev 6:15
Lamb stood on the *m* Zion . . . .Rev 14:1
away, and the *m* were . . . . .Rev 16:20
a great and high *m* . . . . .Rev 21:10

MOUNTING—*rising, ascending*

[*also* MOUNTED, MOUNTS]

for by the *m* up of Luhith . . . . .Is 15:5
the *m*, they are come . . . . .Jer 32:24
m up from the earth in . . . . . . .Ezek 10:19
by casting up *m*, and . . . . .Ezek 17:17

MOURN—*to express grief or sorrow*

Caused by:

Death . . . . .Gen 50:10
Defection 1Sam 15:35
Disobedience . . . . .Ezra 9:4-7
Desolation . . . . .Joel 1:9, 10
Defeat . . . . .Rev 18:11
Discouragement . . . . .Ps 42:9
Disease . . . . .Job 2:5-8

Transformed into:
Gladness ... Is 51:11
Hope ... John 11:23-28
Everlasting joy ... Is 35:10

Signs of:
Tearing of clothing ... 2Sam 3:31,32
Ashes on head ... 2Sam 13:19
Sackcloth ... Gen 37:34
Neglect of appearance ... 2Sam 19:24
Presence of mourners ... John 11:19,31
Apparel ... 2Sam 14:2
Shave head ... Jer 16:6, 7

[*also* MOURN, MOURNED, MOURNETH, MOURNFULLY, MOURNING]

Abraham came to **m** for ... Gen 23:2
The days of **m** for my ... Gen 27:41
loins, and **m** for his son ... Gen 37:34
when the days of his **m** ... Gen 50:4
there they **m** with a ... Gen 50:10
saw the **m** in the floor of ... Gen 50:11
is a grievous **m** to the ... Gen 50:11
evil tidings, they **m** ... Ex 33:4
and the people **m** greatly ... Num 14:39
they **m** for Aaron thirty ... Num 20:29
eaten thereof in my **m** ... Deut 26:14
How long wilt thou **m** ... 1Sam 16:1
And they **m**, and wept ... 2Sam 1:12
sackcloth, and **m** before ... 2Sam 3:31
when the **m** was past ... 2Sam 11:27
And David **m** for his son ... 2Sam 13:37
king weepeth and **m** for ... 2Sam 19:1
day was turned into **m** ... 2Sam 19:2
to the city, to **m** and to ... 1Kin 13:29
and they **m** over him ... 1Kin 13:30
Ephraim their father **m** ... 1Chr 7:22
Judah and Jerusalem **m** ... 2Chr 35:24
he **m** because of the ... Ezra 10:6
I wept, and **m** certain ... Neh 1:4
Lord your God; **m** not ... Neh 8:9
great **m** among the Jews ... Esth 4:3
to joy, and from **m** into ... Esth 9:22
together to come to **m** ... Job 2:11
to raise up their **m** ... Job 3:8
soul within him shall **m** ... Job 14:22
harp also is turned to **m** ... Job 30:31
turned for me my **m** into ... Ps 30:11
as one that **m** for his ... Ps 35:14
I go **m** all the day long ... Ps 38:6
go I **m** because of the ... Ps 43:2
I **m** in my complaint ... Ps 55:2
And thou **m** at the last ... Prov 5:11
a time to **m**, and a time ... Eccl 3:4
go to the house of **m** ... Eccl 7:2
gates shall lament and **m** ... Is 3:26
The fishers also shall **m** ... Is 19:8
call to weeping, and to **m** ... Is 22:12
earth **m** and languisheth ... Is 33:9
unto him and to his **m** ... Is 57:18
like bears, and **m** sore like ... Is 59:11
the days of thy **m** shall ... Is 60:20
appoint unto them that **m** ... Is 61:3
For this shall the earth **m** ... Jer 4:28
make thee **m**, as for an ... Jer 6:26
and being desolate it **m** ... Jer 12:11
not into the house of **m** ... Jer 16:5
swearing the land **m** ... Jer 23:10
I will turn their **m** into ... Jer 31:13
shall **m** for the men of ... Jer 48:31
The ways of Zion do **m** ... Lam 1:4
daughter of Judah **m** ... Lam 2:5
lamentations, and **m**, and ... Ezek 2:10
nor the seller **m** ... Ezek 7:12
neither shalt thou **m** nor ... Ezek 24:16
to cry, make no **m** for ... Ezek 24:17
ye shall not **m** nor weep ... Ezek 24:18
m one toward another ... Ezek 24:18
I Daniel was **m** three ... Dan 10:2
Therefore shall the land **m** ... Hos 4:3
them as the bread of **m** ... Hos 9:4
is wasted, the land **m** ... Joel 1:10
with weeping, and with **m** ... Joel 2:12
the shepherds shall **m** ... Amos 1:2
the husbandman to **m** ... Amos 5:16
your feasts unto **m** ... Amos 8:10
dwell therein shall **m** ... Amos 9:5
like the dragons, and **m** ... Mic 1:8
When ye fasted and **m** ... Zech 7:5
and they shall **m** for him ... Zech 12:10
for him, as one **m** for his ... Zech 12:10
there be a great **m**, in ... Zech 12:11
the **m** of Hadadrimmon ... Zech 12:11
that we have walked **m** ... Mal 3:14
and great **m**, Rachel ... Matt 2:18
Blessed are they that **m** ... Matt 5:4
we have **m** unto you, and ... Matt 11:17
the tribes of the earth **m** ... Matt 24:30
with him, as they **m** and ... Mark 16:10
now! for ye shall **m** and ... Luke 6:25
we have **m** to you, and ... Luke 7:32
and have not rather **m** ... 1Cor 5:2
your **m**, your fervent ... 2Cor 7:7
Be afflicted, and **m**, and ... James 4:9
laughter be turned to **m** ... James 4:9
day, death, and **m**, and ... Rev 18:8

MOURNER—*one who laments*

[*also* MOURNERS]

feign thyself to be a **m** ... 2Sam 14:2
that comforteth the **m** ... Job 29:25
and the **m** go about the ... Eccl 12:5
will make it as the **m** of ... Amos 8:10

MOUSE—*a small rodent*
Accounted unclean ... Lev 11:29
Destructive of crops ... 1Sam 6:5
Eaten by idolatrous Israelites ... Is 66:17

[*also* MICE]

and five golden **m** ... 1Sam 6:4
images of your **m** ... 1Sam 6:5
the coffer with the **m** ... 1Sam 6:11
the golden **m** ... 1Sam 6:18

MOUTH—*the opening in the head for eating and speaking; any opening*

Descriptive of:
Top of a well ... Gen 29:2,3,8
Opening of a sack ... Gen 42:27,28
Man's ... Job 3:1

Exhortations concerning:
Make all acceptable ... Ps 19:14
Keep with a bridle ... Ps 39:1
Set a watch before ... Ps 141:3
Keep the corrupt from ... Eph 4:29
Keep filthy speech from ... Col 3:8

Of unregenerate, source of:
Idolatry ... 1Kin 19:18
Lying ... 1Kin 22:13, 22, 23
Unfaithfulness ... Ps 5:9
Cursing ... Ps 10:7
Pride ... Ps 17:10
Evil ... Ps 50:19
Lies ... Ps 63:11
Vanity ... Ps 144:8, 11
Foolishness ... Prov 15:2, 14

Of regenerate, used for:
Prayer ... 1Sam 1:12
God's Law ... Josh 1:8
Praise ... Ps 34:1
Wisdom ... Ps 37:30
Testimony ... Eph 6:9
Confession ... Rom 10:8-10
Righteousness ... Ps 71:15

[*also* MOUTHS]

hath opened her **m** to ... Gen 4:11
in her **m** was an olive leaf ... Gen 8:11
inquire at her **m** ... Gen 24:57
from the well's **m** ... Gen 29:10
again in the **m** of your ... Gen 43:12
in his sack's **m** ... Gen 44:1
found in our sacks' **m** ... Gen 44:8
it is my **m** that speaketh ... Gen 45:12
Who hath made man's **m**? ... Ex 4:11
put words in his **m** ... Ex 4:15
thee instead of a **m** ... Ex 4:16
law may be in thy **m** ... Ex 13:9
will I speak **m** to **m** ... Num 12:8
earth opened her **m**, and ... Num 16:32
God putteth in my **m** ... Num 22:38
hath put in my **m**? ... Num 23:12
earth opened her **m**, and ... Num 26:10
proceeded out of your **m** ... Num 32:24
of the **m** of the Lord doth ... Deut 8:3
At the **m** of two witnesses ... Deut 17:6
at the **m** of one witness ... Deut 17:6
at the **m** of two witnesses ... Deut 19:15
or at the **m** of three ... Deut 19:15
unto thee, in thy **m** ... Deut 30:14
put it in their **m**, that this ... Deut 31:19
proceed out of your **m** ... Josh 6:10
stones upon the **m** of the ... Josh 10:18
stones in the cave's **m** ... Josh 10:27
putting their hand to their **m** ... Judg 7:6
I have opened my **m** unto ... Judg 11:35
hast opened thy **m** unto ... Judg 11:36
proceeded out of thy **m** ... Judg 11:36
my **m** is enlarged over ... 1Sam 2:1
come out of your **m** ... 1Sam 2:3
put his hand to his **m** ... 1Sam 14:27
thy **m** hath testified ... 2Sam 1:16
words in the **m** of thine ... 2Sam 14:19
is tidings in his **m** ... 2Sam 18:25
And the **m** of it within ... 1Kin 7:31
but the **m** thereof was ... 1Kin 7:31
also upon the **m** of it were ... 1Kin 7:31
spakest also with thy **m** ... 1Kin 8:24
word of the Lord in thy **m** ... 1Kin 17:24
put his **m** upon his **m** ... 2Kin 4:34
judgments of his **m** ... 1Chr 18:12
he spake with his **m** to ... 2Chr 6:4
spirit in the **m** of all ... 2Chr 16:21
Necho from the **m** of God ... 2Chr 35:22
of the Lord by the **m** of ... 2Chr 36:21
of the Lord by the **m** of ... Ezra 1:1
manna from their **m** ... Neh 9:20
out of the king's **m** ... Esth 7:8
from their **m**, and from ... Job 5:15
will not refrain my **m** ... Job 7:11
Till he fill thy **m** with ... Job 8:21
and the **m** taste his ... Job 12:11
Thine own **m** condemneth ... Job 15:6
by the breath of his **m** ... Job 15:30
upon me with their **m** ... Job 16:10
wickedness be sweet in his **m** ... Job 20:12
your hand upon your **m** ... Job 21:5
fill my **m** with arguments ... Job 23:4
their hand on their **m** ... Job 29:9
they opened their **m** wide ... Job 29:23
have I suffered my **m** to ... Job 31:30
I have opened my **m** ... Job 33:2
hath spoken in my **m** ... Job 33:2
Job open his **m** in vain ... Job 35:16
that goeth out of his **m** ... Job 37:2
draw up Jordan into his **m** ... Job 40:23
flame goeth out of his **m** ... Job 41:21
Out of..**m** of babes and ... Ps 8:2
that my **m** shall not ... Ps 17:3
and fire out of his **m** ... Ps 18:8
upon me with their **m** ... Ps 22:13
Save me from the lion's **m** ... Ps 22:21
whose **m** must be held in ... Ps 32:9
by the breath of his **m** ... Ps 33:6
they opened their **m** wide ... Ps 35:21
The words of his **m** are ... Ps 36:3
I opened not my **m** ... Ps 39:9
My **m** shall speak of ... Ps 49:3
my covenant in thy **m**? ... Ps 50:16
my **m** shall show forth ... Ps 51:15
The words of his **m** were ... Ps 55:21
belch out with their **m** ... Ps 59:7
they bless with their **m** ... Ps 62:4
my **m** shall praise thee ... Ps 63:5
and my **m** hath spoken ... Ps 66:14
not the pit shut her **m** ... Ps 69:15
set their **m** against the ... Ps 73:9
I will open my **m** in a ... Ps 78:2
open thy **m** wide, and I ... Ps 81:10
satisfieth thy **m** with good ... Ps 103:5
iniquity shall stop her **m** ... Ps 107:42
For the **m** of the wicked ... Ps 109:2
the **m** of the deceitful ... Ps 109:2
They have **m**, but they ... Ps 115:5
the judgments of thy **m** ... Ps 119:13

The law of thy *m* is better ....Ps 119:72
than honey to my *m* ....Ps 119:103
I opened my *m*, and ....Ps 119:131
any breath in their *m* ....Ps 135:17
to the roof of my *m* ....Ps 137:6
scattered at the grave's *m* .....Ps 141:7
My *m* shall speak the ....Ps 145:21
out of his *m* cometh ....Prov 2:6
from thee a froward *m*........Prov 4:24
not from the words of my *m* ..Prov 5:7
the words of thy *m* ....Prov 6:2
the words of thy *m* ....Prov 6:2
the words of my *m* ....Prov 7:24
All the words of my *m* are ....Prov 8:8
covereth the *m* of the ....Prov 10:6
The *m* of a righteous ....Prov 10:11
covereth the *m* of the ....Prov 10:11
The *m* of the just.............Prov 10:31
A hypocrite with his *m*........Prov 11:9
the *m* of the upright shall .....Prov 12:6
by the fruit of his *m* ....Prov 13:2
In the *m* of the foolish ....Prov 14:3
the *m* of the wicked ....Prov 15:28
wise teacheth his *m* ....Prov 16:23
The words of a man's *m* ......Prov 18:4
A fool's *m* is his..............Prov 18:7
much as bring it to his *m* .....Prov 19:24
his *m* shall be filled with ......Prov 20:17
The *m* of strange women......Prov 22:14
so is a parable in the *m* ....Prov 26:7
flattering *m* worketh ....Prov 26:28
eateth, and wipeth her *m* .....Prov 30:20
Open thy *m* for the dumb .....Prov 31:8
She openeth her *m* with.......Prov 31:26
Be not rash with thy *m* ....Eccl 5:2
labor of man is for his *m*......Eccl 6:7
the words of his *m* ....Eccl 10:13
with the kisses of his *m* ....Song 1:2
And the roof of thy *m* like ....Song 7:9
the *m* of the Lord hath ....Is 1:20
he laid it upon my *m*, and ....Is 6:7
every *m* speaketh folly ....Is 9:17
with the rod of his *m* ....Is 11:4
near me with their *m* ....Is 29:13
my *m* it hath commanded .....Is 34:16
word is gone out of my *m* .....Is 45:23
made my *m* like a sharp ......Is 49:2
kings shall shut their *m* ....Is 52:15
yet he opened not his *m* ......Is 53:7
so he openeth not his *m* ......Is 53:7
goeth forth out of my *m* ......Is 55:11
the *m* of the Lord hath ....Is 58:14
I have put in thy *m*............Is 59:21
not depart out of thy *m* ....Is 59:21
nor out of the *m* of thy ....Is 59:21
nor out of the *m* of thy ....Is 59:21
and touched my *m*.............Jer 1:9
put my words in thy *m*.........Jer 1:9
is cut off from their *m* ....Jer 7:28
the *m* of the Lord hath ....Jer 9:12
thou art near in their *m*.......Jer 12:2
and not out of the *m* of........Jer 23:16
speak with thee *m* to *m* ....Jer 34:3
hast written from my *m* ....Jer 36:6
unto me with his *m* ....Jer 36:18
therein from the *m* of..........Jer 36:32
spoken with your *m* ....Jer 44:25
be named in the *m* of..........Jer 44:26
sides of the hole's *m* ....Jer 48:28
have opened their *m* ....Lam 2:16
Out of the *m* of the ....Lam 3:38
have opened their *m* ....Lam 3:46
open thy *m*, and eat that ......Ezek 2:8
and it was in my *m* as ....Ezek 3:3
to the roof of thy *m* ....Ezek 3:26
abominable flesh into my *m* ..Ezek 4:14
and never open thy *m* any ....Ezek 16:63
thy *m* be opened to him ......Ezek 24:27
shalt hear the word at my *m* ..Ezek 33:7
had opened my *m*, until.......Ezek 33:22
my *m* was opened, and I ....Ezek 33:22
my flock from their *m* ....Ezek 34:10
Thus with your *m* ye have.....Ezek 35:13
near to the *m* of the ....Dan 3:26
and laid upon the *m* of ....Dan 6:17
hath shut the lions' *m*.........Dan 6:22
and a *m* speaking great ....Dan 7:8
came flesh nor wine in my *m* ..Dan 10:3
Baalim out of her *m* ....Hos 2:17
Set the trumpet to thy *m*......Hos 8:1
is cut off from your *m* ....Joel 1:5
out of the *m* of the lion ....Amos 3:12
putteth not into their *m* ....Mic 3:5
m of the Lord of hosts ....Mic 4:4
keep the doors of thy *m* ......Mic 7:5
even fall into the *m* of ....Nah 3:12
tongue be found in their *m* ....Zeph 3:13
weight of lead upon the *m* ....Zech 5:8
his blood out of his *m* ....Zech 9:7
truth was in his *m* ....Mal 2:6
proceedeth out of the *m* ......Matt 4:4
heart the *m* speaketh ....Matt 12:34
unto me with their *m* ....Matt 15:8
which goeth into the *m* ....Matt 15:11
cometh out of the *m*...........Matt 15:11
proceed out of the *m* ....Matt 15:18
in the *m* of two or three ......Matt 18:16
m was opened immediately ....Luke 1:64
proceeded out of his *m* ....Luke 4:22
something out of his *m*........Luke 11:54
I will give you a *m* and ....Luke 21:15
put it to his *m* ....John 19:29
the Holy Ghost by the *m* .....Acts 1:16
by the *m* of all his holy ....Acts 3:21
opened he not his *m*...........Acts 8:32
Then Peter opened his *m* ......Acts 10:34
the Gentiles by my *m* ....Acts 15:7
about to open his *m* ....Acts 18:14
smite him on the *m*............Acts 23:2
Whose *m* is full of cursing.....Rom 3:14
shalt not muzzle the *m*.........1Cor 9:9
our *m* is open unto you 2Cor 6:11
In the *m* of two or three 2Cor 13:1
that I may open my *m* ....Eph 6:19
the spirit of his *m* 2Thess 2:8
delivered out of the *m* of 2Tim 4:17
whose *m* must be stopped .....Titus 1:11
promises, stopped the *m* ......Heb 11:33
bits in the horses *m*...........James 3:3
of the same *m* proceedeth .....James 3:10
guile found in his *m* 1Pet 2:22
m speaketh great swelling .....Jude 16
and out of his *m* went a........Rev 1:16
spew thee out of my *m* ....Rev 3:16
and out of their *m* issued .....Rev 9:17
shall be in thy *m* sweet ....Rev 10:9
proceedeth out of their *m* .....Rev 11:5
earth opened her *m*, and ......Rev 12:16
dragon cast out of his *m* ......Rev 12:16
him a *m* speaking great ....Rev 13:5
And in their *m* was found .....Rev 14:5
come out of the *m* of ....Rev 16:13
and out of the *m* of the ....Rev 16:13
out of the *m* of the false ......Rev 16:13
proceeded out of his *m* ....Rev 19:21

MOVE—*to pass from one location to another; stir; arouse; excite*

Of God's Spirit in:
Creation ....Gen 1:2
Man....................Judg 13:25
Prophets 2Pet 1:21

Of things immovable:
Righteous...............Ps 112:6
City of God.............Ps 46:4, 5
Eternal kingdom ....Ps 96:10

[*also* MOVEABLE, MOVED, MOVEDST, MOVETH, MOVING]

the *m* creature that hath ......Gen 1:20
living creature that *m* ....Gen 1:21
And all flesh died that *m* .....Gen 7:21
upon all that *m* upon the......Gen 9:2
shall not a dog *m* his ....Ex 11:7
all that *m* in the waters ....Lev 11:10
living creature that *m* in ......Lev 11:46
thou shalt not *m* a sickle ......Deut 23:25
They have *m* me to jealousy...Deut 32:21
m his tongue against ....Josh 10:21
she *m* him to ask of her.......Judg 1:14
only her lips *m*, but her 1Sam 1:13
of their own, and *m* no 2Sam 7:10
the king was much *m* 2Sam 18:33
he *m* David against them......2Sam 24:1
the feet of Israel *m* 2Kin 21:8
stable, that it be not *m* 1Chr 16:30
God *m* them to depart 2Chr 18:31
they have *m* sedition..........Ezra 4:15
he stood not up, nor *m* ....Esth 5:9
thou *m* me against him........Job 2:3
the *m* of my lips should ....Job 16:5
is *m* out of his place ....Job 37:1
He *m* his tail like a cedar .....Job 40:17
I shall not be *m* ....Ps 10:6
things shall never be *m* ....Ps 15:5
hand, I shall not be *m* ....Ps 16:8
of the hills *m* ....Ps 18:7
he shall not be *m*.............Ps 21:7
I said, I shall never be *m* .....Ps 30:6
she shall not be *m*: God .....Ps 46:5
the kingdoms were *m* ....Ps 46:6
shall not be greatly *m*.........Ps 62:2
not our feet to be *m* ....Ps 66:9
seas, and every thing that *m*..Ps 69:34
m him to jealousy with........Ps 78:58
that it cannot be *m* ....Ps 93:1
let the earth be *m* ....Ps 99:1
suffer thy foot to be *m*.........Ps 121:3
her ways are *m*, that..........Prov 5:6
righteous shall not be *m* ......Prov 12:3
m his lips he bringeth ....Prov 16:30
the cup, when it *m* itself ......Prov 23:31
and my bowels were *m* for ....Song 5:4
posts of the door *m* at the ....Is 6:4
his heart was *m*, and the ......Is 7:2
trees of the wood are *m*........Is 7:2
Hell from beneath is *m* ....Is 14:9
earth is *m* exceedingly ....Is 24:19
that it should not be *m* ....Is 41:7
and all the hills *m* lightly......Jer 4:24
hammers, that it *m* ....Jer 10:4
whose waters are *m* as the ....Jer 46:7
The earth is *m* at the ....Jer 49:21
that liveth, which *m* ....Ezek 47:9
he was *m* with choler ....Dan 8:7
they shall *m* out of their ......Mic 7:17
was *m* with compassion ....Matt 9:36
servant was *m* with ....Matt 18:27
all the city was *m*, saying .....Matt 21:10
will not *m* them with one .....Matt 23:4
Jesus, *m* with compassion .....Mark 1:41
But the chief priests *m*........Mark 15:11
waiting for the *m* of the.......John 5:3
that I should not be *m* ....Acts 2:25
which believed not, *m* ....Acts 17:5
in him we live, and *m* ....Acts 17:28
And all the city was *m* ....Acts 21:30
and be not *m* away from ....Col 1:23
no man should be *m* by 1Thess 3:3
By faith Noah..*m* with ....Heb 11:7
and island were *m* ....Rev 6:14

MOVER—*one who stirs up a crowd*
and a *m* of sedition ....Acts 24:5

MOWER—*one who binds sheaves*
the *m* filleth not his hand .....Ps 129:7

MOWING—*cutting of grass*
First growth for taxes ....Amos 7:1
Left on the ground ....Ps 72:6

MOZA (mō'zä)—*"origin; offspring"*
1. Descendant of Judah 1Chr 2:46
2. Descendant of Saul 1Chr 8:36, 37

concubine, bare Haran, and *M*.1Chr 2:46
Zimri; and Zimri begat *M*.....1Chr 8:36
M begat Binea; Rapha was his .1Chr 8:37
and Zimri begat *M* 1Chr 9:42
And *M* begat Binea 1Chr 9:43

MOZAH (mō'zä)—*"unleavened"*
A Benjamite town ....Josh 18:21, 26

MUCH—*great in number, quantity, or degree*
for thou art *m* mightier ....Gen 26:16
had *m* cattle, and.............Gen 30:43

Ask me never so ***m*** dowry ... Gen 34:12
was five times so ***m*** ... Gen 43:34
this day, to save ***m*** people ... Gen 50:20
herds, even very ***m*** ... Ex 12:38
remained not so ***m*** as one ... Ex 14:28
gathered ***m*** had nothing ... Ex 16:18
cinnamon half so ***m*** ... Ex 30:23
make it, and too ***m*** ... Ex 36:7
Aaron have, one as ***m*** ... Lev 7:10
if it spread ***m*** abroad in ... Lev 13:22
if the scall spread ***m*** in ... Lev 13:35
Ye take too ***m*** upon you ... Num 16:3
out against him with ***m*** ... Num 20:20
and ***m*** people of Israel ... Num 21:6
not so ***m*** as a foot breadth ... Deut 2:5
carry ***m*** seed out into the ... Deut 28:39
m people, even as the ... Josh 11:4
of Judah was too ***m*** for ... Josh 19:9
with ***m*** riches unto your ... Josh 22:8
with very ***m*** cattle, with ... Josh 22:8
iron, and with very ***m*** ... Josh 22:8
it grieveth me ***m*** for ... Ruth 1:13
then take as ***m*** as thy soul ... 1Sam 2:16
How ***m*** more, if haply the ... 1Sam 14:30
m greater slaughter ... 1Sam 14:30
Saul's son delighted ***m*** in ... 1Sam 19:2
how ***m*** more then if we ... 1Sam 23:3
as thy life was ***m*** set by ... 1Sam 26:24
so let my life be ***m*** set ... 1Sam 26:24
How ***m*** more, when ... 2Sam 4:11
there came ***m*** people by ... 2Sam 13:34
m more now may this ... 2Sam 16:11
the king was ***m*** moved ... 2Sam 18:33
understanding exceeding ***m*** ... 1Kin 4:29
very ***m*** gold, and precious ... 1Kin 10:2
how ***m*** rather then, when ... 2Kin 5:13
there was ***m*** money in ... 2Kin 12:10
innocent blood very ***m*** ... 2Kin 21:16
brought David very ***m*** ... 1Chr 18:8
brought ***m*** cedar wood to ... 1Chr 22:4
Lebanon, as ***m*** as thou ... 2Chr 2:16
they carried away very ***m*** ... 2Chr 14:13
was exceeding ***m*** spoil in ... 2Chr 14:14
spoil, it was so ***m*** ... 2Chr 20:25
Lord is able to give thee ***m*** ... 2Chr 25:9
he had ***m*** cattle, both in ... 2Chr 26:10
So ***m***..the children of ... 2Chr 27:5
assembled at Jerusalem ***m*** ... 2Chr 30:13
gathered ***m*** people together ... 2Chr 32:4
come, and find ***m*** water ... 2Chr 32:4
had exceeding ***m*** riches ... 2Chr 32:27
wrought ***m*** evil in the ... 2Chr 33:6
it is a time of ***m*** rain ... Ezra 10:13
decayed, and there is ***m*** ... Neh 4:10
it yieldeth ***m*** increase ... Neh 9:37
shall there arise too ***m*** ... Esth 1:18
How ***m*** less in them that ... Job 4:19
How ***m*** less man, that ... Job 25:6
hand had gotten ***m*** ... Job 31:25
gave Job twice as ***m*** as he ... Job 42:10
than gold, yea, than ***m*** ... Ps 19:10
praise thee among ***m*** ... Ps 35:18
I am afflicted very ***m*** ... Ps 119:107
With..***m*** fair speech she ... Prov 7:21
M food is in the tillage ... Prov 13:23
of the righteous is ***m*** ... Prov 15:6
How ***m*** better is it to get ... Prov 16:16
m more do his friends ... Prov 19:7
not so ***m*** as bring it to ... Prov 19:24
eat so ***m*** as is sufficient ... Prov 25:16
in ***m*** wisdom is ***m*** grief ... Eccl 1:18
he hath ***m*** sorrow and ... Eccl 5:17
Be not righteous over ***m*** ... Eccl 7:16
sinner destroyed ***m*** ... Eccl 9:18
m study is a weariness ... Eccl 12:12
this day, and ***m*** more ... Is 56:12
nitre, and take thee ***m*** ... Jer 2:22
summer fruits very ***m*** ... Jer 40:12
How ***m*** more when I send ... Ezek 14:21
art infamous and ***m*** ... Ezek 22:5
companies, and ***m*** ... Ezek 26:7
the fruit thereof ***m*** ... Dan 4:12
my cogitations ***m*** troubled ... Dan 7:28
the people shall be ***m*** ... Joel 2:6
and also ***m*** cattle? ... Jon 4:11
and ***m*** pain is in all loins ... Nah 2:10
Ye have sown ***m***, and ... Hag 1:6
have we spoken so ***m*** ... Mal 3:13
be heard for their ***m*** ... Matt 6:7
shall he not ***m*** more ... Matt 6:30
how ***m*** more shall they ... Matt 10:25
where they had not ***m*** ... Matt 13:5
have been sold for ***m*** ... Matt 26:9
began to publish it ***m*** ... Mark 1:45
they could not so ***m*** as ... Mark 3:20
he besought him ***m*** that ... Mark 5:10
and ***m*** people followed ... Mark 5:24
he came out, saw ***m*** ... Mark 6:34
Jesus saw it, he was ***m*** ... Mark 10:14
were rich cast in ***m*** ... Mark 12:41
so ***m*** the more went there ... Luke 5:15
to sinners, to receive as ***m*** ... Luke 6:34
m people of the city was ... Luke 7:12
for she loved ***m*** ... Luke 7:47
from the hill, ***m*** people ... Luke 9:37
how ***m*** more shall your ... Luke 11:13
how ***m*** more are ye better ... Luke 12:24
unto whomsoever ***m*** is ... Luke 12:48
given, of him shall be ***m*** ... Luke 12:48
men have committed ***m*** ... Luke 12:48
And how ***m*** owest thou ... Luke 16:7
least is faithful also in ***m*** ... Luke 16:10
least is unjust also in ***m*** ... Luke 16:10
but he cried so ***m*** the ... Luke 18:39
were ***m*** perplexed ... Luke 24:4
because there was ***m*** ... John 3:23
of the fishes as ***m*** as they ... John 6:11
M people of the Jews ... John 12:9
die it bringeth forth ***m*** ... John 12:24
the same bringeth forth ***m*** ... John 15:5
sold the land for so ***m***? ... Acts 5:8
she said, Yea for so ***m*** ... Acts 5:8
it, no, not so ***m*** as to set ... Acts 7:5
which gave ***m*** alms to the ... Acts 10:2
the church, and taught ***m*** ... Acts 11:26
when there had been ***m*** ... Acts 15:7
for I have ***m*** people in ... Acts 18:10
have not so ***m*** as heard ... Acts 19:2
had given them ***m*** ... Acts 20:2
Now when ***m*** time was ... Acts 27:9
had ***m*** work to come by ... Acts 27:16
So as ***m*** as in me is, I am ... Rom 1:15
M more then, being now ... Rom 5:9
m more the grace of God ... Rom 5:15
grace did ***m*** more abound ... Rom 5:20
how ***m*** more their fullness ... Rom 11:12
as ***m*** as lieth in you, live ... Rom 12:18
who bestowed ***m*** labor ... Rom 16:6
and in fear, and in ***m*** ... 1Cor 2:3
m more things that ... 1Cor 6:3
Priscilla salute you ***m*** in ... 1Cor 16:19
out of ***m*** affliction and ... 2Cor 2:4
in ***m*** patience, in ... 2Cor 6:4
Praying us with ***m*** ... 2Cor 8:4
but now ***m*** more ... 2Cor 8:22
m more bold to speak ... Phil 1:14
Holy Ghost, and in ***m*** ... 1Thess 1:5
gospel of God with ***m*** ... 1Thess 2:2
not given to ***m*** wine ... 1Tim 3:8
coppersmith did me ***m*** ... 2Tim 4:14
not given to ***m*** wine ... Titus 2:3
though I might be ***m*** bold ... Philem 8
made so ***m*** better than ... Heb 1:4
by how ***m*** also he is the ... Heb 8:6
so ***m*** the more, as ye see ... Heb 10:25
we not ***m*** rather be in ... Heb 12:9
m more shall not we ... Heb 12:25
righteous man availeth ***m*** ... James 5:16
being ***m*** more precious ... 1Pet 1:7
the flesh, through ***m*** ... 2Pet 2:18
wept ***m***, because no ... Rev 5:4
How ***m*** she hath glorified ... Rev 18:7
so ***m*** torment and sorrow ... Rev 18:7

MUFFLERS—*elaborate veils*
Worn by women ... Is 3:16, 19

MULBERRY—*a fruit-bearing tree*
Referred to by Jesus ... Luke 17:6

them over against the ***m*** trees ... 2Sam 5:23
in the tops of the ***m*** trees. ... 2Sam 5:24
them over against the ***m*** ... 1Chr 14:14
in the tops of the ***m*** ... 1Chr 14:15

MULE—*offspring of a horse and a donkey*
Breeding of, forbidden ... Lev 19:19
Sign of kingship ... 1Kin 1:33
Used in trade ... Ezek 27:14
Considered stubborn ... Ps 32:9

[*also* MULES, MULES']
found the ***m*** in the ... Gen 36:24
gat him up upon his ***m*** ... 2Sam 13:29
Absalom rode upon a ***m*** ... 2Sam 18:9
the ***m*** went under the ... 2Sam 18:9
m that was under him ... 2Sam 18:9
ride upon the king's ***m*** ... 1Kin 1:44
spices, horses, and ***m*** ... 1Kin 10:25
servant two ***m*** burden of ... 2Kin 5:17
on camels, and on ***m*** ... 1Chr 12:40
spices, horses, and ***m*** ... 2Chr 9:24
their ***m***, two hundred ... Ezra 2:66
their ***m***, two hundred ... Neh 7:68
horseback, and riders on ***m*** ... Esth 8:10
litters, and upon ***m*** ... Is 66:20
of the horse, of the ***m*** ... Zech 14:15

MULTIPLY—*to increase in quantity or quality*

Of good things:
Holy seed ... Jer 30:19
Churches ... Acts 9:31
Word of God ... Acts 12:24
God's wonders ... Ex 7:3
Loaves and fish ... Matt 15:32-39
John 6:1-15

Secret of:
God's:
Promise ... Gen 16:10
Oath ... Gen 26:3, 4
Man's obedience ... Deut 7:12, 13

[*also* MULTIPLIED, MULTIPLIEDST, MULTIPLIETH, MULTIPLYING]
Be fruitful, and ***m***, and ... Gen 1:22
seas, and let fowl ***m*** in ... Gen 1:22
Be fruitful, and ***m***, and ... Gen 1:28
I will greatly ***m*** thy ... Gen 3:16
men began to ***m*** on the ... Gen 6:1
Be fruitful, and ***m***, and ... Gen 9:1
in the earth, and ***m*** ... Gen 9:7
thee, and will ***m*** thee ... Gen 17:2
in ***m*** I will ***m*** thy ... Gen 22:17
I will ***m*** thy seed as the ... Gen 22:17
and ***m*** thy seed for my ... Gen 26:24
be fruitful and ***m***; a ... Gen 35:11
grew, and ***m*** exceedingly ... Gen 47:27
m, and waxed exceeding ... Ex 1:7
lest they ***m***, and it come ... Ex 1:10
people ***m***, and waxed ... Ex 1:20
beast of the field ***m*** ... Ex 23:29
fruitful, and ***m*** you ... Lev 26:9
Lord your God hath ***m*** ... Deut 1:10
that ye may live, and ***m*** ... Deut 8:1
herds and thy flocks ***m*** ... Deut 8:13
silver and thy gold is ***m*** ... Deut 8:13
all that thou hast is ***m*** ... Deut 8:13
he shall not ***m*** horses to ... Deut 17:16
Neither shall he ***m*** wives ... Deut 17:17
m to himself silver and ... Deut 17:17
good, and ***m*** thee above ... Deut 30:5
m his seed, and gave him ... Josh 24:3
all their family ***m*** ... 1Chr 4:27
their cattle were ***m*** in the ... 1Chr 5:9
children also ***m*** thou as ... Neh 9:23
and ***m*** my wounds without ... Job 9:17
If his children be ***m***, it ... Job 27:14
and I shall ***m*** my days ... Job 29:18
us, and ***m*** his words ... Job 34:37
he ***m*** words without ... Job 35:16
Their sorrows shall be ***m*** ... Ps 16:4
also, so that they are ***m*** ... Ps 107:38
me thy days shall be ***m*** ... Prov 9:11
When the wicked are ***m*** ... Prov 29:16
Thou hast ***m*** the nation ... Is 9:3
our transgressions are ***m*** ... Is 59:12
when ye be ***m*** and increased ... Jer 3:16
so will I ***m*** the seed of ... Jer 33:22

M

ye *m* more than the ... Ezek 5:7
I have caused thee to *m* ... Ezek 16:7
passed by, and *m* thy ... Ezek 16:25
thou hast *m* thine ... Ezek 16:51
she *m* her whoredoms ... Ezek 23:19
have *m* your words ... Ezek 35:13
And I will *m* men upon ... Ezek 36:10
I will *m* upon you man ... Ezek 36:11
I will *m* the fruit ... Ezek 36:30
will place them, and *m* ... Ezek 37:26
the earth; Peace be *m* ... Dan 4:1
and oil, and *m* her silver ... Hos 2:8
Judah hath *m* fenced ... Hos 8:14
m visions, and used ... Hos 12:10
Gilgal *m* transgression ... Amos 4:4
m thy merchants above ... Nah 3:16
the disciples was *m* ... Acts 6:1
the people grew and *m* ... Acts 7:17
Holy Ghost, were *m* ... Acts 9:31
m your seed sown, and ... 2Cor 9:10
and *m* I will *m* ... Heb 6:14
and peace, be *m* ... 1Pet 1:2
Grace and peace be *m* ... 2Pet 1:2
peace, and love, be *m* ... Jude 2

MULTITUDE—*a large gathering of people*

Dangers of:
Mixed, source of evil ... Ex 12:38
Follow after in doing evil . Ex 23:2
Sacrifices, vain ... Is 1:11

Christ's compassion upon:
Teaching ... Matt 5:1
Healing ... Matt 12:15
Teaching parables to ... Matt 13:1-3, 34
Feeding ... Matt 14:15-21

Their attitude toward Christ:
Reaction to ... Matt 9:8, 33
Recognition of ... Matt 14:5; Matt 21:46
Reception of ... Matt 21:8-11
Running after ... John 6:2
Rejection of ... Matt 27:20

[*also* MULTITUDES]
be numbered for *m* ... Gen 16:10
thou mayest be a *m* of ... Gen 28:3
increased unto a *m* ... Gen 30:30
be numbered for *m* ... Gen 32:12
I will make of thee a *m* ... Gen 48:4
seed shall become a *m* ... Gen 48:19
According to the *m* of ... Lev 25:16
the mixed *m* that was ... Num 11:4
stars of heaven for *m* ... Deut 1:10
stars of heaven for *m* ... Deut 28:62
upon the seashore in *m* ... Josh 11:4
his chariots and his *m* ... Judg 4:7
grasshoppers for *m* ... Judg 7:12
by the seaside for *m* ... Judg 7:12
the seashore in *m* ... 1Sam 13:5
even among the whole *m* ... 2Sam 6:19
nor counted for *m* ... 1Kin 3:8
be told nor numbered for *m* ... 1Kin 8:5
deliver all this great *m* ... 1Kin 20:28
they are as all the *m* of ... 2Kin 7:13
even as all the *m* of the ... 2Kin 7:13
the remnant of the *m* ... 2Kin 25:11
dust of the earth in *m* ... 2Chr 1:9
and ye be a great *m*, and ... 2Chr 13:8
cometh a great *m* against ... 2Chr 20:2
they looked unto the *m* ... 2Chr 20:24
For a *m* of the people ... 2Chr 30:18
Israel all the mixed *m* ... Neh 13:3
riches, and the *m* of his ... Esth 5:11
not the *m* of words be ... Job 11:2
m of years should teach ... Job 32:7
By reason of the *m* of ... Job 35:9
thy house in the *m* of ... Ps 5:7
no king saved by the *m* of ... Ps 33:16
praise, with a *m* that kept ... Ps 42:4
unto the *m* of thy tender ... Ps 51:1
in the *m* of thy mercy ... Ps 69:13
unto the *m* of the wicked ... Ps 74:19
let the *m* of isles be glad ... Ps 97:1
according to the *m* of his ... Ps 106:45
In the *m* of words there ... Prov 10:19
in the *m* of counselors ... Prov 11:14
In the *m* of people is the ... Prov 14:28
There is gold, and a *m* of ... Prov 20:15
cometh through the *m* of ... Eccl 5:3
For in the *m* of dreams ... Eccl 5:7
and their *m* dried up with ... Is 5:13
The noise of a *m* in the ... Is 13:4
Woe to the *m* of many ... Is 17:12
Moreover the *m* of thy ... Is 29:5
the *m* of the terrible ones ... Is 29:5
So shall the *m* of all the ... Is 29:8
the *m* of the city shall be ... Is 32:14
for the *m* of thy ... Is 47:9
wearied in the *m* of thy ... Is 47:13
and according to the *m* ... Is 63:7
from the *m* of mountains ... Jer 3:23
is a *m* of waters in the ... Jer 10:13
one, for the *m* of thine ... Jer 30:14
a great *m*, even all the ... Jer 44:15
and the *m* of their cattle ... Jer 49:32
covered with the *m* of ... Jer 51:42
the *m* of her transgressions ... Lam 1:5
remain, nor of their *m* ... Ezek 7:11
is touching the whole *m* ... Ezek 7:13
according to the *m* of his ... Ezek 14:4
a voice of a *m* being at ... Ezek 23:42
by reason of the *m* of the ... Ezek 27:16
thy merchant in the *m* of ... Ezek 27:18
making, for the *m* of all ... Ezek 27:18
m of thy merchandise ... Ezek 28:16
he shall take her *m*, and ... Ezek 29:19
make the *m* of Egypt to ... Ezek 30:10
Egypt, and to his *m* ... Ezek 31:2
him fair by the *m* of his ... Ezek 31:9
mighty will I cause thy *m* ... Ezek 32:12
all the *m* thereof shall be ... Ezek 32:12
of man, wail for the *m* of ... Ezek 32:18
draw her and all her *m* ... Ezek 32:20
slain with all her *m* ... Ezek 32:25
comforted over all his *m* ... Ezek 32:31
they bury Gog and all his *m* ... Ezek 39:11
like the voice of a *m* ... Dan 10:6
set forth a great *m* ... Dan 11:11
the *m* shall be given into ... Dan 11:11
shall set forth a *m* ... Dan 11:13
mad, for the *m* of thine ... Hos 9:7
way, in the *m* of thy ... Hos 10:13
M, *m* in the valley of ... Joel 3:14
noise by reason of the *m* ... Mic 2:12
and there is a *m* of slain ... Nah 3:3
the *m* of men and cattle ... Zech 2:4
followed him great *m* of ... Matt 4:25
And seeing the *m*, he went ... Matt 5:1
mountain, great *m* ... Matt 8:1
But when the *m* saw it ... Matt 9:8
But when he saw the *m* ... Matt 9:36
and great *m* followed him ... Matt 12:15
the whole *m* stood on the ... Matt 13:2
Then Jesus sent the *m* ... Matt 13:36
to death, he feared the *m* ... Matt 14:5
send the *m* away, that ... Matt 14:15
he commanded the *m* to sit ... Matt 14:19
disciples to the *m* ... Matt 14:19
while he sent the *m* away ... Matt 14:22
great *m* came unto him ... Matt 15:30
that the *m* wondered ... Matt 15:31
I have compassion on the *m* ... Matt 15:32
as to fill so great a *m*? ... Matt 15:33
disciples to the *m* ... Matt 15:36
they were come to the *m* ... Matt 17:14
And the *m* rebuked them ... Matt 20:31
And the *m* that went before ... Matt 21:9
Then spake Jesus to the *m* ... Matt 23:1
him a great *m* with swords ... Matt 26:47
his hands before the *m* ... Matt 27:24
all the *m* resorted unto him ... Mark 2:13
a great *m*, when they had ... Mark 3:8
on him because of the *m* ... Mark 3:9
And the *m* cometh together ... Mark 3:20
gathered..him a great *m* ... Mark 4:1
and the whole *m* was by the ... Mark 4:1
Thou seest the *m* thronging ... Mark 5:31
those days the *m* being very ... Mark 8:1
saw a great *m* about them ... Mark 9:14
with him a great *m* with ... Mark 14:43
m of the people were ... Luke 1:10
a *m* of the heavenly host ... Luke 2:13
m that came forth to be ... Luke 3:7
great *m* came together to ... Luke 5:15
him in because of the *m* ... Luke 5:19
whole *m* sought to touch ... Luke 6:19
the *m* throng thee and press ... Luke 8:45
disciples to set before the *m* ... Luke 9:16
hearing the *m* pass by ... Luke 18:36
Pharisees..among the *m* ... Luke 19:39
he yet spake, behold a *m* ... Luke 22:47
a great *m* of impotent folk ... John 5:3
a *m* being in that place ... John 5:13
abroad, the *m* came together ... Acts 2:6
m both of men and women ... Acts 5:14
came also a *m* out of the ... Acts 5:16
saying pleased the whole *m* ... Acts 6:5
m of the city was divided ... Acts 14:4
they had gathered the *m* ... Acts 15:30
the devout Greeks a great *m* ... Acts 17:4
drew Alexander out of the *m* ... Acts 19:33
the *m* must needs come ... Acts 21:22
some another, among..*m* ... Acts 21:34
Sadducees: and the *m* was ... Acts 23:7
about whom all the *m* of the ... Acts 25:24
as the stars of the sky in *m* ... Heb 11:12
and shall hide a *m* of sins ... James 5:20
for charity shall cover the *m* ... 1Pet 4:8
a great *m*, which no man ... Rev 7:9
are peoples, and *m*, and ... Rev 17:15

MUNIFICENCE—*generosity in giving*

Measure of on:
God's part ... Mal 3:10
Israel's part ... Ex 36:3-7
Judah's part ... 1Chr 29:3-9
Christian's part ... 2Cor 8:1-5

MUNITION—*rampart; ammunition*
Kept for war ... Nah 2:1

fight against her and her *m* ... Is 29:7

MUPPIM (mŭp'ĭm)—*"obscurities"*
Son of Benjamin ... Gen 46:21
Called Shupham ... Num 26:39
Shuppim and Shephuphan. 1Chr 7:12, 15

MURDER—*the unlawful killing of a human being*

Defined as:
Coming out of the heart . Matt 15:19
Result from anger ... Matt 5:21, 22
Work of the flesh ... Gal 5:19
Excluding from eternal life ... 1John 3:15

Guilt of:
Determined by witnesses . Num 35:30
Not redeemable ... Num 35:30
Not forgiven by flight to the altar ... Ex 21:14

Penalty of:
Ordained by God ... Gen 9:6
Executed by avenger of blood ... Deut 19:6

See HOMICIDE

[*also* MURDERS]
doth he *m* the innocent ... Ps 10:8
ye steal, *m*, and commit ... Jer 7:9
company of priests *m* in the ... Hos 6:9
said, Thou shalt do no *m* ... Matt 19:18
adulteries, forniciations, *m* ... Mark 7:21
committed *m* in the ... Mark 15:7
for *m*, was cast into prison ... Luke 23:19
full of envy, *m*, debate ... Rom 1:29
repented they of their *m* ... Rev 9:21

MURDERER—*one who kills unlawfully*

[*also* MURDERERS]
so that he die, he is a *m* ... Num 35:16
the *m* shall surely be put to ... Num 35:16
die, and he die, he is a *m* ... Num 35:17
the *m* shall surely be put to ... Num 35:17
die, and he die, he is a *m* ... Num 35:18
the *m* shall surely be put to ... Num 35:18
for he is a *m*: the revenger ... Num 35:21

shall slay the *m*, when he .....Num 35:21
satisfaction..life of a *m* ....Num 35:31
son of a *m* hath sent to take ..2Kin 6:32
children of the *m* he slew 2Kin 14:6
m rising with the light ....Job 24:14
lodged in it; but now *m* ....Is 1:21
is wearied because of *m* ....Jer 4:31
bring.. his children to the *m* ...Hos 9:13
and destroyed those *m* ....Matt 22:7
He was a *m* from the ....John 8:44
desired a *m* to be granted .....Acts 3:14
now the betrayers and *m* ......Acts 7:52
profane, for *m* of fathers 1Tim 1:9
m of mothers, for manslayers ..1Tim 1:9
none of you suffer as a *m* 1Pet 4:15
and the abominable, and *m* ...Rev 21:8

MURMUR—*to grumble; sullen dissatisfaction*

Caused by:

Thirst ....Ex 15:24
Hunger ....Ex 16:2, 3, 8
Fear....................Num 14:1-4

Against Christ, because of His:

Practices ....Luke 15:1, 2
Pronouncements ....John 6:41-61

Of Christians:

Provoked ....Acts 6:1
Forbidden ....John 6:43
Excluded ....Phil 2:14

[*also* MURMURED, MURMURINGS]

heareth your *m* against the ....Ex 16:7
for he hath heard your *m* .....Ex 16:9
heard the *m* of the children ...Ex 16:12
and the people *m* against.......Ex 17:3
congregation which *m* ....Num 14:27
heard the *m* of the children ...Num 14:27
which they *m* against me ......Num 14:27
which have *m* against me......Num 14:29
is Aaron, that ye *m* against....Num 16:11
children of Israel *m* against....Num 16:41
quite take away their *m* ....Num 17:10
And ye *m* in your tents, and ..Deut 1:27
all..*m* against the princes .....Josh 9:18
But *m* in their tents, and ......Ps 106:25
that *m* shall learn doctrine ....Is 29:24
m against the goodman of .....Matt 20:11
And they *m* against her ....Mark 14:5
Pharisees *m* against his ....Luke 5:30
the Pharisees and scribes *m* ...Luke 15:2
they saw it, they all *m* ....Luke 19:7
M not among yourselves ......John 6:43
much *m* among the people ....John 7:12
that the people *m* such ....John 7:32
arose a *m* of the Grecians .....Acts 6:1
Neither *m* ye, as some of 1Cor 10:10
as some of them also *m* 1Cor 10:10
Do all things without *m* ....Phil 2:14

MURMURERS—*those who complain*

These are *m*, complainers .....Jude 16

MURRAIN—*pestilence*

Fifth Egyptian plague ....Ex 9:1-6

MUSE—*to question; meditate*

[*also* MUSED, MUSING]

while I was *m* the fire burned. .Ps 39:3
m on the work of thy hands ...Ps 143:5
all men *m* in their hearts of ...Luke 3:15

MUSHI (mōō'shī)—*"drawn out; deserted"*

Son of Merari ....Ex 6:19
Descendants of, called Mushites .... {Num 3:33; Num 26:58}

of Merari; Mehali and *M*......Ex 6:19
their families; Mahli, and *M*...Num 3:20
of Merari; Mahli, and *M* 1Chr 6:19
of Merari; Mahli, and *M* 1Chr 23:21
Merari were Mahli and *M* 1Chr 24:26

MUSIC—*sounds containing rhythm, melody, or harmony*

Used in:

Farewells ....Gen 31:27
Entertainments ....Is 5:12
Weddings ....Jer 7:34
Funerals ....Matt 9:18, 23
Sacred processions 1Chr 13:6-8
Victory celebrations .....Ex 15:20, 21
Coronation services 2Chr 23:11, 13
Dedication services 2Chr 5:11-13

Influence of, upon:

Mental disorders 1Sam 16:14-17, 23
Sorrowful ....Ps 137:1-4

List of instruments of:

Cornet ....Dan 3:5, 7
Cymbal 1Cor 13:1
Dulcimer ....Dan 3:5, 10, 15
Harp 1Sam 16:16, 23
Organ ....Ps 150:4
Pipe ....Is 30:29
Psaltery................1Sam 10:5
Sackbut.................Dan 3:5, 7, 10
Timbrel.................Gen 31:27; Ex 15:20
Trumpet ....Josh 6:4
Viol ....Is 5:12
Complete orchestra 2Sam 6:5

[*also* MUSICAL]

and with instruments of *m*.....1Sam 18:6
with instruments of *m*.........1Chr 15:16
with *m* instruments of God 1Chr 16:42
instruments of *m* of the 2Chr 7:6
skill of instruments of *m* 2Chr 34:12
the *m* instruments of David ...Neh 12:36
m instruments, and that ....Eccl 2:8
all the daughters of *m* ....Eccl 12:4
rising up; I am their *m*........Lam 3:63
young men from their *m* ......Lam 5:14
dulcimer and all kinds of *m* ...Dan 3:10
neither were instruments of *m* .Dan 6:18
themselves instruments of *m* ...Amos 6:5
he heard *m* and dancing ......Luke 15:25

MUSIC IN CHRISTIAN WORSHIP

From heart ....Eph 5:19
Means of teaching ....Col 3:16

MUSICIAN—*a player of a musical instrument*

according to the chief *M* with..Ps 4:*title*
chief *M* ....Ps 9:*title*
To the chief *M*, A Psalm of ...Ps 11:*title*
chief *M* upon Sheminith.......Ps 12:*title*
the chief *M* upon Aijeleth .....Ps 22:*title*
To the chief *M*, Maschil ....Ps 42:*title*
chief *M* upon Shoshannim .....Ps 45:*title*
chief *M* upon Mahalath ....Ps 53:*title*
To the chief *M* upon Jonath ...Ps 56:*title*
To the chief *M*, Al-taschith....Ps 57:*title*
the chief *M* upon Shushan.....Ps 60:*title*
the chief *M* upon Neginah.....Ps 61:*title*
the chief *M*, to Jeduthun ......Ps 62:*title*
the chief *M* upon Gittith ......Ps 81:*title*
of harpers, and *m*, and of .....Rev 18:22

MUSICK—*See* MUSIC

MUST—*imperative; to have to*

Concerning Christ's:

Preaching ....Luke 4:43
Suffering...............Matt 16:21
Death ....John 3:14
Fulfillment of Scripture ..Matt 26:54
Resurrection ....John 20:9
Ascension...............Acts 3:21
Reign 1Cor 15:25

Concerning the believer's:

Belief ....Heb 11:6
Regeneration............John 3:7
Salvation ....Acts 4:12
Worship ....John 4:24
Duty ....Acts 9:6
Suffering...............Acts 9:16
Mission ....Acts 19:21
Moral life..............Titus 1:7
Inner life 2Tim 2:24
Judgment 2Cor 5:10

Concerning prophecy:

Gospel's proclamation ...Mark 13:10
Gentiles' inclusion ....John 10:16
Earth's tribulations ......Matt 24:6
Resurrection 1Cor 15:53

Laban said, It *m* not be so ....Gen 29:26
Thou *m* come in unto me .....Gen 30:16
If it *m* be so now, do this .....Gen 43:11
drew nigh that Israel *m* die....Gen 47:29
for we *m* hold a feast unto ....Ex 10:9
thereof *m* we take to serve ....Ex 10:26
what we *m* serve the Lord ....Ex 10:26
that which every man *m* eat ...Ex 12:16
m walk, and the work that ....Ex 18:20
it *m* be put into water, and....Lev 11:32
ye *m* eat unleavened bread ....Lev 23:6
so he *m* do after the law of ...Num 6:21
m the children of Israel ....Num 18:22
m we fetch you water out of ..Num 20:10
M I not take heed to speak ..Num 23:12
Lord speaketh, that I *m* do?...Num 23:26
again by what way we *m* go ...Deut 1:22
But I *m* die in this land ....Deut 4:22
I *m* not go over Jordan: but ...Deut 4:22
m eat them before the Lord ...Deut 12:18
thou *m* go with this people ....Deut 31:7
the way by which ye *m* go ....Josh 3:4
ye *m* turn away this day from .Josh 22:18
m offer it unto the Lord ......Judg 13:16
There *m* be an inheritance ....Judg 21:17
thou *m* buy it also of Ruth ....Ruth 4:5
mine hand, and, lo, I *m* die ...1Sam 14:43
we *m* needs die, and are as ...2Sam 14:14
ruleth over men *m* be just.....2Sam 23:3
touch them *m* be fenced 2Sam 23:7
sleepeth, and *m* be awaked....1Kin 18:27
Lord *m* be exceeding 1Chr 22:5
mouth *m* be held in with bit...Ps 32:9
hath friends *m* show himself ...Prov 18:24
deliver him, yet thou *m* do ....Prov 19:19
edge, then *m* he put to more ..Eccl 10:10
O Solomon, *m* have a ....Song 8:12
they *m* needs be borne........Jer 10:5
but ye *m* tread down with .....Ezek 34:18
scribes that Elijah *m* first .....Matt 17:10
it *m* needs be that offences ....Matt 18:7
new wine *m* be put into ....Mark 2:22
Son of man *m* suffer many ....Mark 8:31
scribes that Elijah *m* first .....Mark 9:11
for such things *m* needs be ....Mark 13:7
scriptures *m* be fulfilled ....Mark 14:49
I *m* be about my Father's .....Luke 2:49
new wine *m* be put into ....Luke 5:38
Son of man *m* suffer many ....Luke 9:22
Nevertheless I *m* walk today...Luke 13:33
and I *m* needs go and see it ...Luke 14:18
first *m* he suffer many things ..Luke 17:25
for today I *m* abide at thy.....Luke 19:5
these things *m* first come ......Luke 21:9
the passover *m* be killed ......Luke 22:7
m yet be accomplished in .....Luke 22:37
m release one unto them at ...Luke 23:17
Son of man *m* be delivered ....Luke 24:7
He *m* increase, but I *m* ....John 3:30
he *m* needs go through.........John 4:4
I *m* work the works of him ....John 9:4
Son of man *m* be lifted up? ...John 12:34
m needs have been fulfilled ...Acts 1:16
m one be ordained to be a ....Acts 1:22
m through much tribulation ...Acts 14:22
saying, Ye *m* be circumcised...Acts 15:24
Sirs, what *m* I do to be saved? .Acts 16:30
Christ *m* needs have suffered ..Acts 17:3
I *m* by all means keep this ....Acts 18:21
the multitude *m* needs come ...Acts 21:22
so *m* thou bear witness also ...Acts 23:11
thou *m* be brought before .....Acts 27:24
ye *m* needs be subject, not ....Rom 13:5
for then *m* ye needs go out....1Cor 5:10
m be also heresies among 1Cor 11:19
If I *m* needs glory, I will 2Cor 11:30
bishop then *m* be blameless ...1Tim 3:2
m the deacons be grave 1Tim 3:8
laboreth *m* be first partaker ...2Tim 2:6
whose mouths *m* be stopped...Titus 1:11
remaineth that some *m* enter ..Heb 4:6
there *m* also of necessity be ...Heb 9:16

M

m he often have suffered.....Heb 9:26
as they that *m* give account ...Heb 13:17
judgment *m* begin at the 1Pet 4:17
shortly I *m* put off this my 2Pet 1:14
which *m* shortly come to pass..Rev 1:1
things which *m* be hereafter ...Rev 4:1
Thou *m* prophesy again before .Rev 10:11
m in this manner be killed ....Rev 11:5
sword *m* be killed with the ....Rev 13:10
he *m* continue a short space ...Rev 17:10
after that he *m* be loosed a....Rev 20:3

MUSTARD SEED—*a very small seed*
Kingdom compared to ...Matt 13:31
Faith compared to ....Matt 17:20

[*also* MUSTARD]
is like a grain of *m* seed ......Matt 13:31
It is like a grain of *m s* ....Mark 4:31
It is like a grain of *m s* ......Luke 13:19
ye had faith as a grain of *m s* .Luke 17:6

MUSTER—*to assemble*

[*also* MUSTERETH]
which *m* the people of the 2Kin 25:19
Lord of hosts *m* the host of ...Is 13:4
host, who *m* the people of ....Jer 52:25

MUTABILITY—*proneness to change*

Asserted of:
Physical world..........Matt 5:18
Earthly world 1John 2:15-17
Old covenant ....Heb 8:8-13
Present order 2Cor 4:18

Denied of:
God....................Mal 3:6
Christ ....Heb 1:10, 11
Heb 13:8

See IMMUTABILITY; MOVE

MUTH-LABBEN (mŭth'lăb'ĕn)—*"die for the son"*
chief musician according to *M* .Ps 9:*title*

MUTILATION—*maiming; damage; disfigurement*

Object of, forbidden:
On the body ....Lev 19:28
For:
Priesthood ....Lev 21:18
Sacrifice ....Lev 22:22
Mourning ....Jer 41:5-7

Practiced by:
Jews...................Judg 19:29, 30
Philistines..............Judg 16:21
Canaanites ....Judg 1:6, 7
Baal prophets 1Kin 18:28

MUTINY—*revolt against authority*
By Israelites ....Num 14:1-4

MUTTER—*to murmur*

[*also* MUTTERED]
wizards that peep, and that *m* .Is 8:19
tongue hath *m* perverseness ...Is 59:3

MUTUAL—*a common interest*
Spoken of faith..........Rom 1:12

MUZZLING—*covering the mouth (as for an animal)*

Applied:
To oxen ....Deut 25:4
Figuratively, to Christians.1Cor 9:9-11

MY—*See* INTRODUCTION

MYRA (mī'rä)—*"weep"—a town of Lycia*
Paul changes ships here ..Acts 27:5, 6

MYRRH—*an aromatic gum resin*

Dried gum (Heb., mor) of a balsam tree, used:
Given as a sedative ......Mark 15:23
Used for embalming .....John 19:38, 39

Fragrant resin (Heb., lot) used:
In commerce ....Gen 37:25
As presents ....Gen 43:11
In anointing oil..........Ex 30:23
As a perfume ....Ps 45:8
For beauty treatment .....Esth 2:12
Brought as gifts ....Matt 2:11

perfumed my bed with *m* .....Prov 7:17
of *m* is my wellbeloved ....Song 1:13
smoke, perfumed with *m* ......Song 3:6
get me to the mountain of *m* ..Song 4:6
m and aloes, with all the ......Song 4:14
my *m* with my spice; I ....Song 5:1
my hands dropped with *m* .....Song 5:5
with sweet smelling *m*.........Song 5:5

MYRTLE—*a shrub*
Found in mountains;
booths made of ....Neh 8:15
Figurative of the Gospel. .Is 41:19
Used symbolically ....Zech 1:10, 11

shall come up the *m* tree ......Is 55:13
he stood among the *m* trees ...Zech 1:8

MYSELF—*me*
I was naked; and I hid *m* .....Gen 3:10
By *m* have I sworn, saith .....Gen 22:16
and brought you unto *m* ......Ex 19:4
Egypt I sanctified them for *m* .Num 8:17
I the Lord will make *m* ....Num 12:6
I am not able to bear you *m* ..Deut 1:9
I turned *m* and came down....Deut 10:5
times before, and shake *m* ....Judg 16:20
I cannot redeem it for *m*......Ruth 4:6
I forced *m* therefore, and 1Sam 13:12
I may hide *m* in the field 1Sam 20:5
avenging *m* with mine own 1Sam 25:33
surely go forth with you *m* 2Sam 18:2
and have kept *m* from mine ...2Sam 22:24
I will surely show *m* unto 1Kin 18:15
I will disguise *m*, and enter....1Kin 22:30
I bow *m* in the house of 2Kin 5:18
I bow down *m* in the house ...2Kin 5:18
place to *m* for a house of 2Chr 7:12
I will disguise *m*, and will 2Chr 18:29
she had prepared but *m*.......Esth 5:12
do honor more than to *m*? ....Esth 6:6
I would harden *m* in sorrow ...Job 6:10
so that I am a burden to *m*? ..Job 7:20
If I justify *m*, mine own.......Job 9:20
heaviness, and comfort *m* .....Job 9:27
If I wash *m* with snow water ..Job 9:30
leave my complaint upon *m* ...Job 10:1
then I will not hide *m* from ...Job 13:20
mine error remaineth with *m* ..Job 19:4
Whom I shall see for *m* ....Job 19:27
have eaten my morsel *m* ......Job 31:17
or lifted up *m* when evil ......Job 31:29
I abhor *m*, and repent in......Job 42:6
kept *m* from mine iniquity ....Ps 18:23
I behaved *m* as though he .....Ps 35:14
then I would have hid *m* ......Ps 55:12
I *m* will awake early ....Ps 57:8
behave *m* wisely in a perfect ..Ps 101:2
and harp: I *m* will awake .....Ps 108:2
but I give *m* unto prayer ......Ps 109:4
delight *m* in thy statutes ......Ps 119:16
m in thy commandments ......Ps 119:47
Lord; and I have comforted *m* .Ps 119:52
do I exercise *m* in great.......Ps 131:1
behaved and quieted *m* ....Ps 131:2
in mine heart to give *m* ....Eccl 2:3
turned *m* to behold wisdom ...Eccl 2:12
I *m* perceived also that one ...Eccl 2:14
showed *m* wise under the .....Eccl 2:19
now will I lift up *m*..........Is 33:10
still, and refrained *m* ....Is 42:14
people have I formed for *m* ...Is 43:21
spreadeth..the earth by *m* .....Is 44:24
I have sworn by *m*, the ....Is 45:23
I would comfort *m* against ....Jer 8:18
I *m* will fight against you......Jer 21:5
words, I swear by *m*, saith ....Jer 22:5
sworn by *m*, saith the Lord....Jer 49:13
Lord will answer him by *m*....Ezek 14:7
made *m* known unto them ....Ezek 20:5
sight I made *m* known unto ...Ezek 20:9
and I have made it for *m* .....Ezek 29:3
I will make *m* known among ..Ezek 35:11
magnify *m*, and sanctify *m* ....Ezek 38:23
neither did I anoint *m* at all ...Dan 10:3
bow *m* before the high God? ..Mic 6:6
I trembled in *m*, that I........Hab 3:16
separating *m*, as I have ....Zech 7:3
I *m* worthy to come unto .....Luke 7:7
and my feet, that it is I *m*.....Luke 24:39
If I bear witness of *m*, my ....John 5:31
God, or whether I speak of *m* .John 7:17
I am not come of *m*, but he ...John 7:28
Though I bear record of *m* ....John 8:14
one that bear witness of *m* ....John 8:18
and that I do nothing of *m* ....John 8:28
neither came I of *m*, but he ...John 8:42
If I honor *m*, my honor is .....John 8:54
me, but I lay it down of *m* ....John 10:18
For I have not spoken of *m* ...John 12:49
and receive you unto *m* ....John 14:3
unto you I speak not of *m* ....John 14:10
and will manifest *m* to him ....John 14:21
for their sakes I sanctify *m* ....John 17:19
saying, Stand up; I *m* also.....Acts 10:26
count I my life dear unto *m* ...Acts 20:24
cheerfully answer for *m* ....Acts 24:10
And herein do I exercise *m* ...Acts 24:16
would also hear the man *m*....Acts 25:22
I think *m* happy, king.........Acts 26:2
I shall answer for *m* this ......Acts 26:2
I verily thought with *m* ....Acts 26:9
I *m* serve the law of God .....Rom 7:25
wish that *m* were accursed ....Rom 9:3
reserved to *m* seven thousand .Rom 11:4
I *m* also am persuaded of .....Rom 15:14
succorer of many, and of *m* ...Rom 16:2
For I know nothing by *m* 1Cor 4:4
a figure transferred to *m* 1Cor 4:6
all men were even as I *m* 1Cor 7:7
I made *m* servant unto all.....1Cor 9:19
I *m* should be a castaway 1Cor 9:27
I determined this with *m* 2Cor 2:1
Now I Paul *m* beseech you 2Cor 10:1
offence in abasing *m* that 2Cor 11:7
m from being burdensome.....2Cor 11:9
you, and so will I keep *m* 2Cor 11:9
of *m* I will not glory, but 2Cor 12:5
I *m* was not burdensome 2Cor 12:13
I make *m* a transgressor ......Gal 2:18
I also *m* shall come shortly ....Phil 2:24
I count not *m* to have ....Phil 3:13
a partner, receive him as *m* ...Philem 17

MYSIA (mĭsh'ĭ-ä)—*"abominable"—a province in northwestern Asia Minor*
Paul and Silas pass
through..............Acts 16:7, 8

MYSTERY—*something unknown except through divine revelation*

Concerning God's:
Secrets ....Deut 29:29
Providence ....Rom 11:33-36
Sovereignty ....Rom 9:11-23
Prophecies 1Pet 1:10-12
Predestination ....Rom 8:29, 30

Concerning Christianity:
Christ's incarnation 1Tim 3:16
Christ's nature ....Col 2:2
Kingdom of God ....Luke 8:10
Christian faith 1Tim 3:9
Indwelling Christ ....Col 1:26, 27
Union of all believers ....Eph 3:4-9
Israel's blindness ....Rom 11:25
Lawlessness 2Thess 2:7
Harlot Babylon..........Rev 17:5, 7
Resurrection of saints 1Cor 15:51
God's completed purpose .Rev 10:7

[*also* MYSTERIES]
m of the kingdom of heaven...Matt 13:11
m of the kingdom of God .....Mark 4:11
to the revelation of the *m* .....Rom 16:25
the wisdom of God in a *m* 1Cor 2:7
stewards of the *m* of God 1Cor 4:1
and understand all *m* 1Cor 13:2
in the spirit he speaketh *m* 1Cor 14:2
known unto us the *m* of his ...Eph 1:9
made known unto me the *m*...Eph 3:3

my knowledge in the *m* of . . . .Eph 3:4
is the fellowship of the *m* . . . . .Eph 3:9
This is a great *m*: but I . . . . . . .Eph 5:32
make known the *m* of the . . . . .Eph 6:19
to speak the *m* of Christ . . . . . .Col 4:3
The *m* of the seven stars . . . . . .Rev 1:20

MYTHOLOGY, REFERRED TO
Jupiter . . . . .Acts 14:12, 13
Mercurius . . . . .Acts 14:12
Pantheon . . . . .Acts 17:16-23
Diana . . . . .Acts 19:24-41
Castor and Pollox . . . . . . .Acts 28:11

MYTHS—*speculative and philosophical fables or allegories*
Condemned 1Tim 1:4
Fables 1Tim 4:7
False 2Tim 4:4

N

NAAM (nā'ăm)—*"pleasantness"*
Son of Caleb 1Chr 4:15

NAAMAH (nā'ä-mä)—*"beautiful"*
1. Daughter of Lamech . . . .Gen 4:19-22
2. Ammonite wife of Solomon; mother of King Rehoboam 1Kin 14:21, 31
3. Town of Judah . . . . .Josh 15:1, 41

NAAMAN (nā'ä-măn)—*"pleasantness"*
1. Son of Benjamin . . . . .Gen 46:21
2. Captain in the Syrian army 2Kin 5:1-11
Healed of his leprosy 2Kin 5:14-17
Referred to by Christ . . .Luke 4:27

[*also* NAAMAN'S]
sons of Bela were Ard and *N*. .Num 26:40
and she waited on *N* wife 2Kin 5:2
master hath spared *N* this 2Kin 5:20
So Gehazi followed after *N*. . . .2Kin 5:21
when *N* saw him running 2Kin 5:21
N said, Be content, take 2Kin 5:23
leprosy..of *N* shall cleave 2Kin 5:27
Abishua and *N*, and Ahoah . . .1Chr 8:4
N, and Ahiah, and Gera 1Chr 8:7

NAAMATHITE (nā'ä-mă-thīt)—*an inhabitant of Naamah*
Applied to Zophar, Job's friend . . . . .Job 2:11

answered Zophar the *N* . . . . . .Job 11:1
answered Zophar the *N* . . . . . .Job 20:1
Shuhite and Zophar the *N* . . . .Job 42:9

NAAMITES
Descendants of Naaman. .Num 26:40

NAARAH, NAARATH (nā'ä-rä, nā'ä-răth)—*"youthful"*
1. Wife of Ashur 1Chr 4:5, 6
2. Town of Ephraim . . . . . . .Josh 16:7
Same as Naaran 1Chr 7:28

NAARAI (nā'ä-rī)—*"youthful"*
One of David's mighty men 1Chr 11:37

NAASHON—*See* NAHSHON

NAASSON—*See* NAHSHON

NABAL (nā'băl)—*"foolish; wicked"*
Wealthy sheep owner 1Sam 25:2, 3
Refuses David's request . .1Sam 25:4-12
Abigail, wife of, appeases David's wrath against . .1Sam 25:13-35
Drunk, dies of a stroke . .1Sam 25:36-39
Widow of, becomes David's wife 1Sam 25:39-42

[*also* NABAL'S]
Abigail the Carmelitess, *N* 1Sam 27:3
the wife of *N* the Carmelite . . .1Sam 30:5
Abigail *N* wife the Carmelite . .2Sam 2:2
the wife of *N* the Carmelite . . .2Sam 3:3

NABOTH (nā'bŏth)—*"a sprout"*
Owner of vineyard coveted by King Ahab. .1Kin 21:1-4
Accused falsely of blasphemy and disloyalty 1Kin 21:5-16
Murder of, avenged 1Kin 21:17-25

portion of *N* the Jezreelite 2Kin 9:21
portion of the field of *N* 2Kin 9:25
seen yesterday the blood of *N*. .2Kin 9:26

NACHON (nā'kŏn)—*"stroke"*
Threshing floor, site of Uzzah's death 2Sam 6:6, 7

Called:
Perez-uzzah ("breach") . .2Sam 6:8
Chidon 1Chr 13:9

NACHOR—*See* NAHOR

NADAB (nā'dăb)—*"liberal"*
1. Eldest of Aaron's four sons . . . . .Ex 6:23
Takes part in affirming covenant . . . . .Ex 24:1, 9-12
Becomes priest . . . . .Ex 28:1
Consumed by fire . . . . . .Lev 10:1-7
Dies childless . . . . .Num 3:4
2. Judahite 1Chr 2:28, 30
3. Benjamite 1Chr 8:30
4. King of Israel 1Kin 14:20
Killed by Baasha 1Kin 15:25-31

of the sons of Aaron; *N*. . . . . . .Num 3:2
And unto Aaron was born *N* . .Num 26:60
N and Abihu died, when . . . . . .Num 26:61
sons also of Aaron; *N*, and 1Chr 6:3
and Baal, and Ner, and *N*. 1Chr 9:36
of Aaron; *N*, and Abihu 1Chr 24:1
N and Abihu died before 1Chr 24:2

NAGGAI, NAGGE (năg'ī, năg'ī)—*"splendor"*
Ancestor of Christ . . . . . . .Luke 3:25

NAGGING WOMAN
Gets Samson's secret . . . .Judg 16:13-17
Called brawling . . . . .Prov 21:9, 19
Undesirable . . . . .Prov 25:24
Prov 27:15

NAHALAL, NAHALLAL, NAHALOL (nä-hăl'ăl, nä-hăl'lăl, nä-hăl'ŏl)—*"pasture"*
Village of Zebulun . . . . . .Josh 19:10, 15
Assigned to Merarite Levites . . . . .Josh 21:35
Canaanites not driven from . . . . .Judg 1:30

NAHALIEL (nä-hā'lĭ-ĕl)—*"valley of God"*
Israelite camp . . . . .Num 21:19

NAHAM (nā'hăm)—*"comfort"*
Father of Keilah 1Chr 4:19

NAHAMANI (nā-hä-mā'nī)—*"compassionate"*
Returned after the exile . .Neh 7:7

NAHARAI, NAHARI (nā'hä-rī)—*"snorting one"*
Armor-bearer of Joab 2Sam 23:37
1Chr 11:39

NAHASH (nā-hăsh)—*"oracle; serpent"*
1. King of Ammon; makes impossible demands . . .1Sam 11:1-15
2. King of Ammon who treats David kindly 2Sam 10:2
Son of, helps David 2Sam 17:27-29
3. Father of Abigail and Zeruiah, David's half sisters 2Sam 17:25

N the king of the children 1Sam 12:12
N the king of the children 1Chr 19:1
unto Hanun the son of *N* 1Chr 19:2

NAHATH (nā'hăth)—*"lowness"*
1. Edomite chief . . . . .Gen 36:13
2. Kohathite Levite 1Chr 6:26
Called Tohu 1Sam 1:1
3. Levite in Hezekiah's reign 2Chr 31:13

duke *N*, duke Zerah, duke . . . .Gen 36:17
N, Zerah, Shammah, and 1Chr 1:37

NAHBI (nä-bī)—*"Jehovah is protection"*
Spy of Naphtali . . . . .Num 13:14

NAHOR, NACHOR (nā'hôr, nā'kôr)—*"piercer"*
1. Grandfather of Abraham .Gen 11:24-26
2. Son of Terah, brother of Abraham . . . . .Gen 11:27
Marries Milcah, begets eight sons by her and four by concubine . . . . .Gen 11:29
City of Haran . . . . .Gen 24:10
God of . . . . .Gen 31:53

thirty years, and begat *N*. . . . . .Gen 11:22
Serug lived after he begat *N*. . .Gen 11:23
children unto thy brother *N* . . .Gen 22:20
eight Milcah did bear to *N* . . . .Gen 22:23
the wife of *N*, Abraham's . . . . .Gen 24:15
which she bare unto *N* . . . . . . .Gen 24:24
Know ye Laban the son of *N*. .Gen 29:5
Abraham, and the father of *N* .Josh 24:2
Serug, *N*, Terah 1Chr 1:26
which was the son of *N* . . . . . . .Luke 3:34

NAHSHON, NAASHON, NAASSON (nä'-shŏn, nā'sŏn)—*"oracle"*
Judahite leader . . . . .Num 1:4, 7
Aaron's brother-in-law . . .Ex 6:23
Ancestor of David . . . . . . .Ruth 4:20-22
Ancestor of Christ . . . . . . .Matt 1:4

N the son of Amminadab . . . . .Num 2:3
offering the first day was *N* . . .Num 7:12
N the son of Amminadab . . . . .Num 7:17
N the son of Amminadab . . . . .Num 10:14
and Amminadab begat *N*. 1Chr 2:10
N begat Salma, and Salma 1Chr 2:11

NAHUM, NAUM (nā'hŭm, nā'ŭm)—*"comforter"*
Inspired prophet to Judah concerning Nineveh . . . .Nah 1:1
Ancestor of Christ . . . . . . .Luke 3:25

NAHUM, THE BOOK OF—*a book of the Old Testament*
The awesomeness of God .Nah 1:1-15
The destruction of Nineveh . . . . .Nah 2—3

NAIL—*a slender and usually pointed fastener; fingernail*

Significant uses of:
Killing a man . . . . .Judg 4:21, 25
Holding idols in place . . . .Is 41:7
Fastening Christ to cross .John 20:25

Figurative uses of:
Words fixed in the memory . . . . .Eccl 12:11
Revived nation . . . . .Ezra 9:8
Messiah's kingdom . . . . . .Is 22:23, 24
Messiah's death . . . . .Is 22:25
Atonement for man's sin .Col 2:14

[*also* NAILS]
shave her head..pare her *n* . . . .Deut 21:12
and smote the *n* into his . . . . . .Judg 4:21
dead, and the *n* was in his . . . .Judg 4:22
She put her hand to the *n*. . . . .Judg 5:26
iron in abundance for the *n* . . .1Chr 22:3
weight of the *n* was fifty 2Chr 3:9
it with *n* and with hammers . . .Jer 10:4
and his *n* like birds' claws . . . . .Dan 4:33
of iron, and his *n* of brass . . . . .Dan 7:19
of him the *n*, out of him . . . . . .Zech 10:4

NAIN (nā'ĭn)—*"beauty"*
Village south of Nazareth; Jesus raises widow's son here . . . . . .Luke 7:11-17

NAIOTH (nā'ŏth)—*"habitation"*
Prophets school in Ramah . . . . {1Sam 19:18, 19, 22, 23

NAKED—*nude; without customary covering*

Used of man's:
Original state . . . . .Gen 2:25
Sinful state Gen3:7,10,11
State of grace . . . . .Rom 8:35
Disembodied state 2Cor 5:3

Evil of:
Strictly forbidden . . . . .Lev 18:6-20
Brings a curse . . . . .Gen 9:21-25
Judged by God . . . . .Ezek 22:10

Instances of:
Noah guilty of . . . . .Gen 9:21-23
Forbidden, to priests . . . . .Ex 20:26
Michal rebukes David for .2Sam 6:20-23

Putting clothing on:
Indicates a changed life . .Mark 5:15
Promises a reward . . . . . . .Matt 25:34-40
Takes away shame . . . . . . .Rev 3:18
Sign of true faith . . . . .James 2:15-17

Figurative of:
Separation from God . . . .Is 20:3
Israel's unworthiness . . . . .Ezek 16:7-22
Judah's spiritual adultery .Ezek 16:36-38
God's judgment . . . . .Ezek 16:39
Spiritual need . . . . .Hos 2:9
Wickedness . . . . .Nah 3:4, 5
Needy Matt25:36,38
God's knowledge . . . . .Heb 4:13
Unpreparedness . . . . .Rev 16:15

[*also* NAKEDNESS]
to see the *n* of the land . . . . . . .Gen 42:9
breeches to cover their *n* . . . . . .Ex 28:42
saw that the people were *n* . . . .Ex 32:25
had made *n* unto their shame . .Ex 32:25
uncovered his father's *n* . . . . . . .Lev 20:11
see her *n*, and she see his *n* . . .Lev 20:17
uncovered his sister's *n* . . . . . . .Lev 20:17
the *n* of thy mother's sister . . . .Lev 20:19
uncovered his brother's *n* . . . . .Lev 20:21
and in thirst, and in *n* Deut28:48
lay down *n* all that day and . . .1Sam19:24
confusion of thy mother's *n* . . .1Sam20:30
all that were *n* among them . . .2Chr 28:15
N came I out of my . . . . .Job 1:21
stripped the *n* of their . . . . .Job 22:6
n to lodge without clothing . . . .Job 24:7
Hell is *n* before him, and . . . . .Job 26:6
n shall he return to go as . . . . .Eccl 5:15
walking *n* and barefoot . . . . . . .Is 20:2
young and old, *n* and . . . . .Is 20:4
Thy *n* shall be uncovered . . . . .Is 47:3
when thou seest the *n*, that . . .Is 58:7
they have seen her *n*: yea . . . . .Lam 1:8
and shalt make thyself *n* . . . . . .Lam 4:21
hath covered the *n* with a . . . . .Ezek 18:7
These discovered her *n* Ezek23:10
discovered her *n*: then my Ezek23:18
shall leave thee *n* and bare Ezek23:29
n of thy whoredoms shall Ezek23:29
Lest I strip her *n*, and set . . . . .Hos 2:3
the mighty shall flee away *n* . . .Amos 2:16
I will go stripped and *n* . . . . . . .Mic 1:8
thou mayest look on their *n* . . .Hab 2:15
Thy bow was made quite *n* . . . .Hab 3:9
thee in? or *n*, and clothed . . . . .Matt 25:38
n, and ye clothed me not . . . . .Matt 25:43
linen cloth cast about his *n* . . . .Mark 14:51
unto him, (for he was *n*,) . . . . .John 21:7
out of that house *n* and . . . . . . .Acts 19:16
and thirst, and are *n* 1Cor 4:11
fastings often, in cold and *n* . . .2Cor 11:27
and poor, and blind, and *n* . . . .Rev 3:17

NAME—*to give the word by which a person, place, or thing is known; the word by which something is known*

Determined by:
Events of the time . . . . . . .Gen 30:8
Prophetic position . . . . . . .Gen 25:26
Fondness of hope . . . . .Gen 29:32-35
Change of character . . . . .John 1:42
Innate character 1Sam 25:25
Coming events . . . . .Is 8:1-4
Divine mission . . . . .Matt 1:21

Of God, described as:
Great . . . . .Josh 7:9
Secret . . . . .Judg 13:18
Glorious . . . . .Is 63:14
Everlasting . . . . .Ps 135:13
Excellent . . . . .Ps 148:13
Holy . . . . .Is 57:15

Of God, evil acts against:
Taken in vain . . . . .Ex 20:7
Sworn falsely . . . . .Lev 19:12
Lies spoken in . . . . .Zech 13:3
Despised . . . . .Mal 1:6

Of God, proper attitude toward:
Exalt . . . . .Ps 34:3
Praise . . . . .Ps 54:6
Love . . . . .Ps 69:36

Of Christ:
Given before birth . . . . . . .Matt 1:21, 23
Hated by the world . . . . . .Matt 10:22
Deeds done in, rewarded .Matt 10:42
Believers baptized in Acts2:38
Miracles performed by . . .Acts3:16
Believers suffer for Acts5:41
Speaking in Acts9:27, 29
Gentiles called by Acts15:14,17
Final subjection to . . . . . . .Phil 2:9, 10

Of believers:
Called everlasting . . . . . . .Is 56:5
Written in heaven . . . . . . .Luke 10:20
Called evil by world . . . . .Luke 6:22
Known by Christ . . . . .John 10:3
Confessed by Christ . . . . .Rev 3:5
"Called by" . . . . .Is 62:2
Rev 3:12

[*also* NAMED, NAME'S, NAMES, NAMETH]
Adam gave *n* to all cattle . . . . .Gen 2:20
bless thee, and make thy *n* . . . .Gen 12:2
he had *n* in the audience . . . . . .Gen 23:16
the *n* of the sons of Ishmael . . .Gen 25:13
by their *n*, according to . . . . . . .Gen 25:13
called their *n* after the *n* . . . . . .Gen 26:18
What is thy *n*? And he said . . .Gen 32:27
thy *n* shall not be called . . . . . .Gen 35:10
but Israel shall be thy *n* . . . . . . .Gen 35:10
and he called his *n* Israel . . . . .Gen 35:10
n of the dukes that came . . . . . .Gen 36:40
their places, by their *n* . . . . .Gen 36:40
let my name be *n* on them . . . .Gen 48:16
are the *n* of the children . . . . . .Ex 1:1
say to me, What is his *n*? . . . . .Ex 3:13
this is my *n* for ever, and . . . . .Ex 3:15
them the *n* of the children . . . .Ex 28:9
Six of their *n* on one stone . . . .Ex 28:10
n of the rest on the other . . . . .Ex 28:10
bear their *n* before the Lord . .Ex 28:12
n of the children of Israel . . . . .Ex 28:21
twelve, according to their *n* . . .Ex 28:21
sight, and I know thee by *n* . . .Ex 33:17
n of the children of Israel . . . . .Ex 39:6
n of the children of Israel . . . . .Ex 39:14
according to their *n*, like . . . . . .Ex 39:14
with the number of their *n* . . . .Num 1:2
are expressed by their *n* . . . . . .Num 1:17
to the number of the *n* . . . . . . .Num 1:18
are the *n* of the sons of . . . . . . .Num 3:2
the sons of Levi by their *n* . . . .Num 3:17
take the number of their *n* . . . .Num 3:40
put my *n* upon the children . . .Num 6:27
were their *n*: of the tribe . . . . . .Num 13:4
the *n* of the daughters of . . . . . .Num 26:33
the *n* of the tribes of their . . . .Num 26:55
are the *n* of his daughters . . . . .Num 27:1
(their *n* being changed) . . . . . .Num 32:38
gave other *n* unto the cities . . .Num 32:38
These are the *n* of the men . . .Num 34:17
the *n* of the Lord thy God . . . .Deut 5:11
n of them out of that place . . . .Deut 12:3
into an harlot's house, *n* . . . . . .Josh 2:1
are the *n* of his daughters . . . . .Josh 17:3
she *n* the child Ichabod 1Sam4:21
his people for his great *n* 1Sam12:22
the *n* of his two daughters 1Sam14:49
son of Ahitub, *n* Abiathar 1Sam22:20
n of those that were born 2Sam5:14
n is called by the *n* of 2Sam6:2
have made thee a great *n* 2Sam7:9
build an house for my *n* 2Sam7:13
the pillar after his own *n* 2Sam18:18
And these are their *n*: The 1Kin 4:8
build an house unto my *n* 1Kin 5:5
of a far country for thy *n* 1Kin 8:41
call..on the *n* of your gods 1Kin 18:24
of Jacob, whom he *n* Israel . . .2Kin 17:34
mentioned by their *n* were 1Chr 4:38
which are called by their *n* 1Chr 6:65
had six sons, whose *n* are 1Chr 9:44
Glory ye in his holy *n*: let 1Chr 16:10
by number of *n* by their 1Chr 23:24
far country for thy great *n* 2Chr 6:32
which are called by my *n* 2Chr 7:14
What are the *n* of the men . . . .Ezra 5:4
We asked their *n* also, to . . . . .Ezra 5:10
we might write the *n* of the . . .Ezra 5:10
and all of them by their *n* . . . . .Ezra 10:16
away; blessed be the *n* of . . . . .Job 1:21
will sing praise to the *n* . . . . . . .Ps 7:17
nor take up their *n* into my . . .Ps 16:4
of righteousness for his *n* . . . . .Ps 23:3
for thy *n* sake lead me . . . . .Ps 31:3
praise the *n* of God with a . . . .Ps 69:30
His *n* shall endure for ever . . . .Ps 72:17
within me, bless his holy *n* . . . .Ps 103:1
he saved them for his *n* sake . .Ps 106:8
help is in the *n* of the Lord . . .Ps 124:8
Quicken me..for thy *n* sake . . .Ps 143:11
calleth them all by their *n* . . . . .Ps 147:4
and take the *n* of my God in . .Prov 30:9
which hath been is *n* already . .Eccl 6:10
A good *n* is better than . . . . . . .Eccl 7:1
he calleth them all by *n* by . . . .Is 40:26
For my *n* sake will I defer . . . .Is 48:9
my people shall know my *n* . . .Is 52:6
shall be *n* the Priests of the . . .Is 61:6
were not called by thy *n* . . . . . .Is 63:19
us, do thou it for thy *n* sake . .Jer 14:7
my name shall no more be *n* . .Jer 44:26
But I wrought for my *n* Ezek20:9
But I wrought for my *n* Ezek20:14
wrought with you for my *n* Ezek20:44
the *n* of them were Aholah . . .Ezek23:4
their *n*; Samaria is Aholah Ezek23:4
but for mine holy *n* sake Ezek36:22
after the *n* of the tribes Ezek48:31
of the eunuchs gave *n* . . . . .Dan 1:7
the king *n* Belteshazzar . . . . . . .Dan 5:12
people are called by thy *n* . . . . .Dan 9:19
I will take away the *n* of . . . . . .Hos 2:17
are *n* chief of the nations . . . . .Amos 6:1
art *n* the house of Jacob . . . . . .Mic 2:7
cut off the *n* of the idols . . . . . .Zech 13:2
heaven, Hallowed be thy *n* . . . .Matt 6:9
a man, *n* Matthew, sitting . . . . .Matt 9:9
the *n* of the twelve apostles . . . .Matt 10:2
gathered together in my *n* . . . . .Matt 18:20
children, or lands, for my *n* . . .Matt 19:29
many shall come in my *n* . . . . .Matt 24:5
cometh in the *n* of the Lord . . .Mark11:9
hated of all men for my *n* Mark13:13
which was *n* Gethsemane Mark14:32
a certain priest *n* Zechariah . . .Luke1:5
things; and holy is his *n* Luke1:49
which was so *n* of the angel . . .Luke2:21
whom also he *n* apostles Luke6:13
there came a man *n* Jairus Luke8:41
certain beggar *n* Lazarus Luke16:20
kings and rulers for my *n* Luke21:12
there was a man *n* Joseph Luke23:50
Pharisees, *n* Nicodemus . . . . . . .John 3:1
one of them, *n* Caiaphas . . . . . .John 11:49
ye shall ask in my *n* . . . . .John 14:13
they do unto you for my *n* . . . .John 15:21
ye asked nothing in my *n* . . . . .John 16:24
keep through thine own *n* . . . . .John 17:11
number of *n* together . . . . .Acts 1:15
there is none other *n* under . . .Acts 4:12
a certain man *n* Ananias . . . . . .Acts 5:1
at Damascus, *n* Ananias . . . . . .Acts 9:10
he must suffer for my *n* . . . . . . .Acts 9:16

a certain man ***n*** Aeneas ....Acts 9:33
one of them ***n*** Agabus ....Acts 11:28
was there ***n*** Timothy ....Acts 16:1
a woman ***n*** Damaris, and .....Acts 17:34
a certain man's house, ***n*** ......Acts 18:7
man ***n*** Demetrius, a ....Acts 19:24
Judea a certain prophet, ***n*** ....Acts 21:10
calling on the ***n*** of the Lord ...Acts 22:16
other prisoners unto one ***n*** ....Acts 27:1
not where Christ was ***n*** ....Rom 15:20
so much as ***n*** among the 1Cor 5:1
and every name that is ***n*** ......Eph 1:21
in heaven and earth is ***n*** ......Eph 3:15
let it not be once ***n*** among ....Eph 5:3
whose ***n*** are in the book ......Phil 4:3
in the ***n*** of the Lord Jesus .....Col 3:17
that ***n*** the name of Christ 2Tim 2:19
nameth the ***n*** of Christ 2Tim 2:19
are forgiven you for his ***n*** 1John 2:12
believe on the ***n*** of his Son 1John 3:23
believe on the ***n*** of the Son ...1John 5:13
his ***n*** sake they went forth 3John 7
my ***n*** sake hast labored ....Rev 2:3
the stone a new ***n*** written .....Rev 2:17
hast a few ***n*** even in Sardis ....Rev 3:4
full of ***n*** of blasphemy ....Rev 17:3
whose ***n*** were not written in ...Rev 17:8
is called The Word of God ....Rev 19:13
and ***n*** written thereon ....Rev 21:12
them the ***n*** of the twelve ......Rev 21:14

NAMELY—*that is to say*
the flocks, ***n***, of the sheep ....Lev 1:10
Of the children of Joseph, ***n*** ...Num 1:32
slain; ***n***, Evi, and Rekem .....Num 31:8
N, Bezer in the wilderness ....Deut 4:43
n, the Hittites, and the ....Deut 20:17
N, five lords of the ....Judg 3:3
gave the cities of Judah, ***n*** 1Chr 6:57
n, the house of the 1Chr 9:23
n, of the sons of Jeshua the ...Ezra 10:18
n, Zechariah the son *of* ....Neh 12:35
n, upon the thirteenth day ....Esth 8:12
n, riches kept for the ....Eccl 5:13
n, by them beyond the river ....Is 7:20
n, Elnathan the son of ....Jer 26:22
And the second is like, ***n*** .....Mark 12:31
n, Judas surnamed Barsabas ...Acts 15:22
n, Thou shalt love thy ....Rom 13:9

NAMES OF CHRIST—*See* CHRIST

NAOMI (nā'ō-mī, nā-ō'mī)—*"pleasantness; my joy"*
Widow of Elimelech .....Ruth 1:1-3
Returns to Bethlehem with Ruth ....Ruth 1:14-19
Arranges Ruth's marriage to Boaz ....Ruth 3—4
Considers Ruth's child (Obed) her own ....Ruth 4:16, 17

And *N* said unto her two .....Ruth 1:8
N said, Turn again, my ....Ruth 1:11
Call me not *N*, call me ....Ruth 1:20
So *N* returned, and Ruth ......Ruth 1:22
N had a kinsman of her ....Ruth 2:1
that came back with *N* ....Ruth 2:6
And *N* said unto her ....Ruth 2:20
N said unto her, The man .....Ruth 2:20
N said unto Ruth her ....Ruth 2:22

NAPHISH (nā'fĭsh)—*"numerous"*
Ishmael's eleventh son ...Gen 25:15
See NEPHISH

NAPHTALI (năf'tä-lī)—*"that struggles"*
1. Son of Jacob by Bilhah ..Gen 30:1, 8
Sons of, form tribe ......Gen 46:24
Receives Jacob's blessing.Gen 49:21, 28
2. Tribe of ....Num 1:42
Stationed last ....Num 2:29-31
Territory assigned by ....Josh 19:32-39
Canaanites not driven out by ....Judg 1:33
Barak becomes famous ..Judg 4:6, 14-16
Bravery of, praised......Judg 5:18
Warriors of, under Gideon ....Judg 7:23
Warriors of, help David .1Chr 12:34
Conquered by wars 1Kin 15:20
Taken captive 2Kin 15:29
Prophecy of a great light in ....Is 9:1-7
Fulfilled in Christ's ministry in ....Matt 4:12-16

handmaid; Dan, and *N*........Gen 35:25
Dan, and *N*, Gad, and ....Ex 1:4
Of *N*, Ahira the son of ....Num 1:15
prince of the children of *N* ....Num 7:78
Of the tribe of *N*, Nahbi ......Num 13:14
These are the families of *N*....Num 26:50
and Zebulun, Dan, and *N*.....Deut 27:13
all *N*, and the land of.........Deut 34:2
in Galilee in mount *N* ....Josh 20:7
the tribe of *N*, Kedesh in .....Josh 21:32
Zebulun and *N* to Kedesh.....Judg 4:10
unto Zebulun, and unto *N* ....Judg 6:35
Ahimaaz was in *N*, he also 1Kin 4:15
widow's son of the tribe of *N*..1Kin 7:14
Joseph, and Benjamin, *N* 1Chr 2:2
And out of the tribe of *N* 1Chr 6:76
Issachar and Zebulun and *N*...1Chr 12:40
all the store cities of *N*........2Chr 16:4
Zebulun, and the princes of *N* .Ps 68:27
west side, a portion for *N* .....Ezek 48:3
gate of Asher, one gate of *N* ..Ezek 48:34

NAPHTUHIM (năf-tū'hĭm)
Fourth son of Mizraim; probably refers to a district in Egypt also ...Gen 10:13

NAPKIN—*a cloth*
I have kept laid up in a ***n*** .....Luke 19:20
was bound about with a ***n***.....John 11:44
n, that was about his head ....John 20:7

NARCISSUS (när-sĭs'ŭs)—*meaning unknown*
Christian in Rome ....Rom 16:11

NARROW—*small in width; exclusive*

[*also* NARROWED, NARROWER, NARROWLY]
and stood in a ***n*** place ....Num 22:26
mount Ephraim be too ***n*** for ..Josh 17:15
made windows of ***n*** lights 1Kin 6:4
made ***n*** rests round about 1Kin 6:6
and lookest ***n*** unto all my .....Job 13:27
a strange woman is a ***n*** pit ....Prov 23:27
that see thee shall ***n*** look .....Is 14:16
covering ***n*** than that he can ....Is 28:20
now be too ***n*** by reason of ....Is 49:19
n windows to the little ....Ezek 40:16
n windows and palm trees .....Ezek 41:26
is the gate, and ***n*** is the way ..Matt 7:14

NATHAN (nā'thăn)—*"gift"*
1. Son of David 2Sam 5:14
Mary's lineage traced through ....Zech 12:12
2. Judahite 1Chr 2:36
3. Prophet under David and Solomon 1Chr 29:29
Reveals God's plan to David 2Sam 7:2-29
Rebukes David's sin 2Sam 12:1-15
Renames Solomon as Jedidiah 2Sam 12:24, 25
Reveals Adonijah's plot .1Kin 1:10-46
Sons of, in official positions 1Kin 4:1, 2, 5
4. Father of Igal 2Sam 23:36
5. A chief among returnees .Ezra 8:16
6. One who divorced his foreign wife ....Ezra 10:34, 39

N the prophet, and Shimei 1Kin 1:8
Shimea and Shobab, and *N*....1Chr 3:5
Joel the brother of *N* 1Chr 11:38
Shobab, *N* and Solomon 1Chr 14:4
David said to *N* the 1Chr 17:1
N said unto David, Do all.....1Chr 17:2
word of God came to *N*.......1Chr 17:3
so did *N* speak unto David 1Chr 17:15
the book of *N* the prophet 2Chr 9:29
seer, and *N* the prophet.......2Chr 29:25
N the prophet came unto him. .Ps 51:*title*
which was the son of *N* ....Luke 3:31

NATHANAEL (nä-thăn'ā-ĕl)—*"God has given"*
One of Christ's disciples. .John 1:45-51

NATHAN-MELECH (nā-thăn-mē'lĕk)—*"king's gift"*
An official in Josiah's reign ....2 Kin 23:11

NATION—*group of people under a sovereign government; a community of people; a tribe*

Of the world:
Descendants of Noah's sons ....Gen 10:32
Originate in a person ....Gen 19:37, 38
Made of one blood ......Acts 17:26
Separated by God ....Deut 32:8
Inherit separate characteristics ....Gen 25:23
Laden with iniquity ......Is 1:4
Destroyed by corruption .Lev 18:26-28
Exalted by righteousness .Prov 14:34
Father of many nations ..Gen 17:4
LORD will set you high above all ....Deut 28:1
Subject to repentance ....Jer 18:7-10
Judged by God..........Gen 15:14
Under God's control.....Jer 25:8-14
Future of, revealed ......Dan 2:27-45
Gospel to be preached to all....................Matt 24:14
Sarah shall be mother of many ....Gen 17:16

Of Israel:
Descendants of Abraham .Gen 12:2
John 8:33, 37
Designated..............Ex 19:6
Given blessings..........Deut 4:7, 8
Rom 9:4, 5
Punished by God ....Jer 25:1-11
Scattered among nations. .Neh 1:8
Luke 21:24
Christ died for ....John 11:51

Of the true people of God:
Described as righteous ...Is 26:2
Born in a day ....Is 66:8
Accounted fruitful ....Matt 21:43
Believers are ....1 Pet 2:9

[*also* NATIONS]
Tidal king of ***n***...............Gen 14:1
with Tidal king of ***n*** ....Gen 14:9
father of many ***n*** have I.......Gen 17:5
I will make ***n*** of thee ....Gen 17:6
will make him a great ***n*******.......Gen 17:20
a great and mighty ***n*** ....Gen 18:18
n of the earth..be blessed .....Gen 18:18
slay also a righteous ***n***? ....Gen 20:4
I will make him a great ***n*** .....Gen 21:18
n of the earth be blessed ......Gen 22:18
princes according to their ***n*** ...Gen 25:16
n of the earth be blessed ......Gen 26:4
n and a company of ***n*** ....Gen 35:11
make of thee a great ***n***.......Gen 46:3
become a multitude of ***n*** ......Gen 48:19
Egypt since it became a ***n***.....Ex 9:24
sell her unto a strange ***n*** ......Ex 21:8
this ***n*** is thy people ....Ex 33:13
cast out the ***n*** before thee .....Ex 34:24
the ***n*** are defiled ....Lev 18:24
walk in the manners of the ***n***. Lev 20:23
make of thee a greater ***n***......Num 14:12
the ***n*** which have heard the ...Num 14:15
not be reckoned among the ***n*** .Num 23:9
he shall eat up the ***n***.........Num 24:8
n that are under the whole ....Deut 2:25
Surely this great ***n*** is a wise ...Deut 4:6
unto all ***n*** under the whole ....Deut 4:19
scatter you among the ***n*** ......Deut 4:27

a ***n*** from the midst of..***n*** ......Deut 4:34
To drive out ***n*** from before ....Deut 4:38
hath cast out many ***n*** before ...Deut 7:1
seven ***n*** greater ....Deut 7:1
God will put out those ***n*** ......Deut 7:22
n greater and mightier ....Deut 9:1
make of thee a ***n*** mightier .....Deut 9:14
Lord drive out all these ***n*** .....Deut 11:23
n which ye shall possess ....Deut 12:2
n that are upon the earth .....Deut 14:2
shalt lend unto many ***n*** ....Deut 15:6
shalt reign over many ***n*** ....Deut 15:6
abominations of those ***n*** ....Deut 18:9
God hath cut off the ***n*** ....Deut 19:1
and became there a ***n*** ....Deut 26:5
make thee high above all ***n*** ....Deut 26:19
lend unto many ***n*** ....Deut 28:12
unto a ***n*** which neither ....Deut 28:36
Lord shall bring a ***n*** against ...Deut 28:49
a ***n*** whose tongue thou shalt ...Deut 28:49
among..***n*** shalt thou find no .. Deut 28:65
serve the gods of these ***n*** ......Deut 29:18
mind among all the ***n*** ....Deut 30:1
destroy these ***n*** from..thee ....Deut 31:3
Most High divided to the ***n*** ...Deut 32:8
anger with a foolish ***n*** ....Deut 32:21
Rejoice, O ye ***n*** with his ....Deut 32:43
king of the ***n*** of Gilgal ....Josh 12:23
divided unto you by lot these ***n***.Josh 23:4
n that I have cut off ....Josh 23:4
great ***n*** and strong ....Josh 23:9
drive out any of these ***n*** ....Josh 23:13
n..Joshua left when he died ...Judg 2:21
these are the ***n***..Lord left .....Judg 3:1
to judge us like all the ***n*** 1Sam 8:5
those ***n*** were of old 1Sam 27:8
what one ***n*** in the earth 2Sam 7:23
from the ***n*** and their gods? 2Sam 7:23
his fame was in all ***n*** 1Kin 4:31
abominations of the ***n*** 1Kin 14:24
there is no ***n*** or kingdom 1Kin 18:10
oath of the kingdom and ***n*** 1Kin 18:10
n which thou hast removed 2Kin 17:26
every ***n*** made gods of their 2Kin 17:29
every ***n*** in their cities 2Kin 17:29
So these ***n*** feared the Lord 2Kin 17:41
gods of the ***n*** delivered 2Kin 19:12
more evil than did the ***n*** 2Kin 21:9
fear of him upon all ***n*** 1Chr 14:17
when they went from ***n*** to ***n***...1Chr 16:20
marvelous works among all ***n***..1Chr 16:24
let men say among the ***n*** 1Chr 16:31
what one ***n*** in the earth is 1Chr 17:21
by driving out ***n*** from before ..1Chr 17:21
brought from all these ***n*** 1Chr 18:11
and a byword among all ***n*** 2Chr 7:20
n was destroyed of ***n*** 2Chr 15:6
the gods of the ***n*** of those 2Chr 32:13
gods of the ***n*** of other lands ...2Chr 32:17
the rest of the ***n*** whom the ....Ezra 4:10
among many ***n*** was..no king ...Neh 13:26
He increaseth the ***n*** ....Job 12:23
done against a ***n***, or against ...Job 34:29
all the ***n*** that forget God ......Ps 9:17
kindreds of the ***n***..worship ....Ps 22:27
Blessed is the ***n*** whose God ....Ps 33:12
the ***n*** under our feet ....Ps 47:3
his eyes behold the ***n*** ....Ps 66:7
n be glad and sing for joy .....Ps 67:4
govern the ***n*** upon earth ......Ps 67:4
all ***n*** shall call him blessed ....Ps 72:17
cut them off from being a ***n*** ...Ps 83:4
All ***n*** whom thou hast made ...Ps 86:9
rejoice in the gladness of thy ***n***.Ps 106:5
seed also among the ***n*** ....Ps 106:27
praises unto thee among the ***n*** .Ps 108:3
Lord is high above all ***n*** ....Ps 113:4
praise the Lord, all ye ***n*** ......Ps 117:1
smote great ***n***, and slew ....Ps 135:10
not dealt so with any ***n*** ....Ps 147:20
people curse, ***n*** shall abhor ....Prov 24:24
all ***n*** shall flow unto it ....Is 2:2
he shall judge among the ***n*** ....Is 2:4
n..lift up sword against ***n*** ......Is 2:4
lift up an ensign to the ***n*** ......Is 5:26

Thou hast multiplied the ***n*** ....Is 9:3
against a hypocritical ***n*** ....Is 10:6
to destroy and cut off ***n*** ....Is 10:7
kingdoms of ***n*** gathered ....Is 13:4
all the kings of the ***n*** ....Is 14:9
the kings of the ***n***, even all ....Is 14:18
and to the rushing of ***n*** ....Is 17:12
a ***n*** scattered and peeled ......Is 18:2
n meted out and trodden ......Is 18:7
and she is a mart of ***n*** ....Is 23:3
veil..spread over all ***n*** ....Is 25:7
thou hast increased the ***n*** .....Is 26:15
hast increased the ***n*** ....Is 26:15
multitude of all the ***n*** be ......Is 29:8
the ***n*** were scattered ....Is 33:3
of the Lord is upon all ***n*** ....Is 34:2
gods of the ***n*** delivered ....Is 37:12
n are as a drop of a bucket ...Is 40:15
gave the ***n*** before him ....Is 41:2
to subdue ***n*** before him ....Is 45:1
give ear unto me, O my ***n*** ....Is 51:4
in the eyes of all the ***n*** ....Is 52:10
call a ***n*** that thou knowest .....Is 55:5
n that knew not thee ....Is 55:5
as a ***n*** that did righteousness ..Is 58:2
small one a strong ***n*** ....Is 60:22
spring forth before all the ***n*** ...Is 61:11
n..not called by my name .....Is 65:1
I will gather all ***n*** and.........Is 66:18
Lord out of all ***n*** ....Is 66:20
ordained..prophet unto the ***n*** ..Jer 1:5
n changed their gods ....Jer 2:11
all the ***n*** shall be gathered......Jer 3:17
heritage of the hosts of ***n***? ....Jer 3:19
Make ye mention to the ***n*** ....Jer 4:16
I will bring a ***n*** upon you .....Jer 5:15
it is a mighty ***n***..ancient ***n*** .....Jer 5:15
a ***n*** whose language thou ......Jer 5:15
a great ***n*** shall be raised.......Jer 6:22
n that obeyeth not the voice...Jer 7:28
soul be avenged on shall a ***n*** ..Jer 9:9
These ***n*** are uncircumcised ....Jer 9:26
not fear thee, O King of ***n***? ...Jer 10:7
among all..men of the ***n*** ......Jer 10:7
pluck up and destroy that ***n*** ...Jer 12:17
n shall pass by this city ......Jer 22:8
made all the ***n*** to drink ....Jer 25:17
controversy with the ***n*** ....Jer 25:31
evil shall go forth from ***n*** to ***n*** .Jer 25:32
all ***n*** shall serve him ....Jer 27:7
many ***n*** and great kings ....Jer 27:7
n and kingdom which will not .Jer 27:8
that ***n*** will I punish, saith .....Jer 27:8
from the neck of all ***n*** ....Jer 28:11
gather you from all the ***n*** .....Jer 29:14
I make a full end of all ***n*** .....Jer 30:11
the word of the Lord, O ye ***n*** .Jer 31:10
cease from being a ***n*** ....Jer 31:36
and against all the ***n*** ....Jer 36:2
among all..***n*** of the earth?.....Jer 44:8
full end of all the ***n*** ....Jer 46:28
cut it off from being a ***n*** ......Jer 48:2
n whither the outcasts ....Jer 49:36
an assembly of great ***n*** ....Jer 50:9
desolation among the ***n***! ....Jer 50:23
a great ***n***, and many kings .....Jer 50:41
n have drunken of her wine ...Jer 51:7
therefore the ***n*** are mad ....Jer 51:7
blow the trumpet among the ***n*** .Jer 51:27
prepare the ***n*** against her .....Jer 51:27
astonishment among the ***n***! ....Jer 51:41
that was great among the ***n*** ...Lam 1:1
n that could not save ....Lam 4:17
rebellious ***n*** that..rebelled .....Ezek 2:3
set it in..midst of the ***n*** ....Ezek 5:5
multiplied more than the ***n*** ....Ezek 5:7
to the judgments of the ***n*** .....Ezek 5:7
a reproach among the ***n*** ....Ezek 5:14
escape the sword among the ***n*** .Ezek 6:8
scatter them among the ***n*** .....Ezek 12:15
n set against him on every ....Ezek 19:8
cause many ***n*** to come up .....Ezek 26:3
the terrible of the ***n*** ....Ezek 28:7
exalt..any more above the ***n*** ...Ezek 29:15
no more rule over the ***n*** ......Ezek 29:15

the Egyptians among the ***n*** ....Ezek 30:26
the terrible of the ***n*** ....Ezek 31:12
like a young lion of the ***n*** .....Ezek 32:2
the terrible of the ***n*** ....Ezek 32:12
daughters of the famous ***n*** .....Ezek 32:18
and hast bereaved thy ***n*** ......Ezek 36:13
cause thy ***n*** to fall ....Ezek 36:15
they shall be no more two ***n***...Ezek 37:22
brought forth out of the ***n*** .....Ezek 38:8
known in the eyes of many ***n*** ..Ezek 38:23
O people, ***n***, and languages ...Dan 3:4
every people, ***n***, and ....Dan 3:29
unto all people, ***n***, and.........Dan 4:1
him, all people, ***n*** and ....Dan 5:19
wrote unto all people, ***n*** ......Dan 6:25
that all people, ***n***, and ....Dan 7:14
stand up out of the ***n*** ....Dan 8:22
was since there was a ***n*** ....Dan 12:1
have hired among the ***n*** ....Hos 8:10
be wanderers among the ***n*** ....Hos 9:17
n is come up upon my land ....Joel 1:6
I will also gather all ***n*** ....Joel 3:2
named chief of the ***n*** ....Amos 6:1
will raise up against you a ***n***...Amos 6:14
many ***n*** shall come, and say ...Mic 4:2
rebuke strong ***n*** afar off.......Mic 4:3
n..not lift..sword against ***n*** ....Mic 4:3
many ***n*** are gathered against...Mic 4:11
n through her whoredoms .....Nah 3:4
that bitter and hasty ***n*** ....Hab 1:6
continually to slay the ***n***? .....Hab 1:17
thou hast spoiled many ***n*** .....Hab 2:8
O ***n*** not desired ....Zeph 2:1
n of the Cherethites!..........Zeph 2:5
all the beasts of the ***n***.........Zeph 2:14
determination is to gather..***n*** ..Zeph 3:8
And I will shake all ***n*** ....Hag 2:7
desire of all ***n*** shall come .....Hag 2:7
people, and so is this ***n*** ....Hag 2:14
n which spoiled you ....Zech 2:8
the ***n*** whom they knew not ....Zech 7:14
of all languages of the ***n*** ......Zech 8:23
n against Jerusalem ....Zech 14:2
n..came against Jerusalem .....Zech 14:16
even this whole ***n***.............Mal 3:9
n shall rise against ***n*** ....Matt 24:7
ye shall be hated of all ***n*** .....Matt 24:9
him shall be gathered all ***n*** .....Matt 25:32
therefore, and teach all ***n*** .....Matt 28:19
a Syrophoenician by ***n*** ....Mark 7:26
called of all ***n*** the house of ....Mark 11:17
published among all ***n*** ....Mark 13:10
he loveth our ***n***, and he ....Luke 7:5
n of the world seek after ......Luke 12:30
upon the earth distress of ***n*** ...Luke 21:25
fellow perverting the ***n*** ....Luke 23:2
in his name among all ***n*** ......Luke 24:47
take away..our place and ***n***....John 11:48
whole ***n*** perish not ....John 11:50
Thine own ***n*** and the chief ....John 18:35
out of every ***n*** under heaven ..Acts 2:5
report among all the ***n*** ....Acts 10:22
in every ***n*** he that feareth .....Acts 10:35
had destroyed seven ***n*** ....Acts 13:19
all ***n*** to walk in their own .....Acts 14:16
a judge unto this ***n*** ....Acts 24:10
mine own ***n*** at Jerusalem.......Acts 26:4
to the faith among all ***n***........Rom 1:5
become the father of many ***n*** ..Rom 4:18
by a foolish ***n*** I will anger. ....Rom 10:19
equals in mine own ***n*** ....Gal 1:14
thee shall all ***n*** be blessed .....Gal 3:8
crooked and perverse ***n*** ....Phil 2:15
I give power over the ***n*** ....Rev 2:26
tongue and people, and ***n*** .....Rev 5:9
man could number, of all ***n*** ...Rev 7:9
many peoples, and ***n***, and .....Rev 10:11
the ***n*** were angry, and thy .....Rev 11:18
kindreds, and tongues, and ***n*** ..Rev 13:7
n shall come and worship .....Rev 15:4
peoples..multitudes, and ***n*** ....Rev 17:15
were all ***n*** deceived ....Rev 18:23
deceive the ***n*** no more ....Rev 20:3
n of them which are saved ....Rev 21:24
for the healing of the ***n*** ....Rev 22:2

NATIONAL DUTIES—*See* CITIZEN, CITIZENSHIP

NATIONS, TABLE OF—*the list of the descendants of Noah's sons*
Record ....Gen 10:1-32

NATIVE—*belonging to a particular place by birth*
nor see his *n* country ....Jer 22:10

NATIVITY—*birth; origin*
in the land of his *n* ....Gen 11:28
and the land of thy *n* ....Ruth 2:11
to the land of our *n* ....Jer 46:16
n is of the land of Canaan ....Ezek 16:3
in the land of thy *n*..........Ezek 21:30

NATURAL—*the physical rather than the spiritual*

Described as:
Physical origin ....James 1:23
Normal ....Rom 1:26
Unregenerate 1Cor 2:14
Unnatural..............2Pet 2:12
Temporal 1Cor 15:46

Contrasted with:
Acquired ....Rom 11:21, 24
Perverted ....Rom 1:26, 27
Spiritual (life) 1Cor 2:14
Spiritual (body) 1Cor 15:44-46

NATURAL MAN—*sinful man*
Does not accept things of God..................1Cor 2:14
Contrasted with spiritual. .1Cor 15:44-46

NATURAL RELIGION—*nature's witness to God*

Contents of, God's:
Glory ....Ps 19:1-3
Nature ....Rom 1:19, 20
Sovereignty ....Acts 17:23-31
Goodness...............Acts 14:15-17

Characteristics of:
Original ....Rom 1:19, 20
Universal ....Rom 10:18
Inadequate..............Rom 2:12-15
Corrupted ....Rom 1:21-32
Valuable...............Dan 5:18-23

NATURALIZATION—*the process of becoming a citizen of an adopted country*
Natural level, rights of . . .Acts 22:25-28
Spiritual level, blessings of...................Eph 2:12-19

NATURALLY—*that which might be expected*
will *n* care for your state ......Phil 2:20
know *n*, as brute beasts ....Jude 10

NATURE—*the physical universe; man's original or natural condition*

Descriptive of:
Right order of things ....Rom 1:26
Natural sense of right ....Rom 2:14
Physical origin ....Rom 2:27
Non-existence ....Gal 4:8
Man's natural depravity . .Eph 2:3
Divine..................2Pet 1:4

Of man's unregenerate, described as:
Under wrath ....Eph 2:3
Source of:
Iniquity...............James 3:6
Corruption 2Pet 2:12

olive tree which is wild by *n*. . .Rom 11:24
wert grafted contrary to *n* ....Rom 11:24
Doth not even *n* itself teach . . .1Cor 11:14
We who are Jews by *n*........Gal 2:15
not on him the *n* of angels ....Heb 2:16

NATURE, BEAUTIES OF
Reveal God's glory ......Ps 19:1-6
Greater than outward appearance ....Matt 6:28-30
Descriptive of spiritual blessings ....Is 35:1, 2

NAUGHT—*See* NOUGHT

NAUGHTY—*very bad*

[*also* NAUGHTINESS]
giveth ear to a *n* tongue ......Prov 17:4
other basket had very *n* figs . . .Jer 24:2
filthiness and superfluity of *n* . .James 1:21

NAUGHTY PERSON—*one who does evil or wrong*
Wrongly ascribed 1Sam 17:28
Descriptive of the wicked .Prov 6:12
Downfall of ....Prov 11:6

NAUM—*See* NAHUM

NAVEL—*the point at which the umbilical cord was attached*

Used literally of:
Lover's appeal ....Song 7:2

Used figuratively of:
Inward self.............Prov 3:8
Israel's wretched condition ....Ezek 16:4

is in the *n* of his belly ....Job 40:16
n is like a round goblet ....Song 7:2

NAVES—*hubs of wheels*
axletrees, and their *n* 1Kin 7:33

NAVY—*a country's warships*
Solomon's 1Kin 9:26
Jehoshaphat's 1Kin 22:48

sent in the *n* his servants 1Kin 9:27
the *n* also of Hiram, that 1Kin 10:11
n of Tharshish with the *n* of. . .1Kin 10:22
three years came the *n* of 1Kin 10:22

NAY—*no*
N; but thou didst laugh ....Gen 18:15
said, *N*, I pray thee...........Gen 33:10
N, but to see the nakedness . . .Gen 42:12
do..unto thee? and he said, *N*. .Num 22:30
said, *N*; but as captain of .....Josh 5:14
If he said, *N* ....Judg 12:5
N, my brethren, *n*, I pray .....Judg 19:23
n, my daughters, for it........Ruth 1:13
N; but thou shalt give it me . . .1Sam 2:16
N; but we will have a king 1Sam 8:19
N; but a king shall reign 1Sam 12:12
N, my brother, do not force . . .2Sam 13:12
Hushai said, unto Absalom, *N*. .2Sam 16:18
(for he will not say thee *n*,) . . .1Kin 2:17
I pray thee, say me not *n* 1Kin 2:20
for I will not say thee *n*.......1Kin 2:20
other woman said, *N* 1Kin 3:22
Israel said unto him. *N* 2Kin 3:13
n, but let the shadow return . . .2Kin 20:10
n..not at all ashamed ....Jer 6:15
be, Yea, yea; *N*, *n* ....Matt 5:37
I tell you, *N*; but rather.......Luke 12:51
And he said, *N*, father ....Luke 16:30
N; but he deceiveth the people .John 7:12
n verily; but let them come . . .Acts 16:37
N: but by the law of faith .....Rom 3:27
N, in all these things we are . . .Rom 8:37
N, ye do wrong, and defraud . .1Cor 6:8
should be yea yea, and *n n*? . . .2Cor 1:17
not yea and *n*, but in him 2Cor 1:19
yea be yea, and your *n*, *n* .....James 5:12

NAZARENE (năz-ä-rēn')—*a native of Nazareth*
Jesus to be called........Matt 2:23
Descriptive of Jesus' followers...............Acts 24:5

NAZARETH (năz'ä-rěth)—*"sanctified"*

Town in Galilee:
Considered obscure ......John 1:46
City of Jesus' parents ....Matt 2:23
Early home of Jesus .....Luke 2:39-51
Jesus departs from.......Mark 1:9
Jesus rejected by ....Luke 4:16-30

As a title of honor descriptive of Jesus:
Anointed by the Spirit . . .Acts 10:38
Risen Lord ....Acts 22:8

And leaving *N*, he came ......Matt 4:13
Jesus the prophet of *N*........Matt 21:11
was also with Jesus of *N*......Matt 26:71
thou Jesus of *N*? ....Mark 1:24
heard that it was Jesus of *N*. . .Mark 10:47
wast with Jesus of *N*..........Mark 14:67
Ye seek Jesus of *N* ....Mark 16:6
city of Galilee, named *N* ......Luke 1:26
Galilee, out of the city of *N*. . .Luke 2:4
with thee thou Jesus of *N*? ....Luke 4:34
told him, that Jesus of *N*......Luke 18:37
Concerning Jesus of *N* ....Luke 24:19
Jesus of *N*, the son of Joseph . .John 1:45
answered him, Jesus of *N* .....John 18:5
Jesus of *N*..King of the Jews . .John 19:19
Jesus of *N*..approved of God . .Acts 2:22
name of Jesus Christ of *N*.....Acts 3:6
name of Jesus Christ of *N*.....Acts 4:10
to the name of Jesus of *N*.....Acts 26:9

NAZARITE (năz'ă-rīt)—*one especially consecrated to God*

Methods of becoming, by:
Birth ....Judg 13:5, 7
Vow...................Num 6:2

Requirements of:
Separation ....Num 6:4
No:
Strong drink ....Num 6:3, 4
Shaving...............Num 6:5
Defilement............Num 6:6, 7
Corruption ....Amos 2:11, 12
Holiness ....Num 6:8

Examples of:
Samson ....Judg 16:17
Samuel 1Sam 1:11-28
John the Baptist.........Luke 1:13, 15
Christians 2Cor 6:17

[*also* NAZARITE, NAZARITES]
is the law of the *N* ....Num 6:13
N shall shave the head ....Num 6:18
upon the hands of the *N* ......Num 6:19
after that the *N* may drink ....Num 6:20
law of the *N* who hath vowed .Num 6:21
N were purer than snow ......Lam 4:7

NEAH (nē'ä)—*"moved"*
Town in Zebulun ....Josh 19:13

NEAPOLIS (nĕ-ăp'ō-lĭs)—*"the new city"*
Seaport of Philippi ......Acts 16:11

NEAR—*close at hand (in place or time)*

Of dangers, from:
Prostitute ....Prov 7:8
Destruction ....Prov 10:14
God's judgment ....Joel 3:14

Of the Messianic salvation, as:
Promised ....Is 50:8
Available ....Is 51:5

Of Christ's return, described by:
Christ ....Matt 24:33
Paul ....Rom 13:11

[*also* NEARER]
n to enter into Egypt ....Gen 12:11
came *n* to break the door .....Gen 19:9
city is *n* to flee unto ....Gen 19:20
Abimelech had not come *n*....Gen 20:4
Jacob went *n* unto Isaac ......Gen 27:22
Bring it *n* to me, and I ....Gen 27:25
he brought it *n* to him ....Gen 27:25
he came *n*, and kissed him ....Gen 27:27
n, and rolled the stone........Gen 29:10
came *n* to his brother ....Gen 33:3
with her children came *n*......Gen 33:7
Joseph *n* and Rachel..........Gen 33:7
came *n* to the steward of......Gen 43:19
brethren, Come *n* to me ......Gen 45:4
they came *n*, And he said .....Gen 45:4
brought them *n* unto him .....Gen 48:10
let him come *n* and keep......Ex 12:48
one came not *n* the other .....Ex 14:20
which come *n* to the Lord.....Ex 19:22
Moses alone shall come *n* .....Ex 24:2
n to the altar to minister ......Ex 30:20

congregation drew *n* ....Lev 9:5
So they went *n*, and carried ...Lev 10:5
thy father's *n* kinswoman......Lev 18:12
are her *n* kinswomen ....Lev 18:17
that is *n* unto him ....Lev 21:2
Bring the tribe of Levi *n* ......Num 3:6
cause him to come *n*..........Num 16:5
will he cause to come *n* ....Num 16:5
brought thee *n* to him ....Num 16:10
cometh any thing *n* unto ......Num 17:13
Moab by Jordan *n* Jericho ....Num 26:63
came *n* unto Moses...........Num 31:48
they came *n* unto him ....Num 32:16
Moab by Jordan *n* Jericho ....Num 33:50
n and spake before Moses.....Num 36:1
ye came *n* unto me ....Deut 1:22
that ye came *n* unto me ....Deut 5:23
any trees *n* unto the altar .....Deut 16:21
wife of the one draweth *n* .....Deut 25:11
come not *n* unto it ....Josh 3:4
Come *n* put your feet upon ...Josh 10:24
they came *n*, and put their ....Josh 10:24
all that lay *n* Ashdod ....Josh 15:46
came *n* before Eleazar ....Josh 17:4
n the hill that lieth on the.....Josh 18:13
in the houses *n* to Micah's ....Judg 18:22
children of Israel came *n*......Judg 20:24
man is *n* of kin unto us ....Ruth 2:20
true that I am thy *n* kinsman ..Ruth 3:12
child, *n* to be delivered 1Sam 4:19
Saul drew *n* to Samuel.........1Sam 9:18
tribe of Benjamin to come *n* ..1Sam 10:20
Draw ye *n* hither, all the......1Sam 14:38
drew *n* to the Philistine 1Sam 17:40
David came *n* to the people ...1Sam 30:21
Go *n*, and fall upon him 2Sam 1:15
came apace, and drew *n* 2Sam 18:25
Come *n* hither, that I may 2Sam 20:16
land of the enemy, far or *n* ...1Kin 8:46
people, Come *n* unto me......1Kin 18:30
people came *n* unto him 1Kin 18:30
it is *n* unto my house 1Kin 21:2
Gehazi came *n* to thrust 2Kin 4:27
a land far off or *n* 2Chr 6:36
were *n* the Ethiopians 2Chr 21:16
Esther drew *n* and touched ....Esth 5:2
a prince would I go *n* ....Job 31:37
One is so *n* to another ....Job 41:16
for trouble is *n* ....Ps 22:11
good for me to draw *n* to God .Ps 73:28
n unto the gates of death .....Ps 107:18
Thou art *n*, O Lord; and all ...Ps 119:151
Let my cry come *n* before.....Ps 119:169
Israel, a people *n* unto him ...Ps 148:14
a neighbor that is *n*...........Prov 27:10
her time is *n* to come ....Is 13:22
draw *n* me with their mouth ...Is 29:13
Come *n*, ye nations, to hear ...Is 34:1
let them come *n*; then let .....Is 41:1
let us come *n* together ....Is 41:1
draw *n* together, ye that ......Is 45:20
Come ye *n* unto me, hear ye ..Is 48:16
My righteousness is *n* ....Is 51:5
shall not come *n* thee ....Is 54:14
call..upon him while he is *n* ...Is 55:6
salvation is *n* to come.........Is 56:1
is far off, and to him that is *n* .Is 57:19
thou art *n* in their mouth .....Jer 12:2
will cause him to draw *n* ......Jer 30:21
draw *n* to battle ....Jer 46:3
land of Moab, far or *n*........Jer 48:24
Thou drewest *n* in the day ....Lam 3:57
n shall fall by the sword ......Ezek 6:12
the day draweth *n* ....Ezek 7:12
come not *n* any man ....Ezek 9:6
n to a menstruous woman .....Ezek 18:6
Those that be *n*, and those ....Ezek 22:5
For the day is *n*, even the.....Ezek 30:3
the day of the Lord is *n* ......Ezek 30:3
shall not come *n* unto me .....Ezek 44:13
n to any of my holy things ....Ezek 44:13
n to me to minister unto me ..Ezek 44:15
come *n* to minister unto the ...Ezek 45:4
certain Chaldeans came *n* .....Dan 3:8
came *n*, and spake before .....Dan 6:12
I came *n* unto one of them....Dan 7:16
unto all Israel, that are *n* .....Dan 9:7
let all the men of war draw *n*. .Joel 3:9
seat of violence to come *n* ....Amos 6:3
day of the Lord is *n* upon .....Obad 15
she drew not *n* to her God ....Zeph 3:2
I will come *n* to you ....Mal 3:5
time of the fruit drew *n* ....Matt 21:34
ye know that summer is *n*......Mark 13:28
Then drew *n* unto him all .....Luke 15:1
when he was come *n*; he ......Luke 19:41
n unto Jesus to kiss him ......Luke 22:47
in Aenon *n* to Salim ....John 3:23
country *n* to the wilderness ....John 11:54
drew *n* to behold it ....Acts 7:31
he came *n* Damascus ....Acts 9:3
chief captain came *n* ....Acts 21:33
drew *n* to some country ....Acts 27:27
draw *n* with a true heart ......Heb 10:22

NEARIAH (nē-ä-rī'ä)—*"Jehovah drives away"*
1. Descendant of David 1Chr 3:22, 23
2. Simeonite captain 1Chr 4:42

NEARNESS OF GOD—*God's presence*

Old Testament:
In sense of time ....Is 46:13
Zeph 1:14
In prayer ....Is 55:6

New Testament:
In sense of time ....Rev 1:1-3
Rev 22:10
In prayer ....Phil 4:5-9

NEARSIGHTED—*unable to see at a distance*
Metaphorically descriptive of certain Christians ...2Pet 1:8, 9

NEBAI (nē'bī)—*"projecting"*
Leader who signs the sealed covenant ....Neh 10:19

NEBAIOTH (nĕ-bā'yŏth)—*"husbandry"*
Eldest son of Ishmael ....Gen 25:13
Descendants of, form Arabian tribe ....Is 60:7

[*also* NEBAJOTH]
the sister of *N*................Gen 28:9
sister of *N* ....Gen 36:3

NEBALLAT (nĕ-băl'ăt)—*"prophecy"*
Postexilic town of Benjamin ....Neh 11:31, 34

NEBAT (nē'băt)—*"cultivation"*
Father of Jeroboam......1Kin 11:26

Jeroboam the son of *N*........1Kin 12:2
Jeroboam the son of *N*........1Kin 15:1
Jeroboam the son of *N*........1Kin 16:26
Jeroboam the son of *N*........1Kin 21:22
Jeroboam the son of *N*........2Kin 3:3
Jeroboam the son of *N*........2Kin 10:29
Jeroboam the son of *N*........2Kin 14:24
Jeroboam the son of *N* king ...2Kin 17:21
Jeroboam the son of *N*? 2Chr 9:29
Jeroboam the son of *N*........2Chr 10:15

NEBO (nē'bō)—*"height"*
1. Babylonian god of literature and science ..Is 46:1
2. Mountain peak near Jericho ....Num 33:47
Name of Pisgah's summit.Deut 34:1
3. Moabite town near Mt. Nebo ....Num 32:3
Restored by Reubenites. .Num 32:37, 38
Mentioned in the prophecy ....Is 15:2
4. Town in Judah ....Ezra 2:29

mount *N*..in the land of.......Deut 32:49
dwelt in Aroer even unto *N* ...1Chr 5:8
the sons of *N*; Jeiel ....Ezra 10:43
men of the other *N* ....Neh 7:33
Woe unto *N*! ....Jer 48:1
upon *N* and upon Beth ....Jer 48:22

NEBUCHADNEZZAR (nĕb-ū-kăd-nĕz'er)—*"may the god Nabu guard my boundary stones"—monarch of the Neo-Babylonian Empire (605-562 B.C.)*

Life of:
Defeats Pharaoh Necho at Carchemish .... 2Chr 35:20; Jer 46:2
Besieges Jerusalem; carries captives to Babylon ....Dan 1:1, 2
Crushes Jehoiachin's revolt (597 B.C.) 2Kin 24:10-17
Carries sacred vessels to Babylon 2Kin 24:13
Destroys Jerusalem; captures Zedekiah (587 B.C.) ....Jer 39:5, 6
Leads attack on Tyre ....Ezek 26:7

Features concerning:
Builder of Babylon ......Dan 4:30
First of four great empires..............Dan 2:26-48
Instrument of God's judgment ....Jer 27:8
Called God's servant.....Jer 25:9
Afflicted with insanity ...Dan 4:28-37

Prophecies concerning his:
Conquest of Judah and Jerusalem.............Jer 21:7, 10
Destruction of Jerusalem .Jer 32:28-36
Conquest of other nations.Jer 27:7-9
Conquest of Egypt ......Jer 43:10-13
Destruction of Tyre......Ezek 26:7-12
Utter destruction ....Is 14:4-27

[*also* NEBUCHADREZZAR]
N king of Babylon came up ...2Kin 24:1
N king of Babylon came 2Kin 25:1
the nineteenth year of king *N*. .2Kin 25:8
N king of Babylon had 2Kin 25:22
Jerusalem by the hand of *N* ...1Chr 6:15
Against him came up *N* 2Chr 36:6
N also carried of the vessels ...2Chr 36:7
rebelled against king *N*........2Chr 36:13
N had brought forth ....Ezra 1:7
gave..into the hand of *N* .....Ezra 5:12
N took..out of the temple .....Ezra 6:5
N the king of Babylon had ....Neh 7:6
N the king of Babylon had ....Esth 2:6
N..of Babylon maketh war ....Jer 21:2
hand of *N* king of Babylon ....Jer 22:25
N king of Babylon had.......Jer 24:1
first year of *N* king ....Jer 25:1
lands into the hand of *N* ......Jer 27:6
N king of Babylon took not ...Jer 27:20
break the yoke of *N* ....Jer 28:11
N had carried away captive....Jer 29:1
deliver..into the hand of *N* ....Jer 29:21
eighteenth year of *N* ....Jer 32:1
when *N* king of Babylon ......Jer 34:1
when *N* king of Babylon ......Jer 35:11
whom *N* king of Babylon .....Jer 37:1
came *N* king of Babylon ......Jer 39:1
Judah into the hand of *N* .....Jer 44:30
N king of Babylon should .....Jer 46:13
N king of Babylon shall ....Jer 49:28
N..of Babylon hath broken ....Jer 50:17
N the king of Babylon hath ...Jer 51:34
N king of Babylon came ......Jer 52:4
nineteenth year of *N* king .....Jer 52:12
the people whom *N* carried....Jer 52:28
In the eighteenth year of *N* ...Jer 52:29
twentieth year of *N* ....Jer 52:30
N..Babylon caused his army ...Ezek 29:18
to cease by the hand of *N*.....Ezek 30:10
brought them in before *N* .....Dan 1:18
second year of..reign of *N*.....Dan 2:1
N dreamed dreams ....Dan 2:1
N..made an image of gold.....Dan 3:1
N..sent to gather together ....Dan 3:2
image which *N* the king ....Dan 3:2
image that *N* the king had ....Dan 3:3
image that *N* had set up ......Dan 3:3
image that *N*..had set up ......Dan 3:5
image that *N* the king had ....Dan 3:7

N in his rage and fury ....Dan 3:13
O *N* we are not careful to .....Dan 3:16
N the king was astonished .....Dan 3:24
N spake and said, Blessed .....Dan 3:28
N was at rest in mine house ...Dan 4:4
This dream I king *N* have .....Dan 4:18
father *N* had taken out ....Dan 5:2
God gave *N* thy father a ......Dan 5:18

NEBUSHASBAN (nĕb-ū-shăs'băn)—*"Nabu delivers me"*
Babylonian officer ....Jer 39:13

NEBUZAR-ADAN (nĕb-ū-zär-ā'dăn)—*"the god Nabu has given seed"*
Nebuchadnezzar's captain at siege of Jerusalem ..2Kin 25:8-20
Carries out Nebuchadnezzar's commands 2Kin 25:8-20
Protects Jeremiah ....Jer 39:11-14

N the captain of the guard ....Jer 39:9
N the captain of the guard left .Jer 39:10
N the captain of the guard ....Jer 40:1
N the captain of the guard ....Jer 43:6
N, captain of the guard ....Jer 52:12
N the captain of the guard ....Jer 52:15
N the captain of the guard ....Jer 52:26
N the captain of the guard ....Jer 52:30

NECESSARY—*something imperative; essential*

As applied to God's plan:
Preaching to the Jews first ....Acts 13:46
Change of the Law ......Heb 7:12
Of Christ's sacrifice ......Heb 8:3

In the Christian's life:
Wise decisions 2Cor 9:5
Personal needs ....Acts 20:34

See MUST

[*also* NECESSITIES, NECESSITY]
more than my *n* food ....Job 23:12
For of *n* he must release one. .Luke 23:17
burden than these *n* things ....Acts 15:28
such things as were *n* ....Acts 28:10
to the *n* of saints ....Rom 12:13
in his heart, having no *n* 1Cor 7:37
for *n* is laid upon me 1Cor 9:16
seem to be more feeble, are *n* .1Cor 12:22
in affliction, in *n* 2Cor 6:4
not grudgingly, or of *n* 2Cor 9:7
in *n*, in persecutions 2Cor 12:10
n to send to you ....Phil 2:25
once and again unto my *n* ......Phil 4:16
good works for *n* uses ....Titus 3:14
not be as it were of *n* ....Philem 14
also of *n* be the death ....Heb 9:16
was therefore *n* that the ......Heb 9:23

NECHO, NECHOH (nē'kō)—*Pharaoh of Egypt who fought Josiah at Megiddo*
N king of Egypt 2Chr 35:20
words of *N* from the mouth ...2Chr 35:22
N took Jehoahaz his brother...2Chr 36:4

See PHARAOH-NECHO

NECK—*that which connects the head with the body*

Uses of:
Ornaments ....Ezek 16:11
Beauty ....Song 4:4
Authority ....Gen 41:42

Significant acts performed by:
Emotional salutation .....Gen 45:14
Subjection of enemies ....Josh 10:24

Figurative of:
Servitude ....Gen 27:40
Severe punishment ......Is 8:8
Rescue ....Is 52:2

See YOKE

[*also* NECKS]
upon the smooth of his *n* .....Gen 27:16
fell on his *n*, and kissed him ..Gen 33:4
fell on his *n*..wept on his *n* ....Gen 46:29
in the *n* of thine enemies .....Gen 49:8
then thou shalt break his *n* ....Ex 13:13
wring off..head from his *n* ....Lev 5:8
strike off the heifer's *n* ....Deut 21:4
rebellion, and thy stiff *n* ......Deut 31:27
n of them that take ....Judg 5:30
were on their camels *n* ....Judg 8:21
and his *n* brake, and he died ..1Sam 4:18
the *n* of mine enemies 2Sam 22:41
but hardened their *n* 2Kin 17:14
like to the *n* of their fathers ...2Kin 17:14
he stiffened his *n* 2Chr 36:13
put not their *n* to the work ....Neh 3:5
but hardened their *n* ....Neh 9:17
hardened their *n*, and would ..Neh 9:29
upon him, even on his *n* ......Job 15:26
thou clothed his *n* with ....Job 39:19
given me the *n* of mine ....Ps 18:40
speak not with a stiff *n* ....Ps 75:5
and chains about thy *n* ....Prov 1:9
thy soul, and grace to thy *n* ...Prov 3:22
reproved hardeneth his *n* ......Prov 29:1
thy *n* with chains of gold ......Song 1:10
with one chain of thy *n* ....Song 4:9
walk with stretched forth *n* ....Is 3:16
yoke from off thy *n* ....Is 10:27
reach to the midst of the *n* ....Is 30:28
as if he cut off a dog's *n* ......Is 66:3
but hardened their *n* ....Jer 7:26
have hardened their *n* ....Jer 19:15
and put them upon thy *n* .....Jer 27:2
bring their *n* under the yoke ..Jer 27:11
n of all nations within the .....Jer 28:11
a yoke of iron upon the *n* .....Jer 28:14
come up upon my *n* ....Lam 1:14
n are under persecution ....Lam 5:5
the *n* of them that are slain ...Ezek 21:29
chain of gold about his *n* ......Dan 5:7, 29
chain of gold about thy *n* .....Dan 5:16
shall not remove your *n* ....Mic 2:3
foundation unto the *n* ....Hab 3:13
were hanged about his *n* ......Matt 18:6
were hanged about his *n* ......Mark 9:42
fell on his *n*, and kissed him ..Luke 15:20
upon the *n* of the disciples ....Acts 15:10
and fell on Paul's *n* ....Acts 20:37
life laid down their own *n* .....Rom 16:4

NECKLACE—*an ornament worn around the neck*
Signifying rank ....Gen 41:41, 42
Worn by animals ....Judg 8:26

NECROMANCER—*one who inquires of the dead*
Strongly condemned .....Deut 18:10, 11
Consulted by King Saul ..1Sam 28:7-19
Consultation with, rebuked ....Is 8:19

NEDABIAH (nĕd'ă-bī-ä)—*"Jehovah is willing"*
Son of King Jeconiah 1Chr 3:18

NEED—*necessary; to require*

Physical necessity, arising from lack of:
Food ....Deut 15:8
Provisions 2Chr 2:16

Moral necessity, arising from:
Spiritual immaturity .....Heb 5:12
Order of things..........Matt 3:14
Spiritual need ....Luke 10:42

Promises concerning supply of:
Promised ....Matt 6:8, 32
Provided ....Acts 2:45
Fulfilled ....Rev 21:23

Caused by:
Riotous living ....Luke 15:14

Provision against, by:
Help of others 2Cor 9:12

Reaction to, shown in:
Humble submission to God's will ....Phil 4:11, 12

See MUST; NECESSARY

[*also* NEEDED, NEEDEST, NEEDETH, NEEDFUL, NEEDS]
thou wouldst *n* be gone ....Gen 31:30
What *n* it? let me find ....Gen 33:15
Have I *n* of mad men, that....1Sam 21:15
For we must *n* die 2Sam 14:14
not *n* to fight in this 2Chr 20:17
they have *n* of, both ....Ezra 6:9
n for the house of thy God ....Ezra 7:20
shall have no *n* of spoil ....Prov 31:11
they must *n* be borne ....Jer 10:5
be whole *n* not a physician ....Matt 9:12
They *n* not depart; give ye ....Matt 14:16
must *n* be that offenses ....Matt 18:7
The Lord hath *n* of them .....Matt 21:3
n have we of witnesses? ....Matt 26:65
no *n* of the physician ....Mark 2:17
the Lord hath *n* of him ....Mark 11:3
for such things must *n* be .....Mark 13:7
n we any further witnesses? ....Mark 14:63
whole *n* not a physician ....Luke 5:31
give him as many as he *n* .....Luke 11:8
have *n* of these things ....Luke 12:30
must *n* go and see it ....Luke 14:18
the Lord hath *n* of him ....Luke 19:31
n we any further witnesses? ...Luke 22:71
n not that any should testify...John 2:25
n go through Samaria ....John 4:4
n not save to wash his feet ....John 13:10
n of against the feast ....John 13:29
n not that any man should ask .John 16:30
this scripture must *n* ....Acts 1:16
according as he had *n* ....Acts 4:35
was *n* to circumcise them .....Acts 15:5
as though he *n* any thing ......Acts 17:25
multitude must *n* come ....Acts 21:22
ye must *n* be subject ....Rom 13:5
business she hath *n* of you ....Rom 16:2
must ye *n* go out of the 1Cor 5:10
n so require, let him do what..1Cor 7:36
I have no *n* of thee 1Cor 12:21
I have no *n* of you 1Cor 12:21
or *n* we, as some others 2Cor 3:1
If I must *n* glory, ...2Cor 11:30
to give to him that *n* ....Eph 4:28
abide in the flesh is more *n* ...Phil 1:24
God shall supply all your *n* ....Phil 4:19
n not to speak any thing 1Thess 1:8
n not that I write unto you 1Thess 4:9
n that I write unto you 1Thess 5:1
that *n* not to be ashamed 2Tim 2:15
grace to help in time of *n* .....Heb 4:16
n was there that another ......Heb 7:11
Who *n* not daily as those .....Heb 7:27
which are *n* to the body.......James 2:16
now for a season, if *n* be 1Pet 1:6
n not that any man teach you. .1John 2:27
seeth his brother have *n* 1John 3:17
n for me to write unto you ....Jude 3
and have *n* of nothing ....Rev 3:17
city had no *n* of the sun ......Rev 21:23
n no candle, neither light .....Rev 22:5

NEEDLE—*a sharp instrument used in sewing or embroidering*
Product of, used in tabernacle ....Ex 26:36
Figurative of something impossible ....Matt 19:24

[*also* NEEDLE'S]
go through the eye of a *n* .....Matt 19:24
go through the eye of a *n* .....Mark 10:25
go through a *n* eye ....Luke 18:25

NEEDLEWORK—*embroidery*
Of the tabernacle...... Ex 26:36; Ex 28:39; Ex 38:18

linen wrought with *n* ....Ex 26:36
linen, wrought with *n* ....Ex 27:16
make the girdle of *n* ....Ex 28:39
fine twined linen of *n* ....Ex 36:37
gate of the court was *n* ....Ex 38:18
and purple, and scarlet, of *n* ..Ex 39:29

N

a prey of divers colors of *n*. . . .Judg 5:30
unto the king in raiment of *n*. . .Ps 45:14

NEEDY—*the poor; destitute*

Evil treatment of:
Oppression. . . . . .Amos 4:1
Injustice toward . . . . .Is 10:2

Promise toward:
God's:
Remembrance of . . . . . .Ps 9:18
Deliverance . . . . .Ps 35:10
Salvation of . . . . .Ps 72:4-13
Exaltation of . . . . .Ps 113:7
Strength of . . . . .Is 25:4

Right treatment of:
Recommended . . . . .Deut 24:14, 15
Remembered . . . . .Jer 22:16
Rewarded . . . . .Matt 25:34-40

See POOR; POVERTY

thy poor, and to thy *n* . . . . .Deut 15:11
turn the *n* out of the way . . . . .Job 24:4
light killeth the poor and *n* . . . .Job 24:14
for the sighing of the *n* . . . . . . .Ps 12:5
to cast down the poor and *n* . .Ps 37:14
But I am poor and *n* . . . . .Ps 40:17
am poor and *n*: make haste . . .Ps 70:5
poor and *n* praise thy name . . .Ps 74:21
Deliver the poor and *n* . . . . . . .Ps 82:4
for I am poor and *n* . . . . .Ps 86:1
For I am poor and *n* . . . . .Ps 109:22
the *n* from among men . . . . . . .Prov 30:14
forth her hands to the *n* . . . . . .Prov 31:20
n shall lie down in safety . . . . . .Is 14:30
and the steps of the *n* . . . . .Is 26:6
poor and *n* seek water . . . . .Is 41:17
the right of the *n* do they . . . . .Jer 5:28
hand of the poor and *n* . . . . . . .Ezek 16:49
vexed the poor and *n* . . . . .Ezek 22:29
O ye that swallow up the *n* . . .Amos 8:4
n for a pair of shoes . . . . .Amos 8:6

NEESINGS—*See* SNEEZE

NEGEV (něg'ěv)—*"dry; parched"—denotes southern Palestine*
Hebron located in . . . . . . .Num 13:22

NEGINAH (ně-gē'nä)—*"stringed instrument"*
chief Musician upon *N* . . . . .Ps 61:*title*

NEGINOTH (něg'ĭ-nŏth)—*same as Neginah*
chief Musician on *N* . . . . .Ps 54:*title*

NEGLECT—*to fail to respond to duties*

Of material things:
One's appearance 2Sam 19:24
Needs of the body . . . . . . .Col 2:23

Of spiritual things:
Gospel . . . . .Matt 22:2-5
Salvation . . . . .Heb 2:1-3

Consequences of:
Kept out . . . . .Matt 25:1-13
Sent to hell . . . . .Matt 25:24-30
Reward lost 1Cor 3:10-15

[*also* NEGLECTED]
if he shall *n* to hear them . . . . .Matt 18:17
if he *n* to hear the church . . . . .Matt 18:17
n in the daily ministration . . . . .Acts 6:1
N not the gift that is in thee . . .1Tim 4:14

NEGLIGENT—*given to neglect*
My sons, be not now *n* 2Chr 29:11
will not be *n* to put you 2Pet 1:12

NEHELAMITE (nē-hěl'ă-mīt)
Term applied to
Shemaiah, a false
prophet . . . . .Jer 29:24-32

NEHEMIAH (nē-hě-mī'ä)—*"Jehovah is consolation"*
1. Leader in the postexilic community . . . . .Ezra 2:2
2. Postexilic workman . . . . .Neh 3:16

NEHEMIAH (nē-hě-mī'ä)—*"Jehovah is consolation"—the Governor of Jerusalem who helped rebuild the city*

Life of:
Son of Hachaliah . . . . .Neh 1:1
Cupbearer to the Persian King Artaxerxes I (465—424 B.C.) . . . . . . .Neh 1:11
Grieves over Jerusalem's desolation . . . . .Neh 1:4-11
Appointed governor . . . . .Neh 5:14
Sent to rebuild Jerusalem .Neh 2:1-8
Unwelcome by non-Jews .Neh 2:9, 10
Views walls at night . . . . .Neh 2:11-20
Gives list of builders . . . . .Neh 3:1-32
Continues work in spite of opposition . . . . .Neh 4:1-23
Makes reforms among Jews . . . . .Neh 5:1-19
Opposition continues, but work completed . . . . . . .Neh 6:1-19
Introduces law and order .Neh 7:1-73
Participates with Ezra in restored worship . . . . . .Neh 8—10
Registers inhabitants . . . . .Neh 11:1-36
Registers priests and Levites . . . . .Neh 12:1-26
Returns to Artaxerxes; revisits Jerusalem . . . . . .Neh 13:6, 7
Institutes reforms . . . . .Neh 13:1-31

Character of:
Patriotic . . . . .Neh 1:1-4
Prayerful . . . . .Neh 1:5-11
Perceptive . . . . .Neh 2:17-20
Persistent . . . . .Neh 4:1-23
Persuasive . . . . .Neh 5:1-13
Pure in motives . . . . .Neh 5:14-19
Persevering . . . . .Neh 6:1-19

See the following article

NEHEMIAH, THE BOOK OF—*a book of the Old Testament*
Nehemiah's prayer . . . . . . .Neh 1:4-11
Inspection of the wall . . . .Neh 2:11-16
Rebuilding the wall . . . . . .Neh 3:1-32
The enemies' plot . . . . . . .Neh 6:1-14
The reading of the Law . .Neh 8:1-18
Confession of the priests .Neh 9:4-38
Nehemiah's reform . . . . . .Neh 13:7-31

NEHILOTH—*wind instruments*
Title of a psalm . . . . .Ps 5:*title*

NEHUM (nē'hŭm)—*"pity"*
Postexilic returnee . . . . . . .Neh 7:7
Called Rehum . . . . .Ezra 2:2

NEHUSHTA (ně-hŭsh'tă)—*"basis; ground"*
Wife of King Jehoiakim . .2Kin 24:8

NEHUSHTAN (ně-hŭsh'tăn)—*"piece of brass"*
Applied to brazen serpent 2Kin 18:4

NEIEL (ně-ī'ěl)—*"commotion of God"*
Town in Asher . . . . .Josh 19:24, 27

NEIGH—*the cry of a horse*

Used of:
Horses . . . . .Jer 8:16
Lustful desires . . . . .Jer 5:8
Rendered, "bellow" . . . . .Jer 50:11

[*also* NEIGHINGS]
thine adulteries, and thy *n* . . . .Jer 13:27

NEIGHBOR—*fellow human being; one living near another*

Sins against, forbidden:
False witness . . . . .Ex 20:16
Coveting . . . . .Ex 20:17
Lying . . . . .Lev 6:2-5
Hating . . . . .Deut 19:11-13
Despising . . . . .Prov 14:21
Enticing . . . . .Prov 16:29
Deception . . . . .Prov 26:19
Flattery . . . . .Prov 29:5
Failure to pay . . . . .Jer 22:13
Adultery . . . . .Jer 29:23

Duties toward, encouraged:
Love . . . . .Rom 13:9, 10
Speak truth to . . . . .Eph 4:25
Teach . . . . .Jer 31:34
Show mercy to . . . . .Luke 10:29, 37

[*also* NEIGHBOR'S, NEIGHBORS, NEIGHBORS']
woman shall borrow of her *n* . .Ex 3:22
man borrow of his *n* . . . . .Ex 11:2
n next unto his house . . . . .Ex 12:4
presumptuously upon his *n* . . . .Ex 21:14
deliver unto his *n* money . . . . . .Ex 22:7
put into his hand unto his *n* . . .Ex 22:8
man deliver unto his *n* . . . . .Ex 22:10
take thy *n* raiment . . . . .Ex 22:26
and every man his *n* . . . . .Ex 32:27
not lie carnally with thy *n* . . . . .Lev 18:20
shalt not defraud thy *n* . . . . .Lev 19:13
against the blood of thy *n* . . . . .Lev 19:16
shalt love thy *n* as thyself . . . . .Lev 19:18
man cause a blemish in his *n* . .Lev 24:19
sell ought unto thy *n* . . . . .Lev 25:14
buyest ought of thy *n* hand . . . .Lev 25:14
should kill his *n* unawares . . . . .Deut 4:42
false witness against thy *n* . . . . .Deut 5:20
thou desire thy *n* wife . . . . .Deut 5:21
thou covet thy *n* house . . . . .Deut 5:21
or any thing that is thy *n* . . . . .Deut 5:21
lendeth ought unto his *n* . . . . . .Deut 15:2
shall not exact it of his *n* . . . . . .Deut 15:2
killeth his *n* ignorantly . . . . .Deut 19:4
into the wood with his *n* . . . . . .Deut 19:5
lighteth upon his *n* . . . . .Deut 19:5
But if any man hate his *n* . . . . . .Deut 19:11
not remove thy *n* landmark . . .Deut 19:14
he hath humbled his *n* wife . . .Deut 22:24
man riseth against his *n* . . . . . . .Deut 22:26
comest into thy *n* vineyard . . . .Deut 23:24
standing corn of thy *n* . . . . .Deut 23:25
unto thy *n* standing corn . . . . . .Deut 23:25
removeth his *n* landmark . . . . . .Deut 27:17
smiteth his *n* secretly . . . . .Deut 27:24
heard that they were their *n* . . .Josh 9:16
smote his *n* unwittingly . . . . . . .Josh 20:5
and gave it to his *n* . . . . .Ruth 4:7
women her *n* gave it a name . .Ruth 4:17
given it to a *n* of thine 1Sam 15:28
given it to thy *n*, even to 1Sam 28:17
and give them unto thy *n* 2Sam 12:11
man trespass against his *n* 1Kin 8:31
unto his *n* in the word 1Kin 20:35
vessels abroad of all thy *n* 2Kin 4:3
If a man sin against his *n* 2Chr 6:22
I am as one mocked of his *n* . .Job 12:4
as a man pleadeth for his *n*! . . .Job 16:21
laid wait at my *n* door . . . . .Job 31:9
speak vanity..with his *n* . . . . . . .Ps 12:2
nor doeth evil to his *n* . . . . .Ps 15:3
up a reproach against his *n* . . . .Ps 15:3
speak peace to their *n* . . . . .Ps 28:3
but especially among my *n* . . . .Ps 31:11
us a reproach to our *n* . . . . .Ps 44:13
become a reproach to our *n* . . .Ps 79:4
makest us a strife unto our *n* . .Ps 80:6
he is a reproach to his *n* . . . . . .Ps 89:41
privily slandereth his *n* . . . . . . .Ps 101:5
Say not unto thy *n*, Go . . . . . . .Prov 3:28
goeth in to his *n* wife . . . . .Prov 6:29
mouth destroyeth his *n* . . . . .Prov 11:9
more excellent than his *n* . . . . .Prov 12:26
is hated even of his own *n* . . . .Prov 14:20
n cometh and searcheth . . . . . . .Prov 18:17
poor is separated from his *n* . . .Prov 19:4
n findeth no favor in his eyes . .Prov 21:10
Be not a witness against thy *n* .Prov 24:28
n hath put thee to shame . . . . .Prov 25:8
Debate thy cause with thy *n* . . .Prov 25:9
thy foot from thy *n* house . . . . .Prov 25:17
false witness against his *n* . . . . .Prov 25:18
better is a *n* that is near . . . . . .Prov 27:10
a man is envied of his *n* . . . . . .Eccl 4:4
and every one by his *n* . . . . .Is 3:5
and every one against his *n* . . .Is 19:2
helped every one his *n* . . . . .Is 41:6
neighed after his *n* wife . . . . . . .Jer 5:8
n and his friend shall perish . . .Jer 6:21
between a man and his *n* . . . . .Jer 7:5
heed every one of his *n* . . . . . . .Jer 9:4

n will walk with slanders . . . . . .Jer 9:4
every one her *n* lamentation . . .Jer 9:20
against all mine evil *n* . . . . .Jer 12:14
say every man to his *n* . . . . .Jer 22:8
useth his *n* service without . . . .Jer 22:13
tell every man to his *n* . . . . .Jer 23:27
ye say every one to his *n* . . . . .Jer 23:35
liberty every man to his *n* . . . . .Jer 34:15
his brethren, and his *n* . . . . . . .Jer 49:10
Gomorrah and the *n* cities . . . .Jer 49:18
the Egyptians thy *n*, great . . . . .Ezek 16:26
hath defiled his *n* wife . . . . .Ezek 18:6
abomination with his *n* wife . . .Ezek 22:11
greedily gained of thy *n* . . . . . . .Ezek 22:12
on the Assyrians her *n* . . . . .Ezek 23:5
defile every one his *n* wife . . . .Ezek 33:26
unto him that giveth his *n* . . . . .Hab 2:15
ye call every man his *n* . . . . . . .Zech 3:10
every one against his *n* . . . . .Zech 8:10
every one on the hand of his *n*.Zech 14:13
against the hand of his *n* . . . . . .Zech 14:13
Thou shalt love thy *n* . . . . .Matt 5:43
love thy *n* as thyself . . . . .Matt 19:19
n and her cousins heard . . . . . . .Luke 1:58
and thy *n* as thyself . . . . .Luke 10:27
thy kinsmen, nor thy rich *n* . . .Luke 14:12
calleth..his friends and *n* . . . . . .Luke 15:6
The *n* therefore, and they . . . . .John 9:8
he that did his *n* wrong . . . . . . .Acts 7:27
every one of us please his *n* . . .Rom 15:2
love thy *n* as thyself . . . . .Gal 5:14
speak..truth with his *n* . . . . .Eph 4:25
not teach every man his *n* . . . . .Heb 8:11
love thy *n* as thyself . . . . .James 2:8

NEITHER—*See* Introduction

NEKEB (nē′kĕb)—*"a narrow pass"*
Village in Naphtali . . . . . .Josh 19:33

NEKODA (nĕ-kō′dä)—*"herdsman"*
Founder of a family of
Temple servants . . . . . . .Ezra 2:48
Genealogy of, rejected . . .Ezra 2:59, 60

the children of *N* . . . . .Neh 7:50
children of *N*, six hundred . . . .Neh 7:62

NEMUEL (nĕm′ū-ĕl)—*"God is speaking"*
1. Brother of Dathan and
Abiram . . . . .Num 26:9
2. Eldest son of Simeon 1Chr 4:24
Head of Nemuelites . . . . .Num 26:12
Called Jemuel . . . . .Gen 46:10

NEPHEG (nē′fĕg)—*"sprout; shoot"*
1. Izhar's son; Korah's
brother . . . . .Ex 6:21
2. David's son born in
Jerusalem 2Sam 5:13-15

Nogah, and *N*, and Japhia 1Chr 3:7

NEPHEW—*archaic for grandson*
Applied to:
Abdon's . . . . .Judg 12:14
Widow's 1Tim 5:4
Used as a curse . . . . .Is 14:22

have son nor *n* among . . . . . . .Job 18:19

NEPHISH (nē′fĭsh)—*"numerous"—a tribe descended from Ishmael*
Hagarites, with Jetur, and *N* . .1Chr 5:19

NEPHISHESIM (nĕ-fĭsh′ĕ-sĭm)—*"expansions"*

[*also* nephusim]
the children of *N* . . . . .Ezra 2:50
the children of *N* . . . . .Neh 7:52

NEPHTHALIM (nĕf′thä-lim)—*the same as Naphtali*
borders of Zabulon and *N* . . . . .Matt 4:13
N were sealed twelve thousand .Rev 7:6

NEPHTOAH (nĕf-tō′ä)—*"open"*
Border town between
Judah and Benjamin . . .Josh 15:9

NEPHUSIM—*See* Nephishesim

NEPOTISM—*putting relatives in public office*
Joseph's . . . . .Gen 47:11, 12
Saul's 1Sam 14:50
David's 2Sam 8:16-18
Nehemiah's . . . . .Neh 7:2

NER (nûr)—*"light"*
Father of Abner;
grandfather of Saul 1Sam 14:50, 51

N the father of Abner 1Sam 14:51
Abner the son of *N* 1Sam 26:5
Abner the son of *N* 1Sam 26:14
Abner the son of *N* 2Sam 2:8
son of *N* came to the king 2Sam 3:23
blood of Abner..son of *N* 2Sam 3:28
Abner the son of *N* 1Kin 2:5
N begat Kish, and Kish 1Chr 8:33
Kish, and Baal, and *N* 1Chr 9:36
N begat Kish; and Kish 1Chr 9:39
Abner the son of *N* 1Chr 26:28

NEREUS (nē′rūs)—*"lamp"*
Christian at Rome . . . . . . .Rom 16:15

NERGAL (nûr-găl)—*a Babylonian god of war*
Worshiped by men of
Cuth 2Kin 17:30

NERGAL-SHAREZER (nûr-găl-shä-rē′zer)—*"may the god Nergal defend the prince"*
Babylonian prince during
capture of Jerusalem . . .Jer 39:3, 13

NERI (nē′rī)—*"whose lamp is Jehovah"*
Ancestor of Christ . . . . . . .Luke 3:27

NERIAH (nĕ-rī′ä)—*"whose lamp is Jehovah"*
Father of Baruch . . . . .Jer 32:12

called Baruch the son of *N* . . . .Jer 36:4
son of *N* took the roll . . . . .Jer 36:14
son of *N* setteth thee . . . . .Jer 43:3
spake unto Baruch..son of *N* . .Jer 45:1
Seraiah the son of *N* . . . . .Jer 51:59

NEST—*a place of rest, retreat, or lodging, often used to describe a bird's house*
Kinds of:
Eagle's . . . . .Job 39:27
Swallow's . . . . .Ps 84:3
Great owl . . . . .Is 34:15
Dove's . . . . .Jer 48:28
Figurative of:
False security . . . . .Num 24:21, 22
Lord's resting place . . . . . .Matt 8:20
Full maturity . . . . .Job 29:18
Something out of place . .Prov 27:8
Helplessness . . . . .Is 10:14

[*also* nests]
bird's *n* chance to be . . . . .Deut 22:6
eagle stirreth up her *n* . . . . .Deut 32:11
birds make their *n* . . . . .Ps 104:17
bird cast out of the *n* . . . . .Is 16:2
makest thy *n* in the cedars . . . .Jer 22:23
thy *n* as high as the eagle . . . . .Jer 49:16
thy *n* among the stars . . . . .Obad 4
he may set his *n* on high . . . . . .Hab 2:9
birds of the air have *n* . . . . .Matt 8:20

NET—*a meshed fabric used to capture insects, birds, fish, or other animals*
Kinds of:
Design in a structure . . . .Ex 27:4, 5
Trapping a bird or animal.Prov 1:17
Catching fish . . . . .John 21:6-11
Figurative of:
Plots of evil men . . . . .Ps 9:15
Predatory men . . . . .Ps 31:4
God's chastisements . . . . .Job 19:6
Flattery . . . . .Prov 29:5
God's sovereign plan . . . .Ezek 12:13
Ezek 17:20

[*also* nets]
n of checker work 1Kin 7:17
cast into a *n* by his own feet . .Job 18:8
draweth him into his *n* . . . . .Ps 10:9
pluck my feet out of the *n* . . . .Ps 25:15
hid for me their *n* in a pit . . . . .Ps 35:7
n that he hath hid catch . . . . . . .Ps 35:8
prepared a *n* for my steps . . . . .Ps 57:6
broughtest us into the *n* . . . . . . .Ps 66:11
spread a *n* by the wayside . . . . .Ps 140:5
wicked fall into their own *n* . . .Ps 141:10
desireth the *n* of evil men . . . . .Prov 12:12
heart is snares and *n* . . . . .Eccl 7:26
fishes..taken in an evil *n* . . . . . .Eccl 9:12
spread *n* upon the waters . . . . .Is 19:8
as a wild bull in a *n* . . . . .Is 51:20
spread a *n* for my feet . . . . .Lam 1:13
spread their *n* over him . . . . . . .Ezek 19:8
place for the spreading of *n* . . .Ezek 26:5
place to spread *n* upon . . . . .Ezek 26:14
therefore spread out my *n* . . . . .Ezek 32:3
shall bring thee up in my *n* . . . .Ezek 32:3
be a place to spread forth *n* . . .Ezek 47:10
n spread upon Tabor . . . . .Hos 5:1
his brother with a *n* . . . . .Mic 7:2
they catch them in their *n* . . . . .Hab 1:15
shall they..empty their *n* . . . . . .Hab 1:17
casting a *n* into the sea . . . . . . .Matt 4:18
they straightway left their *n* . . .Matt 4:20
their father, mending their *n* . .Matt 4:21
of heaven is like unto a *n*. . . . .Matt 13:47
casting a *n* into the sea . . . . . . .Mark 1:16
they forsook their *n* . . . . .Mark 1:18
in the ship mending their *n* . . . .Mark 1:19
and were washing their *n* . . . . .Luke 5:2
let down..*n* for a draught . . . . .Luke 5:4
I will let down the *n* . . . . .Luke 5:5
of fishes: and their *n* brake . . . .Luke 5:6

NETHANEEL (nĕ-thăn′ĕ-ĕl)—*"God gives"*
1. Leader of Issachar . . . . .Num 1:8
2. Jesse's fourth son 1Chr 2:13, 14
3. Levite trumpeter 1Chr 15:24
4. Levite scribe 1Chr 24:6
5. Obed-edom's fifth son . .1Chr 26:4
6. Prince sent to teach
Judah 2Chr 17:7
7. Levite chief 2Chr 35:9
8. Priest who married a
foreign wife . . . . .Ezra 10:18-22
9. Priest in Joiakim's time .Neh 12:21
10. Levite musician in
dedication service . . . .Neh 12:36

N the son of Zuar shall be . . . .Num 2:5
second day *N* the son of Zuar .Num 7:18
offering of *N*..son of Zuar . . . . .Num 7:23
was *N* the son of Zuar . . . . .Num 10:15

NETHANIAH (nĕth-ä-nī′ä)—*"Jehovah gives"*
1. Son of Asaph 1Chr 25:2, 12
2. Levite teacher in
Jehoshaphat's reign . . .2Chr 17:8
3. Father of Jehudi . . . . .Jer 36:14
4. Father of Ishmael, struck
down Gedaliah 2Kin 25:23, 25

Ishmael the son of *N* . . . . .Jer 40:8
son of *N* to slay thee? . . . . .Jer 40:14
slay Ishmael the son of *N* . . . . .Jer 40:15
Ishmael the son of *N* . . . . .Jer 41:1
son of *N* went forth . . . . .Jer 41:6
son of *N* slew them . . . . .Jer 41:7
son of *N* filled it with . . . . .Jer 41:9
son of *N* carried them . . . . .Jer 41:10
son of *N* had done . . . . .Jer 41:11
to fight with..son of *N* . . . . .Jer 41:12
son of *N* escaped . . . . .Jer 41:15
from Ishmael the son of *N* . . . .Jer 41:16
son of *N* had slain Gedaliah . . .Jer 41:18

NETHER—*situated down or below*

[*also* nethermost]
at the *n* part of the mount . . . .Ex 19:17
and the *n* springs . . . . .Josh 15:19
side of the *n* Beth-horon . . . . . .Josh 18:13
springs and the *n* springs . . . . . .Judg 1:15
n chamber was five cubits 1Kin 6:6
and Beth-horon the *n* 1Kin 9:17
built Beth-horon the *n* 1Chr 7:24

to the *n* parts of the earth ....Ezek 31:14
in the *n* parts of the earth.....Ezek 31:16
Eden unto the *n* parts of......Ezek 31:18
n parts of the earth...........Ezek 32:18
n parts of the earth...........Ezek 32:24

NETHINIM (něth'ĭ-nĭm)—*"given"—the name given to those who were set apart to do the menial tasks of the sanctuary*

Described as:
Servants of the Levites...Ezra 8:20

Probable origin of:
Midianites ....Num 31:2, 41
Gibeonites ....Josh 9:23, 27
Solomon's slaves 1Kin 9:20, 21

Characteristics of:
Governed by captains ....Neh 11:21
Assigned certain cities ...1Chr 9:2
Exempt from taxes ......Ezra 7:24
Zealous for Israel's covenant..............Neh 10:28, 29
Assigned important jobs. .Ezra 8:17
Returned from exile in large numbers.........Ezra 2:43-54

See MEHUNIM

All the *N*, and the children....Ezra 2:58
N, dwelt in their cities ....Ezra 2:70
the *N*, unto Jerusalem ....Ezra 7:7
the *N* dwelt in Ophel ....Neh 3:26
unto the place of the *N* ....Neh 3:31
N: the children of Ziha ....Neh 7:46
All the *N*, and the children....Neh 7:60
the *N*, and all Israel ....Neh 7:73
and the *N*, and the children ...Neh 11:3

NETOPHATHITE (nē-tō'fă-thīt)—*an inhabitant of Netophah*
Town of Judah near Jerusalem .... Ezra 2:22; Neh 7:26
Occupied by returning Levites 1Chr 9:16
Applied to two of David's mighty men 2Sam 23:28, 29
Loyalty of, demonstrated .2Kin 25:23, 24

[*also* NETOPHAH, NETOPHATHI]
the son of Baanah, a *N* 2Sam 23:29
Maharai the *N*, Heled the 1Chr 11:30
the son of Baanah the *N* 1Chr 11:30
was Maharai the *N* 1Chr 27:13
was Heldai the *N*.............1Chr 27:15
the men of *N*, fifty and six ....Ezra 2:22
the men of Beth-lehem and *N* .Neh 7:26
and from the village of *N* .....Neh 12:28
sons of Ephai the *N*, and .....Jer 40:8

NETTLES—*thorn bushes*
Sign of:
Indolence ....Prov 24:31
Desolation ....Is 34:13
Retreat for cowards .....Job 30:7

silver, *n* shall possess them ....Hos 9:6
breeding of *n*, and saltpits.....Zeph 2:9

NETWORK—*artistic handwork*
Tabernacle ....Ex 27:4
Temple 2Kin 7:18-41

[*also* NETWORKS]
altar, a brazen grate of *n* .....Ex 38:4
round about upon the one *n*...1Kin 7:18
the belly which was by the *n* ..1Kin 7:20
two *n*, to cover the two 1Kin 7:41
pomegranates for one *n* 1Kin 7:42
pomegranates for the two *n* ...1Kin 7:42
they that weave *n*, shall be ....Is 19:9
n and pomegranates upon the. .Jer 52:22
pomegranates upon the *n* .....Jer 52:23

NEUTRALITY—*not engaged on either side of a question*
Impossibility of, taught...Matt 6:24; Matt 12:30
Invitation to, rejected....Josh 24:15, 16

NEVER—*not ever*

Concerning God's spiritual promises:
Satisfaction ....John 4:14
Stability ....Ps 55:22
Security ....John 10:28

Concerning God's threats:
Chastisement............2Sam 12:10
Desolation ....Is 13:20
Forgiveness ....Mark 3:29

n saw in all the land..........Gen 41:19
it shall *n* go out ....Lev 6:13
upon which *n* came yoke ......Num 19:2
poor shall *n* cease ....Deut 15:11
n break my covenant with.....Judg 2:1
withes that were *n* dried ......Judg 16:7
ropes that were *n* occupied ....Judg 16:11
infants which *n* saw light ......Job 3:16
n eateth with pleasure ....Job 21:25
I shall *n* be in adversity.......Ps 10:6
he will *n* see it ....Ps 10:11
these things..*n* be moved......Ps 15:5
let me *n* be ashamed ....Ps 31:1
charming *n* so wisely..........Ps 58:5
let me *n* be put to............Ps 71:1
righteous..*n* be removed ......Prov 10:30
destruction are *n* full ....Prov 27:20
eyes of man are *n* satisfied ....Prov 27:20
It shall *n* be inhabited ....Is 13:20
seed of evildoers shalt *n* ......Is 14:20
it shall *n* be built ....Is 25:2
n hold their peace day ....Is 62:6
n want a man to sit upon .....Jer 33:17
n open thy mouth any more ...Ezek 16:63
n shalt be any more ....Ezek 27:36
which shall *n* be destroyed ....Dan 2:44
my people shall *n* be ....Joel 2:26
n forget any of..works ....Amos 8:7
judgment doth *n* go forth .....Hab 1:4
I *n* knew you: depart from me .Matt 7:23
n read, Out of the mouth .....Matt 21:16
yet I will *n* be offended ....Matt 26:33
n saw it on this fashion ....Mark 2:12
n read what David did ....Mark 2:25
fire that *n*..be quenched ......Mark 9:43
man if he had *n* been born ....Mark 14:21
thou *n* gavest me a kid ....Luke 15:29
and the wombs that *n* bare ....Luke 23:29
paps which *n* gave suck ....Luke 23:29
n man before was laid ....Luke 23:53
cometh to me..*n* hunger ....John 6:35
believeth on me..*n* thirst ......John 6:35
N man spake like this man ....John 7:46
he shall *n* see death ....John 8:51
shall *n* taste of death ....John 8:52
believeth in me shall *n*........John 11:26
wherein was *n* man yet laid ...John 19:41
n eaten any thing..common....Acts 10:14
Charity *n* faileth..............1Cor 13:8
n able to come to..knowledge. .2Tim 3:7
n with those sacrifices.........Heb 10:1
I will *n* leave thee, nor ....Heb 13:5
these things, ye shall *n* fall 2Pet 1:10

NEVERTHELESS—*however*
n in the day when I visit ......Ex 32:34
N these shall ye not eat ....Lev 11:4
N the people be strong........Num 13:28
n the firstborn of man ....Num 18:15
n it shall be purified ....Num 31:23
N these ye shall not eat ....Deut 14:7
N the children of Israel ....Josh 13:13
n the inhabitants of...........Judg 1:33
N the people refused to 1Sam 8:19
N Saul spake not any thing....1Sam 20:26
N David took the stronghold ..2Sam 5:7
n he would not drink 2Sam 23:16
N thou shalt not build 1Kin 8:19
n Asa's heart was perfect 1Kin 15:14
n the high places were not 1Kin 22:43
n, if thou see me when I am ..2Kin 2:10
N they departed not from 2Kin 13:6
N David took the castle of 1Chr 11:5
N they shall be his servants ...2Chr 12:8
N there are good things 2Chr 19:3
N the people did sacrifice 2Chr 33:17
N we made our prayer ....Neh 4:9
N for thy great mercies' ....Neh 9:31
N Haman refrained himself....Esth 5:10
n thou heardest the voice .....Ps 31:22
N I am continually with thee ..Ps 73:23
N my loving-kindness will .....Ps 89:33
N he regarded..affliction ......Ps 106:44
n the counsel of the Lord .....Prov 19:21
n the poor man's wisdom .....Eccl 9:16
N the dimness shall not be ....Is 9:1
N in those days, saith the .....Jer 5:18
N hear thou now this word ....Jer 28:7
N I will remember my ....Ezek 16:60
N I withdrew mine hand ......Ezek 20:22
N leave the stump of his ......Dan 4:15
N the men rowed hard to .....Jon 1:13
n for the oath's sake..........Matt 14:9
n I say unto you, Hereafter ...Matt 26:64
n not what I will, but what....Mark 14:36
n at thy word I will let........Luke 5:5
N when the Son of man.......Luke 18:8
n let us go unto him ....John 11:15
N among the chief rulers ......John 12:42
N he left not himself..........Acts 14:17
N death reigned from Adam...Rom 5:14
N, to avoid fornication 1Cor 7:2
N he that standeth steadfast ...1Cor 7:37
N neither is the man..........1Cor 11:11
N, when it shall turn to the ...2Cor 3:16
n, being crafty, I caught 2Cor 12:16
n I live; yet not I, but ....Gal 2:20
N, let every one of you ....Eph 5:33
N to abide in the flesh ....Phil 1:24
n I am not ashamed 2Tim 1:12
n afterward it yieldeth ....Heb 12:11
N we, according to..promise ...2Pet 3:13
N I have..against thee ....Rev 2:4

NEW—*something recently come into existence*
Commandment ....John 13:34
Covenant ....Jer 31:31
Creature 2Cor 5:17
Fruit ....Ezek 47:12
Earth...................Is 65:17
Spirit ....Ezek 11:19
Heaven ....Is 66:22
Jerusalem ....Rev 21:2
Name ....Is 62:2
Man....................Eph 2:15
Song ....Is 42:10
New thing (Christ's birth).Jer 31:22
All things new ....Rev 21:5

[*also* NEWLY, NEWNESS]
n meat offering unto..Lord ....Lev 23:16
if the Lord make a *n* thing ....Num 16:30
that hath built a *n* house ......Deut 20:5
a man hath taken a *n* wife ....Deut 24:5
n gods that came *n* up ....Deut 32:17
which we filled, were *n* ....Josh 9:13
They chose *n* gods............Judg 5:8
had but *n* set the watch ....Judg 7:19
found a *n* jawbone of an ass ..Judg 15:15
Delilah..took *n* ropes ....Judg 16:12
Now therefore make a *n* cart ..1Sam 6:7
Tomorrow is the *n* moon.......1Sam 20:18
ark of God upon a *n* cart 2Sam 6:3
girded with a *n* sword.........2Sam 21:16
clad..with a *n* garment 1Kin 11:29
Bring me a *n* cruse, and put...2Kin 2:20
ark of God in a *n* cart 1Chr 13:7
on the *n* moons, and on the ...2Chr 2:4
the Lord, before the *n* court ..2Chr 20:5
offering, both of the *n* moons. .Ezra 3:5
sabbaths, of the *n* moons .....Neh 10:33
tithes of..corn, the *n* wine.....Neh 13:5
ready to burst like *n* bottles ...Job 32:19
Sing unto him a *n* song ....Ps 33:3
put a *n* song in my mouth.....Ps 40:3
sing unto the Lord a *n* song ...Ps 98:1
Sing unto the Lord a *n* song...Ps 149:1
burst out with *n* wine ....Prov 3:10
no *n* thing under the sun......Eccl 1:9
pleasant fruits, *n* and old.....Song 7:13
the *n* moons and sabbaths.....Is 1:13
n wine mourneth, the vine ....Is 24:7

n things do I declare ....Is 42:9
Behold, I will do a *n* thing ....Is 43:19
showed thee *n* things from ....Is 48:6
n wine is found in the ....Is 65:8
in the entry of the *n* gate .....Jer 26:10
at the entry of the *n* gate .....Jer 36:10
They are *n* every morning .....Lam 3:23
a *n* heart and a *n* spirit ....Ezek 18:31
n heart also will I give you ....Ezek 36:26
feasts, and in the *n* moons ....Ezek 45:17
sabbaths and in the *n* moons . .Ezek 46:3
feast days, her *n* moons ....Hos 2:11
n wine take away the heart ....Hos 4:11
because of the *n* wine ....Joel 1:5
shall drop down *n* wine ....Joel 3:18
When will the *n* moon be gone. Amos 8:5
upon the *n* wine, and upon ....Hag 1:11
and *n* wine the maids ....Zech 9:17
n cloth unto an old garment ...Matt 9:16
put *n* wine into old bottles ....Matt 9:17
they put *n* wine into ....Matt 9:17
treasure things *n* and old ......Matt 13:52
blood of the *n* testament ......Matt 26:28
laid it in his own *n* tomb ......Matt 27:60
What *n* doctrine is this? ....Mark 1:27
n cloth on an old garment .....Mark 2:21
else the *n* piece that filled .....Mark 2:21
n wine into old bottles ....Mark 2:22
else the *n* wine doth burst .....Mark 2:22
n wine must be put into *n* .....Mark 2:22
drink it *n* in the kingdom ......Mark 14:25
a *n* garment upon an old ....Luke 5:36
both the *n* maketh a rent .....Luke 5:36
n agreeth not with the old ....Luke 5:36
n wine into old bottles ....Luke 5:37
else the *n* wine will burst .....Luke 5:37
n wine must be put into *n* .....Luke 5:38
cup is the *n* testament ....Luke 22:20
garden a *n* sepulcher ....John 19:41
men are full of *n* wine ....Acts 2:13
know what this *n* doctrine .....Acts 17:19
or to hear some *n* thing ....Acts 17:21
should serve in *n* of spirit .....Rom 7:6
that ye may be a *n* lump 1Cor 5:7
ministers of the *n* testament ...2Cor 3:6
but a *n* creature ....Gal 6:15
that ye put on the *n* man .....Eph 4:24
have put on the *n* man ....Col 3:10
I will make a *n* covenant ......Heb 8:8
n covenant, he hath made .....Heb 8:13
mediator of the *n* testament ...Heb 9:15
By a *n* and living way, which . .Heb 10:20
mediator of the *n* covenant ....Heb 12:24
n heavens and a *n* earth 2Pet 3:13
I write no *n* commandment 1John 2:7
n commandment I write unto . .1John 2:8
I wrote a *n* commandment 2John 5
in the stone a *n* name written .Rev 2:17
which is *n* Jerusalem ....Rev 3:12
write upon him my *n* name ....Rev 3:12
sung as it were a *n* song ......Rev 14:3
n heaven and a *n* earth ....Rev 21:1

NEW BIRTH—*regeneration; becoming a Christian*

Described as:
One heart ....Ezek 11:19
Resurrection ....Rom 6:4-10
New creature 2Cor 5:17
Circumcision ....Deut 30:6
Holy seed 1John 3:9
Begotten 1Pet 1:3
Name written in heaven . .Luke 10:20

Productive of:
Growth 1Pet 2:1, 2
Knowledge 1Cor 2:12-16
Change 2Cor 3:18
Fruitfulness ....John 15:1-8
Victory 1John 5:4
Discipline ....Heb 12:3-11

See Bcpn Again

NEW COVENANT—*God's final, everlasting covenant with His people, in which His grace expressed in Christ is made available to all who believe*

Described as:
Everlasting ....Is 55:3
Of peace ....Ezek 34:25
Of life ....Mal 2:5

Elements of:
Author—God ....Eph 2:4
Cause—God's love ......John 3:16
Mediator—Christ 1Tim 2:5
Time originated—in eternity ....Rom 8:29, 30
Time instituted—at man's sin ....Gen 3:15
Time realized—at Christ's death ....Eph 2:13-22
Time consummated—in eternity ....Eph 2:7
Duties—faith and repentance ....Mark 1:15

Ratification of, by:
God's promise ....Gen 3:15
God's oath ....Is 54:9, 10
Christ's blood ....Heb 9:12-26
Spirit's sealing 2Cor 1:22

Superiority of, to the old:
Hope ....Heb 7:19
Priesthood ....Heb 7:20-28
Covenant ....Heb 8:6
Sacrifice ....Heb 9:23

NEW GATE—*a Temple gate*
Princes meet at ....Jer 26:10

NEW JERUSALEM—*the capital city of God's new creation*
Vision, seen by Abraham . Heb 11:10, 16
Reality of, experienced by believers ....Gal 4:26, 31
Consummation of, awaits eternity ....Heb 13:14

NEW MAN—*See* New Birth

NEW MOON—*beginning of the month*
A festival day ....Ps 81:3
Col 2:16
A point of reference .....Is 66:23

NEW TESTAMENT—*See* New Covenant

NEW YEAR—*beginning of the year*
Erection of the tabernacle on ....Ex 40:17, 18

NEWBORN—*recently born*
As *n* babies, desire 1Pet 2:22

NEWS—*a report of recent events*

Kinds of:
Distressing ....Gen 32:6-8
Disturbing ....Josh 22:11-20
Alarming 1Sam 4:13-22
Agonizing 2Sam 18:31-33
Sorrowful ....Neh 1:2-11
Joyful ....Luke 2:8-18
Good 1Kin 1:42
Fatal 1Sam 4:19

Of salvation:
Out of Zion ....Is 40:9
By a person ....Is 41:27
Bringer of peace ....Is 52:7
By Christ ....Is 61:1-3

good *n* from a far country .....Prov 25:25

NEXT—*immediately before or after*
set time in the *n* year ....Gen 17:21
neighbor *n* unto his house .....Ex 12:4
that do pitch *n* unto him ......Num 2:5
night, and all the *n* day ....Num 11:32
kinsman that is *n* to him ......Num 27:11
is *n* unto the slain man ....Deut 21:3
that are *n* unto the slain ......Deut 21:6
unto us, one of our *n* kinsmen . Ruth 2:20
n unto him Abinadab, and the . 1Sam 17:13
Israel, I shall be *n* unto 1Sam 23:17
the evening of the *n* day 1Sam 30:17
I said unto her on the *n* day . .2Kin 6:29
the chief, and Shapham the *n*. .1Chr 5:12
And *n* to him was Jehohanan . .2Chr 17:15
n him was Amasiah the son of . 2Chr 17:16
And *n* him was Jehozabad 2Chr 17:18
Elkanah that was *n* to the king. 2Chr 28:7
Shimei his brother was..*n* 2Chr 31:12
and *n* him were Eden, and 2Chr 31:15
n unto him builded the men ...Neh 3:2
n to them builded Zaccur .....Neh 3:2
N..repaired Meremoth ....Neh 3:4
N..repaired Meshullam ....Neh 3:4
n unto them repaired Zadok . .Neh 3:4
n unto them repaired Melatiah . Neh 3:7
N unto him repaired Uzziel . . .Neh 3:8
N..also repaired Hananiah .....Neh 3:8
n unto them repaired Jedaiah. .Neh 3:10
n unto him repaired Hattush . .Neh 3:10
N unto him repaired Hashabiah Neh 3:17
n to them was Hanan ....Neh 13:13
n unto him was Carshena .....Esth 1:14
the morning rose the *n* day ....Jon 4:7
Now the *n* day, that followed . .Matt 27:62
Let us go into the *n* towns ....Mark 1:38
that on the *n* day, when they . .Luke 9:37
n day John seeth Jesus ....John 1:29
On the *n* day much people ....John 12:12
them in hold unto the *n* day ...Acts 4:3
preached..the *n* sabbath ....Acts 13:42
n day he departed with ....Acts 14:20
n day over against Chios ......Acts 20:15
n day we arrived at Samos ....Acts 20:15
n day we came to Miletus .....Acts 20:15
n day purifying himself ....Acts 21:26
n day we touched at Sidon ....Acts 27:3

NEZIAH (nĕ-zī'ä)—*"preeminent"*
Head of a Nethinim family ....Ezra 2:43, 54

NEZIB (nē'zĭb)—*"standing-place"*
Town of Judah ....Josh 15:1, 43

NIBHAZ (nĭb'hăz)
Idol of Avites 2Kin 17:31

NIBSHAN (nĭb'shăn)—*"prophecy"*
Town of Judah ....Josh 15:1, 62

NICANOR (nī-kā'nôr)—*"conqueror"*
One of the seven men chosen as deacons .....Acts 6:1-5

NICODEMUS (nĭk-ō-dē'mŭs)—*"innocent blood"*
Pharisee; converses with Jesus ....John 3:1-12
Protests unfairness of Christ's trial ....John 7:50-52
Brings gifts to anoint Christ's body ....John 19:39, 40

NICOLAITANS (nĭk-ō-lā'ĭ-tănz)—*an early Christian sect*
Group teaching moral looseness ....Rev 2:6-15

NICOLAS (nĭk'ŏ-lăs)—*"conqueror of the people"*
Non-Jewish proselyte deacon ....Acts 6:5

NICOPOLIS (nĭ-cŏp'ō-lĭs)—*"the city of victory"*
Town in Epirus (near Actium) ....Titus 3:12

NIGER (nī'jer)
Latin surname of Simeon, a teacher in Antioch . . .Acts 13:1

NIGH—*near*
drew *n* that Israel must die ....Gen 47:29
Draw not *n* hither: put off ....Ex 3:5
but they shall not come *n* .....Ex 24:2
he came *n* unto the camp .....Ex 32:19
were afraid to come *n* him ....Ex 34:30
sanctified..that come *n* ....Lev 10:3
n to offer the offerings ....Lev 21:21
not come *n* to offer..bread ....Lev 21:21
any that is *n* of kin unto ......Lev 25:49
stranger that cometh *n* ....Num 1:51

children of Israel come *n*......Num 8:19
a stranger shall not come *n*....Num 18:4
come *n* the tabernacle of......Num 18:22
unto all the places *n*..........Deut 1:7
who hath God so *n* unto them .Deut 4:7
are come *n* unto the battle ....Deut 20:2
brother be not *n* unto thee ....Deut 22:2
and drew *n*, and came ....Josh 8:11
and drew *n* to meet David 1Sam 17:48
Joab drew *n*, and the people ..2Sam 10:13
why went ye *n* the wall? 2Sam 11:21
days of David drew *n*.........1Kin 2:1
they that were *n* them 1Chr 12:40
Ahasuerus, both *n* and far ....Esth 9:20
shall not come *n* unto him ....Ps 32:6
Draw *n* unto my soul, and ....Ps 69:18
salvation is *n* them that ....Ps 85:9
but it shall not come *n* thee ...Ps 91:7
draw *n* that follow after.......Ps 119:150
n unto all them that call ......Ps 145:18
not *n* the door of her house ...Prov 5:8
nor the years draw *n* ....Eccl 12:1
Holy One of Israel draw *n* ....Is 5:19
draweth *n* unto me with their..Matt 15:8
they drew *n* unto Jerusalem ...Matt 21:1
not come *n* unto him for the ..Mark 2:4
and he was *n* unto the sea ....Mark 5:21
to pass, know that it is *n*......Mark 13:29
came and drew *n* to the house .Luke 15:25
he was *n* to Jerusalem ....Luke 19:11
when he was come *n*, even ....Luke 19:37
your redemption draweth *n*....Luke 21:28
kingdom of God is *n* at hand ..Luke 21:31
drew *n* unto the village ....Luke 24:28
feast of the Jews, was *n*.......John 6:4
n unto the place where they ...John 6:23
Jews' passover was *n* at hand ..John 11:55
sepulcher was *n* at hand ......John 19:42
time of the promise drew *n* ...Acts 7:17
drew *n* unto the city, Peter....Acts 10:9
n..was the city of Lasea.......Acts 27:8
word is *n* thee, even in thy....Rom 10:8
n by the blood of Christ ......Eph 2:13
he was sick *n* unto death......Phil 2:27
and is *n* unto cursing ....Heb 6:8
Draw *n* to God..will draw *n*...James 4:8

NIGHT—*from dusk to dawn; dark*

Important facts concerning:
Made by God...........Ps 104:20
Named at creation.......Gen 1:5
Begins at sunset.........Gen 28:11
Established by God's covenant.........Gen 8:22
Displays God's glory.....Ps 19:2
Designed for rest........Ps 104:23
Wild beasts creep in .....Ps 104:20-22
None in heaven ....Zech 14:7
Divided into "watches" and hours.............Mark 13:35

Special events in:
Jacob's wrestling ....Gen 32:22-31
Egypt's greatest plague...Ex 12:12-31
Ordinance of the Passover..............Ex 12:42
King's sleeplessness......Esth 6:1
Nehemiah's vigil.........Neh 2:11-16
Belshazzar slain ....Dan 5:30
Angelic revelation ....Luke 2:8-15
Nicodemus' talk ....John 3:2
Release from prison .....Acts 5:19
Paul's escape............Acts 9:24, 25
Wonderful conversion....Acts 16:25-33
Lord's return............Mark 13:35

Good acts in:
Toil ....Luke 5:5
Prayer..................1Sam 15:11; Luke 6:12
Song ....Job 35:10; Ps 42:8
Flight from evil ....1Sam 19:10; Matt 2:14
Dreams.................Matt 2:12, 13, 19

Evil acts in:
Drunkenness ....Is 5:11
Thievery................Obad 5; Matt 27:64
Debauchery 1Thess 5:2-7
Betrayal ....Matt 26:31, 34, 46-50
Death ....Luke 12:20

Figurative of:
Present age ....Rom 13:11, 12
Death ....John 9:4
Unregenerate state 1Thess 5:5, 7
Judgment ....Mic 3:6

[*also* NIGHTS]
divide the day from the *n*.....Gen 1:14
over the day and over the *n*...Gen 1:18
earth forty days and forty *n*...Gen 7:4
he and his servants, by *n*......Gen 14:15
tarry all *n*, and wash your.....Gen 19:2
abide in the street all *n* ....Gen 19:2
father drink wine that *n*.......Gen 19:33
father drink wine that *n*.......Gen 19:35
with him, and tarried all *n* ....Gen 24:54
appeared unto him the same *n* .Gen 26:24
he lay with her that *n*.........Gen 30:16
by day, or stolen by *n* ....Gen 31:39
and tarried all *n* in the........Gen 31:54
lodged that *n* in the company..Gen 32:21
each man his dream in one *n*..Gen 40:5
in the visions of the *n* ....Gen 46:2
all that day, and all that *n* ....Ex 10:13
eat the flesh in that *n*.........Ex 12:8
by *n* in a pillar of fire ....Ex 13:21
light; to go by day and *n*......Ex 13:21
it gave light by *n* to these .....Ex 14:20
not near the other all the *n* ...Ex 14:20
strong east wind all that *n*.....Ex 14:21
forty days and forty *n*.........Ex 24:18
burning upon the altar all *n* ...Lev 6:9
day and *n* seven days ....Lev 8:35
abide with thee all *n*..........Lev 19:13
appearance of fire by *n* ....Num 9:16
fell upon the camp in the *n* ...Num 11:9
and the people wept that *n*.....Num 14:1
unto them, Lodge here this *n*..Num 22:8
God came unto Balaam at *n* ..Num 22:20
in fire by *n*, to show you ......Deut 1:33
forty days and forty *n*.........Deut 9:9
forty days and forty *n*.........Deut 9:18
forty days and forty *n*.........Deut 10:10
forth out of Egypt by *n* ....Deut 16:1
remain all *n* upon the tree ....Deut 21:23
thou shalt fear day and *n* .....Deut 28:66
meditate therein day and *n*....Josh 1:8
where ye shall lodge this *n*....Josh 4:3
Joshua lodged that *n* among...Josh 8:9
went up from Gilgal all *n* .....Josh 10:9
came to pass the same *n* ......Judg 6:25
by day, that he did it by *n* ....Judg 6:27
And God did so that *n* ....Judg 6:40
Now therefore up by *n*.........Judg 9:32
laid wait for him all *n* ....Judg 16:2
were quiet all the *n*...........Judg 16:2
I pray you tarry all *n* ....Judg 19:9
places to lodge all *n* ....Judg 19:13
round about upon me by *n*....Judg 20:5
Tarry this *n*, and it shall ......Ruth 3:13
his ox with him that *n* 1Sam 14:34
Lord hath said to me this *n* ...1Sam 15:16
wall unto us both by *n* and....1Sam 25:16
came to the woman by *n*......1Sam 28:8
rose up, and went away that *n* .1Sam 28:25
three days and three *n* 1Sam 30:12
his men walked all that *n* 2Sam 2:29
through the plain all *n* 2Sam 4:7
went in, and lay all *n* upon....2Sam 12:16
Lodge not this *n* in the 2Sam 17:16
the beasts of the field by *n*....2Sam 21:10
open toward this house *n* 1Kin 8:29
forty days and forty *n*.........1Kin 19:8
and he arose by *n*, and smote .2Kin 8:21
men of war fled by *n* 2Kin 25:4
in that work day and *n* 1Chr 9:33
In that *n* did God appear 2Chr 1:7
appeared to Solomon by *n* 2Chr 7:12
and the fat until *n* 2Chr 35:14
before thee now, day and *n* ...Neh 1:6
against them day and *n* ....Neh 4:9
in the *n* they may be a guard..Neh 4:22
the *n* will they come to slay ...Neh 6:10
the pillar of fire by *n* ....Neh 9:19
drink three days, *n* or day ....Esth 4:16
seven days and seven *n* ....Job 2:13
n in which it was said.........Job 3:3
let that *n* be solitary ....Job 3:7
from the visions of the *n*......Job 4:13
I arise, and the *n* be gone?....Job 7:4
away as a vision of the *n*......Job 20:8
day and *n* come to an end ....Job 26:10
dew lay all *n* upon my branch .Job 29:19
dream, in a vision of the *n*....Job 33:15
who giveth songs in the *n*......Job 35:10
doth he meditate day and *n*...Ps 1:2
instruct me in the *n* seasons ...Ps 16:7
hast visited me in the *n* ....Ps 17:3
and in the *n* season, and ......Ps 22:2
weeping may endure for a *n*...Ps 30:5
day and *n* thy hand was heavy .Ps 32:4
have been my meat day and *n* .Ps 42:3
Day and *n* they go about it ...Ps 55:10
thine, the *n* also is thine ......Ps 74:16
my sore ran in the *n*..........Ps 77:2
n with a light of fire ....Ps 78:14
past, and as a watch in the *n*..Ps 90:4
afraid for the terror by *n*......Ps 91:5
faithfulness every *n* ....Ps 92:2
fire to give light in the *n*......Ps 105:39
eyes prevent the *n* watches ....Ps 119:148
by day, nor the moon by *n*....Ps 121:6
by *n* stand in the house ....Ps 134:1
moon and stars to rule by *n*...Ps 136:9
n shall be light about me......Ps 139:11
but the *n* shineth as the day...Ps 139:12
in the black and dark *n* ....Prov 7:9
candle goeth not out by *n*.....Prov 31:18
taketh not rest in the *n* ....Eccl 2:23
lie all *n* betwixt my breasts....Song 1:13
because of fear in the *n*.......Song 3:8
of a flaming fire by *n*.........Is 4:5
n Ar of Moab is laid waste....Is 15:1
n Kir of Moab is laid waste ...Is 15:1
n of my pleasure hath ....Is 21:4
set in my ward whole *n* ....Is 21:8
morning cometh, and..*n*.......Is 21:12
I desired thee in the *n* ....Is 26:9
I will keep it *n* and day ....Is 27:3
be as a dream of a *n* vision ...Is 29:7
not be quenched *n* nor day....Is 34:10
at noonday as in the *n*.........Is 59:10
hold their peace day nor *n* ....Is 62:6
Arise, and let us go by *n* .....Jer 6:5
aside to tarry for a *n*? ....Jer 14:8
serve other gods day and *n*....Jer 16:13
and my covenant of the *n*.....Jer 33:20
day and *n* in their season .....Jer 33:20
and in the *n* to the frost ......Jer 36:30
if thieves by *n*, they will ......Jer 49:9
She weepeth sore in the *n*.....Lam 1:2
Arise, cry out in the *n*........Lam 2:19
unto Daniel in a *n* vision......Dan 2:19
and passed the *n* fasting ......Dan 6:18
I saw in my vision by *n* ....Dan 7:2
I saw in the *n* visions ....Dan 7:7
fall with thee in the *n*.........Hos 4:5
lie all *n* in sackcloth ....Joel 1:13
maketh the day dark with *n* ...Amos 5:8
in a *n*, and perished in a *n* ...Jon 4:10
I saw by *n*, and behold a .....Zech 1:8
forty days and forty *n*.........Matt 4:2
three *n* in the whale's belly....Matt 12:40
three *n* in..heart of the earth ..Matt 12:40
fourth watch of the *n* Jesus....Matt 14:25
His disciples came by *n* ....Matt 28:13
n and day, he was in the ......Mark 5:5
fourth watch of the *n* ....Mark 6:48
because of me this *n*..........Mark 14:27
this day, even in this *n*........Mark 14:30
and prayers *n* and day ....Luke 2:37
in that *n* there shall be two ...Luke 17:34

cry day and *n* unto him .... Luke 18:7
at *n* he went out, and abode .. Luke 21:37
he that came to Jesus by *n* .... John 7:50
But if a man walk in the *n* .... John 11:10
immediately out: and it was *n* . John 13:30
first came to Jesus by *n* .... John 19:39
that *n* they caught nothing .... John 21:3
same *n* Peter was sleeping ..... Acts 12:6
appeared to Paul in the *n* ..... Acts 16:9
sent away Paul and Silas by *n* . Acts 17:10
Lord to Paul in the *n* .... Acts 18:9
warn every one *n* and day ..... Acts 20:31
n following the Lord stood .... Acts 23:11
him by *n* to Antipatris .... Acts 23:31
serving God day and *n* .... Acts 26:7
by me this *n* the angel .... Acts 27:23
fourteenth *n* was come .... Acts 27:27
same *n*..he was betrayed 1Cor 11:23
a *n* and a day I have been 2Cor 11:25
laboring *n* and day, because 1Thess 2:9
N and day praying exceedingly . 1Thess 3:10
labor and travail *n* and day 2Thess 3:8
supplications and prayers *n* 1Tim 5:5
in my prayers *n* and day 2Tim 1:3
come as a thief in the *n* 2Pet 3:10
they rest not day and *n* .... Rev 4:8
of it, and the *n* likewise .... Rev 8:12
they have no rest day nor *n* .. Rev 14:11
there shall be no *n* there ...... Rev 21:25
there shall be no *n* there ...... Rev 22:5

NIGHT MONSTER—*a nocturnal creature*
Dwells in ruins .... Is 34:14

NIGHTHAWK—*a swift woodland bird*
Unclean bird .... Lev 11:16

NILE (nīl)—*"dark blue"—the great river of Egypt*

Called:
Sihor .... Is 23:3
Stream of Egypt .... Is 27:12
Sea .... Nah 3:8

Characteristics of:
Has seven streams .... Is 11:15
Overflows annually ...... Jer 46:8
Source of Egyptian wealth .... Is 19:5-8

Events connected with:
Drowning of male children .... Ex 1:22
Moses placed in .... Ex 2:3
Water of, turned to blood Ex 7:15, 20

Figurative of:
Judgment .... Ezek 30:12; Amos 9:5
Army .... Jer 46:7-9

NIMRAH (nĭm'rä)—*an abbreviation of Beth-Nimrah*
Town in Gilead .... Num 32:3, 36

NIMRIM (nĭm'rĭm)—*"bitterness"*
Place in south Moab ..... Is 15:6

NIMROD (nĭm'rŏd)—*"valiant; strong"*
Ham's grandson .... Gen 10:6-8
Becomes a mighty hunter . Gen 10:8, 9
Establishes cities .... Gen 10:10-12
Land of Assyria, thus described .... Mic 5:6

NIMSHI (nĭm'shī)—*"Jehovah reveals"*
Grandfather of King Jehu. 2Kin 9:2, 14
Called Jehu's father 2Kin 9:20

against Jehu the son of *N* 2Chr 22:7

NINE

[*also* NINTH]
Adam lived were *n* hundred ... Gen 5:5
n hundred and twelve .... Gen 5:8
were *n* hundred and ten ...... Gen 5:14
were *n* hundred sixty and *n* ... Gen 5:27
two hundred and *n* years ...... Gen 11:19
ninety years old and *n* .... Gen 17:1
was twenty and *n* talents ...... Ex 38:24
in the *n* day of the month .... Lev 23:32
unto thee forty and *n* years ... Lev 25:8
old fruit until the *n* year ...... Lev 25:22
were fifty and *n* thousand ..... Num 1:23
the *n* day Abidan the son of .. Num 7:60
n cubits was the length .... Deut 3:11
inheritance unto the *n* tribes .. Josh 13:7
the cities are twenty and *n* .... Josh 15:32
n cities with their villages ..... Josh 15:54
n hundred chariots of iron .... Judg 4:3
at the end of *n* months 2Sam 24:8
reigned twenty and *n* years 2Kin 14:2
n and thirtieth year of 2Kin 15:17
In the *n* year of Hoshea 2Kin 17:6
reigned twenty and *n* years 2Kin 18:2
is the *n* year of Hoshea king .. 2Kin 18:10
in the *n* year of his reign 2Kin 25:1
n day of the fourth month 2Kin 25:3
Eliada, and Eliphelet, *n* 1Chr 3:8
eighth, Elzabad the *n* 1Chr 12:12
n to Jeshua, the tenth 1Chr 24:11
n to Mattaniah, he, his sons ... 1Chr 25:16
n captain for the *n* month 1Chr 27:12
Asa in the thirty and *n* year ... 2Chr 16:12
silver, *n* and twenty knives .... Ezra 1:9
n hundred seventy .... Ezra 2:36
It was the *n* month, on the .... Ezra 10:9
n hundred and thirty .... Neh 7:38
n parts to dwell in other ...... Neh 11:1
king of Judah, in the *n* month . Jer 36:9
winter house in the *n* month .. Jer 36:22
n year of Zedekiah king of .... Jer 39:1
the *n* day of the month .... Jer 39:2
in the *n* year of his reign ...... Jer 52:4
in the *n* day of the month ..... Jer 52:6
Again in the *n* year .... Ezek 24:1
twentieth day of the *n* .... Hag 2:10
fourth day of the *n* month .... Zech 7:1
he not leave the ninety and *n*. . Matt 18:12
about the sixth and *n* hour .... Matt 20:5
all the land unto the *n* hour ... Matt 27:45
whole land until the *n* hour ... Mark 15:33
the *n* hour Jesus cried .... Mark 15:34
ninety and *n* in..wilderness .... Luke 15:4
but where are the *n*? .... Luke 17:17
over all the earth until the *n* .. Luke 23:44
at the *n* hour I prayed .... Acts 10:30
eighth, beryl; the *n*, a topaz ... Rev 21:20

NINETEEN

[*also* NINETEENTH]
a hundred and *n* years .... Gen 11:25
n cities with their villages ..... Josh 19:38
David's servants *n* men 2Sam 2:30
which is the *n* year of king 2Kin 25:8
The *n* to Pethahiah 1Chr 24:16
The *n* to Mallothi 1Chr 25:26

NINETY

Enos lived *n* years .... Gen 5:9
hundred *n* and five years ...... Gen 5:30
Sarah, that is *n* years old ..... Gen 17:17
Eli was *n* and eight years 1Sam 4:15
Ater of Hezekiah *n* and eight. . Ezra 2:16
three hundred *n* and two ...... Ezra 2:58
Ater of Hezekiah *n* and eight. . Neh 7:21
three hundred *n* and two ...... Neh 7:60
n and six pomegranates .... Jer 52:23
length thereof *n* cubits .... Ezek 41:12

NINEVE—*an early spelling of Nineveh*

NINEVEH (nĭn'ĕ-vä)—*meaning unknown*

History of:
Built by Asshur .... Gen 10:11, 12
Capital of Assyria 2Kin 19:36
Jonah preaches to .... Jon 1:1, 2
Citizens of:
Repent .... Jon 3:5-9
At the judgment seat .... Matt 12:41

Prophecies concerning its:
Destruction by Babylon .. Nah 2:1-4
Internal weakness .... Nah 3:11-17
Utter desolation .... Nah 3:18, 19

Described as:
Great city .... Jon 3:2, 3
Wealthy .... Nah 2:9
Fortified .... Nah 3:8, 12
Wicked .... Jon 1:2
Idolatrous .... Nah 1:14
Careless .... Zeph 2:15
Full of lies .... Nah 3:1

returned and dwelt at *N* ...... Is 37:37
and *N* shall be overthrown .... Jon 3:4
should not I spare *N* .... Jon 4:11
will make *N* a desolation ...... Zeph 2:13
The men of *N* shall rise up .... Luke 11:32

NINEVITES—*the inhabitants of Nineveh*
Jonah was a sign unto the *N* .. Luke 11:30

NINTH—*See* NINE

NINTH HOUR—*three p.m.*
Time of Christ's death ... Matt 27:46
Customary hour of prayer. Acts 3:1
Time of Cornelius' vision . Acts 10:1, 3

NISAN (nī'săn)—*"beginning"*
Name of Abib (first month of Jewish year) after the exile .... Neh 2:1
See JEWISH CALENDAR

NISROCH (nĭz'rŏk)—*"eagle; hawk"*
Sennacherib's god 2Kin 19:37

NITRE—*carbonate of soda; lye*
Figurative of agitation ... Prov 25:20
As a cleansing agent ..... Jer 2:22

NO—*See* INTRODUCTION

NO (nō)—*"stirring up"—the Egyptian city of Thebes*
punish the multitude of *N* ..... Jer 46:25
execute judgments in *N* .... Ezek 30:14
cut off the multitude of *N* ..... Ezek 30:15
N shall be rent asunder .... Ezek 30:16
better than populous *N* .... Nah 3:8

NOADIAH (nō'ä'dī-ä)—*"Jehovah assembles"*
1. Levite in Ezra's time .... Ezra 8:33
2. Prophetess who tries to frighten Nehemiah .... Neh 6:14

NOAH (nō'ä)—*"rest"—the patriarch chosen to build the ark*

Life of:
Son of Lamech .... Gen 5:28, 29
Father of Shem, Ham and Japheth .... Gen 5:32
Finds favor with God .... Gen 6:8
Lives in the midst of corruption .... Gen 6:1-13
Instructed to build the ark .... Gen 6:13-22
Preacher of righteousness . 2Pet 2:5
Enters ark with family and animals .... Gen 7:1-24
Preserved during flood ... Gen 8:1-17
Builds an altar .... Gen 8:18-22
Covenant established with. Gen 9:1-19
Plants a vineyard; becomes drunk .... Gen 9:20, 21
Pronounces curse and blessings .... Gen 9:22-27
Dies at 950 .... Gen 9:28, 29

Character of:
Righteous .... Gen 6:9
Obedient .... Heb 11:7
In fellowship with God ... Gen 6:9
Notable in history .... Ezek 14:14, 20

[*also* NOE]
N five hundred .... Gen 5:30
generations of the sons of *N* ... Gen 10:1
families of the sons of *N* ...... Gen 10:32
N, Shem, Ham, and Japheth .. 1Chr 1:4
is as the waters of *N* .... Is 54:9
waters of *N* should no more ... Is 54:9
as the days of *N* were, so ..... Matt 24:37
day that *N* entered into the ... Matt 24:38
which was the son of *N* ...... Luke 3:36
as it was in the days of *N* ..... Luke 17:26

N

day that *N* entered into the ...Luke 17:27
God waited in the days of *N* ..1Pet 3:20

NOAH—*"flattery; movement"*
Daughter of Zelophehad .Num 26:33

daughters; Mahlah, *N*.........Num 27:1
N, the daughters of..........Num 36:11
daughters, Mahlah, and *N*.....Josh 17:3

NOB (nōb)—*"prophecy"*
City of priests; David flees to 1Sam 21:1-9
Priests of, killed by Saul .1Sam 22:9-23
Near Jerusalem..........Is 10:32
Reinhabited after the exile ....Neh 11:32

NOBAH (nō'bä)—*"prominent"*
1. Manassite leader........Num 32:42
2. Town in Gad...........Judg 8:11

NOBLE—*possessing outstanding qualities; aristocratic; expression of respect*
the great and *n* Asnappar .....Ezra 4:10
the king's most *n* princes......Esth 6:9
I had planted thee a *n* vine ...Jer 2:21
in all places, most *n* Felix .....Acts 24:3
I am not mad, most *n* Festus ..Acts 26:25
not many *n*, are called 1Cor 1:26

NOBLEMAN—*a man of high rank*
Heals son of ....John 4:46-54
Cites in parable ....Luke 19:12-27

[*also* NOBLES]
n of the children of Israel .....Ex 24:11
n of the people digged it......Num 21:18
dominion over the *n* among ...Judg 5:13
the *n* that were in the city 1Kin 21:8
elders and the *n* who were 1Kin 21:11
captains of hundreds..the *n*....2Chr 23:20
their *n* put not their necks ....Neh 3:5
rose up, and said unto the *n* ..Neh 4:14
And I said unto the *n* ....Neh 4:19
rebuked the *n*, and the rulers..Neh 5:7
the *n* of Judah sent many .....Neh 6:17
heart to gather together the *n* .Neh 7:5
clave to..brethren, their *n* .....Neh 10:29
I contended with the *n* of .....Neh 13:17
n and princes of..provinces ....Esth 1:3
the *n* held their peace ....Job 29:10
Make their *n* like Oreb ....Ps 83:11
their *n* with fetters of iron .....Ps 149:8
By me princes rule, and *n*.....Prov 8:16
when thy king is the son of *n*..Eccl 10:17
go into the gates of the *n* .....Is 13:2
call the *n* thereof to the.......Is 34:12
brought down all their *n* ......Is 43:14
n have sent their little ones ...Jer 14:3
n of Judah and Jerusalem .....Jer 27:20
n shall be of themselves......Jer 30:21
slew all the *n* of Judah........Jer 39:6
decree of the king and his *n*...Jon 3:7
n shall dwell in the dust.......Nah 3:18

NOD (nōd)—*"vagabond"*
Place (east of Eden) of Cain's abode ....Gen 4:16, 17

NODAB (nō'dăb)—*"nobility"*
Arabian tribe 1Chr 5:19

NOE—*See* NOAH

NOGAH (nō'gä)—*"splendor"*
One of David's sons 1Chr 3:1, 7

NOHAH (nō'hä)—*"rest"*
Benjamin's fourth son ...1Chr 8:1, 2

NOISE—*sound; to make a sound*
Kinds of:
Sea.....................Ps 65:7
Battle ....Is 13:4
Jer 47:3
Songs ....Ezek 26:13
Amos 5:23
Mourners ....Matt 9:23
Crying..................1Sam 4:13, 14
Revelry.................Ex 32:17, 18
Dog.....................Ps 59:6
God's glory ....Ezek 43:2
Figurative of:
Strong opposition........Is 31:4
Worthlessness ....Jer 46:17

[*also* NOISED]
and the *n* of the trumpet......Ex 20:18
make any *n* with your voice ...Josh 6:10
his fame was *n* throughout ....Josh 6:27
from the *n* of archers ....Judg 5:11
heard the *n* of the shout 1Sam 4:6
n of this great shout 1Sam 4:6
n that was in the host.........1Sam 14:19
n of the city being in an 1Kin 1:41
the *n* that ye have heard 1Kin 1:45
to hear a *n* of chariots 2Kin 7:6
n of horses even the *n* of a....2Kin 7:6
heard the *n* of the guard 2Kin 11:13
making a *n* with psalteries.....1Chr 15:28
Athaliah heard the *n* 2Chr 23:12
n of the shout of joy ....Ezra 3:13
n of the weeping of the ....Ezra 3:13
the *n* was heard afar off ......Ezra 3:13
or the *n* of his tabernacle? ....Job 36:29
n..showeth concerning it ......Job 36:33
Hear..the *n* of his voice ....Job 37:2
play skillfully with a loud *n* ...Ps 33:3
at the *n* of thy waterspouts ....Ps 42:7
my complaint, and make a *n* ..Ps 55:2
make a *n* like a dog ....Ps 59:14
Make a joyful *n* unto God ....Ps 66:1
joyful *n* unto the God of......Ps 81:1
than the *n* of many waters ....Ps 93:4
make a joyful *n* to the rock ...Ps 95:1
n unto him with psalms ....Ps 95:2
joyful *n* unto the lord.........Ps 98:4
make a loud *n* and rejoice ....Ps 98:4
a joyful *n* before the Lord ....Ps 98:6
Make a joyful *n* unto the Lord.Ps 100:1
warrior is with confused *n*.....Is 9:5
grave, and the *n* of thy viols ..Is 14:11
a *n* like the *n* of the seas .....Is 17:12
n of them that rejoice ....Is 24:8
fleeth from the *n* of the fear ..Is 24:18
bring down the *n* of strangers .Is 25:5
earthquake, and great *n*.......Is 29:6
At the *n* of the tumult ....Is 33:3
A voice of *n* from the city ....Is 66:6
heart maketh a *n* in me ....Jer 4:19
for the *n* of the horsemen .....Jer 4:29
Behold the *n* of the bruit .....Jer 10:22
with the *n* of a great tumult ..Jer 11:16
n shall come even to the ......Jer 25:31
moved at the *n* of their fall ...Jer 49:21
at the cry the *n*..was heard ....Jer 49:21
n of the taking of Babylon ....Jer 50:46
n of their voice is uttered ....Jer 51:55
n in the house of the Lord ....Lam 2:7
heard the *n* of their wings.....Ezek 1:24
like the *n* of great waters .....Ezek 1:24
as the *n* of a host ....Ezek 1:24
also the *n* of the wings........Ezek 3:13
the *n* of the wheels over ......Ezek 3:13
a *n* of a great rushing.........Ezek 3:13
by the *n* of his roaring ....Ezek 19:7
at the *n* of the horsemen......Ezek 26:10
I prophesied there was a *n* ....Ezek 37:7
Like the *n* of chariots ....Joel 2:5
like the *n* of a flame of fire ...Joel 2:5
make great *n* by reason ....Mic 2:12
n of a whip and the *n* of......Nah 3:2
n of a cry from the fish gate ..Zeph 1:10
it was *n* that he was in the ....Mark 2:1
all these sayings were *n*.......Luke 1:65
when this was *n* abroad ....Acts 2:6
pass away with a great *n* 2Pet 3:10
as it were the *n* of thunder ....Rev 6:1

NOISOME—*something evil or deadly*
Hurtful beasts...........Ezek 14:15, 21
Deadly pestilence........Ps 91:3
Foul sore ....Rev 16:2

NOMAD—*wanderer*
Life style of patriarchs ...Gen 12:1-9
Gen 13:1-18
Israel's history ....Deut 26:5

NON—*See* NUN

NONE—*not any; no one*
n of us shall withhold from....Gen 23:6
is *n* other but the house of ....Gen 28:17
is *n* greater in this house ......Gen 39:9
there was *n* of the men of.....Gen 39:11
n that could interpret ....Gen 41:6
is *n* that can interpret it.......Gen 41:15
was *n* that could declare it ....Gen 41:24
n so discreet and wise as ......Gen 41:39
n like unto the Lord our God. .Ex 8:10
there is *n* like me in all ....Ex 9:14
n like it in all the land of .....Ex 9:24
such as there was *n* like it.....Ex 11:6
n of you shall go out at the ...Ex 12:22
n of these diseases upon ......Ex 15:26
in it there shall be *n* ....Ex 16:26
gather, and they found *n*......Ex 16:27
n shall appear before me......Ex 23:15
n shall appear before me......Ex 34:20
N of you shall approach.......Lev 18:6
n of it until the morrow.......Lev 22:30
down, and *n* shall make you...Lev 26:6
they shall fall when *n* ....Lev 26:36
N devoted, which shall be .....Lev 27:29
sons of Kohath he gave *n* .....Num 7:9
there was *n* left him alive .....Num 21:35
n of the men that came ....Num 32:11
of every city, we left *n* to .....Deut 2:34
God there is *n* else beside.....Deut 4:35
have *n* other gods before......Deut 5:7
and there was *n* to save ....Deut 22:27
have *n* assurance of thy life ...Deut 28:66
n like unto the God of........Deut 33:26
Israel; *n* went out, and *n*.....Josh 6:1
n of you be freed from ....Josh 9:23
therein; he let *n* remain ....Josh 10:28
he had left him *n* remaining ...Josh 10:33
therein; he left *n* remaining ..Josh 10:39
they left them *n* remaining ....Josh 11:8
n of the Anakim left in the ...Josh 11:22
gave *n* inheritance among .....Josh 14:3
let us be going. But *n* ....Judg 19:28
were *n* of the inhabitants.....Judg 21:9
is *n* to redeem it beside ....Ruth 4:4
There is *n* holy as the Lord ...1Sam 2:2
for there is *n* besides thee.....1Sam 2:2
n like him among all the 1Sam 10:24
David said, There is *n* like 1Sam 21:9
is *n* that showeth me that 1Sam 22:8
is *n* of you that is sorry 1Sam 22:8
for there is *n* like thee 2Sam 7:22
n can turn to the right hand ..2Sam 14:19
Beware that *n* touch the 2Sam 18:12
was *n* like thee before 1Kin 3:12
were of pure gold; *n* were.....1Kin 10:21
all Judah; *n* was exempted 1Kin 15:22
I will receive *n*. And he.......2Kin 5:16
there shall be *n* to bury 2Kin 9:10
he left him *n* remaining 2Kin 10:11
be here with you *n* of the 2Kin 10:23
was *n* left but the tribe of.....2Kin 17:18
n remained, save the poorest ..2Kin 24:14
N ought to carry the ark 1Chr 15:2
Eliezer had *n* other sons 1Chr 23:17
such as *n* of the kings have....2Chr 1:12
were of pure gold; *n* were.....2Chr 9:20
let *n* go out or come in to 2Chr 16:1
fallen to the earth and *n* 2Chr 20:24
that *n* which was unclean 2Chr 23:19
there *n* of the sons of Levi ....Ezra 8:15
n of us put off our clothes ....Neh 4:23
n did compel; for so the ......Esth 1:8
is *n* like him in the earth......Job 1:8
and *n* spake a word unto.....Job 2:13
there is *n* that can deliver .....Job 10:7
tabernacle, because it is *n*.....Job 18:15
and him that had *n* to help....Job 29:12
n saith, Where is God my.....Job 35:10

N is so fierce that dare stir ....Job 41:10
while there is *n* to deliver .....Ps 7:2
works there is *n* that doeth ....Ps 14:1
but there was *n* to save ....Ps 18:41
and *n* can keep alive his ......Ps 22:29
devices of the people of *n* .....Ps 33:10
n of his steps shall slide ....Ps 37:31
pieces, and there be *n* to......Ps 50:22
there is *n* that doeth good.....Ps 53:3
take pity, but there was *n* .....Ps 69:20
comforters, but I found *n* .....Ps 69:20
for there is *n* to deliver ....Ps 71:11
n of the men of might have ....Ps 76:5
and Israel would *n* of me .....Ps 81:11
fell down, and there was *n* ....Ps 107:12
and would *n* of my reproof....Prov 1:25
N that go unto her return .....Prov 2:19
and *n* is barren among ....Song 4:2
and *n* shall quench them ......Is 1:31
N shall be weary nor ....Is 5:27
n shall slumber nor sleep......Is 5:27
there was *n* that moved the ...Is 10:14
n shall be alone in his ....Is 14:31
he shall open, and *n* shall .....Is 22:22
he shall shut, and *n* shall......Is 22:22
n shall pass through it for .....Is 34:10
fail, *n* shall want her mate ....Is 34:16
yea, there is *n* that showeth ...Is 41:26
there is *n* that declareth.......Is 41:26
there is *n* that heareth your ...Is 41:26
are for a prey, and *n* ....Is 42:22
for a spoil and *n* saith ....Is 42:22
n considereth in his heart .....Is 44:19
that there is *n* beside me......Is 45:6
I am the Lord, and there is *n* .Is 45:6
I am the Lord; and there is *n* .Is 45:18
I am God, and there is *n* .....Is 45:22
for I am God, and there is *n* ..Is 46:9
I am God, and there is *n* .....Is 46:9
thou hast said, *n* seeth me ....Is 47:10
I am, and *n* else beside ....Is 47:10
I called, was there *n* to ....Is 50:2
n considering that the ....Is 57:1
n calleth for justice, nor ......Is 59:4
people there was *n* with.......Is 63:3
that there was *n* to uphold ....Is 63:5
I called, *n* did answer.........Is 66:4
and burn that *n* can quench ...Jer 4:4
n shall fray them away........Jer 7:33
that *n* passeth through? ......Jer 9:12
is *n* like unto thee, O Lord ...Jer 10:6
there is *n* to stretch forth .....Jer 10:20
they shall have *n* to bury......Jer 14:16
n doth return from ....Jer 23:14
n shall make him afraid ....Jer 30:10
n should serve himself of......Jer 34:9
unto this day they drink *n* .....Jer 35:14
n of them shall remain or .....Jer 42:17
n of the remnant of Judah ....Jer 44:14
n shall return but such as ....Jer 44:14
n shall tread with shouting ....Jer 48:33
and *n* shall dwell therein ......Jer 50:3
for, and there shall be *n* ......Jer 50:20
and fall, and *n* shall raise .....Jer 50:32
she hath *n* to comfort her .....Lam 1:2
of the enemy, and *n* did help ..Lam 1:7
I sigh: there is *n* to comfort ...Lam 1:21
is *n* that doth deliver us.......Lam 5:8
n of them shall remain ....Ezek 7:11
peace, and there shall be *n*....Ezek 7:25
N eye pitied thee, to do.......Ezek 16:5
pledge hath spoiled *n* by ......Ezek 18:7
end that *n* of all the trees .....Ezek 31:14
that *n* shall pass through ......Ezek 33:28
and *n* shall make them ....Ezek 34:28
left *n* of them any more.......Ezek 39:28
was found *n* like Daniel.......Dan 1:19
n can stay his hand, or say ....Dan 4:35
n that could deliver the ....Dan 8:7
n that holdeth with me in .....Dan 10:21
to his end, and *n* shall help ...Dan 11:45
and *n* shall deliver her out ....Hos 2:10
n among them that calleth ....Hos 7:7
n iniquity in me that were.....Hos 12:8
the Lord your God, and *n* ....Joel 2:27
there is *n* to raise her up......Amos 5:2
there is *n* understanding ......Obad 7
n that shall cast a cord by .....Mic 2:5
n shall make them afraid ......Mic 4:4
there is *n* upright among ......Mic 7:2
cry; but *n* shall look back .....Nah 2:8
and *n* made them afraid? ......Nah 2:11
I am, and there is *n* beside ....Zeph 2:15
waste, that *n* passeth by ......Zeph 3:6
that there is *n* inhabitant ......Zeph 3:6
ye clothe you, but there is *n* ..Hag 1:6
let *n* of you imagine evil ......Zech 7:10
let *n* deal treacherously ....Mal 2:15
seeking rest and findeth *n* .....Matt 12:43
commandment of God of *n*....Matt 15:6
there is *n* good but one ....Matt 19:17
But found *n*; yea, though .....Matt 26:60
witnesses came..found they *n* ..Matt 26:60
Making..word of God of *n* ....Mark 7:13
is *n* good but one..God ....Mark 10:18
is *n* other commandment ....Mark 12:31
him to death; and found *n* ....Mark 14:55
is *n* of thy kindred that is .....Luke 1:61
impart to him that hath *n* .....Luke 3:11
n of them was Elijah sent .....Luke 4:26
seeking rest; and finding *n* ....Luke 11:24
sought fruit..and found *n*......Luke 13:6
on this fig tree, and find *n* ....Luke 13:7
n is good, save one..God .....Luke 18:19
that there was *n* other boat ...John 6:22
n of you keepeth the law? ....John 7:19
saw *n* but the woman, he .....John 8:10
the works which *n* other ......John 15:24
n of you asketh me, Whither ..John 16:5
and *n* of them is lost, but .....John 17:12
thou gavest me have I lost *n* ..John 18:9
n of the disciples durst ask ....John 21:12
Silver and gold have I *n* ......Acts 3:6
n other name under heaven ...Acts 4:12
he gave him *n* inheritance .....Acts 7:5
n of these things which ye.....Acts 8:24
word to *n* but unto the Jews ..Acts 11:19
Gallio cared for *n* of those ....Acts 18:17
But *n* of these things move....Acts 20:24
forbid *n* of his acquaintance ...Acts 24:23
but if there be *n* of these .....Acts 25:11
they brought *n* accusation .....Acts 25:18
saying *n* other things than .....Acts 26:22
n righteous, no, not one ......Rom 3:10
is *n* that understandeth........Rom 3:11
is *n* that seeketh after God ....Rom 3:11
and the promise made of *n*....Rom 4:14
Spirit of Christ, he is *n* ....Rom 8:9
word of God hath taken *n* ....Rom 9:6
n of us liveth to himself.......Rom 14:7
thank God that I baptized *n*...1Cor 1:14
n of the princes of this........1Cor 2:8
wives be as though they had *n* .1Cor 7:29
there is *n* other God, but 1Cor 8:4
But I have used *n* of these 1Cor 9:15
Give *n* offense, neither to 1Cor 10:32
n of them is without 1Cor 14:10
write *n* other things unto 2Cor 1:13
of the apostles saw I *n* ....Gal 1:19
make the promise of *n* effect ..Gal 3:17
ye will be *n* otherwise ....Gal 5:10
n render evil for evil unto 1Thess 5:15
n occasion to the adversary....1Tim 5:14
let *n* of you suffer as a........1Pet 4:15
is *n* occasion of stumbling 1John 2:10
Fear *n* of those things ....Rev 2:10

NOON—*midday*

Time of:
Eating ....Gen 43:16, 25
Resting 2Sam 4:5
Praying ....Ps 55:17
Complain and murmur ...Ps 55:17
Drunkenness 1Kin 20:16
Destruction ....Ps 91:6
Death 2Kin 4:20

Figurative of:
Blindness ....Deut 28:29
Cleansing ....Job 11:17

[*also* NOONDAY, NOONTIDE]
from morning even until *n* 1Kin 18:26
grope in the *n* as in the night..Job 5:14
and thy judgment as the *n* ....Ps 37:6
makest thy flock to rest at *n* ..Song 1:7
night in the midst of the *n* ....Is 16:3
thy darkness be as the *n* ......Is 58:10
we stumble at *n* day as in .....Is 59:10
arise, and let us go up at *n*....Jer 6:4
and the shouting at *n* ....Jer 20:16
the sun to go down at *n* ....Amos 8:9
drive out Ashdod at the *n* day .Zeph 2:4
unto Damascus about *n* ....Acts 22:6

NOPH (nŏf)—*the Hebrew name of the Egyptian city of Memphis*
princes of *N* are deceived .....Is 19:13
children of *N* and Tahapanes ..Jer 2:16
at Tahpanhes and at *N*........Jer 44:1
publish in *N* and in Tahpanhes .Jer 46:14
N shall be waste and desolate .Jer 46:19
images to cease out of *N*......Ezek 30:13
and *N* shall have distresses ....Ezek 30:16

NOPHAH (nō'fä)—*"fearful"*
Moabite town ....Num 21:29, 30

NOR—*See* INTRODUCTION

NORTH—*the direction opposite south; from the north*

Refers to:
A geographical direction..Gen 28:14
Ps 107:3
Invading forces ....Is 14:31
Jer 6:1

[*also* NORTHERN, NORTHWARD]
the place where thou art *n* ....Gen 13:14
n side there shall be twenty ...Ex 26:20
for the *n* side in length ....Ex 27:11
which is toward the *n* ....Ex 36:25
for the *n* side the hangings ....Ex 38:11
side of the tabernacle *n* ....Ex 40:22
on the side of the altar *n* .....Lev 1:11
Dan shall be on the *n* side ....Num 2:25
the side of the tabernacle *n* ...Num 3:35
this shall be your *n* border ....Num 34:7
on the *n* side two thousand....Num 35:5
long enough; turn you *n* ....Deut 2:3
thine eyes westward, and *n*.....Deut 3:27
pitched on the *n* side of Ai....Josh 8:11
on the *n* of the mountains.....Josh 11:2
the borders of Ekron *n* ....Josh 13:3
border in the *n* quarter ....Josh 15:5
n, looking toward Gilgal ......Josh 15:7
which is Chesalon, on the *n* ...Josh 15:10
sea to Michmethah on the *n*...Josh 16:6
on the *n* side of the river .....Josh 17:9
n it was Manasseh's and .....Josh 17:10
abide in their coasts on the *n*..Josh 18:5
their border on the *n* side .....Josh 18:12
side of Jericho on the *n* side ..Josh 18:12
And was drawn from the *n*....Josh 18:17
side over against Arabah *n* ....Josh 18:18
compasseth it on the *n* side ...Josh 19:14
on the *n* side of the hill of ....Josh 24:30
n side of the hill Gaash ....Judg 2:9
Midianites were on the *n*......Judg 7:1
together, and went *n* ....Judg 12:1
is on the *n* side of Beth-el ....Judg 21:19
situate *n* over..Michmash......1Sam 14:5
three looking toward the *n* 1Kin 7:25
on the *n* side of the altar 2Kin 16:14
toward the east, west, *n* 1Chr 9:24
three looking toward the *n* 2Chr 4:4
He stretcheth out the *n* ....Job 26:7
weather cometh out of the *n* ..Job 37:22
Zion, on the sides of the *n*....Ps 48:2
n and the south thou hast .....Ps 89:12
The *n* wind driveth away rain. .Prov 25:23
turneth about unto the *n*......Eccl 1:6
the south, or toward the *n* ....Eccl 11:3
Awake, O *n* wind; and come ..Song 4:16
in the sides of the *n* ....Is 14:13
raised up one from the *n*......Is 41:25
I will say to the *n*, Give up ...Is 43:6

these from the ***n*** and from the .Is 49:12
face thereof is toward the ***n*** . . .Jer 1:13
families..kingdoms of the ***n*** . . . .Jer 1:15
these words toward the ***n*** . . . . .Jer 3:12
bring evil from the ***n***, and . . . . .Jer 4:6
evil appeareth out of the ***n*** . . . .Jer 6:1
commotion out of the ***n*** . . . . . . .Jer 10:22
them that come from the ***n*** . . . .Jer 13:20
Shall iron break the ***n*** iron . . . .Jer 15:12
Israel from the land of the ***n*** . .Jer 16:15
of Israel out of the ***n*** . . . . .Jer 23:8
take all the families of the ***n*** . .Jer 25:9
will bring them from the ***n*** . . . .Jer 31:8
and fall toward the ***n*** by . . . . . .Jer 46:6
it cometh out of the ***n*** . . . . .Jer 46:20
waters rise up out of the ***n*** . . . .Jer 47:2
out of the ***n*** there cometh up . .Jer 50:3
people shall come from the ***n*** . .Jer 50:41
come unto her from the ***n*** . . . . .Jer 51:48
a whirlwind came out of the ***n***. .Ezek 1:4
that looketh toward the ***n*** . . . . .Ezek 8:3
now the way toward the ***n*** . . . .Ezek 8:5
eyes the way toward the ***n*** . . . .Ezek 8:5
n at the gate of the altar . . . . . .Ezek 8:5
which lieth toward the ***n*** . . . . . .Ezek 9:2
faces from the south to the ***n*** . .Ezek 20:47
flesh from the south to the ***n*** . .Ezek 21:4
a king of kings from the ***n*** . . . .Ezek 26:7
There be the princes of the ***n*** . .Ezek 32:30
Togarmah of the ***n*** quarters . . .Ezek 38:6
thee to come up from ***n*** parts. .Ezek 39:2
cubits eastward and ***n*** . . . . .Ezek 40:19
court that looked toward the ***n*** .Ezek 40:20
brought me to the ***n*** gate . . . . .Ezek 40:35
at the side of the ***n*** gate . . . . . .Ezek 40:44
the prospect toward the ***n*** . . . . .Ezek 40:44
one door toward the ***n***, and . . .Ezek 41:11
court, the way toward the ***n*** . . .Ezek 42:1
the building toward the ***n*** . . . . .Ezek 42:1
their doors toward the ***n*** . . . . . .Ezek 42:4
n chambers and the south . . . . .Ezek 42:13
me the way of the ***n*** gate . . . . .Ezek 44:4
entereth in by the way of the ***n*** Ezek 46:9
go forth by the way of the ***n*** . .Ezek 46:9
of the way of the gate ***n*** . . . . . .Ezek 47:2
land toward the ***n*** side . . . . .Ezek 47:15
of Damascus, and the ***n n*** . . . . .Ezek 47:17
And this is the ***n*** side . . . . .Ezek 47:17
From the ***n*** end to the coast . . .Ezek 48:1
the border of Damascus ***n*** . . . . .Ezek 48:1
n side four thousand and . . . . . .Ezek 48:16
of the city on the ***n*** side . . . . . .Ezek 48:30
the ram..westward, and ***n*** . . . . .Dan 8:4
come to the king of the ***n*** . . . . .Dan 11:6
years than the king of the ***n*** . . .Dan 11:8
For the king of the ***n*** shall . . . .Dan 11:13
and the king of the ***n*** shall . . . .Dan 11:40
off from you the ***n*** army . . . . . .Joel 2:20
and from the ***n*** even to the . . . .Amos 8:12
out his hand against the ***n*** . . . . .Zeph 2:13
flee from the land of the ***n*** . . . .Zech 2:6
therein go forth into the ***n*** . . . .Zech 6:6
these that go toward the ***n*** . . . .Zech 6:8
shall remove toward the ***n*** . . . . .Zech 14:4
from the ***n***, and from the . . . . .Luke 13:29
toward the south west and ***n*** . .Acts 27:12
the ***n*** three gates; on the . . . . . .Rev 21:13

NOSE—*the organ on the face used for breathing and smelling*

Used literally for:
Breathing . . . . .Gen 2:7
Smelling . . . . .Amos 4:10
Ornamentation . . . . .Is 3:21
Bondage . . . . .Is 37:29
Blood (forced) . . . . .Prov 30:33
Behemoth . . . . .Job 40:15-24
Idols . . . . .Ps 115:6
Nosebleeding produced by wringing . . . . .Prov 30:33

Used figuratively of:
Man's life . . . . .Job 27:3
God's:
Power . . . . .Ex 15:8
Sovereign control 2Kin 19:28
Overindulgence . . . . . . .Num 11:20
National hope (Zedekiah) . . . . .Lam 4:20

[*also* NOSES]
or he that hath a flat ***n*** . . . . . . .Lev 21:18
put an hook into his ***n***? . . . . . . .Job 41:2
thy ***n*** is as the tower of . . . . . . .Song 7:4
and the smell of thy ***n*** like . . . .Song 7:8
put the branch to their ***n*** . . . . . .Ezek 8:17
they shall take away thy ***n*** . . . .Ezek 23:25
it shall stop the ***n*** of the . . . . . .Ezek 39:11

NOSE RING—*a ring put into the nose*
Worn by women . . . . .Is 3:21
Put in swine's snout . . . . .Prov 11:22

NOSTRIL—*opening in the nose*

[*also* NOSTRILS]
in whose ***n*** was the breath . . . .Gen 7:22
went up a smoke out of his ***n***. . .2Sam 22:9
blast of the breath of his ***n*** 2Sam 22:16
by the breath of his ***n*** are . . . . .Job 4:9
spirit of God is in my ***n*** . . . . . . .Job 27:3
glory of his ***n*** is terrible . . . . . . .Job 39:20
Out of his ***n*** goeth smoke . . . . .Job 41:20
up a smoke out of his ***n*** . . . . . . .Ps 18:8
whose breath is in his ***n*** . . . . . . .Is 2:22
The breath of our ***n***, the . . . . . .Lam 4:20
to come up unto your ***n*** . . . . . . .Amos 4:10

NOT—*See* INTRODUCTION

NOTED—*remarkable; prominent*

[*also* NOTABLE, NOTE]
a table and ***n*** it in a book . . . . .Is 30:8
goat had a ***n*** horn between . . . .Dan 8:5
is ***n*** in the scripture of truth . . .Dan 10:21
n prisoner called Barabbas . . . .Matt 27:16
great and ***n*** day of the Lord . . .Acts 2:20
indeed a ***n*** miracle hath been . .Acts 4:16
of ***n*** among the apostles . . . . . . .Rom 16:7
n that man, and have no 2Thess 3:14

NOTHING—*not any thing*

Things classified as:
Service without:
Christ . . . . .John 15:5
Love 1Cor 13:3
Circumcision 1Cor 7:19
Flesh . . . . .John 6:63

n will be restrained from . . . . . .Gen 11:6
only unto these men do ***n*** . . . . .Gen 19:8
have done unto thee ***n*** but . . . .Gen 26:29
and here also have I done ***n*** . . .Gen 40:15
n die of all that is the . . . . .Ex 9:4
ye shall let ***n*** of it remain . . . . .Ex 12:10
that gathered much had ***n*** . . . . .Ex 16:18
he shall go out free for ***n*** . . . . .Ex 21:2
If he have ***n***, then he shall . . . .Ex 22:3
There shall ***n*** cast their . . . . . . .Ex 23:26
eat ***n*** that is made of the . . . . . .Num 6:4
n at all, beside this manna . . . .Num 11:6
and touch ***n*** of theirs, lest . . . . .Num 16:26
Let ***n***, I pray thee, hinder . . . . .Num 22:16
thee; thou hast lacked ***n*** . . . . . .Deut 2:7
save alive ***n*** that breatheth . . . .Deut 20:16
the damsel thou shalt do ***n*** . . . .Deut 22:26
he hath ***n*** left him in the . . . . . .Deut 28:55
left ***n*** undone of all that . . . . . . .Josh 11:15
such as before knew ***n*** . . . . .Judg 3:2
is ***n*** else save the sword . . . . . . .Judg 7:14
and he had ***n*** in his hand . . . . .Judg 14:6
every whit, and hid ***n*** from 1Sam 3:18
father will do ***n*** either great 1Sam 20:2
servant knew ***n*** of all this 1Sam 22:15
so that ***n*** was missed of all 1Sam 25:21
there is ***n*** better for me than . .1Sam 27:1
And there was ***n*** lacking 1Sam 30:19
But the poor man had ***n*** 2Sam 12:3
that which doth cost me ***n*** 2Sam 24:24
in his month; they lacked ***n*** . . .1Kin 4:27
There was ***n*** in the ark 1Kin 8:9
n accounted of in the days 1Kin 10:21
country? And he answered, ***N*** . .1Kin 11:22
looked, and said, There is ***n*** . . .1Kin 18:43
tell me ***n*** but that which is 1Kin 22:16
fall unto the earth ***n*** of the 2Kin 10:10
there was ***n*** in his house 2Kin 20:13
n shall be left, saith the 2Kin 20:17
There was ***n*** in the ark save . . .2Chr 5:10
n hid from Solomon which 2Chr 9:2
thou say ***n*** but the truth to 2Chr 18:15
this is ***n*** else but sorrow of . . . .Neh 2:2
and found ***n*** to answer . . . . .Neh 5:8
unto them for whom ***n*** is . . . . . .Neh 8:10
so that they lacked ***n*** . . . . .Neh 9:21
required ***n*** but what Hegai . . . .Esth 2:15
Yet all this availeth me ***n*** . . . . .Esth 5:13
There is ***n*** done for him . . . . . . .Esth 6:3
they go to ***n***, and perish . . . . . .Job 6:18
now ye are ***n***; ye see my . . . . . .Job 6:21
of yesterday, and know ***n*** . . . . .Job 8:9
make my speech ***n*** worth? . . . . .Job 24:25
hangeth the earth upon ***n*** . . . . .Job 26:7
It profiteth a man ***n*** that he . . .Job 34:9
is ***n*** hid from the heat . . . . .Ps 19:6
and mine age is as ***n*** before . . .Ps 39:5
dieth he shall carry ***n*** away . . . .Ps 49:17
and ***n*** shall offend them . . . . . . .Ps 119:165
is ***n*** froward or perverse in . . . .Prov 8:8
is simple, and knoweth ***n*** . . . . . .Prov 9:13
of wickedness profit ***n*** . . . . .Prov 10:2
sluggard desireth and hath ***n*** . . .Prov 13:4
beg in harvest and have ***n*** . . . . .Prov 20:4
If thou hast ***n*** to pay, why . . . . .Prov 22:27
There is ***n*** better for a man . . .Eccl 2:24
n can be put to it, nor any . . . .Eccl 3:14
and there is ***n*** in his hand . . . . .Eccl 5:14
and shall take ***n*** of his . . . . .Eccl 5:15
that he wanteth ***n*** for his . . . . . .Eccl 6:2
man should find ***n*** after him . . .Eccl 7:14
all her princes shall be ***n*** . . . . . .Is 34:12
there was ***n*** in his house . . . . . .Is 39:2
nations before him are as ***n*** . . .Is 40:17
counted to him less than ***n*** . . . .Is 40:17
confounded..shall be as ***n*** . . . . .Is 41:11
against thee shall be as ***n*** . . . . .Is 41:12
ye are of ***n***, and your work . . . .Is 41:24
vanity; their works are ***n*** . . . . . .Is 41:29
that is profitable for ***n***? . . . . . . .Is 44:10
lest thou bring me to ***n*** . . . . . . .Jer 10:24
it was profitable for ***n*** . . . . .Jer 13:7
there is ***n*** too hard for thee . . .Jer 32:17
thee a thing; hide ***n*** from . . . . .Jer 38:14
of the people, which had ***n*** . . . .Jer 39:10
will keep ***n*** back from you . . . .Jer 42:4
her utterly, let ***n*** of her be . . . .Jer 50:26
Is it ***n*** to you, all ye that . . . . . .Lam 1:12
own spirit, and have seen ***n***! . . .Ezek 13:3
the earth are reputed as ***n*** . . . . .Dan 4:35
yea, and ***n*** shall escape . . . . . . .Joel 2:3
his den, if he have taken ***n***? . . .Amos 3:4
the Lord God will do ***n***, but . . .Amos 3:7
in comparison of it as ***n***? . . . . . .Hag 2:3
it is..good for ***n***, but to . . . . . . .Matt 5:13
n covered, that shall not . . . . . .Matt 10:26
three days, and have ***n*** to eat. .Matt 15:32
n shall be impossible unto . . . . .Matt 17:20
found ***n*** thereon, but leaves . . .Matt 21:19
swear by the temple, it is ***n*** . . .Matt 23:16
unto him, Answerest thou ***n*** . . .Matt 26:62
and elders, he answered ***n*** . . . .Matt 27:12
thou ***n*** to do with that just . . . .Matt 27:19
saw that he could prevail ***n*** . . . .Matt 27:24
See thou say ***n*** to any man . . . .Mark 1:44
there is ***n*** hid, which shall . . . .Mark 4:22
was ***n*** bettered, but rather . . . . .Mark 5:26
take ***n*** for their journey . . . . . . .Mark 6:8
There is ***n*** from without . . . . . .Mark 7:15
and having ***n*** to eat, Jesus . . . . .Mark 8:1
kind can come forth by ***n*** . . . . .Mark 9:29
came to it, he found ***n*** but . . . .Mark 11:13
saying, Answerest thou ***n***? . . . .Mark 14:60
things, but he answered ***n*** . . . . .Mark 15:3
n shall be impossible . . . . .Luke 1:37
in those days he did eat ***n*** . . . . .Luke 4:2
the night and have taken ***n*** . . . .Luke 5:5
and lend, hoping for ***n*** . . . . .Luke 6:35
when they had ***n*** to pay . . . . . . .Luke 7:42
n is secret, that shall not . . . . . .Luke 8:17
Take ***n*** for your journey . . . . . .Luke 9:3

n shall by any means hurt .....Luke 10:19
I have *n* to set before him? ...Luke 11:6
n covered, that shall not ......Luke 12:2
thing? And they said, *N* ......Luke 22:35
but he answered him *n*........Luke 23:9
this man hath done *n* amiss ...Luke 23:41
man can receive *n*, except.....John 3:27
Sir, thou hast *n* to draw.......John 4:11
The Son can do *n* of himself ..John 5:19
that remain, that *n* be lost ....John 6:12
the flesh profiteth *n* ....John 6:63
and they say *n* unto him ......John 7:26
I am he, and that I do *n* of ...John 8:28
not of God, he could do *n* ....John 9:33
them, Ye know *n* at all ....John 11:49
Perceive ye how ye prevail *n* ..John 12:19
world cometh and hath *n* .....John 14:30
for without me ye can do *n* ...John 15:5
that day ye shall ask me *n* ....John 16:23
and in secret have I said *n* ....John 18:20
that night they caught *n*.......John 21:3
could say *n* against it ....Acts 4:14
go with them, doubting *n* .....Acts 10:20
n common or unclean hath ....Acts 11:8
spent their time in *n* else......Acts 17:21
to be quiet, and to do *n* ......Acts 19:36
back *n* that was profitable .....Acts 20:20
concerning thee, are *n* ....Acts 21:24
eat *n* until we have slain Paul .Acts 23:14
committed *n* worthy of........Acts 25:25
This man doeth *n* worthy .....Acts 26:31
fasting, having taken *n* ....Acts 27:33
committed *n* against the.......Acts 28:17
that there is *n* unclean ....Rom 14:14
to *n* the understanding 1Cor 1:19
For I know *n* by myself 1Cor 4:4
judge *n* before the time 1Cor 4:5
he knoweth *n* yet as he 1Cor 8:2
gospel, I have *n* to glory 1Cor 9:16
have not charity, I am *n* 1Cor 13:2
as having *n*, and yet 2Cor 6:10
receive damage by us in *n*.....2Cor 7:9
had gathered much had *n* 2Cor 8:15
for in *n* am I behind the 2Cor 12:11
chiefest apostles..I be *n* 2Cor 12:11
we can do *n* against the.......2Cor 13:8
in conference added *n* to......Gal 2:6
Christ shall profit you *n*.......Gal 5:2
in *n* I shall be ashamed ....Phil 1:20
n be done through strife ......Phil 2:3
careful for *n*, but in every.....Phil 4:6
that ye may have lack of *n* 1Thess 4:12
God is good, and *n* to be 1Tim 4:4
doing *n* by partiality 1Tim 5:21
He is proud, knowing *n*........1Tim 6:4
For we brought *n* into this 1Tim 6:7
certain we can carry *n* out 1Tim 6:7
defiled and unbelieving is *n* ..Titus 1:15
that *n* be wanting unto........Titus 3:13
thy mind would I do *n*........Philem 14
he left *n* that is not put ....Heb 2:8
which tribe Moses spake *n* ....Heb 7:14
and entire, wanting *n* ....James 1:4
taking *n* of the Gentiles 3John 7
goods, and have need of *n* ....Rev 3:17

NOTICE—*attention; news*
all the people took *n* of it 2Sam 3:36
bounty, whereof ye had *n* 2Cor 9:5

NOTWITHSTANDING—*nevertheless; however; although*
N they hearkened not unto ....Ex 16:20
N the cities of the Levites .....Lev 25:32
N the children of Korah ......Num 26:11
N ye would not go up, but .....Deut 1:26
N, if the land of your ....Josh 22:19
n the journey that thou ....Judg 4:9
N they hearkened not.........1Sam 2:25
n the princes of the...........1Sam 29:9
N the king's word prevailed ...2Sam 24:4
N in thy days I will not do 1Kin 11:12
N they would not hear 2Kin 17:14
N thou shalt not build the.....2Chr 6:9
n I have spoken unto you .....Jer 35:14
N the children rebelled........Ezek 20:21
N the land shall be desolate ...Mic 7:13
n being warned of God in a ...Matt 2:22
N lest we should offend ....Matt 17:27
n be ye sure of this, that ....Luke 10:11
N it pleased Silas to abide .....Acts 15:34
n, every way, whether in......Phil 1:18
N she shall be saved in 1Tim 2:15
N the Lord stood with me.....2Tim 4:17
n ye give them not those ......James 2:16
N I have a few things against ..Rev 2:20

NOUGHT—*nothing*
Descriptive of:
Something:
Fruitless ....Is 49:24
Without payment ......Gen 29:15
Vain ....Mal 1:10
Nothing ....Is 41:24

Time of:
Past ....Neh 4:15
Present ....Amos 6:13
Future ....Ps 33:10

Things that will come to:
Wicked ....Job 8:22
Wicked counsel ....Is 8:10
Babylon ....Rev 18:17

[*also* NAUGHT]
cleave *n* of the cursed ....Deut 13:17
and to bring you to *n* ....Deut 28:63
water is *n* and the ground 2Kin 2:19
Doth Job fear God for *n*......Job 1:9
mountain falling cometh to *n* ..Job 14:18
ye have set at *n* all my........Prov 1:25
It is *n*, it is *n*, saith ....Prov 20:14
aside the just for a thing of *n*. .Is 29:21
have sold yourselves for *n*.....Is 52:3
and a thing of *n* and the ......Jer 14:14
Beth-el shall come to *n* ....Amos 5:5
things, and be set at *n* ....Mark 9:12
men of war set him at *n* ......Luke 23:11
stone which was set at *n* of....Acts 4:11
of men, it will come to *n* .....Acts 4:38
why dost thou set at *n* thy ....Rom 14:10
not, to bring to *n* things 1Cor 1:28
this world, that come to *n*.....1Cor 2:6
eat any man's bread for *n* 2Thess 3:8

NOURISH—*to provide means of growth*
Descriptive of the growth or care of:
Children ....Acts 7:20, 21
Animals 2Sam 12:3
Plants ....Is 44:14
Family.................Gen 45:11
Country ....Acts 12:20

Figurative of:
Protection ....Is 1:2
Provision ....Ruth 4:15
Pampering ....James 5:5
Preparedness 1Tim 4:6

[*also* NOURISHED, NOURISHETH, NOURISHING, NOURISHMENT]
Joseph *n* his father and ....Gen 47:12
I will *n* you and your little ....Gen 50:21
a man shall *n* a young cow ....Is 7:21
n her whelps among young ....Ezek 19:2
so *n* them three years, that....Dan 1:5
n and cherisheth it, even ......Eph 5:29
having *n* ministered, and ......Col 2:19
place, where she is *n* for ......Rev 12:14

NOURISHER—*one who provides the means of growth*
and a *n* of thine old age ......Rom 4:15

NOVICE—*one who is inexperienced; a recent Christian convert*
Bishops, not to be 1Tim 3:1, 6

NOW—*the present time*
As contrasted with:
Old Testament ....John 4:23
Past ....John 9:25
Future ....John 13:7, 19
Two conditions ....Luke 16:25

In Christ's life, descriptive of His:
Atonement..............Rom 5:11
Humiliation ....Heb 2:8
Resurrection 1Cor 15:20
Glorification ....John 13:31
Intercession ....Heb 9:24
Return 1John 2:28

In the Christian's life, descriptive of:
Salvation ....Rom 13:11
Regeneration............John 5:25
Reconciliation ....Col 1:21, 22
Justification ....Rom 5:9
Victory ....Gal 2:20
Worship ....John 4:23
Suffering 1Pet 1:6-8
Hope ....Rev 12:10
Glorification ....Rom 8:21, 22; 1John 3:2

Descriptive of the present age as:
Time of:
Opportunity 2Cor 6:2
Evil 1Thess 2:6
God's:
Greater revelation .....Eph 3:5
Completed redemption .Col 1:26, 27
Final dealing with mankind ....Heb 12:26

See INTRODUCTION

NUISANCE—*an irritation*
Descriptive of:
Widow ....Luke 18:2-5

NUMBER—*a mathematical unit*
Symbolic of:
One—unity ....Deut 6:4; Matt 19:6
Two—unity ....Gen 1:27
Two—division ....1Kin 18:21; Matt 7:13, 14
Three—the Trinity .....Matt 28:19; 2Cor 13:14
Three—resurrection.... Hos 6:1, 2; Matt 12:40; Luke 13:32
Three—completion 1Cor 13:13
Three—testing ....Judg 7:16
Four—completion...... Matt 13:4-8; Matt 25:2; John 4:35
Five—incompletion .....Matt 25:15-20
Six—man's testing ......Gen 1:27, 31; Rev 13:18
Seven—completion .....Ex 20:10
Seven—fulfillment ......Josh 6:4
Seven—perfection ....Rev 1:4
Eighth—new beginning...Ezek 43:27; 1Pet 3:20
Ten—completion 1Cor 6:9, 10
Tenth—God's part ......Gen 14:20; Mal 3:10
Twelve—God's purpose ..John 11:9; Rev 21:12-17
Forty—testing ....Jon 3:4; Matt 4:2
Forty—judgment ....Num 14:33; Ps 95:10
Seventy—God's completed purpose .. Jer 25:11; Dan 9:24

NUMBER—*to enumerate; count; the total or sum*
[*also* NUMBERED, NUMBEREST, NUMBERING]
man can *n* the dust of the .....Gen 13:16
shall thy seed also be *n* ....Gen 13:16
stars, if thou be able to *n* ......Gen 15:5
cannot be *n* for multitude .....Gen 32:12
being few in *n*, they shall .....Gen 34:30
very much, until he left *n* .....Gen 41:49
it according to the *n* of ....Ex 12:4
according to the *n* of your ....Ex 16:16
the *n* of thy days I will ....Ex 23:26

the LORD, when thou *n*........Ex 30:12
among them that are *n*........Ex 30:13
every one that went to be *n*...Ex 38:26
he shall *n* to himself seven ....Lev 15:13
seventh sabbath shall ye *n*.....Lev 23:16
shalt *n* seven sabbaths of......Lev 25:8
to the *n* of years after the.....Lev 25:15
unto the *n* of years of the.....Lev 25:15
be according unto the *n* of....Lev 25:50
n them in the wilderness......Num 1:19
fathers, those that were *n*......Num 1:22
These are those that were *n*...Num 1:44
which Moses and Aaron *n*....Num 1:44
they that were *n* were six.....Num 1:46
those that were *n* of them.....Num 2:4
that were *n* in the camp of....Num 2:9
and those that were *n* of......Num 2:13
those that were *n* of them.....Num 2:19
those that were *n* of them.....Num 2:26
were *n* of the children of......Num 2:32
all those that were *n* of the...Num 2:32
Levites were not *n* among.....Num 2:33
N the children of Levi after...Num 3:15
old and upward shalt thou *n*...Num 3:15
n of them, according to.......Num 3:22
n of them were seven.........Num 3:22
In the *n* of all the males......Num 3:28
that were *n* of the Levites.....Num 3:39
which Moses and Aaron *n*....Num 3:39
N all the first-born of the....Num 3:40
and take the *n* of their........Num 3:40
those that were *n* of them.....Num 3:43
odd *n* of them is to be........Num 3:48
shalt *n* them after their.......Num 4:29
those that were *n* of them.....Num 4:35
Moses and Aaron did *n*.......Num 4:37
those that were *n* of the.....Num 4:38
were *n* of the families of......Num 4:41
Even those that were *n* of.....Num 4:44
those that were *n* of the......Num 4:45
Moses and Aaron *n*..........Num 4:45
that were *n* of the Levites.....Num 4:46
and the chief of Israel *n*......Num 4:46
n by the hand of Moses.......Num 4:49
thus were they *n* of him.......Num 4:49
all that were *n* of you........Num 14:29
according to your whole *n*......Num 14:29
According to the *n* that ye....Num 15:12
one according to their *n*.....Num 15:12
the *n* of the fourth part.......Num 23:10
that were *n* of them..........Num 26:18
that were *n* of them were.....Num 26:41
those that were *n* of them.....Num 26:47
n of the children of Israel.....Num 26:51
are they that were *n* of the....Num 26:57
that were *n* of them were.....Num 26:62
were not *n* among the children.Num 26:62
they that were *n* by Moses.....Num 26:63
n the children of Israel........Num 26:63
Moses and Aaron the priest *n*.Num 26:64
n the children of Israel........Num 26:64
according to their *n*, after.....Num 29:18
n three hundred thousand.....Num 31:36
be left few in *n* among the....Deut 4:27
ye were more in *n* than any...Deut 7:7
Seven weeks shalt thou *n*.....Deut 16:9
begin to *n* the seven weeks....Deut 16:9
ye shall be left few in *n*.......Deut 28:62
n of the tribes of the children..Josh 4:5
and *n* the people, and went...Josh 8:10
camels were without *n*........Judg 6:5
camels were without *n*........Judg 7:12
children of Benjamin were *n*..Judg 20:15
n four hundred thousand.....Judg 20:17
n of the lords of the.........1Sam 6:4
when he *n* them in Bezek.....1Sam 11:8
N now, and see who is.......1Sam 14:17
when they had *n*, behold......1Sam 14:17
by *n* twelve of Benjamin......2Sam 2:15
David *n* the people that.......2Sam 18:1
Go, *n* Israel and Judah.......2Sam 24:1
Beer-sheba, and *n* ye the.....2Sam 24:2
I may know the *n* of the......2Sam 24:2
the sum of the *n* of the.......2Sam 24:9
to the *n* of the tribes of......1Kin 18:31
he *n* the young men of the....1Kin 20:15
year that Ben-hadad *n* the....1Kin 20:26
the same time, and *n* all......2Kin 3:6
whose *n* was in the days of....1Chr 7:2
n throughout the genealogy...1Chr 7:40
the *n* of the bands that.......1Chr 12:23
and provoked David to *n*.....1Chr 21:1
n Israel from Beer-sheba......1Chr 21:2
and bring the *n* of them to....1Chr 21:2
commanded the people to be *n*.1Chr 21:17
the iron, there is no *n*.........1Chr 22:16
counted by *n* of names by.....1Chr 23:24
the Levites were *n* from......1Chr 23:27
the *n* of the workmen.........1Chr 25:1
of Israel after their *n*.........1Chr 27:1
son of Zeruiah began to *n*....1Chr 27:24
the *n* put in the account......1Chr 27:24
Solomon *n* all..strangers......2Chr 2:17
David his father had *n* them...2Chr 2:17
the *n* wherewith David his....2Chr 2:17
people were without *n* that....2Chr 12:3
the *n* of them according to....2Chr 17:14
he *n* them from twenty.......2Chr 25:5
whole *n* of the chief of the....2Chr 26:12
n of priests sanctified.........2Chr 30:24
n them unto Sheshbazzar......Ezra 1:8
And this is the *n* of them.....Ezra 1:9
daily burnt offerings by *n*.....Ezra 3:4
n and by weight of every......Ezra 8:34
n, I say, of the men of the....Neh 7:7
n of those that were slain.....Esth 9:11
according to the *n* of them....Job 1:5
not come into the *n* of the....Job 3:6
and wonders without *n*........Job 9:10
for now thou *n* my steps......Job 14:16
the *n* of years is hidden......Job 15:20
there any *n* of his armies?.....Job 25:3
mighty men without *n*........Job 34:24
because the *n* of thy days.....Job 38:21
Who can *n* the clouds in.....Job 38:37
Canst thou *n* the months......Job 39:2
are more than can be *n*.......Ps 40:5
for I know not the *n*..........Ps 71:15
So teach us to *n* our days.....Ps 90:12
caterpillars..without *n*.........Ps 105:34
more in *n* than the sand......Ps 139:18
telleth the *n* of the stars......Ps 147:4
is wanting cannot be *n*........Eccl 1:15
and virgins without *n*.........Song 6:8
the residue of the *n* of........Is 21:17
n the houses of Jerusalem.....Is 22:10
n with the transgressors.......Is 53:12
drink offering unto that *n*.....Is 65:11
will I *n* you to the sword......Is 65:12
according to the *n* of thy......Jer 2:28
For according to the *n* of.....Jer 11:13
host of heaven cannot be *n*....Jer 33:22
a small *n* that escape the.....Jer 44:28
according to the *n* of the......Ezek 4:4
according to the *n* of the......Ezek 4:9
God hath *n* thy kingdom......Dan 5:26
books the *n* of the years......Dan 9:2
n of the children of Israel.....Hos 1:10
cannot be measured nor *n*.....Hos 1:10
land, strong, and without *n*....Joel 1:6
and a great *n* of carcases......Nah 3:3
hairs of your head are all *n*...Matt 10:30
disciples and a great *n* of....Mark 10:46
n with the transgressors.......Mark 15:28
hairs of your head are all *n*...Luke 12:7
being of the *n* of the twelve...Luke 22:3
sat down, in *n* about five.....John 6:10
the *n* of names together.......Acts 1:15
For he was *n* with us, and....Acts 1:17
to whom a *n* of men, about...Acts 5:36
the *n* of the disciples was.....Acts 6:1
the *n* of the disciples.........Acts 6:7
and a great *n* believed, and...Acts 11:21
the *n* of the children of.......Rom 9:27
make ourselves of the *n*.......2Cor 10:12
widow be taken into the *n*....1Tim 5:9
n of them was ten thousand...Rev 5:11
I heard the *n* of them........Rev 7:4
which no man could *n*.........Rev 7:9
the *n* of the army of the......Rev 9:16
and I heard the *n* of them....Rev 9:16
beast, or the *n* of his name....Rev 13:17
count the *n* of the beast.......Rev 13:18
mark, and over the *n* of his...Rev 15:2
n of whom is as the sand.....Rev 20:8

NUMBERS, THE BOOK OF—*a book of the Old Testament*
The census.............Num 1:1—4:49
Cleansing of Levites.....Num 8:5-22
The cloud and the tabernacle............Num 9:15-23
The provision of manna..Num 11:4-9
The spies...............Num 13:1—14:45
The rebellion of Korah..Num 16:1-35
The sin of Moses........Num 20:1-13
Aaron's death...........Num 20:22-29
Balaam and Balak.......Num 22:2—24:25
Offerings and feasts.....Num 28:1—29:40
Settlements in Gilead....Num 32:1-42
Preparation for Canaan..Num 33:50—35:34

NUN, NON (nŭn, nŏn)—*"continuation; fish"*
1. Father of Joshua, Israel's military leader........Josh 1:1
   Called Non.............1Chr 7:27
2. Letter in the Hebrew alphabet...........Ps 119:105-112

servant Joshua the son of *N*...Ex 33:11
Joshua the son of *N*, the......Num 11:28
Moses called Oshea..of *N*....Num 13:16
Joshua the son of *N*..........Num 14:30
Joshua the son of *N*..........Num 26:65
Joshua the son of *N*..........Num 32:12
and Joshua the son of *N*......Num 34:17
But Joshua the son of *N*......Deut 1:38
and Hoshea the son of *N*.....Deut 32:44
Joshua the son of *N* sent.....Josh 2:1
to Joshua the son of *N*.......Josh 2:23
and Joshua the son of *N*......Josh 14:1
to Joshua the son of *N*........Josh 19:49
unto Joshua the son of *N*.....Josh 21:1
Joshua the son of *N*, the......Judg 2:8
spake by Joshua the son of *N*..1Kin 16:34
days of Jeshua the son of *N*...Neh 8:17

NURSE—*one who provides nourishment and protection to the young; to provide nourishment or protection*

Duties of:
Provide nourishment.....Gen 21:7
Protect.................2Kin 11:2
Called "guardian".......2Kin 10:1, 5

Figurative of:
Judgment...............Lam 4:4
Provision...............Num 11:12
Gentleness..............1Thess 2:7

[*also* NURSED, NURSING]
to thee a *n* of the Hebrew....Ex 2:7
that she may *n* the child......Ex 2:7
took the child, and *n* it.......Ex 2:9
her bosom, and became *n*.....Ruth 4:16
and his *n* took him up, and...2Sam 4:4
his *n* in a bedchamber.......2Chr 22:11
And kings shall be thy *n*......Is 49:23
and their queens thy *n*........Is 49:23
daughters shall be *n* at thy....Is 60:4

NURTURE *training*
n and admonition of the Lord.Eph 6:4

NUTS—*hard-shelled dried fruits or seeds*
Provided as gifts.........Gen 43:11
Grown in gardens.......Song 6:11

NYMPHAS (nĭm'făs)—*"bridegroom"*
Christian of Laodicea....Col 4:15

O

O—*See* INTRODUCTION

OAK—*a large and strong tree*

Uses of:
Landmarks .....Judg 6:11, 19
Burial place .....Gen 35:8
Place of rest 1Kin 13:14
Place of idolatry .....Is 44:14
For oars .....Ezek 27:6

Figurative of:
Strength .....Amos 2:9
Judgment .....Is 1:29, 30
Haughtiness .....Is 2:11, 13

[*also* OAKS]
Jacob hid them under the *o* .....Gen 35:4
set it up there under an *o* .....Josh 24:26
the thick boughs of a great *o* ..2Sam 18:9
head caught hold of the *o* 2Sam 18:9
Absalom hanged in an *o* 2Sam 18:10
alive in the midst of the *o* 2Sam 18:14
their bones under the *o* 1Chr 10:12
o, whose substance is in .....Is 6:13
and under every thick *o* .....Ezek 6:13
hills under *o* and poplars .....Hos 4:13
howl, O ye *o* of Bashan .....Zech 11:2

OARS—*wooden blades used for rowing*
Made of oak .....Ezek 27:6, 29
Used on galleys .....Is 33:21

OATH—*solemn promise*

Expressions descriptive of:
"As the Lord liveth" 1Sam 19:6
"God is witness" .....Gen 31:50
"The Lord..be witness" ..Jer 42:5
"God judge between us" .Gen 31:53
"The Lord make thee like" .....Jer 29:22
"I adjure thee" .....Matt 26:63
"I call God for a record" .2Cor 1:23

Purposes of:
Confirm covenant .....Gen 26:28
Insure protection .....Gen 31:44-53
Establish truth .....Ex 22:11
Confirm fidelity .....Num 5:19-22
Guarantee duties .....Gen 24:3, 4
Sign a covenant 2Chr 15:12-15
Fulfill promises .....Neh 5:12, 13

Sacredness of:
Obligatory .....Num 30:2-16
Maintained even in deception .....Josh 9:20
Upheld by Christ .....Matt 26:63, 64
Rewarded 2Chr 15:12-15
Maintained in fear 1Sam 14:24, 26

Prohibitions concerning, not:
In idol's name .....Josh 23:7
In creature's name .....Matt 5:34-36

[*also* OATH'S, OATHS]
be clear from this my *o* .....Gen 24:8
be clear from this my *o* .....Gen 24:41
shalt be clear from my *o* .....Gen 24:41
I will perform the *o* which .....Gen 26:3
Joseph took an *o* of the .....Gen 50:25
shall pronounce with an *o* .....Lev 5:4
the woman with an *o* of .....Num 5:21
make thee a curse and an *o* .....Num 5:21
he would keep the *o* which .....Deut 7:8
into his *o*, which the Lord .....Deut 29:12
this covenant and this *o* .....Deut 29:14
blameless of this thine *o* .....Josh 2:17
we will be quit of thine *o* .....Josh 2:20
had made a great *o* concerning .Judg 21:5
charged the people with the *o* .1Sam 14:27
charged the people with an *o* ..1Sam 14:28
Lord's *o* that was between 2Sam 21:7
not kept the *o* of the Lord 1Kin 2:43
an *o* be laid upon him to 1Kin 8:31
o come before thine altar 1Kin 8:31
took an *o* of them in the 2Kin 11:4
Abraham, and of his *o* unto ...1Chr 16:16
an *o* be laid upon him to 2Chr 6:22
the *o* come before the altar ...2Chr 6:22
into a curse, and into an *o* .....Neh 10:29
Abraham, and his *o* unto .....Ps 105:9
in regard of the *o* of God .....Eccl 8:2
as he that feareth an *o* .....Eccl 9:2
That I may perform the *o* .....Jer 11:5
despised the *o* in breaking .....Ezek 16:59
him, and hath taken an *o* .....Ezek 17:13
whose *o* he despised, and .....Ezek 17:16
surely mine *o* that he hath .....Ezek 17:19
to them that have sworn *o* .....Ezek 21:23
the *o* that is written in the .....Dan 9:11
according to the *o* of the .....Hab 3:9
neighbor; and love no false *o* ..Zech 8:17
perform unto the Lord thine *o* .Matt 5:33
he promised with an *o* to .....Matt 14:7
nevertheless for the *o* sake .....Matt 14:9
he denied with an *o*, I do .....Matt 26:72
yet for his *o* sake, and for .....Mark 6:26
God had sworn with an *o* .....Acts 2:30
bound themselves with an *o* ...Acts 23:21
an *o* for confirmation is to .....Heb 6:16
counsel confirmed it by an *o* ..Heb 6:17
earth, neither by any other *o* ..James 5:12

OATHS OF GOD—*God's promises*

Made in Old Testament concerning:
Promise to Abraham .....Gen 50:24
Davidic covenant 2Sam 7:10-16
Messianic priesthood .....Ps 110:4, 5

Fulfilled in New Testament in Christ's:
Birth .....Luke 1:68-73
Kingship on David's throne .....Luke 1:32, 33
Priesthood .....Heb 7:20-28
See SWEARING

OBADIAH (ō-bä-dī'ä)—*"servant of Jehovah"*
1. King Ahab's steward ...1Kin 18:3-16
2. Descendant of David ...1Chr 3:21
3. Chief of Issachar 1Chr 7:3
4. Descendant of Saul 1Chr 8:38
5. Gadite captain 1Chr 12:8, 9
6. Man of Zebulun 1Chr 27:19
7. Prince sent by Jehoshaphat to teach .2Chr 17:7
8. Levite overseer 2Chr 34:12
9. Leader in the postexilic community .....Ezra 8:9
10. Priest who signs the covenant .....Neh 10:5
11. Levite 1Chr 9:16
 Called Abda .....Neh 11:17
12. Postexilic porter .....Neh 12:25
13. Prophet of Judah .....Obad 1

And Ahab called *O*, which 1Kin 18:3
Now *O* feared the Lord 1Kin 18:3
And Ahab said unto *O*, Go ...1Kin 18:5
And as *O* was in the way 1Kin 18:7
sons of Arnan, the sons of *O* ..1Chr 3:21
and Sheariah, and *O*, and 1Chr 8:38
and Sheariah, and *O*, and 1Chr 9:44
Ishmaiah the son of *O* 1Chr 27:19
and to *O*, and to Zechariah ...2Chr 17:7
O the son of Jehiel, and .....Ezra 8:9
Harim, Meremoth, *O* .....Neh 10:5
The vision of *O*, Thus saith ...Obad 1

OBADIAH, THE BOOK OF—*a book of the Old Testament*
Against Edom .....Obad 1-9
Edom against Judah .....Obad 10-14
The day of the Lord .....Obad 15, 16
Zion's victory .....Obad 17-21

OBAL (ō'băl)—*"bare"*
Descendants of Joktan ...Gen 10:28
See EBAL 2

OBDURACY—*resistance to pleadings of mercy*

Expressed by:
"Stiffnecked" .....Ex 33:3, 5
"Uncircumcised" .....Lev 26:41
"Impenitent" .....Rom 2:5
"Harden your hearts" 1Sam 6:6
"Neither will I let" .....Ex 5:1, 2
"I will not hear" .....Jer 22:21
"Seek not" .....John 5:44
"He trespass yet more" ..2Chr 28:22-25
"Being past feeling" .....Eph 4:18, 19
"God gave them up" .....Rom 1:24-28
"Therefore they could not believe" .....John 12:39
"That cannot cease from sin" 2Pet 2:14
"They were appointed" ..1Pet 2:8
"Let him be unjust still" .Rev 22:11
See HARDNESS OF HEART; IMPENITENCE

OBED (ō'bĕd)—*"servant"*
1. Son of Ephial 1Chr 2:37, 38
2. Son of Boaz and Ruth ..Ruth 4:17-22
3. One of David's mighty men 1Chr 11:47
4. Korhite porter 1Chr 26:7
5. Father of Azariah 2Chr 23:1

Boaz begat *O*, and *O* begat 1Chr 2:12
begat *O* of Ruth; and *O* .....Matt 1:5
which was the son of *O* .....Luke 3:32

OBED-EDOM (ō-bĕd-ē'dŏm)—*"servant of (the god) Edom"*
1. Philistine from Gath; ark of the Lord left in his house 2Sam 6:10-12; 1Chr 13:13, 14
2. Overseer of the storehouse 1Chr 26:4-8, 15
3. Levitical musician 1Chr 16:5
4. Guardian of the sacred vessels 2Chr 25:24

O, and Jeiel, the porters 1Chr 15:18
O, and Jeiel, and Azaziah 1Chr 15:21
O and..were doorkeepers 1Chr 15:24
Lord out of the house of *O* ...1Chr 15:25
O with their brethren 1Chr 16:38
O also the son of Jeduthun 1Chr 16:38

OBEDIENCE—*See* OBEY

OBEDIENCE OF CHRIST
To death .....Phil 2:5-11
Learned .....Heb 5:7-10
Submissive .....Matt 26:39, 42

OBEDIENCE TO CIVIL GOVERNMENT
Meet obligation .....Mark 12:13-17
Of God .....Rom 13:1-7
Duty .....Titus 3:1
For Lord's sake 1Pet 2:13-17

OBEISANCE—*bending or bowing*

As an act of:
Respect .....Ex 18:7
Reverence .....Matt 2:11
Flaunting fidelity 2Sam 1:2-16
Fawning favor 2Sam 14:2-4
Feigned flattery 2Sam 15:5, 6

and made *o* to my sheaf .....Gen 37:7
moon and..stars made *o* .....Gen 37:9
their heads, and made *o* .....Gen 43:28
Bath-sheba bowed, and did *o* ..1Kin 1:16
of Judah, and made *o* to 2Chr 24:17

OBEY—*to submit to authority*

Relationship involved:
God—man .....Acts 5:29
Parent—child .....Gen 28:7; Eph 6:1
Husband—wife 1Cor 14:34, 35
Master—slave .....Eph 6:5
Ruler—subject .....Titus 1:1
Leader—follower .....Acts 5:36, 37
Pastor—people .....Heb 13:17
Man—nature .....James 3:3
God—nature .....Matt 8:27
God—demons .....Mark 1:27

Spiritual objects of:
God .....Acts 5:29
Christ .....Heb 5:9

O

Truth ....Gal 5:7
Faith ....Acts 6:7

In the Christian's life:
Comes from the heart ...Rom 6:17
Needs testing 2Cor 2:4
Aided by the Spirit 1Pet 1:22
Manifested in Gentiles ...Rom 15:18
In pastoral relations 2Cor 7:15

Lack of, brings:
Rejection 1Sam 15:20-26
Captivity................2Kin 18:11, 12
Death 1Kin 20:36
Retribution 2Thess 1:8

Examples of:
Noah ....Gen 6:22
Abram ....Gen 12:1-4
Israelites................Ex 12:28
Caleb and Joshua........Num 32:12
David ....Ps 119:106
Asa 1Kin 15:11, 14
Elijah 1Kin 17:5
Hezekiah 2Kin 18:6
Josiah 2Kin 22:2
Zerubbabel ....Hag 1:12
Christ ....Rom 5:19
Paul....................Acts 26:19
Christians...............Phil 2:12

[*also* OBEDIENCE, OBEDIENT, OBEYED, OBEYEDST, OBEYETH, OBEYING]

because thou hast *o* my ....Gen 22:18
that Abraham *o* my voice .....Gen 26:5
o my voice according to ....Gen 27:8
only *o* my voice, and go ......Gen 27:13
my son, *o* my voice; and ......Gen 27:43
o his voice to let Israel go?....Ex 5:2
if ye will *o* my voice indeed ...Ex 19:5
Beware of him, and *o* his .....Ex 23:21
said will we do, and be *o* .....Ex 24:7
children of Israel may be *o*....Num 27:20
and shalt be *o* unto his........Deut 4:30
ye would not be *o* unto the ...Deut 8:20
if ye *o* the commandments ....Deut 11:27
commandments, and *o* his .....Deut 13:4
will not *o* the voice of his .....Deut 21:18
o the voice of the Lord thy....Deut 27:10
wouldest not *o* the voice of....Deut 28:62
shalt *o* his voice according.....Deut 30:2
and that thou mayest *o* his ....Deut 30:20
o not the voice of the Lord ...Josh 5:6
o my voice in all that I ....Josh 22:2
and his voice will we *o*........Josh 24:24
but ye have not *o* my voice ...Judg 2:2
o the commandments of the ...Judg 2:17
but ye have not *o* my ....Judg 6:10
refused to *o* the voice of 1Sam 8:19
serve him, and *o* his voice.....1Sam 12:14
didst thou not *o* the voice 1Sam 15:19
o not the voice of the Lord ...1Sam 28:18
handmaid hath *o* thy voice 1Sam 28:21
they hear, they shall be *o* 2Sam 22:45
prospered; and all Israel *o* 1Chr 29:23
o the words of the Lord.......2Chr 11:4
refused to *o*, neither were .....Neh 9:17
If they *o* and serve him ....Job 36:11
hear of me, they shall *o* me ...Ps 18:44
have not *o* the voice of my ....Prov 5:13
wise reprover upon an *o* ear...Prov 25:12
despiseth to *o* his mother .....Prov 30:17
If ye be willing and *o*, ye .....Is 1:19
children of Ammon shall *o* ....Is 11:14
neither were they *o* unto ......Is 42:24
o the voice of his servant .....Is 50:10
have not *o* my voice, saith ....Jer 3:13
O my voice, and I will be .....Jer 7:23
nation that *o* not the voice ....Jer 7:28
and have not *o* my voice ......Jer 9:13
O my voice, and do them .....Jer 11:4
Yet they *o* not, nor inclined ...Jer 11:8
if they will not *o*, I will ....Jer 12:17
they *o* not, neither inclined....Jer 17:23
my sight, that it *o* not my .....Jer 18:10
that thou *o* not my voice ......Jer 22:21
o the voice of the Lord your ..Jer 26:13
but they *o* not thy voice.......Jer 32:23
more, then they *o*, and let ....Jer 34:10
we *o* the voice of Jonadab ....Jer 35:8
but *o* their father's ....Jer 35:14
o the commandment of ....Jer 35:18
O, I beseech thee, the voice ...Jer 38:20
the Lord, and have not *o* .....Jer 40:3
o the voice of the Lord our ...Jer 42:6
we *o* the voice of the Lord ...Jer 42:6
not *o* the voice of the Lord ...Jer 42:21
o not the voice of the Lord ...Jer 43:4
not *o* the voice of the Lord ...Jer 44:23
dominions shall serve and *o* ...Dan 7:27
Neither have we *o* the voice ...Dan 9:10
that they might not *o* thy .....Dan 9:11
She *o* not the voice; she ......Zeph 3:2
diligently *o* the voice of the ...Zech 6:15
the wind and the sea *o* him? ..Mark 4:41
winds and water, and they *o*...Luke 8:25
in the sea; and it should *o* ....Luke 17:6
our fathers would not *o* ....Acts 7:39
o to the faith among all ....Rom 1:5
and do not *o* the truth, but....Rom 2:8
ye should *o* it in the lusts .....Rom 6:12
of *o* unto righteousness ....Rom 6:16
have not all *o* the gospel ......Rom 10:16
For your *o* is come abroad ....Rom 16:19
nations for the *o* of faith ......Rom 16:26
ye be *o* in all things 2Cor 2:9
thought to the *o* of Christ 2Cor 10:5
when your *o* is fulfilled 2Cor 10:6
ye should not *o* the truth......Gal 3:1
ye should not *o* the truth?.....Gal 5:7
Children, *o* your parents in....Eph 6:1
Children, *o* your parents in ....Col 3:20
o not the gospel of our Lord ..2Thess 1:8
if any man *o* not our word 2Thess 3:14
o to their own husbands ......Titus 2:5
o unto their own masters ......Titus 2:9
to *o* magistrates, to be ....Titus 3:1
Having confidence in thy *o*....Philem 21
salvation unto all them that *o*..Heb 5:9
By faith Abraham..*o*..........Heb 11:8
mouths, that they may *o* ......James 3:3
o and sprinkling of the 1Pet 1:2
o children, not fashioning 1Pet 1:14
if any *o* not the word, they....1Pet 3:1
Even as Sarah *o* Abraham 1Pet 3:6
o not the gospel of God? 1Pet 4:17

OBIL (ō'bĭl)—*"camel-keeper; lender"*
Ishmaelite in charge of camels................1Chr 27:30

OBITUARY—*an account of a person's life; a death notice*
Written of Moses ....Deut 34:1-12

OBJECT—*to oppose verbally*
o, if they had ought against ...Acts 24:19

OBJECTORS—*those who oppose something*
Argue against God's:
Power ....Ex 14:10-15
Provision ....Ex 16:2-17
Promises...............Num 14:1-10

Overcome by:
Prophecies cited ....Jer 26:8-19
Promises claimed ....Acts 4:23-31

OBLATION—*something offered in worship or devotion*

[*also* OBLATIONS]

thou bring an *o* of a meat .....Lev 2:4
for the *o* of the first fruits.....Lev 2:12
And if his *o* be a sacrifice of ..Lev 3:1
one out of the whole *o* for ....Lev 7:14
of Israel to offer their *o*.....Lev 7:38
that will offer his *o* for all.....Lev 22:18
every *o* of theirs, every ....Num 18:9
We have..brought an *o*........Num 31:50
distribute the *o* of the Lord ...2Chr 31:14
Bring no more vain *o* ....Is 1:13
and shall do sacrifice and *o*....Is 19:21
impoverished that he hath no *o*.Is 40:20
he that offereth an *o*, as if ....Is 66:3
burnt offering and an *o* ....Jer 14:12
and the first fruits of your *o*...Ezek 20:40
every *o* of all, of every sort ...Ezek 44:30
of every sort of your *o*........Ezek 44:30
offer an *o* unto the Lord ......Ezek 45:1
of the *o* of the holy portion ...Ezek 45:7
give this *o* for the prince ......Ezek 45:16
The *o* that ye shall offer ......Ezek 48:9
this *o* of the land that is ......Ezek 48:12
All the *o* shall be five and ....Ezek 48:20
offer the holy *o* foursquare ....Ezek 48:20
on the other of the holy *o*.....Ezek 48:21
twenty thousand of the *o*......Ezek 48:21
and it shall be the holy *o* .....Ezek 48:21
offer an *o* and sweet odors ....Dan 2:46
sacrifice and the *o* to cease ....Dan 9:27

OBLIVION—*the state of being forgotten or wiped out*
God's punishment on the wicked ....Ps 34:16

OBOTH (ō'bŏth)—*"desires"*
Israelite camp ....Num 21:10, 11
Num 33:43, 44

OBSCURE—*dark; darkness*

[*also* OBSCURITY]

be put out in *o* darkness ......Prov 20:20
the blind shall see out of *o*....Is 29:18
then shall thy light rise in *o* ...Is 58:10
wait for light, but behold *o*....Is 59:9

OBSERVE—*to keep; remember; see*
Descriptive of:
Remembrance ....Gen 37:11
Laws ....Ex 31:16
Obedience ....Matt 28:20
Watchfulness ....Jer 8:7
Mark 6:20
False rituals.............Gal 4:10

Blessings of proper:
Material prosperity ......Deut 6:3
Righteousness ....Deut 6:25
Elevation ....Deut 28:1, 13
Loving-kindness ....Ps 107:43

Manner of proper:
Carefully ....Deut 12:28
Without change ....Deut 12:32
Diligently ....Deut 24:8
Forever.................2Kin 17:37
Without preference 1Tim 5:21

[*also* OBSERVATION, OBSERVED, OBSERVEST, OBSERVETH]

o the feast of unleavened .....Ex 12:17
ye *o* this day in your..........Ex 12:17
shall *o* this thing for an ....Ex 12:24
is a night to be much *o* ....Ex 12:42
night of the Lord to be *o* of...Ex 12:42
O thou that which I command .Ex 34:11
ye use enchantment, nor *o* ....Lev 19:26
not *o* all these commandments .Num 15:22
shall ye *o* to offer unto me ....Num 28:2
shall *o* to do..as the Lord .....Deut 5:32
shall ye *o* to do ....Deut 8:1
o to do all the statutes ....Deut 11:32
which ye shall *o* to do in ....Deut 12:1
o..all these commandments ....Deut 15:5
O the month of Abib, and .....Deut 16:1
o the feast of tabernacles......Deut 16:13
shalt *o* to do according........Deut 17:10
to *o*..his commandments ......Deut 28:15
wilt not *o* to do all the........Deut 28:58
o to do all the words of.......Deut 31:12
command your children to *o*...Deut 32:46
they have *o* thy word, and ....Deut 33:9
mayest *o* to do according......Josh 1:7
I commanded her let her *o*....Judg 13:14
pass, when Joab *o* the city 2Sam 11:16
the man did diligently *o*.......1Kin 20:33
through the fire, and *o*........2Kin 21:6
only if they will *o* to do 2Kin 21:8
shalt *o* my statutes and........2Chr 7:17
also he *o* times, and used 2Chr 33:6
and *o* his commandments .....Neh 1:5
o..all the commandments......Neh 10:29
they might *o* his statutes ......Ps 105:45
I shall *o* it with my whole ....Ps 119:34

let thine eyes *o* my ways ......Prov 23:26
He that *o* the wind shall ......Eccl 11:4
many things, but thou *o*.......Is 42:20
neither *o* their judgments .....Ezek 20:18
and *o* my statutes, and do.....Ezek 37:24
leopard by the way will I *o*.....Hos 13:7
I have heard him, and *o* ......Hos 14:8
They that *o* lying vanities .....Jon 2:8
whatsoever they bid you *o* ....Matt 23:3
that *o* and do; but do not.....Matt 23:3
all these have I *o* from my ....Mark 10:20
of God cometh not with *o*......Luke 17:20
to receive, neither to *o*........Acts 16:21
that they *o* no such thing......Acts 21:25

OBSERVER—*one who witnesses an action*

[*also* OBSERVERS]
o of times, or an enchanter....Deut 18:10
hearkened unto *o* of times ....Deut 18:14

OBSOLETE WORDS—*words no longer used*

Words* (examples) *not now used:
"Astonied"
("perplexed") ....Dan 5:9
"Leasing" ("lie") ....Ps 4:2, 5:6
"Neesings" ("sneezings") .Job 41:18
"Trow" ("think") ....Luke 17:9
"Wist" ("knew") ....Ex 16:15
"Wit" ("know")..........Ex 2:4
"Wot" ("know")........Ex 32:1, 23

Words* (examples only) *with changed meanings:
"Communicate"
("share") ....Gal 6:6
"Conversation"
("manner of life") .....Eph 4:22
"Let" ("hinder") ....Rom 1:13
"Prevent" ("precede") ...1Thess 4:15
"Suffer" ("allow").......Mat 3:15
"Vile" ("lowly")........Phil 3:21

OBSTACLES—*obstructions*

Eliminated by:
God's help..............Is 45:2
Christ's help ....Is 49:9-11
Spirit's help ....Zech 4:6, 7

OBSTACLES TO FAITH
Men's honor ....John 5:44
Highmindedness ....Rom 11:20

OBSTINACY—*stubbornness*
Continuing in sin 2Chr 28:22, 23
Rejecting counsel........1Kin 12:12-15
Refusing to change ......Jer 44:15-27

[*also* OBSTINATE]
and made his heart *o* ....Deut 2:30
I knew that thou art *o* ....Is 48:4

OBSTRUCT—*to hamper progress*
Attempted ....Ezra 4:1-5
Condemned 3John 9, 10

OBTAIN—*to bring into one's possession*

Of material things:
Advancement ....Esth 2:9-17

Of spiritual things:
Favor ....Prov 8:35
Joy and gladness ....Is 35:10
Heaven ....Luke 20:35-38
Divine help ....Acts 26:22
Salvation ....Rom 11:7
Better resurrection ......Heb 11:35
Faith 2Pet 1:1

[*also* OBTAINED, OBTAINETH, OBTAINING]
certain days *o* I leave of ......Neh 13:6
that she *o* favor in his ....Esth 5:2
A good man *o* favor of the ....Prov 12:2
and *o* favor of the Lord.......Prov 18:22
shall *o* gladness and joy ....Is 51:11
and *o* the kingdom by ....Dan 11:21
her that had not *o* mercy......Hos 2:23
merciful: for they shall *o*......Matt 5:7
o part of this ministry.........Acts 1:17
great sum *o* I this freedom ....Acts 22:28
they had *o* their purpose .....Acts 27:13
o mercy through their unbelief .Rom 11:30
mercy they also may *o* ....Rom 11:31
hath *o* mercy of the Lord 1Cor 7:25
So run, that ye may *o* 1Cor 9:24
we have *o* an inheritance......Eph 1:11
to *o* salvation by our Lord 1Thess 5:9
o of the glory of our Lord 2Thess 2:14
but I *o* mercy, because I 1Tim 1:13
may also *o* the salvation 2Tim 2:10
by inheritance *o* a more.......Heb 1:4
that we may *o* mercy, and.....Heb 4:16
endured, he *o* the promise ....Heb 6:15
he *o* a more excellent ....Heb 8:6
o eternal redemption for us ..Heb 9:12
the elders *o* a good report.....Heb 11:2
o promises, stopped the ....Heb 11:33
to have, and cannot *o*.........James 4:2
which had not *o* mercy........1Pet 2:10
but now have *o* mercy 1Pet 2:10

OCCASION—*an opportunity or circumstance*

[*also* OCCASIONED, OCCASIONS]
he may seek *o* against us......Gen 43:18
give *o* of speech against ....Deut 22:14
them as thou shalt find *o*......Judg 9:33
thou do as *o* serve thee 1Sam 10:7
o the death of all the persons..1Sam 22:22
given great *o* to the enemies...2Sam 12:14
which thou shalt have *o* to ....Ezra 7:20
he findeth *o* against me ....Job 33:10
in her *o* who can turn her.....Jer 2:24
have *o* any more to use this ...Ezek 18:3
to find *o* against Daniel ....Dan 6:4
they could find none *o* nor ....Dan 6:4
taking *o* by the commandment .Rom 7:8
o to fall in his brother's ....Rom 14:13
give you *o* to glory on our 2Cor 5:12
by *o* of the forwardness of 2Cor 8:8
o from them which desire *o* ...2Cor 11:12
use not liberty for an *o* to.....Gal 5:13
none *o* to the adversary 1Tim 5:14
is none *o* of stumbling in......1John 2:10

OCCULTISM—*pertaining to supernatural, especially evil, influences*

Forms of:
Astrology ....Is 47:13
Charming ....Deut 18:11
Consulting with spirits ...Deut 18:11
Divination ....Deut 18:14
Magic ....Gen 41:8
Necromancy ....Deut 18:11
Soothsaying ....Is 2:6
Sorcery ....Ex 22:8
Witchcraft ....Deut 18:10
Wizardry ....Deut 18:11

Attitude toward:
Forbidden ....Deut 18:10, 11
Jer 27:9
Punished by death ....Ex 22:18
Lev 20:6, 27
Forsaken ....Acts 19:18-20

OCCUPATION—*vocation; activity*
shall say, What is your *o*? .....Gen 46:33
brethren, What is your *o*? .....Gen 47:3
o they were tentmakers ....Acts 18:3
with the workmen of like *o*....Acts 19:25

OCCUPIERS—*those who use*
the *o* of thy merchandise ......Ezek 27:27

OCCUPY—*to fill up; reside in; make use of*

[*also* OCCUPIED, OCCUPIETH]
gold that was *o* for the work ..Ex 38:24
ropes that never were *o*.......Judg 16:11
thee to *o* thy merchandise .....Ezek 27:9
they *o* with thee in lambs .....Ezek 27:21
said unto them, *O* till I come ..Luke 19:13
o the room of unlearned 1Cor 14:16
them that have been *o* ....Heb 13:9

OCCURRENT—*occurring at present*
neither adversary nor evil *o* ...1Kin 5:4

OCRAN (ŏk'răn)—*"troubler"*
Man of Asher...........Num 1:13
Num 2:27

Pagiel the son of *O*, prince ....Num 7:72
of Pagiel the son of *O* ....Num 7:77
was Pagiel the son of *O* ....Num 10:26

ODD—*excess; left over*
o number of them is to be ....Num 3:48

ODED (ō'dĕd)—*"aiding; restorer"*
1. Father of Azariah the prophet 2Chr 15:1
2. Prophet of Samaria 2Chr 28:9-15

ODIOUS—*hateful*
had made themselves *o* to 1Chr 19:6
o woman when she is ....Prov 30:23

ODORS—*a pleasing scent*
so shall they burn *o* for ....Jer 34:5
cinnamon, and *o*, and ....Rev 18:13

ODORS, SWEET—*pleasant smelling odors*

Used literally of:
Sacrificial incense ....Lev 26:31
Ointment fragrance ......John 12:3

Used figuratively of:
New life ....Hos 14:7
Prayers ....Rev 5:8
Christian service ....Phil 4:18
which was filled with sweet *o* ..2Chr 16:14
six months with sweet *o*.......Esth 2:12
oblation and sweet *o* unto .....Dan 2:46

OF—*See* INTRODUCTION

OFF—*See* INTRODUCTION

OFFEND—*to transgress moral or divine law; cause difficulty, discomfort or injury*

Causes of:
Christ ....Matt 11:6
Persecution ....Matt 13:21
Matt 24:10
The cross 1Cor 1:23
Physical parts ....Matt 18:8, 9

Causes of, in Christ's:
Lowly position ....Matt 13:54-57
Teaching................Matt 18:8, 9
Being the Rock ....Is 8:14
Being the Bread.........John 6:58-66
Being crucified 1Cor 1:23
Being the righteousness of God ....Rom 9:31-33

Christians forbidden to give:
In anything 2Cor 6:3
By their liberty..........1Cor 8:9, 13
At any time.............Phil 1:10

See STUMBLE

[*also* OFFENSE, OFFENSES, OFFENDED]
what have I *o* thee, that ......Gen 20:9
baker had *o* their lord the.....Gen 40:1
o of heart unto my lord 1Sam 25:31
I have *o*; return from me 2Kin 18:14
have *o* against the Lord 2Chr 28:13
I will not *o* any more ....Job 34:31
I should *o* against the ....Ps 73:15
law and nothing shall *o* ....Ps 119:165
A brother *o* is harder to be ...Prov 18:19
yielding pacifieth great *o* ......Eccl 10:4
all that devour him shall *o* ....Jer 2:3
What have I *o* against thee ....Jer 37:18
We *o* not, because they have ..Jer 50:7
greatly *o*, and revenged ....Ezek 25:12
harlot, yet let not Judah *o* ....Hos 4:15
they acknowledge their *o*, and..Hos 5:15
but when he *o* in Baal, he ....Hos 13:1
he shall pass over, and *o*......Hab 1:11
right eye *o* thee, pluck it......Matt 5:29
whosoever shall not be *o* in ...Matt 11:6
kingdom all things that *o*......Matt 13:41
that the Pharisees were *o* .....Matt 15:12
thout art an *o* unto me........Matt 16:23
lest we should *o* them, go .....Matt 17:27
shall *o* one of these little ......Matt 18:6
the world because of *o*! ....Matt 18:7

for it must needs be that *o* .... Matt 18:7
man by whom the *o* cometh! .. Matt 18:7
thine eye *o* thee, pluck it ..... Matt 18:9
ye shall be *o* because of .... Matt 26:31
Though all men shall be *o* ..... Matt 26:33
thee, yet will I never be *o* ..... Matt 26:33
immediately they are *o* .... Mark 4:17
with us? And they were *o* ...... Mark 6:3
o one of these little ones ...... Mark 9:42
And if thy foot *o* thee, cut .... Mark 9:45
All ye shall be *o* because of ... Mark 14:27
whosoever shall not be *o* in ... Luke 7:23
impossible but that *o* will ..... Luke 17:1
should *o* one of these little .... Luke 17:2
said unto them, Doth this *o* ... John 6:61
you, that ye should not be *o* .. John 16:1
conscience void of *o* toward ... Acts 24:16
have I *o* any thing at all ...... Acts 25:8
Who was delivered for our *o* .. Rom 4:25
as the *o*, so also is the free .... Rom 5:15
o of one many be dead .... Rom 5:15
free gift is of many *o* unto .... Rom 5:16
as by the *o* of one judgment ... Rom 5:18
that man who eateth with *o* ... Rom 14:20
brother stumbleth, or is *o* ..... Rom 14:21
which cause divisions and *o* ... Rom 16:17
I make my brother to *o* 1Cor 8:13
Give none *o*, neither to the ... 1Cor 10:32
committed an *o* in abasing 2Cor 11:7
weak? who is *o*, and I burn ... 2Cor 11:29
is the *o* of the cross ceased .... Gal 5:11
whole law, and yet *o* in one ... James 2:10
For in many things we *o* all ... James 3:2
If any man *o* not in word ..... James 3:2
stumbling, and a rock of *o* 1Pet 2:8

OFFENDER—*one who transgresses; sinner*

[also **OFFENDERS**]
Solomon shall be counted *o* ... 1Kin 1:21
That make a man an *o* for a .. Is 29:21
if I be an *o*, or have .... Acts 25:11

OFFERING—*something given as a part of worship; something given voluntarily*

Characteristics of:
Made to God alone ...... Ex 22:20
Limitation of .... Heb 9:9
Prescribed under the Law. Mark 1:44

Thing offered must be:
Perfect .... Lev 22:21
Ceremonially clean ...... Lev 27:11, 27
Best .... Mal 1:14

Offerer must:
Not delay .... Ex 22:29, 30
Offer in righteousness .... Mal 3:3
Offer with thanksgiving .. Ps 27:6

Classification of:
Private and public .... Lev 4:1-12
Physical and spiritual .... Lev 5:1-13
Voluntary and required .. Lev 1:3
Accepted and rejected ... Judg 6:17-24
Purified and perverted ... Mal 3:3, 4
Passing and permanent ... Jer 7:21-23
Jew and Gentile .... Ps 96:8
Typical and fulfilled ..... Gen 22:2, 13

[*also* **OFFER, OFFERED, OFFERETH, OFFERINGS**]
ground an *o* unto the Lord .... Gen 4:3
to his *o* he had not respect .... Gen 4:5
offered burnt *o* on the altar ... Gen 8:20
the wood for the burnt *o* ...... Gen 22:3
took the wood of the burnt *o* .. Gen 22:6
himself a lamb for a burnt *o* .. Gen 22:8
o sacrifice upon the mount .... Gen 31:54
and he poured a drink *o* ...... Gen 35:14
o sacrifices unto the God of ... Gen 46:1
also sacrifices and burnt *o* ..... Ex 10:25
a burnt *o* and sacrifices for .... Ex 18:12
sacrifice thereon thy burnt *o* .. Ex 20:24
thy peace *o*, thy sheep, and ... Ex 20:24
o the blood of my sacrifice .... Ex 23:18
which *o* burnt *o*, and .... Ex 24:5
sacrificed peace *o* of oxen ..... Ex 24:5
that they bring me an *o* .... Ex 25:2
his heart ye shall take my *o* ... Ex 25:2
the camp: it is a sin *o* .... Ex 29:14
is a burnt *o* unto the Lord .... Ex 29:18
an *o* made by fire unto the .... Ex 29:18
the altar for a burnt *o* .... Ex 29:25
an *o* made by fire unto the .... Ex 29:25
the breast of the wave *o* ...... Ex 29:27
shoulder of the heave *o* .... Ex 29:27
Israel; for it is a heave *o* ..... Ex 29:28
be a heave *o* from the .... Ex 29:28
sacrifice of their peace *o* ...... Ex 29:28
their heave *o* unto the .... Ex 29:28
shalt *o* every day a bullock .... Ex 29:36
lamb thou shalt *o* in the .... Ex 29:39
other lamb thou shalt *o* .... Ex 29:39
an hin of wine for a drink *o* ... Ex 29:40
the meat *o* of the morning .... Ex 29:41
according to the drink *o* ...... Ex 29:41
an *o* made by fire unto the .... Ex 29:41
o no strange incense .... Ex 30:9
burnt sacrifice, nor meat *o* .... Ex 30:9
neither shall ye pour drink *o* .. Ex 30:9
shekel shall be the *o* of the .... Ex 30:13
give an *o* unto the Lord .... Ex 30:15
altar of burnt *o* with all .... Ex 30:28
the altar of burnt *o* with all ... Ex 31:9
morrow, and *o* burnt *o* .... Ex 32:6
brought peace *o*; and the ...... Ex 32:6
o the blood of my sacrifice .... Ex 34:25
you an *o* unto the Lord .... Ex 35:5
let him bring it, an *o* of the ... Ex 35:5
they brought the Lord's *o* ..... Ex 35:21
every man that *o* *o* an *o* of .... Ex 35:22
that did *o* an *o* of silver and ... Ex 35:24
brass brought the Lord's *o* .... Ex 35:24
received of Moses all the *o* .... Ex 36:3
of burnt *o* of shittim wood .... Ex 38:1
brass of the *o* was seventy ..... Ex 38:29
set the altar of the burnt *o* .... Ex 40:6
altar of burnt *o* by the door ... Ex 40:29
o upon it the burnt *o* .... Ex 40:29
and the meat *o* .... Ex 40:29
bring an *o* unto the Lord ...... Lev 1:2
ye shall bring your *o* of the ... Lev 1:2
the head of the burnt *o* .... Lev 1:4
o made by fire, of a sweet .... Lev 1:9
o made by fire, of a sweet .... Lev 1:13
his *o* to the Lord be of fowls .. Lev 1:14
bring his *o* of turtledoves ...... Lev 1:14
any will *o* a meat offering ..... Lev 2:1
his *o* shall be of fine flour ..... Lev 2:1
meat *o* shall be Aaron's .... Lev 2:3
meat *o* baken in a pan, it ..... Lev 2:5
o baken in a frying pan .... Lev 2:7
shall take from the meat *o* .... Lev 2:9
it is an *o* made by fire, of .... Lev 2:9
o of the Lord made by fire .... Lev 2:10
No meat *o*, which ye shall ..... Lev 2:11
in any *o* of the Lord made .... Lev 2:11
meat *o* shalt thou season ...... Lev 2:13
be lacking from thy meat *o* .... Lev 2:13
thine offerings thou shalt *o* .... Lev 2:13
o a meat *o* of thy first fruits ... Lev 2:14
o for the meat *o* of thy .... Lev 2:14
thereon: it is a meat *o* .... Lev 2:15
o made by fire unto the .... Lev 2:16
be a sacrifice of peace *o* ...... Lev 3:1
if he *o* it of the herd .... Lev 3:1
shall *o* it without blemish ..... Lev 3:1
hand upon the head of his *o* ... Lev 3:2
the sacrifice of the peace *o* .... Lev 3:3
an *o* made by fire unto the .... Lev 3:3
if his *o* for a sacrifice of .... Lev 3:6
of peace *o* unto the Lord ..... Lev 3:6
shall *o* it without blemish ..... Lev 3:6
he *o* a lamb for his offering ... Lev 3:7
shall he *o* it before the lord ... Lev 3:7
hand upon the head of his *o* ... Lev 3:8
of the peace *o* an *o* made by .. Lev 3:9
if his *o* be a goat, then he ..... Lev 3:12
he shall *o* it before the Lord .. Lev 3:12
he shall *o* thereof his *o* .... Lev 3:14
an *o* made by fire unto the .... Lev 3:14
unto the Lord for a sin *o* ..... Lev 4:3
of the sacrifice of peace *o* ..... Lev 4:10
shall *o* a young bullock for .... Lev 4:14
of the altar of the burnt *o* ..... Lev 4:18
with the bullock for a sin *o* .... Lev 4:20
sin *o* for the congregation ..... Lev 4:21
he shall bring his *o*, a kid ..... Lev 4:23
where they kill the burnt *o* .... Lev 4:24
the Lord: it is a sin *o* .... Lev 4:24
take of the blood of the sin *o* . Lev 4:25
horns of the altar of burnt *o* ... Lev 4:25
bottom of the altar of burnt *o* . Lev 4:25
he shall bring his *o*, a kid ..... Lev 4:28
upon the head of the sin *o* .... Lev 4:29
slay the sin *o* in the place ..... Lev 4:29
in the place of the burnt *o* .... Lev 4:29
horns of the altar of burnt *o* .. Lev 4:30
off the sacrifice of peace *o* .... Lev 4:31
he bring a lamb for a sin *o* .... Lev 4:32
upon the head of the sin *o* .... Lev 4:33
slay it for a sin *o*, in the ...... Lev 4:33
where they kill the burnt *o* .... Lev 4:33
of the sin *o* with his finger .... Lev 4:34
of the altar of burnt *o* .... Lev 4:34
the sacrifice of the peace *o* .... Lev 4:35
the *o* made by fire unto the ... Lev 4:35
sanctuary, for a trespass *o* ..... Lev 5:15
the ram of the trespass *o* ...... Lev 5:16
estimation, for a trespass *o* .... Lev 5:18
It is a trespass *o*: he hath ..... Lev 5:19
in the day of his trespass *o* .... Lev 6:5
his trespass *o* unto the Lord ... Lev 6:6
estimation, of a trespass *o* ..... Lev 6:6
is the law of the burnt *o* ...... Lev 6:9
It is the burnt *o*, because of ... Lev 6:9
burnt *o* on the altar, and ...... Lev 6:10
burnt *o* in order upon it .... Lev 6:12
the fat of the peace *o* .... Lev 6:12
is the law of the meat *o* .... Lev 6:14
shall *o* it before the Lord ..... Lev 6:14
the flour of the meat *o*, and ... Lev 6:15
which is upon the meat *o* ..... Lev 6:15
most holy, as is the sin *o* ...... Lev 6:17
and as the trespass *o* .... Lev 6:17
o of the Lord made by fire .... Lev 6:18
is the *o* of Aaron and of his ... Lev 6:20
flour for a meat *o* perpetual ... Lev 6:20
baked pieces of the meat *o* .... Lev 6:21
shalt thou *o* for a sweet .... Lev 6:21
meat *o* for the priest shall ..... Lev 6:23
This is the law of the sin *o* .... Lev 6:25
where the burnt *o* is killed .... Lev 6:25
o be killed before the Lord .... Lev 6:25
The priest that *o* it for sin ..... Lev 6:26
o, whereof any of the blood ... Lev 6:30
is the law of the trespass *o* .... Lev 7:1
where they kill the burnt *o* .... Lev 7:2
they kill the trespass *o* .... Lev 7:2
he shall *o* of it all the fat ..... Lev 7:3
the altar for an *o* made by .... Lev 7:5
the Lord: it is a trespass *o* .... Lev 7:5
sin *o* is, so is the trespass *o* ... Lev 7:7
that *o* any man's burnt *o* ...... Lev 7:8
the burnt *o* which he hath *o* ... Lev 7:8
meat *o* that is baked in the .... Lev 7:9
meat *o*, mingled with oil .... Lev 7:10
If he *o* it for a thanksgiving ... Lev 7:12
o with the sacrifice of .... Lev 7:12
o for his *o* leavened bread ..... Lev 7:13
thanksgiving of his peace *o* .... Lev 7:13
o one out of the whole .... Lev 7:14
a heave *o* unto the Lord ...... Lev 7:14
sacrifice of his peace *o* .... Lev 7:15
if the sacrifice of his *o* be ..... Lev 7:16
or a voluntary *o*, it shall be ... Lev 7:16
o an *o* made by fire unto ...... Lev 7:25
the sacrifice of his peace *o* .... Lev 7:29
for a wave *o* before the Lord .. Lev 7:30
heave *o* of the sacrifices of .... Lev 7:32
sacrifices of your peace *o* ..... Lev 7:32
sacrifices of their peace *o* ..... Lev 7:34
this is the law of the burnt *o* .. Lev 7:37
the meat *o*, and of the sin *o* ... Lev 7:37
and of the trespass *o* .... Lev 7:37
the sacrifice of the peace *o* .... Lev 7:37
o their oblations unto the ..... Lev 7:38
and a bullock for the sin *o* .... Lev 8:2
the bullock for the sin *o* ...... Lev 8:14

the ram for the burnt *o* ....Lev 8:18
an *o* made by fire unto the ....Lev 8:21
a wave *o* before the Lord .....Lev 8:27
the altar upon the burnt *o*.....Lev 8:28
an *o* made by fire unto the ....Lev 8:28
waved it for a wave *o* before ..Lev 8:29
a young calf for a sin *o* ....Lev 9:2
and a ram for a burnt *o*........Lev 9:2
kid of the goats for a sin *o*....Lev 9:3
blemish, for a burnt *o* ....Lev 9:3
meat *o* mingled with oil ....Lev 9:4
altar, and *o* thy sin *o* ....Lev 9:7
and thy burnt *o*, and make ....Lev 9:7
o the *o* of the people ....Lev 9:7
slew the calf of the sin *o* ......Lev 9:8
above the liver of the sin *o*....Lev 9:10
he slew the burnt *o*; and ......Lev 9:12
presented the burnt *o* unto ....Lev 9:13
the burnt *o* on the altar ....Lev 9:14
he brought the people's *o* ......Lev 9:15
goat, which was the sin *o* .....Lev 9:15
slew it, and *o* it for sin........Lev 9:15
he brought the burnt *o*........Lev 9:16
he brought the meat *o*, and ...Lev 9:17
for a sacrifice of peace *o* ......Lev 9:18
waved for a wave *o* before ....Lev 9:21
and came down from *o* ....Lev 9:22
of the sin *o*, and the ....Lev 9:22
and the burnt *o*, and peace ....Lev 9:22
upon the altar the burnt *o*.....Lev 9:24
o strange fire before the ......Lev 10:1
the meat *o* that remaineth .....Lev 10:12
o of the Lord made by fire ....Lev 10:12
o made by fire of the fat ......Lev 10:15
wave it for a wave *o* before ...Lev 10:15
sought the goat of the sin *o* ...Lev 10:16
have ye not eaten the sin *o*....Lev 10:17
have they *o* their sin *o* ....Lev 10:19
burnt *o* before the Lord.......Lev 10:19
if I had eaten the sin *o* ....Lev 10:19
the first year for a burnt *o* ....Lev 12:6
or a turtledove, for a sin *o* ....Lev 12:6
shall *o* it before the Lord .....Lev 12:7
the one for the burnt *o* ....Lev 12:8
and the other for a sin *o* ......Lev 12:8
of fine flour for a meat *o* .....Lev 14:10
o him for a trespass *o*.........Lev 14:12
a wave *o* before the Lord .....Lev 14:12
where he shall kill the sin *o* ...Lev 14:13
burnt *o*, in the holy place .....Lev 14:13
as the sin *o* is the priest's .....Lev 14:13
the trespass *o*: it is most ......Lev 14:13
the blood of the trespass *o* ....Lev 14:14
the blood of the trespass *o* ....Lev 14:17
priest shall *o* the sin *o* ....Lev 14:19
he shall kill the burnt *o* ....Lev 14:19
shall *o* the burnt *o*............Lev 14:20
the meat *o* upon the altar .....Lev 14:20
lamb for a trespass *o* to be ....Lev 14:21
with oil for a meat *o*..........Lev 14:21
and the one shall be a sin *o* ..Lev 14:22
and the other a burnt *o* ....Lev 14:22
the lamb of the trespass *o*.....Lev 14:24
a wave *o* before the Lord .....Lev 14:24
the lamb of the trespass *o* .....Lev 14:25
the blood of the trespass *o* ....Lev 14:25
blood of the trespass *o* ....Lev 14:28
to get, the one for a sin *o*.....Lev 14:31
and the other for a burnt *o*....Lev 14:31
meat *o*: and the priest ....Lev 14:31
And the priest shall *o* them ...Lev 15:15
the one for a sin *o* ....Lev 15:15
and the other for a burnt *o*....Lev 15:15
offer the one for a sin *o* ......Lev 15:30
and the other for a burnt *o*....Lev 15:30
when they *o* before the Lord ..Lev 16:1
a young bullock for a sin *o*....Lev 16:3
and a ram for a burnt *o*.......Lev 16:3
kids of the goats for a sin *o* ...Lev 16:5
and one ram for a burnt *o* ....Lev 16:5
o his bullock of the sin *o*......Lev 16:6
and *o* him for a sin *o* ....Lev 16:9
kill the bullock of the sin *o*....Lev 16:11
he kill the goat of the sin *o* ...Lev 16:15
and *o* his burnt *o*............Lev 16:24
the burnt *o* of the people .....Lev 16:24
fat of the sin *o* shall he ....Lev 16:25
bullock for the sin *o* ....Lev 16:27
and the goat for the sin *o* .....Lev 16:27
to *o* an *o* unto the Lord.......Lev 17:4
which they *o* in the open......Lev 17:5
o them for peace *o* ....Lev 17:5
o their sacrifices unto ....Lev 17:7
o a burnt *o* or sacrifice........Lev 17:8
to *o* it unto the Lord; even....Lev 17:9
o a sacrifice of peace *o*........Lev 19:5
Lord, ye shall *o* it at your .....Lev 19:5
bring his trespass *o* unto ......Lev 19:21
even a ram for a trespass *o*....Lev 19:21
the ram of the trespass *o*.......Lev 19:22
of their God, they do *o* ....Lev 21:6
o the bread of thy God: he....Lev 21:8
o the *o* of the Lord ....Lev 21:21
to *o* the bread of his God .....Lev 21:21
not eat of an *o* of the holy .....Lev 22:12
which they *o* unto the Lord ...Lev 22:15
that will *o* his oblation ....Lev 22:18
o unto the Lord for a burnt *o* .Lev 22:18
blemish, that shall ye not *o*....Lev 22:20
a sacrifice of peace *o* unto ....Lev 22:21
or a freewill *o* in beeves or....Lev 22:21
nor make an *o* by fire of......Lev 22:22
thou *o* for a freewill *o* ....Lev 22:23
neither shall ye make any *o* ...Lev 22:24
ye *o* the bread of your God ...Lev 22:25
an *o* made by fire unto the ....Lev 22:27
when ye will *o* a sacrifice of ..Lev 22:29
the Lord, *o* it at your own ....Lev 22:29
ye shall *o* an *o* made by fire ..Lev 23:8
for a burnt *o* unto the ....Lev 23:12
meat *o* thereof shall be two ...Lev 23:13
an *o* made by fire unto the ....Lev 23:13
drink *o* thereof shall be of ....Lev 23:13
brought an *o* unto your God ..Lev 23:14
the sheaf of the wave *o* ....Lev 23:15
o a new meat *o* unto..........Lev 23:16
a burnt *o* unto the Lord.......Lev 23:18
with their meat *o*, and their ..Lev 23:18
an *o* made by fire, of sweet ...Lev 23:18
for a sacrifice of peace *o* ......Lev 23:19
kid of the goats for a sin *o* ....Lev 23:19
a wave *o* before the Lord ......Lev 23:20
an *o* made by fire unto the ....Lev 23:25
an *o* made by fire unto the ....Lev 23:36
an *o* made by fire unto the ....Lev 23:37
unto the Lord, a burnt *o* ......Lev 23:37
and a meat *o*, a sacrifice ......Lev 23:37
beside all your freewill *o* ......Lev 23:38
an *o* made by fire unto the ....Lev 24:7
bring an *o* unto the Lord......Lev 27:9
o strange fire before the ......Num 3:4
and the daily meat *o*..........Num 4:16
every *o* of all the holy ....Num 5:9
he shall bring her *o* for her....Num 5:15
for it is an *o* of jealousy ......Num 5:15
o of memorial, bringing ....Num 5:15
o of memorial in her hands....Num 5:18
which is the jealousy *o* ....Num 5:18
wave the *o* before the Lord ...Num 5:25
the Lord, and *o* it upon the ...Num 5:25
take a handful of the *o* ....Num 5:26
shall *o* the one for a sin *o*.....Num 6:11
and the other for a burnt *o*....Num 6:11
first year for a trespass *o*......Num 6:12
o his *o* unto the Lord ....Num 6:14
blemish for a burnt *o*, and ....Num 6:14
without blemish for a sin *o*....Num 6:14
meat *o*, and their drink ....Num 6:15
o his sin *o*, and his burnt *o*....Num 6:16
for a sacrifice of peace *o* ......Num 6:17
o also his meat *o*, and his .....Num 6:17
the sacrifice of the peace *o*....Num 6:18
a wave *o* before the Lord .....Num 6:20
o unto the Lord for...........Num 6:21
for a sacrifice of peace *o* ......Num 7:83
bullock with his meat *o* ....Num 8:8
shalt thou take for a sin *o*.....Num 8:8
Aaron shall *o* the Levites .....Num 8:11
for an *o* of the children of .....Num 8:11
thou shalt *o* the one for a sin *o*.Num 8:12
other for a burnt *o*, unto......Num 8:12
o them for an *o* unto the Lord .Num 8:13
and *o* them for an *o* ....Num 8:15
and Aaron *o* them as an ......Num 8:21
as an *o* before the Lord.......Num 8:21
we may not *o* an *o* of the Lord.Num 9:7
not the *o* of the Lord ....Num 9:13
trumpets over your burnt *o*....Num 10:10
sacrifices of your peace *o* .....Num 10:10
will make an *o* by fire unto ...Num 15:3
a burnt *o*, or a sacrifice in .....Num 15:3
in a freewill *o*, or in your .....Num 15:3
that *o* his *o* unto the Lord.....Num 15:4
a meat *o* of a tenth deal of....Num 15:4
hin of wine for a drink *o*......Num 15:5
with the burnt *o* or sacrifice ...Num 15:5
for a meat *o* two tenth ....Num 15:6
a drink *o* thou shalt *o* the third.Num 15:7
a bullock for a burnt *o*........Num 15:8
o of three tenth deals of ....Num 15:9
drink *o* half a hin of wine .....Num 15:10
o made by fire, of a sweet ....Num 15:10
in *o* an *o* made by fire, of a ...Num 15:13
o up a heave *o* unto the Lord .Num 15:19
of your dough for a heave *o*...Num 15:20
o of the threshing floor ....Num 15:20
o one young bullock for a .....Num 15:24
his meat *o*, and his drink *o*....Num 15:24
kid of the goats for a sin *o*....Num 15:24
they shall bring their *o*........Num 15:25
their sin *o* before the Lord ....Num 15:25
Respect not thou their *o*; I ....Num 16:15
fifty men that *o* incense ....Num 16:35
they that were burnt had *o*....Num 16:39
near to *o* incense before ......Num 16:40
heave *o* of all the hallowed....Num 18:8
every meat *o* of theirs ....Num 18:9
and every sin *o* of theirs ......Num 18:9
every trespass *o* of theirs ......Num 18:9
they shall *o* unto the Lord ....Num 18:12
fat for an *o* made by fire ......Num 18:17
All the heave *o* of the holy....Num 18:19
o as a heave *o* unto the Lord ..Num 18:24
ye shall offer up a heave *o*....Num 18:26
shall *o* a heave *o* unto the ....Num 18:28
Lord's heave *o* to Aaron the ..Num 18:28
Balak *o* oxen and sheep.......Num 22:40
Balaam *o* on every altar a.....Num 23:2
Balak, Stand by thy burnt *o*...Num 23:3
o a bullock and a ram on .....Num 23:14
he stood by his burnt *o* ....Num 23:17
o strange fire before the ......Num 26:61
My *o*, and my bread for my ...Num 28:2
o unto me in their due........Num 28:2
This is the *o* made by fire .....Num 28:3
for a continual burnt *o*........Num 28:3
lamb shalt thou *o* in the......Num 28:4
other lamb shalt thou *o* at.....Num 28:4
a continual burnt *o*, which ....Num 28:6
the drink *o* thereof shall be ...Num 28:7
unto the Lord for a drink *o* ...Num 28:7
other lamb shalt thou *o* at.....Num 28:8
the meat *o* of the morning .....Num 28:8
drink *o* thereof, thou shalt *o* it .Num 28:8
deals of flour for a meat *o* ....Num 28:9
with oil, and the drink *o* .....Num 28:9
burnt *o* of every sabbath ......Num 28:10
the continual burnt *o* ....Num 28:10
and his drink *o*..............Num 28:10
deals of flour for a meat *o* ....Num 28:12
for a meat *o* unto one lamb ...Num 28:13
burnt *o* of a sweet savor, a ....Num 28:13
kid of the goats for a sin *o*....Num 28:15
unto the Lord shall be *o* ....Num 28:15
the continual burnt *o* ....Num 28:15
and his drink *o*..............Num 28:15
o a sacrifice made by fire .....Num 28:19
o shall be of flour mingled ....Num 28:20
tenth deal shalt thou *o* for ....Num 28:21
the burnt *o* in the morning ....Num 28:23
is for a continual burnt *o*......Num 28:23
manner ye shall *o* daily ....Num 28:24
the continual burnt *o* ....Num 28:24
and his drink *o*..............Num 28:24
burnt *o* for a sweet savor .....Num 28:27

O

thou up to *o* sacrifice .... Is 57:7
furnish the drink *o* unto .... Is 65:11
he that *o* an oblation, as if .... Is 66:3
oblation, as if he *o* swine's .... Is 66:3
bring an *o* in a clean vessel .... Is 66:20
burnt *o* are not acceptable .... Jer 6:20
unto whom they *o* incense ..... Jer 11:12
anger in *o* incense unto Baal .. Jer 11:17
o burnt *o* and an .... Jer 14:12
south, bringing burnt *o* .... Jer 17:26
and sacrifices, and meat *o* ..... Jer 17:26
drink *o* unto other gods .... Jer 19:13
have *o* incense unto Baal ...... Jer 32:29
before me to *o* burnt *o* .... Jer 33:18
to kindle meat *o*,and to do .... Jer 33:18
to pour out drink *o* unto ...... Jer 44:17
poured out drink *o* unto ...... Jer 44:19
o in the high places, and ...... Jer 48:35
they did *o* sweet savor .... Ezek 6:13
o there their sacrifices .... Ezek 20:28
the provocation of their *o* ..... Ezek 20:28
out there their drink *o* .... Ezek 20:28
For when ye *o* your gifts ...... Ezek 20:31
to slay thereon the burnt *o* .... Ezek 40:39
to slay..the sin *o* and .... Ezek 40:39
to slay..the trespass *o* .... Ezek 40:39
hewn stone for the burnt *o* .... Ezek 40:42
burnt *o* and the sacrifice ...... Ezek 40:42
things, and the meat *o* .... Ezek 42:13
and the sin *o*, and the .... Ezek 42:13
trespass *o*; for the place ...... Ezek 42:13
make it, to *o* burnt *o* .... Ezek 43:18
bullock also of the sin *o* .... Ezek 43:21
thou shalt *o* a young bullock .. Ezek 43:23
o them before the Lord .... Ezek 43:24
o them up for a burnt *o* .... Ezek 43:24
shall make your burnt *o* .... Ezek 43:27
altar, and your peace *o* .... Ezek 43:27
o my bread, the fat and the ... Ezek 44:7
they shall slay the burnt *o* ..... Ezek 44:11
he shall *o* his sin *o* .... Ezek 44:27
They shall eat the meat *o* ..... Ezek 44:29
They shall eat..the sin *o* ...... Ezek 44:29
shall eat..the trespass *o* .... Ezek 44:29
o an oblation unto the Lord ... Ezek 45:1
ye shall *o* the tenth part of .... Ezek 45:14
of Israel; for a meat *o* .... Ezek 45:15
a burnt *o*, and for peace ...... Ezek 45:15
prince's part to give burnt *o* ... Ezek 45:17
and meat *o* and drink *o* .... Ezek 45:17
he shall prepare the sin *o* ..... Ezek 45:17
shall prepare..the meat *o* ...... Ezek 45:17
shall prepare..the burnt *o* ..... Ezek 45:17
o, to make reconciliation ...... Ezek 45:17
land a bullock for a sin *o* ..... Ezek 45:22
a burnt *o* to the Lord .... Ezek 45:23
the goats daily for a sin *o* ..... Ezek 45:23
prepare a meat *o* of an .... Ezek 45:24
days, according to the sin *o* ... Ezek 45:25
according to the burnt *o* ...... Ezek 45:25
according to the meat *o* .... Ezek 45:25
the burnt *o* that the prince .... Ezek 46:4
that the prince shall *o* .... Ezek 46:4
o shall be an ephah for .... Ezek 46:5
meat *o* for the lambs as he .... Ezek 46:5
o shall be an ephah to a ...... Ezek 46:11
prepare a voluntary burnt *o* ... Ezek 46:12
or peace *o* voluntarily unto .... Ezek 46:12
he shall prepare his burnt *o* ... Ezek 46:12
offering and his peace *o*, as ... Ezek 46:12
shalt prepare a meat *o* .... Ezek 46:14
a meat *o* continually by a ..... Ezek 46:14
the lamb, and the meat *o* ..... Ezek 46:15
for a continual burnt *o* .... Ezek 46:15
shall boil the trespass *o* .... Ezek 46:20
priests shall boil..the sin *o* ..... Ezek 46:20
they shall bake the meat *o* .... Ezek 46:20
o which ye shall *o* .... Ezek 48:8
oblation of the land that is *o* .. Ezek 48:12
o the holy oblation .... Ezek 48:20
o an oblation and sweet .... Dan 2:46
reproach *o* by him to cease .... Dan 11:18
of God more than burnt *o* .... Hos 6:6
not *o* wine *o* to the Lord ...... Hos 9:4
The meat *o* and the .... Joel 1:9
o is cut off from the house .... Joel 1:9
my God: for the meat *o* and .. Joel 1:13
drink *o* is withholden from .... Joel 1:13
behind him; even a meat *o* .... Joel 2:14
o unto the Lord your God .... Joel 2:14
And *o* a sacrifice of .... Amos 4:5
and publish the free *o* .... Amos 4:5
ye *o* me burnt *o* .... Amos 5:22
meat *o*, I will not accept ...... Amos 5:22
peace *o* of your fat beasts ..... Amos 5:22
ye *o* unto me sacrifices and .... Amos 5:25
o a sacrifice unto the Lord .... Jon 1:16
before him with burnt *o* .... Mic 6:6
shall bring mine *o* .... Zeph 3:10
they *o* there is unclean .... Hag 2:14
Ye *o* polluted bread upon ..... Mal 1:7
o the blind for sacrifice .... Mal 1:8
if ye *o* the lame and sick, is ... Mal 1:8
o it now unto thy governor .... Mal 1:8
will I accept an *o* at your ..... Mal 1:10
place incense shall be *o* .... Mal 1:11
thus ye brought an *o* .... Mal 1:13
o an *o* unto the Lord .... Mal 2:12
he regardeth not the *o* any .... Mal 2:13
thee? In tithes and *o* .... Mal 3:8
then come and *o* thy gift ...... Matt 5:24
o the gift that Moses .... Matt 8:4
to *o* a sacrifice according to ... Luke 2:24
o for thy cleansing .... Luke 5:14
on the one cheek *o* also the ... Luke 6:29
will he *o* him a scorpion? ..... Luke 11:12
and *o* sacrifice unto the idol ... Acts 7:41
given, he *o* them money ...... Acts 8:18
ye abstain from meats *o* to .... Acts 15:29
from things *o* to idols .... Acts 21:25
until that an *o* should be *o* .... Acts 21:26
the *o* up of the Gentiles .... Rom 15:16
as touching things *o* unto 1Cor 8:1
eat it as a thing *o* unto an 1Cor 8:7
o in sacrifice to idols 1Cor 10:19
I be *o* upon the sacrifice ...... Phil 2:17
For I am now ready to be *o* ... 2Tim 4:6
ordained to *o* gifts and .... Heb 8:3
have somewhat also to *o* ...... Heb 8:3
which he *o* for himself, and ... Heb 9:7
he should *o* himself often ..... Heb 9:25
once *o* to bear the sins of ..... Heb 9:28
o year by year continually ..... Heb 10:1
not have ceased to be *o*? ...... Heb 10:2
the *o* of the body of Jesus ..... Heb 10:10
these is, there is no more *o* ... Heb 10:18
By faith Abel *o* unto God a ... Heb 11:4
when he was tried, *o* up ...... Heb 11:17
o up his only begotten son .... Heb 11:17
let us *o* the sacrifice of .... Heb 13:15
when he had *o* Isaac his .... James 2:21
to *o* up spiritual sacrifices 1Pet 2:5
o it with the prayers of all .... Rev 8:3

OFFERING OF CHRIST—*Christ's giving of Himself*

Of Himself:

Predicted .... Ps 40:6-8
Prepared .... Heb 5:1-10
Proclaimed .... Heb 10:5-9
Purified .... Heb 9:14
Personalized .... Heb 7:27
Perfected .... Heb 10:11-14
Praised .... Eph 5:2

OFFERINGS OF THE LEADERS—*by heads of twelve tribes*

1. Six wagons and twelve oxen to transport tabernacle .... Num 7:1-89
2. Dedication gift .... Num 7:1-89

OFFICE—*a position of authority, responsibility, or trust*

Holders of:

Butler .... Gen 40:13
Judge .... Deut 17:9
Priest .... Deut 26:3
Ministers of song 1Chr 6:32
Porters 1Chr 9:22
Publican .... Matt 9:9
Bishop 1Tim 3:1

[*also* OFFICES]

the *o* of a midwife to the ..... Ex 1:16
unto me in the priest's *o* ...... Ex 28:3
unto me in the priest's *o* ...... Ex 28:4
unto me in the priest's *o* ...... Ex 28:41
and the priest's *o* shall be ..... Ex 29:9
unto me in the priest's *o* ...... Ex 30:30
minister in the priest's *o* ...... Ex 35:19
unto me in the priest's *o* ...... Ex 40:13
the Lord in the priest's *o* ...... Lev 7:35
minister in the priest's *o* ...... Num 3:3
shall wait on their priest's *o* ... Num 3:10
priest's *o* for every thing ...... Num 18:7
I have given your priest's *o* .... Num 18:7
in the priest's *o* in his stead ... Deut 10:6
into one of the priests' *o* 1Sam 2:36
priest's *o* in the temple that ... 1Chr 6:10
set *o* over the things that 1Chr 9:31
executed the priest's *o* 1Chr 24:2
according to their *o* in 1Chr 24:3
priests waited on their *o* 2Chr 7:6
executing the priest's *o* 2Chr 11:14
the priests, in their set *o* 2Chr 31:15
their *o* was to distribute .... Neh 13:13
of my God, and for the *o* ..... Neh 13:14
and let another take his *o* ..... Ps 109:8
the *o* of a priest unto me ..... Ezek 44:13
he executed the priest's *o* ..... Luke 1:8
Gentiles, I magnify mine *o* .... Rom 11:13
use the *o* of a deacon 1Tim 3:10
have used the *o* of a deacon ... 1Tim 3:13
the *o* of the priesthood .... Heb 7:5

OFFICER—*one appointed to rule over others*

Descriptive of:

Magistrate .... Luke 12:58
Principal officer 1Kin 4:5, 7

Functions of:

Administer justice .... Num 11:16

[*also* OFFICERS]

Potiphar, an *o* of Pharoah's ... Gen 37:36
wroth against two of his *o* ..... Gen 40:2
let him appoint *o* over the .... Gen 41:34
of the people, and their *o* ..... Ex 5:6
o of the children of Israel ..... Ex 5:14
o of the children of Israel ..... Ex 5:19
was wroth with the *o* of the ... Num 31:14
and *o* among your tribes ...... Deut 1:15
the *o* shall speak unto the ..... Deut 20:5
when the *o* have made an ..... Deut 20:9
of your tribes, and your *o* ..... Deut 31:28
Joshua commanded the *o* of ... Josh 1:10
and their elders, and *o* .... Josh 8:33
judges, and for their *o* .... Josh 24:1
Jerubbaal? and Zebul his *o*? ... Judg 9:28
give to his *o*, and to his 1Sam 8:15
had twelve *o* over all Israel 1Kin 4:7
those *o* provided victual for ... 1Kin 4:27
the chief of Solomon's *o* 1Kin 5:16
king of Israel called an *o* 1Kin 22:9
appointed unto her a certain *o* . 2Kin 8:6
the hundreds, the *o* of the 2Kin 11:15
and his princes, and his *o* 2Kin 24:12
six thousand were *o* and 1Chr 23:4
o among them of Israel on 1Chr 26:30
o, and with the mighty 1Chr 28:1
chief of king Solomon's *o* 2Chr 8:10
Levites shall be *o* before 2Chr 19:11
priest's *o* came and emptied ... 2Chr 24:11
the *o* of his house, that .... Esth 1:8
o of the king, helped the ...... Esth 9:3
will also make thy *o* peace .... Is 60:17
be *o* in the house of the ...... Jer 29:26
judge deliver thee to the *o* .... Matt 5:25
chief priests sent *o* to take .... John 7:32
o answered, Never man spake . John 7:46
o of the Jews took Jesus ...... John 18:12
the *o* which stood by struck ... John 18:22
the *o* came, and found .... Acts 5:22

OFFICES OF CHRIST—*Christ's threefold work on earth*

As Prophet .... Deut 18:18, 19; Is 61:1-3
As Priest .... Ps 110:4; Is 53:1-12
As King .... 2Sam 7:12-17; Luke 1:32, 33

OFFSCOURING—*something vile or worthless*
Jews thus described .... Lam 3:45

the *o* of all things unto 1Cor 4:13

OFFSPRING—*progeny, issue (physical or spiritual)*

Used literally of:
Set-apart firstlings .... Ex 13:12; Ex 34:19
Of a donkey you shall redeem .... Ex 13:13; Ex 34:20
Man's issue (children) .... Job 5:25
Man as created by God .... Acts 17:28, 29
Christ as a descendant of David .... Rev 22:16

Used figuratively of:
True believer .... Is 22:24
New Israel .... Is 44:3-5
Gentile church .... Is 61:9
True Church .... Is 65:23

and their *o* before their .... Job 21:8
o shall not be satisfied .... Job 27:14
yea, let my *o* be rooted .... Job 31:8
the *o* of thy bowels like .... Is 48:19

OFTEN—*many times*

[*also* OFT, OFTENER, OFTENTIMES, OFTTIMES]
as *o* as he passed by 2Kin 4:8
How *o* is the candle of .... Job 21:17
things worketh God *o* .... Job 33:29
How *o* did they provoke .... Ps 78:40
He, that being *o* reproved .... Prov 29:1
For *o* also thine own .... Eccl 7:22
feared the Lord spake *o* .... Mal 3:16
the Pharisees fast *o* .... Matt 9:14
for *o* he falleth into the .... Matt 17:15
how *o* shall my brother sin .... Matt 18:21
how *o* would I have .... Matt 23:37
how *o* bound with fetters .... Mark 5:4
they wash their hands *o* .... Mark 7:3
o it hath cast him into .... Mark 9:22
disciples of John fast *o* .... Luke 5:33
o it had caught him .... Luke 8:29
Jesus *o* resorted thither .... John 18:2
he sent for him the *o* .... Acts 24:26
And I punished them *o* in .... Acts 26:11
o I purposed to come .... Rom 1:13
this do ye, as *o* as ye 1Cor 11:25
For as *o* as ye eat this 1Cor 11:26
o proved diligent in man 2Cor 8:22
more frequent in deaths *o* 2Cor 11:23
In journeyings *o*, in perils 2Cor 11:26
watchings *o*, in hunger 2Cor 11:27
fastings *o*, in cold and 2Cor 11:27
whom I have told you *o* .... Phil 3:18
and thine *o* infirmities 1Tim 5:23
he *o* refreshed me, and 2Tim 1:16
in the rain that cometh *o* .... Heb 6:7
should offer himself *o* .... Heb 9:25
with all plagues, as *o* as .... Rev 11:6

OG (ŏg)—*"giant"*
Amorite king of Bashan .... Deut 3:1, 8
Extent of rule .... Deut 3:8, 10
Residences at Ashtaroth and Edrei .... Josh 12:4
Man of great size .... Deut 3:11
Defeated and killed by Israel .... Num 21:32-35
Territory of, assigned to Manasseh .... Deut 3:13
Memory of, long remembered .... Ps 135:11

the kingdom of *O* king of .... Num 32:33
and *O* the king of Bashan .... Deut 1:4
and the land of *O* king of .... Deut 4:47
and *O* the king of Bashan .... Deut 29:7
did to Sihon and to *O* .... Deut 31:4
Sihon and *O*, whom ye .... Josh 2:10
and to *O* king of Bashan .... Josh 9:10
all the kingdom of *O* in .... Josh 13:12
the kingdom of *O* king of .... Josh 13:30
of the kingdom of *O* in .... Josh 13:31
and of *O* king of Bashan 1Kin 4:19
and the land of *O* king of .... Neh 9:22
And *O* the king of Bashan .... Ps 136:20

OH—*an exclamation used to express an emotion*
O let not the Lord be .... Gen 18:30
O, let me escape thither .... Gen 19:20
O my Lord, if the Lord be .... Judg 6:13
O my lord, as thy soul 1Sam 1:26
O that my grief were .... Job 6:2
O that I had given up the .... Job 10:18
O that my words were .... Job 19:23
O that they were printed .... Job 19:23
O that I were as in .... Job 29:2
O that one would hear me! .... Job 31:35
o save me for thy mercies' .... Ps 6:4
O that the salvation of .... Ps 14:7
O that the salvation of .... Ps 53:6
O that my people had .... Ps 81:13
O that thou wouldest rend .... Is 64:1
O that my head were .... Jer 9:1
O, do not this abominable .... Jer 44:4

OHAD (ō'hăd)—*"strength"*
Son of Simeon .... Gen 46:10

OHEL (ō'hĕl)—*"tent"*
Son of Zerubbabel 1Chr 3:19, 20

OIL—*a liquid extracted from olives; to pour oil on an object or person*

Features concerning:
Given by God .... Ps 104:14, 15
Subject to tithing .... Deut 12:17

Uses of:
Food .... Num 11:8
Anointing 1Sam 10:1
Beautification .... Ruth 3:3
Perfume .... Eccl 10:1
Illumination .... Ex 25:6; Ex 30:26-32; Matt 25:3-8

Types of oil:
Anointing .... Ex 25:6
Pure .... Ex 27:20
Baking .... Ex 29:23
Beaten .... Ex 29:40
Olive .... Ex 30:24
Precious 2Kin 20:13
Golden .... Zech 4:12

Figurative of:
Prosperity .... Deut 32:13
Joy and gladness .... Is 61:3
Wastefulness .... Prov 21:17
Brotherly love .... Ps 133:2
Real grace .... Matt 25:4
Holy Spirit 1John 2:20, 27

[*also* OILED]
and poured *o* upon the top .... Gen 28:18
thereon, and he poured *o* .... Gen 35:14
tempered with *o* .... Ex 29:2
anointed with *o* .... Ex 29:2
take the anointing *o* .... Ex 29:7
and of the anointing *o* .... Ex 29:21
and one cake of *o* .... Ex 29:23
make it an *o* of holy .... Ex 30:25
be a holy anointing *o* .... Ex 30:25
the anointing *o*, and sweet .... Ex 31:11
And *o* for the light, and .... Ex 35:8
spices for anointing *o* .... Ex 35:8
and the anointing *o*, and .... Ex 35:15
And spice, and *o* for the .... Ex 35:28
and for the anointing *o* .... Ex 35:28
the holy anointing *o* .... Ex 37:29
vessels thereof, and the *o* .... Ex 39:37
take the anointing *o* .... Ex 40:9
he shall pour *o* upon it .... Lev 2:1
fine flour mingled with *o* .... Lev 2:4
wafers anointed with *o* .... Lev 2:4
it in pieces, and pour *o* .... Lev 2:6
And thou shalt put *o* upon .... Lev 2:15
he shall put no *o* upon it .... Lev 5:11
meat offering, and of the *o* .... Lev 6:15
meat offering, mingled with *o* .... Lev 7:10
cakes mingled with *o* .... Lev 7:12
wafers anointed with *o* .... Lev 7:12
cakes mingled with *o* .... Lev 7:12
and the anointing *o* .... Lev 8:2
of the anointing *o* .... Lev 8:12
a cake of *o* bread, and .... Lev 8:26
offering mingled with *o* .... Lev 9:4
anointing *o* of the Lord is .... Lev 10:7
o, and one log of *o* .... Lev 14:10
some of the log of *o* .... Lev 14:15
his right finger in the *o* .... Lev 14:16
sprinkle of the *o* with his .... Lev 14:16
the remnant of the *o* that .... Lev 14:18
fine flour mingled with *o* .... Lev 14:21
meat offering, and a log of *o* .... Lev 14:21
priest shall pour of the *o* .... Lev 14:26
priest shall put of the *o* .... Lev 14:28
head the anointing *o* was .... Lev 21:10
flour mingled with *o* .... Lev 23:13
pure *o* olive beaten for .... Lev 24:2
snuffdishes, and all the *o* .... Num 4:9
pertaineth the *o* for the .... Num 4:16
and the anointing *o* .... Num 4:16
he shall pour no *o* upon .... Num 5:15
flour mingled with *o* .... Num 6:15
mingled with *o* for a meat .... Num 7:13
flour mingled with *o* .... Num 8:8
as the taste of fresh *o* .... Num 11:8
part of a hin of *o* .... Num 15:4
with half a hin of *o* .... Num 15:9
the best of the *o*, and all .... Num 18:12
of a hin of beaten *o* .... Num 28:5
of flour mingled with *o* .... Num 28:13
flour mingled with *o* .... Num 28:28
be of flour mingled with *o* .... Num 29:3
anointed with the holy *o* .... Num 35:25
thy wine, and thine *o* .... Deut 7:13
a land of *o* olive, and .... Deut 8:8
thy wine, and thine *o* .... Deut 11:14
wine, or of thy *o* .... Deut 12:17
wine, and of thine *o* .... Deut 14:23
wine, and of thine *o* .... Deut 18:4
thyself with the *o* .... Deut 28:40
rock, and *o* out of the .... Deut 32:13
let him dip his foot in *o* .... Deut 33:24
Samuel took a vial of *o* 1Sam 10:1
fill thine horn with *o*, and 1Sam 16:1
been anointed with *o* 2Sam 1:21
anoint not thyself with *o* 2Sam 14:2
priest took a horn of *o* 1Kin 1:39
measures of pure *o* 1Kin 5:11
in a barrel, and a little *o* 1Kin 17:12
did the cruse of *o* 1Kin 17:16
house, save a pot of *o* 2Kin 4:2
Go, sell the *o*, and pay 2Kin 4:7
take this box of *o* in 2Kin 9:1
and he poured the *o* on 2Kin 9:6
a land of *o* olive and of 2Kin 18:32
the wine, and the *o* 1Chr 9:29
raisins and wine, and *o* 1Chr 12:40
over the cellars of *o* was 1Chr 27:28
thousand baths of *o* 2Chr 2:10
store of victual, and of *o* 2Chr 11:11
of corn, wine, and *o*, and 2Chr 31:5
meat, and drink, and *o* .... Ezra 3:7
wine, and *o*, according .... Ezra 6:9
to a hundred baths of *o* .... Ezra 7:22
the corn, the wine, and the *o* .... Neh 5:11
of wine and of *o*, unto the .... Neh 10:37
new wine, and the *o* .... Neh 13:5
wit, six months with *o* .... Esth 2:12
Which make *o* within .... Job 24:11
anointest my head with *o* .... Ps 23:5
anointed thee with..*o* of .... Ps 45:7
words were softer than *o* .... Ps 55:21
with my holy *o* have I .... Ps 89:20
anointed with fresh *o* .... Ps 92:10
water, and like *o* into his .... Ps 109:18
it shall be an excellent *o* .... Ps 141:5
is smoother than *o* .... Prov 5:3

for wine, and for *o*, and . . . . . .Jer 31:12
summer fruits, and *o* . . . . .Jer 40:10
of barley, and of *o*, and . . . . . . .Jer 41:8
I anointed thee with *o* . . . . .Ezek 16:9
hast set mine *o* and mine . . . . .Ezek 16:18
incense and mine *o* . . . . .Ezek 23:41
and honey, and *o*, and . . . . .Ezek 27:17
rivers to run like *o* . . . . .Ezek 32:14
of *o*, the bath of *o* . . . . .Ezek 45:14
according to the *o* . . . . .Ezek 45:25
and a hin of *o* to an . . . . .Ezek 46:5
offering, and the *o* . . . . .Ezek 46:15
and my flax, mine *o* and . . . . . .Hos 2:5
the wine, and the *o* . . . . .Hos 2:22
is dried up, the *o* . . . . .Joel 1:10
overflow with wine and *o* . . . . .Joel 2:24
thousands of rivers of *o* . . . . . . .Mic 6:7
and upon the *o* . . . . .Hag 1:11
pottage, or wine, or *o*, or . . . . .Hag 2:12
anointed with *o* many . . . . .Mark 6:13
My head with *o* thou . . . . .Luke 7:46
his wounds, pouring in *o* . . . . . .Luke 10:34
hundred measures of *o* . . . . .Luke 16:6
anointed thee with..*o* of . . . . . . .Heb 1:9
anointing him with *o* in . . . . . . .James 5:14
thou hurt not the *o* and . . . . . . .Rev 6:6
and wine, and *o*, and fine . . . . .Rev 18:13

OIL TREE—*the olive tree*
Signifies restoration . . . . . .Is 41:17-20

OINTMENT—*a salve made of olive oil and spices*
By special prescription for tabernacle . . . . .Ex 30:23-25
Misuse of, forbidden . . . . .Ex 30:37, 38
Ingredients stirred together . . . . .Job 41:31

Features concerning:
Considered very valuable .2Kin 20:13
Carried or stored in containers . . . . .Matt 26:7
Can be polluted . . . . .Eccl 10:1

Used of:
Cosmetic . . . . .Eccl 9:8
Sign of hospitality . . . . . . .Luke 7:46
Embalming agent . . . . .Luke 23:55, 56
Sexual attraction . . . . .Is 57:9

[*also* OINTMENTS]
priests made the *o* 1Chr 9:30
like the precious *o* upon . . . . . .Ps 133:2
O and perfume rejoice . . . . .Prov 27:9
better than precious *o* . . . . .Eccl 7:1
savor of thy good *o* . . . . .Song 1:3
thy name is as *o* poured . . . . . . .Song 1:3
the smell of thine *o* than . . . . . .Song 4:10
neither mollified with *o* . . . . . . .Is 1:6
and the precious *o* . . . . .Is 39:2
with the chief *o* . . . . .Amos 6:6
she hath poured this *o* on . . . . .Matt 26:12
alabaster box of *o* of . . . . .Mark 14:3
alabaster box of *o* . . . . .Luke 7:37
anointed the Lord with *o* . . . . . .John 11:2
Mary a pound of *o* of . . . . .John 12:3
the odor of the *o* . . . . .John 12:3
Why was not this *o* sold . . . . . . .John 12:5
cinnamon, and odors, and *o* . . .Rev 18:13

OLD—*mature; having many years*

Descriptive of:
Age . . . . .Gen 25:8
Mature person 1Kin 12:6-13
Experienced . . . . .Ezek 23:43
Ancient times . . . . .Mal 3:4
Old Testament age . . . . . .Matt 5:21-33
Old Tesatment 2Cor 3:14
Unregenerate nature . . . . .Rom 6:6

Of man's age, infirmities of:
Waning sexual desire . . . .Luke 1:18
Physical handicaps 1Kin 1:1, 15
Failing strength . . . . .Ps 71:9

Of man's age, dangers of:
Spiritual decline 1Kin 11:4
Not receiving instruction. .Eccl 4:13
Disrespect toward . . . . . . .Deut 28:50

Of man's age, blessing of:
God's care . . . . .Is 46:4
Continued fruitfulness . . . .Ps 92:14
Security of faith . . . . .Prov 22:6
Fulfillment of life's goals. .Is 65:20
Honor . . . . .Lev 19:32
Grandchildren . . . . .Prov 17:6
Men dream dreams . . . . . .Acts 2:17

See LENGTH OF LIFE

[*also* OLDNESS]
five hundred years *o* . . . . .Gen 5:32
men which were of *o* . . . . .Gen 6:4
was six hundred years *o* . . . . . . .Gen 7:6
a hundred years *o* . . . . .Gen 11:10
seventy and five years *o* . . . . . . .Gen 12:4
heifer of three years *o* . . . . .Gen 15:9
goat of three years *o* . . . . .Gen 15:9
ram of three years *o* . . . . .Gen 15:9
fourscore and six years *o* . . . . . .Gen 16:16
was ninety years *o* . . . . .Gen 17:1
is a hundred years *o*? . . . . .Gen 17:17
that is ninety years *o* . . . . .Gen 17:17
was thirteen years *o* . . . . .Gen 17:25
and Sarah were *o* . . . . .Gen 18:11
After I am waxed *o* shall I . . . .Gen 18:12
pleasure, my lord being *o* . . . . .Gen 18:12
house round, both *o* and . . . . . .Gen 19:4
bare a..son in his *o* . . . . .Gen 21:2
a hundred years *o* . . . . .Gen 21:5
and twenty years *o* . . . . .Gen 23:1
Abraham was *o*, and well . . . . .Gen 24:1
an *o* man, and full of . . . . .Gen 25:8
Isaac was forty years *o* . . . . .Gen 25:20
Esau was forty years *o* . . . . .Gen 26:34
when Isaac was *o*, and . . . . .Gen 27:1
people, being *o* and full . . . . . . .Gen 35:29
being seventeen years *o* . . . . . . .Gen 37:2
Joseph was thirty years *o* . . . . . .Gen 41:46
well, the *o* man of whom . . . . .Gen 43:27
We have a father, an *o* . . . . . . .Gen 44:20
Jacob, How *o* art thou? . . . . . . .Gen 47:8
as a lion, and as an *o* lion . . . . .Gen 49:9
hundred and ten years *o* . . . . . . .Gen 50:26
Moses was fourscore years *o* . . .Ex 7:7
fourscore and three years *o* . . . .Ex 7:7
young and with our *o* . . . . .Ex 10:9
from twenty years *o* and . . . . . .Ex 30:14
from twenty years *o* and . . . . . .Ex 38:26
It is an *o* leprosy in the . . . . . . .Lev 13:11
eat yet of *o* fruit until . . . . .Lev 25:22
ye shall eat of the *o* . . . . .Lev 25:22
And ye shall eat *o* store . . . . . . .Lev 26:10
forth the *o* because of . . . . .Lev 26:10
o even unto sixty years *o* . . . . . .Lev 27:3
o even unto twenty years *o* . . . .Lev 27:5
it be from sixty years *o* . . . . . . .Lev 27:7
From twenty years *o* and . . . . . .Num 1:3
male from a month *o* and . . . . .Num 3:15
From thirty years *o* and . . . . . . .Num 4:3
even until fifty years *o* . . . . .Num 4:3
From thirty years *o* and . . . . . . .Num 4:23
until fifty years *o* shalt . . . . . . .Num 4:23
From thirty years *o* and . . . . . . .Num 4:30
even unto fifty years *o* . . . . .Num 4:30
From thirty years *o* and . . . . . . .Num 4:35
even unto fifty years *o* . . . . .Num 4:35
From thirty years *o* and . . . . . . .Num 4:39
even unto fifty years *o* . . . . .Num 4:39
From thirty years *o* and . . . . . . .Num 4:43
even unto fifty years *o* . . . . .Num 4:43
From thirty years *o* and . . . . . . .Num 4:47
even unto fifty years *o* . . . . .Num 4:47
twenty and five years *o* . . . . . . .Num 8:24
from twenty years *o* and . . . . . .Num 14:29
from a month *o* shalt thou . . . .Num 18:16
from twenty years *o* and . . . . . .Num 26:2
males from a month *o* and . . . .Num 26:62
from twenty years *o* and . . . . . .Num 32:11
twenty and three years *o* . . . . . .Num 33:39
giants dwelt therein in *o* . . . . . .Deut 2:20
raiment waxed not *o* upon . . . .Deut 8:4
they of *o* time have set in . . . . .Deut 19:14
clothes are not waxen *o* . . . . . . .Deut 29:5
shoe is not waxen *o* upon . . . . .Deut 29:5

hundred and twenty years *o* . . .Deut 31:2
Remember the days of *o* . . . . . .Deut 32:7
hundred and twenty years *o* . . .Deut 34:7
did eat of the *o* corn of . . . . . . .Josh 5:11
man and woman, young and *o* .Josh 6:21
and took *o* sacks upon . . . . .Josh 9:4
and wine bottles, *o*, and . . . . . .Josh 9:4
And *o* shoes and clouted . . . . . .Josh 9:5
feet, and *o* garments upon . . . .Josh 9:5
Now Joshua was *o* and . . . . .Josh 13:1
Thou art *o* and stricken . . . . . . .Josh 13:1
Forty years *o* was I when . . . . .Josh 14:7
that Joshua waxed *o* and . . . . . .Josh 23:1
side of the flood in *o* . . . . .Josh 24:2
hundred and ten years *o* . . . . . .Judg 2:8
bullock of seven years *o* . . . . . .Judg 6:25
died in a good *o* age . . . . .Judg 8:32
came an *o* man from his . . . . . .Judg 19:16
the *o* man said, Peace . . . . .Judg 19:20
I am too *o* to have . . . . .Ruth 1:12
a nourisher of thine *o* . . . . .Ruth 4:15
Now Eli was very *o*, and 1Sam 2:22
not be an *o* man in thine 1Sam 2:32
ninety and eight years *o* 1Sam 4:15
when Samuel was *o* 1Sam 8:1
I am *o* and grayheaded 1Sam 12:2
went among men for an *o* 1Sam 17:12
nations were of *o*..inhabitants . .1Sam 27:8
she said, An *o* man cometh . . .1Sam 28:14
son was forty years *o* 2Sam 2:10
was five years *o* when the 2Sam 4:4
David was thirty years *o* 2Sam 5:4
even fourscore years *o* 2Sam 19:32
were wont to speak in *o* 2Sam 20:18
dwelt an *o* prophet in 1Kin 13:11
and the *o* prophet came to 1Kin 13:29
was forty and one years *o* 1Kin 14:21
time of his *o* age he was 1Kin 15:23
thirty and five years *o* 1Kin 22:42
and her husband is *o* 2Kin 4:14
Thirty and two years *o* 2Kin 8:17
Seven years *o* was Jehoash 2Kin 11:21
twenty and five years *o* 2Kin 14:2
Sixteen years *o* was he 2Kin 15:2
Twenty years *o* was Ahaz 2Kin 16:2
Twenty and five years *o* 2Kin 18:2
was twelve years *o* 2Kin 21:1
Josiah was eight years *o* 2Kin 22:1
twenty and three years *o* 2Kin 23:31
was eighteen years *o* 2Kin 24:8
was threescore years *o* 1Chr 2:21
had dwelt there of *o* 1Chr 4:40
So when David was *o* and 1Chr 23:1
from twenty years *o* and 1Chr 27:23
And he died in a good *o* 1Chr 29:28
took counsel with the *o* 2Chr 10:6
the counsel of the *o* 2Chr 10:13
was one and forty years *o* 2Chr 12:13
was thirty and five years *o* 2Chr 20:31
was thirty and two years *o* 2Chr 21:5
Forty and two years *o* was 2Chr 22:2
Joash was seven years *o* 2Chr 24:1
But Jehoiada waxed *o* 2Chr 24:15
hundred and thirty years *o* 2Chr 24:15
twenty and five years *o* 2Chr 25:1
who was sixteen years *o* 2Chr 26:1
twenty and five years *o* 2Chr 27:1
was twenty years *o* when 2Chr 28:1
five and twenty years *o* 2Chr 29:1
from three years *o* and 2Chr 31:16
Manasseh was twelve years *o* . .2Chr 33:1
Josiah was eight years *o* 2Chr 34:1
twenty and three years *o* 2Chr 36:2
Jehoiachin was eight years *o* . . .2Chr 36:9
o man, or him that stooped . . .2Chr 36:17
from twenty years *o* and . . . . . .Ezra 3:8
within the same of *o* time . . . . .Ezra 4:15
o gate repaired Jehoiada . . . . . .Neh 3:6
their clothes waxed not *o* . . . . .Neh 9:21
Ephraim, and above the *o* . . . . .Neh 12:39
Jews, both young and *o* . . . . . . .Esth 3:13
o lion perisheth for lack . . . . . . .Job 4:11
root thereof wax *o* in the . . . . .Job 14:8
Knowest thou not this of *o* . . . .Job 20:4
wicked live, become *o* . . . . .Job 21:7

the *o* way which wicked ....Job 22:15
young, and ye are very *o* ......Job 32:6
died, being *o* and full of ......Job 42:17
it waxeth *o* because of all .....Ps 6:7
have been ever of *o* ....Ps 25:6
bones waxed *o* through ....Ps 32:3
days, in the times of *o* ....Ps 44:1
heavens, which were of *o* .....Ps 68:33
I am *o* and grayheaded ....Ps 71:18
hast purchased of *o* ....Ps 74:2
For God is my King of *o* ......Ps 74:12
considered the days of *o* ......Ps 77:5
remember thy wonders of *o* ...Ps 77:11
utter dark sayings of *o* ....Ps 78:2
is established of *o* ....Ps 93:2
Of *o* hast thou laid the........Ps 102:25
thy judgments of *o* ....Ps 119:52
I remember the days of *o* ......Ps 143:5
before his works of *o* ....Prov 8:22
children are the crown of *o*....Prov 17:6
beauty of *o* men is the ....Prov 20:29
when he is *o*, he will not ......Prov 22:6
Remove not the *o* landmark ...Prov 23:10
it hath been already of *o* ......Eccl 1:10
of pleasant fruits, new and *o* ..Song 7:13
a heifer of three years *o* ......Is 15:5
captives, young and *o*..........Is 20:4
walls for the water of the *o* ...Is 22:11
thy counsels of *o* are..........Is 25:1
come the young and *o* lion ....Is 30:6
consider the things of *o* ....Is 43:18
the former things of *o* ....Is 46:9
all shall wax *o* as a ....Is 50:9
earth shall wax *o* like a ....Is 51:6
held my peace even of *o* ......Is 57:11
they shall build the *o* ....Is 61:4
them all the days of *o* ....Is 63:9
remembered the days of *o*......Is 63:11
an *o* man that hath not ....Is 65:20
of *o* time I have broken.......Jer 2:20
and see, and ask for the *o* ....Jer 6:16
me and before thee of *o* ....Jer 28:8
the Lord hath appeared of *o* ..Jer 31:3
both young men and *o* ....Jer 31:13
o cast clouts and *o* rotten .....Jer 38:11
Put now these *o* cast clouts ...Jer 38:12
as in the days of *o*............Jer 46:26
heifer of three years *o* ....Jer 48:34
I break in pieces *o* and ....Jer 51:22
one and twenty years *o* ....Jer 52:1
had in the days of *o* ....Lam 1:7
commanded in the days of *o*...Lam 2:17
The young and the *o* lie.......Lam 2:21
skin hath he made *o* ....Lam 3:4
they that be dead of *o* ....Lam 3:6
renew our days as of *o*........Lam 5:21
Slay utterly *o* and young ......Ezek 9:6
to destroy it for the *o*.........Ezek 25:15
with the people of *o* ....Ezek 26:20
in places desolate of *o* ....Ezek 26:20
settle you after your *o* ....Ezek 36:11
I have spoken in *o* ....Ezek 38:17
threescore and two years *o* ....Dan 5:31
Hear this, ye *o* men, and .....Joel 1:2
your *o* men shall dream ....Joel 2:28
it as in the days of *o*..........Amos 9:11
have been from of *o* ....Mic 5:2
with calves of a year *o*? ....Mic 6:6
Gilead, as in the days of *o* ....Mic 7:14
But Nineveh is of *o* like.......Nah 2:8
yet *o* men and *o* women ......Zech 8:4
from two years *o* and ....Matt 2:16
of new cloth unto an *o*........Matt 9:16
men put new wine into *o*.......Matt 9:17
treasure things new and *o* .....Matt 13:52
of new cloth on an *o* ....Mark 2:21
taketh away from the *o* ....Mark 2:21
conceived a son in her *o* ......Luke 1:36
when he was twelve years *o* ...Luke 2:42
new garment upon an *o* ....Luke 5:36
putteth new wine into *o* ....Luke 5:37
also having drunk *o*............Luke 5:39
for he saith, The *o* is ....Luke 5:39
one of the *o* prophets is.......Luke 9:19
bags which wax not *o* ....Luke 12:33
be born when he is *o*? ....John 3:4
not yet fifty years *o*...........John 8:57
when thou shalt be *o* ....John 21:18
was above forty years *o* ....Acts 4:22
Moses of *o* time hath in.......Acts 15:21
Mnason of Cyprus, an *o* ......Acts 21:16
about a hundred years *o* ......Rom 4:19
Purge out therefore the *o* 1Cor 5:7
not with *o* leaven, neither 1Cor 5:8
in the reading of the *o* 2Cor 3:14
That ye put off..the *o*.........Eph 4:22
that ye have put off the *o* .....Col 3:9
profane and *o* wives fables 1Tim 4:7
shall wax *o* as doth a ....Heb 1:11
he hath made the first *o* ......Heb 8:13
which decayeth and waxeth *o* ..Heb 8:13
the *o* time the holy women 1Pet 3:5
he was purged from his *o* 2Pet 1:9
spared not the *o* world 2Pet 2:5
an *o* commandment which 1John 2:7
o commandment is the word ...1John 2:7
were before of *o* ordained .....Jude 4
that *o* serpent, called the ......Rev 12:9
that *o* serpent, which is ....Rev 20:2

OLD TESTAMENT—*Books in the Bible (39) from Genesis to Malachi; the Scriptures of the Jewish people*

Characteristics of:
Inspired 2Tim 3:16
Authoritative ....John 10:34, 35
Written by the Holy Spirit ....Heb 3:7
Uses many figurative expressions ....Is 55:1, 12, 13
Written for our admonition 1Cor 10:1-11
Israel now blinded to 2Cor 3:14-16
Foreshadows the New....Heb 9:1-28

With the New Testament, unified in:
Authorship..............Heb 1:1
Plan of salvation 1Pet 1:9-12
Presenting Christ (see Messiah, the) ....Luke 24:25-44

OLIVE—*fruit of the olive tree*
sanctuary, and of *o* oil ....Ex 30:24
bring unto thee pure *o* oil .....Lev 24:2
a land of oil *o* and of 2Kin 18:32
cast off his flower as the *o* ....Job 15:33
thy children like *o* plants ......Ps 128:3
my brethren, bear *o* ....James 3:12

OLIVE TREE—*a prolific tree native to Palestine, known for its olives that were used primarily for oil*

Used for:
Oil of, many uses ....Ex 27:20
Temple furniture 1Kin 6:23
Temple construction 1Kin 6:31-33
Booths ....Neh 8:15

Cultivation of:
By grafting.............Rom 11:24
Hindered by disease .....Deut 28:40
Failure of, a great calamity ....Hab 3:17, 18
Poor provided for ....Deut 24:20
Palestine suitable for.....Deut 6:11

Figuratively of:
Peace ....Gen 8:11
Kingship ....Judg 9:8,9
Israel...................Jer 11:16
The righteous ....Ps 52:8
Faithful remnant ....Is 17:6
Gentile believers ....Rom 11:17, 24
True Church ....Rom 11:17, 24
Prophetic symbols ....Zech 4:3, 11, 12

See Oil

OLIVES, MOUNT OF—*hill in eastern Jerusalem*

Described as:
"The mount of Olives" ..Zech 14:4
"The hill that is before Jerusalem"............1Kin 11:7
"The mount of corruption" 2Kin 23:13
"The mount" ....Neh 8:15
"Olivet" ....Acts 1:12

Scene of:
David's flight 2Sam 15:30
Solomon's idolatry 2Kin 23:13
Ezekiel's vision..........Ezek 11:23
Postexilic festivities ......Neh 8:15
Zechariah's prophecy ....Zech 14:4
Triumphal entry ....Matt 21:1
Weeping ....Luke 19:37, 41
Great prophetic discourse.Matt 24:3
Ascension...............Acts 1:12

into the mount of *O* ....Matt 26:30
at the mount of *O* ....Mark 11:1
upon the mount of *O* ....Mark 13:3
into the mount of *O* ....Mark 14:26
called the mount of *O* ....Luke 19:29
called the mount of *O* ....Luke 21:37
to the mount of *O* ....Luke 22:39
unto the mount of *O*..........John 8:1

OLIVET—*See* Olives, Mount of

OLIVEYARD—*a grove of olive trees*
Freely given ....Josh 24:13
Taken in greed 2Kin 5:20, 26

[*also* oliveyards]
vineyards, their *o*, and ....Neh 5:11
o, and fruit trees in...........Neh 9:25

OLYMPAS (ō-lĭm'păs)—*meaning unknown*
Christian in Rome ....Rom 16:15

OMAR (ō'mer)—*"speaker; mountaineer"*
Grandson of Esau ....Gen 36:11, 15; 1Chr 1:36

OMEGA (ō-mĕ'gä)—*the last letter in the Greek alphabet*
Descriptive of Christ's infinity.............Rev 1:8, 11; Rev 21:6; Rev 22:13

OMEN—*a portent*
Forbidden ....Deut 18:10
The Lord causes to fail..Is 44:25

OMER—*dry measure, approximately three quarts equal to one-tenth ephah*

[*also* omers]
an *o* for every man ....Ex 16:16
did mete it with an *o* ....Ex 16:18
two *o* for one man ....Ex 16:22
Fill an *o* of it to be kept ......Ex 16:32
a pot, and put an *o* full ....Ex 16:33
an *o* is the tenth part of.......Ex 16:36

OMISSION, SINS OF—*sins committed out of neglect or apathy*

Concerning ordinances:
Moses' neglect of circumcision...........Ex 4:24-26
Israel's neglect of the tithe...................Mal 3:7-12
Christians neglecting to assemble ....Heb 10:25

Concerning moral duties:
Witnessing ....Ezek 33:1-6
Warning ....Jer 42:1-22
Watchfulness ....Matt 24:42-51; Matt 26:36-46

OMITTED—*neglected; left out*
o the weightier matters of .....Matt 23:23

OMNIPOTENCE—*infinite power*

Of God, expressed by His:
Names ("Almighty," etc.).Gen 17:1
Creative word ....Gen 1:3
Control of:
Nature ....Amos 4:13
Nations ....Amos 1:1—2:3
All things ....Ps 115:3
Power ....Rom 4:17-24
Unweariness ....Is 40:28

Of Christ, expressed by His power over:
Disease ....Matt 8:3
Unclean spirit ....Mark 1:23-27
Devil ....Matt 4:1-11
Death ....John 10:17, 18
Destiny ....Matt 25:31-33

Of the Holy Spirit, expressed by:
Christ's anointing ....Is 11:2
Confirmation of the
Gospel ....Rom 15:19

[*also* OMNIPOTENT]
for the Lord God *o* ....Rev 19:6

OMNIPRESENCE—*universal presence of God*
God ....Jer 23:23, 24
Christ ....Matt 18:20
Holy Spirit ....Ps 139:7-12

OMNISCIENCE—*infinite knowledge of God*
God ....Is 40:14
Christ ....Col 2:2, 3
Holy Spirit 1Cor 2:10-13

OMRI (ŏm′rī)—*"Jehovah apportions; pupil"*
1. Descendant of Benjamin .1Chr 7:8
2. Judahite 1Chr 9:4
3. Chief officer Issachar 1Chr 27:18
4. King of Israel; made king
by Israel's army 1Kin 16:15, 16
Prevails over Zimri and
Tibni 1Kin 16:17-23
Builds Samaria 1Kin 16:24
Reigns wickedly 1Kin 16:25-28

began Ahab the son of *O* 1Kin 16:29
Ahab the son of *O* reigned 1Kin 16:29
Ahab the son of *O* did evil 1Kin 16:30
Athaliah the daughter of *O* 2Chr 22:2
the statutes of *O* are kept .....Mic 6:16

ON—*See* INTRODUCTION

ON (ŏn)—*"sun; strength"*
1. Reubenite leader; joins
Korah's rebellion .....Num 16:1
2. City of Lower Egypt;
center of sun-worship. .Gen 41:45, 50
Called Bethshemesh .....Jer 43:13
See HERES

ONAM (ō′năm)—*"vigorous"*
1. Horite chief ....Gen 36:23
2. Man of Judah 1Chr 2:26, 28

ONAN (ō′năn)—*"vigorous"*
Second son of Judah;
slain for failure to
consummate union .....Gen 38:8-10

she called his name *O* ....Gen 38:4
of Judah; Er, and *O* ....Gen 46:12
and *O* died in the land of .....Gen 46:12
Judah were Er and *O* ....Num 26:19
and *O* died in the land of .....Num 26:19
of Judah; Er, and *O* 1Chr 2:3

ONCE—*one single time; former*
I will speak yet but this *o* .....Gen 18:32
I pray thee, my sin only this *o* .Ex 10:17
upon the horns of it *o* in ......Ex 30:10
o in the year shall he ....Ex 30:10
of Israel for all their sins *o* ....Lev 16:34
Let us go up at *o*, and ....Num 13:30
consume them at *o* ....Deut 7:22
go round about the city *o* .....Josh 6:3
going about it *o* ....Josh 6:11
compassed the city *o* ....Josh 6:14
I will speak but this *o* ....Judg 6:39
but this *o* with the fleece ......Judg 6:39
I pray thee, only this *o* ....Judg 16:28
be at *o* avenged of the ....Judg 16:28
even to the earth at *o* 1Sam 26:8
o in three years came the 1Kin 10:22
saved himself there, not *o* 2Kin 6:10
every three years *o* came 2Chr 9:21
and *o* in ten days store ....Neh 5:18
For God speaketh *o*, yea ....Job 33:14
God hath spoken *o*; twice .....Ps 62:11
in thy sight when *o* thou ......Ps 76:7
his ways shall fall at *o* ....Prov 28:18
destroy and devour at *o* ....Is 42:14
the land at this *o* ....Jer 10:18
I will this *o* cause them ....Jer 16:21
Yet *o*, it is a little ....Hag 2:6
When *o* the master of the .....Luke 13:25
he died unto sin *o* ....Rom 6:10
five hundred brethren at *o* 1Cor 15:6
I beaten with rods, *o* was 2Cor 11:25
the faith which *o* he ....Gal 1:23
let it not be *o* named ....Eph 5:3
o and again unto my ....Phil 4:16
unto you, even I Paul, *o* 1Thess 2:18
for those who were *o* ....Heb 6:4
for this he did *o*, when ....Heb 7:27
the high priest alone *o* ....Heb 9:7
o in the end of the world .....Heb 9:26
So Christ was *o* offered to .....Heb 9:28
the body of Jesus Christ *o* .....Heb 10:10
this word, Yet *o* more ....Heb 12:27
Christ also hath *o* suffered 1Pet 3:18
faith which was *o* delivered ....Jude 3

ONE, ONE'S—*See* INTRODUCTION

ONENESS—*unity*

Of Christ, with:
The Father ....John 10:30
Christians ....Heb 2:11

Among Christians of:
Baptized 1Cor 12:13
Union ....Ezek 37:16-24
Headship ....Ezek 34:23
Faith ....Eph 4:4-6
Mind ....Phil 2:2
Heart ....Acts 4:32
See UNITY OF BELIEVERS

ONESIMUS (ō-nĕs′ĭ-mŭs)—*"useful"*
Slave of Philemon
converted by Paul in
Rome ....Philem 10:17
With Tychicus, carries
Paul's letters to
Colossae and to
Philemon ....Col 4:7-9

O, a faithful and beloved ......Col 4:9
beseech thee for my son *O* ....Philem 10

ONESIPHOROUS (ŏn-ĕ-sĭf′ō-rŭs)—*"profit-bringer"*
Ephesian Christian
commended for his
service 2Tim 1:16-18

the household of *O* 2Tim 4:19

ONION—*a bulbous plant used for food*
Lusted after by Israelites..Num 11:5

ONLY—*alone in its class; however; merely*
his heart was *o* evil ....Gen 6:5
now thy son, thine *o* son ......Gen 22:2
withheld thy son, thine *o* ....Gen 22:16
o let us consent unto ....Gen 34:23
o the land of the priests ....Gen 47:22
o their little ones, and ....Gen 50:8
remain in the river *o* ....Ex 8:11
o he shall pay for the loss .....Ex 21:19
For that is his covering *o* ......Ex 22:27
O he shall not go in unto .....Lev 21:23
O thou shalt not number ......Num 1:49
O rebel not ye against ....Num 14:9
I will *o*, without doing ....Num 20:19
O the gold, and the silver .....Num 31:22
o I will pass through on ....Deut 2:28
O unto the land of the ....Deut 2:37
O take heed to thyself ....Deut 4:9
not live by bread *o* ....Deut 8:3
O ye shall not eat the ....Deut 12:16
O thou shalt not eat the ....Deut 15:23
man *o* that lay with her ....Deut 22:25
with you *o* do I make this .....Deut 29:14
O be thou strong and very ....Josh 1:7
o be strong and of a good .....Josh 1:18
o Rahab the harlot shall ......Josh 6:17
o the spoil thereof, and ......Josh 8:2
none of them, save Hazor *o* ...Josh 11:13
o divide thou it by lot ....Josh 13:6
thou shalt not have one lot *o* ..Josh 17:17
O that the generations ....Judg 3:2
it now be dry *o* upon the .....Judg 6:39
deliver us *o*, we pray thee .....Judg 10:15
and strengthen me..*o* ....Judg 16:28
o her lips moved, but her 1Sam 1:13
o the stump of Dagon was 1Sam 5:4
served the Lord *o* 1Sam 7:4
o be thou valiant for me 1Sam 18:17
o Jonathan and David 1Sam 20:39
king's sons; for Amnon *o* 2Sam 13:32
I will smite the king *o* 2Sam 17:2
O the people sacrificed 1Kin 3:2
o officer which was in 1Kin 4:19
the tribe of Judah *o* 1Kin 12:20
he *o* of Jeroboam shall 1Kin 14:13
even I *o*, remain a 1Kin 18:22
save *o* with the king of 1Kin 22:31
o in Kir-haraseth left 2Kin 3:25
but the tribe of Judah *o* 2Kin 17:18
o if they will observe to do 2Kin 21:8
O the Lord give thee 1Chr 22:12
save *o* to burn sacrifice 2Chr 2:6
the Lord their God *o* 2Chr 33:17
O Jonathan the son of ....Ezra 10:15
wrong to the king *o* ....Esth 1:16
o upon himself put not ....Job 1:12
O do not two things unto .....Job 13:20
Lord, *o* makest me dwell ......Ps 4:8
He *o* is my rock and my ......Ps 62:2
My soul, wait thou *o* ....Ps 62:5
even of thine *o* ....Ps 71:16
O with thine eyes shalt ....Ps 91:8
tender and *o* beloved in ....Prov 4:3
O by pride cometh ....Prov 13:10
An evil man seeketh *o* ....Prov 17:11
diligent tend *o* to ....Prov 21:5
every one that is hasty *o* ......Prov 21:5
this *o* have I found, that ......Eccl 7:29
she is the *o* one of her ....Song 6:9
o let us be called by thy ......Is 4:1
o to understand the ....Is 28:19
O acknowledge thine ....Jer 3:13
children of Judah have *o* ......Jer 32:30
An evil, an *o* evil ....Ezek 7:5
o shall be delivered ....Ezek 14:18
You *o* have I known of ....Amos 3:2
one mourneth for his *o* ....Zech 12:10
God, and him *o* shalt ....Matt 4:10
speak the word *o*, and ....Matt 8:8
with him, but *o* for the ....Matt 12:4
no man, save Jesus *o* ....Matt 17:8
not *o* do this which is ....Matt 21:21
forgive sins but God *o*? ....Mark 2:7
journey, save a staff *o* ....Mark 6:8
God, and him *o* shalt ....Luke 4:8
he had one *o* daughter ....Luke 8:42
for he is mine *o* child ....Luke 9:38
o had broken the sabbath .....John 5:18
And not for that nation *o* .....John 11:52
Lord, not my feet *o*, but ......John 13:9
o they were baptised in ....Acts 8:16
knowing *o* the baptism ....Acts 18:25
ready not to be bound *o* ....Acts 21:13
not *o* thou, but also all ....Acts 26:29
not *o* do the same, but ....Rom 1:32
then upon the circumcision *o* ..Rom 4:9
not to that *o* which is of ......Rom 4:16
not *o* so, but we also joy ......Rom 5:11
And not *o* this; but when .....Rom 9:10
needs be subject, not *o* ....Rom 13:5
To God *o* wise, be glory ......Rom 16:27
to whom she will; *o* in 1Cor 7:39
or came it unto you *o*? 1Cor 14:36
And not by his coming *o* 2Cor 7:7
And not that *o*, but who 2Cor 8:19
not *o* supplieth the want 2Cor 9:12
they had heard *o*, That ....Gal 1:23
This *o* would I learn of ....Gal 3:2
o use not liberty for an ....Gal 5:13
o lest they should suffer ......Gal 6:12
not *o* in this world, but ....Eph 1:21
O let your conversation ....Phil 1:27
not as in my presence *o* ....Phil 2:12

receiving, but ye *o* ....Phil 4:15
These *o* are my fellow workers .Col 4:11
unto you in word *o* 1Thess 1:5
not the gospel of God *o*.......1Thess 2:8
o he who now letteth will 2Thess 2:7
the *o* wise God, be honor 1Tim 1:17
is the blessed and *o*...........1Tim 6:15
there are not *o* vessels of 2Tim 2:20
O Luke is with me 2Tim 4:11
stood *o* in meats and ....Heb 9:10
offered up his *o* begotten .....Heb 11:17
I shake not the earth *o* ....Heb 12:26
word, and not hearers *o* ......James 1:22
not *o* to the good and 1Pet 2:18
and not for ours *o*, but 1John 2:2
not by water *o*, but by 1John 5:6
and not I *o*, but also all.......2John 1:1
denying the *o* Lord God ....Jude 4
o those men which have ......Rev 9:4
for thou *o* art holy: for ....Rev 15:4

ONLY BEGOTTEN—*only one born*

Of Christ's:

Incarnation ....John 1:14
Godhead ....John 1:18
Mission ....John 3:16, 18
1John 4:9

ONO (ō'nō) —*"grief of him"*

Town of Benjamin rebuilt by Shamed............1Chr 8:12
Reinhabited by returnees .Ezra 2:1, 33

villages in the plain of *O* ......Neh 6:2
Lod, and *O*, the valley ....Neh 11:35

ONWARD—*forward*

Israel went *o* in all ....Ex 40:36

ONYCHA—*ingredient in perfume*

Ingredient of incense .....Ex 30:34

ONYX—*"fingernail" (Greek)*

Translation of a Hebrew word indicating a precious stone .... {Job 28:16, Ezek 28:13}
Found in Havilah ....Gen 2:11-12
Places in high priest's ephod ....Ex 28:9-20
Gathered by David 1Chr 29:2

O stones, and stones to ....Ex 25:7
o stones, and stones to be .....Ex 35:9
they wrought *o* stones.........Ex 39:6

OPEN—*to unfasten; to unlock; to expose*

Descriptive of miracles on:

Earth...................Num16:30,32
Eyes ....John 9:10-32
Ears...................Mark7:34,35
Mouth ....Luke 1:64
Prison doors ....Acts 5:19, 23
Death 2Kin 4:35
Graves ....Matt 27:52

Descriptive of spiritual things:

God's provision ....Ps 104:28
God's bounty ....Mal 3:10
Christ's blood ....Zech 13:1
Man's corruption ....Rom 3:13
Spiritual eyesight Luke24:31,32
Door of faith ....Acts 14:27
Opportunity.............1Cor 16:9

[*also* OPENED, OPENEST, OPENETH, OPENING, OPENINGS, OPENLY]

in the *o* firmament of ....Gen 1:20
your eyes shall be *o* ....Gen 3:5
of them both were *o* ....Gen 3:7
which hath *o* her mouth ....Gen 4:11
that Noah *o* the window ......Gen 8:6
Leah was hated, he *o* her .....Gen 29:31
that was *o* by the way side? ...Gen 38:21
Joseph *o* all the storehouses ...Gen 41:56
we *o* our sacks, and ....Gen 43:21
she had *o* it, she saw the ......Ex 2:6
whatsoever *o* the womb ....Ex 13:2
to the Lord all that *o* ....Ex 13:15
if a man shall *o* a pit ....Ex 21:33
living bird loose into the *o* ....Lev 14:7
which they offer in the *o* ......Lev 17:5
all the first-born that *o*........Num 3:12
instead of such as *o*...........Num 8:16
And every *o* vessel, which.....Num 19:15
the Lord *o* the eyes of ....Num 22:31
man whose eyes are *o* ....Num 24:3
man whose eyes are *o* ....Num 24:15
earth *o* her mouth, and ....Deut 11:6
shalt *o* thine hand wide ....Deut 15:8
answer of peace, and *o* ....Deut 20:11
they left the city *o*, and ....Josh 8:17
he *o* not the doors of the .....Judg 3:25
she *o* a bottle of milk, and ....Judg 4:19
hast *o* thy mouth unto the.....Judg 11:36
days; there was no *o* 1Sam 3:1
o the doors of the house of ...1Sam 3:15
are encamped in the *o* 2Sam 11:11
carved with knobs and *o* 1Kin 6:18
palm trees and *o* flowers 1Kin 6:32
thine eyes may be *o* toward ...1Kin 8:29
Lord, I pray thee, *o* his 2Kin 6:17
Lord *o* their eyes, and 2Kin 6:20
Then *o* the door, and flee 2Kin 9:3
And he *o* it 2Kin 13:17
o, Lord, thine eyes, and 2Kin 19:16
and the *o* thereof every 1Chr 9:27
thine eyes may be *o* 2Chr 6:20
Now mine eyes shall be *o* 2Chr 7:15
o the doors of the house 2Chr 29:3
and thine eyes *o*, that thou ....Neh 1:6
Let not the gates..be *o*........Neh 7:3
Ezra *o* the book in the........Neh 8:5
he *o* it, all the people ....Neh 8:5
this *o* Job his mouth ....Job 3:1
speak, and *o* his lips ....Job 11:5
there can be no *o* ....Job 12:14
he *o* his eyes, and he is not ...Job 27:19
but I *o* my doors to the ....Job 31:32
I will *o* my lips and...........Job 32:20
doth Job *o* his mouth in.......Job 35:16
He *o* also their ear to.........Job 36:10
gates of death been *o* ....Job 38:17
their throat is an *o* ....Ps 5:9
they *o* their mouth ....Ps 35:21
dumb man that *o* not his ......Ps 38:13
mine ears hast thou *o* ....Ps 40:6
I will *o* my dark saying ....Ps 49:4
O Lord, *o* thou my lips ....Ps 51:15
I will *o* my mouth in a ....Ps 78:2
o thy mouth wide, and I ......Ps 81:10
righteousness hath he *o* ....Ps 98:2
thou *o* thine hand, they ....Ps 104:28
He *o* the rock, and the ....Ps 105:41
of the deceitful are *o* ....Ps 109:2
O..the gates of ....Ps 118:19
O thou mine eyes, that........Ps 119:18
I *o* my mouth, and panted .....Ps 119:131
in the *o* of the gates ....Prov 1:21
o of my lips shall be right .....Prov 8:6
he that *o* wide his lips ....Prov 13:3
a fool layeth *o* his folly ....Prov 13:16
O rebuke is better than ....Prov 27:5
O thy mouth for the dumb .....Prov 31:8
O thy mouth, judge ....Prov 31:9
She *o* her mouth with.........Prov 31:26
O to me, my sister, my ....Song 5:2
I *o* to my beloved; but........Song 5:6
o her mouth without ....Is 5:14
devour Israel with *o* ....Is 9:12
o not the house of his ....Is 14:17
so he shall *o*, and none ....Is 22:22
shut, and none shall *o* ....Is 22:22
O ye the gates, that the ....Is 26:2
o thine eyes, *o* Lord, and .....Is 37:17
To *o* the blind eyes, to........Is 42:7
o the ears, but he heareth .....Is 42:20
let the earth *o*, and let ....Is 45:8
Lord God hath *o* mine ear .....Is 50:5
afflicted, yet he *o* not his .....Is 53:7
is dumb, so he *o* not his ......Is 53:7
Their quiver is as an *o* ....Jer 5:16
shut up, and none shall *o* .....Jer 13:19
for unto thee have I *o* ....Jer 20:12
evidence which is *o* ....Jer 32:14
utmost border, *o* her..........Jer 50:26
enemies have *o* their..........Lam 2:16
the heavens were *o*, and ......Ezek 1:1
o thy mouth, and eat ....Ezek 2:8
wast cast out in the *o* ....Ezek 16:5
and hast *o* thy feet ....Ezek 16:25
fire all that *o* the womb ....Ezek 20:26
to *o* the mouth in the ....Ezek 21:22
shalt fall upon the *o* ....Ezek 29:5
will give thee the *o* of the .....Ezek 29:21
had *o* my mouth, until ....Ezek 33:22
and my mouth was *o* ....Ezek 33:22
him that is in the *o* field ......Ezek 33:27
I will *o* your graves ....Ezek 37:12
when I have *o* your............Ezek 37:13
shalt fall upon the *o* ....Ezek 39:5
sabbath it shall be *o* ....Ezek 46:1
new moon it shall be *o*.........Ezek 46:1
his windows being *o* ....Dan 6:10
and the books were *o* ....Dan 7:10
the rivers shall be *o* ....Nah 2:6
set wide *o* unto thine ....Nah 3:13
O thy doors, O Lebanon ......Zech 11:1
when they had *o* their ....Matt 2:11
he *o* his mouth, and ....Matt 5:2
shall reward thee *o* ....Matt 6:4
secret shall reward thee *o* .....Matt 6:6
secret, shall reward thee *o* ....Matt 6:18
knocketh it shall be *o* ....Matt 7:8
I will *o* my mouth in...........Matt 13:35
and when thou hast *o* ....Matt 17:27
he saw the heavens *o* ....Mark 1:10
no more *o* enter into the ......Mark 1:45
he spake that saying *o* ....Mark 8:32
his mouth was *o*...............Luke 1:64
Every male that *o* the.........Luke 2:23
And when he had *o* the ....Luke 4:17
knocketh it shall be *o* ....Luke 11:10
they may *o* unto him ....Luke 12:36
while he *o* to us the ....Luke 24:32
shall see heaven *o* ....John 1:51
seeketh to be known *o* ....John 7:4
not *o*, but as it were in ....John 7:10
no man spake *o* of him ....John 7:13
To him the porter *o* ....John 10:3
walked no more *o* among .....John 11:54
I spake *o* to the world ....John 18:20
I see the heavens *o* ....Acts 7:56
his shearer, so *o* he not ....Acts 8:32
Then Philip *o* his mouth ......Acts 8:35
she *o* her eyes; and when .....Acts 9:40
saw heaven *o*, and a ....Acts 10:11
Then Peter *o* his mouth ....Acts 10:34
and showed him *o* ....Acts 10:40
she *o* not the gate for.........Acts 12:14
all the doors were *o* ....Acts 16:26
seeing the prison doors *o*.......Acts 16:27
a door was *o* unto me of 2Cor 2:12
with *o* face beholding as 2Cor 3:18
that I may *o* my mouth ....Eph 6:19
he made a show of them *o* ....Col 2:15
that God would *o* unto........Col 4:3
men's sins are *o* 1Tim 5:24
things are naked and *o*.........Heb 4:13
and put him to an *o* ....Heb 6:6
and his ears are *o* unto 1Pet 3:12
he that *o*, and no man ....Rev 3:7
shutteth and no man *o* ....Rev 3:7
set before thee an *o* ....Rev 3:8
behold, a door was *o* in.......Rev 4:1
Who is worthy to *o* the ....Rev 5:2
worthy to *o* and to read.......Rev 5:4
the book, and to *o* the........Rev 5:9
when the Lamb *o* one of......Rev 6:1
And when he had *o* the ....Rev 6:3
And when he had *o* the ....Rev 6:7
when he had *o* the sixth.......Rev 6:12
And he *o* the bottomless ......Rev 9:2
little book which is *o* ....Rev 10:8
earth *o* her mouth, and ....Rev 12:16
testimony in heaven was *o* ....Rev 15:5
and the books were *o* ....Rev 20:12
another book was *o*............Rev 20:12

OPERATION—*work; performance*

[*also* OPERATIONS]
the Lord, nor the *o* of ....Ps 28:5
neither consider the *o* of ......Is 5:12
through the faith of the *o* .....Col 2:12
there are diversities of *o* 1Cor 12:6

OPHEL (ō'fĕl)—*"small white cloud"*
South extremity of Jerusalem's eastern hill .Neh 3:15-27
Fortified by Jotham and Manasseh 2Chr 27:3
Residence of Nethinim . . .Neh 3:26

and compassed about *O* 2Chr 33:14
Nethinim dwelt in *O* ....Neh 11:21

OPHIR (ō'fĕr)—*"fruitful region"*
1. Son of Joktan ....Gen 10:26, 29
2. Land, probably in southeast Arabia, inhabited by descendants of 1. . . .Gen 10:29, 30
Famous for its gold ......1 Chr 29:4

they came to *O*, and fetched . . .1Kin 9:28
brought gold from *O* 1Kin 10:11
brought in from *O* great 1Kin 10:11
ships of Tharshish to go to *O* . .1Kin 22:48
O, and Havilah, and Jobab 1Chr 1:23
servants of Solomon to *O* 2Chr 8:18
which brought gold from *O* 2Chr 9:10
the gold of *O* as the stones ....Job 22:24
valued with the gold of *O* .....Job 28:16
the queen in gold of *O* ....Ps 45:9
the golden wedge of *O* ....Is 13:12

OPHNI (ŏf'nī)—*"wearisomeness"*
Village of Benjamin......Josh 18:24

OPHRAH (ŏf'rä)—*"a fawn"*
1. Judahite 1Chr 4:14
2. Town in Benjamin near Michmash ....Josh 18:21, 23
3. Town in Manasseh; home of Gideon ....Judg 6:11, 15
Site of Gideon's burial . . .Judg 8:32

it is yet in *O* of the ....Judg 6:24
put it in his city, even in *O* ....Judg 8:27
his father's house at *O* ....Judg 9:5
the way that leadeth to *O* 1Sam 13:17
and Meonothai begat *O* 1Chr 4:14

OPINION—*advice; conviction*

[*also* OPINIONS]
halt ye between two *o*? 1Kin 18:21
not show you mine *o*..........Job 32:6
I also will show mine *o*........Job 32:10
I also will show mine *o*........Job 32:17

OPPORTUNITY—*the best time for something; favorable circumstances*

Kinds of:
Rejected ....Matt 23:37
Spurned ....Luke 14:16-24
Prepared ....Acts 8:35-39
Providential 1Cor 16:9
Good...................Gal 6:10

Loss of, due to:
Unbelief ....Num 14:40-43
Neglect ....Jer 8:20
Unpreparedness ....Matt 24:50, 51
Blindness ....Luke 19:41, 42

time he sought *o* to ....Matt 26:16
sought *o* to betray him ....Luke 22:6
but ye lacked *o*...............Phil 4:10
have had *o* to have ....Heb 11:15

OPPOSE—*stand against*

Of evil things:
Proud ....James 4:6

Of good things:
Truth...................2Tim 3:8

[*also* OPPOSED, OPPOSEST, OPPOSETH]
hand thou *o* thyself ....Job 30:21
And when they *o* ....Acts 18:6
Who *o* and exalteth 2Thess 2:4

and *o* of science falsely 1Tim 6:20
instructing those that *o* 2Tim 2:25

OPPRESSION—*subjection to unjust hardships*

Kinds of:
Personal ....Is 38:14
National ....Ex 3:9
Economic ....Mic 2:1, 2
Messianic ....Is 53:7
Spiritual ....Acts 10:38

Those subject to:
Widows.................Zech 7:10
Hired servant ....Deut 24:14
Poor ....Ps 12:5
People..................Is 3:5
Soul....................Ps 54:3

Evils of, bring:
Guilt ....Is 59:12, 13
Reproach ....Prov 14:31
Poverty ....Prov 22:16
Judgment ....Ezek 18:12, 13

Punishment of:
God's judgment ....Is 49:26
Captivity...............Is 14:2, 4
Destruction of ....Ps 72:4

Protection against:
Sought in prayer.........Deut 26:7
Given by the LORD .....Ps 103:6
Secured in refuge ....Ps 9:9

Agents of:
Nations ....Judg 10:12
Enemy ....Ps 42:9
Ps 106:42
Wicked ....Ps 55:3
Man....................Ps 119:134
Leaders.................Prov 28:16
Sword ....Jer 46:16
Jer 50:16
Devil ....Acts 10:38
Rich....................James 2:6

[*also* OPPRESS, OPPRESSED, OPPRESSETH, OPPRESSING, OPPRESSIONS]
stranger, nor *o* him ....Ex 22:21
Also thou shalt not *o* a........Ex 23:9
ye shall not *o* one ....Lev 25:14
shall not therefore *o* one ....Lev 25:17
against the enemy that *o* ......Num 10:9
thou shalt not *o* him ....Deut 23:16
thou shalt be only *o* and ......Deut 28:29
thou shalt be only *o* and ......Deut 28:33
by reason of them that *o*......Judg 2:18
mightily *o* the children ....Judg 4:3
the hand of all that *o* ....Judg 6:9
and *o* the children of ....Judg 10:8
of them that *o* you 1Sam 10:18
whom have I *o*? or of.........1Sam 12:3
defrauded us, nor *o* us ....1 Sam 12:4
he saw the *o* of Israel.........2Kin 13:4
king of Syria *o* them 2Kin 13:4
Hazael king of Syria *o* 2Kin 13:22
And Asa *o* some of the 2Chr 16:10
that thou shouldest *o* ....Job 10:3
the multitude of *o* ....Job 35:9
they make the *o* to cry ....Job 35:9
openeth their ears in *o* ....Job 36:15
be a refuge for the *o* ....Ps 9:9
the fatherless and the *o* ....Ps 10:18
of the earth may no more *o* . . .Ps 10:18
From the wicked that *o* ....Ps 17:9
because of the *o* of the ....Ps 43:2
forgettest..our *o*? ....Ps 44:24
he fighting daily *o* me.........Ps 56:1
Trust not in *o*, and ....Ps 62:10
wickedly concerning *o*.........Ps 73:8
O let not the *o* return ....Ps 74:21
for all that are *o* ....Ps 103:6
Their enemies also *o*..........Ps 106:42
brought low through *o* ....Ps 107:39
let not the proud *o* ....Ps 119:122
judgment for the *o* ....Ps 146:7
neither *o* the afflicted in ......Prov 22:22
A poor man that *o* the.........Prov 28:3
the *o* that are done under .....Eccl 4:1
tears of such as were *o*........Eccl 4:1
If thou seest the *o* of the.......Eccl 5:8
Surely *o* maketh a wise ....Eccl 7:7
judgment, relieve the *o* ....Is 1:17
the people shall be *o* ....Is 3:5
judgment, but behold *o* ....Is 5:7
no more rejoice, O thou *o* ....Is 23:12
word, and trust in *o* ....Is 30:12
despiseth the gain of *o* ....Is 33:15
O Lord, I am *o* ....Is 38:14
Assyrian *o* them without ......Is 52:4
He was *o*, and he was ....Is 53:7
thou shalt be far from *o*.......Is 54:14
to let the *o* go free, and ......Is 58:6
speaking *o* and revolt ....Is 59:13
she is wholly *o* in the ....Jer 6:6
If ye *o* not the stranger ....Jer 7:6
o, and for violence ....Jer 22:17
I will punish all that *o* ....Jer 30:20
our nativity, from the *o* ....Jer 46:16
for fear of the *o* sword........Jer 50:16
children of Judah were *o* ......Jer 50:33
hath not *o* any, but hath ......Ezek 18:7
Hath *o* the poor and needy....Ezek 18:12
they dealt by *o* with the.......Ezek 22:7
land have used *o* ....Ezek 22:29
have *o* the stranger ....Ezek 22:29
shall no more *o* my ....Ezek 45:8
inheritance by *o* ....Ezek 46:18
Ephraim is *o* and ....Hos 5:11
hand: he loveth to *o* ....Hos 12:7
which *o* the poor, which ......Amos 4:1
polluted, to the *o*.............Zeph 3:1
o the hireling in ....Mal 3:5
all that were *o* of the ....Acts 10:38

OPPRESSOR—*one who exploits others*

[*also* OPPRESSORS]
not the voice of the *o*.........Job 3:18
is hidden to the *o* ....Job 15:20
and the heritage of *o* ....Job 27:13
leave me not to mine *o* ....Ps 119:121
Envy thou not the *o*, and .....Prov 3:31
is also a great *o* ....Prov 28:16
side of their *o* there was ......Eccl 4:1
children are their *o*, and ......Is 3:12
the rod of his *o* ....Is 9:4
o are consumed out of ....Is 16:4
Lord because of the *o* ....Is 19:20
of the fury of the *o*...........Is 51:13
is the fury of the *o*? ....Is 51:13
of the hand of the *o* ....Jer 21:12
of the hand of the *o* ....Jer 22:3
the fierceness of the *o* ....Jer 25:38
no *o* shall pass through ....Zech 9:8
out of him every *o* ....Zech 10:4

OR—*See* INTRODUCTION

ORACLE—*a revelation; a wise saying*

Descriptive of the Holy of Holies:
Place in temple..........1Kin 6:16
Direction of prayer ......Ps 28:2
Source of truth 1Sam 23:9-12

Descriptive of God's Word:
Received by Israel.......Acts 7:38
Test of truth 1Pet 4:11

[*also* ORACLES]
inquired at the *o* of God 2Sam 16:23
temple and of the *o* 1Kin 6:5
And the *o* he prepared in 1Kin 6:19
the *o* in the forepart was 1Kin 6:20
of gold before the *o* 1Kin 6:21
altar that was by the *o* 1Kin 6:22
the *o* he made two 1Kin 6:23
entering of the *o* he 1Kin 6:31
left, before the *o* 1Kin 7:49
his place, into the *o* of........1Kin 8:6
place before the *o* 1Kin 8:8
chains, as in the *o* 2Chr 3:16
manner before the *o* 2Chr 4:20
his place, to the *o* of the......2Chr 5:7
from the ark before the *o* 2Chr 5:9
were committed the *o* of ......Rom 3:2
principles of the *o* ....Heb 5:12

ORATION—*formal discourse*
Character of:
Egotistical .... Acts 12:21-23
Prejudiced .... Acts 24:1-9
Inspired .... Acts 26:1-29

ORATOR—*an eloquent speaker*
and the eloquent *o* .... Is 3:3
a certain *o* named Tertullus ... Acts 24:1

ORCHARD—*a cultivated garden or park*
Source of fruits .... Song 4:13
Source of nuts .... Song 6:11

[*also* ORCHARDS]
I made me gardens and *o* ..... Eccl 2:5

ORCHESTRA—*a group of musicians playing together*
Instituted by David 2Sam 6:5

ORDAIN—*establish; appoint; set; decree*
As appointment to office:
Idolatrous priests 1Kin 13:33
Priesthood .... Lev 8:1-36
Prophet .... Jer 1:5
Royal officer .... Dan 2:24
Apostles .... Mark 3:14
Christ as judge .... Acts 10:42
Elders .... Titus 1:5
Paul as a preacher 1Tim 2:7
Christ as high priest ..... Heb 5:1
As appointment of temporal things:
World order .... Ps 8:3
Institution of:
Passover .... Ps 81:5
Government .... Rom 13:1
Life .... Num 24:23
Ps 139:16
Man's steps .... Prov 20:24
Offering .... Num 28:6
Law .... Acts 7:53
Gal 3:19
As appointment of eternal things:
Covenant .... Ps 111:9
Salvation .... Acts 13:48
Hidden wisdom 1Cor 2:7
Good works .... Eph 2:10
Apostles .... Jude 4

[*also* ORDAINED, ORDAINETH]
And Jeroboam *o* a feast in 1Kin 12:32
o a feast unto the children 1Kin 12:33
had *o* to burn incense 2Kin 23:5
the seer did *o* in their 1Chr 9:22
Also I will *o* a place for 1Chr 17:9
And he *o* him priests for 2Chr 11:15
with singing, as it was *o* 2Chr 23:18
the instruments *o* by 2Chr 29:27
The Jews *o*, and took .... Esth 9:27
he *o* his arrows against .... Ps 7:13
thou *o* strength because .... Ps 8:2
have *o* a lamp for mine .... Ps 132:17
Lord, thou wilt *o* peace .... Is 26:12
Tophet is *o* of old; yea .... Is 30:33
thou hast *o* them for .... Hab 1:12
chosen you, and *o* .... John 15:16
must one be *o* to be a .... Acts 1:22
when they had *o* them .... Acts 14:23
were *o* of the apostles .... Acts 16:4
that man whom he hath *o* ..... Acts 17:31
which was *o* to life, I .... Rom 7:10
And so *o* I in all 1Cor 7:17
Lord *o* that they which 1Cor 9:14
and *o* elders in every city ..... Titus 1:5
every high priest is *o* to ...... Heb 8:3
these things were thus *o* ...... Heb 9:6

ORDER—*harmony; symmetry; in proper places*
As an arrangement in rows:
Wood for sacrifices ...... Gen 22:9
Lamps set orderly .... Ex 27:21
Battle formation 1Chr 12:38
Words logically developed. Job 33:5
Consecutive narrative .... Luke 1:3
Logical defense .... Job 13:18
Absence of .... Job 10:22
As a classification according to work:
Priestly service 2Kin 23:4
Christ's priesthood .... Ps 110:4
Church services 1Cor 11:34
Church officers .... Titus 1:5
Of something prescribed:
Rules and regulations .... Judg 13:12
Ritual regulations 1Chr 15:13
Church regulations 1Cor 14:40
Subjection to 1Chr 25:2, 6
Of preparation for death:
Ahithophel's 2Sam 17:23
Hezekiah's 2Kin 20:1
Figurative of:
God's covenant 2Sam 23:5
Believer's life .... Ps 37:23
Man's sins .... Ps 50:21

[*also* ORDERED, ORDERETH, ORDERINGS, ORDERLY]
set in *o* one against .... Ex 26:17
lamps to be set in *o* .... Ex 39:37
the table, and set in *o* .... Ex 40:4
that are to be set in *o* .... Ex 40:4
And he set the bread in *o* ..... Ex 40:23
lay the wood in *o* upon .... Lev 1:7
shall lay them in *o* .... Lev 1:12
shall Aaron *o* it from .... Lev 24:3
he shall set it in *o* .... Lev 24:8
she had laid in *o* upon .... Josh 2:6
top of this rock, in the *o* ...... Judg 6:26
he put the wood in *o* 1Kin 18:33
he said, Who shall *o* the 1Kin 20:14
according to their *o* 1Chr 6:32
according to the *o* 1Chr 23:31
the *o* of them in their 1Chr 24:19
according to the *o* of 2Chr 8:14
house of the Lord was set in *o*. 2Chr 29:35
I would *o* my cause .... Job 23:4
o our speech by reason .... Job 37:19
be reckoned up in *o* .... Ps 40:5
to him that *o* his .... Ps 50:23
o my steps in thy word .... Ps 119:133
and set in *o* many .... Eccl 12:9
kingdom, to *o* it, and .... Is 9:7
declare it, and set it in *o* ..... Is 44:7
O ye the buckler and .... Jer 46:3
and thirty in *o* .... Ezek 41:6
in *o* a declaration of .... Luke 1:1
before God in the *o* of .... Luke 1:8
expounded it by *o* .... Acts 11:4
and Phrygia in *o* .... Acts 18:23
thyself also walkest *o* .... Acts 21:24
every man in his own *o* 1Cor 15:28
as I have given *o* to the 1Cor 16:1
beholding your *o* .... Col 2:5
ever after the *o* of .... Heb 5:6
ever after the *o* of .... Heb 6:20
rise after the *o* of .... Heb 7:11
not be called after the *o* ...... Heb 7:11

ORDINANCE—*regulation established for proper procedure; law*
Descriptive of:
Ritual observance .... Heb 9:1, 10
God's laws .... Is 24:5
God's laws in nature ..... Jer 31:35
Man's regulations .... Neh 10:32
Man's laws 1Pet 2:13
Apostolic messages 1Cor 11:2
Jewish legalism .... Eph 2:15
Of the Gospel:
Baptism .... Matt 28:19
Lord's Supper 1Cor 11:23-29
Preaching the Word ..... Rom 10:15

[*also* ORDINANCES]
keep it a feast by an *o* .... Ex 12:14
your generations by an *o* ...... Ex 12:17
this thing for an *o* .... Ex 12:24
is the *o* of the passover .... Ex 12:43
therefore keep this *o* in .... Ex 13:10
a statute and an *o* .... Ex 15:25
thou shalt teach them *o* .... Ex 18:20
neither..walk in their *o* .... Lev 18:3
shall ye keep mine *o* .... Lev 18:30
therefore keep mine *o* .... Lev 22:9
all the *o* of the passover ...... Num 9:12
according to the *o* of the ...... Num 9:14
ye shall have one *o* .... Num 9:14
shall be to you for an *o* .... Num 10:8
One *o* shall be both for .... Num 15:15
an *o* for ever in your .... Num 15:15
to thy sons, by an *o* .... Num 18:8
This is the *o* of the law .... Num 19:2
This is the *o* of the law .... Num 31:21
a statute and an *o* in .... Josh 24:25
it a statute and an *o* for 1Sam 30:25
or after their *o*, or after 2Kin 17:34
This is an *o* for ever 2Chr 2:4
and the *o* by the hand 2Chr 33:8
fire according to the *o* 2Chr 35:13
after the *o* of David king ...... Ezra 3:10
Knowest thou the *o* of .... Job 38:33
and the *o* that he gave .... Ps 99:7
according to thine *o* .... Ps 119:91
forsook not the *o* of .... Is 58:2
they ask of me the *o* of .... Is 58:2
not appointed the *o* of .... Jer 33:25
and keep mine *o*, and .... Ezek 11:20
all the *o* thereof, and all ..... Ezek 43:11
and all the *o* thereof, and do. . Ezek 43:11
concerning all the *o* of .... Ezek 44:5
Concerning the *o* of oil .... Ezek 45:14
by a perpetual *o* unto .... Ezek 46:14
gone away from mine *o* .... Mal 3:7
we have kept his *o* .... Mal 3:14
and *o* of the Lord .... Luke 1:6
resisteth the *o* of God .... Rom 13:2
the handwriting of *o* .... Col 2:14

ORDINARY—*usual; routine*
diminished thine *o* food .... Ezek 16:27

OREB (ō'rĕb)—*"a raven"*
1. Midianite prince slain by Gideon .... Judg 7:25
2. Rock on which Oreb was slain .... Judg 7:25

princes of Midian, *O* .... Judg 8:3
their nobles like *O* .... Ps 83:11
Midian at the rock of *O* .... Is 10:26

OREN (ō'rĕn)—*"pine; strength"*
Judahite 1Chr 2:25

ORGAN—*a wind instrument*
Of ancient origin .... Gen 4:21
Used in:
Entertainments .... Job 21:12
God's worship .... Ps 150:4

ORION (ō-rī'ŏn)—*"strong"*
Brilliant constellation .... Job 9:9

loose the bands of *O*? .... Job 38:31
maketh the seven stars and *O* . Amos 5:8

ORNAMENT—*outward adornment of the body or clothes*
Figurative of:
Wisdom's instruction ..... Prov 1:9
Reproof received .... Prov 25:12
God's provisions .... Ezek 16:7-14
Apostasy from God ...... Jer 4:30
See CLOTHING; JEWELS

[*also* ORNAMENTS]
put on him his *o* .... Ex 33:4
themselves of their *o* .... Ex 33:6
and took away the *o* .... Judg 8:21
put on *o* of gold upon 2Sam 1:24
give to thine head an *o* .... Prov 4:9
their tinkling *o* about .... Is 3:18
the *o* of thy molten .... Is 30:22
as with an *o* .... Is 49:18
decketh himself with *o* .... Is 61:10
Can a maid forget her *o* ...... Jer 2:32
for the beauty of his *o* .... Ezek 7:20
deckedst thyself with *o* .... Ezek 23:40
the *o* of a meek and 1Pet 3:4

ORNAN (ôr'năn)—*"active"—Jebusite from whom David bought a piece of land*

threshing floor of *O* 1Chr 21:15
O turned back, and saw 1Chr 21:20
Now *O* was threshing 1Chr 21:20
Then David said to *O*.........1Chr 21:22
So David said to *O*, Nay 1Chr 21:24
threshing floor of *O* the 1Chr 21:28

ORPAH (ôr'pä)—*"fawn; youthful freshness"*
Ruth's sister-in-law ......Ruth 1:4, 14

ORPHANS—*children deprived of parents by death*
Description of...........Lam 5:3
Provision for ....Deut 24:17, 21
Job helps ....Job 29:12
Visitation of commended .James 1:27
Christians not left "orphans" ....John 14:18

OSEE (ō'zē)—*Greek name for the prophet Hosea*
Quoted by Paul ....Rom 9:25

OSHEA (ō-shē'ä)—*"God saves"*
Same as Joshua ....Num 13:8, 16

OSPRAY—*a dark brown eagle*
Unclean bird............Lev 11:13

OSSIFRAGE—*Latin for bone breaker*
Unclean bird (eagle).....Lev 11:13

OSTENTATIOUS—*vain, ambitious*

Manifested in:
Boastfulness ....Luke 18:10-14
Hypocrisy..............Matt 6:1-7, 16
Conceit................2Sam 15:1-6
Egotism ....Acts 12:20-23

OSTRACISM—*exclusion of a person from society*
Accepted ....Luke 6:22
See EXCOMMUNICATION

OSTRICH—*large, flightless bird*
Figurative of cruelty .....Lam 4:3

feathers unto the *o*? ....Job 39:13

OTHER—*second; different; the one left*

[*also* OTHERS]
name of the *o* Zillah..........Gen 4:19
And he stayed yet *o* ....Gen 8:10
the one from the *o* ....Gen 13:11
is none *o* but the house ....Gen 28:17
serve with me yet seven *o* .....Gen 29:27
if thou shalt take *o* wives .....Gen 31:50
seven *o* kine came up ....Gen 41:3
may send away your *o* ....Gen 43:14
of Egypt even to the *o* ....Gen 47:21
and the name of the *o* ....Ex 1:15
turned again as his *o*..........Ex 4:7
one came not near the *o* ....Ex 14:20
one side, and the *o* on ....Ex 17:12
And the name of the *o* ....Ex 18:4
shalt have no *o* gods ....Ex 20:3
the name of *o* gods ....Ex 23:13
and two rings in the *o* ....Ex 25:12
one end, and the *o* ....Ex 25:19
cherub on the *o* end ....Ex 25:19
o five curtains shall be ....Ex 26:3
on the *o* side shall be ....Ex 27:15
the *o* six names of the ....Ex 28:10
of the rest on the *o*...........Ex 28:10
two *o* rings of gold thou ......Ex 28:27
against the *o* coupling.........Ex 28:27
And thou shalt take the *o* .....Ex 29:19
shall ye make any *o* ....Ex 30:32
and on the *o* were they ....Ex 32:15
shalt worship no *o* god ....Ex 34:14
and the *o* five curtains ....Ex 36:10
of the *o* side of the ....Ex 36:32
two rings unto the *o* ....Ex 37:3
out of the *o* side thereof ......Ex 37:18
the *o* side of the court ....Ex 38:15
And they made two *o*..........Ex 39:20
over against the *o* ....Ex 39:20
and the *o* for a burnt ....Lev 5:7
put on *o* garments, and ....Lev 6:11
may be used in any *o* ....Lev 7:24
he brought the *o* ram ....Lev 8:22
But all *o* flying creeping ......Lev 11:23
the *o* for a sin offering ....Lev 12:8
no lower than the *o* ....Lev 13:26
offering, and the *o* a burnt ....Lev 14:22
they shall take *o* stones ....Lev 14:42
and he shall take *o* ....Lev 14:42
and the *o* for a burnt ....Lev 15:15
and the *o* lot for the ....Lev 16:8
beside the *o* in her life ....Lev 18:18
separated you from *o* ....Lev 20:24
the *o* shall not rule with........Lev 25:53
and the *o* for a burnt ....Num 6:11
and the *o* for a burnt ....Num 8:12
and the *o* did set up the ......Num 10:21
and the name of the *o* ....Num 11:26
and pitched on the *o* side .....Num 21:13
o lamb shalt thou offer........Num 28:4
of the sons of the *o*...........Num 36:3
heaven unto the *o* ....Deut 4:32
shalt have none *o* gods ....Deut 5:7
Ye shall not go after *o*........Deut 6:14
that they may serve *o* ....Deut 7:4
walk after *o* gods, and ....Deut 8:19
turn aside, and serve *o*........Deut 11:16
Are they not on the *o* ....Deut 11:30
Let us go after *o* gods ....Deut 13:2
even unto the *o* end of........Deut 13:7
gone and served *o* gods ....Deut 17:3
speak in the name of *o* ....Deut 18:20
to go after *o* gods to serve ....Deut 28:14
earth even unto the *o* ....Deut 28:64
thou shalt serve *o* ....Deut 28:64
went and served *o* gods ....Deut 29:26
and worship *o* gods, and ......Deut 30:17
are turned unto *o* gods........Deut 31:18
will they turn unto *o* ....Deut 31:20
on the *o* side Jordan ....Josh 2:10
the *o* issued out of the ....Josh 8:22
their land on the *o* side ....Josh 12:1
of Moab, on the *o* side ....Josh 13:32
which were on the *o* side......Josh 17:5
out of the *o* half tribe.........Josh 21:27
the *o* half thereof gave ....Josh 22:7
dwelt on the *o* side ....Josh 24:2
they served *o* gods............Josh 24:2
from the *o* side of the ....Josh 24:3
served on the *o* side of........Josh 24:14
Lord, to serve *o* gods ....Josh 24:16
followed *o* gods, of the ....Judg 2:12
in following *o* gods to ....Judg 2:19
to Gideon on the *o* side.......Judg 7:25
that were on the *o* side ....Judg 10:8
and pitched on the *o* side .....Judg 11:18
be like any *o* man ....Judg 16:17
the *o* with his left ....Judg 16:29
kill, as at *o* times, in..........Judg 20:31
name of the *o* Ruth ....Ruth 1:4
and the name of the *o* 1Sam 1:2
and served *o* gods 1Sam 8:8
sharp rock on the *o*............1Sam 14:4
and the name of the *o* 1Sam 14:4
my son will be on the *o*.......1Sam 14:40
hand, as at *o* times 1Sam 18:10
sat upon his seat, as at *o* 1Sam 20:25
went over to the *o*............1Sam 26:13
and put on *o* raiment 1Sam 28:8
were on the *o* side of the 1Sam 31:7
they that were on the *o* 1Sam 31:7
you in scarlet, with *o* 2Sam 1:24
the *o* on the *o* side of the 2Sam 2:13
one rich, and the *o* 2Sam 12:1
but the one smote the *o*........2Sam 14:6
and *o* instruments of 2Sam 24:22
the *o* woman said, Nay 1Kin 3:22
and half to the *o* 1Kin 3:25
cubits the *o* wing of the 1Kin 6:24
uttermost part of the *o*........1Kin 6:24
was it of the *o* cherub 1Kin 6:26
the two leaves of the *o*........1Kin 6:34
of the floor to the *o* 1Kin 7:7
and seven for the *o* 1Kin 7:17
round about upon the *o* 1Kin 7:20
but go and serve *o* gods.......1Kin 9:6
one side and on the *o*.........1Kin 10:20
not go after *o* gods 1Kin 11:10
gone and made thee *o* gods ...1Kin 14:9
over against the *o* 1Kin 20:29
saw the water on the *o*........2Kin 3:22
the priest, and the *o* 2Kin 12:7
shall not fear *o* gods 2Kin 17:35
shall ye fear *o* gods 2Kin 17:38
on the *o* side Jordan 1Chr 6:78
And *o* of their brethren 1Chr 9:32
Eliezer had none *o* sons.......1Chr 23:17
o wing was likewise...........2Chr 3:11
to the wing of the *o* 2Chr 3:11
one wing of the *o* cherub 2Chr 3:12
the *o* wing was five 2Chr 3:12
to the wing of the *o* 2Chr 3:12
shall go and serve *o* 2Chr 7:19
and on the *o* upon the 2Chr 9:19
with them *o* beside 2Chr 20:1
incense unto *o* gods...........2Chr 28:25
took counsel to keep *o*.........2Chr 30:23
they kept *o* seven days 2Chr 30:23
gods of the nations of *o* 2Chr 32:17
and *o* of the Levites, all.......2Chr 34:12
the *o* holy offerings sod 2Chr 35:13
and ten, and *o* vessels ....Ezra 1:10
repaired the *o* piece ....Neh 3:11
o half of them held both ......Neh 4:16
o men have our lands ....Neh 5:5
children of the *o* Elam ....Neh 7:34
the *o* Jews that were in ....Esth 9:16
withereth before any *o* ....Job 8:12
out of the earth shall *o* ....Job 8:19
number, and set *o* in their ....Job 34:24
leave their wealth to *o* ....Ps 49:10
not in trouble as *o*.............Ps 73:5
are they plagued like *o*.........Ps 73:5
thine honor unto *o* ....Prov 5:9
dieth, so dieth the *o* ....Eccl 3:19
one over against the *o* ....Eccl 7:14
likewise hast cursed *o* ....Eccl 7:22
o lords besides thee...........Is 26:13
Yet will I gather *o* to him .....Is 56:8
burned incense unto *o* ....Jer 1:16
shall be turned unto *o* ....Jer 6:12
after *o* gods whom ye ....Jer 7:9
went after *o* gods to ....Jer 11:10
have walked after *o* gods......Jer 16:11
incense in it unto *o* ....Jer 19:4
and worshiped *o* gods ....Jer 22:9
go not after *o* gods to..........Jer 25:6
Israel, and among *o* ....Jer 32:20
go not after *o* gods to..........Jer 35:15
and to serve *o* gods ....Jer 44:3
burning incense unto *o* ....Jer 44:8
the one toward the *o* ....Ezek 1:23
to the *o* he said in mine.......Ezek 9:5
o daubed it with...............Ezek 13:10
Go thee one way or *o* ....Ezek 21:16
on the *o* side, which was ......Ezek 40:40
five cubits on the *o* ....Ezek 41:2
palm tree on the *o* ....Ezek 41:19
two leaves for the *o* ....Ezek 41:24
shall put on *o* garments ....Ezek 42:14
and on the *o* side of the ......Ezek 45:7
length as one of the *o* ....Ezek 48:8
there is none *o* that can ....Dan 2:11
their hats, and their *o*.........Dan 3:21
diverse from all the *o* ....Dan 7:19
of the *o* which came ....Dan 7:20
behold, there stood *o* ....Dan 12:5
who look to *o* gods, and ......Hos 3:1
where is any *o* that may.......Hos 13:10
thou stoodest on the *o*........Obad 11
the *o* upon the left side ....Zech 4:3
I cut asunder mine *o*..........Zech 11:14
he saw *o* two brethren ....Matt 4:21
turn to him the *o*.............Matt 5:39
do ye more than *o*?...........Matt 5:47
one, and love the *o* ....Matt 6:24
one and despise the *o*.........Matt 6:24
to depart unto the *o* side......Matt 8:18
he was come to the *o* ....Matt 8:28
whole, like as the *o*...........Matt 12:13
with himself seven *o* ....Matt 12:45
But *o* fell into good ....Matt 13:8

O

before him unto the *o* ....Matt 14:22
were come to the *o* ....Matt 16:5
and *o*, Jeremiah, or one ......Matt 16:14
went out, and found *o* ....Matt 20:6
the *o* on the left, in thy ....Matt 20:21
he sent *o* servants more ....Matt 21:36
his vineyard unto *o* ....Matt 21:41
Again, he sent forth *o* ....Matt 22:4
and not to leave the *o* ....Matt 23:23
end of heaven to the *o* ....Matt 24:31
be taken, and the *o*...........Matt 24:40
Afterward came also the *o* ....Matt 25:11
and made them *o* five.........Matt 25:16
came and brought *o* five ......Matt 25:20
o smote him with the ....Matt 26:67
Magdalene, and the *o*.........Matt 27:61
restored whole as the *o* ....Mark 3:5
o fell on good ground, and ....Mark 4:8
the lusts of *o* things..........Mark 4:19
were also with him *o* ....Mark 4:36
over unto the *o* side of.........Mark 5:1
again by ship unto the *o* ......Mark 5:21
O said, That it is Elijah ....Mark 6:15
to the *o* side before...........Mark 6:45
And many *o* things there ......Mark 7:4
departed to the *o* ....Mark 8:13
Elijah; and *o*, One of the .....Mark 8:28
hand, and the *o* on thy ....Mark 10:37
killed, and many *o* ....Mark 12:5
is none *o* commandment ......Mark 12:31
right hand, and the *o* ....Mark 15:27
He saved *o*; himself he........Mark 15:31
many *o* things in his ....Luke 3:18
kingdom of God to *o* ....Luke 4:43
which were in the *o* ....Luke 5:7
of publicans and of *o* ....Luke 5:29
restored whole as the *o* ....Luke 6:10
cheek offer also the *o*..........Luke 6:29
hundred pence, and the *o* .....Luke 7:41
And *o* fell on good ....Luke 8:8
but to *o* in parables............Luke 8:10
o say, that one of the ....Luke 9:19
Lord appointed *o* seventy .....Luke 10:1
passed by on the *o* ....Luke 10:32
seven *o* spirits more ....Luke 11:26
and not to leave the *o* ....Luke 11:42
while the *o* is yet a great......Luke 14:32
one, and love the *o*...........Luke 16:13
one, and despise the *o* ....Luke 16:13
unto the *o* part under.........Luke 17:24
taken, and the *o* left..........Luke 17:35
righteous, and despised *o* .....Luke 18:9
Pharisee, and the *o* a ....Luke 18:10
rather than the *o* ....Luke 18:14
o things blasphemously.........Luke 22:65
And there were also two *o* ....Luke 23:32
He saved *o*; let him ....Luke 23:35
But the *o* answering ....Luke 23:40
o women that were with ......Luke 24:10
o men labored, and ye ....John 4:38
stood on the *o* side of ....John 6:22
that there was none *o*..........John 6:22
him on the *o* side of the ......John 6:25
He is a good man: *o*...........John 7:12
This is he: *o* said, He is.......John 9:9
but climbeth up some *o* ....John 10:1
o sheep I have, which..........John 10:16
O said, These are not.........John 10:21
the works which none *o*........John 15:24
Then went out that *o* ....John 18:16
thyself, or did *o* tell it ....John 18:34
crucified him, and two *o* ......John 19:18
to the *o* disciple, whom ....John 20:2
went forth, and that *o* ....John 20:3
Then went in also that *o* ......John 20:8
o disciples therefore ....John 20:25
Zebedee, and two *o* of his ....John 21:2
also many *o* things which......John 21:25
began to speak with *o* ....Acts 2:4
O mocking said, These ....Acts 2:13
with many *o* words did he .....Acts 2:40
salvation in any *o*.............Acts 4:12
none *o* name under ....Acts 4:12
or of some *o* man? ....Acts 8:34
Barnabas, and certain *o* ....Acts 15:2
asunder one from the *o* ....Acts 15:39
Jason, and of the *o* ....Acts 17:9
o some, He seemeth to be ....Acts 17:18
and *o* said, We will hear ......Acts 17:32
anything concerning *o*.........Acts 19:39
Sadducees, and the *o* ....Acts 23:6
saying none *o* things ....Acts 26:22
Paul and certain *o* ....Acts 27:1
o also, which had.............Acts 28:9
also, even as among *o* ....Rom 1:13
nor any *o* creature, shall ......Rom 8:39
I baptized any *o* 1Cor 1:16
Defraud ye not one the *o* 1Cor 7:5
not an apostle unto *o* 1Cor 9:2
as well as *o* apostles 1Cor 9:5
I have preached to *o*...........1Cor 9:27
one taketh before *o* his 1Cor 11:21
With men of *o* tongues.........1Cor 14:21
tongues and *o* lips 1Cor 14:21
of wheat, or of some *o*.........1Cor 15:37
we write none *o* things 2Cor 1:13
or need we, as some *o* 2Cor 3:1
I mean not that *o* men 2Cor 8:13
I robbed *o* churches 2Cor 11:8
and to all *o*, that, if I 2Cor 13:2
any *o* gospel unto you ....Gal 1:8
But *o* of the apostles ....Gal 1:19
bondmaid, the *o* by a ....Gal 4:22
wrath, even as *o*..............Eph 2:3
in *o* ages was not made ....Eph 3:5
palace, and in all *o* ....Phil 1:13
esteem *o* better than ....Phil 2:3
also on the things of *o* ....Phil 2:4
and with *o* my ....Phil 4:3
neither of you, nor yet of *o* ...1Thess 2:6
let us not sleep, as do *o*........1Thess 5:6
you all toward each *o* 2Thess 1:3
that they teach no *o* 1Tim 1:3
before all, that *o* also 1Tim 5:20
be partaker of *o* men 1Tim 5:22
be able to teach *o* 2Tim 2:2
year with blood of *o* ....Heb 9:25
o had trial of cruel ....Heb 11:36
neither by any *o* oath ....James 5:12
a busybody in *o* men's 1Pet 4:15
as they do also the *o* 2Pet 3:16
and *o* save with fear ....Jude 23
will put upon you none *o* .....Rev 2:24
one is, and the *o* is not ....Rev 17:10

OTHERWISE—*in a different way or manner*
o I should have wrought 2Sam 18:13
O it shall come to pass........1Kin 1:21
passover *o* than it was 2Chr 30:18
lest *o* they should rejoice........Ps 38:16
o ye have no reward ....Matt 6:1
if *o*, then both the new ....Luke 5:36
works: *o* grace is no ....Rom 11:6
o thou also shalt be cut ....Rom 11:22
if *o*, yet as a fool receive......2Cor 11:16
that ye will be none *o* ....Gal 5:10
if in any thing ye be *o* ....Phil 3:15
and they that are *o* 1Tim 5:25
o it is of no strength at all ....Heb 9:17

OTHNI (ŏth'nī)—*"Jehovah is power"*
Son of Shemaiah 1Chr 26:7

OTHNIEL (ŏth'nĭ-ĕl)—*"God is power"*
Son of Kenaz, Caleb's youngest brother ......Judg 1:13
Captures Kirjath-sepher; receives Caleb's daughter as wife.......Josh 15:15-17
First judge of Israel .....Judg 3:9-11

And the sons of Kenaz; *O* 1Chr 4:13
and the sons of *O* 1Chr 4:13
the Netophathite, of *O*........1Chr 27:15

OUCHES—*"woven"—a filigree setting for precious stones*
Setting for precious stones worn by the high priest.................Ex 28:11
Fastener or clasp for cords ....Ex 28:13, 14
Same Hebrew word translated "wrought" . .Ps 45:13

fasten in the two *o* ....Ex 28:25
onyx stones inclosed in *o*......Ex 39:6
they were enclosed in *o* ....Ex 39:13
they made two *o* of gold ......Ex 39:16
fastened in the two *o* ....Ex 39:18

OUGHT—*something morally imperative; obligation; at all; anything*

Of duties not properly done:
Use of talents ....Matt 25:27
Accusation ....Acts 24:19
Growth ....Heb 5:12

Of acts wrongly done:
Worship ....John 4:20, 21
Death ....John 19:7
Wrong behavior 2Cor 2:3
Inconsistent speaking ....James 3:10

Of moral duties among Christians:
Witnessing ....Luke 12:12
Prayer ....Luke 18:1
Service ....John 13:14
Obedience 1Thess 4:1
Helping the weak........Rom 15:1
Love toward wife........Eph 5:28
Proper behavior 2Thess 3:7
Holy conduct 2Pet 3:11
Willingness to sacrifice ...1 John 3:16
Love of one another .....1 John 4:11

See MUST; NECESSARY

[*also* AUGHT, OUGHTEST]
which thing *o* not to be ....Gen 34:7
there is not *a* left in the.......Gen 47:18
ye shall not diminish *a* ....Ex 5:8
shall not minish *a* ....Ex 5:19
if a man borrow *a* of his ......Ex 22:14
things which *o* not to ....Lev 4:2
and if *a* remain until the ......Lev 19:6
if thou sell *a* unto thy.........Lev 25:14
or buyest *a* of thy ....Lev 25:14
will at all redeem *a* of his .....Lev 27:31
if *a* be committed by ....Num 15:24
vowed, or uttered *a* out ....Num 30:6
shall ye diminish *a*............Deut 4:2
have I taken away *a* ....Deut 26:14
nor given *a* thereof for........Deut 26:14
failed not *a* of any good ......Josh 21:45
if *a* but death part thee ....Ruth 1:17
taken *a* of any man's 1Sam 12:4
there *a* missing unto 1Sam 25:7
if I taste bread, or *a* else......2Sam 3:35
Whosoever saith *a* 2Sam 14:10
knowest what thou *o* to 1Kin 2:9
know what Israel *o* 1Chr 12:32
O ye not to know that 2Chr 13:5
o ye not to walk in the ....Neh 5:9
unto him that *o* to be ....Ps 76:11
thy brother hath *a* ....Matt 5:23
these *o* ye to have done.......Matt 23:23
do *a* for his father or ....Mark 7:12
forgive, if ye have *a* ....Mark 11:25
these *o* ye to have done.......Luke 11:42
six days in which men *o*.......Luke 13:14
o not this woman, being ......Luke 13:16
that men *o* always to ....Luke 18:1
O not Christ to have..........Luke 24:26
any man brought him *a* ....John 4:33
a of the things which he ......Acts 4:32
tell thee what thou *o* ....Acts 10:6
o not to think that the ....Acts 17:29
laboring ye *o* to support ......Acts 20:35
Who *o* to have been here .....Acts 24:19
object, if they had *o* ....Acts 24:19
that he *o* not to live any .....Acts 25:24
I had *a* to accuse my ....Acts 28:19
should pray for as we *o* ....Rom 8:26
more highly than he *o* ....Rom 12:3
nothing yet as he *o* to 1Cor 8:2
cause *o* the woman to.........1Cor 11:10
ye *o* rather to forgive 2Cor 2:7
o not to lay up for the 2Cor 12:14
may speak boldly, as I *o* ......Eph 6:20
make it manifest, as I *o*.......Col 4:4

how ye *o* to answer..........Col 4:6
know how thou *o* to..........1Tim 3:15
things which they *o*..........1Tim 5:13
things which they *o*..........Titus 1:11
or oweth thee *a*..........Philem 18
o to give the more earnest....Heb 2:1
by reason hereof he *o*..........Heb 5:3
For that ye *o* to say, If.......James 4:15
o himself also so to walk......1John 2:6
We therefore *o* to receive.....3John 8

OUR, OURS—*See* INTRODUCTION

OURSELVES—*we*
to bow down *o* to thee to?....Gen 37:10
we *o* will go ready armed.....Num 32:17
and we will discover *o*........1Sam 14:8
and let us behave *o*..........1Chr 19:13
but we *o* together will........Ezra 4:3
to charge *o* yearly with........Neh 10:32
let us know among *o*..........Job 34:4
Let us take to *o* the..........Ps 83:12
let us solace *o* with love.......Prov 7:18
falsehood have we hid *o*......Is 28:15
Come, and let us join *o* to....Jer 50:5
for we have heard him *o*......John 4:42
will give *o* continually.........Acts 6:4
of the Spirit, even we *o*.......Rom 8:23
groan within *o*, waiting........Rom 8:23
For if we would judge *o*......1Cor 11:31
we *o* are comforted of........2Cor 1:4
sentence of death in *o*........2Cor 1:9
should not trust in *o*..........2Cor 1:9
we are sufficient of *o*.........2Cor 3:5
to think any thing as of *o*.....2Cor 3:5
For we preach not *o*, but......2Cor 4:5
o your servants for Jesus......2Cor 4:5
whether we be beside *o*.......2Cor 5:13
let us cleanse *o* from all.......2Cor 7:1
or compare *o* with some.......2Cor 10:12
stretch not *o* beyond our......2Cor 10:14
think ye that we excuse *o*.....2Cor 12:19
we *o* also are found..........Gal 2:17
we behaved *o* among you.....1Thess 2:10
we *o* glory in you in the......2Thess 1:4
behaved not *o* disorderly......2Thess 3:7
to make *o* an example........2Thess 3:9
we *o* also were sometimes.....Titus 3:3
the assembling of *o*..........Heb 10:25
we deceive *o*, and the.........1John 1:8

OUTCASTS—*dispossessed people*
Israel among the nations .Ps 147:2
Israel as objects of mercy.Is 16:3, 4
New Israel..............Jer 30:17-22

and shall assemble the *o*......Is 11:12
and the *o* in the land of.......Is 27:13
which gathereth the *o* of......Is 56:8
the *o* of Elam shall not.......Jer 49:36

OUTER—*farther out; outside*
was heard even to the *o*.......Ezek 10:5
shall be cast out into *o*........Matt 8:12
and cast him into *o*...........Matt 22:13
servant into *o* darkness........Matt 25:30

OUTGOINGS—*departures; going beyond*
the *o* of it were at the sea.....Josh 17:9
the *o* of it shall be thine......Josh 17:18
o of the border were at the...Josh 18:19
o thereof are in the valley.....Josh 19:14
o of their border were at......Josh 19:22
the *o* thereof are at the sea...Josh 19:29
o thereof were at Jordan......Josh 19:33
the *o* of the morning and.....Ps 65:8

OUTLANDISH—*foreign; bizarre*
did *o* women cause to sin.....Neh 13:26

OUTLIVED—*live longer than*
the elders that *o* Joshua.......Judg 2:7

OUTMOST—*farthest out*
that is *o* in the coupling.......Ex 26:10
o coast of the Salt Sea........Num 34:3
unto the *o* parts of heaven....Deut 30:4
in the *o* fruitful branches......Is 17:6

OUTRAGEOUS—*extremely bad; going beyond bounds of decency*
Descriptive of anger.....Prov 27:4

OUTRUN—*run faster than*
the other disciple did *o* Peter..John 20:4

OUTSIDE—*beyond the boundary or an enclosure*
the *o* of the armed men.......Judg 7:11
I come to the *o* of the camp...Judg 7:17
came unto the *o* of the camp..Judg 7:19
o toward the great court......1Kin 7:9
behold a wall on the *o* of.....Ezek 40:5
ye make clean the *o* of the....Matt 23:25
the *o* of them may be clean...Matt 23:26
make clean the *o* of the cup...Luke 11:39

OUTSTRETCHED—*extended*
a mighty hand, and with an *o* .Deut 26:8
fight against you with an *o*....Jer 21:5

OUTWARD—*away from the center; exterior; external*

[*also* OUTWARDLY]
the wall of the city and *o*.....Num 35:4
man looketh on the *o*.........1Sam 16:7
the *o* business over Israel.....1Chr 26:29
had the oversight of the *o*.....Neh 11:16
Haman was come into the *o*...Esth 6:4
brought he me into the *o*.....Ezek 40:17
the gate of the *o* court........Ezek 40:20
were toward the *o* court......Ezek 40:34
way of the gate of the *o*......Ezek 44:1
indeed appear beautiful *o*.....Matt 23:27
ye also *o* appear righteous.....Matt 23:28
not a Jew, which is one *o*.....Rom 2:28
which is *o* in the flesh........Rom 2:28
though our *o* man perish......2Cor 4:16
after the *o* appearance?.......2Cor 10:7
o adorning of plaiting the.....1Pet 3:3

OUTWENT—*gone out*
out of all the cities, and *o*.....Mark 6:33

OVEN—*a place for baking or cooking*
Characteristics of:
Used for cooking........Ex 8:3
Fuel for, grass..........Matt 6:30
Made on ground........Gen 18:6
Figurative of:
Scarcity in famine.......Lev 26:26
Lust....................Hos 7:4, 6, 7
God's judgments........Ps 21:9
Effects of famine........Lam 5:10

meat offering baked in the *o*..Lev 2:4
that is baken in the *o*.........Lev 7:9
whether it be *o*, or ranges.....Lev 11:35
that shall burn as an *o*........Mal 4:1
tomorrow is cast into the *o*....Luke 12:28

OVER—*See* INTRODUCTION

OVERCAME—*See* OVERCOME

OVERCHARGE—*to fill too full*

[*also* OVERCHARGED]
hearts be *o* with surfeiting.....Luke 21:34
that I may not *o* you all.......2Cor 2:5

OVERCOME—*to conquer*
Means of, by:
Wine..................Jer 23:9
Fleshly desire..........2Pet 2:19, 20
God...................Rom 8:37
Objects of:
World.................John 16:33
Evil...................Rom 12:21
Satan..................1John 2:13, 14
Evil spirits.............1John 4:4
Two witnesses..........Rev 11:7
Evil powers............Rev 17:13, 14
Promises concerning, for Christians:
Eating of the tree of life..Rev 2:7
Exemption from the second death.........Rev 2:11
Power over the nations..Rev 2:26
Clothed in white raiment.Rev 3:5
Made a pillar in God's Temple...............Rev 3:12
Rulership with Christ....Rev 3:21

[*also* OVERCAME, OVERCOMETH]
Gad, a troop shall *o* him......Gen 49:19
but he shall *o* at the last......Gen 49:19
them that cry for being *o*.....Ex 32:18
for we are well able to *o*......Num 13:30
I shall be able to *o* them......Num 22:11
Ahaz, but could not *o* him....2Kin 16:5
me, for they have *o* me.......Song 6:5
them that are *o* with wine!....Is 28:1
come upon him, and *o* him....Luke 11:22
o them, and prevailed.........Acts 19:16
mightest *o* when thou art......Rom 3:4
is born of God *o* the world....1John 5:4
the victory that *o* the world...1John 5:4
Who is he that *o* the world....1John 5:5
To him that *o* will I give......Rev 2:17
o him by the blood of the.....Rev 12:11
the saints, and to *o* them......Rev 13:7
He that *o* shall inherit all.....Rev 21:7

OVERDRIVE—*drive too hard*
If men should *o* them one.....Gen 33:13

OVERFLOW—*inundate; flow over the bounds*

[*also* OVERFLOWED, OVERFLOWETH, OVERFLOWING, OVERFLOWN]
water of the Red Sea to *o*.....Deut 11:4
Jordan *o* all his banks all......Josh 3:15
when it had *o* all his banks....1Chr 12:15
foundation was *o* with a.......Job 22:16
He bindeth the floods from *o*..Job 28:11
watercourse for the *o* of......Job 38:25
waters, where the floods *o*....Ps 69:2
Let not the waterflood *o* me...Ps 69:15
out, and the streams *o*........Ps 78:20
he shall *o* and go over, he....Is 8:8
decreed shall *o* with..........Is 10:22
a flood of mighty waters *o*....Is 28:2
when the *o* scourge shall......Is 28:15
waters shall *o* the hiding......Is 28:17
his breath, as an *o* stream.....Is 30:28
rivers, they shall not *o*........Is 43:2
and shall be an *o* flood.......Jer 47:2
shall *o* the land, and all.......Jer 47:2
there shall be an *o* shower....Ezek 13:11
be an *o* shower in mine.......Ezek 13:13
an *o* rain, and great..........Ezek 38:22
shall certainly come, and *o*....Dan 11:10
shall they be *o* from before....Dan 11:22
him, and his army shall *o*.....Dan 11:26
and shall *o* and pass over.....Dan 11:40
the fats shall *o* with wine......Joel 2:24
press is full, and vats *o*.......Joel 3:13
the *o* of the water passed by..Hab 3:10
was, being *o* with water.......2Pet 3:6

OVERLAY—*superimpose (as with a veneer)*
Materials used:
Gold...................Ex 26:32
Bronze.................Ex 38:2
Silver..................Ex 38:17
Objects overlaid:
Pillar—with gold........Ex 26:32
Board—with gold........Ex 36:34
Altar—with cedar.......1Kin 6:20
Sanctuary—with gold....1Kin 6:21
Cherubim—with gold....1Kin 6:28
Earthen vessel—with silver dross..........Prov 26:23
Images—with silver......Is 30:22

[*also* OVERLAID, OVERLAYING]
shalt *o* it with pure gold.......Ex 25:11
without shalt thou *o* it........Ex 25:11
wood, and *o* them with gold...Ex 25:13
thou shalt *o* it with pure......Ex 25:24
wood, and *o* them with gold...Ex 25:28
thou shalt *o* the boards with...Ex 26:29
thou shalt *o* the bars with....Ex 26:29
o them with gold, and their...Ex 26:37
thou shalt *o* it with brass......Ex 27:2
and *o* them with brass.......Ex 27:6

shalt *o* it with pure gold . . . . . . .Ex 30:3
and *o* them with gold . . . . .Ex 30:5
wood, and *o* them with gold . . .Ex 36:36
and he *o* their chapiters and . . .Ex 36:38
And he *o* it with pure gold . . . .Ex 37:2
wood, and *o* them with gold . . .Ex 37:4
he *o* it with pure gold, and . . .Ex 37:11
o them with gold, to bear . . . . .Ex 37:15
And he *o* it with pure gold . . . .Ex 37:26
wood, and *o* them with gold . . .Ex 37:28
and *o* them with brass . . . . .Ex 38:6
the *o* of their chapiters . . . . . . .Ex 38:19
o their chapiters, and . . . . .Ex 38:28
in the night; because she *o* 1Kin 3:19
whole house he *o* with gold . . .1Kin 6:22
by the oracle he *o* with gold . . .1Kin 6:22
floor of the house he *o* with . . .1Kin 6:30
flowers, and *o* them with 1Kin 6:32
ivory and *o* it with the best 1Kin 10:10
Hezekiah, king of Judah had *o* .2Kin 18:16
to *o* the walls of the houses 1Chr 29:4
and he *o* it within with pure . . .2Chr 3:4
which he *o* with fine gold 2Chr 3:5
He *o* also the house, the 2Chr 3:7
and he *o* it with fine 2Chr 3:8
o the upper chambers with 2Chr 3:9
work, and *o* them with gold . . .2Chr 3:10
o the doors of them with 2Chr 4:9
of ivory, and *o* it with pure . . .2Chr 9:17
ivory *o* with sapphires . . . . .Song 5:14
covenant *o* round about with . .Heb 9:4

OVERLIVED—*outlived*
the elders that *o* Joshua . . . . . . .Josh 24:31

OVERMUCH—*too much*
be swallowed up with *o* 2Cor 2:7

OVERPASS—*pass over; disregard*

[*also* OVERPAST]
until these calamities be *o* . . . . .Ps 57:1
until the indignation be *o* . . . . .Is 26:20
they *o* the deeds of the . . . . . . .Jer 5:28

OVERPLUS—*surplus*
Restoration of, required. .Lev 25:27

OVERRUNNING—*running past*

[*also* OVERRAN]
of the plain, and *o* Cushi 2Sam 18:23
But with an *o* flood he will . . . .Nah 1:8

OVERSEE—*to mistake; to supervise*

[*also* OVERSIGHT]
peradventure it was an *o* . . . . . .Gen 43:12
o of them that keep the . . . . . . .Num 3:32
the *o* of all the tabernacle . . . . .Num 4:16
o of the house of the Lord 2Kin 12:11
had the *o* of the gates of 1Chr 9:23
were appointed to *o* the 1Chr 9:29
and six hundred to *o* them 2Chr 2:2
the *o* of the house of the 2Chr 34:10
had the *o* of the outward . . . . . .Neh 11:16
having the *o* of the chamber . . .Neh 13:4
among you, taking the *o* 1Pet 5:2

OVERSEER—*a leader or supervisor*
Kinds of:
Prime minister . . . . .Gen 39:4, 5
Managers . . . . .Gen 41:34
Elders . . . . .Acts 20:17, 28

[*also* OVERSEERS]
o to set the people a work 2Chr 2:18
o under the hand of 2Chr 31:13
the *o* of them were Jahath 2Chr 34:12
o of all that wrought the 2Chr 34:13
it into the hand of the *o* 2Chr 34:17
son of Zichri was their *o* . . . . . .Neh 11:9
their *o* was Zabdiel, the son . . .Neh 11:14
with Jezrahiah their *o* . . . . .Neh 12:42
having no guide, *o*, or ruler . . .Prov 6:7

OVERSHADOW—*cast a shadow over*

[*also* OVERSHADOWED]
behold, a bright cloud *o* . . . . . .Matt 17:5
there was a cloud that *o* . . . . . .Mark 9:7
power of the Highest shall *o* . . .Luke 1:35
there came a cloud, and *o* . . . . .Luke 9:34
Peter passing by might *o* . . . . . .Acts 5:15

OVERSIGHT—*See* OVERSEE

OVERSPREAD—*spread over or above*

[*also* OVERSPREADING]
them was the whole earth *o* . . .Gen 9:19
for the *o* of abominations . . . . .Dan 9:27

OVERTAKE—*to catch up with; to pass by*

[*also* OVERTAKEN, OVERTAKETH, OVERTOOK]
they *o* him in the mount . . . . . .Gen 31:23
when thou dost *o* them, say . . .Gen 44:4
he *o* them, and he spake . . . . . .Gen 44:6
o them encamping by the . . . . .Ex 14:9
I will pursue, I will *o* . . . . .Ex 15:9
his heart is hot, and *o* . . . . .Deut 19:6
come on thee, and *o* thee . . . . .Deut 28:2
shall pursue thee, and *o* . . . . . . .Deut 28:45
them quickly; for ye shall *o* . . .Josh 2:5
and *o* the children of Dan . . . . .Judg 18:22
but the battle *o* them; and . . . .Judg 20:42
after this troop? shall I *o* 1Sam 30:8
lest he *o* us suddenly, and 2Sam 15:14
and *o* him in the plains of 2Kin 25:5
sword of thine enemies *o* 1Chr 21:12
mine enemies, and *o* them . . . .Ps 18:37
us, neither doth justice *o* . . . . . .Is 59:9
o Zedekiah in the plains . . . . . .Jer 39:5
which ye feared, shall *o* . . . . . . .Jer 42:16
o Zedekiah in the plains of . . . .Jer 52:8
o her between the straits . . . . . .Lam 1:3
lovers, but she shall not *o* . . . . .Hos 2:7
children of iniquity did not *o* . .Hos 10:9
evil shall not *o* nor prevent . . . .Amos 9:10
Brethren, if a man be *o* in . . . .Gal 6:1
that day should *o* you as a 1Thess 5:4

OVERTHROW—*throw down; destroy; take over*
Agents of:
God .Prov 21:12
Evil .Ps 140:11
Wickedness . . . . .Prov 11:11
Evil ruler . . . . .Dan 11:41
Christ . . . . .John 2:15

[*also* OVERTHREW, OVERTHROWETH, OVERTHROWN]
also, that I will not *o* this . . . . .Gen 19:21
And he *o* those cities, and . . . .Gen 19:25
the Lord *o* the Egyptians . . . . . .Ex 14:27
hast *o* them that rose up . . . . . .Ex 15:7
thou shalt utterly *o* them . . . . . .Ex 23:24
ye shall *o* their altars, and . . . . .Deut 12:3
the Lord *o* in his anger . . . . . . .Deut 29:23
therein, like the *o* of Sodom . . .Deut 29:23
many were *o* and wounded . . . .Judg 9:40
to spy it out, and to *o* it? 2Sam 10:3
against the city, and *o* it? 2Sam 11:25
of them be *o* at the first 2Sam 17:9
and to *o*, and to spy out the . . .1Chr 19:3
and the Ethiopians were *o* 2Chr 14:13
spoiled, and *o* the mighty . . . . .Job 12:19
Know now that God hath *o* . . .Job 19:6
to *o* them in the wilderness . . . .Ps 106:26
But *o* Pharaoh and his host . . .Ps 136:15
purposed to *o* my goings . . . . . .Ps 140:4
judges are *o* in stony places . . .Ps 141:6
The wicked are *o*, and are . . . .Prov 12:7
but wickedness *o* the sinner . . .Prov 13:6
house of the wicked..be *o* . . . . .Prov 14:11
to *o* the righteous in . . . . .Prov 18:5
o the words of the transgressor .Prov 22:12
he that receiveth gifts *o* . . . . . . .Prov 29:4
is desolate, as *o* by strangers . .Is 1:7
God *o* Sodom and Gomorrah . .Is 13:19
but let them be *o* before thee. .Jer 18:23
the cities which the Lord *o* . . .Jer 20:16
o of Sodom and Gomorrah . . . .Jer 49:18
God *o* Sodom and Gomorrah . .Jer 50:40
o some of you, as God *o* . . . . . .Amos 4:11
days, and Nineveh shall be *o* . .Jon 3:4
I will *o* the throne of . . . . .Hag 2:22
I will *o* the chariots, and . . . . . .Hag 2:22
o the tables of . . . . .Matt 21:12
o the tables of the . . . . .Mark 11:15
if it be of God, ye cannot *o* . . .Acts 5:39
were *o* in the wilderness 1Cor 10:5
already; and *o* the faith 2Tim 2:18
condemned them with an *o* 2Pet 2:6

OVERTOOK—*See* OVERTAKE

OVERTURN—*to turn over; destroy*

[*also* OVERTURNED, OVERTURNETH]
and *o* it, that the tent lay . . . . .Judg 7:13
which *o* them in his anger . . . . .Job 9:5
out, and they *o* the earth . . . . .Job 12:15
he *o* the mountains by the . . . .Job 28:9
and he *o* them in the night . . . .Job 34:25
will *o*, *o*, *o*, it: and it . . . . .Ezek 21:27

OVERWHELM—*overthrow; crush; upset*

[*also* OVERWHELMED]
Yea, ye *o* the fatherless . . . . . . .Job 6:27
upon me, and horror hath *o* . . .Ps 55:5
thee, when my heart is *o* . . . . . .Ps 61:2
my spirit was *o*. Selah . . . . .Ps 77:3
the sea *o* their enemies . . . . . . .Ps 78:53
afflicted, when he is *o* . . . . .Ps 102:*title*
Then the waters had *o* us . . . . .Ps 124:4
When my spirit was *o* . . . . .Ps 142:3
is my spirit *o* within me . . . . . . .Ps 143:4

OVERWORK—*too much work; make too much use of*
Complaint of Israelites . . .Ex 5:6-21
Solution of, for Moses . . .Ex 18:14-26

OWE—*to be indebted to; be under obligation*
Financial debt . . . . .Matt 18:24, 28
Moral debt . . . . .Philem 18, 19
Spiritual debt . . . . .Rom 13:8

[*also* OWED, OWEST]
one *o* five hundred pence . . . . .Luke 7:41
How much *o* thou unto my . . . .Luke 16:5
another. And how much *o* . . . .Luke 16:7

OWL—*a bird of prey of nocturnal habits*
Varieties of, all unclean . .Lev 11:13-17
Solitary in habit . . . . .Ps 102:6

[*also* OWLS]
the *o*, and the night hawk . . . . .Deut 14:15
little *o*, and the great *o*, and . . .Deut 14:16
and a companion to *o* . . . . .Job 30:29
and *o* shall dwell there . . . . .Is 13:21
the *o* also and the raven . . . . . .Is 34:11
dragons, and a court for *o* . . . . .Is 34:13
shall the great *o* make her . . . .Is 34:15
me, the dragons and the *o* . . . .Is 43:20
the *o* shall dwell therein . . . . . .Jer 50:39
and mourning as the *o* . . . . .Mic 1:8

OWN—*See* INTRODUCTION

OWNER—*one who has possession of something*

[*also* OWNERS]
the *o* of the ox shall be . . . . . . .Ex 21:28
hath been testified to his *o* . . . .Ex 21:29
the *o* thereof being not with . . .Ex 22:14
the name of Shemer, *o* of 1Kin 16:24
the *o* thereof to lose their . . . . .Job 31:39
away the life of the *o* . . . . .Prov 1:19
good is there to the *o* . . . . .Eccl 5:11
The ox knoweth his *o*, and . . . .Is 1:3
the *o* thereof said unto them . .Luke 19:33
the master and the *o* of the . . .Acts 27:11

OWNERSHIP—*having possession of something; owning*
By men, acquired by:
Purchase . . . . .Gen 23:16-18
Inheritance . . . . .Luke 15:12
Covenant . . . . .Gen 26:25-33
By God, of:
World . . . . .Ps 24:1
Souls of men . . . . .Ezek 18:4
Redeemed 1Cor 6:19, 20

OWNETH—*possesses*
he that *o* the house . . . . .Lev 14:35
man that *o* this girdle . . . . .Acts 21:11

OX—*a domestic bovine mammal*

Uses of:
Pulling covered wagons . . Num 7:3
Plowing 1Kin 19:19
Food . . . . . Deut 14:4
Sacrifice . . . . . Ex 20:24
Means of existence . . . . . Job 24:3
Designs in Temple 1Kin 7:25

Laws concerning:
To rest on Sabbath . . . . . Ex 23:12
Not to be:
Yoked with an ass . . . . . Deut 22:10
Muzzled while treading . Deut 25:4
To be restored . . . . . Ex 22:4, 9-13

Figurative of:
Easy victory . . . . . Num 22:4
Youthful rashness . . . . . Prov 7:22
Sumptuous living . . . . . Prov 15:17
Preach the Gospel . . . . . Is 32:20
Minister's support 1Cor 9:9, 10

Descriptive of:
Of great strength . . . . . Num 23:22
Very wild and ferocious . . Job 39:9-12
Frisky in youth . . . . . Ps 29:6

[*also* OXEN]
and he had sheep, and ***o*** . . . . . Gen 12:16
Abimelech took sheep and ***o*** . . Gen 20:14
Abraham took sheep and ***o*** . . . . Gen 21:27
I have ***o***, and asses, flocks . . . . Gen 32:5
their sheep, and their ***o*** . . . . . Gen 34:28
the ***o***, and upon the sheep . . . . Ex 9:3
nor his ***o***, nor his ass, nor . . . . . Ex 20:17
o gore a man or a woman . . . . . Ex 21:28
then the ***o*** shall be surely . . . . . Ex 21:28
the owner of the ***o*** shall be . . . . Ex 21:28
o were wont to push with . . . . . Ex 21:29
the ***o*** shall be stoned, and . . . . . Ex 21:29
If the ***o*** shall push a . . . . . Ex 21:32
and the ***o*** shall be stoned . . . . . Ex 21:32
And if one man's ***o*** hurt . . . . . Ex 21:35
they shall sell the live ***o*** . . . . . Ex 21:35
the dead ***o*** also they shall . . . . . Ex 21:35
the ***o*** hath used to push in . . . . Ex 21:36
he shall surely pay ***o*** for ***o*** . . . . . Ex 21:36
If a man shall steal an ***o*** . . . . . Ex 22:1
restore five ***o*** for an ***o*** . . . . . Ex 22:1
If a man shall steal an ***o*** . . . . . Ex 22:1
meet thine enemy's ***o*** or his . . . Ex 23:4
peace offerings of ***o*** unto the . . Ex 24:5
cattle, whether ***o*** or sheep . . . . . Ex 34:19
eat no manner of fat, of ***o*** . . . . Lev 7:23
that killeth an ***o***, or lamb . . . . . Lev 17:3
whether it be ***o***, or sheep . . . . . Lev 27:26
Two wagons and four ***o*** he . . . . Num 7:7
four wagons and eight ***o*** he . . . . Num 7:8
the ***o*** for the burnt offering . . . . Num 7:87
Balak offered ***o*** and sheep . . . . Num 22:40
and prepare me here seven ***o*** . . Num 23:1
thine ***o***, nor thine ass, nor . . . . . Deut 5:14
his ***o***, or his ass, or any . . . . . Deut 5:21
wild ***o***, and the chamois . . . . . Deut 14:5
for ***o***, or for sheep, or for . . . . . Deut 14:26
sacrifice, whether it be ***o*** . . . . . Deut 18:3
brother's ***o*** or his sheep go . . . . Deut 22:1
brother's ass or his ***o*** fall . . . . . Deut 22:4
Thine ***o*** shall be slain before . . Deut 28:31
and ***o***, and sheep, and ass . . . . . Josh 6:21
his ***o***, and his asses, and . . . . . Josh 7:24
Israel, neither sheep, nor ***o*** . . . . Judg 6:4
he took a yoke of ***o***, and 1Sam 11:7
shall it be done unto his ***o*** 1Sam 11:7
whose ***o*** have I taken? or 1Sam 12:3
which a yoke of ***o*** might 1Sam 14:14
me hither every man his ***o*** 1Sam 14:34
brought every man his ***o*** 1Sam 14:34
infant and suckling ***o*** and 1Sam 15:3
of the sheep, and of the ***o*** 1Sam 15:9
of the sheep and of the ***o*** 1Sam 15:15
o, and asses, and sheep 1Sam 22:19
away the sheep, and the ***o*** 1Sam 27:9
took hold of it: for the ***o*** 2Sam 6:6
be ***o*** for burnt sacrifice 2Sam 24:22
instruments of the ***o*** for 2Sam 24:22
Adonijah slew sheep and ***o*** 1Kin 1:9
hath slain ***o*** and fat cattle 1Kin 1:25
Ten fat ***o***, and twenty ***o*** out . . . 1Kin 4:23
lions, ***o***, and cherubim 1Kin 7:29
and beneath the lions and ***o*** . . . 1Kin 7:29
sacrificing sheep and ***o***, that . . . 1Kin 8:5
took a yoke of ***o***, and slew 1Kin 19:21
with the instruments of the ***o*** . . 1Kin 19:21
vineyards, and sheep, and ***o*** . . . 2Kin 5:26
brazen ***o*** that were under 2Kin 16:17
and on mules, and on ***o***, and . . 1Chr 12:40
wine, and oil, and ***o***, and 1Chr 12:40
thee the ***o*** also for burnt 1Chr 21:23
it was the similitude of ***o*** 2Chr 4:3
It stood upon twelve ***o*** 2Chr 4:4
sacrificed sheep and ***o*** 2Chr 5:6
twenty and two thousand ***o*** 2Chr 7:5
brought seven hundred ***o*** 2Chr 15:11
Ahab killed sheep and ***o*** for . . . 2Chr 18:2
six hundred ***o*** and three 2Chr 29:33
brought in the tithe of ***o*** 2Chr 31:6
cattle, and three hundred ***o*** 2Chr 35:8
And so did they with the ***o*** 2Chr 35:12
was one ***o*** and six choice . . . . . Neh 5:18
and five hundred yoke of ***o*** . . . . Job 1:3
or loweth the ***o*** over his . . . . . Job 6:5
he eateth grass as an ***o*** . . . . . Job 40:15
and a thousand yoke of ***o*** . . . . . Job 42:12
All sheep and ***o***, yea, and . . . . . Ps 8:7
the Lord better than an ***o*** . . . . . Ps 69:31
similitude of an ***o*** that eateth . . Ps 106:20
our ***o*** may be strong to . . . . . Ps 144:14
Where no ***o*** are, the crib is . . . . Prov 14:4
is by the strength of the ***o*** . . . . . Prov 14:4
The ***o*** knoweth his owner . . . . . Is 1:3
for the sending forth of ***o*** . . . . . Is 7:25
lion shall eat straw like the ***o*** . . Is 11:7
joy and gladness, slaying ***o*** . . . . Is 22:13
o likewise and the young . . . . . Is 30:24
He that killeth an ***o*** is as . . . . . Is 66:3
I was like a lamb or an ***o*** . . . . . Jer 11:19
husbandman and his yoke of ***o*** . Jer 51:23
four had the face of an ***o*** . . . . . Ezek 1:10
thee to eat grass as ***o*** . . . . . Dan 4:25
fed him with grass like ***o*** . . . . . Dan 5:21
will one plow there with ***o***? . . . Amos 6:12
my ***o*** and my fatlings are . . . . . Matt 22:4
the sabbath loose his ***o*** or . . . . . Luke 13:15
I have bought five yoke of ***o*** . . Luke 14:19
that sold ***o*** and sheep and . . . . . John 2:14
o and garlands unto the . . . . . Acts 14:13
muzzle the ***o*** that treadeth 1Tim 5:18

OX GOAD—*spike used to drive oxen*
As a weapon . . . . . Judg 3:31

OZEM (ō'zĕm)—*"strength"*
1. Son of Jesse 1Chr 2:13, 15
2. Descendant of Judah 1Chr 2:25

OZIAS (ō-zī'ăs)—*Greek form of Uzziah*
Joram, and Joram begat ***O*** . . . . Matt 1:8
And ***O*** begat Jotham; and . . . . . Matt 1:9

OZNI (ŏz'nī)—*"bright"*
Son of Gad and head of
a family . . . . . Num 26:15, 16
Called Ezbon . . . . . Gen 46:16

OZNITES—*the descendants of Ozni*
Ozni, the family of the ***O*** . . . . . Num 26:16

P

PAARAI (pā'ä-rī)—*"revelation of Jehovah"*
One of David's mighty
men 2Sam 23:35
Called Naarai 1Chr 11:37

PACES—*unit of measurement based on the length of a human step*
of the Lord had gone six ***p*** 2Sam 6:13

PACIFICATION—*allaying anger or agitation; subduing*

Means of:
Gift . . . . . Prov 21:14
Wise man . . . . . Prov 16:14
Yielding . . . . . Eccl 10:4

Examples of:
Esau, by Jacob . . . . . Gen 32:11-19
Lord, toward His people . Ezek 16:63
Ahasuerus, by Haman's
death . . . . . Esth 7:10

[*also* PACIFIED]
was the king's wrath ***p*** . . . . . Esth 7:10
when I am ***p*** toward thee . . . . . Ezek 16:63

PACK ANIMALS—*animals used to carry burdens*
Used by Israelites 1Chr 12:40

PADAN (pā'dăn)—*"plain"—an abbreviated form of "Padan-Aram"*
for me, when I came from ***P*** . . Gen 48:7

PADAN-ARAM (pā-dăn-ā'răm)—*"plain of Aram"—Mesopotamia*
Home of Isaac's wife . . . . Gen 25:20
Jacob flees to . . . . . Gen 28:2-7
Jacob returns from . . . . . Gen 31:17, 18
Same as Mesopotamia . . . Gen 24:10
People of, called Syrians . Gen 31:24
Language of, called
Syrian 2Kin 18:26
See ARAMAIC

Canaan when he came from ***P*** . Gen 33:18
when he came out of ***P*** . . . . . Gen 35:9
which were born to him in ***P*** . . Gen 35:26
she bare unto Jacob in ***P*** . . . . . Gen 46:15

PADDLE—*a spade-like digging instrument*
Part of a soldier's
equipment . . . . . Deut 23:13

PADON (pā'dŏn)—*"redemption"*
Head of Nethinim family . Ezra 2:44

PAGAN GODS—*the gods of the nations around Israel*

Mentioned:
Molech . . . . . Lev 18:21
Chemosh . . . . . Judg 11:24
Dagon . . . . . Judg 16:23
Baal 2Kin 17:16
Nergal 2Kin 17:30
Succoth-benoth 2Kin 17:30
Ashima 2Kin 17:30
Nibhaz 2Kin 17:31
Tartak 2Kin 17:31
Adrammelech 2Kin 17:31
Anammelech 2Kin 17:31
Nisroch . . . . . Is 37:38
Jupiter . . . . . Acts 14:12
Mercurius . . . . . Acts 14:12
Greek Pantheon . . . . . Acts 17:16-23
Diana . . . . . Acts 19:23-37

Worship of condemned:
By apostolic command . . . 1Cor 10:14
By Law . . . . . Ex 20:3, 4
Deut 5:7

PAGIEL (pā'gĭ-ĕl)—*"God's intervention"*
Son of Ocran, chief of
Asher's tribe . . . . . Num 1:13

Asher shall be ***P*** the son of . . . Num 2:27
day ***P*** the son of Ocran . . . . . Num 7:72
the offering of ***P*** the son of . . . Num 7:77
of Asher was ***P*** the son of . . . . Num 10:26

PAHATH-MOAB (pā-hăth-mō'ăb)—*"ruler of Moab"*
Family of postexilic
returnees . . . . . Ezra 2:6
Members of, divorced
foreign wives . . . . . Ezra 10:19, 30
One of, signs covenant . . . Neh 10:1, 14
Hashub, one of, helps
Nehemiah . . . . . Neh 3:11

Of the sons of ***P***; Elihoenai . . . Ezra 8:4
The children of ***P***, of the . . . . . Neh 7:11

PAI—*See* PAU

PAID—*See* PAY

PAIN—*physical or mental suffering*
Kinds of:
Childbirth ....Rev 12:2
Physical fatigue 2Cor 11:27
Physical afflictions ....Job 33:19
Mental disturbance ......Ps 55:4
Characteristics of:
Affects face ....Joel 2:6
Means of chastening .....Job 15:20
Affects the whole person .Jer 4:19
Common to all men .....Rom 8:22
Remedies for:
Balm ....Jer 51:8
Prayer ....Ps 5:17, 18
God's deliverance ....Acts 2:24
Heaven ....Rev 21:4
Figurative of:
Mental anguish ....Ps 48:6
Impending trouble ....Jer 22:23
Distressing news ....Is 21:2, 3
Israel's captivity ....Is 26:17, 18

[*also* PAINED, PAINFUL, PAINS]
travailed; for her *p* came 1Sam 4:19
know this, it was too *p*........Ps 73:16
the *p* of hell gat hold upon ....Ps 116:3
in *p* as a woman that ....Is 13:8
before her *p* came, she was ...Is 66:7
and *p*, as of a woman in ....Jer 6:24
have put themselves to *p*......Jer 12:13
Why is my *p* perpetual, and ...Jer 15:18
fall with *p* upon the head of...Jer 30:23
great *p* shall be in Ethiopia....Ezek 30:4
great *p* shall come upon.......Ezek 30:9
Sin shall have great *p*, and ....Ezek 30:16
Be in *p*, and labor to bring....Mic 4:10
and much *p* is in all loins .....Nah 2:10
gnawed their tongues for *p*....Rev 16:10
because of their *p* and their ...Rev 16:11

PAINFULNESS—*filled with pain*
weariness and, *p*, in watchings .2Cor 11:27

PAINT—*to apply color, paint, or pigment*
Applied to a wide house .Jer 22:14
Used by women 2Kin 9:30
Used especially by prostitutes .... {Jer 4:30; Ezek 23:40}

PAINTING—*a picture*
Of Chaldeans (bas-reliefs).Ezek 23:14
Of animals and idols (on a secret wall) ....Ezek 8:7-12

PAIR—*two of a kind*
Sandals ....Amos 2:6
Turtledoves ....Luke 2:24
Balances ....Rev 6:5

PALACE—*a royal building*
Descriptive of:
King's residence 2Chr 9:11
Foreign city ....Is 25:2
Dwellings in Zion ....Ps 48:3
Heathen king's residence .Ezra 6:2
Residence of the high priest ....Matt 26:3, 58
Fortified place ....Neh 7:2
Characteristics of:
Place of luxury ....Luke 7:25
Subject to destruction ....Is 13:22
Figurative of:
Messiah's Temple ....Ps 45:8, 15
Divine workmanship .....Ps 144:12
Eternal city ....Jer 30:18

[*also* PALACES]
the *p* of the king's house 1Kin 16:18
hard by the *p* of Ahab king ...1Kin 21:1
in the *p* of the king's house ...2Kin 15:25
p of the king of Babylon 2Kin 20:18
p is not for man, but for 1Chr 29:1
burnt all the *p* thereof with....2Chr 36:19
maintenance from the king's *p* .Ezra 4:14
as I was in Shushan the *p* .....Neh 1:1
beams for the gates of the *p*...Neh 2:8
which was in Shushan the *p* ...Esth 1:2
present in Shushan the *p* ......Esth 1:5
the garden of the king's *p* .....Esth 1:5
virgins unto Shushan the *p* ....Esth 2:3
Now in Shushan the *p* ....Esth 2:5
together unto Shushan the *p*...Esth 2:8
was given in Shushan the *p*....Esth 3:15
his wrath went into the *p* .....Esth 7:7
king returned out of the *p*.....Esth 7:8
was given at Shushan the *p*.....Esth 8:14
in Shushan the *p* the Jews .....Esth 9:6
were slain in Shushan the *p* ...Esth 9:11
men in Shushan the *p*.........Esth 9:12
her bulwarks, consider her *p* ..Ps 48:13
his sanctuary like high *p* ......Ps 78:69
and prosperity within thy *p*....Ps 122:7
hands, and is in kings, *p* ......Prov 30:28
build upon her a *p* of silver ...Song 8:9
they raised up the *p* thereof ...Is 23:13
the *p* shall be forsaken ....Is 32:14
thorns shall come up in her *p*..Is 34:13
p of the king of Babylon ......Is 39:7
and let us destroy her *p*.......Jer 6:5
and is entered into our *p*......Jer 9:21
devour the *p* of Jerusalem.....Jer 17:27
consume the *p* of Ben-hadad ..Jer 49:27
hath swallowed up all her *p* ...Lam 2:5
the enemy the walls of her *p* ..Lam 2:7
he knew their desolate *p* ......Ezek 19:7
they shall set their *p* in ....Ezek 25:4
them to stand in the king's *p* ..Dan 1:4
and flourishing in my *p* ....Dan 4:4
he walked in the *p* of the .....Dan 4:29
of the wall of the king's *p* .....Dan 5:5
Then the king went to his *p* ...Dan 6:18
I was at Shushan in the *p* .....Dan 8:2
the tabernacles of his *p* ....Dan 11:45
and it shall devour the *p* ....Hos 8:14
devour the *p* of Ben-hadad ....Amos 1:4
which shall devour the *p* ......Amos 1:7
which shall devour the *p* ......Amos 1:10
which shall devour the *p* ......Amos 1:12
shall devour the *p* thereof .....Amos 1:14
it shall devour the *p* of........Amos 2:2
devour the *p* of Jerusalem.....Amos 2:5
Publish in the *p* at Ashdod ....Amos 3:9
the *p* in the land of Egypt .....Amos 3:9
violence and robbery in their *p*.Amos 3:10
and thy *p* shall be spoiled .....Amos 3:11
shall cast them into the *p* .....Amos 4:3
Jacob, and hate his *p* ....Amos 6:8
he shall tread in our *p* ....Mic 5:5
and the *p* shall be dissolved ...Nah 2:6
Peter sat without in the *p* .....Matt 26:69
even into the *p* of the high ....Mark 14:54
Peter was beneath in the *p* ....Mark 14:66
man armed keepeth his *p* ......Luke 11:21
Jesus into the *p* of the high ...John 18:15
in Christ are manifest..the *p*...Phil 1:13

PALAL (pā'lăl)—*"judge"*
Postexilic laborer ....Neh 3:25

PALE—*lacking color*
Figurative of:
Shame ....Is 29:22

[*also* PALENESS]
all faces are turned into *p*? ....Jer 30:6
looked and behold a *p* horse ..Rev 6:8

PALESTINE, PALESTINA—*"which is covvered"—region between Jordan River and Dead Sea on the east and the Mediterranean on the west*
on the inhabitants of *P*........Ex 15:14
Rejoice not thou, whole *P* ....Is 14:29
city, thou, whole *P*, art ....Is 14:31
Zidon, and all the coasts of *P*?.Joel 3:4
See CANAAN, LAND OF

PALLU, PHALLU (păl'ū, făll'o͞o)—*"distinguished"*
Son of Reuben; head of tribal family......... {Gen 46:9; Ex 6:14; Num 26:5, 8}

PALM—*the center part of the hand*
Used literally of:
Priest's hand ....Lev 14:15, 26
Idol's hand..............1Sam 5:4
Daniel's hand ....Dan 10:10
Soldier's hand ....Matt 26:67

[*also* PALMS]
upon the *p* of my hands.......Is 49:16
strike him with the *p* of their ..Mark 14:65
struck Jesus with the *p* of .....John 18:22
robes, and *p* in their hands ....Rev 7:9

PALM—*a tropical tree*
Uses of:
Fruit of, for food ....Joel 1:12
Figures of, carved on Temple 1Kin 6:29-35
Branches of, for booths ..Lev 23:40-42
Places of, at Elim and Jericho ....Ex 15:27
Site of, for judgeship ....Judg 4:5
Figurative of:
Righteous...............Ps 92:12
Beauty ....Song 7:7
Victory ....John 12:13

threescore and ten *p* trees .....Num 33:9
Jericho, the city of *p* trees ....Deut 34:3
out of the city of *p* trees ......Judg 1:16
cherubim, lions, and *p* 1Kin 7:36
and set thereon *p* trees and ...2Chr 3:5
Jericho, the city of *p* trees 2Chr 28:15
myrtle branches, and *p*........Neh 8:15
I will go up to the *p* tree......Song 7:8
They are upright as the *p* .....Jer 10:5
and upon each post were *p*....Ezek 40:16
their arches, and their *p* ......Ezek 40:22
it had *p* trees, one on this.....Ezek 40:26
p trees were upon the.........Ezek 40:31
made with cherubim and *p* ....Ezek 41:18
that a *p* tree was between a ...Ezek 41:18
toward the *p* tree on the one ..Ezek 41:19
the *p* tree on the other........Ezek 41:19
cherubim and *p* trees ....Ezek 41:20
cherubim and *p* trees, like.....Ezek 41:25

PALMERWORM—*an insect of Palestine*
Name probably designates the locust ....Amos 4:9

That which the *p* hath left.....Joel 1:4
the caterpillar, and the *p* ......Joel 2:25

PALMS, CITY OF
Moabites conquer ....Judg 3:12, 13

PALSY—*loss of bodily motion*
Healed by:
Christ ....Matt 4:24
Christians ....Acts 8:7

lieth at home sick of the *p* ....Matt 8:6
said unto the sick of the *p* ....Matt 9:2
saith he to the sick of the *p* ...Matt 9:6
bed wherein the sick of the *p*..Mark 2:4
he said unto the sick of the *p*..Mark 2:5
to say to the sick of the *p* .....Mark 2:9
saith to the sick of the *p* ......Mark 2:10
which was taken with a *p* .....Luke 5:18

PALTI, PHALTI (păl'tī, făl'tī)—*"Jehovah delivers"*
1. Benjamite spy ....Num 13:9
2. Man to whom Saul gives Michal, David's wife-to-be, in marriage.1Sam 25:44
See PALTIEL

PALTIEL, PHALTIEL (păl'tĭ-ĕl, făl'tĭ-ĕl)—*"God delivers"*
1. Prince of Issachar ....Num 34:26
2. Same as Palti 2 ....2Sam 3:15

PALTITE (păl'tīt)
Native of Beth-palet .....Josh 15:27
Home of one of David's mighty men 2Sam 23:26
Same referred to as the Pelonite 1Chr 11:27

PAMPHYLIA (pam-fil'i-a)—*"a nation made up of every tribe"—coastal region in South Asia Minor*
People from, at Pentecost. Acts 2:10
Paul visits .... Acts 13:13
John Mark returns home from .... Acts 13:13; Acts 15:38
Paul preaches in cities of . Acts 14:24, 25
Paul sails past .... Acts 27:5

PAN—*an open container for cooking*
Offering in .... Lev 2:5
Cooking .... Lev 6:21
Pouring 2Sam 13:9

[*also* PANS]
make his *p* to receive his ...... Ex 27:3
the *p*, shall be the priest's ..... Lev 7:9
baked it in *p*, and made .... Num 11:8
he struck it into the *p*, or 1Sam 2:14
that were made in the *p* 1Chr 9:31
that which is baked in the *p* ... 1Chr 23:29
in caldrons, and in *p*, and 2Chr 35:13
thou unto thee an iron *p* ...... Ezek 4:3

PANGS—*spasms of pain; mental anguish*
p and sorrows shall take ...... Is 13:8
p have taken hold upon .... Is 21:3
the *p* of a woman that .... Is 21:3
and crieth out in her *p* .... Is 26:17
thou be when *p* come upon ... Jer 22:23
heart of a woman in her *p* .... Jer 48:41
heart of a woman in her *p* .... Jer 49:22
and *p* as of a woman in .... Jer 50:43
p have taken thee as a .... Mic 4:9

PANIC—*sudden overpowering fright*

Among Israelites:
At the Red Sea .... Ex 14:10-12
Before the Philistines 1Sam 4:10
Of Judah before Israel ... 2Kin 14:12

Among nations:
Egyptians .... Ex 14:27
Philistines 1Sam 14:22
Syrians 2Kin 7:6, 7
Ammonites and Moabites. 2Chr 20:22-25

PANNAG (pan'ag)—*"sweet"*
Product of Palestine sold in Tyre .... Ezek 27:17

PANT—*to breathe spasmodically; long for*

[*also* PANTED, PANTETH]
My heart *p*, my strength ...... Ps 38:10
the hart *p* after the water ..... Ps 42:1
so *p* my soul after thee, O .... Ps 42:1
I opened my mouth, and *p* .... Ps 119:3
My heart *p*, fearfulness .... Is 21:4
That *p* after the dust of the ... Amos 2:7

PAPER—*material used for writing*
Writing material .... 2 John 12
Descriptive of reeds ..... Is 19:7
See PAPYRUS

PAPHOS (pā'fŏs)—*"that which boils"*
Paul blinds Elymas ...... Acts 13:6-13

PAPS—*breasts*
Prostitute .... Ezek 23:21
Mary the virgin .... Luke 11:27
Women .... Luke 23:29
Son of man (chest) ...... Rev 1:13

PAPYRUS (pă-pī'rŭs)—*a tall marsh plant growing in the Nile river region, used for making paper*
Referred to as bulrush in . Ex 2:3
See PAPER

PARABLE—*short narrative illustrating some aspect of the truth*

Descriptive of:
Prophecy .... Num 23:7, 18
Discourse .... Job 27:1
Wise saying .... Prov 26:7, 9
Prophetic message .... Ezek 17:1-10
Illustration (especially true of Christ's) .... Matt 13:18

Characteristics of:
Numerous .... Mark 4:33, 34
Illustrative .... Luke 12:16-21

Meaning of:
Self-evident .... Mark 12:1-12
Unknown .... Matt 13:36
Explained .... Luke 8:9-15
Prophetic .... Luke 21:29-36

Design of:
Bring under conviction ... 2Sam 12:1-6
Teach a spiritual truth ... Is 5:1-6
Illustrate a point .... Luke 10:25-37
Fulfill prophecy .... Matt 13:34, 35
Conceal truth from the unbelieving .... Matt 13:10-16

Of Christ, classification of:

Concerning God's love in Christ:
Lost sheep .... Luke 15:4-7
Lost money .... Luke 15:8-10
Prodigal son .... Luke 15:11-32
Hidden treasure .... Matt 13:44
Pearl of great price ...... Matt 13:45, 46

Concerning Israel:
Barren fig tree .... Luke 13:6-9
Two sons .... Matt 21:28-32
Wicked husbandman ..... Matt 21:33-46

Concerning Christianity (the Gospel) in this age:
New cloth .... Matt 9:16
New wine .... Matt 9:17
Sower .... Matt 13:3-8
Tares .... Matt 13:24-30
Mustard seed .... Matt 13:31, 32
Leaven .... Matt 13:33
Net .... Matt 13:47-50
Great supper .... Luke 14:16-24
Seed growing secretly .... Mark 4:26-29

Concerning salvation:
House built on the rock .. Matt 7:24-27
Pharisee and publican .... Luke 18:9-14
Two debtors .... Luke 7:36-50
Marriage of the king's Son .... Matt 22:1-14

Concerning Christian life:
Candle under a bushel ... Matt 5:15, 16
Unmerciful servant ...... Matt 18:23-35
Friend at midnight ...... Luke 11:5-13
Importunate widow ...... Luke 18:1-8
Tower .... Luke 14:28-35
Good Samaritan .... Luke 10:25-37
Unjust steward .... Luke 16:1-13
Laborers in the vineyard . Matt 20:1-17

Concerning rewards and punishments:
Ten virgins .... Matt 25:1-13
Talents .... Matt 25:14-30
Pounds .... Luke 19:12-27
Sheep and goats .... Matt 25:31-46
Master and servant ...... Luke 17:7-10
Servants watching .... Mark 13:33-37; Luke 12:36-40
Rich fool .... Luke 12:16-21
Rich man and Lazarus ... Luke 16:19-31

[*also* PARABLES]
And he took up his *p* .... Num 24:3
he took up his *p*, and said .... Num 24:20
took up his *p*, and said .... Num 24:21
took up his *p*, and said .... Num 24:23
Moreover Job continued his *p* . Job 29:1
will incline mine ear to a *p* .... Ps 49:4
I will open my mouth in a *p* ... Ps 78:2
utter a *p* unto the rebellious ... Ezek 24:3
one take up a *p* against .... Mic 2:4
all these take up a *p* against ... Hab 2:6
Jesus had finished these *p* ..... Matt 13:53
Declare unto us this *p* .... Matt 15:15
Now learn a *p* of the fig tree .. Matt 24:32
and said unto them in *p* .... Mark 3:23
taught them many things by *p* . Mark 4:2
twelve asked of him the *p* ..... Mark 4:10
these things are done in *p* ..... Mark 4:11
them, Know ye not this *p*? .... Mark 4:13
then will ye know all *p*? .... Mark 4:13
asked him concerning the *p* ... Mark 7:17
Now learn a *p* of the fig tree .. Mark 13:28
And he spake also a *p* unto ... Luke 5:36
And he spake a *p* unto them .. Luke 6:39
every city, he spake by a *p* .... Luke 8:4
he put forth a *p* to those ...... Luke 14:7
he spake this *p* unto them .... Luke 15:3
he added and spake a *p* .... Luke 19:11
speak to the people this *p* ..... Luke 20:9
had spoken this *p* against ..... Luke 20:19
This *p* spake Jesus unto .... John 10:6

PARACLETE (păr'ä-klēt)—*"a helper called to one's side"*
Greek word translated "Comforter" and "Advocate" .... John 14:16-18; John 15:26; 1 John 2:1

PARADISE—*the Garden of Eden, later applied to Heaven as well*
Applied in the New Testament to heaven . Luke 23:43; 2Cor 12:4; Rev 2:7

PARADOX—*a statement seemingly untrue or contradictory which may in fact be true*
Getting rich by poverty .. Prov 13:7
Dead burying the dead ... Matt 8:22
Finding life by losing it .. Matt 10:39
Not peace, but a sword .. Matt 10:34-38
Wise as serpents; harmless as doves ..... Matt 10:16
Hating and loving .... Luke 14:26
Becoming great by serving .... Mark 10:43
Dying in order to live .... John 12:24, 25
Becoming a fool to be wise 1Cor 3:18

PARAH (pā'rä)—*"increasing"*
City in Benjamin .... Josh 18:23

PARALYTIC—*one unable to move*
Brought to Jesus .... Matt 9:2; Mark 2:3
Healed by Jesus .... Matt 4:24; Luke 5:24
Healed by Jesus, through Peter .... Acts 9:33

PARAMOURS—*illicit lovers*
Applied to the male lover. Ezek 23:20

PARAN (pā'răn)—*"beauty"*
Mountainous country .... Hab 3:3
Residence of exiled Ishmael .... Gen 21:21
Israelites camp in .... Num 10:12
Headquarters of spies .... Num 13:3, 26
Site of David's refuge 1Sam 25:1

in the wilderness of *P* .... Num 12:16
Red Sea, between *P*, and ..... Deut 1:1
shined forth from mount *P* .... Deut 33:2
of Midian and came to *P* 1Kin 11:18
took men with them out of *P* . 1Kin 11:18

PARBAR (pär'bär)—*"a suburb"*
Precinct or colonnade west of the Temple 1Chr 26:18
Same word translated "suburbs" in 2Kin 23:11

PARCEL—*a tract or plot of land*
he bought a *p* of a field .... Gen 33:19
in a *p* of ground which Jacob .. Josh 24:32
selleth a *p* of land, which ..... Ruth 4:3
was a *p* of ground full of 1Chr 11:13
in the midst of that *p* 1Chr 11:14
the *p* of ground that Jacob .... John 4:5

PARCHED—*roasted; dry*
Corn .... Josh 5:11
Pulse 2Sam 17:28

neither bread, nor *p* corn ..... Lev 23:14
he reached her *p* corn, and .... Ruth 2:14
an ephah of this *p* corn 1Sam 17:17
and five measures of *p* corn ... 1Sam 25:18
p ground shall become a ...... Is 35:7
shall inhabit the *p* places ...... Jer 17:6

P

PARCHMENTS—*writing materials made from animal skins*
Paul sends request 2Tim 4:13

PARDON—*to forgive; forgiveness*
Objects of our:
Transgressions..........Ex 23:21
Iniquities ....Ex 34:9
Backslidings............Jer 5:6, 7
God's, described as:
Not granted 2Kin 24:4
Requested ....Num 14:19, 20
Abundant...............Is 55:7
Covering all sins........Jer 33:8
Belonging to the faithful remnant ....Is 40:2
Basis of:
Lord's name ....Ps 25:11
Repentance ....Is 55:7
Seeking the faith ....Jer 5:1
See FORGIVENESS

[*also* PARDONED, PARDONETH]
I pray thee *p* my sin 1Sam 15:25
this thing the Lord *p* thy 2Kin 5:18
Lord *p* thy servant in this 2Kin 5:18
The good Lord *p* every one ...2Chr 30:18
thou art a God ready to *p*.....Neh 9:17
not *p* my transgression ....Job 7:21
rebelled; thou hast not *p* ......Lam 3:42
unto thee, that *p* iniquity......Mic 7:18

PARE—*to trim or shave off*
her head and *p* her nails ......Deut 21:12

PARENTS—*people who raise children*
Kinds of:
Faithful (Abraham) ......Gen 18:18, 19
Neglectful (Moses) ......Ex 4:24-26
Presumptuous (Jephthah) .Judg 11:30-39
Holy (Hannah) 1Sam 1:11
Indulgent (Eli) 1Sam 2:22-29
Distressed (David).......2Sam 18:32, 33
Honored (Jonadab) ......Jer 35:5-10
Arrogant (Haman) ......Esth 3:1-10
Forgiving (prodigal son's father)...............Luke 15:17-24
Duties toward:
Obedience ....Eph 6:1
Honor ....Ex 20:12
Fear...................Lev 19:3
Duties of, toward children:
Protection ....Heb 11:23
Training ....Deut 6:6, 7
Education...............Gen 18:19
Deut 4:9
Correction ....Deut 21:18-21
Provision 2Cor 12:14
Sins of:
Favoritism ....Gen 25:28
Not restraining children ..1Sam 2:27-36
Bad example 1Kin 15:26
Anger ....Eph 6:4
Sins against, by children:
Disobedience............Rom 1:30
Cursing.................Ex 21:17
Mocking ....Prov 30:17
Disrespect ....Gen 9:21-27

shall rise up against their *p* ....Matt 10:21
shall rise up against their *p* ....Mark 13:12
the *p* brought in the child .....Luke 2:27
p went to Jerusalem every.....Luke 2:41
And her *p* were astonished ....Luke 8:56
hath left house, or *p*, or .....Luke 18:29
shall be betrayed both by *p* ...Luke 21:16
did sin, this man, or his *p* .....John 9:2
this man sinned, nor his *p* .....John 9:3
until they called the *p* of ......John 9:18
His *p* answered them and .....John 9:20
These words spake his *p* ......John 9:22
Therefore said his *p*, He is ....John 9:23
obey your *p* in all things .....Col 3:20
home, and to require their *p* ..1Tim 5:4
disobedient to *p*, unthankful ...2Tim 3:2
his three months of his *p*......Heb 11:23

PARLOR—*a room used mainly for entertaining guests*
Upper room in Eglon's home ....Judg 3:20-25
Room or hall for sacrificial meals 1Sam 9:22
Inside room of the temple 1Chr 28:11

PARMASHTA (pär-măsh'tä)—*"stronger"*
Haman's son ....Esth 9:9

PARMENAS (pär'mĕ-năs)—*"steadfast"*
One of the seven deacons. Acts 6:5

PARNACH (pär'năk)—*"gifted"*
Zebulunite ....Num 34:25

PAROSH, PHAROSH (pā'rŏsh, fā'rŏsh)—*"fleeing; fugitive"*
1. Head of a postexilic family .... Ezra 2:3; Ezra 8:3
Members of, divorced foreign wives ....Ezra 10:25
One of, Pedaiah, helps rebuild ....Neh 3:25
2. Chief who seals the covenant ....Neh 10:1, 14

PARSHANDATHA (pär-shăn-dā'thä)—*given by prayer"*
Haman's son ....Esth 9:7

PARSIMONY—*stinginess; living like a miser*
Characteristics of:
Choosing selfishly ....Gen 13:5-11
Living luxuriantly........Amos 6:4-6
Showing greediness ......John 12:5, 6
Withholding God's tithe ..Mal 3:8
Unmerciful toward the needy ....Zech 7:10-12
Punishment of brings:
Poverty ....Prov 11:24, 25
A curse................Prov 11:26
Revenge ....Prov 21:13
The closing of God's kingdom ....Luke 18:22-25

PART—*See* INTRODUCTION

PARTAKE—*to share in; take part in*
Of physical things:
Sacrifices 1Cor 10:18
Suffering...............2Cor 1:7
Benefit 1Tim 6:2
Human nature ....Heb 2:14
Discipline..............Heb 12:8
Bread 1Cor 10:17
Of evil things:
Evil ....Eph 5:3-7
Demonism 1Cor 10:21
Of spiritual things:
Divine nature 2Pet 1:4
Christ ....Heb 3:14
Holy Spirit.............Heb 6:4
Heavenly calling.........Heb 3:1
Grace ....Phil 1:7
Gospel 1Cor 9:23
Spiritual blessings ....Rom 11:17
Future glory 1Pet 5:1
Promise of salvation .....Eph 3:6

PARTAKER—*one who takes part in*
Of physical things:
Sacrifices 1Cor 10:18
Sufferings..............2Cor 1:7
Of evil things:
Sins 1Tim 5:22
Of spiritual things:
Holiness ....Heb 12:10
Communion.............1Cor 10:16, 17
Spiritual things ....Rom 15:27
Inheritance.............Col 1:12

[*also* PARTAKERS]
hast been *p* with adulterers ...Ps 50:18
we would not have been *p* ....Matt 23:30
if I by grace be a *p*, why am ..1Cor 10:30
be thou *p* of the afflictions 2Tim 1:8
must be first *p* of the fruits 2Tim 2:6
are *p* of Christ's sufferings 1Pet 4:13
God speed is *p* of his evil 2John 11
that ye be not *p* of her sins ...Rev 18:4

PARTED, PARTETH—*See* INTRODUCTION

PARTHIANS (pär'thĭ-ănz)—*inhabitants of Parthia*
Some present at Pentecost ....Acts 2:1, 9

PARTIALITY—*favoritism*
Manifested:
In marriages ....Gen 29:30
Among brothers.........Gen 43:30, 34
Between parents and children ....Gen 25:28
In social life ....James 2:1-4
Inconsistent with:
Household harmony .....Gen 37:4-35
Justice in law ....Lev 19:15
Favoritism in:
Ministry 1Tim 5:21
Spiritual things 2Cor 5:16
Restriction of salvation...Acts 10:28-35
Consistent with:
Choice of workers ....Acts 15:36-40
Estimate of friends ......Phil 2:19-22
God's predestination .....Rom 9:6-24
See FAVORITISM

[*also* PARTIAL]
but have been *p* in the law ....Mal 2:9
and good fruits without *p* .....James 3:17

PARTICULAR—*a separate part of a whole; one by one*
[*also* PARTICULARLY]
he declared *p* what ....Acts 21:19
of Christ and members in *p* ...1Cor 12:27
every one of you in *p* so love..Eph 5:33
we cannot now speak *p* ....Heb 9:5

PARTIES—*persons or groups taking one side of a question*
cause of both *p* shall come ....Ex 22:9

PARTING—*place where separating occurs*
Babylon stood at the *p* of .....Ezek 21:21

PARTITION—*a dividing wall*
In the sanctuary 1Kin 6:21
Between people ....Eph 2:11-14

PARTLY—*not completely*
shall be *p* strong and *p*........Dan 2:42
you; and I *p* believe it 1Cor 11:18
P, whilst ye were made a .....Heb 10:33
p, whilst ye became..........Heb 10:33

PARTNER—*an associate*
Crime ....Prov 29:24
Business ....Luke 5:7, 10
Christian work 2Cor 8:23
Philem 17

PARTRIDGE—*a wild bird, meaning "the caller" (in Hebrew)*
Hunted in mountains 1Sam 26:20
Figurative of ill-gotten riches ....Jer 17:11

PARUAH (pä-rōō'ä)—*"blooming"*
Father of Jehoshaphat, an officer of Solomon.....1Kin 4:17

PARVAIM (pä-vā'ĭm)—*"eastern"*
Unidentified place providing gold for Solomon's Temple 2Chr 3:6

PASACH (pā'săk)—*"limping"*
Asherite 1Chr 7:33

PAS-DAMMIM (păs-dăm'ĭm)—*"boundary of blood"*
Philistines gathered here. .1Chr 11:13

PASEAH, PHASEAH (pä-sē'ä, fä-sē'ä)—*"limping"*

1. Judahite 1Chr 4:12
2. Head of a family of Nethinim ....Ezra 2:43, 49
One of, repairs walls ....Neh 3:6
3. A family of Temple servants ....Neh 7:46, 51

PASHUR (păsh'her)—*"splitter; cleaver"*
1. Official opposing Jeremiah .... Jer 21:1; Jer 38:1-13
Descendants of, returnees ....Neh 11:12
2. Priest who put Jeremiah in jail ....Jer 20:1-6
3. Father of Gedaliah, Jeremiah's opponent . .Jer 38:1
4. Priestly family of returnees ....Ezra 2:38
Members of, divorced foreign wives ....Ezra 10:22
5. Priest who signs the covenant ....Neh 10:3

of Jerobam, the son of ***P***......1Chr 9:12
children of ***P***, a thousand .....Neh 7:41

PASS—*to go by; go beyond*

[*also* PASSED, PASSEDST, PASSEST, PASSETH, PASSING, PAST]

wind to ***p*** over the earth ......Gen 8:1
And Abram ***p*** through the ....Gen 12:6
a burning lamp that ***p***.........Gen 15:17
he rose up, and ***p*** over the ....Gen 31:21
with my staff I ***p*** over this.....Gen 32:10
and ***p*** over the ford Jabbok ...Gen 32:22
as he ***p*** over Penuel the ....Gen 32:31
he ***p*** over before them and ....Gen 33:3
p by Midiantes ....Gen 37:28
of his mourning were ***p*** ....Gen 50:4
I will ***p*** through the land ......Ex 12:12
I see..blood, I will ***p*** over .....Ex 12:13
p over the houses of the ......Ex 12:27
with his horn in time ***p***........Ex 21:29
the ox..to push in time ***p***......Ex 21:36
them every one that ***p*** ....Ex 30:13
Every one that ***p*** among ......Ex 30:14
while my glory ***p*** by, that .....Ex 33:22
And the Lord ***p*** by before.....Ex 34:6
whatsoever ***p*** under the ....Lev 27:32
we ***p*** through to search........Num 14:7
until we have ***p*** thy borders ...Num 20:17
until we be ***p*** thy borders .....Num 21:22
We will ***p*** over armed.........Num 32:32
and ***p*** through the midst of ....Num 33:8
are ***p*** over Jordan into the ....Num 33:51
when we ***p*** by from our ....Deut 2:8
and ***p*** by the way of the.......Deut 2:8
Emim dwelt..in times ***p***.......Deut 2:10
the kingdoms whither thou ***p*** . .Deut 3:21
now of the days that are ***p*** ....Deut 4:32
hated him not in times ***p***......Deut 4:42
he hated not in time ***p***........Deut 19:4
he hated him not in time ***p***....Deut 19:6
of this law, when thou art ***p***...Deut 27:3
through the nations which ye ***p***.Deut 29:16
p over Jordan to go to ....Deut 30:18
P through the host, and ....Josh 1:11
ye shall ***p*** over this Jordan ....Josh 1:11
p over, and came to Joshua ...Josh 2:23
lodged there before they ***p*** ....Josh 3:1
ye have not ***p*** this way ....Josh 3:4
p over before you into Jordan. .Josh 3:11
people ***p*** over..against.........Josh 3:16
the Israelites ***p*** over on ....Josh 3:17
people were ***p*** clean over......Josh 3:17
were clean ***p*** over Jordan .....Josh 4:1
when it ***p*** over Jordan, the ....Josh 4:7
and the people hasted and ***p***. . .Josh 4:10
all the people were clean ***p***....Josh 4:11
the ark of the Lord ***p*** over ....Josh 4:11
tribe of Manasseh ***p*** over......Josh 4:12
thousand prepared for war ***p*** . .Josh 4:13
until ye were ***p*** over, as the . . .Josh 4:23
until we were ***p*** over, that.....Josh 5:1
priests..***p*** on before the ....Josh 6:8
Joshua ***p*** from Makkedah .....Josh 10:29
And Joshua ***p*** from Libnah ....Josh 10:31
Lachish Joshua ***p*** unto ....Josh 10:34
and ***p*** along to Zin, and.......Josh 15:3
and ***p*** along to Hezron ....Josh 15:3
thence it ***p*** toward Azmon.....Josh 15:4
p along by the north of ....Josh 15:6
the border ***p*** toward the.......Josh 15:7
and ***p*** along unto the side .....Josh 15:10
and ***p*** on to Timnah ....Josh 15:10
p along to mount Baalah ......Josh 15:11
p along unto the borders of ...Josh 16:2
and ***p*** by it on the east to .....Josh 16:6
men went and ***p*** through ......Josh 18:9
And ***p*** along toward the.......Josh 18:18
And the border ***p*** along to ....Josh 18:19
from thence ***p*** on along on ....Josh 19:13
people through whom we ***p***.....Josh 24:17
and ***p*** beyond the quarries.....Judg 3:26
Gideon came to Jordan and ***p*** .Judg 8:4
children of Ammon ***p*** over ....Judg 10:9
he ***p*** over Gilead and ....Judg 11:29
p over Mizpeh of Gilead ......Judg 11:29
p over unto the children of....Judg 11:29
Jephthah ***p*** over unto the .....Judg 11:32
p thou over to fight against....Judg 12:1
and ***p*** over against the ....Judg 12:3
p thence unto mount..........Judg 18:13
And they ***p*** on and went ....Judg 19:14
p from Beth-lehem-judah......Judg 19:18
And he ***p*** through mount......1Sam 9:4
and ***p*** through the land........1Sam 9:4
they ***p*** through the land 1Sam 9:4
he ***p*** through the land of 1Sam 9:4
p on before us, (and he ***p*** on) .1Sam 9:27
the battle ***p*** over unto.........1Sam 14:23
p on, and gone down 1Sam 15:12
bitterness of death is ***p***........1Sam 15:32
presence, as in times ***p***........1Sam 19:7
p over with the..men 1Sam 27:2
the Philistines ***p*** on by 1Sam 29:2
men ***p*** on in the rearward 1Sam 29:2
p the love of women..........2Sam 1:26
plain, and ***p*** over Jordan 2Sam 2:29
in times ***p*** to be king 2Sam 3:17
in time ***p***, when Saul was 2Sam 5:2
and ***p*** over Jordan 2Sam 10:17
when the mourning was ***p*** 2Sam 11:27
his servants ***p*** on beside 2Sam 15:18
p on before the king 2Sam 15:18
Ittai the Gittite ***p*** over 2Sam 15:22
all the people ***p*** over..........2Sam 15:23
p over the brook Kidron 2Sam 15:23
all the people ***p*** over..........2Sam 15:23
people had done ***p*** out of 2Sam 15:24
If thou ***p*** on with me, then 2Sam 15:33
when David was a little ***p*** 2Sam 16:1
they ***p*** over Jordan 2Sam 17:22
Absalom ***p*** over Jordan, he....2Sam 17:24
they ***p*** over Jordan 2Sam 24:5
p over the brook Kidron 1Kin 2:37
one that ***p*** by it shall be.......1Kin 9:8
men ***p*** by, and saw the........1Kin 13:25
when midday was ***p***...........1Kin 18:29
behold, the Lord ***p*** by and a . .1Kin 19:11
Elijah ***p*** by him and cast his . . .1Kin 19:19
as the king ***p*** by, he cried 1Kin 20:39
Elisha ***p*** to Shunem 2Kin 4:8
that as oft as he ***p*** by, he 2Kin 4:8
which ***p*** by us continually 2Kin 4:9
Gehazi ***p*** on before them......2Kin 4:31
king of Israel was ***p*** by........2Kin 6:26
and he ***p*** by upon the wall 2Kin 6:30
one that ***p*** the account 2Kin 12:4
there ***p*** by a wild beast........2Kin 14:9
his son to ***p*** through..fire 2Kin 16:3
ruler over them in time ***p*** 1Chr 9:20
time ***p***, even when Saul was ...1Chr 11:2
Israel, and ***p*** over Jordan 1Chr 19:17
to every one that ***p*** by it 2Chr 7:21
Solomon ***p*** all the kings 2Chr 9:22
there ***p*** by a wild beast........2Chr 25:18
So the posts ***p*** from city to 2Chr 30:10
children to ***p*** through..fire 2Chr 33:6
Then a spirit ***p*** before my .....Job 4:15
great things ***p*** finding out .....Job 9:10
he ***p*** on also, but I perceive ...Job 9:11
are ***p*** away as the swift........Job 9:26
as waters that ***p*** away ....Job 11:16
until thy wrath be ***p*** ....Job 14:13
ever against him, and he ***p*** ....Job 14:20
no stranger ***p*** among them ....Job 15:19
My days are ***p***, my purposes...Job 17:11
the fierce lion ***p*** by it ....Job 28:8
I were as in months ***p***.........Job 29:2
welfare ***p*** away as a cloud .....Job 30:15
at midnight, and ***p*** away ......Job 34:20
the wind ***p***, and cleanseth .....Job 37:21
p through the paths ....Ps 8:8
his thick clouds ***p***.............Ps 18:12
he shall bring it to ***p***..........Ps 37:5
Yet he ***p*** away, and, lo, he ....Ps 37:36
assembled, they ***p*** by ....Ps 48:4
a wind that ***p*** away, and ....Ps 78:39
Who ***p*** through the valley .....Ps 84:6
as yesterday when it is ***p*** ......Ps 90:4
For the wind ***p*** over it ....Ps 103:16
as a shadow that ***p*** away ......Ps 144:4
p through the street near......Prov 7:8
As the whirlwind ***p***, so is......Prov 10:25
He that ***p*** by, and ....Prov 26:17
One generation ***p*** away ....Eccl 1:4
requireth that which is ***p***......Eccl 3:15
the winter is ***p***, the rain is .....Song 2:11
little that I ***p*** from them.......Song 3:4
he shall ***p*** through Judah ......Is 8:8
Aiath, he is ***p*** to Migron ......Is 10:28
Zidon, that ***p*** over the sea ....Is 23:2
P through thy land..river ......Is 23:10
arise, ***p*** over to Chittim ....Is 23:12
as chaff that ***p*** away ....Is 29:5
p over he will preserve it......Is 31:5
judgment is ***p*** over from ......Is 40:27
He pursued them, and ***p*** ......Is 41:3
When thou ***p*** through the .....Is 43:2
that no man ***p*** through ....Jer 2:6
harvest is ***p***, the summer ......Jer 8:20
that none ***p*** through? ....Jer 9:12
holy flesh is ***p*** from thee? .....Jer 11:15
as the stubble that ***p*** ....Jer 13:24
that ***p*** thereby shall be ....Jer 18:16
that ***p*** thereby shall be ....Jer 19:8
p between the parts thereof ...Jer 34:18
p between the parts of the ....Jer 34:19
he hath ***p*** the time............Jer 46:17
when I ***p*** by thee, and saw ....Ezek 16:6
Now when I ***p*** by thee ....Ezek 16:8
on every one that ***p*** by........Ezek 16:15
to every one that ***p*** by ....Ezek 16:25
cut off from it him that ***p*** .....Ezek 35:7
in the sight of all that ***p***......Ezek 36:34
p through the land to bury ....Ezek 39:14
river that could not be ***p*** ......Ezek 47:5
the smell of fire had ***p*** on .....Dan 3:27
palace, and ***p*** the night........Dan 6:18
p over upon her fair neck .....Hos 10:11
early dew that ***p*** away ....Hos 13:3
thy waves ***p*** over me..........Jon 2:3
have ***p*** through the gate ....Mic 2:13
p by the transgression.........Mic 7:18
wickedness ***p*** continually? .....Nah 3:19
overflowing of the water ***p*** ....Hab 3:10
every one that ***p*** by her ....Zeph 2:15
waste, that none ***p*** by.........Zeph 3:6
caused thine iniquity to ***p*** .....Zech 3:4
no man ***p*** through nor ....Zech 7:14
come to ***p***, that ten men ......Zech 8:23
because of him that ***p*** by ......Zech 9:8
Till heaven and earth ***p*** ....Matt 5:18
into a ship, and ***p*** over........Matt 9:1
And as Jesus ***p*** forth from.....Matt 9:9
and the time is now ***p***.........Matt 14:15
heard that Jesus ***p*** by ....Matt 20:30
Heaven and earth shall ***p***......Matt 24:35
My words shall not ***p*** away ....Matt 24:35
let this cup ***p*** from............Matt 26:39
they that ***p*** by reviled him.....Matt 27:39
as he ***p*** by, he saw Levi ....Mark 2:14
Let us ***p*** over..other side ....Mark 4:35
Jesus was ***p*** over again ....Mark 5:21
now the time is far ***p*** ....Mark 6:35

would have ***p*** by them .... Mark 6:48
when they had ***p*** over .... Mark 6:53
and ***p*** through Galilee .... Mark 9:30
as they ***p*** by, they saw .... Mark 11:20
the hour might ***p*** from .... Mark 14:35
Simon a Cyrenian, who ***p*** by .. Mark 15:21
that ***p*** by railed on him .... Mark 15:29
when the sabbath was ***p*** .... Mark 16:1
he ***p*** through the midst of ..... Luke 4:30
he ***p*** by on the other side ..... Luke 10:31
him, and ***p*** by on the other .... Luke 10:32
which would ***p*** from hence .... Luke 16:26
p through the midst .... Luke 17:11
hearing the multitude ***p*** by .... Luke 18:36
Jesus of Nazareth ***p*** by .... Luke 18:37
entered and ***p*** through Jericho . Luke 19:1
For he was to ***p*** that way ..... Luke 19:4
these things shall come to ***p***? .. Luke 21:7
is ***p*** from death unto life ...... John 5:24
midst of them and so ***p*** by .... John 8:59
as Jesus ***p*** by, he saw a man .. John 9:1
the shadow of Peter ***p*** by ..... Acts 5:15
p through he preached in ..... Acts 8:40
Peter ***p*** throughout all .... Acts 9:32
in times ***p*** suffered all .... Acts 14:16
had ***p*** throughout Pisidia ...... Acts 14:24
p through Phoenecia and ...... Acts 15:3
p by Mysia came down to ..... Acts 16:8
they had ***p*** through Amphipolis. Acts 17:1
For as I ***p*** by, and beheld ..... Acts 17:23
Paul having ***p*** through the ..... Acts 19:1
when he had ***p*** through .... Acts 19:21
hardly ***p*** it, came unto a ...... Acts 27:8
the fast was now already ***p*** .... Acts 27:9
of sins that are ***p*** .... Rom 3:25
so death ***p*** upon all men ...... Rom 5:12
in times ***p*** have not .... Rom 11:30
his ways ***p*** finding out! .... Rom 11:33
if she ***p*** the flower 1Cor 7:36
all ***p*** through the sea 1Cor 10:1
conversation in time ***p*** .... Gal 1:13
persecuted us in times ***p*** ...... Gal 1:23
also told you in time ***p*** .... Gal 5:21
in time ***p*** ye walked .... Eph 2:2
conversation in times ***p*** .... Eph 2:3
being in time ***p*** Gentiles ...... Eph 2:11
of Christ, which ***p*** knowledge .. Eph 3:19
Who being ***p*** feeling have ..... Eph 4:19
which ***p*** all understanding ..... Phil 4:7
that the resurrection is ***p*** 2Tim 2:18
in time ***p*** was..unprofitable .... Philem 11
spake in time ***p*** unto the ...... Heb 1:1
when she was ***p*** age .... Heb 11:11
faith they ***p*** through the .... Heb 11:29
as..grass he shall ***p*** .... James 1:10
Which in time ***p*** were not 1Pet 2:10
the time ***p*** of our life may 1Pet 4:3
heavens shall ***p*** away with 2Pet 3:10
we have ***p*** from death unto 1John 3:14
One woe is ***p***; and behold ..... Rev 9:12
the second woe is ***p***, and ...... Rev 11:14
first earth were ***p*** away .... Rev 21:1
former things are ***p*** away ...... Rev 21:4

PASSAGE—*road; path; channel; course*

[*also* PASSAGES]
Edom refused to give Israel ***p***. . Num 20:21
p of the children of Israel ..... Josh 22:11
Gileadites took the ***p*** of .... Judg 12:5
slew him at the ***p*** of Jordan ... Judg 12:6
out to the ***p*** of Michmash 1Sam 13:23
between the ***p***, by which 1Sam 14:4
They are gone over the ***p*** ..... Is 10:29
cry from the ***p***; for all thy ..... Jer 22:20
And that the ***p*** are stopped .... Jer 51:32

PASSENGERS—*wayfarers; travelers*
p who go right on their .... Prov 9:15
the valley of the ***p*** on the ..... Ezek 39:11
stop the noses of the ***p*** .... Ezek 39:11
land to bury with the ***p*** .... Ezek 39:14
the ***p*** that pass through .... Ezek 39:15

PASSING AWAY—*ceasing to exist*

Things subject to:
Our days .... Ps 90:9
Old things 2Cor 5:17
World's fashion 1Cor 7:31
World's lust 1John 2:17
Heaven and earth 2Pet 3:10

Things not subject to:
Christ's words .... Luke 21:33
Christ's dominion .... Dan 7:14

PASSION—*suffering; Christ's sufferings between the Last Supper and his death; intense emotion; desire*

Descriptive of:
Christ's sufferings .... Acts 1:3
Man's nature .... James 5:17
Lusts .... Rom 1:26

As applied (theologically) to Christ's sufferings:
Predicted .... Is 53:1-12
Portrayed visibly .... Mark 14:3-8
Preached .... Acts 3:12-18; 1Pet 1:10-12

[*also* PASSIONS]
himself alive after his ***p*** .... Acts 1:3
are men of like ***p*** with you .... Acts 14:15
subject to like ***p*** as we are .... James 5:17

PASSOVER—*a Jewish festival commemorating the exodus from Egypt*

Features concerning:
Commemorative of the tenth plague .... Ex 12:3-28
Necessity of blood applied .... Ex 12:7
To be repeated annually. . Ex 12:24-27

Observances of:
At Sinai .... Num 9:1-14
At the conquest .... Josh 5:10-12
By Christ .... Matt 26:18, 19

Typical of the Lord's death (the Lord's Supper):
Lamb without blemish ... 1Pet 1:19
One of their own .... Ex 12:5; Heb 2:14, 17
Lamb chosen .... Ex 12:3; 1Pet 2:4
Slain at God's appointed time .... { Ex 12:6; Acts 2:23 }
Christ is 1Cor 5:7
See LAMB OF GOD, THE

[*also* PASSOVERS]
the ordinance of the ***p*** .... Ex 12:43
keep the ***p*** to the Lord .... Ex 12:48
of the ***p*** be left unto the ..... Ex 34:25
at even is the Lord's ***p*** .... Lev 23:5
is the ***p*** of the Lord .... Num 28:16
on the morrow after the ***p*** ..... Num 33:3
keep the ***p*** unto the Lord ..... Deut 16:1
shalt therefore sacrifice the ***p*** .. Deut 16:2
not sacrifice the ***p*** .... Deut 16:5
sacrifice the ***p*** at even .... Deut 16:6
Keep the ***p*** unto the Lord 2Kin 23:21
not holden such a ***p*** from 2Kin 23:22
this ***p*** was holden to the 2Kin 23:23
to keep the ***p*** unto the 2Chr 30:1
keep the ***p*** in the second 2Chr 30:2
keep the ***p*** unto the Lord 2Chr 30:5
killed the ***p*** on the 2Chr 30:15
the killing of the ***p*** 2Chr 30:17
yet did they eat the ***p*** 2Chr 30:18
Josiah kept a ***p*** unto the 2Chr 35:1
killed the ***p*** on the 2Chr 35:1
kill the ***p***, and sanctify 2Chr 35:6
all for the ***p*** offerings 2Chr 35:7
unto the priests for the ***p*** 2Chr 35:8
unto the Levites for ***p*** 2Chr 35:9
they killed the ***p***, and the 2Chr 35:11
roasted the ***p*** with fire 2Chr 35:13
to keep the ***p***, and to offer 2Chr 35:16
were present kept the ***p*** 2Chr 35:17
was no ***p*** like to that kept 2Chr 35:18
such a ***p*** as Josiah kept 2Chr 35:18
of Josiah was this ***p*** kept 2Chr 35:19
the captivity kept the ***p*** .... Ezra 6:19
killed the ***p*** for all the .... Ezra 6:20
ye shall have the ***p*** .... Ezek 45:21
for thee to eat the ***p***? .... Matt 26:17
days was the feast of the ***p*** .... Mark 14:1
when they killed the ***p*** .... Mark 14:12
thou mayest eat the ***p***? .... Mark 14:12
I shall eat the ***p*** with my ...... Mark 14:14
they made ready the ***p*** .... Mark 14:16
year at the feast of the ***p*** ..... Luke 2:41
which is called the ***P*** .... Luke 22:1
the ***p*** must be killed .... Luke 22:7
Go and prepare us the ***p*** ...... Luke 22:8
I shall eat the ***p*** with my ...... Luke 22:11
they made ready the ***p*** .... Luke 22:13
I have desired to eat this ***p*** ... Luke 22:15
the Jews' ***p*** was at hand .... John 2:13
in Jerusalem at the ***p*** .... John 2:23
the ***p***, a feast of the Jews .... John 6:4
Jews' ***p*** was nigh at hand ..... John 11:55
to Jerusalem before the ***p*** ..... John 11:55
Jesus six days before the ***p*** .... John 12:1
before the feast of the ***p*** ..... John 13:1
that they might eat the ***p*** ...... John 18:28
release unto you one at the ***p***. John 18:39
the preparation of the ***p*** .... John 19:14
Through faith he kept the ***p*** .. Heb 11:28

PASSWORD—*a secret word used to identify friends*
Used by Gileadites ...... Judg 12:5, 6

PASTOR—*shepherd*
To perfect the saints ..... Eph 4:11, 12
Appointed by God .... Jer 3:15
Some rebellious .... Jer 2:8
Unfaithful ones are punished .... Jer 22:22
See SHEPHERD

[*also* PASTORS]
p are become brutish .... Jer 10:21
Many ***p*** have destroyed my .... Jer 12:10
not hastened from being a ***p*** .. Jer 17:16
Woe be unto the ***p*** that ...... Jer 23:1
against the ***p*** that feed my ..... Jer 23:2

PASTURE—*a place for grazing animals*

Used literally of places for:
Cattle to feed .... Gen 47:4
Wild animals to feed ..... Is 32:14
God's material blessings .. Ps 65:11-13

Used figuratively of:
Restoration and peace ... Ezek 34:13-15
True Israel .... Ps 95:7
Kingdom of God .... Is 49:9, 10
Kingdom of Israel .... Jer 25:36
Gospel .... Is 30:23
Abundant provision for salvation .... Ezek 45:15

Of the true Israel (the church), described as:
God's people .... Ps 100:3
Provided for .... John 10:9
Purchased .... Ps 74:1, 2
Thankful .... Ps 79:13
Scattered by false pastors . Jer 23:1
See SHEPHERD

[*also* PASTURES]
twenty oxen out of the ***p*** 1Kin 4:23
to seek ***p*** for their flocks 1Chr 4:39
they found fat ***p*** and good 1Chr 4:40
p there for their flocks 1Chr 4:41
mountains is his ***p*** .... Job 39:8
to lie down in green ***p*** .... Ps 23:2
like harts that find no ***p*** ...... Lam 1:6
have eaten up the good ***p*** ..... Ezek 34:18
the residue of your ***p***? .... Ezek 34:18
flock, the flock of my ***p*** ...... Ezek 34:31
According to their ***p***, so ...... Hos 13:6
because they have no ***p*** .... Joel 1:18
the ***p*** of the wilderness .... Joel 1:19
the ***p*** of the wilderness .... Joel 1:20
the ***p*** of the wilderness do .... Joel 2:22
shall go in and out, and find ***p*** . John 10:9

PATARA (păt'ä-rä)—*"trodden under foot"*
Paul changes ships here .. Acts 21:1, 2

PATE—*the top of the head*
Figurative of retribution . . Ps. 7:16

PATH—*a walk; manner of life*
Of the wicked:
Brought to nothing . . . . . . Job 6:18
Becomes dark . . . . Job 24:13
Is crooked . . . . Is 59:8
Leads to death . . . . Prov 2:18
Filled with wickedness . . . Prov 1:15,16
Is destructive . . . . Is 59:7
Followed by wicked rulers Is 3:12
Made difficult by God . . . Hos. 2:6
Of believers:
Beset with difficulties . . . . Job 19:8
Under God's control . . . . . Job 13:27
Hindered by the wicked . . Job 30:13
Enriched by the Lord . . . . Ps 23:3
Upheld by God . . . . Ps 17:5
Provided with light . . . . . . Ps 119:105
Known by God . . . . Ps 139:3
Like a shining light . . . . . . Prov 4:18
Directed by God . . . . Is 26:7
To be pondered . . . . Prov 4:26
No death at the end . . . . . . Prov 12:28
Sometimes unknown . . . . . Is 42:16
Sometimes seems crooked. Lam 3:9
To be made straight . . . . . Heb 12:13
Of righteousness:
Taught by father . . . . Prov 4:1, 11
Kept . . . . Prov 2:20
Shown to Messiah . . . . Ps 16:11
Acts 2:28
Taught to believers . . . . . . Ps 25:4, 5
Sought by believers . . . . . . Ps 119:35
Is 2:3
Rejected by unbelieving . . Jer 6:16
Jer 18:15
Of the Lord:
True . . . . Ps 25:10
Plain . . . . Ps 27:11
Rich . . . . Ps 65:11
Guarded . . . . Prov 2:8
Upright . . . . Prov 2:13
Living . . . . Prov 2:19
Peaceful . . . . Prov 3:17

[*also* PATHS, PATHWAY]
an adder in the *p*, that . . . . Gen 49:17
angel..stood in a *p* . . . . Num 22:24
So are the *p* of all that . . . . Job 8:13
p which no fowl knoweth . . . . . Job 28:7
he marketh all my *p* . . . . Job 33:11
know the *p* to the house . . . . . . Job 38:20
He maketh a *p* to shine . . . . Job 41:32
through the *p* of the seas . . . . . . Ps 8:8
the *p* of the destroyer . . . . Ps 17:4
thy *p* in the great waters . . . . . . Ps 77:19
thou knewest my *p* . . . . Ps 142:3
yea, every good *p* . . . . Prov 2:9
they froward in their *p* . . . . Prov 2:15
he shall direct thy *p* . . . . Prov 3:6
Enter not into the *p* of the . . . . Prov 4:14
ponder the *p* of life . . . . Prov 5:6
go not astray in her *p* . . . . Prov 7:25
in the places of the *p* . . . . Prov 8:2
the *p* of judgment . . . . Prov 8:20
p thereof..is no death . . . . Prov 12:28
turn aside out of the *p* . . . . Is 30:11
taught him in the *p* of . . . . Is 40:14
a *p* in the mighty waters . . . . . . Is 43:16
The restorer of *p* to dwell . . . . . Is 58:12
walk in *p*, in a way not . . . . Jer 18:15
walk every one in his *p* . . . . Joel 2:8
and we will walk in his *p* . . . . . . Mic 4:2
make his *p* straight . . . . Matt 3:3
make his *p* straight . . . . Mark 1:3
make his *p* straight . . . . Luke 3:4

PATHROS (păth′rŏs)—*"persuasion of ruin"*
Name applied to south (Upper) Egypt . . . . Ezek 29:10-14
Described as a lowly kingdom . . . . Ezek 29:14-16
Refuge for dispersed Jews. Jer 44:1-15
Jews to be regathered from . . . . Is 11:11

PATHRUSIM—*the inhabitants of Pathros*
Hamitic people descending from Mizraim and living in Pathros . . . . Gen 10:14

PATIENCE—*the ability to bear trials without grumbling*
Of the Trinity:
God, the author of . . . . . . Rom 15:5
Christ, the example of . . . 2Thess 3:5
Spirit, the source of . . . . . Gal 5:22
Described as:
Rewarded . . . . Rom 2:7
Endured with joy . . . . Col 1:11
Product of:
Good heart . . . . Luke 8:15
Tribulation . . . . Rom 5:3, 4
Testing of faith . . . . James 1:3
Hope . . . . Rom 8:25
Scriptures . . . . Rom 15:4
Necessary grace, in:
Times of crises . . . . Luke 21:15-19
Dealing with a church . . . 2Cor 12:12
Opposing evil . . . . Rev 2:2
Soundness of faith . . . . . . Titus 2:2
Waiting for Christ's return . . . . James 5:7, 8

[*also* PATIENT, PATIENTLY]
and wait *p* for him . . . . Ps 37:7
I waited *p* for the Lord . . . . Ps 40:1
p in spirit is better than . . . . Eccl 7:8
Lord, have *p* with me . . . . Matt 18:26
Have *p* with me, and I . . . . Matt 18:29
beseech thee to hear me *p* . . . . Acts 26:3
in hope; *p* in tribulation . . . . Rom 12:12
of God, in much *p*, in 2Cor 6:4
and *p* of hope in our Lord 1Thess 1:3
be *p* toward all men 1Thess 5:14
for your *p* and faith in all 2Thess 1:4
p, not a brawler, not 1Tim 3:3
faith, love, *p*, meekness 1Tim 6:11
apt to teach, *p* 2Tim 2:24
long suffering, charity, *p* 2Tim 3:10
faith and *p* inherit the . . . . Heb 6:12
after he had *p* endured . . . . Heb 6:15
for ye have need of *p* . . . . Heb 10:36
let us run with *p* the race . . . . . Heb 12:1
But let *p* have her perfect . . . . . James 1:4
affliction, and of *p* . . . . James 5:10
heard of the *p* of Job . . . . James 5:11
faults, ye shall take it *p*? 1Pet 2:20
ye take it *p*, this is 1Pet 2:20
temperance *p*; and to *p* 2Pet 1:6
kingdom and *p* of Jesus . . . . Rev 1:9
hast *p*, and for my name's . . . . . Rev 2:3
thy *p*. and thy works . . . . Rev 2:19
kept the word of my *p* . . . . Rev 3:10
is the *p* and the faith of . . . . Rev 13:10
Here is the *p* of the saints . . . . . Rev 14:12

PATMOS (păt′mŏs)—*"mortal"*
John banished here, receives the revelation . Rev 1:9

PATRIARCH—*ancient family, or tribal head*
Applied in New Testament, to Abraham, to Jacob's sons, and to David . . . . Heb 7:4

[*also* PATRIARCHS]
speak unto you of the *p* David . Acts 2:29
Jacob begat the twelve *p* . . . . . . Acts 7:8
the *p*, moved with envy . . . . Acts 7:9

PATRIARCHAL AGE—*the time of Abraham, Isaac, and Jacob*
Rulers of:
Kings . . . . Gen 12:15-20
Chiefs . . . . Gen 26:1
Family heads (fathers) . . . Gen 18:18, 19
Business of:
Cattle, etc. . . . . Gen 12:16
Caravans . . . . Gen 37:28-36
Selling, etc . . . . Gen 23:1-20
Contracts . . . . Gen 21:27-30
Business agreements . . . . . Gen 30:28-34
Customs of:
Prevalence of polygamy . . Gen 16:4
Existence of slavery . . . . . Gen 12:16
Son's wife, selected by his father . . . . Gen 24:1-4
Children given significant names . . . . Gen 29:31-35
Religion of:
Existence of idolatry . . . . . Gen 35:1, 2
Worship of God Almighty. Gen 14:19-22
God's covenant recognized . . . . Gen 12:1-3
Circumcision observed . . . Gen 17:10-14
Headship of father . . . . . . Gen 35:2
Obedience primary . . . . . . Gen 18:18, 19
Prayers and sacrifices offered . . . . Gen 12:8
Blessings and curses pronounced by father . . Gen 27:27-40
True faith believed . . . . . . Matt 15:28
Heb 11:8-22

PATRICIDE—*the killing of one's father*
Sennacherib's sons guilty of 2Kin 19:36, 37

PATRIMONY—*inherited possessions*
Applied to Levites' portion . . . . Deut 18:8
Same idea found in . . . . . Luke 12:13
See INHERITANCE, EARTHLY

PATRIOTISM—*love of one's country*
Manifested in:
Willingness to fight for one's country 1Sam 17:26-51
Concern for national survival . . . . Esth 4:13-17
Desire for national revival Neh 1:2-11
Loyalty to national leader. 2Sam 2:10
Respect for national leaders 2Sam 1:18-27

PATROBAS (păt′rō-băs)—*"paternal"*
Christian at Rome . . . . Rom 16:14

PATTERN—*a copy; an example*
Of physical things:
Tabernacle . . . . Heb 8:5
Temple 1Chr 28:11-19
Of spiritual things:
Good works . . . . Titus 2:7
Heavenly originals . . . . Heb 9:23
See EXAMPLE; EXAMPLE OF CHRIST, THE

the *p* of the tabernacle . . . . Ex 25:9
p of all the instruments . . . . Ex 25:9
p..showed thee in the mount . . Ex 25:40
the *p* which the Lord had . . . . . Num 8:4
the *p* of the altar of the . . . . Josh 22:28
altar, and the *p* of it 2Kin 16:10
let them measure the *p* . . . . Ezek 43:10
p to them which should 1Tim 1:16

PAU, PAI (pā′ū, pā′ī)—*"howling"*
Edomite town, residence of King Hadar (Hadad) . . . . {Gen 36:39; 1Chr 1:50}

PAUL (pôl)—*"little"—a Pharisee who was converted and made an apostle to the Gentiles; who wrote several of the letters in the New Testament*
Life of:
From birth to conversion:
Born at Tarsus in Cilicia . Acts 22:3
Born a Roman citizen . . . Acts 22:25-28
Called Saul until changed to Paul . . . . {Acts 9:11; Acts 13:9}
Benjamite Jew . . . . Phil 3:5
Citizen of Tarsus . . . . Acts 21:39
By trade a tentmaker . . . . Acts 18:1, 3
Zealot for Judaism . . . . . . Gal 1:14
Phil 3:5

- Very strict Pharisee ...... Acts 23:6; Phil 3:5, 6
- Educated under Gamaliel . Acts 22:3
- His sister in Jerusalem ... Acts 23:16
- Apparently unmarried or a widower 1Cor 9:5
- Member of Jewish council . Acts 26:10
- Zealous for the Mosaic Law .... Acts 26:4, 5
- Consented to Stephen's death .... Acts 7:58; Acts 8:1; Acts 22:20
- Intensified persecution of Christians .... Acts 9:1-3; Acts 22:3-5; Acts 26:10, 11; Gal 1:13
- Conscientious persecutor . Acts 26:9; 1Tim 1:13

His conversion:

- On road to Damascus .... Acts 9:1-19
- At noon .... Acts 26:13
- Blinded by supernatural vision .... Acts 9:3, 8; 2Cor 12:1-7
- Responded willingly to Jesus' entreaty .... Acts 9:4-9
- Given a divine commission .... Acts 9:6, 10-18; Eph 3:1-8
- Instructed and baptized by Ananias .... Acts 9:6, 10-18
- Repeated his conversion story .... Acts 22:1-16; Acts 26:1-20
- Referred to it often .... 1Cor 9:1, 16; 1Cor 15:8-10; Gal 1:12-16
- Considered himself unworthy .... Eph 3:1-8
- Cites details of his change. Phil 3:4-10
- Regretted former life 1Tim 1:12-16
- Not ashamed of Christ ... Rom 1:16; 2Tim 1:8-12
- Preached Jesus as God's Son and as the Christ (that is, the Messiah) .. Acts 9:19-22
- Persecuted by Jews; went to Arabia ...... Acts 9:23-25; 2Cor 11:32, 33; Gal 1:17
- Returned to Damascus ... Gal 1:17
- Visited Jerusalem briefly . Acts 9:26-29; Gal 1:18, 19
- Received vision of his ministry to Gentiles .... Acts 22:17-21
- Sent by disciples to Tarsus .... Acts 9:29, 30; Gal 1:21
- Brought to Antioch (in Syria) by Barnabas .... Acts 11:22-26
- Sent to Jerusalem with relief .... Acts 11:27-30
- Returned to Antioch ..... Acts 12:25

First Missionary Journey:

- Divinely chosen and commissioned .... Acts 13:1-4; Acts 26:19, 20
- Accompanied by Barnabas and John Mark .... Acts 13:1, 5
- Preached in Cyprus ..... Acts 13:4-12
- Sailed to Perga; Mark left him .... Acts 13:13
- Preached in Antioch (in Pisidia); rejected by Jews .... Acts 13:14-51; 2Tim 3:11
- Rejected in Iconium ..... Acts 13:51, 52; Acts 14:1-5
- Stoned at Lystra .... Acts 14:6-20; 2Tim 3:11
- Went to Derbe .... Acts 14:20, 21
- Returned to Antioch (in Syria) .... Acts 14:21-26
- Told Christians about his work .... Acts 14:27, 28
- Participated in Jerusalem Council .... Acts 15:2-22; Gal 2:1-10
- Rebuked Peter in Antioch for inconsistency .... Gal 2:11-21

Second Missionary Journey:

- Rejected John Mark as companion; took Silas. . Acts 15:36-40
- Strengthened churches in Syria and Cilicia .... Acts 15:41
- Revisited Derbe and Lystra .... Acts 16:1
- Took Timothy as worker . Acts 16:1-5
- Directed by the Spirit where to preach .... Acts 16:6, 7
- Responded to Macedonian vision ..... Acts 16:8, 9
- Joined by Luke ("we") .. Acts 16:10
- Entered Macedonia ...... Acts 16:10, 11
- Converted Lydia at Philippi .... Acts 16:12-15
- Cast into prison; jailer converted .... Acts 16:16-34
- Used Roman citizenship. . Acts 16:35-39
- Preached at Thessalonica .... Acts 17:1-9; 1Thess 1:7; 1Thess 2:2-18
- Received by the Bereans . Acts 17:10-13
- Left Silas and Timothy; went to Athens .... Acts 27:14-17
- Preached on Mars' Hill (the Areopagus) .... Acts 17:18-34
- Arrived in Corinth; stayed with Aquila and Priscilla .... Acts 18:1-5
- Reunited with Silas and Timothy .... Acts 18:5; 1Thess 3:6
- Wrote letters to Thessalonians 1Thess 3:1-6; 2Thess 2:2
- Established a church at Corinth .... Acts 18:5-18
- Stopped briefly at Ephesus .... Acts 18:19-21
- Saluted Jerusalem church; returned to Antioch (in Syria) .... Acts 18:22

Third Missionary Journey:

- Strengthened churches of Galatia and Phrygia ... Acts 18:23
- Gave direction for relief collection 1Cor 16:1
- Ministered three years in Ephesus .... Acts 19:1-12; Acts 20:31
- Saved from angry mob ... Acts 19:13-41
- Probably wrote *Galatians* here .... Gal 1:1
- Wrote *First Corinthians* here 1Cor 5:9
- Went to Troas; failed to meet Titus 2Cor 2:12, 13
- Reunited with Titus in Macedonia .... Acts 20:1; 2Cor 7:5-16
- Wrote *Second Corinthians;* sent Titus to Corinth with this letter 2Cor 8:6-18
- Traveled extensively ..... Acts 20:2; Rom 15:19
- Visited Greece and Corinth .... Acts 20:2, 3
- Wrote *Romans* in Corinth. Rom 1:1
- Returned through Macedonia .... Acts 20:3
- Preached long sermon in Troas .... Acts 20:5-13
- Gave farewell talk to Ephesian elders at Miletus .... Acts 20:14-38
- Arrived in Caesarea ..... Acts 21:1-8
- Warned by Agabus ...... Acts 21:9-14

In Jerusalem and Caesarea:

- Arrived in Jerusalem; welcomed by church ... Acts 21:15-19
- Falsely charged; riot follows .... Acts 21:20-40
- Defended his action; removed by Roman police .... Acts 22:1-30
- Defended his action before Jewish council .. Acts 23:1-10
- Saved from Jewish plot; taken to Caesarea ..... Acts 23:11-35
- Defended himself before Felix .... Acts 24:1-23
- Preached to Felix and Drusilla .... Acts 24:24-26
- Imprisoned for two years . Acts 24:27
- Accused before Festus by Jews .... Acts 25:1-9
- Appealed to Caesar ..... Acts 25:10-12
- Defended himself before Agrippa .... Acts 25:13-27; Acts 26:1-32

Voyage to Rome:

- Sailed from Caesarea to Crete .... Acts 27:1-13
- Ship tossed by storm ..... Acts 27:14-20
- Assured by the Lord ..... Acts 27:21-25
- Ship wrecked; all saved .. Acts 27:26-44
- On island of Melita ...... Acts 28:1-10
- Continued journey to Rome .... Acts 28:11-16
- Rejected by Jews in Rome .... Acts 28:17-29
- Dwelt in Rome two years. Acts 28:30, 31
- Wrote *Ephesians, Colossians, Philippians,* and *Philemon* here ...... Eph 3:1; Eph 6:20; Phil 1:7, 13; Col 4:7-18; Philem 10, 22

Final ministry and death:

- Released from first Roman imprisonment .... Phil 1:25; Phil 2:17, 24; 2Tim 4:16, 17
- Wrote *First Timothy* and *Titus* .... 1Tim 1:1-3; Titus 1:1-5
- Visited Macedonia and other places 2Tim 4:20
- Wrote *Second Timothy* from Roman prison .. 2Tim 1:8; 2Tim 4:6-8
- Sent final news and greetings 2Tim 4:9-22

Missionary methods of:

- Pay his own way .... Acts 18:3; Acts 20:33-35; 2Cor 11:7, 9
- Preach to the Jews first .. Acts 13:46; Acts 17:1-5
- Establish churches in large cities .... Acts 19:1-10; Rom 1:7-15
- Travel with companions . Acts 15:40; Acts 20:4; Col 4:14
- Report work to sending church .... Acts 14:26-28; Acts 21:17-20
- Use his Roman citizenship when necessary .... Acts 16:36-39; Acts 22:24-29; Acts 25:10-12
- Seek to evangelize the world .... Col 1:23-29; 2Tim 4:17

Writings of:

- Inspired by God 2Cor 13:3; 1Thess 2:13; 2Tim 3:15, 16
- Contain difficult things .. 2Pet 3:15, 16
- Written by himself ...... Gal 6:11; 2Thess 3:17
- Sometimes dictated to a scribe .... Rom 16:22
- Considered weighty by some 2Cor 10:10
- His name sometimes forged 2Thess 2:2
- Reveal personal information 2Cor 11:1-33; 2Cor 12:1-11
- Convey personal messages .... Phil 2:19-30; Heb 13:23, 24
- Contain salutation and closing doxology 2Cor 1:2, 3; 2Cor 13:14
- Disclose personal plans .. Phil 2:19-24; Philem 22
- Some complimentary ..... Phil 4:10-19

Some filled with rebuke . . Gal 1:6-8
Gal 5:1-10

Characteristics of:
Consecrated 1Cor 4:1-15
Phil 3:7-14
Cheerful .... Acts 16:25
2Cor 4:8-10
Courageous .... Acts 9:29
Acts 20:22-24
Considerate of others .... Phil 2:25-30
Philem 7-24
Conscientious 2Cor 1:12-17
2Cor 6:3, 4
Christ-centered 2Cor 4:10, 11
Phil 1:20-23
Conciliatory 2Cor 2:1-11
Gal 2:1-15
Composed 2Cor 12:8-10
2Tim 4:7, 8

Saul, (who also is called **P**) .... Acts 13:9
when **P** and his company ...... Acts 13:13
Then **P** stood up, and .... Acts 13:16
followed **P** and Barnabas ...... Acts 13:43
which were spoken by **P** ...... Acts 13:45
P and Barnabas waxed .... Acts 13:46
persecution against **P** .... Acts 13:50
The same heard **P** speak ...... Acts 14:9
people saw what **P** had .... Acts 14:11
P, Mercurius, because he ..... Acts 14:12
apostles, Barnabas and **P** ...... Acts 14:14
stoned **P**, drew him out of .... Acts 14:19
beloved Barnabas and **P** ...... Acts 15:25
P also and Barnabas .... Acts 15:35
P said unto Barnabas .... Acts 15:36
P stood on the stairs, and ..... Acts 21:40
Then said **P**, I stand at .... Acts 25:10
Then Agrippa said unto **P** ..... Acts 26:1
P stretched forth the hand .... Acts 26:1
P, thou art beside thyself ..... Acts 26:24
Agrippa said unto **P**, Almost . . Acts 26:28
P said, I would to God .... Acts 26:29
delivered **P** and certain .... Acts 27:1
Julius courteously entreated **P** . Acts 27:3
P admonished them .... Acts 27:9
things which were spoken by **P**. Acts 27:11
P stood forth in the midst ..... Acts 27:21
Fear not, **P**, thou must be ..... Acts 27:24
P said to the centurion .... Acts 27:31
P besought them all to .... Acts 27:33
willing to save **P** .... Acts 27:43
P had gathered a bundle ...... Acts 28:3
to whom **P** entered in .... Acts 28:8
whom when **P** saw .... Acts 28:15
P was suffered to dwell .... Acts 28:16
days **P** called the chief .... Acts 28:17
after that **P** had spoken .... Acts 28:25
P dwelt two whole years ...... Acts 28:30
P, called to be an apostle 1Cor 1:1
you saith, I am of **P** 1Cor 1:12
was **P** crucified for you? 1Cor 1:13
baptized in the name of **P**? 1Cor 1:13
one saith, I am of **P** 1Cor 3:4
Who then is **P** and who is 1Cor 3:5
Whether **P**, or Apollos 1Cor 3:22
of me **P** with mine own 1Cor 16:21
P an apostle of Jesus 2Cor 1:1
Now I **P** myself beseech 2Cor 10:1
P an apostle of Jesus .... Eph 1:1
P and Timothy, the .... Phil 1:1
P, an apostle of Jesus .... Col 1:1
I **P** am made a minister .... Col 1:23
P, and Silvanus and 1Thess 1:1
P, and Silvanus and 2Thess 1:1
P, an apostle of Jesus 2Tim 1:1
P, a prisoner of Jesus .... Philem 1

PAULINE THEOLOGY—*ideas developed by Paul in his writings*
Given by revelation ...... Gal 1:11, 12
Salvation by grace .... Eph 2:1-10
To Gentiles .... Eph 3:1-12

PAULUS, SERGIUS (pôl'ŭs, sûr'jĭ-ŭs)
Roman proconsul of
Cyprus .... Acts 13:4, 7

PAUPER—*a person unable to support himself*
Richly rewarded in
heaven .... Luke 16:19-23

PAVEMENT—*a terrace made of brick or stones*
God's, made of sapphire . Ex 24:10
Shushan's, made of
precious stones .... Esth 1:5, 6
Of stone 2Kin 16:17
Ezekiel's Temple,
surrounded by .... Ezek 40:17, 18
Judgment place of Pilate . John 19:13
See GABBATHA

[*also* PAVED]
p work of a sapphire .... Ex 24:10
faces to the ground upon the **p**. 2Chr 7:3
being **p** with love .... Song 3:10
p..was for the outer court ..... Ezek 42:3

PAVILION—*a covered place; tent; booth*
Place of refuge .... Ps 27:5
Canopy of God's abode . . Job 36:29
Protective covering
("tabernacle") .... Is 4:6

[*also* PAVILIONS]
made darkness **p** round 2Sam 22:12
he and the kings in the **p** 1Kin 20:12
drinking himself drunk in the **p**. 1Kin 20:16
his **p** round about him .... Ps 18:11
keep them secretly in a **p** ..... Ps 31:20
his royal **p** over them .... Jer 43:10

PAWETH—*to strike the ground with a hoof*
He **p** in the valley .... Job 39:21

PAWS—*the feet of animals having claws*
Descriptive of certain
animals .... Lev 11:27
Of bears and lions 1Sam 17:37

PAY—*to give money or its equivalent in return for something*
Lord's blessing .... Prov 19:17
Punishment .... Matt 5:26
Servitude and forgiveness . Matt 18:23-35
Sign of righteousness .... Ps 37:21
See VOW

[*also* PAID, PAYED]
he shall **p** for the loss of ...... Ex 21:19
he shall **p** as the judges .... Ex 21:22
he shall surely **p** ox for ox .... Ex 21:36
let him **p** double .... Ex 22:7
p double unto his neighbor .... Ex 22:9
p money according to the ..... Ex 22:17
water, then I will **p** for .... Num 20:19
shalt not slack to **p** it .... Deut 23:21
let me go and **p** my vow 2Sam 15:7
else thou shalt **p** a talent 1Kin 20:39
Go, sell the oil, and **p** thy 2Kin 4:7
make to **p** tribute until 2Chr 8:8
children of Ammon **p** 2Chr 27:5
will they not **p** toll .... Ezra 4:13
custom, was **p** unto them ...... Ezra 4:20
will **p** ten thousand talents .... Esth 3:9
Haman had promised to **p** ..... Esth 4:7
thou shalt **p** thy vows .... Job 22:27
p my vows before them .... Ps 22:25
and **p** thy vows unto .... Ps 50:14
I will **p** thee my vows .... Ps 66:13
Vow, and **p** unto the Lord .... Ps 76:11
p my vows unto the Lord ..... Ps 116:14
day have I **p** my vows .... Prov 7:14
If thou hast nothing to **p** ...... Prov 22:27
vow unto God, defer not to **p** . Eccl 5:4
p that which thou hast .... Eccl 5:4
shouldest vow and not **p** ...... Eccl 5:5
so he **p** the fare thereof .... Jon 1:3
I will **p** that which I have ..... Jon 2:9
Doth not your master **p** .... Matt 17:24
ye **p** tithe of mint and .... Matt 23:23
they had nothing to **p** .... Luke 7:42
hast **p** the very last mite ...... Luke 12:59
this cause **p** ye tribute .... Rom 13:6
p tithes in Abraham .... Heb 7:9

PE (pā)
Letter in the Hebrew
alphabet .... Ps 119:129-136

PEACE—*the presence and experience of right relationships*

Kinds of:
International 1Sam 7:14
National 1Kin 4:24
Civil .... Rom 14:19
Domestic 1Cor 7:15
Individual .... Luke 8:48
False 1Thess 5:3
Hypocritical .... James 2:16
Spiritual .... Rom 5:1

Source of:
God .... Phil 4:7
Christ .... John 14:27
Holy Spirit .... Gal 5:22

Of Christ:
Predicted .... Is 9:6, 7
Promised .... Hag 2:9
Announced .... Is 52:7

Lord's relation to, He:
Reveals .... Jer 33:6
Gives .... Ps 29:11
Ordains .... Is 26:12

Among the wicked:
Not known by .... Is 59:8
None for .... Is 48:22

Among believers, truths concerning:
Comes through Christ's
atonement .... Is 53:5
Results from
reconciliation .... Col 1:20
Product of justification . . . Rom 5:1
Obtained by faith .... Is 26:3

Among believers, exhortations regarding:
Should live in 2Cor 13:11
Should pursue 2Tim 2:22

go to thy fathers in **p** .... Gen 15:15
at her held his **p** .... Gen 24:21
sent thee away in **p** .... Gen 26:29
departed from him in **p** .... Gen 26:31
to my father's house in **p** ...... Gen 28:21
Jacob held his **p** until .... Gen 34:5
give Pharaoh an answer of **p** . . Gen 41:16
And he said, **P** be to you ..... Gen 43:23
get you up in **p** unto your ..... Gen 44:17
said to Moses, Go in **p** .... Ex 4:18
and ye shall hold your **p** ...... Ex 14:14
go to their place in **p** .... Ex 18:23
and thy **p** offerings .... Ex 20:24
p offerings of oxen .... Ex 24:5
of their **p** offerings .... Ex 29:28
and brought **p** offerings .... Ex 32:6
a sacrifice of **p** offering .... Lev 3:1
sacrifice of the **p** offering ..... Lev 3:3
a sacrifice of **p** offering .... Lev 3:6
sacrifice of the **p** offering ..... Lev 3:9
sacrifice of **p** offerings .... Lev 4:10
sacrifice of **p** offerings .... Lev 4:26
sacrifice of **p** offerings .... Lev 4:31
sacrifice of the **p** offerings .... Lev 4:35
fat of the **p** offerings .... Lev 6:12
sacrifice of **p** offerings .... Lev 7:11
of his **p** offerings .... Lev 7:13
blood of the **p** offerings ...... Lev 7:14
sacrifice of his **p** offerings .... Lev 7:15
sacrifice of **p** offerings .... Lev 7:20
of his **p** offerings unto .... Lev 7:29
of his **p** offerings .... Lev 7:29
of your **p** offerings .... Lev 7:32
blood of the **p** offerings .... Lev 7:33
of their **p** offerings .... Lev 7:34
of the **p** offerings .... Lev 7:37
a ram for **p** offerings .... Lev 9:4
ram for a sacrifice of **p** .... Lev 9:18
the burnt offering, and **p** ...... Lev 9:22
And Aaron held his **p** .... Lev 10:3
sacrifices of **p** offerings .... Lev 10:14
them for **p** offerings .... Lev 17:5
a sacrifice of **p** offerings ...... Lev 19:5

P

a sacrifice of *p* offerings . . . . Lev 22:21
a sacrifice of *p* offerings . . . . Lev 23:19
I will give *p* in the land . . . . Lev 26:6
blemish for *p* offerings . . . . Num 6:14
a sacrifice of *p* offerings . . . . Num 6:17
sacrifice of the *p* offerings . . . . . Num 6:18
thee, and give thee *p* . . . . Num 6:26
sacrifice of the *p* offerings . . . . . Num 7:88
of your *p* offerings . . . . Num 10:10
vow, or *p* offerings unto . . . . . . Num 15:8
him my covenant of *p* . . . . Num 25:12
and for your *p* offerings . . . . Num 29:39
shall hold his *p* at her . . . . Num 30:4
held his *p* at her in the . . . . Num 30:7
held his *p* at her, and . . . . Num 30:11
hold his *p* at her from . . . . Num 30:14
he held his *p* at her in . . . . Num 30:14
Heshbon with words of *p* . . . . . Deut 2:26
then proclaim *p* unto it . . . . Deut 20:10
make thee answer of *p* . . . . Deut 20:11
if it will make no *p* with . . . . . . Deut 20:12
shalt not seek their *p* . . . . Deut 23:6
shalt offer *p* offerings . . . . Deut 27:7
I shall have *p*, though I . . . . Deut 29:19
sacrificed *p* offerings . . . . Josh 8:31
Joshua made *p* with them . . . . . Josh 9:15
Gibeon had made *p* with . . . . . . Josh 10:1
it hath made *p* with Joshua . . . . Josh 10:4
to Joshua at Makkedah in *p* . . . Josh 10:21
not a city that made *p* . . . . Josh 11:19
or if to offer *p* offerings . . . . Josh 22:23
with our *p* offerings . . . . Josh 22:27
was *p* between Jabin the . . . . . . Judg 4:17
him, *P* be unto thee . . . . Judg 6:23
When I come again in *p* . . . . . . Judg 8:9
I return in *p* from the . . . . Judg 11:31
said unto them, Go in *p* . . . . . . Judg 18:6
unto him, Hold thy *p* . . . . Judg 18:19
the old man said, *P* be . . . . Judg 19:20
and *p* offerings before . . . . Judg 20:26
offerings and *p* offerings . . . . . . Judg 21:4
Eli..said, Go in *p* 1Sam 1:17
sacrifices of *p* offerings 1Sam 10:8
But he held his *p* 1Sam 10:27
sacrifices of *p* offerings 1Sam 11:15
to me, and *p* offerings 1Sam 13:9
thy servant shall have *p* 1Sam 20:7
thou mayest go in *p* 1Sam 20:13
for there is *p* to thee, and 1Sam 20:21
said to David, Go in *p* 1Sam 20:42
P be both to thee 1Sam 25:6
and *p* be to thine house 1Sam 25:6
p be unto all that thou 1Sam 25:6
Go up in *p* to thine house 1Sam 25:35
now return, and go in *p* 1Sam 29:7
and he went in *p* 2Sam 3:21
and he was gone in *p* 2Sam 3:22
and he is gone in *p* 2Sam 3:23
and *p* offerings before the 2Sam 6:17
offerings and *p* offerings 2Sam 6:18
made *p* with Israel, and 2Sam 10:19
hold now thy *p*, my sister 2Sam 13:20
said unto him, Go in *p* 2Sam 15:9
return into the city in *p* 2Sam 15:27
the people shall be in *p* 2Sam 17:3
day he came again in *p* 2Sam 19:24
in *p* unto his own house 2Sam 19:30
shed the blood of war in *p* 1Kin 2:5
go down to the grave in *p* 1Kin 2:6
there be *p* for ever from 1Kin 2:33
offered *p* offerings, and 1Kin 3:15
and he had *p* on all sides 1Kin 4:24
p between Hiram and 1Kin 5:12
a sacrifice of *p* offerings 1Kin 8:63
fat of the *p* offerings 1Kin 8:64
fat of the *p* offerings 1Kin 8:64
p offerings upon the altar 1Kin 9:25
be come out for *p* 1Kin 20:18
man to his house in *p* 1Kin 22:17
of affliction, until I come in *p* . 1Kin 22:27
If thou return at all in *p* 1Kin 22:28
Jehoshaphat made *p* with 1Kin 22:44
I know it; hold ye your *p* 2Kin 2:3
he said unto him, Go in *p* 2Kin 5:19
and we hold our *p* 2Kin 7:9
let him say, Is it *p*? 2Kin 9:17
saith the king, Is it *p*? 2Kin 9:18
hast thou to do with *p*? 2Kin 9:18
saith the king, Is it *p*? 2Kin 9:19
hast thou to do with *p*? 2Kin 9:19
he said, Is it *p*, Jehu? 2Kin 9:22
What *p*, so long 2Kin 9:22
Had Zimri *p*, who slew his 2Kin 9:31
blood of his *p* offerings 2Kin 16:13
the people held their *p* 2Kin 18:36
p and truth be in my days? 2Kin 20:19
into thy grave in *p* 2Kin 22:20
Jesse: *p*, *p* be unto thee 1Chr 12:18
and *p* be to thine helpers 1Chr 12:18
offered..*p* offerings before 1Chr 16:1
and the *p* offerings 1Chr 16:2
made *p* with David, and 1Chr 19:19
burnt offerings and *p* 1Chr 21:26
give *p* and quietness unto 1Chr 22:9
and the fat of *p* offerings 2Chr 7:7
was no *p* to him that went 2Chr 15:5
return..to his house in *p* 2Chr 18:16
until I return in *p* 2Chr 18:26
thou certainly return in *p* 2Chr 18:27
returned to his house in *p* 2Chr 19:1
the fat of the *p* offerings 2Chr 29:35
offering *p* offerings 2Chr 30:22
and for *p* offerings 2Chr 31:2
p offerings and thank 2Chr 33:16
to thy grave in *p* 2Chr 34:28
rest beyond the river, *P* . . . . Ezra 4:17
Unto Darius the king, all *p* . . . . Ezra 5:7
unto Ezra..perfect *p* . . . . Ezra 7:12
their *p* or their wealth . . . . Ezra 9:12
Then held they their *p* . . . . Neh 5:8
Hold your *p*, for the day . . . . Neh 8:11
if thou..holdest thy *p* . . . . Esth 4:14
with words of *p* and truth . . . . . Esth 9:30
speaking *p* to all his seed . . . . . Esth 10:3
shall be at *p* with thee . . . . Job 5:23
tabernacle shall be in *p* . . . . Job 5:24
make men hold their *p*? . . . . Job 11:3
ye would..hold your *p*! . . . . Job 13:5
Hold your *p*, let me alone . . . . . Job 13:13
with him, and be at *p* . . . . Job 22:21
he maketh *p* in his high . . . . Job 25:2
The nobles held their *p* . . . . Job 29:10
hold thy *p*, and I will . . . . Job 33:31
hold thy *p*, and I shall . . . . Job 33:33
both lay me down in *p* . . . . Ps 4:8
unto him that was at *p* . . . . Ps 7:4
speak *p* to their neighbors . . . . . Ps 28:3
seek *p*, and pursue it . . . . Ps 34:14
For they speak not *p* . . . . Ps 35:20
in the abundance of *p* . . . . Ps 37:11
the end of that man is *p* . . . . . . Ps 37:37
silence, I held my *p* . . . . Ps 39:2
hold not thy *p* at my tears . . . . Ps 39:12
delivered my soul in *p* . . . . Ps 55:18
against such as be at *p* . . . . Ps 55:20
bring *p* to the people . . . . Ps 72:3
abundance of *p* so long as . . . . . Ps 72:7
hold not thy *p*, and be not . . . . Ps 83:1
speak *p* unto his people . . . . Ps 85:8
righteousness and *p* have . . . . . . Ps 85:10
Hold not thy *p*, O God . . . . Ps 109:1
Great *p* have they which . . . . . . Ps 119:165
with him that hateth *p* . . . . Ps 120:6
I am for *p*: but when . . . . Ps 120:7
Pray for the *p* of . . . . Ps 122:6
P be within thy walls . . . . Ps 122:7
P be within thee . . . . Ps 122:8
but *p* shall be upon Israel . . . . . Ps 125:5
and *p* upon Israel . . . . Ps 128:6
maketh *p* in thy borders . . . . . . Ps 147:14
and *p*, shall they add to . . . . Prov 3:2
and all her paths are *p* . . . . Prov 3:17
I have *p* offerings with . . . . Prov 7:14
understanding holdeth his *p* . . . Prov 11:12
to the counselors of *p* . . . . Prov 12:20
his enemies to be at *p* . . . . Prov 16:7
when he holdeth his *p* . . . . Prov 17:28
of war, and a time of *p* . . . . Eccl 3:8
he may make *p* with me . . . . . . Is 27:5
he shall make *p* with me . . . . . . Is 27:5
righteousness shall be *p* . . . . . . Is 32:17
the ambassadors of *p* . . . . Is 33:7
they held their *p* . . . . Is 36:21
for *p* I had great . . . . Is 38:17
shall be *p* and truth . . . . Is 39:8
long time holden my *p* . . . . Is 42:14
I make *p*, and create evil . . . . . Is 45:7
then had thy *p* been as a . . . . . . Is 48:18
the covenant of my *p* be . . . . . . Is 54:10
great shall be the *p* of thy . . . . . Is 54:13
and be led forth with *p* . . . . Is 55:12
He shall enter into *p* . . . . Is 57:2
have not I held my *p* . . . . Is 57:11
P, *p* to him that is far off . . . . . Is 57:19
There is no *p*, saith . . . . Is 57:21
The way of *p* they . . . . Is 59:8
make thy officers *p* . . . . Is 60:17
will I not hold my *p* . . . . Is 62:1
hold their *p* day nor . . . . Is 62:6
wilt thou hold thy *p*, and . . . . . . Is 64:12
extend *p* to her like a . . . . Is 66:12
Ye shall have *p*; whereas . . . . . . Jer 4:10
I cannot hold my *p* . . . . Jer 4:19
P, *p*; when there is no *p* . . . . . . Jer 6:14
P, *p*; when there is no *p* . . . . . . Jer 8:11
We looked for *p*, but no . . . . Jer 8:15
if in the land of *p*, wherein . . . . Jer 12:5
no flesh shall have *p* . . . . Jer 12:12
will give you assured *p* in . . . . . Jer 14:13
p, and there is no good . . . . Jer 14:19
taken away my *p* from . . . . Jer 16:5
Lord..said, Ye shall have *p* . . . . Jer 23:17
which prophesieth of *p* . . . . Jer 28:9
seek the *p* of the city . . . . Jer 29:7
in the *p* thereof shall ye have *p*. Jer 29:7
of fear, and not of *p* . . . . Jer 30:5
But thou shalt die in *p* . . . . Jer 34:5
go forth from thence in *p* . . . . . Jer 43:12
my soul far off from *p* . . . . Lam 3:17
they shall seek *p*, and . . . . Ezek 7:25
P; and there was no *p* . . . . Ezek 13:10
see visions of *p* for her . . . . Ezek 13:16
no *p* saith the Lord God . . . . . . Ezek 13:16
with them a covenant of *p* . . . . Ezek 34:25
make a covenant of *p* . . . . Ezek 37:26
and your *p* offerings . . . . Ezek 43:27
and for *p* offerings . . . . Ezek 45:15
and the *p* offerings . . . . Ezek 45:17
and his *p* offerings . . . . Ezek 46:2
offering or *p* offerings . . . . Ezek 46:12
burnt..and his *p* offerings . . . . . Ezek 46:12
P be multiplied unto you . . . . . . Dan 4:1
P be multiplied unto you . . . . . . Dan 6:25
by *p* shall destroy many . . . . Dan 8:25
p be unto thee, be strong . . . . . Dan 10:19
the *p* offerings of your fat . . . . . Amos 5:22
men that were at *p* with . . . . Obad 7
their teeth and cry, *P* . . . . Mic 3:5
this man shall be the *p* . . . . Mic 5:5
tidings, that publisheth *p*! . . . . . Nah 1:15
Hold thy *p* at the presence . . . . Zeph 1:7
the counsel of *p* shall be . . . . . . Zech 6:13
was there any *p* to him . . . . Zech 8:10
judgment of truth and *p* . . . . . . Zech 8:16
love the truth and *p* . . . . Zech 8:19
he shall speak *p* unto the . . . . . Zech 9:10
covenant..of life and *p* . . . . Mal 2:5
he walked with me in *p* . . . . Mal 2:6
let your *p* come upon it . . . . Matt 10:13
let your *p* return to you . . . . Matt 10:13
come to send *p* on earth . . . . . . Matt 10:34
I came not to send *p* . . . . Matt 10:34
they should hold their *p* . . . . Matt 20:31
But Jesus held his *p* . . . . Matt 26:63
Hold thy *p*, and come out . . . . . Mark 1:25
But they held their *p* . . . . Mark 3:4
unto the sea, *P*, be still . . . . Mark 4:39
go in *p*, and be whole . . . . Mark 5:34
but they held their *p* . . . . Mark 9:34
have *p* one with another . . . . . . Mark 9:50
that he should hold his *p* . . . . . . Mark 10:48
held his *p*, and answered . . . . . . Mark 14:61
our feet into the way of *p* . . . . . Luke 1:79
on earth *p*, good will . . . . Luke 2:14
thy servant depart in *p* . . . . Luke 2:29

Hold thy *p*, and come out .....Luke 4:35
faith..saved thee; go in *p* ......Luke 7:50
made thee whole; go in *p* .....Luke 8:48
say, *P* be to this house ....Luke 10:5
if the son of *p* be there ....Luke 10:6
your *p* shall rest upon it.......Luke 10:6
his goods are in *p* ....Luke 11:21
I am come to give *p* ....Luke 12:51
And they held their *p*.........Luke 14:4
desireth conditions of *p* ....Luke 14:32
that he should hold his *p*......Luke 18:39
p in heaven, and glory in the . .Luke 19:38
if these should hold their *p* ....Luke 19:40
belong unto thy *p*! ....Luke 19:42
answer, and held their *p* ......Luke 20:26
P be unto you...................Luke 24:36
in me ye might have *p* ....John 16:33
P be unto you...................John 20:19
again, *P* be unto you ....John 20:21
said, *P* be unto you............John 20:26
preaching *p* by Jesus ....Acts 10:36
held their *p*, and glorified .....Acts 11:18
hand to hold their *p* ....Acts 12:17
desired *p*; because their ....Acts 12:20
after they had held their *p* ....Acts 15:13
were let go in *p* from the .....Acts 15:33
depart, and go in *p* ....Acts 16:36
speak, and hold not thy *p* .....Acts 18:9
Grace to you and *p*.............Rom 1:7
honor, and *p* to every..........Rom 2:10
the way of *p* have they........Rom 3:17
minded is life and *p* ....Rom 8:6
preach the gospel of *p* ....Rom 10:15
righteousness, and *p* ....Rom 14:17
all joy and *p* in believing ......Rom 15:13
the God of *p* be with you .....Rom 15:33
God of *p* shall bruise Satan ...Rom 16:20
Grace be unto you, and *p* 1Cor 1:3
let the first hold his *p*..........1Cor 14:30
confusion, but of *p* 1Cor 14:33
conduct him forth in *p* 1Cor 16:11
to you and *p* from God 2Cor 1:2
Grace be to you and *p*..........Gal 1:3
p be on them, and mercy .....Gal 6:16
Grace be to you, and *p* ....Eph 1:2
For he is our *p*, who hath .....Eph 2:14
new man, so making *p*.........Eph 2:15
preached *p* to you which ......Eph 2:17
Spirit in the bond of *p* ....Eph 4:3
of the gospel of *p* ....Eph 6:15
P be to the brethren ....Eph 6:23
Grace be unto you, and *p*.....Phil 1:2
God of *p* shall be with you ...Phil 4:9
Grace be unto you, and *p* .....Col 1:2
made *p* through the blood .....Col 1:20
the *p* of God rule..hearts......Col 3:15
Grace be unto you, and *p* 1Thess 1:1
be at *p* among yourselves 1Thess 5:13
God of *p* sanctify you 1Thess 5:23
Grace unto you, and *p*.........2Thess 1:2
Lord of *p* himself give you *p* ..2Thess 3:16
mercy, and *p*, from God 1Tim 1:2
mercy, and *p*, from God 2Tim 1:2
mercy, and *p*, from God ......Titus 1:4
Grace to you, and *p* ....Philem 3
which is, King of *p* ....Heb 7:2
received the spies with *p* ......Heb 11:31
Follow *p* with all men.........Heb 12:14
the God of *p*, that brought ....Heb 13:20
in *p* of them that make *p* .....James 3:18
Grace unto you, and *p*.........1Pet 1:2
P be with you all that are 1Pet 5:14
Grace and *p* be multiplied 2Pet 1:2
may be found of him in *p* 2Pet 3:14
Grace be with you..and *p* 2John 3
P be to thee. Our friends 3John 14
p, and love, be multiplied .....Jude 2
Grace be unto you, and *p* .....Rev 1:4
to take *p* from the earth ......Rev 6:4

PEACEABLE—*to be or to live in accord with others*

[*also* PEACEABLY]
These men are *p* with us ......Gen 34:21
not speak *p* unto him ....Gen 37:4
those lands again *p* ....Judg 11:13
to call *p* unto them ....Judg 21:13
and said, Comest thou *p*? 1Sam 16:4
he said, *P*: I am come to......1Sam 16:5
that are *p* and faithful 2Sam 20:19
And she said, Comest thou *p*? .1Kin 2:13
And he said, *P* 1Kin 2:13
wide, and quiet, and *p* 1Chr 4:40
If ye be come *p* unto me 1Chr 12:17
dwell in a *p* habitation ....Is 32:18
one speaketh *p* to his ....Jer 9:8
p habitations are cut down ....Jer 25:37
he shall come in *p*, and ....Dan 11:21
enter *p* even upon the ....Dan 11:24
live *p* with all men ....Rom 12:18
lead a quiet and *p* life in 1Tim 2:2
p fruit of righteousness........Heb 12:11
first pure, then *p*, gentle ......James 3:17

PEACEMAKERS—*those who work for peace*
Christ the great 2Cor 5:18-21
Christians become ....Matt 5:9
Rom 14:19
Rules regarding 1Pet 3:8-13

PEACOCK—*a male peafowl*
Imported by Solomon from Tarshish 1Kin 10:22
Trade item...............2Chr 9:21

[*also* PEACOCKS]
goodly wings unto the *p*?......Job 39:13

PEARL—*a precious gem found in oyster shells*
Used literally of:
Valuable gems ....Rev 18:12, 16
Woman's attire 1Tim 2:9
Used figuratively of:
Spiritual truths ....Matt 7:6
Kingdom ....Matt 13:45, 46
Worldly adornment ......Rev 17:4
Wonders of heaven's glories ....Rev 21:21

[*also* PEARLS]
made of coral, or of *p* ....Job 28:18
every..gate was of one *p* ......Rev 21:21

PECULIAR—*something separated to one's own use*
Applied literally to:
Israel (God's own) ......Ex 19:5
Treasure (Solomon's own) Eccl 2:8
Translated:
"Special" ....Deut 7:6
"Jewels" ....Mal 3:17
Applied figuratively to:
True Israel..............Ps 135:4
Christian................Titus 2:14
True church.............1Pet 2:9

a *p* people unto himself ....Deut 14:2
to be his *p* people ....Deut 26:18

PEDAHEL (pĕd'ä-hĕl)—*"whom God redeems"*
Prince of Naphtali ....Num 34:28

PEDAHZUR (pĕ-dä'zer)—*"the rock delivers"*
Father of Gamaliel ......Num 1:10

Gamaliel the son of *P* ....Num 2:20
Gamaliel the son of *P* ....Num 7:54
of Gamaliel the son of *P*.......Num 7:59
was Gamaliel the son of *P* ....Num 10:23

PEDAIAH (pĕ-dā'yä)—*"Jehovah delivers"*
1. Father of Joel, ruler in David's reign 1Chr 27:20
2. Grandfather of Jehoiakim 2Kin 23:36
3. Son of Jeconiah.........1Chr 3:18, 19
4. Postexilic workman .....Neh 3:25
5. Ezra's Levite attendant . .Neh 8:4
6. Man appointed as treasurer ....Neh 13:13
7. Postexilic Benjamite.....Neh 11:7

PEDIGREES—*lineages*
they declared their *p* after.....Num 1:18

PEELED—*stripped*
a nation scattered and *p* ......Is 18:2
a people scattered and *p* ......Is 18:7
every shoulder was *p* ....Ezek 29:18

PEEP—*to chirp; mutter*

[*also* PEEPED]
and unto wizards that *p* ....Is 8:19
or opened the mouth, or *p* ....Is 10:14

PEKAH (pē'kä)—*"opening"*
Son of Remaliah; usurps Israel's throne 2Kin 15:25-28
Forms alliance with Rezin of Syria against Ahaz . .Is 7:1-9
Alliance defeated; captives returned 2Kin 16:5-9
Territory of, overrun by Tiglath-pileser 2Kin 15:29
Assassinated by Hoshea . .2Kin 15:30

the rest of the acts of *P*.......2Kin 15:31
In the second year of *P* 2Kin 15:32
P the son of Remaliah 2Kin 15:37
the seventeenth year of *P* 2Kin 16:1

PEKAHIAH (pĕk-ä-hī'ä)—*"Jehovah has opened (the eyes)"*
Son of Menahem; king of Israel..................2Kin 15:22-26
Assassinated by Pekah . . .2Kin 15:23-25

PEKOD (pē'kŏd)—*"visitation"*
Aramean tribe during Nebuchadnezzar's reign.Jer 50:21

Chaldeans, *P*, and Shoa ....Ezek 23:23

PELAIAH (pĕ-lā'yä)—*"Jehovah is distinguished"*
1. Judahite................1Chr 3:24
2. Ezra's Levite attendant; reads covenant........Neh 8:7

PELALIAH (pĕl-ä-lī'ä)—*"Jehovah has judged"*
Postexilic priest ....Neh 11:12

PELATIAH (pĕl-ä-tī'ä)—*"Jehovah delivers"*
1. Simeonite captain in war with Amalekites 1Chr 4:42, 43
2. Prince dying while Ezekiel prophesies ....Ezek 11:1-13
3. Descendant of Solomon .1Chr 3:21
4. One who signs the covenant ....Neh 10:1, 22

PELEG, PHALEC (pē'lĕg, fā'lĕc)—*"division"*
Brother of Joktan ....Gen 10:25
Son of Eber ....Luke 3:35

and begat *P*..................Gen 11:16
Eber lived after he begat *P*....Gen 11:17
P lived thirty years, and ......Gen 11:18
P lived after he begat Reu ....Gen 11:19
name of the one was *P* 1Chr 1:19
Eber, *P*, Reu 1Chr 1:25

PELET (pē'lĕt)—*"deliverance"*
1. Judahite................1Chr 2:47
2. Benjamite warrior under David 1Chr 12:3

PELETH (pē'lĕth)—*"flight; haste"*
1. Reubenite, father of On .Num 16:1
2. Judahite................1Chr 2:33

PELETHITES (pĕ'lĕth-īts)—*perhaps a contraction of Philistines*
David's faithful soldiers during Absalom's and Sheba's rebellions 2Sam 15:18-22
See CHERETHITES

Cherethites and the *P*.........2Sam 8:18
the *P*, and all the mighty......2Sam 20:7
and over the *P* 2Sam 20:23
the *P*, went down, and 1Kin 1:38
Cherethites, and the *P* 1Kin 1:44
Cherethites and the *P*.........1Chr 18:17

PELICAN—*"the vomiter"—a large, web-footed bird noted for its large pouchlike beak*

P

Ceremonially unclean bird Lev 11:18
Dwells in wilderness ..... Ps 102:6
Lives in ruins .... Is 34:11
Zeph 2:14

PELONITE (pĕl'ō-nīt)
Descriptive of two of David's mighty men ... 1Chr 11:27, 36
See **Paltite**

was Helez the *P* 1Chr 27:10

PEN—*an instrument for writing*
Figurative of tongue ..... Ps 45:1
Lying .... Jer 8:8
Not preferred 3John 13

they that handle the *p* .... Judg 5:14
graven with an iron *p* .... Job 19:24
write in it with a man's *p* ..... Is 8:1
is written with a *p* of iron ..... Jer 17:1

PENALTIES—*punishments inflicted for wrongdoings*

For sexual sins:
Adultery—death .... Lev 20:10
Incest—death .... Lev 20:11-14
Sodomy—destruction .... Gen 19:13, 17, 24

For bodily sins:
Drunkenness—exclusion . 1Cor 5:11
1Cor 6:9, 10
Murder—death .... Ex 21:12-15
Persecution—God's judgment .... Matt 23:34-36

For following heathen ways:
Human sacrifice—death .. Lev 20:2-5
Witchcraft—death .... Ex 22:18
Idolatry—death .... Ex 22:20

For internal sins:
Ingratitude—punished ... Prov 17:13
Pride—abomination ...... Prov 16:5
Unbelief—exclusion ..... Num 20:12
Swearing—curse .... Jer 23:10
Zech 5:3
Blasphemy—death .... Lev 24:14-16, 23

PENCE—*See* **Penny**

PENIEL (pĕ-nī'ĕl)—*"face of God"*
Place east of Jordan; site of Jacob's wrestling with angel .... Gen 32:24-31
See **Penuel**

PENINNAH (pĕ-nĭn'ä)—*"coral; pearl"*
Elkanah's second wife ... 1Sam 1:2, 4

PENITENCE—*sorrow for one's sins or shortcomings*

Results of:
Forgiveness .... Ps 32:5, 6
Restoration .... Job 22:23-29
Renewed fellowship ..... Ps 51:12, 13

Examples of:
Job .... Job 42:1-6
David .... Ps 51:1-19
Josiah 2Kin 22:1, 19
Publicans .... Luke 18:13
Thief on the cross .... Luke 23:39-42

Elements:
Acknowledgement of sin . Job 33:27, 28
Luke 15:18, 21
Broken heart .... Ps 34:18
Ps 51:17
Plea for mercy .... Luke 18:13
Confession 1John 1:9
See **Repentance**

PENKNIFE—*a scribe's knife*
Used by Jehoiakim on Jeremiah's roll .... Jer 36:23-28

PENNY—*the Roman denarius*
Debt of 100 .... Matt 18:28
Day laborer's pay .... Matt 20:2-13
Roman coin .... Matt 22:19-21
Two, the cost of lodging . Luke 10:35
Ointment, worth 300 ..... John 12:5
Famine prices .... Rev 6:6
See **Jewish Measures**

[*also* **pence**]
bring me a *p*, that I may ...... Mark 12:15
than three hundred *p* .... Mark 14:5
one owed five hundred *p* ...... Luke 7:41
Show me a *p*. Whose image ... Luke 20:24

PENNYWORTH—*the purchasing power of a penny*
buy two hundred *p* of .... Mark 6:37
Two hundred *p* of bread ...... John 6:7

PENTECOST (pĕn'tē-kŏst)—*fiftieth day after Passover*

In the Old Testament:
Called "the Feast of Weeks" .... Ex 34:22, 23
Marks completion of barley harvest .... Lev 23:15, 16
Called "Feast of Harvest". Ex 23:16
Work during, prohibited . Lev 23:21
Two loaves presented .... Lev 23:17, 20
Other sacrifices prescribed .... Lev 23:18
Offerings given by Levites Deut 16:10-14
Time of consecration .... Deut 16:12, 13
Observed during Solomon's time 2Chr 8:12, 13
See **Feasts, Hebrew**

In the New Testament:
Day of the Spirit's coming; the formation of the Christian Church. Acts 2:1-47
Paul desires to attend .... Acts 20:16
Paul plans to stay in Ephesus until 1Cor 16:8

PENUEL (pĕ-nū'ĕl)—*"face of God"*
1. Inhabitants of, slain by Gideon .... Judg 8:8, 9, 17
Later refortified by Jeroboam .... 1 Kin 12:25
Same as Peniel .... Gen 32:24-31
2. Judahite 1Chr 4:4
3. Benjamite 1Chr 8:25

PENURY—*extreme poverty; destitution*
Widow's gift in, commended .... Luke 21:1-4

the lips tendeth only to *p* ..... Prov 14:23

PEOPLE, PEOPLES—*See* **Introduction**

PEOR (pē'ôr)—*"opening"*
1. Mountain of Moab opposite Jericho ...... Num 23:28
Israel's camp seen from . Num 24:2
2. Moabite god called Baalpeor .... Num 25:3, 5, 18
Israelites punished for worship of .... Num 31:16

PERADVENTURE—*perhaps; possibly*
P there be fifty righteous ...... Gen 18:24
P there shall lack five .... Gen 18:28
P there shall be forty .... Gen 18:29
P there shall thirty be .... Gen 18:30
P there shall be twenty .... Gen 18:31
P ten shall be found there ..... Gen 18:32
P thou wouldest take by ...... Gen 31:31
p he will accept of me .... Gen 32:20
Lest *p* he die also, as .... Gen 38:11
Lest *p* mischief befall .... Gen 42:4
p it was an oversight .... Gen 43:12
lest *p* I see the evil that ...... Gen 44:34
Joseph will *p* hate us .... Gen 50:15
Lest *p* the people repent .... Ex 13:17
p I shall make an atonement .. Ex 32:30
p I shall prevail, that we ...... Num 22:6
p I shall be able to .... Num 22:11
p the Lord will come to .... Num 23:3
p it will please God that ...... Num 23:27
P ye dwell among us .... Josh 9:7
p he will lighten his hand 1Sam 6:5
p he can show us our way 1Sam 9:6
p we may find grass to 1Kin 18:5
p he sleepeth, and must be 1Kin 18:27
p he will save thy life 1Kin 20:31
p the Spirit of the Lord 2Kin 2:16
P he will be enticed, and ...... Jer 20:10
yet *p* for a good man some .... Rom 5:7
if God *p* will give them 2Tim 2:25

PERAZIM (pĕr'ä-zĭm)—*"lord of breaches"—a place near the Valley of Rephaim*
rise up as in mount *P* .... Is 28:21

PERCEIVE—*to derive knowledge through one of the senses*
Outward circumstances ... 2Sam 12:19
Acts 27:10
Outward intentions ...... John 6:15
Acts 23:29
Intuition 1Sam 3:8
John 4:19
Unusual manifestations ... 1Sam 12:17, 18
Acts 10:34
Spiritual insight .... Neh 6:12
Acts 14:9
God's blessings 2Sam 5:12
Neh 6:16
Bitter experience .... Eccl 1:17
Eccl 3:22
Obvious implication ..... Matt 21:45
Luke 20:19
God's revelation .... Gal 2:9
1John 3:16
Internal consciousness .... Luke 8:46
Acts 8:23

[*also* **perceived, perceivest, perceiveth, perceiving, perception**]
he *p* not when she lay .... Gen 19:33
given you a heart to *p* .... Deut 29:4
day we *p* that the Lord is ..... Josh 22:31
Gideon *p* that he was an ...... Judg 6:22
p..that your wickedness is 1Sam 12:17
And Saul *p* that it was 1Sam 28:14
p that the king's heart 2Sam 14:1
for this day I *p*, that if 2Sam 19:6
p that it was not the king 1Kin 22:33
I *p* that this is a holy 2Kin 4:9
David *p*..the Lord had 1Chr 14:2
p that it was not the king 2Chr 18:32
p that the portions of the ..... Neh 13:10
Mordecai *p* all that was .... Esth 4:1
on also, but I *p* him not ...... Job 9:11
low, but he *p* it not of them ... Job 14:21
but I cannot *p* him .... Job 23:8
yet man *p* it not .... Job 33:14
thou *p* the breadth .... Job 38:18
to *p* the words of .... Prov 1:2
p not in him the lips .... Prov 14:7
p that her merchandise is ..... Prov 31:18
p also that one event .... Eccl 2:14
see ye indeed, but *p* not ...... Is 6:9
speech than thou canst *p* ...... Is 33:19
have not heard, nor *p* .... Is 64:4
p and heard his word? .... Jer 23:18
for the matter was not *p* ...... Jer 38:27
shall see, and shall not *p* ..... Matt 13:14
when Jesus *p*, he said .... Matt 16:8
Jesus *p* their wickedness ...... Matt 22:18
when Jesus *p* in his spirit ..... Mark 2:8
they may see, and not *p* ...... Mark 4:12
Do ye not *p*, that .... Mark 7:18
p ye not yet, neither .... Mark 8:17
p that he had answered .... Mark 12:28
they *p* that he had seen a ..... Luke 1:22
Jesus *p* their thoughts .... Luke 5:22
p not the beam that is .... Luke 6:41
them, that they *p* it not .... Luke 9:45
Jesus, *p* the thought of .... Luke 9:47
p that he had spoken this ..... Luke 20:19
But he *p* their craftiness ..... Luke 20:23
Sir, I *p* that thou art a .... John 4:19
P ye how ye prevail .... John 12:19
p that they were unlearned .... Acts 4:13
p that the one..were Sadducees. Acts 23:6
ye shall see, and not *p* .... Acts 28:26
p that the same epistle 2Cor 7:8

PERDITION—*the state of the damned; destruction*
Judas Iscariot ....John 17:12
Lost ....Philem 1:28
Antichrist 2Thess 2:3
Rev 17:8, 11

drown men in..*p* 1Tim 6:9
who draw back unto *p* ....Heb 10:39
judgment and *p* of ungodly 2Pet 3:7

PERES—*to split into pieces*
Sentence of doom ....Dan 5:28

PERESH (pē'rĕsh)—*"separate"*
Man of Manasseh 1Chr 7:16

PEREZ, PHAREZ (pē'rĕz, fā'rĕz)—*"bursting through"*
One of Judah's twin sons by Tamar ....Gen 38:24-30
Numbered among Judah's sons ....Gen 46:12
Founder of a tribal family.Num 26:20, 21
Descendants of, notable in later times 1Chr 27:3
Ancestor of David and Christ ....Ruth 4:12-18
See PHARES

of the children of *P* ....Neh 11:4
sons of *P* that dwelt at ....Neh 11:6

PEREZITES (pē'rĕz-īts)
Descendants of Perez ....Num 26:20

PEREZ-UZZA, PEREZ-UZZAH (pē-rĕz-ŭz'ä)—*"a breakthrough of Uzza"—place between Kirjath-jearim and Jerusalem*
name of the place *P* to this 2Sam 6:8
that place is called *P* to 1Chr 13:11

PERFECT—*complete; to complete thoroughly*

[*also* PERFECTED, PERFECTING, PERFECTLY]
Noah was a just man and *p* ...Gen 6:9
before me, and be thou *p* .....Gen 17:1
shalt be *p* with the Lord ......Deut 18:13
the Rock, his work is *p* ....Deut 32:4
God of Israel, Give a *p* lot 1Sam 14:41
As for God, his way is *p* 2Sam 22:31
and he maketh my way *p* 2Sam 22:33
Let your heart..be *p* 1Kin 8:61
his heart was not *p* with.......1Kin 11:4
his heart was not *p* with.......1Kin 15:3
Asa's heart was *p* 1Kin 15:14
truth and with a *p* heart.......2Kin 20:3
came with a *p* heart 1Chr 12:38
serve him with a *p* heart 1Chr 28:9
with *p* heart they offered 1Chr 29:9
Solomon my son a *p* heart 1Chr 29:19
house of the Lord was *p* 2Chr 8:16
heart of Asa was *p* 2Chr 15:17
them whose heart is *p* 2Chr 16:9
and with a *p* heart............2Chr 19:9
the work was *p* by them 2Chr 24:13
but not with a *p* heart 2Chr 25:2
unto Ezra..*p* peace ....Ezra 7:12
man was *p* and upright ....Job 1:1
a *p* and an upright man ....Job 1:8
a *p* and an upright man ....Job 2:3
not cast away a *p* man ....Job 8:20
if I say, I am *p*, it shall ....Job 9:20
Though I were *p*, yet ....Job 9:21
destroyeth the *p* and the ......Job 9:22
thou makest thy ways *p*? ......Job 22:3
and searcheth out all *p* ....Job 28:3
he that is *p* in knowledge .....Job 36:4
which is *p* in knowledge?......Job 37:16
As for God, his way is *p* ......Ps 18:30
and maketh my way *p* ....Ps 18:32
law of the Lord is *p* ....Ps 19:7
Mark the *p* man, and ....Ps 37:37
shoot in secret at the *p* ....Ps 64:4
behave..wisely in a *p* way .....Ps 101:2
my house with a *p* heart ......Ps 101:2
that walketh in a *p* way ......Ps 101:6
will *p* that which ....Ps 138:8
hate them with *p* hatred ......Ps 139:22
the *p* shall remain in it........Prov 2:21
righteousness of the *p* ....Prov 11:5
when the bud is *p* ....Is 18:5
wilt keep him in *p* peace ......Is 26:3
truth and with a *p* heart.......Is 38:3
is blind as he that is *p* ....Is 42:19
ye shall consider it *p* ....Jer 23:20
it was *p* through my ....Ezek 16:14
I am of *p* beauty ....Ezek 27:3
builders have *p* thy beauty ....Ezek 27:4
have made thy beauty *p* ....Ezek 27:11
Thou wast *p* in thy ways ......Ezek 28:15
were made *p* whole ....Matt 14:36
If thou wilt be *p*, go ....Matt 19:21
p understanding of all ....Luke 1:3
that is *p*..as his master ....Luke 6:40
the third day I shall be *p* ......Luke 13:32
him this *p* soundness ....Acts 3:16
the way of God more *p* ....Acts 18:26
p manner of the law ....Acts 22:3
inquire something more *p* .....Acts 23:15
somewhat of him more *p* ......Acts 23:20
more *p* knowledge of ....Acts 24:22
and *p* will of God ....Rom 12:2
ye be *p* joined together 1Cor 1:10
Be *p*, be of good comfort 2Cor 13:11
unto a *p* man, unto the ....Eph 4:13
Let us..as many as be *p* ....Phil 3:15
every man *p* in Christ ....Col 1:28
stand *p* and complete ....Col 4:12
know *p* that the day 1Thess 5:2
being made *p*, he became .....Heb 5:9
the law made nothing *p* ....Heb 7:19
that did the service *p* ....Heb 9:9
and more *p* tabernacle ....Heb 9:11
the comers thereunto *p* ....Heb 10:1
spirits of just men made *p* .....Heb 12:23
every *p* gift is from above .....James 1:17
the *p* law of liberty ....James 1:25
by works was faith made *p*? ...James 2:22
the same is a *p* man ....James 3:2
verily is the love of God *p* 1John 2:5
and his love is *p* in us 1John 4:12
Herein is our love made *p* 1John 4:17
p love casteth out fear 1John 4:18
that feareth is not made *p* 1John 4:18
have not found thy works *p* ...Rev 3:2

PERFECTION—*the state of being entirely without fault or defect*

Applied to natural things:
Day ....Prov 4:18
Gold 2Chr 4:21
Weights ....Deut 25:15
Beauty ....Ezek 28:12
Offering ....Lev 22:21

Applied to spiritual graces:
Patience ....James 1:4
Love ....Col 3:14
Holiness 2Cor 7:1
Praise ....Matt 21:16
Faith 1Thess 3:10
Good works ....Heb 13:21
Unity ....John 17:23
Strength 2Cor 12:9

Means of:
God 1Pet 5:10
Christ ....Heb 10:14
Holy Spirit ....Gal 3:3
God's Word 2Tim 3:16, 17
Ministry ....Eph 4:11, 12
Sufferings ....Heb 2:10

Stages of:
Eternally accomplished ...Heb 10:14
Objective goal ....Matt 5:48
Subjective process 2Cor 7:1
Daily activity 2Cor 13:9
Present possession 1Cor 2:6
Experience not yet reached ....Phil 3:12
Descriptive of the completed Church .....Heb 11:40
Heaven's eternal standard.1Cor 13:10-12

the Almighty unto *p* ....Job 11:7
shall he prolong the *p* ....Job 15:29
Out of Zion, the *p* of beauty ..Ps 50:2
have seen an end of all *p* .....Ps 119:96
come upon thee in their *p* .....Is 47:9
and bring no fruit to *p* ....Luke 8:14
let us go on unto *p* ....Heb 6:1
p were by the..priesthood .....Heb 7:11

PERFORM—*to fulfill; carry out; do according to a prescribed ritual*

[*also* PERFORMANCE, PERFORMED, PERFORMETH, PERFORMING]
I will *p* the oath which I ......Gen 26:3
not able to *p* it thyself ....Ex 18:18
enter in to *p* the service.......Num 4:23
a sacrifice in *p* a vow ....Num 15:3
for a sacrifice in *p* a vow ......Num 15:8
he commanded you to *p* ......Deut 4:13
may *p* the word which ....Deut 9:5
thou shalt keep and *p* ....Deut 23:23
p the duty of a husband's .....Deut 25:5
p the duty of my husband's....Deut 25:7
p unto thee the part ....Ruth 3:13
p against Eli all things 1Sam 3:12
not *p* my commandments......1Sam 15:11
p the commandment of the 1Sam 15:13
p the request of his 2Sam 14:15
p all that the king 2Sam 21:14
then will I *p* my word.........1Kin 6:12
the Lord hath *p* his word 1Kin 8:20
he might *p* his saying 1Kin 12:15
to *p* the words of this 2Kin 23:3
he might *p* the words 2Kin 23:24
Lord..hath *p* his word..........2Chr 6:10
Lord might *p* his word 2Chr 10:15
p the words of the covenant ...2Chr 34:31
that *p* not this promise ....Neh 5:13
and hast *p* thy words ....Neh 9:8
not *p* the commandment ......Esth 1:15
the kingdom it shall be *p*......Esth 5:6
and to *p* my request ....Esth 5:8
shall be *p*, even to the half ....Esth 7:2
hands cannot *p* their ....Job 5:12
p the thing that is appointed...Job 23:14
they are not able to *p*.........Ps 21:11
unto God that *p* all things .....Ps 57:2
I may daily *p* my vows ....Ps 61:8
thee shall the vow be *p* ....Ps 65:1
I have sworn..I will *p* it ....Ps 119:106
heart to *p* thy statutes ....Ps 119:112
Lord of hosts will *p* this.......Is 9:7
Lord hath *p* his whole work ...Is 10:12
vow a vow..and *p* it ....Is 19:21
p the counsel of his ....Is 44:26
shall *p* all my pleasure ....Is 44:28
hasten my word to *p* it........Jer 1:12
p the oath which I have ....Jer 11:5
have *p* the thoughts............Jer 23:20
Lord *p* thy words which ....Jer 28:6
and *p* my good word toward...Jer 29:10
he have *p* the intents ....Jer 30:24
will *p* that good thing ....Jer 33:14
not *p* the words of the ....Jer 34:18
words of Jonadab..are *p* ......Jer 35:14
p the commandment ....Jer 35:16
We will surely *p* our vows .....Jer 44:25
and surely *p* your vows ....Jer 44:25
purpose..shall be *p* ....Jer 51:29
the word, and will *p* it ....Ezek 12:25
Lord have spoken it, and *p* it..Ezek 37:14
Thou wilt *p* the truth ....Mic 7:20
solemn feasts *p* thy vows ......Nah 1:15
shalt *p* unto the Lord ....Matt 5:33
these things shall be *p* ....Luke 1:20
be a *p* of those things.........Luke 1:45
p the mercy promised to ......Luke 1:72
p all things according to.......Luke 2:39
he was able also to *p* ....Rom 4:21
how to *p* that which is ....Rom 7:18
therefore I have *p* this ....Rom 15:28
Now..*p* the doing of it 2Cor 8:11
so there may be a *p* also 2Cor 8:11
will *p* it until the day ....Phil 1:6

PERFUME—*a sweet-smelling scent; fragrance*
Made by:
Apothecary ....Ex 30:25, 35
Combining:
Various ingredients ......Job 41:31
Olive oil with imported aromatics 1Kin 10:10
Uses of:
Incense and ointment for tabernacle ....Ex 30:22-28
Personal adornment .....Prov 27:9
Seduction ....Prov 7:17
Figurative of Christ's:
Glories ....Ps 45:8
Righteousness and intercession ....Song 3:6
Spiritual prostitution .....Is 57:9

PERFUMER—*one who produces pleasant scents*
Great art ....Ex 30:25
Eccl 10:1
Used in tabernacle ......Ex 30:25, 35
Used in embalming 2Chr 16:14
A maker of ointment ....Eccl 10:1
Among returnees ....Neh 3:8

PERGA (pûr'gä)—*"very earthy"—the capital of Pamphylia*
Visited by Paul..........Acts 13:13, 14
Acts 14:25

PERGAMOS (pûr'gä-mŏs)—*"elevation"—a leading city in Mysia in Asia Minor*
One of the seven churches here ....Rev 1:11
Antipas martyred here ...Rev 2:12, 13
Special message to.......Rev 2:12-17

PERHAPS—*possibly*
if *p* the thought of thine ......Acts 8:22
lest *p* such..be swallowed......2Cor 2:7
For *p* he..departed for ....Philem 15

PERIDA (pě-rī'dä)—*"separation"*
Head of a family of Temple servants ....Neh 7:46, 57
Same as Peruda ....Ezra 2:55

PERIL—*physical or spiritual danger*
Escape from, by:
Prayer..................Gen 32:6-12
Pacifying gifts ....Gen 32:13-20
Quick action 1Sam 18:10, 11
Flight ....Matt 2:12-15
Love of Christ ....Rom 8:35
God....................2Cor 1:10

[*also* PERILOUS, PERILS]
bread with the *p* of our ....Lam 5:9
or nakedness, or *p*...........Rom 8:35
in *p* of waters, in *p* of 2Cor 11:26
p by mine own countrymen....2Cor 11:26
p by the heathen, in *p* 2Cor 11:26
in *p* in the wilderness 2Cor 11:26
in *p* in the sea, in *p* among....2Cor 11:26

PERISH—*to become destroyed or ruined*
Applied to:
Universe................Heb 1:11
Old world 2Pet 3:6
Animals ....Ps 49:12, 20
Vegetation ....Jon 4:10
Food ....John 6:27
Gold 1Pet 1:7
Human body 2Cor 4:16
Soul...................Matt 10:28
Safeguards against:
God's:
Power ....John 10:28
Will ....Matt 18:14
Providence ....Luke 21:18
Christ's resurrection 1Cor 15:18, 19
Repentance ....Luke 13:3, 5
See LOST

[*also* PERISHED, PERISHETH, PERISHING]
p not through the famine......Gen 41:36
and many of them *p* ....Ex 19:21
eye of his maid, that it *p*......Ex 21:26
p among the heathen ....Lev 26:38
p from among the congregation.Num 16:33
Behold, we die, we *p*, we all *p*.Num 17:12
he also shall *p* for ever........Num 24:24
shall soon utterly *p* from ......Deut 4:26
so shall ye *p*; because ye ......Deut 8:20
A Syrian ready to *p* was ......Deut 26:5
pursue thee until thou *p* ......Deut 28:22
man *p* not alone ....Josh 22:20
until ye *p* from off this........Josh 23:13
So let all thine enemies *p* .....Judg 5:31
into battle, and *p*.............1Sam 26:10
p one day by the hand of Saul .1Sam 27:1
the weapons of war *p*! 2Sam 1:27
house of Ahab shall *p* 2Kin 9:8
to cause to *p*, all Jews ....Esth 3:13
to be slain, and to *p* ....Esth 7:4
nor the memorial of them *p* ...Esth 9:28
Let the day *p* wherein I ....Job 3:3
who ever *p*, being innocent? ...Job 4:7
The old lion *p* for lack ....Job 4:11
p for ever without any ....Job 4:20
hypocrite's hope shall *p* ....Job 8:13
shall *p* for ever like ....Job 20:7
seen any *p* for want of ....Job 31:19
life from *p* by the sword ......Job 33:18
they shall *p* by the sword .....Job 36:12
way of the ungodly shall *p* ....Ps 1:6
shall fall and *p* ....Ps 9:3
memorial is *p* with them ......Ps 9:6
the wicked shall *p* ....Ps 37:20
and the brutish person *p* ......Ps 49:10
is like the beasts that *p* ....Ps 49:20
that are far from thee shall *p* ..Ps 73:27
Which *p* at En-dor ....Ps 83:10
be put to shame and *p* ....Ps 83:17
They shall *p*, but thou ....Ps 102:26
his thoughts *p* ....Ps 146:4
of the wicked shall *p*..........Prov 10:28
hope of unjust men *p* ....Prov 11:7
the wicked *p*, there is ....Prov 11:10
that speaketh lies shall *p* ......Prov 19:9
when they *p*, the righteous ....Prov 28:28
him that is ready to *p*.........Prov 31:6
But those riches *p* by evil .....Eccl 5:14
just man that *p* in his ....Eccl 7:15
and their envy, is now *p* ....Eccl 9:6
made all their memory to *p* ...Is 26:14
of their wise men shall *p* ......Is 29:14
righteous *p*, and no man ......Is 57:1
not serve thee shall *p* ....Is 60:12
heart of the king shall *p*.......Jer 4:9
truth is *p*, and is cut off.......Jer 7:28
for what the land *p* and is.....Jer 9:12
shall *p* from the earth ....Jer 10:11
the law shall not *p* from.......Jer 18:18
and that ye might *p*...........Jer 27:15
the valley also shall *p* ....Jer 48:8
p from the prudent? ....Jer 49:7
my hope is *p* from the Lord ...Lam 3:18
but the law shall *p* from.......Ezek 7:26
his fellows should not *p* ....Dan 2:18
harvest of the field is *p* ....Joel 1:11
the Philistines shall *p* ....Amos 1:8
houses of ivory shall *p* ....Amos 3:15
upon us, that we *p* not........Jon 1:6
anger, that we *p* not? ....Jon 3:9
is thy counselor *p*? ....Mic 4:9
king shall *p* from Gaza........Zech 9:5
of thy members should *p*......Matt 5:29
and *p* in the waters ....Matt 8:32
and the bottles *p* ....Matt 9:17
shall *p* with the sword ....Matt 26:52
carest thou not that we *p*? .....Mark 4:38
and the bottles shall *p* ....Luke 5:37
saying, Master Master we *p* ...Luke 8:24
p between the altar and ....Luke 11:51
and I *p* with hunger!..........Luke 15:17
believeth..should not *p* ....John 3:15
believeth..should not *p* ....John 3:16
he also *p*; and all ....Acts 5:37
Thy money *p* with thee ....Acts 8:20
shall also *p* without law ....Rom 2:12
them that *p* foolishness........1Cor 1:18
saved, and in them that *p* 2Cor 2:15
are to *p* with the using ....Col 2:22
in them that *p*................2Thess 2:10
By faith..Rahab *p* not.........Heb 11:31
the fashion of it *p* ....James 1:11
p in their own corruption 2Pet 2:12
not willing that any should *p* ..2Pet 3:9
p in the gainsaying of ....Jude 11

PERIZZITES (pěr'ĭ-zīts)—*"dwellers in the open country"*
Descendants of Perez ....Num 26:20
One of seven Canaanite nations ....Deut 7:1
Possessed Palestine in Abraham's time ....Gen 13:7
Land of, promised to Abraham's seed ....Gen 15:18, 20
Jacob's fear of ....Gen 34:30
Israel commanded to utterly destroy ....Deut 20:17
Israel forbidden to intermingle with ....Ex 23:23-25
Defeated by Joshua.......Josh 3:10
Many of, slain by Judah .Judg 1:4, 5
Israel intermarries with ..Judg 3:5-7
Made slaves by Solomon .1Kin 9:20, 21
See CANAANITES

[*also* PERIZZITE]
the *P*, and the Hivites ....Ex 3:8
the *P*, and the Hivites ....Ex 3:17
the Hittite, and the *P*.........Ex 33:2
the Hittite, and the *P*.........Ex 34:11
the Canaanite, the *P*..........Josh 9:1
the Hittite, and the *P*.........Josh 11:3
the *P*, the Hivites ....Josh 12:8
in the land of the *P* ....Josh 17:15
the Amorites, and the *P* ....Josh 24:11
the *P*, and the Hivites 2Chr 8:7
the Hittites, the *P* ....Ezra 9:1
the Amorites, and the *P* ......Neh 9:8

PERJURY—*swearing falsely*
Condemned by the Law ..Lev 19:12
Hated by God ....Zech 8:17
Requires atonement .....Lev 6:2-7
Brings punishment ....Zech 5:3, 4
Mal 3:5
See FALSE WITNESSES

[*also* PERJURED]
for liars, for *p* persons 1Tim 1:10

PERMISSION—*authority to do something*
Speak by 1Cor 7:6

PERMIT—*to allow*

[*also* PERMITTED]
Thou art *p* to speak for ....Acts 26:1
not *p* unto them to speak 1Cor 14:34
with you, if the Lord *p* 1Cor 16:7
this will we do, if God *p* ......Heb 6:3

PERNICIOUS—*destructive; wicked*
shall follow their *p* ways 2Pet 2:2

PERPETUAL—*lasting forever*
Statute ....Ex 27:21
Incense.................Ex 30:8
Covenant ....Ex 31:16
Priesthood ....Ex 40:15
Possession ....Lev 25:34
Allotment...............Num 18:8
Ruins ....Ps 9:6
Ps 74:3
Pain....................Jer 15:18
Hissing ....Jer 18:16
Sleep ....Jer 51:39
Desolation ....Jer 51:62
Mountains ....Hab 3:6

[*also* PERPETUALLY]
you, for *p* generations ....Gen 9:12
theirs for a *p* statute ....Ex 29:9
a *p* statute for your ....Lev 3:17
flour for a meat offering *p* ....Lev 6:20
by fire by a *p* statute ....Lev 24:9
it shall be a *p* statute ....Num 19:21

heart shall be there *p* 1Kin 9:3
heart shall be there *p* 2Chr 7:16
are come to a *p* end ....Ps 9:6
unto the *p* desolations ....Ps 74:3
put them to a *p* reproach .....Ps 78:66
of the sea by a *p* decree ......Jer 5:22
back by a *p* backsliding ....Jer 8:5
desolate, and a *p* hissing ......Jer 18:16
and a *p* shame, which ....Jer 23:40
hissing, and *p* desolations .....Jer 25:9
make it *p* desolations ....Jer 25:12
cities thereof shall be *p* wastes .Jer 49:13
the Lord in a *p* covenant ......Jer 50:5
shall sleep a *p*, sleep and......Jer 51:57
hast had a *p* hatred ....Ezek 35:5
make thee *p* desolations ....Ezek 35:9
by a *p* ordinance unto the .....Ezek 46:14
and his anger did tear *p* ....Amos 1:11
and a *p* desolation ....Zeph 2:9

PERPLEXITY—*bewilderment; inability to see the way out of a situation*
Predicted by Christ ......Luke 21:25

[*also* PERPLEXED]
the city Shushan was *p* ....Esth 3:15
and of *p* by the Lord God ....Is 22:5
the herds of cattle are *p* ....Joel 1:18
now shall be their *p* ....Mic 7:4
And he was *p*, because ....Luke 9:7
as they were much *p* ....Luke 24:4
are *p*, but not in despair 2Cor 4:8

PERSECUTION—*affliction; oppression; torment*

Caused by:
Man's sinful nature ......Gal 4:29
Hatred of God ....John 15:20-23
Ignorance of God ....John 16:1-3
Hatred of Christ.........1Thess 2:15
Rev 12:13
Preaching the cross ......Gal 5:11
Gal 6:12
Godly living ....Matt 13:21
2Tim 3:12
Mistaken zeal ....Acts 13:50
Acts 26:9-11

Christian's attitude under:
Flee from ....Matt 10:23
Rejoice in ....Matt 5:12
Be patient under 1Cor 4:12
Glorify God in 1Pet 4:16
Pray during ....Matt 5:44

[*also* PERSECUTE, PERSECUTED, PERSECUTEST, PERSECUTING, PERSECUTIONS]
hate thee, which *p* thee ....Deut 30:7
Why do ye *p* me as God ....Job 19:22
Why *p* we him, seeing ....Job 19:28
from all them that *p* me.......Ps 7:1
his pride doth *p* the poor .....Ps 10:2
from them that *p* me ....Ps 31:15
against them that *p* me........Ps 35:3
angel of the Lord *p* them .....Ps 35:6
him; *p* and take him ....Ps 71:11
So *p* them with thy ....Ps 83:15
but *p* the poor and needy .....Ps 109:16
judgment on them that *p*......Ps 119:84
they *p* me wrongfully ....Ps 119:86
p me without a cause ....Ps 119:161
nations in anger, is *p* ....Is 14:6
be confounded that *p* me......Jer 17:18
covered with anger, and *p*.....Lam 3:43
P and destroy them in anger ..Lam 3:66
Our necks are under *p* ....Lam 5:5
p for righteousness' sake ......Matt 5:10
revile you, and *p* you ....Matt 5:11
use you, and *p* you ....Matt 5:44
p them from city to city ....Matt 23:34
and lands, with *p* ....Mark 10:30
they shall slay and *p* ....Luke 11:49
hands on you, and *p* you ......Luke 21:12
did the Jews *p* Jesus ....John 5:16
If they have *p* me, they ....John 15:20
have not your fathers *p*? ....Acts 7:52
Saul, why *p* thou me?..........Acts 9:4
I am Jesus whom thou *p* ......Acts 9:5
p that arose about Stephen ....Acts 11:19
p this way unto the death .....Acts 22:4
Saul, why *p* thou me..........Acts 22:7
of Nazareth whom thou *p* .....Acts 22:8
Saul, why *p* thou me?.........Acts 26:14
I am Jesus whom thou *p* ......Acts 26:15
or distress, or *p* ....Rom 8:35
Bless them which *p* you ....Rom 12:14
being *p*, we suffer it 1Cor 4:12
I *p* the church of God 1Cor 15:9
p, but not forsaken; cast 2Cor 4:9
p, in distressses for Christ's....2Cor 12:10
I *p* the church of God ....Gal 1:13
he which *p* us in times ....Gal 1:23
zeal, *p* the church ....Phil 3:6
your *p* and tribulations 2Thess 1:4
p, afflictions, which came 2Tim 3:11
Lystra; what *p* I endured......2Tim 3:11

PERSECUTION PSALM
Of David ....Ps 69

PERSECUTOR—*one who harasses continually*

[*also* PERSECUTORS]
p thou threwest into the deeps .Neh 9:11
his arrows against the *p* ....Ps 7:13
my *p* and mine enemies ....Ps 119:157
deliver me from my *p*.........Ps 142:6
and revenge me of my *p* ......Jer 15:15
my *p* shall stumble ....Jer 20:11
all her *p* overtook her ....Lam 1:3
Our *p* are swifter than ....Lam 4:19
a blasphemer, and a *p* 1Tim 1:13

PERSEVERANCE—*steadfastness; persistence*

Elements involved in:
Spiritual growth ....Eph 4:15
Fruitfulness ....John 15:4-8
God's armor ....Eph 6:11-18
Chastening..............Heb 12:5-13
Assurance 2Tim 1:12
Salvation ....Matt 10:22
Reward..................Gal 6:9

PERSIA (pûr'zhä)—*"cuts or divides"—great empire including all of western Asia and parts of Europe and Africa*

[*also* PERSIAN, PERSIANS]
the kingdom of *P*.............2Chr 36:20
year of Cyrus king of *P* 2Chr 36:22
spirit of Cyrus king of *P* 2Chr 36:22
saith Cyrus king of *P* 2Chr 36:23
year of Cyrus king of *P* ....Ezra 1:1
spirit of Cyrus king of *P* ....Ezra 1:1
Cyrus king of *P* bring forth....Ezra 1:8
the king of *P* hath ....Ezra 4:3
days of Cyrus king of *P*.......Ezra 4:5
reign of Darius king of *P* .....Ezra 4:5
reign of Darius king of *P* .....Ezra 4:24
of Artaxerxes king of *P* ....Ezra 7:1
the reign of Darius the *P* .....Neh 12:22
the power of *P* and Media ....Esth 1:3
the seven princes of *P* ....Esth 1:14
ladies of *P* and Media say .....Esth 1:18
the laws of the *P* and the .....Esth 1:19
They of *P* and of Lud and ....Ezek 27:10
given to the Medes and *P* .....Dan 5:28
law of the Medes and *P*........Dan 6:8
law of the Medes and *P*........Dan 6:15
the reign of Cyrus the *P* ......Dan 6:28
the kings of Media and *P* .....Dan 8:20
of the kingdom of *P* ....Dan 10:13
with the kings of *P* ....Dan 10:13
fight with the prince of *P* .....Dan 10:20

PERSIS (Pûr'sĭs)—*"Persian"*
Christian woman in Rome Rom 16:12

PERSON—*a human being; individual*

[*also* PERSONS]
Abram, Give me the *p*.......Gen 14:21
Joseph was a goodly *p* ....Gen 39:6
no uncircumcised *p* shall ......Ex 12:48
to the number of your *p* ......Ex 16:16
not respect the *p* of the ....Lev 19:15
nor honor the *p* of the ....Lev 19:15
the *p* shall be for the Lord ....Lev 27:2
and that *p* be guilty...........Num 5:6
for an unclean *p* they ....Num 19:17
upon the *p* that were ....Num 19:18
whosoever hath killed any *p* ...Num 31:19
portion of fifty, of the *p* ......Num 31:30
p were sixteen thousand.......Num 31:40
was thirty and two *p* ....Num 31:40
killeth any *p* unawares ....Num 35:15
Whoso killeth any *p* ....Num 35:30
not testify against any *p* ....Num 35:30
respect *p* in judgment ....Deut 1:17
threescore and ten *p* ....Deut 10:22
the clean *p* shall eat it ....Deut 15:22
shall not regard the *p* of ......Deut 28:50
are threescore and ten *p* ......Judg 9:2
hired vain and light *p* ....Judg 9:4
threescore and ten *p* upon.....Judg 9:18
a goodlier *p* than he 1Sam 9:2
which were about thirty *p* 1Sam 9:22
all the *p* of thy father's 1Sam 22:22
and have accepted thy *p* 1Sam 25:35
have slain a righteous *p* 2Sam 4:11
doth God respect any *p* 2Sam 14:14
sons, being seventy *p* 2Kin 10:6
respect of *p*, nor taking 2Chr 19:7
Will ye accept his *p*?...........Job 13:8
if ye do secretly accept *p*......Job 13:10
accept any man's *p* ....Job 32:21
I have not sat with vain *p* .....Ps 26:4
I will not know a wicked *p* ....Ps 101:4
A naughty *p*, a wicked ....Prov 6:12
he that followeth vain *p* is.....Prov 12:11
called a mischievous *p* ....Prov 24:8
vain *p* shall have poverty ......Prov 28:19
The vile *p* shall be no.........Is 32:5
p that Nebuzar-adan ....Jer 43:6
hundred thirty and two *p*......Jer 52:29
hundred forty and five *p* ......Jer 52:30
the *p* were four thousand .....Jer 52:30
respected not the *p* of the .....Lam 4:16
to the loathing of thy *p* ....Ezek 16:5
forts, to cut off many *p* ....Ezek 17:17
shall come at no dead *p* to ....Ezek 44:25
shall stand up a vile *p* ....Dan 11:21
than sixscore thousand *p* ......Jon 4:11
light and treacherous *p*........Zeph 3:4
or accept thy *p*? saith the .....Mal 1:8
will he regard your *p* ....Mal 1:9
regardest not the *p* of.........Matt 22:16
regardest not the *p* ....Mark 12:14
ninety and nine just *p*.........Luke 15:7
thou the *p* of any.............Luke 20:21
God is no respecter of *p* ......Acts 10:34
no respect of *p* with God .....Rom 2:11
yourselves that wicked *p* 1Cor 5:13
by the means of many *p* 2Cor 1:11
it in the *p* of Christ...........2Cor 2:10
accepteth no man's *p* ....Gal 2:6
is there respect of *p* with......Eph 6:9
there is no respect of *p* ....Col 3:25
for liars, for perjured *p* 1Tim 1:10
express image of his *p* ....Heb 1:3
of glory, with respect of *p*.....James 2:1
who without respect of *p*......1Pet 1:17
saved Noah the eighth *p* 2Pet 2:5
what manner of *p* ought 2Pet 3:11
men's *p* in admiration ....Jude 16

PERSONAL DEVOTIONS—*personal, individual worship*

Prayer:
In morning..............Ps 5:3
Ps 119:147
Three times daily ....Ps 55:17
Dan 6:10
Continually 1Thess 3:10
1Tim 5:5

Study:
Daily ....Deut 17:19
For learning ....Acts 17:11
Rom 15:4

PERSUASION—*moving people's minds by argument or entreaty*

Good, to:
Worship .... Acts 18:13
Steadfastness .... Acts 13:43
Belief .... Acts 18:4
Acts 19:8
Turn from idolatry ...... Acts 19:26
Trust Jesus .... Acts 28:23

Evil, to:
Unbelief 2Chr 32:10-19
Unholy alliance 2Chr 18:2
Fatal conflict 1Kin 22:20-22
Turmoil .... Acts 14:19
Error .... Gal 5:8

Objects of:
Hereafter .... Luke 16:31
One's faith in God ...... Rom 4:21
Personal assurance ...... Rom 8:38
Personal liberty 2Tim 1:12
Spiritual stability .... Rom 15:14
Another's faith 2Tim 1:5
God's promises .... Heb 11:13

[*also* PERSUADE, PERSUADED, PERSUADEST, PERSUADETH]
Hezekiah, when he ***p*** you 2Kin 18:32
nor ***p*** you on this manner 2Chr 32:15
forbearing is a prince ***p*** .... Prov 25:15
lest Hezekiah ***p*** you .... Is 36:18
elders ***p*** the multitude .... Matt 27:20
we will ***p*** him, and secure ..... Matt 28:14
they be ***p*** that John was a ..... Luke 20:6
when he would not be ***p*** ...... Acts 21:14
I am ***p*** that none of these ..... Acts 26:26
p me to be a Christian .... Acts 26:28
fully ***p*** in his own mind .... Rom 14:5
am ***p*** by the Lord Jesus .... Rom 14:14
terror of the Lord, we ***p*** 2Cor 5:11
do I now ***p*** men, or God? ..... Gal 1:10
we are ***p*** better things of ...... Heb 6:9

PERTAIN—*belong to*

[*also* PERTAINED, PERTAINETH, PERTAINING]
offerings, that ***p*** unto .... Lev 7:20
which ***p*** to his cleansing .... Lev 14:32
the priest ***p*** the oil for .... Num 4:16
half that ***p*** unto the .... Num 31:43
that which ***p*** unto a man ...... Deut 22:5
were ***p*** unto the children ...... Josh 13:31
a hill that ***p*** to Phinehas ...... Josh 24:33
that ***p*** unto Joash .... Judg 6:11
missed of all that ***p*** unto 1Sam 25:21
if I leave of all that ***p*** to 1Sam 25:22
Ziklag ***p*** unto the kings 1Sam 27:6
which ***p*** to Ish-bosheth 2Sam 2:15
Obed-edom, and all that ***p*** 2Sam 6:12
p unto Mephibosheth 2Sam 16:4
to him ***p*** Sochoh, and all 1Kin 4:10
to him ***p*** the towns of Jair 1Kin 4:13
the vessels that ***p*** unto 1Kin 7:48
p to the king of Egypt 2Kin 24:7
every morning ***p*** to them 1Chr 9:27
every matter ***p*** to God 1Chr 26:32
fenced cities which ***p*** to 2Chr 12:4
things ***p*** to the kingdom .... Acts 1:3
p to the flesh, hath found? .... Rom 4:1
to whom ***p*** the adoption ...... Rom 9:4
things which ***p*** to God .... Rom 15:17
things that ***p*** to this 1Cor 6:3
judgments of things ***p*** to 1Cor 6:4
priest in things ***p*** to God ...... Heb 2:17
spoken ***p*** to another tribe ..... Heb 7:13
as ***p*** to the conscience .... Heb 9:9
all things that ***p*** unto life 2Pet 1:3

PERUDA (pē-rōō'dä)—*"separated"*
One of Solomon's servants whose descendants return from exile .... {Ezra 2:55, Neh 7:57}

PERVERSENESS—*willfully continuing in sinful ways*

Applied to:
Heart .... Prov 12:8
Nation .... Phil 2:15

Source of:
False doctrine .... Acts 20:30

[*also* PERVERSE, PERVERSELY]
thy way is ***p*** before me .... Num 22:32
hath he seen ***p*** in Israel .... Num 23:21
p and crooked generation ..... Deut 32:5
son of the ***p*** rebellious woman . 1Sam 20:30
which thy servant did ***p*** the 2Sam 19:19
sinned, and have done ***p*** 1Kin 8:47
taste discern ***p*** things? .... Job 6:30
for they dealt ***p*** with me ...... Ps 119:78
p lips put far from thee .... Prov 4:24
is nothing froward or ***p*** .... Prov 8:8
p of transgressors shall .... Prov 11:3
is ***p*** in his ways despiseth ...... Prov 14:2
he that is ***p*** in his lips .... Prov 19:1
he that is ***p*** in his ways .... Prov 28:6
p in his ways shall fall .... Prov 28:18
hath mingled a ***p*** spirit .... Is 19:14
trust in oppression and ***p*** ...... Is 30:12
and the city full of ***p*** .... Ezek 9:9
faithless and ***p*** generation ..... Luke 9:41
P disputings of men of 1Tim 6:5

PERVERT—*to cause to turn away from that which is good, true, or morally right*

Evil of, in dealing with:
Man's judgment .... Deut 24:17
God's:
Judgment .... Job 8:3
Word .... Jer 23:36
Ways .... Acts 13:10
Gospel .... Gal 1:7

Caused by:
Drink .... Prov 31:5
Worldly wisdom .... Is 47:10
Spiritual blindness .... Luke 23:2, 14

[*also* PERVERTED, PERVERTETH, PERVERTING]
and ***p*** the words of the .... Ex 23:8
p the words of the righteous ... Deut 16:19
he that ***p*** the judgment .... Deut 27:19
bribes, and ***p*** judgment 1Sam 8:3
and ***p*** that which was right .... Job 33:27
will the Almighty ***p*** .... Job 34:12
that ***p*** his ways shall be .... Prov 10:9
p the ways of judgment .... Prov 17:23
foolishness of man ***p*** .... Prov 19:3
violent ***p*** of judgment .... Eccl 5:8
they have ***p*** their way .... Jer 3:21
and ***p*** all equity .... Mic 3:9
this fellow ***p*** the nation .... Luke 23:2

PESTILENCE—*a plague; a disastrous affliction*
Fifth Egyptian plague .... Ex 9:1-16
Threatened by God ...... Deut 28:21
Sent because of David's sin 2Sam 24:13, 15
Used for man's corrections .... Ezek 38:22
Precedes the Lord's coming .... Hab 3:5

[*also* PESTILENCES, PESTILENT]
he fall upon us with ***p*** .... Ex 5:3
and thy people with ***p*** .... Ex 9:15
send the ***p*** among you .... Lev 26:25
smite them with the ***p*** .... Num 14:12
land famine, if there be ***p*** 1Kin 8:37
even the ***p***, in the land 1Chr 21:12
Lord sent ***p*** upon Israel 1Chr 21:14
if there be ***p***, if there 2Chr 6:28
send ***p*** among my people 2Chr 7:13
judgment, or ***p***, or famine 2Chr 20:9
and from the noisome ***p*** .... Ps 91:3
for the ***p*** that walketh .... Ps 91:6
the famine, and by the ***p*** ...... Jer 14:12
in this city from the ***p*** .... Jer 21:7
famine, and the ***p***, among ..... Jer 24:10
famine, and with the ***p*** .... Jer 27:8
the famine, and by the ***p*** ...... Jer 27:13
the famine, and the ***p*** .... Jer 29:17
the famine, and with the ***p*** .... Jer 29:18
famine, and of the ***p*** .... Jer 32:24
the famine, and by the ***p*** ...... Jer 32:36
the famine, and by the ***p*** ...... Jer 38:2
the famine, and by the ***p*** ...... Jer 42:17
the famine, and by the ***p*** ...... Jer 42:22
the famine, and by the ***p*** ...... Jer 44:13
shall die with the ***p*** .... Ezek 5:12
the famine, and by the ***p*** ..... Ezek 6:11
and the ***p*** and the famine ...... Ezek 7:15
famine and ***p*** shall devour ..... Ezek 7:15
famine, and from the ***p*** .... Ezek 12:16
Or if I send a ***p*** into that ..... Ezek 14:19
I will send into her ***p*** .... Ezek 28:23
caves shall die of the ***p*** .... Ezek 33:27
sent among you the ***p*** .... Amos 4:10
p, and earthquakes, in .... Matt 24:7
and famines, and ***p*** .... Luke 21:11
found this man a ***p*** fellow ..... Acts 24:5

PESTLE—*instrument used for pulverizing material*
Figurative of severe discipline .... Prov 27:22

PETER (pē'ter)—*"stone; rock"—a fisherman who was called to be a disciple and apostle of Christ*

Life of:
Before his call:
Simon Barjona .... Matt 16:17
John 21:15
Brother of Andrew ...... Matt 4:18
Married man .... Mark 1:30
1Cor 9:5
Not highly educated ..... Acts 4:13
Fisherman .... Matt 4:18

From his call to Pentecost:
Brought to Jesus by Andrew .... John 1:40-42
Named Cephas by Christ . John 1:42
Called to discipleship by Christ .... Matt 4:18-22
Mother-in-law healed .... Matt 8:14, 15
Called as apostle .... Matt 10:2-4
Walks on water .... Matt 14:28-33
Confessed Christ's deity .. Matt 16:13-19
Rebuked by Jesus .... Matt 16:21-23
Witnesses transfiguration . Matt 17:1-8
2Pet 1:16-18
Asked important questions .... Matt 18:21
Refused Christ's menial service .... John 13:6-10
Cuts off high priest's slave's ear .... John 18:10, 11
Denied Christ three times. Matt 26:69-75
Wept bitterly .... Matt 26:75
Ran to Christ's sepulcher . John 20:1-8
Returned to fishing ...... John 21:1-14
Witnessed Christ's ascension .... Matt 28:16-20
Returned to Jerusalem ... Acts 1:12-14
Led disciples .... Acts 1:15-26

From Pentecost onward:
Explained Spirit's coming at Pentecost .... Acts 2:1-41
Healed lame man .... Acts 3:1-11
Pronounces judgment .... Acts 5:1-11
Heals .... Acts 5:14-16
Met Paul .... Acts 9:26
Gal 1:17, 18
Raises Dorcas .... Acts 9:36-43
Called to Gentiles .... Acts 10:1-23
Preached the Gospel to Gentiles .... Acts 10:24-46
Explained his action to apostles .... Acts 11:1-18
Imprisoned—delivered ... Acts 12:3-19
Attends Jerusalem Council .... Acts 15:7-14
Rebuked by Paul for inconsistency .... Gal 2:14
Commended Paul's writings 2Pet 3:15, 16

His life contrasted before and after Pentecost, once:
Coward; now courageous ... Matt 26:58, 69-74
Impulsive; now humble ... John 18:10
Ignorant; now enlightened ... Matt 16:21, 22
Deeply inquisitive; now submissive ... John 21:21, 22
Boastful of self; now boastful of Christ ... Matt 26:33, 34
Timid and afraid; now fearless ... Matt 14:28-31

Significance of:
Often the representative for the others ... Matt 17:24-27
Only disciple personally restored by the Lord ... John 21:15-19
Leader in the early church ... Acts 3:12-26

[*also* PETER'S]
answered ***P*** and said ... Matt 15:15
answered ***P*** and said unto ... Matt 19:27
P said unto him, Though ... Matt 26:35
P and the two sons of ... Matt 26:37
Simon he surnamed ***P*** ... Mark 3:16
to follow him, save ***P*** ... Mark 5:37
P answereth and saith ... Mark 8:29
P took him, and began to ... Mark 8:32
he rebuked ***P***, saying ... Mark 8:33
Jesus taketh with him ***P*** ... Mark 9:2
P answered and said to ... Mark 9:5
P began to say unto him ... Mark 10:28
P calling to remembrance ... Mark 11:21
P and James and John ... Mark 13:3
P said unto him ... Mark 14:29
he taketh with him ***P*** ... Mark 14:33
saith unto ***P***, Simon ... Mark 14:37
P followed him afar off ... Mark 14:54
P was beneath in the ... Mark 14:66
when she saw ***P*** warming ... Mark 14:67
again to ***P***, Surely thou ... Mark 14:70
P called to mind the word ... Mark 14:72
tell his disciples and ***P*** ... Mark 16:7
When Simon ***P*** saw it, he ... Luke 5:8
(whom he also named ***P***) ... Luke 6:14
P and they that were with ... Luke 8:45
no man to go in save ***P*** ... Luke 8:51
P answering said, The Christ ... Luke 9:20
he took ***P*** and John and ... Luke 9:28
But ***P*** and they that were ... Luke 9:32
P said unto Jesus, Master ... Luke 9:33
P said unto him, Lord ... Luke 12:41
Then ***P*** said, Lo, we have ... Luke 18:28
And he sent ***P*** and John ... Luke 22:8
I tell thee, ***P***, the cock ... Luke 22:34
house. And ***P*** followed ... Luke 22:54
P sat down among ... Luke 22:55
them. And ***P*** said, Man ... Luke 22:58
P said, Man, I know not ... Luke 22:60
turned, and looked upon ***P*** ... Luke 22:61
P remembered the word ... Luke 22:61
And ***P*** went out, and wept ... Luke 22:62
Then arose ***P***, and ran ... Luke 24:12
the city of Andrew and ***P*** ... John 1:44
Andrew, Simon ***P*** brother ... John 6:8
Simon ***P*** answered him ... John 6:68
Simon ***P*** therefore beckoned ... John 13:24
Simon ***P*** said unto him ... John 13:36
P said unto him, Lord ... John 13:37
said Jesus unto ***P***, Put up ... John 18:11
Simon ***P*** followed Jesus ... John 18:15
P, stood at the door without ... John 18:16
and brought in ***P*** ... John 18:16
that kept the door unto ***P*** ... John 18:17
P stood with them, and ... John 18:18
And Simon ***P*** stood and ... John 18:25
whose ear ***P*** cut off ... John 18:26
P then denied again: and ... John 18:27
P, turning about, seeth ... John 21:20
P, filled with the Holy Ghost ... Acts 4:8
P and John answered and said ... Acts 4:19
P and the other apostles ... Acts 5:29
they sent unto them ***P*** ... Acts 8:14
But ***P*** said unto him, Thy ... Acts 8:20
P passed throughout all ... Acts 9:32
P said unto him, Aeneas ... Acts 9:34
circumcision was unto ***P*** ... Gal 2:7
wrought effectually in ***P*** ... Gal 2:8
But when ***P*** was come to ... Gal 2:11
I said unto ***P*** before them ... Gal 2:14

PETER, THE EPISTLES OF—*two books of the New Testament*

1 Peter
God's salvation ... 1Pet 1:3-12
Obedience and holiness ... 1Pet 1:13-23
Christ the corner stone ... 1Pet 2:4-6
A royal priesthood ... 1Pet 2:9
Christ's example ... 1Pet 2:18-25
Husbands and wives ... 1Pet 3:1-7
Partakers of His suffering ... 1Pet 4:12-19
Be humble before God ... 1Pet 5:6-10

2 Peter
Things pertaining to life ... 2Pet 1:1-4
Diligent growth ... 2Pet 1:5-11
False teachers ... 2Pet 2:1-22
The hope of the day ... 2Pet 3:9, 10

PETHAHIAH (pĕth-ä-hī'ä)—*"Jehovah opens up"*
1. Priest of David's time ... 1Chr 24:16
2. Judahite serving as a Persian official ... Neh 11:24
3. Levite who divorced his foreign wife ... Ezra 10:19, 23
Prays with the other Levites ... Neh 9:4, 5

PETHOR (pē'thôr)—*"soothsayer"—a town in North Mesopotamia*
Balaam's home ... Num 22:5, 7

PETHUEL (pĕ-thū'ĕl)—*"God's opening"*
Father of Joel the prophet ... Joel 1:1

PETITION—*earnest request*

Offered to men:
Treacherous ... Dan 6:7

Offered to God:
Favored ... 1Sam 1:17
Granted ... 1Sam 1:27

[*also* PETITIONS]
I ask one ***p*** of thee, deny ... 1Kin 2:16
desire one small ***p*** of thee ... 1Kin 2:20
What is thy ***p***? and it ... Esth 5:6
My ***p*** and my request is ... Esth 5:7
the king to grant my ***p*** ... Esth 5:8
What is thy ***p***, queen Esther? ... Esth 7:2
life be given me at my ***p*** ... Esth 7:3
now what is thy ***p***? and it ... Esth 9:12
the Lord fulfil all thy ***p*** ... Ps 20:5
shall ask a ***p*** of any God ... Dan 6:12
maketh his ***p*** three times ... Dan 6:13
the ***p*** that we desired ... 1John 5:15

PEULTHAI (pĕ-ŭl'ĕ-thī)—*"Jehovah's seed"*
Levite doorkeeper ... 1Chr 26:5

PHALEC (fā'lĕk)—*Greek form of Peleg*
which was the son of ***P*** ... Luke 3:35

PHALLU—*See* PALLU

PHALTI—*See* PALTI

PHALTIEL (făl'tĭ-ĕl)—*"God delivers"*
Husband of Michal ... 2Sam 3:14, 15

PHANUEL (fă-nū'ĕl)—*"vision of God"*
Father of Anna ... Luke 2:36

PHARAOH (fâr'ō)—*"inhabitant of the palace"—the title of the ruler of Egypt*

Unnamed ones, contemporary of:
Abraham ... Gen 12:15-20
Joseph ... Gen 37:36
Moses (the oppression) ... Ex 1:8-11
Moses (the exodus) ... Ex 5-14
Solomon ... 1Kin 3:1
1Kin 11:17-20
Hezekiah ... 2Kin 18:21

Named ones:
Shishak ... 1Kin 14:25, 26
So ... 2Kin 17:4
Tirhakah ... 2Kin 19:9
Nechoh ... 2Kin 23:29
Hophra ... Jer 44:30
Probably also referred to in ... Jer 37:5, 7, 11

[*also* PHARAOH'S]
Potiphar, an officer of ***P*** ... Gen 39:1
P was wroth against two ... Gen 40:2
he asked ***P*** officers that ... Gen 40:7
P cup was in my hand ... Gen 40:11
pressed them into ***P*** ... Gen 40:11
gave the cup into ***P*** ... Gen 40:11
shall ***P*** lift up thine head ... Gen 40:13
shalt deliver ***P*** cup into ... Gen 40:13
mention of me unto ***P*** ... Gen 40:14
of bakemeats for ***P*** ... Gen 40:17
shall ***P*** lift up thy head ... Gen 40:19
which was ***P*** birthday ... Gen 40:20
the cup into ***P*** hand ... Gen 40:21
years, that ***P*** dreamed ... Gen 41:1
and fat kine. So ***P*** awoke ... Gen 41:4
and ***P*** awoke, and, behold ... Gen 41:7
P told them his dream ... Gen 41:8
interpret them unto ***P*** ... Gen 41:8
the chief butler unto ***P*** ... Gen 41:9
P was wroth with his ... Gen 41:10
Then ***P*** sent and called ... Gen 41:14
and came in unto ***P*** ... Gen 41:14
And ***P*** said unto Joseph ... Gen 41:15
Joseph answered ***P*** ... Gen 41:16
shall give ***P*** an answer of ... Gen 41:16
P said unto Joseph, In my ... Gen 41:17
And Joseph said unto ***P*** ... Gen 41:25
The dream of ***P*** is one ... Gen 41:25
showed ***P*** what he is ... Gen 41:25
I have spoken unto ***P*** ... Gen 41:28
to do he showeth unto ***P*** ... Gen 41:28
doubled unto ***P*** twice ... Gen 41:32
let ***P*** look out a man ... Gen 41:33
Let ***P*** do this, and let him ... Gen 41:34
under the hand of ***P*** ... Gen 41:35
was good in the eyes of ***P*** ... Gen 41:37
P said unto his servants ... Gen 41:38
P said unto Joseph ... Gen 41:39
P said unto Joseph, See ... Gen 41:41
P took off his ring from ... Gen 41:42
And ***P*** said unto Joseph ... Gen 41:44
P called Joseph's name ... Gen 41:45
when he stood before ***P*** ... Gen 41:46
from the presence of ***P*** ... Gen 41:46
the people cried to ***P*** for ... Gen 41:55
P said unto all the ... Gen 41:55
By the life of ***P*** ye shall ... Gen 42:15
by the life of ***P*** surely ye ... Gen 42:16
for thou art even as ***P*** ... Gen 44:18
and the house of ***P*** heard ... Gen 45:2
made me a father to ***P*** ... Gen 45:8
was heard in ***P*** house ... Gen 45:16
pleased ***P*** well, and his ... Gen 45:16
P said unto Joseph, Say ... Gen 45:17
to the commandment of ***P*** ... Gen 45:21
P had sent to carry him ... Gen 46:5
I will go up, and show ***P*** ... Gen 46:31
to pass, when ***P*** shall call ... Gen 46:33
Joseph came and told ***P*** ... Gen 47:1
presented them unto ***P*** ... Gen 47:2
P said unto his brethren ... Gen 47:3
they said unto ***P***, Thy ... Gen 47:3
They said moreover unto ***P*** ... Gen 47:4
P spake unto Joseph ... Gen 47:5
before ***P***: and Jacob blessed ***P*** ... Gen 47:7
P said unto Jacob, How ... Gen 47:8
Jacob said unto ***P***, The ... Gen 47:9
And Jacob blessed ***P***, and ... Gen 47:10
went out from before ***P*** ... Gen 47:10
as ***P*** had commanded ... Gen 47:11
the money into ***P*** house ... Gen 47:14
will be servants unto ***P*** ... Gen 47:19
the land of Egypt for ***P*** ... Gen 47:20
so the land became ***P*** ... Gen 47:20
portion assigned them of ***P*** ... Gen 47:22
portion which ***P*** gave ... Gen 47:22
you this day..for ***P*** ... Gen 47:23

P

give the fifth part unto *P* ......Gen 47:24
and we will be *P* servants .....Gen 47:25
that *P* should have..part ......Gen 47:26
which became not *P* ....Gen 47:26
unto the house of *P* ....Gen 50:4
in the ears of *P* ....Gen 50:4
P said, Go up, and bury ......Gen 50:6
up all the servants of *P* ....Gen 50:7
built for *P* treasure cities ......Ex 1:11
the midwives said unto *P*......Ex 1:19
P charged all his people.......Ex 1:22
daughter of *P* came down .....Ex 2:5
his sister to *P* daughter ....Ex 2:7
And *P* daughter said to ....Ex 2:8
P daughter said unto her ......Ex 2:9
him unto *P* daughter...........Ex 2:10
Now when *P* heard this ....Ex 2:15
Moses fled from the face of *P* .Ex 2:15
I will send thee unto *P*........Ex 3:10
that I should go unto *P* ....Ex 3:11
do all those wonders before *P* .Ex 4:21
thou shalt say unto *P* ....Ex 4:22
Aaron went in, and told *P* ....Ex 5:1
P said, Who is the Lord ......Ex 5:2
P said, Behold, the ....Ex 5:5
And *P* commanded ....Ex 5:6
Thus saith *P*, I will not ....Ex 5:10
P taskmasters had set ....Ex 5:14
came and cried unto *P* ....Ex 5:15
they came forth from *P* ....Ex 5:20
abhorred in the eyes of *P* .....Ex 5:21
I came to *P* to speak in ....Ex 5:23
see what I will do to *P*........Ex 6:1
Go in, spake unto *P* king .....Ex 6:11
how then shall *P* hear me .....Ex 6:12
Israel, and unto *P* king ....Ex 6:13
which speak to *P* king of......Ex 6:27
speak thou unto *P* king ....Ex 6:29
and how shall *P* hearken ......Ex 6:30
made thee a god to *P*.........Ex 7:1
brother shall speak unto *P* ....Ex 7:2
And I will harden *P* heart .....Ex 7:3
But *P* shall not hearken ....Ex 7:4
when they spake unto *P* ....Ex 7:7
When *P* shall speak...........Ex 7:9
rod, and cast it before *P* ......Ex 7:9
went in unto *P* ....Ex 7:10
cast down his rod before *P* ....Ex 7:10
Then *P* also called the ....Ex 7:11
And he hardened *P* heart .....Ex 7:13
P heart is hardened, he ....Ex 7:14
Get thee unto *P* in the........Ex 7:15
river, in the sight of *P* ....Ex 7:20
P heart was hardened.........Ex 7:22
P turned and went into ....Ex 7:23
Go unto *P*, and say unto ......Ex 8:1
P called for Moses............Ex 8:8
Moses said unto *P*, Glory .....Ex 8:9
Aaron went out from *P* ....Ex 8:12
had brought against *P*.........Ex 8:12
when *P* saw that there ....Ex 8:15
magicians said unto *P* ....Ex 8:19
P heart was hardened ....Ex 8:19
and stand before *P* ....Ex 8:20
flies into the house of *P*.......Ex 8:24
P called for Moses............Ex 8:25
P said, I will let you go ....Ex 8:28
flies may depart from *P* ....Ex 8:29
let not *P* deal deceitfully ......Ex 8:29
Moses went out from *P* ....Ex 8:30
swarms of flies from *P* ....Ex 8:31
P hardened his heart..........Ex 8:32
Go in unto *P*, and tell him ....Ex 9:1
P sent, and, behold, there .....Ex 9:7
heart of *P* was hardened ....Ex 9:7
heaven in the sight of *P*.......Ex 9:8
and stood before *P* ....Ex 9:10
hardened the heart of *P*........Ex 9:12
stand before *P*, and say ....Ex 9:13
among the servants of *P* ......Ex 9:20
P sent and called for Moses ...Ex 9:27
out of the city from *P* ....Ex 9:33
when *P* saw that the rain......Ex 9:34
heart of *P* was hardened ......Ex 9:35
Moses, Go in unto *P* ....Ex 10:1
and Aaron came in unto *P* ....Ex 10:3
and went out from *P* ....Ex 10:6
P servants said..How long .....Ex 10:7
were brought again unto *P* ....Ex 10:8
out from *P* presence ....Ex 10:11
P called for Moses............Ex 10:16
he went out from *P*, and ......Ex 10:18
Lord hardened *P* heart.........Ex 10:20
P called unto Moses ....Ex 10:24
P said unto him, Get thee .....Ex 10:28
one plague more upon *P* ......Ex 11:1
in the sight of *P* servants ......Ex 11:3
first-born of *P* that sitteth .....Ex 11:5
out from *P* in a great anger ...Ex 11:8
P shall not hearken ....Ex 11:9
these wonders before *P* ....Ex 11:10
Lord hardened *P* ....Ex 11:10
the first-born of *P* that sat ....Ex 12:29
P rose up in the night ....Ex 12:30
P would hardly let us go ......Ex 13:15
when *P* had let the people ....Ex 13:17
P will say of the children......Ex 14:3
will harden *P* heart, that ......Ex 14:4
I will be honored upon *P* ......Ex 14:4
heart of *P* and of his servants .Ex 14:5
hardened the heart of *P*.......Ex 14:8
horses and chariots of *P* ......Ex 14:9
when *P* drew nigh, the ....Ex 14:10
get me honor upon *P* ....Ex 14:17
me honor upon *P*.............Ex 14:18
sea, even all *P* horses, his .....Ex 14:23
all the host of *P* that came ....Ex 14:28
P chariots and his host hath he.Ex 15:4
the horse of *P* went in ....Ex 15:19
from the sword of *P* ....Ex 18:4
Lord had done unto *P* ....Ex 18:8
and out of the hand of *P*......Ex 18:10
We were *P* bondmen in.......Deut 6:21
sore, upon Egypt, upon *P* .....Deut 6:22
from the hand of *P* king of....Deut 7:8
Lord thy God did unto *P* .....Deut 7:18
midst of Egypt unto *P* ....Deut 11:3
the land of Egypt unto *P*......Deut 29:2
the land of Egypt to *P* ....Deut 34:11
in Egypt in *P* house 1Sam 2:27
P hardened their hearts? 1Sam 6:6
made affinity with *P* king 1Kin 3:1
took *P* daughter, and brought .1Kin 3:1
a house for *P* daughter........1Kin 7:8
P king of Egypt had gone 1Kin 9:16
P daughter came up out 1Kin 9:4
with the daughter of *P* 1Kin 11:1
Hadad said to *P*, Let me......1Kin 11:21
Then *P* said unto him.........1Kin 11:22
under the hand of *P* king 2Kin 17:7
so is *P* king of Egypt unto 2Kin 18:21
silver and the gold to *P* 2Kin 23:35
to the commandment of *P*......2Kin 23:35
Bithiah the daughter of *P* 1Chr 4:18
the daughter of *P* out of 2Chr 8:11
signs and wonders upon *P*.....Neh 9:10
of thee, O Egypt, upon *P* .....Ps 135:9
P and his host in the Red Sea..Ps 136:15
of horses in *P* chariots ....Song 1:9
wise counselors of *P* is ....Is 19:11
how say ye unto *P*, I am ......Is 19:11
in the strength of *P*...........Is 30:2
the strength of *P* be your .....Is 30:3
so is *P* king of Egypt to.......Is 36:6
P king of Egypt, and his ......Jer 25:19
at the entry of *P* house ....Jer 43:9
P king of Egypt is but ....Jer 46:17
multitude of No, and *P* ....Jer 46:25
even *P*, and all them that .....Jer 46:25
before that *P* smote Gaza .....Jer 47:1
shall *P* with his mighty army ..Ezek 17:17
thy face against *P* king........Ezek 29:2
I am against thee, *P* king .....Ezek 29:3
I have broken the arm of *P* ...Ezek 30:21
against *P* king of Egypt ....Ezek 30:22
but I will break *P* arms ....Ezek 30:24
arms of *P* shall fall ....Ezek 30:25
speak unto *P* king of ....Ezek 31:2
This is *P* and all his ....Ezek 31:18
lamentation for *P* king........Ezek 32:2
P shall see them, and ....Ezek 32:31
even *P* and all his army ....Ezek 32:31
P and all his multitude ....Ezek 32:32
sight of *P* king of Egypt.......Acts 7:10
was made known unto *P* ......Acts 7:13
P daughter took him up.......Acts 7:21
scripture saith unto *P* ....Rom 9:17
the son of *P* daughter.........Heb 11:24

PHAROAH-HOPHRA (fâr'ō hōf'rȧ)—*ruler of Egypt (589-570 B.C.)*

I will give *P* king ....Jer 44:30

PHARAOH-NECHO, PHARAOH-NECHOH (fâr'ō nĕ'kō)—*Pharaoh of Egypt (609-594 B.C.)*

P put him in bands at.........2Kin 23:33
P made Eliakim the son 2Kin 23:34
to give it unto *P*..............2Kin 23:35

See Necho; Pharaoh

PHARES, PHAREZ (fā'rēz)—*Greek form of Perez*

his name was called *P* ....Gen 38:29
and Shelah, and *P*, and ....Gen 46:12
sons of *P* were Hezron........Gen 46:12
of *P*, the family of the ....Num 26:20
like the house of *P* ....Ruth 4:12
daughter-in-law bare him *P*....1Chr 2:4
P, Hezron, and Carmi 1Chr 4:1

PHAREZITES (fā'rĕz-īts)

Descendants of Perez ....Num 26:20

PHARISEES (făr'ĭ-sēz)—*"separated ones"—a Jewish sect that upheld the oldest traditions of Israel at the time of Jesus*

Characteristics of:

Jewish sect..............Acts 15:5
Upholders of traditions ..Mark 7:3, 5-8; Gal 1:14
Sticklers for Mosaic Law .Acts 26:5; Phil 3:5
Very careful in outward details ....Matt 23:23; Luke 18:11
Rigid in fasting..........Luke 5:33; Luke 18:12
Zealous for Judaism .....Matt 23:15
Lovers of display ....Matt 23:5-7
Covetous ....Luke 16:14
Cruel persecutors ....Acts 9:1, 2; Phil 3:5, 6

Chief errors of, their:

Outward righteousness ...Luke 7:36-50
Blindness to spiritual things ....John 3:1-10
Emphasis on the ceremonial Law ....Matt 15:1-9
Perversion of Scripture ...Matt 15:1, 9
Self-justification before men..................Luke 16:14, 15
Hindering potential believers.............John 9:16, 22
Refusal to accept Christ. .Matt 12:24-34

Christ's description of:

Vipers ....Matt 12:24, 34
Blind ....Matt 15:12-14
Hypocrites ....Matt 23:13-19
Serpents ....Matt 23:33
Children of the devil.....John 8:13, 44

Attitude of, toward Christ, sought to:

Destroy Him ....Matt 12:14
Tempt Him ....Matt 16:1; Matt 19:3
Entangle Him ....Matt 22:15
Accuse Him ....Luke 11:53, 54

[*also* pharisee, pharisee's, pharisees']

saw many of the *P* and ....Matt 3:7
of the scribes and *P* ....Matt 5:20
when the *P* saw it, they ....Matt 9:11
Why do we and the *P* fast ....Matt 9:14
the *P* said, He casteth out.....Matt 9:34
But when the *P* saw it ....Matt 12:2
the scribes and of the *P*.......Matt 12:38
the leaven of the *P* ....Matt 16:6
of the doctrine of the *P*.......Matt 16:12

P had heard his parables ......Matt 21:45
the *P* had heard that he ....Matt 22:34
the *P* were gathered ....Matt 22:41
scribes and the *P* sit in........Matt 23:2
Thou blind *P*, cleanse.........Matt 23:26
chief priests and *P* came ......Matt 27:62
the scribes and *P* saw him.....Mark 2:16
and of the *P* used to fast......Mark 2:18
of John and of the *P* fast .....Mark 2:18
P said unto him, Behold ......Mark 2:24
the *P* went forth, and ....Mark 3:6
together unto him the *P* ......Mark 7:1
the *P*, and all the Jews........Mark 7:3
P came forth, and began to ...Mark 8:11
beware of the leaven of the *P* .Mark 8:15
the *P* came to him, and.......Mark 10:2
him certain of the *P* ....Mark 12:13
were *P* and doctors of ....Luke 5:17
scribes and the *P* began ....Luke 5:21
scribes and *P* murmured ......Luke 5:30
the disciples of the *P* ....Luke 5:33
certain of the *P* said unto .....Luke 6:2
scribes and *P* watched ....Luke 6:7
P and lawyers rejected ....Luke 7:30
one of the *P* desired him......Luke 7:36
P besought him to dine ....Luke 11:37
do ye *P* make clean the ....Luke 11:39
woe unto you, *P*! for ye.......Luke 11:42
Woe unto you, *P*! for ye love .Luke 11:43
Woe unto you, scribes and *P* ..Luke 11:44
P began to urge him ....Luke 11:53
ye of the leaven of the *P*......Luke 12:1
came certain of the *P*..........Luke 13:31
house of one of the chief *P* ...Luke 14:1
the lawyers and *P* ....Luke 14:3
P and scribes murmured ......Luke 15:2
was demanded of the *P* ....Luke 17:20
the *P* from among the ....Luke 19:39
were sent were of the *P*.......John 1:24
Lord knew how the *P* had ....John 4:1
P heard that the people ....John 7:32
P and..chief priests sent.......John 7:32
the chief priests and *P* ....John 7:45
answered them the *P*, Are ....John 7:47
rulers or of the *P* believed ....John 7:48
P brought unto him a woman..John 8:3
brought to the *P* him ....John 9:13
the *P* also asked him how .....John 9:15
some of the *P* which were .....John 9:40
a *P*, named Gamaliel ....Acts 5:34
Sadducees, and the other *P* ...Acts 23:6
brethren, I am a *P* ....Acts 23:6
son of a *P*: of the hope ....Acts 23:6
dissension between the *P*......Acts 23:7
spirit: but the *P* confess.......Acts 23:8
scribes that were of the *P* .....Acts 23:9
our religion I lived a *P*........Acts 26:5

PHAROSH—*See* Parosh

PHARPAR (fär'pär)—*"that produces fruit"*
One of the two rivers of
Damascus.............2Kin 5:12

PHARZITES (fär'zīts)
Descendants of Pharez ...Num 26:20
See Phares, Pharez

PHASEAH—*See* Paseah

PHEBE—*See* Phoebe

PHENICE, PHENICIA—See Phoenicia

PHICHOL (fī'kŏl)—*"dark water"*
Captain of King
Abimelech's army .....Gen 21:22, 32

PHILADELPHIA (fĭl-ä-dĕl'fĭ-ä)—*"brotherly love"*
City of Lydia in Asia
Minor; church
established here ....Rev 1:11
angel of the church in *P* ....Rev 3:7

PHILANTHROPY—*active effort to promote human welfare*
Manifested by:
Ethiopian ....Jer 38:6-13
Samaritan...............Luke 10:30, 33
Roman centurion ....Luke 7:2-5
Pagans ....Acts 28:2, 7, 10
Christians...............Acts 4:34-37
Precepts concerning:
"Do good unto all"......Gal 6:10
"Love your enemies" ....Matt 5:43-48
"Follow that which is
good" 1Thess 5:15

PHILEMON (fī-lē'mŏn)—*"friendship"*
Christian at Colossae to
whom Paul writes .....Philem 1
Paul appeals to him to
receive Onesimus......Philem 9-21

PHILEMON, THE EPISTLE TO—*a book of the New Testament*
Thanksgiving ....Philem 4-7
Plea for Onesimus.......Philem 10-21
Hope through prayer ....Philem 22

PHILETUS (fī-lē'tus)—*"amiable"*
False teacher...........2Tim 2:17, 18

PHILIP (fĭl'ĭp)—*"lover of horses"*
1. Son of Herod the Great .Matt 14:3
2. One of the twelve
apostles ....Matt 10:3
Brought Nathanael to
Christ...............John 1:43-48
Tested by Christ ....John 6:5-7
Introduced Greeks to
Christ...............John 12:20-22
Gently rebuked by Christ.John 14:8-12
In the upper room ......Acts 1:13
3. One of the seven
deacons ....Acts 6:5
Called an evangelist.....Acts 21:8
Father of four
prophetesses..........Acts 21:8, 9
Preached in Samaria ....Acts 8:5-13
Led the Ethiopian
eunuch to Christ......Acts 8:26-40
Visited by Paul ....Acts 21:8

[*also* PHILIP'S]
and *P*, and Bartholomew......Mark 3:18
Herodias' sake, his brother *P* ..Mark 6:17
his brother *P* tetrarch ....Luke 3:1
Herodias his brother *P* wife ...Luke 3:19
P and Bartholomew ....Luke 6:14

PHILIPPI (fī-lĭp'ī)—*"the same"*
City of Macedonia
(named after Philip of
Macedon) visited by
Paul............... Acts 16:12; Acts 20:6
Paul wrote letter to
church of ....Phil 1:1

[*also* PHILIPPIANS]
the coasts of Caesarea *P* ......Matt 16:13
the towns of Caesarea *P* ......Mark 8:27
Now ye *P* know also, that.....Phil 4:15
as ye know, at *P*, we were 1Thess 2:2

PHILIPPIANS, THE EPISTLE TO THE—*a letter of the apostle Paul*
Thanksgiving ....Phil 1:3-10
Christ is preached ....Phil 1:12-18
To live is Christ ....Phil 1:21
The humility of Christ ...Phil 2:5-11
Lights in the world ......Phil 2:12-16
Perseverance ....Phil 3
Rejoicing in the Lord ....Phil 4:1-13

PHILISTIA (fī-lĭs'tĭ-ä)—*"land of sojourners"—area on southwest coast of Palestine*
"The land of the
Philistines" ....Gen 21:32, 34
"The borders of the
Philistines" ....Josh 13:2
Philistia.................Ps 60:8
behold *P*, and Tyre, with .....Ps 87:4
over *P* will I triumph ....Ps 108:9

PHILISTIM (fī-lĭs'tĭm)—*plural of Philistine*
Race of Canaanites
inhabiting Philistia .....Gen 10:14

PHILISTINES (fī-lĭs'tēns)—*the people of Philistia*
History of:
Descendants of Mizraim. .Gen 10:13, 14
Originally on the island
of Caphtor ....Jer 47:4
Israel commanded to
avoid ....Ex 13:17
Not attacked by Joshua ..Josh 13:1-3
Left to prove Israel......Judg 3:1-4
Israel sold into ....Judg 10:6, 7
Delivered from, by
Samson ....Judg 13—16
Defeat Israel 1Sam 4:1-11
Take ark to house of
Dagon ....1Sam 4—5
Defeated at Mizpeh 1Sam 7:7-14
Champion, Goliath, killed 1Sam 17:1-52
David seeks asylum
among 1Sam 27:1-7
Gather at Aphek; Saul
and sons slain by 1Sam 29:1
Often defeated by David .2Sam 5:17-25
Beseiged by Nadab 1Kin 15:27
War against Jehoram 2Chr 21:16, 17
Defeated by Uzziah 2Chr 26:6, 7
Defeated by Hezekiah ...2Kin 18:8
Prophecies concerning:
Union against Israel .....Is 9:11, 12
Punishment pronounced ..Jer 25:15, 20
Hatred against Israel
revenged ....Ezek 25:15-17
Destruction by Pharaoh ..Jer 47:1-7
Ultimate decay ....Zeph 2:4-6

[*also* PHILISTINE, PHILISTINES']
Abimelech king of the *P* ......Gen 26:1
Abimelech king of the *P* ......Gen 26:8
and the *P* envied him ....Gen 26:14
P had stopped them, and .....Gen 26:15
the *P* had stopped them.......Gen 26:18
unto the sea of the *P* ....Ex 23:31
slew of the *P* six hundred .....Judg 3:31
Ammon, and from the *P*? .....Judg 10:11
the country of the *P* 1Sam 6:1
P called for the priests 1Sam 6:2
of the lords of the *P*...........1Sam 6:4
the lords of the *P* went 1Sam 6:12
five lords of the *P* had 1Sam 6:16
which the *P* returned 1Sam 6:17
number..cities of the *P*........1Sam 6:18
P have brought again the ark ..1Sam 6:21
out of the hand of the *P* 1Sam 7:3
out of the hand of the *P* 1Sam 9:16
the garrison of the *P*..........1Sam 10:5
into the hand of the *P* 1Sam 12:9
smote the garrison of the *P* ...1Sam 13:3
and the *P* heard of it 1Sam 13:3
a garrison of the *P* 1Sam 13:4
abomination with the *P* 1Sam 13:4
the *P* gathered themselves.....1Sam 13:5
P will come down now 1Sam 13:12
but the *P* encamped in 1Sam 13:16
the *P* in three companies......1Sam 13:17
P said, Lest the Hebrews 1Sam 13:19
went down to the *P* 1Sam 13:20
the garrison of the *P*..........1Sam 13:23
go over to the *P* garrison 1Sam 14:1
over unto the *P* garrison 1Sam 14:4
unto the garrison of the *P*.....1Sam 14:11
the *P* said, Behold, the 1Sam 14:11
P went on and increased 1Sam 14:19
Hebrews that were with the *P* .1Sam 14:21
heard that the *P* fled 1Sam 14:22
slaughter among the *P*? 1Sam 14:30
smote the *P* that day 1Sam 14:31
us go down after the *P*........1Sam 14:36
Shall I go down after the *P*? ..1Sam 14:37
from following the *P*..........1Sam 14:46
the *P* went to their 1Sam 14:46
kings..against the *P*...........1Sam 14:47

P

war against the *P* all the 1Sam 14:52
from chasing after the *P* 1Sam 17:53
took the head of the *P*........1Sam 17:54
go forth against the *P*........1Sam 17:55
the slaughter of the *P*........1Sam 17:57
with the head of the *P*........1Sam 17:57
the slaughter of the *P*........1Sam 18:6
let the hand of the *P* be 1Sam 18:17
hand of the *P* may be.........1Sam 18:21
hundred foreskins of the *P* 1Sam 18:25
fall by the hand of the *P*......1Sam 18:25
slew of the *P* two hundred 1Sam 18:27
the princes of the *P* went 1Sam 18:30
his hand, and slew the *P*......1Sam 19:5
fought with the *P*, and........1Sam 19:8
sword of Goliath the *P*........1Sam 21:9
him the sword of Goliath 1Sam 22:10
Behold, the *P* fight 1Sam 23:1
go and smite these *P*? 1Sam 23:2
Go, and smite the *P*, and 1Sam 23:2
the armies of the *P*? 1Sam 23:3
will deliver the *P* into.........1Sam 23:4
and fought with the *P*.........1Sam 23:5
for the *P* have invaded........1Sam 23:27
and went against the *P*........1Sam 23:28
from following the *P*..........1Sam 24:1
in the country of the *P*........1Sam 27:11
P gathered their armies 1Sam 28:1
P gathered themselves 1Sam 28:4
Saul saw the host of the *P* 1Sam 28:5
for the *P* make war against....1Sam 28:15
into the hand of the *P*........1Sam 28:19
into the hand of the *P*........1Sam 28:19
the lords of the *P* passed......1Sam 29:2
said the princes of the *P*......1Sam 29:3
unto the princes of the *P*......1Sam 29:3
of the *P* were wroth with 1Sam 29:4
the princes of the *P* said 1Sam 29:4
displease not..the *P*...........1Sam 29:7
princes of the *P* have 1Sam 29:9
into the land of the *P*.........1Sam 29:11
And the *P* went up to 1Sam 29:11
out of the land of the *P*.......1Sam 30:16
Now the *P* fought against 1Sam 31:1
Israel fled from..the *P* 1Sam 31:1
the *P* followed hard upon 1Sam 31:2
P slew Jonathan, and 1Sam 31:2
and the *P* came and dwelt......1Sam 31:7
when the *P* came to strip 1Sam 31:8
land of the *P* round 1Sam 31:9
that which the *P* had done 1Sam 31:11
the daughters of the *P*........2Sam 1:20
foreskins of the *P*............2Sam 3:14
out of the hand of the *P*......2Sam 3:18
smote the *P*, and subuded.....2Sam 8:1
out of the hand of the *P*......2Sam 8:1
Ammon, and of the *P*.........2Sam 8:12
out of the hand of the *P*......2Sam 19:9
the *P* had hanged them 2Sam 21:12
the *P* had slain Saul 2Sam 21:12
P had yet war again with......2Sam 21:15
fought against the *P* 2Sam 21:15
smote the *P*, and killed 2Sam 21:17
again a battle with the *P*......2Sam 21:18
battle in Gob with the *P*......2Sam 21:19
when they defied the *P* 2Sam 23:9
smote the *P* until his..........2Sam 23:10
P were gathered together 2Sam 23:11
people fled from the *P*........2Sam 23:11
defended it, and slew the *P* ...2Sam 23:12
P pitched in the valley........2Sam 23:13
P was then in Bethlehem.......2Sam 23:14
through the host of the *P*.....2Sam 23:16
unto the land of the *P*........1Kin 4:21
which belonged to the *P*......1Kin 15:27
which belonged to the *P*......1Kin 16:15
in the land of the *P*...........2Kin 8:2
out of the land of the *P*.......2Kin 8:3
(of whom came the *P*)........1Chr 1:12
the *P* fought against 1Chr 10:1
fled from before the *P*........1Chr 10:1
the *P* followed hard after 1Chr 10:2
P slew Jonathan, and 1Chr 10:2
the *P* came and dwelt.........1Chr 10:7
the *P* came to strip 1Chr 10:8
sent into the land of the *P* 1Chr 10:9
all that the *P* had done 1Chr 10:11
the *P* were gathered 1Chr 11:13
fled from before the *P*........1Chr 11:13
delivered it and slew the *P*....1Chr 11:14
host of the *P* encamped.......1Chr 11:15
P garrison was then at 1Chr 11:16
through the host of the *P*.....1Chr 11:18
with the *P* against Saul........1Chr 12:19
lords of the *P* upon...........1Chr 12:19
P heard that David was 1Chr 14:8
all the *P* went up to seek 1Chr 14:8
the *P* came and spread........1Chr 14:9
Shall I go up against the *P*? ...1Chr 14:10
the *P* yet again spread 1Chr 14:13
smite the host of the *P*........1Chr 14:15
smote the host of the *P*.......1Chr 14:16
David smote the *P*, and 1Chr 18:1
out of the hand of the *P*......1Chr 18:1
Ammon, and from the *P*......1Chr 18:11
war at Gezer with the *P* 1Chr 20:4
war again with the *P*..........1Chr 20:5
unto the land of the *P* 2Chr 9:26
P brought Jehoshaphat 2Chr 17:11
the spirit of the *P* 2Chr 21:16
The *P* also had invaded 2Chr 28:18
P with the inhabitants..........Ps 83:7
soothsayers like the *P*.........Is 2:6
shoulders of the *P* toward .....Is 11:14
the daughters of the *P* ....Ezek 16:27
the daughters of the *P* ....Ezek 16:57
remnant of the *P* shall ....Amos 1:8
down to Gath of the *P*........Amos 6:2
P from Caphtor, and ....Amos 9:7
they of the plain the *P*........Obad 19
cut off the pride of the *P* .....Zech 9:6

PHILOLOGUS (fĭ-lŏl′ō-gŭs)—*"a lover of learning"*
Christian at Rome ....Rom 16:15

PHILOSOPHER—*expounder of philosophy*
certain *p* of the Epicureans....Acts 17:18

PHILOSOPHY—*the study of fundamental truths*
any man spoil you through *p* . .Col 2:8

PHINEHAS (fĭn-ĕ′ăs)—*"mouth of brass"*
1. Eleazar's son; Aaron's grandson ....Ex 6:25
Slays an Israelite and a Midianite woman .....Num 25:1-18
Wonderfully rewarded ....Ps 106:30, 31
Fights against Midianites .Num 31:6-12
Settles dispute over memorial altar........Josh 22:11-32
Prays for Israel ....Judg 20:28
2. Younger son of Eli 1Sam 1:3
Worthless man..........1Sam 2:12-25
Slain by Philistines 1Sam 4:11, 17
Wife of, dies in childbirth............1Sam 4:19-22
3. Father of a postexilic priest ....Ezra 8:33

a hill that pertained to *P*......Josh 24:33
sons, on Hophni and *P* 1Sam 2:34
sons of Eli, Hophni and *P* 1Sam 4:4
brother, the son of *P* 1Sam 14:3
Eleazar begat *P*, *P* begat 1Chr 6:4
Aaron; Eleazar his son, *P*.....1Chr 6:50
P the son of Eleazar was......1Chr 9:20
of Abishua, the son of *P*......Ezra 7:5
the sons of *P*; Gershom ....Ezra 8:2

PHLEGON (flē′gŏn)—*"burning"*
Christian at Rome ....Rom 16:14

PHOEBE, PHEBE (fē′bĕ)—*"shining"*
Deaconess of the church at Cenchrea..........Rom 16:1, 2

PHOENECIA (fē-nĭsh′ĭ-ă)—*"purple"*
Mediterranean coastal region including the cities of Ptolemais, Tyre, Zarephath and Sidon; evangelized by early Christians ....Acts 11:19
Jesus preaches here......Matt 15:21

passed through *P* and Samaria .Acts 15:3

PHOENIX (fē′nĭks)—*a harbor in southern Crete*
Paul was to winter there .Acts 27:12
See PHOENICIA

PHRYGIA (frĭj′ĭ-ă)—*"barren"—region of central Asia Minor*
Jews from, at Pentecost . .Acts 2:1, 10
Visited twice by Paul ....Acts 16:6

country of Galatia and *P*......Acts 18:23

PHURAH (fū′rä)—*"beauty"*
Gideon's servant ....Judg 7:10, 11

PHUT, PUT (fŭt, pŭt)—*"bow"*
1. Third son of Ham.......Gen 10:6
2. Warriors (from Africa) allied with Egypt .....Ezek 27:10
Same as Libyans in .....Jer 46:9

PHUVAH, PUA, PUAH (fū′vä, pū′ä)—*"utterance"*
1. Issachar's second son ....Gen 46:13
Descendants of Punites . .Num 26:23
2. Father of Tola, Israel's judge ....Judg 10:1

PHYGELLUS (fĭ′jĕ-lŭs)—*"fugitive"*
Becomes an apostate 2Tim 1:15

PHYLACTERY—*"a charm"*
Scripture verses placed on the forehead; based upon a literal interpretation of.......Ex 13:9-16
Condemned by Christ....Matt 23:5

PHYSICIAN—*trained healer*
God the only true ....Deut 32:39
Practiced embalming......Gen 50:2, 26
Job's friends of no value .Job 13:4
Consulted by Asa 2Chr 16:12
For the sick only ....Matt 9:12
Proverb concerning, quoted ....Luke 4:23
Payment for services of . .Mark 5:26
Luke, "the beloved".....Col 4:14

[*also* PHYSICIANS]
is there no *p* there?..........Jer 8:22
have no need of the *p* ....Mark 2:17
are whole need not a *p* ....Luke 5:31
spent all her living upon *p* ....Luke 8:43

PI-BESETH (pī-bē′sĕth)—*"house of Bast"*
City of Lower Egypt 40 miles north of Memphis. Ezek 30:17

PICK—*to remove piece by piece*
ravens of the valley shall *p* ....Prov 30:17

PICTURES—*drawn or carved representations of scenes*
Descriptive of idolatrous images................Num 33:52
Like a word ....Prov 25:11
"Pleasant pictures" ......Is 2:16

PIECE—*part of a larger whole*
Land ....Gen 33:19
Silver..................1Sam 2:36
Fig cake 1Sam 30:12
Money ....Job 42:11
Fish ....Luke 24:42

[*also* PIECES]
laid each *p* one against........Gen 15:10
passed between those *p* ....Gen 15:17
a thousnd *p* of silver ....Gen 20:16
for twenty *p* of silver ....Gen 37:28
Surely he is torn in *p* ....Gen 44:28
three hundred *p* of silver ......Gen 45:22
Lord, hath dashed in *p*........Ex 15:6
If it be torn in *p*, then ....Ex 22:13
shalt cut the ram in *p*..........Ex 29:17
put them unto his *p*, and......Ex 29:17
beaten out of one *p* made......Ex 37:7
and cut it into his *p* ....Lev 1:6
Thou shalt part it in *p* ....Lev 2:6

the baked *p* of the meat ......Lev 6:21
he cut the ram into *p* ....Lev 8:20
the head, and the *p*, and ......Lev 8:20
with the *p* thereof, and ....Lev 9;13
of a whole *p* shalt thou ....Num 10:2
Shechem for a hundred *p* .....Josh 24:32
threescore and ten *p* ....Judg 9:4
woman cast a *p* of a ....Judg 9:53
eleven hundred *p* of ....Judg 16:5
her bones, into twelve *p* .....Judg 19:29
concubine, and cut her in *p* ...Judg 20:6
shall be broken to *p* 1Sam 2:10
and hewed them in *p* 1Sam 11:7
Samuel hewed Agag in *p* 1Sam 15:33
of bread, and a good *p* of 2Sam 6:19
cast a *p* of a millstone 2Sam 11:21
a *p* of ground full of 2Sam 23:11
and rent it in twelve *p* 1Kin 11:30
and cut it in *p*, and lay 1Kin 18:23
brake in *p* the rocks 1Kin 19:11
and rent them in two *p* 2Kin 2:12
and mar every good *p* of 2Kin 3:19
on every good *p* of land.......2Kin 3:25
six thousand *p* of gold 2Kin 5:5
for fourscore *p* of silver 2Kin 6:25
images brake they in *p* 2Kin 11:18
brake in *p* the brazen 2Kin 18:4
he brake in *p* the images 2Kin 23:14
cut in *p* all the vessels 2Kin 24:13
Chaldees break in *p* 2Kin 25:13
and a good *p* of flesh 1Chr 16:3
and his images in *p* 2Chr 23:17
they all were broken in *p* 2Chr 25:12
cut in *p* the vessels of.........2Chr 28:24
brake the images in *p* 2Chr 31:1
images, he brake in *p* 2Chr 34:4
repaired the other *p*, and .....Neh 3:11
repaired the other *p* ....Neh 3:20
of Henadad another *p* ....Neh 3:24
son of Zalaph, another *p*......Neh 3:30
neck, and shaken me to *p* .....Job 16:12
and break me in *p* with ....Job 19:2
break in *p* mighty men ....Job 34:24
His bones are as strong *p* .....Job 40:18
as a *p* of the..millstone.........Job 41:24
dash them in *p* like a ....Ps 2:9
a lion, rending it in *p* ....Ps 7:2
God, lest I tear you in *p* ......Ps 50:22
let them be as cut in *p* ....Ps 58:7
submit himself with *p* of ......Ps 68:30
break in *p* the oppressor ......Ps 72:4
heads of leviathan in *p* ....Ps 74:14
broken Rahab in *p*, as ....Ps 89:10
They break in *p* thy ....Ps 94:5
brought to a *p* of bread ....Prov 6:26
for a *p* of bread that man .....Prov 28:21
like a *p* of a pomegranate .....Song 4:3
As a *p* of a pomegranate .....Song 6:7
was to bring a thousand *p* .....Song 8:11
ye beat my people to *p* ....Is 3:15
ye shall be broken in *p* ....Is 8:9
ye shall be broken in *p* ....Is 8:9
ye shall be broken in *p* ....Is 8:9
children..be dashed to *p* ......Is 13:16
vessel that is broken in *p*......Is 30:14
I will break in *p* the gates .....Is 45:2
goeth out..be torn in *p*.........Jer 5:6
breaketh the rock in *p*? ....Jer 23:29
give him daily a *p* of bread....Jer 37:21
Merodach is broken in *p* ......Jer 50:2
I break in *p* the nations ....Jer 51:20
break in *p* the horse and ......Jer 51:21
break in *p* the chariot and.....Jer 51:21
will I break in *p* man and .....Jer 51:22
will I break in *p* old and ......Jer 51:22
break in *p* the young man ......Jer 51:22
break in *p* with thee the ......Jer 51:23
will I break in *p* the ....Jer 51:23
I break in *p* captains and......Jer 51:23
and pulled me in *p* ....Lam 3:11
of itself, or is torn in *p* ....Ezek 4:14
barley and for *p* of bread .....Ezek 13:19
Gather the *p* thereof into .....Ezek 24:4
even every good *p* ....Ezek 24:4
ye shall be cut in *p*, and ......Dan 2:5
and the gold, broken to *p* .....Dan 2:35
as iron breaketh in *p* ....Dan 2:40
it break in *p* and bruise ....Dan 2:40
that it break in *p* the iron .....Dan 2:45
Abed-nego shall be cut in *p* . . .Dan 3:29
brake all their bones in *p* .....Dan 6:24
devoured and brake in *p* ......Dan 7:7
tread it..break it in *p* ....Dan 7:23
for fifteen *p* of silver..........Hos 3:2
Samaria shall be broken in *p* . .Hos 8:6
mother was dashed in *p* ....Hos 10:14
infants shall be dashed in *p*....Hos 13:16
the lion two legs, or a *p* ......Amos 3:12
one *p* was rained upon ....Amos 4:7
p whereupon it rained not.....Amos 4:7
images..be beaten to *p* ....Mic 1:7
bones and chop them in *p*.....Mic 3:3
thou shalt beat in *p* many .....Mic 4:13
treadeth..teareth in *p* ....Mic 5:8
He that dasheth in *p* is.........Nah 2:1
children..dashed in *p*..........Nah 3:10
price thirty *p* of silver.........Zech 11:12
tear their claws in *p* ....Zech 11:16
with it shall be cut in *p* ....Zech 12:3
putteth a *p* of new cloth ......Matt 9:16
thou shalt find a *p* of ....Matt 17:27
him for thirty *p* of silver ......Matt 26:15
brought again the thirty *p* .....Matt 27:3
priests took the silver *p* ....Matt 27:6
seweth a *p* of new cloth ....Mark 2:21
the new *p* that filled it ....Mark 2:21
the fetters broken in *p* ....Mark 5:4
putteth a *p* of a new ....Luke 5:36
I have bought a *p* of..........Luke 14:18
what woman having ten *p* .....Luke 15:8
if she lose one *p*, doth not ....Luke 15:8
found it fifty thousand *p* ......Acts 19:19
and some on broken *p* of .....Acts 27:44

PIERCE—*to push a pointed instrument through something*

Used literally of:
Nail in Sisera ....Judg 5:26
Messiah's predicted death.Ps 22:16
Christ's death ....John 19:34, 37

Used figuratively of:
God's destruction........Num 24:8
Egypt's weakness 2Kin 18:21
Harsh words ....Prov 12:18
Great conflict of soul ....Job 30:16, 17
God's Word ....Heb 4:12
Coveted riches 1Tim 6:10

[*also* PIERCED, PIERCETH, PIERCING]
nose *p* through snares.........Job 40:24
leviathan the *p* serpent ....Is 27:1
into his hand, and *p* it ....Is 36:6
me whom they have *p* ....Zech 12:10
shall *p* through thy own ....Luke 2:35
they also which *p* him.........Rev 1:7

PIETY—*holy living*

Aided by:
God's Word 2Tim 3:14-17
Godly parents 1Sam 1:11
Prayer ....James 5:16-18
Good works 1Tim 5:10
Hope of Christ's return . .Titus 2:11-14

Hindered by:
World ....James 4:4
Flesh ....Rom 8:1-13
Satan...................Luke 22:31
Envying and strife 1Cor 3:1-7

Value of:
Profitable now and later. .1Tim 4:8
Safeguard in temptation . .Gen 39:7-9
Rewarded in heaven .....Rev 14:13
See HOLINESS OF CHRISTIANS; SANCTIFICATION

them learn first to show *p* 1Tim 5:4

PIGEON—*bird used for sacrifices*
As a sin offering ....Lev 12:6
As a burnt offering ......Lev 1:14
Offered by Mary ....Luke 2:22, 24
See DOVE

[*also* PIGEONS]
turtledove, and a young *p* .....Gen 15:9
or two young *p*...............Lev 5:7
or two young *p*...............Lev 14:22
or two young *p*...............Lev 15:14
turtles, or two young *p*........Num 6:10
or two young *p*...............Luke 2:24

PI-HAHIROTH (pī-hä-hī′rŏth)—*"the mouth"*
Israelite camp before crossing the Red Sea { Ex 14:2, 9; Num 33:7, 8

PILATE (pī′lăt)—*"marine dart-carrier"*
Procurator of Judea (A.D. 26-36) ....Luke 3:1
Destroyed Galileans .....Luke 13:1
Jesus brought before.....Matt 27:2
Washed hands in mock innocency.............Matt 27:24
Notorious in history .....Acts 3:13
Acts 4:27

said *P* unto him, Hearest......Matt 27:13
P said unto them, Whom .....Matt 27:17
P saith unto them, What ......Matt 27:22
went to *P*, and begged the ....Matt 27:58
P commanded the body to be. .Matt 27:58
Pharisees came..unto *P* ....Matt 27:62
P said unto them, Ye ....Matt 27:65
and delivered him to *P*........Mark 15:1
P asked him, Art thou ....Mark 15:2
And *P* asked him again ....Mark 15:4
so that *P* marveled ....Mark 15:5
P answered them, saying ......Mark 15:9
P answered and said ....Mark 15:12
P said unto them, Why ....Mark 15:14
so *P*, willing to content ....Mark 15:15
went in boldly unto *P*..........Mark 15:43
P marveled if he were ....Mark 15:44
and led him unto *P* ....Luke 23:1
And *P* asked him, saying......Luke 23:3
said *P* to the chief priests .....Luke 23:4
When *P* heard of Galilee......Luke 23:6
sent him again to *P*...........Luke 23:11
P and Herod were made ......Luke 23:12
P, when he had called ....Luke 23:13
P therefore, willing to ....Luke 23:20
P gave sentence that it........Luke 23:24
went unto *P*, and begged......Luke 23:52
P then went out unto ....John 18:29
Then said *P* unto them.......John 18:31
P entered into the..hall ....John 18:33
P answered, Am I a Jew? .....John 18:35
P..said unto him, Art thou ....John 18:37
P saith..What is truth? ....John 18:38
Then *P*..took Jesus ....John 19:1
P therefore went forth ....John 19:4
P saith unto them, Behold ....John 19:5
P saith unto them, Take ......John 19:6
P therefore heard that ....John 19:8
Then saith *P* unto him ....John 19:10
P sought to release ....John 19:12
P therefore heard that ....John 19:13
P saith..Shall I crucify ....John 19:15
P wrote a title, and put ....John 19:19
priests of the Jews to *P* ....John 19:21
P answered, What I have .....John 19:22
besought *P* that their ....John 19:31
besought *P* that he ....John 19:38
of Jesus: and *P* gave ....John 19:38
they *P* that he should be ......Acts 13:28
before Pontius *P* 1Tim 6:13

PILDASH (pĭl′dăsh)—*"flame of fire"*
Son of Nahor and Milcah.Gen 22:20-22

PILE—*a heap*

p thereof is fire and much.....Is 30:33
make the *p* for fire great ......Ezek 24:9

PILEHA (pĭl′ĕ-hä)—*"worship"*
Signer of the covenant . . .Neh 10:24

PILGRIMAGE—*journey through a foreign land; the course of life on earth*
the years of my *p* are ....Gen 47:9
in the days of their *p* ....Gen 47:9

P

the land of their *p* ....Ex 6:4
in the house of my *p* ....Ps 119:54

PILGRIMS—*God's people as exiles or wanderers*

Elements involved in:
Forsaking all for Christ . . Luke 14:26, 27,33
Traveling by faith ....Heb 11:9
Faces set toward Zion . . . Jer 50:5
Encouraged by God's promises ....Heb 11:13
Sustained by God ....Is 35:1-10

Their journey in this world as:
Pilgrims and strangers....1Pet 2:11, 12
Lights ....Phil 2:15
Salt ....Matt 5:13
God's own 1Pet 2:9, 10
Chosen out of the world .John 17:6
1Pet 1:1, 2

See STRANGERS

PILLAGE—*to plunder*
Of the temple, by Nebuzaradan..........2Kin 25:8-17

PILLAR—*a column or support*

Descriptive of:
Memorial sites ....Gen 28:18, 22
Woman turned to salt....Gen 19:26
Altars of idolatry........Deut 12:3
Supports for a building. . Judg 16:25, 26,29
Covenant site ....Ex 24:4-8
Miracles ....Joel 2:30

Figurative of:
God's presence ....Ex 33:9, 10
Earth's supports ....Job 9:6
God's sovereignty over nations ....Is 19:19
Man's legs ....Song 5:15
Important persons ....Gal 2:9
Church 1Tim 3:15
True believers...........Rev 3:12
Angel's feet.............Rev 10:1

[*also* PILLARS]
thou anointedst the *p* ....Gen 31:13
a stone, and set it up for a *p* . . Gen 31:45
heap, and behold this *p* ....Gen 31:51
this *p* be witness, that I ....Gen 31:52
over this heap and this *p* ......Gen 31:52
And Jacob set up a *p* in ......Gen 35:14
talked with him, even a *p* .....Gen 35:14
And Jacob set a *p* upon.......Gen 35:20
the *p* of Rachel's grave ....Gen 35:20
four *p* of shittim wood ....Ex 26:32
five *p* of shittim wood ....Ex 26:37
twenty *p* thereof and..........Ex 27:10
the hooks of the *p*, and ....Ex 27:10
twenty *p* and their twenty .....Ex 27:11
hooks of the *p* and their ......Ex 27:11
their *p* three, and their........Ex 27:14
All the *p* round about the .....Ex 27:17
his *p*, and their sockets ....Ex 35:17
the five *p* of it with their......Ex 36:38
Their *p* were twenty, and .....Ex 38:10
the hooks of the *p* and........Ex 38:10
their *p* were twenty, and ......Ex 38:11
hooks of the *p* and their ......Ex 38:11
their *p* ten, and their ....Ex 38:12
hooks of the *p* and their ......Ex 38:12
their *p* three, and their........Ex 38:14
the sockets for the *p* were .....Ex 38:17
hooks of the *p* and their ......Ex 38:17
all the *p* of the court were ....Ex 38:17
he made hooks for the *p* ......Ex 38:28
his *p*, and his sockets ....Ex 39:40
and the *p* thereof, and the ....Num 3:36
and the *p* thereof............Num 4:31
p that was in Shechem ....Judg 9:6
city with a *p* of smoke ....Judg 20:40
the *p* of the earth are the 1Sam 2:8
reared up for himself a *p*......2Sam 18:18
he called the *p* after his 2Sam 18:18
upon four rows of cedar *p*.....1Kin 7:2
cedar beams upon the *p*.......1Kin 7:2
lay on forty-five *p*, fifteen 1Kin 7:3
And he made a porch of *p* 1Kin 7:6
the other *p* and the thick......1Kin 7:6
upon the tops of the *p* 1Kin 7:16
And he made the *p*, and 1Kin 7:18
chapiters upon the two *p* 1Kin 7:20
set up the right *p*, and 1Kin 7:21
he set up the left *p*, and 1Kin 7:21
top of the *p* was lily work 1Kin 7:22
the work of the *p* finished.....1Kin 7:22
The two *p*, and the two 1Kin 7:41
on the top of the two *p* 1Kin 7:41
upon the top of the *p* 1Kin 7:41
of the almug trees *p* 1Kin 10:12
the king stood by a *p* 2Kin 11:14
king stood by a *p*, and 2Kin 23:3
The two *p*, one sea, and 2Kin 25:16
one *p* was eighteen cubits 2Kin 25:17
p with wreathen work..........2Kin 25:17
brazen sea, and the *p* 1Chr 18:8
before the house two *p* 2Chr 3:15
reared up the *p* before 2Chr 3:17
two *p*, and the pommels 2Chr 4:12
on the top of the two *p* 2Chr 4:12
were on the top of the *p* 2Chr 4:12
the king stood at his *p* 2Chr 23:13
rings and *p* of marble ....Esth 1:6
The *p* of heaven tremble ......Job 26:11
I bear up the *p* of it ....Ps 75:3
wilderness like *p* of smoke ....Song 3:6
He made the *p*..of silver ......Song 3:10
city, and an iron *p*............Jer 1:18
concerning the *p*, and ....Jer 27:19
The two *p*, one sea, and ......Jer 52:20
p was eighteen cubits ....Jer 52:21
The second *p* also and the ....Jer 52:22
and there were *p* by the.......Ezek 40:49
p as the *p* of the courts ....Ezek 42:6
and fire, and *p* of smoke ......Joel 2:30

PILLARS OF CLOUD AND FIRE—*the vehicles by which the Lord directed the children of Israel during the Exodus*

As means of:
Guiding Israel.........{Ex 13:21, 22 / Num 14:14}
Protecting Israel.........Ex 14:19, 24
Regulating Israel's journeys ....Num 9:15-23
Manifesting His glory to Israel...............{Ex 24:16-18 / Num 12:5}
Manifesting His presence .Ex 34:5-8
Deut 31:15
Communicating with Israel.................Ex 33:9, 10

Effect of:
Cause of fear ....Ex 19:9, 16
Repeated in the Temple. .1Kin 8:10, 11
Long remembered ....Ps 99:7
Recalled with gratitude . . Neh 9:12, 19
Repeated in Christ's transfiguration..........Matt 17:5

Figurative of God's:
Wonders ....Joel 2:30
Departure from Jerusalem Ezek 9:3
Presence among believers.Matt 18:20

PILLED—*peeled*
p white strakes in them ....Gen 30:37
rods which he had *p* ....Gen 30:38

PILLOW—*a cushion*
Stone used as ....Gen 28:11, 18
Made of goat's hair......1Sam 19:13, 16
Used on a ship..........Mark 4:38

[*also* PILLOWS]
women that sew *p* in all.......Ezek 13:18
I am against your *p*..........Ezek 13:20

PILOT—*one who guides*
Of Tyre's ships..........Ezek 27:8-29
Shipmaster ....Jon 1:6
Used figuratively ....James 3:4

PILTAI (pĭl'tī)—*"Jehovah causes to escape"*
Priest of Joiakim's time . . Neh 12:12, 17

PIN—*a wooden or metal peg*
Used in a weaver's loom .Judg 16:13, 14
See NAIL

[*also* PINS]
thereof, and all the *p* ....Ex 27:19
p of the court shall be ....Ex 27:19
The *p* of the tabernacle ....Ex 35:18
the *p* of the court, and........Ex 35:18
all the *p* of the tabernacle .....Ex 38:20
all the *p* of the tabernacle .....Ex 38:31
all the *p* of the court ....Ex 38:31
his cords, and his *p*, and ......Ex 39:40
their *p*, and their cords ....Num 3:37
their *p*, and their cords ....Num 4:32
wimples, and the crisping *p*....Is 3:22

PINE—*to waste away*
From disobedience ......Lev 26:14, 16
Egypt ....Is 19:8
Judah ....Is 33:9
Jer 15:9
Jerusalem...............Lam 4:9

[*also* PINETH, PINING]
left of you shall *p* away ....Lev 26:39
they *p* away with them ....Lev 26:39
cut me off with *p* sickness .....Is 38:12
shall *p* away for your ....Ezek 24:23
and we *p* away in them ....Ezek 33:10
with his teeth, and *p* away ....Mark 9:18

PINE TREES—*evergreen trees*
Used in Solomon's Temple 2Chr 3:5
Product of Lebanon .....Is 60:13
Used figuratively ....Is 41:19

PINNACLE—*a summit; highest ledge*
Of the Temple ....Matt 4:5

PINON (pī'nŏn)—*"darkness"*
Edomite chief ....Gen 36:41
1Chr 1:52

PIPE—*to play the flute; the flute*

Descriptive of:
Musical instrument 1Sam 10:5
Player of a flute ....Rev 18:22
Hollow tube ....Zech 4:2, 12

Figurative of:
Joyful deliverance ....Is 30:29
Mournful lamentation ....Jer 48:36
Inconsistent reactions ....Matt 11:17
Spiritual discernment 1Cor 14:7

[*also* PIPED, PIPES]
the people *p* with *p* 1Kin 1:40
tabret, and *p*, and wine ....Is 5:12
thy tabrets and of thy *p* ....Ezek 28:13
We have *p* unto you, and .....Luke 7:32

PIRAM (pī'răm)—*"indomitable; wild"*
Amorite king of Jarmuth .Josh 10:3

PIRATHON (pĭr'ä-thŏn)—*"princely"*
Town in Ephraim........Judg 12:15

PIRATHONITE (pĭr-ä'thŏn-īt)—*inhabitant of Pirathon*

Descriptive of:
Abdon ....Judg 12:13-15
Benaiah 2Sam 23:30

Benjamin, Benaiah the *P* 1Chr 11:31
was Benaiah the *P*............1Chr 27:14

PISGAH (pĭz'gä)—*a mountain peak in the Abarim range in Moab*
Balaam offers sacrifice upon ....Num 23:14
Moses views promised land from ....Deut 3:27
Site of Moses' death .....Deut 34:1-7
Summit of, called Nebo . . Deut 32:49-52
See NEBO

top of *P*, which looketh ....Num 21:20
under the springs of *P* ....Deut 4:49

PISIDIA (pī-sĭd'ĭ-ä)—*"pitch"—a mountainous district in Asia Minor*

Twice visited by Paul ....Acts 13:13, 14
Acts 14:24

PISON (pī'sŏn)—*"changing"*
One of Eden's four rivers.Gen 2:10, 11

PISPAH (pĭs'pä)—*"expansion"*
Asherite 1Chr 7:38

PISS—*urine; to urinate*

[*also* PISSETH]
that *p* against the wall 1Sam 25:22
that *p* against the wall 1Kin 14:10
one that *p* against a wall 1Kin 16:11
Ahab him that *p* against 1Kin 21:21
Ahab him that *p* against 2Kin 9:8
and drink their own *p*.........2Kin 18:27
and drink their own *p*.........Is 36:12

PIT—*a hole*

Figurative of:
Grave ....Ps 30:9
Snare...................Ps 35:7
Harlot ....Prov 23:27
Mouth of strange woman .Prov 22:14
Destruction ....Ps 55:23
Self-destruction..........Prov 28:10
Hell.....................Ps 28:1
Devil's abode ....Rev 9:1, 2, 11
See ABYSS

[*also* PITS]
cast him into some *p*..........Gen 37:20
cast him into this *p* that.......Gen 37:22
and cast him into a *p* ....Gen 37:24
p was empty, there was ....Gen 37:24
returned unto the *p*...........Gen 37:29
Joseph was not in the *p* ....Gen 37:29
if a man shall open a *p* ....Ex 21:33
if a man shall dig a *p* ....Ex 21:33
a fountain or *p* ....Lev 11:36
down quick into the *p* ....Num 16:30
in high places, and in *p* 1Sam 13:6
he is hid now in some *p*.......2Sam 17:9
lion in the midst of a *p* 2Sam 23:20
at the *p* of the shearing 2Kin 10:14
slew a lion in a *p* in a 1Chr 11:22
down to the bars of the *p* .....Job 17:16
back his soul from the *p* ......Job 33:18
going down to the *p* ....Job 33:24
back his soul from the *p* ......Job 33:30
He made a *p*, and digged .....Ps 7:15
that go down into the *p*.......Ps 28:1
when I go down to the *p*?......Ps 30:9
also out of a horrible *p* ....Ps 40:2
they have digged a *p*..........Ps 57:6
that go down into the *p*.......Ps 88:4
the *p* be digged for the ....Ps 94:13
The proud have digged *p*......Ps 119:85
into the fire; into deep *p*......Ps 140:10
that go down into the *p*.......Prov 1:12
Whoso diggeth a *p* shall.......Prov 26:27
person shall flee to the *p*......Prov 28:17
He that diggeth a *p* shall......Eccl 10:8
to the sides of the *p* ....Is 14:15
Fear, and the *p*, and the ......Is 24:17
fear shall fall into the *p* ......Is 24:18
out of the midst of the *p* ......Is 24:18
water withal out of the *p*......Is 30:14
into the *p* cannot hope ....Is 38:18
should not die in the *p*.........Is 51:14
land of deserts and of *p*........Jer 2:6
they came to the *p*, and.......Jer 14:3
digged a *p* for my soul ....Jer 18:20
into the midst of the *p* ....Jer 41:7
Fear, and the *p*, and the ......Jer 48:43
fear shall fall into the *p* ......Jer 48:44
getteth up out of the *p*........Jer 48:44
was taken in their *p* ....Lam 4:20
he was taken in their *p* ....Ezek 19:4
that descend into the *p*........Ezek 26:20
that go down to the *p*.........Ezek 26:20
that go down to the *p*.........Ezek 31:14
that go down into the *p*.......Ezek 32:18
that go down to the *p*.........Ezek 32:24
that go down to the *p*.........Ezek 32:29
the *p* wherein is no water .....Zech 9:11
a *p* on the sabbath day........Matt 12:11
or an ox fallen into a *p* ....Luke 14:5
key of the bottomless *p* ....Rev 9:1
opened the bottomless *p* ....Rev 9:2
a smoke out of the *p* ....Rev 9:2
of the smoke of the *p*.........Rev 9:2
out of the bottomless *p* ....Rev 11:7
key of the bottomless *p* ....Rev 20:1

PITCH—*tar*
Ark covered with........Gen 6:14
In Babel's tower.........Gen 11:3
In Moses' ark ....Ex 2:3
Kings fall in ....Gen 14:10

Shall be turned into *p*.........Is 34:9
Shall become burning *p* ....Is 34:9

PITCH—*to erect and fix in place*

[*also* PITCHED]
Beth-el, and *p* his tent ....Gen 12:8
p his tent in the valley ....Gen 26:17
Jacob had *p* his tent in........Gen 31:25
Laban..*p* in the mount ....Gen 31:25
p his tent before the city ......Gen 33:18
p in Rephidim: and there ......Ex 17:1
and *p* it without the camp .....Ex 33:7
the tabernacle is to be *p* ......Num 1:51
Israel shall *p* their tents ....Num 1:52
p by his own standard ....Num 2:2
congregation shall they *p* ......Num 2:2
those that do *p* next unto .....Num 2:5
p behind the tabernacle ....Num 3:23
Israel *p* their tents ....Num 9:17
and *p* in the wilderness ....Num 12:16
p at Ije-abarim, in the ....Num 21:11
and *p* on the other side ....Num 21:13
and *p* in Succoth ....Num 33:5
and they *p* before Migdol .....Num 33:7
trees; and they *p* there ....Num 33:9
p in Kibroth-hattaavah ....Num 33:16
and *p* in Rimmon-parez ....Num 33:19
Libnah, and *p* at Rissah.......Num 33:21
and *p* in mount Shapher ....Num 33:23
Tahath, and *p* at Tarah ....Num 33:27
p in Hashmonah..............Num 33:29
and *p* in Jotbathah ....Num 33:33
and *p* in mount Hor ....Num 33:37
and *p* in Punon...............Num 33:42
and *p* in Ije-abarim ....Num 33:44
and *p* in the mountains of .....Num 33:47
p by Jordan, from ....Num 33:49
a place to *p* your tents ....Deut 1:33
did Joshua *p* in Gilgal ....Josh 4:20
p on the north side of Ai .....Josh 8:11
p together at the waters.......Josh 11:5
p his tent unto the plain ......Judg 4:11
and *p* beside the well of.......Judg 7:1
p in Jahaz, and fought ....Judg 11:20
and *p* in Kirjath-jearim ....Judg 18:12
and *p* beside Eben-ezer 1Sam 4:1
Philistines *p* in Aphek 1Sam 4:1
p between Shochoh and 1Sam 17:1
And Saul *p* in the hill of 1Sam 26:3
place where Saul had *p* 1Sam 26:5
the people *p* round about 1Sam 26:5
came and *p* in Shunem.........1Sam 28:4
and they *p* in Gilboa..........1Sam 28:4
that David had *p* for it........2Sam 6:17
p in the valley of Rephaim 2Sam 23:13
Israel *p* before them 1Kin 20:27
Jerusalem and *p* against it 2Kin 25:1
ark of God, and *p* it for 1Chr 15:1
and *p* before Medeba 1Chr 19:7
had *p* a tent for it at..........2Chr 1:4
shall the Arabian *p* tent ....Is 13:20
p their tents against her ....Jer 6:3
Jerusalem, and *p* against ......Jer 52:4

PITCHER—*a vessel with handles*

Used for:
Water ....Gen 24:16
Protection of a torch.....Judg 7:16, 19

Figurative of:
Heart ....Eccl 12:6

[*also* PITCHERS]
Let down thy *p*, I pray........Gen 24:14
her *p* upon her shoulder ......Gen 24:15
a little water of thy *p* ....Gen 24:17
emptied her *p* into the ....Gen 24:20
her *p* on her shoulder ....Gen 24:45
brake the *p*, and held the .....Judg 7:20
esteemed as earthen *p* ....Lam 4:2
man bearing a *p* of water .....Mark 14:13
bearing a *p* of water ....Luke 22:10

PITHOM (pī'thŏm)—*"their mouthful"*
Egyptian city built by
Hebrew slaves.........Ex 1:11

PITHON (pī'thŏn)—*"harmless"*
Son of Micah 1Chr 8:35

PITILESSNESS—*showing no mercy*

Examples of:
Rich man 2Sam 12:1-6
Nebuchadnezzar 2Kin 25:6-21
Medes ....Is 13:18
Edom ....Amos 1:11
Heartless creditor ....Matt 18:29, 30
Strict religionists.........Luke 10:30-32
Merciless murderers .....Acts 7:54-58

PITY—*compassion; to show compassion*

Of God, upon:
Heathen ....Jon 4:10, 11
Israel ....Is 63:9
Faithful remnant ....Is 54:8-10
Believer ....James 5:11

Of men:
Pleaded.................Job 19:21
Upon the poor ....Prov 19:17
Upon children...........Ps 103:13
Encouraged 1Pet 3:8
See COMPASSION; MERCY

[*also* PITIED, PITIETH, PITIFUL]
have no *p* upon them ....Deut 7:16
neither shall thine eye *p* him ..Deut 13:8
Thine eye shall not *p* him .....Deut 19:13
thine eye shall not *p* her ......Deut 25:12
because he had no *p* 2Sam 12:6
looked for some to take *p*.....Ps 69:20
so the Lord *p* them that.......Ps 103:13
them also to be *p* of all ....Ps 106:46
I will not *p*, nor spare ....Jer 13:14
who shall have *p* upon ....Jer 15:5
neither have *p*, nor have ......Jer 21:7
of Jacob, and hath not *p* ......Lam 2:2
down, and hath not *p*.........Lam 2:17
hast killed, and not *p* ....Lam 2:21
slain, thou hast not *p* ....Lam 3:43
hands of the *p* women ....Lam 4:10
neither will I have *p* ....Ezek 7:4
neither will I have *p* ....Ezek 7:9
neither will I have *p* ....Ezek 8:18
spare, neither have ye *p* ......Ezek 9:5
neither will I have *p* ....Ezek 9:10
None eye *p* thee, to do ....Ezek 16:5
that which your soul *p* ....Ezek 24:21
I had *p* for mine holy name ...Ezek 36:21
his land, and *p* his people .....Joel 2:18
and did cast off all *p*..........Amos 1:11
shepherds *p* them not ....Zech 11:5
no more *p* the inhabitants .....Zech 11:6
I had *p* on thee? ....Matt 18:33

PLACE, PLACED, PLACES—*See* INTRODUCTION

PLAGUE—*a disastrous affliction or epidemic*

Descriptive of:
Divine judgment ....Ex 9:14
Leprosy ....Lev 13:1-59
Disease ....Mark 3:10
Final judgment ....Rev 9:20

Instances of:
In Egypt.................Ex 11:1
At Kibroth-hattaavah ....Num 11:33, 34
At Kadesh ....Num 14:37
At Peor ....Josh 22:17
Among:
Philistines.............1Sam 5:7

P

Israelites 2Sam 24:15
Sennacherib's soldiers . . Is 37:36

Sent by God:
Because of sin ....Gen 12:17
As final judgments ......Rev 15:1, 8

Remedy against, by:
Judgment ....Ps 106:29, 30
Prayer and confession 1Kin 8:37, 38
Separation ....Rev 18:4
Promise ....Ps 91:10
Obedience ....Rev 22:18

[*also* PLAGUED, PLAGUES]
p shall not be upon you ....Ex 12:13
that there be no *p* among .....Ex 30:12
the Lord *p* the people ....Ex 32:35
if the *p* of leprosy be ....Lev 14:3
whom is the *p* of leprosy ......Lev 14:32
I put the *p* of leprosy in ......Lev 14:34
there is as it were a *p*.........Lev 14:35
go into it to see the *p*.........Lev 14:36
he shall look on the *p* ....Lev 14:37
if the *p* be in the walls ....Lev 14:37
p be spread in the walls ....Lev 14:39
stones in which the *p* is ....Lev 14:40
if the *p* come again, and ......Lev 14:43
if the *p* be spread in the ......Lev 14:44
the *p* hath not spread in ......Lev 14:48
because the *p* is healed ....Lev 14:48
manner of *p* of leprosy ....Lev 14:54
seven times more *p* upon ......Lev 26:21
there be no *p* among the ......Num 8:19
the Lord: the *p* is begun ......Num 16:46
the *p* was begun among ....Num 16:47
and the *p* was stayed ....Num 16:48
they that died in the *p* ....Num 16:49
and the *p* was stayed ....Num 16:50
p was stayed from the ....Num 25:8
that died in the *p* were........Num 25:9
slain in the day of the *p*.......Num 25:18
came to pass after the *p*.......Num 26:1
was a *p* among the ....Num 31:16
Take heed in the *p* of.........Deut 24:8
make thy *p* wonderful.........Deut 28:59
p of thy seed..great *p* ....Deut 28:59
sickness, and every *p* ....Deut 28:61
when they see the *p* of........Deut 29:22
I *p* Egypt, according to ....Josh 24:5
Egyptians with all the *p* 1Sam 4:8
for one *p* was on you all 1Sam 6:4
p may be stayed from the 2Sam 24:21
the *p* was stayed from 2Sam 24:25
that they should be *p* 1Chr 21:17
p may be stayed from the 1Chr 21:22
p will the Lord smite thy 2Chr 21:14
neither are they *p* like ....Ps 73:5
day long have I been *p* ....Ps 73:14
p them that hate him ....Ps 89:23
hiss because of all the *p*.......Jer 19:8
shall hiss at all the *p*..........Jer 49:17
and hiss at all her *p* ....Jer 50:13
O death, I will be thy *p*.......Hos 13:14
this shall be the *p* ....Zech 14:12
be the *p* of the horse ....Zech 14:15
in these tents, as this *p* ......Zech 14:15
there shall be the *p*............Zech 14:18
him, as many as had *p*.........Mark 3:10
she was healed of that *p* ......Mark 5:29
and be whole of thy *p* ....Mark 5:34
many..infirmities and *p*.........Luke 7:21
smite the earth with all *p* .....Rev 11:6
power over these *p* ....Rev 16:9
God because of the *p* of ......Rev 16:21
the *p* thereof was..great ....Rev 16:21
shall her *p* come in one ....Rev 18:8
full of the seven last *p* ....Rev 21:9

PLAIN—*a geographically level area (usually refers to specific regional areas)*
Dry region............Num 22:1; Deut 3:17; Deut 34:3
Low regions ....Jer 17:26; Obad 19

[*also* PLAINS]
found a *p* in the land of.......Gen 11:2
all the *p* of Jordan............Gen 13:10
Lot chose him all the *p* ....Gen 13:11
in the cities of the *p* ....Gen 13:12
dwelt in the *p* of Mamre ......Gen 13:18
dwelt in the *p* of Mamre ......Gen 14:13
him in the *p* of Mamre........Gen 18:1
neither stay..in all the *p*.......Gen 19:17
those cities, and all the *p* .....Gen 19:25
all the land of the *p* ....Gen 19:28
the cities of the *p*.............Gen 19:29
them in the *p* of Moab ....Num 26:3
Israel in the *p* of Moab by ....Num 26:63
camp at the *p* of Moab ....Num 31:12
pitched in the *p* of Moab ......Num 33:48
in the *p* of Moab ....Num 33:49
Moses in the *p* of Moab.......Num 33:50
Moses in the *p* of Moab.......Num 35:1
Israel in the *p* of Moab ....Num 36:13
in the *p* over against the ......Deut 1:1
places nigh..in the *p* ....Deut 1:7
the way of the *p* from ....Deut 2:8
the cities of the *p*, and ....Deut 3:10
p also, and Jordan, and ....Deut 3:17
even unto the sea of the *p* ....Deut 3:17
in the *p* country ....Deut 4:43
p on this side Jordan ....Deut 4:49
unto the sea of the *p* ....Deut 4:49
beside the *p* of Moreh? ....Deut 11:30
Moses went up from the *p* ....Deut 34:1
p of the valley of Jericho ......Deut 34:3
wept for Moses in the *p*.......Deut 34:8
toward the sea of the *p* ....Josh 3:16
battle, to the *p* of Jericho .....Josh 4:13
even in the *p* of Jericho ....Josh 5:10
appointed, before the *p* ....Josh 8:14
p south of Chinneroth ....Josh 11:2
and the valley, and the *p*......Josh 11:16
and all the *p* on the east ......Josh 12:1
the *p* to the Sea of ....Josh 12:3
and unto the sea of the *p* .....Josh 12:3
p, and in the springs ....Josh 12:8
all the *p* of Medeba unto......Josh 13:9
the river, and all the *p*........Josh 13:16
cities that are in the *p* ....Josh 13:17
all the cities of the *p*..........Josh 13:21
in the *p* of Moab ....Josh 13:32
the wilderness upon the *p* ......Josh 20:8
his tent unto the *p* of ....Judg 4:11
by the *p* of the pillar ....Judg 9:6
come along by the *p* of ....Judg 9:37
the *p* of the vineyards.........Judg 11:33
come to the *p* of Tabor 1Sam 10:3
the *p* on the south of 1Sam 23:24
that night through the *p*........2Sam 2:29
them away through the *p*......2Sam 4:7
tarry in the *p* of the 2Sam 15:28
the *p* of the wilderness 2Sam 17:16
ran by the way of the *p* 2Sam 18:23
In the *p* of Jordan did 1Kin 7:46
against them in the *p* 1Kin 20:23
against them in the *p* 1Kin 20:25
unto the sea of the *p* 2Kin 14:25
king went..toward the *p* 2Kin 25:4
him in the *p* of Jericho........2Kin 25:5
trees that were in the low *p* ...1Chr 27:28
In the *p* of Jordan did 2Chr 4:17
that are in the low *p*...........2Chr 9:27
low country, and in the *p* 2Chr 26:10
priests, the men of the *p* ......Neh 3:22
villages in the *p* of Ono ....Neh 6:2
p country round about ....Neh 12:28
Benjamin, and from the *p*.....Jer 17:26
valley, and rock of the *p* ......Jer 21:13
went out the way of the *p*.....Jer 39:4
the *p* shall be destroyed ....Jer 48:8
come upon the *p* country......Jer 48:21
by the way of the *p*...........Jer 52:7
Zedekiah in the *p* of...........Jer 52:8
Arise, go forth into the *p* .....Ezek 3:22
and went forth into the *p* .....Ezek 3:23
vision that I saw in the *p*......Ezek 8:4
set it up in the *p* of Dura .....Dan 3:1
the south and the *p*? ....Zech 7:7
shall be turned as a *p* ....Zech 14:10
and stood in the *p* ....Luke 6:17

PLAIN—*average; normal; clear*
Jacob was a *p* man ....Gen 25:27
lead me in a *p* path...........Ps 27:11
all *p* to him that.............Prov 8:9
way of the righteous is made *p*.Prov 15:19
he hath made *p* the face ......Is 28:25
and the rough places *p* ....Is 40:4
loosed, and he spake *p*........Mark 7:35

PLAINLY—*clearly*

[*also* PLAINNESS]
if the servant shall *p* say ......Ex 21:5
p appear unto the house 1Sam 2:27
He told us *p* that the asses 1Sam 10:16
unto us hath been *p* read .....Ezra 4:18
shall be ready to speak *p*......Is 32:4
be the Christ, tell us *p* ....John 10:24
said Jesus unto them *p*........John 11:14
show you *p* of the Father .....John 16:25
Lo, now speakest thou *p* ......John 16:29
use great *p* of speech 2Cor 3:12
declare *p* that they seek ....Heb 11:14

PLAISTER—*See* PLASTER

PLAIT—*to intertwine*
Of Christ's crown........Matt 27:29
Of woman's hair 1Pet 3:3

[*also* PLAITED]
p a crown of thorns, and ......Mark 15:17
the soldiers *p* a crown ....John 19:2

PLANES—*tools for smoothing or shaping wood*
he fitteth it with *p* and........Is 44:13

PLANETS—*heavenly bodies*
and to the *p*, and to all 2Kin 23:5

PLANKS—*boards*
floor of the house with *p*......1Kin 6:15
thick *p* upon the face of.......Ezek 41:25
of the house, and thick *p* .....Ezek 41:26

PLANS—*methods of action*
Acknowledging God in. . .Prov 3:6
Considering all possibilities ....Luke 14:31-33
Leaving God out ....Luke 12:16-21
Not trusting God ....Ps 52:7

PLANT—*to set or sow with seeds or plants; vegetation*
Created by God ....Gen 1:11, 12
Given as food ....Gen 1:28, 29

[*also* PLANTED, PLANTEDST, PLANTETH, PLANTING, PLANTINGS, PLANTS]
every *p* of the field before ....Gen 2:5
Lord God *p* a garden ....Gen 2:8
Abraham *p* a grove in ....Gen 21:33
bring them in, and *p*..........Ex 15:17
shall have *p* all manner ....Lev 19:23
which the Lord hath *p* ....Num 24:6
trees, which thou *p* not ....Deut 6:11
shalt not *p* thee a grove ....Deut 16:21
man is he that hath *p* a ....Deut 20:6
thou shalt *p* a vineyard........Deut 28:30
Thou shalt *p* vineyards ....Deut 28:39
oliveyards which ye *p* not .....Josh 24:13
Israel, and will *p* 2Sam 7:10
sow ye, and reap, and *p* 2Kin 19:29
that dwelt among *p* and 1Chr 4:23
Israel and will *p* 1Chr 17:9
forth boughs like a *p* ....Job 14:9
shall be like a tree *p* by........Ps 1:3
with thy hand, and *p* ....Ps 44:2
thy right hand hath *p* ....Ps 80:15
that be *p* in the house ....Ps 92:13
He that *p* the ear, shall ....Ps 94:9
sow the fields and *p* ....Ps 107:37
children like olive *p* ....Ps 128:3
our sons may be as *p* ....Ps 144:12
of her hands she *p*............Prov 31:16
I *p* my vineyards ....Eccl 2:4
a time to *p*, and a time ....Eccl 3:2
pluck up that which is *p*.......Eccl 3:2

p it with the choicest ....Is 5:2
Judah his pleasant *p* ....Is 5:7
down the principal *p* ....Is 16:8
shalt thou *p* pleasant ....Is 17:10
thou plant pleasant *p* ....Is 17:10
shalt thou make thy *p* ....Is 17:11
ye, and reap, and *p* ....Is 37:30
will *p* in the wilderness........Is 41:19
he *p* an ash, and the rain .....Is 44:14
that I may *p* the heavens......Is 51:16
him as a tender *p* ....Is 53:2
the branch of my *p*, the ....Is 60:21
the *p* of the Lord, that........Is 61:3
they shall *p* vineyards ....Is 65:21
they shall not *p*, and...........Is 65:22
to build, and to *p* ....Jer 1:10
I had *p* thee a noble vine ......Jer 2:21
into the degenerate *p* ....Jer 2:21
the Lord of hosts, that *p* ....Jer 11:17
Thou hast *p* them, yea ....Jer 12:2
to build and to *p* it ....Jer 18:9
and I will *p* them, and not ....Jer 24:6
p gardens, and eat the fruit ...Jer 29:5
yet *p* vines upon the ....Jer 31:5
the planters shall *p*, and ......Jer 31:5
to build, and to *p* ....Jer 31:28
I will *p* them in this land......Jer 32:41
nor sow seed, nor *p* ....Jer 35:7
I have *p* I will pluck ....Jer 45:4
thy *p* are gone over the ....Jer 48:32
of the land, and *p* it in a......Ezek 17:5
behold, being *p*, shall it ....Ezek 17:10
p it upon a high ....Ezek 17:22
is *p* in the wilderness ....Ezek 19:13
build houses, and *p* ....Ezek 28:26
running round about..*p* ....Ezek 31:4
raise up for them a *p* ....Ezek 34:29
and *p* that that was ....Ezek 36:36
p the tabernacles of his ....Dan 11:45
Tyrus, is *p* in a pleasant.......Hos 9:13
p pleasant vineyards ....Amos 5:11
they shall *p* vineyards ....Amos 9:14
the field, and as *p* of a........Mic 1:6
they shall *p* vineyards ....Zeph 1:13
p, which my heavenly ....Matt 15:13
Father hath not *p*...............Matt 15:13
man *p* a vineyard ....Mark 12:1
had a fig tree *p* in his.........Luke 13:6
the root, and be thou *p* in ....Luke 17:6
they sold, they *p*, they ....Luke 17:28
p together in the likeness ......Rom 6:5
I have *p*, Apollos watered......1Cor 3:6
neither is he that *p* any 1Cor 3:7
who *p* a vineyard, and 1Cor 9:7

PLANTATION—*ground where plants are cultivated*
the furrows of her *p* ....Ezek 17:7

PLANTERS—*those who plant and cultivate crops*
the *p* shall plant, and ....Jer 31:5

PLANTS OF THE BIBLE
Anise ....Matt 23:23
Bramble ....Judg 9:14, 15
Brier ....Judg 8:7, 16
Broom ("juniper") ....Ps 120:4
Calamus ....Song 4:14
Camphire (Henna) ......Song 1:14
Cummin ....Is 28:25, 27
Fitch ....Ezek 4:9
Garlic ....Num 11:5
Gourd 2Kin 4:39
Grass....................Ps 103:15
Hyssop ....Ex 12:22
Lily ....Song 5:13
Mallows ....Job 30:4
Mandrakes...............Gen 30:14-16
Mint ....Matt 23:23
Mustard ....Matt 13:31
Myrtle ....Is 55:13
Rose ....Is 35:1
Rue ....Luke 11:42
Saffron ....Song 4:13, 14
Spikenard ....Song 4:13, 14
Thorn ....Judg 8:7
Vine of Sodom ....Deut 32:32
Wormwood ....Deut 29:18

PLASTER—*a pasty composition*
Building material used on:
Infested walls ....Lev 14:42, 48
Mt. Ebal ....Deut 27:2, 4
Babylon's walls ....Dan 5:5
See LIME; MORTAR
Medicinal material:
Figs applied to Hezekiah's boil ....Is 38:21

[*also* PLASTERED]
and after it is *p* ....Lev 14:43
and lay it for a *p* upon ....Is 38:21

PLAT—*a plot of ground*
I will requite thee in this *p* 2Kin 9:26
cast him into the *p* 2Kin 9:26

PLATE—*a flat, thin piece of material hammered or beaten into various forms*

[*also* PLATES]
thou shalt make a *p* of.........Ex 28:36
the gold into thin *p* ....Ex 39:3
they made the *p* of the........Ex 39:30
did he put the golden *p* ....Lev 8:9
make them broad *p* ....Num 16:38
brazen wheels and *p* of 1Kin 7:30
Silver spread into *p* is ....Jer 10:9

PLATTER—*a large, side plate*
Deep dish or basin ("charger") ....Matt 14:8, 11
Side dish for food ....Matt 23:25, 26
Used figuratively ....Matt 23:25, 26
the cup and the *p* ....Luke 11:39

PLAY—*to perform*
Music 1Sam 16:16-23
Immoral acts ....Ex 32:6
Fighting 2Sam 2:14
Dancing 2Sam 6:5, 21
Fish ....Ps 104:26
Children ....Is 11:8

[*also* PLAYED, PLAYEDST, PLAYETH, PLAYING]
daughter-in-law hath *p* ....Gen 38:24
she profane herself by *p* .....Lev 21:9
to *p* the whore in her ....Deut 22:21
concubine *p* the whore ....Judg 19:2
a man that can *p* well..........1Sam 16:17
another as they *p* 1Sam 18:7
David *p* with his hand 1Sam 19:9
and let us *p* the men for 2Sam 10:12
when the minstrel *p* 2Kin 3:15
David and all Israel *p*..........1Chr 13:8
David dancing and *p*............1Chr 15:29
beasts of the field *p* ....Job 40:20
thou *p* with him as with ....Job 41:5
p skillfully with a loud ....Ps 33:3
p on instruments followed ......Ps 68:25
were the damsels *p* with ....Ps 68:25
p on instruments shall..........Ps 87:7
thou hast made to *p* ....Ps 104:26
wanderest, *p* the harlot ....Jer 2:20
thou hast *p* the harlot..........Jer 3:1
not, but went and *p* the ....Jer 3:8
p the harlot because of........Ezek 16:15
p the harlot thereupon ....Ezek 16:16
Thou hast *p* the whore ....Ezek 16:28
thee to cease from *p* the ......Ezek 16:41
Aholah *p* the harlot when .....Ezek 23:5
in unto a woman that *p* ....Ezek 23:44
p well on an instrument ....Ezek 33:32
For their mother hath *p* ....Hos 2:5
shalt not *p* the harlot ....Hos 3:3
boys and girls *p* in the ....Zech 8:5
drink, and rose up to *p* 1Cor 10:7

PLAYER—*a performer of a musical instrument*

[*also* PLAYERS]
Who is a cunning *p* 1Sam 16:16
p on instruments followed .....Ps 68:25
p on instruments shall be......Ps 87:7

PLEA—*to appeal*
between *p* and *p* and ....Deut 17:8

PLEAD—*to entreat intensely*
Asking for judgment against:
Idolatry..................Judg 6:31, 32
Evil king 1Sam 24:15
Asking for protection of:
Poor ....Prov 22:23
Widows...................Is 1:17
Repentant ....Mic 7:9

[*also* PLEADED, PLEADETH, PLEADINGS]
the Lord that hath *p* 1Sam 25:39
set me a time to *p*? ....Job 9:19
and hearken to the *p* of ....Job 13:6
Who is he that will *p* with.....Job 13:19
one might *p* for a man ....Job 16:21
as a man *p* for his ....Job 16:21
Will he *p* against me with .....Job 23:6
P my cause, O Lord, with.....Ps 35:1
Judge me, O God, and *p* .....Ps 43:1
P my cause, and deliver.......Ps 119:154
he shall *p* their cause ....Prov 23:11
p the cause of the poor ....Prov 31:9
Lord standeth up to *p* ....Is 3:13
let us *p* together..............Is 43:26
that *p* the cause of his ....Is 51:22
nor any *p* for truth ....Is 59:4
will the Lord *p* with all ....Is 66:16
I will yet *p* with you ....Jer 2:9
children will I *p* ....Jer 2:9
Wherefore will ye *p* with......Jer 2:29
thou, O Lord, when I *p*........Jer 12:1
he will *p* with all flesh ....Jer 25:31
none to *p* thy cause...........Jer 30:13
Behold, I will *p* thy cause .....Jer 51:36
thou hast *p* the causes ....Lam 3:58
and will *p* with him there .....Ezek 17:20
Like as I *p* with your ....Ezek 20:36
so will I *p* with you, saith .....Ezek 20:36
will *p* against him with ....Ezek 38:22
P with your mother, *p* ....Hos 2:2
p with them there for ....Joel 3:2
and he will *p* with ....Mic 6:2

PLEASANT—*agreeable; giving pleasure*

[*also* PLEASANTNESS]
every tree that is *p* to the .....Gen 2:9
it was *p* to the eyes, and ......Gen 3:6
the land that it was *p* ....Gen 49:15
were lovely and *p* 2Sam 1:23
very *p* hast thou been 2Sam 1:26
whatsoever is *p* in thine 1Kin 20:6
situation of this city is *p*.......2Kin 2:19
and for all manner of *p* 2Chr 32:27
are fallen unto me in *p* ....Ps 16:6
they despised the *p* land ......Ps 106:24
how *p* it is for brethren to ....Ps 133:1
unto his name; for it is *p*.......Ps 135:3
and knowledge is *p* unto thy...Prov 2:10
Her ways are ways of *p* ....Prov 3:17
eaten in secret is *p* ....Prov 9:17
words of the pure are *p* ....Prov 15:26
P words are as ....Prov 16:24
with all precious and *p* ....Prov 24:4
p thing it is for the eyes.......Eccl 11:7
my beloved, yea, *p* ....Song 1:16
his garden, and eat his *p* ......Song 4:16
gates are all manner of *p* ......Song 7:13
Tarshish, and upon all *p* ....Is 2:16
and dragons in their *p* ....Is 13:22
for the teats, for the *p* ....Is 32:12
all our *p* things are laid ....Is 64:11
and give thee a *p* land, a.......Jer 3:19
p places of the wilderness .....Jer 23:10
son? is he a *p* child? ....Jer 31:20
all her *p* things that she ....Lam 1:7
have given their *p* things ....Lam 1:11
walls, and destroy thy *p* ....Ezek 26:12
song of one that hath a *p* .....Ezek 33:32
east, and toward the *p* ....Dan 8:9
I ate no *p* bread, neither ......Dan 10:3
precious stones, and *p* ....Dan 11:38
p places for their silver.........Hos 9:6
the treasure of all *p* ....Hos 13:15

P

temples my goodly *p* .... Joel 3:5
ye have planted *p* .... Amos 5:11
ye cast out from their *p* .... Mic 2:9
glory out of all the *p* .... Nah 2:9
for they laid the *p* land .... Zech 7:14
and Jerusalem be *p* .... Mal 3:4

PLEASE—*to satisfy*

Applied to God's:
Sovereignty .... Ps 115:3
Election 1Sam 12:22
Method 1Cor 1:21
Reactions to man 1Kin 3:10
Purpose .... Col 1:19
Creative acts 1Cor 12:18
Will .... Matt 3:17

Applied to the unregenerate's:
Behavior .... Rom 8:8
Passions .... Matt 14:6
Ways 1Thess 2:15
Prejudices .... Acts 12:3

Applied to the regenerate's:
Faith .... Heb 11:5, 6
Calling 2Tim 2:4
Concern for others ...... Rom 15:26, 27
Married life 1Cor 7:12, 13
Example, Christ .... John 8:29

[*also* PLEASED, PLEASETH, PLEASING]
do to her as it *p* thee .... Gen 16:6
dwell where it *p* thee .... Gen 20:15
daughters of Canaan *p* .... Gen 28:8
of God, and thou wast *p* ...... Gen 33:10
their words *p* Hamor .... Gen 34:18
and it *p* Pharaoh well .... Gen 45:16
If she *p* not her master .... Ex 21:8
peradventure it will *p* God .... Num 23:27
saw that it *p* the Lord .... Num 24:1
And the saying *p* me well ..... Deut 1:23
of Manasseh spake, it *p* ...... Josh 22:30
If the Lord were *p* to kill ..... Judg 13:23
for me; for she *p* me well ..... Judg 14:3
and she *p* Samson well .... Judg 14:7
hath *p* the Lord to make 1Sam 12:22
Saul, and the thing *p* him 1Sam 18:20
p David well to be the 1Sam 18:26
if it *p* my father to do 1Sam 20:13
notice of it, and it *p* them 2Sam 3:36
the king did *p* all 2Sam 3:36
p thee to bless the house 2Sam 7:29
saying *p* Absalom well 2Sam 17:4
desire which he was *p* to 1Kin 9:1
him; and they *p* him not 1Kin 9:12
else, it if *p* thee, I will 1Kin 21:6
p thee to bless the house 1Chr 17:27
kind to this people, and *p* 2Chr 10:7
the thing *p* the king and 2Chr 30:4
If it *p* the king, and if thy ..... Neh 2:5
it *p* the king to send me ...... Neh 2:6
it *p* the king, let there go a ... Esth 1:19
p the king and the princes ..... Esth 1:21
maiden which *p* the king ...... Esth 2:4
And the thing *p* the king ...... Esth 2:4
it *p* the king to grant my ...... Esth 5:8
And the thing *p* Haman .... Esth 5:14
it *p* the king, and if I have .... Esth 8:5
king, and I be *p* in his .... Esth 8:5
it would *p* God to destroy ..... Job 6:9
children shall seek to *p* .... Job 20:10
Be *p*, O Lord, to deliver ...... Ps 40:13
shalt thou be *p* with the .... Ps 51:19
shall *p* the Lord better .... Ps 69:31
Whatsoever the Lord *p* .... Ps 135:6
When a man's ways *p* the ..... Prov 16:7
whoso *p* God shall escape ..... Eccl 7:26
he doeth whatsoever *p* .... Eccl 8:3
awake my love, till he *p* ...... Song 2:7
awake my love, till he *p* ...... Song 3:5
awake my love, until he *p* ..... Song 8:4
p themselves in the .... Is 2:6
Lord is well *p* for his .... Is 42:21
it *p* the Lord to bruise .... Is 53:10
choose the things that *p* .... Is 56:4
It *p* Darius to set over the .... Dan 6:1
neither shall they be *p* .... Hos 9:4
O Lord, hast done as it *p* ..... Jon 1:14
Lord be *p* with thousands ..... Mic 6:7
will he be *p* with thee, or ..... Mal 1:8
whom my soul is well *p* .... Matt 12:18
in whom I am well *p* .... Matt 17:5
in whom I am well *p* .... Mark 1:11
danced and *p* Herod .... Mark 6:22
in thee I am well *p* .... Luke 3:22
the saying *p* the whole .... Acts 6:5
Then *p* it the apostles .... Acts 15:22
the weak, and not to *p* .... Rom 15:1
Let every one of us *p* his ..... Rom 15:2
Christ *p* not himself .... Rom 15:3
if he be *p* to dwell with 1Cor 7:13
how he may *p* the Lord 1Cor 7:32
how she may *p* her 1Cor 7:34
God was not well *p* 1Cor 10:5
Even as I *p* all men in all 1Cor 10:33
a body as it hath *p* 1Cor 15:38
or do I seek to *p* men .... Gal 1:10
I yet *p* men, I should .... Gal 1:10
the Lord unto all *p* .... Col 1:10
not as *p* men, but God 1Thess 2:4
ought to walk and to *p* 1Thess 4:1
to *p* them well in all .... Titus 2:9
God is well *p* .... Heb 13:16
in whom I am well *p* 2Pet 1:17
those things that are *p* in 1John 3:22

PLEASURE—*desire or inclination; gratification of the senses*

Kinds of:
Physical .... Eccl 2:1-10
Sexual .... Gen 18:12
Worldly .... Luke 8:14
Immoral .... Titus 3:3
Spiritual .... Ps 36:8
Heavenly .... Ps 16:11

God's, described as:
Sovereign .... Eph 1:5, 9
Creative .... Rev 4:11
In righteousness 1Chr 29:17
Purpose .... Luke 12:32
Not in evil .... Ps 5:4
Not in the wicked .... Ezek 18:23, 32
Ezek 33:11

Christian's described as:
Subject to God's will 2Cor 12:10
Inspired by God .... Phil 2:13
Fulfilled by God 2Thess 1:11

The unbeliever's, described as:
Unsatisfying .... Eccl 2:1
Enslaving .... Titus 3:3
Deadening 1Tim 5:6
Judged 2Thess 2:12
Defiant .... Rom 1:32

[*also* PLEASURES]
thy fill at thine own *p* .... Deut 23:24
let the king send his *p* .... Ezra 5:17
fathers and do his *p* .... Ezra 10:11
cattle, at their *p* .... Neh 9:37
to every man's *p* .... Esth 1:8
For what *p* hath he in his ..... Job 21:21
it any *p* to the Almighty ...... Job 22:3
their years in *p* .... Job 36:11
p in the prosperity of .... Ps 35:27
Do good in thy good *p* .... Ps 51:18
thy servants take *p* in her ..... Ps 102:14
his, that do his *p* .... Ps 103:21
bind his princes at his *p* ...... Ps 105:22
of all them that have *p* .... Ps 111:2
taketh not *p* in the legs .... Ps 147:10
Lord taketh *p* in them .... Ps 147:11
the Lord taketh *p* in his .... Ps 149:4
that loveth *p* shall be a .... Prov 21:17
for he hath no *p* in fools ...... Eccl 5:4
shalt say, I have no *p* .... Eccl 12:1
the night of my *p* hath he ..... Is 21:4
shall perform all my *p* .... Is 44:28
I will do all my *p* .... Is 46:10
thou that art given to *p* .... Is 47:8
he will do his *p* on .... Is 48:14
p of the Lord shall .... Is 53:10
your fast ye find *p* .... Is 58:3
from doing thy *p* on my .... Is 58:13
nor finding thine own *p* .... Is 58:13
the wind at her *p* .... Jer 2:24
wherein is no *p*? .... Jer 22:28
liberty at their *p* .... Jer 34:16
vessel wherein is no *p* .... Jer 48:38
whom thou hast taken *p* ...... Ezek 16:37
vessel wherein is no *p* .... Hos 8:8
I will take *p* in it, and I .... Hag 1:8
I have no *p* in you, saith ...... Mal 1:10
show the Jews a *p* .... Acts 24:27
to do the Jews a *p* .... Acts 25:9
lovers of *p* more than 2Tim 3:4
thou hast had no *p* .... Heb 10:6
my soul shall have no *p* .... Heb 10:38
to enjoy the *p* of sin for ...... Heb 11:25
after their own *p* .... Heb 12:10
Ye have lived in *p* on the ..... James 5:5
count it *p* to riot in the 2Pet 2:13

PLEDGE—*something given for security of a debt; a vow*

Of material things:
Garments .... Ex 22:26
Regulations concerning ... Deut 24:10-17
Evil of .... Job 22:6
Restoration of, sign of righteousness .... Ezek 18:7, 16
Unlawfully held back .... Ezek 18:12

Of spiritual things:
The Holy Spirit in the heart 2Cor 1:22
Given by God 2Cor 5:5
Guarantee of future redemption .... Eph 1:13, 14

See BORROW; DEBT; LENDING; SURETY

[*also* PLEDGES]
Wilt thou give me a *p* till ..... Gen 38:17
upper millstone to *p* .... Deut 24:6
taketh a man's life to *p* .... Deut 24:6
and take their *p* 1Sam 17:18
give *p* to my lord the king of .. 2Kin 18:23
widow's ox for a *p* .... Job 24:3
p of him for a strange .... Prov 20:16
a *p* of him for a strange .... Prov 27:13
give *p*, I pray thee, to my ..... Is 36:8
wicked restore the *p* .... Ezek 33:15
clothes laid to *p* by every ..... Amos 2:8

PLEIADES (plē'yä-dēz)—*"cluster of many stars"—a constellation*
Part of God's creation ... Job 9:9
Amos 5:8

sweet influences of *P* .... Job 38:31

PLENTY—*plentiful; ample; full*

Of physical things:
Food .... Gen 41:29-47
Prosperity .... Deut 28:11
Productivity .... Jer 2:7
Rain .... Ps 68:9
Water .... Lev 11:36

Of spiritual things:
God's loving kindness .... Ps 86:5, 15
God's redemption .... Ps 130:7
Recompenses .... Ps 31:23
Souls in need .... Matt 9:37

How to obtain, by:
Industry .... Prov 28:19
Putting God first .... Prov 3:9, 10
Lord's blessing 2Chr 31:10

See ABUNDANCE

[*also* PLENTEOUS, PLENTEOUSNESS, PLENTIFUL, PLENTIFULLY]
the seven years of *p*, that ..... Gen 41:53
make thee *p* in every .... Deut 30:9
Ophir great *p* of almug 1Kin 10:11
gold at Jerusalem as *p* as 2Chr 1:15
and thou shalt have *p* of ...... Job 22:25
hast thou *p* declared the ...... Job 26:3
in judgment and in *p* of .... Job 37:23
slow to anger, and in *p* .... Ps 103:8
diligent tend only to *p* .... Prov 21:5
joy out of the *p* field .... Is 16:10

it shall be fat and *p*..........Is 30:23
for then had we *p* of..........Jer 44:17
is taken from the *p*..........Jer 48:33
And ye shall eat in *p*..........Joel 2:26
and their meat *p*..........Hab 1:16
man brought forth *p*..........Luke 12:16

PLOTTINGS—*secret plans; schemes*

Against:
Poor..........Ps 10:7-11
Perfect..........Ps 64:4-7
Prophets..........Jer 18:18
Persecuted..........Matt 5:11, 12

Inspired by:
Contempt..........Neh 4:1-8
Hatred..........Gen 37:8-20
Devil..........John 13:27
Envy..........Matt 27:18

Examples of:
Esau against Jacob..........Gen 27:41-45
Satan against Job..........Job 1:8-22
Ahab against Naboth..........1Kin 21:1-16
Jews against Jeremiah..........Jer 26:8-15
Haman against the Jews..........Esth 7:3-6
Chaldeans against Daniel..........Dan 6:1-8
Jews against Christ..........Matt 26:1-5
John 11:47-53
Jews against Paul..........Acts 23:12-22

[*also* PLOTTETH]
The wicked *p* against the..........Ps 37:12

PLOUGH—*tool used to till the earth*
having put his hand to the *p*..........Luke 9:62

PLOW—*to dig up the earth*

Used literally of:
Elisha..........1Kin 19:19
Forbidden with mixed animals..........Deut 22:10
Job's sons..........Job 1:14

Used figuratively of:
Proper learning..........Is 28:24, 26
Wrongdoing..........Hos 10:13
Punishment..........Hos 10:11
Affliction..........Ps 129:3
Destruction..........Jer 26:18
Persistent sin..........Job 4:8
Christian labor..........1Cor 9:10
Information from a wife..........Judg 14:18
Constancy in decision..........Luke 9:62
Perverse action..........Amos 6:12

[*also* PLOWED, PLOWING]
a yoke of oxen might *p*..........1Sam 14:14
sluggard will not *p* by..........Prov 20:4
and the *p* of the wicked..........Prov 21:4
Zion for your sake be *p*..........Mic 3:12
having a servant *p* or..........Luke 17:7

PLOWMAN—*a farmer*

Used literally of:
Farming..........Is 28:24

Used figuratively of:
Prosperity..........Amos 9:13
Christian ministry..........1Cor 9:10

[*also* PLOWMEN]
alien shall be your *p*..........Is 61:5
p were ashamed, they..........Jer 14:4

PLOWSHARES—*the hard part of the plow that cuts the furrow*
Made into swords..........Joel 3:10
Swords made into..........Is 2:4

beat their swords into *p*..........Mic 4:3

PLUCK—*to pull or pick off or out*

[*also* PLUCKED, PLUCKETH]
was an olive leaf *p*..........Gen 8:11
p it out of his bosom, and..........Ex 4:7
p away his crop with his..........Lev 1:16
p down all their high..........Num 33:52
thou mayest *p* the ears..........Deut 23:25
ye shall be *p* from off the..........Deut 28:63
a man *p* off his shoe, and..........Ruth 4:7
p the spear out of the..........2Sam 23:21
p the spear out of the..........1Chr 11:23
will I *p* them up by the..........2Chr 7:20
p off the hair of my head..........Ezra 9:3
p off their hair, and made..........Neh 13:25
p the fatherless from the..........Job 24:9
and *p* the spoil out of his..........Job 29:17
he shall *p* my feet out of..........Ps 25:15
p thee out of thy dwelling..........Ps 52:5
p it out of thy bosom..........Ps 74:11
pass by the way do *p*..........Ps 80:12
foolish *p* it down with..........Prov 14:1
time to *p* up that which..........Eccl 3:2
cheeks to them that *p* off..........Is 50:6
for the wicked are not *p*..........Jer 6:29
I will *p* them out of their..........Jer 12:14
and *p* out the house of..........Jer 12:14
I have *p* them out I will..........Jer 12:15
to *p* up, and to pull down..........Jer 18:7
hand, yet would I *p* thee..........Jer 22:24
plant them and not *p*..........Jer 24:6
to *p* up, and to break..........Jer 31:28
it shall not be *p* up, nor..........Jer 31:40
will plant you, and not *p*..........Jer 42:10
have planted I will *p*..........Jer 45:4
to *p* it up by the roots..........Ezek 17:9
she was *p* up in fury, she..........Ezek 19:12
p off thine own breasts..........Ezek 23:34
wings thereof were *p*..........Dan 7:4
the first horns *p* up by..........Dan 7:8
kingdom shall be *p*..........Dan 11:4
a firebrand *p* out of the..........Amos 4:11
p off their skin from off..........Mic 3:2
And I will *p* up thy..........Mic 5:14
not this a brand *p* out of..........Zech 3:2
right eye offend thee, *p* it..........Matt 5:29
and began to *p* the ears..........Matt 12:1
thine eye offend thee, *p*..........Matt 18:9
to *p* the ears of corn..........Mark 2:23
had been *p* asunder by..........Mark 5:4
if thine eye offend thee, *p*..........Mark 9:47
his disciples *p* the ears..........Luke 6:1
Be thou *p* up by the root..........Luke 17:6
any man *p* them out of..........John 10:28
would have *p* out your..........Gal 4:15
twice dead, *p* up by the..........Jude 12

PLUCKT—*See* PLUCK

PLUMBLINE—*a cord with a weight, used to determine exact uprightness*

Figurative of:
Destruction..........2Kin 21:13
God's judgment..........Amos 7:7, 8
God's building..........Zech 4:10

PLUMMET—*same as plumbline*
and the *p* of the house..........2Kin 21:13
righteousness to the *p*..........Is 28:17
shall see the *p* in the..........Zech 4:10

PLUNGE—*to cause to enter quickly into something*
yet shalt thou *p* me in the..........Job 9:31

POCHERETH (pŏk-ĕ-rĕth)—*"binding"*
Descendants of, among Solomon's servants..........Ezra 2:57; Neh 7:59

POETRY, HEBREW

Classified according to form:
Synonymous—repetition of same thoughts..........Ps 19:2
Progressive—advance of thought in second line..........Job 3:17
Synthetic—second line adds something new..........Ps 104:19
Climactic—the thought climbs to a climax..........Ps 121:3, 4
Antithetic—the second line contrasted with first..........Prov 14:1
Comparative—the "as" compared with the "so"..........Prov 10:26
Acrostic—alphabetic..........Ps 119:1-176

Classified according to function:
Didactic (teaching)..........Deut 32:1-43
Book of Job
Lyrics..........Ex 15:1-19
Judg 5:1-31
Elegies..........2Sam 1:17-27
Psalms..........Book of Psalms

POETS—*those who write poetry*
also of your own *p* have..........Acts 17:28

POINT—*to indicate position or direction; place; location; time; tip of something*

[*also* POINTED, POINTS]
I am at the *p* to die..........Gen 25:32
ye shall *p* out for you..........Num 34:7
mount Hor ye shall *p*..........Num 34:8
ye shall *p* out your east..........Num 34:10
sharp *p* things upon the..........Job 41:30
in all *p* as he came, so..........Eccl 5:16
with the *p* of a diamond..........Jer 17:1
have set the *p* of the..........Ezek 21:15
daughter lieth at the *p* of..........Mark 5:23
son: for he was at the *p*..........John 4:47
was in all *p* tempted like..........Heb 4:15

POISON—*a substance that kills, injures, or impairs*
Reptiles..........Deut 32:24
Dragons..........Deut 32:33
Adders..........Ps 140:3
Gourd..........2Kin 4:39
Hemlock..........Hos 10:4
Waters..........Jer 8:14
Asps..........Rom 3:13
Job 20:16

p whereof drinketh up my..........Job 6:4
Their *p* is like the *p* of a..........Ps 58:4
evil, full of deadly *p*..........James 3:8

POLE—*a tall, slender shaft*
and set it upon a *p*..........Num 21:8
and put it upon a *p*..........Num 21:9

POLICY—*a method or course of action*
through his *p* also he shall..........Dan 8:25

POLISHED—*shined*

[*also* POLISHING]
p after the similitude of..........Ps 144:12
hid me, and made me a *p*..........Is 49:2
rubies, their *p* was of..........Lam 4:7
feet like in color to *p*..........Dan 10:6

POLITENESS—*refined manners*

Manifested by:
Kings..........Gen 47:2-11
Hebrews..........Gen 43:26-29
Romans..........Acts 27:3
Pagans..........Acts 28:1, 2
Christians..........Philem 8-21

Counterfeited by:
Trickery..........2Sam 20:9, 10
Deceit..........2Sam 15:1-6
Hypocrisy..........Matt 22:7, 8
Pride..........Luke 14:8-10
Snobbery..........James 2:1-4
Selfishness..........3John 9, 10
See COURTESY

POLITICIANS—*government officials*

Evils manifested by:
Ambition..........2Sam 15:1-6
Flattery..........Dan 6:4-15
Indifference..........Acts 18:12-16
Avarice..........Acts 24:26

Good manifested by:
Provision..........Gen 41:33-49
Protection..........Neh 2:7-11
Piety..........2Chr 34:1-33
Prayer..........2Chr 20:6-12
Praise..........2Chr 20:27-29

POLL—*a counting of votes; to cut the hairy part of the head*

Descriptive of a person:
In a military census..........Num 1:2, 18, 20; Num 3:47

P

Descriptive of cutting off the hair:
Absalom ... 2Sam 14:26
Priests ... Ezek 44:20
Mourning (figurative) ... Mic 1:16

[*also* POLLS]
their number by their **p** ... 1Chr 23:3
of names by their **p** ... 1Chr 23:24

POLLUTE—*to defile*

Described as something unclean:
Morally ... Num 35:33, 34
Spiritually ... Acts 15:20

Means of:
Blood ... Ps 106:38
Idolatry ... Ezek 20:30, 31
Abominations ... Jer 7:30
Unregenerate service ... Ezek 44:7
Wickedness ... Jer 3:1, 2
Contempt of the Lord ... Mal 1:7, 12
Captivity ... Is 47:6
See UNCLEAN

[*also* POLLUTED, POLLUTING, POLLUTION, POLLUTIONS]
upon it, thou hast **p** ... Ex 20:25
neither shall ye **p** the holy ... Num 18:32
the altar, and **p** it ... 2Kin 23:16
p the house of the Lord ... 2Chr 36:14
as **p**, put from the ... Ezra 2:62
as **p**, put from the ... Neh 7:64
should my name be **p**? ... Is 48:11
the sabbath from **p** it ... Is 56:2
thou say, I am not **p** ... Jer 2:23
But ye turned and **p** my ... Jer 34:16
he hath **p** the kingdom ... Lam 2:2
have **p** themselves with ... Lam 4:14
soul hath not been **p**; for ... Ezek 4:14
spoil; and they shall **p** it ... Ezek 7:21
And will ye **p** me among ... Ezek 13:19
neither be **p** any more ... Ezek 14:11
saw thee **p** in thine own ... Ezek 16:6
and wast **p** in thy blood ... Ezek 16:22
should not be **p** before ... Ezek 20:9
sabbaths they greatly **p** ... Ezek 20:13
should not be **p** before ... Ezek 20:14
my statutes, but **p** my ... Ezek 20:16
they **p** my sabbaths: then ... Ezek 20:21
be **p** in the sight of the ... Ezek 20:22
had **p** my sabbaths, and ... Ezek 20:24
I **p** them in their own ... Ezek 20:26
Are ye **p** after the manner ... Ezek 20:30
ye **p** yourselves with all ... Ezek 20:31
was set apart for **p** ... Ezek 22:10
she was **p** with them ... Ezek 23:17
because thou art **p** with ... Ezek 23:30
wherewith they had **p** ... Ezek 36:18
I will not let them **p** my ... Ezek 39:7
shall **p** the sanctuary of ... Dan 11:31
iniquity, and is **p** with blood ... Hos 6:8
and thou shalt die in a **p** ... Amos 7:17
because it is **p**, it shall ... Mic 2:10
that is filthy and **p** ... Zeph 3:1
hath **p** this holy place ... Acts 21:28
have escaped the **p** of the ... 2Pet 2:20

POLLUX (pŏl'ŭks)—*part of the constellation Gemini*
was Castor and **P** ... Acts 28:11

POLYGAMY—*having more than one wife*

Caused by:
Barrenness of first wife ... Gen 16:1-6
Desire for large family ... Judg 8:30
Political ties with other countries ... 1Kin 3:1, 2
Sexual desire ... 2Chr 11:23
Slavery ... Gen 16:1, 3

Contrary to:
God's original Law ... Gen 2:24
Ideal picture of marriage ... Ps 128:1-6
God's commandment ... Ex 20:14
God's equal distribution of the sexes ... Gen 1:27; 1Cor 7:2
Relationship between Christ and the Church ... Eph 5:22-33

Productive of:
Dissension ... Gen 16:1
Discord ... 1Sam 1:6
Degeneracy ... 1Kin 11:1-4
See ADULTERY; FAMILY; FORNICATION; MARRIAGE

POMEGRANATE—*a small tree-bearing an apple-shaped fruit*
Grown in Canaan ... Num 13:23

Ornaments of:
Worn by priests ... Ex 28:33
In Temple ... 1Kin 7:18
Sign of fruitfulness ... Hag 2:19
Used figuratively ... Song 4:3

[*also* POMEGRANATES]
p, a golden bell and a **p** ... Ex 28:34
hems of the robe **p** ... Ex 39:24
the bells between the **p** ... Ex 39:25
about between the **p** ... Ex 39:25
a **p**, a bell and a **p** ... Ex 39:26
or of vines, or of **p** ... Num 20:5
and fig trees, and **p** ... Deut 8:8
under a **p** tree which is in ... 1Sam 14:2
upon the two pillars had **p** ... 1Kin 7:20
p were two hundred ... 1Kin 7:20
And four hundred **p** for the ... 1Kin 7:42
two rows of **p** for one ... 1Kin 7:42
p upon the chapiter ... 2Kin 25:17
and made a hundred **p** ... 2Chr 3:16
hundred **p** on the two ... 2Chr 4:13
two rows of **p** on each ... 2Chr 4:13
are an orchard of **p** ... Song 4:13
As a piece of a **p** are thy ... Song 6:7
vine flourished, and the **p** ... Song 6:11
grape appear, and the **p** ... Song 7:12
of the juice of my **p** ... Song 8:2
p upon the chapiters ... Jer 52:22
and the **p** were like unto ... Jer 52:22
were ninety and six **p** on ... Jer 52:23
and all the **p** upon the ... Jer 52:23
the **p** tree, the palm tree ... Joel 1:12

POMMEL—*round; a bowl*
Round ornament ... 2Chr 4:12, 13
Same as "bowl" ... 1Kin 7:41, 42

POMP—*ostentatious display; splendor; vainglory*
multitude, and their **p** ... Is 5:14
Thy **p** is brought down ... Is 14:11
make the **p** of the strong ... Ezek 7:24
the **p** of her strength ... Ezek 30:18
they shall spoil the **p** of ... Ezek 32:12
the **p** of her strength ... Ezek 33:28
Bernice, with great **p** ... Acts 25:23

PONDER—*to think about, especially quietly, soberly, and deeply*

[*also* PONDERED, PONDERETH]
P the path of thy feet ... Prov 4:26
thou shouldest **p** the path ... Prov 5:6
the Lord, and he **p** all his ... Prov 5:21
eyes: but the Lord **p** the ... Prov 21:2
not he that **p** the heart ... Prov 24:12
things, and **p** them in her ... Luke 2:19

POND—*a reservoir of water*

[*also* PONDS]
rivers, and upon their **p** ... Ex 7:19
the rivers, and over the **p** ... Ex 8:5
make sluices and **p** for fish ... Is 19:10

PONTIUS PILATE—*See* PILATE

PONTUS (pŏn'tŭs)—*"the sea"—a coastal strip of north Asia Minor*
Jews from, at Pentecost ... Acts 2:5, 9
Home of Aquila and Priscilla ... Acts 18:2
Christians of, addressed by Peter ... 1Pet 1:1

POOL—*a reservoir of water*

Used for:
Washing ... 1Kin 22:38
Water supply ... 2Kin 20:20
Irrigation ... Eccl 2:6
Healing ... John 5:2-7

Famous ones:
Gibeon ... 2Sam 2:13
Hebron ... 2Sam 4:12
Samaria ... 1Kin 22:38
Bethesda ... John 5:2
Siloam ... John 9:7
The upper ... Is 7:3
The lower ... Is 22:9, 11
The King's ... Neh 2:14

[*also* POOLS]
and upon all their **p** of ... Ex 7:19
conduit of the upper **p** ... 2Kin 18:17
p of Siloah by the king's ... Neh 3:15
and to the **p** that was ... Neh 3:16
rain also filleth the **p** ... Ps 84:6
for the bittern, and **p** of ... Is 14:23
ground shall become a **p** ... Is 35:7
conduit of the upper **p** ... Is 36:2
make the wilderness a **p** ... Is 41:18
I will dry up the **p** ... Is 42:15
Nineveh is..like a **p** of ... Nah 2:8
Go to the **p** of Siloam ... John 9:11

POOR—*needy; lacking material possessions*

Descriptive of:
Needy ... Luke 21:2
Lower classes ... 2Kin 24:14
Rebellious ... Jer 5:3, 4
Holy remnant ... Zeph 3:12-14

Causes of:
God's sovereignty ... 1Sam 2:7
Sloth ... Prov 6:10, 11
Lack of industry ... Prov 24:30-34
Love of pleasure ... Prov 21:17
Stubbornness ... Prov 13:18
Empty pursuits ... Prov 28:19
Drunkenness ... Prov 23:21

Wrong treatment of:
Reproaches God ... Prov 14:31
Brings punishment ... Prov 21:13
Brings poverty ... Prov 22:16
Regarded by God ... Eccl 5:8
Judged by God ... Is 3:13-15

Legislation designed for protection of:
Daily payment of wages ... Lev 19:13
Sharing of tithes with ... Deut 14:28, 29
Loans to, without interest ... Lev 25:35, 37
Right to glean ... Lev 19:9, 10
Land of, restored in jubilee year ... Lev 25:25-30
Equal participation in feasts ... Lev 16:11, 14
Permanent bondage of, forbidden ... Deut 15:12-15
See NEEDY; POVERTY, SPIRITUAL

[*also* POORER]
p and very ill-favored ... Gen 41:19
any of my people that is **p** ... Ex 22:25
thou countenance a **p** man ... Ex 23:3
the judgment of thy **p** ... Ex 23:6
that the **p** of thy people ... Ex 23:11
more, and the **p** shall not ... Ex 30:15
if he be **p**, and cannot get ... Lev 14:21
the person of the **p** ... Lev 19:15
leave them unto the **p** ... Lev 23:22
by thee be waxen **p** ... Lev 25:39
dwelleth by him wax **p** ... Lev 25:47
if he be **p** than thy ... Lev 27:8
there shall be no **p** among ... Deut 15:4
If there be among you a **p** ... Deut 15:7
thine hand from thy **p** ... Deut 15:7
p shall never cease out of ... Deut 15:11
And if the man be **p**, thou ... Deut 24:12
he is **p**, and setteth his ... Deut 24:15
family is **p** in Manasseh ... Judg 6:15
not young men, whether **p** ... Ruth 3:10
seeing that I am a **p** man ... 1Sam 18:23
one rich, and the other **p** ... 2Sam 12:1
took the **p** man's lamb ... 2Sam 12:4
p of the land to be ... 2Kin 25:12
and gifts to the **p** ... Esth 9:22

he saveth the *p* from the ......Job 5:15
seek to please the *p* ....Job 20:10
p of the earth hide ....Job 24:4
the light killeth the *p* ....Job 24:14
I delivered the *p* that ....Job 29:12
soul grieved for the *p*? ....Job 30:25
withheld the *p* from their .....Job 31:16
the rich more than the *p*? .....Job 34:19
giveth right to the *p* ....Job 36:6
expectation of the *p* shall .....Ps 9:18
pride doth persecute the *p* ....Ps 10:2
wait to catch the *p* ....Ps 10:9
doth catch the *p* when he .....Ps 10:9
p committeth himself ....Ps 10:14
For the oppression of the *p* ...Ps 12:5
the counsel of the *p* ....Ps 14:6
This *p* man cried, and the .....Ps 34:6
deliverest the *p* from..........Ps 35:10
the *p* and the needy from .....Ps 35:10
bow, to cast down the *p* ......Ps 37:14
I am *p* and needy; yet ....Ps 40:17
that considereth the *p*..........Ps 41:1
low and high, rich and *p* ......Ps 49:2
thy goodness for the *p* ....Ps 68:10
But I am *p* and sorrowful .....Ps 69:29
I am *p* and needy: make ......Ps 70:5
and thy *p* with judgment ......Ps 72:2
p also, and him that hath .....Ps 72:12
congregation of thy *p* ....Ps 74:19
Defend the *p* and.............Ps 82:3
hear me: for I am *p* and ......Ps 86:1
Yet setteth he the *p* on ....Ps 107:41
persecuted the *p* and...........Ps 109:16
right hand of the *p* ....Ps 109:31
hath given to the *p* ....Ps 112:9
raiseth up the *p* out of ....Ps 113:7
I will satisfy her *p* with ....Ps 132:15
and the right of the *p* ....Ps 140:12
He becometh *p* that ....Prov 10:4
maketh himself *p* ....Prov 13:7
the tillage of the *p*............Prov 13:23
The *p* is hated even of his.....Prov 14:20
Whoso mocketh the *p*.........Prov 17:5
The *p* useth entreaties ....Prov 18:23
Better is the *p* that ....Prov 19:1
brethren of the *p* do hate .....Prov 19:7
and a *p* man is better ....Prov 19:22
The rich and *p* meet ....Prov 22:2
his bread to the *p* ....Prov 22:9
p, because he is *p* ....Prov 22:22
A *p* man that oppresseth ......Prov 28:3
Better is the *p* that ....Prov 28:6
but the *p* that hath ....Prov 28:11
that giveth unto the *p*.........Prov 28:27
the cause of the *p* ....Prov 29:7
faithfully judgeth the *p*........Prov 29:14
or lest I be *p*, and steal ....Prov 30:9
plead the cause of the *p*.......Prov 31:9
Better is a *p* and a wise ....Eccl 4:13
oppression of the *p* ....Eccl 5:8
what hath the *p*, that ....Eccl 6:8
was found in it a *p* wise.......Eccl 9:15
remembered that same *p* ......Eccl 9:15
the right from the *p* of my ....Is 10:2
shall he judge the *p* ....Is 11:4
first-born of the *p* shall ....Is 14:30
a strength to the *p*............Is 25:4
the feet of the *p*..............Is 26:6
the *p* among men shall ....Is 29:19
destroy the *p* with lying ....Is 32:7
When the *p* and needy ....Is 41:17
p that are cast out to thy.....Is 58:7
that is *p* and of a contrite .....Is 66:2
souls of the *p* innocents ......Jer 2:34
delivered the soul of the *p* ....Jer 20:13
judged the cause of the *p* .....Jer 22:16
guard left of the *p* of the......Jer 39:10
certain of the *p* of the ....Jer 52:15
the hand of the *p* and.........Ezek 16:49
Hath oppressed the *p* and .....Ezek 18:12
and have vexed the *p* and .....Ezek 22:29
silver, and the *p* for a pair ....Amos 2:6
which oppress the *p* ....Amos 4:1
treading is upon the *p* ....Amos 5:11
the *p* of the land to fail ....Amos 8:4
was as to devour the *p* ....Hab 3:14
stranger, nor the *p* ....Zech 7:10
even you, O *p* of the flock ....Zech 11:7
the *p* have the gospel ....Matt 11:5
hast, and give to the *p* ....Matt 19:21
and given to the *p* ....Matt 26:9
hast, and give to the *p* ....Mark 10:21
there came a certain *p* ....Mark 12:42
been given to the *p*...........Mark 14:5
the gospel to the *p* ....Luke 4:18
Blessed be ye *p*; for ....Luke 6:20
to the *p* the gospel is ....Luke 7:22
a feast, call the *p*.............Luke 14:13
distribute unto the *p* ....Luke 18:22
goods I give to the *p* ....Luke 19:8
and given to the *p*? ....John 12:5
p always ye have with you ....John 12:8
give something to the *p* ....John 13:29
p saints which are at ....Rom 15:26
all my goods to feed the *p* 1Cor 13:3
as *p*, yet making many 2Cor 6:10
your sakes he became *p* 2Cor 8:9
hath given to the *p* 2Cor 9:9
should remember the *p* ....Gal 2:10
in also a *p* man in vile ....James 2:2
not God chosen the *p* of ......James 2:5
miserable, and *p*, and ....Rev 3:17
great, rich and *p*, free ....Rev 13:16

POOR IN SPIRIT—*humble; self-effacing*
Promised blessing ....Matt 5:3

POPLAR TREE—*a fast-growing tree of the willow family*
Used in deception of
Laban ....Gen 30:37
Pagan rites among ....Hos 4:13
Probably same as
"willows" in ....Lev 23:40

POPULARITY—*the esteem in which one is held by others*
Obtained by:
Heroic exploits ....Judg 8:21, 22
Unusual wisdom 1Kin 4:29-34
Trickery 2Sam15:1-6
Outward display Matt6:2,5,16

POPULARITY OF JESUS
Factors producing His:
Teaching................Mark1:22,27
Healing.................Mark 5:20
Miracles ....John 12:9-19
Feeding the people ......John 6:15-27
Factors causing decline of His:
High ethical standards ...Mark 8:34-38
Foretells His death ......Matt 16:21-28

POPULATION—*the total inhabitants of a place*
Israel's, increased in
Egypt ....Ex 1:7, 8
Nineveh's, great ....Jon 4:11
Heaven's, vast ....Rev 7:9

[*also* POPULOUS]
great, mighty, and *p* ....Deut 26:5
Art thou better than *p* No ....Nah 3:8

PORATHA (pō-rā'thä)—*"favored"*
One of Haman's sons ....Esth 9:8

PORCH—*entrance; entrance room*
Central court of a house .Matt 26:71
Portico for pedestrians ...John 5:2
Roofed colonnade ....John 10:3
Court of the temple 1Kin 6:3, 6, 7

[*also* PORCHES]
forth through the *p* ....Judg 3:23
p before the temple of the 1Kin 6:3
he made a *p* of pillars 1Kin 7:6
and the *p* was before 1Kin 7:6
Then he made a *p* for the 1Kin 7:7
judge, even the *p* of 1Kin 7:7
court within the *p* 1Kin 7:8
wife, like unto this *p*..........1Kin 7:8
of lily work in the *p* 1Kin 7:19
the pattern of the *p*..........1Chr 28:11
p that was in the front of 2Chr 3:4
had built before the *p*.........2Chr 8:12
that was before the *p* of.......2Chr 15:8
up the doors of the *p* 2Chr 29:7
between the *p* and the ....Ezek 8:16
p of the gate within was.......Ezek 40:7
Then measured he the *p* ......Ezek 40:9
and the *p* of the gate was .....Ezek 40:9
in the *p* of the gate were ......Ezek 40:39
brought me to the *p* of the ....Ezek 40:48
each post of the *p* ....Ezek 40:48
temple, and the *p* of the ......Ezek 41:15
upon the face of the *p* ....Ezek 41:25
by the way of the *p*...........Ezek 44:3
by the way of the *p*...........Ezek 46:2
weep between the *p* and ......Joel 2:17
he went out into the *p* ....Mark 14:68
in the *p* that is called ....Acts 3:11
accord in Solomon's *p* ....Acts 5:12

PORCIUS FESTUS (pôr'shĭ-ŭs fĕs'tŭs)—*"swine-like"*—*successor to Felix*
Paul stands trial before ..Acts 25:1-22
See FESTUS
after two years *P* came........Acts 24:27

PORK—*swine's flesh*
Classified as unclean .....Lev 11:7, 8

PORT—*a harbor*
At Joppa ....Jon 1:3
Fair Havens.............Acts 27:8
Phoenix ....Acts 27:12
Syracuse ....Acts 28:12
Rhegium................Acts 28:13
Puteoli ....Acts 28:13
well, and to the dung *p* ....Neh 2:13

PORTER—*gatekeeper or doorkeeper*
Watchman of a city......2Sam 18:26
Watchman of a house....Mark 13:34
Shepherd's attendant.....John 10:3
Official of the temple 1Chr 23:5
Origin of, in Moses' time .1Chr 9:17-26
Belongs to Levites ....Neh 12:47
Duties of, designed by
David 1Chr 26:1-19
Office of, important 1Chr 9:26

[*also* PORTERS]
and called unto the *p* of.......2Kin 7:10
he called the *p*; and they 2Kin 7:11
and Jeiel, the *p* 1Chr 15:18
Hosah to be *p*...............1Chr 16:38
p also by their courses 2Chr 8:14
the Levites, shall be *p* of 2Chr 23:4
the *p* toward the east 2Chr 31:14
scribes, and officers, and *p* 2Chr 34:13
and the *p* waited at every 2Chr 35:15
children of the *p*; the ....Ezra 2:42
the singers, and the *p* ....Ezra 7:7
and of the *p*; Shallum ....Ezra 10:24
p and the singers and the .....Neh 7:1
the Levites, and the *p* ....Neh 7:73
the Levites, the *p*.............Neh 10:28
Moreover the *p*, Akkub ....Neh 11:19
were *p* keeping the ward ......Neh 12:25
the *p* kept the ward of ....Neh 12:45
the singers, and the *p* ....Neh 13:5

PORTICO—*porch*
Solomon's ....John 10:23
Of Bethesda ....John 5:2

PORTION—*a stipulated part; one's part or share of something*
Of things material:
Inheritance.............Gen 48:22
Of good things:
Spirit 2Kin 2:9
Lord ....Ps 119:57
Spiritual riches ....Is 61:7
Of evil things:
Things of the world......Ps 17:14
Fellowship with the
wicked ....Neh 2:20

P

Of things eternal:
Punishment of the wicked. Ps 11:6
See INHERITANCE

[*also* PORTIONS]
the *p*, of the men which .... Gen 14:24
let them take their *p* .... Gen 14:24
yet any *p* or inheritance .... Gen 31:14
priests had a *p* assigned .... Gen 47:22
did eat their *p* which .... Gen 47:22
unto them for their *p* .... Lev 6:17
is the *p* of the anointing .... Lev 7:35
thou shalt take one *p* of .... Num 31:30
Moses took one *p* of fifty .... Num 31:47
shall have like *p* to eat .... Deut 18:8
a double *p* of all that he .... Deut 21:17
For the Lord's *p* is his .... Deut 32:9
in a *p* of the lawgiver .... Deut 33:21
fell ten *p* to Manasseh .... Josh 17:5
but one lot and one *p* to .... Josh 17:14
of the *p* of the children of .... Josh 19:9
sons and her daughters, *p* 1Sam 1:4
Hannah he gave a worthy *p* 1Sam 1:5
Bring the *p* which I gave 1Sam 9:23
What *p* have we in David? 1Kin 12:16
eat Jezebel in the *p* of 2Kin 9:10
him in the *p* of the field 2Kin 9:25
face of the field in the *p* 2Kin 9:37
saying, What *p* have we 2Chr 10:16
For Ahaz took away a *p* 2Chr 28:21
also the king's *p* of his 2Chr 31:3
daily *p* for their service 2Chr 31:16
give *p* to all the males 2Chr 31:19
have no *p* on this side .... Ezra 4:16
and send *p* unto them .... Neh 8:10
certain *p* should be for .... Neh 11:23
p of the law for the priests .... Neh 12:44
porters, every day his *p* .... Neh 12:47
the *p* of the Levites had .... Neh 13:10
and of sending *p* one to .... Esth 9:19
the *p* of a wicked man .... Job 20:29
their *p* is cursed in the .... Job 24:18
but how little a *p* is heard .... Job 26:14
the *p* of a wicked man .... Job 27:13
what *p* of God is there .... Job 31:2
Lord is the *p* of mine .... Ps 16:5
sword; they shall be a *p* .... Ps 63:10
of my heart, and my *p* .... Ps 73:26
and my *p* in the land of .... Ps 142:5
and a *p* to her maidens .... Prov 31:15
this was my *p* of all my .... Eccl 2:10
works; for that is his *p* .... Eccl 3:22
him: for it is his *p* .... Eccl 5:18
they any more a *p* .... Eccl 9:6
Give a *p* to seven, and also .... Eccl 11:2
This is the *p* of them that .... Is 17:14
I divide him a *p* with .... Is 53:12
the stream is thy *p* .... Is 57:6
p of Jacob is not like them .... Jer 10:16
have trodden my *p* under .... Jer 12:10
pleasant *p* a desolate .... Jer 12:10
the *p* of thy measures .... Jer 13:25
The *p* of Jacob is not like .... Jer 51:19
day a *p* until the day of .... Jer 52:34
The Lord is my *p*, saith .... Lam 3:24
unto the Lord, a holy *p* .... Ezek 45:1
oblation of the holy *p* .... Ezek 45:6
And a *p* shall be for the .... Ezek 45:7
oblation of the holy *p* .... Ezek 45:7
oblation of the holy *p* .... Ezek 45:7
Joseph shall have two *p* .... Ezek 47:13
east and west, a *p* for .... Ezek 48:1
the west side, a *p* for .... Ezek 48:3
the west side, a *p* for .... Ezek 48:5
unto the west side, a *p* .... Ezek 48:7
oblation of the holy *p* .... Ezek 48:18
oblation of the holy *p* .... Ezek 48:18
over against the *p* for .... Ezek 48:21
Simeon shall have a *p* .... Ezek 48:24
west side, Zebulun a *p* .... Ezek 48:26
with the *p* of the king's .... Dan 1:8
did eat the *p* of the king's .... Dan 1:15
let his *p* be with the .... Dan 4:15
they that feed of the *p* .... Dan 11:26
devour them with their *p* .... Hos 5:7
hath changed the *p* of my .... Mic 2:4
by them their *p* is fat .... Hab 1:16
inherit Judah his *p* .... Zech 2:12
him his *p* with the .... Matt 24:51
their *p* of meat in due .... Luke 12:42
give me the *p* of goods .... Luke 15:12

PORTRAY—*to illustrate*

[*also* PORTRAYED]
p upon it the city, even .... Ezek 4:1
p upon the wall round .... Ezek 8:10
saw men *p* upon the wall .... Ezek 23:14
Chaldeans *p* with vermilion .... Ezek 23:14

POSITION—*place of influence*
Sought after by Pharisees . Matt 23:5-7
James and John request . . Mark 10:37
Seeking, denounced .... Luke 14:7-11
Diotrephes sought 3John 9

POSSESS—*to own; acquire*
Objects of:
Promised land .... Deut 4:1, 5
Ruins .... Is 14:21
Spiritual riches .... Is 57:13
Christ .... Prov 8:22
One's:
Soul .... Luke 21:19
Body of wife 1Thess 4:4
Sins .... Job 13:26
Of Canaan:
Promised .... Gen 17:8
Under oath .... Neh 9:15
Israel challenged to .... Num 13:20

[*also* POSSESSED, POSSESSEST, POSSESSETH, POSSESSING, POSSESSION, POSSESSIONS]
shall *p* the gate of his .... Gen 22:17
me a *p* of a burying place .... Gen 23:4
Unto Abraham for a *p* in .... Gen 23:18
let thy seed *p* the gate of .... Gen 24:60
had *p* of flocks, and *p* of .... Gen 26:14
therein, and get you *p* .... Gen 34:10
in the land of their *p* .... Gen 36:43
them a *p* in the land of .... Gen 47:11
and they had *p* therein .... Gen 47:27
for an everlasting *p* .... Gen 48:4
Hittite for a *p* of a .... Gen 49:30
the field for a *p* of a .... Gen 50:13
I give to you for a *p* .... Lev 14:34
of the land of your *p* .... Lev 14:34
give it unto you to *p* it .... Lev 20:24
every man unto his *p* .... Lev 25:10
all the land of your *p* ye .... Lev 25:24
he may return unto his *p* .... Lev 25:27
of the cities of their *p* .... Lev 25:32
city of his *p*, shall go .... Lev 25:33
p among the children of Israel . Lev 25:33
unto the *p* of his fathers .... Lev 25:41
inherit them for a *p* .... Lev 25:46
part of a field of his *p* .... Lev 27:16
of the fields of his *p* .... Lev 27:22
his *p* shall be sold or .... Lev 27:28
Let us go up at once, and *p* .... Num 13:30
his seed shall *p* it .... Num 14:24
p his land from Arnon .... Num 21:24
And Edom shall be a *p* .... Num 24:18
Seir also shall be a *p* .... Num 24:18
the lot shall the *p* .... Num 26:56
Give unto us therefore a *p* .... Num 27:4
family, and he shall *p* .... Num 27:11
thy servants for a *p* .... Num 32:5
land of Gilead for a *p* .... Num 32:29
have *p* among you in the .... Num 32:30
given you the land to *p* .... Num 33:53
the inheritance of their *p* .... Num 35:2
into the land of his *p* .... Num 35:28
daughter, that *p* an .... Num 36:8
p the land which the Lord .... Deut 1:8
give it, and they shall *p* .... Deut 1:39
unto Esau for a *p* .... Deut 2:5
of their land for a *p* .... Deut 2:9
children of Lot for a *p* .... Deut 2:9
children of Ammon any *p* .... Deut 2:19
children of Lot for a *p* .... Deut 2:19
begin to *p* it, and contend .... Deut 2:24
this land which we *p* at .... Deut 3:12
given you this land to *p* .... Deut 3:18
every man unto his *p* .... Deut 3:20
whither ye go over to *p* .... Deut 4:14
ye go over Jordan to *p* it .... Deut 4:26
they *p* his land, and the .... Deut 4:47
which I give them to *p* .... Deut 5:31
land whither ye go to *p* .... Deut 6:1
whither thou goest to *p* .... Deut 7:1
and go in and *p* the land .... Deut 8:1
p nations greater and .... Deut 9:1
heart, dost thou go to *p* .... Deut 9:5
and *p* the land which I .... Deut 9:23
they may go in and *p* the .... Deut 10:11
be strong, and go in and *p* .... Deut 11:8
land, whither ye go to *p* it .... Deut 11:8
whither ye go to *p* it .... Deut 11:11
whither thou goest to *p* .... Deut 11:29
over Jordan to go in to *p* .... Deut 11:31
you, and ye shall *p* it .... Deut 11:31
fathers giveth thee to *p* .... Deut 12:1
whither thou goest to *p* .... Deut 12:29
for an inheritance to *p* .... Deut 15:4
shalt *p* it, and shalt dwell .... Deut 17:14
which thou shalt *p* .... Deut 18:14
giveth thee to *p* it .... Deut 19:2
giveth thee to *p* it .... Deut 21:1
whither thou goest to *p* it .... Deut 23:20
an inheritance to *p* it .... Deut 25:19
and *p* it, and dwellest .... Deut 26:1
whither thou goest to *p* it .... Deut 28:21
which thy fathers *p* .... Deut 30:5
and thou shalt *p* it .... Deut 30:5
Jordan to go to *p* .... Deut 30:18
and thou shalt *p* .... Deut 31:3
go over Jordan to *p* .... Deut 32:47
of Israel for a *p* .... Deut 32:49
p thou the west and the .... Deut 33:23
this Jordan, to go in to *p* .... Josh 1:11
they also have *p* the land .... Josh 1:15
the land of your *p* .... Josh 1:15
p their land on the other .... Josh 12:1
gave it for a *p* unto the .... Josh 12:6
very much land to be *p* .... Josh 13:1
this was the *p* of the half .... Josh 13:29
long are ye slack to go to *p* .... Josh 18:3
edge of the sword, and *p* .... Josh 19:47
son of Jephunneh for his *p* .... Josh 21:12
and they *p* it, and dwelt .... Josh 21:43
unto the land of your *p* .... Josh 22:4
to the land of their *p* .... Josh 22:9
whereof they were *p* .... Josh 22:9
if the land of your *p* be .... Josh 22:19
ye shall *p* their land, as .... Josh 23:5
mount Seir, to *p* it .... Josh 24:4
unto his inheritance to *p* .... Judg 2:6
and *p* the city of palm trees .... Judg 3:13
p all the land of the .... Judg 11:21
p all the coasts of the .... Judg 11:22
and shouldest thou *p* .... Judg 11:23
Wilt not thou *p* that which .... Judg 11:24
us, them will we *p* .... Judg 11:24
to go, and to enter to *p* .... Judg 18:9
Maon, whose *p* were in 1Sam 25:2
p of the vineyard of 1Kin 21:15
is gone down to *p* 1Kin 21:18
and also taken *p* 1Kin 21:19
p Samaria, and dwelt in 2Kin 17:24
their *p* and habitations 1Chr 7:28
that dwelt in their *p* in 1Chr 9:2
p of the king, and of his 1Chr 28:1
that ye may *p* this good 1Chr 28:8
their suburbs and their *p* 2Chr 11:14
to cast us out of thy *p* 2Chr 20:11
every man to his *p*, into 2Chr 31:1
cities, and *p* of flocks and 2Chr 32:29
unto which ye go to *p* .... Ezra 9:11
so they *p* the land of .... Neh 9:22
p houses full of all goods .... Neh 9:25
every one in his *p* in their .... Neh 11:3
I made to *p* months of .... Job 7:3
the earth for thy *p* .... Ps 2:8
got not the land in *p* .... Ps 44:3
there, and have it in *p* .... Ps 69:35
houses of God in *p* .... Ps 83:12

For thou hast *p* my reins ......Ps 139:13
good things in *p* ....Prov 28:10
great *p* of great and ....Eccl 2:7
house of Israel shall *p* ....Is 14:2
also make it a *p* for ....Is 14:23
and the bittern shall *p* it ......Is 34:11
his trust in me shall *p*.........Is 57:13
their land they shall *p*.........Is 61:7
thy holiness have *p* ....Is 63:18
and they shall *p* it ....Jer 30:3
shall be *p* again in this ....Jer 32:15
and they shall *p* their ....Ezek 7:24
is this land given in *p* ....Ezek 11:15
men of the east for a *p* ....Ezek 25:4
shall ye *p* the land? ....Ezek 33:25
mine, and we will *p* ....Ezek 35:10
places are ours in *p* ....Ezek 36:2
might be a *p* unto the ....Ezek 36:3
and they shall *p* thee ....Ezek 36:12
p in Israel: I am their *p* ....Ezek 44:28
for a *p* for twenty ....Ezek 45:5
and of the *p* of the city ....Ezek 45:7
before the *p* of the city ....Ezek 45:7
it shall be their *p* by ....Ezek 46:16
thrust them out of their *p* .....Ezek 46:18
inheritance out of his own *p* ...Ezek 46:18
every man from his *p* ....Ezek 46:18
with the *p* of the city ....Ezek 48:20
from the *p* of the Levites .....Ezek 48:22
and from the *p* of the city .....Ezek 48:22
p the kingdom for ever ....Dan 7:18
saints *p* the kingdom...........Dan 7:22
silver, nettles shall *p* ....Hos 9:6
to *p* the land of the...........Amos 2:10
they may *p* the remnant ....Amos 9:12
of Jacob shall *p* their ....Obad 17
south shall *p* the mount ....Obad 19
they shall *p* the fields of ......Obad 19
and Benjamin shall *p* ....Obad 19
shall *p* that of the ....Obad 20
shall *p* the cities of the.........Obad 20
p the dwelling places that .....Hab 1:6
my people shall *p*.............Zeph 2:9
this people to *p* all these ......Zech 8:12
them that were *p* with ....Mark 1:32
see him that was *p* with ....Mark 5:15
had been *p* with the devil .....Mark 5:18
for he had great *p* ....Mark 10:22
was *p* of the devils was ....Luke 8:36
the things which he *p* ....Luke 12:15
give tithes of all that I *p* ......Luke 18:12
sold their *p* and goods ....Acts 2:45
of the things which he *p* ......Acts 4:32
Sapphira his wife, sold a *p* ....Acts 5:1
give it to him for a *p* ....Acts 7:5
of many that were *p* with them.Acts 8:7
damsel *p* with a spirit of ......Acts 16:16
quarters were *p* of the ....Acts 28:7
buy, as though they *p* not 1Cor 7:30
redemption of the purchased *p* .Eph 1:14

POSSESSOR—*owner; claimant*
[*also* POSSESSORS]

high God, *p* of heaven ....Gen 14:19
Whose *p* slay them, and ......Zech 11:5
p of lands or houses sold......Acts 4:34

POSSIBLE—*that which can exist or happen*

Things possible:
All, with God ....Matt 19:26
All, to the believer ......Mark 9:23
Peaceful living ....Gal 4:15

Things impossible:
Deception of the saints ..Matt 24:24
Removal of the Cross....Matt 26:39
Christ's remaining in the grave ....Acts 2:24
Removal of sins by animal sacrifice........Heb 10:4

with God all things are *p*......Mark 10:27
seduce, if it were *p*, even .....Mark 13:22
if it were *p*, the hour ....Mark 14:35
with men are *p* with God .....Luke 18:27
it were *p* for him, to be at ....Acts 20:16
if it were *p*, to thrust in........Acts 27:39
If it be *p*, as much as lieth ....Rom 12:18

POST—*pillar; column*
Private homes ....Ex 12:7
Tabernacle 1Sam 1:9
Temple 1Kin 6:31, 33

[*also* POSTS]

and on the two side *p*.........Ex 12:23
door, or unto the door *p*......Ex 21:6
write them upon the *p* ....Deut 6:9
write them upon the door *p* ...Deut 11:20
all the doors and *p* were 1Kin 7:5
beams, the *p*, and the walls ...2Chr 3:7
waiting at the *p* of my ....Prov 8:34
the *p* of the door moved ......Is 6:4
the doors also and the *p* ......Is 57:8
and the *p* thereof, two ....Ezek 40:9
made also *p* of threescore .....Ezek 40:14
the *p* of the court round ......Ezek 40:14
p thereof and the arches ......Ezek 40:21
on that side, upon the *p* ......Ezek 40:26
palm trees were upon the *p* ...Ezek 40:31
palm trees were upon the *p* ...Ezek 40:34
p thereof were toward the .....Ezek 40:37
palm trees were upon the *p* ...Ezek 40:37
and measured each *p* of.......Ezek 40:48
there were pillars by the *p* ....Ezek 40:49
measured the *p*, six cubits .....Ezek 41:1
and measured the *p* of the ....Ezek 41:3
The *p* of the temple were .....Ezek 41:21
and their *p* by my *p*, and the ..Ezek 43:8
and put it upon the *p* of ......Ezek 45:19
upon the *p* of the gate of .....Ezek 45:19
and shall stand by the *p*.......Ezek 46:2
the door, that the *p* may ......Amos 9:1

POSTERITY—*descendants*
to preserve you a *p* in the .....Gen 45:7
of your *p* shall be unclean .....Num 9:10
take away the *p* of Baasha 1Kin 16:3
will take away thy *p* 1Kin 21:21
yet their *p* approve their ......Ps 49:13
Let his *p* be cut off, and ......Ps 109:13
and not to his *p*, nor ....Dan 11:4
hooks, and your *p* with ....Amos 4:2

POSTHUMOUS—*after death*
Mary of Bethany ....Matt 26:13
Abel ....Heb 11:4
All believers ....Rev 14:13

POSTS—*runners; couriers; postmen*
Letters sent by 2Chr 30:6, 10
Sent on swift horses .....Esth 3:13, 15
Figurative of speed ......Job 9:25

POT—*a rounded, open-mouthed vessel*

Use of:
Cooking ....Zech 14:21
Refining ....Prov 17:3

Figurative of:
Egyptian slavery.........Ps 81:6
Sudden destruction ......Ps 58:9
Impending national destruction ....Jer 1:13
Merciless punishment ....Mic 3:2, 3
Complete sanctification ..Zech 14:20, 21

[*also* POTS]

when we sat by the flesh *p* ....Ex 16:3
Take a *p* and put an omer ....Ex 16:33
p, and the shovels, and ....Ex 38:3
be sodden in a brazen *p*.......Lev 6:28
it be oven, or ranges for *p* ....Lev 11:35
and he put the broth in a *p* ...Judg 6:19
kettle, or caldron or *p* 1Sam 2:14
the *p*, and the shovels 1Kin 7:45
in the house, save a *p* 2Kin 4:2
shred them into the *p* of 2Kin 4:39
And he cast it into the *p*......2Kin 4:41
there was no harm in the *p*....2Kin 4:41
the *p*, and the shovels 2Kin 25:14
And Huram made the *p* 2Chr 4:11
offerings sod they in *p* 2Chr 35:13
as out of a seething *p*.........Job 41:20
the deep to boil like a *p* ......Job 41:31
sea like a *p* of ointment ....Job 41:31
ye have lain among the *p* .....Ps 68:13
As the fining *p* for silver ......Prov 27:21
of thorns under a *p* ....Eccl 7:6
Rechabites *p* full of wine ......Jer 35:5
Set on a *p*, set it on ....Ezek 24:3
p, brazen vessels, and.........Mark 7:4
was the golden *p* that had .....Heb 9:4

POTENTATE—*a mighty one*
Christ the only absolute ..1Tim 6:15

POTIPHAR (pŏt'ĭ-fer)—*"belonging to the sun-god"*
High Egyptian officer ....Gen 39:1
Puts Joseph in jail ....Gen 39:20

POTI-PHERAH (pō-tĭf'er-ä)—*"given of the sun-god"*
Egyptian priest of On (Heliopolis) ....Gen 41:45-50
Father of Asenath, Joseph's wife ....Gen 46:20

POTSHERD—*a fragment of broken pottery*

Figurative of:
Weakness ....Ps 22:15
Leviathan's underparts ...Job 41:30

Uses of:
Scraping ....Job 2:8
Scooping water ....Is 30:14

[*also* POTSHERDS]

wicked heart are like a *p*......Prov 26:23
Let the *p* strive with the ......Is 45:9

POTSHERD GATE—*a gate of Jerusalem*
By valley of Ben-hinnom .Jer 19:2

POTTAGE—*a thick vegetable soup*
Price of Esau's birthright .Gen 25:29-34
Eaten by Elisha's disciples 2Kin 4:38-41
Ordinary food...........Hag 2:12

POTTER—*one who makes earthenware vessels*

Art of, involves:
Reducing clay to paste ...Is 41:25
Shaping by revolving wheel ....Jer 18:1-4
Molding by hands ....Jer 18:6

Figurative of:
Complete destruction ....Is 30:14
God's sovereignty over men ....Is 64:8
Israel's lack of understanding ....Is 29:16

[*also* POTTER'S, POTTERS]

These were the *p*, and 1Chr 4:23
in pieces like a *p* vessel ....Ps 2:9
get a *p* earthen bottle ....Jer 19:1
work of the hands of the *p* ....Lam 4:2
part of *p* clay, and part of.....Dan 2:41
Cast it unto the *p* ....Zech 11:13
cast them to the *p* in the ......Zech 11:13
not the *p* power over the......Rom 9:21
as the vessels of a *p* shall .....Rev 2:27

POTTER'S FIELD—*burial place for poor people*
Judas' money used for purchase of ....Matt 27:7, 8

POUND—*a Greek measure of weight (12 ounces)*
Used in parable ....Luke 19:12-27

three *p* of gold went to one ...1Kin 10:17
five thousand *p* of silver ......Ezra 2:69
two hundred *p* of silver ....Neh 7:71
p hath gained ten pounds .....Luke 19:16
p of ointment of spikenard ....John 12:3
about a hundred *p* weight .....John 19:39

POUR—*to flow freely from something; to cause to flow*

Applied to:
Rain from clouds ....Amos 9:6
Oil from vessels ....Gen 35:14

P

Blood from animals......Lev 8:15
Water from barrels......1Kin 18:33

Used figuratively of:
Christ's death..........Ps 22:14
Spirit's coming.........Joel 2:28, 29
Holy Spirit.............Ezek 39:29
God's:
Wrath...............2Chr 34:21, 25
Blessings...........Mal 3:10
Sovereignty.........Job 10:9, 10
Prayer and repentance...Lam 2:19
Extreme emotions.......1Sam 1:15

[also POURED, POUREDST, POUREST, POURETH, POURING]

pillar, and ***p*** oil upon the.....Gen 28:18
river, and ***p*** it upon the.......Ex 4:9
the rain was not ***p*** upon.......Ex 9:33
and ***p*** it upon his head........Ex 29:7
shall ye ***p*** drink offering.......Ex 30:9
flesh shall it not be ***p***........Ex 30:32
and he shall ***p*** oil upon it.....Lev 2:1
shall ***p*** all the blood of........Lev 4:7
where the ashes are ***p*** out.....Lev 4:12
shall ***p*** out his blood at.......Lev 4:25
shall ***p*** out all the blood.......Lev 4:34
And he ***p*** of the anointing.....Lev 8:12
p out the blood at the........Lev 9:9
p it into the palm of his.......Lev 14:15
priest shall ***p*** of the oil.......Lev 14:26
the anointing oil was ***p***........Lev 21:10
he shall ***p*** no oil upon it......Num 5:15
p the water out of his.........Num 24:7
strong wine to be ***p***...........Num 28:7
shall ***p*** it upon the earth......Deut 12:16
p out upon the altar of........Deut 12:27
shalt ***p*** it upon the ground.....Deut 15:23
this rock, and ***p*** out the.......Judg 6:20
water, and ***p*** it out before.....1Sam 7:6
vial of oil, and ***p*** it upon......1Sam 10:1
a pan, and ***p*** them out........2Sam 13:9
thereof, but ***p*** it out unto.....2Sam 23:16
are upon it shall be ***p***.........1Kin 13:3
p water on the hands of.......2Kin 3:11
p out into all those vessels....2Kin 4:4
vessels to her; and she ***p***......2Kin 4:5
P out for the people, that.....2Kin 4:41
he ***p*** the oil on his head.......2Kin 9:6
p his drink offering, and......2Kin 16:13
drink of it, but ***p*** it out.......1Chr 11:18
my wrath shall not be ***p***.......2Chr 12:7
roarings are ***p*** out like........Job 3:24
He ***p*** contempt upon..........Job 12:21
p out my gall upon the........Job 16:13
mine eye ***p*** out tears unto.....Job 16:20
the rock ***p*** me out rivers.......Job 29:6
now my soul is ***p*** out upon....Job 30:16
they ***p*** down rain according....Job 36:27
things, I ***p*** out my soul........Ps 42:4
grace is ***p*** into thy lips........Ps 45:2
p out your heart before........Ps 62:8
P out thine indignation........Ps 69:24
p out of the same; but the....Ps 75:8
The clouds ***p*** out water.......Ps 77:17
P out thy wrath upon the.....Ps 79:6
He ***p*** contempt upon..........Ps 107:40
p out my complaint before....Ps 142:2
I will ***p*** out my spirit..........Prov 1:23
mouth of fools ***p*** out..........Prov 15:2
thy name is as ointment ***p*****.....Song 1:3
they ***p*** out a prayer when.....Is 26:16
hath ***p*** out upon you the......Is 29:10
spirit be ***p*** upon us from......Is 32:15
p upon him the fury of........Is 42:25
p water upon him that is......Is 44:3
I will ***p*** my spirit upon........Is 44:3
the skies ***p*** down.............Is 45:8
hath ***p*** out his soul unto.......Is 53:12
hast thou ***p*** a drink...........Is 57:6
p it out upon the children.....Jer 6:11
to ***p*** out drink offerings.......Jer 7:18
my fury shall be ***p*** out........Jer 7:20
P out thy fury upon the.......Jer 10:25
will ***p*** their wickedness........Jer 14:16
p out their blood by the.......Jer 18:21
p out drink offerings..........Jer 19:13
p out drink offerings..........Jer 32:29
and my fury hath been ***p***......Jer 42:18
so shall my fury be ***p***.........Jer 42:18
and mine anger was ***p***.........Jer 44:6
p out drink offerings..........Jer 44:17
he ***p*** out his fury like.........Lam 2:4
p out into their mothers'......Lam 2:12
p out in the top of every......Lam 4:1
I shortly ***p*** out my fury........Ezek 7:8
p out of thy fury upon........Ezek 9:8
and ***p*** out my fury upon it.....Ezek 14:19
p out thy fornications on......Ezek 16:15
thy filthiness was ***p*** out.......Ezek 16:36
I will ***p*** out my fury..........Ezek 20:8
I would ***p*** out my fury........Ezek 20:21
p out there their drink........Ezek 20:28
and with fury ***p*** out...........Ezek 20:34
p out mine indignation........Ezek 21:31
Lord have ***p*** out my fury......Ezek 22:22
and ***p*** their whoredom..........Ezek 23:8
set it on, and also ***p*** water....Ezek 24:3
she ***p*** it not upon the.........Ezek 24:7
And I will ***p*** my fury upon....Ezek 30:15
Wherefore I ***p*** my fury........Ezek 36:18
p out my spirit upon the......Ezek 39:29
p out my wrath upon..........Hos 5:10
p them out upon the face.....Amos 5:8
waters that are ***p*** down........Mic 1:4
I will ***p*** down the stones.......Mic 1:6
his fury is ***p*** out like fire......Nah 1:6
blood shall be ***p*** out as.......Zeph 1:17
to ***p*** upon them mine..........Zeph 3:8
I will ***p*** upon the house.......Zech 12:10
ointment, and ***p*** it on his.......Matt 26:7
the box, and ***p*** it on his.......Mark 14:3
p in oil and wine, and set.....Luke 10:34
and ***p*** out the changers'.......John 2:15
After that he ***p*** water into.....John 13:5
p out of my Spirit upon........Acts 2:17
p out in those days of.........Acts 2:18
p out the gift of the Holy.....Acts 10:45
p out the vials of the.........Rev 16:1
p out his vial upon the........Rev 16:2
p out his vial upon the........Rev 16:4
angel ***p*** out his vial upon......Rev 16:10
angel ***p*** out his vial into.......Rev 16:17

POURTRAY—*See* PORTRAY

POVERTY—*lacking material or spiritual well-being*

that thou hast, come to ***p*****.....Gen 45:11
lest thou come to ***p***...........Prov 20:13
give me neither ***p*** nor.........Prov 30:8
drink and forget his ***p***.........Prov 31:7
deep ***p*** abounded unto the.....2Cor 8:2

POVERTY, SPIRITUAL—*a condition that can describe either humility or immaturity before God*

In a bad sense, of spiritual:
Decay.................Rev 2:9
Immaturity.............1Cor 3:1-3

Used in a good sense, of:
The contrite...........Is 66:2
God's people...........Is 14:32

Caused by:
Hastiness..............Prov 21:5
Greed.................Prov 22:16
Laziness...............Prov 24:30-34

POWDER—*finely-ground particles*

[*also* POWDERS]

and ground it to ***p***............Ex 32:20
the rain of thy land ***p***.........Deut 28:24
and stamped it small to ***p*****.....2Kin 23:6
the ***p*** thereof upon the........2Kin 23:6
graven images into ***p***..........2Chr 34:7
all ***p*** of the merchant?.........Song 3:6
it will grind him to ***p***..........Matt 21:44
it will grind him to ***p***..........Luke 20:18

POWER—*having authority, control, or influence*

[*also* POWERFUL, POWERS]

with all my ***p*** I have..........Gen 31:6
prince hast ***p*** with God........Gen 32:28
the excellency of ***p***...........Gen 49:3
to show in thee my ***p***.........Ex 9:16
is become glorious in ***p***.......Ex 15:6
he shall have no ***p***............Ex 21:8
Egypt with great ***p***............Ex 32:11
the pride of your ***p***...........Lev 26:19
let the ***p*** of my lord be........Num 14:17
now any ***p*** at all to say........Num 22:38
with his mighty ***p*** out of.......Deut 4:37
My ***p***, and the might of.......Deut 8:17
by thy mighty ***p***..............Deut 9:29
he seeth that their ***p*** is........Deut 32:36
p to flee this way or that......Josh 8:20
people, and hast great ***p*****......Josh 17:17
a mighty man of ***p***............1Sam 9:1
until they had no more ***p***......1Sam 30:4
God is my strength and ***p*****.....2Sam 22:33
Egypt with great ***p***...........2Kin 17:36
were of small ***p***..............2Kin 19:26
Joab led forth the ***p*** of the....1Chr 20:1
and the ***p***, and the glory......1Chr 29:11
them that have no ***p***..........2Chr 14:11
thine hand is there not ***p***......2Chr 20:6
no ***p*** to keep still the.........2Chr 22:9
God hath ***p*** to help, and......2Chr 25:8
war with mighty ***p***............2Chr 26:13
Lachish, and all his ***p*** with...2Chr 32:9
them to cease by force and ***p***..Ezra 4:23
his ***p*** and his wrath is.........Ezra 8:22
redeemed by thy great ***p*****......Neh 1:10
is it in our ***p*** to redeem........Neh 5:5
p of Persia and Media..........Esth 1:3
p of the people and...........Esth 8:11
Jews hoped to have ***p***.........Esth 9:1
the acts of his ***p*** and of.......Esth 10:2
that he hath is in thy ***p*****......Job 1:12
in war from the ***p*** of the......Job 5:20
old, yea, are mighty in ***p***?.....Job 21:7
me with his great ***p***?..........Job 23:6
also the mighty with his ***p*****....Job 24:22
helped him that is without ***p***?..Job 26:2
but the thunder of his ***p***......Job 26:14
God exalteth by his ***p***.........Job 36:22
he is excellent in ***p***, and......Job 37:23
conceal his parts nor his ***p***.....Job 41:12
my darling from the ***p*** of......Ps 22:20
voice of the Lord is ***p***.........Ps 29:4
seen the wicked in great ***p*****....Ps 37:35
my soul from the ***p*** of........Ps 49:15
scatter them by thy ***p***.........Ps 59:11
this; that ***p*** belongeth.........Ps 62:11
see thy ***p*** and thy glory.......Ps 63:2
mountains; being girded with ***p***.Ps 65:6
the greatness of thy ***p***.........Ps 66:3
giveth strength and ***p***.........Ps 68:35
thy ***p*** to every one that is......Ps 71:18
by his ***p*** he brought in.........Ps 78:26
to the greatness of thy ***p***......Ps 79:11
knoweth the ***p*** of thine........Ps 90:11
make his mighty ***p*** to be.......Ps 106:8
willing in the day of thy ***p*****....Ps 110:3
his people the ***p*** of his........Ps 111:6
our Lord, and of great ***p*****......Ps 147:5
firmament of his ***p***............Ps 150:1
it is in the ***p*** of thine hand....Prov 3:27
and life are in the ***p*** of the....Prov 18:21
their oppressors there was ***p***...Eccl 4:1
hath given him ***p*** to eat.......Eccl 5:19
God giveth him not ***p*** to.......Eccl 6:2
word of a king is there is ***p***....Eccl 8:4
no man that hath ***p*** over......Eccl 8:8
hath he ***p*** in the day of......Eccl 8:8
inhabitants were of small ***p***....Is 37:27
for that he is strong in ***p***......Is 40:26
horse, the army and the ***p***.....Is 43:17
deliver..from the ***p*** of the.....Is 47:14
redeem? or have I no ***p*** to.....Is 50:2
hath made the earth by his ***p***..Jer 10:12
my great ***p*** and by my.........Jer 27:5
by thy great ***p*** and...........Jer 32:17
without great ***p*** or many.......Ezek 17:9
in thee to their ***p*** to shed.....Ezek 22:6
pride of her ***p*** shall come.....Ezek 30:6
given thee a kingdom, ***p*****......Dan 2:37

bodies the fire had no **p** ....Dan 3:27
kingdom by the might of my **p** .Dan 4:30
Daniel from the **p** of the ......Dan 6:27
unto him in the fury of his **p** ..Dan 8:6
the nation, but not in his **p** ....Dan 8:22
mighty but not by his own **p**...Dan 8:24
shall not retain the **p** of ....Dan 11:6
have **p** over the treasures ......Dan 11:43
to scatter the **p** of the holy ....Dan 12:7
strength he had **p** with God ...Hos 12:3
ransom..from the **p** of the .....Hos 13:14
because it is in the **p** of ....Mic 2:1
I am full of **p** by the spirit ....Mic 3:8
slow to anger and great in **p**...Nah 1:3
loins, strong, fortify thy **p** .....Nah 2:1
be delivered from the **p** of ....Hab 2:9
was the hiding of his **p** ....Hab 3:4
Not by might, nor by **p** ....Zech 4:6
he will smite her **p** in the .....Zech 9:4
kingdom, and the **p**, and ......Matt 6:13
he gave them **p** against........Matt 10:1
scriptures nor the **p** of God ..Matt 22:29
man sitting..right hand of **p** ...Matt 26:64
Son of man hath **p** on earth ...Mark 2:10
And to have **p** to heal ....Mark 3:15
gave them **p** over unclean .....Mark 6:7
neither the **p** of God?.........Mark 12:24
the clouds with great **p**........Mark 13:26
sitting on the right hand of **p** ..Mark 14:62
him in the spirit and **p** ....Luke 1:17
All this **p** will I give thee .....Luke 4:6
p of the Lord was present .....Luke 5:17
amazed at the mighty **p** of God Luke 9:43
unto you **p** to tread on........Luke 10:19
all the **p** of the enemy ....Luke 10:19
hath killed hath **p** to cast......Luke 12:5
unto magistrates, and **p** ....Luke 12:11
p and authority..governor .....Luke 20:20
the **p** of heaven shall be.......Luke 21:26
man coming in a cloud with **p** .Luke 21:27
your hour, and the **p** of.......Luke 22:53
not that I have **p** to crucify ....John 19:10
thee, and have **p** to release ....John 19:10
the Father hath..own **p**........Acts 1:7
by our own **p** or holiness ......Acts 3:12
By what **p**, or by what ....Acts 4:7
it not in thine own **p**?..........Acts 5:4
Stephen, full of faith and **p**....Acts 6:8
man is the great **p** of God.....Acts 8:10
Holy Ghost and with **p**..........Acts 10:38
the **p** of Satan unto God ....Acts 26:18
nor principalities, nor **p** ....Rom 8:38
that I might show my **p** ....Rom 9:17
wrath, and to make his **p** ......Rom 9:22
be subject unto the higher **p**...Rom 13:1
is no **p** but of God; the ....Rom 13:1
p that be are ordained of God .Rom 13:1
not be afraid of the **p**?........Rom 13:3
the **p** of the Holy Ghost ......Rom 15:13
to him that is of **p** to ....Rom 16:25
are saved it is the **p** of God ...1Cor 1:18
are puffed up, but the **p** 1Cor 4:19
the **p** of our Lord Jesus 1Cor 5:4
be brought under the **p** 1Cor 6:12
wife hath not **p** of her own 1Cor 7:4
hath not **p** of his own 1Cor 7:4
Have we not **p** to eat and 1Cor 9:4
have we not **p** to forbear 1Cor 9:6
be partakers of this **p** 1Cor 9:12
we have not used this **p** 1Cor 9:12
the woman to have **p** on her ..1Cor 11:10
rule and all authority and **p** ...1Cor 15:24
excellency of the **p** may be 2Cor 4:7
of truth by the **p** of God 2Cor 6:7
For to their **p**, I bear 2Cor 8:3
beyond their **p** they were.......2Cor 8:3
prince of the **p** of the air......Eph 2:2
effectual working of his **p** .....Eph 3:7
and **p** in heavenly places ......Eph 3:10
Lord, and in the **p** of his......Eph 6:10
principalities, against **p**........Eph 6:12
the **p** of his resurrection.......Phil 3:10
according to his glorious **p** ....Col 1:11
or principalities or **p** ....Col 1:16
of all principality and **p** ....Col 2:10
spoiled principalities and **p** ....Col 2:15
also in **p** and in the Holy 1Thess 1:5
and from the glory of his **p**....2Thess 1:9
all **p** and signs and lying 2Thess 2:9
Not because we have not **p**....2Thess 3:9
be honor and **p** everlasting 1Tim 6:16
of **p**, and of love, and of a 2Tim 1:7
but denying the **p** thereof 2Tim 3:5
him that had the **p** of death ...Heb 2:14
but after the **p** of an ....Heb 7:16
kept by the **p** of God 1Pet 1:5
as his divine **p** hath given 2Pet 1:3
are greater in **p** and might 2Pet 2:11
majesty, dominion and **p** .....Jude 25
will I give **p** over the ....Rev 2:26
glory and honor and **p** ....Rev 4:11
was slain to receive **p** ....Rev 5:12
p was given to him that ....Rev 6:4
p and might, be unto God ....Rev 7:12
unto them was given **p** ....Rev 9:3
p was to hurt men five ....Rev 9:10
I will give **p** unto my two .....Rev 11:3
have **p** to shut heaven ....Rev 11:6
have **p** over waters to ....Rev 11:6
God and the **p** of his Christ ...Rev 12:10
the dragon gave him his **p** .....Rev 13:2
p was given unto him to ......Rev 13:5
he exerciseth all the **p** of ......Rev 13:12
And he had **p** to give life .....Rev 13:15
the altar, which had **p** ....Rev 14:18
of God, and from his **p** ....Rev 15:8
p was given unto him to ......Rev 16:8
receive **p** as kings one ....Rev 17:12
heaven, having great **p** ....Rev 18:1
honor, and **p** unto the Lord ...Rev 19:1
second death have no **p** ....Rev 20:6

POWER OF CHRIST—*the power Christ has exhibited or bestows*

Described as:
Given by God..........John 17:2
Derived from the Spirit ..Luke 4:14
Delegated to others.......Luke 9:1
Determined by Himself ..John 10:18

Manifested as power in:
Creation ....John 1:3, 10
Upholds all things ....Heb 1:3
Miracles ....Luke 4:36
Regeneration...........John 5:21-26
Salvation ....Heb 7:25
Resurrecting believers....John 5:28, 29
His return ....Matt 24:30

Manifested as authority to:
Forgive sins ....Matt 9:6, 8
Teach ....Luke 4:32
Give sonship ....John 1:12
Lay down His life ....John 10:18
Authority ....Matt 28:18

Benefits from, to believers:
Life ....John 17:2
Strength ....Phil 4:13
Effective service 1Tim 1:12
2Tim 4:17
Perfected in weakness....2Cor 12:9
Conquest over temptation.Heb 2:18
Glorification ....Phil 3:20, 21

POWER OF GOD

Manifested in:
Creation ....Jer 51:15
Keeps watch on the nations ....Ps 66:7
Christ's:
Birth ....Luke 1:35
Miracles ....Luke 11:20
Resurrection 2Cor 13:4
Exaltation ....Eph 1:19, 20
Regeneration...........Eph 1:19
Sanctification...........Phil 2:13
Believer's resurrection ...1Cor 6:14

Believer's attitude toward:
Renders praise for.......Ps 21:13
Sings of ....Ps 59:16
Talks of ....Ps 145:11

POWER OF THE HOLY SPIRIT

Manifested in Christ's:
Conception ....Luke 1:35
Ministry ....Luke 4:14
Miracles ....Luke 11:20
Resurrection ....Rom 1:4

Manifested in the believer's:
Regeneration...........Ezek 37:11-14
Effective ministry........Luke 24:49

POWER, SPIRITUAL—*power in the Christian's life*

Sources of:
Holy Spirit.............1Cor 2:4, 5
Christ 1Cor 1:24
Gospel ....Rom 1:16
God's kingdom ....Mark 9:1
God's Word ....Heb 4:12
New life ....Eph 1:19

PRACTICE—*to do something customarily; a customary habit*
Wicked works ....Ps 141:4
Hypocrisy..............Is 32:6
Power ....Dan 8:24
Work evil ....Mic 2:1

[*also* PRACTICED, PRACTICES]
Saul secretly **p** mischief 1Sam 23:9
to **p** hypocrisy and to ....Is 32:6
ground; and it **p** and..........Dan 8:12
exercised with covetous **p** 2Pet 2:14

PRAETORIUM—*See* PRETORIUM

PRAISE—*to laud another's qualities*
whom thy brethren shall **p** ....Gen 49:8
in **p**, and in name, and in .....Deut 26:19
so much **p** as Absalom 2Sam 14:25
p and minister before the 2Chr 8:14
the people running and **p** 2Chr 23:12
such as taught to sing **p** 2Chr 23:13
gold; so is a man to his **p** .....Prov 27:21
the Lord, she shall be **p**.......Prov 31:30
p the dead which are ....Eccl 4:2
the concubines, and they **p** ....Song 6:9
neither my **p** to graven........Is 42:8
Salvation and thy gates **P** .....Is 60:18
garment of **p** for the spirit.....Is 61:3
make Jerusalem a **p** in ....Is 62:7
and for a **p** and for a ....Jer 13:11
shall be no more **p** of ....Jer 48:2
is the city of **p** not left ....Jer 49:25
how is the **p** of the whole .....Jer 51:41
get them **p** and fame in ....Zeph 3:19
whose **p** is not of men, but ....Rom 2:29
shall every man have **p** of 1Cor 4:5
Now I **p** you, brethren 1Cor 11:2
brother, whose **p** is in the 2Cor 8:18
and for the **p** of them that 1Pet 2:14

PRAISE OF GOD—*ascription of honor and glory to God*

Objects of:
God Himself ....Ps 139:14
God's:
Name 1Chr 29:13
Ps 99:3
Power ....Ps 21:13
Wonders..............Ps 89:5
Loving-kindness ....Ps 138:2
Works ....Ps 145:4

Times of:
Daily...................Ps 72:15
Continually ....Ps 71:6
Seven times daily.......Ps 119:164
All the day ....Ps 35:28
At midnight............Ps 119:62
Acts 16:25
While I live ....Ps 146:2

[*also* PRAISE, PRAISED, PRAISES, PRAISING]
Now will I **p** the Lord ....Gen 29:35
fearful in **p**, doing ....Ex 15:11
thy **p**, and he is thy God ......Deut 10:21
Lord, who is worthy to be **p**...2Sam 22:4
and I will sing **p** unto thy 2Sam 22:50

p the Lord God of Israel 1Chr 16:4
Lord, and greatly to be *p* 1Chr 16:25
four thousand *p* the Lord 1Chr 23:5
made, said David, to *p* 1Chr 23:5
thanks and to *p* the Lord 1Chr 25:3
p and thanking the Lord 2Chr 5:13
p the Lord, saying, For 2Chr 5:13
worshiped, and *p* the Lord 2Chr 7:3
the king..to *p* the Lord 2Chr 7:6
stood up to *p* the Lord God 2Chr 20:19
p the beauty of holiness 2Chr 20:21
and to say, *P* the Lord 2Chr 20:21
to sing *p* unto the Lord 2Chr 29:30
And they sang *p* with 2Chr 29:30
Levites and the priest *p* 2Chr 30:21
to *p* in the gates of the 2Chr 31:2
p the Lord, after the ...... Ezra 3:10
p and giving thanks unto the ...... Ezra 3:11
great shout, when they *p* ...... Ezra 3:11
Amen, and *p* the Lord ...... Neh 5:13
above all blessing and *p* ...... Neh 9:5
to *p* and to give thanks ...... Neh 12:24
I will *p* the Lord according ...... Ps 7:17
p to the name of the Lord ...... Ps 7:17
I will *p* thee, O Lord, with ...... Ps 9:1
I will sing *p* to thy name ...... Ps 9:2
Sing *p* to the Lord, which ...... Ps 9:11
Lord, who is worthy to be *p* ...... Ps 18:3
sing *p* unto thy name ...... Ps 18:49
inhabitest the *p* of Israel ...... Ps 22:3
congregation will I *p* thee ...... Ps 22:22
Ye that fear the Lord, *p* ...... Ps 22:23
My *p* shall be of thee ...... Ps 22:25
I will sing *p* unto the Lord ...... Ps 27:6
and with my song will I *p* ...... Ps 28:7
Shall the dust *p* thee? ...... Ps 30:9
p is comely for the upright ...... Ps 33:1
his *p* shall continually be ...... Ps 34:1
I will *p* thee among much ...... Ps 35:18
my mouth, even *p* unto our ...... Ps 40:3
with the voice of joy and *p* ...... Ps 42:4
for I shall yet *p* him, who ...... Ps 42:11
harp will I *p* thee, O God ...... Ps 43:4
day long, and *p* thy name ...... Ps 44:8
shall the people *p* thee for ...... Ps 45:17
Sing *p* to God, sing *p* ...... Ps 47:6
sing *p* unto our King, sing *p* ...... Ps 47:6
greatly to be *p* in the city ...... Ps 48:1
thy *p* unto the ends ...... Ps 48:10
and men will *p* thee ...... Ps 49:18
Whoso offereth *p* glorifieth ...... Ps 50:23
mouth shall show forth thy *p* ...... Ps 51:15
I will *p* thee for ever ...... Ps 52:9
I will *p* thy name, O Lord ...... Ps 54:6
In God I will *p* his word ...... Ps 56:4
In God will I *p* his word ...... Ps 56:10
in the Lord will I *p* his ...... Ps 56:10
O God; I will render *p* ...... Ps 56:12
is fixed; I will sing and..*p* ...... Ps 57:7
I sing *p* unto thy name for ...... Ps 61:8
than life, my lips shall *p* ...... Ps 63:3
P waiteth for thee, O God ...... Ps 65:1
of his name; make his *p* ...... Ps 66:2
Let the people *p* thee, O ...... Ps 67:3
O God; let all the people *p* ...... Ps 67:3
Let the people *p* thee, O ...... Ps 67:5
O God; let all the people *p* ...... Ps 67:5
unto God, sing *p* to his ...... Ps 68:4
p the name of God with a ...... Ps 69:30
will yet *p* thee more and ...... Ps 71:14
the poor and needy *p* thy ...... Ps 74:21
I will sing *p* to the God of ...... Ps 75:9
the wrath of man shall *p* ...... Ps 76:10
p of the Lord, and his ...... Ps 78:4
thy *p* to all generations ...... Ps 79:13
they will be still *p* thee ...... Ps 84:4
I will *p* thee, O Lord my ...... Ps 86:12
shall the dead arise and *p* ...... Ps 88:10
to sing *p* unto thy name ...... Ps 92:1
Lord is great and greatly..*p* ...... Ps 96:4
and rejoice, and sing *p* ...... Ps 98:4
created shall *p* the Lord ...... Ps 102:18
I will sing *p* to my God ...... Ps 104:33
his laws. *P* ye the Lord ...... Ps 105:45
P ye the Lord. O give ...... Ps 106:1
his words; they sang his *p* ...... Ps 106:12
Amen. *P* ye the Lord ...... Ps 106:48
Oh that men would *p* ...... Ps 107:8
I will sing and give *p* ...... Ps 108:1
peace, O God of my *p* ...... Ps 109:1
p the Lord with my ...... Ps 109:30
will *p* him among the ...... Ps 109:30
P ye the Lord, I will ...... Ps 111:1
p the Lord with my whole ...... Ps 111:1
P ye the Lord. Blessed is ...... Ps 112:1
P ye the Lord. *P*, O ye ...... Ps 113:1
p the name of the Lord ...... Ps 113:1
the Lord's name is to be *p* ...... Ps 113:3
The dead *p* not the Lord ...... Ps 115:17
O Jerusalem. *P* ye the Lord ...... Ps 116:19
p the Lord, all ye nations ...... Ps 117:1
ye nations; *p* him all ye ...... Ps 117:1
into them, and I will *p* the ...... Ps 118:19
art my God, and I will *p* ...... Ps 118:28
p thee with uprightness of ...... Ps 119:7
My lips shall utter *p* ...... Ps 119:171
P ye the Lord. *P* ye the name ...... Ps 135:1
p him, O ye servants ...... Ps 135:1
Lord is good; sing *p* unto ...... Ps 135:3
Jerusalem. *P* ye the Lord ...... Ps 135:21
I will *p* thee with my whole ...... Ps 138:1
the gods will I sing *p* unto ...... Ps 138:1
p thy name.. ...... Ps 138:2
the kings of..earth shall *p* ...... Ps 138:4
of prison, that I may *p* ...... Ps 142:7
ten strings will I sing *p* ...... Ps 144:9
David's psalm of *p* ...... Ps 145:*title*
Lord, and greatly to be *p* ...... Ps 145:3
thy works shall *p* thee ...... Ps 145:10
P ye the Lord. *P* the ...... Ps 146:1
all generations. *P* ye ...... Ps 146:10
P ye the Lord;for it is ...... Ps 147:1
it is good to sing *p* unto ...... Ps 147:1
it is pleasant; and *p* is ...... Ps 147:1
P the Lord; O Jerusalem ...... Ps 147:12
p thy God, O Zion ...... Ps 147:12
P ye the Lord. *P* ye the ...... Ps 148:1
p him in the heights ...... Ps 148:1
P ye him, all his angels ...... Ps 148:2
p ye him, all his hosts ...... Ps 148:2
P ye him, sun and moon ...... Ps 148:3
p him, all ye stars of light ...... Ps 148:3
Let them *p* the name of ...... Ps 148:5
Let them *p* the name of ...... Ps 148:13
people, the *p* of all his ...... Ps 148:14
unto him. *P* ye the Lord ...... Ps 148:14
P ye the Lord. Sing unto ...... Ps 149:1
his *p* in the congregation ...... Ps 149:1
sing *p* unto him with the ...... Ps 149:3
his saints. *P* ye the Lord ...... Ps 149:9
P ye the Lord ...... Ps 150:1
P God in his sanctuary ...... Ps 150:1
p him in the firmament ...... Ps 150:1
P him for his mighty acts ...... Ps 150:2
p him according to his ...... Ps 150:2
P him with the sound ...... Ps 150:3
p him with the psaltery ...... Ps 150:3
P him with the timbrel ...... Ps 150:4
p him with stringed ...... Ps 150:4
P him upon the loud cymbals ...... Ps 150:5
p him upon the high-sounding. ...... Ps 150:5
hath breath *p* the Lord ...... Ps 150:6
P ye the Lord ...... Ps 150:6
O Lord, I will *p* thee ...... Is 12:1
I will *p* thy name; for ...... Is 25:1
For the grave cannot *p* ...... Is 38:18
and declare his *p* in the ...... Is 42:12
they shall show forth my *p* ...... Is 43:21
for my *p* will I refrain ...... Is 48:9
show forth the *p* of the Lord ...... Is 60:6
and the *p* of the Lord ...... Is 63:7
house, where our fathers *p* ...... Is 64:11
saved; for thou art my *p* ...... Jer 17:14
p ye the Lord; for he ...... Jer 20:13
p ye, and say, O Lord ...... Jer 31:7
a *p* and an honor before ...... Jer 33:9
P the Lord of hosts: for the ...... Jer 33:11
bring the sacrifice of *p* ...... Jer 33:11
I thank thee, and *p* thee ...... Dan 2:23
p and honored him that ...... Dan 4:34
Now I Nebuchadnezzar *p* ...... Dan 4:37
p the name of the Lord ...... Joel 2:26
earth was full of his *p* ...... Hab 3:3
thou hast perfected *p*? ...... Matt 21:16
and he spake, and *p* God ...... Luke 1:64
heavenly host, *p* God and ...... Luke 2:13
when they saw it, gave *p* ...... Luke 18:43
rejoice and *p* God with a ...... Luke 19:37
temple, *p* and blessing God ...... Luke 24:53
unto him, Give God the *p* ...... John 9:24
P God, and having favor ...... Acts 2:47
walking, and leaping, and *p* ...... Acts 3:8
again, *P* the Lord, all ye ...... Rom 15:11
To the *p* of the glory of ...... Eph 1:6
possession, unto the *p* of ...... Eph 1:14
unto the glory and *p* of God ...... Phil 1:11
if there be any *p*, think on ...... Phil 4:8
the church will I sing *p* ...... Heb 2:12
us offer the sacrifice of *p* ...... Heb 13:15
be found unto *p* and honor 1Pet 1:7
show forth the *p* of him 1Pet 2:9
whom be *p* and dominion 1Pet 4:11
P our God, all ye his ...... Rev 19:5

PRAISE OF MEN—*commendation of human beings*

Worthy:
From another ...... Prov 27:2
For:
Faithfulness ...... Prov 31:28
Obedience ...... Rom 13:3
Works ...... Prov 31:31

Unworthy for:
Wicked ...... Prov 28:4
Disorder 1Cor 11:17, 22
Self-seeking ...... John 12:43

PRANCING—*walking in a spirited matter; strutting*

[*also* PRANCINGS]
by the means of the *p* ...... Judg 5:22
p of their mighty ones ...... Judg 5:22
the *p* horses, and of the ...... Nah 3:2

PRATING—*foolish babbling*

Descriptive of:
Fool ...... Prov 10:8, 10
Diotrephes 3John 10

PRAYER—*communication with God; request of God*

Kinds of:
Secret ...... Matt 6:6
Family ...... Acts 10:2, 30
Group ...... Matt 18:20
Public 1Cor 14:14-17

Parts of:
Adoration ...... Dan 4:34, 35
Confession 1John 1:9
Supplication 1Tim 2:1-3
Intercession ...... James 5:15
Thanksgiving ...... Phil 4:6

Personal requirements of:
Purity of heart ...... Ps 66:18, 19
Believing ...... Matt 21:22
In Christ's name ...... John 14:13
According to God's will 1John 5:14

General requirements of:
Forgiving spirit ...... Matt 6:14
Simplicity ...... Matt 6:5, 6
Humility and repentance. ...... Luke 18:10-14
Unity of believers ...... Matt 18:19, 20
Tenacity ...... Luke 18:1-8
Importunity ...... Luke 11:5-8
Intensity ...... Matt 7:7-11
Confident expectation ...... Mark 11:24
Without many words ...... Matt 6:7
Unceasingly 1Thess 5:17

Answers refused, because of:
Sin ...... Ps 66:18
Selfishness ...... James 4:3
Doubt ...... James 1:5-7
Disobedience ...... Prov 28:9
Inhumanity ...... Prov 21:13
Pride ...... Luke 18:11, 12, 14

Posture for:
Standing ... Neh 9:5
Kneeling ... Ezra 9:5
Sitting ... 1Chr 17:16-27
Bowing ... Ex 34:8
Hands uplifted ... 1Tim 2:8

[*also* PRAY, PRAYED, PRAYERS, PRAYETH, PRAYING]
Say I ***p*** thee, thou art my ... Gen 12:13
Let there be no strife, I ***p*** ... Gen 13:8
I ***p*** thee, go in unto my ... Gen 16:2
pass not away, I ***p*** thee ... Gen 18:3
now, my lords, turn in, I ***p*** ... Gen 19:2
let me I ***p*** you bring ... Gen 19:8
he shall ***p*** for thee and ... Gen 20:7
So Abraham ***p*** unto God ... Gen 20:17
if thou wilt give it, I ***p*** ... Gen 23:13
to Jacob, Feed me, I ***p*** ... Gen 25:30
I ***p*** thee, sit and eat of my ... Gen 27:19
Give me, I ***p*** thee of thy ... Gen 30:14
Deliver me, I ***p*** thee from ... Gen 32:11
Jacob said, Nay, I ***p*** thee ... Gen 33:10
Let my lord, I ***p*** thee ... Gen 33:14
I ***p*** you give her him to ... Gen 34:8
Hear I ***p*** you, this dream ... Gen 37:6
tell me, I ***p*** thee, where ... Gen 37:16
Go to, I ***p*** thee, let me come ... Gen 38:16
to God? tell me them, I ***p*** ... Gen 40:8
I ***p*** thee, let thy servant ... Gen 44:33
Come near to me, I ***p*** you ... Gen 45:4
we ***p*** thee, let thy servants ... Gen 47:4
put I ***p*** thee, thy hand ... Gen 47:29
bury me not, I ***p*** thee, in ... Gen 47:29
speak, I ***p*** you, in the ears ... Gen 50:4
Forgive, I ***p*** thee now the ... Gen 50:17
we ***p*** thee, forgive the ... Gen 50:17
O my Lord, send, I ***p*** thee ... Ex 4:13
let us go, we ***p*** thee, three ... Ex 5:3
forgive, I ***p*** thee, my sin ... Ex 10:17
blot me, I ***p*** thee, out of ... Ex 32:32
therefore, I ***p*** thee, if I ... Ex 33:13
let my Lord, I ***p*** thee go ... Ex 34:9
he said, Leave us not, I ***p*** ... Num 10:31
when Moses ***p*** unto the Lord ... Num 11:2
kill me, I ***p*** thee, out of ... Num 11:15
Hear, I ***p*** you, ye sons of ... Num 16:8
Let us pass, I ***p*** thee ... Num 20:17
p unto the Lord, that he ... Num 21:7
And Moses ***p*** for the ... Num 21:7
therefore, I ***p*** thee, curse ... Num 22:6
therefore I ***p*** thee, curse ... Num 22:17
him, Come, I ***p*** thee, with ... Num 23:13
I ***p*** thee, let me go over ... Deut 3:25
I ***p*** for Aaron also the ... Deut 9:20
I ***p*** you, swear unto me ... Josh 2:12
give, I ***p*** thee, glory to the ... Josh 7:19
Show us we ***p*** thee, the ... Judg 1:24
Give me, I ***p*** thee, a little ... Judg 4:19
Depart not hence, I ***p*** ... Judg 6:18
Give I ***p*** you, loaves of ... Judg 8:5
Speak, I ***p*** you in the ears ... Judg 9:2
deliver us only, we ***p*** thee ... Judg 10:15
Let me, I ***p*** thee, pass ... Judg 11:17
beware, I ***p*** thee, and drink ... Judg 13:4
take her, I ***p*** thee, instead ... Judg 15:2
Tell me, I ***p*** thee, wherein ... Judg 16:6
God, remember me, I ***p*** ... Judg 16:28
strengthen me, I ***p*** thee ... Judg 16:28
Ask counsel, we ***p*** thee ... Judg 18:5
Be content, I ***p*** thee and ... Judg 19:6
evening, I ***p*** you tarry all ... Judg 19:9
nay, I ***p*** you, do not so ... Judg 19:23
I ***p*** you, let me glean and ... Ruth 2:7
p unto the Lord, and wept ... 1Sam 1:10
continued ***p*** before the Lord ... 1Sam 1:12
Hannah ***p***, and said, My ... 1Sam 2:1
Put me, I ***p*** thee, into one ... 1Sam 2:36
I ***p*** thee hide it not from me ... 1Sam 3:17
I will ***p*** for you unto the ... 1Sam 7:5
And Samuel ***p*** unto the Lord ... 1Sam 8:6
Tell me, I ***p*** thee, where ... 1Sam 9:18
Tell me, I ***p*** thee, what ... 1Sam 10:15
P for thy servants ... 1Sam 12:19
see, I ***p*** you how mine ... 1Sam 14:29
I ***p*** thee, pardon my sin ... 1Sam 15:25
Let David, I ***p*** thee, stand ... 1Sam 16:22
now therefore, I ***p*** thee ... 1Sam 19:2
Let me go, I ***p*** thee; for ... 1Sam 20:29
let me get away, I ***p*** thee ... 1Sam 20:29
my mother, I ***p*** thee, come ... 1Sam 22:3
Go, I ***p*** you, prepare yet ... 1Sam 23:22
give, I ***p*** thee, whatsoever ... 1Sam 25:8
Let not my lord, I ***p*** thee ... 1Sam 25:25
let me smite him, I ***p*** thee ... 1Sam 26:8
I ***p*** thee, let my lord the ... 1Sam 26:19
said, I ***p*** thee, divine unto ... 1Sam 28:8
I ***p*** thee, bring me hither ... 1Sam 30:7
went the matter? I ***p*** thee ... 2Sam 1:4
in his heart to ***p*** this ... 2Sam 7:27
heart to pray this ***p*** unto ... 2Sam 7:27
him, I ***p*** thee, let my sister ... 2Sam 13:5
I ***p*** thee, speak unto the ... 2Sam 13:13
p thee, feign thyself to ... 2Sam 14:2
Let thine handmaid, I ***p*** ... 2Sam 14:12
I ***p*** thee, let me go and ... 2Sam 15:7
go over, I ***p*** thee, and take ... 2Sam 16:9
let me, I ***p*** thee also run ... 2Sam 18:22
Let thy servant, I ***p*** thee ... 2Sam 19:37
say, I ***p*** you, unto Joab ... 2Sam 20:16
let thine hand, I ***p*** thee ... 2Sam 24:17
let me, I ***p*** thee, give thee ... 1Kin 1:12
I ***p*** thee, unto Solomon ... 1Kin 2:17
let thy word, I ***p*** thee, be ... 1Kin 8:26
thou respect unto the ***p*** ... 1Kin 8:28
thy servant ***p*** before thee ... 1Kin 8:28
p which thy servant shall ... 1Kin 8:29
confess thy name, and ***p*** ... 1Kin 8:33
when he shall come and ***p*** ... 1Kin 8:42
thou in heaven their ***p*** ... 1Kin 8:45
p unto thee toward their ... 1Kin 8:48
made an end of ***p*** all this ***p*** ... 1Kin 8:54
him, I have heard thy ***p*** ... 1Kin 9:3
p for me, that my hand ... 1Kin 13:6
wife, Arise, I ***p*** thee and ... 1Kin 14:2
Fetch me, I ***p*** thee, a little ... 1Kin 17:10
I ***p*** thee, let this child's ... 1Kin 17:21
Let me, I ***p*** thee, kiss my ... 1Kin 19:20
I ***p*** you, and see how this ... 1Kin 20:7
Ben-hadad saith, I ***p*** thee ... 1Kin 20:32
Inquire, I ***p*** thee, at the ... 1Kin 22:5
O man of God, I ***p*** thee ... 2Kin 1:13
Elisha, Tarry here, I ***p*** ... 2Kin 2:2
said unto him, Tarry I ***p*** ... 2Kin 2:6
Elisha, Behold, I ***p*** ... 2Kin 2:19
chamber, I ***p*** thee, on the ... 2Kin 4:10
Run now, I ***p*** thee, to meet ... 2Kin 4:26
them twain, and ***p*** unto the ... 2Kin 4:33
wherefore consider, I ***p*** ... 2Kin 5:7
I ***p*** thee, be given to thy ... 2Kin 5:17
let us go, we ***p*** thee, unto ... 2Kin 6:2
Elisha ***p***, and said, Lord ... 2Kin 6:17
Smite this people, I ***p*** ... 2Kin 6:18
Let some take, I ***p*** thee ... 2Kin 7:13
therefore, I ***p*** thee, give ... 2Kin 18:23
lift up thy ***p*** for the ... 2Kin 19:4
Hezekiah ***p*** before the Lord ... 2Kin 19:15
to the wall, and ***p***..Lord ... 2Kin 20:2
I have heard thy ***p***, I have ... 2Kin 20:5
let thine hand, I ***p*** thee ... 1Chr 21:17
p which thy servant ... 2Chr 6:19
which thy servant ***p*** ... 2Chr 6:19
to hearken unto the ***p*** ... 2Chr 6:20
p and make supplication ... 2Chr 6:24
if they come and ***p*** in this ... 2Chr 6:32
from the heavens their ***p*** ... 2Chr 6:35
turn and ***p*** unto thee ... 2Chr 6:37
attent unto the ***p*** that is ... 2Chr 6:40
had made an end of ***p*** ... 2Chr 7:1
humble themselves and ***p*** ... 2Chr 7:14
Inquire, I ***p*** thee, at the ... 2Chr 18:4
But Hezekiah ***p*** for them ... 2Chr 30:18
and their ***p*** came up to ... 2Chr 30:27
of Amoz, ***p*** and cried to ... 2Chr 32:20
p unto him, and he was ... 2Chr 33:13
Manasseh, and his ***p*** unto ... 2Chr 33:18
p for the life of the king ... Ezra 6:10
Now when Ezra had ***p*** ... Ezra 10:1
and ***p*** before the God of ... Neh 1:4
hear the ***p*** of thy servant ... Neh 1:6
I ***p*** before thee now, day ... Neh 1:6
attentive to the ***p*** of thy ... Neh 1:11
p of thy servants, who ... Neh 1:11
Nevertheless we made our ***p*** ... Neh 4:9
I ***p*** you, let us leave off ... Neh 5:10
the thanksgiving in ***p*** ... Neh 11:17
Return, I ***p*** you, let it not ... Job 6:29
inquire, I ***p*** thee of the ... Job 8:8
restrainest ***p*** before God ... Job 15:4
mine hands; also my ***p*** is ... Job 16:17
should we have, if we ***p*** ... Job 21:15
Receive I ***p*** thee, the law ... Job 22:22
Thou shalt make thy ***p*** ... Job 22:27
Let me not, I ***p*** you ... Job 32:21
Job, I ***p*** thee, hear my ... Job 33:1
my servant Job shall ***p*** ... Job 42:8
Job, when he ***p*** for his ... Job 42:10
upon me, and hear my ***p*** ... Ps 4:1
God for unto thee will I ***p*** ... Ps 5:2
will I direct my ***p*** unto ... Ps 5:3
the Lord will receive my ***p*** ... Ps 6:9
every one that is godly ***p*** ... Ps 32:6
p returned into mine own ... Ps 35:13
Hear my ***p***, O Lord, and ... Ps 39:12
p unto the God of my life ... Ps 42:8
Hear my ***p***, O God; give ... Ps 54:2
Give ear to my ***p***, O God ... Ps 55:1
morning, and at noon will I ***p*** ... Ps 55:17
O God; attend unto my ***p*** ... Ps 61:1
O God in my ***p*** ... Ps 64:1
O Thou that hearest ***p*** ... Ps 65:2
for me, my ***p*** is unto thee ... Ps 69:13
p also shall be made for ... Ps 72:15
p of David the son of Jesse ... Ps 72:20
against the ***p*** of thy ... Ps 80:4
God of hosts, hear my ***p*** ... Ps 84:8
Let my ***p*** come before ... Ps 88:2
Hear my ***p***, O Lord, and ... Ps 102:1
will regard the ***p*** of the ... Ps 102:17
and not despise their ***p*** ... Ps 102:17
but I give myself unto ***p*** ... Ps 109:4
P for the peace of Jerusalem ... Ps 122:6
Let my ***p*** be set forth ... Ps 141:2
Hear my ***p***, O Lord, give ... Ps 143:1
the ***p*** of the upright is his ... Prov 15:8
when ye make many ***p*** ... Is 1:15
of Judah, judge, I ***p*** you ... Is 5:3
to his sanctuary to ***p*** ... Is 16:12
poured out a ***p*** when ... Is 26:16
Read this, I ***p*** thee; and ... Is 29:11
give pledges, I ***p*** thee, to ... Is 36:8
thy ***p*** for the remnant that ... Is 37:4
Hezekiah ***p*** unto the Lord ... Is 37:15
the wall, and ***p*** unto the ... Is 38:2
I have heard thy ***p***, I have ... Is 38:5
and worshipeth it, and ***p*** ... Is 44:17
and ***p*** unto a god that ... Is 45:20
joyful in my house of ***p*** ... Is 56:7
be called a house of ***p*** ... Is 56:7
p not thou for this people ... Jer 7:16
neither lift up cry nor ***p*** ... Jer 7:16
p not thou for this people ... Jer 11:14
neither lift up a cry or ***p*** ... Jer 11:14
P not for this people for ... Jer 14:11
Inquire, I ***p*** thee of the Lord. ... Jer 21:2
and ***p*** unto the Lord for it ... Jer 29:7
Buy my field, I ***p*** thee ... Jer 32:8
P now unto the Lord our God ... Jer 37:3
hear now I ***p*** thee, O my ... Jer 37:20
let my supplication, I ***p*** ... Jer 37:20
Let me go I ***p*** thee ... Jer 40:15
P for us unto the Lord ... Jer 42:20
Come, I ***p*** you, and hear ... Ezek 33:30
hear, I ***p*** you, all people ... Lam 1:18
he shutteth out my ***p*** ... Lam 3:8
p and gave thanks before ... Dan 6:10
and found Daniel ***p*** and ... Dan 6:11
by ***p*** and supplications ... Dan 9:3
And I ***p*** unto the Lord ... Dan 9:4
God hear the ***p*** of thy ... Dan 9:17
while I was speaking and ***p*** ... Dan 9:20
Tell us, we ***p*** thee, for ... Jon 1:8
my ***p*** came in unto thee ... Jon 2:7
said, I ***p*** thee, O Lord, was ... Jon 4:2
A ***p*** of Habakkuk the ... Hab 3:1

now, I **p** you, consider ... Hag 2:15
to **p** before the Lord ... Zech 7:2
to **p** before the Lord ... Zech 8:21
now, I **p** you, beseech God ... Mal 1:9
p for them..despitefully ... Matt 5:44
P ye therefore the Lord ... Matt 9:38
not out but by **p** and ... Matt 17:21
hands on them and **p** ... Matt 19:13
be called the house of **p** ... Matt 21:13
a pretense make long **p** ... Matt 23:14
p ye that your flight be ... Matt 24:20
that I cannot now **p** to my ... Matt 26:53
they began to **p** him to ... Mark 5:17
p him that he might be ... Mark 5:18
departed into a mountain to **p** . Mark 6:46
by nothing, but by **p** and ... Mark 9:29
all nations the house of **p**? ... Mark 11:17
when ye stand **p**, forgive ... Mark 11:25
a pretense make long **p** ... Mark 12:40
p ye that your flight be ... Mark 13:18
Sit ye here, while I..**p** ... Mark 14:32
p that if it were possible ... Mark 14:35
people were **p** without at ... Luke 1:10
not, Zechariah, for thy **p** ... Luke 1:13
with fastings and **p** night ... Luke 2:37
p him that he would ... Luke 5:3
fast often, and make **p** ... Luke 5:33
p for them which ... Luke 6:28
p ye therefore the Lord ... Luke 10:2
Lord, teach us to **p** ... Luke 11:1
see it; I **p** thee have me ... Luke 14:18
I **p** thee therefore, father ... Luke 16:27
My house is the house of **p** ... Luke 19:46
a show make long **p** ... Luke 20:47
therefore, and **p** always ... Luke 21:36
p for thee, that thy faith ... Luke 22:32
P that ye enter not into ... Luke 22:40
in an agony he **p** more ... Luke 22:44
when he rose up from **p** ... Luke 22:45
his disciples **p** him, saying ... John 4:31
I will **p** the Father, and ... John 14:16
that I will **p** the Father ... John 16:26
And they **p**, and said ... Acts 1:24
breaking of bread and in **p** ... Acts 2:42
the hour of **p**, being the ... Acts 3:1
And when they had **p**, the ... Acts 4:31
ourselves continually to **p** ... Acts 6:4
when they had **p**, they laid ... Acts 6:6
p for them, that they ... Acts 8:15
wickedness, and **p** God ... Acts 8:22
P ye to the Lord for me ... Acts 8:24
Saul, of Tarsus: for..he **p** ... Acts 9:11
kneeled down, and **p** ... Acts 9:40
Thy **p** and thine alms are ... Acts 10:4
upon the housetop to **p** ... Acts 10:9
And said, Cornelius, thy **p** ... Acts 10:31
p they him to tarry ... Acts 10:48
I was in the city of Joppa **p** ... Acts 11:5
but **p** was made without ... Acts 12:5
they had fasted and **p** ... Acts 13:3
p with fasting, they ... Acts 14:23
man of Macedonia, and **p** ... Acts 16:9
kneeled down, and **p** with ... Acts 20:36
while I **p** in the temple ... Acts 22:17
p me to bring this young ... Acts 23:18
I **p** thee that thou wouldest ... Acts 24:4
I **p** you to take some meat ... Acts 27:34
Paul entered in, and **p** ... Acts 28:8
mention..always in my **p** ... Rom 1:9
we should **p** for as we ... Rom 8:26
desire and **p** to God for ... Rom 10:1
continuing instant in **p** ... Rom 12:12
with me in your **p** to God ... Rom 15:30
yourselves to fasting and **p** ... 1Cor 7:5
man **p** or prophesying ... 1Cor 11:4
every woman that **p** or ... 1Cor 11:5
comely that a woman **p** ... 1Cor 11:13
tongue **p** that he may ... 1Cor 14:13
also helping together by **p** ... 2Cor 1:11
we **p** you in Christ's stead ... 2Cor 5:20
P us with much entreaty ... 2Cor 8:4
by their **p** for you, which ... 2Cor 9:14
Now I **p** to God that ye do ... 2Cor 13:7
mention of you in my **p** ... Eph 1:16
P always with all **p** and ... Eph 6:18
Always in every **p** of mine ... Phil 1:4
And this I **p**, that your love ... Phil 1:9
Lord Jesus Christ, **p** always ... Col 1:3
do not cease to **p** for you ... Col 1:9
Continue in **p**, and watch ... Col 4:2
p also for us, that God ... Col 4:3
fervently for you in **p** ... Col 4:12
mention of you in our **p** ... 1Thess 1:2
Night and day **p** ... 1Thess 3:10
I **p** God your whole spirit ... 1Thess 5:23
we **p** always for you, that ... 2Thess 1:11
brethren, **p** for us, that ... 2Thess 3:1
by the word of God and **p** ... 1Tim 4:5
in supplications and **p** ... 1Tim 5:5
remembrance of thee in my **p**. . 2Tim 1:3
I **p** God that it may not ... 2Tim 4:16
of thee always in my **p** ... Philem 4
he had offered up **p** ... Heb 5:7
P for us; for we trust we ... Heb 13:18
p one for another, that ... James 5:16
he **p** earnestly that it ... James 5:17
life; that your **p** be not ... 1Pet 3:7
therefore sober, and..**p** ... 1Pet 4:7
I do not say that he shall **p** ... 1John 5:16
holy faith, **p** in the Holy Ghost. Jude 20
odors, which are the **p** ... Rev 5:8
offer it with the **p** of all ... Rev 8:3

PRAYER MEETINGS—*meetings whose primary purpose is to pray together*

In the upper room ... Acts 1:13, 14
In a house ... Acts 12:5-17
By a river ... Acts 16:13
On a beach ... Acts 21:5

PRAYERS OF CHRIST—*the prayers Jesus prayed on earth*

Their nature:

Adoration ... Matt 11:25-27
Intercession ... John 17:1-26
Thanksgiving ... John 11:41, 42

Their great occasions:

At His baptism ... Luke 3:21, 22
Before selecting the apostles ... Luke 6:12-16
At His transfiguration ... Luke 9:28, 29
In Gethsemane ... Matt 26:36-42

Their times and places:

In secret ... Luke 5:16
Luke 9:18
Early in morning ... Mark 1:35
With others ... Luke 11:1
On mountain ... Matt 14:23

PREACH—*to proclaim the truth; proclaim the gospel*

The Gospel:

Necessity of ... 1Cor 9:16
Without charge ... 1Cor 9:18
Extent of, to all ... Col 1:25
Only one ... Gal 1:8, 9
Centers in the Cross ... 1Cor 1:23
Preacher's importance in. . Rom 10:14, 15

Attitudes toward:

Accepted ... Luke 11:32
Rejected ... 2Pet 2:4, 5
Not perfected by ... Heb 4:2
Perverted ... Gal 1:6-9
Contentious about ... Phil 1:15-18
Counted foolishness ... 1Cor 1:18-21
Ridiculed ... Acts 17:16-18
Not ashamed of ... Rom 1:15, 16

[*also* PREACHED, PREACHEST, PREACHETH, PREACHING]

prophets to **p** of thee at ... Neh 6:7
have **p** righteousness in ... Ps 40:9
anointed me to **p** good ... Is 61:1
p unto it the **p** that I ... Jon 3:2
p in the wilderness of Judea ... Matt 3:1
time Jesus began to **p** ... Matt 4:17
and **p** the gospel of the ... Matt 4:23
and **p** the gospel of the ... Matt 9:35
as ye go, **p** saying, The ... Matt 10:7
to teach and to **p** in their ... Matt 11:1
the poor have the gospel **p** ... Matt 11:5
they repented at the **p** ... Matt 12:41
be **p** in all the world for ... Matt 24:14
this gospel shall be **p** in ... Matt 26:13
p the baptism of repentance ... Mark 1:4
And **p**, saying, There ... Mark 1:7
p the gospel in the kingdom ... Mark 1:14
and he **p** the word unto ... Mark 2:2
might send them forth to **p** ... Mark 3:14
and **p** that men should ... Mark 6:12
this gospel shall be **p** ... Mark 14:9
and **p** the gospel to every ... Mark 16:15
they went forth, and **p** ... Mark 16:20
p the baptism of repentance ... Luke 3:3
exhortation **p** he unto the ... Luke 3:18
to **p** deliverance to the ... Luke 4:18
I must **p** the kingdom of ... Luke 4:43
he **p** in the synagogues ... Luke 4:44
poor the gospel is **p** ... Luke 7:22
p and showing the glad ... Luke 8:1
he sent them to **p** the ... Luke 9:2
p the gospel and healing ... Luke 9:6
the kingdom of God is **p** ... Luke 16:16
in the temple, and **p** the ... Luke 20:1
should be **p** in his name ... Luke 24:47
which before was **p** unto ... Acts 3:20
p through Jesus the ... Acts 4:2
not to teach and **p** Jesus ... Acts 5:42
went every where **p** the ... Acts 8:4
Samaria and **p** Christ ... Acts 8:5
testified and **p** the word ... Acts 8:25
p the gospel in many ... Acts 8:25
he **p** in all the cities, till ... Acts 8:40
he **p** Christ in the ... Acts 9:20
Israel **p** peace by Jesus ... Acts 10:36
baptism which John **p** ... Acts 10:37
he commanded us to **p** ... Acts 10:42
p the word to none but ... Acts 11:19
they **p** the word of God ... Acts 13:5
p unto you the forgiveness ... Acts 13:38
And there they **p** the ... Acts 14:7
and **p** unto you that ye ... Acts 14:15
they had **p** the word in ... Acts 14:25
every city them that **p** ... Acts 15:21
and **p** the word of the Lord ... Acts 15:35
we have **p** the word ... Acts 15:36
Holy Ghost to **p** the word ... Acts 16:6
this Jesus, whom I **p** ... Acts 17:3
the word of God was **p** of ... Acts 17:13
by Jesus whom Paul **p** ... Acts 19:13
Paul **p** unto them ready ... Acts 20:7
as Paul was long **p**, he sunk ... Acts 20:9
P the kingdom of God ... Acts 28:31
that **p** a man should not ... Rom 2:21
word of faith which we **p** ... Rom 10:8
fully **p** the gospel of Christ ... Rom 15:19
so have I strived to **p** the ... Rom 15:20
gospel and the **p** of Jesus ... Rom 16:25
not to baptize, but to **p** the ... 1Cor 1:17
p was not with enticing ... 1Cor 2:4
they which **p** the gospel ... 1Cor 9:14
when I have **p** to others ... 1Cor 9:27
you the gospel which I **p** ... 1Cor 15:1
they, so we **p**, and so ye ... 1Cor 15:11
if Christ be **p** that he rose ... 1Cor 15:12
be not risen, then is our **p** ... 1Cor 15:14
who was **p** among you by ... 2Cor 1:19
I came to Troas to **p** Christ's . . 2Cor 2:12
for we **p** not ourselves ... 2Cor 4:5
to you also in **p** the gospel ... 2Cor 10:14
p the gospel in the regions ... 2Cor 10:16
if he that cometh **p** another ... 2Cor 11:4
Jesus, whom we have not **p** ... 2Cor 11:4
now **p** the faith which ... Gal 1:23
I **p** among the Gentiles ... Gal 2:2
p before the gospel unto ... Gal 3:8
I **p** the gospel unto you ... Gal 4:13
if I yet **p** circumcision ... Gal 5:11
came and **p** peace to you ... Eph 2:17
I should **p** among the ... Eph 3:8
which was **p** to every ... Col 1:23
we **p**, warning every man ... Col 1:28
we **p** unto you the gospel ... 1Thess 2:9
p unto the Gentiles ... 1Tim 3:16
P the word; be instant ... 2Tim 4:2
me the **p** might be fully ... 2Tim 4:17

manifested his word through *p* .Titus 1:3
them that have *p* the 1Pet 1:12
and *p* unto the spirits in.......1Pet 3:19
cause was the gospel *p* 1Pet 4:6
to *p* unto them that dwell .....Rev 14:6

PREACHER—*one who proclaims the gospel publicly*
Author of Ecclesiastes ...Eccl 1:1, 2
Causes to hear ....Rom 10:14
Paul, speaking of himself .1Tim 2:7
2Tim 1:11
Noah, of righteousness ...2Pet 2:5

have I found, saith the *p* ......Eccl 7:27
of vanities, saith the *p* ....Eccl 12:8
p sought to find out ....Eccl 12:10

PRECEPT—*specific charge*

God's:
Commanded ....Heb 9:19
Corrupted ....Matt 15:9
Kept ....Ps 119:56-69
Sought ....Ps 119:40-94
Not forgotten ....Ps 119:93, 141
Loved ....Ps 119:159
Source of understanding. .Ps 119:100, 104

[*also* PRECEPTS]
commandedst them *p* ....Neh 9:14
commanded us to keep thy *p* ..Ps 119:4
I will meditate in thy *p* ....Ps 119:15
understand the way of thy *p* ...Ps 119:27
yet I erred not from thy *p*.....Ps 119:110
so will I keep thy *p*............Ps 119:134
kept thy *p* and thy testimonies .Ps 119:168
p must be upon *p*, *p* upon *p* ...Is 28:10
me is taught by the *p* of ......Is 29:13
and kept all his *p*, and.........Jer 35:18
by departing from thy *p*........Dan 9:5
heart he wrote you this *p* .....Mark 10:5
Moses had spoken every *p* ....Heb 9:19

PRECIOUS—*something extremely valuable*

Applied to spiritual things:
Word of God 1Sam 3:1
Wisdom ....Prov 3:13, 15
Soul..................1Sam 26:21
One's life 2Kin 1:13, 14
Redemption of a soul ....Ps 49:8
God's thoughts toward us.Ps 139:17
Death of God's people ...Ps 72:14
Christ ....Is 28:16
Christ's blood 1Pet 1:19
Faith 2Pet 1:1
Promises...............2Pet 1:4
Trial of faith 1Pet 1:7

Applied figuratively to:
Knowledge.............Prov 20:15
Sons of Zion ....Lam 4:2
Rewards 1Cor 3:12-14
Final harvest ....James 5:7
Worldly pomp..........Rev 17:4
Heaven's glory ....Rev 21:11, 19

to her mother *p* things ....Gen 24:53
for the *p* things of heaven .....Deut 33:13
p fruits brought forth by ......Deut 33:14
p things put forth by the ......Deut 33:14
for the *p* things of the earth ...Deut 33:16
a talent of gold with the *p* 2Sam 12:30
and very much gold, and *p* 1Kin 10:2
almug trees, and *p* stones 1Kin 10:11
the house of his *p* things 2Kin 20:13
the spices, and the *p*..........2Kin 20:13
and there were *p* stones in 1Chr 20:2
all manner of *p* stones, and ...1Chr 29:2
garnished the house with *p* 2Chr 3:6
gold in abundance, and *p* 2Chr 9:1
brought algum trees and *p* 2Chr 9:10
the dead bodies, and *p*........2Chr 20:25
and of gold, and of *p* 2Chr 21:3
and for gold, and for *p* 2Chr 32:27
with beasts, and with *p* ....Ezra 1:6
vessels of fine copper, *p* ......Ezra 8:27
and his eyes seeth every *p*.....Job 28:10
p in the sight of the Lord .....Ps 116:15
and weepeth, bearing *p* ....Ps 126:6
It is like the *p* ointment ....Ps 133:2
We shall find all *p* ....Prov 1:13
adulteress will hunt for *p* ......Prov 6:26
of a diligent man is *p* ....Prov 12:27
A gift is as a *p* stone in ....Prov 17:8
with all *p* and pleasant ....Prov 24:4
name is better than *p* ....Eccl 7:1
a man more *p* than fine ....Is 13:12
them the house of his *p* ....Is 39:2
the spices, and the *p*..........Is 39:2
Since thou wast *p* in my.......Is 43:4
take forth the *p* from the .....Jer 15:19
and all the *p* things ....Jer 20:5
taken the treasure and *p* .....Ezek 22:25
Dedan..thy merchant in *p* .....Ezek 27:20
every *p* stone was thy ....Ezek 28:13
p vessels of silver and of ......Dan 11:8
over all the *p* things of........Dan 11:43
alabaster box of very *p*........Matt 26:7
ointment of spikenard very *p* ..Mark 14:3
but chosen of God, and *p* 1Pet 2:4
which believe he is *p* 1Pet 2:7
silver, and *p* stones, and ......Rev 18:12
manner vessels of most *p*......Rev 18:12
with gold, and *p* stones ....Rev 18:16

PRECIOUS PROMISES—*promises God has made to those who obey Him*

To the troubled by:
Doubts ....Ps 73:1-28
Afflictions ....Ps 34:1-22
Persecution ....Matt 5:11, 12
Anxiety.................Phil 4:6
Temptation 1Cor 10:13
Infirmities 2Cor 12:7-10
Discipline...............Heb 12:3-13

To the sorrowful over:
Death 1Thess 4:13-18
Sickness ....James 5:13-16
Their sins ....Ps 32:1-11
Disappointment ....Rom 8:28

To those troubled by:
World 1John 2:15-17
Flesh ....Gal 5:16-18
Satan..................Luke 22:31, 32
Anxious ....Matt 6:31-34
Sin ....James 1:12-15
Pride 1Pet 5:5-7

To the active Christian in his:
Giving..................Mal 3:10
Zeal....................Phil 4:13
Soul winning ....James 5:20
Fruitfulness ....John 7:38, 39
Graces 2Pet 1:5-11
Prayers ....James 5:16
Perseverance ....Gal 6:9
Watchfulness ....Eph 6:10-20
Assurance ....Rom 8:32-39
Ministry ....Ps 138:8

PREDESTINATION—*God's plan for the eternal salvation of those who choose Him*

Described as:
"Purpose" ....Rom 8:28
"Afore prepared" ....Rom 9:23
"Foreknowledge".......Acts 2:23
"Foreknew" ....Rom 8:29
"Ordained"............Acts 13:48
"Appointed" ....Acts 22:10
"Determined" ....Luke 22:22
"Foreseeing" ....Gal 3:8
"Before the world began".2Tim 1:9

Determined by God's:
Counsel ....Acts 2:23
Foreknowledge ....Acts 2:23
Good pleasure ....Luke 12:32
1Cor 1:21
Will ....Eph 1:5, 9, 11
Purpose ....Eph 3:11
Power ....Is 40:10-17
Rom 9:15-24

Expressed toward the believer in:
Election ....Eph 1:4
Salvation 2Thess 2:13, 14
Justification ....Rom 8:30
Sanctification...........1Thess 2:12, 13
Glorification ....Rom 8:30
Eternal destiny ....Matt 25:34

See FOREKNOWLEDGE OF GOD; ELECT

PREDICT—*to foretell*
Astrologers ....Is 47:13

PREEMINENCE—*being supreme above all*

Of creatures:
Sought by the devil ......Is 14:12-15
Sought by man ....Gen 3:5, 6
Illustrated by Diotrephes .3John 9, 10

Of Christ:
Predicted ....Ps 45:6, 7
Proclaimed.............Luke 1:31-33
Visualized ....Matt 17:4, 5
Realized ....Col 1:19
Acknowledged ....Phil 2:9, 10

a man hath no *p* above a .....Eccl 3:19
things he might have the *p* ....Col 1:18

PREFER—*to promote; choose; set before*

[*also* PREFERRED, PREFERRING]
he *p* her and her maids ....Esth 2:9
If I *p* not Jerusalem ....Ps 137:6
this Daniel was *p* above ....Dan 6:3
cometh after me is *p*..........John 1:15
a man which is *p* before me ...John 1:30
love; in honor *p* one ....Rom 12:10
without *p* one before 1Tim 5:21

PREGNANCY—*the condition of containing the unborn within the body*
Safeguards provided .....Ex 21:22-25
Evidences of ....Luke 1:44
God's call during ....Jer 1:4, 5
Gal 1:15

PREJUDICE—*a biased opinion*

Toward men, based on:
Race ....Acts 19:34
Social position ....James 2:1-4
Jealousy ....Gen 37:3-11

Toward Christ, based on His:
Lowly origin ....Mark 6:3
Residence in Galilee .....John 1:46
Race ....John 4:9
Teaching...............John 9:16-41

See BIGOTRY

PREMEDITATION—*deliberate plan to perform an act*

With:
Evil intent ....Gen 27:41-45
Good intent............Luke 14:28-33
Heavenly sanctions ......James 4:13-17

[*also* PREMEDITATE]
speak, neither do ye *p* ....Mark 13:11

PREPARATION—*action or actions to achieve readiness beforehand; plan or plans*

[*also* PREPARATIONS]
will therefore now make *p* 1Chr 22:5
The *p* of the heart in man, and.Prov 16:1
torches in the day of his *p* ....Nah 2:3
And it was the *p* of the ....John 19:14
because of the Jews' *p* day ....John 19:42
with the *p* of the gospel ....Eph 6:15

PREPARATION DAY—*the day on which the Jews prepared to celebrate the Sabbath*
Evening ....Matt 27:57, 62
Day before Sabbath .....Mark 15:42
Luke 23:54

PREPARE—*to make ready beforehand; plan*

Of spiritual things:
To build an altar ....Josh 22:26
Lord's way.............Matt 8:3

P

God .... Amos 4:12
God's throne .... Ps 9:7
Heart .... Ezra 7:10
Passover .... Luke 22:8, 9
Spiritual provision .... Ps 23:5
Service 2Tim 2:21
Redeemed people .... Rom 9:23, 24

Of eternal things:
Reward .... Matt 20:23
Kingdom .... Matt 25:34
Heaven .... John 14:2, 3
Heavenly city .... Heb 11:16
Everlasting fire .... Matt 25:41

[*also* PREPARED, PREPAREDST, PREPAREST, PREPARETH, PREPARING]

I have *p* the house, and .... Gen 24:31
bread, which she had *p* .... Gen 27:17
neither had they *p* for .... Ex 12:39
and I will *p* him an .... Ex 15:2
they shall *p* that which .... Ex 16:5
place which I have *p* .... Ex 23:20
drink offering shalt thou *p* .... Num 15:5
thou *p* a bullock for a .... Num 15:8
number that ye shall *p* .... Num 15:12
city of Sihon be built and *p* .... Num 21:27
p me here seven oxen and .... Num 23:1
unto him, I have *p* seven .... Num 23:4
Thou shalt *p* thee a way .... Deut 19:3
people, saying, *p* you .... Josh 1:11
he had *p* of the children .... Josh 4:4
p your hearts unto the 1Sam 7:3
I pray you, *p* ye, and 1Sam 23:22
Absalom *p* him chariots 2Sam 15:1
he *p* him chariots and 1Kin 1:5
so they *p* timber and 1Kin 5:18
the oracle he *p* in the 1Kin 6:19
Ahab, *p* thy chariot, and 1Kin 18:44
showbread, to *p* it every 1Chr 9:32
for their brethren had *p* 1Chr 12:39
P a place for the ark of God 1Chr 15:1
place that I have *p* for 1Chr 15:12
And David *p* iron in 1Chr 22:3
I have *p* for the house 1Chr 22:14
Now I have *p* with all my 1Chr 29:2
we have *p* to build thee 1Chr 29:16
and *p* their heart unto thee 1Chr 29:18
place which David had *p* 2Chr 1:4
to *p* me timber in 2Chr 2:9
place that David had *p* 2Chr 3:1
the work of Solomon was *p* 2Chr 8:16
he *p* not his heart to seek 2Chr 12:14
spices *p* by the apothecaries' 2Chr 16:14
thousand ready *p* for the 2Chr 17:18
hast *p* thine heart to seek 2Chr 19:3
people had not *p* their 2Chr 20:33
Uzziah *p* for them 2Chr 26:14
p his ways before the Lord 2Chr 27:6
transgression, have we *p* 2Chr 29:19
That *p* his heart to seek 2Chr 30:19
to *p* chambers in the 2Chr 31:11
of the Lord; and they *p* 2Chr 31:11
p yourselves by the 2Chr 35:4
the service was *p*, and the 2Chr 35:10
brethren the Levites *p* 2Chr 35:15
this when Josiah had *p* 2Chr 35:20
Ezra had *p* his heart to .... Ezra 7:10
was *p* for me daily was .... Neh 5:18
also the fowls were *p* for .... Neh 5:18
for whom nothing is *p* .... Neh 8:10
had *p* for him a great .... Neh 13:5
in *p* him a chamber in the .... Neh 13:7
the banquet that I have *p* .... Esth 5:4
banquet that I shall *p* for .... Esth 5:8
banquet that she had *p* .... Esth 5:12
the gallows that he had *p* .... Esth 6:4
the gallows that he had *p* .... Esth 7:10
p thyself to the search of .... Job 8:8
If thou *p* thine heart, and .... Job 11:13
dust, and *p* raiment as the .... Job 27:16
it; he *p* it, yea, and .... Job 28:27
city, when I *p* my seat in .... Job 29:7
also *p* for him the .... Ps 7:13
thou wilt *p* their hearts .... Ps 10:17
They have *p* a net for my .... Ps 57:6
p themselves without my .... Ps 59:4
O *p* mercy and truth .... Ps 61:7
thou *p* them corn, when .... Ps 65:9
God, hast *p* of thy .... Ps 68:10
thou hast *p* the light and .... Ps 74:16
Thou *p* room before it .... Ps 80:9
they may *p* a city for .... Ps 107:36
hath *p* his throne in the .... Ps 130:19
who *p* rain for the earth .... Ps 147:8
When he *p* the heavens, I .... Prov 8:27
Judgments are *p* for .... Prov 19:29
The horse is *p* against .... Prov 21:31
p thy work without, and .... Prov 24:27
they *p* their meat in the .... Prov 30:25
p slaughter for his .... Is 14:21
p the table, watch in the .... Is 21:5
yea, for the king it is *p* .... Is 30:33
p ye the way of the Lord .... Is 40:3
ye up, *p* the way, take up .... Is 57:14
p the way of the people .... Is 62:10
p for him that waiteth .... Is 64:4
that *p* a table for that .... Is 65:11
p ye war against her .... Jer 6:4
p them for the day of .... Jer 12:3
I will *p* destroyers against .... Jer 22:7
Stand fast, and *p* thee .... Jer 46:14
the watchmen, *p* the .... Jer 51:12
p against her the nations .... Jer 51:28
thou shalt *p* thy bread .... Ezek 4:15
man, *p* thee stuff for .... Ezek 12:3
thy pipes was *p* in thee .... Ezek 28:13
I will *p* thee unto blood .... Ezek 35:6
Be thou *p*, and *p* for thyself .... Ezek 38:7
thou *p* every day a goat .... Ezek 43:25
they shall also *p* a young .... Ezek 43:25
he shall *p* the sin offering .... Ezek 45:17
p a burnt offering to the .... Ezek 45:23
priests shall *p* his burnt .... Ezek 46:2
shall *p* a voluntary burnt .... Ezek 46:12
he shall *p* his burnt .... Ezek 46:12
Thou shalt daily *p* a .... Ezek 46:13
thou shalt *p* it every .... Ezek 46:13
Thus shall they *p* the .... Ezek 46:15
have *p* lying and corrupt .... Dan 2:9
and gold, which they *p* .... Hos 2:8
going forth is *p* as the .... Hos 6:3
p war, wake up the .... Joel 3:9
p a great fish to swallow .... Jon 1:17
And the Lord God *p* a .... Jon 4:6
that God *p* a vehement .... Jon 4:8
they even *p* war against .... Mic 3:5
the defense shall be *p* .... Nah 2:5
Lord hath *p* a sacrifice .... Zeph 1:7
and he shall *p* the way .... Mal 3:1
p ye the way of the Lord .... Matt 3:3
which shall *p* thy way .... Matt 11:10
Behold, I have *p* my .... Matt 22:4
p for thee to eat the .... Matt 26:17
which shall *p* thy way .... Mark 1:2
to them for whom it is *p* .... Mark 10:40
wilt thou that we go and *p* .... Mark 14:12
room furnished and *p* .... Mark 14:15
face of the Lord to *p* his .... Luke 1:76
p before the face of all .... Luke 2:31
p ye the way of the Lord .... Luke 3:4
which shall *p* thy way .... Luke 7:27
his lord's will, and *p* not .... Luke 12:47
p spices and ointments .... Luke 23:56
spices which they had *p* .... Luke 24:1
hath *p* for them that love 1Cor 2:9
who shall *p* himself to 1Cor 14:8
p me also a lodging: for .... Philem 22
but a body hast thou *p* .... Heb 10:5
p an ark to the saving of .... Heb 11:7
while the ark was a *p* 1Pet 3:20
trumpets *p* themselves to .... Rev 8:6
like unto horses *p* unto .... Rev 9:7
where she hath a place *p* .... Rev 12:6
kings of the east might be *p* .... Rev 16:12
p as a bride adorned for .... Rev 21:2

PRESBYTERY—*the Christian eldership acting as a body*
Ordination ascribed to 1Tim 4:14
See ELDERS IN THE CHURCH

PRESCRIBE—*to lay down a rule*

[*also* PRESCRIBED, PRESCRIBING]

and salt without *p* how .... Ezra 7:22
which they have *p* .... Is 10:1

PRESENCE—*being present*

[*also* PRESENT]

dwell in the *p* of all his .... Gen 16:12
in the *p* of the sons of my .... Gen 23:11
died in the *p* of all his .... Gen 25:18
out from the *p* of Isaac .... Gen 27:30
went out from the *p* of .... Gen 41:46
were troubled at his *p* .... Gen 45:3
should we die in thy *p* .... Gen 47:15
driven out from Pharaoh's *p* .... Ex 10:11
departed from the *p* of .... Ex 35:20
Aaron went down from the *p* .... Num 20:6
unto him in the *p* of the .... Deut 25:9
the priests, in the *p* of .... Josh 4:11
p of the children of .... Josh 8:32
the people that were *p* 1Sam 13:15
David avoided out of his *p* 1Sam 18:11
he was in his *p*, as in 1Sam 19:7
hand, or what there is *p* 1Sam 21:3
the mad man in my *p* 1Sam 21:15
I not serve in the *p* of his 2Sam 16:19
served in thy father's *p* 2Sam 16:19
so will I be in thy *p* 2Sam 16:19
days, and be thou here *p* 2Sam 20:4
went out from the *p* of 2Sam 24:4
came into the king's *p* 1Kin 1:28
p of all the congregation 1Kin 8:22
fled from the *p* of king 1Kin 12:2
numbered, and were all *p* 1Kin 20:27
against Naboth in the *p* 1Kin 21:13
that I regard the *p* of 2Kin 3:14
his *p* a leper as white as 2Kin 5:27
cast he them from his *p* 2Kin 13:23
cast them out from his *p* 2Kin 24:20
that were in the king's *p* 2Kin 25:19
Aaron in the *p* of David 1Chr 24:31
joy thy people, which are *p* 1Chr 29:17
p of all the congregation 2Chr 6:12
earth sought the *p* of 2Chr 9:23
p of Solomon the king 2Chr 10:2
in thy *p*, for thy name 2Chr 20:9
all that were *p* with him 2Chr 29:29
that were *p* at Jerusalem 2Chr 30:21
all Israel that were *p* went 2Chr 31:1
altars of Baalim in his *p* 2Chr 34:4
were *p* in Jerusalem 2Chr 34:32
for all that were *p*, to the 2Chr 35:7
Judah and Israel that were *p* 2Chr 35:18
all Israel there *p*, had .... Ezra 8:25
beforetime sad in his *p* .... Neh 2:1
the people that were *p* in .... Esth 1:5
p of Ahasuerus the king .... Esth 1:10
Jews that are *p* in .... Esth 4:16
went out from the *p* of .... Esth 8:15
me in the *p* of mine .... Ps 23:5
strength, a very *p* help in .... Ps 46:1
Lord now in the *p* of all .... Ps 116:14
Go from the *p* of a foolish .... Prov 14:7
surety in the *p* of his .... Prov 17:18
forth thyself in the *p* of .... Prov 25:6
devour it in your *p* .... Is 1:7
the *p* of the priests and of .... Jer 28:1
Hananiah in the *p* of the .... Jer 28:5
and in the *p* of all the .... Jer 28:5
and in the *p* of the .... Jer 32:12
answered in the *p* of the .... Dan 2:27
of the Lord was *p* to heal .... Luke 5:17
There were *p* at that .... Luke 13:1
in the *p* of them that sit .... Luke 14:10
there is joy in the *p* of the .... Luke 15:10
unto you, being yet *p* .... John 14:25
did Jesus in the *p* of his .... John 20:30
denied him in the *p* of .... Acts 3:13
departed from the *p* of the .... Acts 5:41
we all here *p* before God .... Acts 10:33
and all the elders were *p* .... Acts 21:18
all men which are here *p* .... Acts 25:24
thanks to God in the *p* of .... Acts 27:35
because of the *p* rain, and .... Acts 28:2
for to will is *p* with me .... Rom 7:18

sufferings of this *p* time ....Rom 8:18
then at this *p* time also ....Rom 11:5
flesh should glory in his *p* 1Cor 1:29
or things *p*, or things to 1Cor 3:22
unto this *p* hour we both 1Cor 4:11
as absent in body, but *p* 1Cor 5:3
judged..as though I were *p* 1Cor 5:3
that this is good for the *p* 1Cor 7:26
part remain unto this *p* 1Cor 15:6
body, and to be *p* with the 2Cor 5:8
when I am *p* with that 2Cor 10:2
as if I were *p*, the second 2Cor 13:2
deliver us from this *p* evil .....Gal 1:4
not only when I am *p*.........Gal 4:18
obeyed, not as in my *p* ....Phil 2:12
me, having loved this *p* 2Tim 4:10
and godly, in this *p* world .....Titus 2:12
figure for the time then *p* .....Heb 9:9
no chastening for the *p* ....Heb 12:11
and be established in the *p* 2Pet 1:12
in the *p* of the holy angels ....Rev 14:10

PRESENCE, DIVINE—*the truth that God is present*

Described as:
Glory 1Chr 16:27
Joyful ....Ps 16:11
Protective...............Ps 31:20
Everywhere ....Ps 139:7
Guide ....Ex 33:14, 15

the *p* of the Lord God ....Gen 3:8
Cain went out from the *p* .....Gen 4:16
forth from the *p* of the Lord ..Job 1:12
forth from the *p* of the Lord ..Job 2:7
am I troubled at his *p* ....Job 23:15
fall and perish at thy *p*........Ps 9:3
come forth from thy *p* ....Ps 17:2
Cast me not away from thy *p*..Ps 51:11
the wicked perish at the *p*.....Ps 68:2
dropped at the *p* of God ....Ps 68:8
was moved at the *p* of God ...Ps 68:8
his *p* with thanksgiving ....Ps 95:2
wax at the *p* of the Lord ......Ps 97:5
p of the Lord of the ....Ps 97:5
come before his *p* with........Ps 100:2
earth, at the *p* of the Lord ....Ps 114:7
p of the God of Jacob ....Ps 114:7
upright shall dwell in thy *p* ....Ps 140:13
shall be moved at his *p* ....Is 19:1
and the angel of his *p*.........Is 63:9
might flow down at thy *p* .....Is 64:1
flowed down at thy *p* ....Is 64:3
down at the *p* of the Lord ....Jer 4:26
ye not tremble at my *p* ....Jer 5:22
and cast you out of my *p* .....Jer 23:39
cast them out from his *p* ......Jer 52:3
earth, shall shake at my *p*.....Ezek 38:20
earth is burned at his *p* ....Nah 1:5
in the *p* of the Lord God .....Zeph 1:7
stand in the *p* of God.........Luke 1:19
eaten and drunk in thy *p*......Luke 13:26
from the *p* of the Lord........Acts 3:19
from the *p* of the Lord........2Thess 1:9
to appear in the *p* of God.....Heb 9:24
faultless before the *p* of ....Jude 24

PRESENT—*to offer*

As an introduction of:
Joseph's brothers ....Gen 47:2
Joseph to his father......Gen 46:29
Dorcas to her friends ....Acts 9:41
Paul to a governor ......Acts 23:33

Descriptive of the Christian's life as:
Living and holy sacrifice. .Rom 12:1
Chaste virgin 2Cor 11:2
Holy ....Col 1:22
Perfect ....Col 1:28
Without blemish.........Eph 5:27
Resurrected 2Cor 4:14

[*also* PRESENTED, PRESENTING]
Sinai, and *p* thyself there ......Ex 34:2
it is *p* unto the priest ....Lev 2:8
p them to minister unto ....Lev 7:35
sons *p* unto him the blood ....Lev 9:12
sons *p* unto him the blood ....Lev 9:18
p the man that is to be ....Lev 14:11
scapegoat, shall be *p*..........Lev 16:10
shall *p* himself before ....Lev 27:8
p them before Aaron the......Num 3:6
p themselves in the ....Deut 31:14
p themselves before God ......Josh 24:1
p themselves in the ....Judg 20:2
p yourselves before the 1Sam 10:19
evening, and *p* himself 1Sam 17:16
to *p* themselves before ....Job 1:6
to *p* themselves before ....Job 2:1
them to *p* himself before ......Job 2:1
p their supplication ....Jer 36:7
I *p* my supplication ....Jer 38:26
ye sent me to *p* your ....Jer 42:9
they *p* the provocation of .....Ezek 20:28
p our supplications ....Dan 9:18
p my supplication before ......Dan 9:20
treasures, they *p* unto.........Matt 2:11
Jerusalem, to *p* him to ....Luke 2:22
and to *p* you faultless ....Jude 24

PRESENT—*gift*

Offered to:
Brother.................Gen 32:13-20
King ....Is 39:1
Solomon 1Kin 4:21
Foreign nation ....Hos 10:6

Purposes of:
Conceal a treacherous act.Judg 3:15-23
Verify a messenger ......Judg 6:18-24
Secure a message 2Kin 8:7-10
Pay tribute..............2Kin 17:3, 4
Show friendship 2Kin 20:12, 13
Show obedience ....Ps 72:10

See GIFTS OF MAN

[*also* PRESENTS]
then receive my *p* at my ......Gen 33:10
carry down the man a *p*.......Gen 43:11
the *p* against Joseph ....Gen 43:25
is not a *p* to bring to the 1Sam 9:7
and brought him no *p*.........1Sam 10:27
a *p* for you of the spoil 1Sam 30:26
brought every man his *p* 1Kin 10:25
unto thee a *p* of silver 1Kin 15:19
it for a *p* to the king of 2Kin 16:8
agreement with me by a *p*.....2Kin 18:31
all the priests..*p* were 2Chr 5:11
brought every man his *p* 2Chr 9:24
brought to Jehoshaphat *p* 2Chr 17:5
and *p* to Hezekiah king of 2Chr 32:23
shall kings bring *p* unto ....Ps 68:29
bring *p* unto him that ....Ps 76:11
the *p* be brought unto the .....Is 18:7
an agreement with me by a *p*..Is 36:16
for a *p* horns of ivory and.....Ezek 27:15
thou give *p* to Moresheth .....Mic 1:14

PRESENTLY—*immediately*
not fail to burn the fat *p* 1Sam 2:16
A fool's wrath is *p* known.....Prov 12:16
And *p* the fig tree withered ...Matt 21:19
shall *p* give me more ....Matt 26:53
therefore I hope to send *p* ....Phil 2:23

PRESERVATION, GOD'S—*God's keeping his people safe from harm*

As manifested over:
World ....Neh 9:6
King 2Sam 8:6, 14
Animals ....Ps 36:6
Nation.................Gen 45:5, 7
Messiah ....Is 49:8
Apostle................2Tim 4:18
Believers 1Thess 5:23
Faithful................Ps 31:23

Special objects of:
Those who trust Him ....Ps 16:1
Holy ....Ps 86:2
Souls of saints...........Ps 97:10
Simple..................Ps 116:6
Those who love Him ....Ps 145:20
Strangers ....Ps 146:9

Spiritual means of:
Integrity ....Ps 25:21
Lovingkindness ....Ps 40:11
Mercy and truth ....Ps 61:7
Wisdom ....Prov 4:5, 6
Losing one's life ....Luke 17:33
Prophet.................Hos 12:13

PRESERVE—*to keep safe from harm; protect; maintain*

[*also* PRESERVED, PRESERVETH]
we may *p* seed of our ....Gen 19:32
to face, and my life is *p*.......Gen 32:30
that he might *p* us alive ....Deut 6:24
p us in all the way...........Josh 24:17
who hath *p* us, and 1Sam 30:23
Lord *p* David whithersoever ...1Chr 18:6
thy visitation hath *p* my ....Job 10:12
as in the days when God *p* ....Job 29:2
He *p* not the life of the ....Job 36:6
p them from this ....Ps 12:7
thou shalt *p* me from ....Ps 32:7
they are *p* for ever: but ....Ps 37:28
The Lord will *p* him, and .....Ps 41:2
p my life from fear of the .....Ps 64:1
p thou those that are ....Ps 79:11
Lord shall *p* thee from ....Ps 121:7
he shall *p* thy soul ....Ps 121:7
man: *p* me from the ....Ps 140:1
and *p* the way of his saints ....Prov 2:8
Discretion shall *p* thee ....Prov 2:11
the lips of the wise shall *p* ....Prov 14:3
he that keepeth his way *p* .....Prov 16:17
Mercy and truth *p* the king....Prov 20:28
The eyes of the Lord *p* ....Prov 22:12
passing over he will *p*.........Is 31:5
and to restore the *p* of........Is 49:6
children, I will *p* them ....Jer 49:11
new bottles, and both are *p* ...Matt 9:17
new bottles; and both are *p* ...Luke 5:38
and *p* in Jesus Christ ....Jude 1

PRESERVER—*one who keeps safe; protector*
I do unto thee, O thou *P* .....Job 7:20

PRESIDENT—*ruler*
Daniel acted as..........Dan 6:2

[*also* PRESIDENTS]
the *p* and princes sought ......Dan 6:4
All the *p* of the kingdom......Dan 6:7

PRESS—*a machine for extracting the juice from grapes; to apply pressure to*
Used literally ....Neh 13:15
Figurative of appointed time...................Joel 3:13

[*also* PRESSED, PRESSES, PRESSETH]
And he *p* upon them ....Gen 19:3
p them into Pharaoh's ....Gen 40:11
he *p* him: howbeit he 2Sam 13:25
p on by the king's ....Esth 8:14
in me, and thy hand *p* ....Ps 38:2
p shall burst out with ....Prov 3:10
tread out no wine in their *p* ...Is 16:10
there were their breast *p* ......Ezek 23:3
Behold, I am *p* under you.....Amos 2:13
vessels out of the *p* ....Hag 2:16
unto him for the *p*............Mark 2:4
they *p* upon him for to........Mark 3:10
came in the *p* behind, and ....Mark 5:27
good measure, *p* down ....Luke 6:38
not come at him for the *p*.....Luke 8:19
could not for the *p* ....Luke 19:3
Paul was *p* in the spirit ....Acts 18:5
that we were *p* out of.........2Cor 1:8

PRESSFAT—*vat into which the juice was collected when grapes were pressed*
one came to the *p* for to ......Hag 2:16

PRESSURE—*force exerted*

As evil:
Perversion ....Gen 19:9
Enticement ....Judg 16:16

As a good, to:
Hear God's Word ....Luke 5:1

Get into the kingdom ....Luke 16:16
Attain a goal............Phil 3:14

PRESUME—*to speak or act without warrant*

[*also* PRESUMPTUOUSLY]
soul that doeth aught *p* ....Num 15:30
and went *p* up into the........Deut 1:43
man that will do *p*............Deut 17:12
durst *p* in his heart ....Esth 7:5

PRESUMPTION—*speaking or acting without warrant*

Manifested in:
Speaking without divine warrant...............Deut 18:20-22
Acting without God's presence..............Num 14:44, 45
Living without God......Luke 12:19-21
Performing functions without authority......Num 16:3-11
Supposing God will not judge sin ....Ps 73:8, 9
Aspiring to divine titles ..Is 14:12-15
Posing as righteous ......Luke 18:11, 12
Making plans without God..................James 4:13, 14

Judgment upon:
Defeat..................Is 37:23-36
Loss of power...........Judg 16:20
Quick punishment 2Sam 6:6, 7
Rejection 1Sam 15:3, 9-23
Destruction ....Lev 10:1, 2

[*also* PRESUMPTUOUS]
thy servant also from *p* ....Ps 19:13
p are they, self-willed 2Pet 2:10

PRETENSE—*false or counterfeit profession*
Pharisees condemned for .Matt 23:14

for a *p* make long prayers .....Mark 12:40
whether in *p*, or in truth ......Phil 1:18

PRETORIUM—*the governor's official residence*
1. Pilate's, in Jerusalem ....Mark 15:16
Translated "common hall" and "judgment hall"................Matt 27:27
2. Herod's palace at Caesarea ....Acts 23:35
3. Praetorian guard at Rome................Phil 1:13

PREVAIL—*to gain mastery over*

Of physical force:
Waters ....Gen 7:18-24
Enemies.................Num 22:6
Combat..................1Sam 17:50

Of supernatural force in:
Battle ....Ex 17:11
Combat..................1Sam 17:9, 50
Accomplish much 1Sam 26:25
Conquest ....Jer 20:7
Victory ....Rev 5:5

[*also* PREVAILED, PREVAILEST, PREVAILETH]
my sister, and I have *p* ....Gen 30:8
he saw that he *p* not..........Gen 32:25
because the famine *p* ....Gen 47:20
of thy father have *p* ....Gen 49:26
of the house of Joseph *p* ......Judg 1:35
p against Chushan ....Judg 3:10
and *p* against Jabin the ....Judg 4:24
hand of Midian *p* against......Judg 6:2
what means we may *p* ....Judg 16:5
strength shall no man *p* 1Sam 2:9
Surely the men *p* against 2Sam 11:23
the king's word *p* against......2Sam 24:4
people that followed Omri *p*...1Kin 16:22
shalt persuade him, and *p* 1Kin 22:22
the famine *p* in the city 2Kin 25:3
For Judah *p* above his 1Chr 5:2
the king's word *p* against......1Chr 21:4
to Hamath-zobah, and *p* 2Chr 8:3
children of Judah *p*...........2Chr 13:18
God; let not man *p*...........2Chr 14:11
and thou shalt also *p* 2Chr 18:21
Ammonites, and *p*............2Chr 27:5
thou shalt not *p* against ....Esth 6:13
Thou *p* for ever against ....Job 14:20
they shall *p* against him ....Job 15:24
robber shall *p* against ....Job 18:9
Arise, O Lord let not man *p* ..Ps 9:19
With our tongue will we *p* ....Ps 12:4
enemy say, I have *p* ....Ps 13:4
Iniquities *p* against me ....Ps 65:3
yet they have not *p* ....Ps 129:2
if one *p* against him, two......Eccl 4:12
it, but could not *p* against.....Is 7:1
pray; but he shall not *p* ....Is 16:12
he shall *p* against his..........Is 42:13
if so be thou mayest *p* ....Is 47:12
but they shall not *p*............Jer 1:19
themselves, yet can they not *p* .Jer 5:22
enticed, and we shall *p*........Jer 20:10
thee on, and have *p* ....Jer 38:22
my bones, and it *p* against ....Lam 1:13
because the enemy *p*...........Lam 1:16
the saints, and *p* against ......Dan 7:21
against them and shall *p* ......Dan 11:7
over the angels, and *p* ....Hos 12:4
deceived thee, and *p*..........Obad 7
gates of hell shall not *p* ....Matt 16:18
Pilate saw..he could *p*.........Matt 27:24
of the chief priests *p* ....Luke 23:23
Perceive ye how ye *p* ....John 12:19
p against them, so that........Acts 19:16
p not; neither was their ....Rev 12:8

PREVARICATION—*evasion of truth*
Ananias and Sapphira killed for ....Acts 5:1-10
Solemn warning against ..Col 3:9

PREVENT—*to be ready; forestall; precede*

[*also* PREVENTED, PREVENTEST]
the snares of death *p* 2Sam 22:6
Why did the knees *p* me ......Job 3:12
the days of affliction *p* ....Job 30:27
Who hath *p* me, that I........Job 41:11
the snares of death *p* ....Ps 18:5
thou *p* him with the ....Ps 21:3
God of my mercy shall *p*......Ps 59:10
tender mercies speedily *p* .....Ps 79:8
morning shall my prayer *p* ....Ps 88:13
I *p* the dawning of the ....Ps 119:147
Mine eyes *p* the night.........Ps 119:148
p with their bread him ....Is 21:14
shall not overtake nor *p*.......Amos 9:10
into the house, Jesus *p*........Matt 17:25
shall not *p* them which 1Thess 4:15

PREY—*that which is taken by attack*

Used figuratively of:
Enemies ....Gen 49:9
Innocent victims ....Ezek 22:27

children should be a *p* ....Num 14:3
lie down until he eat of the *p*. .Num 23:24
all the spoil, and all the *p* .....Num 31:11
Take the sum of the *p* ....Num 31:26
the *p* which the men of ....Num 31:32
which ye said should be a *p* ...Deut 1:39
we took for a *p* unto ....Deut 2:35
cities, we took for a *p* to......Deut 3:7
ye take for a *p* unto ....Josh 8:2
Israel took for a *p* unto ....Josh 11:14
they not divided the *p* ....Judg 5:30
to Sisera a *p* of divers ....Judg 5:30
p of divers colors of ....Judg 5:30
man the earrings of his *p*......Judg 8:24
they shall become a *p* and.....2Kin 21:14
p in the land of captivity ......Neh 4:4
the spoil of them for a *p* ....Esth 8:11
on the *p* they laid not.........Esth 9:15
lion perisheth for lack of *p* ....Job 4:11
eagle that hasteth to the *p* ....Job 9:26
rising betimes for a *p* ....Job 24:5
Wilt thou hunt the *p* for ......Job 38:39
thence she seeketh the *p* ......Job 39:29
lion that is greedy of his *p* ....Ps 17:12
than the mountains of *p*.......Ps 76:4
lions roar after their *p* ....Ps 104:21
not given us as a *p* to.........Ps 124:6
lieth in wait as for a *p* ....Prov 23:28
lay hold of the *p*, and.........Is 5:29
widows may be their *p* ....Is 10:2
young lion roaring on his *p*...Is 31:4
is the *p* of a great spoil ....Is 33:23
divided; the lame take the *p*..Is 33:23
they are for a *p*, and ....Is 42:22
the *p* be taken from the.......Is 49:24
evil maketh himself a *p* ....Is 59:15
shall be unto him for a *p*......Jer 21:9
p..thee will I give for a *p* .....Jer 30:16
shall have his life for a *p*.....Jer 38:2
thy life shall be for a *p* ....Jer 39:18
I give unto thee for a *p* in ....Jer 45:5
of the strangers for a *p* ....Ezek 7:21
learned to catch the *p*.........Ezek 19:3
roaring lion ravening the *p* ....Ezek 22:25
a *p* of thy merchandise........Ezek 26:12
her spoil, and take her *p* ......Ezek 29:19
my flock became a *p*..........Ezek 34:8
shall no more be a *p* to the ...Ezek 34:28
became a *p* and derision ......Ezek 36:4
a spoil, and to take a *p* ....Ezek 38:12
scatter among them the *p* .....Dan 11:24
forest, when he hath no *p*.....Amos 3:4
filled his holes with *p*, and ....Nah 2:12
robbery; the *p* departeth ......Nah 3:1
day that I rise up to the *p*.....Zeph 3:8

PRICE—*cost*

[*also* PRICES]
thou shalt diminish the *p*......Lev 25:16
give again the *p* of his ....Lev 25:51
the *p* of a dog, into the ....Deut 23:18
surely buy it of thee at a *p*....2Sam 24:24
the linen yarn at a *p*..........1Kin 10:28
grant it me for the full *p* 1Chr 21:22
the linen yarn at a *p*..........2Chr 1:16
Man knoweth not the *p* ....Job 28:13
the *p* of wisdom is above......Job 28:18
thy wealth by their *p* ....Ps 44:12
a *p* in the hand of a fool ......Prov 17:16
the goats are the *p* of the .....Prov 27:26
her *p* is far above rubies ......Prov 31:10
my captives, not for *p* nor.....Is 45:13
money and without *p* ....Is 55:1
give to the spoil without *p* ....Jer 15:13
think good, give me my *p* .....Zech 11:12
p thirty pieces of silver........Zech 11:12
found one pearl of great *p* ....Matt 13:46
because it is the *p* of blood....Matt 27:6
p of the things that were ......Acts 4:34
kept back part of the *p*, his ...Acts 5:2
and they counted the *p* of.....Acts 19:19
For ye are bought with a *p*....1Cor 6:20
Ye are bought with a *p*; be....1Cor 7:23
sight of God of great *p* 1Pet 3:4

PRICKED—*afflicted with anguish, grief or remorse; pierced slightly with a sharp point*

[*also* PRICKING, PRICKS]
be *p* in your eyes, and ....Num 33:55
and I was *p* in my reins ....Ps 73:21
shall be no more a *p* brier ....Ezek 28:24
they were *p* in their heart .....Acts 2:37
thee to kick against the *p* .....Acts 9:5
thee to kick against the *p* .....Acts 26:14

PRIDE—*a conceited sense of one's superiority*

Origin of, in:
Devil ....Is 14:13-15
Ambition ....Dan 5:20-23
Evil heart...............Mark 7:21, 22
World 1John 2:16
Self-righteousness........Luke 18:11, 12
Worldly power ....Ezek 16:49, 56

Evils of:
Hardens the mind ....Dan 5:20
Produces spiritual decay..Hos 7:9, 10
Keeps from real progress .Prov 26:12
Hinders coming to God ..Ps 10:4
Issues in self-deception...Jer 49:16

Makes men reject God's
Word .... Jer 43:2
Leads to ruin .... Prov 16:18

Characteristic of:

Wicked .... Ps 73:6
World rulers .... Hab 2:4, 5
Last days 2Tim 3:2

I will break the ***p*** of your ..... Lev 26:19
I know thy ***p***, and the 1Sam 17:28
humbled himself for the ***p***..... 2Chr 32:26
purpose, and hide ***p*** from ..... Job 33:17
because of the ***p*** of evil .... Job 35:12
His scales are his ***p***, shut ...... Job 41:15
over all the children of ***p***...... Job 41:34
in his ***p*** doth persecute .... Ps 10:2
thy presence from the ***p*** of ..... Ps 31:20
the foot of ***p*** come against ..... Ps 36:11
even be taken in their ***p*******..... Ps 59:12
p, and arrogancy, and the ..... Prov 8:13
p cometh, then cometh........ Prov 11:2
by ***p*** cometh contention .... Prov 13:10
of the foolish is a rod of ***p*** .... Prov 14:3
p shall bring him low .... Prov 29:23
p and stoutness of heart....... Is 9:9
We have heard of the ***p*** of .... Is 16:6
his haughtiness, and his ***p*** ..... Is 16:6
to stain the ***p*** of all glory...... Is 23:9
he shall bring down their ***p***.... Is 25:11
Woe to the crown of ***p***, to .... Is 28:1
The crown of ***p***, the .... Is 28:3
will I mar the ***p*** of Judah ..... Jer 13:9
the great ***p*** of Jerusalem ...... Jer 13:9
secret places for your ***p*** .... Jer 13:17
We have heard the ***p*** of........ Jer 48:29
his arrogancy, and his ***p*** .... Jer 48:29
hath blossomed, ***p*** hath .... Ezek 7:10
and the ***p*** of her power .... Ezek 30:6
those that walk in ***p*** he is ..... Dan 4:37
the ***p*** of Israel doth testify ..... Hos 5:5
p of thine heart hath.......... Obad 3
shall they have for their ***p*** ..... Zeph 2:10
them that rejoice in thy ***p*** ..... Zeph 3:11
off the ***p*** of the Philistines ..... Zech 9:6
the ***p*** of Assyria shall be ...... Zech 10:11
the ***p*** of Jordan is spoiled ..... Zech 11:3
being lifted up with ***p*** he 1Tim 3:6

PRIEST—*authorized minister, especially one who makes sacrificial offerings and mediates between God and man*

Requirements of:

Must be a son of Aaron. . Ex 29:9
Sanctified to office ...... Ex 29:44
Statute perpetual .... Ex 27:21
No physical blemish ..... Lev 21:17-23
Genealogy of, necessary. . Ezra 2:62

Duties of:

Keeping the sanctuary ... Num 3:38
Keep lamp burning
continually .... Ex 27:20, 21
Continuing the sacred fire. Lev 6:12, 13
Covering furniture when
moved .... Num 4:5-15
Burning incense .... Ex 30:7, 8
Offering sacrifices .... Lev 1:1-17
Blessing the people ...... Num 6:23-27
Purifying the unclean .... Lev 15:15-31
Diagnosing leprosy ...... Lev 13:2-59
Blowing the trumpets .... Num 10:1-10
Carrying the ark of the
covenant .... Josh 3:6-17
Teaching the Law .... Lev 10:11

Names of:

Aaron .... Ex 31:10
Abiathar 1Sam 23:9
Ahimelech 1Sam 22:11
Amariah 2Chr 19:11
Ananias .... Acts 23:2
Caiaphas .... Matt 26:3
Christ .... Heb 3:1
Eleazar .... Num 16:39
Eli 1Sam 1:9
Eliashib .... Neh 3:1
Ezekiel Ezek1:3
Ezra .... Ezra 7:11, 12
Hilkiah 2Kin 22:4
Ira 2Sam 20:26
Jehorada 2Kin 11:9
Jehozadak .... Hag 1:1
Joshua .... Zech 3:1
Maaseiah .... Jer 37:3
Mattan (of Baal) 2Kin 11:18
Melchizedek .... Heb 7:1
Pashhur .... Jer 20:1
Phinehas .... Josh 22:30
Sceva .... Acts 19:14
Seraiah 2Kin 25:18
Shelemiah .... Neh 13:13
Urijah 2Kin 16:10
Zabud 1Kin 4:5
Zacharias .... Luke 1:5
Zadok 2Sam 15:27
Zephaniah 2Kin 25:18

See LEVITES

[*also* PRIEST'S, PRIESTS, PRIESTS']

was the ***p*** of the most high .... Gen 14:18
daughter of Poti-pherah ***p***..... Gen 41:45
Poti-pherah ***p*** of On bare ..... Gen 41:50
Poti-pherah ***p*** of On bare ..... Gen 46:20
the land of the ***p*** bought ...... Gen 47:22
p had a portion assigned ...... Gen 47:22
p of Midian had seven .... Ex 2:16
father-in-law, the ***p*** of......... Ex 3:1
Jethro, the ***p*** of Midian .... Ex 18:1
unto me a kingdom of ***p*** ...... Ex 19:6
the ***p*** and the people break..... Ex 19:24
minister unto me in the ***p*** ..... Ex 28:1
minister unto me in the ***p*** ..... Ex 28:41
minister unto me in the ***p*** ..... Ex 29:1
son that is ***p*** in his stead ...... Ex 29:30
minister unto me in the ***p*** ..... Ex 30:30
garments for Aaron the ***p*** ..... Ex 35:19
sons, to minister in the ***p***...... Ex 35:19
son to Aaron the ***p*** .... Ex 38:21
garments for Aaron the ***p*** ..... Ex 39:41
to minister in the ***p*** office ..... Ex 39:41
minister unto me in the ***p*** ..... Ex 40:13
it to Aaron's sons the ***p*** ...... Lev 2:2
p shall burn the memorial ..... Lev 2:2
it is presented unto the ***p*** ..... Lev 2:8
p shall take from the meat .... Lev 2:9
the ***p*** shall burn the.......... Lev 2:16
Aaron's sons the ***p*** shall....... Lev 3:2
the ***p*** shall burn it upon .... Lev 3:11
p shall burn them upon .... Lev 3:16
p that is anointed do sin ...... Lev 4:3
p that is anointed shall........ Lev 4:5
p shall dip his finger in .... Lev 4:6
p shall put some of the .... Lev 4:7
p shall burn them upon .... Lev 4:10
p that is anointed shall........ Lev 4:16
p shall dip his finger in .... Lev 4:17
the ***p*** shall make an.......... Lev 4:20
the ***p*** shall take of the .... Lev 4:25
p shall make an atonement .... Lev 4:26
p shall take of the blood ...... Lev 4:30
p shall make an atonement .... Lev 4:31
p shall take of the blood of ... Lev 4:34
p shall burn them upon .... Lev 4:35
p shall make an atonement .... Lev 4:35
p shall make an atonement .... Lev 5:6
bring them unto the ***p*** .... Lev 5:8
p shall make an atonement .... Lev 5:10
shall he bring it to the ***p*** ...... Lev 5:12
p shall take his handful .... Lev 5:12
p shall make an atonement .... Lev 5:13
the remnant shall be the ***p*** .... Lev 5:13
and give it unto the ***p*** .... Lev 5:16
p shall make an atonement .... Lev 5:16
offering, unto the ***p*** .... Lev 5:18
p shall make atonement .... Lev 5:18
trespass offering, unto the ***p*** .. Lev 6:6
p shall make an atonement .... Lev 6:7
p shall put on his linen........ Lev 6:10
the ***p*** of his sons that is ...... Lev 6:22
offering for the ***p*** shall be .... Lev 6:23
The ***p*** that offereth it for ..... Lev 6:26
the males among the ***p*** .... Lev 6:29
p shall burn them upon .... Lev 7:5
Every male among the ***p*** ...... Lev 7:6
p that maketh atonement...... Lev 7:7
p that offereth any man's ..... Lev 7:8
p shall have to himself .... Lev 7:8
pan, shall be the ***p*** that .... Lev 7:9
p shall burn the fat upon ...... Lev 7:31
ye give unto the ***p*** for an...... Lev 7:32
unto Aaron the ***p*** and unto .... Lev 7:34
unto the Lord in the ***p*** .... Lev 7:35
congregation, unto the ***p*** ...... Lev 12:6
p shall make an atonement .... Lev 12:8
p shall go forth out of the ..... Lev 14:3
p shall look, and, behold ...... Lev 14:3
the ***p*** command to take for .... Lev 14:4
p shall command that one ..... Lev 14:5
p that maketh him clean ...... Lev 14:11
p shall take one he lamb ...... Lev 14:12
as the sin offering is the ***p*** ..... Lev 14:13
p shall take some of the....... Lev 14:14
p shall put it upon the tip ..... Lev 14:14
p shall take some of the....... Lev 14:15
the ***p*** shall dip his right .... Lev 14:16
the ***p*** put upon the tip .... Lev 14:17
the ***p*** shall make an.......... Lev 14:18
p shall offer the sin .... Lev 14:19
the ***p*** shall offer the burnt ..... Lev 14:20
p shall make an atonement .... Lev 14:20
his cleansing unto the ***p*** .... Lev 14:23
the ***p*** shall take the lamb ...... Lev 14:24
the ***p*** shall wave them for ..... Lev 14:24
p shall take some of the....... Lev 14:25
p shall pour of the oil into .... Lev 14:26
the ***p*** shall sprinkle with....... Lev 14:27
the ***p*** shall put of the oil ..... Lev 14:28
p shall make an atonement .... Lev 14:31
shall come and tell the ***p*** ..... Lev 14:35
the ***p*** shall command that ..... Lev 14:36
the ***p*** go into it to see the ..... Lev 14:36
the ***p*** shall go in to see........ Lev 14:36
the ***p*** shall go out of the ...... Lev 14:38
the ***p*** shall come again the .... Lev 14:39
the ***p*** shall command that ..... Lev 14:40
the ***p*** shall come and look ..... Lev 14:44
if the ***p*** shall come in, and .... Lev 14:48
p shall pronounce the .... Lev 14:48
and give them unto the ***p*** ...... Lev 15:14
to minister in the ***p*** office ..... Lev 16:32
an atonement for the ***p*** .... Lev 16:33
unto the ***p***, and offer them .... Lev 17:5
the ***p*** shall sprinkle the .... Lev 17:6
p shall make an atonement .... Lev 19:22
Speak unto the ***p*** the sons ..... Lev 21:1
daughter of any ***p***, if she ...... Lev 21:9
the high ***p*** among his .... Lev 21:10
a sojourner of the ***p***, or an .... Lev 22:10
the ***p*** daughter also be .... Lev 22:12
it unto the ***p*** with the holy .... Lev 22:14
first fruits..unto the ***p*** .... Lev 23:10
the sabbath the ***p*** shall .... Lev 23:11
the ***p*** shall wave them with .... Lev 23:20
holy to the Lord for the ***p*** ..... Lev 23:20
himself before the ***p*** .... Lev 27:8
the ***p*** shall value him .... Lev 27:8
vowed shall the ***p*** value .... Lev 27:8
the beast before the ***p*** .... Lev 27:11
p shall value it, whether ...... Lev 27:12
who art the ***p***, so shall it ...... Lev 27:12
the ***p*** shall estimate it .... Lev 27:14
the ***p*** shall estimate it .... Lev 27:14
p shall reckon unto him .... Lev 27:18
possession..shall be the ***p***... Lev 27:21
Aaron, the ***p*** which were ...... Num 3:3
to minister in the ***p*** office ..... Num 3:3
them before Aaron the ***p***...... Num 3:6
they shall wait on their ***p***...... Num 3:10
the son of Aaron the ***p*** .... Num 3:32
the son of Aaron the ***p*** .... Num 4:16
the son of Aaron the ***p*** .... Num 4:28
even to the ***p***; beside the ...... Num 5:8
they bring unto the ***p*** .... Num 5:9
any man giveth the ***p*** .... Num 5:10
bring his wife unto the ***p*** ..... Num 5:15
the ***p*** shall bring her near ..... Num 5:16
the ***p*** shall take holy water .... Num 5:17

the **p** shall take, and put it .... Num 5:17
the **p** shall set the woman .... Num 5:18
p shall have in his hand .... Num 5:18
the **p** shall charge her by .... Num 5:19
p shall charge the woman .... Num 5:21
the **p** shall say unto the .... Num 5:21
the **p** shall write these .... Num 5:23
p shall take the jealousy .... Num 5:25
p shall take a handful .... Num 5:26
p shall execute upon her .... Num 5:30
young pigeons to the **p** .... Num 6:10
the **p** shall offer the one .... Num 6:11
p shall bring them before .... Num 6:16
p shall offer also his meat .... Num 6:17
p shall take the sodden .... Num 6:19
the **p** shall wave them for .... Num 6:20
this is holy for the **p**, with .... Num 6:20
the son of Aaron the **p** .... Num 7:8
p shall make an atonement .... Num 15:25
p shall make an atonement .... Num 15:28
the son of Aaron the **p** .... Num 16:37
with thee shall keep your **p** .... Num 18:7
I have given your **p** office .... Num 18:7
offering to Aaron the **p** .... Num 18:28
give her unto Eleazar the **p** .... Num 19:3
And Eleazar the **p** shall .... Num 19:4
p shall take cedar wood .... Num 19:6
Then the **p** shall wash his .... Num 19:7
p shall be unclean until .... Num 19:7
son of Aaron the **p**, saw .... Num 25:7
son of Aaron the **p**, hath .... Num 25:11
the son of Aaron the **p** .... Num 26:1
and Eleazar the **p** spake .... Num 26:3
Moses and Eleazar the **p** .... Num 26:63
Moses and Aaron the **p** .... Num 26:64
and before Eleazar the **p** .... Num 27:2
him before Eleazar the **p** .... Num 27:19
stand before Eleazar the **p** .... Num 27:21
him before Eleazar the **p** .... Num 27:22
the son of Eleazar the **p** .... Num 31:6
Moses, and Eleazar the **p** .... Num 31:12
Moses, and Eleazar the **p** .... Num 31:13
Eleazar the **p** said unto .... Num 31:21
and Eleazar the **p**, and the .... Num 31:26
give it unto Eleazar the **p** .... Num 31:29
Eleazar the **p** did as .... Num 31:31
Eleazar the **p**, as the .... Num 31:41
and Eleazar the **p** took the .... Num 31:51
Moses, and to Eleazar the **p** .... Num 32:2
commanded Eleazar the **p** .... Num 32:28
p went up into mount Hor .... Num 33:38
Eleazar the **p**, and Joshua .... Num 34:17
the death of the high **p** .... Num 35:25
the death of the high **p** .... Num 35:28
the death of the high **p** .... Num 35:28
until the death of the **p** .... Num 35:32
his son ministered in the **p** .... Deut 10:6
shalt come unto the **p** the .... Deut 17:9
will not hearken unto the **p** .... Deut 17:12
The **p** the Levites, and all .... Deut 18:1
the **p** due from the people .... Deut 18:3
shall give unto the **p** the .... Deut 18:3
p and the judges, which .... Deut 19:17
p shall approach and .... Deut 20:2
p the sons of Levi shall .... Deut 21:5
p the Levites shall teach .... Deut 24:8
thou shalt go unto the **p** .... Deut 26:3
the **p** the Levites spake .... Deut 27:9
the **p** the sons of Levi .... Deut 31:9
p the Levites bearing it .... Josh 3:3
place where the **p** feet .... Josh 4:3
feet of the **p** which bare .... Josh 4:9
passed over, and the **p** .... Josh 4:11
therefore commanded the **p** .... Josh 4:17
p shall bear before the ark .... Josh 6:4
the **p** shall blow with the .... Josh 6:4
son of Nun called the **p** .... Josh 6:6
let seven **p** bear seven .... Josh 6:6
the **p** that blew with the .... Josh 6:9
p going on, and blowing .... Josh 6:9
seven **p** bearing seven .... Josh 6:13
p going on, and blowing .... Josh 6:13
p blew with the trumpets .... Josh 6:16
that side before the **p** .... Josh 8:33
which Eleazar the **p**, and .... Josh 14:1
near before Eleazar the **p** .... Josh 17:4
which Eleazar the **p**, and .... Josh 19:51
the death of the high **p** .... Josh 20:6
Levites unto Eleazar the **p** .... Josh 21:1
children of Aaron the **p** .... Josh 21:13
children of Aaron, the **p** .... Josh 21:19
the son of Eleazar the **p** .... Josh 22:13
the son of Eleazar the **p** .... Josh 22:31
sons, who became his **p** .... Judg 17:5
young man became his **p** .... Judg 17:12
hired me, and I am his **p** .... Judg 18:4
p stood in the entering of .... Judg 18:17
be to us a father and a **p** .... Judg 18:19
for thee to be a **p** unto the .... Judg 18:19
be a **p** unto a tribe and a .... Judg 18:19
And the **p** heart was glad .... Judg 18:20
had made, and the **p** which .... Judg 18:27
his sons were **p** to the tribe .... Judg 18:30
p of the Lord, were there 1Sam 1:3
the Lord before Eli the **p** 1Sam 2:11
p custom with the people 1Sam 2:13
the **p** servant came, while 1Sam 2:13
Give flesh to roast for the **p** 1Sam 2:15
raise me up a faithful **p** 1Sam 2:35
into one of the **p** offices 1Sam 2:36
neither the **p** of Dagon 1Sam 5:5
Philistines called for the **p** 1Sam 6:2
son of Eli, the Lord's **p** in 1Sam 14:3
Saul talked unto the **p** 1Sam 14:19
Saul said unto the **p** 1Sam 14:19
to Nob to Ahimelech the **p** 1Sam 21:1
the **p** answered David, and 1Sam 21:4
the **p** gave him hallowed 1Sam 21:6
and slay the **p** of the Lord 1Sam 22:17
hand to fall upon the **p** 1Sam 22:17
thou, and fall upon the **p** 1Sam 22:18
and he fell upon the **p** 1Sam 22:18
Saul had slain the Lord's **p** 1Sam 22:21
said to Abiathar the **p** 1Sam 30:7
of Abiathar, were the **p** 2Sam 8:17
Zadok and Abiathar the **p**? 2Sam 15:35
Zadok and Abiathar the **p** 2Sam 15:35
and to Abiathar the **p** 2Sam 17:15
and to Abiathar the **p** 2Sam 19:11
and Abiathar were the **p** 2Sam 20:25
and with Abiathar the **p** 1Kin 1:7
king, and Abiathar the **p** 1Kin 1:19
servant, and Zadok the **p** 1Kin 1:26
Zadok the **p** and Nathan 1Kin 1:34
Zadok the **p**, and Nathan 1Kin 1:38
Zadok the **p** took a horn 1Kin 1:39
with him Zadok the **p**, and 1Kin 1:44
and for Abiathar the **p** 1Kin 2:22
out Abiathar from being **p** 1Kin 2:27
the son of Zadok the **p** 1Kin 4:2
and Abiathar were the **p** 1Kin 4:4
the **p** took up the ark 1Kin 8:3
the **p** brought in the ark 1Kin 8:6
the **p** could not stand to 1Kin 8:11
made **p** of the lowest of the 1Kin 12:31
he offer the **p** of the high 1Kin 13:2
lowest of the people **p** of 1Kin 13:33
one of the **p** of the high 1Kin 13:33
his kinfolks, and his **p** 2Kin 10:11
the **p** give king David's 2Kin 11:10
the **p** commanded the 2Kin 11:15
p had said, Let her not be 2Kin 11:15
Jehoiada the **p** instructed 2Kin 12:2
And Jehoash said to the **p** 2Kin 12:4
p had not repaired the 2Kin 12:6
p consented to receive no 2Kin 12:8
the **p** took a chest, and 2Kin 12:9
of the Lord: it was the **p** 2Kin 12:16
And Urijah the **p** built an 2Kin 16:11
the **p** made it against 2Kin 16:11
Thus did Urijah the **p** 2Kin 16:16
Carry thither one of the **p** 2Kin 17:27
them **p** of the high places 2Kin 17:32
elders of the **p**, covered 2Kin 19:2
Hilkiah the high **p** said 2Kin 22:8
commanded Hilkiah the **p** 2Kin 22:12
the **p**, and the prophets 2Kin 23:2
Hilkiah the high **p** 2Kin 23:4
put down the idolatrous **p** 2Kin 23:5
the **p** out of the cities of 2Kin 23:8
where the **p** had burned 2Kin 23:8
And he slew all the **p** of the 2Kin 23:20
that executed the **p** office 1Chr 6:10
p, Levites, and the 1Chr 9:2
sons of the **p** made the 1Chr 9:30
p and Levites which are in 1Chr 13:2
Zadok and Abiathar the **p** 1Chr 15:11
the **p** did blow with the 1Chr 15:24
and Jahaziel the **p** with 1Chr 16:6
the **p**, and his brethren 1Chr 16:39
and his brethren the **p** 1Chr 16:39
of Abiathar, were the **p** 1Chr 18:16
Israel, with the **p** and the 1Chr 23:2
and Ithamar executed the **p** 1Chr 24:2
princes, and Zadok the **p** 1Chr 24:6
of the fathers of the **p** 1Chr 24:6
son of Jehoiada, a chief **p** 1Chr 27:5
of the **p** and the Levites 1Chr 28:13
and Zadok to be **p** 1Chr 29:22
the sea was for the **p** to 2Chr 4:6
p and the Levites bring 2Chr 5:5
p were come out of the 2Chr 5:11
p that were present were 2Chr 5:11
p could not stand to 2Chr 5:14
p, O Lord God, be clothed 2Chr 6:41
p could not enter into the 2Chr 7:2
p waited on their offices 2Chr 7:6
p sounded trumpets before 2Chr 7:6
courses of the **p** to their 2Chr 8:14
and minister before the **p** 2Chr 8:14
the **p** and the Levites that 2Chr 11:13
from executing the **p** office 2Chr 11:14
cast out the **p** of the Lord 2Chr 13:9
made you **p** after the 2Chr 13:9
be a **p** of them that are no 2Chr 13:9
p with sounding trumpets 2Chr 13:12
without a teaching **p**, and 2Chr 15:3
Elishama and Jehoram, **p** 2Chr 17:8
of the Levites, and of the **p** 2Chr 19:8
the wife of Jehoiada the **p** 2Chr 22:11
the **p** and of the Levites 2Chr 23:4
Jehoiada the **p** had 2Chr 23:8
Jehoiada the **p** dismissed 2Chr 23:8
Jehoiada the **p** brought 2Chr 23:14
slew Mattan the **p** of Baal 2Chr 23:17
by the hand of the **p** the 2Chr 23:18
the days of Jehoiada the **p** 2Chr 24:2
the **p** and the Levites 2Chr 24:5
and the high **p** officer came 2Chr 24:11
the sons of Jehoiada the **p** 2Chr 24:25
Azariah the **p** went in 2Chr 26:17
fourscore **p** of the Lord 2Chr 26:17
to the **p** the sons of Aaron 2Chr 26:18
he was wroth with the **p** 2Chr 26:19
the **p** in the house of the 2Chr 26:19
brought in the **p** and the 2Chr 29:4
the **p** the sons of Aaron to 2Chr 29:21
p killed them, and they 2Chr 29:24
the **p** were too few, so that 2Chr 29:34
other **p** had sanctified 2Chr 29:34
to sanctify..than the **p** 2Chr 29:34
the **p** had not sanctified 2Chr 30:3
the **p** sprinkled the blood 2Chr 30:16
number of **p** sanctified 2Chr 30:24
p the Levites arose and 2Chr 30:27
the courses of the **p** 2Chr 31:2
p and Levites for burnt 2Chr 31:2
questioned with the **p** 2Chr 31:9
Azariah the chief **p** of the 2Chr 31:10
the genealogy of the **p** by 2Chr 31:17
the sons of Aaron the **p** 2Chr 31:19
all the males among the **p** 2Chr 31:19
burnt the bones of the **p** 2Chr 34:5
to Hilkiah the high **p** 2Chr 34:9
p hath given me a book 2Chr 34:18
set the **p** in their charges 2Chr 35:2
unto the people, to the **p** 2Chr 35:8
gave unto the **p** for the 2Chr 35:8
p sprinkled the blood from 2Chr 35:11
themselves, and for the **p** 2Chr 35:14
the **p** the sons of Aaron 2Chr 35:14
the **p** the sons of Aaron 2Chr 35:14
the chief of the **p**, and the 2Chr 36:14
and the **p**, and the Levites .... Ezra 1:5
The **p**: the children of .... Ezra 2:36

till there stood up a *p* with . . . .Ezra 2:63
one hundred *p* garments . . . . . .Ezra 2:69
So the *p*, and the Levites . . . . .Ezra 2:70
his brethren the *p*, and. . . . . . . .Ezra 3:2
set the *p* in their apparel . . . . . .Ezra 3:10
to the appointment of the *p* . . .Ezra 6:9
they set the *p* in their . . . . .Ezra 6:18
p and the Levites were . . . . .Ezra 6:20
for their brethren the *p* . . . . . . .Ezra 6:20
son of Aaron the chief *p* . . . . . .Ezra 7:5
of Israel, and of the *p* . . . . .Ezra 7:7
of the *p*, offering willingly . . . . .Ezra 7:16
whatsoever Ezra the *p*, the . . . .Ezra 7:21
the people and the *p*. . . . . .Ezra 8:15
before the chief of the *p* . . . . . .Ezra 8:29
the son of Uriah the *p* . . . . .Ezra 8:33
people of Israel, and the *p* . . . .Ezra 9:1
Ezra, and made the chief *p*. . . .Ezra 10:5
Ezra the *p* stood up, and . . . . . .Ezra 10:10
to the Jews, nor to the *p* . . . . . .Neh 2:16
up with his brethren the *p* . . . . .Neh 3:1
of Eliashib the high *p* . . . . .Neh 3:20
horse gate repaired the *p* . . . . . .Neh 3:28
Then I called the *p*, and . . . . . .Neh 5:12
p: the children of Jedaiah . . . . .Neh 7:39
till there stood up a *p* with . . . .Neh 7:65
hundred and thirty *p* . . . . .Neh 7:70
So the *p*, and the Levites . . . . .Neh 7:73
Ezra the *p* brought the law . . . .Neh 8:2
the *p*, and the Levites, unto . . .Neh 8:13
on our princes, and on our *p* . .Neh 9:32
Levites, and *p* seal unto it . . . . .Neh 9:38
Shemaiah: these were the *p* . . .Neh 10:8
cast the lots among the *p* . . . . .Neh 10:34
p, to the chambers of the . . . . .Neh 10:37
p the son of Aaron shall be . . .Neh 10:38
and the *p* that minister . . . . .Neh 10:39
p, and the Levites, and . . . . . . .Neh 11:3
p, and the Levites, were in . . . .Neh 11:20
are the *p*, and the Levites . . . . .Neh 12:1
the days of Joiakim were *p* . . . .Neh 12:12
of Ezra the *p*, the scribe . . . . . .Neh 12:26
And the *p* and the Levites . . . .Neh 12:30
the *p* sons with trumpets . . . . . .Neh 12:35
of the law for the *p* and. . . . . . .Neh 12:44
for Judah rejoiced for the *p* . . .Neh 12:44
before this, Eliashib the *p* . . . . .Neh 13:4
and the offerings of the *p* . . . . .Neh 13:5
son of Eliashib the high *p* . . . . .Neh 13:28
Their *p* fell by the sword . . . . . .Ps 78:64
and Aaron among his *p* . . . . . . .Ps 99:6
art a *p* for ever after the . . . . . .Ps 110:4
p be clothed with . . . . .Ps 132:9
to record, Uriah the *p* . . . . .Is 8:2
the people, so with the *p* . . . . . .Is 24:2
the *p* and the prophet have . . . .Is 28:7
elders of the *p* covered . . . . .Is 37:2
take of them for *p* and for . . . .Is 66:21
p that were in Anathoth . . . . . .Jer 1:1
The *p* said not, Where is . . . . . .Jer 2:8
the *p* shall be astonished . . . . . .Jer 4:9
the *p* bear rule by their . . . . . . .Jer 5:31
prophet even unto the *p* . . . . . . .Jer 6:13
the bones of the *p*, and the . . .Jer 8:1
prophet even unto the *p* . . . . . .Jer 8:10
p, and the prophets, and . . . . . .Jer 13:13
and the *p* go about into a . . . . .Jer 14:18
shall not perish from the *p* . . . .Jer 18:18
of the ancients of the *p* . . . . . . .Jer 19:1
the son of Maaseiah the *p* . . . . .Jer 21:1
both prophet and *p* are . . . . . . .Jer 23:11
the *p*, and the people, and . . . .Jer 23:34
the *p* and the prophets and . . . .Jer 26:7
the *p* and to the prophets . . . .Jer 26:16
I spake to the *p* and to all . . . .Jer 27:16
in the presence of the *p* . . . . . . .Jer 28:1
p, and to the prophets . . . . . . .Jer 29:1
son of Maaseiah the *p*, and . . . .Jer 29:25
The Lord hath made thee *p* . . .Jer 29:26
stead of Jehoiada the *p* . . . . . . .Jer 29:26
the soul of the *p* with . . . . .Jer 31:14
their *p*, and their prophets . . . .Jer 32:32
Neither shall the *p* the . . . . . . .Jer 33:18
the eunuchs, and the *p* . . . . .Jer 34:19
into captivity with his *p* . . . . . .Jer 48:7
his *p* and his princes . . . . .Jer 49:3
took Seraiah the chief *p* . . . . . . .Jer 52:24
Zephaniah the second *p* . . . . . . .Jer 52:24
p sigh, her virgins are . . . . .Lam 1:4
anger the king and the *p* . . . . . .Lam 2:6
the iniquities of her *p* . . . . .Lam 4:13
unto Ezekiel the *p* . . . . .Ezek 1:3
shall perish from the *p* . . . . .Ezek 7:26
p have violated my law . . . . . . .Ezek 22:26
is for the *p*, the keepers of . . . .Ezek 40:45
the *p* that approach unto . . . . . .Ezek 42:13
shalt give to the *p* the . . . . .Ezek 43:19
p shall make your burnt . . . . . . .Ezek 43:27
to do the office of a *p* unto . . .Ezek 44:13
But the *p* the Levites, the . . . . .Ezek 44:15
or a widow that had a *p* . . . . . .Ezek 44:22
oblations, shall be the *p* . . . . . . .Ezek 44:30
land shall be for the *p* the . . . . .Ezek 45:4
p shall take of the blood . . . . . .Ezek 45:19
p shall prepare his burnt . . . . . .Ezek 46:2
p shall boil the trespass . . . . . . .Ezek 46:20
even for the *p*, shall be . . . . . . .Ezek 48:10
against the border of the *p* . . . .Ezek 48:13
they that strive with the *p* . . . . .Hos 4:4
be, like people, like *p* . . . . .Hos 4:9
Hear ye this, O *p*; and . . . . .Hos 5:1
the company of *p* murder . . . . .Hos 6:9
the *p* thereof that rejoiced . . . .Hos 10:5
the *p*, the Lord's ministers . . . .Joel 1:9
Let the *p*, the ministers . . . . . . .Joel 2:17
the *p* of Beth-el sent to . . . . . . .Amos 7:10
p thereof teach for hire . . . . . . .Mic 3:11
the Chemarim with the *p* . . . . . .Zeph 1:4
her *p* have polluted the . . . . . . .Zeph 3:4
of Josedech, the high *p* . . . . . . .Hag 2:2
Ask now the *p* concerning . . . . .Hag 2:11
p answered and said, It . . . . . . .Hag 2:13
now, O Joshua the high *p* . . . . .Zech 3:8
of Josedech, the high *p* . . . . . . .Zech 6:11
unto the *p* which were in . . . . . .Zech 7:3
you, O *p*, that despise my . . . . .Mal 1:6
O ye *p*, this commandment . . . .Mal 2:1
the *p* lips should keep . . . . .Mal 2:7
all the chief *p* and scribes . . . . .Matt 2:4
show thyself to the *p*, and . . . . .Matt 8:4
him, but only for the *p*? . . . . . .Matt 12:4
the elders and chief *p* and . . . . .Matt 16:21
betrayed unto the chief *p* . . . . .Matt 20:18
chief *p* and scribes saw . . . . .Matt 21:15
chief *p* and Pharisees had . . . . .Matt 21:45
together the chief *p* . . . . .Matt 26:3
the chief *p* and elders of . . . . . .Matt 26:47
a servant of the high *p* . . . . .Matt 26:51
the high *p* answered and . . . . . .Matt 26:63
the chief *p* and elders of . . . . . .Matt 27:1
the chief *p* took the silver . . . . .Matt 27:6
p and elders persuaded . . . . .Matt 27:20
the chief *p* and Pharisees . . . . . .Matt 27:62
showed unto the chief *p* . . . . . . .Matt 28:11
show thyself to the *p*, and . . . . .Mark 1:44
days of Abiathar the high *p* . . .Mark 2:26
lawful to eat but for the *p* . . . . .Mark 2:26
of the chief *p*, and scribes . . . . .Mark 8:31
delivered unto the chief *p* . . . . .Mark 10:33
the scribes and chief *p* . . . . .Mark 11:18
the chief *p* and the scribes . . . .Mark 14:1
from the chief *p* and the . . . . . .Mark 14:43
a servant of the high *p* . . . . .Mark 14:47
the palace of the high *p* . . . . .Mark 14:54
chief *p* and all the council . . . . .Mark 14:55
the high *p* asked him . . . . .Mark 14:61
the maids of the high *p* . . . . . . .Mark 14:66
p held a consultation with . . . . .Mark 15:1
the chief *p* had delivered . . . . . .Mark 15:10
also the chief *p* mocking . . . . . .Mark 15:31
executed the *p* office before . . .Luke 1:8
Caiaphas being the high *p* . . . . .Luke 3:2
and show thyself to the *p* . . . . .Luke 5:14
lawful to eat but for the *p* . . . . .Luke 6:4
of the elders and chief *p* . . . . . .Luke 9:22
came down a certain *p* . . . . .Luke 10:31
yourselves unto the *p* . . . . .Luke 17:14
But the chief *p* and the . . . . . . .Luke 19:47
the chief *p* and the scribes . . . .Luke 20:1
the chief *p* and scribes . . . . .Luke 22:2
the servant of the high *p* . . . . . .Luke 22:50
Jesus said unto the chief *p* . . . .Luke 22:52
brought him into the high *p* . . .Luke 22:54
said Pilate to the chief *p* . . . . . .Luke 23:4
together the chief *p* and . . . . . . .Luke 23:13
chief *p* and our rulers . . . . .Luke 24:20
Jews sent *p* and Levites . . . . . . .John 1:19
Pharisees and the chief *p* . . . . . .John 7:32
Then gathered the chief *p* . . . . .John 11:47
being the high *p* that same . . . .John 11:49
But the chief *p* consulted . . . . . .John 12:10
the chief *p* and the Pharisees . .John 18:3
and smote the high *p* servant . .John 18:10
was the high *p* that same . . . . . .John 18:13
was known unto the high *p* . . . .John 18:15
into the palace of the high *p* . .John 18:15
high *p* then asked Jesus . . . . . . .John 18:19
unto Caiaphas the high *p* . . . . . .John 18:24
the chief *p* therefore and . . . . . .John 19:6
the chief *p* of the Jews to . . . . .John 19:21
unto the people, the *p* . . . . .Acts 4:1
the high *p*, and Caiaphas . . . . . .Acts 4:6
the kindred of the high *p* . . . . .Acts 4:6
Then the high *p* rose up . . . . . .Acts 5:17
the high *p* and the captain . . . .Acts 5:24
the chief *p* heard these . . . . .Acts 5:24
the *p* were obedient to the . . . .Acts 6:7
Then said the high *p*, Are . . . . .Acts 7:1
Lord, went unto the high *p* . . . .Acts 9:1
authority from the chief *p* . . . . .Acts 9:14
the *p* of Jupiter, Which . . . . . . .Acts 14:13
the high *p* doth bear me . . . . . .Acts 22:5
and commanded the chief *p* . . .Acts 22:30
Revilest thou God's high *p*? . . .Acts 23:4
they came to the chief *p* . . . . . .Acts 23:14
the high *p* descended . . . . .Acts 24:1
high *p* and the chief of the . . . .Acts 25:2
chief *p* and the elders of . . . . . .Acts 25:15
authority from the chief *p* . . . . .Acts 26:10
and faithful high *p* in . . . . .Heb 2:17
we have a great high *p* . . . . .Heb 4:14
Thou art a *p* for ever after . . . .Heb 5:6
made a high *p* for ever . . . . .Heb 6:20
abideth a *p* continually . . . . . . .Heb 7:3
ariseth another *p* . . . . .Heb 7:15
an oath he was made *p* . . . . . . .Heb 7:20
p were made without an . . . . . .Heb 7:21
the *p* went always into the . . . .Heb 9:6
Christ being come a high *p* . . . .Heb 9:11
p standeth daily . . . . .Heb 10:11
sanctuary by the high *p* for . . . .Heb 13:11
unto our God kings and *p* . . . . .Rev 5:10
they shall be *p* of God and . . . .Rev 20:6

PRIESTHOOD—*inherited office that performs the sacrifices for the people*

surely be an everlasting *p* . . . . .Ex 40:15
bear the iniquity of your *p* . . . .Num 18:1
of an everlasting *p* . . . . .Num 25:13
p of the Lord is their . . . . .Josh 18:7
polluted, put from the *p* . . . . . .Neh 7:64
they have defiled the *p* . . . . .Neh 13:29
and the covenant of the *p* . . . . .Neh 13:29
receive the office of the *p* . . . . .Heb 7:5
For the *p* being changed . . . . . .Heb 7:12

PRIESTHOOD OF BELIEVERS—*the doctrine that those who believe in Christ are able to have direct access to God*

Typical of Israel 1Pet 2:9
Predicted in prophecy . . . .Is 61:6
Including all believers . . . .Rev 1:5, 6
Having access to God . . . .Eph 2:18
Body as a living sacrifice .Rom 12:1
Spiritual sacrifices 1Pet 2:5
Praise and good works . . .Heb 13:15, 16
Deeds of kindness . . . . . . .Phil 4:18

PRIESTHOOD OF CHRIST—*one of Christ's offices as the Son of God*

Superior to Aaron as:

Man; Christ the Son of God . . . . .Heb 7:28
Sinner; Christ, sinless . . . .Heb 7:26, 27
Typical; Christ's the fulfillment . . . . .Heb 8:1-6

P

Subject to change;
Christ's unchangeable ... Heb 7:23, 24
Imperfect; Christ's perfect ... Heb 7:11, 25

Christ as priest:
Satisfies God's justice ... Rom 3:24-28
Pacifies God's wrath ... Rom 5:9
Justifies the sinner ... Rom 5:1
Sanctifies the believer ... 1Cor 1:30
See HIGH PRIEST

PRINCE—*a ruler*
Descriptive of:
Ruler ... Judg 5:15
Head or captain ... Ex 2:14
Noble or volunteer ... Ps 47:9

Of the Messiah:
Of David's line ... Ezek 34:23, 24
Reign of, forever ... Ezek 37:24, 25
Time of, determined ... Dan 9:25, 26
Reign of, peaceful ... Is 9:6
Author of life ... Acts 3:15
Exalted to be Savior ... Acts 5:31

[*also* PRINCE'S, PRINCES]
The *p* also of Pharaoh saw ... Gen 12:15
twelve *p* shall he beget ... Gen 17:20
art a mighty *p* among us ... Gen 23:6
twelve *p* according to their ... Gen 25:16
p hast thou power with ... Gen 32:28
p of the country, saw her ... Gen 34:2
p of the tribes of their ... Num 1:16
the *p* of Israel, heads of ... Num 7:2
were the *p* of the tribes ... Num 7:2
p offered for dedicating ... Num 7:10
the *p* offered their offering ... Num 7:10
their offering, each *p* on ... Num 7:11
p of the children of Zebulun ... Num 7:24
p of the children of Simeon ... Num 7:36
p of the children of Ephraim ... Num 7:48
p of the children of Benjamin ... Num 7:60
p of the children of Asher ... Num 7:72
p, which are heads of the ... Num 10:4
and fifty *p* of the assembly ... Num 16:2
thou make thyself..a *p* ... Num 16:13
of all their *p* according to ... Num 17:2
a rod apiece, for each *p* ... Num 17:6
The *p* digged the well, the ... Num 21:18
the *p* of Moab abode with ... Num 22:8
p of Moab rose up, and ... Num 22:14
went with the *p* of Moab ... Num 22:21
and to the *p* that were with ... Num 22:40
he, and all the *p* of Moab ... Num 23:6
a *p* of the chief house among ... Num 25:14
p and all the congregation ... Num 27:2
the *p* of the congregation ... Num 31:13
the *p* of the congregation ... Num 32:2
take one *p* of every tribe ... Num 34:18
the *p* of the children of ... Num 34:23
Moses, and before the *p* ... Num 36:1
p of the congregation ... Josh 9:15
p of the congregation had ... Josh 9:18
murmured against the *p* ... Josh 9:18
p said unto them, Let them ... Josh 9:21
the *p* had promised them ... Josh 9:21
Moses smote with the *p* ... Josh 13:21
of Nun, and before the *p* ... Josh 17:4
him ten *p*, of each chief ... Josh 22:14
of each chief house a *p* ... Josh 22:14
the *p*, returned from the ... Josh 22:32
ye kings; give ear, O ye *p* ... Judg 5:3
two *p* of the Midianites ... Judg 7:25
into your hands the *p* of ... Judg 8:3
unto him the *p* of Succoth ... Judg 8:14
p of Gilead said one to ... Judg 10:18
to set them among *p*, and ... 1Sam 2:8
the *p* of the Philistines ... 1Sam 18:30
the *p* of the Philistines ... 1Sam 29:3
the *p* of the Philistines ... 1Sam 29:3
the *p* of the Philistines ... 1Sam 29:4
p of the Philistines said ... 1Sam 29:4
p and a great man fallen ... 2Sam 3:38
p of the children of ... 2Sam 10:3
regardest neither *p* nor ... 2Sam 19:6
these were the *p* which he ... 1Kin 4:2
p, and his captains, and ... 1Kin 9:22
make him *p* all the days of ... 1Kin 11:34
and made thee *p* over my ... 1Kin 14:7
and made thee *p* over my ... 1Kin 16:2
of the *p* of the provinces ... 1Kin 20:14
p of the provinces went out ... 1Kin 20:17
p and the trumpeters by ... 2Kin 11:14
and his *p*, and his officers ... 2Kin 24:12
p of the children of Judah ... 1Chr 2:10
by their names were *p* ... 1Chr 4:38
he was *p* of the Reubenites ... 1Chr 5:6
of valor, chief of the *p* ... 1Chr 7:40
p of the children of ... 1Chr 19:3
also commanded all the *p* ... 1Chr 22:17
together all the *p* of Israel ... 1Chr 23:2
before the king, and the *p* ... 1Chr 24:6
p of the tribes of Israel ... 1Chr 27:22
David assembled all the *p* ... 1Chr 28:1
p of the tribes, and the ... 1Chr 28:1
p of the tribes of Israel ... 1Chr 29:6
Rehoboam, and to the *p* ... 2Chr 12:5
he sent to his *p*, even to ... 2Chr 17:7
and divers also of the *p* ... 2Chr 21:4
and found the *p* of Judah ... 2Chr 22:8
p and the trumpets by the ... 2Chr 23:13
the *p* and all the people ... 2Chr 24:10
destroyed all the *p* of the ... 2Chr 24:23
and the spoil before the *p* ... 2Chr 28:14
p commanded the Levites ... 2Chr 29:30
taken counsel, and his *p* ... 2Chr 30:2
of the king and of the *p* ... 2Chr 30:12
Hezekiah and the *p* came ... 2Chr 31:8
He took counsel with his *p* ... 2Chr 32:3
p gave willingly unto the ... 2Chr 35:8
of the king, and of his *p* ... 2Chr 36:18
unto Sheshbazzar, the *p* of ... Ezra 1:8
all the king's mighty *p* ... Ezra 7:28
David and the *p* had ... Ezra 8:20
things were done, the *p* ... Ezra 9:1
to the counsel of the *p* ... Ezra 10:8
on our kings, on our *p* ... Neh 9:32
our *p*, Levites, and priests ... Neh 9:38
brought up the *p* of Judah ... Neh 12:31
made a feast unto all his *p* ... Esth 1:3
the people and the *p* her ... Esth 1:11
before the king and the *p* ... Esth 1:16
day unto all the king's *p* ... Esth 1:18
great feast unto all his *p* ... Esth 2:18
set his seat above all the *p* ... Esth 3:1
advanced him above the *p* ... Esth 5:11
of the king's most noble *p* ... Esth 6:9
Or with *p* that had gold ... Job 3:15
He leadeth *p* away spoiled ... Job 12:19
is the house of the *p*? ... Job 21:28
The *p* refrained talking ... Job 29:9
a *p* would I go near unto ... Job 31:37
and to *p*, Ye are ungodly? ... Job 34:18
mayest make *p* in all the ... Ps 45:16
the *p* of Judah and their ... Ps 68:27
the *p* of Zebulun, and the *p* ... Ps 68:27
shall cut off the spirit of *p* ... Ps 76:12
and fall like one of the *p* ... Ps 82:7
yea, all their *p* as Zebah ... Ps 83:11
bind his *p* at his pleasure ... Ps 105:22
poureth contempt upon *p* ... Ps 107:40
That he may set him with *p* ... Ps 113:8
with the *p* of his people ... Ps 113:8
than to put confidence in *p* ... Ps 118:9
P also did sit and speak ... Ps 119:23
Put not your trust in *p*, nor ... Ps 146:3
p, and all judges of the ... Ps 148:11
kings reign, and *p* decree ... Prov 8:15
is the destruction of the *p* ... Prov 14:28
much less do lying lips a *p* ... Prov 17:7
nor to strike *p* for equity ... Prov 17:26
entreat the favor of the *p* ... Prov 19:6
servant to have rule over *p* ... Prov 19:10
in the presence of the *p* ... Prov 25:7
of a land many are the *p* ... Prov 28:2
p that wanteth understanding ... Prov 28:16
nor for *p* strong drink ... Prov 31:4
p walking as servants upon ... Eccl 10:7
thy *p* eat in due season ... Eccl 10:17
thy feet with shoes, O *p* ... Song 7:1
Thy *p* are rebellious, and ... Is 1:23
give children to be their *p* ... Is 3:4
Are not my *p* altogether ... Is 10:8
p of Zoan are fools, the ... Is 19:11
The *p* of Zoan are become ... Is 19:13
p of Noph are deceived ... Is 19:13
arise, ye *p*, and anoint the ... Is 21:5
whose merchants are *p* ... Is 23:8
For his *p* were at Zoan ... Is 30:4
his *p* shall be afraid of the ... Is 31:9
p shall rule in judgment ... Is 32:1
all her *p* shall be nothing ... Is 34:12
bringeth the *p* to nothing ... Is 40:23
upon *p* as upon mortar ... Is 41:25
profaned the *p* of the ... Is 43:28
p also shall worship ... Is 49:7
the *p* thereof, against the ... Jer 1:18
they, their kings, their *p* ... Jer 2:26
and the heart of the *p* ... Jer 4:9
the bones of his *p*, and the ... Jer 8:1
p sitting upon the throne ... Jer 17:25
and their *p*, the men of ... Jer 17:25
the *p* of Judah, with the ... Jer 24:1
kings thereof, and the *p* ... Jer 25:18
the *p* of Judah heard these ... Jer 26:10
Jeremiah unto all the *p* ... Jer 26:12
men, and all the *p*, heard ... Jer 26:21
p of Judah and Jerusalem ... Jer 29:2
their kings, their *p*, their ... Jer 32:32
Now when all the *p* and all ... Jer 34:10
king of Judah and his *p* ... Jer 34:21
by the chamber of the *p* ... Jer 35:4
all the *p* sat there, even ... Jer 36:12
Hananiah, and all the *p* ... Jer 36:12
said the *p* unto Baruch ... Jer 36:19
and brought him to the *p* ... Jer 37:14
the *p* said unto the king ... Jer 38:4
to the king of Babylon's *p* ... Jer 38:18
if the *p* hear that I have ... Jer 38:25
p of the king of Babylon ... Jer 39:3
all the king of Babylon's *p* ... Jer 39:13
the *p* of the king, even ten ... Jer 41:1
our kings, and our *p* ... Jer 44:17
with his priests and his *p* ... Jer 48:7
and his priests and his *p* ... Jer 49:3
of Babylon, and upon her *p* ... Jer 50:35
I will make drunk her *p* ... Jer 51:57
this Seraiah was a quiet *p* ... Jer 51:59
also all the *p* of Judah in ... Jer 52:10
p are become like harts ... Lam 1:6
the kingdom and the *p* ... Lam 2:2
P are hanged up by their ... Lam 5:12
the *p* shall be clothed with ... Ezek 7:27
son of Benaiah, *p* of the ... Ezek 11:1
burden concerneth the *p* ... Ezek 12:10
the king thereof, and the *p* ... Ezek 17:12
a lamentation for the *p* of ... Ezek 19:1
shall be upon all the *p* of ... Ezek 21:12
profane wicked *p* of Israel ... Ezek 21:25
the *p* of Israel, every one ... Ezek 22:6
heads, all of them *p* to look ... Ezek 23:15
all the *p* of the sea shall ... Ezek 26:16
all the *p* of Kedar, they ... Ezek 27:21
say unto the *p* of Tyrus ... Ezek 28:2
no more a *p* in the land of ... Ezek 30:13
her kings, and all her *p* ... Ezek 32:29
servant David a *p* among ... Ezek 34:24
David shall be their *p* ... Ezek 37:25
the chief *p* of Meshech and ... Ezek 38:2
p of Meshech and Tubal ... Ezek 39:1
the blood of the *p* of the ... Ezek 39:18
It is for the *p*; the *p*, he ... Ezek 44:3
a portion shall be for the *p* ... Ezek 45:7
p shall no more oppress ... Ezek 45:8
the *p* part to give burnt ... Ezek 45:17
the *p* prepare for himself ... Ezek 45:22
p shall enter by the way ... Ezek 46:2
when the *p* shall enter, he ... Ezek 46:8
the *p* shall prepare a ... Ezek 46:12
it shall return to the *p* ... Ezek 46:17
residue shall be for the *p* ... Ezek 48:21
of that which is the *p* ... Ezek 48:22
Benjamin, shall be for the *p* ... Ezek 48:22
king's seed, and of the *p* ... Dan 1:3
the *p* of the eunuchs gave ... Dan 1:7
with the *p* of the eunuchs ... Dan 1:9
whom the *p* of the eunuchs ... Dan 1:11

to gather together the *p* ....Dan 3:2
the *p*, governors, and ....Dan 3:27
that the king, and his *p* ....Dan 5:2
an hundred and twenty *p* ......Dan 6:1
above the presidents and *p* ....Dan 6:3
these presidents and *p* ....Dan 6:6
himself even to the *p* of the ...Dan 8:11
stand up against the *P* of *p* ....Dan 8:25
our kings, our *p*, and our .....Dan 9:6
the *p* of the kingdom of.......Dan 10:13
Michael, one of the chief *p* ....Dan 10:13
return to fight with the *p* .....Dan 10:20
lo, the *p* of Grecia shall.......Dan 10:20
be strong, and one of his *p* ....Dan 11:5
a *p* for his own behalf shall ...Dan 11:18
p which standeth for the ......Dan 12:1
a king, and without a *p* ....Hos 3:4
p of Judah were like them ....Hos 5:10
and the *p* with their lies.......Hos 7:3
p shall fall by the sword.......Hos 7:16
have made *p*, and I knew .....Hos 8:4
all their *p* are revolters.......Hos 9:15
Give me a king and *p*? ....Hos 13:10
he and his *p* together ....Amos 1:15
slay all the *p* thereof with .....Amos 2:3
p of the house of Israel ....Mic 3:1
p asketh, and the judge ....Mic 7:3
the *p* shall be a scorn unto ....Hab 1:10
will punish the *p*, and the .....Zeph 1:8
p within her are roaring.......Zeph 3:3
least among the *p* of Judah ....Matt 2:6
devils through the *p* of the ....Matt 9:34
by Beelzebub the *p* of the .....Matt 12:24
that the *p* of the Gentiles .....Matt 20:25
p of the devils casteth he ......Mark 3:22
nor of the *p* of this world 1Cor 2:6
and the *p* of the kings of......Rev 1:5

PRINCE OF THIS WORLD—*a title of Satan*
Satan thus called ....John 14:30
To be cast out ....John 12:31
Is judged ....John 16:11
Source of evil ....Eph 2:2

PRINCESS—*female member of a royal family*
[*also* PRINCESSES]
seven hundred wives, *p* 1Kin 11:3
p among the provinces ....Lam 1:1

PRINCIPAL—*chief; finest; in full*
also unto thee *p* spices ....Ex 30:23
restore it in the *p*, and ....Lev 6:5
his trespass with the *p* ....Num 5:7
the son of Nathan was *p* 1Kin 4:5
the *p* scribe of the host 2Kin 25:19
one *p* household being 1Chr 24:6
p to begin the thanksgiving ....Neh 11:17
Wisdom is the *p* thing ....Prov 4:7
have broken down the *p* ......Is 16:8
cast in the *p* wheat and ....Is 28:25
ashes, ye *p* of the flock ....Jer 25:34
an howling of the *p* of the ....Jer 25:36
p scribe of the host who ......Jer 52:25
shepherds and eight *p* men ....Mic 5:5
and *p* men of the city ....Acts 25:23

PRINCIPALITY—*rulers and governments; angels and demons*
Christians subject to .....Titus 3:1
Created by Christ ....Col 1:16
Subject to Christ ....Eph 1:20, 21
Beholders of God's redemption ....Eph 3:10
Overcome by Christ .....Col 2:15
Fighting against Christians Eph 6:12
Powerless against Christians ....Rom 8:38
[*also* PRINCIPALITIES]
or dominions, or *p*, or ....Col 1:16
head of all *p* and power.......Col 2:10

PRINCIPLES—*elementary Christian truths*
To be maintained........1Tim 5:21
Christians must go beyond ....Heb 5:12
the *p* of the doctrine of ....Heb 6:1

PRINT—*a recognizable sign*
On the body, forbidden ..Lev 19:28
On the hands, desired ...John 20:25
In a book, longed for ....Job 19:23

PRISCILLA, PRISCA (prĭ-sĭl'ä, prĭs'kä)—*"ancient one"*
Wife of Aquila ....Acts 18:1-3
An instructed Christian ..Acts 18:26
One of Paul's helpers ....Rom 16:3
Greetings sent from 1Cor 16:19
Timothy commanded to greet 2Tim 4:19

PRISED—*See* PRIZE

PRISON—*a place of confinement or captivity*
Place of:
Hard labor.............Judg16:21, 25
Confinement ....Jer 52:11
Guards ....Acts 12:3-6
Stocks ....Acts 16:23, 24
Torture ....Acts 22:24, 25
Execution..............Matt 14:10
Notable occupants of:
Joseph.................Gen 40:2, 3
Micaiah................1Kin 22:26-28
Jeremiah...............Jer 32:2, 8, 12
Hanani 2Chr 16:7-10
Zedekiah ....Jer 52:11
John the Baptist.........Luke 3:20
Apostles ....Acts 5:18, 19
Peter ....Acts 12:1-4
Paul...................Acts 16:24
See IMPRISONMENT
[*also* PRISONS]
and put him into the *p*, a .....Gen 39:20
and he was there in the *p* .....Gen 39:20
keeper of the *p* committed ....Gen 39:22
prisoners that were in the *p* ...Gen 39:22
ye shall be kept in *p*, that .....Gen 42:16
up, and bound him in *p* 2Kin 17:4
king of Judah out of *p* 2Kin 25:27
Put this fellow in the *p*........2Chr 18:26
was by the court of the *p* .....Neh 3:25
they stood still in the *p* ....Neh 12:39
Bring my soul out of *p*........Ps 142:7
out of *p* he cometh to reign ...Eccl 4:14
shall be shut up in the *p* ......Is 24:22
the prisoners from the *p* ......Is 42:7
in darkness out of the *p*.......Is 42:7
He was taken from *p* and .....Is 53:8
opening of the *p* to them......Is 61:1
thou shouldest put him in *p* ...Jer 29:26
up in the court of the *p* ....Jer 33:1
they had not put him into *p* ...Jer 37:4
in *p* in the house of ....Jer 37:15
they had made that the *p* .....Jer 37:15
into the court of the *p* ....Jer 37:21
in the court of the *p* ....Jer 37:21
was in the court of the *p* .....Jer 38:6
abode in the court of the *p*....Jer 38:28
out of the court of the *p* ......Jer 39:14
brought him forth out of *p* ....Jer 52:31
that John was cast into *p* ......Matt 4:12
and thou be cast into *p* ....Matt 5:25
John had heard in the *p* the ...Matt 11:2
put him in *p* for Herodias .....Matt 14:3
went and cast him into *p* ......Matt 18:30
I was in *p*, and ye came.......Matt 25:36
and in *p*, and ye visited ....Matt 25:43
that John was put in *p* ....Mark 1:14
in *p* for Herodias' sake........Mark 6:17
officer cast thee into *p* ....Luke 12:58
the synagogues, and into *p* ....Luke 21:12
go with thee, both into *p*......Luke 22:33
murder, was cast into *p* ....Luke 23:19
John was not yet cast into *p* ..John 3:24
to the *p* to have them.........Acts 5:21
The *p* truly found we shut.....Acts 5:23
committed them to *p* ....Acts 8:3
and a light shined in the *p* ....Acts 12:7
foundations of the *p* were .....Acts 16:26
of the *p* awaking out of ....Acts 16:27
seeing the *p* doors open.......Acts 16:27
and have cast us into *p* ....Acts 16:37
delivering into *p* both men ....Acts 22:4
saints did I shut up in *p*.......Acts 26:10
in *p* more frequent, in 2Cor 11:23
unto the spirits in *p*...........1Pet 3:19
cast some of you into *p* ....Rev 2:10
shall be loosed out of his *p*....Rev 20:7

PRISONER—*one confined in jail*
Used literally of:
Criminals ....Matt 27:15, 16
Christians ....Eph 4:1; Col 4:10
Used figuratively of:
Gentiles ....Is 42:6, 7
Those in spiritual darkness ....Is 49:9; Zech 9:11, 1
Righteous in their need ..Ps 69:33; Ps 79:11; Ps 146:7, 8
[*also* PRISONERS]
where the king's *p* were ....Gen 39:20
and took some of them *p* .....Num 21:1
There the *p* rest together......Job 3:18
hear the groaning of the *p* ....Ps 102:20
bow down under the *p* ....Is 10:4
not the house of his *p*? ....Is 14:17
lead away the Egyptians *p*.....Is 20:4
as *p* are gathered in the pit....Is 24:22
feet all the *p* of the earth .....Lam 3:34
released unto them one *p* .....Mark 15:6
unto God: and the *p* heard ....Acts 16:25
Paul the *p* called me unto .....Acts 23:18
unreasonable to send a *p*......Acts 25:27
Paul and certain other *p* ......Acts 27:1
the *p* to the captain of ....Acts 28:16
was I delivered *p* from ....Acts 28:17
Paul, the *p* of Jesus Christ ....Eph 3:1
our Lord, nor of me his *p*......2Tim 1:8
Paul, a *p* of Jesus Christ ......Philem 1

PRIVATE—*secret; hidden; admitted as one's sharing in a secret*
[*also* PRIVATELY, PRIVILY, PRIVY]
or hath his *p* member cut .....Deut 23:1
unto Abimelech *p* ....Judg 9:31
the skirt of Saul's robe *p*......1Sam 24:4
which thine heart is *p* to 1Kin 2:44
his eyes are *p* set against......Ps 10:8
p shoot at the upright in ......Ps 11:2
net that they have laid *p* ......Ps 31:4
of laying snares *p*............Ps 64:5
Whoso *p* slandereth his ....Ps 101:5
have they *p* laid a snare.......Ps 142:3
us lurk *p* for the innocent .....Prov 1:11
entereth into their *p* ....Ezek 21:14
minded to put her away *p*.....Matt 1:19
had *p* called the wise men.....Matt 2:7
disciples came unto him *p* .....Matt 24:3
a desert place by ship *p* ....Mark 6:32
his disciples asked him *p* ......Mark 9:28
and Andrew asked him *p* .....Mark 13:3
aside *p* into a desert place.....Luke 9:10
said *p*, Blessed are the ....Luke 10:23
his wife also being *p* ....Acts 5:2
do they thrust us out *p*?.......Acts 16:37
and went with him aside *p* ....Acts 23:19
but *p* to them which were .....Gal 2:2
came in *p* to spy out our .....Gal 2:4
is of any *p* interpretation 2Pet 1:20
p shall bring in damnable 2Pet 2:1

PRIVILEGES OF BELIEVERS—*spiritual "rights" of those who believe in Christ*
Access to God ....Rom 5:2
Christ's intercession......Heb 7:25, 26
Eternal life ....John 17:2, 3
Growth assured 1Pet 2:2
Intercession of the Spirit .Rom 8:16, 17
Kinship with Christ ......Heb 2:10-14
Membership in God's kingdom 1Cor 6:9-11
Names written in book of life ....Rev 20:15
Partakers of the divine nature 2Pet 1:4

P

Reconciled to God ......Rom 5:10
Suffering with Christ.....Acts 5:41
Trials overcome 1Pet 1:6-8
Victorious living ....Rom 8:37-39

PRIVILEGES OF ISRAEL—*the benefits God granted to Israel when He chose her*

Consisted of:
Chosen by God ....Deut 7:6-8
Entrusted with God's revelation.............Rom 3:1, 2
Blessings bestowed upon .Rom 9:4, 5
Messiah (Christ).........Acts 2:22-39
Gospel first preached to .Acts 3:18-26

Lost because of:
Unbelief ....Matt 8:10-12
Spiritual hardness ....John 12:37-40
Spiritual blindness ....John 9:39-41

Now given to:
Gentiles ....Matt 21:43
Faithful remnant ....Rom 11:1-7
Church 1Pet 2:5-10

PRIZE—*a reward for faithful accomplishment*

Described as crown of:
Righteousness 2Tim 4:8
Glory 1Pet 5:4
Life ....James 1:12

Factors involved in obtaining:
Self-control 1Cor 9:25-27
Following the rules 2Tim 2:5
Pressing toward ....Phil 3:14
Enduring temptation .....James 1:12
Looking to Jesus ....Heb 12:1, 2
Loving His appearing 2Tim 4:8

[*also* PRIZED]
that I was *p* at of them ....Zech 11:13
but one receiveth the *p*? 1Cor 9:24

PROBATION—*a period of testing*

Factors determining:
God's promises..........Matt 21:33-43
Specific time ....Dan 9:24-27
Faith or unbelief ....Acts 13:32-48
Rom 10:1-21

None after death:
No change permitted ....Luke 16:26
Judgment final ....Rev 20:11-15
Destinies eternally fixed..Matt 25:46

PROCEED—*to come forth from a source; move along a course*

[*also* PROCEEDED, PROCEEDETH, PROCEEDING]
The thing *p* from the Lord ....Gen 24:50
p out of the candlestick ....Ex 25:35
that *p* out of his mouth ....Num 30:2
whatsoever *p* out of her ....Num 30:12
hath *p* out of your mouth .....Num 32:24
that *p* out of the mouth of ....Deut 8:3
word *p* out of your mouth.....Josh 6:10
hath *p* out of thy mouth ......Judg 11:36
Wickedness *p* from the........1Sam 24:13
shall *p* out of thy bowels 2Sam 7:12
Elihu also *p*, and said.........Job 36:1
yea, twice; but I will *p* no .....Job 40:5
as an error which *p* from ......Eccl 10:5
I will *p* to do a marvelous .....Is 29:14
for a law shall *p* from me .....Is 51:4
they *p* from evil to evil ....Jer 9:3
them shall *p* thanksgiving .....Jer 30:19
Most High *p* not evil and .....Lam 3:38
wrong judgment *p* ....Hab 1:4
that *p* out of the mouth ....Matt 4:4
which *p* out of the mouth .....Matt 15:18
the heart of men, *p* evil ......Mark 7:21
words which *p* out of his ......Luke 4:22
I *p* forth and came from ......John 8:42
which *p* from the Father ......John 15:26
he *p* further to take Peter .....Acts 12:3
communication *p* out ....Eph 4:29
they shall *p* no further 2Tim 3:9
p blessing and cursing.........James 3:10
of the throne *p* lightnings .....Rev 4:5
fire *p* out of their mouth ......Rev 11:5
sword *p* out of his mouth .....Rev 19:21
p out of the throne of God ....Rev 22:1

PROCESS—*procedure; a series of events from one stage to another*
And in *p* of time it came to ...Gen 4:3
p of time the daughter of .....Gen 38:12
came to pass in *p* of time .....Ex 2:23
came to pass in *p* of time .....Judg 11:4
it came to pass, that in *p* of ...2Chr 21:19

PROCHORUS (prok'o-rus)—*"choir leader"*
One of the seven deacons. Acts 6:5

PROCLAIM—*to announce officially*

Physical objects of:
Idolatrous feast..........Ex 32:4, 5
Holy convocation........Lev 23:2, 4, 21
Year of jubilee ....Lev 25:10
Fast 2Chr 20:3
Release ....Jer 34:17

Spiritual objects of:
God's name ....Ex 33:19
God's Word ....Jer 3:12
Salvation ....Is 62:11

[*also* PROCLAIMED, PROCLAIMETH, PROCLAIMING]
p the name of the Lord ....Ex 34:5
be *p* throughout the camp .....Ex 36:6
against it, then *p* peace ....Deut 20:10
p in the ears of the people ....Judg 7:3
P a fast, and set Naboth 1Kin 21:9
p a fast, and set Naboth 1Kin 21:12
P a solemn assembly for 2Kin 10:20
for Baal. And they *p* it 2Kin 10:20
man of God *p*, who *p* these ...2Kin 23:16
Then I *p* a fast there, at ......Ezra 8:21
publish and *p* in all their ......Neh 8:15
of the city, and *p* before ......Esth 6:9
p before him. Thus shall it ....Esth 6:11
will *p* every one his own ......Prov 20:6
p liberty to the captives ....Is 61:1
p there this word, and say.....Jer 7:2
P all these words in the ....Jer 11:6
p there the words that I.......Jer 19:2
Jerusalem, to *p* liberty ....Jer 34:8
in *p* liberty every man to ......Jer 34:15
p a fast before the Lord.......Jer 36:9
P ye this among the ....Joel 3:9
p and publish the free ....Amos 4:5
and *p* a fast, and put on ....Jon 3:5
be *p* upon the housetops ......Luke 12:3
strong angel *p* with a loud.....Rev 5:2

PROCLAMATION—*an announcement*
king Asa made a *p* 1Kin 15:22
went a *p* throughout the 1Kin 22:36
made a *p* through Judah 2Chr 24:9
make *p* throughout all 2Chr 30:5
he made a *p* throughout all....2Chr 36:22
he made a *p* throughout all....Ezra 1:1
and made a *p* concerning......Dan 5:29

PROCRASTINATION—*to put off; delay*

Manifested in:
Delaying a decision ......Matt 19:22
Putting minor things first .Luke 9:59-62
Presuming on tomorrow..Prov 27:1
Postponing service 2Cor 8:10-14
Rejecting reproof........Prov 29:1

Evils of, missing:
Salvation 2Cor 6:1
Life's importance ....Eccl 12:1
God's opportunity ....Jer 13:16

PROCURE—*to bring about; find*

[*also* PROCURED, PROCURETH]
diligently seeketh good *p* ......Prov 11:27
Hast thou not *p* this unto .....Jer 2:17
way and thy doings have *p* ....Jer 4:18
we *p* great evil against our ....Jer 26:19
all the prosperity that I *p* .....Jer 33:9

PRODIGAL SON—*one who spent lavishly*
Parable concerning ......Luke 15:11-32

PRODUCE—*to set forth; make known*
P your cause, saith the........Is 41:21

PROFANE—*to treat something holy with irreverence*

Manifested in:
Breaking God's Law .....Amos 2:7
Defiling God's house ....Mal 1:12, 13
Not observing the Sabbath ....Neh 13:17, 18
Committing abominations.Mal 2:10, 11
Idolatry.................Lev 18:21
Swearing falsely ....Lev 19:12
Illegal marriages.........Lev 21:14, 15
Blemished service ....Lev 21:21-23

Punishment of:
Excommunication ....Lev 19:8
Death ....Lev 21:9
Destruction ....Ezek 28:16

[*also* PROFANED, PROFANENESS]
and to *p* my holy name ....Lev 20:3
among his people, to *p*........Lev 21:4
wife that is a whore, or *p* .....Lev 21:7
p the sanctuary of his God ....Lev 21:12
they *p* not my holy name ......Lev 22:2
shall not *p* the holy things .....Lev 22:15
thou hast *p* his crown by ......Ps 89:39
I have *p* the princes of the ....Is 43:28
prophet and priest are *p* ......Jer 23:11
prophets of Jerusalem is *p*.....Jer 23:15
p wicked prince of Israel ......Ezek 21:25
and hast *p* my sabbaths ....Ezek 22:8
law, and have *p* mine holy ....Ezek 22:26
between the holy and *p* ....Ezek 22:26
and I am *p* among them ....Ezek 22:26
and have *p* my sabbaths.......Ezek 23:38
day into my sanctuary to *p* ....Ezek 23:39
I will *p* my sanctuary ....Ezek 24:21
sanctuary, when it was *p* ......Ezek 25:3
they went, they *p* my holy ....Ezek 36:20
ye have *p* among the ....Ezek 36:22
which was *p* among the ....Ezek 36:23
ye have *p* in the midst of .....Ezek 36:23
the sanctuary and the *p* ....Ezek 42:20
between the holy and *p* ....Ezek 44:23
a *p* place for the city, for .....Ezek 48:15
priests in the temple *p* the ....Matt 12:5
hath gone about to *p* the......Acts 24:6
sinners, for unholy and *p*......1Tim 1:9
But refuse *p* and old wives 1Tim 4:7
p and vain babblings, and 1Tim 6:20
shun *p* and vain babblings 2Tim 2:16
be any fornicator, or *p*........Heb 12:16

PROFESSION—*a public declaration of one's faith*
Best ....Heb 3:1
Good 1Tim 6:12
Steadfast................Heb 3:14
Commendable 2Cor 9:13
Harmful 1Tim 6:20, 21
Inconsistent ....Titus 1:16
Degrading ....Rom 1:22
Tragic ....Matt 7:23

[*also* PROFESS, PROFESSING]
I *p* this day unto the Lord ....Deut 26:3
women *p* godliness 1Tim 2:10
God, let us hold fast our *p* ....Heb 4:14
Let us hold fast the *p* of ......Heb 10:23

PROFIT—*gain; advantage; to benefit*

Things empty of:
Wickedness ....Prov 10:2
Riches..................Prov 11:4
Labor without God ......Eccl 2:11
Lying words ....Jer 7:8
World ....Matt 16:26
Flesh ....John 6:63
Word without faith ......Heb 4:2
Mere profession ....James 2:14, 16

Things full of:
Spiritual gifts............1Cor 12:7
Godliness 1Tim 4:8
Inspired Word 2Tim 3:16
Youthful service 2Tim 4:11
Good works ....Titus 3:8

[*also* PROFITABLE, PROFITED, PROFITETH, PROFITING]
p shall this birthright ....Gen 25:32
What *p* is it if we slay our ....Gen 37:26
which cannot *p* nor deliver 1Sam 12:21
for the king's *p* to suffer ......Esth 3:8
what *p* should we have, if .....Job 21:15
Can a man be *p* unto God ....Job 22:2
is wise may be *p* unto ....Job 22:2
strength of their hands *p* ......Job 30:2
which was right, and it *p* ......Job 33:27
It *p* a man nothing that he ....Job 34:9
What *p* shall I have, if I ......Job 35:3
What *p* is there in my blood ...Ps 30:9
In all labor there is *p* ....Prov 14:23
What *p* hath a man of all ......Eccl 1:3
p hath he that worketh ....Eccl 3:9
p of the earth is for all..........Eccl 5:9
is *p* to them that see the ....Eccl 7:11
but wisdom is *p* to direct ....Eccl 10:10
a people that could not *p* .....Is 30:5
nor be an help nor *p*, but ......Is 30:5
delectable things shall not *p* ...Is 44:9
image that is *p* for nothing? ...Is 44:10
thou shalt be able to *p*, if .....Is 47:12
which teacheth thee to *p* ......Is 48:17
for they shall not *p* thee ......Is 57:12
after things that do not *p* .....Jer 2:8
for that which doth not *p* .....Jer 2:11
to pain, but shall not *p* ....Jer 12:13
was marred, it was *p* for .....Jer 13:7
wherein there is no *p* ....Jer 16:19
shall not *p* this people ....Jer 23:32
What *p* the graven image .....Hab 2:18
what *p* is it that we have ......Mal 3:14
it is *p* for thee that one ....Matt 5:29
thou mightest be *p* by me .....Matt 15:5
thou mightest be *p* by me .....Mark 7:11
For what shall it *p* a man .....Mark 8:36
back nothing that was *p* ....Acts 20:20
circumcision verily *p*, if ....Rom 2:25
p is there of circumcision? .....Rom 3:1
I speak for your own *p* 1Cor 7:35
not seeking mine own *p* 1Cor 10:33
p of many, that they may 1Cor 10:33
have not charity, it *p* me 1Cor 13:3
what shall I *p* you, except I ...1Cor 14:6
And *p* in the Jews' religion ....Gal 1:14
Christ shall *p* you nothing .....Gal 5:2
that thy *p* may appear to 1Tim 4:15
not about words to no *p* 2Tim 2:14
but now *p* to thee and to .....Philem 11
he for our *p*, that we might ...Heb 12:10
p them that have been ....Heb 13:9

PROFOUND—*deep; all-encompassing*
revolters are *p* to make ....Hos 5:2

PROGENITORS—*forefathers*
blessings of my *p* unto the ....Gen 49:26

PROGNOSTICATORS—*those who profess to know the future*
Help from, vain ....Is 47:13-15

PROHIBITION—*restraints placed against evil*
Against:
Idolatry 1John 5:21
Drunkenness ....Luke 21:34
Uncleanness ....Eph 4:18, 19
Worldiness 1John 2:15-17
Based upon:
Sanctity of the body 1Cor 6:13-20
New life in Christ ....Col 3:1-10
God's holiness 1Pet 1:14-16

PROLONG—*to lengthen a period of time*

[*also* PROLONGED, PROLONGETH]
shall not *p* your days upon ....Deut 4:26
that thy days may be *p* ....Deut 5:16
ye may *p* your days in the .....Deut 5:33
that thy days may be *p* ....Deut 6:2
ye may *p* your days in the .....Deut 11:9
he may *p* his days in his ......Deut 17:20
and that thou mayest *p* ....Deut 22:7
shall not *p* your days upon ....Deut 30:18
ye shall *p* your days in the ....Deut 32:47
that I should *p* my life? ....Job 6:11
shall he *p* the perfection ....Job 15:29
Thou wilt *p* the king's life .....Ps 61:6
fear of the Lord *p* days ....Prov 10:27
state thereof shall be *p* ....Prov 28:2
covetousness shall *p* his ....Prov 28:16
a wicked man that *p* his ....Eccl 7:15
his days be *p*, yet surely I .....Eccl 8:12
neither shall he *p* his days .....Eccl 8:13
her days shall not be *p* ....Is 13:22
seed, he shall *p* his days ......Is 53:10
The days are *p*, and every .....Ezek 12:22
none of my words be *p* any ...Ezek 12:28
lives were *p* for a season ......Dan 7:12

PROMISE—*to pledge oneself to do or not do something; a pledge*

[*also* PROMISED, PROMISEDST, PROMISES, PROMISING]
according as he hath *p* ....Ex 12:25
shall know my breach of *p* ....Num 14:34
place which the Lord hath *p* ...Num 14:40
and bless you, as he hath *p* ...Deut 1:11
God of thy fathers hath *p* .....Deut 6:3
into the land which he *p* ......Deut 9:28
as the Lord thy God *p* him ....Deut 10:9
as he hath *p* thee, and ....Deut 12:20
God blesseth thee, as he *p* ....Deut 15:6
land which he *p* to give ....Deut 19:8
hast *p* with thy mouth ....Deut 23:23
people, as he hath *p* thee .....Deut 26:18
God of thy fathers hath *p* .....Deut 27:3
as the princes had *p* them .....Josh 9:21
unto your brethren, as he *p* ...Josh 22:4
p this goodness unto thy 2Sam 7:28
made me an house, as he *p* ...1Kin 2:24
Solomon wisdom, as he *p* 1Kin 5:12
of Israel, as the Lord *p* 1Kin 8:20
David my father that thou *p* ...1Kin 8:24
as I *p* to David thy father 1Kin 9:5
as he *p* him to give him 2Kin 8:19
p this goodness unto thy 1Chr 17:26
let thy *p* unto David my 2Chr 1:9
p to give a light to him 2Chr 21:7
do according to this *p* ....Neh 5:12
performeth not this *p* ....Neh 5:13
did according to this *p* ....Neh 5:13
p them that they should go ....Neh 9:15
which thou hadst *p* to their ....Neh 9:23
money that Haman had *p* ......Esth 4:7
his *p* fail for evermore? ....Ps 77:8
he remembered his holy *p* .....Ps 105:42
all the good that I have *p* .....Jer 32:42
good thing which I have *p* .....Jer 33:14
his wicked way, by *p* him .....Ezek 13:22
he *p* with an oath to give .....Matt 14:7
and *p* to give him money ......Mark 14:11
perform the mercy *p* to ....Luke 1:72
p, and sought opportunity .....Luke 22:6
but wait for the *p* of the ......Acts 1:4
the *p* of the Holy Ghost ......Acts 2:33
ready, looking for a *p* from ...Acts 23:21
for the hope of the *p* made ....Acts 26:6
p afore by his prophets ....Rom 1:2
For the *p*, that he should .....Rom 4:13
the *p* might be sure to ....Rom 4:16
children of the *p* are ....Rom 9:8
Having therefore these *p* 2Cor 7:1
the *p* of the Spirit through ....Gal 3:14
and his seed were the *p* ....Gal 3:16
the law, it is no more of *p* ....Gal 3:18
gave it to Abraham by *p* ....Gal 3:18
come to whom the *p* was ....Gal 3:19
heirs according to the *p* ....Gal 3:29
the freewoman was by *p* ....Gal 4:23
with that holy Spirit of *p* ......Eph 1:13
from the covenants of *p* ....Eph 2:12
partakers of his *p* in ....Eph 3:6
first commandment with *p* ......Eph 6:2
having *p* of the life that 1Tim 4:8
p being left us of entering .....Heb 4:1
blessed him that had the *p* .....Heb 7:6
established upon better *p* ......Heb 8:6
p of eternal inheritance ....Heb 9:15
he is faithful that *p* ....Heb 10:23
God, ye might receive the *p* ...Heb 10:36
him faithful who had *p* ....Heb 11:11
now he hath *p*, saying, Yet ....Heb 12:26
While they *p* them liberty 2Pet 2:19
the *p* that he hath *p* us 1John 2:25

PROMISES OF GOD—*message that raises real hope*
Described as:
Never failing ....Josh 23:5-15; 1Kin 8:56
Backed by God's oath ...Heb 6:12-20
Fulfilled on schedule .....Acts 7:6, 17; Gal 4:4
Given to Israel ....Rom 9:4
Confirmed by Christ .....Rom 15:8
Centered in Christ 2Cor 1:20; 2Tim 1:1
Kept by faith ....Rom 4:20, 21; Heb 11:13-40
Exceedingly great 2Pet 1:4
Not slow 2Pet 3:4-13
Objects of, for Israel:
Land of Palestine ....Acts 7:5; Heb 11:9
Davidic kingship 2Chr 6:10-16
Messiah ....Acts 13:23-33
Gospel ....Acts 10:43
New heart ....Jer 31:33
Objects of, for Christians:
Holy Spirit ....Luke 24:49
Salvation ....Acts 2:3
Kingdom ....James 2:5
Life eternal ....Titus 1:2
Crown of life ....James 1:12
New earth 2Pet 3:13
See MESSIAH, THE

PROMISES TO BELIEVERS—*See* PRECIOUS PROMISES; PRIVILEGES OF BELIEVERS

PROMOTE—*to advance*

[*also* PROMOTED]
p thee unto great honor ....Num 24:11
go to be *p* over the trees? .....Judg 9:9
did king Ahasuerus *p* ....Esth 3:1
wherein the king had *p* ....Esth 5:11
Then the king *p* Shadrach .....Dan 3:30

PROMOTION—*advancement in status*
Deserved ....Gen 41:38-42
Desirable ....Prov 4:8
Divine ....Ps 75:6, 7
Despicable ....Num 22:17, 37

but shame shall be the *p* ......Prov 3:35

PRONOUNCE—*to declare officially; declare to be; utter*

[*also* PRONOUNCED, PRONOUNCING]
swear, *p* with his lips to ....Lev 5:4
look on him, and *p* him ....Lev 13:3
then the priest shall *p* him ....Lev 13:8
he shall *p* him clean that ......Lev 13:13
then the priest shall *p* him ....Lev 13:17
then the priest shall *p* him ....Lev 13:22
the priest shall *p* him ....Lev 13:25
and the priest shall *p* him .....Lev 13:28
then the priest shall *p* him ....Lev 13:34
priest shall *p* him utterly ......Lev 13:44
and shall *p* him clean, and ....Lev 14:7
he could not frame to *p* it .....Judg 12:6
p this prophecy against ....Neh 6:12
hath *p* evil against thee ....Jer 11:17
p all this great evil ....Jer 16:10
against whom I have *p* ....Jer 18:8
the evil that I have *p* ....Jer 19:15
words which I have *p* ....Jer 25:13
evil that he hath *p* against .....Jer 26:13
for I have *p* the word ....Jer 34:5
evil that I have *p* against ......Jer 35:17
Lord hath *p* against this ....Jer 36:7
evil that I have *p* against ......Jer 36:31
hath *p* this evil upon this ......Jer 40:2

P

PROOF—*piece of evidence*

[*also* PROOFS]
passion by many infallible *p* . . . Acts 1:3
that I might know the *p* of 2Cor 2:9
p of Christ speaking in 2Cor 13:3
But ye know the *p* of him . . . . . Phil 2:22
make full *p* of thy ministry 2Tim 4:5

PROPER—*suitable; excellent; belonging to one*
I have of mine own *p* good 1Chr 29:3
field is called in their *p* . . . . Acts 1:19
every man hath his *p* gift 1Cor 7:7
they saw he was a *p* child . . . . . Heb 11:23

PROPERTY—*material possessions*

Acquired by:
Industry . . . . Gen 31:36-42
Inheritance . . . . Eccl 2:21
Purchase . . . . Gen 23:7-20
Deception 1Kin 21:1-16
Coveting . . . . Josh 7:21
See OWNERSHIP

PROPHECY—*inspired declaration of God's will and purpose*

Characteristics of:
Given by God . . . . Is 41:22, 23
Centered in Christ . . . . Luke 24:26, 27, 44
Inspired by the Spirit 2Pet 1:21
Not of one's own interpretation 2Pet 1:20
Always relevant . . . . Rev 22:10
Must not be changed by man . . . . Rev 22:18, 19

True, based on:
Inspiration . . . . Mic 3:8
Foreknowledge . . . . Is 42:9

False, evidenced by:
Nonfulfillment . . . . Jer 28:1-17
Peaceful message . . . . Jer 23:17-22
Apostasy from God . . . . . . Deut 13:1-5
Lying . . . . Jer 23:25-34
Scoffing 2Pet 3:3, 4

Fulfillment of:
Unconditional . . . . Ezek 12:25-28
Sometimes:
Conditional . . . . Jon 3:1-10
Dated . . . . Dan 9:24-27
Non-literal . . . . Matt 17:10-12
Unrecognized by Jews . . . Acts 13:27-29
Interpretation of, needed . Luke 24:25-44
Often referred to . . . . Matt 1:22, 23
Matt 2:14-23

[*also* PROPHECIES]
p of Ahijah the Shilonite 2Chr 9:29
p of Oded the prophet 2Chr 15:8
he pronounced this *p* . . . . Neh 6:12
son of Jakeh, even the *p* . . . . . . Prov 30:1
them is fulfilled the *p* . . . . Matt 13:14
is given to us, whether *p* . . . . . . Rom 12:6
of miracles: to another *p* 1Cor 12:10
though I have the gift of *p* 1Cor 13:2
whether there be *p*, they 1Cor 13:8
the *p* which went before 1Tim 1:18
which was given thee by *p* 1Tim 4:14
also a more sure word of *p* 2Pet 1:19
hear the words of this *p* . . . . Rev 1:3
in the days of their *p* . . . . Rev 11:6
of Jesus is the spirit of *p* . . . . . . Rev 19:10
the sayings of the *p* of this . . . . Rev 22:7

PROPHESY—*to proclaim by inspiration the will of God*

[*also* PROPHESIED, PROPHESIETH, PROPHESYING, PROPHESYINGS]
rested upon them, they *p* . . . . . Num 11:25
Medad do *p* in the camp . . . . . . Num 11:27
them; and they shall *p* 1Sam 10:5
upon him, and he *p* among 1Sam 10:10
he had made an end of *p* 1Sam 10:13
and he *p* in the midst of 1Sam 18:10
company of the prophets *p* 1Sam 19:20
of Saul, and they also *p* 1Sam 19:20
messengers, and they *p* 1Sam 19:21
the third time, and they *p* 1Sam 19:21
p before Samuel in like 1Sam 19:24
and they *p* until the time 1Kin 18:29
not *p* good concerning me 1Kin 22:8
all the prophets *p* before 1Kin 22:10
who should *p* with harps 1Chr 25:1
p according to the order of 1Chr 25:2
for he never *p* good unto 2Chr 18:7
And all the prophets *p* so 2Chr 18:11
he would not *p* good unto 2Chr 18:17
p..against Jehoshaphat 2Chr 20:37
p unto the Jews that were . . . . . Ezra 5:1
prospered through the *p* of . . . . Ezra 6:14
P not unto us right things . . . . . Is 30:10
smooth things, *p* deceits . . . . Is 30:10
the prophets *p* by Baal . . . . Jer 2:8
The prophets *p* falsely, and . . . . Jer 5:31
P not in the name of the . . . . . . Jer 11:21
The prophets *p* lies in my . . . . . Jer 14:14
p unto you a false vision . . . . . . Jer 14:14
the people to whom they *p* . . . . Jer 14:16
the Lord had sent him to *p* . . . . Jer 19:14
Jeremiah *p* these things . . . . Jer 20:1
they *p* in Baal, and caused . . . . Jer 23:13
of the prophets that *p* . . . . Jer 23:16
p against all the nations . . . . Jer 25:13
p thou against them all . . . . Jer 25:30
p in the name of the Lord . . . . . Jer 26:9
sent me to *p* against this . . . . . . Jer 26:12
Micah the Morasthite *p* in . . . . . Jer 26:18
p in the name of the Lord . . . . . Jer 26:20
who *p* against this city and . . . . Jer 26:20
For they *p* a lie unto you, ... Jer 27:10
Lord, yet they *p* a lie in . . . . . . Jer 27:15
prophets that *p* unto you . . . . . . Jer 27:15
prophets that *p* unto you . . . . . . Jer 27:16
for they *p* a lie unto you . . . . . . Jer 27:16
p falsely unto you in my . . . . . . Jer 29:9
Shemaiah hath *p* unto . . . . Jer 29:31
Wherefore dost thou *p* . . . . Jer 32:3
prophets which *p* unto . . . . Jer 37:19
and thou shalt *p* against it . . . . . Ezek 4:7
of Israel, and *p* against . . . . Ezek 6:2
p against them, *p*, O son of . . . Ezek 11:4
when I *p*, that Pelatiah . . . . Ezek 11:13
p against the prophets of . . . . . . Ezek 13:2
prophets of Israel that *p* . . . . . . Ezek 13:2
unto them that *p* out of . . . . Ezek 13:2
of thy people, which *p* . . . . Ezek 13:17
heart; and *p* thou against . . . . . . Ezek 13:17
p against the forest of the . . . . . Ezek 20:46
and *p* against the land of . . . . . . Ezek 21:2
son of man, *p*, and smite . . . . . . Ezek 21:14
Ammonites, and *p* against . . . . . Ezek 25:2
Zidon, and *p* against . . . . Ezek 28:21
Egypt, and *p* against him . . . . . . Ezek 29:2
Son of man, *p* and say . . . . Ezek 30:2
p against the shepherds . . . . Ezek 34:2
p, and say unto them . . . . Ezek 34:2
mount Seir, and *p* against . . . . . Ezek 35:2
p unto the mountains of . . . . . . Ezek 36:1
p therefore concerning . . . . Ezek 36:6
p upon these bones, and . . . . . . Ezek 37:4
So I *p* as I was commanded . . . Ezek 37:7
and as I *p*, there was a . . . . Ezek 37:7
p and say unto them . . . . Ezek 37:12
and Tubal, and *p* against . . . . . . Ezek 38:2
p in those days many . . . . Ezek 38:17
son of man, *p* against Gog . . . . Ezek 39:1
your daughters shall *p* . . . . Joel 2:28
the prophets, saying, *p* . . . . Amos 2:12
spoken, who can but *p*? . . . . Amos 3:8
and there eat bread, and *p* . . . . Amos 7:12
me, Go, *p* unto my people . . . . Amos 7:15
P ye not, say they to them . . . . Mic 2:6
say they to them that *p* . . . . Mic 2:6
they shall not *p* to them . . . . Mic 2:6
that when any shall yet *p* . . . . . Zech 13:3
him through when he *p* . . . . Zech 13:3
his vision, when he hath *p* . . . . Zech 13:4
Lord, have we not *p* in thy . . . . Matt 7:22
prophets and the law *p* . . . . Matt 11:13
well did Isaiah *p* of you . . . . Matt 15:7
P unto us, thou Christ . . . . Matt 26:68
Well hath Isaiah *p* of you . . . . . Mark 7:6
and to say unto him, *P* . . . . Mark 14:65
the Holy Ghost, and *p* . . . . Luke 1:67
P, who is it that smote . . . . Luke 22:64
he *p* that Jesus should die . . . . . John 11:51
your daughters shall *p* . . . . Acts 2:17
spake with tongues, and *p* . . . . . Acts 19:6
virgins, which did *p* . . . . Acts 21:9
let us *p* according to the . . . . . . Rom 12:6
Every man praying or *p* 1Cor 11:4
p with her head uncovered 1Cor 11:5
we know in part, and we *p* 1Cor 13:9
but rather that ye may *p* 1Cor 14:1
But he that *p* speaketh 1Cor 14:3
but rather that ye *p* 1Cor 14:5
greater is he that *p* than 1Cor 14:5
or by knowledge, or by *p* 1Cor 14:6
For ye may all *p* one by 1Cor 14:31
Despise not *p* 1Thess 5:20
who *p* of the grace that 1Pet 1:10
Adam, *p* of these, saying . . . . . . Jude 14
Thou must *p* again before . . . . . Rev 10:11
in the days shall *p* a thousand . Rev 11:3

PROPHET—*inspired messenger who declares the will of God*

Described as:
God's servants . . . . Zech 1:6
God's messengers 2Chr 36:15
Holy prophets . . . . Luke 1:70
Holy men 2Pet 1:21
Watchmen . . . . Ezek 3:17
Prophets of God . . . . Ezra 5:2

Message of:
Centered in Christ . . . . Luke 10:24
Interpreted by Christ . . . . Luke 24:27, 44
United in testimony . . . . . Acts 3:21, 24
Contains grace and salvation 1Pet 1:9-12
Abiding revelation . . . . Matt 5:17, 18

[*also* PROPHET'S, PROPHETS]
the Lord's people were *p* . . . . . . Num 11:29
If there be a *p* among you . . . . Num 12:6
unto the words of that *p* . . . . . . Deut 13:3
p, which shall presume to . . . . . Deut 18:20
of other gods, even that *p* . . . . . Deut 18:20
When a *p* speaketh in the . . . . . Deut 18:22
p hath spoken it . . . . Deut 18:22
arose not a *p* since in . . . . Deut 34:10
a *P* was before time called 1Sam 9:9
company of *p* coming 1Sam 10:5
he prophesied among the *p* 1Sam 10:11
Is Saul also among the *p*? 1Sam 10:11
saw the company of the *p* 1Sam 19:20
p Gad said unto David 1Sam 22:5
nor by Urim, nor by *p* 1Sam 28:6
the hand of Nathan the *p* 2Sam 12:25
Nathan the *p*, and Shimei 1Kin 1:8
king, Nathan the *p* also 1Kin 1:22
priest, and Nathan the *p* 1Kin 1:32
and Nathan the *p*, and 1Kin 1:38
dwelt an old *p* in Beth-el 1Kin 13:11
unto the *p* that brought 1Kin 13:20
in the city where the old *p* 1Kin 13:25
the *p* took up the carcase 1Kin 13:29
and the old *p* came to the 1Kin 13:29
Ahijah the *p*, which told 1Kin 14:2
Jezebel cut off the *p* of 1Kin 18:4
Obadiah took an hundred *p* . . . 1Kin 18:4
Jezebel slew the *p* of the 1Kin 18:13
men of the Lord's *p* 1Kin 18:13
p of Baal four hundred and . . . 1Kin 18:19
the *p* of the groves four 1Kin 18:19
remain a *p* of the Lord 1Kin 18:22
Baal's *p* are four hundred 1Kin 18:22
them, Take the *p* of Baal 1Kin 18:40
how he had slain all the *p* 1Kin 19:1
came a *p* unto Ahab king 1Kin 20:13
man of the sons of the *p* 1Kin 20:35
the *p* departed, and waited 1Kin 20:38
gathered the *p* together 1Kin 22:6
the *p* prophesied so, saying 1Kin 22:12
mouth of all his *p* 1Kin 22:22
the *p* that were at Beth-el 2Kin 2:3
men of the sons of the *p* 2Kin 2:7

Is there not here a *p* of 2Kin 3:11
thee to the *p* of thy father 2Kin 3:13
to the *p* of thy mother 2Kin 3:13
wives of the sons of the *p* 2Kin 4:1
sons of the *p* were sitting 2Kin 4:38
pottage for the sons of the *p* ...2Kin 4:38
the *p* that is in Samaria 2Kin 5:3
the *p* had bid thee do some 2Kin 5:13
men of the sons of the *p* 2Kin 5:22
the sons of the *p* said unto 2Kin 6:1
but Elisha, the *p* that is in 2Kin 6:12
of the children of the *p* 2Kin 9:1
unto me all the *p* of Baal 2Kin 10:19
against Judah, by all the *p* 2Kin 17:13
to you by my servants the *p* 2Kin 17:13
p Isaiah the son of Amoz 2Kin 20:1
came Isaiah the *p* unto 2Kin 20:14
Lord..by his servants the *p* 2Kin 21:10
the priests, and the *p*, and 2Kin 23:2
p that came out of Samaria.....2Kin 23:18
spake by his servants the *p* 2Kin 24:2
and do my *p* no harm.........1Chr 16:22
David said to Nathan the *p*....1Chr 17:1
the book of Nathan the *p* 1Chr 29:29
in the story of the *p* Iddo 2Chr 13:22
together of *p* four hundred 2Chr 18:5
not here a *p* of the Lord 2Chr 18:6
the *p* prophesied so, saying....2Chr 18:11
mouth of all his *p* 2Chr 18:21
believe his *p*, so shall ye 2Chr 20:20
to him from Elijah the *p* 2Chr 21:12
Yet he sent *p* to them, to 2Chr 24:19
sent unto him a *p*, which 2Chr 25:15
did Isaiah the *p*, the son 2Chr 26:22
seer, and Nathan the *p*.........2Chr 29:25
of the Lord by his *p* 2Chr 29:25
p Isaiah the son of Amoz 2Chr 32:20
the days of Samuel the *p*......2Chr 35:18
words, and misused his *p*......2Chr 36:16
prophesying of Haggai the *p*...Ezra 6:14
by thy servants the *p* ....Ezra 9:11
also appointed *p* to preach .....Neh 6:7
slew thy *p* which testified .....Neh 9:26
our priests, and on our *p*......Neh 9:32
there is no more any *p*........Ps 74:9
anointed, and do my *p* no .....Ps 105:15
war, the judge, and the *p* .....Is 3:2
the *p* that teacheth lies........Is 9:15
the priest and the *p* have ......Is 28:7
the *p* and your rulers, the .....Is 29:10
to the *p*, Prophesy not unto ...Is 30:10
unto Isaiah the *p* the son......Is 37:2
Isaiah the *p* the son of........Is 38:1
Isaiah the *p* unto king ....Is 39:3
ordained thee a *p* unto the ....Jer 1:5
the *p* prophesied by Baal......Jer 2:8
hath devoured your *p* ....Jer 2:30
astonished, and the *p* shall ....Jer 4:9
the *p* shall become wind ....Jer 5:13
the *p* even unto the priest .....Jer 6:13
you all my servants the *p* .....Jer 7:25
the bones of the *p*, and the ...Jer 8:1
the *p* even unto the priest .....Jer 8:10
the *p* say unto them, Ye ....Jer 14:13
p that prophesy in my ....Jer 14:15
shall those *p* be consumed.....Jer 14:15
both the *p* and the priest......Jer 14:18
nor the word from the *p* ....Jer 18:18
smote Jeremiah the *p* ....Jer 20:2
broken because of the *p* ......Jer 23:9
p and priest are profane ......Jer 23:11
also in the *p* of Jerusalem .....Jer 23:14
of hosts concerning the *p*......Jer 23:15
the *p* of Jerusalem is..........Jer 23:15
shalt thou say to the *p* ....Jer 23:37
Jeremiah the *p* spake unto .....Jer 25:2
you all his servants the *p* ......Jer 25:4
So the priests and the *p*.......Jer 26:7
unto the priests and to the *p* ..Jer 26:16
hearken not ye to your *p*......Jer 27:9
the *p* that prophesy unto ....Jer 27:15
if they be *p*, and if the word ..Jer 27:18
Jeremiah the *p* sent from......Jer 29:1
to the priests, and to the *p* ....Jer 29:1
raised us up *p* in Babylon .....Jer 29:15
which maketh himself a *p* .....Jer 29:27
Jeremiah the *p* was shut ......Jer 32:2
and their *p*, and the men of ...Jer 32:32
Jeremiah the *p* spake all ....Jer 34:6
you all my servants the *p* .....Jer 35:15
Jeremiah the *p* commanded ....Jer 36:8
he spake by the *p* Jeremiah ...Jer 37:2
Lord unto the *p* Jeremiah .....Jer 37:6
Where are now your *p*.........Jer 37:19
done to Jeremiah the *p* ....Jer 38:9
took Jeremiah the *p* unto .....Jer 38:14
said unto Jeremiah the *p* ......Jer 42:2
and Jeremiah the *p*, and ......Jer 43:6
you all my servants the *p* .....Jer 44:4
that Jeremiah the *p* spake .....Jer 45:1
Lord..to Jeremiah the *p*.......Jer 46:1
Lord..to Jeremiah the *p*.......Jer 47:1
to Jeremiah the *p* against .....Jer 49:34
by Jeremiah the *p* ....Jer 50:1
Jeremiah the *p* commanded ...Jer 51:59
her *p* also find no vision ......Lam 2:9
priest and the *p* be slain ......Lam 2:20
For the sins of her *p*, and .....Lam 4:13
there hath been a *p* among ....Ezek 2:5
they seek a vision of the *p* ....Ezek 7:26
face, and cometh to the *p*.....Ezek 14:4
cometh to a *p* to inquire of....Ezek 14:7
if the *p* be deceived when .....Ezek 14:9
Lord have deceived that *p*.....Ezek 14:9
prophesy against the *p* of .....Ezek 13:2
p are like the foxes in the .....Ezek 13:4
p of Israel which prophesy ....Ezek 13:16
conspiracy of her *p* in the .....Ezek 22:25
a *p* hath been among them ....Ezek 33:33
time by my servants the *p* .....Ezek 38:17
Lord came to Jeremiah the *p* ..Dan 9:2
unto thy servants the *p*........Dan 9:6
p also shall fall with thee......Hos 4:5
have I hewed them by the *p*...Hos 6:5
p is a fool, the spiritual ....Hos 9:7
I have also spoken by the *p* ...Hos 12:10
by the ministry of the *p*.......Hos 12:10
p the Lord brought Israel .....Hos 12:13
by a *p* was he preserved ......Hos 12:13
raised up of your sons for *p* ...Amos 2:11
his secret..servants the *p* ......Amos 3:7
I was no *p*, neither..a *p* son ...Amos 7:14
be the *p* of this people ....Mic 2:11
the *p* that make my people ....Mic 3:5
the *p* thereof divine for ....Mic 3:11
prayer of Habakkuk the *p*.....Hab 3:1
Her *p* are light and ....Zeph 3:4
the Lord by Haggai the *p* .....Hag 1:1
the words of Haggai the *p*.....Hag 1:12
the Lord by the *p* Haggai .....Hag 2:1
the former *p* have cried ....Zech 1:4
to the *p*, saying, Should ....Zech 7:3
his spirit by the former *p*......Zech 7:12
by the mouth of the *p* ....Zech 8:9
the *p* and the unclean.........Zech 13:2
shall say, I am no *p*, I am.....Zech 13:5
will send you Elijah the *p* .....Mal 4:5
thus it is written by the *p* .....Matt 2:5
spoken by Jeremiah the *p* .....Matt 2:17
which was spoken by the *p* ....Matt 2:23
spoken of by the *p* Isaiah .....Matt 3:3
spoken by Isaiah the *p*........Matt 4:14
so persecuted they the *p* ......Matt 5:12
this is the law and the *p* ......Matt 7:12
spoken by Isaiah the *p*........Matt 8:17
p in the name of a *p* shall .....Matt 10:41
ye out for to see? A *p*? ....Matt 11:9
unto you, and more than a *p* ..Matt 11:9
For all the *p* and the law......Matt 11:13
spoken by Isaiah the *p*........Matt 12:17
many *p* and righteous men ....Matt 13:17
which was spoken by the *p* ....Matt 13:35
they counted him as a *p*.......Matt 14:5
but the sign of the *p* Jonah ....Matt 16:4
Jeremiah, or one of the *p* .....Matt 16:14
which was spoken by the *p* ....Matt 21:4
for all hold John as a *p* ....Matt 21:26
hang all the law and the *p* ....Matt 22:40
ye build the tombs of the *p* ...Matt 23:29
of them which killed the *p* ....Matt 23:31
thou that killed the *p* ....Matt 23:37
And many false *p* shall rise....Matt 24:11
of the *p* might be fulfilled .....Matt 26:56
spoken by Jeremiah the *p* .....Matt 27:9
which was spoken by the *p* ....Matt 27:35
As it is written in the *p* ....Mark 1:2
A *p* is not without honor......Mark 6:4
prophet, or as one of the *p*....Mark 6:15
and others, One of the *p*......Mark 8:28
John, that he was a *p* ....Mark 11:32
spoken of by Daniel the *p*.....Mark 13:14
false Christs and false *p* ....Mark 13:22
called the *p* of the Highest ....Luke 1:76
the words of Isaiah the *p*......Luke 3:4
the book of the *p* Isaiah ......Luke 4:17
in the time of Elisha the *p* ....Luke 4:27
their fathers unto the *p* ....Luke 6:23
a great *p* is risen up among ...Luke 7:16
This man, if he were a *p*......Luke 7:39
one of the old *p* was risen.....Luke 9:8
but the sign of Jonah the *p*....Luke 11:29
the sepulchers of the *p*........Luke 11:47
That the blood of all the *p* ....Luke 11:50
all the *p*, in the kingdom ......Luke 13:28
a *p* perish out of Jerusalem....Luke 13:33
law and the *p* were until ......Luke 16:16
hear not Moses and the *p* .....Luke 16:31
that are written by the *p* ......Luke 18:31
persuaded that John was a *p* ..Luke 20:6
was a *p* mighty in deed ....Luke 24:19
Art thou that *p*? And he ......John 1:21
Christ, nor Elijah..that *p*? .....John 1:25
and the *p*, did write, Jesus ....John 1:45
perceive that thou art a *p* .....John 4:19
p that should come into the ...John 6:14
Of a truth this is the *P*........John 7:40
It is written in the *p*, And.....John 6:45
Abraham is dead, and the *p*...John 8:52
eyes? He said, He is a *p* ......John 9:17
of Isaiah the *p* might be.......John 12:38
was spoken by the *p* Joel .....Acts 2:16
by the mouth of all his *p*......Acts 3:18
p shall the Lord your God ....Acts 3:22
p shall the Lord your God ....Acts 7:37
written in the book of the *p*...Acts 7:42
chariot read Isaiah the *p* ......Acts 8:28
whom speaketh the *p* this? ....Acts 8:34
him give all the *p* witness .....Acts 10:43
came *p* from Jerusalem ....Acts 11:27
sorcerer, a false *p*, a Jew......Acts 13:6
reading of the law and the *p* ..Acts 13:15
agree the words of the *p* ......Acts 15:15
written in the law and in the *p*.Acts 24:14
which the *p* and Moses did ....Acts 26:22
Holy Ghost by Isaiah the *p*....Acts 28:25
p in the holy scriptures........Rom 1:2
witnessed by the law and the *p*.Rom 3:21
Lord, they have killed thy *p*...Rom 11:3
the scriptures of the *p* ....Rom 16:26
the *p* speak two or three 1Cor 14:29
man think himself to be a *p*...1Cor 14:37
holy apostles and *p* by the ....Eph 3:5
some, apostles; and some, *p*...Eph 4:11
Lord Jesus, and their own *p*...1Thess 2:15
even a *p* of their own, said....Titus 1:12
unto the fathers by the *p*......Heb 1:1
and Samuel, and of the *p* .....Heb 11:32
the *p*, who have spoken in ....James 5:10
forbade the madness of the *p*..2Pet 2:16
spoken before by the holy *p*...2Pet 3:2
many false *p* are gone out.....1John 4:1
to his servants the *p* ....Rev 10:7
these two *p* tormented them...Rev 11:10
the blood of saints and *p*......Rev 16:6
of the mouth of the false *p*....Rev 16:13
and ye holy apostles and *p* ....Rev 18:20
the beast and the false *p* ......Rev 20:10
God of the holy *p*, sent ....Rev 22:6

PROPHETESS—*a female prophet*

Good:

Miriam ....Ex 15:20, 21
Deborah ....Judg 4:4, 5
Huldah 2Kin 22:12-20

Isaiah's wife ....Is 8:1-3
Anna ....Luke 2:36
Daughters of Philip ......Acts 21:8, 9
Prophecy concerning .....Joel 2:28

False:
Women of Judah ....Ezek 13:17
Noadiah ....Neh 6:14
Jezebel ....Rev 2:20

PROPHETS IN THE NEW TESTAMENT

Office of, based upon:
Christ's prophetic office ..Deut 18:15, 18
Old Testament prediction.Joel 2:28
Acts 2:18
Holy Spirit's coming .....John 16:7, 13
Divine institution 1Cor 12:28

Functions of:
Strengthen ....Acts 15:32
Define God's will.........Acts 13:1-3
Predict the future........Acts 21:10, 11

PROPHETS, NAMES OF THE
Enoch ....Gen 5:21, 24
Noah...................Gen 9:25-27
Abraham ....Gen 20:1, 7
Jacob...................Gen 49:1
Aaron...................Ex 7:1
Moses ....Deut 18:18
Joshua..................1Kin 16:34
One sent to Israel ....Judg 6:8-10
One sent to Eli 1Sam 2:27-36
Samuel 1Sam 3:20
David ....Acts 2:25, 30
Nathan 2Sam 7:2
Zadok 2Sam 15:27
Gad 2Sam 24:11-14
Ahijah 1Kin 11:29
One of Judah 1Kin 13:1
Iddo....................2Chr 9:29; 12:15
Shemaiah 2Chr 12:5, 7, 15
Azariah.................2Chr 15:1-8
Hanani 2Chr 16:7-10
Jehu....................1Kin 16:1, 7, 12
Elijah 1Kin 17:1
Elisha 2Kin 19:16
Micaiah.................1Kin 22:7, 8
Jonah 2Kin 14:25
Isaiah 2Kin 19:2
Hosea ....Hos 1:1
Amos ....Amos 1:1
Micah ....Mic 1:1
Oded...................2Chr 28:9
Nahum ....Nah 1:1
Joel ....Joel 1:1
Zephaniah ....Zeph 1:1
Jeduthun 2Chr 35:15
Jeremiah................2Chr 36:12, 21
Habakkuk ....Hab 1:1
Obadiah ....Obad 1
Ezekiel ....Ezek 1:3
Daniel..................Matt 24:15
Haggai ....Ezra 5:1
Zechariah............{Ezra 5:1; Zech 1:1; Luke 1:67}
Malachi.................Mal 1:1
John the Baptist ....Luke 7:26-28
Agabus ....Acts 11:28
Paul....................1Tim 4:1
Peter 2Pet 2:1, 2
John ....Rev 1:1

PROPITIATION—*appeasing or conciliating*

Elements in Christ's:
Dying for man's sins 1Pet 1:18, 19
Satisfying God's justice ..Rom 3:25, 26
Becoming the mercy seat .Rom 3:25
Reconciling God and man.2Cor 5:18, 19
Offering believing sinner perfect righteousness ...2Cor 5:20, 21

he is the ***p*** for our sins 1John 2:2
his Son to be the ***p*** for our 1John 4:10

PROPORTION—*the relation of one part to another or to the whole*
according to the ***p*** of every 1Kin 7:36
power, nor his comely ***p*** ......Job 41:12
according to the ***p*** of faith.....Rom 12:6

PROSELYTE—*a convert to Judaism*

Regulations imposed upon:
Circumcision ....Gen 17:13
Observance of the Law ..Ex 12:48, 49
Obedience to the covenant ....Deut 29:10-13
Association with Israel ...Ruth 1:16
Separation from heathenism ....Ezra 6:21
Participation in feasts ....John 12:20
Acts 8:27

Special significance of:
Typical of Gentile converts ....Is 56:3-8
Concerned about Christ ..John 12:20
Among early converts....Acts 6:5
Source of Gentile church .Acts 13:42-46

[*also* PROSELYTES]
sea and land to make one ***p*** ...Matt 23:15

PROSPECT—*view*
and their ***p*** was toward the ....Ezek 40:44
the ***p*** toward the north ....Ezek 40:44
p is toward the north ....Ezek 40:46
whose ***p*** is toward the east ....Ezek 42:15
gate whose ***p*** is toward the ....Ezek 43:4

PROSPERITY—*a state of material or spiritual abundance*

Kinds of:
Material 1Cor 16:2
National ....Ezek 16:13, 14
Personal ....Dan 6:28
Deceitful 1Kin 22:12, 15
Evil ....Ps 73:12
Spiritual 3John 2
Divine..................Is 53:10

Of the righteous:
Promised ....Ps 1:3
Prayed for ....Neh 1:11
Perplexed...............Jer 12:1-3

Of the wicked:
Lack of understanding over..................Ps 73:3-12
Righteous must not fret over..................Ps 37:7
Terrible end of..........Jer 20:11

Hindrances to:
Transgression 2Chr 24:20
Hiding one's sins ....Prov 28:13
Distrust of the Lord .....Jer 2:36, 37

True secrets of:
Lord's blessings ....Ps 35:27
Keeping God's Law ......Josh 1:7, 8
God's guidance ....Gen 24:40-56
Trust in God............Neh 2:20
Dedication to God 2Chr 31:20, 21
Listening to God's prophets ....Ezra 6:14
Belief in God's Word 2Chr 20:20

Perils of:
Forgetting God ....Deut 8:10-12
Prov 30:7-9
Destruction ....Prov 1:32
Rebellion ....Jer 22:21

[*also* PROSPER, PROSPERED, PROSPERETH, PROSPEROUS, PROSPEROUSLY]
had made his journey ***p*** or ....Gen 24:21
Joseph, and he was a ***p*** ....Gen 39:2
did the Lord made it to ***p*** .....Gen 39:23
Lord? but it shall not ***p*** ....Num 14:41
their peace nor their ***p*** ....Deut 23:6
and thou shalt not ***p*** in thy ....Deut 28:29
that ye may ***p*** in all that ......Deut 29:9
the children of Israel ***p***........Judg 4:24
say to him that liveth in ***p*** 1Sam 25:6
did, and how the war ***p*** 2Sam 11:7
mayest ***p*** in all that thou 1Kin 2:3
and ***p*** exceedeth the fame 1Kin 10:7
and he ***p*** whithersoever he 2Kin 18:7
p thou, and build the house ...1Chr 22:11
Then shalt thou ***p***, if thou 1Chr 22:13
of David his father, and ***p*** 1Chr 29:23
fathers; for ye shall not ***p*** 2Chr 13:12
side. So they built and ***p*** 2Chr 14:7
to Ramoth-gilead, and ***p*** 2Chr 18:11
Lord, God made him to ***p*** 2Chr 26:5
and Hezekiah ***p*** in all his 2Chr 32:30
on, and ***p*** in their hands ......Ezra 5:8
of thy righteousness ***p***..........Job 8:6
against him, and hath ***p*** ....Job 9:4
p the destroyer shall come ....Job 15:21
shall spend their days in ***p*****.....Job 36:11
my ***p*** I said, I shall never .....Ps 30:6
majesty ride ***p*** because of .....Ps 45:4
I beseech thee, send now ***p*****....Ps 118:25
they shall ***p*** that love thee .....Ps 122:6
and ***p*** within thy palaces ......Ps 122:7
it turneth, it ***p***................Prov 17:8
In the day of ***p*** be joyful ......Eccl 7:14
knowest not whether shall ***p*** ...Eccl 11:6
he shall make his way ***p***.......Is 48:15
formed against thee shall ***p*** ....Is 54:17
p in the thing whereto I.......Is 55:11
the fatherless, yet they ***p*** ......Jer 5:28
therefore they shall not ***p*** .....Jer 10:21
no man of his seed shall ***p*** ....Jer 22:30
a King shall reign and ***p***........Jer 23:5
Chaldeans, ye shall not ***p*** .....Jer 32:5
the ***p*** that I procure unto ......Jer 33:9
the chief, her enemies ***p*** ......Lam 1:5
off from peace: I forgat ***p*** .....Lam 3:17
being planted, shall it ***p***? ......Ezek 17:10
Shall he ***p***? shall he escape ....Ezek 17:15
and it practiced, and ***p*** ....Dan 8:12
cause craft to ***p*** in his ....Dan 8:25
it shall not ***p***: for yet the ......Dan 11:27
My cities through ***p*** shall ......Zech 1:17
was inhabited and in ***p*** ....Zech 7:7
For the seed shall be ***p***........Zech 8:12
I might have a ***p*** journey by ...Rom 1:10

PROSTITUTE—*to engage in sexual activity for money*
Forbidden ....Lev 19:29

PROSTITUTION—*See* HARLOT

PROTECTION—*help; aid*
you, and be your ***p*** ....Deut 32:38

PROTECTION, DIVINE—*God's protective work for us*

Characteristics of:
Continuous ....Ps 121:3-8
Unfailing ....Josh 1:5
Assuring................Is 41:10
Persevering ....John 10:29-30
Satisfying 2Cor 12:9, 10
Necessary...............Ps 124:1-5

Provided against:
Evil 2Thess 3:3
Temptation 1Cor 10:13
Persecution ....Rev 3:10
Enemies ....Ps 56:9
Falling.................Judg 24
Dangers ....Ps 91:3-7
Calamities ....Ps 57:1

PROTEST—*to declare one's disapproval*

[*also* PROTESTED, PROTESTING]
The man did solemnly ***p*** ......Gen 43:3
howbeit yet ***p*** solemnly........1Sam 8:9
by the Lord, and ***p*** unto 1Kin 2:42
I earnestly ***p*** unto your........Jer 11:7
rising early and ***p***, saying ......Jer 11:7
angel of the Lord ***p***...........Zech 3:6
I ***p*** by your rejoicing which 1Cor 15:31

PROUD—*haughty; defiant; possessing inordinate self-esteem*

Descriptive of:
Moabites ....Jer 48:29
Babylonians............Jer 50:29-32

Wicked ... Ps 17:9, 10
Scoffers ... Prov 21:24

God's attitude toward:
Does not respect ... Ps 40:4
Rebukes ... Ps 119:21
Resists ... James 4:6

See PRIDE

[*also* PROUDLY]
thing wherein they dealt **p** ... Ex 18:11
no more so exceeding **p** ... 1Sam 2:3
that they dealt **p** against ... Neh 9:10
yet they dealt **p** and ... Neh 9:29
p helpers do stoop under ... Job 9:13
he smiteth through the **p** ... Job 26:12
here shall thy **p** waves be ... Job 38:11
behold every one that is **p** ... Job 40:11
that speaketh **p** things ... Ps 12:3
speak grievous things **p** ... Ps 31:18
plentifully rewarded the **p** ... Ps 31:23
the **p** are risen against me ... Ps 86:14
render a reward to the **p** ... Ps 94:2
look and a **p** heart will not ... Ps 101:5
p have had me greatly in ... Ps 119:51
Let the **p** be ashamed; for ... Ps 119:78
let not the **p** oppress me ... Ps 119:122
with the contempt of the **p** ... Ps 123:4
p waters had gone over our ... Ps 124:5
the **p** he knoweth afar off ... Ps 138:6
p have hid a snare for me ... Ps 140:5
A **p** look, a lying tongue ... Prov 6:17
destroy the house of the **p** ... Prov 15:25
Every one that is **p** in heart ... Prov 16:5
high look, and a **p** heart, ... Prov 21:4
is of a **p** heart stirreth ... Prov 28:25
better than the **p** in spirit ... Eccl 7:8
upon every one that is **p** ... Is 2:12
the child..behave himself **p** ... Is 3:5
arrogancy of the **p** to cease ... Is 13:11
pride of Moab; he is very **p** ... Is 16:6
me, and give ear; be not **p** ... Jer 13:15
all the **p** men, saying unto ... Jer 43:2
p in the day of distress ... Obad 12
he is a **p** man, neither ... Hab 2:5
now we call the **p** happy ... Mal 3:15
all the **p**, yea, and all that ... Mal 4:1
the **p** in the imagination of ... Luke 1:51
despiteful, **p**, boasters ... Rom 1:30
He is **p**, knowing nothing ... 1Tim 6:4
p, blasphemers, disobedient ... 2Tim 3:2
God resisteth the **p**, and ... 1Pet 5:5

PROVE—*to show something to be true*

Descriptive of:
Testing physically ... 1Sam 17:39
Luke 14:19
Testing morally ... John 6:6
Showing something to be true ... Gen 42:15, 16

Objects of, among Christians:
Love ... 2Cor 8:8
Sacrifice ... Rom 12:2
Faith ... 2Cor 13:5
Works ... Gal 6:4
Abilities ... 1Tim 3:10

[*also* PROVED, PROVETH, PROVING]
ordinance, and there he **p** them Ex 15:25
that I may **p** them, whether ... Ex 16:4
Fear not: for God is come to **p**. Ex 20:20
humble thee, and to **p** thee ... Deut 8:2
the Lord your God **p** you ... Deut 13:3
thou didst **p** at Massah ... Deut 33:8
them I may **p** Israel ... Judg 2:22
to **p** Israel by them, even as ... Judg 3:1
me **p**, I pray thee, but this ... Judg 6:39
p him with hard questions ... 1Kin 10:1
to **p** Solomon with hard ... 2Chr 9:1
perfect, it shall also **p** me ... Job 9:20
Thou hast **p** mine heart ... Ps 17:3
Examine me, O Lord, and **p** ... Ps 26:2
thou, O God has **p** us ... Ps 66:10
I **p** thee at the waters of ... Ps 81:7
p me, and saw my work ... Ps 95:9
All this have I **p** by wisdom ... Eccl 7:23
P thy servants, I beseech ... Dan 1:12
this matter, and **p** them ten ... Dan 1:14
p me now herewith, saith ... Mal 3:10
p that this is very Christ ... Acts 9:22
Paul, which they could not **p** ... Acts 25:7
we have before **p** both Jews ... Rom 3:9
p diligent in many things ... 2Cor 8:22
P what is acceptable unto ... Eph 5:10
P all things; hold fast that ... 1Thess 5:21
your fathers tempted me, **p** ... Heb 3:9

PROVENDER—*food for animals*
Supplied for animals ... Gen 24:25, 32
Gen 42:27

and he gave their asses **p** ... Gen 43:24
is both straw and **p** for our ... Judg 19:19
house, and gave **p** unto the ... Judg 19:21
ground shall eat clean **p** ... Is 30:24

PROVERB—*a short, wise saying*

Descriptive of:
Wise saying ... 1Sam 24:13
Something generally accepted ... Ezek 12:22, 23
Object of taunt ... Deut 28:37
Figurative language ... John 16:25, 29

Characteristics of:
Brief ... 1Sam 10:12
Striking statement ... Luke 4:23
Authoritative ... Prov 1:1-6
Emphasis by repetition ... Prov 3:17

[*also* PROVERBS]
they that speak in **p** ... Num 21:27
spake three thousand **p** ... 1Kin 4:32
Israel shall be a **p** and a ... 1Kin 9:7
be a **p** and a byword among ... 2Chr 7:20
and I became a **p** to them ... Ps 69:11
These are also **p** of Solomon ... Prov 25:1
and set in order many **p** ... Eccl 12:9
up this **p** against the king ... Is 14:4
to be a reproach and a **p**, a ... Jer 24:9
make him a sign and a **p** ... Ezek 14:8
every one that useth **p** ... Ezek 16:44
use this **p** against thee ... Ezek 16:44
use this **p** concerning the ... Ezek 18:2
a taunting **p** against him ... Hab 2:6
according to the true **p** ... 2Pet 2:22

PROVERBS, THE BOOK OF—*a book of the Old Testament*
Tribute to wisdom ... Prov 1—2
Against immorality ... Prov 5:1-23
Parental counsel ... Prov 6—7
Miscellaneous proverbs ... Prov 10—24
Proverbs of Agur and Lemuel ... Prov 30:1—31:9
The worthy woman ... Prov 31:10-31

PROVIDE—*a preparation beforehand*
Provide for own house ... 1Tim 5:8
Provide for poor ... Is 58:7

[*also* PROVIDED, PROVIDETH, PROVIDING, PROVISION]
God will **p** himself a lamb ... Gen 22:8
shall I **p** for mine own house ... Gen 30:30
and to give them **p** for the ... Gen 42:25
gave them **p** for the way ... Gen 45:21
p out of all the people able ... Ex 18:21
And he **p** the first part for ... Deut 33:21
their **p** was dry and mouldy ... Josh 9:5
have **p** me a king among ... 1Sam 16:1
P me now a man that can ... 1Sam 16:17
p the king of sustenance ... 2Sam 19:32
p victuals for the king and ... 1Kin 4:7
month in a year made **p** ... 1Kin 4:7
prepared great **p** for them ... 2Kin 6:23
for the which I have made **p** ... 1Chr 29:19
whom David my father did **p** ... 2Chr 2:7
he **p** him cities, and ... 2Chr 32:29
p for the raven his food? ... Job 38:41
corn, when thou hast so **p** ... Ps 65:9
can he **p** flesh for his ... Ps 78:20
I will abundantly bless her **p** ... Ps 132:15
P her meat in the summer ... Prov 6:8
them a daily **p** of the king's ... Dan 1:5
P neither gold, nor silver ... Matt 10:9
things be, which thou hast **p**? ... Luke 12:20
p yourselves bags which ... Luke 12:33
And **p** them beasts, that ... Acts 23:24
P things honest in the ... Rom 12:17
make not **p** for the flesh ... Rom 13:14
P for honest things, not ... 2Cor 8:21
But if any **p** not for his own ... 1Tim 5:8
God having **p** some better ... Heb 11:40

PROVIDENCE—*divine guidance of human destiny*

Described as:
Universal ... Ps 103:19
Purposive ... Gen 45:5-8
Righteous ... Ps 145:17
Something mysterious ... Job 11:7-9
Irresistible ... Dan 4:35

Manifested, in the world, in God's:
Preserving the world ... Neh 9:6
Providing for His possessions ... Ps 104:27, 28
Guiding world events ... Acts 17:26, 27
Ruling over the elements ... Is 50:2, 3
Preserving nature ... Gen 8:22
Ordering man's life ... Ps 75:6, 7
Controlling minute details. Matt 10:29, 30

Attitude of believers toward:
Acknowledge in prosperity ... 1Chr 29:11, 12; Prov. 3:6
Humble himself before in adversity ... Job 1:21; Ps 119:75
Remember God's hand ... Ps 37:1-40
Ps 139:10

PROVINCE—*a government district*

Ruled by:
Governors ... Esth 3:12
Proconsuls ... Acts 13:4, 7

Characteristics of:
Numerous ... Esth 1:1
Ruled by one man ... Dan 2:48, 49
Justice perverted in ... Eccl 5:8
People, citizens of ... Acts 23:34
News spreads to ... Esth 9:4

Of the Roman Empire:
Achaia ... Acts 18:12
Asia ... Acts 19:10
Bithynia ... Acts 16:7
Cappadocia ... Acts 2:9
Cyprus ... Acts 13:4
Egypt ... Matt 2:13
Galatia ... Acts 16:6
Macedonia ... Acts 16:12
Pamphylia ... Acts 13:13
Lycia ... Acts 27:5
Syria ... Matt 4:24

[*also* PROVINCES]
men of the princes of the **p** ... 1Kin 20:14
princes of the **p** went out ... 1Kin 20:17
the children of the **p** that ... Ezra 2:1
hurtful unto kings and **p** ... Ezra 4:15
we went into the **p** of Judea ... Ezra 5:8
is in the **p** of the Medes ... Ezra 6:2
in all the **p** of Babylon ... Ezra 7:16
that are left..in the **p** ... Neh 1:3
are the children of the **p** ... Neh 7:6
are the chief of the **p** that ... Neh 11:3
nobles and princes of the **p** ... Esth 1:3
into all the king's **p** ... Esth 1:22
into every **p** according to ... Esth 1:22
in all the **p** of his kingdom ... Esth 2:3
in all the **p** of thy kingdom ... Esth 3:8
in every **p**, whithersoever ... Esth 4:3
the people of the king's **p** ... Esth 4:11
Jews..in all the king's **p** ... Esth 8:5
unto every **p** according to ... Esth 8:9
rulers of the **p** which are ... Esth 8:9
hundred twenty and seven **p** ... Esth 8:9
given in every **p** ... Esth 8:13
p of the king Ahasuerus ... Esth 9:2
in the rest of the king's **p** ... Esth 9:12
Jews..in the king's **p** ... Esth 9:16
family, every **p**, and every ... Esth 9:28
and seven **p** of the kingdom ... Esth 9:30
of kings and of the **p** ... Eccl 2:8

and princess among the *p* .....Lam 1:1
on every side from the *p* ....Ezek 19:8
plain of Dura, in the *p* of .....Dan 3:1
rulers of the *p*, to come ....Dan 3:2
Abed-nego, in the *p* of........Dan 3:30
which is the *p* of Elam ....Dan 8:2
the fattest places of the *p* .....Dan 11:24
letter, he asked of what *p* .....Acts 23:34
Festus was come into the *p*....Acts 25:1

PROVISION—*See* PROVIDE

PROVOKE—*to irritate or agitate another*

Between people:
Two women 1Sam 1:7
Satan and man 1Chr 21:1
Peoples (nations) ....Rom 10:19
Christians 2Cor 9:2
Father and children ......Eph 6:4

Causes of, between God and man:
Evil ....Deut 4:25
Sins 1Kin 16:2
Whoredoms ....Ezek 16:26

[*also* PROVOCATION, PROVOCATIONS, PROVOKED, PROVOKEDST, PROVOKETH, PROVOKING]

and obey his voice, *p* him .....Ex 23:21
How long will this people *p* ...Num 14:11
of them that *p* me see it ....Num 14:23
that these men have *p* the .....Num 16:30
thou *p* the Lord thy God to ...Deut 9:7
in Horeb ye *p* the Lord to ....Deut 9:8
Lord, to *p* him to anger.......Deut 9:18
and serve them, and *p* me.....Deut 31:20
p him to jealousy with ....Deut 32:16
because of the *p* of his sons ...Deut 32:19
p me to anger with their ......Deut 32:21
I will *p* them to anger with....Deut 32:21
and *p* the Lord to anger ......Judg 2:12
her adversary also *p* her 1Sam 1:6
molten images, to *p* me to 1Kin 14:9
their groves, *p* the Lord to 1Kin 14:15
they *p* him to jealousy with ...1Kin 14:22
Israel sin, by his *p* 1Kin 15:30
p the Lord God of Israel to ...1Kin 15:30
in *p* him to anger with the 1Kin 16:7
p the Lord God of Israel to ...1Kin 16:13
to *p* the Lord God of Israel ...1Kin 16:33
for the *p* wherewith thou 1Kin 21:22
thou hast *p* me to anger.......1Kin 21:22
p to anger the Lord God of ...1Kin 22:53
things to *p* the Lord to........2Kin 17:11
Lord, to *p* him to anger.......2Kin 21:6
have *p* me to anger, since 2Kin 21:15
they might *p* me to anger 2Kin 22:17
had made to *p* the Lord to 2Kin 23:19
of all the *p* that Manasseh.....2Kin 23:26
that Manasseh had *p* him 2Kin 23:26
p to anger the Lord God 2Chr 28:25
Lord, to *p* him to anger.......2Chr 33:6
they might *p* me to anger 2Chr 34:25
p the God of heaven unto .....Ezra 5:12
have *p* thee to anger before ...Neh 4:5
and had wrought great *p* ......Neh 9:18
they that *p* God are secure ....Job 12:6
eye continue in their *p*? ....Job 17:2
by *p* the Most High in the ....Ps 78:17
p him in the wilderness ....Ps 78:40
tempted and *p* the most.......Ps 78:56
not your heart, as in the *p* ....Ps 95:8
but *p* him at the sea, even ....Ps 106:7
Because they *p* his spirit ......Ps 106:33
p him to anger sinneth ....Prov 20:2
p the Holy One of Israel......Is 1:4
Lord, to *p* the eyes of his .....Is 3:8
people that *p* me to anger .....Is 65:3
they may *p* me to anger ....Jer 7:18
Do they *p* me to anger?.......Jer 7:19
not *p* themselves to the ....Jer 7:19
p me to anger with their ......Jer 8:19
p me to anger in offering .....Jer 11:17
p me not to anger with the....Jer 25:6
unto other gods, to *p* me to ..Jer 32:29
Israel have only *p* me to ......Jer 32:30
have committed to *p* me to....Jer 44:3
returned to *p* me to anger.....Ezek 8:17
presented the *p* of their ......Ezek 20:28
Ephraim *p* him to anger ......Hos 12:14
when your fathers *p* me to ....Zech 8:14
to *p* him to speak of many ....Luke 11:53
Gentiles, for to *p* them to .....Rom 11:11
p the Lord to jealousy? 1Cor 10:22
is not easily *p*, thinketh no 1Cor 13:5
p one another, envying one ...Gal 5:26
p not your children to ....Col 3:21
not your hearts, as in the *p* ...Heb 3:8
they had heard, did *p*.........Heb 3:16
to *p* unto love and to good ....Heb 10:24

PRUDENCE—*wisdom applied to practical matters; caution; shrewdness*

Characteristics of:
Dwells with widsom .....Prov 8:12
Observant ....Prov 14:15
Foresees evil ....Prov 22:3
Regards reproof ....Prov 15:5
Conceals knowledge .....Prov 12:23
Crowned with knowledge .Prov 14:18
Keeps silent.............Amos 5:13

Descriptive of:
David 1Sam 16:18
Solomon 2Chr 2:12
Messiah ....Is 52:13
Wife ....Prov 19:14
Believers ....Hos 14:9
Worldly-wise ....Matt 11:25

Examples of:
Jacob...................Gen 32:3-23
Joseph..................Gen 41:39-49
Gideon ....Judg 8:1-3

[*also* PRUDENT]

a *p* man covereth shame ......Prov 12:16
p man dealeth with ....Prov 13:16
wisdom of the *p* is to ....Prov 14:8
wise in heart shall be called *p*. .Prov 16:21
the *p* getteth knowledge.......Prov 18:15
A *p* man foreseeth the evil ....Prov 27:12
and the *p*, and the ancient ....Is 3:2
and *p* in their own sight.......Is 5:21
for I am *p*: and I have ....Is 10:13
understanding of their *p*.......Is 29:14
counsel perished from the *p*? ..Jer 49:7
things from the wise and *p* ....Luke 10:21
Sergius Paulus, a *p* man.......Acts 13:7
the understanding of the *p* 1Cor 1:19
us in all wisdom and *p* ....Eph 1:8

PRUNE—*to cut back plants for the purpose of producing more growth*
Vineyards...............Lev 25:3, 4
Figurative of God's care. .Is 5:6
John 15:2

Instruments used to:
Hooks ....Is 2:4
Knives..................Is 18:5

PRUNINGHOOKS—*knives or hooks*
and your *p* into spears ....Joel 3:10
and their spears into *p* ....Mic 4:3

PSALM—*a sacred song or poem used in worship*
Some written by David ..2Sam 23:1
Prophetic of Christ ......Luke 24:44
Used in worship ....Ps 95:2
Used in church 1Cor 14:26

[*also* PSALMS]

David delivered first this *p* 1Chr 16:7
Sing unto him, sing *p* unto 1Chr 16:9
A *P* of David, when he fled ...Ps 3:*title*
Neginoth, A *P* of David ......Ps 4:*title*
Sheminith, A *P* of David......Ps 6:*title*
Gittith, A *P* of David.........Ps 8:*title*
upon Muth-labben, A *P* of ....Ps 9:*title*
chief Musician, A *P* of........Ps 11:*title*
A *P* of David ....Ps 15:*title*
A *P* of David, Michtam ....Ps 16:*title*
Aijeleth Shahar, A *P* of ......Ps 22:*title*
A *P* and Song at the..........Ps 30:*title*
the chief Musician, A *P* of ....Ps 31:*title*
A *P* of David, Maschil ....Ps 32:*title*
A *P* of David, when he ....Ps 34:*title*
A *P* of David ....Ps 35:*title*
A *P* of David the servant .....Ps 36:*title*
A *P* of David, to bring to .....Ps 38:*title*
even to Jeduthun, A *P* of .....Ps 39:*title*
chief Musician, A *P* of........Ps 40:*title*
P for the sons of Korah ....Ps 47:*title*
A *P* of Asaph ....Ps 50:*title*
A *P* of David, when ....Ps 51:*title*
A *P* of David, when Doeg ....Ps 52:*title*
Mahalath, Maschil, A *P*.......Ps 53:*title*
A *P* of David, when the ....Ps 54:*title*
Maschil, A *P* of David ....Ps 55:*title*
Neginah, A *P* of David ....Ps 61:*title*
Jeduthun, A *P* of David ......Ps 62:*title*
A *P* of David, when he ....Ps 63:*title*
A *P* and Song of David ....Ps 65:*title*
Shoshannim, A *P* of ....Ps 69:*title*
A *P* of David, to bring to .....Ps 70:*title*
A *P* for Solomon ....Ps 72:*title*
Gittith, A *P* of Asaph ....Ps 81:*title*
A *P* or Song for the sons .....Ps 87:*title*
A *P* or Song for the ....Ps 92:*title*
A *P* of praise ....Ps 100:*title*
Sing unto him, sing *p* unto ....Ps 105:2
chief Musician, A *P* of........Ps 139:*title*
David's *P* of praise ....Ps 145:*title*
saith in the book of *P* ....Luke 20:42
is written in the book of *P* ....Acts 1:20
written in the second *p*........Acts 13:33
he saith also in another *p* .....Acts 13:35
Speaking to yourselves in *p*....Eph 5:19
admonishing one another in *p*. .Col 3:16
any merry? let him sing *p* .....James 5:13

PSALMS, THE BOOK OF—*a book of the Old Testament*
Book I—The Genesis
Book Concerning Man..Ps 1—41
Blessed are the righteous ....Ps 1
The holy hill ....Ps 15
The creation of God ..Ps 19
Messianic Psalm ....Ps 22
Prayer for God's help..Ps 28
Book II—The Exodus
Book Concerning Israel as a Nation ....Ps 42—72
Psalm of longing ......Ps 42
Prayer for cleansing ...Ps 51
Prayer for deliverance .Ps 70
Book III—The Leviticus
Book Concerning the Sanctuary ....Ps 73—89
Prayer for restoration . .Ps 80
Book IV—The Numbers
Book Concerning Israel and the Nation......Ps 90—106
The Lord reigns ....Ps 93
God's wondrous works .Ps 105
Book V—The Deuteronomy
Book Concerning God and His word ....Ps 107—150
On God's Commandments ....Ps 119
Psalm of faithfulness...Ps 128
God is gracious ....Ps 145
Psalms of praise ....Ps 149
Ps 150

PSALTERY—*musical instrument*

Used in:
Prophecy 1Sam 10:5
Processions 2Sam 6:5
Worship ....Ps 150:3
Government proclamations ....Dan 3:5, 7

[*also* PSALTERIES]

harps also and *p* for singers ...1Kin 10:12
and with harps, and with *p*....1Chr 13:8
p and harp and cymbals........1Chr 15:16
with *p* on Alamoth 1Chr 15:20
making a noise with *p* and 1Chr 15:28

and Jeiel with *p* and with 1Chr 16:5
prophesy with harps, with *p* ...1Chr 25:1
with cymbals, *p*, and harps 1Chr 25:6
having cymbals and *p* and 2Chr 5:12
and harps and *p* for singers....2Chr 9:11
came to Jerusalem with *p* 2Chr 20:28
with *p*, and with harps 2Chr 29:25
with cymbals, *p*, and with .....Neh 12:27
sing unto him with the *p* ......Ps 33:2
awake, *p* and harp............Ps 57:8
also praise thee with the *p* ....Ps 71:22
pleasant harp with the *p* ......Ps 81:2
ten strings, and upon the *p* ....Ps 92:3
Awake, *p* and harp ....Ps 108:2
upon a *p* and an instrument ...Ps 144:9
p and dulcimer, and all ....Dan 3:10

PTOLEMAIS (tŏl-ĕ-mā'ĭs)—*"hot sand"—a seaport city south of Tyre*
Paul lands at ....Acts 21:7
Same as Accho ....Judg 1:31

PUAH, PUA (pū'ä)—*"utterance"—same as Phuvah*
Father of Tola ....Judg 10:1

the name of the other *P* ......Ex 1:15
Issachar were, Tola and *P*.....1Chr 7:1

PUBLIC—*accessible or visible to all*

[*also* PUBLICLY]
to make her a *p* example......Matt 1:19
the Jews, and that *p* ....Acts 18:28
you, and have taught you *p* ...Acts 20:20

PUBLIC OPINION—*the viewpoint of the public at large*
Rescues Jonathan 1Sam 14:45
Delays John's death .....Matt 14:1-5
Protects the apostles .....Acts 5:26
Makes Saul sin 1Sam 15:24
Increases Pilate's guilt ...Matt 27:21-26
Incites persecution ....Acts 12:1-3

PUBLICAN—*Jew engaged in tax collecting*
Description of:
Collector of taxes........Luke 5:27
Often guilty of extortion .Luke 3:12, 13
Classed with lowest sinners ....Matt 9:10, 11; Matt 21:31, 32
Do not even, the same...Matt 5:46
Thomas and Matthew, the ....Matt 10:3
Thank thee I am not ....Luke 18:11
As an heathen and a ....Matt 18:17
Spiritual attitude of:
Often conscientious ......Luke 19:2, 8
Often hospitable.........Luke 5:29
Received John's baptism .Matt 21:32
Listened to Jesus ....Luke 15:1
Conscious of their sins ...Luke 18:13, 14
Many sat with him ......Mark 2:15
Why do ye eat with .....Luke 5:30
A friend of ....Matt 11:19
Luke 7:34

[*also* PUBLICANS]
others? do not even the *p* .....Matt 5:47
a friend of *p* and sinners ......Matt 11:19
eat with *p* and sinners ....Mark 2:16
and drinketh with *p* and ......Mark 2:16
eat and drink with *p* and ......Luke 5:30
the *p*, justified God, being ....Luke 7:29
Pharisee, and the other a *p*....Luke 18:10

PUBLICK—*See* PUBLIC

PUBLISH—*to proclaim publicly*
Descriptive of:
Victory 1Sam 31:9
Message of doom........Jon 3:7
Royal decree ....Esth 1:20, 22
Good news ....Mark 1:45
Objects of:
Peace ....Is 52:7
Doom ....Jer 4:5, 15, 16
Gospel ....Mark 13:10
God's Word ....Acts 13:49

[*also* PUBLISHED, PUBLISHETH]
I will *p* the name of the.......Deut 32:3
p it not in the streets of.......2Sam 1:20
p and proclaim in all their.....Neh 8:15
province was *p* unto all ....Esth 3:14
was *p* unto all people ....Esth 8:13
I may *p* with the voice of .....Ps 26:7
company of those that *p* ......Ps 68:11
house of Jacob, and *p* it in ....Jer 5:20
p ye, praise ye, and say ....Jer 31:7
Declare ye in Egypt, and *p* in .Jer 46:14
and *p* in Noph and in ....Jer 46:14
among the nations, and *p* .....Jer 50:2
up a standard; *p*, and ....Jer 50:2
P in the palaces at............Amos 3:9
proclaim and *p* the free ....Amos 4:5
good tidings, that *p* peace! ....Nah 1:15
began to *p* in Decapolis ....Mark 5:20
more a great deal they *p* ......Mark 7:36
p throughout the whole ....Luke 8:39
which was *p* throughout all ....Acts 10:37

PUBLIUS (pŭb'lĭ-ŭs)—*"common; first"*
Roman official; entertains Paul..................Acts 28:7, 8

PUDENS (pū'dĕnz)—*"shamefaced"*
Believer at Rome........2Tim 4:21

PUFFED—*proud or conceited*

[*also* PUFFETH]
for all his enemies, he *p* at ....Ps 10:5
safety from him that *p* at......Ps 12:5
that no one of you be *p* up....1Cor 4:6
Now some are *p* up, as 1Cor 4:18
of them which are *p* up 1Cor 4:19
ye are *p* up, and have not.....1Cor 5:2
Knowledge *p* up, but charity ..1Cor 8:1
vaunteth not itself, is not *p*....1Cor 13:4
vainly *p* up by his fleshly......Col 2:18

PUHITES (pū'hīts)
Family of Kirjath-jearim. .1Chr 2:53

PUL (pŭl)—*"strong"*
King of Assyria; same as Tiglath-Pilneser........2Kin 15:19

stirred up the spirit of *P* 1Chr 5:26
nations, to Tarshish, *P* ....Is 66:19

PULL—*to attract, compel or influence; remove; tear apart*

[*also* PULLED, PULLING]
p her in unto him into ....Gen 8:9
and *p* Lot into the house ......Gen 19:10
he could not *p* it in again 1Kin 13:4
timber be *p* down from his ....Ezra 6:11
P me out of the net that ......Ps 31:4
thy state shall he *p* thee.......Is 22:19
to root out, and to *p* down ....Jer 1:10
p them out like sheep for .....Jer 12:3
to *p* down, and to destroy .....Jer 18:7
them, and not *p* them down ...Jer 24:6
build you, and not *p* you ......Jer 42:10
ways, and *p* me in pieces......Lam 3:11
shall he not *p* up the roots ....Ezek 17:9
no more be *p* up out of ....Amos 9:15
p off the robe with the........Mic 2:8
and *p* away the shoulder ......Zech 7:11
p out the mote out of thine ...Matt 7:4
p out the mote that is in ......Luke 6:42
to *p* out the mote that is ......Luke 6:42
I will *p* down my barns ....Luke 12:18
p him out on the sabbath .....Luke 14:5
Paul should have been *p* in....Acts 23:10
to the *p* down of strong 2Cor 10:4
with fear, *p* them out of ......Jude 23

PULPIT—*a rostrum*
Ezra reads law from .....Neh 8:4-8

PULSE—*a vegetable diet of peas and beans primarily*
Preferred by Daniel .....Dan 1:12, 16

PUNISHMENT—*a penalty; rough or harsh treatment*
Agents of:
State ....Rom 13:1-4
Nation..................Josh 7:25
Prophet.................1Sam 15:33
Witnesses ....John 8:7
Soldiers.................Matt 27:27-35
Kinds of (non-capital):
Imprisonment ....Matt 5:25
Fine ....Ex 21:22
Restitution ....Ex 22:3-6
Retaliation ....Deut 19:21
Scourging ....Acts 22:25
Bondage ....Matt 18:25
Banishment ....Rev 1:9
Torture ....Heb 11:35
Mutilation ....Judg 1:5-7
Kinds of (capital):
Burning ....Gen 38:24
Hanging ....Esth 7:9, 10
Crucifying ....Matt 27:35
Beheading ....Mark 6:16, 27
Stoning ....Lev 24:14
Cutting in pieces ....Dan 2:5
Exposing to lions ....Dan 6:16, 24
Killing with the sword ...Acts 12:2
See CAPITAL PUNISHMENT

[*also* PUNISH, PUNISHED, PUNISHMENTS]
My *p* is greater than I can ....Gen 4:13
hand; he shall be surely *p* .....Ex 21:20
or two, he shall not be *p*......Ex 21:21
I will *p* you seven times ....Lev 26:18
p you yet seven times for .....Lev 26:24
accept of the *p* of their ....Lev 26:41
there shall no *p* happen to 1Sam 28:10
hast *p* us less than our ....Ezra 9:13
bringeth the *p* of the sword ...Job 19:29
strange *p* to the workers of....Job 31:3
an iniquity to be *p* by the .....Job 31:11
an iniquity to be *p* by the .....Job 31:28
upon the heathen, and *p* ......Ps 149:7
to *p* the just is not good ......Prov 17:26
great wrath shall suffer *p*......Prov 19:19
When the scorner is *p*, the ....Prov 21:11
simple pass on, and are *p* .....Prov 22:3
simple pass on, and are *p* .....Prov 27:12
p the fruit of the stout ....Is 10:12
I will *p* the world for their ....Is 13:11
shall *p* the host of the high ....Is 24:21
to *p* the inhabitants of the.....Is 26:21
p leviathan the piercing ....Is 27:1
that I will *p* all them which....Jer 9:25
Behold, I will *p* them ....Jer 11:22
say when he shall *p* thee? .....Jer 13:21
I will *p* you according to ......Jer 21:14
I will even *p* that man and ....Jer 23:34
I will *p* the king of Babylon ...Jer 25:12
that nation will I *p* saith ......Jer 27:8
I will *p* Shemaiah the ....Jer 29:32
I will *p* all that oppress ....Jer 30:20
I will *p* him and his seed ......Jer 36:31
I will *p* them that dwell in ....Jer 44:13
as I have *p* Jerusalem, by .....Jer 44:13
I will *p* you in this place ......Jer 44:29
I will *p* the multitude of No ...Jer 46:25
I will *p* the king of Babylon ...Jer 50:18
have *p* the king of Assyria ....Jer 50:18
And I will *p* Bel in Babylon ...Jer 51:44
a man for the *p* of his sins? ...Lam 3:39
p of the iniquity of the........Lam 4:6
the *p* of the sin of Sodom .....Lam 4:6
p of thine iniquity ....Lam 4:22
bear the *p* of their iniquity ....Ezek 14:10
p of the prophet shall be ......Ezek 14:10
the *p* of him that seeketh .....Ezek 14:10
I will *p* them for their ways ...Hos 4:9
I will not *p* your daughters ....Hos 4:14
p Jacob according to his ......Hos 12:2
will not turn away the *p*.......Amos 1:3
not turn away the *p* ....Amos 2:1
I will *p* you for all your ....Amos 3:2
I will *p* the princes, and.......Zeph 1:8
will I *p* all those that leap ....Zeph 1:9
p the men that are settled .....Zeph 1:12
not be cut off, howsoever I *p*..Zeph 3:7

As I thought to *p* you, when . . Zech 8:14
the shepherds, and I *p* the . . . . Zech 10:3
This shall be the *p* of Egypt . . . Zech 14:19
the *p* of all nations that . . . . Zech 14:19
go away into everlasting *p* . . . . . Matt 25:46
how they might *p* them . . . . Acts 4:21
unto Jerusalem, for to be *p* . . . Acts 22:5
I *p* them oft in every . . . . Acts 26:11
Sufficient to..man is this *p* 2Cor 2:6
p with everlasting destruction . . 2Thess 1:9
how much sorer *p*, suppose . . . . Heb 10:29
sent by him for the *p* of. 1Pet 2:14
the day of judgment to be *p* . . . 2Pet 2:9

PUNISHMENT, EVERLASTING—*See* HELL; ETERNAL; EVERLASTING

PUNITES (pū'nīts)—*a family of the tribe of Issachar*
Descendants of Pua . . . . . . Num 26:23

PUNON (pū'nŏn)—*"precious stone"*
Israelite camp . . . . Num 33:42, 43

PUR (po͞or)—*"a lot"*
Cast for Jews' slaughter . . Esth 3:7
Origin of Purim . . . . Esth 9:24-26

PURCHASE—*to buy*

Used literally of:
Cave . . . . Gen 49:32
Field . . . . Jer 32:9-16
Wife . . . . Ruth 4:10

Used figuratively of:
Israel's redemption . . . . . . Ex 15:16
God's gifts . . . . Acts 8:20
Church . . . . Acts 20:28

[*also* PURCHASED]
if a man *p* of the Levites . . . . . . Lev 25:33
which thou hast *p* of old . . . . . . Ps 74:2
which his right hand had *p* . . . . Ps 78:54
p a field with the reward . . . . . . Acts 1:18
redemption of the *p* . . . . Eph 1:14
p to themselves a good 1Tim 3:13

PURE—*uncontaminated; not containing any mixture of evil; unmixed*

Descriptive of:
Chastity 1Tim 5:2
Uncontaminated 1Kin 5:11
Innocent . . . . Acts 20:26
Regenerated . . . . Titus 1:15

Applied figuratively to God's:
Law . . . . Ps 19:8
Word . . . . Ps 119:140
Wisdom . . . . James 3:17

Applied figuratively to the believer's:
Heart . . . . Ps 24:4
Mind 2Pet 3:1
Conscience 1Tim 3:9
Language . . . . Zeph 3:9
Body . . . . Heb 10:22

Applied to the Christian's life:
Source . . . . Titus 1:15
Command 1Tim 4:12
Means . . . . Phil 4:8
Outward manifestation . . . James 1:27
Inward evidence 1Tim 1:5
Goal 1John 3:3
Reward . . . . Matt 5:8
False . . . . Prov 20:9

Applied symbolically to:
New Jerusalem . . . . Rev 21:18, 21

[*also* PURELY, PURENESS, PURER, PURITY]
thou shalt overlay it with *p* . . . . Ex 25:11
make a mercy seat of *p* gold . . Ex 25:17
thou shalt overlay it with *p* . . . . Ex 25:24
of *p* gold shalt thou make . . . . . Ex 25:29
make a candlestick of *p* gold . . Ex 25:31
be one beaten work of *p* gold . Ex 25:36
thereof, shall be of *p* gold . . . . . Ex 25:38
a talent of *p* gold shall he . . . . . Ex 25:39
p olive oil beaten for the . . . . . . Ex 27:20
two chains of *p* gold at the . . . . Ex 28:14
ends of wreathen work of *p* . . . Ex 28:22
thou shalt make a plate of *p* . . . Ex 28:36
shalt overlay it with *p* gold . . . . Ex 30:3
of *p* myrrh five hundred . . . . . . Ex 30:23
spices with *p* frankincense . . . . . Ex 30:34
tempered together, *p* and . . . . . Ex 30:35
and the *p* candlestick with . . . . . Ex 31:8
he overlaid it with *p* gold . . . . . Ex 37:2
he made the mercy seat of *p* . . Ex 37:6
And he overlaid it with *p* . . . . . Ex 37:11
covers to cover withal, of *p* . . . Ex 37:16
the candlestick of *p* gold . . . . . . Ex 37:17
one beaten work of *p* gold . . . . Ex 37:22
his snuffdishes, of *p* gold . . . . . . Ex 37:23
Of a talent of *p* gold made . . . . Ex 37:24
he overlaid it with *p* gold . . . . . Ex 37:26
and the *p* incense of sweet . . . . Ex 37:29
wreathen work of *p* gold . . . . . . Ex 39:15
they made bells of *p* gold . . . . . Ex 39:25
plate of the holy crown of *p* . . . Ex 39:30
p candlestick, with the . . . . Ex 39:37
bring unto thee *p* oil olive . . . . . Lev 24:2
the lamps upon the *p* . . . . Lev 24:4
upon the *p* table before the . . . Lev 24:6
p frankincense upon which . . . . Lev 24:7
drink the *p* blood of the . . . . . . Deut 32:14
the *p* thou wilt show thyself *p*. . 2Sam 22:27
he overlaid it with *p* gold 1Kin 6:20
house within with *p* gold 1Kin 6:21
candlesticks of *p* gold, five 1Kin 7:49
spoons, and the censers of *p* . . . 1Kin 7:50
p gold for the fleshhooks 1Chr 28:17
he overlaid it within with *p* 2Chr 3:4
before the oracle, of *p* gold . . . 2Chr 4:20
the censers, of *p* gold 2Chr 4:22
overlaid it with *p* gold 2Chr 9:17
of Lebanon were of *p* gold 2Chr 9:20
in order upon the *p* table 2Chr 13:11
all of them were *p*, and . . . . Ezra 6:20
more *p* than his Maker? . . . . . . Job 4:17
If thou wert *p* and upright . . . . Job 8:6
said, My doctrine is *p* . . . . Job 11:4
also my prayer is *p* . . . . Job 16:17
delivered by the *p* of thine . . . . Job 22:30
the stars are not *p* in his . . . . . . Job 25:5
it be valued with *p* gold . . . . Job 28:19
words of the Lord are *p*. . . . . . . Ps 12:6
the *p* thou wilt show thyself *p* . Ps 18:26
settest a crown of *p* gold . . . . . . Ps 21:3
the words of the *p* are . . . . Prov 15:26
whether his work be *p*, and . . . Prov 20:11
but as for the *p*, his work is . . . Prov 21:8
Every word of God is *p* . . . . Prov 30:5
a generation that are *p* in . . . . . Prov 30:12
p purge away thy dross . . . . Is 1:25
Her Nazarites were *p* than . . . . Lam 4:7
hair of his head like the *p* . . . . . Dan 7:9
Shall I count them *p* with . . . . . Mic 6:11
art of *p* eyes than to behold . . . Hab 1:13
unto my name, and a *p* . . . . Mal 1:11
All things indeed are *p* . . . . Rom 14:20
By *p*, by knowledge, by 2Cor 6:6
in spirit, in faith, in *p* 1Tim 4:12
men's sins; keep theyself *p* 1Tim 5:22
my forefathers with *p* 2Tim 1:3
call on the Lord out of a *p* 2Tim 2:22
in *p* and white linen . . . . Rev 15:6

PURGE—*to cleanse thoroughly*

Used, in the Old Testament, ceremonially of:
Cleansing . . . . Ezek 20:38
Separation from idolatry . 2Chr 34:3, 8

Used, in the Old Testament, figuratively of:
Reformation . . . . Ezek 24:13
Regeneration . . . . Is 4:4
Sanctification . . . . Is 1:25
Forgiveness . . . . Ps 51:7
Consecration . . . . Is 6:7
Atonement . . . . Mal 3:3, 4
Judgment . . . . Is 22:14

[*also* PURGED, PURGETH, PURGING]
not be *p* with sacrifice 1Sam 3:14
thou shalt *p* them away . . . . Ps 65:3
deliver us, and *p* away our . . . . Ps 79:9
and truth iniquity is *p* . . . . Prov 16:6
the iniquity of Jacob be *p* . . . . . . Is 27:9
thou cleanse and *p* it . . . . Ezek 43:20
Seven days shall they *p* the . . . . Ezek 43:26
to *p*, and to make them . . . . Dan 11:35
will thoroughly *p* his floor . . . . . Matt 3:12
the draught, *p* all meats? . . . . . . Mark 7:19
will thoroughly *p* his floor . . . . . Luke 3:17
he *p* it, that it may bring . . . . . . John 15:2
P out therefore the old 1Cor 5:7
a man therefore *p* himself 2Tim 2:21
had by himself *p* our sins . . . . . Heb 1:3
p your conscience from . . . . Heb 9:14
by the law *p* with blood . . . . Heb 9:22
worshipers once *p* should . . . . . . Heb 10:2
that he was *p* from his old 2Pet 1:9

PURIFICATION—*ceremonial or spiritual cleansing*

Objects of:
Israelites at Sinai . . . . Ex 19:10
Priests at ordination . . . . . Ex 29:4
Levites at ordination . . . . . Num 8:6, 7
Offerings 2Chr 4:6
High priest . . . . Lev 16:4, 24
People unclean . . . . Lev 15:2-13
Nazarite after vow . . . . Acts 21:24, 26

Accomplished by:
Sprinkling . . . . Num 19:13-18
Washing parts of the body . . . . Ex 30:18, 19
Washing the whole body . Lev 8:6
Running water . . . . Lev 15:13

Figurative of:
Christ's atonement . . . . Mal 3:3
Regeneration . . . . Acts 15:9
Sanctification . . . . James 4:8
Obedience 1Pet 1:22

[*also* PURIFICATIONS]
separation: it is a *p* for sin . . . . Num 19:9
to the *p* of the sanctuary 2Chr 30:19
God, and the ward of the *p* . . . Neh 12:45
their things for *p* be given . . . . . Esth 2:3
of their *p* accomplished . . . . Esth 2:12
for the *p* of the women . . . . Esth 2:12
And when the days of her *p* . . . Luke 2:22
this hope in him *p* himself 1John 3:3

PURIFIER—*one who cleanses*
shall sit as a refiner and *p* . . . . . Mal 3:3

PURIFY—*to cleanse*

[*also* PURIFIED, PURIFIETH, PURIFYING]
his finger, and *p* the altar . . . . . Lev 8:15
of her *p* three and thirty . . . . . . Lev 12:4
days of her *p* be fulfilled . . . . . . Lev 12:4
blood of her *p* threescore . . . . . Lev 12:5
days of her *p* are fulfilled . . . . . Lev 12:6
And the Levites were *p* . . . . Num 8:21
p himself with it on the third . . . . Num 19:12
he *p* not himself the third . . . . . Num 19:12
the seventh day he shall *p* . . . . . . Num 19:19
unclean, and shall not *p* . . . . . . Num 19:20
p both yourselves and your . . . . Num 31:19
p all your raiment, and all . . . . Num 31:20
nevertheless it shall be *p* . . . . . . Num 31:23
p from her uncleanness 2Sam 11:4
in the *p* of all holy things 1Chr 23:28
and the Levites were *p* . . . . Ezra 6:20
the Levites *p* themselves . . . . . . Neh 12:30
of breakings they *p* . . . . Job 41:25
furnace of earth, *p* seven . . . . . . Ps 12:6
and *p* themselves in the . . . . Is 66:17
purge the altar and *p* it . . . . Ezek 43:26
Many shall be *p*, and made . . . . Dan 12:10
of the *p* of the Jews . . . . John 2:6
and the Jews about *p* . . . . John 3:25
passover, to *p* themselves . . . . . John 11:55
next day *p* himself with . . . . Acts 21:26
Asia found me *p* in the . . . . Acts 24:18
p unto himself a peculiar . . . . . . Titus 2:14
sanctifieth to the *p* of the . . . . . Heb 9:13
heavens should be *p* with . . . . . Heb 9:23

PURIM (pūr'ĭm)—*"lots"*
Jewish festival celebrating being rescued from Haman's plot ....Esth 9:26-28

PURLOINING—*stealing*
Forbidden ....Titus 2:10

PURPLE—*a color, or cloth dyed that color*
Used in the tabernacle ...Ex 25:4
Sign of riches ....Luke 16:19
Worn by royalty.........Judg 8:26
Lydia, seller of..........Acts 16:14

blue, and *p*, and scarlet ....Ex 26:1
of the tent, of blue, and *p* ....Ex 26:36
cubits, of blue, and *p* ....Ex 27:16
gold, and blue, and *p*, and ....Ex 28:5
even of gold, of blue, and *p*...Ex 28:8
of blue, and of *p* ....Ex 28:33
And blue, and *p*, and scarlet ..Ex 35:6
both of blue, and of *p* ....Ex 35:25
twined linen, and blue, and *p*..Ex 36:8
tabernacle door blue, and *p* ...Ex 36:37
needlework, of blue, and *p*....Ex 38:18
the blue, and *p*, and scarlet ...Ex 39:1
it in the blue, and in the *p* ....Ex 39:3
and *p*, and scarlet, and fine ...Ex 39:8
twined linen, and blue, and *p*..Ex 39:29
and spread a *p* cloth thereon ..Num 4:13
and in iron, and in *p*, and.....2Chr 2:7
of blue, and *p*, and crimson ...2Chr 3:14
cords of fine linen and *p* ......Esth 1:6
garment of fine linen and *p* ...Esth 8:15
her clothing is silk and *p* ......Prov 31:22
the covering of it of *p*, the ....Song 3:10
hair of thine head like *p* ......Song 7:5
blue and *p* is their clothing ....Jer 10:9
blue and *p* from the isles of ...Ezek 27:7
they clothed him with *p*, and ..Mark 15:17
they took off the *p* from him ..Mark 15:20
and they put on him a *p* robe .John 19:2
crown of thorns, and the *p* ....John 19:5
arrayed in *p* and scarlet ....Rev 17:4
fine linen, and *p*, and silk .....Rev 18:12

PURPOSE—*object or end; propose as an aim*

[*also* PURPOSED, PURPOSES, PURPOSETH, PURPOSING]
doth comfort himself, *p* to ....Gen 27:42
the handfuls of *p* for her ......Ruth 2:16
ye *p* to keep under the........2Chr 28:10
they had made for the *p* ......Neh 8:4
my *p* are broken off, even ....Job 17:11
withdraw man from his *p*......Job 33:17
Without counsel *p* are ....Prov 15:22
p is established by counsel ....Prov 20:18
every *p* under the heaven .....Eccl 3:1
Because to every *p* there is....Eccl 8:6
To what *p* is the multitude ....Is 1:11
I have *p*, so shall it stand .....Is 14:24
shall be broken in the *p*.......Is 19:10
help in vain, and to no *p*......Is 30:7
I have *p* it, I will also.........Is 46:11
To what *p* cometh there to ....Jer 6:20
which I *p* to do unto them ....Jer 26:3
evil which I *p* to do unto......Jer 36:3
p against the inhabitants ......Jer 49:20
and his *p*, that he hath........Jer 49:20
p of the Lord shall be ....Jer 51:29
The Lord hath *p* to destroy ...Lam 2:8
To what *p* is this waste ....Matt 26:8
with *p* of heart they would ....Acts 11:23
Paul *p* in the spirit, when .....Acts 19:21
he *p* to return through ....Acts 20:3
appeared unto thee for this *p*..Acts 26:16
they had obtained their *p* ......Acts 27:13
oftentimes I *p* to come unto ...Rom 1:13
called according to his *p*.......Rom 8:28
Even for this same *p* have I ...Rom 9:17
according as he *p* in his 2Cor 9:7
which he hath *p* in himself ....Eph 1:9
p of him who worketh all ......Eph 1:11
which he *p* in Christ Jesus.....Eph 3:11
unto you for the same *p* ......Eph 6:22
unto you for the same *p* ......Col 4:8
but according to his own *p* 2Tim 1:9
p the Son of God was 1John 3:8

PURPOSES OF GOD—*God's goals or intentions*

Characteristics of:
Centered in Christ.......Eph 3:11
Irresistible ....Is 14:26, 27
Unknown to the wise ....Is 19:11, 12
Made known ....Jer 50:45
Irreversible ....Jer 4:28
Planned ....Is 23:9
Fulfilled ....Rom 9:11
Victorious 2Chr 32:2-22

PURPOSES OF MAN—*mankind's goals or intentions*

Good:
Hindered by evil men....Ezra 4:5
Known by others 2Tim 3:10
Permitted ....Dan 1:8-16
Accomplished 1Kin 5:5
Determine ....Ps 17:3
Delayed ....Acts 19:21
Not vacillating 2Cor 1:17

Evil:
Known by God..........Jer 49:30
Designed against the righteous ....Ps 140:4
Hindered ....Dan 6:17-23

PURSE—*a bag for carrying items*
One, forbidden..........Prov 1:14
Disciples forbidden to take ....Luke 10:4

[*also* PURSES]
silver, nor brass in your *p* .....Matt 10:9
bread, no money in their *p* ....Mark 6:8
I sent you without *p*, and .....Luke 22:35
that hath a *p*, let him ....Luke 22:36

PURSUE—*to go after*
"Enemy said, I will".....Ex 15:9
"Shall flee when none" ..Lev 26:17
"I will arise and".......2Sam 17:1
"Seek peace, and" ......Ps 34:14
"Blood shall" ....Ezek 35:6

[*also* PURSUED, PURSUETH, PURSUING]
eighteen, and *p* them unto ....Gen 14:14
and *p* them unto Hobah ....Gen 14:15
p after him seven days ....Gen 31:23
hast so hotly *p* after me ....Gen 31:36
did not *p* after the sons of ....Gen 35:5
he *p* after the children ....Ex 14:8
the Egyptians *p* after them ....Ex 14:9
And the Egyptians *p*, and .....Ex 14:23
shall fall when none *p* ....Lev 26:36
overflow them as they *p* ......Deut 11:4
avenger of the blood *p* the ....Deut 19:6
they shall *p* thee until thou ....Deut 28:22
p after them quickly; for ......Josh 2:5
the men *p* after them the .....Josh 2:7
they which *p* after them ....Josh 2:7
called together to *p* after ......Josh 8:16
and they *p* after Joshua ....Josh 8:16
open, and *p* after Israel ....Josh 8:17
the avenger of blood *p* after ..Josh 20:5
the Egyptians *p* after your....Josh 24:6
they *p* after him, and ....Judg 1:6
Barak *p* after the chariots .....Judg 4:16
and *p* after the Midianites .....Judg 7:23
p Midian, and brought ....Judg 7:25
were with him, faint, yet *p* ....Judg 8:4
he *p* after them and took .....Judg 8:12
p hard after them unto.........Judg 20:45
and *p* the Philistines and 1Sam 7:11
and *p* the Philistines 1Sam 17:52
he *p* after David in the 1Sam 23:25
Saul returned from *p* after 1Sam 23:28
after whom dost thou *p*? 1Sam 24:14
Yet a man is risen to *p* thee...1Sam 25:29
my lord thus *p* after his 1Sam 26:18
Shall I *p* after this troop? 1Sam 30:8
P: for thou shalt surely 1Sam 30:8
David *p* he and four 1Sam 30:10
And Asahel *p* after Abner 2Sam 2:19
and *p* after Israel no more 2Sam 2:28
and Joab came from *p* a 2Sam 3:22
from *p* after Israel 2Sam 18:16
lord's servants and *p* after 2Sam 20:6
p after Sheba the son of 2Sam 20:7
Abishai his brother *p* after 2Sam 20:10
I have *p* mine enemies and....2Sam 22:38
thine enemies, while they *p* ...2Sam 24:13
he is talking or he is *p* or 1Kin 18:27
Syrians fled, and Israel *p*......1Kin 20:20
they turned back from *p* 1Kin 22:33
of the Chaldees *p* after the 2Kin 25:5
Abijah *p* after Jeroboam 2Chr 13:19
were with him *p* them unto....2Chr 14:13
turned back again from *p* 2Chr 18:32
and wilt thou *p* the dry ....Job 13:25
they *p* my soul as the ....Job 30:15
I have *p* mine enemies and ....Ps 18:37
tendeth to life; so he that *p* ...Prov 11:19
p it to his own death ....Prov 11:19
Evil *p* sinners but to the ......Prov 13:21
he *p* them with words, yet ....Prov 19:7
wicked flee when no man *p* ...Prov 28:1
they that *p* you be swift.......Is 30:16
He *p* them and passed ....Is 40:13
Chaldeans' army *p* after.......Jer 39:5
the sword shall *p* thee ....Jer 48:2
Chaldeans *p* after the king ....Jer 52:8
p us upon the mountains ......Lam 4:19
and blood shall *p* thee ....Ezek 35:6
the enemy shall *p* him ....Hos 8:3
did *p* his brother with the .....Amos 1:11
and darkness shall *p* his ....Nah 1:8

PURSUER—*one who goes after another or others*

[*also* PURSUERS]
mountain, lest the *p* meet .....Josh 2:16
until the *p* be returned ....Josh 2:16
until the *p* were returned......Josh 2:22
p sought them throughout all ..Josh 2:22
turned back upon the *p* ....Josh 8:20
without strength before the *p* ..Lam 1:6

PURTENANCE—*entrails*
his legs, and with the *p* ....Ex 12:9

PUSH—*to press with force; make a strong effort*

[*also* PUSHED, PUSHING]
ox were wont to *p* with ....Ex 21:29
ox hath used to *p* in time .....Ex 21:36
p the people together ....Deut 33:17
shalt thou *p* the Syrians 1Kin 22:11
p Syria until they be 2Chr 18:10
they *p* away my feet ....Job 30:12
we *p* down our enemies ....Ps 44:5
p all the diseased with ....Ezek 34:21
saw the ram *p* westward ......Dan 8:4
king of the south *p* at him ....Dan 11:40

PUT—*See* PHUT

PUT—*to place; lay; send*

[*also* PUTTEST, PUTTETH, PUTTING]
p it on her shoulder, and......Gen 21:14
P, I pray thee, thy hand ......Gen 24:2
p any of it upon a stranger ....Ex 30:33
p them..the head of the ....Lev 16:21
that God *p* in my mouth ......Num 22:38
thou *p* thy nest in a rock......Num 24:21
that then *p* thou hands ....Deut 12:18
thou *p* thine hand unto ....Deut 15:10
and *p* forth her hand, and.....Deut 25:11
and *p* it in a secret place .....Deut 27:15
he shall be *p* to death.........Josh 1:18
lapped, *p* their hand to ....Judg 7:6
himself as he that *p* it off 1Kin 20:11
which thou *p* on me will I.....2Kin 18:14
Thou *p* my feet also in........Job 13:27
he *p* no trust in his saints .....Job 15:15
p forth his hand upon..........Job 28:9
He *p* my feet in the stocks ....Job 33:11
He that *p* not out his ....Ps 15:5
he *p* down one, and ....Ps 75:7
let them be *p* to shame ....Ps 83:17

P

Thou *p* away all the .... Ps 119:119
p his trust in the Lord .... Prov 28:25
whoso *p* his trust in the .... Prov 29:25
fig tree *p* forth her .... Song 2:13
p away the evil of your .... Is 1:16
I have *p* my spirit upon .... Is 42:1
he that *p* his trust in me ...... Is 57:13
p forth of the finger, and ..... Is 58:9
as a shepherd *p* on his .... Jer 43:12
p the stumbling block of ...... Ezek 14:4
P ye in the sickle .... Joel 3:13
that *p* thy bottle to him .... Hab 2:15
that he hateth *p* away .... Mal 2:16
p a piece of new cloth .... Matt 9:16
Jesus *p* forth his hand .... Matt 8:3
is yet tender, and *p* forth ..... Matt 24:32
no man *p* new wine into .... Mark 2:22
he *p* in the sickle .... Mark 4:29
tender, and *p* forth leaves ..... Mark 13:28
p a piece of a new garment ... Luke 5:36
or *p* it under a bed .... Luke 8:16
having *p* his hand to the ...... Luke 9:62
a candle, *p* it in a secret ...... Luke 11:33
Whosoever *p* away his wife .... Luke 16:18
he *p* forth his own sheep ...... John 10:4
coming in and *p* his hand on .. Acts 9:12
he *p* him in prison .... Acts 12:19
the Jews *p* him forward .... Acts 19:33
as *p* you in mind, because ..... Rom 15:15
p away from yourselves 1Cor 5:13
p all enemies under his feet ... 1Cor 15:25
must *p* on incorruption 1Cor 15:53
p all things under his .... Eph 1:22
p off the old man which is .... Eph 4:22
p on the new man, which ..... Eph 4:24
bitterness and wrath..be *p* .... Eph 4:31
p off all these, anger, wrath .. Col 3:8
p on the breastplate of faith ... 1Thess 5:8
counted me faithful, *p* me into . 1Tim 1:12
some having *p* away concerning 1Tim 1:19
if thou *p* the brethren in 1Tim 4:6
by the *p* on of my hands 2Tim 1:6
p my laws into their mind ..... Heb 8:10
p away sin by the sacrifice .... Heb 9:26
p bits in horses mouths .... James 3:3
by *p* you in remembrance 2Pet 1:13
must *p* off this my tabernacle .. 2Pet 1:14
will *p* you in remembrance .... Jude 5
will *p* upon you none other .... Rev 2:24
God hath *p* in their hearts to .. Rev 17:17

PUTEOLI (pū-tē'ō-lī)—*"sulphurous wells"*
Seaport of Italy .... Acts 28:13

PUTIEL (pū'tĭ-ĕl)—*God enlightens*
Father-in-law of Eleazar. . Ex 6:25

PYGARG (pī'gärg)—*a white-rumped antelope*
Clean animal .... Deut 14:5

Q

QUAILS—*small game birds*
Sent to satisfy hunger .... Ex 16:12, 13
Sent as a judgment ...... Num 11:31-34

at even the *q* came up .... Ex 16:13
asked, and he brought *q* ...... Ps 105:40

QUAKE—*to shake*

[*also* QUAKED, QUAKING]
and the whole mount *q* .... Ex 19:18
trembled, and the earth *q* 1Sam 14:15
eat thy bread with *q* .... Ezek 12:18
a great *q* fell upon them ...... Dan 10:7
The earth shall *q* before ...... Joel 2:10
The mountains *q* at him .... Nah 1:5
earth did *q*, and the rocks ..... Matt 27:51
I exceedingly fear and *q* ...... Heb 12:21

QUANTITY—*an amount or number*
all vessels of small *q* .... Is 22:24

QUARANTINE—*restriction of a person's contacts with others*
Required of lepers .... Lev 13:45, 46
Miriam consigned .... Num 12:14-16
Imposed under King Azariah 2Kin 15:1-5

QUARREL—*a dispute*
Caused by:
Flesh .... James 4:1, 2
Hatred .... Mark 6:18, 19
Productive of:
Friction .... Matt 20:20-24
Separation .... Acts 15:37-40
Cured by:
Gentleness 2Tim 2:24-26
Forgiveness .... Col 3:13
Unity of mind .... Phil 2:3, 4
See CONTENTION; STRIFE

avenge the *q* of my covenant. . Lev 26:25
see how he seeketh a *q* 2Kin 5:7

QUARRY—*a site of excavation or mining*
Israelites flee to ("Shebarim") .... Josh 7:5
Some near Gilgal .... Judg 3:19, 26
Same word translated "graven images" in .... Deut 7:5, 25

QUARTER—*fourth part; division or district*

[*also* QUARTERS]
the people from every *q* ...... Gen 19:4
seen with thee in all thy *q* ..... Ex 13:7
q shall be from the .... Num 34:3
the four *q* of thy vesture ...... Deut 22:12
north *q* was from the bay ..... Josh 15:5
this was the west *q* .... Josh 18:14
In four *q* were the porters 1Chr 9:24
wander every one to his *q* ..... Is 47:15
for his gain, from his *q* .... Is 56:11
winds from the four *q* of ...... Jer 49:36
Togarmah of the north *q* ...... Ezek 38:6
to him from every *q* .... Mark 1:45

QUARTUS (kwôr'tŭs)—*"fourth"*
Christian at Corinth ..... Rom 16:23

QUATERNION—*a company of four soldiers*
Peter guarded by four ... Acts 12:4

QUEEN—*a king's wife; a female ruler*
Applied to:
Queen regent 1Kin 10:1-13
Queen mother 1Kin 15:13
Heathen deity .... Jer 44:15-30
Mystical Babylon .... Rev 18:7
Names of:
Of Sheba 1Kin 10:1
Vashti .... Esth 1:9
Esther .... Esth 5:3
Of Heaven .... Jer 7:18
Of the South .... Matt 12:42

[*also* QUEENS]
sister of Tahpenes the *q* 1Kin 11:19
and the children of the *q* 2Kin 10:13
q of Sheba heard of the 2Chr 9:1
q of Sheba gave king Solomon . 2Chr 9:9
removed her from being *q* 2Chr 15:16
(the *q* also sitting by him) ..... Neh 2:6
Vashti the *q* made a feast ..... Esth 1:9
bring Vashti the *q* before ..... Esth 1:11
do unto the *q* Vashti .... Esth 1:15
deed of the *q* shall come ...... Esth 1:17
Vashti the *q* to be brought .... Esth 1:17
pleaseth the king be *q* .... Esth 2:4
told it unto Esther the *q* ...... Esth 2:22
q exceedingly grieved .... Esth 4:4
Esther the *q* standing in .... Esth 5:2
q did let no man come in ..... Esth 5:12
banquet with Esther the *q* ..... Esth 7:1
Esther the *q* answered .... Esth 7:3
before the king and the *q* ...... Esth 7:6
enemy unto Esther the *q* ...... Esth 8:1
king said unto Esther the *q* .... Esth 9:12
Esther the *q* had enjoined ..... Esth 9:31
hand did stand the *q* .... Ps 45:9
are threescore *q*, and .... Song 6:8
q thy nursing mother .... Is 49:23
the king and to the *q* .... Jer 13:18
king, and the *q*, and the ...... Jer 29:2
the *q* by reason of the .... Dan 5:10
q and spake said, O king ...... Dan 5:10
The *q* of the south shall .... Luke 11:31
under Candace *q* of the .... Acts 8:27

QUENCH—*to extinguish*
Applied literally to:
Fire .... Num 11:2
Thirst .... Ps 104:11
Applied figuratively to:
Love .... Song 8:7
God's wrath 2Kin 22:17
Spirit 1Thess 5:19
Persecution .... Heb 11:34

[*also* QUENCHED]
they shall *q* my coal which 2Sam 14:7
that thou *q* not the light of 2Sam 21:17
place, and shall not be *q* 2Chr 34:25
are *q* as the fire of thorns ..... Ps 118:12
and none shall *q* them .... Is 1:31
It shall not be *q* night nor ..... Is 34:10
flax shall he not *q* .... Is 42:3
extinct, they are *q* as tow ..... Is 43:17
neither shall their fire be *q* .... Is 66:24
burn that none can *q* it .... Jer 4:4
burn, and shall not be *q* ...... Jer 7:20
and it shall not be *q* .... Jer 17:27
burn that none can *q* it .... Jer 21:12
flame shall not be *q* .... Ezek 20:47
be none to *q* it in Bethel ...... Amos 5:6
flax shall he not *q* .... Matt 12:20
fire that never shall be *q* ...... Mark 9:43
fire that never shall be *q* ...... Mark 9:45
not, and the fire is not *q* ...... Mark 9:48
Q not the Spirit 1Thess 5:19

QUESTION—*an inquiry*
Asked by:
Wicked .... Matt 22:16-40
John 18:33-38
Sincere .... Matt 18:1-6
Acts 1:6
Jesus .... Matt 22:41-45

[*also* QUESTIONED, QUESTIONING, QUESTIONS]
to prove him with hard *q* 1Kin 10:1
Solomon with hard *q* at 2Chr 9:1
Hezekiah *q* with the 2Chr 31:9
ask him any more *q* .... Matt 22:46
began to *q* with him .... Mark 8:11
q one with another what ...... Mark 9:10
scribes, What *q* ye with .... Mark 9:16
will also ask of you one *q* ..... Mark 11:29
durst ask him any *q* .... Mark 12:34
them, and asking them *q* ...... Luke 2:46
not ask him any *q* at .... Luke 20:40
he *q* with him in many .... Luke 23:9
there arose a *q* between .... John 3:25
and elders about this *q* .... Acts 15:2
if it be a *q* of words and ...... Acts 18:15
danger to be called in *q* .... Acts 19:40
the dead I am called in *q* ..... Acts 23:6
to be accused of *q* of their .... Acts 23:29
I am called in *q* by you .... Acts 24:21
But had certain *q* against ...... Acts 25:19
in all customs and *q* .... Acts 26:3
to be accused of *q* of their .... Acts 23:29
I am called in *q* by you .... Acts 24:21
But had certain *q* against ...... Acts 25:19
in all customs and *q* .... Acts 26:3
no *q* for conscience sake 1Cor 10:25
no *q* for conscience sake 1Cor 10:27
which minister *q* 1Tim 1:4
q and strifes of words 1Tim 6:4
foolish and unlearned *q* 2Tim 2:23
avoid foolish *q*, and .... Titus 3:9

QUICKEN—*to revive again; come alive*
Descriptive of:
Spiritual revival .... Ps 71:20
Physical resurrection ..... John 5:21

Spiritual resurrection (regeneration) ....Eph 2:5

Accomplished by:
God 1Tim 6:13
Christ 1Cor 15:45
Holy Spirit ....John 6:63
God's Word ....Ps 119:25, 50
God's precepts ....Ps 119:93

[*also* QUICK, QUICKENED, QUICKENETH, QUICKENING]
there be *q* raw flesh ....Lev 13:10
go down *q* into the pit ....Num 16:30
them go down *q* into hell .....Ps 55:15
q us, and we will call upon ....Ps 80:18
and *q* thou me in thy way .....Ps 119:37
Q me after thy ....Ps 119:88
for with them thou hast *q* .....Ps 119:93
q me according to thy.........Ps 119:149
q me according to thy.........Ps 119:156
had swallowed us up *q* ....Ps 124:3
Q me, O Lord, for thy ....Ps 143:11
him of *q* understanding ....Is 11:3
the Judge of *q* and dead ......Acts 10:42
even God, who *q* the dead ....Rom 4:17
also *q* your mortal bodies .....Rom 8:11
thou sowest is not *q* 1Cor 15:36
you hath he *q*, who were ......Eph 2:1
flesh, hath he *q* together ......Col 2:13
shall judge the *q* and the 2Tim 4:1
the word of God is *q* ....Heb 4:12
flesh, but *q* by the Spirit 1Pet 3:18
ready to judge the *q* and 1Pet 4:5

QUICKLY—*speedily; fast*
Make ready *q* three ....Gen 18:6
thou hast found it so *q* ....Gen 27:20
turned aside *q* out of the ......Ex 32:8
go *q* unto the congregation ....Num 16:46
out, and destroy them *q* ......Deut 9:3
get thee down *q* from ....Deut 9:12
they are *q* turned aside ....Deut 9:12
lest ye perish *q* from off ......Deut 11:17
and until thou perish *q* ....Deut 28:20
pursue after them *q*; for ......Josh 2:5
the ambush arose *q* out of ....Josh 8:19
come up to us *q*, and save ....Josh 10:6
ye shall perish *q* from off .....Josh 23:16
they turned *q* out of the ......Judg 2:17
thou shalt go down *q* 1Sam 20:19
Now therefore send *q*, and 2Sam 17:16
both of them away *q* 2Sam 17:18
pass *q* over the water 2Sam 17:21
king said, Come down *q* 2Kin 1:11
Fetch *q* Micaiah the son 2Chr 18:8
cord is not *q* broken ....Eccl 4:12
Agree with thine adversary *q* ..Matt 5:25
go *q*, and tell his disciples .....Matt 28:7
departed *q* from the ....Matt 28:8
they went out *q*, and fled .....Mark 16:8
Go out *q* into the streets ......Luke 14:21
sit down *q*, and write fifty .....Luke 16:6
she arose *q*, and came ....John 11:29
That thou doest, do *q* ....John 13:27
up, saying, Arise up *q* ....Acts 12:7
get thee *q* out of Jerusalem ...Acts 22:18
I will come unto thee *q* ....Rev 2:5
I will come unto thee *q* ....Rev 2:16
Behold, I come *q*: hold ....Rev 3:11
the third woe cometh *q* ....Rev 11:14
Behold, I come *q*: blessed ....Rev 22:7
I come *q*; and my reward .....Rev 22:12
saith, Surely I come *q* ....Rev 22:20

QUICKSAND—*sand which engulfs*
Endangers Paul's ship ....Acts 27:17

QUIET—*calm; free from noise; to calm; still*

Descriptive of:
Man ....Jer 51:59
People ....Judg 18:7, 27
City 2Kin 11:20
Nation 2Chr 14:1, 5
Earth ....Is 14:7

Realization of:
Predicted ....Is 32:17, 18
Comes from God 1Chr 22:9
Preferred ....Prov 17:1
To be sought 1Thess 4:11
Undeniable ....Acts 19:36
Commanded 2Thess 3:12
Obtainable ....Ps 131:2
Very valuable 1Pet 3:4
Rewarded ....Is 30:15

[*also* QUIETED, QUIETETH, QUIETLY, QUIETNESS]
country was in *q* forty ....Judg 8:28
were *q* all the night, saying ....Judg 16:2
the land was wide, and *q* 1Chr 4:40
realm of Jehoshaphat was *q* ...2Chr 20:30
the city was *q*, after that 2Chr 23:21
have lain still and been *q* .....Job 3:13
not feel *q* in his belly ....Job 20:20
wholly at ease and *q* ....Job 21:23
When he giveth *q*, who ....Job 34:29
he *q* the earth by the south ...Job 37:17
them that are *q* in the land ....Ps 35:20
glad because they be *q* ....Ps 107:30
behaved and *q* myself ....Ps 131:2
be *q* from fear of evil ....Prov 1:33
Better is a handful with *q* .....Eccl 4:6
men are heard in *q* more ......Eccl 9:17
Jerusalem a *q* habitation ......Is 33:20
shall be in rest, and be *q* ......Jer 30:10
will it be ere thou be *q* ....Jer 47:6
the sea; it cannot be *q* ....Jer 49:23
q wait for the salvation ....Lam 3:26
be *q*, and will be no more .....Ezek 16:42
Though they be *q*, and ....Nah 1:12
have *q* my spirit in the ....Zech 6:8
by thee we enjoy great *q* ......Acts 24:2
lead a *q* and peaceable life 1Tim 2:2

QUIT—*to forsake; acquit; leave*
Unworthy ....Luke 9:62
Believers should not .....Gal 6:9
2Thess 3:13
Press on ....Phil 3:12-14

he that smote him be *q* ....Ex 21:19
we will be *q* of thine oath .....Josh 2:20
and *q* yourselves like men 1Sam 4:9
q you like men, be strong 1Cor 16:13

QUITE—*completely*
and hath *q* devoured also .....Gen 31:15
q break down their images ....Ex 23:24
q take away their murmurings. .Num 17:10
q plucked down all their ......Num 33:52
away, and he is *q* gone? 2Sam 3:24
driven *q* from me? ....Job 6:13
bow was made *q* naked ....Hab 3:9

QUIVER—*a case for carrying arrows; to shake or tremble*

Used by:
Hunters ....Gen 27:3
Soldiers ....Job 39:23
Is 22:6

Figurative of:
Children ....Ps 127:5
Messiah ....Is 49:2

[*also* QUIVERED]
q is as an open sepulcher .....Jer 5:16
of his *q* to enter into my ......Lam 3:13
my lips *q* at the voice ....Hab 3:16

QUOTATIONS—*words repeated or referred to*

Introduced by:
"The Holy Spirit" ....Acts 28:25
"As it is written" ....Rom 15:9
"The Scripture" ....Gal 3:8
Old Testament writer ....Rom 10:5-20

Purposes of:
Cite fulfillment ....Matt 1:22, 23
Confirm a truth ....Matt 4:4
Prove a doctrine ....Rom 4:7, 8
Show the true meaning ..Acts 2:25-36

R

RAAMAH (rā'ä-mä)—*"trembling"*
Son of Cush ....Gen 10:6, 7
Father of Sheba and Dedan ....Gen 10:7
Noted traders ....Ezek 27:22

and Sabta, and *R* 1Chr 1:9
the sons of *R*; Sheba, and 1Chr 1:9

RAAMIAH (rā-ä-mī'ä)—*"Jehovah causes trembling"*
Postexilic chief ....Neh 7:7
Same as Reelaiah ....Ezra 2:2

RAAMSES, RAMESES (rā-ăm'sēz, răm'ĕ-sez)—*"child of the sun"*
Part of Egypt inhabited by Jacob ....Gen 47:11
Treasure city built by Hebrew slaves ....Ex 1:11

the land, in the land of *R* .....Gen 47:11
from *R* to Succoth ....Ex 12:37
they departed from *R* ....Num 33:3
children..removed from *R* .....Num 33:5

RABBAH, RABBATH (răb'ăth)—*"great"*
1. Town of Judah ....Josh 15:60
2. Capital of Ammon ......Amos 1:14
Bedstead of Og here ......Deut 3:11
On Gad's boundary .....Josh 13:25
Besieged by Joab 2Sam 12:26
Defeated and enslaved by David 2Sam 12:29-31
Destruction of, foretold. .Jer 49:2, 3

the son of Nahash of *R* 2Sam 17:27
and came and besieged *R* 1Chr 20:1
smote *R*, and destroyed 1Chr 20:1
the sword may come to *R* .....Ezek 21:20

RABBI (răb'ī)—*"my master"*

Applied to:
John the Baptist ....John 3:26
Jewish leader ....John 3:2
Jesus Christ ....John 1:38, 49

Significance of:
Coveted title ....Matt 23:6, 7
Forbidden by Christ .....Matt 23:8
Expressive of imperfect faith .... Mark 14:45, John 20:16
Translated "Master" .....Mark 14:45

RABBITH (răb'ĭth)—*"great"*
Frontier town of Issachar .Josh 19:20

RABBLE, THE—*disorderly crowd of people*
Cause of discord ....Num 11:4-6
Clamors for Jesus' death. .Matt 26:47
Seeks Paul's life ....Acts 17:1-8

RABBONI (rä-bō'nī)—*Aramaic form of Rabbi*
Mary addresses Christ as .John 20:16

RAB-MAG (răb'măg)—*head of the Magi*
Title applied to Nergal-sharezer ....Jer 39:3, 13

RAB-SARIS (răb'sä-rĭs)—*head chamberlain*

Title applied to:
Assyrian officials sent by Sennacherib 2Kin 18:17
Babylonian Nebushasban .Jer 39:13
Babylonian prince ....Jer 39:3

Office of:
Considered important ....Dan 1:7

RAB-SHAKEH (răb'shä-kĕ)—*head of the cupbearers*
Sent 2Kin 18:17
King of Assyria sent .....Is 36:2
And told him the words of ....Is 36:22
Hear all the words 2Kin 19:4

R said unto them, Speak ye ...2Kin 18:19
unto *R*, Speak, I pray thee 2Kin 18:26

R said unto them, Hath my . . .2Kin 18:27
Then ***R*** stood and cried 2Kin 18:28
told him the words of ***R*** 2Kin 18:37
hear all the words of ***R*** 2Kin 19:4
So ***R*** returned, and found 2Kin 19:8
R said unto them, Say ye . . . . .Is 36:4
R, speak, I pray thee . . . . .Is 36:11
R said, Hath my master . . . . . . .Is 36:12
R stood, and cried with a . . . . .Is 36:13
will hear the words of ***R*** . . . . . .Is 37:4
So ***R*** returned, and found . . . . .Is 37:8

RACA (rä-kä')—*a term of insult*
Use of, forbidden by
Christ . . . . .Matt 5:21, 22

RACE—*a contest; a course*
patience the *r* that is set . . . . . .Heb 12:1

RACE, CHRISTIAN—*the Christian life*
Requirements of:
Discipline 1Cor 9:24-27
Patience . . . . .Eccl 9:11
Steadfastness . . . . .Gal 5:7

RACE, HUMAN—*humanity*
Unity of . . . . .Gen 3:20
Divisions of . . . . .Gen 10:1-32
Scattering of . . . . .Gen 11:1-9
Bounds of . . . . .Acts 17:26
Depravity of . . . . .Rom 1:18-32
Salvation of . . . . .John 3:16

RACE RELATIONS—*the relationship between the races*
Salvation is for all . . . . . . .Eph 2:11-22
Eph 3:7-9
All are same in Christ . . .Col 3:9-11

RACHAB—*See* Rahab

RACHAL (rā'kăl)—*"to whisper"*
City in Judah 1Sam 30:29

RACHEL, RAHEL (rā'chĕl, rā'hĕl)—*"ewe"*
Laban's younger daughter; Jacob's favorite wife . . . . .Gen 29:28-30
Supports her husband's position . . . . .Gen 31:14-16
Mother of Joseph and Benjamin . . . . .Gen 30:22-25
Prophecy concerning, quoted . . . . {Jer 31:15; Matt 2:18}

[*also* rachel's]
R his daughter cometh . . . . .Gen 29:6
R came with her father's . . . . . .Gen 29:9
Jacob saw ***R*** the daughter . . . . .Gen 29:10
Jacob kissed ***R***, and lifted . . . . . .Gen 29:11
And Jacob told ***R*** that he . . . . .Gen 29:12
name of the younger was ***R*** . . .Gen 29:16
R was beautiful and well . . . . . .Gen 29:17
Jacob loved ***R***; and said . . . . . . .Gen 29:18
serve thee seven years for ***R*** . . .Gen 29:18
Jacob served seven years for ***R***.Gen 29:20
did I not serve with thee for ***R***?.Gen 29:25
but ***R*** was barren . . . . .Gen 29:31
when ***R*** saw that she bare . . . . .Gen 30:1
R envied her sister; and . . . . . . .Gen 30:1
kindled against ***R*** . . . . .Gen 30:2
R said, God hath judged . . . . . .Gen 30:6
Bilhah ***R*** maid conceived . . . . . .Gen 30:7
And ***R*** said, With great . . . . . . .Gen 30:8
R said to Leah, Give me . . . . . .Gen 30:14
And ***R*** said, Therefore he . . . . .Gen 30:15
called ***R*** and Leah . . . . .Gen 31:4
R had stolen the images . . . . . .Gen 31:19
knew not that ***R*** had . . . . .Gen 31:32
and entered into ***R*** tent . . . . . . .Gen 31:33
R had taken the images . . . . . . .Gen 31:34
Leah, and unto ***R*** . . . . .Gen 33:1
R and Joseph hindermost . . . . .Gen 33:2
came Joseph near and ***R*** . . . . . .Gen 33:7
and ***R*** travailed, and she . . . . . .Gen 35:16
the pillar of ***R*** grave unto . . . . .Gen 35:20
sons of ***R***; Joseph, and . . . . .Gen 35:24
of Bilhah, ***R*** handmaid . . . . .Gen 35:25
sons of ***R***, Jacob's wife . . . . .Gen 46:19
These are the sons of ***R*** . . . . . . .Gen 46:22
Laban gave unto ***R*** his . . . . .Gen 46:25
R died by me in the land . . . . . .Gen 48:7
like ***R*** and like Leah . . . . .Ruth 4:11
two men by ***R*** sepulcher 1Sam 10:2

RACHEL, TOMB OF—*the place where Rachel was buried*
Near Bethlehem—first mention of in Bible . . . .Gen 35:19

RADDAI (răd'ā-ī)—*"Jehovah subdues; beating down"*
One of David's brothers. .1Chr 2:14

RADIANCE IN LIFE—*a joyful countenance or attitude toward life*
Caused by:
Wisdom . . . . .Prov 4:7-9
Soul-winning . . . . .Dan 12:3
Transfiguration . . . . .Matt 17:2
Beholding the Lord . . . . . .Ps 34:5
2Cor 3:7-18

RAFTERS—*timbers used to support a roof*
Made of fir . . . . .Song 1:17

RAGAU (rā'gô)—*See* Reu

RAGE—*violent and raving madness or anger; to be filled with violent anger*
Descriptive of:
Sea .Luke 8:24
Strong drink . . . . .Prov 20:1
Anger . . . . .Dan 3:13
Heathen . . . . .Ps 2:1
Caused by:
Insanity 2Chr 16:7-10
Supposed insult 2Kin 5:11, 12
Jealousy . . . . .Prov 6:34
Insolence against God . . .2Kin 19:27, 28

[*also* raged, rageth, raging]
slain them in a *r* that 2Chr 28:9
with fierceness and *r* . . . . .Job 39:24
Cast abroad the *r* of thy . . . . . .Job 40:11
of the *r* of mine enemies . . . . . .Ps 7:6
heathen *r*, the kingdoms . . . . . .Ps 46:6
rulest the *r* of the sea . . . . .Ps 89:9
fool *r*, and is confident . . . . . . .Prov 14:16
whether he *r* or laugh . . . . .Prov 29:9
in, and thy *r* against me . . . . . . .Is 37:28
Because thy *r* against me . . . . . .Is 37:29
ye horses; and *r*, ye . . . . .Jer 46:9
Nebuchadnezzar in his *r* . . . . . .Dan 3:13
for the *r* of their tongue . . . . . .Hos 7:16
the sea ceased from her *r* . . . . .Jon 1:15
The chariots shall *r* in the . . . . .Nah 2:4
Why did the heathen *r* . . . . .Acts 4:25
R waves of the sea . . . . .Jude 13

RAGGED—*jagged*
the tops of the *r* rocks . . . . .Is 2:21

RAGS—*tattered and spoiled clothing*
Used as cushions . . . . .Jer 38:11-13
Reward of drowsiness . . . .Prov 23:21
Man's righteousness like. .Is 64:6

RAGUEL (rä-gū'ĕl)—*another name for Jethro, the father-in-law of Moses*
Hobab, the son of ***R*** the . . . . . .Num 10:29

RAHAB, RACHAB (rā'hăb, rā'kăb)—*"violence"—a woman of Jericho whose hospitality was rewarded with God's blessing*
Prostitute living in Jericho Josh 2:1
Concealed Joshua's spies .Josh 2:1-24
Spared by invading Israelites . . . . .Josh 6:17-25
Included among the faithful . . . . .Heb 11:31
Cited as an example . . . . .James 2:25
Ancestress of Christ . . . . .Matt 1:5

RAHAB—*a figure of speech*
Used figuratively of Egypt . . . . .Ps 87:4
Translated "the proud" . .Job 9:13
hast broken ***R*** in pieces . . . . . . .Ps 89:10
not it that hath cut ***R*** . . . . .Is 51:9

RAHAM (rā'hăm)—*"pity; love"*
Descendant of Caleb 1Chr 2:44

RAHEL—*See* Rachel

RAILER—*rebellious person*
or a *r*, or a drunkard 1Cor 5:11

RAILING—*acting insolently against one another*
Manifested by:
Rebellious 2Sam 16:5-8
Unbelieving . . . . .Mark 15:29-32
False teachers 2Pet 2:10-12
Sin of:
Excludes from Christian fellowship 1Cor 5:11
Forbidden 1Pet 3:8, 9

[*also* rail, railed, railings]
master; and he *r* on them 1Sam 25:14
letters to *r* on the Lord 2Chr 32:17
that passed by *r* on him . . . . . . .Mark 15:29
were hanged *r* on him . . . . .Luke 23:39
evil for evil, or *r* for *r* 1Pet 3:9
bring not *r* accusation 2Pet 2:11
him a *r* accusation . . . . .Jude 9

RAIMENT—*clothing*
Indicative of:
Plenty . . . . .Gen 24:53
Position . . . . .Judg 8:26
Provision . . . . .Matt 6:28
Poverty . . . . .James 2:2
Personality . . . . .Gen 27:15, 27
Regulations concerning:
Not to be kept . . . . .Ex 22:26
To be divided . . . . .Josh 22:8
To be purified . . . . .Num 31:20
Not to be multiplied 1Tim 6:8
Figurative of:
Redemption . . . . .Is 63:3
Imputation of righteousness . . . . .Zech 3:4
Purity . . . . .Rev 3:5, 18
Honor of position . . . . . . .Ps 45:14

bread to eat and *r* to put . . . . .Gen 28:20
changed his *r*, and came . . . . . .Gen 41:14
gave each man changes of *r* . . .Gen 45:22
silver, and five changes of *r* . . .Gen 45:22
and jewels of gold, and *r* . . . . .Ex 3:22
and jewels of gold, and *r* . . . . .Ex 12:35
her food, her *r*, and her . . . . . .Ex 21:10
for ass, for sheep, for *r* . . . . .Ex 22:9
it is his *r* for his skin . . . . .Ex 22:27
any vessel of wood, or *r* . . . . . . .Lev 11:32
Thy *r* waxed not old upon . . . .Deut 8:4
in giving him food and *r* . . . . . .Deut 10:18
the *r* of her captivity from . . . .Deut 21:13
shalt thou do with his *r* . . . . . . .Deut 22:3
may sleep in his own *r* . . . . .Deut 24:13
a widow's *r* to pledge . . . . .Deut 24:17
his *r* upon his right . . . . .Judg 3:16
and put thy *r* upon thee . . . . . . .Ruth 3:3
put on other *r*, and he 1Sam 28:8
and ten changes of *r* 2Kin 5:5
gold, and *r*, and went and 2Kin 7:8
vessels of gold, and *r* 2Chr 9:24
sent *r* to clothe Mordecai . . . . .Esth 4:4
and prepare *r* as the clay . . . . . .Job 27:16
as the *r* of those that are . . . . . .Is 14:19
thy *r* was of fine linen . . . . .Ezek 16:13
John had his *r* of camel's . . . . .Matt 3:4
and the body than *r*? . . . . .Matt 6:25
A man clothed in soft *r*? . . . . . . .Matt 11:8
his *r* was white as the . . . . .Matt 17:2
put his own *r* on him, and . . . .Matt 27:31
and his *r* white as snow . . . . . . .Matt 28:3
his *r* became shining . . . . .Mark 9:3
A man clothed in soft *r*? . . . . . . .Luke 7:25
his *r* was white and . . . . .Luke 9:29
the body is more than *r* . . . . .Luke 12:23
they parted his *r*, and cast . . . .Luke 23:34
They parted my *r* among . . . . . .John 19:24
he shook his *r*, and said . . . . . . .Acts 18:6

kept the *r* of them that ....Acts 22:20
clothed in white *r* ....Rev 4:4

RAIN—*drops of water falling from the sky; to fall as drops of water from the sky*

Features concerning:

Sent by God ....Jer 14:22
Sent on all mankind .....Matt 5:45
Sign of God's goodness ..Deut 28:12
Controlled by God's decrees .... Job 28:26; Job 37:6
Withheld because of sin ..Deut 11:17
Sent as a result of judgment ....Gen 7:4
Former and latter ....Jer 5:24
To be prayed for 1Kin 8:35, 36

Figurative of:

God's Word ....Is 55:10, 11
Spiritual blessing ....Ps 72:6
Righteousness ....Hos 10:12
Final judgment ....Matt 7:24-27
Hell ....Ps 11:6
Earth's ingathering ......James 5:7

[*also* RAINED, RAINY]

not caused it to *r* upon ....Gen 2:5
the *r* was upon the earth ......Gen 7:12
the *r* from heaven was ....Gen 8:2
r upon Sodom and Gomorrah. .Gen 19:24
cause it to *r*..grievous hail .....Ex 9:18
r hail upon the land of........Ex 9:23
r was not poured upon the ....Ex 9:33
Pharaoh saw that the *r*........Ex 9:34
will *r* bread from heaven ....Ex 16:4
I will give you *r* in due ....Lev 26:4
drinketh water of the *r* of .....Deut 11:11
I will give you the *r* of........Deut 11:14
the first *r* and the latter *r* .....Deut 11:14
make the *r* of thy land ....Deut 28:24
shall drop as the *r* ....Deut 32:2
r upon the tender herb........Deut 32:2
shall send thunder and *r* 1Sam 12:17
neither let there be *r* 2Sam 1:21
by clear shining after *r*........2Sam 23:4
shall not be dew nor *r* 1Kin 17:1
the Lord sendeth *r* upon 1Kin 17:14
and I will send *r* upon 1Kin 18:1
that the *r* stop thee not 1Kin 18:44
neither shall ye see *r* 2Kin 3:17
shut up, and there is no *r* 2Chr 6:26
heaven that there be no *r* 2Chr 7:13
and for the great *r* ....Ezra 10:9
Who giveth *r* upon the earth ..Job 5:10
r it upon him while he is ......Job 20:23
waited for me as for the *r*.....Job 29:23
wide as for the latter *r*........Job 29:23
pour down *r* according to .....Job 36:27
To cause it to *r* on the earth ..Job 38:26
didst send a plentiful *r*........Ps 68:9
r down manna upon them .....Ps 78:24
r also filleth the pools ....Ps 84:6
He gave them hail for *r*........Ps 105:32
lightnings for the *r* ....Ps 135:7
who prepareth *r* for the ....Ps 147:8
as a cloud of the latter *r*......Prov 16:15
clouds and wind without *r*.....Prov 25:14
and as *r* in harvest, so ....Prov 26:1
sweeping *r* which leaveth......Prov 28:3
If the clouds be full of *r* ......Eccl 11:3
clouds return after the *r* ......Eccl 12:2
is past, the *r* is over and ......Song 2:11
from storm and from *r*........Is 4:6
the clouds that they *r* no ......Is 5:6
shall he give the *r* of thy ......Is 30:23
and the *r* doth nourish it ......Is 44:14
hath been no latter *r* ....Jer 3:3
he maketh lightnings with *r* ...Jer 10:13
was no *r* in the earth ....Jer 14:4
maketh lightnings with *r* ......Jer 51:16
the cloud in the day of *r*......Ezek 1:28
r upon in the day of ....Ezek 22:24
I will *r* upon him, and ....Ezek 38:22
overflowing *r*, and great ......Ezek 38:22
come unto us as the *r*.........Hos 6:3
as the latter and former *r* .....Hos 6:3
r righteousness upon ....Hos 10:12
the former *r* moderately ......Joel 2:23
come down for you the *r*......Joel 2:23
the former *r*, and the latter *r* ..Joel 2:23
have withholden the *r*.........Amos 4:7
I caused it to *r* upon one .....Amos 4:7
it not to *r* upon another.......Amos 4:7
one piece was *r* upon ....Amos 4:7
Ask ye of the Lord *r* in the ...Zech 10:1
the latter *r*; so the Lord.......Zech 10:1
give them showers of *r*........Zech 10:1
r fire and brimstone from .....Luke 17:29
gave us *r* from heaven ....Acts 14:17
because of the present *r* ......Acts 28:2
earth which drinketh in the *r* ..Heb 6:7
receive..early and latter *r* .....James 5:7
r not on the earth by the .....James 5:17
and the heaven gave *r* ....James 5:18
it *r* not in the days of.........Rev 11:6

RAINBOW—*an arc in the sky that exhibits the colors of the spectrum by reflection from moisture in the air*

Appears after the flood. .Gen 9:12, 13
Sign of God's covenant ..Gen 9:16, 17
Around angel's head .....Rev 10:1
Over God's throne ......Rev 4:3

RAISE—*to lift up*

[*also* RAISED, RAISETH, RAISING]

and *r* up seed to thy..........Gen 38:8
for this cause have I *r* ....Ex 9:16
shalt not *r* a false report ....Ex 23:1
God will *r* up unto thee.......Deut 18:15
to *r* up unto his brother.......Deut 25:7
he *r* up in their stead ....Josh 5:7
r over him a great heap of ....Josh 7:26
r thereon a..heap of stones ....Josh 8:29
Lord *r* up judges ....Judg 2:16
r up a deliverer ....Judg 3:9
r up the name of the dead ....Ruth 4:5
He *r* up the poor 1Sam 2:8
r me up a faithful priest.........1Sam 2:35
r up evil against thee 2Sam 12:11
man who was *r* up on high 2Sam 23:1
r a levy out of all Israel.......1Kin 5:13
levy which King Solomon *r*.....1Kin 9:15
Lord shall *r* him up a king 1Kin 14:14
r up thy seed after thee 1Chr 17:11
and *r* it up to the towers 2Chr 32:5
r it up a very great height.....2Chr 33:14
whose spirit God had *r* ....Ezra 1:5
r up their mourning ....Job 3:8
not be *r* out of their sleep.....Job 14:12
they *r* up against me ....Job 30:12
When he *r* up himself.........Job 41:25
unto me, and *r* me up ....Ps 41:10
and *r* the stormy wind ....Ps 107:25
r up the poor out of the dust ..Ps 113:7
r up all those..be bowed ......Ps 145:14
r them that are bowed ....Ps 146:8
I *r* thee up under the ....Song 8:5
r up from their thrones ....Is 14:9
r up a cry of destruction ......Is 15:5
they *r* up the palaces ....Is 23:13
will *r* forts against thee ....Is 29:3
r up the righteous man........Is 41:2
will *r* up the decayed ....Is 44:26
r him up in righteousness .....Is 45:13
servant to *r* up the tribes......Is 49:6
shalt *r* up the foundation ......Is 58:12
shall *r* up..desolations ....Is 61:4
a great nation shall be *r*.......Jer 6:22
r unto David a righteous ......Jer 23:5
great whirlwind shall be *r* .....Jer 25:32
hath *r* us up prophets ....Jer 29:15
I will *r* up unto them ....Jer 30:9
I will *r* and cause to come ....Jer 50:9
many kings shall be *r* up ......Jer 50:41
r up against Babylon...........Jer 51:1
Lord hath *r* up the spirit ......Jer 51:11
r up thy lovers against ....Ezek 23:22
will *r* up for them a plant .....Ezek 34:29
it *r* up itself on one side ......Dan 7:5
third day he will *r* us up ......Hos 6:2
r after he hath kneaded ....Hos 7:4
r them out of the place ....Joel 3:7
I *r* up of your sons ....Amos 2:11
there is none to *r* her up......Amos 5:2
I will *r* up against you ....Amos 6:14
I *r* up the tabernacle..........Amos 9:11
I will *r* up his ruins ....Amos 9:11
we *r* against him seven........Mic 5:5
r up strife and contention .....Hab 1:3
is *r* up out of his holy ....Zech 2:13
and *r* up thy sons............Zech 9:13
will *r* up a shepherd ....Zech 11:16
Joseph being *r* from sleep .....Matt 1:24
to *r* up children unto ....Matt 3:9
the lepers, *r* the dead ....Matt 10:8
the dead are *r* up.............Matt 11:5
r again the third day..........Matt 16:21
third day he shall be *r* ....Matt 17:23
r up seed unto his brother ....Matt 22:24
r up seed unto his brother ....Mark 12:19
r up a horn of salvation ....Luke 1:69
to *r* up children unto ....Luke 3:8
deaf hear, the dead are *r* .....Luke 7:22
and be *r* the third day ....Luke 9:22
r up seed unto his brother ....Luke 20:28
Now that the dead are *r* ......Luke 20:37
three days I will *r* it up ....John 2:19
Father *r* up the dead ....John 5:21
r it up again at the last ....John 6:39
whom he *r* from the dead .....John 12:1
Whom God hath *r* up..........Acts 2:24
r up Christ to sit on his ....Acts 2:30
God hath *r* from the dead.....Acts 3:15
Lord your God *r* up unto .....Acts 3:22
God *r* from the dead ....Acts 4:10
of our fathers *r* up Jesus ......Acts 5:30
Lord your God *r* up unto .....Acts 7:37
God *r* up the third day ....Acts 10:40
r him up, saying, Arise up ....Acts 12:7
he *r* up unto them David .....Acts 13:22
God *r* him from the dead .....Acts 13:30
r him up from the dead ......Acts 13:34
r persecution against Paul .....Acts 13:50
r him from the dead ....Acts 17:31
neither *r* up the people ....Acts 24:12
God should *r* the dead? ....Acts 26:8
believe on him that *r* up ......Rom 4:24
as Christ was *r* up ....Rom 6:4
who is *r* from the dead ....Rom 7:4
r up Jesus from the dead......Rom 8:11
he that *r* up Christ ....Rom 8:11
same purpose have I *r* ....Rom 9:17
hath *r* him from the dead .....Rom 10:9
hath both *r* up the Lord 1Cor 6:14
r up us by his own power 1Cor 6:14
God that he *r* up Christ.......1Cor 15:15
whom he *r* not up 1Cor 15:15
if the dead *r* not 1Cor 15:16
Christ be not *r*, your faith.....1Cor 15:17
it is *r* in incorruption 1Cor 15:42
it is *r* in power 1Cor 15:43
shall be *r* incorruptible 1Cor 15:52
God which *r* the dead 2Cor 1:9
which *r* up the Lord 2Cor 4:14
shall *r* up us also by Jesus.....2Cor 4:14
who *r* him from the dead .....Gal 1:1
he *r* him from the dead ....Eph 1:20
hath *r* us up together ....Eph 2:6
r him from the dead ....Col 2:12
whom he *r* from the dead 1Thess 1:10
seed of David was *r* 2Tim 2:8
God was able to *r* him up .....Heb 11:19
dead *r* to life again ....Heb 11:35
Lord shall *r* him up...........James 5:15
r him up from the dead 1Pet 1:21

RAISER—*a collector*

in his estate a *r* of taxes ......Dan 11:20

RAISINS—*dried grapes*

Nourishing food 1Sam 25:18
Provided for David 2Sam 16:1

figs, and two clusters of *r* 1Sam 30:12
of figs, and bunches of *r* 1Chr 12:40

RAKEM (rā'kĕm)—*"friendship"*

Manassite 1Chr 7:16

R

RAKKATH (răk'ăth)—*"empty"*
Fortified city of Naphtali .Josh 19:32,35

RAKKON (răk'ŏn)—*"void"*
Danite village ....Josh 19:40,46

RAM, ARAM—*"exalted"*
1. Ancestor of David ......Ruth 4:19
Ancestor of Christ ......Matt 1:3, 4
2. Man of Judah 1Chr 2:25, 27

RAM—*a male sheep*
Used as food............Gen 31:38
Used in offerings ....Gen 22:13
Appointed for certain offerings ....Lev 5:15
Skin of, used as coverings. Ex 26:14
Horns of, used as trumpets ....Josh 6:4-13

[*also* RAMS, RAMS']
and a *r* of three years old .....Gen 15:9
r which leaped upon the ......Gen 31:10
ewes, and twenty *r* ....Gen 32:14
r skins dyed red, and ....Ex 25:5
two *r* without blemish.........Ex 29:1
shalt also take one *r* ....Ex 29:15
upon the head of the *r*........Ex 29:15
shalt cut the *r* in pieces ....Ex 29:17
shalt take the other *r* ....Ex 29:19
upon the head of the *r*........Ex 29:19
shalt take of the *r* the fat .....Ex 29:22
it is a *r* of consecration ....Ex 29:22
the *r* of the consecration ......Ex 29:27
shall eat the flesh of the *r*.....Ex 29:32
r skins dyed red, and ....Ex 35:7
skins of *r*, and badgers' ....Ex 35:23
tent of *r* skins dyed red ....Ex 36:19
covering of *r* skins dyed.......Ex 39:34
with the *r* of the trespass......Lev 5:16
r without blemish out of ......Lev 6:6
sin offering, and two *r* ....Lev 8:2
r for the burnt offering ....Lev 8:18
upon the head of the *r*.........Lev 8:18
burnt the whole *r* upon ....Lev 8:21
the other *r*, the *r* of ....Lev 8:22
upon the head of the *r*.........Lev 8:22
a *r* for a burnt offering ....Lev 9:2
the *r* for a sacrifice of ....Lev 9:18
a *r* for a burnt offering ....Lev 16:3
a *r* for a trespass offering .....Lev 19:21
one young bullock, and two *r*. .Lev 23:18
the *r* of the atonement ....Num 5:8
one *r* without blemish for .....Num 6:14
offer the *r* for a sacrifice ......Num 6:17
sodden shoulder of the *r* ......Num 6:19
young bullock, one *r*..........Num 7:15
four bullocks, the *r* sixty ......Num 7:88
for a *r*, thou shalt prepare ....Num 15:6
seven oxen and seven *r* ....Num 23:1
altar a bullock and a *r* ....Num 23:2
and a *r* on every altar ....Num 23:14
two young bullocks, and one *r* .Num 28:11
part of a hin unto a *r*.........Num 28:14
two tenth deals for a *r* ....Num 28:20
tenth deals unto one *r* ....Num 28:28
one young bullock, one *r* .....Num 29:2
one young bullock, one *r* .....Num 29:8
young bullocks, two *r*, and ....Num 29:13
deals to each *r* of the two *r* ...Num 29:14
young bullocks, two *r*..........Num 29:17
for the bullocks, for the *r* .....Num 29:18
eleven bullocks, two *r* ....Num 29:20
for the bullocks, for the *r* .....Num 29:21
day ten bullocks two *r* ....Num 29:23
for the bullocks, for the *r* .....Num 29:24
day nine bullocks, two *r* ....Num 29:26
for the bullocks, for the *r* .....Num 29:27
eight bullocks, two *r*, and .....Num 29:29
for the bullocks, for the *r* .....Num 29:30
seven bullocks, two *r*, and ....Num 29:32
for the bullocks, for the *r* .....Num 29:33
for the bullock, for the *r* ......Num 29:37
r of the breed of Bashan ......Deut 32:14
hearken than the fat of *r*......1Sam 15:22
an hundred thousand *r*........2Kin 3:4
bullocks and seven *r* 1Chr 15:26
bullocks, a thousand *r* 1Chr 29:21
bullock and seven *r* 2Chr 13:9
and seven hundred *r* 2Chr 17:11
bullocks, and seven *r* 2Chr 29:21
an hundred *r*, and two 2Chr 29:32
young bullocks, and *r*.........Ezra 6:9
this money bullocks, *r* ....Ezra 7:17
ninety and six *r*, seventy ......Ezra 8:35
a *r* of the flock for their ......Ezra 10:19
bullocks and seven *r* ....Job 42:8
with the incense of *r*..........Ps 66:15
mountains skipped like *r* ......Ps 114:4
of the burnt offerings of *r*......Is 1:11
the fat of the kidneys of *r*.....Is 34:6
the *r* of Nebaioth shall ....Is 60:7
like *r* with he goats ....Jer 51:40
occupied..in lambs, and *r* .....Ezek 27:21
between the *r* and the he .....Ezek 34:17
of *r*, of lambs and of goats ....Ezek 39:18
a *r* out of the flock without ...Ezek 43:23
seven *r* without blemish ....Ezek 45:23
and an ephah for a *r*, and .....Ezek 45:24
and a *r* without blemish ....Ezek 46:4
and six lambs, and a *r* ....Ezek 46:6
the river a *r* which had ....Dan 8:3
came to the *r* that had ....Dan 8:6
come close unto the *r*.........Dan 8:7
smote the *r*, and brake........Dan 8:7
was no power in the *r* to......Dan 8:7
with thousands of *r* ....Mic 6:7

RAM—*an instrument of war*
Used to destroy gates and walls ....Ezek 4:2
Used by Babylonians ....Ezek 21:22

RAMAH, RAMA (rā'ma)—*"elevated"*
1. Town of Asher ....Josh 19:24,29
2. City of Naphtali ....Josh 19:32,36
3. Benjamite city near Jerusalem ....Josh 18:21,25
Deborah's palm near here ....Judg 4:5
Fortress built 1Kin 15:17-22
Gathering of captives....Jer 40:1
Reinhabited after exile ..Ezra 2:26
Probable site of Rachel's tomb 1Sam 10:2
Samuel's headquarters ...1Sam 7:15,17
David flees to 1Sam 19:18-23
4. Town called Ramothgilead.........2Kin 8:28, 29

lodge..in Gibeah, or in *R* .....Judg 19:13
Elkanah went to *R* to his 1Sam 2:11
came to Samuel unto *R* 1Sam 8:4
Then Samuel went to *R* 1Sam 15:34
Samuel rose up, and went to *R*.1Sam 16:13
David fled from Naioth in *R* ..1Sam 20:1
Gibeah under a tree in *R* 1Sam 22:6
buried..in his house at *R* 1Sam 25:1
buried him in *R*, even in 1Sam 28:3
Judah, and built *R*............2Chr 16:1
he left off building of *R*.......2Chr 16:5
away the stones of *R* 2Chr 16:6
wounds..given him at *R* 2Chr 22:6
men of *R* and Gaba, six.......Neh 7:30
Hazor, *R*, Gittaim ....Neh 11:33
R is afraid; Gibeah of.........Is 10:29
A voice was heard in *R* ....Jer 31:15
In *R* was there a voice ....Matt 2:18

RAMATH OF THE SOUTH
A town of Simeon ....Josh 19:8
Same as Baalath-beer ....Josh 19:8

RAMATHAIM-ZOPHIM (rā-mä-thā-ĭm-zō'fĭm)—*town where Samuel was born*
Home of Elkanah 1Sam 1:1
Also called "Ramah" 1Sam 1:19
See RAMAH

RAMATHITE (rā-mä-thīt)—*an inhabitant of Ramah*
Shimei called...........1Chr 27:27

RAMATH-LEHI (rā-măth-lē'hī)—*"jawbone"—location in Judah where Samson slew many Philistines*
and called that place *R*.......Judg 15:17

RAMATH-MIZPEH (rā-măth-mĭz'pĕ)—*"place of the watchtower"*
An inheritance of Gad ...Josh 13:24-26

RAMESES—*See* RAAMSES

RAMIAH (rä-mī'ä)—*"Jehovah is high"—an Israelite who married a foreign wife during the Exile*
sons of Parosh; *R*............Ezra 10:25

RAMOTH (rā'mŏth)—*"high places; heights"*
1. Town of Issachar; possibly same as Remeth and Jarmuth ..1Chr 6:73
2. Same as Ramath ....Josh 19:8
3. Town of Gilead ....Deut 4:43

R in Gilead with her suburbs ..Josh 21:38
which were in south *R* 1Sam 30:27
Know ye that *R* in Gilead 1Kin 22:3
And *R* with her suburbs 1Chr 6:73
Jashub, and Sheal, and *R* .....Ezra 10:29

RAMOTH-GILEAD (rā-mŏth-gĭl'ĕ-ăd)—*"heights of Gilead"*

City of refuge east of Jordan..............Deut 4:43; Josh 20:8; 1Chr 6:80
Site of Ahab's fatal conflict with Syrians ...1Kin 22:1-39
Called Ramah and Ramoth ....Deut 4:43; 2Kin 8:29

Shall I go to *R* to battle.......1Kin 22:6
The son of Geber, in *R*; to....1Kin 4:13
Hazael king of Syria in *R* 2Kin 8:28
oil in thine hand, and go to *R* .2Kin 9:1
Now Joram had kept *R* 2Kin 9:14
to go up with him to *R* 2Chr 18:2
Shall we go to *R* to battle 2Chr 18:5
Shall we go to *R* to battle 2Chr 18:14
king of Judah went up to *R* ...2Chr 18:28

RAMPART—*a city's outer fortification*
Around:
Certain cities............2Sam 20:15
Jerusalem ....Ps 48:13

the *r* and the wall to..........Lam 2:8
whose *r* was the sea, and .....Nah 3:8

RAN—*See* RUN

RANG—*sounded out*
so that the earth *r* again 1Sam 4:5

RANGE—*the extent of something; stove or oven*

[*also* RANGES, RANGING]
it be oven, or *r* for pots.......Lev 11:35
that cometh within the *r* 2Kin 11:8
Have her forth of the *r* 2Chr 23:14
The *r* of the mountains ....Job 39:8
roaring lion, and a *r* bear .....Prov 28:15

RANK—*foul; row of people; line of soldiers*

[*also* RANKS]
up upon one stalk, *r* and ......Gen 41:5
set forth in the second *r* ......Num 2:16
against light in three *r* 1Kin 7:4
which could keep *r* 1Chr 12:33
shall not break their *r* ....Joel 2:7
And they sat down in *r*, by ...Mark 6:40

RANSOM—*to redeem by a payment*
Of man, for:
Israelites.................Ex 30:12-16
Murderer, forbidden .....Num 35:31,32
Some, unpayable ....Prov 6:34, 35
Brother, impossible ......Ps 49:7, 8
Of Christ:
For all...................Matt 20:28
From grave ....Hos 13:14
From Satan ....Jer 31:11
Cause of joy ....Is 35:10

[*also* RANSOMED]
the *r* of his life whatsoever ....Ex 21:30
the pit: I have found a *r* ......Job 33:24

a great *r* cannot deliver . . . . . . .Job 36:18
The *r* of a man's life are . . . . . .Prov 13:8
The wicked shall be a *r* . . . . . . .Prov 21:18
I gave Egypt for thy *r* . . . . .Is 43:3
way for the *r* to pass over? . . . .Is 51:10
to give his life a *r* for . . . . .Mark 10:45
Who gave himself a *r* for 1Tim 2:6

RAPACITY—*seizing others' goods; covetousness*
Descriptive of Satan 1Pet 5:8
Characteristic of false teachers . . . . .Luke 11:39

RAPE—*forced sexual relations*
Features concerning:
Death penalty for . . . . . . .Deut 22:25-27
Captives subjected to . . . .Is 13:16
Example of:
Tamar by Amnon 2Sam 13:6-29

RAPHA, RAPHAH (rā'fä)—*"fearful"*
1. Benjamin's fifth son 1Chr 8:1, 2
But not listed . . . . .Gen 46:21
2. Descendant of Jonathan .1Chr 8:37
Called Rephaiah in 1Chr 9:43
3. Same word translated "giant" 2Sam 21:16-20

RAPHU (rā'fū)—*"feared; one healed"*
Benjamite . . . . .Num 13:9

RAPTURE, THE—*the translation of the redeemed to a glorified state at Christ's return*
Not all will sleep . . . .{1Cor 15:51; 1Thess 4:15, 17}
Dead in Christ will rise . .{1Cor 15:52; 1Thess 4:13, 14, 16}
Living to be transformed .1Cor 15:51-53
Saints caught up 1Thess 4:16, 17

RARE—*unusual*
a *r* thing that the king . . . . .Dan 2:11

RASE—*raze; demolish*
R it, *r* it, even to the . . . . .Ps 137:7

RASHNESS—*ill-advised and hasty action*
Examples of:
Moses' killing the Egyptian . . . . .Ex 2:11, 12
Jephthah's vow . . . . .Judg 11:30-39
Israel's vow against the Benjamites . . . . .Judg 21:1-6
Josiah's war against Necho 2Chr 35:20-24
Peter's cutting off the ear of Malchus . . . . .John 18:10

[*also* RASH, RASHLY]
Be not *r* with thy mouth . . . . . .Eccl 5:2
r shall understand . . . . .Is 32:4
quiet, and to do nothing *r* . . . . .Acts 19:36

RASOR—*See* RAZOR

RATE—*a fixed quantity*
gather a certain *r* every . . . . . . .Ex 16:4
horses, and mules, a *r* year 1Kin 10:25
of the king, a daily *r* for 2Kin 25:30
a certain *r* every day 2Chr 8:13
horses, and mules, a *r* year 2Chr 9:24

RATHER—*instead of; more properly*
have not *r* done it for fear . . . .Josh 22:24
hath not David *r* sent his 2Sam 10:3
how much *r* then, when he 2Kin 5:13
and death *r* than my life . . . . . .Job 7:15
he justified himself *r* than . . . . .Job 32:2
lying *r* than to speak . . . . .Ps 52:3
I had *r* be a doorkeeper in . . . .Ps 84:10
knowledge *r* than choice gold . .Prov 8:10
understanding *r* to be . . . . .Prov 16:16
a man, *r* than a fool in his . . . .Prov 17:12
name is *r* to be chosen . . . . .Prov 22:1
loving favor *r* than silver . . . . . .Prov 22:1
But go *r* to the lost sheep . . . . .Matt 10:6
r than having two hands . . . . . .Matt 18:8
go ye *r* to them that sell . . . . . .Matt 25:9
that *r* a tumult was made . . . . .Matt 27:24
nothing bettered, but *r* . . . . .Mark 5:26
should *r* release Barabbas . . . . .Mark 15:11
r rejoice, because your . . . . .Luke 10:20
Yea *r*, blessed are they . . . . . . .Luke 11:28
But *r* seek ye the kingdom . . . .Luke 12:31
will not *r* say unto him . . . . .Luke 17:8
his house justified *r* than . . . . . .Luke 18:14
loved darkness *r* than . . . . .John 3:19
ought to obey God *r* than . . . . .Acts 5:29
And not *r*, as we be . . . . .Rom 3:8
died, yea *r*, that is risen . . . . . . .Rom 8:34
r through their fall salvation . . .Rom 11:11
but *r* give place unto . . . . .Rom 12:19
but judge this *r*, that no . . . . . .Rom 14:13
and have not *r* mourned 1Cor 5:2
do ye not *r* take wrong? 1Cor 6:7
r suffer yourselves to be 1Cor 6:7
be made free, use it *r* 1Cor 7:21
over you, are not we *r*? 1Cor 9:12
r that ye may prophesy 1Cor 14:1
ye ought *r* to forgive him 2Cor 2:7
of the spirit be *r* glorious? 2Cor 3:8
r to be absent from the 2Cor 5:8
will I *r* glory in my 2Cor 12:9
known God, or *r* are . . . . .Gal 4:9
but *r* let him labor . . . . .Eph 4:28
convenient: but *r* giving . . . . . . .Eph 5:4
fallen out *r* unto the . . . . .Phil 1:12
r than godly edifying 1Tim 1:4
exercise thyself *r* unto 1Tim 4:7
but *r* do them service 1Tim 6:2
love's sake I *r* beseech . . . . .Philem 9
Choosing *r* to suffer . . . . .Heb 11:25
r be in subjection unto . . . . .Heb 12:9
But I beseech you the *r* to . . . .Heb 13:19
Wherefore the *r*, brethren 2Pet 1:10

RATIONING—*limits prescribed for necessities*
By Joseph, to save Egypt .Gen 41:35-57

RATTLING—*noisy*
[*also* RATTLETH]
The quiver *r* against him . . . . . .Job 39:23
the noise of the *r* of the . . . . . .Nah 3:2

RAVEN—*a black, flesh-eating bird*
Characteristics of:
Unclean for food . . . . .Lev 11:15
Solitary in habit . . . . .Is 34:11
Flesh-eating . . . . .Prov 30:17
Black . . . . .Song 5:11
Special features concerning:
First creature sent from the ark . . . . .Gen 8:7
Elijah fed by 1Kin 17:4-7
Fed by God . . . . .Luke 12:24

[*also* RAVENS]
every *r* after his kind . . . . .Deut 14:14
Who provideth for the *r* . . . . . .Job 38:41
food, and to the young *r* . . . . . .Ps 147:9

RAVENOUS—*greedy for food; destructive*
[*also* RAVENING, RAVIN]
Benjamin shall *r* as a wolf . . . .Gen 49:27
as a *r* and a roaring lion . . . . . .Ps 22:13
any *r* beast shall go up . . . . .Is 35:9
Calling a *r* bird from the . . . . . .Is 46:11
like a roaring lion *r* the . . . . . . .Ezek 22:25
give thee unto the *r* birds . . . . .Ezek 39:4
prey, and his dens with *r* . . . . . .Nah 2:12
they are *r* wolves . . . . .Matt 7:15
full of *r* and wickedness . . . . . . .Luke 11:39

RAVISHED—*overcome with emotion; raped or violated*
be thou *r* always with her . . . . .Prov 5:19
Thou hast *r* my heart . . . . .Song 4:9
thou hast *r* my heart with . . . . .Song 4:9
spoiled, and their wives *r* . . . . .Is 13:16
They *r* women in Zion . . . . .Lam 5:11
rifled, and the women *r* . . . . . . .Zech 14:2

RAW—*not cooked*
Eat not of it *r*, nor sodden . . . .Ex 12:9
be quick *r* flesh in the . . . . .Lev 13:10
for the *r* flesh is unclean . . . . . .Lev 13:15
flesh of thee, but *r* 1Sam 2:15

RAZE—*See* RASE

RAZOR—*a sharp instrument used for cutting hair*
Forbidden to:
Nazarites . . . . .Num 6:1-5
Samson . . . . .Judg 13:5
Mentioned in Hannah's vow 1Sam 1:11
Used by barbers . . . . .Ezek 5:1
See HAIR; KNIFE

[*also* RASOR]
no *r* come upon his head . . . . . .Num 6:5
no *r* shall come on his . . . . .Judg 13:5
hath not come a *r* upon . . . . . . .Judg 16:17
no *r* come upon his head 1Sam 1:11
like a sharp *r*, working . . . . .Ps 52:2
with a *r* that is hired . . . . .Is 7:20
take thee a barber's *r* . . . . .Ezek 5:1

REACH—*to thrust; stretch for; extend*
[*also* REACHED, REACHETH, REACHING]
tower, whose top may *r* . . . . . . .Gen 11:4
the top of it *r* to heaven . . . . . .Gen 28:12
boards shall *r* from end to . . . .Ex 26:28
unto the thighs they shall *r* . . . .Ex 28:42
threshing shall *r* unto the . . . . .Lev 26:5
vintage shall *r* unto . . . . .Lev 26:5
which *r* unto Medeba . . . . .Num 21:30
shall *r* unto the side of the . . . .Num 34:11
shall *r* from the wall of . . . . . . .Num 35:4
and *r* to Dabbasheth . . . . .Josh 19:11
r to the river..before Jokneam .Josh 19:11
And the coast *r* to Tabor . . . . .Josh 19:22
and *r* to Carmel westward . . . . .Josh 19:26
and *r* to Zebulun, and to . . . . .Josh 19:27
and *r* to Zebulun on the . . . . . .Josh 19:34
r to Asher on the west . . . . .Josh 19:34
he *r* her parched corn . . . . .Ruth 2:14
r to the wall of the house 2Chr 3:11
r to the wing of the other 2Chr 3:11
cubits, *r* to the wall of the 2Chr 3:12
in a rage that *r* up unto 2Chr 28:9
head *r* unto the clouds . . . . .Job 20:6
thy faithfulness *r* unto . . . . .Ps 36:5
and thy truth *r* unto the . . . . . . .Ps 108:4
r forth her hands to the . . . . . . .Prov 31:20
shall *r* even to the neck . . . . . . .Is 8:8
the sword *r* unto the soul . . . . .Jer 4:10
it *r* unto thine heart . . . . .Jer 4:18
they *r* even to the sea of . . . . . .Jer 48:32
judgment *r* unto heaven . . . . . . .Jer 51:9
the height thereof *r* unto . . . . . .Dan 4:11
whose height *r* unto the . . . . . . .Dan 4:20
is grown, and *r* unto . . . . .Dan 4:22
mountains shall *r* unto . . . . .Zech 14:5
R hither thy finger, and . . . . . . .John 20:27
r hither thy hand, and . . . . .John 20:27
a measure to *r* even unto 2Cor 10:13
as though we *r* not unto 2Cor 10:14
r forth unto those things . . . . . .Phil 3:13
for her sins have *r* unto . . . . . . .Rev 18:5

READ—*to understand the meaning of printed material*
[*also* READEST, READETH, READING]
r therein all the days of . . . . . . .Deut 17:19
shalt *r* this law before all . . . . . .Deut 31:11
he *r* all the words of the law . .Josh 8:34
the king of Israel had *r* 2Kin 5:7
the messengers, and *r* it 2Kin 19:14
he *r* in their ears all the 2Kin 23:2
And Shaphan *r* it before 2Chr 34:18
he *r* in their ears all the 2Chr 34:30
been plainly *r* before me . . . . . .Ezra 4:18
he *r* therein before the . . . . .Neh 8:3
to understand the *r* . . . . .Neh 8:8
he *r* in the book of the law . . .Neh 8:18
r in the book of the law . . . . . .Neh 9:3
they were *r* before the . . . . .Esth 6:1
R this, I pray thee: and . . . . . . .Is 29:11

R

book of the Lord, and *r* ...... Is 34:16
the messengers, and *r* it ...... Is 37:14
the priest *r* this letter .... Jer 29:29
go thou, and *r* in the roll ..... Jer 36:6
shalt *r* them in the ears of .... Jer 36:6
r in the book..words of .... Jer 36:8
when Baruch *r* the book ...... Jer 36:13
roll wherein thou hast *r* .... Jer 36:14
Sit down now, and *r* it in ..... Jer 36:15
So Baruch *r* it in their ears .... Jer 36:15
shalt *r* all these words .... Jer 51:61
made an end of *r* this book .. Jer 51:63
shall *r* this writing .... Dan 5:7
should *r* this writing .... Dan 5:15
I will *r* the writing .... Dan 5:17
that he may run that *r* it ...... Hab 2:2
Have ye not *r* what David .... Matt 12:3
Have ye not *r*, that he .... Matt 19:4
have ye never *r*, Out of the .. Matt 21:16
have ye not *r* that which ...... Matt 22:31
whoso *r*, let him .... Matt 24:15
And have ye not *r* this .... Mark 12:10
him that *r* understand .... Mark 13:14
and stood up for to *r* .... Luke 4:16
Have ye not *r* so much as ..... Luke 6:3
the law? how *r* thou? .... Luke 10:26
This title then *r* many of ...... John 19:20
in his chariot *r* Isaiah .... Acts 8:28
the *r* of the law and the .... Acts 13:15
prophets which are *r* every .... Acts 13:27
being *r* in the synagogues ..... Acts 15:21
governor had *r* the letter ...... Acts 23:34
ye *r* or acknowledge 2Cor 1:13
known and *r* of all men 2Cor 3:2
r of the old testament 2Cor 3:14
when ye *r*, ye may .... Eph 3:4
epistle is *r* among you .... Col 4:16
r the epistle from Laodicea .... Col 4:16
be *r* unto all..brethren 1Thess 5:27
give attendance to *r* 1Tim 4:13
worthy to open and to *r* ...... Rev 5:4

READINESS—*being prepared for action*

Descriptive of:
Being prepared .... Matt 22:4, 8
Being responsive 2Cor 8:11, 19

Objects of:
Willing people .... Luke 1:17
Passover .... Luke 22:12, 13
Lord's return .... Matt 24:44
Preaching the Gospel .... Rom 1:15

READING THE BIBLE

Blessings of:
Brings repentance 2Kin 22:8-20
Reminds us of duties .... Neh 8:12, 13
Produces reformation .... Neh 13:1-3
Gives knowledge of prophecy .... Rev 1:3

Reactions to:
Responsiveness .... Ex 24:7
Rejection .... Jer 36:21-28
Rebellion .... Luke 4:16-30
Request for more light ... Acts 8:29-35
Research .... Acts 17:10, 11

READY—*prepared; to prepare*
Make *r* quickly three .... Gen 18:6
and slay, and make *r* .... Gen 43:16
And Joseph made *r* his .... Gen 46:29
he made *r* his chariot .... Ex 14:6
be almost *r* to stone me .... Ex 17:4
be *r* against the third day ..... Ex 19:11
And be *r* in the morning ...... Ex 34:2
ourselves will go *r* armed ..... Num 32:17
ye were *r* to go up into .... Deut 1:41
Syrian *r* to perish was my ..... Deut 26:5
the city, but be ye all *r* .... Josh 8:4
Gideon..made *r* a kid .... Judg 6:19
shall have made *r* a kid .... Judg 13:15
and five sheep *r* dressed 1Sam 25:18
thy servants are *r* to do 2Sam 15:15
thou hast no tidings *r*? 2Sam 18:22
of stone made *r* before 1Kin 6:7
And Joram said, Make *r* 2Kin 9:21
his chariot was made *r* 2Kin 9:21
bands that were *r* armed 1Ch 12:23
made *r* for the building 1Chr 28:2
thousand *r* prepared for 2Chr 17:18
made *r* for themselves 2Chr 35:14
a *r* scribe in the law .... Ezra 7:6
thou art a God *r* to pardon ... Neh 9:17
be *r* against that day .... Esth 3:14
Jews should be *r* against ...... Esth 8:13
are *r* to raise up their .... Job 3:8
He that is *r* to slip with .... Job 12:5
darkness is *r* at his hand ...... Job 15:23
are *r* to become heaps .... Job 15:28
the graves are *r* for me .... Job 17:1
destruction shall be *r* at .... Job 18:12
him that was *r* to perish .... Job 29:13
it is *r* to burst like new .... Job 32:19
bent his bow, and made it *r* ... Ps 7:12
make *r* their arrow upon ...... Ps 11:2
make *r* thine arrows .... Ps 21:12
I am *r* to halt, and my .... Ps 38:17
is the pen of a *r* writer .... Ps 45:1
good, and *r* to forgive .... Ps 86:5
r to die from my youth .... Ps 88:15
that are *r* to be slain .... Prov 24:11
him that is *r* to perish .... Prov 31:6
be more *r* to hear, than to .... Eccl 5:1
r to perish in..Assyria .... Is 27:13
be..as a breach *r* to fall .... Isa 30:13
shall be *r* to speak plainly ..... Is 32:4
Lord was *r* to save me .... Is 38:20
It is *r* for the sodering .... Is 41:7
as if he were *r* to destroy? .... Is 51:13
even to make all *r* .... Ezek 7:14
if ye be *r* that at what .... Dan 3:15
made *r* their heart like an ..... Hos 7:6
they that were *r* went in ...... Matt 25:10
they made *r* the passover ..... Matt 26:19
there make *r* for us .... Mark 14:15
The spirit truly is *r*, but .... Mark 14:38
was sick, and *r* to die .... Luke 7:2
to make *r* for him .... Luke 9:52
Be ye therefore *r* also .... Luke 12:40
for all things are now *r* .... Luke 14:17
Make *r* wherewith I may ...... Luke 17:8
Lord, I am *r* to go with .... Luke 22:33
but your time is alway *r* .... John 7:6
they made *r*, he fell into a .... Acts 10:10
r to depart on the morrow .... Acts 20:7
I am *r* not to be bound .... Acts 21:13
he come near, are *r* to kill .... Acts 23:15
Make *r* two hundred .... Acts 23:23
Achaia was *r* a year ago 2Cor 9:2
that the same might be *r* 2Cor 9:5
line of things made *r* to 2Cor 10:16
third time I am *r* to come 2Cor 12:14
works, *r* to distribute 1Tim 6:18
For I am now *r* to be 2Tim 4:6
to be *r* to every good work .... Titus 3:1
waxeth old is *r* to vanish ...... Heb 8:13
r to be revealed in the last 1Pet 1:5
and be *r* always to give an 1Pet 3:15
r to judge the quick and 1Pet 4:5
lucre, but of a *r* mind 1Pet 5:2
remain, that are *r* to die ...... Rev 3:2
woman..*r* to be delivered ..... Rev 12:4
wife hath made herself *r* ...... Rev 19:7

REAIAH, REAIA (rē-ā'yä)—*"Jehovah sees"*
1. Reubenite 1Chr 5:5
2. Founder of Nethinim family .... Ezra 2:47
3. Calebite family 1Chr 4:2

The children of *R*, the .... Neh 7:50

REAL PROPERTY—*land that is owned*

Characteristic features of:
Property desired .... Gen 23:4
Price stipulated .... Gen 33:19
Posts erected .... Deut 19:14
Posterity remembered .... Num 33:54
Publicity required .... Ruth 4:1-4
Proof documented .... Jer 32:10-17

Unusual examples of:
Monopoly of land established .... Gen 47:20
Sale as a prophetic proof . Jer 32:6-44
Mark of beast required .. Rev 13:16, 17

REALM—*kingdom*
the *r* of Jehoshaphat was 2Chr 20:30
priests and Levites, in my *r* ... Ezra 7:13
astrologers..in all his *r* .... Dan 1:20
to set him over the whole *r* ... Dan 6:3
the *r* of the Chaldeans .... Dan 9:1
against the *r* of Grecia .... Dan 11:2

REAP—*to harvest*

Provisions concerning:
Areas restricted .... Lev 19:9, 10
Times restricted .... Lev 25:1-11
Sin hinders .... Jer 12:13

Figurative of:
Harvest of souls .... John 4:35-38
Trust in God .... Matt 6:2
Gospel age .... Amos 9:13-15
Injustice .... Matt 25:26
Payment for services 1Cor 9:11
Blessings 2Cor 9:6
Reward for righteousness . Gal 6:8, 9
Punishment for sin ...... Hos 10:13
Judgment on the world .. Rev 14:14-16
Final judgment .... Matt 13:30-43

[*also* REAPED, REAPEST, REAPETH; REAPING]
and shall *r* the harvest .... Lev 23:10
of thy field when thou *r* .... Lev 23:22
the field that they do *r* .... Ruth 2:9
r their wheat harvest 1Sam 6:13
and to *r* his harvest 1Sam 8:12
third year sow ye, and *r* 2Kin 19:29
wickedness, *r* the same .... Job 4:8
r every one his corn in the .... Job 24:6
sow in tears shall *r* in joy ..... Ps 126:5
iniquity shall *r* vanity .... Prov 22:8
the clouds shall not *r* .... Eccl 11:4
r the ears with his arm .... Is 17:5
third year sow ye, and *r* ...... Is 37:30
shall *r* the whirlwind .... Hos 8:7
righteousness, *r* in mercy ...... Hos 10:12
sow, but thou shalt not *r* ...... Mic 6:15
r where thou hast not .... Matt 25:24
for they neither sow nor *r* ..... Luke 12:24
r that thou didst not sow ...... Luke 19:21
and *r* that I did not sow ...... Luke 19:22
soweth, that shall he also *r* ... Gal 6:7
have *r* down your fields .... James 5:4
of them which have *r* .... James 5:4

REAPERS—*harvesters*
in the field after the *r* .... Ruth 2:3
servant..set over the *r* .... Ruth 2:5
the *r* among the sheaves ...... Ruth 2:7
out to his father to the *r* 2Kin 4:18

REAR—*to build, erect*

[*also* REARED]
shalt *r* up the tabernacle ...... Ex 26:30
the tabernacle was *r* up .... Ex 40:17
Moses *r* up the tabernacle ..... Ex 40:18
bars thereof, and *r* up his ..... Ex 40:18
neither *r* you up..image .... Lev 26:1
the tabernacle was *r* up .... Num 9:15
r up for himself a pillar 2Sam 18:18
Go up, *r* an altar unto the 2Sam 24:18
he *r* up an altar for Baal 1Kin 16:32
her *r* up altars for Baal 2Kin 21:3
And he *r* up the pillars 2Chr 3:17
he *r* up altars for Baalim 2Chr 33:3
wilt thou *r* it up in three ...... John 2:20

REARWARD—*at the back of something*
which was the *r* of all .... Num 10:25
the *r* came after the ark .... Josh 6:9
in the *r* with Achish 1Sam 29:2
God of Israel will be your *r* ... Is 52:12
the Lord shall be thy *r* .... Is 58:8

REASON—*good cause; to think logically*

Faculty of:
Makes men sane .... Dan 4:36
Prepares for salvation .... Is 1:18
Makes men guilty .... Mark 11:31-33

Inadequacy of:
Biased against the truth . . Mark 2:6-8
Gospel not explained by. . 1Cor 1:18-31
1Cor 2:1-14

[*also* REASONED, REASONING, REASONS]
in the land by *r* of that . . . . Gen 41:31
Canaan fainted by *r* of . . . . Gen 47:13
Israel sighed by *r* of the . . . . Ex 2:23
by *r* of their taskmasters . . . . . . Ex 3:7
corrupted by *r* of..flies . . . . Ex 8:24
be unclean by *r* of a dead . . . . . Num 9:10
by *r* of the anointing . . . . Num 18:8
were afraid by *r* of the fire . . . . Deut 5:5
that is not clean by *r* . . . . Deut 23:10
old by *r* of..journey . . . . Josh 9:13
by *r* of them that . . . . Judg 2:18
may *r* with you before 1Sam 12:7
this is the *r* of the levy 1Kin 9:15
stand to minister by *r* of 2Chr 5:14
by *r* of this..multitude 2Chr 20:15
fall out by *r* of..sickness 2Chr 21:15
which are blackish by *r* . . . . Job 6:16
my words to *r* with him? . . . . . . Job 9:14
and I desire to *r* with God . . . . Job 13:3
Hear now my *r*, and . . . . Job 13:6
r with unprofitable talk? . . . . . . Job 15:3
eye also is dim by *r* of . . . . Job 17:7
and by *r* of his highness I . . . . . Job 31:23
I gave ear to your *r* . . . . Job 32:11
By *r* of the multitude of . . . . . . Job 35:9
cry out by *r* of the arm of . . . . . Job 35:9
speech by *r* of darkness . . . . Job 37:19
by *r* of the disquietness . . . . Ps 38:8
by *r* of the enemy and . . . . Ps 44:16
that shouteth by *r* of wine . . . . . Ps 78:65
mourneth by *r* of affliction . . . . Ps 88:9
if by *r* of strength they be . . . . . Ps 90:10
By *r* of the voice of my . . . . Ps 102:5
not plow by *r* of the cold . . . . . Prov 20:4
men that can render a *r* . . . . Prov 26:16
and the *r* of things . . . . Eccl 7:25
bring forth your strong *r* . . . . . . Is 41:21
by *r* of the inhabitants . . . . Is 49:19
full of branches by *r* . . . . Ezek 19:10
terrors by *r* of the sword . . . . . . Ezek 21:12
By *r* of the abundance of . . . . . Ezek 26:10
thy merchant by *r* of the . . . . . . Ezek 27:12
by *r* of thy brightness . . . . Ezek 28:17
by *r* of the words of the . . . . . . Dan 5:10
by *r* of transgression . . . . Dan 8:12
I cried by *r* of..affliction . . . . . Jon 2:2
by *r* of the multitude . . . . Mic 2:12
they *r* among themselves . . . . . . Matt 16:7
why *r* ye among yourselves . . . . Matt 16:8
they *r* with themselves . . . . Matt 21:25
they *r* among themselves . . . . . . Mark 8:16
Why *r* ye, because ye . . . . Mark 8:17
heard them *r* together . . . . Mark 12:28
the Pharisees began to *r* . . . . . . Luke 5:21
there arose a *r* among . . . . Luke 9:46
they *r* with themselves . . . . Luke 20:5
they communed together and *r*. Luke 24:15
sea arose by *r* of a great . . . . . . John 6:18
by *r* of him many..Jews . . . . John 12:11
It is not *r* that we should . . . . . Acts 6:2
r with them out of the . . . . Acts 17:2
r in the synagogue every . . . . . . Acts 18:4
r would that I should bear . . . . Acts 18:14
as he *r* of righteousness . . . . Acts 24:25
great *r* among themselves . . . . . Acts 28:29
by *r* of him who hath . . . . Rom 8:20
by *r* of the glory that 2Cor 3:10
by *r* hereof he ought, as . . . . . . Heb 5:3
to continue by *r* of death . . . . . Heb 7:23
a *r* of the hope that is in 1Pet 3:15
by *r* of whom the way of 2Pet 2:2
earth by *r* of the other . . . . Rev 8:13
by *r* of the smoke of the pit . . . Rev 9:2
sea by *r* of her costliness . . . . . . Rev 18:19

REASONABLE—*possessing sound judgment*
which is your *r* service . . . . Rom 12:1

REBA (rē'bä)—*"fourth part; sprout; offspring"*
Midianite chief slain by Israelites . . . . Num 31:8; Josh 13:21

REBEKAH, REBECCA (rĕ-bĕk'ä)—*"flattering"*
Daughter of Bethuel . . . . . Gen 22:20-23
Becomes Isaac's wife . . . . Gen 24:15-67
Mother of Esau and Jacob . . . . Gen 25:21-28
Poses as Isaac's sister . . . . Gen 26:6-11
Disturbed by Esau's marriages . . . . Gen 26:34, 35
Causes Jacob to deceive Isaac . . . . Gen 27:1-29
Urges Jacob to leave home . . . . Gen 27:42-46
Burial of, in Machpelah . . Gen 49:31
Mentioned by Paul . . . . . . Rom 9:10

[*also* REBEKAH'S]
and that he was *R* son . . . . Gen 29:12
Deborah *R* nurse died . . . . Gen 35:8

REBEL—*to actively oppose authority; one who actively opposes authority*

Against:
God . . . . Dan 9:5, 9
God's Word . . . . Num 20:24
Davidic kingship 1Kin 12:19
Constituted priesthood . . . Num 17:1-10
Spirit . . . . Is 63:10

Evil of:
Keeps from blessings . . . . Num 20:24
Increases sin . . . . Job 34:37
Needs to be confessed . . . Dan 9:4-12
Characterizes a people . . . Is 65:2

See INSURRECTION

[*also* REBELLED, REBELLEST, REBELLION, REBELLIOUS, REBELS]
the thirteenth year they *r* . . . . . Gen 14:4
r not ye against the Lord . . . . . Num 14:9
Hear now, ye *r*; must we . . . . . Num 20:10
ye *r* against my . . . . Num 27:14
but *r* against the . . . . Deut 1:26
ye have been *r* against . . . . Deut 9:7
ye *r* against the commandment . Deut 9:23
a stubborn and *r* son . . . . Deut 21:18
I know thy *r*, and thy . . . . Deut 31:27
been *r* against the Lord . . . . Deut 31:27
doth *r* against thy . . . . Josh 1:18
r this day against the Lord? . . . Josh 22:16
r not against the Lord . . . . Josh 22:19
Lord, nor *r* against us . . . . Josh 22:19
if it be in *r*, or if in . . . . Josh 22:22
not *r* against the 1Sam 12:14
For *r* is as..witchcraft 1Sam 15:23
of the perverse *r* woman 1Sam 20:30
Moab *r* against Israel 2Kin 1:1
Moab *r* against..Israel 2Kin 3:5
he *r* against..Assyria 2Kin 18:7
that thou *r* against me? 2Kin 18:20
turned and *r* against him 2Kin 24:1
And Israel *r* against the 2Chr 10:19
hath *r* against his lord 2Chr 13:6
he also *r* against king 2Chr 36:13
the *r* and the bad city . . . . Ezra 4:12
r and sedition have been . . . . . . Ezra 4:19
ye do? will ye *r* against . . . . Neh 2:19
thou and the Jews think to *r* . . Neh 6:6
in their *r* appointed a . . . . Neh 9:17
disobedient, and *r* against . . . . . Neh 9:26
that *r* against the light . . . . Job 24:13
they have *r* against thee . . . . Ps 5:10
let not the *r* exalt . . . . Ps 66:7
the *r* dwell in a dry land . . . . . . Ps 68:6
stubborn and *r* generation . . . . . Ps 78:8
r not against his word . . . . Ps 105:28
they *r* against..God . . . . Ps 107:11
evil man seeketh only *r* . . . . Prov 17:11
they have *r* against me . . . . Is 1:2
But if ye refuse and *r*, ye . . . . . Is 1:20
princes are *r*, and . . . . Is 1:23
Woe to the *r* children . . . . Is 30:1
that thou *r* against me? . . . . Is 36:5
I was not *r*, neither turned . . . . Is 50:5
she hath been *r* against . . . . Jer 4:17
a revolting and a *r* heart . . . . . . Jer 5:23
taught *r* against the Lord . . . . . . Jer 28:16
taught *r* against the Lord . . . . . . Jer 29:32
Zedekiah *r* against the . . . . Jer 52:3
r against his commandment . . . . Lam 1:18
transgressed and have *r* . . . . Lam 3:42
to a *r* nation that hath *r* . . . . . . Ezek 2:3
nation that hath *r* against . . . . . Ezek 2:3
though they be a *r* house . . . . . Ezek 2:6
thou *r* like that *r* house . . . . Ezek 2:8
though they be a *r* house . . . . . Ezek 3:9
for they are a *r* house . . . . Ezek 3:27
in the midst of a *r* house . . . . . . Ezek 12:2
for they are a *r* house . . . . Ezek 12:2
Israel, the *r* house . . . . Ezek 12:9
Say now to the *r* house . . . . Ezek 17:12
he *r* against him in . . . . Ezek 17:15
they *r* against me, and . . . . Ezek 20:8
the children *r* against me . . . . . . Ezek 20:21
purge out..the *r* . . . . Ezek 20:38
parable unto the *r* house . . . . . . Ezek 24:3
thou shalt say to the *r* . . . . Ezek 44:6
and they *r* against me . . . . Hos 7:14
hath *r* against her God . . . . Hos 13:16

REBUILDING JERUSALEM—*the activity that followed the return from the Exile*
Permitted by proclamation . . . . Ezra 1:1-4
Opposed . . . . Ezra 4:1-6
Neh 4:1-3
Temple . . . . Ezra 5:1, 2
Ezra 6:14, 15
Walls . . . . Neh 6:15, 16

REBUKE—*to reprimand sharply*

Jesus' power to restrain:
Sea . . . . Matt 8:26
Demons . . . . Matt 17:18
Fever . . . . Luke 4:39
Peter . . . . Mark 8:33

[*also* REBUKED, REBUKES, REBUKETH, REBUKING]
his father *r* him, and said . . . . . Gen 37:10
any wise *r* thy neighbor . . . . Lev 19:17
cursing, vexation, and *r* . . . . Deut 28:20
glean them, and *r* her not . . . . . Ruth 2:16
at the *r* of the Lord 2Sam 22:16
a day of trouble, and of *r* 2Kin 19:3
fathers look thereon, and *r* it . . 1Chr 12:17
and I *r* the nobles, and the . . . . Neh 5:7
O Lord, *r* me not in..anger . . . Ps 6:1
Thou hast *r* the heathen . . . . . . Ps 9:5
were discovered at thy *r* . . . . . . Ps 18:15
O Lord, *r* me not in thy . . . . . . Ps 38:1
R the company of . . . . Ps 68:30
At thy *r*, O God of Jacob . . . . . Ps 76:6
perish at the *r* of thy . . . . Ps 80:16
At thy *r* they fled; at the . . . . . Ps 104:7
He *r* the Red Sea also, and . . . Ps 106:9
hast *r* the proud that are . . . . . . Ps 119:21
he that *r* a wicked man . . . . Prov 9:7
r a wise man, and he will . . . . . Prov 9:8
a scorner heareth not *r* . . . . Prov 13:1
them that *r* him shall be . . . . . . Prov 24:25
He that *r* a man afterwards . . . Prov 28:23
better to hear the *r* of the . . . . . Eccl 7:5
and shall *r* many people . . . . . . Is 2:4
God shall *r* them, and . . . . Is 17:13
r of his people shall he . . . . Is 25:8
shall flee at the *r* of one . . . . . . Is 30:17
the *r* of five shall ye flee . . . . . . Is 30:17
day of trouble, and of *r* . . . . Is 37:3
behold, at my *r* I dry up . . . . . . Is 50:2
Lord, the *r* of thy God . . . . Is 51:20
with thee, nor *r* thee . . . . Is 54:9
his *r* with flames of fire . . . . Is 66:15
for thy sake..suffered *r* . . . . Jer 15:15
in fury and in furious *r* . . . . Ezek 5:15
upon them with furious *r* . . . . . . Ezek 25:17
desolate in the day of *r* . . . . Hos 5:9
They hate him that *r* in . . . . Amos 5:10
r strong nations afar off . . . . Mic 4:3
He *r* the sea, and maketh . . . . . Nah 1:4
The Lord *r* thee, O Satan . . . . . Zech 3:2

R

chosen Jerusalem *r* thee .... Zech 3:2
and began to *r* him .... Matt 16:22
and the disciples *r* them .... Matt 19:13
the multitude *r* them .... Matt 20:31
and Jesus *r* him, saying .... Mark 1:25
he arose, and *r* the wind ...... Mark 4:39
him, and began to *r* him ...... Mark 8:32
he *r* Peter, saying, Get .... Mark 8:33
he *r* the foul spirit, saying ..... Mark 9:25
his disciples *r* those that ...... Mark 10:13
And Jesus *r* him, saying .... Luke 4:35
he *r* then, suffered them ...... Luke 4:41
he arose, and *r* the wind ...... Luke 8:24
Jesus *r* the unclean spirit ...... Luke 9:42
trespass against thee, *r* him .... Luke 17:3
disciples saw it, they *r* .... Luke 18:15
Master, *r* thy disciples .... Luke 19:39
other answering *r* him .... Luke 23:40
the sons of God, without *r* .... Phil 2:15
R not an elder, but entreat 1Tim 5:1
Wherefore *r* them sharply ..... Titus 1:13
when thou art *r* of him .... Heb 12:5
But was *r* for his iniquity 2Pet 2:16
but said, The Lord *r* thee ..... Jude 9
many as I love, I *r* and .... Rev 3:19

REBUKE FOR SIN—*a reprimand for sin*

Manner of:
Before all 1Tim 5:20
With longsuffering 2Tim 4:2
Sharply .... Titus 2:15
With all authority .... Titus 2:15

Examples of:
Isaac by Abimelech ...... Gen 26:6-11
Laban by Jacob .... Gen 31:36-42
Saul by Samuel 1Sam 13:13
Ahab by Elijah 1Kin 21:20
Judah by Zechariah 2Chr 24:20
Israel by Ezra .... Ezra 10:10, 11
David by God .... Ps 39:11
Peter by Paul .... Gal 2:11-14

REBUKER—*one who reprimands*
have been a *r* of them .... Hos 5:2

RECAH (rē'kä)—*"uttermost part"—a village in Judah (same as Rechah)*
These are the men of ***R*** 1Chr 4:12

RECALL—*call back*
This I *r* to my mind .... Lam 3:21

RECEIPT—*refers to place where taxes were collected*
Matthew..at the *r* of custom ... Matt 9:9
Alphaeus..at the *r* of custom .. Mark 2:14
Levi..at the *r* of custom .... Luke 5:27

RECEIVE—*to take into one's possession*

Good things:
Word .... James 1:21
Holy Spirit .... Acts 2:38
Christ Jesus .... Col 2:6
Forgiveness .... Acts 26:18
Petitions 1John 3:22
Reward 1Cor 3:8, 14

Evil things:
Punishment .... Rom 1:27
Wrong .... Col 3:25
Beast's mark .... Rev 13:16
Reward for unrighteousness 2Pet 2:13

[*also* RECEIVED, RECEIVEDST, RECEIVEST, RECEIVETH, RECEIVING]

to *r* thy brother's blood .... Gen 4:11
then *r* my present at .... Gen 33:10
to *r* his pledge from the .... Gen 38:20
thou shalt *r* them of .... Ex 29:25
let her be *r* in again .... Num 12:14
ye *r* of the children of .... Num 18:28
I have *r* commandment .... Num 23:20
have *r* their inheritance .... Num 34:14
half tribe have *r* their .... Num 34:15
whereunto they are *r* .... Num 36:3
shall *r* of thy words .... Deut 33:3
Gadites have *r* their .... Josh 13:8
had not yet *r* their .... Josh 18:2
would not have *r* a burnt ..... Judg 13:23
man that *r* me to house .... Judg 19:18
which thou shalt *r* of 1Sam 10:4
hand have I *r* any bribe 1Sam 12:3
So David *r* of her hand 1Sam 25:35
r a thousand skekels of 2Sam 18:12
and thou shalt *r* them 1Kin 5:9
too little to *r* the burnt 1Kin 8:64
merchants *r* the..yarn 1Kin 10:28
I stand, I will *r* none 2Kin 5:16
not *r* at his hands that 2Kin 5:20
r no more money of your 2Kin 12:7
Hezekiah *r* the letter of 2Kin 19:14
David *r* them, and made 1Chr 12:18
merchants *r* the linen yarn 2Chr 1:16
r and held..baths 2Chr 4:5
not able to *r* the burnt 2Chr 7:7
and the priests *r* the blood 2Chr 29:22
they *r* of the hand of the 2Chr 30:16
from him: but he *r* it not ..... Esth 4:4
we *r* good at the hand of ..... Job 2:10
and shall we not *r* evil? ...... Job 2:10
and mine ear *r* a little .... Job 4:12
R, I pray thee, the law .... Job 22:22
shall *r* of the Almighty .... Job 27:13
what *r* he of thine hand? ...... Job 35:7
the Lord will *r* my prayer ..... Ps 6:9
r the blessing from the Lord ... Ps 24:5
grave; for he shall *r* me .... Ps 49:15
thou hast *r* gifts for men ...... Ps 68:18
afterward *r* me to glory .... Ps 73:24
shall *r* the congregation .... Ps 75:2
To *r* the instruction of .... Prov 1:3
if thou wilt *r* my words .... Prov 2:1
Hear..and *r* my sayings .... Prov 4:10
R my instruction, and not ..... Prov 8:10
wise..will *r* commandments .... Prov 10:8
Hear..and *r* instruction .... Prov 19:20
he *r* knowledge .... Prov 21:11
looked.. and *r* instruction ..... Prov 24:32
but he that *r* gifts .... Prov 29:4
And Hezekiah *r* the letter ..... Is 37:14
she hath *r* of the Lord's .... Is 40:2
they *r* no correction .... Jer 2:30
refused to *r* correction .... Jer 5:3
nor *r* correction .... Jer 7:28
your ear *r* the word of his ..... Jer 9:20
hear, nor *r* instruction .... Jer 17:23
not hearkened..to *r* instruction Jer 32:33
Will ye not *r* instruction to .... Jer 35:13
thee *r* in thine heart .... Ezek 3:10
when thou shalt *r* thy .... Ezek 16:61
not *r* usury nor increase .... Ezek 18:17
shall *r* no more reproach ...... Ezek 36:30
ye shall *r* of me gifts and ..... Dan 2:6
Ephraim shall *r* shame .... Hos 10:6
and *r* us graciously .... Hos 14:2
she *r* not correction; she ...... Zeph 3:2
or *r* it with good will at .... Mal 2:13
every one that asketh *r* .... Matt 7:8
ye have *r*, freely give .... Matt 10:8
whosoever shall not *r* you ..... Matt 10:14
He that *r* you *r* me .... Matt 10:40
r me *r* him that sent me ...... Matt 10:40
He that *r* a prophet in the .... Matt 10:41
shall *r* a prophet's reward ..... Matt 10:41
he that *r* a righteous man ..... Matt 10:41
shall *r* a righteous man's ...... Matt 10:41
blind *r* their sight, and .... Matt 11:5
he which *r* seed by the .... Matt 13:19
anon with joy *r* it .... Matt 13:20
r seed among the thorns ...... Matt 13:22
they that *r* tribute money ..... Matt 17:24
child in my name *r* me .... Matt 18:5
they *r* every man a penny ..... Matt 20:9
they should have *r* more ...... Matt 20:10
they likewise *r* every man ..... Matt 20:10
And when they had *r* it .... Matt 20:11
ask..believing, ye shall *r* ...... Matt 21:22
r the greater damnation .... Matt 23:14
he that had *r* the five .... Matt 25:16
But he that had *r* one .... Matt 25:18
that had *r* two talents .... Matt 25:22
have *r* mine own with .... Matt 25:27
was no room to *r* them .... Mark 2:2
r it with gladness .... Mark 4:16
whosoever shall not *r* you ..... Mark 6:11
which they have *r* to hold ..... Mark 7:4
shall *r* one of such children .... Mark 9:37
in my name, *r* me .... Mark 9:37
shall *r* me, *r* not me, but ...... Mark 9:37
shall not *r* the kingdom of .... Mark 10:15
that I might *r* my sight .... Mark 10:51
immediately he *r* his sight ..... Mark 10:52
believe that ye *r* them .... Mark 11:24
r from the husbandmen .... Mark 12:2
myrrh: but he *r* it not .... Mark 15:23
he was *r* up into heaven ...... Mark 16:19
have *r* your consolation .... Luke 6:24
of whom ye hope to *r* .... Luke 6:34
to *r* as much again .... Luke 6:34
r the word with joy .... Luke 8:13
the people gladly *r* him .... Luke 8:40
whosoever will not *r* you ...... Luke 9:5
he *r* them, and spake unto .... Luke 9:11
r this child in my name *r* me .. Luke 9:48
shall *r* me *r* him that sent me . Luke 9:48
ye enter, and they *r* you ...... Luke 10:8
Martha *r* him into..house ..... Luke 10:38
This man *r* sinners, and .... Luke 15:2
r him safe and sound .... Luke 15:27
r me into their houses .... Luke 16:4
in thy lifetime *r* thy good ..... Luke 16:25
shall not *r* the kingdom of .... Luke 18:17
immediately he *r* his sight ..... Luke 18:43
that I may *r* my sight .... Luke 18:41
came down, and *r* him .... Luke 19:6
to *r* for himself a kingdom .... Luke 19:12
shall *r* greater damnation ...... Luke 20:47
for we *r* the due reward .... Luke 23:41
and his own *r* him not .... John 1:11
his fullness have all we *r* ...... John 1:16
and ye *r* not our witness ...... John 3:11
no man *r* his testimony .... John 3:32
that hath *r* his testimony ...... John 3:33
he that reapeth *r* wages .... John 4:36
the Galileans *r* him .... John 4:45
But I *r* not testimony .... John 5:34
name, and ye *r* me not .... John 5:43
name, him ye will *r* .... John 5:43
they willingly *r* him into ...... John 6:21
day *r* circumcision .... John 7:23
washed, and I *r* sight .... John 9:11
blind, and *r* his sight .... John 9:18
him that had *r* his sight .... John 9:18
commandment have I *r* of ..... John 10:18
and *r* not my words, hath ..... John 12:48
r whomsoever I send *r* me .... John 13:20
he that *r* me *r* him that ...... John 13:20
He then having *r* the sop ..... John 13:30
and *r* you unto myself .... John 14:3
for he shall *r* of mine .... John 16:14
they have *r* them, and .... John 17:8
having *r* a band of men .... John 18:3
Jesus..*r* the vinegar .... John 19:30
R ye the Holy Ghost .... John 20:22
But ye shall *r* power, after .... Acts 1:8
a cloud *r* him out of their ..... Acts 1:9
having *r* of the Father .... Acts 2:33
expecting to *r* something ...... Acts 3:5
feet..bones *r* strength .... Acts 3:7
r the lively oracles to give ..... Acts 7:38
Lord Jesus, *r* my spirit .... Acts 7:59
Samaria had *r* the word .... Acts 8:14
might *r* the Holy Ghost .... Acts 8:15
that he might *r* his sight ...... Acts 9:12
he *r* sight forthwith, and ...... Acts 9:18
vessel was *r* up again into ..... Acts 10:16
shall *r* remission of sins .... Acts 10:43
Gentiles had also *r*..word ..... Acts 11:1
they were *r* of the church ..... Acts 15:4
not lawful for us to *r* .... Acts 16:21
having *r* such a charge .... Acts 16:24
whom Jason hath *r*: and ...... Acts 17:7
r a commandment unto .... Acts 17:15
exhorting the disciples to *r* .... Acts 18:27
Have ye *r* the Holy Ghost ..... Acts 19:2
which I have *r* of the Lord .... Acts 20:24
blessed to give than to *r* ...... Acts 20:35
the brethren *r* us gladly .... Acts 21:17

from whom also I *r* letters .... Acts 22:5
Brother Saul, *r* thy sight .... Acts 22:13
r authority from..priests .... Acts 26:10
fire, and *r* us every one .... Acts 28:2
We neither *r* letters out .... Acts 28:21
r grace and apostleship .... Rom 1:5
r the sign of circumcision .... Rom 4:11
have now *r* the atonement .... Rom 5:11
r abundance of grace .... Rom 5:17
have not *r* the spirit of .... Rom 8:15
r the Spirit of adoption .... Rom 8:15
shall the *r* of them be .... Rom 11:15
r to themselves damnation .... Rom 13:2
that is weak in the faith *r* .... Rom 14:1
for God hath *r* him .... Rom 14:3
r ye one another, as Christ .... Rom 15:7
as Christ also *r* us to the .... Rom 15:7
That ye *r* her in the Lord .... Rom 16:2
have *r*, not the spirit of 1Cor 2:12
the natural man *r* not 1Cor 2:14
that thou didst not *r*? 1Cor 4:7
didst *r* it, why..glory 1Cor 4:7
as if thou hadst not *r* it? 1Cor 4:7
all, but one *r* the prize? 1Cor 9:24
I have *r* of the Lord that 1Cor 11:23
church may *r* edifying 1Cor 14:5
which also ye have *r*, and 1Cor 15:1
as we have *r* mercy, we 2Cor 4:1
r the things done in..body 2Cor 5:10
ye *r* not the grace of God 2Cor 6:1
R us; we have wronged 2Cor 7:2
fear..trembling ye *r* him 2Cor 7:15
that we would *r* the gift 2Cor 8:4
or if ye *r* another spirit 2Cor 11:4
which ye have not *r* 2Cor 11:4
you than that ye have *r* .... Gal 1:9
R ye the Spirit by..works .... Gal 3:2
might *r* the promise of the .... Gal 3:14
we might *r* the adoption .... Gal 4:5
but *r* me as an angel of .... Gal 4:14
shall he *r* of the Lord .... Eph 6:8
R him..in the Lord .... Phil 2:29
have both learned, and *r* .... Phil 4:9
concerning giving and *r* .... Phil 4:15
r the reward of the .... Col 3:24
whom ye *r* commandments .... Col 4:10
if he come unto you *r* him .... Col 4:10
r the word in..affliction 1Thess 1:6
ye *r* the word of God 1Thess 2:13
ye *r* it not as the word of 1Thess 2:13
as ye have *r* of us how ye 1Thess 4:1
r not the love of the truth 2Thess 2:10
tradition which he *r* of us 2Thess 3:6
world, *r* up into glory 1Tim 3:16
God hath created to be *r* 1Tim 4:3
be *r* with thanksgiving 1Tim 4:4
elder *r* not an accusation 1Tim 5:19
thou therefore *r* him, that is .... Philem 12
a partner, *r* him as myself .... Philem 17
r a just recompense of .... Heb 2:2
r blessing from God .... Heb 6:7
who *r* the office of the .... Heb 7:5
from them *r* tithes of .... Heb 7:6
but there he *r* them, of .... Heb 7:8
might *r* the promise of .... Heb 9:15
r the knowledge of..truth .... Heb 10:26
ye might *r* the promise .... Heb 10:36
after *r* for an inheritance .... Heb 11:8
Sarah herself *r* strength to .... Heb 11:11
he that had *r* the promises .... Heb 11:17
she had *r* the spies with .... Heb 11:31
through faith, *r* not the .... Heb 11:39
every son whom he *r* .... Heb 12:6
we *r* a kingdom which .... Heb 12:28
r anything of the Lord .... James 1:7
had *r* the messengers .... James 2:25
shall *r*..condemnation .... James 3:1
Ye ask, and *r* not, because .... James 4:3
until he *r* the early and .... James 5:7
R the end of your faith 1Pet 1:9
vain conversation *r* by 1Pet 1:18
every man hath *r* the gift 1Pet 4:10
r a crown of glory that 1Pet 5:4
he *r* from God the Father 2Pet 1:17
anointing which ye have *r* 1John 2:27
If we *r* the witness of men 1John 5:9
have *r* a commandment 2John 4
but that we *r* a full reward 2John 8
therefore ought to *r* such 3John 8
among them, *r* us not 3John 9
saving he that *r* it .... Rev 2:17
even as I *r* of my Father .... Rev 2:27
thou hast *r* and heard .... Rev 3:3
to *r* glory and honor and .... Rev 4:11
Lamb..slain to *r* power .... Rev 5:12
r a mark in their right hand .... Rev 13:16
r his mark in his forehead .... Rev 14:9
whosoever *r* the mark of .... Rev 14:11
which have *r* no kingdom .... Rev 17:12
but *r* power as kings one .... Rev 17:12
ye *r* not of her plagues .... Rev 18:4
that had *r* the mark of the .... Rev 19:20
r his mark upon their .... Rev 20:4

RECEIVER—*one who takes possession, one who receives*

the scribe? where is the *r* .... Is 33:18

RECHAB (rē'kăb)—*"companionship"*

1. Assassin of Ish-bosheth .. 2Sam 4:2, 6
2. Father of Jehonadab, founder of the Rechabites 2Kin 10:15-23
   Related to the Kenites .. 1Chr 2:55
3. Postexilic ruler .... Neh 3:14

R our father commanded .... Jer 35:6
Jonadab the son of ***R*** .... Jer 35:14
son of ***R*** shall not want .... Jer 35:19

RECHABITES (rē'kăb-īts)—*descendants of Rechab*

Kenite clan fathered by Rechab and believing in the simple life .... Jer 35:1-19

RECIPROCATION—*mutual interchange*

Gentiles to Jews .... Rom 15:27
Students to teachers .... Gal 6:6

RECKON—*to assign; compute; consider; judge*

[*also* RECKONED, RECKONETH, RECKONING]

he shall *r* with him that .... Lev 25:50
r unto him the money .... Lev 27:18
shall *r* the instruments .... Num 4:32
offering shall be *r* unto .... Num 18:27
shall not be *r* among the .... Num 23:9
Beeroth also was *r* to 2Sam 4:2
they *r* not with the men 2Kin 12:15
was no *r* made with them 2Kin 22:7
genealogy is not to be *r* 1Chr 5:1
were *r* by genealogies in 1Chr 5:17
r in all by..genealogies 1Chr 7:5
were *r* by genealogies 1Chr 9:1
they were in one *r* 1Chr 23:11
were *r* by genealogies 2Chr 31:19
that were *r* by genealogy .... Ezra 2:62
him were *r* by genealogy .... Ezra 8:3
might be *r* by genealogy .... Neh 7:5
cannot be *r* up in order .... Ps 40:5
I *r* till morning, that, as .... Is 38:13
they shall *r* unto him .... Ezek 44:26
when he had begun to *r* .... Matt 18:24
cometh, and *r* with them .... Matt 25:19
was *r* among the .... Luke 22:37
the reward not *r* of grace .... Rom 4:4
How was it then *r*? .... Rom 4:10
r ye also yourselves to be .... Rom 6:11
I *r* that the sufferings .... Rom 8:18

RECOMMENDED—*entrusted; committed*

been *r* to the grace of God .... Acts 14:26
being *r* by the brethren .... Acts 15:40

RECOMPENSE—*to pay back in kind*

On the righteous:

Even now .... Prov 11:31
According to one's righteousness .... Ps 18:20, 24
Eagerly expected .... Heb 10:35

On the unrighteous:

Justly deserved .... Rom 1:27
Belongs to God only .... Heb 10:30
Will surely come .... Jer 51:56
To the next generation .... Jer 32:18
Fully at the second advent 2Thess 1:6

[*also* RECOMPENSED, RECOMPENSES, RECOMPENSING]

he shall *r* his trespass .... Num 5:7
trespass be *r* unto the Lord .... Num 5:8
vengeance, and *r* .... Deut 32:35
The Lord *r* thy work, and .... Ruth 2:12
king *r* it me with such a 2Sam 19:36
of my hands hath he *r* me 2Sam 22:21
by *r* his way upon his own 2Chr 6:23
for vanity shall be his *r* .... Job 15:31
he will *r* it, whether thou .... Job 34:33
the *r* of a man's hands .... Prov 12:14
Say not thou, I will *r* evil .... Prov 20:22
year of *r* for..controversy .... Is 34:8
even God with a *r* .... Is 35:4
his adversaries, *r* to his .... Is 59:18
he will repay *r* .... Is 59:18
r even *r* into their bosom .... Is 65:6
rendereth *r* to his enemies .... Is 66:6
I will *r* their iniquity .... Jer 16:18
Shall evil be *r* for good? .... Jer 18:20
r them according to their .... Jer 25:14
r her according to her work .... Jer 50:29
will render unto her a *r* .... Jer 51:6
Render unto them a *r* .... Lam 3:64
will *r* upon thee all thine .... Ezek 7:3
will *r* thee for all thine .... Ezek 7:8
will *r* their way upon .... Ezek 9:10
r their way upon their own .... Ezek 11:21
will *r* thy way upon .... Ezek 16:43
will I *r* upon his own head .... Ezek 17:19
have I *r* upon, their heads .... Ezek 22:31
shall *r* your lewdness .... Ezek 23:49
the days of *r* are come .... Hos 9:7
to his doings will he *r* him .... Hos 12:2
will ye render me a *r*? .... Joel 3:4
if ye *r* me, swiftly and .... Joel 3:4
return your *r* upon .... Joel 3:4
and a *r* be made thee .... Luke 14:12
they cannot *r* thee: for .... Luke 14:14
be *r* at the resurrection .... Luke 14:14
stumbling block, and a *r* unto .... Rom 11:9
shall be *r* unto him again? .... Rom 11:35
R to no man evil for evil .... Rom 12:17
Now for a *r* in the same 2Cor 6:13
received a just *r* of reward .... Heb 2:2
unto the *r* of the reward .... Heb 11:26

RECONCILIATION—*making peace between enemies*

Effected on men while:

Helpless .... Rom 5:6
Sinners .... Rom 5:8
Enemies of God .... Rom 5:10
God-haters .... Col 1:21

Accomplished by:

God in Christ 2Cor 5:18
Christ's death .... Rom 5:10
Christ's blood .... Eph 2:13

Productive of:

Peace with God .... Rom 5:1
Access to God .... Rom 5:2
Union of Jews and Gentiles .... Eph 2:14

[*also* RECONCILE, RECONCILED, RECONCILING]

r withal in the holy place .... Lev 6:30
sanctified it, to make *r* .... Lev 8:15
made an end of *r* the holy .... Lev 16:20
r himself unto his master? 1Sam 29:4
made *r* with their blood 2Chr 29:24
to make *r* for them .... Ezek 45:15
so shall ye *r* the house .... Ezek 45:20
and to make *r* for iniquity .... Dan 9:24
first be *r* to thy brother .... Matt 5:24
be the *r* of the world .... Rom 11:15
or be *r* to her husband 1Cor 7:11
r the world unto himself 2Cor 5:19
in Christ's stead, be ye *r* 2Cor 5:20
r both unto God in one .... Eph 2:16

r all things unto himself . . . . . . .Col 1:20
make r for the sins of the . . . . .Heb 2:17

RECORD—*to set down in writing; a written recollection of past events*

[*also* RECORDED, RECORDS]
where I r my name I will . . . . .Ex 20:24
and earth to r this day . . . . . . .Deut 30:19
and earth to r against . . . . . . .Deut 31:28
and to r, and to thank and 1Chr 16:4
made in the book of the r . . . . .Ezra 4:15
and therein was a r thus . . . . . .Ezra 6:2
were r chief of the fathers . . . . .Neh 12:22
book of r of the chronicles . . . .Esth 6:1
and my r is on high . . . . .Job 16:19
faithful witnesses to r . . . . .Is 8:2
And this is the r of John . . . . . .John 1:19
bare r that this is the Son . . . . .John 1:34
Thou bearest r of thyself . . . . . .John 8:13
thyself; thy r is not true . . . . . . .John 8:13
Though I bear r of myself . . . . .John 8:14
myself, yet my r is true . . . . . . .John 8:14
from the dead, bare r . . . . .John 12:17
And he that saw it bare r . . . . .John 19:35
his r is true: and he . . . . .John 19:35
I take you to r this day . . . . . . .Acts 20:26
bear them r that they . . . . .Rom 10:2
I call God for a r upon 2Cor 1:23
I bear r, yea, and beyond 2Cor 8:3
I bear you r, that, if it . . . . .Gal 4:15
For God is my r, how . . . . .Phil 1:8
For I bear him r, that he . . . . .Col 4:13
that bear r in heaven 1John 5:7
r that God gave of his Son 1John 5:10
this is the r, that God 1John 5:11
yea, and we also bear r 3John 12
and ye know that our r is 3John 12
Who bare r of the word of . . . .Rev 1:2

RECORDER—*high court official*
Records events 2Sam 8:16
Represents the king 2Kin 18:18
Repairs the Temple 2Chr 34:8

the son of Ahilud, the r 1Kin 4:3
the son of Ahilud, r 1Chr 18:15
and Joah, Asaph's son, the r . .Is 36:3
Joah, the son of Asaph, the r. .Is 36:22

RECOUNT—*narrate*
He shall r his worthies . . . . .Nah 2:5

RECOVER—*to restore lost things; become well*

Of sickness:
By remedy 2Kin 20:7
By a miracle 2Kin 5:3-14
Sought from idols 2Kin 1:2-17
Prayed for . . . . .Is 38:16

Of physical things:
Defeat in war 2Chr 13:19, 20
Conquered territory 2Sam 8:3
2Kin 13:25
Captured people . . . . .Jer 41:16

[*also* RECOVERED, RECOVERING]
did ye not r them within . . . . . .Judg 11:26
and without fail r all 1Sam 30:8
r all that the Amalekites 1Sam 30:18
the spoil that we have r 1Sam 30:22
Shall I r of this disease? 2Kin 8:8
thou shouldest surely r 2Kin 8:14
how he r Damascus, and 2Kin 14:28
king of Syria r Elath 2Kin 16:6
could not r themselves 2Chr 14:13
that I may r strength . . . . .Ps 39:13
r the remnant of his people . . .Is 11:11
was r of his sickness . . . . .Is 38:9
had been sick, and was r . . . . . .Is 39:1
daughter of my people r? . . . . .Jer 8:22
will r my wool and my . . . . .Hos 2:9
sick, and they shall r . . . . .Mark 16:18
r of sight to the blind . . . . .Luke 4:18
may r themselves out of 2Tim 2:26

RECTITUDE—*uprightness of life*
True way of living . . . . . . .Prov 4:23-27

RED—*a color whose hue resembles blood*
Blood 2Kin 3:22
Wine . . . . .Prov 23:31
Complexion . . . . .Lam 4:7

[*also* REDDISH, REDNESS]
first came out r, all over . . . . . .Gen 25:25
His eyes shall be r with . . . . . . .Gen 49:12
rams' skins dyed r, and . . . . . . .Ex 25:5
of rams' skins dyed r . . . . .Ex 26:14
rams' skins dyed r, and . . . . . . .Ex 35:7
of rams' skins dyed r . . . . .Ex 36:19
of rams' skins dyed r . . . . .Ex 39:34
white, and somewhat r . . . . .Lev 13:19
white r sore..a leprosy . . . . .Lev 13:42
be greenish or r in the . . . . .Lev 13:49
strakes, greenish or r . . . . .Lev 14:37
bring thee a r heifer . . . . .Num 19:2
pavement of r, and blue . . . . . .Esth 1:6
cup, and the wine is r . . . . .Ps 75:8
who hath r of eyes? . . . . .Prov 23:29
though..be r like crimson . . . . .Is 1:18
A vineyard of r wine . . . . .Is 27:2
art thou r in thine apparel . . . .Is 63:2
of his mighty men is made r . . .Nah 2:3
man riding upon a r horse . . . .Zech 1:8
were there r horses . . . . .Zech 1:8
In..chariot were r horses . . . . . .Zech 6:2
weather: for the sky is r . . . . . .Matt 16:2
another horse that was r . . . . . .Rev 6:4
behold a great r dragon . . . . . . .Rev 12:3

RED DRAGON—*another name for Satan*
Seen in John's vision . . . .Rev 12:3-17

RED HEIFER—*See* HEIFER

RED HORSE—*symbol of war*
Seen in John's vision . . . .Rev 6:4

RED SEA—*sea of reeds*
Boundary of promised land . . . . .Ex 23:31
Israelites camp by . . . . . . .Num 33:10, 11
Ships built on 1Kin 9:26
Locusts destroyed . . . . . . .Ex 10:19
Divided by God . . . . .Ex 14:21
Crossed by Israel . . . . .Ex 14:22, 29
Egyptians drowned . . . . . .Ex 15:4, 21

cast them into the R S . . . . .Ex 10:19
the wilderness of the R S . . . . .Ex 13:18
by the way of the R S . . . . .Num 14:25
Hor by the way of the R S . . . .Num 21:4
and encamped by the R S . . . . .Num 33:10
the plain over against the R S .Deut 1:1
by the way of the R S . . . . .Deut 2:1
dried up the water of the R S .Josh 2:10
your God did to the R S . . . . . .Josh 4:23
horsemen unto the R S . . . . . . .Josh 24:6
the wilderness unto the R S . . .Judg 11:16
their cry by the R S . . . . .Neh 9:9
him at the sea, even at the R S.Ps 106:7
He rebuked the R S also . . . . . .Ps 106:9
terrible things by the R S into .Ps 106:22
which divided the R S . . . . .Ps 136:13
was heard in the R S . . . . .Jer 49:21
Egypt, and in the R S . . . . .Acts 7:36
passed through the R S as by . .Heb 11:29

REDEEM—*to save from distress*

[*also* REDEEMED, REDEEMEDST, REDEEMETH, REDEEMING]
angel which r me from all . . . . .Gen 48:16
r you with a stretched out . . . . .Ex 6:6
of an ass thou shalt r . . . . .Ex 13:13
if thou wilt not r it, then . . . . . .Ex 13:13
first-born..shalt thou r . . . . .Ex 13:13
people which thou has r . . . . . . .Ex 15:13
then shall he let her be r . . . . . .Ex 21:8
of an ass thou shalt r . . . . .Ex 34:20
if thou r him not, then . . . . .Ex 34:20
first-born..thou shalt r . . . . .Ex 34:20
not at all r, nor freedom . . . . . .Lev 19:20
any of his kin come to r it . . . .Lev 25:25
he r that which his brother . . . .Lev 25:25
if the man have none to r . . . . .Lev 25:26
himself be able to r it . . . . .Lev 25:26
he may r it within a..year . . . . .Lev 25:29
within a..year may he r it . . . . .Lev 25:29
r within the space of..year . . . .Lev 25:30
he is sold he may be r . . . . .Lev 25:48
his brethren may r him . . . . . . .Lev 25:48
uncle's son, may r him . . . . .Lev 25:49
his family may r him . . . . .Lev 25:49
able, he may r himself . . . . .Lev 25:49
But if he will at all r it . . . . . .Lev 27:13
the field will..r it . . . . .Lev 27:19
man, it shall not be r . . . . .Lev 27:20
he shall r it according to . . . . .Lev 27:27
thing..shall be sold or r . . . . . . .Lev 27:28
holy; it shall not be r . . . . .Lev 27:33
those that are to be r of . . . . . .Num 3:46
were r by the Levites . . . . .Num 3:49
of man shalt thou..r . . . . .Num 18:15
beasts shalt thou r . . . . .Num 18:15
that are to be r from a . . . . .Num 18:16
goat, thou shalt not r . . . . .Num 18:17
thou hast r through thy . . . . . . .Deut 9:26
r you out of..bondage . . . . .Deut 13:5
the Lord thy God r thee . . . . . .Deut 15:15
Israel, whom thou hast r . . . . . .Deut 21:8
the Lord thy God r thee . . . . . .Deut 24:18
If thou wilt r it, r it . . . . .Ruth 4:4
If thou wilt not r it . . . . .Ruth 4:4
is none to r it beside . . . . .Ruth 4:4
And he said, I will r it . . . . .Ruth 4:4
I cannot r it for myself . . . . . . .Ruth 4:6
r thou my right to thyself . . . . .Ruth 4:6
for I cannot r it . . . . .Ruth 4:6
concerning r and . . . . .Ruth 4:7
hath r my soul out of all 2Sam 4:9
whom God went to r for 2Sam 7:23
which thou r to thee 2Sam 7:23
hath r my soul out of all 1Kin 1:29
God went to r to be his 1Chr 17:21
whom thou hast r out of 1Chr 17:21
hast r by thy power . . . . .Neh 1:10
it in our power to r them . . . . .Neh 5:5
r our brethern the Jews . . . . . . .Neh 5:8
he shall r thee from death . . . . .Job 5:20
R me from the hand..mighty . .Job 6:23
R Israel, O God, out of all . . . .Ps 25:22
r me, and be merciful . . . . .Ps 26:11
hast r me, O Lord God . . . . . . .Ps 31:5
Lord r the soul of his . . . . .Ps 34:22
r us for thy mercies . . . . .Ps 44:26
can..r his brother . . . . .Ps 49:7
unto my soul, and r it . . . . .Ps 69:18
soul, which thou hast r . . . . .Ps 71:23
He shall r their soul from . . . . .Ps 72:14
hast with thine arm r thy . . . . . .Ps 77:15
r them from the hand . . . . .Ps 106:10
Let the r of the Lord say . . . . .Ps 107:2
hath r from the hand . . . . .Ps 107:2
r Israel from..iniquities . . . . . . .Ps 130:8
Zion shall be r with . . . . .Is 1:27
Lord, who r Abraham . . . . .Is 29:22
but the r shall walk there . . . . .Is 35:9
Fear not: for I have r thee . . . .Is 43:1
unto thee for I have r thee . . . .Is 44:22
The Lord hath r..Jacob . . . . . . .Is 48:20
at all, that it cannot r . . . . .Is 50:2
shall be r without money . . . . . .Is 52:3
he hath r Jerusalem . . . . .Is 52:9
people, The r of the Lord . . . . .Is 62:12
the year of my r is come . . . . .Is 63:4
I will r thee out of the . . . . .Jer 15:21
the Lord hath r Jacob . . . . .Jer 31:11
thou hast r my life . . . . .Lam 3:58
though I have r them, yet . . . . .Hos 7:13
shall r thee from the hand . . . .Mic 4:10
r thee out of the house of . . . . .Mic 6:4
visited and r his people . . . . . . .Luke 1:68
should have r Israel . . . . .Luke 24:21
R the time, because the . . . . . . .Eph 5:16
are without, r the time . . . . .Col 4:5
r us to God by thy blood . . . . .Rev 5:9

REDEEMER—*one who saves others from distress; a Messianic title for Jesus*
I know that my R liveth . . . . . . .Job 19:25
Lord, my strength, and my r . .Ps 19:14

and the high God their *r* ...... Ps 78:35
For their *R* is mighty; he ...... Prov 23:11
saith the Lord, and thy *R* ..... Is 41:14
saith the Lord, your *R* .... Is 43:14
his *R* the Lord of hosts .... Is 44:6
As for our *R*, the Lord of ..... Is 47:4
Thus saith the Lord, thy *R* .... Is 48:17
the *R* of Israel, and his .... Is 49:7
thy *R* the Holy One of Israel .. Is 54:5
the *R* shall come to Zion ...... Is 59:20
thy Savior and thy *R* .... Is 60:16
Lord, art our father, our *r* .... Is 63:16
Their *R* is strong .... Jer 50:34

REDEMPTION—*salvation accomplished by paying the price for sin*

Defined as deliverance from:
Curse of the Law .... Gal 3:13
Bondage of the Law ..... Gal 4:5
Iniquity .... Titus 2:14
Enemies .... Ps 136:24
Destruction .... Ps 103:4
Death .... Hos 13:14
Grave .... Ps 49:15
Vain conversation 1Pet 1:18
Present evil world .... Gal 1:4

Accomplished by:
God's power .... Deut 7:8
Christ's blood .... Eph 1:7
God's grace .... Rom 3:24, 25

Benefits of:
Forgiveness .... Col 1:14
Justification .... Rom 3:24
Adoption .... Gal 4:4, 5
God's possession 1Cor 6:20
God's people .... Titus 2:14
Purification .... Titus 2:14
Sealing .... Eph 4:30
Inheritance .... Heb 9:15
Heaven's glory .... Rev 14:3, 4

grant a *r* for the land .... Lev 25:24
again the price of his *r* .... Lev 25:52
Moses took the *r* money ...... Num 3:49
He sent *r* unto his people ..... Ps 111:9
with him is plenteous *r* .... Ps 130:7
the right of *r* is thine to .... Jer 32:7
looked for *r* in Jerusalem ..... Luke 2:38
for your *r* draweth nigh .... Luke 21:28
adoption..the *r* of our body ... Rom 8:23
and sanctification, and *r* 1Cor 1:30
obtained eternal *r* for us ...... Heb 9:12

REDOUND—*to add or increase*
thanksgiving of many *r* to 2Cor 4:15

REED—*tall grass growing in marshes*

Figurative of:
Weakness .... Is 36:6
Instability .... Matt 11:7
God's measure .... Ezek 40:3
Davidic line .... Is 42:3

[*also* REEDS]
r is shaken in the water 1Kin 14:15
the staff of this bruised *r* 2Kin 18:21
in the covert of the *r* .... Job 40:21
up: the *r* and flags shall .... Is 19:6
grass with *r* and rushes .... Is 35:7
the *r* they have burned .... Jer 51:32
measuring *r* of six cubits ...... Ezek 40:5
breadth of the building one *r* .. Ezek 40:5
and the height, one *r* .... Ezek 40:5
which was one *r* broad .... Ezek 40:6
which was one *r* broad .... Ezek 40:6
r long, and one *r* broad .... Ezek 40:7
full *r* of six great cubits ...... Ezek 41:8
side with the measuring *r* ..... Ezek 42:16
reed, five hundred *r* .... Ezek 42:16
measuring *r* round about ...... Ezek 42:16
r, with the measuring *r* .... Ezek 42:18
hundred *r* with the measuring *r*. Ezek 42:19
five hundred *r* long .... Ezek 42:20
five and twenty thousand *r* .... Ezek 45:1
five and twenty thousand *r* .... Ezek 48:8
A bruised *r* shall he not .... Matt 12:20
and a *r* in his right hand ...... Matt 27:29
smote him..with a *r* .... Mark 15:19
r shaken with the wind .... Luke 7:24
given me a *r* like unto a ...... Rev 11:1
with me had a golden *r* to .... Rev 21:15

REEL—*walk or move unsteadily*
They *r* to and fro, and .... Ps 107:27
shall *r* to and fro like a .... Is 24:20

REELAIAH (rē-ĕl-ā'yä)—*returned to Palestine with Zerubbabel*
Seraiah, *R*, Mordecai .... Ezra 2:2
See RAAMIAH

REFINE—*to become pure or perfected*

[*also* REFINED]
the altar of incense *r* gold 1Chr 28:18
talents of *r* silver 1Chr 29:4
of wines on the lees well *r* .... Is 25:6

REFINER—*one who purifies things by smelting*

[*also* REFINER'S]
for he is like a *r* fire, and ..... Mal 3:2
sit as a *r* and purifier of .... Mal 3:3

REFINING, SPIRITUAL—*purifying of the spirit*
By afflictions .... Is 48:10
By fire .... Zech 13:9
For a purpose .... John 15:2
More precious than gold . 1Peter 1:7

REFLECTION—*contemplation on*
Past .... Mark 14:72
Present .... Luke 14:31-33
Future .... Acts 21:12-14

REFORMATIONS, RELIGIOUS—*return to original purity of worship and life*

Manifested by or in:
Recovery of the Law 2Kin 22:8-20
Resolving to follow the Lord .... Ezra 10:1-17
Religious zeal for the Lord .... Neh 13:11-31
Restoration of judges 2Chr 19:1-11

[*also* REFORMATION, REFORMED]
if ye will not be *r* by me ...... Lev 26:23
them until the time of *r* .... Heb 9:10

REFRAIN—*to curb; restrain; keep oneself from doing*

[*also* REFRAINED, REFRAINETH]
r himself, and said .... Gen 43:31
Joseph could not *r* himself .... Gen 45:1
Haman *r* himself .... Esth 5:10
I will not *r* my mouth .... Job 7:11
The princes *r* talking, and ..... Job 29:9
not *r* my lips, O Lord .... Ps 40:9
r my feet from every evil ..... Ps 119:101
r thy foot from their path ..... Prov 1:15
he that *r* his lips is wise .... Prov 10:19
to *r* from embracing .... Eccl 3:5
been still, and *r* myself .... Is 42:14
praise will I *r* for thee .... Is 48:9
Wilt thou *r* thyself for .... Is 64:12
they have not *r* their feet ..... Jer 14:10
R thy voice from weeping ..... Jer 31:16
R from these men, and .... Acts 5:38
let him *r* his tongue from 1Pet 3:10

REFRESH—*to renew; restore*

Spiritual:
In the spirit 1Cor 16:18
In the heart .... Philem 7, 20
Often needed 2Tim 1:16
Mutual .... Rom 15:32
Special times .... Acts 3:19
Refused .... Is 28:12

[*also* REFRESHED, REFRESHETH]
the stranger, may be *r* .... Ex 23:12
he rested, and was *r* .... Ex 31:17
so Saul was *r*, and was 1Sam 16:23
weary, and *r* themselves 2Sam 16:14
home with me, and *r* 1Kin 13:7
speak, that I may be *r* .... Job 32:20
r the soul of his masters ...... Prov 25:13
unto his friends to *r* .... Acts 27:3
because his spirit was *r* 2Cor 7:13

REFUGE—*a shelter from harm*

Divine:
In the Lord .... Ps 142:5
From storms .... Is 4:5, 6
Time of trouble .... Ps 9:9
Place of protection ...... Ps 91:9, 10
Always ready .... Ps 46:1

The eternal God is thy *r* ...... Deut 33:27
my high tower, and my *r* 2Sam 22:3
because the Lord is his *r* ...... Ps 14:6
known in her palaces for a *r* .. Ps 48:3
wings will I make my *r* .... Ps 57:1
r in the day of my trouble .... Ps 59:16
my strength, and my *r* is ...... Ps 62:7
but thou art my strong *r* ...... Ps 71:7
Lord, He is my *r* and my ..... Ps 91:2
God is the rock of my *r* .... Ps 94:22
high hills are a *r* for the ...... Ps 104:18
r failed me; no man cared ..... Ps 142:4
children..have a place of *r* .... Prov 14:26
a *r* from the storm, a .... Is 25:4
we have made lies our *r* ...... Is 28:15
r in the day of affliction .... Jer 16:19
fled for *r* to lay hold .... Heb 6:18

REFUGE, CITIES OF—*places where one who had killed could find sanctuary*
shall be six cities for *r* .... Num 35:6
be unto you cities for *r* .... Num 35:12
which shall be cities of *r* ...... Num 35:14
him to the city of his *r* .... Num 35:25
of the city of his *r* .... Num 35:27
fled to the city of his *r* .... Num 35:32
Appoint..you cities of *r* .... Josh 20:2
city of *r* for the slayer .... Josh 21:13
Hebron, the city of *r*, and 1Chr 6:57

REFUSE—*to reject or decline; remainder*

Of things, physical:
Marriage .... Ex 22:17
Passage .... Num 20:21
King 1Sam 16:7
Display .... Esth 1:12
Leader .... Acts 7:35
Martyrdom .... Acts 25:11
Fables 1Tim 4:7
Adoption .... Heb 11:24

Of things, spiritual:
Hardness of heart .... Ex 7:14
Disobedience .... Ex 16:28
Obedience 1Sam 8:19
Messiah .... Ps 118:22
Salvation .... Is 8:6
Shame .... Jer 3:3
Repentance .... Hos 11:5
Healing .... Jer 15:18
God .... Heb 12:25

[*also* REFUSED, REFUSETH]
but he *r* to be comforted ...... Gen 37:35
he *r*, and said unto his .... Gen 39:8
his father *r*, and said .... Gen 48:19
if thou *r* to let him go .... Ex 4:23
if thou *r* to let them go .... Ex 8:2
if thou *r* to let them go .... Ex 9:2
long wilt thou *r* to humble .... Ex 10:3
Lord *r* to give me leave .... Num 22:13
My husband's brother *r* to .... Deut 25:7
thing that was vile and *r* 1Sam 15:9
r, and said, I will not eat 1Sam 28:23
he *r* to turn aside 2Sam 2:23
him; but he *r* to eat 2Sam 13:9
And the man *r* to smite 1Kin 20:35
which he *r* to give thee 1Kin 21:15
him to take it; but he *r* 2Kin 5:16
r to obey, neither were .... Neh 9:17
that my soul *r* to touch .... Job 6:7
whether thou *r*, or .... Job 34:33
soul *r* to be comforted .... Ps 77:2
of God, and *r* to walk in ...... Ps 78:10
I have called, and ye *r* .... Prov 1:24
and be wise, and *r* it not ...... Prov 8:33

R

he that *r* reproof erreth ....Prov 10:17
to him that *r* instruction ......Prov 13:18
r instruction despiseth.........Prov 15:32
they *r* to do judgment ....Prov 21:7
But if ye *r* and rebel, ye ......Is 1:20
may know to *r* the evil........Is 7:15
youth, when thou wast *r* ......Is 54:6
r to receive correction ....Jer 5:3
hold fast deceit, they *r*.........Jer 8:5
through deceit they *r* to.......Jer 9:6
which *r* to hear my words .....Jer 11:10
which *r* to hear my words .....Jer 13:10
r to take the cup at thine .....Jer 25:28
r to be comforted for her .....Jer 31:15
But if thou *r* to go forth ......Jer 38:21
they *r* to let them go ....Jer 50:33
and *r* in the midst of the ......Lam 3:45
they have *r* my judgments .....Ezek 5:6
sell the *r* of the wheat? ....Amos 8:6
But they *r* to hearken.........Zech 7:11
God is..nothing to be *r* 1Tim 4:4
But the younger widows *r* 1Tim 5:11

REFUSE GATE—*a gate of Jerusalem*
Nehemiah viewed city
from ....Neh 2:13
Wall dedicated near .....Neh 12:31

REGARD—*to consider; think of highly*
Honors God ....Is 17:7, 8
Honors God's Word .....Ps 119:6, 15, 117
Rejects the unbelieving . .Gen 4:4, 5

[*also* REGARDED, REGARDEST, REGARDETH, REGARDING]
Also *r* not your stuff..........Gen 45:20
let them not *r* vain words .....Ex 5:9
r not the word of the Lord ....Ex 9:21
R not them that have ....Lev 19:31
r not persons, nor taketh......Deut 10:17
not *r* the person of the old ....Deut 28:50
neither did she *r* it 1Sam 4:20
thee, *r* this man of Belial 1Sam 25:25
brother, *r* not this thing 2Sam 13:20
thou *r* neither princes nor 2Sam 19:6
to answer, nor any that *r* 1Kin 18:29
r the presence of Jehoshaphat .2Kin 3:14
r me according to the 1Chr 17:17
not God *r* it from above ......Job 3:4
I stand up, and thou *r* me.....Job 30:20
nor *r* the rich more than ......Job 34:19
neither will the Almighty *r* ....Job 35:13
Take heed, *r* not iniquity .....Job 36:21
r he the crying of the ....Job 39:7
r not the works of the Lord ...Ps 28:5
hatred them that *r* lying.......Ps 31:6
If I *r* iniquity in my heart .....Ps 66:18
the God of Jacob *r* it ....Ps 94:7
r..prayer of the destitute ......Ps 102:17
he *r* their affliction ....Ps 106:44
out my hand, and no man *r* ...Prov 1:24
thou mayest *r* discretion ......Prov 5:2
He will not *r* any ransom .....Prov 6:35
man *r* the life of his beast.....Prov 12:10
r reproof..be honored.........Prov 13:18
that *r* reproof is prudent ......Prov 15:5
but the wicked *r* not to ....Prov 29:7
higher than the highest *r*......Eccl 5:8
in *r* of the oath of God ....Eccl 8:2
r the clouds shall not reap ....Eccl 11:4
r not the work of the Lord ....Is 5:12
which shall not *r* silver........Is 13:17
despised the cities, he *r* not ..Is 33:8
he will no more *r* them ....Lam 4:16
O king, have not *r* thee ....Dan 3:12
Judah *r* not thee, O king......Dan 6:13
r the god of his fathers ....Dan 11:37
of women, nor *r* any god .....Dan 11:37
will I *r* the peace offerings ....Amos 5:22
r, and wonder marvelously ....Hab 1:5
will he *r* your persons.........Mal 1:9
he *r* not the offering any ......Mal 2:13
r not the person of men.......Matt 22:16
r not the person of men.......Mark 12:14
feared not God, neither *r* .....Luke 18:2
I fear not God, nor *r* man ....Luke 18:4
to him they had *r* ....Acts 8:11
the Lord he doth not *r* it .....Rom 14:6
r the day, *r* it unto..Lord .....Rom 14:6
r not the day, to the Lord ....Rom 14:6
unto death, not *r* his life ......Phil 2:30
r them not, saith the Lord ....Heb 8:9

REGEM (rē'gĕm)—*"friendship"*
Calebite 1Chr 2:47

REGEM-MELECH (rē-gĕm-mē'lĕk)—*"royal friend"*
Sent in deputation to
Zechariah.............Zech 7:2

REGENERATION—*new birth; renewal of moral and spiritual nature; restoration of all things*
the *r* when the Son of man ....Matt 19:28
saved us, by the washing of *r*. .Titus 3:5
See BORN AGAIN; NEW BIRTH

REGION—*area or district*

[*also* REGIONS]
r of Argob, the kingdom ......Deut 3:4
in all the *r* of Dor 1Kin 4:11
the *r* round about Jordan .....Matt 3:5
sat in the *r* and shadow of ....Matt 4:16
the *r* round about Galilee .....Mark 1:28
through that whole *r*..........Mark 6:55
of the *r* of Trachonitis ....Luke 3:1
through all the *r* round ....Luke 4:14
throughout all the *r*...........Luke 7:17
throughout the *r* of Judea .....Acts 8:1
throughout all the *r*...........Acts 13:49
unto the *r* that lieth ....Acts 14:6
and the *r* of Galatia ....Acts 16:6
preach the gospel in the *r* 2Cor 10:16
boasting in the *r* of Achaia 2Cor 11:10
I came into the *r* of Syria .....Gal 1:21

REGISTER—*a record of genealogies*
Priests not recorded in . . .Ezra 2:62
Excluded from priesthood.Neh 7:63-65
Those recorded in ....Neh 7:5-62

sought their *r* among ....Ezra 2:62
found a *r* of the genealogy ....Neh 7:5

REHABIAH (rē-hä-bī'ä)—*"Jehovah is a widener"*
Grandson of Moses 1Chr 23:17
Concerning *R*: of the sons of *R*.1Chr 24:21
R his son, and Jeshaiah 1Chr 26:25

REHEARSE—*to repeat; recite aloud*

[*also* REHEARSED]
r it in the ears of Joshua ......Ex 17:14
r the righteous acts of ....Judg 5:11
r them in the ears of the Lord .1Sam 8:21
they *r* them before Saul 1Sam 17:31
Peter *r* the matter from ....Acts 11:4
r all that God had done ....Acts 14:27

REHOB (rē'hŏb)—*"width"*
1. Two cities of Asher .....Josh 19:24, 28
One assigned to
Levites...............Josh 21:31
Delayed conquest of
one ....Judg 1:31
2. Northern city visited by
Joshua's spies.........Num 13:21
Defeated by David....2Sam 10:8
Called Beth-rehob 2Sam 10:6
3. Father of Hadadezer 2Sam 8:3, 12
4. Signer of the covenant . .Neh 10:11

and *R* with her suburbs 1Chr 6:75

REHOBOAM, ROBOAM (rē-hō-bō'ăm, rō-bō'ăm)—*"freer of the people"*
Son and successor of
Solomon..............1Kin 11:43
Refuses reformatory
measures 1Kin 12:1-15
Ten tribes revolt from ...1Kin 12:16-24
Temporary prosperity of .2Chr 11:5-23
Lapses into idolatry......1Kin 14:21-24
Kingdom of, invaded by
Egypt 1Kin 14:25-28
Reigns 17 years 1Kin 14:21
Death of................1Kin 14:29-31
In Christ's genealogy ....Matt 1:7

unto *R* king of Judah 1Kin 12:27
again to *R* king of Judah 1Kin 12:27
was war between *R* and 1Kin 15:6
Solomon's son was *R* 1Chr 3:10
R his son reigned in his 2Chr 9:31
and *R* went to Shechem 2Chr 10:1
R took counsel with the 2Chr 10:6
R forsook the counsel of 2Chr 10:13
R sent Hadoram that was 2Chr 10:18
R was come to Jerusalem 2Chr 11:1
the kingdom again to *R* 2Chr 11:1
R had established the 2Chr 12:1
Shemaiah the prophet to *R* 2Chr 12:5
R strengthened himself 2Chr 12:13
R was one and forty years.....2Chr 12:13
Now the acts of *R*, first 2Chr 12:15
between *R* and Jeroboam 2Chr 12:15
strengthened..against *R* 2Chr 13:7
R was young and 2Chr 13:7
begat *R*; and *R* begat Abijah . .Matt 1:7

REHOBOTH (rĕ-hō'bŏth)—*"spaces"*
1. Name of a well dug by
Isaac..................Gen 26:22
2. City "by the river" ......Gen 36:37
3. Built by Asshur ....Gen 10:11

REHUM (rē'hŭm)—*"pity"*
1. Persian officer ....Ezra 4:8-23
2. Postexilic returnee ....Ezra 2:2
3. Priest who returns with
Zerubbabel...........Neh 12:3, 7
Same as Harim ....Neh 12:15
4. Signer of the covenant . .Neh 10:25
5. Postexilic Levite ....Neh 3:17

REI (rē'ī)—*"friendly"*
One of David's faithful
officers 1Kin 1:8

REIGN—*to rule over*
Descriptive of the rule of:
Man....................Gen 36:31
God....................Ps 47:8
Christ ....Rev 20:4, 6
Believers ....Rev 5:10
Sin.....................Rom 5:21
Death ....Rom 5:14, 17
Grace ....Rom 5:21
Of Christ's rule:
Predicted ....Is 32:1
Described..............Jer 23:5, 6
Announced ....Luke 1:31-33
Rejected...............Luke 19:14, 27
Fulfilled ....Rom 15:12
Enthroned 1Cor 15:25
Eternal ....Rev 11:15-17

[*also* REIGNED, REIGNEST, REIGNETH, REIGNING]
before there *r* any king ....Gen 36:31
and Jobab..*r* in his stead ......Gen 36:33
and Hadad..*r* in his stead .....Gen 36:35
and Saul..*r* in his stead ....Gen 36:37
and Hadar *r* in his stead ......Gen 36:39
thou indeed *r* over us?.........Gen 37:8
The Lord shall *r* for ever .....Ex 15:18
that hate you shall *r* over .....Lev 26:17
shalt *r* over many nations .....Deut 15:6
they shall not *r* over thee .....Deut 15:6
And *r* in mount Hermon ......Josh 12:5
which *r* in Heshbon..........Josh 13:10
the Amorites, which *r* in ......Josh 13:21
king of Canaan, that *r* in......Judg 4:2
and ten persons *r* over ....Judg 9:2
of that one *r* over you? ....Judg 9:2
fig tree, Come thou, and *r* ....Judg 9:10
bramble, Come thou, and *r* ...Judg 9:14
Abimelech had *r* three ....Judg 9:22
that I should not *r* over 1Sam 8:7
the king that shall *r* over 1Sam 8:11
shall *r* over my people 1Sam 9:17
Shall Saul *r* over us?..........1Sam 11:12
a king shall *r* over us 1Sam 12:12

the king that *r* over you.......1Sam 12:14
Saul *r* one year; and when 1Sam 13:1
r two years over Israel........1Sam 13:1
him from *r* over Israel?.......1Sam 16:1
r over Israel, and *r*..........2Sam 2:10
r over all that thine heart.....2Sam 3:21
r, and he *r* forty years........2Sam 5:4
r over Judah seven years.......2Sam 5:5
r thirty and three years.......2Sam 5:5
David *r* over all Israel........2Sam 8:15
Hanun his son *r* in his........2Sam 10:1
Absalom *r* in Hebron.........2Sam 15:10
whose stead thou hast *r*.......2Sam 16:8
that Adonijah..doth *r*.........1Kin 1:11
Solomon thy son shall *r*.......1Kin 1:13
why then doth Adonijah *r*.....1Kin 1:13
now, behold, Adonijah *r*......1Kin 1:18
Adonijah shall *r* after me.....1Kin 1:24
that David *r* over Israel.......1Kin 2:11
seven years *r* he in Hebron....1Kin 2:11
years *r* he in Jerusalem.......1Kin 2:11
on me, that I should *r*........1Kin 2:15
Solomon *r* over all...........1Kin 4:21
year of Solomon's *r* over......1Kin 6:1
and *r* in Damascus...........1Kin 11:24
r according to all that thy.....1Kin 11:37
Solomon *r* in Jerusalem........1Kin 11:42
Rehoboam *r* over them.......1Kin 12:17
he warred, and how he *r*......1Kin 14:19
days which Jeroboam *r*........1Kin 14:20
Nadab his son *r* in his........1Kin 14:20
Rehoboam..*r* in Judah........1Kin 14:21
old when he began to *r*.......1Kin 14:21
he *r* seventeen years in.......1Kin 14:21
son of Nebat *r* Abijam over...1Kin 15:1
Asa his son *r* in his stead.....1Kin 15:8
years *r* he in Jerusalem.......1Kin 15:10
Nadab..began to *r* over Israel .1Kin 15:25
r over Israel two years........1Kin 15:25
it came to pass, when he *r*....1Kin 15:29
Elah his son *r* in his stead.....1Kin 16:6
Elah..to *r* over Israel in.......1Kin 16:8
did Zimri *r* seven days in.....1Kin 16:15
so Tibni died, and Omri *r*.....1Kin 16:22
Ahab his son *r* in his stead....1Kin 16:28
Ahab..to *r* over Israel........1Kin 16:29
Ahaziah his son *r* in his.......1Kin 22:40
Jehoshaphat..to *r* over........1Kin 22:41
Jehoram his son *r* in his.......1Kin 22:50
Ahaziah..to *r* over Israel......1Kin 22:51
Jehoram *r* in his stead........2Kin 1:17
Jehoram..began to *r* over Israel 2Kin 3:1
king of Judah and *r*..........2Kin 3:1
should have *r* in his stead.....2Kin 3:27
Jehoram the son..began to *r*...2Kin 8:16
r eight years in Jerusalem.....2Kin 8:17
did Ahaziah..begin to *r*.......2Kin 8:25
r one year in Jerusalem.......2Kin 8:26
Ahaziah to *r* over Judah......2Kin 9:29
Jehoahaz his son *r* in his......2Kin 10:35
And Athaliah did *r* over......2Kin 11:3
Jehoash began to *r*..........2Kin 12:1
and forty years *r* he in........2Kin 12:1
began to *r* over Israel.........2Kin 13:1
Samaria, and *r* seventeen.....2Kin 13:1
in Samaria, and *r* sixteen......2Kin 13:10
r Amaziah the son of Joash...2Kin 14:1
old when he began to *r*.......2Kin 14:2
Jeroboam his son *r* in his.....2Kin 14:16
Zachariah his son *r* in his....2Kin 14:29
king of Judah to *r*...........2Kin 15:1
he *r* two and fifty years.......2Kin 15:2
Zachariah..*r* over Israel.......2Kin 15:8
and slew him, and *r* in his....2Kin 15:10
and slew him, and *r* in his....2Kin 15:14
son of Gadi to *r* over Israel...2Kin 15:17
Pekahiah his son *r* in his......2Kin 15:22
he killed him, and *r* in his....2Kin 15:25
Pekah..to *r* over Israel.......2Kin 15:27
and slew him, and *r* in his....2Kin 15:30
when he began to *r*..........2Kin 15:33
Ahaz his son *r* in his stead....2Kin 15:38
son of Jotham..began to *r*.....2Kin 16:1
and *r* sixteen years in.........2Kin 16:2
Hoshea..to *r* in Samaria.......2Kin 17:1
that Hezekiah..began to *r*.....2Kin 18:1
r twenty and nine years.......2Kin 18:2
Esarhaddon his son *r* in his...2Kin 19:37
Manasseh his son *r* in his.....2Kin 20:21
years old..he began to *r*.......2Kin 21:1
r fifty and five years in.......2Kin 21:1
r two years in Jerusalem......2Kin 21:19
old when he began to *r*.......2Kin 22:1
he *r* thirty and one years......2Kin 22:1
old when he began to *r*.......2Kin 23:31
he *r* three months in..........2Kin 23:31
old when he began to *r*.......2Kin 23:36
Jehoiachin his son *r* in his.....2Kin 24:6
old when he began to *r*.......2Kin 24:8
he *r* in Jerusalem three.......2Kin 24:8
old when he began to *r*.......2Kin 24:18
the ninth year of his *r*........2Kin 25:1
that *r* in the land of Edom....1Chr 1:43
Jobab the son..*r* in his........1Chr 1:44
Hadad the son..*r* in his.......1Chr 1:46
Shaul of Rehoboth..*r* in.......1Chr 1:48
was dead. Hadad *r* in his.....1Chr 1:50
he *r* seven years and six.......1Chr 3:4
r thirty and three years.......1Chr 3:4
cities unto the *r* of David.....1Chr 4:31
the nations, the Lord *r*........1Chr 16:31
so David *r* over all Israel.....1Chr 18:14
his son *r* in his stead..........1Chr 19:1
David the son..*r* over all......1Chr 29:26
he *r* over Israel was forty.....1Chr 29:27
seven years *r* he in Hebron....1Chr 29:27
years *r* he in Jerusalem.......1Chr 29:27
all his *r* and his might........1Chr 29:30
hast made me to *r* in his......2Chr 1:8
and *r* over Israel............2Chr 1:13
the fourth year of his *r*.......2Chr 3:2
And he *r* over all the kings...2Chr 9:26
Rehoboam his son *r* in his....2Chr 9:31
Rehoboam *r* over them.......2Chr 10:17
himself in Jerusalem and *r*....2Chr 12:13
old when he began to *r*.......2Chr 12:13
he *r* seventeen years in.......2Chr 12:13
Abijah to *r* over Judah.......2Chr 13:1
r three years in Jerusalem.....2Chr 13:2
Asa his son *r* in his stead.....2Chr 14:1
year of the *r* of Asa..........2Chr 15:10
year of the *r* of Asa..........2Chr 16:1
and fortieth year of his *r*......2Chr 16:13
Jehoshaphat *r* over Judah.....2Chr 17:1
third year of his *r* he sent.....2Chr 17:7
Jehoshaphat..*r* over Judah.....2Chr 20:31
five..when he began to *r*......2Chr 20:31
he *r* twenty and five years.....2Chr 20:31
Jehoram his son *r* in his.......2Chr 21:1
two..when he began to *r*......2Chr 21:5
r in Jerusalem eight years.....2Chr 21:20
Jehoram king of Judah *r*......2Chr 22:1
Ahaziah when he began to *r*..2Chr 22:2
the king's son shall *r*..........2Chr 23:3
seven..when he began to *r*....2Chr 24:1
five..when he began to *r*......2Chr 25:1
r fifty and two years in.......2Chr 26:3
Jotham his son *r* in his stead..2Chr 26:23
years old when he began to *r*..2Chr 27:1
he *r* sixteen years in Jerusalem.2Chr 27:1
and Ahaz his son *r* in his.....2Chr 27:9
old when he began to *r*.......2Chr 28:1
he *r* sixteen years in..........2Chr 28:1
Hezekiah began to *r* when....2Chr 29:1
he *r* nine and twenty years....2Chr 29:1
old when he began to *r*.......2Chr 33:1
he *r* fifty and five............2Chr 33:1
r two years in Jerusalem......2Chr 33:21
eight..when he began to *r*.....2Chr 34:1
he *r* in Jerusalem one and.....2Chr 34:1
eighteenth year of his *r*.......2Chr 34:8
year of the *r* of Josiah........2Chr 35:19
old when he began to *r*.......2Chr 36:2
he *r* three months in..........2Chr 36:2
Jehoiachin his son *r* in his.....2Chr 36:8
eight..when he began to *r*.....2Chr 36:9
and *r* eleven years in.........2Chr 36:11
r of the kingdom of Persia....2Chr 36:20
r of Darius king of Persia.....Ezra 4:5
And in the *r* of Ahasuerus....Ezra 4:6
in the beginning of his *r*......Ezra 4:6
second year of the *r* of Darius .Ezra 4:24
sixth year of the *r* of Darius...Ezra 6:15
the *r* of Artaxerxes king......Ezra 7:1
in the *r* of Artaxerxes the.....Ezra 8:1
r of Darius of Persia..........Neh 12:22
this is Ahasuerus which *r*.....Esth 1:1
In the third year of his *r*......Esth 1:3
the seventh year of his *r*......Esth 2:16
That the hypocrite *r* not......Job 34:30
The Lord *r*, he is clothed.....Ps 93:1
heathen that the Lord *r*.......Ps 96:10
Lord *r*; let the earth..........Ps 97:1
Lord *r*; let the people.........Ps 99:1
The Lord shall *r* for ever.....Ps 146:10
By me kings *r*, and...........Prov 8:15
For a servant when he *r*......Prov 30:22
of prison he cometh to *r*......Eccl 4:14
The Lord of hosts shall *r* in...Is 24:23
Esar-haddon his son *r* in......Is 37:38
saith unto Zion, Thy God *r*...Is 52:7
thirteenth year of his *r*........Jer 1:2
r instead of Josiah his........Jer 22:11
Shalt thou *r*, because thou....Jer 22:15
of the *r* of Jehoiakim........Jer 26:1
of the *r* of Jehoiakim........Jer 27:1
of the *r* of Zedekiah..........Jer 28:1
a son to *r* upon his throne....Jer 33:21
Zedekiah..*r* instead of........Jer 37:1
the *r* of Zedekiah king of.....Jer 49:34
in the fourth year of his *r*.....Jer 51:59
old when he began to *r*.......Jer 52:1
he *r* eleven years in.........Jer 52:1
first year of his *r* lifted.......Jer 52:31
of the *r* of Jehoiakim.........Dan 1:1
r of Nebuchadnezzar..........Dan 2:1
Daniel prospered in the *r*.....Dan 6:28
r of Cyrus the Persian........Dan 6:28
the *r* of King Belshazzar......Dan 8:1
first year of his *r* I Daniel.....Dan 9:2
r over them in mount Zion....Mic 4:7
Archelaus did *r* in Judea......Matt 2:22
of the *r* of Tiberius Caesar....Luke 3:1
Let not sin..*r* in your.........Rom 6:12
rise to *r* over the Gentiles.....Rom 15:12
have *r* as kings without us.....1Cor 4:8
I would to God ye did *r*......1Cor 4:8
we also might *r* with you......1Cor 4:8
we shall also *r* with him.......2Tim 2:12
which *r* over the kings of.....Rev 17:18
they shall *r* for ever and......Rev 22:5

REINS—*kidneys; loins; heart; mind*
he cleaveth my *r* asunder.....Job 16:13
my *r* be consumed within.....Job 19:27
God trieth the hearts and *r*....Ps 7:9
my *r* also instruct me in.......Ps 16:7
try my *r* and my heart........Ps 26:2
I was pricked in my *r*.........Ps 73:21
thou hast possessed my *r*......Ps 139:13
my *r* shall rejoice, when......Prov 23:16
the girdle of his *r*.............Is 11:5
triest the *r* and the heart......Jer 11:20
and far from their *r*..........Jer 12:2
the heart, I try the *r*..........Jer 17:10
seest the *r* and the heart......Jer 20:12
quiver to enter into my *r*......Lam 3:13
which searcheth the *r* and.....Rev 2:23

REJECT—*to refuse; disown*
Man's rejection of:
God....................1Sam 8:7
God's Word............1Sam 15:23, 26
God's knowledge........Hos 4:6
Christ..................Mark 8:31
God's rejection of man, as:
Unbeliever..............John 12:48
Heretic................Titus 3:10
Unfruitful...............Heb 6:8
Reprobate..............Heb 12:17

[*also* REJECTED]
have this day *r* your God.....1Sam 10:19
r him from reigning over......1Sam 16:1
And they *r* his statutes........2Kin 17:15
is despised and *r* of men......Is 53:3

R

REJOICE

Lord hath *r* thy confidences ... Jer 2:37
nor to my law, but *r* it .... Jer 6:19
Lord hath *r* and forsaken ..... Jer 7:29
r the word of the Lord .... Jer 8:9
thou utterly *r* Judah? .... Jer 14:19
thou hast utterly *r* us .... Lam 5:22
thou hast *r* knowledge .... Hos 4:6
stone which the builders *r* ..... Matt 21:42
him, he would not *r* her ...... Mark 6:26
r the commandment of God ... Mark 7:9
stone which the builders *r* ..... Mark 12:10
r the counsel of God .... Luke 7:30
r of the elders and chief ...... Luke 9:22
be *r* of this generation .... Luke 17:25
which the builders *r* .... Luke 20:17
ye despised not, nor *r* .... Gal 4:14

REJOICE—*to be glad*

Kinds of:
Gloating .... Mic 7:8
Vindictive .... Rev 18:20
Marital .... Prov 5:18
Defiant .... Is 8:6
Prophetic .... John 8:56
Future .... Phil 2:16
Rewarded .... Ps 126:6

Caused by:
God's blessing .... Ex 18:9
God's Word .... Jer 15:16
Assurance .... Luke 10:20
Salvation .... Luke 15:6-10
Persecution .... Acts 5:41
Reunion of believers ..... Phil 2:28
Exaltation .... James 1:9
Christ's return 1Pet 4:13

Sphere of, in:
God's salvation .... Ps 21:1
God's protection .... Ps 63:7
God's blessings .... Ps 106:5
Lord Himself .... Hab 3:18

Agents of:
Heart 1Chr 16:10
Soul .... Ps 35:9
Earth .... Ps 97:1
God's people .... Ps 118:24
Believing spirit .... Luke 1:47

[*also* REJOICED, REJOICEST, REJOICETH, REJOICING]

r before the Lord your .... Lev 23:40
r in all that ye put your .... Deut 12:7
r before the Lord your .... Deut 12:18
and thou shalt *r*, thou .... Deut 14:26
r before the Lord thy .... Deut 16:11
thou shalt surely *r* .... Deut 16:15
shalt *r* in every good thing .... Deut 26:11
r before the Lord thy God .... Deut 27:7
Lord *r* over you to do you .... Deut 28:63
Lord will *r* over you to .... Deut 28:63
again *r* over thee for good .... Deut 30:9
as he *r* over thy fathers .... Deut 30:9
R, O ye nations, with his ..... Deut 32:43
R, Zebulun, in thy going ..... Deut 33:18
then *r* ye in Abimelech .... Judg 9:19
and let him also *r* in you ...... Judg 9:19
Dagon their god, and to *r* ..... Judg 16:23
saw him, he *r* to meet him .... Judg 19:3
My heart *r* in the Lord 1Sam 2:1
I *r* in thy salvation 1Sam 2:1
saw the ark, and *r* to see it ... 1Sam 6:13
the men of Israel *r* greatly ... 1Sam 11:15
thou sawest it, and didst *r* 1Sam 19:5
daughters of the Philistines *r* .. 2Sam 1:20
and *r* with great joy 1Kin 1:40
come up from thence *r* 1Kin 1:45
of Solomon, that he *r* greatly .. 1Kin 5:7
the people of the land *r* 2Kin 11:14
glad, and let the earth *r* 1Chr 16:31
the people *r*, for that they 1Chr 29:9
David..also *r* with great joy ... 1Chr 29:9
let thy saints *r* in goodness 2Chr 6:41
all Judah *r* at the oath 2Chr 15:15
to *r* over their enemies 2Chr 20:27
the people of the land *r* 2Chr 23:13
with *r* and with singing 2Chr 23:18
princes and all the people *r* ... 2Chr 24:10
And Hezekiah *r* and all 2Chr 29:36
that dwelt in Judah *r* 2Chr 30:25
great sacrifices, and *r* .... Neh 12:43
them *r* with great joy .... Neh 12:43
also and the children *r* .... Neh 12:43
Shushan *r* and was glad .... Esth 8:15
Which *r* exceedingly, and ..... Job 3:22
and thy lips with *r* .... Job 8:21
and he shall not *r* therein ..... Job 20:18
r at the sound of the organ .... Job 21:12
I *r* because my wealth was .... Job 31:25
and *r* in his strength .... Job 39:21
and *r* with trembling .... Ps 2:11
put their trust in thee *r* .... Ps 5:11
I will be glad and *r* in thee .... Ps 9:2
me *r* when I am moved .... Ps 13:4
Jacob shall *r*, and Israel .... Ps 14:7
heart is glad and my glory *r* ... Ps 16:9
r as a strong man to run ...... Ps 19:5
Lord are right, *r* the .... Ps 19:8
We will *r* in thy salvation ..... Ps 20:5
how greatly shall he *r*, ... Ps 21:1
my heart greatly *r* .... Ps 28:7
not made my foes to *r* over ... Ps 30:1
be glad and *r* in thy mercy .... Ps 31:7
Be glad in the Lord, and *r* .... Ps 32:11
R in the Lord, O ye .... Ps 33:1
in mine adversity they *r* .... Ps 35:15
enemies wrongfully *r* over ..... Ps 35:19
that *r* at mine hurt .... Ps 35:26
they should *r* over me .... Ps 38:16
all those that seek thee *r* ...... Ps 40:16
r shall they be brought .... Ps 45:15
Let mount Zion *r*, let the ..... Ps 48:11
thou hast broken may *r* .... Ps 51:8
Jacob shall *r*, and Israel .... Ps 53:6
righteous shall *r* when he ..... Ps 58:10
r, I will divide Shechem .... Ps 60:6
the morning and evening to *r* .. Ps 65:8
there did we *r* in him .... Ps 66:6
let them *r* before God .... Ps 68:3
let them exceedingly *r* .... Ps 68:3
JAH, and *r* before him .... Ps 68:4
all those that seek thee *r* ...... Ps 70:4
My lips shall greatly *r* .... Ps 71:23
thy people may *r* in thee? ..... Ps 85:6
R the soul of thy servant ...... Ps 86:4
and Hermon shall *r* in thy ..... Ps 89:12
made all his enemies to *r* ..... Ps 89:42
r and be glad all our days ..... Ps 90:14
Let the heavens *r*, and let ..... Ps 96:11
the daughters of Judah *r* ...... Ps 97:8
R in the Lord, ye .... Ps 97:12
make a loud noise, and *r* ..... Ps 98:4
Lord shall *r* in his works ...... Ps 104:31
them *r* that seek the Lord ..... Ps 105:3
declare his works with *r* .... Ps 107:22
righteous shall see it, and *r* ... Ps 107:42
r, I will divide Shechem .... Ps 108:7
but let thy servant *r* .... Ps 109:28
voice of *r* and salvation .... Ps 118:15
r in the way of thy .... Ps 119:14
they are the *r* of my heart .... Ps 119:111
I *r* at thy word, as one .... Ps 119:162
Israel *r* in him that made ..... Ps 149:2
r to do evil, and delight .... Prov 2:14
r with the wife of thy youth ... Prov 5:18
delight, *r* always before .... Prov 8:30
the righteous, the city *r* .... Prov 11:10
light of the righteous *r* .... Prov 13:9
light of the eyes *r* .... Prov 15:30
my heart shall *r*, even mine ... Prov 23:15
of the righteous shall..*r* .... Prov 23:24
R not when thine enemy ...... Prov 24:17
Ointment and perfume *r* ...... Prov 27:9
When righteous men do *r* ..... Prov 28:12
in authority, the people *r* ..... Prov 29:2
Whoso loveth wisdom *r* .... Prov 29:3
heart *r* in all my labor .... Eccl 2:10
a man to *r*, and to do good ... Eccl 3:12
that come after shall not *r* .... Eccl 4:16
and to *r* in his labor .... Eccl 5:19
years, and *r* in them all .... Eccl 11:8
will be glad and *r* in thee ..... Song 1:4
he that *r*, shall descend .... Is 5:14
r in Rezin and Remaliah's ..... Is 8:6
men *r* when they divide .... Is 9:3
them that *r* in my highness .... Is 13:3
Yea, the fir trees *r* at thee .... Is 14:8
Thou shalt no more *r*, O .... Is 23:12
noise of them that *r* endeth ... Is 24:8
glad and *r* in his salvation ..... Is 25:9
poor among men shall *r* .... Is 29:19
and the desert shall *r* .... Is 35:1
thou shalt *r* in the Lord .... Is 41:16
shall *r* in their portion .... Is 61:7
the bridegroom *r* over the ..... Is 62:5
so shall thy God *r* over .... Is 62:5
him that *r* and worketh .... Is 64:5
my servants shall *r*, but .... Is 65:13
I create Jerusalem a *r* .... Is 65:18
And I will *r* in Jerusalem ..... Is 65:19
R ye with Jerusalem, and ..... Is 66:10
r for joy with her, all ye ...... Is 66:10
doest evil, then thou *r* .... Jer 11:15
of the mockers, nor *r* .... Jer 15:17
the virgin *r* in the dance ...... Jer 31:13
r over them to do them good .. Jer 32:41
ye were glad, because ye *r* .... Jer 50:11
drunken, that they may *r* ..... Jer 51:39
thine enemy to *r* over .... Lam 2:17
R and be glad, O daughter .... Lam 4:21
let not the buyer *r*, nor .... Ezek 7:12
r in heart with all thy .... Ezek 25:6
When the whole earth *r* .... Ezek 35:14
didst *r* at the inheritance ...... Ezek 35:15
R not, O Israel, for joy, as .... Hos 9:1
the priests thereof that *r* ...... Hos 10:5
O land; be glad and *r* .... Joel 2:21
r in a thing of nought .... Amos 6:13
have *r* over the children ...... Obad 12
R not against me, O mine ..... Mic 7:8
they *r* and are glad .... Hab 1:15
their *r* was as to devour .... Hab 3:14
r city that dwelt carelessly ..... Zeph 2:15
them that *r* in thy pride .... Zeph 3:11
will *r* over thee with joy ...... Zeph 3:17
r, O daughter of Zion .... Zech 2:10
shall *r*, and shall see the ...... Zech 4:10
R greatly, O daughter of ...... Zech 9:9
heart shall *r* as through .... Zech 10:7
heart shall *r* in the Lord ...... Zech 10:7
r with exceeding great joy ..... Matt 2:10
R, and be exceeding glad ..... Matt 5:12
he *r* more of that sheep .... Matt 18:13
many shall *r* at his birth .... Luke 1:14
R ye in that day, and leap .... Luke 6:23
that hour Jesus *r* in spirit .... Luke 10:21
r for all the glorious things .... Luke 13:17
it on his shoulders, *r* .... Luke 15:5
began to *r* and praise God .... Luke 19:37
r..because of the bridegroom's . John 3:29
that reapeth may *r* together ... John 4:36
a season to *r* in his light ...... John 5:35
If ye loved me, ye would *r* .... John 14:28
but the world shall *r* .... John 16:20
Therefore did my heart *r* ...... Acts 2:26
r in the works of their own .... Acts 7:41
he went on his way *r* .... Acts 8:39
they *r* for the consolation ..... Acts 15:31
meat before them, and *r* ...... Acts 16:34
r in hope of the glory of ...... Rom 5:2
R in hope; patient in .... Rom 12:12
R with them that do *r* .... Rom 12:15
R, ye Gentiles, with his ...... Rom 15:10
that *r* as though they *r* 1Cor 7:30
all the members *r* with it 1Cor 12:26
R not in iniquity 1Cor 13:6
but *r* in the truth 1Cor 13:6
r which I have in Christ 1Cor 15:31
our *r* is this, the testimony 2Cor 1:12
of whom I ought to *r* 2Cor 2:3
sorrowful, yet always *r* 2Cor 6:10
so that I *r* the more 2Cor 7:7
I *r*, not that ye were made 2Cor 7:9
R, thou barren that .... Gal 4:27
shall he have *r* in himself ..... Gal 6:4
r may be more abundant ...... Phil 1:26
may *r* in the day of Christ .... Phil 2:16

my brethren, *r* in the Lord ....Phil 3:1
R in the Lord always ....Phil 4:4
But I *r* in the Lord greatly ....Phil 4:10
now *r* in my sufferings ....Col 1:24
hope, or joy, or crown of *r* ...1Thess 2:19
R evermore 1Thess 5:16
r of the hope firm unto the ...Heb 3:6
mercy *r* against judgment .....James 2:13
ye *r* in your boastings.........James 4:16
boastings all such *r* is evil .....James 4:16
Wherein ye greatly *r*..........1Pet 1:6
I *r* greatly that I found........2John 4
For I *r* greatly, when the......3John 3
upon the earth shall *r*.........Rev 11:10
r, ye heavens, and ye that.....Rev 12:12
R over her, thou heaven ......Rev 18:20
Let us be glad and *r*, and .....Rev 19:7

REKEM (rē'kĕm)—*"friendship"*
1. Midianite king slain by Moses ....Num 31:8
2. Descendant of Caleb 1Chr 2:43, 44
3. City of Benjamin ....Josh 18:27

RELAPSE—*to turn back to sin*
Danger of, explained ....Heb 6:4-6

RELATIVES—*kin*

Good derived from:
Encouragement..........Esth 4:12-17
Salvation ....John 1:40-42

Evil derived from:
Strife ....Gen 31:1-42
Persecution ....Mark 13:12
Jealousy ....Gen 37:3-11

RELEASE—*to set free*

[*also* RELEASED]
thou shalt make a *r*...........Deut 15:1
brother thine hand shall *r* .....Deut 15:3
solemnity of the year of *r* .....Deut 31:10
he made a *r* to the provinces ..Esth 2:18
r unto the people a prisoner...Matt 27:15
twain will ye that I *r* unto .....Matt 27:21
r he Barabbas unto them.......Matt 27:26
r unto them one prisoner .....Mark 15:6
I *r* unto you the King of ......Mark 15:9
chastise him, and *r* him ....Luke 23:16
and *r* unto us Barabbas ....Luke 23:18
And he *r* unto them him ......Luke 23:25
r unto you one at the ....John 18:39
I *r* unto you the King of ......John 18:39
and have power to *r* thee? ....John 19:10

RELIED—*See* RELY

RELIEF—*aid; service*
In early church ....Acts 4:32-37
Determined to send .....Acts 11:29
Fulfilled at Christ's return. 2Thess 1:7

[*also* RELIEVE, RELIEVED, RELIEVETH]
then thou shalt *r* him ....Lev 25:35
seek judgment, *r* the..........Is 1:17
for meat to *r* the soul.........Lam 1:11
their meat to *r* their soul......Lam 1:19
let them *r* them, and let 1Tim 5:16
r them that are widows 1Tim 5:16

RELIGION—*system of attitudes toward, beliefs about, and practices of worship*

[*also* RELIGIOUS]
the Jews and *r* proselytes .....Acts 13:43
of our *r* I lived a Pharisee.....Acts 26:5
in time past in the Jews' *r*.....Gal 1:13
among you seem to be *r* ......James 1:26
heart, this man's *r* is vain .....James 1:26

RELIGION, FALSE—*religion that is not true to the teaching of the Scriptures*

Characterized by:
Apostasy 2Thess 2:3, 4
Backsliding ....Jer 5:23-31
Ceremonialism ....Mark 7:3-13
Display ....Matt 6:5
Ease 1Kin 12:27-31
Formalism 2Tim 3:5

RELY—*depend*

[*also* RELIED]
they *r* upon the Lord God 2Chr 13:18
hast *r* on the king of Syria 2Chr 16:7
not *r* on the Lord thy God 2Chr 16:7
thou didst *r* on the Lord 2Chr 16:8

REMAIN—*to stay in the same place; abide; be left over*

[*also* REMAINED, REMAINEST, REMAINETH, REMAINING]
Noah only *r* alive, and they ...Gen 7:23
the earth *r*, seedtime ....Gen 8:22
r fled to the mountain ....Gen 14:10
R a widow at thy father's .....Gen 38:11
may *r* in the river only?.......Ex 8:9
r unto you from the hail ......Ex 10:5
r not any green thing ....Ex 10:15
of it *r* until the morning.......Ex 12:10
r of it until the morning.......Ex 12:10
there *r* not so much as one ....Ex 14:28
which *r* over lay up for you ...Ex 16:23
the fat of my sacrificer *r* ......Ex 23:18
that *r* of the curtains..........Ex 26:12
half curtain that *r*, shall ....Ex 26:12
bread, *r* unto the morning.....Ex 29:34
that which *r* of the flesh ......Lev 8:32
the meat offering that *r* ....Lev 10:12
r among them in the midst ....Lev 16:16
ought *r* until the third day ....Lev 19:6
r in the hand of him that .....Lev 25:28
to the years that *r*............Lev 27:18
the tabernacle, *r* thereon ......Num 9:22
r two of the men in the camp .Num 11:26
shall destroy him that *r* ....Num 24:19
which ye let *r* of them ....Num 33:55
r in the city of his refuge .....Num 35:28
inheritance *r* in the tribe ......Num 36:12
city, we left none to *r* ....Deut 2:34
none was left to him *r* ....Deut 3:3
only Og king of Bashan *r* .....Deut 3:11
have *r* long in the land........Deut 4:25
r all night until the ....Deut 16:4
r shall hear, and fear ....Deut 19:20
and shall *r* in thine house .....Deut 21:13
r in the land which Moses.....Josh 1:14
r any more courage in any ....Josh 2:11
none of them *r* or escape .....Josh 8:22
heap of stones, that *r* unto ....Josh 8:29
the rest which *r* of them ......Josh 10:20
r until this very day ....Josh 10:27
were therein; he let none *r*....Josh 10:30
he had left him none *r*........Josh 10:33
he left none *r*; as he had......Josh 10:39
they left them none *r* ....Josh 11:8
and in Ashdod, there *r* ....Josh 11:22
there *r* yet very much land ....Josh 13:1
who *r* of the remnant of the...Josh 13:12
r among the children of ....Josh 18:2
r of the children of Kohath....Josh 21:20
r of the families of the ....Josh 21:40
by lot these nations that *r*.....Josh 23:4
even these that *r* among ......Josh 23:12
him that *r* have dominion .....Judg 5:13
why did Dan *r* in ships?.......Judg 5:17
and there *r* ten thousand ......Judg 7:3
wives for them that *r* ....Judg 21:7
stone *r* unto this day..........1Sam 6:18
which *r* were scattered 1Sam 11:11
There *r* yet the youngest 1Sam 16:11
r in a mountain in the 1Sam 23:14
r in the sides of the cave 1Sam 24:3
Tamar *r* desolate in her 2Sam 13:20
r in any of the coasts of.......2Sam 21:5
For six months did Joab *r*.....1Kin 11:16
r a prophet of the Lord 1Kin 18:22
r in the days of his father 1Kin 22:46
five of the horses that *r* 2Kin 7:13
Jehu slew all that *r* of the 2Kin 10:11
r the grove also in Samaria 2Kin 13:6
none *r*, save the poorest 2Kin 24:14
people that *r* in the land 2Kin 25:22
r in the chambers were 1Chr 9:33
ark of God *r* with the.........1Chr 13:14
the covenant of the Lord *r* 1Chr 17:1
for we *r* yet escaped, as it.....Ezra 9:15
nor any *r* in his dwellings .....Job 18:19
mine error *r* with myself .....Job 19:4
and shall *r* in the tomb ....Job 21:32
answers there *r* falsehood .....Job 21:34
r of him shall be buried.......Job 27:15
dens, and *r* in their places.....Job 37:8
in his neck *r* strength, and ....Job 41:22
and *r* in the wilderness........Ps 55:7
the perfect shall *r* in it........Prov 2:21
r in the congregation of.......Prov 21:16
also my wisdom *r* with me .....Eccl 2:9
he that *r* in Jerusalem ....Is 4:3
shall he *r* at Nob that day.....Is 10:32
righteousness *r* in the ....Is 32:16
it may *r* in the house ....Is 44:13
Which *r* among the graves ....Is 65:4
make, shall *r* before me.......Is 66:22
your seed and your name *r*....Is 66:22
that *r* of this evil family.......Jer 8:3
this city shall *r* for ever ....Jer 17:25
Jerusalem, that *r* in this ....Jer 24:8
r still in their own land ....Jer 27:11
vessels that *r* in the house .....Jer 27:21
palace shall *r* after the ....Jer 30:18
r of the cities of Judah........Jer 34:7
there *r* but wounded men .....Jer 37:10
Jeremiah *r* in the court ....Jer 37:21
r in this city shall die by ......Jer 38:2
war that *r* in this city ....Jer 38:4
Jeremiah *r* in the court ....Jer 38:13
people that *r* in the city.......Jer 39:9
people that *r* in Mizpah ....Jer 41:10
none of them shall *r*..........Jer 42:17
to leave you none to *r* ....Jer 44:7
Zidon every helper that *r* .....Jer 47:4
his taste *r* in him ....Jer 48:11
they have *r* in their holds .....Jer 51:30
that none shall *r* in it ....Jer 51:62
people that *r* in the city.......Jer 52:15
anger none escaped nor *r* .....Lam 2:22
Thou, O Lord, *r* for ever .....Lam 5:19
r and is besieged shall die .....Ezek 6:12
none of them shall *r*, nor .....Ezek 7:11
that *r* shall be scattered ....Ezek 17:21
the fowls of the heaven *r* .....Ezek 31:13
fowls of the heaven to *r*.......Ezek 32:4
r upon the face of the earth...Ezek 39:14
there *r* no strength in me .....Dan 10:8
there *r* no strength in me .....Dan 10:17
r ten men in one house ....Amos 6:9
r in the day of distress ....Obad 14
any *r* of the house of Esau ....Obad 18
so my spirit *r* among you .....Hag 2:5
r in the midst of his house ....Zech 5:4
All the families that *r*.........Zech 12:14
would have *r* until this day ....Matt 11:23
that *r* twelve baskets..........Matt 14:20
them, and *r* speechless ....Luke 1:22
r to them twelve baskets ......Luke 9:17
And in the same house *r*......Luke 10:7
Spirit descending, and *r* on ....John 1:33
the fragments that *r* ....John 6:12
r over and above unto ....John 6:13
that my joy might *r* in you ....John 15:11
not *r* upon the cross ....John 19:31
r, was it not thine own.........Acts 5:4
stuck fast, and *r* unmovable ...Acts 27:41
depart, let her *r* unmarried 1Cor 7:11
it *r*, that both they that 1Cor 7:29
part *r* unto this present 1Cor 15:6
that which *r* is glorious........2Cor 3:11
poor: his righteousness *r* 2Cor 9:9
r unto the coming of the Lord .1Thess 4:15
shall perish; but thou *r*........Heb 1:11
it *r* that some must enter......Heb 4:6
r no more sacrifice for sins ....Heb 10:26
cannot be shaken may *r*.......Heb 12:27
from the beginning shall *r*.....1John 2:24
seed *r* in him; and he 1John 3:9
strengthen the things which *r* ..Rev 3:2

REMAINDER—*remaining group or part*
shalt burn the *r* with fire ......Ex 29:34

R

r thereof shall Aaron and .....Lev 6:16
the *r* of it shall be eaten ......Lev 7:16
name nor *r* upon the earth 2Sam 14:7
the *r* of wrath shalt thou ......Ps 76:10

REMALIAH (rĕm-ä-lī'ä)—*"Jehovah increases; whom Jehovah has adorned"*
Father of Pekah 2Kin 15:25

[*also* REMALIAH'S]
against Pekah the son of ***R*** 2Kin 15:30
and Pekah the son of ***R*** 2Kin 15:37
year of Pekah the son of ***R*** 2Kin 16:1
the son of ***R*** slew in Judah 2Chr 28:6
the son of ***R***, king of Israel....Is 7:1
Ephraim, and the son of ***R*** ....Is 7:5
head of Samaria is ***R*** son......Is 7:9
rejoice in Rezin and ***R*** son ....Is 8:6

REMEDY—*a cure*
Without ....Prov 6:15
Right kind 1John 1:7

people, till there was no *r*.....2Chr 36:16
and that without *r* ....Prov 29:1

REMEMBER—*to call to mind again*
Aids to:
Rainbow ....Gen 9:15, 16
Covenant ....Ex 2:24
Passover ....Ex 13:3
Sabbath ....Ex 20:8
Offering ....Num 5:15
Son (child)..............2Sam 18:18
Prophet's presence 1Kin 17:18
Book ....Mal 3:16
Lord's Supper ....Luke 22:19
Epistle 2Pet 3:1
See MEMORY

[*also* REMEMBERED, REMEMBEREST, REMEMBERETH, REMEMBERING, REMEMBRANCE, REMEMBRANCES]
God *r* Noah, and every ....Gen 8:1
God *r* Abraham, and sent .....Gen 19:29
God *r* Rachel, and God ....Gen 30:22
the chief butler *r* Joseph ......Gen 40:23
I do *r* my faults this ....Gen 41:9
And Joseph *r* the dreams ....Gen 42:9
God *r* his covenant with ......Ex 2:24
and I have *r* my covenant .....Ex 6:5
put out the *r* of Amalek ....Ex 17:14
R Abraham, Isaac and ....Ex 32:13
r my covenant with Jacob .....Lev 26:42
with Abraham will I *r* ....Lev 26:42
and I will *r* the land ....Lev 26:42
shall be *r* before the Lord .....Num 10:9
We *r* the fish, which we did ...Num 11:5
r all the commandments ......Num 15:39
r that thou wast a servant .....Deut 5:15
thou well *r* what the Lord .....Deut 7:18
thou shalt *r* all the way ....Deut 8:2
R, and forget not, how thou ...Deut 9:7
r that thou wast a bondman ...Deut 15:15
mayest *r* the day when ....Deut 16:3
R what the Lord thy God .....Deut 24:9
R what Amalek did unto ....Deut 25:17
blot out the *r* of Amalek ......Deut 25:19
R the days of old, consider ....Deut 32:7
make the *r* of them to cease...Deut 32:26
r the word which Moses ......Josh 1:13
of Israel *r* not the Lord ....Judg 8:34
r also that I am your bone ....Judg 9:2
r me, I pray thee, and ....Judg 16:28
r me, and not forget thine 1Sam 1:11
his wife, and the Lord *r*.......1Sam 1:19
I *r* that which Amalek did 1Sam 15:2
then *r* thine handmaid 1Sam 25:31
king *r* the Lord thy God 2Sam 14:11
r how that when I and thou ...2Kin 9:25
r now how I have walked 2Kin 20:3
the king *r* not the kindness 2Chr 24:22
R, I beseech thee, the ....Neh 1:8
r the Lord, which is great .....Neh 4:14
R me, O my God, concerning .Neh 13:14
R them, O my God, because ..Neh 13:29
r Vashti, and what she had ....Esth 2:1
days should be *r* and kept .....Esth 9:28
R, I pray thee, who ever ......Job 4:7
o *r* that my life is wind ....Job 7:7
R, I beseech thee, that........Job 10:9
r it as waters that pass ....Job 11:16
Your *r* are like unto ashes ....Job 13:12
a set time, and *r* me ....Job 14:13
His *r* shall perish from the ....Job 18:17
Even when I *r* I am afraid ....Job 21:6
he shall be no more *r*; and ....Job 24:20
R that thou magnify his ....Job 36:24
upon him, *r* the battle, do ....Job 41:8
For in death there is no *r* .....Ps 6:5
inquisition for blood, he *r*.....Ps 9:12
R all thy offerings, and ....Ps 20:3
ends of the world shall *r* ......Ps 22:27
R, O Lord, thy tender ....Ps 25:6
at the *r* of his holiness ....Ps 30:4
cut off the *r* of them from ....Ps 34:16
When I *r* these things, I ....Ps 42:4
to be *r* in all generations ......Ps 45:17
I *r* thee upon my bed ....Ps 63:6
Psalm of David, to bring to *r*..Ps 70:*title*
R thy congregation, which.....Ps 74:2
I *r* God, and was troubled ....Ps 77:3
r my song in the night ....Ps 77:6
r the years of the right........Ps 77:10
r that God was their rock .....Ps 78:35
They *r* not his hand, nor ......Ps 78:42
r not against us former........Ps 79:8
Israel may be no more in *r*....Ps 83:4
whom thou *r* no more ....Ps 88:5
R how short my time is ....Ps 89:47
at the *r* of his holiness ....Ps 97:12
He hath *r* his mercy and ......Ps 98:3
thy *r* unto all generations .....Ps 102:12
he *r* that we are dust ....Ps 103:14
that *r* his commandments .....Ps 103:18
R his marvelous works ....Ps 105:5
He hath *r* his covenant........Ps 105:8
R me, O Lord, with the.......Ps 106:4
r not the multitude of thy .....Ps 106:7
iniquity of his fathers be *r*.....Ps 109:14
wonderful works to be *r* ......Ps 111:4
shall be in everlasting *r* ....Ps 112:6
R the word unto thy servant...Ps 119:49
I *r* thy judgments of old ......Ps 119:52
r David and all his ....Ps 132:1
Who *r* us in our low estate ....Ps 136:23
we wept, when we *r* Zion .....Ps 137:1
If I do not *r* thee, let my .....Ps 137:6
I *r* the days of old; I ....Ps 143:5
and *r* his misery no more .....Prov 31:7
is no *r* of former things ....Eccl 1:11
any *r* of things that are to.....Eccl 1:11
there is no *r* of the wise ......Eccl 2:16
much *r* the days of his life ....Eccl 5:20
no man *r* that same poor......Eccl 9:15
r the days of darkness ....Eccl 11:8
R now thy Creator in the .....Eccl 12:1
r thy love more than wine.....Song 1:4
songs, that thou mayest be *r* ..Is 23:16
name, and to the *r* of thee ....Is 26:8
R now, O Lord, I beseech ....Is 38:3
R ye not the former things ....Is 43:18
Put me in *r*: let us plead ......Is 43:26
R these, O Jacob and ....Is 44:21
R this, and show ....Is 46:8
neither didst *r* the latter ......Is 47:7
shalt not *r* the reproach ....Is 54:4
hast thou set up thy *r*.........Is 57:8
lied, and hast not *r* me ......Is 57:11
Then he *r* the days of old .....Is 63:11
that *r* thee in thy ways ....Is 64:5
the former shall not be *r* ....Is 65:17
I *r* thee, the kindness of ......Jer 2:2
neither shall they *r* it ....Jer 3:16
name may be no more *r* ......Jer 11:19
will now *r* their iniquity ....Jer 14:10
r me, and visit me, and ....Jer 15:15
children *r* their altars ....Jer 17:2
R that I stood before thee.....Jer 18:20
him, I do earnestly *r* him .....Jer 31:20
did not the Lord *r* them ......Jer 44:21
r the Lord afar off, and let....Jer 51:50
Jerusalem *r* in the days of.....Lam 1:7
she *r* not her last end ....Lam 1:9
r not his footstool in the ......Lam 2:1
R mine affliction and my ......Lam 3:19
soul hath them still in *r* ....Lam 3:20
R, O Lord, what is come .....Lam 5:1
hath done shall not be *r* ......Ezek 3:20
r me among the nations ....Ezek 6:9
r the days of thy youth ....Ezek 16:22
I will *r* my covenant ....Ezek 16:60
there shall ye *r* your ways .....Ezek 20:43
will call to *r* the iniquity ......Ezek 21:23
your iniquity to be *r* ....Ezek 21:24
to *r* the days of her youth.....Ezek 23:19
nor *r* Egypt any more..........Ezek 23:27
Ammonites may not be *r* .....Ezek 25:10
their iniquity to *r*.............Ezek 29:16
righteousness..not be *r* ......Ezek 33:13
ye *r* your own evil ways.......Ezek 36:31
no more be *r* by their name ...Hos 2:17
I *r* all their wickedness.........Hos 7:2
will he *r* their iniquity ....Hos 8:13
he will *r* their iniquity ....Hos 9:9
r not the brotherly covenant...Amos 1:9
r now what Balak king of .....Mic 6:5
known; in wrath *r* mercy ......Hab 3:2
r me in far countries ....Zech 10:9
they shall no more be *r* ....Zech 13:2
a book of *r* was written ....Mal 3:16
R ye the law of Moses my ....Mal 4:4
r that thy brother hath ....Matt 5:23
neither *r* the five loaves ....Matt 16:9
Peter *r* the word of Jesus .....Matt 26:75
we *r* that that deceiver ....Matt 27:63
ye not and do ye not *r*? ....Mark 8:18
Peter calling to *r* saith ....Mark 11:21
Israel in *r* of his mercy........Luke 1:54
to *r* his holy covenant..........Luke 1:72
r that thou in thy lifetime .....Luke 16:25
R Lot's wife ....Luke 17:32
for you: this do in *r* of me ....Luke 22:19
Peter *r* the word of the Lord ..Luke 22:61
r me when thou comest ....Luke 23:42
r how he spake unto you.......Luke 24:6
And they *r* his words ....Luke 24:8
r that it was written ....John 2:17
r they that these things ....John 12:16
bring all things to your *r* ......John 14:26
ye may *r* that I told you of....John 16:4
thine alms are had in *r*........Acts 10:31
r I the word of the Lord ......Acts 11:16
r that by the space of ....Acts 20:31
bring you into *r* of my ways ...1Cor 4:17
that ye *r* me in all things 1Cor 11:2
for you: this do in *r* of me 1Cor 11:24
r the obedience of you all 2Cor 7:15
that we should *r* the poor .....Gal 2:10
r, that ye being in time ....Eph 2:11
thank my God upon every *r*...Phil 1:3
R my bonds. Grace be ....Col 4:18
R without ceasing your........1Thess 1:3
r, brethren, our labor 1Thess 2:9
that ye have good *r* of us 1Thess 3:6
R ye not, that, when I was 2Thess 2:5
the brethren in *r* of these 1Tim 4:6
r of thee in my prayers 2Tim 1:3
R that Jesus Christ of the 2Tim 2:8
things put them in *r* 2Tim 2:14
iniquities will I *r* no more .....Heb 8:12
is a *r* again made of sins ......Heb 10:3
sins and iniquities will I *r* .....Heb 10:17
R them that are in bonds .....Heb 13:3
always in *r* of these things.....2Pet 1:12
these things always in *r* 2Pet 1:15
r his deeds which he doeth 3John 10
therefore put you in *r*.........Jude 5
r ye the words which were ....Jude 17
R therefore from whence ......Rev 2:5
R..how thou hast received .....Rev 3:3
came in *r* before God ....Rev 16:19
God hath *r* her iniquities ......Rev 18:5

REMETH (rē'mĕth)—*"height"*
Frontier town of Issachar .Josh 19:21
See RAMOTH

REMISSION—*forgiveness*

Based upon:
Christ's death .... Matt 26:28
Faith in Christ .... Acts 10:43
Repentance .... Mark 1:4

Significance of:
Shows God's righteousness .... Rom 3:25
Makes salvation real .... Luke 1:77
Must be preached .... Luke 24:47

[*also* REMIT, REMITTED]
for the *r* of sins .... Luke 3:3
Whosesoever sins ye *r* .... John 20:23
they are *r* unto them .... John 20:23
Christ for the *r* of sins .... Acts 2:38
shedding of blood is no *r* .... Heb 9:22
Now where *r* of these is .... Heb 10:18

REMMON—*See* RIMMON

REMMON-METHOAR (rĕm-ŏn-mĕth'ō-är)—*"Remmon to Neah"*
City of Zebulun .... Josh 19:10, 13
Same as Rimmon 1Chr 6:77

REMNANT—*that which is left over*

Used literally of:
Cloth left over .... Ex 26:12
Race left remaining .... Deut 3:11
Nation still surviving .... Amos 1:8

Used spiritually of the faithful Israel:
Punished .... Is 1:9
Protected .... Is 37:31-33
Scattered .... Ezek 5:10
Gathered .... Is 10:20-22
Repentant .... Jer 31:7-9
Forgiven .... Mic 7:18
Saved .... Jer 23:3-8
Rom 9:27
Blessing .... Mic 5:7, 8
Holy .... Zeph 3:12, 13
Elected .... Rom 11:5

r of the meat offering shall .... Lev 2:3
the *r* shall be the priest's .... Lev 5:13
r of his children which he .... Deut 28:54
was of the *r* of the giants .... Josh 12:4
of the *r* of the giants .... Josh 13:12
unto the *r* of these nations .... Josh 23:12
of the *r* of the Amorites 2Sam 21:2
to the *r* of the people 1Kin 12:23
r of the house of Jeroboam 1Kin 14:10
r of the sodomites, which 1Kin 22:46
thy prayer for the *r* 2Kin 19:4
the *r* of mine inheritance 2Kin 21:14
the *r* of the multitude 2Kin 25:11
r of the sons of Kohath 1Chr 6:70
and he will return to the *r* 2Chr 30:6
and of all the *r* of Israel 2Chr 34:9
r of their brethren the .... Ezra 3:8
our God, to leave us a *r* to .... Ezra 9:8
r..left of the captivity .... Neh 1:3
the *r* of them the fire .... Job 22:20
a *r* of them shall return .... Is 10:22
the name, and *r*, and son .... Is 14:22
upon the *r* of the land .... Is 15:9
r shall be very small and .... Is 16:14
and the *r* of Syria .... Is 17:3
thy prayer for the *r* .... Is 37:4
r of the house of Israel .... Is 46:3
glean the *r* of Israel as a .... Jer 6:9
shall be no *r* of them .... Jer 11:23
it shall be well with thy *r* .... Jer 15:11
Ekron, and the *r* of Ashdod .... Jer 25:20
the *r* of the people that .... Jer 39:9
had left a *r* of Judah .... Jer 40:11
r of the people whom he .... Jer 41:16
God, even for all this *r* .... Jer 42:2
took all the *r* of Judah .... Jer 43:5
I will take the *r* of Judah .... Jer 44:12
r of the country of Caphtor .... Jer 47:4
I leave a *r*, that ye may .... Ezek 6:8
full end of the *r* of Israel? .... Ezek 11:13
shall be left a *r* that shall .... Ezek 14:22
r shall fall by the sword .... Ezek 23:25
the *r* of the sea coast .... Ezek 25:16
r whom the Lord shall .... Joel 2:32
be gracious unto the *r* of .... Amos 5:15
possess the *r* of Edom .... Amos 9:12
gather the *r* of Israel .... Mic 2:12
make her that halted a *r* .... Mic 4:7
r of his brethren shall .... Mic 5:3
r of the people shall spoil .... Hab 2:8
I will cut off the *r* of Baal .... Zeph 1:4
r of the house of Judah .... Zeph 2:7
with all the *r* of the people .... Hag 1:12
eyes of the *r* of this people .... Zech 8:6
r took his servants .... Matt 22:6
the *r* were affrighted, and .... Rev 11:13
war with the *r* of her seed .... Rev 12:17
r were slain with the sword .... Rev 19:21

REMORSE—*distress arising from guilt*
Of a renegade .... Matt 27:3-5
Of a disciple .... Luke 22:62
In flame .... Luke 16:24

REMOVE—*to get rid of; to take from one place to another*

[*also* REMOVED, REMOVETH, REMOVING]
Noah *r*..covering of the ark .... Gen 8:13
he *r*..unto a mountain .... Gen 12:8
Then Abram *r* his tent .... Gen 13:18
r from thence, and digged .... Gen 26:22
r..all the speckled .... Gen 30:32
he *r* that day the he goats .... Gen 30:35
he *r* them to cities from .... Gen 47:21
r it from Ephraim's head .... Gen 48:17
he *r* the swarms of flies .... Ex 8:31
angel..*r* and went behind .... Ex 14:19
the people saw it, they *r* .... Ex 20:18
people *r* from Hazeroth .... Num 12:16
they *r* and pitched .... Num 21:12
of Israel *r* from Rameses .... Num 33:5
r from Marah and came .... Num 33:9
they *r* from the Red Sea .... Num 33:11
r from the desert of Sinai .... Num 33:16
r from mount Shapher .... Num 33:24
they *r* from Makheloth .... Num 33:26
they *r* from Bene-jaakan .... Num 33:32
they *r* from Ezion-gaber .... Num 33:36
they *r* from Dibon-gad .... Num 33:46
of Israel *r* from tribe to .... Num 36:7
not *r* thy neighbor's .... Deut 19:14
r his neighbor's landmark .... Deut 27:17
he *r* into all the kingdoms .... Deut 28:25
they *r* from Shittim and .... Josh 3:1
ye shall *r* from your place .... Josh 3:3
then would I *r* Abimelech .... Judg 9:29
why his hand is not *r* from 1Sam 6:3
Saul *r* him from him, and 1Sam 18:13
David would not *r* the ark 2Sam 6:10
he *r* Amasa out of the 2Sam 20:12
r all the idols that his 1Kin 15:12
high places were not *r* 1Kin 15:14
high places were not *r* 2Kin 15:4
r the laver from off them 2Kin 16:17
r them out of his sight 2Kin 17:18
He *r* the high places and 2Kin 18:4
r Judah also out of my sight 2Kin 23:27
as I have *r* Israel and will 2Kin 23:27
they *r* them to Manahath 1Chr 8:6
he *r* her from being queen 2Chr 15:16
more *r* the foot of Israel 2Chr 33:8
they *r* the burnt offerings 2Chr 35:12
r the mountains and .... Job 9:5
r away the speech of the .... Job 12:20
rock is *r* out of his place .... Job 14:18
rock be *r* out of his place? .... Job 18:4
hope hath he *r* like a tree .... Job 19:10
Some *r* the landmarks .... Job 24:2
would he have *r* thee out .... Job 36:16
hand of the wicked *r* me .... Ps 36:11
though the earth be *r* .... Ps 46:2
I *r* his shoulder from the .... Ps 81:6
he *r* our transgressions .... Ps 103:12
should not be *r* for ever .... Ps 104:5
R from me reproach .... Ps 119:22
Zion, which cannot be *r* .... Ps 125:1
left; *r* thy foot from evil .... Prov 4:27
R thy way far from her .... Prov 5:8
righteous shall never be *r* .... Prov 10:30
R not the ancient landmark .... Prov 22:28
R not the old landmark .... Prov 23:10
r stones shall be hurt .... Eccl 10:9
r sorrow from thy heart .... Eccl 11:10
Lord have *r* men far away .... Is 6:12
r the bounds of the people .... Is 10:13
in the sure place be *r* .... Is 22:25
shall be *r* like a cottage .... Is 24:20
r it far unto all the ends .... Is 26:15
r their heart far from .... Is 29:13
shall not thy teachers be *r* .... Is 30:20
stakes thereof shall ever be *r* .... Is 33:20
r from me as a shepherd's .... Is 38:12
his place shall he not *r* .... Is 46:7
depart, and the hills be *r* .... Is 54:10
then shalt thou not *r* .... Jer 4:1
to be *r* into all kingdoms .... Jer 15:4
be *r* into all the kingdoms .... Jer 24:9
r you far from your land .... Jer 27:10
to be *r* to all the kingdoms .... Jer 29:18
r it from before my face .... Jer 32:31
be *r* into all the kingdoms .... Jer 34:17
shall *r*, they shall depart .... Jer 50:3
sinned; therefore she is *r* .... Lam 1:8
hast *r* my soul far off from .... Lam 3:17
and their gold shall be *r* .... Ezek 7:19
prepare thee stuff for *r* .... Ezek 12:3
r by day in their sight .... Ezek 12:3
r from thy place to another .... Ezek 12:3
R the diadem and take off .... Ezek 21:26
them to be *r* and spoiled .... Ezek 23:46
uncleanness of a *r* woman .... Ezek 36:17
r violence and spoil and .... Ezek 45:9
he *r* kings and setteth up .... Dan 2:21
like them that *r* the bound .... Hos 5:10
r far off from you the .... Joel 2:20
r them far from their border .... Joel 3:6
themselves shall be *r* .... Amos 6:7
shall not *r* your necks .... Mic 2:3
how hath he *r* it from me! .... Mic 2:4
shall the decree be far *r* .... Mic 7:11
r the iniquity of that land .... Zech 3:9
mountain shall *r* toward .... Zech 14:4
R hence to yonder place .... Matt 17:20
Be thou *r* and be thou .... Matt 21:21
Be thou *r* and be thou .... Mark 11:23
willing, *r* this cup from me .... Luke 22:42
he *r* him into this land .... Acts 7:4
he had *r* him, he raised .... Acts 13:22
that I could *r* mountains 1Cor 13:2
marvel that ye are so soon *r* .... Gal 1:6
r..things that are shaken .... Heb 12:27
r thy candlestick out of his .... Rev 2:5

REMPHAN (rĕm'făn)—*a name for Kiyyan, a Babylonian astral deity*
Worshiped by Israelites .... Acts 7:41-43

REND—*to tear apart by force*

Used literally of:
Garments .... Ezra 9:3, 5
Clothing .... Esth 4:1
Rocks .... Matt 27:51
Veil .... Matt 27:51
Flesh .... Matt 7:6
Body .... Mark 9:26

Figuratively of:
Repentance .... Joel 2:13
Harlotry .... Jer 4:30
Destruction .... Hos 13:8
Dissolution of the old economy .... Mark 15:38
Joy 1Kin 1:40

[*also* RENDING, RENT, RENTEST]
pit, and he *r* his clothes .... Gen 37:29
they *r* their clothes and .... Gen 44:13
habergeon that it be not *r* .... Ex 28:32
hole, that it should not *r* .... Ex 39:23
neither *r* your clothes; lest .... Lev 10:6
his clothes shall be *r* and .... Lev 13:45
r it out of the garment .... Lev 13:56
his head, nor *r* his clothes .... Lev 21:10
the land *r* their clothes .... Num 14:6
Joshua *r* his clothes and .... Josh 7:6

R

and wine bottles, old, and *r* . . .Josh 9:4
her, that he *r* his clothes . . . . . .Judg 11:35
and he *r* him as he would . . . . .Judg 14:6
day with his clothes *r* 1Sam 4:12
of his mantle and it *r* 1Sam 15:27
Lord hath *r* the kingdom 1Sam 28:17
Saul with his clothes *r* 2Sam 1:2
R your clothes and gird 2Sam 3:31
r her garment of divers 2Sam 13:19
meet him with his coat *r* 2Sam 15:32
r the kingdom from thee 1Kin 11:11
not *r* away all the kingdom 1Kin 11:13
and *r* it in twelve pieces 1Kin 11:30
altar shall be *r*, and 1Kin 13:3
And *r* the kingdom away 1Kin 14:8
wind *r* the mountains 1Kin 19:11
words that he *r* his clothes 1Kin 21:27
and *r* them in two pieces 2Kin 2:12
letter that he *r* his clothes 2Kin 5:7
that he *r* his clothes 2Kin 6:30
Athaliah *r* her clothes and 2Kin 11:14
r Israel from the house of 2Kin 17:21
with their clothes *r* 2Kin 18:37
that he *r* his clothes 2Kin 19:1
law, that he *r* his clothes 2Kin 22:11
Athaliah *r* her clothes 2Chr 23:13
law, that he *r* his clothes 2Chr 34:19
r thy clothes and weep 2Chr 34:27
Job arose and *r* his mantle . . . .Job 1:20
r every one his mantle . . . . .Job 2:12
cloud is not *r* under them . . . . .Job 26:8
my soul like a lion *r* it in . . . . .Ps 7:2
time to *r*, and a time to sew . . .Eccl 3:7
and instead of a girdle a *r* . . . . .Is 3:24
Hezekiah with..clothes *r* . . . . . .Is 36:22
that he *r* his clothes . . . . .Is 37:1
wouldest *r* the heavens . . . . .Is 64:1
thou *r* thy face with painting . .Jer 4:30
nor *r* their garments . . . . .Jer 36:24
shaven and their clothes *r* . . . . .Jer 41:5
a stormy wind shall *r* it . . . . . . .Ezek 13:11
and *r* all their shoulder . . . . . . .Ezek 29:7
and No shall be *r* asunder . . . . .Ezek 30:16
and turn again and *r* you . . . . . .Matt 7:6
and the *r* is made worse . . . . . . .Matt 9:16
high priest *r* his clothes . . . . . . .Matt 26:65
and the *r* is made worse . . . . . . .Mark 2:21
high priest *r* his clothes . . . . . . .Mark 14:63
both the new maketh a *r* . . . . . .Luke 5:36
veil of the temple was *r* . . . . . . .Luke 23:45
Let us not *r* it, but cast . . . . . . .John 19:24
they *r* their clothes and . . . . . . .Acts 14:14
the magistrates *r* off their . . . . .Acts 16:22

RENDER—*to deliver; give; yield; restore*

[*also* RENDERED, RENDEREST, RENDERETH, RENDERING]
which they shall *r* unto me . . . .Num 18:9
will *r* vengeance to mine . . . . . .Deut 32:41
r the wickedness of . . . . .Judg 9:56
did God *r* upon their heads . . .Judg 9:57
r to every man his 1Sam 26:23
r unto the king of Israel 2Kin 3:4
r unto every man according . . .2Chr 6:30
Hezekiah *r* not again 2Chr 32:25
r unto man his . . . . .Job 33:26
work of a man shall he *r* . . . . . .Job 34:11
r to them their desert . . . . .Ps 28:4
They also that *r* evil for . . . . . . .Ps 38:20
I will *r* praises unto . . . . .Ps 56:12
r to every man according to . . .Ps 62:12
r unto our neighbors . . . . .Ps 79:12
r a reward to the proud . . . . . . .Ps 94:2
What shall I *r* unto the . . . . . . .Ps 116:12
man's hands shall be *r* . . . . .Prov 12:14
not he *r* to every man . . . . .Prov 24:12
seven men that can *r* a . . . . .Prov 26:16
that *r* recompense to his . . . . . .Is 66:6
to *r* his anger with fury . . . . . . .Is 66:15
he will *r* unto her a . . . . .Jer 51:6
R unto them a recompense . . . .Lam 3:64
so will we *r* the calves of . . . . . .Hos 14:2
will ye *r* me a recompense . . . .Joel 3:4
that I will *r* double unto . . . . . .Zech 9:12
r him the fruits in their . . . . . . .Matt 21:41
R therefore unto Caesar . . . . . .Matt 22:21
R to Caesar the things that . . . .Mark 12:17
R therefore unto Caesar the . . .Luke 20:25
will *r* to every man . . . . .Rom 2:6
R therefore to all their . . . . .Rom 13:7
Let the husband *r* unto the 1Cor 7:3
thanks can we *r* to God 1Thess 3:9
that none *r* evil for evil 1Thess 5:15
Not *r* evil for evil 1Pet 3:9

RENEW—*to restore; make new*

[*also* RENEWED, RENEWEST]
and *r* the kingdom there 1Sam 11:14
and *r* the altar of the Lord 2Chr 15:8
my bow was *r* in my hand . . . . .Job 29:20
r a right spirit within me . . . . . .Ps 51:10
thy youth is *r* like the . . . . .Ps 103:5
Lord shall *r* their strength . . . . .Is 40:31
and let the people *r* their . . . . .Is 41:1
r our days as of old . . . . .Lam 5:21
the inward man is *r* day by 2Cor 4:16
be *r* in the spirit of your . . . . . .Eph 4:23
which is *r* in knowledge . . . . . . .Col 3:10
to *r* them again unto . . . . .Heb 6:6

RENEWAL OF STRENGTH

Sources of:
Holy Spirit . . . . .Titus 3:5
Wait for the Lord . . . . . . .Is 40:31
Cleansing from sin . . . . . . .Ps 51:10

Objects of:
Youthfulness . . . . .Ps 103:5
Peoples . . . . .Is 41:1
Inward man 2Cor 4:16
New man . . . . .Col 3:10
Mind . . . . .Rom 12:2

RENOWN—*of great reputation*
Man .Gen 6:4
City .Ezek 26:17
God .Dan 9:15
Plant . . . . .Ezek 34:29

[*also* RENOWNED]
the *r* of the congregation . . . . . .Num 1:16
evildoers shall never be *r* . . . . .Is 14:20
rulers great lords and *r* . . . . . . .Ezek 23:23

RENT, RENTEST—*See* REND

RENUNCIATION—*giving up the right to do something; rejection*

Blessings of:
True discipleship . . . . .Luke 14:33
True reward . . . . .Mark 10:28-31
Future reward . . . . .Luke 18:28-30

[*also* RENOUNCED]
have *r* the hidden things of 2Cor 4:2

REPAID—*See* REPAY

REPAIR—*restore what has been destroyed*

[*also* REPAIRED, REPAIRING]
r the cities and dwelt in . . . . . . .Judg 21:23
and *r* the breaches of the 1Kin 11:27
r the altar of the Lord that 1Kin 18:30
them *r* the breaches of the 2Kin 12:5
not *r* the breaches of the 2Kin 12:6
to *r* the breaches of the 2Kin 12:8
to *r* the breaches of the 2Kin 22:5
Joab *r* the rest of the city 1Chr 11:8
Joash was minded to *r* the 2Chr 24:4
money to *r* the house of 2Chr 24:5
and carpenters to *r* the 2Chr 24:12
the *r* of the house of God 2Chr 24:27
house of the Lord, and *r* 2Chr 29:3
r Millo in the city of David . . .2Chr 32:5
he *r* the altar of the Lord 2Chr 33:16
to *r* the house of the Lord 2Chr 34:8
to *r* the desolations . . . . .Ezra 9:9
the old gate *r* Jehoiada the . . . .Neh 3:6
next unto him *r* Uzziel . . . . .Neh 3:8
After him *r* Nehemiah . . . . .Neh 3:16
After him *r* their brethren . . . . . .Neh 3:18
Zabbai earnestly *r* the . . . . .Neh 3:20
after him *r* the priests . . . . .Neh 3:22
above the horse gate *r* the . . . .Neh 3:28
After him *r* Hananiah the . . . . .Neh 3:30
the sheep gate *r* the . . . . .Neh 3:32
they shall *r* the waste . . . . .Is 61:4

REPAIRER—*one who restores damaged things*
The *r* of the breach . . . . .Is 58:12

REPAY—*to return payment; refund; requite*

[*also* REPAID, REPAYETH]
r them that hate him to . . . . . . .Deut 7:10
he will *r* him to his face . . . . . . .Deut 7:10
shall *r* him what he hath . . . . . .Job 21:31
that I should *r* him? . . . . .Job 41:11
righteous good shall be *r* . . . . . .Prov 13:21
accordingly he will *r* fury . . . . . .Is 59:18
the islands he will *r* . . . . .Is 59:18
when I come again, I will *r* . . .Luke 10:35
I will *r*, saith the Lord . . . . .Rom 12:19
own hand, I will *r* it . . . . .Philem 19

REPEATETH—*to do again*
he that *r* a matter . . . . .Prov 17:9

REPENT—*turn away from sin and change one's behavior*

Described as:
"Turned" . . . . .Acts 9:35
"Repent" . . . . .Acts 8:22
"Return" 1Sam 7:3
"Conversion" . . . . .Acts 15:3

Kinds of:
National . . . . .Joel 3:5-8
Internal . . . . .Ps 51:10-13
Unavailing . . . . .Heb 12:16, 17
True . . . . .Acts 9:1-20
Unreal . . . . .Ex 9:27-35

Derived from gift of:
God .Acts 11:18
Christ . . . . .Acts 5:31
Spirit . . . . .Zech 12:10

Things leading to:
God's long-suffering 2Pet 3:9
God's goodness . . . . .Rom 2:4
Conviction of sin . . . . .Acts 2:37, 38

Productive of:
Life .Acts 11:18
Remission of sins . . . . .Mark 1:4
New spirit . . . . .Ezek 18:31
New heart . . . . .Ezek 18:31
Joy .Luke 15:7, 10

Signs of:
Reformation of life . . . . . .Matt 3:8
Restitution . . . . .Luke 19:8
Godly sorrow 2Cor 7:9, 10
See CONVERSION

[*also* REPENTANCE, REPENTED, REPENTEST, REPENTETH, REPENTING, REPENTINGS]
r the Lord that he had . . . . .Gen 6:6
r me that I have made them . . .Gen 6:7
the people *r* when they see . . . .Ex 13:17
r of this evil against thy . . . . . . .Ex 32:12
Lord *r* of the evil which he . . . .Ex 32:14
son of man that he should *r* . . .Num 23:19
r himself for his servants . . . . . .Deut 32:36
for it *r* the Lord because . . . . . .Judg 2:18
children of Israel *r* . . . . .Judg 21:6
r me that I have set up 1Sam 15:11
of Israel will not lie nor *r* 1Sam 15:29
a man that he should *r* 1Sam 15:29
Lord *r* that he had made 1Sam 15:35
the Lord *r* him of the evil 2Sam 24:16
and *r* and make 1Kin 8:47
and he *r* him of the evil 1Chr 21:15
and *r* in dust and ashes . . . . . . .Job 42:6
it *r* thee concerning thy . . . . . . .Ps 90:13
r according to the . . . . .Ps 106:45
hath sworn and will not *r* . . . . .Ps 110:4
r himself concerning his . . . . . . .Ps 135:14
purposed it, and will not *r* . . . .Jer 4:28
no man *r* him of his . . . . .Jer 8:6
I am weary with *r* . . . . .Jer 15:6
r of the evil that I thought . . . .Jer 18:8
the Lord overthrew and *r* . . . .Jer 20:16
that I may *r* me of the evil . . . .Jer 26:3

and the Lord will *r* him of ... Jer 26:13
the Lord *r* him of the evil ... Jer 26:19
that I was turned I *r* ... Jer 31:19
r me of the evil that I ... Jer 42:10
R, and turn..from your ... Ezek 14:6
R and turn yourselves ... Ezek 18:30
I spare, neither will I *r* ... Ezek 24:14
my *r* are kindled together ... Hos 11:8
r shall be hid from mine ... Hos 13:14
and *r* him of the evil ... Joel 2:13
if he will return and *r* ... Joel 2:14
Lord *r* for this; It shall not ... Amos 7:3
Lord *r* for this; This also ... Amos 7:6
tell if God will turn and *r* ... Jon 3:9
God *r* of the evil, that he ... Jon 3:10
and *r* thee of the evil ... Jon 4:2
Lord of hosts and I *r* not ... Zech 8:14
R ye; for the kingdom ... Matt 3:2
fruits meet for *r* ... Matt 3:8
baptize you with water unto *r* ... Matt 3:11
R for the kingdom of ... Matt 4:17
righteous, but sinners to *r* ... Matt 9:13
because they *r* not ... Matt 11:20
would have *r* long ago in ... Matt 11:21
they *r* at the preaching of ... Matt 12:41
but afterward he *r* ... Matt 21:29
ye had seen it, *r* not ... Matt 21:32
that he was condemned, *r* ... Matt 27:3
preach the baptism of *r* ... Mark 1:4
r ye and believe the ... Mark 1:15
righteous, but sinners to *r* ... Mark 2:17
preached that men should *r* ... Mark 6:12
preaching the baptism of *r* ... Luke 3:3
fruits worthy of *r* ... Luke 3:8
righteous, but sinners to *r* ... Luke 5:32
had a great while ago *r* ... Luke 10:13
they *r* at the preaching of ... Luke 11:32
except ye *r*, ye shall all ... Luke 13:3
persons, which need no *r* ... Luke 15:7
from the dead, they will *r* ... Luke 16:30
and if he *r*, forgive him ... Luke 17:3
r and remission of sins ... Luke 24:47
R ye..and be converted ... Acts 3:19
to give *r* to Israel ... Acts 5:31
to the Gentiles granted *r* ... Acts 11:18
the baptism of *r* to all ... Acts 13:24
all men everywhere to *r* ... Acts 17:30
with the baptism of *r* ... Acts 19:4
r toward God, and faith ... Acts 20:21
that they should *r* and turn ... Acts 26:20
and do works meet for *r* ... Acts 26:20
of God leadeth thee to *r*? ... Rom 2:4
of God are without *r* ... Rom 11:29
I do not *r*, though I did *r* ... 2Cor 7:8
but that ye sorrowed to *r* ... 2Cor 7:9
godly sorrow worketh *r* ... 2Cor 7:10
to salvation not to be *r* of ... 2Cor 7:10
not *r* of the uncleanness ... 2Cor 12:21
will give them *r* ... 2Tim 2:25
again the foundation of *r* ... Heb 6:1
renew them again unto *r* ... Heb 6:6
Lord sware and will not *r* ... Heb 7:21
for he found no place of *r* ... Heb 12:17
that all should come to *r* ... 2Pet 3:9
thou art fallen and *r* ... Rev 2:5
of his place, except thou *r* ... Rev 2:5
to *r* of her fornication ... Rev 2:21
fornication; and she *r* not ... Rev 2:21
and hold fast and *r* ... Rev 3:3
r not of the works of their ... Rev 9:20
Neither *r* they of their ... Rev 9:21
r not to give him glory ... Rev 16:9
and *r* not of their deeds ... Rev 16:11

REPETITIONS—*empty phrases*
ye pray, use not vain *r* ... Matt 6:7

REPHAEL (rē′fā-ĕl)—*"God has healed"*
Levite porter ... 1Chr 26:7

REPHAH (rē′fä)—*"healing; support"*
Ancestor of Joshua ... 1Chr 7:25-27

REPHAIAH (rĕ-fā′yä)—*"Jehovah is healing"*
1. Man of Issachar ... 1Chr 7:2
2. Descendant of Jonathan ... 1Chr 9:43
Called Rapha ... 1Chr 8:37
3. Simeonite prince ... 1Chr 4:42, 43
4. Postexilic ruler ... Neh 3:9
5. Descendant of David ... 1Chr 3:21

REPHAIM (rĕf′ā-ĭm)—*giants*
1. Early race of giants in Palestine ... Gen 14:5
Among doomed nations ... Gen 15:20
See GIANTS
2. Valley near Jerusalem ... 2Sam 23:13, 14
Very fertile ... Is 17:5
Scene of Philistine defeats ... 2Sam 5:18-22

in the valley of *R* ... 1Chr 11:15
in the valley of *R* ... 1Chr 14:9

REPHIDIM (rĕf′ĭ-dĭm)—*"beds"*
Israelite camp ... Num 33:12-15
Moses struck rock ... Ex 17:1-7
Amalek defeated ... Ex 17:8-16

they were departed from *R* ... Ex 19:2

REPLENISH—*to supply; nourish; fill up again*

[*also* REPLENISHED]
multiply and *r* the earth ... Gen 1:28
multiply and *r* the earth ... Gen 9:1
they be *r* from the east ... Is 2:6
pass over the sea, have *r* ... Is 23:2
I have *r* every sorrowful ... Jer 31:25
I shall be *r*, now she is ... Ezek 26:2
wast *r* and made very ... Ezek 27:25

REPLIEST—*give answer to*
who art thou that *r* against ... Rom 9:20

REPORT—*a transmitted account*

Kinds of:
True ... 1Kin 10:6
Good ... Prov 15:30
False ... Ex 23:1
Defaming ... Jer 20:10
Slanderous ... Rom 3:8
Evil ... 2Cor 6:8

Good, obtained by:
Fear ... Deut 2:25
Just life ... Acts 10:22
Devout life ... Acts 22:12
Outsiders ... 1Tim 3:7
Faith ... Heb 11:2, 39
Friends ... 3John 12

[*also* REPORTED]
unto his father their evil *r* ... Gen 37:2
shalt not raise a false *r* ... Ex 23:1
brought up an evil *r* of the ... Num 13:32
bring up the evil *r* upon ... Num 14:37
for it is no good *r* that ... 1Sam 2:24
was a true *r* which I heard ... 2Chr 9:5
It is *r* among the heathen ... Neh 6:6
have matter for an evil *r* ... Neh 6:13
they *r* his good deeds ... Neh 6:19
when it shall be *r* ... Esth 1:17
a good *r* maketh the bones ... Prov 15:30
the *r* concerning Egypt ... Is 23:5
pained at the *r* of Tyre ... Is 23:5
to understand the *r* ... Is 28:19
Who hath believed our *r* ... Is 53:1
R, say they, and we will *r* ... Jer 20:10
Babylon hath heard the *r* ... Jer 50:43
by his side *r* the matter ... Ezek 9:11
r among the Jews ... Matt 28:15
who hath believed our *r*? ... John 12:38
r all that the chief priests ... Acts 4:23
seven men of honest *r* ... Acts 6:3
well *r* of by the brethren ... Acts 16:2
who hath believed our *r*? ... Rom 10:16
It is *r* commonly that there ... 1Cor 5:1
r that God is in you of a ... 1Cor 14:25
and dishonor, by evil *r* ... 2Cor 6:8
things are of good *r* ... Phil 4:8
he must have a good *r* of ... 1Tim 3:7
Well *r* of for good works ... 1Tim 5:10
elders obtained a good *r* ... Heb 11:2
a good *r* through faith ... Heb 11:39
which are now *r* unto you ... 1Pet 1:12
Demetrius hath good *r* of ... 3John 12

REPROACH—*blame or discredit*

Objects of:
God ... 2Kin 19:4-23
God's people ... Neh 6:13
Messiah ... Rom 15:3
Christians ... Luke 6:22

Agents of:
Enemies ... Neh 4:4
Foolish ... Ps 74:22
Scorner ... Prov 22:10
Satan ... 1Tim 5:14, 15
1Tim 3:7

Evil causes of:
Unbelief ... Jer 6:10
Idolatry ... Ezek 22:4
Breaking God's Law ... Num 15:30, 31
Sin ... Prov 14:34

Good causes of:
Faith in God's promises ... Heb 11:24-26
Living for Christ ... 1Pet 4:14
Suffering for Christ ... Heb 13:13

Of God's people:
Permitted by God ... Jer 15:15

[*also* REPROACHED, REPROACHES, REPROACHEST, REPROACHETH, REPROACHFULLY]
God hath taken away my *r* ... Gen 30:23
for that were a *r* unto us ... Gen 34:14
the same *r* the Lord ... Num 15:30
have I rolled away the *r* of ... Josh 5:9
among the sheaves, and *r* ... Ruth 2:15
lay it for a *r* upon all ... 1Sam 11:2
taketh away the *r* from ... 1Sam 17:26
pleaded the cause of my *r* ... 1Sam 25:39
hast thou *r* and blasphemed ... 2Kin 19:22
in great affliction and *r* ... Neh 1:3
that we be no more a *r* ... Neh 2:17
the *r* of the heathen our ... Neh 5:9
me upon the cheek *r* ... Job 16:10
ten times have ye *r* me ... Job 19:3
plead against me my *r* ... Job 19:5
heard the check of my *r* ... Job 20:3
my heart shall not *r* me so ... Job 27:6
up a *r* against his ... Ps 15:3
r of men, and despised ... Ps 22:6
I was a *r* among all mine ... Ps 31:11
make me not the *r* of the ... Ps 39:8
bones, mine enemies *r* me ... Ps 42:10
makest us a *r* to our ... Ps 44:13
For the voice of him that *r* ... Ps 44:16
it was not an enemy that *r* ... Ps 55:12
save me from the *r* of him ... Ps 57:3
for thy sake I have borne *r* ... Ps 69:7
The *r* of them that *r* thee ... Ps 69:9
Thou hast known my *r* ... Ps 69:19
he covered with *r* and ... Ps 71:13
long shall the adversary *r*? ... Ps 74:10
this, that the enemy hath *r* ... Ps 74:18
how the foolish man *r* thee ... Ps 74:22
put them to a perpetual *r* ... Ps 78:66
a *r* to our neighbors ... Ps 79:4
into their bosom their *r* ... Ps 79:12
they have *r* thee, O Lord ... Ps 79:12
he is a *r* to his ... Ps 89:41
the *r* of thy servants ... Ps 89:50
thine enemies have *r* ... Ps 89:51
they have *r* the footsteps ... Ps 89:51
Mine enemies *r* me all the ... Ps 102:8
I became also a *r* unto ... Ps 109:25
Remove from me *r* and ... Ps 119:22
Turn away my *r* which I ... Ps 119:39
to answer him that *r* me ... Ps 119:42
his *r* shall not be wiped ... Prov 6:33
the poor *r* his Maker ... Prov 14:31
but sin is a *r* to any people ... Prov 14:34
the poor *r* his Maker ... Prov 17:5
and with ignominy *r* ... Prov 18:3
shame, and bringeth *r* ... Prov 19:26
strife and *r* shall cease ... Prov 22:10
may answer him that *r* me ... Prov 27:11
name, to take away our *r* ... Is 4:1
but a shame, and also a *r* ... Is 30:5
sent to *r* the living God ... Is 37:4
thou *r* and blasphemed? ... Is 37:23

the curse, and Israel to *r* ...... Is 43:28
fear ye not the *r* of men ...... Is 51:7
the *r* of thy widowhood .... Is 54:4
the Lord is unto them a *r* ..... Jer 6:10
of the Lord was made a *r* ..... Jer 20:8
an everlasting *r* upon you ..... Jer 23:40
to be a *r* and a proverb .... Jer 24:9
an hissing and a *r* among ..... Jer 29:18
I did bear the *r* of my .... Jer 31:19
and a curse and a *r* .... Jer 42:18
a *r* among all the nations ..... Jer 44:8
become a desolation a *r* .... Jer 49:13
because we have heard *r* ...... Jer 51:51
he is filled full with *r* .... Lam 3:30
Thou hast heard their *r* .... Lam 3:61
consider and behold our *r* ..... Lam 5:1
r among the nations .... Ezek 5:14
it shall be a *r* and a taunt ..... Ezek 5:15
of thy *r* of the daughters ...... Ezek 16:57
and concerning their *r* .... Ezek 21:28
I made thee a *r* unto the ...... Ezek 22:4
bear the *r* of the people .... Ezek 36:15
become a *r* to all that are ..... Dan 9:16
cause the *r* offered by him .... Dan 11:18
without his own *r* he shall ..... Dan 11:18
his *r* shall his Lord return ..... Hos 12:14
not thine heritage to *r* .... Joel 2:17
make you a *r* among the ...... Joel 2:19
ye shall bear the *r* of my ...... Mic 6:16
I have heard the *r* of .... Zeph 2:8
they have *r* my people .... Zeph 2:8
to whom the *r* of it was a ..... Zeph 3:18
to take away my *r* among ..... Luke 1:25
and shall *r* you, and cast ...... Luke 6:22
Master, thus saying thou *r* .... Luke 11:45
The *r* of them that *r* thee ..... Rom 15:3
I speak as concerning *r* 2Cor 11:21
in infirmities, in *r* 2Cor 12:10
fall into *r* and..snare of 1Tim 3:7
both labor and suffer *r* 1Tim 4:10
to the adversary to speak *r* 1Tim 5:14
both by *r* and afflictions ...... Heb 10:33
Esteeming the *r* of Christ ..... Heb 11:26
the camp, bearing his *r* .... Heb 13:13
ye be *r* for the name of 1Pet 4:14

REPROBATE—*rejected as worthless; depraved*

Causes of:
Not having Christ 2Cor 13:3-5
Rejecting the faith 2Tim 3:8
Spiritual barrenness ...... Heb 6:7, 8
Lack of discipline 1Cor 9:24-27
Rejection by the Lord .. Jer 6:30

Consequences of, given up to:
Evil .... Rom 1:24-32
Delusion 2Thess 2:11, 12
Blindness .... Matt 13:13-15
Destruction 2Pet 2:9-22

[*also* REPROBATES]
R silver shall men call .... Jer 6:30
God gave them over to a *r* .... Rom 1:28
is in you, except ye be *r*? 2Cor 13:5
know that we are not *r* 2Cor 13:6
honest, though we be as *r* 2Cor 13:7
r concerning the faith 2Tim 3:8
unto every good work *r* .... Titus 1:16

REPROOF—*a cutting rebuke for misconduct*

Sources of:
God .... Ps 50:8, 21
Backslidings .... Jer 2:19
God's Word 2Tim 3:16
John the Baptist .... Luke 3:16, 19

Examples of:
Samuel 1Sam 13:13
Daniel .... Dan 5:22, 23
John the Baptist .... Matt 3:7-12
Stephen .... Acts 7:51
Paul .... Gal 2:11

[*also* REPROOFS]
astonished at his *r* .... Job 26:11
in whose mouth are no *r* ...... Ps 38:14
Turn you at my *r*, behold ..... Prov 1:23
they despised all my *r* .... Prov 1:30
and my heart despised *r* ...... Prov 5:12
r of instruction are the way ... Prov 6:23
he that refuseth *r* erreth ...... Prov 10:17
but he that hateth *r* .... Prov 12:1
that regardeth *r* shall be ...... Prov 13:18
but he that regardeth *r* .... Prov 15:5
The ear that heareth the *r* .... Prov 15:31
A *r* entereth more into a ...... Prov 17:10
The rod and *r* give wisdom .... Prov 29:15

REPROVE—*to rebuke; express disapproval of*
Designed for good .... Heb 12:5
Accomplished in love .... Rev 3:19

[*also* REPROVED, REPROVETH]
thus she was *r* .... Gen 20:16
Abraham *r* Abimelech .... Gen 21:25
will *r* the words 2Kin 19:4
he *r* kings for their sakes 1Chr 16:21
doth your arguing *r*? .... Job 6:25
He will surely *r* you .... Job 13:10
Will he *r* thee for fear .... Job 22:4
he that *r* God, let him .... Job 40:2
he *r* kings for their sakes ...... Ps 105:14
and let him *r* me .... Ps 141:5
He that *r* a scorner .... Prov 9:7
R not a scorner .... Prov 9:8
scorner loveth not one that *r* .. Prov 15:12
and *r* one that hath .... Prov 19:25
being often *r* hardeneth .... Prov 29:1
lest he *r* thee, and thou be .... Prov 30:6
r after the hearing .... Is 11:3
a snare for him that *r* in ...... Is 29:21
r the words which the Lord ... Is 37:4
hast thou not *r* Jeremiah ...... Jer 29:27
let no man strive, nor *r* .... Hos 4:4
shall answer when I am *r* ..... Hab 2:1
his deeds should be *r* .... John 3:20
is come, he will *r* the world ... John 16:8
darkness, but rather *r* them ... Eph 5:11
that are *r* are made .... Eph 5:13
r, rebuke, exhort with all 2Tim 4:2

REPROVER—*one who rebukes*
wise *r* upon an obedient ear ... Prov 25:12
shalt not be to them a *r* .... Ezek 3:26

REPTILES

Facts concerning:
Created by God .... Gen 1:24, 25
Made to praise God ..... Ps 148:7, 10
Placed under man's power .... Gen 1:26
Classified as unclean ..... Lev 11:31-43
Seen in a vision .... Acts 10:11-14
Worshiped by pagans .... Rom 1:23
Likeness of, forbidden ... Deut 4:16, 18
Portrayed on walls .... Ezek 8:10

List of:
Adder .... Prov 23:32
Asp .... Rom 3:13
Chameleon .... Lev 11:30
Cockatrice .... Is 11:8
Dragon .... Deut 32:33
Ferret .... Lev 11:30
Frog .... Rev 16:13
Leviathan .... Job 41:1, 2
Lizard .... Lev 11:30
Scorpion .... Deut 8:15
Serpents .... Matt 10:7
Snake .... Matt 7:10
Snail .... Ps 58:8
Tortoise .... Lev 11:29
Viper .... Acts 28:3

REPUTATION—*public esteem; fame*

Good:
Wonderful asset .... Prov 22:1
Based on integrity 2Cor 8:18-24
Hated by wicked .... Dan 6:4-8
Required of church officials .... Acts 6:3
Worthy of trust .... Acts 16:2

Dangers of:
Universal praise .... Luke 6:26
Flattering speech .... Rom 16:18
Worldly friendship .... James 4:4
Worldly praise 1John 4:5, 6
Undue deference toward . Gal 2:6

[*also* REPUTED]
r vile in your sight? .... Job 18:3
is in *r* for wisdom .... Eccl 10:1
of the earth are *r* .... Dan 4:35
had in *r* among all .... Acts 5:34
to them which were of *r* ...... Gal 2:2
But made himself of no *r* ..... Phil 2:7

REQUEST—*to ask for something; something asked for*

[*also* REQUESTED, REQUESTS]
I would desire a *r* of you ..... Judg 8:24
golden earrings that he *r* ...... Judg 8:26
the *r* of his handmaid 2Sam 14:15
he *r* for himself that he 1Kin 19:4
that which he *r* 1Chr 4:10
king granted him all his *r* ..... Ezra 7:6
what dost thou make *r*? .... Neh 2:4
make *r* before him for her .... Esth 4:8
and what is thy *r*? .... Esth 5:3
My petition and my *r* .... Esth 5:7
and what is thy *r*? .... Esth 7:2
Haman stood up to make *r* .... Esth 7:7
what is thy *r* further? .... Esth 9:12
Oh that I might have my *r* .... Job 6:8
not withholden the *r* .... Ps 21:2
he gave them their *r* .... Ps 106:15
he *r* of the prince .... Dan 1:8
Then Daniel *r* of the king ..... Dan 2:49
Making *r*, if by any means .... Rom 1:10
for you all making *r* .... Phil 1:4
let your *r* be made known ..... Phil 4:6

REQUIRE—*to request; demand as necessary*

[*also* REQUIRED, REQUIREST, REQUIRETH, REQUIRING]
your lives will I *r* .... Gen 9:5
every beast will I *r* it .... Gen 9:5
will I *r* the life of man .... Gen 9:5
my hand didst thou *r* it .... Gen 31:39
behold, also his blood is *r* ..... Gen 42:22
my hand shalt thou *r* him ..... Gen 43:9
such things as they *r* .... Ex 12:36
the Lord thy God *r* of thee ... Deut 10:12
in my name, I will *r* it .... Deut 18:19
thy God will surely *r* it .... Deut 23:21
let the Lord himself *r* it ...... Josh 22:23
to thee all that thou *r* .... Ruth 3:11
the Lord even *r* it 1Sam 20:16
the king's business *r* haste 1Sam 21:8
but one thing I *r* of thee 2Sam 3:13
r his blood of your hand 2Sam 4:11
when he *r*, they set bread 2Sam 12:20
whatsoever thou shalt *r* 2Sam 19:38
as the matter shall *r* 1Kin 8:59
as every day's work *r* 1Chr 16:37
doth my lord *r* this thing? 1Chr 21:3
the duty of every day *r* 2Chr 8:14
thou not *r* of the Levites 2Chr 24:6
look upon it, and *r* it 2Chr 24:22
as the duty of every day *r* ..... Ezra 3:4
the God of heaven, shall *r* .... Ezra 7:21
to *r* of the king a band .... Ezra 8:22
and will *r* nothing of them .... Neh 5:12
r not I the bread .... Neh 5:18
she *r* nothing .... Esth 2:15
Thou wilt not *r* it .... Ps 10:13
offering hast thou not *r* .... Ps 40:6
captive *r* of us a song .... Ps 137:3
they that wasted us *r* of us ... Ps 137:3
Two things have I *r* of thee ... Prov 30:7
God *r* that which is past ...... Eccl 3:15
r this at your hand .... Is 1:12
blood will I *r* .... Ezek 3:18
there will I *r* your offerings ... Ezek 20:40
blood will I *r* .... Ezek 33:6
I will *r* my flock .... Ezek 34:10
rare thing that the king *r* ...... Dan 2:11
and what doth the Lord *r* ..... Mic 6:8
may be *r* of this generation .... Luke 11:50
thy soul shall be *r* of thee ..... Luke 12:20
have *r* mine own .... Luke 19:23

r that he..be crucified .... Luke 23:23
it should be as they *r* .... Luke 23:24
the Jews *r* a sign 1Cor 1:22
it is *r* in stewards 1Cor 4:2
and need so *r*, let him do 1Cor 7:36

REQUITE—*to repay; retaliate*

[*also* REQUITED, REQUITING]
and will certainly *r* us .... Gen 50:15
Do ye thus *r* the Lord .... Deut 32:6
so God hath *r* me .... Judg 1:7
and he hath *r* me evil 1Sam 25:21
and I also will *r* you this 2Sam 2:6
the Lord will *r* me good 2Sam 16:12
I will *r* thee in this plat 2Kin 9:26
by *r* the wicked 2Chr 6:23
to *r* it with thy hand .... Ps 10:14
raise me up, that I may *r* ..... Ps 41:10
God of..shall surely *r* .... Jer 51:56
and to *r* their parents 1Tim 5:4

REREWARD—*See* REARWARD

RESCUE—*to save or deliver from something perilous*

[*also* RESCUED, RESCUETH]
shalt have none to *r* them ..... Deut 28:31
So the people *r* Jonathan 1Sam 14:45
and David *r* his two wives 1Sam 30:18
r my soul from their .... Ps 35:17
He delivereth and *r* .... Dan 6:27
and none shall *r* him .... Hos 5:14
came I with an army and *r* .... Acts 23:27

RESEMBLE—*to look like; compare*

[*also* RESEMBLANCE, RESEMBLED]
each one *r* the children .... Judg 8:18
r through all the earth .... Zech 5:6
whereunto shall I *r* it? .... Luke 13:18

RESEN (rē'sĕn)—*"bride"*
City built by Asshur ..... Gen 10:11, 12

RESERVE—*to keep back; set aside or apart*

[*also* RESERVED, RESERVETH]
thou not *r* a blessing .... Gen 27:36
things, *r* from the fire .... Num 18:9
r not to each man his wife .... Judg 21:22
gave to her that she had *r* ..... Ruth 2:18
r of them for..chariots 2Sam 8:4
but *r* of them..chariots 1Chr 18:4
r to the day of destruction? .. Job 21:30
I have *r* against the time ..... Job 38:23
he *r* his anger for ever? .... Jer 3:5
r unto us the appointed .... Jer 5:24
I will pardon..whom I *r* .... Jer 50:20
and he *r* wrath for his .... Nah 1:2
be *r* unto the hearing .... Acts 25:21
I have *r* to myself .... Rom 11:4
r in heaven for you 1Pet 1:4
to be *r* unto judgment 2Pet 2:4
to *r* the unjust unto the day .. 2Pet 2:9
r unto fire against the day 2Pet 3:7
hath *r* in everlasting chains .... Jude 6

RESERVOIR—*place where water is stored*
Family cisterns .... Is 36:16
Garden pools .... Eccl 2:6

RESH (rĕsh)
Letter of the Hebrew alphabet .... Ps 119:153-160

RESHEPH (rē'shĕf)—*the name of a Canaanite deity; meaning unknown*
Descendant of Ephraim .. 1Chr 7:23-25

RESIDUE—*a remnant; remainder*

Used literally of:
Survivors .... Jer 8:3

Used spiritually of:
Faithful remnant .... Is 28:5
Promised seed .... Zech 8:11-13

r of that which is escaped ..... Ex 10:5
And the *r* of the families 1Chr 6:66
r of Israel, of the priests ...... Neh 11:20
the *r* of the number .... Is 21:17
am deprived of the *r* .... Is 38:10
r thereof he maketh a god .... Is 44:17
the *r* of them will I deliver .... Jer 15:9
the *r* of Jerusalem .... Jer 24:8
the *r* of the vessels .... Jer 27:19
unto the *r* of the elders .... Jer 29:1
the *r* of the princes of .... Jer 39:3
all the *r* of the people .... Jer 41:10
r of the people that .... Jer 52:15
wilt thou destroy all the *r* ..... Ezek 9:8
thy *r* shall be devoured .... Ezek 23:25
the *r* of your pastures? .... Ezek 34:18
foul the *r* with your feet? ..... Ezek 34:18
unto the *r* of the heathen ..... Ezek 36:3
And the *r* in length over ...... Ezek 48:18
stamped the *r* with the feet .... Dan 7:7
r of my people shall spoil ..... Zeph 2:9
and to the *r* of the people ..... Hag 2:2
r of the people shall not be ... Zech 14:2
the *r* of the spirit .... Mal 2:15
and told it unto the *r* .... Mark 16:13
r of men might seek .... Acts 15:17

RESIGNATION—*patient submission to*
Disquieting problem ..... Josh 22:9-34
Tragic death 2Sam 19:1-8
God's chastening .... Job 2:10
Cross .... Mark 14:36
Sufferings ahead .... Acts 21:11-14
Pain 2Cor 12:7-10
Want .... Phil 4:11, 12

RESIST—*to stand against*

Of evil things:
Sin .... Heb 12:4
Adversaries .... Luke 21:15

Of good things:
God's will .... Rom 9:19
Holy Spirit .... Acts 7:51
Truth 2Tim 3:8
Wisdom .... Acts 6:10
Constituted authority .... Rom 13:2

[*also* RESISTED, RESISTETH]
at his right hand to *r* him ..... Zech 3:1
say unto you, That ye *r* not ... Matt 5:39
For who hath *r* his will? ...... Rom 9:19
not yet *r* unto blood .... Heb 12:4
God *r* the proud .... James 4:6
R the devil, and he will .... James 4:7
and he doth not *r* you .... James 5:6
God *r* the proud 1Pet 5:5
r steadfast in the faith 1Pet 5:9

RESOLVED—*reached a firm decision about*
I am *r* what to do, that .... Luke 16:4

RESORT—*to go, especially frequently or habitually*

[*also* RESORTED]
r to him out of all 2Chr 11:13
r ye thither unto us .... Neh 4:20
I may continually *r* .... Ps 71:3
the multitude *r* unto him ...... Mark 2:13
and the people *r* unto him .... Mark 10:1
many *r* unto him .... John 10:41
Jesus ofttimes *r* thither .... John 18:2
whither the Jews always *r* ..... John 18:20
unto the women which *r* ...... Acts 16:13

RESPECT—*honor manifested toward the worthy; to consider worthy of high regard*

Wrong kind:
Favoring the wealthy .... James 2:3, 9

Right kind:
Rejects the proud .... Ps 40:4

On God's part:
Regards the lowly .... Ps 138:6
Honors His covenant 2Kin 13:23
Makes God just 1Pet 1:17

[*also* RESPECTED, RESPECTETH]
And the Lord had *r* .... Gen 4:4
God had *r* unto them .... Ex 2:25
r the person of the poor ...... Lev 19:15
For I will have *r* unto you .... Lev 26:9
R not thou their offering ...... Num 16:15
shall not *r* persons .... Deut 1:17
thou shalt not *r* persons .... Deut 16:19
doth God *r* any person 2Sam 14:14
have thou *r* unto the prayer ... 1Kin 8:28
Have *r*..to the prayer of 2Chr 6:19
nor *r* of persons 2Chr 19:7
r not any that are wise .... Job 37:24
Have *r* unto the covenant ..... Ps 74:20
have *r* unto all..commandments Ps 119:6
r unto thy statutes .... Ps 119:117
r of persons in judgment ...... Prov 24:23
To have *r* of persons .... Prov 28:21
have *r* to the Holy One .... Is 17:7
r that which his fingers .... Is 17:8
r unto him that fashioned ..... Is 22:11
r not..the priests .... Lam 4:16
there is no *r* of persons .... Rom 2:11
no glory in this *r* 2Cor 3:10
is there *r* of persons .... Eph 6:9
Not that I speak in *r* .... Phil 4:11
or in *r* of a holy day .... Col 2:16
there is no *r* of persons .... Col 3:25
r unto the recompense .... Heb 11:26
Lord of glory, with *r* .... James 2:1

RESPECTER—*one who makes distinctions*
God is no *r* of persons .... Acts 10:34

RESPITE—*reprieve; delay or rest*
Pharaoh saw that there was *r* .. Ex 8:15
Give us seven days' *r* 1Sam 11:3

RESPONSIBILITY—*accountability for one's actions*

Shifting of, by:
Blaming another .... Gen 3:12
Claiming innocency ...... Matt 27:24
Blaming a people .... Ex 32:21-24

Cannot be excused by:
Ignorance .... Acts 17:30, 31
Unbelief .... John 3:18-20
Previous good .... Ex 33:12, 13
One's ancestors .... Matt 3:9, 10

Is increased by:
Sight .... John 9:39-41
Privilege .... John 15:22, 24
Opportunity .... Matt 11:20-24
Continuance in sin .... Matt 23:31-35
Rejection .... Matt 10:11-15

REST—*sleep; freedom from activity; the remainder*

Descriptive of:
Physical relaxation .... Gen 18:4
Sinful laziness .... Matt 26:45
Confidence .... Hab 3:16-19
Completion of salvation .. Heb 4:3, 8-11

Need of:
Recognized in God's Law. Ex 20:10, 11
Recognized by Christ .... Mark 6:31
Longed after .... Ps 55:6
Provided for .... Rev 6:11
Enjoyed after death ..... Job 3:13, 17; Rev 14:13

Source of, in:
Christ .... Matt 11:28, 29
Trust .... Ps 37:7
Returning to God .... Is 30:15

Disturbance of, by:
Sin .... Is 57:20
Rebellion .... Is 28:12
Persecution .... Acts 9:23
Anxiety 2Cor 2:13

See QUIETNESS

[*also* RESTED, RESTEST, RESTETH, RESTING]
he *r* on the seventh day .... Gen 2:2
the ark *r* in the seventh .... Gen 8:4
no *r* for the sole of her .... Gen 8:9
Jacob fed the *r* of Laban's .... Gen 30:36
he saw that *r* was good .... Gen 49:15
r from their burdens .... Ex 5:5
and *r* in all the coasts .... Ex 10:14
r of the holy sabbath unto .... Ex 16:23
r on the seventh day .... Ex 16:30
thou shalt let it *r* .... Ex 23:11
names of the *r* on the other ... Ex 28:10

R

seventh is the sabbath of *r* . . . .Ex 31:15
on the seventh day he *r* . . . . . . .Ex 31:17
and I will give thee *r* . . . . .Ex 33:14
seventh day thou shalt *r* . . . . . .Ex 34:21
in harvest thou shalt *r* . . . . .Ex 34:21
a sabbath of *r* to the Lord . . . .Ex 35:2
r of the blood shall be wrung . .Lev 5:9
r of the oil..in his hand . . . . . . .Lev 14:17
shall be a sabbath of *r* . . . . .Lev 16:31
is the sabbath of *r* . . . . .Lev 23:3
sabbath of *r* unto the land . . . .Lev 25:4
then shall the land *r* . . . . .Lev 26:34
as it lieth..it shall *r* . . . . .Lev 26:35
did not *r* in your sabbaths . . . . .Lev 26:35
they *r* in their tents . . . . .Num 9:18
the cloud *r* in the wilderness . .Num 10:12
to search out a *r* place . . . . .Num 10:33
when the spirit *r* upon them . . .Num 11:25
the *r* of them that were . . . . . . .Num 31:8
the *r* of Gilead . . . . .Deut 3:13
maidservant may *r* as well . . . . .Deut 5:14
are not as yet come to the *r* . . .Deut 12:9
God hath given thee *r* . . . . .Deut 25:19
the sole of thy foot have *r* . . . .Deut 28:65
God hath given you *r* . . . . .Josh 1:13
r in the waters of Jordan . . . . . .Josh 3:13
the *r* which remained . . . . .Josh 10:20
the land *r* from war . . . . .Josh 11:23
the *r* of the kingdom . . . . .Josh 13:27
And the land had *r* . . . . .Josh 14:15
the *r* of the children . . . . .Josh 17:2
the *r* of the children . . . . .Josh 21:5
Lord gave them *r* . . . . .Josh 21:44
r unto your brethren . . . . .Josh 22:4
the Lord had given *r* . . . . .Josh 23:1
the land had *r* forty years . . . . .Judg 3:11
the land had *r* forty years . . . . .Judg 5:31
the *r* of the people bowed . . . . .Judg 7:6
that ye may find *r* . . . . .Ruth 1:9
shall I not seek *r* for thee . . . . .Ruth 3:1
the *r* of the people he sent 1Sam 13:2
the *r* we have..destroyed 1Sam 15:15
Let it *r* on the head of Joab . . .2Sam 3:29
the Lord had given him *r* 2Sam 7:1
r of the people he delivered . . .2Sam 10:10
gather the *r* of the people 2Sam 12:28
the birds of the air to *r* 2Sam 21:10
my God hath given me *r* 1Kin 5:4
they *r* on the house 1Kin 6:10
hath given *r* unto his people . . .1Kin 8:56
the *r* of the acts of Solomon . . .1Kin 11:41
the *r* of the acts of Jeroboam . .1Kin 14:19
smote the *r* of the Amalekites .1Chr 4:43
after that the ark had *r* 1Chr 6:31
Joab repaired the *r* 1Chr 11:8
r also..were of one heart 1Chr 12:38
and the *r* that were chosen 1Chr 16:41
r of the people he delivered . . .1Chr 19:11
who shall be a man of *r* 1Chr 22:9
hath given *r* unto his people . . .1Chr 23:25
r of the sons of Levi 1Chr 24:20
build a house of *r* 1Chr 28:2
O Lord God, into thy *r* place .2Chr 6:41
Now the *r* of the acts 2Chr 9:29
And the *r* of the acts 2Chr 13:22
for the land had *r* 2Chr 14:6
the Lord had given him *r* 2Chr 14:6
for we *r* on thee, and in thy . . .2Chr 14:11
Lord gave them *r* 2Chr 15:15
his God gave him *r* 2Chr 20:30
they brought the *r* of 2Chr 24:14
Now the *r* of the acts 2Chr 25:26
the *r* of the acts of Uzziah 2Chr 26:22
the *r* or the acts of Jotham 2Chr 27:7
r of his acts and of all 2Chr 28:26
r themselves upon the words . .2Chr 32:8
the *r* of the acts of Hezekiah . .2Chr 32:32
the *r* of the acts of Manasseh . .2Chr 33:18
the *r* of the acts of Josiah 2Chr 35:26
the *r* of the acts of Jehoiakim .2Chr 36:8
the *r* of the chief . . . . .Ezra 4:3
the *r* of their companions . . . . .Ezra 4:9
r of the nations . . . . .Ezra 4:10
r that are on this side . . . . .Ezra 4:10
r of their companions . . . . .Ezra 4:17
and unto the *r* beyond . . . . .Ezra 4:17
r of the children . . . . .Ezra 6:16
the *r* of the silver . . . . .Ezra 7:18
the *r* that did the work . . . . . . .Neh 2:16
to the *r* of the people . . . . .Neh 4:14
and the *r* of our enemies . . . . . .Neh 6:1
the *r* of the people gave . . . . . .Neh 7:72
But after they had *r* . . . . .Neh 9:28
the *r* of the people . . . . .Neh 10:28
the *r* of the people also . . . . . . .Neh 11:1
the *r* of the..provinces? . . . . . . .Esth 9:12
fourteenth day of the same *r* . .Esth 9:17
r from their enemies . . . . .Esth 9:22
There the prisoners *r* . . . . .Job 3:18
thou shalt take thy *r* . . . . .Job 11:18
Turn from him, that he may *r* .Job 14:6
our *r* together is in the dust . .Job 17:16
be in safety, whereon he *r* . . . .Job 24:23
my sinews take no *r* . . . . .Job 30:17
My bowels boiled, and *r* not . .Job 30:27
my flesh also shall *r* . . . . .Ps 16:9
the *r* of their substance . . . . . . .Ps 17:14
neither is there any *r* . . . . .Ps 38:3
r from the days of adversity . . .Ps 94:13
they should not enter..my *r* . . .Ps 95:11
Return unto thy *r* . . . . .Ps 116:7
rod of the wicked shall not *r* . .Ps 125:3
Arise, O Lord, into thy *r* . . . . .Ps 132:8
neither will he *r* content . . . . . .Prov 6:35
Wisdom *r* in the heart . . . . .Prov 14:33
spoil not his *r* place . . . . .Prov 24:15
rage or laugh, there is no *r* . . . .Prov 29:9
his heart taketh not *r* . . . . .Eccl 2:23
this hath more *r* . . . . .Eccl 6:5
for anger *r* in the bosom . . . . . .Eccl 7:9
makest thy flock to *r* . . . . .Song 1:7
shall *r* all of them . . . . .Is 7:19
r of the trees of his forest . . . . .Is 10:19
spirit of the Lord shall *r* . . . . . .Is 11:2
give thee *r* from thy sorrow . . .Is 14:3
I will take my *r*, and I will . . . .Is 18:4
also shalt thou have no *r* . . . . . .Is 23:12
the hand of the Lord *r* . . . . .Is 25:10
and in quiet *r* places . . . . .Is 32:18
screech owl also shall *r* . . . . . . .Is 34:14
for herself a place of *r* . . . . .Is 34:14
my judgment to *r* for a light . . .Is 51:4
they shall *r* in their beds . . . . . .Is 57:2
Jerusalem's sake I will not *r* . . .Is 62:1
the Lord caused him to *r* . . . . .Is 63:14
where is the place of my *r*? . . .Is 66:1
and ye shall find *r* . . . . .Jer 6:16
and shall be in *r* . . . . .Jer 30:10
I went to cause him to *r* . . . . . .Jer 31:2
the *r* of the people . . . . .Jer 39:9
my sighing, and I find no *r* . . . .Jer 45:3
return, and be in *r* . . . . .Jer 46:27
into thy scabbard, *r* . . . . .Jer 47:6
he may give *r* to the land . . . . .Jer 50:34
and the *r* of the multitude . . . . .Jer 52:15
the heathen, she findeth no *r* . .Lam 1:3
day and night: give..no *r* . . . . . .Lam 2:18
we labor, and have no *r* . . . . . .Lam 5:5
my fury to *r* upon them . . . . . . .Ezek 5:13
my fury toward thee to *r* . . . . . .Ezek 16:42
I will cause my fury to *r* . . . . . .Ezek 21:17
my fury to *r* upon thee . . . . . . .Ezek 24:13
go to them that are at *r* . . . . . . .Ezek 38:11
blessing to *r* in thine house . . . .Ezek 44:30
r of the land shall they . . . . .Ezek 45:8
As for the *r* of the tribes . . . . . .Ezek 48:23
the *r* of the wise men . . . . .Dan 2:18
Nebuchadnezzar was at *r* . . . . . .Dan 4:4
As..the *r* of the beasts . . . . .Dan 7:12
thou shalt *r* and stand . . . . .Dan 12:13
for this is not your *r* . . . . .Mic 2:10
he will *r* in his love . . . . .Zeph 3:17
the earth..is at *r* . . . . .Zech 1:11
Damascus shall be the *r* . . . . .Zech 9:1
r eat every one the flesh . . . . . .Zech 11:9
seeking *r*, and findeth none . . .Matt 12:43
The *r* said, Let be . . . . .Matt 27:49
Sleep on now and take your *r* .Mark 14:41
your peace shall *r* upon it . . . . .Luke 10:6
through dry places, seeking *r* . .Luke 11:24
take ye thought for the *r*? . . . . .Luke 12:26
and *r* the sabbath day . . . . .Luke 23:56
the eleven, and to all the *r* . . . .Luke 24:9
had spoken of taking of *r* . . . . .John 11:13
my flesh shall *r* in hope . . . . . . .Acts 2:26
of the *r* durst no man join . . . .Acts 5:13
what is the place of my *r*? . . . .Acts 7:49
the churches *r* throughout . . . . .Acts 9:31
And the *r*, some on boards . . . .Acts 27:44
art called a Jew, and *r* . . . . .Rom 2:17
and the *r* were blinded . . . . .Rom 11:7
But to the *r* speak I 1Cor 7:12
r will I set in order 1Cor 11:34
I had no *r* in my spirit 2Cor 2:13
Macedonia, our flesh had no *r* .2Cor 7:5
Christ may *r* upon me 2Cor 12:9
to you who are troubled *r* 2Thess 1:7
They shall not enter..my *r* . . . .Heb 3:11
left us of entering..his *r* . . . . . . .Heb 4:1
believed do enter into *r* . . . . . . .Heb 4:3
they shall enter into my *r* . . . . .Heb 4:3
they shall enter into my *r* . . . . .Heb 4:5
Jesus had given them *r* . . . . .Heb 4:8
he that is entered into his *r* . . .Heb 4:10
live the *r* of his time 1Pet 4:2
spirit of glory and of God *r* . . .1Pet 4:14
I say, and unto the *r* . . . . .Rev 2:24
they *r* not day and night . . . . . .Rev 4:8
r of the men which were not . .Rev 9:20
and they have no *r* . . . . .Rev 14:11
the *r* of the dead lived not . . . .Rev 20:5

RESTINGPLACE—*a location where one can find renewal and strength*
they have forgotten their *r* . . . .Jer 50:6

RESTITUTION—*act of restoring*
Time of . . . . .Acts 3:21
Of damaged property . . . .Ex 22:3-12

to his substance shall the *r* . . . .Job 20:18

RESTORATION—*renewal of something to its former state*

Miraculous, from:
Death 2Kin 8:1, 5
Dried hand 1Kin 13:4, 6
Withered hand . . . . .Mark 3:5
Blindness . . . . .Mark 8:25

Natural of:
Man's wife . . . . .Gen 20:7, 14
Man's position . . . . .Gen 40:13, 21
Land 2Sam 9:7
Visit . . . . .Heb 13:19

Spiritual:
Joy . . . . .Ps 51:11, 12
Recovery . . . . .Jer 30:17
God's blessings . . . . .Joel 2:25
Christ . . . . .Is 49:6

[*also* RESTORE, RESTORED, RESTORETH]
me he *r* unto mine office . . . . . .Gen 41:13
r every man's money . . . . .Gen 42:25
My money is *r* . . . . .Gen 42:28
he shall *r* five oxen . . . . .Ex 22:1
r that which he took . . . . .Lev 6:4
that killeth..shall *r* it . . . . .Lev 24:21
r the overplus unto the . . . . . . .Lev 25:27
r him to the city . . . . .Num 35:25
and thou shalt *r* it to him . . . . .Deut 22:2
and shall not be *r* to thee . . . . .Deut 28:31
r those lands again . . . . .Judg 11:13
had *r* the eleven hundred . . . . . .Judg 17:3
now therefore I will *r* it . . . . . . .Judg 17:3
taken from Israel were *r* 1Sam 7:14
and I will *r* it you 1Sam 12:3
And he shall *r* the lamb 2Sam 12:6
r me the kingdom of my 2Sam 16:3
from thy father, I will *r* 1Kin 20:34
whose son he had *r* to life 2Kin 8:1
R all that was hers 2Kin 8:6
He built Elath, and *r* it 2Kin 14:22
which Huram had *r* 2Chr 8:2
be *r*, and brought again . . . . . . .Ezra 6:5
R, I pray you, to them . . . . .Neh 5:11
and his hands shall *r* . . . . .Job 20:10
He *r* my soul: he leadeth me . .Ps 23:3

I *r* that which I took . . . . .Ps 69:4
he be found, he shall *r*. . . . . . . .Prov 6:31
I will *r* thy judges . . . . .Is 1:26
and none saith, *R* . . . . .Is 42:22
r comforts unto him . . . . .Is 57:18
and *r* them to this place . . . . . . .Jer 27:22
but hath *r* to the debtor . . . . . . .Ezek 18:7
If the wicked *r* the pledge . . . . .Ezek 33:15
to *r* and to build . . . . .Dan 9:25
r whole, like as the other . . . . .Matt 12:13
and *r* all things . . . . .Mark 9:12
his hand was *r* whole . . . . .Luke 6:10
false accusation, I *r* him . . . . . .Luke 19:8
r such a one in the spirit . . . . . .Gal 6:1

RESTORATION OF ISRAEL—*returning the nation Israel to its homeland and to its proper relationship with God*
Promised in the prophets .Is 11:11
Seen in John's ministry . .Matt 17:11
Anticipated by Caiaphas .John 11:49-52
Questioned by the disciples . . . . .Acts 1:6
Realized at Pentecost . . . .Joel 2:28-32
Fulfilled in the Church . . .Eph 2:11-22
Perfected in Heaven . . . . .Heb 12:22-28

RESTORER—*one who returns something to its former state*
shall be unto thee a *r* . . . . .Ruth 4:15
The *r* of paths to dwell in . . . . .Is 58:12

RESTRAIN—*to keep back*

[*also* RESTRAINED, RESTRAINEST, RESTRAINT]
the people were *r* . . . . .Ex 36:6
vile, and he *r* them not 1Sam 3:13
there is no *r* to the Lord 1Sam 14:6
r prayer before God . . . . .Job 15:4
dost thou *r* wisdom . . . . .Job 15:8
toward me? are they *r*? . . . . . . .Is 63:15
and I *r* the floods . . . . .Ezek 31:15
scarce *r* they the people . . . . . . .Acts 14:18

RESTRAINTS, DIVINE—*God's prevention or limitation of actions or their consequences*
On:
Man's wrath . . . . .Ps 76:10
Man's designs . . . . .Gen 11:6
Natural forces . . . . .Gen 8:2
Childbearing . . . . .Gen 16:2
Wicked 2Kin 19:28
Antichrist 2Thess 2:3-7

RESTS—*supporting ledges*
For the beams of the Temple 1Kin 6:6

RESURRECTION—*act of rising from the dead*
Doctrine of:
Looked for in faith . . . . .Job 19:25-27
Taught in Old Testament .Is 26:19; Dan 12:2, 3, 13
Denied by Sadducees . . . .Matt 22:23-28; Acts 23:6, 8
Affirmed by Christ . . . . .{John 5:28, 29; John 6:39, 40, 44}
Illustrated by the Lazarus .John 11:23-44
Explained away by false teachers 2Tim 2:18
Questioned by some 1Cor 15:12
Mocked at by heathen . . .Acts 17:32
Proclaimed by Paul . . . . . .Acts 24:14, 15
Accomplished by:
God's power . . . . .Matt 22:28, 29
Christ . . . . .John 5:28, 29
Holy Spirit . . . . .Rom 8:11
Proof of, based on:
God's power 1Cor 6:14
Union with Christ . . . . . . .Rom 8:11
Christ's resurrection 1Cor 15:12-56
Time of, at:
Last day . . . . .John 6:39-44
Christ's return 1Thess 4:13-18
Last trumpet 1Cor 15:51-55
Nature of:
Incorruptible 1Cor 15:42, 54
Glorious 1Cor 15:43
Spiritual 1Cor 15:44
Transforming 1Cor 15:51
Like angels . . . . .Matt 22:30
Like Christ . . . . .Phil 3:21
Of the wicked:
Predicted . . . . .Dan 12:2
Described . . . . .John 5:28, 29
Simultaneous . . . . .Acts 24:15

which say there is no *r* . . . . .Mark 12:18
be recompensed at the *r* . . . . . .Luke 14:14
deny that there is any *r* . . . . . . .Luke 20:27
and the *r* from the dead . . . . . .Luke 20:35
through Jesus the *r* . . . . .Acts 4:2
unto them Jesus, and the *r* . . . .Acts 17:18
in the likeness of his *r* . . . . .Rom 6:5
of *r* of the dead . . . . .Heb 6:2
might obtain a better *r* . . . . .Heb 11:35
hope by the *r* of Jesus 1Pet 1:3
by the *r* of Jesus 1Pet 3:21

RESURRECTION OF CHRIST—*the return of Christ to bodily life following His death*
Features concerning:
Foretold in the Psalms . . .Ps 16:10, 11; Acts 13:34, 35
Presented in prophecy . . .Is 53:10-12; 1Cor 15:4
Announced by Christ . . . .Mark 9:9, 10; John 2:19-22
Proclaimed by the apostles . . . .{Acts 2:32; Acts 3:15}
Accomplished by:
God's power . . . . .Acts 2:24
Christ's power . . . . .John 10:18
Spirit's power . . . . .Rom 8:11
Proven by:
Empty tomb . . . . .John 20:1-9
Angelic testimony . . . . . . .Matt 28:5-7
His enemies . . . . .Matt 28:11-15
Many infallible proofs . . . .John 20:20, 27; Acts 1:3
Apostolic preaching . . . . . .Acts 1:22; Acts 4:33
Lord's Day (first day of the week) . . . .{John 20:1, 19; 1Cor 16:2}
Purposes of:
Fulfill Scripture . . . . .Luke 24:45, 46
Forgive sins 1Cor 15:17
Justify the sinner . . . . .Rom 4:25; Rom 8:34
Give hope 1Cor 15:18, 19
Make faith real 1Cor 15:14-17
Prove His Sonship . . . . . . .Ps 2:7; Rom 1:4
Set Him on David's throne . . . . .Acts 2:30-32
Insure His exaltation . . . . .Acts 4:10, 11; Phil 2:9, 10
Guarantee the coming judgment . . . . .Acts 17:31
Seal the believer's resurrection . . . .{Acts 26:23; 1Cor 15:20, 23}
Appearances of, to:
Mary Magdalene . . . . .Mark 16:9
Other women . . . . .Matt 28:9
Two disciples . . . . .Luke 24:13-15
Simon Peter . . . . .Luke 24:34
Ten apostles . . . . .John 20:19, 24
Eleven apostles . . . . .John 20:26
Apostles at Sea of Tiberias . . . . .John 21:1
Apostles in Galilee . . . . . .Matt 28:16, 17
500 brethren 1Cor 15:6
All the apostles . . . . .Luke 24:51; Acts 1:9
Paul 1Cor 15:8
James 1Cor 15:7

RESURRECTION, SPIRITUAL—*that which occurs to an individual who becomes a Christian*
Accomplished by power of:
God . . . . .Eph 1:19
Christ . . . . .Eph 5:14
Holy Spirit . . . . .Ezek 11:19
Features concerning:
Takes place now . . . . .John 5:25
Gives eternal life . . . . .John 5:24
Delivers from spiritual death . . . . .Rom 6:4, 13
Changes life . . . . .Is 32:15
Issues in immortality . . . . .John 11:25, 26
Delivers from Satan's power . . . . .Acts 26:18
Realized in new life . . . . . .Phil 3:10, 11
Called "first" . . . . .Rev 20:5, 6

RESURRECTIONS OF THE BIBLE—*returning to life of people other than Jesus*
Widow's son 1Kin 17:17-22
Shunammite's son 2Kin 4:32-35
Unnamed man 2Kin 13:20, 21
Jairus' daughter . . . . .Matt 9:23-25
Widow's only son . . . . .Luke 7:11-15
Lazarus of Bethany . . . . . .John 11:43, 44
Many saints . . . . .Matt 27:52, 53
Dorcas . . . . .Acts 9:36-40
In symbolism . . . . .Rev 11:8, 11

RETAIN—*to keep in possession or use*

[*also* RETAINED, RETAINETH]
and *r* those three hundred . . . . .Judg 7:8
the damsel's father *r* him . . . . . .Judg 19:4
Dost thou still *r* . . . . .Job 2:9
happy is..one that *r* her . . . . . . .Prov 3:18
Let thine heart *r* my words . . . .Prov 4:4
A gracious woman *r* honor . . . .Prov 11:16
and strong men *r* riches . . . . . . .Prov 11:16
over the spirit to *r* the . . . . .Eccl 8:8
and I *r* no strength . . . . .Dan 10:8
shall not *r* the power . . . . .Dan 11:6
he *r* not his anger for ever . . . . .Mic 7:18
sins ye *r*, they are *r* . . . . .John 20:23
to *r* God in their knowledge . . .Rom 1:28
Whom I would have *r* . . . . .Philem 13

RETALIATION—*to return like for like; repay in kind*
Forbidden . . . . .Luke 9:54, 55
Return good, not evil . . . .Prov 25:21, 22
God's responsibility . . . . . .Prov 20:22
Christ's teaching on . . . . . .Matt 5:39-44

RETIRE—*to withdraw from*

[*also* RETIRED]
the men of Israel *r* . . . . .Judg 20:39
and *r* ye from him 2Sam 11:15
they *r* from the city 2Sam 20:22
r, stay not: for I will . . . . .Jer 4:6

RETRIBUTION—*something given or exacted in recompense*
Expressed by:
God's wrath . . . . .Rom 1:18
Lamb's wrath . . . . .Rev 6:16, 17
Vengeance . . . . .Jude 7
Punishment 2Thess 1:6-9
Corruption 2Pet 2:9-22
Due to the sinner's:
Sin . . . . .Rom 2:1-9
Evil works . . . . .Ex 32:34
Persecution of the righteous 2Thess 1:6
Rejection of Christ . . . . . .Heb 10:29, 30
Deliverance from, by:
Christ 1Thess 1:10
God's appointment 1Thess 5:9

RETURN—*to go back; come back*
Descriptive of:
Going back home . . . . . . .Gen 31:3, 13
Repentance 2Chr 6:24, 38
Vengeance or retribution .1Kin 2:33, 44
Divine visitation . . . . .Joel 2:14
Christ's advent . . . . .Acts 15:16
Death . . . . .Gen 3:19

R

[*also* RETURNED, RETURNETH, RETURNING]
waters *r* from off the earth .... Gen 8:3
r not again unto him .... Gen 8:12
they *r*, and came to .... Gen 14:7
his *r* from the slaughter .... Gen 14:17
R to thy mistress .... Gen 16:9
I will certainly *r* unto thee .... Gen 18:10
Abraham *r* unto his place ..... Gen 18:33
r into..the Philistines .... Gen 21:32
Abraham *r* unto his young men Gen 22:19
and *r* unto his place .... Gen 31:55
the messengers *r* to Jacob ..... Gen 32:6
R unto thy country .... Gen 32:9
Esau *r* that day on his way .... Gen 33:16
And Reuben *r* unto the pit .... Gen 37:29
r to Judah, and said, I cannot . Gen 38:22
r to them again, and .... Gen 42:24
we had *r* this second time ..... Gen 43:10
every man..*r* to the city .... Gen 44:13
And Joseph *r* into Egypt ...... Gen 50:14
Moses went and *r* to Jethro ... Ex 4:18
r unto my brethren which ..... Ex 4:18
thou goest to *r* into Egypt ..... Ex 4:21
And Moses *r* unto the Lord ... Ex 5:22
they see war, and they *r* ...... Ex 13:17
and the sea *r* to his strength ... Ex 14:27
Moses *r* the words .... Ex 19:8
And Moses *r* unto the Lord ... Ex 32:31
rulers of the congregation *r* ... Ex 34:31
r unto her father's house ...... Lev 22:13
r every man unto his .... Lev 25:10
shall *r* every man unto his ..... Lev 25:10
that he may *r* unto his .... Lev 25:27
and shall *r* unto his own ...... Lev 25:41
of his fathers shall he *r* .... Lev 25:41
the field shall *r* unto him ...... Lev 27:24
R, O Lord, unto the many .... Num 10:36
they *r* from searching .... Num 13:25
for us to *r* into Egypt? .... Num 14:3
to search the land, who *r* ..... Num 14:36
Aaron *r* unto Moses .... Num 16:50
R unto Balak, and thus .... Num 23:5
he *r* unto him, and, lo, he .... Num 23:6
went and *r* to his place .... Num 24:25
We will not *r* unto our .... Num 32:18
slayer shall *r* into the land .... Num 35:28
And ye *r* and wept .... Deut 1:45
r every man unto his .... Deut 3:20
nor cause the people to *r* ..... Deut 17:16
henceforth *r* no more .... Deut 17:16
go and *r* to his house .... Deut 20:5
go and *r* unto his house .... Deut 20:7
shalt *r* unto the Lord .... Deut 30:2
thou shalt *r* and obey .... Deut 30:8
r unto the land of your .... Josh 1:15
until the pursuers be *r* .... Josh 2:16
waters of Jordan *r* unto their .. Josh 4:18
once, and *r* into the camp ..... Josh 6:14
And they *r* to Joshua .... Josh 7:3
that all the Israelites *r* .... Josh 8:24
Joshua *r*, and all Israel .... Josh 10:15
then shall the slayer *r* .... Josh 20:6
therefore now *r* ye, and get ... Josh 22:4
half tribe of Manasseh *r* ...... Josh 22:9
they *r*, and corrupted .... Judg 2:19
she *r* answer to herself .... Judg 5:29
let him *r* and depart early ..... Judg 7:3
r of the people twenty .... Judg 7:3
the son of Joash *r* from .... Judg 8:13
I *r* in peace from the .... Judg 11:31
that she *r* unto her father ..... Judg 11:39
And after a time he *r* to ...... Judg 14:8
r unto their inheritance .... Judg 21:23
r from the country of Moab ... Ruth 1:6
Go, *r* each to her mother's .... Ruth 1:8
r thou after thy sister .... Ruth 1:15
So Naomi *r*, and Ruth the ..... Ruth 1:22
r out of the county of Moab ... Ruth 1:22
worshiped..the Lord, and *r* 1Sam 1:19
any wise *r* him a trespass 1Sam 6:3
ye *r* him for a trespass 1Sam 6:8
r to Ekron the same day 1Sam 6:16
And his *r* was to Ramah 1Sam 7:17
Come, and let us *r* 1Sam 9:5
I will not *r* with thee 1Sam 15:26
David went and *r* from Saul ... 1Sam 17:15
r from the slaughter of 1Sam 18:6
Saul *r* from pursuing after 1Sam 23:28
r from..the Philistines 1Sam 24:1
hath *r* the wickedness of 1Sam 25:39
r, my son David: for I will 1Sam 26:21
and Saul *r* to his place 1Sam 26:25
r, and came to Achish 1Sam 27:9
Make this fellow *r*, that he 1Sam 29:4
to *r* into the land of the 1Sam 29:11
was *r* from the slaughter 2Sam 1:1
r from following their 2Sam 2:26
r from following Abner 2Sam 2:30
unto him, Go, *r*. And he *r* 2Sam 3:16
r to bless his household 2Sam 6:20
he *r* from smiting of the 2Sam 8:13
beards be grown, and then *r* .. 2Sam 10:5
Joab *r* from the children 2Sam 10:14
and she *r* unto her house 2Sam 11:4
but he shall not *r* to me 2Sam 12:23
people *r* unto Jerusalem 2Sam 12:31
So Absalom *r* to his own 2Sam 14:24
r to thy place and abide 2Sam 15:19
r into the city in peace 2Sam 15:27
r upon thee all the blood 2Sam 16:8
seekest is as if all *r* 2Sam 17:3
the people *r* from pursuing 2Sam 18:16
R thou, and all thy servants ... 2Sam 19:14
king *r*, and came to Jordan 2Sam 19:15
Joab *r* to Jerusalem unto 2Sam 20:22
people *r* after him only to 2Sam 23:10
r to him that sent me 2Sam 24:13
r his blood upon his own 1Kin 2:32
r unto thee with..heart 1Kin 8:48
r every man to his house 1Kin 12:24
r to depart, according to 1Kin 12:24
r not by the way..he came 1Kin 13:10
I may not *r* with thee 1Kin 13:16
r on thy way to the 1Kin 19:15
And he *r* back from him 1Kin 19:21
r of the year the king 1Kin 20:22
r every man to his house 1Kin 22:17
and from thence he *r* to 2Kin 2:25
and *r* to their own land 2Kin 3:27
he *r*, and walked in the house . 2Kin 4:35
he *r* to the man of God 2Kin 5:15
And the messengers *r*, and told 2Kin 7:15
that the woman *r* out of the ... 2Kin 8:3
king Joram was *r* to be 2Kin 9:15
hostages, and *r* to Samaria 2Kin 14:14
I have offended; *r* from me ... 2Kin 18:14
and shall *r* to his own 2Kin 19:7
r, and found the king 2Kin 19:8
shadow *r* backward ten degrees. 2Kin 20:10
upon them, and *r* to Jerusalem. 2Kin 23:20
David *r* to bless his house 1Chr 16:43
beards be grown, and then *r* .. 1Chr 19:5
the people *r* to Jerusalem 1Chr 20:3
r and confess thy name 2Chr 6:24
Jeroboam *r* out of Egypt 2Chr 10:2
ye me to *r* answer to this 2Chr 10:6
r every man to his house 2Chr 11:4
r from going against 2Chr 11:4
abundance, and *r* to Jerusalem . 2Chr 14:15
let them *r*..every man to his ... 2Chr 18:16
the king of Judah *r* 2Chr 19:1
r, every man of Judah 2Chr 20:27
And he *r* to be healed in 2Chr 22:6
And they *r* home in great 2Chr 25:10
then they *r* to Samaria 2Chr 28:15
he will *r* to the remnant 2Chr 30:6
all the children of Israel *r* 2Chr 31:1
he *r* with shame of face to 2Chr 32:21
land of Israel, he *r* to 2Chr 34:7
and then they *r* answer .... Ezra 5:5
and when wilt thou *r*? .... Neh 2:6
gate of the valley, and so *r* .... Neh 2:15
places whence ye shall *r* ...... Neh 4:12
we *r* all of us to the wall ...... Neh 4:15
to *r* to their bondage .... Neh 9:17
yet when they *r*, and cried .... Neh 9:28
the morrow she *r* into the ..... Esth 2:14
Esther bade them *r* Mordecai .. Esth 4:15
king *r* out of the palace .... Esth 7:8
should *r* upon his own head ... Esth 9:25
and naked shall I *r* thither .... Job 1:21
R, I pray you, let it not .... Job 6:29
r again, my righteousness ..... Job 6:29
He shall *r* no more to his ..... Job 7:10
I go whence I shall not *r* ...... Job 10:21
believeth not that he shall *r* .. Job 15:22
way whence I shall not *r* ...... Job 16:22
for you all, do ye *r*, and come . Job 17:10
If thou *r* to the Almighty ..... Job 22:23
shall *r* to the days of his ...... Job 33:25
that they *r* from iniquity ...... Job 36:10
go forth, and *r* not unto ...... Job 39:4
R, O Lord, deliver my soul ... Ps 6:4
sakes therefore *r* thou on ..... Ps 7:7
my prayer *r* into mine own .... Ps 35:13
They *r* at evening: they make . Ps 59:6
Therefore his people *r* .... Ps 73:10
let not the oppressed *r* .... Ps 74:21
r and inquired early after ..... Ps 78:34
R, we beseech thee, O God ... Ps 80:14
and sayest, ***R***, ye children ..... Ps 90:3
shall *r* unto righteousness ..... Ps 94:15
die, and *r* to their dust .... Ps 104:29
R unto thy rest, O my soul .... Ps 116:7
goeth forth, he *r* to his .... Ps 146:4
None that go unto her *r* ...... Prov 2:19
As a dog *r* to his vomit .... Prov 26:11
so a fool *r* to his folly .... Prov 26:11
rolleth a stone, it will *r* .... Prov 26:27
the wind *r* again according .... Eccl 1:6
rivers come, thither they *r* .... Eccl 1:7
So I *r*, and considered all ..... Eccl 4:1
shall he *r* to go as he came .... Eccl 5:15
I *r*, and saw under the sun .... Eccl 9:11
nor the clouds *r* after the ..... Eccl 12:2
R, ***r***, O Shulamite .... Song 6:13
r, *r*, that we may look upon ... Song 6:13
it shall be..it shall *r* .... Is 6:13
The remnant shall *r*, even ..... Is 10:21
shall *r* even to the Lord .... Is 19:22
inquire, inquire ye: *r*, come ... Is 21:12
r and rest shall ye be saved ... Is 30:15
ransomed of the Lord shall *r* .. Is 35:10
rumor, and *r* to his own land .. Is 37:7
Rabshakeh *r*, and found the ... Is 37:8
So the sun *r* ten degrees ...... Is 38:8
r..for I have redeemed .... Is 44:22
in righteousness..not *r* .... Is 45:23
redeemed of the Lord shall *r* .. Is 51:11
and let him *r* unto the Lord ... Is 55:7
heaven, and *r* not thither ..... Is 55:10
R for thy servants' sake .... Is 63:17
shall he *r* unto her again? ..... Jer 3:1
r again unto me, saith the ..... Jer 3:1
thou unto me. But she *r* not .. Jer 3:7
If thou wilt *r*, O Israel .... Jer 4:1
Lord, *r* to me: and if thou .... Jer 4:1
they have refused to *r* .... Jer 5:3
shall he turn away, and not *r*? . Jer 8:4
plucked them out I will *r* ..... Jer 12:15
r with their vessels empty ..... Jer 14:3
since they *r* not from .... Jer 15:7
r, then will I bring thee .... Jer 15:19
let them *r* unto thee .... Jer 15:19
but *r* not thou unto them ..... Jer 15:19
r ye now every one from his .. Jer 18:11
for he shall *r* no more .... Jer 22:10
whereunto they desire to *r* .... Jer 22:27
thither shall they not *r* .... Jer 22:27
none doth *r* from his .... Jer 23:14
r unto me with their whole .... Jer 24:7
in causing you to *r* to this .... Jer 29:10
I will cause them to *r* to ...... Jer 30:3
anger of the Lord shall not *r* .. Jer 30:24
a great company shall *r* .... Jer 31:8
cause their captivity to *r* ...... Jer 32:44
the captivity of Israel to *r* ..... Jer 33:7
cause their captivity to *r* ...... Jer 33:26
they had let go free, to *r* ...... Jer 34:11
them to *r* to this city .... Jer 34:22
R ye now every man from his . Jer 35:15
r every man from his evil ..... Jer 36:3
r to Egypt into their own ..... Jer 37:7
to *r* to Jonathan's house ...... Jer 38:26
Even all the Jews *r* out of ..... Jer 40:12

from Mizpah cast about and *r* .Jer 41:14
cause you to *r* to your own....Jer 42:12
that were *r* from all nations ...Jer 43:5
r into the land of Judah.......Jer 44:14
desire to *r* to dwell there......Jer 44:14
r but such as shall escape .....Jer 44:14
Jacob shall *r*, and be in rest ...Jer 46:27
none shall *r* in vain...........Jer 50:9
living creatures ran and *r* .....Ezek 1:14
the seller shall not *r* to........Ezek 7:13
multitude..which shall not *r* ...Ezek 7:13
have *r* to provoke me to ......Ezek 8:17
should not *r* from his ....Ezek 13:22
r to their former estate ....Ezek 16:55
r to your former estate........Ezek 16:55
he should *r* from his ways.....Ezek 18:23
it shall not *r* any more ....Ezek 21:5
r into the land of Pathros .....Ezek 29:14
passeth out and him that *r* ....Ezek 35:7
and thy cities shall not *r* ......Ezek 35:9
not *r* by the way of the gate...Ezek 46:9
r to the brink of the river .....Ezek 47:6
Now when I had *r*, behold ....Ezek 47:7
mine understanding *r* unto me .Dan 4:34
now will I *r* to fight ....Dan 10:20
shall *r* into his own land ......Dan 11:9
king of the north shall *r*.......Dan 11:13
r into his land..riches ....Dan 11:28
and *r* to his own land ....Dan 11:28
he shall be grieved, and *r* .....Dan 11:30
r, and have intelligence ....Dan 11:30
I will go and *r* to my first .....Hos 2:7
the children of Israel *r*.........Hos 3:5
I will go and *r* to my place ....Hos 5:15
Come, and let us *r* unto the ...Hos 6:1
I *r* the captivity of my ....Hos 6:11
do not *r* to the Lord their.....Hos 7:10
they shall *r* to Egypt..........Hos 8:13
Ephraim shall *r* to Egypt......Hos 9:3
shall not *r* into the land ....Hos 11:5
because they refused to *r* .....Hos 11:5
reproach shall his Lord *r*......Hos 12:14
O Israel, *r* unto the Lord .....Hos 14:1
will I *r* your recompense ......Joel 3:4
have ye not *r* unto me ....Amos 4:6
thy reward shall *r* upon ....Obad 15
r to the hire of a harlot ....Mic 1:7
of his brethren shall *r*........Mic 5:3
and they *r* and said, Like as...Zech 1:6
no man passed through nor *r*..Zech 7:14
I am *r* unto Zion, and will ....Zech 8:3
because of him that *r*.........Zech 9:8
r and build the desolate ....Mal 1:4
R unto me, and I will *r* unto ..Mal 3:7
ye said, Wherein shall we *r*? ..Mal 3:7
that they should not *r* to ......Matt 2:12
let your peace *r* to you ....Matt 10:13
will *r* into my house from .....Matt 12:44
as he *r* into the city, he ....Matt 21:18
him which is in the field *r*.....Matt 24:18
when he *r*, he found them ....Mark 14:40
and *r* to her own house ....Luke 1:56
shepherds *r*, glorifying and ....Luke 2:20
as they *r*, the child Jesus ......Luke 2:43
Jesus *r* in the power of ....Luke 4:14
r to the house, found the .....Luke 7:10
R to thine own house, and ....Luke 8:39
pass, that, when Jesus was *r*...Luke 8:40
apostles, when they were *r*....Luke 9:10
And the seventy *r* again ......Luke 10:17
r unto my house whence I .....Luke 11:24
will *r* from the wedding ....Luke 12:36
r to give glory to God ....Luke 17:18
let him likewise not *r* back ....Luke 17:31
a kingdom and to *r*...........Luke 19:12
to pass, that when he was *r* ..Luke 19:15
smote their breasts, and *r* ....Luke 23:48
r from the sepulcher, and .....Luke 24:9
r to Jerusalem with..joy ....Luke 24:52
r they unto Jerusalem from....Acts 1:12
not in the prison, they *r* ......Acts 5:22
r to Jerusalem, and preached ..Acts 8:25
Was *r*, and sitting in his.......Acts 8:28
Saul *r* from Jerusalem ....Acts 12:25
John departing from them *r* ...Acts 13:13
now no more to *r* to..........Acts 13:34
they *r* again to Lystra.........Acts 14:21
but I will *r* again unto you ....Acts 18:21
to *r* through Macedonia ....Acts 20:3
and they *r* home again ....Acts 21:6
with him, and *r* to the castle ..Acts 23:32
and *r* again unto Damascus....Gal 1:17
r from the slaughter of........Heb 7:1
had opportunity to have *r*.....Heb 11:15
are now *r* unto the Shepherd ..1Pet 2:25

REU (rē'ū)—*"friendship"*
Descendant of Shem.....Gen 11:10-21
Called Ragau ....Luke 3:35

REUBEN (ro͞o'bĕn)—*"behold, a son"*
Jacob's eldest son ....Gen 29:31, 32
Guilty of misconduct; loses preeminence .....Gen 35:22
Proposes plan to save Joseph's life...........Gen 37:21-29
Offers sons as pledge ....Gen 42:37
Father of four sons ......Gen 46:8, 9
Pronounced unstable.....Gen 49:3, 4
Descendants of..........Num 26:5-11

And *R* went in the days of ....Gen 30:14
R answered them, saying ......Gen 42:22
as *R* and Simeon they shall....Gen 48:5
R, Simeon, Levi and Judah....Ex 1:2
sons of *R* the first-born ....Ex 6:14
these be the families of *R* ......Ex 6:14
prince of the children of *R* ....Num 7:30
standard of the camp of *R* ....Num 10:18
tribe of *R*, Shammua the son ..Num 13:4
son of Peleth, sons of *R*.......Num 16:1
tribe of the children of *R* .....Num 34:14
sons of Eliab, the son of *R* ....Deut 11:6
R, Gad, and Asher, and ......Deut 27:13
Let *R* live, and not die........Deut 33:6
And the children of *R* ....Josh 4:12
unto the tribe..of *R*...........Josh 13:15
border of the children of *R*....Josh 13:23
the inheritance of..*R*..........Josh 13:23
stone of Bohan the son of *R* ..Josh 15:6
and Gad, and *R*, and half .....Josh 18:7
plain out of the tribe of *R*.....Josh 20:8
out of the tribe of *R*..........Josh 21:7
of *R* and the children ....Josh 22:9
the sons of Israel; *R* 1Chr 2:1
the sons of *R* the first-born 1Chr 5:1
sons of *R*, and the Gadites 1Chr 5:18
out of the tribe of *R*..........1Chr 6:63
west side, a portion for *R* .....Ezek 48:6
one gate of *R*, one gate of ....Ezek 48:31
of *R* were sealed twelve ....Rev 7:5

REUBENITE (ro͞o'bĕn-īt)—*descendant of Reuben*
Divided into four tribal families...............Num 26:5-11
Elizur, warrior ....Num 1:5
Census of, at Sinai ......Num 1:18-21
Census of, at conquest ...Num 26:7
Place of, in march ....Num 2:10
Seek inheritance east of Jordan................Num 32:1-42
Join in war against Canaanites ....Josh 1:12-18
Altar erected by, misunderstood.........Josh 22:10-34
Criticized by Deborah ...Judg 5:15, 16
Enslaved by Assyria 2Kin 15:29

[*also* REUBENITES]
cities..gave I unto the *R* ......Deut 3:12
the plain country, of the *R* ....Deut 4:43
an inheritance unto the *R* .....Deut 29:8
a possession unto the *R* ....Josh 12:6
the *R* and the Gadites ....Josh 13:8
Then Joshua called the *R* .....Josh 22:1
the Gadites and the *R* 2Kin 10:33
he was prince of the *R* 1Chr 5:6
the son of Shiza the *R* 1Chr 11:42
a captain of the *R* 1Chr 11:42
of Jordan, of the *R* 1Chr 12:37
made rulers over the *R* 1Chr 26:32
the ruler of the *R* 1Chr 27:16

REUEL (ro͞o'ĕl)—*"God is his friend"*
1. Son of Esau ....Gen 36:2-4
2. Moses' father-in-law .....Ex 2:18
   See JETHRO
3. Benjamite 1Chr 9:8
4. Gadite leader ....Num 2:14
   Called Deuel ....Num 7:42, 47

R the son of Bashemath ......Gen 36:10
these are the sons of *R* ....Gen 36:17
dukes that came of *R* ....Gen 36:17
sons of Esau; Eliphaz, *R* 1Chr 1:35

REUMAH (roo'mä)—*"exalted"*
Nahor's concubine ....Gen 22:24

REVEAL—*to make known*

[*also* REVEALED, REVEALETH]
those things which are *r*.......Deut 29:29
word of the Lord yet *r*........1Sam 3:7
hast *r* to thy servant 2Sam 7:27
The heaven shall *r* his ....Job 20:27
A talebearer *r* secrets ....Prov 11:13
a talebearer *r* secrets ....Prov 20:19
it was *r* in mine ears...........Is 22:14
glory of the Lord shall be *r* ...Is 40:5
my righteousness to be *r* ....Is 56:1
for unto thee have I *r* ....Jer 11:20
r unto them the abundance ....Jer 33:6
secret *r* unto Daniel ....Dan 2:19
He *r* the deep and secret......Dan 2:22
he that *r* secrets maketh ......Dan 2:29
seeing thou couldst *r* this......Dan 2:47
a thing was *r* unto Daniel .....Dan 10:1
he *r* his secret unto his........Amos 3:7
covered, that shall not be *r*....Matt 10:26
hast *r* them unto babes ....Matt 11:25
the Son will *r* him ....Matt 11:27
and blood hath not *r* it ....Matt 16:17
r unto him by the Holy Ghost .Luke 2:26
hast *r* them unto babes ....Luke 10:21
to whom the Son will *r* ....Luke 10:22
covered that shall not be *r* ....Luke 12:2
the Son of man is *r*...........Luke 17:30
the arm of the Lord been *r*? ..John 12:38
righteousness of God *r*.........Rom 1:17
the glory which shall be *r* .....Rom 8:18
hath *r* them unto us by his 1Cor 2:10
it shall be *r* by fire 1Cor 3:13
If any thing be *r* to another ...1Cor 14:30
To *r* his Son in me ....Gal 1:16
should afterwards be *r* ....Gal 3:23
r unto his holy apostles ....Eph 3:5
God shall *r* even this ....Phil 3:15
Lord Jesus shall be *r* 2Thess 1:7
and that man of sin be *r* 2Thess 2:3
shall that Wicked be *r* 2Thess 2:8
to be *r* in the last time........1Pet 1:5
when his glory shall be *r*......1Pet 4:13
of the glory that shall be *r* 1Pet 5:1

REVEALER—*one who makes known*
and a *r* of secrets, seeing......Dan 2:47

REVELATION—*an uncovering of something hidden*

Source of:
God....................Dan 2:28-47
Christ ....John 1:18
The Spirit..............1Cor 2:10
Not in man ....Matt 16:17

Objects of:
God....................Matt 11:25, 27
Christ 2Thess 1:7
Man of sin 2Thess 2:3, 6, 8

Instruments of:
Prophets 1Pet 1:12
Daniel..................Dan 10:1
Christ ....Heb 1:1, 2
Apostles 1Cor 2:10
Paul....................Gal 1:16

Of the first advent:
Predicted ....Is 40:5
Revealed ....Is 53:1
Rejected................John 12:38-41

R

Of God's righteousness ... Is 56:1
Of peace and truth ... Jer 33:6-8
Eph 2:11-17

Time of the second advent:
Uncovering ... Matt 10:26
Judgment ... Luke 17:26-30
Victory ... 2Thess 2:3, 6, 8
Glory ... 1Pet 5:1
Resurrection ... Rom 8:18, 19
Reward ... 1Cor 3:13
Glorification ... 1John 3:2
Grace ... 1Pet 1:5, 13
Joy ... 1Pet 4:13

Of divine truth, characteristics of:
God-originated ... Dan 2:47
Verbal ... Heb 1:1
In the created world ... Ps 19:1, 2
Illuminative ... Eph 1:17
Now revealed ... Rom 16:26
Truth communicating ... Eph 3:3, 4

[*also* REVELATIONS]
and *r* of the righteous ... Rom 2:5
the *r* of the mystery ... Rom 16:25
speak to you either by *r* ... 1Cor 14:6
come to visions and *r* ... 2Cor 12:1
it but by the *r* of Jesus ... Gal 1:12
And I went up by *r*, and ... Gal 2:2
the *R* of Jesus Christ ... Rev 1:1

REVELATION, THE—*a book of the New Testament*
Vision of the Son of Man. Rev 1:9-20
Message to the seven churches ... Rev 2:1—3:22
The book of seven seals . Rev 4:1—6:17
The judgment ... Rev 7:1—9:21
The two beasts ... Rev 13
Babylon doomed ... Rev 17:1—18:24
The marriage supper ... Rev 19:6-10
The judgment of the wicked ... Rev 20:11-15
New heaven and new earth ... Rev 21:1-8
The new Jerusalem ... Rev 21:9—22:5
Christ's coming ... Rev 22:6-21

REVELLINGS—*carousings*
drunkenness, *r* and such ... Gal 5:21
r, banquetings, and ... 1Pet 4:3

REVENGE—*to take vengeance; retaliation*
Manifestation of:
Belongs to God ... Rev 18:20
Performed by rulers ... Rom 13:4
Righteously allowed ... 1Kin 20:42
Pleaded for ... Jer 11:20
Disallowed among men .. Prov 20:22
Forbidden to disciples ... Luke 9:54, 55

Antidotes of:
Overcome by kindness ... 1Sam 25:30-34
Exhibit love ... Luke 6:35
Bless ... Rom 12:14
Forbear wrath ... Rom 12:19
Manifest forbearance ... Matt 5:38-41
Flee from ... Gen 27:41-45

Examples of:
Simeon and Levi ... Gen 34:25
Joseph ... Gen 42:9-24
Samson ... Judg 16:28-30
Joab ... 2Sam 3:27, 30
Jezebel ... 1Kin 19:2
Ahab ... 1Kin 22:26, 27
Haman ... Esth 3:8-15
Philistines ... Ezek 25:15-17
Herodias ... Mark 6:19-24
Jews ... Acts 7:54, 59

[*also* REVENGES, REVENGETH, REVENGING]
r upon the enemy ... Deut 32:42
r of the blood ... Ps 79:10
r me of my persecutors ... Jer 15:15
and we shall take our *r* ... Jer 20:10
God is jealous and the Lord *r* . Nah 1:2
what zeal, yea, what *r* ... 2Cor 7:11
to *r* all disobedience ... 2Cor 10:6

REVENGER—*one who retaliates*

[*also* REVENGERS]
The *r* of blood himself ... Num 35:19
between the slayer and the *r* .. Num 35:24
the *r* of blood find him ... Num 35:27
and the *r* of blood kill ... Num 35:27
suffer the *r* of blood ... 2Sam 14:11

REVENUE—*income*

[*also* REVENUES]
shalt endamage the *r* ... Ezra 4:13
my *r* than choice silver ... Prov 8:19
r of the wicked is trouble ... Prov 15:6
then great *r* without right ... Prov 16:8
of the river is her *r* ... Is 23:3
shall be ashamed of your *r* ... Jer 12:13

REVERENCE—*a feeling of deep respect, love, awe, and esteem; to show feelings of respect and esteem*
Manifested toward:
God ... Ps 89:7
God's house ... Lev 19:30
Christ ... Matt 21:37
Kings ... 1Kin 1:31
Parents ... Heb 12:9
Husbands ... Eph 5:33

[*also* REVERENCED]
my sabbaths and *r* ... Lev 26:2
fell on his face and did *r* ... 2Sam 9:6
bowed, and *r* Haman ... Esth 3:2
bowed not, nor did him *r* ... Esth 3:2
bowed not, nor did him *r* ... Esth 3:5
They will *r* my son ... Mark 12:6
r him when they see him ... Luke 20:13

REVEREND—*worthy of reverence*
Applied only to God in the Scriptures ... Ps 111:9

REVERSE—*to turn around; to annul*
and I cannot *r* it ... Num 23:20
to *r* the letters devised ... Esth 8:5

REVILE—*to speak of another abusively*
Christ, object of ... Matt 27:39
Christ, submissive under. . 1Pet 2:23
Christians, objects of ... Matt 5:11
Right attitude toward ... 1Cor 4:12
Punishment of ... 1Cor 6:10
False teachers ... 2Pet 2:10-12

[*also* REVILED, REVILEST, REVILINGS]
Thou shalt not *r* the gods ... Ex 22:28
neither be ye afraid of..*r* ... Is 51:7
the *r* of the children ... Zeph 2:8
crucified with him *r* him ... Mark 15:32
Then they *r* him, and said ... John 9:28
R thou God's high priest? ... Acts 23:4

REVILERS—*slanderers*
nor *r*, nor extortioners ... 1Cor 6:10

REVIVAL—*renewed zeal to worship and obey God*
Conditions for:
Humility ... 2Chr 7:14
Prayer ... 2Chr 7:14
James 5:16
Broken heart ... Ps 34:18
Confession ... Ps 66:18
Repentance ... 2Cor 7:10
Turning from sin ... 2Chr 7:14
2Tim 2:19
Complete surrender ... Acts 9:5, 6
Rom 12:1, 2

REVIVE—*to restore to consciousness or life*
Descriptive of:
Renewed strength ... Gen 45:27
Refreshment ... Judg 15:19
Restoration ... Neh 4:2
Resurrection ... 1Kin 17:22

Of the Spirit:
Given to the humble ... Is 57:15
Source of joy ... Ps 85:6
Possible even in trouble .. Ps 138:7
Source of fruitfulness ... Hos 6:2, 3
Hos 14:7

[*also* REVIVED, REVIVING]
the bones of Elisha, he *r* ... 2Kin 13:21
give us a little *r* ... Ezra 9:8
r thy work in the midst ... Hab 3:2
commandment came, sin *r* ... Rom 7:9
both died, and rose, and *r* ... Rom 14:9

REVOLT—*to rebel; a rebellion*

[*also* REVOLTED, REVOLTING]
r from under the hand ... 2Kin 8:20
r from under the hand ... 2Kin 8:22
Libnah *r* at the same time ... 2Kin 8:22
In his days the Eodmites *r* ... 2Chr 21:8
r from under his hand ... 2Chr 21:10
will *r* more and more ... Is 1:5
children of Israel have..*r* ... Is 31:6
speaking oppression and *r* ... Is 59:13
r and a rebellious heart ... Jer 5:23

REVOLTERS—*those who rebel*
They are all grievous *r* ... Jer 6:28
the *r* are profound ... Hos 5:2
all their princes are *r* ... Hos 9:15

REWARD—*that which is given in return for good or evil; to recompense*

[*also* REWARDED, REWARDETH, REWARDS]
thy exceeding great *r* ... Gen 15:1
have ye *r* evil for good? ... Gen 44:4
r for your service ... Num 18:31
the *r* of divination ... Num 22:7
not persons, nor taketh *r* ... Deut 10:17
r to slay an innocent person .. Deut 27:25
and will *r* them that hate ... Deut 32:41
thou hast *r* me good ... 1Sam 24:17
whereas I have *r* thee evil ... 1Sam 24:17
Lord *r* thee good for that ... 1Sam 24:19
have given him a *r* for his ... 2Sam 4:10
recompense..with such a *r*? ... 2Sam 19:36
Lord *r* me according to ... 2Sam 22:21
I will give thee a *r* ... 1Kin 13:7
I say, how they *r* us ... 2Chr 20:11
r for me of your substance? .. Job 6:22
looketh for the *r* of his ... Job 7:2
r him and he shall know it ... Job 21:19
I have *r* evil unto him ... Ps 7:4
r against the innocent ... Ps 15:5
Lord *r* me according ... Ps 18:20
and plentifully *r* the proud ... Ps 31:23
They *r* me evil for good ... Ps 35:12
them be desolate for a *r* ... Ps 40:15
r evil unto mine enemies ... Ps 54:5
a *r* for the righteous ... Ps 58:11
for a *r* of their shame ... Ps 70:3
render a *r* to the proud ... Ps 94:2
r us according to ... Ps 103:10
r me evil for good ... Ps 109:5
this be the *r* of mine ... Ps 109:20
fruit of the womb is his *r* ... Ps 127:3
r thee as thou hast served ... Ps 137:8
Whoso *r* evil for good ... Prov 17:13
a *r* in the bosom strong ... Prov 21:14
Then there shall be a *r* ... Prov 24:14
all things both *r* the fool ... Prov 26:10
and *r* transgressors ... Prov 26:10
a good *r* for their labor ... Eccl 4:9
have they any more a *r* ... Eccl 9:5
and followeth after *r* ... Is 1:23
r evil unto themselves ... Is 3:9
r of his hands shall be given .. Is 3:11
justify the wicked for *r* ... Is 5:23
behold his *r* is with him ... Is 40:10
not for price nor *r* ... Is 45:13
r is with him, and his work ... Is 62:11
for thy work shall be *r* ... Jer 31:16
gave him victuals and a *r* ... Jer 40:5
in that thou givest a *r* ... Ezek 16:34
no *r* is given unto thee ... Ezek 16:34
receive of me gifts and *r* ... Dan 2:6

give thy *r* to another ....Dan 5:17
These are my *r* that my ....Hos 2:12
and *r* them their doings ....Hos 4:9
a *r* upon every cornfloor ......Hos 9:1
r shall return upon thine ......Obad 15
heads thereof judge for *r* ......Mic 3:11
the judge asketh for a *r* ....Mic 7:3
shall receive a prophet's *r* .....Matt 10:41
a righteous man's *r* ....Matt 10:41
he shall *r* every man ....Matt 16:27
he shall not lose his *r* ....Mark 9:41
behold your *r* is great ....Luke 6:23
we receive the due *r* ....Luke 23:41
with the *r* of iniquity ....Acts 1:18
do this thing..I have a *r* 1Cor 9:17
no man beguile you of your *r* .Col 2:18
is worthy of his *r* 1Tim 5:18
a just recompense of *r* ....Heb 2:2
a great recompense of *r* ....Heb 10:35
the recompense of the *r* ....Heb 11:26
the *r* of unrighteousness 2Pet 2:13
that we receive a full *r* 2John 8
the error of Balaam for *r* .....Jude 11

REWARD OF THE RIGHTEOUS—*that which is given the People of God*

Described as:
Sure ....Prov 11:18
Full ....Ruth 2:12
Remembered 2Chr 15:7
Great ....Matt 5:12
Open ....Matt 6:4, 6, 18

Obtained by:
Keeping God's commandments ....Ps 19:11
Sowing righteousness ....Prov 11:18
Fearing God's commandments ....Prov 13:13
Feeding an enemy ....Prov 25:21, 22
Simple service ....Matt 6:1
Grace through faith ......Rom 4:4, 5, 16
Faithful service ....Col 3:23, 24
Seeking God diligently ...Heb 11:6

At Christ's return:
After the resurrection ....Rev 11:18
Tested by fire 1Cor 3:8-14
According to works ......Rev 22:12

See CROWNS OF CHRISTIANS; HIRE; WAGES

REWARD OF THE WICKED—*that which is given to those who do not fear the Lord*

Visited upon:
Now ....Ps 91:8
At the judgment 2Tim 4:14

Measure of:
By retribution ....Rev 18:6
According to the wickedness 2Sam 3:39
Plentifully ....Ps 31:23

REWARDER—*one who gives what is deserved*
a *r* of them that diligently .....Heb 11:6

REZEPH (rē'zĕf)—*"pavement"*
Place destroyed by the Assyrians 2Kin 19:12

REZIA (rĕ-zī'ä)—*"Jehovah is pleasing"*
Asherite 1Chr 7:39

REZIN (rē'zĭn)—*"dominion"*
1. King of Damascus; joins Pekah against Ahaz ...2Kin 15:37
Confederacy of, inspires Isaiah's great Messianic prophecy ....Is 7:1—9:12
2. Head of a Nethinim family ....Ezra 2:48

R king of Syria and Pekah 2Kin 16:5
of Reaiah, the children of ***R*** ...Neh 7:50

REZON (rē'zŏn)—*"prince; noble"*
Son of Eliada; establishes Syrian kingdom 1Kin 11:23-25

RHEGIUM (rē'jĭ-ŭm)—*"fracture"—a town in southern Italy*
Paul's ship arrived at ....Acts 28:13

RHESA (rē'sä)—*"head"*
Ancestor of Christ ....Luke 3:27

RHODA (rōdä)—*"rose"*
Servant girl ....Acts 12:13-16

RHODES (rōdz)—*"rose"—an island off the southwest coast of Asia*
Paul's ship passes by .....Acts 21:1

RIB—*a curved bone in the chest area*
Eve formed of Adam's ...Gen 2:22

[*also* RIBS]
took one of his *r* ....Gen 2:21
smote him under the fifth *r* ...2Sam 2:23
there under the fifth *r* 2Sam 3:27
smote him under the fifth *r* ...2Sam 4:6
smote him..the fifth *r* 2Sam 20:10
three *r* in the mouth of it .....Dan 7:5

RIBAI (rī'bī)—*"Jehovah contends"*
One of David's mighty men 2Sam 23:29

RIBBAND—*a ribbon*
On the fringe of garments.Num 15:38

RIBLAH (rĭb'lä)—*"quarrel"*
1. Town on Israel's eastern border ....Num 34:11
2. Town in the land of Hamath 2Kin 23:33
Headquarters of:
Pharaoh Nechoh 2Kin 23:31-35
Nebuchadnezzar 2Kin 25:6, 20
Zedekiah blinded here ..Jer 39:5-7

to ***R*** in the land of Hamath ...Jer 52:9
the king of Babylon to ***R*** ......Jer 52:26

RICH—*wealthy*

Spiritual handicaps of:
Selfishly satisfied ....Luke 6:24
Reluctant to leave riches .Luke 18:22-25
Forgetful of God ....Luke 12:15-21
Indifferent to others' needs ....Luke 16:19-31
Easily tempted 1Tim 6:9
Hindered spiritually ......Matt 19:23, 24
Misplaced trust ....Prov 11:28

Applied, spiritually, to:
God ....Eph 2:4
Christ ....Rom 10:12
Christians ....James 2:5
True riches 2Cor 8:9
Good works 1Tim 6:18
Worldly people ....Jer 5:27, 28
Self-righteous ....Hos 12:8
Synagogue of Satan ......Rev 2:9

[*also* RICHER]
And Abram was very *r* ....Gen 13:2
I have made Abram *r* ....Gen 14:23
The *r* shall not give more .....Ex 30:15
sojourner or stranger wax *r* ...Lev 25:47
men, whether poor or *r* ....Ruth 3:10
maketh poor, and maketh *r* ...1Sam 2:7
one *r*, and the other poor 2Sam 12:1
He shall not be *r* ....Job 15:29
The *r* man shall lie down .....Job 27:19
nor regardeth the *r* more ......Job 34:19
r among the people ....Ps 45:12
low and high, *r* and poor .....Ps 49:2
of the diligent maketh *r* ....Prov 10:4
of the Lord, it maketh *r* ......Prov 10:22
the *r* hath many friends ....Prov 14:20
r man's wealth is his ....Prov 18:11
wine and oil shall not be *r* ....Prov 21:17
The *r* and poor meet ....Prov 22:2
he that giveth to the *r* ....Prov 22:16
Labor not to be *r* ....Prov 23:4
perverse..though he be *r* ......Prov 28:6
that maketh haste to be *r* .....Prov 28:20
abundance of the *r* ....Eccl 5:12
the *r* sit in low place ....Eccl 10:6
with the *r* in his death ....Is 53:9
not the *r* man glory ....Jer 9:23
in chests of *r* apparel ....Ezek 27:24
shall be far *r* than they ....Dan 11:2

r men..are full of violence .....Mic 6:12
be the Lord; for I am *r* ....Zech 11:5
there came a *r* man of ....Matt 27:57
for a *r* man to enter into ......Mark 10:25
many that were *r* cast in ......Mark 12:41
the *r* he hath sent empty ......Luke 1:53
nor thy *r* neighbors ....Luke 14:12
publicans, and he was *r* ....Luke 19:2
r men casting their gifts ....Luke 21:1
ye are full, now ye are *r* 1Cor 4:8
yet making many *r* 2Cor 6:10
r, in that he is made low ......James 1:10
shall the *r* man fade away .....James 1:11
Go to now, ye *r* men ....James 5:1
thou sayest, I am *r* ....Rev 3:17
the *r* men, and the chief ......Rev 6:15
r and poor, free and bond ....Rev 13:16
merchants..are waxed *r* ....Rev 18:3
made *r* all that had ships ......Rev 18:19

RICHES—*material and spiritual joys of life*

Material:

Described as:
Spiritually valueless ......Ps 49:6, 7
Inferior ....Heb 11:26
Fleeting ....Prov 23:5
Unsatisfying ....Eccl 4:8
Hurtful ....Eccl 5:13, 14
Deceitful ....Matt 13:22
Choking ....Luke 8:14
Uncertain 1Tim 6:17
Corrupted ....James 5:2

Proper attitude toward:
Not to:
Put first 1Kin 3:11, 13
Be trusted ....Ps 52:7
Set heart upon ....Ps 62:10
Be desired ....Prov 30:8
Not forever ....Prov 27:24
Use in giving 2Cor 8:2
Remember God's supply. .Phil 4:19

Spiritual:

Source of, in:
God's Law ....Ps 119:14
Divine wisdom ....Prov 3:13, 14
Unselfish service ....Prov 13:7
Reverential fear ....Prov 22:4
Fulfillment ....Rom 11:12
Christ ....Col 1:27
Assurance ....Col 2:2
Christ's Word ....Col 3:16

r which God hath taken ....Gen 31:16
r were more than that ....Gen 36:7
Return with much *r* ....Josh 22:8
enrich him with great *r* 1Sam 17:25
kings of the earth for *r* 1Kin 10:23
Both *r* and honor come 1Chr 29:12
not asked *r*, wealth 2Chr 1:11
kings of the earth in *r* 2Chr 9:22
he had *r* and honor 2Chr 17:5
Jehoshaphat had *r* 2Chr 18:1
both *r* with the dead 2Chr 20:25
Hezekiah had exceeding much *r* .2Chr 32:27
r of his glorious kingdom .....Esth 1:4
the glory of his *r* ....Esth 5:11
He hath swallowed down *r* ....Job 20:15
Will he esteem thy *r*? ....Job 36:19
better than the *r* of many .....Ps 37:16
he heapeth up *r* ....Ps 39:6
they increase in *r* ....Ps 73:12
the earth is full of thy *r* ....Ps 104:24
and *r* shall be in his house ....Ps 112:3
in her left hand *r* ....Prov 3:16
R and honor are with me .....Prov 8:18
r and righteousness ....Prov 8:18
R profit not in the day ....Prov 11:4
He that trusteth in his *r* ....Prov 11:28
poor, yet hath great *r* ....Prov 13:7
of the wise is their *r* ....Prov 14:24
r are the inheritance ....Prov 19:14
be chosen than great *r* ....Prov 22:1
precious and pleasant *r* ....Prov 24:4
whom God hath given *r* ....Eccl 6:2
not yet *r* to men ....Eccl 9:11

r of Damascus and the spoil ... Is 8:4
a nest the *r* of the people ... Is 10:14
their *r* upon the shoulders ..... Is 30:6
hidden *r* of secret places ...... Is 45:3
eat the *r* of the Gentiles ...... Is 61:6
rich man glory in his *r* .... Jer 9:23
he that getteth *r* .... Jer 17:11
r..he hath gotten are perished . Jer 48:36
make a spoil of thy *r* .... Ezek 26:12
r and thy fairs .... Ezek 27:27
thou hast gotten thee *r* .... Ezek 28:4
lifted up because of thy *r* ..... Ezek 28:5
prey, and spoil, and *r* .... Dan 11:24
the deceitfulness of *r* .... Mark 4:19
they that have *r* .... Mark 10:23
Or despisest thou the *r* .... Rom 2:4
make known the *r* of his .... Rom 9:23
the *r* of his grace .... Eph 1:7
show the exceeding *r* .... Eph 2:7
unsearchable *r* of Christ .... Eph 3:8
to receive power and *r* .... Rev 5:12
great *r* is come to nought ...... Rev 18:17

RICHES, MANAGEMENT OF—*the way in which one uses material blessings*
Reflects spiritual attitude . Luke 16:10-12
Demands budget .... Luke 14:28-30

RICHLY—*in full measure*
Word of Christ dwell in you *r* . Col 3:16
who giveth us *r* all things 1Tim 6:17

RID—*to make free of*

[*also* RIDDANCE]
might *r* him out of their hands . Gen 37:22
will *r* you out..their bondage .. Ex 6:6
clean *r* of the corners .... Lev 23:22
r evil beasts out of the land ... Lev 26:6
r them out of the hand .... Ps 82:4
r me, and deliver me .... Ps 144:7
make even a speedy *r* .... Zeph 1:18

RIDDEN—*See* RIDE

RIDDLE—*a problem to be solved or guessed*
Samson's famous .... Judg 14:12-19
Classed as a parable ..... Ezek 17:2
Avoided by God .... Num 12:8

RIDE—*to travel in or on a means of transportation; be carried*

[*also* RIDDEN, RIDETH, RIDING, RODE]
they *r* upon the camels .... Gen 24:61
he made him to *r* .... Gen 41:43
what saddle soever he *r* .... Lev 15:9
Now he was *r* upon his ass .... Num 22:22
which thou hast *r* ever .... Num 22:30
He made him *r* on the high ... Deut 32:13
who *r* upon the heaven .... Deut 33:26
Speak, ye that *r* on white ..... Judg 5:10
had thirty sons that *r* .... Judg 10:4
And it was so, as she *r* 1Sam 25:20
men, which *r* upon camels 1Sam 30:17
the king's household to *r* 2Sam 16:2
Absalom *r* upon a mule 2Sam 18:9
that I may *r* thereon 2Sam 19:26
cause Solomon my son to *r* 1Kin 1:33
to *r* upon the king's 1Kin 1:44
and he *r* thereon 1Kin 13:13
slack not thy *r* for me 2Kin 4:24
So Jehu *r* in a chariot 2Kin 9:16
So they made him *r* 2Kin 10:16
save the beast that I *r* .... Neh 2:12
the horse that the king *r* ...... Esth 6:8
posts that *r* upon mules .... Esth 8:14
causest me to *r* upon it .... Job 30:22
he *r* upon a cherub .... Ps 18:10
And in thy majesty *r* .... Ps 45:4
caused men to *r* over our ..... Ps 66:12
r upon the heavens .... Ps 68:4
Lord *r* upon a swift cloud ..... Is 19:1
We will *r* upon the swift ...... Is 30:16
and I will cause thee to *r* ..... Is 58:14
they *r* upon horses .... Jer 6:23
r in chariots and on horses .... Jer 17:25
r in chariots and on horses .... Jer 22:4
they shall *r* upon horses .... Jer 50:42
horsemen *r* upon horses .... Ezek 23:6
all of them *r* upon horses ..... Ezek 23:23
all of them *r* upon horses ..... Ezek 38:15
I will make Ephraim to *r* ..... Hos 10:11
we will not *r* upon horses ..... Hos 14:3
he that *r* the horse deliver .... Amos 2:15
didst *r* upon thine horses ...... Hab 3:8
those that *r* in them .... Hag 2:22
a man *r* upon a red horse ..... Zech 1:8
lowly, and *r* upon an ass ...... Zech 9:9

RIDER—*one who rides*

[*also* RIDERS]
So that his *r* shall fall .... Gen 49:17
horse and his *r* .... Ex 15:01
thy part to set *r* upon them ... 2Kin 18:23
r on mules, camels .... Esth 8:10
the horse and his *r* .... Job 39:18
thy part to set *r* upon them ... Is 36:8
break..the horse and his *r* ...... Jer 51:21
pieces the chariot and his *r* .... Jer 51:21
and their *r* shall come .... Hag 2:22
r on horses..confounded ...... Zech 10:5
and his *r* with madness .... Zech 12:4

RIDGES—*a raised strip (as of plowed ground)*
Thou waterest the *r* .... Ps 65:10

RIDICULE—*See* MOCKING

RIE—*See* RYE

RIFLED—*ransacked*
be taken and the houses *r* ..... Zech 14:2

RIGHT—*that which is just and fair; privilege; in a direct line or course; correct*

Things that are:
God's Law .... Ps 19:8
God's Word .... Ps 33:4
God's Way .... Ps 107:7
Thoughts of the righteous. Prov 12:5
Work of the pure .... Prov 21:8
Obedience to God .... Acts 4:19, 20
Obedience to parents .... Eph 6:1

Things that are not:
False riches .... Jer 17:11
Injustice to the poor ..... Is 10:2
Man's way .... Prov 21:2
Man's heart .... Ps 78:37

[*also* RIGHTLY]
Judge of all the earth do *r*? ... Gen 18:25
which had led me in the *r* ..... Gen 24:48
Is not he *r* named Jacob? ..... Gen 27:36
that which is *r* in his sight ..... Ex 15:26
daughters..speak *r* .... Num 27:7
do that which is *r* and good ... Deut 6:18
whatsoever is *r* in his own ..... Deut 12:8
that which is good and *r* ...... Deut 12:28
to do that which is *r* .... Deut 13:18
r in the sight of the Lord ..... Deut 21:9
without iniquity, just and *r* .... Deut 32:4
good and *r* unto thee .... Josh 9:25
not frame to pronounce it *r* ... Judg 12:6
man did that which was *r* ..... Judg 17:6
man did that which was *r* ..... Judg 21:25
redeem thou my *r* to thyself ... Ruth 4:6
teach you the good and the *r* .. 1Sam 12:23
thy matters are good and *r* 2Sam 15:3
What *r* therefore have I 2Sam 19:28
do that which is *r* 1Kin 11:33
and do that is *r* in my sight ... 1Kin 11:38
to do that only which was *r* ... 1Kin 14:8
David did that which was *r* 1Kin 15:5
Asa did that which was *r* 1Kin 15:11
Is thine heart *r*, as my heart ... 2Kin 10:15
executing that which is *r* 2Kin 10:30
that which was *r* in 2Kin 12:2
did that which was *r* 2Kin 14:3
that which was *r* in 2Kin 15:3
did not that which was *r* 2Kin 16:2
things that were not *r* 2Kin 17:9
did that which was *r* 2Kin 18:3
And..that which was *r* in 2Kin 22:2
was *r* in the eyes of all 1Chr 13:4
that which was good and *r* 2Chr 14:2
that which was *r* 2Chr 20:32
Joash did that which was *r* 2Chr 24:2
did that which was *r* 2Chr 25:2
did that which was *r* 2Chr 26:4
did that which was *r* 2Chr 27:2
did not that which was *r* 2Chr 28:1
did that which was *r* 2Chr 29:2
that which was good and *r* 2Chr 31:20
did that which was *r* 2Chr 34:2
God, to seek of him a *r* way .. Ezra 8:21
ye have no portion, nor *r* ..... Neh 2:20
gavest them *r* judgments ...... Neh 9:13
the thing seem *r* before the ... Esth 8:5
How forcible are *r* words ..... Job 6:25
perverted that which was *r* .... Job 33:27
upon man more than *r* .... Job 34:23
thinkest thou this to be *r* ...... Job 35:2
but giveth *r* to the poor ...... Job 36:6
of me the thing that is *r* ...... Job 42:7
maintained my *r* and my cause . Ps 9:4
in the throne judging *r* .... Ps 9:4
Hear the *r*, O Lord .... Ps 17:1
shall help her, and that *r* ...... Ps 46:5
renew a *r* spirit within .... Ps 51:10
that thy judgments are *r* ...... Ps 119:75
the afflicted and the *r* .... Ps 140:12
I have led thee in *r* paths ..... Prov 4:11
opening of my lips..be *r* ...... Prov 8:6
go *r* on their ways .... Prov 9:15
a way which seemeth *r* .... Prov 14:12
great revenues without *r* ...... Prov 16:8
pure, and whether it be *r* ..... Prov 20:11
when thy lips speak *r* .... Prov 23:16
that giveth a *r* answer .... Prov 24:26
travail and every *r* work ...... Eccl 4:4
Prophesy not unto us *r* .... Is 30:10
when the needy speaketh *r* ..... Is 32:7
a noble vine, wholly a *r* seed .. Jer 2:21
r of the needy do they .... Jer 5:28
and their force is not *r* .... Jer 23:10
r of redemption is thine .... Jer 32:7
and had done *r* in my sight .... Jer 34:15
be driven out every man *r* .... Jer 49:5
turn aside the *r* of a man ..... Lam 3:35
that which is lawful and *r* ..... Ezek 18:5
that which is lawful and *r* ..... Ezek 33:14
ways of the Lord are *r* .... Hos 14:9
they know not to do *r* .... Amos 3:10
poor in the gate from their *r* .. Amos 5:12
aside the stranger from his *r* .. Mal 3:5
whatsoever is *r* I will give ..... Matt 20:4
and in his *r* mind .... Mark 5:15
Thou hast *r* judged .... Luke 7:43
clothed, and in his *r* mind ..... Luke 8:35
Thou hast answered *r* .... Luke 10:28
judge ye not what is *r*? .... Luke 12:57
sayest and teachest *r* .... Luke 20:21
thy heart is not *r* .... Acts 8:21
to pervert the *r* ways .... Acts 13:10
r dividing the word 2Tim 2:15
they have no *r* to eat .... Heb 13:10
have forsaken the *r* way 2Pet 2:15
have *r* to the tree of life ...... Rev 22:14

RIGHT—*the direction opposite of left*
then I will go to the *r* .... Gen 13:9
thou depart to the *r* hand ..... Gen 13:9
Ephraim in his *r* hand .... Gen 48:13
toward Israel's *r* hand .... Gen 48:13
r hand upon the head .... Gen 48:17
on their *r* hand .... Ex 14:22
Thy *r* hand, O Lord, is .... Ex 15:6
thy *r* hand, O Lord, hath ..... Ex 15:6
upon the tip of the *r* ear ...... Ex 29:20
the tip of the *r* ear of his ..... Ex 29:20
the thumb of their *r* hand ..... Ex 29:20
great toe of their *r* foot .... Ex 29:20
r shoulder shall ye give .... Lev 7:32
the tip of Aaron's *r* ear .... Lev 8:23
thumb of his *r* hand .... Lev 8:23
great toe of his *r* foot .... Lev 8:23
upon the tip of their *r* ear ..... Lev 8:24
thumbs of their *r* hands .... Lev 8:24
great toes of their *r* feet ...... Lev 8:24
upon the *r* shoulder .... Lev 8:26

r shoulder Aaron waved ..... Lev 9:21
upon the tip of the *r* ear ..... Lev 14:14
the thumb of his *r* hand ..... Lev 14:14
the great toe of his *r* foot ..... Lev 14:14
the tip of the *r* ear ..... Lev 14:17
the thumb of his *r* hand ..... Lev 14:17
the great toe of his *r* foot ..... Lev 14:17
the tip of the *r* ear ..... Lev 14:25
the thumb of his *r* hand ..... Lev 14:25
the great toe of his *r* foot ..... Lev 14:25
upon the tip of the *r* ear ..... Lev 14:28
the thumb of his *r* hand ..... Lev 14:28
the great toe of his *r* foot ..... Lev 14:28
the *r* shoulder are thine ..... Num 18:18
will not turn to the *r* hand ..... Num 20:17
the *r* hand or to the left ..... Num 22:26
turn unto the *r* hand ..... Deut 2:27
the *r* hand or to the left ..... Deut 5:32
the *r* hand, nor to the left ..... Deut 17:11
the *r* hand, or to the left ..... Deut 28:14
his *r* hand went a fiery law ..... Deut 33:2
from it to the *r* hand ..... Josh 1:7
people passed over *r* ..... Josh 3:16
along on the *r* hand ..... Josh 17:7
therefrom to the *r* hand ..... Josh 23:6
raiment upon his *r* thigh ..... Judg 3:16
r hand to the workmen's ..... Judg 5:26
trumpets in their *r* hands ..... Judg 7:20
one with his *r* hand ..... Judg 16:29
not aside to the *r* hand 1Sam 6:12
thrust out all your *r* eyes 1Sam 11:2
turned not to the *r* hand 2Sam 2:19
none can turn to the *r* 2Sam 14:19
men were on his *r* hand 2Sam 16:6
with the *r* hand to kiss 2Sam 20:9
r side of the city that lieth 2Sam 24:5
mother, and she sat on his *r* 1Kin 2:19
the *r* side of the house 1Kin 6:8
he set up the *r* pillar 1Kin 7:21
on the *r* side of the house 1Kin 7:39
standing by him on his *r* 1Kin 22:19
the *r* corner of the temple 2Kin 11:11
turned not aside to the *r* hand 2Kin 22:2
the *r* hand of the mount 2Kin 23:13
stood on his *r* hand 1Chr 6:39
could use both the *r* hand 1Chr 12:2
one on the *r* hand 2Chr 3:17
on the *r* hand Jachin 2Chr 3:17
put five on the *r* hand 2Chr 4:6
five on the *r* side, and five 2Chr 4:8
standing on his *r* hand 2Chr 18:18
the *r* side of the temple 2Chr 23:10
declined neither to the *r* hand 2Chr 34:2
Masseiah, on his *r* hand ..... Neh 8:4
one went on the *r* hand ..... Neh 12:31
hideth himself on the *r* hand ..... Job 23:9
Upon my *r* hand rise ..... Job 30:12
Should I lie against my *r* ..... Job 34:6
thine own *r* hand can save ..... Job 40:14
he is at my *r* hand ..... Ps 16:8
savest by thy *r* hand ..... Ps 17:7
thy *r* hand hath holden me up ..... Ps 18:35
saving strength of his *r* hand ..... Ps 20:6
thy *r* hand shall find out ..... Ps 21:8
r hand is full of bribes ..... Ps 26:10
thy *r* hand, and thine arm ..... Ps 44:3
thy *r* hand shall teach thee ..... Ps 45:4
thy *r* hand did stand ..... Ps 45:9
r hand is full of ..... Ps 48:10
save with thy *r* hand ..... Ps 60:5
thy *r* hand upholdeth ..... Ps 63:8
holden me by my *r* hand ..... Ps 72:23
even thy *r* hand? ..... Ps 74:11
the *r* hand of the Most High ..... Ps 77:10
thy *r* hand hath planted ..... Ps 80:15
high is thy *r* hand ..... Ps 89:13
r hand of his adversaries ..... Ps 89:42
ten thousand at thy *r* hand ..... Ps 91:7
his *r* hand, and his holy arm ..... Ps 98:1
thy *r* hand, and answer ..... Ps 108:6
Satan stand at his *r* hand ..... Ps 109:6
Sit thou at my *r* hand ..... Ps 110:1
r hand of the Lord ..... Ps 118:15
The *r* hand of the Lord ..... Ps 118:16
thy shade upon thy *r* hand ..... Ps 121:5
my *r* hand forget her ..... Ps 137:5
thy *r* hand shall save ..... Ps 138:7
thy *r* hand shall hold me ..... Ps 139:10
I looked on my *r* hand ..... Ps 142:4
a *r* hand..of falsehood ..... Ps 144:8
days is in her *r* hand ..... Prov 3:16
the ointment of his *r* hand ..... Prov 27:16
man's heart is at his *r* hand ..... Eccl 10:2
his *r* hand doth embrace ..... Song 2:6
his *r* hand should embrace ..... Song 8:3
snatch on the *r* hand ..... Is 9:20
r hand of my righteousness ..... Is 41:10
lie in my *r* hand? ..... Is 44:20
Cyrus, whose *r* hand I have ..... Is 45:1
r hand..spanned ..... Is 48:13
break forth on the *r* hand ..... Is 54:3
hath sworn by his *r* hand ..... Is 62:8
the *r* hand of Moses ..... Is 63:12
the signet upon my *r* hand ..... Jer 22:24
drawn back his *r* hand ..... Lam 2:3
a lion, on the *r* side ..... Ezek 1:10
lie again on thy *r* side ..... Ezek 4:6
cherubim stood on the *r* side ..... Ezek 10:3
dwelleth at thy *r* hand ..... Ezek 16:46
either on the *r* hand ..... Ezek 21:16
all out of thy *r* hand ..... Ezek 39:3
the *r* side of the house ..... Ezek 47:1
held up his *r* hand ..... Dan 12:7
discern between their *r* hand ..... Jon 4:11
cup of the Lord's *r* hand ..... Hab 2:16
standing at his *r* hand ..... Zech 3:1
the *r* side of the bowl ..... Zech 4:3
and upon his *r* eye ..... Zech 11:17
his *r* eye shall be ..... Zech 11:17
r hand and on the left ..... Zech 12:6
thy *r* eye offend thee ..... Matt 5:29
what thy *r* hand doeth ..... Matt 6:3
Sit thou on my *r* hand ..... Matt 22:44
the sheep on his *r* hand ..... Matt 25:33
man sitting on the *r* hand ..... Matt 26:64
a reed in his *r* hand ..... Matt 27:29
sit, one on thy *r* hand ..... Mark 10:37
Sit thou on my *r* hand ..... Mark 12:36
man sitting on the *r* hand ..... Mark 14:62
one on his *r* hand ..... Mark 15:27
sitting on the *r* side ..... Mark 16:5
on the *r* side of the altar ..... Luke 1:11
r hand was withered ..... Luke 6:6
Sit thou on my *r* hand ..... Luke 20:42
cut off his *r* ear ..... Luke 22:50
one on the *r* hand ..... Luke 23:33
cut off his *r* ear ..... John 18:10
the *r* side of the ship ..... John 21:6
for he is on my *r* hand ..... Acts 2:25
he took him by the *r* hand ..... Acts 3:7
exalted with his *r* hand ..... Acts 5:31
on the *r* hand of God ..... Acts 7:55
even at the *r* hand of God ..... Rom 8:34
righteousness on the *r* hand 2Cor 6:7
r hands of fellowship ..... Gal 2:9
at his own *r* hand ..... Eph 1:20
on the *r* hand of God ..... Col 3:1
the *r* hand of the Majesty ..... Heb 1:3
on the *r* hand of the throne ..... Heb 8:1
sat down on the *r* hand of God ..... Heb 10:12
r hand of the throne of God ..... Heb 12:2
on the *r* hand of God 1Pet 3:22
his *r* hand seven stars ..... Rev 1:16
seven stars in his *r* hand ..... Rev 2:1
in the *r* hand of him ..... Rev 5:1
his *r* foot upon the sea ..... Rev 10:2
a mark in their *r* hand ..... Rev 13:16

RIGHTEOUS—*without guilt before God; acting in accord with God's laws*

Applied to:

God ..... John 17:25
Christ 1John 2:1
Messiah ..... Is 53:11
Christians ..... Matt 25:37, 46

Blessings of:

Prayers of, heard ..... Prov 15:29
Safely guarded ..... Prov 18:10
Bold as a lion ..... Prov 28:1
Shine forth ..... Matt 13:43

[*also* RIGHTEOUSLY]

have I seen *r* before me ..... Gen 7:1
thou also destroy the *r* ..... Gen 18:23
wilt thou slay also a *r* nation? ..... Gen 20:4
hath been more *r* than I ..... Gen 38:26
Lord is *r* and I and my people ..... Ex 9:27
and *r* slay thou not ..... Ex 23:7
the death of the *r* and ..... Num 23:10
judge *r* between every man ..... Deut 1:16
pervert the words of the *r* ..... Deut 16:19
they shall justify the *r* ..... Deut 25:1
the *r* acts of the Lord ..... Judg 5:11
r acts toward the inhabitants ..... Judg 5:11
all the *r* acts of the Lord 1Sam 12:7
to David, Thou art more *r* 1Sam 24:17
men have slain a *r* person 2Sam 4:11
who fell upon two men more *r* 1Kin 2:32
justifying the *r* to give 1Kin 8:32
all the people, Ye be *r* 2Kin 10:9
justifying the *r* by giving 2Chr 6:23
they said, The Lord is *r* 2Chr 12:6
thy words; for thou art *r* ..... Neh 9:8
were the *r* cut off? ..... Job 4:7
though I were *r*, yet would I ..... Job 9:15
r, yet will I not lift up ..... Job 10:15
woman, that he should be *r*? ..... Job 15:14
The *r* also shall hold on ..... Job 17:9
Almighty, that thou art *r*? ..... Job 22:3
the *r* might dispute with him ..... Job 23:7
he was *r* in his own eyes ..... Job 32:1
For Job hath said, I am *r* ..... Job 34:5
If thou be *r* what givest ..... Job 35:7
eyes from the *r* ..... Job 36:7
that thou mayest be *r*? ..... Job 40:8
in the congregation of the *r* ..... Ps 1:5
thou, Lord, wilt bless the *r* ..... Ps 5:12
for the *r* God trieth ..... Ps 7:9
what can the *r* do? ..... Ps 11:3
the generation of the *r* ..... Ps 14:5
true and *r* altogether ..... Ps 19:9
contemptuously against the *r* ..... Ps 31:18
in the Lord and rejoice, ye *r* ..... Ps 32:11
Rejoice in the Lord, O ye *r* ..... Ps 33:1
of the Lord are upon the *r* ..... Ps 34:15
be glad that favor my *r* ..... Ps 35:27
little that a *r* man hath ..... Ps 37:16
Lord upholdeth the *r* ..... Ps 37:17
the *r* showeth mercy, and ..... Ps 37:21
yet have I not seen the *r* ..... Ps 37:25
r shall inherit the land ..... Ps 37:29
The *r* also shall see ..... Ps 52:6
never suffer the *r* to be ..... Ps 55:22
The *r* shall rejoice ..... Ps 58:10
there is a reward for the *r* ..... Ps 58:11
The *r* shall be glad in the ..... Ps 64:10
shalt judge the people *r* ..... Ps 67:4
let the *r* be glad; let them ..... Ps 68:3
not be written with the *r* ..... Ps 69:28
shall the *r* flourish ..... Ps 72:7
of the *r* shall be exalted ..... Ps 75:10
The *r* shall flourish like ..... Ps 92:12
against the soul of the *r* ..... Ps 94:21
he shall judge the people *r* ..... Ps 96:10
Light is sown for the *r* ..... Ps 97:11
The *r* shall see it and rejoice ..... Ps 107:42
full of compassion, and *r* ..... Ps 112:4
r shall be in everlasting ..... Ps 112:6
Gracious is the Lord, and *r* ..... Ps 116:5
the tabernacles of the *r* ..... Ps 118:15
into which the *r* shall enter ..... Ps 118:20
learned thy *r* judgments ..... Ps 119:7
R art thou, O Lord, and ..... Ps 119:137
rest upon the lot of the *r* ..... Ps 125:3
lest the *r* put forth ..... Ps 125:3
Lord is *r*; he hath cut ..... Ps 129:4
r shall give thanks ..... Ps 140:13
Let the *r* smite me; it ..... Ps 141:5
the *r* shall compass me ..... Ps 142:7
Lord is *r* in all his ways ..... Ps 145:17
the Lord loveth the *r* ..... Ps 146:8
sound wisdom for the *r* ..... Prov 2:7
his secret is with the *r* ..... Prov 3:32
soul of the *r* to famish ..... Prov 10:3
mouth of a *r* man is a well ..... Prov 10:11
the *r* tendeth to life ..... Prov 10:16

lips of the *r* feed many........Prov 10:21
the *r* shall be granted........Prov 10:24
the *r* is an everlasting........Prov 10:25
r shall never be removed......Prov 10:30
The *r* is delivered out of......Prov 11:8
the *r* shall be recompensed....Prov 11:31
A *r* man regardeth the life....Prov 12:10
A *r* man hateth lying; but.....Prov 13:5
the *r* good shall be repaid.....Prov 13:21
the *r* there is favor..........Prov 14:9
the *r* hath hope in his death...Prov 14:32
the *r* is much treasure........Prov 15:6
R lips are the delight.........Prov 16:13
overthrow the *r* in judgment...Prov 18:5
r man wisely considereth......Prov 21:12
father of the *r* shall greatly....Prov 23:24
the dwelling of the *r*..........Prov 24:15
unto the wicked, Thou art *r*...Prov 24:24
A *r* man falling down before..Prov 25:26
causeth the *r* to go astray.....Prov 28:10
perish, the *r* increase........Prov 28:28
the *r* are in authority........Prov 29:2
Open thy mouth, judge *r*.....Prov 31:9
God shall judge the *r*.........Eccl 3:17
Be not *r* over much; neither...Eccl 7:16
to the work of the *r*..........Eccl 8:14
that the *r* and the wise........Eccl 9:1
there is one event to the *r*....Eccl 9:2
ye to the *r*, that it shall.......Is 3:10
righteousness of the *r*.........Is 5:23
even glory to the *r*...........Is 24:16
r nation which keepeth the....Is 26:2
He that walketh *r*............Is 33:15
Who raised up the *r* man.....Is 41:2
r perisheth, and no man......Is 57:1
the *r* is taken away..........Is 57:1
people also shall be all *r*.....Is 60:21
of hosts, that judgest the *r*....Jer 11:20
R art thou, O Lord...........Jer 12:1
Lord of hosts, that triest the *r*.Jer 20:12
raise unto David a *r* Branch...Jer 23:5
Lord is *r*; for I have..........Lam 1:18
When a *r* man doth turn......Ezek 3:20
if thou warn the *r* man........Ezek 3:21
that the *r* sin not, and he.....Ezek 3:21
the heart of the *r* sad.........Ezek 13:22
they are more *r* than thou.....Ezek 16:52
the righteousness of the *r*.....Ezek 18:20
when the *r* turneth away......Ezek 18:24
a *r* man turneth away.........Ezek 18:26
from thee the *r* and the wicked.Ezek 21:3
r men, they shall judge.......Ezek 23:45
righteousness of the *r*.........Ezek 33:12
I shall say to the *r*............Ezek 33:13
r turneth from his............Ezek 33:18
Lord our God is *r* in all.......Dan 9:14
they sold the *r* for silver......Amos 2:6
compass about the *r*..........Hab 1:4
the man that is more *r*........Hab 1:13
between the *r* and the wicked.Mal 3:18
I am not come to call the *r*...Matt 9:13
a *r* man in the name of a *r*....Matt 10:41
r men have desired to see.....Matt 13:17
also outwardly appear *r*.......Matt 23:28
I came not to call the *r*.......Mark 2:17
And they were both *r* before..Luke 1:6
I came not to call the *r*.......Luke 5:32
in themselves that they were *r*.Luke 18:9
Certainly this was a *r* man....Luke 23:47
appearance, but judge *r*.......John 7:24
revelation of the *r* judgment...Rom 2:5
There is none *r*, no, not......Rom 3:10
for a *r* man will one die.......Rom 5:7
token of the *r* judgment......2Thess 1:5
law is not made for a *r*.......1Tim 1:9
the Lord, and *r* judge, shall...2Tim 4:8
we should live soberly, *r*......Titus 2:12
witness that he was *r*.........Heb 11:4
prayer of a *r* man availeth....James 5:16
to him that judgeth *r*.........1Pet 2:23
the Lord are over the *r*.......1Pet 3:12
if the *r* scarcely be saved......1Pet 4:18
that *r* man dwelleth...........2Pet 2:8
vexed his *r* soul.............2Pet 2:8
If ye know that he is *r*........1John 2:29
r, even as he is *r*.............1John 3:7
were evil, and his brother's *r*..1John 3:12
Thou art *r*, O Lord...........Rev 16:5
r are his judgments...........Rev 19:2
filthy still: and he that is *r*....Rev 22:11
let him be *r* still and he.......Rev 22:11

RIGHTEOUSNESS—*inherent or imputed guiltlessness before God*

Kinds of:

Created....................Eph 4:24
Legal......................Phil 3:6
Personal...................Phil 3:9
Imputed....................Phil 3:9
Experimental...............Heb 5:13
Actual.....................Heb 11:33
Real.......................1John 2:29

Of Christ, He:

Is the believer's.........Jer 33:16
Loves.....................Heb 1:9
Judges with...............Is 11:4
Is girded with............Is 11:5
Brings in.................Is 46:13
Fulfills all..............Matt 3:15
Confers upon believers...Is 61:10

[*also* RIGHTEOUSNESS', RIGHTEOUSNESSES]

he counted it to him for *r*.....Gen 15:6
shall my *r* answer for me......Gen 30:33
but in *r* shalt thou judge......Lev 19:15
it shall be our *r*.............Deut 6:25
r the Lord hath brought......Deut 9:4
Not for thy *r*, or for the......Deut 9:5
it shall be *r* unto thee.........Deut 24:13
shall offer sacrifices of *r*......Deut 33:19
render to every man his *r*.....1Sam 26:23
according to my *r*............2Sam 22:21
before thee in truth and in *r*..1Kin 3:6
give him according to his *r*....1Kin 8:32
according to his *r*............2Chr 6:23
return again my *r* is in it......Job 6:29
the habitation of thy *r*........Job 8:6
My *r* I hold fast.............Job 27:6
put on *r*, and it clothed me...Job 29:14
render unto man his *r*........Job 33:26
My *r* is more than God's?.....Job 35:2
will ascribe *r* to my Maker....Job 36:3
I call O God of my *r*.........Ps 4:1
Lead me, O Lord, in thy *r*....Ps 5:8
Lord, according to my *r*.....Ps 7:8
judge the world in *r*..........Ps 9:8
For the..Lord loveth *r*........Ps 11:7
uprightly and worketh *r*.......Ps 15:2
I will behold thy face in *r*.....Ps 17:15
me according to my *r*.........Ps 18:20
shall declare his *r*............Ps 22:31
leadeth me in the paths of *r*...Ps 23:3
r from the God of his.........Ps 24:5
deliver me in thy *r*...........Ps 31:1
He loveth *r* and judgment.....Ps 33:5
my God, according to thy *r*...Ps 35:24
shall speak of thy *r*..........Ps 35:28
Thy *r* is like..mountains.......Ps 36:6
bring forth thy *r* as the.......Ps 37:6
I have preached *r* in the.......Ps 40:9
truth and meekness and *r*.....Ps 45:4
lovest *r*, and hatest..........Ps 45:7
right hand is full of *r*.........Ps 48:10
shall declare his *r*............Ps 50:6
shall sing aloud of thy *r*.......Ps 51:14
lying rather than to speak *r*...Ps 52:3
speak *r*, O congregation......Ps 58:1
r wilt thou answer us.........Ps 65:5
them not come into thy *r*.....Ps 69:27
Deliver me in thy *r*...........Ps 71:2
show forth thy *r*..............Ps 71:15
make mention of thy *r*........Ps 71:16
Thy *r* also, O God...........Ps 71:19
tongue..shall talk of thy *r*.....Ps 71:24
r unto the king's son.........Ps 72:1
r and peace have kissed.......Ps 85:10
R shall go before him.........Ps 85:13
thy *r* in the land.............Ps 88:12
r shall they be exalted........Ps 89:16
judgment shall return..*r*.......Ps 94:15
judge the world with *r*........Ps 96:13
r..are the habitation..........Ps 97:2
r hath he openly showed......Ps 98:2
with *r* shall he judge..........Ps 98:9
executest judgment and *r*.....Ps 99:4
Lord executeth *r*.............Ps 103:6
his *r* unto children's.........Ps 103:17
he that doeth *r*..............Ps 106:3
counted unto him for *r*........Ps 106:31
his *r* endureth for ever........Ps 111:3
his *r* endureth for ever........Ps 112:3
his *r* endureth for ever........Ps 112:9
Open to me the gates of *r*....Ps 118:19
quicken me in thy *r*..........Ps 119:40
is an everlasting *r*...........Ps 119:142
thy commandments are *r*......Ps 119:172
priests be clothed with *r*......Ps 132:9
answer me and in thy *r*.......Ps 143:1
thy *r* sake bring my soul......Ps 143:11
goodness..sing of thy *r*........Ps 145:7
shalt thou understand *r*.......Prov 2:9
the words..are in *r*..........Prov 8:8
r delivereth from death.......Prov 10:2
r delivereth from death.......Prov 11:4
r of the perfect..direct........Prov 11:5
to him that soweth *r*..........Prov 11:18
As *r* tendeth to life...........Prov 11:19
truth showeth forth *r*.........Prov 12:17
In the way of *r* is life........Prov 12:28
R keepeth him...............Prov 13:6
R exalteth a nation...........Prov 14:34
loveth him. .after *r*..........Prov 15:9
Better is a little with *r*........Prov 16:8
throne is established by *r*.....Prov 16:12
found in the way of *r*.........Prov 16:31
mercy findeth life, *r*..........Prov 21:21
shall be established in *r*.......Prov 25:5
the place of *r*, that...........Eccl 3:16
man that perisheth in his *r*....Eccl 7:15
r lodged in it.................Is 1:21
r, the faithful city...........Is 1:26
her converts with *r*...........Is 1:27
oppression, for *r*.............Is 5:7
the *r* of the righteous.........Is 5:23
shall overflow with *r*..........Is 10:22
judgment and hasting *r*.......Is 16:5
the world will learn *r*.........Is 26:9
and *r* to the plummet.........Is 28:17
a king shall reign in *r*.........Is 32:1
work of *r* shall be peace......Is 32:17
the effect of *r* quietness.......Is 32:17
Zion with judgment and *r*.....Is 33:5
the right hand of my *r*.........Is 41:10
have called thee in *r*..........Is 42:6
is well pleased for his *r*.......Is 42:21
let the skies pour down *r*.....Is 45:8
let *r* spring up together.......Is 45:8
I the Lord speak *r*............Is 45:19
in the Lord have I *r*..........Is 45:24
that are far from *r*............Is 46:12
but not in truth, nor in *r*......Is 48:1
ye that follow after *r*.........Is 51:1
My *r* is near; my salvation....Is 51:5
r shall not be abolished.......Is 51:6
but my *r* shall be for ever.....Is 51:8
In *r*..be established...........Is 54:14
my *r* to be revealed..........Is 56:1
I will declare thy *r*..........Is 57:12
as a nation that did *r*.........Is 58:2
thy *r* shall go before thee.....Is 58:8
his *r*, it sustained him.........Is 59:16
peace and thine exactors *r*....Is 60:17
might be called trees of *r*.....Is 61:3
Lord God will cause *r*.........Is 61:11
r thereof go forth............Is 62:1
I that speak in *r*, mighty......Is 63:1
rejoiceth and worketh *r*.......Is 64:5
our *r* are as filthy rags........Is 64:6
in judgment and in *r*..........Jer 4:2
lovingkindness..and *r*.........Jer 9:24
Execute ye judgment and *r*....Jer 22:3
be called, The Lord Our *R*....Jer 23:6
Branch of *r* to grow up.......Jer 33:15
execute judgment and *r*.......Jer 33:15
be called, The Lord our *r*.....Jer 33:16
hath brought forth our *r*......Jer 51:10

man doth turn from his *r* .....Ezek 3:20
his *r* which he hath done ......Ezek 3:20
their own souls by their *r* .....Ezek 14:14
the *r* of the righteous ....Ezek 18:20
in his *r* that he hath done .....Ezek 18:22
turneth away from his *r* ....Ezek 18:24
All his *r* that he hath done ....Ezek 18:24
man turneth away from his *r* ..Ezek 18:26
r of the righteous ....Ezek 33:12
be able to live for his *r* ....Ezek 33:12
r shall not be remembered ....Ezek 33:13
and break off thy sins by *r* ....Dan 4:27
r belongeth unto thee ....Dan 9:7
according to all thy *r* ....Dan 9:16
supplications..for our *r* ....Dan 9:18
to bring in everlasting *r* ....Dan 9:24
that turn many to *r* ....Dan 12:3
betroth thee unto me in *r* .....Hos 2:19
sow to yourselves in *r*.........Hos 10:12
till he come and rain *r* ....Hos 10:12
and leave off *r* in the earth....Amos 5:7
fruit of *r* into hemlock ....Amos 6:12
know the *r* of the Lord ....Mic 6:5
and I shall behold his *r* ....Mic 7:9
seek *r*, seek meekness ....Zeph 2:3
God, in truth and in *r* ....Zech 8:8
the Lord an offering in *r*......Mal 3:3
Sun of *r* arise with healing ....Mal 4:2
hunger and thirst after *r* ......Matt 5:6
persecuted for *r* sake ....Matt 5:10
That except your *r* ....Matt 5:20
shall exceed the *r*.............Matt 5:20
kingdom of God and his *r*.....Matt 6:33
unto you in the way of *r* ......Matt 21:32
holiness and *r* before him .....Luke 1:75
world of sin and of *r* ....John 16:8
feareth him and worketh *r* ....Acts 10:35
thou enemy of all *r* ....Acts 13:10
will judge the world in *r* ......Acts 17:31
as he reasoned of *r* ....Acts 24:25
is the *r* of God revealed ......Rom 1:17
keep the *r* of the law ....Rom 2:26
commend the *r* of God ....Rom 3:5
r of God without the law .....Rom 3:21
his *r* for the remission ....Rom 3:25
counted unto him for *r*.........Rom 4:3
unto whom God imputeth *r* ...Rom 4:6
seal of the *r* of the faith ......Rom 4:11
that *r* might be imputed.........Rom 4:11
it was imputed to him for *r* ...Rom 4:22
receive..the gift of *r* ....Rom 5:17
the *r* of one the free gift ......Rom 5:18
grace reign through *r* ....Rom 5:21
of *r* unto God ....Rom 6:13
became the servants of *r* ......Rom 6:18
your members servants to *r* ...Rom 6:19
ye were free from *r*............Rom 6:20
r of the law..be fulfilled.......Rom 8:4
cut it short in *r*................Rom 9:28
not after *r* have attained to *r* ..Rom 9:30
the *r* which is of faith ....Rom 9:30
after the law of *r* ....Rom 9:31
attained to the law of *r* ....Rom 9:31
ignorant of God's *r* ....Rom 10:3
establish their own *r* ....Rom 10:3
unto the *r* of God ....Rom 10:3
Christ..end of the law for *r*....Rom 10:4
describeth the *r* which is ......Rom 10:5
man believeth unto *r* ....Rom 10:10
r and peace and joy in the ....Rom 14:17
unto us wisdom and *r*.........1Cor 1:30
Awake to *r*, and sin not 1Cor 15:34
r exceed in glory 2Cor 3:9
the *r* of God in him 2Cor 5:21
the armor of *r* on the right 2Cor 6:7
what fellowship hath *r* 2Cor 6:14
his *r* remaineth for ever 2Cor 9:9
as the ministers of *r* 2Cor 11:15
if *r* come by the law ....Gal 2:21
accounted to him for *r* ....Gal 3:6
r..have been by the law ....Gal 3:21
the hope of *r* by faith ....Gal 5:5
is in all goodness and *r* ....Eph 5:9
the breastplate of *r* ....Eph 6:14
filled with the fruits of *r* ......Phil 1:11
follow after *r*, godliness 1Tim 6:11
r, faith, charity, peace 2Tim 2:22
for instruction in *r*............2Tim 3:16
there is..a crown of *r* 2Tim 4:8
Not by works of *r* ....Titus 3:5
a scepter of *r* is the...........Heb 1:8
interpretation King of *r* ....Heb 7:2
heir of the *r*..by faith ....Heb 11:7
the peaceable fruit of *r* ....Heb 12:11
worketh not the *r* of God .....James 1:20
imputed unto him for *r* ....James 2:23
the fruit of *r* is..peace ....James 3:18
dead to sins..live unto *r*.......1Pet 2:24
suffer for *r* sake 1Pet 3:14
the *r* of God and our Savior...2Pet 1:1
a preacher of *r* 2Pet 2:5
new earth wherein dwelleth *r* ..2Pet 3:13
that doeth *r* is righteous 1John 3:7
whosoever doeth not *r* 1John 3:10
the fine linen is the *r* ....Rev 19:8

RIGHTLY—*See* RIGHT

RIGOR—*harsh inflexibility; severity*
children..to serve with *r*.......Ex 1:13
Thou shalt not rule..with *r* ....Lev 25:43
other shall not rule with *r*.....Lev 25:53

RIMMON, REMMON (rĭm'ŏn, rĕm'ŏn)—*"pomegranate; exalted; greatness"*
1. Benjamite 2Sam 4:2-9
2. Rock near Gibeah.......Judg 20:45-47
   Benjamites hide here....Judg 21:13-23
3. Town in south Judah ....Josh 15:1, 32
   Assigned to Simeon .....Josh 19:7, 8
   Mentioned in prophecy ..Zech 14:10
   Called En-rimmon ....Neh 11:29
4. Syrian God (meaning "thunderer")
   worshiped by Naaman .2Kin 5:18
5. City of Zebulun ....Josh 19:13
   Levitical city............1Chr 6:77
   Called Dimnah ....Josh 21:35

See REMMON-METHOAR

RIMMON-PAREZ (rĭm-ŏn-pē'rĕz)—*"pomegranates of the wrath"*
Israelite camp ....Num 33:19, 20

RING—*a circular band*

Article of furniture, for:
Staves of the ark ....Ex 25:12-15
Curtains ....Ex 26:29
Priest's ephod ....Ex 28:23-28
Incense altar ....Ex 30:4
Drapery ....Esth 1:6

Article of apparel:
Symbol of authority .....Gen 41:42
Sealing royal documents. .Esth 3:12
Gifts ....Ex 35:22
Feminine adornment .....Is 3:16, 21
Expressive of position....Luke 15:22
Sign of social status......James 2:2

[*also* RINGS]
shalt make for it four *r* ....Ex 25:26
the *r* in the four corners ......Ex 25:26
the head of it unto one *r*......Ex 26:24
r in the four corners ....Ex 27:4
the head thereof, to one *r*.....Ex 36:29
made their *r* of gold ....Ex 36:34
And he cast for it four *r* ......Ex 37:3
two *r* upon the one side.......Ex 37:3
two *r* upon the other side .....Ex 37:3
And he cast for it four *r* ......Ex 37:13
r upon the four corners ....Ex 37:13
two *r* of gold for it ....Ex 37:27
four *r* for the four ends ....Ex 38:5
of gold, and two gold *r* ....Ex 39:16
the two *r* in the two ends .....Ex 39:16
they made two *r* of gold ......Ex 39:19
bind the breastplate by his *r*...Ex 39:21
unto the *r* of the ephod ....Ex 39:21
chains, and bracelets, *r* ....Num 31:50
the king took his *r* ....Esth 3:10
the king took off his *r* ....Esth 8:2
sealed it with the king's *r* .....Esth 8:10
His hands are as gold *r* ....Song 5:14
their *r*, they were so high .....Ezek 1:18
their *r* were full of eyes ....Ezek 1:18

RINGLEADER—*the leader of a mob*
Paul contemptuously called ....Acts 24:5

RINGSTRAKED—*marked with circular stripes*
he goats that were *r* ....Gen 30:35
of the flocks toward the *r* .....Gen 30:40
The *r* shall be thy hire ....Gen 31:8
then bare all the cattle *r* ......Gen 31:8
upon the cattle are *r*..........Gen 31:12

RINNAH (rĭn'ä)—*"praise to God; strength"*
Son of Shimon 1Chr 4:20

RINSED—*to cleanse by washing lightly or pouring*
scoured, and *r* in water ....Lev 6:28
and hath not *r* his hands ......Lev 15:11

RIOT—*a violent public disorder; wantonness; to engage in unruly behavior*
Pacified by town clerk ...Acts 19:20-41

[*also* RIOTING]
not in *r* and drunkenness......Rom 13:13
children not accused of *r*......Titus 1:6
same excess of *r*..............1Pet 4:4
count it pleasure to *r* 2Pet 2:13

RIOTOUS—*living without restraint*
Loose living..............Luke 15:13
Gluttonous eaters ....Prov 23:20, 21
Sexual promiscuity.......Rom 13:13

RIP—*to tear or split apart or open*

[*also* RIPPED]
r up their women............2Kin 8:12
with child he *r* up 2Kin 15:16
child shall be *r* up ....Hos 13:16
have *r* up the women ....Amos 1:13

RIPE—*fully grown; fully developed*

[*also* RIPENING]
brought forth *r* grapes ....Gen 40:10
first of thy *r* ....Ex 22:29
the sour grape is *r*............Is 18:5
figs that are first *r*...........Jer 24:2
for the harvest is *r* ....Joel 3:13
harvest of the earth is *r*.......Rev 14:15

RIPHATH (rī'făth)—*"spoken"*
Son of Gomer...........Gen 10:3
Called Diphath 1Chr 1:6

RISE—*to assume a standing position; get up from a resting position*

Of resurrection:
Christ's ....Mark 8:31
Believers' (spiritually)....Col 2:12
Believers' (physically) ....John 11:23, 24

Of Christ's resurrection:
Predicted ....Mark 14:28
Fulfilled ....Matt 28:6, 7
Remembered............John 2:22
Evidenced ....John 21:14
Preached 1Cor 15:11-15
Misunderstood ....Mark 9:9, 10

[*also* RISEN, RISEST, RISETH, RISING, ROSE]
r up against Abel............Gen 4:8
Lot seeing them *r* up ....Gen 19:1
and ye shall *r* up early ....Gen 19:2
sun was *r* upon the earth......Gen 19:23
Abraham *r* up early ....Gen 21:14
Abraham *r* up early ....Gen 22:3
they *r* up and went ....Gen 22:19
drink and *r* up ....Gen 25:34
Jacob *r* up early.............Gen 28:18
he *r* up and passed over ......Gen 31:21
cannot *r* up before thee ....Gen 31:35
he *r* up that night ....Gen 32:22
r up to comfort him ....Gen 37:35
r up from Beer-sheba ....Gen 46:5
R up early in the morning.....Ex 8:20
r any from his place for.......Ex 10:23
R up, and get you forth ....Ex 12:31

R

overthrown them that *r* up ....Ex 15:7
If the sun be *r* upon him ......Ex 22:3
And Moses *r* up..............Ex 24:13
And they *r* up early ....Ex 32:6
drink and *r* up to play ....Ex 32:6
r up and worshiped...........Ex 33:10
skin of his flesh a *r*...........Lev 13:2
if the *r* be white..............Lev 13:10
quick raw flesh in the *r*........Lev 13:10
it is a *r* of the burning ....Lev 13:28
for a *r* and for a scab ....Lev 14:56
r up before the hoary head....Lev 19:32
east side toward the *r*.........Num 2:3
R up, Lord and let thine ......Num 10:35
r up early in the morning .....Num 14:40
Moses *r* up and went unto ....Num 16:25
princes of Moab *r* up ....Num 22:14
R up, Balak, and hear ....Num 23:18
shall *r* up as a great lion .....Num 23:24
Scepter shall *r* out of Israel ...Num 24:17
And Balaam *r* up, and went...Num 24:25
r up in your father's stead.....Num 32:14
Now *r* up, said I ....Deut 2:13
R ye up, take your journey....Deut 2:24
and when thou *r* up ....Deut 6:7
and when thou *r* up ....Deut 11:19
r up against him..............Deut 19:11
false witness *r* up against......Deut 19:16
r against his neighbor ....Deut 22:26
thine enemies that *r* up ....Deut 28:7
children that shall *r* up........Deut 29:22
let them *r* up and help you....Deut 32:38
and *r* up from Seir ....Deut 33:2
of them that *r* against him ....Deut 33:11
that they *r* not again..........Deut 33:11
Joshua *r* early................Josh 3:1
waters..*r* up upon an heap ....Josh 3:16
r early about the dawning .....Josh 6:15
r up and buildeth this city.....Josh 6:26
r up from the ambush ....Josh 8:7
Joshua *r* up early.............Josh 8:10
toward the *r* of the sun ....Josh 12:1
shall *r* and go through ....Josh 18:4
and there *r* up fire ....Judg 6:21
r up early, and pitched........Judg 7:1
R thou and fall upon us ....Judg 8:21
r up against my father's ....Judg 9:18
and Abimelech *r* up ....Judg 9:35
he *r* up to depart.............Judg 19:5
but he *r* up and departed .....Judg 19:10
the man *r* up, and gat him ....Judg 19:28
the children of Israel *r* up .....Judg 20:19
flame with smoke *r*............Judg 20:38
the people *r* early ....Judg 21:4
she was *r* up to glean ....Ruth 2:15
she *r* up before one ....Ruth 3:14
r up after they had eaten 1Sam 1:9
when Samuel *r* early..........1Sam 15:12
David *r* up early 1Sam 17:20
he should *r* against me 1Sam 22:13
man is *r* to pursue thee 1Sam 25:29
Then they *r* up, and went 1Sam 28:25
r up early in the morning 1Sam 29:10
didst *r* and eat bread 2Sam 12:21
family is *r* against thine 2Sam 14:7
And Absalom *r* up early 2Sam 15:2
them that *r* up 2Sam 22:40
r up, and went every man 1Kin 1:49
I *r* in the morning 1Kin 3:21
I am *r* up in the room 1Kin 8:20
r up early in the morning 2Kin 3:22
of God was *r* early 2Kin 6:15
they *r* up in the twilight.......2Kin 7:5
which *r* up against me 2Kin 16:7
r up in the room of David 2Chr 6:10
r early in the morning 2Chr 20:20
r up to the kingdom 2Chr 21:4
r up..smote the Edomites 2Chr 21:9
expressed by name *r* up 2Chr 28:15
r up betimes, and sending 2Chr 36:15
r up the chief of the ....Ezra 1:5
Ezra *r* up from before ....Ezra 10:6
Let us *r* up and build ....Neh 2:18
Eliashib the high priest *r*......Neh 3:1
from the *r* of the morning.....Neh 4:21
r up early in the morning .....Job 1:5
the sun, and it *r* not ....Job 9:7
man lieth down and *r* not .....Job 14:12
my leanness *r* up in me ....Job 16:8
earth shall *r* up against........Job 20:27
murderer *r* with the light......Job 24:14
r up and no man is sure ......Job 24:22
shall I do when God *r* up? ....Job 31:14
that *r* up against me ....Ps 3:1
they were not able to *r* ....Ps 18:38
under me those that *r* up .....Ps 18:39
but we are *r*, and stand ....Ps 20:8
war should *r* against me.......Ps 27:3
False witnesses did *r* up.......Ps 35:11
shall not be able to *r* ....Ps 36:12
that *r* up against us ....Ps 44:5
earth from the *r* of the sun ....Ps 50:1
r up against me ....Ps 54:3
those that *r* up against ....Ps 74:23
strangers *r* up for me against ..Ps 94:16
vain for you to *r* up early .....Ps 127:2
grieved with those that *r* ......Ps 139:21
falleth..and *r* up again ....Prov 24:16
calamity shall *r* suddenly ......Prov 24:22
r early in the morning ....Prov 27:14
When the wicked *r*, men ......Prov 28:28
r also while it is yet night .....Prov 31:15
spirit of the ruler *r* up ....Eccl 10:4
r up at the voice of the bird...Eccl 12:4
R up, my love, my fair one ...Song 2:10
r up to open to my beloved ...Song 5:5
Woe unto them that *r* up .....Is 5:11
I will *r* up against them ....Is 14:22
they shall not *r*...............Is 26:14
R up, ye women that are at ...Is 32:9
from the *r* of the sun ....Is 41:25
they shall not *r*...............Is 43:17
not know from whence it *r*....Is 47:11
thy light *r* in obscurity ....Is 58:10
glory from the *r* of the sun ....Is 59:19
glory of the Lord is *r* ....Is 60:1
r up early and speaking ....Jer 7:13
r early and protesting ....Jer 11:7
r early and sending ....Jer 25:4
and fall and *r* no more ....Jer 25:27
r up certain of the elders......Jer 26:17
r up early and sending ....Jer 29:19
r early and speaking ....Jer 35:14
r up early and sending ....Jer 35:15
Egypt *r* up like a flood ....Jer 46:8
r up out of the north ....Jer 47:2
that *r* up against me ....Jer 51:1
I am not able to *r* up ....Lam 1:14
lips of those that *r* up.........Lam 3:62
sitting down and their *r* up ....Lam 3:63
Violence is *r* up into a rod ....Ezek 7:11
and *r* up in haste ....Dan 3:24
another shall *r* after them .....Dan 7:24
I *r* up and did the king's ......Dan 8:27
she shall no more *r*...........Amos 5:2
r against the house of.........Amos 7:9
r up wholly as a flood ....Amos 8:8
r up wholly like a flood ....Amos 9:5
r up against her in battle......Obad 1
r up to flee unto Tarshish .....Jon 1:3
is *r* up as an enemy ....Mic 2:8
r up against her mother ....Mic 7:6
shall not *r* up the second......Nah 1:9
Shall they not *r* up ....Hab 2:7
they *r* early, and corrupted ....Zeph 3:7
I *r* up to the prey ....Zeph 3:8
r up against the hand ....Zech 14:13
r of the sun even unto ....Mal 1:11
he maketh his sun to *r*........Matt 5:45
children shall *r* up against .....Matt 10:21
r a greater than John ....Matt 11:11
Nineveh shall *r* in judgment ...Matt 12:41
he is *r* from the dead ....Matt 14:2
third day he shall *r* again .....Matt 20:19
shall *r* against nation..........Matt 24:7
false prophets shall *r*.........Matt 24:11
But after I am *r* again ....Matt 26:32
After three days I will *r*.......Matt 27:63
He is *r* from the dead ....Matt 27:64
r up a great while ....Mark 1:35
Satan *r* up against himself .....Mark 3:26
and *r* night and day ....Mark 4:27
John the Baptist was *r* ....Mark 6:14
third day he shall *r* again .....Mark 10:34
r and came to Jesus ....Mark 10:50
when they shall *r*.............Mark 12:23
the dead that they *r* ....Mark 12:26
shall *r* against nation..........Mark 13:8
r up against their parents .....Mark 13:12
and false prophets shall *r* .....Mark 13:22
R up, let us go; lo, he ....Mark 14:42
at the *r* of the sun ....Mark 16:2
he is *r*; he is not here.........Mark 16:6
seen him after he was *r* ....Mark 16:14
r again of many in Israel ......Luke 2:34
r up, and thrust him out ......Luke 4:29
or to say, ***R*** up and walk?.....Luke 5:23
r up, and followed him ....Luke 5:28
prophet is *r* up among us .....Luke 7:16
John was *r* from the dead .....Luke 9:7
old prophets is *r* again ....Luke 9:19
I cannot *r* and give thee ......Luke 11:7
he will not *r* and give him.....Luke 11:8
he will *r* and give him ....Luke 11:8
r up in the judgment ....Luke 11:32
cloud *r* out of the west........Luke 12:54
master of the house is *r* up....Luke 13:25
third day he shall *r* again .....Luke 18:33
shall *r* against nation..........Luke 21:10
when he *r* up from prayer.....Luke 22:45
r and pray, lest ye enter ......Luke 22:46
He is not here, but is *r* ....Luke 24:6
and the third day *r* again......Luke 24:7
to *r* from the dead ....Luke 24:46
R, take up thy bed ....John 5:8
Thy brother shall *r* again......John 11:23
that she *r* up hastily ....John 11:31
He *r* from supper, and laid ....John 13:4
r again from the dead.........John 20:9
of Nazareth *r* up ....Acts 3:6
Then the high priest *r* up .....Acts 5:17
After this man *r* up Judas .....Acts 5:37
R, Peter, kill and eat ....Acts 10:13
he *r* up, and came into ....Acts 14:20
Peter *r* up, and said ....Acts 15:7
r again from the dead.........Acts 17:3
r and stand upon thy feet .....Acts 26:16
should *r* from the dead ....Acts 26:23
the king *r* up................Acts 26:30
yea rather, that is *r* again .....Rom 8:34
Christ both died and *r* ....Rom 14:9
r to reign over the Gentiles ...Rom 15:12
and drink and *r* up to play 1Cor 10:7
he *r* from the dead 1Cor 15:12
be that the dead *r* not 1Cor 15:15
Christ *r* from the dead 1Cor 15:20
if the dead *r* not at all? 1Cor 15:29
died for them, and *r* again 2Cor 5:15
If ye then be *r* with Christ ....Col 3:1
Jesus died and *r* again 1Thess 4:14
in Christ shall *r* first 1Thess 4:16
priest should *r* after ....Heb 7:11
sun is no sooner *r* with ....James 1:11
R, and measure the temple ....Rev 11:1
beast *r* up out of the sea ......Rev 13:1
her smoke *r* up for ever.......Rev 19:3

RISSAH (rĭs'ä)—*"dew"*
Israelite camp ....Num 33:21, 22

RITES—*ceremonial acts*
according to all the *r* of it.....Num 9:3

RITHMAH (rĭth'mä)—*"noise"*
Israelite camp ....Num 33:18, 19

RIVALRY—*competition*
Between man and neighbor ....Eccl 4:4

RIVER—*a large, running stream of water*
Uses of:
Water ....Jer 2:18
Irrigation ....Gen 2:10
Bathing..................Ex 2:5
Baptisms.................Matt 3:6
Healing.................2Kin 5:10

List of:
Abana 2Kin 5:12
Arnon . . . . Josh 12:1
Chebar . . . . Ezek 10:15, 20
Euphrates . . . . Gen 2:14
Gihon . . . . Gen 2:13
Gozan 2Kin 17:6
Hiddekel . . . . Gen 2:14
Jabbok . . . . Deut 2:37
Jordan . . . . Josh 3:8
Kanah . . . . Josh 16:8
Kishon . . . . Judg 5:21
Nile (Sihor) . . . . Jer 2:18
Pharpar 2Kin 5:12
Pison . . . . Gen 2:11
Ulai . . . . Dan 8:2, 16

Figurative of:
Prosperity of saints . . . . . . Ps 1:3
Affliction . . . . Ps 124:4
Christ . . . . Is 32:1, 2
God's presence . . . . Is 33:21
Peace . . . . Is 66:12
Holy Spirit . . . . John 7:38, 39

[*also* RIVER'S, RIVERS]
this land, the *r* of Egypt . . . . . . Gen 15:18
great *r*, the *r* Euphrates . . . . Gen 15:18
and passed over the *r* . . . . Gen 31:21
Saul of Rehoboth by the *r* . . . . Gen 36:37
he stood by the *r* . . . . Gen 41:1
after them out of the *r* . . . . Gen 41:3
upon the brink of the *r* . . . . Gen 41:3
upon the bank of the *r* . . . . Gen 41:17
ye shall cast into the *r* . . . . Ex 1:22
in the flags by the *r* brink . . . . . Ex 2:3
take of the water of the *r* . . . . . Ex 4:9
thou takest out of the *r* . . . . Ex 4:9
shalt stand by the *r* brink . . . . . Ex 7:15
waters which are in the *r* . . . . . . Ex 7:17
that is in the *r* shall die . . . . . . Ex 7:18
and the *r* shall stink . . . . Ex 7:18
drink of the water of the *r* . . . . Ex 7:18
streams, upon their *r* . . . . Ex 7:19
waters that were in the *r* . . . . . . Ex 7:20
fish that was in the *r* died . . . . . Ex 7:21
r stank, and the Egyptians . . . . Ex 7:21
the water of the *r* . . . . Ex 7:21
digged round about the *r* . . . . . . Ex 7:24
the water of the *r* . . . . Ex 7:24
r shall bring forth frogs . . . . . . Ex 8:3
they shall remain in the *r* . . . . . Ex 8:11
from the desert unto the *r* . . . . Ex 23:31
in the seas, and in the *r* . . . . Lev 11:9
by the *r* of the land of . . . . Num 22:5
as gardens by the *r* side . . . . Num 24:6
Azmon unto the *r* of Egypt . . . Num 34:5
great *r*, the *r* Euphrates . . . . Deut 1:7
is by the brink of the *r* . . . . Deut 2:36
the city that is by the *r* . . . . Deut 2:36
r of Arnon unto mount . . . . Deut 3:8
even unto the *r* Arnon . . . . Deut 3:16
even unto the *r* Jabbok . . . . Deut 3:16
a land of *r* of waters . . . . Deut 10:7
the *r*, the *r* Euphrates . . . . Deut 11:24
great *r*, the *r* Euphrates . . . . Josh 1:4
bank of the *r* Arnon . . . . Josh 12:2
from the middle of the *r* . . . . . . Josh 12:2
even unto the *r* Jabbok . . . . Josh 12:2
bank of the *r* Arnon . . . . Josh 13:9
in the midst of the *r* . . . . Josh 13:9
bank of the *r* Arnon . . . . Josh 13:16
in the midst of the *r* . . . . Josh 13:16
on the south side of the *r* . . . . . Josh 15:7
westward unto the *r* Kanah . . . . Josh 16:8
southward of the *r* . . . . Josh 17:9
the north side of the *r* . . . . Josh 17:9
to the *r* Kishon Sisera . . . . Judg 4:7
unto the *r* of Kishon . . . . Judg 4:13
at the *r* Euphrates 2Sam 8:3
will draw in into the *r* 2Sam 17:13
from the *r* unto the land 1Kin 4:21
region on this side the *r* 1Kin 4:24
kings on this side the *r* 1Kin 4:24
scatter them beyond the *r* 1Kin 14:15
which is by the *r* Arnon 2Kin 10:33
Habor by the *r* of Gozan 2Kin 18:11
up all the *r* of besieged 2Kin 19:24
from the *r* of Egypt 2Kin 24:7
unto the *r* Euphrates 2Kin 24:7
Shaul of Rehoboth by the *r* . . . 1Chr 1:48
and to the *r* Gozan 1Chr 5:26
that were beyond the *r* 1Chr 19:16
unto the *r* of Egypt 2Chr 7:8
that are on this side the *r* . . . . . Ezra 4:10
portion on this side the *r* . . . . . . Ezra 4:16
countries beyond the *r* . . . . Ezra 4:20
on this side the *r* . . . . Ezra 5:6
governor beyond the *r* . . . . Ezra 6:6
which are beyond the *r* . . . . Ezra 6:6
governor on this side the *r* . . . . Ezra 6:13
people that are beyond the *r* . . Ezra 7:25
at the *r* of Ahava . . . . Ezra 8:21
governors on this side the *r* . . . Ezra 8:36
governors beyond the *r* . . . . Neh 2:7, 9
He shall not see the *r* . . . . Job 20:17
r among the rocks . . . . Job 28:10
poured me out *r* of oil . . . . Job 29:6
drinketh up a *r*, and hasteth . . Job 40:23
of the *r* of thy pleasures . . . . . . Ps 36:8
There is a *r*, the streams . . . . . . Ps 46:4
enrichest it with..*r* of God . . . . Ps 65:9
thou driedst up mighty *r* . . . . . . Ps 74:15
waters to run down like *r* . . . . . Ps 78:16
her branches unto the *r* . . . . Ps 80:11
his right hand in the *r* . . . . Ps 89:25
r into a wilderness . . . . Ps 107:33
R of waters run down . . . . Ps 119:136
By the *r* of Babylon . . . . Ps 137:1
r of waters in the streets . . . . . . Prov 5:16
All the *r* run into the sea . . . . . Eccl 1:7
from whence the *r* come . . . . . . Eccl 1:7
eyes of doves by the *r* . . . . Song 5:12
part of the *r* of Egypt . . . . Is 7:18
by them beyond the *r* . . . . Is 7:20
shake his hand over the *r* . . . . . Is 11:15
land the *r* have spoiled! . . . . Is 18:2
the *r* shall be wasted . . . . Is 19:5
shall turn the *r* far away . . . . . . Is 19:6
through thy land as a *r* . . . . Is 23:10
r and streams of waters . . . . Is 30:25
r of the besieged places . . . . Is 37:25
will open *r* in high places . . . . . Is 41:18
will make the *r* islands . . . . Is 42:15
and through the *r* . . . . Is 43:2
and *r* in the desert . . . . Is 43:19
and I will dry up thy *r* . . . . Is 44:27
thy peace been as a *r* . . . . Is 48:18
I make the *r* a wilderness . . . . . Is 50:2
her roots by the *r* . . . . Jer 17:8
to walk by the *r* of waters . . . . . Jer 31:9
north by the *r* Euphrates . . . . . . Jer 46:6
waters are moved like the *r* . . . . Jer 46:8
let tears run down like a *r* . . . . Lam 2:18
runneth down with *r* . . . . Lam 3:48
captives by the *r* of Chebar . . . Ezek 1:1
dwelt by the *r* of Chebar . . . . . . Ezek 3:15
to the *r* and to the valleys . . . . . Ezek 6:3
I saw by the *r* of Chebar . . . . . . Ezek 10:22
My *r* is mine own . . . . Ezek 29:3
will cause the fish of thy *r* . . . . Ezek 29:4
out of the midst of thy *r* . . . . . . Ezek 29:4
fish of thy *r* shall stick . . . . Ezek 29:4
The *r* is mine . . . . Ezek 29:9
and against thy *r* . . . . Ezek 29:10
And I will make the *r* dry . . . . . Ezek 30:12
r running round about . . . . Ezek 31:4
little *r* unto all the trees . . . . . . Ezek 31:4
camest forth with thy *r* . . . . Ezek 32:2
and fouledst their *r* . . . . Ezek 32:2
their *r* to run like oil . . . . Ezek 32:14
in all thy *r*, shall they . . . . Ezek 35:8
I saw by the *r* Chebar . . . . Ezek 43:3
r that I could not pass over . . . Ezek 47:5
r that could not be passed . . . . . Ezek 47:5
bank of the *r* were very . . . . Ezek 47:7
the *r* shall come . . . . Ezek 47:9
by the *r* upon the bank . . . . Ezek 47:12
r toward the Great Sea . . . . Ezek 48:28
stood before the *r* a ram . . . . . . Dan 8:3
by the side of the great *r* . . . . . Dan 10:4
of the bank of the *r* . . . . Dan 12:5
r of waters are dried up . . . . Joel 1:20
r of Judah shall flow . . . . Joel 3:18
r of the wilderness . . . . Amos 6:14
fortress even to the *r* . . . . Mic 7:12
drieth up all the *r* . . . . Nah 1:4
situate among the *r* . . . . Nah 3:8
displeased against the *r*? . . . . . . Hab 3:8
thine anger against the *r*? . . . . . Hab 3:8
beyond the *r* of Ethiopia . . . . . . Zeph 3:10
r even to the ends . . . . Zech 9:10
baptized of him in the *r* . . . . Mark 1:5
out of the city by a *r* side . . . . . Acts 16:13
the third part of the *r* . . . . Rev 8:10
in the great *r* Euphrates . . . . . . Rev 9:14
out his vial upon the *r* . . . . Rev 16:4
the great *r* Euphrates . . . . Rev 16:12
pure *r* of water of life . . . . Rev 22:1

RIZPAH (rĭz'pä)—*"variegated; hot stone"*
Saul's concubine taken by Abner 2Sam 3:6-8
Sons of, killed 2Sam 21:8, 9
Grief-stricken, cares for corpses 2Sam 21:10-14

ROAD—*a figure of speech for "a raid"*
have ye made a *r* today? 1Sam 27:10

ROAR—*deep, animal cry*

[*also* ROARED, ROARETH, ROARING, ROARINGS]
lion *r* against him . . . . Judg 14:5
Let the sea *r* 1Chr 16:32
r are poured out like the . . . . . . Job 3:24
The *r* of the lion . . . . Job 4:10
After it a voice *r*; he . . . . Job 37:4
from the words of my *r*? . . . . Ps 22:1
bones waxed old through my *r* . Ps 32:3
r by reason of the . . . . Ps 38:8
waters..*r* and be troubled . . . . . Ps 46:3
enemies *r* in the midst of . . . . . Ps 74:4
sea *r* and the fullness . . . . Ps 96:11
sea *r*, and the fullness . . . . Ps 98:7
lions *r* after their prey . . . . Ps 104:21
wrath is as the *r* of a lion . . . . . Prov 19:12
r lion and a ranging bear . . . . . . Prov 28:15
Their *r* shall be like a lion . . . . Is 5:29
shall *r* like young lions . . . . Is 5:29
shall *r*, and lay hold of . . . . Is 5:29
they shall *r* against them . . . . . . Is 5:30
like the *r* of the sea . . . . Is 5:30
young lion *r* on his prey . . . . . . Is 31:4
he shall cry, yea, *r* . . . . Is 42:13
the sea, whose waves *r* . . . . Is 51:15
We *r* all like bears . . . . Is 59:11
young lions *r* upon him . . . . Jer 2:15
they *r*, yet can they not . . . . Jer 5:22
their voice *r* like the sea . . . . . . Jer 6:23
shall *r* from on high . . . . Jer 25:30
r upon his habitation . . . . Jer 25:30
voice shall *r* like the sea . . . . . . Jer 50:42
waves do *r* like great waters . . . Jer 51:55
by the noise of his *r* . . . . Ezek 19:7
he shall *r* like a lion . . . . Hos 11:10
shall *r*, then the children . . . . . . Hos 11:10
also shall *r* out of Zion . . . . Joel 3:16
The Lord will *r* from Zion . . . . . Amos 1:2
The lion hath *r* . . . . Amos 3:8
within her are *r* lions . . . . Zeph 3:3
a voice of the *r* of..lions . . . . . . Zech 11:3
the sea and the waves *r* . . . . Luke 21:25
as a *r* lion, walketh about 1Pet 5:8
as when a lion *r* . . . . Rev 10:3

ROAST—*to cook food by heating in an oven*

[*also* ROASTED, ROASTETH]
in that night, *r* with fire . . . . . . Ex 12:8
thou shalt *r* and eat it . . . . Deut 16:7
flesh to *r* for the priest 1Sam 2:15
And they *r* the passover 2Chr 35:13
slothful man *r* not that . . . . Prov 12:27
he *r* *r*, and is satisfied . . . . Is 44:16
I have *r* flesh and eaten it . . . . . Is 44:19
king of Babylon *r* in the . . . . . . Jer 29:22

R

ROB—*to take something belonging to someone else*

Used literally of:
Plundering 1Sam 23:1
Taking from the poor ....Prov 22:22
Robbers ....Judg 9:25

Used figuratively of:
Dishonest riches ....Ps 62:10
Holding back from God ..Mal 3:8, 9
False teachers ....John 10:1, 8
Taking wages 2Cor 11:8

[*also* ROBBED, ROBBERY, ROBBETH]
neighbor, neither *r* him ....Lev 19:13
r you of your children ....Lev 26:22
r all that came along.........Judg 9:25
r the threshing floors 1Sam 23:1
as a bear *r* of her whelps 2Sam 17:8
the wicked have *r* me ....Ps 119:61
Let a bear *r* of her whelps ....Prov 17:12
The *r* of the wicked shall .....Prov 21:7
R not the poor ....Prov 22:22
r his father or his mother .....Prov 28:24
they may *r* the fatherless! .....Is 10:2
and have *r* their treasures .....Is 10:13
the lot of them that *r* us ......Is 17:14
a people *r* and spoiled ....Is 42:22
I hate *r* for burnt offering .....Is 61:8
and they shall be *r* ....Jer 50:37
oppression, and exercised *r*....Ezek 22:29
give again that he had *r*........Ezek 33:15
and *r* those that *r* them ....Ezek 39:10
and *r* in their palaces ....Amos 3:10
it is all full of lies and *r*.......Nah 3:1
Will a man *r* God? ....Mal 3:8
Now Barabbas was a *r*........John 18:40
of waters, in perils of *r* 2Cor 11:26
r to be equal with God ....Phil 2:6

ROBBER—*one who steals*

[*also* ROBBERS]
r swalloweth up their ....Job 5:5
tabernacles of *r* prosper ....Job 12:6
r shall prevail against him .....Job 18:9
and Israel to the *r*? ....Is 42:24
a den of *r* in your eyes? ......Jer 7:11
the *r* shall enter into it........Ezek 7:22
beget a son that is a *r* ....Ezek 18:10
r of thy people shall exalt .....Dan 11:14
troops of *r* wait for a man ....Hos 6:9
troop of *r* spoileth without ....Hos 7:1
came to thee, if *r* by night ....Obad 5
are neither *r* of churches ......Acts 19:37

ROBE—*a long, flowing outer garment*

[*also* ROBES]
r, and a embroidered coat .....Ex 28:4
upon the hem of the *r* ....Ex 28:34
and the *r* of the ephod.........Ex 29:5
r of the ephod of woven ......Ex 39:22
upon the hems of the *r* ....Ex 39:24
about the hem of the *r*.........Ex 39:26
clothed him with the *r* ....Lev 8:7
stripped himself of the *r* 1Sam 18:4
skirt of thy *r* in my hand 1Sam 24:11
I cut off the skirt of thy *r* 1Sam 24:11
such *r* were the king's 2Sam 13:18
having put on their *r* 1Kin 22:10
David was clothed with a *r* 1Chr 15:27
clothed in their *r* 2Chr 18:9
my judgment was as a *r*.......Job 29:14
will clothe him with thy *r* .....Is 22:21
and lay away their *r* ....Ezek 26:16
and he laid his *r* from him ....Jon 3:6
the *r* with the garment ....Mic 2:8
put on him a scarlet *r*.........Matt 27:28
took the *r* off from him ....Matt 27:31
Bring forth the best *r* ....Luke 15:22
desire to walk in long *r* ....Luke 20:46
arrayed him in a gorgeous *r* ...Luke 23:11
put on him a purple *r*.........John 19:2
thorns, and the purple *r* ......John 19:5
white *r* were given unto ....Rev 6:11
are arrayed in white *r*?........Rev 7:13

ROBOAM—*See* REHOBOAM

ROCK—*stone*

Used for:
Altars ....Judg 6:20, 26
Idol worship ....Is 57:5
Protection 1Sam 13:6
Shade ....Is 32:2
Inscriptions ....Job 19:24
Executions 2Chr 25:12
Foundations.............Matt 7:24, 25
Shelter ....Job 24:8
Tomb ....Matt 27:60

Miracles connected with:
Water from ....Ex 17:6
Fire from ....Judg 6:21
Broken by wind 1Kin 19:11
Rent at Christ's death ...Matt 27:51

Figurative of Christ, as:
Refuge ....Is 32:2
Foundation of the Church.Matt 16:18
Source of blessings 1Cor 10:4
Stone of stumbling ......Is 8:14
Foundation of faith ......Matt 7:24, 25

[*also* ROCKS]
shalt stand upon a *r* ....Ex 33:21
the *r* before their eyes ....Num 20:8
them water out of the *r*.......Num 20:8
together before the *r* ....Num 20:10
water out of this *r*? ....Num 20:10
from the top of the *r* ....Num 23:9
puttest thy nest in a *r*.........Num 24:21
water out of the *r* of flint .....Deut 8:15
suck honey out of the *r* ....Deut 32:13
and oil out of the flinty *r* .....Deut 32:13
Of the ***R*** that begat thee ......Deut 32:18
their *r* is not as our ***R*** ....Deut 32:31
from the *r*, and upward ....Judg 1:36
Oreb upon the *r* Oreb ....Judg 7:25
dwelt in the top of the *r* ......Judg 15:8
him up from the *r* ....Judg 15:13
unto the *r* Rimmon ....Judg 20:47
abode in the *r* Rimmon ....Judg 20:47
there any *r* like our God 1Sam 2:2
sharp *r* on the one side 1Sam 14:4
sharp *r* on the other side 1Sam 14:4
the *r* of the wild goats 1Sam 24:2
spread it for her upon the *r* ...2Sam 21:10
The God of my *r*; in him 2Sam 22:3
and blessed be my *r* 2Sam 22:47
of the *r* of my salvation 2Sam 22:47
down to the *r* to David 1Chr 11:15
them out of the *r*.............Neh 9:15
the *r* is removed out of his ....Job 14:18
the *r* be removed out of his ...Job 18:4
forth his hand upon the *r* .....Job 28:9
rivers among the *r*............Job 28:10
wild goats of the *r* bring ......Job 39:1
and abideth on the *r*...........Job 39:28
upon the crag of the *r* ....Job 39:28
The Lord is my *r*, and my ....Ps 18:2
who is a *r* save our God? .....Ps 18:31
and blessed be my *r* ....Ps 18:46
shall set me up upon a *r* ......Ps 27:5
will I cry, O Lord my *r* ....Ps 28:1
be thou my strong *r* ....Ps 31:2
my *r* and my fortress ....Ps 31:3
I will say unto God my *r*........Ps 42:9
my *r* and my salvation ....Ps 62:2
my *r* and my salvation ....Ps 62:6
the *r* of my strength ....Ps 62:7
my *r* and my fortress ....Ps 71:3
He clave the *r* in ....Ps 78:15
streams also out of the *r* ......Ps 78:16
God was their *r* ....Ps 78:35
the *r* of my salvation ....Ps 89:26
he is my *r* and there is no .....Ps 92:15
God is the *r* of my refuge .....Ps 94:22
to the *r* of our salvation.......Ps 95:1
He opened the *r* ....Ps 105:41
way of a serpent upon a *r*.....Prov 30:19
make..their houses in the *r*....Prov 30:26
in the clefts of the *r* ....Song 2:14
Enter into the *r*, and hide .....Is 2:10
go into the holes of the *r* .....Is 2:19
go into the clefts of the *r* .....Is 2:21
the tops of the ragged *r*........Is 2:21
of Midian at the *r* of Oreb ....Is 10:26
for himself in a *r*? ....Is 22:16
shall be the munitions of *r* ....Is 33:16
inhabitants of the *r* sing.......Is 42:11
waters to flow out of the *r* ....Is 48:21
he clave the *r* also ....Is 48:21
and climb up upon the *r* ......Jer 4:29
faces harder than a *r* ....Jer 5:3
from the *r* of the field? ....Jer 18:14
that breaketh the *r* ....Jer 23:29
in the clefts of the *r* ....Jer 49:16
roll thee down from the *r* .....Jer 51:25
set it upon the top of a *r* .....Ezek 24:7
her like the top of a *r* ....Ezek 26:4
horses run upon the *r*?........Amos 6:12
dwellest in the clefts of the *r* ..Obad 3
r are thrown down by him ....Nah 1:6
was hewn out of a *r* ....Mark 15:46
laid the foundation on a *r*.....Luke 6:48
it was founded upon a *r*.......Luke 6:48
And some fell upon a *r*.......Luke 8:6
They on the *r* are they........Luke 8:13
should have fallen upon *r* .....Acts 27:29
a stumbling stone and *r*.......Rom 9:33
r of offense, even to them 1Pet 2:8
in the *r* of the mountains .....Rev 6:15

ROD—*a staff or stick*

Used for:
Sign of authority ....Ex 4:17, 20
Egyptians' staffs ....Ex 7:12
Punishment ....Ex 21:20
Club 1Sam 14:27
Correction of children ...Prov 13:24

Figurative of:
Christ ....Is 11:1
Christ's rule.............Ps 2:9
Authority ....Is 14:5, 29
The Gospel ....Ps 110:2

[*also* RODS]
took him *r* of green poplar ....Gen 30:37
which was in the *r*............Gen 30:37
conceived before the *r* ....Gen 30:39
Jacob laid the *r* before ....Gen 30:41
conceive among the *r* ....Gen 30:41
And he said, A *r*..............Ex 4:2
Take thy *r*, and cast it ....Ex 7:9
Aaron cast down his *r* ....Ex 7:10
r..turned to a serpent ....Ex 7:15
Say unto Aaron, Take thy *r* ...Ex 7:19
thine hand with thy *r* ....Ex 8:5
his hand with his *r* ....Ex 8:17
his *r* over the land............Ex 10:13
and thy *r*..thou smotest ....Ex 17:5
passeth under the *r*...........Lev 27:32
every one of them a *r* ....Num 17:2
of their fathers, twelve *r* ......Num 17:2
man's name upon his *r*........Num 17:2
Aaron's name upon the *r* .....Num 17:3
one *r* shall be for the head ....Num 17:3
princes gave him a *r* apiece ...Num 17:6
houses even twelve *r*..........Num 17:6
r of Aaron was among their *r* .Num 17:6
Moses brought out all the *r* ...Num 17:9
took every man his *r* ....Num 17:9
Take the *r* and gather ....Num 20:8
r he smote the rock twice .....Num 20:11
r that was in mine hand.......1Sam 14:43
chasten him with the *r* 2Sam 7:14
take his *r* away from me ......Job 9:34
r and thy staff..comfort me ....Ps 23:4
the *r* of thine inheritance......Ps 74:2
transgression with the *r* ....Ps 89:32
the *r* of the wicked ....Ps 125:3
r is for the back of him ....Prov 10:13
foolish is a *r* of pride ....Prov 14:3
r of correction shall drive .....Prov 22:15
beat him with the *r*...........Prov 23:14
The *r* and reproof give........Prov 29:15
the *r* of his oppression ....Is 9:4
r should shake itself ....Is 10:15

his *r* was upon the sea ....Is 10:26
smite the earth with the *r* .....Is 11:4
the cummin with a *r* ....Is 28:27
a *r* of an almond tree ....Jer 1:11
and the beautiful *r* ....Jer 48:17
by the *r* of his wrath..........Lam 3:1
the *r* hath blossomed ....Ezek 7:10
strong *r* for the scepters.......Ezek 19:11
out of a *r* of her branches.....Ezek 19:14
to pass under the *r* ....Ezek 20:37
sword contemn even the *r*?....Ezek 21:13
judge of Israel with a *r* ....Mic 5:1
Feed thy people with thy *r* ....Mic 7:14
come unto you with a *r* 1Cor 4:21
Thrice was I beaten with *r* 2Cor 11:25
Aaron's *r* that budded ....Heb 9:4
rule them with a *r* of iron .....Rev 2:27
nations with a *r* of iron ....Rev 12:5

RODANIM—*See* **Dodanim**

RODE—*See* **Ride**

ROE—*deer; gazelle*

Described as:
Fit for food ....Deut 12:15, 22
Cheerful ....Prov 5:19
Swift 1Chr 12:8
Wild 2Sam 2:18
Hunted by men ....Prov 6:5
In Solomon's provisions ..1Kin 4:23

Figurative of:
Timidity ....Is 13:14
Swiftness 2Sam 2:18
Good wife ....Prov 5:19
Church ....Song 4:5
Christ ....Song 2:9, 17

See **Hart; Hind**

[*also* **roebuck, roes**]
The hart, and the *r* ....Deut 14:5
as the *r*, and as the hart ......Deut 15:22
by the *r*, and by the hinds ....Song 2:7
by the *r*, and by the hinds ....Song 3:5
young *r* that are twins ....Song 7:3
to a *r* or to a young hart ......Song 8:14

ROGELIM (ro'gĕ'lĭm)—*"footmen"*
Town in Gilead 2Sam 17:27

came down from *R* 2Sam 19:31

ROGUE—*mischievous or evil individual*
Descriptive of the fraudulent ....Is 32:5, 7

ROHGAH (rō'gä)—*"outcry; alarm"*
Asherite 1Chr 7:34

ROLL—*a book; a written document*
Called a volume ....Ps 40:7
State documents written on ....Ezra 6:2
Scripture written on .....Is 8:1

[*also* **rolls**]
made in the house of the *r* ....Ezra 6:1
Take thee a *r* of a book ......Jer 36:2
and read in the *r* ....Jer 36:6
Take in thine hand the *r* ......Jer 36:14
took the *r* in his hand ....Jer 36:14
sent Jehudi to fetch the *r* .....Jer 36:21
he would not burn the *r* ......Jer 36:25
Take thee again another *r*.....Jer 36:28
words that were in the first *r* ..Jer 36:28
took Jeremiah another *r* ......Jer 36:32
a *r* of a book was therein .....Ezek 2:9
caused me to eat that *r* ....Ezek 3:2
and behold a flying *r* ....Zech 5:1

ROLL—*to move by revolving*

[*also* **rolled, rolleth, rolling**]
r the stone from the well's ....Gen 29:3
and till they *r* the stone ....Gen 29:8
I *r* away the reproach of ......Josh 5:9
R great stones upon the ....Josh 10:18
r a great stone unto me 1Sam 14:33
they *r* themselves upon me ....Job 30:14
he that *r* a stone ....Prov 26:27
and garments *r* in blood ......Is 9:5
a *r* thing before the ....Is 17:13
r thee down from the rocks ...Jer 51:25
of Aphrah *r* thyself ....Mic 1:10
r a great stone to the door ....Matt 27:60
and *r* back the stone from.....Matt 28:2
r a stone unto the door ....Mark 15:46
r us away the stone ....Mark 16:3
that the stone was *r* away .....Mark 16:4
stone *r* away from the ....Luke 24:2
as a scroll when it is *r* ....Rev 6:14

ROLLER—*a bandage*
to put a *r* to bind it ....Ezek 30:21

ROMAMTI-EZER (rō'măm-tĭ-ē'zer)—*"highest help"*
Son of Heman 1Chr 25:4, 31

ROMAN—*pertaining to Rome; citizen of Rome*
1. Inhabitant of Rome .....Acts 2:10
2. Official agent of the Roman government ...John 11:46
3. Person possessing Roman citizenship ....Acts 16:21-38

[*also* **romans**]
scourge a man that is a *R* .....Acts 22:25
for this man is a *R* ....Acts 22:26
Tell me, art thou a *R*? ....Acts 22:27
knew that he was a *R*.........Acts 22:29
understood that he was a *R* ...Acts 23:27
not the manner of the *R* ......Acts 25:16
into the hands of the *R* ....Acts 28:17

ROMANS, THE EPISTLE TO THE—*a book of the New Testament*
The power of the Gospel .Rom 1:16
The pagans condemned ..Rom 1:17-32
The Jews condemned ....Rom 2:1-9
The advantages of the Jews ....Rom 3:1-8
None righteous ....Rom 3:9-20
Righteousness through faith.................Rom 3:21-31
Abraham justified ....Rom 4
The second Adam ....Rom 5:12-21
On baptism ....Rom 6
The pull of sin ....Rom 7
The spiritual life.........Rom 8
The destiny of the Jews ..Rom 9—11
Life as worship..........Rom 12:1, 2
Serving the body ....Rom 12:3-21
Bearing with one another.Rom 14, 15
Greetings ....Rom 16:1-24

ROME (rōm)—*"City of Romulus"*
Jews expelled from ......Acts 18:2
Paul:
Writes to Christians of .Rom 1:7
Desires to go to ....Acts 19:21
Comes to ....Acts 28:14
Imprisoned in ....Acts 28:16

bear witness also at *R*.........Acts 23:11
gospel to you that are at *R* ....Rom 1:15
when he was in *R* 2Tim 1:17

ROOF—*the top of a building; a covering*

[*also* **roofs**]
under the shadow of my *r*.....Gen 19:8
a battlement for thy *r*.........Deut 22:8
up to the *r* of the house ......Josh 2:6
laid in order upon the *r*.......Josh 2:6
upon the *r* about three........Judg 16:27
the *r* of the king's house 2Sam 11:2
the *r* he saw a woman 2Sam 11:2
watchman went up to the *r*....2Sam 18:24
upon the *r* of his house ....Neh 8:16
cleaved to the *r*..mouth ....Job 29:10
cleaved to the *r* of..mouth ....Ps 137:6
r of thy mouth like the ....Song 7:9
whose *r* they have burned .....Jer 19:13
whose *r* they have offered .....Jer 32:29
cleaveth to the *r* of..mouth ....Lam 4:4
cleave to the *r* of..mouth......Ezek 3:26
r of the one little chamber ....Ezek 40:13
shouldest come under my *r*....Matt 8:8
uncovered the *r* where he .....Mark 2:4
enter under my *r* ....Luke 7:6

ROOM—*a space inside a building, set aside for particular uses*

[*also* **rooms**]
r thou make in the ark........Gen 6:14
r in thy father's house ....Gen 24:23
and *r* to lodge in ....Gen 24:25
and *r* for the camels ....Gen 24:31
Lord hath made *r* for us ......Gen 26:22
in the *r* of Joab 2Sam 19:13
in his *r* over the host 1Kin 2:35
king in the *r* of his father 1Kin 5:1
I am risen up in the *r*.........1Kin 8:20
put captains in their *r*.........1Kin 20:24
and reigned in his *r*...........2Kin 15:25
and dwelt in their *r*...........1Chr 4:41
king in the *r* of his father 2Chr 26:1
preparedst *r* before it ....Ps 80:9
A man's gift maketh *r* ....Prov 18:16
shall not be *r* enough ....Mal 3:10
in the *r* of his father ....Matt 2:22
love the uppermost *r* ....Matt 23:6
no *r* to receive them ....Mark 2:2
uppermost *r* at feasts ....Mark 12:39
there was no *r* for them.......Luke 2:7
chose out the chief *r*..........Luke 14:7
down in the highest *r* ....Luke 14:8
go sit down in the lowest *r* ....Luke 14:10
show you a large upper *r* .....Luke 22:12
went up into an upper *r*.......Acts 1:13
the *r* of the unlearned 1Cor 14:16

ROOT—*the underground part of a plant; source or origin*

Used figuratively of:
Material foundation......Jer 12:2
Remnant ....Judg 5:14
National existence ....Is 14:30
National source ....Rom 11:16-18
Source of evil 1Tim 6:10
Judgment and destruction.1Kin 14:15
Restoration 2Kin 19:30
Spiritual life ....Hos 14:5
Spiritual foundation......Eph 3:17
Messiah ....Is 11:1, 10

[*also* **rooted, roots**]
r that beareth gall ....Deut 29:18
r them out of their land.......Deut 29:28
pluck them up by the *r* 2Chr 7:20
seen the foolish taking *r* .....Job 5:3
His *r* are wrapped about .....Job 8:17
the *r* thereof wax old ....Job 14:8
His confidence shall be *r*......Job 18:14
the *r* of the matter is ....Job 19:28
mountains by the *r* ....Job 28:9
r was spread out by the ....Job 29:19
let my offspring be *r* out .....Job 31:8
r out all mine increase ....Job 31:12
and *r* thee out of the land.....Ps 52:5
cause it to take deep *r*........Ps 80:9
transgressors shall be *r*........Prov 2:22
r of the righteous............Prov 12:3
r shall be as rottenness.......Is 5:24
shall be a *r* of Jesse ....Is 11:10
out of the serpent's *r* ....Is 14:29
of Jacob to take *r* ....Is 27:6
Judah shall again take *r*.......Is 37:31
their stock shall not take *r* ....Is 40:24
to *r* out, and to pull down ....Jer 1:10
spreadeth out her *r* by ....Jer 17:8
r thereof were under him .....Ezek 17:6
shall he not pull up the *r* .....Ezek 17:9
to pluck it up by the *r* ....Ezek 17:9
r was by great waters ....Ezek 31:7
stump of his *r* in the earth ....Dan 4:15
stump of the tree *r* ....Dan 4:26
out of a branch of her *r*.......Dan 11:7
their *r* is dried up ....Hos 9:16
and his *r* from beneath........Amos 2:9
and Ekron shall be *r*..........Zeph 2:4
neither *r* nor branch ....Mal 4:1
axe is laid unto the *r* ....Matt 3:10
because they had no *r* ....Matt 13:6

R

hath he not *r* in himself .... Matt 13:21
not planted, shall be *r* .... Matt 15:13
because it had no *r* .... Mark 4:6
fig tree dried up from the *r* ... Mark 11:20
axe is laid unto the *r* .... Luke 3:9
these have no *r* .... Luke 8:13
thou plucked up by the *r* .... Luke 17:6
There shall be a *r* of Jesse .... Rom 15:12
R and built up in him .... Col 2:7
lest any *r* of bitterness .... Heb 12:15
plucked up by the *r* .... Jude 12
of Judah, the ***R*** of David ..... Rev 5:5
the *r* and the offspring of ..... Rev 22:16

ROPE—*a strong cord of fibers twisted or braided together*

[*also* ROPES]
bind me fast with new *r* .... Judg 16:11
Israel bring *r* to that city 2Sam 17:13
and *r* upon our heads 1Kin 20:31
as it were with a cart *r* .... Is 5:18
cut off the *r* of the boat .... Acts 27:32

ROSE—*a flowering plant*
Used symbolically of
Sharon .... Song 2:1
Desert shall blossom ..... Is 35:1

ROSE—*See* RISE

ROSH (rŏsh)—*"head"*
1. Benjamin's son .... Gen 46:21
2. Northern people connected with Meshech and Tubal ... Ezek 38:2

ROT—*to decay*
Used literally of:
Sickness .... Num 5:21-27
Hardwood trees .... Is 40:20
Used figuratively of:
Wicked .... Prov 10:7
Foolish wife .... Prov 12:4

[*also* ROTTEN, ROTTENNESS]
as a *r* thing, consumeth .... Job 13:28
brass as *r* wood .... Job 41:27
envy the *r* of the bones .... Prov 14:30
so their root shall be as *r* ..... Is 5:24
clouts and old *r* rags .... Jer 38:11
clouts and *r* rags .... Jer 38:12
the house of Judah as *r* .... Hos 5:12
seed is *r* under their clods ..... Joel 1:17
r entered into my bones .... Hab 3:16

ROUGH—*uneven; harsh*

[*also* ROUGHLY]
and spake *r* unto them .... Gen 42:7
spake *r* to us, and took us .... Gen 42:30
heifer unto a *r* valley .... Deut 21:4
thy father answer thee *r* 1Sam 20:10
answered the people *r* 1Kin 12:13
king answered them *r* 2Chr 10:13
the rich answereth *r* .... Prov 18:23
his *r* wind in the day .... Is 27:8
and the *r* places plain .... Is 40:4
as the *r* caterpillars .... Jer 51:27
the *r* goat is the king of .... Dan 8:21
a *r* garment to deceive .... Zech 13:4
r ways shall be made smooth .. Luke 3:5

ROUND—*around; circular*
compassed the house *r* .... Gen 19:4
cities that were *r* about .... Gen 35:5
was *r* about every city .... Gen 41:48
digged *r* about the river .... Ex 7:24
there lay a small *r* thing .... Ex 16:14
crown of gold *r* about .... Ex 25:11
an handbreadth *r* about .... Ex 25:25
pillars *r* about the court .... Ex 27:17
scarlet *r* about the hem .... Ex 28:33
between them *r* about .... Ex 28:33
hem of the robe *r* about .... Ex 28:34
sprinkle it *r* about upon .... Ex 29:16
the sides thereof *r* about .... Ex 30:3
a crown of gold *r* about .... Ex 30:3
a crown of gold *r* about .... Ex 37:11
a handbreadth *r* about .... Ex 37:12
for the border..*r* about .... Ex 37:12
a crown of gold *r* about .... Ex 37:26
and of the court *r* about .... Ex 38:20
of the court *r* about .... Ex 38:31
pins of the court *r* about .... Ex 38:31
r about between the .... Ex 39:25
set up the court *r* about .... Ex 40:8
the blood *r* about .... Lev 1:5
upon the altar *r* about .... Lev 3:2
the blood..upon the altar *r* .... Lev 3:13
horns of the altar *r* about ..... Lev 8:15
r about upon the altar .... Lev 9:12
house to be scraped..*r* about .. Lev 14:41
not *r* the corners of your ...... Lev 19:27
the heathen that are *r* .... Lev 25:44
r about the tabernacle .... Num 1:50
and by the altar *r* about .... Num 3:26
by the altar *r* about .... Num 4:26
r about the tabernacle .... Num 11:24
r about the camp .... Num 11:32
that were *r* about them .... Num 16:34
of the country *r* about .... Num 32:33
suburbs for the cities *r* .... Num 35:2
the people which are *r* .... Deut 6:14
the people which are *r* .... Deut 13:7
thine enemies *r* about .... Deut 25:19
go *r* about the city .... Josh 6:3
children of Judah *r* about ..... Josh 15:12
r about these cities .... Josh 19:8
suburbs *r* about them .... Josh 21:42
their enemies *r* about .... Josh 23:1
that were *r* about them .... Judg 2:12
place *r* about the camp .... Judg 7:21
beset the house *r* about .... Judg 20:5
the Benjamites *r* about .... Judg 20:43
from the country *r* about 1Sam 14:21
pitched *r* about him 1Sam 26:5
of the Philistines *r* about 1Sam 31:9
And David built *r* about 2Sam 5:9
pavilions *r* about him 2Sam 22:12
wall of Jerusalem *r* about 1Kin 3:1
peace on all sides *r* 1Kin 4:24
house he built chambers *r* 1Kin 6:5
the walls of the house *r* 1Kin 6:5
made chambers *r* about 1Kin 6:5
walls of the house *r* about 1Kin 6:29
two rows *r* about upon 1Kin 7:18
it was *r* all about 1Kin 7:23
cubits did compass it *r* 1Kin 7:23
the brim of it *r* about 1Kin 7:24
compassing the sea *r* 1Kin 7:24
the mouth thereof was *r* 1Kin 7:31
foursquare, not *r* 1Kin 7:31
and additions *r* about 1Kin 7:36
ran *r* about the altar 1Kin 18:35
chariots of fire *r* about 2Kin 6:17
r about the king 2Kin 11:11
places *r* about Jerusalem 2Kin 23:5
against the city *r* about 2Kin 25:4
upon the chapiter *r* about 2Kin 25:17
villages that were *r* about 1Chr 4:33
r about the house of God 1Chr 9:27
the city *r* about 1Chr 11:8
of all the chambers *r* 1Chr 28:12
brim to brim, *r* in compass 2Chr 4:2
cubits did compass it *r* 2Chr 4:2
which did compass it *r* 2Chr 4:3
compassing the sea *r* about 2Chr 4:3
gave them rest *r* about 2Chr 15:15
gave him rest *r* about 2Chr 20:30
by the king *r* about 2Chr 23:10
plain country *r* about .... Neh 12:28
fashioned me together *r* .... Job 10:8
r about my tabernacle .... Job 19:12
r about by his counsels .... Job 37:12
themselves against me *r* .... Ps 3:6
Bashan have beset me *r* .... Ps 22:12
encampeth *r* about them .... Ps 34:7
and go *r* about her .... Ps 48:12
go *r* about the city .... Ps 59:6
r about their habitations .... Ps 78:28
them that are *r* about us .... Ps 79:4
faithfulness *r* about thee .... Ps 89:8
burneth up his enemies *r* .... Ps 97:3
mountains are *r* about .... Ps 125:2
is *r* about his people .... Ps 125:2
navel is like a *r* goblet .... Song 7:2
r tires like the moon .... Is 3:18
I will camp against thee *r* ..... Is 29:3
Lift up thine eyes *r* about ..... Is 49:18
against all the walls..*r* .... Jer 1:15
tents against her *r* about .... Jer 6:3
devour all things *r* about it .... Jer 21:14
for fear was *r* about .... Jer 46:5
against Babylon *r* about .... Jer 50:14
camp against it *r* about .... Jer 50:29
be against her *r* about .... Jer 51:2
were by the city *r* about .... Jer 52:7
upon the chapiters *r* about .... Jer 52:22
adversaries should be *r* .... Lam 1:17
a solemn day my terrors *r* ..... Lam 2:22
full of eyes *r* about them ...... Ezek 1:18
appearance of fire *r* about ..... Ezek 1:27
it had brightness *r* about ...... Ezek 1:27
rams against it *r* about .... Ezek 4:2
that are *r* about her .... Ezek 5:6
nations that are *r* about .... Ezek 5:7
nations that are *r* about .... Ezek 5:14
idols *r* about their altars .... Ezek 6:13
were full of eyes *r* about ...... Ezek 10:12
gather them *r* about .... Ezek 16:37
all that are *r* about .... Ezek 16:57
despise thee *r* about .... Ezek 16:57
upon thy walls *r* about .... Ezek 27:11
despise them *r* about them .... Ezek 28:26
her company is *r* about .... Ezek 32:23
graves are *r* about him .... Ezek 32:25
places *r* about my hill .... Ezek 34:26
that are *r* about .... Ezek 36:4
to pass by them *r* about .... Ezek 37:2
court *r* about the gate .... Ezek 40:14
within the gate *r* about .... Ezek 40:16
windows were *r* about .... Ezek 40:16
and in the arches..*r* about ..... Ezek 40:25
arches *r* about were five .... Ezek 40:30
windows to it *r* about .... Ezek 40:36
r about the house on every .... Ezek 41:5
upward *r* about the house ..... Ezek 41:7
twenty cubits *r* about the ...... Ezek 41:10
five cubits thick *r* about ...... Ezek 41:12
r about on their three .... Ezek 41:16
ceiled with wood *r* about ..... Ezek 41:16
all the house *r* about .... Ezek 41:19
measuring reed *r* about .... Ezek 42:16
the whole limit..*r* about .... Ezek 43:12
upon the border *r* about .... Ezek 43:20
in breadth, square *r* about ..... Ezek 45:2
and fifty cubits *r* about .... Ezek 45:2
a row of building *r* about ..... Ezek 46:23
r about them four .... Ezek 46:23
places under the rows *r* .... Ezek 46:23
yourselves together *r* about .... Joel 3:11
be even *r* about the land ..... Amos 3:11
depth closed me *r* about .... Jon 2:5
had the waters *r* about it ...... Nah 3:8
wall of fire *r* about .... Zech 2:5
all the people *r* about .... Zech 12:2
wealth of all the heathen *r* .... Zech 14:14
region *r* about Jordan .... Matt 3:5
and hedged it *r* about .... Matt 21:33
region *r* about Galilee .... Mark 1:28
he looked *r* about on them .... Mark 3:34
went *r* about the villages ...... Mark 6:6
that whole region *r* about ..... Mark 6:55
Jesus looked *r* about .... Mark 10:23
dwelt *r* about them .... Luke 1:65
all the region *r* about .... Luke 4:14
looking *r* about upon .... Luke 6:10
the Gadarenes *r* about .... Luke 8:37
compass thee *r*, and keep ..... Luke 19:43
the Jews *r* about him .... John 10:24
r about unto Jerusalem .... Acts 5:16
region that lieth *r* about .... Acts 14:6
great light *r* about me .... Acts 22:6
shining *r* about me .... Acts 26:13
r about unto Illyricum .... Rom 15:19
overlaid *r* about with gold ..... Heb 9:4
rainbow *r* about the .... Rev 4:3
and *r* about the throne .... Rev 4:6
stood *r* about the throne .... Rev 7:11

ROUSE—*to awaken*
who shall *r* him up? . . . . .Gen 49:9

ROVERS—*robbers; roving warriors*
against the band of the *r* 1Chr 12:21

ROW—*numerous objects arranged in a straight line*

[*also* ROWS]
even four *r* of stones . . . . .Ex 28:17
r shall be a sardius . . . . .Ex 28:17
this shall be the first *r* . . . . .Ex 28:17
the third *r* a ligure . . . . .Ex 28:19
set in it four *r* of stones . . . . . . .Ex 39:10
the first *r* was a sardius . . . . . . .Ex 39:10
this was the first *r* . . . . .Ex 39:10
the third *r*, a ligure . . . . .Ex 39:12
them in two *r*, six on a *r* . . . . . .Lev 24:6
three *r* of hewed stone 1Kin 6:36
and a *r* of cedar beams 1Kin 6:36
were windows in three *r* 1Kin 7:4
and a *r* of cedar beams 1Kin 7:12
two *r* round about upon 1Kin 7:18
knobs were cast in two *r* 1Kin 7:24
Two *r* of oxen were cast 2Chr 4:3
three *r* of great stones . . . . .Ezra 6:4
and a *r* of new timber . . . . .Ezra 6:4
comely with *r* of jewels . . . . . . .Song 1:10
a *r* of building round . . . . .Ezek 46:23
boiling places under the *r* . . . . .Ezek 46:23

ROWERS—*those who propel a boat with oars*
Thy *r* have brought thee . . . . . .Ezek 27:26

ROWING—*navigating a boat with oars*
Against odds . . . . .Jon 1:13
With much labor . . . . .Mark 6:48

[*also* ROWED]
r about five and twenty . . . . . . .John 6:19

ROYAL—*belonging or pertaining to a king*

Used literally of:
King's children 2Kin 11:1
Robes of royalty . . . . .Esth 6:8
City of a king 2Sam 12:26

Used spiritually of:
True Israel . . . . .Is 62:3
True Church 1Pet 2:9

shall yield *r* dainties . . . . .Gen 49:20
one of the *r* cities . . . . .Josh 10:2
dwell in the *r* city 1Sam 27:5
and took the *r* city 2Sam 12:26
gave her of his *r* bounty 1Kin 10:13
of Elishama, the seed *r* 2Kin 25:25
such *r* majesty as had not 1Chr 29:25
r of the house of Judah 2Chr 22:10
r wine in abundance . . . . .Esth 1:7
king with the crown *r* . . . . .Esth 1:11
go a *r* commandment . . . . .Esth 1:19
king give her *r* estate . . . . .Esth 1:19
he set the *r* crown upon . . . . . . .Esth 2:17
put on her *r* apparel . . . . .Esth 5:1
r throne in the *r* house . . . . .Esth 5:1
in *r* apparel of blue . . . . .Esth 8:13
of Elishama, of the seed *r* . . . . .Jer 41:1
to establish a *r* statute . . . . .Dan 6:7
arrayed in *r* apparel . . . . .Acts 12:21
If ye fulfill the *r* law . . . . .James 2:8

RUBBING—*moving back and forth with friction*
r them in their hands . . . . .Luke 6:1

RUBBISH—*trash; garbage*
r which are burned? . . . . .Neh 4:2

RUBIES—*precious stones, red in color*
Very valuable . . . . .Prov 3:15
Wisdom more valuable than . . . . .Job 28:18
Good wife above price of.Prov 31:10
Reddish color . . . . .Lam 4:7

wisdom is better than *r* . . . . . . .Prov 8:11
and a multitude of *r* . . . . .Prov 20:15

RUDDER—*steering apparatus of a ship*
Literally . . . . .Acts 27:40
Figuratively . . . . .James 3:4

RUDDY—*reddish*
Now he was *r* 1Sam 16:12
he was but a youth, and *r* 1Sam 17:42
My beloved is white and *r* . . . .Song 5:10
r in body than rubies . . . . .Lam 4:7

RUDE—*unskilled*
though I be *r* in speech 2Cor 11:6

RUDENESS—*discourtesy*

Shown toward:
Christ . . . . .Matt 26:67, 68
Paul .Acts 23:2

RUDIMENTS—*principles*
after the *r* of the world . . . . . . .Col 2:8

RUE—*a pungent perennial shrub*
Tithed by Pharisees . . . . . .Luke 11:42

RUFUS (ro͞o'fŭs)—*"red"*
1. Son of Simon of Cyrene .Mark 15:21
2. Christian of Rome . . . . . .Rom 16:13
Probably the same as 1

RUHAMAH (ro͞o-hä'mä)—*"pitied"*
Symbolic name for Israel .Hos 2:1

RUIN—*to destroy; remains of something destroyed*

[*also* RUINED, RUINOUS, RUINS]
fenced cities into *r* heaps 2Kin 19:25
his strongholds to *r* . . . . .Ps 89:40
knoweth the *r* of them . . . . .Prov 24:22
let this *r* be under thy hand . . .Is 3:6
For Jerusalem is *r* . . . . .Is 3:8
and it shall be a *r* heap . . . . . . .Is 17:1
of a defensed city a *r* . . . . .Is 25:2
iniquity shall not be your *r* . . . .Ezek 18:30
and their *r* be multiplied . . . . . .Ezek 21:15
Upon his *r*..all the fowls . . . . . .Ezek 31:13
r cities are become fenced . . . . .Ezek 36:35
and I will raise up his *r* . . . . . . .Amos 9:11
r of that house was great . . . . . .Luke 6:49
I will build again the *r* . . . . .Acts 15:16

RULE—*to govern; exercise authority; principle*

Of natural things:
Sun and moon . . . . .Gen 1:16, 18
Sea .Ps 89:9

Among men:
Man over woman . . . . . . .Gen 3:16
King over people . . . . . . .Ezra 4:20
Diligent over the lazy . . . .Prov 12:24
Servant over a son . . . . . .Prov 17:2
Rich over poor . . . . .Prov 22:7
Servants over a people . . .Neh 5:15

Of the Messiah:
Predicted . . . . .Is 40:9, 10
Promised . . . . .Zech 6:13
Victorious . . . . .Ps 110:2
Announced . . . . .Matt 2:6
Established . . . . .Rev 12:5
Described . . . . .Rev 2:27

[*also* RULED, RULEST, RULETH, RULING]
thou shalt *r* over him . . . . .Gen 4:7
r over all that he had . . . . .Gen 24:2
shall all my people be *r* . . . . . . .Gen 41:40
r over him with rigor . . . . .Lev 25:43
r with rigor over him in . . . . . . .Lev 25:53
and *r* from Aroer . . . . .Josh 12:2
R thou over us, both . . . . .Judg 8:22
I will not *r* over you . . . . .Judg 8:23
shall my son *r* over you . . . . . . .Judg 8:23
the Lord shall *r* over you . . . . .Judg 8:23
days when the judges *r* . . . . . . .Ruth 1:1
r over men must be just 2Sam 23:3
r in the fear of God 2Sam 23:3
which *r* over the people 1Kin 5:16
bare *r* over the people 1Kin 9:23
r throughout the house 1Chr 26:6
bare *r* over the people 2Chr 8:10
r not thou over all the 2Chr 20:6
r in his own house . . . . .Esth 1:22
Jews had *r* over them . . . . .Esth 9:1
know that God *r* in Jacob . . . . .Ps 59:13
kingdom *r* over all . . . . .Ps 103:19
hated them *r* over them . . . . . . .Ps 106:41
The sun to *r* by day . . . . .Ps 136:8
By me princes *r* . . . . .Prov 8:16
r his spirit than he that . . . . . . .Prov 16:32
to have *r* over princes . . . . .Prov 19:10
the wicked beareth *r* . . . . .Prov 29:2
have *r* over all my labor . . . . . .Eccl 2:19
one man *r* over another . . . . . . .Eccl 8:9
babes shall *r* over them . . . . . . .Is 3:4
r over their oppressors . . . . .Is 14:2
he that *r* the nations in . . . . . . .Is 14:6
r this people which is in . . . . . . .Is 28:14
arm shall *r* for him . . . . .Is 40:10
r over them make them . . . . . . .Is 52:5
bear *r* by their means . . . . .Jer 5:31
and *r* any more in Judah . . . . . .Jer 22:30
Servants have *r* over us . . . . . . .Lam 5:8
of them that bare *r* . . . . .Ezek 19:11
will I *r* over you . . . . .Ezek 20:33
cruelty have ye *r* them . . . . .Ezek 34:4
bear *r* over all the earth . . . . . .Dan 2:39
that the most High *r* . . . . .Dan 4:17
r in the kingdom of men . . . . . .Dan 5:21
r with great dominion . . . . .Dan 11:3
but Judah yet *r* with God . . . . .Hos 11:12
should *r* over them . . . . .Joel 2:17
to *r* over the Gentiles . . . . .Mark 10:42
he that *r*, with diligence . . . . . . .Rom 12:8
have put down all *r* 1Cor 15:24
r which God hath distributed . .2Cor 10:13
walk according to this *r* . . . . . . .Gal 6:16
let us walk by the same *r* . . . . .Phil 3:16
God *r* in your hearts . . . . .Col 3:15
that *r* well his own house 1Tim 3:4
not how to *r* his own house . . .1Tim 3:5
r their children and their 1Tim 3:12
which have the *r* over you . . . .Heb 13:7
that have..*r* over you . . . . .Heb 13:24
r them with a rod of iron . . . . .Rev 19:15

RULER—*one who governs or exercises authority*

Good characteristics of:
Upholding the good . . . . .Rom 13:3
Believing . . . . .Matt 9:18, 23
Chosen by God 2Sam 7:8

Bad characteristics of:
Men-pleasers . . . . .John 12:42, 43
Ignorant . . . . .Acts 3:17
Hostile . . . . .Acts 4:26
Loving bribes . . . . .Hos 4:18

Respect toward:
Commanded . . . . .Ex 22:28
Illustrated . . . . .Acts 23:5

[*also* RULER'S, RULERS]
him *r* over all the land . . . . .Gen 41:43
a *r* throughout all the . . . . .Gen 45:8
make them *r* over my cattle . . .Gen 47:6
r of the congregation . . . . .Ex 16:22
r of thousands, and *r* . . . . .Ex 18:21
r of fifties, and *r* of tens . . . . . .Ex 18:21
r of thousands, *r* . . . . .Ex 18:25
r of fifties, and *r* of tens . . . . . .Ex 18:25
r brought onyx stones . . . . .Ex 35:27
When a *r* hath sinned . . . . .Lev 4:22
one a *r* among them . . . . .Num 13:2
make them *r* over you . . . . .Deut 1:13
Zebul the *r* of the city . . . . .Judg 9:30
Philistines are *r* over us? . . . . . .Judg 15:11
thee *r* over Israel 1Sam 25:30
r over the people 2Sam 6:21
David's sons were chief *r* 2Sam 8:18
Jairite was a chief *r* about 2Sam 20:26
to be *r* over Israel 1Kin 1:35
unto the *r* of Jezreel 2Kin 10:1
took the *r* over hundreds 2Kin 11:19
he made Gedaliah..*r* 2Kin 25:22
of him came the chief *r* 1Chr 5:2
was the *r* over them 1Chr 9:20
r over my people Israel 1Chr 17:7
to the *r* of the people 1Chr 21:2
was Mikloth also the *r* 1Chr 27:4
the *r* of the substance 1Chr 27:31
Judah to be the *r* 1Chr 28:4

R

r over my people Israel 2Chr 6:5
r among his brethren 2Chr 11:22
scribe and Maaseiah the *r* 2Chr 26:11
gathered the *r* of the city 2Chr 29:20
r of the house of God 2Chr 31:13
r hath been chief ....Ezra 9:2
r knew not whither I went ....Neh 2:16
the nobles, nor to the *r* ....Neh 2:16
r of the half part of ....Neh 3:9
r of part of Beth-haccerem ....Neh 3:14
the *r* of the half part of ....Neh 3:16
the *r* of the half part of ....Neh 3:18
the nobles, and to the *r* ....Neh 4:14
the nobles, and to the *r* ....Neh 4:19
of the Jews and *r* ....Neh 5:17
Hananiah the *r* of the ....Neh 7:2
r of the people dwelt ....Neh 11:1
contended I with the *r* ....Neh 13:11
to the *r* of every people ....Esth 3:12
the *r* of the provinces ....Esth 9:3
r take counsel together ....Ps 2:2
r of all his substance ....Ps 105:21
no guide, overseer, or *r* ....Prov 6:7
wicked *r* over the poor ....Prov 28:15
Many seek the *r* favor ....Prov 29:26
the spirit of the *r* rise ....Eccl 10:4
ye *r* of Sodom ....Is 1:10
our *r*, and let this ruin ....Is 3:6
Send ye the lamb to the *r* .....Is 16:1
All thy *r* are fled together .....Is 22:3
to a servant of *r* ....Is 49:7
r over the seed of Abraham ...Jer 33:26
all the *r* thereof ....Jer 51:28
in the land, *r* against *r* ....Jer 51:46
with blue, captains and *r* ......Ezek 23:6
captains and *r*, great lords .....Ezek 23:23
is no king, lord, nor *r* ....Dan 2:10
r over the whole province .....Dan 2:48
the *r* of the provinces ....Dan 3:2
third *r* in the kingdom ....Dan 5:29
that is to be *r* in Israel ....Mic 5:2
that have no *r* over them? ....Hab 1:14
came a certain *r* ....Matt 9:18
r over all his goods ....Matt 24:47
r of the synagogue ....Mark 5:22
r of the synagogue's ....Mark 5:35
r of the synagogue ....Mark 5:38
r of the synagogue ....Luke 8:41
r over his household ....Luke 12:42
the *r* of the synagogue ....Luke 13:14
r for my name's sake ....Luke 21:12
the *r* also with them ....Luke 23:35
r of the feast had tasted ....John 2:9
Do the *r* know indeed ....John 7:26
their *r*, and elders ....Acts 4:5
made thee a *r* and a judge ....Acts 7:27
thee a *r* and a judge? ....Acts 7:35
to be a *r* and a deliverer .....Acts 7:35
the *r* of the synagogue ....Acts 13:15
of the Jews with their *r* ....Acts 14:5
unto the *r* of the city ....Acts 17:6
chief *r* of the synagogue ......Acts 18:8
the *r* of the darkness ....Eph 6:12

RUMAH (rōō'mä)—*"exalted"*
Residence of Pedaiah 2Kin 23:36

RUMBLING—*low, heavy rolling sound*
at the *r* of his wheels ....Jer 47:3

RUMOR—*a message; an unverifiable report*

[*also* RUMORS]
and he shall hear a *r* 2Kin 19:7
he shall hear a *r* ....Is 37:7
I have heard a *r* ....Jer 49:14
r that shall be heard ....Jer 51:46
a *r* shall both come one ....Jer 51:46
another year shall come a *r* ...Jer 51:46
and *r* shall be upon *r* ....Ezek 7:26
heard a *r* from the Lord ......Obad 1
of wars and *r* of wars ....Matt 24:6
of wars and *r* of wars ....Mark 13:7
this *r* of him went forth ....Luke 7:17

RUMP—*backside of an animal*
ram the fat and the *r* ....Ex 29:22
the fat..and the whole *r* ....Lev 3:9
the *r*, and the fat ....Lev 7:3
took the fat, and the *r* ....Lev 8:25
and of the ram, the *r* ....Lev 9:19

RUN—*to move fast in galloping fashion; flee*
Used literally of:
Man ....Num 11:27
Water ....Ps 105:41
Fire ....Ex 9:23
Race 1Cor 9:24
Used figuratively of:
Eagerness in:
Evil ....Prov 1:16
Good ....Ps 119:32
Joy of salvation ....Ps 23:5
Christian life 1Cor 9:26

[*also* RAN, RUNNEST, RUNNETH, RUNNING]
branches *r* over the wall ......Gen 49:22
vessel over *r* water ....Lev 14:5
killed over the *r* water ....Lev 14:6
and in the *r* water ....Lev 14:51
a *r* issue out of his flesh ......Lev 15:2
his flesh *r* with his issue ....Lev 15:3
or hath a *r* issue ....Lev 22:4
r water shall be put ....Num 19:17
angry fellows *r* upon thee .....Judg 18:25
shall *r* before his chariots 1Sam 8:11
he might *r* to Beth-lehem 1Sam 20:6
fifty men to *r* before 2Sam 15:1
also *r* after Cushi 2Sam 18:22
Wherefore wilt thou *r* 2Sam 18:22
said he, let me *r* 2Sam 18:23
And he said unto him, *R* 2Sam 18:23
behold a man *r* alone 2Sam 18:24
saw another man *r* 2Sam 18:26
Behold another man *r* alone ...2Sam 18:26
the *r* of the foremost 2Sam 18:27
the *r* of Ahimaaz 2Sam 18:27
fifty men to *r* before him 1Kin 1:5
I may *r* to the man of God 2Kin 4:22
r after him, and take 2Kin 5:20
Naaman saw him *r* after 2Kin 5:21
eyes of the Lord *r* to 2Chr 16:9
people *r* and praising 2Chr 23:12
river that *r* to Ahava ....Ezra 8:15
He *r* upon him ....Job 15:26
I have *r* through a troop ......Ps 18:29
which *r* continually ....Ps 58:7
to *r* down like rivers ....Ps 78:16
which *r* among the hills ....Ps 104:10
waters *r* down mine eyes ......Ps 119:136
his word *r* very swiftly ....Ps 147:15
and when thou *r* ....Prov 4:12
r waters out of thine own .....Prov 5:15
the righteous *r* into ....Prov 18:10
rivers *r* into the sea ....Eccl 1:7
we will *r* after thee ....Song 1:4
as the *r* to and fro ....Is 33:4
shall he *r* upon them ....Is 33:4
that knew not thee shall *r* .....Is 55:5
R..to and fro through ....Jer 5:1
hast *r* with the footmen ....Jer 12:5
eyes *r* down with tears ....Jer 14:17
suddenly make him *r* away ....Jer 49:19
shall *r* to meet another ....Jer 51:31
eye *r* down with water ....Lam 1:16
tears *r* down like a river ......Lam 2:18
shall thy tears *r* down ....Ezek 24:16
r round about his plants ....Ezek 31:4
many shall *r* to and fro ....Dan 12:4
horsemen, so shall they *r* .....Joel 2:4
r to and fro in the city ....Joel 2:9
r upon the wall, they ....Joel 2:9
r down as waters ....Amos 5:24
shall *r* to and fro ....Amos 8:12
r like the lightnings ....Nah 2:4
may *r* that readeth it ....Hab 2:2
ye *r* every man unto his ....Hag 1:9
R, speak to this young man ...Zech 2:4
and the wine *r* out ....Matt 9:17
r to bring his disciples ....Matt 28:8
and *r* to him saluted him ......Mark 9:15
there came one *r* ....Mark 10:17
shaken together, and *r* ....Luke 6:38
Then she *r*, and cometh ....John 20:2
r under a certain island ....Acts 27:16
nor of him that *r* ....Rom 9:16
I should *r*, or had *r* ....Gal 2:2
that I have not *r* in vain ......Phil 2:16
let us *r* with patience ....Heb 12:1
ye *r* not with them 1Pet 4:4
many horses *r* to battle ....Rev 9:9

RUSH—*a marsh plant; move with haste or energy*
Cut off from Israel;
rendered "bulrush" ....Is 9:14
Concerning growth of ....Job 8:11
Signifying restoration ....Is 35:7

[*also* RUSHED, RUSHETH, RUSHING]
r forward, and stood ....Judg 9:44
and *r* upon Gibeah ....Judg 20:37
and to the *r* of nations ....Is 17:12
make a *r* like the *r* of ....Is 17:12
r like the *r* of many waters ....Is 17:13
head or tail, branch or *r* ......Is 19:15
horse *r* into the battle ....Jer 8:6
at the *r* of his chariots ....Jer 47:3
voice of a great *r* ....Ezek 3:12
as of a *r* mighty wind ....Acts 2:2
they *r* with one accord ....Acts 19:29

RUST—*corrosion of metals*
Destruction of earthly
treasures ....Matt 6:19, 20
Of gold and silver ....James 5:3

RUTH (rōōth)—*"friendship; companion"*
Moabites ....Ruth 1:4
Follows Naomi ....Ruth 1:6-18
Marries Boaz ....Ruth 4:9-13
Ancestress of Christ .....Ruth 4:13, 21, 22

I am *R* thine ....Ruth 3:9
also of *R* the Moabitess ....Ruth 4:5
Boaz begat Obed of *R* ....Matt 1:5

RUTH, THE BOOK OF—*a book of the Old Testament*
Naomi's misfortunes .....Ruth 1:1-14
Ruth's loyalty ....Ruth 1:14-22
The favor of Boaz ....Ruth 2:1-23
Boaz redeems ....Ruth 3:8—4:12
The generations of Ruth. .Ruth 4:13-22

RYE, RIE—*an edible grain*
wheat and the *r* were not .....Ex 9:32
barley and the *r* ....Is 28:25

S

SABACHTHANI (sä-bäk'tä-nē)—*Aramaic for "hast thou forsaken me?"*
Christ's cry on the cross. .Matt 27:46

saying Eloi, Eloi, lama *s*? .....Mark 15:34

SABAOTH—*Hebrew for "hosts"*
God as Lord of ....Rom 9:29
James 5:4

SABBATH—*the Jewish day of rest and worship*
History of:
Instituted at creation .....Gen 2:2, 3
Observed before Sinai ...Ex 16:22-30
Commanded at Sinai .....Ex 20:8-11
Repeated at Canaan's
entry ....Deut 5:12-15
References to 2Kin 4:23
Proper observance of,
described ....Is 56:2-7
Postexilic Jews
encouraged to keep ....Neh 10:31
Perversion of, condemned
by Christ ....Luke 13:14-17
Christ teaches on ....Mark 6:2
Paul preached on ....Acts 13:14
First day kept as, by
Christians ....John 20:19

Facts concerning:
Commemorative of creation ... Ex 20:8-11
Seventh day during the Old Testament ... Deut 5:14
Observance of, a perpetual covenant ... Ex 31:16, 17
Made for man's good ... Mark 2:27
Christ's Lordship over ... Luke 6:5

Regulations concerning:
Work prohibited on ... Lev 23:3
Cattle must rest on ... Ex 20:10
Business forbidden on ... Jer 17:21, 22
To last from evening until evening ... Lev 23:32
Worship on ... Ezek 46:3
Works of mercy on ... Matt 12:12
Necessities lawful on ... Luke 13:15, 16

See FIRST DAY OF THE WEEK

[*also* SABBATHS]
Verily my *s* ye shall keep ... Ex 31:13
Ye shall keep the *s* ... Ex 31:14
seventh is the *s* of rest ... Ex 31:15
doeth any work in the *s* ... Ex 31:15
a *s* of rest to the Lord ... Ex 35:2
upon the *s* day ... Ex 35:3
be a *s* of rest unto you ... Lev 16:31
and keep my *s* ... Lev 19:3
Ye shall keep my *s* ... Lev 19:30
after the *s* the priest ... Lev 23:11
the morrow after the *s* ... Lev 23:15
seven *s* shall be complete ... Lev 23:15
morrow after the seventh *s* ... Lev 23:16
shall ye have a *s* ... Lev 23:24
first day shall be a *s* ... Lev 23:39
eighth day shall be a *s* ... Lev 23:39
s he shall set it in order ... Lev 24:8
the land keep a *s* unto ... Lev 25:2
a *s* of rest unto the land ... Lev 25:4
a *s* for the Lord ... Lev 25:4
number seven *s* of years ... Lev 25:8
the space of the seven *s* ... Lev 25:8
and shall enjoy her *s* ... Lev 26:43
sticks upon the *s* day ... Num 15:32
the *s* day two lambs ... Num 28:9
that enter in on the *s* ... 2Kin 11:5
were to come in on the *s* ... 2Kin 11:9
should go out on the *s* ... 2Kin 11:9
to prepare it every *s* ... 1Chr 9:32
unto the Lord in the *s* ... 1Chr 23:31
on the *s*, and on the new ... 2Chr 2:4
on the *s*, and on the new ... 2Chr 8:13
entering on the *s* ... 2Chr 23:4
were to come in on the *s* ... 2Chr 23:8
were to go out on the *s* ... 2Chr 23:8
burnt offerings for the *s* ... 2Chr 31:3
land had enjoyed her *s* ... 2Chr 36:21
lay desolate she kept *s* ... 2Chr 36:21
madest known..thy holy *s* ... Neh 9:14
the *s*, of the new moons ... Neh 10:33
wine presses on the *s* ... Neh 13:15
into Jerusalem on the *s* ... Neh 13:15
and profane the *s* day? ... Neh 13:17
to be dark before the *s* ... Neh 13:19
opened till after the *s* ... Neh 13:19
brought in on the *s* day ... Neh 13:19
came..no more on the *s* ... Neh 13:21
to sanctify the *s* day ... Neh 13:22
the new moons and *s* ... Is 1:13
away thy foot from the *s* ... Is 58:13
and call the *s* a delight ... Is 58:13
from one *s* to another ... Is 66:23
of this city on the *s* day ... Jer 17:24
but hallow the *s* day, to ... Jer 17:24
unto me to hallow the *s* ... Jer 17:27
Jerusalem on the *s* day ... Jer 17:27
and did mock at her *s* ... Lam 1:7
s to be forgotten in ... Lam 2:6
also I gave them my *s* ... Ezek 20:12
but polluted my *s* ... Ezek 20:16
they polluted my *s*: then ... Ezek 20:21
and hast profaned my *s* ... Ezek 22:8
and have profaned my *s* ... Ezek 23:38
they shall hallow my *s* ... Ezek 44:24
new moons, and in the *s* ... Ezek 45:17
but on the *s* it shall be ... Ezek 46:1
unto the Lord in the *s* ... Ezek 46:4
as he did on the *s* day ... Ezek 46:12
her new moons, and her *s* ... Hos 2:11
and the *s*, that we may ... Amos 8:5
Jesus went on the *s* day ... Matt 12:1
how that on the *s* days ... Matt 12:5
the temple profane the *s* ... Matt 12:5
to heal on the *s* day ... Matt 12:10
to do well on the *s* days ... Matt 12:12
neither on the *s* day ... Matt 24:20
In the end of the *s*, as it ... Matt 28:1
s day he entered..the ... Mark 1:21
through..fields on the *s* ... Mark 2:23
on the *s* day that which is ... Mark 2:24
is Lord also of the *s* ... Mark 2:28
heal him on the *s* day ... Mark 3:2
the day before the *s* ... Mark 15:42
And when the *s* was past ... Mark 16:1
synagogue on the *s* day ... Luke 4:16
taught them on the *s* days ... Luke 4:31
on the second *s* after the ... Luke 6:1
not lawful..on the *s* days? ... Luke 6:2
to pass also on another *s* ... Luke 6:6
lawful on the *s* days to ... Luke 6:9
in..synagogues on the *s* ... Luke 13:10
to eat bread on the *s* day ... Luke 14:1
pull him out on the *s* ... Luke 14:5
and the *s* drew on ... Luke 23:54
the same day was the *s* ... John 5:9
these things on the *s* day ... John 5:16
on the *s* day circumcise ... John 7:22
on the *s* day receive ... John 7:23
whit whole on the *s* day? ... John 7:23
s day when Jesus made ... John 9:14
upon the cross on the *s* day ... John 19:31
s day was a high day ... John 19:31
prophets..read every *s* ... Acts 13:27
preached to them the next *s* ... Acts 13:42
next *s* day came almost ... Acts 13:44
synagogues every *s* day ... Acts 15:21
on the *s* we went out of ... Acts 16:13
three *s* days reasoned ... Acts 17:2
reasoned..every *s* ... Acts 18:4
moon, or of the *s* days ... Col 2:16

SABBATH DAY'S JOURNEY—*distance one could travel on the Sabbath (about 3,100 feet)*
Between Mt. Olivet and Jerusalem ... Acts 1:12

SABBATICAL YEAR—*a rest every seventh year*

Purpose of:
Rest the land ... Ex 23:10, 11
Emancipate slaves ... Ex 21:2-6
Remit debts ... Deut 15:1-6

Allusions to, in history, in:
Time of the judges ... Ruth 4:1-10
Pre-exilic times ... Jer 32:6-16
Postexilic times ... Neh 10:31

Spiritual significance of:
Punishment for nonobservance ... Lev 26:33-35
Illustrative of spiritual release ... Is 61:1-3; Luke 4:18-21
Figurative of spiritual rest ... Heb 4:1-11

See JUBILEE, YEAR OF

SABEANS (sä-bē'ănz)—*descendants of Sheba*
Job's property attacked by ... Job 1:13-15
Subject to Israel ... Is 45:14
See SHEBA 4, 5, 6

brought *S* from the ... Ezek 23:42
shall sell them to the *S* ... Joel 3:8

SABTAH (săb'tä)—*"striking"*
Son of Cush and grandson of Ham ... Gen 10:7

[*also* SABTA]
Seba, and Havilah, and *S* ... 1Chr 1:9

SABTECHA (săb'tĕ-kä)—*"striking"*
Son of Cush and grandson of Ham ... Gen 10:7

SACAR (sā'kär)—*"hired"*
1. Ahiam's father ... 1Chr 11:35
   Called Sharar ... 2Sam 23:33
2. Father of gatekeepers ... 1Chr 26:4

SACK—*a bag for carrying items*

[*also* SACK'S, SACKS, SACKS']
commanded to fill their *s* ... Gen 42:25
man's money into his *s* ... Gen 42:25
it was in his *s* mouth ... Gen 42:27
lo, it is even in my *s* ... Gen 42:28
in the mouth of your *s* ... Gen 43:12
we opened our *s*, and ... Gen 43:21
in the mouth of his *s* ... Gen 43:21
you treasure in your *s* ... Gen 43:23
saying, Fill the men's *s* ... Gen 44:1
money in his *s* mouth ... Gen 44:1
found in our *s* mouths ... Gen 44:8
down every man his *s* to ... Gen 44:11
opened every man his *s* ... Gen 44:11
or raiment, or skin, or *s* ... Lev 11:32
old *s* upon their asses ... Josh 9:4

SACKBUT—*a musical instrument*
Mistranslation for "harp" in the Babylonian orchestra ... Dan 3:5-15

SACKCLOTH—*a coarse fabric made of goat's hair*

Worn by:
Kings ... 2Kin 6:30
Prophets ... Is 20:2
John ... Matt 3:4
People ... Luke 10:13
Women ... Is 32:11

Expressive of:
Sorrow ... Gen 37:34
Repentance ... Joel 1:8, 13
Subjection ... 1Kin 20:31, 32
Fasting ... Is 58:5
Protest ... Esth 4:1-4

Symbolic of:
Severe judgment ... Is 50:3
God's judgment ... Rev 6:12

[*also* SACKCLOTHES]
and gird you with *s* ... 2Sam 3:31
the daughter of Aiah took *s* ... 2Sam 21:10
and put *s* upon his flesh ... 1Kin 21:27
and fasted, and lay in *s* ... 1Kin 21:27
covered himself with *s* ... 2Kin 19:1
who were clothed in *s* ... 1Chr 21:16
with fasting, and with *s* ... Neh 9:1
sewed *s* upon my skin ... Job 16:15
thou hast put off my *s* ... Ps 30:11
sick, my clothing was *s* ... Ps 35:13
made *s* also my garment ... Ps 69:11
stomacher a girding of *s* ... Is 3:24
gird themselves with *s* ... Is 15:3
and to girding with *s* ... Is 22:12
covered himself with *s* ... Is 37:1
gird you with *s*, lament ... Jer 4:8
gird thee with *s*, and ... Jer 6:26
and upon the loins *s* ... Jer 48:37
gird you with *s*; lament ... Jer 49:3
girded themselves with *s* ... Lam 2:10
gird themselves with *s* ... Ezek 7:18
and gird them with *s* ... Ezek 27:31
with fasting, and *s*, and ... Dan 9:3
I will bring up *s* upon ... Amos 8:10
a fast, and put on *s* ... Jon 3:5
beast be covered with *s* ... Jon 3:8
repented long ago in *s* ... Matt 11:21
days, clothed in *s* ... Rev 11:3

SACRED PLACES—*places where God is worshiped*
Chosen by God ... Deut 12:11
Not to trust in ... John 4:20-24

SACRIFICE—*an offering made to God or the false gods*

S

Requirements of:
Upon altar only ... Ex 20:24
Clean animals ... Gen 8:20
To God alone ... Ex 22:20
Perfect animals ... Lev 22:19
At place divinely established ... Deut 12:6
By appointed priests ... 1Sam 2:28
In faith ... Gen 4:4
In obedience ... 1Sam 15:22

Perversion of, in offering:
To demons ... 1Cor 10:20
To idols ... 2Chr 34:25
Defective animals ... Mal 1:13, 14
Without respect ... 1Sam 2:29

Inadequacy of:
Could not atone for sins . Ps 40:6
Limited to legal purification ... Heb 9:13, 22

Figurative of:
Christ's sacrifice ... 1Cor 5:7
Prayer ... Ps 141:2
Worship ... 1Pet 2:5
Righteousness ... Ps 51:19

Of Christ to:
Redeem from the curse ... Gal 3:13
Secure our redemption ... Matt 20:28
Reconcile God and man . Rom 5:10

[*also* SACRIFICED, SACRIFICEDST, SACRIFICES, SACRIFICETH, SACRIFICING]

Jacob offered *s* upon the ... Gen 31:54
offered *s* unto the God ... Gen 46:1
we may *s* to the Lord ... Ex 3:18
s unto the Lord our God ... Ex 5:3
go and do *s* to the Lord ... Ex 5:17
may do *s* unto the Lord ... Ex 8:8
shall *s* the abomination ... Ex 8:26
we *s* the abomination of ... Ex 8:26
ye may *s* to the Lord ... Ex 8:28
s and burnt offerings ... Ex 10:25
we may *s* unto the Lord ... Ex 10:25
the *s* of the Lord's passover ... Ex 12:27
I *s* to the Lord all that ... Ex 13:15
burnt offering and *s* for ... Ex 18:12
s thereon thy burnt ... Ex 20:24
not offer the blood of my *s* ... Ex 23:18
the fat of my *s* remain ... Ex 23:18
s peace offerings of oxen ... Ex 24:5
of the *s* of..offerings ... Ex 29:28
incense thereon, nor burnt *s* .. Ex 30:9
it, and have *s* thereunto ... Ex 32:8
and do *s* unto their gods ... Ex 34:15
and thou eat of his *s* ... Ex 34:15
the blood of my *s* with ... Ex 34:25
the *s* of the feast of ... Ex 34:25
offering be a burnt *s*, of ... Lev 1:3
the goats, for a burnt *s* ... Lev 1:10
burnt *s* for his offering ... Lev 1:14
oblation be a *s* of peace ... Lev 3:1
altar upon the burnt *s* ... Lev 3:5
offer of the *s* of the peace ... Lev 3:9
bullock of the *s* of peace ... Lev 4:10
from off the *s* of peace ... Lev 4:31
law of the *s* of peace ... Lev 7:11
the *s* of thanksgiving ... Lev 7:13
if the *s* of his offering ... Lev 7:16
day that he offereth his *s* ... Lev 7:16
flesh of the *s* of his peace ... Lev 7:18
offereth the *s* of his peace ... Lev 7:29
s of your peace offerings ... Lev 7:32
s of the peace offerings ... Lev 7:37
burnt *s* for a sweet ... Lev 8:21
to *s* before the Lord ... Lev 9:4
beside the burnt *s* of the ... Lev 9:17
the ram for a *s* of peace ... Lev 9:18
s of the Lord made by ... Lev 10:13
Israel may bring their *s* ... Lev 17:5
a burnt offering or *s* ... Lev 17:8
if ye offer a *s* of peace ... Lev 19:5
offereth a *s* of peace ... Lev 22:21
ye shall *s* one kid of the ... Lev 23:19
year for a *s* of peace ... Lev 23:19
they do not offer a *s* unto ... Lev 27:11
the ram for a *s* of peace ... Num 6:17
all the oxen for the *s* of ... Num 7:88
s of your peace offerings ... Num 10:10
s in performing a vow ... Num 15:3
s in performing a vow ... Num 15:8
he stood by his burnt *s* ... Num 23:6
the people unto the *s* of ... Num 25:2
my bread for my *s* made ... Num 28:2
a *s* made by fire unto ... Num 28:6
a *s* made by fire unto the ... Num 28:13
the meat of the *s* made ... Num 28:24
a *s* made by fire unto the ... Num 29:6
your *s*, and your tithes ... Deut 12:6
blood of thy *s* shall be ... Deut 12:27
shalt not *s* it unto the ... Deut 15:21
therefore *s* the passover ... Deut 16:2
which thou *s* the first day ... Deut 16:4
Thou mayest not *s* the ... Deut 16:5
shalt *s* the passover at ... Deut 16:6
shalt not *s* unto the Lord ... Deut 17:1
people..that offer a *s* ... Deut 18:3
They *s* unto devils, not to ... Deut 32:17
did eat the fat of their *s* ... Deut 32:38
burnt *s* upon thine altar ... Deut 33:10
offer *s* of righteousness ... Deut 33:19
the Lord, and *s* peace ... Josh 8:31
s of the Lord..of Israel ... Josh 13:14
burnt offering, nor for *s* ... Josh 22:26
with our *s*, and with our ... Josh 22:27
meat offerings, or for *s* ... Josh 22:29
s there unto the Lord ... Judg 2:5
offer a burnt *s* with the ... Judg 6:26
a great *s* unto Dagon ... Judg 16:23
to *s* unto the Lord of ... 1Sam 1:3
when any man offered *s* ... 1Sam 2:13
said to the man that *s* ... 1Sam 2:15
not be purged with *s* ... 1Sam 3:14
s of the people today in ... 1Sam 9:12
to *s* *s* of peace offerings ... 1Sam 10:8
they *s* *s* of peace offerings ... 1Sam 11:15
oxen, to *s* unto the Lord ... 1Sam 15:15
s unto the Lord thy God ... 1Sam 15:21
say, I am come to *s* to ... 1Sam 16:2
I am come to *s* unto the ... 1Sam 16:5
come with me to the *s* ... 1Sam 16:5
and called them to the *s* ... 1Sam 16:5
there is a yearly *s* there ... 1Sam 20:6
he *s* oxen and fatlings ... 2Sam 6:13
Giloh, while he offered *s* ... 2Sam 15:12
here be oxen for burnt *s* ... 2Sam 24:22
Only the people *s* in high ... 1Kin 3:2
king went to Gibeon to *s* ... 1Kin 3:4
s sheep and oxen, that ... 1Kin 8:5
offered *s* before the Lord ... 1Kin 8:62
incense and *s* unto their ... 1Kin 11:8
this people go up to do *s* ... 1Kin 12:27
offering of the evening *s* ... 1Kin 18:29
offering of the evening *s* ... 1Kin 18:36
burnt offering nor *s* unto ... 2Kin 5:17
a great *s* to do to Baal ... 2Kin 10:19
they went in to offer *s* ... 2Kin 10:24
people still *s* and burnt ... 2Kin 12:3
as yet the people did *s* ... 2Kin 14:4
people *s* and burnt incense ... 2Kin 15:4
he *s* and burnt incense ... 2Kin 16:4
and the king's burnt *s* ... 2Kin 16:15
and all the blood of the *s* ... 2Kin 16:15
which *s* for them in the ... 2Kin 17:32
nor serve them, nor *s* to ... 2Kin 17:35
they offered burnt *s* and ... 1Chr 16:1
the Jebusite, then he *s* ... 1Chr 21:28
they *s* *s* unto the Lord ... 1Chr 29:21
and *s* in abundance for all ... 1Chr 29:21
save only to burn *s* ... 2Chr 2:6
s sheep and oxen, which ... 2Chr 5:6
burnt offerings and the *s* ... 2Chr 7:1
Solomon offered a *s* ... 2Chr 7:5
to *s* unto the Lord God ... 2Chr 11:16
every evening burnt *s* ... 2Chr 13:11
He *s* also and burnt incense ... 2Chr 28:4
will I *s* to them, that ... 2Chr 28:23
bring *s* and thank offerings ... 2Chr 29:31
congregation brought in *s* ... 2Chr 29:31
s thereon peace offerings ... 2Chr 33:16
people did *s*..in the high ... 2Chr 33:17
graves of them that had *s* ... 2Chr 34:4
we do *s* unto him since ... Ezra 4:2
place where they offered *s* ... Ezra 6:3
astonished until..evening *s* ... Ezra 9:4
will they *s*? will they ... Neh 4:2
they offered great *s* ... Neh 12:43
Offer the *s* of ... Ps 4:5
accept thy burnt *s* ... Ps 20:3
a covenant with me by *s* ... Ps 50:5
not reprove thee for thy *s* ... Ps 50:8
For thou desirest not *s* ... Ps 51:16
The *s* of God are a ... Ps 51:17
I will freely *s* unto thee ... Ps 54:6
unto thee burnt *s* of ... Ps 66:15
and ate the *s* of the dead ... Ps 106:28
s their sons and their ... Ps 106:37
And let them *s* the *s* of ... Ps 107:22
thee..*s* of thanksgiving ... Ps 116:17
bind the *s* with cords ... Ps 118:27
s of the wicked is an ... Prov 15:8
house full of *s* with strife ... Prov 17:1
acceptable to the Lord than *s* .. Prov 21:3
hear, than to give the *s* ... Eccl 5:1
him that *s*, and to him ... Eccl 9:2
the multitude of your *s* ... Is 1:11
day, and shall do *s* and ... Is 19:21
to year; let them kill *s* ... Is 29:1
the Lord hath a *s* in ... Is 34:6
honored me with thy *s* ... Is 43:23
s shall be accepted upon ... Is 56:7
wentest thou up to offer *s* ... Is 57:7
s in gardens, and burneth ... Is 65:3
he that *s* a lamb, as if he ... Is 66:3
nor your *s* sweet unto me ... Jer 6:20
burnt offerings or *s* ... Jer 7:22
burnt offerings, and *s* ... Jer 17:26
and bringing *s* of praise ... Jer 17:26
bring the *s* of praise ... Jer 33:11
God of hosts hath a *s* in ... Jer 46:10
thou *s* unto them to be ... Ezek 16:20
they offered there their *s* ... Ezek 20:28
to my *s* that I do *s* for you ... Ezek 39:17
s upon the mountains of ... Ezek 39:17
s which I have *s* for you ... Ezek 39:19
burnt offering and the *s* ... Ezek 40:42
offering and the *s* for the ... Ezek 44:11
boil the *s* of the people ... Ezek 46:24
daily *s* was taken away ... Dan 8:11
concerning the daily *s* ... Dan 8:13
s and the oblation to ... Dan 9:27
take away the daily *s* ... Dan 11:31
daily *s* shall be taken ... Dan 12:11
without a *s*, and without ... Hos 3:4
s upon the tops of the ... Hos 4:13
ashamed because of their *s* ... Hos 4:19
I desired mercy, and not *s* ... Hos 6:6
They *s* flesh for the ... Hos 8:13
their *s* shall be unto them ... Hos 9:4
they *s* unto Baalim, and ... Hos 11:2
they *s* bullocks in Gilgal ... Hos 12:11
the men that *s* kiss the ... Hos 13:2
bring your *s* every morning ... Amos 4:4
a *s* of thanksgiving with ... Amos 4:5
a *s* unto the Lord ... Jon 1:16
will *s* unto thee with ... Jon 2:9
they *s* unto their net ... Hab 1:16
Lord hath prepared a *s* ... Zeph 1:7
they that *s* shall come ... Zech 14:21
ye offer the blind for *s* ... Mal 1:8
s unto the Lord a corrupt ... Mal 1:14
have mercy, and not *s* ... Matt 9:13
have mercy, and not *s* ... Matt 12:7
every *s* shall be salted ... Mark 9:49
burnt offerings and *s* ... Mark 12:33
to offer a *s* according to ... Luke 2:24
had mingled with their *s* ... Luke 13:1
offered *s* unto the idol ... Acts 7:41
to me slain beasts and *s* ... Acts 7:42
would have done *s* with ... Acts 14:13
your bodies a living *s* ... Rom 12:1
Christ our passover is *s* ... 1Cor 5:7
offered in *s* unto idols ... 1Cor 8:4
which eat of the *s* ... 1Cor 10:18
is offered in *s* to idols ... 1Cor 10:19
offered in *s* unto idols ... 1Cor 10:28

for us an offering and a *s* .....Eph 5:2
the *s* and service of your ......Phil 2:17
s acceptable..to God..........Phil 4:18
may offer both gifts and *s* .....Heb 5:1
offer up *s*, first for his ....Heb 7:27
to offer gifts and *s*...........Heb 8:3
offered both gifts and *s* ....Heb 9:9
put away sin by the *s*.........Heb 9:26
can never with those *s* ....Heb 10:1
in those *s* there is a ....Heb 10:3
S and offering thou ....Heb 10:5
In burnt offerings and *s*.......Heb 10:6
after he had offered one *s*.....Heb 10:12
a more excellent *s* than ....Heb 11:4
with such *s* God is well ....Heb 13:16
eat things *s* unto idols ....Rev 2:14

SACRILEGE—*profaning of holy things*

Done by:
Defaming God's name ...2Kin 18:28-35
Profaning the Sabbath ...Neh 13:15-21
Debauching holy things ..John 2:14-16

Those guilty of:
People...................1Sam 6:19
Pagans ....Dan 5:1-4
Priests ....Lev 10:1-7
Pharisees ....Matt 23:16-22

dost thou commit *s*? ....Rom 2:22

SAD—*downcast; filled with unhappiness*

[*also* SADLY, SADNESS]
and, behold, they were *s*......Gen 40:6
Wherefore look ye so *s* ....Gen 40:7
countenance was no more *s* ...1Sam 1:18
Why is thy spirit so *s* 1Kin 21:5
s in his presence..............Neh 2:1
my countenance be *s* ....Neh 2:3
the *s* of the countenance ......Eccl 7:3
heart of the righteous *s* ....Ezek 13:22
whom I have not made *s*......Ezek 13:22
of a *s* countenance ....Matt 6:16
he was *s* at that saying.......Mark 10:22
as ye walk, and are *s*? ....Luke 24:17

SADDLE—*cloth or leather seat for a rider; to put a saddle on*
Balaam's...............Num 22:21

[*also* SADDLED]
morning, and *s* his ass ....Gen 22:3
what *s* soever he rideth ....Lev 15:9
with him two asses *s*.........Judg 19:10
with a couple of asses *s*.......2Sam 16:1
I will *s* me an ass, that I 2Sam 19:26
arose, and *s* his ass 1Kin 2:40
unto his sons, *S* me the ass....1Kin 13:13
that he *s* for him the ass 1Kin 13:23
Then she *s* an ass, and........2Kin 4:24

SADDUCEES (săd'ū-sēz)—*"followers of Zadok"—priestly artistocratic party; often opposed to the Pharisees*
Rejected by John........Matt 3:7
Tempted Jesus ....Matt 16:1-12
Silenced by Jesus ....Matt 22:23-34
Disturbed by teaching of resurrection ....Acts 4:1, 2
Opposed apostles ....Acts 5:17-40

come unto him the *S* which ...Mark 12:18
came to him certain of the *S* ..Luke 20:27
that the one part were *S* ......Acts 23:6
the Pharisees and the *S* ....Acts 23:7
S say that..no resurrection ....Acts 23:8

SADOC (sā'dŏk)—*Greek form of Zadok; "righteous"*
Ancestor of Christ.......Matt 1:14

SAFE—*living without fear or harm*

False means of:
Wickedness ....Job 21:7-9, 17
Folly ....Job 5:2-4
False hope 1Thess 5:3

True means of:
Lord ....Ps 4:8
Lord's protection ....Deut 33:12
Apostolic admonition ....Phil 3:1

[*also* SAFELY, SAFETY]
dwell in the land in *s* ....Lev 25:18
and dwell in your land *s* ......Lev 26:5
so that ye dwell in *s* ....Deut 12:10
Israel then shall dwell in *s* ....Deut 33:28
side, and ye dwelled *s* 1Sam 12:11
Is the young man Absalom *s*? .2Sam 18:29
Judah and Israel dwelt *s* 1Kin 4:25
I was not in *s*, neither ....Job 3:26
may be exalted to *s*...........Job 5:11
be given him to be in *s* ....Job 24:23
set him in *s* from him.........Ps 12:5
horse is a vain thing for *s* .....Ps 33:17
he led them on *s* so ....Ps 78:53
Hold..and I shall be *s*..........Ps 119:117
unto me shall dwell *s* ....Prov 1:33
of counselors there is *s*........Prov 11:14
runneth into it, and is *s*.......Prov 18:10
of counselors there is *s*........Prov 24:6
her husband doth *s* trust ......Prov 31:11
shall carry it away *s* ....Is 5:29
needy shall lie down in *s*......Is 14:30
pursued them, and passed *s* ...Is 41:3
and Israel shall dwell *s*........Jer 23:6
Jerusalem shall dwell *s*........Jer 33:16
And they shall dwell *s* ....Ezek 28:26
shall be *s* in their land ....Ezek 34:27
they shall dwell *s*, and ....Ezek 34:28
are at rest, that dwell *s* ....Ezek 38:11
they dwelt *s* in their land .....Ezek 39:26
make them to lie down *s*......Hos 2:18
shall be *s* inhabited ....Zech 14:11
and lead him away *s*..........Mark 14:44
received him *s* and sound .....Luke 15:27
found we shut with all *s*.......Acts 5:23
the jailor to keep them *s*......Acts 16:23
bring him *s* unto Felix ....Acts 23:24
they escaped all *s* to land .....Acts 27:44

SAFEGUARD—*safekeeping*
me thou shalt be in *s* 1Sam 22:23

SAFFRON—*a variety of crocus; used as a perfume or medicine*
Figurative of the bride ...Song 4:14

SAID, SAIDST—*See* INTRODUCTION

SAIL—*expanse of cloth which catches the wind and propels a ship; to navigate a boat or ship*

Figurative of:
Enemies' weakness ......Is 33:23
The pride of Tyre ....Ezek 27:7

[*also* SAILED, SAILING]
as they *s* he fell asleep........Luke 8:23
from thence they *s* to ....Acts 13:4
took Mark, and *s* unto ....Acts 15:39
And he *s* from Ephesus ....Acts 18:21
about to *s* into Syria ....Acts 20:3
we *s* away from Philippi ......Acts 20:6
we *s* thence, and came ....Acts 20:15
s over into Phoenicia ....Acts 21:2
and *s* into Syria ....Acts 21:3
we should *s* into Italy ....Acts 27:1
we had *s* over the sea of ......Acts 27:5
a ship..*s* into Italy ....Acts 27:6
when we had *s* slowly.........Acts 27:7
we *s* under Crete, over ....Acts 27:7
struck *s*, and so were ....Acts 27:17

SAILORS—*mariners*
Skilled..................1Kin 9:27
Fearful ....Jon 1:5
Cry bitterly ....Ezek 27:8-36
Storm-tossed ....Acts 27:18-31

s, and as many as trade ....Rev 18:17

SAINTS—*all of God's redeemed people*

Descriptive of:
Old Testament believers. .Matt 27:52
Christians ....Acts 9:32, 41
Christian martyrs ....Rev 16:6
Present with Christ at His return 1Thess 3:13

Their weaknesses, subject to:
Needs 2Cor 9:1, 12
Rom 12:13
Persecution ....Dan 7:21, 25

Their duty to:
Keep God's Word ....Jude 3
Grow spiritually ....Eph 4:12
Avoid evil ....Eph 5:3
Judge Christians 1Cor 6:1, 2
Pray for others ....Eph 6:18
Minister to others ....Heb 6:10

God's protection of, He:
Forsakes them not.......Ps 37:28
Gathers them ....Ps 50:5
Keeps them 1Sam 2:9
Counts them precious ....Ps 116:15
Intercedes for them......Rom 8:27
Will glorify them 2Thess 1:10

[*also* SAINT, SAINTS']
with ten thousands of *s* ....Deut 33:2
and let thy *s* rejoice in 2Chr 6:41
to which of the *s* wilt ....Job 5:1
But to the *s* that are in ....Ps 16:3
love the Lord, all ye his *s*.....Ps 31:23
O fear the Lord, ye his *s* .....Ps 34:9
it is good before thy *s* ....Ps 52:9
his people, and to his *s* ....Ps 85:8
in the assembly of the *s*.......Ps 89:7
the souls of his *s* ....Ps 97:10
Aaron the *s* of the Lord ......Ps 106:16
her *s* shall shout aloud ....Ps 132:16
the praise of all his *s* ....Ps 148:14
Let the *s* be joyful in ....Ps 149:5
the way of his *s* ....Prov 2:8
the *s* of the most High........Dan 7:18
judgment was given to the *s*...Dan 7:22
that the *s* possessed the ....Dan 7:22
wear out the *s* of the ....Dan 7:25
the *s* of the most High........Dan 7:27
I heard one *s* speaking ....Dan 8:13
another *s* said unto that.......Dan 8:13
said unto that certain *s*........Dan 8:13
is faithful with the *s* ....Hos 11:12
and all the *s* with thee ....Zech 14:5
evil he hath done to thy *s*.....Acts 9:13
of the *s* did I shut up in ......Acts 26:10
beloved..called to be *s* ....Rom 1:7
to minister unto the *s*.........Rom 15:25
may be accepted of the *s*......Rom 15:31
the Lord, as becometh *s* ......Rom 16:2
Christ Jesus, called to be *s* 1Cor 1:2
in all churches of the *s*........1Cor 14:33
the collection for the *s*........1Cor 16:1
all the *s* which are in all 2Cor 1:1
ministering to the *s*............2Cor 8:4
All the *s* salute you...........2Cor 13:13
to the *s*..at Ephesus ....Eph 1:1
and love unto all the *s*........Eph 1:15
his inheritance in the *s*........Eph 1:18
fellow citizens with the *s* ......Eph 2:19
than the least of all *s* ....Eph 3:8
to comprehend with all *s*......Eph 3:18
all the *s* in Christ Jesus ....Phil 1:1
Salute every *s* in Christ ....Phil 4:21
s and faithful brethren ....Col 1:2
the love..to all the *s* ....Col 1:4
the inheritance of the *s* ....Col 1:12
made manifest to his *s* ....Col 1:26
she have washed the *s* feet 1Tim 5:10
Jesus, and toward all *s*........Philem 5
the bowels of the *s* are........Philem 7
over you, and all the *s*........Heb 13:24
ten thousands of his *s*.........Jude 14
are the prayers of *s*...........Rev 5:8
with the prayers of all *s*.......Rev 8:3
with the prayers of the *s* ......Rev 8:4
to make war with the *s* ....Rev 13:7
is the patience of the *s*........Rev 14:12
thy ways, thou King of *s* ....Rev 15:3
with the blood of the *s*........Rev 17:6
of prophets, and of *s* ....Rev 18:24
the camp of the *s*.............Rev 20:9

SAITH—*See* INTRODUCTION

SAKE—*end; purpose; good of*
[*also* SAKES]
is the ground for thy *s* ....Gen 3:17
well with me for thy *s* ....Gen 12:13
all the place for their *s* ....Gen 18:26
not do it for forty's *s* ....Gen 18:29
not destroy if for ten's *s* ......Gen 18:32
for my servant Abraham's *s* ...Gen 26:24
house for Joseph's *s* ....Gen 39:5
Egyptians for Israel's *s* ....Ex 18:8
go free for his tooth's *s* ....Ex 21:27
for their *s* remember..........Lev 26:45
Enviest thou for my *s*? ....Num 11:29
the plague for Peor's *s* ....Num 25:18
angry with me for your *s* ......Deut 1:37
angry with me for your *s* ......Deut 4:21
unto them for our *s* ....Judg 21:22
me much for your *s* ....Ruth 1:13
for his great name's *s* 1Sam 12:22
for his people Israel's *s* 2Sam 5:12
for Jonathan's *s*? 2Sam 9:1
gently for my *s* with the.......2Sam 18:5
country for thy name's *s* 1Kin 8:41
for David my servant's *s* 1Kin 11:13
Jerusalem's *s* which I 1Kin 11:13
for my servant David's *s* 1Kin 11:32
Jerusalem's *s*, the city.........1Kin 11:32
for David's *s* did the Lord 1Kin 15:4
for David his servant's *s* 2Kin 8:19
save it, for mine own *s* 2Kin 19:34
my servant David's *s*..........2Kin 19:34
this city for mine own *s* 2Kin 20:6
for my servant David's *s* 2Kin 20:6
reproved kings for their *s* 1Chr 16:21
for thy great mercies' *s* ....Neh 9:31
for the children's *s* of my .....Job 19:17
for their *s* therefore ....Ps 7:7
for his name's *s* ....Ps 23:3
For thy name's *s*, O Lord .....Ps 25:11
save me for thy mercies' *s*.....Ps 31:16
us for thy mercies' *s* ....Ps 44:26
be ashamed for my *s* ....Ps 69:6
be confounded for my *s*........Ps 69:6
Lord, for thy name's *s* ....Ps 109:21
and companions' *s* ....Ps 122:8
servant David's *s* turn.........Ps 132:10
O Lord, for thy name's *s* ......Ps 143:11
righteousness' *s* bring ....Ps 143:11
to save it for mine own *s* .....Is 37:35
for my servant David's *s* ......Is 37:35
For your *s* I have sent to .....Is 43:14
name's *s* will I defer ....Is 48:9
Zion's *s* will I not hold ....Is 62:1
I do for my servants' *s*........Is 65:8
do thou it for thy name's *s* ....Jer 14:7
for thy *s* I have suffered ......Jer 15:15
wrought for my name's *s*.......Ezek 20:9
I do not this for your *s* ....Ezek 36:22
for mine holy name's *s*.........Ezek 36:22
for their *s* that shall ....Dan 2:30
desolate, for the Lord's *s* .....Dan 9:17
my *s* this great tempest ....Jon 1:12
shall Zion for your *s* be ....Mic 3:12
the devourer for your *s* ....Mal 3:11
for righteousness' *s* ....Matt 5:10
and kings for my *s* ....Matt 10:18
loseth his life for my *s* ....Matt 10:39
for the oath's *s*................Matt 14:9
kingdom of heaven's *s* ....Matt 19:12
nations for my name's *s*.......Matt 24:9
ariseth for the word's *s* ....Mark 4:17
yet for his oath's *s*, and ....Mark 6:26
and for their *s* which sat ......Mark 6:26
for my *s*, and the gospel's .....Mark 10:29
all men for my name's *s* ....Mark 13:13
for the Son of man's *s* ....Luke 6:22
the kingdom of God's *s* ....Luke 18:29
hated..for my name's *s*.........Luke 21:17
glad for your *s* that I ....John 11:15
came not for Jesus' *s* ....John 12:9
down thy life for my *s*? ....John 13:38
you for my name's *s* ....John 15:21
for their *s* I sanctify ....John 17:19
suffer for my name's *s* ....Acts 9:16
not written for his *s* alone .....Rom 4:23
are enemies for your *s* ....Rom 11:28
beloved for the fathers' *s*......Rom 11:28
but also for conscience *s* ......Rom 13:5
and to Apollos for your *s* 1Cor 4:6
are fools for Christ's *s* 1Cor 4:10
it altogether for our *s*? 1Cor 9:10
For our *s*, no doubt, this.......1Cor 9:10
question for conscience *s* 1Cor 10:25
for conscience *s*: for the 1Cor 10:28
for your *s* forgave I it.........2Cor 2:10
your servants for Jesus' *s*.....2Cor 4:5
all things are for your *s* 2Cor 4:15
your *s* he became poor........2Cor 8:9
distresses for Christ's *s* 2Cor 12:10
Christ's *s* hath forgiven ....Eph 4:32
also to suffer for his *s* ....Phil 1:29
my flesh for his body's *s* ......Col 1:24
among you for your *s*.........1Thess 1:5
joy for your *s* before our......1Thess 3:9
wine for thy stomach's *s* 1Tim 5:23
endure..for the elect's *s* 2Tim 2:10
not, for filthy lucre's *s* ....Titus 1:11
Yet for love's *s* I rather.......Philem 9
of man for the Lord's *s* 1Pet 2:13
you for his name's *s* 1John 2:12
For the truth's *s*, which 2John 2
for his name's *s* they..........3John 7
name's *s* hast labored ....Rev 2:3

SALAH, SALA (sā'lä)—*the son of Arphaxad*
Arphaxad begat *S*; and *S* .....Gen 10:24
lived after he begat *S* ....Gen 11:13
S lived after he begat ....Gen 11:15
See SHELAH

SALAMIS (săl'ä-mĭs)—*"shaken"—a town of Cyprus*
Paul preaches here ......Acts 13:4, 5

SALATHIEL (sä-lā'thĭ-ĕl)—*Greek form of Shealtiel*
Jechoniah begat *S* ....Matt 1:12
and *S* begat Zorobabel........Matt 1:12
which was the son of *S* ....Luke 3:27

SALCHAH, SALCAH (săl'kä)—*"thy lifting up"*
City in Bashan ....Deut 3:10
in mount Hermon, and in *S* ...Josh 12:5
the land of Bashan unto *S* 1Chr 5:11

SALE—*transfer of ownership from one person to another*
count the years of the *s* ....Lev 25:27
price of his *s* shall be ....Lev 25:50
of the *s* of his patrimony ......Deut 18:8

SALEM (sā'lĕm)—*"perfect peace"*
Jerusalem's original name.Gen 14:18
Used poetically..........Ps 76:2
Melchisedek king of *S* ....Heb 7:1
after that also King of *S* ......Heb 7:2

SALIM (sā'lĭm)—*"path"*
Place near Aenon ....John 3:23

SALIVA—*spittle*
Used figuratively for a short time ....Job 7:19

SALLAI (săl'ā-ī)—*"rejecter"*
1. Benjamite chief.........Neh 11:8
2. Priestly family ....Neh 12:20
Called Sallu ....Neh 12:7

SALLU (săl'ū)—*"weighed; dear"*
Benjamite family 1Chr 9:7

SALMA (săl'mä)—*"strength; clothing"*
Son of Hur 1Chr 2:50, 51
begat *S*, and *S* begat.........1Chr 2:11
sons of *S*; Beth-lehem 1Chr 2:54

SALMON (săl-mōn)—*"strength; clothing"*
Father of Boaz ....Ruth 4:20, 21
Ancestor of Christ.......Matt 1:4, 5
was white as snow in *S* ....Ps 68:14
Boaz, which was the son of *S* .Luke 3:32

SALMONE (săl-mō'nĕ)—*"peace"*
Crete, over against *S* ....Acts 27:7

SALOME (sä-lō'mĕ)—*"strength; clothing"*
1. Among ministering women...............Mark 15:40, 41
Visits empty tomb ......Mark 16:1
2. Herodias' daughter (not named in the Bible)...Matt 14:6-11

SALT—*a compound that gives flavor*
Uses of:
Seasoning:
Food ....Job 6:6
Sacrifice ....Lev 2:13
Everlasting covenant .....Num 18:19
Rubbed on infants at birth ....Ezek 16:4
Making land unproductive.Judg 9:45
Miracles connected with:
Lot's wife becomes pillar of....................Gen 19:26
Elisha purified water with.2Kin 2:19-22
Figurative of:
God's everlasting covenant..............Num 18:19
Barrenness and desolation.Deut 29:23
Good influence..........Matt 5:13
Peace in the heart ....Mark 9:50
Wise speech ....Col 4:6
Final judgment ....Mark 9:49
Reprobation ....Ezek 47:9, 11

Edomites in the valley of *s* 1Chr 18:12
sons by a covenant of *s* 2Chr 13:5
went to the valley of *s* 2Chr 25:11
wheat, *s*, wine, and oil........Ezra 6:9
s without prescribing..........Ezra 7:22
Edom in the valley of *s* ....Ps 60:*title*
s land and not inhabited ......Jer 17:6
priests shall cast *s* upon ....Ezek 43:24
S is good: but if the *s*.........Luke 14:34
yield *s* water and fresh........James 3:12

SALT, CITY OF—*a city near En-gedi*
City in the wilderness of Judah ....Josh 15:62

SALT SEA—*the Dead Sea*
Old Testament name for the Dead Sea .... Gen 14:3; Num 34:3, 12
the plain, even the *S S*........Deut 3:17
the plain, even the *S S*........Josh 3:16
the plain, even the *S S*........Josh 12:3
the shore of the *S S* ....Josh 15:2
east border was the *S S* ....Josh 15:5
north bay of the *S S*..........Josh 18:19

SALT, VALLEY OF—*a valley south of the Dead Sea*
Site of:
David's victory 2Sam 8:13
Amaziah's victory 2Kin 14:7

SALTPITS—*mines for producing salt*
breeding of nettles, and *s* .....Zeph 2:9

SALU (sā'lū)—*"miserable; unfortunate"*
Simeonite prince ....Num 25:14

SALUTATION—*greetings from one person to another*
Normal:
Between:
Brothers 1Sam 17:22
Social ranks...........Gen 47:7
Strangers 1Sam 10:3, 4
Christians............Acts 18:22
On visits...............Rom 16:21-23
Examples of forms used in:
"God be gracious" ......Gen 43:29
"Peace be with thee" ....Judg 19:20
"The LORD be with you".Ruth 2:4
"The LORD bless thee ...Ruth 2:4
"Blessed be thou" ....Ruth 3:10
"Hail"..................Luke 1:28
"All hail"...............Matt 28:9
See BENEDICTION

[*also* SALUTATIONS]
s in the marketplace ....Mark 12:38
what manner of *s* this ....Luke 1:29
Elisabeth heard the *s* of ....Luke 1:41
s of me Paul with mine 1Cor 16:21
The *s* by the hand of me ......Col 4:18
The *s* of Paul with mine 2Thess 3:17

SALUTE—*to show respect or goodwill*

[*also* SALUTED, SALUTETH]
that he might *s* him 1Sam 13:10
of the wilderness to *s* our 1Sam 25:14
to the people, he *s* them 1Sam 30:21
unto king David, to *s* him 2Sam 8:10
meet any man, *s* him not 2Kin 4:29
and if any *s* thee, answer 2Kin 4:29
to *s* the children of the 2Kin 10:13
he *s* him and said to him 2Kin 10:15
And if ye *s* your brethren .....Matt 5:47
come into an house, *s* it ......Matt 10:12
running to him *s* him ....Mark 9:15
began to *s* him, Hail ....Mark 15:18
and *s* Elisabeth ....Luke 1:40
voice of thy *s* sounded in .....Luke 1:44
and *s* no man by the way .....Luke 10:4
up, and *s* the church, he ......Acts 18:22
and *s* the brethren, and ....Acts 21:7
when he had *s* them, he ....Acts 21:19
unto Caesarea to *s* Festus .....Acts 25:13
S my well-beloved ....Rom 16:5
S Andronicus and Junia ....Rom 16:7
S Urbane, our helper ....Rom 16:9
S Apelles approved in ....Rom 16:10
S them..of Aristobulus' ....Rom 16:10
S Herodion my kinsman ......Rom 16:11
S Tryphena and Tryphosa .....Rom 16:12
S the beloved Persis ....Rom 16:12
S Rufus chosen in the ....Rom 16:13
S Asyncritus, Phlegon ....Rom 16:14
S Philologus, and Julia ....Rom 16:15
S one another with an ....Rom 16:16
churches of Christ *s* you ......Rom 16:16
Sosipater, my kinsmen, *s* you ..Rom 16:21
churches of Asia *s* you 1Cor 16:19
Aquila and Priscilla *s* you 1Cor 16:19
All the saints *s* you 2Cor 13:13
S every saint in Christ ....Phil 4:21
All the saints *s* you ....Phil 4:22
Aristarchus..*s* you, and ....Col 4:10
who is one of you..*s* you ......Col 4:12
S the brethren..in ....Col 4:15
S Prisca and Aquila 2Tim 4:19
All that are with me *s* thee ....Titus 3:15
There *s* thee Epaphras ....Philem 23
S all them that have the ......Heb 13:24
They of Italy *s* you ....Heb 13:24
at Babylon..*s* you 1Pet 5:13
Our friends *s* thee 3John 14

SALVATION—*the total work of God in affecting a right relationship between mankind and himself*

Descriptive of:
National deliverance .....Ex 14:13
Deliverance from enemies. 2Chr 20:17
Messiah ....Matt 1:21

Source of, in:
God's grace ....Eph 2:5, 8
God's love ....Rom 5:8
God's mercy ....Titus 3:5
Christ alone ....Acts 4:12
Cross 1Cor 1:18

History of:
Promised to Adam ......Gen 3:15
Announced to Abram ....Gen 12:1-3
Revealed to the prophets . 1Pet 1:10-12
Longed for the saints ....Ps 119:81, 174
Promised to Gentiles ....Is 45:21, 22
To be realized by the Messiah ....Is 59:16, 17
Seen in Christ's birth ....Luke 1:69, 77
Christ, the author ....Heb 5:9
Appeared to all men .....Titus 2:11
Proclaimed to Israel .....Zech 9:9
Accomplished on the cross ....John 3:14, 15
Preached through the Gospel ....Eph 1:13
Rejected by Israel ....Acts 13:26-46
Extended to Gentiles ....Acts 28:28
This age, day of 2Cor 6:2
God's long-suffering in ...2Pet 3:9
Final, nearer each day ...Rom 13:11
Consummated in the second advent ....Heb 9:28
Praise for, in heaven .....Rev 7:10

Requirements of:
Confession ....Acts 2:21
Repentance ....Mark 1:15
Faith ....John 3:14-18
Regeneration ....John 3:38
Holy scripture 2Tim 3:15

Negative blessings of, deliverance from:
Sin ....Matt 1:21
Satan's power ....Heb 2:14, 15
Wrath ....Rom 5:9
Eternal death ....John 3:16, 17

Positive blessings of:
Chosen to 2Thess 2:13
Appointed to 1Thess 5:9
Kept unto 1Pet 1:5
Rejoiced in 1Pet 4:13
To be worked out ....Phil 2:12

Temporal aspects of:
Past ....Eph 2:8
Present 1Cor 1:18
Future ....Heb 9:28

I have waited for thy *s* ....Gen 49:18
and he is become my *s* ....Ex 15:2
the Rock of his *s* ....Deut 32:15
because I rejoice in thy *s* 1Sam 2:1
wrought this great *s* in 1Sam 14:45
and the horn of my *s* 2Sam 22:3
God of the rock of my *s* 2Sam 22:47
this is all my *s*, and all 2Sam 23:5
from day to day his *s* 1Chr 16:23
priests..be clothed with *s* 2Chr 6:41
He also shall be my *s* ....Job 13:16
S belongeth unto the Lord ....Ps 3:8
I will rejoice in thy *s* ....Ps 9:14
shall rejoice in thy *s* ....Ps 13:5
Oh that the *s* of Israel ....Ps 14:7
and the horn of my *s* ....Ps 18:2
me the shield of my *s* ....Ps 18:35
God of my *s* be exalted ....Ps 18:46
We will rejoice in thy *s* ....Ps 20:5
and in thy *s* how..shall ....Ps 21:1
glory is great in thy *s* ....Ps 21:5
thou art the God of my *s* .....Ps 25:5
Lord is my light and my *s* .....Ps 27:1
me, O God of my *s* ....Ps 27:9
it shall rejoice in his *s* ....Ps 35:9
s of the righteous is of ....Ps 37:39
help me, O Lord my *s* ....Ps 38:22
thy faithfulness and thy *s* ......Ps 40:10
love thy *s* say continually .....Ps 40:16
Restore..joy of thy *s* ....Ps 51:12
Oh that the *s* of Israel ....Ps 53:6
He only is my rock and my *s* ..Ps 62:2
In God is my *s* and my ....Ps 62:7
us, O God of our *s* ....Ps 65:5
God is the God of *s* ....Ps 68:20
let thy *s*, O God, set me up ...Ps 69:29
righteousness and thy *s* ....Ps 71:15
trusted not in his *s* ....Ps 78:22
Turn us, O God of our *s* ......Ps 85:4
his *s* is nigh them that ....Ps 85:9
and the rock of my *s* ....Ps 89:26
noise to the rock of our *s* .....Ps 95:1
hath made known his *s* ....Ps 98:2
O visit me with thy *s* ....Ps 106:4
I will take the cup of *s* ....Ps 116:13
and is become my *s* ....Ps 118:14
and art become my *s* ....Ps 118:21
O Lord, even thy *s* ....Ps 119:41
S is far from the wicked ......Ps 119:155
I have hoped for thy *s* ....Ps 119:166
clothe her priests with *s* ....Ps 132:16
the strength of my *s* ....Ps 140:7
It is he that giveth *s* ....Ps 144:10
beautify the meek with *s* ......Ps 149:4
God is my *s*; I will trust ......Is 12:2
he also is become my *s* ....Is 12:2
the God of thy *s* ....Is 17:10
s will God appoint for ....Is 26:1
times, and strength of *s* ....Is 33:6
with an everlasting *s* ....Is 45:17
be far off, and my *s* shall .....Is 46:13
I will place *s* in Zion for ......Is 46:13
my *s* is gone forth, and ....Is 51:5
but my *s* shall be for ever .....Is 51:6
good, that publisheth *s* ....Is 52:7
see the *s* of our God ....Is 52:10
for my *s* is near to come ......Is 56:1
for *s*, but it is far off ....Is 59:11
shalt call thy walls *S* ....Is 60:18
with the garments of *s* ....Is 61:10
s thereof as a lamp that ....Is 62:1
Behold, thy *s* cometh ....Is 62:11
arm brought *s* unto me ....Is 63:5
Truly in vain is *s* hoped ....Jer 3:23
Lord our God is the *s* of ....Jer 3:23
quietly wait for the *s* of ....Lam 3:26
vowed, *S* is of the Lord ....Jon 2:9
wait for the God of my *s* .....Mic 7:7
and thy chariots of *s*? ....Hab 3:8
for the *s* of thy people ....Hab 3:13
for *s* with thine anointed ......Hab 3:13
eyes have seen thy *s* ....Luke 2:30
shall see the *s* of God ....Luke 3:6
This day is *s* come to this .....Luke 19:9
for *s* is of the Jews ....John 4:22
be for *s* unto the ends of ......Acts 13:47
unto us the way of *s* ....Acts 16:17
power of God unto *s* to ....Rom 1:16
confession is made unto *s* .....Rom 10:10
s is come unto the Gentiles ...Rom 11:11
your consolation and *s* 2Cor 1:6
worketh repentance to *s* 2Cor 7:10
And take the helmet of *s* .....Eph 6:17
turn to my *s* through ....Phil 1:19
but to you of *s*, and that ......Phil 1:28
an helmet, the hope of *s* 1Thess 5:8
also obtain the *s* which is 2Tim 2:10
who shall be heirs of *s*? ....Heb 1:14
if we neglect so great *s* ....Heb 2:3
captain of their *s* perfect ......Heb 2:10
things that accompany *s* ....Heb 6:9
your faith, even the *s* of 1Pet 1:9
long-suffering..is *s* 2Pet 3:15
you of the common *s* ....Jude 3
is come *s*, and strength ....Rev 12:10
Alleluia; *S*, and glory ....Rev 19:1

SAMARIA (sä-mâr'ĭ-ä)—*"watch mountain"*
1. Capital of Israel 1Kin 16:24-29
   Israel's "crown of pride". Is 28:1
   Besieged twice by Benhadad 1Kin 20:1-22
   Miraculously saved 2Kin 6:8-23
   Worshipers of Baal destroyed 2Kin 10:1-28
   Threatened with divine judgment ....Amos 3:11, 12
   Repopulated with foreigners 2Kin 17:24-41
2. Name of Northern Kingdom 1Kin 21:1
3. District of Palestine in Christ's time ....Luke 17:11-19
   Preaching in, forbidden by Christ ....Matt 10:5
   Gospel preached ....Acts 1:8
   Churches established there ....Acts 9:31
   Paul preached there .....Acts 15:3

are in the cities of *S* 1Kin 13:32
which he had built in *S* 1Kin 16:32
was a sore famine in *S* 1Kin 18:2
my father made in *S* 1Kin 20:34
and came to *S* 1Kin 20:43
of Israel, which is in *S* 1Kin 21:18

S

entrance of the gate of *S* 1Kin 22:10
and was brought to *S* 1Kin 22:37
buried the king in *S* 1Kin 22:37
reign over Israel in *S* the......1Kin 22:51
chamber that was in *S* 2Kin 1:2
thence he returned to *S* 2Kin 2:25
Jehoram went out of *S* 2Kin 3:6
went up, and beseiged *S* 2Kin 6:24
was a great famine in *S* 2Kin 6:25
in the gate of *S* 2Kin 7:1
this time in the gate of *S* 2Kin 7:18
they buried him in *S* 2Kin 10:35
reigned over Israel in *S* 2Kin 10:36
the grove also in *S* 2Kin 13:6
to reign over Israel in *S* 2Kin 13:10
and returned to *S* 2Kin 14:14
began to reign in *S* 2Kin 14:23
reigned a full month in *S* 2Kin 15:13
Tirzah, and came to *S* 2Kin 15:14
the son of Jabesh in *S* 2Kin 15:14
reign over Israel in *S* 2Kin 15:23
to reign over Israel in *S* 2Kin 15:27
up to *S*, and besieged it 2Kin 17:5
came up against *S* 2Kin 18:9
they delivered *S* out of.........2Kin 18:34
prophet that came out of *S* 2Kin 23:18
went down to Ahab to *S* 2Chr 18:2
for he was hid in *S* 2Chr 22:9
also, and returned to *S* 2Chr 25:24
the host that came to *S* 2Chr 28:9
set in the cities of *S* ....Ezra 4:10
and the army of *S* ....Neh 4:2
head of Ephraim is *S* ....Is 7:9
head of *S* is Remaliah's ....Is 7:9
and the inhabitant of *S* ....Is 9:9
is not *S* as Damascus? ....Is 10:9
they delivered *S* out of........Is 36:19
in the prophets of *S* ....Jer 23:13
from *S*, even fourscore ....Jer 41:5
thine elder sister is *S* ....Ezek 16:46
captivity of *S* and her ....Ezek 16:53
S is Aholah, and ....Ezek 23:4
and the wickedness of *S* ......Hos 7:1
calf of *S* shall be broken ......Hos 8:6
As for *S*, her king is cut ......Hos 10:7
upon the mountains of *S* ......Amos 3:9
in the mountain of *S*..........Amos 4:1
that sware by the sin of *S* .....Amos 8:14
and the fields of *S*............Obad 19
concerning *S* and Jerusalem ...Mic 1:1
will make *S* as an heap ....Mic 1:6
must needs go through *S* ......John 4:4
a woman of *S* to draw ....John 4:7
saith the woman of *S* ....John 4:9
regions of Judea and *S*........Acts 8:1
bewitched the people of *S*.....Acts 8:9

SAMARITAN (sä-măr'ĭ-tăn)—*inhabitant of Samaria*
Made of mixed races 2Kin 17:24-41
Seek alliance with Jews ..Ezra 4:1-4
Help of, rejected by Nehemiah ....Neh 4:1, 2
Christ and the woman of .John 4:5-42
Story of "the good Samaritan" ....Luke 10:30-37
Beliefs of ....John 4:25
Converts among ....Acts 8:5-25

[*also* SAMARITANS]
city of the *S* enter..not........Matt 10:5
into a village of the *S*.........Luke 9:52
and he was a *S*..............Luke 17:16
that thou art a *S* ....John 8:48

SAME—*See* INTRODUCTION

SAMECH (sä'mĕk)
Letter of the Hebrew alphabet ....Ps 119:113-120

SAMGAR-NEBO (săm-gär-nē'bō)—*"be gracious, Nebo"*
Prince of Nebuchadnezzar.Jer 39:3

SAMLAH (săm'lä)—*"garment"*
Edomite king ....Gen 36:36, 37

S of Masrekah reigned 1Chr 1:47
S was dead, Shaul of 1Chr 1:48

SAMOS (sā'mŏs)—*"full of gravel"—an island off the coast of Lydia*
Visited by Paul..........Acts 20:15

SAMOTHRACIA (săm-ō-thrā-shĭ-ä)—*"of the Samians and Thracians"—an island in the Aegean Sea*
Visited by Paul..........Acts 16:11

SAMSON (săm'sŭn)—*"distinguished; strong"—a judge of Israel for twenty years whose great strength made famous*

Life of:
Birth of, predicted.......Judg 13:2-23
God's Spirit moves him ..Judg 13:24, 25
Desired a Philistine wife .Judg 14:1-9
Propounded a riddle .....Judg 14:10-14
Betrayed, kills 30 men ..Judg 14:15-20
Enticed by Delilah, loses strength ....Judg 16:4-20
Blinded and bound ......Judg 16:21
Destroyed over 3,000 in his death ....Judg 16:22-31; Heb 11:32

Contrasts of his life:
Parents' concern; his unconcern ....Judg 13:8
Obedient, victorious; disobedient, defeated ..Judg 15:14
Seeks revenge; is revenged.............Judg 15:1-8
Spirit-moved; animated by lust................Judg 15:14
Physically strong; morally weak ....Judg 16:3, 12
Greater victory in death than in life..........Judg 16:29, 30; Heb 11:32

To bind *S* are we come ......Judg 15:10
said to *S*, Knowest thou ......Judg 15:11
S said unto them, Sware ......Judg 15:12
S said, With the jawbone .....Judg 15:16
Then went *S* to Gaza ....Judg 16:1
saying, *S* is come hither ....Judg 16:2

SAMUEL (săm'ū-el)—*"asked of God; heard of God"—a prophet, and the last judge, of Israel*

Life of:
Born in answer to Hannah's prayer.......1Sam 1:5-21
Dedicated to God before his birth 1Sam 1:11, 22
Brought to Shiloh 1Sam 1:24-28
His mother praised God for 1Sam 2:1-10
Received a revelation concerning Eli's house .1Sam 3:1-19
Recognized as a prophet .1Sam 3:20, 21
Became a circuit judge...1Sam 7:15-17
Organized porter service .1Chr 9:22; 1Chr 26:28
Called Israel to repentance............1Sam 7:3-6
Anointed Saul as king ...1Sam 10:1
Lamented in death 1Sam 25:1

Character of:
Inspired as a writer 1Chr 29:29
Inspired as a prophet ....Acts 3:24
Diligent as a judge 1Sam 7:15-17
Faithful to God ....Heb 11:32-34
Industrious in service 1Chr 9:22
Devout in life ....Jer 15:1
Powerful in prayer.......Ps 99:6
Remembered in death ...1Sam 25:1

But *S* ministered before 1Sam 2:18
the child *S* grew before 1Sam 2:21
the child *S* grew on, and 1Sam 2:26
word of *S* came to all.........1Sam 4:1
of Israel said to *S* 1Sam 7:8
And *S* took a sucking..........1Sam 7:9
S cried unto the Lord for 1Sam 7:9
as *S* was offering up the 1Sam 7:10
Then *S* took a stone 1Sam 7:12
all the days of *S* 1Sam 7:13
when *S* was old, that he 1Sam 8:1
came to *S* unto Ramah 1Sam 8:4
the thing displeased *S*.........1Sam 8:6
S prayed unto the Lord 1Sam 8:6
the Lord said unto *S*..........1Sam 8:7
S told all the words of 1Sam 8:10
to obey the voice of *S* 1Sam 8:19
S heard all the words 1Sam 8:21
Lord said to *S*, Hearken 1Sam 8:22
And *S* said unto the men 1Sam 8:22
behold, *S* came out 1Sam 9:14
Now the Lord had told *S* 1Sam 9:15
when *S* saw Saul 1Sam 9:17
Saul drew near to *S* in 1Sam 9:18
S answered Saul, and said.....1Sam 9:19
And *S* took Saul and his 1Sam 9:22
And *S* said unto the cook 1Sam 9:23
S said, Behold that which 1Sam 9:24
So Saul did eat with *S* 1Sam 9:24
S communed with Saul.........1Sam 9:25
S called Saul to the top 1Sam 9:26
both of them, he and *S* 1Sam 9:26
S said to Saul, Bid the 1Sam 9:27
turned..to go from *S*..........1Sam 10:9
no where, we came to *S* 1Sam 10:14
Tell me..what *S* said 1Sam 10:15
whereof *S* spake..............1Sam 10:16
And *S* called the people 1Sam 10:17
when *S* had caused all 1Sam 10:20
S said to all the people 1Sam 10:24
S told the people the 1Sam 10:25
And *S* sent all the people 1Sam 10:25
after Saul and after *S* 1Sam 11:7
the people said unto *S* 1Sam 11:12
said *S* to the people 1Sam 11:14
S said unto all Israel..........1Sam 12:1
S said unto..people, It is 1Sam 12:6
sent..Jephthah, and *S* 1Sam 12:11
So *S* called unto the Lord 1Sam 12:18
feared the Lord and *S* 1Sam 12:18
S said unto the people 1Sam 12:20
the set time that *S* had........1Sam 13:8
but *S* came not to Gilgal 1Sam 13:8
And *S* said, What hast 1Sam 13:11
S arose, and gat him 1Sam 13:15
S also said unto Saul, The 1Sam 15:1
And it grieved *S*; and he 1Sam 15:11
S rose early to meet Saul 1Sam 15:12
was told *S*, saying, Saul 1Sam 15:12
S said, What meaneth 1Sam 15:14
And *S* said, When thou 1Sam 15:17
S said, Hath the Lord 1Sam 15:22
S said unto Saul, I will........1Sam 15:26
And *S* said..The Lord 1Sam 15:28
Then said *S*, Bring ye.........1Sam 15:32
S said, As thy sword hath 1Sam 15:33
S hewed Agag in pieces 1Sam 15:33
S came no more to see 1Sam 15:35
nevertheless *S* mourned 1Sam 15:35
S said, How can I go? 1Sam 16:2
Lord said unto *S*, Look 1Sam 16:7
his sons to pass before *S* 1Sam 16:10
S said unto Jesse, The 1Sam 16:10
S said unto Jesse, Are 1Sam 16:11
S said unto Jesse, Send 1Sam 16:11
S took the horn of oil 1Sam 16:13
S rose up, and went to........1Sam 16:13
escaped, and came to *S* 1Sam 19:18
he and *S* went and dwelt......1Sam 19:18
Where are *S* and David? 1Sam 19:22
Now *S* was dead, and all......1Sam 28:3
when the woman saw *S* 1Sam 28:12
And *S* said to Saul, Why......1Sam 28:15
of the words of *S*.............1Sam 28:20
sons of *S*; the first-born 1Chr 6:28
word of the Lord by *S* 1Chr 11:3
days of *S* the prophet 2Chr 35:18
until *S* the prophet ....Acts 13:20

SAMUEL, THE BOOKS OF—*books of the Old Testament*

1Samuel:
Birth of Samuel 1Sam 1:19-28
Hannah's song 1Sam 2:1-10

The ark captured 1Sam 4:1-11
The ark returned 1Sam 6:1-21
Saul chosen as king 1Sam 9:1-27
Saul anointed 1Sam 10:1-27
Saul against the Philistines 1Sam 13:1-4
Saul is rejected 1Sam 15:10-31
David is anointed.........1Sam 16:1-13
David and Goliath........1Sam 17:23-58
Jonathan's love 1Sam 19:1-7
Saul against David.......1Sam 23:6-29
David spares Saul 1Sam 24:1-8
1Sam 26:1-16
The medium of En-dor ..1Sam 28:7-25
David against the Amalekites 1Sam 30:1-31
Death of Saul 1Sam 31:1-13

2Samuel:

David's lament 2Sam 1:17-27
David anointed as king ..2Sam 2:1-7
The ark in Zion 2Sam 6:1-19
David plans the Temple..2Sam 7:1-29
The kingdom expands....2Sam 8:1-18
David and Bath-sheba ...2Sam 11:1-27
Nathan rebukes David ...2Sam 12:1-12
David repents 2Sam 12:13, 14
David's child dies........2Sam 12:15-23
Amnon and Tamar 2Sam 13:1-19
The mighty men.........2Sam 23:8-39
David takes a census 2Sam 24:1-25

SANBALLAT (săn-băl'ăt)—*"strong"*

Influential Samaritan.....Neh 2:10
Opposes Nehemiah's plans ....Neh 4:7, 8
Seeks to assassinate Nehemiah.............Neh 6:1-4
Fails in intimidation .....Neh 6:5-14
His daughter marries Eliashib, the high priest Neh 13:4, 28

SANCTIFICATION—*state of growing in divine grace*

Produced by:

God 1Thess 5:23
Christ ....Heb 2:11
Holy Spirit..............1Pet 1:2
Truth....................John 17:17, 19
Christ's blood ....Heb 9:14
Prayer 1Tim 4:4, 5

See GODLINESS; HOLINESS OF CHRISTIANS; PIETY

s, and redemption 1Cor 1:30
will of God, even your *s* 1Thess 4:3
vessel in *s* and honor 1Thess 4:4
to salvation through *s* of 2Thess 2:13

SANCTIFY—*to set apart for holy purposes*

[*also* SANCTIFIED, SANCTIFIETH]

the seventh day, and *s* it ......Gen 2:3
S unto me all the.............Ex 13:2
and *s* them today and.........Ex 19:10
unto the people, and *s*........Ex 19:14
the mount, and *s* it ....Ex 19:23
consecrate..and *s* them........Ex 28:41
s the breast of the wave.......Ex 29:27
shalt anoint it, to *s* it ....Ex 29:36
shall be *s* by my glory ....Ex 29:43
I will *s* the tabernacle.........Ex 29:44
I will *s* also both Aaron.......Ex 29:44
Lord that doth *s* you ....Ex 31:13
anoint the laver..and *s* it ......Ex 40:11
all that was therein, and *s*.....Lev 8:10
laver and his foot, to *s*........Lev 8:11
s Aaron, and..garments ....Lev 8:30
therefore *s* yourselves ....Lev 11:44
the Lord which *s* you ....Lev 20:8
Thou shalt *s* him ....Lev 21:8
I the Lord, which *s* you ....Lev 21:8
for I the Lord do *s* them......Lev 21:23
I the Lord do *s* them ....Lev 22:9
man shall *s* his house ....Lev 27:14
he that *s* it will redeem ....Lev 27:15
If he *s* his field from..........Lev 27:17
if a man *s* unto the Lord......Lev 27:22
had anointed it, and *s* it ......Num 7:1
had anointed them and *s*......Num 7:1
S yourselves against ....Num 11:18
and he was *s* in them ....Num 20:13
s me at the water before ......Num 27:14
Keep the sabbath day to *s* it ..Deut 5:12
ye *s* me not in the midst ......Deut 32:51
the people, *S* yourselves ......Josh 3:5
Up, *s* the people, and say .....Josh 7:13
S yourselves against ....Josh 7:13
s Eleazar his son to keep 1Sam 7:1
s yourselves, and come........1Sam 16:5
it were *s* this day in the 1Sam 21:5
s yourselves, both ye and 1Chr 15:12
priests and..Levites *s* 1Chr 15:14
priests..were *s*................2Chr 5:11
house, which I have *s* for 2Chr 7:20
Levites, *s* now yourselves 2Chr 29:5
s the house of the Lord 2Chr 29:5
so they *s* the house of the 2Chr 29:17
priests had *s* themselves 2Chr 29:34
upright in heart to *s* 2Chr 29:34
which he hath *s* forever 2Chr 30:8
that were not *s*...............2Chr 30:17
they *s* themselves in 2Chr 31:18
passover, and *s* yourselves.....2Chr 35:6
they *s* it, and set up the.......Neh 3:1
tower of Meah they *s* it ....Neh 3:1
they *s* holy things unto........Neh 12:47
s them unto the children ......Neh 12:47
to *s* the sabbath day ....Neh 13:22
Job sent and *s* them ....Job 1:5
be *s* in righteousness..........Is 5:16
S the Lord of hosts ....Is 8:13
they shall *s* my name ....Is 29:23
s the Holy One of Jacob ......Is 29:23
out of the womb I *s* thee .....Jer 1:5
am the Lord that *s* them ......Ezek 20:12
will be *s* in you before ....Ezek 20:41
be *s*..in the sight of the ....Ezek 28:25
I the Lord do *s* Israel.........Ezek 37:28
when I shall be *s* in thee ......Ezek 38:16
shall not *s* the people ....Ezek 44:19
priests that are *s* of the ....Ezek 48:11
S ye a fast, call a solemn .....Joel 1:14
s a fast, call a solemn ....Joel 2:15
temple that *s* the gold? ....Matt 23:17
the altar that *s* the gift?.......Matt 23:19
whom the Father hath *s*.......John 10:36
among all them which are *s* ...Acts 20:32
being *s* by the Holy Ghost ....Rom 15:16
them that are *s* in Christ 1Cor 1:2
husband is *s* by the 1Cor 7:14
unbelieving wife is *s* by 1Cor 7:14
might *s* and cleanse it.........Eph 5:26
s, and meet for the 2Tim 2:21
that *s* and they who are ....Heb 2:11
s to the purifying of the.......Heb 9:13
we are *s* through ....Heb 10:10
perfected..them that are *s*.....Heb 10:14
wherewith he was *s*...........Heb 10:29
he might *s* the people.........Heb 13:12
them that are *s* by God ....Jude 1

SANCTIMONIOUSNESS—*assumed and pretended holiness*

Condemned by Christ....Matt 6:5

SANCTUARY—*a holy place*

[*also* SANCTUARIES]

s, O Lord, which thy ....Ex 15:17
let them make me a *s*.........Ex 25:8
the shekel of the *s*............Ex 30:13
for the service of the *s*........Ex 36:1
all the work of the *s*..........Ex 36:4
after the shekel of the *s*.......Ex 38:24
after the shekel of the *s*.......Ex 38:26
before the veil of the *s*........Lev 4:6
the *s* out of the camp ....Lev 10:4
atonement for the holy *s*......Lev 16:33
to defile my *s*, and to ....Lev 20:3
Neither..go out of the *s*.......Lev 21:12
profane the *s* of his God ......Lev 21:12
that he profane not my *s*......Lev 21:23
after the shekel of the *s*.......Lev 27:3
the charge of the *s* ....Num 3:28
keep the charge of the *s* ......Num 3:32
shekel of the *s* shalt ....Num 3:47
they minister in the *s* ....Num 4:12
an end of covering the *s* ......Num 4:15
all the vessels of the *s* ....Num 4:15
the service of the *s* ....Num 7:9
after the shekel of the *s*.......Num 7:85
come nigh unto the *s* ....Num 8:19
the iniquity of the *s* ....Num 18:1
keep the charge of the *s* ......Num 18:5
defiled the *s* of the Lord ......Num 19:20
was by the *s* of the Lord ......Josh 24:26
the instruments of the *s*.......1Chr 9:29
the governors of the *s* 1Chr 24:5
a *s* therein for thy name 2Chr 20:8
for the *s*, and for Judah.......2Chr 29:21
the purification of the *s*.......2Chr 30:19
are the vessels of the *s*........Neh 10:39
Send thee help from the *s*.....Ps 20:2
God, my King, in the *s*.......Ps 68:24
done wickedly in the *s*........Ps 74:3
way, O God, is in the *s*.......Ps 77:13
built his *s* like high ....Ps 78:69
from the height of his *s* ....Ps 102:19
Lift up your hands in the *s*....Ps 134:2
he shall be for a *s*; but........Is 8:14
the princes of the *s* ....Is 43:28
trodden down thy *s* ....Is 63:18
is the place of our *s* ....Jer 17:12
strangers are come into the *s*..Jer 51:51
entered into her *s* ....Lam 1:10
he hath abhorred his *s* ....Lam 2:7
the *s* are poured out in ....Lam 4:1
thou hast defiled my *s* ....Ezek 5:11
go far off from my *s*? ....Ezek 8:6
and begin at my *s* ....Ezek 9:6
to them as a little *s*...........Ezek 11:16
defiled my *s* in the same ......Ezek 23:38
I will profane my *s* ....Ezek 24:21
Thou hast defiled thy *s* ......Ezek 28:18
set my *s* in the midst ....Ezek 37:26
and the face of the *s*..........Ezek 41:21
separation between the *s* ......Ezek 42:20
gate of the outward *s* ....Ezek 44:1
have brought into my *s* ....Ezek 44:7
be in my *s*, to pollute it.......Ezek 44:7
shall enter into my *s* ....Ezek 44:9
kept the charge of my *s*.......Ezek 44:15
shall enter into my *s* ....Ezek 44:16
that he goeth into the *s* ....Ezek 44:27
to minister in the *s* ....Ezek 44:27
for the *s* five hundred..........Ezek 45:2
the *s* and the most holy ....Ezek 45:3
the ministers of the *s* ....Ezek 45:4
a holy place for the *s* ....Ezek 45:4
and cleanse the *s* ....Ezek 45:18
they issued out of the *s* ....Ezek 47:12
s shall be in the midst ....Ezek 48:8
s of the Lord shall be ....Ezek 48:10
place of his *s* was cast ....Dan 8:11
shall the *s* be cleansed ....Dan 8:14
face to shine upon thy *s*.......Dan 9:17
destroy the city and the *s* .....Dan 9:26
pollute the *s* of strength.......Dan 11:31
the *s* of Israel shall be ....Amos 7:9
priests have polluted the *s*.....Zeph 3:4
A minister of the *s*, and ......Heb 8:2
service, and a worldly *s* ....Heb 9:1
which is called the *s* ....Heb 9:2
blood is brought into the *s* ....Heb 13:11

See HOLY OF HOLIES; TABERNACLE

SAND—*a loose granular soil*

Figurative uses of:

One's posterity ....Gen 22:17
Weight ....Job 6:3
Large number of people. .Josh 11:4
God's thoughts toward us. Ps 139:17, 18

seed as the *s* of the sea ....Gen 32:12
corn as the *s* of the sea ....Gen 41:49
and hid him in the *s* ....Ex 2:12
treasures hid in the *s* ....Deut 33:19
the *s* by the seaside ....Judg 7:12
as the *s* which is on the 1Sam 13:5
the *s* that is by the sea........2Sam 17:11

S

many as the *s* which is 1Kin 4:20
s that is on the seashore 1Kin 4:29
multiply my days as the *s* .....Job 29:18
fowls like as the *s* of the ......Ps 78:27
heavy, and the *s* weighty ......Prov 27:3
people Israel be as the *s* ......Is 10:22
seed also had been as the *s* ...Is 48:19
the *s* for the bound of ....Jer 5:22
above the *s* of the seas........Jer 15:8
s of the sea measured.........Jer 33:22
Israel shall be as the *s* ....Hos 1:10
the captivity as the *s*..........Hab 1:9
built his house upon the *s*.....Matt 7:26
be as the *s* of the sea ....Rom 9:27
s which is by the seashore .....Heb 11:12
upon the *s* of the sea ....Rev 13:1
is as the *s* of the sea.........Rev 20:8

SANDALS—*coverings for the foot*

Characteristics of:
Worn on the feet........1Kin 2:5
Tied by a latchet ....Gen 14:23
Some considered worthless ....Amos 2:6
Used for dress occasions. .Luke 15:22
Worn as adornment .....Song 7:1
Worn out after a journey .Josh 9:5, 13
Preserved supernaturally. .Deut 29:5
Worn by Christ's disciples.Mark 6:9

Symbolism of:
Taking on—readiness for a journey ....Ex 12:11
Putting off—reverence before God .... Ex 3:5; Josh 5:15
Want of—mourning......2Sam 15:30
Giving to another—manner of attestation in Israel ....Ruth 4:7, 8
To unloose another's—act of homage ....Luke 3:16

Figurative of:
Preparation for service ...Eph 6:15
Alertness ....Is 5:27

and bind on thy *s* ....Acts 12:8

SANG—*See* Sing

SANITATION AND HYGIENE

Laws relating to:
Dead bodies ....Lev 11:24-40
Contagion ....Num 9:6, 10
Leprosy ....Lev 13:2-59
Menstruation............Lev 15:19-30
Women in childbirth .....Lev 12:2-8
Man's discharge ....Lev 15:2-18

Provisions for health:
Washing ....Deut 23:10, 11
Burning ....Num 31:19-23
Isolation ....Lev 13:2-5, 31-33
Destruction ....Lev 14:39-45
Covering excrement ......Deut 23:12, 13

SANK—*See* Sink

SANSANNAH (săn-săn'ä)—*"branch"*
Town in south Judah ....Josh 15:31

SAP—*the circulating fluid of plants*
Lord's trees full of ......Ps 104:16

SAPH (saf)—*"preserver"*
Philistine giant 2Sam 21:18
Called Sippai............1Chr 20:4

SAPHIR (sā'fer)—*"delightful"*
Town of Judah ....Mic 1:11

SAPPHIRA (să-fī'rä)—*"beautiful; sapphire"*
Wife of Ananias.........Acts 5:1
Struck dead for lying ....Acts 5:1-11

SAPPHIRE—*a precious stone*
Worn by high priest .....Ex 28:18
John's vision ....Rev 21:19

[*also* sapphires]
row, an emerald, a *s*..........Ex 39:11
of it are the place of *s* ....Job 28:6
precious onyx, or the *s*........Job 28:16
ivory overlaid with *s* ....Song 5:14
lay thy foundations with *s* .....Is 54:11
their polishing was of *s* ....Lam 4:7
appearance of a *s* stone ....Ezek 1:26
them as it were a *s* stone .....Ezek 10:1
jasper, the *s*, the emerald .....Ezek 28:13

SARAH, SARA, SARAI (sâr'ä, sâr'ä-ī)—*"princess"*
Wife of Abram ....Gen 11:29-31
Abraham's half-sister ....Gen 20:11-13
Represented as Abram's sister ....Gen 12:10-20
Barren ....Gen 11:30
Gave Abram her maid ...Gen 16:1-3
Promised a son..........Gen 17:15-21; Rom 9:9
Gave birth to Isaac ......Gen 21:1-8

[*also* sarah's, sarai's]
Abram took *S* his wife ....Gen 12:5
S said unto Abram, My ....Gen 16:5
Abram said unto *S*, Behold ...Gen 16:6
when *S* dealt hardly with......Gen 16:6
he said, Hagar, *S* maid ....Gen 16:8
face of my mistress *S* ....Gen 16:8
into the tent unto *S*, and......Gen 18:6
Where is *S* thy wife? ....Gen 18:9
lo, *S* thy wife shall have ......Gen 18:10
S heard it in the tent ....Gen 18:10
Abraham and *S* were old .....Gen 18:11
with *S* after the manner.......Gen 18:11
S laughed within herself.......Gen 18:12
Wherefore did *S* laugh ....Gen 18:13
and *S* shall have a son ....Gen 18:14
S denied, saying, I ....Gen 18:15
Abraham said of *S* his ....Gen 20:2
king..sent, and took *S* ....Gen 20:2
restored him *S* his wife ....Gen 20:14
unto *S* he said, Behold.......Gen 20:16
of *S* Abraham's wife ....Gen 20:18
And *S* saw the son of.........Gen 21:9
in all that *S* hath said ....Gen 21:12
S was an hundred and ....Gen 23:1
years of the life of *S*..........Gen 23:1
S died in Kirjath-arba........Gen 23:2
came to mourn for *S* ....Gen 23:2
Abraham buried *S* his wife ....Gen 23:19
S my master's wife bare.......Gen 24:36
into his mother *S* tent ....Gen 24:67
Abraham buried, and *S* ....Gen 25:10
S handmaid, bare unto........Gen 25:12
buried Abraham and *S*.........Gen 49:31
daughter of Asher was *S* ......Num 26:46
unto *S* that bare you..........Is 51:2
the deadness of *S* womb ......Rom 4:19
S herself received.............Heb 11:11
as *S* obeyed Abraham 1Pet 3:6

SARAPH (sā'răf)—*"burning"*
Descendant of Judah 1Chr 4:22

SARCASM—*ridicule; mocking*

Purposes of, to:
Recall injustice ....Judg 9:7-19
Remind of duty neglected.1Sam 26:15
Mock idolaters 1Kin 18:27
Deflate pride............1Kin 20:10, 11
Warn of defeat 2Kin 14:8-12

Uttered by:
Friend ....Job 11:2-12
Enemies ....Neh 4:2, 3
Persecutors ....Matt 27:28, 29
Apostle ....Acts 23:1-5
God ....Jer 25:27

SARDINE—*a stone of translucent orange-red quartz*
a jasper and a *s* stone ....Rev 4:3

SARDIS (sär'dĭs)—*"prince of joy"—the chief city of Lydia in Asia Minor*
One of the seven churches ....Rev 1:11
of the church in *S* write ....Rev 3:1
a few names even in *S* ....Rev 3:4

SARDITES (sär'dīts)
Descendants of Sered ....Num 26:26

SARDIUS—*a precious stone*
Used in "breastplate" ....Ex 28:15-17
In the garden of Eden ...Ezek 28:13
Worn by Priest ....Ex 28:17

sardonyx; the sixth, *s* ....Rev 21:20

SARDONYX—*a precious stone*
In John's vision ....Rev 21:19, 20

SAREPTA (sä-rĕp'tä)—*a city located midway between Tyre and Sidon*
unto *S*, a city of Sidon ....Luke 4:26
See Zarephath

SARGON (sär'gŏn)—*"(the god) Sargon has established the king(ship)"*
King of Assyria ....Is 20:1

SARID (sā'rĭd)—*"survivor"*
Village of Zebulun ......Josh 19:10, 12

SARON (sā'rŏn)—*the Greek form of Sharon*
Inhabitants turn to the Lord ....Acts 9:35

SARSECHIM (sär'sĕ-kĭm)—*"chief of the eunuchs"*
Prince of Nebuchadnezzar.Jer 39:3

SARUCH (sā'rŭk)—*See* Serug

SAT, SATEST—*See* Sit

SATAN (sā'tăn)—*"adversary"*

Names of:
See Devil

Designs of, to:
Undo God's work ....Mark 4:15
Make men turn away from God.............Job 2:4, 5
Instigate evil ....John 13:2, 27
Secure men's worship ....Luke 4:6-8; 2Thess 2:3, 4

Character of:
Deceiver................Rev 12:9
Father of lies ....John 8:44
Adversary 1Pet 5:9

Methods of:
Disguises himself 2Cor 11:14
Insinuates doubt.........Gen 3:1
Misuses Scripture ....Matt 4:6
Uses schemes 2Cor 2:11
Afflicts believers ....Luke 13:16

Judgment upon:
Bound..................Mark 3:27
Cast out ....John 12:31
Judged ....John 16:11
Bruised.................Rom 16:20
Assigned to hell ....Matt 25:41

[*also* satan's]
S stood up against Israel 1Chr 21:1
and *S* came also among ....Job 1:6
unto *S*, Whence comest ....Job 1:7
S answered the Lord..........Job 1:7
S answered the Lord..........Job 1:9
Lord said unto *S*, Behold .....Job 1:12
S went forth from the.........Job 1:12
Lord said unto *S*, From ....Job 2:2
S answered the Lord..........Job 2:2
the Lord said unto *S*..........Job 2:3
Lord said unto *S*, Behold .....Job 2:6
went *S* forth from the.........Job 2:7
let *S* stand at his right ....Ps 109:6
S standing at his right.........Zech 3:1
the Lord said unto *S*..........Zech 3:2
Lord rebuke thee, O *S*........Zech 3:2
Get thee hence, *S* ....Matt 4:10
And if *S* cast out *S*, he ....Matt 12:26
Get thee behind me, *S*........Matt 16:23
forty days, tempted of *S* ......Mark 1:13
How can *S* cast out *S*? ....Mark 3:23
S rise up against himself ......Mark 3:26
Get thee behind me, *S* ....Mark 8:33
I beheld *S* as lightning ....Luke 10:18
S also be divided against ......Luke 11:18
entered *S* into Judas ....Luke 22:3

S hath desired to have ....Luke 22:31
why hath *S* filled thine ....Acts 5:3
from the power of *S* unto .....Acts 26:18
deliver such a one unto *S* 1Cor 5:5
that *S* tempt you not for 1Cor 7:5
the messenger of *S* to 2Cor 12:7
but *S* hindered us 1Thess 2:18
after the working of *S* 2Thess 2:9
I have delivered unto *S* 1Tim 1:20
turned aside after *S*..........1Tim 5:15
are the synagogue of *S*.........Rev 2:9
dwellest, even where *S* seat ...Rev 2:13
you, where *S* dwelleth ....Rev 2:13
known the depths of *S*.........Rev 2:24
of the synagogue of *S*.........Rev 3:9
which is the Devil, and *S* .....Rev 20:2
S shall be loosed out of ....Rev 20:7

SATIATE—*to satisfy fully or to excess*
Scorners and fools shall be..................Prov 1:22, 31
The sword shall be ......Jer 46:10

[*also* SATIATED]
s the soul of the priests ....Jer 31:14
I have *s* the weary soul ....Jer 31:25

SATIRE—*wit, irony, or sarcasm used to expose and discredit vice or folly*
Jesus' devastating use of. .Matt 23:1-33

SATISFACTION—*that which completely fulfills*

Of physical things:
Sexual pleasures ....Prov 5:19
Bread of heaven.........Ps 105:40
Long life ....Ps 91:16

Of spiritual things, God's:
Mercy ....Ps 90:14
Presence ....Ps 17:15

Of things empty of:
Labor ....Is 55:2
Sinful ways ....Ezek 16:28, 29
Persecution ....Job 19:22

no *s* for the life..murderer ....Num 35:31
no *s* for him that is fled.......Num 35:32

SATISFY—*gratify to the fullest*

[*also* SATISFIED, SATISFIEST, SATISFIETH, SATISFYING]
my lust shall be *s* upon ....Ex 15:9
shall eat, and not be *s* ....Lev 26:26
and shall eat and be *s* ....Deut 14:29
O Naphtali, *s* with favor ......Deut 33:23
shall not be *s* with bread ......Job 27:14
his flesh! We cannot be *s* .....Job 31:31
s the desolate and waste ......Job 38:27
meek shall eat and be *s* ....Ps 22:26
shall be abundantly *s* ....Ps 36:8
famine they shall be *s*.........Ps 37:19
My soul shall be *s* as with.....Ps 63:5
be *s* with the goodness of .....Ps 65:4
rock should I have *s* thee .....Ps 81:16
s thy mouth with good ....Ps 103:5
is *s* with the fruit of thy.......Ps 104:13
he *s* the longing soul..........Ps 107:9
I will *s* her poor with ....Ps 132:15
s the desire of every ....Ps 145:16
if he steal to *s* his soul........Prov 6:30
tilleth his land shall be *s* ......Prov 12:11
eateth to the *s* of his soul .....Prov 13:25
good man shall be *s* from .....Prov 14:14
hath it shall abide *s*..........Prov 19:23
A man's belly shall be *s*.......Prov 18:20
eyes of man are never *s*.......Prov 27:20
things that are never *s* ....Prov 30:15
eye is not *s* with seeing ....Eccl 1:8
neither is his eye *s* with ....Eccl 4:8
loveth silver shall not be *s* ....Eccl 5:10
and they shall not be *s*........Is 9:20
his soul, and shall be *s*........Is 53:11
labor for that which *s* not? ....Is 55:2
and *s* the afflicted soul........Is 58:10
my people shall be *s* with .....Jer 31:14
his soul shall be *s* upon ....Jer 50:19
to be *s* with bread ....Lam 5:6

shall not *s* their souls ....Ezek 7:19
ye shall be *s* therewith ....Joel 2:19
water; but they were not *s* ....Amos 4:8
shalt eat, but not be *s* ....Mic 6:14
death, and cannot be *s*........Hab 2:5
can a man *s* these men........Mark 8:4
to the *s* of the flesh ....Col 2:23

SATRAP (sā'trăp)—*"protector of the land"*
Officials appointed over the kingdom ....Dan 6:1

SATYR—*"he-goat; hairy one"*—*Greek mythological figure*
Objects of worship ("devils") 2Chr 11:15

[*also* SATYRS]
and *s* shall dance there........Is 13:21
s shall cry to his fellow ....Is 34:14

SAUL (sôl)—*"asked"*—*the first king of Israel*
Son of Kish; first king of Israel.................1Sam 9:1, 2
Seeks his father's asses...1Sam 9:3-14
Meets Samuel 1Sam 9:16-27
Anointed as king 1Sam 10:1-16
Victories and family 1Sam 14:47-52
Fights against Philistines; becomes jealous of David 1Sam 17:1-58; 1Sam 18:6-13
Promises his daughter to David 1Sam 18:14-30
Seeks to murder David ..1Sam 19:1-24
Pursues David...........1Sam 23:1-28
His life spared by David .1Sam 26:1-25
Defeated, commits suicide 1Sam 31:1-6
Burial of................1Sam 31:7-13
David's lament over 2Sam 1:17-27
Sin of, exposed..........2Sam 21:1-9

[*also* SAUL'S]
And *S* died, and ....Gen 36:38
asses of Kish *S* father 1Sam 9:3
a day before *S* came 1Sam 9:15
S uncle said unto him.........1Sam 10:14
S uncle said, Tell me, I 1Sam 10:15
S the son of Kish was.........1Sam 10:21
S also went home to 1Sam 10:26
messengers to Gibeah of *S* 1Sam 11:4
S came after the herd.........1Sam 11:5
S said, What aileth the........1Sam 11:5
Spirit of God came upon *S*....1Sam 11:6
cometh not forth after *S* 1Sam 11:7
that *S* put the people in.......1Sam 11:11
Shall *S* reign over us?.........1Sam 11:12
S said, There shalt not........1Sam 11:13
made *S* king before the 1Sam 11:15
there *S* and all the men 1Sam 11:15
S reigned one year 1Sam 13:1
S chose him three thousand ...1Sam 13:2
two thousand were with *S*.....1Sam 13:2
S blew the trumpet 1Sam 13:3
S had smitten a garrison 1Sam 13:4
together after *S* to Gilgal 1Sam 13:4
As for *S*, he was yet in 1Sam 13:7
And *S* said, Bring hither 1Sam 13:9
S went out to meet him 1Sam 13:10
S said, Because I saw 1Sam 13:11
Samuel said to *S*, Thou 1Sam 13:13
S numbered the people 1Sam 13:15
S, and Jonathan his son 1Sam 13:16
people that were with *S*.......1Sam 13:22
S and with Jonathan 1Sam 13:22
Jonathan the son of *S*.........1Sam 14:1
S tarried in the uttermost 1Sam 14:2
watchmen of *S* in Gibeah 1Sam 14:16
said *S* unto the people 1Sam 14:17
S said unto Ahiah, Bring......1Sam 14:18
S talked unto the priest 1Sam 14:19
S said unto the priest 1Sam 14:19
And *S* and all the people 1Sam 14:20
Israelites that were with *S*.....1Sam 14:21
S had adjured the people 1Sam 14:24
Then they told *S*, saying 1Sam 14:33
S said, Disperse yourselves 1Sam 14:34
S built an altar unto the 1Sam 14:35

S said, Let us go down 1Sam 14:36
S asked counsel of God 1Sam 14:37
S said, Draw ye near 1Sam 14:38
the people said unto *S*, Do....1Sam 14:40
S said unto the Lord God 1Sam 14:41
S and Jonathan were taken....1Sam 14:41
S said, Cast lots between......1Sam 14:42
S said to Jonathan, Tell 1Sam 14:43
S answered, God do so and ...1Sam 14:44
people said unto *S*, Shall......1Sam 14:45
Then *S* went up from 1Sam 14:46
of *S* wife was Ahinoam 1Sam 14:50
the son of Ner, *S* uncle 1Sam 14:50
Samuel also said unto *S*.......1Sam 15:1
S gathered the people.........1Sam 15:4
S came to a city of Amalek ...1Sam 15:5
And *S* said unto the Kenites ..1Sam 15:6
S smote the Amalekites 1Sam 15:7
S and the people spared 1Sam 15:9
me that I have set up *S* 1Sam 15:11
rose early to meet *S* in........1Sam 15:12
Samuel, saying, *S* came to 1Sam 15:12
Samuel came to *S*: and *S* 1Sam 15:13
S said, They have brought 1Sam 15:15
Samuel said unto *S*, Stay......1Sam 15:16
S said unto Samuel, Yea, I....1Sam 15:20
S said unto Samuel, I have 1Sam 15:24
And Samuel said unto *S*, I 1Sam 15:26
turned again after *S* 1Sam 15:31
S worshiped the Lord 1Sam 15:31
S went up to his house........1Sam 15:34
his house to Gibeah of *S*......1Sam 15:34
came no more to see *S* 1Sam 15:35
Samuel mourned for *S* 1Sam 15:35
that he had made *S* king 1Sam 15:35
wilt thou mourn for *S*.........1Sam 16:1
S hear it, he will kill me 1Sam 16:2
the Lord departed from *S* 1Sam 16:14
S servants said unto him 1Sam 16:15
S said unto his servants 1Sam 16:17
S sent messengers unto 1Sam 16:19
by David his son unto *S* 1Sam 16:20
And David came to *S*, and 1Sam 16:21
S sent to Jesse, saying 1Sam 16:22
from God was upon *S* 1Sam 16:23
so *S* was refreshed, and 1Sam 16:23
an end of speaking unto *S* 1Sam 18:1
S took him that day, and 1Sam 18:2
whithersoever *S* sent..........1Sam 18:5
S set him over the men of 1Sam 18:5
and also in the sight of *S* 1Sam 18:5
there was a javelin in *S* 1Sam 18:10
S daughter should have 1Sam 18:19
Michal *S* daughter loved 1Sam 18:20
S servants spake those 1Sam 18:23
that Michal *S* daughter........1Sam 18:28
Jonathan *S* son delighted......1Sam 19:2
he slipped away out of *S*......1Sam 19:10
and Abner sat by *S* side 1Sam 20:25
S spake not anything that 1Sam 20:26
and *S* said unto Jonathan 1Sam 20:27
And Jonathan answered *S*.....1Sam 20:28
Then *S* anger was kindled.....1Sam 20:30
Jonathan answered *S* his 1Sam 20:32
S cast a javelin at him to 1Sam 20:33
man of the servants of *S* 1Sam 21:7
herdmen that belonged to *S* ...1Sam 21:7
fled that day for fear of *S*.....1Sam 21:10
S hath slain his thousands 1Sam 21:11
S heard that David was 1Sam 22:6
S abode in Gibeah under 1Sam 22:6
S said unto his servants 1Sam 22:7
set over the servants of *S* 1Sam 22:9
And *S* said, Hear now 1Sam 22:12
And *S* said unto him, Why 1Sam 22:13
that *S* had slain the Lord's 1Sam 22:21
that he would surely tell *S* 1Sam 22:22
Jonathan *S* son arose, and 1Sam 23:16
S was returned from 1Sam 24:1
S took three thousand 1Sam 24:2
and *S* went in to cover his 1Sam 24:3
and cut off the skirt of *S*......1Sam 24:4
because he had cut off *S*......1Sam 24:5
them not to rise against *S*.....1Sam 24:7
S rose up out of the cave 1Sam 24:7

S

cried after *S*, saying, My ... 1Sam 24:8
when *S* looked behind him ... 1Sam 24:8
And David said to *S* ... 1Sam 24:9
these words unto *S* ... 1Sam 24:16
S said, Is this thy voice ... 1Sam 24:16
S lifted up his voice, and ... 1Sam 24:16
sware unto *S*. And *S* ... 1Sam 24:22
S had given Michal his ... 1Sam 25:44
the cruse of water from *S* ... 1Sam 26:12
one day by the hand of *S* ... 1Sam 27:1
S shall despair of me, to ... 1Sam 27:1
S that David was fled to ... 1Sam 27:4
And *S* had put away those ... 1Sam 28:3
and *S* gathered all Israel ... 1Sam 28:4
S saw the host of the ... 1Sam 28:5
S inquired of the Lord ... 1Sam 28:6
said *S* unto his servants ... 1Sam 28:7
S disguised himself, and ... 1Sam 28:8
thou knowest what *S* hath ... 1Sam 28:9
S sware to her by the Lord ... 1Sam 28:10
the woman spake to *S* ... 1Sam 28:12
deceived me? for thou art *S* ... 1Sam 28:12
said unto *S*, I saw gods ... 1Sam 28:13
S perceived that it was ... 1Sam 28:14
Samuel said to *S*, Why ... 1Sam 28:15
S answered, I am sore ... 1Sam 28:15
S fell straightway all ... 1Sam 28:20
the woman came unto *S* ... 1Sam 28:21
she brought it before *S* ... 1Sam 28:25
David, the servant of *S* ... 1Sam 29:3
S slew his thousands, and ... 1Sam 29:5
and Melchi-shua, *S* sons ... 1Sam 31:2
pass after the death of *S* ... 2Sam 1:1
out of the camp from *S* ... 2Sam 1:2
S and Jonathan his son ... 2Sam 1:4
S and Jonathan his son ... 2Sam 1:5
S leaned upon his spear ... 2Sam 1:6
fasted until even, for *S* ... 2Sam 1:12
were they that buried *S* ... 2Sam 2:4
this kindness..unto *S* ... 2Sam 2:5
for your master *S* is dead ... 2Sam 2:7
But Abner..captain of *S* ... 2Sam 2:8
Ish-bosheth the son of *S* ... 2Sam 2:8
Ish-bosheth *S* son was ... 2Sam 2:10
Ish-bosheth the son of *S* ... 2Sam 2:12
Ish-bosheth the son of *S* ... 2Sam 2:15
war between the house of *S* ... 2Sam 3:1
the house of *S* waxed ... 2Sam 3:1
war between the house of *S* ... 2Sam 3:6
strong for the house of *S* ... 2Sam 3:6
S had a concubine, whose ... 2Sam 3:7
unto the house of *S* ... 2Sam 3:8
from the house of *S* ... 2Sam 3:10
bring Michal *S* daughter ... 2Sam 3:13
to Ish-bosheth *S* son ... 2Sam 3:14
S son heard that Abner ... 2Sam 4:1
And *S* son had two men ... 2Sam 4:2
Jonathan, *S* son, had a son ... 2Sam 4:4
came of *S* and Jonathan ... 2Sam 4:4
Ish-bosheth the son of *S* ... 2Sam 4:8
my lord..this day of *S* ... 2Sam 4:8
saying, Behold, *S* is dead ... 2Sam 4:10
when *S* was king over us ... 2Sam 5:2
Michal *S* daughter looked ... 2Sam 6:16
the daughter of *S* came out ... 2Sam 6:20
the daughter of *S* had no ... 2Sam 6:23
as I took it from *S*, whom ... 2Sam 7:15
is left of the house of *S* ... 2Sam 9:1
was of the house of *S* ... 2Sam 9:2
yet any of the house of *S* ... 2Sam 9:3
of Jonathan, the son of *S* ... 2Sam 9:6
thee all the land of *S* thy ... 2Sam 9:7
the king called to Ziba, *S* ... 2Sam 9:9
all that pertained to *S* ... 2Sam 9:9
thee out of the hand of *S* ... 2Sam 12:7
family of the house of *S* ... 2Sam 16:5
blood of the house of *S* ... 2Sam 16:8
servant of the house of *S* ... 2Sam 19:17
Mephibosheth son of *S* ... 2Sam 19:24
the concubine of *S* ... 2Sam 21:11
and took the bones of *S* ... 2Sam 21:12
Philistines had slain *S* in ... 2Sam 21:12
thence the bones of *S* and ... 2Sam 21:13
bones of *S* and Jonathan ... 2Sam 21:14
and out of the hand of *S* ... 2Sam 22:1
days of *S* they made war ... 1Chr 5:10
Kish, and Kish begat *S* ... 1Chr 8:33
and *S* begat Jonathan ... 1Chr 8:33
Kish; and Kish begat *S* ... 1Chr 9:39
and *S* begat Jonathan ... 1Chr 9:39
followed hard after *S* ... 1Chr 10:2
Malchi-shua, the sons of *S* ... 1Chr 10:2
battle went sore against *S* ... 1Chr 10:3
said *S* to his armor-bearer ... 1Chr 10:4
S took a sword, and fell ... 1Chr 10:4
armor-bearer saw that *S* ... 1Chr 10:5
So *S* died, and his three ... 1Chr 10:6
and that *S* and his sons ... 1Chr 10:7
they found *S* and his sons ... 1Chr 10:8
Philistines had done to *S* ... 1Chr 10:11
took away the body of *S* ... 1Chr 10:12
So *S* died for his ... 1Chr 10:13
even when *S* was king ... 1Chr 11:2
himself close because of *S* ... 1Chr 12:1
S brethren of Benjamin ... 1Chr 12:2
the Philistines against *S* ... 1Chr 12:19
will fall to his master *S* ... 1Chr 12:19
to turn the kingdom of *S* ... 1Chr 12:23
Benjamin, the kindred of *S* ... 1Chr 12:29
ward of the house of *S* ... 1Chr 12:29
not at it in the days of *S* ... 1Chr 13:3
Michal the daughter of *S* ... 1Chr 15:29
and *S* the son of Kish ... 1Chr 26:28
and from the hand of *S* ... Ps 18:*title*
Gibeah of *S* is fled ... Is 10:29

SAUL (sôl)—*"asked"—the original name of the Apostle Paul*

whose name was *S* ... Acts 7:58
S was consenting unto his ... Acts 8:1
As for *S*, he made havoc ... Acts 8:3
S, yet breathing out ... Acts 9:1
S, *S*, why persecutest ... Acts 9:4
S arose from the earth ... Acts 9:8
of Judas for one called *S* ... Acts 9:11
Brother *S*, the Lord, even ... Acts 9:17
S certain days with the ... Acts 9:19
S increased the more in ... Acts 9:22
await was known of *S* ... Acts 9:24
S was come to Jerusalem ... Acts 9:26
to Tarsus, for to seek *S* ... Acts 11:25
hands of Barnabas and *S* ... Acts 11:30
S returned from Jerusalem ... Acts 12:25
Herod the tetrarch and *S* ... Acts 13:1
Separate me Barnabas and *S* ... Acts 13:2
called for Barnabas and *S* ... Acts 13:7
S, who also is called ... Acts 13:9
gave unto them *S* the son ... Acts 13:21
S, *S*, why persecutest ... Acts 22:7
me, Brother *S*, receive thy ... Acts 22:13
S, *S*, why persecutest ... Acts 26:14

SAVE—*to bring into a state of well-being; except*

[*also* SAVED, SAVEST, SAVETH, SAVING]

but they will *s* thee alive ... Gen 12:12
unto me in *s* my life ... Gen 19:19
s the bread which he ... Gen 39:6
to *s* your lives by a great ... Gen 45:7
Thou hast *s* our lives ... Gen 47:25
to *s* much people alive ... Gen 50:20
but *s* the men children ... Ex 1:17
daughter ye shall *s* alive ... Ex 1:22
Lord *s* Israel that day ... Ex 14:30
any god, *s* unto the Lord ... Ex 22:20
be *s* from your enemies ... Num 10:9
s Caleb the son of ... Num 14:30
Have ye *s* all the women ... Num 31:15
S Caleb the son of ... Num 32:12
S Caleb the son of ... Deut 1:36
your enemies, to *s* you ... Deut 20:4
there was none to *s* her ... Deut 22:27
and no man shall *s* thee ... Deut 28:29
O people *s* by the Lord ... Deut 33:29
ye will *s* alive my father ... Josh 2:13
Joshua *s* Rahab the harlot ... Josh 6:25
none of them, *s* Hazor ... Josh 11:13
in the land, *s* cities to ... Josh 14:4
shalt *s* Israel from the ... Judg 6:14
shall I *s* Israel? ... Judg 6:15
Baal? will ye *s* him? ... Judg 6:31
own hand hath *s* me ... Judg 7:2
that lapped will I *s* you ... Judg 7:7
which they had *s* alive ... Judg 21:14
it may *s* us out of the ... 1Sam 4:3
he may *s* my people out ... 1Sam 9:16
s you out of all your ... 1Sam 10:19
and said, God *s* the king ... 1Sam 10:24
How shall this man *s* us? ... 1Sam 10:27
restraint to the Lord to *s* ... 1Sam 14:6
So the Lord *s* Israel that ... 1Sam 14:23
liveth, which *s* Israel ... 1Sam 14:39
for there is no other *s* ... 1Sam 21:9
David *s* the inhabitants ... 1Sam 23:5
s four hundred young men ... 1Sam 30:17
s to every man his wife ... 1Sam 30:22
David I will *s* my people ... 2Sam 3:18
God *s* the king, God *s* ... 2Sam 16:16
this day have *s* thy life ... 2Sam 19:5
thou *s* me from violence ... 2Sam 22:3
be *s* from mine enemies ... 2Sam 22:4
who is God, *s* the Lord? ... 2Sam 22:32
who is a rock, *s* our God? ... 2Sam 22:32
but there was none to *s* ... 2Sam 22:42
thou mayest *s* thine own ... 1Kin 1:12
God *s* king Solomon ... 1Kin 1:34
s we two in the house ... 1Kin 3:18
s only in the matter of ... 1Kin 15:5
he will *s* thy life ... 1Kin 20:31
and *s* himself there, not ... 2Kin 6:10
if they *s* us alive, we ... 2Kin 7:4
S that the high places ... 2Kin 15:4
s thou us out of his hand ... 2Kin 19:19
s the poorest sort of the ... 2Kin 24:14
s them by a great ... 1Chr 11:14
ye, *S* us, O God of our ... 1Chr 16:35
s only to burn sacrifice ... 2Chr 2:6
s only with the king of ... 2Chr 18:30
said, God *s* the king ... 2Chr 23:11
Thus the Lord *s* Hezekiah ... 2Chr 32:22
s the beast that I rode ... Neh 2:12
s that every one put them ... Neh 4:23
s them out of the hand ... Neh 9:27
thine hand; but *s* his life ... Job 2:6
he *s* the poor from the ... Job 5:15
he shall *s* the humble ... Job 22:29
how *s* thou the arm that ... Job 26:2
s me, O my God: for thou ... Ps 3:7
oh *s* me for thy mercies' ... Ps 6:4
s me from all them that ... Ps 7:1
God, which *s* the upright ... Ps 7:10
O thou that *s* by thy ... Ps 17:7
be *s* from mine enemies ... Ps 18:3
thou wilt *s* the afflicted ... Ps 18:27
who is God *s* the Lord ... Ps 18:31
who is a rock *s* our God? ... Ps 18:31
the Lord *s* his anointed ... Ps 20:6
s strength of his right ... Ps 20:6
S, Lord: let the king ... Ps 20:9
S thy people, and bless ... Ps 28:9
s me for thy mercies' ... Ps 31:16
is no king *s* by the ... Ps 33:16
s him out of all his troubles ... Ps 34:6
s such as be of a contrite ... Ps 34:18
did their own arm *s* them ... Ps 44:3
thou hast *s* us from our ... Ps 44:7
s me, O God, by thy ... Ps 54:1
and the Lord will *s* me ... Ps 55:16
s me from the reproach ... Ps 57:3
s me from bloody men ... Ps 59:2
s with thy right hand, and ... Ps 60:5
thy *s* health among all ... Ps 67:2
s me, O God; for the ... Ps 69:1
For God will *s* Zion, and ... Ps 69:35
commandment to *s* me ... Ps 71:3
he shall *s* the children of ... Ps 72:4
s the souls of the needy ... Ps 72:13
to *s* all the meek of the ... Ps 76:9
and come and *s* us ... Ps 80:2
shine; and we shall be *s* ... Ps 80:3
shine; and we shall be *s* ... Ps 80:7
s thy servant that ... Ps 86:2
and *s* the son of ... Ps 86:16
he *s* them for his name's ... Ps 106:8
he *s* them out of their ... Ps 107:13

s with thy right hand ....Ps 108:6
O *s* me according to thy ......Ps 109:26
to *s* him from those that ......Ps 109:31
I am thine, *s* me; for I........Ps 119:94
right hand shall *s* me ....Ps 138:7
hear their cry, and will *s* ......Ps 145:19
and he shall *s* thee ....Prov 20:22
walketh uprightly shall be *s* ...Prov 28:18
s the beholding of them.......Eccl 5:11
for him, and he will *s* us ......Is 25:9
and rest shall ye be *s* ....Is 30:15
he will come and *s* you ....Is 35:4
defend this city to *s* it ....Is 37:35
But Israel shall be *s* in........Is 45:17
unto a god that cannot *s* ......Is 45:20
s thee from these things.......Is 47:13
and I will *s* thy children.......Is 49:25
righteousness, mighty to *s* .....Is 63:1
angel of his presence *s* ....Is 63:9
will say, Arise, and *s* us.......Jer 2:27
that thou mayest be *s*.........Jer 4:14
shall not *s* them at all in ......Jer 11:12
I am with thee to *s* thee ......Jer 15:20
save me, and I shall be *s*......Jer 17:14
he shall be *s* out of it.........Jer 30:7
I will *s* thee from afar ....Jer 30:10
s thy people, the remnant .....Jer 31:7
I will *s* thee from afar ....Jer 46:27
nation that could not *s* us .....Lam 4:17
wicked way, to *s* his life ......Ezek 3:18
to *s* the souls alive that ....Ezek 13:19
will I *s* my flock, and ....Ezek 34:22
but I will *s* them out of ....Ezek 37:23
s of thee, O king, he shall ....Dan 6:7
will *s* them by the Lord ....Hos 1:7
s thee in all thy cities? ....Hos 13:10
s that I will not..destroy ......Amos 9:8
and thou wilt not *s* ....Hab 1:2
he will *s*, he will rejoice.......Zeph 3:17
I will *s* my people from ....Zech 8:7
their God shall *s* them in .....Zech 9:16
Lord also shall *s* the tents .....Zech 12:7
shall *s* his people from ....Matt 1:21
him, saying, Lord, *s* us ....Matt 8:25
to the end shall be *s*..........Matt 10:22
the Father, *s* the Son ....Matt 11:27
cried, saying, Lord, *s* me.......Matt 14:30
will *s* his life shall lose ....Matt 16:25
they saw no man, *s* Jesus .....Matt 17:8
to *s* that which was lost ....Matt 18:11
saying, *s* they to whom it .....Matt 19:11
end, the same shall be *s* ......Matt 24:13
there should no flesh be *s* .....Matt 24:22
in three days, *s* thyself ....Matt 27:40
He *s* others; himself he ....Matt 27:42
himself he cannot *s* ....Matt 27:42
to *s* life, or to kill? ....Mark 3:4
s that he laid his hands ....Mark 6:5
whosoever will *s* his life ....Mark 8:35
the same shall *s* it ....Mark 8:35
saw no man any more, *s* Jesus .Mark 9:8
Who then can be *s*? ....Mark 10:26
the same shall be *s* ....Mark 13:13
no flesh should be *s* ....Mark 13:20
S thyself, and come down .....Mark 15:30
He *s* others; himself he ....Mark 15:31
is baptized shall be *s*..........Mark 16:16
we should be *s* from our ......Luke 1:71
s unto Sarepta, a city of ......Luke 4:26
cleansed, *s* Naaman...........Luke 4:27
s life, or to destroy it? ....Luke 6:9
Thy faith hath *s* thee; go ......Luke 7:50
no man to go in, *s* Peter ......Luke 8:51
whosoever will *s* his life ....Luke 9:24
the same shall *s* it ....Luke 9:24
lives, but to *s* them ....Luke 9:56
are there few that be *s*? ....Luke 13:23
to God, *s* this stranger ....Luke 17:18
shall seek to *s* his life ....Luke 17:33
none is good, *s* one, that......Luke 18:19
Who then can be *s*? ....Luke 18:26
thy faith hath *s* thee ....Luke 18:42
seek and to *s* that which ......Luke 19:10
He *s* others; let him *s* himself. .Luke 23:35
thou be Christ, *s* thyself ......Luke 23:39
through him might be *s* ....John 3:17
that ye might be *s* ....John 5:34
s that one whereinto his ......John 6:22
enter in, he shall be *s*.........John 10:9
Father, *s* me from this ....John 12:27
world, but to *s* the world .....John 12:47
needeth not *s* to wash his .....John 13:10
of the Lord shall be *s*.........Acts 2:21
S youselves from this ....Acts 2:40
such as should be *s* ....Acts 2:47
whereby we must be *s* ....Acts 4:12
Moses, ye cannot be *s* ....Acts 15:1
Christ we shall be *s*...........Acts 15:11
what must I do to be *s*?.......Acts 16:30
thou shalt be *s*, and thy.......Acts 16:31
s only that they keep ....Acts 21:25
hope that we should be *s* .....Acts 27:20
willing to *s* Paul ....Acts 27:43
shall be *s* from wrath ....Rom 5:9
we shall be *s* by his life ....Rom 5:10
For we are *s* by hope ....Rom 8:24
a remnant shall be *s* ....Rom 9:27
that they might be *s* ....Rom 10:1
of the Lord shall be *s*.........Rom 10:13
flesh, and might *s* some ....Rom 11:14
so all Israel shall be *s*.........Rom 11:26
unto us which are *s* it is.......1Cor 1:18
preaching to *s* them that 1Cor 1:21
s the spirit of man which 1Cor 2:11
but he himself shall be *s* 1Cor 3:15
the spirit may be *s* in the 1Cor 5:5
thou shalt *s* thy husband 1Cor 7:16
thou shalt *s* thy wife 1Cor 7:16
by all means *s* some 1Cor 9:22
that they may be *s* 1Cor 10:33
By which also ye are *s* 1Cor 15:2
in them that are *s*, and 2Cor 2:15
forty stripes *s* one 2Cor 11:24
none, *s* James the Lord's......Gal 1:19
by grace ye are *s* ....Eph 2:5
grace are ye *s* through ....Eph 2:8
that they might be *s* 1Thess 2:16
that they might be *s* 2Thess 2:10
into the world to *s* sinners 1Tim 1:15
will have all men to be *s* 1Tim 2:4
she shall be *s* in 1Tim 2:15
thou shalt both *s* thyself 1Tim 4:16
hath *s* us, and called..........2Tim 1:9
to his mercy he *s* us ....Titus 3:5
that was able to *s* him ....Heb 5:7
also to *s* them to the ....Heb 7:25
that believe to the *s* of........Heb 10:39
is able to *s* your souls.........James 1:21
works? can faith *s* him ....James 2:14
who is able to *s* and to ....James 4:12
prayer..shall *s* the sick ....James 5:15
his way shall *s* a soul ....James 5:20
souls were *s* by water 1Pet 3:20
baptism doth also now *s* 1Pet 3:21
righteous scarcely be *s* 1Pet 4:18
but *s* Noah the eighth.........2Pet 2:5
s the people out of the........Jude 5
others *s* with fear ....Jude 23
knoweth *s* he that ....Rev 2:17
s he that had the mark........Rev 13:17
s shall walk in the light ....Rev 21:24

SAVIOR—*one who brings salvation*

Applied to:
God ....Ps 106:21
Christ 2Tim 1:10

[*also* SAVIORS]

and my refuge, my *s*..........2Sam 22:3
the Lord gave Israel a *s*.........2Kin 13:5
thou gavest them *s*, who ......Neh 9:27
he shall send them a *s*, and ...Is 19:20
beside me there is no *s* ....Is 43:11
a just God and a *S*; there .....Is 45:21
I the Lord am thy *S* ....Is 60:16
the *S* thereof in time of ....Jer 14:8
there is no *s* beside me ....Hos 13:4
s shall come..on mount Zion ..Obad 21
hath rejoiced in God my *S* ....Luke 1:47
in the city of David a *S* ....Luke 2:11
the Christ, the *S* of the ....John 4:42
raised unto Israel a *S* ....Acts 13:23
he is the *s* of the body ....Eph 5:23
look for the *S*, the Lord ......Phil 3:20
commandment of God our *S* ..1Tim 1:1
in the sight of God our *S* 1Tim 2:3
commandment of God our *S* ..Titus 1:3
the doctrine of God our *S*.....Titus 2:10
great God and our *S* Jesus ....Titus 2:13
and love of God our *S* ....Titus 3:4
of God and our *S* Jesus 2Pet 1:1
of the Lord and *S* 2Pet 2:20
of our Lord and *S* 2Pet 3:18
To the only wise God our *S* ...Jude 25

SAVIOR, JESUS—*Jesus as the one who brings salvation*

Characteristics of:
Only ....Acts 4:10, 12
Complete ....Col 2:10
Powerful ....Jude 24
Authoritative............John 10:18
Universal 1Tim 4:10

Announcement of, by:
Prophets ....Is 42:6, 7
Angels ....Matt 1:20, 21
John the Baptist.........John 1:29
Christ ....John 12:44-50
Peter ....Acts 5:31
Paul 1Tim 1:15
John 1John 4:14

Office of, involves His:
Becoming man ....Heb 2:14
Perfect righteousness.....Heb 5:8, 9
Perfect obedience ....Rom 5:19, 20
Dying for us 1Pet 1:18-20

Saves us from:
Wrath ....Rom 5:9
Sin ....John 1:29
Death ....John 11:25, 26

SAVOR—*a particular smell or flavor; to enjoy*

[*also* SAVOREST, SAVORS, SAVORY]

Lord smelled a sweet *s*........Gen 8:21
make me *s* meat, such as I ....Gen 27:4
I will make them *s* meat for ...Gen 27:9
she gave the *s* meat and ......Gen 27:17
ye have made our *s* to be .....Ex 5:21
sweet *s* before the Lord ....Ex 29:25
of a sweet *s* unto the Lord ....Lev 1:9
of a sweet *s* unto the Lord ....Lev 2:9
of a sweet *s* unto the Lord ....Lev 3:5
a sweet *s* unto the Lord.......Lev 4:31
a sweet *s* unto the Lord.......Lev 6:21
consecrations for a sweet *s* ....Lev 8:28
the Lord for a sweet *s* ....Lev 23:13
smell the *s* of your sweet......Lev 26:31
a sweet *s* unto the Lord.......Num 15:3
of a sweet *s* unto the Lord ....Num 15:10
a sweet *s* unto the Lord.......Num 15:24
by fire, for a sweet *s* ....Num 28:2
of a sweet *s* unto the Lord ....Num 28:8
of a sweet *s* unto the Lord ....Num 28:24
for a sweet *s* unto the Lord ...Num 29:2
unto the Lord for a sweet *s* ...Num 29:8
of a sweet *s* unto the Lord ....Num 29:36
sweet *s* unto the God of ......Ezra 6:10
to send..a stinking *s* ....Eccl 10:1
s of thy good ointments ....Song 1:3
sweet *s* to all their idols.......Ezek 6:13
they made their sweet *s* ....Ezek 20:28
and his ill *s* shall come up.....Joel 2:20
if the salt have lost his *s* ......Matt 5:13
s not the things that be ....Matt 16:23
s not the things that be ....Mark 8:33
If the salt have lost his *s* .....Luke 14:34
the *s* of his knowledge 2Cor 2:14
God a sweet *s* of Christ.......2Cor 2:15
the *s* of death unto death 2Cor 2:16
God for a sweet-smelling *s* ....Eph 5:2

SAW, SAWEST—*See* SEE

SAW—*a tool used to cut hard material*
Stones 1Kin 7:9
Wood ....Is 10:15
For torture..............1Chr 20:3

S

[*also* SAWS]
and put them under *s*, and 2Sam 12:31

SAWED—*cut with a back-and-forth motion*

[*also* SAWN]
s with saws, within and 1Kin 7:9
stoned, they were *s* asunder ...Heb 11:37

SAY, SAYEST, SAYING—*See* INTRODUCTION

SCAB—*blemish; natural covering of a wound; sign of plague or disease*
Disqualifies an offering ..Lev 22:21, 22
Priest observes ....Lev 13:6-8
Israel threatened with ....Deut 28:27

[*also* SCABBED]
rising, a *s*, or bright spot ......Lev 13:2
or *s*, or hath his stones ....Lev 21:20
will smite with a *s* the ....Is 3:17

SCABBARD—*a sheath*
For God's Word.........Jer 47:6

SCAFFOLD—*a platform*
had made a brazen *s*, of 2Chr 6:13

SCALES—*instruments to measure weight*
weighed the mountains in *s*....Is 40:12

SCALES—*outer covering of a fish*
whatsoever hath fins and *s* ....Lev 11:9
hath no fins nor *s* in ....Lev 11:12
have fins and *s* shall ye eat ....Deut 14:9
His *s* are his pride, shut.......Job 41:15
fish..to stick unto thy *s* ....Ezek 29:4
fish..shall stick unto thy *s* .....Ezek 29:4
his eyes as it had been *s* ......Acts 9:18

SCALETH—*to climb*
wise man *s* the city of the .....Prov 21:22

SCALL—*a scabby disorder (as of the scalp)*
a dry *s*, even a leprosy ....Lev 13:30
look on the plague of the *s*....Lev 13:31
shut up him that hath..the *s*...Lev 13:31
behold, if the *s* spread not ....Lev 13:32
s be not in sight deeper ....Lev 13:32
the *s* shall he not shave ....Lev 13:33
shut up him that hath the *s* ...Lev 13:33
priest shall look on the *s* ......Lev 13:34
s be not spread in the skin .....Lev 13:34
s be spread in the skin ....Lev 13:36
But if the *s* be in his sight ....Lev 13:37
s is healed, he is clean ....Lev 13:37
of plague of leprosy, and *s* ....Lev 14:54

SCALP—*the part of the human head covered with hair*
hairy *s* of such a one as ....Ps 68:21

SCANDAL—*disgraceful conduct*
Priesthood 1Sam 2:22-24
Family...................2Sam 13:1-22

SCANT MEASURE—*a small amount of something*
Abomination ....Mic 6:10

SCAPEGOAT—*a goat which symbolically bears the sins of the people*
Bears sin away ....Lev 16:8-22
Typical of Christ ....Is 53:6, 11, 12

goat for the *s* shall wash ......Lev 16:26

SCARCE—*hardly; barely; a deficiency in quantity*

[*also* SCARCELY, SCARCENESS]
Jacob was yet *s* gone out......Gen 27:30
shalt eat bread without *s* ......Deut 8:9
s restrained they the ....Acts 14:18
s were come over against .....Acts 27:7
s for a righteous man will .....Rom 5:7
if the righteous *s* be saved 1Pet 4:18

SCAREST—*to frighten*
Then thou *s* me with dreams ..Job 7:14

SCARLET—*a brilliant crimson*

Literal uses of, for:
Tabernacle ....Ex 26:1, 31, 36
Identification............Gen 38:28, 30

Symbolic uses of:
Royalty.................Matt 27:28
Prosperity...............2Sam 1:24
Conquest ....Nah 2:3
Deep sin................Is 1:18

and *s*, and fine linen..........Ex 25:4
of blue, and purple, and *s*.....Ex 27:16
and *s*, and fine linen ....Ex 28:5
of blue, and purple, and *s*.....Ex 28:8
blue, and purple, and *s* ....Ex 35:6
blue, and purple, and *s* ....Ex 36:8
of blue, and purple, and *s*.....Ex 38:18
blue, and purple, and *s* ....Ex 39:1
cedar wood, and *s*, and ....Lev 14:4
cedar wood, and *s*, and ....Lev 14:49
hyssop, and with the *s* ....Lev 14:52
upon them a cloth of *s*........Num 4:8
shalt bind this line of *s*........Josh 2:18
are clothed with *s* ....Prov 31:21
lips are like a thread of *s* .....Song 4:3
that were brought up in *s* .....Lam 4:5
shall be clothed with *s* ....Dan 5:7
they clothed Daniel with *s* ....Dan 5:29
and *s* wool, and hyssop ....Heb 9:19
sit upon a *s* colored beast .....Rev 17:3
purple, and silk, and *s* ....Rev 18:12

SCATTER—*to disperse abroad*

Applied to:
Nations ....Gen 11:8, 9
Christians ....Acts 8:1, 4

Caused by:
Sin 1Kin 14:15, 16
Persecution ....Acts 11:19

[*also* SCATTERED, SCATTERETH, SCATTERING]
s abroad upon the face of .....Gen 11:4
in Jacob, and *s* them in ....Gen 49:7
people were *s* abroad ....Ex 5:12
s you among the heathen .....Lev 26:33
and let thine enemies be *s* ....Num 10:35
and *s* thou the fire yonder ....Num 16:37
s you among the nations ......Deut 4:27
the Lord thy God hath *s* ......Deut 30:3
said, I would *s* them into .....Deut 32:26
which remained were *s*.........1Sam 11:11
and the people were *s* from ...1Sam 13:8
the battle was there *s* over 2Sam 18:8
he sent out arrows, and *s* 2Sam 22:15
I saw all Israel *s* upon the.....1Kin 22:17
and all his army were *s* 2Kin 25:5
all Israel *s* upon the 2Chr 18:16
s you abroad among the ......Neh 1:8
certain people *s* abroad ....Esth 3:8
lion's whelps are *s* abroad ....Job 4:11
brimstone shall be *s* upon .....Job 18:15
he *s* his bright cloud ....Job 37:11
s the east wind upon the ......Job 38:24
sent out his arrows, and *s* .....Ps 18:14
and hast *s* us among the ......Ps 44:11
God hath *s* the bones of ......Ps 53:5
s them by thy power; and .....Ps 59:11
cast us off, thou hast *s*.........Ps 60:1
arise, let his enemies be *s* .....Ps 68:1
s thou the people that ....Ps 68:30
thou hast *s* thine enemies .....Ps 89:10
of iniquity shall be *s* ....Ps 92:9
and to *s* them in the lands ....Ps 106:27
Our bones are *s* at the ....Ps 141:7
Cast forth lightning, and *s*.....Ps 144:6
he *s* the hoar frost like........Ps 147:16
There is that *s*, and ye ....Prov 11:24
s away all evil with his ....Prov 20:8
to a nation *s* and peeled ......Is 18:2
s abroad the inhabitants.......Is 24:1
fitches, and *s* the cummin .....Is 28:25
s, and tempest, and...........Is 30:30
thyself the nations were *s* .....Is 33:3
and the whirlwind shall *s*......Is 41:16
hast *s* thy ways to the.........Jer 3:13
s them also among the ....Jer 9:16
all their flocks shall be *s* ......Jer 10:21
s them as with an east ....Jer 18:17
destroy and *s* the sheep ....Jer 23:1
Ye have *s* my flock, and ......Jer 23:2
nations whither I have *s* ......Jer 30:11
He that *s* Israel will ....Jer 31:10
unto thee should be *s*.........Jer 40:15
I will *s* into all winds them ....Jer 49:32
Israel is a *s* sheep; the ....Jer 50:17
and all his army was *s* ....Jer 52:8
third part thou shalt *s* in ......Ezek 5:2
s your bones..about your......Ezek 6:5
shall be *s* through the ....Ezek 6:8
and *s* them over the city ......Ezek 10:2
have *s* them among the ....Ezek 11:16
I will *s* toward every wind.....Ezek 12:14
shall be *s* toward all winds ....Ezek 17:21
would *s* them among the ......Ezek 20:23
countries wherein ye are *s*.....Ezek 20:34
I will *s* thee among the ....Ezek 22:15
among whom they are *s*.......Ezek 28:25
I will *s* the Egyptians ....Ezek 29:12
whither they were *s*...........Ezek 29:13
will *s* the Egyptians...........Ezek 30:23
And they were *s*, because .....Ezek 34:5
field, when they were *s* ....Ezek 34:5
And I *s* them among the ......Ezek 36:19
s every man from his ....Ezek 46:18
off his leaves, and *s* his ....Dan 4:14
he shall *s* among them the ....Dan 11:24
to *s* the power of the holy ....Dan 12:7
have *s* among the nations .....Joel 3:2
is *s* upon the mountains........Nah 3:18
mountains were *s*..............Hab 3:6
as a whirlwind to *s* me ....Hab 3:14
the horns which have *s*.........Zech 1:19
over the land of Judah to *s*....Zech 1:21
I *s* them with a whirlwind .....Zech 7:14
and the sheep shall be *s*.......Zech 13:7
were *s* abroad as sheep ....Matt 9:36
gathereth not with me *s*.......Matt 12:30
of the flock shall be *s*.........Matt 26:31
and the sheep shall be *s*.......Mark 14:27
s the proud in the ....Luke 1:51
gathereth not with me *s*.......Luke 11:23
them, and *s* the sheep ....John 10:12
children of God that were *s* ..John 11:52
come, that ye shall be *s*.......John 16:32
s, and brought to nought......Acts 5:36
twelve tribes which are *s*......James 1:1
strangers *s* throughout 1Pet 1:1

SCENT—*odor; fragrance*
through the *s* of water it ......Job 14:9
and his *s* is not changed.......Jer 48:11
s thereof shall be as the.......Hos 14:7

SCEPTER—*a royal staff*
Sign of authority ....Esth 4:11
Of Judah's tribe ....Gen 49:10
Promise concerning ......Num 24:17
Fulfilled in Christ........Heb 1:8

[*also* SCEPTERS]
out to Esther the golden *s* ....Esth 5:2
touched the top of the *s* ......Esth 5:2
golden *s* toward Esther ....Esth 8:4
of thy kingdom is a right *s* ....Ps 45:6
and the *s* of the rulers ....Is 14:5
strong rods for the *s* of ....Ezek 19:11
him that holdeth the *s* ....Amos 1:5
the *s* of Egypt shall depart ....Zech 10:11

SCEPTRE—*See* SCEPTER

SCEVA (sē'vä)—*"fitted"*
Jewish priest at Ephesus .Acts 19:14

SCHEMES OF SATAN—*the Devil's divisive plans*
Known by Christians.....2Cor 2:11
Warnings against 2Cor 11:3, 13-15
Armor provided against ..Eph 6:11
World falls before ....Rev 13:1-18

SCHIN (shīn)
Letter of the Hebrew alphabet ....Ps 119:161-168

SCHISM—*a division within the church*
Prohibition concerning ...1Cor 12:25

Translated "rent" and "division" ....Matt 9:16

SCHOLARS—*those who specialize in learning*
Numbered by David 1Chr25:1,7,8
God's judgment against ..Mal 2:12
Moses, an expert ....Acts 7:22
Gamaliel, famous as .....Acts 5:34

SCHOOL—*an institution of learning*
Home ....Deut 6:6-10
Temple 1Chr 25:7, 8
In Ephesus..............Acts 19:1, 9
Levites, teachers of......2Chr 17:7-9
Best subjects of ....Is 50:4

SCHOOLMASTER—*a tutor*
Applied to the Mosaic law...................Gal 3:24, 25

SCIENCE—*knowledge or understanding (modern understandings of science are more technical than the way the Bible uses the term)*
Implied reference to:
Architecture 2Chr 2:1-18
Astronomy..............Gen 15:5
Biology.................Ps 139:13-16
Carpentry...............Gen 6:14-16
Medicine ....Ps 103:3
Meteorology ....Job 38:22-38
Surveying ....Ezek 40:5, 6
Significance of, to:
Manifest God's existence .Ps 19:1-6
Prove God's prophecies ..Jer 25:12
Illustrate heaven's glory ..Rev 21:9-23
Point to Christ as source of...................Col 2:3

and understanding *s* ....Dan 1:4
oppositions of *s* falsely so 1Tim 6:20

SCOFF—*to mock*
they shall *s* at the kings ....Hab 1:10

SCOFFERS—*persons who show contempt of others*
come in the last days *s*........2Pet 3:3

SCORCH—*to parch or burn*
[*also* SCORCHED]
sun was up, they were *s*.......Matt 13:6
the sun was up, it was *s*.......Mark 4:6
him to *s* men with fire ....Rev 16:8
were *s* with great heat ....Rev 16:9

SCORN—*to reject with contempt; disdain; derision*
[*also* SCORNEST, SCORNETH, SCORNFUL, SCORNING]
thee, and laughed thee to *s* ...2Kin 19:21
but they laughed them to *s*....2Chr 30:10
they laughed us to *s* ....Neh 2:19
s to lay hands on Mordecai....Esth 3:6
man is laughed to *s*...........Job 12:4
My friends *s* me: but mine ....Job 16:20
innocent laugh them to *s*......Job 22:19
drinketh up *s* like water?......Job 34:7
He *s* the multitude of the .....Job 39:7
sitteth in the seat of the *s*.....Ps 1:1
that see me laugh me to *s*.....Ps 22:7
a *s* and a derision to them ....Ps 44:13
a *s* and derision to them ......Ps 79:4
s of those that are at ease.....Ps 123:4
Surely he *s* the scorners ....Prov 3:34
if thou *s*, thou alone shalt.....Prov 9:12
S men bring a city into a......Prov 29:8
the word of the Lord, ye *s*....Is 28:14
and laughed thee to *s*.........Is 37:22
harlot, in that thou *s* hire .....Ezek 16:31
thou shalt be laughed to *s*.....Ezek 23:32
princes shall be a *s* unto ......Hab 1:10
they laughed him to *s*.........Matt 9:24
and they laughed him to *s*.....Mark 5:40
they laughed him to *s*.........Luke 8:53

SCORNER—*one who shows arrogant disdain*
Classified among:
Fools ....Prov 1:22
Wicked ....Prov 9:7
Described as:
Unwilling to take rebuke .Prov 9:7, 8
Incorrigible ....Prov 15:12
Abomination ....Prov 24:9
[*also* SCORNERS]
s delight in their scorning .....Prov 1:22
but a *s* heareth not rebuke ....Prov 13:1
A *s* seeketh wisdom, and .....Prov 14:6
Smite a *s*, and the simple .....Prov 19:25
are prepared for *s* ....Prov 19:29
When the *s* is punished ....Prov 21:11
Cast out the *s*, and ....Prov 22:10
the *s* is consumed, and all.....Is 29:20
out his hand with *s* ....Hos 7:5

SCORPION—*an eight-legged creature having a poisonous tail*
Used literally of:
Desert creatures ....Deut 8:15
Poisonous creatures ......Luke 10:19
Used figuratively of:
Heavy burdens 1Kin 12:11
Agents of antichrist ......Rev 9:3, 5, 10
[*also* SCORPIONS]
I will chastise you with *s* 2Chr 10:11
thou dost dwell among *s* ......Ezek 2:6
egg, will he offer him a *s*? ....Luke 11:12

SCOURED—*scrubbed*
pot, it shall be both *s*.........Lev 6:28

SCOURGING—*whipping severely*
Objects of:
Christ ....John 19:1
Christians ....Matt 10:17
Paul....................Gal 6:17
Inflicted by:
Roman government ......Acts 22:25-29
[*also* SCOURGE, SCOURGED, SCOURGES, SCOURGETH, SCOURGINGS]
she shall be *s*; they shall ......Lev 19:20
s in your sides, and thorns ....Josh 23:13
from the *s* of the tongue ......Job 5:21
If the *s* slay suddenly, he .....Job 9:23
of hosts shall stir up a *s*.......Is 10:26
overflowing *s* shall pass ....Is 28:15
and to *s*, and to crucify ....Matt 20:19
some of them shall ye *s* in ....Matt 23:34
and when he had *s* Jesus ......Matt 27:26
shall *s* him, and shall spit .....Mark 10:34
had *s* him, to be crucified .....Mark 15:15
they shall *s* him, and put......Luke 18:33
he had made a *s* of small .....John 2:15
should be examined by *s* ......Acts 22:24
of cruel mockings and *s*.......Heb 11:36
s every son whom he ....Heb 12:6

SCRABBLED—*scratched or clawed frantically*
and *s* on the doors of the 1Sam 21:13

SCRAPE—*to grate harshly*
[*also* SCRAPED]
cause the house to be *s* ....Lev 14:41
the dust that they *s* off........Lev 14:41
a potsherd to *s* himself........Job 2:8
I will also *s* her dust from.....Ezek 26:4

SCREECH OWL—*a nocturnal bird*
Dwells in ruins ....Is 34:14

SCRIBE—*an expert in legal matters*
Employment of:
Transcribers of legal contracts.............Jer 32:12
Keepers of records ......Jer 36:25, 26
Advisers in state affairs ..1Chr 27:32
Custodians of draft records 2Kin 25:19
Collectors of Temple revenue...............2Kin 12:10
Teacher of the Law......Ezra 7:6, 10, 12
Characteristics of, in New Testament times, their:
Righteousness external ...Matt 5:20
Teaching without authority..............Matt 7:29
Their attitude toward Christ:
Accusing Him of blasphemy ....Mark 2:6-7
Seeking to accuse........Luke 6:7
Questioning His authority.Luke 20:1, 2
Christ's attitude toward:
Exposes them ....Matt 23:13-36
Condemns them ....Luke 20:46, 47
Calls them hypocrites ....Matt 15:1-9
[*also* SCRIBE'S, SCRIBES]
and Seraiah was the *s*.........2Sam 8:17
the sons of Shisha, *s* 1Kin 4:3
Shebna the *s*, and Joah 2Kin 18:18
the son of Meshullam, the *s*...2Kin 22:3
Shaphan the *s* came to the 2Kin 22:9
And Shaphan the *s*, and 2Kin 22:12
the families of the *s* which 1Chr 2:55
and Shavsha was *s*............1Chr 18:16
a wise man, and a *s* 1Chr 27:32
king's *s* and the high priest's ..2Chr 24:11
of the Levites there were *s*....2Chr 34:13
said to Shaphan the *s* 2Chr 34:15
Shaphan the *s*, and Asaiah 2Chr 34:20
and Shimshai the *s* wrote .....Ezra 4:8
and to Shimshai the *s*.........Ezra 4:17
Rehum, and Shimshai the *s* ...Ezra 4:23
unto Ezra the priest, the *s* ....Ezra 7:11
even a *s* of the words ....Ezra 7:11
they spake unto Ezra the *s*....Neh 8:1
and Ezra the priest the *s*......Neh 8:9
of Ezra the priest, the *s*.......Neh 12:26
and Zadok the *s*..............Neh 13:13
Then were the king's *s*........Esth 3:12
Where is the *s*? where is ......Is 33:18
Shebna the *s*, and Joah ....Is 36:22
the pen of the *s* is in vain .....Jer 8:8
son of Shaphan the *s* ....Jer 36:10
king's house, into the *s* ....Jer 36:12
chamber of Elishama the *s* ....Jer 36:20
it out of Elishama the *s*.......Jer 36:21
gave it to Baruch the *s*........Jer 36:32
house of Jonathan the *s*.......Jer 37:20
chief priests and *s* of the ......Matt 2:4
And a certain *s* came, and ....Matt 8:19
certain of the *s* said ....Matt 9:3
certain of the *s* and of the ....Matt 12:38
and chief priests and *s* ....Matt 16:21
Why then say the *s* that.......Matt 17:10
priests and unto the *s*.........Matt 20:18
chief priests and *s* saw ....Matt 21:15
s and the Pharisees sit in......Matt 23:2
chief priests, and the *s*........Matt 26:3
mocking him, with the *s* ......Matt 27:41
authority, and not as the *s* ....Mark 1:22
s which came down from......Mark 3:22
and certain of the *s*...........Mark 7:1
the chief priests, and *s*........Mark 8:31
Why say the *s* that Elijah .....Mark 9:11
and the *s* questioning with ....Mark 9:14
he asked the *s*, What ....Mark 9:16
priests, and unto the *s* ....Mark 10:33
And the *s* and chief priests ....Mark 11:18
And one of the *s* came ....Mark 12:28
the *s* said unto him, Well .....Mark 12:32
Beware of the *s* which love....Mark 12:38
chief priests and the *s*........Mark 14:1
and the elders and the *s* ......Mark 14:53
with the elders and *s* ....Mark 15:1
s and the Pharisees began to ..Luke 5:21
and chief priests and *s* ....Luke 9:22
Woe unto you, *s* and ....Luke 11:44
Pharisees and *s* murmured ....Luke 15:2
chief priests and the *s*.........Luke 19:47
chief priests and the *s*.........Luke 20:19
the chief priests and *s*.........Luke 22:2
And the chief priests and *s*....Luke 23:10
s and Pharisees brought ....John 8:3
rulers, and elders, and *s* ......Acts 4:5
and the elders, and the *s*......Acts 6:12

S

s that were of the ....Acts 23:9
is the wise? where is the *s*? ...1Cor 1:20

SCRIBE'S KNIFE—*a knife used to sharpen reed pens*
Used by Jehoiakim on
Jeremiah's scroll.......Jer 36:23-28

SCRIP—*a traveler's bag; a wallet*

Used by:
Shepherds 1Sam 17:40
Travelers ....Luke 9:3

Nor *s* for your journey........Matt 10:10
no *s*, no bread, no money.....Mark 6:8
Carry neither purse, nor *s*.....Luke 10:4
without purse, and *s*, and .....Luke 22:35
take it, and likewise his *s* .....Luke 22:36

SCRIPTURE—*God's written record of his revelation*

Called:
Word of God ....Heb 4:12
Word of truth..........James 1:18
Oracles of God.........Rom 3:2
Word..................James 1:21-23
Holy Scriptures..........Rom 1:2
Sword of the Spirit ......Eph 6:17
Scriptures of the prophets.Rom 16:26

Described as:
Authoritative............1Pet 4:11
Inspired 2Tim 3:16
Effectual in life 1Thess 2:13
True ....Ps 119:160
Perfect ....Ps 19:7
Sharp ....Heb 4:12
Pure....................Prov 30:5

Inspiration of, proved by:
External evidence ....Heb 2:1-4
Internal nature 2Tim 3:16, 17
Infallibility ....John 10:35
Fulfillment of prophecy ..John 5:39, 45-47

Understanding of, by:
Spirit's illumination 1Cor 2:10-14
Searching ....John 5:39
Reasoning ....Acts 17:2
Comparing..............2Pet 1:20, 21
Human help ....Acts 17:10-12

Proper uses of:
Regeneration............1Pet 1:23
Salvation 2Tim 3:15
Producing life ....John 20:31
Searching our hearts .....Heb 4:12
Spiritual growth ....Acts 20:32
Sanctification............John 17:17
Illumination.............Ps 119:105
Keeping from sin ....Ps 119:9, 11
Defeating Satan ....Eph 6:16, 17
Proving truth............Acts 18:28

Misuses of, by:
Satan...................Matt 4:6
Hypocrites ....Matt 22:23-29

Positive attitudes toward:
Let dwell in richly ....Col 3:16
Search daily.............Acts 17:11
Hide in the heart........Ps 119:11
Delight in...............Ps 1:2
Love ....Ps 119:97, 113, 167
Receive with meekness...James 1:21
Teach to children........Deut 11:19
Obey ....James 1:22
Read ....Deut 17:19

Negative attitudes toward, not to:
Add to or subtract from. .Deut 4:2
Handle deceitfully 2Cor 4:2
Wrest 2Pet 3:16
Invalidating by traditions .Mark 7:9-13

Fulfillment of, cited to show:
Christ's:
Mission ....Luke 4:16-21
Death ....Luke 24:27, 45-47
Rejection ....Acts 28:25-29
Resurrection ....Acts 2:24-31
Spirit's descent ....John 14:16-21
Faith ....Rom 4:3

Distortion of:
Condemned ....Prov 30:5, 6
Rev 22:18-20
Predicted 2Tim 4:3, 4

Memorization of:
Keeps from sin ....Ps 119:11
Gives understanding .....Ps 119:130
Facilitates prayer ....John 15:7

[*also* SCRIPTURES]
which is noted in the *s* of .....Dan 10:21
Did ye never read in the *s* ....Matt 21:42
how then shall the *s* be ....Matt 26:54
s of the prophets might ....Matt 26:56
have ye not read this *s*........Mark 12:10
because ye know not the *s* ....Mark 12:24
but the *s* must be fulfilled .....Mark 14:49
the *s* was fulfilled, which ......Mark 15:28
while he opened to us the *s* ...Luke 24:32
they believed the *s*, and.......John 2:22
as the *s* hath said, out of.....John 7:38
Hath not the *s* said, That .....John 7:42
that the *s* may be fulfilled ....John 13:18
the *s* might be fulfilled ....John 17:12
the *s* might be fulfilled ....John 19:24
the *s* might be fulfilled ....John 19:28
s should be fulfilled...........John 19:36
again another *s* saith..........John 19:37
yet they knew not the *s* ....John 20:9
s must needs have been ....Acts 1:16
The place of the *s* which ......Acts 8:32
began at the same *s*, and......Acts 8:35
man, and mighty in the *s* .....Acts 18:24
the *s* saith unto Pharaoh ......Rom 9:17
the *s* saith, Whosoever be .....Rom 10:11
Wot ye not what the *s* saith ...Rom 11:2
and comfort of the *s* we.......Rom 15:4
our sins according to the *s* 1Cor 15:3
day according to the *s* 1Cor 15:4
the *s*, foreseeing that God.....Gal 3:8
the *s* hath concluded all.......Gal 3:22
what saith the *s* ....Gal 4:30
the *s* saith, Thou shalt not 1Tim 5:18
law according to the *s* ....James 2:8
And the *s* was fulfilled........James 2:23
ye think that the *s* saith in ....James 4:5
it is contained in the *s* 1Pet 2:6

SCRIPTURES, DEVOTIONAL READINGS—*inspirational Bible selections*

For personal needs:
Comfort ....Ps 43:1-5
Rom 8:26-28
Courage ....Ps 46:1-11
2Cor 4:7-18
Direction ....Heb 4:16
James 1:5, 6
Peace ....Ps 4:1-8
Phil 4:4-7
Relief ....Ps 91:1-16
2Cor 12:8-10
Rest...................Matt 11:28-30
Rom 8:31-39
Temptation............Ps 1:1-6
1Cor 10:6-13
James 1:12-16

For instruction:
Sermon on the mount....Matt 5:1—7:29
Prayer..................Matt 6:5-15
Phil 4:6, 7
Golden rule ....Matt 7:12
Great commandment ....Matt 22:36-40
Salvation ....John 3:1-36
Good shepherd.........John 10:1-18
Spiritual fruit ....John 15:1-17
Gal 5:22, 23
Guilt ....Rom 8:1
Righteousness ....Rom 3:19-28
Justification ....Rom 5:1-21
Christian service ....Rom 12:1-21
Rom 13:1-14
Love 1Cor 13:1-13
Stewardship 2Cor 8:1-24
2Cor 9:1-15
Regeneration............Eph 2:1-10
Christ's exaltation ....Phil 2:5-11
Resurrection 1Thess 4:13-18
Judgment ....Rev 20:10-15
New heaven and earth ...Rev 21:1-27
Rev 22:1-5

SCRIPTURES, DISTORTION OF—*inaccurate interpretations*
Condemned ....Prov 30:5, 6
Turning unto fables......2Tim 4:3, 4
By unlearned 2Pet 3:15-17
God will punish ....Rev 22:18-20

SCROLL—*a papyrus or leather roll*
Applied to the heavens ..Is 34:4
Sky split apart like a.....Rev 6:14

SCRUPLES—*doubts regarding one's actions*
Manifested by Jews ......John 18:28

SCULL—*See* SKULL

SCUM—*a foul, filmy covering*
Used figuratively ....Ezek 24:6-12

SCURVY—*most likely an itch, rather than a disease*
blemish in his eye, or be *s* ....Lev 21:20
or having a wen, or *s* ....Lev 22:22

SCYTHIANS (sĭth'ĭ-ăns)—*natives of Scythia*
In the Christian church ..Col 3:11

SEA—*a large body of water*

Described as:
Created by God ....Acts 4:24
Deep ....Ps 68:22
Turbulent and dangerous .Ps 89:9
All rivers run into ....Eccl 1:7
Bound by God's decree ..Jer 5:22
Manifesting God's works .Ps 104:24, 25

List of, in the Bible:
Great Sea
(Mediterranean) ....Ezek 47:10
Salt or Dea Sea ....Gen 14:3
Red Sea ....Ex 10:19
Sea of Galilee
(Chinnereth) ....Num 34:11
Adriatic ....Acts 27:27

Figurative of:
Extension of the Gospel. .Is 11:9
Righteousness ....Is 48:18
False teachers ....Jude 13

[*also* SEAS]
of the waters called he *S*......Gen 1:10
over the fish of the *s* ....Gen 1:26
all the fishes of the *s* ....Gen 9:2
sand which is upon the *s*......Gen 22:17
corn as the sand of the *s*......Gen 41:49
cast them into the Red *S*......Ex 10:19
between Migdol and the *s*.....Ex 14:2
it shall ye encamp by the *s*....Ex 14:2
out thine hand over the *s* .....Ex 14:16
through the midst of the *s*.....Ex 14:16
out his hand over the *s* ....Ex 14:21
s to go back by a strong .....Ex 14:21
and made the *s* dry land ......Ex 14:21
them to the midst of the *s* ....Ex 14:23
forth his hand over the *s*......Ex 14:27
s returned to his strength .....Ex 14:27
in the midst of the *s*..........Ex 14:27
land in the midst of the *s* .....Ex 14:29
hath he thrown into the *s* .....Ex 15:1
hath he cast into the *s* ....Ex 15:4
are drowned in the Red *s* .....Ex 15:4
wind, the *s* covered them .....Ex 15:10
his horsemen into the *s* ....Ex 15:19
the waters of the *s* upon ......Ex 15:19
land in the midst of the *s* .....Ex 15:19
Israel from the Red *S*.........Ex 15:22
thy bounds from the Red *s*....Ex 23:31
the *s* of the Philistines ....Ex 23:31
in the waters, in the *s* ....Lev 11:9
fish of the *s* be gathered ......Num 11:22

Canaanites dwell by the *s* .....Num 13:29
by the way of the Red *S* ......Num 21:4
midst of the *s* into the ....Num 33:8
removed from the Red *S* ......Num 33:11
out of it shall be at the *s* ......Num 34:5
great *s* ye shall point out ......Num 34:7
over against the Red *S* ....Deut 1:1
by the way of the Red *S* ......Deut 1:40
the *s* of the plain..salt *s* ....Deut 3:17
the Red *s* to overflow them ...Deut 11:4
Neither is it beyond the *s* .....Deut 30:13
who shall go over the *s* for ....Deut 30:13
of the abundance of the *s* .....Deut 33:19
unto the great *s* toward ....Josh 1:4
the *s* of the plain..salt *s* ....Josh 3:16
which were by the *s* ....Josh 5:1
the sand that is upon the *s* ....Josh 11:4
to the *s* of Chinneroth on .....Josh 12:3
and unto the *s* of the plain ....Josh 12:3
even the salt *s* on the east ....Josh 12:3
from the shore of the salt *s* ...Josh 15:2
east border was the salt *s* .....Josh 15:5
s at the uttermost part of .....Josh 15:5
border was to the great *s* .....Josh 15:12
great *s*, and the border ....Josh 15:47
out thereof are at the *s* ....Josh 16:3
out thereof were at the *s* ......Josh 16:8
the *s* is his border ....Josh 17:10
the north bay of the salt *s* .....Josh 18:19
at the *s* from the coast to .....Josh 19:29
and ye came unto the *s* ....Josh 24:6
horsemen unto the Red *S* .....Josh 24:6
and brought the *s* upon ....Josh 24:7
Asher continued on the *s* .....Judg 5:17
wilderness unto the Red *S* ....Judg 11:16
the sand which is on the *s* 1Sam 13:5
the sand that is by the *s* 2Sam 17:11
sand which is by the *s* 1Kin 4:20
from Lebanon unto the *s* 1Kin 5:9
I will convey them by *s* in 1Kin 5:9
compassing the *s* round 1Kin 7:24
he set the *s* on the right 1Kin 7:39
on the shore of the Red *S* 1Kin 9:26
king had at *s* a navy of 1Kin 10:22
little cloud out of the *s* 1Kin 18:44
Hamath unto the *s* of the 2Kin 14:25
the brazen *s* that was in 2Kin 25:13
Let the *s* roar, and the 1Chr 16:32
to thee in floats by *s* to 2Chr 2:16
compassing the *s* round 2Chr 4:3
s was for the priests to 2Chr 4:6
One *s*, and twelve oxen 2Chr 4:15
had knowledge of the *s* 2Chr 8:18
from Lebanon to the *s* of .....Ezra 3:7
the *s*, and all that is ....Neh 9:6
their cry by the Red *S* ....Neh 9:9
thou didst divide the *s* ....Neh 9:11
through the midst of the *s* .....Neh 9:11
upon the isles of the *s* ....Esth 10:1
than the sand of the *s* ....Job 6:3
upon the waves of the *s* ....Job 9:8
the fishes of the *s* shall ....Job 12:8
He divideth the *s* with his .....Job 26:12
the bottom of the *s* ....Job 36:30
into the springs of the *s*? ......Job 38:16
the fish of the *s*, and ....Ps 8:8
through the paths of the *s* .....Ps 8:8
hath founded it upon the *s* ....Ps 24:2
into the midst of the *s* ....Ps 46:2
stilleth the noise of the *s* ......Ps 65:7
He turned the *s* into dry ......Ps 66:6
the *s*, and everything that .....Ps 69:34
dominion also from *s* to *s* .....Ps 72:8
Thy way is in the *s*, and ....Ps 77:19
like as the sand of the *s* ....Ps 78:27
out her boughs unto the *s* .....Ps 80:11
set his hand also in the *s* ......Ps 89:25
The *s* is his, and he made .....Ps 95:5
let the *s* roar, and the ....Ps 98:7
at the *s*, even at the Red *S* ....Ps 106:7
things by the Red *S* ....Ps 106:22
The *s* saw it, and fled ....Ps 114:3
the *s*, and all deep places .....Ps 135:6
which divided the Red *S* ......Ps 136:13
uttermost parts of the *s* ....Ps 139:9

When he gave to the *s* his ....Prov 8:29
ship in the midst of the *s* .....Prov 30:19
like the roaring of the *s* ....Is 5:30
Israel be..sand of the *s* ....Is 10:22
from the islands of the *s* ......Is 11:11
tongue of the Egyptian *s* ......Is 11:15
like the noise of the *s* ....Is 17:12
ambassadors by the *s* ....Is 18:2
of the desert of the *s* ....Is 21:1
for the *s* hath spoken ....Is 23:4
even the strength of the *s* .....Is 23:4
shall cry aloud from the *s* .....Is 24:14
the dragon that is in the *s* .....Is 27:1
maketh a way in the *s* ....Is 43:16
at my rebuke I dry up the *s* ...Is 50:2
not it which hath dried the *s* ..Is 51:10
made the depths of the *s* ......Is 51:10
are like the troubled *s* ....Is 57:20
brought them up out of the *s* ..Is 63:11
voice roareth like the *s* ....Jer 6:23
above the sand of the *s* ....Jer 15:8
concerning the *s*, and ....Jer 27:19
the sand of the *s* measured ....Jer 33:22
plants are gone over the *s* .....Jer 48:32
they reach even to the *s* of ....Jer 48:32
there is sorrow on the *s* ....Jer 49:23
I will dry up her *s*, and ....Jer 51:36
the brazen *s* that was in ....Jer 52:17
breach is great like the *s* ......Lam 2:13
remnant of the *s* coast ....Ezek 25:16
nets in the midst of the *s* .....Ezek 26:5
which wast strong in the *s* .....Ezek 26:17
at the entry of the *s* ....Ezek 27:3
are in the midst of the *s* ......Ezek 27:4
thee in the midst of the *s* .....Ezek 27:26
all the pilots of the *s* shall .....Ezek 27:29
went forth out of the *s* ....Ezek 27:33
God in the midst of the *s* .....Ezek 28:2
art as a whale in the *s* ....Ezek 32:2
So that the fishes of the *s* .....Ezek 38:20
desert, and go into the *s* ......Ezek 47:8
brought forth into the *s* ......Ezek 47:8
north side from the great *s* ....Ezek 47:15
the border unto the east *s* .....Ezek 47:18
also shall be the great *s* ....Ezek 47:20
strove upon the great *s* ....Dan 7:2
of his palace between the *s* ....Dan 11:45
Israel shall..sand of the *s* ......Hos 1:10
his face toward the east *s* .....Joel 2:20
for the waters of the *s* ....Amos 5:8
sight in the bottom of the *s* ...Amos 9:3
out a great wind into the *s* ....Jon 1:4
a mighty tempest in the *s* .....Jon 1:4
which hath made the *s* ....Jon 1:9
that the *s* may be calm ....Jon 1:11
for the *s* wrought, and was ....Jon 1:11
cast me forth into the *s* ....Jon 1:12
so shall the *s* be calm unto ....Jon 1:12
cast him forth into the *s* ......Jon 1:15
in the midst of the *s* ....Jon 2:3
from *s* to *s*, and from ....Mic 7:12
He rebuketh the *s*, and ....Nah 1:4
whose rampart was the *s* ......Nah 3:8
her wall was from the *s* ....Nah 3:8
men as the fishes of the *s* .....Hab 1:14
as the waters cover the *s* ......Hab 2:14
walk through the *s* with ....Hab 3:15
and the fishes of the *s* ....Zeph 1:3
the *s* coast shall be ....Zeph 2:6
and the earth, and the *s* ......Hag 2:6
smite her power in the *s* ......Zech 9:4
pass through the *s* with ....Zech 10:11
smite the waves in the *s* ....Zech 10:11
them toward the former *s* .....Zech 14:8
them toward the hinder *s* .....Zech 14:8
which is upon the *s* coast .....Matt 4:13
walking by the *s* of Galilee ....Matt 4:18
casting a net into the *s* ....Matt 4:18
the winds and the *s* ....Matt 8:26
steep place into the *s* ....Matt 8:32
that was cast into the *s* ....Matt 13:47
them, walking on the *s* ....Matt 14:25
nigh unto the *s* of Galilee .....Matt 15:29
in the depth of the *s* ....Matt 18:6
ye compass *s* and land to .....Matt 23:15

walked by the *s* of Galilee ....Mark 1:16
casting a net into the *s* ....Mark 1:16
with his disciples to the *s* .....Mark 3:7
a ship, and sat in the *s* ....Mark 4:1
multitude was by the *s* on .....Mark 4:1
wind and the *s* obey him? .....Mark 4:41
a steep place into the *s* ....Mark 5:13
and were choked in the *s* .....Mark 5:13
he was nigh unto the *s* ....Mark 5:21
was in the midst of the *s* ......Mark 6:47
him walking upon the *s* ....Mark 6:49
and he were cast into the *s* ....Mark 9:42
be thou planted in the *s* ....Luke 17:6
Jesus went over the *s* ....John 6:1
Galilee, which is the *s* of ......John 6:1
went over the *s* toward ....John 6:17
see Jesus walking on the *s* ....John 6:19
on the other side of the *s* ....John 6:25
did cast himself into the *s* .....John 21:7
in the Red *s*, and in the ......Acts 7:36
to go as it were to the *s* ......Acts 17:14
down the boat into the *s* ......Acts 27:30
themselves unto the *s* ....Acts 27:40
a place where two *s* met ......Acts 27:41
he hath escaped the *s*, yet .....Acts 28:4
be as the sand of the *s* ....Rom 9:27
all passed through the *s* 1Cor 10:1
perils in the *s*, in perils 2Cor 11:26
is like a wave of the *s* ....James 1:6
such as are in the *s*, and ......Rev 5:13
on the earth nor on the *s* .....Rev 7:1
the earth, neither the *s* ....Rev 7:3
fire was cast into the *s* ....Rev 8:8
part of the *s* became blood ....Rev 8:8
his right foot upon the *s* ......Rev 10:2
the *s* and the things which ....Rev 10:6
s of the earth and of the *s* ....Rev 12:12
upon the sand of the *s* ....Rev 13:1
a beast rise up out of the *s* ....Rev 13:1
were a *s* of glass mingled .....Rev 15:2
stand on the *s* of glass ....Rev 15:2
out his vial upon the *s* ....Rev 16:3
living soul died in the *s* ....Rev 16:3
all that had ships in the *s* .....Rev 18:19
is as the sand of the *s* ....Rev 20:8
and there was no more *s* ......Rev 21:1

SEA, MOLTEN—*a large bronze vessel made by Hinam of Tyre and placed in Solomon's Temple*
Vessel in the Temple 1Kin 7:23

SEA OF GLASS—*an object in a vision of John, in which a state of absolute holiness is anticipated, apparently drawing on a picture of the tabernacle laver*
Before the throne of God.Rev 4:6

SEAFARING—*descriptive of sailors*
that wast inhabited of *s* ....Ezek 26:17

SEAL—*instrument used to authenticate ownership; visible mark of ownership; to confirm or make secure*

Used literally to:
Guarantee business deals .Jer 32:11-14
Ratify covenants.........Neh 10:1
Insure a prophecy ....Dan 9:24
Protect books ....Rev 5:2, 5, 9
Lock doors ....Matt 27:66

Used figuratively of:
Ownership of married love .... Song 4:12; Song 8:6
Hidden things ....Is 29:11
Acceptance of Christ ....John 3:33
God's witness to Christ ..John 6:27
Believer's security 2Cor 1:22
Assurance ....Eph 4:30
God's ownership of His people ....Rev 7:3-8

[*also* SEALED, SEALEST, SEALETH, SEALS]
and *s* up among my ....Deut 32:34
and *s* them with his *s* 1Kin 21:8
Levites, and priests, *s* unto ....Neh 9:38
and *s* with the king's ring .....Esth 3:12
s it with the king's ring ....Esth 8:8

S

s it with the king's ring ....Esth 8:10
and *s* up the stars ....Job 9:7
My transgression is *s* up ......Job 14:17
and *s* their instruction.........Job 33:16
He *s* up the hand of every ....Job 37:7
is turned as clay to the *s* ......Job 38:14
together as with a close *s* .....Job 41:15
s the law among my ....Is 8:16
the evidence, and *s* it ....Jer 32:10
subscribe evidences, and *s*.....Jer 32:44
Thou *s* up the sum, full of ....Ezek 28:12
the king *s* it with his own .....Dan 6:17
shut up the words, and *s* ......Dan 12:4
up and *s* till the time of.......Dan 12:9
s the stone, and ....Matt 27:66
s of the righteousness of ......Rom 4:11
this, and have *s* to them ......Rom 15:28
s of mine apostleship are 1Cor 9:2
standeth sure, having this *s*....2Tim 2:19
backside *s* with seven ....Rev 5:1
Lamb opened one of the *s* ....Rev 6:1
he had opened the second *s* ...Rev 6:3
he had opened the third *s* .....Rev 6:5
he had opened the fourth *s*....Rev 6:7
he had opened the fifth *s* .....Rev 6:9
he had opened the sixth *s* .....Rev 6:12
the *s* of the living God........Rev 7:2
had opened the seventh *s* ......Rev 8:1
s of God in their foreheads....Rev 9:4
S up those things which ....Rev 10:4
shut him up, and set a *s* ......Rev 20:3
S not the sayings of the ....Rev 22:10

SEAM—*the joint of two pieces of cloth or material*
now the coat was without *s*....John 19:23

SEAMSTRESS—*a dressmaker*
Dorcas known as ....Acts 9:36-42

SEARCH—*to investigate; look for*
Applied literally to:
Land ....Num 13:2-32
Lost article ....Gen 31:34-37
Records ....Ezra 4:15, 19
Child ....Matt 2:8
Scriptures ....John 5:39
Enemy 1Sam 23:23
Applied figuratively to:
Man's heart ....Ps 139:1, 23
Understanding ....Prov 2:4
Conscience ....Prov 20:27
Self-examination ....Judg 5:16

[*also* SEARCHED, SEARCHEST, SEARCHETH, SEARCHING, SEARCHINGS]
Laban *s* all the tent, but ......Gen 31:34
thou hast *s* all my stuff ....Gen 31:37
He shall not *s* whether it ......Lev 27:33
to *s* out a resting place........Num 10:33
s the land from the ....Num 13:21
they returned from *s* of ....Num 13:25
were of them that *s* the ....Num 14:6
we passed through to *s* it .....Num 14:7
the men that went to *s*........Num 14:38
and they shall *s* us out the ....Deut 1:22
the valley of Eshcol, and *s* ....Deut 1:24
thou inquire, and make *s* .....Deut 13:14
Israel to *s* out the country.....Josh 2:2
there were great *s* of heart ....Judg 5:16
out the land, and to *s* it.......Judg 18:2
said unto them, Go, *s* the .....Judg 18:2
to *s* the city, and to spy 2Sam 10:3
they shall *s* thine house 1Kin 20:6
S, and look that there be 2Kin 10:23
come unto thee for to *s* 1Chr 19:3
for the Lord *s* all hearts.......1Chr 28:9
be *s* made in the king's ....Ezra 5:17
s was made in the house ......Ezra 6:1
Lo this, we have *s* it, so ......Job 5:27
to the *s* of their fathers ....Job 8:8
mine iniquity, and *s* after .....Job 10:6
thou by *s* find out God ....Job 11:7
Is it good that he should *s* ....Job 13:9
and *s* out all perfection ....Job 28:3
he prepared it, yea, and *s*.....Job 28:27
cause which I knew not I *s*....Job 29:16
whilst ye *s* out what to say ....Job 32:11
number of his years be *s* ......Job 36:26
walked in the *s* of the ....Job 38:16
and he *s* after every green ....Job 39:8
shall not God *s* this out ....Ps 44:21
They *s* out iniquities ....Ps 64:6
accomplish a diligent *s* ....Ps 64:6
and *s* for her as for hid ....Prov 2:4
neighbor cometh and *s*.........Prov 18:17
of kings is to *s* out a..........Prov 25:2
hath understanding *s* him ......Prov 28:11
seek and *s* out by wisdom .....Eccl 1:13
s of his understanding.........Is 40:28
not found it by secret *s* ....Jer 2:34
shall *s* for me with all.........Jer 29:13
foundations of the earth *s* .....Jer 31:37
though it cannot be *s* ....Jer 46:23
Let us *s* and try our ways .....Lam 3:40
none did *s* or seek after.......Ezek 34:6
I will both *s* my sheep ....Ezek 34:11
will *s* and take them out ......Amos 9:3
the things of Esau *s* out.......Obad 6
I will *s* Jerusalem with ....Zeph 1:12
S, and look: for out of........John 7:52
s the scriptures daily ....Acts 17:11
And he that *s* the hearts ......Rom 8:27
for the Spirit *s* all things 1Cor 2:10
inquired and *s* diligently 1Pet 1:10
S what, or what manner of 1Pet 1:11
he which *s* the reins and ......Rev 2:23

SEARED—*burned; scorched*
conscience *s* with a hot 1Tim 4:2

SEASHORE—*coastline*
upon the *s* in multitude ....Josh 11:4
sand which is on the *s* 1Sam 13:5
and against the *s* ....Jer 47:7
sand which is by the *s* ....Heb 12:12

SEASON—*a period of time; to add spices*
Descriptive of:
Period of the year ....Gen 1:14
Revealed times..........1Thess 5:1
Prophetic period.........Rev 6:11
Right time ....Deut 11:14
Short period ....Philem 15
Appointed time ....Num 9:2, 3, 7
Of the year:
Guaranteed by God .....Gen 8:22
Proof of God's providence ....Acts 14:17
Indicated by the moon ...Ps 104:19

[*also* SEASONED, SEASONS]
and they continued a *s* in .....Gen 40:4
ordinance in his *s* from ....Ex 13:10
judge the people at all *s* ......Ex 18:22
offering shalt thou *s* with.......Lev 2:13
ye shall proclaim in their *s* ....Lev 23:4
will give you rain in due *s*.....Lev 26:4
Lord in his appointed *s* ....Num 9:13
unto me in their due *s* ....Num 28:2
the *s* that thou camest ....Deut 16:6
in the wilderness a long *s* .....Josh 24:7
About this *s*, according to.....2Kin 4:16
a long *s* Israel hath been 2Chr 15:3
of corn cometh in in his *s* .....Job 5:26
forth Mazzaroth in his *s*.......Job 38:32
forth his fruit in his *s* ....Ps 1:3
instruct me in the night *s* .....Ps 16:7
appointed the moon for *s* .....Ps 104:19
them their meat in due *s*......Ps 104:27
a word spoken in due *s* ....Prov 15:23
To every thing there is a *s* ....Eccl 3:1
how to speak a word in *s* .....Is 50:4
and the latter, in his *s* ....Jer 5:24
to come down in his *s* ....Ezek 34:26
the times and the *s* ....Dan 2:21
were prolonged for a *s*........Dan 7:12
and my wine in the *s* ....Hos 2:9
him the fruits in their *s* ....Matt 21:41
to give them meat in due *s*? ...Matt 24:45
wherewith will ye *s* it? ....Mark 9:50
shall be fulfilled in their *s* .....Luke 1:20
portion of meat in due *s* ......Luke 12:42
wherewith shall it be *s*? ....Luke 14:34
at the *s* he sent a servant .....Luke 20:10
at a certain *s* into the pool ....John 5:4
to know the times or the *s* ....Acts 1:7
not seeing the sun for a *s* .....Acts 13:11
have been with you at all *s*....Acts 20:18
when I have a convenient *s* ...Acts 24:25
though it were but for a *s* 2Cor 7:8
for in due *s* we shall reap .....Gal 6:9
be always with grace, *s* ....Col 4:6
the word; be instant in *s* 2Tim 4:2
pleasures of sin for a *s*.........Heb 11:25
rejoice, though now for a *s*....1Pet 1:6
must be loosed a little *s*.......Rev 20:3

SEAT—*a place of authority or prominence; a place to sit*
Descriptive of:
Inner court ....Ezek 8:3
Assembly ....Matt 23:6
Figurative of:
God's throne ....Job 23:3
Association with evil.....Ps 1:1
Satanic power ....Rev 13:2

[*also* SEATED, SEATS]
a mercy *s* of pure gold ....Ex 25:17
even of the mercy *s* shall......Ex 25:19
the mercy *s* with their ....Ex 25:20
toward the mercy *s* shall ......Ex 25:20
from above the mercy *s*.......Ex 25:22
before the mercy *s* that is .....Ex 30:6
thereof, with the mercy *s* .....Ex 35:12
two ends of the mercy *s*........Ex 37:7
out of the mercy *s* made he ...Ex 37:8
thereof, and the mercy *s* ......Ex 39:35
the veil before the mercy *s* ....Lev 16:2
the cloud upon the mercy *s* ...Lev 16:2
finger upon the mercy *s*.......Lev 16:14
and before the mercy *s* ....Lev 16:14
it upon the mercy *s*...........Lev 16:15
and before the mercy *s* ....Lev 16:15
from off the mercy *s* that .....Num 7:89
of the lawgiver, was he *s*......Deut 33:21
And he arose out of his *s* .....Judg 3:20
Eli the priest sat upon a *s*.....1Sam 1:9
he fell from off the *s* 1Sam 4:18
the king sat upon his *s*........1Sam 20:25
The Tachmonite..in the *s* 2Sam 23:8
s to be set for the king's 1Kin 2:19
of the place of the mercy *s* 1Chr 28:11
and set his *s* above all the.....Esth 3:1
I prepared my *s* in the ....Job 29:7
on a *s* in the high places ......Prov 9:14
the *s* of the image of ....Ezek 8:3
cause the *s* of violence to .....Amos 6:3
and the *s* of them that sold....Matt 21:12
Pharisees sit in Moses' *s* ......Matt 23:2
and the *s* of them that sold....Mark 11:15
uppermost *s* in the synagogues .Luke 11:43
highest *s* in the synagogues ....Luke 20:46
down in the judgment *s*........John 19:13
him to the judgment *s* ....Acts 18:12
him before the judgment *s* ....Acts 18:17
sitting on the judgment *s*......Acts 25:6
I sat on the judgment *s* ....Acts 25:17
the judgment *s* of Christ ......Rom 14:10
the judgment *s* of Christ 2Cor 5:10
you before the judgment *s*? ...James 2:6
even where Satan's *s* is ....Rev 2:13
were four and twenty *s* ....Rev 4:4
upon the *s* I saw four and .....Rev 4:4
sat before God on their *s* .....Rev 11:16
vial upon the *s* of the beast ...Rev 16:10

SEATWARD—*facing the seat*
to the mercy *s* were the ....Ex 37:9

SEBA (sē'bä)—*"drunkard"*
Cush's oldest son ....Gen 10:7
See SABEANS

S, and Havilah, and Sabta 1Chr 1:9
of Sheba and *S* shall offer.....Ps 72:10
Ethiopia and *S* for thee ....Is 43:3

SEBAT (sē'băt)
Eleventh month of the Hebrew year ....Zech 1:7

SECACAH (sĕ-kā'kă)—*"thicket"*
Village of Judah . . . . Josh 15:1, 61

SECHU (sē'kū)—*"defense"*
Village near Ramah 1Sam 19:22

SECOND—*next to first in place or time*
Descriptive of:
Next in order . . . . Gen 1:8
Repetition 1Kin 18:34
Second advent . . . . Heb 9:28
Used figuratively and spiritually of:
Christ 1Cor 15:47
Finality . . . . Titus 3:10
New covenant . . . . Heb 8:7
Death . . . . Rev 2:11

the *s* river is Gihon . . . . Gen 2:13
in the *s* month . . . . Gen 7:11
out of heaven the *s* time . . . . . . Gen 22:15
maid bare Jacob a *s* son . . . . . . Gen 30:12
and dreamed the *s* time . . . . . . Gen 41:5
the *s* called he Ephraim . . . . . . Gen 41:52
came unto him the *s* year . . . . . Gen 47:18
he went out the *s* day . . . . Ex 2:13
in the coupling of the *s* . . . . Ex 26:4
which coupleth the *s* . . . . Ex 26:10
s row shall be an emerald . . . . . Ex 28:18
in the coupling of the *s* . . . . Ex 36:12
the *s* row, an emerald . . . . Ex 39:11
the *s* for a burnt offering . . . . . Lev 5:10
first day of the *s* month . . . . . . Num 1:1
s year after they were . . . . Num 1:1
set forth in the *s* rank . . . . Num 2:16
first month of the *s* year . . . . . . Num 9:1
blow an alarm the *s* time . . . . . Num 10:6
day of the *s* month . . . . Num 10:11
the *s* year, that the cloud . . . . . Num 10:11
of Israel the *s* time . . . . Josh 5:2
took it on the *s* day . . . . Josh 10:32
s bullock of seven years . . . . . . Judg 6:25
s bullock was offered . . . . Judg 6:28
out of Gibeah the *s* day . . . . Judg 20:25
name of his *s*, Abiah 1Sam 8:2
eat no meat the *s* day 1Sam 20:34
his *s*, Chileab, of Abigail 2Sam 3:3
Zif, which is the *s* month 1Kin 6:1
the *s* year of Asa king 1Kin 15:25
And they did it the *s* time 1Kin 18:34
in the *s* year of Jehoram 2Kin 1:17
wrote a letter the *s* time 2Kin 10:6
In the *s* year of Pekah 2Kin 15:32
the priests of the *s* order 2Kin 23:4
Zephaniah the *s* priest 2Kin 25:18
Abinadab the *s*, and Shimma . . 1Chr 2:13
s Jehoiakim, the third 1Chr 3:15
Ashbel the *s*, and Aharah 1Chr 8:1
the first, Obadiah the *s*, Eliab . 1Chr 12:9
the chief and Zizah the *s* 1Chr 23:11
the first, and Jesiah the *s* 1Chr 23:20
the first, Amariah the *s* 1Chr 24:23
Jediael the *s*, Zebadiah 1Chr 26:2
Hilkiah the *s*, Tebaliah 1Chr 26:11
king the *s* time 1Chr 29:22
s day of the *s* month 2Chr 3:2
passover in the *s* month 2Chr 30:2
day of the *s* month 2Chr 30:15
silver basins of a *s* . . . . Ezra 1:10
s year of their coming . . . . Ezra 3:8
in the *s* month, began . . . . Ezra 3:8
the *s* day were gathered . . . . . . Neh 8:13
Bakbukiah the *s* among . . . . . . Neh 11:17
returned into the *s* house . . . . . Esth 2:14
unto Esther on the *s* day . . . . . Esth 7:2
name of the *s*, Kezia . . . . Job 42:14
and there is not a *s* . . . . Eccl 4:8
his hand again the *s* time . . . . . Is 11:11
came unto me the *s* time . . . . . Jer 1:13
unto Jeremiah the *s* time . . . . . Jer 33:1
s pillar also and the . . . . Jer 52:22
the *s* face was the face . . . . Ezek 10:14
in the *s* year of . . . . Dan 2:1
unto Jonah the *s* time . . . . Jon 3:1
shall not rise up the *s* . . . . Nah 1:9
and a howling from the *s* . . . . . Zeph 1:10
In the *s* year of Darius . . . . Hag 1:1
in the *s* year of Darius . . . . Hag 2:10
s chariot black horses . . . . Zech 6:2
came to the *s*, and said . . . . Matt 21:30
s is like unto it, Thou shalt . . . . Matt 22:39
the *s* took her, and died . . . . . . Mark 12:21
s time the cock crew . . . . Mark 14:72
to pass on the *s* sabbath . . . . . . Luke 6:1
s came, saying, Lord, thy . . . . . Luke 19:18
s time into his mother's . . . . John 3:4
to him again the *s* time . . . . John 21:16
s time Joseph was made . . . . . . Acts 7:13
the first and the *s* ward . . . . Acts 12:10
also written in the *s* psalm . . . . Acts 13:33
might have a *s* benefit 2Cor 1:15
were present, the *s* time 2Cor 13:2
first and *s* admonition . . . . Titus 3:10
been sought for the *s* . . . . Heb 8:7
And after the *s* veil . . . . Heb 9:3
that he may establish the *s* . . . . Heb 10:9
and the *s* beast like a calf . . . . . Rev 4:7
he had opened the *s* seal . . . . . . Rev 6:3
I heard the *s* beast say . . . . Rev 6:3
And the *s* angel sounded . . . . . . Rev 8:8
The *s* woe is past, and behold . Rev 11:14
s angel poured out his vial . . . . Rev 16:3
s death hath no power . . . . Rev 20:6
of fire.This is the *s* death . . . . . Rev 20:14
which is the *s* death . . . . Rev 21:8
jasper; the *s*, sapphire . . . . Rev 21:19

SECOND COMING OF CHRIST—*His return to earth, this time in glory*
Described as Day of:
The Lord 1Thess 5:2
Lord Jesus 1Cor 5:5
God 2Pet 3:12
That day 2Thess 1:10
Last day . . . . John 12:48
Purposes of, to:
Fulfill His Word . . . . John 14:3
Raise the dead 1Thess 4:13-18
Destroy death 1Cor 15:25, 26
Gather the elect . . . . Matt 24:31
Judge the world . . . . Matt 25:32-46
Glorify believers . . . . Col 3:4
Reward God's people . . . . Matt 16:27
Time of:
Unknown to us . . . . Matt 24:27, 36
After the Gospel's proclamation to all . . . . Matt 24:14
After the rise of antichrist 2Thess 2:2, 3
At the last trump 1Cor 15:51, 52
In days like Noah's . . . . . . Matt 24:37-47
Manner of:
In the clouds . . . . Matt 24:30
In flaming fire 2Thess 1:7, 8
With the angels . . . . Matt 25:31
As a thief 1Thess 5:2, 3
In His glory . . . . Matt 25:31
Believer's attitude toward, to:
Wait for 1Cor 1:7
Look for . . . . Titus 2:13
Be ready for . . . . Matt 24:42-51
Love 2Tim 4:8
Be busy until . . . . Luke 19:13-18
Pray for . . . . Rev 22:20

SECONDARILY—*in the second place*
First apostles, *s* prophets 1Cor 12:28

SECRET—*something hidden from others*
To be kept . . . . Prov 25:9
Sign of faithfulness . . . . . . Prov 11:13
To those who expose, condemned . . . . Prov 20:19

[*also* SECRETLY, SECRETS]
didst thou flee away *s* . . . . Gen 31:27
come not thou into their *s* . . . . Gen 49:6
entice thee *s*, saying . . . . Deut 13:6
and taketh him by the *s* . . . . Deut 25:11
and putteth it in a *s* place . . . . . Deut 27:15
for want of all things *s* . . . . Deut 28:57
Shittim two men to spy *s* . . . . . . Josh 2:1
I have a *s* errand . . . . Judg 3:19
my name, seeing it is *s*? . . . . Judg 13:18
emerods in their *s* parts 1Sam 5:9
Commune with David *s* 1Sam 18:22
and abide in a *s* place 1Sam 19:2
For thou didst it *s* 2Sam 12:12
children of Israel did *s* 2Kin 17:9
was *s* brought to me . . . . Job 4:12
show thee the *s* of wisdom . . . . Job 11:6
thou wouldest keep me *s* . . . . . . Job 14:13
Is there any *s* thing . . . . Job 15:11
s of God was upon my . . . . Job 29:4
heart hath been *s* enticed . . . . . Job 31:27
s places doth he murder . . . . . . Ps 10:8
He lieth in wait *s* as a lion . . . . Ps 10:9
darkness his *s* place . . . . Ps 18:11
cleanse thou me from *s* faults . . Ps 19:12
The *s* of the Lord is with . . . . . Ps 25:14
in the *s* of his tabernacle . . . . . . Ps 27:5
in the *s* of thy presence . . . . Ps 31:20
knoweth the *s* of the heart . . . . Ps 44:21
shoot in *s* at the perfect . . . . Ps 64:4
s sins in the light of thy . . . . Ps 90:8
dwelleth in the *s* place . . . . Ps 91:1
when I was made in *s* . . . . Ps 139:15
s is with the righteous . . . . Prov 3:32
eaten in *s* is pleasant . . . . Prov 9:17
A gift in *s* pacifieth anger . . . . . Prov 21:14
discover not a *s* to . . . . Prov 25:9
better than *s* love . . . . Prov 27:5
judgment, with every *s* thing . . Eccl 12:14
s places of the stairs . . . . Song 2:14
will discover their *s* parts . . . . . . Is 3:17
I have not spoken in *s* . . . . Is 45:19
not found it by *s* search . . . . Jer 2:34
weep in *s* places for your . . . . . Jer 13:17
hide himself in *s* places . . . . Jer 23:24
asked him *s* in his house . . . . . . Jer 37:17
spake to Gedaliah in Mizpah *s* . Jer 40:15
uncovered his *s* places . . . . Jer 49:10
and as a lion in *s* places . . . . . . Lam 3:10
shall pollute my *s* place . . . . Ezek 7:22
is no *s* that they can hide . . . . . Ezek 28:3
heaven concerning this *s* . . . . . . Dan 2:18
the deep and *s* things . . . . Dan 2:22
God in heaven that revealeth *s* . Dan 2:28
that revealeth *s* maketh . . . . Dan 2:29
s is not revealed to me . . . . Dan 2:30
and no *s* troubleth thee . . . . Dan 4:9
revealeth his *s* unto his . . . . Amos 3:7
as to devour the poor *s* . . . . Hab 3:14
thine alms may be in *s* . . . . Matt 6:4
Father which seeth in *s* . . . . Matt 6:4
thy Father which is in *s* . . . . Matt 6:18
which seeth in *s*, shall . . . . Matt 6:18
which have been kept *s* . . . . Matt 13:35
he is in the *s* chambers . . . . Matt 24:26
neither was any thing kept *s* . . . Mark 4:22
For nothing is *s*, that shall . . . . Luke 8:17
putteth it in a *s* place . . . . Luke 11:33
that doeth any thing in *s* . . . . . . John 7:4
but as it were in *s* . . . . John 7:10
called Mary her sister *s* . . . . John 11:28
in *s* have I said nothing . . . . John 18:20
shall judge the *s* of men . . . . . . Rom 2:16
s since the world began . . . . Rom 16:25
s of his heart made manifest . . . 1Cor 14:25
are done of them in *s* . . . . Eph 5:12

SECRET DISCIPLES—*those who kept hidden their belief in Christ*
Among Jewish leaders . . . John 12:42
Fearful of Jewish disfavor . John 19:38

SECRET PRAYER—*private prayer*
Commended by Christ . . . Matt 6:6
Practiced by:
Christ . . . . Mark 1:35
Peter . . . . Acts 10:9

SECRET THINGS—*mysteries*
Known by God . . . . Deut 29:29
See MYSTERY

SECT—*religious movements in Judaism*
Pharisees . . . . Acts 15:5
Sadducees . . . . Acts 5:17
Herodians . . . . Matt 22:16
Christians described as . . . Acts 24:5

S

straitest *s* of our religion ....Acts 26:5
for as concerning this *s* ....Acts 28:22

SECUNDUS (sĕ-kŭn'dŭs)—*"second"*
Thessalonian Christian ...Acts 20:4

SECURE—*confident; without fear; something given as a pledge to fulfill a promise*

[*also* SECURELY, SECURITY]
for the host was *s* ....Judg 8:11
Zidonians, quiet and *s* ....Judg 18:7
that were at quiet and *s* ....Judg 18:27
thou shalt be *s*, because ....Job 11:18
that provoke God are *s* ....Job 12:6
he dwelleth *s* by thee ....Prov 3:29
pass by *s* as men averse ....Mic 2:8
persuade him, and *s* you ......Matt 28:14
had taken *s* of Jason ....Acts 17:9

SECURITY OF THE SAINTS—*the secure salvation of those who believe in Christ*

Expressed by:
"Shall never perish" .....John 10:28
"None of them is lost"..John 17:12
"Protected by the power of God" 1Pet 1:5

Guaranteed by:
Spirit's sealing...........2Cor 1:21, 22
Christ's intercession......Rom 8:34-39
God's power ....Jude 24

See ASSURANCE

SEDITION—*incitement to revolt against lawful authority*
Miriam and Aaron, against Moses ....Num 12:1-13

[*also* SEDITIONS]
that they have moved *s* ....Ezra 4:15
certain *s* made in the city .....Luke 23:19
a mover of *s* among all ....Acts 24:5
wrath, strife, *s* ....Gal 5:20

SEDUCE—*to lead astray through lust*

[*also* SEDUCED, SEDUCETH]
way of the wicked *s* them .....Prov 12:26
they have also *s* Egypt ....Is 19:13
they have *s* my people ....Ezek 13:10
them that *s* you 1John 2:26

SEDUCER—*one who leads another astray*

Agent of:
Evil spirits 1Tim 4:1
False teachers ....Mark 13:22
Evil leaders 2Kin 21:9

Characteristics of:
Grow worse.............2Tim 3:13
Self-deceived ....Prov 12:26
Lead to evil.............Rev 2:20
Preach false message.....Ezek 13:9, 10

[*also* SEDUCERS]
and *s* shall wax worse 2Tim 3:13

SEE—*to look at; perceive; observe*

[*also* SAW, SAWEST, SEEING, SEEN, SEEST, SEETH]
I *s* righteous before me ....Gen 7:1
shall be *s* in the cloud ....Gen 9:14
all the land which thou *s* ......Gen 13:15
give me, *s* I go childless.......Gen 15:2
looked after him that *s* me? ...Gen 16:13
Lot *s* them rose up to meet ...Gen 19:1
What *s* thou, that thou hast ...Gen 20:10
Esau *s* that the daughters .....Gen 28:8
when Jacob *s* Rachel ....Gen 29:10
s that Leah was hated ....Gen 29:31
Rachel *s* that she bare Jacob ..Gen 30:1
and *s* in a dream ....Gen 31:10
s all that Laban doeth ....Gen 31:12
and all that thou *s* is mine ....Gen 31:43
I have *s* God face to face .....Gen 32:30
I have *s* thy face ....Gen 33:10
I had *s* the face of God ....Gen 33:10
since I have *s* thy face ....Gen 46:30
surely *s* the affliction ....Ex 3:7
s that which is done to you....Ex 3:16
or deaf, or the *s*..............Ex 4:11
when he *s* thee, he will be ....Ex 4:14
s my face thou shalt die.......Ex 10:28
no leavened bread be *s* ....Ex 13:7
shall there be leaven *s* ....Ex 13:7
Ye have *s* what I did unto ....Ex 19:4
driven away, no man *s* it......Ex 22:10
I have *s* this people ....Ex 32:9
any man be *s* throughout......Ex 34:3
he hath *s* or known of it ......Lev 5:1
holy place, *s* it is most holy ...Lev 10:17
hath been *s* of the priest ......Lev 13:7
when the priest *s* it ....Lev 13:20
Lord art *s* face to face ....Num 14:14
s all the people were in ....Num 15:26
hath he *s* perverseness in......Num 23:21
s him not, and cast it upon....Num 35:23
s the sons of the Anakim .....Deut 1:28
s all that the Lord your ....Deut 3:21
which thine eyes have *s* ....Deut 4:9
and when thou *s* the sun ......Deut 4:19
I have *s* this people...........Deut 9:13
not *s* the chastisement ....Deut 11:2
be no leavened bread *s* ....Deut 16:4
and *s* horses, and chariots .....Deut 20:1
s all that the Lord did ....Deut 29:2
s their abominations ....Deut 29:17
s that their power is gone .....Deut 32:36
s I am a great people ....Josh 17:14
s all that the Lord ....Josh 23:3
had *s* all the great works ....Judg 2:7
s an angel of the Lord face....Judg 6:22
s the shadow of the.............Judg 9:36
my name, *s* it is secret? ....Judg 13:18
because we have *s* God ....Judg 13:22
we have *s* the land ....Judg 18:9
s that this man is come ....Judg 19:23
s the women are destroyed ....Judg 21:16
s the Lord hath testified ......Ruth 1:21
of the Philistines had *s* it......1Sam 6:16
s I have rejected him from 1Sam 16:1
for the Lord *s* not as man.....1Sam 16:7
not as man *s*, for man 1Sam 16:7
Have ye *s* this man 1Sam 17:25
s that I am a poor man 1Sam 18:23
Saul *s* and knew..the Lord 1Sam 18:28
Israel: thou *s* it, and didst.....1Sam 19:5
s the company of the prophets .1Sam 19:20
David *s* that Saul was come ...1Sam 23:15
s how that the Lord had 1Sam 24:10
s the Lord hath withholden....1Sam 25:26
Amnon, *s* he was dead..........2Sam 13:39
s to come into the city 2Sam 17:17
s that thou hast no tidings.....2Sam 18:22
was *s* upon the wings of.......2Sam 22:11
mine eyes even *s* it 1Kin 1:48
ends of the staves were *s*......1Kin 8:8
were not *s* without 1Kin 8:8
and mine eyes had *s* it 1Kin 10:7
s what way the man of God ...1Kin 13:12
S thou how Ahab humbleth ...1Kin 21:29
is pleasant, as my lord *s* 2Kin 2:19
s yesterday the blood of 2Kin 9:26
s your master's sons are.......2Kin 10:2
they *s* in thine house? 2Kin 20:15
when he had *s* him 2Kin 23:29
s there is no wrong 1Chr 12:17
I *s* with joy thy people 1Chr 29:17
s the heaven and heaven 2Chr 2:6
staves were *s* from the ark 2Chr 5:9
they were not *s* without 2Chr 5:9
and mine eyes had *s* it 2Chr 9:6
had *s* the first house ....Ezra 3:12
s that thou our God hast......Ezra 9:13
sad, *s* thou art not............Neh 2:2
as I have *s*, they that plow ....Job 4:8
eye of him that hath *s* me .....Job 7:8
and *s* the place of stones ......Job 8:17
or *s* thou as man seeth? ....Job 10:4
ghost, and no eye had *s* me! ..Job 10:18
he *s* wickedness also ....Job 11:11
s his days are determined .....Job 14:5
I have *s* I will declare.........Job 15:17
s he judgeth those that........Job 21:22
all ye yourselves have *s* it .....Job 27:12
his eye *s* every precious ....Job 28:10
S it is hid from the eyes ......Job 28:21
s under the whole heaven .....Job 28:24
have *s* any perish for want ....Job 31:19
that it cannot be *s* ....Job 33:21
bones that were not *s* stick ....Job 33:21
and he *s* all his goings ....Job 34:21
s the treasures of the hail .....Job 38:22
Thou hast *s* it; for thou ....Ps 10:14
s he delighted in him ....Ps 22:8
aha, our eye hath *s* it.........Ps 35:21
s that his day is coming ....Ps 37:13
have I not *s* the righteous .....Ps 37:25
s the wicked in great power ...Ps 37:35
They *s* it..they marveled ......Ps 48:5
When thou *s* a thief ....Ps 50:18
mine eye hath *s* his desire.....Ps 54:7
when he *s* the vengeance ......Ps 58:10
s thee in the sanctuary ....Ps 63:2
wherein we have *s* evil.........Ps 90:15
s an end of all perfection .....Ps 119:96
s he hath no heart to ....Prov 17:16
S thou a man diligent.........Prov 22:29
whom thine eyes have *s*.......Prov 25:7
S thou a man wise in his ......Prov 26:12
S thou a man that is hasty ....Prov 29:20
eye is not satisfied with *s* .....Eccl 1:8
s all the works that are done ..Eccl 1:14
not *s* the evil work that ....Eccl 4:3
s the oppression of the poor ..Eccl 5:8
Behold that which I have *s* ....Eccl 5:18
he hath not *s* the sun ....Eccl 6:5
S there be many things ....Eccl 6:11
s in the days of my vanity.....Eccl 7:15
neither day nor night *s* sleep ..Eccl 8:16
This wisdom have I *s* also .....Eccl 9:13
s servants upon horses ....Eccl 10:7
mine eyes have *s* the King ....Is 6:5
is *s* that Moab is weary ....Is 16:12
I was dismayed at the *s* ....Is 21:3
Let him declare what he *s*.....Is 21:6
and they say, Who *s* us? ......Is 29:15
I have *s* thy tears ....Is 38:5
they *s* in thine house? ....Is 39:4
in mine house have they *s*.....Is 39:4
S many things, but thou ......Is 42:20
thy shame shall be *s* ....Is 47:3
thou hast said, None *s* me ....Is 47:10
say they, and thou *s* not? .....Is 58:3
glory shall be *s* upon thee .....Is 60:2
who hath *s* such things? ....Is 66:8
Jeremiah, what *s* thou? ....Jer 1:11
Thou hast well *s*; for I ....Jer 1:12
even I have *s* it, saith..........Jer 7:11
S thou not what they do ......Jer 7:17
s she hath wrought lewdness...Jer 11:15
I have *s* thine adulteries ....Jer 13:27
s also in the prophets of ......Jer 23:14
What *s* thou, Jeremiah? ....Jer 24:3
have I *s* them dismayed ....Jer 46:5
have *s* her nakedness ....Lam 1:8
have *s* vain and foolish.........Lam 2:14
s for thee false burdens ....Lam 2:14
I am the man that hath *s* .....Lam 3:1
s all their vengeance ....Lam 3:60
I *s* visions of God ....Ezek 1:1
which I *s* by the river ....Ezek 3:23
s thou what they do? ....Ezek 8:6
s what the ancients of.........Ezek 8:12
The Lord *s* us not ....Ezek 8:12
vision that I had *s* went up ....Ezek 11:24
he *s* is for many days ....Ezek 12:27
s vanity and lying.............Ezek 13:6
spoken vanity, and *s* lies ......Ezek 13:8
s thou doest all these ....Ezek 16:30
S then that I will cut off ......Ezek 21:4
s the sword come upon the ....Ezek 33:3
as thou *s*, deal with thy ....Dan 1:13
dream which I have *s* ....Dan 2:26
s thou couldst reveal this......Dan 2:47
Nebuchadnezzar have *s* ....Dan 4:18
I Daniel, had *s* the vision .....Dan 8:15
s thou hast forgotten the ......Hos 4:6
I have *s* a horrible thing ......Hos 6:10
me, Amos, what *s* thou? ......Amos 7:8
unto me, what *s* thou? ....Zech 4:2
have I *s* with mine eyes ....Zech 9:8

diviners have *s* a lie .... Zech 10:2
have *s* his star in the east ..... Matt 2:2
When they *s* the star .... Matt 2:10
s the young child with Mary ... Matt 2:11
he *s* many of the Pharisees .... Matt 3:7
s the Spirit of God .... Matt 3:16
heart: for they shall *s* God .... Matt 5:8
they may *s* your good works ... Matt 5:16
men, to be *s* of them .... Matt 6:1
Father which *s* in secret .... Matt 6:4
they may be *s* of men .... Matt 6:5
which *s* in secret, shall .... Matt 6:18
things which ye do hear and *s* . Matt 11:4
Master, we would *s* a sign ..... Matt 12:38
because they seeing *s* not ..... Matt 13:13
ye shall *s*, and shall not .... Matt 13:14
and have not *s* them .... Matt 13:17
till they *s* the Son of man ..... Matt 16:28
they do for to be *s* of men .... Matt 23:5
shall *s* the Son of man .... Matt 24:30
Come, *s* the place where the .. Matt 28:6
s they may *s*, and not perceive . Mark 4:12
s the multitude thronging ..... Mark 5:31
s the tumult, and them .... Mark 5:38
having eyes, *s* ye not? .... Mark 8:18
and said, I *s* men as trees ..... Mark 8:24
what things they had *s* .... Mark 9:9
Jesus *s* that the people .... Mark 9:25
s one casting out devils .... Mark 9:38
they *s* the Fig tree dried ...... Mark 11:20
and had been *s* of her .... Mark 16:11
that he had *s* a vision in ...... Luke 1:22
this be, *s* I know not a man? .. Luke 1:34
that they had heard and *s* ..... Luke 2:20
eyes have *s* thy salvation ...... Luke 2:30
We have *s* strange things ...... Luke 5:26
John what things ye have *s* .... Luke 7:22
Simon, *S* thou this woman? ... Luke 7:44
s they might not *s*, and .... Luke 8:10
till they *s* the kingdom of God . Luke 9:27
and have not *s* them .... Luke 10:24
s Abraham afar off .... Luke 16:23
S here; or, s there: go not .... Luke 17:23
to have *s* some miracle .... Luke 23:8
that they had *s* a spirit .... Luke 24:37
John *s* Jesus coming unto ..... John 1:29
s the Spirit descending .... John 1:33
shalt *s* greater things than ..... John 1:50
s that thou doest these .... John 2:18
testify that we have *s* .... John 3:11
what he hath *s* and heard ..... John 3:32
Come, *s* a man, which told me . John 4:29
voice at any time, nor *s* his ... John 5:37
thou then, that we may *s*? .... John 6:30
ye also have *s* me, and .... John 6:36
every one which *s* the Son .... John 6:40
man hath *s* the Father .... John 6:46
I have *s* with my Father .... John 8:38
Abraham rejoiced to *s* my ..... John 8:56
s him that he was blind .... John 9:8
Thou hast both *s* him .... John 9:37
they which *s* not might *s* ...... John 9:39
s the wolf coming, and .... John 10:12
Sir, we would *s* Jesus .... John 12:21
eyes..that they should not *s* ... John 12:40
s me *s* him that sent me ...... John 12:45
know him, and have *s* him .... John 14:7
s me hath *s* the Father .... John 14:9
the world *s* me no more .... John 14:19
they both *s* and hated both me . John 15:24
and *s* the linen clothes .... John 20:6
that she had *s* the Lord .... John 20:18
We have *s* the Lord .... John 20:25
because thou hast *s* me .... John 20:29
are they that have not *s* .... John 20:29
s the disciple whom Jesus ..... John 21:20
Peter *s* him saith to Jesus ..... John 21:21
being *s* of them forty days .... Acts 1:3
s him go into heaven .... Acts 1:11
s it is but the third hour ...... Acts 2:15
Who *s* Peter and John about .. Acts 3:3
we have *s* and heard .... Acts 4:20
I have *s* the affliction .... Acts 7:34
s the miracles which .... Acts 8:6
hath *s* in a vision a man ...... Acts 9:12
vision which he had *s* .... Acts 10:17
had *s* the grace of God .... Acts 11:23
not *s* the sun for a season ..... Acts 13:11
after he had *s* the vision ...... Acts 16:10
s the prison doors open .... Acts 16:27
s he giveth to all life .... Acts 17:25
Thou *s*, brother, how many ... Acts 21:20
had *s* before with him .... Acts 21:29
thou hast *s* and heard .... Acts 22:15
S that by thee we enjoy .... Acts 24:2
things which thou hast *s* ...... Acts 26:16
the world are clearly *s* .... Rom 1:20
S it is one God, which shall ... Rom 3:30
hope that is *s* is not hope ..... Rom 8:24
for what a man *s*, why .... Rom 8:24
eyes that they should not *s* .... Rom 11:8
not spoken of, they shall *s* .... Rom 15:21
Eye hath not *s*, nor ear 1Cor 2:9
have I not *s* Jesus Christ 1Cor 9:1
s he understandeth not 1Cor 14:16
that he was *s* of Cephas 1Cor 15:5
s of about five hundred 1Cor 15:6
that, he was *s* of James 1Cor 15:7
S then that we have such 2Cor 3:12
at the things which are *s* 2Cor 4:18
things which are not *s* 2Cor 4:18
which are *s* are temporal 2Cor 4:18
which are not *s* are eternal 2Cor 4:18
S that many glory after 2Cor 11:18
that which he *s* me to be 2Cor 12:6
heard, and *s* in me, do .... Phil 4:9
not *s* my face in the flesh ..... Col 2:1
s that ye have put off .... Col 3:9
S it is a righteous thing 2Thess 1:6
in the Spirit, *s* of angels 1Tim 3:16
whom no man hath *s*, nor 1Tim 6:16
but we *s* Jesus, who was made . Heb 2:9
S therefore it remaineth .... Heb 4:6
s ye are dull of hearing .... Heb 5:11
s he ever liveth to make ...... Heb 7:25
S..thou make all things .... Heb 8:5
evidence of things not *s* .... Heb 11:1
are *s* were not made .... Heb 11:3
but having *s* them afar off ..... Heb 11:13
as *s* him who is invisible ...... Heb 11:27
S thou how faith wrought ..... James 2:22
s the end of the Lord .... James 5:11
having not *s*, ye love 1Pet 1:8
S ye have purified your 1Pet 1:22
he that will..*s* good days 1Pet 3:10
among them, in *s* and hearing . 2Pet 2:8
s that ye look for..things 2Pet 3:14
have *s* with our eyes 1John 1:1
we have *s* and heard 1John 1:3
for we shall *s* him as he is 1John 3:2
s his brother have need 1John 3:17
No man hath *s* God 1John 4:12
brother whom he hath *s* 1John 4:20
God whom he hath not *s*? 1John 4:20
doeth evil hath not *s* God 3John 11
and every eye shall *s* .... Rev 1:7
What thou *s*, write in a .... Rev 1:11
the things..thou hast *s* .... Rev 1:19
with eyesalve, that thou..*s* ..... Rev 3:18
when I had heard and *s* .... Rev 22:8

SEED—*the particle of matter that transmits life; one's descendants*

Descriptive of:
One's ancestry .... Gen 12:7
Messianic line .... Gen 21:12
Nation 2Kin 17:20
Christ .... Gal 3:16, 19

Figurative of true believers:
Born of God 1Pet 1:23
Abraham's true children. . Gal 3:29
Children of promise ..... Rom 9:7, 8
Including Israel's faithful . Rom 9:29

Sowing of, figurative of:
God's Word .... Matt 13:3, 32
Spiritual blessings 1Cor 9:11
Christ's death .... John 12:24
Christian's body 1Cor 15:36-49

[*also* SEED'S, SEEDS]
the herb yielding *s* .... Gen 1:11
whose *s* is in itself .... Gen 1:11
and herb yielding *s* after ...... Gen 1:12
whose *s* was in itself .... Gen 1:12
every herb bearing *s* .... Gen 1:29
fruit of a tree yielding *s* .... Gen 1:29
between thy *s* and her *s* .... Gen 3:15
s alive upon the face of all .... Gen 7:3
and with your *s* after you ..... Gen 9:9
give it, and to thy *s* for ever .. Gen 13:15
make thy *s* as the dust of ..... Gen 13:16
thy *s* also be numbered .... Gen 13:16
to me thou hast given no *s* .... Gen 15:3
thy *s* shall be a stranger .... Gen 15:13
multiply thy *s* exceedingly ..... Gen 16:10
me and thee and thy *s* .... Gen 17:7
and to thy *s* after thee .... Gen 17:7
and thy *s* after thee in .... Gen 17:9
which is not of thy *s* .... Gen 17:12
preserve *s* of our father .... Gen 19:32
a nation, because he is thy *s* .. Gen 21:13
multiply thy *s* as the stars ..... Gen 22:17
s shall possess the gate .... Gen 22:17
Unto thy *s* will I give this ..... Gen 24:7
unto thee, and unto thy *s* ..... Gen 26:3
s to multiply as the stars ...... Gen 26:4
give unto thy *s* all these .... Gen 26:4
and in thy *s* shall all the ...... Gen 26:4
and to thy *s* with thee .... Gen 28:4
thy *s* shall be as the dust ...... Gen 28:14
and in thy *s* shall all the ...... Gen 28:14
to thy *s* after thee will I .... Gen 35:12
the *s* should not be his .... Gen 38:9
should give *s* to his brother ... Gen 38:9
all his *s* brought he with ...... Gen 46:7
here is *s* for you, and ye ...... Gen 47:23
give this land to thy *s* .... Gen 48:4
s shall become a multitude .... Gen 48:19
and it was like coriander *s* .... Ex 16:31
to him and to his *s* .... Ex 30:21
I will multiply your *s* .... Ex 32:13
will I give unto your *s* .... Ex 32:13
fall upon any sowing *s* .... Lev 11:37
woman have conceived *s* ...... Lev 12:2
is the *s* of copulation .... Lev 15:17
whose *s* goeth from him ...... Lev 15:32
thy field with mingled *s* ...... Lev 19:19
he hath given of his *s* .... Lev 20:3
shall he profane his *s* .... Lev 21:15
hath a blemish of the *s* .... Lev 21:21
What man soever of the *s* ..... Lev 22:4
whose *s* goeth from him ...... Lev 22:4
be according to the *s* .... Lev 27:16
barley *s* shall be valued .... Lev 27:16
and shall conceive *s* .... Num 5:28
and his *s* shall possess it ...... Num 14:24
and to thy *s* with thee .... Num 18:19
s shall be in many waters ..... Num 24:7
unto them and to their *s* ...... Deut 1:8
chose their *s* after them .... Deut 10:15
where thou sowedst thy *s* ..... Deut 11:10
vineyard with divers *s* .... Deut 22:9
fruit of thy *s* which thou ...... Deut 22:9
and upon thy *s* for ever .... Deut 28:46
and the heart of thy *s* .... Deut 30:6
of the mouths of their *s* ...... Deut 31:21
between my *s* and thy *s* 1Sam 20:42
day of Saul, and of his *s* 2Sam 4:8
and to his *s* for evermore 2Sam 22:51
and upon the head of his *s* 1Kin 2:33
David, and upon his *s* 1Kin 2:33
of the king's *s* in Edom 1Kin 11:14
contain two measures of *s* 1Kin 18:32
and unto thy *s* for ever 2Kin 5:27
destroyed all the *s* royal 2Kin 11:1
of Elishama, of the *s* royal 2Kin 25:25
ye *s* of Israel his servant 1Chr 16:13
it to the *s* of Abraham 2Chr 20:7
father's house, and their *s* ..... Ezra 2:59
father's house, nor their *s* ..... Neh 7:61
I say, to his *s*, and hast .... Neh 9:8
be of the *s* of the Jews .... Esth 6:13
perish from their *s* .... Esth 9:28
peace to all his *s* .... Esth 10:3

that thy *s* shall be great ....Job 5:25
s is established in their........Job 21:8
he will bring home thy *s* ....Job 39:12
and to his *s* for evermore .....Ps 18:50
all ye the *s* of Jacob, glorify ...Ps 22:23
all ye the *s* of Israel ....Ps 22:23
s shall inherit the earth ....Ps 25:13
nor his *s* begging bread ....Ps 37:25
and his *s* is blessed ....Ps 37:26
s also of his servants shall .....Ps 69:36
s will I establish for ever .....Ps 89:4
His *s* also will I make to ......Ps 89:29
s shall be established ....Ps 102:28
overthrow their *s* also ....Ps 106:27
weepeth, bearing precious *s* ...Ps 126:6
but the *s* of the righteous .....Prov 11:21
In the morning sow thy *s* .....Eccl 11:6
a *s* of evildoers, children ....Is 1:4
holy *s* shall be the substance ..Is 6:13
make thy *s* to flourish ....Is 17:11
he give the rain of thy *s* ......Is 30:23
bring thy *s* from the east ......Is 43:5
not unto the *s* of Jacob ....Is 45:19
s also had been as the ....Is 48:19
s shall inherit the Gentiles ....Is 54:3
s of the adulterer and the .....Is 57:3
of the mouth of thy *s* ....Is 59:21
s shall be known among the ...Is 61:9
s which the Lord hath blessed..Is 61:9
s of the blessed of the Lord ...Is 65:23
noble vine, wholly a right *s* ...Jer 2:21
cast out, he and his *s* ....Jer 22:28
s of the house of Israel ....Jer 23:8
s from the land of their ....Jer 30:10
s of Israel also shall cease .....Jer 31:36
I multiply the *s* of David ......Jer 33:22
cast away the *s* of Jacob ....Jer 33:26
I will not take any of his *s* ....Jer 33:26
over the *s* of Abraham ....Jer 33:26
vineyard, nor field, nor *s*......Jer 35:9
of Elishama, of the *s* royal ....Jer 41:1
his *s* is spoiled, and his ....Jer 49:10
also of the *s* of the land.......Ezek 17:5
s of the house of Jacob ....Ezek 20:5
of the *s* of the house of ....Ezek 44:22
of the king's *s*, and of ....Dan 1:3
of the *s* of the Medes ....Dan 9:1
The *s* is rotten under their ....Joel 1:17
grapes him that soweth *s* ......Amos 9:13
Is the *s* yet in the barn? ......Hag 2:19
the *s* shall be prosperous ......Zech 8:12
I will corrupt your *s* ....Mal 2:3
s fell by the way side ....Matt 13:4
received *s* by the way side ....Matt 13:19
the *s* into stony places ....Matt 13:20
s into the good ground........Matt 13:23
sow good *s* in thy field?.......Matt 13:27
good *s* is the Son of man .....Matt 13:37
as a grain of mustard *s*........Matt 17:20
cast *s* into the ground.........Mark 4:26
like a grain of mustard *s* ......Mark 4:31
less than all the *s* that ....Mark 4:31
and dying left no *s* ....Mark 12:20
had her, and left no *s*.........Mark 12:22
to Abraham, and to his *s* .....Luke 1:55
The *s* is the word of God .....Luke 8:11
as a grain of mustard *s*........Luke 17:6
Christ cometh of the *s* of .....John 7:42
that ye are Abraham's *s* ......John 8:37
in thy *s* shall all the ....Acts 3:25
his *s* should sojourn in a ......Acts 7:6
made of the *s* of David ....Rom 1:3
might be sure to all the *s* .....Rom 4:16
of the *s* of Abraham ....Rom 11:1
ministereth *s* to the sower 2Cor 9:10
and multiply your *s* sown 2Cor 9:10
Christ of the *s* of David.......2Tim 2:8
on him the *s* of Abraham .....Heb 2:16
Isaac shall thy *s* be called .....Heb 11:18
again, not of corruptible *s*.....1Pet 1:23
his *s* remaineth in him 1John 3:9
with the remnant of her *s* .....Rev 12:17

SEEDTIME—*time for sowing seeds*
s and harvest, and cold ....Gen 8:22

SEEING—*See* SEE

SEEK—*to look for; attempt to obtain*

Things of the world:
Worldly things ....Matt 6:32
One's life ....Luke 17:33
One's selfish interest .....Phil 2:21

Things of the Spirit:
True wisdom ....Prov 2:4
God's kingdom ....Matt 6:33
Another's benefit 2Cor 12:14
Peace 1Pet 3:11
Heavenly country........Heb 11:14

[*also* SEEKEST, SEEKETH, SEEKING, SOUGHT]
saying, What *s* thou? ....Gen 37:15
I *s* my brethren: tell me.......Gen 37:16
he *s* to slay Moses ....Ex 2:15
shall not *s* for yellow hair .....Lev 13:36
s not after your own heart ....Num 15:39
s ye the priesthood also? ......Num 16:10
to *s* for enchantments ....Num 24:1
thou shalt *s* the Lord ....Deut 4:29
s him with all thy heart ....Deut 4:29
his habitation shall ye *s* ....Deut 12:5
until thy brother *s* after it .....Deut 22:2
Thou shalt not *s* their peace ...Deut 23:6
the man whom thou *s*.........Judg 4:22
shall I not *s* rest for thee......Ruth 3:1
and arise, go *s* the asses 1Sam 9:3
he said, To *s* the asses 1Sam 10:14
Saul my father *s* to kill 1Sam 19:2
Saul *s* to smite David 1Sam 19:10
that *s* my life *s* thy life.......1Sam 22:23
come out to *s* his life 1Sam 23:15
to *s* David and his men 1Sam 24:2
Behold, David *s* thy hurt?......1Sam 24:9
pursue thee, and to *s* thy soul .1Sam 25:29
is come out to *s* a flea 1Sam 26:20
S me a woman that hath 1Sam 28:7
came up to *s* David...........2Sam 5:17
of my bowels, *s* my life 2Sam 16:11
the man whom thou *s*..........2Sam 17:3
thou *s* to destroy a city 2Sam 20:19
Achish to *s* his servants 1Kin 2:40
s to go to thine own 1Kin 11:22
they *s* my life, to take 1Kin 19:10
how this man *s* mischief.......1Kin 20:7
thee, and *s* thy master 2Kin 2:16
he *s* a quarrel against me 2Kin 5:7
s pasture for their flocks 1Chr 4:39
rejoice that *s* the Lord 1Chr 16:10
S the Lord and his strength ...1Chr 16:11
s his face continually..........1Chr 16:11
s for all the commandments ...1Chr 28:8
s my face, and turn from......2Chr 7:14
not his heart to *s* 2Chr 12:14
we have *s* the Lord our God ..2Chr 14:7
s him, he will be found 2Chr 15:2
would not *s* the Lord 2Chr 15:13
set himself to *s* the Lord 2Chr 20:3
s the Lord..all his heart 2Chr 22:9
his heart to *s* God 2Chr 30:19
began to *s* after the God 2Chr 34:3
for we *s* your God, as ye do ..Ezra 4:2
to *s* the law of the Lord ......Ezra 7:10
them for good that *s* him .....Ezra 8:22
to *s* the welfare of the ....Neh 2:10
s the wealth of his people .....Esth 10:3
I would *s* unto God ....Job 5:8
wouldest *s* unto God..........Job 8:5
thence she *s* the prey ....Job 39:29
and *s* after leasing? ....Ps 4:2
will not *s* after God ....Ps 10:4
understand, and *s* God ....Ps 14:2
of them that *s* him ....Ps 24:6
that *s* thy face, O Jacob.......Ps 24:6
saidst, *S* ye my face ....Ps 27:8
Thy face, Lord, will I *s* ....Ps 27:8
I *s* the Lord, and he ....Ps 34:4
s peace, and pursue it ....Ps 34:14
righteous, and *s* to slay him ...Ps 37:32
s after my life lay snares ......Ps 38:12
that *s* my hurt speak ....Ps 38:12
those that *s* thee rejoice ......Ps 40:16
oppressors *s* after my soul .....Ps 54:3
that *s* my soul, to destroy .....Ps 63:9
heart shall live that *s* God .....Ps 69:32
those that *s* thee rejoice ......Ps 70:4
unto shame, that *s* my hurt....Ps 71:24
my trouble I *s* the Lord ....Ps 77:2
s their meat from God ....Ps 104:21
S the Lord, and his strength...Ps 105:4
s his face evermore ....Ps 105:4
that *s* him with the whole .....Ps 119:2
for they *s* not thy statutes .....Ps 119:155
God I will *s* thy good ....Ps 122:9
they shall *s* me early ....Prov 1:28
If thou *s* her as silver ....Prov 2:4
s me early shall find me.......Prov 8:17
s good procureth favor ....Prov 11:27
he that *s* mischief, it ....Prov 11:27
understanding *s* knowledge ....Prov 15:14
evil man *s* only rebellion ......Prov 17:11
s and intermeddleth with ......Prov 18:1
that go to *s* mixed wine ....Prov 23:30
s the Lord understand ....Prov 28:5
Many *s* the ruler's favor ......Prov 29:26
She *s* wool, and flax ....Prov 31:13
heart to *s* and search out ......Eccl 1:13
I *s* in mine heart to give ......Eccl 2:3
Which yet my soul *s*, but I ....Eccl 7:28
man labor to *s* it out ....Eccl 8:17
will *s* him whom my soul......Song 3:2
s judgment, relieve the........Is 1:17
S unto them that have ....Is 8:19
people *s* unto their God? .....Is 8:19
to it shall the Gentiles *s*.......Is 11:10
judging, and *s* judgment ......Is 16:5
will I *s* thee early.............Is 26:9
Israel, neither *s* the Lord! .....Is 31:1
s unto him a cunning ....Is 40:20
Thou shalt *s* them and shalt ...Is 41:12
poor and needy *s* water ....Is 41:17
ye that *s* the Lord ....Is 51:1
s me daily, and delight........Is 58:2
that *s* her will not weary ......Jer 2:24
thee, they will *s* thy life ....Jer 4:30
judgment, that *s* the truth .....Jer 5:1
s thy life, saying, Prophesy ....Jer 11:21
and they that *s* their lives .....Jer 19:9
hand of them that *s* thy life ...Jer 22:25
ye shall *s* me, and find me ....Jer 29:13
them that *s* their life ....Jer 34:20
s not the welfare of this.......Jer 38:4
these men that *s* thy life ....Jer 38:16
s thou great things for ....Jer 45:5
for thyself? *s* them not ....Jer 45:5
them that *s* their life ....Jer 49:37
people sigh, they *s* bread......Lam 1:11
to the soul that *s* him ....Lam 3:25
they shall *s* peace, and there ..Ezek 7:25
punishment of him that *s*......Ezek 14:10
search or *s* after them ....Ezek 34:6
so will I *s* out my sheep.......Ezek 34:12
s by prayer and supplications ..Dan 9:3
she shall *s* them, but..........Hos 2:7
their herds to *s* the Lord ......Hos 5:6
offense, and *s* my face ....Hos 5:15
they will *s* me early...........Hos 5:15
for it is time to *s* the Lord ....Hos 10:12
S ye me, and ye shall live .....Amos 5:4
S the Lord, and ye shall ......Amos 5:6
S good, and not evil ....Amos 5:14
I *s* comforters for thee? ....Nah 3:7
S ye the Lord, all ye meek ....Zeph 2:3
s righteousness, *s* meekness ...Zeph 2:3
to *s* the Lord of hosts.........Zech 8:21
shall *s* the young one ....Zech 11:16
s the law at his mouth ....Mal 2:7
and the Lord, whom ye *s* .....Mal 3:1
s the young child to ....Matt 2:13
s, and ye shall find ....Matt 7:7
and he that *s* findeth ....Matt 7:8
generation *s* after a sign ......Matt 12:39
s rest, and findeth none ....Matt 12:43
generation *s* after a sign ......Matt 16:4
s that which is gone astray? ...Matt 18:12
s to lay hands on him.........Matt 21:46
s false witness..Jesus ....Matt 26:59

ye *s* Jesus, which was . . . . .Matt 28:5
All men *s* for thee . . . . .Mark 1:37
s of him a sign from . . . . .Mark 8:11
generation *s* after a sign? . . . . .Mark 8:12
scribes *s*..might take him . . . . . .Mark 14:1
Ye *s* Jesus of Nazareth . . . . .Mark 16:6
again to Jerusalem, *s* him . . . . .Luke 2:45
How is it that ye *s* me? . . . . . . .Luke 2:49
multitude *s* to touch him . . . . . .Luke 6:19
s, and ye shall find . . . . .Luke 11:9
and he that *s* findeth . . . . .Luke 11:10
s to catch something out . . . . . .Luke 11:54
s not ye what ye shall eat . . . . .Luke 12:29
nations of the world *s* . . . . .Luke 12:30
s ye the kingdom of God . . . . .Luke 12:31
three years I come *s* fruit . . . . .Luke 13:7
will *s* to enter in, and . . . . .Luke 13:24
s diligently till she find . . . . . . .Luke 15:8
s and to save that which . . . . . .Luke 19:10
unto them, What *s* ye? . . . . .John 1:38
Father *s* such to worship . . . . . .John 4:23
no man said, What *s* thou? . . . .John 4:27
I *s* not mine own will . . . . .John 5:30
s not the honor that . . . . .John 5:44
to Capernaum, *s* for Jesus . . . . .John 6:24
Ye *s* me, not because ye . . . . . .John 6:26
himself *s* his own glory . . . . .John 7:18
s his glory that sent him . . . . . .John 7:18
whom they *s* to kill? . . . . .John 7:25
ye shall *s* me, and shall . . . . . . .John 8:21
But now ye *s* to kill me . . . . . . .John 8:40
I *s* not mine own glory . . . . .John 8:50
Ye shall *s* me: and as I . . . . . . .John 13:33
said unto them Whom *s* ye? . . .John 18:4
he them again, Whom *s* ye? . . .John 18:7
Pilate *s* to release him . . . . .John 19:12
weepest thou? whom *s* thou? . .John 20:15
Behold, three men *s* thee . . . . .Acts 10:19
Tarsus, for to *s* Saul . . . . .Acts 11:25
When Herod had *s* for him . . . .Acts 12:19
s to turn away the deputy . . . . .Acts 13:8
might *s* after the Lord . . . . .Acts 15:17
they should *s* the Lord . . . . .Acts 17:27
in well doing *s* for glory . . . . . . .Rom 2:7
none that *s* after God . . . . .Rom 3:11
they *s* it not by faith . . . . .Rom 9:32
Greeks *s* after wisdom 1Cor 1:22
s not to be loosed 1Cor 7:27
from a wife? *s* not a wife 1Cor 7:27
Let no man *s* his own 1Cor 10:24
not *s* mine own profit 1Cor 10:33
unseemly, *s* not her own 1Cor 13:5
s that ye may excel to 1Cor 14:12
ye *s* a proof of Christ 2Cor 13:3
or do I *s* to please men? . . . . . .Gal 1:10
s to be justified by Christ . . . . .Gal 2:17
s those things which are above .Col 3:1
he *s* me out very diligently 2Tim 1:17
them that diligently *s* him . . . . .Heb 11:6
he *s* it carefully with tears . . . . .Heb 12:17
but we *s* one to come . . . . .Heb 13:14
s whom he may devour 1Pet 5:8
in those days..men *s* death . . . .Rev 9:6

SEEM—*to give the impression of being*

[*also* SEEMED, SEEMETH]
he *s* as one that mocked . . . . . .Gen 19:14
s to him as a deceiver . . . . .Gen 27:12
It *s* to me there is as . . . . .Lev 14:35
S it but a small thing . . . . .Num 16:9
not *s* hard unto thee . . . . .Deut 15:18
as it *s* good and right . . . . .Josh 9:25
s evil unto you to serve . . . . . . .Josh 24:15
s good unto thee . . . . .Judg 10:15
Do what *s* thee good 1Sam 1:23
all that *s* good unto you 1Sam 11:10
Do what *s* good unto thee 1Sam 14:40
shall *s* good unto thee 1Sam 24:4
all that *s* good to Israel 2Sam 3:19
do that which *s* him good 2Sam 10:12
What *s* you best I will do 2Sam 18:4
shall *s* good unto thee 2Sam 19:37
if it *s* good to thee 1Kin 21:2
If it *s* good unto you 1Chr 13:2
if it *s* good to the king . . . . .Ezra 5:17
not all the trouble *s* little . . . . .Neh 9:32
as it *s* good to thee . . . . .Esth 3:11
If it *s* good unto the king . . . . .Esth 5:4
which *s* right unto a man . . . . . .Prov 14:12
in his own cause *s* just . . . . . . .Prov 18:17
and it *s* great unto me . . . . .Eccl 9:13
as *s* good to the potter . . . . .Jer 18:4
do with me as *s* good . . . . .Jer 26:14
s good unto thee to come . . . . . .Jer 40:4
s ill unto thee to come . . . . .Jer 40:4
it *s*..convenient unto . . . . .Jer 40:5
S it a small thing unto you . . . .Ezek 34:18
they shall *s* like torches . . . . . . .Nah 2:4
so it *s* good in thy sight . . . . . . .Matt 11:26
It *s* good to me also . . . . .Luke 1:3
that which he *s* to have . . . . . . .Luke 8:18
words *s* to them as idle . . . . . . .Luke 24:11
s good unto us, being . . . . .Acts 15:25
He *s* to be a setter forth . . . . . .Acts 17:18
s to be wise in this world 1Cor 3:18
man *s* to be contentious 1Cor 11:16
s to be more feeble 1Cor 12:22
not *s* as if I would terrify 2Cor 10:9
these who *s* to be somewhat . . .Gal 2:6
who *s* to be pillars . . . . .Gal 2:9
s to come short of it . . . . .Heb 4:1
present *s* to be joyous . . . . .Heb 12:11
you *s* to be religious . . . . .James 1:26

SEEMLY—*appropriate*
Delight is not *s* for a fool . . . . .Prov 19:10

SEEN—*See* **SEE**

SEER—*prophet*
Amos . . . . .Amos 7:12
Asaph 2Chr 29:30
Gad .2Sam 24:11
Heman 1Chr 25:5
Samuel 1Sam 9:19
Zadok 2Sam 15:27
Iddo 2Chr 9:29
Hanani 2Chr 16:7
Jeduthun 2Chr 35:15

[*also* SEER'S, SEERS]
and let us go to the *s* 1Sam 9:9
beforetime called a *S* 1Sam 9:9
where the *s* house is 1Sam 9:18
prophets, and by all the *s* 2Kin 17:13
David and Samuel the *s* 1Chr 9:22
unto Gad, David's *s* 1Chr 21:9
all that Samuel the *s* 1Chr 26:28
book of Samuel the *s* 1Chr 29:29
the book of Gad the *s* 1Chr 29:29
Iddo the *s* concerning 2Chr 12:15
Asa was wroth with the *s* 2Chr 16:10
of Hanani the *s* went out 2Chr 19:2
and of Gad the king's *s* 2Chr 29:25
words of the *s* that spake 2Chr 33:18
among the sayings of the *s* 2Chr 33:19
the *s* hath he covered . . . . .Is 29:10
say to the *s*, See not . . . . .Is 30:10
shall the *s* be ashamed . . . . .Mic 3:7

SEEST, SEETH—*See* **SEE**

SEETHE—*to boil*

[*also* SEETHING]
and *s* that ye will *s* . . . . .Ex 16:23
not *s* a kid in his mother's . . . .Ex 23:19
and *s* his flesh in the holy . . . . .Ex 29:31
not *s* a kid in his mother's . . . .Deut 14:21
while the flesh was in *s* 1Sam 2:13
s pottage for the sons 2Kin 4:38
as out of a *s* pot or caldron . . .Job 41:20
I see a *s* pot; and the face . . . .Jer 1:13
let them *s* the bones of it . . . . .Ezek 24:5
and take of them, and *s* . . . . . . .Zech 14:21

SEGUB (sē'gŭb)—*"might; protection"*
1. Son of Hiel 1Kin 16:34
2. Son of Hezron 1Chr 2:21, 22

SEIR (sē'ĭr)—*"rough; wooded"*
1. Mt. Seir . . . . .Gen 14:6
   Home of Esau . . . . .Gen 32:3
   Mountain range of Edom.Gen 36:21
   Horites dispossessed by Esau's descendants . . . .Deut 2:12
   Refuge of Amalekite remnant 1Chr 4:42, 43
   Desolation of . . . . .Ezek 35:15
2. Landmark on Judah's boundary . . . . .Josh 15:10

I come unto my lord unto *S* . . .Gen 33:14
dwelt Esau in mount *S* . . . . .Gen 36:8
the sons of *S* the Horite . . . . . .Gen 36:20
dukes in the land of *S* . . . . .Gen 36:30
S also shall be a possession . . . .Num 24:18
by the way of mount *S* . . . . .Deut 1:2
we compassed mount *S* . . . . . . .Deut 2:1
given mount *S* unto Esau . . . . .Deut 2:5
of Esau, which dwelt in *S* . . . . .Deut 2:8
rose up from *S* unto them . . . . .Deut 33:2
that goeth up to *S* . . . . .Josh 11:17
gave unto Esau mount *S* . . . . . .Josh 24:4
thou wentest out of *S* . . . . .Judg 5:4
the sons of *S*; Lotan, and 1Chr 1:38
and Moab and mount *S* 2Chr 20:10
inhabitants of mount *S* 2Chr 20:23
of the inhabitants of *S* 2Chr 20:23
gods of the children of *S* 2Chr 25:14
He calleth to me out of *S* . . . . .Is 21:11
that Moab and *S* do say . . . . . . .Ezek 25:8
Behold, O mount *S*, I am . . . . .Ezek 35:3

SEIRATH (sē-ī'răth)—*"tempest"*
Ehud's refuge . . . . .Judg 3:26

SEIZE—*to take by force; keep fast; hold*
Let darkness . . . . .Job 3:6
Let us kill him and . . . . . .Matt 21:38

[*also* SEIZED]
and *s* upon the city . . . . .Josh 8:7
Let death *s* upon them . . . . .Ps 55:15
and fear hath *s* on her . . . . .Jer 49:24

SELAH (sē'lä)—*"a rock"*
Place in Edom 2Kin 14:7

[*also* SELA]
from *S* to the wilderness . . . . . .Is 16:1

SELAH (sē'lä)—*a musical term, possibly indicating an intended pause*
out of his holy hill. *S* . . . . .Ps 3:4
seek after leasing? *S* . . . . .Ps 4:2
honor in the dust. *S* . . . . .Ps 7:5
to be but men. *S* . . . . .Ps 9:20
the request of his lips. *S* . . . . . .Ps 21:2
he is the King of glory. *S* . . . . .Ps 24:10
iniquity of my sin. *S* . . . . .Ps 32:5
is altogether vanity. *S* . . . . .Ps 39:5
thy name for ever. *S* . . . . .Ps 44:8
Jacob is our refuge. *S* . . . . .Ps 46:7
establish it for ever. *S* . . . . .Ps 48:8
for he shall receive me. *S* . . . . .Ps 49:15
speak righteousness. *S* . . . . .Ps 52:3
set God before them. *S* . . . . .Ps 54:3
that abideth of old. *S* . . . . .Ps 55:19
fallen themselves. *S* . . . . .Ps 57:6
the ends of the earth. *S* . . . . . . .Ps 59:13
the covert of thy wings. *S* . . . . .Ps 61:4
God is a refuge for us. *S* . . . . . .Ps 62:8
exalt themselves. *S* . . . . .Ps 66:7
face to shine upon us; *S* . . . . . .Ps 67:1
through the wilderness: *S* . . . . .Ps 68:7
praises unto the Lord; *S* . . . . . .Ps 68:32
bear up the pillars of it. *S* . . . . .Ps 75:3
sword, and the battle. *S* . . . . . . .Ps 76:3
spirit was overwhelmed. *S* . . . . .Ps 77:3
of Jacob and Joseph. *S* . . . . . . .Ps 77:15
of the wicked? *S* . . . . .Ps 82:2
be still praising thee. *S* . . . . .Ps 84:4
covered all their sin. *S* . . . . .Ps 85:2
man was born there. *S* . . . . .Ps 87:6
arise and praise thee? *S* . . . . . . .Ps 88:10
faithful witness in heaven. *S* . . .Ps 89:37
the hand of the grave? *S* . . . . . .Ps 89:48
have set gins for me. *S* . . . . . . .Ps 140:5
thee, as a thirsty land. *S* . . . . . .Ps 143:6
One from Mount Paran *S* . . . . . .Hab 3:3
oaths of the tribes..word. *S* . . .Hab 3:9
foundation unto the neck. *S* . . .Hab 3:13

S

SELA-HAMMAH-LEKOTH (sē-lä-hă-mä'lĕ-kŏth)—*"rock of divisions"*
Cliff on the Wilderness of Maon 1Sam 23:28

SELED (sē'lĕd)—*"exultation"*
Judahite 1Chr 2:30

SELEUCIA (sĕ-lū'shĭ-ä)—*"beaten by the waves"—a seaport in Syria located about 5 miles (8 km.) north of the mouth of the Orontes River*
Paul and Barnabas embark from .... Acts 13:4

SELF—*the person; one's being*

[*also* SELVES]
swarest by thine own *s* .... Ex 32:13
own *s* that summer is now .... Luke 21:30
of mine own *s* do nothing .... John 5:30
thou me with thine own *s* .... John 17:5
your own *s* shall men arise .... Acts 20:30
judge not mine own *s* 1Cor 4:3
their own *s* to the Lord 2Cor 8:5
faith: prove your own *s* 2Cor 13:5
Know ye not your own *s* 2Cor 13:5
be lovers of their own *s* 2Tim 3:2
unto me even thine own *s* .... Philem 19
only, deceiving..own *s* .... James 1:22
his own *s* bare our sins 1Pet 2:24

SELF-ABASEMENT—*destruction to or humiliation of oneself*
Jacob, before Esau .... Gen 33:3-10
Moses, before God .... Ex 3:11
Roman, before Christ .... Luke 7:7-9
Christ, true example of .... Phil 2:5-8

SELF-ACCEPTANCE—*believing in oneself*
Based on, by Christians:
Planned before birth by God .... Ps 139:13-16
Workmanship of God .... Ps 138:8
Eph 2:10
Christ has provided life .... John 10:10
God desires man's fellowship .... John 17:3
God's love .... Rom 5:8
Living epistle of God 2Cor 3:2
Complete in Christ .... Col 2:10
Chosen by God 1Pet 2:9
Hindered by, false attitudes:
Looking on outward appearance 1Sam 16:7
Questioning God's direction .... Is 45:9
Doubting God's grace 2Cor 12:9, 10

SELF-CONDEMNATION—*declaring one's own character or actions wrong*
Caused by one's:
Heart 1John 3:20
Conscience .... John 8:7-9
Sins 2Sam 24:17
Mouth .... Job 9:20
Evil works .... Matt 23:31

SELF-CONTROL—*restraint or discipline exercised over one's behavior*
Origin of:
Brought about by Christ .... Luke 8:35
Christian grace 2Pet 1:6
Elements involved in:
Ruling one's spirit .... Prov 16:32
Soberness .... Rom 12:3
Control of the body 1Cor 9:27
Hindered by:
Fleshly lusts 1Pet 2:11
Tongue .... Ps 39:1, 2
Drink .... Prov 23:29-35
Sexual sins 1Thess 4:3, 4
Unclean spirit .... Mark 5:2-16
Self-expressionism .... Prov 25:28

SELF-DECEPTION—*being dishonest with oneself*
Factors contributing to:
Scoffers 2Pet 3:3, 4
Wordliness .... Matt 24:48-51
False teaching 1Thess 5:3
Self-deception .... Prov 14:12
Examples of:
Babylon .... Is 47:7-11
Jewish women .... Jer 44:16-19
Jewish leaders .... John 8:33, 41

SELF-DENIAL—*limitation of one's desires*
Expressed by:
"Denying" .... Titus 2:12
"Abstaining" 1Pet 4:2
"Forsaketh not" .... Luke 14:33
"Taking up the cross" .... Matt 10:38
"Crucifying the flesh" .... Gal 5:24
"Put off" .... Eph 4:22
"Mortify" .... Col 3:5
Objects of:
Appetite .... Prov 23:2
Sinful pleasures .... Heb 11:25, 26
Worldly ambitions .... Matt 16:24-26
Willingness to, manifested by:
Judah .... Gen 44:33
Moses .... Ex 32:32
Paul .... Acts 20:22-24
Commended as:
Christian duty .... Rom 12:1, 2
Rewardable .... Luke 18:28-30

SELF-EXALTATION—*taking excessive pride in oneself*
Manifested by:
Satan .... Is 14:12-15
Antichrist 2Thess 2:4
Wicked .... Ps 73:9
Evils of, seen in:
Self-abasement .... Matt 23:12
Pride .... Prov 16:18
Antidotes of:
Humility .... Prov 15:33
Christ's example .... Phil 2:5-8
See PRIDE

SELF-EXAMINATION—*considering one's attitudes or actions*
Purposes of, to:
Test one's faith 2Cor 13:5
Prepare for the Lord's Supper 1Cor 11:28-32
Prove one's work .... Gal 6:4
Prove all things 1Thess 5:21
Means of:
God Himself .... Ps 26:2
God's Word .... Heb 4:12
Christ's example .... Heb 12:1, 2

SELFISHNESS—*loving oneself above all others*
Exemplified in:
Self-love 2Tim 3:2
Self-seeking .... Phil 2:21
Avoidance of, by:
Seeking the good of others 1Cor 10:24
Putting Christ first .... Phil 1:21, 22
Manifesting love 1Cor 13:5
Examples of:
Nabal 1Sam 25:3, 11
Haman .... Esth 6:6
James and John .... Mark 10:35-37
Jewish people .... John 6:26
Solomon .... Eccl 2:10, 11
Rich fool .... Luke 12:16-21
Rich man .... Luke 16:19-25
Consequences of:
Poverty .... Prov 23:21
Sin .... Rom 13:13, 14
Loss of spirituality .... Gal 5:16, 17

SELF-RIGHTEOUSNESS—*narrow-minded boasting of one's beliefs*
Described as:
Objectionable .... Deut 9:4-6
Self-condemned .... Job 9:20
Unprofitable .... Is 57:12
Like filthy rags .... Is 64:6
Offensive .... Is 65:5
External .... Matt 23:25-28
One-sided .... Luke 11:42
Boastful .... Luke 18:11, 12
Insufficient .... Phil 3:4-9
Condemned because it:
Cannot make pure .... Prov 30:12
Cannot save .... Matt 5:20
Rejects God's righteousness .... Rom 10:3
Examples of:
Saul 1Sam 15:13-21
Young man .... Matt 19:16-20
Lawyer .... Luke 10:25, 29
Pharisees .... Luke 11:39

SELFSAME—*same; identical to*
the *s* day entered Noah .... Gen 7:13
the *s* day was Abraham .... Gen 17:26
this *s* day have I brought .... Ex 12:17
came to pass the *s* day .... Ex 12:51
s day that ye have brought .... Lev 23:14
unto Moses that *s* day .... Deut 32:48
parched corn in the *s* day .... Josh 5:11
s day the hand of the Lord .... Ezek 40:1
was healed in the *s* hour .... Matt 8:13
that one and the *s* Spirit 1Cor 12:11
wrought us for the *s* thing 2Cor 5:5

SELF-WILL—*stubborn adherence to one's own wishes*
Manifested in:
Presumption .... Num 14:40-45
Unbelief 2Kin 17:14
Evil heart .... Jer 7:24
Disobeying parents .... Deut 21:18-20
Pride .... Neh 9:16, 29
Stubbornness .... Is 48:4-8
Rejecting God's messengers .... Jer 44:16
Resisting God's Spirit .... Acts 7:51
False teaching 2Pet 2:10
Sin of, among Christians:
Illustrated .... Acts 15:36-40
Warned against .... Heb 3:7-12
Examples of:
Simeon and Levi .... Gen 49:5, 6
Israelites .... Ex 32:9
Saul 1Sam 15:19-23
David 2Sam 24:4
See PRIDE

[*also* SELF-WILLED]
s they digged down a wall .... Gen 49:6
not *s*, not soon angry .... Titus 1:7
Presumptuous are they, *s* 2Pet 2:10

SELL—*to give something to another for money or consideration*

[*also* SELLEST, SELLETH, SOLD]
S me this day thy birthright .... Gen 25:31
he *s* his birthright .... Gen 25:33
s his daughter to be a .... Ex 21:7
stealeth a man, and *s* him .... Ex 21:16
they shall *s* the live ox .... Ex 21:35
shall be *s* for his theft .... Ex 22:3
s aught unto thy neighbor .... Lev 25:14
fruits doth he *s* unto thee .... Lev 25:16
s himself unto the stranger .... Lev 25:47
s me meat for money .... Deut 2:28
not *s* her at all for money .... Deut 21:14
merchandise of him, or *s* him .... Deut 24:7
the Lord shall *s* Sisera .... Judg 4:9
s a parcel of land .... Ruth 4:3
did *s* himself to work 1Kin 21:25
Go, *s* the oil, and pay thy 2Kin 4:7
ye even *s* your brethren? .... Neh 5:8
s thy people for nought .... Ps 44:12
head of him that *s* it .... Prov 11:26
Buy the truth, and *s* it not .... Prov 23:23

fine linen, and *s* it . . . . .Prov 31:24
s the land into the hand . . . . . . .Ezek 30:12
And I will *s* your sons . . . . .Joel 3:8
s them to the Sabeans . . . . .Joel 3:8
that we may *s* corn? . . . . .Amos 8:5
s nations through her . . . . .Nah 3:4
they that *s* them say . . . . .Zech 11:5
two sparrows, *s* for a farthing .Matt 10:29
and *s* all that he hath . . . . .Matt 13:44
go and *s* that thou hast . . . . . . .Matt 19:21
s whatsoever thou hast . . . . .Mark 10:21
S that ye have, and give . . . . . .Luke 12:33
let him *s* his garment . . . . .Luke 22:36
I am carnal, *s* under sin . . . . . . .Rom 7:14
and *s*, and get gain . . . . .James 4:13
no man might buy or *s* . . . . .Rev 13:17

SELLER—*one who offers something for sale*

[*also* SELLERS]
a *s* of all kinds of . . . . .Neh 13:20
the buyer, so with the *s* . . . . . . .Is 24:2
rejoice, nor the *s* mourn . . . . . .Ezek 7:12
s shall not return to that . . . . . .Ezek 7:13
Lydia, a *s* of purple . . . . .Acts 16:14

SELVEDGE—*the edge of a fabric*
from the *s* in the coupling . . . . .Ex 26:4

SELVES—*See* SELF

SEM (sĕm)—*Greek form of Shem*
In Christ's ancestry . . . . . .Luke 3:36

SEMACHIAH (sĕm-ä-kī'ä)—*"Jehovah supports"*
Levite porter 1Chr 26:7

SEMEI (sĕm'ĕ-ī)—*Greek form of Shimei*
In Christ's ancestry . . . . . .Luke 3:26

SENAAH (sĕ-nā'ä)—*"thorny"*
Family of returnees . . . . . .Neh 7:38
Ezra 2:35
See HASSENAAH

SENATE—*the Jewish Sanhedrin*
Disturbed by miracle . . . .Acts 5:18-21

SENATORS—*men who serve as advisors*
instructed by Joseph . . . . .Ps 105:17-23

SEND—*to cause to go; deliver; transmit; summon*

[*also* SENDEST, SENDETH, SENDING, SENT, SENTEST]
God *s* him forth from . . . . .Gen 3:23
s his angel before thee . . . . .Gen 24:7
will *s* his angel with thee . . . . . .Gen 24:40
s me away that I may . . . . .Gen 24:56
s me away, that I may . . . . .Gen 30:25
I will *s* thee a kid from . . . . . . .Gen 38:17
me a pledge, till thou *s* it? . . . .Gen 38:17
If thou wilt *s* our brother . . . . .Gen 43:4
S the lad with me . . . . .Gen 43:8
For God did *s* me before . . . . .Gen 45:5
will *s* thee unto Pharaoh . . . . . .Ex 3:10
I Am hath *s* me unto you . . . . .Ex 3:14
O my Lord, *s*, I pray thee . . . .Ex 4:13
of him whom thou wilt *s* . . . . . .Ex 4:13
I will *s* swarms of flies . . . . . . .Ex 8:21
S therefore now, and . . . . .Ex 9:19
thou *s* forth thy wrath . . . . .Ex 15:7
I *s* an angel before thee . . . . . . .Ex 23:20
And I will *s* hornets . . . . .Ex 23:28
thou wilt *s* with me . . . . .Ex 33:12
s him away by the hand . . . . . . .Lev 16:21
s the pestilence among you . . . .Lev 26:25
S thou men, that..may . . . . .Num 13:2
Moses *s* to spy out the land . . .Num 13:16
land whither thou *s* us . . . . .Num 13:27
Lord *s* fiery serpents among . . .Num 21:6
s unto thee to call thee? . . . . . .Num 22:37
We will *s* men before us . . . . . .Deut 1:22
I will *s* grass in thy fields . . . . .Deut 11:15
s him out free from thee . . . . . .Deut 15:13
s her out of his house . . . . .Deut 24:1
Lord shall *s* against thee . . . . . .Deut 28:48
thou *s* us, we will . . . . .Josh 1:16
Joshua *s* men from Jericho . . . .Josh 7:2
I will *s* them, and they . . . . .Josh 18:4
s come again unto us . . . . .Judg 13:8
S away the ark of the God 1Sam 5:11
s away the ark of the God 1Sam 6:3
s it not empty; but in 1Sam 6:3
s thee a man out of the land . .1Sam 9:16
s messengers unto all 1Sam 11:3
Lord *s* me to anoint thee 1Sam 15:1
s thee to Jesse the 1Sam 16:1
S me David thy son 1Sam 16:19
it thee, and *s* thee away 1Sam 20:13
s and fetch him unto me 1Sam 20:31
whom thou didst *s* 1Sam 25:25
S me Uriah the Hittite 2Sam 11:6
evil in *s* me away is greater . . .2Sam 13:16
ye shall *s* unto me every 2Sam 15:36
which thou *s* to me for 1Kin 5:8
thou shalt *s* them 1Kin 8:44
day that the Lord *s* rain 1Kin 17:14
s, and gather to me all 1Kin 18:19
didst *s* for to thy servant 1Kin 20:9
s to inquire of Baal-zebub 2Kin 1:6
he said, Ye shall not *s* 2Kin 2:16
S me, I pray thee, one of 2Kin 4:22
s unto me to recover a man . . .2Kin 5:7
and let us *s* and see 2Kin 7:13
began to *s* against Judah 2Kin 15:37
s abroad unto our brethren 1Chr 13:2
and didst *s* him cedars to 2Chr 2:3
S me also cedar trees 2Chr 2:8
s rain upon thy land 2Chr 6:27
s pestilence among my 2Chr 7:13
Assyria *s* his servants to 2Chr 32:9
rising up betimes, and *s* 2Chr 36:15
let the king *s* his pleasure . . . . .Ezra 5:17
wouldest *s* me unto Judah . . . . .Neh 2:5
s portions unto them for . . . . . .Neh 8:10
s portions one to another . . . . .Esth 9:19
s waters upon the fields . . . . . .Job 5:10
he *s* them out, and they . . . . . . .Job 12:15
and *s* him away . . . . .Job 14:20
s forth their little ones . . . . .Job 21:11
S thee help from the . . . . .Ps 20:2
He shall *s* from heaven . . . . . . .Ps 57:3
God shall *s* forth his mercy . . . .Ps 57:3
didst *s* a plentiful rain . . . . .Ps 68:9
s evil angels among them . . . . . .Ps 78:49
He *s* the springs into the . . . . . .Ps 104:10
Thou *s* forth thy spirit . . . . .Ps 104:30
s the rod of thy strength . . . . . .Ps 110:2
S thine hand from above . . . . . .Ps 144:7
s forth his commandment . . . . .Ps 147:15
sluggard to them that *s* him . . .Prov 10:26
messenger to them that *s* . . . . . .Prov 25:13
s a message by the hand . . . . . .Prov 26:6
s forth a stinking savor . . . . .Eccl 10:1
s forth the smell . . . . .Song 1:12
Whom shall I *s*, and who . . . . .Is 6:8
Here am I; *s* me . . . . .Is 6:8
be for the *s* forth of oxen . . . . .Is 7:25
s among his fat ones . . . . .Is 10:16
s ambassadors by the sea . . . . . .Is 18:2
shall *s* them a savior . . . . .Is 19:20
I will *s* a blast upon him . . . . . .Is 37:7
his Spirit, hath *s* me . . . . .Is 48:16
I will *s* those that escape . . . . . .Is 66:19
to all that I shall *s* thee . . . . . .Jer 1:7
rising up early and *s* them . . . . .Jer 7:25
s serpents, cockatrices . . . . .Jer 8:17
s for cunning women . . . . .Jer 9:17
I will *s* for many fishers . . . . . . .Jer 16:16
will I *s* for many hunters . . . . . .Jer 16:16
I will *s* the sword . . . . .Jer 24:10
s and take all the families . . . . .Jer 25:9
sword that I will *s* among . . . . .Jer 25:16
up early, and *s* them . . . . .Jer 26:5
Lord *s* me to prophesy . . . . .Jer 26:12
s them to the king of Edom . . .Jer 27:3
S to all them of the . . . . .Jer 29:31
rising up early and *s* them . . . . .Jer 35:15
God, to whom we *s* thee . . . . . .Jer 42:6
will *s* unto him wanderers . . . . .Jer 48:12
is *s* unto the heathen . . . . .Jer 49:14
s unto Babylon fanners . . . . .Jer 51:2
I *s* thee to the children of . . . . .Ezek 2:3
s upon them the evil arrows . . .Ezek 5:16
I will *s* to destroy you . . . . .Ezek 5:16
will I *s* upon you famine . . . . . .Ezek 5:17
and will *s* famine upon it . . . . . .Ezek 14:13
s my four sore judgments . . . . .Ezek 14:21
in *s* his ambassadors into . . . . . .Ezek 17:15
I will *s* a fire on Magog . . . . . . .Ezek 39:6
My God hath *s* his angel . . . . . .Dan 6:22
s a fire upon his cities . . . . .Hos 8:14
I will *s* you corn, and wine . . . .Joel 2:19
s a fire into the house of . . . . . .Amos 1:4
I will *s* a fire on the wall . . . . . .Amos 1:10
I will *s* a fire upon Moab . . . . .Amos 2:2
s a famine in the land . . . . .Amos 8:11
Lord of hosts hath *s* me . . . . . . .Zech 2:9
even *s* a curse upon you . . . . . .Mal 2:2
s you Elijah the prophet . . . . . .Mal 4:5
and *s* rain on the just . . . . .Matt 5:45
s forth laborers into his . . . . . . .Matt 9:38
These twelve Jesus *s* forth . . . . .Matt 10:5
I *s* you forth as sheep in . . . . . .Matt 10:16
I am come to *s* peace on . . . . . .Matt 10:34
I came not to *s* peace, but . . . .Matt 10:34
I *s* my messenger before . . . . . .Matt 11:10
he *s* forth judgment unto . . . . . .Matt 12:20
Son of man shall *s* forth . . . . . .Matt 13:41
s the multitude away . . . . .Matt 14:15
S her away; for she . . . . .Matt 15:23
I am not *s* but unto the lost . . .Matt 15:24
I will not *s* them away . . . . .Matt 15:32
straightway he will *s* . . . . .Matt 21:3
behold, I *s* unto you . . . . .Matt 23:34
I *s* my messenger before . . . . . .Mark 1:2
he might *s* them forth to . . . . .Mark 3:14
that he would not *s* them . . . . .Mark 5:10
S us into the swine, that . . . . . .Mark 5:12
to *s* them forth by two . . . . . . .Mark 6:7
if I *s* them away fasting to . . . .Mark 8:3
he *s* forth two of his . . . . .Mark 11:1
straightway he will *s* him . . . . . .Mark 11:3
beat him, and *s* him away . . . . .Mark 12:3
s unto him certain of the . . . . . .Mark 12:13
And he *s* forth two of his . . . . .Mark 14:13
Gabriel and am *s* to speak . . . .Luke 1:19
for therefore am I *s* . . . . .Luke 4:43
I *s* my messenger before . . . . . .Luke 7:27
Jesus *s* them two and two . . . . .Luke 10:1
s forth laborers into . . . . .Luke 10:2
s you forth as lambs . . . . .Luke 10:3
I will *s* them prophets . . . . .Luke 11:49
he *s* an ambassage, and . . . . . . .Luke 14:32
s him into his fields to feed . .Luke 15:15
s Lazarus, that he may . . . . .Luke 16:24
I will *s* my beloved son . . . . . .Luke 20:13
I *s* the promise of my . . . . .Luke 24:49
was a man *s* from God, whose .John 1:6
God *s* not his Son to condemn .John 3:17
the Father which hath *s* him . . .John 5:23
He hath *s* him, him ye believe .John 5:38
He that *s* me is true whom ye .John 7:28
He that *s* me is with me . . . . . .John 8:29
which is by interpretation *S* . . .John 9:7
believeth on Him that *s* me . . .John 12:44
Father which *s* me, he gave . . .John 12:49
whomsoever I *s* receiveth . . . . .John 13:20
whom the Father will *s* in . . . . .John 14:26
I will *s* unto you from the . . . . .John 15:26
I go my way to him that *s* me .John 16:5
but if I depart, I will *s* . . . . .John 16:7
Jesus Christ whom thou hast *s* .John 17:3
that thou didst *s* me . . . . .John 17:8
may believe that thou..*s* me . . .John 17:21
hath sent me, even so *s* I . . . . .John 20:21
he shall *s* Jesus Christ . . . . .Acts 3:20
the same did God *s* to be . . . . .Acts 7:35
nothing, for I have *s* them . . . .Acts 10:20
angel to *s* for thee into . . . . . . .Acts 10:22
S therefore to Joppa, and call. .Acts 10:32
word which God *s* unto . . . . . . .Acts 10:36
S men to Joppa, and call . . . . . .Acts 11:13
so they, being *s* forth by the . .Acts 13:4
s chosen men of their own . . . .Acts 15:22
to *s* chosen men unto you . . . . .Acts 15:25
excellent governor Felix *s* . . . . .Acts 23:26
he would *s* for him to . . . . .Acts 25:3
determined to *s* him . . . . .Acts 25:25

S

unto whom now I *s* ....Acts 26:17
God *s* his own Son in the .....Rom 8:3
they preach except they be *s* ..Rom 10:15
will I *s* to bring your 1Cor 16:3
God hath *s* forth the Spirit ....Gal 4:6
to *s* Timothy shortly ....Phil 2:19
necessary to *s* to you ....Phil 2:25
God shall *s* them strong.......2Thess 2:11
When I shall *s* Artemas ....Titus 3:12
fountain *s* forth at the ....James 3:11
God *s* his only begotten.......1John 4:9
s it unto the seven............Rev 1:11
and shall *s* gifts one to........Rev 11:10

SENEH (sē'nĕ)—*"enemy"*
Sharp rock between
Michmash and Gibeah. .1Sam 14:4, 5

SENIR, SHENIR (sē'nĭr, shē'nĭr)—*"mount of light"*
Amorite name of Mt.
Hermon ....Deut 3:9
Noted for firs ....Ezek 27:5

Baal-hermon and *S* 1Chr 5:23
from the top of *S* and Hermon.Song 4:8

SENNACHERIB (sĕ-năk'er-ĭb)—*"(the god) Sin has substituted for my brother"*
Assyrian king (705-681
B.C.); son and successor
of Sargon II 2Kin 18:13
Death of, by assassination.2Kin 19:37

and hear the words of *S* 2Kin 19:16
prayed to me against *S*........2Kin 19:20
So *S* king of Assyria 2Kin 19:36
S king of Assyria came 2Chr 32:1
Hezekiah saw that *S* was 2Chr 32:2
this did *S* king of Assyria 2Chr 32:9
Thus saith *S* king of 2Chr 32:10
the hand of *S* the king 2Chr 32:22
that *S* king of Assyria.........Is 36:1
hear all the words of *S*........Is 37:17
prayed to me against *S*........Is 37:21
so *S* king of Assyria ....Is 37:37

SENSE—*intended meaning*
and gave the *s* ....Neh 8:8

SENSES—*the faculties of feeling: sight, smell, taste, touch, and sound*
Described figuratively ....Eccl 12:3-6
Used by Isaac ....Gen 27:21-27
Impaired in Barzillai 2Sam 19:32-35
Use of, as evidence ......John 20:26-29
Proper use of ....Heb 5:14

SENSES, SPIRITUAL
Taste ....Ps 34:8
Sight ....Eph 1:18
Hearing ....Gal 3:2

SENSUAL—*worldly; fleshly; carnal*
Descriptive of:
Unregenerate ....Jude 19
Worldly wisdom ....James 3:15
Same as "natural" 1Cor 2:14
Rebellious against God . .Rom 8:7

SENSUALIST—*one whose chief desire is to satisfy the physical senses*
Illustrated by:
Nabal 1Sam 25:36
Rich fool ....Luke 12:16-20

SENT, SENTEST—*See* SEND

SENTENCE—*a riddle or difficult saying; legal pronouncement*

[*also* SENTENCES]
shall show thee the *s* of.......Deut 17:9
According to the *s* of the .....Deut 17:11
from the *s* which they.........Deut 17:11
Let my *s* come forth from .....Ps 17:2
divine *s* is in the lips of ....Prov 16:10
s against an evil work is.......Eccl 8:11
also will I give *s* against.......Jer 4:12
showing of hard *s*, and........Dan 5:12
understanding dark *s*..........Dan 8:23
Pilate gave *s* that it ....Luke 23:24

my *s* is, that we trouble ....Acts 15:19
we had the *s* of death in 2Cor 1:9

SENUAH (sĕ nū'ä)—*a descendant of Benjamin*
son of *S* was second over .....Neh 11:9
See HASSENUAH

SEORIM (sĕ-ō'rĭm)—*"fear; distress"*
Name of a priestly course.1Chr 24:1-8

SEPARATE PLACE—*the Temple yard*
Of Ezekiel's Temple .....Ezek 41:12

the *s p*, and the ....Ezek 41:13
the *s p* which was ....Ezek 41:15
over against the *s p*...........Ezek 42:10
which are before the *s p* ......Ezek 42:13

SEPARATION—*set apart; removal from*
As a good act from:
Unclean ....Lev 15:31
Evil workers ....Num 16:21
Heathen filthiness ....Ezra 6:21
Pagan intermarriages.....Ezra 9:1, 2
Foreigners ....Neh 13:3
Strong drink ....Num 6:2-6
As an evil act by:
False teachers ....Luke 6:22
Separatists ....Jude 19
Whisperers..............Prov 16:28
Gossipers ....Prov 17:9
As descriptive of:
God's judgment ....Deut 29:21
God's sovereignty ....Deut 32:8
Israel's uniqueness.......Lev 20:24
Choice of the Levites ....Num 8:14
Nazarite vow ....Num 6:2-6
Christian obedience 2Cor 6:17
Union with Christ ....Rom 8:35, 39
Christ's purity ....Heb 7:26
Final separation ....Matt 25:32

[*also* SEPARATE, SEPARATED, SEPARATETH, SEPARATING]
s thyself, I pray thee.........Gen 13:9
they *s* themselves the one .....Gen 13:11
people shall be *s* ....Gen 25:23
And Jacob did *s* the ....Gen 30:40
him that was *s* from his ....Gen 49:26
so shall we be *s*, I and thy ....Ex 33:16
the days of the *s* for ....Lev 12:2
she lieth upon in her *s*........Lev 15:20
out of the time of her *s* ....Lev 15:25
beyond the time of her *s*......Lev 15:25
be as the days of her *s*........Lev 15:25
her as the bed of her *s*........Lev 15:26
uncleanness of her *s* ....Lev 15:26
shall ye *s* the children of ......Lev 15:31
I have *s* from you as..........Lev 20:25
s themselves from the ....Lev 22:2
the days of his *s* he is.........Num 6:8
Lord the days of his *s* ....Num 6:12
be lost, because his *s* was .....Num 6:12
shave the head of his *s* at .....Num 6:18
hair of the head of his *s* ......Num 6:18
unto the Lord for his *s*.........Num 6:21
after the law of his *s*..........Num 6:21
God of Israel hath *s* you ....Num 16:9
Israel for a water of *s*.........Num 19:9
water of *s* hath not been ......Num 19:20
sprinkleth the water of *s* ......Num 19:21
that toucheth..water of *s* ......Num 19:21
time the Lord *s* the tribe ......Deut 10:8
Thou shalt *s* three cities.......Deut 19:2
him that was *s* from his ....Deut 33:16
the *s* cities for the ....Josh 16:9
s them from among all 1Kin 8:53
there *s* themselves unto 1Chr 12:8
s to the service of the sons 1Chr 25:1
Then Amaziah *s* them, to 2Chr 25:10
Then I *s* twelve of the ....Ezra 8:24
s from the congregation ....Ezra 10:8
s yourselves from the ....Ezra 10:11
we are *s* upon the wall........Neh 4:19
all they that had *s* ....Neh 10:28
and a whisperer *s* chief ....Prov 16:28

repeateth a matter *s* very .....Prov 17:9
desire a man, having *s* ....Prov 18:1
the poor is *s* from his ....Prov 19:4
Lord hath utterly *s* me ....Is 56:3
to *s* himself thence in the .....Jer 37:12
which *s* himself from me ......Ezek 14:7
to make a *s* between the ......Ezek 42:20
themselves are *s* with ....Hos 4:14
s themselves unto that ....Hos 9:10
s myself, as I have done ......Zech 7:3
S me Barnabas and Saul ......Acts 13:2
and *s* the disciples ....Acts 19:9
apostle, *s* unto the gospel .....Rom 1:1
who *s* me from my mother's . . .Gal 1:15
he withdrew and *s* himself.....Gal 2:12

SEPHAR (sē'fär)—*"scribe"*
Place on Joktan's
boundary ....Gen 10:30

SEPHARAD (sĕ-fā'răd)—*"a book descending"*
Place inhabited by exiles .Obad 20

SEPHARVAIM, SEPHARVITES (sef-är-vā'ĭm, sef-är'īts)—*"the two scribes"—an Assyrian city*
People of, sent to
Samaria 2Kin 17:24, 31

where are the gods of *S*.......2Kin 18:34
the king of the city of *S*.......2Kin 19:13
are the gods of *S*? ....Is 36:19
the king of the city of *S*.......Is 37:13

SEPULCHER—*a place of burial; a tomb*
Used literally of:
Place of burial ....Gen 23:6
Christ's grave ....John 19:41, 42
Used figuratively of:
Hypocrisy...............Matt 23:27

[*also* SEPULCHERS]
man knoweth of his *s* ....Deut 34:6
and was buried in the *s* of ....Judg 8:32
two men by Rachel's *s* 1Sam 10:2
buried him in the *s* of his 2Sam 2:32
was buried in the *s* of his 2Sam 17:23
not come unto the *s* of thy 1Kin 13:22
him in his *s* with his 2Kin 9:28
in his *s* in the garden of.......2Kin 21:26
he spied the *s* that were.......2Kin 23:16
took the bones out of the *s* ...2Kin 23:16
buried him in his own *s* 2Kin 23:30
buried him in his own *s* 2Chr 16:14
buried him not in the *s* 2Chr 24:25
the chiefest of the *s* 2Chr 32:33
place of my fathers' *s* ....Neh 2:3
place over against the *s* ....Neh 3:16
their throat is an open *s* ......Ps 5:9
hast hewed thee out a *s*.......Is 22:16
that heweth him out a *s*.......Is 22:16
quiver is as an open *s*..........Jer 5:16
garnish the *s* of the ....Matt 23:29
stone to the door of the *s* .....Matt 27:60
s be made sure until the ......Matt 27:64
other Mary to see the *s* ....Matt 28:1
laid him in a *s* which was .....Mark 15:46
unto the door of the *s* ....Mark 15:46
they came unto the *s* at ....Mark 16:2
And entering into the *s* ....Mark 16:5
for ye build the *s* of the.......Luke 11:47
laid it in a *s* that was ....Luke 23:53
they came unto the *s* ....Luke 24:1
returned from the *s*, and ....Luke 24:9
which were early at the *s* .....Luke 24:22
yet dark, unto the *s* ....John 20:1
taken away from the *s* ....John 20:1
came to the *s* ....John 20:3
and went into the *s*, and ......John 20:6
stood without at the *s*..........John 20:11
and looked in the *s* ....John 20:11
his *s* is with us unto this ......Acts 2:29
and laid in the *s* that ....Acts 7:16
and laid him in a *s* ....Acts 13:29
Their throat is an open *s*......Rom 3:13

SEPULCHRE—*See* Sepulcher

SERAH (sĕ'rä)—*"extension"*
Daughter of Asher ......Gen 46:17
Called Sarah ....Num 26:46

SERAIAH (sĕ-rā'yä)—*"Jehovah is prince; Jehovah has prevailed"*
1. David's secretary 2Sam 8:17
   Called Sheva, Shisha, and Shavsha 2Sam 20:25; 1Kin 4:3; 1Chr 18:16
2. Son of Tanhumeth 2Kin 25:23
3. Son of Kenaz 1Chr 4:13, 14
4. Simeonite 1Chr 4:35
5. Chief priest ....Jer 52:24, 27
6. Postexilic leader ....Neh 12:1, 12
7. Signer of the covenant .Neh 10:2
8. Postexilic priest ....Neh 11:11
9. Officer of King Jehoiakim ....Jer 36:26
11. Prince of Judah; carries Jeremiah's prophecy to Babylon ....Jer 51:59, 61

guard took *S* the chief 2Kin 25:18
begat *S*, and *S* begat..........1Chr 6:14
Jeshua, Nehemiah, *S* ....Ezra 2:2
Ezra the son of *S*, the ....Ezra 7:1
and *S* the son of ....Jer 40:8

SERAPHIM (sĕr'ä-fĭm)—*"burning ones"*
Type of angels ....Is 6:1, 2

Then flew one of the *s* ....Is 6:6

SERED (sē'rĕd)—*"escape; deliverance"*
Son of Zebulun; founder of Sardites ....Gen 46:14

of *S*, the family of the ....Num 26:26

SERGIUS PAULUS (sûr'jĭ-ŭs pô'lŭs)
Roman proconsul of Cyprus converted by Paul ....Acts 13:7-12

SERGEANTS—*military men who guarded Paul and Silas*
magistrates sent the *s* ....Acts 16:35
the *s* told these words ....Acts 16:38

SERMON—*a discourse on a biblical theme*
A prolonged message ....Acts 20:7

SERMON ON THE MOUNT—*the name given to Jesus' discourse to his followers on a hillside near Capernaum*
Preached by Christ ......Matt 5—7
Those blessed ....Matt 5:3-12
Salt and light ....Matt 5:13-16
The law fulfilled ....Matt 5:17-20
On anger ....Matt 5:21-26
On adultery and divorce .Matt 5:27-32
Oaths ....Matt 5:33-37
Love your enemies ......Matt 5:38-48
The religious life ....Matt 6:1-4
Matt 6:5-15
How to pray ....Matt 6:16-18
Undivided devotion ......Matt 6:19-34
Judging others ....Matt 7:1-6
Encouragement to pray ..Matt 7:7-12
Entering the kingdom ....Matt 7:13-23
Two foundations ....Matt 7:24-27

SERPENT—*snake*

Characteristics of:
Created by God ....Job 26:13
Subtle ....Gen 3:1
Some poisonous ....Num 21:6
Live on rocks, walls, etc. .Prov 30:19
Cursed by God ....Gen 3:14, 15

Miracles connected with:
Aaron's rod turned into ..Ex 7:9, 15
Israelites cured by looking at .... Num 21:6-9; John 3:14, 15
Power over, given to apostles ....Mark 16:18
Healing from bite of .....Acts 28:5, 6

Figurative of:
Intoxication ....Prov 23:31, 32
Wisdom ....Matt 10:16
Malice ....Ps 58:4
Unexpected evil ....Eccl 10:8
Enemies ....Is 14:29
Christ ....John 3:14-16
Satan ....Rev 20:2
Dan's treachery ....Gen 49:17
Sting of wine ....Prov 23:31, 32
Wickedness of sinners ....Ps 58:3, 4

[*also* serpent's, serpents]
woman said unto the *s* ....Gen 3:2
s said unto the woman ....Gen 3:4
and it became a *s* ....Ex 4:3
it shall become a *s* ....Ex 7:9
and it became a *s* ....Ex 7:10
and they became *s* ....Ex 7:12
wherein were fiery *s* ....Deut 8:15
with the poison of *s* of ....Deut 32:24
tongues like a *s* ....Ps 140:3
s will bite without ....Eccl 10:11
out of the *s* root shall ....Is 14:29
leviathan the piercing *s* ....Is 27:1
that crooked *s* ....Is 27:1
and fiery flying *s* ....Is 30:6
and dust shall be the *s* ....Is 65:25
I will send *s*, cockatrices ......Jer 8:17
shall go like a *s* ....Jer 46:22
hand on the wall, and a *s* .....Amos 5:19
will I command the *s* ....Amos 9:3
lick the dust like a *s* ....Mic 7:17
will he give him a *s*? ....Matt 7:10
Ye *s*, ye generation of ....Matt 23:33
power to tread on *s* and ......Luke 10:19
a fish give him a *s*? ....Luke 11:11
were destroyed of *s* 1Cor 10:9
as the *s* beguiled Eve 2Cor 11:3
of *s*, and of things in ....James 3:7
tails were like unto *s* ....Rev 9:19
old *s*, called the Devil ....Rev 12:9
from the face of the *s* ....Rev 12:14
the *s* cast out of his ....Rev 12:15

SERUG, SARUCH (sē'rŭg, sā'rŭk)—*"strength; firmness"*
Descendant of Shem .....Gen 11:20-23
In Christ's ancestry ......Luke 3:35

SERVANT—*one who serves others*

Descriptive of:
Slave ....Gen 9:25
Social inferior ....Gen 19:2
Worshiper of God 1Sam 3:9
Messenger of God ....Josh 1:2
Messiah ....Is 42:1
Follower of Christ 2Tim 2:24

Applied distinctively to:
Prophets ....Zech 1:6
Messiah ....Zech 3:8
Moses ....Mal 4:4
Christians ....Acts 2:18
Glorified saints ....Rev 22:3

See Slave

[*also* servant's, servants, servants']
s trade hath been about ....Gen 43:34
Pharaoh, and into his *s* ....Ex 8:24
Lord; for thy *s* heareth 1Sam 3:9
hast spoken also of thy *s* 2Sam 7:19
thy *s* an understanding 1Kin 3:9
to thy son for David my *s* 1Kin 11:13
life for David my *s* 1Kin 11:34
for David his *s* sake 2Kin 8:19
ye seed of Israel his *s* 1Chr 16:13
hast also spoken of thy *s* 1Chr 17:17
Lord, for thy *s* sake, and 1Chr 17:19
my *s* shall be with thy *s* 2Chr 2:8
I called my *s*, and he gave ....Job 19:16
by them thy *s* is warned ....Ps 19:11
put not thy *s* away in anger ...Ps 27:9
redeemeth the soul of his *s* ....Ps 34:22
O Lord, truly I am thy *s* ......Ps 116:16
bountifully with thy *s* ....Ps 119:17
heritage unto Israel his *s* ......Ps 136:22
and the borrower is *s* to ......Prov 22:7
as with the *s*, so with his ......Is 24:2
unto thee, Thou art my *s* .....Is 41:9
For Jacob my *s* sake, and .....Is 45:4
hath redeemed his *s* Jacob ....Is 48:20
shall my righteous *s* ....Is 53:11
Return, for thy *s* sake ....Is 63:17
so will I do for my *s* sake .....Is 65:8
and my *s* shall dwell there ....Is 65:9
Is Israel a *s*? is he a ....Jer 2:14
unto you all my *s* ....Jer 35:15
his *s* was healed in the ....Matt 8:13
nor the *s* above his lord ....Matt 10:24
as his master, and the *s* ....Matt 10:25
among you, let him be your *s* .Matt 20:27
is a faithful and wise *s* ....Matt 24:45
good and faithful *s* ....Matt 25:21
the unprofitable *s* into ....Matt 25:30
be last of all, and *s* ....Mark 9:35
chiefest, shall be *s* of all ......Mark 10:44
that *s*, which knew his ....Luke 12:47
hired *s* of my father's ....Luke 15:17
No *s* can serve two masters ...Luke 16:13
which of you having a *s* ....Luke 17:7
say, We are unprofitable *s* ....Luke 17:10
s abideth not in the house .....John 8:35
The *s* is not greater than ......John 13:16
Henceforth I call you not *s* ....John 15:15
The *s* is not greater than ......John 15:20
The *s* name was Malchus ....John 18:10
the mouth of thy *s* David .....Acts 4:25
his *s* ye are to whom ye ....Rom 6:16
free from sin, and become *s* ...Rom 6:22
that judgest another man's *s* ..Rom 14:4
which is a *s* of the church .....Rom 16:1
Art thou called being a *s* 1Cor 7:21
price, be not ye the *s* of 1Cor 7:23
yet have I made myself *s* 1Cor 9:19
s be obedient to your masters .Eph 6:5
him the form of a *s* ....Phil 2:7
masters, give unto your *s* .....Col 4:1
maliciousness, but as the *s* 1Pet 2:16
they themselves are the *s* 2Pet 2:19
Praise our God, all ye his *s* ...Rev 19:5

SERVE—*to respond to the needs of others*

[*also* served, servedst, servest, serveth, serving]
they *s* Chedorlaomer ....Gen 14:4
is not theirs, and shall *s* ....Gen 15:13
and the elder, shall *s* the ......Gen 25:23
Let people *s* thee, and ....Gen 27:29
thou therefore *s* me for ....Gen 29:15
Jacob *s* seven years for ....Gen 29:20
did not I *s* with thee for ......Gen 29:25
s with him yet seven other ....Gen 29:30
for whom I have *s* ....Gen 30:26
all my power have I *s* ....Gen 31:6
in his sight, and he *s* ....Gen 39:4
with them, and he *s* ....Gen 40:4
children of Israel to *s* ....Ex 1:13
ye shall *s* God upon this ......Ex 3:12
that he may *s* me ....Ex 4:23
they may *s* me in the ....Ex 7:16
that they may *s* me ....Ex 8:1
that they may *s* me ....Ex 9:1
that they may *s* me ....Ex 10:3
ye that are men, and *s* ....Ex 10:11
we take to *s* the Lord our .....Ex 10:26
not with what ye must *s* ....Ex 10:26
go, *s* the Lord, as ye ....Ex 12:31
let Israel go from *s* ....Ex 14:5
that we may *s* the ....Ex 14:12
better for us to *s* the ....Ex 14:12
thyself to them, nor *s* ....Ex 20:5
six years he shall *s* ....Ex 21:2
down to their gods, nor *s* .....Ex 23:24
if thou *s* their gods, it ....Ex 23:33
compel him to *s* as a ....Lev 25:39
thereof, and all that *s* ....Num 3:36
and shall *s* no more ....Num 8:25
and ye shall *s* ....Num 18:7
to worship them, and *s* ....Deut 4:19
thyself unto them, nor *s* ......Deut 5:9
Lord thy God, and *s* him ......Deut 6:13
me, that they may *s* other .....Deut 7:4
other gods, and *s* ....Deut 8:19
to *s* the Lord thy God ....Deut 10:12

S

and to *s* him with all your.....Deut 11:13
ye shall possess *s* their........Deut 12:2
How did these nations *s* ......Deut 12:30
and let us *s* them.............Deut 13:2
Let us go and *s* other.........Deut 13:6
and *s* thee six years..........Deut 15:12
thee, in *s* thee six years.......Deut 15:18
And hath gone and *s* ....Deut 17:3
and they shall *s* thee.........Deut 20:11
go after other gods to *s*.......Deut 28:14
s not the Lord thy God ....Deut 28:47
thou *s* thine enemies..........Deut 28:48
and *s* the gods of these ....Deut 29:18
went and *s* other gods ....Deut 29:26
worship other gods, and *s* .....Deut 30:17
unto other gods, and *s*........Deut 31:20
unto this day, and *s* under ....Josh 16:10
and to *s* him with all your.....Josh 22:5
neither *s* them, nor bow ......Josh 23:7
and have gone and *s* other .....Josh 23:16
and they *s* other gods.........Josh 24:2
and *s* him in sincerity and .....Josh 24:14
and *s* ye the Lord ....Josh 24:14
it seem evil unto you to *s* .....Josh 24:15
day whom ye will *s*............Josh 24:15
we will *s* the Lord............Josh 24:15
we also *s* the Lord ....Josh 24:18
Lord, and *s* strange gods......Josh 24:20
the Lord, to *s* him............Josh 24:22
people *s* the Lord all the ......Judg 2:7
following other gods to *s*......Judg 2:19
to their sons, and *s* their ......Judg 3:6
s Cushan-rishathaim ....Judg 3:8
him, Why hast thou *s* us ......Judg 8:1
that we should *s* him ....Judg 9:28
s the men of Hamor the ......Judg 9:28
for why should we *s* ....Judg 9:28
and *s* Baalim, and ....Judg 10:6
forsook the Lord, and *s*.......Judg 10:6
forsaken me, and *s* other......Judg 10:13
unto the Lord, and *s* him 1Sam 7:3
and Ashtaroth, and *s* the......1Sam 7:4
forsaken me, and *s* other......1Sam 8:8
that thou do as occasion *s*.....1Sam 10:7
we will *s* thee 1Sam 11:1
and have *s* Baalim and........1Sam 12:10
and we will *s* thee 1Sam 12:10
but *s* the Lord with all........1Sam 12:20
our servants, and *s* 1Sam 17:9
the Lord, saying, Go, *s* 1Sam 26:19
peace with Israel, and *s*.......2Sam 10:19
I will *s* the Lord.............2Sam 15:8
whom should I *s*? 2Sam 16:19
should I not *s* in the 2Sam 16:19
as I have *s* in thy father's 2Sam 16:19
s Solomon all the days of 1Kin 4:21
go and *s* other gods, and 1Kin 9:6
worshiped them, and *s*........1Kin 9:9
thou the grievous *s* of thy 1Kin 12:4
went and *s* Baal, and 1Kin 16:31
For he *s* Baal, and 1Kin 22:53
unto them, Ahab *s* Baal 2Kin 10:18
but Jehu shall *s* him 2Kin 10:18
For they *s* idols, whereof......2Kin 17:12
and *s* their own gods 2Kin 17:33
nor *s* them, nor sacrifice 2Kin 17:35
king of Assyria, and *s* 2Kin 18:7
host of heaven, and *s*.........2Kin 21:3
land, and *s* the king of........2Kin 25:24
and their officers that *s* 1Chr 27:1
s him with a perfect heart 1Chr 28:9
and shall go and *s* other 2Chr 7:19
worshiped them, and *s*........2Chr 7:22
and we will *s* thee 2Chr 10:4
s groves and idols 2Chr 24:18
stand before him, to *s* 2Chr 29:11
So the *s* of the house of 2Chr 29:35
and *s* the Lord your God 2Chr 30:8
host of heaven, and *s* 2Chr 33:3
commanded Judah to *s*........2Chr 33:16
present in Israel to *s*.........2Chr 34:33
s the Lord their God 2Chr 34:33
s now the Lord your God 2Chr 35:3
have not *s* thee in their ......Neh 9:35
s in the presence of...........Esth 1:10

that we should *s* him ....Job 21:15
If they obey and *s* him........Job 36:11
unicorn be willing to *s*........Job 39:9
S the Lord with fear, and .....Ps 2:11
I have not known shall *s*......Ps 18:43
A seed shall *s* him; it ....Ps 22:30
all nations shall *s*............Ps 72:11
be all they that *s* graven ......Ps 97:7
S the Lord with gladness......Ps 100:2
perfect way, he shall *s* ....Ps 101:6
and the kingdoms, to *s*........Ps 102:22
And they *s* their idols.........Ps 106:36
thee as thou hast *s* ....Ps 137:8
the king himself is *s* by ....Eccl 5:9
thou wast made to *s* ....Is 14:3
the Egyptians shall *s*..........Is 19:23
caused thee to *s* with an ......Is 43:23
the Lord, to *s* him............Is 56:6
that will not *s* thee shall ......Is 60:12
and *s* strange gods in your ....Jer 5:19
so shall ye *s* strangers in ......Jer 5:19
whom they have *s* ....Jer 8:2
went after other gods to *s*.....Jer 11:10
walk after other gods, to *s* ....Jer 13:10
other gods and have *s* them ...Jer 16:11
ye *s* other gods day and.......Jer 16:13
will cause thee to *s* thine......Jer 17:4
other gods, and *s* them ....Jer 22:9
after other gods to *s* ....Jer 25:6
kings shall *s* themselves ....Jer 25:14
have I given him also to *s*.....Jer 27:6
And all nations shall *s* ....Jer 27:7
kings shall *s* themselves ....Jer 27:7
Ye shall not *s* the king of .....Jer 27:9
and *s* him and his people .....Jer 27:12
Ye shall not *s* the king of .....Jer 27:14
that they may *s* ....Jer 28:14
and they shall *s* him: and .....Jer 28:14
no more *s* themselves ....Jer 30:8
none should *s* himself of ......Jer 34:9
and when he hath *s* thee ......Jer 34:14
after other gods to *s*..........Jer 35:15
Fear not to *s* the ....Jer 40:9
s the king of Babylon.........Jer 40:9
to *s* other gods, whom ....Jer 44:3
s the king of Babylon ....Jer 52:12
countries, to *s* wood and .....Ezek 20:32
all of them in the land, *s*......Ezek 20:40
army to serve a great *s* ....Ezek 29:18
of those that *s* themselves .....Ezek 34:27
for food unto them that *s* .....Ezek 48:18
that *s* the city shall *s* it.......Ezek 48:19
they *s* not thy gods, nor.......Dan 3:12
God whom we *s* is able to ....Dan 3:17
might not *s* nor worship.......Dan 3:28
Thy God whom thou *s*.........Dan 6:16
languages, should *s* him ......Dan 7:14
dominions shall *s* and ....Dan 7:27
Israel *s* for a wife, and........Hos 12:12
Lord, to *s* him with one.......Zeph 3:9
said, It is vain to *s* ....Mal 3:14
his own son that *s*............Mal 3:17
him only shalt thou *s* ....Matt 4:10
No man can *s* two ....Matt 6:24
Ye cannot *s* God and mammon. Matt 6:24
might *s* him without fear .....Luke 1:74
s God with fastings and ......Luke 2:37
him only shalt thou *s* ....Luke 4:8
cumbered about much *s*.......Luke 10:40
sister hath left me to *s*........Luke 10:40
will come forth and *s* ....Luke 12:37
many years do I *s* ....Luke 15:29
No servant can *s* two ....Luke 16:13
Ye cannot *s* God and ....Luke 16:13
gird thyself, and *s* ....Luke 17:8
chief, as he that doth *s* ....Luke 22:26
meat, or he that *s*? ....Luke 22:27
among you as he that *s* ....Luke 22:27
supper; and Martha *s*.........John 12:2
If any man *s* me, let him......John 12:26
if any man *s* me, him will .....John 12:26
word of God, and *s* ....Acts 6:2
come forth, and *s* me in ......Acts 7:7
after he had *s* his own ....Acts 13:36
S the Lord with all ....Acts 20:19

s God day and night..........Acts 26:7
whose I am, and whom I *s*....Acts 27:23
whom I *s* with my spirit.......Rom 1:9
and *s* the creature more.......Rom 1:25
we should not *s* sin ....Rom 6:6
we should *s* in newness ....Rom 7:6
The elder shall *s* the..........Rom 9:12
fervent in spirit; *s* the.........Rom 12:11
he that in these things *s*.......Rom 14:18
such *s* not our Lord Jesus .....Rom 16:18
but prophesying *s*, not 1Cor 14:22
Wherefore then *s* the law? ....Gal 3:19
did *s* unto them which by .....Gal 4:8
flesh, but by love *s* one ....Gal 5:13
he hath *s* with me in the ......Phil 2:22
for ye *s* the Lord Christ.......Col 3:24
idols to *s* the living and 1Thess 1:9
whom I *s* from my 2Tim 1:3
s divers lusts and ....Titus 3:3
Who *s* unto the example ......Heb 8:5
dead works to *s* the living .....Heb 9:14
we may *s* God acceptably .....Heb 12:28
right to eat which *s* the ....Heb 13:10
s him day and night in ....Rev 7:15
his servants shall *s*............Rev 22:3

SERVICE—*occupation or function of serving; employment as a servant; the act of serving*
For the *s* which thou shalt ....Gen 29:27
knowest my *s* which I.........Gen 30:26
and in all manner of *s* in......Ex 1:14
all their *s*..was with rigor......Ex 1:14
ye shall keep this *s* ....Ex 12:25
thou shalt keep this *s* in.......Ex 13:5
the tabernacle in all the *s* .....Ex 27:19
the *s* of the tabernacle ....Ex 30:16
And the cloth of *s*, and ....Ex 31:10
The cloth of *s*, to do ....Ex 35:19
to do *s* in the holy place ......Ex 35:19
for any work of the *s* ....Ex 35:24
of work for the *s* of the.......Ex 36:1
than enough for the *s* of ......Ex 36:5
for the *s* of the Levites, by ....Ex 38:21
they made cloth of *s*..........Ex 39:1
do *s* in the holy place, and ....Ex 39:1
The cloth of *s* to do ....Ex 39:41
to do *s* in the holy place ......Ex 39:41
to do the *s* of the ....Num 3:7
hanging, and all the *s*.........Num 3:31
shall be the *s* of the sons of ...Num 4:4
to perform the *s*..............Num 4:23
Gershonites to *s*..............Num 4:24
instruments of their *s* ....Num 4:26
s of the sons of the ....Num 4:27
and in all their *s* ....Num 4:27
entereth into the *s*...........Num 4:30
with all their *s* ....Num 4:32
s of the families..of...........Num 4:33
according to all their *s*........Num 4:33
that might do *s* in the.........Num 4:37
that might do *s* in the.........Num 4:41
came to do the *s* of the ....Num 4:47
s of the burden in the ....Num 4:47
may be to do the *s* of the .....Num 7:5
according to his *s*............Num 7:5
according unto their *s*........Num 7:8
they may execute the *s* of ....Num 8:11
do the *s* of the children of ....Num 8:19
wait upon the *s* of the ....Num 8:24
and shall do no *s*.............Num 8:26
the *s* of the tabernacle ....Num 16:9
the *s* of the tabernacle ....Num 18:4
office unto you as a *s*.........Num 18:7
their *s* which they serve ......Num 18:21
the *s* of the tabernacle ....Num 18:21
reward for your *s* in the.......Num 18:31
that we might do the *s* of .....Josh 22:27
we will *s* thee 1Kin 12:4
work of the *s* of the house 1Chr 9:13
work for the *s* of the 1Chr 23:24
for the *s* of the house of 1Chr 23:28
work of the *s* of the house 1Chr 23:28
their offices in their *s*........1Chr 24:3
separated to the *s* of the 1Chr 25:1
according to their *s* 1Chr 25:1

for strength for the *s* 1Chr 26:8
work of the *s* of the house 1Chr 28:13
vessels of *s* in the house 1Chr 28:13
of all manner of *s* 1Chr 28:14
of every kind of *s* 1Chr 28:14
for all the *s* of the house 1Chr 28:21
for any manner of *s* 1Chr 28:21
to consecrate his *s* 1Chr 29:5
priests to their *s* 2Chr 8:14
that they may know my *s* 2Chr 12:8
s of the kingdoms of the 2Chr 12:8
did the work of the *s* 2Chr 24:12
according to his *s* 2Chr 31:2
began in the *s* of the 2Chr 31:21
work in any manner of *s* 2Chr 34:13
encouraged them to the *s* 2Chr 35:2
depart from their *s* 2Chr 35:15
their courses, for the *s* ....Ezra 6:18
had appointed for the *s* of ....Ezra 8:20
of a shekel for the *s* ....Neh 10:32
cattle, and herb for the *s* ......Ps 104:14
caused his army to *s* a ....Ezek 29:18
the *s* that he had served ......Ezek 29:18
think that he doeth God *s* .....John 16:2
and the *s* of God, and the ....Rom 9:4
is your reasonable *s* ....Rom 12:1
s which I have for ....Rom 15:31
administration of this *s* 2Cor 9:12
of them, to do you *s* 2Cor 11:8
With good will doing *s* ....Eph 6:7
sacrifice and *s* of your ....Phil 2:17
but rather do them *s* 1Tim 6:2
ordinances of divine *s* ....Heb 9:1
make him that did the *s* ....Heb 9:9
and charity, and *s* ....Rev 2:19

SERVICE TO GOD—*actions done for God's sake*

Requirements of:
Fear.....................Ps 2:11
Upright walking ....Ps 101:6
Absolute loyalty..........Matt 6:24
Regeneration............Rom 7:6
Serve the Lord ....Rom 12:11
Humility ....Acts 20:19
Love ....Gal 5:13

Rewards of:
Divine honor............John 12:26
Acceptance before God ..Rom 14:18
Inheritance..............Col 3:24
Eternal blessedness ......Rev 7:15
Rev 22:3

SERVILE—*laborious; subservient*
ye shall do no *s* work ....Lev 23:7, 8
Ye shall do no *s* work ....Lev 23:25
do no manner of *s* work ......Num 28:18
ye shall do no *s* work ....Num 28:26
ye shall do no *s* work ....Num 29:1
ye shall do no *s* work ....Num 29:35

SERVITOR—*servant*
And his *s* said, What should...2Kin 4:43

SERVITUDE—*status of a servant*
the grievous *s* of 2Chr 10:4
and because of great *s* ....Lam 1:3

SET, SETTEST, SETTETH, SETTING—*See* INTRODUCTION

SETH (sĕth)—*"compensation; sprout"*
Third son of Adam ......Gen 4:25
In Christ's ancestry ......Luke 3:38

called his name *S* ....Gen 5:3
S lived an hundred and ....Gen 5:6
And all the days of *S* ....Gen 5:8

SETHUR (sē'ther)—*"secreted; hidden"*
Asherite spy ....Num 13:2, 13

SETTER—*proponent*
to be a *s* forth of strange .....Acts 17:18

SETTING—*mounting for jewelry*
For precious stones worn by the high priest .....Ex 28:11
Corded chains on filigree .Ex 28:13, 14
Same Hebrew word translated "interwoven".Ps 45:13

[*also* SETTINGS]
set it in *s* of stones ....Ex 28:17
their *s* of their threshold ......Ezek 43:8

SETTLE—*to place; decide; establish; ledge*

[*also* SETTLED, SETTLEST]
a *s* place for thee to abide 1Kin 8:13
he *s* his countenance 2Kin 8:11
I will *s* him in mine house 1Chr 17:14
thou *s* the furrows ....Ps 65:10
O Lord, thy word is *s* in ......Ps 119:89
the mountains were *s* ....Prov 8:25
he hath *s* on his lees, and ......Jer 48:11
will *s* you after your old ......Ezek 36:11
the lower *s* shall be two ....Ezek 43:14
the lesser *s* even to the ....Ezek 43:14
greater *s* shall be four ....Ezek 43:14
four corners of the *s* ....Ezek 43:20
the men that are *s* on ....Zeph 1:12
S it therefore in your ....Luke 21:14
the faith grounded and *s* ......Col 1:23
stablish, strengthen, *s* 1Pet 5:10

SEVEN

Of social customs:
Serving for a wife ....Gen 29:20, 27
Bowing ....Gen 33:3
Mourning ....Gen 50:10
Feast ....Judg 14:12, 17
Fasting 1Sam 31:13

Of things:
Days ....Gen 2:3
Weeks ....Dan 9:25
Months ....Lev 23:24-44
Years ....Gen 41:1-57
Nations ....Deut 7:1
Ways ....Deut 28:7
Women ....Is 4:1
Brethren ....Mark 12:20-22
Spirits ....Matt 12:45
Men ....Acts 6:3-5
Churches ....Rev 1:4, 20

Of rituals:
Victims of sacrifices .....Lev 23:18
Sprinkling of blood ......Lev 4:6
Sprinkling of oil ....Lev 14:16
Passover ....Ex 12:15
Consecration ....Ex 29:30, 35
Defilement..............Lev 12:2
Convocation ....Lev 23:24-44
Jubilee ....Lev 25:8

Miracles:
Plagues ....Ex 7:25
Jericho's fall ....Josh 6:4, 8, 13
Naaman's baths 2Kin 5:10
Loaves ....Matt 15:34
Baskets ....Matt 15:37

Of symbols:
Purification ....Ps 12:6
Worship ....Ps 119:164
Gospel light.............Is 30:26
Spirits ....Rev 1:4
Seals ....Rev 5:1
Angels ....Rev 8:2
Heads and crowns ....Rev 13:1
Plagues ....Rev 15:6
Vials ....Rev 15:7
Kings ....Rev 17:10

[*also* SEVENS, SEVENTH]
s day God ended his work ....Gen 2:2
rested on the *s* day from ......Gen 2:2
Enos eight hundred and *s* .....Gen 5:7
Lamech *s* hundred eighty .....Gen 5:26
days of Lamech were *s* ....Gen 5:31
seventy and *s* years: and ......Gen 5:31
shalt take to thee by *s* ....Gen 7:2
fowls also of the air by *s* ......Gen 7:3
s days, and I will cause it .....Gen 7:4
it came to pass after *s* ....Gen 7:10
the ark rested in the *s* ....Gen 8:4
he stayed yet other *s* days .....Gen 8:12
Serug two hundred and *s* ......Gen 11:21
What mean these *s* ewe ....Gen 21:29
was an hundred and *s* ....Gen 23:1
will serve thee *s* years for .....Gen 29:18
serve with me yet *s* other .....Gen 29:27
pursued after him *s* days' .....Gen 31:23
himself to the ground *s* ....Gen 33:3
priest of Midian had *s* ....Ex 2:16
hundred and thirty and *s* ......Ex 6:20
the first day until the *s* ....Ex 12:15
S days thou shalt eat ....Ex 13:6
s day shall be a feast to ....Ex 13:6
people on the *s* day for ....Ex 16:27
people rested on the *s* ....Ex 16:30
s day is the sabbath of ....Ex 20:10
and rested the *s* day ....Ex 20:11
s days it shall be with ....Ex 22:30
s year thou shalt let it ....Ex 23:11
s day he called unto ....Ex 24:16
shalt make the *s* lamps ....Ex 25:37
on the *s* day he rested ....Ex 31:17
S days thou shalt eat ....Ex 34:18
s day there shall be to ....Ex 35:2
and *s* hundred and thirty ......Ex 38:24
the thousand *s* hundred ....Ex 38:28
thereof upon the altar *s* ....Lev 8:11
of the congregation in *s* ....Lev 8:33
for *s* days shall he ....Lev 8:33
that hath the plague *s* ....Lev 13:4
shall look on him the *s* ....Lev 13:5
shall shut him up *s* days.......Lev 13:5
shall look upon him the *s* .....Lev 13:27
plague of the scall *s* ....Lev 13:31
that hath the plague *s* ....Lev 13:50
the plague on the *s* day ....Lev 13:51
from the leprosy *s* times ......Lev 14:7
is in his left hand *s* times .....Lev 14:27
and shut up the house *s* ....Lev 14:38
shall come again the *s* ....Lev 14:39
number to himself *s* ....Lev 15:13
he shall be unclean *s* ....Lev 15:24
blood with his finger *s* ....Lev 16:14
it shall be *s* days under ....Lev 22:27
fire unto the Lord *s* days ......Lev 23:8
the *s* day is a holy ....Lev 23:8
s sabbath shall ye ....Lev 23:16
But in the *s* year shall be .....Lev 25:4
What shall we eat the *s* ....Lev 25:20
I will punish you *s* times ......Lev 26:18
and will punish you yet *s* ......Lev 26:24
were fifty and *s* thousand .....Num 1:31
were fifty and *s* thousand .....Num 2:8
and two thousand and *s* ....Num 2:26
numbered of them were *s* .....Num 3:22
on the *s* day shall he ....Num 6:9
s lamps shall give light ....Num 8:2
she not be ashamed *s* ....Num 12;14
out from the camp *s* ....Num 12:14
Hebron was built *s* years ......Num 13:22
fourteen thousand and *s* ....Num 16:49
congregation *s* times ....Num 19:4
and on the *s* day he shall .....Num 19:12
the *s* day he shall not be ......Num 19:12
tent shall be unclean *s* ....Num 19:14
and on the *s* day ....Num 19:19
and on the *s* day he shall .....Num 19:19
Build me here *s* altars ....Num 23:1
s oxen and *s* rams ....Num 23:1
built *s* altars, and offered .....Num 23:14
Build me here *s* altars ....Num 23:29
s bullocks and *s* rams ....Num 23:29
and three thousand and *s* .....Num 26:7
a thousand *s* hundred ....Num 26:51
s lambs of the first year ....Num 28:11
s days shall unleavened ....Num 28:17
throughout the *s* lambs........Num 28:21
throughout the *s* days ....Num 28:24
throughout the *s* lambs........Num 28:29
in the *s* month, on the ....Num 29:1
s lambs of the first year ....Num 29:2
s lambs of the first year ....Num 29:8
fifteenth day of the *s* ....Num 29:12
feast unto the Lord *s* days ....Num 29:12
s lambs of the first year ....Num 29:36
abide without the camp *s* .....Num 31:19

third day, and on the *s* .... Num 31:19
thirty thousand and *s* .... Num 31:43
the *s* day is the sabbath .... Deut 5:14
s years thou shalt make .... Deut 15:1
s year thou shalt let him .... Deut 15:12
s days shalt thou eat .... Deut 16:3
S weeks shalt thou .... Deut 16:9
begin to number the *s* .... Deut 16:9
S days shalt thou keep .... Deut 16:15
flee *s* ways before .... Deut 28:25
the *s* day ye shall compass .... Josh 6:4
let *s* priests bear *s* .... Josh 6:6
after the same manner *s* .... Josh 6:15
they compassed the city *s* .... Josh 6:15
came to pass at the *s* .... Josh 6:16
the children of Israel *s* .... Josh 18:2
describe the land into *s* .... Josh 18:6
into the hand of Midian *s* .... Judg 6:1
thousand and *s* hundred .... Judg 8:26
And he judged Israel *s* .... Judg 12:9
came to pass on the *s* .... Judg 14:15
s day before the sun went .... Judg 14:18
If they bind me with *s* .... Judg 16:7
weavest the *s* locks of my .... Judg 16:13
numbered *s* hundred .... Judg 20:15
better to thee than *s* .... Ruth 4:15
barren hath born *s* 1Sam 2:5
s days shalt thou tarry 1Sam 10:8
Give us *s* days' respite 1Sam 11:3
And he tarried *s* days 1Sam 13:8
the house of Judah was *s* 2Sam 2:11
over Judah *s* years and 2Sam 5:5
chariots, and *s* hundred 2Sam 8:4
slew the man of *s* 2Sam 10:18
on the *s* day, that the 2Sam 12:18
s men of his sons be 2Sam 21:6
the Hittite: thirty and *s* 2Sam 23:39
s years of famine come 2Sam 24:13
s years reigned he in 1Kin 2:11
and the third was *s* 1Kin 6:6
and *s* for the other chapiter 1Kin 7:17
Ethanim, which is the *s* 1Kin 8:2
s days and *s* days, even 1Kin 8:65
he had *s* hundred wives 1Kin 11:3
did Zimri reign *s* days in 1Kin 16:15
And he said, Go again *s* 1Kin 18:43
came to pass at the *s* 1Kin 18:44
I have left me *s* thousand 1Kin 19:18
over against the other *s* 1Kin 20:29
a compass of *s* days' 2Kin 3:9
the child sneezed *s* times 2Kin 4:35
dipped himself *s* times in 2Kin 5:14
land of the Philistines *s* 2Kin 8:2
s year Jehoiada sent and 2Kin 11:4
S years old was Jehoash 2Kin 11:21
in the thirty and *s* year 2Kin 13:10
which was the *s* year of 2Kin 18:9
in the *s* month, that 2Kin 25:25
pass in the *s* and thirtieth 2Kin 25:27
on the *s* and twentieth day 2Kin 25:27
sixth, David the *s* 1Chr 2:15
he reigned *s* years and six 1Chr 3:4
Zia, and Heber, *s* 1Chr 5:13
fourscore and *s* thousand 1Chr 7:5
to come after *s* days from 1Chr 9:25
war, *s* thousand and one 1Chr 12:25
and spear thirty and *s* 1Chr 12:34
s thousand horsemen 1Chr 18:4
s to Hakkoz, the eighth 1Chr 24:10
Elioenai the *s* 1Chr 26:3
thousand and *s* hundred 1Chr 26:30
The *s* captain for the *s* 1Chr 27:10
s thousand talents of 1Chr 29:4
feast which was in the *s* 2Chr 5:3
Solomon kept the feast *s* 2Chr 7:8
dedication of the altar *s* 2Chr 7:9
and the feast *s* days 2Chr 7:9
s hundred oxen and *s* 2Chr 15:11
s thousand and *s* hundred 2Chr 17:11
in the *s* year Jehoiada 2Chr 23:1
and *s* thousand and five 2Chr 26:13
brought *s* bullocks, and *s* 2Chr 29:21
and *s* lambs, and *s* he 2Chr 29:21
eat throughout the feast *s* 2Chr 30:22
to keep other *s* days 2Chr 30:23
kept other *s* days with 2Chr 30:23
unleavened bread *s* days 2Chr 35:17
Arah, *s* hundred seventy .... Ezra 2:5
s hundred and forty and .... Ezra 2:25
hundred forty and *s* .... Ezra 2:38
there were *s* thousand .... Ezra 2:65
hundred thirty and *s* .... Ezra 2:65
thousand *s* hundred and .... Ezra 2:67
And when the *s* month .... Ezra 3:1
the *s* year of Artaxerxes .... Ezra 7:7
king, and of his *s* .... Ezra 7:14
Zaccai, *s* hundred and .... Neh 7:14
threescore and *s* .... Neh 7:19
Ono, *s* hundred twenty .... Neh 7:37
whom there were *s* .... Neh 7:67
hundred thirty and *s* .... Neh 7:67
s hundred and twenty .... Neh 7:69
and when the *s* month .... Neh 7:73
in the feast of the *s* .... Neh 8:14
kept the feast *s* days .... Neh 8:18
over an hundred and *s* .... Esth 1:1
s day, when the heart of .... Esth 1:10
s chamberlains that .... Esth 1:10
s maidens, which were .... Esth 2:9
hundred twenty and *s* .... Esth 9:30
were born unto him *s* .... Job 1:2
the ground *s* days and *s* .... Job 2:13
you now *s* bullocks and *s* .... Job 42:8
s are an abomination .... Prov 6:16
For a just man falleth *s* .... Prov 24:16
are *s* abominations in .... Prov 26:25
Give a portion to *s*, and .... Eccl 11:2
shall smite it in the *s* .... Is 11:15
that hath borne *s* .... Jer 15:9
died the same year in the *s* .... Jer 28:17
s men of them that were .... Jer 52:25
in the *s* year three .... Jer 52:28
s and thirtieth year of the .... Jer 52:31
astonished among them *s* .... Ezek 3:15
came to pass in the *s* .... Ezek 20:1
pass in the *s* and .... Ezek 29:17
s months shall the house .... Ezek 39:12
they went up into it by *s* .... Ezek 40:22
the breadth of the door, *s* .... Ezek 41:3
S days shall they purge .... Ezek 43:26
shalt do the *s* day of the .... Ezek 45:20
the passover, a feast of *s* .... Ezek 45:21
s days of the feast he .... Ezek 45:23
s bullocks and *s* rams .... Ezek 45:23
daily the *s* days .... Ezek 45:23
the furnace one *s* times .... Dan 3:19
field, till *s* times pass .... Dan 4:23
the Prince shall be *s* .... Dan 9:25
that maketh the *s* .... Amos 5:8
we raise against him *s* .... Mic 5:5
In the *s* month, in the one .... Hag 2:1
upon one stone shall be *s* .... Zech 3:9
top of it, and his *s* lamps .... Zech 4:2
and *s* pipes to the *s* lamps .... Zech 4:2
mourned in the fifth and *s* .... Zech 7:5
And he took the *s* loaves .... Matt 15:36
Neither the *s* loaves of .... Matt 16:10
and I forgive him? till *s* .... Matt 18:21
say not unto thee, Until *s* .... Matt 18:22
but, Until seventy times *s* .... Matt 18:22
the third, unto the *s* .... Matt 22:26
shall she be of the *s*? .... Matt 22:28
And they said, *S* .... Mark 8:5
meat that was left *s* .... Mark 8:8
when the *s* among four .... Mark 8:20
And they said, *S* .... Mark 8:20
for the *s* had her to wife .... Mark 12:23
out of whom he had cast *s* .... Mark 16:9
with an husband *s* .... Luke 2:36
him *s* other spirits more .... Luke 11:26
against thee *s* times in a .... Luke 17:4
and *s* times in a day turn .... Luke 17:4
and in like manner the *s* .... Luke 20:31
the *s* hour the fever left .... John 4:52
destroyed *s* nations in the .... Acts 13:19
where we abode *s* days .... Acts 20:6
which was one of the *s* .... Acts 21:8
tarry with them *s* .... Acts 28:14
to myself *s* thousand men .... Rom 11:4
of the *s* day on this wise .... Heb 4:4
rest the *s* day from all his .... Heb 4:4
were compassed about *s* .... Heb 11:30
And Enoch also, the *s* from .... Jude 14
the *s* churches which are .... Rev 1:11
in the midst of the *s* .... Rev 1:13
he had in his right hand *s* .... Rev 1:16
that holdeth the *s* stars .... Rev 2:1
midst of the *s* golden .... Rev 2:1
there were *s* lamps of fire .... Rev 4:5
which are the *s* Spirits of .... Rev 4:5
and to loose the *s* seals .... Rev 5:5
having *s* horns and *s* .... Rev 5:6
which are the *s* Spirits of .... Rev 5:6
when he had opened the *s* .... Rev 8:1
And I saw the *s* angels .... Rev 8:2
s angels which had the *s* .... Rev 8:6
s thunders had uttered .... Rev 10:4
which the *s* thunders .... Rev 10:4
were slain of men *s* .... Rev 11:13
And the *s* angel sounded .... Rev 11:15
having *s* heads and ten .... Rev 12:3
s crowns upon his heads .... Rev 12:3
the *s* plagues of the *s* .... Rev 15:8
saying to the *s* angels .... Rev 16:1
s angels which had the *s* .... Rev 17:1
hath the *s* heads and ten .... Rev 17:7
and is of the *s*, and goeth .... Rev 17:11
came unto me one of the *s* .... Rev 21:9
s vials full of the *s* last .... Rev 21:9
the *s*, chrysolite; the .... Rev 21:20

SEVEN SAYINGS FROM THE CROSS—*Jesus' words from the cross*

1. "Father, forgive them" .... Luke 23:34
2. "Today shalt thou be with me in paradise" .... Luke 23:43
3. "Woman, behold thy son" .... John 19:26
4. "My God, my God" .... Matt 27:46, Mark 15:34
5. "I thirst" .... John 19:28
6. "It is finished" .... John 19:30
7. "Father, into thy hands" .... Luke 23:46

SEVENFOLD—*seven times*

be taken on him *s* .... Gen 4:15
If Cain shall be avenged *s* .... Gen 4:24
Lamech seventy and *s* .... Gen 4:24
our neighbors *s* .... Ps 79:12
found, he shall restore *s* .... Prov 6:31
of the sun shall be *s* .... Is 30:26

SEVENTEEN

[*also* SEVENTEENTH]
month, the *s* day of the .... Gen 7:11
on the *s* day of the month .... Gen 8:4
Joseph, being *s* years old .... Gen 37:2
in the land of Egypt *s* .... Gen 47:28
even threescore and *s* men .... Judg 8:14
reigned *s* years in 1Kin 14:21
Israel in Samaria the *s* 1Kin 22:51
Samaria, and reigned *s* 2Kin 13:1
the *s* year of Pekah the 2Kin 16:1
s thousand and two 1Chr 7:11
The *s* to Hezir, the 1Chr 24:15
The *s* to Joshbekashah 1Chr 25:24
he reigned *s* years in 2Chr 12:13
Harim, a thousand and *s* .... Ezra 2:39
Harim, a thousand and *s* .... Neh 7:42
the money, even *s* shekels .... Jer 32:9

SEVENTY

Elders appointed .... Ex 24:1, 9
Years in Babylon .... Dan 9:2
Weeks in prophetic vision .... Dan 9:24
In forgiveness .... Matt 18:22
Disciples went forth .... Luke 10:1

truly Lamech *s* and .... Gen 4:24
seven hundred *s* and seven .... Gen 5:31
and Abram was *s* and five .... Gen 12:4
the loins of Jacob were *s* .... Ex 1:5
seven hundred *s* and five .... Ex 38:28
bowl of *s* shekels .... Num 7:13
shekels, each bowl *s* .... Num 7:85
me *s* men of the elders of .... Num 11:16
gave it unto the *s* .... Num 11:25

father, in slaying his *s* ....Judg 9:56
to Beer-sheba *s* thousand 2Sam 24:15
And Ahab had *s* sons in 2Kin 10:1
the king's sons, and slew *s* 2Kin 10:7
there fell of Israel *s* 1Chr 21:14
thousand an hundred *s* ....Ezra 2:3
of Arab, seven hundred *s* .....Ezra 2:5
children of Hodaviah, *s* ....Ezra 2:40
Zabbud, and with them *s* .....Ezra 8:14
thousand an hundred *s* ....Neh 7:8
Jeshua, nine hundred *s* ....Neh 7:39
gates, were an hundred *s* ......Neh 11:19
of their foes *s* and five ....Esth 9:16
Tyre shall be forgotten *s* ......Is 23:15
end of *s* years shall Tyre ......Is 23:15
serve the king of..*s* years ......Jer 25:11
after *s* years be ....Jer 29:10
before them *s* men of the ......Ezek 8:11
toward the west was *s* ....Ezek 41:12
even those *s* years, did ye .....Zech 7:5
And the *s* returned again .....Luke 10:17

SEVER—*to cut out; cut off*

[*also* SEVERED]
s in that day the land ....Ex 8:22
shall *s* between the cattle .....Ex 9:4
and have *s* you from other ....Lev 20:26
s three cities on this side ......Deut 4:41
had *s* himself from the ....Judg 4:11
they shall *s* out men of ....Ezek 39:14
s the wicked from among .....Matt 13:49

SEVERAL—*separate; individual*

[*also* SEVERALLY]
a *s* tenth deal of flour ....Num 28:13
A *s* tenth deal unto one ....Num 28:29
And a *s* tenth deal to each ....Num 29:15
death, and dwelt in a *s* 2Kin 15:5
And in every *s* city he 2Chr 11:12
in every *s* city of Judah 2Chr 28:25
man according to his *s* ....Matt 25:15
dividing to every man *s* 1Cor 12:11
every *s* gate was of one ....Rev 21:21

SEVERITY—*strictness in judgment or discipline*
the goodness and *s* of God ....Rom 11:22
on them which fell, *s* ....Rom 11:22

SEW—*to stitch*

[*also* SEWED, SEWEST, SEWETH]
they *s* fig leaves together ......Gen 3:7
and thou *s* up mine ....Job 14:17
I have *s* sackcloth upon ....Job 16:15
and a time to *s* ....Eccl 3:7
Woe to the women that *s* .....Ezek 13:18
s a piece of new cloth ....Mark 2:21

SEXES—*male and female*

Creation of:
By God ....Gen 1:27
For:
Union ....Gen 2:23-25
Helpfulness ....Gen 2:18
Procreation ....Gen 4:1
Sexual needs ....Prov 5:17-19

Regulations concerning:
Distinctive clothing for ...Deut 22:5
Subordination of 1Cor 11:3-16
Equality in Christ ....Gal 3:28
Different functions of 1Tim 2:8-15
Love between ....Eph 5:22-33

SEXUAL LOVE—*physical tenderness or intercourse*
Good and holy ....Gen 1:27, 28
Gen 2:24, 25
For procreation ....Gen 4:1
In marriage only ....Prov 5:15-20
Expression of love ....Song 1:12-15
Song 3:1-5
Mutual responsibility.....1Cor 7:3-5

SEXUAL PERVERSION—*sexual contact condemned in scripture*

Types of:
Adultery ....Deut 22:22-29
Prostitution ....Deut 23:17
Incest ....Lev 18:6-18
Homosexuality ....Rom 1:26, 27
Mankind with beasts .....Deut 27:21

Judgment upon:
Defilement ....Lev 18:22-28
Destruction 1Cor 5:1-5
Death ....Lev 20:13-16

SHAALBIM, SHAALABBIN (shā-ăl'bĭm, shā-ä-lăb'ĭn)—*"place of foxes"*
Amorite city assigned to
Danites ....Josh 19:42
Subdued by house of
Joseph ....Judg 1:35

SHAALBONITE (shā-ăl'bōn-īt)—*an inhabitant of Shaalbim*
Eliahba called 2Sam 23:32

Eliahba the *S*, of the 2Sam 23:32
Baharomite, Eliahba the *S* 1Chr 11:33

SHAAPH (shā'ăf)—*"union; friendship"*
1. Descendant of Caleb 1Chr 2:47
2. Son of Caleb 1Chr 2:49

SHAARAIM (shā-ä-rā'ĭm)—*"gates"*
1. Village in Judah ....Josh 15:36
2. City of Simeon 1Chr 4:31

fell down by the way to *S* 1Sam 17:52

SHAASHGAZ (shā-ăsh'găz)—*"lover of beauty; one eager to learn"*
Persian eunuch ....Esth 2:14

SHABBETHAI (shăb'ĕ-thī)—*"sabbath-born"*
Postexilic Levite ....Ezra 10:15
Interprets the law ....Neh 8:7, 8

And *S* and Jozabad, of ....Neh 11:16

SHACHIA (shä-kī'ä)—*"fame of Jehovah"*
Benjamite 1Chr 8:10

SHADE—*a shelter from sunlight*
Lord is thy *s* upon thy ....Ps 121:5

SHADOW—*a dark figure created by blocking out the light; an imperfect representation*

Used literally of:
Man ....Acts 5:15
Mountain ....Judg 9:36
Sundial 2Kin 20:9-11

Used figuratively of:
Protection ....Ps 91:1
Brevity ....Ps 102:11
Change ....James 1:17
Death ....Matt 4:16
Types ....Col 2:17
Old Testament period ....Heb 10:1

[*also* SHADOWS]
on the earth are as a *s* 1Chr 29:15
s of death stain it; let a ....Job 3:5
earnestly desireth the *s* ....Job 7:2
days upon earth are a *s* ....Job 8:9
of darkness and the *s* of ......Job 10:21
bringeth out to light the *s* .....Job 12:22
he fleeth also as a *s* ....Job 14:2
on my eyelids is the *s* of ......Job 16:16
my members are as a *s* ....Job 17:7
is to them even as the *s* of .....Job 24:17
are in the terrors of the *s* ......Job 24:17
is no darkness, nor *s* of ....Job 34:22
seen the doors of the *s* of .....Job 38:17
cover him with their *s* ....Job 40:22
hide me under the *s* of thy ....Ps 17:8
valley of the *s* of death ....Ps 23:4
trust under the *s* of thy ....Ps 36:7
and covered us with the *s* .....Ps 44:19
lo the *s* of thy wings will ......Ps 57:1
in the *s* of thy wings will ......Ps 63:7
were covered with the *s* ....Ps 80:10
in darkness and in the *s* ....Ps 107:10
I am gone like the *s* when ....Ps 109:23
days are as a *s* that pass ......Ps 144:4
vain life which he spendeth ....Eccl 6:12
his days, which are as *s* ....Eccl 8:13
I sat down under his *s* ....Song 2:3
day break, and the *s* flee .....Song 2:17
the day break, and the *s* ......Song 4:6
tabernacle for a *s* in the ....Is 4:6
dwell in the land of the *s* .....Is 9:2
make thy *s* as the night ....Is 16:3
a *s* from the heat, when ....Is 25:4
trust in the *s* of Egypt ....Is 30:2
s of a great rock in a ....Is 32:2
and gather under her *s* ....Is 34:15
bring again the *s* of the ....Is 38:8
in the *s* of his hand hath ......Is 49:2
in the *s* of mine hand ....Is 51:16
of drought, and of the *s* ....Jer 2:6
s of the evening are ....Jer 6:4
light, he turn it into the *s* .....Jer 13:16
fled stood under the *s* of ......Jer 48:45
Under his *s* we shall live ......Lam 4:20
the *s* of the branches ....Ezek 17:23
under his *s* dwelt all great .....Ezek 31:6
dwelt under his *s* in the ....Ezek 31:17
beasts of the field had *s* ....Dan 4:12
because the *s* thereof ....Hos 4:13
dwell under his *s* shall ....Hos 14:7
the *s* of death into the ....Amos 5:8
sat under it in the *s*, till ....Jon 4:5
air may lodge under the *s* .....Mark 4:32
in darkness and in the *s* ....Luke 1:79
example and *s* of heavenly ....Heb 8:5

SHADOWING—*obscured by shadow*
Woe to the land *s* with ....Is 18:1
with a *s* shroud, and of an ....Ezek 31:3
of glory *s* the mercy seat ......Heb 9:5

SHADRACH (shā'drăk)—*"servant of (the god) Sin"*
Hananiah's Babylonian
name ....Dan 1:3, 7
Cast into the fiery
furnace ....Dan 3:1-28

set *S*, Meshach, and ....Dan 2:49
amiss against the God of *S* ....Dan 3:29
the king promoted *S* ....Dan 3:30

SHADY—*sheltered from the sun's direct rays*
He lieth under the *s* trees .....Job 40:21
The *s* trees cover him with .....Job 40:22

SHAFT—*long handle of a weapon; a pole*
his *s*, and his branches, his ....Ex 25:31
his *s*, and his branch, his ......Ex 37:17
beaten gold, unto the *s* ....Num 8:4
made me a polished *s* ....Is 49:2

SHAGE (shā'gē)—*"erring; wandering"*
Father of one of David's
mighty men 1Chr 11:34

SHAHARAIM (shā-hä-rā'ĭm)—*"double dawn"*
Benjamite 1Chr 8:8-11

SHAHAZIMAH (shā-hä-zī'mä)—*"heights"*
Town of Issachar ....Josh 19:17, 22

SHAKE—*to tremble; totter*

Descriptive of:
Thunder ....Ps 77:1
Earthquakes ....Acts 4:31
Fear ....Matt 28:4

Used figuratively of:
Fear ....Is 14:16
Second advent ....Heb 12:26, 27
Rejection ....Luke 9:5
Acts 18:6

[*also* SHAKED, SHAKEN, SHAKETH, SHAKING, SHOOK]
sound of a *s* leaf chase ....Lev 26:36
before, and *s* myself ....Judg 16:20
hold of it; for the oxen *s* 2Sam 6:6
earth *s* and trembled 2Sam 22:8
Israel, as a reed is *s* in 1Kin 14:15
of Jerusalem hath *s* her 2Kin 19:21
Also I *s* my lap, and said .....Neh 5:13
So God *s* out every man ......Neh 5:13
even thus be he *s* out ....Neh 5:13
made all my bones to *s* ....Job 4:14
s the earth out of her ....Job 9:6
you, and *s* mine head at .....Job 16:4

S

by my neck, and *s* me to......Job 16:12
the wicked might be *s* out.....Job 38:13
he laugheth at the *s* of a......Job 41:29
earth *s* and trembled..........Ps 18:7
hills moved and were *s*........Ps 18:7
shoot out the lip, they *s*.......Ps 22:7
Lord *s* the wilderness ....Ps 29:8
Lord *s* the wilderness of ......Ps 29:8
a *s* of the head among the ....Ps 44:14
breaches thereof; for it *s*......Ps 60:2
The earth *s*, the heavens ......Ps 68:8
loins continually to *s*..........Ps 69:23
upon me they *s* their ....Ps 109:25
ariseth to *s* terribly the........Is 2:19
if the rod should *s* itself.......Is 10:15
shall *s* his hand against........Is 10:32
s the hand, that they may .....Is 13:2
left in it, as the *s* of an ....Is 17:6
the *s* of the hand of the.......Is 19:16
Lord of hosts, which he *s* .....Is 19:16
over the sea, he *s* the.........Is 23:11
shall be as the *s* of an ....Is 24:13
battles of *s* will he fight.......Is 30:32
of Jerusalem hath *s* her ....Is 37:22
all my bones *s*; I am like......Jer 23:9
thy walls shall *s* at the ....Ezek 26:10
suburbs shall *s* at the ....Ezek 27:28
a noise, and behold a *s* ....Ezek 37:7
great *s* in the land of Israel ...Ezek 38:19
of the earth, shall *s* at my.....Ezek 38:20
s off his leaves, and ....Dan 4:14
and the earth shall *s*..........Joel 3:16
door, that the posts may *s* ....Amos 9:1
trees shall be terribly *s*........Nah 2:3
if they be *s*, they shall ....Nah 3:12
while, and I will *s* the ....Hag 2:6
I will *s* the heavens and.......Hag 2:21
I will *s* mine hand upon.......Zech 2:9
or city, *s* off the dust of.......Matt 10:14
to see? A reed *s* with the .....Matt 11:7
powers of the heavens..*s* ......Matt 24:29
s off the dust under your......Mark 6:11
are in heaven shall be *s*.......Mark 13:25
measure, pressed down, *s* .....Luke 6:38
house, and could not *s*........Luke 6:48
to see? A reed *s* with the .....Luke 7:24
the powers of heaven..*s*.......Luke 21:26
s off the dust of their feet.....Acts 13:51
foundations..prison were *s*.....Acts 16:26
he *s* off the beast into the.....Acts 28:5
That ye be not soon *s* in 2Thess 2:2
Whose voice then *s* the ....Heb 12:26
of those things that are *s*......Heb 12:27
which cannot be *s* may........Heb 12:27
when she is *s* of a mighty .....Rev 6:13

SHALEM (shā'lĕm)—*"safe"*
Town near Shechem; can mean "in peace" ....Gen 33:18

SHALIM (shā'lĭm)—*"foxes"—a district in Ephraim*
Mentioned in Saul's pursuit 1Sam 9:4

SHALISHA (shä-lī'shä)—*"the third"—an area near Mount Ephraim, probably northeast of Lydda*
Mentioned in Saul's pursuit 1Sam 9:4

SHALL—*See* INTRODUCTION

SHALLECHETH (shăl'ĕ-kĕth)—*"a casting out"*
Gate of Solomon's temple.1Chr 26:16

SHALLUM (shăl'ŭm)—*"recompenser"*
1. King of Israel 2Kin 15:10-15
2. Husband of Huldah 2Kin 22:14
3. Judahite..............1Chr 2:40, 41
4. Simeonite 1Chr 4:25
5. Father of Hilkiah 1Chr 6:12, 13
6. Naphtali's son 1Chr 7:13
7. Family of porters ......Ezra 2:42
8. Called Shelemiah 1Chr 26:14
9. Father of Jehizkiah 2Chr 28:12
10. One who divorced his foreign wife ....Ezra 10:24
11. Another who divorced his foreign wife ......Ezra 10:42
12. Son of Hallohesh ......Neh 3:12
13. Jeremiah's uncle ....Jer 32:7
14. Father of Maaseiah ....Jer 35:4

the porters were, *S* and 1Chr 9:17
their brethren: *S* was 1Chr 9:17
And *S* the son of Kore 1Chr 9:19
the first-born of *S* the.........1Chr 9:31
the wife of *S* the son of........2Chr 34:22
son of *S*, the son of Zadok....Ezra 7:2
porters: the children of *S* .....Neh 7:45
saith the Lord touching *S* .....Jer 22:11

SHALLUN (shăl'ŭn)—*"recompenser"—one who helped repair the wall of Jerusalem*
of the fountain repaired *S*.....Neh 4:15

SHALMAI (shăl'mī)—*"Jehovah is recompenser"*
Head of a family of Nethinim ....Ezra 2:46

Hagaba, the children of *S* .....Neh 7:48

SHALMAN (shăl'măn)
Contraction of Shalmaneser ....Hos 10:14

SHALMANESER (shăl-măn-ē'zer)—*"(the god) Sulman is chief"*
Assyrian king 2Kin 17:3

that *S* king of Assyria.........2Kin 18:9

SHALT—*See* INTRODUCTION

SHAMA (shā'mä)—*"hearer"*
Son of Hotham..........1Chr 11:44

SHAMARIAH (shăm-ä-rī'ä)—*"whom Jehovah guards"*
Son of Rehoboam 2Chr 11:18, 19

SHAMBLES—*meat market*
Question concerning meat bought in 1Cor 10:25

SHAME—*painful consciousness of guilt; disgrace or disrepute; to disgrace*

Caused by:
Rape 2Sam 13:13
Defeat..................2Chr 32:21
Folly ....Prov 3:35
Idleness ....Prov 10:5
Pride ....Prov 11:2
A wicked wife ....Prov 12:4
Lying...................Prov 13:5
Stubbornness ....Prov 13:18
Haste in speech ....Prov 18:13
Mistreatment of parents ..Prov 19:26
Evil companions.........Prov 28:7
Juvenile delinquency .....Prov 29:15
Nakedness ....Is 47:3
Idolatry................Jer 2:26, 27
Impropriety 1Cor 11:6
Lust ....Phil 3:19

Of the unregenerate:
Hardened in ....Jer 8:12
Pleasure in.............Rom 1:26, 27, 32
Vessels of..............Rom 9:21
Glory in ....Phil 3:19
Like foam ....Jude 13

In the Christian life, of:
Unregenerate's life ......Rom 6:21
Sinful things ....Eph 5:12
Improper behavior.......1Cor 11:14, 22
Christ ....Rom 1:16

[*also* SHAMED, SHAMEFUL, SHAMEFULLY, SHAMETH]

take it to her, lest we be *s* ....Gen 38:23
them naked unto their *s* ......Ex 32:25
that might put them to *s* ......Judg 18:7
his father had done him *s* 1Sam 20:34
hast *s* this day the faces of 2Sam 19:5
shall be clothed with *s* ....Job 8:22
will ye turn my glory into *s*? ..Ps 4:2
Ye have *s* the counsel of......Ps 14:6
put to *s* that seek after my ....Ps 35:4
and put to *s* that wish me .....Ps 40:14
hast put them to *s* that........Ps 44:7
the *s* of my face hath ....Ps 44:15
thou hast put them to *s* ....Ps 53:5
reproach; *s* hath covered ......Ps 69:7
for a reward of their *s* ....Ps 70:3
they are brought unto *s* ....Ps 71:24
Fill their faces with *s* ....Ps 83:16
covered him with *s* ....Ps 89:45
adversaries be clothed, with *s*..Ps 109:29
O Lord, put me not to *s* ......Ps 119:31
enemies will I clothe with *s* ...Ps 132:18
getteth to himself *s* ....Prov 9:7
a prudent man covereth *s* .....Prov 12:16
against him that causeth *s* .....Prov 14:35
over a son that causeth *s*......Prov 17:2
neighbor..put thee to *s*........Prov 25:8
heareth it put thee to *s* ....Prov 25:10
riotous men *s* his father ....Prov 28:7
uncovered, to the *s* of ....Is 20:4
shall be the *s* of thy lord's ....Is 22:18
strength of Pharaoh..*s* ....Is 30:3
not my face from *s* and ....Is 50:6
shalt not be put to *s*..........Is 54:4
shalt forget the *s* of thy ....Is 54:4
For your *s* ye shall have ......Is 61:7
s hath devoured the labor .....Jer 3:24
have ye..altars to that *s* ....Jer 11:13
thy face, that thy *s* may.......Jer 13:26
should be consumed with *s*? ...Jer 20:18
a perpetual *s*, which shall .....Jer 23:40
nations have heard of thy *s*....Jer 46:12
Moab turned the back with *s* ..Jer 48:39
s hath covered our faces ....Jer 51:51
and *s* shall be upon all ....Ezek 7:18
bear thine own *s* for thy ......Ezek 16:52
mayest bear thine own *s* ......Ezek 16:54
any more because of thy *s* ....Ezek 16:63
and bear their *s* with them ....Ezek 32:30
neither bear the *s* of the ......Ezek 34:29
yet have born the *s* of the.....Ezek 36:6
hear in thee the *s* of the ......Ezek 36:15
but they shall bear their *s* .....Ezek 44:13
s and everlasting contempt ....Dan 12:2
conceived them hath done *s* ...Hos 2:5
change their glory into *s* ......Hos 4:7
separated themselves, that *s* ...Hos 9:10
brother Jacob *s* shall cover ....Obad 10
of Saphir, having thy *s*........Mic 1:11
s shall cover her which........Mic 7:10
and the kingdoms thy *s* ....Nah 3:5
hast consulted *s* to thy ....Hab 2:10
s spewing shall be on thy .....Hab 2:16
the unjust knoweth no *s* ......Zeph 3:5
head, and sent him away *s* ....Mark 12:4
begin with *s* to take the ....Luke 14:9
also, and entreated him *s* .....Luke 20:11
worthy to suffer *s* for his......Acts 5:41
write not these things to *s*.....1Cor 4:14
I speak to your *s*. Is it so 1Cor 6:5
s for women to speak in 1Cor 14:35
I speak this to your *s* 1Cor 15:34
and were *s* entreated, as 1Thess 2:2
and put him to an open *s* .....Heb 6:6
the cross, despising the *s*......Heb 12:2
foaming out their own *s*.......Jude 13
s of thy nakedness do not .....Rev 3:18
naked, and they see his *s* .....Rev 16:15

SHAMED (shā'mĕd)—*"destroyer"*
Son of Elpaal 1Chr 8:12

SHAMEFACEDNESS—*modesty*
apparel, with *s* and sobriety ...1Tim 2:9

SHAMELESSLY—*insensible to disgrace*
vain fellows *s* uncovereth......2Sam 6:20

SHAMER (shā'mer)—*"preserver"*
1. Levite.................1Chr 6:46
2. Asherite 1Chr 7:30, 34

SHAMGAR (shăm′gär)—*"cupbearer"*
Judge of Israel; struck down 600 Philistines . . . Judg 3:31
days of *S* the son of Anath . . . . Judg 5:6

SHAMHUTH (shăm′hŭth)—*"fame; renown"*
Commander in David's army 1Chr 27:8

SHAMIR (shā′mer)—*"thorn hedge"*
1. Town in Judah . . . . Josh 15:1, 48
2. Town in Ephraim . . . . Judg 10:1
3. Levite 1Chr 24:24
died, and was buried in *S* . . . . Judg 10:2

SHAMMA (shăm′ă)—*"fame; renown"*
Asherite 1Chr 7:36, 37

SHAMMAH (shăm′ä)—*"fame; renown"*
1. Son of Reuel . . . . Gen 36:13, 17
2. Son of Jesse 1Sam 16:9
Called Shimea 1Chr 2:13
3. One of David's mighty men 2Sam 23:11
Also called Shammoth the Harorite 1Chr 11:27
Abinadab, and the third *S* 1Sam 17:13
S the Harodite, Elika the 2Sam 23:25
S the Hararite, Ahiam 2Sam 23:33
Nahath, Zerah, *S*, and 1Chr 1:37

SHAMMAI (shăm′ā-ī)—*"celebrated"*
1. Grandson of Jerahmeel . . 1Chr 2:28, 32
2. Descendant of Caleb 1Chr 2:44, 45
3. Descendant of Judah 1Chr 4:17

SHAMMOTH (shăm′ŏth)—*"fame; renown"*
One of David's mighty men 1Chr 11:27

SHAMMUA, SHAMMUAH (shă-mū′ä)—*"famous"*
1. Reubenite spy . . . . Num 13:2-4
2. Son of David 2Sam 5:13, 14
3. Levite . . . . Neh 11:17
4. Postexilic priest . . . . Neh 12:1, 18
S, and Shobab, Nathan 1Chr 14:4

SHAMSHERAI (shăm′shĕ-rī)—*"heroic"*
Son of Jeroham 1Chr 8:26

SHAPE—*to create; one's form*
[*also* SHAPEN, SHAPES]
I was *S* in iniquity; and in . . . . . Ps 51:5
a bodily *s* like a dove . . . . Luke 3:22
any time, nor seen his *s* . . . . John 5:37
s of the locust were like . . . . Rev 9:7

SHAPHAM (shā′făm)—*"youthful; vigorous"*
Gadite 1Chr 5:12

SHAPHAN (shā′făn)—*"prudent; sly"*
Scribe under Josiah 2Kin 22:3
Takes book of the Law to Josiah 2Kin 22:8-10
Is sent to Huldah for interpretation 2Kin 22:14
Assists in repairs of temple 2Chr 34:8
Father of notable son . . . . Jer 36:10-12, 25
Ahikam the son of *S*, and 2Kin 22:12
and *S* the scribe, and 2Kin 22:12
of Ahikam, the son of *S* 2Kin 25:22
answered and said to *S* 2Chr 34:15
delivered the book to *S* 2Chr 34:15
And *S* carried the book to 2Chr 34:16
Then *S* the scribe told 2Chr 34:18
And *S* read it before the 2Chr 34:18
and Ahikam the son of *S* 2Chr 34:20
the son of Micah, and *S* 2Chr 34:20
of Ahikam the son of *S* . . . . Jer 26:24
hand of Elasah the son of *S* . . Jer 29:3
of Ahikam the son of *S* . . . . Jer 39:14
of Ahikam the son of *S* . . . . Jer 40:5
son of Ahikam the son of *S* . . Jer 40:9
of Ahikam the son of *S* . . . . Jer 40:11
of Ahikam the son of *S* . . . . Jer 41:2
of Ahikam the son of *S* . . . . Jer 43:6
Jaazaniah the son of *S* . . . . Ezek 8:11

SHAPHAT (shā′făt)—*"judge"*
1. Simeonite spy . . . . Num 13:2-5
2. Son of Shemaiah 1Chr 3:22
3. Gadite chief 1Chr 5:11, 12
4. One of David's herdsmen 1Chr 27:29
5. Father of the prophet Elisha 1Kin 19:16, 19
is Elisha the son of *S* 2Kin 3:11
head of Elisha the son of *S* . . . 2Kin 6:31

SHAPHER (shā′fer)—*"bright"*
Israelite encampment . . . . Num 33:23
removed from mount *S* . . . . Num 33:24

SHARAI (shă-rā′ī)—*"Jehovah is deliverer"*
Divorced his foreign wife . Ezra 10:40

SHARAIM—*See* SHAARAIM

SHARAR (shā′rer)—*"strong"*
Father of Ahiam 2Sam 23:33

SHARE—*a plow*
sharpen every man his *s* 1Sam 13:20

SHARERS—*those who participate in or use something with others*

Of physical things:
Sacrifices 1Cor 10:18
Suffering 2Cor 1:7; 1Pet 4:13

Of evil things:
Sins 1Tim 5:22

Of spiritual things:
Holiness . . . . Heb 12:10
Communion 1Cor 10:16, 17
Spiritual things . . . . Rom 15:27
Inheritance . . . . Col 1:12

SHAREZER, SHEREZER (shă-rē′zer, shĕ-rē′zer)—*"he has protected the king"*
1. Son of Sennacherib . . . . . Is 37:38
2. Sent to Zechariah concerning fasting . . . . . Zech 7:1-3
and *S* his son smote him 2Kin 19:37

SHARON (shăr′ŭn)—*"his song"*
1. Coastal plain between Joppa and Mt. Carmel . 1Chr 27:29
Famed for roses . . . . Song 2:1
2. Pasture east of the Jordan 1Chr 5:16
S is like a wilderness . . . . Is 33:9
excellency of Carmel and *S* . . . . Is 35:2
And *S* shall be a fold of . . . . . . Is 65:10

SHARONITE (shăr′ŭn-īt)—*an inhabitant of Sharon*
Shitrai 1Chr 27:29

SHARP—*keen-edged; biting*

Descriptive of:
Stone . . . . Ex 4:25
Knives . . . . Josh 5:2, 3
Share 1Sam 13:20, 21
Rocks 1Sam 14:4
Arrows . . . . Is 5:28

Used to compare a sword with:
Tongue . . . . Ps 57:4
Adulteress . . . . Prov 5:4
Mouth . . . . Is 49:2
God's Word . . . . Heb 4:12

Figurative of:
Deceitfulness . . . . Ps 52:2
Falsehood . . . . Prov 25:18
Contention . . . . Acts 15:39
Severe rebuke 2Cor 13:10
Christ's conquest . . . . Rev 14:14-18

[*also* SHARPER, SHARPLY, SHARPNESS]
did chide with him *s* . . . . Judg 8:1
S stones are under him . . . . Job 41:30
s pointed things upon the . . . . . Job 41:30
Thine arrows are *s* in the . . . . . Ps 45:5
S arrows of the mighty . . . . Ps 120:4
a new *s* threshing . . . . Is 41:15
take thee a *s* knife, take . . . . . . Ezek 5:1
the most upright is *s* than . . . . . Mic 7:4
present I should use *s* 2Cor 13:10
Wherefore rebuke them *s* . . . . . Titus 1:13
hath the *s* sword with . . . . Rev 2:12
of his mouth goeth a *s* . . . . Rev 19:15

SHARPEN—*to make sharp; make keen*
[*also* SHARPENED, SHARPENETH]
to *s* every man his share 1Sam 13:20
axes, and to *s* the goads 1Sam 13:21
mine enemy *s* his eyes . . . . Job 16:9
They have *s* their tongues . . . . . Ps 140:3
Iron *s* iron; so a man *s* . . . . Prov 27:17
A sword, a sword is *s*, and . . . . Ezek 21:9
It is *s* to make a sore . . . . Ezek 21:10
this sword is *s*, and it is . . . . Ezek 21:11

SHARUHEN (shă-roo′hĕn)—*"gracious house"*
Town of Judah assigned to Simeon . . . . Josh 19:1, 6
Called Shaaraim . . . . Josh 15:36; 1Chr 4:31

SHASHAI (shā′shī)—*"noble; free"*
Divorced his foreign wife . Ezra 10:40

SHASHAK (shā′shăk)—*"assaulter; runner"*
Benjamite 1Chr 8:14, 25

SHAUL (shā′ŭl)—*variant form of Saul*
1. King of Edom . . . . Gen 36:37
2. Son of Simeon . . . . Gen 46:10
Founder of a tribal family . . . . Num 26:13
3. Kohathite Levite 1Chr 6:24
S the son of a Canaanitish . . . . Ex 6:15
when *S* was dead, Baal-hanan . 1Chr 1:49
Jamin, Jarib, Zerah, and *S* 1Chr 4:24

SHAULITES—*of the tribe of Shaul*
Shaul, the family of the *S* . . . . . Num 26:13

SHAVE—*to cut off the hair*

Used worthily to express:
Accommodation . . . . Gen 41:14
Cleansing . . . . Lev 14:8, 9
Commitment . . . . Deut 21:12
Mourning . . . . Job 1:18-20
Sorrow . . . . Jer 41:5

Used unworthily to express:
Defeat of a Nazarite . . . . . Judg 16:19
Contempt 2Sam 10:4
Unnaturalness 1Cor 11:5, 6

[*also* SHAVED, SHAVEN]
the scall shall he not *s* . . . . Lev 13:33
He shall be *s*, but the . . . . Lev 13:33
they *s* off the corner of . . . . Lev 21:5
shall *s* his head in the day . . . . . Num 6:9
seventh day shall he *s* it . . . . Num 6:9
shall *s* the head of his . . . . Num 6:18
hair of his separation is *s* . . . . . Num 6:19
let them *s* all their flesh . . . . Num 8:7
s, then my strength will go . . . . Judg 16:17
grow again after he was *s* . . . . . Judg 16:22
s them, and cut off their 1Chr 19:4
Lord *s* with a razor that is . . . . Is 7:20
Neither shall they *s* their . . . . . . Ezek 44:20
them, that they may *s* . . . . Acts 21:24

SHAVEH (shā′vĕ)—*"the plain"*
Valley near Salem; Abram meets king of Sodom here . . . . Gen 14:17, 18
Emim in *S* Kiriathaim . . . . Gen 14:5

SHAVEH-KIRIATHAIM (shā-vĕ-kĭr-yä-thā′ĭm)—*"plains of Kiriathaim"*
Plain near Kiriathaim inhabited by Emim . . . . Gen 14:5

SHAVSHA, SHISHA (shăv′shä, shī′shä)—*"nobility"*
David's secretary 1Chr 18:14, 16
Serves under Solomon also 1Kin 4:3

SHE—*See* INTRODUCTION

SHEAF—*the stalk and ear of a cereal grass*

[*also* SHEAVES]
we were binding *s* in the ......Gen 37:7
and, lo, my *s* arose, and ......Gen 37:7
behold, your *s* stood ....Gen 37:7
made obeisance to my *s*.......Gen 37:7
bring a *s* of the firstfruits .....Lev 23:10
wave the *s* before the Lord....Lev 23:11
ye wave the *s* an he lamb .....Lev 23:12
brought the *s* of the wave .....Lev 23:15
and hast forgot a *s* in the .....Deut 24:19
reapers among the *s* ....Ruth 2:7
glean even among the *s* ....Ruth 2:15
bringing in *s*, and lading ....Neh 13:15
take away the *s* from the......Job 24:10
rejoicing, bringing his *s* ....Ps 126:6
nor he that bindeth *s* his ......Ps 129:7
is pressed that is full of *s* .....Amos 2:13
gather them as the *s* into......Mic 4:12
a torch of fire in a *s* ....Zech 12:6

SHEAL (shē'ăl)—*"request"*
Divorced his foreign wife .Ezra 10:29

SHEALTIEL (shĕ-ăl'tĭ-ĕl)—*"lent by God"*
Son of King Jeconiah and father of Zerubbabel...1Chr 3:17

Zerubbabel the son of *S* ......Ezra 3:2
Zerubbabel the son of *S* ......Ezra 3:8
Zerubbabel the son of *S* ......Ezra 5:2
Zerubbabel the son of *S* ......Neh 12:1
Zerubbabel the son of *S* ......Hag 1:1
Zerubbabel the son of *S* ......Hag 1:12
of Zerubbabel the son of *S*....Hag 1:14
Zerubbabel the son of *S* ......Hag 2:2
my servant the son of *S*.......Hag 2:23

SHEAR—*to cut off the hair or wool of*

[*also* SHEARING, SHORN]
And Laban went to *s* his......Gen 31:19
up to Timnath to *s* his ....Gen 38:13
nor *s* the firstling of thy.......Deut 15:19
he was *s* his sheep in 1Sam 25:2
that Nabal did *s* his sheep 1Sam 25:4
at the *s* house in the way 2Kin 10:12
at the pit of the *s* house 2Kin 10:14
of sheep that are even *s*.......Song 4:2
it to return into his *s*? ....Ezek 21:30
having *s* his head in ....Acts 18:18
covered, let her also be *s* 1Cor 11:6
shame for a woman to be *s* ...1Cor 11:6

SHEARER—*one who cuts fleece from sheep*

[*also* SHEARERS]
heard that thou hast *s* 1Sam 25:7
I have killed for my *s*.........1Sam 25:11
as a sheep before her *s* is .....Is 53:7
a lamb dumb before his *s* .....Acts 8:32

SHEARIAH (shē-ä-rī'ä)—*"Jehovah is decider"*
Descendant of Saul 1Chr 9:44

SHEAR-JASHUB (shē-är-jä'shŭb)—*"a remnant returns"*
Symbolic name given to Isaiah's son ....Is 7:3

SHEATH—*a covering for a blade*
drew it out of his *s* thereof 1Sam 17:51
upon his loins in the *s* 2Sam 20:8
his sword again into the *s* 1Chr 21:27
my sword out of his *s*.........Ezek 21:3
forth my sword out of his *s* ...Ezek 21:5
thy sword into the *s* ....John 18:11

SHEAVES—*See* SHEAF

SHEBA (shē'bä)—*"oath; covenant"*
1. City in territory assigned to Simeon ....Josh 19:1, 2
2. Benjamite insurrectionist .2Sam 20:1-22
3. Descendant of Cush through Raamah ......Gen 10:7
4. Descendant of Shem ....Gen 10:28
5. Grandson of Abraham and Keturah ....Gen 25:3
6. Gadite chief 1Chr 5:13
7. Land of, occupied by Sabeans, famous traders ....Job 1:15; Ps 72:10
   Queen of, visits Solomon; marvels at his wisdom 1Kin 10:1-13
   Mentioned by Christ ....Matt 12:42

sons of Raamah; *S*, and.......1Chr 1:9
Ebal, and Abimael, and *S*.....1Chr 1:22
sons of Jokshan; *S*, and 1Chr 1:32
queen of *S* heard of the.......2Chr 9:1
queen of *S* had seen the 2Chr 9:3
spice as the queen of *S* 2Chr 9:9
companies of *S* waited for .....Job 6:19
given of the gold of *S*.........Ps 72:15
all they from *S* shall ....Is 60:6
to me incense from *S* ....Jer 6:20
The merchants of *S* and.......Ezek 27:22
the merchants of *S* ....Ezek 27:23
S, and Dedan, and the........Ezek 38:13

SHEBAH (shē'bä)—*"seven"*
Name given to a well and town (Beersheba) .....Gen 26:31-33

SHEBAM (shē'băm)—*"fragrance"—a city east of the Jordan river*
Elealeh, and *S*, and Nebo .....Num 32:3

SHEBANIAH (shĕb-ä-nī'ä)—*"Jehovah is powerful"*
1. Levite trumpeter 1Chr 15:24
2. Levite; offers prayer and signs covenant ....Neh 9:4, 5
3. Levite who signs covenant ....Neh 10:12
4. Priest who signs covenant Neh 10:4

their brethren, *S*, Hodijah.....Neh 10:10
Melicu, Jonathan; of *S*.......Neh 12:14

SHEBARIM (shĕb'ä-rĭm)—*"hopes"*
Place near Ai ....Josh 7:5
See QUARRY

SHEBER (shē'ber)—*"breach"*
Son of Caleb 1Chr 2:48

SHEBNA (shĕb'nä)—*"youthfulness"*
Treasurer under Hezekiah ....Is 22:15
Demoted to position of scribe 2Kin 19:2
Man of pride and luxury; replaced by Eliakim ...Is 22:19-21

S the scribe, and Joah 2Kin 18:18
S, and Joah, unto Rab 2Kin 18:26
S the scribe, and Joah 2Kin 18:37
over the house, and *S* the .....Is 36:3
Then said Eliakim and *S* ....Is 36:11
S the scribe, and the..........Is 37:2

SHEBUEL (shĕ-bū'ĕl)—*"God is renown"*
1. Son of Gershom 1Chr 23:16
2. Son of Heman 1Chr 25:4

SHECANIAH (shĕk-ä-nī'ä)—*"Jehovah is a neighbor"*
1. Descendant of Zerubbabel 1Chr 3:21, 22
2. Postexilic returnee ......Ezra 8:5
3. Descendant of Aaron ...1Chr 24:11
4. Priest 2Chr 31:15
5. Divorced his foreign wife.Ezra 10:2, 3
6. Father of Shemaiah .....Neh 3:29 (Probably same as number 1)
7. Post exilic priest ....Neh 12:3, 7
8. Father-in-law of Tobiah .Neh 6:18

SHECHEM, SICHEM (shĕ'kĕm, sī'kĕm)—*"portion"*
1. Son of Hamor; seduces Dinah, Jacob's daughter ....Gen 34:1-31
2. Son of Gilead; founder of a tribal family......Num 26:31
3. Son of Shemida 1Chr 7:19
4. Ancient city of Ephraim .Gen 33:18
   Abram camps near ......Gen 12:6
   Jacob buys ground here .Gen 33:18, 19
   Hivites, inhabit ....Gen 34:2
   Inhabitants of, slaughtered by Simeon and Levi ....Gen 34:25-29
   Pastures near ....Gen 37:12, 13
   Becomes city of refuge ..Josh 20:7
   Joseph buried here ....Josh 24:32
   Joshua's farewell address here ....Josh 24:1, 25
   Center of idol-worship...Judg 9:1, 4-7
   Town destroyed.........Judg 9:23, 45
   Jeroboam made king here 1Kin 12:1-19
   Name of, used poetically.Ps 108:7

[*also* SHECHEM'S]
the children of Hamor, *S* .....Gen 33:19
and took Dinah out of *S* ......Gen 34:26
the oak, which was by *S* ......Gen 35:4
Hebron, and he came to *S* ....Gen 37:14
and for the children of *S*......Josh 17:2
that lieth before *S* ....Josh 17:7
gave them *S* with her ....Josh 21:21
concubine that was in *S* ....Judg 8:31
ears of all the men of *S*.......Judg 9:2
ears of all the men of *S*.......Judg 9:3
king over the men of *S* ....Judg 9:18
and devour the men of *S*......Judg 9:20
out from the men of *S* ....Judg 9:20
upon the men of *S*, which.....Judg 9:24
And the men of *S* set liers ....Judg 9:25
brethren, and went over *S* ....Judg 9:26
men of *S* put their............Judg 9:26
Abimelech, and who is *S*......Judg 9:28
of Hamor the father of *S* .....Judg 9:28
his brethren be come to *S*.....Judg 9:31
they laid wait against *S* ....Judg 9:34
out before the men of *S* ......Judg 9:39
should not dwell in *S* ....Judg 9:41
men of the tower of *S* ....Judg 9:46
men of the tower of *S* died....Judg 9:49
the evil of the men of *S*.......Judg 9:57
goeth up from Beth-el to *S*....Judg 21:19
Then Jeroboam built *S* in 1Kin 12:25
S in mount Ephraim with 1Chr 6:67
S also and the towns..........1Chr 7:28
And Rehoboam went to *S* 2Chr 10:1
S were all Israel come to......2Chr 10:1
I will divide *S*, and mete ......Ps 60:6
came certain from *S* ....Jer 41:5

SHECHEMITES (shĕ'kĕm-īts)—*the citizens of Shechem*
Shechem, the family of the *S* ..Num 26:31

SHED—*to cause to flow by cutting or wounding; be dispersed*

Descriptive of:
Blood ....Gen 9:6
Bowels 2Sam 20:10
Holy Spirit.............Titus 3:6

As applied to blood, indicative of:
Justifiable execution .....Gen 9:6
Unjustifiable murder.....Gen 37:22
Unacceptable sacrifice ...Lev 17:1-5
Attempted vengeance 1Sam 25:31, 34
Unpardonable 2Kin 24:4
Abomination ....Prov 6:16, 17
Heinous crime ....Is 59:7
New covenant ....Matt 26:28

[*also* SHEDDETH, SHEDDING]
there shall no blood be *s*......Ex 22:2
there shall be blood *s*.........Ex 22:3
be cleansed of the blood..*s*....Num 35:33
by the blood of him that *s* ....Num 35:33
innocent blood be not *s* ....Deut 19:10
Our hands have not *s* this .....Deut 21:7
thee from coming to *s* 1Sam 25:26
this day from coming to *s* 1Sam 25:33
and *s* the blood of war in 1Kin 2:5
innocent blood, which Joab *s*..1Kin 2:31
Manasseh *s* innocent 2Kin 21:16

hast *s* blood abundantly 1Chr 22:8
thou hast *s* much blood ....1 Chr 22:8
Their blood have they *s* ....Ps 79:3
of thy servants which is *s* .....Ps 79:10
s innocent blood, even the ....Ps 106:38
evil, and make haste to *s* .....Prov 1:16
s not innocent blood in ....Jer 7:6
s innocent blood in this ....Jer 22:3
for to *s* innocent blood........Jer 22:17
s the blood of the just in......Lam 4:13
wedlock and *s* blood are ......Ezek 16:38
The city *s* blood in the........Ezek 22:3
thy blood that thou hast *s* .....Ezek 22:4
in thee to their power to *s* ....Ezek 22:6
men that carry tales to *s* ......Ezek 22:9
have they taken gifts to *s* .....Ezek 22:12
ravening the prey, to *s* ....Ezek 22:27
manner of women that *s* ......Ezek 23:45
toward your idol, and *s* ....Ezek 33:25
hast *s* the blood of the ....Ezek 35:5
that they had *s* upon the ......Ezek 36:18
s innocent blood in their ......Joel 3:19
righteous blood *s* upon........Matt 23:35
s for many for the remission...Matt 26:28
testament, which is *s* for ......Mark 14:24
which was *s* from the ....Luke 11:50
in my blood, which is *s* ....Luke 22:20
he hath *s* forth this ....Acts 2:33
thy martyr Stephen was *s* .....Acts 22:20
Their feet are swift to *s* ....Rom 3:15
love of God is *s* abroad ....Rom 5:5
s on us abundantly through....Titus 3:6
and without *s* of blood is......Heb 9:22
For they have *s* the blood .....Rev 16:6

SHEDDER—*one who kills*
son that is a robber, a *s*.......Ezek 18:10

SHEDEUR (shĕd'ē-er)—*"shedder of light"*
Reubenite leader ....Num 1:5

day Elizur the son of *S* ....Num 7:30
of Elizur the son of *S* ....Num 7:35
was Elizur the son of *S* ....Num 10:18

SHEEP—*an animal that was kept as domesticated livestock in biblical days; one easily influenced or led*

Characteristics of:
Domesticated 2Sam 12:3
Gentile ....Jer 11:19
Defenseless ....Mic 5:8
Needful of care ....Ezek 34:5

Uses of, for:
Food 1Sam 25:18
Milk...................1Cor 9:7
Clothing ....Prov 31:13
Coverings ....Ex 26:14
Presents 2Sam 17:29
Tribute 2Kin 3:4
Sacrifice ....Gen 4:4

Uses of, in Levitical system as:
Burnt offering..........Lev 1:10
Sin offering ....Lev 4:32
Guilt offering ....Lev 5:15
Peace offering..........Lev 22:21

Needs of, for:
Protection ....Job 30:1
Shepherd ....John 10:4, 27
Fold...................John 10:1
Pastures ....Ex 3:1
Water ....Gen 29:8-10
Rest...................Ps 23:2
Shearing 1Sam 25:2, 11

Figurative of:
Innocent 2Sam 24:17
Wicked ....Ps 49:14
Jewish people ....Ps 74:1
Backsliders.............Jer 50:6
Lost sinners ....Matt 9:36
Christians..............John 10:1-16
Christ ....John 1:29
Saved ....Matt 26:31-34
Church ....Acts 20:28

See LAMB; LAMB OF GOD

[*also* SHEEP'S]
Abel was a keeper of *s* ....Gen 4:2
he had *s*, and oxen, and ......Gen 12:16
And Abimelech took *s*........Gen 20:14
And Abraham took *s* and .....Gen 21:27
were three flocks of *s* lying....Gen 29:2
daughter cometh with the *s*....Gen 29:6
brown cattle among the *s* .....Gen 30:32
the brown among the *s* ....Gen 30:35
Laban went to shear his *s* .....Gen 31:19
They took their *s*, and ....Gen 34:28
to Timnath to shear his *s* .....Gen 38:13
the oxen, and upon the *s* .....Ex 9:3
take it out from the *s*.........Ex 12:5
offerings, thy *s*, and thine .....Ex 20:24
shall steal an ox, or a *s* ....Ex 22:1
an ox, and four *s* for a *s* ......Ex 22:1
it be for ox, for ass, for *s* .....Ex 22:9
thine oxen, and with thy *s* ....Ex 22:30
whether ox or *s*, that is ....Ex 34:19
of ox, or of *s*, or of ....Lev 7:23
the beeves, of the *s*, or of.....Lev 22:19
When a bullock, or a *s*, or ....Lev 22:27
the firstling of a *s*, or the .....Num 18:17
Balak offered oxen and *s* .....Num 22:40
not as *s* which have no........Num 27:17
of the asses, and of the *s* .....Num 31:28
thousand and five hundred *s*...Num 31:36
thousand and five hundred *s*...Num 31:43
ones, and folds for your *s* .....Num 32:24
and the flocks of thy *s*, in .....Deut 7:13
eat: the ox, the *s*, and the ....Deut 14:4
shear the firstling of thy *s* .....Deut 15:19
bullock, or *s*, wherein is ......Deut 17:1
whether it be ox or *s* ....Deut 18:3
brother's ox or his *s* go ....Deut 22:1
and the flocks of thy *s* ....Deut 28:4
kine, or flocks of thy *s*........Deut 28:51
Butter of kine and milk of *s*...Deut 32:14
and *s*, and ass, with the.......Josh 6:21
his asses, and his *s*, and.......Josh 7:24
Israel, neither *s*, nor ox ....Judg 6:4
take the tenth of your *s*.......1Sam 8:17
and took *s*, and oxen, and 1Sam 14:32
then this bleating of the *s* 1Sam 15:14
people took of the spoil, *s* 1Sam 15:21
behold, he keepeth the *s*......1Sam 16:11
Saul to feed his father's *s* 1Sam 17:15
thou left those few *s* 1Sam 17:28
and *s*, with the edge of 1Sam 22:19
with them keeping the *s* 1Sam 25:16
took away the *s*, and the......1Sam 27:9
Adonijah slew *s* and oxen 1Kin 1:9
and fat cattle and *s* in 1Kin 1:25
a hundred *s*, beside 1Kin 4:23
sacrificing *s* and oxen 1Kin 8:5
as *s* that have not a 1Kin 22:17
and vineyards, and *s* 2Kin 5:26
s two hundred and fifty 1Chr 5:21
oil, and oxen, and *s* 1Chr 12:40
even from following the *s* 1Chr 17:7
for these *s*, what have 1Chr 21:17
sacrificed *s* and oxen..........2Chr 5:6
and twenty thousand *s* 2Chr 7:5
away *s* and camels in 2Chr 14:15
and seven thousand *s* 2Chr 15:11
Ahab killed *s* and oxen 2Chr 18:2
oxen and three thousand *s* 2Chr 29:33
bullocks and seven thousand *s* .2Chr 30:24
bullocks and ten thousand *s* ...2Chr 30:24
in the tithe of oxen and *s* 2Chr 31:6
they builded the *s* gate........Neh 3:1
one ox and six choice *s* ....Neh 5:18
was seven thousand *s* ....Job 1:3
with the fleece of my *s*........Job 31:20
he had fourteen thousand *s*....Job 42:12
All *s* and oxen, yea, and ......Ps 8:7
us like *s* appointed for ....Ps 44:11
people to go forth like *s* ......Ps 78:52
we thy people and *s* of thy ....Ps 79:13
his pasture, and the *s* of ......Ps 95:7
his people, and the *s* of.......Ps 100:3
gone astray like a lost *s*.......Ps 119:176
our *s* may bring forth ....Ps 144:13
teeth are like a flock of *s* .....Song 4:2
Thy teeth are as a flock of *s* ..Song 6:6
a young cow, and two *s*.......Is 7:21
and as a *s* that no man ....Is 13:14
slaying oxen, and killing *s*.....Is 22:13
All we like *s* have gone ....Is 53:6
and as a *s* before her ....Is 53:7
them out like *s* for the........Jer 12:3
and scatter the *s* of my ....Jer 23:1
Israel is a scattered *s* ....Jer 50:17
My *s* wandered through ....Ezek 34:6
I, will both search my *s* ....Ezek 34:11
day that he is among his *s* ....Ezek 34:12
so will I seek out my *s*........Ezek 34:12
and for a wife he kept *s* ......Hos 12:12
the flocks of *s* are made ......Joel 1:18
them together as the *s* ....Mic 2:12
the *s* shall be scattered........Zech 13:7
which come to you in *s* ....Matt 7:15
go rather to the lost *s* of ......Matt 10:6
I send you forth as *s* in ....Matt 10:16
that shall have one *s*, and .....Matt 12:11
is a man better than a *s*.......Matt 12:12
but unto the lost *s* of the .....Matt 15:24
man have an hundred *s* ....Matt 18:12
he rejoiceth more of that *s*....Matt 18:13
divideth his *s* from the ....Matt 25:32
he shall set the *s* on his ....Matt 25:33
were as *s* not having a ....Mark 6:34
s shall be scattered ....Mark 14:27
you, having an hundred *s* .....Luke 15:4
I have found my *s* which ......Luke 15:6
that sold oxen and *s* and ......John 2:14
temple, and the *s*, and ....John 2:15
Jersualem by the *s* market ....John 5:2
is the shepherd of the *s* ....John 10:2
and the *s* hear his voice ....John 10:3
and he calleth his own *s* ....John 10:3
saith unto him, Feed my *s* ....John 21:16
Jesus saith..Feed my *s* ....John 21:17
He was led as a *s* to the ......Acts 8:32
accounted as *s* for the ....Rom 8:36
great shepherd of the *s* ....Heb 13:20
For ye were as *s* going 1Pet 2:25
and beasts, and *s*, and ....Rev 18:13

SHEEP GATE—*a gate of the restored city of Jerusalem*
Repaired ....Neh 3:32
Dedicated...............Neh 12:38, 39

SHEEPCOTE—*an enclosure for sheep*
David chosen while caring for 2Sam 7:8

[*also* SHEEPCOTES]
he came to the *s* by the 1Sam 24:3
I took thee from the *s* 1Chr 17:7

SHEEPFOLD—*a shelter for sheep*
Enclosure for folks ......Num 32:16
Entrance to, only by Christ ....John 10:1

[*also* SHEEPFOLDS]
abodest thou among the *s* .....Judg 5:16
and took him from the *s* ......Ps 78:70

SHEEPMASTER—*owner, dealer, and breeder of sheep*
Mesha, king of Moab 2Kin 3:4

SHEEPSHEARERS—*those who cut sheep's wool*
Employed by Judah .....Gen 38:12
Many employed by Nabal.1Sam 25:7, 11
Used figuratively ....Is 53:7

Absalom had *s* in Baal........2Sam 13:23
now, thy servant hath *s* 2Sam 13:24

SHEEPSKINS—*the skin of sheep*
they wandered about in *s* .....Heb 11:37

SHEET—*a broad piece of cloth*
Large piece of cloth .....Acts 11:5

[*also* SHEETS]
will give you thirty *s* and......Judg 14:12
shall ye give me thirty *s*.......Judg 14:13
great *s* knit at the four........Acts 10:11

S

SHEHARIAH (shē-hä-rī'ä)—*"Jehovah is the dawn"*
Benjamite 1Chr 8:26

SHEKEL—*a Jewish measure (approximately .533 oz.); a coin*

As a weight:
Standard of, defined .....Ex 30:13
Used in weighing ....Josh 7:21
See WEIGHTS

As money:
Used in currency 1Sam 9:8
Fines paid in ....Deut 22:19, 29
Revenues of the sanctuary paid in ......Neh 10:32

[*also* SHEKELS]
worth four hundred *s* of ......Gen 23:15
four hundred *s* of silver ....Gen 23:16
golden earring of half a *s* .....Gen 24:22
unto their master thirty *s* ......Ex 21:32
sanctuary: a *s* is twenty ....Ex 30:13
an half *s* shall be the ....Ex 30:13
pure myrrh five hundred *s* ....Ex 30:23
the *s* of the sanctuary ....Ex 30:24
seven hundred and thirty *s* ....Ex 38:24
the *s* of the sanctuary ....Ex 38:25
every man, that is, half a *s* ....Ex 38:26
the *s* of the sanctuary ....Ex 38:26
with thy estimation by *s* ....Lev 5:15
the *s* of the sanctuary ....Lev 5:15
estimation shall be fifty *s* ......Lev 27:3
according to the *s* of the ......Lev 27:25
gerahs shall be the *s* ....Lev 27:25
even take five *s* apiece by .....Num 3:47
the *s* of the sanctuary ....Num 3:47
the *s* is twenty gerahs ....Num 3:47
hundred and thirty *s* ....Num 7:13
silver bowl of seventy *s* ....Num 7:13
the *s* of the sanctuary ....Num 7:79
for the money of five *s* ....Num 18:16
seven hundred and fifty *s* .....Num 31:52
him in an hundred *s* of ....Deut 22:19
and two hundred *s* of silver ...Josh 7:21
and seven hundred *s* of ....Judg 8:26
The eleven hundred *s* of ......Judg 17:2
mother took two hundred *s* ...Judg 17:4
coat was five thousand *s* 1Sam 17:5
of his head at two hundred *s* ..2Sam 14:26
have give thee ten *s* of 2Sam 18:11
weighed three hundred *s* 2Sam 21:16
and the oxen for fifty *s* of 2Sam 24:24
hundred *s* of gold went 1Kin 10:16
fine flour be sold for a *s* 2Kin 7:1
measures of barley for a *s* 2Kin 7:1
fine flour was sold for a *s* 2Kin 7:16
measures of barley for a *s* 2Kin 7:16
measures of barley for a *s* 2Kin 7:18
measure of fine flour for a *s* ...2Kin 7:18
of each man fifty *s* of 2Kin 15:20
the place six hundred *s* 1Chr 21:25
chariot for six hundred *s* 2Chr 1:17
of the nails was fifty *s* of 2Chr 3:9
hundred *s* of beaten gold 2Chr 9:15
and wine, beside forty *s* ....Neh 5:15
money, even seventeen *s* ......Jer 32:9
be by weight, twenty *s* ....Ezek 4:10
And the *s* shall be twenty .....Ezek 45:12
s, five and twenty *s* ....Ezek 45:12
fifteen *s*, shall be your ....Ezek 45:12
the ephah small, and the *s* ....Amos 8:5

SHEKINAH (shĕ-kī'nä)—*a word expressing the glory and presence of God*

As indicative of God's presence:
In nature ....Ps 18:7-15
In the exodus from Egypt. Ex 13:21, 22
At Sinai ....Ex 24:16-18
In tabernacle ....Ex 40:34-38
Upon the mercy seat ....Ex 25:22
In the wilderness ....Num 9:15-23; Num 10:11-36
In the Temple 2Chr 7:1-3

Illustrated by Christ in His:
Divine nature ....Col 2:9
Incarnation ....Luke 1:35
Nativity ....Luke 2:9
Manifestation to Israel ...Hag 2:9; Zech 2:5
Transfiguration 2Pet 1:17
Ascension ....Acts 1:9
Transforming us by His Spirit 2Cor 3:18; 2Cor 4:6
Return ....Matt 24:44
Eternal habitation with saints ....Rev 21:3

Accompanied by:
Angels ....Is 6:1-4
Cloud ....Num 9:15-23
Fire ....Heb 12:18-21
Earthquake ....Hag 2:21

SHELAH (shē'lä)—*"peace"*
1. Son of Arphaxad 1Chr 1:18
   Called Salah ....Luke 3:35
2. Son of Judah ....Gen 38:1-26
   Founder of the Shelanites ....Num 26:20

and called his name *S* ....Gen 38:5
for she saw that *S* was ....Gen 38:14
Er, and Onan, and *S* ....Gen 46:12
of *S*, the family of the ....Num 26:20
Arphaxad begat *S*, and *S* 1Chr 1:18
Er, and Onan, and *S* 1Chr 2:3
The sons of *S* the son of 1Chr 4:21

SHELANITES—*of the tribe of Shelah*
of *S*, the family of the ....Num 26:20

SHELEMIAH (shĕl-ĕ-mī'ä)—*"Jehovah is recompense"*
1. Father of Hananiah .....Neh 3:30
2. Postexilic priest ....Neh 13:13
3. Father of Irijah ....Jer 37:13
4. Porter 1Chr 26:14
   Called Meshelemiah 1Chr 9:21
5. Ancestor of Jehudi ......Jer 36:14
6. Son of Abdeel ....Jer 36:26
7. Father of Jehucal ....Jer 37:3

lot eastward fell to *S* 1Chr 26:14
And *S*, and Nathan, and ......Ezra 10:39
Hananiah the son of *S* ....Neh 3:30
over the treasuries, *S* the .....Neh 13:13
the son of *S*, the son of ....Jer 36:14
sent Jehucal the son of *S* ......Jer 37:3
and Jucal the son of *S* ....Jer 38:1

SHELEPH (shē'lĕf)—*"drawn out"*
Son of Joktan; head of a tribe 1Chr 1:20

SHELESH (shē'lĕsh)—*"might"*
Asherite 1Chr 7:35

SHELOMI (shĕ-lō'mī)—*"Jehovah is peace"*
Father of an Asherite prince ....Num 34:27

SHELOMITH, SHELOMOTH (shĕ-lō'mĭth, shĕ-lō'mŏth)—*"peacefulness"*
1. Daughter of Dibri; her son executed ....Lev 24:10-23
2. Chief Levite of Moses ...1Chr 23:18
3. Gershonites in David's time 1Chr 23:9
4. Descendant of Moses, had charge of treasures. 1Chr 26:25
5. Son or daughter of King Rehoboam 2Chr 11:20
6. Daughter of Zerubbabel .1Chr 3:19
7. Family who went with Ezra ....Ezra 8:10

S: of the sons of *S* 1Chr 24:22
Which *S* and his brethren 1Chr 26:26
was under the hand of *S* 1Chr 26:28

SHELTER—*something that gives protection or covering*
the rock for want of a *s* ....Job 24:8
been a *s* for me, and a ....Ps 61:3

SHELUMIEL (shĕ-lū'mĭ-ĕl)—*"God is peace"*
Simeonite warrior ....Num 1:6

shall be *S* the son of ....Num 2:12
fifth day *S* the son of ....Num 7:36
of *S* the son of ....Num 7:41
was *S* the son of ....Num 10:19

SHEM (shĕm)—*"name; renown"*
Oldest son of Noah ......Gen 5:32
Escapes the flood ....Gen 7:13
Receives a blessing ......Gen 9:23, 26
Ancestor of Semitic people ....Gen 10:22-32
Ancestor of:
  Abram ....Gen 11:10-26
  Jesus ....Luke 3:36

Noah begat three sons, *S* .....Gen 6:10
forth of the ark, were *S* ....Gen 9:18
dwell in the tents of *S* ....Gen 9:27
the sons of Noah: *S* ....Gen 10:1
Unto *S* also, the father of .....Gen 10:21
Noah, *S*, Ham, and Japheth ...1Chr 1:4
The sons of *S*; Elam, and 1Chr 1:17
S, Arphaxad, Shelah 1Chr 1:24

SHEMA (shē'mä)—*"fame; repute"*
1. Reubenite 1Chr 5:8
2. Benjamite head 1Chr 8:12, 13
3. Ezra's attendant ....Neh 8:4
4. City of Judah ....Josh 15:26
5. Son of Hebron 1Chr 2:43

And *S* begat Raham, the 1Chr 2:44

SHEMAAH (shĕ-mā'ä)—*"the fame"*
Father of two of David's warriors 1Chr 12:3

SHEMAIAH (shĕ-mā'yä)—*"Jehovah is fame; Jehovah hears"*
1. Father of Shimri 1Chr 4:37
2. Reubenite 1Chr 5:4
3. Levite who helped move the ark 1Chr 15:8, 12
4. Scribe in David's time ..1Chr 24:6
5. Son of Obed-edom 1Chr 26:4, 6, 7
6. Prophet of Judah 1Kin 12:22-24
   Explains Shishak's invasion as divine punishment 2Chr 12:5-8
   Records Rehoboam's reign 2Chr 12:15
7. Levite teacher under Jehoshaphat 2Chr 17:8
8. Levite in Hezekiah's reign 2Chr 29:14, 15
9. Levite treasurer 2Chr 31:14, 15
10. Officer of Levites in Josiah's reign 2Chr 35:9
11. Father of Urijah ....Jer 26:20
12. False prophet ....Jer 29:24-28
13. Father of Delaiah ......Jer 36:12
14. Descendant of David ...1Chr 3:22
15. Keeper of the East Gate to Nehemiah ...Neh 3:29
16. Merarite Levite living in Jerusalem 1Chr 9:14
17. Son of Adonikam ......Ezra 8:13
18. Leading man under Ezra ....Ezra 8:16
19. Priest who divorced his foreign wife ....Ezra 10:21
20. Man who divorced his foreign wife ....Ezra 10:31
21. Prophet hired by Sanballat ....Neh 6:10-14
22. Priest who signs covenant ....Neh 10:1, 8
23. Participant in dedication service ....Neh 12:34
24. Postexilic priest ....Neh 12:35
25. Levite musician ....Neh 12:36

And Obadiah the son of *S* 1Chr 9:16
S, and Eliel, and Amminadab. .1Chr 15:11
of the Lord came to *S* 2Chr 11:2
the Levites: *S* the son of ......Neh 11:15
S, and Joiarib, Jedaiah ....Neh 12:6
Of Bilgah, Shammua; of *S* ....Neh 12:18
And Masseiah, and *S* ....Neh 12:42
the Lord concerning *S* ....Jer 29:31

that *S* hath prophesied ....Jer 29:31
I will punish *S* the ....Jer 29:32

SHEMARIAH (shĕm-ä-rī'ä)—*"whom Jehovah guards"*
1. Mighty man of Benjamin.1Chr 12:5
2. Son of Rehoboam.......2Chr 11:18,19
3. Divorced his foreign wife.Ezra 10:31,32

SHEMEBER (shĕm-ē'ber)—*"splendor of heroism"*
King of Zeboiim ....Gen 14:2

SHEMER (shē'mer)—*"watch"*
1. Sells Omri hill on which Samaria is built 1Kin 16:23,24
2. Levite..................1Chr 6:46
3. Asherite 1Chr 7:30, 34

SHEMIDA, SHEMIDAH (shĕ-mī'dä)—*"fame of knowing"*
Descendant of Manasseh; founder of the Shemidaites ....Num 26:29,32

and for the children of *S* ......Josh 17:2
And the sons of *S* were 1Chr 7:19

SHEMINITH (shĕm'ĭ-nĭth)—*"eighth"*
Musical term 1Chr 15:21

on Neginoth upon *S* ....Ps 6:*title*
chief Musician upon *S* ....Ps 12:*title*

SHEMIRAMOTH (shĕ-mĭr'ä-mŏth)—*"fame of the highest"*
1. Levite musician in David's time..........1Chr 15:18,20
2. Levite teacher under Jehoshaphat 2Chr 17:8

SHEMUEL (shĕ-mū'ĕl)—*"asked of God"*
1. Grandson of Issachar....1Chr 7:1, 2
2. Another spelling of Samuel...............1Chr 6:33

Simeon, *S* the son of ....Num 34:20

SHEN (shĕn)—*"tooth; a pointed rock"*
Rock west of Jerusalem ..1Sam 7:12

SHENAZAR (shĕ-năz'är)—*"ivory keeper; Sin (the god) protect"*
Son of Jeconiah 1Chr 3:18

SHENIR (shē'ner)—*"light that sleeps"—the Amorite name for Hermon*
from the top of *S* and ....Song 4:8
See SENIR

SHEPHAM (shē'făm)—*"wild"*
Place near the Sea of Galilee ....Num 34:11

from Hazar-enan to *S*.........Num 34:10

SHEPHATIAH (shĕf-ä-tī'ä)—*"Jehovah is judge"*
1. Benjamite warrior.......1Chr 12:5
2. Son of David 2Sam 3:4
3. Simeonite chief 1Chr 27:16
4. Son of King Jehoshaphat.2Chr 21:2
5. Opponent of Jeremiah..Jer 38:1
6. Descendant of Judah ....Neh 11:4
7. Servant of Solomon whose descendants return from exile .....Ezra 2:57

The fifth, *S* of Abital 1Chr 3:3
Meshullam the son of *S* 1Chr 9:8
The children of *S*, three ......Ezra 2:4
The children of *S*, three ......Neh 7:9
The children of *S*, the ....Neh 7:59

SHEPHERD—*one who tends sheep*

Duties of, toward his flock:
Defend 1Sam 17:34-36
Water ....Gen 29:2-10
Give rest to..............Jer 33:12
Know ....John 10:3-5
Number ....Jer 33:13
Secure pasture for 1Chr 4:39-41
Search for the lost.......Ezek 34:12-16
Luke 15:4, 5

Good, described as:
Faithful................Gen 31:38-40
Fearless 1Sam 17:34-36
Unselfish ....Luke 15:3-6
Considerate ....Gen 33:13,14
Believing ....Luke 2:8-20

Bad, described as:
Unfaithful ....Ezek 34:1-10
Cowardly ....John 10:12,13
Selfish.................Is 56:11, 12
Ruthless ....Ex 2:17, 19
Unbelieving ....Jer 50:6

Descriptive of:
God ....Ps 78:52, 53
Christ ....Heb 13:20
Joshua..................Num 27:16-23
David 2Sam 5:2
Judges 1Chr 17:6
National leaders ....Jer 49:19
Cyrus ....Is 44:28
Jewish leaders...........Matt 9:36
Church elders 1Pet 5:2

[*also* SHEPHERD'S, SHEPHERDS, SHEPHERDS']
every *s* is an abomination .....Gen 46:34
Thy servants are *s*, both ......Gen 47:3
from thence is the *s*, the ......Gen 49:24
put them in a *s* bag which.....1Sam 17:40
now thy *s* which were..........1Sam 25:7
sheep that have not a *s* 1Kin 22:17
as sheep that have no *s* 2Chr 18:16
The Lord is my *s*; I shall......Ps 23:1
Give ear, O *S* of Israel ....Ps 80:1
are given from one *s*..........Eccl 12:11
feed thy kids beside the *s* .....Song 1:8
neither shall the *s* make.......Is 13:20
when a multitude of *s* is ......Is 31:4
is removed from me as a *s* ....Is 38:12
of the sea with the *s* of ....Is 63:11
The *s* with their flocks ....Jer 6:3
And I will set up *s* over.......Jer 23:4
Howl, ye *s*, and cry; and......Jer 25:34
And the *s* shall have no........Jer 25:35
A voice of the cry of the *s* ....Jer 25:36
and keep him, as a *s* doth.....Jer 31:10
as a *s* putteth on his..........Jer 43:12
and who is that *s* that.........Jer 49:19
and who is that *s* that.........Jer 50:44
in pieces with thee the *s* ......Jer 51:23
because there is no *s* ....Ezek 34:5
because there was no *s*........Ezek 34:8
And I will set up one *s* ....Ezek 34:23
and he shall be their *s* ....Ezek 34:23
habitations of the *s* shall ......Amos 1:2
As the *s* taketh out of the.....Amos 3:12
raise against him seven *s* ......Mic 5:5
Thy *s* slumber, O king of .....Nah 3:18
dwellings and cottages for *s* ...Zeph 2:6
because there was no *s*........Zech 10:2
was kindled against the *s*......Zech 10:3
of the howling of the *s*........Zech 11:3
and their own *s* pity them .....Zech 11:5
Three *s* also I cut off in.......Zech 11:8
instruments of a foolish *s* .....Zech 11:15
lo, I will raise up a *s* in ....Zech 11:16
Woe to the idol *s* that ....Zech 11:17
as sheep not having a *s* ....Mark 6:34
I will smite the *s*, and the .....Mark 14:27
in by the door is the *s* of .....John 10:2
returned unto the *S* and 1Pet 2:25

SHEPHERD, JESUS THE GOOD

Described prophetically in His:
Prophetic position (teaching)..............Is 40:10, 11
Priestly position (sacrifice) ....Zech 13:7; Matt 26:31
Kingly position (ruling) ..Ezek 37:24; Matt 2:6

Described typically as:
Good...................John 10:11,14
Chief 1Pet 5:4
Great ....Heb 13:20
One ....John 10:16
Gentle ....Is 40:11
One who separates ......Matt 25:31-46

SHEPHI (shē'fī)—*"unconcern"—a descendant of Seir the Horite*
and Ebal, *S*, Onam 1Chr 1:40

SHEPHO (shē'fō)—*"unconcern"*
Son of Shobal ....Gen 36:23

SHEPHUPHAN (shĕ-fū'făn)—*"obscurities"—a son of Benjamin*
And Gera, and *S*, and 1Chr 8:5

SHERAH (shē'rä)—*"blood-relationship"*
Daughter of Ephraim; builder of cities 1Chr 7:24

SHERD—*fragment of pottery*

[*also* SHERDS]
in the bursting of it a *s* ....Is 30:14
thou shalt break the *s*.........Ezek 23:34
See POTSHERD

SHEREBIAH (shĕr-ĕbī'ä)—*"Jehovah is originator"*
1. Levite family returning with Ezra ....Ezra 8:18
2. Levite who assists Ezra ..Neh 8:7

S Hashabiah, and ten of ......Ezra 8:24
Bunni, *S*, Bani, and ....Neh 9:4
Bani, Hashabniah, *S* ....Neh 9:5
Zaccur, *S*, Shebaniah ....Neh 10:12
Binnui, Kadmiel, *S* ....Neh 12:8
Hashabiah, *S*, and ....Neh 12:24

SHERESH (shē'rĕsh)—*"union"*
Grandson of Manasseh...1Chr 7:16

SHEREZER—*See* SHAREZER

SHERIFFS—*court officials*
Called by Nebuchadnezzar ....Dan 3:2, 3

SHESCHACH, SHESHACH (shē'shăk)—*probably a cryptogram*
Symbolic of Babylon.....Jer 25:26

How is *S* taken! and how .....Jer 31:51

SHESHAI (shē'shī)—*"free; noble"*
Descendant of Anak .....Num 13:22
Driven out by Caleb .....Josh 15:14
Destroyed by Judah .....Judg 1:10

SHESHAN (shē'shăn)—*"free; noble"*
Jerahmeelite 1Chr 2:31-35

SHESHBAZZAR (shĕsh-băz'er)—*"O Shamash (the god) protect the father"*
Prince of Judah ....Ezra 1:8, 11

one, whose name was *S* ....Ezra 5:14
Then came the same *S*........Ezra 5:16

SHETH (shĕth)—*"compensation; sprout"*
1. Son of Adam (same as Seth) 1Chr 1:1
2. Name descriptive of the Moabites ....Num 24:17

SHETHAR (shē'thär)—*"star; commander"*
Persian prince ....Esth 1:14

SHETHAR-BOZNAI (shē-thär-bŏz-nī)—*"starry splendor"*
Official of Persia ....Ezra 5:3, 6

S, and your companions ......Ezra 6:6
S, their companions ....Ezra 6:13

SHEVA (shē'vä)—*"self-satisfying"*
1. Son of Caleb 1Chr 2:43, 49
2. David's scribe 2Sam 20:25

SHEW, SHEWETH, SHEWING—*See* SHOW

SHEWBREAD—*See* SHOWBREAD

SHIBBOLETH (shĭb'bō-lĕth)
Password ....Judg 12:5, 6

[*also* SIBBOLETH]
he said *S*: for he ....Judg 12:6

SHIBMAH (shĭb'mä)—*"to be cold"*
names being changed and *S* ..Num 32:38

S

SHICRON (shĭk′rŏn)—*"drunkenness"*
Town of Judah ....Josh 15:11

SHIELD—*a piece of defensive armor carried on the arm*

Uses of:
Protection 2Chr 14:8
Treasures in war 1Kin 14:25, 26
Riches 2Chr 32:27
Ornamenting public buildings 1Kin 10:17

Figurative of:
God's:
Protection ....Ps 33:20
Favor ....Ps 5:12
Salvation ....Ps 18:35
Truth ....Ps 91:4
Faith ....Eph 6:16
Rulers ....Ps 47:9

[*also* SHIELDS]
not, Abram: I am thy *s* ....Gen 15:1
by the Lord, the *s* of thy ......Deut 33:29
was there a *s* or spear ....Judg 5:8
one bearing a *s* went before ...1Sam 17:7
man that bare the *s* went 1Sam 17:41
a spear, and with a *s* 1Sam 17:45
s of the mighty is vilely 2Sam 1:21
the *s* of Saul, as though he 2Sam 1:21
David took the *s* of gold 2Sam 8:7
he is my *s*, and the horn 2Sam 22:3
given me the *s* of thy 2Sam 22:36
their stead brazen *s* 1Kin 14:27
king David's spears and *s* 2Kin 11:10
nor come before it with *s* 2Kin 19:32
that could handle *s* and 1Chr 12:8
of Judah that bare *s* 1Chr 12:24
with *s* and spear thirty 1Chr 12:34
David took the *s* of gold 1Chr 18:7
three hundred *s* made he 2Chr 9:16
shekels of gold went to one *s* ..2Chr 9:16
several city he puts *s* 2Chr 11:12
he carried away also the *s* 2Chr 12:9
king Rehoboam made *s* 2Chr 12:10
armed men with bow and *s* 2Chr 17:17
spears, and bucklers, and *s* 2Chr 23:9
could handle spear and *s* 2Chr 25:5
throughout all the host *s* 2Chr 26:14
and *s* in abundance 2Chr 32:5
the spears, the *s*, and the .....Neh 4:16
glittering spear and the *s* ......Job 39:23
But thou, O Lord, art a *s* .....Ps 3:3
Lord is my strength and my *s* .Ps 28:7
Take hold of *s* and ....Ps 35:2
them down, O Lord our *s* .....Ps 59:11
arrows of the bow, the *s* ......Ps 76:3
Behold, O God our *s*, and ....Ps 84:9
Lord God is a sun and *s* ......Ps 84:11
he is their help and their *s* ....Ps 115:9
my *s*, and he in whom I ....Ps 144:2
he is a *s* unto them that ....Prov 30:5
bucklers, all *s* of mighty ......Song 4:4
princes, and anoint the *s* ......Is 21:5
and Kir uncovered the *s* ......Is 22:6
nor come before it with *s* .....Is 37:33
ye the buckler and *s* ....Jer 46:3
Libyans, that handle the *s* .....Jer 46:9
the arrows: gather the *s* ....Jer 51:11
buckler and *s* and helmet ....Ezek 23:24
hanged the *s* and helmet ......Ezek 27:10
hanged their *s* upon thy ....Ezek 27:11
company with bucklers and *s* ..Ezek 38:4
all of them with *s* and ....Ezek 38:5
the *s* and the bucklers ....Ezek 39:9
s of his mighty men is ....Nah 2:3

SHIGGAION (shĭ-gā′yŏn)—*"irregular"*
Musical term ....Ps 7:*title*

Plural form:
Shigionoth ....Hab 3:1

SHIHON (shī′hŏn)—*"wall of strength"*
Town of Issachar ....Josh 19:19

SHIHOR (shī′hŏr)—*"blackness"—the east branch of the Nile River*
from *S* of Egypt even 1Chr 13:5

SHIHOR-LIBNATH (shī-hôr-lĭb′năth)—*"black of whiteness"*
Small river in Asher's territory ....Josh 19:26

SHILHI (shĭl′hī)—*"a warrior; one with darts"*
Father of Azubah 1Kin 22:42

SHILHIM (shĭl′hĭm)—*"armed"*
Town in south Judah ....Josh 15:1, 32

SHILLEM (shĭl′ĕm)—*"compensation"*
Son of Naphtali ....Gen 46:24
of *S* the family of the ....Num 26:49

SHILLEMITES (shĭl′ĕm-īts)—*the residents of Shillem*
of Shillem, the family *S* ....Num 26:49

SHILOAH (shĭ-lō′ä)—*"sent"*
A pool of Jerusalem, figurative of God's protection ....Is 8:6
See SILOAM

SHILOH (shī′lō)—*"peace"*
1. Town of Ephraim ....Judg 21:19
Center of religious worship ....Judg 18:31
Canaan divided here ....Josh 18:1, 10
Benjamites seize women here ....Judg 21:19-23
Ark of the covenant taken from 1Sam 4:3-11
Site of Eli's judgeship ...1Sam 4:12-18
Home of Ahijah 1Kin 14:2, 4
Punishment given to ....Jer 7:12-14
2. Messianic title ....Gen 49:10

you before the Lord in *S* ......Josh 18:8
Joshua to the host at *S* ....Josh 18:9
an inheritance by lot in *S* .....Josh 19:51
spake unto them at *S* in ....Josh 21:2
children of Israel out of *S* .....Josh 22:9
together at *S*, to go up to .....Josh 22:12
them unto the camp to *S* .....Judg 21:12
sacrifice unto the Lord..*S* 1Sam 1:3
after they had eaten in *S* 1Sam 1:9
house of the Lord in *S* 1Sam 1:24
they did in *S* unto all the 1Sam 2:14
Lord appeared again in *S* 1Sam 3:21
himself to Samuel in *S* 1Sam 3:21
the Lord's priest in *S* 1Sam 14:3
the house of Eli in *S* 1Kin 2:24
forsook the tabernacle of *S* ....Ps 78:60
make this house like *S* ....Jer 26:6
This house shall be like *S* .....Jer 26:9
certain from Shechem from *S* ..Jer 41:5

SHILONI (shĭ-lō′nī)—*"weapon; armor"*
Father of Zechariah .....Neh 11:5

SHILONITE (shī′lō-nīt)
Native of Shiloh 1Kin 11:29

spake by Ahijah the *S* 1Kin 12:15
his servant Ahijah the *S* 1Kin 15:29
prophecy of Ahijah the *S* 2Chr 9:29
by the hand of Ahijah the *S* ...2Chr 10:15

SHILSHAH (shĭl′shä)—*"might; heroism"*
Asherite 1Chr 7:36, 37

SHIMEA (shĭm′ĕ-ä)—*"fame; rumor"*
1. Gershonite Levite 1Chr 6:39
2. Merarite Levite 1Chr 6:30
3. Brother of David 2Sam 13:3
4. Son of David 1Chr 3:1, 5
5. Benjamite 1Chr 8:1, 32
Called Shimeam 1Chr 9:38

[*also* SHIMEAH, SHIMEAM]
the son of *S* David's 2Sam 13:32
Jonathan the son of *S* 2Sam 21:21
And Mikloth begat *S* 1Chr 9:38
Jonathan the son of *S* 1Chr 20:7

SHIMEATH (shĭm′ĕ-ăth)—*"fame"*
Ammonitess 2Kin 12:21
son of *S* an Ammonitess 2Chr 24:26

SHIMEATHITES (shĭm-ē′ăth-īts)
Family of scribes 1Chr 2:55

SHIMEI (shĭm′ĕ-ī)—*"Jehovah is fame; Jehovah hear me"*
1. Son of Gershon ....Ex 6:17
2. Son of Merari 1Chr 6:29
3. Simeonite 1Chr 4:24-27
4. Levite 1Chr 6:42
5. Benjamite family head .1Chr 8:21
7. Levite musician in David's time 1Chr 25:3, 17
8. Overseer of vineyards under David 1Chr 27:27
9. Benjamite; insults David 2Sam 16:5-13
Pardoned, but confined .2Sam 19:16-23
Breaks parole; executed by Solomon 1Kin 2:39-46
10. Faithful follower of Solomon 1Kin 1:8
11. Levite; assists in purification 2Chr 29:14-16
12. Levite treasurer in Hezekiah's reign 2Chr 31:12, 13
13. Benjamite ancestor of Mordecai ....Esth 2:5
14. Brother of Zerubbabel .1Chr 3:19

[*also* SHIMHI, SHIMI]
S, according to their ....Ex 6:17
hast with thee *S* the son 1Kin 2:8
king sent and called for *S* 1Kin 2:36
S said unto the king 1Kin 2:38
S dwelt in Jerusalem 1Kin 2:38
S the son of Elah, in 1Kin 4:18
his son, Gog his son, *S* 1Chr 5:4
Gershom: Libni, and *S* 1Chr 6:17
Shimrath, the sons of *S* 1Chr 8:21
And the sons of *S* were 1Chr 23:10
four were the sons of *S* 1Chr 23:10
Levites: Jozabad, and *S* ....Ezra 10:23
Jeremai, Manasseh, and *S* .....Ezra 10:33
And Bani, and Binnui, *S* ......Ezra 10:38
the family of *S* a part ....Zech 12:13

SHIMEON (shĭm′ĕ-ŭn)—*"hearing"*
Divorced his foreign wife .Ezra 10:31

SHIMHI—*See* SHIMEI

SHIMI—*See* SHIMEI

SHIMITES (shĭm′īts)—*the family of Shimei*
Libnites..family of the *S* ......Num 3:21

SHIMMA—*See* SHAMMAH

SHIMON (shī′mŏn)—*"trier; valuer"*
Judahite family 1Chr 4:1, 20

SHIMRATH (shĭm′răth)—*"watch"*
Benjamite 1Chr 8:21

SHIMRI (shĭm′rī)—*"Jehovah is watching"*
1. Father of Jediael 1Chr 11:45
2. Merarite Levite 1Chr 26:10
3. Levite; assists in purification 2Chr 29:13

SHIMRITH (shĭm′rĭth)—*"watch"*
Moabitess 2Chr 24:26
Called Shomer 2Kin 12:21

SHIMRON (shĭm′rŏn)—*"watch"*
1. Son of Issachar ....Gen 46:13
2. Town of Zebulun ....Josh 11:1

[*also* SHIMROM]
of *S*, the family of the ....Num 26:24
Kattath, and Nahallal..*S* ......Josh 19:15
and Puah, Jashub, and *S* 1Chr 7:1

SHIMRONITES (shĭm′rŏn-īts)
Shimron, the family of the *S* ..Num 26:24

SHIMRON-MERON (shĭm-rŏn-mē′rŏn)—*"guard of lashing"*
Town conquered by Joshua ....Josh 12:20

SHIMSHAI (shĭm′shī)—*"Jehovah is splendor"*
Scribe opposing the Jews .Ezek 4:8
and *S* the scribe, and the .....Ezra 4:9

to *S* the scribe, and to the ....Ezra 4:17
S the scribe and their ....Ezra 4:23

SHINAB (shī'năb)—*the king of Admah*
Fought against
Chedorlaomer.........Gen 14:1, 12

SHINAR (shī'när)—*"watch of him that sleeps"—the region around Babylon*
Original home of Noah's
sons..................Gen 10:10
Tower built here ....Gen 11:2-9
Amraphel, king of.......Gen 41:1, 9
Home of the remnant
Jews ....Is 11:11

land of *S* to the house of .....Dan 1:2
an house in the land of *S* .....Zech 5:11

SHINE—*to give out or reflect light*

Used literally of:
Sun ....Job 31:26
Moon ....Job 25:5
Star ....Joel 3:15
Earth...................Ezek 43:2
Moses' face ....Ex 34:29-35
Christ's face ....Matt 17:2
Angels ....Acts 12:7
Glorified Christ ....Acts 9:3
Christ's return...........Luke 17:24

Applied figuratively to:
God's blessing...........Num 6:25
God's Word 2Pet 1:19
Christ's first advent ......Is 9:2
John 1:5
Gospel 2Cor 4:4
Believer's life ....Matt 5:16
Regeneration............2Cor 4:6
Believer's glory..........Dan 12:3
Matt 13:43

[*also* SHINED, SHINETH, SHINING, SHONE]
he *s* forth from mount ....Deut 33:2
of the earth by clear *s* 2Sam 23:4
and the sun *s* upon the 2Kin 3:22
neither let the light *s* ....Job 3:4
s upon the counsel of the .....Job 10:3
thou shalt *s* forth, thou ....Job 11:17
spark of his fire shall not *s* ....Job 18:5
the light shall *s* upon thy......Job 22:28
When his candle *s* upon.......Job 29:3
it not to *s* by the cloud ....Job 36:32
light of his cloud to *s*? ....Job 37:15
sneezings a light doth *s* ....Job 41:18
thy face to *s* upon thy ....Ps 31:16
of beauty, God hath *s* ....Ps 50:2
and cause his face to *s* ....Ps 67:1
between the cherubim, *s* ....Ps 80:1
and cause thy face to *s*.........Ps 80:3
oil to make his face to *s* ....Ps 104:15
thy face to *s* upon thy ....Ps 119:135
but the night *s* as the ....Ps 139:12
path of the just is as the *s* ....Prov 4:18
s more and more unto the ....Prov 4:18
man's wisdom..face to *s*.......Eccl 8:1
the *s* of a flaming fire by......Is 4:5
them hath the light *s* ....Is 9:2
cause her light to *s* ....Is 13:10
Arise, *s*; for thy light is ....Is 60:1
They are waxen fat, they *s* ....Jer 5:28
thy face to *s* upon thy ....Dan 9:17
shall withdraw their *s* ....Joel 2:10
at the *s* of thy glittering.......Hab 3:11
Let your light so *s* before .....Matt 5:16
east, and *s* even unto the .....Matt 24:27
And his raiment became *s*.....Mark 9:3
the glory of the Lord *s*........Luke 2:9
bright *s* of a candle doth ......Luke 11:36
men stood by them in *s*.......Luke 24:4
He was a burning and a *s*.....John 5:35
s from heaven a great.........Acts 22:6
s round about me and ....Acts 26:13
of darkness, hath *s* in our 2Cor 4:6
among whom ye *s* as ....Phil 2:15
and the true light now *s*........1John 2:8
was as the sun *s* in his ....Rev 1:16
the day *s* not for a third ......Rev 8:12
light of a candle shall *s* ....Rev 18:23
neither of the moon, to *s* .....Rev 21:23

SHIP—*a large seagoing vessel*

Uses of:
Fishing ....John 21:3-8
Travel ....Jon 1:3
Cargoes ....Acts 27:3, 10, 38
War ....Num 24:24
Commerce ....Ps 107:23

Parts of:
Sign ....Acts 28:11
Lifeboats ....Acts 27:16-32
Anchor ....Acts 27:29, 40
Rudder ....Acts 27:40
Cables..................Acts 27:17
Ropes ....Acts 27:32
Sails....................Is 33:23
Oars ....Ezek 27:6

Notable ones:
Ark ....Gen 7:17, 18
Jonah's ....Jon 1:3, 4
Of Tarshish ....Is 23:1, 14
Christ's ....Matt 8:23-27
Paul's ....Acts 27:1-44

[*also* SHIPS]
shall be for an haven of *s* .....Gen 49:13
into Egypt again with *s* ....Deut 28:68
did Dan remain in *s*? ....Judg 5:17
made a navy of *s* in 1Kin 9:26
Jehoshaphat made *s* of........1Kin 22:48
the *s* were broken at..........1Kin 22:48
hands of his servants *s* 2Chr 8:18
the king's *s* went to...........2Chr 9:21
s of Tarshish bringing 2Chr 9:21
him to make *s* to go to 2Chr 20:36
they made the *s* in 2Chr 20:36
away as the swift *s* ....Job 9:26
Thou breakest the *s* of........Ps 48:7
There go the *s*: there is ....Ps 104:26
way of a *s* in the midst of .....Prov 30:19
is like the merchants *s* ....Prov 31:14
And upon all the *s* of.........Is 2:16
Howl, ye *s* of Tarshish ....Is 23:1
Howl, ye *s* of Tarshish ....Is 23:14
neither shall gallant *s* ....Is 33:21
Chaldeans, whose cry..*s*.......Is 43:14
for me, and the *s* of ....Is 60:9
made all thy *s* boards of ......Ezek 27:5
s of the sea with their ....Ezek 27:9
come down from their *s*.......Ezek 27:29
messengers go forth..*s* ....Ezek 30:9
s of Chittim shall come ....Dan 11:30
he found a *s* going to ....Jon 1:3
wares that were in the *s*.......Jon 1:5
into the sides of the *s*.........Jon 1:5
in a *s* with Zebedee their .....Matt 4:21
immediately left the *s*..........Matt 4:22
he was entered into a *s* ....Matt 8:23
he entered into a *s*, and.......Matt 9:1
so that he went into a *s*.......Matt 13:2
he departed thence by *s*.......Matt 14:13
s was now in the midst of .....Matt 14:24
were come into the *s* ....Matt 14:32
took *s*, and came into the .....Matt 15:39
were in the *s* mending ....Mark 1:19
that a small *s* should..........Mark 3:9
so that he entered into a *s* ....Mark 4:1
with him other little *s*.........Mark 4:36
waves beat into the *s*, so ......Mark 4:37
the hinder part of the *s* ....Mark 4:38
he was come out of the *s* .....Mark 5:2
again by *s* unto the other .....Mark 5:21
into a desert place by *s* ....Mark 6:32
the *s* was in the midst of ......Mark 6:47
were come out of the *s* ....Mark 6:54
straightway he entered..*s* ......Mark 8:10
had they in the *s* with ....Mark 8:14
saw two *s* standing by the .....Luke 5:2
entered into one of the *s*......Luke 5:3
the people out of the *s*.......Luke 5:3
which were in the other *s* .....Luke 5:7
and filled both the *s* ....Luke 5:7
that he went into a *s* with .....Luke 8:22
entered into a *s*, and went ....John 6:17
received him into the *s*........John 6:21
and immediately the *s* was ....John 6:21
and entered into a *s* ....John 21:3
on the right side of the *s*......John 21:6
disciples came in a little *s* .....John 21:8
we went before to *s*, and......Acts 20:13
And finding a *s* sailing ....Acts 21:2
one of another, we took *s*.....Acts 21:6
entering into a *s* of ....Acts 27:2
only of the lading and *s* ....Acts 27:10
And when the *s* was ....Acts 27:15
day they lightened the *s*.......Acts 27:18
but of the *s* ....Acts 27:22
Except these abide in the *s*....Acts 27:31
they lightened the *s*, and ......Acts 27:38
seas met, they ran the *s*.......Acts 27:41
broken pieces of the *s* ....Acts 27:44
we departed in a *s* of ....Acts 28:11
Behold also the *s*, which ......James 3:4
third part of the *s* were ....Rev 8:9
all the company in *s* and ......Rev 18:17

SHIPHI (shī'fī)—*"Jehovah is fullness"*
Simeonite 1Chr 4:37

SHIPHMITE (shĭf'mīt)—*a native of Shiphmoth*
Zabdi called 1Chr 27:27

SHIPHRAH (shĭf'rä)—*"beauty"*
Hebrew midwife.........Ex 1:15

SHIPHTAN (shĭf'tăn)—*"judge"*
Ephraimite..............Num 34:24

SHIPMASTER
s came to him and said ....Jon 1:6
every *s* and all the company ...Rev 18:17

SHIPMEN—*sailor*
s that had knowledge of 1Kin 9:27
s deemed that they drew ......Acts 27:27
the *s* were about to flee ....Acts 27:30

SHIPPING—*boarding a ship*
they also took *s*, and ....John 6:24

SHIPWRECK—*a wreck of a seagoing vessel*
Paul in three 2Cor 11:25
Figurative of apostasy....1Tim 1:19

SHIPYARDS—*places equipped to build and repair ships*
Solomon's, on the Red
Sea 1Kin 9:26

SHISHA (shī'shä)—*"distinction; nobility"*
Father of Solomon's
scribes 1Kin 4:3
Called Shavsha 1Chr 18:16

SHISHAK (shī'shăk)—*another name for Sesconchis I, king of Egypt*
into Egypt, unto *S* king 1Kin 11:40
S king of Egypt came up......1Kin 14:25
S king of Egypt came up......2Chr 12:2
to Jerusalem because of *S*.....2Chr 12:5
left you in the hand of *S* 2Chr 12:5
Jerusalem by the hand of *S* ...2Chr 12:7
S king of Egypt came up......2Chr 12:9

SHITRAI (shĭt'rī)—*"Jehovah is deciding"*
Sharonite overseer of
David's herds 1Chr 27:29

SHITTAH (shĭt'ä)—*the acacia tree*
cedar, the *s* tree, and the .....Is 41:19

SHITTIM (shĭt'ĭm)—*"thorns"*
1. Israel's last camp before
crossing the Jordan ...Josh 3:1
Scene of Balaam's
attempted curse.......Num 22—24
Sin of Baal-peor here ...Num 25:1-18
Site of Joshua's
commission...........Num 27:12-23
War with Midianites here.Num 31:1-54
Reuben and Gad receive
inheritance here ......Num 32:1-42
Scene of Moses' final
addresses............Deut 1—34

Spies sent from . . . . Josh 2:1
2. Valley blessed by the
Lord . . . . Joel 3:18

And Israel abode in *S* . . . . Num 25:1
son of Num sent out of *S* . . . . Josh 2:1
they removed from *S* . . . . Josh 3:1
water the valley of *S* . . . . Joel 3:18
answered him from *S* . . . . Mic 6:5

SHITTIM—*wood of the acacia tree*
Used in:
Making the ark . . . . Ex 25:10, 13
Table of showbread . . . . . Ex 37:10
Altar of incense . . . . Ex 30:1
Altar of burnt offering . . . Ex 38:1, 6
Tabernacle boards . . . . Ex 26:15-37

and badgers' skins, and *s* . . . . . . Ex 25:5
make a table of *s* wood . . . . Ex 25:23
make the staves of *s* wood . . . . Ex 25:28
make an altar of *s* wood . . . . . . Ex 27:1
for the altar, staves of *s* . . . . Ex 27:6
shalt make the staves of *s* . . . . . Ex 30:5
and badgers' skins, and *s* . . . . . . Ex 35:7
with whom was found *s* . . . . Ex 35:24
for the tabernacle of *s* . . . . Ex 36:20
And he made bars of *s* . . . . Ex 36:31
thereunto four pillars of *s* . . . . . Ex 36:36
Bezaleel made the ark of *s* . . . . Ex 37:1
and he made staves of *s* . . . . Ex 37:4
made the table of *s* wood . . . . . Ex 37:10
made the staves of *s* . . . . Ex 37:15
the incense altar of *s* . . . . Ex 37:25
he made the staves of *s* . . . . Ex 37:28
of burnt offering of *s* . . . . Ex 38:1
he made the staves of *s* . . . . Ex 38:6
And I made an ark of *s* . . . . Deut 10:3

SHIVERS—*slivers; pieces*
they be broken to *s* . . . . Rev 2:27

SHIZA (shī'zä)—*"splendor"*
Reubenite 1Chr 11:42

SHOA (shō'ä)—*"kings"*
Race or tribe against
Israel . . . . Ezek 23:23

SHOBAB (shō'băb)—*"returning"*
1. Son of Caleb 1Chr 2:18
2. Son of David 2Sam 5:14

Shimea, and *S*, and 1Chr 3:5
S, Nathan, and Solomon 1Chr 14:4

SHOBACH (shō'băk)—*"expansion"*
Commander of the Syrian
army 2Sam 10:16-18
Spelled Shophach 1Chr 19:16, 18

SHOBAI (shō'bī)—*"Jehovah is glorious"*
Head of a family of
porters . . . . Ezra 2:42

Hatita, the children of *S* . . . . . . Neh 7:45

SHOBAL (shō'băl)—*"wandering"*
1. Son of Seir; a Horite
chief . . . . Gen 36:20-29
2. Judahite, son of Caleb
and ancestor of the
people of Kirjath-jerim. 1Chr 2:50, 52

sons of Seir; Lotan, and *S* 1Chr 1:38
The sons of *S*; Alion, and 1Chr 1:40
Carmi, and Hur, and *S* 1Chr 4:1
Reaiah the son of *S* begat 1Chr 4:2

SHOBEK (shō'bĕk)—*"free"*
Signer of Nehemiah's
sealed covenant . . . . Neh 10:24

SHOBI (shō'bī)—*"Jehovah is glorious"*
Ammonite who brings
food to David 2Sam 17:27, 28

SHOCHO, SHOCHOH (shō'kō)—*"defense"*
gathered together at *S* 1Sam 17:1
between *S* and Azekah 1Sam 17:1
and *S* with the villages 2Chr 28:18

SHOCK—*a pile of sheaves*

[*also* SHOCKS]
and burnt up both the *s* . . . . Judg 15:5
s of corn cometh in in his . . . . . Job 5:26

SHOD—*to put on footgear*
arrayed them, and *s* them 2Chr 28:15
s thee with badgers' skin . . . . . . Ezek 16:10
But be *s* with sandals; and . . . . Mark 6:9
feet *s* with the preparation . . . . Eph 6:15

SHOE—*footwear*
Characteristics of:
Worn on the feet 1Kin 2:5
Tied by a latchet . . . . Gen 14:23
Some considered
worthless . . . . Amos 2:6
Used for dress occasions . Luke 15:22
Worn as adornment . . . . . Song 7:1
Dirty after a trip . . . . Josh 9:5, 13
Preserved supernaturally . Deut 29:5
Symbolism of:
Putting on—readiness for
a journey . . . . Ex 12:11
Putting off—reverence
before God . . . . { Ex 3:5; Josh 5:15 }
Want of—mourning 2Sam 15:30
Giving to
another—renunciation
of Mosaic marriage
rights . . . . Ruth 4:7, 8
To loose another's—act
of homage . . . . Luke 3:16
Figurative of:
Preparation for service . . . Eph 6:15
Protection and provision . Deut 33:25
Alertness . . . . Is 5:27
See SANDALS

[*also* SHOE'S, SHOES]
and loose his *s* from off his . . . Deut 25:9
him that hath his *s* loosed . . . . . Deut 25:10
Edom will I cast out my *s* . . . . . Ps 60:8
Edom will I cast out my *s* . . . . . Ps 108:9
put off thy *s* from thy foot . . . . Is 20:2
put on thy *s* upon thy feet . . . . Ezek 24:17
your *s* upon your feet . . . . Ezek 24:23
the needy for a pair of *s* . . . . . . Amos 8:6
whose *s* I am not worthy . . . . . . Matt 3:11
neither two coats, neither *s* . . . . Matt 10:10
latchet of whose *s* I am not . . . Mark 1:7
purse, nor scrip, nor *s* . . . . Luke 10:4
purse, and scrip, and *s* . . . . Luke 22:35
Put off thy *s* from thy feet . . . . Acts 7:33
s of his feet I am not . . . . Acts 13:25
s latchet I am not worthy . . . . . John 1:27

SHOHAM (shō'hăm)—*"leek-green beryl"*
Merarite Levite 1Chr 24:27

SHOMER (shō'mer)—*"keeper"*
Asherite 1Chr 7:30, 32
Called Shamer 1Chr 7:34

Jehozabad the son of *S* 2Kin 12:21

SHONE—*See* SHINE

SHOOK—*See* SHAKE

SHOOT—*a new growth on a plant*

[*also* SHOOTETH, SHOOTING, SHOT]
and her blossoms *s* forth . . . . . . Gen 40:10
s forth in his garden . . . . Job 8:16
measure, when it *s* forth . . . . . . Is 27:8
branches, and *s* forth sprigs . . . Ezek 17:6
s forth her branches . . . . Ezek 17:7
of waters when he *s* forth . . . . . Ezek 31:5
he hath *s* up his top . . . . Ezek 31:10
s up their top among the . . . . . . Ezek 31:14
s forth your branches . . . . Ezek 36:8
s up of the latter growth . . . . . . Amos 7:1
s out great branches; so . . . . Mark 4:32
When they now *s* forth, ye . . . . Luke 21:30

SHOOT—*to hurl a projectile at*

[*also* SHOOTING, SHOT]
s at him, and hated him . . . . Gen 49:23
be stoned, or *s* through . . . . Ex 19:13
middle bar to *s* through . . . . Ex 36:33
We have *s* at them . . . . Num 21:30
s three arrows on the side 1Sam 20:20
as though I *s* at a mark 1Sam 20:20
now the arrows which I *s* 1Sam 20:36
he *s* an arrow beyond him 1Sam 20:36
arrow which Jonathan had *s* . . . 1Sam 20:37
would *s* from the wall? 2Sam 11:20
And the shooters *s* from off . . . 2Sam 11:24
Elisha said, *S*. And he *s* 2Kin 13:17
city, nor *s* an arrow there 2Kin 19:32
sword, and to *s* with bow 1Chr 5:18
hurling stones and *s* arrows 1Chr 12:2
s arrows and great stones 2Chr 26:15
archers *s* at king Josiah 2Chr 35:23
city, nor *s* an arrow there . . . . . Is 37:33
tongue is as an arrow *s* . . . . Jer 9:8
s at her, spare no arrows . . . . . . Jer 50:14
privily *s* at the upright in . . . . . . Ps 11:2
and he *s* out lightnings . . . . Ps 18:14
they *s* out the lip, they . . . . Ps 22:7
his bow to *s* his arrows . . . . Ps 58:7
bend their bows to *s* their . . . . . Ps 64:3
s in secret at the perfect . . . . . . Ps 64:4
suddenly do they *s* at him . . . . . Ps 64:4
God shall *s* at them with . . . . . . Ps 64:7
s out thine arrows, and . . . . Ps 144:6

SHOOTERS—*persons using bows and arrows*
s shot from off the wall 2Sam 11:24

SHOPHACH—*See* SHOBACH

SHOPHAN (shō'făn)—*"burrow"*
Town in Gad . . . . Num 32:34, 35

SHORE—*the coast*
sand which is upon the sea *s* . . Gen 22:17
dead upon the sea *s* . . . . Ex 14:30
from the *s* of the salt sea . . . . . Josh 15:2
continued on the sea *s* . . . . Judg 5:17
on the *s* of the Red sea 1Kin 9:26
multitude stood on the *s* . . . . . . Matt 13:2
was full, they drew to *s* . . . . Matt 13:48
and drew to the *s* . . . . Mark 6:53
Jesus stood on the *s* . . . . John 21:4
we kneeled down on the *s* . . . . Acts 21:5
a certain creek with a *s* . . . . Acts 27:39
wind, and made toward *s* . . . . . Acts 27:40
See SEASHORE

SHORN—*See* SHEAR

SHORT—*not long; brief*
Descriptive of:
Life . . . . Ps 89:47
Time of the devil on
earth . . . . Rev 12:12
Gospel age 1Cor 7:29
Expressive of God's:
Power . . . . Is 50:2
Plan . . . . Rev 22:6
Provision . . . . Is 59:1, 2
Tribulation . . . . Matt 24:21, 22

[*also* SHORTER, SHORTLY]
God will *s* bring it to pass . . . . . Gen 41:32
the Lord's hand waxed *s*? . . . . . Num 11:23
Lord began to cut Israel *s* 2Kin 10:32
is *s* because of darkness . . . . . . Job 17:12
triumphing of the wicked is *s* . . Job 20:5
bed is *s* than that a man . . . . . . Is 28:20
s be brought again from . . . . . . Jer 27:16
I *s* pour out my fury upon . . . . Ezek 7:8
upper chambers were *s* . . . . Ezek 42:5
himself..depart *s* thither . . . . Acts 25:4
come *s* of the glory of God . . . Rom 3:23
cut it *s* in righteousness . . . . Rom 9:28
a *s* work will the Lord . . . . Rom 9:28
Satan under your feet *s* . . . . Rom 16:20
come to you *s*, if the Lord 1Cor 4:19
to send Timothy *s* unto you . . . Phil 2:19
I also myself shall come *s* . . . . . Phil 2:24
taken from you for a *s* 1Thess 2:17
hoping to come unto thee *s* . . . 1Tim 3:14
diligence to come *s* unto 2Tim 4:9
should seem to come *s* of it . . . Heb 4:1

if he come *s*, I will see ....Heb 13:23
s I must put off this my 2Pet 1:14
I trust I shall *s* see thee 3John 14
must *s* come to pass ....Rev 1:1
he must continue a *s* space ....Rev 17:10
things which must *s* be ....Rev 22:6

SHORTENED—*cut off*
of his youth hast thou *s* ....Ps 89:45
in the way; he *s* my days ......Ps 102:23
years of the wicked..be *s* ......Prov 10:27
Lord had *s* those days ....Mark 13:20
chosen, he hath *s* the days ....Mark 13:20

SHOSHANNIM (shō-shăn'ĭm)—*"lilies"*—*a musical term*
Musical term ....Ps 45:*title*
Ps 69:*title*

SHOSHANNIM-EDUTH (shō-shăn'ĭm-ē'dŭth)—*a musical term*
To the chief musician upon *S* . .Ps 80:*title*

SHOT—*See* Shoot

SHOULD—*See* Introduction

SHOULDER—*the place on the body where the arm and trunk meet*

Of men, used for:
Burdens ....Is 46:7
Supporting clothes ....Ex 12:34

Figurative of:
Notable persons ....Ezek 24:4, 5
Destruction ....Ezek 29:7
Servitude ....Is 10:27
Rebellion ....Zech 7:11
Messianic authority ......Is 9:6
Security ....Deut 33:12

[*also* shoulders]
and laid it upon both their *s*, . .Gen 9:23
Hagar, putting it on her *s* .....Gen 21:14
her pitcher upon her *s* ....Gen 24:15
with her pitcher on her *s* ......Gen 24:45
bowed his *s* to bear, and ......Gen 49:15
stones upon the *s* of the ......Ex 28:12
his two *s* for a memorial ......Ex 28:12
upon them, and the right *s* ....Ex 29:22
the *s* of the heave offering ....Ex 29:27
them on the *s* of the ephod . . .Ex 39:7
right *s* shall ye give unto ......Lev 7:32
shall have the right *s* for ......Lev 7:33
heave *s* have I taken of ....Lev 7:34
their fat, and the right *s* ......Lev 8:25
fat, and upon the right *s* ......Lev 8:26
the right *s* Aaron waved ......Lev 9:21
s shall ye eat in a clean ....Lev 10:14
heave *s* and the wave breast . . .Lev 10:15
the sodden *s* of the ram ....Num 6:19
wave breast and heave *s* ......Num 6:20
should bear upon their *s* ......Num 7:9
breast and as the right *s* ......Num 18:18
give unto the priest the *s* ......Deut 18:3
you a stone upon his *s* ....Josh 4:5
took it, and laid it on his *s* ....Judg 9:48
put them upon his *s*, and .....Judg 16:3
from his *s* and upward he 1Sam 9:2
And the cook took up the *s* . . .1Sam 9:24
a target..between his *s* 1Sam 17:6
ark of God upon their *s* 1Chr 15:15
be a burden upon your *s* 2Chr 35:3
withdrew the *s*, and ....Neh 9:29
arm fall from my *s* blade ......Job 31:22
I would take it upon my *s* .....Job 31:36
I removed his *s* from the ......Ps 81:6
staff of his *s*, the rod of.......Is 9:4
the *s* of the Philistines ....Is 11:14
David will I lay upon his *s* ....Is 22:22
upon the *s* of young asses .....Is 30:6
thou bear it upon thy *s* ....Ezek 12:6
I bare it upon my *s* in their . . .Ezek 12:7
upon his *s* in the twilight ......Ezek 12:12
and every *s* was peeled ....Ezek 29:18
thrust with side and with *s* ....Ezek 34:21
and lay them on men's *s* ......Matt 23:4
it, he layeth it on his *s* ....Luke 15:5

SHOULDERPIECES—*decorations on the priest's robes*
It shall have the two *s* ....Ex 28:7
s of the ephod before it ....Ex 28:25
made *s* for it, to couple it .....Ex 39:4
them on the *s* of the ephod . . .Ex 39:18

SHOULDEST—*See* Introduction

SHOUT—*to utter a loud cry; a loud cry*

Occasions of, in:
Conquest ....Josh 6:5, 16, 20
Choosing a king 1Sam 10:24
Sound of singing ....Ex 32:17, 18
Laying foundation of the Temple ....Ezek 3:11-13

In spiritual things:
At creation ....Job 38:7
In the Messiah's arrival . .Zech 9:9

[*also* shouted, shouteth, shouting, shoutings]
noise of..people as they *s* .....Ex 32:17
all the people saw, they *s* .....Lev 9:24
the *s* of a king is among ......Num 23:21
not *s*, nor make any noise .....Josh 6:10
bid you *s*; then shall ye *s* .....Josh 6:10
s when the priests blew ....Josh 6:20
the people *s* with a great......Josh 6:20
Philistines *s* against him ....Judg 15:14
all Israel *s* with a great *s* 1Sam 4:5
heard the noise of the *s* 1Sam 4:6
noise of this great *s* in the 1Sam 4:6
fight, and *s* for the battle 1Sam 17:20
ark of the Lord with *s* 2Sam 6:15
ark..of the Lord with *s*........1Chr 15:28
the men of Judah gave a *s* 2Chr 13:15
as the men of Judah *s*, it......2Chr 13:15
a loud voice, and with *s*.......2Chr 15:14
people *s* with a great *s*........Ezra 3:11
the noise of the *s* of joy ......Ezra 3:13
the people *s* with a loud *s*.....Ezra 3:13
the captains, and the *s*........Job 39:25
let them ever *s* for joy ....Ps 5:11
s for joy, and be glad.........Ps 35:27
God is gone up with a *s* ......Ps 47:5
that *s* by reason of wine ......Ps 78:65
let thy saints *s* for joy ....Ps 132:9
wicked perish, there is *s* ......Prov 11:10
Cry out and *s*, thou ....Is 12:6
s for thy summer fruits........Is 16:9
neither shall there be *s*........Is 16:10
their vintage *s* to cease........Is 16:10
s, ye lower parts of the ....Is 44:23
and the *s* at noontide ....Jer 20:16
give a *s*, as they that ....Jer 25:30
none shall tread with *s*........Jer 48:33
their *s* shall be no *s* ....Jer 48:33
S against her round about ......Jer 50:15
I cry and *s*, he shutteth ....Lam 3:8
to lift up the voice with *s* .....Ezek 21:22
s in the day of battle ....Amos 1:14
s, O Israel; be glad and ....Zeph 3:14
headstone thereof with *s* ......Zech 4:7
the people gave a *s*, saying ....Acts 12:22
descend from heaven with a *s* .1Thess 4:16

SHOVEL—*an implement for removing the ashes from the altar*
1. Used for removing ashes .Ex 27:3
2. Winnowing tool ....Is 30:24

[*also* shovels]
and the *s*, and the basins......Ex 38:3
the fleshhooks, and the *s*......Num 4:14
made the lavers, and the *s* 1Kin 7:40
the *s*, and the snuffers 2Kin 25:14
made the pots, and the *s*......2Chr 4:11
caldrons also, and the *s* ....Jer 52:18

SHOW—*to exhibit; offer; set forth; point out*

[*also* showed, showedst, showest, showeth, showing]
unto a land that I will *s*.......Gen 12:1
thou hast *s* unto me in........Gen 19:19
kindness which thou shalt *s*....Gen 20:13
and *s* kindness unto my ....Gen 24:12
which thou hast *s* unto ....Gen 32:10
s kindness, I pray thee ....Gen 40:14
God hath *s* Pharaoh what .....Gen 41:25
about to do he *s* unto..........Gen 41:28
I will go up, and *s* Pharaoh . . .Gen 46:31
lo, God hath *s* me also thy....Gen 48:11
you, saying, *S* a miracle ....Ex 7:9
up, for to *s* in thee my........Ex 9:16
I might *s* these my signs ......Ex 10:1
thou shalt *s* thy son in ....Ex 13:8
which he will *s* to you ....Ex 14:13
and the Lord *s* him a tree .....Ex 15:25
shalt *s* them the way..........Ex 18:20
s mercy unto thousands ....Ex 20:6
Acording to all that I *s* ....Ex 25:9
which was *s* thee in the ....Ex 26:30
s me now thy way, that I .....Ex 33:13
I beseech thee, *s* me thy .....Ex 33:18
s mercy on whom I will *s* .....Ex 33:19
reddish, and it be *s* to the.....Lev 13:19
of the Lord might be *s*........Lev 24:12
pattern which the Lord had *s* . .Num 8:4
signs..I have *s* among ....Num 14:11
the Lord will *s* who are ....Num 16:5
and whatsoever he *s* me ......Num 23:3
to *s* you by what way he ......Deut 1:33
to *s* thy servants thy ....Deut 3:24
Unto thee it was *s*, that ....Deut 4:35
to *s* you the word of the ......Deut 5:5
s mercy unto thousands ....Deut 5:10
Lord our God hath *s* us.......Deut 5:24
with them, nor *s* mercy ....Deut 7:2
of his anger, and *s* thee ......Deut 13:17
they shall *s* thee the ....Deut 17:9
Lord shall choose shall *s* ......Deut 17:10
which they shall *s* thee ....Deut 17:11
the old, nor *s* favor to ....Deut 28:50
thy father, and he will *s*.......Deut 32:7
Lord *s* him all the land of.....Deut 34:1
since I have *s* you kindness....Josh 2:12
ye will also *s* kindness ....Josh 2:12
he would not *s* them the ......Josh 5:6
S us, we pray thee, the ....Judg 1:24
the city, and we will *s* thee....Judg 1:24
when he *s* them the entrance . .Judg 1:25
will *s* thee the man whom .....Judg 4:22
s me a sign that thou ....Judg 6:17
s they kindness to the.........Judg 8:35
ran, and *s* her husband ....Judg 13:10
for he hath *s* me all his ....Judg 16:18
It hath fully been *s* me........Ruth 2:11
s more kindness in the ....Ruth 3:10
Samuel feared to *s* Eli 1Sam 3:15
and *s* them the manner 1Sam 8:9
peradventure he can *s* us......1Sam 9:6
and *s* thee what thou 1Sam 10:8
messengers came and *s* it 1Sam 11:9
up to us, and we will *s*........1Sam 14:12
I will *s* thee what thou 1Sam 16:3
Jonathan *s* him all those 1Sam 19:7
or small, but that he will *s* 1Sam 20:2
then I will *s* it thee, and 1Sam 20:13
is none that *s* me that my 1Sam 22:8
or *s* unto me that my son 1Sam 22:8
he fled, and did not *s* it.......1Sam 22:17
s this day how that thou 1Sam 24:18
men, and they will *s* thee 1Sam 25:8
s this kindness unto...........2Sam 2:5
s kindness and truth 2Sam 2:6
s kindness this day unto.......2Sam 3:8
I may *s* him kindness for......2Sam 9:1
surely *s* thee kindness for 2Sam 9:7
I will *s* kindness unto 2Sam 10:2
s David all that Joab had 2Sam 11:22
s me both it, and his 2Sam 15:25
thou wilt *s* thyself 2Sam 22:26
man thou wilt *s* thyself........2Sam 22:26
the pure thou wilt *s* 2Sam 22:27
froward thou wilt *s* thyself 2Sam 22:27
and *s* mercy to his............2Sam 22:51
hast not *s* it unto thy 1Kin 1:27
If he will *s* himself a..........1Kin 1:52
therefore, and *s* thyself 1Kin 2:2

S

and his might that he *s* 1Kin 16:27
saying, Go, *s* thyself unto 1Kin 18:1
I will surely *s* myself..........1Kin 18:15
fell it? And he *s* him 2Kin 6:6
s me which of us is for........2Kin 6:11
s you what the Syrians 2Kin 7:12
Lord hath *s* me that thou 2Kin 8:13
s them all the house of 2Kin 20:13
that Hezekiah *s* them not 2Kin 20:13
Shaphan the scribe *s* the 2Kin 22:10
s forth from day to day his 1Chr 16:23
I will *s* kindness unto 1Chr 19:2
his father *s* kindness to 1Chr 19:2
hast *s* great mercy unto 2Chr 1:8
s mercy unto thy servants 2Chr 6:14
to *s* himself strong in the......2Chr 16:9
could not *s* their father's ......Ezra 2:59
grace hath been *s* from ....Ezra 9:8
could not *s* their father's ......Neh 7:61
And *s* signs and wonders ......Neh 9:10
of fire by night, to *s* them.....Neh 9:19
he *s* the riches of his ....Esth 1:4
to *s* the people..her beauty ....Esth 1:11
that she should not *s* it ....Esth 2:10
Esther had not yet *s* her ......Esth 2:20
to *s* it unto Esther, and to ....Esth 4:8
pity should be *s* from his......Job 6:14
s me wherefore thou ....Job 10:2
thou *s* thyself marvelous ......Job 10:16
s thee the secrets of ....Job 11:6
I will *s* thee, hear me ....Job 15:17
and durst not *s* you mine .....Job 32:6
my part, I also will *s* ....Job 32:17
to *s* unto man his.............Job 33:23
me a little, and I will *s* ....Job 36:2
Then he *s* them their ....Job 36:9
that say, Who will *s* us.........Ps 4:6
s forth all thy marvelous ......Ps 9:1
Thou wilt *s* me the path ......Ps 16:11
S thy marvelous ....Ps 17:7
thou wilt *s* thyself merciful ....Ps 18:25
thou wilt *s* thyself upright .....Ps 18:25
the pure thou wilt *s* thyself ....Ps 18:26
wilt *s* thyself froward ....Ps 18:26
s mercy to his anointed ....Ps 18:50
the firmament *s* his ....Ps 19:1
S me thy ways, O Lord ....Ps 25:4
he hath *s* me his ....Ps 31:21
righteous *s* mercy, and ....Ps 37:21
man walketh in a vain *s*........Ps 39:6
will I *s* the salvation of ....Ps 50:23
my mouth shall *s* forth ....Ps 51:15
shall *s* forth thy ....Ps 71:15
I have *s* thy strength..........Ps 71:18
s to the generation to ....Ps 78:4
his wonders that he had *s* .....Ps 78:11
s forth thy praise to all ....Ps 79:13
S us thy mercy, O Lord........Ps 85:7
S me a token for good ....Ps 86:17
Wilt thou *s* wonders to.........Ps 88:10
him, and *s* him my ....Ps 91:16
s forth thy loving-kindness ....Ps 92:2
vengeance belongeth, *s*........Ps 94:1
s..his salvation from day ....Ps 96:2
They *s* his signs among ....Ps 105:27
who can *s* forth all his ....Ps 106:2
he remembered not to *s* ......Ps 109:16
A good man *s* favor ....Ps 112:5
is the Lord, which hath *s* .....Ps 118:27
He *s* his word unto Jacob .....Ps 147:19
He that speaketh truth *s* ......Prov 12:17
hath friends must *s* ....Prov 18:24
wickedness shall be *s* ....Prov 26:26
I have *s* myself wise ....Eccl 2:19
s himself through the ....Song 2:9
s of their countenance ....Is 3:9
Let favor be *s* to the ....Is 26:10
formed them will *s* them ......Is 27:11
s the lighting down of his .....Is 30:30
s them the house of his ....Is 39:2
dominion, that Hezekiah *s* ....Is 39:2
s to him the way of...........Is 40:14
and *s* us what shall ....Is 41:22
let them *s* the former ....Is 41:22
there is none that *s*, yea ......Is 41:26
this, and *s* us former..........Is 43:9
shall come, let them *s* ....Is 44:7
Remember this, and *s* ....Is 46:8
thou didst *s* them no..........Is 47:6
out of my mouth, and I *s* .....Is 48:3
s thee new things from........Is 48:6
in darkness, *S* yourselves ......Is 49:9
s my people their.............Is 58:1
s forth the praises..Lord ......Is 60:6
then thou *s* me their doings ...Jer 11:18
shalt *s* this people all these ....Jer 16:10
I will *s* them the back ....Jer 18:17
The Lord *s* me, and ....Jer 24:1
Thou *s* lovingkindness ....Jer 32:18
s thee great and mighty ....Jer 33:3
the Lord thy God may *s* ....Jer 42:3
are cruel, and will not *s*.......Jer 50:42
to *s* the king of Babylon ....Jer 51:31
things that the Lord had *s*.....Ezek 11:25
shalt *s* her all her............Ezek 22:2
neither have they *s* ....Ezek 22:26
their mouth they *s* much ......Ezek 33:31
thou not *s* us what thou.......Ezek 37:18
upon all that I shall *s*.........Ezek 40:4
that I might *s* them unto ......Ezek 40:4
s them the form of the........Ezek 43:11
for to *s* the king his ....Dan 2:2
But if ye *s* the dream ....Dan 2:6
therefore *s* me the dream .....Dan 2:6
earth that can *s* the...........Dan 2:10
s the king the ....Dan 2:16
the soothsayers, *s* unto........Dan 2:27
iniquities by *s* mercy..........Dan 4:27
s me the interpretation........Dan 5:7
they could not *s* the ....Dan 5:15
I will *s* thee that which ....Dan 10:21
I will *s* wonders in the ....Joel 2:30
hath the Lord God *s* unto .....Amos 7:1
Thus he *s* me: and, behold ....Amos 7:7
Thus hath the Lord God *s* ....Amos 8:1
He hath *s* thee, O man ....Mic 6:8
I *s* unto him marvelous ....Mic 7:15
I will *s* the nations thy ....Nah 3:5
Why dost thou *s* me ....Hab 1:3
unto me, I will *s* thee.........Zech 1:9
the Lord *s* me four ....Zech 1:20
s him all the kingdom.........Matt 4:8
thy way, *s* thyself to the ......Matt 8:4
shall *s* judgment to the........Matt 12:18
I would *s* them a sign from....Matt 16:1
began Jesus to *s* unto his......Matt 16:21
S me the tribute money ....Matt 22:19
s him the buildings of.........Matt 24:1
shall *s* great signs and........Matt 24:24
and *s* unto the chief ....Matt 28:11
thy way, *s* thyself to the ......Mark 1:44
mighty works do *s* forth.......Mark 6:14
and shall *s* signs and ....Mark 13:22
he will *s* you a large ....Mark 14:15
and to *s* thee these glad.......Luke 1:19
He hath *s* strength with ....Luke 1:51
till the day of his *s* unto ......Luke 1:80
s unto him all the ....Luke 4:5
but go, and *s* thyself to ....Luke 5:14
I will *s* you to whom he.......Luke 6:47
s how great things God ....Luke 8:39
he said, He that *s* mercy .....Luke 10:37
Go *s* yourselves unto the ......Luke 17:14
S me a penny ....Luke 20:24
even Moses *s* at the bush .....Luke 20:37
for a *s* make long prayers .....Luke 20:47
he shall *s* you a large ....Luke 22:12
What sign *s* thou unto us .....John 2:18
s him all things that ....John 5:20
s him greater works than ......John 5:20
things, *s* thyself to the ....John 7:4
good works have I *s* you ......John 10:32
he was, he should *s* it.........John 11:57
s us the Father, and it ....John 14:8
and he will *s* you things ....John 16:13
I shall *s* you plainly of ....John 16:25
Jesus *s* himself again to ....John 21:1
and on this wise *s* he ....John 21:1
To whom also he *s* ....Acts 1:3
s whether of these two ....Acts 1:24
I will *s* wonders in............Acts 2:19
miracle of healing was *s*.......Acts 4:22
land which I shall *s* ....Acts 7:3
s wonders and signs in ....Acts 7:36
For I will *s* him how ....Acts 9:16
s the coats and garments ......Acts 9:39
God hath *s* me that I ....Acts 10:28
he *s* us how he had seen ......Acts 11:13
Go *s* these things unto ....Acts 12:17
s unto us the way of ....Acts 16:17
but have *s* you, and have .....Acts 20:20
thou hast *s* these things ....Acts 23:22
willing to *s* the Jews ....Acts 24:27
should *s* light unto the ....Acts 26:23
people *s* us no little ....Acts 28:2
for God hath *s* it unto them ...Rom 1:19
s the work of the law ....Rom 2:15
runneth, but of God that *s* ....Rom 9:16
that I might *s* my power ......Rom 9:17
eat not for his sake that *s* 1Cor 10:28
ye do *s* the Lord's death 1Cor 11:26
s I unto you a more 1Cor 12:31
I *s* you a mystery; We 1Cor 15:51
Wherefore *s* ye to them 2Cor 8:24
desire to make a fair *s*........Gal 6:12
he might *s* the exceeding ......Eph 2:7
he made a *s* of them..........Col 2:15
s of us what manner of 1Thess 1:9
of God, *s* himself that he 2Thess 2:4
s forth all long-suffering.......1Tim 1:16
learn first to *s* piety at 1Tim 5:4
in his times he shall *s*.........1Tim 6:15
Study to *s* thyself.............2Tim 2:15
s thyself a pattern of..........Titus 2:7
in doctrine *s* uncorruptness ....Titus 2:7
gentle, *s* all meekness.........Titus 3:2
which ye have *s* toward ....Heb 6:10
one of you do *s* the same .....Heb 6:11
mercy, that hath *s* no ....James 2:13
s me thy faith without ....James 2:18
I will *s* thee my faith ....James 2:18
let him *s* out of a good ....James 3:13
should *s* forth the praises 1Pet 2:9
Lord Jesus Christ hath *s* 2Pet 1:14
and *s* unto you that eternal....1John 1:2
to *s* unto his servants ....Rev 1:1
I will *s* thee things which......Rev 4:1
I will *s* thee the bride.........Rev 21:9
and *s* me that great city.......Rev 21:10
the angel which *s* me ....Rev 22:8

SHOWBREAD—*"bread of thy face"—bread kept in the temple or tabernacle*

Provisions concerning:
Provided by the people ..Lev 24:8
Prepared by the Levites ..1Chr 9:32
Placed in two rows ......Ex 25:30
Perennially supplied .....Num 4:7
Presented to the Lord ...Lev 24:7, 8
Provided for priests only .Lev 24:9
Matt 12:4, 5

Table of:
Placed in Holy Place.....Ex 26:35
Heb 9:2
Made of acacia ....Ex 25:23-28
Carried by:
Kohathite Levites .....Num 4:4, 7, 15
High priest..............Num 4:7, 8, 16

Symbolic of:
Twelve tribes ....Ex 28:10-12
Christ ....John 6:48
Church 1Cor 10:17

shalt set upon the table *s* .....Ex 25:30
his vessels, and the *s* ....Ex 35:13
vessels thereof, and the *s* .....Ex 39:36
table of *s* they shall spread ....Num 4:7
no bread there but the *s* 1Sam 21:6
of gold, whereupon the *s*......1Kin 7:48
the *s*, to prepare it 1Chr 9:32
Both for the *s*, and for the 1Chr 23:29
gold for the tables of *s*........1Chr 28:16
and for the continual *s*........2Chr 2:4
the *s* also set they in order 2Chr 13:11
the *s*, and for the continual ...Neh 10:33

eat the *s*, which was not ......Matt 12:4
the *s*, which is not lawful .....Mark 2:26
and did take and eat the *s* ....Luke 6:4
and the table, and the *s*.......Heb 9:2

SHOWERS—*sudden outpourings*

Used literally of rain:
Withheld ....Jer 3:3
Predicted ....Luke 12:54
Requested ....Zech 10:1
Blessing ....Ps 65:10

Used figuratively of:
God's Word ....Deut 32:2
God's wrath ....Ezek 13:11, 13
Messiah's advent ....Ps 72:6
Gospel ....Ezek 34:25, 26
Remnant ....Mic 5:7

the *s* of the mountains ....Job 24:8
can the heavens give *s*? ....Jer 14:22
shall be *s* of blessing..........Ezek 34:26

SHRANK—*withered*
eat not of the sinew which *s*...Gen 32:32
thigh in the sinew that *s* ......Gen 32:32

SHRED—*cut or tear into strips*
s them into the pot of 2Kin 4:39

SHRINES—*places where saints or deities are worshiped*
made silver *s* for Diana ....Acts 19:24

SHROUD—*to cover or shelter*
Used figuratively ....Ezek 31:3

SHRUBS—*brushwood; bushes*
child under one of the *s*.......Gen 21:15

SHUA, SHUAH (shōō'ä)—*"prosperity"*
1. Son of Abraham by Keturah ....Gen 25:1, 2
2. Father of Judah's wife ...Gen 38:2, 12
3. Descendant of Judah 1Chr 4:1, 11
4. Daughter of Heber 1Chr 7:32

and Ishbak, and *S* 1Chr 1:32
daughter of *S* the 1Chr 2:3

SHUAL (shōō'ăl)—*"jackal"*
1. Asherite 1Chr 7:30, 36
2. Region raised by a Philistine company 1Sam 13:17

SHUBAEL, SHEBUEL (shōō'bā-ĕl, shĕ-bū'ĕl)—*"God is renown"*
1. Levite, son of Amram ...1Chr 24:20
2. Levite, son of Herman ..1Chr 25:4

to *S*, he, his sons, and 1Chr 25:20

SHUHAM (shōō'hăm)—*"depression"*
Son of Dan ....Num 26:42
Called Hushim ....Gen 46:23
Head of the Shuhamites. .Num 26:42, 43

S, the family of Shuhamites ...Num 26:42

SHUHAMITES—*of the tribe of Shuham*
the family of the *S* ....Num 26:42
the families of the *S* ....Num 26:43

SHUHITE (shōō'hīt)—*a descendant of Shua*
Bildad called; a descendant of Abraham by Keturah .... {Gen 38:2, 12; Job 2:11}

answered Bildad the *S* ....Job 8:1
answered Bildad the *S* ....Job 25:1

SHULAMITE (shōō'lä-mīt)—*a native of Shulam*
Shepherd's sweetheart ...Song 6:13

SHUMATHITES (shōō'mä-thīts)
Family of Kirjath-jearim. .1Chr 2:53

SHUN—*to hold back; shrink*

[*also* SHUNNED]
not *s* to declare unto you .....Acts 20:27
But *s* profane and vain........2Tim 2:16

SHUNAMMITE (shōō'nä-mīt)—*a native of Shunem*
1. Abishag, David's nurse called 1Kin 1:3, 15
2. Woman who cared for Elisha...............2Kin 4:8-12

he give me Abishag the *S* 1Kin 2:17
Abishag the *S* be given to 1Kin 2:21
ask Abishag the *S for*.........1Kin 2:22
Behold, yonder is that *S* 2Kin 4:25
and said, Call this *S* 2Kin 4:36

SHUNEM (shōō'nĕm)—*"their sleep"*
Border town of Issachar. .Josh 19:18

came and pitched in *S* 1Sam 28:4
that Elisha passed to *S*........2Kin 4:8

SHUNI (shōō'nī)—*"fortunate"*
Son of Gad ....Gen 46:16

of *S*, the family of the ....Num 26:15

SHUNITES (shōō'nīts)—*Shuni's descendants*
Shuni, the family of the *S*.....Num 26:15

SHUPHAM (shōō'făm)—*"obscurities"—a son of Benjamin*
S, the family of the...........Num 26:39

SHUPHAMITES (shōō'făm-īts)—*descendants of Shupham*
the family of the *S*,...........Num 26:39

SHUPPIM (shŭp'ĭm)—*"serpent"*
Levite porter 1Chr 26:16

S also, and Huppim, the 1Chr 7:12
the sister of Huppim and *S*....1Chr 7:15

SHUR (shōōr)—*"wall"*
Wilderness in south Palestine.............Gen 16:7
Israel went from Red Sea to ....Ex 15:22
On Egypt's border 1Sam 15:7
Hagar flees to ....Gen 16:7

between Kadesh and *S* ....Gen 20:1
from Havilah unto *S* ....Gen 25:18
as thou goest to *S*, even 1Sam 27:8

SHUSHAN (shōō'shăn)—*"a lily"*
Residence of Persian monarchs ....Esth 1:2
Located on river Ulai ......Dan 8:2
Court of Ahasuerus here .Esth 1:2, 5

as I was in *S* the palace ....Neh 1:1
fair young virgins unto *S* ......Esth 2:3
gathered together unto *s* ......Esth 2:8
decree was given in *S* the .....Esth 3:15
city *S* was perplexed ....Esth 3:15
Jews that are present in *S*.....Esth 4:16
the city of *S* rejoiced and .....Esth 8:15
of those..slain in *S* ....Esth 9:11
the Jews which are in *S* ....Esth 9:13
the Jews that were in *S* ....Esth 9:15
three hundred men at *S* ....Esth 9:15

SHUSHAN-EDUTH (shōō'shăn-ē'dŭth)—*"lily of the testimony"—a musical term*
chief musician upon *S*........Ps 60:*title*

SHUT—*to close securely*

Applied literally to:
Ark ....Gen 7:16
Door ....Gen 19:6, 10
Leper ....Lev 13:4-44
Animals ....Dan 6:22
Court ....Jer 33:1
Prison ....Acts 26:10

Applied figuratively to:
Womb 1Sam 1:5, 6
God's mercies ....Ps 77:9
Finality of salvation......Matt 25:10
Union with Christ ....Song 4:12
Spiritual blindness ....Is 6:10
Awe....................Is 52:15
Heaven's glory ....Is 60:11
God's Word ....Jer 20:9
Vision ....Dan 12:4
Secret prayer...........Matt 6:6
Christ's sovereignty ......Rev 3:7, 8

[*also* SHUTTETH, SHUTTING]
wilderness hath *s* them ....Ex 14:3
s up it that hath the plague ...Lev 13:50
s up the house seven days.....Lev 14:38
be *s* out from the camp ....Num 12:14
s up the heaven, that there....Deut 11:17
nor *s* thine hand from thy .....Deut 15:7
the Lord had *s* them up?.......Deut 32:30
the time of *s* of the gate ......Josh 2:5
gone out, they *s* the gate......Josh 2:7
s the doors of the parlor ......Judg 3:23
of the city, and *s* it to them ...Judg 9:51
s up their calves at home 1Sam 6:10
s up unto the day of their 2Sam 20:3
When heaven is *s* up, and.....1Kin 8:35
is *s* up and left in Israel.......1Kin 21:21
thou shalt *s* the door upon 2Kin 4:4
s the door upon him and 2Kin 4:21
s the door, and hold him......2Kin 6:32
for there was not any *s* up 2Kin 14:26
When the heaven is *s* up 2Chr 6:26
s up the doors of the house ...2Chr 28:24
Mehetabeel who was *s* ....Neh 6:10
s the doors of the temple .....Neh 6:10
that the gate should be *s* ......Neh 13:19
s not up the doors of my......Job 3:10
he *s* up a man, and there .....Job 12:14
s up the sea with doors ....Job 38:8
s me up into the hand of......Ps 31:8
pit *s* her mouth upon me ......Ps 69:15
I am *s* up, and I cannot.......Ps 88:8
He *s* his eyes to devise........Prov 16:30
s his lips is esteemed ....Prov 17:28
the doors shall be *s* in ....Eccl 12:4
open and none shall *s*.........Is 22:22
he shall *s* and none shall .....Is 22:22
every house is *s* up, that ......Is 24:10
be *s* up in the prison ....Is 24:22
s thy doors about thee ....Is 26:20
s his eyes from seeing evil.....Is 33:15
for he hath *s* their eyes ....Is 44:18
the gates shall not be *s* ....Is 45:1
forth, and *s* the womb? ....Is 66:9
cities..shall be *s* up ....Jer 13:19
Jeremiah..was *s* up in the .....Jer 32:2
For Zedekiah..had *s* him ......Jer 32:3
saying, I am *s* up; I ....Jer 36:5
shout, he *s* out my prayer .....Lam 3:8
Go, *s* thyself within thine .....Ezek 3:24
This gate shall be *s*, it ....Ezek 44:2
s the six working days ....Ezek 46:1
gate shall not be *s* until ....Ezek 46:2
forth one shall *s* the gate......Ezek 46:12
s thou up the vision ....Dan 8:26
s the doors for nought? ....Mal 1:10
s up the kingdom of heaven ...Matt 23:13
he *s* up John in prison ....Luke 3:20
heaven was *s* up three ....Luke 4:25
the door is now *s* and my .....Luke 11:7
up, and hath *s* to the door ....Luke 13:25
doors were *s* where the ....John 20:19
Jesus the doors being *s* ....John 20:26
prison truly found we *s* ....Acts 5:23
the doors were *s* ....Acts 21:30
s up unto the faith which .....Gal 3:23
s up his bowels of 1John 3:17
openeth and no man *s* ....Rev 3:7
s and no man openeth ....Rev 3:7
have power to *s* heaven ....Rev 11:6
bottomless pit, and *s* him .....Rev 20:3
gates of it shall not be *s* ......Rev 21:25

SHUTHELAH (shōō'thĕ-lä)—*"setting of Telah"*
1. Son of Ephraim; head of a family ....Num 26:35, 36
2. Ephraimite 1Chr 7:20, 21

SHUTTLE—*a tool used in weaving*
Our days swifter than ....Job 7:6

SIA, SIAHA (sī'ä, sī'ä-hä)—*"congregation"*
Family of returning Nethinim .... {Ezra 2:43, 44; Neh 7:47}

S

SIBBECAI, SIBBECHAI (sĭb'ĕ-kī)—*"Jehovah is intervening"*
One of David's mighty men ...1Chr 11:29
Slays a Philistine giant ...2Sam 21:18
Commander of a division .1Chr 27:11

SIBBOLETH—*See* **SHIBBOLETH**

SIBMAH (sĭb'mä)—*"to be cold"*
Town of Reuben ...Num 32:3, 38
Famous for wines ...Is 16:8, 9

O vine of *S*, I will weep ...Jer 48:32

SIBRAIM (sĭb-rā'ĭm)—*"twofold hope"*
Place in north Palestine ..Ezek 47:16

SICHEM (sī'kĕm)—*"portion"*
land unto the place of *S* ...Gen 12:6

SICK—*ill*

Caused by:
Age ...Gen 48:1, 10
Accident ...2Kin 1:2
Wine ...Hos 7:5
Sins ...Mic 6:13
Despondency ...Prov 13:12
Prophetic visions ...Dan 8:27
Love ...Song 2:5
God's judgment ...2Chr 21:14-19
God's sovereignty ...John 11:4

Healing of, by:
Figs ...2Kin 20:7
Miracle ...1Kin 17:17-23
Prayer ...James 5:14, 15
God's mercy ...Phil 2:25-30
See **DISEASES; HEALING**

[*also* SICKLY, SICKNESS, SICKNESSES]
that is *s* of her flowers ...Lev 15:33
a woman having her *s* ...Lev 20:18
take away from thee all *s* ...Deut 7:15
s and of long continuance ...Deut 28:59
every *s*, and every plague ...Deut 28:61
s which the Lord hath laid ...Deut 29:22
David, she said, He is *s* ...1Sam 19:14
three days agone I fell *s* ...1Sam 30:13
David, and it was very *s* ...2Sam 12:15
that he fell *s* for his sister ...2Sam 13:2
and made himself *s* ...2Sam 13:6
whatsoever *s* there be ...1Kin 8:37
son of Jeroboam fell *s* ...1Kin 14:1
his *s* was so sore, that ...1Kin 17:17
Jezreel, because he was *s* ...2Kin 8:29
Now Elisha was fallen *s* ...2Kin 13:14
Hezekiah *s* unto death ...2Kin 20:1
or whatsoever *s* there be ...2Chr 6:28
Ahab..because he was *s* ...2Chr 22:6
Hezekiah was *s* to the ...2Chr 32:24
sad, seeing thou art not *s*? ...Neh 2:2
they were *s*, my clothing ...Ps 35:13
make all his bed in his *s* ...Ps 41:3
thou say, and I was not *s* ...Prov 23:35
and wrath with his *s* ...Eccl 5:17
ye tell him, I am *s* of love ...Song 5:8
the whole head is *s*, and ...Is 1:5
shall not say, I am *s* ...Is 33:24
was Hezekiah *s* unto death ...Is 38:1
was recovered of his *s* ...Is 38:9
cut me off with pining *s* ...Is 38:12
heard that he had been *s* ...Is 39:1
that are *s* with famine! ...Jer 14:18
healed that which was *s* ...Ezek 34:4
When Ephraim saw his *s* ...Hos 5:13
if ye offer the lame and *s* ...Mal 1:8
healing all manner of *s* ...Matt 4:23
brought unto him all *s* ...Matt 4:24
at home *s* of the palsy ...Matt 8:6
mother laid..*s* of a fever ...Matt 8:14
and healed all that were *s* ...Matt 8:16
infirmities and bare our *s* ...Matt 8:17
a man *s* of the palsy ...Matt 9:2
unto the *s* of the palsy ...Matt 9:2
but they that are *s* ...Matt 9:12
healing every *s* and every ...Matt 9:35
to heal all manner of *s* ...Matt 10:1
Heal the *s*, cleanse the ...Matt 10:8
and he healed their *s* ...Matt 14:14
I was *s*, and ye visited me ...Matt 25:36
saw we thee *s*, or in prison ...Matt 25:39
naked, or *s*, or in prison ...Matt 25:44
wife's mother lay *s* of a ...Mark 1:30
healed many that were *s* ...Mark 1:34
bringing one *s* of the palsy ...Mark 2:3
unto the *s* of the palsy ...Mark 2:5
saith to the *s* of the palsy ...Mark 2:10
but they that are *s* ...Mark 2:17
to have power to heal *s* ...Mark 3:15
his hands upon a few *s* ...Mark 6:5
in beds those that were *s* ...Mark 6:55
shall lay hands on the *s* ...Mark 16:18
that had any *s* with divers ...Luke 4:40
but they that are *s* ...Luke 5:31
was *s* and ready to die ...Luke 7:2
whole that had been *s* ...Luke 7:10
of God and to heal the *s* ...Luke 9:2
And heal the *s* that are ...Luke 10:9
son was *s* at Capernaum ...John 4:46
brother. Lazarus was *s* ...John 11:2
he whom thou lovest is *s* ...John 11:3
This *s* is not unto death ...John 11:4
had heard..that he was *s* ...John 11:6
they brought forth the *s* ...Acts 5:15
and was *s* of the palsy ...Acts 9:33
brought unto the *s* ...Acts 19:12
father of Publius lay *s* of ...Acts 28:8
have I left at Miletus *s* ...2Tim 4:20

SICKLE—*an instrument used for cutting grain*
Literally ...Deut 16:9
Figuratively ...Mark 4:29
Rev 14:14-19

not move a *s* unto thy ...Deut 23:25
that handleth the *s* in the ...Jer 50:16
Put ye in the *s*, for the ...Joel 3:13

SIDDIM, VALE OF (sĭd'ĭm)—*"the tilled field"*
Valley of bitumen pits near the Dead Sea ...Gen 14:3, 8, 10

SIDE—*object or direction to either right or left*

[*also* SIDES]
ark shalt thou set in the *s* ...Gen 6:16
along by the river's *s* ...Ex 2:5
lintel and the two *s* posts ...Ex 12:22
one *s*..on the other *s* ...Ex 17:12
rings shall be in the one *s* ...Ex 25:12
two rings in the other *s* ...Ex 25:12
rings by the *s* of the ark ...Ex 25:14
shall come out of the *s* ...Ex 25:32
candlestick out of..one *s* ...Ex 25:32
candlestick out of..other *s* ...Ex 25:32
cubit on the one *s* and a ...Ex 26:13
s of that which remaineth ...Ex 26:13
the *s* of the tabernacle ...Ex 26:13
on this *s* and on that *s* ...Ex 26:13
second *s* of the tabernacle ...Ex 26:20
the north *s* there shall be ...Ex 26:20
tabernacle in the two *s* ...Ex 26:23
other *s* of the tabernacle ...Ex 26:27
the *s* of the tabernacle ...Ex 26:27
s of the tabernacle toward ...Ex 26:35
the table on the north *s* ...Ex 26:35
upon the two *s* of the altar ...Ex 27:7
for the south *s* southward ...Ex 27:9
cubits long for one *s* ...Ex 27:9
west *s* shall be hangings ...Ex 27:12
The hangings of one *s* of ...Ex 27:14
the *s* of the ephod inward ...Ex 28:26
the *s* thereof round about ...Ex 30:3
written on both their *s* ...Ex 32:15
the one *s* and on the other ...Ex 32:15
man his sword by his *s* ...Ex 32:27
s of another curtain ...Ex 36:11
other *s* of the tabernacle ...Ex 36:25
tabernacle in the two *s* ...Ex 36:28
other *s* of the tabernacle ...Ex 36:32
two rings upon the the *s* ...Ex 37:3
two rings upon the other *s* ...Ex 37:3
rings by the *s* of the ark ...Ex 37:5
cherub on..end on this *s* ...Ex 37:8
on the other end on that *s* ...Ex 37:8
out of the one *s* thereof ...Ex 37:18
out of the other *s* thereof ...Ex 37:18
rings on the *s* of the altar ...Ex 38:7
s southward the hangings ...Ex 38:9
the west *s* were hangings ...Ex 38:12
hangings of the one *s* of ...Ex 38:14
was on the *s* of the ephod ...Ex 39:19
the *s* of the tabernacle ...Ex 40:22
it on the *s* of the altar ...Lev 1:11
sin offering upon the *s* of ...Lev 5:9
east *s* toward the rising ...Num 2:3
the west *s* shall be the ...Num 2:18
the *s* of the tabernacle ...Num 3:29
camps..on the south *s* ...Num 10:6
a days journey on this *s* ...Num 11:31
journey on the other *s* ...Num 11:31
and Abiram on every *s* ...Num 16:27
on the other *s* of Arnon ...Num 21:13
Moab on this *s* Jordan by ...Num 22:1
gardens by the river's *s* ...Num 24:6
on yonder *s* Jordan ...Num 32:19
is fallen..on this *s* Jordan ...Num 32:19
eyes, and thorns in your *s* ...Num 33:55
on the east *s* of Ain ...Num 34:11
s of the sea of Chinnereth ...Num 34:11
east *s* two thousand cubits ...Num 35:5
south *s* two thousand cubits ...Num 35:5
west *s* two thousand cubits ...Num 35:5
north *s* two thousand cubits ...Num 35:5
all Israel on this *s* Jordan ...Deut 1:1
south, and by the sea *s* ...Deut 1:7
land..on this *s* Jordan ...Deut 3:8
one *s* of heaven unto the ...Deut 4:32
this *s* Jordan, in the valley ...Deut 4:46
not on the other *s* Jordan ...Deut 11:30
s of the ark of the covenant ...Deut 31:26
Moses gave..this *s* Jordan ...Josh 1:14
on the other *s* Jordan ...Josh 2:10
the *s* of Jordan westward ...Josh 5:1
on the east *s* of Beth-el ...Josh 7:2
Ai, on the west *s* of Ai ...Josh 8:9
and Ai, on the west *s* of ...Josh 8:12
Of Israel, some on this *s* ...Josh 8:22
on that *s*; and they smote ...Josh 8:22
stood on this *s* the ark ...Josh 8:33
s before the priests the ...Josh 8:33
were on this *s* Jordan ...Josh 9:1
other *s* Jordan toward the ...Josh 12:1
other *s* Jordan eastward ...Josh 13:27
tribe on the other *s* Jordan ...Josh 14:3
s to Maaleh-acrabbim ...Josh 15:3
s unto Kadesh-barnea ...Josh 15:3
south *s* of the Jebusite ...Josh 15:8
unto the *s* of mount Jearim ...Josh 15:10
Chesalon, on the north *s* ...Josh 15:10
inheritance on the east *s* ...Josh 16:5
were on the other *s* Jordan ...Josh 17:5
border on the north *s* was ...Josh 18:12
went up to the *s* of Jericho ...Josh 18:12
of Jericho on the north *s* ...Josh 18:12
s of Luz, which is Beth-el ...Josh 18:13
s of the nether Beth-horon ...Josh 18:13
the *s* over against Arabah ...Josh 18:18
border of it on the east *s* ...Josh 18:20
the north *s* to Hannathon ...Josh 19:14
to Zebulun on the south *s* ...Josh 19:34
to Asher on the west *s* ...Josh 19:34
other *s* Jordan by Jericho ...Josh 20:8
you on the other *s* Jordan ...Josh 22:4
and scourges in your *s* ...Josh 23:13
fathers dwelt..other *s* ...Josh 24:2
dwelt on the other *s* Jordan ...Josh 24:8
the other *s* of the flood ...Josh 24:15
be as thorns in your *s* ...Judg 2:3
on the north *s* of the hill ...Judg 2:9
by the sea *s* for multitude ...Judg 7:12
to Gideon on the other *s* ...Judg 7:25
their enemies on every *s* ...Judg 8:34
were on the other *s* Jordan ...Judg 10:8
east *s* of the land of Moab ...Judg 11:18
on the other *s* or Arnon ...Judg 11:18
the *s* of mount Ephraim ...Judg 19:1
on the north *s* of Beth-el ...Judg 21:19
the east *s* of the highway ...Judg 21:19
by the *s* of the gate ...1Sam 4:18

a coffer by the *s* thereof 1Sam 6:8
your enemies on every *s* 1Sam 12:11
garrison..on the other *s* 1Sam 14:1
sharp rock on the one *s* 1Sam 14:4
sharp rock on the other *s* 1Sam 14:4
all Israel, Be ye on one *s* 1Sam 14:40
son will be on the other *s* 1Sam 14:40
a mountain on the one *s* 1Sam 17:3
mountain on the other *s* 1Sam 17:3
three arrows on the *s* 1Sam 20:20
and Abner sat by Saul's *s* 1Sam 20:25
on this *s* of the mountain 1Sam 23:26
on that *s* of the mountain 1Sam 23:26
in the *s* of the cave 1Sam 24:3
Israel..on the other *s* 1Sam 31:7
on the other *s* Jordan 1Sam 31:7
on the one *s* of the pool 2Sam 2:13
on the other *s* of the pool 2Sam 2:13
way of the hill *s* behind 2Sam 13:34
Shimei went..on the hill's *s* 2Sam 16:13
on the right *s* of the city 2Sam 24:5
region on this *s* the river 1Kin 4:24
kings on this *s* the river 1Kin 4:24
had peace on all *s* round 1Kin 4:24
given me rest on every *s* 1Kin 5:4
lintel and *s* posts were a 1Kin 6:31
at the *s* of every addition 1Kin 7:30
on the right *s* of the house 1Kin 7:39
on the left *s* of the house 1Kin 7:39
on the right *s* of the house 1Kin 7:39
were stays on either *s* on 1Kin 10:19
water on the other *s* as red 2Kin 3:22
on the north *s* of the altar 2Kin 16:14
to the *s* of Lebanon 2Kin 19:23
the east *s* of the valley 1Chr 4:39
other *s* Jordan by Jericho 1Chr 6:78
the east *s* of Jordan were 1Chr 6:78
we, David, and on thy *s* 1Chr 12:18
given you rest on every *s* 1Chr 22:18
five on the right *s* and 2Chr 4:8
sea *s* in the land of Edom 2Chr 8:17
lions stood..on the one *s* 2Chr 9:19
the sea on this *s* Syria 2Chr 20:2
right *s* of the temple to 2Chr 23:10
to the left *s* of the temple 2Chr 23:10
west *s* of the city of David 2Chr 32:30
are on this *s* the river ....Ezra 4:10
portion on this *s* the river .....Ezra 4:16
were on this *s* the river ....Ezra 5:6
the governors on this *s* the ....Ezra 8:36
of the governor on this *s* ......Neh 3:7
that he hath on every *s*? ......Job 1:10
be ready at his *s* ....Job 18:12
wicked walk on every *s* ....Ps 12:8
mount Zion, on the *s* of ......Ps 48:2
hills rejoice on every *s* ....Ps 65:12
shall fall at thy *s* ....Ps 91:7
Lord who was on our *s* ....Ps 124:1
in the *s* of the north ....Is 14:13
to the *s* of Lebanon ....Is 37:24
be raised from the *s* of the ....Jer 6:22
of many, fear on every *s* ......Jer 20:10
their calamity from all *s* ....Jer 49:32
six pomegranates on a *s* ....Jer 52:23
their wings on their four *s* .....Ezek 1:8
face of a lion..right *s* ....Ezek 1:10
face of an ox on the left *s* .....Ezek 1:10
which covered on this *s* ....Ezek 1:23
which covered on that *s* ....Ezek 1:23
lie again on thy right *s* ....Ezek 4:6
thou shalt lie upon thy *s* ......Ezek 4:9
writer's inkhorn by his *s* ......Ezek 9:3
cherubim..on the right *s* ....Ezek 10:3
went upon their four *s* ....Ezek 10:11
come unto thee on every *s* ....Ezek 16:33
against thee on every *s* ....Ezek 23:22
sword upon her on every *s* ....Ezek 28:23
swallowed you..on every *s* .....Ezek 36:3
yourselves on every *s* ....Ezek 39:17
this *s*, and three on that *s* .....Ezek 40:10
this *s* and on that *s* ....Ezek 40:10
was one cubit on this *s* ....Ezek 40:12
was one cubit on that *s* ....Ezek 40:12
s, and six cubits on that *s* .....Ezek 40:12
this *s* and three on that *s* .....Ezek 40:21
this *s*, and on that *s* ....Ezek 40:34
s without as one goeth up .....Ezek 40:40
and on the other *s*, which .....Ezek 40:40
s..four tables on that *s* ....Ezek 40:41
by the *s* of the gate; eight .....Ezek 40:41
at the *s* of the north gate .....Ezek 40:44
at the *s* of the east gate ....Ezek 40:44
s..five cubits on that *s* ....Ezek 40:48
three cubits on that *s* ....Ezek 40:48
cubits broad on the one *s* ......Ezek 41:1
cubits broad on the other *s* ....Ezek 41:1
five cubits on the one *s* ....Ezek 41:2
five cubits on the other *s* ......Ezek 41:2
the *s* of the door were five ....Ezek 41:2
of every *s* chamber ....Ezek 41:5
the house on every *s* ....Ezek 41:5
s chambers were three ....Ezek 41:6
house for the *s* chambers ......Ezek 41:6
the foundations of the *s* ....Ezek 41:8
for the *s* chamber without .....Ezek 41:9
place of the *s* chambers ....Ezek 41:9
doors of the *s* chambers ....Ezek 41:11
galleries thereof on the one *s* ..Ezek 41:15
other *s*, an hundred cubits ....Ezek 41:15
palm tree on the one *s* ....Ezek 41:19
palm tree on the other *s* ......Ezek 41:19
palm trees on the one *s* ....Ezek 41:26
other *s*, on the sides of ....Ezek 41:26
s chambers of the house ....Ezek 41:26
was the entry on the east *s* ....Ezek 42:9
north *s*, five hundred reeds ....Ezek 42:17
turned..to the west *s* ....Ezek 42:19
measured it by the four *s* .....Ezek 42:20
the prince on the one *s* ....Ezek 45:7
other *s* of the oblation of .....Ezek 45:7
from the west *s* westward .....Ezek 45:7
from the east *s* eastward ......Ezek 45:7
was at the *s* of the gate ....Ezek 46:19
the right *s* of the house ....Ezek 47:1
at the south *s* of the altar .....Ezek 47:1
many trees on the one *s* ....Ezek 47:7
bank thereof, on this *s* ....Ezek 47:12
that *s*, shall grow all trees .....Ezek 47:12
And this is the north *s* ....Ezek 47:17
east *s* ye shall measure ....Ezek 47:18
And this is the east *s* ....Ezek 47:18
the south *s* southward ....Ezek 47:19
is the south *s* southward ......Ezek 47:19
The west *s* also shall be ....Ezek 47:20
This is the west *s* ....Ezek 47:20
are his *s* east and west ....Ezek 48:1
of Dan from the east *s* ....Ezek 48:2
west *s*, a portion for Asher ....Ezek 48:2
east *s* unto the west *s* ....Ezek 48:4
east *s* unto the west *s* ....Ezek 48:7
the north *s* four thousand .....Ezek 48:16
the south *s* four thousand .....Ezek 48:16
the east *s* four thousand ......Ezek 48:16
the west *s* four thousand ......Ezek 48:16
east *s* unto the west *s* ....Ezek 48:23
the city on the north *s* ....Ezek 48:30
the south *s* four thousand .....Ezek 48:33
up itself on the one *s* ....Dan 7:5
shall not stand on his *s* ....Dan 11:17
s of the bank of the river .....Dan 12:5
other on that *s* of the bank ....Dan 12:5
is by the *s* of the house ....Amos 6:10
stoodest on the other *s* ....Obad 11
into the *s* of the ship ....Jon 1:5
on the east *s* of the city ....Jon 4:5
the right *s* of the bowl ....Zech 4:3
the other upon the left *s* ......Zech 4:3
right *s* of the candlestick ......Zech 4:11
upon the left *s* thereof ....Zech 4:11
be cut off as on this *s* ....Zech 5:3
be cut off as on that *s* ....Zech 5:3
to depart unto the other *s* .....Matt 8:18
house and sat by the sea *s* ....Matt 13:1
seeds fell by the way *s* ....Matt 13:4
received seed by the way *s* ....Matt 13:19
disciples..to the other *s* ....Matt 16:5
he went..by the sea *s* ....Mark 2:13
some fell by the way *s* ....Mark 4:4
over unto the other *s* ....Mark 4:35
by ship unto the other *s* ....Mark 5:21
departed to the other *s* ....Mark 8:13
sat by the highway *s* ....Mark 10:46
on the right *s* of the altar .....Luke 1:11
Those by the way *s* are ....Luke 8:12
passed by on the other *s* ......Luke 10:31
sat by the way *s* begging ......Luke 18:35
on the other *s* of the sea .....John 6:22
other with him, on either *s* ....John 19:18
with a spear pierced his *s* .....John 19:34
them his hands and his *s* ......John 20:20
and thrust it into my *s* ....John 20:27
house is by the sea *s* ....Acts 10:6
smote Peter on the *s* and .....Acts 12:7
are troubled on every *s* 2Cor 4:8
on either *s* of the river ....Rev 22:2

SIDON (sī'dŏn)—*"hunting"*
Canaanite city 20 miles north of Tyre ....Gen 10:15,19
Israel's northern boundary ....Josh 19:28
Canaanites not expelled from ....Judg 1:31
Israelites oppressed by ...Judg 10:12
Gods of, entice Israelites .1Kin 11:5, 33
Judgments pronounced on ....Is 23:12
Israelites sold as slaves by.Joel 3:4-6
People from, hear Jesus ..Luke 6:17
Visited by Jesus ....Matt 15:21
Paul visits at ....Acts 27:3

tolerable for Tyre and *S* ......Matt 11:22
they about Tyre and *S* ....Mark 3:8
borders of Tyre and *S* ....Mark 7:24
unto Sarepta, a city of *S* ......Luke 4:26
been done in Tyre and *S* .....Luke 10:13
with them of Tyre and *S* ......Acts 12:20
See ZIDON

SIDONIANS—*of the tribe of Sidon*
Which Hermon the *S* call .....Deut 3:9
that is beside the *S* ....Josh 13:4
the Canaanites and the *S* ......Judg 3:3
timber like unto the *S* 1Kin 5:6

SIEGE—*a military blockade of a city*
Methods employed in:
Supplies cut off 2Kin 19:24
Ambushes laid ....Judg 9:34
Battering rams used .....Ezek 4:2
Arrows shot 2Kin 19:32
Suffering of:
Famine 2Kin 6:26-29
Pestilence ....Jer 21:6
Examples of:
Jericho ....Josh 6:2-20
Jerusalem 2Kin 24:10,11
See WAR

to employ them in the *s* ....Deut 20:19
hath nothing left in the *s* ......Deut 28:55
Israel laid *s* to Gibbethon 1Kin 15:27
laid *s* against Lachish 2Chr 32:9
in the *s* in Jerusalem? 2Chr 32:10
and will lay *s* against thee .....Is 29:3
flesh of his friend in the *s* .....Jer 19:9
thou shalt lay *s* against ....Ezek 4:3
toward the *s* of Jerusalem .....Ezek 4:7
ended the days of thy *s* ....Ezek 4:8
troops; he hath laid *s* ....Mic 5:1
Draw thee waters for the *s* ....Nah 3:14
the *s* both against Judah ......Zech 12:2

SIEVE—*a screen used to separate coarser material from finer particles*
nations with the *s* of vanity....Is 30:28

SIFT—*to separate with a sieve*
Used figuratively of:
God's judgment ....Amos 9:9
Satan's temptation ....Luke 22:31

s the nation with the sieve ....Is 30:28

SIGH—*to take a deep, audible breath*
[*also* SIGHED, SIGHEST, SIGHETH, SIGHING, SIGHS]
my *s* cometh before I eat .....Job 3:24

S

poor, for the *s* of the needy . . . Ps 12:5
and my years with *s* . . . . Ps 31:10
the *s* of the prisoner come . . . . Ps 79:11
the *s* thereof have I made . . . . . Is 21:2
all the merryhearted do *s* . . . . . Is 24:7
fainted in my *s*, and I find . . . . Jer 45:3
s, her virgins are afflicted . . . . . Lam 1:4
s and turneth backward . . . . Lam 1:8
They have heard that I *s* . . . . . . Lam 1:21
s are many, and my heart . . . . . Lam 1:22
foreheads of the men that *s* . . . Ezek 9:4
S..thou son of man, with . . . . . . Ezek 21:6
with bitterness *s* before . . . . Ezek 21:6
Say unto thee, Wherefore *s* . . . Ezek 21:7
looking up to heaven he *s* . . . . . Mark 7:34
he *s* deeply in his spirit . . . . Mark 8:12

SIGHT—*something seen; the ability to see; field of vision*

[*also* SIGHTS]
tree..is pleasant to the *s* . . . . . . Gen 2:9
hath found grace in thy *s* . . . . . Gen 19:19
not be grievous in thy *s* . . . . Gen 21:12
bury my dead out of my *s* . . . . . Gen 23:8
grace in the *s* of my lord . . . . . . Gen 33:8
grace in the *s* of my lord . . . . . . Gen 33:15
found grace in his *s* . . . . Gen 39:4
left in the *s* of my lord . . . . Gen 47:18
have found grace in thy *s* . . . . . Gen 47:29
aside and see this great *s* . . . . . . Ex 3:3
signs in the *s* of the people . . . . Ex 4:30
river, in the *s* of Pharaoh . . . . . Ex 7:20
in the *s* of his servants . . . . Ex 7:20
in the *s* of the Egyptians . . . . . . Ex 11:3
s of Pharaoh's servants . . . . Ex 11:3
and in the *s* of the people . . . . . Ex 11:3
that which is right in his *s* . . . . . Ex 15:26
in the *s* of all the people . . . . . . Ex 19:11
found grace in my *s* . . . . Ex 33:12
have found grace in thy *s* . . . . . Ex 33:13
I may find grace in thy *s* . . . . . . Ex 33:13
hast found grace in my *s* . . . . . . Ex 33:17
s of all the house of Israel . . . . Ex 40:38
in the *s* of the Lord . . . . Lev 10:19
in *s* be not deeper than the . . . Lev 13:4
in *s* lower then the skin . . . . Lev 13:20
in *s* deeper than the skin . . . . . . Lev 13:31
in *s* deeper than the skin . . . . . . Lev 13:34
which in *s* are lower than . . . . . Lev 14:37
rule..over him in thy *s* . . . . Lev 25:53
s of Aaron their father . . . . Num 3:4
have found favor in thy *s* . . . . . Num 11:15
and so we were in their *s* . . . . . Num 13:33
s of all the congregation . . . . . . Num 20:27
woman in the *s* of Moses . . . . . . Num 25:6
s of all the congregation . . . . . . Num 25:6
have found grace in thy *s* . . . . . Num 32:5
the *s* of all the Egyptians . . . . . Num 33:3
in the *s* of the nations . . . . Deut 4:6
brought thee out in his *s* . . . . . . Deut 4:37
in the *s* of the Lord to . . . . Deut 9:18
right in the *s* of the Lord . . . . . Deut 12:28
in the *s* of the Lord . . . . Deut 17:2
for the *s* of thine eyes . . . . Deut 28:34
in the *s* of all Israel . . . . Deut 31:7
in the *s* of all Israel . . . . Deut 34:12
in the *s* of all Israel . . . . Josh 3:7
he said in the *s* of Israel . . . . . . Josh 10:12
those great signs in our *s* . . . . . . Josh 24:17
evil in the *s* of the Lord . . . . . . Judg 2:11
again in the *s* of the Lord . . . . . Judg 3:12
evil in the *s* of the Lord . . . . . . Judg 3:12
evil in the *s* of the Lord . . . . . . Judg 6:1
of the Lord..out of his *s* . . . . . . Judg 6:21
evil..in the *s* of the Lord . . . . . . Judg 13:1
whose *s* I shall find grace . . . . . Ruth 2:2
find grace in thy *s* 1Sam 1:18
wast little in thine own *s* 1Sam 15:17
hath found favor in my *s* 1Sam 16:22
was accepted in the *s* of 1Sam 18:5
in the *s* of Saul's servants 1Sam 18:5
thou art good in my *s* 1Sam 29:9
will be base in mine own *s* 2Sam 6:22
yet a small thing in thy *s* 2Sam 7:19
wives in the *s* of this sun 2Sam 12:11
a couple of cakes in my *s* 2Sam 13:6
have found grace in thy *s* 2Sam 14:22
concubines in the *s* of all 2Sam 16:22
fail thee a man in my *s* 1Kin 8:25
evil in the *s* of the Lord 1Kin 11:6
do that is right in my *s* 1Kin 11:38
evil in the *s* of the Lord 1Kin 15:26
evil in the *s* of the Lord 1Kin 16:19
evil in the *s* of the Lord 1Kin 21:20
evil in the *s* of the Lord 1Kin 22:52
be precious in thy *s* 2Kin 1:13
evil in the *s* of the Lord 2Kin 3:2
evil in the *s* of the Lord 2Kin 8:18
right in the *s* of the Lord 2Kin 12:2
evil in the *s* of the Lord 2Kin 13:11
right in the *s* of the Lord 2Kin 14:3
evil in the *s* of the Lord 2Kin 14:24
evil in the *s* of the Lord 2Kin 15:9
right in the *s* of the Lord 2Kin 15:34
evil in the *s* of the Lord 2Kin 17:2
removed them out of his *s* 2Kin 17:18
Israel out of his *s* 2Kin 17:23
which was good in thy *s* 2Kin 20:3
in the *s* of the Lord 2Kin 21:6
evil in the *s* of the Lord 2Kin 21:16
right in the *s* of the Lord 2Kin 22:2
evil in the *s* of the Lord 2Kin 23:32
evil in the *s* of the Lord 2Kin 24:9
evil in the *s* of the Lord 1Chr 2:3
blood upon..earth in my *s* 1Chr 22:8
in the *s* of all Israel 1Chr 29:25
not fail thee a man in my *s* . . . 2Chr 6:16
right in the *s* of the Lord 2Chr 20:32
right in the *s* of the Lord 2Chr 24:2
right in the *s* of the Lord 2Chr 26:4
right in the *s* of the Lord 2Chr 27:2
right in the *s* of the Lord 2Chr 29:2
evil in the *s* of the Lord 2Chr 33:2
evil in the *s* of the Lord 2Chr 33:22
evil in the *s* of the Lord 2Chr 36:5
evil in the *s* of the Lord 2Chr 36:12
the *s* of the kings of Persia . . . . Ezra 9:9
mercy in the *s* of this man . . . . Neh 1:11
in the *s* of all the people . . . . . . Neh 8:5
s of all them that looked . . . . . . Esth 2:15
obtained favor in his *s* . . . . Esth 5:2
favor in thy *s*, O king . . . . Esth 7:3
heavens are not clean in his *s* . Job 15:15
I am an alien in their *s* . . . . Job 19:15
stars are not pure in his *s* . . . . . Job 25:5
down even at the *s* of him? . . . Job 41:9
shall not stand in thy *s* . . . . Ps 5:5
are far above out of his *s* . . . . . Ps 10:5
done this evil in thy *s* . . . . Ps 51:4
who may stand in thy *s* . . . . Ps 76:7
the heathen in our *s* . . . . Ps 79:10
in the *s* of the heathen . . . . Ps 98:2
Precious in the *s* of the Lord . . Ps 116:15
net is spread in the *s* of . . . . Prov 1:17
in the *s* of my mother . . . . Prov 4:3
man that is good in his *s* . . . . . . Eccl 2:26
hasty to go out of his *s* . . . . Eccl 8:3
prudent in their own *s*! . . . . Is 5:21
we been in thy *s*, O Lord . . . . . Is 26:17
wast precious in my *s* . . . . Is 43:4
abominations out of my *s* . . . . . Jer 4:1
have done evil in my *s* . . . . Jer 7:30
If it do evil in my *s*, that . . . . . . Jer 18:10
break the bottle in the *s* of . . . . Jer 19:10
had done right in my *s* . . . . Jer 34:15
done in Zion in your *s* . . . . Jer 51:24
out of man in their *s* . . . . Ezek 4:12
in the *s* of all that pass . . . . Ezek 5:14
up from the earth in my *s* . . . . . Ezek 10:19
remove by day in their *s* . . . . . . Ezek 12:3
another place in their *s* . . . . Ezek 12:3
thy stuff by day in their *s* . . . . . Ezek 12:4
go forth at even in their *s* . . . . . Ezek 12:4
In their *s* shalt thou bear . . . . . . Ezek 12:6
in the *s* of many women . . . . Ezek 16:41
whose *s* I brought them . . . . Ezek 20:14
be polluted in the *s* of the . . . . Ezek 20:22
in whose *s* I brought them . . . . Ezek 20:22
false divination in their *s* . . . . . . Ezek 21:23
s of all them that behold . . . . . . Ezek 28:18
loathe..in your own *s* . . . . Ezek 36:31
in the *s* of many nations . . . . . . Ezek 39:27
s thereof to the end of all . . . . . Dan 4:11
whoredoms out of her *s* . . . . Hos 2:2
and we shall live in his *s* . . . . . . Hos 6:2
they be hid from my *s* . . . . Amos 9:3
I am cast out of thy *s* . . . . Jon 2:4
good in the *s* of the Lord . . . . . Mal 2:17
their eyes received *s* . . . . Matt 20:34
Lord..I might receive my *s* . . . . Mark 10:51
he received his *s* . . . . Mark 10:52
great in the *s* of the Lord . . . . . Luke 1:15
that were blind he gave *s* . . . . . Luke 7:21
against heaven and in thy *s* . . . . Luke 15:21
Lord that I may receive my *s* . . Luke 18:41
he received his *s* . . . . Luke 18:43
fearful *s* and great signs . . . . Luke 21:11
he vanished out of their *s* . . . . . Luke 24:31
washed and I received *s* . . . . John 9:11
blind and received his *s* . . . . John 9:18
of him that..received his *s* . . . . . John 9:18
received him out of their *s* . . . . Acts 1:9
wisdom in the *s* of Pharaoh . . . Acts 7:10
not right in the *s* of God . . . . . . Acts 8:21
he might receive his *s* . . . . Acts 9:12
he received *s* forthwith . . . . Acts 9:18
Saul, receive thy *s* . . . . Acts 22:13
no flesh be justified in his *s* . . . Rom 3:20
honest in the *s* of all . . . . Rom 12:17
s of God speak we in Christ . . . 2Cor 2:17
walk by faith, not be *s* 2Cor 5:7
only in the *s* of the Lord 2Cor 8:21
the law in the *s* of God . . . . Gal 3:11
unreproveable in his *s* . . . . Col 1:22
s of God and our Father 1Thess 1:3
the *s* of God our Savior 1Tim 2:3
is not manifest in his *s* . . . . Heb 4:13
is well-pleasing in his *s* . . . . Heb 13:21
in the *s* of the Lord . . . . James 4:10
s of God of great price 1Pet 3:4
that are pleasing in his *s* 1John 3:22
in *s* like unto an emerald . . . . . Rev 4:3
to do in the *s* of the beast . . . . Rev 13:14

SIGN—*a remarkable or miraculous event given to indicate God's presence, favor, work or judgment*

Descriptive of:
Heavenly bodies . . . . Gen 1:14
Rainbow . . . . Gen 9:12-17
Circumcision . . . . Gen 17:11
Bloodshed . . . . Ex 12:13
God's wonders . . . . Ps 65:8
Covenant . . . . Rom 4:11
Miracles . . . . Deut 26:8
Memorial . . . . Num 16:38
Symbolic act . . . . Is 8:18
Witness . . . . Is 19:19, 20
Outward display . . . . John 4:48

Purposes of, to:
Authenticate a prophecy . Deut 13:1
1Sam 2:31, 34
Strengthen faith . . . . Judg 6:17
Is 7:11
Recall God's blessings . . . Josh 24:15-17
Confirm God's Word 2Kin 19:28, 29
Heb 2:4
Insure a promise 2Kin 20:5, 9-11
Confirm a prophecy 1Kin 13:3-5

Concerning Christ in His:
Nativity . . . . Luke 2:12
Ministry . . . . John 20:30
Acts 2:22
Resurrection . . . . Matt 12:38-40

Value of:
Discounted as such . . . . . . Matt 16:1-4
Demanded unnecessarily . John 6:30
Demonstrated by apostles. Acts 5:12
Displayed by Paul . . . . Rom 15:19

In prophecy, concerning:
Christ's first advent . . . . . . Is 7:11, 14
Matt 1:21-23
Second advent . . . . Matt 24:3, 30

Antichrist 2Thess 2:9
End .... Rev. 15:1

As assurance of:
Presence .... Ex 3:12
Judgment upon sin ...... Num 17:10
Goodness .... Ps 86:17

[*also* SIGNED, SIGNS]
to the voice of the first *s* .... Ex 4:8
the voice of the latter *s* .... Ex 4:8
believe also these two *s* .... Ex 4:9
s which he had commanded ... Ex 4:28
s and..wonders in the land .... Ex 7:3
my *s* which I have done .... Ex 10:2
s unto thee upon thine .... Ex 13:9
a *s* between me and the .... Ex 31:17
the *s* which I have showed .... Num 14:11
men; and they became a *s* .... Num 26:10
by *s* and by wonders, and ..... Deut 4:34
for a *s* upon thine hand .... Deut 6:8
s, and the wonders, and ...... Deut 7:19
for a *s* upon your hand .... Deut 11:18
the *s* or the wonder come ..... Deut 13:2
be upon thee for a *s* .... Deut 28:46
s, and those great miracles .... Deut 29:3
all the *s* and the wonders ..... Deut 34:11
may be a *s* among you .... Josh 4:6
there was an appointed *s* ...... Judg 20:38
when these *s* are come 1Sam 10:7
and this shall be a *s* unto 1Sam 14:10
be the *s* that the Lord 2Kin 20:8
and he gave him a *s* 2Chr 32:24
s and wonders upon .... Neh 9:10
set up their ensigns for *s* ...... Ps 74:4
How he had wrought his *s* .... Ps 78:43
s and wonder upon Egypt ..... Is 20:3
this shall be a *s* unto thee ..... Is 37:30
this shall be a *s* unto thee ..... Is 38:7
for an everlasting *s* that .... Is 55:13
s of fire in Beth-haccerem ..... Jer 6:1
not dismayed at the *s* of ...... Jer 10:2
land of Egypt with *s* .... Jer 32:21
be a *s* to the house of Israel... Ezek 4:3
s unto the house of Israel ..... Ezek 12:6
Say, I am your *s*; like as ...... Ezek 12:11
s between me and them .... Ezek 20:12
Ezekiel is unto you a *s* .... Ezek 24:24
shall he set up a *s* by it .... Ezek 39:15
it good to show the *s* .... Dan 4:2
s the writing, that it be .... Dan 6:8
king Darius *s* the writing ...... Dan 6:9
knew that the writing was *s* ... Dan 6:10
Hast thou not *s* a decree ...... Dan 6:12
the decree that thou hast *s* .... Dan 6:13
worketh *s* and wonders in ..... Dan 6:27
show great *s* and wonders ..... Matt 24:24
betrayed him gave them a *s* ... Matt 26:48
seeking of him a *s* from .... Mark 8:11
generation seek after a *s*? ..... Mark 8:12
no *s* be given unto this........ Mark 8:12
be the *s* when all these .... Mark 13:4
shall show *s* and wonders ..... Mark 13:22
And these *s* shall follow ...... Mark 16:17
confirming the word with *s* .... Mark 16:20
they made *s* to his father ...... Luke 1:62
a *s* which shall be spoken ..... Luke 2:34
generation; they seek a *s* ...... Luke 11:29
there shall no *s* be given ...... Luke 11:29
the *s* of Jonah the prophet .... Luke 11:29
what *s* will there be when ..... Luke 21:7
there shall be *s* in the sun ..... Luke 21:25
What *s* showest thou unto ..... John 2:18
s in the earth beneath .... Acts 2:19
wonders and *s* were done ..... Acts 2:43
that *s* and wonders may be .... Acts 4:30
showed wonders and *s* in ...... Acts 7:36
granted *s* and wonders to ..... Acts 14:3
s was Castor and Pollux .... Acts 28:11
the *s* of circumcision .... Rom 4:11
For the Jews require a *s* 1Cor 1:22
tongues are for a *s* 1Cor 14:22
Truly the *s* of an apostle 2Cor 12:12
in *s*, and wonders, and 2Cor 12:12

SIGNET—*a seal used to give personal authority to a document*

[*also* SIGNETS]
Thy *s* and thy bracelets .... Gen 38:18
like the engravings of a *s* ..... Ex 28:11
like the engravings of a *s* ..... Ex 28:36
of gold, graven as *s* are .... Ex 39:6
like the engravings of a *s* ..... Ex 39:14
to the engravings of a *s* .... Ex 39:30
s upon my right hand .... Jer 22:24
sealed it with his own *s* .... Dan 6:17
and with the *s* of his lords .... Dan 6:17
will make thee as a *s* .... Hag 2:23

SIGNIFY—*to show; imply; have significance*

Concerning men:
Peter's death .... John 21:19
Ritual performed .... Acts 21:26
Jewish scheme .... Acts 23:15

Concerning predicted events:
New dispensation .... Heb 9:8
Christ's death .... John 12:33
Christ's sufferings 1Pet 1:11
Gospel age .... Rev 1:1
Famine .... Acts 11:28
World's end .... Heb 12:27

[*also* SIGNIFICATION, SIGNIFIED, SIGNIFIETH, SIGNIFYING]
spake, *s* what death he .... John 18:32
s by the Spirit .... Acts 11:28
s the crimes laid against .... Acts 25:27
none of them is without *s* 1Cor 14:10
s the removing of those .... Heb 12:27

SIHON (sī'hŏn)—*"great; bold"*
Amorite king residing at Heshbon .... Num 21:26-30
Victorious over Moabites . Num 21:26-30
Ruler of five Midianite princes .... Josh 13:21
Refused Israel's request for passage .... Deut 2:26-28
Defeated by Israel .... Num 21:21-32
Territory of, assigned to Reuben and Gad ...... Num 32:1-38
Victory over, long celebrated .... Deut 31:4

as thou didst unto *S* king ..... Num 21:34
After he had slain *S*, the ...... Deut 1:4
thine hand *S* the Amorite ..... Deut 2:24
S king of Heshbon would ..... Deut 2:30
S came out against us .... Deut 2:32
as we did unto *S* king of ...... Deut 3:6
S the king of Heshbon .... Deut 29:7
the other side Jordan, *S* ...... Josh 2:10
S king of the Amorites .... Josh 12:2
S king of the Amorites .... Josh 13:10
of *S* king of Heshbon .... Josh 13:27
sent messengers unto *S* .... Judg 11:19
But *S* trusted not Israel .... Judg 11:20
S gathered all his people ...... Judg 11:20
of *S* king of the Amorites 1Kin 4:19
possessed the land of *S* .... Neh 9:22
S king of the Amorites .... Ps 135:11
S king of the Amorites .... Ps 136:19
flame from the midst of *S* ..... Jer 48:45

SIHOR, SHIHOR (sī'hŏr)—*"blackness"*
Name given to the Nile .. Is 23:3
Israel's southwestern border .... Josh 13:3; 1Chr 13:5

to drink the waters of *S*? ...... Jer 2:18

SILAS, SILVANUS (sī'läs, sĭl-vā'nŭs)—*"forest; woody; third; asked"*
Leader in the Jerusalem church .... Acts 15:22
Christian prophet .... Acts 15:32
Sent on a mission ...... Acts 15:22-35
Became Paul's companion. Acts 15:36-41
Roman citizen .... Acts 16:25-39
Paul commended his work at Corinth 2Cor 1:19
Called Silvanus 1Thess 1:1
Associated in Paul's writings 2Thess 1:1
Peter's helper 1Pet 5:12

they caught Paul and *S* .... Acts 16:19
consorted with Paul and *S* ..... Acts 17:4
S and Timothy abode .... Acts 17:14
S and Timothy were .... Acts 18:5

SILENCE—*the absence of sound; secrecy*

Kinds of:
Will of God .... Rev 8:1; 1Pet 2:15
Troubled .... Jer 20:9

Virtue of:
Suitable time for .... Eccl 3:7
Commanded 1Cor 14:34
Sign of prudence .... Prov 21:23
Sign of wisdom .... Prov 17:28

Forbidden to God's:
Watchmen .... Is 62:6
Messengers .... Acts 5:27-4
Praisers .... Ps 30:12

Considered as:
Blessing .... Zech 2:13
Curse 1Sam 2:9
Judgment .... Jer 8:14
Punishment .... Is 15:1

Of God:
Broken in judgment ..... Ps 50:3
Misunderstood by men ... Ps 50:21, 23

Of Christ:
Predicted .... Is 53:7
Before:
Sinners .... John 8:6
High priest .... Matt 26:62, 63
Pilate .... Matt 27:14
Herod .... Luke 23:9

[*also* SILENT]
O king; who said, Keep *s* ..... Judg 3:19
was *s*, and I heard a voice .... Job 4:16
that I kept *s*, and went not .... Job 31:34
night season and am not *s* ..... Ps 22:2
O Lord my rock; be not *s* ..... Ps 28:1
thou be *s* to me, I become .... Ps 28:1
let them be *s* in the grave ..... Ps 31:17
lying lips be put to *s* .... Ps 31:18
keep not *s*, O Lord, be not ... Ps 35:22
I was dumb with *s*, I held ..... Ps 39:2
Keep not thou *s*, O God .... Ps 83:1
soul had almost dwelt in *s* ..... Ps 94:17
that go down into *s* .... Ps 115:17
Keep *s* before me, O .... Is 41:1
Sit thou *s*, and get thee .... Is 47:5
I will not keep *s*, but will ..... Is 65:6
cities and let us be *s* .... Jer 8:14
the ground, and keep *s* .... Lam 2:10
sitteth along and keepeth *s* .... Lam 3:28
the prudent shall keep *s* ...... Amos 5:13
cast them forth with *s* .... Amos 8:3
let all the earth keep *s* .... Hab 2:20
put the Sadducees to *s* .... Matt 22:34
all the multitude kept *s* .... Acts 15:12
them, they kept the more *s* ... Acts 22:2
him keep *s* in the church 1Cor 14:28
woman learn in *s* with all 1Tim 2:11
the man, but to be in *s* 1Tim 2:12

SILK—*a cloth derived from the silkworm*

Sign of:
Luxury .... Ezek 16:10, 13
Wantonness .... Rev 18:12

clothing is *s* and purple .... Prov 31:22

SILLA (sĭl'ä)—*"exalting"*
Quarter of suburb of Jerusalem 2Kin 12:20

SILLY—*foolish; simple; idle*
envy slayeth the *s* one .... Job 5:2
Ephraim..is like a *s* dove ...... Hos 7:11
captive *s* women laden with ... 2Tim 3:6

SILOAM, SILOAH (sĭ-lō'ăm, sĭ-lō'äh)—*"sent"*
Pool at Jerusalem .... Neh 3:15
Tower of, kills 18 people . Luke 13:4
Blind man washes in ..... John 9:1-11

SILVANUS—*See* SILAS

SILVER—*a precious metal*

Features concerning:

Mined from the earth....Job 28:1
Melted by fire..........Ezek 22:22
Sign of wealth..........Gen 13:2
Used as money..........Gen 23:15, 16
Article of commerce.....Ezek 27:12
Given as presents........1Kin 10:25
Used in:
Tabernacle............Ex 38:19
Temple...............2Kin 12:13
Christ sold for 30 pieces of..................Zech 11:12; Matt 26:15
Peter devoid of.........Acts 3:6

Figurative of:

God's Word............Ps 12:6
God's people............Zech 13:9
Understanding..........Prov 3:13, 14
Degeneration..........Is 1:22
Rejection...............Jer 6:30

a thousand pieces of *s*........Gen 20:16
flocks, and herds, and *s*.......Gen 24:35
for twenty pieces of *s*.........Gen 37:28
s cup, in the sack's mouth.....Gen 44:2
three hundred pieces of *s*.....Gen 45:22
in her house, jewels of *s*......Ex 3:22
the Egyptians jewels of *s*......Ex 12:35
master thirty shekels of *s*......Ex 21:32
forty sockets of *s* under.......Ex 26:19
and their sockets of *s*.........Ex 26:25
their fillets shall be of *s*.......Ex 27:10
shall be filleted with *s*........Ex 27:17
their hooks shall be of *s*......Ex 27:17
the Lord; gold, and *s*, and....Ex 35:5
to work in gold, and in *s*......Ex 35:32
their forty sockets of *s*.........Ex 36:26
for them four sockets of *s*.....Ex 36:36
and their fillets of *s*...........Ex 38:11
and their fillets of *s*...........Ex 38:17
of their chapiters of *s*.........Ex 38:17
court were filleted with *s*......Ex 38:17
the *s* of them that were.......Ex 38:25
estimation by shekels of *s*.....Lev 5:15
the male five shekels of *s*.....Lev 27:6
female..three shekels of *s*.....Lev 27:6
And his offering was one *s*....Num 7:13
his offering one *s* charger.....Num 7:19
s bowl of seventy shekels.....Num 7:19
offering was one *s* charger....Num 7:25
one *s* bowl of seventy.........Num 7:25
His offering was one *s*........Num 7:31
one *s* bowl of seventy.........Num 7:31
offering was one *s* charger....Num 7:37
one *s* bowl of seventy.........Num 7:37
His offering was one *s*........Num 7:43
a *s* bowl of seventy shekels....Num 7:43
His offering was one *s*........Num 7:49
one *s* bowl of seventy.........Num 7:49
His offering was one *s*........Num 7:55
one *s* bowl of seventy.........Num 7:55
offering was one *s* charger....Num 7:61
s bowl of seventy shekels.....Num 7:61
His offering was one *s*........Num 7:67
s bowl of seventy shekels.....Num 7:67
His offering was one *s*........Num 7:73
one *s* bowl of seventy shekels.Num 7:73
His offering was one *s*........Num 7:79
s bowl of seventy shekels.....Num 7:79
chargers of *s*, twelve *s*........Num 7:84
Each charger of *s* weighing....Num 7:85
s vessels weighed two.........Num 7:85
give me his house full of *s*....Num 22:18
Only the gold, and the *s*......Num 31:22
thou shalt not desire the *s*.....Deut 7:25
multiply to himself *s* and......Deut 17:17
father fifty shekels of *s*........Deut 22:29
But all the *s*, and gold, and...Josh 6:19
two hundred shekels of *s*......Josh 7:21
midst of my tent, and the *s*...Josh 7:21
and the *s*, and the garment....Josh 7:24
for a hundred pieces of *s*......Josh 24:32
eleven hundred shekels of *s*...Judg 17:2
mine ears, behold, the *s* is....Judg 17:2
dedicated the *s* unto the......Judg 17:3
give thee ten shekels of *s*.....Judg 17:10
to him for a piece of *s*........1Sam 2:36
brought..him vessels of *s*......2Sam 8:10
thee ten shekels of *s*..........2Sam 18:11
We will have no *s* nor gold....2Sam 21:4
even the *s*, and the gold......1Kin 7:51
bringing gold, and *s*, ivory....1Kin 10:22
s to be in Jerusalem as........1Kin 10:27
the house of the Lord, *s*......1Kin 15:15
unto thee a present of *s*.......1Kin 15:19
Thy *s* and thy gold is mine....1Kin 20:3
for my *s*, and for my gold.....1Kin 20:7
with him ten talents of *s*......2Kin 5:5
bound two talents of *s* in......2Kin 5:23
for fourscore pieces of *s*......2Kin 6:25
dung for five pieces of *s*......2Kin 6:25
of the Lord bowls of *s*........2Kin 12:13
of gold, or vessels of *s*........2Kin 12:13
a thousand talents of *s*........2Kin 15:19
Ahaz took the *s* and gold......2Kin 16:8
Hezekiah gave him all the *s*...2Kin 18:15
may sum the *s* which is.......2Kin 22:4
Jehoiakim gave the *s* and.....2Kin 23:35
exacted the *s* and the gold....2Kin 23:35
of vessels of gold and *s*.......1Chr 18:10
sent a thousand talents of *s*...1Chr 19:6
Of the gold, the *s*, and the....1Chr 22:16
of all manner of service; *s*.....1Chr 28:14
for all instruments of *s* by.....1Chr 28:14
s for the tables of *s*...........1Chr 28:16
every basin; and likewise *s*....1Chr 28:17
weight for every basin of *s*....1Chr 28:17
and the *s* for things of *s*.......1Chr 29:2
talents of refined *s*...........1Chr 29:4
of *s* ten thousand talents......1Chr 29:7
s and gold..as plenteous.......2Chr 1:15
to work in gold, and in *s*......2Chr 2:7
the *s*, and the gold, and.......2Chr 5:1
pure gold: none were of *s*.....2Chr 9:20
vessels of *s*, and vessels of....2Chr 9:24
dedicated, *s*, and gold, and....2Chr 15:18
behold, I have sent thee *s*.....2Chr 16:3
gave them great gifts of *s*.....2Chr 21:3
for a hundred talents of *s*.....2Chr 25:6
a hundred talents of *s*.........2Chr 27:5
in a hundred talents of *s*......2Chr 36:3
his place help him with *s*......Ezra 1:4
a thousand chargers of *s*......Ezra 1:9
vessels of gold and of *s*.......Ezra 1:11
vessels also of gold and *s*.....Ezra 5:14
to carry the *s* and gold........Ezra 7:15
with the rest of the *s* and.....Ezra 7:18
weighed unto them the *s*.......Ezra 8:25
and fifty talents of *s*..........Ezra 8:26
and *s* vessels a hundred.......Ezra 8:26
weight of the *s*, and the.......Ezra 8:30
beside forty shekels of *s*......Neh 5:15
two thousand pound of *s*.......Neh 7:72
to *s* rings and pillars of.......Esth 1:6
the beds were of gold and *s*...Esth 1:6
s is given to thee, the.........Esth 3:11
filled their houses with *s*......Job 3:15
Though he heap up *s* as........Job 27:16
s be weighed for the price.....Job 28:15
thou hast tried us, as *s* is.....Ps 66:10
of a dove covered with *s*......Ps 68:13
them forth also with *s*.........Ps 105:37
thousands of gold and *s*........Ps 119:72
If thou seekest her as *s*.......Prov 2:4
my instruction, and not *s*......Prov 8:10
of the just is as choice *s*......Prov 10:20
fining pot is for *s*, and the....Prov 17:3
away the dross from the *s*.....Prov 25:4
a potsherd covered with *s*.....Prov 26:23
I gathered me also *s* and......Eccl 2:8
He that loveth *s* shall not.....Eccl 5:10
not be satisfied with *s*.........Eccl 5:10
of gold with studs of *s*........Song 1:11
upon her a palace of *s*.........Song 8:9
Their land also is full of *s*.....Is 2:7
shall cast his idols of *s*.......Is 2:20
of thy graven images of *s*.....Is 30:22
the *s*, and the gold, and the...Is 39:2
and weigh *s* in the balance....Is 46:6
their *s* and their gold with.....Is 60:9
They deck it with *s* and.......Jer 10:4
seventeen shekels of *s*.........Jer 32:9
cast their *s* in the streets......Ezek 7:19
their *s* and their gold shall....Ezek 7:19
of my gold and of my *s*........Ezek 16:17
they gather *s*, and brass.......Ezek 22:20
and *s* into thy treasures.......Ezek 28:4
breast and his arms of *s*.......Dan 2:32
brass, the clay, the *s*, and.....Dan 2:45
the gods of gold, and of *s*.....Dan 5:4
their precious vessels of *s*.....Dan 11:8
treasures of gold and of *s*.....Dan 11:43
multiplied her *s* and gold......Hos 2:8
their *s* and their gold have....Hos 8:4
molten images of their *s*......Hos 13:2
have taken my *s* and my......Joel 3:5
sold the righteous for *s*.......Amos 2:6
Take ye the spoil of *s*, take...Nah 2:9
laid over with gold and *s*......Hab 2:19
all they that bear *s* are cut....Zeph 1:11
s is mine, and the gold is.....Hag 2:8
Then take *s* and gold, and....Zech 6:11
heaped up *s* as the dust.......Zech 9:3
I took the thirty pieces of *s*...Zech 11:13
a refiner and purifier of *s*.....Mal 3:3
purge them as gold and *s*.....Mal 3:3
gold, nor *s*, nor brass in......Matt 10:9
the thirty pieces of *s* to.......Matt 27:3
the chief priests took the *s*....Matt 27:6
woman having ten pieces..*s*....Luke 15:8
Godhead..unto gold, or *s*.....Acts 17:29
make *s* shrines for Diana......Acts 19:24
this foundation gold, *s*........1Cor 3:12
vessels of gold and of *s*.......2Tim 2:20
Your gold and *s* is cankered...James 5:3
corruptible things, as *s* and....1Pet 1:18
and idols of gold, and *s*.......Rev 9:20
merchandise of gold, and *s*....Rev 18:12

SILVERLINGS—*silver shekels*

vines at a thousand *s*.........Is 7:23

SILVERSMITH—*a worker with silver*

Demetrius, an Ephesian..Acts 19:24-41

SIMEON (sĭm'ĕ-ŭn)—*"hearing"*

1. Son of Jacob by Leah...Gen 29:33
   Joined Levi in massacre of Shechemites.......Gen 34:25-31
   Held as hostage by Joseph...............Gen 42:24, 36
   Denounced by Jacob....Gen 34:30
   Sons of................Gen 46:10
2. Tribe of, descendants of Jacob's son...........Gen 46:10
   Number of, at first census...............Num 1:23
   Number of, at second census...............Num 26:12-14
   Position of, on Mt. Gerizim..............Deut 27:12
   Inheritance of, within Judah's..............Josh 19:1-9
   With Judah, fought Canaanites...........Judg 1:1, 3, 17
   Victory over Ham and Amalekites...........1Chr 4:24-43
   Recognized in Ezekiel's vision................Ezek 48:24-33
3. Ancestor of Christ......Luke 3:30
4. Righteous man; blessed the child Jesus........Luke 2:25-35
5. Christian prophet at Antioch.............Acts 13:1
6. Simon Peter............Acts 15:14

S, and Levi, and Judah.......Gen 35:23
he brought *S* out unto them...Gen 43:23
Reuben and *S*, they shall be...Gen 48:5
Reuben, *S*, Levi, and Judah...Ex 1:2
And the sons of *S*; Jemuel....Ex 6:15
these are the families of *S*.....Ex 6:15
Of *S*; Shelumiel the son of....Num 1:6
shall be the tribe of *S*.........Num 2:12
captain of the children of *S*...Num 2:12
tribe of the children of *S*......Num 10:19

tribe of the children of *S* ......Num 34:20
and out of the tribe of *S* ......Josh 21:4
tribe of the children of *S* ......Josh 21:9
Reuben, *S*, Levi, and Judah ...1Chr 2:1
tribe of the children of *S* 1Chr 6:65
and Manasseh..out of *S* 2Chr 15:9
and *S*, even unto Naphtali 2Chr 34:6
the tribe of *S* were sealed .....Rev 7:7

SIMEONITES—*descendants of Simeon*
chief house among the *S* ......Num 25:14
are the families of the *S* ......Num 26:14
of the *S*, Shephatiah the 1Chr 27:16

SIMILITUDE—*likeness of two things*

Expressive of:
Physical 2Chr 4:3
Typical ....Rom 5:14
Literary (simile) ....Ps 144:12
Spiritual ....James 3:9

Expressed by:
"Like" ....James 1:6
"As" 1Pet 2:5
"Likeness" ....Rom 6:5
"Liken" ....Matt 7:24, 26

[*also* SIMILITUDES]
the *s* of the Lord shall he .....Num 12:8
the words, but saw no *s* ....Deut 4:12
ye saw no manner of *s* on .....Deut 4:15
the *s* of any figure, the ....Deut 4:16
their glory into the *s* of ....Ps 106:20
s of the sons of men touched ..Dan 10:16
and used *s*, by the ministry ....Hos 12:10
the *s* of Melchisedec there ....Heb 7:15

SIMON (sī'mŭn)—*"hearing"*
1. Simon Peter ....Matt 4:18
   See PETER
2. One of the Twelve; called "the Canaanite".Matt 10:4
3. One of Jesus' brothers ..Matt 13:55
4. The leper ....Matt 26:6
5. Pharisee ....Luke 7:36-40
6. Man of Cyrene ....Matt 27:32
7. Father of Judas Iscariot. .John 6:71
8. Sorcerer ....Acts 8:9-24
9. Tanner in Joppa ....Acts 9:43

[*also* SIMON'S]
S, who is called Peter ....Matt 10:2
S Peter answered and said ....Matt 16:16
Blessed art thou, *S* Bar-jona ..Matt 16:17
What thinkest thou, *S*? ....Matt 17:25
he saw *S* and Andrew his .....Mark 1:16
S wife's mother lay sick ....Mark 1:30
S and they that were with .....Mark 1:36
and *S* the Canaanite ....Mark 3:18
Joses, and of Judah, and *S*? ...Mark 6:3
in the house of *S* the leper ....Mark 14:3
compel one *S* a Cyrenian .....Mark 15:21
and entered into *S* house ......Luke 4:38
of the ships, which was *S* .....Luke 5:3
said unto *S*, Launch out ......Luke 5:4
When *S* Peter saw it, he ......Luke 5:8
which were partners with *S* ....Luke 5:10
Jesus said unto *S*, Fear ....Luke 5:10
of Alphaeus, and *S* called .....Luke 6:15
S answered and said, I ....Luke 7:43
S, *S*, behold, Satan hath ......Luke 22:31
they laid hold upon one *S* .....Luke 23:26
and hath appeared to *S* ....Luke 24:34
was Andrew, *S* Peter's ....John 1:40
Thou art *S* the son of Jona ....John 1:42
S Peter answered him, Lord ...John 6:68
Judas Iscariot, *S* son ....John 12:4
of Judas Iscariot, *S* son ....John 13:2
Then cometh he to *S* Peter ....John 13:6
S Peter therefore beckoned ....John 13:24
S Peter said unto him, Lord ...John 13:36
S Peter followed Jesus, and ...John 18:15
and cometh to *S* Peter ....John 20:2
There were together *S* Peter ...John 21:2
when *S* Peter heard that it ....John 21:7
Jesus saith to *S* Peter, *S* ......John 21:15
S Zelotes, and Judas the ......Acts 1:13
for one *S*, whose surname .....Acts 10:5
made inquiry for *S* house .....Acts 10:17
S, which was surnamed Peter ..Acts 10:18
hither *S*, whose surname is ....Acts 10:32
house of one *S* a tanner by ....Acts 10:32
S Peter, a servant and an 2Pet 1:1

SIMONY—*using religious offices as means of profit*
Simon Magus guilty of ...Acts 8:18, 19
Peter's condemnation of. .Acts 8:20-23

SIMPLE—*foolish; those who do not possess wisdom or knowledge*
Enlightened by God's Word ....Ps 119:105; Ps 19:7
Able to understand ......Prov 1:4
Receptive of correction ..Prov 19:25
Void of understanding ...Prov 7:7
Easily tempted ....Prov 9:4, 16
Gullible ....Prov 14:15
Inherit folly ....Prov 14:18
Unmindful of danger ....Prov 22:3
The Lord preserves ......Ps 116:6

understanding unto the *s* ......Ps 119:130
How long, ye *s* ones, will ye ..Prov 1:22
the turning away of the *s* .....Prov 1:32
O ye *s*, understand wisdom ....Prov 8:5
Whoso is *s*, let him turn in ....Prov 9:4
she is *s*, and knoweth ....Prov 9:13
is punished, the *s* is made .....Prov 21:11
the *s* pass on, and are ....Prov 27:12
and for him that is *s* ....Ezek 45:20
deceive the hearts of the *s* ....Rom 16:18
is good, and *s* concerning .....Rom 16:19

SIMPLICITY—*purity; lack of ostentation; foolishness*

Necessary in:
Prayer ....Matt 6:5-15
Dress 1Pet 3:3-5
Conduct 2Cor 1:12
Giving ....Rom 12:8
Preaching 1Thess 2:3-7

Purposes of, to:
Avoid outward display ...Matt 6:1-4
Defeat Satan 2Cor 11:3, 4
Remain pure in an evil world ....Rom 16:19

and they went in their *s* 2Sam 15:11

SIMRI (sĭm'rī)—*"Jehovah is watching"*—*gatekeeper of the tabernacle in David's day*
had sons; *S* the chief 1Chr 26:10

SIN—*thoughts or behavior which are contrary to the glory or character of God; to commit an offense against God's laws*

Defined as:
Transgression 1John 3:4
Unrighteousness 1John 5:17
Omission of known duty .James 4:17
Not from faith ....Rom 14:23
Thought of foolishness ...Prov 24:9

Sources of, in:
Satan ....John 8:44
Man's heart ....Matt 15:19, 20
Lust ....James 1:15
Adam's transgression ....Rom 5:12, 16
Natural birth ....Ps 51:5

Kinds of:
National ....Prov 14:34
Personal ....Josh 7:20
Secret ....Ps 90:8
Presumptuous ....Ps 19:13
Open 1Tim 5:24
Shameless ....Is 3:9
Youthful ....Ps 25:7
Public 2Sam 24:10, 17
Unforgiveable ....Matt 12:21, 32; John 8:24
Of ignorance ....Lev 4:2
Willfully ....Heb 10:26

Consequences of, among the unregenerate:
Blindness ....John 9:41
Servitude ....John 8:34
Irreconcilable 1Tim 3:1-7
Death ....Rom 6:23

God's attitude toward:
Withholds men from .....Gen 20:6
Punishes for ....Ex 32:34
Provides a fountain for...Zech 13:1
Blots out ....Is 44:22
Casts away ....Mic 7:19
Forgives ....Ex 34:7
Remembers no more ....Jer 31:34

Christ's relationship to:
Free of 1John 3:5
Knew no 2Cor 5:21
Makes men conscious of. .John 15:22, 24
Died for our 1Cor 15:3
As an offering for ....Is 53:10; Heb 9:28
Substitutionary ....Is 53:5, 6; Matt 26:28
Takes it away ....John 1:29
Saves His people from ...Matt 1:21
Has power to forgive ....Matt 9:6
Makes reconciliation for. .Heb 2:17
Purges our ....Heb 1:3
Cleanses us from 1John 1:7, 9
Washes us from ....Rev 1:5

Regenerate must:
Acknowledge ....Ps 32:5
Confess ....Ps 51:3, 4
Be sorry for ....Ps 38:18
Not serve ....Rom 6:6
Not obey ....Rom 6:6, 12
Subdue ....Rom 6:14-22
Lay aside ....Heb 12:1
Resist ....Heb 12:4
Keep from ....Ps 19:13

Helps against:
Use God's Word ....Ps 119:11
Guard the tongue ....Ps 39:1
Walk in the Spirit ....Rom 8:1-14
Avoid evil companions ...1Tim 5:22
Confess to the Lord 1John 1:8, 9
Exercise love 1Pet 4:8
Go to the Advocate 1John 2:1

[*also* SINFUL, SINNED, SINNEST, SINNETH, SINNING, SINS]
doest not well, *s* lieth at ......Gen 4:7
and on my kingdom a great *s*? .Gen 20:9
and *s* against God? ....Gen 39:9
of thy brethren, and their *s* ...Gen 50:17
unto them, I have *s* this.......Ex 9:27
s yet more, and hardened .....Ex 9:34
I have *s* against the Lord .....Ex 10:16
forgive..my *s* only this once ...Ex 10:17
they make thee *s* against ......Ex 23:33
every day a bullock for a *s* ....Ex 29:36
so great a *s* upon them? ......Ex 32:21
people, Ye have *s* a great *s* ...Ex 32:30
an atonement for your *s* ......Ex 32:30
thou wilt forgive their *s* ....Ex 32:32
Whosoever hath *s* against me ..Ex 32:33
our iniquity and our *s*.........Ex 34:9
priest..is anointed do *s* ....Lev 4:3
according to the *s* of the ......Lev 4:3
for his *s*, which he hath *s* .....Lev 4:3
the Lord for a *s* offering ......Lev 4:3
Israel *s* through ignorance .....Lev 4:13
When the *s*, which they have *s*.Lev 4:14
a young bullock for the *s* .....Lev 4:14
a *s* offering for the ....Lev 4:21
if his *s*, wherein he hath *s*.....Lev 4:23
before the Lord: it is a *s*......Lev 4:24
for him as concerning his *s* ....Lev 4:26
Or if his *s*, which he hath *s* ...Lev 4:28
for his *s* which he hath *s* ......Lev 4:28
slay the *s* offering in the ......Lev 4:29
the head of the *s* offering .....Lev 4:33
slay it for a *s* offering in ......Lev 4:33
an atonement for his *s* ....Lev 4:35
a soul *s*, and hear the voice ...Lev 5:1
shall confess that he hath *s* ....Lev 5:5
for his *s* which he hath *s* ......Lev 5:6
the goats, for a *s* offering .....Lev 5:6

for him concerning his *s* . . . . . .Lev 5:6
which is for the *s* offering . . . . .Lev 5:8
the blood of the *s* offering . . . .Lev 5:9
altar: it is a *s* offering . . . . .Lev 5:9
for his *s* which he hath *s* . . . . . .Lev 5:10
that *s* shall bring for his . . . . . . .Lev 5:11
fine flour for a *s* offering . . . . . .Lev 5:11
for it is a *s* offering . . . . .Lev 5:11
touching his *s* that he hath . . . .Lev 5:13
And if a soul *s*, and commit . . .Lev 5:17
If a soul *s*, and commit a . . . . .Lev 6:2
these that a man doeth, *s* . . . . .Lev 6:3
because he hath *s*, and is . . . . .Lev 6:4
is the law of the *s* offering . . . .Lev 6:25
the *s* offering be killed . . . . .Lev 6:25
no *s* offering, whereof any . . . .Lev 6:30
of the *s* offering, and of . . . . . . .Lev 7:37
bullock for the *s* offering . . . . . .Lev 8:2
of the bullock for the *s* . . . . . . .Lev 8:14
a kid of the goats for a *s* . . . . . .Lev 9:3
and slew the calf of the *s* . . . . .Lev 9:8
was the *s* offering for the . . . . .Lev 9:15
slew it, and offered it for *s* . . . .Lev 9:15
the goat of the *s* offering . . . . . .Lev 10:16
offered their *s* offering . . . . .Lev 10:19
the other for a *s* offering . . . . . .Lev 12:8
he shall kill the *s* offering . . . . .Lev 14:13
s offering is the priest's . . . . . . .Lev 14:13
and the one shall be a *s* . . . . . . .Lev 14:22
the one for a *s* offering . . . . . . .Lev 15:15
a young bullock for a *s* . . . . . . .Lev 16:3
offer his bullock of the *s* . . . . . .Lev 16:6
bring the bullock of the *s* . . . . .Lev 16:11
kill the bullock of the *s* . . . . . . .Lev 16:11
transgressions in all their *s* . . . .Lev 16:16
fat of the *s* offering shall . . . . . .Lev 16:25
And the bullock for the *s* . . . . .Lev 16:27
and the goat for the *s* . . . . .Lev 16:27
all your *s* before the Lord . . . . . .Lev 16:30
his *s* which he hath done . . . . . .Lev 19:22
they shall bear their *s* . . . . .Lev 20:20
lest they bear *s* for it . . . . .Lev 22:9
his God shall bear his *s* . . . . . . .Lev 24:15
seven times more for your *s* . . .Lev 26:18
yet seven times for your *s* . . . . .Lev 26:24
commit any *s* that men . . . . .Num 5:6
the one for a *s* offering . . . . . . .Num 6:11
for him, for that he *s* by . . . . . .Num 6:11
shall offer his *s* offering . . . . . .Num 6:16
the kids of the goats for *s* . . . . .Num 7:87
shalt offer the one for a *s* . . . . .Num 8:12
lay not the *s* upon us . . . . .Num 12:11
hath promised: for we have *s* . .Num 14:40
kid of the goats for a *s* . . . . . . .Num 15:24
if any soul *s* through . . . . .Num 15:27
of the first year for a *s* . . . . .Num 15:27
the soul that *s* ignorantly . . . . . .Num 15:28
s by ignorance before the . . . . .Num 15:28
shall one man *s*, and wilt . . . . .Num 16:22
every *s* offering of theirs . . . . . .Num 18:9
shall bear no *s* by reason . . . . . .Num 18:32
heifer of purification for *s* . . . . .Num 19:17
I have *s*; for I knew not . . . . . .Num 22:34
kid of the goats for a *s* . . . . . . .Num 28:15
beside the *s* offering of . . . . . . .Num 29:11
one goat for a *s* offering . . . . . .Num 29:22
an increase of *s* men, to . . . . . .Num 32:14
sure your *s* will find you . . . . . .Num 32:23
have *s* against the Lord . . . . . . .Deut 1:41
of all your *s* which ye *s* . . . . . . .Deut 9:18
took your *s*, the calf which . . . .Deut 9:21
thee, and it be *s* unto thee . . . .Deut 15:9
for any *s*, in any *s* that he *s* . . .Deut 19:15
if a man have committed a *s* . .Deut 21:22
and it would be *s* in thee . . . . .Deut 23:21
not cause the land to *s* . . . . .Deut 24:4
put to death for his own *s* . . . . .Deut 24:16
Israel hath *s*, and they . . . . .Josh 7:11
transgressions nor your *s* . . . . . .Josh 24:19
saying, We have *s* against . . . . .Judg 10:10
I have not *s* against thee . . . . . .Judg 11:27
the *s* of the young men was . . .1Sam 2:17
one man *s* against another 1Sam 2:25
but if a man *s* against the 1Sam 2:25
We have *s* against the Lord . . .1Sam 7:6

God forbid that I should *s* 1Sam 12:23
people *s* against the Lord 1Sam 14:33
see wherein this *s* hath 1Sam 14:38
rebellion is as the *s* of 1Sam 15:23
said unto Samuel, I have *s* 1Sam 15:24
I pray thee, pardon my *s* 1Sam 15:25
Let not the king *s* against 1Sam 19:4
he hath not *s* against thee 1Sam 19:4
what is my *s* before thy 1Sam 20:1
Then said Saul, I have *s* 1Sam 26:21
Nathan, I have *s* against 2Sam 12:13
Lord..hath put away thy *s* 2Sam 12:13
I have *s* greatly in that I 2Sam 24:10
they have *s* against thee 1Kin 8:33
forgive the *s* of thy people 1Kin 8:34
and forgive the *s* of thy 1Kin 8:36
If they *s* against thee 1Kin 8:46
(for there is no man..*s* not) . . .1Kin 8:46
We have *s*, and have done 1Kin 8:47
And this thing became a *s* 1Kin 12:30
s of Jeroboam, who did *s* 1Kin 14:16
and who made Israel to *s* 1Kin 14:16
he walked in all the *s* of 1Kin 15:3
of his father, and in his *s* 1Kin 15:26
he made Israel to *s* 1Kin 15:26
s of Jeroboam which he *s* 1Kin 15:30
which he made Israel *s* 1Kin 15:30
Jeroboam, and in his *s* 1Kin 15:34
he made Israel to *s* 1Kin 15:34
me to anger with their *s* 1Kin 16:2
s of Baasha, and the *s* of Elah .1Kin 16:13
they made Israel to *s* 1Kin 16:13
his *s* which he *s* in doing 1Kin 16:19
of Jeroboam, and in his *s* 1Kin 16:19
to make Israel to *s* 1Kin 16:19
of Jeroboam..and in his *s* 1Kin 16:26
he made Israel to *s* 1Kin 16:26
walk in the *s* of Jeroboam 1Kin 16:31
and made Israel to *s* 1Kin 21:22
he cleaved unto the *s* of 2Kin 3:3
which made Israel to *s* 2Kin 3:3
not from the *s* of Jeroboam . . .2Kin 10:31
which made Israel to *s* 2Kin 10:31
s of the house of Jeroboam . . .2Kin 13:6
who made Israel *s* 2Kin 13:11
from all the *s* of Jeroboam 2Kin 14:24
who made Israel to *s* 2Kin 14:24
Israel had *s* against the 2Kin 17:7
and made them *s* a great *s* 2Kin 17:21
in all the *s* of Jeroboam 2Kin 17:22
beside his *s* wherewith he 2Kin 21:16
he made Judah to *s* 2Kin 21:16
who made Israel to *s* 2Kin 23:15
unto God, I have *s* greatly 1Chr 21:8
If a man *s* against his 2Chr 6:22
because they have *s* against . . .2Chr 6:24
and turn from their *s* 2Chr 6:26
If they *s* against thee 2Chr 6:36
thy people which have *s* 2Chr 6:39
man shall die for his own *s* 2Chr 25:4
s against the Lord your God?. .2Chr 28:10
for the *s* offering before 2Chr 29:23
all his *s*, and his trespass 2Chr 33:19
and for a *s* offering for all . . . .Ezra 6:17
and confess the *s* of the . . . . . . .Neh 1:6
we have *s* against thee . . . . .Neh 1:6
my father's house have *s* . . . . . .Neh 1:6
let not their *s* be blotted . . . . . .Neh 4:5
over us because of our *s* . . . . . .Neh 9:37
s offerings to make an . . . . .Neh 10:33
Solomon king of Israel *s* . . . . . .Neh 13:26
outlandish women cause to *s* . .Neh 13:26
may be that my sons have *s* . . .Job 1:5
all this did not Job *s* with . . . . .Job 2:10
I have *s*; what shall I do . . . . . .Job 7:20
and searchest after my *s*? . . . . .Job 10:6
are mine iniquities and *s*? . . . . .Job 13:23
my transgression and my *s* . . . .Job 13:23
bones are full of the *s* of . . . . . .Job 20:11
grave those which have *s* . . . . . .Job 24:19
rebellion unto his *s* . . . . .Job 34:37
If thou *s*, what doest thou . . . . .Job 35:6
Stand in awe, and *s* not . . . . . . .Ps 4:4
pain; and forgive all my *s* . . . . .Ps 25:18
is forgiven, whose *s* is . . . . .Ps 32:1

my bones because of my *s* . . . .Ps 38:3
s offering hast thou not . . . . . . .Ps 40:6
soul; for I have *s* against . . . . . .Ps 41:4
and cleanse me from my *s* . . . .Ps 51:2
Hide thy face from my *s* . . . . . .Ps 51:9
transgression, nor for my *s* . . . .Ps 59:3
and my *s* are not hid from . . . .Ps 69:5
they *s* yet more against him . . .Ps 78:17
us, and purge away our *s* . . . . .Ps 79:9
hast covered all their *s* . . . . . . .Ps 85:2
dealt with us after our *s* . . . . . . .Ps 103:10
We have *s* with our fathers . . . .Ps 106:6
let not the *s* of his mother . . . .Ps 109:14
with the cords of his *s* . . . . .Prov 5:22
but love covereth all *s* . . . . .Prov 10:12
fruit of the wicked to *s* . . . . . . .Prov 10:16
Fools make a mock at *s* . . . . . . .Prov 14:9
hasteth with his feet *s* . . . . .Prov 19:2
clean, I am pure from my *s*? . .Prov 20:9
plowing of the wicked, is *s* . . . .Prov 21:4
covereth his *s* shall not . . . . .Prov 28:13
to cause thy flesh to *s* . . . . .Eccl 5:6
that doeth good, and *s* not . . . .Eccl 7:20
Ah *s* nation, a people laden . . .Is 1:4
though your *s* be as scarlet . . . .Is 1:18
and *s* as it were with a cart . . .Is 5:18
the fruit to take away his *s* . . .Is 27:9
have made unto you for a *s* . . .Is 31:7
hand double for all her *s* . . . . . .Is 40:2
he against whom we have *s*? . .Is 42:24
will not remember thy *s* . . . . . . .Is 43:25
he bare the *s* of many, and . . . .Is 53:12
the house of Jacob their *s* . . . . .Is 58:1
and our *s* testify against us . . . .Is 59:12
art wroth; for we have *s* . . . . . .Is 64:5
thou sayest, I have not *s* . . . . . .Jer 2:35
and your *s* have withholden . . .Jer 5:25
because we have *s* against . . . . .Jer 8:14
for we have *s* against thee . . . . .Jer 14:20
that for all thy *s*, even in . . . . .Jer 15:13
what is our *s* that we have . . . .Jer 16:10
s of Judah is written with . . . . .Jer 17:1
blot out their *s* from thy . . . . . .Jer 18:23
because thy *s* were increased . .Jer 30:15
to cause Judah to *s* . . . . .Jer 32:35
they have *s* against me . . . . .Jer 33:8
whereby they have *s* . . . . .Jer 33:8
ye have *s* against the Lord . . . .Jer 44:23
she hath *s* against the Lord . . . .Jer 50:14
filled with *s* against the . . . . . . .Jer 51:5
Jerusalem hath grievously *s* . . . .Lam 1:8
for the punishment of his *s*? . . .Lam 3:39
the punishment of the *s* of . . . .Lam 4:6
Edom; he will discover thy *s* . .Lam 4:22
unto us, that we have *s* . . . . . . .Lam 5:16
he shall die in his *s* . . . . .Ezek 3:20
when the land *s* against me . . . .Ezek 14:13
committed half of thy *s* . . . . . . .Ezek 16:51
seeth all his father's *s* . . . . .Ezek 18:14
soul that *s*, it shall die . . . . .Ezek 18:20
and in his *s* that he hath *s* . . . .Ezek 18:24
all your doings your *s* do . . . . . .Ezek 21:24
transgressions and our *s* be . . . .Ezek 33:10
wherein they have *s* . . . . .Ezek 37:23
burnt offering and the *s* . . . . . . .Ezek 40:39
a young bullock for a *s* . . . . . . .Ezek 43:19
without blemish for a *s* . . . . . . .Ezek 43:22
he shall offer his *s* offering . . . .Ezek 44:27
shall prepare the *s* offering . . . .Ezek 45:17
the land a bullock for a *s* . . . . .Ezek 45:22
days, according to the *s* . . . . . . .Ezek 45:25
off thy *s* by righteousness . . . . .Dan 4:27
We have *s*, and have . . . . .Dan 9:5
because we have *s* against . . . . .Dan 9:11
to make an end of *s*, and to . . .Dan 9:24
so they *s* against me . . . . .Hos 4:7
They eat up the *s* of my . . . . . .Hos 4:8
hath made many altars to *s* . . . .Hos 8:11
altars shall be unto him to *s* . . .Hos 8:11
iniquity, and visit their *s* . . . . . .Hos 8:13
iniquity in me that were *s* . . . . .Hos 12:8
Ephraim is bound up; his *s* . . .Hos 13:12
transgressions..mighty *s* . . . . . . .Amos 5:12
swear by the *s* of Samaria . . . . .Amos 8:14
Lord God are upon the *s* . . . . .Amos 9:8

for the *s* of the house of ......Mic 1:5
is the beginning of the *s* ......Mic 1:13
body for the *s* of my soul? ....Mic 6:7
Lord, because I have *s*........Mic 7:9
their *s* into the depths of......Mic 7:19
people, and hath *s* against.....Hab 2:10
have *s* against the Lord ....Zeph 1:17
save his people from their *s* ...Matt 1:21
thy *s* be forgiven thee.........Matt 9:2
power on earth to forgive *s* ...Matt 9:6
manner of *s* and blasphemy ...Matt 12:31
shall my brother *s* against .....Matt 18:21
I have *s* in that I have ....Matt 27:4
for the remission of *s* ....Mark 1:4
Son, thy *s* be forgiven thee....Mark 2:5
palsy, Thy *s* be forgiven ......Mark 2:9
s shall be forgiven unto the ...Mark 3:28
their *s* should be forgiven .....Mark 4:12
adulterous and *s* generation ...Mark 8:38
the remission of their *s* ....Luke 1:77
for the remission of *s* ....Luke 3:3
from me; for I am a *s* man....Luke 5:8
Man, thy *s* are forgiven ....Luke 5:20
forgive *s*, but God alone? .....Luke 5:21
Say, Thy *s* be forgiven thee ...Luke 5:23
upon earth to forgive *s*........Luke 5:24
Her *s*, which are many, are ...Luke 7:47
he said unto her, Thy *s* are ...Luke 7:48
Who is this that forgiveth *s*....Luke 7:49
forgive us our *s*; for we also...Luke 11:4
Father, I have *s* against ....Luke 15:18
delivered into the hands of *s* ..Luke 24:7
remission of *s* should be ......Luke 24:47
s no more, lest a worse ....John 5:14
that is without *s* among you ...John 8:7
and shall die in your *s* ....John 8:21
of you convinceth me of *s*?....John 8:46
Master, who did *s*, this man ...John 9:2
Neither hath this man *s* ....John 9:3
wast altogether born in *s*......John 9:34
will reprove the world of *s* ....John 16:8
Of *s*, because they believe ....John 16:9
hath the greater *s* ....John 19:11
Whosesoever *s* ye remit ....John 20:23
whosesoever *s* ye retain ....John 20:23
Christ for the remission of *s*...Acts 2:38
that your *s* may be blotted ....Acts 3:19
Israel, and forgiveness of *s* ....Acts 5:31
lay not this *s* to their ....Acts 7:60
shall receive remission of *s* ....Acts 10:43
you the forgiveness of *s* ....Acts 13:38
and wash away thy *s*..........Acts 22:16
receive forgiveness of *s* ....Acts 26:18
For as many as have *s* ....Rom 2:12
and as many as have *s* in .....Rom 2:12
that they are all under *s* ......Rom 3:9
law is the knowledge of *s* .....Rom 3:20
For all have *s*, and come ......Rom 3:23
for the remission of *s* that.....Rom 3:25
forgiven, and whose *s* are .....Rom 4:7
Lord will not impute *s* ....Rom 4:8
until the law *s* was in the .....Rom 5:13
s is not imputed when ....Rom 5:13
that had not *s* after the ....Rom 5:14
where *s* abounded, grace ......Rom 5:20
as *s* hath reigned unto ....Rom 5:21
we continue in *s*, that.........Rom 6:1
we that are dead to *s* ....Rom 6:2
that is dead is freed from *s*....Rom 6:7
that he died, he died unto *s* ...Rom 6:10
to be dead indeed unto *s*......Rom 6:11
of unrighteousness unto *s* .....Rom 6:13
the motions of *s*, which were ..Rom 7:5
Is the law *s*? God forbid ......Rom 7:7
I had not known *s*, but by ....Rom 7:7
But *s*, taking occasion by .....Rom 7:8
For without the law *s* was .....Rom 7:8
the commandment came, *s* ....Rom 7:9
For *s*, taking occasion by......Rom 7:11
s, that it might appear *s*.......Rom 7:13
that *s* by the commandment ...Rom 7:13
might become exceeding *s*.....Rom 7:13
I am carnal, sold under *s* .....Rom 7:14
it, but *s* that dwelleth in ......Rom 7:17
captivity to the law of *s*.......Rom 7:23
with the flesh the law of *s*.....Rom 7:25
I shall take away their *s*.......Rom 11:27
Every *s* that a man doeth is ...1Cor 6:18
fornication *s* against his 1Cor 6:18
thou marry, thou hast not *s* ...1Cor 7:28
virgin marry, she hath not *s* ...1Cor 7:28
when ye *s* so against the 1Cor 8:12
conscience, ye *s* against 1Cor 8:12
vain: ye are yet in your *s* 1Cor 15:17
to righteousness, and *s* not 1Cor 15:34
The sting of death is *s* 1Cor 15:56
and the strength of *s* is 1Cor 15:56
many which have *s* already 2Cor 12:21
which heretofore have *s*.......2Cor 13:2
Who gave himself for our *s* ...Gal 1:4
Christ the minister of *s*? ......Gal 2:17
hath concluded all under *s* ....Gal 3:22
forgiveness of *s*, according ....Eph 1:7
dead in trespasses and *s*.......Eph 2:1
Even when we were dead in *s* .Eph 2:5
Be ye angry, and *s* not.......Eph 4:26
even the forgiveness of *s* ......Col 1:14
off the body of the *s* of the ...Col 2:11
you, being dead in your *s* .....Col 2:13
be saved, to fill up their *s*.....1Thess 2:16
that man of *s* be revealed 2Thess 2:3
Them that *s* rebuke before 1Tim 5:20
silly women laden with *s* 2Tim 3:6
is such is subverted, and *s*.....Titus 3:11
the deceitfulness of *s* ....Heb 3:13
not with them that had *s* ....Heb 3:17
as we are, yet without *s*.......Heb 4:15
gifts and sacrifices for *s* ....Heb 5:1
for himself, to offer for *s* .....Heb 5:3
for his own *s*, and then ....Heb 7:27
their *s* and their iniquities .....Heb 8:12
he appeared to put away *s* ....Heb 9:26
no more conscience of *s* ......Heb 10:2
remembrance again made of *s* .Heb 10:3
goats should take away *s*......Heb 10:4
and sacrifices for *s*............Heb 10:6
and offering for *s*.............Heb 10:8
which can never take away *s* ..Heb 10:11
offered one sacrifice for *s* .....Heb 10:12
s and iniquities will I ....Heb 10:17
is no more offering for *s* ......Heb 10:18
enjoy the pleasures of *s*.......Heb 11:25
by the high priest for *s*.......Heb 13:11
of persons, ye commit *s*.......James 2:9
if he have committed *s*........James 5:15
shall hide a multitude of *s*.....James 5:20
Who did no *s*, neither was 1Pet 2:22
own self bare our *s* in his 1Pet 2:24
that we, being dead to *s* 1Pet 2:24
Christ..once suffered for *s*.....1Pet 3:18
flesh hath ceased from *s* 1Pet 4:1
was purged from his old *s*.....2Pet 1:9
not the angels that *s* 2Pet 2:4
that cannot cease from *s* 2Pet 2:14
Son cleanseth us from all *s*....1John 1:8
the propitiation for our *s*......1John 2:2
for the *s* of the whole world...1John 2:2
because your *s* are forgiven ...1John 2:12
Whosoever abideth in him *s*...1John 3:6
whosoever *s* hath not seen 1John 3:6
He that committeth *s* is of 1John 3:8
of God doth not commit *s* 1John 3:9
he cannot *s*, because he is.....1John 3:9
the propitiation for our *s*......1John 4:10
any man see his brother *s* 1John 5:16
a *s* which is not unto death....1John 5:16
them that *s* not unto death 1John 5:16
There is a *s* unto death 1John 5:16
whosoever is born of God *s* ...1John 5:18
be not partakers of her *s*......Rev 18:4
her *s* have reached unto ......Rev 18:5

SIN (sĭn)—*"bush"*
1. Wilderness between the Red Sea and Sinai ....Ex 16:1
2. City of Egypt ....Ezek 30:15, 16

unto the wilderness of *S* ....Ex 16:1
from the wilderness of *S* ......Ex 17:1
out of the wilderness of *S* .....Num 33:12

SINAI, SINA (sī′nī, sī′nä)—*"a bush"*
Mountain (same as Horeb) where the Law was given ....Ex 19:1-25
Used allegorically by Paul.Gal 4:24, 25
See Horeb

is between Elim and *S*, on ....Ex 16:1
Lord abode upon mount *S* ....Ex 24:16
him upon mount *S*, two ....Ex 31:18
the morning unto mount *S* ....Ex 34:2
came down from mount *S*.....Ex 34:29
Moses in mount *S*, in ....Lev 7:38
unto Moses in mount *S* ....Lev 25:1
of Israel in mount *S* by ....Lev 26:46
Moses in the wilderness of *S* ..Num 1:1
spake with Moses in mount *S*..Num 3:1
Moses in the wilderness of *S* ..Num 3:14
even in the wilderness of *S*....Num 9:5
in the wilderness of *S*.........Num 26:64
The Lord came from *S*........Deut 33:2
even that *S* from before.......Judg 5:5
down also upon mount *S*......Neh 9:13
even *S* itself was moved at ....Ps 68:8
is among them, as in *S*........Ps 68:17
the wilderness of mount *S*.....Acts 7:30
spake to him in the mount *S* ..Acts 7:38

SIN-BEARER—*one who takes the sins of another upon himself*
Typical—the scapegoat...Lev 16:6-19
Real—Jesus Christ.......Heb 9:11-28

SINCE—*subsequently*
Lord hath blessed thee *s* ......Gen 30:30
Let me die, *s* I have seen .....Gen 46:30
nor *s* thou hast spoken unto ...Ex 4:10
in Egypt *s* the foundation .....Ex 9:18
hast ridden ever *s* I was.......Num 22:30
s the day that God created ....Deut 4:32
s I have showed you ....Josh 2:12
which they have done *s* the ...1Sam 8:8
about these three days, *s* I 1Sam 21:5
s the day of thy coming 1Sam 29:6
s the time that I brought 2Sam 7:6
S the day that I brought 1Kin 8:16
field *s* the day that she........2Kin 8:6
s the day that I brought.......1Chr 17:5
S the day that I brought 2Chr 6:5
S the people began to bring ...2Chr 31:10
s the days of Esar-haddon.....Ezra 4:2
s the days of our fathers ......Ezra 9:7
s the days of Jeshua the.......Neh 8:17
s man was placed upon earth ..Job 20:4
S thou art laid down, no ......Is 14:8
S thou wast precious in my....Is 43:4
s the beginning of the.........Is 64:4
S the day that your fathers ....Jer 7:25
For *s* I spake, I cried out .....Jer 20:8
for *s* I spake against him ......Jer 31:20
for *s* thou spakest of him .....Jer 48:27
s thou hast not hated blood ...Ezek 35:6
as never was *s* there was a ....Dan 12:1
S those days were, when ......Hag 2:16
not *s* the beginning of the .....Matt 24:21
How long is it ago *s* this ......Mark 9:21
have been *s* the world began ..Luke 1:70
s that time the kingdom of ....Luke 16:16
S the world began was it ......John 9:32
holy prophets *s* the world .....Acts 3:21
twelve days *s* I went up to ....Acts 24:11
was kept secret *s* the world....Rom 16:25
For *s* by man came death 1Cor 15:21
S ye seek a proof of Christ....2Cor 13:3
S we heard of your faith in....Col 1:4
s the day we heard it, do .....Col 1:9
of the oath, which was *s* ......Heb 7:28
s the fathers fell asleep 2Pet 3:4
such as was not *s* men were ...Rev 16:18

SINCERITY—*without deceit; genuineness*
Descriptive of:
God's Word 1Pet 2:2
Faith 1Tim 1:5
Believer's love 2Cor 8:8, 24
Should characterize:
Young men ....Titus 2:6, 7

Worship ....John 4:23, 24
Preaching 2Cor 2:17
Believer's life 2Cor 1:12
Public relationships ......Judg 9:16, 19

Examples of:
Nathanael...............John 1:47
Christ 1Pet 2:22
Paul 1Thess 2:3-5

[*also* SINCERE, SINCERELY]
and serve him in *s* and in .....Josh 24:14
the unleavened bread of *s* 1Cor 5:8
our Lord Jesus Christ in *s* .....Eph 6:24
ye may be *s* and without ......Phil 1:10
Christ of contention, not *s* ....Phil 1:16

SINEW—*tendon of an animal or man*

[*also* SINEWS]
eat not of the *s* which ....Gen 32:32
Jacob's thigh in the *s* that .....Gen 32:32
fenced me with bones and *s* ..Job 10:11
the *s* of his stones are ....Job 40:17
and thy neck is an iron *s* ......Is 48:4
And I will lay *s* upon you .....Ezek 37:6

SING—*See* SINGING

SINGED—*lightly burnt*
nor..hair of their head *s* ......Dan 3:27

SINGERS—*vocal musicians*
Leaders of 1Chr 25:2-6
Under teachers 1Chr 15:22, 27
Mixed 2Chr 35:15, 25

[*also* SINGER]
also and psalteries for *s* 1Kin 10:12
Heman a *s*, the son of Joel....1Chr 6:33
these are the *s*, chief of 1Chr 9:33
So the *s*, Heman, Asaph 1Chr 15:19
Levites which were the *s* 2Chr 5:12
harps and psalteries for *s* 2Chr 9:11
the *s* with instruments of 2Chr 23:13
and the *s* sang, and the 2Chr 29:28
s: the children of Asaph ......Ezra 2:41
and the Levites, and the *s*.....Ezra 7:7
Of the *s* also; Eliashib ....Ezra 10:24
the *s* and the Levites were ....Neh 7:1
and the porters, and the *s*.....Neh 7:73
the porters, and the *s*.........Neh 10:39
portion should be for the *s* ....Neh 11:23
s had builded them villages ....Neh 12:29
both the *s* and the porters.....Neh 12:45
gave the portions of the *s* .....Neh 12:47
the Levites, and the *s*, that....Neh 13:10
s went before, the players .....Ps 68:25
As well the *s* as the players ...Ps 87:7
I gat me men *s* and women *s* ..Eccl 2:8
the chambers of the *s* in ......Ezek 40:44
the chief *s* on my stringed .....Hab 3:19

SINGING—*producing music with the voice*

Descriptive of:
Birds ....Ps 104:12
Trees 1Chr 16:33
Believers ....Eph 5:19
Redeemed ....Rev 5:9
Morning stars ....Job 38:7

Occasions of:
Times of:
Victory ....Ex 15:1, 21
Revelry..............Ex 32:18
Imprisonment ....Acts 16:25
Joy...................James 5:13
Lord's Supper ....Matt 26:30

Manner of, with:
Thanksgiving ....Ps 147:7
Joy ....Ps 27:6
Gladness................Jer 31:7
Spirit 1Cor 14:15
Grace ....Col 3:16

Objects of:
God's:
Power ....Ps 59:16
Mercies..............Ps 89:1
Righteousness ....Ps 51:14
New song ....Rev 14:3

[*also* SANG, SING, SINGETH, SUNG]
Then *s* Moses and the ....Ex 15:1
Then Israel *s* this song ....Num 21:17
Spring up, O well; *s* ye ....Num 21:17
Then *s* Deborah and Barak ...Judg 5:1
I, even I, will *s* unto the ......Judg 5:3
will *s* praise to the Lord ......Judg 5:3
of Israel, *s* and dancing 1Sam 18:6
s one to another of him in 1Sam 21:11
this David, of whom they *s*....1Sam 29:5
the voice of *s* men and *s* 2Sam 19:35
I will *s* praises unto thy 2Sam 22:50
of the congregation with *s*.....1Chr 6:32
S unto him, *s* psalms 1Chr 16:9
began to *s* and to praise 2Chr 20:22
such as taught to *s* praise 2Chr 23:13
with rejoicing and with *s* 2Chr 23:18
the singers *s*, and the 2Chr 29:28
to *s* praise unto the Lord 2Chr 29:30
all the *s* men and the *s* 2Chr 35:25
two hundred *s* men and *s* .....Ezra 2:65
And they *s* together by ....Ezra 3:11
five *s* men and *s* women ......Neh 7:67
the singers *s* loud, with ....Neh 12:42
widow's heart to *s* for joy .....Job 29:13
morning stars *s* together ......Job 38:7
David, which he *s* unto ....Ps 7:*title*
will *s* praise to the name ......Ps 7:17
S praises to the Lord ....Ps 9:11
I will *s* unto the Lord ....Ps 13:6
and *s* praises unto thy ....Ps 18:49
so will we *s* and praise thy ....Ps 21:13
S unto the Lord, O ye ....Ps 30:4
s unto him with the psaltery ...Ps 33:2
S praises to God, *s* praises ....Ps 47:6
s praises unto our King, *s* .....Ps 47:6
is fixed: I will *s* and give ......Ps 57:7
So will I *s* praise unto thy.....Ps 61:8
S forth the honor of his ....Ps 66:2
worship thee, and shall *s* ......Ps 66:4
they shall *s* to thy name.......Ps 66:4
the nations be glad and *s* .....Ps 67:4
S unto God, *s* praises to ......Ps 68:4
S unto God, ye kingdoms .....Ps 68:32
O *s* praises unto the Lord .....Ps 68:32
I will *s* praises to the God ....Ps 75:9
and to *s* praises unto thy......Ps 92:1
O *s* unto the Lord a new ....Ps 96:1
s unto the Lord, all the ......Ps 96:1
O *s* unto the Lord a new .....Ps 98:1
S unto the Lord with the......Ps 98:5
before his presence with *s*.....Ps 100:2
s of mercy and judgment......Ps 101:1
unto thee, O Lord, will I *s* ....Ps 101:1
s unto the Lord as long as ....Ps 104:33
I will *s* praise to my God .....Ps 104:33
S unto him, *s* psalms ....Ps 105:2
I will *s* praises unto thee .....Ps 108:3
S us one of the songs of ......Ps 137:3
gods will I *s* praise unto.......Ps 138:1
will *s* a new song unto thee ...Ps 144:9
ten strings will I *s* praises .....Ps 144:9
I will *s* praises unto..God .....Ps 146:2
good to *s* praises unto our ....Ps 147:1
s praises unto him with ....Ps 149:3
let them *s* aloud upon their ...Ps 149:5
so is he that *s* songs to........Prov 25:20
the righteous doth *s* and ......Prov 29:6
of the *s* of birds is come ......Song 2:12
will I *s* to my well-beloved ....Is 5:1
S unto the Lord; for he ....Is 12:5
they break forth into *s* ....Is 14:7
shall Tyre *s* as a harlot........Is 23:15
shall *s* for the majesty of......Is 24:14
day shall this song be *s* in......Is 26:1
Awake and *s*, ye that dwell ...Is 26:19
In that day *s* ye unto her .....Is 27:2
rejoice even with joy and *s*....Is 35:2
the tongue of the dumb *s* .....Is 35:6
S unto the Lord a new song ...Is 42:10
S, O ye heavens; for the ......Is 44:23
with a voice of *s* declare ......Is 48:20
return, and come with *s*.......Is 51:11
voice together shall they *s*.....Is 52:8
S, O barren, thou that ....Is 54:1
forth before you into *s* ....Is 55:12
servants shall *s* for joy of .....Is 65:14
S unto the Lord, praise ye ....Jer 20:13
come and *s* in the height of ..Jer 31:12
ships of Tarshish did *s* of .....Ezek 27:25
she shall *s* there, as in ....Hos 2:15
voice shall *s* in the ....Zeph 2:14
will joy over thee with *s* ......Zeph 3:17
S and rejoice, O daughter.....Zech 2:10
when they had *s* a hymn ......Mark 14:26
prayed, and *s* praises unto ....Acts 16:25
Gentiles, and *s* unto thy ......Rom 15:9
the church will I *s* praise ......Heb 2:12
any merry? let him *s* psalms ..James 5:13
s as it were a new song ....Rev 14:3
And they *s* the song of Moses..Rev 15:3

SINGLE—*sound; of one purpose*

[*also* SINGLENESS]
if therefore thine eye be *s* .....Matt 6:22
when thine eye is *s*, thy ....Luke 11:34
gladness and *s* of heart........Acts 2:46
in *s* of your heart, as unto ....Eph 6:5
in *s* of heart, fearing God .....Col 3:22

SINGULAR—*something special; set apart*
Descriptive of a vow .....Lev 27:2

SINIM, SINITES (sī′nĭm, sī′nīts)—*people from a far land, possibly from the land of Sin*
1. Canaanite people ....Gen 10:15-18
2. Distant land from which people will return .....Is 49:7-12

SINK—*to submerge; become partly buried; become engulfed*

Used literally of:
Stone 1Sam 17:49
Army ....Ex 15:4, 5, 10
Boat ....Luke 5:7
Man...................Matt 14:30

[*also* SANK, SUNK]
they *s* into the bottom as a ....Ex 15:5
stone *s* into his forehead 1Sam 17:49
heathen are *s* down in the.....Ps 9:15
I *s* in deep mire, where ....Ps 69:2
the mire, and let me not *s* ....Ps 69:14
mire: so Jeremiah *s* in the.....Jer 38:6
Thus shall Babylon *s*, and .....Jer 51:64
Her gates are *s* into the ....Lam 2:9
sayings *s* down into your ......Luke 9:44
preaching, he *s* down with ....Acts 20:9

SINLESSNESS—*See* HOLINESS OF CHRIST; PERFECTION

SINNER—*one who is unregenerate transgressing God's law*

Descriptive of:
Wicked city ....Gen 13:13
Race 1Sam 15:18
Wicked Israelites ....Amos 9:8, 10
Jewish people ....Matt 26:45, 47
Man under conviction....Luke 5:8
Luke 18:13
Human race ....Rom 5:8, 19

Characteristics of:
Hostile to God ....Jude 15
Scheme wickedly ....Ps 26:9, 10
Easily ensnared ....Eccl 7:26
Righteous enticed by ....Prov 1:10
Law made for 1Tim 1:9
Conscious of sin ....Luke 18:13
Able to repent ....Luke 15:7, 10
Conversion of ....James 5:20
In need of cleansing .....James 4:8

Punishment of:
Pursued by evil..........Prov 13:21
Overthrown by evil ......Prov 13:6
Wealth of, acquired by the just ....Prov 13:22
Sorrow given to ....Ezek 18:20
Will be punished ....Prov 11:31
Will be consumed ....Ps 104:35

Christ's relationship to:
Came to call ....Luke 5:32

Friend of ....Luke 7:34
Receives such ....Luke 15:1, 2
Endures hostility from ...Heb 12:3
Separate from ....Heb 7:26

[*also* SINNERS]
The censers of these *s* ....Num 16:38
nor standeth in the way of *s*...Ps 1:1
therefore will he teach *s* ......Ps 25:8
s shall be converted unto......Ps 51:13
the wicked and the *s*..........Prov 11:31
overthroweth the *s* ....Prov 13:6
Let not thine heart envy *s*.....Prov 23:17
to the *s* he giveth travail ......Eccl 2:26
but the *s* shall be taken by ....Eccl 7:26
Though a *s* do evil ....Eccl 8:12
as is the good, so is the *s* .....Eccl 9:2
transgressors and of the *s* .....Is 1:28
and he shall destroy the *s* .....Is 13:9
The *s* in Zion are afraid ......Is 33:14
the *s* being a hundred.........Is 65:20
publicans and *s* sat also ....Matt 9:10
Master with publicans and *s*? ..Matt 9:11
the righteous, but *s* to ....Matt 9:13
a friend of publicans and *s* ....Matt 11:19
publicans and *s* sat also ....Mark 2:15
eat with publicans and *s* ......Mark 2:16
drinketh with publicans and *s*? .Mark 2:16
but *s* to repentance ....Mark 2:17
betrayed into the hands of *s*...Mark 14:41
with publicans and *s*? ....Luke 5:30
for *s* also love those that ......Luke 6:32
ye? for *s* also do even the .....Luke 6:33
s also lend to *s*, to receive ....Luke 6:34
the city, which was a *s*.........Luke 7:37
s above all the Galileans ......Luke 13:2
were *s* above all men that .....Luke 13:4
over one *s* that repenteth .....Luke 15:7
God be merciful to me a *s* ....Luke 18:13
with a man that is a *s*.........Luke 19:7
man that is a *s* do such ....John 9:16
that God heareth not *s*........John 9:31
am I also judged as a *s*? ......Rom 3:7
by nature, and not *s* of ....Gal 2:15
into the world to save *s* 1Tim 1:15
converteth the *s* from the .....James 5:20

SION—*See* ZION

SIPHMOTH (sĭf'mŏth)—*"fruitful"—a place in southern Judah frequented by David*
David shares spoils with. .1Sam 30:26-28

SIPPAI (sĭp'ī)—*"Jehovah is preserver"*
Philistine giant 1Chr 20:4
Called Saph.............2Sam 21:18

SIR—*a form of address to men*

[*also* SIRS]
O *s*, we came indeed down....Gen 43:20
S, didst not thou sow good ....Matt 13:27
S, we remember that that .....Matt 27:63
S, thou hast nothing to ....John 4:11
S, I perceive..thou art a ......John 4:19
S, I have no man, when the ...John 5:7
S, if thou have borne him .....John 20:15
S, ye are brethren; why do ....Acts 7:26
S, what must I do to be.......Acts 16:30
S, I perceive that this.........Acts 27:10
s, be of good cheer ....Acts 27:25
I said unto him, *S*, thou ......Rev 7:14

SIRAH (sī'rä)—*"turning aside"*
Well near Hebron 2Sam 3:26

SIRION (sĭ'rŏn)—*"breastplate"*
Sidonian name for Mt. Hermon ....Deut 3:9
Lebanon and *S* like a ....Ps 29:6

SISAMAI (sĭs'ä-mī)—*"Jehovah is distinguished"*
Judahite 1Chr 2:40

SISERA (sĭs'er-ä)—*"mediation; array"*
1. Canaanite commander of Jabin's army; slain by Jael..................Judg 4:2-22
2. Ancestor of postexilic Nethinim ....Ezra 2:43, 53

courses fought against *S*.......Judg 5:20
the hammer she smote *S* ....Judg 5:26
The mother of *S* looked ....Judg 5:28
S a prey of divers colors ......Judg 5:30
them into the hand of *S*.......1Sam 12:9
the children of *S*, the ....Neh 7:55
as to *S*, as to Jabin, at ....Ps 83:9

SISTER—*a female having the same parents as another; of the same tribe; a female believer in Christ*

Descriptive of:
Female relative ....Gen 24:30-60
Woman of the same tribe.Num 25:18

Features concerning:
Protected by:
Brothers ....Gen 34:13-31
Laws ....Lev 18:9-13, 18
Friction between ....Luke 10:39, 40
Loved by Jesus..........John 11:5

Figurative of:
Samaria and Jerusalem...Ezek 23:1-49
Christian................Matt 12:50
Christian woman ....Rom 16:1
Church ....2 John 13

[*also* SISTER'S, SISTERS]
the *s* of Tubal-cain was ....Gen 4:22
I pray thee, thou art my *s*.....Gen 12:13
Sarah his wife, She is my *s*....Gen 20:2
And yet indeed she is my *s* ...Gen 20:12
the *s* to Laban the Syrian .....Gen 25:20
said, She is my *s*; for he ......Gen 26:7
the *s* of Nebajoth, to be his ...Gen 28:9
tidings of Jacob his *s* son......Gen 29:13
Rachel envied her *s* ....Gen 30:1
Ishmael's daughter, *s* ....Gen 36:3
Beriah, and Serah their *s* .....Gen 46:17
And his *s* stood afar off.......Ex 2:4
Jochebed his father's *s* ....Ex 6:20
the prophetess, the *s*..........Ex 15:20
if a man shall take his *s*.......Lev 20:17
he hath uncovered his *s*.......Lev 20:17
nakedness of thy mother's *s* ...Lev 20:19
of thy father's *s*; for he ....Lev 20:19
And for his *s* a virgin ....Lev 21:3
his brother, or for his *s* ....Num 6:7
Moses, and Miriam their *s* ....Num 26:59
be he that lieth with his *s* .....Deut 27:22
and my brethren, and my *s*....Josh 2:13
not her younger *s* fairer.......Judg 15:2
son of David had a fair *s* 2Sam 13:1
my brother Absalom's *s*.......2Sam 13:4
let Tamar my *s* come, and 2Sam 13:6
hold now thy peace, my *s*.....2Sam 13:20
the day that he forced his *s* ...2Sam 13:32
to wife the *s* of his own 1Kin 11:19
wife, the *s* of Tahpenes the ...1Kin 11:19
Jehosheba..*s* of Ahaziah 2Kin 11:2
Timna was Lotan's *s*..........1Chr 1:39
Whose *s* were Zeruiah, and ...1Chr 2:16
and Shelomith their *s* 1Chr 3:19
of his wife Hodiah the *s* 1Chr 4:19
his *s* Hammoleketh bare 1Chr 7:18
Hotham, and Shua their *s*.....1Chr 7:32
she was the *s* of Ahaziah......2Chr 22:11
called for their three *s* to .....Job 1:4
wisdom, Thou art my *s* ....Prov 7:4
ravished my heart, my *s* ......Song 4:9
A garden inclosed is my *s*.....Song 4:12
saying, Open to me, my *s*.....Song 5:2
We have a little *s*, and she ....Song 8:8
what shall we do for our *s* ....Song 8:8
her treacherous *s* Judah ....Jer 3:7
her treacherous *s* Judah ....Jer 3:10
and thou art the *s* of thy ......Ezek 16:45
thine elder *s* is Samaria ....Ezek 16:46
younger *s*, that dwelleth ......Ezek 16:46
the iniquity of thy *s* Sodom ...Ezek 16:49
which hast judged thy *s*.......Ezek 16:52
thy *s*, Sodom and her ....Ezek 16:55
thee hath humbled his *s*.......Ezek 22:11
or for *s* that hath had no......Ezek 44:25
Ammi; and to your *s* ....Hos 2:1
And his *s*, are they not all ....Matt 13:56
is my brother, and my *s*.......Mark 3:35
and are not his *s* here with ....Mark 6:3
houses, and brethren, and *s* ...Mark 10:30
she had a *s* called Mary ....Luke 10:39
not care that my *s* hath ....Luke 10:40
and brethren, and *s*...........Luke 14:26
the town of Mary and her *s* ...John 11:1
Therefore his *s* sent unto ......John 11:3
called Mary her *s* secretly .....John 11:28
Martha, the *s* of him that .....John 11:39
when Paul's *s* son heard of ....Acts 23:16
and Julia, Nereus, and his *s* ...Rom 16:15
brother or a *s* is not under 1Cor 7:15
power to lead about a *s*.......1Cor 9:5
Marcus, *s* son to Barnabas ....Col 4:10
the younger as *s*, with all 1Tim 5:2
If a brother or *s* be naked ....James 2:15

SISTER-IN-LAW—*the sister of one's spouse*
thy *s* is gone back ....Ruth 1:15
return thou after thy *s* ....Ruth 1:15

SIT—*to rest, dwell*

Descriptive of:
Partridge ....Jer 17:11
Man....................Gen 18:1
Judge ....Ex 18:13, 14
Priest...................Zech 6:13
King ....Deut 17:15, 18
God....................Ps 2:4
Messiah ....Ps 110:1

Purposes of, to:
Eat.....................Matt 26:20, 21
Rest....................John 4:6
Mourn..................Neh 1:4
Teach ....Matt 26:55
Transact business ....Matt 9:9
Beg ....Luke 18:35
Learn ....Mark 5:15
Ride ....Matt 21:5
Worship ....Acts 2:2

Figurative of Christ's
Session ....Heb 1:3
Rule ....Matt 19:28
Judgment ....Matt 25:31

[*also* SAT, SATEST, SITTEST, SITTETH, SITTING]
he *s* in the tent door in ....Gen 18:1
And she *s* over against him ...Gen 21:16
s and eat of my venison.......Gen 27:19
the images..and *s* upon ....Gen 31:34
s in an open place, which .....Gen 38:14
himself, and *s* upon the bed ...Gen 48:2
Midian: and he *s* down by ....Ex 2:15
Pharaoh that *s* upon his ....Ex 11:5
when we *s* by the flesh pots ...Ex 16:3
that Moses *s* to judge the .....Ex 18:13
every thing, whereon he *s*.....Lev 15:4
whereon he *s* that hath the ....Lev 15:6
every thing also that she *s*.....Lev 15:20
any thing whereon she *s* ......Lev 15:23
go to war, and shall ye *s*......Num 32:6
them when thou *s* in thine ....Deut 6:7
them when thou *s* in thine ....Deut 11:19
the dam *s* upon the young ....Deut 22:6
they *s* down at thy feet ....Deut 33:3
ye that *s* in judgment, and ....Judg 5:10
and *s* under an oak which .....Judg 6:11
And they *s* down, and did ....Judg 19:6
wept, and *s* there before ......Judg 20:26
she *s* beside the reapers ....Ruth 2:14
S still, my daughter, until ....Ruth 3:18
And he turned aside, and *s* ...Ruth 4:1
city, and said, *S* ye down ....Ruth 4:2
Eli the priest *s* upon a seat....1Sam 1:9
them *s* in the chiefest 1Sam 9:22
as he *s* in his house with 1Sam 19:9
to *s* with the king at meat.....1Sam 20:5
king *s* upon his seat, as 1Sam 20:25
Abner *s* by Saul's side, and ...1Sam 20:25
they *s* down, the one on the...2Sam 2:13
David in, and *s* before 2Sam 7:18
the king arose, and *s* in.......2Sam 19:8

Behold, the king doth *s* in 2Sam 19:8
and he shall *s* upon my 1Kin 1:13
shall *s* on the throne of my....1Kin 1:20
should *s* on the throne of 1Kin 1:27
may come and *s* upon my 1Kin 1:35
Solomon *s* on the throne 1Kin 1:46
and *s* down on his throne 1Kin 2:19
she *s* on his right hand........1Kin 2:19
reign, as soon as he *s* on 1Kin 16:11
children of Beliah, and *s* 1Kin 21:13
I saw the Lord *s* on his 1Kin 22:19
behold, he *s* on the top of 2Kin 1:9
But Elisha *s* in his house 2Kin 6:32
house, and the elders *s* 2Kin 6:32
s we here until we die? 2Kin 7:3
shall *s* on the throne of 2Kin 10:30
and Jeroboam *s* upon his......2Kin 13:13
me to the men which *s* on 2Kin 18:27
to pass, as David *s* in his 1Chr 17:1
Solomon my son to *s* upon the .1Chr 28:5
Solomon *s* on the throne 1Chr 29:23
s upon the throne of Israel 2Chr 6:16
table, and the *s* of his 2Chr 9:4
s either of them on his.........2Chr 18:9
and they *s* in a void place 2Chr 18:9
I saw the Lord *s* upon his 2Chr 18:18
of my beard, and *s* down .....Ezra 9:3
s in the street of the house .....Ezra 10:9
I *s* down and wept, and ....Neh 1:4
unto me, (the queen also *s* ....Neh 2:6
king Ahasuerus *s* on the ......Esth 1:2
Mordecai *s* in the king's ......Esth 2:19
king and Haman *s* down to....Esth 3:15
Mordecai..*s* at the king's ......Esth 5:13
and he *s* down among the .....Job 2:8
I chose out their way, and *s*...Job 29:25
nor *s* in the seat of the ....Ps 1:1
s in the throne judging ....Ps 9:4
He *s* in the lurking places .....Ps 10:8
I have not *s* with vain ....Ps 26:4
and will not *s* with the ....Ps 26:5
The Lord *s* upon the flood ....Ps 29:10
yea, the Lord *s* King for ......Ps 29:10
Thou *s* and speakest ....Ps 50:20
s between the cherubim ....Ps 99:1
Such as *s* in darkness and .....Ps 107:10
Princes also did *s* and speak ...Ps 119:23
also *s* upon thy throne ....Ps 132:12
of Babylon, there we *s*.........Ps 137:1
For she *s* at the door of her ...Prov 9:14
When thou *s* to eat with a ....Prov 23:1
he *s* among the elders ....Prov 31:23
and the rich *s* in low..........Eccl 10:6
the king *s* at his table..........Song 1:12
I *s* down under his shadow ....Song 2:3
desolate shall *s* upon the ......Is 3:26
saw also the Lord *s* upon .....Is 6:1
he shall *s* upon it in truth .....Is 16:5
to him that *s* in judgment .....Is 28:6
to the men that *s* upon the....Is 36:12
Come down, and *s* in the .....Is 47:1
Babylon, *s* on the ground .....Is 47:1
I shall not *s* as a widow.......Is 47:8
arise, and *s* down; O ....Is 52:2
In the ways hast thou *s* ....Jer 3:2
Why do we *s* still?............Jer 8:14
queen, humble yourselves, *s*...Jer 13:18
I *s* not in the assembly of .....Jer 15:17
I *s* alone because of thy.......Jer 15:17
that *s* upon the throne of ......Jer 22:2
s upon the throne of David ...Jer 22:30
s upon the throne of David ...Jer 29:16
that *s* in the court of the ......Jer 32:12
want a man to *s* upon the .....Jer 33:17
Now the king *s* in the.........Jer 36:22
have none to *s* upon the ......Jer 36:30
and *s* in the middle gate ......Jer 39:3
doth the city *s* solitary ....Lam 1:1
He *s* alone and keepeth ....Lam 3:28
Behold their *s* down, and .....Lam 3:63
and I *s* where they *s*..........Ezek 3:15
elders of Judah *s* before ......Ezek 8:1
elders..unto me, and *s* ....Ezek 14:1
s upon a stately bed ....Ezek 23:41
shall *s* upon the ground ....Ezek 26:16
they *s* before thee as my ......Ezek 33:31
but Daniel *s* in the gate of ....Dan 2:49
the Ancient of days did *s* .....Dan 7:9
will I *s* to judge all the ....Joel 3:12
sackcloth, and *s* in ashes ....Jon 3:6
and *s* on the east side of ....Jon 4:5
booth, and *s* under it in.......Jon 4:5
shall *s* every man under ....Mic 4:4
all the earth *s* still, and ....Zech 1:11
thy fellows that *s* before ......Zech 3:8
he shall *s* as a refiner and .....Mal 3:3
people which *s* in darkness ....Matt 4:16
which *s* in the region and .....Matt 4:16
as Jesus *s* at meat in the ......Matt 9:10
s down with him and his ......Matt 9:10
unto children *s* in the ....Matt 11:16
he went into a ship, and *s*.....Matt 13:2
which *s* with him at meat .....Matt 14:9
multitude to *s* down on the....Matt 14:19
multitude to *s* down on the....Matt 15:35
these my two sons may *s*.......Matt 20:21
two blind men *s* by the way ...Matt 20:30
S thou on my right hand ......Matt 22:44
Pharisees *s* in Moses' seat .....Matt 23:2
of God, and by him that *s* ....Matt 23:22
s upon the mount of Olives ...Matt 24:3
come, he *s* down with the .....Matt 26:20
S ye here, while I go and .....Matt 26:36
and *s* with the servants.........Matt 26:58
Son of man *s* on the right .....Matt 26:64
Mary, *s* over against the ......Matt 27:61
stone from the door, and *s* ....Matt 28:2
certain of the scribes *s* ....Mark 2:6
as Jesus *s* at meat in his ......Mark 2:15
sinners *s* also together with....Mark 2:15
looked..on them which *s* ......Mark 3:34
Herod and them that *s* with ...Mark 6:22
to make all *s* down by ....Mark 6:39
they *s* down in ranks, by ......Mark 6:40
people to *s* down on ....Mark 8:6
unto us that we may *s* ....Mark 10:37
But to *s* on my right hand ....Mark 10:40
s by the highway side ....Mark 10:46
on him; and he *s* upon him ...Mark 11:7
S thou on my right hand ......Mark 12:36
they *s* and did eat, Jesus ......Mark 14:18
S ye here, while I shall ......Mark 14:32
Son of man *s* on the right .....Mark 14:62
unto the eleven as they *s*......Mark 16:14
light to them that *s* in ....Luke 1:79
s in the midst of the ....Luke 2:46
to the minister, and *s* down ...Luke 4:20
s at the receipt of custom .....Luke 5:27
of others that *s* down with ....Luke 5:29
house, and *s* down to meat ....Luke 7:36
And they that *s* at meat.......Luke 7:49
s at the feet of Jesus..........Luke 8:35
Make them *s* down by ....Luke 9:14
did so, and made them all *s* ...Luke 9:15
Mary which also *s* at Jesus'....Luke 10:39
and make them to *s* down.....Luke 12:37
s down in the kingdom of .....Luke 13:29
s not down in the highest .....Luke 14:8
and *s* down in the lowest......Luke 14:10
of them that *s* at meat ....Luke 14:10
s not down first, and ....Luke 14:28
s down quickly and write......Luke 16:6
the field, Go and *s* down .....Luke 17:7
blind man *s* by the way side ...Luke 18:35
Lord..*S* thou on my right .....Luke 20:42
hour was come, he *s* down ....Luke 22:14
is greater, he that *s* at ....Luke 22:27
is not he that *s* at meat? ......Luke 22:27
s on thrones judging the ......Luke 22:30
maid beheld him as he *s* ....Luke 22:56
Son of man *s* on the right .....Luke 22:69
his journey, *s* thus on the .....John 4:6
Jesus said, Make the men *s* ...John 6:10
So the men *s* down, in.........John 6:10
Is not this he that *s* and.......John 9:8
that *s* at the table with........John 12:2
s down in the judgment ....John 19:13
two angels in white *s* ....John 20:12
of fire, and it *s* upon each ....Acts 2:3
raise up Christ to *s* on his .....Acts 2:30
Lord..*S* thou on my right .....Acts 2:34
all that *s* in the council ....Acts 6:15
s in his chariot read Isaiah ....Acts 8:28
he would come up and *s* ......Acts 8:31
s upon his throne, and ....Acts 12:21
s a certain man at Lystra......Acts 14:8
And there *s* in a window a ....Acts 20:9
s thou to judge me after ......Acts 23:3
next day *s* on the judgment ......Acts 25:6
Bernice..they that *s* with .....Acts 26:30
s at meat in the idol's.........1Cor 8:10
people *s* down to eat and 1Cor 10:7
revealed to another that *s* 1Cor 14:30
made us *s* together in ....Eph 2:6
as God *s* in the temple of 2Thess 2:4
s down on the right hand .....Heb 1:3
S on my right hand until .....Heb 1:13
him, *S* thou here in a good....James 2:3
s here under my footstool .....James 2:3
to *s* with me in my throne ....Rev 3:21
heaven, and one *s* on the .....Rev 4:2
four and twenty elders *s* ......Rev 4:4
thanks to him that *s* on the ...Rev 4:9
hand of him that *s* on the .....Rev 5:1
unto him that *s* upon the......Rev 5:13
he that *s* on him had a bow ...Rev 6:2
s on him had a pair of ....Rev 6:5
to our God which *s* upon the ..Rev 7:10
and them that *s* on them ......Rev 9:17
one *s* like unto the Son ....Rev 14:14
whore that *s* upon many .....Rev 17:1
woman *s* upon a scarlet ....Rev 17:3
the whore *s*, are peoples ......Rev 17:15
I *s* a queen, and am no ....Rev 18:7
s upon him was called ....Rev 19:11
of them that *s* on them ....Rev 19:18
sword of him that *s* upon .....Rev 19:21
throne, and him that *s* on .....Rev 20:11

SITH—*See* SINCE

SITNAH (sĭt'nä)—*"hatred"*
Well dug by Isaac near Gerar ....Gen 26:21

SITUATE—*to locate; location*
one was *s* northward over 1Sam 14:5
art *s* at the entry of the ....Ezek 27:3
No, that was *s* among the .....Nah 3:8

SITUATION—*location*
s of this city is pleasant 2Kin 2:19
Beautiful for *s*, the joy........Ps 48:2

SIVAN (sĕ-vän')
Third month of the Jewish and Babylonian years ....Esth 8:9

SIX

[*also* SIXTH]
and the morning were the *s* ...Gen 1:31
Noah was *s* hundred years ....Gen 7:6
in the *s* hundredth and first ...Gen 8:13
Abram was fourscore and *s* ...Gen 16:16
and *s* years for thy cattle ......Gen 31:41
s hundred thousand on foot ...Ex 12:37
on the *s* day they shall ....Ex 16:5
S days ye shall gather it.......Ex 16:26
the *s* day the bread of two ....Ex 16:29
s days the Lord made ....Ex 20:11
s years thou shalt sow thy .....Ex 23:10
and the cloud covered it *s*.....Ex 24:16
the *s* branches that come......Ex 25:33
s curtains by themselves.......Ex 26:9
S of their names on one ......Ex 28:10
s names of the rest on the ....Ex 28:10
s days the Lord made ....Ex 31:17
S days shall work be done ....Ex 35:2
westward he made *s* boards ...Ex 36:27
the *s* branches going out of....Ex 37:19
for *s* hundred thousand ....Ex 38:26
set them in two rows, *s* ....Lev 24:6
S years thou shalt sow thy ....Lev 25:3
s years thou shalt prune ....Lev 25:3
blessing upon you in the *s*.....Lev 25:21
s thousand and five hundred...Num 1:21
thousand and *s* hundred.......Num 1:27

thousand and *s* hundred ....Num 2:4
s thousand and five hundred ...Num 2:11
thousand and *s* hundred ....Num 2:31
thousand and *s* hundred ....Num 3:28
thousand and *s* hundred ....Num 4:40
On the *s* day Eliasaph ....Num 7:42
s hundred thousand ....Num 11:21
s hundred thousand ....Num 26:51
s hundred and threescore .....Num 31:37
thirty and *s* thousand ....Num 31:44
s cities shall ye have for ......Num 35:13
S days thou shalt labor ....Deut 5:13
in serving thee *s* years ....Deut 15:18
shalt thou do *s* days ....Josh 6:3
smote..thirty and *s* men ....Josh 7:5
The *s* lot came out to ....Josh 19:32
of the Philistines *s* hundred ....Judg 3:31
s hundred men appointed .....Judg 18:11
twenty and *s* thousand ....Judg 20:15
s measures of barley ....Ruth 3:15
and *s* thousand horsemen 1Sam 13:5
about *s* hundred men 1Sam 14:2
spear's head weighed *s* 1Sam 17:7
passed..with the *s* hundred 1Sam 27:2
seven years and *s* months 2Sam 2:11
the *s*, Ithream, by Eglah 2Sam 3:5
ark..had gone *s* paces 2Sam 6:13
on every hand *s* fingers 2Sam 21:20
and on every foot *s* toes 2Sam 21:20
the middle was *s* cubits 1Kin 6:6
Solomon in one year was *s* 1Kin 10:14
threescore and *s* talents 1Kin 10:14
The throne had *s* steps 1Kin 10:19
s hundred shekels of silver 1Kin 10:29
In the twenty and *s* year 1Kin 16:8
s years reigned he in Tirzah ...1Kin 16:23
s thousand pieces of gold 2Kin 5:5
smitten five or *s* times 2Kin 13:19
in the *s* year of Hezekiah 2Kin 18:10
Ozem the *s*, David the 1Chr 2:15
s were born unto him in 1Chr 3:4
seven years and *s* months 1Chr 3:4
sons and *s* daughters 1Chr 4:27
s and thirty thousand men 1Chr 7:4
And Azel had *s* sons 1Chr 8:38
nine hundred and fifty and *s* ..1Chr 9:9
Attai the *s*, Eliel the 1Chr 12:11
s thousand and eight hundred .1Chr 12:24
eight thousand and *s* hundred .1Chr 12:35
s hundred shekels of gold 1Chr 21:25
and Mattithiah, *s*, under 1Chr 25:3
The *s* to Bukkiah, he 1Chr 25:13
Ammiel the *s*, Issachar 1Chr 26:5
a chariot for *s* hundred 2Chr 1:17
three thousand and *s* 2Chr 2:17
amounting to *s* hundred 2Chr 3:8
Solomon in one year was *s* 2Chr 9:13
threescore and *s* talents 2Chr 9:13
were *s* steps to the throne 2Chr 9:18
s and thirtieth year of 2Chr 16:1
two thousand and *s* hundred ...2Chr 26:12
s hundred small cattle 2Chr 35:8
of Bani, *s* hundred forty ......Ezra 2:10
Adonikam, *s* hundred ....Ezra 2:13
Netophah, fifty and *s* ....Ezra 2:22
a hundred fifty and *s* ....Ezra 2:30
s hundred fifty and two ....Ezra 2:60
s thousand seven hundred .....Ezra 2:67
s year of the reign of ....Ezra 6:15
Israel, ninety and *s* ....Ezra 8:35
Hanun the *s* son of Zalaph ....Neh 3:30
one ox and *s* choice ....Neh 5:18
Binnui, *s* hundred forty ....Neh 7:15
Adonikam *s* hundred ....Neh 7:18
Gaba, *s* hundred twenty ....Neh 7:30
s hundred thirty and *s* ....Neh 7:68
to wit, *s* months with oil ......Esth 2:12
and *s* months with sweet ......Esth 2:12
He shall deliver thee in *s* .....Job 5:19
s things doth the Lord hate ...Prov 6:16
each one had *s* wings ....Is 6:2
hath served thee *s* years ......Jer 34:14
thousand and *s* hundred ....Jer 52:30
the *s* part of an hin ....Ezek 4:11
s men came from the way .....Ezek 9:2
leave but the *s* part ....Ezek 39:2
s cubits on this side, and *s* ....Ezek 40:12
s cubits broad on the one .....Ezek 41:1
wall of the house, *s* cubits .....Ezek 41:5
the *s* part of an ephah ....Ezek 45:13
shut the *s* working days ....Ezek 46:1
blemish, and *s* lambs ....Ezek 46:6
breadth thereof *s* cubits ....Dan 3:1
Darius the king in the *s* month.Hag 1:1
after *s* days Jesus taketh ......Matt 17:1
the *s* and ninth hour ....Matt 20:5
after *s* days Jesus taketh ......Mark 9:2
when the *s* hour was ....Mark 15:33
the *s* month the angel ....Luke 1:26
shut up three years and *s* .....Luke 4:25
it was about the *s* hour ....Luke 23:44
set there *s* waterpots ....John 2:6
it was about the *s* hour ....John 4:6
s days before the passover ....John 12:1
to pray about the *s* hour ......Acts 10:9
s brethren accompanied ....Acts 11:12
three years and *s* months ......James 5:17
each of them *s* wings ....Rev 4:8
had opened the *s* seal ....Rev 6:12
Saying to the *s* angel ....Rev 9:14
S hundred threescore and *s* ....Rev 13:18
thousand and *s* hundred ....Rev 14:20
sardonyx; the *s* sardius ....Rev 21:20

SIXSCORE—*one hundred twenty*
the king *s* talents of gold 1Kin 9:14
more than *s* thousand ....Jon 4:11

SIXTEEN

[*also* SIXTEENTH]
bare unto Jacob, even *s* ....Gen 46:18
sockets of silver, *s* sockets .....Ex 26:25
s thousand and five hundred ...Num 26:22
And *s* thousand persons ....Num 31:46
s cities with their villages ......Josh 15:41
Samaria, and reigned *s* years ..2Kin 13:10
S years old was he when 2Kin 15:2
reigned *s* years in 2Kin 16:2
Shimei had *s* sons and six 1Chr 4:27
to Bilgah, the *s* to Immer 1Chr 24:14
two sons and *s* daughters 2Chr 13:21
S years old was Uzziah 2Chr 26:3
s years in Jerusalem 2Chr 27:8
in the *s* day of the first 2Chr 29:17
threescore and *s* souls ....Acts 27:37

SIXTY
Mahalaleel lived *s* and five ....Gen 5:15
Jared were nine hundred *s* ....Gen 5:20
Enoch were three hundred *s* ...Gen 5:23
years old even unto *s* ....Lev 27:3
the rams *s*, the he goats *s* .....Num 7:88
lambs of the first year *s* ....Num 7:88
Adonikam, six hundred *s* .....Ezra 2:13
hundredfold, some *s* ....Matt 13:23
some thirty, and some *s* ....Mark 4:8

SIXTYFOLD—*sixty times*
some *s*, some thirtyfold ....Matt 13:8

SIZE—*the extent; dimensions*
curtains were all of one *s* .....Ex 36:9
one measure and one *s* 1Kin 6:25
manner of measure and *s* 1Chr 23:29

SKELETON—*the bones of the body*
Cremated ....Amos 2:1

SKEPTICAL—*inquiring; unbelieving*
Thomas, the doubter ....John 20:24-28

SKIES—*See* SKY

SKILL—*possessing special abilities*

Required of:
Soldiers 1Chr 5:18
Craftsmen 2Chr 2:7, 14
Musicians 2Chr 34:12

Obtained by:
Spirit's help ....Ex 31:2-5
God's Word ....Ps 119:98-100
Lord's help ....Ps 144:1

[*also* SKILLFUL, SKILLFULLY, SKILLFULNESS]
can *s* to hew timber like 1Kin 5:6
song, because he was *s* 1Chr 15:22
every willing *s* man, for 1Chr 28:21
thy servants can *s* to cut 2Chr 2:8
song; play *s* with a loud ....Ps 33:3
by the *s* of his hands ....Ps 78:72
nor yet favor to men of *s* .....Eccl 9:11
of brutish men, and *s* to ......Ezek 21:31
and *s* in all wisdom ....Dan 1:4
and *s* in all learning and ......Dan 1:17
thee *s* and understanding ......Dan 9:22
as are *s* of lamentation ....Amos 5:16

SKIN—*the external layer of a person's or animal's body; a hide or pelt*

Of animals, used for:
Clothing ....Gen 3:21
Deception ....Gen 27:16
Coverings ....Ex 26:14
Bottles ....Josh 9:4

Of man:
Diseased ....Lev 13:1-46
Sign of race ....Jer 13:23
Seal of death ....Job 19:26

[*also* SKINS]
she put the *s* of the kids ......Gen 27:16
is his raiment for his *s* ....Ex 22:27
of the bullock, and his *s* ......Ex 29:14
that the *s* of his face ....Ex 34:29
s of Moses' face shone ....Ex 34:35
s dyed red, and badgers *s* .....Ex 35:7
s of rams, and badgers' *s* ......Ex 35:23
tent of rams' *s* dyed red ....Ex 36:19
a covering of badgers' *s* ....Ex 36:19
of rams' *s* dyed red ....Ex 39:34
the covering of badgers' *s* .....Ex 39:34
And the *s* of the bullock ......Lev 4:11
vessel of wood..or *s* ....Lev 11:32
in a *s*, or..made of *s* ....Lev 13:48
in the garment, or in the *s* ....Lev 13:49
woof, or in any thing of *s* .....Lev 13:49
or in the woof, or in a *s* ......Lev 13:51
work that is made of *s* ....Lev 13:51
or any thing of *s*, wherein .....Lev 13:52
garment, or out of the *s* ....Lev 13:56
woof, or in any thing of *s* .....Lev 13:57
or whatsoever thing of *s* ......Lev 13:58
woof, or any thing of *s* ....Lev 13:59
the covering of badgers' *s* .....Num 4:6
covering of badgers' *s* ....Num 4:10
a covering of badgers' *s* ....Num 4:12
covering of the badgers' *s* .....Num 4:25
heifer in his sight; her *s* ....Num 19:5
S for *s*, yea, all that ....Job 2:4
hast clothed me with *s* ....Job 10:11
devour the strength of his *s* ...Job 18:13
My bone cleaveth to my *s* .....Job 19:20
escaped with the *s* of my ......Job 19:20
My *s* is black upon me ....Job 30:30
my bones cleave to my *s* ......Ps 102:5
Ethiopian change his *s* ....Jer 13:23
flesh and my *s*..made old .....Lam 3:4
Our *s* was black like an ....Lam 5:10
shod thee with badgers' *s* .....Ezek 16:10
and the *s* covered them ....Ezek 37:8
pluck off their *s* from off ......Mic 3:2
a girdle of a *s* about his ....Mark 1:6

SKIP—*to leap and bound*

[*also* SKIPPED, SKIPPEDST, SKIPPING]
them also to *s* like a calf ......Ps 29:6
mountains *s* like rams ....Ps 114:4
that ye *s* like rams ....Ps 114:6
s upon the hills ....Song 2:8
of him, thou *s* for ....Jer 48:27

SKIRT—*robe; garment*

[*also* SKIRTS]
nor discover his father's *s* .....Deut 22:30
spread therefore thy *s* ....Ruth 3:9
laid hold upon the *s* of 1Sam 15:27
he had cut off Saul's *s* 1Sam 24:5
see the *s* of thy robe in 1Sam 24:11
I cut off the *s* of thy 1Sam 24:11
down to the *s* of his ....Ps 133:2
Also in thy *s* is found ....Jer 2:34

S

iniquity are thy *s* . . . . . Jer 13:22
I discover thy *s* upon thy . . . . . Jer 13:26
Her filthiness is in her *s* . . . . . Lam 1:9
and bind them in thy *s* . . . . . Ezek 5:3
and I spread my *s* over . . . . . Ezek 16:8
will discover thy *s* upon . . . . . Nah 3:5
holy flesh in the *s* of his . . . . . Hag 2:12
and with his *s* do touch . . . . . Hag 2:12
hold of the *s* of him that . . . . . Zech 8:23

SKULL—*skeleton of the head*
Abimelech's crushed by a woman . . . . . Judg 9:53
Jezebel's left by dogs 2Kin 9:30-37
They brought Him to a place called . . . . . Mark 15:22
Another name for Golgotha . . . . . Matt 27:33
See GOLGOTHA
called the place of a *s* . . . . . John 19:17

SKY—*the expanse of the heavens*
Place of:
Stars . . . . . Heb 11:12
Expansion . . . . . Job 37:18
Weather changes . . . . . Matt 16:2, 3
Thunder . . . . . Ps 77:17
Figurative of:
God's abode . . . . . Ps 18:11
Righteousness . . . . . Is 45:8
Ultimate judgment . . . . . Jer 51:9

[*also* SKIES]
his excellency on the *s* . . . . . Deut 33:26
thick clouds of the *s* 2Sam 22:12
thick clouds of the *s* . . . . . Ps 18:11
s pour down righteousness . . . . Is 45:8
is lifted up even to the *s* . . . . . Jer 51:9
discern the face of the *s* . . . . . Luke 12:56

SLACK—*negligent; slow*

[*also* SLACKED, SLACKNESS]
not be *s* to him that . . . . . Deut 7:10
S not thy hand from thy . . . . . Josh 10:6
s not thy riding for me 2Kin 4:24
dealeth with a *s* hand . . . . . Prov 10:4
Let not thine hands be *s* . . . . . Zeph 3:16
the law is *s* and judgment . . . . . Hab 1:4
The Lord is not *s* 2Pet 3:9
as some men count *s* 2Pet 3:9

SLAIN—*See* SLAY

SLANDER—*a malicious and defamatory statement; to defame*
Described as:
Destructive . . . . . Prov 11:9
Deceitful . . . . . Ps 52:2
Deluding . . . . . Prov 10:18
Devouring . . . . . Prov 16:27-30
Hurled against:
Joseph . . . . . Gen 39:14-19
David 2Sam 10:3
Jews . . . . . Ezra 4:7-16
Christ . . . . . Matt 26:59-61
Paul . . . . . Acts 24:5, 6
Stephen . . . . . Acts 6:11
Christians 1Pet 2:12
Hurled against the righteous by:
Devil . . . . . Job 1:9-11
Revilers 1Pet 3:16
Hypocrites . . . . . Prov 11:9
False leaders 3John 9, 10
Charged against Christ as:
Winebibber . . . . . Matt 11:19
Blasphemer . . . . . Matt 9:3
Demonized . . . . . John 8:48, 52
Rebel . . . . . Luke 23:5
Insurrectionist . . . . . Luke 23:2
Christians:
Warned against . . . . . Titus 3:1, 2
Must endure . . . . . Matt 5:11, 12
Must lay aside . . . . . Eph 4:31

[*also* SLANDERED, SLANDEREST, SLANDERETH, SLANDEROUSLY, SLANDERS]
by bringing up a *s* upon . . . . . Num 14:36
hath *s* thy servant unto 2Sam 19:27
For I have heard the *s* . . . . . Ps 31:13
s thine own mother's son . . . . . Ps 50:20
Whoso privily *s* his neighbor . . Ps 101:5
revolters, walking with *s* . . . . . Jer 6:28
neighbor will walk with *s* . . . . . Jer 9:4
as we be *s* reported, and . . . . . Rom 3:8

SLANDERERS—*defamers*
wives be grave, not *s* 1Tim 3:11

SLANG—*See* SLING

SLAUGHTER—*to butcher; massacre*
from the *s* of Chedorlaomer . . . Gen 14:17
slew them with a great *s* . . . . . Josh 10:10
with a very great *s* . . . . . Judg 11:33
there was a very great *s* 1Sam 4:10
of the people with a great *s* . . . 1Sam 6:19
been now a much greater *s* 1Sam 14:30
David..returned from the *s* 1Sam 18:6
smote them with a great *s* 1Sam 23:5
David was returned from the *s* . 2Sam 1:1
there was there a great *s* 2Sam 18:7
slew them with a great *s* 2Chr 13:17
smote him with a great *s* 2Chr 28:5
the sword, and *s*, and . . . . . Esth 9:5
as an ox goeth to the *s* . . . . . Prov 7:22
according to..*s* of Midian . . . . . Is 10:26
according to the *s* of them . . . . Is 27:7
delivered them to the *s* . . . . . Is 34:2
s in the land of Idumea . . . . . Is 34:6
shall all bow down to the *s* . . . . Is 65:12
but the valley of *s* . . . . . Jer 7:32
out like sheep for the *s* . . . . . Jer 12:3
but The valley of *s* . . . . . Jer 19:6
men are gone..to the *s* . . . . . Jer 48:15
down like lambs to the *s* . . . . . Jer 51:40
every man a *s* weapon in . . . . . Ezek 9:2
it is wrapped up for the *s* . . . . . Ezek 21:15
for the *s* it is furnished . . . . . Ezek 21:28
are profound to make *s* . . . . . Hos 5:2
Esau may be cut off by *s* . . . . . Obad 9
Feed the flock of the *s* . . . . . Zech 11:4
led as a sheep to the *s* . . . . . Acts 8:32
as sheep for the *s* . . . . . Rom 8:36
from the *s* of the kings . . . . . Heb 7:1
hearts, as in a day of *s* . . . . . James 5:5

SLAVE—*servant considered as property*
Acquired by:
Purchase . . . . . Gen 17:12
Voluntary service . . . . . Ex 21:5-6
Birth . . . . . Ex 21:2-4
Capture . . . . . Deut 20:11-14
Debt 2Kin 4:1
Arrest . . . . . Ex 22:2, 3
Inheritance . . . . . Lev 25:46
Gift . . . . . Gen 29:24, 29
Rights of:
Sabbath rest . . . . . Ex 20:10
Share in religious feasts . . Deut 12:12, 18
Membership in covenant . Gen 17:10-14
Refuge for fugitive . . . . . Deut 23:15, 16
Murder of, punishable . . . Ex 21:12
Freedom of, if maimed . . Ex 21:26, 27
Entitled to justice . . . . . Job 31:13-15
Privileges of:
Entrusted with missions . . Gen 24:1-14
Advice of, heeded 1Sam 9:5-10
Marriage in master's house 1Chr 2:34, 35
Rule over sons . . . . . Prov 17:2
May become heir . . . . . Gen 15:1-4
May secure freedom . . . . . Ex 21:2-6
State of, under Christianity:
Union "in Christ" . . . . . Gal 3:28
Treatment of with justice . Eph 6:9
Duties of, as pleasing God . . . . . Eph 6:5-8
See BONDSLAVE; SERVANT

[*also* SLAVES]
is he a homeborn *s* . . . . . Jer 2:14
chariots, and *s*, and souls . . . . . Rev 18:13

SLAY—*to kill violently or in great numbers*

[*also* SLAIN, SLAYETH, SLAYING, SLEW, SLEWEST]
his brother and *s* him . . . . . Gen 4:8
findeth me shall *s* me . . . . . Gen 4:14
whosoever *s* Cain . . . . . Gen 4:15
I have *s* a man to my . . . . . Gen 4:23
s the righteous with the . . . . . Gen 18:25
s also a righteous nation? . . . . . Gen 20:4
s me for my wife's sake . . . . . Gen 20:11
the knife to *s* his son . . . . . Gen 22:10
I *s* my brother Jacob . . . . . Gen 27:41
and *s* all the males . . . . . Gen 34:25
against me, and *s* me . . . . . Gen 34:30
let us *s* him, and cast him . . . . Gen 37:20
What profit is it if we *s* . . . . . Gen 37:26
and the Lord *s* him . . . . . Gen 38:7
S my two sons, if I bring . . . . . Gen 42:37
their anger they *s* a man . . . . . Gen 49:6
he *s* the Egyptian, and hid . . . . Ex 2:12
he sought to *s* Moses . . . . . Ex 2:15
I will *s* thy son..first-born . . . . . Ex 4:23
in their hand to *s* us . . . . . Ex 5:21
his neighbor, to *s* him . . . . . Ex 21:14
innocent and righteous *s* . . . . . Ex 23:7
out, to *s* them in the . . . . . Ex 32:12
s the sin offering in the . . . . . Lev 4:29
And he *s* it; and Moses . . . . . Lev 8:15
s the calf of the sin . . . . . Lev 9:8
s it, and offered it for sin . . . . . Lev 9:15
he shall *s* the lamb in the . . . . . Lev 14:13
in the blood of the *s* bird . . . . . Lev 14:51
flocks and the herds be *s* . . . . . Num 11:22
one shall *s* her before his . . . . . Num 19:3
one that is *s* with a sword . . . . . Num 19:16
now also I had *s* thee . . . . . Num 22:33
the Israelite that was *s* . . . . . Num 25:14
was *s* in the day of the . . . . . Num 25:18
Moses; and they *s* all the . . . . . Num 31:7
they *s* the kings of Midian . . . . Num 31:8
son of Beor they *s* with . . . . . Num 31:8
hath touched any *s* . . . . . Num 31:19
shall *s* the murderer . . . . . Num 35:19
he shall *s* him . . . . . Num 35:19
he had *s* Sihon the king of . . . . Deut 1:4
s them in the wilderness . . . . . Deut 9:28
be found *s* in the land . . . . . Deut 21:1
known who hath *s* him . . . . . Deut 21:1
is next unto the *s* man . . . . . Deut 21:3
his neighbor, and *s* him . . . . . Deut 22:26
reward to *s* an innocent . . . . . Deut 27:25
Thine ox shall be *s* before . . . . Deut 28:31
and *s* the men of Ai . . . . . Josh 8:21
end of *s* all the inhabitants . . . . Josh 8:24
s them with a great . . . . . Josh 10:10
had made an end of *s* . . . . . Josh 10:20
smote them, and *s* them . . . . . Josh 10:26
deliver them up all *s* . . . . . Josh 11:6
Israel *s* with the sword . . . . . Josh 13:22
s of them in Bezek ten . . . . . Judg 1:4
and they *s* Sheshai, and . . . . . Judg 1:10
they *s* of Moab at that . . . . . Judg 3:29
they *s* Oreb upon the . . . . . Judg 7:25
and Zeeb they *s* at the . . . . . Judg 7:25
were they whom ye *s* at . . . . . Judg 8:18
I would not *s* you . . . . . Judg 8:19
s his brethren..sons of . . . . . Judg 9:5
and have *s* his sons . . . . . Judg 9:18
in the fields, and *s* them . . . . . Judg 9:44
Draw thy sword, and *s* me . . . . Judg 9:54
say not of me A woman *s* . . . . . Judg 9:54
in *s* his seventy brethren . . . . . Judg 9:56
s thirty men of them . . . . . Judg 14:19
which *s* many of us . . . . . Judg 16:24
the dead which he *s* at . . . . . Judg 16:30
than they which he *s* in . . . . . Judg 16:30
of the woman that was *s* . . . . . Judg 20:4
they *s* a bullock, and 1Sam 1:25
because the Lord would *s* 1Sam 2:25
and Phinehas, were *s* 1Sam 4:11
that it *s* us not, and our 1Sam 5:11
s the Ammonites until 1Sam 11:11
calves, and *s* them on the 1Sam 14:32
but *s* both man and woman . . . 1Sam 15:3
and smote him, and *s* him 1Sam 17:35

Thy servant *s* both the lion 1Sam 17:36
the Philistine, and *s* him 1Sam 17:50
s of the Philistines two 1Sam 18:27
liveth, he shall not be *s* 1Sam 19:6
and *s* them with a great 1Sam 19:8
to *s* him in the morning 1Sam 19:11
me iniquity, *s* me thyself 1Sam 20:8
Wherefore shall he be *s*? 1Sam 20:32
of his father to *s* David 1Sam 20:33
whom thou *s* in the valley 1Sam 21:9
Turn, and *s* the priests of 1Sam 22:17
Saul had *s* the Lord's 1Sam 22:21
Saul *s* his thousands, and 1Sam 29:5
Philistines *s* Jonathan 1Sam 31:2
came to strip the *s* 1Sam 31:8
Stand..upon me, and *s* me 2Sam 1:9
stood upon him, and *s* him 2Sam 1:10
s the Lord's anointed 2Sam 1:16
From the blood of the *s* 2Sam 1:22
s their brother Asahel 2Sam 3:30
smote him, and *s* him 2Sam 4:7
and they *s* them, and cut 2Sam 4:12
David *s* of the Syrians 2Sam 8:5
s him with the sword of 2Sam 12:9
s all the young men the 2Sam 13:32
one smote the other, and *s* 2Sam 14:6
smote Absalom, and *s* him 2Sam 18:15
Saul sought to *s* them in 2Sam 21:2
Philistines had *s* Saul in 2Sam 21:12
Sibbechai..*s* Saph 2Sam 21:18
brother of David *s* him 2Sam 21:21
and *s* the Philistines 2Sam 23:12
he *s* two lionlike men of 2Sam 23:20
and *s* a lion in the midst 2Sam 23:20
And he *s* an Egyptian, a 2Sam 23:21
s him with his own spear 2Sam 23:21
Adonijah *s* sheep and 1Kin 1:9
s oxen and fat cattle 1Kin 1:19
not *s* his servant with the 1Kin 1:51
s them with the sword 1Kin 2:32
child, and in no wise *s* it 1Kin 3:27
gone up to bury the *s* 1Kin 11:15
David *s* them of Zobah 1Kin 11:24
s all the house of Baasha 1Kin 16:11
and hath also *s* the king 1Kin 16:16
and to *s* my son? 1Kin 17:18
whom I sojourn, by *s* her 1Kin 17:20
find thee, he shall *s* me 1Kin 18:12
when Jezebel *s* the prophets ... 1Kin 18:13
s thy prophets with 1Kin 19:10
of Hazael shall Jehu *s* 1Kin 19:17
of Jehu shall Elisha *s* 1Kin 19:17
yoke of oxen, and *s* them 1Kin 19:21
they *s* every one his man 1Kin 20:20
and *s* they Syrians with a 1Kin 20:21
lion found him, and *s* him 1Kin 20:36
the kings are surely *s* 2Kin 3:23
young men wilt thou *s* 2Kin 8:12
Zimri..who *s* his master? 2Kin 9:31
king's sons, and *s* seventy 2Kin 10:7
my master, and *s* him 2Kin 10:9
but who *s* all these? 2Kin 10:9
s them at the pit of the 2Kin 10:14
king's sons which were *s* 2Kin 11:2
so that he was not *s* 2Kin 11:2
Let her not be *s* in the 2Kin 11:15
s Mattan..priest of Baal 2Kin 11:18
and *s* Joash in the house 2Kin 12:20
which had *s* the king 2Kin 14:5
murderers he *s* not 2Kin 14:6
to Lachish, and *s* him 2Kin 14:19
s him, and reigned in his 2Kin 15:30
which *s* some of them 2Kin 17:25
s them, because they 2Kin 17:26
s all them that had 2Kin 21:24
he *s* all the priests of the 2Kin 23:20
he *s* him at Megiddo 2Kin 23:29
s them at Riblah in the 2Kin 25:21
there fell down many *s* 1Chr 5:22
Philistines *s* Jonathan 1Chr 10:2
Philistines..strip the *s* 1Chr 10:8
and *s* the Philistines 1Chr 11:14
he *s* two lionlike men of 1Chr 11:22
s a lion in a pit in a 1Chr 11:22
he *s* an Egyptian, a man 1Chr 11:23
s him with his own spear 1Chr 11:23
s of the Edomites in the 1Chr 18:12
Sibbechai..*s* Sippai 1Chr 20:4
David's brother *s* him 1Chr 20:7
Abijah and his people *s* 2Chr 13:17
fell down *s* of Israel five 2Chr 13:17
utterly to *s* and destroy 2Chr 20:23
camp had *s* all the eldest 2Chr 22:1
to Ahaziah, he *s* them 2Chr 22:8
king's sons that were *s* 2Chr 22:11
her, let him be *s* with the 2Chr 23:14
king's house, they *s* her 2Chr 23:15
kindness..but *s* his son 2Chr 24:22
he *s* his servants that had 2Chr 25:3
Lachish after him, and *s* 2Chr 25:27
s Maaseiah the king's son 2Chr 28:7
ye have *s* them in a rage 2Chr 28:9
s him in his own house 2Chr 33:24
who *s* their young men 2Chr 36:17
and *s* them and cause the ..... Neh 4:11
they will come to *s* thee .... Neh 6:10
will they come to *s* thee .... Neh 6:10
and *s* thy prophets which ...... Neh 9:26
to be destroyed, to be *s* .... Esth 7:4
s, and to cause to perish ...... Esth 8:11
Jews *s* and destroyed five ..... Esth 9:6
The Jews have *s* and .... Esth 9:12
s three hundred men at .... Esth 9:15
s the servants with the .... Job 1:15
and envy *s* the silly .... Job 5:2
If the scourge *s* suddenly ...... Job 9:23
viper's tongue shall *s* him ..... Job 20:16
Evil shall *s* the wicked .... Ps 34:21
and seeketh to *s* him .... Ps 37:32
S them not, lest my .... Ps 59:11
ye shall be *s* all of you .... Ps 62:3
s the fattest of them, and ..... Ps 78:31
in pieces, as one that is *s* ..... Ps 89:10
blood, and *s* their fish .... Ps 105:29
might even *s* the broken ...... Ps 109:16
And *s* famous kings; for ...... Ps 136:18
the simple shall *s* them .... Prov 1:32
men have been *s* by her .... Prov 7:26
that are ready to be *s* .... Prov 24:11
they shall fall under the *s* ..... Is 10:4
lips shall be *s* the wicked ...... Is 11:4
thy land, and *s* thy people .... Is 14:20
s oxen, and killing sheep ...... Is 22:13
no more cover her *s* .... Is 26:21
he shall *s* the dragon that ..... Is 27:1
he *s* according to the .... Is 27:7
of them that are *s* by him? .... Is 27:7
s the children in the valleys ... Is 57:5
an ox as if he *s* a man .... Is 66:3
the *s* of the Lord shall be ..... Is 66:16
of the forest shall *s* them ..... Jer 5:6
the *s* of the daughter of .... Jer 9:1
young men be *s* by the .... Jer 18:21
counsel against me to *s* me .... Jer 18:23
he *s* me not from the .... Jer 20:17
he shall *s* them before .... Jer 29:21
whom I have *s* in mine anger .. Jer 33:5
Babylon *s* the sons of .... Jer 39:6
Babylon *s* all the nobles ...... Jer 39:6
and I will *s* Ishmael the .... Jer 40:15
wherefore should he *s* .... Jer 40:15
Ishmael also *s* all the Jews .... Jer 41:3
s them not among their .... Jer 41:8
s because of Gedeliah .... Jer 41:9
it with them that were *s* .... Jer 41:9
Nethaniah had *s* Gedaliah ..... Jer 41:18
S all her bullocks; let .... Jer 50:27
her *s* shall fall in the .... Jer 51:47
caused the *s* of Israel .... Jer 51:49
fall the *s* of all the earth ...... Jer 51:49
Babylon *s* the sons of .... Jer 52:10
he *s* also all the princes .... Jer 52:10
s all that were pleasant to ..... Lam 2:4
priest and the prophet be *s* .... Lam 2:20
hast *s*, thou hast not pitied .... Lam 3:43
They that be *s* with the .... Lam 4:9
down your *s* men before ...... Ezek 6:4
when their *s* men shall .... Ezek 6:13
S utterly old and young .... Ezek 9:6
they went forth and *s* in ...... Ezek 9:7
while they were *s* them .... Ezek 9:8
have multiplied your *s* in ...... Ezek 11:6
filled the streets..with the *s* .... Ezek 11:6
thou hast *s* my children .... Ezek 16:21
time, the sword of the *s* .... Ezek 21:14
the great men that are *s* ...... Ezek 21:14
they had *s* their children ...... Ezek 23:39
they shall *s* their sons .... Ezek 23:47
he shall *s* thy people .... Ezek 26:11
s in the midst of the seas ..... Ezek 28:8
before him that *s* thee .... Ezek 28:9
hand of him that *s* thee .... Ezek 28:9
fill the land with the *s* .... Ezek 30:11
with them that be *s* by .... Ezek 31:18
lie uncircumcised, *s* by .... Ezek 32:21
all of them *s*, fallen by .... Ezek 32:23
bed in the midst of the *s* ...... Ezek 32:25
uncircumcised, *s* by the .... Ezek 32:25
midst of them that be *s* .... Ezek 32:25
that are *s* with the sword ...... Ezek 32:28
gone down with the *s* .... Ezek 32:30
that be *s* by the sword .... Ezek 32:30
them that are *s* with the ...... Ezek 32:32
mountains with his *s* men ..... Ezek 35:8
they fall that are *s* with .... Ezek 35:8
they *s* their sacrifices .... Ezek 40:41
they shall *s* the burnt .... Ezek 44:11
wise men should be *s* .... Dan 2:13
sought Daniel..to be *s* .... Dan 2:13
the flame of the fire *s* .... Dan 3:22
even till the beast was *s* .... Dan 7:11
a dry land, and *s* her with ..... Hos 2:3
s them by the words of .... Hos 6:5
will *s* all the princes .... Amos 2:3
young men have I *s* with ...... Amos 4:10
sword, and it shall *s* them ..... Amos 9:4
there is a multitude of *s* .... Nah 3:3
continually to *s* the nations? ... Hab 1:17
ye shall be *s* by my sword ..... Zeph 2:12
s all the children .... Matt 2:16
spitefully, and *s* them .... Matt 22:6
be *s*, and be raised the .... Luke 9:22
Siloam fell and *s* them .... Luke 13:4
hands have crucified and *s* .... Acts 2:23
raised up Jesus whom ye *s* .... Acts 5:30
ye offered to me *s* beasts ..... Acts 7:42
Arise, Peter; *s* and eat .... Acts 11:7
Pilate that he should be *s* ..... Acts 13:28
raiment of them that *s* him .... Acts 22:20
deceived me, and by it *s* me ... Rom 7:11
cross, having *s* the enmity ..... Eph 2:16
were *s* with the sword .... Heb 11:37
wicked one, and *s* his brother . 1John 3:12
thou wast *s*..redeemed .... Rev 5:9
s for the word of God .... Rev 6:9
for to *s* the third part .... Rev 9:15
the Lamb *s* from the .... Rev 13:8
remnant were *s* with the ...... Rev 19:21

SLAYER—*one who kills*

the *s* may flee thither .... Num 35:11
shall deliver the *s* .... Num 35:25
revenger of blood kill the *s* .... Num 35:27
the *s* might flee thither .... Deut 4:42
this is the case of the *s* .... Deut 19:4
That the *s* that killeth .... Josh 20:3
then shall the *s* return .... Josh 20:6
into the hand of the *s* .... Ezek 21:11

SLEEP—*a state of complete or partial unconsciousness; used figuratively of death*

Descriptive of:

Slumber .... Prov 6:4, 10
Desolation .... Jer 51:39, 57
Unregeneracy 1Thess 5:6, 7
Death .... John 11:11-14
Spiritual indifference ..... Matt 25:5
Prophetic vision .... Dan 8:18

Beneficial:

When given by God ..... Ps 3:5
Ps 127:2
While trusting God ...... Ps 4:8
While obeying parents ... Prov 6:20-22
When following wisdom .. Prov 3:21-24
To the working man ..... Eccl 5:12

S

After duty is done . . . . . . .Ps 132:1-5
During a pleasant dream .Jer 31:23-26

Condemned:
When excessive . . . . .Prov 6:9-11
During harvest . . . . .Prov 10:5
In times of danger . . . . . . .Matt 26:45-47

Inability to:
Caused by worry . . . . .Dan 2:1
Produced by insomnia . . .Esth 6:1
Brought on by overwork .Gen 31:40

[*also* SLEEPEST, SLEEPETH, SLEEPING, SLEPT]
s to fall upon Adam, and he *s* .Gen 2:21
a deep *s* fell upon Abram . . . . .Gen 15:12
down in that place to *s* . . . . . . .Gen 28:11
Jacob awaked out of his *s* . . . . .Gen 28:16
my *s* departed from mine . . . . .Gen 31:40
poor, thou shalt not *s* with . . . .Deut 24:12
shalt *s* with thy fathers . . . . .Deut 31:16
And he awaked out of *s* . . . . . .Judg 16:14
he awoke out of his *s* . . . . .Judg 16:20
Samuel was laid down to *s* 1Sam 3:3
Saul lay *s* within the trench . . .1Sam 26:7
and thou shalt *s* with thy 2Sam 7:12
Uriah *s* at the door of the 2Sam 11:9
the king shall *s* with his 1Kin 1:21
David *s* with his fathers 1Kin 2:10
David *s* with his fathers 1Kin 11:21
he *s* with his fathers, and 1Kin 14:20
And Abijam *s* with his 1Kin 15:8
So Baasha *s* with his 1Kin 16:6
peradventure he *s* and 1Kin 18:27
lay and *s* under a juniper 1Kin 19:5
Jehoshaphat *s* with his 1Kin 22:50
Joram *s* with his fathers 2Kin 8:24
And Jehoahaz *s* with his 2Kin 13:9
And Jehoash *s* with his 2Kin 14:16
And Jeroboam *s* with his 2Kin 14:29
And Menahem *s* with his 2Kin 15:22
Ahaz *s* with his fathers 2Kin 16:20
And Manasseh *s* with his 2Kin 21:18
Solomon *s* with his 2Chr 9:31
So Abijah *s* with his 2Chr 14:1
Jehoshaphat *s* with his 2Chr 21:1
So Uzziah *s* with his 2Chr 26:23
Ahaz *s* with his fathers 2Chr 28:27
So Manasseh *s* with his 2Chr 33:20
quiet, I should have *s* . . . . .Job 3:13
be raised out of their *s* . . . . .Job 14:12
mine eyes, lest I *s* the *s* . . . . . . .Ps 13:3
why *s* thou O Lord? . . . . .Ps 44:23
spoiled, they have *s* their *s* . . . .Ps 76:5
cast into a dead *s* . . . . .Ps 76:6
awaked as one out of *s* . . . . . . .Ps 78:65
neither slumber nor *s* . . . . .Ps 121:4
For they *s* not, except . . . . .Prov 4:16
their *s* is taken away . . . . .Prov 4:16
folding of the hands to *s* . . . . . .Prov 6:10
slothfulness into a deep *s* . . . . .Prov 19:15
Love not *s*, lest thou . . . . .Prov 20:13
a little *s*, a little slumber . . . . . .Prov 24:33
folding of the hands to *s* . . . . . .Prov 24:33
nor night seeth *s* . . . . .Eccl 8:16
I *s*, but my heart waketh . . . . . .Song 5:2
none shall slumber nor *s* . . . . . .Is 5:27
the spirit of deep *s* . . . . .Is 29:10
s..loving to slumber . . . . .Is 56:10
and *s* in the woods . . . . .Ezek 34:25
his *s* went from him . . . . .Dan 6:18
then was I in a deep *s* . . . . .Dan 10:9
many of them that *s* . . . . .Dan 12:2
their baker *s* all the night . . . . .Hos 7:6
man is wakened out of his *s* . . .Zech 4:1
Joseph being raised from *s* . . . .Matt 1:24
maid is not dead, but *s* . . . . . . .Matt 9:24
while men *s*, his enemy . . . . . . .Matt 13:25
they all slumbered and *s* . . . . . .Matt 25:5
bodies of the saints which *s* . . .Matt 27:52
stole him away while we *s* . . . . .Matt 28:13
And should *s* and rise . . . . .Mark 4:27
damsel is not dead, but *s* . . . . . .Mark 5:39
Suddenly he find you *s* . . . . .Mark 13:36
and findeth them *s* . . . . .Mark 14:37
unto Peter, Simon, *s* thou? . . . .Mark 14:37
S on now, and take your rest . .Mark 14:41
she is not dead, but *s* . . . . .Luke 8:52
with him were heavy with *s* . . .Luke 9:32
found them *s* for sorrow . . . . . .Luke 22:45
Why *s* ye? rise and pray . . . . . .Luke 22:46
Our friend Lazarus *s* . . . . .John 11:11
Lord, if he *s*, he shall . . . . .John 11:12
Peter was *s* between two . . . . . .Acts 12:6
fell on *s*, and was laid . . . . .Acts 13:36
awaking out of his *s* . . . . .Acts 16:27
being fallen into a deep *s* . . . . .Acts 20:9
he sunk down with *s* . . . . .Acts 20:9
time to awake out of *s* . . . . .Rom 13:11
among you, and many *s* 1Cor 11:30
first fruits of them that *s* 1Cor 15:20
We shall not all *s* 1Cor 15:51
Awake thou that *s* . . . . .Eph 5:14
them also which *s* in Jesus 1Thess 4:14
whether we wake or *s* 1Thess 5:10

SLEEPER—*one who sleeps*
What meanest thou, O *s*? . . . . .Jon 1:6

SLEIGHT—*cunning; artifice*
Christians, beware of . . . .Eph 4:14

SLEPT—*See* SLEEP

SLEW, SLEWEST—*See* SLAY

SLIDE—*to slip*

[*also* SLIDDEN, SLIDETH]
their foot shall *s* in due . . . . . . .Deut 32:35
therefore I shall not *s* . . . . .Ps 26:1
none of his steps shall *s* . . . . . . .Ps 37:31
people of Jerusalem *s* back . . . .Jer 8:5
s back as a..heifer . . . . .Hos 4:16

SLIGHTLY—*lightly; not seriously*
daughter of my people *s* . . . . . .Jer 6:14

SLIME—*soft, moist earth or clay*
Used in Babel's tower . . .Gen 11:3

daubed it with *s* . . . . .Ex 2:3

SLIMEPITS—*holes in the ground*
Siddim was full of *s* . . . . .Gen 14:10

SLING—*an instrument for throwing stones; to hurl*

Used by:
Warriors . . . . .Judg 20:16
David 1Sam 17:40-50

Figurative of:
God's punishment 1Sam 25:29
Captivity . . . . .Jer 10:18
Foolishness . . . . .Prov 26:8

[*also* SLINGS, SLANG]
took..a stone, and *s* it 1Sam 17:49
bows, and *s* to cast stones 2Chr 26:14

SLINGERS—*men who used slings in battle*
the *s* went about it, and 2Kin 3:25

SLINGSTONES—*stones used in a sling*
s are turned with him . . . . .Job 41:28
and subdue with *s* . . . . .Zech 9:15

SLIP—*to steal away; to slide or fall*

[*also* SLIPPED, SLIPPERY, SLIPPETH]
head *s* from the helve . . . . .Deut 19:5
he *s* away out of Saul's 1Sam 19:10
my feet did not *s* 2Sam 22:37
He that is ready to *s* with . . . . .Job 12:5
that my footsteps *s* not . . . . .Ps 17:5
that my feet did not *s* . . . . .Ps 18:36
their way be dark and *s* . . . . .Ps 35:6
when my foot *s*, they . . . . .Ps 38:16
my steps had well-nigh *s* . . . . . .Ps 73:2
set them in *s* pieces . . . . .Ps 73:18
When I said, My foot *s* . . . . . . .Ps 94:18
way shall be..as *s* ways . . . . .Jer 23:12
we should let them *s* . . . . .Heb 2:1

SLIPS—*cuttings made from a plant*
set it with strange *s* . . . . .Is 17:10

SLOTHFUL—*lazy; indolent*

Sources of, in:
Excessive sleep . . . . .Prov 6:9-11
Laziness . . . . .Prov 19:15, 24
Indifference . . . . .Judg 18:9
Desires . . . . .Prov 21:25
Fearful imaginations . . . . .Prov 22:13

Way of:
Brings hunger . . . . .Prov 19:15
Leads to poverty . . . . .Prov 20:4
Produces waste . . . . .Prov 18:9
Causes decay . . . . .Eccl 10:18
Results in forced labor . . .Prov 12:25

Antidotes of, in:
Faithfulness . . . . .Matt 25:26-30
Fervent spirit . . . . .Rom 12:11
Following the faithful . . . .Heb 6:12

[*also* SLOTHFULNESS]
The *s* man roasteth not . . . . . . .Prov 12:27
way of the *s* man is as . . . . .Prov 15:19
I went by the field of the *s* . . . .Prov 24:30
The *s* man saith, There is . . . . .Prov 26:13
s hideth his hand in his . . . . . . .Prov 26:15

SLOW—*sluggish; not hasty*

[*also* SLOWLY]
s of speech, and of a *s* . . . . .Ex 4:10
s to anger and of great . . . . .Neh 9:17
s to anger, and plenteous . . . . .Ps 103:8
He that is *s* to wrath . . . . .Prov 14:29
He that is *s* to anger . . . . .Prov 16:32
s to anger, and of great . . . . . . .Joel 2:13
s to anger, and of great . . . . . . .Jon 4:2
The Lord is *s* to anger . . . . .Nah 1:3
O fools, and *s* of heart . . . . .Luke 24:25
when we had sailed *s* . . . . .Acts 27:7
s to speak, *s* to wrath . . . . .James 1:19

SLOW BELLIES—*lazy gluttons*
Paul calls Cretians such . .Titus 1:12

SLUGGARD—*a lazy person*
Go to the ant, thou *s* . . . . .Prov 6:6
so is the *s* to them . . . . .Prov 10:26
The soul of the *s* desireth . . . . .Prov 13:4
The *s* is wiser in his own . . . . . .Prov 26:16

SLUICES—*artificial passages for water, usually equipped with floodgates to measure the flow*
that make *s* and ponds . . . . .Is 19:10

SLUMBER—*to sleep*

[*also* SLUMBERED, SLUMBERETH, SLUMBERINGS]
in *s* upon the bed . . . . .Job 33:15
keepeth thee will not *s* . . . . .Ps 121:3
shall neither *s* nor sleep . . . . . . .Ps 121:4
eyes, or *s* to mine eyelids . . . . .Ps 132:4
eyes, nor *s* to thine eyelids . . . .Prov 6:4
a little sleep, a little *s* . . . . .Prov 24:33
none shall *s* nor sleep . . . . .Is 5:27
Thy shepherds *s*, O king . . . . . .Nah 3:18
tarried, they all *s* and slept . . . .Matt 25:5
given them the spirit of *s* . . . . .Rom 11:8
and their damnation *s* not 2Pet 2:3

SMALL—*little in size; few in number*

Applied to God's:
Choice . . . . .Num 16:5, 9
Faithful remnant . . . . .Is 1:9

Applied to man's:
Sin . . . . .Ezek 16:20
Unconcern . . . . .Zech 4:10

[*also* SMALLEST]
blindness, both *s* and great . . . .Gen 19:11
shall become *s* dust in all . . . . .Ex 9:9
lay a *s* round thing . . . . .Ex 16:14
as *s* as the hoarfrost on the . . .Ex 16:14
s matter they judged . . . . .Ex 18:26
beat some of it very *s* . . . . .Ex 30:36
sweet incense beaten *s* . . . . .Lev 16:12
s thing that thou hast . . . . .Num 16:13
took the *s* towns thereof . . . . . .Num 32:41
hear the *s* as well as..great . . . .Deut 1:17
it, and ground it very *s* . . . . . . .Deut 9:21
until it was as *s* as dust . . . . . . .Deut 9:21
measures, a great and a *s* . . . . .Deut 25:14
men of the city both *s* and 1Sam 5:9

s of the tribes of Israel? ... 1Sam 9:21
slew not any..great or *s* ... 1Sam 30:2
this was yet a *s* thing ... 2Sam 7:19
beat them as *s* as the dust ... 2Sam 22:43
I desire one *s* petition ... 1Kin 2:20
Fight neither with *s* nor ... 1Kin 22:31
their inhabitants were of *s* ... 2Kin 19:26
stamped it *s* to powder ... 2Kin 23:6
this was a *s* thing in thine ... 1Chr 17:17
as well the *s* as the great ... 1Chr 26:13
death, whether *s* or great ... 2Chr 15:13
came with a *s* company ... 2Chr 24:24
all the people, great and *s* ... 2Chr 34:30
five thousand *s* cattle ... 2Chr 35:9
both unto great and *s* ... Esth 1:5
The *s* and great are there ... Job 3:19
consolations of God *s* ... Job 15:11
likewise to the *s* rain ... Job 37:6
did I beat them *s* as the ... Ps 18:42
fear the Lord, both *s* ... Ps 115:13
thy strength is *s* ... Prov 24:10
of great and *s* cattle ... Eccl 2:7
Is it a *s* thing for you ... Is 7:13
all vessels of *s* quantity ... Is 22:24
inhabitants were of *s* ... Is 37:27
and beat them *s* ... Is 41:15
for a *s* moment..forsaken ... Is 54:7
Both the great and the *s* ... Jer 16:6
a *s* number that escape ... Jer 44:28
I will make thee *s* among ... Jer 49:15
Seemeth it a *s* thing unto ... Ezek 34:18
strong with a *s* people ... Dan 11:23
Jacob arise? for he is *s* ... Amos 7:2
wheat making the ephah *s* ... Amos 8:5
thee *s* among the heathen ... Obad 2
that a *s* ship should wait ... Mark 3:9
they had a few *s* fishes ... Mark 8:7
made a scourge of *s* cords ... John 2:15
barley loaves..two *s* fishes ... John 6:9
s stir among the soldiers ... Acts 12:18
no *s* dissension and ... Acts 15:2
arose no *s* stir about that ... Acts 19:23
no *s* gain unto the ... Acts 19:24
witnessing both to *s* ... Acts 26:22
no *s* tempest lay on us ... Acts 27:20
it is a very *s* thing ... 1Cor 4:3
judge the *s* matters? ... 1Cor 6:2
about with a very *s* helm ... James 3:4
fear thy name, *s* and great ... Rev 11:18
both *s* and great, rich ... Rev 13:16
fear him, both *s* and great ... Rev 19:5
bond, both *s* and great ... Rev 19:18
I saw the dead, *s* and great ... Rev 20:12

SMART—*to feel or endure distress*
a stranger shall *s* for it ... Prov 11:15

SMELL—*to detect odors; odor; aroma*

[*also* SMELLED, SMELLETH, SMELLING]
the Lord *s* a sweet savor ... Gen 8:21
he *s* the *s* of his raiment ... Gen 27:27
s of my son is as the *s* ... Gen 27:27
make like unto that, to *s* ... Ex 30:38
will not *s* the savor ... Lev 26:31
nor hear, nor eat, nor *s* ... Deut 4:28
he *s* the battle afar off ... Job 39:25
thy garments *s* of myrrh ... Ps 45:8
noses have they, but they *s* ... Ps 115:6
sendeth forth the *s* ... Song 1:12
the *s* of thine ointments ... Song 4:10
the *s* of thy garments ... Song 4:11
like the *s* of Lebanon ... Song 4:11
with sweet *s* myrrh ... Song 5:5
The mandrakes give a *s* ... Song 7:13
instead of sweet *s* there ... Is 3:24
the *s* of fire had passed ... Dan 3:27
hearing, where were the *s*? ... 1Cor 12:17

SMITE—*to attack or afflict suddenly and with injury*

Descriptive of:
Curse ... Gen 8:21
Plagues ... Ex 3:20
Miracle ... Ex 17:5, 6
God's punishments ... Deut 28:22-28
Defeat ... 1Sam 4:2, 10
Death ... 2Sam 4:6, 7
Fear ... Dan 5:6
Slapping ... Matt 5:39

Expressive of God's judgment on:
Philistines ... 1Sam 5:6, 9
Pagan nation ... 2Chr 14:12
King's house ... 2Chr 21:5-19
Jews ... Jer 14:19

Used Messianically of Christ's:
Scourging ... Is 50:6
Bearing our sins ... Is 53:4
Death ... Zech 13:7
Judgment ... Is 11:4

[*also* SMITEST, SMITETH, SMITING, SMITTEN, SMOTE, SMOTEST]
and *s* the Rephaim in ... Gen 14:5
and *s* them, and pursued ... Gen 14:15
come to the one..and *s* it ... Gen 32:8
he will come and *s* me ... Gen 32:11
s Midian in the field ... Gen 36:35
an Egyptian *s* an Hebrew ... Ex 2:11
Wherefore *s* thou thy ... Ex 2:13
I will *s* with the rod ... Ex 7:17
s the waters..in the river ... Ex 7:20
the Lord had *s* the river ... Ex 7:25
hail *s* throughout the land ... Ex 9:25
and the rie were not *s* ... Ex 9:32
will *s* all the first-born ... Ex 12:12
to *s* the Egyptians ... Ex 12:23
unto your houses to *s* you ... Ex 12:23
when he *s* the Egyptians ... Ex 12:27
rod..thou *s* the river ... Ex 17:5
s a man, so that he die ... Ex 21:12
s his father, or his mother ... Ex 21:15
if a man *s* his servant ... Ex 21:20
he *s* out his manservant's ... Ex 21:27
that I *s* all the first-born ... Num 3:13
Lord *s* the people with a ... Num 11:33
I will *s* them with the ... Num 14:12
not *s* before your enemies ... Num 14:42
with his rod he *s* the rock ... Num 20:11
they *s* him, and his sons ... Num 21:35
wall: and he *s* her again ... Num 22:25
thou *s* thine ass these three ... Num 22:32
he *s* his hands together ... Num 24:10
shall *s* the corners of Moab ... Num 24:17
if he *s* him with ... Num 35:16
Or in enmity *s* him ... Num 35:21
he that *s* him shall surely ... Num 35:21
lest ye be *s* before your ... Deut 1:42
we *s* him, and his sons ... Deut 2:33
the children of Israel *s* ... Deut 4:46
thou shalt *s* them ... Deut 7:2
s him mortally that he die ... Deut 19:11
thou shalt *s* every male ... Deut 20:13
the hand of him that *s* him ... Deut 25:11
s before thine enemies ... Deut 28:25
The Lord shall *s* thee ... Deut 28:35
battle, and we *s* them ... Deut 29:7
men go up and *s* Ai ... Josh 7:3
men of Ai *s* of them ... Josh 7:5
s them in the going down ... Josh 7:5
s it with the edge of ... Josh 8:24
s them to Azekah, and ... Josh 10:10
s the hindmost of them ... Josh 10:19
s it with the..sword ... Josh 10:28
s it with the..sword ... Josh 10:32
s it with the..sword ... Josh 10:35
Joshua *s* all the country ... Josh 10:40
who *s* them and chased ... Josh 11:8
s the king..with the sword ... Josh 11:10
s them with the..sword ... Josh 11:12
kings he took, and *s* them ... Josh 11:17
the children of Israel *s* ... Josh 12:1
these did Moses *s* and cast ... Josh 13:12
whom Moses *s* with the ... Josh 13:21
He that *s* Kirjath-sepher ... Josh 15:16
he *s* his neighbor ... Josh 20:5
s it with the..sword ... Judg 1:8
He that *s* Kirjath-sepher ... Judg 1:12
they *s* the city with the ... Judg 1:25
s the nail into his temples ... Judg 4:21
the hammer she *s* Sisera ... Judg 5:26
she *s* off his head ... Judg 5:26
s the Midianites as one ... Judg 6:16
Gideon..*s* the host ... Judg 8:11
Israel, and they *s* them ... Judg 11:21
men of Gilead *s* Ephraim ... Judg 12:4
s them with the..sword ... Judg 18:27
Benjamin..they were *s* ... Judg 20:36
s all the city with the edge ... Judg 20:37
Benjamin began to *s* ... Judg 20:39
hath the Lord *s* us ... 1Sam 4:3
Gods that *s* the Egyptians ... 1Sam 4:8
fought, and Israel was *s* ... 1Sam 4:10
s the men of the city ... 1Sam 5:9
were *s* with the emerods ... 1Sam 5:12
he *s* the men of ... 1Sam 6:19
the Lord had *s* many of the ... 1Sam 6:19
s the garrison of the ... 1Sam 13:3
Saul had *s* a garrison ... 1Sam 13:4
and *s* the Amalekites ... 1Sam 14:48
Now go and *s* Amalek ... 1Sam 15:3
I went out after him, and *s* ... 1Sam 17:35
s the Philistine ... 1Sam 17:49
I will *s* David even to the ... 1Sam 18:11
he *s* the javelin into ... 1Sam 19:10
Saul cast a javelin..*s* him ... 1Sam 20:33
Shall I go and *s* these ... 1Sam 23:2
Go, and *s* the Philistines ... 1Sam 23:2
s them with a great ... 1Sam 23:5
the Lord *s* Nabal, that he ... 1Sam 25:38
let me *s* him, I pray thee ... 1Sam 26:8
I will not *s* him the second ... 1Sam 26:8
David *s* them from the ... 1Sam 30:17
he *s* him that he died ... 2Sam 1:15
should I *s* thee to the ... 2Sam 2:22
David..*s* of Benjamin ... 2Sam 2:31
s him there under the fifth ... 2Sam 3:27
they *s* him, and slew him ... 2Sam 4:7
s the Jebusites, and the ... 2Sam 5:8
s the Philistines from Geba ... 2Sam 5:25
David *s* the Philistines ... 2Sam 8:1
David *s* also Hadadezer ... 2Sam 8:3
against Hadadezer, and *s* ... 2Sam 8:10
from *s* of the Syrians ... 2Sam 8:13
from him, that he may be *s* ... 2Sam 11:15
Who *s* Abimelech the son ... 2Sam 11:21
Deliver him that *s* his ... 2Sam 14:7
I will *s* the king only ... 2Sam 17:2
he *s* him..in the fifth rib ... 2Sam 20:10
s the Philistines until his ... 2Sam 23:10
the angel that *s* the people ... 2Sam 24:17
When thy people Israel he *s* ... 1Kin 8:33
the Lord shall *s* Israel ... 1Kin 14:15
cities of Israel, and *s* Ijon ... 1Kin 15:20
he *s* all..of Jeroboam ... 1Kin 15:29
s the horses and chariots ... 1Kin 20:21
the man refused to *s* him ... 1Kin 20:35
that in *s* he wounded him ... 1Kin 20:37
s Micaiah on the cheek ... 1Kin 22:24
mantle..and *s* the waters ... 2Kin 2:8
he also had *s* the waters ... 2Kin 2:14
ye shall *s* every..city ... 2Kin 3:19
up and *s* the Moabites ... 2Kin 3:24
forward *s* the Moabites ... 2Kin 3:24
s them with blindness ... 2Kin 6:18
S this people, I pray ... 2Kin 6:18
I *s* them? shall I *s* them? ... 2Kin 6:21
Thou shalt not *s* them ... 2Kin 6:22
thou *s* those whom thou ... 2Kin 6:22
s Jehoram between his ... 2Kin 9:24
S him also in the chariot ... 2Kin 9:27
Hazael *s* them in all the ... 2Kin 10:32
he *s* thrice, and stayed ... 2Kin 13:18
Israel, *S* upon the ground ... 2Kin 13:18
shouldest have *s* five ... 2Kin 13:19
s Syria till..consumed it ... 2Kin 13:19
s him before the people ... 2Kin 15:10
Then Menahem *s* Tiphsah ... 2Kin 15:16
him, and *s* him in Samaria ... 2Kin 15:25
s the Philistines, even ... 2Kin 18:8
his sons *s* him with the ... 2Kin 19:37
with him, and *s* Gedaliah ... 2Kin 25:25
s Midian in the field ... 1Chr 1:46
Whosoever *s* the Jebusites ... 1Chr 11:6
against Uzza, and he *s* him ... 1Chr 13:10
and David *s* them there ... 1Chr 14:11
s the host of the Philistines ... 1Chr 14:15

David *s* the Philistines 1Chr 18:1
David *s* Hadarezer king of 1Chr 18:3
David had *s* all the host........1Chr 18:9
therefore he *s* Israel 1Chr 21:7
God *s* Jeroboam and all 2Chr 13:15
They *s* also the tents of cattle .2Chr 14:15
and they *s* Ijon, and Dan 2Chr 16:4
s the king of Israel 2Chr 18:33
Judah; and they were *s* 2Chr 20:22
Lord *s* him in his bowels 2Chr 21:18
s of the children of Seir 2Chr 25:11
thou hast *s* the Edomites 2Chr 25:19
they *s* him, and carried 2Chr 28:5
who *s* him with a great 2Chr 28:5
Edomites had come and *s* 2Chr 28:17
s certain of them, and ....Neh 13:25
Jews *s* all their enemies ....Esth 9:5
s the four corners of the ......Job 1:19
have *s* me upon the cheek ....Job 16:10
he *s* through the proud ....Job 26:12
s all mine enemies ....Ps 3:7
and *s* of Edom in the ....Ps 60:*title*
s down the chosen men ....Ps 78:31
And he *s* his enemies ....Ps 78:66
My heart is *s*, and withered ...Ps 102:4
He *s* their vines also ....Ps 105:33
The sun shall not *s* thee.......Ps 121:6
s the first-born of Egypt ......Ps 135:8
s Egypt in their first-born .....Ps 136:10
s me, they wounded me ....Song 5:7
Lord will *s* with a scab........Is 3:17
them, and hath *s* them ....Is 5:25
turneth not unto him that *s* ...Is 9:13
stay upon him that *s* them ....Is 10:20
he shall *s* thee with a rod .....Is 10:24
rod of him that *s* thee ....Is 14:29
the Lord shall *s* Egypt ....Is 19:22
he shall *s* and heal it ....Is 19:22
he *s* him, as he *s* those ....Is 27:7
those that *s* him? or is he .....Is 27:7
s in the camp of the ....Is 37:36
him that *s* the anvil...........Is 41:7
s with the fist of wickedness...Is 58:4
for in my wrath I *s* thee ......Is 60:10
In vain have I *s* your ....Jer 2:30
s him with the tongue.........Jer 18:18
Pashur *s* Jeremiah ....Jer 20:2
he shall *s* them ....Jer 21:7
ye had *s* the whole army ......Jer 37:10
wroth with Jeremiah, and *s*....Jer 37:15
King of Babylon *s* in the ......Jer 46:2
s the land of Egypt ....Jer 46:13
the king of Babylon *s* them ...Jer 52:27
to him that *s* him.............Lam 3:30
s about it with a knife ....Ezek 5:2
I am the Lord that *s*...........Ezek 7:9
through the city, and *s*........Ezek 9:5
s thine hands together ....Ezek 21:14
have *s* mine hand at thy ......Ezek 22:13
I shall *s* all them that ....Ezek 32:15
after that the city was *s* ....Ezek 40:1
s the image upon his feet .....Dan 2:34
s one against another ....Dan 5:6
he hath *s*, and he will bind ....Hos 6:1
I will *s* the winter house .....Amos 3:15
I have *s* you with blasting .....Amos 4:9
S the lintel of the door ....Amos 9:1
s the gourd that it withered ...Jon 4:7
s the judge of Israel ....Mic 5:1
I make thee sick in *s* thee .....Mic 6:13
the knees *s* together and ......Nah 2:10
s you with blasting and ....Hag 2:17
s the waves in the sea ....Zech 10:11
s every horse with ....Zech 12:4
s every horse of the people....Zech 12:4
Lord will *s* all the people .....Zech 14:12
Lord will *s* the heathen ....Zech 14:18
come and *s* the earth ....Mal 4:6
s his fellowservants ....Matt 24:49
priest's, and *s* off his ear ......Matt 26:51
Who is he that *s* thee?.........Matt 26:68
I will *s* the shepherd ....Mark 14:27
s a servant of the..priest ......Mark 14:47
s thee on the one cheek.......Luke 6:29
s upon his breast, saying ......Luke 18:13
shall we *s* with the sword? ....Luke 22:49
held Jesus mocked him *s* ......Luke 22:63
s their breasts, and ....Luke 23:48
s the high priest's servant .....John 18:10
if well, why *s* thou me? ....John 18:23
and *s* the Egyptian ....Acts 7:24
angel of the Lord *s* him ....Acts 12:23
to *s* him on the mouth ....Acts 23:2
s contrary to the law..........Acts 23:3
if a man *s* you on the face 2Cor 11:20
part of the sun was *s* ....Rev 8:12
s the earth with all plagues ....Rev 11:6

SMITERS—*those who hit others*
I gave my back to the *s*.......Is 50:6

SMITH—*a metal worker*
Blacksmith 1Sam 13:19, 20
Workers in iron ....Is 44:12
Tubal-cain, first ....Gen 4:22
Demetrius, silversmith ...Acts 19:24-27
Alexander, coppersmith ..2Tim 4:14

[*also* SMITHS]
all the craftsmen and *s*........2Kin 24:14
created the *s* that bloweth.....Is 54:16
the carpenters and *s*, from ....Jer 24:1

SMITING, SMITTEN—*See* SMITE

SMOKE—*to emit visible columns of combusted materials; exhaust from fire*

Resulting from:
Destruction ....Gen 19:28
God's presence ....Is 6:4
God's vengeance ....Is 34:8-10
Babylon's end ....Rev 14:8-11
World's end.............Is 51:6

Figurative of:
God's anger.............Deut 29:20
Our life ....Ps 102:3
Spiritual distress ....Ps 119:83
Something offensive .....Is 65:5
Spirit's advent..........Joel 2:29, 30

[*also* SMOKING]
behold a *s* furnace, and a .....Gen 15:17
Sinai was altogether on a *s* ....Ex 19:18
the *s* thereof ascended ....Ex 19:18
as the *s* of a furnace ....Ex 19:18
and the mountain *s* ....Ex 20:18
the *s* of the city ascended .....Josh 8:20
the *s* of the city ascended .....Josh 8:21
great flame with *s* rise ....Judg 20:38
a *s* out of his nostrils 2Sam 22:9
Out of his nostrils goeth *s*.....Job 41:20
a *s* out of his nostrils ....Ps 18:8
s shall they consume ....Ps 37:20
As *s* is driven away, so ....Ps 68:2
the hills, and they *s* ....Ps 104:32
mountains and they shall *s* ....Ps 144:5
teeth, and as *s* to the eyes ....Prov 10:26
like pillars of *s* ....Song 3:6
a cloud and *s* by day ....Is 4:5
tails of these *s* firebrands......Is 7:4
like the lifting up of *s*..........Is 9:18
come from the north a *s* ......Is 14:31
s flax shall he not quench .....Is 42:3
the *s* out of the chimney ......Hos 13:3
fire, and pillars of *s* ....Joel 2:30
burn her chariots in the *s* .....Nah 2:13
s flax shall he not quench .....Matt 12:20
fire, and vapor of *s*...........Acts 2:19
And the *s* of the incense ......Rev 8:4
arose a *s* out of the pit ....Rev 9:2
as the *s* of a great furnace ....Rev 9:2
darkened by reason of the *s* ...Rev 9:2
fire and *s* and brimstone ......Rev 9:17
the *s* of their torment ....Rev 14:11
s from the glory of God.......Rev 15:8
see the *s* of her burning.......Rev 18:9
saw the *s* of her burning ......Rev 18:18
And her *s* rose up forever.....Rev 19:3

SMOOTH—*to free from obstruction; polish*

[*also* SMOOTHER, SMOOTHETH]
a hairy man, and I am a *s* ....Gen 27:11
upon the *s* of his neck ....Gen 27:16
chose him five *s* stones........1Sam 17:40
mouth were *s* than butter .....Ps 55:21
her mouth is *s* than oil........Prov 5:3
speak unto us *s* things ....Is 30:10
he that *s* with the hammer ....Is 41:7
Among the *s* stones of the ....Is 57:6
rough ways shall be made *s* ...Luke 3:5

SMOTE, SMOTEST—*See* SMITE

SMYRNA (smûr'nä)—*"myrrh"*
One of the seven churches ....Rev 1:11

angel of the church in *S*.......Rev 2:8

SNAIL—*a small creeping mollusk with an external shell*
Creature in a spiral shell .Ps 58:8

and the lizard, and the *s* ......Lev 11:30

SNAKE CHARMER—*one who supposedly has power over venomous snakes*
Alluded to ....Ps 58:4, 5

SNARE—*trap; to trap*

Uses of:
Catch birds ....Prov 7:23

Figurative of:
Pagan nations ....Josh 23:12, 13
Idols ....Judg 2:3
God's representative .....Ex 10:7
Words ....Prov 6:2
Wicked works ....Ps 9:16
Fear of man ....Prov 29:25
Immoral woman ....Eccl 7:26
Christ ....Is 8:14, 15
Sudden destruction ......Luke 21:34, 35
Riches..................1Tim 6:9, 10
Devil's trap 2Tim 2:26

[*also* SNARED, SNARES]
it will surely be a *s* unto ......Ex 23:33
it be for a *s* in the midst ......Ex 34:12
that will be a *s* unto thee .....Deut 7:16
lest thou be *s* therein ....Deut 7:25
be not *s* by following them ....Deut 12:30
became a *s* unto Gideon ......Judg 8:27
she may be a *s* to him 1Sam 18:21
the *s* of death prevented 2Sam 22:6
he walketh upon a *s* ....Job 18:8
s are round about thee........Job 22:10
wicked he shall rain *s*..........Ps 11:6
s of death prevented me ......Ps 18:5
after my life lay *s* for me .....Ps 38:12
they commune of laying *s* .....Ps 64:5
Let their table become a *s* ....Ps 69:22
from the *s* of the fowler........Ps 91:3
idols: which were a *s* ....Ps 106:36
wicked have laid a *s* for me ...Ps 119:110
the *s* of the fowlers ....Ps 124:7
s is broken, and we are ....Ps 124:7
The proud have hid a *s* ....Ps 140:5
the *s* which they have..........Ps 141:9
they privily laid a *s* for me ....Ps 142:3
is *s* by the transgression.......Prov 12:13
depart from the *s* of death ....Prov 13:14
lips are the *s* of his soul.......Prov 18:7
Thorns and *s* are in the ....Prov 22:5
and get a *s* to thy soul ....Prov 22:25
of an evil man there is a *s* ....Prov 29:6
men bring a city into a *s*......Prov 29:8
birds..caught in the *s* ....Eccl 9:12
men *s* in an evil time ....Eccl 9:12
the *s*, are upon thee ....Is 24:17
and be broken, and *s* and .....Is 28:13
lay a *s* for him that ....Is 29:21
they are all of them *s* in ......Is 42:22
wait, as he that setteth *s* ......Jer 5:26
me, and hid *s* for my feet .....Jer 18:22
the pit, and the *s*, shall be ....Jer 48:43
I have laid a *s* for thee ....Jer 50:24
Fear and a *s* is come ....Lam 3:47
he shall be taken in my *s* .....Ezek 12:13
have been a *s* on Mizpah .....Hos 5:1
a bird fall in a *s* upon the.....Amos 3:5
shall one take up a *s* from ....Amos 3:5
Let their table be..a *s*.........Rom 11:9

not that I may cast a *s* 1Cor 7:35
reproach and the *s* of the 1Tim 3:7
out of the *s* of the devil 2Tim 2:26

SNATCH—*seize*
And he shall *s* on the right ....Is 9:20

SNEEZE—*sudden expiration of breath*
Seven times 2Kin 4:35

SNORTING—*noise made by forcing air through the nose*
s of his horses was heard ......Jer 8:16

SNOUT—*a long, projecting nose*
jewel of gold in a swine's *s* ....Prov 11:22

SNOW—*precipitation in the form of crystalized water vapor*
Characteristics of:
Comes in winter ....Prov 26:1
Sent by God ....Job 37:6
Waters the earth ....Is 55:10
Melts with heat ....Job 6:16, 17
Notable event during 2Sam 23:20
Whiteness illustrative of:
Leprosy ....Ex 4:6
Converted sinner ....Ps 51:7
Is 1:18
Nazarite's purity ....Lam 4:7
Angel ....Matt 28:3
Risen Christ ....Rev 1:14

[*also* SNOWY]
became leprous, white as *s* ....Num 12:10
a leper as white as *s* 2Kin 5:27
slew a lion..in a *s* day 1Chr 11:22
I wash myself with *s* water ....Job 9:30
heat consume the *s* waters ....Job 24:19
into the treasures of the *s*? ....Job 38:22
it was white as *s* in Salmon ....Ps 68:14
and hail, *s*, and vapors ....Ps 148:8
She is not afraid of the *s* ......Prov 31:21
Will a man leave the *s* of .....Jer 18:14
garment was white as *s* ....Dan 7:9
exceeding white as *s* ....Mark 9:3

SNUFFDISHES—*articles used in attending the altar in the tabernacle and the temple*
his *s* of pure gold ....Ex 37:23
and his tongs, and his *s* ....Num 4:9
See SNUFFERS

SNUFFED—*sniffed*

[*also* SNUFFETH]
s up the wind at her ....Jer 2:24
s up the winds like dragons ...Jer 14:6
have *s* at it, saith the Lord ....Mal 1:13

SNUFFERS—*articles used in attending the altar in the tabernacle and the temple*
Used for trimming wicks
in lamps ....Ex 37:23
Dishes used to catch snuff
of lamps ....Ex 25:38

his seven lamps, and his *s* .....Ex 37:23
the bowls, and the *s*, and 1Kin 7:50
the Lord bowls of silver, *s* 2Kin 12:13
and the shovels, and the *s* 2Kin 25:14
And the *s* and the basins 2Chr 4:22
and the *s*, and the bowls ......Jer 52:18

SO—*See* INTRODUCTION

SO (sō)—*"vizier"*
Egyptian king 2Kin 17:4

SOAKED—*drenched*
their land shall be *s* with ......Is 34:7

SOAP—*a cleansing agent*
Figuratively in ....Mal 3:2

and take thee much *s* ....Jer 2:22
fire, and like fullers' *s* ....Mal 3:2

SOBER—*marked by moderation, temperance, or seriousness*
Described as:
Sanity 2Cor 5:13
Soberness (not drunk) ...1Tim 3:2, 11
Temperate nature ....Titus 1:8
Humble mind ....Rom 12:3
Moral rectitude ....Titus 2:12
Self-control ....Gal 5:23
1Cor 7:9
Incentives to, found in:
Lord's return 1Thess 5:1-7
Nearness of the end 1Pet 4:7
Satan's attacks 1Cor 7:5
Required of:
Christians 1Thess 5:6, 8
Church officers 1Tim 3:2, 3
Wives of church officers .1Tim 3:11
Aged men ....Titus 2:2
Young women ....Titus 2:4
Young men ....Titus 2:6
Women 1Tim 2:9
Children 1Tim 2:15
Evangelists 2Tim 4:5
See TEMPERANCE

SOCHO, SHOCO, SHOCOH (sō'kō, shō'kō)
1. Son of Heber 1Chr 4:18
2. City in Judah 2Chr 11:7; 28:18
See SOCOH

SOCIABILITY—*friendly relationships in gatherings of people*
Manifested in:
Family life ....John 12:1-9
National life ....Neh 8:9-18
Church life ....Acts 2:46
Christian's kind, governed by:
No fellowship with evil...2Cor 6:14-18
Righteous living ....Titus 2:12
Honesty in all things .....Col 3:9-14

SOCKET—*pivot for the doors of the tabernacle*

[*also* SOCKETS]
forty *s* of silver under the .....Ex 26:19
two *s* under one board for ....Ex 26:19
and two *s* under another ......Ex 26:19
And their forty *s* of silver ....Ex 26:21
two *s* under one board ....Ex 26:21
and two *s* under another ......Ex 26:21
their *s* of silver, sixteen *s* .....Ex 26:25
two *s* under one board ....Ex 26:25
and two *s* under another ......Ex 26:25
cast five *s* of brass for them ...Ex 26:37
their twenty *s* shall be of ......Ex 27:10
pillars ten, and their *s* ten .....Ex 27:12
be four, and their *s* four ......Ex 27:16
linen, and their *s* of brass .....Ex 27:18
his pillars and their *s* ....Ex 35:17
forty *s* of silver he made ......Ex 36:24
two *s* under one board for ....Ex 36:24
two *s* under another board ....Ex 36:24
And their forty *s* of silver .....Ex 36:26
two *s* under one board ....Ex 36:26
and two *s* under another ......Ex 36:26
s were sixteen *s* of silver ......Ex 36:30
under every board two *s* ....Ex 36:30
their five *s* were of brass ......Ex 36:38
and their *s* of brass twenty ....Ex 38:11
three, and their *s* three ....Ex 38:14
the *s* for the pillars were ......Ex 38:17
talents, a talent for a *s* ....Ex 38:27
cast the *s* of the sanctuary .....Ex 38:27
and the *s* of the veil ....Ex 38:27
s of the hundred talents ....Ex 38:27
And the *s* of the court round ..Ex 38:31
and the *s* of the court gate ....Ex 38:31
and his pillars, and his *s* ......Ex 39:33
fastened his *s*, and set up .....Ex 40:18
thereof, and the *s* thereof .....Num 3:36
the pillars thereof, and *s* ......Num 4:31
set upon *s* of fine gold ....Song 5:15

SOCOH (sō'kō)—*"defense"*
1. Town in south Judah ....Josh 15:1, 35
Where David killed
Goliath 1Sam 17:1, 49
2. Town in Judah's hill
country ....Josh 15:1, 48

SOD—*heavy with moisture; boiled; to boil; make heavy*

[*also* SODDEN]
Jacob *s* pottage: and Esau .....Gen 25:29
nor *s* at all with water ....Ex 12:9
vessel wherein it is *s* ....Lev 6:28
if it be *s* in a brazen pot ......Lev 6:28
shall take the *s* shoulder ......Num 6:19
will not have *s* flesh of thee ...1Sam 2:15
holy offerings *s* they in pots ...2Chr 35:13
have *s* their own children .....Lam 4:10

SODERING—*soldering*
It is ready for the *s* ....Is 41:7

SODI (sō'dī)—*"Jehovah determines"*
Father of the Zebulunite
spy ....Num 13:10

SODOM (sŏd'ĭm)—*"their secret"—one of the five Cities of the Plain, destroyed because of its wickedness*
History of:
Located in Jordan plain ..Gen 13:10
Became Lot's residence ..Gen 13:11-13
Wickedness of, notorious .Gen 13:13
Plundered by
Chedorlaomer ....Gen 14:9-24
Abraham interceded for ..Gen 18:16-33
Destroyed by God ....Gen 19:1-28
Lot sent out of ....Gen 19:29, 30
Destruction of, illustrative of:
God's wrath ....Deut 29:23
Sudden destruction ......Lam 4:6
Total destruction ....Jer 49:18
Future judgment ....Matt 11:23, 24
Example to the ungodly ..2Pet 2:6
Sin of, illustrative of:
Shamelessness ....Is 3:9
Obduracy ....Jer 23:14
Unnaturalness ....Jude 7
Figuratively of:
Wickedness ....Deut 32:32
Jerusalem ....Is 1:9, 10
Judah ....Ezek 16:46-63

goest, unto *S*, and Gomorrah ..Gen 10:19
war with Bera king of *S* ....Gen 14:2
there went out the king of *S* ..Gen 14:8
As when God overthrew *S* ....Is 13:19
As God overthrew *S* and ....Jer 50:40
God overthrew *S* and ....Amos 4:11
Moab shall be as *S*, and the ...Zeph 2:9
tolerable for the land of *S* .....Matt 10:15
shall be more tolerable for *S* ..Mark 6:11
tolerable in that day for *S* .....Luke 10:12
day that Lot went out of *S* ....Luke 17:29
we had been as *S* ....Rom 9:29
which spiritually is called *S* ....Rev 11:8

SODOMA—*See* SODOM

SODOMITE (sŏd'ŭm-īt)—*a male cult prostitute; a man who practices sexual activities with other men*
Prohibition of ....Deut 23:17, 18
Prevalence of, under
Rehoboam 1Kin 14:24
Asa's removal of 1Kin 15:11, 12
Jehoshaphat's riddance of.1Kin 22:46
Josiah's reforms against ..2Kin 23:7
Result of unbelief ....Rom 1:27

SOEVER—*of any kind which may be specified*
what saddle *s* he rideth upon ..Lev 15:9
s there be of the house of .....Lev 17:3
What man *s* of the seed ....Lev 22:4
What thing *s* I command you ..Deut 12:32
what thing *s* thou shalt hear ...2Sam 15:35
the people, how many *s* they ..2Sam 24:3
prayer and supplication *s* 1Kin 8:38
or what supplication *s* 2Chr 6:29
And what cause *s* shall come ..2Chr 19:10
blasphemies wherewith *s* ......Mark 3:28
what place *s* ye enter into .....Mark 6:10
What things *s* ye desire ....Mark 11:24
for what things *s* he doeth ....John 5:19
what things *s* the law saith ....Rom 3:19

SOFT—*delicate in texture; compliant; not hard*

[*also* SOFTER, SOFTLY]
I will lead on *s* according .....Gen 33:14
and went *s* unto him..........Judg 4:21
came *s* and uncovered his .....Ruth 3:7
lay in sackcloth, and went *s* ...1Kin 21:27
For God maketh my heart *s* ...Job 23:16
speak *s* words unto thee? .....Job 41:3
his words were *s* than oil......Ps 55:21
makest it *s* with showers ......Ps 65:10
A *s* answer turneth away......Prov 15:1
and a *s* tongue breaketh the ...Prov 25:15
waters of Shiloah that go *s* ....Is 8:6
I shall go *s* all my years.......Is 38:15
A man clothed in *s* raiment? ..Matt 11:8
they that wear *s* clothing ......Matt 11:8
A man clothed in *s* raiment? ..Luke 7:25
when the south wind blew *s* ...Acts 27:13

SOIL—*dirt*
It was planted in good ...Ezek 17:8
Uzziah loved it..........2Chr 26:10

SOJOURN—*to reside temporarily*

Descriptive of:
Abram in Egypt.........Gen 12:10
Jacob with Laban........Gen 32:4
Israel in Egypt ....Gen 47:4
Stranger ....Ex 12:48, 49
Wandering Levite ....Deut 18:6
Naomi in Moab ....Ruth 1:1
Remnant in Egypt ....Jer 42:15-23
Jews in captivity.........Ezra 1:4

Characterized by:
Simplicity of living.......Heb 11:9
Being among enemies....2Kin 8:1, 2
Lord's blessing ....Gen 26:2, 3

Figurative of:
Righteous in the world...1Chr 29:15
Christian in the world....1Pet 1:17
See FOREIGNERS; STRANGERS

[*also* SOJOURNED, SOJOURNETH, SOJOURNING]
This one fellow came to a *s* ...Gen 19:9
Kadesh and Shur, and *s* in ....Gen 20:1
land wherein thou hast *s* ....Gen 21:23
s in the Philistines' land.......Gen 21:34
where Abraham and Isaac *s* ...Gen 35:27
of her that *s* in her house .....Ex 3:22
s of the children of Israel .....Ex 12:40
stranger that *s* among you .....Lev 16:29
strangers which *s* among ......Lev 17:8
strangers that *s* among ....Lev 17:10
any stranger that *s* among .....Lev 17:12
any stranger that *s* among .....Lev 18:26
if a stranger *s* with thee ......Lev 19:33
strangers that *s* in Israel ......Lev 20:2
stranger that *s* with thee ......Lev 25:6
strangers that do *s* among .....Lev 25:45
if a stranger shall *s* among ....Num 9:14
if a stranger *s* with you ....Num 15:14
stranger that *s* with you ....Num 15:15
stranger that *s* with you ....Num 15:16
the stranger that *s* among .....Num 15:26
the stranger that *s* among .....Num 15:29
the stranger that *s* among .....Num 19:10
and *s* there with a few ....Deut 26:5
the stranger that *s* among .....Josh 20:9
who was a Levite, and he *s* ...Judg 17:7
to *s* where he could find ......Judg 17:8
s where I may find a place ....Judg 17:9
certain Levite *s* on the side....Judg 19:1
and he *s* in Gibeah ....Judg 19:16
the widow with whom I *s* 1Kin 17:20
Jacob *s* in the land of Ham ...Ps 105:23
Woe is me that I *s* in Mesech .Ps 120:5
shall carry her afar off to *s* ....Is 23:7
aforetime into Egypt to *s* .....Is 52:4
Go not into Egypt to *s* there ..Jer 43:2
the land of Egypt to *s* ....Jer 44:12
They shall no more *s* there ....Lam 4:15
or of the stranger that *s*.......Ezek 14:7
of the country where thy *s* ....Ezek 20:38
strangers that *s* among you ....Ezek 47:22
what tribe the stranger *s* ......Ezek 47:23
should *s* in a strange land .....Acts 7:6

SOJOURNER—*a traveler*

[*also* SOJOURNERS]
a stranger and a *s* with you ...Gen 23:4
s of the priest, or a hired .....Lev 22:10
are strangers and *s* with.......Lev 25:23
he be a stranger, or a *s* ....Lev 25:35
a hired servant, and as a *s* ....Lev 25:40
s or stranger wax rich.........Lev 25:47
unto the stranger or *s*.........Lev 25:47
and for the *s* among them .....Num 35:15
were *s* there until this day.....2Sam 4:3
and a *s*, as all my fathers .....Ps 39:12

SOLACE—*to console; delight*
let us *s* ourselves with loves ...Prov 7:18

SOLD—*See* SELL

SOLDIER—*a person engaged in military service*

Good characteristics of:
Obedience ....Matt 8:9
Devotion ....Acts 10:7
Subduing riots...........Acts 21:31-35
Guarding prisoners ......Acts 12:4-6

Bad characteristics of:
Cowardice ....Deut 20:8
Discontent and violence ..Luke 3:14
Rashness ....Acts 27:42
Bribery ....Matt 28:12
Irreligion ....John 19:2, 3, 23

Figurative of:
Christians...............2Tim 2:4
Christian workers........Phil 2:25
Spiritual armor ....Eph 6:1-18

[*also* SOLDIERS, SOLDIERS']
were bands of *s* for war.......1Chr 7:4
thousand and two hundred *s*...1Chr 7:11
the *s* of the army which 2Chr 25:13
of the king a band of *s* ....Ezra 8:22
armed *s* of Moab..cry out .....Is 15:4
s of the governor took Jesus...Matt 27:27
the whole band of *s* ....Matt 27:27
s led him away into the hall ...Mark 15:16
having under me *s*............Luke 7:8
the *s* also mocked him ....Luke 23:36
s, when they had crucified ....John 19:23
things therefore the *s* did .....John 19:24
Then came the *s*, and brake ...John 19:32
one of the *s* with a spear......John 19:34
no small stir among the *s* .....Acts 12:18
commanded the *s* to go ....Acts 23:10
Make ready two hundred *s* ....Acts 23:23
s, as it was commanded ....Acts 23:31
the centurion and to the *s*.....Acts 27:31
the *s* cut off the ropes of......Acts 27:32
the *s* counsel was to kill.......Acts 27:42
by himself with a *s* that ....Acts 28:16
as a good *s* of Jesus Christ 2Tim 2:3

SOLE—*undersurface of a foot*

[*also* SOLES]
no rest for the *s* of her foot ...Gen 8:9
s of your feet shall tread ......Deut 11:24
from the *s* of thy foot unto ....Deut 28:35
to set the *s* of her foot upon ..Deut 28:56
shall the *s* of thy foot have ....Deut 28:65
s of your foot shall tread......Josh 1:3
s of the feet of the priests .....Josh 3:13
s of the priests' feet were .....Josh 4:18
the *s* of his foot even to 2Sam 14:25
put them under the *s* of his ...1Kin 5:3
with the *s* of my feet have I ...2Kin 19:24
s of his foot unto his crown ...Job 2:7
s of the foot even unto ....Is 1:6
with the *s* of my feet have I ...Is 37:25
down at the *s* of thy feet.......Is 60:14
s of their feet was like the *s*...Ezek 1:7
place of the *s* of my feet ......Ezek 43:7
under the *s* of your feet.......Mal 4:3

SOLEMN—*serious; earnest*

[SOLEMNLY]
The man did *s* protest unto ...Gen 43:3
it is a *s* assembly: and ye .....Lev 23:36
and in your *s* days............Num 10:10
in your *s* feasts, to make ......Num 15:3
shall have a *s* assembly ....Num 29:35
seventh day shall be a *s*.......Deut 16:8
thou keep a *s* feast unto ......Deut 16:15
yet protest *s* unto them 1Sam 8:9
a *s* assembly for Baal 2Kin 10:20
on the *s* feasts of the Lord 2Chr 2:4
they made a *s* assembly 2Chr 7:9
and on the *s* feasts 2Chr 8:13
the eighth day was a *s* ....Neh 8:18
on our *s* feast day ....Ps 81:3
the harp with a *s* sound ....Ps 92:3
it is iniquity, even the *s*........Is 1:13
none come to the *s* feasts .....Lam 1:4
hath caused the *s* feasts ....Lam 2:6
as in the day of a *s* feast ......Lam 2:7
as in a *s* day my terrors........Lam 2:22
Jerusalem in her *s* feasts ......Ezek 36:38
the Lord in the *s* feasts ....Ezek 46:9
her sabbaths and all her *s* .....Hos 2:11
What will ye do in the *s* ......Hos 9:5
as in the days of the *s* ....Hos 12:9
a fast, call a *s* assembly ....Joel 1:14
a fast, call a *s* assembly ....Joel 2:15
in your *s* assemblies ....Amos 5:21
keep thy *s* feasts, perform .....Nah 1:15
are sorrowful for the *s* ....Zeph 3:18
the dung of your *s* feasts ......Mal 2:3

SOLEMNITY—*a feast*

[*also* SOLEMNITIES]
s of the year of release ....Deut 31:10
night when a holy *s* is kept....Is 30:29
Zion, the city of our *s* ....Is 33:20
all *s* of the house of Israel ....Ezek 45:17
in the *s* the meat offering .....Ezek 46:11

SOLITARY—*being, living, or going alone*

[*also* SOLITARILY]
Lo, let that night be *s* ....Job 3:7
For want..they were *s*.........Job 30:3
setteth the *s* in families ....Ps 68:6
the wilderness in a *s* way......Ps 107:4
s place shall be glad ....Is 35:1
How doth the city sit *s*........Lam 1:1
which dwell *s* in the wood.....Mic 7:14
and departed into a *s* place....Mark 1:35

SOLITUDE—*aloneness*

For:
Adam, not good.........Gen 2:18
Prayer, good ....Matt 6:6
Matt 14:23
Rest, necessary..........Mark 6:30, 31

SOLOMON (sŏl'ō-mŭn)—*"peace"—David's son by Bathsheba and David's successor as king of unified Israel*

Life of:
David's son by Bathsheba.2Sam 12:24
Name of, significant 1Chr 22:9
Anointed over opposition.1Kin 1:5-48
Spared Adonijah 1Kin 1:49-53
Received dying instruction from David .1Kin 2:1-10
Purged his kingdom of corrupt leaders 1Kin 2:11-46
Prayer of, for wisdom....1Kin 3:1-15
Organized his kingdom...1Kin 4:1-28
Fame of, worldwide 1Kin 4:29-34
Built the Temple 1Kin 5–6
Dedicated the Temple ...1Kin 8:22-66
Built personal palace 1Kin 7:1-12
Lord reappeared to 1Kin 9:1-9
Strengthened his kingdom.1Kin 9:10-28
Received queen of Sheba .1Kin 10:1-13
Encouraged commerce ...1Kin 10:14-29
Falls into polygamy and idolatry 1Kin 11:1-8
God warned him 1Kin 11:9-13

Adversaries arise against him 1Kin 11:14-40
Reign and death.........1Kin 11:41-43
Good features of:
Chooses an understanding heart 1Kin 3:5-9
Exhibited sound judgment 1Kin 3:16-28
Excels in wisdom 1Kin 4:29-34
Great writer 1Kin 4:32
Writer of Psalms ....Ps 72:*title*
Bad features of:
Loves luxury ....Eccl 2:1-11
Marries pagans 1Kin 11:1-3
Turns to idolatry 1Kin 11:4-8
Enslaves Israel 1Kin 12:1-4

[*also* SOLOMON'S]
Shobab, and Nathan and *S* 2Sam 5:14
And *S* provision for one day ..1Kin 4:22
S wisdom excelled the 1Kin 4:30
S builders, and Hiram's 1Kin 5:18
king *S* sent and fetched 1Kin 7:13
he came to king *S*, and 1Kin 7:14
work that he made king *S* 1Kin 7:40
Hiram made to king *S* 1Kin 7:45
S left all the vessels 1Kin 7:47
And *S* made all the vessels 1Kin 7:48
the work that king *S* made 1Kin 7:51
S brought in the things........1Kin 7:51
S assembled the elders 1Kin 8:1
unto king *S* in Jerusalem 1Kin 8:1
assembled..unto king *S*........1Kin 8:2
king *S* and all the 1Kin 8:5
Then spake *S*, The Lord 1Kin 8:12
S desire which he was 1Kin 9:1
officers that were over *S* 1Kin 9:23
all king *S* drinking vessels 1Kin 10:21
men, that stood before *S*......1Kin 12:6
Rehoboam the son of *S* 1Kin 12:21
Rehoboam the son of *S* 1Kin 12:23
Rehoboam the son of *S* 1Kin 14:21
of gold which *S* had made.....1Kin 14:26
said to David, and to *S* 2Kin 21:7
S the king of Israel had 2Kin 23:13
the vessels of gold which *S* 2Kin 24:13
bases which *S* had made for ...2Kin 25:16
Shobab, and Nathan, and *S* ...1Chr 3:5
S son was Rehoboam 1Chr 3:10
that *S* built in Jerusalem 1Chr 6:10
S had built the house of 1Chr 6:32
and Shobab, Nathan, and *S* ...1Chr 14:4
S made the brazen sea 1Chr 18:8
S my son is young and 1Chr 22:5
Then he called for *S* his son...1Chr 22:6
David said to *S*, My son 1Chr 22:7
princes of Israel to help *S* 1Chr 22:17
S his son king over Israel 1Chr 23:1
chosen *S* my son to sit upon...1Chr 28:5
S thy son he shall build my ...1Chr 28:6
S..know thou the God 1Chr 28:9
David gave to *S* his son 1Chr 28:11
David said to *S* his son, Be ...1Chr 28:20
S my son, whom alone God ...1Chr 29:1
give unto *S* my son a perfect ..1Chr 29:19
made *S* the son of David......1Chr 29:22
S sat on the throne of 1Chr 29:23
submitted themselves unto *S*...1Chr 29:24
the Lord magnified *S* 1Chr 29:25
and *S* his son reigned in 1Chr 29:28
And *S*..was strengthened 2Chr 1:1
Then *S* spake unto all Israel...2Chr 1:2
S, and all the congregation 2Chr 1:3
and *S* and the congregation ...2Chr 1:5
S went up thither to the 2Chr 1:6
did God appear unto *S* 2Chr 1:7
And *S* said unto God, Thou ...2Chr 1:8
And God said to *S*, Because ..2Chr 1:11
S came from his journey 2Chr 1:13
And *S* gathered chariots 2Chr 1:14
S had horses brought out of ...2Chr 1:16
S determined to build a 2Chr 2:1
And *S* told out threescore 2Chr 2:2
S sent to Huram the king of...2Chr 2:3
writing, which he sent to *S* 2Chr 2:11
S numbered all the strangers ..2Chr 2:17
S began to build the house 2Chr 3:1
wherein *S* was instructed 2Chr 3:3
was to make for king *S* 2Chr 4:11
his father make to king *S* 2Chr 4:16
S made all these vessels 2Chr 4:18
S made all the vessels that 2Chr 4:19
all the work that *S* made 2Chr 5:1
S brought in all the things.....2Chr 5:1
S assembled the elders of 2Chr 5:2
S, and all the congregation 2Chr 5:6
Then said *S*, The Lord hath ...2Chr 6:1
For *S* had made a brazen 2Chr 6:13
S had made an end of praying .2Chr 7:1
S offered a sacrifice of 2Chr 7:5
S hallowed the middle of......2Chr 7:7
altar which *S* had made 2Chr 7:7
S kept the feast seven days....2Chr 7:8
S finished the house 2Chr 7:11
all that came into *S* heart 2Chr 7:11
S had built the house 2Chr 8:1
Huram had restored to *S*......2Chr 8:2
S built them, and caused 2Chr 8:2
all the store cities that *S* 2Chr 8:6
all that *S* desired to build 2Chr 8:6
did *S* make no servants 2Chr 8:9
S offered burnt offerings 2Chr 8:12
Then went *S* to Ezion-geber ...2Chr 8:17
with the servants of *S*.........2Chr 8:18
brought them to king *S* 2Chr 8:18
heard of the fame of *S*........2Chr 9:1
she came to prove *S* with 2Chr 9:1
when she was come to *S* 2Chr 9:1
S told her all her 2Chr 9:2
nothing hid from *S* which 2Chr 9:2
queen of Sheba gave king *S* ...2Chr 9:9
S gave to the queen of Sheba .2Chr 9:12
brought gold and silver to *S* ...2Chr 9:14
drinking vessels of king *S* 2Chr 9:20
accounted of in the days of *S*..2Chr 9:20
sought the presence of *S* 2Chr 9:23
they brought unto *S* horses 2Chr 9:28
S reigned in Jerusalem over ...2Chr 9:30
fled from the presence of *S* ...2Chr 10:2
unto Rehoboam the son of *S* ..2Chr 11:3
Rehoboam the son of *S*........2Chr 11:17
in the way of David and *S* 2Chr 11:17
the servant of *S* the son of 2Chr 13:6
since the time of *S* the son 2Chr 30:26
which *S* the son of David 2Chr 35:3
The children of *S* servants.....Ezra 2:55
The children of *S* servants.....Neh 7:57
and the children of *S* ....Neh 11:3
of David, and of *S* his son ....Neh 12:45
Did not *S* king of Israel sin ...Neh 13:26
A Song of degrees for *S* ......Ps 127:*title*
The proverbs of *S* the son of ..Prov 1:1
These are also proverbs of *S* ..Prov 25:1
song of songs, which is *S*......Song 1:1
Kedar, as the curtains of *S* ....Song 1:5
king *S* with the crown ....Song 3:11
O *S*, must have a thousand....Song 8:12
S had made in the house ......Jer 52:20
and David the king begat *S* ...Matt 1:6
S in all his glory was not ......Matt 6:29
to hear the wisdom of *S* ......Matt 12:42
a greater than *S* is here ....Matt 12:42
to hear the wisdom of *S* ......Luke 11:31
a greater than *S* is here ....Luke 11:31
S in all his glory was not ......Luke 12:27
walked in the temple in *S* .....John 10:23
the porch that is called *S*......Acts 3:11
But *S* built him a house.......Acts 7:47

SOME—*an indefinite amount*
lest *s* evil take me, and I die ..Gen 19:19
and cast him into *s* pit ....Gen 37:20
he took *s* of his brethren ......Gen 47:2
gathered, *s* more, *s* less ....Ex 16:17
went out *s* of the people ......Ex 16:27
the priest shall put *s* of ....Lev 4:7
put *s* of the blood upon the ...Lev 4:18
priest shall take *s* of the ......Lev 14:15
hath sold away *s* of his........Lev 25:25
s man have lain with thee .....Num 5:20
shalt put *s* of thine honor .....Num 27:20
hath found *s* uncleanness ......Deut 24:1
s on this side, and *s* on ....Josh 8:22
whole congregation sent *s* .....Judg 21:13
and *s* shall run before his 1Sam 8:11
and *s* bade me kill thee 1Sam 24:10
there fell *s* of the people 2Sam 11:17
now in *s* pit, or in *s* other 2Sam 17:9
s of them be overthrown 2Sam 17:9
in him there is found *s* good ..1Kin 14:13
cast him upon *s* mountain 2Kin 2:16
bid thee do *s* great thing 2Kin 5:13
Let *s* take, I pray thee, five ...2Kin 7:13
among them, which slew *s* 2Kin 17:25
s of them, even of the sons ...1Chr 4:42
s of the sons of the priests 1Chr 9:30
grant them *s* deliverance 2Chr 12:7
Also *s* of the Philistines 2Chr 17:11
s of the chief of the fathers ...Ezra 2:68
went up *s* of the children .....Ezra 7:7
I and *s* few men with me .....Neh 2:12
s of our daughters are ....Neh 5:5
s of the chief of the fathers ...Neh 7:70
singers and *s* of the people ....Neh 7:73
s appointed over the ....Neh 12:44
s of my servants set I at ......Neh 13:19
S remove the landmarks ......Job 24:2
S trust in chariots..*s* in ....Ps 20:7
unless they cause *s* to fall .....Prov 4:16
they not leave *s* gleaning ......Jer 49:9
have *s* that shall escape the ...Ezek 6:8
it cast down *s* of the host .....Dan 8:10
awake, *s* to everlasting life ....Dan 12:2
s to shame and everlasting ....Dan 12:2
I have overthrown *s* of you....Amos 4:11
would they not leave *s* ....Obad 5
s seeds fell by the way side....Matt 13:4
s fell among thorns; and the...Matt 13:7
forth fruit, *s* a hundredfold ....Matt 13:8
s sixtyfold, *s* thirtyfold ....Matt 13:8
hundredfold, *s* sixty, *s* thirty...Matt 13:23
S say that thou art John ......Matt 16:14
s, Elijah; and others, Jeremiah.Matt 16:14
For there are *s* eunuchs ....Matt 19:12
and there are *s* eunuchs ......Matt 19:12
s of them ye shall kill.........Matt 23:34
s of them shall ye scourge .....Matt 23:34
s of the watch came into ......Matt 28:11
into Capernaum after *s* ....Mark 2:1
s fell on stony ground.........Mark 4:5
and *s* fell among thorns ....Mark 4:7
and brought forth, *s* thirty ....Mark 4:8
s sixty, and *s* a hundred.......Mark 4:8
forth fruit, *s* thirtyfold ....Mark 4:20
s sixty, and *s* a hundred.......Mark 4:20
s say, Elijah; and others ......Mark 8:28
beating *s*, and killing *s* ....Mark 12:5
And *s* began to spit on him ...Mark 14:65
s fell by the way side ....Luke 8:5
And *s* fell among thorns ....Luke 8:7
And of *s*, that Elijah had .....Luke 9:8
there be *s* standing here ......Luke 9:27
s of them they shall slay ......Luke 11:49
s of the Pharisees from ....Luke 19:39
s of you shall they cause to ...Luke 21:16
have seen *s* miracle done......Luke 23:8
between *s* of John's disciples ..John 3:25
for *s* said, He is a good man ..John 7:12
s said, Shall Christ come ......John 7:41
s of them would have taken ...John 7:44
said *s* of the Pharisees, This ...John 9:16
but climbeth up *s* other way...John 10:1
s of them went their ways ....John 11:46
Then said *s* of his disciples ....John 16:17
might overshadow *s* of them...Acts 5:15
except *s* man should guide ....Acts 8:31
s of them were men of Cyprus .Acts 11:20
And *s* days after Paul said ....Acts 15:36
s said, What will this babbler ..Acts 17:18
tell, or to hear *s* new thing....Acts 17:21
after he had spent *s* time......Acts 18:23
s cried one thing, *s* another ...Acts 21:34
I pray you to take *s* meat .....Acts 27:34
And the rest, *s* on boards .....Acts 27:44
and *s* on broken pieces ....Acts 27:44
were spoken and *s* believed ...Acts 28:24

unto you *s* spiritual gift ....Rom 1:11
what if *s* did not believe? .....Rom 3:3
good man *s* would even dare ..Rom 5:7
s of the branches be broken ...Rom 11:17
s are puffed up, as though 1Cor 4:18
s with conscience of the idol...1Cor 8:7
be ye idolaters, as were *s* 1Cor 10:7
Christ, as *s* of them also 1Cor 10:9
hath set *s* in the church 1Cor 12:28
say *s* among you that there 1Cor 15:12
s man will say, How are the ...1Cor 15:35
or need we, as *s* others 2Cor 3:1
or compare ourselves with *s* ...2Cor 10:12
there be *s* that trouble you ....Gal 1:7
he gave *s*, apostles; and *s* .....Eph 4:11
and *s*, evangelists; and *s* ......Eph 4:11
S indeed preach Christ ....Phil 1:15
and *s* also of good will ....Phil 1:15
the which ye also walked *s* ....Col 3:7
lest by *s* means the tempter ...1Thess 3:5
s which walk among you 2Thess 3:11
s that they teach no other 1Tim 1:3
s having put away..faith 1Tim 1:19
s are already turned aside 1Tim 5:15
and *s* men they follow after ...1Tim 5:24
which while *s* coveted after 1Tim 6:10
and overthrow the faith of *s* ...2Tim 2:18
and of earth; *s* to honor 2Tim 2:20
every house is builded by *s* ....Heb 3:4
it remaineth that *s* must ....Heb 4:6
provided *s* better thing ....Heb 11:40
s strange thing happened 1Pet 4:12
as *s* men count slackness 2Pet 3:9
s have compassion ....Jude 22

SOMEBODY—*a person of unspecified identity*
Jesus said, *S* hath touched ....Luke 8:46
boasting himself to be *s* ....Acts 5:36

SOMETHING—*an unspecified thing*
S hath befallen him 1Sam 20:26
that *s* should be given her .....Mark 5:43
catch *s* out of his mouth ......Luke 11:54
should give *s* to the poor ......John 13:29
expecting to receive *s* of ......Acts 3:5
who hath *s* to say unto ....Acts 23:18
man think himself to be *s* .....Gal 6:3

SOMETIME—*an unspecified time*

[*also* SOMETIMES]
who *s* were far off are made ..Eph 2:13
For ye were *s* darkness ....Eph 5:8
you, that were *s* alienated .....Col 1:21
we ourselves also were *s* ......Titus 3:3
Which *s* were disobedient 1Pet 3:20

SOMEWHAT—*something; in some degree or measure*
they have done *s* against ......Lev 4:13
while he doeth *s* against ......Lev 4:27
bright spot..*s* reddish ....Lev 13:19
bright spot, *s* reddish ....Lev 13:24
the skin, but it be *s* dark ......Lev 13:28
I have *s* to say unto thee 1Kin 2:14
run after him, and take *s* 2Kin 5:20
ease thou *s* the grievous 2Chr 10:4
but make thou it *s* lighter 2Chr 10:10
Simon, I have *s* to say ....Luke 7:40
inquire *s* of him more ....Acts 23:20
I might have *s* to write........Acts 25:26
I be *s* filled with your.........Rom 15:24
ye may have *s* to answer 2Cor 5:12
these who seemed to be *s* .....Gal 2:6
who seemed to be *s* in ....Gal 2:6
that this man have *s* also ....Heb 8:3
I have *s* against thee ....Rev 2:4

SON—*a male child or man*

Descriptive of:
Male child ....Gen 4:25, 26
Half-brothers ....Gen 25:9
Grandson ....Gen 29:5
Disciple ....Prov 7:1
One possessing a certain character 1Sam 2:12
One destined to a certain end ....John 17:12
Messiah ....Is 7:14
Christian...............John 1:12
Angels ....Job 1:6

Characteristics of, sometimes:
Jealous ....Judg 9:2, 18
Quite different ....Gen 9:18-27
Disloyal ....Luke 15:25-30
Unlike their father 2Sam 13:30-39
Spiritually different .....Gen 25:22-34

Admonitions addressed to, concerning:
Instruction ....Prov 1:8
Sinners ....Prov 1:10-19
Wisdom ....Prov 3:13-35
Correction ....Prov 3:11, 12
Immorality.............Prov 5:1-23
Life's dangers ....Prov 6:1-35

[*also* SON'S, SONS, SONS']
she bare a *s*, and called his....Gen 4:25
Noah begat three *s*, Shem .....Gen 6:10
and thy *s* wives with thee .....Gen 6:18
and thy *s* wives with thee .....Gen 8:16
God blessed Noah and his *s* ...Gen 9:1
Lot the *s* of Haran his *s s* .....Gen 11:31
Abraham a *s* in his old age.....Gen 21:2
the *s* of this bondwoman ......Gen 21:10
with my *s*, nor with my *s s* ....Gen 21:23
bound Isaac his *s*, laid and ....Gen 22:9
raiment of her eldest *s* ....Gen 27:15
I will eat of my *s* venison .....Gen 27:25
thy mother's *s* bow down .....Gen 27:29
I have born him three *s* ....Gen 29:34
Give me..of thy *s* mandrakes ..Gen 30:14
take away my *s* mandrakes ....Gen 30:15
thee tonight for thy *s* ....Gen 30:15
kissed his *s* and his ....Gen 31:55
whether it be thy *s* coat ....Gen 37:32
unto Joseph were born two *s* ..Gen 41:50
s of Israel came to buy corn ...Gen 42:5
Slay my two *s*, if I bring ......Gen 42:37
Joseph my *s* is yet alive ....Gen 45:28
His *s*, and his *s s* with him ....Gen 46:7
daughters, and his *s* daughters .Gen 46:7
Moses took his wife and his *s* .Ex 4:20
his *s*, and his *s* garments ......Ex 29:21
of Aaron shall be his *s*........Ex 29:29
their daughters unto thy *s* .....Ex 34:16
shall be Aaron's and his *s* .....Lev 2:3
Aaron's *s* shall sprinkle ....Lev 3:8
and upon his *s* hands ....Lev 8:27
and upon his *s* garments with ..Lev 8:30
they be thy due, and thy *s* ....Lev 10:14
one of his *s* the priests ....Lev 13:2
The nakedness of thy *s* ....Lev 18:10
thou take her *s* daughter ......Lev 18:17
shall be Aaron's and his *s* .....Lev 24:9
If a man die, and have no *s* ...Num 27:8
teach them thy *s*, and thy *s s* .Deut 4:9
thou, and thy *s*, and thy *s s* ...Deut 6:2
thou, and thy *s*, and thy *s s* ...Judg 8:22
she also bare him a *s* ....Judg 8:31
Gideon the *s* of Joash died ....Judg 8:32
gave her *s* suck until she 1Sam 1:23
I called not, my *s*; lie down ...1Sam 3:6
Send me David thy *s*, which ...1Sam 16:19
I am the *s* of a stranger 2Sam 1:13
not one hair of thy *s* fall 2Sam 14:11
O Absalom, my *s*, my *s*! 2Sam 19:4
dead is thy *s*..living is my *s* 1Kin 3:22
the kingdom out of his *s* 1Kin 11:35
we boiled my *s*, and did eat ...2Kin 6:29
Give thy *s*, that we may eat ...2Kin 6:29
and she hath hid her *s* 2Kin 6:29
s of Reuben the first-born 1Chr 5:1
s, and *s s*, a hundred and 1Chr 8:40
Saul and his *s* were dead 1Chr 10:7
Solomon thy *s*, he shall 1Chr 28:6
have chosen him to be my *s* ...1Chr 28:6
into bondage our *s* and our ....Neh 5:5
Haman's ten *s* be hanged .....Esth 9:13
s, and his *s s*, even four.......Job 42:16
said unto me, Thou art my *S* ..Ps 2:7
s of man, that thou makest ....Ps 144:3
My *s* forget not my law ....Prov 3:1
My *s*, despise not the ....Prov 3:11
spareth his rod hateth his *s* ....Prov 13:24
Chasten thy *s* while there .....Prov 19:18
and what is his *s* name........Prov 30:4
shall conceive, and bear a *s* ...Is 7:14
she conceived, and bare a *s* ...Is 8:3
unto us a *s* is given ....Is 9:6
and of the *s* of man which ....Is 51:12
Thy *s* have fainted, they lie ...Is 51:20
and his *s*, and his *s s* ....Jer 27:7
The precious *s* of Zion ....Lam 4:2
s bear the iniquity of ....Ezek 18:19
thereof shall be his *s*..........Ezek 46:16
fourth is like the *S* of God ....Dan 3:25
called my *s* out of Egypt .....Hos 11:1
mourning of an only *s* ....Amos 8:10
s dishonoreth the father ....Mic 7:6
a *s* honoreth his father ....Mal 1:6
as a man spareth his own *s*.....Mal 3:17
think ye of Christ? whose *s* ...Matt 22:42
conceived a *s* in her old age ...Luke 1:36
forth her firstborn *s* ....Luke 2:7
this my *s* was dead, and is ....Luke 15:24
Woman, behold thy *s*! ....John 19:26
no more a servant, but a *s* ....Gal 4:7
if a *s*, then an heir of God ....Gal 4:7
that, as a *s* with the father ....Phil 2:22
offered up his only begotten *s* .Heb 11:17
offered Isaac his *s* upon the ...James 2:21
and he shall be my *s*..........Rev 21:7

SON OF GOD—*a title indicating Christ's deity*

Descriptive of Christ as:
Eternally begotten ....Ps 2:7
Heb 1:5
Messianic King ....Ps 89:26, 27
Virgin-born ....Luke 1:31-35
Trinity-member..........Matt 28:19
Priest-king ....Heb 1:8
Heb 5:5, 6

Witnesses of, by:
Father ....Matt 17:5
Angels ....John 1:51
Demons ....Mark 5:7
Satan...................Matt 4:3, 6
Men....................Matt 16:16
Christ Himself ....John 9:35-37
His resurrection ....Rom 1:1-4
Christians...............Acts 2:36
Scriptures...............John 20:31
Inner witness............1 John 5:10-13

Significance of, as indicating:
Cost of man's reconciliation..........Rom 5:6-11
Greatness of God's love. .John 3:16
Sin of unbelief ....Heb 10:28, 29
Worship due Christ ......Rev 4:11
Dignity of human nature .Rom 8:3
Heb 2:14
Humanity of Christ ......Gal 4:4
Pattern of glorification ...Rom 8:29
Phil 3:21
Destruction of Satan 1John 3:8
Uniqueness of Christ ....Heb 1:5-9

Belief in Christ as:
Derived from the Scriptures............John 20:31
Necessary for eternal life .John 3:18, 36
Source of eternal life ....John 6:40
Foundation of the faith ..Acts 9:20
Affirmation of deity 1John 2:23, 24
Illustrated..............John 11:14-44

Powers of Christ as, to:
Have life in Himself .....John 5:26
Reveal the Father ....Matt 11:27
Glorify the Father ....John 17:1
Do the Father's works ...John 5:19, 20
Redeem men............Gal 4:4, 5
Give freedom ....John 8:36
Raise the dead ....John 5:21, 25
Judge men ....John 5:22

This is my beloved *S*, in ......Matt 3:17
be the *S* of God, command ...Matt 4:3
thou be the *S* of God, cast ....Matt 4:6
Jesus, thou *S* of God? ....Matt 8:29
and no man knoweth the *S*....Matt 11:27
the Father, save the *S* ....Matt 11:27
the *S* will reveal him..........Matt 11:27
thou art the *S* of God ....Matt 14:33
the *S* of the living God ....Matt 16:16
This is my beloved *S*, in ......Matt 17:5
the Christ, the *S* of God ......Matt 26:63
If thou be the *S* of God.......Matt 27:40
he said, I am the *S* of God....Matt 27:43
Truly this was the *S* of God ...Matt 27:54
Thou art my beloved *S* ....Mark 1:11
S of the most high God? ......Mark 5:7
which was the *S* of God.......Luke 3:38
If thou be the *S* of God.......Luke 4:3
Jesus, thou *S* of God most ....Luke 8:28
This is my beloved *S*: hear ....Luke 9:35
Art thou then the *S* of God? ..Luke 22:70
that this is the *S* of God ......John 1:34
Rabbi, thou art the *S* of God..John 1:49
name of the only begotten *S* ..John 3:18
The Father loveth the *S*.......John 3:35
He that believeth on the *S* ....John 3:36
the Father loveth the *S* ....John 5:20
all men should honor the *S*....John 5:23
Christ, the *S* of the living .....John 6:69
Dost thou believe on the *S*....John 9:35
S of God might be glorified ...John 11:4
thou art the Christ, the *S* .....John 11:27
made himself the *S* of God....John 19:7
hath glorified his *S* Jesus ......Acts 3:13
having raised up his *S* Jesus ...Acts 3:26
that he is the *S* of God ....Acts 9:20
his *S* Jesus Christ our Lord....Rom 1:3
declared to be the *S* of God...Rom 1:4
God sending his own *S* in the .Rom 8:3
spared not his own *S*, but .....Rom 8:32
I live by the faith of the *S* ....Gal 2:20
God sent forth his *S* ....Gal 4:4
knowledge of the *S* of God....Eph 4:13
heavens, Jesus the *S* of God...Heb 4:14
they crucify..the *S* of God.....Heb 6:6
trodden under foot the *S*......Heb 10:29
this purpose the *S* of God 1John 3:8
believeth that Jesus is the *S* ...1John 5:5
record that God gave of his *S* .1John 5:10
These things saith the *S* of ....Rev 2:18

SON OF MAN—*Jesus' most common name for Himself and in which He asserted His Messiahship*

Title of, applied to:
Ezekiel ....Ezek 2:1, 3, 6
Daniel..................Dan 8:17
Messiah ....Dan 7:13
Christ:
By Himself ....Matt 8:20
By only Stephen elsewhere ....Acts 7:56
In John's vision ....Rev 1:13

As indicative of Christ's:
Self-designation ....Matt 16:13
Humanity...............Matt 11:19
Messiahship ....Luke 18:31
Lordship ....Matt 12:8
Sovereignty ....Matt 13:41
Obedience ....Phil 2:8
Suffering................Mark 9:12
Death ....Matt 12:40
Resurrection ....Matt 17:9-23
Regal power ....Matt 16:28
Return ....Matt 24:27-37
Glorification ....Heb 2:6-10

Christ's powers as, to:
Forgive sins ....Matt 9:6
Save men ....Luke 19:10
Redeem men............Matt 20:28
Reward men ....Matt 16:27
Reward men ....Matt 19:28
Rule His Church ....Col 1:17, 18

till the *S* of man be come .....Matt 10:23
a word against the *S* of man...Matt 12:32
good seed is the *S* of man.....Matt 13:37
For the *S* of man is come .....Matt 18:11
S of man shall be betrayed ....Matt 20:18
the coming of the *S* of man ...Matt 24:37
not the *S* of man cometh......Matt 24:44
S of man must suffer many ....Mark 8:31
shall the *S* of man be ashamed .Mark 8:38
S of man were risen from the. .Mark 9:9
S of man is delivered into .....Mark 9:31
S of man indeed goeth ....Mark 14:21
S of man is betrayed into .....Mark 14:41
S of man sitting on the right ..Mark 14:62
S of man is come eating and ..Luke 7:34
S of man must suffer many ....Luke 9:22
shall the *S* of man be ashamed .Luke 9:26
S of man shall be delivered ...Luke 9:44
S of man is not come to ......Luke 9:56
S of man hath not where to ...Luke 9:58
S of man cometh at an hour...Luke 12:40
day when the *S* of man is .....Luke 17:30
For the *S* of man is come to ..Luke 19:10
see the *S* of man coming in ...Luke 21:27
betrayest thou the *S* of man ...Luke 22:48
S of man which is in heaven...John 3:13
eat the flesh of the *S* of man ..John 6:53
see the *S* of man ascend up ...John 6:62
who is this *S* of man?.........John 12:34
one like unto the *S* of man?...Rev 1:13
sat like unto the *S* of man ....Rev 14:14

SONG—*a musical composition*

Described as:
New....................Rev 5:9
Spiritual ....Eph 5:19

Uses of, as:
Witness.................Deut 31:19-22
Torment ....Ps 137:3
March ....Num 21:17, 18
Processional............1Chr 13:7, 8

Expressive of:
Triumph ....Judg 5:12
Physical joy ....Gen 31:27
Spiritual joy ....Ps 119:54
Deliverance ....Ps 32:7
Hypocrisy...............Amos 5:23
Derision ....Ps 69:12

Figurative of:
Passover (the Lord's Supper)............ Is 30:29; Matt 26:26-30
Messiah's advent ....Is 42:10
Gospel age..............Is 26:1, 2

[*also* SONGS]
Israel this *s* unto the Lord ....Ex 15:1
The Lord is my strength and *s* .Ex 15:2
Israel the words of this *s* ......Deut 31:30
all the words of this *s*.........Deut 32:44
the Lord the words of this *s* ...2Sam 22:1
set over the service of *s* 1Chr 6:31
of the Levites, was for *s* 1Chr 15:22
he instructed about the *s*......1Chr 15:22
hands of their father for *s*.....1Chr 25:6
in the *s* of the Lord 1Chr 25:7
s of the Lord began also 2Chr 29:27
s of praise and thanksgiving ...Neh 12:46
And now am I their *s*, yea ....Job 30:9
who giveth *s* in the night......Job 35:10
Lord the words of this *s* ......Ps 18:*title*
A Psalm and *S* at the ....Ps 30:*title*
put a new *s* in my mouth .....Ps 40:3
Maschil, A *S* of loves ....Ps 45:*title*
A *S* and Psalm for the ....Ps 48:*title*
the chief Musician, A *S*........Ps 66:*title*
Musician, A Psalm or *S*........Ps 68:*title*
A Psalm or *S* of Asaph ....Ps 75:*title*
I call to remembrance my *s* ...Ps 77:6
Psalm or *S* for the sons ....Ps 87:*title*
A Psalm or *S* for the ....Ps 92:*title*
sing unto the Lord a new *s*....Ps 98:1
Lord is my strength and *s* .....Ps 118:14
A *S* of degrees ....Ps 121:*title*
A *S* of degrees ....Ps 123:*title*
A *S* of degrees ....Ps 125:*title*
A *S* of degrees for Solomon ...Ps 127:*title*
A *S* of degrees ....Ps 129:*title*
A *S* of degrees of David ......Ps 131:*title*
A *S* of degrees of David ......Ps 133:*title*
Sing us one of the *s* of........Ps 137:3
shall we sing the Lord's *s* .....Ps 137:4
Sing unto the Lord a new *s* ...Ps 149:1
singeth *s* to an heavy heart ....Prov 25:20
man to hear the *s* of fools.....Eccl 7:5
The *s* of *s*, which is...........Song 1:1
sing to my well-beloved a *s*....Is 5:1
sweet melody, sing many *s* ....Is 23:16
not drink wine with a *s* ....Is 24:9
Zion with *s* and everlasting....Is 35:10
and their *s* all the day ....Lam 3:14
the noise of thy *s* to cease ....Ezek 26:13
unto them as a very lovely *s*...Ezek 33:32
the *s* of the temple shall ......Amos 8:3
hymns and spiritual *s* ....Col 3:16
sung as it were a new *s* ....Rev 14:3
no man could learn that *s*.....Rev 14:3
they sing the *s* of Moses ......Rev 15:3
and the *s* of the Lamb ....Rev 15:3

SONG OF SOLOMON—*a book of the Old Testament*
The bride and the bridegroom ....Song 1
Song of the bride........Song 2:8—3:5
Song of the bridegroom ..Song 4:1-15
The bride meditates .....Song 4:16—6:3
The bridegroom appeals. .Song 6:4—7:9
Lovers united ....Song 7:10—8:14

SONG WRITER—*a musical composer*
Solomon, famous as 1Kin 4:32

SON-IN-LAW—*a daughter's husband*

[*also* SONS-IN-LAW]
s, and thy sons, and thy.......Gen 19:12
spake unto his *s*, which ....Gen 19:14
that mocked unto his *s*........Gen 19:14
Samson, the *s* of the Timnite ..Judg 15:6
father said unto his *s* ....Judg 19:5
I should be *s* to the king? 1Sam 18:18
shalt this day be my *s*.........1Sam 18:21
as David..the king's *s* 1Sam 22:14
he was the *s* of Shechaniah....Neh 6:18

SONSHIP OF BELIEVERS—*Christians made sons of God*

Evidences of, seen in:
New nature 1John 3:9-12
Possession of the Spirit ..Rom 8:15-17
Chastisement ....Heb 12:5-8

Blessedness of, manifested in:
Regeneration...........John 1:12
Adoption ....Gal 4:5, 6
Glorification ....Rom 8:19-21

SOON—*at once; quickly*

[*also* SOONER]
as *s* as he had left ....Gen 18:33
s as the morning was light.....Gen 44:3
is it that ye are come so *s*.....Ex 2:18
as *s* as he came nigh unto .....Ex 32:19
ye shall *s* utterly perish ....Deut 4:26
as *s* as they which pursued ....Josh 2:7
as *s* as the soles of the feet....Josh 3:13
as *s* as the sun was down .....Josh 8:29
as *s* as Gideon was dead ......Judg 8:33
As *s* as ye be come into 1Sam 9:13
as *s* as the lad was gone 1Sam 20:41
as *s* as David had made 2Sam 6:18
As *s* as ye hear the sound.....2Sam 15:10
as *s* as he sat on his throne ...1Kin 16:11
as *s* as thou art departed 1Kin 20:36
as *s* as he was departed 1Kin 20:36
as *s* as this letter cometh 2Kin 10:2
s as the kingdom was 2Kin 14:5
s as the commandment came ..2Chr 31:5
my Maker would *s* take me ...Job 32:22
s as they hear of me, they .....Ps 18:44
go astray as *s* as they be .....Ps 58:3
s have subdued their enemies..Ps 81:14
They *s* forgat his works ....Ps 106:13

S

that is *s* angry dealeth ....Prov 14:17
s as Zion travailed, she ....Is 66:8
s as she saw them with her ....Ezek 23:16
How *s* is the fig tree ....Matt 21:20
And as *s* as he had spoken ....Mark 1:42
and as *s* as ye be entered .....Mark 11:2
s as the days of his ....Luke 1:23
s as it was sprung up ....Luke 8:6
And as *s* as it was day ....Luke 22:66
as *s* as she heard that ....John 11:20
but as *s* as she is delivered ....John 16:21
s then as they were come .....John 21:9
as *s* as I was sent for ....Acts 10:29
so *s* removed from him ....Gal 1:6
so *s* as I shall see how ....Phil 2:23
That ye be not *s* shaken 2Thess 2:2
not *s* angry, not given to ......Titus 1:7
be restored to you the *s*........Heb 13:19
as *s* as I had eaten it ....Rev 10:10
for to devour her child as *s* ...Rev 12:4

SOOTHSAYER—*a diviner; a fortune teller*
Among Philistines ....Is 2:6
At Babylon ....Dan 2:27
At Philippi..............Acts 16:12, 16
Unable to interpret ......Dan 4:7
Forbidden in Israel ......Mic 5:12
See DIVINATION

[*also* SOOTHSAYERS]
also the son of Beor, the *s* ....Josh 13:22
the Chaldeans, and the *s* ......Dan 5:7
astrologers, Chaldeans, and *s* ..Dan 5:11

SOP—*a small portion of food*
Christ gives to Judas .....John 13:26-30

SOPATER (sō'pä-tĕr)—*"one who defends the father"*
One of Paul's companions.Acts 20:4

SOPE—*See* SOAP

SOPHERETH (sō-fē'rĕth)—*"learning"*
Descendants of Solomon's servants ....Neh 7:57

SORCERER—*supposed possessor of supernatural powers*

Prevalence of, in:
Assyria ....Neh 3:4, 5
Egypt ....Ex 7:11
Babylon ....Is 47:9-13
Palestine................Acts 8:9-24
Last days ....Rev 9:21

Punishment of, described:
Legally ....Deut 18:10-12
Prophetically ....Mal 3:5
Symbolically ....Rev 21:8
See DIVINATION; MAGIC; MAGICIAN

[*also* SORCERERS]
nor to your *s* which speak .....Jer 27:9
the *s*, and the Chaldeans ......Dan 2:2
they found a certain *s*.........Acts 13:6
But Elymas the *s* for so is .....Acts 13:8
For without are dogs, and *s* ...Rev 22:15

SORCERESS—*a female sorcerer*
hither, ye sons of the *s* ....Is 57:3

SORCERY—*the practice of magic*
Forbidden in Israel ......Deut 18:10
Condemned by the prophets ....Mic 5:12
Practiced by Manasseh ...2Chr 33:6
Work of the flesh ....Gal 5:20

[*also* SORCERIES]
for the multitude of thy *s* .....Is 47:9
the multitude of thy *s*.........Is 47:12
had bewitched them with *s* ....Acts 8:11
murders, nor of their *s*........Rev 9:21
by thy *s* were all nations ......Rev 18:23

SORE—*a boil or welt; causing pain or distress*

[*also* SORES]
when they were *s*, that two....Gen 34:25
smote Job with *s* boils ....Job 2:7
bruises, and putrifying *s*.......Is 1:6
laid at his gate, full of *s*.......Luke 16:20
a noisome and grievous *s* .....Rev 16:2
their pains and their *s* ....Rev 16:11

SORE—*extreme*

[*also* SORELY, SORER]
they pressed *s* upon the ....Gen 19:9
and the men were *s* afraid ....Gen 20:8
s longedst after thy father's....Gen 31:30
And the famine was *s* in ......Gen 43:1
famine is *s* in the land of .....Gen 47:4
archers have *s* grieved him ....Gen 49:23
and very *s* lamentation ....Gen 50:10
Moab was *s* afraid of ....Num 22:3
and wonders, great and *s* .....Deut 6:22
s sicknesses, and of long ......Deut 28:59
were *s* afraid of our lives......Josh 9:24
Israel was *s* distressed.........Judg 10:9
And he was *s* athirst..........Judg 15:18
up their voices, and wept *s* ....Judg 21:2
also provoked her *s*...........1Sam 1:6
his hand is *s* upon us 1Sam 5:7
fled..and were *s* afraid 1Sam 17:24
Saul answered, I am *s* 1Sam 28:15
saw that he was *s* troubled 1Sam 28:21
the battle went *s* against 1Sam 31:3
he was *s* wounded of the 1Sam 31:3
there was a very *s* battle 2Sam 2:17
and his sickness was so *s*......1Kin 17:17
that the battle was too *s* 2Kin 3:26
And Hezekiah wept *s*..........2Kin 20:3
the battle went *s* against 1Chr 10:3
whatsoever *s* or whatsoever ...2Chr 6:28
so he died of *s* diseases 2Chr 21:19
for I am *s* wounded 2Chr 35:23
for the people wept very *s* ....Ezra 10:1
Then I was very *s* afraid ......Neh 2:2
and vex them in his *s*.........Ps 2:5
be ashamed and *s* vexed ....Ps 6:10
I am feeble and *s* broken .....Ps 38:8
s broken us in the place of ....Ps 44:19
showed me..*s* troubles ....Ps 71:20
Thou hast thrust *s* at me ......Ps 118:13
s travail hath God given ......Eccl 1:13
a *s* evil which I have seen .....Eccl 5:13
be *s* pained at the report......Is 23:5
his *s* and great and strong .....Is 27:1
and mourn *s* like doves ....Is 59:11
and afflict us very *s*? ....Is 64:12
and mine eye shall weep *s* ....Jer 13:17
shall be *s* confounded ....Jer 50:12
She weepeth *s* in the night ....Lam 1:2
send my four *s* judgments .....Ezek 14:21
and their kings shall be *s*......Ezek 27:35
even with a *s* destruction ......Mic 2:10
s displeased with your ....Zech 1:2
very *s* displeased with ....Zech 1:15
they were *s* displeased ....Matt 21:15
s amazed in themselves ....Mark 6:51
cried, and rent him *s* ....Mark 9:26
and they were *s* afraid ....Luke 2:9
they all wept *s*, and fell ....Acts 20:37
how much *s* punishment ....Heb 10:29

SOREK (sō'rĕk)—*"vine"*
Valley, home of Delilah. .Judg 16:4

SORROW—*grief or sadness; to feel grief or sadness*

Kinds of:
Hypocritical.............Matt 14:9
Unfruitful...............Matt 19:22
Temporary ....John 16:6, 20-22
Continual ....Rom 9:2
Fruitful 2Cor 7:8-11
Christian................1Thess 4:13

Caused by:
Sin ....Gen 3:16, 17
Death ....John 11:33-35
Drunkenness ....Prov 23:29-35
Love of money ....1 Tim 6:10
Apostasy ....Ps 16:4
Persecution ....Esth 9:22
Hardship of life ....Ps 90:10
Knowledge ....Eccl 1:18
Distressing news ....Acts 20:37, 38

Of the righteous:
Not like the world's 1Thess 4:13
Sometimes intense ....Ps 18:4, 5
Seen in the face ....Neh 2:2-4
None in God's blessings ..Prov 10:22
Shown in repentance 2Cor 7:10
To be removed ....Is 25:8
None in heaven ....Rev 21:4
Shall flee away ....Is 51:11
See GRIEF

[*also* SORROWED, SORROWETH, SORROWFUL, SORROWING, SORROWS]
my gray hairs with *s* to the ....Gen 42:38
my gray hairs with *s* to the ....Gen 44:29
for I know their *s* ....Ex 3:7
s shall take hold on the ....Ex 15:14
and cause *s* of heart ....Lev 26:16
failing of eyes and *s* of mind ..Deut 28:65
I am a woman of a *s* spirit 1Sam 1:15
s for you, saying, What shall ..1Sam 10:2
s of hell compassed me about .2Sam 22:6
Because I bare him with *s*.....1Chr 4:9
turned unto them from *s* ......Esth 9:22
nor hid *s* from mine eyes .....Job 3:10
refused to touch are as my *s* ..Job 6:7
I am afraid of all my *s*........Job 9:28
also is dim by reason of *s* ......Job 17:7
having *s* in my heart daily? ....Ps 13:2
s shall be to the wicked ....Ps 32:10
and my *s* was stirred..........Ps 39:2
mischief..and *s* are in ....Ps 55:10
But I am poor and *s*..........Ps 69:29
I found trouble and *s* ....Ps 116:3
late, to eat the bread of *s* .....Ps 127:2
with the eye causeth *s* ....Prov 10:10
in laughter the heart is *s* ......Prov 14:13
s of the heart the spirit is .....Prov 15:13
a fool doeth it to his *s* ....Prov 17:21
days are *s*, and his travail .....Eccl 2:23
s and wrath with his ....Eccl 5:17
S is better than laughter ......Eccl 7:3
behold darkness and *s* ....Is 5:30
s shall take hold of them ......Is 13:8
of grief and of desperate *s* ....Is 17:11
and *s* and sighing shall flee ....Is 35:10
s and mourning shall flee .....Is 51:11
griefs, and carried our *s*.......Is 53:4
comfort myself against *s* ......Jer 8:18
shall not *s* take thee ....Jer 13:21
s is incurable for the ....Jer 30:15
rejoice from their *s* ....Jer 31:13
I have replenished every *s*.....Jer 31:25
there is *s* on the sea ....Jer 49:23
be any *s* like unto my *s* ....Lam 1:12
Give them *s* of heart ....Lam 3:65
with drunkenness and *s* ....Ezek 23:33
vision my *s* are turned ....Dan 10:16
s a little for the burden ....Hos 8:10
s of a travailing woman ....Hos 13:13
are *s* for the solemn ....Zeph 3:18
shall see it, and be very *s* .....Zech 9:5
are the beginning of *s*.........Matt 24:8
they were exceeding *s*.........Matt 26:22
and began to be *s* and very ...Matt 26:37
My soul is exceeding *s* ....Matt 26:38
are the beginnings of *s* ....Mark 13:8
And they began to be *s* ....Mark 14:19
My soul is exceeding *s* ....Mark 14:34
and I have sought thee *s* ......Luke 2:48
he heard this, he was very *s* ...Luke 18:23
Jesus saw that he was very *s* ..Luke 18:24
found them sleeping for *s* .....Luke 22:45
and ye shall be *s*, but ....John 16:20
s from them of whom I ought .2Cor 2:3
be swallowed up with..*s* 2Cor 2:7
As *s*, yet always rejoicing 2Cor 6:10
that ye *s* to repentance 2Cor 7:9
lest I should have *s* upon *s* ....Phil 2:27
and that I may be the less *s* ...Phil 2:28
so much torment and *s*........Rev 18:7
and shall see no *s* ....Rev 18:7

SORRY—*expressing grief, pain, or penitence*
none of you that is *s* for me ...1Sam 22:8
neither be ye *s*; for the joy ....Neh 8:10

I will be *s* for my sin ....Ps 38:18
who shall be *s* for thee?.......Is 51:19
And they were exceeding *s*....Matt 17:23
was done, they were very *s*....Matt 18:31
the king was exceeding *s*......Mark 6:26
if I make you *s*, who is he 2Cor 2:2
the same which is made *s*.....2Cor 2:2

SORT—*a kind; a type*

[*also* SORTS]
of every *s* shalt thou bring ....Gen 6:19
every bird of every *s*..........Gen 7:14
wear a garment of divers *s* ....Deut 22:11
the poorest *s* of the people 2Kin 24:14
divided by lot, one *s* with 1Chr 24:5
long time in such *s* as it.......2Chr 30:5
silver basins of a second *s*.....Ezra 1:10
in ten days store of all *s*......Neh 5:18
four times after this *s*.........Neh 6:4
He sent divers *s* of flies.......Ps 78:45
instruments, and that of all *s*..Eccl 2:8
thy merchants in all *s* of ......Ezek 27:24
ravenous birds of every *s*......Ezek 39:4
which are of your *s*?.........Dan 1:10
lewd fellows of the baser *s*....Acts 17:5
boldly unto you in some *s*.....Rom 15:15
every man's work of what *s*...1Cor 3:13
sorrowed after a godly *s*......2Cor 7:11
this *s* are they which creep 2Tim 3:6
journey after a godly *s*........3John 6

SOSIPATER (sō-sĭp'ä-ter)—*"one who defends the father"*
Kinsman of Paul ....Rom 16:21

SOSTHENES (sŏs'thĕ-nēz)—*"strong; powerful"*
1. Ruler of the synagogue at Corinth ....Acts 18:17
2. Paul's Christian brother. .1Cor 1:1

SOTAI (sō'tī)—*"Jehovah is turning aside"*
Head of a family of servants ....Ezra 2:55

SOTTISH—*thick-headed*
Judah thus called ....Jer 4:22

SOUGHT—*See* INTRODUCTION

SOUL—*that which animates man; the living being; the self*

Descriptive of:
Man's life..............1Sam 24:11
People.................Acts 2:41, 43
Sinner.................James 5:20
Emotional life..........1Sam 18:1, 3
Spiritual life ....Ps 42:1, 2, 4
Disembodied state ....Rev 6:9
Rev 20:4

Characteristics of:
Made by God..........Gen 2:7
Belongs to God ....Ezek 18:3, 4
Possesses immortality ....Matt 10:28
Most vital asset ....Matt 16:26
Leaves body at death ....Gen 35:18

Abilities of, able to:
Believe ....Heb 10:39
Love God ....Luke 10:27
Sin....................Mic 6:7
Prosper 3John 2
Survive death ....Matt 10:28

Duties of, to:
Keep itself.............Deut 4:9
Seek the Lord..........Deut 4:29
Love the Lord ....Deut 6:5
Serve the Lord ....Deut 10:12
Store God's Word ....Deut 11:18
Keep God's Law ....Deut 26:16
Obey God ....Deut 30:2, 6, 10
Get wisdom............Prov 19:8

Enemies of, seen in:
Fleshly lusts............1Pet 2:11
Evil environment 2Pet 2:8
Sin....................Lev 5:4, 15, 17
Adultery...............Prov 6:32
Evil men ....Prov 22:24, 25
Ignorance ....Prov 8:36
Hell ....Prov 23:14

Of the righteous:
Kept by God...........Ps 121:7
Vexed by sin 2Pet 2:8
Subject to authorities ....Rom 13:1
Purified by obedience 1Pet 1:22
Not allowed to famish ...Prov 10:3
Restored...............Ps 23:1, 3
Enriched...............Prov 11:25
Satisfied ....Prov 13:25
Reign with Christ........Rev 20:4

Of the wicked:
Desires evil ....Prov 21:10
Delights in abominations .Is 66:3
Has nothing............Prov 13:4
Required ....Luke 12:19, 20
To be punished ....Rom 2:9

[*also* SOUL'S, SOULS]
and the *s* that they had ....Gen 12:5
and my *s* shall live because ....Gen 12:13
and my *s* shall live ....Gen 19:20
that thy *s* may bless me ....Gen 27:19
that thy *s* may bless me ....Gen 27:31
The *s* of my son Shechem .....Gen 34:8
saw the anguish of his *s*.......Gen 42:21
the *s* of his sons and his ......Gen 46:15
all the *s* were fourteen ....Gen 46:22
the *s* that came with Jacob ....Gen 46:26
in Egypt were two *s* ....Gen 46:27
all the *s* that came out ....Ex 1:5
loins of Jacob were seventy *s*..Ex 1:5
that *s* shall be cut off from ....Ex 12:15
man a ransom for his *s* ....Ex 30:12
atonement for your *s* ....Ex 30:15
that *s* shall be cut off from ....Ex 31:14
If a *s* shall sin through ....Lev 4:2
a *s* sin, and hear the voice ....Lev 5:1
If a *s* sin, and commit ....Lev 6:2
the *s* that eateth of the flesh ..Lev 7:20
even that *s* shall be cut off ....Lev 7:20
the *s* that shall touch any .....Lev 7:21
even that *s* shall be cut off ....Lev 7:21
Whatsoever *s* it be that ....Lev 7:27
even that *s* shall be cut off ....Lev 7:27
ye shall afflict your *s*, and .....Lev 16:29
an atonement for your *s* ......Lev 17:11
an atonement for the *s*........Lev 17:11
every *s* that eateth that ....Lev 17:15
s that turneth after such ......Lev 20:6
set my face against that *s* .....Lev 20:6
make your *s* abominable ......Lev 20:25
The *s* which hath touched .....Lev 22:6
s it be that shall not be ....Lev 23:29
whatsoever *s* it be that........Lev 23:30
same *s* will I destroy from.....Lev 23:30
ye shall afflict your *s* ....Lev 23:32
your *s* abhor my judgments ...Lev 26:15
s abhorred my statutes ....Lev 26:43
same *s* shall be cut off from ...Num 9:13
any *s* sin through ignorance ...Num 15:27
But the *s* that doeth ought ....Num 15:30
that *s* shall be cut off from ....Num 15:30
sinners against their own *s* ....Num 16:38
that *s* shall be cut off from ....Num 19:13
s that toucheth it shall be .....Num 19:22
and our *s* loatheth this ....Num 21:5
an oath to bind his *s* with .....Num 30:2
she hath bound her *s* ....Num 30:4
she hath bound her *s* ....Num 30:4
wherewith she bound her *s*....Num 30:6
wherewith she bound her *s*....Num 30:8
they have bound their *s*.......Num 30:9
wherewith she bound her *s*....Num 30:11
binding oath to afflict the *s*....Num 30:13
heart and with all your *s*......Deut 11:13
your heart and in your *s* ......Deut 11:18
whatsoever thy *s* lusteth.......Deut 12:15
because thy *s* longeth to eat ...Deut 12:20
whatsoever thy *s* lusteth.......Deut 12:20
which is as thine own *s* ....Deut 13:6
whatsoever thy *s* lusteth.......Deut 14:26
whatsoever thy *s* desireth .....Deut 14:26
the *s* that were therein........Josh 10:28
the *s* that were therein........Josh 10:35
the *s* that were therein........Josh 10:37
the *s* that were therein........Josh 10:37
all the *s* that were therein .....Josh 11:11
heart and with all your *s*......Josh 22:5
O my *s*, thou hast trodden ....Judg 5:21
his *s* was grieved for the ......Judg 10:16
so that his *s* was vexed........Judg 16:16
she was in bitterness of *s*......1Sam 1:10
as thy *s* liveth, my lord, I 1Sam 1:26
As thy *s* liveth, O king 1Sam 17:55
loved him as his own *s*........1Sam 18:3
as thy *s* liveth, there is but 1Sam 20:3
loved him as..his own *s* 1Sam 20:17
thou huntest my *s* to take 1Sam 24:11
and to seek thy *s*............1Sam 25:29
s of my lord shall be bound ...1Sam 25:29
the *s* of thine enemies 1Sam 25:29
the *s* of all the people was 1Sam 30:6
who hath redeemed my *s* 2Sam 4:9
as thy *s* liveth, I will not 2Sam 11:11
As thy *s* liveth, my lord.......2Sam 14:19
redeemed my *s* out of all 1Kin 1:29
heart and with all their *s*......1Kin 2:4
to all that thy *s* desireth.......1Kin 11:37
the *s* of the child came into ...1Kin 17:22
Lord liveth, and as thy *s*......2Kin 2:2
Lord liveth, and as thy *s*......2Kin 4:30
his heart, and with all his *s*....2Kin 23:25
set your heart and your *s* 1Chr 22:19
heart and with all their *s*......2Chr 6:38
his heart, and with all his *s*....2Chr 34:31
and life unto the bitter in *s*....Job 3:20
the bitterness of my *s*.........Job 7:11
yet would I not know my *s*....Job 9:21
My *s* is weary of my life .....Job 10:1
in the bitterness of my *s* .....Job 10:1
and his *s* within him shall .....Job 14:22
How long will ye vex my *s*....Job 19:2
and what his *s* desireth........Job 23:13
who hath vexed my *s* ....Job 27:2
pursue my *s* as the wind ......Job 30:15
was not my *s* grieved ....Job 30:25
keepeth back his *s* from.......Job 33:18
his *s* draweth near unto ....Job 33:22
To bring back his *s* from ......Job 33:30
there be which say of my *s*....Ps 3:2
Return, O Lord, deliver my *s* .Ps 6:4
the enemy persecute my *s*.....Ps 7:5
loveth violence his *s* hateth....Ps 11:5
O my *s*, thou hast said........Ps 16:2
deliver my *s* from the wicked ..Ps 17:13
Deliver my *s* from the sword ..Ps 22:20
can keep alive his own *s* ......Ps 22:29
O Lord, do I lift up my *s* .....Ps 25:1
O keep my *s*, and deliver me ..Ps 25:20
brought up my *s* from ....Ps 30:3
with grief, yea, my *s*.........Ps 31:9
Our *s* waiteth for the Lord ....Ps 33:20
The Lord redeemeth the *s* ....Ps 34:22
shame that seek after my *s*....Ps 35:4
my *s* shall be joyful in the ....Ps 35:9
I humbled my *s* with fasting ....Ps 35:13
seek after my *s* to destroy.....Ps 40:14
heal my *s*; for I have sinned...Ps 41:4
art thou cast down, O my *s*? ..Ps 42:5
art thou cast down, O my *s*? ..Ps 42:11
art thou cast down, O my *s*? ..Ps 43:5
For our *s* is bowed down......Ps 44:25
redemption of their *s* is ....Ps 49:8
he lived he blessed his *s* ......Ps 49:18
them that uphold my *s*........Ps 54:4
when they wait for my *s* ....Ps 56:6
for my *s* trusteth in thee ......Ps 57:1
my steps; my *s* is bowed ......Ps 57:6
Truly my *s* waiteth ....Ps 62:1
my *s* thirsteth for thee ....Ps 63:1
My *s* followeth hard after .....Ps 63:8
Which holdeth our *s* in life ....Ps 66:9
are come in unto my *s*........Ps 69:1
Draw nigh unto my *s* ....Ps 69:18
they that lay wait for my *s* ....Ps 71:10
my *s*, which thou hast ....Ps 71:23
save the *s* of the needy ....Ps 72:13

S

not the *s* of thy turtledove .... Ps 74:19
not their *s* from death .... Ps 78:50
Preserve my *s*; for I am .... Ps 86:2
Rejoice the *s* of thy servant ... Ps 86:4
O Lord, do I lift up my *s* ..... Ps 86:4
men..sought after my *s* .... Ps 86:14
why castest thou off my *s*? .... Ps 88:14
my *s* had almost dwelt .... Ps 94:17
the *s* of the righteous .... Ps 94:21
Bless the Lord, O my *s* .... Ps 103:2
Bless the Lord, O my *s* .... Ps 104:1
sent leanness into their *s* ..... Ps 106:15
he satisfieth the longing *s* ..... Ps 107:9
the hungry *s* with goodness .... Ps 107:9
their *s* is melted because of ... Ps 107:26
those that condemn his *s* ...... Ps 109:31
Return unto thy rest, O my *s*.. Ps 116:7
s breaketh for the longing ..... Ps 119:20
My *s* melteth for heaviness .... Ps 119:28
My *s* is continually in my ..... Ps 119:109
s hath kept thy testimonies .... Ps 119:167
Deliver my *s*, O Lord .... Ps 120:2
Our *s* is exceedingly filled ..... Ps 123:4
had gone over our *s* .... Ps 124:4
Our *s* is escaped as a bird ..... Ps 124:7
My *s* waiteth for the Lord ..... Ps 130:6
me with strength in my *s* ...... Ps 138:3
my trust; leave not my *s* ...... Ps 141:8
Bring my *s* out of prison ...... Ps 142:7
my *s* thirsteth after thee ...... Ps 143:6
bring my *s* out of trouble ...... Ps 143:11
Praise the Lord, O my *s* ...... Ps 146:1
is pleasant unto thy *s* .... Prov 2:10
they be life unto thy *s* .... Prov 3:22
if he steal to satisfy his *s* ...... Prov 6:30
doeth good to his own *s* ...... Prov 11:17
he that winneth *s* is wise ...... Prov 11:30
The *s* of the transgressors ...... Prov 13:2
accomplished is sweet to the *s*. Prov 13:19
despiseth his own *s* .... Prov 15:32
his way preserveth his *s* ...... Prov 16:17
honeycomb, sweet to the *s* .... Prov 16:24
lips are the snare of his *s* ..... Prov 18:7
that the *s* be without .... Prov 19:2
and an idle *s* shall suffer ...... Prov 19:15
keepeth his own *s* .... Prov 19:16
thy *s* spare for his crying ...... Prov 19:18
sinneth against his own *s* ...... Prov 20:2
keepeth his *s* from troubles .... Prov 21:23
he that doth keep his *s* .... Prov 22:5
spoil the *s* of those that .... Prov 22:23
he that keepeth thy *s* .... Prov 24:12
of wisdom be unto thy *s* ...... Prov 24:14
he refresheth the *s* of his ...... Prov 25:13
cold waters to a thirsty *s* ...... Prov 25:25
The full *s* loatheth .... Prov 27:7
to the hungry *s* every bitter ... Prov 27:7
but the just seek his *s* .... Prov 29:10
a thief hateth his own *s* .... Prov 29:24
he should make his *s* enjoy .... Eccl 2:24
wanteth nothing for his *s* ...... Eccl 6:2
Which yet my *s* seeketh .... Eccl 7:28
O thou whom my *s* loveth .... Song 1:7
him whom my *s* loveth .... Song 3:2
him whom my *s* loveth .... Song 3:4
my *s* made me like the .... Song 6:12
your appointed feasts my *s* .... Is 1:14
his fruitful field, both *s* .... Is 10:18
With my *s* have I desired ..... Is 26:9
and his *s* is empty .... Is 29:8
and his *s* hath appetite .... Is 29:8
in the bitterness of my *s* ...... Is 38:15
in whom my *s* delighteth ...... Is 42:1
which have said to thy *s* ...... Is 51:23
see of the travail of his *s* ...... Is 53:11
let your *s* delight itself .... Is 55:2
and the *s* which I have .... Is 57:16
have we afflicted our *s* .... Is 58:3
thou draw out thy *s* to the .... Is 58:10
and satisfy the afflicted *s* ...... Is 58:10
my *s* shall be joyful .... Is 61:10
blood of the *s* of the poor ..... Jer 2:34
sword reacheth unto the *s* ..... Jer 4:10
s is wearied because of .... Jer 4:31
lest my *s* depart from thee .... Jer 6:8

the dearly beloved of my *s* .... Jer 12:7
hath thy *s* lothed Zion? .... Jer 14:19
he hath delivered the *s* .... Jer 20:13
great evil against our *s* .... Jer 26:19
I will satiate the *s* of the ...... Jer 31:14
I have satiated the weary *s* .... Jer 31:25
replenished every sorrowful *s*.. Jer 31:25
Lord..that made us this *s* ..... Jer 38:16
well unto thee, and thy *s* ...... Jer 38:20
deliver every man his *s* .... Jer 51:45
meat to relieve the *s* .... Lam 1:11
their meat to relieve their *s* ... Lam 1:19
when their *s* was poured ...... Lam 2:12
My *s* hath them .... Lam 3:20
to the *s* that seeketh him ...... Lam 3:25
thou hast delivered thy *s* ...... Ezek 3:19
my *s* hath not been polluted ... Ezek 4:14
shall not satisfy their *s* .... Ezek 7:19
of every stature to hunt *s* ..... Ezek 13:18
ye hunt the *s* of my people .... Ezek 13:18
will ye save the *s* alive .... Ezek 13:18
the *s* that should not die ...... Ezek 13:19
to save the *s* alive that .... Ezek 13:19
there hunt the *s* to make ...... Ezek 13:20
and will let the *s* go .... Ezek 13:20
s that ye hunt to make .... Ezek 13:20
but deliver their own *s* .... Ezek 14:20
he shall save his *s* alive .... Ezek 18:27
they have devoured *s* .... Ezek 22:25
shall deliver his *s* .... Ezek 33:5
bread for their *s* shall not ..... Hos 9:4
me about, even to the *s* .... Jon 2:5
When my *s* fainted within ...... Jon 2:7
my *s* desired the first ripe ..... Mic 7:1
his *s* which is lifted up .... Hab 2:4
hast sinned against thy *s* ...... Hab 2:10
and my *s* loathed them .... Zech 11:8
their *s* also abhorred me ...... Zech 11:8
shall find rest unto your *s* ..... Matt 11:29
whom my *s* is well pleased .... Matt 12:18
heart, and with all thy *s* .... Matt 22:37
My *s* is exceeding sorrowful ... Matt 26:38
and lose his own *s*? .... Mark 8:36
thy heart, and with all thy *s* .. Mark 12:30
My *s* is exceeding sorrowful ... Mark 14:34
My *s* doth magnify the Lord ... Luke 1:46
pierce through thy own *s* ...... Luke 2:35
patience possess ye your *s* ..... Luke 21:19
Now is my *s* troubled .... John 12:27
thou wilt not leave my *s* ...... Acts 2:27
his *s* was not left in hell ...... Acts 2:31
about three thousand *s* .... Acts 2:41
every *s*, which will not hear ... Acts 3:23
one heart and of one *s* .... Acts 4:32
the *s* of the disciples .... Acts 14:22
hundred..and sixteen *s* .... Acts 27:37
Adam was made a living *s* 1Cor 15:45
for a record upon my *s* 2Cor 1:23
but also our own *s* 1Thess 2:8
your whole spirit and *s* 1Thess 5:23
dividing asunder of *s* .... Heb 4:12
as an anchor of the *s* .... Heb 6:19
s shall have no pleasure .... Heb 10:38
for they watch for your *s* ...... Heb 13:17
is able to save your *s* .... James 1:21
the salvation of your *s* 1Pet 1:9
purified your *s* in obeying 1Pet 1:22
and Bishop of your *s* 1Pet 2:25
is eight *s* were saved by 1Pet 3:20
the keeping of their *s* 1Pet 4:19
beguiling unstable *s* 2Pet 2:14
the altar the *s* of them .... Rev 6:9
and every living *s* died .... Rev 16:3
and slaves, and *s* of men ..... Rev 18:13
fruits that thy *s* lusted .... Rev 18:14

SOUL WINNING—*bringing individuals to Christ*

Importance of .... James 5:20
Christ's command .... Matt 4:19
Our reward .... Dan 12:3

SOUND—*to make a noise; a noise; whole; steadfast; sensible*

[*also* SOUNDED, SOUNDETH, SOUNDING, SOUNDS]

when the trumpet *s* long ...... Ex 19:13
his *s* shall be heard when ...... Ex 28:35
trumpet of the jubilee to *s* .... Lev 25:9
trumpet *s* throughout all ...... Lev 25:9
but ye shall not *s* an alarm .... Num 10:7
ye hear the *s* of the trumpet .. Josh 6:5
when I have *s* my father 1Sam 20:12
s of a going in the tops 2Sam 5:24
hear the *s* of the trumpet 2Sam 15:10
the earth rent with the *s* 1Kin 1:40
when Ahijah heard the *s* of ... 1Kin 14:6
s of his master's feet 2Kin 6:32
hear a *s* of going in the tops .. 1Chr 14:15
harps and cymbals, *s*, by 1Chr 15:16
and with *s* of the cornet 1Chr 15:28
those that should make a *s* 1Chr 16:42
priests *s* with trumpets 2Chr 5:12
one *s* to be heard in 2Chr 5:13
priests *s* trumpets before 2Chr 7:6
and *s* with trumpets 2Chr 23:13
he that *s* the trumpet was ..... Neh 4:18
hear the *s* of the trumpet ..... Neh 4:20
A dreadful *s* is in his ears ..... Job 15:21
the *s* that goeth out of his ..... Job 37:2
the Lord with the *s* of a ...... Ps 47:5
that know the joyful *s* .... Ps 89:15
trumpets and *s* of cornet ...... Ps 98:6
with the *s* of the trumpet ..... Ps 150:3
upon the high *s* cymbals ...... Ps 150:5
He layeth up *s* wisdom for .... Prov 2:7
Counsel is mine, and *s* .... Prov 8:14
when the *s* of the grinding .... Eccl 12:4
my bowels shall *s* like an ...... Is 16:11
the *s* of thy bowels and of .... Is 63:15
the *s* of the trumpet .... Jer 4:19
Hearken to the *s* of the .... Jer 6:17
s of the millstones, and the .... Jer 25:10
heart shall *s* for Moab .... Jer 48:36
heart shall *s* like pipes for ..... Jer 48:36
A *s* of a cry cometh from ..... Jer 51:54
not the *s* again of the .... Ezek 7:7
the *s* of the cherubim's wings .. Ezek 10:5
the isles shake at the *s* of ..... Ezek 26:15
nations to shake at the *s* ...... Ezek 31:16
heard the *s* of the trumpet .... Ezek 33:5
ye hear the *s* of the cornet .... Dan 3:5
that shall hear the *s* of the .... Dan 3:10
s an alarm in my holy .... Joel 2:1
with the *s* of the trumpet ...... Amos 2:2
do not *s* a trumpet before ..... Matt 6:2
with a great *s* of a trumpet .... Matt 24:31
of thy salutation *s* in mine .... Luke 1:44
received him safe and *s* .... Luke 15:27
thou hearest the *s* thereof ..... John 3:8
there came a *s* from heaven ... Acts 2:2
s, and found it twenty .... Acts 27:28
s went into all the earth .... Rom 10:18
I am become as *s* brass, or 1Cor 13:1
things without life giving *s* 1Cor 14:7
give a distinction in the *s* 1Cor 14:7
give an uncertain *s* 1Cor 14:8
the trumpet shall *s*, and the ... 1Cor 15:52
s out the word of the Lord 1Thess 1:8
of love, and of a *s* mind 2Tim 1:7
they may be *s* in the faith ..... Titus 1:13
s in faith, in charity, in .... Titus 2:2
S speech, that cannot be ...... Titus 2:8
And the *s* of a trumpet, and .. Heb 12:19
his voice as the *s* of many ..... Rev 1:15
prepared themselves to *s* ...... Rev 8:6
The first angel *s*, and there .... Rev 8:7
the third angel *s*, and there ... Rev 8:10
the fifth angel *s*, and I saw .... Rev 9:1
and the *s* of their wings was ... Rev 9:9
as the *s* of chariots of many ... Rev 9:9
And the seventh angel *s* .... Rev 11:15
s of a millstone shall be .... Rev 18:22

SOUND DOCTRINE—*doctrine that is free from error*

Manifested in:

Heart's prayer .... Ps 119:80

Speech 2Tim 1:13
Righteous living 1Tim 1:10
Need of:
For exhortation ....Titus 1:9
For the faith ....Titus 1:13
Denied by some 2Tim 4:3

they will not endure *s **d*** 2Tim 4:3
he may be able by *s **d*** both ....Titus 1:9
things which become *s **d*** ....Titus 2:1

SOUNDNESS—*freedom from injury or disease; firmness; stability*
no *s* in my flesh because of ....Ps 38:3
unto the head there is no *s* ....Is 1:6
given him this perfect *s* ....Acts 3:16

SOUR—*bitter taste*
Their drink is *s*; they have ....Hos 4:18

SOUR GRAPES—*unripened grapes*
Used proverbially ....Jer 31:29, 30

[*also* SOUR GRAPE]
and the *s **g*** is ripening ....Is 18:5
The fathers have eaten *s **g*** ....Ezek 18:2

SOUTH—*the opposite direction from north*

[*also* SOUTHWARD]
going on still toward the *s* ....Gen 12:9
journeys from the *s* even to ....Gen 13:3
s, and eastward, and ....Gen 13:14
he dwelt in the *s* country ....Gen 24:62
twenty boards on the *s* side *s* ....Ex 26:18
for the *s* side *s* there shall be ....Ex 27:9
twenty boards for the *s* side *s* ....Ex 36:23
side of the tabernacle *s* ....Ex 40:24
s side shall be the standard ....Num 2:10
side of the tabernacle *s* ....Num 3:29
And they ascended by the *s* ....Num 13:22
which dwelt in the *s* ....Num 21:1
your *s* quarter shall be ....Num 34:3
your *s* border shall be the ....Num 34:3
turn from the *s* to the ....Num 34:4
the *s* to Kadesh-barnea ....Num 34:4
in the vale, and in the *s* ....Deut 1:7
northward, and *s* and ....Deut 3:27
the *s*, and the plain of the ....Deut 34:3
of the hills, and of the *s* ....Josh 10:40
all the *s* country, and all ....Josh 11:16
and in the *s* country ....Josh 12:8
the wilderness of Zin *s* was ....Josh 15:1
the uttermost part of the *s* ....Josh 15:1
s side to Maaleh-acrabbim ....Josh 15:3
s side unto Kadesh-barnea ....Josh 15:3
is on the *s* side of the river ....Josh 15:7
for thou hast given me a *s* ....Josh 15:19
toward the coast of Edom *s* ....Josh 15:21
S it was Ephraim's, and ....Josh 17:10
hill that lieth on the *s* side ....Josh 18:13
the corner of the sea *s* ....Josh 18:14
lieth before Beth-horon *s* ....Josh 18:14
the side of Jebusi on the *s* ....Josh 18:16
sea at the *s* end of Jordan ....Josh 18:19
of Jordan: this was the *s* ....Josh 18:19
to Zebulun on the *s* side ....Josh 19:34
the mountain, and in the *s* ....Judg 1:9
which lieth in the *s* of Arad ....Judg 1:16
other *s* over against Gibeah 1Sam 14:5
out of a place toward the *s* 1Sam 20:41
plain on the *s* of Jeshimon 1Sam 23:24
Against the *s* of Judah 1Sam 27:10
the *s* of the Jerahmeelites 1Sam 27:10
against the *s* of the Kenites 1Sam 27:10
the *s* of the Cherethites 1Sam 30:14
and upon the *s* of Caleb 1Sam 30:14
went out to the *s* of Judah 2Sam 24:7
three looking toward the *s* 1Kin 7:25
eastward over against the *s* 1Kin 7:39
the east, west, north, and *s* 1Chr 9:24
To Obed-edom *s*; and to 1Chr 26:15
three looking toward the *s* 2Chr 4:4
low country, and of the *s* of 2Chr 28:18
and the chambers of the *s* ....Job 9:9
quieteth the earth by the *s* ....Job 37:17
the west, nor from the *s* ....Ps 75:6
and the *s* thou hast created ....Ps 89:12
as the streams in the *s* ....Ps 126:4
wind goeth toward the *s* ....Eccl 1:6
wind; and come, thou *s* ....Song 4:16
As whirlwinds in the *s* pass ....Is 21:1
to the *s*, Keep not back ....Is 43:6
cities of the *s* shall be shut ....Jer 13:19
and in the cities of the *s* ....Jer 32:44
set thy face toward the *s* ....Ezek 20:46
drop thy word toward the *s* ....Ezek 20:46
the forest of the *s* field ....Ezek 20:46
say to the forest of the *s* ....Ezek 20:47
all faces from the *s* to the ....Ezek 20:47
the frame of a city on the *s* ....Ezek 40:2
brought me toward the *s* ....Ezek 40:24
behold a gate toward the *s* ....Ezek 40:24
the inner court toward the *s* ....Ezek 40:27
gate to gate toward the *s* ....Ezek 40:27
inner court by the *s* gate ....Ezek 40:28
he measured the *s* gate ....Ezek 40:28
prospect was toward the *s* ....Ezek 40:45
that were toward the *s* ....Ezek 42:12
measured the *s* side, five ....Ezek 42:18
go by the way of the *s* gate ....Ezek 46:9
And the *s* side *s*, from ....Ezek 47:19
And this is the *s* side *s* ....Ezek 47:19
the *s* side four thousand ....Ezek 48:16
of Gad, at the *s* side *s* ....Ezek 48:28
and northward, and *s* ....Dan 8:4
toward the *s*, and toward ....Dan 8:9
the king's daughter of the *s* ....Dan 11:6
of the *s* shall be moved ....Dan 11:11
arms of the *s* shall not ....Dan 11:15
against the king of the *s* ....Dan 11:25
king of the *s* shall be ....Dan 11:25
the king of the *s* push at ....Dan 11:40
of the *s* shall possess the ....Obad 19
go forth toward the *s* country ....Zech 6:6
go with whirlwinds of the *s* ....Zech 9:14
to Rimmon *s* of Jerusalem ....Zech 14:10
queen of the *s* shall rise up ....Matt 12:42
queen of the *s* shall rise up ....Luke 11:31
the *s*, and shall sit down ....Luke 13:29
Arise, and go toward the *s* ....Acts 8:26
the *s* wind blew softly ....Acts 27:13
three gates; on the *s* three ....Rev 21:13

SOW—*female pig*
s that was washed to her 2Pet 2:22

SOW—*to plant or scatter seed*
Restrictions upon, regarding:
Sabbath year ....Lev 25:3-22
Mingled seed ....Lev 19:19
Weather ....Eccl 11:4, 6
Figurative of evil things:
Iniquity ....Job 4:8
Wind ....Hos 8:7
Discord ....Prov 6:14, 19
Strife ....Prov 16:28
False teaching ....Matt 13:25, 39
Sin ....Gal 6:7, 8
Figurative of good things:
God's Word ....Is 55:10
Reward 2Cor 9:6, 10
Gospel ....Matt 13:3, 4, 37
Gospel messengers ....John 4:36, 37
Resurrection 1Cor 15:36-44
Eternal life ....Gal 6:7-9

[*also* SOWED, SOWEDST, SOWETH, SOWING, SOWN]
Then Isaac *s* in that land ....Gen 26:12
for you, and ye shall *s* the ....Gen 47:23
six years thou shalt *s* thy ....Ex 23:10
thou hast *s* in the field ....Ex 23:16
s seed which is to be *s* ....Lev 11:37
shall reach unto the *s* time ....Lev 26:5
ye shall *s* your seed in vain ....Lev 26:16
where thou *s* thy seed, and ....Deut 11:10
which is neither eared nor *s* ....Deut 21:4
s thy vineyard with divers ....Deut 22:9
thy seed which thou hast *s* ....Deut 22:9
burning, that it is not *s* ....Deut 29:23
so it was when Israel had *s* ....Judg 6:3
down the city, and *s* it with ....Judg 9:45
in the third year *s* ye, and 2Kin 19:29
Then let me *s*, and let ....Job 31:8
Light is *s* for the righteous ....Ps 97:11
s the fields, and plant ....Ps 107:37
that *s* in tears shall reap ....Ps 126:5
him that *s* righteousness ....Prov 11:18
that *s* iniquity shall reap ....Prov 22:8
every thing *s* by the brooks ....Is 19:7
plowman plow all day to *s*? ....Is 28:24
Blessed are ye that *s* beside ....Is 32:20
yea they shall not be *s* ....Is 40:24
that are *s* in it to spring ....Is 61:11
in a land that was not *s* ....Jer 2:2
and *s* not among thorns ....Jer 4:3
shall ye build house, nor *s* ....Jer 35:7
ye shall be tilled and *s* ....Ezek 36:9
I will *s* her unto me in the ....Hos 2:23
treader of grapes him that *s* ....Amos 9:13
shalt *s*, but thou shalt not ....Mic 6:15
no more of thy name be *s* ....Nah 1:14
I will *s* them among the ....Zech 10:9
of the air: for they *s* not ....Matt 6:26
a sower went forth to *s* ....Matt 13:3
And when he had *s* ....Matt 13:4
which was *s* in his heart ....Matt 13:19
unto a man which *s* good ....Matt 13:24
which a man took, and *s* in ....Matt 13:31
He that *s* the good seed is ....Matt 13:37
that I reap where I *s* not ....Matt 25:26
there went out a sower to *s* ....Mark 4:3
as he *s*, some fell by the ....Mark 4:4
The sower *s* the word ....Mark 4:14
side, where the word is *s* ....Mark 4:15
the word that was *s* in their ....Mark 4:15
are *s* on stony ground; who ....Mark 4:16
they which are *s* on good ....Mark 4:20
But when it is *s*, it groweth ....Mark 4:32
A sower went out to *s* his ....Luke 8:5
as he *s*, some fell by the ....Luke 8:5
reapest that thou didst not *s* ....Luke 19:21
have *s* unto you spiritual 1Cor 9:11
fruit of righteousness is *s* ....James 3:18

SOWER—*one who sows*
Cut off the *s* from Babylon ....Jer 50:16
a *s* went forth to sow ....Matt 13:3
there went out a *s* to sow ....Mark 4:3
The *s* soweth the word ....Mark 4:14
s went out to sow his seed ....Luke 8:5

SPACE—*a period of time; a specified area*
abode with him the *s* of a ....Gen 29:14
the *s* of the seven sabbaths ....Lev 25:8
And the *s* in which we came ....Deut 2:14
shall be a *s* between you ....Josh 3:4
a great *s* being between 1Sam 26:13
a little *s* grace hath been ....Ezra 9:8
the *s* of two full years ....Jer 28:11
s also before the little ....Ezek 40:12
s was one cubit on that side ....Ezek 40:12
the *s* of one hour after ....Luke 22:59
about the *s* of three hours ....Acts 5:7
s of four hundred and fifty ....Acts 13:20
they had tarried there a *s* ....Acts 15:33
for the *s* of three months ....Acts 19:8
the *s* of two hours cried ....Acts 19:34
the *s* of three years and six ....James 5:17
And I gave her *s* to repent ....Rev 2:21
s of a thousand and six ....Rev 14:20

SPAIN—*a country in southwestern Europe*
Paul desires to visit ....Rom 15:24, 28

SPAKE, SPAKEST—*See* SPEAK

SPAN—*a unit of measurement; to form an arch over*

[*also* SPANNED]
a *s* shall be the length ....Ex 28:16
a *s* shall be the breadth ....Ex 28:16
a *s* was the length thereof ....Ex 39:9
and a *s* the breadth thereof ....Ex 39:9
height was six cubits and a *s* 1Sam 17:4
meted out heaven with the *s* ....Is 40:12
right hand hath *s* the ....Is 48:13
and children of a *s* long? ....Lam 2:20
round about shall be a *s* ....Ezek 43:13

SPARE—*to refrain from punishing, destroying, or harming*

[*also* SPARED, SPARETH, SPARING]

destroy and not *s* the place ... Gen 18:24
pity him, neither shalt thou *s* ... Deut 13:8
they have, and *s* them not ... 1Sam 15:3
Saul and the people *s* Agag ... 1Sam 15:9
he *s* to take of his own flock ... 2Sam 12:4
my master hath *s* Naaman ... 2Kin 5:20
s me according to the ... Neh 13:22
let him not *s*; for I have ... Job 6:10
he *s* it, and forsake it not ... Job 20:13
me, and *s* not to spit in my ... Job 30:10
O *s* me, that I may recover ... Ps 39:13
he *s* not their soul from ... Ps 78:50
not *s* in the day of vengeance. ... Prov 6:34
He that *s* his rod hateth his ... Prov 13:24
righteous giveth and *s* not ... Prov 21:26
no man shall *s* his brother ... Is 9:19
pieces; he shall not *s* ... Is 30:14
Cry aloud, *s* not, lift up thy ... Is 58:1
I will not pity, nor *s*, nor ... Jer 13:14
he shall not *s* them, neither ... Jer 21:7
s ye not her young men ... Jer 51:3
neither shall mine eye *s* ... Ezek 5:11
And mine eye shall not *s* ... Ezek 7:9
let not your eye *s*, neither ... Ezek 9:5
mine eye *s* them from ... Ezek 20:17
not go back, neither will I *s* ... Ezek 24:14
S thy people, O Lord, and ... Joel 2:17
should not I *s* Nineveh, that ... Jon 4:11
not *s* continually to slay the ... Hab 1:17
I will *s* them, as a man ... Mal 3:17
s his own son that serveth ... Mal 3:17
bread enough and not to *s* ... Luke 15:17
wolves enter..not *s* the ... Acts 20:29
He that *s* not his own Son ... Rom 8:32
take heed lest he also *s* not ... Rom 11:21
trouble in the flesh: but I *s* ... 1Cor 7:28
to *s* you I came not as yet ... 2Cor 1:23
if I come again, I will not *s* ... 2Cor 13:2
if God *s* not the angels that ... 2Pet 2:4

SPARINGLY—*marked by restraint*
soweth *s* shall reap also *s* ... 2Cor 9:6

SPARK—*a small particle of a burning substance*

[*also* SPARKLED, SPARKS]

trouble, as the *s* fly upward ... Job 5:7
s of his fire shall not shine ... Job 18:5
and *s* of fire leap out ... Job 41:19
and the maker of it as a *s* ... Is 1:31
yourselves about with *s* ... Is 50:11
the *s* that ye have kindled ... Is 50:11
s like the color of ... Ezek 1:7

SPARROW—*a small bird*
Value of ... Matt 10:29, 31

[*also* SPARROWS]

the *s* hath found a house ... Ps 84:3
a *s* alone upon the housetop ... Ps 102:7
s sold for two farthings ... Luke 12:6
of more value than many *s* ... Luke 12:7

SPAT—*See* SPIT

SPEAK—*to communicate with the voice*

[*also* SPAKE, SPAKEST, SPEAKEST, SPEAKETH, SPEAKING, SPEAKINGS, SPOKEN]

as the Lord had *s* unto ... Gen 12:4
for the which thou hast *s* ... Gen 19:21
which God had *s* to him ... Gen 21:2
before he had done *s* ... Gen 24:15
cannot *s* unto thee bad or ... Gen 24:50
done that which I have *s* ... Gen 28:15
word that Joseph had *s* ... Gen 44:2
it is my mouth that *s* ... Gen 45:12
thou hast *s* unto thy ... Ex 4:10
Lord had *s* unto Moses ... Ex 9:12
Thou hast *s* well, I will ... Ex 10:29
all this land that I have *s* ... Ex 32:13
a man *s* unto his friend ... Ex 33:11
also that thou hast *s* ... Ex 33:17
till Moses had done *s* with ... Ex 34:33
before the Lord to *s* with him ... Ex 34:34
which the Lord hath *s* ... Lev 10:11
the Lord had *s* unto Moses ... Num 1:48
was gone..to *s* with him ... Num 7:89
the Lord indeed *s* only by ... Num 12:2
hath he not *s* also by us? ... Num 12:2
will I *s* mouth to mouth ... Num 12:8
as ye have *s* in mine ears ... Num 14:28
for we have *s* against the ... Num 21:7
What hath the Lord *s*? ... Num 23:17
All that the Lord *s*, that ... Num 23:26
thing which thou hast *s* is ... Deut 1:14
God *s* out of the midst of ... Deut 4:33
our God shall *s* unto thee ... Deut 5:27
which they have *s* unto ... Deut 5:28
said all that they have *s* ... Deut 5:28
thee, as the Lord hath *s* ... Deut 6:19
I *s* not with your children ... Deut 11:2
s of them when thou sittest ... Deut 11:19
me, They have well *s* ... Deut 18:17
that which they have *s* ... Deut 18:17
When a prophet *s* in the ... Deut 18:22
which the Lord hath not *s* ... Deut 18:22
the prophet hath *s* it ... Deut 18:22
officers shall *s* unto the people ... Deut 20:5
call him, and *s* unto him ... Deut 25:8
the Levites shall *s*, and say ... Deut 27:14
Moses made an end of *s* ... Deut 32:45
when Joshua had *s* unto ... Josh 6:8
that *s* unto the woman? ... Judg 13:11
he had made an end of *s* ... Judg 15:17
and *s* of also in mine ears ... Judg 17:2
take advice, and *s* your minds ... Judg 19:30
with her, then she left *s* ... Ruth 1:18
for that thou hast *s* friendly ... Ruth 2:13
grief have I *s* hitherto ... 1Sam 1:16
wherefore then *s* thou so ... 1Sam 9:21
he had made an end of *s* ... 1Sam 18:1
thou and I have *s* of ... 1Sam 20:23
words which thou *s* unto me ... 1Sam 28:21
unless thou hadst *s* ... 2Sam 2:27
which thou hast *s* of ... 2Sam 6:22
thou hast *s* concernng ... 2Sam 7:25
I pray thee, *s* unto the king ... 2Sam 13:13
he had made an end of *s* ... 2Sam 13:36
my lord the king hath *s* ... 2Sam 14:19
s comfortably unto thy ... 2Sam 19:7
Why *s* thou any more of thy ... 2Sam 19:29
if Adonijah have not *s* this ... 1Kin 2:23
thou *s* also with thy ... 1Kin 8:24
thou *s* unto thy servant ... 1Kin 8:26
as thou *s* by the hand of ... 1Kin 8:53
which the Lord hath *s* ... 1Kin 13:3
for the Lord hath *s* it ... 1Kin 14:11
said, Thus *s* Ben-hadad ... 1Kin 20:5
Jezreelite had *s* to him ... 1Kin 21:4
the Lord hath not *s* by ... 1Kin 22:28
Lord which Elijah had *s* ... 2Kin 1:17
words that thou *s* in thy ... 2Kin 6:12
the man of God had *s* to ... 2Kin 7:18
the thing that he hath *s* ... 2Kin 20:9
also *s* of thy servant's ... 1Chr 17:17
which my lord hath *s* of ... 2Chr 2:15
s with thy mouth, and ... 2Chr 6:15
hast *s* unto thy servant ... 2Chr 6:17
the Lord hath *s* evil ... 2Chr 18:22
and to *s* against him ... 2Chr 32:17
the prophet *s* from the ... 2Chr 36:12
word..*s* by the mouth of ... 2Chr 36:22
we had *s* unto the king ... Ezra 8:22
words that he had *s* ... Neh 2:18
and *s* with them from ... Neh 9:13
could not *s* in the Jews' ... Neh 13:24
fail of all..thou hast *s* ... Esth 6:10
people, and *s* peace to all ... Esth 10:3
While he was yet *s*, there ... Job 1:16
Thou *s* as one of the ... Job 2:10
of the foolish women *s* ... Job 2:10
If I *s* of strength, lo ... Job 9:19
I will *s* in the bitterness ... Job 10:1
s to the earth, and it shall ... Job 12:8
I also could *s* as ye do ... Job 16:4
and after that I have *s* ... Job 21:3
lips shall not *s* wickedness ... Job 27:4
Days should *s*, and multitude ... Job 32:7
no more: they left off *s* ... Job 32:15
I will *s*, that I may be ... Job 32:20
my tongue hath *s* in my ... Job 33:2
God *s* once, yea twice ... Job 33:14
s without knowledge ... Job 34:35
Lord had *s* these words ... Job 42:7
for ye have not *s* of me ... Job 42:7
the tongue that *s* proud ... Ps 12:3
mouth they *s* proudly ... Ps 17:10
which *s* peace to their ... Ps 28:3
s grievous things proudly ... Ps 31:18
and thy lips from *s* guile ... Ps 34:13
mouth of the righteous *s* ... Ps 37:30
to see me, he *s* vanity ... Ps 41:6
even the Lord, hath *s* ... Ps 50:1
sittest and *s* against thy ... Ps 50:20
be justified when thou *s* ... Ps 51:4
hath *s* in his holiness ... Ps 60:6
God hath *s* once; twice ... Ps 62:11
Glorious things are *s* of ... Ps 87:3
Then thou *s* in vision to ... Ps 89:19
hath *s* in his holiness ... Ps 108:7
s against me with a lying ... Ps 109:2
therefore have I *s* ... Ps 116:10
whose mouth *s* vanity ... Ps 144:11
the man that *s* froward ... Prov 2:12
A false witness that *s* lies ... Prov 6:19
I will *s* of excellent things ... Prov 8:6
He that *s* truth showeth ... Prov 12:17
a deceitful witness *s* lies ... Prov 14:25
a word *s* in due season ... Prov 15:23
he that *s* lies shall not ... Prov 19:5
man that heareth *s* ... Prov 21:28
all words that are *s* ... Eccl 7:21
those that are asleep to *s* ... Song 7:9
when she shall be *s* for? ... Song 8:8
for the Lord hath *s* ... Is 1:2
and every mouth *s* folly ... Is 9:17
word that the Lord hath *s* ... Is 16:13
God of Israel hath *s* it ... Is 21:17
for the sea hath *s*, even ... Is 23:4
for the Lord hath *s* it ... Is 25:8
another tongue will he *s* ... Is 28:11
shalt *s* out of the ground ... Is 29:4
s unto us smooth things ... Is 30:10
and *s* uprightly ... Is 33:15
S, I pray thee, unto thy ... Is 36:11
word which the Lord hath *s* ... Is 37:22
hath both *s* unto me ... Is 38:15
mouth of the Lord hath *s* it ... Is 40:5
O Jacob, and *s*, O ... Is 40:27
I have *s* it, I will also ... Is 46:11
I have not *s* in secret ... Is 48:16
how to *s* a word in season ... Is 50:4
the finger, and *s* vanity ... Is 58:9
your lips have *s* lies, your ... Is 59:3
s oppression and revolt ... Is 59:13
I that *s* in righteousness ... Is 63:1
thou hast *s* and done evil ... Jer 3:5
shalt *s* all these words unto ... Jer 7:27
shot out; it *s* deceit ... Jer 9:8
one *s* peaceably to his ... Jer 9:8
mouth of the Lord hath *s* ... Jer 9:12
I have not *s* to them, yet ... Jer 23:21
and I have *s* unto you ... Jer 25:3
heard Jeremiah *s* these ... Jer 26:7
commanded him to *s* unto ... Jer 26:8
the Lord hath *s* against ... Jer 27:13
Thus *s* the Lord of hosts ... Jer 28:2
Thus *s* the Lord God of ... Jer 30:2
the words that I have *s* ... Jer 30:2
shall *s* with him mouth ... Jer 32:4
what this people have *s* ... Jer 33:24
he shall *s* with thee mouth ... Jer 34:3
you, rising early and *s* ... Jer 35:14
because I have *s* unto ... Jer 35:17
which he had *s* unto him ... Jer 36:4
which I *s* unto thee ... Jer 38:20
So they left off *s* with him ... Jer 38:27
thou *s* falsely of Ishmael ... Jer 40:16
Jeremiah, Thou *s* falsely ... Jer 43:2
the word that thou hast *s* ... Jer 44:16
as the Lord hath *s* ... Jer 48:8
for since thou *s* of him ... Jer 48:27
thou shalt *s* my words unto ... Ezek 2:7
go *s* unto the house of ... Ezek 3:1

Lord have *s* it in my zeal .....Ezek 5:13
I the Lord have *s* it ....Ezek 5:15
I the Lord have *s* it ....Ezek 5:17
Almighty God when he *s* .....Ezek 10:5
not *s* a lying divination........Ezek 13:7
albeit I have not *s*? ....Ezek 13:7
when he hath *s* a thing........Ezek 14:9
I the Lord have *s* and ....Ezek 17:24
I the Lord have *s* it, and......Ezek 22:14
I have *s* it, saith the Lord .....Ezek 23:34
for I have *s* it, saith the.......Ezek 26:5
for I have *s* it, saith the.......Ezek 28:10
I the Lord have *s* it ....Ezek 34:24
of my jealousy have I *s* ....Ezek 36:5
I the Lord have *s* it ....Ezek 36:36
he of whom I have *s* in ....Ezek 38:17
for I have *s* it, saith the.......Ezek 39:5
S unto every feathered fowl ...Ezek 39:17
I heard him *s* unto me out ....Ezek 43:6
to thee it is *s* ....Dan 4:31
a mouth *s* great things ....Dan 7:8
he shall *s* great words.........Dan 7:25
Now as he was *s* with me .....Dan 8:18
the words that I *s* ....Dan 10:11
when he had *s* such...........Dan 10:15
yet they have *s* lies ....Hos 7:13
also *s* by the prophets ....Hos 12:10
for the Lord hath *s* it ....Joel 3:8
the Lord hath *s* against ....Amos 3:1
the Lord hath *s*, who can .....Amos 3:8
him that *s* uprightly...........Amos 5:10
with you, as ye have *s* ....Amos 5:14
thou have *s* proudly ....Obad 12
the Lord of hosts hath *s* ......Mic 4:4
at the end it shall *s*...........Hab 2:3
Thus *s* the Lord of hosts ......Hag 1:2
Thus *s* the Lord of hosts ......Zech 6:12
the idols have *s* vanity ....Zech 10:2
thou *s* lies in the name of .....Zech 13:3
What have we *s* so much .....Mal 3:13
which was *s* of the Lord ......Matt 1:22
which was *s* by Jeremiah ......Matt 2:17
was *s* of by the prophet ....Matt 3:3
heard for their much *s* ....Matt 6:7
s the word only, and my ......Matt 8:8
which was *s* by Isaiah ....Matt 8:17
of your Father which *s*........Matt 10:20
whosoever *s* a word ....Matt 12:32
whosoever *s* against the ....Matt 12:32
Why *s* thou..in parables?......Matt 13:10
was *s* by the prophet ....Matt 13:35
was *s* unto you by God ....Matt 22:31
He hath *s* blasphemy ....Matt 26:65
was *s* by the prophet ....Matt 27:35
And as soon as he had *s* ......Mark 1:42
hear, and the dumb to *s* ......Mark 7:37
had *s* the parable against......Mark 12:12
be *s* of for a memorial of .....Mark 14:9
things which were *s* of ....Luke 2:33
suffered them not to *s* ....Luke 4:41
Now when he had left *s*.......Luke 5:4
which *s* blasphemies? ....Luke 5:21
ye have *s* in darkness ....Luke 12:3
ye have *s* in the ear in ....Luke 12:3
Lord, *s* thou this parable......Luke 12:41
And when he had thus *s* ......Luke 19:28
that the prophets have *s* ......Luke 24:25
earth is earthly, and *s* of ......John 3:31
word that Jesus had *s*.........John 4:50
He that *s* of himself ....John 7:18
I *s* that which I have seen.....John 8:38
When he *s* a lie, he *s* of ......John 8:44
had *s* of taking of rest in......John 11:13
the word that I have *s* ....John 12:48
These things have I *s* ....John 14:25
the word which I have *s* ......John 15:3
If I had not come and *s*.......John 15:22
s unto you in proverbs ....John 16:25
Lo, now *s* thou plainly.........John 16:29
plainly, and *s* no proverb .....John 16:29
When Jesus had *s* these ....John 18:1
If I have *s* evil, bear..........John 18:23
And when he had *s* this........John 21:19
s of the things pertaining......Acts 1:3
when he had *s* these ....Acts 1:9
For David *s* concerning ....Acts 2:25
God hath *s* by the mouth .....Acts 3:21
these things which ye have *s*...Acts 8:24
is *s* of in the prophets ....Acts 13:40
who, *s* to them, persuaded ....Acts 13:43
first have been *s* to you ....Acts 13:46
same heard Paul *s*: who ....Acts 14:9
whereof thou *s*, is? ....Acts 17:19
these things cannot be *s*.......Acts 19:36
s perverse things, to draw .....Acts 20:30
when he had thus *s*, he ....Acts 20:36
And when he had thus *s* ......Acts 26:30
he had thus *s*, he took ....Acts 27:35
the things which were *s* ....Acts 28:24
that your faith is *s* of ....Rom 1:8
which is of faith *s* on ....Rom 10:6
your good be evil *s* of ....Rom 14:16
we *s* wisdom among them 1Cor 2:6
I *s* to your shame 1Cor 6:5
why am I evil *s* of for 1Cor 10:30
no man *s* by the Spirit 1Cor 12:3
do all *s* with tongues?.........1Cor 12:30
he that *s* in an unknown 1Cor 14:2
s not unto men, but unto 1Cor 14:2
the spirit he *s* mysteries 1Cor 14:2
s in an unknown tongue 1Cor 14:4
be unto him that *s* a..........1Cor 14:11
and he that *s* shall be a 1Cor 14:11
in the sight of God *s* we in....2Cor 2:17
and therefore have I *s* 2Cor 4:13
which I *s*, I *s* it not after 2Cor 11:17
we *s* before God in Christ.....2Chr 12:19
a proof of Christ *s* in me......2Cor 13:3
s the truth in love, may ....Eph 4:15
s every man truth with ....Eph 4:25
a shame even to *s* of those ....Eph 5:12
s to yourselves in psalms ......Eph 5:19
s the mystery of Christ.......Col 4:3
the Spirit *s* expressly 1Tim 4:1
s lies in hypocrisy 1Tim 4:2
adversary to *s* reproachfully ...1Tim 5:14
last days *s* unto us by his .....Heb 1:2
began to be *s* by the Lord ....Heb 2:3
have *s* of another day.........Heb 4:8
we have *s* this is the sum .....Heb 8:1
by it he being dead yet *s*......Heb 11:4
should not be *s* to them.......Heb 12:19
that *s* better things than.......Heb 12:24
ye refuse not him that *s*.......Heb 12:25
him that *s* from heaven ....Heb 12:25
He that *s* evil of his ....James 4:11
s evil of the law, and ....James 4:11
who have *s* in the name.......James 5:10
and envies, and all evil *s*......1Pet 2:1
they *s* against you as..........1Pet 2:12
same excess of riot, *s* evil 1Pet 4:4
If any man *s*, let him *s*........1Pet 4:11
their part he is evil *s* 1Pet 4:14
of truth shall be evil *s* 2Pet 2:2
s evil of the things............2Pet 2:12
dumb ass *s* with man's voice...2Pet 2:16
s before by the holy 2Pet 3:2
these *s* evil of those things ....Jude 10
ungodly sinners have *s* ....Jude 15
mouth *s* great swelling ....Jude 16
were *s* before of the ....Jude 17
a mouth *s* great things ....Rev 13:5
the beast should both *s* ....Rev 13:15

SPEAKER—*a formal announcer*
an evil *s* be established ....Ps 140:11
he was the chief *s* ....Acts 14:12

SPEAKING—*See* SPEAK

SPEAR—*a long-handled, sharp-pointed weapon*

[*also* SPEAR'S, SPEARS]
Stretch out the *s* that is in ....Josh 8:18
Joshua stretched out the *s*.....Josh 8:18
a shield or *s* seen among......Judg 5:8
make them swords or *s* 1Sam 13:19
neither sword nor *s* found 1Sam 13:22
s head weighed six hundred ...1Sam 17:7
with a sword, and with a *s* 1Sam 17:45
here under thine hand *s* or 1Sam 21:8
his *s* struck in the ground 1Sam 26:7
the *s* that is at his bolster 1Sam 26:11
now see where the king's *s*....1Sam 26:16
Saul leaned upon his *s*........2Sam 1:6
end of the *s* smote him 2Sam 2:23
the *s* came out behind him 2Sam 2:23
of whose *s* was like a 2Sam 21:19
his *s* against eight hundred 2Sam 23:8
Egyptian had a *s* in his hand ..2Sam 23:21
s out of the Egyptian's hand...2Sam 23:21
and slew him with his own *s*...2Sam 23:21
king David's *s* and shields 2Kin 11:10
s against three hundred 1Chr 11:11
a *s* like a weaver's beam 1Chr 11:23
the *s* out of the Egyptian's 1Chr 11:23
slew him with his own *s*.......1Chr 11:23
with shield and *s* thirty........1Chr 12:34
city he put shields and *s* 2Chr 11:12
the captains of hundreds *s*......2Chr 23:9
could handle *s* and shield 2Chr 25:5
their swords, their *s*, and......Neh 4:13
half of them held the *s* from ..Neh 4:21
or his head with fish *s*? ....Job 41:7
at the shaking of a *s*..........Job 41:29
Draw out also the *s* ....Ps 35:3
teeth are *s* and arrows ....Ps 57:4
their *s* into pruninghooks.......Is 2:4
shall lay hold on bow and *s* ...Jer 6:23
furbish the *s*, and put on......Jer 46:4
the handstaves, and the *s* .....Ezek 39:9
your pruninghooks into *s*......Joel 3:10
their *s* into pruninghooks......Mic 4:3
sword and the glittering *s* .....Nah 3:3
shining of thy glittering *s*......Hab 3:11

SPEARMEN—*infantrymen armed with spears*
One of, pierces Christ's side ....John 19:34
Paul's military escort.....Acts 23:23, 24

SPECIAL—*unique, particular; especially*

[*also* SPECIALLY]
S the day that thou ....Deut 4:10
a *s* people unto himself ....Deut 7:6
God wrought *s* miracles ....Acts 19:11
and *s* before thee, O king .....Acts 25:26
s of those that believe 1Tim 4:10
and *s* for those of his own 1Tim 5:8
s they of the circumcision .....Titus 1:10
brother beloved, *s* to me ......Philem 16

SPECKLED—*spotted*
Spotted (of goats) ....Gen 30:32-39
Colored (of birds) ....Jer 12:9

The *s* shall be thy wages ......Gen 31:8
then all the cattle bare *s* ......Gen 31:8
were ring-streaked, *s*, and .....Gen 31:10
are ring-streaked, *s*, and ......Gen 31:12
there red horses, *s*, and ....Zech 1:8

SPECTACLE—*public display*
made a *s* unto the world 1Cor 4:9

SPED—*See* SPEED

SPEECH—*spoken communication*

Of the wicked, consisting of:
Lies ....Ps 58:3
Cursing ....Ps 59:12
Enticements.............Prov 7:21
Blasphemies ....Dan 7:25
Earthly things ....John 3:31
Deception ....Rom 16:18

Of the righteous, consisting of:
God's righteousness......Ps 35:28
Wisdom 1Cor 2:6, 7
God's Word ....Ps 119:172
Truth...................Eph 4:25
Mystery of Christ........Col 4:3, 4
Sound doctrine ....Titus 2:1, 8

[*also* SPEECHES]
hearken unto my *s*: for I ......Gen 4:23
understand one another's *s* ....Gen 11:7
and not in dark *s*............Num 12:8
occasions of *s* against her .....Deut 22:14
my *s* shall distil as the ....Deut 32:2

S

about this form of *s* hath 2Sam 14:20
s pleased the Lord, that 1Kin 3:10
loud voice in the Jews' *s* 2Chr 32:18
spake half in the *s* of ....Neh 13:24
and the *s* of one that is ....Job 6:26
He removeth away the *s* of....Job 12:20
s wherewith he can do no .....Job 15:3
Hear diligently my *s*, and .....Job 21:2
and my *s* dropped upon them .Job 29:22
answer him with your *s* ....Job 32:14
Job, I pray thee, hear my *s* ...Job 33:1
ear unto me, and hear my *s* ...Ps 17:6
There is no *s* nor language ....Ps 19:3
With her much fair *s* she ......Prov 7:21
and thy *s* is comely ....Song 4:3
hearken, and hear my *s* ....Is 28:23
thy *s* shall be low out of ......Is 29:4
thy *s* shall whisper out ....Is 29:4
a people of a deeper *s* ....Is 33:19
use this *s* in the land of ....Jer 31:23
the voice of *s*, as the ....Ezek 1:24
many people of a strange *s* ...Ezek 3:6
O Lord, I have heard thy *s* ...Hab 3:2
for thy *s* betrayeth thee ....Matt 26:73
an impediment in his *s* ....Mark 7:32
do ye not understand my *s*? ...John 8:43
in the *s* of Lycaonia ....Acts 14:11
with excellency of *s* or 1Cor 2:1
not the *s* of them which.......1Cor 4:19
use great plainness of *s* 2Cor 3:12
and his *s* contemptible 2Cor 10:10
Let your *s* be alway with ......Col 4:6
hard *s* which ungodly sinners ..Jude 15

SPEECHLESS—*not able to speak*
garment? And he was *s* ....Matt 22:12
unto them, and remained *s* ....Luke 1:22
journeyed with him stood *s*....Acts 9:7

SPEED—*quickness; swiftness*
"Let him make" ....Is 5:19
"They will come with" ...Is 5:26

[*also* SPED, SPEEDILY, SPEEDY]
send me good *s* this day ......Gen 24:12
they *s* took down every ....Gen 44:11
Have they not *s*? have ....Judg 5:30
Make *s*, haste, stay not 1Sam 20:38
I should *s* escape into the 1Sam 27:1
make *s* to depart, lest he 2Sam 15:14
wilderness, but *s* pass over 2Sam 17:16
Rehoboam made *s* to get 1Kin 12:18
Rehoboam made *s* to get 2Chr 10:18
divided them *s* among all 2Chr 35:13
let it be done with *s* ....Ezra 6:12
had sent, so they did *s* ....Ezra 6:13
thou mayest buy *s* with ....Ezra 7:17
a *s* riddance of all them ....Zeph 1:18
come to him with all *s* ....Acts 17:15
neither bid him God *s* 2John 10
biddeth him God *s* is 2John 11

SPEND—*paying for things; using up*
Wastefully, on:
Harlots ....Luke 15:30
Physicians...............Mark 5:26
Wisely:
In Christ's service 2Cor 12:15

[*also* SPENDEST, SPENDETH, SPENT]
water was *s* in the bottle ......Gen 21:15
how that our money is *s* ......Gen 47:18
shall be *s* in vain ....Lev 26:20
I will *s* mine arrows upon .....Deut 32:23
Jebus, the day was far *s*.......Judg 19:11
for the bread is *s* in our.......1Sam 9:7
and are *s* without hope ....Job 7:6
They *s* their days in ....Job 21:13
shall *s* their days in ....Job 36:11
For my life is *s* with grief .....Ps 31:10
we *s* our years as a tale ....Ps 90:9
a foolish man *s* it up..........Prov 21:20
harlots *s* his substance ....Prov 29:3
vain life which he *s* as a ......Eccl 6:12
I have *s* my strength for ......Is 49:4
do ye *s* money for that.........Is 55:2
bread in the city were *s* ....Jer 37:21
the day was now far *s* ....Mark 6:35
which had *s* all her living .....Luke 8:43
whatsoever thou *s* more ....Luke 10:35
when he had *s* all, there ......Luke 15:14
and the day is far *s* ....Luke 24:29
there *s* their time in ....Acts 17:21
after he had *s* some time ......Acts 18:23
he would not *s* the time ....Acts 20:16
when much time was *s* ....Acts 27:9
night is far *s*, the day ....Rom 13:12
I will very gladly *s* and........2Cor 12:15

SPENT—*See* SPEND

SPEWING—*See* SPUE

SPICE—*aromatic vegetable compound*
Uses of:
Food ....Song 8:2
Incense ....Ex 30:34-38
Fragrance ....Song 4:10
Features concerning:
Used as presents ....Gen 43:11
Objects of commerce .....Gen 37:25
Tokens of royal favor 1Kin 10:2
Stored in the temple 1Chr 9:29
Sign of wealth...........2Kin 20:13

[*also* SPICES]
s for anointing oil, and........Ex 25:6
thee principal *s* of pure ....Ex 30:23
s for anointing oil, and........Ex 35:8
s, and oil for the light ....Ex 35:28
pure incense of sweet *s* ....Ex 37:29
and of *s* very great store 1Kin 10:10
such abundance of *s* as........1Kin 10:10
traffic of the *s* merchants......1Kin 10:15
and armor, and *s* 1Kin 10:25
the ointment of the *s* 1Chr 9:30
and camels that bare *s* 2Chr 9:1
of *s* great abundance...........2Chr 9:9
there any such *s* as the........2Chr 9:9
harness, and *s*, horses.........2Chr 9:24
and divers kinds of *s*..........2Chr 16:14
precious stones, and for *s* 2Chr 32:27
with all the chief *s*............Song 4:14
my myrrh with my *s* ....Song 5:1
cheeks are as a bed of *s* ......Song 5:13
upon the mountains of *s* ......Song 8:14
and the gold, and the *s* ....Is 39:2
the flesh, and *s* it well ....Ezek 24:10
fairs with chief of all *s* ....Ezek 27:22
Salome, had bought sweet *s* ...Mark 16:1
and prepared *s* and ....Luke 23:56
bringing the *s* which they .....Luke 24:1
linen clothes with the *s* ....John 19:40

SPIDER—*an eight-legged insect that spins a web to ensnare its prey*
Web of, figurative of:
Insecurity ....Is 59:5
Godless.................Job 8:14
the *s* taketh hold with ....Prov 30:28

SPIED, SPIES—*See* SPY

SPIKENARD—*a fragrant ointment*
Used as a perfume ......Song 1:12
Mary uses it in anointing Jesus .... Mark 14:3; John 12:3
fruits; camphire, with *s* ....Song 4:13
s and saffron; calamus ....Song 4:14

SPILL—*to flow forth; accidentally flow forth*
Water 2Sam 14:14
Wine ....Luke 5:37

[*also* SPILLED, SPILT]
he *s* it on the ground ....Gen 38:9
water *s* on the ground 2Sam 14:14
bottles, and the wine is *s*......Mark 2:22

SPIN—*to twist fibers together into yarn or thread*
Work done by women ...Ex 35:25
Sign of industry ....Prov 31:19
As an illustration ....Matt 6:28

[*also* SPUN]
up in wisdom *s* goat's hair ....Ex 35:26
they toil not, they *s* not ....Luke 12:27

SPINDLE—*wooden hub that holds yarn during spinning*
layeth her hands to the *s*......Prov 31:19

SPIRIT—*the inner part of a person; God's agency*
Descriptive of:
Holy Spirit..............Gen 1:2
Angels ....Heb 1:7, 14
Man's immaterial nature .1Cor 2:11
Evil 1Sam 16:14-23
Believer's immaterial nature 1Cor 5:3, 5
Controlling influence .....Is 29:10
Inward reality ....Rom 2:29
Disembodied state ....Heb 12:23; 1Pet 3:19
Characteristics of, in man:
Center of emotions 1Kin 21:5
Source of passions ....Ezek 3:14
Cause of volitions (will) ..Prov 16:32
Subject to divine influence............ Deut 2:30; Is 19:14
Leaves body at death ....Eccl 12:7; James 2:26
See SOUL; HOLY SPIRIT

[*also* SPIRITS]
My *s* shall not always ....Gen 6:3
in whom the *s* of God is? .....Gen 41:38
Moses for anguish of *s* ....Ex 6:9
filled him with the *s* of........Ex 31:3
filled him with the *s* of........Ex 35:31
that have familiar *s* ....Lev 19:31
that hath a familiar *s* ....Lev 20:27
s of jealousy come ....Num 5:14
take of the *s* which is ....Num 11:17
took of the *s* that was ....Num 11:25
when the *s* rested upon ....Num 11:25
Lord would put his *s* ....Num 11:29
God of the *s* of all flesh ......Num 16:22
and the *s* of God came ....Num 24:2
a man in whom is the *s* ....Num 27:18
consulter with familiar *s*.......Deut 18:11
of Nun was full of the *s*.......Deut 34:9
was there *s* in them any.......Josh 5:1
the *s* of the Lord came ....Judg 3:10
Then God sent an evil *s* ......Judg 9:23
s of the Lord began to ....Judg 13:25
the *s* of the Lord came ....Judg 14:19
his *s* came again, and he ......Judg 15:19
woman of a sorrowful *s* 1Sam 1:15
and the *s* of God came 1Sam 10:10
the *s* of the Lord came 1Sam 16:13
evil *s* from God came 1Sam 18:10
evil *s* from the Lord was 1Sam 19:9
the *s* of God was upon........1Sam 19:23
those that had familiar *s* 1Sam 28:3
that hath a familiar *s* 1Sam 28:7
that hath a familiar *s* 1Sam 28:7
his *s* came again to him 1Sam 30:12
The *s* of the Lord spake 2Sam 23:2
there was no more *s* in 1Kin 10:5
And there came forth a *s* 1Kin 22:21
I will be a lying *s* in the 1Kin 22:22
hath put a lying *s* in the 1Kin 22:23
double portion of thy *s* be 2Kin 2:9
S of the Lord hath taken......2Kin 2:16
familiar *s* and wizards.........2Kin 21:6
up the *s* of Pul king 1Chr 5:26
the *s* of Tilgath-pilneser 1Chr 5:26
Then the *S* came upon 1Chr 12:18
there was no more *s* in 2Chr 9:4
Then there came out a *s* 2Chr 18:20
hath put a lying *s* in the 2Chr 18:22
came the *S* of the Lord in.....2Chr 20:14
the *s* of God came upon 2Chr 24:20
up the *s* of Cyrus king 2Chr 36:22
up the *s* of Cyrus king of .....Ezra 1:1
gavest also thy good *s* to ......Neh 9:20
Then a *s* passed before ....Job 4:15
in the anguish of my *s* ....Job 7:11

S

not given us the *s* of 2Tim 1:7
Christ be with your *s* .... Philem 25
asunder of soul and *s* .... Heb 4:12
done despite unto the *S* .... Heb 10:29
unto the Father of *s* .... Heb 12:9
s that dwelleth in us .... James 4:5
sanctification of the *S* 1Pet 1:2
the truth through the *S* 1Pet 1:22
but quickened by the *S* 1Pet 3:18
s of glory and of God 1Pet 4:14
by the *S* which he hath 1John 3:24
try the *s* whether they 1John 4:1
he hath given us of his *S* 1John 4:13
it is the *S* that beareth 1John 5:6
because the *S* is truth 1John 5:6
sensual, having not the *S* ...... Jude 19
the seven *S* which are .... Rev 1:4
the *S* on the Lord's day .... Rev 1:10
the *S* saith unto the .... Rev 2:29
I was in the *s* .... Rev 4:2
which are the seven *S* .... Rev 5:6
Yea, saith the *S*, that .... Rev 14:13
they are the *s* of devils .... Rev 16:14
the hold of every foul *s* .... Rev 18:2
me away in the *s* to .... Rev 21:10

SPIRIT, HOLY—*the third Person of the triune God—See* HOLY SPIRIT

SPIRIT OF CHRIST—*the spirit that indwelled Christ*

Descriptive of the Holy Spirit as:
Dwelling in Old Testament prophets 1Pet 1:10-11
Sent by God .... Gal 4:6
Given to believers .... Rom 8:9
Supplying believers ...... Phil 1:19
Produces boldness .... Acts 4:29-31
Commanded .... Eph 5:18

Christ's human spirit (consciousness), of His:
Perception .... Mark 2:8
Emotions .... Mark 8:12
Life .... Luke 23:46

SPIRITS, DISTINGUISHING—*discerning the spirits that are active in a given moment or event*

Described as:
Spiritual gift 1Cor 12:10
Necessary 1Thess 5:19-21

Tests of:
Christ's:
Deity 1Cor 12:3
Humanity 1John 4:1-6
Christian fellowship 1John 2:18, 19

SPIRITUAL—*that which originates from God or pertains to God's unique work in the universe and in the lives of believers*

Applied to:
Gifts 1Cor 12:1
Law .... Rom 7:14
Things .... Rom 15:27
Christians 1Cor 3:1
Resurrected body 1Cor 15:44-46
Evil forces .... Eph 6:12

Designating, Christians:
Ideal state 1Cor 3:1
Discernment 1Cor 2:13-15
Duty .... Gal 6:1
Manner of life .... Col 3:16

a fool, the *s* man is mad ...... Hos 9:7
impart..some *s* gift .... Rom 1:11
made partakers of their *s* ..... Rom 15:27
sown unto you *s* things 1Cor 9:11
all eat the same *s* meat 1Cor 10:3
drink the same *s* drink 1Cor 10:4
drank of that *s* Rock that 1Cor 10:4
and desire *s* gifts 1Cor 14:1
ye are zealous of *s* gifts 1Cor 14:12
to be a prophet, or *s* 1Cor 14:37
with all *s* blessings in .... Eph 1:3
and hymns and *s* songs .... Eph 5:19
and *s* understanding .... Col 1:9
are built up a *s* house 1Pet 2:5
to offer up *s* sacrifices 1Pet 2:5

SPIRITUAL GIFTS—*See* GIFTS, SPIRITUAL

SPIRITUALLY—*related to the spirit*
Source of .... Gal 5:22-26
Expression of 1Cor 13:1-13
Growth in 2Pet 1:4-11
Enemies of 1John 2:15-17

but to be *s* minded is life ..... Rom 8:6
they are *s* discerned 1Cor 2:14
which *s* is called Sodom .... Rev 11:8

SPIT—*to eject from the mouth; saliva*

Symbolic of:
Contempt .... Num 12:14
Rejection .... Matt 26:67
Uncleanness .... Lev 15:8

Miraculous uses of, to heal:
Dumb man .... Mark 7:33-35
Blind man .... Mark 8:23-25
Man born blind .... John 9:6, 7

[*also* SPAT, SPITTED, SPITTING, SPITTLE]
and *s* in his face, and .... Deut 25:9
let his *s* fall down upon 1Sam 21:13
I swallow down my *s*? .... Job 7:19
spare not to *s* in my face ...... Job 30:10
face from shame and *s* .... Is 50:6
And they *s* upon him .... Matt 27:30
And some began to *s* on ...... Mark 14:65
did *s* upon him, and .... Mark 15:19
entreated, and *s* on .... Luke 18:32

SPITE—*petty ill-will or hatred combined with the intention to injure*
Of vexation of grief ..... Ps 10:14
Inflicted upon Christ ..... Matt 22:6

SPOIL—*looting and plundering; the booty of such looting*
Clothing .... Ex 3:22
Cattle .... Josh 8:2
Sheep .... Num 31:32
House .... Mark 3:27
Silver and gold .... Nah 2:9
Camp 1Sam 17:53

[*also* SPOILED, SPOILEST, SPOILETH, SPOILING, SPOILS]
the slain, and *s* the city .... Gen 34:27
he shall divide the *s* .... Gen 49:27
they *s* the Egyptians .... Ex 12:36
I will divide the *s* .... Ex 15:9
took the *s* of all their .... Num 31:9
and the *s*, unto Moses .... Num 31:12
the *s* of the cities which .... Deut 2:35
gather all the *s* of it .... Deut 13:16
all the *s* thereof, shalt .... Deut 20:14
the *s* of thine enemies .... Deut 20:14
and *s* evermore .... Deut 28:29
among the *s* a goodly .... Josh 7:21
s of that city Israel took ..... Josh 8:27
spoilers that *s* them .... Judg 2:14
of them that take the *s*? ...... Judg 5:30
eaten..today of the *s* 1Sam 14:30
and *s* them until the 1Sam 14:36
of them that *s* them 1Sam 14:48
the people took of the *s* 1Sam 15:21
neither *s*, nor any thing 1Sam 30:19
give them aught of the *s* 1Sam 30:22
of the *s* unto the elders 1Sam 30:26
present for you of the *s* 1Sam 30:26
brought in a great *s* with 2Sam 3:22
he brought forth the *s* of 2Sam 12:30
therefore, Moab, to the *s* 2Kin 3:23
out, and *s* the tents of 2Kin 7:16
also exceeding much *s* 1Chr 20:2
the *s* won in battles did 1Chr 26:27
carried away very much *s* 2Chr 14:13
and they *s* all the cities 2Chr 14:14
of the *s* which they had 2Chr 15:11
came to take away the *s* 2Chr 20:25
in gathering of the *s* 2Chr 20:25
of them, and took much *s* 2Chr 25:13
took also away much *s* 2Chr 28:8
and brought the *s* to 2Chr 28:8
with the *s* clothed all 2Chr 28:15
to a *s*, and to confusion .... Ezra 9:7
to take the *s* of them for ...... Esth 3:13
on the *s* laid they not .... Esth 9:10
counselors away *s* .... Job 12:17
and plucked the *s* out of ...... Job 29:17
from him that *s* him? .... Ps 35:10
evil for good to the *s* of .... Ps 35:12
at home divided the *s* .... Ps 68:12
The stout-hearted are *s* .... Ps 76:5
All that pass by the way *s* ..... Ps 89:41
let the strangers *s* his .... Ps 109:11
one that findeth great *s* .... Ps 119:162
fill our houses with *s* .... Prov 1:13
than to divide the *s* with ...... Prov 16:19
s the soul of those that .... Prov 22:23
the soul of those that *s* .... Prov 22:23
s not his resting place .... Prov 24:15
have no need of *s* .... Prov 31:11
foxes, that *s* the vines .... Song 2:15
s of the poor is in your .... Is 3:14
when they divide the *s* .... Is 9:3
shall *s* them of the east .... Is 11:14
their houses shall be *s* .... Is 13:16
portion of them that *s* .... Is 17:14
land the rivers have *s* .... Is 18:7
and the spoiler *s* .... Is 21:2
because of the *s* of the .... Is 22:4
together with the *s* of .... Is 25:11
Woe to thee that *s* .... Is 33:1
and thou wast not *s* .... Is 33:1
to *s*, thou shalt be *s* .... Is 33:1
your *s* shall be gathered .... Is 33:4
for a *s*, and none saith .... Is 42:22
a people robbed and *s* .... Is 42:22
Who gave Jacob for a *s* .... Is 42:24
divide the *s* with the .... Is 53:12
slave? why is he *s* .... Jer 2:14
for the whole land is *s* .... Jer 4:20
suddenly are my tents *s* .... Jer 4:20
wolf of the evenings shall *s* .... Jer 5:6
of Zion, How are we *s* .... Jer 9:19
My tabernacle is *s*, and .... Jer 10:20
treasures..to the *s* .... Jer 15:13
which shall *s* them, and .... Jer 20:5
deliver him that is *s* out .... Jer 21:12
for the Lord hath *s* their ...... Jer 25:36
they that *s* thee shall .... Jer 30:16
shall be a *s*, and all that ...... Jer 30:16
cometh to *s* all the .... Jer 47:4
for the Lord will *s* the .... Jer 47:4
s and great destruction .... Jer 48:3
Moab is *s*, and gone up .... Jer 48:15
Howl, O Heshbon, for Ai is *s* . Jer 49:3
to Kedar, and *s* the men ...... Jer 49:28
And Chaldea shall be a *s* ..... Jer 50:10
all that *s* her shall be .... Jer 50:10
Lord hath *s* Babylon .... Jer 51:55
hath *s* none by violence .... Ezek 18:7
s his brother by violence ...... Ezek 18:18
will deliver thee for a *s* .... Ezek 25:7
they shall make a *s* of .... Ezek 26:12
they shall *s* the pomp of ...... Ezek 32:12
Art thou come to take a *s*? ... Ezek 38:13
goods, to take a great *s*? ...... Ezek 38:13
shall *s* those that *s* them ...... Ezek 39:10
remove violence and *s* .... Ezek 45:9
them the prey, and *s* .... Dan 11:24
the troop of robbers *s* .... Hos 7:1
he shall *s* their images .... Hos 10:2
thy fortresses shall be *s* .... Hos 10:14
as Shalman *s* Beth-arbel ...... Hos 10:14
he shall *s* the treasure .... Hos 13:15
thy palaces shall be *s* .... Amos 3:11
the *s* against the strong .... Amos 5:9
that the *s* shall come .... Amos 5:9
and say, We be utterly *s* ...... Mic 2:4
cankerworm *s*, and flieth ...... Nah 3:16
for *s* and violence are .... Hab 1:3
hast *s* many nations .... Hab 2:8
the people shall *s* thee .... Hab 2:8
the nations which *s* you .... Zech 2:8
my people shall *s* them .... Zeph 2:9
be a *s* to their servants .... Zech 2:9
for their glory is *s* .... Zech 11:3

the pride of Jordan is *s* ....Zech 11:3
thy *s* shall be divided in.......Zech 14:1
and *s* his goods...............Matt 12:29
then he will *s* his house ....Matt 12:29
and divideth his *s*.............Luke 11:22
lest any man *s* you ....Col 2:8
having *s* principalities ....Col 2:15
gave the tenth of the *s*........Heb 7:4
took joyfully the *s* of ....Heb 10:34

SPOILER—*one who plunders during wartime*

[*also* SPOILERS]
hands of *s* that spoiled ....Judg 2:14
s came out of the camp 1Sam 13:17
them into the hand of *s* 2Kin 17:20
from the face of the *s*.........Is 16:4
s are come upon all high ......Jer 12:12
the *s* shall come upon.........Jer 48:8
s is fallen upon thy ....Jer 48:32
from me shall *s* come ....Jer 51:53

SPOKEN—*See* SPEAK

SPOKES—*rods connecting hub with rim*
their felloes and their *s* 1Kin 7:33

SPOKESMAN—*one who speaks on behalf of others*
Aaron deputed to be ....Ex 4:14-16

SPONGE—*a very absorbent sea animal*
Full of vinegar, offered to Christ ....Matt 27:48

ran and filled a *s* full of.......Mark 15:36
and they filled a *s* with ....John 19:29

SPOON—*an instrument for eating resembling a very small bowl with a handle*

[*also* SPOONS]
dishes thereof, and *s*..........Ex 25:29
the dishes, and the *s*, ...Num 4:7
One *s* of ten shekels of ....Num 7:14
One *s* of gold of ten ....Num 7:20
golden *s* were twelve ....Num 7:86
the gold of the *s* was a........Num 7:86
the *s*, and the censers.........1Kin 7:50
the snuffers, and the *s* 2Kin 25:14
the *s*, and the censers.........2Chr 4:22
s, and vessels of gold 2Chr 24:14
the bowls, and the *s*, and .....Jer 52:18
candlesticks, and the *s* ....Jer 52:19

SPORT—*to play; a diversion; amusement; sexual play*

[*also* SPORTING]
Isaac was *s* with Rebekah .....Gen 26:8
that he may make us *s*........Judg 16:25
and he made them *s*..........Judg 16:25
it is as *s* to a fool to do.......Prov 10:23
and saith, Am not I in *s*? .....Prov 26:19
whom do ye *s* yourselves? .....Is 57:4
s themselves with their 2Pet 2:13

SPOT—*a blemish; a marking*

Descriptive of:
Blemish on the face .....Job 11:15
Imperfection of the body .Song 4:7
Mixed colors ....Gen 30:32-39
Leopard's spots ....Jer 13:23

Figuratively ("spotless") of:
Sin ....Jude 23
False teachers 2Pet 2:13
Christ's death 1Pet 1:19
Believer's perfection 2Pet 3:14
Glorified Church ....Eph 5:27
Perfect offering..........Num 19:2
Obedience 1Tim 6:14

[*also* SPOTS]
a scab, or bright *s* ....Lev 13:2
rising, or a bright *s* ....Lev 13:19
have a white bright *s* ....Lev 13:24
hair in the bright *s* ....Lev 13:26
if the bright *s* in the skin......Lev 13:39
it is a freckled *s* that.........Lev 13:39
a red heifer without *s*.........Num 19:2
lambs..first year without *s*.....Num 28:3
lambs..first year without *s*.....Num 28:11
their *s* is not the *s* of his ......Deut 32:5
himself without *s* to God ......Heb 9:14
These are *s* in your ....Jude 12

SPOUSE—*one's marriage partner*

[*also* SPOUSES]
from Lebanon, my *s* ....Song 4:8
my heart, my sister, my *s* .....Song 4:9
love, my sister, my *s*..........Song 4:10
Thy lips, O my *s*, drop as .....Song 4:11
is my sister, my *s*.............Song 4:12
garden, my sister, my *s* ....Song 5:1
and your *s* shall commit.......Hos 4:13
your *s* when they commit .....Hos 4:14

SPRANG—*See* SPRING

SPREAD—*to open; expand; distribute*

[*also* SPREADEST, SPREADETH, SPREADING, SPREADINGS]
the Canaanites *s* abroad.......Gen 10:18
where he had *s* his tent ....Gen 33:19
I will *s* abroad my hands ......Ex 9:29
the cherubim *s* out their ......Ex 37:9
and the plague *s* not in ....Lev 13:6
the scab *s* in the skin ....Lev 13:8
if it *s* much abroad in.........Lev 13:22
As an eagle..*s* abroad.........Deut 32:11
they *s* a garment, and.........Judg 8:25
s therefore thy skirt ....Ruth 3:9
were *s* abroad upon all........1Sam 30:16
and *s* themselves in the 2Sam 5:18
s a covering over the 2Sam 17:19
s ground corn thereon 2Sam 17:19
street, and did *s* them 2Sam 22:43
and *s* gold upon the 1Kin 6:32
s forth his hand toward 1Kin 8:22
with his hand *s* up to 1Kin 8:54
and *s* it on his face, so........2Kin 8:15
came and *s* themselves 1Chr 14:9
cherubim, that *s* out 1Chr 28:18
wings of these cherubim *s* 2Chr 3:13
and *s* forth his hands 2Chr 6:12
s forth his hands in this 2Chr 6:29
his name *s* far abroad.........2Chr 26:15
Which alone *s* out the ....Job 9:8
My root was *s* out by the .....Job 29:19
the *s* of the clouds............Job 36:29
Behold, he *s* his light ....Job 36:30
s himself like..bay tree ....Ps 37:35
He *s* a cloud for a covering ...Ps 105:39
they have *s* a net by the ......Ps 140:5
in vain the net is *s* in the .....Prov 1:17
his neighbor *s* a net for ....Prov 29:5
when ye *s* forth your ....Is 1:15
they that *s* nets upon ....Is 19:8
And he shall *s* forth his ....Is 25:11
that swimmeth *s* forth.........Is 25:11
the Lord, and *s* it before ......Is 37:14
s them out as a tent to........Is 40:22
to *s* sackcloth and ashes.......Is 58:5
that *s* her hands, saying ....Jer 4:31
they shall *s* them before ......Jer 8:2
he shall *s* his royal ....Jer 43:10
and *s* his wings over ....Jer 49:22
adversary hath *s* out ....Lam 1:10
Zion *s* forth her hands ....Lam 1:17
And he *s* it before me ....Ezek 2:10
My net also will I *s* upon .....Ezek 12:13
s vine of low stature ....Ezek 17:6
And I will *s* my net upon .....Ezek 17:20
shalt be a place to *s* nets ......Ezek 26:14
which thou *s* forth to be ......Ezek 27:7
a place to *s* forth nets ....Ezek 47:10
and a net *s* upon Tabor ....Hos 5:1
His branches shall *s* ....Hos 14:6
s upon the mountains ....Joel 2:2
horsemen shall *s*.............Hab 1:8
prosperity..be *s* abroad........Zech 1:17
s dung upon your faces ....Mal 2:3
s abroad his fame in all ....Matt 9:31
s their garments in the ....Matt 21:8
his fame *s* abroad ....Mark 1:28
many *s* their garments ....Mark 11:8
they *s* their clothes in ....Luke 19:36
it *s* no further among ....Acts 4:17
faith..is *s* abroad 1Thess 1:8

SPRIGS—*small shoots; twigs*
cut off the *s* with pruning .....Is 18:5
and shot forth *s* ....Ezek 17:6

SPRING—*place where water flows forth from the ground*
found there a well of *s* water . .Gen 26:19
the plain, under the *s* of ......Deut 4:49
and of the *s*, and all their .....Josh 10:40
upper *s* and the nether *s* ......Josh 15:19
give me also *s* of water ....Josh 15:19
give me also *s* of water ....Judg 1:15
forth unto the *s* of the 2Kin 2:21
into the *s* of the sea? ....Job 38:16
fountain, and a corrupt *s*......Prov 25:26
a *s* shut up, a fountain ....Song 4:12
and the thirsty land *s* ....Is 35:7
s of water shall he guide ......Is 49:10
sea, and make her *s* dry ......Jer 51:36
his *s* shall become dry ....Hos 13:15

SPRING—*to jump, dart, or shoot*

[*also* SPRANG, SPRINGETH, SPRINGING, SPRINGS, SPRUNG]
the east wind *s* up after ....Gen 41:6
the east wind, *s* up after ......Gen 41:23
a leprosy *s* up in his bald .....Lev 13:42
sang this song, *S* up, O ....Num 21:17
and depths that *s* out of.......Deut 8:7
when the day began to *s* ......Judg 19:25
to pass about the *s* of the 1Sam 9:26
doth trouble *s* out of the ......Job 5:6
blessest the *s* thereof ....Ps 65:10
Truth shall *s* out of the ....Ps 85:11
all my *s* are in thee ....Ps 87:7
second year..*s* of the same ....Is 37:30
that which *s* of the same ......Is 37:30
before they *s* forth I tell ......Is 42:9
they shall *s* up as among ......Is 44:4
thine health shall *s* forth ......Is 58:8
are sown in it to *s* forth.......Is 61:11
praise to *s* forth before ....Is 61:11
in all the leaves of her *s* ......Ezek 17:9
thus judgment *s* up ....Hos 10:4
pastures of the wilderness do *s* .Joel 2:22
of death light is *s*.............Matt 4:16
and forthwith they *s* up ....Matt 13:5
immediately it *s* up ....Mark 4:5
yield fruit that *s* up...........Mark 4:8
seed should *s* and grow up ....Mark 4:27
soon as it was *s* up, it ....Luke 8:6
and the thorns *s* up with ......Luke 8:7
on good ground, and *s* up.....Luke 8:8
for a light, and *s* in...........Acts 16:29
our Lord *s* out of Judah ......Heb 7:14
Therefore *s* there..of one .....Heb 11:12

SPRINGTIME—*the season of nature's rebirth*
Symbolically described ...Song 2:11-13

SPRINKLE—*to scatter; wet with drops*

Used literally of:
Water ....Num 8:7
Oil ....Lev 14:16
Human blood 2Kin 9:33

Of blood, used in:
Passover ....Ex 12:21, 22
Sinaitic covenant ....Ex 24:8; Heb 9:19, 21
Sin offering ....Lev 4:6
New covenant ....Heb 12:24

Used figuratively of:
Regeneration............Heb 10:22
Purification 1Pet 1:2

[*also* SPRINKLED, SPRINKLETH, SPRINKLING]
let Moses *s* it toward the......Ex 9:8
Moses *s* it up toward ....Ex 9:10
half of the blood he *s* on......Ex 24:6
s the blood upon the ....Ex 29:20
s the blood round about ......Lev 1:5
shall *s* the blood upon ....Lev 3:2
s the blood thereof upon ......Lev 3:13
s it seven times before ....Lev 4:17

S

there is *s* of the blood ....Lev 6:27
it was *s* in the holy place......Lev 6:27
he *s* round about upon........Lev 7:2
priest's that *s* the blood ....Lev 7:14
Moses *s* the blood upon.......Lev 8:19
he *s* round about upon........Lev 9:12
s upon him that is to be ......Lev 14:7
s with his right finger ....Lev 14:27
and *s* it with his finger ....Lev 16:14
he *s* of the blood with his .....Lev 16:14
he shall *s* of the blood ....Lev 16:19
priest shall *s* the blood ....Lev 17:6
shalt *s* their blood upon ....Num 18:17
water..was not *s* upon ....Num 19:13
s it upon the tent, and ....Num 19:18
water..hath not been *s* upon ...Num 19:20
he that *s* the water of.........Num 19:21
s the blood of his peace 2Kin 16:13
s upon it all the blood 2Kin 16:15
blood, and *s* it on the.........2Chr 29:22
they *s* the blood upon 2Chr 29:22
the priests *s* the blood 2Chr 35:11
s dust upon their heads ....Job 2:12
So shall he *s* many ....Is 52:15
be *s* upon my garments ....Is 63:3
will I *s* clean water upon ......Ezek 36:25
thereon, and to *s* blood ....Ezek 43:18
ashes of an heifer *s* the ....Heb 9:13
and the *s* of blood............Heb 11:28

SPROUT—*to grow or spring up*
down, that it will *s* again......Job 14:7

SPRUNG—*See* SPRING

SPUE—*to vomit*

[*also* SPEWING, SPUED]
That the land *s* not you ....Lev 18:28
as it *s* out the nations.........Lev 18:28
therein, *s* you not out.........Lev 20:22
be drunken, and *s*, and ....Jer 25:27
shameful *s* shall be on ....Hab 2:16
I will *s* thee out of my ....Rev 3:16

SPUN—*See* SPIN

SPUNGE—*See* SPONGE

SPY—*one who watches secretly to obtain information*

Purpose of, to:
Search out Canaan ......Num 13:1-33
Prepare for invasion .....Josh 2:1-21
Search out new land .....Judg 18:2-17
Make false charges ......Luke 20:20

Men accused of, falsely:
Jacob's sons.............Gen 42:9-34
David's servants 2Sam 10:3

[*also* SPIED, SPIES]
And he *s* an Egyptian ....Ex 2:11
came by the way of the *s* .....Num 21:1
And Moses sent to *s* out ......Num 21:32
had *s* out the country ....Josh 6:22
young men that were *s*........Josh 6:23
Joshua sent to *s* out ....Josh 6:25
the *s* saw a man come ....Judg 1:24
David..sent out *s*, and 1Sam 26:4
Absalom sent *s* throughout 2Sam 15:10
Go and *s* where he is 2Kin 6:13
he *s* the company of 2Kin 9:17
he *s* the sepulchers that 2Kin 23:16
she had received the *s* ....Heb 11:31

SQUARE—*an object having four equal sides*
Altar ....Ex 27:1
Breastplate.............Ex 39:8, 9
City of God.............Rev 21:16

[*also* SQUARED, SQUARES]
doors and posts were *s*........1Kin 7:5
posts of the temple were *s* ....Ezek 41:21
s in the four *s* thereof ....Ezek 43:16
broad in the four *s* ....Ezek 43:17
breadth, *s* round about........Ezek 45:2

STAB—*to pierce with a knife*
Asahel by Abner 2Sam 2:22, 23
Abner by Joab 2Sam 3:27
Amasa by Joab..........2Sam 20:10

STABLE—*firm; unmoveable*

[*also* STABILITY]
the world also shall be *s* 1Chr 16:30
be the *s* of thy times..........Is 33:6

STABLE—*a place to keep animals*
Rabbah a *s* for camels ....Ezek 25:5

STABLISH—*to establish*

[*also* STABLISHED, STABLISHETH]
I will *s* the throne of his 2Sam 7:13
will *s* his throne for ever 1Chr 17:12
Then will I *s* the throne 2Chr 7:18
the Lord *s* the kingdom 2Chr 17:5
To *s* this among them.........Esth 9:21
world also is *s*, that...........Ps 93:1
He hath also *s* them for.......Ps 148:6
and *s* a city by iniquity........Hab 2:12
to *s* you according to ....Rom 16:25
he which *s* us with you........2Cor 1:21
and *s* in the faith, as ye ....Col 2:7
he may *s* your hearts 1Thess 3:13
and *s* you in every good 2Thess 2:17
patient; *s* your hearts ....James 5:8
perfect, *s*, strengthen 1Pet 5:10

STACHYS (stā'kĭs)—*"ear of corn"*
One whom Paul loved ...Rom 16:9

STACKS—*piles*
so that the *s* of corn ....Ex 22:6

STACTE—*used as incense*
unto thee sweet spices, *s* ......Ex 30:34

STAFF—*a long stick or rod*
A traveler's support .....Gen 32:10
Denotes food support ....Lev 26:26
A military weapon.......Is 10:24

[*also* STAVES]
s that is in thine hand ....Gen 38:18
your *s* in your hand ....Ex 12:11
walk abroad upon his *s* ....Ex 21:19
make *s* of shittim wood ....Ex 25:13
s shall be in the rings ....Ex 25:15
shalt make the *s* of ....Ex 25:28
s of shittim wood, and ....Ex 27:6
the *s* shall be put into ....Ex 27:7
the *s* shall be upon the........Ex 27:7
shalt make the *s* of ....Ex 30:5
The table, and his *s*, and.......Ex 35:13
grate, his *s*, and all his........Ex 35:16
put the *s* into the rings........Ex 37:5
And he made the *s* of ....Ex 37:15
And he made the *s* of ....Ex 37:28
And he made the *s* ....Ex 38:6
and the *s* thereof ....Ex 39:35
the ark, and set the *s* on ......Ex 40:20
shall put in the *s* thereof ......Num 4:6
shall put to the *s* thereof ......Num 4:11
it between two upon a *s* ......Num 13:23
lawgiver, with their *s* ....Num 21:18
the end of the *s* that was......Judg 6:21
the *s* of his spear was 1Sam 17:7
comest to me with *s*? 1Sam 17:43
or that leaneth on a *s*.........2Sam 3:29
with iron and the *s* of a.......2Sam 23:7
covered the ark and the *s* 1Kin 8:7
they drew out the *s*, that......1Kin 8:8
s were seen out in the 1Kin 8:8
and take my *s* in thine 2Kin 4:29
lay my *s* upon the face........2Kin 4:29
trustest upon the *s* of 2Kin 18:21
down to him with a *s* 1Chr 11:23
shoulders with the *s* 1Chr 15:15
covered the ark and the *s* 2Chr 5:8
drew out the *s* of the ark 2Chr 5:9
ends of the *s* were seen 2Chr 5:9
rod and thy *s* they............Ps 23:4
Judah the stay and the *s* ......Is 3:1
s in their hand is mine ....Is 10:5
the *s* should lift up itself ......Is 10:15
are beaten out with a *s* ....Is 28:27
thou trusteth in the *s* ....Is 36:6
is the strong *s* broken.........Jer 48:17
will break the *s* of bread ......Ezek 4:16
break the *s* of the bread ......Ezek 14:13

their *s* declareth unto ....Hos 4:12
strike through with his *s* ....Hab 3:14
every man with his *s* in ....Zech 8:4
I took unto me two *s* ....Zech 11:7
neither shoes, nor yet *s* ....Matt 10:10
with swords and *s* ....Matt 26:47
journey, save a *s* only ....Mark 6:8
multitude with swords and *s*...Mark 14:43
neither *s*, nor scrip ....Luke 9:3
upon the top of his *s* ....Heb 11:21

STAGGER—*to totter; waver in purpose or action*

[*also* STAGGERED, STAGGERETH]
to *s* like a drunken man.......Job 12:25
s like a drunken man ....Ps 107:27
as a drunken man *s* in ....Is 19:14
they *s*, but not with ....Is 29:9
He *s* not at the promise.......Rom 4:20

STAIN—*to soil; discolor*
the shadow of death *s* it ......Job 3:5
to *s* the pride of all glory .....Is 23:9

STAIRS—*a series or flight of steps*
him on the top of the *s* 2Kin 9:13
the *s* that go down from ......Neh 3:15
up by the *s* of the city of .....Neh 12:37
the secret places of the *s*......Song 2:14
went up the *s* thereof ....Ezek 40:6
when he came upon the *s* .....Acts 21:35

STAIRS, WINDING
Part of Solomon's Temple.1Kin 6:8

STAKES—*pointed pieces of wood driven into the ground for support*
not one of the *s* thereof.......Is 33:20
and strengthen thy *s* ....Is 54:2

STALK—*the main stem of a plant*

[*also* STALKS]
corn came up upon one *s* .....Gen 41:5
seven ears..in one *s*..........Gen 41:22
whirlwind: it hath no *s*.........Hos 8:7

STALL—*quarters for animals; to bog down or stop*
40,000 in Solomon's time .1Kin 4:26

[*also* STALLED, STALLS]
had four thousand *s* for 2Chr 9:25
and *s* for all manner of 2Chr 32:28
than a *s* ox and hatred ....Prov 15:17
out of the midst of the *s* ......Amos 6:4
be no herd in the *s* ....Hab 3:17
grow up as calves of the *s*.....Mal 4:2
ox or his ass from the *s* ....Luke 13:15

STAMMERER—*one who stutters*
Used of judicial punishment ....Is 28:11
Of the Gospel age ....Is 32:1, 4

[*also* STAMMERING]
s shall be ready to speak ......Is 32:4
of a *s* tongue, that thou ....Is 33:19

STAMP—*to pound; strike or beat with the foot*

[*also* STAMPED, STAMPING]
it with fire, and *s* it...........Deut 9:21
I did *s* them as the mire 2Sam 22:43
s it small to powder, and......2Kin 23:6
down her idol, and *s* it........2Chr 15:16
noise of the *s* of the hoofs ....Jer 47:3
thine hand, and *s* with ....Ezek 6:11
and *s* with the feet, and.......Ezek 25:6
s the residue with the ....Dan 7:7
ground, and *s* upon him ......Dan 8:7
ground, and *s* upon them .....Dan 8:10

STANCHED—*stopped a flow*
her issue of blood *s*...........Luke 8:44

STAND—*to support oneself erectly on one's feet; remain in place*

[*also* STANDEST, STANDETH, STANDING, STOOD, STOODEST]
three men *s* by him...........Gen 18:2
Abraham *s* yet before.........Gen 18:22

And they said, *S* back ....Gen 19:9
Abraham *s* up before ....Gen 23:3
he *s* by the camels at the .....Gen 24:30
wherefore *s* thou without? .....Gen 24:31
Behold, I *s* by the well of .....Gen 24:43
and also *s* upright ....Gen 37:7
sheaves *s* round about ....Gen 37:7
s by the other kine upon ......Gen 41:3
when he *s* before Pharaoh .....Gen 41:46
and *s* before Joseph ....Gen 43:15
before all them that *s* by ......Gen 45:1
there *s* no man with him ......Gen 45:1
his sister *s* afar off, to ....Ex 2:4
Moses *s* up and helped ....Ex 2:17
place whereon thou *s* is ....Ex 3:5
Moses..who *s* in the way ......Ex 5:20
shalt *s* by the river's ....Ex 7:15
magicians could not *s* ....Ex 9:11
Fear ye not, *s* still, and ....Ex 14:13
face, and *s* behind them ......Ex 14:19
I will *s* on the top of the ......Ex 17:9
the people *s* by Moses ....Ex 18:13
removed, and *s* afar off ....Ex 20:18
of corn, or the *s* corn ....Ex 22:6
Moses *s* in the gate of ....Ex 32:26
s at the door of the ....Ex 33:9
pillar *s* at the tabernacle ......Ex 33:10
of shittim wood, *s* up ....Ex 36:20
drew near and *s* before ....Lev 9:5
shall any woman *s* before .....Lev 18:23
rear you up a *s* image ....Lev 26:1
power to *s* before your ....Lev 26:37
thy estimation it shall *s* ....Lev 27:17
of the men that shall *s* ....Num 1:5
that they may *s* there ....Num 11:16
And the people *s* up all ....Num 11:32
thy cloud *s* over them ....Num 14:14
and *s* in the door of the ....Num 16:18
s between the dead and ....Num 16:48
angel of the Lord *s* in ....Num 22:23
angel of the Lord *s* in a ....Num 22:24
I knew not that thou *s* in .....Num 22:34
S by thy burnt offering ....Num 23:3
lo, he *s* by his burnt ....Num 23:6
And they *s* before Moses .....Num 27:2
shall *s* before Eleazar ....Num 27:21
then all her vows shall *s* ......Num 30:4
bound her soul shall *s* ....Num 30:4
bound her soul shall *s* ....Num 30:5
then her vows shall *s* ....Num 30:7
bound her soul shall *s* ....Num 30:7
then all her vows shall *s* ......Num 30:11
bound her soul shall *s* ....Num 30:11
until he *s* before the ....Num 35:12
Nun, which *s* before thee .....Deut 1:38
day that thou *s* before ....Deut 4:10
near and *s* under the ....Deut 4:11
But as for thee, *s* thou ....Deut 5:31
can *s* before the children ......Deut 9:2
no man be able to *s* ....Deut 11:25
which *s* there before ....Deut 18:7
comest into the *s* corn ....Deut 23:25
Thou shalt *s* abroad, and ......Deut 24:11
s upon mount Gerizim ....Deut 27:12
Ye *s* this day all of you ....Deut 29:10
him that *s* here with us ....Deut 29:15
pillar of the cloud *s* over ......Deut 31:15
man be able to *s* before ....Josh 1:5
shall *s* upon a heap ....Josh 3:13
waters..from above *s* ....Josh 3:16
the priests' feet *s* firm ....Josh 4:3
which bare the ark *s* in ....Josh 4:10
place whereon thou *s* is ....Josh 5:15
sun, *s* thou still upon ....Josh 10:12
And the sun *s* still, and ....Josh 10:13
so the sun *s* still in the ....Josh 10:13
until he *s* before the ....Josh 20:6
until he *s* before the ....Josh 20:9
could not..*s* before their ......Judg 2:14
all that *s* by him went out .....Judg 3:19
And they *s* every man in ......Judg 7:21
s in the entering of the ....Judg 9:35
into the *s* corn of the ....Judg 15:5
and also the *s* corn ....Judg 15:5
whereupon the house *s* ....Judg 16:26
Dan, *s* by the entering of .....Judg 18:16
Aaron *s* before it in those .....Judg 20:28
woman that *s* by thee 1Sam 1:26
women that *s* by her said 1Sam 4:20
Who is able to *s* before 1Sam 6:20
when he *s* among the 1Sam 10:23
Now therefore *s* still, that 1Sam 12:7
will *s* still in our place 1Sam 14:9
the Philistines *s* on a 1Sam 17:3
Israel *s* on a mountain 1Sam 17:3
to the men that *s* by 1Sam 17:26
I will go out and *s* beside 1Sam 19:3
Samuel *s* as appointed 1Sam 19:20
servants were *s* about 1Sam 22:6
his servants that *s* about 1Sam 22:7
and *s* on the top of a hill 1Sam 26:13
S, I pray thee, upon me 2Sam 1:9
So I *s* upon him, and slew 2Sam 1:10
s on the top of a hill 2Sam 2:25
s by with their clothes 2Sam 13:31
the king *s* by the gate 2Sam 18:4
one of Joab's men *s* by 2Sam 20:11
that all the people *s* still 2Sam 20:12
that came by him *s* still 2Sam 20:12
he *s* in the midst of the 2Sam 23:12
let her *s* before the king 1Kin 1:2
presence, and *s* before 1Kin 1:28
king, and *s* before him 1Kin 3:16
congregation of Israel *s* 1Kin 8:14
And he *s*, and blessed all 1Kin 8:55
which *s* continually 1Kin 10:8
twelve lions *s* there on 1Kin 10:20
and which *s* before him 1Kin 12:8
way, and the ass *s* by it 1Kin 13:24
lion also *s* by the carcase 1Kin 13:24
and the lion *s* by the 1Kin 13:25
liveth, before whom I *s* 1Kin 18:15
host of heaven *s* by him 1Kin 22:19
and *s* before the Lord 1Kin 22:21
went, and *s* to view afar 2Kin 2:7
and they two *s* by Jordan 2Kin 2:7
liveth, before whom I *s* 2Kin 3:14
and *s* in the border 2Kin 3:21
her, she *s* in the door 2Kin 4:15
came, and *s* before him 2Kin 5:15
liveth, before whom I *s* 2Kin 5:16
came and *s* before him 2Kin 8:9
Behold, two kings *s* not 2Kin 10:4
how then shall we *s*? 2Kin 10:4
went out, and *s*, and said 2Kin 10:9
behold, the king *s* by a 2Kin 11:14
and *s* by the conduit of 2Kin 18:17
the king *s* by a pillar 2Kin 23:3
all the people *s* to the 2Kin 23:3
who *s* on his right hand 1Chr 6:39
And Satan *s* up against 1Chr 21:1
angel of the Lord *s* 1Chr 21:15
David the king *s* up upon 1Chr 28:2
and they *s* on their feet 2Chr 3:13
harps, *s* at the east end of 2Chr 5:12
the priests could not *s* to 2Chr 5:14
he *s* before the altar of 2Chr 6:12
them, and all Israel *s* 2Chr 7:6
place, and two lions *s* by 2Chr 9:18
twelve lions *s* there on 2Chr 9:19
old men that had *s* before 2Chr 10:6
and Abijah *s* up upon 2Chr 13:4
Jehoshaphat *s* in the 2Chr 20:5
we *s* before this house 2Chr 20:9
s up to praise the Lord 2Chr 20:19
Moab *s* up against the 2Chr 20:23
priest, which *s* above the 2Chr 24:20
chosen you to *s* before 2Chr 29:11
Levites *s* with the 2Chr 29:26
the king *s* in his place 2Chr 34:31
s in the holy place 2Chr 35:5
till there *s* up a priest ....Ezra 2:63
Then *s* Jeshua with his ....Ezra 3:9
we cannot *s* before thee ....Ezra 9:15
of all the congregation *s* ......Ezra 10:14
while they *s* by, let them ......Neh 7:3
till there *s* up a priest ....Neh 7:65
Ezra the scribe *s* upon a ....Neh 8:4
beside him *s* Mattithiah ....Neh 8:4
and the people *s* in their ......Neh 8:7
they *s* up in their place ....Neh 9:3
they *s* still in the prison ....Neh 12:39
Mordecai's matters would *s* ....Esth 3:4
s in the inner court of ....Esth 5:1
Esther the queen *s* in the .....Esth 5:2
Behold, Haman *s* in the ......Esth 6:5
Haman *s* up to make ....Esth 7:7
and *s* for their lives ....Esth 9:16
the hair of my flesh *s* up ......Job 4:15
but it shall not *s* ....Job 8:15
the aged arose, and *s* up ......Job 29:8
I *s* up, and thou ....Job 30:20
spake not, but *s* still ....Job 32:16
unto this, O Job: *s* still ....Job 37:14
is able to *s* before me? ....Job 41:10
nor *s* in the way of ....Ps 1:1
the ungodly shall not *s* ....Ps 1:5
foolish shall not *s* in thy ......Ps 5:5
Why *s* thou afar off, O ....Ps 10:1
shall *s* in his holy place? ......Ps 24:3
inhabitants..*s* in awe ....Ps 33:8
commanded, and it *s* fast .....Ps 33:9
counsel of the Lord *s* for ......Ps 33:11
and my friends *s* aloof ....Ps 38:11
my kinsmen *s* afar off ....Ps 38:11
where there is no *s* ....Ps 69:2
Their eyes *s* out with ....Ps 73:7
made the waters to *s* as ....Ps 78:13
not made him to *s* in the ......Ps 89:43
his chosen *s* before him ....Ps 106:23
let Satan *s* at his right ....Ps 109:6
They *s* fast forever and ....Ps 111:8
the rock into a *s* water ....Ps 114:8
my heart *s* in awe of ....Ps 119:161
O Lord, who shall *s*? ....Ps 130:3
Ye that *s* in the house of .....Ps 135:2
She *s* in the top of high ....Prov 8:2
of the righteous shall *s* ....Prov 12:7
he shall *s* before kings ....Prov 22:29
he shall not *s* before ....Prov 22:29
is able to *s* before envy? ......Prov 27:4
second child that shall *s* ....Eccl 4:15
he *s* behind our wall, he ......Song 2:9
The Lord *s* up to plead ....Is 3:13
Above it *s* the seraphim ......Is 6:2
It shall not *s*, neither ....Is 7:7
s for an ensign of the ....Is 11:10
I *s*..upon the watchtower ......Is 21:8
with hell shall not *s* ....Is 28:18
Then Rabshakeh *s*, and cried ..Is 36:13
word of our God shall *s* ....Is 40:8
in his place, and he *s* ....Is 46:7
My counsel shall *s*, and ....Is 46:10
prognosticators, *s* up ....Is 47:13
let us *s* together: who is ....Is 50:8
and justice *s* afar off ....Is 59:14
strangers shall *s* and feed .....Is 61:5
S ye in the ways, and see .....Jer 6:16
come and *s* before me in ....Jer 7:10
Moses and Samuel *s* before ...Jer 15:1
thou shalt *s* before me ....Jer 15:19
and he *s* in the court ....Jer 19:14
But if they had *s* ....Jer 23:22
S in the court of the ....Jer 26:2
prince which *s* beside ....Jer 36:21
whose words shall *s* ....Jer 44:28
and *s* forth with your ....Jer 46:4
they *s* not, because the ....Jer 46:15
they did not *s*, because ....Jer 46:21
that shepherd that will *s* ......Jer 49:19
go away, *s* not still ....Jer 51:50
he *s* with his right hand ....Lam 2:4
when those *s*, these *s* ....Ezek 1:21
when they *s*, and had let ......Ezek 1:25
Son of man, *s* upon thy ....Ezek 2:1
there *s* before them ....Ezek 8:11
in the midst of them *s* ....Ezek 8:11
the cherubim *s* on the ....Ezek 10:3
and *s* beside the wheels ....Ezek 10:6
s over the cherubim ....Ezek 10:18
s upon the mountain ....Ezek 11:23
his covenant it might *s* ....Ezek 17:14
shall *s* upon the land ....Ezek 27:29
their trees *s* up in their ....Ezek 31:14
and *s* up upon their feet ......Ezek 37:10

S

and the man *s* by me ....Ezek 43:6
shall *s* before them to........Ezek 44:11
they shall *s* in judgment.......Ezek 44:24
the fishers shall *s* upon........Ezek 47:10
to *s* in the king's palace.......Dan 1:4
s they before the king ....Dan 1:19
excellent, *s* before thee ....Dan 2:31
and it shall *s* for ever ....Dan 2:44
thousand *s* before him ....Dan 7:10
one of them that *s* by ....Dan 7:16
no beasts might *s* before ......Dan 8:4
seen *s* before the river ....Dan 8:6
s before me as the............Dan 8:15
whereas four *s* up for it ....Dan 8:22
four kingdoms shall *s* up ......Dan 8:22
shall also *s* up against.........Dan 8:25
said unto him that *s* ....Dan 10:16
there shall *s* up yet three ......Dan 11:2
when he shall *s* up, his.........Dan 11:4
her roots shall one *s* up ....Dan 11:7
none shall *s* before him ....Dan 11:16
he shall *s* in the glorious ......Dan 11:16
s up in his estate a raiser .....Dan 11:20
but he shall not *s*.............Dan 11:25
time shall Michael *s* up ....Dan 12:1
s for the children of ....Dan 12:1
behold, there *s* other two .....Dan 12:5
there they *s*: the battle........Hos 10:9
shall he *s* that handleth ....Amos 2:15
I saw the Lord *s* upon ....Amos 9:1
day that thou *s* on the ....Obad 11
have *s* in the crossway ....Obad 14
receive of you his *s*...........Mic 1:11
he shall *s* and feed in the .....Mic 5:4
Who can *s* before his ....Nah 1:6
S, *s* shall they cry; but ....Nah 2:8
s upon my watch, and set me..Hab 2:1
the high priest *s* before ....Zech 3:1
Satan *s* at his right hand ......Zech 3:1
those that *s* before him ....Zech 3:4
among these that *s* by ....Zech 3:7
nor feed that that *s* still ....Zech 11:16
his feet shall *s* in that.........Zech 14:4
s over where the young ....Matt 2:9
s in the synagogues ....Matt 6:5
then his kingdom *s*? ....Matt 12:26
the whole multitude *s* on......Matt 13:2
others *s* idle in the ....Matt 20:3
why *s* ye here all the day .....Matt 20:6
unto him they that *s* by ....Matt 26:73
of them that *s* there ....Matt 27:47
withered hand, *S* forth ....Mark 3:3
that house cannot *s*...........Mark 3:25
and, *s* without, sent unto......Mark 3:31
some of them that *s* here .....Mark 9:1
that *s* by drew a sword.........Mark 14:47
to say to them that *s* by.......Mark 14:69
some of them that *s* by ....Mark 15:35
s on the right side of the......Luke 1:11
that *s* in the presence of ......Luke 1:19
and *s* up for to read ....Luke 4:16
he *s* by the lake of ....Luke 5:1
them, and *s* in the plain.......Luke 6:17
s at his feet behind him ....Luke 7:38
thy brethren *s* without ....Luke 8:20
there be some *s* here ....Luke 9:27
a certain lawyer *s* up ....Luke 10:25
how shall his kingdom *s*?......Luke 11:18
Pharisee *s* and prayed.........Luke 18:11
Zaccheus *s*, and said..........Luke 19:8
to *s* before the Son of ....Luke 21:36
scribes *s* and..accused ....Luke 23:10
s afar off, beholding ....Luke 23:49
Jesus..*s* in the midst of.........Luke 24:36
but there *s* one among ....John 1:26
which *s* and heareth him ......John 3:29
Jesus *s* and cried, saying ......John 7:37
and the woman *s* in the ....John 8:9
people therefore, that *s* ....John 12:29
But Peter *s* at the door ....John 18:16
and officers *s* there ....John 18:18
Peter *s* with them, and.........John 18:18
Peter *s* and warmed ....John 18:25
Mary *s* without at the.........John 20:11
back, and saw Jesus *s*..........John 20:14
s in the midst, and said ....John 20:26
men *s* by them in white ....Acts 1:10
why *s* ye gazing up into ....Acts 1:11
Peter, *s* up with the ....Acts 2:14
And he leaping up *s*, and .....Acts 3:8
Go, *s* and speak in the........Acts 5:20
keepers *s* without before ......Acts 5:23
Then *s* there up one in ....Acts 5:34
place where thou *s* is ....Acts 7:33
Jesus *s* on the right and.......Acts 7:55
all the widows *s* by him ....Acts 9:39
S up; I myself also am ....Acts 10:26
which *s* and said unto ....Acts 11:13
told how Peter *s* before ....Acts 12:14
the disciples *s* round ....Acts 14:20
Paul *s* in the midst of.........Acts 17:22
unto me, and *s*, and said......Acts 22:13
I also was *s* by, and ....Acts 22:20
them that *s* by him to.........Acts 23:2
the Lord *s* by him ....Acts 23:11
from Jerusalem *s* round ....Acts 25:7
I *s* at Caesar's judgment ......Acts 25:10
rise, and *s* upon thy feet ......Acts 26:16
Paul *s* forth in the midst ......Acts 27:21
this grace wherein we *s* ....Rom 5:2
and thou *s* by faith ....Rom 11:20
for God is able to make ......Rom 14:4
to his own master he *s*........Rom 14:4
we shall all *s* before the.......Rom 14:10
not *s* in the wisdom of 1Cor 2:5
he that *s* steadfast in his 1Cor 7:37
flesh while the world *s*........1Cor 8:13
that thinketh he *s* take 1Cor 10:12
why *s* we in jeopardy 1Cor 15:30
s fast in the faith, quit 1Cor 16:13
joy: for by faith ye *s*..........2Cor 1:24
for I *s* in doubt of you ....Gal 4:20
S fast therefore in the ....Gal 5:1
may be able to *s* against ....Eph 6:11
S therefore, having your ......Eph 6:14
so *s* fast in the Lord, my ......Phil 4:1
ye may *s* perfect and ....Col 4:12
if ye *s* fast in the Lord 1Thess 3:8
s fast, and hold the 2Thess 2:15
foundation of God *s* sure 2Tim 2:19
answer no man *s* with me 2Tim 4:16
first tabernacle was yet *s*......Heb 9:8
Which *s* only in meats ....Heb 9:10
every priest *s* daily ....Heb 10:11
S thou there, or sit here ......James 2:3
judge *s* before the door ....James 5:9
grace of God wherein ye *s* 1Pet 5:12
earth *s* out of the water.......2Pet 3:5
Behold, I *s* at the door ....Rev 3:20
s a lamb as it had been ....Rev 5:6
who shall be able to *s*? ....Rev 6:17
four angels *s* on the four ......Rev 7:1
angels *s* round about the ......Rev 7:11
angels which *s* before God ....Rev 8:2
angel which I saw *s* upon .....Rev 10:5
the angel which *s* upon ....Rev 10:8
angel *s*, saying, Rise ....Rev 11:1
the dragon *s* before the ....Rev 12:4
a Lamb *s* on the mount.........Rev 14:1
S afar off for..fear of her .....Rev 18:10
shall *s* afar off for the ....Rev 18:15

STANDARD—*a banner used as an emblem, marker, or rallying point; an ensign*

[*also* STANDARDS]
every man by his own *s*.......Num 1:52
they of the *s* of the camp .....Num 2:3
in his place by their *s*.........Num 2:17
be the *s* of the camp of ....Num 2:18
so they pitched by their *s* .....Num 2:34
went the *s* of the camp ....Num 10:14
the *s* of the camp.............Num 10:22
and set up my *s* to the ....Is 49:22
lift up a *s* for the people ......Is 62:10
Set up the *s* toward Zion .....Jer 4:6
publish, and set up a *s*........Jer 50:2
Set ye up a *s* in the land ......Jer 51:27

STANDARD-BEARER—*one who carries an ensign into battle*
as when the *s* fainteth ....Is 10:18

STANK—*See* STINK

STAR—*a luminous body visible in the sky at night*

Features concerning:
Created by God ....Gen 1:16
Ordained by God........Ps 8:3
Set in the expanse ....Gen 1:17
Follow fixed ordinance ...Jer 31:35, 36
Named by God..........Ps 147:4
Established forever ......Ps 148:3, 6
Of vast numbers.........Gen 15:5
Manifest God's power ...Is 40:26
Of different proportions..1Cor 15:41
Very high...............Job 22:12

Worship of:
Forbidden ....Deut 4:19
Punished...............Deut 17:3-7
Introduced by Manasseh .2Kin 21:3
Condemned by the prophets .... Jer 8:2; Zeph 1:4, 5

List of, in Bible:
Arcturus................Job 9:9
Mazzaroth ....Job 38:32
Orion ....Job 9:9
Pleiades ....Job 9:9
Chambers of the south...Job 9:9
Of Bethlehem ....Matt 2:2, 9, 10

Figurative of Christ's
First advent ....Num 24:17
Second advent ....Rev 22:16
Angels ....Rev 1:16, 20
Judgment ....Ezek 32:7
False security ....Obad 4
Glorified saints ....Dan 12:3
Apostates ....Jude 13

[*also* STARS]
thy seed as the *s* of the ....Gen 22:17
eleven *s* made obeisance ......Gen 37:9
seed as the *s* of heaven ....Ex 32:13
as the *s* of heaven for.........Deut 1:10
made thee as the *s* of ....Deut 10:22
the *s* in their courses ....Judg 5:20
Israel like to the *s* of the......1Chr 27:23
till the *s* appeared ....Neh 4:21
Let the *s* of the twilight........Job 3:9
and sealeth up the *s* ....Job 9:7
yea, the *s* are not pure........Job 25:5
The moon and *s* to rule ....Ps 136:9
the *s*, be not darkened........Eccl 12:2
For the *s* of heaven and the ...Is 13:10
my throne above the *s* ....Is 14:13
s shall withdraw their shining ..Joel 2:10
s shall withdraw their shining ..Joel 3:15
that maketh the seven *s*.......Amos 5:8
above the *s* of heaven ....Nah 3:16
what time the *s* appeared .....Matt 2:7
and the *s* shall fall from.......Matt 24:29
the *s* of heaven shall fall ......Mark 13:25
in the moon, and in the *s* .....Luke 21:25
and the *s* of your god..........Acts 7:43
sun nor *s* in many days ....Acts 27:20
for one *s* differeth from 1Cor 15:41
differeth from another *s*.......1Cor 15:41
as the *s* of the sky in ....Heb 11:12
the day *s* arise in your 2Pet 1:19
holdeth the seven *s* in ....Rev 2:1
give him the morning *s* ....Rev 2:28
God, and the seven *s* ....Rev 3:1
the *s* of heaven fell unto ......Rev 6:13
there fell a great *s* from.......Rev 8:10
the *s* is called Wormwood .....Rev 8:11
the third part of the *s*.........Rev 8:12
I saw a *s* fall from heaven.....Rev 9:1
head a crown of twelve *s*......Rev 12:1
the third part of the *s* of ......Rev 12:4

STARE—*to look at fixedly*
they look and *s* upon me......Ps 22:17

STARGAZERS—*astrologers*
the astrologers, the *s* ....Is 47:13

STATE—*an established government; condition*

Agents of:
Under God's control.....Dan 4:17, 25
Jon 19:10, 11
Sometimes evil..........Mark 6:14-29
Sometimes good.........Neh 2:1-9
Protectors of the Law....Rom 13:1-4
Duties of Christians to:
Pray for...............1Tim 2:1, 2
Pay taxes to...........Matt 22:17-21
Be subject to...........Rom 13:5, 6
Resist (when evil).......Acts 4:17-21

house of God in his *s*.........2Chr 24:13
to the *s* of the king...........Esth 1:7
from thy *s* shall he pull.......Is 22:19
the last *s* of that man is.......Matt 12:45
the last *s* of that man is.......Luke 11:26
when I know your *s*..........Phil 2:19
in whatsoever *s* I am.........Phil 4:11

STATELY—*dignified; impressive; grand*
satest upon a *s* bed, and......Ezek 23:41

STATION—*place where one is assigned to stand*
I will drive thee from thy *s*....Is 22:19

STATURE—*one's physical height*
Used physically of:
Giants..................Num 13:32
Sabeans................Is 45:14
Significance of:
Normal, in human growth.Luke 2:52
Cannot be changed......Matt 6:27
Not indicative of greatness.............1Sam 16:7
In spiritual things........Eph 4:13

a man of great *s*, that.........2Sam 21:20
a man of great *s*, five.........1Chr 11:23
This thy *s* is like to a.........Song 7:7
high ones of *s* shall be........Is 10:33
of every *s* to hunt souls.......Ezek 13:18
spreading vine of low *s*.......Ezek 17:6
her *s* was exalted among......Ezek 19:11
shroud.. of a high *s*...........Ezek 31:3
add to his *s* one cubit?........Luke 12:25
because he was little of *s*......Luke 19:3

STATUTE—*law*

[*also* STATUTES]
my commandments, my *s*.....Gen 26:5
he made for them a *s*.........Ex 15:25
commandments and keep..his *s*.Ex 15:26
it shall be a *s* for ever........Ex 28:43
his sons by a *s* for ever.......Ex 29:28
It shall be a perpetual *s*.......Lev 3:17
it is a *s* for ever unto.........Lev 6:22
a *s* for ever throughout.......Lev 7:36
all the *s* which the Lord.......Lev 10:11
thee, by a *s* for ever..........Lev 10:15
souls by a *s* for ever..........Lev 16:31
This shall be a *s* for ever......Lev 17:7
therefore keep my *s* and......Lev 18:26
shall ye observe all my *s*......Lev 19:37
therefore keep all my *s*.......Lev 20:22
a *s* for ever throughout.......Lev 23:14
a *s* for ever throughout.......Lev 23:31
it shall be a *s* for ever........Lev 24:3
If ye walk in my *s* and........Lev 26:3
their soul abhorred my *s*......Lev 26:43
thee, by a *s* for ever..........Num 18:11
them for a *s* for ever..........Num 19:10
children of Israel a *s* of.......Num 27:11
These are the *s*, which........Num 30:16
unto the *s* and unto the.......Deut 4:1
shall hear all these *s*..........Deut 4:6
that time to teach you *s*.......Deut 4:14
testimonies and the *s*.........Deut 4:45
commandments and the *s*.....Deut 5:31
all his *s* and his.............Deut 6:2
testimonies and the *s*.........Deut 6:20
commandments and the *s*.....Deut 7:11
his *s*, which I command.......Deut 10:13
observe to do all the *s*.........Deut 11:32
thee to do these *s*............Deut 26:16
commandments and his *s*......Deut 27:10
commandments and his *s*......Deut 28:45
set them a *s* and an..........Josh 24:25
as for his *s*, I did not.........2Sam 22:23
his ways, to keep his *s*........1Kin 2:3
s and..commandments........1Kin 3:14
commandments and his *s*......1Kin 8:58
my *s* and my judgments.......1Kin 9:4
my covenant and my *s*.........1Kin 11:11
commandments and my *s*.....1Kin 11:34
in the *s* of the heathen........2Kin 17:8
And they rejected his *s*.......2Kin 17:15
do they after their *s*..........2Kin 17:34
his testimonies and his *s*......2Kin 23:3
heed to fulfill the *s* and.......1Chr 22:13
observe my *s* and my.........2Chr 7:17
s and judgments, ye..........2Chr 19:10
testimonies and his *s*..........2Chr 34:31
to teach in Israel *s* and.......Ezra 7:10
commandments nor..*s*.........Neh 1:7
s, and laws, by the hand......Neh 9:14
I did not put away his *s*.......Ps 18:22
The *s* of the Lord are..........Ps 19:8
to do to declare my *s*..........Ps 50:16
they might observe his *s*......Ps 105:45
directed to keep thy *s*!........Ps 119:5
I will keep thy *s*, O..........Ps 119:8
delight myself in thy *s*........Ps 119:16
did meditate in thy *s*..........Ps 119:23
heardest me: teach me thy *s*...Ps 119:26
I will meditate in thy *s*........Ps 119:48
s have been my songs.........Ps 119:54
mercy: teach me thy *s*........Ps 119:64
that I might learn thy *s*.......Ps 119:71
yet do I not forget thy *s*......Ps 119:83
have respect unto thy *s*.......Ps 119:117
and teach me thy *s*...........Ps 119:124
Lord; I will keep thy *s*........Ps 119:145
hast taught me thy *s*..........Ps 119:171
nor in my *s*, that I set........Jer 44:10
my *s* more than the..........Ezek 5:6
my judgments and my *s*.......Ezek 5:6
have not walked in my *s*......Ezek 11:12
Hath walked in my *s*..........Ezek 18:9
hath kept all my *s* and........Ezek 18:19
And I gave them my *s*.........Ezek 20:11
walked not in my *s* but........Ezek 20:16
your God; walk in my *s*.......Ezek 20:19
but had despised my *s*........Ezek 20:24
walk in the *s* of life...........Ezek 33:15
and observe my *s*, and do.....Ezek 37:24
to establish a royal *s*..........Dan 6:7

STAVES—*See* STAFF

STAY—*to remain; stop; restrain; portion*

[*also* STAYED, STAYETH]
s yet other seven days........Gen 8:10
neither *s* thou in all..........Gen 19:17
and *s* there until now.........Gen 32:4
and ye shall *s* no longer.......Ex 9:28
plague..be at a *s*.............Lev 13:5
be in his sight at a *s*..........Lev 13:37
I *s* in the mount..............Deut 10:10
still, and the moon *s*..........Josh 10:13
And *s* ye not, but pursue.....Josh 10:19
would ye *s* for them from.....Ruth 1:13
S, and I will tell thee.........1Sam 15:16
thou hast *s* three days........1Sam 20:19
that were left behind *s*........1Sam 30:9
Ahimaaz *s* by En-rogel........2Sam 17:17
the plague was *s* from........2Sam 24:25
the king was *s* up in his.......1Kin 22:35
And the oil *s*................2Kin 4:6
s not there in the land........2Kin 15:20
It is enough, *s* now thine......1Chr 21:15
plague may be *s* from.........1Chr 21:22
king..*s* himself up in his.......2Chr 18:34
will not *s* them when his......Job 37:4
thy proud waves by *s*?.........Job 38:11
pit; let no man *s* him.........Prov 28:17
S me with flagons............Song 2:5
from Judah the *s* and.........Is 3:1
the whole *s* of bread...........Is 3:1
s upon him that smote........Is 10:20
shall *s* upon the Lord.........Is 10:20
whose mind is *s* on thee......Is 26:3
he *s* his rough wind in........Is 27:8
S yourselves, and wonder.....Is 29:9
s on horses and trust in.......Is 31:1
and *s* upon his God..........Is 50:10
Zion; retire, *s* not............Jer 4:6
and no hands *s* on her........Lam 4:6
the great waters were *s*.......Ezek 31:15
he should not *s* long in.......Hos 13:13
heaven..is *s* from dew.........Hag 1:10
and the earth is *s* from........Hag 1:10
s him, that he should not.....Luke 4:42
he himself *s* in Asia for.......Acts 19:22

STAY—*a support*

[*also* STAYS]
but the Lord was my *s*........2Sam 22:19
lions stood beside the *s*.......1Kin 10:19
s on each side of the.........2Chr 9:18
lions standing by the *s*........2Chr 9:18
but the Lord was my *s*........Ps 18:18
the whole *s* of water..........Is 3:1

STEAD—*location; place*

[*also* STEADS]
in the *s* of his son............Gen 22:13
Husham..reigned in his *s*......Gen 36:34
Hadad..reigned in his *s*.......Gen 36:35
Saul..reigned in his *s*.........Gen 36:37
Hadar reigned in his *s*........Gen 36:39
that is priest in his *s*..........Ex 29:30
sons..anointed in his *s*.........Lev 6:22
and dwelt in their *s*...........Deut 2:12
and dwelt in their *s*...........Deut 2:23
he raised up in their *s*........Josh 5:7
Hanun..reigned in his *s*.......2Sam 10:1
upon my throne in my *s*......1Kin 1:30
Rehoboam..reigned in his *s*...1Kin 11:43
Abijam..reigned in his *s*......1Kin 14:31
Jehoshaphat..in his *s*..........1Kin 15:24
Elah..reigned in his *s*.........1Kin 16:6
Ahaziah..reigned in his *s*......1Kin 22:40
Jehoram..reigned in his *s*......2Kin 1:17
Hazael reigned in his *s*........2Kin 8:15
Jehoahaz..reigned in his *s*.....2Kin 10:35
Joash..reigned in his *s*........2Kin 13:9
Jeroboam..reigned in his *s*....2Kin 14:16
Jotham..reigned in his *s*.......2Kin 15:7
Menahem..reigned in his *s*.....2Kin 15:14
Pekahiah..reigned in his *s*.....2Kin 15:22
Ahaz..reigned in his *s*..........2Kin 15:38
Esarhaddon..reigned in his *s*...2Kin 19:37
Amon..reigned in his *s*.........2Kin 21:18
Josiah..reigned in his *s*........2Kin 21:26
Jehoiachin..reigned in his *s*....2Kin 24:6
Jobab..reigned in his *s*........1Chr 1:44
Hadad..reigned in his *s*........1Chr 1:46
Shaul..reigned in his *s*........1Chr 1:48
Hadad reigned in his *s*.........1Chr 1:50
dwelt in their *s* until..........1Chr 5:22
me to reign in his *s*............2Chr 1:8
Asa..reigned in his *s*...........2Chr 14:1
Jehoram..reigned in his *s*......2Chr 21:1
Amaziah..reigned in his *s*.....2Chr 24:27
Hezekiah..reigned in his *s*.....2Chr 28:27
Amon..reigned in his *s*.........2Chr 33:20
king in his father's *s*..........2Chr 36:1
soul were in my soul's *s*.......Job 16:4
and set others in their *s*.......Job 34:24
Esar-haddon..reigned in his *s*..Is 37:38
thee priest in the *s* of.........Jer 29:26
in thy *s* he might have........Philem 13

STEADFASTNESS—*firmness, persistence, and determination in one's endeavors*
In human things, following:
Person..................Ruth 1:18
Leader.................Jer 35:1-19
Principle................Dan 1:8
In spiritual things:
Enduring chastisement...Heb 12:7
Bearing persecution......Rom 8:35-37
Maintaining perseverance.Heb 3:6, 14
Stability of faith.........Col 2:5
Persevering in service....1Cor 15:58
Resisting Satan..........1Pet 5:9

S

Defending Christian liberty ... Gal 5:1

Elements of, seen in:
Having a goal ... Phil 3:12-14
Discipline ... 1Cor 9:25-27
Run the race ... Heb 12:1, 2
Never give up ... Rev 3:10, 21

[*also* STEADFAST, STEADFASTLY]
settled his countenance *s* ... 2Kin 8:11
yea, thou shalt be *s*, and ... Job 11:15
whose spirit was not *s* ... Ps 78:8
God, and *s* for ever ... Dan 6:26
s set his face to go to ... Luke 9:51
they looked *s* toward ... Acts 1:10
they continued *s* in the ... Acts 2:42
looking *s* on him, saw his ... Acts 6:15
who *s* beholding him ... Acts 14:9
he that standeth *s* in his ... 1Cor 7:37
and our hope of you is *s* ... 2Cor 1:7
could not *s* behold the ... 2Cor 3:7
anchor..both sure and *s* ... Heb 6:19
fall from your own *s* ... 2Pet 3:17

STEADY—*firm; unshaking*
his hands were *s* until ... Ex 17:12

STEAL—*to take something which belongs to someone else*
Common on earth ... Matt 6:19
Forbidden in:
Law ... Ex 20:15
Gospel ... Rom 13:9
Christians not to do ... Eph 4:28
Excludes from heaven ... 1Cor 6:9, 10
None in heaven ... Matt 6:20

[*also* STEALETH, STEALING, STOLE, STOLEN]
be counted *s* with me ... Gen 30:33
Rachel had *s* the images ... Gen 31:19
Jacob *s* away unawares ... Gen 31:20
thou hast *s* away unawares ... Gen 31:26
and *s* away from me ... Gen 31:27
hast thou *s* my gods? ... Gen 31:30
that Rachel had *s* them ... Gen 31:32
s by day, or *s* by night ... Gen 31:39
I was *s* away out of the ... Gen 40:15
should we *s* out of thy ... Gen 44:8
he that *s* a man, and ... Ex 21:16
If a man shall *s* an ox ... Ex 22:1
it be *s* out of the man's ... Ex 22:7
if it be *s* from him, he ... Ex 22:12
Ye shall not *s*, neither ... Lev 19:11
Neither shalt thou *s* ... Deut 5:19
If a man be found *s* any ... Deut 24:7
also *s*, and dissembled ... Josh 7:11
Absalom *s* the hearts of ... 2Sam 15:6
the men of Judah *s* thee ... 2Sam 19:41
had *s* them from the ... 2Sam 21:12
s him from among the ... 2Chr 22:11
tempest *s* him away in ... Job 27:20
S waters are sweet and ... Prov 9:17
Will ye *s*, murder, and ... Jer 7:9
lying, and killing, and *s* ... Hos 4:2
not have *s* till they have ... Obad 5
for every one that *s* shall ... Zech 5:3
Thou shalt not *s*, Thou ... Matt 19:18
s him away while we ... Matt 28:13
Do not kill, Do not *s* ... Mark 10:19
should not *s*, dost thou *s*? ... Rom 2:21
Let him that *s* *s* no ... Eph 4:28

STEALTH—*secrecy; furtiveness*
them by *s* that day into ... 2Sam 19:3

STEDFAST—*See* STEADFAST

STEEL—*iron processed into a durable metal*
bow of *s* is broken by ... 2Sam 22:35
and the bow of *s* shall ... Job 20:24
bow of *s* is broken by ... Ps 18:34
northern iron and the *s*? ... Jer 15:12

STEEP—*precipitous place*
s places shall fall, and ... Ezek 38:20
poured down a *s* place ... Mic 1:4
ran violently down a *s* ... Matt 8:32
ran violently down a *s* ... Mark 5:13
ran violently down a *s* ... Luke 8:33

STEM—*a line of ancestry*
rod out of the *s* of Jesse ... Is 11:1

STEP—*stride; stair; way*

[*also* STEPPED, STEPPETH, STEPS]
up by *s* unto mine altar ... Ex 20:26
s between me and death ... 1Sam 20:3
hast enlarged my *s* under ... 2Sam 22:37
The throne had six *s* ... 1Kin 10:19
And there were six *s* to ... 2Chr 9:18
thou numberest my *s* ... Job 14:16
My foot hath held his *s* ... Job 23:11
and count all my *s*? ... Job 31:4
If my *s* hath turned out ... Job 31:7
compassed us in our *s* ... Ps 17:11
The *s* of a good man are ... Ps 37:23
have our *s* declined from ... Ps 44:18
prepared a net for my *s* ... Ps 57:6
set us in the way of his *s* ... Ps 85:13
thy *s* shall not be ... Prov 4:12
the Lord directeth his *s* ... Prov 16:9
and the *s* of the needy ... Is 26:6
walketh to direct his *s* ... Jer 10:23
They hunt our *s*, that we ... Lam 4:18
up unto it by seven *s* ... Ezek 40:22
going up to it had eight *s* ... Ezek 40:31
Ethiopians..be at his *s* ... Dan 11:43
troubling of the water *s* ... John 5:4
coming, another *s* down ... John 5:7
walk in the *s* of that faith ... Rom 4:12
we not in the same *s*? ... 2Cor 12:18
ye should follow his *s* ... 1Pet 2:21

STEPHANAS (stĕf'ä-năs)—*"crown"*
Corinthian Christian ... 1Cor 1:16
First convert of Achaia ... 1Cor 16:15
Visits Paul ... 1Cor 16:17

STEPHEN (stē'vĕn)—*"crown"—a deacon who became the first Christian martyr*
One of the seven deacons. Acts 6:1-8
Accused falsely by Jews ... Acts 6:9-15
Spoke before the Jewish Sanhedrin ... Acts 7:2-53
Became first Christian martyr ... Acts 7:54-60
Saul (Paul) involved in death of ... Acts 7:58
devout men carried *S* to ... Acts 8:2
persecution that arose about *S* . Acts 11:19
blood of thy martyr *S* ... Acts 22:20

STERN—*the rear*
four anchors out of the *s* ... Acts 27:29

STEWARD—*one employed as a custodian or manager*

Descriptive of:
One over Joseph's household ... Gen 43:19
Curator or guardian ... Matt 20:8
Manager ... Luke 16:2, 3
Management of entrusted duties ... 1Cor 9:17

Duties of, to:
Expend monies ... Rom 16:23
Serve wisely ... Luke 12:42

Of spiritual things, based on:
Lord's ownership ... Ps 24:1, 2; Rom 14:8
Our redemption ... 1Cor 6:20
Gifts bestowed upon us ... Matt 25:14, 15; 1Pet 4:10
Offices given to us ... Eph 3:2-10; Titus 1:7
Faithful in responsibilities. Luke 16:1-3

[*also* STEWARDS]
the *s* of my house is this ... Gen 15:2
the *s* of his house ... Gen 44:1
Arza *s* of his house in ... 1Kin 16:9
s over all the substance ... 1Chr 28:1
wife of Chuza Herod's *s* ... Luke 8:3
commended the unjust *s* ... Luke 16:8
s of the mysteries of God ... 1Cor 4:1
it is required in *s* that a ... 1Cor 4:2
s of the manifold grace of ... 1Pet 4:10

STEWARDSHIP—*use of one's resources*

Basic principles:
Settling accounts ... Rom 14:12
God's ownership ... Ps 24:1; Rom 14:7, 8
Finances and spirituality inseparable ... 1Cor 6:20; Matt 19:16-22; Luke 16:10-13; 2Cor 8:3-8
Needs will be provided ... Matt 6:24-34; Phil 4:19
Content with what God provides ... Ps 37:25; 1Tim 6:6-10; Heb 13:5
Righteousness ... Prov 16:8; Rom 12:17
Avoid debt ... Prov 22:7; Rom 13:8
Do not co-sign ... Prov 6:1-5; Prov 22:26
Inheritance uncertain ... Prov 17:2; Prov 20:21
Proper priority ... Matt 6:19-21, 33
Prosperity is from God ... Deut 29:9; Ps 1:1-3; 3John 2
Saving ... Prov 21:20
Laziness condemned ... Prov 24:30, 31; Heb 6:12
Giving is encouraged ... Prov 3:9, 10; Mal 3:10-12; 2Cor 9:6-8

give an account of thy *s* ... Luke 16:2
away from me the *s* ... Luke 16:3
I am put out of the *s* ... Luke 16:4

STICK—*to prick; adhere to; stay close by*

[*also* STICKETH, STUCK]
spear *s* in the ground ... 1Sam 26:7
bones that were not seen *s* ... Job 33:21
they *s* together, that ... Job 41:17
For thine arrows *s* fast ... Ps 38:2
I have *s* unto thy ... Ps 119:31
is a friend that *s* closer ... Prov 18:24
fish of thy rivers to *s* ... Ezek 29:4
fish of thy rivers shall *s* ... Ezek 29:4
the forepart *s* fast, and ... Acts 27:41

STICKS—*small pieces of wood*
Gathering on Sabbath condemned ... Num 15:32-35
Necessary ... 1Kin 17:10-12
Miracle producing ... 2Kin 6:6
Two become one ... Ezek 37:16-22
Viper in bundle of ... Acts 28:3

STIFF—*rigid*

[*also* STIFFENED]
rebellion and thy *s* neck ... Deut 31:27
but he *s* his neck ... 2Chr 36:13
speak not with a *s* neck ... Ps 75:5
but made their neck *s* ... Jer 17:23

STIFFHEARTED—*stubborn*
impudent children and *s* ... Ezek 2:4

STIFFNECKED—*rebellious; unteachable*

Indicative of Israel's rebelliousness at:
Sinai ... Ex 32:9
Conquest ... Deut 9:6, 13
Captivity ... 2Chr 36:13
Christ's first advent ... Acts 7:51

Remedies of, seen in:
Circumcision (regeneration) ... Deut 10:16
Yield to God ... 2Chr 30:8

for thou art a *s* people ... Ex 33:3
Ye are a *s* people, I will ... Ex 33:5
us; for it is a *s* people ... Ex 34:9

STILL—*progressively; nevertheless; yet*
going on *s* toward the ... Gen 12:9
they were *s* ill-favored ... Gen 41:21
appear *s* in the garment ... Lev 13:57

search the land lived *s* ....Num 14:38
if ye shall *s* do wickedly........1Sam 12:25
and also shalt *s* prevail........1Sam 26:25
But David tarried *s* at 2Sam 11:1
to pass as they *s* went 2Kin 2:11
the people *s* sacrificed 2Kin 12:3
and burned incense *s* in........2Kin 15:35
did sacrifice *s* in the high 2Chr 33:17
s he holdeth fast his ....Job 2:3
That he should *s* live for ......Ps 49:9
For all this they sinned *s* ......Ps 78:32
They shall *s* bring forth ....Ps 92:14
he *s* taught the people ....Eccl 12:9
hand is stretched out *s* ....Is 5:25
hand is stretched out *s* ....Is 10:4
let remain *s* in their own ......Jer 27:11
If ye will *s* abide in this ....Jer 42:10
soul hath them *s* in ....Lam 3:20
thy people *s* are talking ....Ezek 33:30
winding about *s* upward ....Ezek 41:7
house went *s* upward ....Ezek 41:7
breadth..was *s* upward ....Ezek 41:7
he abode *s* in Galilee ....John 7:9
abode two days *s* in the ....John 11:6
Silas to abide there *s* ....Acts 15:34
Timothy abode there *s* ....Acts 17:14
abide not *s* in unbelief ....Rom 11:23
to abide *s* at Ephesus 1Tim 1:3

STILL—*quiet; without motion*

Indicative of:
God's voice 1Kin 19:12
God's presence ....Ps 139:18
Fright ....Ex 15:16
Fixed character ....Rev 22:11
Peace ....Jer 47:6
Quietness ....Num 13:30

Accomplished by:
God ....Ps 107:29
Christ ....Mark 4:39
Submission ....Ps 46:10
Communion ....Ps 4:4

[*also* STILLED, STILLEST, STILLETH]
not, stand *s* and see the ....Ex 14:13
shalt let it rest and lie *s* ....Ex 23:11
them, Stand *s*, and I will ......Num 9:8
Caleb *s* the people ....Num 13:30
ye shall stand *s* in Jordan .....Josh 3:8
And the sun stood *s*, and .....Josh 10:13
So the sun stood *s* in the ......Josh 10:13
cities that stood *s* in their .....Josh 11:13
it is..good and are ye *s*? .....Judg 18:9
but stand thou *s* a while 1Sam 9:27
down and died stood *s* 2Sam 2:23
turned aside and stood *s* 2Sam 18:30
the people stood *s* 2Sam 20:12
that came by him stood *s* 2Sam 20:12
is ours, and we be *s* 1Kin 22:3
stand ye *s* and see the 2Chr 20:17
s in the prison gate ....Neh 12:39
should I have lain *s* ....Job 3:13
but keep it *s* within his ....Job 20:13
stand *s* and consider the ......Job 37:14
mightest *s* the enemy ....Ps 8:2
me beside the *s* waters ....Ps 23:2
Which *s* the noise of the ......Ps 65:7
earth feared, and was *s* ....Ps 76:8
and be not *s*, O God ....Ps 83:1
waves..arise, thou *s* them .....Ps 89:9
Their strength is to sit *s* ....Is 30:7
Why do we sit *s*? ....Jer 8:14
go away, stand not *s* ....Jer 51:50
sun and moon stood *s* in ......Hab 3:11
all the earth sitteth *s* ....Zech 1:11
Jesus stood *s* and called ....Matt 20:32
Jesus stood *s* and ....Mark 10:49
that bare him stood *s* ....Luke 7:14
Mary sat *s* in the house ....John 11:20
the chariot to stand *s* ....Acts 8:38

STING—*to prick painfully; painful prick*

[*also* STINGETH, STINGS]
and *s* like an adder ....Prov 23:32
O death, where is thy *s*? 1Cor 15:55
The *s* of death is sin 1Cor 15:56
were *s* in their tails ....Rev 9:10

STINK—*to smell offensively*

Caused by:
Dead fish ....Ex 7:18, 21
Corpse ....John 11:39
Wounds ....Ps 38:5

Figurative of:
Hostility toward one .....Gen 34:30
Hell ....Is 34:3, 4

[*also* STANK, STINKETH, STINKING]
heaps and the land *s* ....Ex 8:14
and it bred worms and *s* ......Ex 16:20
it did not *s*, neither was ....Ex 16:24
saw that they *s* before 2Sam 10:6
to send forth a *s* savor ....Eccl 10:1
smell there shall be *s* ....Is 3:24
their fish *s* because there ......Is 50:2
his *s* shall come up and ....Joel 2:20
made the *s* of your camps .....Amos 4:10

STIR—*to rouse to activity; agitate*

[*also* STIRRED, STIRRETH, STIRS]
whose heart *s* him up to ......Ex 36:2
who shall *s* him up? ....Num 24:9
As an eagle *s* up her nest .....Deut 32:11
hath *s* up my servant against ..1Sam 22:8
Lord have *s* thee up 1Sam 26:19
Jezebel his wife *s* up 1Kin 21:25
God..*s* up the spirit 1Chr 5:26
Lord *s* up against Jehoram 2Chr 21:16
innocent shall *s* up himself ....Job 17:8
S up thyself, and awake ....Ps 35:23
and my sorrow was *s* ....Ps 39:2
and Manasseh *s* up thy ....Ps 80:2
is of a proud heart *s* up ....Prov 28:25
An angry man *s* up strife .....Prov 29:22
ye *s* not up, nor awake ....Song 2:7
ye *s* not up, nor awake ....Song 8:4
it *s* up the dead for thee ......Is 14:9
Thou that art full of *s*, a ......Is 22:2
he shall *s* up jealousy ....Is 42:13
his sons shall be *s* up ....Dan 11:10
shall he return and be *s* up ....Dan 11:10
He *s* up the people, teaching ..Luke 23:5
no small *s* among the ....Acts 12:18
Jews *s* up the Gentiles ....Acts 14:2
also, and *s* up the people .....Acts 17:13
his spirit was *s* in him ....Acts 17:16
no small *s* about that ....Acts 19:23
s up all the people, and ....Acts 21:27
s up your pure minds 2Pet 3:1

STIR UP—*to provoke or incite*

Of strife, etc., by:
Wrath ....Prov 15:18
Hatred ....Prov 10:12
Grievous words ....Prov 15:1
Unbelief ....Acts 13:50
Agitators ....Acts 6:12
Kings ....Dan 11:2, 25

Of good things:
Generosity ....Ex 35:21, 26
Repentance ....Is 64:7
Ministry 2Tim 1:6
Memory 2Pet 1:13

Of God's sovereignty in:
Punishment 1Kin 11:14, 23
Fulfilling His Word ......2Chr 36:22; Ezra 1:1
Accomplishing His purpose .... Is 13:17; Hag 1:14

STOCK—*log or block of wood; trunk of a plant; family lineage*
to the *s* of the stranger's ......Lev 25:47
the *s* thereof die in the ....Job 14:8
their *s* shall not take root .....Is 40:24
down to the *s* of a tree? ......Is 44:19
Saying to a *s*, Thou art ....Jer 2:27
the *s* is a doctrine of..........Jer 10:8
of the *s* of Abraham ....Acts 13:26
of the *s* of Israel ....Phil 3:5

STOCKS—*a device for publicly punishing offenders*
Instrument of punishment. Acts 16:19, 24
Punishment ....Job 33:11

my feet also in the *s* ....Job 13:27
to the correction of the *s* ......Prov 7:22
with stones and with *s* ....Jer 3:9
put him in the *s* that ....Jer 20:2
Jeremiah out of the *s* ....Jer 20:3
in prison, and in the *s* ....Jer 29:26
ask counsel at their *s* ....Hos 4:12

STOICS—*"pertaining to a colonnade or porch"*
Sect of philosophers founded by Zeno around 308 B.C. ....Acts 17:18

STOLE, STOLEN,—*See* STEALING

STOMACHER—*a garment, usually a robe*
Rich, festive robe ....Is 3:24

STOMACH'S—*concerning the digestive organ; the belly*
a little wine for thy *s* 1Tim 5:23

STONE—*piece of rock*

Natural uses of:
Weighing ....Lev 19:36
Knives ....Ex 4:25
Weapons 1Sam 17:40-50
Holding water ....Ex 7:19
Covering wells ....Gen 29:2
Covering tombs ....Matt 27:60
Landmarks ....Deut 19:14
Writing inscriptions ......Ex 24:12
Buildings ....Matt 24:1, 2
Missiles ....Ex 21:18

Religious uses of:
Altars ....Ex 20:25
Grave ....Josh 7:26
Memorial ....Josh 4:20
Witness ....Josh 24:26, 27
Inscriptions ....Deut 27:4, 8
Idolatry ....Lev 26:1

Figurative of:
Reprobation 1Sam 25:37
Contempt 2Sam 16:6, 13
Christ's rejection ....Ps 118:22
Christ as foundation .....Is 28:16
Desolation ....Jer 51:26
Unregeneracy ....Ezek 11:19
Christ's advent ....Dan 2:34, 35
Conscience ....Hab 2:11
Insensibility ....Zech 7:12
Gentiles ....Matt 3:9
Christ as Head ....Matt 21:42-44
Good works 1Cor 3:12
Christians 1Pet 2:5
Spirit's witness ....Rev 2:17

See ROCK

[*also* STONE'S, STONES, STONY]
And they had brick for *s* ......Gen 11:3
and he took of the *s* of ....Gen 28:11
s that he had put for his ....Gen 28:18
s which I have set for a ....Gen 28:22
rolled the *s* from the ....Gen 29:3
put the *s* again upon the ......Gen 29:3
roll the *s* from the well's ......Gen 29:8
And Jacob took a *s* and ....Gen 31:45
they took *s* and made ....Gen 31:46
him, even a pillar of *s* ....Gen 35:14
the *s* of Israel ....Gen 49:24
sank into the bottom as a *s* ...Ex 15:5
shall be as still as a *s* ....Ex 15:16
they took a *s* and put it ....Ex 17:12
work of a sapphire *s* ....Ex 24:10
Onyx *s*, and *s* to be set ....Ex 25:7
shalt take two onyx *s* ....Ex 28:9
Six of their names on one *s* ...Ex 28:10
six names..on the other *s* .....Ex 28:10
work of an engraver in *s* ......Ex 28:11
put the two *s* upon the ....Ex 28:12
for *s* of memorial unto ....Ex 28:12
the *s* shall be with the ....Ex 28:21

S

in cutting of *s*, to set ... Ex 31:5
of testimony, tables of *s* ... Ex 31:18
Hew thee two tables of *s* ... Ex 34:1
two tables of *s* like unto ... Ex 34:4
hand the two tables of *s* ... Ex 34:4
onyx *s*, and *s* to be set ... Ex 35:9
rulers brought onyx *s* ... Ex 35:27
and *s* to be set, for the ... Ex 35:27
wrought onyx *s* inclosed ... Ex 39:6
set in it four rows of *s* ... Ex 39:10
away the *s* in which the ... Lev 14:40
they shall take other *s* ... Lev 14:42
in the place of those *s* ... Lev 14:42
hath taken away the *s* ... Lev 14:43
down the house, the *s* of it ... Lev 14:45
him with throwing a *s* ... Num 35:17
upon two tables of *s* ... Deut 4:13
them in two tables of *s* ... Deut 5:22
a land whose *s* are iron ... Deut 8:9
to receive the tables of *s* ... Deut 9:9
unto me two tables of *s* ... Deut 9:10
me the two tables of *s* ... Deut 9:11
two tables of *s* like unto ... Deut 10:1
hewed two tables of *s* ... Deut 10:3
thy God, an altar of *s* ... Deut 27:5
Lord thy God of whole *s* ... Deut 27:6
other gods, wood and *s* ... Deut 28:36
idols, wood and *s*, silver ... Deut 29:17
feet stood firm, twelve *s* ... Josh 4:3
up every man of you a *s* ... Josh 4:5
these *s* shall be for a ... Josh 4:7
Joshua set up twelve *s* in ... Josh 4:9
What mean these *s*? ... Josh 4:21
him a great heap of *s* ... Josh 7:26
a great heap of *s* ... Josh 8:29
he wrote there upon the *s* ... Josh 8:32
Roll great *s* upon the ... Josh 10:18
up to the *s* of Bohan ... Josh 15:6
descended to the *s* of ... Josh 18:17
ten persons, upon one *s* ... Judg 9:5
ten persons, upon one *s* ... Judg 9:18
could sling *s* at a hair ... Judg 20:16
there was a great *s* ... 1Sam 6:14
even unto the great *s* of ... 1Sam 6:18
which *s* remaineth unto ... 1Sam 6:18
Then Samuel took a *s* ... 1Sam 7:12
roll a great *s* unto me ... 1Sam 14:33
remain by the *s* Ezel ... 1Sam 20:19
gold with the precious *s* ... 2Sam 12:30
be not one small *s* found ... 2Sam 17:13
a very great heap of *s* ... 2Sam 18:17
at the great *s* which is ... 2Sam 20:8
by the *s* of Zoheleth ... 1Kin 1:9
brought great *s*, costly *s* ... 1Kin 5:17
hewed *s*, to lay the ... 1Kin 5:17
there was no *s* seen ... 1Kin 6:18
All these were of costly *s* ... 1Kin 7:9
the measures of hewed *s* ... 1Kin 7:9
of costly *s*, even great *s* ... 1Kin 7:10
s of ten cubits and *s* of ... 1Kin 7:10
above were costly *s* ... 1Kin 7:11
measures of hewed *s* ... 1Kin 7:11
save the two tables of *s* ... 1Kin 8:9
gold and precious *s* ... 1Kin 10:2
trees, and precious *s* ... 1Kin 10:11
to be in Jerusalem as *s* ... 1Kin 10:27
Elijah took twelve *s* ... 1Kin 18:31
the wood, and the *s*, and ... 1Kin 18:38
good piece of land with *s* ... 2Kin 3:19
cast every man his *s* ... 2Kin 3:25
masons and hewers of *s* ... 2Kin 12:12
but timber and hewed *s* ... 2Kin 12:12
it upon a pavement of *s* ... 2Kin 16:17
buy timber and hewn *s* ... 2Kin 22:6
and the left in hurling *s* ... 1Chr 12:2
masons to hew wrought *s* ... 1Chr 22:2
timber also and *s* have I ... 1Chr 22:14
onyx *s* and *s* to be set ... 1Chr 29:2
glistering *s* and of divers ... 1Chr 29:2
precious *s* and marble *s* ... 1Chr 29:2
as plenteous as *s* ... 2Chr 1:15
brass, in iron, in *s*, and in ... 2Chr 2:14
gold..and precious *s* ... 2Chr 9:1
brought..precious *s* ... 2Chr 9:10
they carried away the *s* ... 2Chr 16:6
and slings to cast *s* ... 2Chr 26:14
arrows and great *s* withal ... 2Chr 26:15
is builded with great *s* ... Ezra 5:8
they revive the *s* out of ... Neh 4:2
break down their *s* wall ... Neh 4:3
be in league with the *s* ... Job 5:23
the strength of *s*? ... Job 6:12
and seeth the place of *s* ... Job 8:17
gold of Ophir as the *s* ... Job 22:24
is molten out of the *s* ... Job 28:2
are hid as with a *s* ... Job 38:30
the sinews of his *s* are ... Job 40:17
Sharp *s* are under him ... Job 41:30
clouds passed, hail *s* and ... Ps 18:12
dash thy foot against a *s* ... Ps 91:12
take pleasure in her *s* ... Ps 102:14
overthrown in *s* places ... Ps 141:6
may be as corner *s* ... Ps 144:12
A gift is as a precious *s* ... Prov 17:8
As he that bindeth a *s* in ... Prov 26:8
s is heavy and the sand ... Prov 27:3
A time to cast away *s* ... Eccl 3:5
time to gather *s* together ... Eccl 3:5
and gathered out the *s* ... Is 5:2
that go down to the *s* ... Is 14:19
of confusion and the *s* of ... Is 34:11
thy borders of pleasant *s* ... Is 54:12
Among the smooth *s* of ... Is 57:6
brass, and for *s* iron ... Is 60:17
gather out the *s* ... Is 62:10
and to a *s*, Thou hast ... Jer 2:27
adultery with *s* and ... Jer 3:9
his throne upon these *s* ... Jer 43:10
my ways with hewn *s* ... Lam 3:9
my teeth with gravel *s* ... Lam 3:16
of a sapphire *s* ... Ezek 1:26
the color of a beryl *s* ... Ezek 10:9
take the *s* heart out of ... Ezek 11:19
to serve wood and *s* ... Ezek 20:32
they shall lay thy *s* and ... Ezek 26:12
every precious *s* was thy ... Ezek 28:13
the midst of the *s* of fire ... Ezek 28:14
away the *s* heart out of ... Ezek 36:26
tables were of hewn *s* ... Ezek 40:42
the *s* was cut out of the ... Dan 2:45
iron, of wood, and of *s* ... Dan 5:4
And a *s* was brought, and ... Dan 6:17
and with precious *s* and ... Dan 11:38
built houses of hewn *s* ... Amos 5:11
I will pour down the *s* ... Mic 1:6
to the dumb *s*, Arise it ... Hab 2:19
a *s* was laid upon a *s* in ... Hag 2:15
behold the *s* that I have ... Zech 3:9
upon one *s* shall be seven ... Zech 3:9
timber thereof and the *s* ... Zech 5:4
they shall be as the *s* of ... Zech 9:16
Jerusalem a burdensome *s* ... Zech 12:3
these *s* be made bread ... Matt 4:3
thy foot against a *s* ... Matt 4:6
will he give him a *s*? ... Matt 7:9
Some fell upon *s* places ... Matt 13:5
the seed into *s* places ... Matt 13:20
sealing the *s* and setting ... Matt 27:66
rolled back the *s* from ... Matt 28:2
some fell on *s* ground ... Mark 4:5
are sown on *s* ground ... Mark 4:16
cutting himself with *s* ... Mark 5:5
s which the builders ... Mark 12:10
see what manner of *s* ... Mark 13:1
not be left one *s* upon ... Mark 13:2
rolled a *s* unto the door ... Mark 15:46
roll us away the *s* from ... Mark 16:3
they saw that the *s* was ... Mark 16:4
able of these *s* to raise ... Luke 3:8
command this *s* that it ... Luke 4:3
thy foot against a *s* ... Luke 4:11
will he give him a *s*? ... Luke 11:11
one *s* upon another ... Luke 19:44
s which the builders ... Luke 20:17
shall fall upon that *s* ... Luke 20:18
adorned with goodly *s* ... Luke 21:5
not be left one *s* upon ... Luke 21:6
from them about a *s* cast ... Luke 22:41
sepulcher that was hewn in *s* ... Luke 23:53
they found the *s* rolled ... Luke 24:2
there six waterpots of *s* ... John 2:6
let him..cast a *s* at her ... John 8:7
Then took they up *s* to ... John 8:59
Jews took up *s* again ... John 10:31
It was a cave and a *s* lay ... John 11:38
Take ye away the *s* ... John 11:39
they took away the *s* ... John 11:41
seeth the *s* taken away ... John 20:1
This is the *s* which was ... Acts 4:11
unto gold, or silver, or *s* ... Acts 17:29
not in tables of *s*, but in ... 2Cor 3:3
written and engraven in *s* ... 2Cor 3:7
as unto a living *s* ... 1Pet 2:4
in Zion a chief corner *s* ... 1Pet 2:6
s which the builders ... 1Pet 2:7
And a *s* of stumbling ... 1Pet 2:8
silver, and brass, and *s* ... Rev 9:20
every *s* about the weight ... Rev 16:21
with gold and precious *s* ... Rev 17:4
silver and precious *s* ... Rev 18:12
with gold, and precious *s* ... Rev 18:16
angel took up a *s* like a ... Rev 18:21
unto a *s* most precious ... Rev 21:11
like a jasper *s*, clear as ... Rev 21:11
all manner of precious *s* ... Rev 21:19

STONE—*execution by pelting with stones*

Punishment inflicted for:

Sacrificing children ... Lev 20:2-5
Divination ... Lev 20:27
Blasphemy ... Lev 24:15-23
Sabbath-breaking ... Num 15:32-36
Apostasy ... Deut 13:1-10
Idolatry ... Deut 17:2-7
Juvenile rebellion ... Deut 21:18-21
Adultery ... Deut 22:22

Examples of:

Achan ... Josh 7:20-26
Adoram ... 1Kin 12:18
Naboth ... 1Kin 21:13
Zechariah ... 2Chr 24:20, 21
Stephen ... Acts 7:59
Paul ... Acts 14:19
Prophets ... Heb 11:37

[*also* STONED, STONEST, STONING]

and will they not *s* us ... Ex 8:26
be almost ready to *s* me ... Ex 17:4
but he shall surely be *s* ... Ex 19:13
the ox shall be surely *s* ... Ex 21:28
the ox shall be *s*, and his ... Ex 21:29
and the ox shall be *s* ... Ex 21:32
all the congregation *s* him ... Lev 24:14
men of his city shall *s* him ... Deut 21:21
s her with stones that she ... Deut 22:21
people spake of *s* him ... 1Sam 30:6
all Israel *s* him with ... 1Kin 12:18
s him with stones, that ... 1Kin 21:13
that Naboth was *s* ... 1Kin 21:15
children of Israel *s* him ... 2Chr 10:18
company shall *s* them ... Ezek 23:47
another, and *s* another ... Matt 21:35
s them which are sent ... Matt 23:37
s them that are sent unto ... Luke 13:34
all the people will *s* us ... Luke 20:6
us, that such should be *s* ... John 8:5
stones again to *s* him ... John 10:31
those works do ye *s* me? ... John 10:32
good work we *s* thee not ... John 10:33
Jews..sought to *s* thee ... John 11:8
they should have been *s* ... Acts 5:26
of the city, and *s* him ... Acts 7:58
and to *s* them ... Acts 14:5
having *s* Paul, drew him ... Acts 14:19
it shall be *s*, or thrust ... Heb 12:20

STONES—*an euphemism for testicles*

or hath his *s* broken ... Lev 21:20
He that is wounded in the *s* ... Deut 23:1

STONES, PRECIOUS—*gems*

Jacinth ... Ex 28:19
Ligure ... Ex 28:19
Onyx ... Gen 2:12
Ruby ... Ex 28:17
Sapphire ... Job 28:6, 16
Sardius ... Rev 4:3

Sardonyx ....Rev 21:20
Topaz ....Job 28:19
Agate ....Is 54:12
Amethyst ....Rev 21:20
Beryl ....Dan 10:6
Chalcedony ....Rev 21:19
Chrysolite...............Rev 21:20
Crystal ....Rev 22:1
Diamond ....Jer 17:1
Emerald ....Ex 28:17
Jasper ....Rev 4:3

STONESQUARERS—*stone workers*
the *s*: so they prepared 1Kin 5:18

STONY—*See* **STONE**

STOOD, STOODEST—*See* **STAND**

STOOL—*a low seat, usually without a back or arms*
Birthstool ....Ex 1:16

a bed, and a table, and a *s*....2Kin 4:10

STOOP—*to bend the body down*

[*also* STOOPED, STOOPETH, STOOPING]
he *s* down, he couched........Gen 49:9
David *s* with his face to.......1Sam 24:8
he *s* with his face to the 1Sam 28:14
or him that *s* for age 2Chr 36:17
proud helpers do *s* under .....Job 9:13
heart of man maketh it *s*......Prov 12:25
Bel boweth down, Nebo *s*.....Is 46:1
They *s*, they bow down ....Is 46:2
not worthy to *s* down ....Mark 1:7
and *s* down, he beheld ....Luke 24:12
But Jesus *s* down and ....John 8:6
again he *s* down, and ....John 8:8
he *s* down, and looking ....John 20:5
she *s* down, and looked ....John 20:11

STOP—*to prevent; cease; block*

[*also* STOPPED, STOPPETH]
windows of heaven were *s*.....Gen 8:2
Philistines had *s* them.........Gen 26:15
for the Philistines had *s* ....Gen 26:18
or his flesh be *s* from his......Lev 15:3
that the rain *s* thee not 1Kin 18:44
s all wells of water, and.......2Kin 3:19
and they *s* all the wells 2Kin 3:25
to *s* the waters of the 2Chr 32:3
who *s* all the fountains 2Chr 32:4
s the upper watercourse of 2Chr 32:30
the breaches began to be *s* ....Neh 4:7
hope, and iniquity *s* her.......Job 5:16
and *s* the way against them....Ps 35:3
like the deaf adder that *s* .....Ps 58:4
that speak lies shall be *s* ......Ps 63:11
and all iniquity shall *s* ....Ps 107:42
Whoso *s* his ears at the cry....Prov 21:13
that *s* his ears from hearing ...Is 33:15
and it shall *s* the noses ....Ezek 39:11
s their ears, that they ....Zech 7:11
s their ears, and ran upon .....Acts 7:57
every mouth may be *s*, and ...Rom 3:19
no man shall *s* me of this 2Cor 11:10
Whose mouths must be *s*......Titus 1:11
s the mouths of lions ....Heb 11:33

STORE—*to lay away for a future time; that which is kept for future use*
of herds and great *s* of........Gen 26:14
ye shall eat of the old *s* ....Lev 25:22
be thy basket and thy *s* ....Deut 28:5
cities of *s* that Solomon 1Kin 9:19
of spices very great *s*, and.....1Kin 10:10
all this *s* that we have 1Chr 29:16
all the *s* cities, which he 2Chr 8:4
s of victual, and of oil 2Chr 11:11
castles, and cities of *s*.........2Chr 17:12
is left is this great *s*...........2Chr 31:10
affording all manner of *s* ......Ps 144:13
fathers have laid up in *s* ......Is 39:6
s up violence and robbery .....Amos 3:10
there is none end of the *s*.....Nah 2:9
Laying up in *s* for 1Tim 6:19
the same word are kept in *s*...2Pet 3:7

STOREHOUSE—*building for storing provisions*

Descriptive of:
Barn ....Deut 28:8
Warehouse ....Gen 41:56
Temple ....Mal 3:10
God's portion 1Cor 16:2

Used for storing:
Grain 2Chr 32:28
The tithe ....Mal 3:10
Treasures 2Kin 20:17

[*also* STOREHOUSES]
over the *s* in the fields 1Chr 27:25
layeth up the depth in *s*.......Ps 33:7
utmost border, open her *s*.....Jer 50:26
which neither have *s* nor ......Luke 12:24

STORIES—*See* **STORY**

STORK—*a large, long-necked, migratory bird*
Nesting of ....Ps 104:17
Migration of ....Jer 8:7
Ceremonially unclean ....Lev 11:19

And the *s*, and the heron .....Deut 14:18
wings like the wings of a *s* ....Zech 5:9

STORM—*a violent atmospheric upheaval marked by wind and precipitation*

Described as:
Grievous................Ex 9:23-25
Sent by God ....Josh 10:11
Destructive ....Matt 7:27

Effects of, upon:
Israelites................Ex 19:16, 19
Philistines...............1Sam 7:10
Mariners................Jon 1:4-14
Animals ....Ps 29:3-9
Disciples................Mark 4:37-41
Soldiers and sailors ......Acts 27:14-44
Nature ....Ps 29:3, 5, 8

[*also* STORMY]
chaff that the *s* carrieth ....Job 21:18
my escape from the windy *s*...Ps 55:8
raiseth the *s* wind, which......Ps 107:25
He maketh the *s* a calm, so ...Ps 107:29
s wind fulfilling his word ......Ps 148:8
for a covert from *s* and ....Is 4:6
refuge from the *s*, a shadow...Is 25:4
is as a *s* against the wall ......Is 25:4
great noise, with *s* and........Is 29:6
and a *s* wind shall rend it .....Ezek 13:11
rend it with a *s* wind in ....Ezek 13:13
ascend and come like a *s*......Ezek 38:9
the whirlwind and in the *s* ....Nah 1:3
there came down a *s* of ....Luke 8:23

STORY—*an account of events or incidents; floor of a building*

[*also* STORIES]
and third *s* shalt thou make ...Gen 6:16
s of the prophet of Iddo 2Chr 13:22
in the *s* of the book of the 2Chr 24:27
against gallery in three *s* ......Ezek 42:3
that buildeth his *s* in the ......Amos 9:6

STOUT—*strong; brave; bold*

[*also* STOUTNESS]
the *s* lion's whelps are ....Job 4:11
say in the pride and *s* of ......Is 9:9
punish the fruit of the *s*.......Is 10:12
look was more *s* than his......Dan 7:20
words have been *s* against.....Mal 3:13

STOUTHEARTED—*courageous*
The *s* are spoiled, they........Ps 76:5
Hearken unto me, ye *s*, that ..Is 46:12

STRAIGHT—*immediately; forthwith; not crooked*

[*also* STRAIGHTWAY]
ascend up every man *s*........Josh 6:5
city, every man *s* before him ..Josh 6:20
the kine took the *s* way 1Sam 6:12
into the city, ye shall *s*........1Sam 9:13
Saul fell *s* all along on 1Sam 28:20
brought it *s* down to the 2Chr 32:30
make thy way *s* before my ....Ps 5:8
let thine eyelids look *s* ....Prov 4:25
He goeth after her *s*, as an....Prov 7:22
crooked cannot be made *s* ....Eccl 1:15
for who can make that *s* ......Eccl 7:13
make *s* in the desert a ....Is 40:3
them, and crooked things *s*....Is 42:16
make the crooked places *s* ....Is 45:2
river of waters in a *s* way .....Jer 31:9
their feet were *s* feet ....Ezek 1:7
they went every one *s* ....Ezek 1:12
s there remained no strength ..Dan 10:17
the Lord, make his paths *s*....Matt 3:3
went up *s* out of the water ....Matt 3:16
s Jesus constrained his ....Matt 14:22
s ye shall find an ass..........Matt 21:2
and *s* took his journey ....Matt 25:15
the Lord, make his paths *s*....Mark 1:3
And *s* coming up out of the ...Mark 1:10
And *s* they forsook their ......Mark 1:18
And *s* he called them ....Mark 1:20
s many were gathered.........Mark 2:2
s the fountain of her blood ....Mark 5:29
And she came in *s* with ....Mark 6:25
out of the ship, *s* they ....Mark 6:54
s he entered into a ship ....Mark 8:10
he saw him, *s* the spirit ....Mark 9:20
and *s* he will send him ....Mark 11:3
s in the morning the chief .....Mark 15:1
the Lord, make his paths *s*....Luke 3:4
drunk old wine *s* desireth .....Luke 5:39
s ye say, There cometh a .....Luke 12:54
immediately she was made *s*...Luke 13:13
Make *s* the way of the Lord...John 1:23
and shall *s* glorify him ....John 13:32
Then fell she down *s* at ....Acts 5:10
street which is called *S*........Acts 9:11
with a *s* course to ....Acts 16:11
baptized, he and all his, *s*.....Acts 16:33
came with a *s* course unto.....Acts 21:1
I sent *s* to thee, and gave .....Acts 23:30
And make *s* paths for your....Heb 12:13
s forgetteth what manner......James 1:24

STRAIGHTFORWARDNESS—*the path of righteousness*
Commanded ....Matt 7:13, 14

STRAIN—*to filter out*
blind guides, which *s* at ....Matt 23:24

STRAIT—*a narrow passage; situation of perplexity or distress; to secure; strictly*

[*also* STRAITLY, STRAITNESS, STRAITS]
The man asked us *s* of our ....Gen 43:7
had *s* sworn the children .....Ex 13:19
in the siege, and in the *s*......Deut 28:53
secretly in the siege and *s* .....Deut 28:57
Jericho was *s* shut up ....Josh 6:1
saw that they were in a *s* 1Sam 13:6
Thy father *s* charged the 1Sam 14:28
unto Gad, I am in a great *s* ...2Sam 24:14
sufficiency he shall be in *s* ....Job 20:22
place, where there is no *s* ....Job 36:16
friend in the siege and *s* ......Jer 19:9
overtook her between the *s* ...Lam 1:3
Jesus *s* charged them, saying ..Matt 9:30
he *s* charged him, and ....Mark 1:43
And he *s* charged them that...Mark 3:12
he charged them *s* that no ....Mark 5:43
he *s* charged them, and ....Luke 9:21
Strive to enter in at the *s* .....Luke 13:24
Let us *s* threaten them, that...Acts 4:17
Did not we *s* command you ...Acts 5:28
For I am in a *s* betwixt ....Phil 1:23

STRAITEN—*to make strait or narrow*

[*also* STRAITENED, STRAITENETH, STRAITEST]
the nations, and *s* them ....Job 12:23
of his strength shall be *s* ......Job 18:7
breadth of the waters is *s* .....Job 37:10
thy steps shall not be *s*.........Prov 4:12
seek their lives, shall *s*........Jer 19:9
the building was *s* more ....Ezek 42:6

S

the spirit of the Lord *s*? . . . . Mic 2:7
am I *s* till it be . . . . Luke 12:50
that after the most *s* sect . . . . . . Acts 26:5
Ye are not *s* in us, but ye 2Cor 6:12
but ye are *s* in your own 2Cor 6:12

STRAKE—*band of planking*

[*also* STRAKES]
and pilled white *s* in them . . . . . Gen 30:37
of the house with hollow *s* . . . . Lev 14:37
s sail, and so were driven . . . . . Acts 27:17

STRANGE—*not native; foreign; different*

[*also* STRANGELY]
Put away the *s* gods . . . . Gen 35:2
but made himself *s* unto . . . . . . Gen 42:7
been a stranger in a *s* land . . . . Ex 2:22
sell her unto a *s* nation . . . . Ex 21:8
and offered *s* fire before . . . . . . Lev 10:1
they offered *s* fire before . . . . . . Num 3:4
and there was no *s* god . . . . Deut 32:12
should behave themselves *s* . . . . Deut 32:27
the Lord, and serve *s* gods . . . . Josh 24:20
put away the *s* gods from . . . . . Judg 10:16
put away the *s* gods and 1Sam 7:3
Solomon loved many *s* women . 1Kin 11:1
have digged and drunk *s* 2Kin 19:24
away the altars of the *s* 2Chr 14:3
have taken *s* wives of the . . . . . Ezra 10:2
land, and from the *s* wives . . . . Ezra 10:11
men that had taken *s* wives . . . Ezra 10:17
these had taken *s* wives . . . . Ezra 10:44
in marrying *s* wives? . . . . Neh 13:27
ye make yourselves *s* to me . . . Job 19:3
a *s* punishment to the . . . . Job 31:3
out..hands to a *s* god . . . . Ps 44:20
There shall no *s* god be . . . . Ps 81:9
shalt thou worship any *s* . . . . . . Ps 81:9
the Lord's song in a *s* . . . . Ps 137:4
deliver thee from the *s* woman . Prov 2:16
son, be ravished with a *s* . . . . . . Prov 5:20
keep thee from the *s* woman . . Prov 7:5
way of man is froward and *s* . . Prov 21:8
and a *s* woman is a narrow . . . . Prov 23:27
a pledge of him for a *s* . . . . Prov 27:13
and shalt set it with *s* . . . . Is 17:10
he may do his work, his *s* . . . . . Is 28:21
bring to pass his act, his *s* . . . . . Is 28:21
degenerate plant of a *s* . . . . Jer 2:21
images, and with *s* vanities? . . . Jer 8:19
not sent to a people of a *s* . . . . Ezek 3:5
strongholds with a *s* god . . . . . Dan 11:39
they have begotten *s* . . . . Hos 5:7
the daughter of a *s* god . . . . Mal 2:11
We have seen *s* things to day . . Luke 5:26
seed should sojourn in a *s* . . . . . Acts 7:6
certain *s* things to our . . . . Acts 17:20
think it *s*..ye run not 1Pet 4:4
think it not *s* concerning 1Pet 4:12
some *s* thing happened unto . . . 1Pet 4:12
and going after *s* flesh . . . . Jude 7

STRANGE WOMAN—*adulteress; prostitute*
deliver thee from the *s w* . . . . . Prov 2:16

STRANGER—*foreigner in a land not of his origin*

Descriptive of:
- Non-Jews . . . . Ex 12:48
- Foreigners . . . . Matt 17:25
- Transients . . . . Luke 24:18
- Visitors . . . . Acts 2:10
- Christians 1Pet 1:1

Positive laws, to:
- Love them . . . . Lev 19:34
- Relieve them . . . . Lev 25:35
- Provide for them . . . . Deut 10:18
- Share in left-overs . . . . Deut 24:19-22
- Treat fairly . . . . Deut 24:14, 17
- Share in religious festivals. Deut 16:11, 14
- Hear the law . . . . Deut 31:12

See FOREIGNERS; SOJOURN; SOJOURNER

[*also* STRANGER'S, STRANGERS, STRANGERS']
be a *s* in a land that is . . . . Gen 15:13
bought with money of any *s* . . . Gen 17:12
I am a *s* and a sojourner . . . . . . Gen 23:4
we not counted of him *s*? . . . . . Gen 31:15
land wherein they were *s* . . . . . . Gen 36:7
wherein his father was a *s* . . . . . Gen 37:1
I have been a *s* in a . . . . Ex 2:22
wherein they were *s* . . . . Ex 6:4
There shall no *s* eat . . . . Ex 12:43
the *s* that sojourneth . . . . Ex 12:49
Thou shalt neither vex a *s* . . . . . Ex 22:21
thou shalt not oppress a *s* . . . . . Ex 23:9
ye know the heart of a *s* . . . . . . Ex 23:9
ye were *s* in the land of . . . . Ex 23:9
but a *s* shall not eat . . . . Ex 29:33
a *s* that sojourneth among . . . . . Lev 16:29
s which sojourn among you . . . Lev 17:8
of your own country, or a *s* . . . Lev 17:15
them for the poor and *s* . . . . Lev 19:10
But the *s* that dwelleth . . . . Lev 19:34
of the *s* that sojourn in . . . . Lev 20:2
daughter..married unto a *s* . . . . Lev 22:12
Neither from a *s* hand . . . . Lev 22:25
unto the poor, and to the *s* . . Lev 23:22
as well for the *s*, as for . . . . Lev 24:22
ye are *s* and sojourners . . . . Lev 25:23
sojourner or *s* wax rich . . . . Lev 25:47
sell himself unto the *s* . . . . Lev 25:47
or to the stock of the *s* . . . . Lev 25:47
s that cometh nigh shall . . . . Num 1:51
if a *s* shall sojourn among . . . . . Num 9:14
for the *s*, and for him that . . . . Num 9:14
for the *s* that sojourneth . . . . . . Num 15:15
so shall the *s* be before . . . . Num 15:15
the *s* that sojourneth among . . . Num 15:26
be born in the land, or a *s* . . . . Num 15:30
a *s* shall not come nigh . . . . Num 18:4
s that sojourneth among . . . . . . Num 19:10
brother, and the *s* that is . . . . . . Deut 1:16
nor thy *s* that is within . . . . Deut 5:14
ye were *s* in the land of . . . . Deut 10:19
shalt give it unto the *s* . . . . Deut 14:21
mayest not set a *s* over . . . . Deut 17:15
because thou wast a *s* in . . . . . . Deut 23:7
Unto a *s* thou mayest lend . . . . Deut 23:20
the judgment of the *s* . . . . Deut 24:17
it shall be for the *s*, for . . . . Deut 24:19
not marry without unto a *s* . . . . Deut 25:5
and the *s* that is among . . . . Deut 26:11
unto the *s*, to the fatherless . . . Deut 26:13
The *s* that is within thee . . . . . . Deut 28:43
the *s* that shall come from . . . . Deut 29:22
after the gods of the *s* of . . . . . . Deut 31:16
as well the *s*, as he that . . . . . . Josh 8:33
s that were conversant . . . . Josh 8:35
hither into the city of a *s* . . . . . Judg 19:12
of me, seeing I am a *s*? . . . . Ruth 2:10
I am the son of a *s* 2Sam 1:13
S shall submit themselves 2Sam 22:45
was no *s* with us in the 1Kin 3:18
all that the *s* calleth to 1Kin 8:43
but few, even a few, and *s* 1Chr 16:19
For we are *s* before thee 1Chr 29:15
Solomon numbered all the *s* . . . 2Chr 2:17
moreover concerning the *s* 2Chr 6:32
the *s* that came out of the 2Chr 30:25
separated..from all *s* . . . . Neh 9:2
and no *s* passed among them . Job 15:19
The *s* did not lodge in the . . . . Job 31:32
s shall submit themselves . . . . . . Ps 18:44
I am a *s* with thee, and a . . . . . Ps 39:12
s are risen up against me . . . . . . Ps 54:3
slay the widow and the *s* . . . . . . Ps 94:6
and let the *s* spoil his . . . . Ps 109:11
from the *s* which flattereth . . . . Prov 2:16
lest *s* be filled with thy . . . . Prov 5:10
thine own, and not *s* with . . . . . Prov 5:17
embrace the bosom of a *s*? . . . . Prov 5:20
the *s* which flattereth with . . . . . Prov 7:5
a *s* doth not intermeddle . . . . . . Prov 14:10
a *s*, and not thine own lips . . . . Prov 27:2
eat thereof, but a *s* eateth . . . . . Eccl 6:2
s devour it in your presence . . . Is 1:7
desolate, as overthrown by *s* . . Is 1:7
the fat ones shall *s* eat . . . . Is 5:17
a palace of *s* to be no city . . . . Is 25:2
multitude of thy *s*..be like . . . . . Is 29:5
let the son of the *s*, that . . . . . . Is 56:3
s shall stand and feed your . . . . Is 61:5
the sons of the *s* shall not . . . . . Is 62:8
for I have loved *s*, and . . . . Jer 2:25
so shall ye serve *s* in a . . . . Jer 5:19
If ye oppress not the *s* . . . . Jer 7:6
do no violence to the *s* . . . . Jer 22:3
in the land where ye be *s* . . . . . Jer 35:7
inheritance is turned to *s* . . . . . . Lam 5:2
into the hands of the *s* for . . . . Ezek 7:21
the *s* that sojourneth in . . . . Ezek 14:7
taketh *s* instead of her . . . . Ezek 16:32
have oppressed the *s* . . . . Ezek 22:29
by the hand of *s* . . . . Ezek 28:10
And *s*, the terrible of the . . . . . Ezek 31:12
s, uncircumcised in heart . . . . . . Ezek 44:9
of any *s* that is among the . . . . Ezek 44:9
to the *s* that sojourn among . . . Ezek 47:22
S have devoured his . . . . Hos 7:9
shall no *s* pass through . . . . Joel 3:17
s carried away captive his . . . . . Obad 11
the day that he became a *s* . . . . Obad 12
nor the fatherless, the *s* . . . . Zech 7:10
turn aside the *s* from his . . . . . . Mal 3:5
Peter saith unto him, Of *s* . . . . Matt 17:26
I was a *s*, and ye took me . . . . Matt 25:35
I was a *s*, and ye took me . . . . Matt 25:43
potter's field, to bury *s* . . . . Matt 27:7
glory to God, save this *s* . . . . . . Luke 17:18
know not the voice of *s* . . . . John 10:5
And a *s* will they not . . . . John 10:5
was a *s* in the land of . . . . Acts 7:29
dwelt as *s* in..land of . . . . Acts 13:17
s which were there spent . . . . . . Acts 17:21
s from the covenants of . . . . Eph 2:12
ye are no more *s* and . . . . Eph 2:19
if she have lodged *s* 1Tim 5:10
confessed that they were *s* . . . . Heb 11:13
forgetful to entertain *s* . . . . Heb 13:2
I beseech you as *s* and 1Pet 2:11
to the brethren, and to *s* 3John 5

STRANGLING—*choking to death by compressing the throat*

[*also* STRANGLED]
So that my soul chooseth *s* . . . . Job 7:15
whelps, and *s* for his . . . . Nah 2:12
and from things *s* . . . . Acts 15:20
blood, and from things *s* . . . . . . Acts 15:29
and from *s*, and from . . . . Acts 21:25

STRATAGEM—*a plan designed to deceive an enemy*
- Joshua's famous . . . . Josh 8:1-22
- Gibeonites' trickery . . . . . . Josh 9:2-27
- Hushai's successful 2Sam 17:6-14

STRAW—*the stalk of wheat or barley; to scatter*
- Used for animals . . . . Gen 24:25, 32
- Used in making bricks . . . Ex 5:7-18
- Eaten by a lion . . . . Is 11:7
- Something worthless . . . . . Job 41:27-29

[*also* STRAWED]
Yet there is both *s* and . . . . Judg 19:19
Barley also and *s* for the 1Kin 4:28
and the lion shall eat *s* . . . . Is 11:7
even as *s* is trodden down . . . . . Is 25:10
lion shall eat *s* like the . . . . Is 65:25
the trees, and *s* them in . . . . Matt 21:8
where thou hast not *s* . . . . Matt 25:24
gather where I have not *s* . . . . . Matt 25:26
the trees, and *s* them in . . . . Mark 11:8

STRAY ANIMALS—*animals that have wandered from their masters*
- Must be returned . . . . Ex 23:4
- Saul's pursuit of 1Sam 9:3-5

STREAM—*a body of running water*

[*also* STREAMS]
of Egypt, upon their *s* . . . . Ex 7:19
at the *s* of the brooks that . . . . Num 21:15
as the *s* of brooks they . . . . Job 6:15
the *s* whereof shall make . . . . . . Ps 46:4
gushed out, and the *s* . . . . Ps 78:20

us, the *s* had gone over ....Ps 124:4
waters, and *s* from Lebanon ...Song 4:15
smite it in the seven *s* ....Is 11:15
of the river unto the *s* ....Is 27:12
breath, as an overflowing *s* ....Is 30:28
place of broad rivers and *s* ....Is 33:21
break out, and *s* in the ....Is 35:6
the smooth stones of the *s* ....Is 57:6
A fiery *s* issued and came .....Dan 7:10
righteousness as a mighty *s* ....Amos 5:24
the *s* beat vehemently upon ...Luke 6:48
against which the *s* did ....Luke 6:49

STREET—*principal thoroughfare*

Uses of:
Display ....Matt 6:5
Teaching................Luke 13:26
Parades.................Esth 6:9, 11
Proclamations ....Neh 8:3-5
Healing.................Mark 6:56

Dangers of, from:
Fighting ....Josh 2:19
Prostitutes ....Prov 7:6-23
Wicked ....Ps 55:11
Assault ....Judg 19:15-26

[*also* STREETS]
we will abide in the *s* all ......Gen 19:2
it into the midst of the *s* ......Deut 13:16
publish it not in the *s* of 2Sam 1:20
them from the *s* of 2Sam 21:12
them as the mire of the *s* 2Sam 22:43
shalt make *s* for thee in 1Kin 20:34
together into the east *s* 2Chr 29:4
s that was before the ....Neh 8:1
and in the *s* of the water ......Neh 8:16
in the *s* of the gate of ....Neh 8:16
to Mordecai unto the *s* of .....Esth 4:6
shall have no name in the *s* ...Job 18:17
did not lodge in the *s* ....Job 31:32
cast them out..in the *s* ....Ps 18:42
and ten thousands in our *s* ....Ps 144:13
be no complaining in our *s* ....Ps 144:14
uttereth her voice in the *s* .....Prov 1:20
rivers of waters in the *s* ....Prov 5:16
through the *s* near her ....Prov 7:8
I shall be slain in the *s* ....Prov 22:13
shall be shut in the *s* ....Eccl 12:4
go about the city in the *s* .....Song 3:2
torn in the midst of the *s* .....Is 5:25
In their *s* they shall gird ......Is 15:3
in their *s*, every one shall .....Is 15:3
voice to be heard in the *s* .....Is 42:2
at the head of all the *s* ....Is 51:20
truth is fallen in the *s* ....Is 59:14
and fro through the *s* of ......Jer 5:1
the young men from the *s* .....Jer 9:21
Judah, and in the *s* of ....Jer 11:6
be cast out in the *s* of ....Jer 14:16
of Judah and in the *s* of ......Jer 44:6
Judah, and in the *s* of ....Jer 44:17
of Moab, and in the *s* ....Jer 48:38
her young men fall in the *s* ....Jer 50:30
thrust through in her *s* ....Jer 51:4
lie on the ground in the *s* .....Lam 2:21
are desolate in the *s* ....Lam 4:5
wandered..in the *s* ....Lam 4:14
cast their silver in the *s* ....Ezek 7:19
a high place in every *s* ....Ezek 16:24
he tread down all thy *s* ....Ezek 26:11
the *s* shall be built again ......Dan 9:25
Wailing shall be in all the *s* ...Amos 5:16
down as the mire of the *s* .....Mic 7:10
shall rage in the *s* ....Nah 2:4
I made their *s* waste, that .....Zeph 3:6
old women dwell in the *s* .....Zech 8:4
s of the city shall be full ......Zech 8:5
and girls playing in the *s* ......Zech 8:5
in the mire of the *s* in ....Zech 10:5
synagogues and in the *s* ......Matt 6:2
man hear his voice in the *s* ....Matt 12:19
go your ways out into the *s* ...Luke 10:10
Go out quickly into the *s* .....Luke 14:21
forth the sick into the *s* .....Acts 5:15
the *s* which is called ....Acts 9:11
passed on through one *s* ......Acts 12:10
the *s* of the city was pure .....Rev 21:21
In the midst of the *s* of it .....Rev 22:2

STRENGTH—*power*

Kinds of:
Physical ....Prov 20:29
Constitutional ....Ps 90:10
Hereditary ....Gen 49:3
Angelic ....Ps 103:20
Military.................Dan 2:37
Spiritual ....Ps 138:3
Superhuman ....Judg 16:5, 6, 19
Divine ....Is 63:1

Dissipation of, by:
Iniquity ....Ps 31:10
Hunger 1Sam 28:20, 22
Sexual looseness ....Prov 31:3
Age ....Ps 71:9
Visions ....Dan 10:8, 16, 17

Increase of:
From:
God ....Is 41:10
Christ 2Tim 4:17
Spirit ....Eph 3:16
Brothers ....Luke 22:32
By:
Wisdom ....Eccl 7:19
Waiting on the LORD ..Is 40:31
Lord's grace 2Cor 12:9

not..yield unto thee her *s* .....Gen 4:12
by *s* of hand the Lord ....Ex 13:3
The Lord is my *s* and song ....Ex 15:2
And your *s* shall be spent .....Lev 26:20
hath as it were the *s* of ....Num 23:22
is the beginning of his *s* ....Deut 21:17
that stood still in their *s* ....Josh 11:13
thou hast trodden down *s* .....Judg 5:21
as the man is, so is his *s* ......Judg 8:21
wherein thy great *s* lieth ......Judg 16:15
and his *s* went from him ......Judg 16:19
stumbled are girded with *s* 1Sam 2:4
and he shall give *s* unto 1Sam 2:10
the *S* of Israel will not 1Sam 15:29
God is my *s* and power: and ..2Sam 22:33
and went in the *s* of that 1Kin 19:8
drew a bow with his full *s* 2Kin 9:24
Seek the Lord and his *s* 1Chr 16:11
unto the Lord glory and *s* 1Chr 16:28
make great, and to give *s* 1Chr 29:12
was *s* in his kingdom 2Chr 1:1
thou, and the ark of thy *s* 2Chr 6:41
the kingdom, and had *s* 2Chr 12:1
The *s* of the bearers of ....Neh 4:10
What is my *s*, that I should ...Job 6:11
in heart, and mighty in *s* ......Job 9:4
With him is wisdom and *s* .....Job 12:13
weakeneth the *s* of the ....Job 12:21
His *s* shall be hunger-bitten ...Job 18:12
It shall devour the *s* of........Job 18:13
death shall devour his *s* ....Job 18:13
No; but he would put *s* ....Job 23:6
the *s* of their hands profit .....Job 30:2
nor all the forces of *s* ....Job 36:19
trust him, because his *s* is .....Job 39:11
and rejoiceth in his *s* ....Job 39:21
In his neck remaineth *s* ....Job 41:22
hast thou ordained *s* ....Ps 8:2
will love thee, O Lord, my *s* ..Ps 18:1
my God, my *s*, in whom I will .Ps 18:2
God that girded me with *s* ....Ps 18:32
thou hast girded me with *s* ....Ps 18:39
O Lord, my *s*, and my ....Ps 19:14
saving *s* of his right hand .....Ps 20:6
king shall joy in thy *s* ....Ps 21:1
My *s* is dried up like a ....Ps 22:15
O my *s*, haste thee to help ....Ps 22:19
Lord is the *s* of my life ....Ps 27:1
The Lord is my *s* and my ......Ps 28:7
The Lord is their *s*, and he....Ps 28:8
is the saving *s* of his ....Ps 28:8
Lord will give *s* unto his ......Ps 29:11
for me: for thou art my *s* .....Ps 31:4
is not delivered by much *s* ....Ps 33:16
deliver any by his great *s* .....Ps 33:17
is their *s* in the time of ....Ps 37:39
heart panteth, my *s* faileth ....Ps 38:10
thou art the God of my *s* .....Ps 43:2
God is our refuge and *s* ....Ps 46:1
man that made not God his *s* ..Ps 52:7
Because of his *s* will I ....Ps 59:9
is the *s* of mine head ....Ps 60:7
the rock of my *s*, and my .....Ps 62:7
Ascribe ye *s* unto God ....Ps 68:34
Israel, and his *s* is in the ......Ps 68:34
forsake me not when my *s* ....Ps 71:9
I will go in the *s* of the ....Ps 71:16
I have showed thy *s* unto .....Ps 71:18
but God is the *s* of my.........Ps 73:26
declared thy *s* among the .....Ps 77:14
chief of their *s* in the ....Ps 78:51
and Manasseh stir up my *s* ....Ps 80:2
Sing aloud unto God our *s* ....Ps 81:1
is the man whose *s* is in.......Ps 84:5
They go from *s* to *s*, every ....Ps 84:7
give thy *s* unto thy servant ....Ps 86:16
art the glory of their *s* ....Ps 89:17
the Lord is clothed with *s* .....Ps 93:1
the *s* of the hills is his ....Ps 95:4
s and beauty are in his........Ps 96:6
unto the Lord glory and *s* .....Ps 96:7
He weakened my *s* in the way .Ps 102:23
Seek the Lord, and his *s* ......Ps 105:4
Ephraim..is the *s* of mine .....Ps 108:8
The Lord is my *s* and song ....Ps 118:14
thou, and the ark of thy *s* .....Ps 132:8
s me with *s* in my soul ....Ps 138:3
The Lord, the *s* of my ....Ps 140:66
Blessed be the Lord my *s* .....Ps 144:1
am understanding; I have *s* ....Prov 8:14
The way of the Lord is *s* ......Prov 10:29
increase is by the *s* of the .....Prov 14:4
and casteth down the *s* of .....Prov 21:22
of knowledge increaseth *s* .....Prov 24:5
day of adversity, thy *s* is ......Prov 24:10
with *s*, and *s* her arms ....Prov 31:17
S and honor are her clothing .Prov 31:25
Wisdom is better than *s* ....Eccl 9:16
eat in due season, for *s* ....Eccl 10:17
men of *s* to mingle strong .....Is 5:22
By the *s* of my hand I have ...Is 10:13
Jehovah is my *s* and my.......Is 12:2
hath spoken, even the *s* of ....Is 23:4
Tarshish: for your *s* is ....Is 23:14
For thou hast been a *s* to .....Is 25:4
a *s* to the needy in his ....Is 25:4
let him take hold of my *s* .....Is 27:5
themselves in the *s* of.........Is 30:2
Their *s* is to sit still...........Is 30:7
of thy times, and *s* of.........Is 33:6
they could not well *s* their ....Is 33:23
and there is not *s* to bring ....Is 37:3
no might he increaseth *s* ......Is 40:29
the people renew their *s* ......Is 41:1
worketh it with the *s* of ....Is 44:12
he is hungry, and his *s* ....Is 44:12
I have spent my *s* for ....Is 49:4
awake, put on *s*, O arm of ....Is 51:9
and by the arm of his *s* ....Is 62:8
bring down their *s* to the......Is 63:6
O Lord, my *s*, and my fortress .Jer 16:19
fortify the height of her *s* .....Jer 51:53
they are gone without *s* ....Lam 1:6
My *s* and my hope is ....Lam 3:18
excellency of your *s*, the ......Ezek 24:21
upon Sin, the *s* of Egypt ......Ezek 30:15
and the pomp of her *s* shall ...Ezek 33:28
shall be in it of the *s* of.......Dan 2:41
shall there be any *s* to ....Dan 11:15
pollute the sanctuary of *s* .....Dan 11:31
have devoured his *s* ....Hos 7:9
the vine do yield their *s*.......Joel 2:22
and feed in the *s* of the ....Mic 5:4
and Egypt were her *s* ....Nah 3:9
The Lord God is my *s*, and he .Hab 3:19
destroy the *s* of the ....Hag 2:22
shall be my *s* in the Lord .....Zech 12:5

S

thy mind, and with all thy *s* . . .Mark 12:30
the soul, and with all the *s* . . . .Mark 12:33
He hath showed *s* with his . . . .Luke 1:51
thy soul, and with all thy *s* . . . .Luke 10:27
and ankle bones received *s* . . . .Acts 3:7
increased the more in *s* . . . . . . .Acts 9:22
when we were yet without *s* . . .Rom 5:6
is sin; and the *s* of sin is 1Cor 15:56
out of measure, above *s* 2Cor 1:8
S with all might, according . . . .Col 1:11
of no *s* at all while the . . . . .Heb 9:17
Sara herself received *s* to . . . . .Heb 11:11
the sun shineth in his *s* . . . . . . .Rev 1:16
thou hast a little *s*, and . . . . . . .Rev 3:8
and riches, and wisdom, and *s* .Rev 5:12
Now is come salvation, and *s* . .Rev 12:10
their power and *s* unto the . . . .Rev 17:13

STRENGTHEN—*to increase one's power*

[*also* STRENGTHENED, STRENGTHENEDST, STRENGTHENETH, STRENGTHENING]
Israel *s* himself, and sat . . . . . . .Gen 48:2
But his bow abode in *s* and . . .Gen 49:24
encourage him, and *s* him . . . .Deut 3:28
Lord *s* Eglon the king of . . . . . .Judg 3:12
shall thine hands be *s* to . . . . . .Judg 7:11
s me, I pray thee, only . . . . . . .Judg 16:28
the wood, and *s* his hand in . . .1Sam 23:16
now let your hands be *s* 2Sam 2:7
Go, *s* thyself, and mark 1Kin 20:22
and there is not *s* to bring 2Kin 19:3
s themselves with him in his . . .1Chr 11:10
s themselves against 2Chr 13:7
s himself, and slew all his 2Chr 21:4
God in his state, and *s* it 2Chr 24:13
for he *s* himself 2Chr 26:8
Also he *s* himself, and built . . .2Chr 32:5
s their hands with vessels . . . . .Ezra 1:6
s their hands in the work . . . . .Ezra 6:22
s their hands for this good . . . .Neh 2:18
Therefore, O God, *s* my hands.Neh 6:9
and thou hast *s* the weak . . . . .Job 4:3
s himself against the . . . . .Job 15:25
I would *s* you with my mouth .Job 16:5
and *s* thee out of Zion . . . . .Ps 20:2
courage, and he shall *s* your . . .Ps 31:24
and *s* himself in his . . . . .Ps 52:7
by..*s* setteth fast the . . . . .Ps 65:6
s, O God, that which thou . . . .Ps 68:28
and bread which *s* man's . . . . . .Ps 104:15
s..me according unto thy . . . . . .Ps 119:28
he *s* the fountains of the . . . . . .Prov 8:28
robe, and *s* him with thy . . . . . .Is 22:21
the oak, which he *s* for . . . . . . .Is 44:14
thy cords, and *s* thy stakes . . . .Is 54:2
and *s* the hands of the . . . . .Ezek 13:22
s the arms of the king of . . . . . .Ezek 30:24
s the arms of the king of . . . . . .Ezek 30:25
and will *s* that which was . . . . .Ezek 34:16
of a man, and he *s* me . . . . .Dan 10:18
had spoken unto me, I was *s* . .Dan 10:19
speak; for thou hast *s* me . . . . .Dan 10:19
stood to confirm and to *s* . . . . .Dan 11:1
but he shall not be *s* by it . . . . .Dan 11:12
I have bound and *s* their . . . . . .Hos 7:15
and the strong shall not *s* . . . . .Amos 2:14
s the spoiled against the . . . . . .Amos 5:9
And I will *s* the house of . . . . .Zech 10:6
an angel..from heaven, *s* . . . . . .Luke 22:43
had received meat, he was *s* . . .Acts 18:23
order, *s* all the disciples . . . . . . .Acts 18:23
through Christ which *s* me . . . .Phil 4:13
perfect, stablish, *s*, settle 1Pet 5:10
and *s* the things which . . . . .Rev 3:2

STRETCH—*to reach out; extend*

[*also* STRETCHED, STRETCHEDST, STRETCHEST, STRETCHETH, STRETCHING]
And Israel *s* out his right . . . . .Gen 48:14
s out my hand, and smite . . . . .Ex 3:20
will redeem you with a *s* . . . . . .Ex 6:6
s out thine hand upon the . . . . .Ex 7:19
S out thy rod, and smite . . . . . .Ex 8:16
Aaron *s* out his hand with . . . .Ex 8:17
S..thine hand toward heaven . .Ex 9:22
Moses *s* forth his rod over . . . .Ex 10:13
S out thine hand toward . . . . . .Ex 10:21
Moses *s* out his hand over . . . .Ex 14:21
S out thine hand over the . . . . .Ex 14:26
Thou *s* out thy right hand . . . . .Ex 15:12
a mighty hand, and by a *s* . . . .Deut 4:34
mighty hand, and the *s* . . . . . . .Deut 7:19
mighty hand, and his *s* out . . . .Deut 11:2
S out the spear that is in . . . . . .Josh 8:18
Joshua *s* out the spear that . . . .Josh 8:18
back, wherewith he *s* out . . . . .Josh 8:26
s forth mine hand against 1Sam 24:6
s..mine hand against the 1Sam 26:11
not afraid to *s* forth thine 2Sam 1:14
s forth the wings of the 1Kin 6:27
he *s* himself upon the child 1Kin 17:21
and he *s* himself upon the 2Kin 4:34
with great power and a *s* 2Kin 17:36
I will *s* over Jerusalem 2Kin 21:13
s out over Jerusalem 1Chr 21:16
s out thine hands toward . . . . . .Job 11:13
he *s* out his hand against . . . . . .Job 15:25
He *s* out the north over . . . . . . .Job 26:7
or who hath *s* the line upon . . .Job 38:5
s her wings toward the . . . . .Job 39:26
s..our hands to a strange . . . . . .Ps 44:20
Ethiopia shall soon *s* out . . . . . .Ps 68:31
I have *s* out my hands unto . . .Ps 88:9
s out the heavens like a . . . . . . .Ps 104:2
To him that *s* out the . . . . .Ps 136:6
I *s* forth my hands unto . . . . . . .Ps 143:6
I have *s* out my hand, and . . . .Prov 1:24
She *s* out her hand to the . . . . .Prov 31:20
and walk with *s* forth necks . . .Is 3:16
s forth his hand against . . . . . . .Is 5:25
away, but his hand is *s* . . . . .Is 5:25
the *s* out of his wings . . . . .Is 8:8
away, but his hand is *s* . . . . .Is 10:4
his hand is *s* out, and . . . . .Is 14:27
He *s* out his hand over . . . . . . .Is 23:11
than that a man can *s* . . . . .Is 28:20
s out upon it the line of . . . . . . .Is 34:11
s out the heavens as a . . . . .Is 40:22
the heavens, and *s* them . . . . . .Is 42:5
The carpenter *s* out his . . . . . . .Is 44:13
my hands, have *s* out the . . . . .Is 45:12
shadows of the..are *s* out . . . . .Jer 6:4
s..my hand upon the . . . . .Jer 6:12
s out the heavens by his . . . . . .Jer 10:12
will I *s* out my hand . . . . .Jer 15:6
by thy great power and *s* . . . . . .Jer 32:17
and hath *s* out the heaven . . . . .Jer 51:15
So will I *s* out my hand . . . . . . .Ezek 6:14
And one cherub *s* forth . . . . . . .Ezek 10:7
then will I *s* out mine . . . . .Ezek 14:13
and with a *s* out arm, and . . . . .Ezek 20:33
also *s* out mine hand upon . . . .Ezek 25:13
s it out upon the land of . . . . . .Ezek 30:25
He shall *s* forth his hand . . . . . .Dan 11:42
he *s* out his hand with . . . . .Hos 7:5
s themselves upon their . . . . . . .Amos 6:4
also *s* out mine hand upon . . . .Zeph 1:4
he to the man, *S* forth . . . . .Matt 12:13
Jesus *s* forth his hand, and . . . .Matt 14:31
unto the man, *S* forth . . . . .Mark 3:5
And he *s* it out: and his . . . . . .Mark 3:5
ye *s* forth no hands . . . . .Luke 22:53
old, thou shalt *s* forth thy . . . . .John 21:18
By *s* forth thine hand to . . . . . .Acts 4:30
I have *s* forth my hands . . . . . . .Rom 10:21
we *s* not ourselves beyond 2Cor 10:14

STREWED—*scattered*
s it upon the graves of them . . .2Chr 34:4

STRIFE—*bitter conflict or dissension; a fight*
Sources of, in:
Hatred . . . . .Prov 10:12
Perverseness . . . . .Prov 16:28
Transgression . . . . .Prov 17:19
Scorner . . . . .Prov 22:10
Anger . . . . .Prov 29:22
Flesh . . . . .Gal 5:19, 20
Actual causes of, seen in:
Self-seeking . . . . .Luke 22:24
Dispute between men . . . .Gen 13:7-11
Contentious man . . . . .Prov 26:21
Being carnal 1Cor 3:3
Disputes 1Tim 6:4
Avoidance of, by:
Being slow to anger . . . . .Prov 15:18
Simplicity of life . . . . .Prov 17:1
See CONTENTION; QUARREL

[*also* STRIFES]
of Zin, in the *s* of the . . . . .Num 27:14
and your burden, and your *s*? .Deut 1:12
my people were at great *s* . . . . .Judg 12:2
a pavilion from the *s* of . . . . . . .Ps 31:20
have seen violence and *s* in . . .Ps 55:9
us a *s* unto our neighbors . . . .Ps 80:6
angered..at the waters of *s* . . . .Ps 106:32
The beginning of *s* is as . . . . . . .Prov 17:14
for a man to cease from *s* . . . . .Prov 20:3
meddleth with *s* belonging . . . . .Prov 26:17
proud heart stirreth up *s* . . . . . .Prov 28:25
of wrath bringeth forth *s* . . . . . .Prov 30:33
Behold, ye fast for *s* and . . . . . .Is 58:4
unto the waters of *s* in . . . . .Ezek 48:28
wantonness, not in *s* and . . . . . .Rom 13:13
envyings, wraths, *s* 2Cor 12:20
Christ even of envy and *s* . . . . .Phil 1:15
nothing be done through *s* . . . .Phil 2:3
about questions and *s* of 1Tim 6:4
to them an end of all *s* . . . . . . .Heb 6:16
envying and *s* in your . . . . .James 3:14
For where envying and *s* is . . . .James 3:16

STRIKE—*to afflict; attack; hit*
Descriptive of:
Smeared blood . . . . .Ex 12:7, 22
Advance in age . . . . .Luke 1:7, 18
Slapping . . . . .John 18:22
God's judgment . . . . .Ps 39:10
Of divine punishment, upon:
Christ . . . . .Is 53:4, 8
Sinners . . . . .Prov 7:23
World . . . . .Ps 110:5
Rebellious . . . . .Is 14:6
Israel . . . . .Is 30:26

[*also* STRICKEN, STRIKETH, STRUCK]
Sarah were old and well *s* . . . . .Gen 18:11
shall *s* off the heifer's . . . . .Deut 21:4
Now Joshua was old and *s* in . .Josh 13:1
Thou art old and *s* in years . . .Josh 13:1
Joshua waxed old and *s* in . . . .Josh 23:1
and *s* through his temples . . . . .Judg 5:26
And he *s* it into the pan 1Sam 2:14
the Lord *s* the child that 2Sam 12:15
the ground, and *s* him not 2Sam 20:10
king David was old and *s* 1Kin 1:1
s his hand over the place 2Kin 5:11
and the Lord *s* him, and he . . .2Chr 13:20
is he that will *s* hands . . . . .Job 17:3
bow of steel shall *s* him . . . . . . .Job 20:24
He *s* them as wicked men in . .Job 34:26
hast *s* thy hand with a . . . . .Prov 6:1
void of understanding *s* . . . . . . .Prov 17:18
good, nor to *s* princes for . . . . .Prov 17:26
one of them that *s* hands . . . . . .Prov 22:26
Why should ye be *s* any . . . . . . .Is 1:5
yet we did esteem him *s* . . . . . .Is 53:4
thou hast *s* them, but they . . . .Jer 5:3
s through for want of the . . . . .Lam 4:9
didst *s* through with his . . . . . . .Hab 3:14
s a servant of the high . . . . .Matt 26:51
did *s* him with the palms . . . . . .Mark 14:65
both were now well *s* in . . . . . . .Luke 1:7
man, and my wife well *s* . . . . . .Luke 1:18
they *s* him on the face . . . . .Luke 22:64
s Jesus with the palm of . . . . . . .John 18:22
a scorpion, when he *s* a . . . . . . .Rev 9:5

STRIKER—*a contentious person*
Disqualifies for church office 1Tim 3:3
not given to wine, no *s* . . . . . . .Titus 1:7

STRING—*a small cord*

[*also* STRINGED, STRINGS]
their arrow upon the *s* ....Ps 11:2
arrows upon thy *s* against .....Ps 21:12
and an instrument of ten *s* ....Ps 33:2
praise him with *s* ....Ps 150:4
songs to the *s* instrument......Is 38:20
chief singer on my *s* ....Hab 3:19
the *s* of his tongue was ....Mark 7:35

STRIP—*to remove clothing or covering*

[*also* STRIPPED, STRIPT]
they *s* Joseph out of his ....Gen 37:23
children of Israel *s* ....Ex 33:6
s Aaron of his garments ......Num 20:26
Moses *s* Aaron of his ....Num 20:28
Jonathan *s* himself of the 1Sam 18:4
Philistines came to *s* the 1Sam 31:8
off his head, and *s* off his 1Sam 31:9
Philistines came to *s* the 1Chr 10:8
when they had *s* him, they 1Chr 10:9
which they *s* off for..........2Chr 20:25
He hath *s* me of my glory.....Job 19:9
s you, and make you bare.....Is 32:11
shall *s* thee also of thy........Ezek 16:39
Lest I *s* her naked, and set....Hos 2:3
and howl, I will go *s* and .....Mic 1:8
And they *s* him, and put on...Matt 27:28
which *s* him of his raiment ....Luke 10:30

STRIPE—*a blow with a rod or whip*
Limit of ....Deut 25:1-4
Because of sin ....Ps 89:32
Upon the Messiah, healing .... { Is 53:5; 1Pet 2:24 }
Uselessness of, on a fool .Prov 17:10
Paul's experience with ...Acts 16:23, 33; 2Cor 11:23

[*also* STRIPES]
wound for wound, *s* for *s* .....Ex 21:25
with the *s* of the children 2Sam 7:14
and *s* for the back of fools ....Prov 19:29
so do *s* the inward parts ......Prov 20:30
shall be beaten with many *s*...Luke 12:47
commit things worthy of *s*.....Luke 12:48
shall be beaten with few *s*.....Luke 12:48
In *s*, in imprisonments, in 2Cor 6:5
times received I forty *s* 2Cor 11:24

STRIPLING—*an adolescent boy*
Inquire..whose son this *s* is....1Sam 17:56

STRIVE—*to contend; endeavor*

[*also* STRIVED, STRIVEN, STRIVETH, STRIVINGS, STROVE]
My spirit shall not..*s* with .....Gen 6:3
because they *s* with him.......Gen 26:20
and for that they *s* not........Gen 26:22
men of the Hebrews *s* ....Ex 2:13
if men *s* together, and one ....Ex 21:18
of Israel *s* together in the .....Lev 24:10
children of Israel *s* with ....Num 20:13
who *s* against Moses and ......Num 26:9
when they *s* against the ....Num 26:9
men *s* together one with ......Deut 25:11
did he ever *s* against..........Judg 11:25
they two *s* together in the 2Sam 14:6
delivered me from the *s*.......2Sam 22:44
Why dost thou *s* against ......Job 33:13
delivered me from the *s*.......Ps 18:43
Lord, with them that *s*........Ps 35:1
he *s* with Aram-naharaim .....Ps 60:*title*
S not with a man without .....Prov 3:30
they that *s* with thee..........Is 41:11
unto him that *s* with his.......Is 45:9
thou hast *s* against the ....Jer 50:24
four winds of the heaven *s* ....Dan 7:2
no man *s*, nor reprove ....Hos 4:4
He shall not *s*, nor cry........Matt 12:19
Jews..*s* among themselves .....John 6:52
showed himself..as they *s* .....Acts 7:26
Pharisees' part arose, and *s* ...Acts 23:9
so have I *s* to preach the......Rom 15:20
every man that *s* for the 1Cor 9:25
if a man also *s* for...........2Tim 2:5
except he *s* lawfully..........2Tim 2:5
s not about words to no.......2Tim 2:14
contentions, and *s* about ......Titus 3:9

STRIVING, SPIRITUAL—*efforts made to serve God*
To enter the strait gate ..Luke 13:24
Against sin..............Heb 12:4
With divine help ....Col 1:29
In prayer ....Rom 15:30
For the faith of the Gospel ....Phil 1:27

STROKE—*a blow*
With an ax..............Deut 19:5
With a sword ....Esth 9:5

[*also* STROKES]
between *s* and *s*, being matters.Deut 17:8
controversy and every *s* be ....Deut 21:5
s is heavier than my ....Job 23:2
Remove thy *s* away from me ..Ps 39:10
and his mouth calleth for *s*....Prov 18:6
in wrath with a continual *s*....Is 14:6
of thine eyes with a *s*.........Ezek 24:16

STRONG—*possessing great moral, spiritual, or physical power*

[*also* STRONGER, STRONGEST, STRONGLY]
shall be *s* than the other ......Gen 25:23
were Laban's, and the *s*.......Gen 25:42
Issachar is a *s* ass............Gen 49:14
a *s* hand shall he let them.....Ex 6:1
a *s* hand shall he drive........Ex 6:1
Lord turned a mighty *s* west...Ex 10:19
sea to go back by a *s* east....Ex 14:21
whether they be *s* or weak ....Num 13:18
people be *s* that dwell in......Num 13:28
people; for they are *s*.........Num 13:31
the children of Ammon was *s* .Num 21:24
was not one city too *s* for.....Deut 2:36
Be *s* and of a good courage ...Deut 31:6
be *s* and of good courage .....Josh 10:25
of Israel were waxen *s* ....Josh 17:13
to Ramah, and to the *s* city ....Josh 19:29
to pass, when Israel was *s*....Judg 1:28
was a *s* tower within the ......Judg 9:51
out of the *s* came forth ....Judg 14:14
honey? and what is *s* than.....Judg 14:18
when Saul saw any *s* man 1Sam 14:52
eagles, they were *s* than 2Sam 1:23
but David waxed *s* and *s*......2Sam 3:1
Abner made himself *s* for 2Sam 3:6
If the Syrians be too *s* for.....2Sam 10:11
children of Ammon be too *s* ..2Sam 10:11
And the conspiracy was *s* 2Sam 15:12
delivered me from my *s*.......2Sam 22:18
be thou *s* therefore, and 1Kin 2:2
and *s* wind rent the...........1Kin 19:11
therefore they were *s* than 1Kin 20:23
surely we shall be *s* than 1Kin 20:23
thy servants fifty *s* men 2Kin 2:16
all that were *s* and apt for 2Kin 24:16
If the Syrians be too *s* for....1Chr 19:12
children of Ammon be too *s* ..1Chr 19:12
whose brethren were *s* men ...1Chr 26:7
the sanctuary: be *s*, and do....1Chr 28:10
the son of Solomon *s* 2Chr 11:17
show himself *s* in..behalf 2Chr 16:9
helped, till he was *s* 2Chr 26:15
Be *s* and courageous, be not ..2Chr 32:7
foundations thereof be *s* ......Ezra 6:3
that ye may be *s*, and eat ......Ezra 9:12
great power, and by thy *s*.....Neh 1:10
of thy mouth be like a *s* ......Job 8:2
clean hands shall be *s* and *s*...Job 17:9
with thy *s* hand thou.........Job 30:21
out the sky, which is *s*........Job 37:18
His bones are as *s* pieces......Job 40:18
the poor may fall by his *s*.....Ps 10:10
delivered me from my *s*.......Ps 18:17
for they were too *s* for me .....Ps 18:17
and rejoiceth as a *s* man .....Ps 19:5
s bulls of Bashan have ....Ps 22:12
The Lord *s* and mighty, the ...Ps 24:8
my mountain to stand *s* ....Ps 30:7
be thou my *s* rock, for a ......Ps 31:2
marvelous kindness in a *s* .....Ps 31:21
are lively, and they are *s*......Ps 38:19
and a *s* tower from the ....Ps 61:3
Be thou my *s* habitation ......Ps 71:3
but thou art my *s* refuge ......Ps 71:7
whom thou madest *s* for ......Ps 80:17
who is a *s* Lord like unto .....Ps 89:8
thine enemies with thy *s* ......Ps 89:10
s is thy hand, and high........Ps 89:13
made them *s* than their ....Ps 105:24
bring me into the *s* city? ......Ps 108:10
With a *s* hand, and with a ....Ps 136:12
for they are *s* than I ....Ps 142:6
many *s* men have been slain...Prov 7:26
rich man's wealth is his *s*.....Prov 10:15
honor: and *s* men retain ......Prov 11:16
The name of the Lord is a *s*...Prov 18:10
harder to be won than a *s*.....Prov 18:19
a reward in the bosom *s* ......Prov 21:14
A wise man is *s*; yea, a man ..Prov 24:5
The ants are a people not *s* ...Prov 30:25
A lion which is *s* among ......Prov 30:30
nor the battle to the *s* ....Eccl 9:11
for love is *s* as death ....Song 8:6
And the *s* shall be as tow .....Is 1:31
men of strength to mingle *s* ...Is 5:22
spake thus to me with a *s*.....Is 8:11
shall the *s* people glorify ......Is 25:3
great and *s* sword shall........Is 27:1
Lord God will come with *s*....Is 40:10
bring forth your *s* reasons .....Is 41:21
will fill ourselves with *s* ....Is 56:12
the neighing of his *s* ones .....Jer 8:16
thou art *s* than I, and hast ....Jer 20:7
hand of him that was *s* than...Jer 31:11
wonders, and with a *s* hand ...Jer 32:21
mighty and *s* men for the .....Jer 48:14
the habitation of the *s* ....Jer 49:19
thy face *s* against their ....Ezek 3:8
forehead *s* against their ....Ezek 3:8
hand of the Lord was *s* upon ..Ezek 3:14
she had *s* rods for the ....Ezek 19:11
she hath no *s* rod to be ....Ezek 19:14
s garrisons shall go down......Ezek 26:11
to make it *s* to hold the.......Ezek 30:21
s among the mighty shall......Ezek 32:21
kingdom shall be *s* as iron ....Dan 2:40
The tree grew, and was *s* .....Dan 4:11
that art grown and become *s* ..Dan 4:22
when he was *s*, the great......Dan 8:8
of the south shall be *s* ....Dan 11:5
become *s* with a small ....Dan 11:23
know their God shall be *s*.....Dan 11:32
is come up upon my land, *s* ...Joel 1:6
as a *s* people set in battle .....Joel 2:5
let the weak say, I am *s* ......Joel 3:10
the spoiled against the *s* ......Amos 5:9
was cast far off a *s* nation .....Mic 4:7
the mortar, make *s* the ....Nah 3:14
yet now be *s*, O Zerubbabel...Hag 2:4
be *s*, O Joshua, son of.........Hag 2:4
and be *s*, all ye people of .....Hag 2:4
Let your hands be *s*, ye ....Zech 8:9
s nations shall come to........Zech 8:22
one enter into a *s* man's ......Matt 12:29
except he first bind the *s*......Matt 12:29
can enter into a *s* man's.......Mark 3:27
will first bind the *s* man.......Mark 3:27
child grew, and waxed *s* .....Luke 2:40
s man armed keepeth his......Luke 11:21
when a *s* than he shall ....Luke 11:22
name hath made this man *s* ...Acts 3:16
was *s* in faith, giving..........Rom 4:20
that are *s* ought to bear ....Rom 15:1
the weakness of God is *s*......1Cor 1:25
we are weak, but ye are *s*.....1Cor 4:10
jealousy? are we *s* than he? ...1Cor 10:22
quit you like men, be *s* 1Cor 16:13
we are weak, and ye are *s* 2Cor 13:9
my brethren, be *s* in the ......Eph 6:10
God shall send them *s* 2Thess 2:11
my son, be *s* in the grace 2Tim 2:1
with *s* crying and tears ....Heb 5:7
But *s* meat belongeth to ......Heb 5:14

S

out of weakness were made *s* . . Heb 11:34
young men, because ye are *s* . . 1John 2:14
I saw a *s* angel proclaiming . . . . Rev 5:2
s is the Lord God who . . . . Rev 18:8

STRONG DRINK—*a powerful intoxicant*
Do not drink wine nor *s d* . . . . Lev 10:9
himself from wine and *s d* . . . . Num 6:3
or vinegar of *s d* . . . . Num 6:3
thou cause the *s* wine to be . . . Num 28:7
or for wine, or for *s d* . . . . Deut 14:26
now drink no wine nor *s d* . . . . Judg 13:7
drunk neither wine nor *s* 1Sam 1:15
Give *s d* unto him that . . . . Prov 31:6
through *s d* are out of . . . . Is 28:7
have erred through *s d* . . . . Is 28:7
of the way through *s d* . . . . Is 28:7
but not with *s d* . . . . Is 29:9
drink neither wine nor *s d* . . . . . Luke 1:15
See DRUNKENNESS

STRONGHOLD—*a fortress*
David captured 2Sam 5:7
The Lord is . . . . Nah 1:7

[*also* STRONGHOLDS]
whether in tents, or in *s* . . . . . . Num 13:19
mountains..caves, and *s* . . . . Judg 6:2
dwelt in *s* at En-gedi 1Sam 23:29
David took the *s* of Zion 2Sam 5:7
And came to the *s* of Tyre 2Sam 24:7
their *s* wilt thou set on 2Kin 8:12
he fortified the *s*, and put 2Chr 11:11
hast brought his *s* to ruin . . . . . Ps 89:40
city, to destroy the *s* . . . . Is 23:11
shall pass over to his *s* . . . . Is 31:9
and he shall destroy thy *s* . . . . . Jer 48:18
s of the daughter of Judah . . . . Lam 2:2
his devices against the *s* . . . . Dan 11:24
and throw down all thy *s* . . . . . . Mic 5:11
s in the day of trouble . . . . Nah 1:7
s shall be like fig trees . . . . Nah 3:12
shall deride every *s* . . . . Hab 1:10
Turn you to the *s*, ye . . . . Zech 9:12
pulling down of *s* 2Cor 10:4

STROVE—*See* STRIVE

STROWED—*See* STREWN

STRUCK—*See* STRIKE

STRUGGLED—*contested*
children *s* together within her . . Gen 25:22

STUBBLE—*the part of a grain which remains in the ground after harvest*
to gather *s* instead of . . . . Ex 5:12
wilt thou pursue the dry *s*? . . . . Job 13:25
are turned with him into *s* . . . . Job 41:28
as the *s* before the wind . . . . . . Ps 83:13
fire devoureth the *s* . . . . Is 5:24
ye shall bring forth *s* . . . . Is 33:11
sword, and as driven *s* to . . . . . Is 41:2
scatter them as the *s* . . . . Jer 13:24
that devoureth the *s* . . . . Joel 2:5
house of Esau for *s* . . . . Obad 18
shall be devoured as *s* . . . . Nah 1:10
do wickedly, shall be *s* . . . . Mal 4:1
stones, wood, hay, *s* 1Cor 3:12

STUBBORN—*unyielding; obstinate*

[*also* STUBBORNNESS]
man have a *s* and . . . . Deut 21:18
doings, nor from their *s* . . . . Judg 2:19
She is loud and *s*; her . . . . Prov 7:11

STUCK—*See* STICK

STUDS—*ornaments*
Of silver . . . . Song 1:11

STUDY—*to read with the intent of acquiring knowledge*
Of the Scriptures . . . . Acts 17:10, 11
2Tim 3:16, 17

[*also* STUDIETH]
of the righteous *s* to . . . . Prov 15:28
For their heart *s* . . . . Prov 24:2
much *s* is a weariness of . . . . . . Eccl 12:12
that ye *s* to be quiet, and 1Thess 4:11
S to show thyself 2Tim 2:15

STUFF—*personal property; possessions*
thou hast searched all my *s* . . . . Gen 31:37
all thy household *s*? . . . . Gen 31:37
neighbor money or *s* . . . . Ex 22:7
among their own *s* . . . . Josh 7:11
himself among the *s* 1Sam 10:22
that tarrieth by the *s* 1Sam 30:24
forth all the household *s* . . . . . . Neh 13:8
prepare thee *s* for . . . . Ezek 12:3
thou bring forth thy *s* . . . . Ezek 12:4
in their sight, as *s* for . . . . Ezek 12:4
I brought forth my *s* by . . . . Ezek 12:7
as *s* for captivity, and in . . . . . . Ezek 12:7
housetop, and his *s* in . . . . Luke 17:31

STUMBLE—*to trip over some obstacle*
Occasions of, found in:
Strong drink . . . . Is 28:7
God's Word 1Pet 2:8
Christ . . . . Rom 9:32, 33
Christ crucified 1Cor 1:23
Christian liberty 1Cor 8:9
Avoidance of, by:
Following wisdom . . . . Prov 3:21, 23
See OFFEND, OFFENSE

[*also* STUMBLED, STUMBLETH, STUMBLING]
that *s* are girded with 1Sam 2:4
the ark; for the oxen *s* 1Chr 13:9
eat up my flesh, they *s* . . . . Ps 27:2
thou shalt not *s* . . . . Prov 4:12
heart be glad when he *s* . . . . Prov 24:17
shall be weary nor *s* . . . . Is 5:27
for a stone of *s* and for a . . . . . Is 8:14
among them shall *s* . . . . Is 8:15
we *s* at noonday as in . . . . Is 59:10
feet *s* upon the dark . . . . Jer 13:16
my persecutors shall *s* . . . . Jer 20:11
shall *s*, and fall toward . . . . Jer 46:6
shall *s* and fall, and not . . . . Dan 11:19
they shall *s* in their walk . . . . . . Nah 2:5
have caused many to *s* at . . . . . Mal 2:8
man walk in the day, he *s* . . . . . John 11:9
they *s* at that *s* stone . . . . Rom 9:32
whereby thy brother *s* . . . . Rom 14:21
And a stone of *s*, and 1Pet 2:8
there is none occasion of *s* 1John 2:10

STUMBLING BLOCK—*an impediment to belief or understanding*

[*also* STUMBLING BLOCKS]
deaf, nor put a *s b* before . . . . . Lev 19:14
take up the *s b* out of the way . Is 57:14
I will lay *s b* before this . . . . Jer 6:21
iniquity, and I lay a *s b* . . . . Ezek 3:20
put the *s b* of their iniquity . . . . Ezek 14:3
the *s b* with the wicked . . . . Zeph 1:3
made a snare, and..a *s b* . . . . . . Rom 11:9
no man put a *s b* or an . . . . Rom 14:13
to cast a *s b* before the . . . . Rev 2:14

STUMP—*remains of a cut tree; remains of a crushed idol*
only the *s* of Dagon was 1Sam 5:4
leave the *s* of his roots . . . . Dan 4:15
to leave the *s* of the tree . . . . . . Dan 4:26

SUAH (sū'ä)—*"riches; distinction"*
An Asherite 1Chr 7:36

SUBDUE—*to conquer; vanquish*

[*also* SUBDUED, SUBDUEDST, SUBDUETH]
the earth, and *s* it . . . . Gen 1:28
the land be *s* before . . . . Num 32:22
with thee, until it be *s* . . . . Deut 20:20
was Midian *s* before the . . . . . . Judg 8:28
So the Philistines were *s* 1Sam 7:13
Philistines, and *s* them 2Sam 8:1
against me hast thou *s* 2Sam 22:40
Moreover I will *s*..thine 1Chr 17:10
and the land is *s* before 1Chr 22:18
and thou *s* before them . . . . Neh 9:24
me, and *s* the people . . . . Ps 18:47
in pieces and *s* all things . . . . . . Dan 2:40
devour, and *s* with sling . . . . Zech 9:15
to *s* all things unto . . . . Phil 3:21

SUBJECTION—*the state of being under another's control*
Of domestic and civil relationships:
Servants to masters 1Pet 2:18
Citizens to government . . . Rom 13:1-6
Children to parents 1Tim 3:4
Wives to husbands . . . . Eph 5:24
Younger to elder 1Pet 5:5
Of spiritual relationships:
Creation to sin . . . . Rom 8:20, 21
Demons to the disciples . . Luke 10:17, 20
Believers to the Gospel . . 2Cor 9:13
Christians to one another . 1Pet 5:5
Christians to God . . . . Heb 12:9
Creation to Christ . . . . Heb 2:5, 8
Church to Christ . . . . Eph 5:24
Christ to God 1Cor 15:28

[*also* SUBJECT]
brought into *s* under . . . . Ps 106:42
brought them into *s* for . . . . Jer 34:11
brought them into *s* . . . . Jer 34:16
Nazareth, and was *s* unto . . . . . Luke 2:51
for it is not *s* to the law . . . . Rom 8:7
and bring it into *s* 1Cor 9:27
the prophets are *s* to the 1Cor 14:32
your professed *s* unto the 2Cor 9:13
we gave place by *s*, no . . . . Gal 2:5
the world, are ye *s* to . . . . Col 2:20
in silence with all *s* 1Tim 2:11
in mind to be *s* to . . . . Titus 3:1
all their lifetime *s* to . . . . Heb 2:15
in *s* to your own husbands 1Pet 3:1
s unto their own husbands 1Pet 3:5
powers being made *s* 1Pet 3:22

SUBJUGATION—*the state of being subdued by force*
Physical force 1Sam 13:19-23
Spiritual power . . . . Mark 5:1-15

SUBMISSION—*yielding to authority; obedience to another's will*
Each other . . . . Eph 5:21
Husbands . . . . Eph 5:22
Rulers 1Pet 2:13
Elders 1Pet 5:5
Christian leaders . . . . Heb 13:17
God . . . . James 4:7

SUBMIT—*to yield to governance or authority*

[*also* SUBMITTED]
s thyself under her hands . . . . . Gen 16:9
s themselves unto Solomon 1Chr 29:24
strangers shall *s* . . . . Ps 18:44
shall thine enemies *s* . . . . Ps 66:3
s himself with pieces of . . . . Ps 68:40
should have *s* themselves . . . . . . Ps 81:15
have not *s* themselves . . . . Rom 10:3
That ye *s* yourselves unto 1Cor 16:16
Wives, *s* yourselves unto . . . . . . Col 3:18

SUBORNED—*induced to give false testimony*
Then they *s* men, which . . . . . . Acts 6:11

SUBSCRIBE—*to attest by signing*

[*also* SUBSCRIBED]
s with his hand unto the . . . . . . Is 44:5
I *s* the evidence, and . . . . Jer 32:10
witnesses that *s* the book . . . . . . Jer 32:12
and *s* evidences, and seal . . . . . Jer 32:44

SUBSTANCE—*material from which something is made; one's possessions*
living *s* that I have made . . . . . . Gen 7:4
And every living *s* was . . . . Gen 7:23
all their *s* that they had . . . . Gen 12:5
for their *s* was great, so . . . . Gen 13:6
come out with great *s* . . . . Gen 15:14
their cattle and their *s* . . . . Gen 34:23
all his *s*, which he had got . . . . Gen 36:6
s that was in their . . . . Deut 11:6
Bless, Lord, his *s*, and . . . . Deut 33:11
cattle and for their *s* . . . . Josh 14:4

rulers of the *s* which was 1Chr 27:31
stewards over all the *s* 1Chr 28:1
away all the *s* that was 2Chr 21:17
portion of his *s* for the 2Chr 31:3
God had given him *s* very 2Chr 32:29
these were of the king's *s* 2Chr 35:7
ones, and for all our *s* ...... Ezra 8:21
elders, all his *s* should be ...... Ezra 10:8
His *s* also was seven ...... Job 1:3
and his *s* is increased in ...... Job 1:10
swalloweth up their *s* ...... Job 5:5
reward for me of your *s* ...... Job 6:22
rich, neither shall his *s* ...... Job 15:29
according to his *s* shall ...... Job 20:18
Whereas our *s* is not cut ...... Job 22:20
and dissolvest my *s* ...... Job 30:22
the rest of their *s* to their ...... Ps 17:14
and ruler of all his *s* ...... Ps 105:21
My *s* was not hid from ...... Ps 139:15
Thine eyes did see my *s* ...... Ps 139:16
shall find all precious *s* ...... Prov 1:13
Honor the Lord with thy *s* ...... Prov 3:9
he shall give all the *s* of ...... Prov 6:31
love me to inherit *s* ...... Prov 8:21
casteth away the *s* of the ...... Prov 10:3
the *s* of a diligent man is ...... Prov 12:27
gain increaseth his *s* ...... Prov 28:8
harlots spendeth his *s* ...... Prov 29:3
give all the *s* of his house ...... Song 8:7
as an oak, whose *s* is in ...... Is 6:13
holy seed shall be the *s* ...... Is 6:13
Thy *s* and thy treasures ...... Jer 15:13
I will give thy *s* and all ...... Jer 17:3
I have found me out *s* ...... Hos 12:8
laid hands on their *s* in ...... Obad 13
their *s* unto the Lord of ...... Mic 4:13
unto him of their *s* ...... Luke 8:3
wasted his *s* with riotous ...... Luke 15:13
better and an enduring *s* ...... Heb 10:34
faith is the *s* of things ...... Heb 11:1

SUBSTITUTION—*replacing one person or thing for another*
Ram for the man ...... Gen 22:13
Offering for the offerer ...... Lev 16:21, 22
Levites for the first-born ...... Num 3:12-45
Christ for the sinner ...... Is 53:4-6
1Pet 2:24

SUBTLETY—*craftiness*
Satan ...... Gen 3:1
Wicked ...... Acts 13:10
Jewish leaders ...... Matt 26:3, 4
Jacob ...... Gen 27:35

[*also* SUBTIL, SUBTILLY, SUBTILTY]
that he dealeth very *s* 1Sam 23:22
Jonadab was a very *s* man 2Sam 13:3
But Jehu did it in *s* 2Kin 10:19
to deal *s* with his servants ...... Ps 105:25
To give *s* to the simple ...... Prov 1:4
attire of a harlot, and *s* of ...... Prov 7:10
The same dealt *s* with our ...... Acts 7:19
beguiled Eve through his *s* 2Cor 11:3

SUBURBS—*open areas around a town, used as a pasture*
of the *s* of their cities ...... Lev 25:34
unto the Levites *s* for the ...... Num 35:2
and the *s* of them shall be ...... Num 35:3
the *s* of the cities, which ...... Num 35:4
shall be to them the *s* ...... Num 35:5
shall ye give with their *s* ...... Num 35:7
their *s* for their cattle ...... Josh 14:4
s thereof for our cattle ...... Josh 21:2
these cities and their *s* ...... Josh 21:3
these cities with their *s* ...... Josh 21:8
eight cities with their *s* ...... Josh 21:41
every one with their *s* ...... Josh 21:42
which was in the *s* 2Kin 23:11
in all the *s* of Sharon 1Chr 5:16
s thereof round about it 1Chr 6:55
in their cities and *s* 1Chr 13:2
left their *s* and their 2Chr 11:14
of the *s* of their cities 2Chr 31:19
The *s* shall shake at the ...... Ezek 27:28
round about for the *s* ...... Ezek 45:2
for dwelling, and for *s* ...... Ezek 48:15
the *s* of the city shall be ...... Ezek 48:17

SUBVERT—*to corrupt or pervert*

[*also* SUBVERTED, SUBVERTING]
To *s* a man in his cause ...... Lam 3:36
with words, *s* your souls ...... Acts 15:24
but to the *s* of the hearers 2Tim 2:14
who *s* whole houses ...... Titus 1:11
he that is such is *s* ...... Titus 3:11

SUCCESS—*attainment of a desired object or end*

Rules of:
Put God first ...... Matt 6:32-34
Follow the Book ...... Josh 1:7-9
Seek the goal ...... Phil 3:13, 14
Never give up ...... Gal 6:9
Do all for Christ ...... Phil 1:20, 21

Hindrances of, seen in:
Unbelief ...... Heb 4:6, 11
Enemies ...... Neh 4:1-23
Sluggishness ...... Prov 24:30-34
Love of the world ...... Matt 16:26

[*also* SUCCEED, SUCCEEDED, SUCCEEDEST]
children of Esau *s* them ...... Deut 2:12
they *s* them, and dwelt ...... Deut 2:21
shall *s* in the name of his ...... Deut 25:6

SUCCOR—*something or someone that gives relief or aid; to aid*

[*also* SUCCORED, SUCCORER]
Syrians..came to *s* 2Sam 8:5
thou *s* us out of the city 2Sam 18:3
the son of Zeruiah *s* him 2Sam 21:17
she hath been a *s* of many ...... Rom 16:2
is able to *s* them that are ...... Heb 2:18

SUCCOTH (sŭk'ŏth)—*"tents"*
1. Place east of the Jordan ...... Judg 8:4, 5
Jacob's residence here ...... Gen 33:17
2. Israel's first camp ...... Ex 12:37

took their journey from *S* ...... Ex 13:20
Rameses, and pitched in *S* ...... Num 33:5
they departed from *S* ...... Num 33:6
men of *S*, Give, I pray you ...... Judg 8:5
the princes of *S* said ...... Judg 8:6
men of *S* had answered ...... Judg 8:8
a young man of the men of *S* ...... Judg 8:14
the princes of *S* ...... Judg 8:14
came unto the men of *S* ...... Judg 8:15
he taught the men of *S* ...... Judg 8:16
between *S* and Zarthan 1Kin 7:46
between *S* and Zeredathah 2Chr 4:17
mete out the valley of *S* ...... Ps 60:6
mete out the valley of *S* ...... Ps 108:7

SUCCOTH-BENOTH (sū-kŏth'bĕ-nŏth)—*"tabernacles of girls"*
Idol set up in Samaria by Babylonians 2Kin 17:30

SUCH—*of the kind indicated*
the father of *s* as dwell ...... Gen 4:20
and of *s* as have cattle ...... Gen 4:20
father of all *s* as handle ...... Gen 4:21
meat, *s* as I love ...... Gen 27:4
daughters of Heth, *s* as ...... Gen 27:46
and of *s* shall be my hire ...... Gen 30:32
s as I never saw in all ...... Gen 41:19
Can we find *s* a one as ...... Gen 41:38
wot ye not that *s* a man as ...... Gen 44:15
there were no *s* locusts as ...... Ex 10:14
after them shall be *s* ...... Ex 10:14
lent unto them *s* things as ...... Ex 12:36
s as fear God, men of truth ...... Ex 18:21
and place *s* over them ...... Ex 18:21
s as have not been done in ...... Ex 34:10
that on which *s* water ...... Lev 11:34
be drunk in every *s* vessel ...... Lev 11:34
s as he is able to get ...... Lev 14:22
pigeons *s* as he can get ...... Lev 14:30
Even *s* as he is able to get ...... Lev 14:31
turneth after *s* as have ...... Lev 20:6
touched any *s* shall be ...... Lev 22:6
man giveth of *s* unto the ...... Lev 27:9
there were *s* a heart ...... Deut 5:29
no more any *s* wickedness ...... Deut 13:11
s abomination is wrought ...... Deut 13:14
s time as thou beginnest ...... Deut 16:9
s abomination is wrought ...... Deut 17:4
commit no more any *s* evil ...... Deut 19:20
For all that do *s* things ...... Deut 25:16
s as before knew nothing ...... Judg 3:2
have told us *s* things as ...... Judg 13:23
that thou comest with *s* ...... Judg 18:23
not been *s* a thing 1Sam 4:7
servants to *s* and *s* 1Sam 21:2
for he is *s* a son of Belial 1Sam 25:17
given unto thee *s* and *s* 2Sam 12:8
no *s* thing ought to be 2Sam 13:12
then hast thou thought *s* 2Sam 14:13
that *s* as be faint in the 2Sam 16:2
with *s* a reward? 2Sam 19:36
s abundance of spices 1Kin 10:10
came to *s* almug trees 1Kin 10:12
In *s*..a place shall be my 2Kin 6:8
s a place shall be my camp 2Kin 6:8
might *s* a thing be? 2Kin 7:19
I am bringing *s* evil upon 2Kin 21:12
s things as were of gold 2Kin 25:15
s as went forth to battle 1Chr 12:33
s as none of the kings 2Chr 1:12
s spice as the queen of 2Chr 9:9
s as set their hearts to 2Chr 11:16
Jehoiada gave it to *s* as 2Chr 24:12
long time in *s* sort as it 2Chr 30:5
side the river, and at *s* ...... Ezra 4:10
all *s* as had separated ...... Ezra 6:21
all *s* as know the laws ...... Ezra 7:25
and of *s* as lay in wait ...... Ezra 8:31
and *s* as are born of ...... Ezra 10:3
are no *s* things done as ...... Neh 6:8
with *s* things as belonged ...... Esth 2:9
the kingdom for *s* a time ...... Esth 4:14
upon all *s* as joined ...... Esth 9:27
knoweth not *s* things ...... Job 12:3
lettest *s* words go out of ...... Job 15:13
s are the dwellings of the ...... Job 18:21
truth unto *s* as keep his ...... Ps 25:10
s as be of a contrite ...... Ps 34:18
s as be blessed of him ...... Ps 37:22
let *s* as love thy salvation ...... Ps 40:16
against *s* as be at peace ...... Ps 55:20
let *s* as love thy salvation ...... Ps 70:4
To *s* as keep his covenant ...... Ps 103:18
for *s* as turn aside unto ...... Ps 125:5
people, that is in *s* a ...... Ps 144:15
s as are upright in their ...... Prov 11:20
S is the way of an ...... Prov 30:20
shall not be *s* as was in ...... Is 9:1
s is our expectation ...... Is 20:6
s a fast that I have chosen ...... Is 58:5
Who hath heard *s* a thing ...... Is 66:8
who hath seen *s* things ...... Is 66:8
see if there be *s* a thing ...... Jer 2:10
soul be avenged on *s* a ...... Jer 9:9
Lord; *S* as are for death ...... Jer 15:2
and *s* as for the sword ...... Jer 15:2
and *s* as are for the famine ...... Jer 15:2
s as are for the captivity ...... Jer 15:2
s as are left in this city ...... Jer 21:7
deliver *s* as are for death ...... Jer 43:11
s as are for captivity to ...... Jer 43:11
s as are for the sword ...... Jer 43:11
he escape that doeth *s* ...... Ezek 17:15
s as had ability in them ...... Dan 1:4
he had spoken *s* words ...... Dan 10:15
s as never was since there ...... Dan 12:1
and *s* as are skillful of ...... Amos 5:16
s as they have not heard ...... Mic 5:15
and all *s* as are clothed ...... Zeph 1:8
given *s* power unto men ...... Matt 9:8
s is the kingdom of heaven ...... Matt 19:14
in *s* an hour as ye think ...... Matt 24:44
s as hear the word ...... Mark 4:18
many *s* parables spake ...... Mark 4:33
s like things ye do ...... Mark 7:8
receive one of *s* children ...... Mark 9:37
for *s* things must needs be ...... Mark 13:7
of whom I hear *s* things ...... Luke 9:9

S

eat *s* things as are set ... Luke 10:8
they suffered *s* things ... Luke 13:2
Father seeketh *s* to ... John 4:23
that *s* should be stoned ... John 8:5
church daily *s* as should ... Acts 2:47
gave no *s* commandment ... Acts 15:24
I will be no judge of *s* ... Acts 18:15
s a fellow from the earth ... Acts 22:22
I doubted of *s* manner of ... Acts 25:20
they laded us with *s* ... Acts 28:10
s things are worthy of ... Rom 1:32
judgest them which do *s* ... Rom 2:3
s fornication as is not so ... 1Cor 5:1
with *s* a one, no, not to eat ... 1Cor 5:11
under bondage in *s* cases ... 1Cor 7:15
taken you but *s* as is ... 1Cor 10:13
s are they also that are ... 1Cor 15:48
s are they also that are ... 1Cor 15:48
ye them that are *s* ... 1Cor 16:18
Sufficient to *s* a man is ... 2Cor 2:6
s trust have we through ... 2Cor 3:4
Let *s* a one think this ... 2Cor 10:11
s as we are in word by ... 2Cor 10:11
s will we be also in deed ... 2Cor 10:11
s a one caught up to the ... 2Cor 12:2
Of *s* a one will I glory ... 2Cor 12:5
I shall not find you *s* as ... 2Cor 12:20
found unto you *s* as ye ... 2Cor 12:20
which do *s* things shall not ... Gal 5:21
restore *s* a one in the ... Gal 6:1
and hold *s* in reputation ... Phil 2:29
is the avenger of all *s* ... 1Thess 4:6
that are *s* we command ... 2Thess 3:12
power thereof: from *s* turn ... 2Tim 3:5
he that is *s* is subverted ... Titus 3:11
being *s* a one as Paul ... Philem 9
s as have need of milk ... Heb 5:12
We have *s* a high priest ... Heb 8:1
him that endured *s* ... Heb 12:3
s sacrifices God is well ... Heb 13:16
we will go into *s* a city ... James 4:13
there came *s* a voice to him ... 2Pet 1:17
We..ought to receive *s* ... 3John 8
and *s* as are in the sea ... Rev 5:13
s as was not since men ... Rev 16:18
on *s* the second death hath ... Rev 20:6

SUCHATHITES (sū'kā-thīts)
Descendants of Caleb ... 1Chr 2:42, 55

SUCK—*to draw milk into the mouth through suction*

Characteristics of:
True among animals ... 1Sam 7:9
Normal for human mothers ... Job 3:12
Figurative of Israel's restoration ... Is 60:16
Figurative of wicked ... Job 20:16

[*also* SUCKED, SUCKING]
have given children *s*? ... Gen 21:7
father beareth the *s* child ... Num 11:12
s of the abundance of the ... Deut 33:19
He shall *s* the poison of ... Job 20:16
Her young ones also *s* up ... Job 39:30
that *s* the breasts of my ... Song 8:1
the *s* child shall play on ... Is 11:8
That ye may *s*, and be ... Is 66:11
they give *s* to their young ... Lam 4:3
The tongue of the *s* child ... Lam 4:4
shalt even drink it and *s* ... Ezek 23:34
those that *s* the breasts ... Joel 2:16
and to them that give *s* ... Matt 24:19
to them that give *s* in ... Mark 13:17
paps which thou hast *s* ... Luke 11:27
to them that give *s*, in ... Luke 21:23

SUCKLING—*young, unweaned person or animal*

[*also* SUCKLINGS]
the *s* also with the man of ... Deut 32:25
infant and *s*, ox and sheep ... 1Sam 15:3
women, children and *s* ... 1Sam 22:19
mouth of babes and *s* ... Ps 8:2
and woman, child and *s* ... Jer 44:7
s swoon in the streets ... Lam 2:11
mouth of babes and *s* ... Matt 21:16

SUDDEN—*happening quickly or unexpectedly*

[*also* SUDDENLY]
if any man die very *s* by ... Num 6:9
if he thrust him *s* without ... Num 35:22
and destroy thee *s* ... Deut 7:4
came unto them *s*, and ... Josh 10:9
lest he overtake us *s*, and ... 2Sam 15:14
for the thing was done *s* ... 2Chr 29:36
s I cursed his habitation ... Job 5:3
and *s* fear troubleth thee ... Job 22:10
return and be ashamed *s* ... Ps 6:10
s shall they be wounded ... Ps 64:7
Be not afraid of *s* fear ... Prov 3:25
shall his calamity come *s* ... Prov 6:15
their calamity shall rise *s* ... Prov 24:22
shall come upon thee *s* ... Is 47:11
s are my tents spoiled ... Jer 4:20
him to fall upon it *s* ... Jer 15:8
s make him run away ... Jer 49:19
Babylon is *s* fallen and ... Jer 51:8
s, when they had looked ... Mark 9:8
s there was with the angel ... Luke 2:13
s there came a sound from ... Acts 2:2
s there was a great ... Acts 16:26
or fallen down dead *s* ... Acts 28:6
then *s* destruction cometh ... 1Thess 5:3
Lay hands *s* on no man ... 1Tim 5:22

SUE—*to bring an action against*
man will *s* thee at the law ... Matt 5:40

SUFFER—*to allow*
s I thee not to touch her ... Gen 20:6
not *s* me to kiss my sons ... Gen 31:28
will not *s* the destroyer to ... Ex 12:23
shalt thou *s* the salt ... Lev 2:13
Or *s* them to bear the ... Lev 22:16
Sihon would not *s* Israel ... Num 21:23
and *s* thee to hunger ... Deut 8:3
s them not to enter into ... Josh 10:19
would not *s* them to come ... Judg 1:34
Moab, and *s* not a man to ... Judg 3:28
S me that I may feel the ... Judg 16:26
s them not to rise against ... 1Sam 24:7
not *s* the revengers of ... 2Sam 14:11
s neither the birds of the ... 2Sam 21:10
that he might not *s* any to ... 1Kin 15:17
He *s* no man to do them ... 1Chr 16:21
king's profit to *s* them ... Esth 3:8
s me to take my breath ... Job 9:18
Neither have I *s* my mouth ... Job 31:30
s not our feet to be moved ... Ps 66:9
proud heart will not I *s* ... Ps 101:5
He *s* no man to do them ... Ps 105:14
will not *s* the..righteous ... Prov 10:3
S not thy mouth to cause ... Eccl 5:6
nor *s* their locks to grow ... Ezek 44:20
said unto him, *S* it to be so ... Matt 3:15
Then he *s* him ... Matt 3:15
s us to go away into the ... Matt 8:31
the kingdom of heaven *s* ... Matt 11:12
S little children, and ... Matt 19:14
have *s* his house to be ... Matt 24:43
s not the devils to speak ... Mark 1:34
s many things of many ... Mark 5:26
how long shall I *s* you? ... Mark 9:19
s to write a bill of ... Mark 10:4
S the little children to ... Mark 10:14
s them not to speak ... Luke 4:41
he *s* no man to go in ... Luke 8:51
I be with you, and *s* you? ... Luke 9:41
wilt thou *s* thine Holy One ... Acts 2:27
but the Spirit *s* them not ... Acts 16:7
the disciples *s* him not ... Acts 19:30
s me to speak unto the ... Acts 21:39
wind not *s* us, we sailed ... Acts 27:7
yet vengeance *s* not to live ... Acts 28:4
Paul was *s* to dwell by ... Acts 28:16
rather *s* yourselves to be ... 1Cor 6:7
not *s* you to be tempted ... 1Cor 10:13
s not a woman to teach ... 1Tim 2:12
s the word of exhortation ... Heb 13:22
thou *s* that woman Jezebel ... Rev 2:20

SUFFER—*endure pain, distress or death*

[*also* SUFFERED, SUFFEREST, SUFFERETH, SUFFERING, SUFFERINGS]
winepresses, and *s* thirst ... Job 24:11
my trouble which I *s* of ... Ps 9:13
do lack, and *s* hunger ... Ps 34:10
I *s* thy terrors I am ... Ps 88:15
idle soul shall *s* hunger ... Prov 19:15
that for thy sake I have *s* ... Jer 15:15
also the Son of man *s* of ... Matt 17:12
they *s* such things? ... Luke 13:2
But first must he *s* many ... Luke 17:25
with you before I *s* ... Luke 22:15
seeing one of them *s* ... Acts 7:24
great things he must *s* ... Acts 9:16
s he their manners in the ... Acts 13:18
so be that we *s* with him ... Rom 8:17
be burned, he shall *s* loss ... 1Cor 3:15
Charity *s* long, and is kind ... 1Cor 13:4
nor for his cause that *s* ... 2Cor 7:12
For ye *s*, if a man bring ... 2Cor 11:20
thrice I *s* shipwreck ... 2Cor 11:25
I have *s* the loss of all ... Phil 3:8
Who now rejoice in my *s* ... Col 1:24
even after that we had *s* ... 1Thess 2:2
s like things of your ... 1Thess 2:14
we should *s* tribulation ... 1Thess 3:4
of God, for which ye also *s* ... 2Thess 1:5
cause I also *s* these things ... 2Tim 1:12
If we *s*, we shall also reign ... 2Tim 2:12
were not *s* to continue by ... Heb 7:23
must he often have *s* ... Heb 9:26
Choosing rather to *s* ... Heb 11:25
his own blood, *s* without ... Heb 13:12
beforehand the *s* of Christ ... 1Pet 1:11
if ye *s* for righteousness ... 1Pet 3:14
as Christ hath *s* for us in ... 1Pet 4:1
for he that hath *s* in the ... 1Pet 4:1
let none of you *s* as a ... 1Pet 4:15
let them that *s* according ... 1Pet 4:19
things which thou shalt *s* ... Rev 2:10

SUFFERING FOR CHRIST
Necessary in Christian living ... 1Cor 12:26; Phil 1:29
Blessed privilege ... Acts 5:41
Never in vain ... Gal 3:4
After Christ's example ... Phil 3:10; 1Pet 2:20, 21
Of short duration ... 1Pet 5:10
Not comparable to heaven's glory ... Rom 8:18; 1Pet 4:13

SUFFERINGS OF CHRIST

Features concerning:
Predicted ... 1Pet 1:11
Announced ... Mark 9:12
Explained ... Luke 24:26, 46
Fulfilled ... Acts 3:18
Witnessed ... 1Pet 5:1
Proclaimed ... Acts 17:2, 3

Benefits of, to Christ:
Preparation for priesthood ... Heb 2:17, 18
Learned obedience ... Heb 5:8
Way to glory ... Heb 2:9, 10

Benefits of, to Christians:
Brought to God ... 1Pet 3:18
Our:
Sins atoned ... Heb 9:26-28
Example ... 1Pet 2:21-23
Fellowship ... Phil 3:10
Comfort ... 2Cor 1:5-7

SUFFICE—*to meet or satisfy a need*

[*also* SUFFICED, SUFFICETH]
be slain for them, to *s* ... Num 11:22
Lord said unto me, Let it *s* ... Deut 3:26
reserved after she was *s* ... Ruth 2:18
Samaria shall *s* for handfuls ... 1Kin 20:10
the Father and it *s* us ... John 14:8
past of our life may *s* us ... 1Pet 4:3

SUFFICIENT—*enough to meet one's needs*

[*also* SUFFICIENCY, SUFFICIENTLY]
stuff they had was *s* for .... Ex 36:7
sanctified themselves *s* 2Chr 30:3
In the fullness of his *s* he ..... Job 20:22
eat *s*, and for durable .... Is 23:18
S unto the day is the evil ..... Matt 6:34
he have *s* to finish it? .... Luke 14:28
of bread is not *s* for .... John 6:7
S to such a man is this 2Cor 2:6
Not that we are *s* of 2Cor 3:5
but our *s* is of God 2Cor 3:5
having all *s* in all things 2Cor 9:8

SUICIDE—*taking of one's own life*

Thought of, induced by:
Life's weariness .... Job 3:20-23
Life's vanity .... Eccl 2:17
Anger .... Jon 4:3, 8, 9

Brought on by:
Hopelessness .... Judg 16:29, 30
Sin 1Kin 16:18, 19
Disappointment 2Sam 17:23
Betrayal of Christ .... Matt 27:3-5

Principles prohibiting, found in:
Body's sacredness 1Cor 6:19
Prohibition against murder .... Ex 20:13
Faith's expectancy 2Tim 4:6-8, 18

Other thoughts concerning:
Desired by some .... Rev 9:6
Attempted but prevented . Acts 16:27, 28
Imputed to Christ .... John 8:22
Satan tempts Christ to ... Luke 4:9

SUIT—*a set of clothing*
a *s* of apparel, and thy .... Judg 17:10

SUKKIM (sŭk'ĭ-ĭm)—*"booth-dwellers"*
African people in Shishak's army 2Chr 12:3

SUM—*an amount of money; the whole amount of something*
laid on him a *s* of money ..... Ex 21:30
takest the *s* of the .... Ex 30:12
the *s* of the tabernacle .... Ex 38:21
Take ye the *s* of all the .... Num 1:2
Levi, neither take the *s* of .... Num 1:49
Take the *s* of all the .... Num 26:2
Take the *s* of the people ...... Num 26:4
have taken the *s* of the .... Num 31:49
the *s* of the number of the 2Sam 24:9
that he may *s* the silver 2Kin 22:4
the *s* of the number of the 1Chr 21:5
the *s* of the money that .... Esth 4:7
Thou sealest up the *s* .... Ezek 28:12
told the *s* of the matters ...... Dan 7:1
Abraham bought for a *s* of .... Acts 7:16
have spoken this is the *s* ...... Heb 8:1

SUMMER—*the warmest season of the year*
Made by God .... Ps 74:17
Sign of God's covenant .. Gen 8:22
Time of:
Fruit harvest 2Sam 16:1, 2
Sowing and harvest .... Prov 6:6-8
Figurative of:
Industry .... Prov 10:5
Opportunity .... Jer 8:20
Preceded by spring ...... Matt 24:32

he was sitting in a *s* .... Judg 3:20
his feet in his *s* chamber ...... Judg 3:24
into the drought of *s* .... Ps 32:4
As snow in *s*, and as rain ..... Prov 26:1
their meat in the *s* .... Prov 30:25
shouting for thy *s* fruits .... Is 16:9
hasty fruit before the *s* .... Is 28:4
gather ye wine, and *s* .... Jer 40:10
is fallen upon thy *s* .... Jer 48:32
the chaff of the *s* .... Dan 2:35
winter house with the *s* .... Amos 3:15
I said, A basket of *s* fruit ..... Amos 8:2
gathered the *s* fruits .... Mic 7:1
in *s* and in winter shall it ..... Zech 14:8
ye know that *s* is near .... Mark 13:28

SUMPTUOUSLY—*luxuriously; extravagantly*
and fared *s* every day .... Luke 16:19

SUN—*the luminous solar body that provides light and heat for the earth*

Characteristics of:
Created by God .... Gen 1:14, 16
Under God's control ..... Ps 104:19
Matt 5:45
Made to rule .... Gen 1:16
Necessary for fruit .... Deut 33:14
Given for light .... Jer 31:35
Made for God's glory .... Ps 148:3
Causes:
Scorching .... Jon 4:8
Sunstroke 2Kin 4:18, 19

Miracles connected with:
Stands still .... Josh 10:12, 13
Shadows of, turned back . 2Kin 20:9-11
Darkening of, at crucifixion .... Luke 23:44-49
Going down at noon ..... Amos 8:9

Worship of:
Forbidden .... Deut 4:19
By Manasseh 2Kin 21:3, 5
By Jews .... Jer 8:2

Figurative of:
God's presence .... Ps 84:11
Earth's sphere of action . . Eccl 1:3, 9, 14
God's Law .... Ps 19:4-7
Future glory .... Matt 13:43
Christ's glory .... Matt 17:2

when the *s* was going down ... Gen 15:12
The *s* was risen upon the ..... Gen 19:23
over Penuel the *s* rose .... Gen 32:31
the *s* waxed hot, it melted .... Ex 16:21
If the *s* be risen upon .... Ex 22:3
toward the rising of the *s* ..... Num 2:3
where the *s* goeth down .... Deut 11:30
either the *s* or moon .... Deut 17:3
when the *s* goeth down .... Deut 24:13
shall the *s* go down upon it ... Deut 24:15
brought forth by the *s* .... Deut 33:14
as soon as the *s* was down .... Josh 8:29
the going down of the *s* .... Josh 10:27
the *s* when he goeth forth ..... Judg 5:31
as soon as the *s* is up .... Judg 9:33
the *s* went down upon .... Judg 19:14
in the sight of this *s* 2Sam 12:11
when the *s* riseth 2Sam 23:4
the going down of the *s* 1Kin 22:36
s shone upon the water 2Kin 3:22
Judah had given to the *s* 2Kin 23:11
the chariots of the *s* 2Kin 23:11
time of the *s* going down 2Chr 18:34
opened until the *s* be hot ..... Neh 7:3
He is green before the *s* ...... Job 8:16
mourning without the *s* .... Job 30:28
from the rising of the *s* .... Ps 50:1
they may not see the *s* .... Ps 58:8
as long as the *s* .... Ps 72:17
the light and the *s* .... Ps 74:16
and his throne as the *s* .... Ps 89:36
The *s* ariseth, they gather ..... Ps 104:22
The *s* shall not smite thee ..... Ps 121:6
The *s* to rule by day .... Ps 136:8
s also ariseth and the *s* .... Eccl 1:5
was no profit under the *s* ..... Eccl 2:11
I had taken under the *s* .... Eccl 2:18
which I took under the *s* ...... Eccl 2:20
under the *s* the place of .... Eccl 3:16
that is done under the *s* .... Eccl 4:3
which walk under the *s* .... Eccl 4:15
he taketh under the *s* .... Eccl 5:18
he hath not seen the *s* .... Eccl 6:5
to them that see the *s* .... Eccl 7:11
better thing under the *s* .... Eccl 8:15
giveth him under the *s* .... Eccl 8:15
that are done under the *s* ..... Eccl 9:3
given thee under the *s* .... Eccl 9:9
thou takest under the *s* .... Eccl 9:9
wisdom..under the *s* .... Eccl 9:13
the eyes to behold the *s* .... Eccl 11:7

While the *s*, or the light ...... Eccl 12:2
s shall be darkened .... Is 13:10
as the light of the *s* .... Is 30:26
the *s* shall be sevenfold .... Is 30:26
is gone down in the *s* dial ..... Is 38:8
s returned ten degrees .... Is 38:8
from the rising of the *s* .... Is 45:6
from the rising of the *s* .... Is 59:19
s shall no more go down ..... Is 60:20
her *s* is gone down .... Jer 15:9
they worshiped the *s* .... Ezek 8:16
I will cover the *s* with a .... Ezek 32:7
going down of the *s* .... Dan 6:14
the *s* and the moon shall ...... Joel 2:10
s and the moon shall be .... Joel 3:15
and the *s* shall go down .... Mic 3:6
when the *s* ariseth they .... Nah 3:17
the *s* and moon stood still ..... Hab 3:11
from the rising of the *s* .... Mal 1:11
S of righteousness arise .... Mal 4:2
And when the *s* was up .... Matt 13:6
shall the *s* be darkened .... Matt 24:29
when the *s* did set, they .... Mark 1:32
the *s* shall be darkened .... Mark 13:24
Now when the *s* was setting ... Luke 4:40
shall be signs in the *s* .... Luke 21:25
s shall be turned into .... Acts 2:20
the brightness of the *s* .... Acts 26:13
There is one glory of the *s* 1Cor 15:41
s go down upon your wrath ... Eph 4:26
s is no sooner risen .... James 1:11
s shineth in his strength .... Rev 1:16
neither shall the *s* light .... Rev 7:16
the *s* and the air were .... Rev 9:2
woman clothed with the *s* ..... Rev 12:1
angel standing in the *s* .... Rev 19:17
neither light of the *s* .... Rev 22:5

SUNDAY—*See* FIRST DAY OF WEEK

SUNDER—*to sever*

[*also* SUNDERED]
that they cannot be *s* .... Job 41:17
cutteth the spear in *s* .... Ps 46:9
cut the bars of iron in *s* .... Ps 107:16
that are beaten in *s* .... Is 27:9
will burst thy bonds in *s* ...... Nah 1:13
and will cut him in *s* .... Luke 12:46

SUNDIAL—*a timepiece which utilizes a shadow cast by the sun*
Miracle of .... Is 38:8

SUNDRY—*in many parts*
Applied to God's revelation .... Heb 1:1

SUNG—*See* SING

SUNK—*See* SINK

SUNRISING—*sunrise*
before Moab, toward the *s* .... Num 21:11
Jordan toward the *s* .... Deut 4:41
side Jordan toward the *s* ...... Josh 1:15
eastward toward the *s* .... Josh 19:12
upon Jordan toward the *s* ..... Josh 19:34
against Gibeah toward the *s* .. Judg 20:43

SUNSTROKE—*stricken by the sun's heat*
Child dies of 2Kin 4:18-20

SUP—*to eat the evening meal*

[*also* SUPPED]
faces shall *s* up as the .... Hab 1:9
Make ready wherewith I may *s*. Luke 17:8
took the cup, when he had *s* .. 1Cor 11:25

SUPERFLUOUS—*exceeding what is necessary or sufficient*

[*also* SUPERFLUITY]
flat nose, or anything *s* .... Lev 21:18
any thing *s* or lacking .... Lev 22:23
it is *s* for me to write 2Cor 9:1
and *s* of naughtiness .... James 1:21

SUPERSCRIPTION—*something inscribed on an object*
Roman coin .... Mark 12:16
Cross of Christ .... Luke 23:38

S

Whose is this image and *s*? . . . .Matt 22:20
the *s* of his accusation . . . . .Mark 15:26
Whose image and *s* hath it? . . .Luke 20:24

SUPERSTITION—*a belief or practice resulting from ignorance, fear, or trust in something other than God*

Causes of, in wrong views of:
God .1Kin 20:23
Holy objects 1Sam 4:3
God's providence . . . . .Jer 44:15-19

Manifestations of, in:
Seeking illogical causes . . .Acts 28:4
Ignorance of the true God . . . . .Acts 17:22
Perverting true religion . .Mark 7:1-16

SUPPER—*a meal, usually in the evening*
made a *s* to his lords . . . . .Mark 6:21
makest a dinner or a *s* . . . . .Luke 14:12
also the cup after *s* . . . . .Luke 22:20
There they made him a *s* . . . . .John 12:2
He riseth from *s*, and laid . . . . .John 13:4
not to eat the Lord's *s* 1Cor 11:20
marriage *s* of the Lamb . . . . . . .Rev 19:9
See LORD'S SUPPER

SUPPLANT—*to supercede by force or treachery*

[*also* SUPPLANTED]
he hath *s* me these two . . . . . . .Gen 27:36
brother will utterly *s* . . . . .Jer 9:4

SUPPLE—*to cleanse*
thou washed in water to *s* . . . . .Ezek 16:4

SUPPLIANTS—*those who implore*
rivers of Ethiopia my *s* . . . . .Zeph 3:10

SUPPLICATION—*a humble entreaty*

[*also* SUPPLICATIONS]
I have not made *s* unto 1Sam 13:12
thy servant, and to his *s* 1Kin 8:28
make *s* unto thee in this 1Kin 8:33
their prayer and their *s* 1Kin 8:45
their prayer and their *s* 1Kin 8:49
unto the *s* of thy servant 1Kin 8:52
the *s* of thy people Israel 1Kin 8:52
made *s* before the Lord 1Kin 8:59
thy servant, and to his *s* 2Chr 6:19
unto the *s* of thy servant 2Chr 6:21
what *s* soever shall be 2Chr 6:29
heard his *s*, and brought 2Chr 33:13
to make *s* unto him . . . . .Esth 4:8
thy *s* to the Almighty . . . . .Job 8:5
Will he make many *s* unto . . . .Job 41:3
The Lord hath heard my *s* . . . .Ps 6:9
Hear the voice of my *s* . . . . . . .Ps 28:2
heardest the voice of my *s* . . . .Ps 31:22
hide not thyself from my *s* . . . .Ps 55:1
heard my voice and my *s* . . . . .Ps 116:1
hear the voice of my *s* . . . . .Ps 140:6
Lord did I make my *s* . . . . .Ps 142:1
they shall make *s* unto . . . . .Is 45:14
and *s* of the children of . . . . . . .Jer 3:21
present their *s* before the . . . . .Jer 36:7
I presented my *s* before . . . . . . .Jer 38:26
me to present your *s* . . . . .Jer 42:9
making *s* before his God . . . . . .Dan 6:11
to seek by prayer and *s* . . . . . . .Dan 9:3
we do not present our *s* . . . . .Dan 9:18
and made *s* unto him . . . . .Hos 12:4
spirit of grace and of *s* . . . . .Zech 12:10
accord in prayer and *s* . . . . .Acts 1:14
prayer and *s* in the Spirit . . . . .Eph 6:18
and *s* for all saints . . . . .Eph 6:18
and *s* with thanksgiving . . . . . .Phil 4:6
first of all, *s*, prayers 1Tim 2:1
offered up prayers and *s* . . . . . .Heb 5:7

SUPPLY—*to provide for; satisfy; provisions*

[*also* SUPPLIED, SUPPLIETH]
on your part they have *s* 1Cor 16:17
may be a *s* for their want 2Cor 8:14
may be a *s* for your want 2Cor 8:14
s the want of the saints 2Cor 9:12
came from Macedonia *s* 2Cor 11:9
by that which every joint *s* . . . . .Eph 4:16
the *s* of the Spirit of Jesus . . . .Phil 1:19
God shall *s* all your need . . . . .Phil 4:19

SUPPORT—*to aid; uphold*
ye ought to *s* the weak . . . . .Acts 20:35
s the weak, be patient 1Thess 5:14

SUPPOSE—*to believe; hold an opinion*

[*also* SUPPOSED, SUPPOSING]
not my lord *s* that they 2Sam 13:32
s that they should have . . . . . . .Matt 20:10
they *s* it had been a spirit . . . . .Mark 6:49
they, *s* him to have been in . . .Luke 2:44
(as was *s*) the son of Joseph . . .Luke 3:23
I *s* that he, to whom he . . . . . . .Luke 7:43
S ye that these Galileans . . . . . .Luke 13:2
s him to be the gardener . . . . . .John 20:15
I *s* that even the world . . . . .John 21:25
not drunken, as ye *s* . . . . .Acts 2:15
For he *s* his brethren . . . . .Acts 7:25
the city, *s* he had been dead . .Acts 14:19
of such things as I *s* . . . . .Acts 25:18
s that they had obtained . . . . . .Acts 27:13
I *s* therefore that this is 1Cor 7:26
I *s* I was not a whit 2Cor 11:5
s to add affliction to my . . . . . .Phil 1:16
I *s* it necessary to send to . . . . .Phil 2:25
s that gain is godliness 1Tim 6:5
sorer punishment, *s* ye . . . . .Heb 10:29
a faithful brother..as I *s* 1Pet 5:12

SUPREME—*highest in authority*
it be to the king, as *s* 1Pet 2:13

SUR (sûr)—*"rebellion"*
Name given to a gate 2Kin 11:6
Called "Gate of the Foundation" 2Chr 23:5

SURE—*secure; certain*

Descriptive of divine things:
God's law . . . . .Ps 19:7
Messianic line 2Sam 23:5
Messiah . . . . .Is 22:23, 25
New covenant . . . . .Acts 13:34
God's:
Prophecies 2Pet 1:19
Promises . . . . .Rom 4:16
Purposes 2Tim 2:19

Applied to the believer's:
Calling and election 2Pet 1:10
Faith . . . . .John 6:69
Dedication . . . . .Neh 9:38
Life of faith . . . . .Is 32:18
Confidence in God's Word . . . . .Luke 1:1
Reward . . . . .Prov 11:18

[*also* SURELY]
thereof thou shalt *s* die . . . . . . .Gen 2:17
s your blood..will I require . . . .Gen 9:5
that thou shalt *s* die . . . . .Gen 20:7
borders..were made *s* . . . . .Gen 23:17
made *s* unto Abraham . . . . .Gen 23:20
wife shall *s* be put to death . . .Gen 26:11
I will *s* give the tenth . . . . .Gen 28:22
S the Lord hath looked . . . . . . .Gen 29:32
s thou hadst sent me away . . . .Gen 31:42
of Pharaoh *s* ye are spies . . . . .Gen 42:16
S he is torn in pieces . . . . .Gen 44:28
God will *s* visit you . . . . .Gen 50:24
S this thing is known . . . . .Ex 2:14
I have *s* visited you . . . . .Ex 3:16
I am *s*..the king of Egypt . . . . .Ex 3:19
he shall *s* thrust you out . . . . . .Ex 11:1
saying, God will *s* visit . . . . .Ex 13:19
but he shall *s* be stoned . . . . . . .Ex 19:13
mother, shall be *s* put to . . . . . .Ex 21:15
mother, shall be *s* put to . . . . . .Ex 21:17
he shall be *s* punished . . . . .Ex 21:22
he shall *s* pay ox for ox . . . . . . .Ex 21:36
he shall *s* make it good . . . . . . .Ex 22:14
with a beast shall *s* be put . . . .Ex 22:19
shalt *s* bring it back to . . . . .Ex 23:4
s be a snare unto thee . . . . .Ex 23:33
he shall *s* be put to death . . . . .Ex 31:15
he shall *s* be put to death . . . . .Lev 20:2
adulteress shall *s* be put . . . . . . .Lev 20:10
shall *s* be put to death . . . . .Lev 20:12
he shall *s* be put to death . . . . .Lev 20:15
shall *s* be put to death . . . . .Lev 20:27
any man shall *s* be put to . . . . .Lev 24:17
s it floweth with milk and . . . . .Num 13:27
I will *s* do it unto all this . . . . .Num 14:35
shalt thou *s* redeem . . . . .Num 18:15
S there is no enchantment . . . . .Num 23:23
thou shalt *s* give them a . . . . . . .Num 27:7
s your sin will find you out . . . .Num 32:23
s be put to death . . . . .Num 35:16
shall be *s* put to death . . . . .Num 35:31
that ye shall *s* perish . . . . .Deut 8:19
be *s* that thou eat not the . . . . .Deut 12:23
s smite the inhabitants . . . . .Deut 13:15
Thou shalt *s* give him . . . . .Deut 15:10
s help him to lift them up . . . . .Deut 22:4
that ye shall *s* perish . . . . .Deut 30:18
S I will be with thee . . . . .Judg 6:16
We shall *s* die, because we . . . .Judg 13:22
S they are smitten down . . . . . .Judg 20:39
S we will return with thee . . . . .Ruth 1:10
I will build him a *s* house 1Sam 2:35
cometh *s* to pass 1Sam 9:6
for thou shalt *s* die 1Sam 14:44
S the Lord's anointed is 1Sam 16:6
clean; *s* he is not clean 1Sam 20:26
Thou shalt *s* die 1Sam 22:16
that thou shalt *s* be king 1Sam 24:20
make my lord a *s* house 1Sam 25:28
s there had not been left 1Sam 25:34
S, as the Lord liveth 1Sam 29:6
I was *s* that he could not 2Sam 1:10
S the men prevailed 2Sam 11:23
born unto thee shall *s* die 2Sam 12:14
I will *s* go forth with you 2Sam 18:2
s buy it of thee at a price 2Sam 24:24
I have *s* built thee 1Kin 8:13
I will *s* rend the kingdom 1Kin 11:11
and build thee a *s* house 1Kin 11:38
I will *s* show myself unto 1Kin 18:15
they said, *S* it is the king 1Kin 22:32
art gone up, but shalt *s* die 2Kin 1:4
the kings are *s* slain 2Kin 3:23
me that he shall *s* die 2Kin 8:10
S I have seen yesterday 2Kin 9:26
S there was not holden 2Kin 23:22
shalt *s* fall before him . . . . .Esth 6:13
s now he would awake for . . . .Job 8:6
He will *s* reprove you . . . . .Job 13:10
S such are the dwellings . . . . . .Job 18:21
no man is *s* of life . . . . .Job 24:22
S there is a vein for the . . . . . . .Job 28:1
S thou hast spoken in mine . . .Job 33:8
S it is meet to be said . . . . .Job 34:31
s he shall be swallowed up . . . .Job 37:20
testimony of the Lord is *s* . . . . .Ps 19:7
S goodness and mercy . . . . .Ps 23:6
S every man walketh in a . . . . .Ps 39:6
s they are disquieted in . . . . . . .Ps 39:6
S men of low degree are . . . . . .Ps 62:9
S the wrath of man shall . . . . . .Ps 76:10
S his salvation is nigh . . . . .Ps 85:9
his commandments are *s* . . . . . .Ps 111:7
S he shall not be moved . . . . . .Ps 112:6
S I will not come into . . . . .Ps 132:3
S thou wilt slay the . . . . .Ps 139:19
S in vain the net is . . . . .Prov 1:17
and make *s* thy friend . . . . .Prov 6:3
uprightly walketh *s* . . . . .Prov 10:9
hateth suretyship is *s* . . . . .Prov 11:15
For *s* there is an end . . . . .Prov 23:18
S the churning of milk . . . . .Prov 30:33
S this also is vanity . . . . .Eccl 4:16
s I know it shall be well . . . . . .Eccl 8:12
s ye shall not be . . . . .Is 7:9
s they are stricken . . . . .Is 16:7
S this iniquity shall not . . . . . . .Is 22:14
He will *s* violently turn . . . . . . .Is 22:18
stone, a *s* foundation . . . . .Is 28:16
his waters shall be *s* . . . . .Is 33:16
Lord will *s* deliver us . . . . .Is 36:15
S God is in thee . . . . .Is 45:14
shalt *s* clothe thee with . . . . . . .Is 49:18

they shall *s* gather .... Is 54:15
the *s* mercies of David .... Is 55:3
S I will no more give thy ..... Is 62:8
s his anger shall turn from .... Jer 2:35
s thou hast greatly deceived ... Jer 4:10
S these are poor; they are ..... Jer 5:4
S our fathers have inherited ... Jer 16:19
s then shalt thou be ashamed .. Jer 22:22
saying, Thou shalt *s* die .... Jer 26:8
I have *s* heard Ephraim .... Jer 31:18
s have mercy upon him .... Jer 31:20
not escape..but shalt *s* be ..... Jer 34:3
Chaldeans shall *s* depart ...... Jer 37:9
not *s* put me to death? .... Jer 38:15
will *s* perform our vows .... Jer 44:25
s accomplish your vows .... Jer 44:25
and *s* perform your vows ...... Jer 44:25
S as Tabor is among .... Jer 46:18
S the least of the flock .... Jer 49:20
s..make their habitations ...... Jer 49:20
S the least of the flock .... Jer 50:45
s..make their habitation .... Jer 50:45
of recompenses shall *s* .... Jer 51:56
S against me is he turned ..... Lam 3:3
S, had I sent thee to them .... Ezek 3:6
not sin, he shall *s* live .... Ezek 3:21
s in the place where the king .. Ezek 17:16
he is just, he shall *s* live ...... Ezek 18:9
his father, he shall *s* live ...... Ezek 18:17
s live, he shall not die .... Ezek 18:21
he shall *s* deal with him .... Ezek 31:11
that he shall *s* live .... Ezek 33:13
s live, he shall not die .... Ezek 33:15
s they that are in the wastes ... Ezek 33:27
S in the fire of my jealousy ... Ezek 36:5
S in that day there shall .... Ezek 38:19
interpretation thereof *s* .... Dan 2:45
kingdom shall be *s* unto .... Dan 4:26
that which shall *s* be .... Hos 5:9
S the Lord God will do .... Amos 3:7
Israel shall *s* be led away ..... Amos 7:11
I will *s* assemble, O Jacob .... Mic 2:12
s come, it will not tarry .... Hab 2:3
S Moab shall be as Sodom .... Zeph 2:9
S thou also art one of .... Matt 26:73
sepulcher be made *s* until ..... Matt 27:64
made the sepulcher *s* .... Matt 27:66
S thou art one of them .... Mark 14:70
s say unto me this proverb .... Luke 4:23
s of this, that the kingdom .... Luke 10:11
we *s* that thou knowest .... John 16:30
known *s* that I came out ...... John 17:8
s that the judgment of God ... Rom 2:2
I am *s* that, when I come ..... Rom 15:29
S blessing I will bless .... Heb 6:14
soul, both *s* and stedfast ...... Heb 6:19
saith, *S* I come quickly .... Rev 22:20

SURETY—*certainty; guarantee; legal liability assumed for another's debt*

Descriptive of:
Certainty .... Gen 15:13
Guarantee .... Gen 43:9
Our Lord .... Heb 7:22

Features concerning:
Risks involved in .... Prov 11:15
Warning against .... Prov 6:1-5

[*also* SURETIES]
Shall I of a *s* bear a child ..... Gen 18:13
of a *s* she is thy wife .... Gen 26:9
servant became *s* for the ...... Gen 44:32
put me in a *s* with thee .... Job 17:3
Be *s* for thy servant for .... Ps 119:122
s in the presence of his .... Prov 17:18
that is *s* for a stranger .... Prov 20:16
them that are *s* for debts ...... Prov 22:26
that is *s* for a stranger .... Prov 27:13
know of a *s*, that the Lord .... Acts 12:11

SURETYSHIP—*legally liable for a debt*
he that hateth *s* is sure .... Prov 11:15

SURFEITING—*gluttonous indulgence*
Christ warns against ..... Luke 21:34

SURMISINGS—*imaginings or inferences*
strife railings, evil *s* 1Tim 6:4

SURNAME—*one's family name*

Descriptive of:
Simon Peter .... Acts 10:5, 32
John Mark .... Acts 12:12, 25
Judas Iscariot .... Luke 22:3
Judas Barsabas .... Acts 15:22
Joses Barnabas .... Acts 4:36
James and John Boanerges .... Mark 3:17

Figurative of God's:
Call of Gentiles .... Is 44:5
Sovereignty over kings ... Is 45:4

[*also* SURNAMED]
whose *s* was Thaddeus .... Matt 10:3
And Simon he *s* Peter .... Mark 3:16
Barsabas, who was *s* Justus .... Acts 1:23
Simon, which was *s* Peter ..... Acts 10:18
Simon, whose *s* is Peter .... Acts 11:13
John, whose *s* was Mark ...... Acts 15:37

SURPRISED—*unexpected; astonished*
hath *s* the hypocrites .... Is 33:14
the strongholds are *s* .... Jer 48:41
praise of the whole earth *s* .... Jer 51:41

SUSANCHITES (sōō'săn-kīts)—*inhabitants of Susa of Elam*
the *S*, the Dehavites, and ..... Ezra 4:9

SUSANNA (sū-zăn'ä)—*"lily"*
Believing woman ministering to Christ ... Luke 8:2, 3

SUSI (sū'sī)—*"Jehovah is swift or rejoicing"*
Mannassite spy .... Num 13:11

SUSPICION—*distrust of others*

Kinds of:
Unjustified .... Josh 22:9-31
Pretended .... Gen 42:7-12
Unsuspected .... John 13:21-28

Objects of:
Esau by Jacob .... Gen 32:3-12
Jeremiah by officials ..... Jer 37:12-15
Jews by Haman .... Esth 3:8, 9
Mary by Joseph .... Matt 1:18-25
Peter by a damsel .... Matt 26:69-74

SUSTENANCE—*nourishment; relief*
Israel by the Lord .... Neh 9:21
Elijah by ravens and a widow 1Kin 17:1-9
Believer by the Lord .... Ps 3:5

[*also* SUSTAIN, SUSTAINED]
and wine have I *s* him .... Gen 27:37
left no *s* for Israel, neither .... Judg 6:4
provided the king of *s* 2Sam 19:32
Lord, and he shall *s* thee ..... Ps 55:22
spirit of a man will *s* his ...... Prov 18:14
his righteousness, it *s* him ..... Is 59:16
our fathers found no *s* .... Acts 7:11

SWADDLING—*bandages; wrapping*
Figurative of Jerusalem .. Ezek 16:3, 4
Jesus wrapped in .... Luke 2:7

[*also* SWADDLED, SWADDLINGBAND]
thick darkness a *s* for it .... Job 38:9
I have *s* and brought up ...... Lam 2:22
babe wrapped in *s* clothes ..... Luke 2:12

SWALLOW—*a long-winged, migratory bird*
Nesting in the sanctuary . Ps 84:3
Noted for chattering ..... Is 38:14

SWALLOW—*to take through the mouth; engulf; overwhelm*

Applied miraculously to:
Aaron's rod .... Ex 7:12
Red Sea .... Ex 15:12
Earth .... Num 16:30-34
Great fish .... Jon 1:17

Applied figuratively to:
God's judgments .... Ps 21:9
Conquest .... Jer 51:34, 44
Captivity .... Hos 8:7, 8
Sorrow 2Cor 2:7
Resurrection .... Is 25:8

[*also* SWALLOWED, SWALLOWETH]
s them up together with .... Num 26:10
s them up, and their .... Deut 11:6
lest the king be *s* up 2Sam 17:16
thou *s* up the inheritance 2Sam 20:19
I should *s* up or destroy 2Sam 20:20
the robber *s* up their .... Job 5:5
my words are *s* up .... Job 6:3
till I *s* down my spittle? .... Job 7:19
He hath *s* down riches .... Job 20:15
and shall not *s* it down .... Job 20:18
surely he shall be *s* up .... Job 37:20
He *s* the ground with .... Job 39:24
Lord shall *s* them up in .... Ps 21:9
not say, We have *s* him .... Ps 35:25
O God: for man would *s* ...... Ps 56:1
enemies would daily *s* me ..... Ps 56:2
of him that would *s* me .... Ps 57:3
neither let the deep *s* me ..... Ps 69:15
the *s* a nest for herself .... Ps 84:3
The earth opened and *s* up .... Ps 106:17
they had *s* us up quick .... Ps 124:3
us *s* them up alive as the ...... Prov 1:12
the lips of a fool will *s* .... Eccl 10:12
they are *s* up of wine, they .... Is 28:7
that *s* thee up shall be far ..... Is 49:19
hath *s* me up like a dragon .... Jer 51:34
that which he hath *s* up .... Jer 51:44
Lord hath *s* up all the .... Lam 2:2
he hath *s* up Israel .... Lam 2:5
hath *s* up all her palaces ...... Lam 2:5
have *s* her up: certainly .... Lam 2:16
and *s* you up on every side .... Ezek 36:3
O ye that *s* up the needy ..... Amos 8:4
and they shall *s* down .... Obad 16
a great fish to *s* up Jonah ..... Jon 1:17
at a gnat, and *s* a camel ...... Matt 23:24
Death is *s* up in victory 1Cor 15:54
might be *s* up of life 2Cor 5:4
s up the flood which the ...... Rev 12:16

SWAN—*a long-necked aquatic bird*
Should be translated "horned owl" .... Lev 11:18
the great owl, and the *s* .... Deut 14:16

SWARE—*See* SWEARING

SWARM—*to mass together; a mass*

[*also* SWARMS]
shall be full of *s* of flies .... Ex 8:21
no *s* of flies shall be there ..... Ex 8:22
came a grievous *s* of flies ..... Ex 8:24
by reason of the *s* of flies ..... Ex 8:24
the *s* of flies may depart ...... Ex 8:29
he removed the *s* of flies ...... Ex 8:31
was *s* of bees and honey ...... Judg 14:8

SWEARING—*taking an oath*

Kinds of:
Proclamatory .... Ex 17:16
Protective .... Gen 21:23
Personal 1Sam 20:17
Purificatory .... Neh 13:25-30
Promissory .... Luke 1:73
Prohibited .... James 5:12

Of God, objects of:
God's purpose .... Is 14:24, 25
God's covenant .... Is 54:9, 10
Messianic priesthood ..... Heb 7:21
See OATHS

[*also* SWARE, SWAREST, SWEAR, SWEARETH, SWORN]
Abraham said, I will *s* .... Gen 21:24
because there they *s* both ..... Gen 21:31
have I *s*, saith the Lord ...... Gen 22:16
s to him concerning that ...... Gen 24:9
my master made me *s* .... Gen 24:37
I *s* unto Abraham thy .... Gen 26:3
Jacob *s* by the fear of his ..... Gen 31:53
And he said, *S* unto me ...... Gen 47:31
as he made thee *s* .... Gen 50:6
the land which he *s* to .... Gen 50:24

S

s to give it to Abraham ....Ex 6:8
s the children of Israel ....Ex 13:19
thou s by thine own self ......Ex 32:13
the land which I s unto ....Ex 33:1
and hear the voice of s ....Lev 5:1
if a soul s, pronouncing ....Lev 5:4
concerning it, and s falsely ....Lev 6:3
which he hath s falsely........Lev 6:5
land which thou s unto........Num 11:12
the land which he s unto ....Num 14:16
I s to make you dwell ....Num 14:30
s an oath to bind his soul .....Num 30:2
which I s unto Abraham ......Num 32:11
land which the Lord s ....Deut 1:8
land, which I s to give ....Deut 1:35
s that I should not go.........Deut 4:21
he s unto thy fathers..........Deut 6:10
and shalt s by his name ....Deut 6:13
he s unto our fathers ....Deut 6:23
the oath which he had s.......Deut 7:8
land which he s unto thy ......Deut 7:13
his covenant which he s ....Deut 8:18
I s unto their fathers..........Deut 10:11
hath s unto thy fathers ....Deut 19:8
Lord s unto our fathers ....Deut 26:3
as thou s unto our fathers .....Deut 26:15
hath s unto thy fathers ....Deut 29:13
Lord s unto thy fathers ....Deut 30:20
into the land which I s.........Deut 31:21
which I s unto Abraham ......Deut 34:4
I s unto their fathers..........Josh 1:6
s unto me by the Lord ....Josh 2:12
thou hast made us to s........Josh 2:20
Lord s that he would not .....Josh 5:6
land, which the Lord s.........Josh 5:6
of the congregation s ....Josh 9:15
princes..had s unto them ......Josh 9:18
And Moses s on that day .....Josh 14:9
he s unto their fathers ....Josh 21:44
the Lord had s unto them .....Judg 2:15
unto them, S unto me ....Judg 15:12
we have s by the Lord ....Judg 21:7
s unto the house of Eli 1Sam 3:14
And David s unto Saul 1Sam 24:22
S unto me by God, that........1Sam 30:15
the Lord hath s to David 2Sam 3:9
it was yet day, David s 2Sam 3:35
I s by the Lord, if thou 2Sam 19:7
Then the men of David s 2Sam 21:17
s unto thine handmaid 1Kin 1:13
s by the Lord thy God 1Kin 1:17
s, and said, As the Lord 1Kin 1:29
I s to him by the Lord 1Kin 2:8
make thee to s by the Lord ...1Kin 2:42
Gedaliah s to them, and to ...2Kin 25:24
upon him to make him s 2Chr 6:22
s unto the Lord with a 2Chr 15:14
had s with all their heart 2Chr 15:15
to s that they should do ....Ezra 10:5
to this word. And they s ......Ezra 10:5
in Judah s unto him ....Neh 6:18
He that s to his own hurt .....Ps 15:4
vanity, nor s deceitfully ....Ps 24:4
that s by him shall glory ......Ps 63:11
have I s by my holiness ......Ps 89:35
s unto David in thy truth? ....Ps 89:49
I s in my wrath that ....Ps 95:11
mad against me are s ....Ps 102:8
have s, and I will perform.....Ps 119:106
that s, as he that feareth ......Eccl 9:2
In that day shall he s ....Is 3:7
The Lord of hosts hath s......Is 14:24
and s to the Lord of hosts ....Is 19:18
bow, every tongue shall s .....Is 45:23
s by the name of the Lord ....Is 48:1
s that the waters of Noah .....Is 54:9
I s that I would not be........Is 54:9
s in the earth shall swear......Is 65:16
earth shall s by the God of....Is 65:16
shalt s, The Lord liveth ....Jer 4:2
s by them that are no gods ....Jer 5:7
adultery, and s falsely ....Jer 7:9
s by my name, The Lord......Jer 12:16
my people to s by Baal ....Jer 12:16
s by myself, saith the Lord ....Jer 22:5
because of s the land ....Jer 23:10
s to their fathers to give ......Jer 32:22
So Zedekiah the king s ....Jer 38:16
have s by my great name .....Jer 44:26
Lord of hosts hath s by ....Jer 51:14
I s unto thee, and entered ....Ezek 16:8
to them that have s oath ......Ezek 21:23
s by him that liveth for ....Dan 12:7
s, and lying, and killing ....Hos 4:2
nor s, The Lord liveth ....Hos 4:15
s falsely in making............Hos 10:4
Lord God hath s by his ....Amos 4:2
s by the excellency of.........Amos 8:7
hast s unto our fathers ....Mic 7:20
and that s by the Lord ....Zeph 1:5
that s shall be cut off as ......Zech 5:3
that s falsely by my name .....Zech 5:4
S not at all; neither by........Matt 5:34
shall s by the temple..........Matt 23:16
s by the gold of the temple....Matt 23:16
shall s by the altar, it ....Matt 23:18
s by the gift that is ....Matt 23:18
s by it, and by all things ......Matt 23:20
shall s by the temple..........Matt 23:21
s by it, and by him that.......Matt 23:21
s by the throne of God ....Matt 23:22
he to curse and to s ....Matt 26:74
he s unto her, Whatsoever ....Mark 6:23
began to curse and to s ....Mark 14:71
oath which he s to our ....Luke 1:73
God had s with an oath to ....Acts 2:30
So I s in my wrath, They .....Heb 3:11
As I have s in my wrath ......Heb 4:3
he could s by no greater ......Heb 6:13
greater, he s by himself ....Heb 6:13
men verily s by the greater ....Heb 6:16
s by him that liveth for ....Rev 10:6

SWEARERS—*those who make vows*
and against false s, and ....Mal 3:5

SWEAT—*perspiration*
Penalty of man's sin .....Gen 3:18, 19
Cause of, avoided ....Ezek 44:18
Of Jesus, in prayer ......Luke 22:44

SWEEP—*to remove with a brush; wipe out*

[*also* SWEEPING, SWEPT]
river of Kishon s them ....Judg 5:21
like a s rain that leaveth no ...Prov 28:3
will s it with the besom ....Is 14:23
hail shall s away the refuge....Is 28:17
thy valiant men s away? ......Jer 46:15
findeth it empty, s, and ....Matt 12:44
findeth it s and garnished .....Luke 11:25
a candle, and s the house .....Luke 15:8

SWEET—*something pleasing to the taste or smell; something personally pleasing*

Descriptive, literally, of:
Water ....Ex 15:25
Honey..................Judg 14:18
Incense ....Ex 25:6
Perfumes ....Esth 2:12

Descriptive, figuratively, of:
God's Law ....Ps 19:10
God's Word ....Ps 119:103
Spiritual fellowship ......Ps 55:14
Meditation ....Ps 104:34
Pleasant words ....Prov 16:24
Sleep ....Prov 3:24
Christians 2Cor 2:15
Christian service ....Eph 5:2

[*also* SWEETER, SWEETLY, SWEETNESS]
And the Lord smelled a s .....Gen 8:21
it is a s savor, an offering .....Ex 29:18
s savor before the Lord ....Ex 29:25
for a s savor, an offering ......Ex 29:41
s cinnamon half so much ......Ex 30:23
of s calamus two hundred .....Ex 30:23
Take unto thee s spices ....Ex 30:34
s spices with pure ....Ex 30:34
anointing oil..s incense ....Ex 35:8
anointing oil, and for the s....Ex 35:28
anointing oil, and the s ....Ex 39:38
s savor unto the ....Lev 1:9
s savor unto the Lord.........Lev 2:9
s savor unto the Lord.........Lev 3:5
of the altar of s incense ....Lev 4:7
the altar for a s savor.........Lev 6:15
sacrifice for a s savor ....Lev 8:21
his hands full of s incense .....Lev 16:12
the Lord for a s savor ....Lev 23:13
savor of your s odors ....Lev 26:31
light, and the s incense ....Num 4:16
s savor unto the Lord.........Num 15:7
s savor unto the Lord.........Num 15:14
s savor unto the Lord..........Num 18:17
mount Sinai for a s savor .....Num 28:6
burnt offering of a s savor ....Num 28:13
s savor unto the Lord..........Num 28:27
s savor unto the Lord..........Num 29:2
the Lord for a s savor ....Num 29:8
a s savor unto the Lord ....Num 29:36
Should I forsake my s ....Judg 9:11
the strong came forth s ....Judg 14:14
the s psalmist of Israel 2Sam 23:1
burn before him s incense 2Chr 2:4
bed..filled with s odors.........2Chr 16:14
s savors unto the God of......Ezra 6:10
the fat, and drink the s ....Neh 8:10
be s in his mouth.............Job 20:12
worm shall feed s on him .....Job 24:20
bind the s influences of ....Job 38:31
yea, s than honey to my ......Ps 119:103
my words; for they are s ......Ps 141:6
Stolen waters are s, and ......Prov 9:17
desire accomplished is s ....Prov 13:19
s of the lips increaseth ....Prov 16:21
Bread of deceit is s to a ......Prov 20:17
honeycomb, which is s.........Prov 24:13
the s of a man's friend by.....Prov 27:9
sleep of a..man is s...........Eccl 5:12
his fruit was s to my taste .....Song 2:3
with s smelling myrrh ....Song 5:5
bed of spices, as s flowers.....Song 5:13
dropping s smelling myrrh.....Song 5:13
goeth down s, causing ....Song 7:9
instead of s smell there shall ..Is 3:24
make s melody, sing many ....Is 23:16
own blood, as with s wine......Is 49:26
s cane from a far country? ....Jer 6:20
my sleep was s unto me ....Jer 31:26
my mouth as honey for s......Ezek 3:3
they made their s savor ....Ezek 20:28
oblation and s odors unto .....Dan 2:46
mountains shall drop s ....Amos 9:13
s wine, but shalt not drink ....Mic 6:15
had bought s spices ....Mark 16:1
an odor of a s smell ....Phil 4:18
same place s water ....James 3:11
in thy mouth s as honey ....Rev 10:9
in my mouth s as honey.......Rev 10:10

SWEET-SMELLING—*with pleasant aroma*
to God for a s savour ....Eph 5:2

SWELL—*to distend or puff up; expand in size, volume, or numbers; behave pompously*

[*also* SWELLED, SWELLING, SWELLINGS, SWOLLEN]
rot, and thy belly to s ....Num 5:21
belly shall s, and her thigh ....Num 5:27
neither did thy foot s ....Deut 8:4
old, and their feet s not.......Neh 9:21
mountains shake with the s....Ps 46:3
thou do in the s of Jordan? ...Jer 12:5
a lion from the s of Jordan....Jer 50:44
when he should have s.........Acts 28:6
backbitings, whisperings, s 2Cor 12:20
great s words of vanity........2Pet 2:18
speaketh great s swords ....Jude 16

SWEPT—*See* SWEEP

SWERVED—*turned aside*
which some having s have 1Tim 1:6

SWIFT—*quick*

[*also* SWIFTER, SWIFTLY]
as s as the eagle flieth ....Deut 28:49
they were s than eagles 2Sam 1:23
were as s as the roes upon 1Chr 12:8

days are *s* than a weaver's ....Job 7:6
passed away as the *s* ships ....Job 9:26
his word runneth very *s* ....Ps 147:15
be *s* in running to mischief ....Prov 6:18
shall come with speed *s* ....Is 5:26
We will ride upon the *s* ....Is 30:16
mules, and upon *s* beasts......Is 66:20
thou art a *s* dromedary ....Jer 2:23
horses are *s* than eagles ....Jer 4:13
perscutors are *s* than the ......Lam 4:19
caused to fly *s*, touched ....Dan 9:21
s and speedily will I ....Joel 3:4
shall perish from the *s* ....Amos 2:14
the chariot to the *s* beast......Mic 1:13
are *s* than the leopards........Hab 1:8
be a *s* witness against the .....Mal 3:5
feet are *s* to shed blood ....Rom 3:15
let every man be *s* to hear ....James 1:19
themselves *s* destruction.......2Pet 2:1

SWIM—*to propel oneself through water*
Miraculously, of iron 2Kin 6:6
Naturally, of people .....Acts 27:42, 43
Figuratively, of tears .....Ps 6:6

[*also* SWIMMEST, SWIMMETH]
spreadeth..his hands to *s* ......Is 25:11
that *s* spreadeth forth his......Is 25:11
the land wherein thou *s* ....Ezek 32:6
were risen, waters to *s* ....Ezek 47:5

SWINE—*hogs; pigs*

Features concerning:
Classed as unclean.......Lev 11:7, 8
Eating of, abominable ...Is 65:4
Caring of, a degradation .Luke 15:16
Herd of, drowned ....Matt 8:30-32

Figurative of:
Abominable things ......Is 65:4
False teachers 2Pet 2:22
Indiscrete woman........Prov 11:22
Reprobate ....Matt 7:6

[*also* SWINE'S]
the *s*, because it divideth ......Deut 14:8
as if he offered *s* blood ....Is 66:3
the midst, eating *s* flesh ....Is 66:17
a great herd of *s* feeding ......Mark 5:11
and entered into the *s* ....Mark 5:13
and also concerning the *s* .....Mark 5:16
a herd of many *s* feeding......Luke 8:32
into his fields to feed *s*........Luke 15:15

SWOLLEN—*See* SWELL

SWOON—*to faint*

[*also* SWOONED]
sucklings *s* in the streets ......Lam 2:11
they *s* as the wounded ....Lam 2:12

SWORD—*a weapon of war*

Described as:
Having haft and blade ...Judg 3:22
Worn in a sheath 1Sam 17:15
Fastened at the waist 2Sam 20:8

Used for:
Defense ....Luke 22:36, 38
Fighting in war ....Josh 6:21
Executing criminals 1Sam 15:33
Suicide ....Acts 16:27

Figurative of:
Divine retribution ....Deut 32:41
Divine victory ....Josh 5:13
God's judgment 1Chr 21:12
An adulteress ....Prov 5:3, 4
Anguish of soul ....Luke 2:35
State ....Rom 13:4
God's Word ....Eph 6:17

[*also* SWORDS]
a flaming *s* which turned ......Gen 3:24
captives taken with the *s* ......Gen 31:26
son with the edge of the *s*.....Gen 34:26
pestilence, or with the *s*.......Ex 5:3
I will draw my *s*, my hand ....Ex 15:9
me from the *s* of Pharaoh .....Ex 18:4
man his *s* by his side ....Ex 32:27
s go through your land........Lev 26:6
fall before you by the *s* ....Lev 26:8
will draw out a *s* after ....Lev 26:33
it were before a *s*, when ......Lev 26:37
this land, to fall by the *s* ......Num 14:3
slain with a *s* in the open .....Num 19:16
with the edge of the *s* ....Num 21:24
were a *s* in mine hand ....Num 22:29
Beor they slew with the *s* .....Num 31:8
city with the edge of the *s* ....Deut 13:15
with the edge of the *s* ....Deut 20:13
The *s* without, and terror .....Deut 32:25
and my *s* shall devour ....Deut 32:42
with the edge of the *s* ....Josh 6:21
fallen on the edge of the *s* ....Josh 8:24
of Israel slew with the *s*.......Josh 10:11
king thereof with the *s*........Josh 11:10
with the edge of the *s* ....Josh 11:12
of Israel slay with the *s* ....Josh 13:22
thy *s*, nor with thy bow ....Josh 24:12
with the edge of the *s* ....Judg 1:8
edge of the *s* before Barak ....Judg 4:15
upon the edge of the *s*........Judg 4:16
else save the *s* of Gideon .....Judg 7:14
s of the Lord, and of Gideon..Judg 7:20
thousand men that drew *s*.....Judg 8:10
Draw thy *s*, and slay me ......Judg 9:54
footmen that drew *s* ....Judg 20:2
thousand men that drew *s*.....Judg 20:17
men; all these drew the *s* .....Judg 20:35
men that drew the *s* ....Judg 20:46
with the edge of the *s* ....Judg 21:10
the Hebrews make them *s*......1Sam 13:19
was neither *s* nor spear 1Sam 13:22
with the edge of the *s* 1Sam 15:8
his *s* upon his armor 1Sam 17:39
Lord saveth not with *s* 1Sam 17:47
Philistine and took his *s*.......1Sam 17:51
thine hand spear or *s*? 1Sam 21:8
have neither brought my *s* 1Sam 21:8
gave him the *s* of Goliath 1Sam 22:10
he with the edge of the *s* 1Sam 22:19
with the edge of the *s* 1Sam 22:19
ye on every man his *s* 1Sam 25:13
girded on every man his *s*.....1Sam 25:13
David also girded on his *s*.....1Sam 25:13
Draw thy *s*, and thrust me 1Sam 31:4
Saul took a *s*, and fell 1Sam 31:4
they were fallen by the *s* 2Sam 1:12
the *s* of Saul returned not 2Sam 1:22
Shall the *s* devour for ever? ...2Sam 2:26
for the *s* devoureth one as 2Sam 11:25
the Hittite with the *s* 2Sam 12:9
hast slain him with the *s* 2Sam 12:9
city with the edge of the *s* 2Sam 15:14
people that day than the *s* 2Sam 18:8
being girded with a new *s* 2Sam 21:16
men that drew the *s* 2Sam 24:9
slay his servant with the *s* 1Kin 1:51
and slew them with the *s*......1Kin 2:32
king said, Bring me a *s* 1Kin 3:24
brought a *s* before the king ...1Kin 3:24
slain..prophets with the *s*......1Kin 19:10
escapeth the *s* of Hazael 1Kin 19:17
escapeth from the *s* of Jehu ...1Kin 19:17
hundred men that drew *s* 2Kin 3:26
taken captive with thy *s*.......2Kin 6:22
with the edge of the *s* 2Kin 10:25
slew Ahtaliah with the *s* 2Kin 11:20
sons smote him with the *s*.....2Kin 19:37
to bear buckler and *s* 1Chr 5:18
Draw thy *s* and thrust me 1Chr 10:4
So Saul took a *s* and fell 1Chr 10:4
thousand men that drew *s*.....1Chr 21:5
thousand men that drew *s*.....1Chr 21:5
a drawn *s* in his hand 1Chr 21:16
his *s* again into the sheath.....1Chr 21:27
evil cometh upon us as the *s* ..2Chr 20:9
him be slain with the *s*........2Chr 23:14
fathers have fallen by the *s* 2Chr 29:9
slew..men with the *s* in 2Chr 36:17
to the *s*, to captivity and ......Ezra 9:7
their families with their *s*......Neh 4:13
every one had his *s* girded ....Neh 4:18
with the stroke of the *s* ....Esth 9:5
with the edge of the *s* ....Job 1:15
from the power of the *s*.......Job 5:20
be ye afraid of the *s* for.......Job 19:29
punishments of the *s*..........Job 19:29
multiplied, it is for the *s* ......Job 27:14
from perishing by the *s* ....Job 33:18
turneth..back from the *s* ......Job 39:22
s of him that layeth at ....Job 41:26
turn not, he will whet his *s*....Ps 7:12
Deliver my soul from the *s*....Ps 22:20
s shall enter into their own ....Ps 37:15
possession by their own *s* .....Ps 44:3
Gird thy *s* upon thy thigh .....Ps 45:3
yet were they drawn *s* ....Ps 55:21
They shall fall by the *s*........Ps 63:10
bow, the shield, and the *s*.....Ps 76:3
Their priests fell by the *s* .....Ps 78:64
servant from the hurtful *s* .....Ps 144:10
two-edged *s* in their hand .....Ps 149:6
like the piercing of a *s* ....Prov 12:18
whose teeth are as *s* ....Prov 30:14
hold *s*, being expert war ......Song 3:8
man hath his *s* upon his thigh .Song 3:8
be devoured with the *s*........Is 1:20
beat their *s* into plowshares ...Is 2:4
men shall fall by the *s* ....Is 3:25
thrust through with a *s*........Is 14:19
from the drawn *s* and ....Is 21:15
strong *s* shall punish ....Is 27:1
Assyrian fall with the *s* ....Is 31:8
the *s* not of a mean man ......Is 31:8
he shall flee from the *s* ....Is 31:8
s of the Lord is filled ....Is 34:6
smote him with the *s* ....Is 37:38
my mouth like a sharp *s* ......Is 49:2
will I number you to the *s* ....Is 65:12
your own *s* hath devoured.....Jer 2:30
shall we see *s* nor famine .....Jer 5:12
for the *s* of the enemy ....Jer 6:25
men shall die by the *s* ....Jer 11:22
consume them by the *s* ....Jer 14:12
S and famine shall not be .....Jer 14:15
s and famine shall those ......Jer 14:15
of the famine and the *s* ....Jer 14:16
behold the slain with the *s* ....Jer 14:18
s to slay and the dogs to .....Jer 15:3
be consumed by the *s*.........Jer 16:4
blood by the force of the *s* ....Jer 18:21
men be slain by the *s* ....Jer 18:21
fall by the *s* of their enemies ..Jer 20:4
slay them with the *s* ....Jer 20:4
s and from the famine ....Jer 21:7
with the edge of the *s* ....Jer 21:7
And I will send the *s*, the .....Jer 24:10
s that I will send among ....Jer 25:16
call for a *s* upon all the ....Jer 25:29
who slew him with the *s* ......Jer 26:23
thy people, by the *s* ....Jer 27:13
persecute them with the *s* .....Jer 29:18
because of the *s* and of ....Jer 32:24
the mounts and by the *s* ......Jer 33:4
to the *s*, to the pestilence .....Jer 34:17
shalt not fall by the *s* ....Jer 39:18
the *s*, which ye feared ....Jer 42:16
that ye shall die by the *s* ......Jer 42:22
s and by the famine ....Jer 44:12
been consumed by the *s* ......Jer 44:18
number that escape the *s*......Jer 44:28
s shall devour round about ....Jer 46:14
from the oppressing *s* ....Jer 46:16
the *s* shall pursue thee ....Jer 48:2
and I will send the *s* after .....Jer 49:37
A *s* is upon the Chaldeans ....Jer 50:35
A *s* is upon the liars; and .....Jer 50:36
s is upon her mighty men .....Jer 50:36
A *s* is upon their horses.......Jer 50:37
a *s* is upon her treasures ......Jer 50:37
abroad the *s* bereaveth, at ....Lam 1:20
that be slain with the *s*........Lam 4:9
I will draw out a *s* after.......Ezek 5:2
part shall fall by the *s* ....Ezek 5:12
I will draw out a *s* after.......Ezek 5:12
I will bring a *s* upon you ......Ezek 6:3
fall by the *s*, by the famine....Ezek 6:11
The *s* is without and the ......Ezek 7:15

S

Ye have feared the *s*; and .....Ezek 11:8
bring a *s* upon you, saith......Ezek 11:8
draw out the *s* after them .....Ezek 12:14
I bring a *s* upon that land .....Ezek 14:17
S, go through the land ....Ezek 14:17
thee through with their *s* ......Ezek 16:40
bands shall fall by the *s* ....Ezek 17:21
my *s* go forth out of his........Ezek 21:4
Say, A *s*, a *s* is sharpened .....Ezek 21:9
terrors by reason of the *s* .....Ezek 21:12
let the *s* be doubled the.......Ezek 21:14
time, the *s* of the slain; it .....Ezek 21:14
s of the great men that are ....Ezek 21:14
s of the king of Babylon ......Ezek 21:19
The *s*, the *s* is drawn ....Ezek 21:28
remnant shall fall by the *s*.....Ezek 23:25
Dedan shall fall by the *s* ......Ezek 25:13
slay with the *s*..daughters .....Ezek 26:8
s against the beauty of ....Ezek 28:7
in the midst of her by the *s* ...Ezek 28:23
s shall come upon Egypt ......Ezek 30:4
they fall in it by the *s*.........Ezek 30:6
make it strong to hold the *s* ...Ezek 30:21
and put my *s* in his hand......Ezek 30:24
that be slain with the *s*........Ezek 31:17
brandish my *s* before them ....Ezek 32:10
By the *s* of the mighty will ....Ezek 32:12
that are slain by the *s*.........Ezek 32:20
slain by the *s* ....Ezek 32:21
slain, fallen by the *s* ....Ezek 32:23
slain by the *s* ....Ezek 32:26
that were slain by the *s* ....Ezek 32:29
his army slain by the *s* ....Ezek 32:31
I bring the *s* upon a land .....Ezek 33:2
s come and take him away ....Ezek 33:4
watchman see the *s* come .....Ezek 33:6
s come and take any person ...Ezek 33:6
wastes shall fall by the *s* ......Ezek 33:27
that are slain with the *s*........Ezek 35:8
all of them handling *s*.........Ezek 38:4
call for a *s* against him........Ezek 38:21
so fell they all by the *s* ....Ezek 39:23
yet they shall fall by the *s*.....Dan 11:33
save them by bow, nor by *s* ...Hos 1:7
princes shall fall by the *s*......Hos 7:16
they shall fall by the *s* ....Hos 13:16
when they fall upon the *s* .....Joel 2:8
Beat your plowshares into *s* ...Joel 3:10
pursue..brother with the *s*.....Amos 1:11
have I slain with the *s* ....Amos 4:10
Jeroboam shall die by the *s* ...Amos 7:11
the last of them with the *s* ....Amos 9:1
of my people..die by the *s* ....Amos 9:10
not lift up a *s* against ....Mic 4:3
beat their *s* into plowshares ...Mic 4:3
will I give up to the *s*.........Mic 6:14
s shall devour thy young lions .Nah 2:13
s shall cut thee off, it ....Nah 3:15
ye shall be slain by my *s* ......Zeph 2:12
one of the *s* of his brother ....Hag 2:22
as the *s* of a mighty man ......Zech 9:13
O *s*, against my shepherd .....Zech 13:7
not to send peace but a *s* .....Matt 10:34
a great multitude with *s*.......Matt 26:47
Put up again thy *s* into his ....Matt 26:52
for all they that take the *s* ....Matt 26:52
shall perish with the *s*.........Matt 26:52
as against a thief with *s* ....Matt 26:55
a great multitude with *s*.......Mark 14:43
that stood by drew a *s* ....Mark 14:47
fall by the edge of the *s*.......Luke 21:24
shall we smite with the *s*? .....Luke 22:49
as against a thief, with *s* .....Luke 22:52
Simon Peter having a *s* ....John 18:10
Peter, Put up thy *s* into ....John 18:11
killed James..with the *s* ....Acts 12:2
nakedness or peril, or *s*? ......Rom 8:35
sharper than any two-edged *s*..Heb 4:12
were slain with the *s*..........Heb 11:37
went a sharp two-edged *s* .....Rev 1:16
with the *s* of my mouth ....Rev 2:16
kill with *s* and with hunger ....Rev 6:8
he that killeth with the *s*......Rev 13:10
must be killed with the *s* ......Rev 13:10
out of his mouth..sharp *s* .....Rev 19:15
were slain with the *s*..........Rev 19:21
s proceeded out of his ....Rev 19:21

SWORN—*See* **SWEARING**

SYCAMINE—*the black mulberry*
Referred to by Jesus.....Luke 17:6

SYCAMORE—*a fig-bearing tree (not the same as the American sycamore)*
Overseers appointed to care for..............1Chr 27:28
Abundant in Palestine ...1Kin 10:27
Amos, a gatherer of .....Amos 7:14
Zacchaeus climbs up .....Luke 19:4

[*also* SYCOMORE, SYCOMORES]
made he as the *s* trees 2Chr 1:15
made he as the *s* trees 2Chr 9:27
and their *s* trees with frost ....Ps 78:47
the *s* are cut down, but we ....Is 9:10

SYCHAR (sī'kär)—*"end"*
City of Samaria; Jesus talks to woman near ...John 4:5-39

SYCHEM (sī'kĕm)—*"shoulder, ridge"*
were carried over into *s*.......Acts 7:16

SYENE (sī-ē'nē)—*"a bush"*
An Egyptian city ....Ezek 29:10; Ezek 30:6

SYMBOLS—*a word, object, or action which stands for something else; representative of spiritual reality or truth in Scripture*

Of things:
Names..................Is 7:3, 14
Numbers................Rev 13:18
Garments ....Zech 3:3-9
Metals..................1Cor 3:12
Animals ....Dan 7:1-8

Of acts (gestures):
Tearing:
Mantle 1Sam 15:27, 28
Garment...............1Kin 11:30-32
Veil ....Matt 27:51
Wearing a yoke ....Jer 27:2-12
Buying a field ....Jer 32:6-15
Boring the ear ....Ex 21:6
Surrendering the shoe....Ruth 4:7
Going naked ....Is 20:2, 3

Of spiritual truths:
Bow—God's covenant ...Gen 9:12, 13
Circumcision—God's covenant............Gen 17:1-14; Rom 4:11
Passover—Christ ....Ex 12:3-28; 1Cor 5:7
Mercy seat—Christ ......Ex 25:17-22; Rom 3:25
Rock—Christ 1Cor 10:4
Blood sprinkled—Christ's blood...............Ex 12:21, 22; 1Pet 1:18, 19
Bronze serpent—Christ ..Num 21:8, 9; John 3:14
Lamb—Christ...........John 1:29
Bread and wine—the new covenant ....Matt 26:26-28; 1Cor 11:23-29

SYMPATHY—*sharing the feelings or experiences of another*

Manifested in:
Bearing others' burdens ..Gal 6:2; Heb 13:3
Expressing sorrow ....John 11:19-33
Offering help in need ....Luke 10:33-35
Helping the weak........Acts 20:35

Expressed by:
Servant for a prophet ....Jer 38:7-13
King for a king..........2Sam 10:2
A maid for a general 2Kin 5:1-4
Old man for a king 2Sam 19:31-39
Pagan for a Jew ....Dan 6:18-23

SYNAGOGUE (sy̆n'ä-gŏg)—*"gathering; congregation"—a house of worship for Jews following the Exile in Babylon*

Organization of:
Under elders ....Luke 7:3-5
Ruler in charge ....Mark 5:22
Attendant...............Luke 4:17, 20
Chief seats of, coveted ...Matt 23:6
Expulsion from ....John 9:22, 34

Purposes of, for:
Prayer.................Matt 6:5
Reading Scripture ....Acts 13:15
Hearing expositions......Acts 13:14, 15
Discipline...............Acts 9:2

Christ's relation to:
Teaches often in.........John 18:20
Worships in ....Luke 4:16-21
Performs miracles in .....Matt 12:9, 10
Expelled from ....Luke 4:22-30

[*also* SYNAGOGUE'S, SYNAGOGUES]
burned up all the *s* of God ....Ps 74:8
teaching in their *s*, and ....Matt 4:23
teaching in their *s*, and ....Matt 9:35
will scourge you in their *s*.....Matt 10:17
he taught them in their *s*......Matt 13:54
the chief seats in the *s* ....Matt 23:6
shall ye scourge in your *s* .....Matt 23:34
day he entered into the *s* .....Mark 1:21
were come out of the *s* ....Mark 1:29
he preached in their *s*.........Mark 1:39
entered again into the *s* ....Mark 3:1
one of the rulers of the *s* ......Mark 5:22
the ruler of the *s* house ....Mark 5:35
unto the ruler of the *s*, Be ....Mark 5:36
house of the ruler of the *s* ....Mark 5:38
he began to teach in the *s*.....Mark 6:2
the chief seats in the *s* ....Mark 12:39
in the *s* ye shall be beaten ....Mark 13:9
he taught in their *s*, being.....Luke 4:15
in the *s* there was a man ......Luke 4:33
he arose out of the *s*, and.....Luke 4:38
he entered into the *s* and .....Luke 6:6
he was a ruler of the *s*........Luke 8:41
the ruler of the *s* house ....Luke 8:49
uppermost seats in the *s* ......Luke 11:43
they bring you unto the *s* .....Luke 12:11
teaching in one of the *s* ....Luke 13:10
ruler of the *s* answered ....Luke 13:14
delivering you up to the *s* .....Luke 21:12
things said he in the *s* ....John 6:59
should be put out of the *s*.....John 12:42
shall put you out of the *s* .....John 16:2
arose certain of the *s* ....Acts 6:9
the *s* of the Libertines ....Acts 6:9
preached Christ in the *s*.......Acts 9:20
the word of God in the *s* .....Acts 13:5
Jews were gone out of the *s*...Acts 13:42
being read in the *s* every......Acts 15:21
where was a *s* of the Jews.....Acts 17:1
in the *s* with the Jews.........Acts 17:17
house joined hard to the *s* ....Acts 18:7
the chief ruler of the *s*........Acts 18:17
to speak boldly in the *s* ....Acts 18:26
beat in every *s* them that .....Acts 22:19
in the *s*, nor in the city ....Acts 24:12
but are the *s* of Satan.........Rev 2:9

SYNTYCHE (sĭn'tĭ-chē)—*"fortunate"*
Philippian woman exhorted by Paul ......Phil 4:2

SYRACUSE (sĭr'ä-kūs)—*"that draws violently"—a city on the east coast of Sicily*
Visited by Paul..........Acts 28:12

SYRIA (sĭr'ĭ-ä)—*"the Aramaeans"—the nation to the north and east of Israel*
Descendants of Aram, Shem's son ....Gen 10:22
Related to the Hebrews ..Deut 26:5
Intermarriage of, with Hebrews............Gen 24:4, 10-67
Called Syrians...........2Sam 10:11
Speak Syriac (Aramaic) ..Dan 2:4
Idolatrous..............2Kin 5:18
Subdued by David 2Sam 8:11-13
Elijah anointed king over.1Kin 19:15
Army of, routed.........2Kin 7:5-7
Joined Israel against Jerusalem............2Kin 16:5

Taken captive by Assyria . 2Kin 16:9
Destruction of, foretold . . Is 17:1-3
Governed by Romans . . . . Luke 2:2
Gospel preached to . . . . . . Acts 15:23, 41

[*also* SYRIANS]
the *S* of Padan-aram . . . . Gen 25:20
the sister to Laban the *S* . . . . . . Gen 25:20
unawares to Laban the *S* . . . . . . Gen 31:20
God came to Laban the *S* . . . . . Gen 31:24
S of Damascus came to 2Sam 8:5
David slew of the *S* two 2Sam 8:5
put garrisons in *S* of 2Sam 8:6
hired the *S* of Beth-rehob 2Sam 10:6
and the *S* of Zoba, twenty 2Sam 10:6
in array against the *S* 2Sam 10:9
the battle against the *S* 2Sam 10:13
the *S* saw that they were 2Sam 10:15
S set themselves in array 2Sam 10:17
the *S* fled before Israel 2Sam 10:18
hundred chariots of the *S* 2Sam 10:18
I abode at Geshur in *S* 2Sam 15:8
and for the kings of *S* 1Kin 10:29
son of Hezlon, king of *S* 1Kin 15:18
Ben-hadad the king of *S* 1Kin 20:1
S fled; and Israel pursued 1Kin 20:20
king of *S* will come up 1Kin 20:22
Ben-hadad numbered the *S* 1Kin 20:26
S have said, The Lord 1Kin 20:28
without war between *S* 1Kin 22:1
shalt thou push the *S* 1Kin 22:11
king of *S* commanded his 1Kin 22:31
the host of the king of *S* 2Kin 5:1
given deliverance unto *S* 2Kin 5:1
spared Naaman this *S* 2Kin 5:20
king of *S* warred against 2Kin 6:8
bands of *S* came no more 2Kin 6:23
king of *S* gathered all 2Kin 6:24
unto the host of the *S* 2Kin 7:4
host of the *S* to hear 2Kin 7:6
what the *S* have done to 2Kin 7:12
the *S* had cast away 2Kin 7:15
Ben-hadad the king of *S* 2Kin 8:7
thou shalt be king over *S* 2Kin 8:13
the *S* wounded Joram 2Kin 8:28
against Hazael king of *S* 2Kin 8:29
wounds which the *S* had 2Kin 9:15
with Hazael king of *S* 2Kin 9:15
sent it to Hazael king of *S* 2Kin 12:18
king of *S* oppressed them 2Kin 13:4
of deliverance from *S* 2Kin 13:17
shalt smite the *S* in Aphek 2Kin 13:17
then hadst thou smitten *S* 2Kin 13:19
now thou shalt smite *S* 2Kin 13:19
So Hazael king of *S* died 2Kin 13:24
Judah Rezin the king of *S* 2Kin 15:37
Rezin king of *S* recovered 2Kin 16:6
recovered Elath to *S* and 2Kin 16:6
hands of the *S* and bands 2Kin 24:2
the *S* of Damascus came 1Chr 18:5
David slew of the *S* two 1Chr 18:5
in array against the *S* 1Chr 19:10
the *S* unto the battle 1Chr 19:14
S saw that they were put 1Chr 19:16
S that were beyond the 1Chr 19:16
the *S* fled before Israel 1Chr 19:18
David slew of the *S* seven 1Chr 19:18
the kings of *S*, by their 2Chr 1:17
relied on the king of *S* 2Chr 16:7
king of *S* escaped out of 2Chr 16:7
king of *S* had commanded 2Chr 18:30
his chariot against the *S* 2Chr 18:34
against Hazael king of *S* 2Chr 22:5
host of *S* came up against 2Chr 24:23
army of the *S* came with a 2Chr 24:24
gods of the kings of *S* 2Chr 28:23
letter was written in the *S* . . . . . Ezra 4:7
interpreted in the *S* tongue . . . . Ezra 4:7
Rezin the king of *S*, and . . . . . . Is 7:1
anger of Rezin with *S* . . . . Is 7:4
Because *S*, Ephraim, and . . . . . . Is 7:5
the head of *S* is Damascus . . . . Is 7:8
S before, and the . . . . Is 9:12
servant in the *S* language . . . . . Is 36:11
fear of the army of the *S* . . . . . Jer 35:11
of the daughters of *S* . . . . Ezek 16:57
fled into the country of *S* . . . . . Hos 12:12
S shall go into captivity . . . . Amos 1:5
and the *S* from Kir? . . . . Amos 9:7
and sailed thence into *S* . . . . Acts 18:18
was about to sail into *S* . . . . Acts 20:3
sailed into *S* and landed . . . . . . Acts 21:3
came into the regions of *S* . . . . Gal 1:21

SYRIAC—*language based on an Aramaic dialect*
Chaldeans to the king in *S* . . . . Dan 2:4

SYRIA-DAMASCUS (sĭr′ĭ-ä-dä-măs′kŭs)—*Damascus of Syria*
David put garrisons in *S* 1Chr 18:6

SYRIA-MAACHAH (sĭr′ĭ-ä-mā′ä-kä)
out of *S* and out of Zobah 1Chr 19:6

SYROPHOENICIAN (sī′rō-fĭ-nĭsh′ăn)—*an inhabitant of Phoenicia*
Daughter of, freed of demon . . . . Mark 7:25-31

SYSTEM—*an orderly method or procedure*
Orderly writing . . . . Luke 1:3
Governing people . . . . Ex 18:13-27
Church government . . . . . . Acts 6:1-7
Priestly ministry . . . . Luke 1:8, 9
Giving 1Cor 16:1, 2

T

TAANACH (tā′ä-năk)—*"who humbles thee"*
Canaanite city conquered by Joshua . . . . Josh 12:21
Assigned to Manasseh . . . Josh 17:11
Assigned to Kohathite Levites . . . . Josh 21:25
Canaanites not expelled from . . . . Josh 17:12, 13
Site of Canaanite defeat . Judg 5:19-22

nor *T* and her towns nor . . . . . . Judg 1:27
pertained *T* and Megiddo 1Kin 4:12
T and her towns, Megiddo 1Chr 7:29

TAANATH-SHILOH (tā-ä-năth-shī′lō)—*"breaking down a fig tree"*
City of Ephraim . . . . Josh 16:5, 6

TABBAOTH (tă-bā′ŏth)—*"spots; rings"*
Ancestor of a Nethinim family . . . . Ezra 2:43

TABBATH (tăb′äth)—*"celebrated"*
Refuge of Midianites . . . . Judg 7:22

TABEEL (tā′bĕ-ĕl)—*"God is good"*
Persian official . . . . Ezra 4:7
Father of a puppet king put forth by Rezin and Pekah . . . . Is 7:1, 6

TABERAH (tăb′ĕ-rä)—*"burning"*
Israelite camp; fire destroys many here . . . . Num 11:1-3

TABERING—*drumming (a tabret)*
Beating the breasts in sorrow . . . . Nah 2:7

TABERNACLE—*the tent where God met with His people after the Exodus*

Descriptive of:
Moses' administrative office . . . . Ex 33:7-11
Structure erected at Sinai . Ex 40:2, 35-38
Portable shrine containing an idol . . . . Acts 7:43
Tent prepared for the ark by David 1Chr 16:1-43
Lord's incarnate Word . . . John 1:14
Heavenly prototype . . . . . . Heb 8:2, 5; Heb 9:11, 24
Holy city . . . . Rev 21:3

Sinaitic, constructed:
By divine revelation . . . . . Ex 25:27; Heb 8:5
By craftsmen inspired by the Spirit . . . . Ex 31:1-11
Out of contributions willingly supplied . . . . . . Ex 25:1-9
For the manifestation of God's glory . . . . Ex 25:8; Ex 29:42, 43
In two parts—holy place and Holiest of all . . . . Ex 26:33, 34; Heb 9:2-7
With surrounding court . . Ex 40:8
Within a year's time . . . . . Ex 40:2, 17

History of:
Set up at Sinai . . . . Ex 40:1-38
Sanctified and dedicated. . Ex 40:9-16
Moved by priests and Levites . . . . Num 4:1-49
Camped at Gilgal . . . . Josh 5:10, 11
Set up at Shiloh . . . . Josh 18:1
Israel's center of worship . Judg 18:31; 1Sam 1:3, 9, 24
Ark of, taken by Philistines 1Sam 4:1-22
Worship not confined to. . 1Sam 7:1, 2, 15-17
Located at Nob during Saul's reign 1Sam 21:1-6
Moved to Gibeon 1Kin 3:4
Ark of, brought to Jerusalem by David 2Sam 6:17
Brought to the Temple by Solomon 1Kin 8:1, 4, 5

Typology of, seen in:
Christ . . . . John 1:14
God's household . . . . Eph 2:19
Believer 1Cor 6:19
Heaven . . . . Heb 9:23, 24

Typology of, seen in Christ:
Candlestick—His enlightening us . . . . Rev 1:13
Sacred bread—His sustaining us . . . . John 6:27-59
Altar of incense—His intercession for us . . . John 17:1-26; Heb 7:25
Veil—His flesh . . . . Heb 10:20
Ark (wood and gold)—His humanity and deity. John 1:14

[*also* TABERNACLES]
shalt make the *t* with ten . . . . . . Ex 26:1
to be a covering upon the *t* . . . Ex 26:7
over the backside of the *t* . . . . . Ex 26:12
boards for the *t* of shittim . . . . . Ex 26:15
make the boards for the *t* . . . . . Ex 26:18
And for the sides of the *t* . . . . . Ex 26:22
of the one side of the *t* . . . . Ex 26:26
of the other side of the *t* . . . . . . Ex 26:27
boards of the side of the *t* . . . . . Ex 26:27
the side of the *t* toward the . . . Ex 26:35
make the court of the *t* . . . . Ex 27:9
In the *t* of the congregation . . . Ex 27:21
unto the *t* of..congregation . . . . Ex 28:43
door of the *t* of the . . . . Ex 29:4
door of the *t* of the . . . . Ex 29:11
the *t* of the congregation . . . . . . Ex 29:32
sanctify the *t* of the . . . . Ex 29:44
service of the *t* of the . . . . Ex 30:16
go into the *t* of the . . . . Ex 30:20
testimony in the *t* of the . . . . . . Ex 30:36
The *t*, his tent, and his . . . . Ex 35:11
The pins of the *t*, and the . . . . . Ex 35:18
wrought the work of the *t* . . . . . Ex 36:8
for the tent over the *t* . . . . Ex 36:14
all the boards of the *t* . . . . Ex 36:22
for the other side of the *t* . . . . . Ex 36:25
for the corners of the *t* . . . . Ex 36:28
of the other side of the *t* . . . . . . Ex 36:32
made an hanging for the *t* . . . . . Ex 36:37
the *t* of the congregation . . . . . . Ex 38:8
This is the sum of the *t* . . . . Ex 38:21
even of the *t* of testimony . . . . . Ex 38:21
and all the pins of the *t* . . . . Ex 38:31
t of the tent of the . . . . Ex 39:32
and the hanging for the *t* . . . . . Ex 39:38
the *t* of the congregation . . . . . . Lev 1:1
door of the *t* of the . . . . Lev 1:5
of the *t* of the congregation . . . Lev 3:2

before the *t* of the .... Lev 3:8
of the *t* of the congregation ... Lev 4:4
the *t* of the congregation ...... Lev 4:7
door of the *t* of the .... Lev 4:7
blood to the *t* of the .... Lev 4:16
in the *t* of the congregation ... Lev 4:18
door of the *t* of the .... Lev 4:18
court of the *t* of the .... Lev 6:16
the *t* of the congregation ...... Lev 6:30
door of the *t* of the .... Lev 8:3
door of the *t* of the .... Lev 8:31
before the *t* of the .... Lev 9:5
door of the *t* of the .... Lev 10:7
the *t* of the congregation ...... Lev 12:6
door of the *t* of the .... Lev 14:23
of the *t* of the congregation ... Lev 15:29
door of the *t* of the .... Lev 16:7
no man in the *t* of the .... Lev 16:17
come into the *t* of .... Lev 16:23
door of the *t* of the .... Lev 17:4
the Lord before the *t* of the ... Lev 17:4
of the *t* of the congregation ... Lev 19:21
feast of *t* for seven days .... Lev 23:34
the *t* of the congregation ...... Lev 24:3
will set my *t* among you .... Lev 26:11
Sinai in the *t* of the .... Num 1:1
Levites over the *t* of .... Num 1:50
shall bear the *t*, and all .... Num 1:50
encamp round about the *t* ..... Num 1:50
when the *t* setteth forward .... Num 1:51
when the *t* is to be pitched .... Num 1:51
about the *t* of testimony ...... Num 1:53
charge of the *t* of testimony ... Num 1:53
the *t* of the congregation ...... Num 2:2
before the *t* of the .... Num 3:7
to do the service of the *t* ...... Num 3:7
the *t* of the congregation ...... Num 3:8
to do the service of the *t* ...... Num 3:8
the *t* of the congregation ...... Num 3:25
be the *t* and the tent .... Num 3:25
door of the *t* of the .... Num 3:25
the side of the *t* southward .... Num 3:29
be the boards of the *t* .... Num 3:36
the *t* toward the east .... Num 3:38
before the *t* of the .... Num 3:38
is in the floor of the *t* .... Num 5:17
the *t* of the congregation ...... Num 6:10
door of the *t* of the .... Num 6:18
Moses..fully set up the *t* ...... Num 7:1
brought them before the *t* ..... Num 7:3
the *t* of the congregation ...... Num 7:5
gone into the *t* of the .... Num 7:89
before the *t* of the .... Num 8:9
Israel in the *t* of the .... Num 8:19
service of the *t* of the .... Num 8:24
brethren in the *t* of .... Num 8:26
And on the day that the *t* ..... Num 9:15
the cloud covered the *t* .... Num 9:15
was taken up from the *t* .... Num 9:17
tarried long upon the *t* .... Num 9:19
cloud tarried upon the *t* .... Num 9:22
door of the *t* of the .... Num 10:3
the *t* was taken down .... Num 10:17
forward, bearing the *t* .... Num 10:17
unto the *t* of..congregation .... Num 11:16
went not out unto the *t* .... Num 11:26
the *t* of the congregation ...... Num 12:4
departed from off the *t* .... Num 12:10
appeared in the *t* of .... Num 14:10
service of the *t* of the Lord .... Num 16:9
the *t* of the congregation ...... Num 16:19
get up from the *t* of Korah .... Num 16:27
the *t* of the congregation ...... Num 16:43
the *t* of the congregation ...... Num 17:4
Moses went into the *t* of ...... Num 17:8
minister before the *t* of .... Num 18:2
the *t* of the congregation ...... Num 18:4
for all the service of the ...... Num 18:4
service of the *t* of the .... Num 18:21
of the *t* of the congregation ... Num 18:23
the *t* of the congregation ...... Num 19:4
door of the *t* of the .... Num 20:6
O Jacob and thy *t*, O Israel ... Num 24:5
of the *t* of the congregation ... Num 25:6
door of the *t* of the .... Num 27:2
charge of the *t* of the Lord .... Num 31:30
the *t* of the congregation ...... Num 31:54
observe the feast of *t* seven ... Deut 16:13
of release in the feast of *t* .... Deut 31:10
yourselves in the *t* of .... Deut 31:14
the *t* of the congregation ...... Deut 31:14
Lord appeared in the *t* in ..... Deut 31:15
over the door of the *t* .... Deut 31:15
the *t* of the congregation ...... Josh 18:1
of the *t* of the congregation ... Josh 19:51
the Lord's *t* dwelleth .... Josh 22:19
door of the *t* of the 1Sam 2:22
in a tent and in a *t* 2Sam 7:6
horn of oil out of the *t* 1Kin 1:39
fled unto the *t* of the Lord 1Kin 2:28
came to the *t* of the Lord 1Kin 2:30
the *t* of the congregation 1Chr 6:32
of the gates of the *t* 1Chr 9:19
house of the *t*, by wards 1Chr 9:23
and from one *t* to another 1Chr 17:5
t of the Lord, which Moses 1Chr 21:29
shall no more carry the *t* 1Chr 23:26
the *t* of the congregation 2Chr 1:3
was at the *t* of the 2Chr 1:6
the *t* of the congregation 2Chr 5:5
vessels that were in the *t* 2Chr 5:5
Israel, for the *t* of witness 2Chr 24:6
kept also the feast of *t* .... Ezra 3:4
thy *t* shall be in peace .... Job 5:24
fire shall consume the *t* of ..... Job 15:34
shall be dark in his *t* .... Job 18:6
it shall dwell in his *t* .... Job 18:15
encamp round about my *t* ..... Job 19:12
him that is left in his *t* .... Job 20:26
secret of God was upon my *t* .. Job 29:4
the men of my *t* said not ...... Job 31:31
or the noise of his *t* .... Job 36:29
who shall abide in thy *t* .... Ps 15:1
hath he set a *t* for the sun .... Ps 19:4
In the secret of his *t* shall .... Ps 27:5
thy holy hill, and to thy *t* ..... Ps 43:3
will abide in thy *t* for ever .... Ps 61:4
In Salem also is his *t*, and ..... Ps 76:2
strength in the *t* of Ham ...... Ps 78:51
he forsook the *t* of Shiloh .... Ps 78:60
amiable are thy *t*, O Lord ..... Ps 84:1
not come into the *t* of my ..... Ps 132:3
We will go into his *t*; we ...... Ps 132:7
the *t* of the upright shall ..... Prov 14:11
a *t* for a shadow in the .... Is 4:6
in truth in the *t* of David ..... Is 16:5
a *t* that shall not be taken ..... Is 33:20
My *t* is spoiled, and all my .... Jer 10:20
t of the daughter of Zion ..... Lam 2:4
My *t* also shall be with them .. Ezek 37:27
plant the *t* of his palace .... Dan 11:45
thorns shall be in their *t* ...... Hos 9:6
the *t* of your Moloch and ..... Amos 5:26
to keep the feast of *t* .... Zech 14:16
scholar out of..*t* of Jacob ...... Mal 2:12
let us make there three *t* ...... Matt 17:4
make three *t*; one for thee .... Mark 9:5
make three *t*; one for thee .... Luke 9:33
Jews' feast of *t* was at hand ... John 7:2
fathers had the *t* of witness .... Acts 7:44
build again the *t* of David ..... Acts 15:16
our earthly house of this *t* 2Cor 5:1
we that are in this *t* do 2Cor 5:4
first *t* was yet standing .... Heb 9:8
sprinkled with blood..the *t* .... Heb 9:21
dwelling in *t* with Isaac .... Heb 11:9
to eat which serve the *t* .... Heb 13:10
as long as I am in this *t* 2Pet 1:13
I must put off this my *t* 2Pet 1:14
blaspheme his name..his *t* ..... Rev 13:6
temple of the *t* of the .... Rev 15:5
t of God is with men and he .. Rev 21:3

TABERNACLE, FEAST OF—*See* FEASTS, HEBREW

TABITHA (tăb'ĭ-thä)—*"gazelle"*
a certain disciple named *T* .... Acts 9:36
to the body said, *T*, arise ..... Acts 9:40

TABLE—*a piece of furniture; a tablet*

Descriptive of:
Article of furniture ...... Matt 15:27
For showbread .... Heb 9:2
Small writing tablet ...... Luke 1:63
Tablet of wood or stone. . Ex 24:12

Figurative of:
Human heart .... Prov 3:3
Christian's heart 2Cor 3:3
God's provision .... Ps 23:5
Intimate fellowship ...... Luke 22:30
Lord's Supper 1Cor 10:21

[*also* TABLES]
make a *t* of shittim wood ..... Ex 25:23
t may be borne with them ..... Ex 25:28
set the *t* without the veil ...... Ex 26:35
over against the *t* .... Ex 26:35
put the *t* on the north side ..... Ex 26:35
t of testimony, *t* of stone ..... Ex 31:18
t of the testimony were .... Ex 32:15
t were written on both their ... Ex 32:15
t were the work of God .... Ex 32:16
writing of God..upon the *t* .... Ex 32:16
t of stone like unto the .... Ex 34:1
I will write upon these *t* .... Ex 34:1
in the first *t*, which thou ...... Ex 34:1
two *t* of stone like unto .... Ex 34:4
his hand the two *t* of stone .... Ex 34:4
two *t* of testimony in .... Ex 34:29
made the *t* of shittim wood .... Ex 37:10
with gold, to bear the *t* .... Ex 37:15
The *t* and all the vessels ...... Ex 39:36
shalt bring in the *t* .... Ex 40:4
put the *t* in the tent .... Ex 40:22
pure *t* before the Lord .... Lev 24:6
shall be the ark, and the *t* ..... Num 3:31
he wrote them upon two *t* ..... Deut 4:13
to receive the *t* of stone .... Deut 9:9
t of the covenant which ...... Deut 9:9
gave me the two *t* of stone .... Deut 9:11
the *t* of the covenant .... Deut 9:11
took the two *t* and cast .... Deut 9:17
write on the *t* the words ...... Deut 10:2
first *t* which thou brakest ...... Deut 10:2
two *t* of stone like unto ...... Deut 10:3
the two *t* in mine hand .... Deut 10:3
put the *t* in the ark which ..... Deut 10:5
their meat under my *t* .... Judg 1:7
not unto the king's *t* 1Sam 20:29
shalt eat bread at my *t* 2Sam 9:7
he shall eat at my *t* 2Sam 9:11
did eat at thine own *t* 2Sam 19:28
of those that eat at thy *t* 1Kin 2:7
of gold and the *t* of gold 1Kin 7:48
save the two *t* of stone 1Kin 8:9
pass, as they sat at the *t* 1Kin 13:20
him there a bed, and a *t* 2Kin 4:10
for the *t* of showbread 1Chr 28:16
showbread, for every *t* 1Chr 28:16
silver for the *t* of silver 1Chr 28:16
He made also ten *t* 2Chr 4:8
in the ark save the two *t* 2Chr 5:10
the meat of his *t* and the 2Chr 9:4
and the showbread *t* 2Chr 29:18
at my *t* a hundred and .... Neh 5:17
should be set on thy *t* .... Job 36:16
preparest a *t* before me .... Ps 23:5
God furnish a *t* in the .... Ps 78:19
upon the *t* of thine heart ...... Prov 3:3
also furnished her *t* .... Prov 9:2
the king sitteth at his *t* .... Song 1:12
Prepare the *t*, watch in .... Is 21:5
prepare a *t* for that troop ..... Is 65:11
upon the *t* of their heart ...... Jer 17:1
of the gate were two *t* .... Ezek 40:39
and two *t* on that side .... Ezek 40:39
north gate, were two *t* .... Ezek 40:40
of the gate were two *t* .... Ezek 40:40
Four *t* were on this side .... Ezek 40:41
and four *t* on that side .... Ezek 40:41
eight *t*, whereupon they .... Ezek 40:41
upon the *t* was the flesh .... Ezek 40:43
t that is before the Lord ...... Ezek 41:22
and make it plain upon *t* ...... Hab 2:2

t of the money changers ......Matt 21:12
brazen vessels and of *t* ....Mark 7:4
dogs under the *t* eat of........Mark 7:28
is with me on the *t* ....Luke 22:21
and overthrew the *t*..........John 2:15
that sat at the *t* with him......John 12:2
word of God and serve *t* ......Acts 6:2
let their *t* be made a snare ....Rom 11:9
living God; not in *t* of stone...2Cor 3:3
the *t* and the showbread ......Heb 9:2
and the *t* of the covenant .....Heb 9:4

TABLETS—*pieces of gold jewelry or small perfume bottles worn around the neck*
earrings, and rings and *t* ......Ex 35:22
rings, earrings, and *t*..........Num 31:50
headbands, and the *t* ....Is 3:20

TABOR (tă'bĕr)—*"purity"*
1. Mountain on borders of Zebulun and Issachar. .Josh 19:12, 22
Great among mountains. .Jer 46:18
Scene of rally against Sisera .... Judg 4:6, 12, 14
2. Town of Zebulun 1Chr 6:77
3. Oak of, near Ramah 1Sam 10:3

the coast reacheth to *T* ....Josh 19:22
draw toward mount *T*..........Judg 4:6
went down from mount *T* .....Judg 4:14
come to the plain of *T* 1Sam 10:3
T with her suburbs 1Chr 6:77
T and Hermon shall rejoice ...Ps 89:12
T is among the mountains .....Jer 46:18
a net spread upon *T* ....Hos 5:1

TABRET—*a musical instrument (timbrel)*
Used by:
Prophets 1Sam 10:5
People.................Gen 31:27

[*also* TABRETS]
with *t* and with harp? ....Gen 31:27
t, and a pipe, and a harp 1Sam 10:5
to meet king Saul, with *t*......1Sam 18:6
aforetime I was as a *t*.........Job 17:6
the *t*, and pipe, and wine .....Is 5:12
The mirth of *t* ceaseth ....Is 24:8
be adorned with thy *t*.........Jer 31:4
workmanship of thy *t* ....Ezek 28:13

TABRIMMON (tăb'rĭm-ŏn)—*"(the god) Rimmon is good"*
Father of Ben-hadad 1Kin 15:18

TACHES—*hooks or clasps*
Couplings for curtains....Ex 26:6, 11, 33

his *t*, and his boards ....Ex 35:11
he made fifty *t* of gold ....Ex 36:13
unto another with the *t* ....Ex 36:13
made fifty *t* of brass to........Ex 36:18
furniture, his *t*, his boards .....Ex 39:33

TACHMONITE (tăk'mō-nīt)—*"wise"*
Descriptive of one of David's heroes 2Sam 23:8
Same as Hachmonite in . .1Chr 11:11

TACKLING—*ropes, cord, line*
Ship's ropes ....Is 33:23
All of a ship's removable gear ....Acts 27:19

TACTFULNESS—*skill and grace in dealing with individuals and situations*
Manifested in:
Appeasing hatred........Gen 32:4, 5, 13-21
Settling disputes 1Kin 3:24-28
Obtaining one's wishes ...Esth 5:1-8; Esth 7:1-6

Illustrated by Christ, in:
Rebuking a Pharisee .....Luke 7:39-50
Teaching humility ....Mark 10:35-44
Forgiving a sinner........John 8:1-11
Rebuking His disciples ...John 21:15-23

TADMOR (tăd'môr)—*"bitterness"*
Trading center near Damascus 2Chr 8:4
A desert town 1Kin 9:18

TAHAN (tā'hăn)—*"graciousness"*
Ephraimite; founder of the Tahanites .... Num 26:35; 1Chr 7:25

TAHANITES—*of the tribe of Tahan*
Tahan, the family of the *T*.....Num 26:35

TAHATH (tā'hăth)—*"depression; humility"*
1. Kohathite Levite 1Chr 6:24
2, 3. Two descendants of Ephraim 1Chr 7:20
4. Israelite encampment ....Num 33:26, 27

TAHPANHES, TEHAPHNEHES (tä'păn-hēz, tĕ-hä'făn-hēz)—*"secret temptation"*
City of Egypt; refuge of fleeing Jews......... Jer 2:16; Jer 44:1; Ezek 30:18

came they even to *T* ....Jer 43:7
Lord unto Jeremiah in *T* ......Jer 43:8
of Pharaoh's house in *T* ....Jer 43:9
publish in Noph and in *T* ......Jer 46:14

TAHPENES (tä'pē-nēz)—*the wife of the pharoah who received Solomon's enemy, Hadad*
Egyptian queen 1Kin 11:19, 20

TAHREA (tä'rē-ä)—*"flight"*
Descendant of Saul 1Chr 9:41
Called Tarea 1Chr 8:33, 35

TAHTIM-HODSHI (tä-tĭm-hŏd'shī)—*"lowlands of Hodshi"*
Place visited by census-taking Joab 2Sam 24:6

TAIL—*the appendage at the rear end of animals*

[*also* TAILS]
and take it by the *t*...........Ex 4:4
the head, and not the *t* ....Deut 28:13
turned *t* to *t*, and put a ....Judg 15:4
the midst between two *t* ......Judg 15:4
moveth his *t* like a cedar ......Job 40:17
two *t* of these smoking ....Is 7:4
from Israel head and *t* ....Is 9:14
which the head or *t*, branch ...Is 19:15
t like unto scorpions ....Rev 9:10
were stings in their *t*..........Rev 9:10
mouth, and in their *t* ....Rev 9:19
t were like unto serpents ......Rev 9:19
his *t* drew the third part.......Rev 12:4

TAILORING—*the art of making clothes*
For Aaron's garments....Ex 39:1

TAKE—*to get possession*

[*also* TAKEN, TAKEST, TAKETH, TAKING, TOOKEST]
God had *t* from man..........Gen 2:22
for out of it wast thou *t*.......Gen 3:19
vengeance shall be *t* ....Gen 4:15
woman was *t* into............Gen 12:15
have *t* her to me to wife ......Gen 12:19
his brother was *t* captive ......Gen 14:14
t upon me to speak unto ......Gen 18:27
woman which thou hast *t*......Gen 20:3
had violently *t* away ....Gen 21:25
he that hath *t* venison.........Gen 27:33
t away thy blessing ....Gen 27:35
thou hast *t* my husband? ......Gen 30:15
Jacob hath *t* away all ....Gen 31:1
hath *t* from our father ....Gen 31:16
Rachel had *t* the images ....Gen 31:34
the water which thou *t* out ....Ex 4:9
hast thou *t* us away to die .....Ex 14:11
that *t* his name in vain ....Ex 20:7
shall not be *t* from it ....Ex 25:15
cloud was *t* up from over .....Ex 40:36
if the cloud were not *t* up .....Ex 40:37
the day that it was *t* up ....Ex 40:37
was *t* off from the bullock .....Lev 4:10
fat of the lamb is *t* away ......Lev 4:35
a thing *t* away by violence.....Lev 6:2
heave shoulder have I *t* ....Lev 7:34
hath *t* away the stones ....Lev 14:43
t from the children of.........Lev 24:8
t the Levites from among .....Num 3:12
have I *t* them unto me ....Num 8:16
cloud was *t* up from the.......Num 9:17
cloud was *t* up in the ....Num 9:21
that the cloud was *t* up ....Num 9:21
the cloud was *t* up from.......Num 10:11
not *t* one ass from them.......Num 16:15
I have *t* your brethren ....Num 18:6
t all..land out of his hand .....Num 21:26
sum of the prey that was *t* ....Num 31:26
servants have *t* the sum ....Num 31:49
t from the inheritance.........Num 36:3
inheritance be *t* away ....Num 36:4
the Lord hath *t* you ....Deut 4:20
that *t* his name in vain ....Deut 5:11
and hath not *t* her? ....Deut 20:7
hast *t* them captive ....Deut 21:10
a man hath *t* a wife...........Deut 24:1
man hath *t* a new wife ....Deut 24:5
wife which he hath *t*..........Deut 24:5
t a man's life to pledge ....Deut 24:6
have I *t* away aught ....Deut 26:14
t reward to slay an innocent ...Deut 27:25
shall be violently *t* away ......Deut 28:31
t of the accursed thing ....Josh 7:11
tribe which the Lord *t* ....Josh 7:14
tribe of Judah was *t* ....Josh 7:16
Zerah..of Judah, was *t*........Josh 7:18
when ye have *t* the city ....Josh 8:8
ambush had *t* the city ....Josh 8:21
how Joshua had *t* Ai..........Josh 10:1
Jerusalem, and had *t* it........Judg 1:8
Kirjath-sepher, and *t* it........Judg 1:12
journey that thou *t* shall ......Judg 4:9
Lord hath *t* vengeance for.....Judg 11:36
t the honey out of the ....Judg 14:9
because he had *t* his wife .....Judg 15:6
of silver..*t* from thee..........Judg 17:2
Ye have *t* away my gods ......Judg 18:24
the ark of God was *t* 1Sam 4:11
the ark of God was *t* 1Sam 4:19
for the ark of God is *t*........1Sam 4:22
cities..the Philistines had *t*.....1Sam 7:14
tribe of Benjamin was *t* 1Sam 10:20
the family of Matri was *t*......1Sam 10:21
the son of Kish was *t* 1Sam 10:21
whose ox have I *t*? 1Sam 12:3
or whose ass have I *t*? 1Sam 12:3
and Jonathan were *t* 1Sam 14:41
t away the reproach from 1Sam 17:26
t from before the Lord 1Sam 21:6
day when it was *t* away 1Sam 21:6
daughters, were *t* captives 1Sam 30:3
spoil that they had *t* 1Sam 30:16
t his wife to be thy wife.......2Sam 12:9
t the city of waters 2Sam 12:27
art *t* in thy mischief...........2Sam 16:8
t up between the heaven 2Sam 18:9
cannot be *t* with hands........2Sam 23:6
whom he had *t* to wife 1Kin 7:8
t hold upon other gods........1Kin 9:9
had gone up, and *t* Gezer 1Kin 9:16
as a man *t* away dung.........1Kin 14:10
saw that the city was *t* 1Kin 16:18
and also *t* possession? 1Kin 21:19
places were not *t* away 1Kin 22:43
I be *t* away from thee.........2Kin 2:9
Lord hath *t* him up 2Kin 2:16
when he had *t* him 2Kin 4:20
t captive with thy sword.......2Kin 6:22
high places were not *t* 2Kin 12:3
which he had *t* out of.........2Kin 13:25
places were not *t* away........2Kin 14:4
Israel, Samaria was *t*..........2Kin 18:10
king of Babylon had *t*.........2Kin 24:7
t heed to fulfill the statutes 1Chr 22:13
household being *t*.............1Chr 24:6
and one *t* for Ithamar 1Chr 24:6
cities which he had *t*..........2Chr 15:8
Asa his father had *t* 2Chr 17:2
hast *t* away the groves 2Chr 19:3

T

persons, nor *t* of gifts 2Chr 19:7
places were not *t* away 2Chr 20:33
t captive of your brethren 2Chr 28:11
had *t* Beth-shemesh 2Chr 28:18
the king had *t* counsel 2Chr 30:2
t away his high places 2Chr 32:12
t of their daughters .... Ezra 9:2
t strange wives of the .... Ezra 10:2
and have *t* strange wives ...... Ezra 10:10
that had *t* strange wives .... Ezra 10:17
had *t* strange wives .... Ezra 10:44
t of them bread and wine ..... Neh 5:15
had *t* the daughter .... Neh 6:18
t her for his daughter .... Esth 2:15
he had *t* from Haman .... Esth 8:2
the Lord hath *t* away .... Job 1:21
seen the foolish *t* root .... Job 5:3
t it even out of the thorns ..... Job 5:5
t away, who can hinder .... Job 9:12
He *t* away the heart of the .... Job 12:24
also *t* me by my neck .... Job 16:12
t the crown from my head ..... Job 19:9
hath..*t* away a house .... Job 20:19
t a pledge from thy brother ... Job 22:6
are *t* out of the way as all ..... Job 24:24
t away my judgment .... Job 27:2
when God *t* away his soul? .... Job 27:8
Iron is *t* out of the earth ...... Job 28:2
affliction have *t* hold .... Job 30:16
t away my judgment .... Job 34:5
mighty shall be *t* away .... Job 34:20
hid is their own foot *t* .... Ps 9:15
them be *t* in the devices .... Ps 10:2
t up a reproach against .... Ps 15:3
iniquities have *t* hold .... Ps 40:12
even be *t* in their pride .... Ps 59:12
They have *t* crafty counsel .... Ps 83:3
t away all thy wrath .... Ps 85:3
though thou *t* vengeance .... Ps 99:8
thou *t* away their breath ...... Ps 104:29
Lord *t* my part with them ..... Ps 118:7
by *t* heed..according to thy .... Ps 119:9
Horror hath *t* hold upon ...... Ps 119:53
anguish have *t* hold .... Ps 119:143
t not pleasure in the legs ...... Ps 147:10
the Lord *t* pleasure in his ..... Ps 149:4
t away the life of the owners .. Prov 1:19
keep thy foot from being *t* .... Prov 3:26
and their sleep is *t* away ...... Prov 4:16
t with the words of thy .... Prov 6:2
hath *t* a bag of money .... Prov 7:20
transgressors shall be *t* .... Prov 11:6
t a gift out of the bosom ...... Prov 17:23
that *t* a dog by the ears .... Prov 26:17
labor which he *t* under .... Eccl 1:3
nor any thing *t* from it .... Eccl 3:14
labor that he *t* under the ...... Eccl 5:18
sinner shall be *t* by her .... Eccl 7:26
thou *t* under the sun .... Eccl 9:9
the fishes that are *t* in an ..... Eccl 9:12
he had *t* with the tongs .... Is 6:6
have *t* evil counsel against ..... Is 7:5
spoil of Samaria shall be *t* ..... Is 8:4
and be snared, and be *t* .... Is 8:15
burden shall be *t* away .... Is 10:27
t up their lodging at Geba ..... Is 10:29
sheep that no man *t* up .... Is 13:14
Damascus is *t* away from ...... Is 17:1
pangs have *t* hold upon me .... Is 21:3
t this counsel against Tyre ..... Is 23:8
pit shall be *t* in the snare ..... Is 24:18
broken, and snared, and *t* ..... Is 28:13
shall not be *t* down .... Is 33:20
Hezekiah hath *t* away .... Is 36:7
have *t* from the ends of .... Is 41:9
t the cypress and the oak ..... Is 44:14
prey be *t* from the mighty ..... Is 49:24
have *t* out of thine hand ...... Is 51:22
t away for nought? .... Is 52:5
He was *t* from prison .... Is 53:8
t hold of my covenant .... Is 56:6
merciful men are *t* away ...... Is 57:1
righteous is *t* away from ...... Is 57:1
and thou *t* no knowledge? ..... Is 58:3
the wind, have *t* us away ...... Is 64:6
with the wife shall be *t* .... Jer 6:11
are dismayed and *t* .... Jer 8:9
yea, they have *t* root .... Jer 12:2
t away my peace from this .... Jer 16:5
them shall be *t* up a curse ..... Jer 29:22
shalt surely be *t*, and .... Jer 34:3
shalt be *t* by..the king of ...... Jer 38:23
when Jerusalem was *t* .... Jer 38:28
and when they had *t* him ...... Jer 39:5
had *t* him being bound in ..... Jer 40:1
is confounded and *t* .... Jer 48:1
t from the plentiful field ..... Jer 48:33
pit shall be *t* in the snare .... Jer 48:44
hath *t* against Edom .... Jer 49:20
Babylon hath *t* counsel .... Jer 49:30
Babylon is *t*, Bel is .... Jer 50:2
thou art also *t* O Babylon .... Jer 50:24
noise of the *t* of Babylon ...... Jer 50:46
Babylon that his city is *t* ..... Jer 51:31
mighty men are *t* .... Jer 51:56
t away his tabernacle .... Lam 2:6
Lord, was *t* in their pits ...... Lam 4:20
shall be *t* in my snare .... Ezek 12:13
t thereof to do any work? ..... Ezek 15:3
also *t* thy fair jewels of .... Ezek 16:17
t thy embroidered garments ... Ezek 16:18
which *t* strangers instead ...... Ezek 16:32
thou hast *t* pleasure .... Ezek 16:37
t the king thereof .... Ezek 17:12
t of the king's seed .... Ezek 17:13
hath *t* an oath of him .... Ezek 17:13
t the mighty of the land .... Ezek 17:13
hath *t* any increase .... Ezek 18:8
t off his hand from the .... Ezek 18:17
he was *t* in their pit .... Ezek 19:4
that they may be *t* .... Ezek 21:23
they *t* gifts to shed blood ...... Ezek 22:12
t usury and increase .... Ezek 22:12
of Judah by *t* vengeance ...... Ezek 25:12
t vengeance with a .... Ezek 25:15
t cedars from Lebanon .... Ezek 27:5
he that *t* warning shall deliver . Ezek 33:5
is *t* away in his iniquity .... Ezek 33:6
t up in the lips of talkers ..... Ezek 36:3
had *t* out of the temple .... Dan 5:2
was *t* up out of the den .... Dan 6:23
their dominion *t* away .... Dan 7:12
daily sacrifice was *t* away ..... Dan 8:11
t away the multitude .... Dan 11:12
sacrifice shall be *t* away .... Dan 12:11
also shall be *t* away .... Hos 4:3
t them by their arms .... Hos 11:3
t my silver and my gold .... Joel 3:5
if he have *t* nothing? .... Amos 3:4
t out of the mouth of the ..... Amos 3:12
have *t* away your horses ...... Amos 4:10
Have we not *t* to us horns .... Amos 6:13
have ye *t* away my glory ...... Mic 2:9
pangs have *t* thee as a .... Mic 4:9
t away thy judgments .... Zeph 3:15
the city shall be *t* .... Zech 14:2
t him up into the holy city .... Matt 4:5
t with divers diseases .... Matt 4:24
t heed that ye do not your .... Matt 6:1
t no thought for your life ..... Matt 6:25
Which of you by *t* thought .... Matt 6:27
bridegroom shall be *t* from .... Matt 9:15
t from the garment .... Matt 9:16
t my yoke upon you and learn . Matt 11:29
t with himself seven other ..... Matt 12:45
shall be *t* away even that ...... Matt 13:12
we have *t* no bread .... Matt 16:7
t heed that no man deceive .... Matt 24:4
one shall be *t*, and the .... Matt 24:40
t the talent from him, and give . Matt 25:28
Joseph had *t* the body .... Matt 27:59
shall be *t* away from .... Mark 2:20
t away from the old .... Mark 2:21
he *t* the father and the .... Mark 5:40
had *t* the five loaves .... Mark 6:41
let him *t* up his cross and ..... Mark 8:34
wheresoever he *t* him .... Mark 9:18
as many have *t* in hand .... Luke 1:1
and have *t* nothing .... Luke 5:5
which was *t* with a palsy ...... Luke 5:18
arise, *t* up thy bed .... Luke 5:24
that was *t* out of the new ..... Luke 5:36
t away thy cloke forbid .... Luke 6:29
t away the word out of .... Luke 8:12
from him shall be *t* even ...... Luke 8:18
was *t* up of fragments .... Luke 9:17
t from him all his armor ...... Luke 11:22
t away the key of knowledge .. Luke 11:52
t thine ease, eat, drink, be .... Luke 12:19
t away from me the .... Luke 16:3
one shall be *t*, and the .... Luke 17:36
t any thing..by false .... Luke 19:8
t up that thou layedst .... Luke 19:21
t up that I laid not down ...... Luke 19:22
they could not *t* hold of his ... Luke 20:26
them would have *t* him .... John 7:44
a woman *t* in adultery .... John 8:3
Jesus said, *T* ye away the stone. John 11:39
had *t* his garments .... John 13:12
beareth not fruit he *t* away .... John 15:2
Pilate said, *T* ye him and judge. John 18:31
they might be *t* away .... John 19:31
seeth the stone *t* away .... John 20:1
have *t* away my Lord .... John 20:13
t bread, and giveth them ...... John 21:13
in which he was *t* up .... Acts 1:2
same day that he was *t* .... Acts 1:22
and many *t* with palsies .... Acts 8:7
life is *t* from the earth .... Acts 8:33
and was *t* up dead .... Acts 20:9
man was *t* of the Jews .... Acts 23:27
be saved was then *t* away ..... Acts 27:20
had *t* up the anchors .... Acts 27:40
who *t* vengeance? .... Rom 3:5
t occasion by the .... Rom 7:8
the word of God hath *t* .... Rom 9:6
t heed how he buildeth there .. 1Cor 3:10
t the wise in their own 1Cor 3:19
deed might be *t* away 1Cor 5:2
thinketh he standest *t* heed lest. 1Cor 10:12
hath no temptation *t* you 1Cor 10:13
t my leave of them 2Cor 2:13
t the shield of faith .... Eph 6:16
t the helmet of salvation and .. Eph 6:17
t from you for a short time 1Thess 2:17
t vengeance on them 2Thess 1:8
until he be *t* out of the way ... 2Thess 2:7
widow be *t* into the number ... 1Tim 5:9
who are *t* captive by him 2Tim 2:26
high priest *t* from among ...... Heb 5:1
t this honor unto himself ...... Heb 5:4
to be *t* and destroyed 2Pet 2:12
t nothing of the Gentiles 3John 7
when he had *t* the book .... Rev 5:8
t to thee thy great power ...... Rev 11:17
the beast was *t*, and with ...... Rev 19:20
God shall *t* away his part out .. Rev 22:19

TAKER—*receiver*
as with the *t* of usury, so ...... Is 24:2

TALE—*number; story*
Stipulated quantity ...... Ex 5:8, 18
Brief meditation .... Ps 90:9
Nonsensical talk .... Luke 24:11

[*also* TALES]
them in full *t* to the king 1Sam 18:27
bring them in and out by *t* 1Chr 9:28
carry *t* to shed blood .... Ezek 22:9

TALEBEARER—*one who gossips*
Reveals secrets .... Prov 11:13
Injures character .... Prov 18:8
Creates strife .... Prov 26:20

t among thy people .... Lev 19:16
a *t* revealeth secrets .... Prov 20:19
of a *t* are as wounds .... Prov 26:22

TALENT—*a unit of weight of approximately 75 lbs (34.02 kg)*
Of gold .... Ex 37:24
Of silver 2Kin 5:5, 22, 23
Of bronze .... Ex 38:29
Of iron 1Chr 29:7
Of brass 1Chr 29:7

Parable of .... Matt 25:14-30
See JEWISH MEASURES

[*also* TALENTS]
Of a *t* of pure gold .... Ex 25:39
was twenty and nine *t* .... Ex 38:24
of the hundred *t* of silver ...... Ex 38:27
hundred *t*, a *t* for a socket .... Ex 38:27
t of gold with the precious 2Sam 12:30
king sixscore *t* of gold 1Kin 9:14
and twenty *t* of gold 1Kin 10:10
Shemer for two *t* of silver 1Kin 16:24
shalt pay a *t* of silver 1Kin 20:39
Pul a thousand *t* of silver 2Kin 15:19
three hundred *t* 2Kin 18:14
silver and thirty *t* of gold 2Kin 18:14
silver, and a *t* of gold 2Kin 23:33
sent a thousand *t* of silver 1Chr 19:6
to weigh a *t* of gold 1Chr 20:2
thousand *t* of gold 1Chr 22:14
thousand *t* of silver 1Chr 22:14
three thousand *t* of gold 1Chr 29:4
thousand *t* of refined silver 1Chr 29:4
to six hundred *t* 2Chr 3:8
and twenty *t* of gold 2Chr 9:9
a hundred *t* of silver 2Chr 25:6
a hundred *t* of silver 2Chr 27:5
of silver and a *t* of gold 2Chr 36:3
a hundred *t* of silver .... Ezra 7:22
and fifty *t* of silver .... Ezra 8:26
vessels a hundred *t* .... Ezra 8:26
of gold a hundred *t* .... Ezra 8:26
ten thousand *t* of silver .... Esth 3:9
was lifted up a *t* of lead .... Zech 5:7
owed him ten thousand *t* ...... Matt 18:24
about the weight of a *t* .... Rev 16:21

TALITHA-CUMI (tăl'ĭ-thă-ko͞o'mē)—*an Aramaic expression meaning, "damsel, arise"*
Jairus' daughter thus
addressed .... Mark 5:41

TALK—*to express oneself in speech; speak*
Described as:
Divine .... Ex 33:9
Deceitful .... Job 13:7
Proud 1Sam 2:3
Mischievous .... Prov 24:2
Vain .... Titus 1:10
Foolish .... Eph 5:4
Of good things, God's:
Law .... Deut 6:7
Judgment .... Ps 37:30, 31
Righteousness .... Ps 71:24
Power .... Ps 145:11

[*also* TALKED, TALKEST, TALKETH, TALKING]
And Cain *t* with Abel .... Gen 4:8
And he left off *t* with him ..... Gen 17:22
place where he *t* with him ..... Gen 35:13
his brethren *t* with him .... Gen 45:15
t with you from heaven .... Ex 20:22
shone while he *t* with him ..... Ex 34:29
come down and *t* with .... Num 11:17
t with you face to face .... Deut 5:4
that God doth *t* with man ..... Deut 5:24
t of them when thou sittest .... Deut 6:7
sign that thou *t* with me .... Judg 6:17
and *t* with the woman .... Judg 14:7
Saul *t* unto the priest 1Sam 14:19
t there with the king 1Kin 1:14
she yet *t* with the king 1Kin 1:22
he is *t*, or he is pursuing 1Kin 18:27
they still went on, and *t* 2Kin 2:11
the king *t* with Gehazi 2Kin 8:4
and *t* not..in the Jews' 2Kin 18:26
t ye of all his wondrous 1Chr 16:9
as he *t* with him 2Chr 25:16
they were yet *t* with him ...... Esth 6:14
a man full of *t* be justified .... Job 11:2
with unprofitable *t*? .... Job 15:3
The princes refrained *t* .... Job 29:9
they *t* to the grief of those .... Ps 69:26
and *t* of thy doings .... Ps 77:12
t ye of all his wondrous .... Ps 105:2
I *t* of thy wondrous works ..... Ps 119:27
it shall *t* with thee .... Prov 6:22
end of his *t* is mischievous .... Eccl 10:13
t with thee of..judgments ...... Jer 12:1
I have *t* with thee .... Jer 38:25
I will there *t* with thee .... Ezek 3:22
people still are *t* against .... Ezek 33:30
and *t* with me, and .... Dan 9:22
t with this my lord? .... Dan 10:17
angel that *t* with me said ...... Zech 1:9
said unto the angel that *t* ..... Zech 1:19
angel that *t* with me came ...... Zech 4:1
the angel that *t* with me .... Zech 4:5
angel that *t* with me .... Zech 5:10
he yet *t* to the people .... Matt 12:46
Moses and Elijah *t* with .... Matt 17:3
entangle him in his *t* .... Matt 22:15
immediately *t* with them ...... Mark 6:50
they were *t* with Jesus .... Mark 9:4
t with him two men .... Luke 9:30
t together of all these .... Luke 24:14
he *t* with us by the way .... Luke 24:32
he *t* with the woman .... John 4:27
Why *t* thou with her? .... John 4:27
it is he that *t* with thee .... John 9:37
I will not *t* much with .... John 14:30
as he *t* with him, he went ..... Acts 10:27
t between themselves .... Acts 26:31
of a trumpet *t* with me .... Rev 4:1
t with me, saying unto me ..... Rev 17:1
t with me had a golden .... Rev 21:15

TALKERS—*used negatively of vain speakers*
taken up in the lips of *t* .... Ezek 36:3
many unruly and vain *t* .... Titus 1:10

TALL—*of a high stature*

[*also* TALLER]
greater and *t* than we .... Deut 1:28
great, and many, and *t* .... Deut 2:10
A people great and *t* .... Deut 9:2
cut down the *t* cedar trees 2Kin 19:23
I will cut down the *t* cedars ... Is 37:24

TALMAI (tăl'mī)—*"bold; spirited"*
1. Son of Anak driven out
by Caleb .... Josh 15:14
2. King of Geshur whose
daughter, Maacah,
becomes David's wife. . 2Sam 3:3

Ahiman, Sheshai, and *T* ...... Num 13:22
and Ahiman, and *T* .... Judg 1:10
fled, and went to *T* 2Sam 13:37
of *T* king of Geshur 1Chr 3:2

TALMON (tăl'mŏn)—*"oppressor; violent"*
Levite porter 1Chr 9:17
Descendants of, return
from exile .... Ezra 2:42
Members of, become
Temple porters .... Neh 11:19

TAMAH (tā'mä)—*"combat"—one whose descendants returned from the Exile*
the children of *T* .... Neh 7:55

TAMAR (tā'mer)—*"palm"*
1. Wife of Er and mother
of Perez and Zerah ... Gen 38:6-30
Ancestress of tribal
families .... Num 26:20, 21
2. Absalom's sister 2Sam 13:1-32
3. Absalom's daughter 2Sam 14:27
4. Place south of the Dead
Sea .... Ezek 47:19

whom *T* bare unto Judah ..... Ruth 4:12
whose name was *T* 2Sam 13:1
sick for his sister *T* 2Sam 13:2
I love *T*, my brother 2Sam 13:4
let my sister *T* come 2Sam 13:5
let *T* my sister come 2Sam 13:6
David sent home to *T* 2Sam 13:7
So *T* went to her brother 2Sam 13:8
And Amnon said unto *T* 2Sam 13:10
T took the cakes which 2Sam 13:10
T put ashes on her head 2Sam 13:19
So *T* remained desolate 2Sam 13:20
he forced his sister *T* 2Sam 13:32
T his daughter in law 1Chr 2:4
from *T* even to the waters ..... Ezek 47:19
begat Pharez and Zerah of *T* .. Matt 1:3

TAME—*humble; subdue; domesticate*

[*also* TAMED]
could any man *t* him .... Mark 5:4
things in the sea, is *t* .... James 3:7
hath been *t* of mankind .... James 3:7
tongue can no man *t* .... James 3:8

TAMMUZ (tăm'ŭs)—*a Babylonian god*
Mourned by women of
Jerusalem .... Ezek 8:14

TANACH (tā'năk)—*"battlement"*
T with her suburbs .... Josh 21:25

TANHUMETH (tăn-hū'mĕth)—*"comfort"*
Father of Seraiah 2Kin 25:23

Seraiah the son of *T* .... Jer 40:8

TANNER—*dresser of hides*
Joppa with one Simon a *t* ..... Acts 9:43
with one Simon a *t* .... Acts 10:6
and call hither Simon a *t* ...... Acts 10:32

TAPESTRY—*hand-woven coverings*
Symbolic of:
Licentiousness .... Prov 7:16
Diligence .... Prov 31:22

TAPHATH (tā'făth)—*"ornament"*
Daughter of Solomon 1Kin 4:11

TAPPUAH (tăp-pū'ä)—*"apple; hill place"*
1. Town of Judah .... Josh 15:1, 34
2. Town of Ephraim .... Josh 16:8, 9
3. Son of Hebron 1Chr 2:43

The king of *T*, one .... Josh 12:17
had the land of *T* .... Josh 17:8
but *T* on the border of .... Josh 17:8

TARAH (tā'rä)—*"wretch"*
Israelite encampment .... Num 33:1, 27

they removed from *T* .... Num 33:28

TARALAH (tăr'ä-lä)—*"strength"*
City of Benjamin .... Josh 18:21, 27

TARE—*See* TEAR

TARE—*a weed resembling wheat*
Sown among wheat ...... Matt 13:24-40

TAREA (tā'rē-ä)—*"flight"*

Melech, and *T*, and Ahaz 1Chr 8:35

TARGET—*a small, round shield*

[*also* TARGETS]
t of brass between his 1Sam 17:6
hundred *t* of beaten 1Kin 10:16
of gold went to one *t* 1Kin 10:16
hundred *t* of beaten gold 2Chr 9:15
beaten gold went to one *t* 2Chr 9:15
army of men that bare *t* 2Chr 14:8

TARPELITES (tär'pĕ-līts)
People transported to
Samaria by the
Assyrians .... Ezra 4:9

TARRY—*to delay; remain*
Of human things:
Prolonged visit .... Acts 9:43
Unnecessary delay 1Sam 1:23
Sinful delay 2Sam 11:1, 2
Embarrassed delay 2Sam 10:5
Indulgence in wine ...... Prov 23:30
Of divine things:
Heavenly visitation ...... Judg 6:18
God's salvation .... Is 46:13
Divine visitation .... Hab 2:3
Spirit's coming .... Luke 24:49
Christ's return .... Heb 10:37

[*also* TARRIED, TARRIEST, TARRIETH, TARRYING]
t all night, and wash your ..... Gen 19:2
with him, and *t* all night ...... Gen 24:54

favor in thine eyes, *t*.........Gen 30:27
t all night in the mount.......Gen 31:54
of Egypt, and could not *t*.....Ex 12:39
t long upon the tabernacle....Num 9:19
t ye also here this night.......Num 22:19
t till they were ashamed.......Judg 3:25
why *t* the wheels of his.......Judg 5:28
t all night, and let thine.......Judg 19:6
t until afternoon..............Judg 19:8
would not *t* that night...........Judg 19:10
t for them till they were.......Ruth 1:13
she *t* a little in the house......Ruth 2:7
seven days shalt thou *t*........1Sam 10:8
part be that *t* by the stuff.....1Sam 30:24
T here today also.............2Sam 11:12
t in a place that was far.......2Sam 15:17
may not *t* thus with thee......2Sam 18:14
t longer than the set time.....2Sam 20:5
T here, I pray thee...........2Kin 2:2
T, I pray thee, here...........2Kin 2:6
again to him, for he *t* at......2Kin 2:18
t till the morning light........2Kin 7:9
and flee, and *t* not...........2Kin 9:3
T at Jericho until your........1Chr 19:5
make no *t*, O my God...........Ps 40:17
O Lord, make no *t*............Ps 70:5
telleth lies shall not *t*.........Ps 101:7
aside to *t* for a night?.........Jer 14:8
that *t* not for man............Mic 5:7
While the bridegroom *t*........Matt 25:5
t ye here, and watch with.....Matt 26:38
t ye yere, and watch..........Mark 14:34
that he *t* so long in the.......Luke 1:21
went in to *t* with them........Luke 24:29
and there he *t* with them......John 3:22
he would *t* with them..........John 4:40
prayed they him to *t* certain...Acts 10:48
after they had *t* there.........Acts 15:33
These going before *t*..........Acts 20:5
disciples, we *t* there seven.....Acts 21:4
now why *t* thou? arise........Acts 22:16
he had *t* among them more....Acts 25:6
at Syracuse, we *t* there........Acts 28:12
to eat, *t* one for another......1Cor 11:33
will *t* at Ephesus until........1Cor 16:8
But if I *t* long, that thou......1Tim 3:15

TARSHISH, THARSHISH (tär'shĭsh, thär'shĭsh)—*"hard; contemplation"*
1. Son of Javan and great grandson of Noah.....Gen 10:4
2. City at a great distance from Palestine........Jon 1:3
   Minerals imported from, by Phoenicians........1Kin 10:22
   Ships of, noted in commerce............Ps 48:7
   Ships of, sent by Jehoshaphat..........1Kin 22:48
3. Benjamite.............1Chr 7:10
4. Persian prince...........Esth 1:14

of Javan, Elishah and *T*.......1Chr 1:7
king's ships went to *T*.........2Chr 9:21
ships of *T* bringing gold.......2Chr 9:21
were not able to go to *T*......2Chr 20:37
breakest the ships of *T*........Ps 48:7
upon all the ships of *T*........Is 2:16
Pass ye over to *T*............Is 23:6
Howl, ye ships of *T*..........Is 23:14
unto the nations, to *T*........Is 66:19
plates is brought from *T*......Jer 10:9
T was thy merchant by........Ezek 27:12
and the merchants of *T*.......Ezek 38:13
I fled before unto *T*..........Jon 4:2

TARSUS (tär'sŭs)—*"winged"—the capital of the Roman province of Cilicia*
Paul's birthplace........Acts 21:39
Saul sent to............Acts 9:30
Visited by Barnabas.....Acts 11:25

one called Saul, of *T*........Acts 9:11
am a Jew, born in *T*..........Acts 22:3

TARTAK (tär'tăk)—*"hero of darkness"*
Deity worshiped by the Avites...............2Kin 17:31

TARTAN (tär'tăn)—*the title of Assyria's commander*
Sent to fight against Jerusalem............2Kin 18:17

TASK—*assigned work*

[*also* TASKS]
your works, your daily *t*......Ex 5:13
fulfilled your *t* in making.....Ex 5:14
your bricks of your daily *t*.....Ex 5:19

TASKMASTER—*a foreman; one who imposes work on another*
Over sons of Israel......Ex 1:11

[*also* TASKMASTERS]
cry by reason of their *t*.......Ex 3:7
commanded the same day the *t*.Ex 5:6
t of the people went out......Ex 5:10
t had set over them..........Ex 5:14

TASTE—*to ascertain the flavor; perceive or recognize; the flavor of something*

Of divine things:
God's Word...........Ps 119:103
Lord..................Ps 34:8
Heavenly gift..........Heb 6:4

Of material things:
Honey..................1Sam 14:29, 43
Manna.................Ex 16:31
Food..................1Sam 14:24
Wine..................John 2:9
Vinegar................Matt 27:34
Death.................Heb 2:9

[*also* TASTED, TASTETH]
t of it was as the *t*...........Num 11:8
more also, if I *t* bread........2Sam 3:35
t in the white of an egg?......Job 6:6
the mouth *t* his meat?........Job 12:11
as the mouth *t* meat..........Job 34:3
which is sweet to thy *t*........Prov 24:13
fruit was sweet to my *t*........Song 2:3
his *t* remained in him.........Jer 48:11
while he *t* the wine...........Dan 5:2
herd nor flock, *t* any..........Jon 3:7
which shall not *t* of death.....Matt 16:28
which shall not *t* of death.....Mark 9:1
which shall not *t* of death.....Luke 9:27
shall *t* of my supper..........Luke 14:24
he shall never *t* of death......John 8:52
touch not; *t* not.............Col 2:21
t the good word of God.......Heb 6:5
t that the Lord is............1Pet 2:3

TATNAI (tăt'nī)—*"gift"*
Persian governor opposing the Jews.....Ezra 5:3, 6

T, governor beyond the.......Ezra 6:6
T, governor on this side.......Ezra 6:13

TATTLERS—*gossipers*
but *t* also and busy bodies.....1Tim 5:13

TATTOOING—*marking the skin indelibly*
Forbidden by God.......Lev 19:28

TAU (tou; to͞o)
Letter in the Hebrew alphabet.............Ps 119:169-176

TAUGHT—*See* TEACH

TAUNT—*scornful challenge; insult*
Goliath against David....1Sam 17:43, 44
David against Abner.....1Sam 26:14-16
Rabshakeh against the Jews.................2Kin 18:28-35
Soldiers and people against Christ.........Matt 27:28-41

[*also* TAUNTING]
proverb, a *t* and a curse.......Jer 24:9
be a reproach and a *t*.........Ezek 5:15

TAVERNS, THE THREE—*a station on the Appian Way*
Place about 30 miles south of Rome........Acts 28:15

TAXED—*having paid money, goods, or labor to a government*

[*also* TAXING]
t the land to give the.........2Kin 23:35
all the world should be *t*......Luke 2:1
To be *t* with Mary...........Luke 2:5
t was first made when........Luke 2:2
in the days of the *t*..........Acts 5:37

TAXES—*money, goods, or labor paid to a government*

Derived from:
People's possessions.....1Sam 8:10-18
Poor..................Amos 5:11

Paid by:
Forced labor............Deut 20:11
Foreigners..............1Chr 22:2
Captured people.........2Sam 8:6, 14
Forced labor............1Kin 5:13-17
All except Levites.......Ezra 7:24

Used for:
Sanctuary...............Ex 30:11-16
King's household........1Kin 4:7-19
Tribute to foreign nations.2Kin 15:17-22
Authorities..............Rom 13:6, 7

Abuses of:
Lead to rebellion........1Kin 12:1-19
Burden people with debts.Neh 5:1-13
Bring enslavement.......Neh 9:36, 37

[*also* TAXATION]
one according to his *t*.........2Kin 23:35

TAX-GATHERERS—*Jews engaged in tax collecting*

Features concerning:
Collector of taxes.......Luke 5:27
Often guilty of extortion..Luke 3:12, 13
Classed with lowest sinners............Matt 9:10, 11; Matt 21:31, 32
Do not even, do the same.................Matt 5:46
Thomas and Matthew, the...................Matt 10:3
"Thank thee that I am not"...................Luke 18:11
As a heathen and a......Matt 18:17

Spiritual attitude of:
Often conscientious......Luke 19:2, 8
Often hospitable.........Luke 5:29
Received John's beliefs..Matt 21:32
Listened to Jesus........Luke 15:1
Conscious of their sins...Luke 18:13, 14
Many sat with Him......Mark 2:15
Why do ye eat with.....Luke 5:30
A friend of.............Matt 11:19; Luke 7:34

TEACH—*to instruct*

Those able to teach:
Parents.................Deut 11:19
Levites.................Lev 10:11
Ancestors...............Jer 9:14
Disciples...............Matt 28:19, 20
Older women............Titus 2:3
Nature.................1Cor 11:14

Significance of teaching:
Combined with preaching.Matt 4:23
Divine calling...........Eph 4:11
Necessary for bishops....1Tim 3:2
Necessary for the Lord's bond-servants.........2Tim 2:24-26
From house to house....Acts 20:20
By sharing..............Gal 6:6
Not granted to women...1Tim 2:12

Authority of, in divine things:
Derived from Christ.....Matt 28:19, 20
Empowered by the Spirit.John 14:26
Taught by the Lord......Is 54:13
Originates in revelation..Gal 1:12

Objects of, in divine things, concerning:
God's way.............Ps 27:11
God's path............Ps 25:4, 5
God's law.............Ps 119:12, 26, 66
God's will.............Ps 143:10

Holiness .... Titus 2:12
Spiritual truths .... Heb 8:11, 12

Perversion of, by:
False prophets .... Is 9:15
False priests .... Mic 3:11
Traditionalists .... Matt 15:9
False teachers 1Tim 4:1-3
Judaizers .... Acts 15:1
False believers 2Tim 4:3, 4

[*also* TAUGHT, TEACHEST, TEACHETH, TEACHING]
t thee what thou shalt say ..... Ex 4:12
shalt *t* them ordinances .... Ex 18:20
in his heart that he may *t* ..... Ex 35:34
t when it is unclean, and ...... Lev 14:57
judgments, which I *t* you ...... Deut 4:1
I have *t* you statutes and ...... Deut 4:5
they may *t* their children ...... Deut 4:10
which thou shalt *t* them .... Deut 5:31
shalt *t* them diligently .... Deut 6:7
which they shall *t* thee .... Deut 17:11
the Levites shall *t* you .... Deut 24:8
t Jacob thy judgments .... Deut 33:10
might know, to *t* them war .... Judg 3:2
I will *t* you the good and 1Sam 12:23
He *t* my hands to war 2Sam 22:35
t them the manner of the 2Kin 17:27
t them how they should 2Kin 17:28
without a *t* priest 2Chr 15:3
t in the cities of Judah 2Chr 17:7
they *t* in Judah, and had 2Chr 17:9
and *t* the people 2Chr 17:9
t the good knowledge of 2Chr 30:22
Levites that *t* the people ...... Neh 8:9
T me, and I will hold my ..... Job 6:24
and they shall *t* thee .... Job 12:7
any *t* God knowledge? .... Job 21:22
of years should *t* wisdom ...... Job 32:7
which I see not *t* thou .... Job 34:32
t us more than the beasts ..... Job 35:11
his power; who *t* like him? .... Job 36:22
He *t* my hands to war .... Ps 18:34
he *t* sinners in the way .... Ps 25:8
meek will he *t* his way .... Ps 25:9
instruct thee and *t* thee .... Ps 32:8
t you the fear of the Lord ..... Ps 34:11
right hand shall *t* thee .... Ps 45:4
I *t* transgressors thy ways ..... Ps 51:13
Michtam of David, to *t* .... Ps 60:*title*
t me from my youth .... Ps 71:17
T me thy way, O Lord .... Ps 86:11
t us to number our days .... Ps 90:12
and *t* him out of thy law ...... Ps 94:12
and *t* his senators wisdom ..... Ps 105:22
T me, O Lord, the way of .... Ps 119:33
t me thy statutes .... Ps 119:68
and *t* me thy statutes .... Ps 119:124
hast *t* me thy statutes .... Ps 119:171
that I shall *t* them .... Ps 132:12
which *t* my hands to war ...... Ps 144:1
He *t* me also, and said, ... Prov 4:4
t thee in the way of wisdom ... Prov 4:11
he *t* with his fingers .... Prov 6:13
that his mother *t* him .... Prov 31:1
t the people knowledge .... Eccl 12:9
discretion, and doth *t* him ..... Is 28:26
fear toward me is *t* by the ..... Is 29:13
t him in the path of .... Is 40:14
t him knowledge, and .... Is 40:14
also *t* the wicked ones .... Jer 2:33
t their tongue to speak .... Jer 9:5
t them to be captains .... Jer 13:21
t rebellion against the Lord .... Jer 29:32
rising up early and *t* .... Jer 32:33
be *t* not to do after your ...... Ezek 23:48
t my people the difference .... Ezek 44:23
might *t* the learning .... Dan 1:4
t us of his ways, and we ...... Mic 4:2
Arise, it shall *t*! Behold .... Hab 2:19
t me to keep cattle from ...... Zech 13:5
his mouth, and *t* them .... Matt 5:2
and shall *t* men so, he .... Matt 5:19
shall do and *t* them .... Matt 5:19
he *t* them as one having .... Matt 7:29
t in their synagogues .... Matt 9:35
to *t* and to preach in their ..... Matt 11:1
t them in their synagogue ..... Matt 13:54
came unto him as he was *t* .... Matt 21:23
t the way of God in truth ..... Matt 22:16
with you *t* in the temple ...... Matt 26:55
for he *t* them as one that ..... Mark 1:22
unto him, and he *t* them ...... Mark 2:13
to *t* by the seaside .... Mark 4:1
he *t* them many things by ..... Mark 4:2
round about the villages, *t* .... Mark 6:6
and what they had *t* .... Mark 6:30
to *t* them many things .... Mark 6:34
t for doctrines the .... Mark 7:7
For he *t* his disciples .... Mark 9:31
wont, he *t* them again .... Mark 10:1
t the way of God in truth ..... Mark 12:14
while he *t* in the temple .... Mark 12:35
with you in the temple *t* ...... Mark 14:49
t in their synagogues .... Luke 4:15
t the people out of the .... Luke 5:3
certain day, as he was *t* .... Luke 5:17
Lord, *t* us to pray .... Luke 11:1
John also *t* his disciples .... Luke 11:1
he was *t* in one of the .... Luke 13:10
cities and villages, *t* .... Luke 13:22
t daily in the temple .... Luke 19:47
sayest and *t* rightly .... Luke 20:21
t the way of God truly .... Luke 20:21
t throughout all Jewry .... Luke 23:5
shall be all *t* of God .... John 6:45
into the temple, and *t* .... John 7:14
and *t* the Gentiles? .... John 7:35
sat down, and *t* them .... John 8:2
as my Father hath *t* me .... John 8:28
and dost thou *t* us? .... John 9:34
began both to do and *t* .... Acts 1:1
that they *t* the people .... Acts 4:2
and *t* the people .... Acts 5:25
should not *t* in this name? ..... Acts 5:28
and *t* much people .... Acts 11:26
t and preaching the word ...... Acts 15:35
t customs, which are not ...... Acts 16:21
t the word of God among ..... Acts 18:11
t diligently the things of .... Acts 18:25
t all the Jews which are .... Acts 21:21
t all men every where .... Acts 21:28
t according to the perfect ..... Acts 22:3
t those things which .... Acts 28:31
which *t* another, thou not ..... Rom 2:21
or he that *t* on *t* .... Rom 12:7
which man's wisdom *t* 1Cor 2:13
which the Holy Ghost *t* 1Cor 2:13
I *t* every where in every 1Cor 4:17
I might *t* others also 1Cor 14:19
and have been *t* by him .... Eph 4:21
and *t* every man in all .... Col 1:28
as ye have been *t* .... Col 2:7
which ye have been *t* 2Thess 2:15
t no other doctrine 1Tim 1:3
things command and *t* 1Tim 4:11
These things *t* and exhort 1Tim 6:2
be able to *t* others also 2Tim 2:2
word as he hath been *t* .... Titus 1:9
t things which they ought ..... Titus 1:11
t the young women to be ..... Titus 2:4
need that one *t* you .... Heb 5:12
not that any man *t* you 1John 2:27
same anointing *t* you of all 1John 2:27
even as it hath *t* you 1John 2:27
t Balak to cast a .... Rev 2:14
t and to seduce my servants ... Rev 2:20

TEACHER—*one who instructs*

[*also* TEACHERS]
the *t* as the scholar 1Chr 25:8
than all my *t* .... Ps 119:99
not obeyed the voice of my *t* .. Prov 5:13
t be removed into a corner .... Is 30:20
thine eyes shall see thy *t* ...... Is 30:20
image, and a *t* of lies .... Hab 2:18
art a *t* come from God .... John 3:2
certain prophets and *t* .... Acts 13:1
a *t* of babes, which hast .... Rom 2:20
prophets, thirdly *t* 1Cor 12:28
Desiring to be *t* of the law 1Tim 1:7
t of the Gentiles in faith 1Tim 2:7
t of good things .... Titus 2:3
time ye ought to be *t* .... Heb 5:12
be false *t* among you 2Pet 2:1

TEAR—*to pull apart by force; to wound*

[*also* TARE, TEARETH, TORN]
which was *t* of beasts .... Gen 31:39
Surely he is *t* in pieces .... Gen 44:28
If it be *t* in pieces, then .... Ex 22:13
good that which was *t* .... Ex 22:13
flesh that is *t* of beasts .... Ex 22:31
which is *t* with beasts .... Lev 7:24
or is *t* with beasts .... Lev 22:8
t the arm with the crown ...... Deut 33:20
will *t* your flesh with the ...... Judg 8:7
lion, which hath *t* him 1Kin 13:26
He *t* me in his wrath .... Job 16:9
t my soul like a lion .... Ps 7:2
lest I *t* you in pieces .... Ps 50:22
carcases were *t* in the .... Is 5:25
shall be *t* in pieces .... Jer 5:6
slay, and the dogs to *t* .... Jer 15:3
or is *t* in pieces .... Ezek 4:14
t them from your arms .... Ezek 13:20
I, will *t* and go away .... Hos 5:14
for he hath *t*, and he will ..... Hos 6:1
anger did *t* perpetually .... Amos 1:11
down, and *t* in pieces .... Mic 5:8
did *t* in pieces enough for ..... Nah 2:12
and *t* their claws in pieces ..... Zech 11:16
that which was *t* .... Mal 1:13
unclean spirit had *t* him .... Mark 1:26
straightway the spirit *t* .... Mark 9:20
t him that he foameth again ... Luke 9:39
threw him down, and *t* him ... Luke 9:42

TEARS—*drops of salty water that moisten and clean the eyes*

Kinds of:
Agonizing .... Ps 6:6
Rewarded .... Ps 126:5
Repentant .... Luke 7:38, 44
Insincere .... Heb 12:17
Intense .... Heb 5:6-8
Woman's .... Esth 8:3

Caused by:
Remorse .... Gen 27:34
Approaching death 2Kin 20:1-5
Oppression .... Eccl 4:1
Defeat .... Is 16:9
Affliction and anguish ... 2Cor 2:4
Christian service .... Acts 20:19, 31

mine eye poureth out *t* .... Job 16:20
hold not thy peace at my *t* .... Ps 39:12
My *t* have been my meat ...... Ps 42:3
put..my *t* into thy bottle ...... Ps 56:8
feedest..with the bread of *t* .... Ps 80:5
them *t* to drink in great .... Ps 80:5
mine eyes from *t*, and my ..... Ps 116:8
God will wipe away *t* from .... Is 25:8
prayer, I have seen thy *t* ...... Is 38:5
mine eyes a fountain of *t* ...... Jer 9:1
and run down with *t* .... Jer 13:17
and thine eyes from *t* .... Jer 31:16
her *t* are on her cheeks .... Lam 1:2
let *t* run down like a river ..... Lam 2:18
altar of the Lord with *t* .... Mal 2:13
with *t*, Lord, I believe .... Mark 9:24
being mindful of thy *t* 2Tim 1:4
God shall wipe away all *t* ..... Rev 7:17
God shall wipe away all *t* ..... Rev 21:4

TEATS—*breasts*
shall lament for the *t* .... Is 32:12
in bruising thy *t* by the .... Ezek 23:21

TEBAH (tē'bä)—*"thick; strong"*
Son of Nahor .... Gen 22:24

TEBALIAH (tĕb-ä-lī'ä)—*"Jehovah is protector; Jehovah has purified"*
Merarite Korahite 1Chr 26:11

TEBETH (tē'bĕth)—*the name of the Hebrew tenth month*
Esther becomes queen in .Esth 2:16, 17

TEDIOUS—*tiresome; boring*
be not further *t* unto thee .....Acts 24:4

TEETH—*See* TOOTH

TEHAPHNEHES—*an important city in the time of Jeremiah*
At *T*..day shall be darkened ...Ezek 30:18

TEHINNAH (tĕ-hĭn'ä)—*"entreaty; supplication"*
Judahite 1Chr 4:12

TEIL—*linden tree*
as a *t* tree, and as an oak .....Is 6:13

TEKEL (tē'käl)—*"weighed"*
Descriptive of Babylon's judgment ....Dan 5:25

TEKOA, TEKOAH (tĕ-kō'ä)— *"that is confirmed"*
Ashur the father of 1Chr 2:24
1Chr 4:5
Fortress city of Judah 2Chr 20:20
Home of a wise woman ..2Sam 14:2, 4, 9
Fortified by Rehoboam ..2Chr 11:6
Home of Amos ....Amos 1:1

blow the trumpet in *T* ....Jer 6:1

TEKOITE (tē-kō'īt)—*an inhabitant of Tekoa*
Ikkesh thus called 2Sam 23:26
Among postexilic workmen ....Neh 3:5, 27

TEL-ABIB (tĕl-ā'bĭb)—*"heap of new grain"*
Place in Babylonia ....Ezek 3:15

TELAH (tē'lä)—*"vigor"*
Ephraimite 1Chr 7:25

TELAIM (tē-lā'ĭm)—*"lambs"—a place in extreme southern Judah*
Saul assembles his army here 1Sam 15:4

TELASSAR, THELASAR (tĕ-lăs'er, thĕ-lăs'-er)—*"taking away"*
City of Mesopotamia 2Kin 19:12
Children of Eden in .....Is 37:12

TELEM (tē'lĕm)—*"their shadow"*
Town in south Judah ....Josh 15:24
Divorced his foreign wife .Ezra 10:24

TEL-HARESHA (tĕl-här-ĕsh'ä)— *"suspension of the plow"*
Babylonian town ....Neh 7:61

TEL-HARSA (tĕl-här'sȧ)— *"mound of workmanship"*
went up from Tel-melah, *T*....Ezra 2:59

TELL—*to declare; relate*

[*also* TELLEST, TELLETH, TELLING, TOLD]
t thee that thou wast..........Gen 3:11
not *t* me that she was thy .....Gen 12:18
t Abram the Hebrew ....Gen 14:13
neither didst thou *t* me........Gen 21:26
of which God had *t* him.......Gen 22:3
that it was *t* Abraham ....Gen 22:20
art thou? *t* me, I pray ....Gen 24:23
I have *t* mine errand..........Gen 24:33
with my master, *t* me ....Gen 24:49
t me; that I may turn ....Gen 24:49
t him concerning the well .....Gen 26:32
Jacob *t* Rachel that he was ....Gen 29:12
t Laban all these things ....Gen 29:13
t me, what shall thy wages ....Gen 29:15
t Laban on the third day ......Gen 31:22
I have sent to *t* my lord ....Gen 32:5
t it his brethren, and..........Gen 37:9
t me, I pray thee, where ......Gen 37:16
was *t* Tamar, saying ....Gen 38:13
t his dream to Joseph ....Gen 40:9
t him, and he interpreted .....Gen 41:12
t him all that befell unto ....Gen 42:29
to *t* the man whether ye ......Gen 43:6
we *t* him the words of my .....Gen 44:24
t my father of all my glory ....Gen 45:13
t him all the words of.........Gen 45:27
that one *t* Joseph, Behold .....Gen 48:1
Moses *t* Aaron all the..........Ex 4:28
unto Pharaoh, and *t* him ......Ex 9:1
it was *t* the king of Egypt .....Ex 14:5
word that we did *t* thee ....Ex 14:12
Moses *t* his father-in-law ......Ex 18:8
Moses came and *t* the.........Ex 24:3
come and *t* the priest ....Lev 14:35
Moses *t* it unto Aaron ....Lev 21:24
t the people the words of .....Num 11:24
t him, and said, We came .....Num 13:27
t it to the inhabitants of.......Num 14:14
showeth me I will *t* thee ......Num 23:3
Balak, *T* not I thee ....Num 23:26
And it be *t* thee, and thou ....Deut 17:4
which they shall *t* thee ....Deut 17:11
t the king of Jericho ....Josh 2:2
t me now what thou hast ......Josh 7:19
certainly *t* thy servants ....Josh 9:24
which our fathers *t* us.........Judg 6:13
heard the *t* of the dream ......Judg 7:15
they *t* it to Jotham ....Judg 9:7
and they *t* Abimelech ....Judg 9:42
came and *t* her husband........Judg 13:6
neither *t* he me his name......Judg 13:6
and *t* his father and his ....Judg 14:2
he *t* not them that he had .....Judg 14:9
I have not *t* it my father ......Judg 14:16
and shall I *t* it thee? ....Judg 14:16
seventh day, that he *t* her .....Judg 14:17
she *t* the riddle to the.........Judg 14:17
mocked me, and *t* me lies .....Judg 16:10
now *t* me, I pray thee ....Judg 16:10
That he *t* her all his heart .....Judg 16:17
T us, how was this ....Judg 20:3
he will *t* thee what thou.......Ruth 3:4
t her all that the man had .....Ruth 3:16
t him that I will judge 1Sam 3:13
Samuel *t* him every whit 1Sam 3:18
came in hastily, and *t* Eli 1Sam 4:14
t us wherewith we shall 1Sam 6:2
Lord had *t* Samuel in his 1Sam 9:15
T me, I pray thee where 1Sam 9:18
T me, I pray thee, what.......1Sam 10:15
He *t* us plainly that the 1Sam 10:16
Samuel spake, he *t* him not ...1Sam 10:16
t the tidings in the ears 1Sam 11:4
But he *t* not his father 1Sam 14:1
T me what thou hast done 1Sam 14:43
Jonathan *t* him, and said 1Sam 14:43
t thee what the Lord hath 1Sam 15:16
liveth, O king, I cannot *t* 1Sam 17:55
they *t* Saul, and the thing 1Sam 18:20
t David these words 1Sam 18:26
and Jonathan *t* David 1Sam 19:2
I see, that I will *t* thee 1Sam 19:3
t him all that Saul had 1Sam 19:18
when it was *t* Saul, he sent 1Sam 19:21
would not I *t* it thee? 1Sam 20:9
Who shall *t* me?..............1Sam 20:10
he would surely *t* Saul 1Sam 22:22
they *t* David, saying 1Sam 23:1
beseech thee, *t* thy servant 1Sam 23:11
was *t* Saul that David was 1Sam 23:13
they *t* David: wherefore 1Sam 23:25
t him all those sayings 1Sam 25:12
t not her husband Nabal 1Sam 25:19
had *t* him these things 1Sam 25:37
Lest they should *t* on us 1Sam 27:11
I pray thee, *t* me 2Sam 1:4
young man that *t* him 2Sam 1:5
the young man that *t* him 2Sam 1:13
they *t* Joab, saying Abner 2Sam 3:23
And it was *t* king David 2Sam 6:12
Go and *t* my servant David 2Sam 7:5
Also the Lord *t* thee that 2Sam 7:11
was *t* David, he gathered......2Sam 10:17
when they had *t* David........2Sam 11:10
t the matters of the war 2Sam 11:19
feared to *t* him that the 2Sam 12:18
if we *t* him that the child......2Sam 12:18
wilt thou not *t* me? 2Sam 13:4
to the king, and *t* him 2Sam 14:33
shalt *t* it to Zadok and 2Sam 15:35
send quickly, and *t* David 2Sam 17:16
wench went and *t* them 1Sam 17:17
went and *t* king David 2Sam 17:17
went and *t* king David 2Sam 17:21
unto the man that *t* him.......2Sam 18:11
Go *t* the king what thou 2Sam 18:21
And it was *t* Joab, Behold 2Sam 19:1
t David what Rizpah the 2Sam 21:11
t them who shall sit on the 1Kin 1:20
t the king, saying, Behold 1Kin 1:23
t king Solomon that Joab 1Kin 2:29
t Solomon that Shimei had 1Kin 2:41
Solomon *t* her all her 1Kin 10:3
king, which he *t* her not 1Kin 10:3
the half was not *t* me 1Kin 10:7
sons came and *t* him all 1Kin 13:11
t also to their father 1Kin 13:11
t me that I should be king 1Kin 14:2
t thee what shall become 1Kin 14:3
t Jeroboam, Thus saith the 1Kin 14:7
t thy lord, Behold, Elijah 1Kin 18:8
when I come and *t* Ahab 1Kin 18:12
to meet Ahab, and *t* him......1Kin 18:16
T my lord the king, All 1Kin 20:9
sent out, and they *t* him 1Kin 20:17
t me nothing but that which ...1Kin 22:16
t you these words? 2Kin 1:7
t me, what hast thou in the ...2Kin 4:2
and hath not *t* me 2Kin 4:27
one went in, and *t* his lord 2Kin 5:4
t the king of Israel 2Kin 6:12
was *t* him, saying, Behold 2Kin 6:13
t the king's household.........2Kin 7:9
t it to the king's house 2Kin 7:11
T me, I pray thee, all the 2Kin 8:4
as he was *t* the king how 2Kin 8:5
the woman, she *t* him.........2Kin 8:6
t me that thou shouldest 2Kin 8:14
It is false; *t* us now 2Kin 9:12
to go to *t* it in Jezreel 2Kin 9:15
t, saying, He came even 2Kin 9:20
a messenger, and *t* him 2Kin 10:8
gave the money, being *t* 2Kin 12:11
t Hezekiah the captain 2Kin 20:5
T the man that sent you 2Kin 22:15
the men of the city *t* him 2Kin 23:17
Go and *t* David my servant ...1Chr 17:4
t thy servant that thou 1Chr 17:25
it was *t* David; and he 1Chr 19:17
Go and *t* David, saying 1Chr 21:10
Solomon *t* out threescore......2Chr 2:2
Solomon *t* her all her 2Chr 9:2
Solomon which he *t* her 2Chr 9:2
t thee that he would not 2Chr 18:17
some that *t* Jehoshaphat 2Chr 20:2
T ye the man that sent........2Chr 34:23
t them what they should ....Ezra 8:17
t I any man what my God.....Neh 2:12
I *t* them of the hand of ....Neh 2:18
who *t* it unto Esther ....Esth 2:22
t Haman, to see whether ......Esth 3:4
t them that he was a Jew .....Esth 3:4
And Mordecai *t* him of all .....Esth 4:7
t to Mordecai Esther's ....Esth 4:12
Mordecai had *t* of Bigthana ...Esth 6:2
Esther had *t* what he was .....Esth 8:1
escaped alone to *t* thee ....Job 1:15
teach thee, and *t* thee.........Job 8:10
and they shall *t* thee ....Job 12:7
have *t* from their fathers ......Job 15:18
of understanding *t* me.........Job 34:34
I may *t* all my bones ....Ps 22:17
t of all thy wondrous ....Ps 26:7
our fathers have *t* us..........Ps 44:1
t the towers thereof...........Ps 48:12
I would not *t* thee ....Ps 50:12
Thou *t* my wanderings ....Ps 56:8
our fathers have *t* us..........Ps 78:3
years as a tale that is *t*........Ps 90:9
t the number of the stars ......Ps 147:4
name, if thou canst *t*?..........Prov 30:4
a thousand years twice *t* ......Eccl 6:6
t a man what shall be ....Eccl 6:12
t him when it shall be?........Eccl 8:7

cannot *t* what shall be ....Eccl 10:14
after him, who can *t* him? .....Eccl 10:14
T me, O thou whom my ....Song 1:7
ye *t* him, that I am sick ....Song 5:8
I will *t* you what I will do .....Is 5:5
t this people, Hear ye.........Is 6:9
t the house of David..........Is 7:2
let them *t* thee now...........Is 19:12
t you from the beginning? .....Is 40:21
forth I *t* you of them ....Is 42:9
T ye, and bring them near ....Is 45:21
t it from that time? ....Is 45:21
t this, utter it even to the .....Is 48:20
t them, Thus saith the ....Jer 15:2
words that I shall *t* thee.......Jer 19:2
they *t* every man to his ....Jer 23:27
do *t* them, and cause my ......Jer 23:32
Go and *t* Hananiah ....Jer 28:13
hands of him that *t* them ......Jer 33:13
king of Judah, and *t* him ......Jer 34:2
Go and *t* the men of Judah ...Jer 35:13
We will surely *t* the king ......Jer 36:16
t all the words in the ears .....Jer 36:20
t ye it in Arnon that Moab ....Jer 48:20
unto them, and *t* them ....Ezek 3:11
T them therefore, Thus ....Ezek 12:23
t them, Behold, the king ......Ezek 17:12
t us what these things are .....Ezek 24:19
t thy servants the dream ......Dan 2:4
t me the dream, and I ....Dan 2:9
I *t* the dream before them.....Dan 4:7
t me the visions of my ....Dan 4:9
t the sum of the matters ......Dan 7:1
which was *t* is true ....Dan 8:26
T ye your children of it ....Joel 1:3
T us, we pray thee ....Jon 1:8
because he had *t* them ....Jon 1:10
believe, though it be *t* you ....Hab 1:5
and have *t* false dreams ....Zech 10:2
See thou *t* no man............Matt 8:4
city, and *t* every thing ....Matt 8:33
What I *t* you in darkness ......Matt 10:27
and went and *t* Jesus ....Matt 14:12
t no man that he was Jesus ....Matt 16:20
T the vision to no man........Matt 17:9
t him his fault between........Matt 18:15
T ye the daughter of Zion .....Matt 21:5
one thing, which if ye *t* ....Matt 21:24
t you by what authority ....Matt 21:24
and said, We cannot *t* ....Matt 21:27
t I you by what authority .....Matt 21:27
T them which are bidden......Matt 22:4
T us therefore, What ....Matt 22:17
T us, when shall these ....Matt 24:3
I have *t* you before ....Matt 24:25
t us whether thou be the ......Matt 26:63
t his disciples that he is ....Matt 28:7
see him: lo, I have *t* you ......Matt 28:7
went to *t* his disciples ....Matt 28:9
anon they *t* him of her ....Mark 1:30
t it in the city, and in ....Mark 5:14
t them how great things ....Mark 5:19
and *t* him all the truth ....Mark 5:33
they should *t* no man ....Mark 7:36
nor *t* it to any in the town ....Mark 8:26
should *t* no man of him ....Mark 8:30
t no man what things ....Mark 9:9
he answered and *t* them ....Mark 9:12
and began to *t* them what .....Mark 10:32
t you by what authority ....Mark 11:29
unto Jesus, We cannot *t* ......Mark 11:33
Neither do I *t* you by what ....Mark 11:33
T us, when shall these ....Mark 13:4
t his disciples and Peter ....Mark 16:7
t it unto the residue ....Mark 16:13
t her from the Lord ....Luke 1:45
t them by the shepherds ......Luke 2:18
charged him to *t* no man ......Luke 5:14
t John what things ye ....Luke 7:22
it was *t* him by certain ....Luke 8:20
which saw it *t* them by ....Luke 8:36
t no man what was done ......Luke 8:56
to *t* no man that thing ....Luke 9:21
I *t* you of a truth, there be ....Luke 9:27
t no man in those days........Luke 9:36
For I *t* you, that many ....Luke 10:24
I *t* you, Nay; but rather ....Luke 12:51
I *t* you, Nay: but, except ....Luke 13:3
Go ye, and *t* that fox ....Luke 13:32
I *t* you, in that night..........Luke 17:34
t you that he will avenge ......Luke 18:8
they *t* him, that Jesus of ......Luke 18:37
t you that, if these should .....Luke 19:40
T us, by what authority ....Luke 20:2
could not *t* whence it was .....Luke 20:7
I *t* thee, Peter, the cock.......Luke 22:34
Art thou the Christ? *t* us ......Luke 22:67
If I *t* you, ye will not ....Luke 22:67
t these things unto the ....Luke 24:10
t you earthly things ....John 3:12
he will *t* us all things ....John 4:25
t me all that ever I did.........John 4:39
and *t* the Jews that it was .....John 5:15
cannot *t* whence I come ....John 8:14
I *t* you the truth, ye ....John 8:45
I have *t* you already ....John 9:27
be the Christ, *t* us plainly .....John 10:24
t them what things Jesus ......John 11:46
cometh and *t* Andrew..........John 12:22
Andrew and Philip *t* Jesus.....John 12:22
I *t* you before it come ....John 13:19
have *t* you before it come .....John 14:29
things have I *t* you ....John 16:4
that I *t* you of them ....John 16:4
others *t* it thee of me? ....John 18:34
t me where thou hast laid .....John 20:15
t the disciples that she ....John 20:18
T me whether ye sold.........Acts 5:8
they returned, and *t* ....Acts 5:22
t thee what thou must do .....Acts 9:6
t thee what thou oughtest .....Acts 10:6
Who shall *t* thee words ....Acts 11:14
t you the same things by ......Acts 15:27
keeper of the prison *t* this.....Acts 16:36
either to *t*, or to hear ....Acts 17:21
be *t* thee of all things ....Acts 22:10
T me, art thou a Roman? .....Acts 22:27
into the castle, and *t*..........Acts 23:16
certain thing to *t* him ....Acts 23:17
t no man that thou hast ....Acts 23:22
be even as it was *t* me ....Acts 27:25
t us your earnest desire 2Cor 7:7
in the body, I cannot *t* 2Cor 12:2
out of the body, I cannot *t* 2Cor 12:2
of the body, I cannot *t*........2Cor 12:3
I *t* you the truth?............Gal 4:16
which I *t* you before ....Gal 5:21
also *t* you in time past ....Gal 5:21
whom I have *t* you often ......Phil 3:18
t you even weeping ....Phil 3:18
we *t* you before that we.......1Thess 3:4
I *t* you these things? 2Thess 2:5
t you there should be ....Jude 18
t thee the mystery of the ......Rev 17:7

TEL-MELAH (tĕl-mē'lä)—*"hill of salt"*
Place in Babylonia.......Ezra 2:59

TEMA (tē'mä)—*"south; sunburnt"*
Son of Ishmael ....Gen 25:15
Descendants of Abraham .1Chr 1:30
Troops of...............Job 6:19
Remote from Palestine ...Jer 25:23
On trade route through Arabia ....Is 21:13, 14

TEMAN (tē'măn)—*"southern"*
1. Grandson of Esau; duke of Edom ....Gen 36:11, 15
2. Another duke of Edom..Gen 36:42
3. Judgment pronounced against ....Amos 1:12
God appears from ......Hab 3:3
of Eliphaz; *T*, and Omar 1Chr 1:36
Duke Kenaz, duke *T* 1Chr 1:53
Is wisdom no more in *T*? .....Jer 49:7
the inhabitants of *T*..........Jer 49:20
make it desolate from *T* ......Ezek 25:13
And thy mighty men, O *T* ....Obad 9

TEMANI (tē'măn-ī)
Tribe in northeast Edom .Gen 36:34

TEMANITE (tē'măn-īt)—*an inhabitant of Teman*
Job's friend, Eliphaz .....Job 42:7, 9
[*also* TEMANITES]
of the land of the *T* 1Chr 1:45
Eliphaz the *T*, and Bildad .....Job 2:11
Eliphaz the *T* answered ....Job 4:1
answered Eliphaz the *T* ....Job 15:1
Eliphaz the *T* answered ....Job 22:1

TEMENI (tĕm'ĕ-nī)—*"fortunate"*
Son of Ashur 1Chr 4:5, 6

TEMPERANCE—*moderation, restraint*

Needed in:
Eating ....Prov 23:1-3
Sexual appetites 1Cor 7:1-9
All things...............1Cor 9:25-27

Helped by:
Self-control ....Prov 16:32
God's Spirit.............Gal 5:23
Spiritual growth 2Pet 1:6

In the use of wine, total recommended by:
Solomon ....Prov 23:31-35
Angel ....Judg 13:3-5
Nazarite vow ....Num 6:2, 3
First, among Rechabites. .Jer 35:1-10

See SELF-CONTROL; SOBER

[*also* TEMPER, TEMPERATE, TEMPERED]
t together, pure and holy......Ex 30:35
to *t* with the fine flour ....Ezek 46:14
of righteousness, *t* ....Acts 24:25
God hath *t* the body 1Cor 12:24
men, sober, just, holy, *t* ....Titus 1:8
men be sober, grave, *t*........Titus 2:2

TEMPEST—*violent storm*

Literal uses of:
At Sinai ....Heb 12:18-21
Jonah's ship tossed by ...Jon 1:4-15
Calmed by Christ........Matt 8:23-27
Paul's ship destroyed by. .Acts 27:14-20

Figurative of:
Destructiveness..........Is 28:2
God's wrath ....Jer 30:23
God's chastening ....Job 9:17
Furious troubles ....Ps 55:8
God's judgments ....Ps 83:15
Hell's torments ....Ps 11:6
Raging destructiveness ...2Pet 2:17
Destruction by war ......Amos 1:14

t stealeth him away in ....Job 27:20
noise, with storm and *t* ....Is 29:6
and *t*, and hailstones..........Is 30:30
and a covert from the *t* ....Is 32:2
afflicted, tossed with *t* ....Is 54:11

TEMPESTUOUS—*stormy*
very *t* round about him ....Ps 50:3
sea wrought, and was *t*........Jon 1:11
and was *t* against them........Jon 1:13
arose against it a *t* wind.......Acts 27:14

TEMPLE—*space on either side of human forehead*
smote the nail into his *t*.......Judg 4:21
the nail was in his *t*...........Judg 4:22
stricken through his *t* ....Judg 5:26
t are like a piece of a ....Song 4:3
pomegranate are thy *t* ....Song 6:7

TEMPLE—*place of worship*
[*also* TEMPLES]
seat by a post of the *t* 1Sam 1:9
out in the *t* of the Lord 1Sam 3:3
worship toward thy holy *t* .....Ps 5:7
The Lord is in his holy *t* ......Ps 11:4
my voice out of his *t*..........Ps 18:6
to inquire in his *t*.............Ps 27:4
t doth every one speak ....Ps 29:9
God, in the midst of thy *t*.....Ps 48:9
house, even of thy holy *t*......Ps 65:4
thy *t* at Jerusalem shall ....Ps 68:29
holy *t* have they defiled ....Ps 79:1
worship toward thy holy *t* .....Ps 138:2
his train filled the *t* ....Is 6:1

T

the *t*, Thy foundation shall .... Is 44:28
voice from the *t*, a voice ..... Is 66:6
saying, The *t* of the Lord ..... Jer 7:4
t of the Lord, The *t* .... Jer 7:4
were set before the *t* .... Jer 24:1
the vengeance of his *t* .... Jer 50:28
the vengeance of his *t* .... Jer 51:11
at the door of the *t* .... Ezek 8:16
backs toward the *t* of the ..... Ezek 8:16
he brought me to the *t* .... Ezek 41:1
with the inner *t* and the .... Ezek 41:15
The posts of the *t* were .... Ezek 41:21
on the doors of the *t* .... Ezek 41:25
t were a hundred cubits .... Ezek 42:8
t which was in Jerusalem ...... Dan 5:2
have carried into your *t* my ... Joel 3:5
songs of the *t* shall be .... Amos 8:3
again toward thy holy *t* .... Jon 2:4
the Lord from his holy *t* ...... Mic 1:2
the Lord is in his holy *t* .... Hab 2:20
upon a stone in the *t* of the ... Hag 2:15
build the *t* of the Lord .... Zech 6:12
for a memorial in the *t* .... Zech 6:14
that the *t* might be built .... Zech 8:9
suddenly come to his *t* .... Mal 3:1
t of the great goddess .... Acts 19:27
sit at meat in the idol's *t* 1Cor 8:10
of the things of the *t* ? 1Cor 9:13
I make a pillar in the *t* .... Rev 3:12
day and night in his *t* .... Rev 7:15
measure the *t* of God .... Rev 11:1
the *t* of God was opened ...... Rev 11:19
was seen in his *t* the ark ...... Rev 11:19
angel came out of the *t* .... Rev 14:15
t of the tabernacle of the ...... Rev 15:5
t was filled with smoke .... Rev 15:8
able to enter into the *t* .... Rev 15:8
a great voice out of the *t* .... Rev 16:1
I saw no *t* therein: for the ..... Rev 21:22
Lamb are the *t* of it .... Rev 21:22

TEMPLE, HEROD'S—*temple rebuilt prior to Christ's birth*

Zechariah received vision in .... Luke 1:5-22
Infant Jesus greeted here by Simeon and Anna .. Luke 2:22-39
Jesus visited at 12 .... Luke 2:42-52
Jesus visited and cleansed. John 2:15-17
Construction of, specified. John 2:19, 20
Jesus taught in .... John 8:20
Jesus cleansed again ..... Matt 21:12-16
Jesus spoke parables in .. Matt 21:23-46
Jesus exposes Pharisees in Matt 23:1-39
Destruction of, foretold .. Matt 24:1, 2
Veil of, rent at Christ's death .... { Matt 27:51 / Heb 10:20 }
Christians worshiped here. Acts 2:46
Apostles taught here ...... Acts 3:1-26
Stephen's teaching on the true .... Acts 7:46-50
Apostles understand prophecy concerning ... Acts 15:14-18
Paul accused of profaning. Acts 21:20-30

on a pinnacle of the *t* .... Matt 4:5
priests in the *t* profane .... Matt 12:5
you teaching in the *t* .... Matt 26:55
to destroy the *t* of God .... Matt 26:61
pieces of silver in the *t* .... Matt 27:5
that destroyest the *t* .... Matt 27:40
Jerusalem, and into the *t* ...... Mark 11:11
Jesus went into the *t* .... Mark 11:15
sold and bought in the *t* .... Mark 11:15
as he was walking in the *t* ..... Mark 11:27
while he taught in the *t* .... Mark 12:35
as he went out of the *t* .... Mark 13:1
daily with you in the *t* .... Mark 14:49
destroy this *t*..made with ...... Mark 14:58
that destroyest the *t* .... Mark 15:29
veil of the *t* was rent .... Mark 15:38
on a pinnacle of the *t* .... Luke 4:9
the altar and the *t* .... Luke 11:51
up into the *t* to pray .... Luke 18:10
And he went into the *t* .... Luke 19:45
the people in the *t* .... Luke 20:1
as some spake of the *t* .... Luke 21:5
morning to him in the *t* .... Luke 21:38
and captains of the *t* .... Luke 22:52
daily with you in the *t* .... Luke 22:53
veil of the *t* was rent .... Luke 23:45
continually in the *t* .... Luke 24:53
in the *t* those that sold .... John 2:14
Jesus findeth him in the *t* ..... John 5:14
Jesus went up into the *t* .... John 7:14
he came again into the *t* ...... John 8:2
Jesus walked in the *t* .... John 10:23
as they stood in the *t* .... John 11:56
synagogue, and in the *t* .... John 18:20
and the captain of the *t* .... Acts 4:1
speak in the *t* to the .... Acts 5:20
the captain of the *t* .... Acts 5:24
daily in the *t*, and in .... Acts 5:42
in *t* made with hands .... Acts 17:24
while I prayed in the *t* .... Acts 22:17
about to profane the *t* .... Acts 24:6
found me purified in the *t* ..... Acts 24:18
neither against the *t* .... Acts 25:8
Jews caught me in the *t* .... Acts 26:21

TEMPLE, SOLOMON'S—*original temple in Jerusalem; constructed during Solomon's reign*

Features regarding:
Site of, on Mt. Moriah ... 2Sam 24:18-25
Conceived by David 2Sam 7:1-3
Building of, forbidden to David 1Chr 22:5-16
David promised a greater house 2Sam 7:4-29
Pattern of, given to Solomon by David 1Chr 28:1-21
Provisions for, given to Solomon 1Chr 29:1-19
Supplies furnished by Hiram 1Kin 5:1-18
Construction of, by Solomon .... 2Chr 3—4
Dedication of, by Solomon 2Chr 6
Seven years in building .. 1Kin 6:38
No noise in building 1Kin 6:7
Date of building 1Kin 6:1, 37, 38
Workmen employed in ... 1Kin 5:15-17

History of:
Ark brought into 1Kin 8:1-9
Filled with God's glory ... 1Kin 8:10, 11
Treasures taken away 1Kin 14:25, 26
Repaired by Jehoash 2Kin 12:4-14
Treasures of, given to Arameans by Jehoash .. 2Kin 12:17, 18
Treasures of, given to Assyrians by Ahaz 2Kin 16:14, 18
Worship of, restored by Hezekiah 2Chr 29:3-35
Treasures of, given by Hezekiah to Assyrians . 2Kin 18:13-16
Desecrated by Manasseh's idolatry 2Kin 21:4-7
Repaired and purified by Josiah 2Kin 23:4-12
Plundered and burned by Babylonians 2Kin 25:9-17

the porch before the *t* 1Kin 6:3
the *t* before it, was forty 1Kin 6:17
in the porch of the *t* 1Kin 7:21
in the *t* of the Lord 2Kin 11:10
right corner of the *t* 2Kin 11:11
to the left corner of the *t* 2Kin 11:11
by the altar and the *t* 2Kin 11:11
in the *t* of the Lord 2Kin 24:13
office in the *t* that Solomon ... 1Chr 6:10
the right side of the *t* 2Chr 23:10
to the left side of the *t* 2Chr 23:10
along by the altar and the *t* ... 2Chr 23:10
went into the *t* of the Lord 2Chr 26:16
entered not into the *t* 2Chr 27:2
Josiah had prepared the *t* 2Chr 35:20

TEMPLE, SPIRITUAL

Descriptive of:
Christ's body .... John 2:19, 21
Believer's body 1Cor 6:19
True Church 1Cor 3:16, 17
Apostate church 2Thess 2:4

Believers as, described as:
Indwelt by God 2Cor 6:16
Indwelt by Christ .... Eph 3:17, 18
Indwelt by the Spirit ..... Eph 2:21, 22
Priests 1Pet 2:5
Offering spiritual sacrifices .... Heb 3:15, 16

TEMPLE, ZERUBBABEL'S—*built after the Jews' return from Babylon*
By the order of Cyrus ... Ezra 1:1-4
Temple vessels restored for .... Ezra 1:7-11
Worship of, restored ..... Ezra 3:3-13
Work of rebuilding hindered .... Ezra 4:1-24
Building of, completed .. Ezra 6:13-18
Inferiority of .... Ezra 3:12

[*also* TEMPLE]
the *t* that is in Jerusalem ...... Ezra 5:15
t which is at Jerusalem .... Ezra 6:5
house of God, within the *t* .... Neh 6:10
shut the doors of the *t* .... Neh 6:10

TEMPORAL—*pertaining to earthly life*
Things that are seen 2Cor 4:18

TEMPORAL BLESSINGS—*those which are given to supply the needs of those alive on earth*

Consisting of:
Rain .... Matt 5:45
Seedtime and harvest .... Gen 8:22
Food and raiment .... Luke 12:22-31
Prosperity .... Deut 8:7-18
Children .... Ps 127:3-5
Preservation of life 2Tim 4:16-18
Providential guidance .... Gen 24:12-14, 42-44

God's supply of:
Promised .... Prov 3:9, 10
Provided .... Neh 9:15
Prayed for .... Matt 6:11
Acknowledged .... Ps 23:1-5
Explained .... Deut 8:2, 3
Contingent upon obedience .... { Mal 3:7-11 / Matt 6:25-34 }
Object of praise .... Ps 103:1-5

TEMPTATION—*testing; enticement to do wrong*

Of God:
Forbidden .... Matt 4:7
By Israel .... Ps 78:18-56, Heb 3:9
Not possible .... James 1:13

Of Christ by:
The devil .... Matt 4:1-10
Jewish leaders .... Matt 16:1
His disciples .... Matt 16:23
Like us, but without sin .. Heb 4:15
Design of .... Heb 2:18

Of Satan, against:
Job .... Job 1:6-12
David 1Chr 21:1
Joshua .... Zech 3:1-5
Jesus .... Luke 4:1-13
Ananias and Sapphira .... Acts 5:1-3
Christians 1Cor 7:5

Of Christians by:
Lust .... James 1:13-15
Riches 1Tim 6:9
Liability to .... Gal 6:1
Warnings against .... Matt 26:41
Prayer against .... Matt 6:13
Limitation of 1Cor 10:13
Deliverance from 2Pet 2:9

Of men by:
Eve .... Gen 3:6

Potiphar's wife .... Gen 39:1-19
Delilah .... Judg 16:6-20
Jezebel 1Kin 21:7
Job's wife .... Job 2:9
Adulteress .... Prov 7:5-27
Herodias' daughter .... Mark 6:22-29

[*also* TEMPT, TEMPTATIONS, TEMPTED, TEMPTETH, TEMPTING]

that God did *t* Abraham .... Gen 22:1
do ye *t* the Lord? .... Ex 17:2
because they *t* the Lord .... Ex 17:7
t me now these ten times .... Num 14:22
by *t*, by signs and by .... Deut 4:34
as ye *t* him in Massah .... Deut 6:16
t which thine eyes saw .... Deut 7:19
t which thine eyes have .... Deut 29:3
day of *t* in the wilderness .... Ps 95:8
When your fathers *t* me .... Ps 95:9
and *t* God in the desert .... Ps 106:14
neither will I *t* the Lord .... Is 7:12
t God are even delivered .... Mal 3:15
came unto him *t* him .... Matt 19:3
Why *t* ye me, ye hypocrites? .... Matt 22:18
him a question *t* him .... Matt 22:35
forty days, *t* of Satan .... Mark 1:13
sign from heaven, *t* him .... Mark 8:11
put away his wife? *t* him .... Mark 10:2
unto them, Why *t* ye me? .... Mark 12:15
lest ye enter into *t* .... Mark 14:38
in time of *t* fall away .... Luke 8:13
stood up and *t* him .... Luke 10:25
lead us not into *t* .... Luke 11:4
t him, sought of him a sign .... Luke 11:16
said unto them, Why *t* ye me? .... Luke 20:23
Pray..ye enter not into *t* .... Luke 22:40
lest ye enter into *t* .... Luke 22:46
This they said, *t* him .... John 8:6
t the Spirit of the Lord? .... Acts 5:9
therefore why *t* ye God .... Acts 15:10
Neither let us *t* Christ 1Cor 10:9
as some of them also *t* 1Cor 10:9
t which was in my flesh .... Gal 4:14
means the tempter have *t* you 1Thess 3:5
day of the *t* in the wilderness .... Heb 3:8
sawn asunder, were *t* .... Heb 11:37
when ye fall into divers *t* .... James 1:2
the man that endureth *t* .... James 1:12
through manifold *t* 1Pet 1:6
deliver the godly out of *t* 2Pet 2:9
keep thee from the hour of *t* .... Rev 3:10

TEMPTER—*one who tempts*

And when the *t* came to him .... Matt 4:3
means the *t* have tempted you 1Thess 3:5

TEN

Descriptive of:

Brothers .... Gen 42:3
Cubits .... Ex 26:16
Pillars and sockets .... Ex 27:12
Commandments .... Ex 34:28
Shekels .... Num 7:14
Years .... Ruth 1:4
Loaves 1Sam 17:17
Tribes 1Kin 11:31, 35
Degrees 2Kin 20:9-11
Virgins .... Matt 25:1-13
Talents .... Matt 25:28
Lepers .... Luke 17:11-19
Pieces of money .... Luke 19:12-27
Horns .... Rev 12:3

Expressive of:

Representation .... Ruth 4:2
Intensity .... Num 14:22
Sufficiency .... Neh 4:12
Magnitude .... Dan 1:20
Remnant .... Amos 5:3
Completion .... Dan 7:7, 20, 24
Perfection .... Luke 19:16-24

[*also* TEN'S, TENS, TENTH]

nine hundred and *t* years .... Gen 5:14
until the *t* month .... Gen 8:5
in the *t* month on the first .... Gen 8:5
Abram had dwelt *t* years .... Gen 16:3
t shall be found .... Gen 18:32
not destroy it for *t* sake .... Gen 18:32
servant took *t* camels .... Gen 24:10
few days, at the least *t* .... Gen 24:55
changed my wages *t* times .... Gen 31:7
forty kine, and *t* bulls .... Gen 32:15
she asses, and *t* foals .... Gen 32:15
t asses laden with the good .... Gen 45:23
t she asses laden with .... Gen 45:23
Egypt, were threescore and *t* .... Gen 46:27
for him threescore and *t* .... Gen 50:3
hundred and *t* years old .... Gen 50:26
In the *t* day of this month .... Ex 12:3
threescore and *t* palm trees .... Ex 15:27
of fifties and rulers of *t* .... Ex 18:21
t curtains of fine twined .... Ex 26:1
one lamb a *t* deal of flour .... Ex 29:40
t curtains of fine twined .... Ex 36:8
t, and their sockets *t* .... Ex 38:12
t part of an ephah of fine .... Lev 5:11
three *t* deals of fine flour .... Lev 14:10
on the *t* day of the month .... Lev 16:29
wave loaves of two *t* deals .... Lev 23:17
two *t* deals shall be in one .... Lev 24:5
put *t* thousand to flight .... Lev 26:8
the female *t* shekels .... Lev 27:5
t shall be holy unto the .... Lev 27:32
t part of an ephah of barley .... Num 5:15
spoon of gold of *t* shekels .... Num 7:20
weighing *t* shekels apiece .... Num 7:86
least gathered *t* homers .... Num 11:32
of a *t* deal of flour .... Num 15:4
three *t* deals of flour .... Num 15:9
of Levi all the *t* in Israel .... Num 18:21
a *t* part of an ephah of .... Num 28:5
t deals of flour for a meat .... Num 28:12
and two *t* deals of flour .... Num 28:12
three *t* deals shall ye offer .... Num 28:20
two *t* deals for a ram .... Num 28:20
t deals unto one bullock .... Num 28:28
two *t* deals unto one ram .... Num 28:28
three *t* deals for a bullock .... Num 29:3
two *t* deals for a ram .... Num 29:3
t day of this seventh month .... Num 29:7
three *t* deals to a bullock .... Num 29:9
two *t* deals to one ram .... Num 29:9
three *t* deals unto every .... Num 29:14
two *t* deals to each ram .... Num 29:14
fourth day *t* bullocks .... Num 29:23
threescore and *t* palm trees .... Num 33:9
fifties, and captains over *t* .... Deut 1:15
even *t* commandments .... Deut 4:13
with threescore and *t* .... Deut 10:22
even to his *t* generation .... Deut 23:2
put *t* thousand to flight .... Deut 32:30
with *t* thousands of saints .... Deut 33:2
t day of the first month .... Josh 4:19
t portions to Manasseh .... Josh 17:5
tribe of Manasseh, *t* cities .... Josh 21:5
t princes, of each chief .... Josh 22:14
hundred and *t* years old .... Josh 24:29
in Bezek *t* thousand men .... Judg 1:4
hundred and *t* years old .... Judg 2:8
about *t* thousand men .... Judg 3:29
with thee *t* thousand men .... Judg 4:6
Gideon took *t* men of his .... Judg 6:27
there remained *t* thousand .... Judg 7:3
threescore and *t* sons .... Judg 8:30
threescore and *t* persons .... Judg 9:2
threescore and *t* persons .... Judg 9:5
threescore and *t* sons .... Judg 9:24
he judged Israel *t* years .... Judg 12:11
thee *t* shekels of silver .... Judg 17:10
t men of a hundred .... Judg 20:10
out of *t* thousand .... Judg 20:10
better to thee than *t* sons? 1Sam 1:8
and threescore and *t* 1Sam 6:19
take the *t* of your seed 1Sam 8:15
t thousand men of Judah 1Sam 15:4
David his *t* thousands 1Sam 18:7
David his *t* thousands? 1Sam 21:11
sent out *t* young men 1Sam 25:5
David his *t* thousands? 1Sam 29:5
the king left *t* women 2Sam 15:16
art worth *t* thousand 2Sam 18:3
have *t* parts in the king 2Sam 19:43
king took the *t* women 2Sam 20:3
T fat oxen and twenty 1Kin 4:23
t thousand a month by 1Kin 5:14
t cubits was the breadth 1Kin 6:3
the other were *t* cubits 1Kin 6:24
cherub was *t* cubits 1Kin 6:26
stones of *t* cubits 1Kin 7:10
t in a cubit, compassing 1Kin 7:24
he made the *t* bases 1Kin 7:37
he *t* lavers of brass 1Kin 7:38
every one of the *t* bases 1Kin 7:38
him *t* talents of silver 2Kin 5:5
and *t* changes of raiment 2Kin 5:5
horsemen and *t* chariots 2Kin 13:7
and *t* thousand footmen 2Kin 13:7
valley of salt *t* thousand 2Kin 14:7
t years in Samaria 2Kin 15:17
t thousand captives 2Kin 24:14
his reign in the *t* month 2Kin 25:1
in the *t* day of the month 2Kin 25:1
t men with him, and smote 2Kin 25:25
Manasseh by lot, *t* cities 1Chr 6:61
Jeremiah the *t*, Machbanai 1Chr 12:13
t thousand men that drew 1Chr 21:5
t to Shimei, he, his sons 1Chr 25:17
and *t* thousand drams 1Chr 29:7
silver *t* thousand talents 1Chr 29:7
t thousand men to bear 2Chr 2:2
and *t* cubits the height 2Chr 4:1
t in a cubit, compassing 2Chr 4:3
t candlesticks of gold 2Chr 4:7
the land was quiet *t* years 2Chr 14:1
of Seir *t* thousand 2Chr 25:11
t thousand measures of 2Chr 27:5
and *t* thousand of barley 2Chr 27:5
threescore and *t* bullocks 2Chr 29:32
and *t* thousand sheep 2Chr 30:24
three months and *t* days 2Chr 36:9
sort four hundred and *t* .... Ezra 1:10
a hundred and *t* males .... Ezra 8:12
first day of the *t* month .... Ezra 10:16
once in *t* days store of all .... Neh 5:18
bring one of *t* to dwell in .... Neh 11:1
house royal in the *t* month .... Esth 2:16
t thousand talents of silver .... Esth 3:9
The *t* sons of Haman .... Esth 9:10
Haman's *t* sons be hanged .... Esth 9:13
t times have ye reproached .... Job 19:3
t thousands of people .... Ps 3:6
instrument of *t* strings .... Ps 33:2
threescore years and *t* .... Ps 90:10
t thousand at thy right .... Ps 91:7
instrument of *t* strings .... Ps 92:3
instrument of *t* strings .... Ps 144:9
more than *t* mighty men .... Eccl 7:19
chiefest among *t* thousand .... Song 5:10
Ahaz, *t* degrees backward .... Is 38:8
sun returned *t* degrees .... Is 38:8
even *t* men with him came .... Jer 41:1
But *t* men were found among .... Jer 41:8
came to pass after *t* days .... Jer 42:7
his reign, in the *t* month .... Jer 52:4
in the *t* day of the month .... Jer 52:4
in the *t* day of the month .... Jer 52:12
the *t* day of the month .... Ezek 20:1
ninth year, in the *t* month .... Ezek 24:1
t day of the month .... Ezek 24:1
t year, in the *t* month .... Ezek 29:1
t month, in the fifth day .... Ezek 33:21
entry of the gate *t* cubits .... Ezek 40:11
breadth of the door was *t* .... Ezek 41:2
chambers was a walk of *t* .... Ezek 42:4
breadth shall be *t* thousand .... Ezek 45:1
t thousand of breadth .... Ezek 45:5
the *t* part of a homer .... Ezek 45:11
is a homer of *t* baths .... Ezek 45:14
t baths are a homer .... Ezek 45:14
t thousand in breadth .... Ezek 48:9
t thousand in breadth .... Ezek 48:10
t thousand in breadth .... Ezek 48:13
t thousand eastward .... Ezek 48:18
t thousand westward .... Ezek 48:18
Prove thy servants..*t* days .... Dan 1:12
t days their countenances .... Dan 1:15
t thousand times *t* .... Dan 7:10

T

down many *t* thousands ....Dan 11:12
t men in one house ....Amos 6:9
measures, there were but *t* ....Hag 2:16
threescore and *t* years?........Zech 1:12
breadth thereof *t* cubits ....Zech 5:2
t men shall take hold out .....Zech 8:23
him *t* thousand talents ....Matt 18:24
the *t* heard it, they were ......Matt 20:24
when the *t* heard it ....Mark 10:41
t thousand to meet him ....Luke 14:31
having *t* pieces of silver ....Luke 15:8
horsemen threescore and *t* ....Acts 23:23
them more than *t* days ....Acts 25:6
t thousand instructors 1Cor 4:15
t thousand words in an........1Cor 14:19
t thousands of his saints ......Jude 14
have tribulation *t* days ....Rev 2:10
the *t* part of the city fell ......Rev 11:13
seven heads and *t* horns ....Rev 13:1
upon his horns *t* crowns ....Rev 13:1
seven heads and *t* horns ....Rev 17:3
t horns..thou sawest are *t* .....Rev 17:12
the *t*, a chrysoprasus ....Rev 21:20

TEN COMMANDMENTS—*the ethical instructions given by God to Moses at Mount Sinai*

Facts concerning:
Given at Sinai..........Ex 20:1-17
Written on stone ....Ex 24:12
Written by God ....Ex 31:18
First stones broken ......Ex 32:19
Another copy given......Ex 34:1
Put in the ark ....Deut 10:1-5
Called a covenant ....Ex 34:28
Given in a different form .Deut 5:6-21
The greatest of these ....Matt 22:35-40
Rom 13:8-10

Allusions to, in Scripture:
First...................Acts 17:23
Second 1Kin 18:17-40
Third...................Matt 5:33-37
Fourth..................Jer 17:21-27
Fifth ....Deut 21:18-21
Eph 6:1-3
Sixth ....Num 35:16-21
Seventh.................Num 5:12-31
Matt 5:27-32
Eighth..................Matt 19:18
Ninth...................Deut 19:16-21
Tenth ....Rom 7:7

TEND—*to incline toward; attend to*

[*also* TENDETH]
labor of the righteous *t* ....Prov 10:16
As righteousness *t* to life ......Prov 11:19
talk of the lips *t* only to.......Prov 14:23
fear of the Lord *t* to life ......Prov 19:23

TENDER—*young; gentle; compassionate*

Used of physical things:
Animal ....Gen 18:7
Grass...................2Sam 23:4
Son ....Prov 4:3
Weak eyes ....Gen 29:17
Small children..........Gen 33:13
Women.................Deut 28:56
Instability ....Deut 28:54

Used of spiritual things:
Messiah ....Is 53:2
Compassion ....Eph 4:32
God's mercy ....Luke 1:78
Man's heart 2Kin 22:19
Christ's return..........Matt 24:32
Babylon's destruction ....Is 47:1

small rain upon the *t* herb.....Deut 32:2
Solomon..is young and *t* 1Chr 22:5
is yet young and *t* 1Chr 29:1
Because thine heart was *t* 2Chr 34:27
t branch thereof will not ......Job 14:7
the bud of the *t* herb ....Job 38:27
O Lord, thy *t* mercies..........Ps 25:6
not thou thy *t* mercies ....Ps 40:11
multitude of thy *t* mercies .....Ps 69:16
let thy *t* mercies speedily ......Ps 79:8
Let thy *t* mercies come........Ps 119:77
t mercies are over all his ......Ps 145:9
t mercies of the wicked ....Prov 12:10
t grape give a good smell .....Song 2:13
the *t* grape appear ....Song 7:12
his young twigs a *t* one ....Ezek 17:22
Daniel into favor and *t*........Dan 1:9

TENDERHEARTED—*indecisive; timid; gentle*
Rehoboam was young and *t* ...2Chr 13:7
kind to one another, *t* ....Eph 4:32

TENDERNESS—*expressing feeling or sympathy*
Shown toward the young .Gen 33:13
Expressed toward an enemy 1Sam 30:11-15
Illustrated by a Samaritan.Luke 10:33-36
Manifested by a father ...Luke 15:11-24

TENONS—*projections in a piece of wood used to make a joint*
t shall there be in one board ..Ex 26:17
one board for his two *t* ......Ex 26:19
board for his two *t* ....Ex 26:19
one board for his two *t* ......Ex 36:24
board for his two *t* ....Ex 36:24

TENOR—*the purport of something spoken or written*
the *t* of these words ....Gen 43:7
the *t* of these words ....Ex 34:27

TENT—*portable cloth or animal-hide dwellings*

Used by:
People..................1Chr 17:5
Shepherds ....Is 38:12
Armies 1Sam 13:2
Rechabites ....Jer 35:7, 10
Women.................Gen 24:67
Maidservants ....Gen 31:33

Features concerning:
Fastened by cords ....Is 54:2
Door provided ....Gen 18:1
Used for the ark 2Sam 7:1-6

Figurative of:
Shortness of life ....Is 38:12
2Cor 5:1
Heavens ....Is 40:22
Enlarge ....Is 54:2

[*also* TENTS]
of such as dwell in *t* ....Gen 4:20
uncovered within his *t* ....Gen 9:21
place where his *t* had been ....Gen 13:3
had flocks, and herds, and *t* ...Gen 13:5
Then Abram removed his *t*....Gen 13:18
meet them from the *t* door ....Gen 18:2
said, Behold, in the *t* ....Gen 18:9
plain man, dwelling in *t* ....Gen 25:27
t in the valley of Gerar ....Gen 26:17
Jacob had pitched his *t*........Gen 31:25
Laban searched all the *t* ......Gen 31:34
he had spread his *t* ....Gen 33:19
of the curtains of the *t* ....Ex 26:12
a covering for the *t* of ....Ex 26:14
every man at his *t* door ......Ex 33:8
The tabernacle, his *t*, and .....Ex 35:11
to couple the *t* together ......Ex 36:18
the *t* of the congregation ......Ex 39:32
t of the congregation.........Ex 39:40
t of the congregation..........Ex 40:7
t over the tabernacle ....Ex 40:19
the covering of the *t* ....Ex 40:19
candlestick in the *t* of ....Ex 40:24
t of the congregation..........Ex 40:29
the *t* of the congregation ......Ex 40:32
t of the congregation..........Ex 40:34
abroad out of his *t* seven ......Lev 14:8
Israel shall pitch their *t* ....Num 1:52
tabernacle, and the *t*..........Num 3:25
they rested in their *t* ....Num 9:18
of Israel abode in their *t* ......Num 9:22
man in the door of his *t*.......Num 11:10
whether in *t*, or in strong .....Num 13:19
stood in the door of their *t* ....Num 16:27
when a man dieth in a *t*.......Num 19:14
t, and all that is in the *t*.......Num 19:14
How goodly are thy *t*, O ......Num 24:5
man of Israel into the *t* ....Num 25:8
ye murmured in your *t*........Deut 1:27
Get you into your *t* again .....Deut 5:30
and go unto thy *t* ....Deut 16:7
removed from their *t* ....Josh 3:14
in the midst of my *t* ....Josh 7:21
they ran unto the *t*; and......Josh 7:22
in his *t*, and the silver ....Josh 7:22
his *t*, and all that he had .....Josh 7:24
they went unto their *t*.........Josh 22:6
much riches unto your *t* ....Josh 22:8
his *t* unto the plain of.........Judg 4:11
in unto her into the *t* ....Judg 4:18
wife took a nail of the *t*.......Judg 4:21
be above women in the *t*......Judg 5:24
Midian and came unto a *t*.....Judg 7:13
not any of us go to his *t* ......Judg 20:8
fled every man into his *t* 1Sam 4:10
and they spoiled their *t* 1Sam 17:53
put his armor in his *t* 1Sam 17:54
fled every one to his *t* 2Sam 18:17
city, every man to his *t* 2Sam 20:22
their *t* joyful and glad.........1Kin 8:66
to your *t*, O Israel: now.......1Kin 12:16
departed unto their *t*..........1Kin 12:16
their *t*, and their horses 2Kin 7:7
they went into one *t* 2Kin 7:8
entered into another *t*.........2Kin 7:8
and spoiled the *t* of the 2Kin 7:16
Israel dwelt in their *t* 2Kin 13:5
and pitched for it a *t* 1Chr 15:1
it in the midst of the *t* 1Chr 16:1
a *t* for it at Jerusalem.........2Chr 1:4
people away into their *t*.......2Chr 7:10
all Israel went to their *t*.......2Chr 10:16
abode we in *t* three days ......Ezra 8:15
let none dwell in their *t* ....Ps 69:25
t which he placed among ......Ps 78:60
in the *t* of wickedness.........Ps 84:10
dwell in the *t* of Kedar! ....Ps 120:5
as the *t* of Kedar ....Song 1:5
shall the Arabian pitch *t* ......Is 13:20
suddenly are my *t* spoiled .....Jer 4:20
none to stretch forth my *t*.....Jer 10:20
the captivity of Jacob's *t* ......Jer 30:18
up every man in his *t* ....Jer 37:10
Their *t* and their flocks ....Jer 49:29
save the *t* of Judah first ....Zech 12:7

TENTH—*See* TEN

TENTMAKERS
occupation they were *t*........Acts 18:3

TENTMAKING—*the craft of making tents*

The occupation of:
Aquila and Priscilla......Acts 18:2, 3
Paul...................Acts 18:2, 3

TERAH, THARA (tē'rä, thā'rä)—*"turning; duration"*
Father of Abram ....Gen 11:26
Idolater................Josh 24:2
Dies in Haran ....Gen 11:25-32

TERAPHIM (těr'ă-fĭm)—*household idols used by neighboring tribes and by apostate Israel*
Laban's, stolen by Rachel.Gen 31:19-35
Used in idolatry ....Hos 3:4
made an ephod, and *t* ....Judg 17:5
houses an ephod, and *t* ....Judg 18:14
the ephod, and the *t*..........Judg 18:17
the ephod, and the *t*..........Judg 18:18
took the ephod, and the *t* .....Judg 18:20

TERESH (tē'rĕsh)—*"strictness; reverence"*
King's official ....Esth 2:21
told of Bigthana and *T*........Esth 6:2

TERMED—*called*
no more be *t* Forsaken ....Is 62:4
any more be *t* Desolate ....Is 62:4

TERRACES—*raised embankment with a leveled top*
of the algum trees *t*..........2Chr 9:11

TERRESTRIAL—*belonging to the earth*
Spoken of bodies 1Cor 15:40

TERRIBLE—*bad; awesome*

[*also* TERRIBLENESS, TERRIBLY]
a *t* thing that I will do . . . . Ex 34:10
great and *t* wilderness . . . . Deut 1:19
great and *t* wilderness . . . . Deut 8:15
these great and *t* things . . . . . . Deut 10:21
and with great *t*, and with . . . . . Deut 26:8
of an angel of God, very *t* . . . . . Judg 13:6
a name of greatness and *t* 1Chr 17:21
heaven, the great and *t* God . . . Neh 1:5
the mighty, and the *t* God . . . . Neh 9:32
with God is *t* majesty . . . . Job 37:22
teeth are *t* round about . . . . Job 41:14
For the Lord most high is *t* . . . Ps 47:2
t things in righteousness . . . . Ps 65:5
God, How *t* art thou in thy . . . Ps 66:3
he is *t* in his doing toward . . . . Ps 66:5
God, thou art *t* out of thy . . . . . Ps 68:35
he is *t* to the kings of the . . . . . Ps 76:12
them praise thy great and *t* . . . . Ps 99:3
t things by the Red Sea . . . . Ps 106:22
speak of the might of thy *t* . . . . Ps 145:6
t as an army with banners . . . . . Song 6:4
he ariseth to shake *t* the . . . . . . Is 2:19
the haughtiness of the *t* . . . . Is 13:11
from a people *t* from their . . . . Is 18:7
the *t* nations shall fear . . . . Is 25:3
branch of the *t* ones shall . . . . . Is 25:5
For the *t* one is brought to . . . . Is 29:20
didst *t* things which we . . . . Is 64:3
thee out of the hand of the *t* . . Jer 15:21
because of the *t* famine . . . . Lam 5:10
was as the color of the *t* . . . . . . Ezek 1:22
him, the *t* of the nations . . . . . . Ezek 30:11
t of the nations, all of them . . . Ezek 32:12
and the form thereof was *t* . . . . Dan 2:31
fir trees shall be *t* shaken . . . . . Nah 2:3
t by your adversaries . . . . Phil 1:28

TERRIFY—*to fill with intense fear*

[*also* TERRIFIED, TERRIFIEST]
neither be ye *t* because of . . . . . Deut 20:3
the blackness of the day *t* it . . . . Job 3:5
the contempt of families *t* me . . Job 31:34
I would *t* you by letters 2Cor 10:9
in nothing *t* by your . . . . Phil 1:28

TERROR—*intense fear*

Caused by:
Lord's presence . . . . Heb 12:21
Fear . . . . Job 9:34
Death . . . . Job 24:17
Arrogance and pride . . . . . Jer 49:16
War . . . . Ezek 21:12
Fright . . . . Luke 24:37
Persecutors 1Pet 3:14

Sent as a means of:
Protection . . . . Gen 35:5
Punishment . . . . Lev 26:16

Safeguards against, found in:
God's promise . . . . Ps 91:5
God's plan . . . . Luke 21:9

[*also* TERRORS]
out arm, and by great *t* . . . . Deut 4:34
sword without, and *t* within . . . Deut 32:25
that your *t* is fallen upon us . . . Josh 2:9
the *t* of God do set themselves . Job 6:4
T shall make him afraid on . . . . Job 18:11
bring him to the king of *t* . . . . . Job 18:14
out of his gall: *t* are upon him . Job 20:25
T take hold on him as waters . . Job 27:20
T are turned upon me: they . . . Job 30:15
destruction from God was a *t* . . Job 31:23
t of death are fallen upon me . . Ps 55:4
utterly consumed with *t* . . . . Ps 73:19
suffer thy *t* I am distracted . . . . Ps 88:15
shall lop the bough with *t* . . . . . Is 10:33
heart shall meditate *t* . . . . Is 33:18
it suddenly, and *t* upon the city . Jer 15:8
Be not a *t* unto me: thou art . . Jer 17:17
out arm, and with great *t* . . . . . Jer 32:21
solemn day my *t* round about . . Lam 2:22
cause their *t* to be on all that . . Ezek 26:17
thou shalt be a *t* and never . . . . Ezek 27:36
caused *t* in the land of the . . . . Ezek 32:23
though their *t* was caused in . . . Ezek 32:25
they were the *t* of the mighty . . Ezek 32:27
have caused my *t* in the land . . Ezek 32:32
rulers are not a *t* to good . . . . . Rom 13:3
Knowing..the *t* of the Lord 2Cor 5:11

TERTIUS (tûr'shĭ-ŭs)—*"third"*
Paul's scribe . . . . Rom 16:22

TERTULLUS (ter-tŭl'ŭs)—*"third"*
Orator who accuses Paul . Acts 24:1-8

TEST—*a trial that manifests a person's real character*

By:
Difficult demands . . . . Gen 12:1, 2
Severe trials . . . . Job 1:6-22
Prosperity of the wicked . Ps 73:1-28
Hardships 2Cor 11:21-33

Kinds of:
Given to Solomon 1Kin 10:1-3
Physical 1Sam 17:38, 39
Supernatural . . . . Ex 7—11
Spiritual . . . . Dan 6:1-28
National . . . . Ex 32:1-35

Purposes of, to:
Test obedience . . . . Gen 3:1-8
Gen 22:1-18
Learn God's will . . . . Judg 6:36-40
Accept good diet . . . . Dan 1:12-16
Refute Satan's claims . . . . Job 1:6-22
Destroy idolatry 1Kin 18:22-24

Descriptive of:
Testing physically 1Sam 17:39
Testing morally . . . . John 6:6
Showing something to be true . . . . Gen 42:15, 16

Objects of, among Christians:
Faith 2Cor 13:5
Abilities 1Tim 3:10

TESTAMENT—*a covenant; a will*
Descriptive of a person's will . . . . Heb 9:15-17
New covenant . . . . Matt 26:28
New Testament dispensation 2Cor 3:6
Superiority of the new . . . Heb 8:6-13

is my blood of the new *t* . . . . . . Mark 14:24
This cup is the new *t* in my . . . Luke 22:20
This cup is the new *t* in my . . . 1Cor 11:25
made a surety of a better *t* . . . . Heb 7:22
neither the first *t* was . . . . Heb 9:18
is the blood of the *t* which . . . . Heb 9:20
his temple the ark of his *t* . . . . . Rev 11:19

TESTATOR—*one who leaves a will or testament in force at his death*
be the death of the *t* . . . . Heb 9:16
strength at all while the *t* . . . . . Heb 9:17

TESTIFY—*to bear witness on behalf of a person or cause*

[*also* TESTIFIED, TESTIFIEDST, TESTIFIETH, TESTIFYING]
it hath been *t* to his owner . . . . Ex 21:29
witness shall not *t* against . . . . . Num 35:30
t, and his statutes, which he . . . Deut 6:17
I *t* against you this day . . . . Deut 8:19
t against him that which . . . . Deut 19:16
hath *t* falsely against his . . . . Deut 19:18
words which I *t* among you . . . . Deut 32:46
the Lord hath *t* against me . . . . Ruth 1:21
Lord *t* against Israel, and 2Kin 17:13
testimonies which he *t* 2Kin 17:15
Lord; and they *t* against 2Chr 24:19
prophets which *t* against . . . . . . Neh 9:26
t against them, that thou . . . . . . Neh 9:29
t against them by thy spirit . . . . Neh 9:30
thou didst *t* against them . . . . . . Neh 9:34
thine own lips *t* against . . . . Job 15:6
Israel, and I will *t* against . . . . . Ps 50:7
my people, and I will *t* unto . . . Ps 81:8
our iniquities *t* against us . . . . . . Jer 14:7
of Israel doth *t* to his face . . . . . . Hos 5:5
pride of Israel *t* to his face . . . . . Hos 7:10
and *t* in the house of Jacob . . . . Amos 3:13
that he may *t* unto them . . . . . . Luke 16:28
that any should *t* of man . . . . . . John 2:25
and *t* that we have seen . . . . John 3:11
seen and heard, that he *t* . . . . . John 3:32
of the woman, which *t* . . . . John 4:39
they are they which *t* of me . . . John 5:39
it hateth, because I *t* of it . . . . . John 7:7
troubled in spirit, and *t* . . . . John 13:21
the Father, he shall *t* of me . . . John 15:26
disciple which *t* of these . . . . John 21:24
words did he *t* and exhort . . . . . Acts 2:40
they had *t* and preached the . . . Acts 8:25
hast *t* of me in Jerusalem . . . . . Acts 23:11
if they would *t*, that after . . . . . Acts 26:5
we have *t* of God that he 1Cor 15:15
the *t* of our conscience 2Cor 1:12
For I *t* again to every man . . . . Gal 5:3
t in the Lord, that ye . . . . Eph 4:17
have forewarned you and *t* 1Thess 4:6
ransom for all, to be *t* in due . . 1Tim 2:6
But one in a certain place *t* . . . Heb 2:6
For he *t*, Thou art a priest . . . . Heb 7:17
was righteous, God *t* of his . . . . Heb 11:4
t beforehand the sufferings 1Pet 1:11
t that this is the true grace 1Pet 5:12
t that the Father sent the 1John 4:14
which he hath *t* of his Son 1John 5:9
and *t* of the truth that is in 3John 3
sent mine angel to *t* unto . . . . . Rev 22:16
I *t* unto every man that . . . . Rev 22:18
He which *t* these things . . . . Rev 22:20

TESTIMONY—*witness borne on behalf of something*

Necessary elements of, seen in:
Verbal expression 2Sam 1:16
Witnesses . . . . Neh 13:15
John 8:17

Means of:
Prophets . . . . Acts 10:42, 43
Messengers . . . . Acts 20:21, 24
Song . . . . Deut 31:21
Our sins . . . . Is 59:12

Reaction to:
Believed 2Thess 1:10
Confirmed 1Cor 1:6

Purpose of, to:
Establish the Gospel . . . . . Acts 10:42
Prove Jesus was the Christ . . . . Acts 18:5
Lead to repentance . . . . . . Acts 20:21

[*also* TESTIMONIES]
Aaron laid it up before the *T* . . Ex 16:34
the ark thou shalt put the *t* . . . . Ex 25:21
the veil the ark of the *t* . . . . Ex 26:33
veil, which is before the *t* . . . . . Ex 27:21
that is by the ark of the *t* . . . . . Ex 30:6
mercy seat that is over the *t* . . . Ex 30:6
the *t* in the tabernacle . . . . Ex 30:36
tables of *t*, tables of stone . . . . . Ex 31:18
the two tables of *t* in Moses' . . Ex 34:29
ark of the *t*, and the staves . . . . Ex 39:35
before the ark of the *t* . . . . Ex 40:5
and covered the ark of the *t* . . . Ex 40:21
seat that is upon the *t* . . . . Lev 16:13
Without the veil of the *t*, in . . . Lev 24:3
over the tabernacle of *t* . . . . Num 1:50
veil, and cover the ark of *t* . . . . Num 4:5
namely, the tent of the *t* . . . . . . Num 9:15
congregation before the *t* . . . . . . Num 17:4
are the *t*, and the statutes . . . . . Deut 4:45
t, and his statutes, which he . . . Deut 6:17
What mean the *t*, and the . . . . . Deut 6:20
that bear the ark of the *t* . . . . . Josh 4:16
and this was a *t* in Israel . . . . . . Ruth 4:7
his judgments, and his *t* 1Kin 2:3
him, and gave him the *t* 2Kin 11:12
his *t* which he *t* against 2Kin 17:15
thy commandments, thy *t* 1Chr 29:19
crown, and gave him the *t* 2Chr 23:11

T

commandments, and his *t* 2Chr 34:31
commandments and thy *t*......Neh 9:34
the *t* of the Lord is sure ......Ps 19:7
keep his covenant and his *t*....Ps 25:10
ordained in Joseph for a *t*.....Ps 81:5
Thy *t* are very sure ....Ps 93:5
are they that keep his *t* ....Ps 119:2
for I have kept thy *t*..........Ps 119:22
stuck unto thy *t*: O Lord ......Ps 119:31
I will speak of thy *t* also ......Ps 119:46
that have known thy *t* ....Ps 119:79
thy *t* are my meditation ....Ps 119:99
therefore I love thy *t* ....Ps 119:119
Thy *t* are wonderful ....Ps 119:129
The righteousness of thy *t*.....Ps 119:144
Concerning thy *t*, I have ......Ps 119:152
My soul hath kept thy *t*........Ps 119:167
unto the *t* of Israel, to give....Ps 122:4
Bind up the *t*, seal the law ....Is 8:16
in his statutes, nor in his *t* ....Jer 44:23
commanded, for a *t* unto......Mark 1:44
your feet for a *t* against.......Mark 6:11
for my sake, for a *t* against....Mark 13:9
commanded, for a *t* unto......Luke 5:14
your feet for a *t* against ......Luke 9:5
it shall turn to you for a *t*.....Luke 21:13
and no man receiveth his *t* ....John 3:32
I receive not *t* from man ......John 5:34
we know that his *t* is true .....John 21:24
to whom also he gave *t*, and ..Acts 13:22
not receive thy *t* concerning ...Acts 22:18
unto you the *t* of God 1Cor 2:1
of the *t* of our Lord 2Tim 1:8
a *t* of those things which ......Heb 3:5
this *t*, that he pleased God ....Heb 11:5
God, and of the *t* of Jesus ....Rev 1:2
for the *t* which they held ......Rev 6:9
and by the word of their *t*.....Rev 12:11
God, and have the *t* of Jesus ..Rev 12:17
the tabernacle of the *t* in......Rev 15:5
brethren that have the *t* of ....Rev 19:10
t of Jesus is the spirit of ......Rev 19:10
He which *t* these things ....Rev 22:20

TETH (tĕth)
Letter in the Hebrew alphabet ....Ps 119:65-72

TETRARCH—*a ruler over a fourth part of a kingdom*

Herod the *t* heard of the fame .Matt 14:1
Herod being *t* of Galilee ......Luke 3:1
brother Philip *t* of Ituraea ......Luke 3:1
Lysanias the *t* of Abilene .....Luke 3:1
Herod the *t*, being reproved ...Luke 3:19
the *t* heard of all that was .....Luke 9:7
brought up with Herod the *t* ..Acts 13:1

THADDAEUS (thă-dē'ŭs)—*"breast"*
One of the twelve disciples ....Mark 3:18
See JUDAS 2

whose surname was *T*.........Matt 10:3

THAHASH (thā'hăsh)—*"reddish"*
Son of Nahor ....Gen 22:24

THAMAH—*See* TAMAH

THAMAR—*See* TAMAR

THAN—*See* INTRODUCTION

THANK—*to express gratitude*

[*also* THANKED, THANKING, THANKS]
bowed himself, and *t* the 2Sam 14:22
Therefore I will give *t* unto....2Sam 22:50
to *t* and praise the Lord God ..1Chr 16:4
Give *t* unto the Lord, call 1Chr 16:8
we may give *t* to thy holy 1Chr 16:35
to *t* and praise the Lord.......1Chr 23:30
t and to praise the Lord.......1Chr 25:3
our God, we *t* thee, and 1Chr 29:13
in praising and *t* the Lord 2Chr 5:13
t offerings into the house......2Chr 29:31
sacrifices and *t* offerings 2Chr 29:31
to minister, and to give *t*......2Chr 31:2
peace offerings and *t* offerings .2Chr 33:16
and giving *t* unto the Lord ....Ezra 3:11
to praise and to give *t* ....Neh 12:24
company of them that gave *t* ..Neh 12:38
grave who shall give thee *t*? ...Ps 6:5
give *t* at the remembrance.....Ps 30:4
t in the great congregation ....Ps 35:18
thee, O God, do we give *t* ....Ps 75:1
unto thee do we give *t*: for ....Ps 75:1
thing to give *t* unto the Lord ..Ps 92:1
O give *t* unto the Lord; call ...Ps 105:1
give *t* unto thy holy name .....Ps 106:47
O give *t* unto the Lord........Ps 118:1
t unto the name of the Lord...Ps 122:4
O give *t* unto the God of .....Ps 136:2
O give *t* unto the God of .....Ps 136:26
Sing unto the Lord with *t* .....Ps 147:7
I *t* thee, and praise thee, O ...Dan 2:23
and gave *t* before his God.....Dan 6:10
I *t* thee, O Father, Lord ......Matt 11:25
gave *t*, and brake them ....Matt 15:36
he took the cup, and gave *t* ...Matt 26:27
the seven loaves, and gave *t*...Mark 8:6
t likewise unto the Lord ......Luke 2:38
which love you, what *t* have ...Luke 6:32
do good to you, what *t* have ..Luke 6:33
ye hope to receive, what *t*.....Luke 6:34
I *t* thee, O Father, Lord .....Luke 10:21
he *t* that servant because ......Luke 17:9
God, I *t* thee, that I am not...Luke 18:11
he took the cup, and gave *t* ...Luke 22:17
t to God in presence of them ..Acts 27:35
t God, and took courage ......Acts 28:15
I *t* my God through Jesus .....Rom 1:8
God be *t*, that ye were the ....Rom 6:17
Lord, for he giveth God *t* .....Rom 14:6
eateth not, and giveth God *t* ..Rom 14:6
I *t* my God always on your....1Cor 1:4
for that for which I give *t*? 1Cor 10:30
say Amen at thy giving of *t* ...1Cor 14:16
thou verily givest *t* well 1Cor 14:17
I *t* my God, I speak with 1Cor 14:18
t may be given by many on ...2Cor 1:11
Now *t* be unto God, which 2Cor 2:14
But *t* be to God, which put ...2Cor 8:16
but rather giving of *t* ....Eph 5:4
t to God and the Father ....Col 1:3
Giving *t* unto the Father ......Col 1:12
t to God and the Father by ...Col 3:17
what *t* can we render to God ..1Thess 3:9
We are bound to *t* God 2Thess 1:3
I *t* Christ Jesus our Lord 1Tim 1:12
and giving of *t*, be made for all 1Tim 2:1
I *t* God, whom I serve from ...2Tim 1:3
I *t* my God, making mention ..Philem 4
our lips giving *t* to his name ...Heb 13:15
t to him that sat on the ....Rev 4:9
We give thee *t*, O Lord God ..Rev 11:17

THANKFULNESS—*gratefulness expressed to another*

Described as:
Spiritual sacrifice ....Ps 116:17
Duty 2Thess 2:13
Unceasing ....Eph 1:16
Spontaneous ....Phil 1:3
In Christ's name.........Eph 5:20
God's will 1Thess 5:18
Heaven's theme ....Rev 7:12

Expressed for:
Food ....John 6:11, 23
Wisdom ....Dan 2:23
Converts...............1Thess 1:2
Prayer answered ....John 11:41
Victory 1Cor 15:57
Salvation 2Cor 9:15
Lord's Supper 1Cor 11:24
Changed lives 1Thess 2:13

Expressed by:
Healed Samaritan ....Luke 17:12-19
Righteous ....Ps 140:13

[*also* THANKFUL]
be *t* unto him, and bless his ...Ps 100:4
most noble Felix, with all *t*....Acts 24:3
not as God, neither were *t* ....Rom 1:21
in one body; and be ye *t* ......Col 3:15

THANKSGIVING—*act of expressing gratitude*

[*also* THANKSGIVINGS]
If he offer it for a *t*, then he ..Lev 7:12
sacrifice of *t* unleavened .....Lev 7:12
offerings for *t* shall be ....Lev 7:15
principal to begin the *t* in .....Neh 11:17
of praise and *t* unto God......Neh 12:46
publish with the voice of *t*.....Ps 26:7
God *t*; and pay thy vows ......Ps 50:14
will magnify him with *t* ....Ps 69:30
before his presence with *t* .....Ps 95:2
Enter into his gates with *t*.....Ps 100:4
to thee the sacrifice of *t*.......Ps 116:17
shall be found therein, *t* ....Is 51:3
out of them shall proceed *t*....Jer 30:19
a sacrifice of *t* with leaven ....Amos 4:5
unto thee with the voice of *t* ..Jon 2:9
through the *t* of many redound.2Cor 4:15
causeth through us *t* to God ...2Cor 9:11
also by many *t* unto God......2Cor 9:12
and supplication with *t* let.....Phil 4:6
abounding therein with *t* ......Col 2:7
watch in the same with *t* ......Col 4:2
received with *t* of them 1Tim 4:3

THANKWORTHY—*deserving gratitude*
is *t*, if a man for conscience ...1Pet 2:19

THARA (thā'rä)—*See* TERAH

THARSHISH—*See* TARSHISH

THAT—*See* INTRODUCTION

THE—*See* INTRODUCTION

THEATER—*a place of public assembly*
Paul kept from entering ..Acts 19:29-31

THEBEZ (thē'bĕz)—*"muddy"*
Fortified city near Shechem..............Judg 9:50-55
the wall, that he died in *T*? ...2Sam 11:21

THEE—*See* INTRODUCTION

THEE-WARD—*directed to you*
his works have been to *t* 1Sam 19:4

THEFT—*the act of stealing*

Kinds of:
Imputed ....Gen 44:1-17
Improbable ....Matt 28:11-13
Real...................Acts 5:1-3

Characteristics of:
Done often at night .....Jer 49:9
Comes unexpectedly .....Luke 12:39
Purpose of, to steal......John 10:10
Window used by ....John 10:1

Objects of:
Idol ....Gen 31:19-35
Food ....Prov 6:30
Traveler ....Luke 10:30, 36
Money ....John 12:6

Evil of:
Condemned ....Ex 22:1-12
Punished...............Josh 7:21-26
Inconsistent with truth ..Jer 7:9, 10
Defiles a man ....Matt 15:19, 20
Excludes from heaven ...1Cor 6:10
Not to be among Christians............Eph 4:28
See STEALING

THEIR—*See* INTRODUCTION

THEIRS—*belonging to them*
in a land that is not *t* ....Gen 15:13
times so much as any of *t* .....Gen 43:34
priest's office shall be *t* for ....Ex 29:9
t is thine own nakedness ......Lev 18:10
and touch nothing of *t*, lest....Num 16:26
the fire: every oblation of *t*....Num 18:9
every meat offering of *t* ......Num 18:9
and every sin offering of *t*......Num 18:9
every trespass offering of *t* ....Num 18:9
had: for *t* was the first lot ....Josh 21:10

the Kohathites: for *t* was 1Chr 6:54
I pray thee, be like one of *t*...2Chr 18:12
multitude, nor of any of *t*.....Ezek 7:11
thing in Israel shall be *t*.......Ezek 44:29
dwelling places that are not *t*..Hab 1:6
t is the kingdom of heaven ....Matt 5:3
Christ our Lord, both *t* and ...1Cor 1:2

THELASAR—*See* TELASSAR

THEM, THEMSELVES—*See* INTRODUCTION

THEN—*See* INTRODUCTION

THENCEFORTH—*from now on*
t it shall be accepted for an ...Lev 22:27
sight of all nations from *t*......2Chr 32:23
it is *t* good for nothing, but ...Matt 5:13
t Pilate sought to release ......John 19:12

THEOCRACY—*government by God*
Evident under Moses ....Ex 19:3-6
Continued under Joshua. .Josh 1:1-8
Rejected by Israel 1Sam 8:4-9
To be restored ....Is 2:2-4
Is 9:6, 7

THEOPHANY—*an appearance of God*
Of God:
At Sinai ....Ex 24:9-12
In the tabernacle ....Ex 40:34-38
In the Temple...........1Kin 8:10, 11
To Isaiah ....Is 6:1-9
Of Christ as "the angel," to:
Abraham ....Gen 18:1-8
Jacob..................Gen 31:11, 13
Moses ....Ex 3:1-11
Joshua..................Josh 5:13-15
Israel...................Judg 2:1-5
Gideon ....Judg 6:11-24
Manoah ....Judg 13:2-25
Paul....................Acts 27:23, 24
Of Christ, as incarnate, in:
Old Testament 1Cor 10:4, 9
Nativity................John 1:14, 18
His:
Resurrected form......John 20:26-29
Ascended form........Acts 7:55, 56
Return in glory........Rev 1:7, 8
Glorified form ....Matt 17:1-15

THEOPHILUS (thĕ-ŏf'ĭ-lŭs)—*"loved by God"*
Luke addresses his writings to .... { Luke 1:3 / Acts 1:1 }

THERE—*See* INTRODUCTION

THEREABOUT—*near*
were much perplexed *t*........Luke 24:4

THEREAT—*at that place or occurrence*
hands and their feet *t*.........Ex 30:19
their hands and their feet *t*....Ex 40:31
there be which go in *t* ....Matt 7:13

THEREBY—*by that means*
that ye should be defiled *t* .....Lev 11:43
t good shall come unto.........Job 22:21
whosoever is deceived *t* is .....Prov 20:1
wood shall be endangered *t* ...Eccl 10:9
shall gallant ship pass *t*........Is 33:21
that passeth *t* shall be ....Jer 18:16
doth any son of man pass *t*....Jer 51:43
their sight, and carry out *t* ....Ezek 12:5
he shall not fall *t* in the day ...Ezek 33:12
and right, he shall live *t*.......Ezek 33:19
Hamath also shall border *t* ....Zech 9:2
of God might be glorified *t*....John 11:4
having slain the enmity *t*......Eph 2:16
them which are exercised *t* ....Heb 12:11
t some have entertained ....Heb 13:2
word, that ye may grow *t* 1Pet 2:2

THEREFORE—*See* INTRODUCTION

THEREFROM—*from that*
ye turn not aside *t* to the .....Josh 23:6
to sin; he departed not *t* 2Kin 3:3
to sin; he departed not *t* 2Kin 13:2

THEREIN—*See* INTRODUCTION

THEREINTO—*into there*
are in the countries enter *t* ....Luke 21:21

THEREOF—*See* INTRODUCTION

THEREON—*See* INTRODUCTION

THEREOUT—*from it*
he shall take *t* his handful .....Lev 2:2
jaw, and there came water *t*...Judg 15:19

THERETO—*See* INTRODUCTION

THEREUNTO—*to that*
it, and have sacrificed *t* ....Ex 32:8
t a crown of gold round ....Ex 37:11
all the places nigh *t*, in........Deut 1:7
and watching *t* with all ....Eph 6:18
make the comers *t* perfect.....Heb 10:1
knowing that ye are *t* 1Pet 3:9

THEREUPON—*on that or it*
and the mercy seat that is *t* ...Ex 31:7
and playedst the harlot *t* ......Ezek 16:16
of Judah they shall feed *t* .....Zeph 2:7
heed how he buildeth *t* 1Cor 3:10

THEREWITH—*with that; thereupon; forthwith*
or the field, be consumed *t*....Ex 22:6
t he made the sockets to the ..Ex 38:30
that maketh atonement *t* ......Lev 7:7
from him, and is defiled *t* .....Lev 15:32
not eat to defile himself *t* .....Lev 22:8
thou eat unleavened bread *t*...Deut 16:3
and slew a thousand men *t* ....Judg 15:15
bribe to blind mine eyes *t*? 1Sam 12:3
and thrust me through *t*.......1Sam 31:4
smote him *t* in the fifth rib 2Sam 20:10
t sent Naaman my servant.....2Kin 5:6
and thrust me through *t*.......1Chr 10:4
built *t* Geba and Mizpah 2Chr 16:6
great treasure and trouble *t* ...Prov 15:16
dry morsel, and quietness *t*....Prov 17:1
of man to be exercised *t* ......Eccl 1:13
stones shall be hurt *t* ....Eccl 10:9
against him that heweth *t*? ....Is 10:15
shalt prepare thy bread *t* ......Ezek 4:15
and ye shall be satisfied *t* .....Joel 2:19
raiment let us be *t* content 1Tim 6:8
T bless we God, even the .....James 3:9
t curse we men, which are ....James 3:9

THESE—*See* INTRODUCTION

THESSALONIANS (thĕs-ä-lō'nĭ-ăns)—*dwellers in Thessalonica*
and of the *T*, Aristarchus .....Acts 20:4
unto the church of the *T* 1Thess 1:1
the church of the *T* in God....2Thess 1:1

THESSALONIANS, THE EPISTLES TO THE—*two books of the New Testament*
1 Thessalonians:
Commendation 1Thess 1:2-10
Paul's apostolic ministry..1Thess 2:1-20
Timothy as envoy 1Thess 3:1-10
The quiet life 1Thess 4:11, 12
The second coming 1Thess 4:13-18
Sons of light, not darkness 1Thess 5:4-7
Christian conduct 1Thess 5:12-24
2 Thessalonians:
Encouragement in suffering 2Thess 1:3-12
The man of sin 2Thess 2:3-10
Steadfastness 2Thess 2:15-17
Maintaining order 2Thess 3:1-15

THESSALONICA (thĕs-ä-lō-nī'kä)—*"victory at sea"—city situated on the Macedonian coast*
Paul preaches in ....Acts 17:1-13
Paul writes letters to churches of 1Thess 1:1

For even in *T* ye sent once ....Phil 4:16
and is departed unto *T*.......2Tim 4:10

THEUDAS (thū'däs)—*"the gift of God"*
Leader of an unsuccessful revolt ....Acts 5:36

THEY—*See* INTRODUCTION

THICK—*dense; wide; heavy*
[*also* THICKER, THICKNESS]
was a *t* darkness in all the.....Ex 10:22
a *t* cloud upon the mount .....Ex 19:16
and the boughs of *t* trees......Lev 23:40
clouds, and *t* darkness ....Deut 4:11
waxen fat, thou art grown *t* ...Deut 32:15
the *t* boughs of a great oak....2Sam 18:9
and the *t* beam were before ...1Kin 7:6
he would dwell in the *t* 1Kin 8:12
shall be *t* than my father's.....1Kin 12:10
a *t* cloth, and dipped it in 2Kin 8:15
t of it was an handbreadth 2Chr 4:5
he would dwell in the *t* 2Chr 6:1
shall be *t* than my father's.....2Chr 10:10
and branches of *t* trees, to ....Neh 8:15
t bosses of his bucklers........Job 15:26
the waters in his *t* clouds .....Job 26:8
t darkness a swaddling band ..Job 38:9
dark waters and *t* clouds of....Ps 18:11
lifted up axes upon the *t* ......Ps 74:5
blotted out, as a *t* cloud.......Is 44:22
t thereof was four fingers .....Jer 52:21
tree, and under every *t* oak ...Ezek 6:13
was exalted among the *t* ......Ezek 19:11
his top was among the *t*.......Ezek 31:3
up their top among the *t* ......Ezek 31:14
The *t* of the wall, which was ..Ezek 41:9
building was five cubits *t* ......Ezek 41:12
of the house, and *t* planks.....Ezek 41:26
chambers were in the *t* of .....Ezek 42:10
clouds and of *t* darkness ......Joel 2:2
ladeth himself with *t* clay! .....Hab 2:6
of clouds and *t* darkness ......Zeph 1:15
people were gathered *t*........Luke 11:29

THICKET—*a dense growth of shrubbery*
[*also* THICKETS]
a ram caught in a *t* by his .....Gen 22:13
in caves, and in *t*.............1Sam 13:6
in the *t* of the forests ....Is 9:18
shalt cut down the *t* of the ....Is 10:34
lion is come up from his *t*.....Jer 4:7
they shall go into the *t*, and ..Jer 4:29

THIEF—*one who steals*
[*also* THIEVES]
If a *t* be found breaking up ...Ex 22:2
If the *t* be not found, then ....Ex 22:8
him; then that *t* shall die ......Deut 24:7
and in the night is as a *t* ......Job 24:14
thou sawest a *t*, then thou.....Ps 50:18
Men do not despise a *t*, if.....Prov 6:30
and companions of *t* ....Is 1:23
As the *t* is ashamed when .....Jer 2:26
was he found among *t*? ....Jer 48:27
the *t* cometh in, and the ......Hos 7:1
in at the windows like a *t* .....Joel 2:9
If *t* came to thee, if robbers ...Obad 5
enter into the house of the *t*...Zech 5:4
where *t* break through and ....Matt 6:19
ye have made it a den of *t* ....Matt 21:13
in what watch the *t* would .....Matt 24:43
two *t* crucified with him ....Matt 27:38
T, covetousness, wickedness ...Mark 7:22
ye have made it a den of *t* ....Mark 11:17
ye come out, as against a *t* ....Mark 14:48
Jericho, and fell among *t*......Luke 10:30
where no *t* approacheth ....Luke 12:33
ye have made it a den of *t* .....Luke 19:46
Be ye come out, as against a *t* .Luke 22:52
way, the same is a *t* and a ....John 10:1
ever came before me are *t* ....John 10:8
but because he was a *t*, and ..John 12:6
Nor *t*, nor covetous, nor 1Cor 6:10
Lord so cometh as a *t* in the ..1Thess 5:2
as a murderer, or as a *t*.......1Pet 4:15
Lord will come as a *t* in the ...2Pet 3:10
I will come on thee as a *t*.....Rev 3:3
fornication, nor of their *t* .....Rev 9:21

THIGH—*the portion of the leg between the knee and the hip*

[*also* THIGHS]
thee, thy hand under my *t* ....Gen 24:2
touched the hollow of his *t* ....Gen 32:25
and he halted upon his *t* ......Gen 32:31
is upon the hollow of the *t* ....Gen 32:32
the hollow of Jacob's *t* in .....Gen 32:32
the lions even unto the *t* ......Ex 28:42
Lord doth make thy *t* to rot ...Num 5:21
swell, and her *t* shall rot ......Num 5:27
his raiment upon his right *t*....Judg 3:16
he smote them hip and *t* ......Judg 15:8
Gird thy sword upon thy *t* .....Ps 45:3
the joints of thy *t* are like .....Song 7:1
smite therefore upon thy *t*.....Ezek 21:12
his belly and his *t* of brass ....Dan 2:32
and on his *t* a name written ...Rev 19:16

THIMNATHAH—*See* TIMNAH

THIN—*lean; scanty; not dense or thick*
seven *t* ears and blasted ....Gen 41:6
seven ears, withered, *t* ....Gen 41:23
the seven *t* and ill-favored.....Gen 41:27
they did beat the gold into *t*...Ex 39:3
and there be in it a yellow *t*...Lev 13:30
of Jacob shall be made *t* ......Is 17:4

THINE—*See* INTRODUCTION

THING, THINGS—*See* INTRODUCTION

THINK—*to form an idea or image of something in the mind*

[*also* THINKEST, THINKETH, THINKING, THOUGHT, THOUGHTEST]
I *t*, Surely the fear of God ....Gen 20:11
t on me when it shall be ......Gen 40:14
I had not *t* to see thy face ....Gen 48:11
evil which he *t* to do unto ......Ex 32:14
I *t* to promote thee unto ......Num 24:11
marry to whom they *t*.........Num 36:6
I verily *t* that thou hadst ......Judg 15:2
t to advertise thee, saying .....Ruth 4:4
Eli *t* she had been drunken....1Sam 1:13
Saul *t* to make David fall 1Sam 18:25
t to have brought good........2Sam 4:10
t that I would have given 2Sam 4:10
T thou that David doth 2Sam 10:3
t that all the king's sons.......2Sam 13:33
hast thou *t* such a thing 2Sam 14:13
Me *t* the running of the 2Sam 18:27
and to do what he *t* good 2Sam 19:18
I *t*, He will surely come 2Kin 5:11
T thou that David doth 1Chr 19:3
for he *t* to make him king 2Chr 11:22
And now ye *t* to withstand 2Chr 13:8
T upon me, my God, for......Neh 5:19
they *t* to do me mischief ......Neh 6:2
God, *t* thou upon Tobiah .....Neh 6:14
t scorn to lay hands on........Esth 3:6
T not with thyself that ....Esth 4:13
should I *t* upon a maid?.......Job 31:1
T thou this to be right ....Job 35:2
yet the Lord *t* upon me ....Ps 40:17
t of thy lovingkindness ....Ps 48:9
thou *t* that I was altogether ...Ps 50:21
I *t* on my ways, and turned ...Ps 119:59
he *t* in his heart, so is he ....Prov 23:7
a wise man *t* to know it.......Eccl 8:17
neither doth his heart *t* so .....Is 10:7
as I have *t*, so shall it come ...Is 14:24
evil that I *t* to do unto them ..Jer 18:8
t to cause my people to ....Jer 23:27
and thou shalt *t* an evil thought Ezek 38:10
I *t* it good to show the signs...Dan 4:2
if so be that God will *t* ....Jon 1:6
Lord of hosts *t* to do unto ....Zech 1:6
again have I *t* in these days ...Zech 8:15
If ye *t* good, give me my ......Zech 11:12
Lord, and that *t* upon his .....Mal 3:16
while he *t* on these things .....Matt 1:20
t not to say within ....Matt 3:9
t that they shall be heard .....Matt 6:7
T not that I am come to ......Matt 10:34
saying, What *t* thou, Simon? ..Matt 17:25
what *t* ye? A certain man .....Matt 21:28
an hour as ye *t* not the Son ...Matt 24:44
T thou that I cannot now .....Matt 26:53
the blasphemy: what *t* ye?.....Mark 14:64
t I myself worthy to come .....Luke 7:7
now of these three, *t* thou.....Luke 10:36
ye *t* ye have eternal life ....John 5:39
they *t* that he had spoken .....John 11:13
t ye, that he will not come ....John 11:56
hast *t* that the gift of God.....Acts 8:20
While Peter *t* on the vision ....Acts 10:19
Whom *t* ye that I am? I am ...Acts 13:25
Paul *t* not good to take him ...Acts 15:38
I *t* myself happy, king ....Acts 26:2
I verily *t* with myself, that.....Acts 26:9
to hear of thee what thou *t*....Acts 28:22
And *t* thou this, O man ....Rom 2:3
t of himself more highly.......Rom 12:3
highly than he ought to *t*......Rom 12:3
t soberly, according as God ...Rom 12:3
not to *t* of men above that 1Cor 4:6
any man *t* that he behaveth ...1Cor 7:36
any man *t* that he knoweth 1Cor 8:2
let him that *t* he standeth 1Cor 10:12
we *t* to be less honorable 1Cor 12:23
as a child, I *t* as a child 1Cor 13:11
t any thing as of ourselves.....2Cor 3:5
I *t* it necessary to exhort 2Cor 9:5
I *t* to be bold against some 2Cor 10:2
t of us as if we walked 2Cor 10:2
Let such an one *t* this..........2Cor 10:11
man should *t* of me above.....2Cor 12:6
if a man *t* himself to be ....Gal 6:3
above all that we ask or *t* .....Eph 3:20
is meet for me to *t* this of.....Phil 1:7
t it not robbery to be equal ...Phil 2:6
If any other man *t* that he ....Phil 3:4
we *t* it good to be left at......1Thess 3:1
shall he be *t* worthy, who .....Heb 10:29
man *t* that he shall receive ....James 1:7
t it strange that ye run not 1Pet 4:4
Yea, I *t* it meet, as long 2Pet 1:13

THIRD

[*also* THIRDLY]
the morning were the *t* day....Gen 1:13
and *t* stories shalt thou........Gen 6:16
told Laban on the *t* day ....Gen 31:22
came to pass on the *t* day .....Gen 34:25
said unto them the *t* day ......Gen 42:18
In the *t* month, when the .....Ex 19:1
And be ready against the *t* ....Ex 19:11
t day the Lord will come ......Ex 19:11
it came to pass on the *t* day ...Ex 19:16
the *t* row a ligure, an agate ...Ex 28:19
the *t* row, a ligure, an agate ...Ex 39:12
the sacrifice on the *t* day ......Lev 7:17
if aught remain until the *t* .....Lev 19:6
go forward in the *t* rank ......Num 2:24
t and fourth generation ....Num 14:18
the *t* part of an hin of wine ...Num 15:7
himself with it on the *t* day....Num 19:12
purify not himself the *t* day ...Num 19:12
t part of an hin unto a ram....Num 28:14
your captives on the *t* day.....Num 31:19
t and fourth generation ....Deut 5:9
of thine increase the *t* year ....Deut 26:12
their cities on the *t* day ....Josh 9:17
Benjamin on the *t* day ....Judg 20:30
Samuel again the *t* time 1Sam 3:8
messengers again the *t* time ...1Sam 19:21
any time, or the *t* day 1Sam 20:12
even to pass on the *t* day 2Sam 1:2
sent forth a *t* part of the 2Sam 18:2
a *t* part under the hand of 2Sam 18:2
t part under the hand of 2Sam 18:2
the *t* day after that I was......1Kin 3:18
out of the middle into the *t* ...1Kin 6:8
to Rehoboam the *t* day 1Kin 12:12
Come to me again the *t* day...1Kin 12:12
t year of Asa king of Judah ...1Kin 15:33
he said, Do it the *t* time 1Kin 18:34
And they did it the *t* time.....1Kin 18:34
come to pass in the *t* year.....1Kin 22:2
sent again a captain of the *t*...2Kin 1:13
t captain of fifty went up......2Kin 1:13
a *t* part shall be at the gate ...2Kin 11:6
a *t* part at the gate behind 2Kin 11:6
in the *t* year sow ye, and......2Kin 19:29
the house of the Lord the *t* ...2Kin 20:8
second, and Shimma the *t*.....1Chr 2:13
t Zedekiah, the fourth 1Chr 3:15
second, and Eliphelet the *t*....1Chr 8:39
the *t*, and Jekameam the 1Chr 23:19
Jehaziel the *t*, Jekameam......1Chr 24:23
Zebadiah the *t*, Jathniel the ...1Chr 26:2
Tebaliah the *t*, Zechariah 1Chr 26:11
t captain of the host for the 1Chr 27:5
t month was Benaiah the 1Chr 27:5
to Rehoboam on the *t* day 2Chr 10:12
Come again to me on the *t*....2Chr 10:12
in the *t* year of his reign he ...2Chr 17:7
t part shall be at the king's....2Chr 23:5
t part at the gate of the 2Chr 23:5
t month they began to lay.....2Chr 31:7
house was finished on the *t*....Ezra 6:15
t part of a shekel for the ......Neh 10:32
In the *t* year of his reign ......Esth 1:3
called at that time in the *t* ....Esth 8:9
of the *t*, Keren-happuch.......Job 42:14
shall Israel be the *t* with ......Is 19:24
t entry that is in the house ....Jer 38:14
shalt burn with fire a *t* part ...Ezek 5:2
thou shalt take a *t* part ....Ezek 5:2
a *t* part thou shalt scatter .....Ezek 5:2
A *t* part of thee shall die......Ezek 5:12
a *t* part shall fall by the ....Ezek 5:12
I will scatter a *t* part into .....Ezek 5:12
sword be doubled the *t* time...Ezek 21:14
the *t* part of an hin of oil .....Ezek 46:14
t year of the reign of ....Dan 1:1
shall be the *t* ruler in the .....Dan 5:7
t year of the reign of king.....Dan 8:1
t day he will raise us up.......Hos 6:2
the *t* chariot white horses .....Zech 6:3
the *t* part through the fire .....Zech 13:9
be raised again the *t* day ......Matt 16:21
went out about the *t* hour .....Matt 20:3
the *t*, unto the seventh........Matt 22:26
made sure until the *t* day .....Matt 27:64
killed, he shall rise the *t* day ..Mark 9:31
seed: and the *t* likewise ......Mark 12:21
was the *t* hour, and they ......Mark 15:25
and be raised the *t* day ....Luke 9:22
t day I shall be perfected......Luke 13:32
And again he sent a *t*: and ....Luke 20:12
said unto them the *t* time .....Luke 23:22
is the *t* day since these ....Luke 24:21
t day there was a marriage ....John 2:1
saith unto him the *t* time......John 21:17
he said unto him the *t* time ...John 21:17
but the *t* hour of the day......Acts 2:15
fell down from the *t* loft ......Acts 20:9
And the *t* day we cast out.....Acts 27:19
prophets, *t* teachers...........1Cor 12:28
he rose again the *t* day........1Cor 15:4
caught up to the *t* heaven 2Cor 12:2
is the *t* time I am coming 2Cor 13:1
t beast had a face as a man ...Rev 4:7
he had opened the *t* seal ......Rev 6:5
I heard the *t* beast say ....Rev 6:5
the *t* part of the sea became...Rev 8:8
the *t* part of the creatures .....Rev 8:9
t part of the ships were ....Rev 8:9
And the *t* angel sounded ......Rev 8:10
fell upon the *t* part of the .....Rev 8:10
the *t* part of the waters ....Rev 8:11
the *t* part of the sun was ......Rev 8:12
and the *t* part of the moon ....Rev 8:12
and the *t* part of the stars .....Rev 8:12
t part of them was darkened...Rev 8:12
the day shone not for a *t*......Rev 8:12
three was the *t* part of men ...Rev 9:18
tail drew the *t* part of the .....Rev 12:4
t angel poured out his vial ....Rev 16:4

THIRST—*craving for drink; to crave drink*
Caused by:
Wilderness drought ......Ex 17:3
Unbelief ....Deut 28:47, 48

Siege 2Chr 32:11
Travels 2Cor 11:27
Extreme pain ....John 19:28
Flame ....Luke 16:24

Figurative of:
Salvation ....Is 55:1
Righteousness ....Matt 5:6
Holy Spirit..............John 7:37-39
Serving Christ ....Matt 25:35-42

Satisfaction of:
By a miracle ....Neh 9:15, 20
Longed for...............Ps 63:1
In Christ alone ....John 6:35
Final invitation ....Rev 22:17
Perfectly fulfilled ....Is 49:10
Rev 7:16

[*also* THIRSTED, THRISTETH, THIRSTY]
to add drunkenness to *t*.......Deut 29:19
water to drink; for I am *t*.....Judg 4:19
and now shall I die for *t*......Judg 15:18
winepresses, and suffer *t*......Job 24:11
My soul *t* for God, for the ....Ps 42:2
t they gave me vinegar to .....Ps 69:21
and *t*, their soul fainted ....Ps 107:5
my soul *t* after thee, as a *t*....Ps 143:6
he be *t*, give him water to.....Prov 25:21
multitude dried up with *t*......Is 5:13
water to him that was *t*.......Is 21:14
as when a *t* man dreameth ....Is 29:8
will cause the drink of the *t*...Is 32:6
t land springs of water ....Is 35:7
their tongue faileth for *t* ......Is 41:17
water upon him that is *t* ......Is 44:3
And they *t* not when he led ...Is 48:21
is no water, and dieth for *t*....Is 50:2
and thy throat from *t* ....Jer 2:25
the roof of his mouth for *t* ....Lam 4:4
wilderness, in a dry and *t* .....Ezek 19:13
dry land, and slay her with *t* ..Hos 2:3
famine of bread, nor a *t* for ...Amos 8:11
drinketh of this water shall *t*...John 4:13
give me this water, that I *t*....John 4:15
feed him; if he *t*, give him ....Rom 12:20
both hunger, and *t*, and are ...1Cor 4:11

THIRTEEN

[*also* THIRTEENTH]
in the *t* year they rebelled.....Gen 14:4
his son was *t* years old ....Gen 17:25
and threescore and *t*..........Num 3:43
t young bullocks, two rams ....Num 29:13
t cities and their villages ......Josh 19:6
tribe of Benjamin, *t* cities .....Josh 21:4
t cities with their suburbs .....Josh 21:19
building his own house *t* 1Kin 7:1
their families were *t* cities 1Chr 6:60
t to Huppah, the fourteenth ...1Chr 24:13
brethren of Hosah were *t* 1Chr 26:11
scribes called on the *t* day.....Esth 3:12
the *t* day of the twelfth ....Esth 8:12
t day of the month Adar ....Esth 9:17
in the *t* year of his reign ......Jer 1:2
length of the gate, *t* cubits ....Ezek 40:11

THIRTY

[*also* THIRTIETH]
Adam lived a hundred and *t*...Gen 5:3
Jared eight hundred and *t*.....Gen 5:16
Arphaxad lived five and *t* .....Gen 11:12
And Eber lived four and *t* ....Gen 11:16
And Peleg lived *t* years ....Gen 11:18
And Serug lived *t* years ....Gen 11:22
T milch camels with their .....Gen 32:15
his daughters were *t* and ......Gen 46:15
hundred *t* and seven ....Ex 6:16
hundred and *t* and seven ....Ex 6:20
four hundred and *t* years ......Ex 12:41
curtain shall be *t* cubits ....Ex 26:8
hundred and *t* shekels.........Ex 38:24
were *t* and two thousand ......Num 1:35
were *t* and two thousand ......Num 2:21
t years old and upward.........Num 4:3
From *t* years old and ....Num 4:43
mourned for Aaron *t* days.....Num 20:29
them, *t* and two thousand .....Num 26:37
t and two thousand persons ...Num 31:35
beeves were *t* and six ....Num 31:38
the Lord's tribute was *t* ....Num 31:40
And *t* and six thousand ....Num 31:44
Zered, was *t* and eight ....Deut 2:14
smote of them about *t* and ....Josh 7:5
all the kings *t* and one ....Josh 12:24
t sons that rode on *t* ass......Judg 10:4
they had *t* cities, which ....Judg 10:4
t sons, and *t* daughters ....Judg 12:9
took in *t* daughters from ......Judg 12:9
they brought *t* companions ....Judg 14:11
t sheets and *t* change of ....Judg 14:13
field, about *t* men of Israel ...Judg 20:31
fell of Israel *t* thousand 1Sam 4:10
men of Judah *t* thousand 1Sam 11:8
David was *t* years old when ...2Sam 5:4
men of Israel, *t* thousand 2Sam 6:1
honorable than the *t* 2Sam 23:23
the Hittite: *t* and seven in 2Sam 23:39
t and three years reigned 1Kin 2:11
levy was *t* thousand men 1Kin 5:13
height thereof *t* cubits.........1Kin 7:2
line of *t* cubits did compass....1Kin 7:23
t and eighth year of Asa 1Kin 16:29
two hundred and *t* two.........1Kin 20:15
t and two captains that........1Kin 22:31
T and two years old was 2Kin 8:17
t and eighth year of 2Kin 15:8
nine and *t* year of Uzziah 2Kin 15:13
reigned *t* and one years 2Kin 22:1
and *t* year of the captivity 2Kin 25:27
reigned *t* and three years......1Chr 3:4
and two thousand and *t* 1Chr 7:7
honorable among the *t*.........1Chr 11:25
of the Reubenites, and *t* 1Chr 11:42
a hundred and *t* 1Chr 15:7
age of *t* years and upward.....1Chr 23:3
was *t* and eight thousand 1Chr 23:3
t and three years reigned......1Chr 29:27
pillars of *t* and five cubits 2Chr 3:15
t year of the reign of Asa 2Chr 15:19
Asa in the *t* and ninth year....2Chr 16:12
Jehoram was *t* and two 2Chr 21:5
hundred and *t* years old.......2Chr 24:15
number of *t* thousand 2Chr 35:7
t chargers of gold.............Ezra 1:9
and six hundred and *t*.........Ezra 2:35
three hundred *t* and seven.....Ezra 2:65
camels, four hundred *t* ....Ezra 2:67
and *t* year of Artaxerxes ......Neh 5:14
nine hundred and *t* ....Neh 7:38
three hundred *t* and seven.....Neh 7:67
camels, four hundred *t*........Neh 7:69
the king these *t* days..........Esth 4:11
Take from hence *t* men ....Jer 38:10
t year of the captivity ....Jer 52:31
came to pass in the *t* year .....Ezek 1:1
t chambers were upon the .....Ezek 40:17
of forty cubits long and *t*......Ezek 46:22
God or man for *t* days.........Dan 6:7
hundred and five and *t*.........Dan 12:12
price *t* pieces of silver.........Zech 11:12
some sixty, some *t*............Matt 13:23
some *t*, and some sixty........Mark 4:8
be about *t* years of age ....Luke 3:23
infirmity *t* and eight years .....John 5:5
about five and twenty or *t*.....John 6:19
four hundred and *t* years ......Gal 3:17

THIRTY HEROES, THE—*men who served David*
Served David 1Chr 12:1-40

THIRTY PIECES OF SILVER—*money paid to Judas to betray Christ*
Price of slave ....Ex 21:32
Given to Judas ....Matt 26:14-16
Buys field...............Matt 27:3-10

THIRTYFOLD—*thirty times*
some sixtyfold, some *t* ....Matt 13:8
fruit, some *t*, some sixty ......Mark 4:20

THIS—*See* INTRODUCTION

THISTLE—*a prickly plant*

[*also* THISTLES]
and *t* shall it bring forth to ....Gen 3:18
The *t* that was in Lebanon 2Kin 14:9
and trode down the *t* 2Kin 14:9
The *t* that was in Lebanon 2Chr 25:18
and trode down the *t* 2Chr 25:18
t grow instead of wheat ....Job 31:40
t shall come up on their.......Hos 10:8
of thorns, or figs of *t* ? ....Matt 7:16

THITHER—*toward that place*
t were all the flocks ....Gen 29:3
had brought him down *t* ....Gen 39:1
get you down *t*, and buy for...Gen 42:2
the Lord, until we come *t*.....Ex 10:26
bring in *t* within the veil ......Ex 26:33
that he may flee *t* ....Num 35:6
unawares may flee *t* ....Num 35:15
Thou also shalt not go in *t* ....Deut 1:37
they shall go in *t*, and unto....Deut 1:39
seek, and *t* thou shalt come ...Deut 12:5
t shall ye bring all that I ......Deut 12:11
every slayer may flee *t*........Deut 19:3
shalt not go *t* unto the land ...Deut 32:52
all the people to labor *t*.......Josh 7:3
and unwittingly may flee *t*.....Josh 20:3
Israel went *t* a whoring ....Judg 8:27
they turned in *t*, and said .....Judg 18:3
they turned aside *t*, to go .....Judg 19:15
thou art come *t* to the city 1Sam 10:5
the man should yet come *t* 1Sam 10:22
they went down *t* to him 1Sam 22:1
So David went up *t*, and his...2Sam 2:2
were divided hither and *t* 2Kin 2:8
he turned in *t* to eat bread 2Kin 4:8
fell on a day, that he came *t* ..2Kin 4:11
for *t* the Syrians are come 2Kin 6:9
And when thou comest *t*.......2Kin 9:2
of the trumpet, resort ye *t* ....Neh 4:20
t brought I again the..........Neh 13:9
naked shall I return *t* ....Job 1:21
rivers come, *t* they return .....Eccl 1:7
with bows shall men come *t* ...Is 7:24
forth *t* the feet of the ox ......Is 32:20
t wentest thou up to offer .....Is 57:7
company shall return *t* ....Jer 31:8
they went, *t* was their spirit ...Ezek 1:20
upon me, and brought me *t* ...Ezek 40:1
Herod, he was afraid to go *t* ..Matt 2:22
ran afoot *t* out of all cities ....Mark 6:33
and where I am, *t* ye cannot ..John 7:34
and goest thou *t* again? ....John 11:8
cometh *t* with lanterns and ....John 18:3
ran *t* to him, and heard him ...Acts 8:30
women which resorted *t*.......Acts 16:13
came *t* also, and stirred ....Acts 17:13

THITHERWARD—*to there*
And they turned *t*, and came ..Judg 18:15
to Zion with their faces *t*......Jer 50:5
to be brought on my way *t* ....Rom 15:24

THOMAS (tŏm'ăs)—*"twin"—one of the twelve apostles of Jesus*
Apostle of Christ ....Matt 10:3
Ready to die with Christ .John 11:16
In need of instruction ....John 14:1-6
Not present when Christ appears ....John 20:19-24
States terms of belief ....John 20:25
Christ appears again and convinces him ....John 20:26-29; John 21:1, 2
In the upper room.......Acts 1:13

T, and James the son of ......Mark 3:18
T, James the son of ....Luke 6:15

THONGS—*leather straps*
Used to bind Paul ....Acts 22:25

THORN—*a plant with sharp projections on its stems*

Used literally of:
Earth's produce ....Gen 3:18

T

Land under judgment ....Is 34:13
Christ's crown ....John 19:2

Used figuratively of:

Unbelief ....Is 32:13-15
Judgments ....Hos 2:6
Pain ....Prov 26:9
False prophets ....Matt 7:15, 16
Agent of Satan 2Cor 12:7
Barrenness ....Matt 13:7, 22

[*also* THORNS]

break out, and catch in *t* ......Ex 22:6
eyes, and *t* in your sides ......Num 33:55
sides, and *t* in your eyes ......Josh 23:13
shall be as *t* in your sides .....Judg 2:3
and *t* of the wilderness and ....Judg 8:16
be all of them as *t* thrust 2Sam 23:6
took Manasseh among the *t* ...2Chr 33:11
taketh it even out of the *t* .....Job 5:5
his jaw through with a *t*? ......Job 41:2
your pots can feel the *t* ....Ps 58:9
quenched as the fire of *t* ......Ps 118:12
man is as an hedge of *t* ....Prov 15:19
all grown over with *t*, and .....Prov 24:31
crackling of *t* under a pot .....Eccl 7:6
lily among *t*, so is my love ....Song 2:2
shall come up briers and *t* .....Is 5:6
even be for briers and *t* ....Is 7:23
the fear of briers and *t* ....Is 7:25
shall burn and devour his *t* ....Is 10:17
t cut up shall they be ....Is 33:12
of the *t* shall come up the .....Is 55:13
and sow not among *t* ....Jer 4:3
grieving *t* of all that are ....Ezek 28:24
t shall be in their ....Hos 9:6
the *t* and the thistle shall ......Hos 10:8
is sharper than a *t* hedge ......Mic 7:4
be folden together as *t* ....Nah 1:10
had platted a crown of *t* ......Matt 27:29
And some fell among *t* ....Mark 4:7
t grew up, and choked it ....Mark 4:7
a crown of *t*, and put it ....Mark 15:17
of *t* men do not gather figs ....Luke 6:44
And some fell among *t* ....Luke 8:7
t sprang up with it, and ....Luke 8:7
that which fell among *t* are ....Luke 8:14
wearing the crown of *t* ....John 19:5
beareth *t* and briers ....Heb 6:8

THOROUGHLY—*completely*

cause him to be *t* healed ......Ex 21:19
images brake they in pieces *t* ..2Kin 11:18
shall *t* glean the remnant ......Jer 6:9
if ye *t* amend your ways ....Jer 7:5
if ye *t* execute judgment ....Jer 7:5
I *t* washed away thy blood ....Ezek 16:9
will *t* purge his floor ....Matt 3:12
he will *t* purge his floor ....Luke 3:17
been *t* made manifest 2Cor 11:6

THOSE—*See* INTRODUCTION

THOU—*See* INTRODUCTION

THOUGH—*although*

t thou wouldest needs be ......Gen 31:30
and it was as *t* it budded ......Gen 40:10
t he wist it not, yet is he ......Lev 5:17
t he be a stranger or a ....Lev 25:35
t I walk in the imagination ....Deut 29:19
t they have iron chariots ......Josh 17:18
and *t* they be strong ....Josh 17:18
T thou detain me, I will.......Judg 13:16
T ye have done this, yet ......Judg 15:7
t I be not like unto one of ....Ruth 2:13
t it be in Jonathan my son 1Sam 14:39
t it were sanctified this day 1Sam 21:5
as *t* he had not anointed 2Sam 1:21
t they would have fetched 2Sam 4:6
t he be not cleansed 2Chr 30:19
t there were of you cast out ...Neh 1:9
t it was turned to the ....Esth 9:1
T thy beginning was small .....Job 8:7
T I were perfect, yet would ...Job 9:21
t man be born like a wild .....Job 11:12
T the root thereof wax old ....Job 14:8
T I speak, my grief is not .....Job 16:6
and *t* I forbear, what am I .....Job 16:6
And *t* after my skin worms ....Job 19:26
T his excellency mount up.....Job 20:6
T wickedness be sweet in .....Job 20:12
mouth, *t* he hide it under .....Job 20:12
T it be given him to be in.....Job 24:23
T he hath gained, when God ..Job 27:8
T he heap up silver as the.....Job 27:16
young ones, as *t* they were ....Job 39:16
t I walk through the valley ....Ps 23:4
T an host should encamp.......Ps 27:3
t war should rise against ......Ps 27:3
T he fall, he shall not ....Ps 37:24
t the earth be removed ....Ps 46:2
and *t* the mountains be ....Ps 46:2
T the waters thereof roar .....Ps 46:3
t the mountains shake ....Ps 46:3
T ye have lain among the .....Ps 68:13
t thou tookest vengeance ......Ps 99:8
T I walk in the midst ....Ps 138:7
t thou givest many gifts ....Prov 6:35
t hand join in hand, he ....Prov 16:5
in his ways, *t* he be rich.......Prov 28:6
t he live a thousand years .....Eccl 6:6
t a man labor to seek it ....Eccl 8:17
t a wise man think to know ...Eccl 8:17
t your sins be as scarlet ....Is 1:18
t they be red like crimson .....Is 1:18
t thou wast angry with me.....Is 12:1
men, *t* fools, shall not err .....Is 35:8
t thou hast not known me .....Is 45:5
t Abraham be ignorant of us ..Is 63:16
For *t* thou wash thee with .....Jer 2:22
T thou clothest thyself ....Jer 4:30
t thou deckest thee with ....Jer 4:30
t thou rentest thy face with....Jer 4:30
t the waves thereof toss ....Jer 5:22
t they roar, yet can they ......Jer 5:22
t they speak fair words........Jer 12:6
T Moses and Samuel stood .....Jer 15:1
t I make a full end of all ......Jer 30:11
t I taught them, rising up .....Jer 32:33
t thou shouldest make thy .....Jer 49:16
T Babylon should mount up ...Jer 51:53
t he cause grief, yet will.......Lam 3:32
t briers and thorns be with ....Ezek 2:6
t they be a rebellious house ...Ezek 2:6
t they cry in mine ears with ...Ezek 8:18
not see it, *t* he shall die ......Ezek 12:13
T these three men were in it ..Ezek 14:16
t thou be sought for, yet ......Ezek 26:21
t their terror was caused ......Ezek 32:25
t they were the terror of ......Ezek 32:27
t thou knowest all this ....Dan 5:22
T thou, Israel, play the ....Hos 4:15
t I have redeemed them........Hos 7:13
Yea, *t* they have hired ....Hos 8:10
yea, *t* they bring forth, yet ....Hos 9:16
T he be fruitful among ....Hos 13:15
T ye offer me burnt ....Amos 5:22
T they dig into hell, thence....Amos 9:2
t they climb up to heaven .....Amos 9:2
t they hide themselves in ......Amos 9:3
t they be hid from my sight ...Amos 9:3
t they go into captivity ....Amos 9:4
T thou exalt thyself as ....Obad 4
t thou set thy nest among .....Obad 4
Beth-lehem Ephratah, *t* thou ..Mic 5:2
T they be quiet, and ....Nah 1:12
T I have afflicted thee, I ......Nah 1:12
not believe, *t* it be told ....Hab 1:5
Zidon, *t* it be very wise ....Zech 9:2
t all the people of the earth ...Zech 12:3
T all me shall be offended ....Matt 26:33
t many false witnesses came ...Matt 26:60
was as *t* he would go to ....Luke 9:53
t one rose from the dead ......Luke 16:31
t he bear long with them? .....Luke 18:7
T Jesus himself baptized ......John 4:2
T I bear record of myself .....John 8:14
t he were dead, yet shall he ...John 11:25
as *t* by our own power or ......Acts 3:12
t a man declare it unto you ...Acts 13:41
t he be not far from every ....Acts 17:27
as *t* they would inquire........Acts 23:20
whom, *t* he hath escaped ......Acts 28:4
t they be not circumcised......Rom 4:11
t she be married to another ...Rom 7:3
T the number of the ....Rom 9:27
t ye have ten thousand 1Cor 4:15
as *t* I were present 1Cor 5:3
weep, as *t* they wept not 1Cor 7:30
as *t* they rejoiced not 1Cor 7:30
buy, as *t* they possessed.......1Cor 7:30
For *t* I preach the gospel......1Cor 9:16
T I speak with the tongues 1Cor 13:1
And *t* I have the gift of 1Cor 13:2
t I have all faith, so that 1Cor 13:2
t I bestow all my goods to 1Cor 13:3
and *t* I give my body to be 1Cor 13:3
t our outward man perish 2Cor 4:16
as *t* God did beseech you 2Cor 5:20
t I made you sorry with a 2Cor 7:8
not repent, *t* I did repent 2Cor 7:8
t it were but for a season 2Cor 7:8
t he was rich, yet for your 2Cor 8:9
t I should boast somewhat.....2Cor 10:8
t I be rude in speech, yet 2Cor 11:6
t I would desire to glory 2Cor 12:6
t the more abundantly I 2Cor 12:15
t we be as reprobates 2Cor 13:7
But *t* we, or an angel from ....Gal 1:8
a servant, *t* he be lord ....Gal 4:1
T I might also have ....Phil 3:4
t I be absent in the flesh ......Col 2:5
t I might be much bold in .....Philem 8
T he were a Son, yet learned ..Heb 5:8
t they come out of the loins ...Heb 7:5
t a man say he hath faith .....James 2:14
ye greatly rejoice, *t* now 1Pet 1:6
t now ye see him not, yet 1Pet 1:8
of these things, *t* ye know 2Pet 1:12
not as *t* I wrote a new 2John 5
in remembrance, *t* ye once ....Jude 5

THOUGHT—*See* THINK

THOUGHT—*the process of thinking; an idea*

Of the wicked, described as:

Evil ....Gen 6:5
Abominable ....Prov 15:26
Sinful ....Is 59:7
Devoid of God ....Ps 10:4
Known by God 1Cor 3:20
In need of repentance ...Acts 8:22
Sinful ....Is 59:7
Devoid of God ....Ps 10:4

Of the believer:

Comprehended by God ..1Chr 28:9
Ps 139:2
Captivated by Christ 2Cor 10:5
Criticized by God's Word.Heb 4:12
In need of examination ..Ps 139:23

Of God:

Not like man's ....Is 55:8, 9
To believer, good ....Ps 139:17

[*also* THOUGHTS]

not a *t* in thy wicked heart ....Deut 15:9
there were great *t* of heart ....Judg 5:15
t of the heart of thy people ...1Chr 29:18
t from the visions of the .....Job 4:13
despised in the *t* of him ....Job 12:5
my *t* cause me to answer ......Job 20:2
t of his heart to all ....Ps 33:11
and thy *t* which are to us .....Ps 40:5
t are against me for evil.......Ps 56:5
the inward *t* of every one .....Ps 64:6
and thy *t* are very deep ....Ps 92:5
The Lord knoweth the *t* ......Ps 94:11
I hate vain *t*: but thy law .....Ps 119:113
that very day his *t* perish ......Ps 146:4
The *t* of the righteous are .....Prov 12:5
thy *t* shall be established ......Prov 16:3
The *t* of foolishness is sin .....Prov 24:9
the king, no not in thy *t* ......Eccl 10:20
unrighteous man his *t* ....Is 55:7
good, after their own *t* ....Is 65:2
How long shall thy vain *t* .....Jer 4:14
performed the *t* of his heart ...Jer 23:20
I know the *t* that I think ......Jer 29:11
t of peace, and not of evil.....Jer 29:11

thou shalt think an evil *t* ......Ezek 38:10
O king, thy *t* came into thy ...Dan 2:29
t upon my bed and the........Dan 4:5
one hour, and his *t* troubled...Dan 4:19
let not thy *t* trouble thee ......Dan 5:10
unto man what is his *t* ....Amos 4:13
know not the *t* of the Lord....Mic 4:12
taking *t* can add one cubit.....Matt 6:27
take no *t*, saying, What ....Matt 6:31
Take..no *t* for the morrow ....Matt 6:34
morrow shall take *t* for the ....Matt 6:34
Jesus knowing their *t* said .....Matt 9:4
of the heart proceed evil *t*.....Matt 15:19
of men, proceed evil *t* ....Mark 7:21
take no *t* beforehand what ....Mark 13:11
t of many hearts may be ......Luke 2:35
he knew their *t*, and said......Luke 6:8
take ye no *t* how or what .....Luke 12:11
Take no *t* for your life ....Luke 12:22
why take ye *t* for the rest? ....Luke 12:26
do *t* arise in your hearts? .....Luke 24:38
and their *t* the mean while ....Rom 2:15
a discerner of the *t* and ....Heb 4:12
become judges of evil *t*? ......James 2:4

THOUSAND

[*also* THOUSANDS]
brother a *t* pieces of silver ....Gen 20:16
the mother of *t* of millions ....Gen 24:60
six hundred *t* on foot that .....Ex 12:37
be rulers of *t*, and rulers ......Ex 18:21
showing mercy unto *t* of them .Ex 20:6
a *t* seven hundred and ....Ex 38:25
t seven hundred seventy.......Ex 38:28
you shall put ten *t* to flight ....Lev 26:8
fathers, heads of *t* in Israel ....Num 1:16
forty and six *t* and five........Num 1:21
and five *t* six hundred..........Num 1:25
fifty and four *t* and four.......Num 1:29
forty *t* and five hundred.......Num 1:33
thirty and five *t* and four.......Num 1:37
forty and one *t* and five ....Num 1:41
were six hundred *t* and........Num 1:46
three *t* and five hundred ......Num 1:46
fifty and four *t* and four.......Num 2:6
hundred *t* and fourscore *t* .....Num 2:9
six *t* and four hundred ....Num 2:9
fifty and nine *t* and three .....Num 2:13
a hundred *t* and fifty..........Num 2:16
one *t* and four hundred ....Num 2:16
thirty and two *t* and two ....Num 2:21
a hundred *t* and eight *t* ....Num 2:24
forty and one *t* and five ....Num 2:28
Dan were a hundred *t* ....Num 2:31
fifty and seven *t* and six.......Num 2:31
hosts were six hundred *t* ......Num 2:32
three *t* and five hundred ......Num 2:32
eight *t* and six hundred ....Num 3:28
were twenty and two *t* ....Num 3:39
t three hundred and ....Num 3:50
two *t* and six hundred and ....Num 4:40
eight *t* and five hundred ......Num 4:48
unto the many *t* of Israel......Num 10:36
are six hundred *t* footmen .....Num 11:21
were twenty and four *t*.........Num 25:9
twenty and two *t* and two .....Num 26:14
sixteen *t* and five hundred.....Num 26:22
threescore *t* and five ....Num 26:27
thirty and two *t* and five ......Num 26:37
four *t* and four hundred........Num 26:43
forty and five *t* and four ......Num 26:50
of Israel, six hundred *t*........Num 26:51
t seven hundred and thirty ....Num 26:51
every tribe a *t*, throughout ....Num 31:4
of Israel, a *t* of every tribe ....Num 31:5
every tribe, twelve *t*, armed ...Num 31:5
with the captains over *t* ....Num 31:14
caught, was six hundred *t* .....Num 31:32
seventy *t* and five *t* sheep .....Num 31:32
And threescore and one *t* .....Num 31:34
number three hundred *t*.......Num 31:36
thirty *t* and five hundred ......Num 31:36
thirty *t* and five hundred ......Num 31:39
was three hundred *t* ....Num 31:43
and thirty *t* and seven *t* ....Num 31:43
And thirty *t* asses and five ....Num 31:45
were over *t* of the host........Num 31:48
captains of *t*, and captains .....Num 31:48
sixteen *t* seven hundred ....Num 31:52
gold of the captains of *t*.......Num 31:54
the east side two *t* cubits ......Num 35:5
south side two *t* cubits ....Num 35:5
west side two *t* cubits ....Num 35:5
north side two *t* cubits ....Num 35:5
make you a *t* times so ....Deut 1:11
over you, captains over *t* ......Deut 1:15
mercy unto *t* of them ....Deut 5:10
How should one chase a *t* ......Deut 32:30
and two put ten *t* to flight.....Deut 32:30
came with ten *t* of saints ......Deut 33:2
are the ten *t* of Ephraim ......Deut 33:17
they are the *t* of Manasseh ....Deut 33:17
two *t* cubits by measure ....Josh 3:4
about two or three *t* men .....Josh 7:3
out thirty *t* mighty men ....Josh 8:3
men and women, were twelve *t*.Josh 8:25
among the *t* of Israel ....Josh 22:14
the *t* of Israel which were .....Josh 22:30
slew of them in Bezek ten *t* ...Judg 1:4
ten *t* men of the children......Judg 4:6
Tabor, and ten *t* men after ....Judg 4:14
people twenty and two *t* ......Judg 7:3
them, about fifteen *t* men .....Judg 8:10
twenty *t* men that drew ....Judg 8:10
a *t* and seven hundred ....Judg 8:26
Ephraimites forty and two *t* ...Judg 12:6
took it, and slew a *t* men .....Judg 15:15
three *t* men and women ....Judg 16:27
and a hundred of a *t*..........Judg 20:10
t out of ten *t*, to fetch ....Judg 20:10
four hundred *t* men that ......Judg 20:17
of Israel again eighteen *t* ......Judg 20:25
and five *t* and a hundred ......Judg 20:35
in the highways five *t* men ....Judg 20:45
Gidom, and slew two *t* men ...Judg 20:45
twelve *t* men of the ....Judg 21:10
in the field about four *t* 1Sam 4:2
fifty *t* and threescore and 1Sam 6:19
appoint him captains over *t*....1Sam 8:12
of Israel were three hundred *t* .1Sam 11:8
the men of Judah thirty *t* 1Sam 11:8
Saul chose him three *t* men ...1Sam 13:2
two *t* were with Saul in 1Sam 13:2
a *t* were with Jonathan in 1Sam 13:2
Israel, thirty *t* chariots 1Sam 13:5
six *t* horsemen, and people 1Sam 13:5
two hundred *t* footmen........1Sam 15:4
and ten *t* men of Judah 1Sam 15:4
was five *t* shekels of brass 1Sam 17:5
unto the captain of their *t* 1Sam 17:18
Saul hath slain his *t*...........1Sam 18:7
and David his ten *t*............1Sam 18:7
ascribed unto David ten *t* 1Sam 18:8
they have ascribed but *t*.......1Sam 18:8
Saul hath slain his *t*...........1Sam 21:11
and David his ten *t*? 1Sam 21:11
out throughout all the *t* of 1Sam 23:23
Saul took three *t* chosen 1Sam 24:2
three *t* chosen men of Israel ...1Sam 26:2
Saul slew his *t*................1Sam 29:5
and David his ten *t*? 1Sam 29:5
men of Israel, thirty *t*.........2Sam 6:1
took from him a *t* chariots 2Sam 8:4
and twenty *t* footmen 2Sam 8:4
salt, being eighteen *t* men 2Sam 8:13
of Zoba, twenty *t* footmen 2Sam 10:6
of king Maacah a *t* men.......2Sam 10:6
of Ish-tob twelve *t* men 2Sam 10:6
choose out twelve *t* men 2Sam 17:1
set captains of *t* and captains ..2Sam 18:1
thou art worth ten *t* of us 2Sam 18:3
receive a *t* shekels of silver 2Sam 18:12
eight hundred *t* valiant men ...2Sam 24:9
were five hundred *t* men 1Sam 24:9
t burnt offerings did 1Kin 3:4
Solomon had forty *t* stalls 1Kin 4:26
and twelve *t* horsemen 1Kin 4:26
he spake three *t* proverbs 1Kin 4:32
songs were a *t* and five 1Kin 4:32
the levy was thirty *t* men......1Kin 5:13
and ten *t* that bare burdens ...1Kin 5:15
fourscore *t* hewers in the 1Kin 5:15
three *t* and three hundred 1Kin 5:16
two and twenty *t* oxen 1Kin 8:63
a hundred and twenty *t* 1Kin 8:63
had a *t* and four hundred 1Kin 10:26
twelve *t* horsemen, whom 1Kin 10:26
left me seven *t* in Israel 1Kin 19:18
a hundred *t* footmen 1Kin 20:29
Israel a hundred *t* lambs 2Kin 3:4
hundred *t* rams, with 2Kin 3:4
chariots, and ten *t* footmen....2Kin 13:7
Pul a *t* talents of silver 2Kin 15:19
fourscore and five *t* 2Kin 19:35
men of might, even seven *t*....2Kin 24:16
craftsmen and smiths a *t* 2Kin 24:16
and forty *t* seven hundred 1Chr 5:18
of their camels fifty *t* 1Chr 5:21
two hundred and fifty *t* 1Chr 5:21
and of asses two *t* 1Chr 5:21
and of men a hundred *t*.......1Chr 5:21
war, six and thirty *t* men 1Chr 7:4
and two *t* and thirty 1Chr 7:7
were seventeen *t* and two 1Chr 7:11
a *t* and seven hundred and 1Chr 9:13
captains of the *t* that were 1Chr 12:20
six *t* and eight hundred 1Chr 12:24
children of Levi four *t* and 1Chr 12:26
the kindred of Saul, three *t* ...1Chr 12:29
of Manasseh eighteen *t*........1Chr 12:31
of Naphtali a *t* captains 1Chr 12:34
spear thirty and seven *t* 1Chr 12:34
expert in war, forty *t* 1Chr 12:36
the captains over *t*, went 1Chr 15:25
to a *t* generations.............1Chr 16:15
David took from him a *t* 1Chr 18:4
seven *t* horsemen and twenty *t* .1Chr 18:4
valley of salt eighteen *t* 1Chr 18:12
thirty and two *t* chariots 1Chr 19:7
of the Syrians seven *t* men 1Chr 19:18
and forty *t* footmen...........1Chr 19:18
they of Israel were a *t* *t* 1Chr 21:5
hundred *t* men that drew......1Chr 21:5
threescore and ten *t* men......1Chr 21:5
hundred *t* talents of gold 1Chr 22:14
and a *t* *t* talents of silver 1Chr 22:14
four *t* were to set forward 1Chr 23:4
six *t* were officers and 1Chr 23:4
four *t* were porters 1Chr 23:5
four *t* praised the Lord........1Chr 23:5
two *t* and seven hundred 1Chr 26:32
captains of *t* and hundreds 1Chr 27:1
were twenty and four *t*........1Chr 27:2
Even three *t* talents of gold ...1Chr 29:4
seven *t* talents of refined 1Chr 29:4
the captains of *t* and of 1Chr 29:6
of God of gold five *t* talents ...1Chr 29:7
and ten *t* drams 1Chr 29:7
and of silver ten *t* talents......1Chr 29:7
of brass eighteen *t* talents 1Chr 29:7
hundred *t* talents of iron 1Chr 29:7
even a *t* bullocks, a *t* rams 1Chr 29:21
a *t* lambs, with their drink 1Chr 29:21
to the captains of *t* and of.....2Chr 1:2
had a *t* and four hundred 2Chr 1:14
twelve *t* horsemen, which 2Chr 1:14
ten *t* men to bear burdens.....2Chr 2:2
fourscore *t* to hew in the 2Chr 2:2
three *t* and six hundred to.....2Chr 2:2
twenty *t* measures of..........2Chr 2:10
and twenty *t* measures of......2Chr 2:10
and twenty *t* baths of wine 2Chr 2:10
and twenty *t* baths of oil 2Chr 2:10
a hundred and fifty *t*..........2Chr 2:17
three *t* and six hundred 2Chr 2:17
ten *t* of them to be bearers....2Chr 2:18
fourscore *t* to be hewers 2Chr 2:18
three *t* and six hundred 2Chr 2:18
of twenty and two *t* oxen 2Chr 7:5
hundred and twenty *t* sheep ...2Chr 7:5
and twelve *t* horsemen 2Chr 9:25
and threescore *t* horsemen 2Chr 12:3
four hundred *t* chosen men 2Chr 13:3
eight hundred *t* chosen men ...2Chr 13:3
of Judah three hundred *t*......2Chr 14:8

hundred and fourscore *t* 2Chr 14:8
oxen and seven *t* sheep 2Chr 15:11
seven *t* and seven hundred 2Chr 17:11
hundred and fourscore *t* 2Chr 17:15
and shield two hundred *t* 2Chr 17:17
made them captains over *t* 2Chr 25:5
three hundred *t* choice men ...2Chr 25:5
the children of Seir ten *t* 2Chr 25:11
and smote three *t* of them 2Chr 25:13
valor were two *t* and six 2Chr 26:12
an army, three hundred *t* 2Chr 26:13
seven *t* and five hundred 2Chr 26:13
ten *t* measures of wheat 2Chr 27:5
ten *t* of barley. So much 2Chr 27:5
brethren two hundred *t* 2Chr 28:8
oxen and three *t* sheep 2Chr 29:33
t bullocks and ten *t* sheep 2Chr 30:24
to the number of thirty *t* 2Chr 35:7
three *t* bullocks: these 2Chr 35:7
offerings five *t* small cattle 2Chr 35:9
gold, a *t* chargers of silver .....Ezra 1:9
were five *t* and four hundred ..Ezra 1:11
two *t* eight hundred and ......Ezra 2:6
t two hundred twenty and .....Ezra 2:12
a *t* two hundred fifty and .....Ezra 2:31
children of Immer, a *t* fifty ....Ezra 2:37
Harim, a *t* and seventeen .....Ezra 2:39
seven *t* three hundred ....Ezra 2:65
and one *t* drams of gold ....Ezra 2:69
and five *t* pounds of silver .....Ezra 2:69
a *t* cubits on the wall unto ....Neh 3:13
two *t* and eight hundred ......Neh 7:11
two *t* three hundred twenty....Neh 7:17
a *t* two hundred fifty and .....Neh 7:34
of Immer, a *t* fifty and two ....Neh 7:40
Harim, a *t* and seventeen .....Neh 7:42
were seven *t* three hundred ....Neh 7:67
treasure a *t* drams of gold .....Neh 7:70
twenty *t* drams of gold ....Neh 7:71
t and two hundred pounds ....Neh 7:71
was twenty *t* drams of gold ....Neh 7:72
and two *t* pounds of silver .....Neh 7:72
pay ten *t* talents of silver ......Esth 3:9
also was seven *t* sheep ....Job 1:3
three *t* camels, and five ....Job 1:3
a *t*, to show unto man ....Job 33:23
for he had fourteen *t* sheep ...Job 42:12
sheep, and six *t* camels ....Job 42:12
and a *t* yoke of oxen, and a ...Job 42:12
of oxen, and a *t* she asses .....Job 42:12
be afraid of ten *t* of people ....Ps 3:6
the cattle upon a *t* hills ....Ps 50:10
chariots of God are twenty *t* ...Ps 68:17
thy courts is better than a *t* ...Ps 84:10
a *t* years in thy sight are ......Ps 90:4
t shall fall at thy side ....Ps 91:7
and ten *t* at thy right hand ....Ps 91:7
than *t* of gold and silver ....Ps 119:72
and ten *t* in our streets ....Ps 144:13
though he live a *t* years ....Eccl 6:6
one man among a *t* have I ....Eccl 7:28
there hang a *t* bucklers ....Song 4:4
bring a *t* pieces of silver ....Song 8:11
t vines at a *t* silverlings ....Is 7:23
will give thee two *t* horses .....Is 36:8
little one shall become a *t* .....Is 60:22
loving-kindness unto *t* ....Jer 32:18
three *t* Jews and three and ....Jer 52:28
the breadth shall be ten *t* .....Ezek 45:1
length of five and twenty *t* ....Ezek 45:3
breadth of ten *t*: and in ....Ezek 45:3
five and twenty *t* of length ....Ezek 45:5
and the ten *t* of breadth ....Ezek 45:5
of the city five *t* broad ....Ezek 45:6
and five and twenty *t* long ....Ezek 45:6
Again he measured a *t* ....Ezek 47:4
twenty *t* reeds in breadth ......Ezek 48:8
five and twenty *t* in length ....Ezek 48:10
the west ten *t* in breadth ......Ezek 48:10
the east ten *t* in breadth ......Ezek 48:10
five and twenty *t* in length ....Ezek 48:10
shall be five and twenty *t* .....Ezek 48:13
five *t*, that are left in ....Ezek 48:15
the five and twenty *t* ....Ezek 48:15
holy portion shall be ten *t* .....Ezek 48:18
and ten *t* westward; and it ....Ezek 48:18
five and twenty *t* of the ....Ezek 48:21
the five and twenty *t* ....Ezek 48:21
four *t* and five hundred ....Ezek 48:32
feast to a *t* of his lords ....Dan 5:1
and drank wine before the *t* ...Dan 5:1
t t ministered unto him ....Dan 7:10
ten *t* times ten *t* stood ....Dan 7:10
t two hundred and ninety ....Dan 12:11
went out by a *t* shall leave ....Amos 5:3
sixscore *t* persons that ....Jon 4:11
little among the *t* of Judah ....Mic 5:2
be pleased with *t* of rams .....Mic 6:7
with ten *t* of rivers of oil? .....Mic 6:7
five loaves of the five *t* ....Matt 16:9
owed him ten *t* talents ....Matt 18:24
they were about two *t* ....Mark 5:13
eaten were about four *t* ....Mark 8:9
the seven among four *t* ....Mark 8:20
they were about five *t* men ....Luke 9:14
against him with twenty *t* ? ....Luke 14:31
in number about five *t* ....John 6:10
them about three *t* souls ......Acts 2:41
it fifty *t* pieces of silver ....Acts 19:19
t of Jews there are which .....Acts 21:20
reserved to myself seven *t* .....Rom 11:4
ten *t* instructors in Christ 1Cor 4:15
ten *t* words in an unknown 1Cor 14:19
with ten *t* of his saints ....Jude 14
ten *t* times ten, *t*, and *t* of *t* ...Rev 5:11
forty and four *t* of all the .....Rev 7:4
were two hundred *t t* ....Rev 9:16
a *t* two hundred and ....Rev 11:3
a *t* two hundred and ....Rev 12:6
hundred forty and four *t* ......Rev 14:1
t and six hundred furlongs .....Rev 14:20
the reed, twelve *t* furlongs ....Rev 21:16

THOUSAND YEARS
As one day 2Pet 3:8
Millennial reign ....Rev 20:1-7

THREAD—*a filament or group of filaments twisted together in a continuous strand*
Refused by Abram ......Gen 14:23
Tied to hand ....Gen 38:28
Tied in window ....Judg 2:18
Lips like scarlet ....Song 4:3

had the scarlet *t* upon his .....Gen 38:30
bind this line of scarlet *t* ......Josh 2:18
a *t* of tow is broken when .....Judg 16:9

THREATEN—*to menace another by words or actions*
Purposes of, to:
Silence a prophet 1Kin 19:1, 2
Hinder a work ....Neh 6:1-14
Hinder the Gospel ....Acts 4:17, 21
Exemplified by:
Jehoram against Elisha ...2Kin 6:31
Jews against Christians ...Acts 4:29
Saul against Christians ...Acts 9:1

[*also* THREATENED, THREATENINGS]
let us straitly *t* them ....Acts 4:17
unto them, forbearing *t* ....Eph 6:9
when he suffered, he *t* not 1Pet 2:23

THREE
Methuselah *t* hundred ....Gen 5:22
Noah begat *t* sons, Shem ......Gen 6:10
t wives of his sons with ....Gen 7:13
flood *t* hundred and fifty ......Gen 9:28
four hundred and *t* years ......Gen 11:15
a heifer of *t* years old ....Gen 15:9
a she goat of *t* years old ......Gen 15:9
a ram of *t* years old, and a ....Gen 15:9
t measures of fine meal ....Gen 18:6
I have born him *t* sons ....Gen 29:34
pass about *t* months after .....Gen 38:24
The *t* branches are *t* days ....Gen 40:12
I had *t* white baskets on ......Gen 40:16
t days shall Pharaoh lift ....Gen 40:19
together into ward *t* days ......Gen 42:17
t hundred pieces of silver ......Gen 45:22
child, she hid him *t* months ...Ex 2:2
t days' journey into the ....Ex 5:3
fourscore and *t* years old ......Ex 7:7
the land of Egypt *t* days ......Ex 10:22
t days in the wilderness ....Ex 15:22
T times thou shalt keep a .....Ex 23:14
t branches of the ....Ex 25:32
T bowls made like unto ....Ex 25:33
t bowls made like almonds ....Ex 25:33
t, and their sockets *t* ....Ex 27:14
t branches of the ....Ex 37:18
T bowls made after the ....Ex 37:19
t bowls made like almonds ....Ex 37:19
t, and their sockets *t* ....Ex 38:14
purifying *t* and thirty days .....Lev 12:4
t years shall it be as ....Lev 19:23
be *t* shekels of silver ....Lev 27:6
thousand and *t* hundred ....Num 1:23
hundred thousand and *t* ....Num 1:46
and *t* thousand and four ....Num 2:30
t hundred and threescore ......Num 3:50
mount of the Lord *t* days .....Num 10:33
them in the *t* days' journey ....Num 10:33
ye *t* unto the tabernacle ....Num 12:4
And they *t* came out ....Num 12:4
smitten me these *t* times? .....Num 22:28
from me these *t* times ....Num 22:33
forty and *t* thousand and ......Num 26:7
were fifty and *t* thousand ......Num 26:47
t tenth deals of flour for ......Num 28:12
t tenth deals unto one ....Num 28:28
t tenth deals to a bullock ......Num 29:9
t hundred thousand and ....Num 31:36
t days' journey in the ....Num 33:8
t cities on this side Jordan .....Num 35:14
t cities shall ye give in ....Num 35:14
Moses severed *t* cities on ....Deut 4:41
T times in a year shall all .....Deut 16:16
separate *t* cities for thee ......Deut 19:2
to inherit, into *t* parts ....Deut 19:3
add *t* cities more for thee .....Deut 19:9
t days ye shall pass over ......Josh 1:11
abode there *t* days, until ......Josh 2:22
two or *t* thousand men go .....Josh 7:3
to pass at the end of *t* days ...Josh 9:16
towns, even *t* countries ....Josh 17:11
with her suburbs; *t* cities ......Josh 21:32
thence the *t* sons of Anak .....Judg 1:20
t hundred men that lapped ....Judg 7:7
t hundred men into *t* ....Judg 7:16
the *t* hundred blew the ....Judg 7:22
had reigned *t* years over ......Judg 9:22
Israel twenty and *t* years ......Judg 10:2
of Arnon, *t* hundred years? ...Judg 11:26
not in *t* days expound the .....Judg 14:14
t thousand men of Judah ......Judg 15:11
t thousand men and women ...Judg 16:27
with her, with *t* bullocks 1Sam 1:24
t sons and two daughters 1Sam 2:21
thee *t* men going up to God ...1Sam 10:3
one carrying *t* kids, and 1Sam 10:3
carrying *t* loaves of bread 1Sam 10:3
the people in *t* companies 1Sam 11:11
Philistines in *t* companies 1Sam 13:17
t eldest sons of Jesse went 1Sam 17:13
names of his *t* sons that 1Sam 17:13
thou hast stayed *t* days 1Sam 20:19
and bowed himself *t* times 1Sam 20:41
t thousand chosen men 1Sam 24:2
t thousand chosen men of 1Sam 26:2
t days agone I fell sick 1Sam 30:13
Saul and his *t* sons fallen 1Sam 31:8
were *t* sons of Zeruiah 2Sam 2:18
reigned thirty and *t* years 2Sam 5:5
and was there *t* years 2Sam 13:38
he took *t* darts in his hand 2Sam 18:14
in the days of David *t* years ...2Sam 21:1
one of the *t* mighty men 2Sam 23:9
the *t* mighty men brake 2Sam 23:16
Zeruiah, was chief among *t* 2Sam 23:18
spear against *t* hundred 2Sam 23:18
and had the name among *t* 2Sam 23:18
not most honorable of *t*? 2Sam 23:19
attained not unto the first *t* 2Sam 23:19
attained not to the first *t* 2Sam 23:23
wilt thou flee *t* months 2Sam 24:13

thirty and *t* years reigned 1Kin 2:11
spake *t* thousand proverbs.....1Kin 4:32
with *t* rows of hewed stone 1Kin 6:36
were windows in *t* rows 1Kin 7:4
against light in *t* ranks 1Kin 7:4
t looking toward the north 1Kin 7:25
t looking toward the west 1Kin 7:25
t looking toward the south 1Kin 7:25
t looking toward the east......1Kin 7:25
t times in a year did 1Kin 9:25
t hundred shields of beaten....1Kin 10:17
t pound of gold went to one...1Kin 10:17
and *t* hundred concubines 1Kin 11:3
T years reigned he in 1Kin 15:2
continued *t* years without 1Kin 22:1
sought *t* days, but found 2Kin 2:17
to him two or *t* eunuchs.......2Kin 9:32
the *t* and twentieth year of 2Kin 13:1
and besieged it *t* years 2Kin 17:5
t hundred talents of silver 2Kin 18:14
Jehoahaz was twenty and *t* 2Kin 23:31
he reigned *t* months in 2Kin 23:31
he reigned in Jerusalem *t* 2Kin 24:8
the *t* keepers of the door......2Kin 25:18
had *t* and twenty cities 1Chr 2:22
Hezekiah, and Azrikam, *t*.....1Chr 3:23
Saul died, and his *t* sons 1Chr 10:6
was one of the *t* mighties 1Chr 11:12
t brake through the host 1Chr 11:18
Joab, he was chief of the *t* 1Chr 11:20
spear against *t* hundred 1Chr 11:20
had a name among the *t* 1Chr 11:20
Of the *t*, he was more 1Chr 11:21
attained not to the first *t*......1Chr 11:21
kindred of Saul, *t* thousand....1Chr 12:29
in his house *t* months 1Chr 13:14
Either *t* years' famine 1Chr 21:12
t months to be destroyed.......1Chr 21:12
t days the sword of the Lord ..1Chr 21:12
and Zetham, and Joel, *t* 1Chr 23:8
and Haziel, and Haran, *t*......1Chr 23:9
The *t* and twentieth to 1Chr 24:18
thirty and *t* years reigned 1Chr 29:27
t thousand and six hundred....2Chr 2:2
and *t* thousand and six 2Chr 2:18
oxen, *t* looking toward the 2Chr 4:4
t looking toward the west 2Chr 4:4
t looking toward the south 2Chr 4:4
t looking toward the east......2Chr 4:4
t and twentieth day of the.....2Chr 7:10
solemn feasts, *t* times in 2Chr 8:13
t hundred shields made he 2Chr 9:16
t hundred shekels of gold 2Chr 9:16
again unto me after *t* days 2Chr 10:5
of Solomon strong, *t* years 2Chr 11:17
for *t* years they walked in 2Chr 11:17
Judah *t* hundred thousand.....2Chr 14:8
men of valor *t* hundred 2Chr 17:14
them *t* hundred thousand......2Chr 25:5
t hundred thousand and 2Chr 26:13
t years old and upward........2Chr 31:16
cattle, and *t* hundred oxen 2Chr 35:8
was twenty and *t* years old 2Chr 36:2
he reigned *t* months in 2Chr 36:2
t hundred seventy and ....Ezra 2:4
t hundred twenty and *t*........Ezra 2:17
a hundred twenty and *t* ....Ezra 2:21
two hundred twenty and *t*.....Ezra 2:28
Jericho, *t* hundred forty ....Ezra 2:34
hundred seventy and *t* ....Ezra 2:36
two thousand *t* hundred ....Ezra 2:64
t rows of great stones ....Ezra 6:4
abode we in tents *t* days ......Ezra 8:15
not come within *t* days.........Ezra 10:8
and was there *t* days...........Neh 2:11
two thousand *t* hundred ....Neh 7:17
Bezai, *t* hundred twenty.......Neh 7:23
a hundred twenty and *t* ....Neh 7:32
Jericho, *t* hundred forty ....Neh 7:36
nine hundred seventy and *t*....Neh 7:39
thousand *t* hundred and ....Neh 7:66
eat nor drink *t* days ....Esth 4:16
on the *t* and twentieth day ....Esth 8:9
slew *t* hundred men at ....Esth 9:15
and *t* thousand camels ....Job 1:3
Job's *t* friends heard of all ....Job 2:11
against his *t* friends was ....Job 32:3
seven sons and *t* daughters ....Job 42:13
t things that are never ....Prov 30;15
For *t* things the earth is ....Prov 30:21
a heifer of *t* years old.........Is 15:5
two or *t* berries in the top.....Is 17:6
is the *t* and twentieth year ....Jer 25:3
as a heifer of *t* years old ......Jer 48:34
t thousand Jews and *t* and.....Jer 52:28
t hundred and ninety days.....Ezek 4:5
these *t* men, Noah, Daniel ....Ezek 14:14
t on this side, and *t* on that ...Ezek 40:10
they *t* were of one measure ...Ezek 40:10
the gate was *t* cubits on ....Ezek 40:48
this side, and *t* cubits on ......Ezek 40:48
about on their *t* stories........Ezek 41:16
against gallery in *t* stories .....Ezek 42:3
t gates northward; one ....Ezek 48:31
measures: and *t* gates ....Ezek 48:33
nourishing them *t* years ....Dan 1:5
Did not we cast *t* men ....Dan 3:24
his knees *t* times a day........Dan 6:10
it had *t* ribs in the mouth .....Dan 7:5
and before whom *t* fell........Dan 7:20
thousand and *t* hundred ....Dan 8:14
till *t* whole weeks were........Dan 10:3
thousand *t* hundred and ....Dan 12:12
For *t* transgressions of ....Amos 1:3
t transgressions of Tyrus ......Amos 1:9
For *t* transgressions of the.....Amos 1:13
t transgressions of Judah ......Amos 2:4
your tithes after *t* years ....Amos 4:4
two or *t* cities wandered ......Amos 4:8
the fish *t* days and *t* nights ....Jon 1:17
T shepherds also I cut off .....Zech 11:8
was *t* days and *t* nights........Matt 12:40
hid in *t* measures of meal .....Matt 13:33
make here *t* tabernacles ....Matt 17:4
two or *t* are gathered ....Matt 18:20
and buildest it in *t* days ....Matt 27:40
now been with me *t* days......Mark 8:2
let us make *t* tabernacles ......Mark 9:5
within *t* days I will build ......Mark 14:58
with her about *t* months ......Luke 1:56
shut up *t* years and six ....Luke 4:25
let us make *t* tabernacles ......Luke 9:33
Which now of these *t* ....Luke 10:36
t against two, and two..*t* ......Luke 12:52
hid in *t* measures of meal .....Luke 13:21
containing two or *t* firkins.....John 2:6
thou rear it up in *t* days? .....John 2:20
a hundred and fifty and *t* ......John 21:11
about *t* thousand souls ....Acts 2:41
father's house *t* months ....Acts 7:20
Behold, *t* men seek thee ......Acts 10:19
t men already come unto......Acts 11:11
for the space of *t* months ......Acts 19:8
And there abode *t* months ....Acts 20:3
after *t* days he ascended ......Acts 25:1
And after *t* months we ....Acts 28:11
Forum, and The *T* Taverns....Acts 28:15
day *t* and twenty thousand 1Cor 10:8
faith, hope, charity, these *t*....1Cor 13:13
by two, or at the most by *t*....1Cor 14:27
two or *t* witnesses shall 2Cor 13:1
after *t* years I went up to .....Gal 1:18
before two or *t* witnesses......1Tim 5:19
under two or *t* witnesses ......Heb 10:28
space of *t* years and six ....James 5:17
are *t* that bear record in 1John 5:7
and these *t* are one 1John 5:7
are *t* that bear witness in......1John 5:8
and these *t* agree in one 1John 5:8
t measures of barley for a .....Rev 6:6
By these *t* was the third.......Rev 9:18
after *t* days and a half the.....Rev 11:11
was divided into *t* parts ....Rev 16:19
On the east *t* gates ....Rev 21:13
on the north *t* gates ....Rev 21:13
on the south *t* gates ....Rev 21:13
and on the west *t* gates ....Rev 21:13

THREEFOLD—*three times*

t cord is not quickly ....Eccl 4:12

THREESCORE—*sixty*

a hundred *t* and fifteen ....Gen 25:7
the souls were *t* and six ....Gen 46:26
mourned for him *t* and ten ....Gen 50:3
and *t* and ten palm trees ......Ex 15:27
of her purifying *t* and six......Lev 12:5
t and fourteen thousand.......Num 1:27
t and fourteen thousand.......Num 2:4
two hundred and *t* and.......Num 3:43
and *t* and five shekels.........Num 3:50
t and four thousand and ......Num 26:25
were *t* and four thousand .....Num 26:43
t and one thousand asses......Num 31:34
Lord's tribute was *t* and.......Num 31:38
and *t* and ten palm trees ......Num 33:9
t cities, all the region ....Deut 3:4
are in Bashan *t* cities ....Josh 13:30
T and ten kings, having ....Judg 1:7
had *t* and ten sons of his ......Judg 8:30
they gave him *t* and ten.......Judg 9:4
slain his sons, *t* and ten ....Judg 9:18
that rode on *t* and ten ass .....Judg 12:14
fifty thousand and *t* and.......1Sam 6:19
three hundred and *t* men......2Sam 2:31
t great cities with walls........1Kin 4:13
had *t* and ten thousand 1Kin 5:15
hundred *t* and six talents 1Kin 10:14
and *t* men of the people of....2Kin 25:19
he married when he was *t*.....1Chr 2:21
seven hundred and *t* 1Chr 5:18
with their brethren *t* and 1Chr 16:38
t and two of Obed-edom 1Chr 26:8
t and ten thousand men to 2Chr 2:2
first measure was *t* cubits 2Chr 3:3
wives and *t* concubines........2Chr 11:21
sons and *t* daughters 2Chr 11:21
and *t* thousand horsemen......2Chr 12:3
to fulfill *t* and ten years 2Chr 36:21
seven hundred and *t* ....Ezra 2:9
t and one thousand drams.....Ezra 2:69
breadth thereof *t* cubits ....Ezra 6:3
and with them *t* males ....Ezra 8:13
seven hundred and *t* ....Neh 7:14
two thousand *t* and seven .....Neh 7:19
and *t* and seven priests' ....Neh 7:72
years are *t* years and ten ......Ps 90:10
t valiant men are about it .....Song 3:7
within *t* and five years ....Is 7:8
and *t* men of the people of....Jer 52:25
made also posts of *t* cubits ....Ezek 40:14
whose height was *t* cubits .....Dan 3:1
weeks, and *t* and two weeks...Dan 9:25
indignation these *t* and ten ....Zech 1:12
from Jerusalem about *t* ....Luke 24:13
his kindred, *t* and fifteen......Acts 7:14
two hundred *t* and sixteen......Acts 27:37
the number under *t* years 1Tim 5:9
two hundred and *t* days ....Rev 11:3
is Six hundred *t* and six ....Rev 13:18

THRESHING—*separating kernels of grain from the husks*

Characteristics of:

Done by a stick ....Is 28:27
By cart wheels also ......Is 28:27, 28
By the feet of oxen......Hos 10:11
Large and roomy place ..Gen 50:10

Figurative of:

God's judgments ....Jer 51:33
Minister's labor 1Cor 9:9, 10

[*also* THRESH, THRESHED]

your *t* shall reach unto ....Lev 26:5
Gideon *t* wheat by the ....Judg 6:11
and *t* instruments and 2Sam 24:22
them like the dust by *t*.........2Kin 13:7
Now Ornan was *t* wheat 1Chr 21:20
O my *t*, and the corn ....Is 21:10
a new sharp *t* instrument ......Is 41:15
thou shalt *t* the mountains.....Is 41:15
they have *t* Gilead with ....Amos 1:3
with *t* instruments of iron ....Amos 1:3
Arise and *t*, O daughter of ....Mic 4:13
thou didst *t* the heathen.......Hab 3:12

T

THRESHING FLOOR—*place where grain was threshed, usually beaten earth or an area paved with stones*

[*also* THRESHING FLOORS]
heave offering of the *t f*.......Num 15:20
as the increase of the *t f*......Num 18:30
barley tonight in the *t f*.......Ruth 3:2
Keiliah, and they rob the *t f*...1Sam 23:1
they came to Nachon's *t f*.....2Sam 6:6
David said, To buy the *t f*....2Sam 24:21
came unto the *t f* of Chidon...1Chr 13:9
the Lord in the *t f* of Ornan...1Chr 21:18
Grant me the place of this *t f* .1Chr 21:22
prepared in the *t f* of Ornan...2Chr 3:1
the chaff of the summer *t f*....Dan 2:35

THRESHING PLACE—*threshing floor*
of the Lord was by the *t p* 2Sam 24:16

THRESHOLD—*the stone, plank, or piece of timber that lies under a door*

[*also* THRESHOLDS]
her hands were upon the *t* ....Judg 19:27
were cut off upon the *t* 1Sam 5:4
came to the *t* of the door 1Kin 14:17
ward at the *t* of the gates .....Neh 12:25
was, to the *t* of the house .....Ezek 9:3
from off the *t* of the house ....Ezek 10:18
measured the *t* of the gate ....Ezek 40:6
and the other *t* of the gate ....Ezek 40:6
setting of their *t* by my *t* ......Ezek 43:8
issued out from under the *t* ...Ezek 47:1
all those that leap on the *t* ....Zeph 1:9
desolation shall be in the *t* ....Zeph 2:14

THREW, THREWEST—*See* THROW

THRICE—*three times*
Males of Israel assemble. .Ex 34:23, 24
Peter's denial ....Luke 22:34, 61
Vessel's appearance......Acts 10:16
Paul's shipwrecks 2Cor 11:25
Paul's petitions 2Cor 12:8

he smote *t* and stayed.........2Kin 13:18
crow, thou shalt deny me *t*....Matt 26:34
twice, thou shalt deny me *t*....Mark 14:30
till thou hast denied me *t* .....John 13:38

THROAT—*the front part of the neck; the part of the body used for swallowing*
Glutton's warning ....Prov 23:2
Thirsty one ....Ps 69:3
Source of evil ....Ps 5:9

and thy *t* from thirst ....Jer 2:25
and took him by the *t* ....Matt 18:28
t is an open sepulcher.........Rom 3:13

THRONE—*the seat and symbol of kingly authority*

Of men:
Under God's sovereignty..Dan 5:18-21
Established on
righteousness..........Prov 16:12
Upheld by mercy ....Prov 20:28
Subject to:
Succession 2Chr 6:10, 16
Termination...........Jer 22:4-30

Of God:
Resplendent in glory.....Is 6:1-3
Relentless in power......Dan 2:44
Ruling over all ....Dan 4:25, 34, 35
Righteous in execution...Ps 9:4, 7, 8
Regal throughout eternity.Rev 22:1, 3

Of Christ:
Based upon the Davidic
covenant..............2Sam 7:12-16
Of eternal duration ......Ps 89:4, 29, 36
Dan 7:13, 14
Explained in its nature...Is 9:6, 7
Symbolized in its
functions ....Zech 6:12, 13
Promised to Christ ......Luke 1:31-33
Christ rises to possess....Heb 8:1
Christ now rules from....Eph 1:20-22
1Pet 3:20-22
Shares with the Godhead .Rev 5:12-14
Shares with believers ....Luke 22:30
Rev 3:21
Judges men from ....Matt 25:31

[*also* THRONES]
in the *t* will I be greater ......Gen 41:40
that sitteth upon his *t* ....Ex 11:5
sitteth upon the *t* of his ....Deut 17:18
them inherit the *t* of glory.....1Sam 2:8
the *t* of David over Israel 2Sam 3:10
king and his *t* be guiltless 2Sam 14:9
and he shall sit upon my *t*?....1Kin 1:13
sit on the *t* of my lord 1Kin 1:20
sit on the *t* of my lord 1Kin 1:27
come and sit upon my *t* 1Kin 1:35
and make his *t* greater 1Kin 1:37
t of my lord king David 1Kin 1:37
his *t* greater than thy *t* 1Kin 1:47
a man on the *t* of Israel.......1Kin 2:4
and sat down on his *t* and.....1Kin 2:19
upon his *t* shall there be 1Kin 2:33
him a son to sit on his *t*.......1Kin 3:6
he made a porch for the *t*.....1Kin 7:7
to sit on the *t* of Israel........1Kin 8:25
will establish the *t* of thy 1Kin 9:5
man upon the *t* of Israel 1Kin 9:5
the king made a great *t* of 1Kin 10:18
The *t* had six steps and 1Kin 10:19
the top of the *t* was round 1Kin 10:19
of Judah sat each on his *t*.....1Kin 22:10
set him on his father's *t*.......2Kin 10:3
And he sat on the *t* of the 2Kin 11:19
sons shall sit on the *t* of.......2Kin 15:12
I will stablish his *t* for 1Chr 17:12
establish the *t* of his 1Chr 22:10
sat on the *t* of the Lord 1Chr 29:23
will I stablish the *t* of thy 2Chr 7:18
the king made a great *t* of 2Chr 9:17
were six steps to the *t* 2Chr 9:18
were fastened to the *t*.........2Chr 9:18
the Lord sitting upon his *t* 2Chr 18:18
unto the *t* of the governor.....Neh 3:7
Ahasuerus sat on the *t*........Esth 1:2
back the face of his *t* ....Job 26:9
kings are they on the *t*.........Job 36:7
the Lord's *t* is in heaven ......Ps 11:4
Thy *t*, O God, is for ever .....Ps 45:6
are the habitation of thy *t*.....Ps 89:14
and cast his *t* down to the.....Ps 89:44
Thy *t* is established of old .....Ps 93:2
are the habitation of his *t* .....Ps 97:2
there are set *t* of judgment ....Ps 122:5
t of the house of David ....Ps 122:5
body will I set upon thy *t* .....Ps 132:11
A king that sitteth in the *t* ....Prov 20:8
his *t* shall be established ......Prov 25:5
raised up from their *t* all ......Is 14:9
exalt my *t* above the stars .....Is 14:13
a glorious *t* to his father's .....Is 22:23
The heaven is my *t*, and ......Is 66:1
set every one his *t* at the......Jer 1:15
that sit upon David's *t* ....Jer 13:13
A glorious high *t* from the ....Jer 17:12
sittest upon the *t* of David ....Jer 22:2
sitteth upon the *t* of David ....Jer 29:16
a son to reign upon his *t* ......Jer 33:21
will set his *t* upon these ....Jer 43:10
set his *t* above the *t* of the ....Jer 52:32
t from generation to ....Lam 5:19
was the likeness of a *t* ....Ezek 1:26
upon the likeness of the *t* .....Ezek 1:26
come down from their *t*.......Ezek 26:16
the place of my *t* and the .....Ezek 43:7
I beheld till the *t* were cast....Dan 7:9
t was like the fiery flame ......Dan 7:9
and he arose from his *t* ....Jon 3:6
I will overthrow the *t* of ......Hag 2:22
by heaven; for it is God's *t*....Matt 5:34
man shall sit in the *t* of ....Matt 19:28
shall sit upon twelve *t*.........Matt 19:28
sweareth by the *t* of God .....Matt 23:22
up Christ to sit on his *t* ....Acts 2:30
Heaven is my *t* and earth .....Acts 7:49
apparel, sat upon his *t* ....Acts 12:21
they be *t* or dominions........Col 1:16
Thy *t*, O God, is for ever .....Heb 1:8
come boldly unto the *t* of .....Heb 4:16
right hand of the *t* of God ....Heb 12:2
which are before his *t*.........Rev 1:4
to sit with me in my *t*.........Rev 3:21
a *t* was set in heaven ....Rev 4:2
and one sat on the *t* ....Rev 4:2
about the *t* were four and .....Rev 4:4
out of the *t* proceeded ....Rev 4:5
fire burning before the *t* ......Rev 4:5
before the *t* there was a.......Rev 4:6
and in the midst of the *t* ......Rev 4:6
and round about the *t* ....Rev 4:6
him that sat on the *t*..........Rev 4:10
their crowns before the *t* ....Rev 4:10
in the midst of the *t* and ......Rev 5:6
angels round about the *t* ......Rev 5:11
of him that sitteth on the *t* ....Rev 6:16
stood before the *t*, and........Rev 7:9
which sitteth upon the *t* ....Rev 7:10
stood round about the *t*........Rev 7:11
and fell before the *t* on ....Rev 7:11
they before the *t* of God ......Rev 7:15
he that sitteth on the *t*........Rev 7:15
is in the midst of the *t* ....Rev 7:17
which was before the *t*.........Rev 8:3
up unto God, and to his *t*.....Rev 12:5
a new song before the *t*.......Rev 14:3
from the *t* saying, It is ....Rev 16:17
a voice came out of the *t* ....Rev 19:5
I saw *t* and they sat upon .....Rev 20:4
I saw a great white *t* and......Rev 20:11
he that sat upon the *t* said ....Rev 21:5

THRONG—*to crowd together in great numbers*

[*also* THRONGED, THRONGING]
lest they should *t* him ....Mark 3:9
people followed him and *t*.....Mark 5:24
seest the multitude *t* ....Mark 5:31
But as he went the people *t* ...Luke 8:42
the multitude *t* thee and ......Luke 8:45

THROUGH—*by way of; by means of; from one end or side to the other; because of*

[*also* THROUGHOUT]
is filled with violence *t* ....Gen 6:13
walk *t* the land in the ....Gen 13:17
great plenty *t* all the land .....Gen 41:29
perish not *t* the famine.........Gen 41:36
and a ruler *t* all the land ......Gen 45:8
t all the land of Egypt ....Ex 5:12
was blood *t* all the land of ....Ex 7:21
lice *t* all the land of Egypt ....Ex 8:17
declared *t* all the earth ....Ex 9:16
hail smote *t* all the land of ....Ex 9:25
of the field, *t* all the land .....Ex 10:15
Lord *t* your generations ....Ex 12:14
t to smite the Egyptians ....Ex 12:23
t the way of the ....Ex 13:18
Egyptians *t* the pillar of ....Ex 14:24
break *t* unto the Lord..........Ex 19:21
shall bore his ear *t* with ....Ex 21:6
Lord *t* your generations ....Ex 30:8
seed *t* their generations ....Ex 30:21
you *t* your generations ....Ex 31:13
the sabbath *t* their ....Ex 31:16
be seen *t* all the mount ....Ex 34:3
be proclaimed *t* the camp .....Ex 36:6
priesthood *t* their ....Ex 40:15
your generations *t* all your ....Lev 3:17
soul shall sin *t* ignorance ......Lev 4:2
somewhat *t* ignorance ....Lev 4:22
and sin *t* ignorance ....Lev 5:15
a statute for ever *t* your.......Lev 10:9
a statute for ever *t* your.......Lev 23:14
a statute for ever *t* your.......Lev 23:31
proclaim liberty *t* all the ......Lev 25:10
neither shall the sword go *t* ...Lev 26:6
t their generations ....Num 1:42
camp of Judah pitch *t*..........Num 2:3
hundred and fifty *t* their ......Num 2:16
numbered of the camps *t*......Num 2:32
Gershon *t* the houses of.......Num 4:22

 THROUGH

numbered of them *t* their .....Num 4:40
ordinance for ever *t* your......Num 10:8
weep *t* their families..........Num 11:10
t which we have gone to ......Num 13:32
any soul sin *t* ignorance ....Num 15:27
a statute for ever *t* your.......Num 18:23
I pray thee, *t* thy country .....Num 20:17
we will not pass *t* the fields ....Num 20:17
or *t* the vineyards, neither ....Num 20:17
said, Thou shalt not go *t* ......Num 20:20
Let me pass *t* thy land ....Num 21:22
and pierce them *t* with his.....Num 24:8
and thrust both of them *t* .....Num 25:8
and the woman *t* her belly ....Num 25:8
every month *t* the months .....Num 28:14
ye shall offer daily *t* the.......Num 28:24
for one lamb, *t* the seven .....Num 29:4
shall make go *t* the fire .....Num 31:23
fire ye shall make go *t* the ....Num 31:23
you *t* your generations ....Num 35:29
t all that great and terrible ....Deut 1:19
to pass *t* the coast of ....Deut 2:4
thy walking *t* this great........Deut 2:7
Thou art to pass over *t*, Ar ...Deut 2:18
drink; only I will pass *t* on ....Deut 2:28
t that great and terrible ....Deut 8:15
and thrust it *t* his ear unto ....Deut 15:17
thy God giveth thee, *t* thy.....Deut 16:18
thou trustedst *t* all thy ....Deut 28:52
thee in all thy gates *t* all ......Deut 28:52
t the nations which ye ....Deut 29:16
t this thing ye shall ....Deut 32:47
t the host and command ......Josh 1:11
pursuers sought them *t* all.....Josh 2:22
the officers went *t* the host ....Josh 3:2
Jericho *t* mount Beth-el ....Josh 16:1
Go and walk *t* the land ....Josh 18:8
went up *t* the mountains ......Josh 18:12
and led him *t* all the land .....Josh 24:3
t them I may prove Israel ....Judg 2:22
and the travelers walked *t*.....Judg 5:6
and cried *t* the lattice ....Judg 5:28
messengers *t* all Manasseh.....Judg 6:35
messengers *t* all mount.........Judg 7:24
t the wilderness unto the ......Judg 11:16
along *t* the wilderness ....Judg 11:18
trusted not Israel to pass *t* ....Judg 11:20
t all the tribes of Israel ....Judg 20:10
a deadly destruction *t* all 1Sam 5:11
passed *t* mount Ephraim 1Sam 9:4
t the land of Shalisha 1Sam 9:4
t the land of Shalim 1Sam 9:4
t the land of the Benjamites ...1Sam 9:4
Saul blew the trumpet *t* 1Sam 13:3
out *t* all the thousands of 1Sam 23:23
sword and thrust me *t* 1Sam 31:4
come and thrust me *t* 1Sam 31:4
walked all that night *t* 2Sam 2:29
and went *t* all Bithron 2Sam 2:29
daughter looked *t* a window ...2Sam 6:16
t all Edom put he 2Sam 8:14
t the heart of Absalom.........2Sam 18:14
strife *t* all the tribes of 2Sam 19:9
T the brightness before 2Sam 22:13
brake *t* the host of the 2Sam 23:16
So when they had gone *t*.......2Sam 24:8
for a fair damsel *t* all the 1Kin 1:3
made a proclamation *t* all 1Kin 15:22
there went a proclamation *t* ...1Kin 22:36
Ahaziah fell down *t* a 2Kin 1:2
break *t* even unto the king 2Kin 3:26
and made his son to pass *t* 2Kin 16:3
of Assyria came up *t* all.......2Kin 17:5
he made his son pass *t* 2Kin 21:6
t the anger of the Lord it 2Kin 24:20
and *t* all the land of his 2Chr 8:6
run to and fro *t* the whole 2Chr 16:9
fenced cities *t* all Judah 2Chr 17:19
he went out again *t* the 2Chr 19:4
and proclaimed a fast *t* all.....2Chr 20:3
made a proclamation *t* 2Chr 24:9
t all the host shields 2Chr 26:14
the king and his princes *t* 2Chr 30:6
did Hezekiah *t* all Judah 2Chr 31:20
that ran *t* the midst of the.....2Chr 32:4
a proclamation *t* all his........2Chr 36:22
a proclamation *t* all his........Ezra 1:1
they prospered *t* the ....Ezra 6:14
they went *t* the midst of.......Neh 9:11
shall be published *t* all his.....Esth 1:20
him on horseback *t* the ....Esth 6:9
cities *t* all the provinces of ....Esth 9:2
kept *t* every generation ....Esth 9:28
and terrifiest me *t* visions .....Job 7:14
of steel shall strike him *t* ......Job 20:24
In the dark they dig *t*.........Job 24:16
light I walked *t* darkness ......Job 29:3
his nose pierceth *t* snares......Job 40:24
passeth *t* the paths of the .....Ps 8:8
For by thee I have run *t* ......Ps 18:29
t the mercy of the Most High..Ps 21:7
my bones waxed old *t* my .....Ps 32:3
T thee will we push down .....Ps 44:5
t thy name will we tread ......Ps 44:5
t the greatness of thy ....Ps 66:3
we went *t* fire and *t* water.....Ps 66:12
and moon endure, *t* all........Ps 72:5
tongue walketh *t* the ....Ps 73:9
he went out *t* the land of .....Ps 81:5
Lord, hast made me glad *t* ....Ps 92:4
brought low *t* oppression ......Ps 107:39
knees are weak *t* fasting ......Ps 109:24
neither speak they *t* their .....Ps 115:7
T thy precepts I get ....Ps 119:104
O Lord *t* all generations ......Ps 135:13
people *t* the wilderness........Ps 136:16
I looked *t* my casement ....Prov 7:6
a dart strike *t* his liver ....Prov 7:23
T desire a man, having........Prov 18:1
a dream cometh *t* the ....Eccl 5:3
t idleness of the hands the ....Eccl 10:18
the house droppeth *t*..........Eccl 10:18
showing himself *t* the ....Song 2:9
And he shall pass *t* Judah .....Is 8:8
T the wrath of the Lord.......Is 9:19
thrust *t* with a sword..........Is 14:19
whirlwinds in the south pass *t*. .Is 21:1
I would go *t* them, I would....Is 27:4
But they also have erred *t*.....Is 28:7
t strong drink are out of ......Is 28:7
have erred *t* strong drink ......Is 28:7
are out of the way *t* strong ....Is 28:7
For *t* the voice of the Lord....Is 30:31
none shall pass *t* it for ever ...Is 34:10
When thou passest *t* the waters.Is 43:2
t the rivers they shall not .....Is 43:2
thou walkest *t* the fire ....Is 43:2
so that no man went *t* thee ....Is 60:15
That led them *t* the deep.......Is 63:13
that led us *t* the wilderness ....Jer 2:6
t a land of deserts and of .....Jer 2:6
t a land of drought and of.....Jer 2:6
t a land that no man..*t*........Jer 2:6
Run ye to and fro *t* the ....Jer 5:1
up, so that none can pass *t*....Jer 9:10
places *t* the wilderness ....Jer 12:12
high places for sin *t* all........Jer 17:3
their daughters to pass *t* ....Jer 32:35
t all her land the wounded ....Jer 51:52
prayer should not pass *t*........Lam 3:44
the cup also shall pass *t*........Lam 4:21
and blood shall pass *t* thee ....Ezek 5:17
Go *t* the midst of the city .....Ezek 9:4
t the midst of Jerusalem ......Ezek 9:4
Dig thou *t* the wall in their....Ezek 12:5
they shall dig *t* the wall ....Ezek 12:12
noisome beasts to pass *t* ....Ezek 14:15
no man may pass *t* because....Ezek 14:15
for it was perfect *t* my ....Ezek 16:14
t thy whoredoms with ....Ezek 16:36
and disperse them *t* the ....Ezek 20:23
make your sons to pass *t*......Ezek 20:31
No foot of man shall pass *t*....Ezek 29:11
foot of beast shall pass *t* ......Ezek 29:11
will disperse them *t* the ....Ezek 30:23
My sheep wandered *t* all ......Ezek 34:6
against him *t* all my ....Ezek 38:21
passing *t* the land to bury .....Ezek 39:14
made *t* all the house round ....Ezek 41:19
brought me *t* the waters.......Ezek 47:3
brought me *t* the waters.......Ezek 47:4
and brought me *t*..............Ezek 47:4
And *t* his policy also he ....Dan 8:25
strength *t* his riches he ....Dan 11:2
no strangers pass *t* her ....Joel 3:17
led you forty years *t* the ......Amos 2:10
and published *t* Nineveh ......Jon 3:7
and have passed *t* the gate ....Mic 2:13
down, when he shall pass *t* ....Nah 1:12
nations *t* her whoredoms ......Nah 3:4
families *t* her witchcrafts ......Nah 3:4
shall march *t* the breadth......Hab 1:6
Thou didst strike *t* with ....Hab 3:14
didst walk *t* the sea with ......Hab 3:15
t the heap of great waters ......Hab 3:15
sent to walk to and fro *t* ......Zech 1:10
My cities *t* prosperity shall ....Zech 1:17
t the two golden pipes ....Zech 4:12
might walk to and fro *t* ....Zech 6:7
walk to and fro *t* the ....Zech 6:7
So they walked to and fro *t* ...Zech 6:7
no oppressor shall pass *t* ......Zech 9:8
heart shall rejoice as *t* ....Zech 10:7
him shall thrust him *t*.........Zech 13:3
his fame went *t* all Syria ......Matt 4:24
where thieves break *t* and .....Matt 6:19
devils *t* the prince of the ......Matt 9:34
he walketh *t* dry places ....Matt 12:43
fame spread abroad *t* all ......Mark 1:28
t the corn fields on the........Mark 2:23
God of none effect *t* your .....Mark 7:13
and passed *t* Galilee ....Mark 9:30
carry any vessel *t* the ....Mark 11:16
be preached *t* the whole ......Mark 14:9
t all the hill country of........Luke 1:65
T the tender mercy of our.....Luke 1:78
fame of him *t* all the region ...Luke 4:14
let him down *t* the tiling ......Luke 5:19
of him went forth *t* all ....Luke 7:17
and *t* all the region round .....Luke 7:17
he went *t* every city and ....Luke 8:1
and went *t* the towns ....Luke 9:6
out devils *t* Beelzebub the.....Luke 11:15
he walketh *t* dry places ....Luke 11:24
t the cities and villages........Luke 13:22
t the midst of Samaria ....Luke 17:11
Jesus entered..passed *t*........Luke 19:1
teaching *t* all Jewry ....Luke 23:5
men *t* him might believe ......John 1:7
must needs go *t* Samaria ......John 4:4
ye are clean *t* the word ....John 15:3
Sanctify them *t* thy truth ......John 17:17
believe on me *t* their word .....John 17:20
might have life *t* his name .....John 20:31
that he *t* the Holy Ghost ......Acts 1:2
I wot that *t* ignorance ye ......Acts 3:17
t laying on of the apostles' ....Acts 8:18
Peter passed *t* all quarters .....Acts 9:32
was published *t* all Judea ......Acts 10:37
t his name whosoever ....Acts 10:43
when they had gone *t* the .....Acts 13:6
published *t* all the region......Acts 13:49
t much tribulation enter ....Acts 14:22
we believe that *t* the grace ....Acts 15:11
as they went *t* the cities ....Acts 16:4
they had gone *t* Phrygia ....Acts 16:6
which had believed *t* grace ....Acts 18:27
had passed *t* Macedonia ....Acts 19:21
said to Paul *t* the Spirit ....Acts 21:4
all the Jews *t* the world ....Acts 24:5
I thank my God *t* Jesus ....Rom 1:8
is spoken of *t* the whole.......Rom 1:8
t breaking the law ....Rom 2:23
abounded *t* my lie unto his ....Rom 3:7
propitiation *t* faith in his ......Rom 3:25
t the forbearance of God......Rom 3:25
make void the law *t* faith? ....Rom 3:31
Abraham or to his seed, *t*......Rom 4:13
but *t* the righteousness of .....Rom 4:13
peace with God *t* our Lord ....Rom 5:1
in God *t* our Lord Jesus ......Rom 5:11
reign *t* righteousness ....Rom 5:21
God is eternal life *t* Jesus .....Rom 6:23
it was weak *t* the flesh ....Rom 8:3
conquerors *t* him that ....Rom 8:37

now obtained mercy *t* their ....Rom 11:30
and *t* him and to him, are .....Rom 11:36
we *t* patience and comfort .....Rom 15:4
I may glory *t* Jesus Christ .....Rom 15:17
be glory *t* Jesus Christ for .....Rom 16:27
Christ *t* the will of God 1Cor 1:1
t thy knowledge shall the 1Cor 8:11
we see *t* a glass, darkly 1Cor 13:12
I shall pass *t* Macedonia 1Cor 16:5
for I do pass *t* Macedonia 1Cor 16:5
trust have we *t* Christ to 2Cor 3:4
t his poverty might be rich 2Cor 8:9
gospel *t* all the churches 2Cor 8:18
but mighty *t* God to the.......2Cor 10:4
t a window in a basket was....2Cor 11:33
was crucified *t* weakness 2Cor 13:4
I *t* the law am dead to the ....Gal 2:19
would justify the heathen *t* ....Gal 3:8
Gentiles *t* Jesus Christ ....Gal 3:14
the promise of the Spirit *t* .....Gal 3:14
t infirmity of the flesh I ....Gal 4:13
confidence in you *t* the.........Gal 5:10
redemption *t* his blood ....Eph 1:7
grace are ye saved *t* faith .....Eph 2:8
a habitation of God *t* the .....Eph 2:22
church by Christ Jesus *t*.........Eph 3:21
t the ignorance that is in ......Eph 4:18
salvation *t* your prayer ....Phil 1:19
that which is *t* the faith of.....Phil 3:9
I can do all things *t* Christ ....Phil 4:13
redemption *t* his blood ....Col 1:14
body of his flesh *t* death ......Col 1:22
risen with him *t* the faith ......Col 2:12
salvation *t* sanctification 2Thess 2:13
pierced themselves *t* with.......1Tim 6:10
immortality to light *t* the 2Tim 1:10
manifested his word *t* ....Titus 1:3
that *t* your prayers I shall .....Philem 22
their salvation perfect *t* ....Heb 2:10
t fear of death were all ....Heb 2:15
who *t* faith and patience ......Heb 6:12
t the offering of the body .....Heb 10:10
T faith we understand.........Heb 11:3
T faith he kept the ....Heb 11:28
Who *t* faith subdued ....Heb 11:33
or thrust *t* with a dart.........Heb 12:20
in his sight, *t* Jesus Christ .....Heb 13:21
the strangers scattered *t* 1Pet 1:1
t sanctification of the 1Pet 1:2
t manifold temptations 1Pet 1:6
glorified *t* Jesus Christ 1Pet 4:11
us *t* the righteousness 2Pet 1:1
t the knowledge of him 2Pet 1:3
t covetousness shall they 2Pet 2:3
they allure *t* the lusts of.......2Pet 2:18
t much wantonness, those 2Pet 2:18
that we might live *t* him.......1John 4:9
an angel flying *t* the midst.....Rev 8:13
may enter in *t* the gates ....Rev 22:14

THROUGHLY—*See* THOROUGHLY

THROW—*to hurl; toss; fling*

[*also* THROWING, THROWN, THREW, THREWEST]

rider hath he *t* into the sea ....Ex 15:1
if he smite him with *t* a ....Num 35:17
ye shall *t* down their altars ....Judg 2:2
because he hath *t* down his ....Judg 6:32
t stones at him and cast 2Sam 16:13
battered the wall, to *t* it.......2Sam 20:15
his head shall be *t* to thee 2Sam 20:21
t down thine altars 1Kin 19:10
And he said, *T* her down 2Kin 9:33
So they *t* her down 2Kin 9:33
t down the high places 2Chr 31:1
persecutors thou *t* into the ....Neh 9:11
to destroy and to *t* down ......Jer 1:10
nor *t* down any more for ......Jer 31:40
are fallen her walls are *t* ....Jer 50:15
t down in his wrath the ....Lam 2:2
shall *t* down thine eminent ....Ezek 16:39
thee *t* into the wilderness .....Ezek 29:5
and *t* down all thy strong .....Mic 5:11
and the rocks are *t* down......Nah 1:6
shall build, but I will *t* ....Mal 1:4
that shall not be *t* down.......Matt 24:2
and she *t* in two mites ....Mark 12:42
that shall not be *t* down.......Mark 13:2
the devil had *t* him in the .....Luke 4:35
devil *t* him down, and tare ....Luke 9:42
and *t* dust into the air ....Acts 22:23
great city Babylon be *t*........Rev 18:21

THRUST—*to shove; pierce*

[*also* THRUSTETH]

he shall surely *t* you out ......Ex 11:1
she *t* herself unto the wall.....Num 22:25
But if he *t* him of hatred......Num 35:20
to *t* thee out of the way.......Deut 13:5
t it through his ear unto.......Deut 15:17
right thigh and *t* it into ....Judg 3:21
Zebul *t* out Gaal and his ......Judg 9:41
they *t* out Jephthah and.......Judg 11:2
I may *t* out all your right 1Sam 11:2
come and *t* me through 1Sam 31:4
t his sword in his fellow's 2Sam 2:16
be all of them as thorns *t* 2Sam 23:6
So Solomon *t* out Abiathar 1Kin 2:27
Gehazi came near to *t* her 2Kin 4:27
t me through therewith........1Chr 10:4
and they *t* him out from 2Chr 26:20
God *t* him down, not man ....Job 32:13
hast *t* sore at me that I ....Ps 118:13
t thee through with their ......Ezek 16:40
to *t* them out of their ....Ezek 46:18
Neither shall one *t*............Joel 2:8
begat him shall *t* him ....Zech 13:3
and *t* him out of the city ......Luke 4:29
shall be *t* down to hell ....Luke 10:15
and you yourselves *t* out ......Luke 13:28
t my hand into his side........John 20:25
neighbor wrong *t* him ....Acts 7:27
t them into the inner ....Acts 16:24
it were possible, to *t* in ....Acts 27:39
or *t* through with a dart.......Heb 12:20
T in thy sickle and reap.......Rev 14:15
T in thy sharp sickle and......Rev 14:18

THUMB—*the digit at the base of the human hand*

Anointing of, as an act of consecration ....Lev 8:23, 24
As an act of purification. .Lev 14:14, 17, 25, 28
Cutting off of, an act of subjugation ....Judg 1:6, 7

the *t* of their right hand ....Ex 29:20

THUMMIN—*See* URIM and THUMMIN

THUNDER—*the loud sound that follows lightning; to produce a loud noise; shout*

Supernaturally brought:

Upon the Egyptians .....Ex 9:22-34
At Sinai ....Ex 19:16
Against the Philistines ...1Sam 7:10
At David's deliverance ...2Sam 22:14, 15

Figurative of:

God's:
Power ....Job 26:14
Control ....Ps 104:7
Majesty...............Rev 4:5
Visitations of judgment ..Rev 11:19

[*also* THUNDERED, THUNDERETH, THUNDERINGS, THUNDERS]

all the people saw the *t* ....Ex 20:18
Lord, and he shall send *t* 1Sam 12:17
the Lord sent *t* and rain.......1Sam 12:18
for the lightning of the *t* ......Job 28:26
t with the voice of his.........Job 37:4
way for the lightning of *t*......Job 38:25
clothed his neck with *t*? ....Job 39:19
thou *t* with a voice like ....Job 40:9
The Lord also *t* in the ....Ps 18:13
the God of glory *t*; the.........Ps 29:3
voice of thy *t* was in the ......Ps 77:18
in the secret place of *t* ....Ps 81:7
of the Lord of hosts with *t* ....Is 29:6
Boanerges..The sons of *t*.......Mark 3:17
and heard it, said that it *t*......John 12:29
as it were the noise of *t*.......Rev 6:1
there were voices and *t* ....Rev 8:5
seven *t* uttered their voices ....Rev 10:3
t had uttered their voices......Rev 10:4
which the seven *t* uttered .....Rev 10:4
and as the voice of a great *t*...Rev 14:2
were voices and *t*, and ....Rev 16:18
as the voice of mighty *t* ....Rev 19:6

THUNDERBOLTS—*sudden roar caused by thunder*

and their flocks to hot *t*.......Ps 78:48

THUS—*See* INTRODUCTION

THY—*See* INTRODUCTION

THYATIRA (thī-ä-tī'rä)—*"sacrifice of labor"—an important town in the Roman province of Asia*

Residence of Lydia ......Acts 16:14
One of the seven churches ....Rev 2:18-24
Home of Jezebel ....Rev 2:20

THYINE—*a small, cone-bearing tree*

Wood of, used for furniture ....Rev 18:12

THYSELF—*yourself*

separate *t*, I pray thee ....Gen 13:9
submit *t* under her hands......Gen 16:9
keep that thou hast unto *t*.....Gen 33:9
exaltest thou *t* against.........Ex 9:17
take heed to *t*, see my ....Ex 10:28
not able to perform it *t* ....Ex 18:18
Thou shalt not bow down *t*....Ex 20:5
Take heed to *t*, lest thou ......Ex 34:12
make an atonement for *t* ......Lev 9:7
with any beast to defile *t*......Lev 18:23
thou shalt love him as *t* ....Lev 19:34
that thou bear it not *t* ....Num 11:17
take heed to *t*, and keep ......Deut 4:9
and mightier than *t* ....Deut 9:1
Take heed to *t* that thou ......Deut 12:19
shalt thou take unto *t*.........Deut 20:14
thou mayest not hide *t* ....Deut 22:3
wherewith thou coverest *t* .....Deut 22:12
thou shalt not anoint *t* ....Deut 28:40
cut down for *t* there in.........Josh 17:15
Wash *t*..and anoint thee........Ruth 3:3
make not *t* known unto the ...Ruth 3:3
take heed to *t* until the 1Sam 19:2
a secret place, and hide *t* 1Sam 19:2
where thou didst hide *t* 1Sam 20:19
then thou shalt bestir *t* 2Sam 5:24
thy bed, and make *t* sick 2Sam 13:5
I pray thee, feign *t* to be 2Sam 14:2
and anoint not *t* with oil 2Sam 14:2
thou *t* wouldest have set 2Sam 18:13
have set *t* against me 2Sam 18:13
merciful thou wilt show *t*......2Sam 22:26
man thou wilt show *t* 2Sam 22:26
the pure thou wilt show *t* 2Sam 22:27
froward thou wilt show *t* 2Sam 22:27
strong therefore and show *t* ...1Kin 2:2
not asked for *t* long life 1Kin 3:11
hast asked riches for *t* 1Kin 3:11
t understanding to discern 1Kin 3:11
and disguise *t*, that thou 1Kin 14:2
hide *t* by the brook Cherith ...1Kin 17:3
strengthen *t*, and mark 1Kin 20:22
sold *t* to work evil in the......1Kin 21:20
hast humbled *t* before..........2Kin 22:19
advise *t* what word I shall 1Chr 21:12
and knowledge for *t* 2Chr 1:11
thou hast joined *t* with 2Chr 20:37
and thou didst humble *t*........2Chr 34:27
humblest *t* before me 2Chr 34:27
Think not with *t* that thou ....Esth 4:13
prepare *t* to the search of .....Job 8:8
thou restrain wisdom to *t*? ....Job 15:8
hand thou opposest *t* ....Job 30:21
Deck *t* now with majesty......Job 40:10
and array *t* with glory and.....Job 40:10
lift up *t* because of the........Ps 7:6
merciful thou wilt show *t*.......Ps 18:25
thou wilt show *t* upright.......Ps 18:25
the pure thou wilt show *t* .....Ps 18:26

froward thou wilt show *t* ......Ps 18:26
Fret not *t* because of ....Ps 37:1
fret not *t* because of him ......Ps 37:7
when thou doest well to *t* .....Ps 49:18
boastest thou *t* in mischief.....Ps 52:1
O turn *t* to us again ....Ps 60:1
thou madest strong for *t* ......Ps 80:17
Lord? Wilt thou hide *t* ....Ps 89:46
Lift up *t*, thou judge of ....Ps 94:2
now, my son, and deliver *t* ....Prov 6:3
humble *t*, and make sure ....Prov 6:3
thou shalt be wise for *t* ....Prov 9:12
and make it fit for *t* in........Prov 24:27
Boast not *t* of tomorrow ......Prov 27:1
over much; neither make *t* ....Eccl 7:16
thou *t* likewise hast cursed ....Eccl 7:22
hide *t* as it were for ....Is 26:20
thou art a God that hidest *t* ...Is 45:15
Shake *t* from the dust.........Is 52:2
loose *t* from the bands of .....Is 52:2
off, and didst debase *t* ....Is 57:9
Then shalt thou delight *t* ......Is 58:14
thou refrain *t* for these........Is 64:12
not procured this unto *t*.......Jer 2:17
Though thou clothest *t* ....Jer 4:30
in vain shalt thou make *t*......Jer 4:30
And thou, even *t*, shalt ....Jer 17:4
thou closest *t* in cedar ....Jer 22:15
thou great things for *t* ....Jer 45:5
how long wilt thou cut *t*.......Jer 47:5
give *t* no rest; let not the .....Lam 2:18
and shalt make *t* naked ....Lam 4:21
me, Go, shut *t* within thine ...Ezek 3:24
defiled *t* in thine idols ....Ezek 22:4
whom thou didst wash *t*........Ezek 23:40
eyes, and deckedst *t* with .....Ezek 23:40
and prepare for *t*, thou ....Ezek 38:7
Let thy gifts be to *t*, and ......Dan 5:17
chasten *t* before thy God ......Dan 10:12
Though thou exalt *t* as the ....Obad 4
house of Aphrah roll *t* in .....Mic 1:10
t many as the cankerworm ....Nah 3:15
Deliver *t*, O Zion, that ....Zech 2:7
Son of God, cast *t* down ......Matt 4:6
show *t* to the priest, and ......Matt 8:4
love thy neighbor as *t*.........Matt 22:39
show *t* to the priest, and ......Mark 1:44
Save *t*, and come down ....Mark 15:30
of God, cast *t* down from .....Luke 4:9
but go, and show *t* to the .....Luke 5:14
Lord, trouble not *t*: for ....Luke 7:6
and gird *t*, and serve me ......Luke 17:8
If thou be Christ, save *t*.......Luke 23:39
What sayest thou of *t*? ....John 1:22
Thou bearest record of *t* ......John 8:13
being a man, makest *t* God ...John 10:33
Sayest thou this thing of *t* ....John 18:34
Go near, and join *t* to this ....Acts 8:29
Do *t* no harm: for we are .....Acts 16:28
and purify *t* with them ....Acts 21:24
thou *t* also walkest orderly ....Acts 21:24
permitted to speak for *t*.......Acts 26:1
another, thou condemnest *t* ...Rom 2:1
t art a guide of the blind ......Rom 2:19
love thy neighbor as *t*.........Rom 13:9
love thy neighbor as *t*.........Gal 5:14
to behave *t* in the house of....1Tim 3:15
give *t* wholly to them 1Tim 4:15
Take heed unto *t*, and unto ...1Tim 4:16
this thou shalt both save *t*.....1Tim 4:16
of other men's sins: keep *t* 1Tim 5:22
Study to show *t* approved 2Tim 2:15
showing *t* a pattern of ....Titus 2:7
love thy neighbor as *t*.........James 2:8

TIBERIAS (tī-bēr'ĭ-ăs)—*"good vision"—a city on the west coast of the Sea of Galilee*
Galilee, which is the sea of *T*. .John 6:1
came other boats from *T* .....John 6:23
disciples at the sea of *T* ....John 21:1

TIBERIUS (tī-bēr'ĭ-ŭs)—*"son of (the river) Tiber"—third emperor of the Roman Empire*
of the reign of *T* Caesar ......Luke 3:1

TIBHATH (tĭb'hăth)—*"extension"*
Town in the kingdom of Zobah 1Chr 18:8

TIBNI (tĭb'nī)—*"intelligent"*
Son of Ginath 1Kin 16:21, 22

TIDAL (tī'dăl)—*"splendor; renown"*
King allied with Chedorlaomer ....Gen 14:1, 9

TIDINGS—*items of news*

Descriptive of:
Joyful ....Gen 29:13
Good 1Kin 1:42
Bad 1Sam 11:4-6
Foreboding ....Jer 37:5
Distressing 2Sam 4:4
Fatal 1Sam 4:19

Of salvation:
Out of Zion ....Is 40:9
By a person............Is 41:27
Bringer of peace ....Is 52:7
By Christ ....Is 61:1-3

people heard these evil *t* ......Ex 33:4
alive, to bring *t* to Gath.......1Sam 27:11
to have brought good *t*........2Sam 4:10
him a reward for his *t* 2Sam 4:10
that *t* came to David..........2Sam 13:30
run, and bear the king *t*.......2Sam 18:19
Thou shalt not bear *t* this 2Sam 18:20
thou shalt bear *t* another 2Sam 18:20
day thou shalt bear no *t*.......2Sam 18:20
there is *t* in his mouth 2Sam 18:25
and cometh with good *t* 2Sam 18:27
Then *t* came to Joab: for......1Kin 2:28
sent to thee with heavy *t* 1Kin 14:6
this day is a day of good *t* 2Kin 7:9
to carry *t* unto their idols 1Chr 10:9
not be afraid of evil *t* ....Ps 112:7
brought *t* to my father ....Jer 20:15
for they have heard evil *t* .....Jer 49:23
shalt answer, For the *t* ....Ezek 21:7
But *t* out of the east and ......Dan 11:44
of him that bringeth good *t*....Nah 1:15
to show thee these glad *t*......Luke 1:19
showing the glad *t* of the ......Luke 8:1
t of these things came ....Acts 11:22
t came unto the chief ....Acts 21:31
and bring glad *t* of good ......Rom 10:15
us good *t* of your faith 1Thess 3:6

TIE—*to fasten; attach*

[*also* TIED]
t unto it a lace of blue ....Ex 39:31
and *t* the kine to the cart 1Sam 6:7
milch kine, and *t* them to 1Sam 6:10
but horses *t*, and asses *t*.......2Kin 7:10
and *t* them about thy neck ....Prov 6:21
ye shall find an ass *t* ....Matt 21:2
ye shall find a colt *t* ....Mark 11:2
ye shall find a colt *t* ....Luke 19:30

TIGLATH-PILESER (tĭg-lăth-pĭ-lē'zer)—*"my trust is in the son of Asharra"*
Powerful Assyrian king who invades Samaria ..2Kin 15:29

[*also* TILGATH-PILNESER]
Ahaz sent messengers to *T* 2Kin 16:7
to Damascus to meet *T* 2Kin 16:10
whom *T* king of Assyria 1Chr 5:6
spirit of *T* king of Assyria 1Chr 5:26
T king of Assyria came 2Chr 28:20

TIKVAH (tĭk'vä)—*"hope"*
1. Father-in-law of Huldah .2Kin 22:14
Called Tikvath 2Chr 34:22
2. Father-in-law of Jahaziah.Ezra 10:15

TILE—*flat pieces of clay or stone used for roofs or floors*
Large brick of soft clay ..Ezek 4:1
Earthen roof ....Luke 5:19

TILGATH-PILNESER—*See* TIGLATH-PILESER

TILL—*to cultivate the ground*

[*also* TILLAGE, TILLED, TILLEST, TILLETH]
not a man to *t* the ground.....Gen 2:5
to *t* the ground from whence ..Gen 3:23
When thou *t* the ground ......Gen 4:12
the work of the field for *t*.....1Chr 27:26
in all the cities of our *t* ....Neh 10:37
He that *t* his land shall.........Prov 12:11
Much food is in the *t* of the ...Prov 13:23
t his land shall have plenty ....Prov 28:19
and ye shall be *t* and sown ....Ezek 36:9
the desolate land shall be *t* ....Ezek 36:34

TILL—*until*
t thou return unto the ....Gen 3:19
I cannot do any thing *t* ....Gen 19:22
t Shelah my son be grown.....Gen 38:11
t thy people pass over, O .....Ex 15:16
t the people pass over ....Ex 15:16
laid it up *t* the morning ....Ex 16:24
t the day that it was taken ....Ex 40:37
stone them with stones, *t*......Deut 17:5
t all the people that were .....Josh 5:6
t we have drawn them ....Josh 8:6
they tarried *t* they were ....Judg 3:25
t thou come to Minnith ....Judg 11:33
where her lord was, *t* it ....Judg 19:26
tarry for them *t* they were.....Ruth 1:13
t I know what God will do 1Sam 22:3
or aught else, *t* the sun be 2Sam 3:35
taketh away dung, *t* it be 1Kin 14:10
they urged him *t* he was 2Kin 2:17
if we tarry *t* the morning......2Kin 7:9
t he had filled Jerusalem 2Kin 21:16
t there was no remedy 2Chr 36:16
t there stood up a priest ......Ezra 2:63
us *t* thou hadst consumed .....Ezra 9:14
over *t* I come into Judah ......Neh 2:7
the morning *t* the stars........Neh 4:21
opened *t* after the sabbath ....Neh 13:19
alone *t* I swallow down my ....Job 7:19
t he shall accomplish, as ......Job 14:6
I wait, *t* my change comes ....Job 14:14
Elihu had waited *t* Job had....Job 32:4
out his wickedness *t* thou ....Ps 10:15
t every one submit himself ....Ps 68:30
t a dart strike through ....Prov 7:23
t I might see what was ....Eccl 2:3
nor awake my love, *t* he ......Song 2:7
field to field, *t* there be ....Is 5:8
purged from you *t* ye die......Is 22:14
t ye be left as a beacon ....Is 30:17
t he have set judgment in .....Is 42:4
give him no rest, *t* he ....Is 62:7
t he make Jerusalem a ....Is 62:7
bury in Tophet, *t* there be ....Jer 7:32
t there be no place to.........Jer 19:11
t they be consumed from......Jer 24:10
t I have consumed them ......Jer 49:37
in prison *t* the day of his ......Jer 52:11
T the Lord look down, and ...Lam 3:50
t thou hast ended the days ....Ezek 4:8
t I have caused my fury to ....Ezek 24:13
t ye have scattered them ......Ezek 34:21
And ye shall eat fat *t* ye ......Ezek 39:19
and drink blood *t* ye be ....Ezek 39:19
before me, *t* the time be ......Dan 2:9
t seven times pass over........Dan 4:23
t his hairs were grown like ....Dan 4:33
t he knew that the most.......Dan 5:21
t the wings thereof were ......Dan 7:4
beheld even *t* the beast was ...Dan 7:11
t the indignation be...........Dan 11:36
go thou thy way *t* the end.....Dan 12:13
t they acknowledge their ......Hos 5:15
not have stolen *t* they had.....Obad 5
t he might see what would ....Jon 4:5
gnaw not the bones *t* the ......Zeph 3:3
not *t* she had brought forth....Matt 1:25
T heaven and earth pass ......Matt 5:18
pass from the law, *t* all be ....Matt 5:18
and there abide *t* ye go ....Matt 10:11
t he send forth judgment ......Matt 12:20

T

t they see the Son of man ..... Matt 16:28
t he should pay the debt ...... Matt 18:30
t I make thine enemies thy .... Matt 22:44
pass, *t* all these things be ..... Matt 24:34
abide *t* ye depart from that .... Mark 6:10
t the Son of man were risen ... Mark 9:9
t all these things be done ..... Mark 13:30
t the day of his showing .... Luke 1:80
t it be accomplished .... Luke 12:50
t I shall dig about it, and ..... Luke 13:8
and seek diligently *t* she ...... Luke 15:8
them, Occupy *t* I come .... Luke 19:13
not pass away, *t* all be .... Luke 21:32
crow, *t* thou hast denied ...... John 13:38
T another king arose .... Acts 7:18
even *t* break of day, so he .... Acts 20:11
t they had killed Paul .... Acts 23:12
kept *t* I might send him to .... Acts 25:21
Lord's death *t* he come 1Cor 11:26
t the seed shall come to .... Gal 3:19
offense *t* the day of Christ .... Phil 1:10
T I come, give attendance 1Tim 4:13
already hold fast *t* I come ..... Rev 2:25
t the seven plagues of the ..... Rev 15:8

TILLER—*a farmer*
Man's first job .... Gen 2:5
Sin's handicap on .... Gen 4:12
Industry in, commended. . Prov 12:11

Cain was a *t* of the ground .... Gen 4:2

TILON (tī'lŏn)—*"mockery; scorn"*
Son of Shimon 1Chr 4:20

TIMAEUS (tī-mē'ŭs)—*"honorable"*
Father of Bartimaeus .... Mark 10:46

TIMBER—*wood suitable for building*
in carving of *t*, to work .... Ex 31:5
the stones of it, and the *t* ..... Lev 14:45
can skill to hew *t* like 1Kin 5:6
thy desire concerning *t* of 1Kin 5:8
and concerning *t* of fir 1Kin 5:8
prepared *t* and stones to 1Kin 5:18
rested on the house with *t* 1Kin 6:10
to buy *t* and hewed stone 2Kin 12:12
t of cedars, with masons 1Chr 14:1
and workers of stone and *t* 1Chr 22:15
skill to cut *t* in Lebanon 2Chr 2:8
the hewers that cut *t* 2Chr 2:10
stones of Ramah, and the *t* 2Chr 16:6
and *t* is laid in the walls .... Ezra 5:8
let *t* be pulled down from ..... Ezra 6:11
give me *t* to make beams ..... Neh 2:8
thy stones and thy *t* and ...... Ezek 26:12
beam out of the *t* shall .... Hab 2:11
t thereof and the stones .... Zech 5:4

TIMBREL—*a small hand drum*

Used in:
Entertainment .... Gen 31:27
Worship .... Ps 81:1-4

[*also* TIMBRELS]
took a *t* in her hand .... Ex 15:20
went out after her with *t* ...... Ex 15:20
out to meet him with *t* .... Judg 11:34
and on psalteries, and on *t* 2Sam 6:5
with psalteries, and with *t* 1Chr 13:8
They take the *t* and harp ...... Job 21:12
the damsels playing with *t* ..... Ps 68:25
and bring hither the *t* .... Ps 81:2
praises unto him with the *t* .... Ps 149:3
Praise him with the *t* and ..... Ps 150:4

TIME—*a continuum of past, present, and future events*

Computation of, by:
Years .... Gen 15:13
Months 1Chr 27:1
Weeks .... Dan 10:2
Days .... Gen 8:3
Moments .... Ex 33:5
Sundial 2Kin 20:9-11

Events of, dated by:
Succession of families .... Gen 5:1-32
Lives of great men ...... Gen 7:6, 11
Succession of kings 1Kin 11:42, 43
Earthquakes .... Amos 1:1
Important events (the Exodus) 1Kin 6:1
Important emperors ..... Luke 3:1

Periods of, stated in years:
Bondage in Egypt .... Acts 7:6
Wilderness wanderings ... Deut 1:3
Judges .... Judg 11:26
Captivity .... Dan 9:2
Seventy weeks (490 years) Dan 9:24-27

Sequence of prophetic events in, indicated by:
"The time is fulfilled" (Christ's advent) ...... Mark 1:15
"The fullness of the time" (Christ's advent) .. Gal 4:4
"The times of the Gentiles" (the Gospel age) .... Luke 21:24
"The day of salvation" (the Gospel age) 2Cor 6:2
"In the last days" (the Gospel age) .... Acts 2:17
"In the last days" (the time before Christ's return) 2Tim 3:1; 2Pet 3:3
"The last day" (Christ's return) .... John 6:39, 54; John 12:48
"New heavens" (eternity). 2Pet 3:13

Importance of, indicated by:
Shortness of life .... Ps 89:47
Making the most of it .... Eph 5:16
Purpose of, for salvation. . 2Pet 3:9, 15
Uncertainty of .... Luke 12:16-23
Our goal, eternity .... Heb 11:10, 13-16
God's plan in .... Acts 14:15-17

For everything:
To give birth, to die ..... Eccl 3:1-8, 17

[*also* TIMES]
hated him not in *t* past .... Deut 4:42
or an observer of *t* .... Deut 18:10
fire and observed *t*, and 2Kin 21:6
understanding of the *t* 1Chr 12:32
the *t* that went over him 1Chr 29:30
also he observed *t*, and 2Chr 33:6
come at appointed *t* .... Ezra 10:14
at *t* appointed year by .... Neh 10:34
men, which knew the *t* .... Esth 1:13
a refuge in *t* of trouble .... Ps 9:9
bless the Lord at all *t* .... Ps 34:1
Trust in him at all *t*; ye .... Ps 62:8
righteousness at all *t* .... Ps 106:3
thy judgments at all *t* .... Ps 119:20
breasts satisfy thee at all *t* .... Prov 5:19
alone in his appointed *t* .... Is 14:31
ancient *t*, that I have .... Is 37:26
knoweth her appointed *t* ...... Jer 8:7
prophesieth of the *t* that ...... Ezek 12:27
not discern the signs of the *t* .. Matt 16:3
you to know the *t* or the ...... Acts 1:7
until the *t* of restitution ...... Acts 3:21
t before appointed .... Acts 17:26
in *t* past have not believed .... Rom 11:30
persecuted us in *t* past .... Gal 1:23
days, and months, and *t* ...... Gal 4:10
of the fullness of *t* .... Eph 1:10
of the *t* and the seasons 1Thess 5:1
latter *t* some shall depart 1Tim 4:1
Which in his *t* he shall 1Tim 6:15
hath in due *t* manifested ...... Titus 1:3
who at sundry *t* and in .... Heb 1:1
manifest in these last *t* 1Pet 1:20

TIME—*occasions; instance*

[*also* TIMES]
supplanted me these two *t* ..... Gen 27:36
changed my wages ten *t* .... Gen 31:7
to the ground seven *t* .... Gen 33:3
three *t* thou shalt keep a ...... Ex 23:14
of the blood seven *t* .... Lev 4:6
upon the altar seven *t* .... Lev 8:11
oil with his finger seven *t* ..... Lev 14:16
sprinkle the house seven *t* ..... Lev 14:51
with his finger seven *t* .... Lev 16:14
enchantment, nor observe *t* .... Lev 19:26
punish you seven *t* more ...... Lev 26:18
punish you yet seven *t* for ..... Lev 26:24
me now these ten *t* .... Num 14:22
smitten me these three *t*? ..... Num 22:28
from me these three *t* .... Num 22:33
blessed them these three *t* ..... Num 24:10
you a thousand *t* so many ..... Deut 1:11
compass the city seven *t* ...... Josh 6:4
the same manner seven *t* ...... Josh 6:15
compassed the city seven *t* .... Josh 6:15
began to move him at *t* in ..... Judg 13:25
I will go out as at other *t* ..... Judg 16:20
and kill, as at other *t* .... Judg 20:31
and called as other *t*, Samuel .. 1Sam 3:10
his presence, as in *t* past 1Sam 19:7
bowed himself three *t* 1Sam 20:41
sought for David in *t* past 2Sam 3:17
his people Israel at all *t* 1Kin 8:59
upon the child three *t* 1Kin 17:21
How many *t* shall I adjure 1Kin 22:16
the child sneezed seven *t* 2Kin 4:35
wash in Jordan seven *t* 2Kin 5:10
dipped himself seven *t* 2Kin 5:14
Three *t* did Joash beat 2Kin 13:25
the *t* that went over him 1Chr 29:30
three *t* in the year, even 2Chr 8:13
How many *t* shall I adjure 2Chr 18:15
they said unto us ten *t* .... Neh 4:12
many *t* didst thou deliver ...... Neh 9:28
ten *t* have ye reproached ...... Job 19:3
seeing *t* are not hidden .... Job 24:1
earth, purified seven *t* .... Ps 12:6
a just man falleth seven *t* ..... Prov 24:16
do evil a hundred *t* .... Eccl 8:12
he found them ten *t* better .... Dan 1:20
furnace one seven *t* more ..... Dan 3:19
till seven *t* pass over him ...... Dan 4:23
his knees three *t* a day .... Dan 6:10
ten thousand *t* ten .... Dan 7:10
and think to change *t* and ..... Dan 7:25
a time and *t* and the .... Dan 7:25
strengthened her in these *t* .... Dan 11:6
shall be for a *t*, *t*, and .... Dan 12:7
unto thee, Until seven *t* .... Matt 18:22
but, Until seventy *t* seven ..... Matt 18:22
trespass against thee seven *t* ... Luke 17:4
seven *t* in a day turn again .... Luke 17:4
And this was done three *t* ..... Acts 11:10
five *t* received I forty 2Cor 11:24
was ten thousand *t* ten .... Rev 5:11
for a *t*, and *t*, and half .... Rev 12:14

TIMIDITY—*lacking in courage or boldness*
Nicodemus .... John 3:1, 2
Joseph of Arimathea ..... John 19:38
Certain people .... John 9:18-23

TIMNA (tĭm'nä)—*"allotted portion; restraining"*
1. Concubine of Eliphaz ... Gen 36:12, 22
2. Duke of Edom .... Gen 36:40

Gatam, Kenaz, and *T*, and 1Chr 1:36
and *T* was Lotan's sister 1Chr 1:39

TIMNAH, TIMNATH, THIMNATHAH (tĭm'nä, tĭm'năth, thĭm'năth-äh)—*"portion; image"*
1. Town of Judah .... Josh 15:10
   Assigned to Dan .... Josh 19:40, 43
   Captured by Philistines . . 2Chr 28:18
2. Town in Judah's hill country .... Josh 15:57

his sheepshearers to *T* .... Gen 38:12
which is by the way to *T* ...... Gen 38:14
Samson went down to *T* ...... Judg 14:1
a woman in *T* of the .... Judg 14:1
and his mother, to *T* .... Judg 14:5
to the vineyards of *T* .... Judg 14:5
dukes of Edom were; duke *T* . . 1Chr 1:51

TIMNATH-HERES—*See* TIMNATH-SERAH

TIMNATH-SERAH (tĭm-năth-sē'rä)—*"image of the sun"*

Village in Ephraim's hill country ....Josh 19:50
Place of Joshua's burial . .Josh 24:29, 30
Called Timnath-heres ....Judg 2:9

TIMNITE (tĭm-nīt)—*an inhabitant of Timnah*
Samson thus called ......Judg 15:6

TIMON (tī-mŏn)—*"honorable"*
One of the seven deacons. Acts 6:1-5

TIMOTHEUS—*See* TIMOTHY

TIMOTHY (tĭm'ō-thĭ)—*"honored of God"—a young friend and convert of Paul*

Life of:
Of mixed parentage .....Acts 16:1, 3
Faith of, from childhood .2Tim 1:5; 2Tim 3:15
Becomes Paul's companion ....Acts 16:1-3
Ordained by the presbytery 1Tim 4:14
Left behind at Troas .....Acts 17:14
Sent by Paul to Thessalonica 1Thess 3:1, 2, 6
Rejoined Paul at Corinth . Acts 18:1-5
Preached Christ to Corinthians 2Cor 1:19
Sent by Paul into Macedonia ....Acts 19:22
Sent by Paul to Corinth . .1Cor 4:17
Returned with Paul to Jerusalem ....Acts 20:1-5
With Paul in Rome ......Phil 1:1; Phil 2:19, 23
Set free ....Heb 13:23
Left at Ephesus by Paul .1Tim 1:3
Paul summoned him to Rome 2Tim 4:9, 11, 21

Character of:
Devout from childhood . .2Tim 3:15
Faithful in service ....Phil 2:22
Beloved by Paul 1Tim 1:2, 18
Follows Paul's way 1Cor 4:17
In need of instruction 1Tim 4:12-16
Of sickly nature 1Tim 5:23
Urged to remain faithful .1Tim 6:20, 21

T my workfellow, and ....Rom 16:21
if *T* come, see that he 1Cor 16:10
T our brother, unto the 2Cor 1:1
Paul and *T*, the servants ......Phil 1:1
Jesus to send *T* shortly ....Phil 2:19
will of God, and *T* our........Col 1:1
Silvanus, and *T*, unto 1Thess 1:1
Silvanus, and *T*, unto 2Thess 1:1

TIMOTHY, THE EPISTLES TO—*books of the New Testament*

1 Timothy:
Toward true doctrine 1Tim 1:3-7
Paul's ministry 1Tim 1:12-17
Christ, the Mediator 1Tim 2:5, 6
Instructions to women . . .1Tim 2:9-15
Church officials 1Tim 3:1-13
The good minister 1Tim 4:6-16
Fight the good fight 1Tim 6:11-21

2 Timothy:
Call to responsibility 2Tim 1:6-18
Call for strength 2Tim 2:1-13
Against apostasy 2Tim 3:1-9
The Scriptures called inspired 2Tim 3:14-17
Charge to Timothy 2Tim 4:1-8
Paul's personal concerns .2Tim 4:9-18

TIN—*a bluish-white, malleable metal obtained by smelting*
Used in early times ......Num 31:22
Brought from Tarshish . . .Ezek 27:12
Figurative of degeneracy .Is 1:25

all they are brass, and *t* ....Ezek 22:18
and iron, and lead, and *t* ......Ezek 22:20

TINGLE—*to feel a ringing or stinging sensation*
that heareth it shall *t* 1Sam 3:11
of it, both his ears shall *t* 2Kin 21:12
heareth, his ears shall *t* ....Jer 19:3

TINKLING—*jingling; clinking*
making a *t* with their feet .....Is 3:16
their *t* ornaments about ....Is 3:18
brass, or a *t* cymbal 1Cor 13:1

TIP—*end of something*
the *t* of the right ear of ....Ex 29:20
the *t* of Aaron's right ear .....Lev 8:23
upon the *t* of the right ear ....Lev 14:14
upon the *t* of the right ear ....Lev 14:25
may dip the *t* of his finger ....Luke 16:24

TIPHSAH (tĭf'sä)—*"passage"*
1. Place designating Solomon's northern boundary............1Kin 4:24
2. Unidentified town attacked by Menahem .2Kin 15:16

TIRAS (tī'răs)—*"longing"*
Son of Japheth ....Gen 10:2

TIRATHITES (tī'rä-thīts)
Family of scribes 1Chr 2:55

TIRE—*an ornamental headdress*

Worn by:
Ezekiel ....Ezek 24:17, 23
Daughters of Zion ....Is 3:18
Jezebel 2Kin 9:30

TIRED—*adorned with an ornament*
t her head, and looked 2Kin 9:30

TIRHAKAH (tûr'hä-kä)—*a king of Ethiopia and Egypt who aided Hezekiah*
Opposes Sennacherib 2Kin 19:9

TIRHANAH (tûr-hä-nä)—*"kindness"*
Son of Caleb 1Chr 2:42, 48

TIRIA (tĭr'ĭ-ä)—*"foundation"*
Son of Jehaleleel 1Chr 4:16

TIRSHATHA (tûr-shä'thä)—*"reverend"—a title of the governor of Judea under Persian rule*
Perisan title used of Zerubbabel ....Ezra 2:63
Applied to Nehemiah ....Neh 8:9

the *T* said unto them ....Ezra 2:63
the *T* said unto them ....Neh 7:65
T gave to the treasure a.......Neh 7:70
were, Nehemiah, the *T* ....Neh 10:1

TIRZAH (tûr'zä)—*"delight"*
1. Zelophehad's youngest daughter ....Num 26:33
2. Town near Samaria .....Josh 12:24
Seat of Jeroboam's rule .1Kin 14:17
Israel's kings rule here down to Omri 1Kin 16:6-23
Famous for its beauty . . .Song 6:4

and Milcah, and *T*............Num 27:1
Mahlah, *T*, and Hoglah ....Num 36:11
Hoglah, Milcah, and *T*........Josh 17:3
of Ramah, and dwelt in *T*.....1Kin 15:21
reign over all Israel in *T* 1Kin 15:33
of Gadi went up from *T* 2Kin 15:14
coasts thereof from *T* 2Kin 15:16

TISHBITE (tĭsh'bīt)—*an inhabitant of Tishbeh*
Elijah thus called 1Kin 17:1

came to Elijah the *T*.........1Kin 21:17
Lord said to Elijah the *T* 2Kin 1:3
he said, It is Elijah the *T* 2Kin 1:8
his servant Elijah the *T* 2Kin 9:36

TITHE—*the tenth of one's income; to pay a tenth of one's income*
Given by Abraham to Melchizedek ....Heb 7:1, 2, 6
Promised by Jacob ......Gen 28:22
Belongs to the Lord .....Lev 27:30-33
Given to Levites ....Num 18:21-24
Given by Levites to priests ....Num 18:25, 26
Taken to Temple ....Deut 12:5-19
Rules regarding ....Deut 14:22-29
Honesty in, required .....Deut 26:13-15
Of animals, every tenth . .Lev 27:32, 33
Recognition of, by Jews . .Neh 13:5, 12
Promise regarding ....Mal 3:7-12
Pharisaic legalism on, condemned ....Luke 18:9-14

[*also* TITHES, TITHING]
And he gave him *t* of all ......Gen 14:20
unto the Lord of all your *t* ....Num 18:28
made an end of *t* all the *t* .....Deut 26:12
which is the year of *t* ....Deut 26:12
the *t* of all things brought 2Chr 31:5
brought in the *t* of oxen.......2Chr 31:6
the *t* of holy things which 2Chr 31:6
in the offerings and the *t*......2Chr 31:12
the *t* of our ground unto ......Neh 10:37
have the *t* in all the cities .....Neh 10:37
when the Levites take *t* ....Neh 10:38
shall bring up the *t* of the *t*....Neh 10:38
first fruits, and for the *t*.......Neh 12:44
brought all Judah the *t* of ....Neh 13:12
your *t* after three years ....Amos 4:4
for ye pay *t* of mint and ....Matt 23:23
ye *t* mint and rue and all......Luke 11:42
to take *t* of the people ....Heb 7:5
men that die receive *t*.........Heb 7:8
receiveth *t*, paid *t* in ....Heb 7:9

TITLE—*an appellation of honor; inscription*
Condemned by Christ ....Matt 23:1-8

[*also* TITLES]
What *t* is that that I see? 2Kin 23:17
let me give flattering *t* ....Job 32:21
not to give flattering *t* ....Job 32:22
And Pilate wrote a *t*, and .....John 19:19
This *t* then read many of......John 19:20

TITTLE—*a mark distinguishing similar letters in the Hebrew alphabet*
Figurative of minute requirements ....Matt 5:18
See JOT

pass, than one *t* of the law ....Luke 16:17

TITUS (tī'tŭs)—*"pleasant"*
Greek Christian and Paul's companion ......Titus 1:4
Sent by Paul to Corinth . .2Cor 7:13, 14
Organized Corinthian relief fund 2Cor 8:6-23
Met Paul in Macedonia . .2Cor 7:6, 7
Accompanied Paul to Crete ....Titus 1:5
Sent by Paul to Dalmatia .2Tim 4:10

I found not *T* my brother 2Cor 2:13
I desired *T*, and with him 2Cor 12:18
Did *T* make a gain of you?....2Cor 12:18
and took *T* with me also ......Gal 2:1
But neither *T*, who was ....Gal 2:3

TITUS, THE EPISTLE TO—*a book of the New Testament*
Qualifications of an elder .Titus 1:5-9
Against false teachings . . .Titus 1:10-16
Domestic life ....Titus 2:1-10
Godly living ....Titus 3:3-8

TIZITE (tī'zīt)
Description of Joha, David's mighty man . . .1Chr 11:45

TO—*See* INTRODUCTION

TO WIT—*namely; that is to say*
Used by Paul twice 2Cor 5:19; 8:1

TOAH (tō'ä)—*"depression; humility"—an ancestor of Samuel the prophet*
son of Eliel, the son of *T* 1Chr 6:34

TOB (tŏb)—*"good"*
Jephthah's refuge east of the Jordan ....Judg 11:3, 5

TOBADONIJAH (tŏb-ăd-ō-nī'jä)—*"the Lord Jehovah is good"*
Levite teacher 2Chr 17:7, 8

TOBIAH (tō-bī'ä)—*"Jehovah is good"*
1. Founder of a postexilic family . . . . .Ezra 2:60
2. Ammonite servant; ridiculed the Jews . . . . .Neh 2:10
3. Levite teacher 2Chr 17:7, 8
4. Came from Babylon . . . . .Zech 6:10, 14

[*also* TOBIJAH]
Now *T* the Ammonite was . . . .Neh 4:3
when Sanballat, and *T* . . . . .Neh 4:7
when Sanballat, and *T* . . . . .Neh 6:1
for *T* and Sanballat had . . . . . . .Neh 6:12
upon *T* and Sanballat . . . . .Neh 6:14
sent many letters unto *T* . . . . . .Neh 6:17
letters of *T* came unto . . . . .Neh 6:17
T sent letters to put me . . . . . . .Neh 6:19
the children of *T*, the . . . . .Neh 7:62
God, was allied unto *T* . . . . . . .Neh 13:4
evil that Eliashib did for *T* . . . .Neh 13:7
the household stuff of *T* . . . . . .Neh 13:8

TOCHEN (tō'kĕn)—*"middle"*
Town of Simeon 1Chr 4:32

TODAY—*the present time*
I will pass through..flock *t* . . . .Gen 30:32
ye are come so soon *t* . . . . .Ex 2:18
which he will show to you *t* . . .Ex 14:13
Consecrate yourselves *t* . . . . . . .Ex 32:29
hath the Lord smitten us *t* 1Sam 4:3
here *t* also, and tomorrow 2Sam 11:12
T if ye will hear his voice . . . . .Ps 95:7
grass of the field, which *t* is . . .Matt 6:30
foul weather *t*: for the sky . . . .Matt 16:3
Son, go work *t* in my vineyard .Matt 21:28
We have seen strange things *t* .Luke 5:26
grass, which is *t* in the field . . .Luke 12:28
I do cures *t* and tomorrow . . . .Luke 13:32
t I must abide at thy house . . . .Luke 19:5
t shall thou be..in paradise . . . .Luke 23:43
t is the third day since . . . . .Luke 24:21
T if ye will hear his voice . . . . .Heb 3:7
while it is called *T* . . . . .Heb 3:13
T if ye will hear his voice . . . . .Heb 3:15
T, after so long a time . . . . .Heb 4:7
t have I begotten thee . . . . .Heb 5:5
the same yesterday, and *t* . . . . .Heb 13:8
T or tomorrow we will go . . . . .Jas 4:13

TOE—*a digit at the end of the foot*
Aaron's, anointed . . . . . . .Ex 29:20
Of captives, amputated . .Judg 1:6, 7
Of an image . . . . .Dan 2:41, 42

[*also* TOES]
great *t* of his right foot . . . . .Lev 8:23
great *t* of his right foot . . . . .Lev 14:14
and on every foot six *t* 2Sam 21:20
whose fingers and *t* were 1Chr 20:6

TOGARMAH (tō-gär'mä)—*"all bone"*
Northern country inhabited by descendants of Gomer .Gen 10:3

and Riphath, and *T* 1Chr 1:6
the house of *T* traded in . . . . . .Ezek 27:14
house of *T* of the north . . . . . . .Ezek 38:6

TOGETHER—*in or into one; in a body*
rich and poor meet *t*, the . . . . .Prov 22:2
three are gathered *t* in my . . . .Matt 18:20
gathered thy children *t* . . . . .Matt 23:37
therefore God hath joined *t* . . .Mark 10:9
all that believed were *t* . . . . .Acts 2:44
had gathered the church *t* . . . . .Acts 14:27
that all things work *t* for . . . . . .Rom 8:28
We then, as workers *t* with 2Cor 6:1
not unequally yoked *t* 2Cor 6:14
assembling of ourselves *t* . . . . . .Heb 10:25

TOHU (tō'hū)—*"depression; humility"*
son of Elihu, the son of *T* 1Sam 1:1

TOI, TOU (tō'ĕ, tō'ōō)—*"error; wandering"*
King of Hamath; sends embassy to salute David 2Sam 8:9-12

TOIL—*to work long and hard; hard work*

[*also* TOILED, TOILING]
our work and *t* of our . . . . .Gen 5:29
made me forget all my *t* . . . . . .Gen 41:51
they *t* not, neither do they . . . .Matt 6:28
he saw them *t* in rowing . . . . . .Mark 6:48
Master, we have *t* all the . . . . . .Luke 5:5
grow: they *t* not, they . . . . .Luke 12:27

TOKEN—*a visible sign*

Descriptive of:
Rainbow . . . . .Gen 9:12-17
Circumcision . . . . .Gen 17:11
Bloodshed . . . . .Ex 12:13
God's wonders . . . . .Ps 65:8

As assurance of:
God's:
Presence . . . . .Ex 3:12
Judgment upon sin . . . .Num 17:10
Goodness . . . . .Ps 86:17
Guarantee . . . . .Josh 2:12, 18, 21
Identification . . . . .Mark 14:44
Genuineness 2Thess 3:17
Coming judgment 2Thess 1:5

[*also* TOKENS]
shall be for a *t* upon thine . . . .Ex 13:16
t of the damsel's virginity . . . . .Deut 22:15
are the *t* of my daughter's . . . . .Deut 22:17
t of virginity be not found . . . . .Deut 22:20
do ye not know their *t* . . . . .Job 21:29
sent *t* and wonders into . . . . . . .Ps 135:9
the *t* of the liars . . . . .Is 44:25
an evident *t* of perdition . . . . . .Phil 1:28

TOLA (tō'lä)—*"warm; crimson"*
1. Son of Issachar and family head . . . . .Gen 46:13
2. Son of Puah; a judge of Israel . . . . .Judg 10:1

sons of Issachar were, *T* 1Chr 7:1
sons of *T*; Uzzi, and 1Chr 7:2
father's house, to wit, of *T* 1Chr 7:2

TOLAD (tō'lăd)—*"kindred of God"*
Simeonite town 1Chr 4:29
Called Eltolad . . . . .Josh 19:4

TOLAITES—*descendants of Tola*
Tola, the family of the *T* . . . . . .Num 26:23

TOLD—*See* TELL

TOLERABLE—*capable of being endured*
It shall be more *t* for the . . . . . .Matt 10:15
It shall be more *t* for Tyre . . . .Matt 11:22
It shall be more *t* for the . . . . . .Matt 11:24
It shall be more *t* for . . . . .Mark 6:11
It shall be more *t* in that . . . . . .Luke 10:12
It shall be more *t* for Tyre . . . .Luke 10:14

TOLERANCE—*an attitude of sympathy or indulgence toward opposing views*

Approved in dealing with:
Disputes among brothers .Mark 9:38-40
Weaker brother . . . . .Rom 14:1-23
Repentant brother 2Cor 2:4-11

Condemned in dealing with:
Sin .1Cor 5:1-13
Evil 2Cor 6:14-18
Sin in ourselves . . . . .Mark 9:43-48
Error 2John 10, 11

TOLL—*taxes*
Imposed by Jews . . . . .Ezra 4:20
Imposed upon Jews . . . . . .Ezra 4:13
Levites excluded from . . .Ezra 7:24

TOMB—*a place of burial*
John's body placed in . . . .Mark 6:25-29
Christ's body placed in Joseph's . . . . .Matt 25:57-60

[*also* TOMBS]
and shall remain in the *t* . . . . . .Job 21:32
devils, coming out of the *t* . . . .Matt 8:28
the *t* of the prophets . . . . .Matt 23:29
laid it in his own new *t* . . . . . . .Matt 27:60
there met him out of the *t* . . . .Mark 5:2
his dwelling among the *t* . . . . . .Mark 5:3
and in the *t*, crying, and . . . . . .Mark 5:5
in any house, but in the *t* . . . . .Luke 8:27

TOMORROW—*the day after today*
And he said, *T*. And he . . . . . .Ex 8:10
and from his people, *t* . . . . .Ex 8:29
T is the rest of the holy . . . . . . .Ex 16:23
t I will stand on the top . . . . . . .Ex 17:9
Sanctify them today and *t* . . . . .Ex 19:10
Sanctify yourselves against *t* . . .Num 11:18
t the Lord will show . . . . .Num 16:5
and they, and Aaron, *t* . . . . . . .Num 16:16
for *t* the Lord will do . . . . .Josh 3:5
t about this time will . . . . .Josh 11:6
Lord that *t* he will be . . . . .Josh 22:18
t get you early on your . . . . . . .Judg 19:9
T about this time I will 1Sam 9:16
T, by that time the sun 1Sam 11:9
tonight, *t* thou shalt be 1Sam 19:11
my father about *t* any 1Sam 20:12
t I will let thee depart 2Sam 11:12
of them by *t* about this 1Kin 19:2
be *t* about this time 2Kin 7:18
me to Jezreel by *t* this 2Kin 10:6
t go ye down against 2Chr 20:16
and *t* am I invited unto . . . . .Esth 5:12
to do *t* also according . . . . .Esth 9:13
come again and *t* I will . . . . . . .Prov 3:28
drink for *t* we shall . . . . .Is 22:13
is, and *t* is cast into the . . . . . . .Matt 6:30
I do cures today and *t* . . . . .Luke 13:32
him down unto you *t* . . . . .Acts 23:15
T, said he, thou shalt . . . . .Acts 25:22
us eat and drink; for *t* 1Cor 15:32
Today or *t* we will go . . . . .James 4:13

TONGS—*a tool used for grasping*
t thereof, and the . . . . .Ex 25:38
his *t*, and his snuffdishes . . . . . .Num 4:9
lamps, and the *t* of gold 1Kin 7:49
the lamps, and the *t*, made 2Chr 4:21
smith with the *t* both . . . . .Is 44:12

TONGUE—*the primary organ used for speech and tasting; a language*

Descriptive of:
Language . . . . .Gen 10:5, 20, 21
Speech . . . . .Ex 4:10
The physical organ . . . . . .Judg 7:5
Externalism 1John 3:18
People or race . . . . .Is 66:18
Spiritual gift 1Cor 12:10-30
Submission . . . . .Is 45:23

Kinds of:
Backbiting . . . . .Prov 25:23
As of fire . . . . .Acts 2:3
Deceitful . . . . .Mic 6:12
Double 1Tim 3:8
False . . . . .Ps 120:3
Flattering . . . . .Prov 6:24
Just .Prov 10:20
Lying . . . . .Prov 21:6
Muttering . . . . .Is 59:3
New .Mark 16:17
Perverse . . . . .Prov 17:20
Sharpened . . . . .Ps 140:3
Slow . . . . .Ex 4:10
Soft .Prov 25:15
Stammering . . . . .Is 33:19
Wholesome . . . . .Prov 15:4
Wise . . . . .Prov 15:2

Characteristics of:
Small but important . . . . .James 3:5
Untameable . . . . .James 3:6
Source of trouble . . . . .Prov 21:23
Means of sin . . . . .Ps 39:1
Known by God . . . . .Ps 139:4

Proper employment of, in:
Speaking:
God's righteousness....Ps 35:28
Wisdom ....Ps 37:30
God's Word ....Ps 119:172
Singing praises ....Ps 126:2
Kindness................Prov 31:26
Confessing Christ........Phil 2:11
See SLANDER

[*also* TONGUES]
shall not a dog move his *t*.....Ex 11:7
whose *t* thou shalt not ....Deut 28:49
none moved his *t* against ......Josh 10:21
and his word was in my *t* 2Sam 23:2
was written in the Syrian *t* ....Ezra 4:7
interpreted in the Syrian *t*.....Ezra 4:7
I had held my *t* ....Esth 7:4
from the scourge of the *t*......Job 5:21
Is there iniquity in my *t*.......Job 6:30
thou choosest the *t* of the .....Job 15:5
viper's *t* shall slay him ....Job 20:16
their *t* cleaved to the roof .....Job 29:10
or his *t* with a cord which .....Job 41:1
they flatter with their *t*........Ps 5:9
the *t* that speaketh proud .....Ps 12:3
backbiteth not with his *t* ......Ps 15:3
from the strife of *t* ....Ps 31:20
Keep thy *t* from evil, and .....Ps 34:13
then spake I with my *t*.........Ps 39:3
my *t* is the pen of a ready.....Ps 45:1
and thy *t* frameth deceit ......Ps 50:19
Thy *t* deviseth mischiefs ....Ps 52:2
O Lord, and divide their *t* ....Ps 55:9
and their *t* a sharp sword .....Ps 57:4
shall make their own *t* to .....Ps 64:8
the *t* of thy dogs in the ....Ps 68:23
their *t* walketh through........Ps 73:9
lied unto him with their *t* .....Ps 78:36
against me with a lying *t* ......Ps 109:2
and from a deceitful *t*.........Ps 120:2
let my *t* cleave to the roof ....Ps 137:6
A proud look, a lying *t* ......Prov 6:17
froward *t* shall be cut out .....Prov 10:31
the *t* of the wise is health .....Prov 12:18
The *t* of the wise useth ....Prov 15:2
answer of the *t*, is from ....Prov 16:1
giveth ear to a naughty *t* ......Prov 17:4
are in the power of the *t*......Prov 18:21
A lying *t* hateth those.........Prov 26:28
that flattereth with the *t* .....Prov 28:23
and milk are under thy *t* ......Song 4:11
their *t* and their doings........Is 3:8
another *t* will he speak to .....Is 28:11
the *t* of the stammerers ....Is 32:4
the *t* of the dumb sing ....Is 35:6
me the *t* of the learned ....Is 50:4
every *t* that shall rise ....Is 54:17
they bend their *t* like ....Jer 9:3
taught their *t* to speak ....Jer 9:5
Their *t* is as an arrow shot ....Jer 9:8
us smite him with the *t* ....Jer 18:18
that use their *t*, and say ......Jer 23:31
make thy *t* cleave to the ......Ezek 3:26
the *t* of the Chaldeans ....Dan 1:4
holdest thy *t* when the ....Hab 1:13
a deceitful *t* be found ....Zeph 3:13
their *t* shall consume ....Zech 14:12
spit, and touched his *t* ....Mark 7:33
his *t* loosed, and he spake .....Luke 1:64
in the Hebrew *t* Bethesda .....John 5:2
is called in their proper *t*......Acts 1:19
every man in our own *t* ....Acts 2:8
hear them speak in our *t* ......Acts 2:11
they spake with *t*, and ....Acts 19:6
unto them in the Hebrew *t* ....Acts 21:40
with their *t* they have ....Rom 3:13
every *t* shall confess to ....Rom 14:11
and bridleth not his *t* ....James 1:26
the *t* can no man tame ....James 3:8
him refrain his *t* from evil 1Pet 3:10
of every kindred, and *t* ....Rev 5:9
and people, and *t*, stood ......Rev 7:9
the Hebrew *t* is Abaddon .....Rev 9:11
people and kindreds and *t*.....Rev 11:9
gnawed their *t* for pain........Rev 16:10
in the Hebrew *t* Armageddon..Rev 16:16

TONGUES, SPEAKING IN—*glossolalia or ecstatic utterances*

At Pentecost:
Opposite of Babel ....Gen 11:6-9
Sign of the Spirit's coming ....Acts 2:3, 4
External manifestation ...Acts 2:4, 5
Meaning of, interpreted by Peter ....Acts 2:14-40

At Corinth:
Spiritual gift (last rank) ..1Cor 12:8-10, 28-30
Interpreter of, required ..1Cor 14:27, 28
Love superior to 1Cor 13:1-13
Subject to abuse.........1Cor 14:22-26

speaketh in an unknown *t* 1Cor 14:2
that ye all spake with *t*........1Cor 14:5
he that speaketh with *t*........1Cor 14:5
ye utter by the *t* words........1Cor 14:9
if I pray in an unknown *t* 1Cor 14:14
I speak with *t* more than 1Cor 14:18
words in an unknown *t*........1Cor 14:19
With men of other *t* and 1Cor 14:21
forbid not to speak with *t* 1Cor 14:39

TOO—*also*
Is any thing *t* hard for the.....Gen 18:14
the household be *t* little ....Ex 12:4
to make it, and *t* much ....Ex 36:7
it is *t* heavy for me ....Num 11:14
ye take *t* much upon you......Num 16:7
cause that is *t* hard for........Deut 1:17
his name there be *t* far........Deut 12:21
way be *t* long for thee ....Deut 14:24
place be *t* far from thee ....Deut 14:24
Ephraim be *t* narrow for ......Josh 17:15
went out *t* little for them......Josh 19:47
they were *t* strong for.........Judg 18:26
I am *t* old to have a ....Ruth 1:12
Zeruiah be *t* hard for me 2Sam 3:39
If the Syrians be *t* strong......2Sam 10:11
Ammon be *t* strong for 2Sam 10:11
they were *t* strong for me 2Sam 22:18
my lord the king say so *t*......1Kin 1:36
It is *t* much for you to go 1Kin 12:28
the battle was *t* sore for.......2Kin 3:26
If the Syrians be *t* strong......1Chr 19:12
But the priests were *t* few 2Chr 29:34
arise *t* much contempt ....Esth 1:18
things *t* wonderful for me .....Job 42:3
they were *t* strong for me .....Ps 18:17
burden they are *t* heavy ....Ps 38:4
or in things *t* high for me .....Ps 131:1
Wisdom is *t* high for a ....Prov 24:7
ye are *t* superstitious ....Acts 17:22

TOOK, TOOKEST—*See* INTRODUCTION

TOOL—*an instrument used or worked by hand*
Anvil...................Is 41:7
Awl....................Deut 15:17
Axe....................1Chr 20:3
Bellows.................Jer 6:29
Brickkiln 2Sam 12:31
Compass.................Is 44:13
Fining pot ....Prov 17:3
Fleshhook ....Ex 27:3
Fork 1Sam 2:13
Furnace ....Prov 17:3
Goad 1Sam 13:21
Graving tool ....Ex 32:4
Hammer.................Ps 74:6
Inkhorn ....Ezek 9:2
Knife...................Gen 22:6
Mattock 1Sam 13:21
Ox-goad ....Judg 3:31
Pan ....Ex 27:3
Plane...................Is 44:13
Plowshare...............Is 2:4
Plumb line ....Amos 7:8
Pruning hook ....Is 2:4
Razor ....Num 6:5
Saw 2Sam 12:31
Shovel..................Ex 27:3
Sickle ....Deut 16:9
Wheel ....Eccl 12:6

thou lift up thy *t* upon it ......Ex 20:25
not lift up any iron *t* upon ....Deut 27:5
any *t* of iron heard in the 1Kin 6:7

TOOTH—*hard bony appendage in the mouth used for chewing food*

Used for:
Eating..................Num 11:33
Showing hatred..........Acts 7:54

Figurative of:
Destruction ....Job 4:10
Holding on to life ....Job 13:14
God's chastening ....Job 16:9
Escaped with the "skin of my teeth" ....Job 19:20
Judgment ....Ps 3:7
Hatred ....Ps 35:16
Persecution ....Ps 57:4
Corporate guilt ....Jer 31:29, 30
Greediness..............Dan 7:5, 7, 19
Starvation...............Amos 4:6
Hired prophets ....Mic 3:5
Remorse ....Matt 13:42, 50

[*also* TEETH, TOOTH'S]
his *t* white with milk ....Gen 49:12
Eye for eye, *t* for *t* ....Ex 21:24
out his manservant's *t*.........Ex 21:27
or his maidservant's *t* ....Ex 21:27
go free for his *t* sake ....Ex 21:27
eye for eye, *t* for *t*............Lev 24:20
t for *t*, hand for hand ....Deut 19:21
also send the *t* of beasts.......Deut 32:24
of three *t* in his hand 1Sam 2:13
the spoil out of his *t* ....Job 29:17
t are terrible round about .....Job 41:14
upon him with his *t*...........Ps 37:12
Break their *t*, O God ....Ps 58:6
break out the great *t*..........Ps 58:6
us as a prey to their *t*.........Ps 124:6
As vinegar to the *t* ....Prov 10:26
trouble is like a broken *t*......Prov 25:19
their jaw *t* as knives ....Prov 30:14
t are like a flock of sheep .....Song 4:2
Thy *t* are as a flock of ....Song 6:6
instrument having *t* ....Is 41:15
hiss and gnash the *t* ....Lam 2:16
the children's *t* are set ....Ezek 18:2
t are the *t* of a lion ....Joel 1:6
cheek *t* of a great lion ....Joel 1:6
an eye..and a *t* for a *t* ....Matt 5:38
and gnashing of *t*.............Matt 8:12
and gnashing of *t*.............Matt 13:42
and gnashing of *t*.............Matt 22:13
and gnashing of *t*.............Matt 24:51
and gnashing of *t*.............Matt 25:30
cast the same in his *t* ....Matt 27:44
gnasheth with his *t* ....Mark 9:18
and gnashing of *t*.............Luke 13:28
t were as the *t* of lions ....Rev 9:8

TOP—*the summit; crown; pinnacle*

[*also* TOPS]
t of the mountains seen ....Gen 8:5
whose *t* may reach unto ....Gen 11:4
poured oil upon the *t* of it ....Gen 28:18
stand on the *t* of the hill ......Ex 17:9
on the *t* of the mount ....Ex 19:20
called Moses up to the *t* of ....Ex 19:20
be a hole in the *t* of it ....Ex 28:32
me in the *t* of the mount ......Ex 34:2
into the *t* of the mountain .....Num 14:40
died there in the *t* of the ......Num 20:28
from the *t* of the rocks I ......Num 23:9
Balaam unto the *t* of Peor ....Num 23:28
upon the *t* of the head ....Deut 33:16
to the *t* of the mountain ......Josh 15:8
upon the *t* of this rock ....Judg 6:26
in the *t* of the mountains......Judg 9:25
up to the *t* of the tower ....Judg 9:51
went to the *t* of the rock ......Judg 15:11

T

with Saul upon the *t* of the 1Sam 9:25
stood on the *t* of a hill 1Sam 26:13
stood on the *t* of a hill 2Sam 2:25
the *t* of the mulberry trees 2Sam 5:24
past the *t* of the hill 2Sam 16:1
upon the *t* of the pillars 1Kin 7:16
upon the *t* of the pillars 1Kin 7:17
upon the *t* of the pillars 1Kin 7:19
in the *t* of the base was 1Kin 7:35
on the *t* of the base the 1Kin 7:35
on the *t* of the two pillars 1Kin 7:41
upon the *t* of the pillars 1Kin 7:41
t of the throne was round 1Kin 10:19
up to the *t* of Carmel 1Kin 18:42
the grass on the house *t*........2Kin 19:26
t of the upper chamber of 2Kin 23:12
t of the mulberry trees 1Chr 14:15
that was on the *t* of each......2Chr 3:15
on the *t* of the two pillars 2Chr 4:12
on the *t* of the pillars 2Chr 4:12
unto the *t* of the rock..........2Chr 25:12
from the *t* of the rock 2Chr 25:12
the *t* of the scepter ....Esth 5:2
the *t* of the mountains ....Ps 72:16
in the *t* of high places..........Prov 8:2
look from the *t* of Amana .....Song 4:8
in the *t* of the mountains ......Is 2:2
on the *t* of their houses ....Is 15:3
upon the *t* of a mountain .....Is 30:17
in the *t* of every street ....Lam 2:19
all the *t* of the mountains .....Ezek 6:13
the *t* of his young twigs ....Ezek 17:4
set it upon the *t* of a rock.....Ezek 24:7
her like the *t* of a rock.........Ezek 26:4
his *t* was among the thick .....Ezek 31:3
t among the thick boughs .....Ezek 31:14
the *t* of the mountains ....Hos 4:13
on the *t* of the mountains .....Joel 2:5
t of Carmel shall wither ....Amos 1:2
in the *t* of the mountains ......Mic 4:1
at the *t* of all the streets ......Nah 3:10
a bowl upon the *t* of it ....Zech 4:2
are upon the *t* thereof ....Zech 4:2
in twain from the *t* to the .....Matt 27:51
in twain from the *t* to the .....Mark 15:38
seam, woven from the *t*.......John 19:23
upon the *t* of his staff.........Heb 11:21

TOPAZ—*a precious stone*
Used in breastplate ......Ex 39:10
Of great value ....Job 28:19
In Eden ....Ezek 28:13
In New Jerusalem ....Rev 21:2, 20

TOPHEL (tō'fĕl)—*"ruin"*
Israelite camp ....Deut 1:1

TOPHET (tō'fĕt)—*"a drum"*
Place of human sacrifice
in the valley of Hinnon.Jer 7:31, 32

T is ordained of old; yea ......Is 30:33
shall no more be called ***T***.....Jer 19:6
they shall bury them in ***T***.....Jer 19:11
even make this city as ***T***......Jer 19:12
defiled as the place of ***T***......Jer 19:13
came Jeremiah from ***T***.........Jer 19:14

TORCH—*a burning object used to give light*
[*also* TORCHES]
chariots..with flaming *t*........Nah 2:3
they shall seem like *t*, they ....Nah 2:4
like a *t* of fire in a sheaf ......Zech 12:6
with lanterns and *t* and ....John 18:3

TORMENT—*extreme physical, mental or spiritual anguish; to inflict such anguish*
Kinds of:
Physical ....Matt 8:6
Eternal ....Rev 20:10
Means of:
Official ....Matt 18:34
Persecutors ....Heb 11:35
Fear......................1John 4:18
Flame ....Luke 16:23-25
God ....Rev 14:9-11

[*also* TORMENTED, TORMENTS]
with divers diseases and *t* .....Matt 4:24
come hither to *t* us before .....Matt 8:29
by God, that thou *t* me not ...Mark 5:7
I beseech thee, *t* me not ......Luke 8:28
come into this place of *t* ......Luke 16:28
being destitute, afflicted, *t*.....Heb 11:37
fear, because fear hath *t* 1John 4:18
should be *t* five months ....Rev 9:5
their *t* was as the *t* of a ....Rev 9:5
these two prophets *t* them.....Rev 11:10
smoke of their *t* ascendeth ....Rev 14:11
so much *t* and sorrow give ....Rev 18:7
off for the fear of her *t* ....Rev 18:10
off for the fear of her *t* ....Rev 18:15

TORMENTORS—*whoever causes anguish*
delivered him to the *t*.........Matt 18:34

TORN—*See* TEAR

TORTOISE—*the great lizard*
Classed as unclean.......Lev 11:29

TORTURED—*inflicted with extreme pain*
and others were *t*, not ....Heb 11:35

TOSS—*to fling about*
[*also* TOSSED, TOSSINGS]
I am full of *t* to and fro.......Job 7:4
I am *t* up and down as........Ps 109:23
a vanity *t* and fro of ....Prov 21:6
turn and *t* thee like a ....Is 22:18
O thou afflicted, *t* ....Is 54:11
waves thereof *t* themselves ....Jer 5:22
of the sea, *t* with waves ....Matt 14:24
t with a tempest ....Acts 27:18
t to and fro, and carried ......Eph 4:14
driven with the wind and *t* ....James 1:6

TOTTERING—*wobbling*
ye be, and as a *t* fence........Ps 62:3

TOU—*See* TOI

TOUCH—*to make physical contact with something, especially with one's hands*
Kinds of:
Unclean ....Lev 5:2, 3
Angelic.................1Kin 19:5, 7
Queenly ....Esth 5:2
Divine...................Job 19:21
Cleansing ....Is 6:7
Healing..................Matt 8:3
Sexual...................1Cor 7:1
Satanic 1John 5:18
Purposes of, to:
Purify ....Is 6:7
Strengthen ....Dan 10:10-18
Harm ....Zech 2:8
Heal ....Mark 5:27-31
Receive a blessing ....Mark 10:13
Restore to life ....Luke 7:14
Manifest faith ....Luke 7:39-50

[*also* TOUCHED, TOUCHETH, TOUCHING]
neither shall ye *t* it, lest ....Gen 3:3
He that *t* this man or his ......Gen 26:11
as we have not *t* thee ....Gen 26:29
thy brother Esau, as *t* thee ....Gen 27:42
he *t* the hollow of Jacob's .....Gen 32:32
or *t* the border of it ....Ex 19:12
whosoever *t* the mount.........Ex 19:12
whatsoever *t* them shall ....Ex 30:29
that *t* them shall be holy ......Lev 6:18
t the flesh thereof shall be ....Lev 6:27
soul that shall *t* any...........Lev 7:21
carcase shall ye not *t* ....Lev 11:8
whosoever *t* the carcase ....Lev 11:24
whoso *t* their carcase ....Lev 11:27
he that *t* the carcase ....Lev 11:39
she shall *t* no hallowed.........Lev 12:4
he that *t* the flesh of him .....Lev 15:7
whomsoever he *t* that ....Lev 15:11
whosoever *t* her shall be ......Lev 15:19
whosoever *t* any thing that ....Lev 15:22
whosoever *t* those things ......Lev 15:27
whosoever *t* any creeping .....Lev 22:5
The soul which hath *t* any.....Lev 22:6

they shall not *t* any holy ......Num 4:15
the Levites *t* their charge......Num 8:26
He that *t* the dead body of....Num 19:11
whosoever *t* one that is ....Num 19:16
upon him that *t* a bone ....Num 19:18
unclean person *t* shall be ......Num 19:22
the soul that *t* it shall be ......Num 19:22
nor *t* their dead carcase ....Deut 14:8
therefore we may not *t* them ..Josh 9:19
t the flesh and..cakes ....Judg 6:21
that they shall not *t* thee?.....Ruth 2:9
whose hearts God had *t*.......1Sam 10:26
And as *t* the matter which 1Sam 20:23
shall not *t* thee any more 2Sam 14:10
that shall *t* them must be.....2Sam 23:7
the wing of the one *t* the......1Kin 6:27
other cherub *t* the other 1Kin 6:27
their wings *t* one another......1Kin 6:27
let down and *t* the bones......2Kin 13:21
As *t* the words which thou 2Kin 22:18
T not mine anointed, and 1Chr 16:22
that *t* any of the priests ....Ezra 7:24
and *t* all that he hath, and ....Job 1:11
it *t* thee, and thou art.........Job 4:5
there shall no evil *t* thee ......Job 5:19
T the Almighty, we cannot ....Job 37:23
which I have made *t* the ......Ps 45:1
T not mine anointed, and .....Ps 105:15
t her shall not be innocent ....Prov 6:29
my beloved *t* his vineyard .....Is 5:1
t no unclean thing ....Is 52:11
forth his hand, and *t* my ......Jer 1:9
t all their wickedness ....Jer 1:16
that *t* the inheritance ....Jer 12:14
saith the Lord *t* Shallum ......Jer 22:11
not *t* their garments ....Lam 4:14
creatures that *t* one ....Ezek 3:13
the vision is *t* the whole.......Ezek 7:13
when the east wind *t* it?.......Ezek 17:10
out, and blood *t* blood ....Hos 4:2
God of hosts is he that *t* ......Amos 9:5
with his skirt do *t* bread.......Hag 2:12
he *t* her hand, and the ....Matt 8:15
t the hem of his garment......Matt 9:20
If I may but *t* his garment.....Matt 9:21
many as *t* were made ....Matt 14:36
Jesus came and *t* them ....Matt 17:7
shall agree on earth as *t*.......Matt 18:19
on them, and *t* their eyes .....Matt 20:34
upon him for to *t* him ....Mark 3:10
t if it were but the border .....Mark 6:56
as many as *t* him were made ..Mark 6:56
he spit, and *t* his tongue ......Mark 7:33
as *t* the dead, that they ....Mark 12:26
forth his hand, and *t* him .....Luke 5:13
multitude sought to *t* him .....Luke 6:19
and *t* the border of his........Luke 8:44
Jesus said, Who *t* me? ....Luke 8:45
sayest thou, Who *t* me? ....Luke 8:45
Somebody hath *t* me ....Luke 8:46
what cause she had *t* him .....Luke 8:47
t not the burdens with ....Luke 11:46
that he would *t* them ....Luke 18:15
in this man *t* those things .....Luke 23:14
saith unto her, ***T*** me not ......John 20:17
intend to do as *t* these men ...Acts 5:35
T the resurrection of the ......Acts 24:21
next day we *t* at Sidon ....Acts 27:3
but as *t* the election, they .....Rom 11:28
for a man not to *t* a woman ...1Cor 7:1
as *t* things offered unto 1Cor 8:1
t not the unclean thing........2Cor 6:17
as *t* the ministering to.........2Cor 9:1
Hebrews: as *t* the law, a ......Phil 3:5
T not; taste not: handle ....Col 2:21
Barnabas, *t* whom ye ....Col 4:10
t brotherly love ye need.......1Thess 4:9
have confidence in the Lord *t* .2Thess 3:4
t with the feeling of our.......Heb 4:15
the firstborn should *t* ....Heb 11:28
mount that might be *t* ....Heb 12:18
if so much as a beast *t* the ....Heb 12:20

TOW—*a short or broken fiber*
as a thread of *t* is broken .....Judg 16:9

the strong shall be as *t* ....Is 1:31
they are quenched as *t* ....Is 43:17

TOWARD—*in the direction of*
pitched his tent *t* Sodom ......Gen 13:12
his face *t* the ground..........Gen 19:1
And he looked *t* Sodom ......Gen 19:28
t all the land of the plain .....Gen 19:28
and went *t* Haran.............Gen 28:10
was not *t* him as before ....Gen 31:2
face *t* the mount Gilead........Gen 31:21
right hand *t* Israel's...........Gen 48:13
left hand *t* Israel's right ....Gen 48:13
that they looked *t* the.........Ex 16:10
t the forepart thereof ....Ex 28:27
is *t* the north corner ....Ex 36:25
lifted up his hand *t* the........Lev 9:22
side *t* the rising of the ....Num 2:3
looked *t* the tabernacle........Num 16:42
which looketh *t* Jeshimon .....Num 21:20
his face *t* the wilderness.......Num 24:1
eastward *t* the sunrising ....Num 34:15
Jordan *t* the sunrising ....Deut 4:41
shall be evil *t* his brother......Deut 28:54
and *t* the wife of his bosom ...Deut 28:54
t the remnant of his ....Deut 28:54
be evil *t* the husband of.......Deut 28:56
and *t* her son, and *t* her.......Deut 28:56
t her young one that...........Deut 28:57
t her children which she.........Deut 28:57
sea *t* the going down of the ...Josh 1:4
came down *t* the sea of ....Josh 3:16
that is in thy hand *t* Ai ....Josh 8:18
had in his hand *t* the city .....Josh 8:18
Lebanon, *t* the sunrising ......Josh 13:5
border went up *t* Debir ....Josh 15:7
northward looking *t* Gilgal ....Josh 15:7
passed *t* the waters of.........Josh 15:7
went out *t* the sea to ....Josh 16:6
and went forth *t* Geliloth......Josh 18:17
border went up *t* the sea ......Josh 19:11
their border was *t* Jezreel .....Josh 19:18
t the sunrising to ....Josh 19:27
t the north side of ....Josh 19:27
fords of Jordan *t* Moab ....Judg 3:28
heart is *t* the governors ....Judg 5:9
anger was abated *t* him ....Judg 8:3
day draweth *t* evening ....Judg 19:9
over against Gibeah *t* the .....Judg 20:43
the valley of Zeboim *t* the 1Sam 13:18
David hasted, and ran *t* the ...1Sam 17:48
arose out of a place *t* the 1Sam 20:41
heart was *t* Absalom...........2Sam 14:1
servants coming on *t* him......2Sam 24:20
outside *t* the great court 1Kin 7:9
three looking *t* the north 1Kin 7:25
three looking *t* the west 1Kin 7:25
three looking *t* the south 1Kin 7:25
three looking *t* the east 1Kin 7:25
forth his hands *t* heaven 1Kin 8:22
eyes may be opened *t* this.....1Kin 8:29
t the place of which thou......1Kin 8:29
shall make *t* this place 1Kin 8:29
if they pray *t* this place 1Kin 8:35
and pray *t* this house 1Kin 8:42
Lord *t* the city which 1Kin 8:44
and *t* the house that I.........1Kin 8:44
good thing *t* the Lord God 1Kin 14:13
I would not look *t* thee 2Kin 3:14
t the east, west, north 1Chr 9:24
a day, and *t* Assupim two 1Chr 26:17
three looking *t* the north 2Chr 4:4
and three looking *t* the........2Chr 4:4
three looking *t* the south 2Chr 4:4
three looking *t* the east 2Chr 4:4
prayeth *t* this place 2Chr 6:20
they pray *t* this place 2Chr 6:26
pray *t* their land, which 2Chr 6:38
t the city which thou hast 2Chr 6:38
and *t* the house which I 2Chr 6:38
came *t* the watch tower 2Chr 20:24
good in Israel, both *t* God 2Chr 24:16
and *t* his house 2Chr 24:16
mercy endureth for ever *t* .....Ezra 3:11
against the water gate *t* ....Neh 3:26
manner *t* all that knew ....Esth 1:13
upon their heads *t* heaven .....Job 2:12
her wings *t* the south? ....Job 39:26
worship *t* thy holy temple .....Ps 5:7
hands *t* thy holy oracle........Ps 28:2
cause thine anger *t* us to ......Ps 85:4
is his mercy *t* them that.......Ps 103:11
kindness is great *t* us ....Ps 117:2
king's favor is *t* a wise ....Prov 14:35
wind goeth *t* the south ....Eccl 1:6
if the tree fall *t* the south .....Eccl 11:3
t the north, in the place ......Eccl 11:3
Lebanon, which looketh *t* .....Song 7:4
went up *t* Jerusalem to ....Is 7:1
fear *t* me is taught by the .....Is 29:13
with their face *t* the earth .....Is 49:23
and of thy mercies *t* me?......Is 63:15
be known *t* his servants ....Is 66:14
indignation *t* his enemies ......Is 66:14
face thereof is *t* the north .....Jer 1:13
Set up the standard *t* Zion ....Jer 4:6
tried mine heart *t* thee ....Jer 12:3
perform my good word *t* you ..Jer 29:10
thine heart *t* the highway......Jer 31:21
t the north by the river ....Jer 46:6
lift up thy hands *t* him for.....Lam 2:19
straight, the one *t* the other ...Ezek 1:23
thy face *t* the mountains ......Ezek 6:2
that looketh *t* the north ....Ezek 8:3
now the way *t* the north ....Ezek 8:5
eyes the way *t* the north ......Ezek 8:5
backs *t* the temple of the......Ezek 8:16
and their faces *t* the east ......Ezek 8:16
worshiped the sun *t* the ....Ezek 8:16
scatter *t* every wind all ....Ezek 12:14
branches turned *t* him.........Ezek 17:6
did bend her roots *t* him .....Ezek 17:7
shot forth her branches *t* him ..Ezek 17:7
set thy face *t* the south........Ezek 20:46
drop thy word *t* the south .....Ezek 20:46
set thy face *t* Jerusalem ....Ezek 21:2
thy word *t* the holy places.....Ezek 21:2
lift up your eyes *t* your idols ..Ezek 33:25
court that looked *t* the ....Ezek 40:20
gate *t* the north, and *t* ....Ezek 40:23
he brought me *t* the south.....Ezek 40:24
behold a gate *t* the south......Ezek 40:24
the inner court *t* the south ....Ezek 40:27
gate to gate *t* the south ....Ezek 40:27
arches..were *t* the utter ....Ezek 40:31
arches..were *t* the outward ....Ezek 40:34
prospect was *t* the south ......Ezek 40:44
the prospect *t* the north ....Ezek 40:44
prospect is *t* the north is ......Ezek 40:46
were *t* the place that was......Ezek 41:11
one door *t* the north ....Ezek 41:11
another door *t* the south ......Ezek 41:11
separate place *t* the east ......Ezek 41:14
was *t* the palm tree ....Ezek 41:19
young lion *t* the palm tree .....Ezek 41:19
court, the way *t* the north .....Ezek 42:1
the building *t* the north ....Ezek 42:1
t the utter court on the ....Ezek 42:7
chambers which were *t* the ....Ezek 42:11
before the wall *t* the east......Ezek 42:12
me forth *t* the gate ....Ezek 42:15
prospect is *t* the east..........Ezek 42:15
gate that looketh *t* the east ....Ezek 43:1
stairs shall look *t* the east .....Ezek 43:17
sanctuary which looketh *t* ......Ezek 44:1
inner court..*t* the east..........Ezek 46:1
which looked *t* the north ......Ezek 46:19
waters issued out *t* the east....Ezek 47:8
t the north five and twenty ....Ezek 48:10
t the west ten thousand in .....Ezek 48:10
t the east ten thousand in .....Ezek 48:10
t the south five and twenty ....Ezek 48:10
the oblation *t* the east ....Ezek 48:21
and twenty thousand *t* the .....Ezek 48:21
God hath wrought *t* me ....Dan 4:2
ones *t* the four winds of.......Dan 8:8
exceeding great, *t* the south ...Dan 8:9
t the east, and *t* the ....Dan 8:9
on my face *t* the ground ......Dan 8:18
and my face *t* the ground ......Dan 10:9
divided *t* the four winds ....Dan 11:4
and come *t* the south ....Dan 11:29
t the children of Israel ....Hos 3:1
his face *t* the east sea ....Joel 2:20
hinder part *t* the utmost.......Joel 2:20
will look again *t* thy holy......Jon 2:4
grizzled go forth *t* the south ...Zech 6:6
Israel, shall be *t* the Lord .....Zech 9:1
t the east and *t* the west ......Zech 14:4
shall remove *t* the north ......Zech 14:4
and half of it *t* the south ......Zech 14:4
half of them *t* the former .....Zech 14:8
half of them *t* the hinder ......Zech 14:8
his hand *t* his disciples ....Matt 12:49
to dawn *t* the first day of .....Matt 28:1
with compassion *t* them ....Mark 6:34
peace, good will *t* men ....Luke 2:14
journeying *t* Jerusalem ....Luke 13:22
over the sea *t* Capernaum ....John 6:17
looked steadfastly *t* heaven ....Acts 1:10
Greeks, repentance *t* God .....Acts 20:21
And have hope *t* God, which ..Acts 24:15
offense *t* God and *t* men ......Acts 24:16
wind, and made *t* shore ....Acts 27:40
their lust one *t* another ....Rom 1:27
t thee, goodness, if thou ......Rom 11:22
likeminded one *t* another......Rom 15:5
uncomely *t* his virgin..........1Cor 7:36
brought on my way *t* Judea ...2Cor 1:16
confirm your love *t* him 2Cor 2:8
your fervent mind *t* me 2Cor 7:7
all grace abound *t* you 2Cor 9:8
absent am bold *t* you 2Cor 10:1
mighty in me *t* the Gentiles ...Gal 2:8
hath abounded *t* us in all......Eph 1:8
your lack of service *t* me ......Phil 2:30
Walk in wisdom *t* them ....Col 4:5
in love one *t* another 1Thess 3:12
ye do it *t* all the brethren 1Thess 4:10
weak, be patient *t* all men 1Thess 5:14
all *t* each other aboundeth 2Thess 1:3
Savior *t* man appeared ....Titus 3:4
thou hast *t* the Lord Jesus.....Philem 5
Lord Jesus, and *t* all saints ....Philem 5
works, and of faith *t* God .....Heb 6:1
for conscience *t* God..........1Pet 2:19
have we confidence *t* God......1John 3:21

TOWEL—*a cloth used to dry something*
Used by Christ ....John 13:4, 5

TOWER—*a tall structure; bulwark*

Purposes of, for:
Protection ....Matt 21:33
Watchmen 2Kin 9:17
Safeguarding people 2Chr 26:10, 15

Partial list of:
Babel ....Gen 11:4, 9
David ....Song 4:4
Lebanon................Song 7:4
Penuel..................Judg 8:17
Shechem...............Judg 9:40, 47, 49
Siloam.................Luke 13:4

[*also* TOWERS]
us build us a city and a *t*......Gen 11:4
to see the city and the *t*.......Gen 11:5
tent beyond the *t* of Edar .....Gen 35:21
I will break down this *t* ....Judg 8:9
men of the *t* of Shechem ......Judg 9:46
a strong *t* within the city ......Judg 9:51
up to the top of the *t* ....Judg 9:51
Abimelech came unto the *t*....Judg 9:52
unto the door of the *t* to .....Judg 9:52
my high *t*, and my refuge 2Sam 22:3
He is the *t* of salvation........2Sam 22:51
when he came to the *t*, he 2Kin 5:24
the *t* of the watchmen 2Kin 17:9
about them walls, and *t* 2Chr 14:7
toward the watch *t* in 2Chr 20:24
built *t* in Jerusalem 2Chr 26:9
he built castles and *t*..........2Chr 27:4
and raised it up to the *t*.......2Chr 32:5
even unto the *t* of Meah ......Neh 3:1
sanctified it, unto the *t* of ....Neh 3:1

t which lieth out from the .....Neh 3:25
against the great *t* that ....Neh 3:27
and the *t* of Hananeel ....Neh 12:39
and the *t* of Meah, even ......Neh 12:39
her: tell the *t* thereof ....Ps 48:12
high *t*, and my deliverer ......Ps 144:2
of the Lord is a strong *t* ......Prov 18:10
and my breasts like *t* ....Song 8:10
And upon every high *t*........Is 2:15
they set up the *t* thereof ......Is 23:13
the forts and *t* shall be ....Is 32:14
I have set thee for a *t* and ....Jer 6:27
and break down her *t*.........Ezek 26:4
Gammadim were in thy *t*......Ezek 27:11
from the *t* of Syene even ......Ezek 29:10
And thou, O *t* of the flock ....Mic 4:8
and set me upon the *t* ....Hab 2:1
and against the high *t*.........Zeph 1:16
from the *t* of Hananeel ....Zech 14:10
the wine vat, and built a *t*.....Mark 12:1
intending to build a *t* ....Luke 14:28

TOWER OF FURNACES—*a tower of Jerusalem*
Rebuit by Nehemiah .....Neh 3:11

TOWN—*a settled area, usually recognized by a name*

[*also* TOWNS]
their names, by their *t* ....Gen 25:16
went and took the small *t* .....Num 32:41
beside unwalled *t* a great......Deut 3:5
house was upon the *t* wall .....Josh 2:15
t of Jair, which are in.........Josh 13:30
Ashdod with her *t* and her ....Josh 15:47
Gaza with her *t* and her ......Josh 15:47
Beth-shean and her *t* ....Josh 17:11
and Ibleam and her *t* ....Josh 17:11
of Dor and her *t* ....Josh 17:11
of En-dor and her *t*...........Josh 17:11
of Taanach and her *t* ....Josh 17:11
of Megiddo and her *t* ....Josh 17:11
of Beth-shean and her *t*.......Judg 1:27
nor Taanach and her *t* ....Judg 1:27
of Dor and her *t* ....Judg 1:27
of Ibleam and her *t*...........Judg 1:27
of Megiddo and her *t* ....Judg 1:27
in Heshbon and her *t* ....Judg 11:26
and in Aroer and her *t*........Judg 11:26
the elders of the *t* trembled ...1Sam 16:4
a place in some *t* in the 1Sam 27:5
pertained the *t* of Jair the 1Kin 4:13
Aram, with the *t* of Jair.......1Chr 2:23
Kenath, and the *t* thereof 1Chr 2:23
Beth-el and the *t* thereof 1Chr 7:28
Gezer, with the *t* thereof......1Chr 7:28
Shechem..the *t* thereof 1Chr 7:28
Gaza and the *t* thereof.........1Chr 7:28
Beth-shean and her *t* 1Chr 7:29
Taanach and her *t*.............1Chr 7:29
Megiddo and her *t*.............1Chr 7:29
Dor and her *t* 1Chr 7:29
her *t* out of the hand of.......1Chr 18:1
Beth-el with the *t* thereof 2Chr 13:19
Jeshanah with the *t* thereof.....2Chr 13:19
Ephraim with the *t* thereof 2Chr 13:19
dwelt in the unwalled *t*........Esth 9:19
city and upon all her *t* ....Jer 19:15
him that buildeth a *t* with .....Hab 2:12
inhabited as *t* without ....Zech 2:4
city or *t* ye shall enter ....Matt 10:11
Let us go into the next *t* ......Mark 1:38
and led him out of the *t* ......Mark 8:23
Neither go into the *t*, nor .....Mark 8:26
nor tell it to any in the *t* ......Mark 8:26
into the *t* of Caesarea ....Mark 8:27
were come out of every *t* of ...Luke 5:17
went through the *t*............Luke 9:6
they may go into the *t* and ....Luke 9:12
out of the *t* of Bethlehem .....John 7:42
not yet come into the *t* ....John 11:30

TOWN CLERK—*a keeper of court records*
Appeases the people .....Acts 19:35

TRACHONITIS (trăk-ŏ-nī'tĭs)—*"strong"*
Volcanic region southeast of Damascus ....Luke 3:1

TRADE—*commerce; to exchange items*
Objects of, such as:
Gold 1Kin 9:28
Timber 1Kin 5:6, 8, 9
Hardwood 1Kin 10:11, 12
Spices 1Kin 10:10, 15
Property ....Ruth 4:3, 4
Slaves ....Joel 3:6
Means of, by:
Wagons ....Gen 46:5, 6
Kines..................1Sam 6:7, 8
Floats 1Kin 5:7-9
Camels 1Kin 10:1, 2
Asses..................Num 22:21-33
Horses 1Kin 20:20
Caravans ....Gen 37:25-36
Centers of, in:
Tyre...................Ezek 27:1-36
Jerusalem ....Neh 13:15-21

[*also* TRADED, TRADING]
dwell and *t* ye herein ....Gen 34:10
for their *t* hath been to ....Gen 46:32
went and *t* with the same .....Matt 25:16
man had gained by *t*..........Luke 19:15
and as many as *t* by sea.......Rev 18:17

TRADES AND CRAFTS
Baker ....Gen 40:1
Brick makers............Ex 5:7
Carpenter...............Is 41:7
Engineers ....Gen 11:3, 4
Farmers ....Ps 104:13-15
Fishermen ....Matt 4:18-22
Lawyers ....Luke 5:17
Millers ....Ex 11:5
Physician ....Col 4:14
Smiths.................Is 44:12

TRADITIONS—*precepts or customs passed down from past generations*
Christian described as:
Inspired by the Spirit ....John 15:26, 27
Handed down by apostles.2Thess 3:6, 7
Based on eyewitnesses ...2Pet 1:16, 19
Classed as Scripture 1Tim 5:18
2Pet 3:16
Once for all delivered....Jude 3
Consisting of fundamental truths 1Cor 15:1-3
Originating with Christ...Matt 28:20
1Cor 11:1-23

[*also* TRADITION]
the *t* of the elders? ....Matt 15:2
of none effect by your *t*........Matt 15:6
holding the *t* of the elders .....Mark 7:3
to the *t* of the elders..........Mark 7:5
none effect through your *t* ....Mark 7:13
of the *t* of my fathers ....Gal 1:14
hold the *t* which ye have been .2Thess 2:15
by *t* from your fathers 1Pet 1:18

TRAFFIC—*to carry on trade*
and ye shall *t* in the land......Gen 42:34
t of the spice merchants 1Kin 10:15
carried it into a land of *t*......Ezek 17:4
by the iniquity of thy *t*........Ezek 28:18

TRAFFICKERS—*traders*
t are the honorable of ....Is 23:8

TRAIN—*that which trails behind*
Monarch's retinue 1Kin 10:2
Trailing robe ....Is 6:1

TRAIN—*to educate; prepare*

[*also* TRAINED]
he armed his *t* servants ....Gen 14:14
T up a child in the way he ....Prov 22:6

TRAITOR—*one who betrays a trust*
Descriptive of:
Judas...................Luke 6:16
End-time people.........2Tim 3:4

TRAMPLE—*to tread heavily so as to injure or destroy*
and *t* them in my fury ....Is 63:3
lest they *t* them under ....Matt 7:6

TRANCE—*a state of being during which the individual appears to be hypnotized*
Peter's on a housetop ....Acts 10:10
into a *t*, but having his........Num 24:4
and in a *t* I saw a vision ......Acts 11:5
the temple, I was in a *t* ....Acts 22:17

TRANQUILITY—*freedom from agitation or turmoil*
be a lengthening of thy *t* ......Dan 4:27

TRANSFERRED—*passed from one to another*
in a figure *t* to myself.........1Cor 4:6

TRANSFIGURATION—*a radical transformation in appearance*
Moses ....Ex 34:29-35
Christ, on a high mountain ....Matt 17:1-17
Christ, remembered 2Pet 1:16-18
Stephen ....Acts 6:15

[*also* TRANSFIGURED]
and he was *t* before them .....Mark 9:2

TRANSFORMED—*changed in character or condition*

[*also* TRANSFORMING]
ye *t* by the renewing of ....Rom 12:2
t themselves into the..........2Cor 11:13
Satan himself is *t* into an angel.2Cor 11:14
be *t* as the ministers of........2Cor 11:15

TRANSGRESSION—*a violation of God's law*
Described as:
Personal 1Tim 2:14
Public ....Rom 5:14
Political ....Esth 3:3
Premeditated ....Josh 7:11-25
Caused by:
Law ....Rom 4:15
Sin 1John 3:4
Wine ....Hab 2:5
Idolatry.................1Chr 5:25
Intermarriage ....Ezra 10:10, 13
Fear of the people 1Sam 15:24
Productive of:
Powerlessness ....Judg 2:20-23
Unfaithfulness...........1Chr 9:1
Death 1Chr 10:13
Destruction ....Ps 37:38
Curse ....Is 24:5, 6
Punishment of, by:
Defeat..................2Chr 12:1-5
Disease.................2Chr 26:16-21
Captivity................Neh 1:8
Affliction ....Ps 107:17
Death in hell............Is 66:24
Reaction to, by:
Further disobedience.....Num 14:41-45
Covering up ....Job 31:33
Repentance ....Ezra 9:4-7
Forgiveness of:
Difficult ....Josh 24:19
Out of God's mercy .....Ex 34:7
By:
Confession ....Ps 32:1, 5
Removal..............Ps 103:12
Blotting out ....Is 44:22
Christ's relation to:
Wounded for our ....Is 53:5
Stricken for our ....Is 53:8
Make intercession for ....Is 53:12
Provided a Redeemer for.Rom 11:26, 27
Died for our ....Heb 9:15
See SIN

[*also* TRANSGRESS, TRANSGRESSED, TRANSGRESSEST, TRANSGRESSETH, TRANSGRESSING, TRANSGRESSIONS]
he will not pardon your *t* .....Ex 23:21
of their *t* in all their sins ......Lev 16:16

forgiving iniquity and *t* ....Num 14:18
thy God, in *t* his covenant ....Deut 17:2
have not *t* thy commandments .Deut 26:13
or if in *t* against the Lord .....Josh 22:22
ye have *t* the covenant of the ..Josh 23:16
forgive your *t* nor your sins ...Josh 24:19
make the Lord's people to *t* ...1Sam 2:24
Ye have *t*: roll a great 1Sam 14:33
evil nor *t* in mine hand 1Sam 24:11
all their *t* wherein they........1Kin 8:50
they have *t* against thee 1Kin 8:50
God, but *t* his covenant 2Kin 18:12
who *t* in the thing accursed....1Chr 2:7
t ye the commandments 2Chr 24:20
t sore against the Lord........2Chr 28:19
did cast away in his *t* 2Chr 29:19
people, *t* very much after 2Chr 36:14
mourned because of the *t* .....Ezra 10:6
to *t* against our God in ....Neh 13:27
Why *t* thou the king's..........Esth 3:3
dost thou not pardon my *t* ....Job 7:21
make me to know my *t* and ...Job 13:23
If I covered my *t* as Adam ....Job 31:33
I am clean without *t*, I am ....Job 33:9
if thy *t* be multiplied..........Job 35:6
their *t* that they have ....Job 36:9
in the multitude of their *t* .....Ps 5:10
that my mouth shall not *t* .....Ps 17:3
innocent from the great *t*......Ps 19:13
ashamed which *t* without ......Ps 25:3
sins of my youth, nor my *t* ....Ps 25:7
The *t* of the wicked saith......Ps 36:1
Deliver me from all my *t*......Ps 39:8
For I acknowledge my *t*.......Ps 51:3
as for our *t*, thou shalt........Ps 65:3
visit their *t* with the rod.......Ps 89:32
wicked is snared by the *t*......Prov 12:13
mouth *t* not in judgment ......Prov 16:10
loveth *t* that loveth strife ......Prov 17:19
For the *t* of a land many ......Prov 28:2
of bread that man will *t*.......Prov 28:21
t of an evil man there is ......Prov 29:6
man aboundeth in *t*..........Prov 29:22
t thereof shall be heavy ....Is 24:20
blotteth out thy *t* for mine ....Is 43:25
teachers have *t* against ....Is 43:27
your *t* is your mother put .....Is 50:1
are ye not children of *t* ....Is 57:4
t are multiplied before ....Is 59:12
for our *t* are with us; and .....Is 59:12
In *t* and lying against the......Is 59:13
that turn from *t* in Jacob ......Is 59:20
pastors also *t* against me ......Jer 2:8
thou saidst, I will not *t*........Jer 2:20
hast *t* against the Lord ....Jer 3:13
because their *t* are many ......Jer 5:6
the men that have *t* my ....Jer 34:18
for the multitude of her *t* .....Lam 1:5
done unto me for all my *t*.....Lam 1:22
We have *t* and have rebelled ..Lam 3:42
fathers have *t* against me......Ezek 2:3
any more with all their *t* ......Ezek 14:11
away from all his *t* that he ....Ezek 18:28
Cast away from you all your *t* .Ezek 18:31
them that *t* against me ....Ezek 20:38
If our *t* and our sins be ....Ezek 33:10
him in the day of his *t* ....Ezek 33:12
according to their *t* have I.....Ezek 39:24
sacrifice by reason of *t* ....Dan 8:12
Yea, all Israel have *t* thy ......Dan 9:11
finish the *t*, and to make ......Dan 9:24
they like men have *t* the ......Hos 6:7
they have *t* against me ....Hos 7:13
For three *t* of Damascus ......Amos 1:3
For three *t* of Gaza, and ......Amos 1:6
For three *t* of Tyrus, and .....Amos 1:9
For three *t* of Edom, and .....Amos 1:11
For three *t* of the children ....Amos 1:13
For three *t* of Moab, and .....Amos 2:1
For three *t* of Judah, and .....Amos 2:4
For three *t* of Israel, and......Amos 2:6
shall visit the *t* of Israel.......Amos 3:14
Come to Beth-el, and *t* ....Amos 4:4
your manifold *t* and your......Amos 5:12
For the *t* of Jacob is all ....Mic 1:5
What is the *t* of Jacob? ....Mic 1:5
the *t* of Israel were found .....Mic 1:13
give my first-born for my *t* ....Mic 6:7
thou hast *t* against me ....Zeph 3:11
disciples *t* the tradition........Matt 15:2
neither *t* I at any time thy.....Luke 15:29
from which Judas by *t* fell.....Acts 1:25
circumcision dost *t* the law? ...Rom 2:27
It was added because of *t* .....Gal 3:19
every *t* and disobedience ......Heb 2:2
for sin is the *t* of the law 1John 3:4
Whosoever *t*, and abideth 2John 9

TRANSGRESSOR—*one who goes beyond prescribed limits*

[*also* TRANSGRESSORS]
will I teach *t* thy ways ....Ps 51:13
I beheld the *t*, and was ....Ps 119:158
and the *t* shall be rooted ......Prov 2:22
t shall be taken in their ....Prov 11:6
but the way of *t* is hard ....Prov 13:15
and the *t* for the upright ......Prov 21:18
the words of the *t* ....Prov 22:12
the fool, and rewardeth *t*......Prov 26:10
destruction of the *t* and ....Is 1:28
called a *t* from the womb .....Is 48:8
the *t* are come to the full .....Dan 8:23
but the *t* shall fall therein .....Hos 14:9
was numbered with the *t* ......Mark 15:28
reckoned among the *t*.........Luke 22:37
I make myself a *t*............Gal 2:18
convinced of the law as *t*......James 2:9
art become a *t* of the law .....James 2:11

TRANSITORY—*passing quickly away; fleeting*

Descriptive of man's:
Life ....Ps 39:4, 5
Pleasures ....Is 47:8, 9
Plans ....Luke 12:16-21

Caused by:
World's passing away 1John 2:15-17
Our mortality ....Ps 90:3-12
Impending future world ..2Cor 4:17, 18

TRANSLATE—*to change something or someone from one condition to another*
Enoch ....Heb 11:5
Elijah 2Kin 2:1-11
Christians 1Thess 4:16, 17

[*also* TRANSLATED]
To *t* the kingdom from the 2Sam 3:10
hath *t* us into the kingdom ....Col 1:13
By faith Enoch was *t* that .....Heb 11:5
because God had *t* him ....Heb 11:5

TRANSPARENT—*something that can be seen through*
gold, as it were *t* glass ....Rev 21:21

TRAP—*a snare*

[*also* TRAPS]
shall be snares and *t* unto .....Josh 23:13
and a *t* for him in the way ....Job 18:10
welfare, let it become a *t* .....Ps 69:22
set a *t*, they catch men........Jer 5:26
made a snare, and a *t*.........Rom 11:9

TRAVAIL—*the labor pains of childbirth; to toil hard*

Descriptive of:
Childbirth pains ....Gen 38:27
Anguish ....Is 53:11

Of a woman's, described as:
Fearful ....Ps 48:6
Painful ....Is 13:8
Hazardous ....Gen 35:16-19
Joyful afterwards ....John 16:21

Figurative of:
New Israel ....Is 66:7, 8
Messiah's birth ....Mic 4:9, 10
Redemption ....Mic 5:3
New birth...............Gal 4:19
Creation's rebirth ....Rom 8:22

[*also* TRAVAILED, TRAVAILEST, TRAVAILETH, TRAVAILING]
pass in the time of her *t* ......Gen 38:27
to pass, when she *t* ....Gen 38:28
all the *t* that had come........Ex 18:8
the *t* that hath befallen........Num 20:14
man *t* with pain all his ....Job 15:20
he *t* with iniquity, and ....Ps 7:14
pain, as of a woman in *t* ......Ps 48:6
this sore *t* hath God given.....Eccl 1:13
to the sinner he giveth *t*.......Eccl 2:26
I considered all *t*, and ....Eccl 4:4
vanity, yea, it is a sore *t* .....Eccl 4:8
pangs of a woman that *t* ......Is 21:3
I *t* not, nor bring forth........Is 23:4
will I cry like a *t* woman .....Is 42:14
didst not *t* with child.........Is 54:1
voice as of a woman in *t*......Jer 4:31
sorrows..as a woman in *t*?.....Jer 13:21
a man doth *t* with child? ......Jer 30:6
and her that *t* with child ......Jer 31:8
her, as a woman in *t*.........Jer 49:24
me with gall and *t* ....Lam 3:5
The sorrows of a *t* woman ....Hos 13:13
and cry, thou that *t* not ....Gal 4:27
brethren our labor and *t* 1Thess 2:9
as *t* upon a woman with.......1Thess 5:3
with labor and *t* night.........2Thess 3:8
child cried, *t* in birth..........Rev 12:2

TRAVEL—*to journey*

[*also* TRAVELED, TRAVELETH, TRAVELING]
poverty come as one that *t* ....Prov 6:11
poverty come as one that *t* ....Prov 24:34
O ye *t* companies of ....Is 21:13
t in the greatness of his ....Is 63:1
man *t* into a far country.......Matt 25:14
Stephen *t* as far as............Acts 11:19
Paul's companions in *t* ....Acts 19:29
of the churches to *t* with 2Cor 8:19

TRAVELER—*one who journeys*

[*also* TRAVELERS]
that *t* walked through ....Judg 5:6
there came a *t* unto the 2Sam 12:4
opened my doors to the *t* .....Job 31:32

TRAVERSING—*moving back and forth or from side to side*
dromedary *t* her ways ....Jer 2:23

TREACHERY—*betrayal of a trust*

Manifested by:
People ....Josh 9:3-15
Woman ....Judg 4:18-21
King 2Sam 11:14, 15
Son 2Sam 13:28, 29
Enemy ....Esth 3:8-15
Disciple ....Matt 26:47-50

Accompanied by:
Deceit ....Gen 34:13-31
Soothing words ....Judg 9:1-5
Professed favor 1Sam 18:17-19
Pretense ....Dan 6:1-8

[*also* TREACHEROUS, TREACHEROUSLY]
Shechem dealt *t* with ....Judg 9:23
There is *t*, O Ahaziah 2Kin 9:23
the *t* dealer dealeth *t* ....Is 21:2
the *t* dealers have dealt *t*......Is 24:16
t dealers have dealt very *t*.....Is 24:16
not spoiled; and dealest *t* .....Is 33:1
they dealt not *t* with thee .....Is 33:1
make an end to deal *t* ....Is 33:1
they shall deal *t* with thee .....Is 33:1
her *t* sister Judah saw it.......Jer 3:7
her *t* sister Judah feared ......Jer 3:8
t sister Judah hath not ....Jer 3:10
herself more than *t* Judah .....Jer 3:11
as a wife *t* departeth from .....Jer 3:20
so have ye dealt *t* with me ....Jer 3:20
an assembly of *t* men ....Jer 9:2
happy that deal very *t*? ....Jer 12:1
have dealt *t* with her..........Lam 1:2
dealt *t* against the Lord ....Hos 5:7
upon them that deal *t*.........Hab 1:13

T

prophets are light and *t* ....Zeph 3:4
we deal *t* every man ....Mal 2:10
whom thou hast dealt *t* ....Mal 2:14
spirit, that ye deal not *t*.......Mal 2:16

TREAD—*to beat or press with the feet; walk on or over*

[*also* TREADETH, TREADING, TRODDEN, TRODE]
land that he hath *t* upon ......Deut 1:36
of your feet shall *t* shall.......Deut 11:24
ox when he *t* out the corn.....Deut 25:4
t upon their high places ....Deut 33:29
sole of your feet shall *t* ....Josh 1:3
thy feet have *t* shall ....Josh 14:9
thou hast *t* down strength .....Judg 5:21
vineyards, and *t* the grapes ....Judg 9:27
t on the threshold of Dagon ...1Sam 5:5
t upon him in the gate 2Kin 7:17
and *t* down the thistle.........2Kin 14:9
and *t* down the thistle.........2Chr 25:18
t upon the waves of the sea ...Job 9:8
which wicked men have *t*? ....Job 22:15
t their winepresses, and ....Job 24:11
let him *t* down my life ....Ps 7:5
shall *t* down our enemies ......Ps 60:12
it is that shall *t* down our .....Ps 108:13
your hand, to *t* my courts? ....Is 1:12
and it shall be *t* down.........Is 5:5
for the *t* of lesser cattle ....Is 7:25
mountains *t* him under ....Is 14:25
meted out and *t* down ....Is 18:2
Moab shall be *t* down.........Is 25:10
straw is *t* down for the........Is 25:10
The foot shall *t* it down.......Is 26:6
shall be *t* under feet ....Is 28:3
and as the potter *t* clay ....Is 41:25
I have *t* the winepress alone ...Is 63:3
I will *t* down the people in ....Is 63:6
they have *t* my portion........Jer 12:10
as they that *t* the grapes ......Jer 25:30
hath *t* under foot all my.......Lam 1:15
he *t* down all thy streets ......Ezek 26:11
ye have *t* with your feet.......Ezek 34:19
shall *t* it down, and break .....Dan 7:23
loveth to *t* out the corn ....Hos 10:11
t upon the high places of......Amos 4:13
your *t* is upon the poor ....Amos 5:11
t upon the high places of......Mic 1:3
shall she be *t* down as the.....Mic 7:10
clay, and *t* the mortar.........Nah 3:14
which *t* down their enemies ...Zech 10:5
shall *t* down the wicked ....Mal 4:3
be *t* under the foot of men ....Matt 5:13
it was *t* down, and the ....Luke 8:5
they *t* one upon another ......Luke 12:1
the ox that *t* out the corn 1Cor 9:9
muzzle the ox that *t* out.......1Tim 5:18
who hath *t* under foot the .....Heb 10:29
city shall they *t* under.........Rev 11:2
winepress was *t* without ....Rev 14:20

TREADER—*one who smashes grapes*

[*also* TREADERS]
t shall tread out no wine ......Is 16:10
the *t* of grapes him that ....Amos 9:13

TREASON—*betrayal of one's country*

Instances of:
Rahab against Jericho....Josh 2:1-24
Israelites against
Rehoboam............1Kin 12:16-19
Absalom against David ..2Sam 15:1-14
Sheba against David 2Sam 20:1-22
Athaliah against Judah ...2Kin 11
2Chr 22:10-12

Characterized by:
Conspiracy..............1Kin 16:9-11, 20
Giving secrets 1Sam 30:15, 16
Falling out 2Sam 3:6-21
Jealousy ....Num 12:1-11

See CONSPIRACY; TREACHERY

TREASURE—*something of great value; hoarded wealth; to cherish or store*

Descriptive of:
Storage cities............Ex 1:11
Storehouses 1Kin 7:51
Places for storing archives.Ezra 5:17
Offering boxes ....Luke 21:1

Figurative of:
Earth's productive capacity ....Ps 17:14
Wisdom ....Prov 2:4
People of God ....Ex 19:5
Man's spiritual possibilities ....Matt 12:35
New life in Christ 2Cor 4:6, 7
Christ as the divine depository ....Col 2:3, 9
Future rewards ....Matt 6:19, 20

[*also* TREASURED, TREASURES, TREASUREST]
open unto thee his good *t* .....Deut 28:12
sealed up among my *t*? ....Deut 32:34
he took away the *t* of the 1Kin 14:26
the *t* of the king's house 1Kin 14:26
in the *t* of the house of 1Kin 15:18
and the *t* of the king's 1Kin 15:18
the *t* of the house of the 2Kin 12:18
the *t* of the king's house 2Kin 16:8
all that was found in his *t* 2Kin 20:13
all the *t* of the house of.......2Kin 24:13
the *t* of the king's house 2Kin 24:13
over the *t* of the house of 1Chr 26:22
were over all the *t* of the 1Chr 26:26
among the *t* of the house 2Chr 5:1
took away the *t* of the 2Chr 12:9
the *t* of the king's house 2Chr 12:9
the *t* of the king's house 2Chr 25:24
the *t* of the house of the 2Chr 36:18
unto the *t* of the work ....Ezra 2:69
gave to the *t* a thousand ......Neh 7:70
chambers, into the *t* house ....Neh 10:38
the chambers for the *t* ....Neh 12:44
into the *t* of the snow.........Job 38:22
thou seen the *t* of the.........Job 38:22
Israel for his peculiar *t*.........Ps 135:4
and I will fill their *t* ....Prov 8:21
T of wickedness profit ....Prov 10:2
the righteous is much *t*........Prov 15:6
There is *t* to be desired ....Prov 21:20
the peculiar *t* of kings.........Eccl 2:8
is there any end of their *t* .....Is 2:7
shall not be *t* nor laid up......Is 23:18
their *t* upon the bunches ......Is 30:6
fear of the Lord is his *t* ....Is 33:6
there is nothing among my *t*...Is 39:4
forth the wind out of his *t*....Jer 10:13
and all thy *t* to the spoil ......Jer 17:3
we have *t* in the field, of......Jer 41:8
trusted in her *t*, saying ....Jer 49:4
abundant in *t*, thine end ....Jer 51:13
they have taken the *t* and .....Ezek 22:25
gold and silver into thy *t* .....Ezek 28:4
vessels into the *t* house of.....Dan 1:2
power over the *t* of gold ......Dan 11:43
spoil the *t* of all pleasant ......Hos 13:15
yet the *t* of wickedness.........Mic 6:10
they had opened their *t* ....Matt 2:11
where your *t* is, there ....Matt 6:21
heaven is like unto *t* hid ......Matt 13:44
and thou shalt have *t* in.......Matt 19:21
and thou shalt have *t* in.......Mark 10:21
good *t* of his heart............Luke 6:45
he that layeth up *t* for ....Luke 12:21
where your *t* is, there will .....Luke 12:34
shalt have *t* in heaven.........Luke 18:22
t up unto thyself wrath........Rom 2:5
riches than the *t* in Egypt .....Heb 11:26
heaped *t* together for the......James 5:3

TREASURER—*a custodian of funds*

Under:
David, Ahijah...........1Chr 26:20
Solomon, Jehiel 1Chr 29:7, 8
Hezekiah, Shebna ....Is 22:15
Cyrus, Mithredath ....Ezra 1:8
Candace, the Ethiopian eunuch ....Acts 8:27
At Corinth, Erastus .....Rom 16:23

[*also* TREASURERS]
the *t* which are beyond the ....Ezra 7:21
And I made *t* over the ....Neh 13:13
the *t*, the counselors ....Dan 3:2

TREASURY—*a place where items of worth are kept*

[*also* TREASURIES]
into the *t* of the Lord ....Josh 6:19
and *t* of the house of God 1Chr 9:26
and of the *t* thereof...........1Chr 28:11
the *t* of the house of God 1Chr 28:12
t of the dedicated things 1Chr 28:12
made himself *t* for silver 2Chr 32:27
wine and the oil unto the *t* ....Neh 13:12
made treasurer over the *t* .....Neh 13:13
bring it into the king's *t*.......Esth 3:9
the wind out of his *t*..........Ps 135:7
of the king under the *t*.........Jer 38:11
to put them into the *t*.........Matt 27:6
sat over against the *t* ....Mark 12:41
cast money into the *t* ....Mark 12:41
which have cast into the *t* .....Mark 12:43
spake Jesus in the *t*...........John 8:20

TREATISE—*a systematic written account*
The former *t* have I made .....Acts 1:1

TREE—*a woody perennial plant used for fruit, shade, or wood*

Characteristics of:
Created by God ....Gen 1:11, 12
Of fixed varieties ....Gen 1:12, 29
Can be grafted ....Rom 11:24
Subject to God's judgments ....Hab 2:17, 19

Used for:
Shade ....Gen 18:4
Burial sites..............Gen 35:8
Food ....Deut 20:19, 20
Cross ....Acts 5:30
Buildings 1Kin 5:10
Idolatry.................Is 44:14, 17
Fuel....................Is 44:15, 16, 19

List of, in Bible:
Aloe ....Ps 45:8
Ash ....Is 44:14
Bay ....Ps 37:35
Cedar 1Kin 10:27
Chestnut ....Ezek 31:8
Cypress ....Is 44:14
Elm ....Hos 4:13
Fig......................Deut 8:8
Fir 2Sam 6:5
Hazel ....Gen 30:37
Juniper 1Kin 19:4, 5
Mulberry 2Sam 5:23
Myrtle...................Is 41:19
Oak ....Is 1:30
Olive ....Judg 9:9
Palm ....Ex 15:27
Pomegranate ....Deut 8:8
Poplar...................Hos 4:13
Shittim ....Ex 36:20
Sycamore ....Amos 7:14
Willow ....Is 44:4

Figurative of:
Righteous...............Ps 1:1-3
Believer's life ....Prov 11:30
Wisdom ....Prov 3:18
Basic character ....Matt 7:17-19
Continued prosperity ....Is 65:22
Judgment ....Luke 23:31
Eternal life ....Rev 22:14
Covenant ....Rom 11:24

[*also* TREES]
every *t* of the garden thou ....Gen 2:16
of the *t* of the knowledge .....Gen 2:17
ye shall not eat of every *t* .....Gen 3:1
eat of the fruit of the *t*.........Gen 3:2
saw that the *t* was good ....Gen 3:6
a *t* to be desired to make .....Gen 3:6
she gave me of the *t*, and .....Gen 3:12
take also of the *t* of life ....Gen 3:22
stood by them under the *t*.....Gen 18:8

all the *t* that were in the ...... Gen 23:17
shall hang thee on a *t* .... Gen 40:19
brake every *t* of the field ...... Ex 9:25
all the fruit of the *t* which ...... Ex 10:15
not any green thing in the *t* ... Ex 10:15
the Lord showed him a *t* ...... Ex 15:25
planted all manner of *t* for .... Lev 19:23
the boughs of goodly *t* .... Lev 23:40
branches of palm *t* .... Lev 23:40
and the boughs of thick *t* ..... Lev 23:40
the *t* of the land yield .... Lev 26:20
fruit of the *t*, is the Lord's .... Lev 27:30
made of the vine *t* .... Num 6:4
t of lign aloes which the .... Num 24:6
cedar *t* beside the waters ...... Num 24:6
vineyards and olive *t* .... Deut 6:11
and under every green *t* .... Deut 12:2
thee a grove of any *t* near ..... Deut 16:21
the axe to cut down the *t* ..... Deut 19:5
and thou hang him on a *t* .... Deut 21:22
thee in the way in any *t* .... Deut 22:6
olive *t* throughout all thy ...... Deut 28:40
Jericho, the city of palm *t* .... Deut 34:3
king of Ai he hanged on a *t* ... Josh 8:29
carcase down from the *t* ...... Josh 8:29
and hanged them on five *t* .... Josh 10:26
hanging upon the *t* until ...... Josh 10:26
out of the city of palm *t* ...... Judg 1:16
dwelt under the palm *t* .... Judg 4:5
t went forth on a time to ...... Judg 9:8
But the olive *t* said unto ...... Judg 9:9
the *t* said to the fig *t* .... Judg 9:10
But the fig *t* said unto .... Judg 9:11
said the *t* unto the vine .... Judg 9:12
all the *t* unto the bramble ..... Judg 9:14
down a bough from the *t* ...... Judg 9:48
under a pomegranate *t* 1Sam 14:2
buried them under a *t* at 1Sam 31:13
cedar *t*, and carpenters 2Sam 5:11
the tops of the mulberry *t* 2Sam 5:24
vine and under his fig *t* 1Kin 4:25
spake of *t*, from the cedar 1Kin 4:33
cedar *t* out of Lebanon 1Kin 5:6
two cherubim of olive *t* 1Kin 6:23
of cherubim and palm *t* 1Kin 6:29
doors also were of olive *t* 1Kin 6:32
of cherubim and palm *t* 1Kin 6:32
and upon the palm *t* 1Kin 6:32
two doors were of fir *t* 1Kin 6:34
cherubim and palm *t* 1Kin 6:35
Solomon with cedar *t* and fir *t* . 1Kin 9:11
of the almug *t* pillars 1Kin 10:12
came no such almug *t*, nor 1Kin 10:12
and under every green *t* 1Kin 14:23
shall fell every good *t* 2Kin 3:19
and felled all the good *t* 2Kin 3:25
and under every green *t* 2Kin 17:10
cut down the tall cedar *t* 2Kin 19:23
and the choice fir *t* thereof 2Kin 19:23
against the mulberry *t* 1Chr 14:14
the *t* of the wood sing 1Chr 16:33
Also cedar *t* in abundance 1Chr 22:4
olive *t* and they sycamore *t* 1Chr 27:28
and cedar *t* made he as 2Chr 1:15
the sycamore *t* that are in 2Chr 1:15
house he cieled with fir *t* 2Chr 3:5
set thereon palm *t* and 2Chr 3:5
of the algum *t* terraces 2Chr 9:11
cedar *t* made he as the 2Chr 9:27
he as the sycamore *t* that 2Chr 9:27
to bring cedar *t* from .... Ezra 3:7
and branches of thick *t* .... Neh 8:15
of all fruit of all *t* .... Neh 10:35
were both hanged on a *t* ...... Esth 2:23
For there is hope of a *t* .... Job 14:7
shall be broken as a *t* .... Job 24:20
He lieth under the shady *t* .... Job 40:21
like a green olive *t* in the ..... Ps 52:8
up axes upon the thick *t* ...... Ps 74:5
flourish like the palm *t* .... Ps 92:12
the *t* of the wood rejoice ...... Ps 96:12
the fir *t* are her house .... Ps 104:17
brake the *t* of their coasts ..... Ps 105:33
cometh, it is a *t* of life .... Prov 13:12
Whoso keepeth the fig *t* ...... Prov 27:18
I planted *t* in them of all ...... Eccl 2:5
the *t* fall toward the south ..... Eccl 11:3
place where the *t* falleth ...... Eccl 11:3
As the apple *t* among the *t* .... Song 2:3
stature is like to a palm *t* ..... Song 7:7
thee up under the apple *t* ..... Song 8:5
as a teil *t*, and as an oak ...... Is 6:13
as the *t* of the wood are ...... Is 7:2
the fir *t* rejoice at thee .... Is 14:8
the shaking of an olive *t* ...... Is 24:13
and every one of his fig *t* ..... Is 36:16
and the choice fir *t* thereof .... Is 37:24
a *t* that will not rot .... Is 40:20
O forest, and every *t* .... Is 44:23
all the *t* of the field shall ...... Is 55:12
shall come up the fir *t* .... Is 55:13
shall come up the myrtle *t* .... Is 55:13
idols under every green *t* ...... Is 57:5
come unto thee, the fir *t* ...... Is 60:13
the pine *t*, and the box .... Is 60:13
behind one *t* in the midst ..... Is 66:17
I see a rod of an almond *t* .... Jer 1:11
and under every green *t* .... Jer 3:6
up thy vines and thy fig *t* ..... Jer 5:17
upon the *t* of the field .... Jer 7:20
nor figs on the fig *t*, and ...... Jer 8:13
are upright as the palm *t* ...... Jer 10:5
Let us destroy the *t* with ...... Jer 11:19
under every green *t*, and ...... Ezek 6:13
which is among the *t* of .... Ezek 15:2
As the vine *t* among the ...... Ezek 15:6
t of the field shall know .... Ezek 17:24
brought down the high *t* ...... Ezek 17:24
have exalted the low *t*, ... Ezek 17:24
have dried up the green *t* ..... Ezek 17:24
have made the dry *t* .... Ezek 17:24
rod of my son, as every *t* ..... Ezek 21:10
boards of fir *t* of Senir .... Ezek 27:5
above all the *t* of the field .... Ezek 31:5
so that all the *t* of Eden ...... Ezek 31:9
of all the *t* by the waters ...... Ezek 31:14
neither their *t* stand up in ..... Ezek 31:14
the *t* of Eden, the choice ...... Ezek 31:16
among the *t* of Eden? .... Ezek 31:18
down with the *t* of Eden ...... Ezek 31:18
t of the field shall yield .... Ezek 34:27
arches, and their palm *t* .... Ezek 40:22
palm *t* were upon the .... Ezek 40:31
a palm *t* was between a .... Ezek 41:18
toward the palm *t* on the ...... Ezek 41:19
cherubim and palm *t* .... Ezek 41:20
windows and palm *t* on the .... Ezek 41:26
shall grow all *t* for meat ...... Ezek 47:12
Hew down the *t*, and cut ...... Dan 4:14
Hew the *t* down, and destroy .. Dan 4:23
her vines and her fig *t* .... Hos 2:12
firstripe in the fig *t* .... Hos 9:10
I am like a green fir *t* .... Hos 14:8
and barked my fig *t* .... Joel 1:7
and the fig *t* languisheth ...... Joel 1:12
pomegranate *t*, the palm *t* ..... Joel 1:12
the apple *t*, even all the .... Joel 1:12
even all the *t* of the field ...... Joel 1:12
for the *t* beareth her fruit ..... Joel 2:22
the fig *t* and the vine do ...... Joel 2:22
vineyards and your fig *t* .... Amos 4:9
vine and under his fig *t* .... Mic 4:4
the fir *t* shall be terribly .... Nah 2:3
the fig *t* shall not blossom ..... Hab 3:17
stood among the myrtle *t* ..... Zech 1:8
stood among the myrtle *t* ..... Zech 1:11
vine and under the fig *t* .... Zech 3:10
What are these two olive *t* .... Zech 4:11
Howl, fir *t*; for the cedar ...... Zech 11:2
laid unto the root of the *t* ..... Matt 3:10
every *t* which bringeth .... Matt 3:10
Either make the *t* good .... Matt 12:33
or else make the *t* corrupt ..... Matt 12:33
t is known by his fruit .... Matt 12:33
herbs, and becometh a *t* ...... Matt 13:32
when he saw a fig *t* in the ..... Matt 21:19
the fig *t* withered away .... Matt 21:19
which is done to the fig *t* ..... Matt 21:21
I see men as *t*, walking .... Mark 8:24
seeing a fig *t* afar off .... Mark 11:13
fig *t* which thou cursedst is .... Mark 11:21
learn a parable of the fig *t* .... Mark 13:28
laid unto the root of the *t* ..... Luke 3:9
every *t* therefore which .... Luke 3:9
good *t* bringeth not forth ...... Luke 6:43
corrupt *t* bring forth good ..... Luke 6:43
man had a fig *t* planted .... Luke 13:6
and waxed a great *t* .... Luke 13:19
up into a sycamore *t* to .... Luke 19:4
Behold the fig *t*, and all .... Luke 21:29
I saw thee under the fig *t* ..... John 1:50
Took branches of palm *t* ...... John 12:13
slew and hanged on a *t* .... Acts 10:39
took him down from the *t* ..... Acts 13:29
thou, being a wild olive *t* ..... Rom 11:17
and fatness of the olive *t* ...... Rom 11:17
one that hangeth on a *t* .... Gal 3:13
Can the fig *t*, my brethren .... James 3:12
in his own body on the *t* 1Pet 2:24
t whose fruit withereth .... Jude 12
I give to eat of the *t* .... Rev 2:7
on the sea, nor on any *t* .... Rev 7:1
These are the two olive *t* ...... Rev 11:4

TREE OF LIFE—*so-called because its fruit gives immortality to the one who eats it*

In Eden .... Gen 2:9
In New Jerusalem .... Rev 22:1, 2

TREMBLE—*to shake*

Expressive of:

Deep concern .... Gen 27:33
Fear .... Mark 16:8
Filial trust .... Is 66:2, 5
Apprehension 1Sam 16:4
Infirmity .... Eccl 12:3
Obedience .... Phil 2:12

Applied to:

People .... Dan 6:26
Earth .... Ps 97:4
Nations .... Is 64:2
Heart .... Deut 28:65
Flesh .... Ps 119:120
Servants .... Eph 6:5
Christians 1Cor 2:3

Caused by:

Physical change .... Luke 8:47
Earthquake .... Acts 16:29

[*also* TREMBLED, TREMBLETH, TREMBLING]

t shall take hold upon .... Ex 15:15
people..in the camp *t* .... Ex 19:16
shall *t*, and be in anguish ...... Deut 2:25
earth *t*, and the heavens ...... Judg 5:4
his heart *t* for the ark of 1Sam 4:13
the people followed him *t* 1Sam 13:7
there was *t* in the host 1Sam 14:15
the spoilers, they also *t* 1Sam 14:15
so it was a very great *t* 1Sam 14:15
and his heart greatly *t* 1Sam 28:5
the earth shook and *t* 2Sam 22:8
every one that *t* at the .... Ezra 9:4
those that *t* at the .... Ezra 10:3
Fear came upon me, and *t* .... Job 4:14
and the pillars thereof *t* .... Job 9:6
At this also my heart *t* .... Job 37:1
fear, and rejoice with *t* .... Ps 2:11
the earth shook and *t* .... Ps 18:7
hast made the earth to *t* ...... Ps 60:2
on the earth, and it *t* .... Ps 104:32
T, thou earth, at the .... Ps 114:7
the hills did *t*, and their .... Is 5:25
that made the earth to *t* .... Is 14:16
T, ye women that are at ...... Is 32:11
the dregs of the cup of *t* ...... Is 51:17
mountains, and, lo, they *t* ..... Jer 4:24
ye not *t* at my presence .... Jer 5:22
wrath the earth shall *t* .... Jer 10:10
We have heard a voice of *t* .... Jer 30:5
they shall fear and *t* for all .... Jer 33:9
drink thy water with *t* .... Ezek 12:18
shall *t* at every moment .... Ezek 26:16
shall *t* at every moment .... Ezek 32:10
t and feared before him .... Dan 5:19
word unto me, I stood *t* .... Dan 10:11
children shall *t* from the ...... Hos 11:10

T

When Ephraim spake *t*, he ....Hos 13:1
inhabitants of the land *t*.....Joel 2:1
Shall not the land *t* for.......Amos 8:8
of the land of Midian did *t*....Hab 3:7
saw thee, and they *t*..........Hab 3:10
When I heard, my belly *t*.....Hab 3:16
I *t* in myself, that I might.....Hab 3:16
make Jerusalem a cup of *t*....Zech 12:2
the woman fearing and *t*......Mark 5:33
they *t* and were amazed.......Mark 16:8
Then Moses *t*, and durst......Acts 7:32
he *t* and astonished said.......Acts 9:6
Felix *t*, and answered, Go.....Acts 24:25
with fear and *t* ye received....2Cor 7:15
devils also believe, and *t*......James 2:19

TRENCH—*a ditch*
he came to the *t*, as the.......1Sam 17:20
lay sleeping within the *t*.......1Sam 26:7
city, and it stood in the *t*.......2Sam 20:15
the water that was in the *t*....1Kin 18:38
enemies shall cast a *t*.........Luke 19:43

TRESPASS—*to transgress; transgression*

[*also* TRESPASSED, TRESPASSES, TRESPASSING]
What is my *t*? what is my .....Gen 31:36
the *t* of thy brethren, and .....Gen 50:17
forgive the *t* of thy ....Gen 50:17
For all manner of *t*...........Ex 22:9
shall bring his *t* offering.......Lev 5:6
If a soul commit a *t*, and......Lev 5:15
shall bring for his *t* unto......Lev 5:15
sanctuary, for a *t* offering.....Lev 5:15
for a *t* offering, unto the......Lev 5:18
t against the Lord............Lev 5:19
commit a *t* against the Lord...Lev 6:2
bring his *t* offering unto.......Lev 6:6
for a *t* offering unto the.......Lev 6:6
he hath done in *t* therein......Lev 6:7
the law of the *t* offering.......Lev 7:1
Lord: it is a *t* offering........Lev 7:5
of the *t* offering, and of.......Lev 7:37
offer him for a *t* offering......Lev 14:12
the blood of the *t* offering.....Lev 14:14
one lamb for a *t* offering......Lev 14:21
the lamb of the *t* offering.....Lev 14:25
the blood of the *t* offering.....Lev 14:25
the blood of the *t* offering.....Lev 14:28
bring his *t* offering unto.......Lev 19:21
evan a ram for a *t* offering....Lev 19:21
to bear the iniquity of *t*.......Lev 22:16
to do a *t* against the Lord.....Num 5:6
against whom he hath *t*........Num 5:7
kinsman to recompense the *t*...Num 5:8
t be recompensed unto the....Num 5:8
have done *t* against her.......Num 5:27
every *t* offering of theirs......Num 18:9
Because ye *t* against me.......Deut 32:51
of Israel committed a *t* in.....Josh 7:1
commit a *t* in the accursed....Josh 22:20
return him a *t* offering........1Sam 6:3
return him for a *t* offering.....1Sam 6:8
forgive the *t* of thine..........1Sam 25:28
any man *t* against his.........1Kin 8:31
t money and sin money.........2Kin 12:16
this do, and ye shall not *t*......2Chr 19:10
Jerusalem for this their *t*......2Chr 24:18
to our sins and to our *t*.......2Chr 28:13
our *t* is great, and there.......2Chr 28:13
he *t* yet more against the......2Chr 28:22
t against the Lord God.........2Chr 30:7
all his sins, and his *t*..........2Chr 33:19
we been in a great *t* unto.....Ezra 9:7
to increase the *t* of Israel.....Ezra 10:10
as goeth on still in his *t*.......Ps 68:21
sinneth against me by *t*.......Ezek 14:13
in his *t* that he hath..........Ezek 18:24
because they *t* against me.....Ezek 39:23
their *t* whereby they have *t*....Ezek 39:26
offering and the *t* offering.....Ezek 40:39
offering, and the *t* offering....Ezek 44:29
their *t* that they have *t*.......Dan 9:7
and *t* against my law..........Hos 8:1
if ye forgive men their *t*.......Matt 6:14
forgive not men their *t*........Matt 6:15
Father forgive your *t*..........Matt 6:15
brother shall *t* against.........Matt 18:15
may forgive you your *t*........Mark 11:25
brother *t* against thee........Luke 17:3
if he *t* against thee seven......Luke 17:4

TRIAL—*a hardship or temptation that tests one's faith*

Characteristics of:
Some very severe........2Cor 1:8-10
Cause of, sometimes unknown ....Job 1:7-22
Sometimes physical 2Cor 12:7-10
Enduarble 1Cor 10:13
Rewardable ....Matt 5:10-12

Design of, to:
Test faith ....Gen 22:1-18
Purify faith ....Mal 3:3, 4 1Pet 1:6-9
Increase patience ....James 1:3, 4, 12
Bring us to a better place.Ps 66:10-12
Chasten us ....Is 48:10
Glorify God 1Pet 4:12-16

[*also* TRIALS]
at the *t* of the innocent ....Job 9:23
Because it is a *t*, and what ....Ezek 21:13
in a great *t* of affliction 2Cor 8:2
had *t* of cruel mockings ....Heb 11:36

TRIBE—*a large clan*

[*also* TRIBES]
to the twelve *t* of Israel ....Ex 24:4
according to the twelve *t*......Ex 28:21
the son of Hur, of the *t*.......Ex 31:2
Ahisamach, of the *t* of Dan ...Ex 31:6
of Hur, of the *t* of Judah .....Ex 35:30
Ahisamach, of the *t* of Dan ...Ex 35:34
of Hur, of the *t* of Judah .....Ex 38:22
of the *t* of Dan..............Ex 38:23
of Dibri, of the *t* of Dan ....Lev 24:11
shall be a man of every *t*......Num 1:4
of the *t* of Reuben; Elizur.....Num 1:5
of the *t* of their fathers ....Num 1:16
even of the *t* of Reuben.......Num 1:21
even of the *t* of Simeon ....Num 1:23
even of the *t* of Gad..........Num 1:25
even of the *t* of Judah ....Num 1:27
even of the *t* of Issachar ......Num 1:29
even of the *t* of Zebulum ......Num 1:31
even of the *t* of Ephraim......Num 1:33
even of the *t* of Manasseh.....Num 1:35
even of the *t* of Benjamin .....Num 1:37
even of the *t* of Dan..........Num 1:39
even of the *t* of Asher ....Num 1:41
even of the *t* of Naphtali ......Num 1:43
Levites after the *t* of their.....Num 1:47
not number the *t* of Levi......Num 1:49
Cut ye not off the *t* of the ....Num 4:18
were the princes of the *t* .....Num 7:2
also of the *t* of Levi ....Num 18:2
t of thy father, bring thou .....Num 18:2
tents according to their *t* ......Num 24:2
names of the *t* of their........Num 26:55
unto the heads of the *t*.........Num 30:1
Of every *t* a thousand.........Num 31:4
all the *t* of Israel ....Num 31:4
a thousand of every *t* ....Num 31:5
a thousand of every *t* ....Num 31:6
chief fathers of the *t* of ....Num 32:28
to the *t* of your fathers........Num 33:54
to give unto the nine *t*........Num 34:13
The two *t* and the half *t*.......Num 34:15
of the sons of the other *t* .....Num 36:3
to the inheritance of the *t*.....Num 36:3
the inheritance of the *t*........Num 36:4
of the *t* of our fathers.........Num 36:4
t of the sons of Joseph ....Num 36:5
t of their father shall they .....Num 36:6
Israel remove from *t* to *t*......Num 36:7
of the *t* of his fathers ....Num 36:7
in any *t* of the children ....Num 36:8
of the family of the *t* ....Num 36:8
from one *t* to another *t* ....Num 36:9
every one of the *t* of the ......Num 36:9
the *t* of the family of their ....Num 36:12
and known among your *t*......Deut 1:13
the chief of your *t*, wise.......Deut 1:15
and officers among your *t*.....Deut 1:15
men of you, one of a *t*........Deut 1:23
all the heads of your *t* ....Deut 5:23
choose out of all your *t* ....Deut 12:5
choose in one of thy *t* ....Deut 12:14
thee, throughout thy *t* ....Deut 16:18
chosen him out of all thy *t* ....Deut 18:5
captains of your *t*, your ....Deut 29:10
or woman, or family, or *t* .....Deut 29:18
out of all the *t* of Israel ....Deut 29:21
all the elders of your *t* ....Deut 31:28
t of Israel were gathered ....Deut 33:5
men out of the *t* of Israel .....Josh 3:12
out of every *t* a man..........Josh 3:12
out of every *t* a man..........Josh 4:2
out of every *t* a man..........Josh 4:4
to the number of the *t* ....Josh 4:5
the number of the *t*...........Josh 4:8
according to your *t* ....Josh 7:14
that the *t* which the Lord .....Josh 7:14
brought Israel by their *t*.......Josh 7:16
their divisions by their *t*.......Josh 11:23
gave unto the *t* of Israel ......Josh 12:7
inheritance unto the nine *t* ....Josh 13:7
the fathers of the *t* of.........Josh 14:1
nine *t*, and for the half *t* ......Josh 14:2
the inheritance of two *t* ....Josh 14:3
a half *t* on the other side......Josh 14:3
of Joseph were two *t* ....Josh 14:4
there remained..seven *t* ....Josh 18:2
the fathers of the *t* of.........Josh 19:51
the fathers of the *t* of.........Josh 21:1
cities out of those two *t* ....Josh 21:16
all the *t* of Israel ....Josh 22:14
an inheritance for your *t* ......Josh 23:4
gathered all the *t* of Israel.....Josh 24:1
unto them among the *t*........Judg 18:1
be a priest unto a *t* and a .....Judg 18:19
priests to the *t* of Dan ....Judg 18:30
even of all the *t* of Israel......Judg 20:2
throughout all the *t* of ....Judg 20:10
t of Israel sent men...........Judg 20:12
all the *t* of Benjamin ....Judg 20:12
one *t* lacking in Israel?........Judg 21:3
among all the *t* of Israel ......Judg 21:5
There is one *t* cut off ....Judg 21:6
is there of the *t* of Israel .....Judg 21:8
a breach in the *t* of Israel .....Judg 21:15
a *t* be not destroyed out of....Judg 21:17
every man to his *t* and to .....Judg 21:24
out of all the *t* of Israel 1Sam 2:28
smallest of the *t* of Israel?.....1Sam 9:21
of the *t* of Benjamin?..........1Sam 9:21
before the Lord by your *t* 1Sam 10:19
all the *t* of Israel to come 1Sam 10:20
t of Benjamin was taken 1Sam 10:20
caused the *t* of Benjamin......1Sam 10:21
made the head of the *t*.......1Sam 15:17
came all the *t* of Israel to 2Sam 5:1
with any of the *t* of Israel 2Sam 7:7
is of one of the *t* of Israel.....2Sam 15:2
all the *t* of Israel 2Sam 15:10
all the *t* of Israel 2Sam 19:9
through all the *t* of Israel 2Sam 24:2
son of the *t* of Naphtali 1Kin 7:14
and all the heads of the *t* 1Kin 8:1
will give one *t* to thy son......1Kin 11:13
will give ten *t* to thee 1Kin 11:31
have one *t* for my servant 1Kin 11:32
it unto thee, even ten *t* 1Kin 11:35
his son will I give one *t* 1Kin 11:36
but the *t* of Judah only 1Kin 12:20
with the *t* of Benjamin 1Kin 12:21
the *t* of the sons of Jacob 1Kin 18:31
none left but the *t* of Judah ...2Kin 17:18
out of all *t* of Israel 2Kin 21:7
over the *t* of Israel 1Chr 27:16
Israel..princes of the *t* 1Chr 28:1
and all the heads of the *t* 2Chr 5:2
out of all the *t* of Israel 2Chr 11:16
before all the *t* of Israel.......2Chr 33:7
number of the *t* of Israel ......Ezra 6:17

t of Israel to dwell in . . . . Ps 78:55
the *t* go up, the *t* of the . . . . . . Ps 122:4
that are the stay of the *t* . . . . . Is 19:13
the *t* of thine inheritance . . . . . Is 63:17
the *t* of Israel his fellows . . . . . Ezek 37:19
to the twelve *t* of Israel . . . . . . Ezek 47:13
you among the *t* of Israel . . . . . Ezek 47:22
in what *t* the stranger . . . . Ezek 47:23
it out of all the *t* of Israel . . . . Ezek 48:19
by lot unto the *t* of Israel . . . . . Ezek 48:29
among the *t* of Israel have . . . . Hos 5:9
to the oaths of the *t* . . . . Hab 3:9
as of all the *t* of Israel . . . . Zech 9:1
the twelve *t* of Israel . . . . Matt 19:28
Phanuel, of the *t* of Asher . . . . Luke 2:36
the twelve *t* of Israel . . . . Luke 22:30
a man of the *t* of Benjamin . . . Acts 13:21
promise our twelve *t* . . . . Acts 26:7
of the *t* of Benjamin . . . . Rom 11:1
of the *t* of Benjamin . . . . Phil 3:5
pertaineth to another *t* . . . . Heb 7:13
of which *t* Moses spake . . . . Heb 7:14
the Lion of the *t* of Judah . . . . . Rev 5:5
all the *t* of the children . . . . . . Rev 7:4
Of the *t* of Judah were . . . . Rev 7:5
Of the *t* of Reuben were . . . . . . Rev 7:5
Of the *t* of Gad were sealed . . . Rev 7:5
Of the *t* of Asher were sealed . Rev 7:6
Of the *t* of Naphtali were . . . . . Rev 7:6
Of the *t* of Manasseh were . . . . Rev 7:6
Of the *t* of Simeon were . . . . . . Rev 7:7
Of the *t* of Levi were . . . . Rev 7:7
Of the *t* of Issachar . . . . Rev 7:7
Of the *t* of Zebulun were . . . . . Rev 7:8
Of the *t* of Joseph were . . . . Rev 7:8
Of the *t* of Benjamin were . . . . Rev 7:8
names of the twelve *t* of the . . . Rev 21:12

TRIBES OF ISRAEL—*the families that descended from each of Jacob's twelve sons*
Twelve in number . . . . Gen 49:28
Descended from Jacob's sons . . . . Gen 35:22-26
Jacob forecasted future of. Gen 49:3-27
Moses foretold future of. . Deut 33:6-35
Numbered . . . . Num 1:44-46
Camped by standards . . . . Num 2:2-31
Canaan divided among . . . Josh 15-17
Names of, engraven . . . . . Ex 39:14
United until Rehoboam's rebellion 1Kin 12:16-20
Returned after exile . . . . . Ezra 8:35
Typical of Christians . . . . . James 1:1

TRIBULATION—*state or time of great affliction*
Descriptive of:
National distress . . . . Deut 4:30
Afflictions 1Sam 10:19
Persecutions 1Thess 3:4
Severe testings . . . . Rev 2:10, 22
Christian's attitude toward:
Must expect . . . . Acts 14:22
Glory in . . . . Rom 5:3
Overcome . . . . Rom 8:35-37
Patient in . . . . Rom 12:12
Joyful in 2Cor 7:4
Faint not at . . . . Eph 3:13

[*also* TRIBULATIONS]
you in the time of your *t* . . . . . . Judg 10:14
deliver me out of all *t* 1Sam 26:24
for when *t* or persecution . . . . . Matt 13:21
after the *t* of those days . . . . . . Matt 24:29
after that *t*, the sun . . . . Mark 13:24
world ye shall have *t* . . . . John 16:33
T and anguish upon every . . . . . Rom 2:9
comforteth us in all our *t* 2Cor 1:4
persecutions and *t* that ye 2Thess 1:4
t to them that trouble your 2Thess 1:6
brother, and companion in *t* . . . Rev 1:9
thy works, and *t*, and . . . . Rev 2:9
which came out of great *t* . . . . . Rev 7:14

TRIBUTARY—*one who pays tribute money*
[*also* TRIBUTARIES]
shall be *t* unto thee . . . . Deut 20:11
among them and became *t* . . . . Judg 1:30
Beth-anath became *t* unto . . . . . Judg 1:33
so that they became *t* . . . . Judg 1:35
how is she become *t*! . . . . Lam 1:1

TRIBUTE—*a tax imposed on a subjugated nation*
Israelites 2Kin 23:33
Christ settles question concerning . . . . Matt 22:17-21
Paul's admonitons concerning . . . . Rom 13:6, 7

became a servant unto *t* . . . . Gen 49:15
levy a *t* unto the Lord of . . . . . . Num 31:28
Lord's *t* was threescore . . . . Num 31:38
Lord's *t* was thirty and . . . . Num 31:40
a *t* of a freewill offering . . . . . . Deut 16:10
this day, and serve under *t* . . . . Josh 16:10
put the Canaanites to *t* . . . . Judg 1:28
Adoram was over the *t* 2Sam 20:24
of Abda was over the *t* 1Kin 4:6
who was over the *t* 1Kin 12:18
put the land to a *t* of 2Kin 23:33
make to pay *t* until this day . . . 2Chr 8:8
that was over the *t* 2Chr 10:18
will they not pay toll, *t*, and . . . Ezra 4:13
even of the *t* beyond the . . . . . . Ezra 6:8
money for the king's *t* . . . . Neh 5:4
laid a *t* upon the land . . . . Esth 10:1
slothful shall be under *t* . . . . . . Prov 12:24
Is it lawful to give *t* to . . . . Mark 12:14
to give *t* unto Caesar . . . . Luke 20:22
forbidding to give *t* to . . . . Luke 23:2
for this cause pay ye *t* . . . . Rom 13:6

TRIBUTE MONEY—*the Temple tax*
Levied yearly upon all Jews . . . . Matt 17:24-27; Matt 22:17-21

TRICKERY—*use of guile or deceit*
By Gibeonites . . . . Josh 9:3-6
By Saul 1Sam 28:7-10
By Amnon 2Sam 13:1-15
Christians, beware of . . . . Eph 4:14

TRICKLETH—*falling in drops*
Mine eye *t* down, and . . . . Lam 3:49

TRIED, TRIEST, TRIETH—*See* TRY

TRIFLES—*things of slight importance*
Pharisees obsessed by . . . . Matt 23:23-25
Avoidance of, by Christians . . . . Titus 3:9

TRIMMED—*adjusted; cared for*
[*also* TRIMMEST]
his feet, nor *t* his beard 2Sam 19:24
Why *t* thou thy way to . . . . Jer 2:33
arose, and *t* their lamps . . . . Matt 25:7

TRINITY, THE—*God the Father, Son, and Holy Spirit*
Revealed in the Old Testament:
At Creation . . . . Gen 1:1-3, 26
In the personality of the Spirit . . . . Is 40:13; Is 48:16
By:
Divine angel . . . . Judg 13:8-23
Personification of Wisdom . . . . Prov 8:22-31
Threefold "Holy" . . . . . Is 6:3
Aaronic benediction . . . Num 6:24-27
Revealed in the New Testament:
At Christ's baptism . . . . . . Matt 3:16, 17
In:
Christ's teaching . . . . John 14:26; John 15:26
Baptismal formula . . . . . Matt 28:19
Apostolic benediction . . 2Cor 13:14
Apostolic teaching . . . . . Gal 4:4-6

TRIUMPH—*to obtain victory; prevail*
[*also* TRIUMPHED, TRIUMPHING]
for he hath *t* gloriously . . . . Ex 15:1
for he hath *t* gloriously . . . . Ex 15:21
of the uncircumcised *t* 2Sam 1:20
That the *t* of the wicked . . . . . . Job 20:5
let not mine enemies *t* . . . . Ps 25:2
mine enemy doth not *t* . . . . Ps 41:11
God with the voice of *t* . . . . Ps 47:1
t thou because of me . . . . Ps 60:8
I will *t* in the works of . . . . Ps 92:4
long shall the wicked *t*? . . . . Ps 94:3
and to *t* in thy praise . . . . Ps 106:47
over Philistia will I *t* . . . . Ps 108:9

TRIUMPHAL ENTRANCE—*Jesus' entry into Jerusalem in the last week of his earthly ministry*
Prophesied . . . . Zech 9:9
Fulfilled . . . . Matt 21:2-11

TROAS (trō'ăs)—*"penetrated"—an important city on the coast of Mysia*
Paul received vision here . Acts 16:8-11

before tarried for us at *T* . . . . . Acts 20:5
to *T* to preach Christ's 2Cor 2:12
cloke that I left at *T* with 2Tim 4:13

TRODDEN, TRODE—*See* TREAD

TROGYLLIUM (trō-jĭl'ĭ-ŭm)—*"fruit port"—a rocky projection of the ridge of Mycale and a town*
Paul's ship tarried here . . Acts 20:15

TROOP—*group of soldiers*
Place in fortified cities . . . 2Chr 17:2
Come together and camp . Job 19:12
"Daughter of troops" . . . . Mic 5:1

[*also* TROOPS]
Leah said, A *t* cometh . . . . Gen 30:11
a *t* shall overcome him . . . . Gen 49:19
Shall I pursue after this *t*? 1Sam 30:8
Abner and became one *t* 2Sam 2:25
I have run through a *t* 2Sam 22:30
the *t* of the Philistines 2Sam 23:13
The *t* of Tema looked, the . . . . Job 6:19
I have run through a *t* . . . . Ps 18:29
prepare a table for that *t* . . . . . . Is 65:11
assembled themselves by *t* . . . . . Jer 5:7
bring a *t* suddenly upon . . . . Jer 18:22
as *t* of robbers wait for a . . . . . . Hos 6:9
the *t* of robbers spoileth . . . . . . Hos 7:1
founded his *t* in the earth . . . . . Amos 9:6
invade them with his *t* . . . . Hab 3:16

TROPHIMUS (trŏf'ĭ-mŭs)—*"a foster child"*
One of Paul's companions Acts 20:4

with him in the city *T* an . . . . . . Acts 21:29
T have I left at Miletum 2Tim 4:20

TROUBLE—*that which causes concern or distress; to cause concern or distress*
Kinds of:
Physical, of nature . . . . Ps 46:3
Mental . . . . Dan 5:9
Spiritual, of the wicked . . Is 57:20
Spiritual, of the righteous. Ps 77:3
National . . . . Jer 30:7
Domestic . . . . Prov 11:29
Caused by:
Misdeeds of sons . . . . Gen 34:30
Mysterious dream . . . . Dan 2:1, 3
Unexpected news 1Sam 28:21
Sin . . . . Josh 7:25
Evil spirits 1Sam 16:14, 15
Enemies . . . . Ezra 4:4
Physical malady . . . . Job 4:5
God's:
Presence . . . . Job 23:15
Withdrawal . . . . Ps 30:7
Wrath . . . . Ps 78:49
Our sins . . . . Ps 38:4-6
Mouth . . . . Prov 21:23
Angel visitant . . . . Luke 1:12, 29
Wars, etc . . . . Mark 13:7
Trials 2Cor 7:5
Afflicted 2Thess 1:7
God's help to His saints in, to:
Hide . . . . Ps 27:5
Deliver . . . . Ps 50:15
Help . . . . Ps 46:1

T

Attend ....Ps 91:15
Revive ....Ps 138:7

[*also* TROUBLED, TROUBLEDST, TROUBLES, TROUBLEST, TROUBLETH, TROUBLING, TROUBLINGS]

were *t* at his presence ....Gen 45:3
and *t* the host of the ....Ex 14:24
and *t* shall befall them Deut31:17
of Israel a curse, and *t* it ......Josh 6:18
art one of them that *t* me .....Judg 11:35
My father hath *t* the land 1Sam14:29
all the Israelites were *t*.........2Sam 4:1
Art thou he that *t* Israel? 1Kin 18:17
I have not *t* Israel 1Kin 18:18
king of Syria was sore *t* 2Kin 6:11
This day is a day of *t*, and 2Kin 19:3
in my *t* I have prepared 1Chr 22:14
they in their *t* did turn 2Chr 15:4
them, and to *t* them 2Chr 32:18
and in the time of their *t*......Neh 9:27
the wicked cease from *t*.......Job 3:17
was I quiet; yet *t* came.........Job 3:26
Yet man is born unto *t*, as ....Job 5:7
shall deliver thee in six *t* ......Job 5:19
T and anguish shall make .....Job 15:24
should not my spirit be *t*? .....Job 21:4
and sudden fear *t* thee ....Job 22:10
weep for him that was in *t*? ...Job 30:25
the people shall be *t* at ....Job 34:20
against the time of *t* ....Job 38:23
they increased that *t* me ......Ps 3:1
consider my *t* which I ....Ps 9:13
those that *t* me rejoice ....Ps 13:4
far from me; for *t* is near .....Ps 22:11
The *t* of my heart are ....Ps 25:17
thou hast considered my *t* .....Ps 31:7
shalt preserve me from *t* ......Ps 32:7
saved him out of all his *t*......Ps 34:6
deliver him in time of *t* ....Ps 41:1
delivered me out of all *t* ......Ps 54:7
refuge in the day of my *t* .....Ps 59:16
spoken, when I was in *t*.......Ps 66:14
me great and sore *t*...........Ps 71:20
They are not in *t* as other .....Ps 73:5
I am so *t* that I cannot........Ps 77:4
the depths also were *t* ....Ps 77:16
vanity, and their years in *t* ....Ps 78:33
Thou calledst in *t*, and I ......Ps 81:7
and by thy wrath are we *t*......Ps 90:7
I will be with him in *t*; I ......Ps 91:15
unto the Lord in their *t*........Ps 107:6
soul is melted because of *t* ....Ps 107:26
Give us help from *t*: for.......Ps 108:12
T and anguish have ....Ps 119:143
I showed before him my *t*.....Ps 142:2
sake bring my soul out of *t*....Ps 143:11
is delivered out of *t*...........Prov 11:8
he that is cruel *t* his own .....Prov 11:17
revenues of the wicked is *t* ....Prov 15:6
is greedy of gain *t* his own ....Prov 15:27
unfaithful man in time of *t* ....Prov 25:19
wicked is as a *t* fountain ......Prov 25:26
they are a *t* unto me; I am ....Is 1:14
behold at eveningtide *t*........Is 17:14
Lord, in *t* have they ....Is 26:16
are at east; be *t*, ye..........Is 32:11
also in the time of *t* ....Is 33:2
nor save him out of his *t* ......Is 46:7
the former *t* are forgotten .....Is 65:16
in the time of their *t* they .....Jer 2:27
of health, and behold *t*........Jer 8:15
cry unto me for their *t* ....Jer 11:14
of healing, and behold *t*.......Jer 14:19
my bowels are *t* for him.......Jer 31:20
for in the day of *t* they ....Jer 51:2
my bowels are *t*; mine ....Lam 1:20
have heard of my *t* ....Lam 1:21
come, the day of *t* is near .....Ezek 7:7
people of..land shall be *t*......Ezek 7:27
they shall be *t* in their ....Ezek 27:35
t the waters with thy feet .....Ezek 32:2
hoofs of beasts *t* them ....Ezek 32:13
the visions of my head *t* me ...Dan 4:5
thee, and no secret *t* thee .....Dan 4:9
interpretation thereof, *t* ....Dan 4:19
his thoughts *t* him, so ....Dan 5:6
visions of my head *t* me.......Dan 7:15
the wall, even in *t* times ......Dan 9:25
of the north shall *t* him ....Dan 11:44
stronghold in the day of *t* .....Nah 1:7
might in the day of *t*..........Hab 3:16
a day of *t* and distress ....Zeph 1:15
they were *t*, because there ....Zech 10:2
these things, he was *t* ....Matt 2:3
see that ye be not *t*: for........Matt 24:6
Why *t* ye the woman? ....Matt 26:10
why *t* thou the Master ....Mark 5:35
all saw him, and were *t* ....Mark 6:50
shall be famines and *t*.........Mark 13:8
her alone; why *t* ye her? ......Mark 14:6
Lord, *t* not thyself ....Luke 7:6
careful and *t* about many......Luke 10:41
answer and say, *T* me not .....Luke 11:7
because this widow *t* me ......Luke 18:5
the pool, and *t* the water......John 5:4
groaned in the spirit and was *t*.John 11:33
he was *t* in spirit, and.........John 13:21
Let not your heart be *t* ....John 14:27
sentence is, that we *t* not them.Acts 15:19
us have *t* you with words.......Acts 15:24
T not yourselves; for his ......Acts 20:10
shall have *t* in the flesh 1Cor 7:28
them which are in any *t*.......2Cor 1:4
We are *t* on every side........2Cor 4:8
there be some that *t* you ......Gal 1:7
he that *t* you shall bear ....Gal 5:10
henceforth let no man *t* me ...Gal 6:17
to them that *t* you 2Thess 1:6
or be *t*, neither by spirit 2Thess 2:2
Wherein I suffer *t*, as an 2Tim 2:9
of bitterness springing up *t* ....Heb 12:15
their terror, neither be *t* 1Pet 3:14

TROUBLER—*tormenter*
Achar, the *t* of Israel, who 1Chr 2:7

TROUGH—*receptacle containing drinking water for animals*

[*also* TROUGHS]

her pitcher into the *t* ....Gen 24:20
watering *t* when the flocks ....Gen 30:38
filled the *t* to water their ......Ex 2:16

TROW—*to believe; think*
commanded him? I *t* not ......Luke 17:9

TRUCE—*a temporary cessation of warfare*
With good results........2Sam 2:25-31

TRUCEBREAKERS—*violators of agreements*
Characteristic of the last days...................2Tim 3:1, 3

TRUE—*reliable; trustworthy*

Applied to:
God...................John 17:3
Christ ....Rev 3:7, 14
God's:
Word.................John 21:24
Judgments ....Rev 16:7
Believer's heart 2Cor 6:8
Worshipers..............John 4:23

Proof of:
Given by men ....John 5:32
Based upon testimony ...John 8:13-18
Recognized by men......John 10:41

See TRUTH

[*also* TRULY]

deal kindly and *t* with my .....Gen 24:49
we are *t* men, thy servants ....Gen 42:11
we are *t* men, we are no ......Gen 42:31
but that ye are *t* men ....Gen 42:34
but *t* his younger brother......Gen 48:19
But as *t* as I live, all the ......Num 14:21
Thou shalt *t* tithe all the ......Deut 14:22
it be *t*, and the thing ....Deut 17:4
and give me a *t* token ....Josh 2:12
deal kindly and *t* with.........Josh 2:14
if ye have done *t* and ....Judg 9:16
it is *t* that I am thy near ......Ruth 3:12
but *t* as the Lord liveth 1Sam 20:3
God, and thy words be *t* 2Sam 7:28
It was a *t* report that I........1Kin 10:6
It was a *t* report which I 2Chr 9:5
judgments, and *t* laws.........Neh 9:13
For *t* my words shall not ....Job 36:4
judgments of the Lord are *t* ...Ps 19:9
T my soul waiteth upon ....Ps 62:1
O Lord, *t* I am thy servant ....Ps 116:16
that dealt *t* are his delight .....Prov 12:22
A *t* witness delivereth.........Prov 14:25
T the light is sweet, and ......Eccl 11:7
T in vain is salvation..........Jer 3:23
But the Lord is the *t* God .....Jer 10:10
I said, *T* this is a grief ....Jer 10:19
hath executed *t* judgment .....Ezek 18:8
my judgments, to deal *t*.......Ezek 18:9
The thing is *t*, according ......Dan 6:12
and the thing was *t*, but.......Dan 10:1
The harvest *t* is plenteous .....Matt 9:37
T this was the Son of God ....Matt 27:54
we know that thou art *t*.......Mark 12:14
The spirit *t* is ready, but ......Mark 14:38
The harvest *t* is great, but.....Luke 10:2
your trust the *t* riches?........Luke 16:11
teachest the way of God *t*.....Luke 20:21
That was the *t* Light ....John 1:9
to his seal that God is *t*.......John 3:33
in that saidest thou *t*..........John 4:18
herein is that saying *t* ....John 4:37
my witness is not *t* ....John 5:31
giveth you the *t* bread ....John 6:32
sent him, the same is *t*........John 7:18
but he that sent me is *t* ....John 7:28
he that sent me is *t*; and ......John 8:26
I am the *t* vine, and my.......John 15:1
record, and his record is *t* .....John 19:35
knoweth that he saith *t* ....John 19:35
For John *t* baptized with ......Acts 1:5
prison *t* found we shut ....Acts 5:23
it was *t* which was done ....Acts 12:9
But as God is *t*, our word 2Cor 1:18
T the signs of an apostle 2Cor 12:12
and *t* holiness ....Eph 4:24
thee also, *t* yokefellow ....Phil 4:3
whatsoever things are *t*.........Phil 4:8
serve the living and *t* God.....1Thess 1:9
This is a *t* saying, If a 1Tim 3:1
This witness is *t* ....Titus 1:13
they *t* were many priests ......Heb 7:23
and of the *t* tabernacle ....Heb 8:2
are the figures of the *t*........Heb 9:24
draw near with a *t* heart ......Heb 10:22
t our fellowship is with........1John 1:3
the *t* light now shineth 1John 2:8
may know him that is *t* 1John 5:20
we are in him that is *t* 1John 5:20
This is the *t* God, and 1John 5:20
know that our record is *t*......3John 12
O Lord, holy and *t* ....Rev 6:10
just and *t* are thy ways........Rev 15:3
t and righteous are his ....Rev 19:2
are the *t* sayings of God ......Rev 19:9
was called Faithful and *T* .....Rev 19:11
words are *t* and faithful ....Rev 21:5
sayings are faithful and *t* ......Rev 22:6

TRUMPET—*a wind musical instrument*

Features concerning:
Instrument of music 1Chr 13:8
Made of ram's horn .....Josh 6:4

Uses of, in Israel, to:
Signal God's presence....Ex 19:16, 19
Regulate marchings ......Num 10:2, 5, 6
Call assemblies ....Num 10:2, 3, 7
Announce a feast........Lev 23:23-25
Gather the nation ....Judg 3:27
Alert against an enemy ..Neh 4:18, 20
Herald a new king.......1Kin 1:34-41
Hail a religious event 1Chr 13:8
Assist in worship ....Neh 12:35-41

Uses of, at Christ's return, to:
Herald Christ's coming...Matt 24:31
Signal prophetic events...Rev 8:2, 6, 13
Rev 9:14
Raise the dead 1Thess 4:16

[*also* TRUMP, TRUMPETS]
when the *t* soundeth long .....Ex 19:13
and the noise of the *t*.........Ex 20:18
cause the *t* of the jubilee to ...Lev 25:9
make the *t* sound throughout ..Lev 25:9
they blow but with one *t*......Num 10:4
shall blow with the *t*..........Num 10:8
blow with the *t* over your .....Num 10:10
the *t* to blow in his hand ......Num 31:6
hear the sound of the *t*.......Josh 6:5
seven *t* of rams' horns ....Josh 6:6
bearing the seven *t* ....Josh 6:8
Lord, and blew with the *t*.....Josh 6:8
that blew with the *t*...........Josh 6:9
and blowing with the *t*........Josh 6:9
priests bearing seven *t* ....Josh 6:13
and blew with the *t*...........Josh 6:13
and blowing with the *t*........Josh 6:13
priests blew with the *t*........Josh 6:20
heard the sound of the *t*......Josh 6:20
Gideon, and he blew a *t*......Judg 6:34
in their hand, and their *t*......Judg 7:8
When I blow with a *t*, I and...Judg 7:18
they blew the *t*, and brake ....Judg 7:19
three companies blew the *t*....Judg 7:20
t in their right hands to ......Judg 7:20
Saul blew the *t* throughout 1Sam 13:3
So Joab blew a *t*, and all......2Sam 2:28
ye hear the sound of the *t*.....2Sam 15:10
blew a t, and said, We have...2Sam 20:1
with *t*, saying, Jehu is king 2Kin 9:13
basins, *t*, and vessels of 2Kin 12:13
did blow with the *t* before.....1Chr 15:24
of the cornet, and with *t*......1Chr 15:28
with *t* and cymbals for 1Chr 16:42
priests sounding with *t*........2Chr 5:12
priests sounded *t* before.......2Chr 7:6
priests sounded with the *t*.....2Chr 13:14
harps and *t* unto the house 2Chr 20:28
the princes and the *t* by the ...2Chr 23:13
rejoiced, and sounded with *t* ..2Chr 23:13
song..began also with the *t*....2Chr 29:27
in their apparel with *t*.........Ezra 3:10
of the priests' sons with *t* .....Neh 12:35
that it is the sound of the *t*....Job 39:24
He saith among the *t*, Ha, ha. .Job 39:25
Lord with the sound of a *t*....Ps 47:5
With *t* and sound of cornet....Ps 98:6
him with the sound of the *t*...Ps 150:3
he bloweth a *t*, hear ye ....Is 18:3
lift up thy voice like a *t*.......Is 58:1
Blow ye the *t* in the land .....Jer 4:5
hear the sound of the *t*? ......Jer 4:21
to the sound of the *t*..........Jer 6:17
the *t* among the nations ....Jer 51:27
They have blown the *t*........Ezek 7:14
heareth the sound of the *t*.....Ezek 33:4
watchman..blow not the *t* .....Ezek 33:6
in Gibeah, and the *t* in ....Hos 5:8
Blow ye the *t* in Zion, and ....Joel 2:1
and with the sound of the *t* ...Amos 2:2
the *t* and alarm against the ....Zeph 1:16
Lord God shall blow the *t*.....Zech 9:14
do not sound a *t* before thee ..Matt 6:2
t give an uncertain sound 1Cor 14:8
of an eye, at the last *t* 1Cor 15:52
and with the *t* of God 1Thess 4:16
sound of a *t*, and the voice ....Heb 12:19
me a great voice, as of a *t* ....Rev 1:10
were of a *t* talking with me....Rev 4:1

TRUMPETERS—*those who blow trumpets*
princes and the *t* by the.......2Kin 11:14
as the *t* and singers were 2Chr 5:13
sang, and the *t* sounded.......2Chr 29:28
and of pipers, and *t* ....Rev 18:22

TRUST—*to put one's confidence in*

Not to be placed in:
Weapons ....Ps 44:6
Wealth ....Ps 49:6, 7
Leaders..................Ps 146:3
Man.....................Jer 17:5
Works ....Jer 48:7
One's own righteousness. .Ezek 33:13

To be placed in:
God's:
Name ....Ps 33:21
Word.................Ps 119:42
Christ ....Matt 12:17-21

Benefits of:
Joy.....................Ps 5:11
Deliverance ....Ps 22:4, 5
Triumph ....Ps 25:2, 3
God's goodness ....Ps 31:19
Mercy ....Ps 32:10
Provision ....Ps 37:3, 5
Blessedness ....Ps 40:4
Safety ....Ps 56:4, 11
Usefulness ....Ps 73:28
Guidance ....Prov 3:5, 6
Inheritance..............Is 57:13

[*also* TRUSTED, TRUSTEDST, TRUSTEST, TRUSTETH, TRUSTING, TRUSTY]
come down, wherein thou *t* ...Deut 28:52
their rock in whom they *t* .....Deut 32:37
put your *t* in my shadow ......Judg 9:15
Sihon *t* not Israel to pass......Judg 11:20
wings thou art come to *t* ......Ruth 2:12
of my rock; in him will I *t* 2Sam 22:3
He *t* in the Lord God of 2Kin 18:5
is this wherein thou *t*? 2Kin 18:19
Now on whom dost thou *t* 2Kin 18:20
We *t* in the Lord our God 2Kin 18:22
make you *t* in the Lord 2Kin 18:30
God in whom thou *t* deceive ..2Kin 19:10
they put their *t* in him 1Chr 5:20
he put no *t* in his servants.....Job 4:18
away the speech of the *t* ......Job 12:20
he slay me, yet will I *t* in .....Job 13:15
that is deceived *t* in vanity ....Job 15:31
Wilt thou *t* him, because his...Job 39:11
he *t* that he can draw up ......Job 40:23
all they that put their *t*........Ps 2:12
and put your *t* in the Lord ....Ps 4:5
God, in thee do I put my *t*....Ps 7:1
thy name will put their *t* in....Ps 9:10
In the Lord put I my *t*........Ps 11:1
But I have *t* in thy mercy .....Ps 13:5
for in thee do I put my *t*......Ps 16:1
which put their *t* in thee ......Ps 17:7
strength, in whom I will *t* .....Ps 18:2
to all those that *t* in him ......Ps 18:30
Some *t* in chariots, and ....Ps 20:7
For the king *t* in the Lord.....Ps 21:7
He *t* on the Lord that he .....Ps 22:8
for I put my *t* in thee ....Ps 25:20
I have *t* also in the Lord .....Ps 26:1
O Lord, do I put my *t*; let ....Ps 31:1
vanities: but I *t* in the Lord ...Ps 31:6
But I *t* in thee, O Lord: I.....Ps 31:14
blessed is the man that *t* in....Ps 34:8
none of them that *t* in him ....Ps 34:22
children of men put their *t* ....Ps 36:7
save them, because they *t* in...Ps 37:40
fear, and shall *t* in the Lord ...Ps 40:3
familiar friend, in whom I *t* ...Ps 41:9
They that *t* in their wealth ....Ps 49:6
I *t* in the mercy of God for ...Ps 52:8
but I will *t* in thee ....Ps 55:23
I am afraid, I will *t* in thee....Ps 56:3
I will *t* in the covert of thy ....Ps 61:4
T in him at all times; ye ......Ps 62:8
T not in oppression, and ......Ps 62:10
O Lord, do I put my *t*: let ....Ps 71:1
thou art my *t* from my youth ..Ps 71:5
and *t* not in his salvation .....Ps 78:22
blessed is the man that *t* in....Ps 84:12
my God; in him will I *t* ....Ps 91:2
under his wings shalt thou *t* ...Ps 91:4
heart is fixed, *t* in the Lord ..Ps 112:7
so is every one that *t* in.......Ps 115:8
O Israel, *t* thou in the Lord ..Ps 115:9
Ye that fear the Lord, *t* in ....Ps 115:11
is better to *t* in the Lord ......Ps 118:8
They that *t* in the Lord ....Ps 125:1
in thee is my *t*; leave not .....Ps 141:8
in thee do I *t*: cause me to ....Ps 143:8
shield, and he in whom I *t* ....Ps 144:2
He that *t* in his riches shall....Prov 11:28
thy *t* may be in the Lord, I ...Prov 22:19
He that *t* in his own heart is ..Prov 28:26
putteth his *t* in the Lord ......Prov 29:25
husband doth safely *t* in.......Prov 31:11
I will *t*, and not be afraid .....Is 12:2
thee: because he *t* in thee .....Is 26:3
T ye in the Lord for ever .....Is 26:4
t in the shadow of Egypt ......Is 30:3
and *t* in chariots, because .....Is 31:1
is this wherein thou *t*? ....Is 36:4
king of Egypt to all that *t*.....Is 36:6
t on Egypt for chariots and....Is 36:9
not thy God, in whom thou *t*..Is 37:10
that *t* in graven images........Is 42:17
hast *t* in thy wickedness ....Is 47:10
on mine arm shall they *t* ......Is 51:5
t in vanity, and speak lies .....Is 59:4
fenced cities, wherein thou *t*...Jer 5:17
T ye not in lying words ....Jer 7:4
ye *t*, and unto the place.......Jer 7:14
forgotten me, and *t* in ....Jer 13:25
Blessed is the man that *t* in ...Jer 17:7
thou makest this people to *t* ..Jer 28:15
thou hast put thy *t* in me .....Jer 39:18
that *t* in her treasures ....Jer 49:4
and let thy widows *t* in me ....Jer 49:11
his servants that *t* in him ......Dan 3:28
because thou didst *t* in thy ....Hos 10:13
and *t* in the mountain of ......Amos 6:1
T ye not in a friend, put ye ...Mic 7:5
knoweth them that *t* in him ...Nah 1:7
the maker of his work *t*.......Hab 2:18
she *t* not in the Lord; she .....Zeph 3:2
t in the name of the Lord .....Zeph 3:12
He *t* in God; let him deliver...Matt 27:43
for them that *t* in riches.......Mark 10:24
all his armor wherein he *t*.....Luke 11:22
commit to your *t* the true .....Luke 16:11
we *t* that it had been he ......Luke 24:21
even Moses, in whom ye *t* ....John 5:45
in him shall the Gentiles *t*.....Rom 15:12
but I *t* to tarry a while........1Cor 16:7
should not *t* in ourselves 2Cor 1:9
I *t* ye shall acknowledge 2Cor 1:13
I *t* also are made manifest.....2Cor 5:11
I *t* that ye shall know that.....2Cor 13:6
glory, who first *t* in Christ.....Eph 1:12
t in the Lord Jesus to send ....Phil 2:19
he might *t* in the flesh ....Phil 3:4
put in *t* with the gospel 1Thess 2:4
was committed to my *t*........1Tim 1:11
and desolate, *t* in God 1Tim 5:5
nor *t* in uncertain riches.......1Tim 6:17
t that through your prayers ....Philem 22
I will put my *t* in him.........Heb 2:13
women also, who *t* in God 1Pet 3:5
but I *t* to come unto you 2John 12
t I shall shortly see thee.......3John 14

TRUTH—*that which is reliable, trustworthy, and consistent with the character and revelation of God*

Ascribed to:
God's Law ....Ps 119:142-160
Christ ....John 14:6
Holy Spirit..............John 14:17
God's Word ....John 17:17, 19
Gospel ....Gal 2:5, 14

Effects of, to:
Make free ....John 8:31, 32
Sanctify.................John 17:17-19
Purify 1Pet 1:22
Establish.................Eph 4:15

Wrong attitudes toward, to:
Change into a lie ....Rom 1:25
Disobey ....Rom 2:8
Walk contrary to ....Gal 2:17
Love not 2Thess 2:10
Believe not 2Thess 2:12
Be destitute of 1Tim 6:5
Never come to 2Tim 3:7
Resist 2Tim 3:8
Turn from 2Tim 4:4

T

Right attitudes toward, to:
Speak ....Eph 4:25
Walk in 3John 3, 4
Declare ....Acts 26:25
Worship in ....John 4:23, 24
Come to 1Tim 2:4
Believe and know 1Tim 4:3
Handle accurately 2Tim 2:15
Obey 1Pet 1:22
Be established 2Pet 1:12

[*also* TRUTH'S]
of his mercy and his *t* ....Gen 24:27
whether there be any *t* in .....Gen 42:16
such as fear God, men of *t* ....Ex 18:21
if it be *t*, and the thing ....Deut 13:14
him in sincerity and in *t* ....Josh 24:14
in *t* ye anoint me king over ...Judg 9:15
serve him in *t* with all your 1Sam 12:24
show kindness and *t* unto 2Sam 2:6
walk before me in *t* with all ...1Kin 2:4
the Lord in thy mouth is *t* 1Kin 17:24
Of a *t*, Lord, the kings of 2Kin 19:17
peace and *t* be in my days? ...2Kin 20:19
thou say nothing but the *t* 2Chr 18:15
with words of peace and *t* .....Esth 9:30
I know it is so of a *t*: but .....Job 9:2
Lead me in thy *t*, and teach ...Ps 25:5
and I have walked in thy *t* ....Ps 26:3
shall it declare thy *t*? ....Ps 30:9
me, O Lord God of *t* ....Ps 31:5
all his works are done in *t* ....Ps 33:4
thy *t* from the great ....Ps 40:10
t continually preserve me ....Ps 40:11
send out thy light and thy *t* ...Ps 43:3
desirest *t* in the inward ....Ps 51:6
forth his mercy and his *t* ....Ps 57:3
and thy *t* unto the clouds .....Ps 57:10
displayed because of the *t* .....Ps 60:4
in the *t* of thy salvation ....Ps 69:13
Mercy and *t* are met ....Ps 85:10
Lord; I will walk in thy *t* ......Ps 86:11
and *t* shall go before thy ......Ps 89:14
his *t* shall be thy shield ......Ps 91:4
his mercy and his *t* ....Ps 98:3
his *t* endureth to all ....Ps 100:5
t reacheth unto the clouds .....Ps 108:4
mercy, and for thy *t* sake .....Ps 115:1
the *t* of the Lord endureth ....Ps 117:2
I have chosen the way of *t* ....Ps 119:30
the word of *t* utterly out ......Ps 119:43
Lord hath sworn in *t* unto .....Ps 132:11
all that call upon him in *t* .....Ps 145:18
therein is: which keepeth *t* ....Ps 146:6
Let not mercy and *t* forsake ...Prov 3:3
He that speaketh *t* showeth ...Prov 12:17
t shall be to them that ....Prov 14:22
Mercy and *t* preserve the ....Prov 20:28
certainty of the words of *t* .....Prov 22:21
answer the words of *t* ....Prov 22:21
upright, even words of *t* ......Eccl 12:10
Of a *t* many houses shall ......Is 5:9
sit upon it in *t* in the ....Is 16:5
keepeth the *t* may enter in ....Is 26:2
walked before thee in *t* and ...Is 38:3
shall make known thy *t* ....Is 38:19
bring forth judgment unto *t* ...Is 42:3
in *t*, nor in righteousness ......Is 48:1
for *t* is fallen in the street ......Is 59:14
I will direct their work in *t* ....Is 61:8
bless himself in the God of *t* ..Is 65:16
shall swear by the God of *t* ...Is 65:16
The Lord liveth, in *t*, in ....Jer 4:2
not thine eyes upon the *t* .....Jer 5:3
not valiant for the *t* upon .....Jer 9:3
of a *t* the Lord hath sent me ..Jer 26:15
Of a *t* it is, that your God ....Dan 2:47
and asked him the *t* of all .....Dan 7:16
it cast down the *t* to the ......Dan 8:12
noted in the scripture of *t* .....Dan 10:21
there is no *t*, nor mercy ....Hos 4:1
Thou wilt perform the *t* to ....Mic 7:20
shall be called a city of *t* ......Zech 8:3
Speak ye every man the *t* to ...Zech 8:16
execute the judgment of *t* .....Zech 8:16
t thou art the Son of God .....Matt 14:33
teachest the way of God in *t* ..Matt 22:16
him, and told him all the *t* ....Mark 5:33
Master, thou hast said the *t* ...Mark 12:32
I tell you of a *t*, many ....Luke 4:25
Of a *t* I say unto you, that ....Luke 12:44
Of a *t* this fellow also was .....Luke 22:59
Father, full of grace and *t* .....John 1:14
and *t* came by Jesus Christ ....John 1:17
he that doeth *t* cometh to .....John 3:21
he bare witness unto the *t* .....John 5:33
Of a *t* this is the Prophet .....John 7:40
that hath told you the *t* ....John 8:40
and abode not in the *t* ....John 8:44
because there is no *t* in him ..John 8:44
I tell you the *t*, ye believe .....John 8:45
I say the *t*, why do ye not .....John 8:46
Father, even the Spirit of *t* ....John 15:26
the Spirit of *t*, is come, he ....John 16:13
he will guide you into all *t* ....John 16:13
bear witness unto the *t* ....John 18:37
Every one that is of the *t* .....John 18:37
of a *t* against thy holy child ...Acts 4:27
Of a *t* I perceive that God is ..Acts 10:34
the *t* in unrighteousness ....Rom 1:18
Who changed the *t* of God .....Rom 1:25
of God is according to *t* ....Rom 2:2
knowledge and of the *t* in .....Rom 2:20
if the *t* of God hath more .....Rom 3:7
I say the *t* in Christ, I lie .....Rom 9:1
circumcision for the *t* of God ..Rom 15:8
bread of sincerity and *t* 1Cor 5:8
but rejoiceth in the *t* 1Cor 13:6
that God is in you of a *t* 1Cor 14:25
by manifestation of the *t* 2Cor 4:2
word of *t*, by the power of 2Cor 6:7
spake all things to you in *t* 2Cor 7:14
before Titus, is found a *t* 2Cor 7:14
As the *t* of Christ is in me 2Cor 11:10
a fool; for I will say the *t* 2Cor 12:6
against the *t*, but for the *t* 2Cor 13:8
ye should not obey the *t* ......Gal 3:1
ye should not obey the *t*? ......Gal 5:7
that ye heard the word of *t* ....Eph 1:13
by him, as the *t* is in Jesus ....Eph 4:21
and righteousness and *t* ....Eph 5:9
in pretense, or in *t*, Christ ....Phil 1:18
word of the *t* of the gospel ....Col 1:5
it is in *t*, the word of God 1Thess 2:13
Spirit and belief of the *t* 2Thess 2:13
(I speak the *t* in Christ, and ...1Tim 2:7
pillar and ground of the *t* 1Tim 3:15
Who concerning the *t* have 2Tim 2:18
the acknowledging of the *t* 2Tim 2:25
t which is after godliness ......Titus 1:1
of men, that turn from the *t* ...Titus 1:14
the knowledge of the *t* ....Heb 10:26
he us with the word of *t* ......James 1:18
and lie not against the *t* ....James 3:14
any of you do err from the *t* ..James 5:19
of *t* shall be evil spoken of 2Pet 2:2
we lie, and do not the *t* 1John 1:6
is a liar, and the *t* is not 1John 2:4
because ye know not the *t* 1John 2:21
and that no lie is of the *t* 1John 2:21
but in deed and in *t* 1John 3:18
know we the spirit of *t* 1John 4:6
whom I love in the *t* 2John 1
they that have known the *t* 2John 1
t sake, which dwelleth in us ...2John 2
of thy children walking in *t* 2John 4
Gaius, whom I love in the *t* ...3John 1
be fellow helpers to the *t* 3John 8
of all men, and of the *t* 3John 12

TRUTHFULNESS—*adhering to or abiding by what is true*
Commanded ....Ps 15:2
Exemplified by Levi .....Mal 2:6
Should characterize
Christians ....Eph 4:25

TRY—*to put to test or put on trial*
[*also* TRIED, TRIEST, TRIETH, TRYING]
and every stroke be *t* ....Deut 21:5
will *t* them for thee there .....Judg 7:4
the word of the Lord is *t* 2Sam 22:31
God, that thou *t* the heart 1Chr 29:17
God left him, to *t* him 2Chr 32:31
and *t* him every moment ......Job 7:18
when he hath *t* me, I shall ....Job 23:10
For the ear *t* words, as the ....Job 34:3
for the righteous God *t* the ....Ps 7:9
t the children of men ....Ps 11:4
The Lord *t* the righteous ......Ps 11:5
as silver *t* in a furnace of ......Ps 12:6
the word of the Lord is *t* ......Ps 18:30
the word of the Lord *t* him ....Ps 105:19
t me, and know my thoughts ..Ps 139:23
but the Lord *t* the hearts ......Prov 17:3
and a *t* stone, a precious ......Is 28:16
thou mayest know and *t* ......Jer 6:27
t the reins and the heart ......Jer 11:20
t mine heart toward thee ......Jer 12:3
Lord search the heart, I *t* .....Jer 17:10
t the righteous, and seest ......Jer 20:12
us search and *t* our ways ......Lam 3:40
to *t* them, and to purge, and ..Dan 11:35
and made white, and *t* ....Dan 12:10
will try them as gold is *t* ......Zech 13:9
will *t* them as gold is *t* ....Zech 13:9
the fire shall *t* every man's 1Cor 3:13
God, which *t* our hearts 1Thess 2:4
he was *t*, offered up Isaac .....Heb 11:17
t of your faith worketh ....James 1:3
he is *t*, he shall receive ....James 1:12
it be *t* with fire, might be 1Pet 1:7
fiery trial which is to *t* 1Pet 4:12
t the spirits whether they 1John 4:1
hast *t* them which say they ....Rev 2:2
t them that dwell upon the ....Rev 3:10
to buy of me gold *t* in the .....Rev 3:18

TRYPHAENA (trī-fē'nä)—*"dainty"*
Woman at Rome
commended by Paul ...Rom 16:12

TRYPHOSA (trī-fō'sä)—*"delicate"*
Woman at Rome
commended by Paul ...Rom 16:12

TUBAL (tū'bǎl)—*a son of Japheth and a tribe in eastern Asia Minor*
1. Son of Japheth ....Gen 10:2
2. Tribe associated with
Javan and Meshech ...Is 66:19
In Gog's army ....Ezek 38:2, 3
Punishment of ....Ezek 32:26, 27

and *T*, and Meshech, and 1Chr 1:5
T, and Meshech, they were ....Ezek 27:13
prince of Meshech and ***T*** ......Ezek 39:1

TUBAL-CAIN (tū-bǎl-kān)—*"Tubal, the smith"*
Son of Lamech ....Gen 4:19-22

TUMBLED—*rolled into*
bread *t* into the host of ....Judg 7:13

TUMULT—*a confused uproar*
Against:
God ....Is 37:29
Christ ....Matt 27:24
Paul ....Acts 19:29, 40
Paul pleads innocent of ..Acts 24:18

[*also* TUMULTS, TUMULTUOUS]
meaneth the noise of this *t* 1Sam 4:14
I saw a great *t*, but I knew 2Sam 18:29
me and thy *t* is come up 2Kin 19:28
and the *t* of the people ....Ps 65:7
lo, thine enemies make a *t* ....Ps 83:2
a *t* noise of the kingdoms of ...Is 13:4
art full of stirs, a *t* city ....Is 22:2
of the *t* the people fled ....Is 33:3
noise of a great *t* he hath .....Jer 11:16
of the head of the *t* ones ......Jer 48:45
a *t* arise among thy people ....Hos 10:14
Moab shall die with *t*, with ....Amos 2:2
the great *t* in the midst ....Amos 3:9
t from the Lord shall be ......Zech 14:13
seeth the *t*, and them that .....Mark 5:38
the certainty for the *t* ....Acts 21:34

in imprisonments, in *t*, in 2Cor 6:5
whisperings, swellings, *t* 2Cor 12:20

TURN—*to go in a new direction; reverse*

[*also* TURNED, TURNEST, TURNETH, TURNING]

flaming sword which *t* every ... Gen 3:24
my lords, *t* in, I pray you ..... Gen 19:2
they *t* in unto him, and .... Gen 19:3
until thy brother's fury *t* ...... Gen 27:44
he *t* unto her by the way ...... Gen 38:16
I will now *t* aside, and see .... Ex 3:3
Lord saw that he *t* aside to .... Ex 3:4
the rod which was *t* to a ...... Ex 7:15
the river were *t* to blood ...... Ex 7:20
he *t* himself, and went out .... Ex 10:6
servants was *t* against the ..... Ex 14:5
thine enemies *t* their backs .... Ex 23:27
Moses *t*, and went down .... Ex 32:15
the hair in the plague is *t* ..... Lev 13:3
and it have *t* the hair .... Lev 13:10
Or if the raw flesh *t* again ..... Lev 13:16
the plague be *t* into white ..... Lev 13:17
hair in the bright spot be *t* .... Lev 13:25
the soul that *t* after such ...... Lev 20:6
Tomorrow *t* you, and get ...... Num 14:25
ye are *t* away from the Lord .. Num 14:43
will not *t* into the fields .... Num 21:22
they *t* and went up by the ..... Num 21:33
way to *t* either to the .... Num 22:26
and the ass saw me, and *t* ..... Num 22:33
unless she had *t* from me ..... Num 22:33
hath *t* my wrath away from .... Num 25:11
t again unto Pi-hahiroth .... Num 33:7
your border shall *t* from the ... Num 34:4
T you, and take your .... Deut 1:7
t and went up into the .... Deut 1:24
enough: *t* you northward ...... Deut 2:3
we *t* and passed by the way ... Deut 2:8
thou *t* to the Lord thy God ... Deut 4:30
will *t* away thy son from ...... Deut 7:4
quickly *t* aside out of the ...... Deut 9:12
t aside quickly out of the ...... Deut 9:16
t aside out of the way .... Deut 11:28
Lord may *t* from the .... Deut 13:17
and thou shalt *t* in the .... Deut 16:7
that he *t* not aside from .... Deut 17:20
Lord thy God *t* the curse ..... Deut 23:5
in thee, and *t* away from ...... Deut 23:14
heart *t* away this day from .... Deut 29:18
t unto the Lord thy God ...... Deut 30:10
will they *t* unto other gods .... Deut 31:20
t not from it to the right ...... Josh 1:7
Israel *t* their backs before ..... Josh 7:8
t their backs before their ...... Josh 7:12
fled to the wilderness *t* .... Josh 8:20
Joshua at that time *t* back ..... Josh 11:10
then the coast *t* to Ramah ..... Josh 19:29
and the coast *t* to Hosah ...... Josh 19:29
t from following the Lord ..... Josh 22:23
ye *t* not aside therefrom to .... Josh 23:6
they *t* quickly out of the ...... Judg 2:17
T in, my lord, *t* in to me ...... Judg 4:18
And when he had *t* in unto ... Judg 4:18
t aside to see the carcass ...... Judg 14:8
they *t* in thither, and said ..... Judg 18:3
So they *t* and departed .... Judg 18:21
t and went back unto his ...... Judg 18:26
t into this city of the .... Judg 19:11
we any of us *t* into his .... Judg 20:8
when the men of Israel *t* ...... Judg 20:41
t and fled toward the .... Judg 20:45
the men of Israel *t* again ...... Judg 20:48
And Naomi said, *T* again ..... Ruth 1:11
man was afraid, and *t* .... Ruth 3:8
such a one! *t* aside, sit .... Ruth 4:1
t not aside to the right 1Sam 6:12
shalt be *t* into another 1Sam 10:6
t not aside from following 1Sam 12:20
company *t* unto the way 1Sam 13:17
another company *t* the way 1Sam 13:18
another company *t* to the 1Sam 13:18
t thee; behold, I am with 1Sam 14:7
whithersoever he *t* himself 1Sam 14:47
as Samuel *t* about to go 1Sam 15:27
t again with me, that I 1Sam 15:30
he *t* from him toward 1Sam 17:30
T thou, and fall upon the 1Sam 22:18
David's young men *t* their 1Sam 25:12
bow of Jonathan *t* not back ... 2Sam 1:22
T thee aside to thy right 2Sam 2:21
not *t* aside from following 2Sam 2:21
T thee aside from following ... 2Sam 2:22
none can *t* to the right 2Sam 14:19
t the counsel of Ahithophel ... 2Sam 15:31
he *t* aside, and stood still 2Sam 18:30
I pray thee, *t* back again 2Sam 19:37
and *t* not again until I had 2Sam 22:38
and whithersoever thou *t* 1Kin 2:3
howbeit the kingdom is *t* 1Kin 2:15
Joab had *t* after Adonijah 1Kin 2:28
he *t* not after Absalom 1Kin 2:28
shall *t* again to thee, and 1Kin 8:33
at all *t* from following 1Kin 9:6
t and went to her own 1Kin 10:13
wives *t* away his heart 1Kin 11:4
heart of this people t 1Kin 12:27
t again to go by the way 1Kin 13:17
t not aside from any thing 1Kin 15:5
thou hast *t* their heart 1Kin 18:37
a man *t* aside, and brought 1Kin 20:39
they *t* aside to fight 1Kin 22:32
T thine hand, and carry 1Kin 22:34
he *t* not aside from it 1Kin 22:43
the messengers *t* back unto 2Kin 1:5
Go, *t* again unto the king 2Kin 1:6
t back, and looked on them ... 2Kin 2:24
he *t* into the chamber, and 2Kin 4:11
t again from his chariot 2Kin 5:26
with peace? *t* thee behind 2Kin 9:18
the king of Assyria *t* back 2Kin 15:20
wilt thou *t* away the face of ... 2Kin 18:24
he *t* his face to the wall 2Kin 20:2
T again, and tell Hezekiah 2Kin 20:5
wiping it, and *t* it upside 2Kin 21:13
Josiah *t* himself, he spied 2Kin 23:16
Lord *t* not from the 2Kin 23:26
he *t* and rebelled against 2Kin 24:1
t the kingdom unto David 1Chr 10:14
t the kingdom of Saul to 1Chr 12:23
t his face, and blessed 2Chr 6:3
thy name, and *t* from their 2Chr 6:26
t not away..face of thine 2Chr 6:42
But if ye *t* away, and 2Chr 7:19
wrath of the Lord *t* from 2Chr 12:12
T thine hand, that thou 2Chr 18:33
t from them, and destroyed ... 2Chr 20:10
and at the *t* of the wall 2Chr 26:9
t away their faces from 2Chr 29:6
Lord, and *t* their backs 2Chr 29:6
that his fierce wrath may *t* 2Chr 29:10
of his wrath may *t* away 2Chr 30:8
if ye *t* again unto the Lord 2Chr 30:9
not *t* away his face from 2Chr 30:9
t the heart of the king of ...... Ezra 6:22
But if ye *t* unto me, and ...... Neh 1:9
and viewed the wall, and *t* .... Neh 2:15
the armory at the *t* of the ..... Neh 3:19
Azariah unto the *t* of the ..... Neh 3:24
against them to *t* them to ..... Neh 9:26
God *t* the curse into a .... Neh 13:2
when every maid's *t* was ...... Esth 2:12
it was *t* to the contrary .... Esth 9:1
of the saints wilt thou *t*? ...... Job 5:1
of their way are *t* aside .... Job 6:18
t thy spirit against God .... Job 15:13
I loved are *t* against me .... Job 19:19
mind, and who can *t* him? .... Job 23:13
and under it is *t* up as it ...... Job 28:5
harp also is *t* to mourning ..... Job 30:31
shall *t* again unto dust .... Job 34:15
Because they *t* back from ..... Job 34:27
It is *t* as clay to the seal ..... Job 38:14
t he back from the sword ..... Job 39:22
are *t* with him into stubble .... Job 41:28
mine enemies are *t* back ...... Ps 9:3
wicked shall be *t* into hell ..... Ps 9:17
I *t* again till they were .... Ps 18:37
and *t* unto the Lord .... Ps 22:27
t for me my mourning into .... Ps 30:11
let them be *t* back and .... Ps 35:4
nor such as *t* aside to lies ..... Ps 40:4
then shall mine eyes *t* back .... Ps 56:9
He *t* the sea into dry land ..... Ps 66:6
hath not *t* away my prayer .... Ps 66:20
t unto me according to the .... Ps 69:16
let them be *t* backward, and ... Ps 70:2
t back in the day of battle ..... Ps 78:9
t back and tempted God ...... Ps 78:41
But *t* back, and dealt .... Ps 78:57
T us again, O God of hosts ... Ps 80:7
t my hand against their .... Ps 81:14
T us, O God of our .... Ps 85:4
O *t* unto me, and have .... Ps 86:16
hast also *t* the edge of his ..... Ps 89:43
Thou *t* man to destruction ..... Ps 90:3
t not again to cover the .... Ps 104:9
t their waters into blood ...... Ps 105:29
t rivers into a wilderness ...... Ps 107:33
t the rock into a standing ..... Ps 114:8
T away mine eyes from .... Ps 119:37
t my feet unto thy .... Ps 119:59
those that fear thee t unto .... Ps 119:79
T again our captivity, O ...... Ps 126:4
and *t* back that hate Zion ..... Ps 129:5
will not *t* from it; Of the ...... Ps 132:11
the way of the wicked he *t* .... Ps 146:9
T you at my reproof .... Prov 1:23
t away of the simple shall ..... Prov 1:32
T not to the right hand .... Prov 4:27
A soft answer *t* away wrath ... Prov 15:1
t it whithersoever he will ...... Prov 21:1
he *t* away his wrath from ...... Prov 24:18
that *t* away his ear from ...... Prov 28:9
but wise men *t* away wrath .... Prov 29:8
beasts, and *t* not away for ..... Prov 30:30
south, and *t* about unto the ... Eccl 1:6
t myself to behold wisdom .... Eccl 2:12
and all *t* to dust again .... Eccl 3:20
should I be as one that *t* ...... Song 1:7
t, my beloved, and be thou .... Song 2:17
whither is thy beloved *t* .... Song 6:1
And I will *t* my hand upon .... Is 1:25
all this his anger is not *t* ...... Is 5:25
people *t* not unto him that .... Is 9:13
his anger is not *t* away .... Is 10:4
every man *t* to his own .... Is 13:14
they shall *t* the rivers far ...... Is 19:6
my pleasure hath he *t* into .... Is 21:4
Tyre, and she shall *t* to her .. Is 23:17
t of things upside down .... Is 29:16
Lebanon..*t* into a fruitful ...... Is 29:17
and *t* aside the just for a ...... Is 29:21
when ye *t* to the right .... Is 30:21
and when ye *t* to the left ...... Is 30:21
wilt thou *t* away the face ...... Is 36:9
Hezekiah *t* his face toward .... Is 38:2
a deceived heart hath *t* him .. Is 44:20
that *t* wise men backward ..... Is 44:25
have *t* every one to his own .. Is 53:6
t away thy foot from the ...... Is 58:13
he was *t* to be their enemy .... Is 63:10
thou *t* into the degenerate .... Jer 2:21
occasion who can *t* her way? . Jer 2:24
these things, *T* thou unto ..... Jer 3:7
Judah hath not *t* unto me ..... Jer 3:10
and shalt not *t* away from ..... Jer 3:19
Your iniquities have *t* away .. Jer 5:25
t back thine hand as a .... Jer 6:9
every one *t* to his course ...... Jer 8:6
he *t* it into the shadow of ..... Jer 13:16
wayfaring man that *t* aside .... Jer 14:8
to *t* away thy wrath from ...... Jer 18:20
t them from their evil way .... Jer 23:22
T ye again now every one ..... Jer 25:5
and *t* every man from his ..... Jer 26:3
will *t* away your captivity ...... Jer 29:14
t thou me, and I shall be ...... Jer 31:18
thou me, and I shall be *t* ...... Jer 31:18
have *t* unto me the back ...... Jer 32:33
that I will not *t* away from ... Jer 32:40
now *t*, and had done right ...... Jer 34:15
and they are *t* away back ..... Jer 38:22
also are *t* back, and are .... Jer 46:21
Flee ye, *t* back, dwell deep .... Jer 49:8
t them away on the .... Jer 50:6

sigheth, and *t* backward ....Lam 1:8
my feet, he hath *t* me back....Lam 1:13
mine heart is *t* within me .....Lam 1:20
to *t* away thy captivity ....Lam 2:14
Surely against me is he *t* ......Lam 3:3
and *t* again to the Lord ....Lam 3:40
Our inheritance is *t* to ....Lam 5:2
O Lord, and we shall be *t*.....Lam 5:21
they *t* not when they went ....Ezek 1:9
t not from his wickedness .....Ezek 3:19
shalt not *t* thee from one......Ezek 4:8
t thee yet again, and thou .....Ezek 8:6
t thee yet again, and thou .....Ezek 8:15
they *t* not as they went ....Ezek 10:11
they *t* not as they went ....Ezek 10:11
and *t* yourselves from your ....Ezek 14:6
t away your face from all .....Ezek 14:6
whose branches *t* toward ......Ezek 17:6
t away from his ....Ezek 18:24
t away from all his ....Ezek 18:28
t yourselves from all your .....Ezek 18:30
the wicked of his way to *t*.....Ezek 33:9
if he do not *t* from his way....Ezek 33:9
but that the wicked *t* from ....Ezek 33:11
t ye, *t* ye from your evil.......Ezek 33:11
t from his righteousness ....Ezek 33:18
the wicked *t* from his ....Ezek 33:19
I will *t* thee back, and put ....Ezek 38:4
I will *t* thee back ....Ezek 39:2
two leaves apiece, two *t*.......Ezek 41:24
He *t* about to the west side ...Ezek 42:19
might *t* from our iniquities ....Dan 9:13
anger and thy fury be *t* ....Dan 9:16
my sorrows are *t* upon me .....Dan 10:16
t his face unto the isles ....Dan 11:18
he shall cause it to *t* upon.....Dan 11:18
t many to righteousness ....Dan 12:3
doings to *t* unto their God ....Hos 5:4
Ephraim is a cake not *t* ....Hos 7:8
words, and *t* to the Lord ......Hos 14:2
anger is *t* away from him......Hos 14:4
t ye even to me with all.......Joel 2:12
The sun shall be *t* into ....Joel 2:31
will not *t* away the ....Amos 1:3
I will not *t* away the ....Amos 1:9
t aside the way of the meek ...Amos 2:7
and *t* the shadow of death......Amos 5:8
t aside the poor in the ....Amos 5:12
have *t* judgment into gall......Amos 6:12
let them *t* every one from .....Jon 3:8
if God will *t* and repent.......Jon 3:9
and *t* away from his fierce.....Jon 3:9
they *t* from their evil way .....Jon 3:10
t away he hath divided our ....Mic 2:4
He will *t* again, he will........Mic 7:19
t away the excellency of.......Nah 2:2
Lord's right hand shall be *t*....Hab 2:16
are *t* back from the Lord......Zeph 1:6
and *t* away their captivity .....Zeph 2:7
I *t* back your captivity ....Zeph 3:20
t not to me, saith the Lord ....Hag 2:17
T ye unto me, saith the ....Zech 1:3
I will *t* unto you, saith ....Zech 1:3
Then I *t*, and lifted up ....Zech 5:1
T you to the stronghold ....Zech 9:12
t mine hand upon the little ....Zech 13:7
And the land shall be *t* ....Zech 14:10
t many away from iniquity ....Mal 2:6
t the heart of the fathers ......Mal 4:6
t aside into the parts of ....Matt 2:22
t to him the other also ....Matt 5:39
and *t* again and rend you .....Matt 7:6
But Jesus *t* him about, and ....Matt 9:22
t, and said unto Peter.........Matt 16:23
t him about in the press.......Mark 5:30
is in the field not *t* back ......Mark 13:16
Israel shall be *t* to the ....Luke 1:16
t back again to Jerusalem ....Luke 2:45
he *t* to the woman, and said...Luke 7:44
it shall *t* to you again ....Luke 10:6
t him unto his disciples........Luke 10:23
t back, and with a loud ....Luke 17:15
t to you for a testimony ....Luke 21:13
But Jesus *t* unto them said ....Luke 23:28
Jesus *t*, and saw them.........John 1:38
she *t* herself back, and saw ....John 20:14
t about, seeth the disciple .....John 21:20
shall be *t* into darkness ....Acts 2:20
in *t* away every one of you ....Acts 3:26
God *t*, and gave them up to ...Acts 7:42
and *t* unto the Lord ....Acts 11:21
t away the deputy from the....Acts 13:8
ye should *t* from these ....Acts 14:15
t and said to the spirit ....Acts 16:18
and *t* away much people ......Acts 19:26
should repent and *t* to God ...Acts 26:20
t away ungodliness from ......Rom 11:26
when it shall *t* to the Lord 2Cor 3:16
how *t* ye again to the weak....Gal 4:9
this shall *t* to my salvation ....Phil 1:19
ye *t* to God from idols to 1Thess 1:9
t aside unto vain jangling 1Tim 1:6
in Asia be *t* away from me 2Tim 1:15
power thereof: from such *t* 2Tim 3:5
men, that *t* from the truth.....Titus 1:14
t to flight the armies of ....Heb 11:34
we *t* away from him that ......Heb 12:25
neither shadow of *t* ....James 1:17
and we *t* about their whole ....James 3:3
t about with a very small......James 3:4
to *t* from the holy 2Pet 2:21
dog is *t* to his own vomit......2Pet 2:22
t the grace of our God ....Jude 4
I *t* to see the voice that ....Rev 1:12
And being *t*, I saw seven......Rev 1:12
waters to *t* them to blood .....Rev 11:6

TURTLE—*same as turtledove*

[*also* TURTLES]
shall take unto her two *t*......Lev 15:29
day he shall bring two *t*.......Num 6:10
the *t* and the crane and the ...Jer 8:7

TURTLEDOVE—*a dove or pigeon*
Migratory bird ....Song 2:12
Term of affection.........Ps 74:19
Offering of the poor .....Lev 12:2, 6-8
Luke 2:24

[*also* TURTLEDOVES]
a *t*, and a young pigeon ....Gen 15:9
bring his offering of *t* ....Lev 1:14
two *t*, or two young pigeons ...Lev 5:7
be not able to bring two *t*.....Lev 5:11
two *t*, or two young pigeons ...Lev 14:22
shall offer the one of the *t* ....Lev 14:30

TUTORS—*instructors of children*
Referred to by Paul .....Gal 4:2

TWAIN—*two*
in the one of the *t*............1Sam 18:21
shut the door upon them *t* 2Kin 4:33
with *t* he covered his face .....Is 6:2
with *t* he covered his feet .....Is 6:2
and with *t* he did fly ....Is 6:2
when they cut the calf in *t* .....Jer 34:18
both *t* shall come forth.........Ezek 21:19
go a mile, go with him *t* ....Matt 5:41
they are no more *t*, but ....Matt 19:6
Whether of the *t* will ye.......Matt 27:21
they *t* shall be one flesh.......Mark 10:8
so then they are no more *t* ....Mark 10:8
make in himself of *t* one ......Eph 2:15

TWELVE
Angels ....Rev 21:12
Apostles ....Rev 21:14
Baskets ....John 6:13
Brazen bulls ....Jer 52:20
Brethren...............Gen 42:32
Cakes ....Lev 24:5
Cities..................1Chr 6:63
Cubits 1Kin 7:15
Foundations............Rev 21:14
Fountains ....Num 33:9
Fruits ....Rev 22:2
Gates ....Rev 21:12
Golden spoons ....Num 7:86
He goats...............Ezra 8:35
Hours ....John 11:9
Legions of angels ....Matt 26:53
Lions 1Kin 10:20
Men...................Josh 3:12
Months ....Dan 4:29
Officers................1Kin 4:7
Oxen 2Chr 4:15
Patriarchs ....Acts 7:8
Pieces 1Kin 11:30
Pillars ....Ex 24:4
Princes ....Gen 17:20
Rods ....Num 17:2
Silver bowls ....Num 7:84
Sons of Jacob ....Gen 35:22
Spoons ....Num 7:86
Stars ....Rev 12:1
Stones 1Kin 18:31
Thousand 2Sam 17:1
Thrones ....Matt 19:28
Tribes ....Luke 22:30
Wells ....Ex 15:27
Years of age ....Luke 2:42

[*also* TWELFTH]
nine hundred and *t* years......Gen 5:8
T years they served ....Gen 14:4
t princes according to ....Gen 25:16
Thy servants are *t* brethren....Gen 42:13
and the *t* tribes of Israel ......Gen 49:28
the children of Israel, *t* ....Ex 28:21
according to the *t* tribes.......Ex 28:21
the children of Israel, *t* ....Ex 39:14
according to the *t* tribes.......Ex 39:14
princes of Israel, being *t* ......Num 1:44
covered wagons, and *t* oxen ...Num 7:3
On the *t* day Ahira the son ...Num 7:78
t bullocks, the rams *t* ....Num 7:87
lambs of the first year *t* ....Num 7:87
goats for sin offering *t* ....Num 7:87
houses, even *t* rods ....Num 17:6
offer *t* young bullocks..........Num 29:17
t thousand armed for war .....Num 31:5
threescore and *t* thousand .....Num 31:33
tribute was threescore and *t* ...Num 31:38
I took *t* men of you, one of ...Deut 1:23
take you *t* men out of the .....Josh 3:12
Take you *t* men out of the ....Josh 4:2
t stones, and ye shall ....Josh 4:3
Joshua called the *t* men ....Josh 4:4
t stones out of the midst ......Josh 4:8
Joshua set up *t* stones in ......Josh 4:9
And those *t* stones, which .....Josh 4:20
t cities with their villages......Josh 18:24
tribe of Zebulun, *t* cities ......Josh 21:7
her bones, into *t* pieces ......Judg 19:29
by number *t* of Benjamin 2Sam 2:15
t of the servants of David 2Sam 2:15
and *t* thousand horsemen......1Kin 4:26
It stood upon *t* oxen 1Kin 7:25
and *t* oxen under the sea 1Kin 7:44
t thousand horsemen, whom ...1Kin 10:26
reign over Israel, *t* years 1Kin 16:23
plowing with *t* yoke of oxen ...1Kin 19:19
him, and he with the *t* 1Kin 19:19
of Judah, and reigned *t* years ..2Kin 3:1
In the *t* year of Joram 2Kin 8:25
Manasseh was *t* years old 2Kin 21:1
in the *t* month, on the seven ..2Kin 25:27
brethren a hundred and *t* 1Chr 15:10
Eliashib, the *t* to Jakim 1Chr 24:12
brethren and sons were *t*......1Chr 25:9
his brethren, were *t*...........1Chr 25:10
t captain for the *t* month 1Chr 27:15
and *t* thousand horsemen......2Chr 1:14
t lions stood there on the 2Chr 9:19
With *t* hundred chariots 2Chr 12:3
in the *t* year he began to 2Chr 34:3
eight hundred and *t*...........Ezra 2:6
t he goats, according to ....Ezra 6:17
I separated *t* of the chief ......Ezra 8:24
t day of the first month ....Ezra 8:31
t years, I and my brethren ....Neh 5:14
that she had been *t* months....Esth 2:12
t year of king Ahasuerus ......Esth 3:7
to the *t* month, that is, the ....Esth 3:7
thirteenth day of the *t* ....Esth 8:12
the valley of salt *t* ....Ps 60:*title*
a fillet of *t* cubits did ....Jer 52:21

TWENTY

[*also* TWENTIETH, TWENTY'S]

TWICE—*two times*

t have I heard this ....Ps 62:11
he live a thousand years *t* .....Eccl 6:6
before the cock crow *t* ....Mark 14:30
I fast *t* in the week, I give ....Luke 18:12
fruit, *t* dead, plucked up ......Jude 12

TWIGS—*small shoots or branches*
off the top of his young *t* .....Ezek 17:4

TWILIGHT—*the light of early morning or late evening*
David smote them from the *t*..1Sam 30:17
they rose up in the *t*, to go....2Kin 7:5
the stars of the *t* thereof ......Job 3:9
In the *t*, in the evening ....Prov 7:9
carry it forth in the *t* ....Ezek 12:6
upon his shoulder in the *t*.....Ezek 12:12

TWINED—*twisted together*
ten curtains of fine *t* linen .....Ex 26:1
scarlet, and fine *t* linen ....Ex 26:36
hangings..of fine *t* linen ....Ex 27:9
five cubits of fine *t* linen ......Ex 27:18
scarlet, and fine *t* linen ....Ex 28:8
curtains of fine *t* linen ....Ex 36:8
scarlet, and fine *t* linen ....Ex 36:37
about were of fine *t* linen .....Ex 38:16
scarlet, and fine *t* linen ....Ex 39:2
breeches of fine *t* linen........Ex 39:28

TWINKLING—*an instant*
moment, in the *t* of an eye 1Cor 15:52

TWINS
Esau and Jacob ....Gen 25:24-26
Pharez and Zarah ....Gen 38:27-30

whereof every one bear *t*......Song 4:2
two young roes that are *t* .....Song 4:5
every one beareth *t*, and ......Song 6:6
two young roes that are *t* .....Song 7:3

TWO
Lights ....Gen 1:16
Tables of stone..........Ex 34:1, 4
Goats ....Lev 16:7, 8
Spies ....Josh 2:1, 4
Wives 1Sam 1:2
Evils ....Jer 2:13
Masters..................Matt 6:24
Witnesses ....Matt 18:16
People agreeing ....Matt 18:19, 20
Commandments ....Matt 22:40
Thieves ....Matt 27:38
Covenants ....Gal 4:24
Become one ....Eph 5:31
Hard-pressed from both directions ....Phil 1:23

God made *t* great lights ....Gen 1:16
in *t* and *t* unto Noah ....Gen 7:9
ark, *t* and *t* of all flesh ....Gen 7:15
told his *t* brethren ....Gen 9:22
came *t* angels to Sodom ....Gen 19:1
hand of his *t* daughters........Gen 19:16
took *t* of his young men.......Gen 22:3
T nations are in thy womb ....Gen 25:23
Laban had *t* daughters ....Gen 29:16
t of the sons of Jacob ....Gen 34:25
Slay my *t* sons, if I bring......Gen 42:37
my wife bare me *t* sons ....Gen 44:27
t years hath the famine ....Gen 45:6
t side posts with the blood ....Ex 12:22
the bread of *t* days ....Ex 16:29
t sockets under one board .....Ex 26:19
tabernacle in the *t* sides ....Ex 26:23
t sides of the altar ....Ex 27:7
shalt take *t* onyx stones ....Ex 28:9
t chains of pure gold...........Ex 28:14
t lambs of the first year ....Ex 29:38
Hew thee *t* tables of stone ....Ex 34:1
made *t* cherubims of gold .....Ex 37:7
t ends of the mercy seat.......Ex 37:7
cleansed *t* birds alive..........Lev 14:4
take *t* he lambs without ....Lev 14:7
death of the *t* sons of ....Lev 16:1
shalt set them in *t* rows ....Lev 24:6
or *t* young pigeons............Num 6:10
weighed *t* thousand ....Num 7:85
it were *t* days, or a ....Num 9:22
Make thee *t* trumpets ....Num 10:2
The *t* tribes and the half ......Num 34:15
done unto these *t* kings ....Deut 3:21
upon *t* tables of stone ....Deut 4:13
Lord gave me *t* tables.........Deut 9:11
t tables of the covenant ....Deut 9:15
out of my *t* hands, and........Deut 9:17
mouth of *t* witnesses ....Deut 19:15
t kings of the Amorites ....Josh 2:10
dagger which had *t* edges .....Judg 3:16
the *t* kings of Midian ....Judg 8:12
bound..with *t* new cords ......Judg 15:13
Philistines for my *t* eyes ......Judg 16:28
slew *t* thousand men of them ..Judg 20:45
her *t* daughters-in-law with ....Ruth 1:7
t went until they came to .....Ruth 1:19
give thee *t* loaves of bread 1Sam 10:4
David's *t* wives were taken 1Sam 30:5
and *t* clusters of raisins........1Sam 30:12
Saul's son had *t* men that 2Sam 4:2
handmaid had *t* sons 2Sam 14:6
your *t* sons with you 2Sam 15:27
came there *t* women, that 1Kin 3:16
Divide the living child in *t* 1Kin 3:25
t doors were of fir tree........1Kin 6:34
cast *t* pillars of brass 1Kin 7:15
ark save the *t* tables of........1Kin 8:9
Solomon made *t* hundred 1Kin 10:16
t were alone in the field.......1Kin 11:29
Israel divided into *t* parts 1Kin 16:21
I am gathering *t* sticks 1Kin 17:12
they *t* stood by Jordan 2Kin 2:7
t went over on dry ground 2Kin 2:8
rent them in *t* pieces..........2Kin 2:12
Lay ye them in *t* heaps 2Kin 10:8
images, even *t* calves 2Kin 17:16
slew *t* lionlike men of Moab ...1Chr 11:22
T rows of oxen were cast 2Chr 4:3
ark save the *t* tables 2Chr 5:10
t courts of the house..Lord 2Chr 33:5
t vessels of fine copper ....Ezra 8:27
a work of one day or *t*........Ezra 10:13
mules, *t* hundred forty and ....Neh 7:68
Only do not *t* things unto .....Job 13:20
T things have I required of ....Eccl 4:9
if *t* lie together, then ....Eccl 4:11
ditch between the *t* walls ......Is 22:11
to open..the *t* leaved gates ....Is 45:1
people have committed *t* ......Jer 2:13
t baskets of figs were set ......Jer 24:1
These *t* nations and ....Ezek 35:10
t countries shall be mine ......Ezek 35:10
divided into *t* kingdoms ....Ezek 37:22
sanctuary had *t* doors ....Ezek 41:23
Joseph shall have *t* portions ...Ezek 47:13
ram which had *t* horns ....Dan 8:3
After *t* days..revive us ....Hos 6:2
Can *t* walk together ....Amos 3:3
are the *t* anointed ones ....Zech 4:14
from *t* years old and under ....Matt 2:16
No man can serve *t* masters ...Matt 6:24
t possessed with devils ....Matt 8:28
t blind men followed him .....Matt 9:27
he sent *t* of his disciples.......Matt 11:2
t eyes to be cast into hell .....Matt 18:9
if *t* of you shall agree on ......Matt 18:19
my *t* sons may sit.............Matt 20:21
t blind man sitting by the .....Matt 20:30
sent Jesus *t* disciples ....Matt 21:1
A certain man had *t* sons .....Matt 21:28
On these *t* commandments ....Matt 22:40
shall *t* be in the field ....Matt 24:40
T women shall be grinding ....Matt 24:41
he that had received *t*.........Matt 25:17
gained the other *t* ....Matt 25:17
received *t* talents came ....Matt 25:22
gained *t* other talents ....Matt 25:22
after *t* days is the feast ......Matt 26:2
the *t* sons of Zebedee ....Matt 26:37
came *t* false witnesses ....Matt 26:60
send them forth by *t* and *t* ....Mark 6:7
not put on *t* coats ....Mark 6:9
t hundred pennyworth of ......Mark 6:37
Five, and *t* fishes ....Mark 6:38
loaves and the *t* fishes ....Mark 6:41
t hands go into hell ....Mark 9:43
t feet to be cast into hell .....Mark 9:45
t eyes to be cast into hell .....Mark 9:47
sendeth forth *t*..disciples ......Mark 11:1
where *t* ways met.............Mark 11:4
she threw in *t* mites ....Mark 12:42
sendeth forth *t* of his ....Mark 14:13
they crucify *t* thieves..........Mark 15:27
He that hath *t* coats, let.......Luke 3:11
saw *t* ships standing by........Luke 5:2
unto him *t* of his disciples .....Luke 7:19
which had *t* debtors...........Luke 7:41
have *t* coats apiece ....Luke 9:3
five loaves and *t* fishes ....Luke 9:13
talked with him *t* men ....Luke 9:30
t men that stood with him.....Luke 9:32
seventy..sent them *t* ....Luke 10:1
he took out *t* pence...........Luke 10:35
sparrows..for *t* farthings ....Luke 12:6
three against *t*, and ....Luke 12:52
certain man had *t* sons ....Luke 15:11
No servant..serve *t* masters ....Luke 16:13
shall be *t* men in one bed .....Luke 17:34
T women shall be grinding ....Luke 17:35
T men shall be in the field ....Luke 17:36
T men went up into the ....Luke 18:10
sent *t* of his disciples..........Luke 19:29
widow casting..*t* mites.........Luke 21:2
here are *t* swords ....Luke 22:38
t other, malefactors ....Luke 23:32
t men stood by them in ....Luke 24:4
t of them went that same .....Luke 24:13
John stood, and *t* of his ....John 1:35
t disciples heard him speak ....John 1:37
t which heard John ....John 1:40
he abode there *t* days ....John 4:40
t days he departed thence .....John 4:43
T..pennyworth of bread ....John 6:7
loaves, and *t* small fishes ......John 6:9
testimony of *t* men is true .....John 8:17
he abode *t* days still in.........John 11:6
crucified him..*t* other with .....John 19:18
seeth *t* angels in white ....John 20:12
t other of his disciples ....John 21:2
t men stood by them in white .Acts 1:10
appointed *t*, Joseph called .....Acts 1:23
these *t* thou hast chosen ......Acts 1:24
where he begat *t* sons.........Acts 7:29
sent unto him *t* men ....Acts 9:38
called *t* of his..servants........Acts 10:7
sleeping between *t* soldiers ....Acts 12:6
bound with *t* chains ....Acts 12:6
by the space of *t* years ....Acts 19:10
sent into Macedonia *t* of ......Acts 19:22
space of *t* hours cried out .....Acts 19:34
bound with *t* chains...........Acts 21:33
unto him *t* centurions ....Acts 23:23
ready *t* hundred soldiers ......Acts 23:23
place where *t* seas meet ....Acts 27:41
Paul dwelt *t* whole years ......Acts 28:30
for *t*..shall be one flesh 1Cor 6:16
let it be by *t*, or at the........1Cor 14:27
prophets speak *t* or three 1Cor 14:29
mouth of *t* or three 2Cor 13:1
Abraham had *t* sons, the ......Gal 4:22
these are the *t* covenants ......Gal 4:24
t shall be one flesh ....Eph 5:31
before *t*..witnesses 1Tim 5:19
t immutable things, in.........Heb 6:18
mercy under *t* or three ....Heb 10:28
sword with *t* edges............Rev 2:12
come *t* woes more hereafter ...Rev 9:12
power unto my *t* witnesses ....Rev 11:3
These are the *t* olive trees.....Rev 11:4
t candlesticks standing ....Rev 11:4
t prophets tormented them ....Rev 11:10
t wings of a great eagle ....Rev 12:14
had *t* horns like a lamb ....Rev 13:11

TWO-EDGED—*sharp on both sides*
and a *t* sword in their hand ...Ps 149:6
wormwood, sharp as a *t* sword .Prov 5:4
sharper than any *t* sword ......Heb 4:12
mouth went a sharp *t* sword ...Rev 1:16

TWOFOLD—*twice as much*
t more the child of hell … Matt 23:15

TYCHICUS (tĭk'ĭ-kŭs)—*"fortunate"*
Asian Christian and companion … Acts 20:4
Carried Paul's letter to Colossians … Col 4:7
Carried letter to Ephesians … Eph 6:21, 22
Accompanied Onesimus to his master … Col 4:7
Later sent to Ephesus by Paul … 2Tim 4:12

Artemas unto thee, or *T* … Titus 3:12

TYPE—*person or thing which foreshadows or prefigures something else*

***May be*:**
Ceremony—Passover … 1Cor 5:7
Event—wilderness journeys … 1Cor 10:1-11
Institution—priesthood … Heb 9:11
Person—Adam … Rom 5:14
Thing—veil … Heb 10:20

TYRANNUS (tī-răn'ŭs)—*"tyrant"*
Paul teaches in his school. Acts 19:9

TYRE (tīr)—*"rock"*
Ancient city … Josh 19:29
Noted for commerce … Ezek 27:1-36
King of, helped Solomon . 1Kin 5:1-10
Denounced by prophets … Joel 3:4-6
Fall of, predicted … Ezek 26:1-21
Jesus visited … Matt 15:21-28

[*also* TYRUS]
Hiram king of *T* sent … 2Sam 5:11
came to the stronghold of *T* … 2Sam 24:7
and fetched Hiram out of *T* … 1Kin 7:13
king of *T* had furnished … 1Kin 9:11
Hiram king of *T* sent … 1Chr 14:1
sent to Huram the king of *T* … 2Chr 2:3
his father was a man of *T* … 2Chr 2:14
them of *T*, to bring cedar … Ezra 3:7
There dwelt men of *T* also … Neh 13:16
daughter of *T* shall be … Ps 45:12
Philistia, and *T*, with … Ps 87:4
The burden of *T*. Howl, ye … Is 23:1
this counsel against *T* … Is 23:8
T shall be forgotten … Is 23:15
shall *T* sing as a harlot … Is 23:15
And all the kings of *T* … Jer 25:22
cut off from *T* and Zidon … Jer 47:4
say unto the prince of *T* … Ezek 28:2
a great service against *T* … Ezek 29:18
as I saw *T*, is planted in … Hos 9:13
to do with me, O *T* … Joel 3:4
three transgressions of *T* … Amos 1:9
T, and Zidon, though it be … Zech 9:2
been done in *T* and Sidon … Matt 11:21
the coasts of *T* and Sidon … Matt 15:21
about *T* and Sidon, a great … Mark 3:8
from the coasts of *T* and … Mark 7:31
from the seacoast of *T* … Luke 6:17
be more tolerable for *T* … Luke 10:14
displeased with them of *T* … Acts 12:20
finished our course from *T* … Acts 21:7

TZADDI (tsăd'ē, tsä-dē')
Letter of the Hebrew Alphabet … Ps 119:137-144

U

UCAL (ū'kăl)—*"signs of God"*
Proverbs addressed to … Prov 30:1

UEL (ū'ĕl)—*"will of God"*
Divorced his foreign wife . Ezra 10:34

ULAI (ū'lī)—*"pure water"*
Scene of Daniel's visions . . Dan 8:2-16

ULAM (ū'lăm)—*"solitary; preceding"*
Manassite … 1Chr 7:16, 17
were, *U* his first-born … 1Chr 8:39
sons of *U* were mighty men … 1Chr 8:40

ULLA (ŭl'ä)—*"elevation; burden"*
Descendant of Asher … 1Chr 7:30, 39

UMMAH (ŭm'ä)—*"darkened"*
Asherite town … Josh 19:24, 30

UNACCUSTOMED—*not used to*
as a bullock *u* to the yoke … Jer 31:18

UNADVISEDLY—*rashly*
he spake *u* with his lips … Ps 106:33

UNAWARES—*without premeditation; suddenly; unexpectedly*
Jacob stole away *u* to Laban … Gen 31:20
hast stolen away *u* to me … Gen 31:26
killeth any person at *u* … Num 35:11
killeth any person *u* may … Num 35:15
should kill his neighbor *u* … Deut 4:42
that killeth any person *u* … Josh 20:3
killeth any person at *u* … Josh 20:9
destruction come..at *u* … Ps 35:8
so that day come upon you *u* … Luke 21:34
false brethren *u* brought in … Gal 2:4
have entertained angels *u* … Heb 13:2
and certain men crept in *u* … Jude 4

UNBELIEF—*refusal to accept and appropriate God's truth*

***Caused by*:**
Sin … John 16:9
Satan … John 8:43-47
Evil heart … Heb 3:12
Honor from one another . John 5:44
Not belonging to Christ … John 10:26
Judicial blindness … John 12:37-40

***Manifested in*:**
Questioning God's Word . Gen 3:1-6; 2Pet 3:4, 5
Turning from God … Heb 3:12
Questioning God's power . Ps 78:19, 20
Hating God's messengers . Acts 7:54, 57
Resisting the Spirit … Acts 7:51, 52
Discounting evidence … John 12:37
Opposing the Gospel … 1Thess 2:14-16
Rejecting Christ … John 12:48; John 16:9

***Consequences of, seen in*:**
Hindering miracles … Matt 13:58
Exclusion from blessings . Heb 3:15-19
Condemnation … John 3:18, 19
Rejection … Rom 11:20
Judgment … John 12:48
Death … John 8:24, 25
Destruction … 2Thess 1:8, 9
God's wrath … John 3:36

***Those guilty, described as*:**
Stiffnecked … Acts 7:51
Uncircumcised … Jer 6:10
Blinded … Eph 4:18
Rebels … Num 17:10

[*also* UNBELIEVING]
unto them, Because of your *u* . Matt 17:20
marveled because of their *u* … Mark 6:6
upbraided them with their *u* … Mark 16:14
the *u* Jews stirred up the … Acts 14:2
their *u* make the faith of … Rom 3:3
promise of God through *u* … Rom 4:20
they abide not still in *u* … Rom 11:23
mercy through their *u* … Rom 11:30
God hath concluded..in *u* … Rom 11:32
u husband is sanctified by … 1Cor 7:14
u wife is sanctified by the … 1Cor 7:14
I did it ignorantly in *u* … 1Tim 1:13
and *u* is nothing pure … Titus 1:15
entered not in because of *u* … Heb 4:6
after the same example of *u* … Heb 4:11
But the fearful, and *u* … Rev 21:8

UNBELIEVERS—*those who are not Christians*
Condemnation of … Mark 16:16
Intermarriage with Christians, forbidden … 2Cor 6:14, 15
him his portion with the *u* … Luke 12:46
and that before the *u* … 1Cor 6:6
that are unlearned, or *u* … 1Cor 14:23

UNBLAMABLE—*blameless; without guilt*

[*also* UNBLAMABLY]
to present you holy and *u* … Col 1:22
u we behaved ourselves … 1Thess 2:10
stablish your hearts *u* in … 1Thess 3:13

UNCERTAIN—*not sure*

[*also* UNCERTAINLY]
the trumpet gave an *u* sound … 1Cor 14:8
nor trust in *u* riches … 1Tim 6:17
I therefore so run, not as *u* … 1Cor 9:26

UNCERTAINTIES—*things which may or may not happen*

***Caused by*:**
Unknown future … Prov 27:1
Divine Providence … James 4:13-17
Our lack of knowledge … John 21:18-23

***Need not affect our*:**
Assurance … 1Cor 9:26
Trust in God … Rom 4:19-21
Plans … Acts 21:11-15

UNCHANGEABLE—*permanent; eternal*
ever, hath an *u* priesthood … Heb 7:24

UNCHARITABLENESS—*a critical spirit; unforgiving*
Condemning others … Matt 7:1-4; James 4:11, 12
Passing false judgments … Luke 7:39
Assuming superior holiness … John 8:1-11
Not forgiving readily … Luke 15:25-32; 2Cor 2:6-11
Imputing evil to others … 1Sam 1:14-17

UNCIRCUMCISED—*not circumcised; outside of God's covenant*

***Descriptive of*:**
Gentiles … Gal 2:7
Unregenerate state … Col 2:13
Unregenerate Jews and Gentiles … Jer 9:25, 26

***State of, in the Old Testament, excludes from*:**
Covenant … Ex 17:14
Passover … Ex 12:48
Land … Josh 5:7
Sanctuary … Ezek 44:7, 9
Holy city … Is 52:1

***State of, in the New Testament*:**
Has no spiritual value … Gal 5:6
Need not be changed … 1Cor 7:18, 19
Explained … Rom 2:25-29

[*also* UNCIRCUMCISION]
the *u* man child whose flesh … Gen 17:14
our sister to one that is *u* … Gen 34:14
hear me, who am of *u* lips? … Ex 6:12
I am of *u* lips, and how … Ex 6:30
count the fruit thereof as *u* … Lev 19:23
their *u* hearts be humbled … Lev 26:41
wife of the *u* Philistines? … Judg 14:3
the garrison of these *u* … 1Sam 14:6
this *u* Philistine shall be … 1Sam 17:36
lest these *u* come and … 1Sam 31:4
the daughters of the *u* … 2Sam 1:20
lest these *u* come and abuse … 1Chr 10:4
ear is *u*, and they cannot … Jer 6:10
die the deaths of the *u* … Ezek 28:10
lie in the midst of the *u* … Ezek 31:18
be thou laid with the *u* … Ezek 32:19
they lie *u*, slain by the … Ezek 32:21
are gone down *u* into the … Ezek 32:24
All of them *u*, slain by the … Ezek 32:25
all of them *u*, slain by the … Ezek 32:26
that are fallen of the *u* … Ezek 32:27
in the midst of the *u* … Ezek 32:28
they shall lie with the *u* … Ezek 32:29
and they lie *u* with them … Ezek 32:30
laid in the midst of the *u* … Ezek 32:32
Ye stiffnecked and *u* in … Acts 7:51
Thou wentest in to men *u* … Acts 11:3

faith, and *u* through faith .....Rom 3:30
or upon the *u* also? for we ....Rom 4:9
in circumcision, or in *u*? ......Rom 4:10
circumcision, but in *u* ....Rom 4:10
which he had yet being *u* ....Rom 4:11
which he had being yet *u* .....Rom 4:12
who are called *U* by that ......Eph 2:11

UNCLE—*the brother of one's father or mother*

[*also* UNCLE'S]
of Uzziel the *u* of Aaron ......Lev 10:4
shall lie with his *u* wife ....Lev 20:20
uncovered his *u* nakedness ....Lev 20:20
Either his *u*, or his *u* son .....Lev 25:49
Saul's *u* said unto him and 1Sam 10:14
Saul's *u* said, Tell me, I.......1Sam 10:15
Saul said unto his *u*, He 1Sam 10:16
the son of Ner, Saul's *u*.......1Sam 14:50
David's *u* was a counselor 1Chr 27:32
Hanameel..thine *u* shall come .Jer 32:7
Hanameel mine *u* son came to .Jer 32:8
field of Hanammel my *u* son . .Jer 32:9
sight of Hanameel mine *u* son .Jer 32:12
And a man's *u* shall take .....Amos 6:10

UNCLEAN—*contaminated by ritual, physical, moral, or spiritual impurity*

Descriptive of:
Men and women ....Deut 23:10
Lev. 15:1-33
Not of the Lord ....Is 52:1

Transformation of, by:
Purification ....Is 6:5-7
Separation 2Cor 6:17
Knowledge in Jesus ......Rom 14:14
Prayer 1Tim 4:3-5

See CLEAN; POLLUTE; SANITATION AND HYGIENE

[*also* UNCLEANNESS, UNCLEANESSES]
if a soul touch any *u* thing ....Lev 5:2
be a carcase of an *u* beast.....Lev 5:2
a carcase of *u* cattle, or ....Lev 5:2
carcase of *u* creeping things ...Lev 5:2
he also shall be *u*.............Lev 5:2
Or if he touch the *u* of man...Lev 5:3
whatsoever *u* it be that a......Lev 5:3
that toucheth any *u* thing .....Lev 7:19
Lord, having his *u* upon him . .Lev 7:20
shall touch any *u* thing........Lev 7:21
of man, or any *u* beast........Lev 7:21
or any abominable *u* thing ....Lev 7:21
as the *u* of man, or any *u* .....Lev 7:21
and between *u* and clean ......Lev 10:10
not the cud; he is *u* to you....Lev 11:7
for these ye shall be *u* ....Lev 11:24
shall be *u* until the even ......Lev 11:24
cheweth the cud, are *u* unto...Lev 11:26
toucheth them shall be *u* ......Lev 11:26
and be *u* until the even ....Lev 11:28
even: they are *u* unto you.....Lev 11:28
are *u* to you among all that ...Lev 11:31
shall be *u* until the even ......Lev 11:31
is in it shall be *u* ....Lev 11:33
carcase faileth shall be *u* ......Lev 11:35
are *u*, and shall be *u* unto.....Lev 11:35
it shall be *u* unto you ....Lev 11:38
and be *u* until the even ....Lev 11:40
difference between the *u* ......Lev 11:47
she shall be *u* seven days .....Lev 12:2
infirmity shall she be *u*........Lev 12:2
him, and pronounce him *u* ....Lev 13:3
priest shall pronounce him *u* . .Lev 13:11
shut him up: for he is *u*.......Lev 13:11
and pronounce him to be *u* ...Lev 13:15
for the raw flesh is *u* ....Lev 13:15
for yellow hair: he is *u*........Lev 13:36
He is a leprous man, he is *u* . .Lev 13:44
pronounce him utterly *u* ....Lev 13:44
shall be defiled; he is *u* ......Lev 13:46
plague be not spread; it is *u*. .Lev 13:55
to be cleansed from his *u* .....Lev 14:19
in the house be not made *u* ...Lev 14:36
the city into an *u* place ....Lev 14:41
because of his issue he is *u*....Lev 15:2
that hath the issue, is *u* ....Lev 15:4
he sitteth, shall be *u* ....Lev 15:4
u of the children of Israel .....Lev 16:16
in the midst of their *u* ....Lev 16:16
and be *u* until the even ....Lev 17:15
she is put apart for her *u* .....Lev 18:19
between clean beasts and *u*....Lev 20:25
between *u* fowls and clean ....Lev 20:25
separated from you as *u* ......Lev 20:25
having his *u* upon him ....Lev 22:3
whereby he may be made *u* ...Lev 22:5
man of whom he may take *u* . .Lev 22:5
whatsoever *u* he hath ....Lev 22:5
if it be any *u* beast ....Lev 27:11
hast not gone aside to *u* ......Num 5:19
not make himself *u* for his ....Num 6:7
the firstling of the *u* beasts ....Num 18:15
shall be *u* until the even ......Num 19:8
man shall be *u* seven days.....Num 19:11
his *u* is yet upon him ....Num 19:13
in the tent, shall be *u*.........Num 19:14
shall be *u* seven days ....Num 19:16
shall sprinkle upon the *u* ......Num 19:19
the man that shall be *u* ....Num 19:20
sprinkled upon him; he is *u* ...Num 19:20
the *u* person toucheth...........Num 19:22
person toucheth shall be *u* ....Num 19:22
toucheth it shall be *u* ....Num 19:22
u and the clean may eat ......Deut 12:15
they are *u* unto you ....Deut 14:7
not eat; it is *u* unto you......Deut 14:10
u and the clean person........Deut 15:22
he hath found some *u* in her . .Deut 24:1
ought thereof for any *u* use ...Deut 26:14
land of your possession be *u* . .Josh 22:19
and eat not any *u* thing ....Judg 13:4
drink, nor eat any *u* thing.....Judg 13:14
she was purified from her *u* ...2Sam 11:4
none which was *u* in any 2Chr 23:19
all the *u* that they found 2Chr 29:16
u land with the filthiness ......Ezra 9:11
and to another with their *u*....Ezra 9:11
a clean thing out of an *u*?.....Job 14:4
the clean, and to the *u*........Eccl 9:2
the *u* shall not pass over ......Is 35:8
thence, touch no *u* thing ......Is 52:11
them, Depart ye; it is *u*.......Lam 4:15
between the *u* and the clean...Ezek 22:26
save you from all your *u* ......Ezek 36:29
they shall eat *u* things in ......Hos 9:3
If one that is *u* by a dead .....Hag 2:13
any of these, shall it be *u*? ....Hag 2:13
and said, It shall be *u* ....Hag 2:13
Jerusalem for sin and for *u*....Zech 13:1
u spirit to pass out of the .....Zech 13:2
power against *u* spirits ....Matt 10:1
men's bones, and of all *u* .....Matt 23:27
a man with an *u* spirit ....Mark 1:23
commandeth he..*u* spirits......Mark 1:27
said, He hath an *u* spirit ......Mark 3:30
Come out..thou *u* spirit ....Mark 5:8
them power over *u* spirits .....Mark 6:7
had a spirit of an *u* devil .....Luke 4:33
were vexed with *u* spirits......Luke 6:18
Jesus rebuked the *u* spirit .....Luke 9:42
were vexed with *u* spirits......Acts 5:16
thing that is common or *u*.....Acts 10:14
nothing common or *u* hath at. .Acts 11:8
God also gave them up to *u*...Rom 1:24
your members servants to *u* ...Rom 6:19
have not repented of the *u* 2Cor 12:21
Adultery, fornication, *u* ....Gal 5:19
work all *u* with greediness.....Eph 4:19
But fornication, and all *u* .....Eph 5:3
nor *u* person, nor covetous ....Eph 5:5
the earth; fornication, *u*.......Col 3:5
not of deceit, nor of *u* 1Thess 2:3
a heifer sprinkling the *u* ......Heb 9:13
the flesh in the lust of *u* 2Pet 2:10
I saw three *u* spirits like ......Rev 16:13
of every *u* and hateful bird ....Rev 18:2

UNCLOTHED—*refers to being without one's physical body*
not for that we would be *u*....2Cor 5:4

UNCOMELY—*inappropriately; unattractive*
behaveth himself *u* toward 1Cor 7:36
our *u* parts have more 1Cor 12:23

UNCONDEMNED—*not convicted of a crime*
have beaten us openly *u* ......Acts 16:37
man that is a Roman, and *u*? . .Acts 22:25

UNCONDITIONAL SURRENDER—*unreserved commitment to Christ*
Required by Christ ......Luke 14:26, 27
As sacrifice ....Rom 12:1

UNCORRUPTIBLE—*not subject to perversion or decay*

[*also* UNCORRUPTNESS]
the glory of the *u* God........Rom 1:23
showing *u*, gravity ....Titus 2:7

UNCOVER—*to make known; bring to light; reveal*

[*also* UNCOVERED, UNCOVERETH]
he was *u* within his tent.......Gen 9:21
u not your heads ....Lev 10:6
to *u* their nakedness ....Lev 18:6
mother, shalt thou not *u* ......Lev 18:7
thou shalt not *u* her ....Lev 18:7
thou shalt not *u* ....Lev 18:9
not *u* the nakedness of........Lev 18:12
not *u* the nakedness of........Lev 18:14
u the nakedness of thy ....Lev 18:15
thou shalt not *u* her ....Lev 18:15
not *u* the nakedness ....Lev 18:17
daughter, to *u* her ....Lev 18:17
unto a woman to *u* her ....Lev 18:19
wife hath *u* his father's........Lev 20:11
she hath *u* the fountain ....Lev 20:18
unto a woman to *u* her ....Lev 20:19
u the nakedness of thy ....Lev 20:19
u the woman's head ....Num 5:18
because he *u* his father's ......Deut 27:20
and *u* his feet, and lay ....Ruth 3:4
u his feet and laid ....Ruth 3:7
who *u* himself today 2Sam 6:20
fellows shamelessly *u* 2Sam 6:20
with their buttocks *u*..........Is 20:4
and grind meal: *u* thy locks ...Is 47:2
make bare the leg, *u* ....Is 47:2
Thy nakedness shall be *u* .....Is 47:3
I have *u* his secret places .....Jer 49:10
thine arm shall be *u* ....Ezek 4:7
let thy foreskin be *u* ....Hab 2:16
for he shall *u* the cedar ....Zeph 2:14
they *u* the roof where he......Mark 2:4
prophesieth with her head *u*...1Cor 11:5
woman pray unto God *u*? 1Cor 11:13

UNCTION—*an anointing*
With the Holy Spirit.....1John 2:20, 27

an *u* from the Holy One 1John 2:20

UNDEFILED—*untainted*
Such persons are blessed .Ps 119:1
Christ is ....Heb 7:26
Describes marriage act ...Heb 13:4
Applied to true religion . .James 1:27
Our inheritance thus called 1Pet 1:4

my love, my dove, my *u* ......Song 5:2
My dove, my *u* is but one.....Song 6:9

UNDER—*beneath*
u the firmament ....Gen 1:7
life, from *u* heaven ....Gen 6:17
u the whole heaven ....Gen 7:19
submit thyself *u* her hands ....Gen 16:9
rest yourselves *u* the tree .....Gen 18:4
came they *u* the shadow ......Gen 19:8
cast the child *u*..shrubs........Gen 21:15
Jacob hid them *u* the oak .....Gen 35:4
thing that was *u* his hand .....Gen 39:23
lay up corn *u* the hand........Gen 41:35
thy hand *u* my thigh ....Gen 47:29
blessings..that lieth *u* ....Gen 49:25
out from *u* the burdens ....Ex 6:6
a stone, and put it *u* him .....Ex 17:12
from *u* the hand of the ....Ex 18:10

the water *u* the earth .... Ex 20:4
he die *u* his hand .... Ex 21:20
lying *u* his burden .... Ex 23:5
an altar *u* the hill .... Ex 24:4
u two branches of the .... Ex 25:35
silver *u* the twenty boards .... Ex 26:19
two sockets *u* one board .... Ex 26:19
two sockets *u* another .... Ex 26:19
two sockets *u* one board .... Ex 26:25
two sockets *u* another .... Ex 26:25
make to it *u* the crown .... Ex 30:4
u the twenty boards .... Ex 36:24
two sockets *u* one board .... Ex 36:24
two sockes *u* another .... Ex 36:24
u every board two sockets .... Ex 36:30
u two branches of the .... Ex 37:21
grate of network *u* the .... Ex 38:4
any thing that was *u* him .... Lev 15:10
seven days *u* the dam .... Lev 22:27
passeth *u* the rod .... Lev 27:32
u the custody and charge .... Num 3:36
u the hand of Ithamar .... Num 4:28
which is *u* the sacrifice .... Num 6:18
u the hand of Ithamar .... Num 7:8
clave asunder that was *u* .... Num 16:31
she fell down *u* Balaam .... Num 22:27
men of war which are *u* .... Num 31:49
u the hand of Moses .... Num 33:1
u the whole heaven .... Deut 2:25
sea, *u* Ashdoth-pisgah .... Deut 3:17
stood *u* the mountain .... Deut 4:11
u the springs of Pisgah .... Deut 4:49
their name from *u* heaven .... Deut 7:24
their name from *u* heaven .... Deut 9:14
u every green tree .... Deut 12:2
of Amalek from *u* heaven .... Deut 25:19
earth that is *u* thee .... Deut 28:23
his name from *u* heaven .... Deut 29:20
of my tent, and the silver *u* .... Josh 7:21
to the Hivite *u* Hermon .... Josh 11:3
south, *u* Ashdoth-pisgah .... Josh 12:3
this day, serve *u* tribute .... Josh 16:10
their meat *u* my table .... Judg 1:7
u the hand of Israel .... Judg 3:30
sat *u* an oak which was in .... Judg 6:11
to God this people were *u* .... Judg 9:29
u whose wings thou art .... Ruth 2:12
they came *u* Beth-car 1Sam 7:11
what is *u* thine hand? 1Sam 21:3
here *u* thine hand spear 1Sam 21:8
buried them *u* a tree 1Sam 31:13
smote him *u* the fifth rib 2Sam 2:23
smote him *u* the fifth rib 2Sam 4:6
were therein, and put them *u* .. 2Sam 12:31
u harrows of iron, and *u* 2Sam 12:31
people *u* the hand of 2Sam 18:2
u the hand of Abishai 2Sam 18:2
u the hand of Ittai 2Sam 18:2
mule went *u* the..boughs 2Sam 18:9
the mule that was *u* him 2Sam 18:9
darkness was *u* his feet 2Sam 22:10
they are fallen *u* my feet 2Sam 22:39
bringeth down the people *u* 2Sam 22:48
u his vine and *u* his fig 1Kin 4:25
put them *u*..his feet 1Kin 5:3
u the laver were 1Kin 7:30
twelve oxen *u* the sea 1Kin 7:44
found him sitting *u* an oak 1Kin 13:14
and put no fire *u* 1Kin 18:23
sat down *u* a juniper tree 1Kin 19:4
Edom revolted from *u* 2Kin 8:20
he trode her *u* foot 2Kin 9:33
the name of Israel from *u* 2Kin 14:27
brazen oxen that were *u* it 2Kin 16:17
u every green tree 2Kin 17:10
u the oak in Jabesh 1Chr 10:12
their manner, *u* Aaron 1Chr 24:19
u the hands of their father 1Chr 25:3
u the hands of Shelomith 1Chr 26:28
u it was the similitude 2Chr 4:3
u the wings of the cherubim 2Chr 5:7
u the dominion of 2Chr 21:8
u the hand of Judah 2Chr 21:10
revolt from *u* his hand 2Chr 21:10
u their hand was an army 2Chr 26:13
u the children of Judah 2Chr 28:10
the beast that was *u* me .... Neh 2:14
helpers do stoop *u* him .... Job 9:13
formed from *u* the waters .... Job 26:5
u it is turned up as it were .... Job 28:5
u the nettles they were .... Job 30:7
He lieth *u* the shady trees .... Job 40:21
Sharp stones are *u* him .... Job 41:30
put all things *u* his feet .... Ps 8:6
hide me *u* the shadow .... Ps 17:8
enlarged my steps *u* me .... Ps 18:36
subdued *u* me those .... Ps 18:39
we tread them *u* that rise .... Ps 44:5
subdue the people *u* us .... Ps 47:3
and the nations *u* our feet .... Ps 47:3
u his wings shalt thou .... Ps 91:4
dragon shalt thou trample *u* .... Ps 91:13
poison is *u* their lips .... Ps 140:3
slothful shall be *u* tribute .... Prov 12:24
he taketh *u* the sun? .... Eccl 1:3
all things that are done *u* .... Eccl 1:13
should do *u* the heaven .... Eccl 2:3
work..wrought *u* the sun .... Eccl 2:17
wise *u* the sun .... Eccl 2:19
labored *u* the sun .... Eccl 2:22
that are done *u* the sun .... Eccl 4:1
I saw vanity *u* the sun .... Eccl 4:7
evil..I have seen *u* the sun .... Eccl 5:13
evil..I have seen *u* the sun .... Eccl 6:1
thorns *u* a pot .... Eccl 7:6
no better thing *u* the sun .... Eccl 8:15
God giveth him *u* the sun .... Eccl 8:15
all things that are *u* .... Eccl 9:3
hath given thee *u* the sun .... Eccl 9:9
thou takest *u* the sun .... Eccl 9:9
wisdom..also *u* the sun .... Eccl 9:13
I sat down *u* his shadow .... Song 2:3
milk are *u* thy tongue .... Song 4:11
u the apple tree .... Song 8:5
this ruin be *u* thy hand .... Is 3:6
bow down *u* the prisoners .... Is 10:4
they shall fall *u* the slain .... Is 10:4
worm is spread *u* thee .... Is 14:11
tread him *u* foot .... Is 14:25
defiled *u* the inhabitants .... Is 24:5
shall be trodden *u* feet .... Is 28:3
gather *u* her shadow .... Is 34:15
idols *u* every green tree .... Is 57:5
valleys *u* the clifts .... Is 57:5
high hill and *u* every green .... Jer 2:20
strangers *u* every..tree .... Jer 3:13
trodden my portion *u* foot .... Jer 12:10
bring their neck *u* the yoke .... Jer 27:11
pass again *u* the hands .... Jer 33:13
u thine armholes *u* .... Jer 38:12
bulls that were *u* the bases .... Jer 52:20
trodden *u* foot all..men .... Lam 1:15
anger from *u* the heavens .... Lam 3:66
necks are *u* persecution .... Lam 5:5
hands..*u* their wings .... Ezek 1:8
u every green tree .... Ezek 6:13
u every thick oak .... Ezek 6:13
hand *u* their wings .... Ezek 10:8
hands of a man was *u* their .... Ezek 10:21
u it shall dwell all fowl .... Ezek 17:23
burn also the bones *u* it .... Ezek 24:5
u his branches did all the .... Ezek 31:6
u his shadow dwelt .... Ezek 31:6
swords *u* their heads .... Ezek 32:27
boiling places *u* the rows .... Ezek 46:23
u the threshold .... Ezek 47:1
waters came down from *u* .... Ezek 47:1
beasts..had shadow *u* it .... Dan 4:12
beasts get away from *u* .... Dan 4:14
the kingdom *u* the whole .... Dan 7:27
gone a whoring from *u* .... Hos 4:12
They that dwell *u* his .... Hos 14:7
The seed is rotten *u* their .... Joel 1:17
I am pressed *u* you .... Amos 2:13
laid a wound *u* thee .... Obad 7
sat *u* it in the shadow .... Jon 4:5
mountains..molten *u* him .... Mic 1:4
u the vine and *u* the fig .... Zech 3:10
be ashes *u* the soles of your .... Mal 4:3
from two years old and *u* .... Matt 2:16
candle, and put it *u* a bushel .... Matt 5:15
shouldest come *u* my roof .... Matt 8:8
I am a man *u* authority .... Matt 8:9
having soldiers *u* me .... Matt 8:9
u a bushel, or *u* a bed? .... Mark 4:21
the dust *u* your feet .... Mark 6:11
shouldest enter *u* my roof .... Luke 7:6
a man set *u* authority .... Luke 7:8
having *u* me soldiers .... Luke 7:8
neither *u* a bushel .... Luke 11:33
the one part *u* heaven .... Luke 17:24
the other part *u* heaven .... Luke 17:24
thou wast *u* the fig tree .... John 1:48
every nation *u* heaven .... Acts 2:5
great authority *u* Candace .... Acts 8:27
bound..*u* a great curse .... Acts 23:14
we sailed *u* Crete, over .... Acts 27:7
u color as though they .... Acts 27:30
they are all *u* sin .... Rom 3:9
them who are *u* the law .... Rom 3:19
not *u* the law, but *u* grace .... Rom 6:15
bruise Satan *u* your feet .... Rom 16:20
be brought *u* the power 1Cor 6:12
u the law, as *u* the law 1Cor 9:20
them that are *u* the law 1Cor 9:20
I keep *u* my body, and bring .. 1Cor 9:27
to be *u* obedience 1Cor 14:34
all things are put *u* him 1Cor 15:27
put all things *u* him 1Cor 15:27
the governor *u* Aretas 2Cor 11:32
works of the law are *u* the .... Gal 3:10
we were kept *u* the law .... Gal 3:23
u tutors and governors .... Gal 4:2
made *u* the law .... Gal 4:4
desire to be *u* the law .... Gal 4:21
all things *u* his feet .... Eph 1:22
things *u* the earth .... Phil 2:10
every creature whch is *u* .... Col 1:23
number *u* threescore 1Tim 5:9
subjection *u* his feet .... Heb 2:8
in subjection *u* him .... Heb 2:8
is not put *u* him .... Heb 2:8
all things put *u* him .... Heb 2:8
transgressions..*u* the .... Heb 9:15
trodden *u* foot the Son .... Heb 10:29
sit here *u* my footstool .... James 2:3
u the mighty hand of God 1Pet 5:6
in everlasting chains *u* .... Jude 6
neither *u* the earth .... Rev 5:3
I saw *u* the altar .... Rev 6:9
the moon *u* her feet .... Rev 12:1

UNDERGIRDING—*making secure underneath*
they used helps, *u* the ship .... Acts 27:17

UNDERNEATH—*beneath*
two sides of the ephod *u* .... Ex 28:27
two sides of the ephod *u* .... Ex 39:20
u are the everlasting arms .... Deut 33:27

UNDERSETTERS—*supports*
Supports placed under the laver 1Kin 7:30, 34

UNDERSTAND—*to grasp something's nature and significance; perception; common sense*

Means of, by:
God's:
Gift 1Kin 3:9-12
Revelation .... Rom 1:20
Word .... Ps 119:104, 130
Books .... Dan 9:2, 23
Holy Spirit .... Ex 31:3
Christ 1John 5:20
Prayer .... Ps 119:34-125
Faith .... Heb 11:3
Enlightening .... Eph 1:18
Interpretation .... Neh 8:2-13
Explanation .... Luke 24:45
Reproof .... Prov 15:32
Later event .... Ps 73:17

Limitations on, by:
Unbelief .... John 8:43
Unregeneracy .... Eph 4:18

Spiritual blindness ....Is 6:9, 10
Judicial punishment ......Is 44:18, 19
Difficulties 2Pet 3:16

[*also* UNDERSTANDEST, UNDERSTANDETH, UNDERSTANDING, UNDERSTOOD]
u one another's speech ....Gen 11:7
u a dream to interpret ....Gen 41:15
not that Joseph *u* them ....Gen 42:23
in wisdom, in *u* ....Ex 35:31
Lord put wisdom and *u* ....Ex 36:1
u that these men have ....Num 16:30
Take you wise men, and *u* ....Deut 1:13
your *u* in the sight of ....Deut 4:6
a wise and *u* people ....Deut 4:6
U therefore this day ....Deut 9:3
thou shalt not *u* ....Deut 28:49
wise, that they *u* this ....Deut 32:29
they *u* that the ark 1Sam 4:6
She was a woman of good *u*...1Sam 25:3
u that Saul was come in.......1Sam 26:4
all Israel *u* that...............2Sam 3:37
for thyself *u* to discern 1Kin 3:11
God gave Solomon..*u*...........1Kin 4:29
language; for we *u* it 2Kin 18:26
were men that had *u* 1Chr 12:32
u all the imaginations 1Chr 28:9
Lord made me *u* in writing....1Chr 28:19
endued with prudence and *u* ..2Chr 2:12
who had *u* in the visions 2Chr 26:5
for Elnathan, men of *u* ....Ezra 8:16
knowledge, and having *u* ......Neh 10:28
u of the evil that Eliashib .....Neh 13:7
u wherein I have erred........Job 6:24
I have *u* as well as you ....Job 12:3
he hath counsel and *u* ....Job 12:13
ear hath heard and *u* it ....Job 13:1
what *u* thou, which is not ....Job 15:9
hid their heart from *u* ....Job 17:4
by his *u* he smiteth ....Job 26:12
his power who can *u*?.........Job 26:14
God *u* the way thereof........Job 28:23
to depart from evil is *u* ....Job 28:28
unto me, ye men of *u* ....Job 34:10
Let men of *u* tell me ....Job 34:34
u the spreadings of the........Job 36:29
or who hath given *u* ....Job 38:36
I uttered that I *u* not ....Job 42:3
if there were any that did *u* ...Ps 14:2
Who can *u* his errors? ....Ps 19:12
mule, which have no *u*..........Ps 32:9
of my heart shall be of *u*.......Ps 49:3
is honor, and *u* not ....Ps 49:20
if there were any that did *u* ...Ps 53:2
a language that I *u* not ....Ps 81:5
neither will they *u* ....Ps 82:5
neither doth a fool *u* ....Ps 92:6
u the loving-kindness ....Ps 107:43
a good *u* have all they ....Ps 111:10
u the way of thy precepts .....Ps 119:27
I *u* more than the ancients ....Ps 119:100
give me *u*, and I shall live ....Ps 119:144
thou *u* my thought afar off ....Ps 139:2
his *u* is infinite ....Ps 147:5
perceive the words of *u* ....Prov 1:2
To *u* a proverb, and the ......Prov 1:6
apply thine heart to *u*.........Prov 2:2
u the fear of the Lord ....Prov 2:5
cometh knowledge and *u* ....Prov 2:6
thou *u* righteousness ....Prov 2:9
good *u* in the sight of God ....Prov 3:4
the man that getteth *u* ....Prov 3:13
father and attend to know *u*...Prov 4:1
with all thy getting get *u* ......Prov 4:7
call *u* thy kinswoman ....Prov 7:4
u put forth her voice? ....Prov 8:1
O ye simple, *u* wisdom ....Prov 8:5
all plain to him that *u* ....Prov 8:9
I am *u*; I have strength ....Prov 8:14
go in the way of *u*.............Prov 9:6
lips of him that hath *u* ....Prov 10:13
him that is void of *u*...........Prov 10:13
a man of *u* holdeth his........Prov 11:12
Good *u* giveth favor ....Prov 13:15
prudent is to *u* his way ....Prov 14:8
heart of him that hath *u* ......Prov 14:33
a man of *u* walketh ....Prov 15:21
u rather to be chosen ....Prov 16:16
A man void of *u* striketh......Prov 17:18
is before him that hath *u*......Prov 17:24
Lips is esteemed a man of *u*..Prov 17:28
he that keepeth *u* ....Prov 19:8
he will *u* knowledge ....Prov 19:25
a man of *u* will draw it out....Prov 20:5
how can a man then *u* ....Prov 20:24
no wisdom nor *u* nor counsel ..Prov 21:30
and by *u* it is established ......Prov 24:3
a man of *u* and knowledge ....Prov 28:2
Evil men *u* not judgment .....Prov 28:5
they that seek the Lord *u* ......Prov 28:5
The prince that wanteth *u*......Prov 28:16
though he *u* he will not ....Prov 29:19
nor yet riches to men of *u* ....Eccl 9:11
spirit of wisdom and *u* ....Is 11:2
it is a people of no *u* ....Is 27:11
whom shall he make to *u* .....Is 28:9
framed it. He had no *u*? ......Is 29:16
the rash shall *u* knowledge ....Is 32:4
Syrian language; for we *u* .....Is 36:11
showed to him the way of *u*? ..Is 40:14
not *u* from the foundations ....Is 40:21
is no searching of his *u* ....Is 40:28
u that I am he ....Is 43:10
have not known nor *u* ....Is 44:18
shepherds that cannot *u* ....Is 56:11
feed you with..and *u*..........Jer 3:15
neither *u* what they say ....Jer 5:15
foolish people..without *u* ......Jer 5:21
the wise man, that may *u* .....Jer 9:12
he *u* and knoweth me..........Jer 9:24
words thou canst not *u*.........Ezek 3:6
with thine *u* thou hast ....Ezek 28:4
in knowledge, and *u* ....Dan 1:4
matters of wisdom and *u* ......Dan 1:20
mine *u* returned unto me .....Dan 4:34
u, interpreting of dreams ......Dan 5:12
make this man to *u*............Dan 8:16
u dark sentences ....Dan 8:23
the vision, but none *u* it ......Dan 8:27
iniquities, and *u* thy truth .....Dan 9:13
Know therefore and *u* ....Dan 9:25
and he *u* the thing, and had ...Dan 10:1
had *u* of the vision ....Dan 10:1
didst set thine heart to *u* ......Dan 10:12
that *u* among the people ......Dan 11:33
none of the wicked shall *u* ....Dan 12:10
but the wise shall *u*...........Dan 12:10
people that doth not *u* ....Hos 4:14
according to their own *u* ......Hos 13:2
there is none *u* in him ....Obad 7
neither *u* they his counsel .....Mic 4:12
hear not, neither do they *u*....Matt 13:13
hear, and shall not *u* ....Matt 13:14
should *u* with their heart ......Matt 13:15
word of the Kingdom and *u* ...Matt 13:19
Have ye *u* all these things?....Matt 13:51
said unto them Hear, and *u* ...Matt 15:10
Are ye also yet without *u*? ....Matt 15:16
Do not ye yet *u*, that ....Matt 15:17
Do ye not yet *u*, neither ......Matt 16:9
How is it that ye do not *u* ....Matt 16:11
the disciples *u* that he ....Matt 17:13
(whoso readeth, let him *u*:) ...Matt 24:15
they may hear, and not *u* .....Mark 4:12
every one of you, and *u* ......Mark 7:14
Are ye so without *u* also? .....Mark 7:18
ye not yet, neither *u*? ....Mark 8:17
they *u* not that saying.........Mark 9:32
(let him that readeth *u*,) ......Mark 13:14
perfect *u* of all things ....Luke 1:3
astonished at his *u*............Luke 2:47
u not the saying which he .....Luke 2:50
hearing they might not *u* ......Luke 8:10
u none of these things ....Luke 18:34
u not that he spake ....John 8:27
These things *u* not his ....John 12:16
nor *u* with their heart..........John 12:40
his brethren would have *u*.....Acts 7:25
U thou what thou readest? ....Acts 8:30
u that he was a Roman ....Acts 23:27
he *u*..he was of Cilicia ....Acts 23:34
Because that thou mayest *u*,...Acts 24:11
u with their heart, and ....Acts 28:27
Without *u*, covenantbreakers ..Rom 1:31
There is none that *u* ....Rom 3:11
have not heard shall *u* ....Rom 15:21
nothing the *u* of the prudent ..1Cor 1:19
Wherefore I give you to *u* 1Cor 12:3
I *u* as a child, I thought as a ..1Cor 13:11
for no man *u* him; howbeit....1Cor 14:2
words easy to be *u* 1Cor 14:9
I will pray with the *u* 1Cor 14:15
I will sing with the *u* 1Cor 14:15
five words with my *u* 1Cor 14:19
be not children in *u* 1Cor 14:20
children, but in *u* be men 1Cor 14:20
u my knowledge in..mystery ...Eph 3:4
u what the will of the Lord ...Eph 5:17
I would ye should *u* ....Phil 1:12
peace..which passeth all *u* .....Phil 4:7
wisdom and spiritual *u* ....Col 1:9
u neither what they say 1Tim 1:7
Lord give thee *u* in all 2Tim 2:7
Through faith we *u* that the ...Heb 11:3
evil of things that they *u* not ..2Pet 2:12
come, and hath given us an *u* .1John 5:20
him that hath *u* count.........Rev 13:18

UNDERTAKE—*to take on; take responsibility for*

[*also* UNDERTOOK]
Jews *u* to do as they had......Esth 9:23
I am oppressed; *u* for me .....Is 38:14

UNDO—*to unloose; rein*

[*also* UNDONE]
thou art *u*, O people ....Num 21:29
he left nothing *u* of all.........Josh 11:15
Woe is me! for I am *u* ....Is 6:5
to *u* the heavy burdens ....Is 58:6
I will *u* all that afflict ....Zeph 3:19
not to leave the other *u*.......Matt 23:23
not to leave the other *u*.......Luke 11:42

UNDRESSED—*not cultivated or tended*
the grapes of thy vine *u*.......Lev 25:5
grapes in it of thy vine *u*......Lev 25:11

UNEQUAL—*not just; not even*

[*also* UNEQUALLY]
are not your ways *u*? ....Ezek 18:25
not *u* yoked together with.....2Cor 6:14

UNFAITHFUL—*not faithful; untrustworthy*

[*also* UNFAITHFULLY]
dealt *u* like their fathers ......Ps 78:57
Confidence in an *u* man ......Prov 25:19

UNFAITHFULNESS—*failure to fulfill promises*
Marriage vows ....Mal 2:14, 15
Use of talents ....Matt 25:24-30
Unfruitful service ....John 15:2, 4, 6
Abusing vows ....Judg 16:16-20
Rom 2:17-24

UNFEIGNED—*genuine; sincere*
the Holy Ghost, by love *u* 2Cor 6:6
conscience, and of faith *u* 1Tim 1:5
the *u* faith that is in thee 2Tim 1:5
Spirit unto *u* love............1Pet 1:22

UNFRUITFUL—*unproductive*

Caused by:
Unfaithfulness ....Is 5:1-7
Worldliness ....James 4:1-4
Negligence ....Luke 19:20-27

Punished by:
God's judgments ....Matt 3:10
Rejection:
Now ....John 15:2, 4, 6
Hereafter ....Heb 6:8

he becometh *u* ....Matt 13:22
it becometh *u* ....Mark 4:19
my understanding is *u* 1Cor 14:14
the *u* works of darkness.......Eph 5:11

that they be not *u* ... Titus 3:14
nor *u* in the knowledge ... 2Pet 1:8

UNGIRDED—*released from a restraining band or girdle*
he *u* his camels ... Gen 24:32

UNGODLINESS—*disregard for God's truth*
Described as:
Prospering in the world ... Ps 73:12
Growing worse ... 2Tim 2:16
Perverting God's grace ... Jude 4
Abounding in the last days ... Jude 18
Christ died for ... Rom 5:6
Judgments upon, by:
Flood ... 2Pet 2:5, 6
Law ... 1Tim 1:9
God's decree ... Jude 4
God's revelation ... Rom 1:18
Christ's return ... Jude 14, 15
World's end ... 2Pet 3:7
Final judgment ... Ps 1:4-6

[*also* UNGODLY]
floods of *u* men made me ... 2Sam 22:5
Shouldest thou help the *u* ... 2Chr 19:2
delivered me to the *u* ... Job 16:11
to princes, Ye are *u*? ... Job 34:18
the counsel of the *u* ... Ps 1:1
broken the teeth of the *u* ... Ps 3:7
cause against an *u* nation ... Ps 43:1
An *u* man diggeth up evil ... Prov 16:27
An *u* witness scorneth ... Prov 19:28
him that justifieth the *u* ... Rom 4:5
turn away *u* from Jacob ... Rom 11:26
denying *u* and worldly ... Titus 2:12
the *u* and the sinner ... 1Pet 4:18

UNHOLY—*wicked; showing disregard for holiness*
between holy and *u* ... Lev 10:10
for *u* and profane ... 1Tim 1:9
to parents, unthankful, *u* ... 2Tim 3:2
sanctified, an *u* thing ... Heb 10:29

UNICORN—*the wild ox*
Of great strength ... Num 23:22
Very wild and ferocious ... Job 39:9-12
Frisky in youth ... Ps 29:6

[*also* UNICORNS]
the strength of a *u* ... Num 24:8
are like the horns of *u* ... Deut 33:17
the horns of the *u* ... Ps 22:21
like the horn of a *u* ... Ps 92:10
the *u* shall come down ... Is 34:7

UNINTENTIONALLY—*without premeditation*
Concerning an innocent killer ... Josh 20:3-5

UNION—*joining of two or more things into one*
Of:
Godhead ... John 17:21, 22
Christ and believers ... John 15:1-7
God and man ... Acts 17:28, 29
Mankind ... Acts 17:26
Satan and the unsaved ... John 8:44
Believers in prayer ... Matt 18:19, 20
See ONENESS

UNION WITH CHRIST—*refers to believers' oneness with Christ*
Compared to:
Head and the body ... Eph 4:15, 16
Marriage bond ... Eph 5:23, 30
Building ... Eph 2:21, 22
Parts of the body ... 1Cor 12:12, 27
Vine and branches ... John 15:4, 5
Food and the body ... John 6:56, 57
Illustrated in the "togethers":
Crucified ... Rom 6:6
Buried ... Rom 6:4
Made alive ... Eph 2:5
Sitting ... Eph 2:6
Suffering ... Rom 8:17
Reigning ... 2Tim 2:12
Glorified ... Rom 8:17
Manifested in, oneness:
Of mind ... 1Cor 2:16
Of spirit ... 1Cor 6:17
In suffering ... Phil 3:10
In worship ... 1Cor 10:16, 17
In ministry ... 2Cor 5:18-21

UNITE—*to join*

[*also* UNITED]
be not thou *u* ... Gen 49:6
u my heart to fear ... Ps 86:11

UNITY—*joined relationship*
brethren to dwell together in *u* ... Ps 133:1
keep the *u* of the Spirit ... Eph 4:3
we all come in the *u* ... Eph 4:13

UNITY OF BELIEVERS—*believers' oneness with each other and with their common purpose*
Based upon:
Indwelling Spirit ... 1Cor 3:16, 17; 1Cor 6:19
New birth ... 2Cor 5:17
Union with Christ ... 2Cor 13:5
Expressed by oneness of:
Mind ... 1Pet 3:8
Unity of Spirit ... Ps 133:1-3
Faith ... Eph 4:4-6
Fellowship ... Acts 2:42-47
Concern ... 1Cor 12:25, 26
Consistent with such differences as:
Physical ... 1Pet 3:1-7
Social ... Eph 6:5-9
Mental ... 1Cor 1:26-29

UNJUST—*characterized by injustice*
Described as:
Abomination ... Prov 29:27
Recipient of God's blessings ... Matt 5:45
Saveable ... 1Pet 3:18
Judgment of:
In the resurrection ... Acts 24:15
Will be punished ... 2Pet 2:9
Will perish ... Prov 11:7

[*also* UNJUSTLY]
the deceitful and *u* man ... Ps 43:1
How long will ye judge *u* ... Ps 82:2
u gain increaseth his ... Prov 28:8
uprightness will he deal *u* ... Is 26:10
the *u* knoweth no shame ... Zeph 3:5
the lord commended the *u* ... Luke 16:8
Hear what the *u* judge ... Luke 18:6
men are, extortioners, *u* ... Luke 18:11
go to law before the *u* ... 1Cor 6:1
He that is *u*, let him be *u* ... Rev 22:11

UNKNOWN—*that which is not known or understood*
speaketh in an *u* tongue ... 1Cor 14:2
speaketh in an *u* tongue ... 1Cor 14:13
words in an *u* tongue ... 1Cor 14:19
As *u*, and yet well known ... 2Cor 6:9
u by face unto the churches ... Gal 1:22

UNKNOWN GOD—*mentioned by Paul in his Mars' Hill discourse*
Altar to ... Acts 17:22, 23

UNLADE—*to unload*
ship was to *u* her burden ... Acts 21:3

UNLAWFUL—*not lawful; not right*
an *u* thing for a man ... Acts 10:28
to day with their *u* deeds ... 2Pet 2:8

UNLEARNED—*uneducated; not understanding the truth*
they were *u* and ignorant men ... Acts 4:13
the *u* say Amen at thy giving ... 1Cor 14:16
believeth not, or one *u* ... 1Cor 14:24
foolish and *u* questions ... 2Tim 2:23
that are *u* and unstable ... 2Pet 3:16

UNLEAVENED—*that which has not been caused to rise with yeast or leaven*
Used of bread in the passover ... Ex 12:8-20; Mark 14:1, 12
Typical of Christians ... 1Cor 5:7, 8

did bake *u* bread, and they ... Gen 19:3
Seven days shall ye eat *u* ... Ex 12:15
ye shall eat *u* bread, until ... Ex 12:18
they baked *u* cakes of the ... Ex 12:39
U bread shall be eaten ... Ex 13:7
thou shalt eat *u* bread ... Ex 23:15
u bread, and cakes *u* ... Ex 29:2
wafers *u* anointed with oil ... Ex 29:2
feast of *u* bread shalt thou ... Ex 34:18
thou shalt eat *u* bread ... Ex 34:18
u cakes of fine flour ... Lev 2:4
oil, or *u* wafers anointed ... Lev 2:4
with *u* bread shall it be ... Lev 6:16
u cakes mingled with oil ... Lev 7:12
u wafers anointed with oil ... Lev 7:12
the basket of *u* bread ... Lev 8:26
he took one *u* cake, and a ... Lev 8:26
the feast of *u* bread unto ... Lev 23:6
ye must eat *u* bread ... Lev 23:6
and a basket of *u* bread ... Num 6:15
wafers of *u* bread anointed ... Num 6:15
u cake out of the basket ... Num 6:19
one *u* wafer, and shall put ... Num 6:19
seven days shall *u* bread ... Num 28:17
shalt thou eat *u* bread ... Deut 16:3
in the feast of *u* bread ... Deut 16:16
u cakes, and parched corn ... Josh 5:11
and *u* cakes of an ephah ... Judg 6:19
the flesh and the *u* cakes ... Judg 6:21
the flesh and the *u* cakes ... Judg 6:21
and did bake *u* bread ... 1Sam 28:24
did eat of the *u* bread ... 2Kin 23:9
for the *u* cakes, and for ... 1Chr 23:29
in the feast of *u* bread ... 2Chr 8:13
the feast of *u* bread ... 2Chr 30:21
the feast of *u* bread ... Ezra 6:22
u bread shall be eaten ... Ezek 45:21
Now the feast of *u* bread ... Matt 26:17
the feast of *u* bread drew ... Luke 22:1
were the days of *u* bread ... Acts 12:3

UNLESS—*except*
u he wash his flesh with ... Lev 22:6
u she had turned from me ... Num 22:33
u thou hadst spoken surely ... 2Sam 2:27
u I had believed to see the ... Ps 27:13
U thy law had been my ... Ps 119:92
u they cause some to fall ... Prov 4:16
u ye have believed in vain ... 1Cor 15:2

UNLOOSE—*untie*
to stoop down and *u* ... Mark 1:7
I am not worthy to *u* ... Luke 3:16
I am not worthy to *u* ... John 1:27

UNMARRIED—*not having a spouse*
say therefore to the *u* ... 1Cor 7:8
He that is *u* careth ... 1Cor 7:32

UNMERCIFUL—*lacking mercy*
Shown by Simeon and Levi ... Gen 34:25-31
By Pharaoh ... Ex 5:4-19
By creditor ... Matt 18:28-30

affection, implacable, *u* ... Rom 1:31

UNMINDFUL—*inattentive; forgetful*
that begat thee thou art *u* ... Deut 32:18

UNMOVABLE—*not able to be moved*
stuck fast, and remained *u* ... Acts 27:41
brethren, be ye steadfast, *u* ... 1Cor 15:58

UNNI (ŭn'ī)—*"answering is with Jehovah"*
Levite musician ... 1Chr 15:18

Jehiel, and *U*, and Eliab ... 1Chr 15:20
Also Bakbukiah and *U* ... Neh 12:9

UNOCCUPIED—*not busy*
the highways were *u* ... Judg 5:6

UNPARDONABLE SIN—*a sin against the Holy Spirit; the details of this are not clearly defined in Scripture*
Sin not forgivable ... Matt 12:31, 32; Luke 12:10

UNPERFECT—*imperfect*
my substance, yet being *u* .....Ps 139:16

UNPREPARED—*not ready*
with me, and find you *u* 2Cor 9:4

UNPROFITABLE—*useless; not fruitful*

[*also* UNPROFITABLENESS]
reason with *u* talk? or ....Job 15:3
cast ye the *u* servant..........Matt 25:30
you, say, We are *u* servants ...Luke 17:10
are together become *u* ....Rom 3:12
for they are *u* and vain ....Titus 3:9
in time past was to thee *u*.....Philem 11
for the weakness and *u* ....Heb 7:18
for that is *u* for you ....Heb 13:17

UNPUNISHED—*not punished*
the wicked shall not be *u* .....Prov 11:21
calamities shall not be *u* ......Prov 17:5
should ye be utterly *u*? ....Jer 25:29
Ye shall not be *u*: for I will ...Jer 25:29
leave thee altogether *u*........Jer 30:11
shall altogether go *u*? ....Jer 49:12
thou shalt not go *u*, but.......Jer 49:12

UNQUENCHABLE—*not able to be extinguished*
burn up..chaff with *u* fire .....Matt 3:12
he will burn with fire *u* ....Luke 3:17

UNREASONABLE—*not conforming to reason or logic; unfair*
u to send a prisoner ....Acts 25:27
u and wicked men 2Thess 3:2

UNREBUKABLE—*unable to be reproached*
commandment without spot, *u* .1Tim 6:14

UNREPROVABLE—*not able to be refuted or rebuked*
unblamable and *u* in his sight..Col 1:22

UNREST—*a state of agitation*
Of the nations ....Luke 21:25, 26
Of the wicked...........Is 57:20
Remedy given by Christ .Matt 11:28
Available to Christians ...Phil 4:7

UNRIGHTEOUSNESS—*not justified before God; sinfulness; wickedness*
Attitude toward, by the wicked, they:
Suppress the truth in ....Rom 1:18
Are filled with ....Rom 1:29
Obey it.................Rom 2:8
Love the wages of.......2Pet 2:15
Take pleasure in 2Thess 2:12
Receive the reward of ...2Pet 2:13
Shall not inherit the kingdom..............1Cor 6:9
Relation of believers toward:
They are cleansed from ..1John 1:9
God is merciful toward their ....Heb 8:12
Must not fellowship with .2Cor 6:14
All the world guilty......Rom 3:1-20

[*also* UNRIGHTEOUS, UNRIGHTEOUSLY]
wicked to be an *u* witness .....Ex 23:1
shall do no *u* in judgment .....Lev 19:15
shall do no *u* in judgment .....Lev 19:35
all that do *u* are an...........Deut 25:16
riseth up against me as the *u* ..Job 27:7
of the *u* and cruel man ....Ps 71:4
my rock, and there is no *u* ....Ps 92:15
that decree *u* decrees ....Is 10:1
the *u* man his thoughts........Is 55:7
buildeth his house by *u* ....Jer 22:13
friends of the mammon of *u*...Luke 16:9
faithful in the *u* mammon .....Luke 16:11
same is true, and no *u* is in ...John 7:18
if our *u* commend the.........Rom 3:5
Is God *u* who taketh ....Rom 3:5
as instruments of *u* unto ......Rom 6:13
Is there *u* with God? ....Rom 9:14
deceivableness of *u* in them ...2Thess 2:10
God is not *u* to forget ....Heb 6:10
All *u* is sin: and there is a 1John 5:17

UNRIPE—*not ripe*
shake off his *u* grape ....Job 15:33

UNRULY—*ungovernable; headstrong; willful*
warn them that are *u* 1Thess 5:14
not accused of riot or *u* ....Titus 1:6
many *u* and vain talkers ......Titus 1:10
it is an *u* evil ....James 3:8

UNSATIABLE—*not able to be satisfied*
because thou wast *u* ....Ezek 16:28

UNSAVORY—*unpleasant to taste or smell*
thou wilt show thyself *u*.......2Sam 22:27
that which is *u* be eaten.......Job 6:6

UNSEARCHABLE—*inscrutable*
doeth great things and *u* ......Job 5:9
and his greatness is *u* ....Ps 145:3
and the heart of kings is *u* ....Prov 25:3
how *u* are his judgments ......Rom 11:33
Gentiles the *u* riches of ....Eph 3:8

UNSEEMLY—*improper; immoral*
working that which is *u* ....Rom 1:27
Doth not behave itself *u* 1Cor 13:5

UNSELFISHNESS—*not putting self first*
Christ, an example of, in His:
Mission.................John 6:38
Suffering................Matt 26:39, 42
Concern ....John 19:26, 27
Death ....Phil 2:5-8
In the believer, prompted by:
Christ's example.........Phil 2:3-8
Love 1Cor 13:4, 5
Concern 1Cor 10:23-33
Christian service.........Phil 2:25-30
Sacrifice ....Rev 12:11
Examples of:
Abram ....Gen 13:8-12
Moses ....Num 14:12-29
Gideon ....Judg 8:22, 23
Jonathan................1Sam 18:4
David 1Chr 21:17
Nehemiah...............Neh 5:14-19
Daniel..................Dan 5:17
Christians...............Acts 4:34, 35
Paul....................1Cor 9:19-23
Onesiphorus 2Tim 1:16-18

UNSHOD—*without shoes*
thy foot from being *u* ....Jer 2:25

UNSKILLFUL—*having a lack of skill*
one that useth milk is *u* ....Heb 5:13

UNSPEAKABLE—*not able to be expressed*
God's Gift 2Cor 9:15

paradise and heard *u* words ...2Cor 12:4
joy *u* and full of glory 1Pet 1:8

UNSPOTTED—*untainted; untouched*
to keep himself *u* from.........James 1:27

UNSTABLE—*wavering; vacillating*
u as water, thou shalt not .....Gen 49:4
A double minded man is *u* ....James 1:8
from sin; beguiling *u* souls 2Pet 2:14
are unlearned and *u* wrest.....2Pet 3:16

UNSTOPPED—*unplugged*
ears of the deaf shall be *u* ....Is 35:5

UNTAKEN—*not taken away*
remaineth the same veil *u* 2Cor 3:14

UNTEMPERED MORTAR—*whitewash*
Figurative of false prophets ....Ezek 13:10, 14

daub it with *u m* ....Ezek 13:11
daubed it with *u m* ....Ezek 13:15
daubed them with *u m* ....Ezek 22:28

UNTHANKFUL—*not properly grateful*
is kind unto the *u* and to .....Luke 6:35
disobedient to parents, *u* 2Tim 3:2

UNTIL—*up to the time that; till such time as*
u the tenth month ....Gen 8:5
and grew *u* he became very ...Gen 26:13
U thy brother's anger turn ....Gen 27:45
u all the flocks be gathered ...Gen 29:8
with him *u* the breaking of....Gen 32:24
u I come unto my lord unto...Gen 33:14
by her, *u* his lord came ....Gen 39:16
from our youth even *u* now ...Gen 46:34
foundation thereof even *u*.....Ex 9:18
keep it up *u* the fourteenth....Ex 12:6
nothing of it remain *u* ....Ex 12:10
which remaineth of it *u* ....Ex 12:10
first day *u* the seventh day ....Ex 12:15
u the one and twentieth.......Ex 12:18
left of it *u* the morning ....Ex 16:20
u they came to a land ....Ex 16:35
u they came unto the ....Ex 16:35
sacrifice remain *u* the ....Ex 23:18
u thou be increased and ......Ex 23:30
u he was gone into the........Ex 33:8
u he went in to speak with ....Ex 34:35
not leave any of it *u* the .....Lev 7:15
them shall be unclean *u* the ...Lev 11:24
shall be unclean *u* the even ...Lev 11:27
shall be unclean *u* the even ...Lev 11:31
shall be unclean *u* the even ...Lev 11:39
and be unclean *u* the even ....Lev 11:40
shall be unclean *u* the even ...Lev 14:46
shall be unclean *u* the even ...Lev 15:10
u he come out, and have......Lev 16:17
remain *u* the third day ....Lev 19:6
holy things *u* he be clean .....Lev 22:4
leave none of it *u* the morrow .Lev 22:30
old fruit *u* the ninth year......Lev 25:22
u the year of jubilee ....Lev 25:28
even *u* fifty years old ....Num 4:3
u the days be fulfilled in ......Num 6:5
u it come out at your ....Num 11:20
u your carcases be wasted.....Num 14:33
be unclean *u* the even ....Num 19:8
shall be unclean *u* even ....Num 19:21
u we have passed thy ....Num 20:17
u there was none left him .....Num 21:35
u Asshur shall carry thee......Num 24:22
u we have brought them ......Num 32:17
u he hath driven out his ......Num 32:21
u the death of the high ....Num 35:28
went *u* ye came into this ......Deut 1:31
u we were come over the .....Deut 2:14
u all the generation of the ....Deut 2:14
u I shall pass over Jordan .....Deut 2:29
U the Lord have given rest ....Deut 3:20
u they be destroyed ....Deut 7:23
u ye came unto this place .....Deut 9:7
u ye came into this place......Deut 11:5
thee *u* thy brother seek ....Deut 22:2
to do, *u* thou be destroyed ....Deut 28:20
and *u* thou perish quickly ....Deut 28:20
pursue thee *u* thou perish .....Deut 28:22
u he have destroyed thee .....Deut 28:48
land, *u* thou be destroyed .....Deut 28:51
u he have destroyed thee .....Deut 28:51
thee, *u* thou be destroyed .....Deut 28:61
song, *u* they were ended ......Deut 31:30
U the Lord hath given your ...Josh 1:15
u the pursuers were returned ..Josh 2:22
u every thing was finished.....Josh 4:10
u ye were passed over, as .....Josh 4:23
us, *u* we were gone over ......Josh 4:23
u the day I bid you shout .....Josh 6:10
u ye take away the accursed...Josh 7:13
u he had utterly destroyed ....Josh 8:26
u the people had avenged .....Josh 10:13
which remain *u* this very day ..Josh 10:27
u they left them none.........Josh 11:8
u they had destroyed them .....Josh 11:14
u he stand before the ....Josh 20:6
u the death of the high ....Josh 20:6
we are not cleansed *u* this.....Josh 22:17
u he have destroyed you ......Josh 23:15
u they had destroyed Jabin ....Judg 4:24
u I come unto thee and ....Judg 6:18
u the day of the captivity .....Judg 18:30
her all the night *u* the ....Judg 19:25
went *u* they came to ....Ruth 1:19
gleaned in the field *u* even ....Ruth 2:17
u he shall have done eating ...Ruth 3:3

she lay at his feet *u* the .... Ruth 3:14
u thou know how the matter .. Ruth 3:18
u he have finished the .... Ruth 3:18
up *u* the child be weaned 1Sam 1:22
tarry *u* thou have weaned 1Sam 1:23
son suck *u* she weaned him ... 1Sam 1:23
u they came under Beth-car ... 1Sam 7:11
Ammonites *u* the heat of 1Sam 11:11
eateth any food *u* evening 1Sam 14:24
u thou comest to Shur 1Sam 15:7
Saul *u* the day of his death 1Sam 15:35
to thyself *u* the morning 1Sam 19:2
another, *u* David exceeded 1Sam 20:41
u they had no more power 1Sam 30:4
and fasted *u* even, for 2Sam 1:12
from Geba *u* thou come to 2Sam 5:25
u all the people had done 2Sam 15:24
u there be not one small 2Sam 17:13
king departed *u* the day 2Sam 19:24
not again *u* I had consumed ... 2Sam 22:38
u he had made an end of 1Kin 3:1
u the Lord put them under 1Kin 5:3
u I came, and mine eyes 1Kin 10:7
in Egypt *u* the death of 1Kin 11:40
u the day that the Lord 1Kin 17:14
u the time of the offering 1Kin 18:29
affliction, *u* I come in peace ... 1Kin 22:27
u an ass's head was sold 2Kin 6:25
left the land, even *u* now 2Kin 8:6
of the gate *u* the morning 2Kin 10:8
u he had cast them out of 2Kin 17:20
U I come and take you 2Kin 18:32
steads *u* the captivity 1Chr 5:22
u it was a great host, like 1Chr 12:22
u thou hast finished all 1Chr 28:20
make to pay tribute *u* this 2Chr 8:8
u I came, and mine eyes 2Chr 9:6
push Syria *u* they be 2Chr 18:10
the Syrians *u* the even 2Chr 18:34
u they had made an end 2Chr 24:10
u the other priests had 2Chr 29:34
u the wrath of the Lord 2Chr 36:16
u the land had enjoyed 2Chr 36:21
u the reign of Darius .... Ezra 4:5
u now hath it been in .... Ezra 5:16
sat astonished *u* the evening ... Ezra 9:4
be opened *u* the sun be hot ... Neh 7:3
u the days of Johanan the ..... Neh 12:23
u thy wrath be past .... Job 14:13
u his iniquity be found .... Ps 36:2
u I have showed thy strength .. Ps 71:18
his labor *u* the evening .... Ps 104:23
u I make thine enemies .... Ps 110:1
u that he have mercy .... Ps 123:2
take our fill of love *u* .... Prov 7:18
U the day break and the ...... Song 2:17
U the day break and the ...... Song 4:6
that continue *u* night till ...... Is 5:11
u the indignation be .... Is 26:20
U I come and take you .... Is 36:17
u the righteousness thereof go . Is 62:1
u he have executed .... Jer 23:20
u I have consumed them ...... Jer 27:8
shall not return *u* he .... Jer 30:24
u he hath performed the ...... Jer 30:24
u all the roll was consumed ... Jer 36:23
u the day that Jerusalem ...... Jer 38:28
a portion *u* the day of his ..... Jer 52:34
u he come whose right .... Ezek 21:27
shall not be shut *u* the .... Ezek 46:2
u thou know that the .... Dan 4:32
u a time and times and the ... Dan 7:25
dough, *u* it be leavened .... Hos 7:4
u the time that she which ..... Mic 5:3
u the day that I rise up to .... Zeph 3:8
u the carrying away into ...... Matt 1:17
there *u* the death of Herod .... Matt 2:15
law prophesied *u* John .... Matt 11:13
together *u* the harvest .... Matt 13:30
U seventy times seven .... Matt 18:22
know not *u* the flood came .... Matt 24:39
made sure *u* the third day ..... Matt 27:64
u that day that I drink it ..... Mark 14:25
u the day that these things .... Luke 1:20
which is lost, *u* he find it? .... Luke 15:4
u the day that Noah entered .. Luke 17:27
u it be fulfilled in the .... Luke 22:16
earth *u* the ninth hour .... Luke 23:44
kept the good wine *u* now .... John 2:10
U the day in which he .... Acts 1:2
u the times of restitution ...... Acts 3:21
u Samuel the prophet .... Acts 13:20
u..an offering should be .... Acts 21:26
u we have slain Paul .... Acts 23:14
For *u* the law sin was in ...... Rom 5:13
u the fullness of the Gentiles .. Rom 11:25
u the Lord come, who both ... 1Cor 4:5
u this day remaineth the 2Cor 3:14
u the time appointed of .... Gal 4:2
u the redemption of the .... Eph 1:14
from the first day *u* now ...... Phil 1:5
let, *u* he be taken out of 2Thess 2:7
u the appearing of our Lord ... 1Tim 6:14
u I make thine enemies .... Heb 1:13
u he receive the early and .... James 5:7
u the day dawn, and the 2Pet 1:19
in darkness even *u* now 1John 2:9
u their fellow servants .... Rev 6:11
u the thousand years were .... Rev 20:5

UNTIMELY—*unseasonably; prematurely*
hidden *u* birth I had not ...... Job 3:16
like the *u* birth of a .... Ps 58:8
that an *u* birth is better .... Eccl 6:3
fig tree casteth her *u* figs ...... Rev 6:13

UNTO—*See* INTRODUCTION

UNTOWARD—*unruly*
from this *u* generation .... Acts 2:40

UNWALLED—*having no walls*
beside *u* towns a great many .. Deut 3:5
that dwelt in the *u* towns ..... Esth 9:19
to the land of *u* villages .... Ezek 38:11

UNWASHEN—*not washed*
to eat with *u* hands defileth ... Matt 15:20
that is to say, with *u* hands .... Mark 7:2
but eat bread with *u* hands? ... Mark 7:5

UNWEIGHED—*not weighed*
Solomon left all the vessels *u* .. 1Kin 7:47

UNWISE—*lacking wisdom*
O foolish people and *u*? ...... Deut 32:6
he is an *u* son; for he .... Hos 13:13
to the wise and to the *u* ...... Rom 1:14
Wherefore be ye not *u*, but ... Eph 5:17

UNWITTINGLY—*unknowingly; inadvertently*
Concerning an innocent killer .... Josh 20:3-5
eat of the holy thing *u* .... Lev 22:14

UNWORLDLINESS—*not tied to earthly preoccupations*
Negatively expressed in, not:
Loving the world 1John 2:15-17
Fellowshiping with evil ... 2Cor 6:14-18
Mixing in worldly affairs . 2Tim 2:4
Positively expressed in:
Seeking God's kingdom first .... Matt 6:33, 34
Living for Jesus .... Gal 2:20
Becoming a living sacrifice .... Rom 12:1, 2
Having a heavenly mind . Col 3:1, 2
Looking for Jesus .... Titus 2:11-15
Looking to Jesus .... Heb 12:1, 2

UNWORTHINESS—*not being fit; lacking merit*
Caused by a sense of:
Failure .... Gen 32:10
Social difference 1Sam 18:18, 23
Sin .... Luke 15:19, 21
Inferiority .... John 1:27
Examples of:
Moses .... Ex 4:10
Centurion .... Matt 8:8
Peter .... Luke 5:8
Paul 1Cor 15:9

[*also* UNWORTHILY, UNWORTHY]
u of everlasting life .... Acts 13:46
u to judge the smallest 1Cor 6:2
drink this cup of the Lord *u* .. 1Cor 11:27
that eateth and drinketh *u* 1Cor 11:29

UP—*See* INTRODUCTION

UPBRAID—*to criticize; find fault with*
[*also* UPBRAIDED, UPBRAIDETH]
with whom ye did *u* me .... Judg 8:15
Then began he to *u* the .... Matt 11:20
and *u* them with their .... Mark 16:14
men liberally and *u* not .... James 1:5

UPHARSIN (ū-fär'sĭn)—*Chaldean for "and divided"*
Interpreted by Daniel .... Dan 5:5, 25, 28
See MENE, MENE, TEKEL, UPHARSIN

UPHAZ (ū'făz)—*"pure gold"*
Unidentified place of fine gold .... Jer 10:9
girded with fine gold of *U* ..... Dan 10:5

UPHOLD—*to give support to; lift up*
[*also* UPHELD, UPHOLDEN, UPHOLDEST, UPHOLDETH, UPHOLDING]
Thy words have *u* him .... Job 4:4
the Lord *u* the righteous ...... Ps 37:17
u me in mine integrity .... Ps 41:12
u me with thy free spirit ...... Ps 51:12
thy right hand *u* me .... Ps 63:8
U me according unto thy ...... Ps 119:116
throne is *u* by mercy .... Prov 20:28
honor shall *u* the humble ..... Prov 29:23
I will *u* thee with the .... Is 41:10
and my fury, it *u* me .... Is 63:5
there was none to *u* .... Is 63:5
They also that *u* Egypt .... Ezek 30:6
u all things by the word .... Heb 1:3

UPON—*See* INTRODUCTION

UPPER—*higher*
[*also* UPPERMOST]
u basket there was of all ...... Gen 40:17
u door post of the houses ..... Ex 12:7
a covering upon his *u* lip ...... Lev 13:45
nether or the *u* millstone ...... Deut 24:6
he gave her the *u* springs ..... Josh 15:19
unto Beth-horon the *u* .... Josh 16:5
gave her the *u* springs .... Judg 1:15
by the conduit of the *u* pool ... 2Kin 18:17
the nether, and the *u* 1Chr 7:24
and of the *u* chambers 1Chr 28:11
overlaid the *u* chamber 2Chr 3:9
he built Beth-horon the *u* 2Chr 8:5
stopped the *u* watercourse 2Chr 32:30
the conduit of the *u* pool ..... Is 7:3
berries in the top of the *u* ..... Is 17:6
bough and an *u* branch .... Is 17:9
stood by the conduit of the *u* .. Is 36:2
u chambers were shorter ...... Ezek 42:5
shall lodge in the *u* lintels ..... Zeph 2:14
love the *u* rooms at feasts ..... Matt 23:6
and the *u* rooms at feasts ..... Mark 12:39
love the *u* seats in .... Luke 11:43
passed through the *u* coasts ... Acts 19:1

UPPER ROOM—*a chamber; usually built on a roof*
Ahaziah fell from 2Kin 1:2
Ahaz's 2Kin 23:12
Disciples prepared for Christ .... Mark 14:14-16
Dorcas placed in .... Acts 9:36, 37
Paul preached in .... Acts 20:7, 8

UPRIGHTNESS—*character and behavior approved by God*
Descriptive of:
God's nature .... Is 26:7
Man's state .... Eccl 7:29
Devout .... Job 1:1, 8
Of God, manifested in His:
Works .... Ps 111:8

U

Judgments ....Ps 119:137
Delights 1Chr 29:17

Blessings of, for saints:
Temporal blessings ......Ps 84:11
Lord's blessings ....Ps 11:7
Prosperity...............Prov 14:11
Deliverance ....Prov 11:3, 6, 11
Salvation ....Ps 7:10
God's presence ....Ps 140:13
Light in darkness ....Ps 112:4
Answered prayer ....Prov 15:8
Righteousness ....Ps 36:10
Joy......................Ps 32:11
Glory ....Ps 64:10
Final dominion ....Ps 49:14

Attitude of wicked toward, they:
Are devoid of ....Hab 2:4
Leave the path of ....Prov 2:13
Hate ....Prov 29:10
Persecute ....Ps 37:14
Laugh to scorn ....Job 12:4

[*also* UPRIGHT, UPRIGHTLY]
sheaf arose and also stood *u*...Gen 37:7
floods stood *u* as a heap ......Ex 15:8
yoke, and made you go *u* .....Lev 26:13
or for the *u* of thine heart ....Deut 9:5
thou hast been *u*, and thy 1Sam 29:6
was also *u* before him 2Sam 22:24
merciful, and with the *u* man ..2Sam 22:26
thou wilt show thyself *u* 2Sam 22:26
in *u* of heart with thee 1Kin 3:6
integrity of heart, and in *u* 1Kin 9:4
the Levites were more *u* 2Chr 29:34
a perfect and an *u* man ....Job 2:3
and the *u* of thy ways?........Job 4:6
If thou wert pure and *u*.......Job 8:6
U men shall be astonished.....Job 17:8
be of the *u* of my heart ....Job 33:3
to show unto man his *u* ....Job 33:23
may privily shoot at the *u* .....Ps 11:2
He that walketh *u* and ....Ps 15:2
I was also *u* before him ....Ps 18:23
merciful; with an *u* man ......Ps 18:25
thou wilt show thyself *u*.......Ps 18:25
then shall I be *u* and ....Ps 19:13
we are risen, and stand *u* .....Ps 20:8
Good and *u* is the Lord ......Ps 25:8
Let integrity and *u* preserve ...Ps 25:21
praise is comely for the *u* .....Ps 33:1
do ye judge *u*, O ye sons .....Ps 58:1
congregation I will judge *u*....Ps 75:2
show that the Lord is *u* ....Ps 92:15
u in heart shall follow it ......Ps 94:15
and gladness for the *u* in......Ps 97:11
in the assembly of the *u* ......Ps 111:1
the *u* shall be blessed ....Ps 112:2
I will praise thee with *u*........Ps 119:7
to them that are *u* in their ....Ps 125:4
me into the land of *u* ....Ps 143:10
to them that walk *u* ....Prov 2:7
For the *u* shall dwell in ....Prov 2:21
Lord is strength to the *u* ......Prov 10:29
are *u* in their way are his .....Prov 11:20
mouth of the *u* shall ....Prov 12:6
keepeth him that is *u* in........Prov 13:6
He that walketh in his *u* ......Prov 14:2
of understanding walketh *u*....Prov 15:21
The highway of the *u* is to ....Prov 16:17
transgressor for the *u* ....Prov 21:18
as for the *u*, he directeth ......Prov 21:29
poor that walketh in his *u* ......Prov 28:6
the *u* shall have good things ...Prov 28:10
walketh *u* shall be saved ......Prov 28:18
is *u* in the way is ....Prov 29:27
which was written was *u* ......Eccl 12:10
more than wine: the *u* love....Song 1:4
The way of the just is *u*.......Is 26:7
land of *u* will he deal ....Is 26:10
righteously, and speaketh *u* ...Is 33:15
each one walking in his *u* .....Is 57:2
touched me, and set me *u*......Dan 8:18
unto thee, and stand *u*........Dan 10:11
kingdom, and *u* ones with.....Dan 11:17
abhor him that speaketh *u* ....Amos 5:10
to him that walketh *u*?........Mic 2:7
there is none *u* among men ...Mic 7:2
u is sharper than a thorn ......Mic 7:4
Stand *u* on thy feet ....Acts 14:10
they walked not *u* according...Gal 2:14

UPRISING—*getting up*
downsitting and mine *u* ....Ps 139:2

UPROAR—*commotion; violent disturbance*
the city being in an *u*? 1Kin 1:41
be an *u* among the people ....Matt 26:5
there be an *u* of the people ...Mark 14:2
set all the city on an *u* ....Acts 17:5
after the *u* was ceased, Paul ...Acts 20:1
these days madest an *u* ....Acts 21:38

UPSIDE—*the top side*
wiping it and turning it *u* down.2Kin 21:13
wicked he turneth *u* down......Ps 146:9
waste, and turneth it *u* down ..Is 24:1
turning of things *u* down ......Is 29:16
turned the world *u* down ......Acts 17:6

UPWARD—*from lower to higher*
Fifteen cubits *u* did the ....Gen 7:20
twenty years old and *u* ....Ex 38:26
twenty years old and *u*........Num 1:3
from a month old and *u* ......Num 3:15
and five years old and *u* ....Num 8:24
twenty years old and *u*.........Num 32:11
from the rock, and *u* ....Judg 1:36
from his shoulders and *u* 1Sam 9:2
from his shoulders and *u* 1Sam 10:23
to put on armor, and *u* 2Kin 3:21
downward, and bear fruit *u* ...2Kin 19:30
thirty years and *u* 1Chr 23:3
of twenty years and *u*.........1Chr 23:24
from three years old and *u* 2Chr 31:16
twenty years old and *u*.........2Chr 31:17
twenty years old and *u*........Ezra 3:8
as the sparks fly *u* ....Job 5:7
the spirit of man that goeth *u* .Eccl 3:21
their God, and look *u* ....Is 8:21
downward, and bear fruit *u* ...Is 37:31
eyes fail with looking *u* ....Is 38:14
wings were stretched *u*........Ezek 1:11
from his loins even *u*, as ......Ezek 8:2
a winding about still *u* to .....Ezek 41:7
went still *u* round about ......Ezek 41:7
of the house was still *u* ....Ezek 41:7
consider from this day and *u* ..Hag 2:15

UR (ûr)—*"flame; light"*
Father of Eliphal 1Chr 11:35
Called Ahasbai..........2Sam 23:34

UR OF THE CHALDEES—*"fire"—city in the highlands of Mesopotamia*
City of Abram's early life.Gen 11:28-31
Gen 15:7
Located in Mesopotamia by Stephen ....Acts 7:2, 4

URBANE (ûr'bān)—*"pleasant; witty"*
A Christian saluted by Paul..................Rom 16:9

URGE—*to entreat; solicit*

[*also* URGED]
and he *u* him, and he took ....Gen 33:11
with her words, and *u* him ....Judg 16:16
u him till he was ashamed.....2Kin 2:17
he *u* him, and bound two 2Kin 5:23
Pharisees began to *u* him .....Luke 11:53

URGENT—*pressing; strict*
the Egyptians were *u* ....Ex 12:33
king's commandment was *u* ...Dan 3:22

URI (ū'rī)—*"enlightened; my light"*
1. Father of Bezaleel 1Chr 2:20
2. Father of Geber 1Kin 4:19
3. Divorced his foreign wife.Ezra 10:24

Bezaleel the son of *U*.........Ex 31:2
And Bezaleel the son of *U* ....Ex 38:22
that Bezaleel the son of *U* 2Chr 1:5

URIAH (ū-rī'ä)—*"Jehovah is my light"*
1. Hittite and one of David's warriors 2Sam 23:39
Condemned to death by David................2Sam 11:1-27
2. Priest ....Ezra 8:33
3. Prophet in Jeremiah's time ....Jer 26:20-23
4. Stands with Ezra........Neh 8:4

[*also* URIAH'S]
killed *U* the Hittite with 2Sam 12:9
taken the wife of *U* the 2Sam 12:10
the child that *U* wife 2Sam 12:15
matter of *U* the Hittite........1Kin 15:5
U the Hittite, Zabad the 1Chr 11:41
Meremoth the son of *U* ....Ezra 8:33
witnesses to record, *U* ....Is 8:2
had been the wife of *U* ....Matt 1:6

URIAS—*See* URIAH

URIEL (ū'rĭ-ĕl)—*"God is my light"*
1. Kohathite Levite 1Chr 6:22, 24
2. Man of Gibeah 2Chr 13:2

Kohath, *U* the chief 1Chr 15:5
and for the Levites, for *U* 1Chr 15:11

URIJAH (ū-rī'jä)—*"Jehovah is my light"*
1. High priest in Ahaz' time.2Kin 16:10-16
2. Postexilic priest 2Kin 16:10-16
3. Prophet in Jeremiah's time ....Jer 26:20
4. Stands with Ezra........Neh 8:4

Meremoth the son of *U*.......Neh 3:21

URIM AND THUMMIN (ū'rĭm, thŭm'ĭm)—*"lights and perfections"—priestly objects of uncertain description*
Placed in the breastplate of the high priest ......Ex 28:30
Method of consulting God .... {Num 27:21, 1Sam 14:3-37}
Use of, confined to priests ....Deut 33:8
Answer by, refused 1Sam 28:6

of judgment the *U* and the *T* ..Ex 28:30
breastplate the *U* and the *T* ...Lev 8:8
Let thy *T* and thy *U* be with ..Deut 33:8
a priest with *U* and with *T* ....Ezra 2:63
stood up a priest with *U* and *T*.Neh 7:65

US—*See* INTRODUCTION

USE—*to apply; employ*

[*also* USED, USES, USEST, USETH, USING]
the ox hath *u* to push in ......Ex 21:36
be *u* in any other *u*...........Lev 7:24
mayest *u* them for the ....Num 10:2
or that *u* divination, or an ....Deut 18:10
thereof for any unclean *u* .....Deut 26:14
a beast, for so *u* the young ....Judg 14:10
whom he had *u* as his friend ..Judg 14:20
Judah the *u* of the bow 2Sam 1:18
and *u* divination and..........2Kin 17:17
times, and *u* enchantments 2Kin 21:6
u both the right hand 1Chr 12:2
times, and *u* enchantments 2Chr 33:6
u witchcraft, and dealt 2Chr 33:6
which the king *u* to ....Esth 6:8
as thou *u* to do unto those ....Ps 119:132
wise *u* knowledge aright ....Prov 15:2
The poor *u* entreaties ....Prov 18:23
A wild ass *u* to the ....Jer 2:24
u his neighbor's service ....Jer 22:13
that *u* their tongues, and ......Jer 23:31
in vain shalt thou *u* many .....Jer 46:11
more *u* it as a proverb in .....Ezek 12:23
one that *u* proverbs shall .....Ezek 16:44
u this proverb concerning .....Ezek 18:2
two ways, to *u* divination .....Ezek 21:21
people..have *u* oppression .....Ezek 22:29
envy which thou hast *u* out....Ezek 35:11
visions, and *u* similitudes ......Hos 12:10
which despitefully *u* you ......Matt 5:44
of the Pharisees *u* to fast......Mark 2:18
which despitefully *u* you ......Luke 6:28

in the same city *u* sorcery .....Acts 8:9
to *u* them despitefully.........Acts 14:5
also which *u* curious arts ......Acts 19:19
they *u* helps, ungirding........Acts 27:17
did change the natural *u* ......Rom 1:26
tongues they have *u* deceit ....Rom 3:13
mayest be made free, *u* it 1Cor 7:21
we have not *u* this power 1Cor 9:12
I have *u* none of these 1Cor 9:15
minded, did I *u* lightness? 2Cor 1:17
present I should *u* sharpness...2Cor 13:10
u not liberty for an ....Gal 5:13
good to the *u* of edifying......Eph 4:29
to perish with the *u* ....Col 2:22
u we flattering words 1Thess 2:5
if a man *u* it lawfully 1Tim 1:8
u a little wine for thy 1Tim 5:23
meat for the master's *u* 2Tim 2:21
works for necessary *u* ....Titus 3:14
For one that *u* milk is ....Heb 5:13
those who by reason of *u* .....Heb 5:14
of them that were so *u*........Heb 10:33
not *u* your liberty for a 1Pet 2:16
U hospitality one to 1Pet 4:9

USURER—*one who charges interest on money lent*
not be to him as a *u*.........Ex 22:25

USURPATION—*seizing authority illegally*
Methods of, by:
Intrigue.................2Sam 15:1-12
Defying God's Law......1Sam 13:8-14
Changing God's worship .2Kin 16:10-17
Conspiracy..............1Kin 15:27, 28
Assuming dictatorial rights.................3John 9, 10
Consequences of, seen in:
Defeat and death........2Kin 11:1-6
Another conspiracy 2Kin 15:10-15
Defeat and conditional forgiveness............1Kin 1:5-53
Spirit of, manifested in:
Man's transgression ......Gen 3:1-7
Satan's fall..............Is 14:12-14
Woman's weakness 1Tim 2:12
Antichrist's desire ....2Thess 2:3, 4; Rev 13:1-18

USURY—*charging excessive interest on money lent*
shalt thou lay upon him *u* .....Ex 22:25
Take thou no *u* of him, or ....Lev 25:36
lend upon *u* to thy brother ....Deut 23:19
u of money, *u* of victuals .....Deut 23:19
u of any thing that is lent .....Deut 23:19
anything that is lent upon *u* ...Deut 23:19
thou mayest lend upon *u*......Deut 23:20
thou shalt not lend upon *u*.....Deut 23:20
Ye exact *u*, every one of......Neh 5:7
not out his money to *u* ....Ps 15:5
He that by *u* and unjust ......Prov 28:8
as with the taker of *u*.........Is 24:2
so with the giver of *u* to ......Is 24:2
have lent to me on *u* ....Jer 15:10
Hath given forth upon *u* ......Ezek 18:13
hath not received *u* nor ....Ezek 18:17
received mine own with *u* .....Matt 25:27
required mine own with *u*? ....Luke 19:23

USWARD—*us*
thy thoughts which are to *u* ...Ps 40:5
power to *u* who believed ......Eph 1:19
but is longsuffering to *u*.......2Pet 3:9

UTENSILS, KITCHEN
Bowls ....Amos 6:6
Charger ....Matt 14:11
Cruse 1Kin 17:12
Cup and platter ....Matt 23:25
Fork (tongs) 1Sam 2:13, 14
Iron pan...............Ezek 4:3
Kettle (pot)............1Sam 2:14
Kneading trough ....Ex 8:3
Millstones..............Is 47:2
Pan ....Lev 2:5

UTHAI (ū'thī)—*"my iniquity; Jehovah is help"*
1. Judahite................1Chr 9:4
2. Postexilic returnee ......Ezra 8:14

UTMOST—*at the farthest or most distant point; the extreme limit; the most possible*
[*also* UTTERMOST]
in the *u* edge of another ......Ex 26:4
the *u* edge of the curtain......Ex 36:17
in the *u* parts of the camp ....Num 11:1
which is in the *u* coast ....Num 22:36
shalt see but the *u* part ....Num 23:13
unto the *u* sea shall your......Deut 11:24
of Judah, unto the *u* sea ......Deut 34:2
was the *u* part of the ....Josh 15:1
u cities of the tribe of ....Josh 15:21
in the *u* part of Gibeah 1Sam 14:2
the *u* part of the one wing 1Kin 6:24
wing unto the *u* part of 1Kin 6:24
the *u* part of the camp of 2Kin 7:5
the *u* part of the heaven ......Neh 1:9
the *u* parts of the earth ....Ps 2:8
in the *u* parts of the sea ......Ps 139:9
the *u* part of the rivers........Is 7:18
that are in the *u* corners ......Jer 9:26
that are in the *u* corners ......Jer 49:32
part toward the *u* sea ....Joel 2:20
hast paid the *u* farthing ....Matt 5:26
the *u* part of the earth ....Mark 13:27
to the *u* part of heaven ....Mark 13:27
u parts of the earth to ....Luke 11:31
the *u* part of the earth ....Acts 1:8
I will know the *u* of your .....Acts 24:22
wrath..upon them to the *u* 1Thess 2:16
to save them to the *u*.........Heb 7:25

UTTER—*See* OUTER

UTTER—*to speak*
[*also* UTTERED, UTTERETH, UTTERING]
if he do not *u* it, then he .....Lev 5:1
vowed, or *u* aught out of .....Num 30:6
yours, if ye *u* not this our .....Josh 2:14
awake, awake, *u* a song.......Judg 5:12
Jephthah *u* all his words ......Judg 11:11
and the Most High *u* his 2Sam 22:14
appointed to *u* destruction 1Kin 20:42
and *u* my words to him ....Neh 6:19
u words out of their heart? ....Job 8:10
mouth *u* thine iniquity ....Job 15:5
whom hast thou *u* words? .....Job 26:4
nor my tongue *u* deceit ....Job 27:4
lips shall *u* knowledge ....Job 33:3
Day unto day *u* speech ....Ps 19:2
he *u* his voice, the earth ....Ps 46:6
I will *u* dark sayings of ....Ps 78:2
long shall they *u* and ....Ps 94:4
Who can *u* the mighty acts ....Ps 106:2
abundantly *u* the memory .....Ps 145:7
u her voice in the streets ......Prov 1:20
and he that *u* a slander ....Prov 10:18
false witness will *u* lies ....Prov 14:5
shall *u* perverse things ....Prov 23:33
A fool *u* all his mind: but .....Prov 29:11
labor; man cannot *u* it ....Eccl 1:8
u any thing before God ....Eccl 5:2
u error against the Lord ......Is 32:6
u it even to the end of the ....Is 48:20
conceiving and *u* from ....Is 59:13
I will *u* my judgments ....Jer 1:16
When he *u* his voice, there ....Jer 10:13
have they *u* their voice........Jer 48:34
u a parable unto the ....Ezek 24:3
brought me forth into the *u* ...Ezek 42:1
toward the *u* court on ....Ezek 42:7
them from the *u* court ....Ezek 42:9
go forth into the *u* court ......Ezek 44:19
even into the *u* court of.......Ezek 44:19
brought me forth into the *u* ...Ezek 46:21
Lord shall *u* his voice ....Joel 2:11
u his voice from Jerusalem ....Amos 1:2
u his mischievous desire.......Mic 7:3
the deep *u* his voice, and .....Hab 3:10
he will make an *u* end of .....Nah 1:8
be no more *u* destruction .....Zech 14:11

u things which have been .....Matt 13:35
groanings which cannot be *u* ..Rom 8:26
ye *u* by the tongue words 1Cor 14:9
not lawful for a man to *u* 2Cor 12:4
to say, and hard to be *u* ......Heb 5:11
thunders *u* their voices........Rev 10:3
thunders had *u* their voices....Rev 10:4
the seven thunders *u*..........Rev 10:4

UTTERANCE—*speaking*
as the Spirit gave them *u* .....Acts 2:4
enriched by him, in all *u* 1Cor 1:5
faith, and *u*, and knowledge ...2Cor 8:7
that *u* may be given unto .....Eph 6:19
open unto us a door of *u* .....Col 4:3

UTTERLY—*totally*
u put out the remembrance ...Ex 17:14
he shall be *u* destroyed ....Ex 22:20
pronounce him *u* unclean .....Lev 13:44
soul shall be *u* cut off.........Num 15:31
they *u* destroyed them ....Num 21:3
and *u* destroyed the men......Deut 2:34
And we *u* destroyed them.....Deut 3:6
u destroying the men ....Deut 3:6
ye shall soon *u* perish.........Deut 4:26
but shall *u* be destroyed ......Deut 4:26
but thou shalt *u* detest it ......Deut 7:26
and thou shalt *u* abhor it......Deut 7:26
destroying it *u*, and all........Deut 13:15
ye will *u* corrupt yourselves ...Deut 31:29
Og, whom ye *u* destroyed .....Josh 2:10
until he had *u* destroyed ......Josh 8:26
the king..he *u* destroyed ......Josh 10:28
therein he *u* destroyed ....Josh 10:35
and *u* destroyed all the ....Josh 10:39
sword, *u* destroying them .....Josh 11:11
that he might destroy them *u* ..Josh 11:20
and did not *u* drive them .....Josh 17:13
Zephath, and *u* destroyed it ...Judg 1:17
that thou hadst *u* hated ....Judg 15:2
u destroy all that they 1Sam 15:3
and would not *u* destroy 1Sam 15:9
that they destroyed *u* 1Sam 15:9
Go and *u* destroy the 1Sam 15:18
should have been *u* destroyed .1Sam 15:21
heart of a lion, shall *u* melt ...2Sam 17:10
were not able *u* to destroy 1Kin 9:21
by destroying them *u* 2Kin 19:11
destroyed them *u* unto 1Chr 4:41
Seir, *u* to slay and destroy 2Chr 20:23
my fathers *u* destroyed........2Chr 32:14
thou didst not *u* consume .....Neh 9:31
he shall not be *u* cast down ...Ps 37:24
will I not *u* take from him ....Ps 89:33
word of truth *u* out of my.....Ps 119:43
it would *u* be contemned......Song 8:7
idols he shall *u* abolish........Is 2:18
shall *u* destroy the tongue .....Is 11:15
earth is *u* broken down ....Is 24:19
by destroying them *u* ....Is 37:11
u separated me from his ......Is 56:3
brother will *u* supplant........Jer 9:4
thou *u* rejected Judah?........Jer 14:19
and will *u* destroy them ....Jer 25:9
should ye be *u* unpunished ....Jer 25:29
waste and *u* destroy after .....Jer 50:21
destroy ye *u* all her host ......Jer 51:3
thou hast *u* rejected us........Lam 5:22
Slay *u* old and young ....Ezek 9:6
make themselves *u* bald.......Ezek 27:31
destroy, and *u* to make ....Dan 11:44
Israel; but I will *u* take ....Hos 1:6
I will not *u* destroy the ....Amos 9:8
through thee; he is *u* cut off...Nah 1:15
will *u* consume all things ......Zeph 1:2
his right eye shall be *u*........Zech 11:17
there is *u* a fault among.......1Cor 6:7
shall *u* perish in their 2Pet 2:12
she shall be *u* burned ....Rev 18:8

UTTERMOST—*See* UTMOST

UZ (ŭz)—*"counsel; firmness"*
1. Descendant of Shem ....Gen 10:23
2. Descendant of Seir ......Gen 36:28
3. Son of Nahor...........Gen 22:20, 21

4. Place in south Edom; residence of Job ......Job 1:1

Aram, and *U*, and Hul, and ...1Chr 1:17
The sons of Dishan; *U* 1Chr 1:42
the kings of the land of *U* .....Jer 25:20
dwellest in the land of *U* ......Lam 4:21

UZAI (ū'zī)—*"hoped for"*
Father of Palal ....Neh 3:25

UZAL (ū'zăl)—*"wandering"*
Son of Joktan ....Gen 10:27

UZZA, UZZAH (ŭz'ä)—*"strength"*
1. Son of Shimei 1Chr 6:29
2. Descendant of Ehud 1Chr 8:7
3. Head of a returning Temple servant family .Ezra 2:49
4. Name of a garden.......2Kin 21:18, 26
5. Son of Abinadab struck down for touching the ark of the covenant ...2Sam 6:3-11

and *U* and Ahio drove the 1Chr 13:7
was kindled against *U*.........1Chr 13:10
made a breach upon *U*........1Chr 13:11
The children of *U*, the ....Ezra 2:49
the children of *U*, the ....Neh 7:51

UZZEN-SHERAH (ŭz'ĕn-shĕr'ră)—*"ear of the flesh"*
Town built by Sherah, Ephraim's daughter 1Chr 7:24

UZZI (ŭz'ī)—*"Jehovah is strong; my strength"*
1. Descendant of Aaron ...1Chr 6:5, 51
2. Descendant of Issachar ..1Chr 7:1-3
3. Son of Bela 1Chr 7:7
4. Levite overseer ....Neh 11:22
5. Postexilic priest ....Neh 12:19, 42

U begat Zerahiah and.........1Chr 6:6
Bukki his son, *U* his son 1Chr 6:51
and Elah the son of *U* 1Chr 9:8
Zerahiah, the son of *U*........Ezra 7:4

UZZIA (ŭ-zī'ä)—*"Yahweh is strong"*
One of David's mighty men 1Chr 11:44

UZZIAH (ŭ-zī'ä)—*"Jehovah is strong; my strength is Jehovah"*
1. Kohathite Levite 1Chr 6:24
2. Father of Jehonathan....1Chr 27:25
3. King of Judah, called Azariah .... {2Kin 14:21; 2Kin 15:1-7}
   - Reigned 52 years 2Kin 15:1, 2
   - Reigned righteously 2Chr 26:4, 5
   - Conquered the Philistines.2Chr 26:6-8
   - Strengthened Jerusalem ..2Chr 26:9
   - Developed agriculture ...2Chr 26:10
   - Usurped priestly function; stricken with leprosy...............2Chr 26:16-21
   - Life of, written by Isaiah.2Chr 26:22, 23
   - Earthquake in the days of ....Amos 1:1
   - Death of, time of Isaiah's vision ....Is 6:1
4. Priest who divorced his foreign wife ....Ezra 10:19, 21
5. Judahite................Neh 11:4

and thirtieth year of *U* 2Kin 15:13
Jotham the son of *U* 2Kin 15:30
Jotham the son of *U* king 2Kin 15:32
to all that his father *U* 2Kin 15:34
people of Judah took *U* 2Chr 26:1
Sixteen years old was *U* 2Chr 26:3
U had an host of fighting 2Chr 26:11
U prepared for them..shields ..2Chr 26:14
according to all his father *U* ...2Chr 27:2
in the days of *U*, Jotham ......Is 1:1
of Jotham, the son of *U*.......Is 7:1
in the days of *U*, Jotham ......Hos 1:1
earthquake in the days of *U* ...Zech 14:5

UZZIEL (ŭ-zē'ĕl)—*"God is my strength; God is strong"*
1. Levite, son of Kohath and family head ......Ex 6:18, 22
2. Son of Bela 1Chr 7:7
3. Simeonite captain 1Chr 4:41-43
4. Levite musician 1Chr 25:3, 4
5. Levite assisting in Hezekiah's reforms....2Chr 29:14-19
6. Goldsmith working on Jerusalem's wall ......Neh 3:8

the sons of *U* the uncle ....Lev 10:4
Izehar, Hebron, and *U*........Num 3:19
Elizaphan the son of *U* ....Num 3:30
Izhar, and Hebron, and *U*.....1Chr 6:2
Izhar and Hebron and *U* 1Chr 6:18
sons of *U*; Amminadab 1Chr 15:10
Izhar, Hebron and *U* 1Chr 23:12
Of the sons of *U*; Michah 1Chr 23:20
of the sons of *U*; Michah......1Chr 24:24

UZZIELITES (ŭ-zī'ĕl-īts)—*members of the family of Uzziel*
and the family of the *U* ....Num 3:27
the Hebronites, and the *U* 1Chr 26:23

V

VAGABOND—*an aimless wanderer*
Curse on Cain ....Gen 4:12, 14
Curse upon the wicked...Ps 109:10
Professional exorcists thus called ....Acts 19:13

VAIL—*See* VEIL; VEIL, WOMAN'S

VAIN—*useless; conceited; empty; to no end*

Applied to physical things:
Beauty ....Prov 31:30
Life ....Eccl 6:12
Customs ....Jer 10:3
Men ....Job 11:12
Adornment ....Jer 4:30
Healing.................Jer 46:11
Sacrifice ....Is 1:13
Protection 1Sam 25:21
Safety ....Ps 33:17
World's creation.........Is 45:18, 19

Applied to spiritual things:
Obedience ....Deut 32:46, 47
Chastisement...........Jer 2:30
Visions ....Ezek 13:7
Serving God ....Mal 3:14
Faith 1Cor 15:17
Words..................Eph 5:6
Imaginations ....Rom 1:21
Babblings 2Tim 2:16

Applied to possibilities:
God's grace 1Cor 15:10
Christ's death ....Gal 2:21
Scriptures ....James 4:5
Faith 1Cor 15:2-17
Religion ....James 1:26
Worship ....Is 45:19
Labor 1Thess 3:5
Reception...............1Thess 2:1, 2
Sufferings ....Gal 3:4

[*also* VAINLY]
let them not regard *v* words ...Ex 5:9
of the Lord thy God in *v* .....Ex 20:7
that taketh his name in *v*......Ex 20:7
shall sow your seed in *v*.......Lev 26:16
strength shall be spent in *v* ...Lev 26:20
name of the Lord..in *v*........Deut 5:11
that taketh his name in *v*.......Deut 5:11
Abimelech hired *v* and ....Judg 9:4
were gathered *v* men to ....Judg 11:3
should ye go after *v* things 1Sam 12:21
nor deliver; for they are *v*.....1Sam 12:21
one of the *v* fellows 2Sam 6:20
became *v*, and went after 2Kin 17:15
but they are but *v* words 2Kin 18:20
gathered unto him *v* men 2Chr 13:7
why then labor I in *v*? ....Job 9:29
For he knoweth *v* men ....Job 11:11
wise man utter *v* knowledge ...Job 15:2
Shall *v* words have an end ....Job 16:3
then comfort ye me in *v* ......Job 21:34
are ye thus altogether *v*? ......Job 27:12
Job open his mouth in *v* ......Job 35:16
her labor is in *v* without ......Job 39:16
the hope of him is in *v*........Job 41:9
people imagine a *v* thing? .....Ps 2:1
not sat with *v* persons.........Ps 26:4
An horse is a *v* thing for ......Ps 33:17
every man walketh in a *v* .....Ps 39:6
they are disquieted in *v* ......Ps 39:6
for *v* is the help of man ....Ps 60:11
cleansed my heart in *v* ....Ps 73:13
for *v* is the help of man ....Ps 108:12
I hate *v* thoughts: but ....Ps 119:113
they labor in *v* that build......Ps 127:1
watchman waketh but in *v* ....Ps 127:1
enemies take thy name in *v* ...Ps 139:20
Surely in *v* the net is ....Prov 1:17
that followeth *v* persons ....Prov 12:11
the name of my God in *v* .....Prov 30:9
Egyptians shall help in *v* ......Is 30:7
(but they are but *v* words) ....Is 36:5
I have labored in *v* ....Is 49:4
for nought, and in *v* ....Is 49:4
They shall not labor in *v*......Is 65:23
vanity, and are become *v*? ....Jer 2:5
in *v* is salvation hoped for.....Jer 3:23
thy *v* thoughts lodge ....Jer 4:14
the founder melteth in *v* ......Jer 6:29
certainly in *v* made he it ......Jer 8:8
pen of the scribes is in *v* ......Jer 8:8
unto you: they make you *v*....Jer 23:16
none shall return in *v* ....Jer 50:9
people shall labor in *v* ....Jer 51:58
seen *v* and foolish things ......Lam 2:14
yet failed for our *v* help.......Lam 4:17
said in *v* that I would do ......Ezek 6:10
be no more any *v* vision ......Ezek 12:24
dreams; they comfort in *v* .....Zech 10:2
pray, use not *v* repetitions.....Matt 6:7
in *v* they do worship me ......Matt 15:9
in *v* they do worship me ......Mark 7:7
people imagine *v* things? ......Acts 4:25
beareth not the sword in *v* ....Rom 13:4
the wise, that they are *v* 1Cor 3:20
your labor is not in *v* in......1Cor 15:58
the grace of God in *v* 2Cor 6:1
boasting..should be in *v* 2Cor 9:3
run, or had run, in *v* ....Gal 2:2
upon you labor in *v* ....Gal 4:11
in *v*, neither labored in *v*.......Phil 2:16
philosophy and *v* deceit ....Col 2:8
v puffed up by his fleshly .....Col 2:18
have turned aside unto *v* 1Tim 1:6
profane and *v* babblings 1Tim 6:20
and *v* talkers and deceivers ....Titus 1:10
are unprofitable and *v* ....Titus 3:9
O *v* man, that faith without ..James 2:20
from your *v* conversation 1Pet 1:18

VAINGLORY—*conceit*
Very offensive in the Christian's life....... {Gal 5:26; Phil 2:3}

VAJEZATHA (vä-jĕz'ä-thä)—*"born of Ized; given-of-the-best-one"*
One of Haman's sons ....Esth 9:9

VALE—*valley*
in the *v* of Siddim ....Gen 14:3
v of Siddim was full of ....Gen 14:10
in the hills, and in the *v* ......Deut 1:7
of the south, and of the *v* .....Josh 10:40
trees that are in the *v*.........1Kin 10:27
trees that are in the *v*.........2Chr 1:15
in the cities of the *v* ....Jer 33:13

VALIANT—*possessing courage*

[*also* VALIANTEST, VALIANTLY]
and Israel shall do *v* ....Num 24:18
thousand men of the *v* ....Judg 21:10
strong man, or any *v* man 1Sam 14:52
only be thou *v* for me, and....1Sam 18:17
All the *v* men arose, and......1Sam 31:12
strengthened, and be ye *v* 2Sam 2:7

be courageous, and be *v* 2Sam 13:28
he also that is *v*, whose 2Sam 17:10
they be with him are *v* men . . .2Sam 17:10
hundred thousand *v* men 2Sam 24:9
for thou art a *v* man 1Kin 1:42
tribe of Manasseh, of *v* men . . .1Chr 5:18
of Issachar were *v* men of 1Chr 7:5
son of a *v* man of Kabzeel 1Chr 11:22
let us behave ourselves *v* 1Chr 19:13
v men, unto Jerusalem 1Chr 28:1
an army of *v* men of war 2Chr 13:3
day, which were all *v* men 2Chr 28:6
threescore and eight *v* men . . . .Neh 11:6
Through God we shall do *v* . . .Ps 60:12
Through God we shall do *v* . . .Ps 108:13
hand of the Lord doeth *v* . . . . .Ps 118:15
hand of the Lord doeth *v* . . . . .Ps 118:16
threescore *v* men are . . . . .Song 3:7
inhabitants like a *v* man . . . . . . .Is 10:13
are not *v* for the truth . . . . .Jer 9:3
the *v* men are in scarlet . . . . . . .Nah 2:3
waxed *v* in fight, turned . . . . . . .Heb 11:34

VALLEY—*a depression in the land between hills or mountains*

[*also* VALLEYS]
at the *v* of Shaveh, which . . . . .Gen 14:17
servants digged in the *v* . . . . . . .Gen 26:19
Canaanites dwelt in the *v* . . . . .Num 14:25
from Bamoth in the *v* . . . . .Num 21:20
As the *v* are they spread . . . . . .Num 24:6
came unto the *v* of Eshcol . . . .Deut 1:24
So we abode in the *v* over . . . .Deut 3:29
depths that spring out of the *v* .Deut 8:7
heifer unto a rough *v* . . . . .Deut 21:4
heifer's neck there in the *v* . . . .Deut 21:4
plain of the *v* of Jericho . . . . . . .Deut 34:3
them unto the *v* of Achor . . . . .Josh 7:24
v between them and Ai . . . . . . .Josh 8:11
in the hills, and in the *v* . . . . . .Josh 9:1
Moon, in the *v* of Ajalon . . . . .Josh 10:12
the *v* of Mizpeh eastward . . . . .Josh 11:8
land of Goshen, and the *v* . . . .Josh 11:16
of Israel, and the *v* of the . . . . .Josh 11:16
in the *v* of Lebanon . . . . .Josh 12:7
And in the *v*, Beth-aram . . . . . .Josh 13:27
v of the son of Hinnom . . . . . . .Josh 15:8
v of Hinnom westward . . . . .Josh 15:8
v of the giants northward . . . . .Josh 15:8
land of the *v* have chariots . . . .Josh 17:16
who are of the *v* of Jezreel . . . .Josh 17:16
v of the son of Hinnom . . . . . . .Josh 18:16
v of the giants on the north . . .Josh 18:16
to the *v* of Hinnom . . . . .Josh 18:16
are in the *v* of Jiphthah-el . . . .Josh 19:14
in the south, and in the *v* . . . . .Judg 1:9
to come down to the *v* . . . . .Judg 1:34
pitched in the *v* of Jezreel . . . . .Judg 6:33
was beneath him in the *v* . . . . .Judg 7:8
a woman in the *v* of Sorek . . . .Judg 16:4
wheat harvest in the *v* 1Sam 6:13
and laid wait in the *v* 1Sam 15:5
was a *v* between them 1Sam 17:3
until thou come to the *v* 1Sam 17:52
on the other side of the *v* 1Sam 31:7
in the *v* of Rephaim 2Sam 5:18
in the *v* of Rephaim 2Sam 23:13
he is not God of the *v* 1Kin 20:28
mountain, or into some *v* 2Kin 2:16
v shall be filled with water 2Kin 3:17
v of the children of Hinnom . . .2Kin 23:10
father of the *v* of Charashim . .1Chr 4:14
Israel that were in the *v* 1Chr 10:7
to flight all them of the *v* 1Chr 12:15
in the *v* of Rephaim 1Chr 14:9
Edomites in the *v* of salt 1Chr 18:12
in array in the *v* of 2Chr 14:10
in the *V* of Berachah 2Chr 20:26
called, The *V* of Berachah 2Chr 20:26
at the *v* gate, and at the 2Chr 26:9
the *v* of the son of Hinnom . . .2Chr 33:6
fight in the *v* of Megiddo 2Chr 35:22
by the gate of the *v* . . . . .Neh 2:15
v gate repaired Hanun . . . . .Neh 3:13
unto the *v* of Hinnom . . . . .Neh 11:30
Ono, the *v* of craftsmen . . . . . . .Neh 11:35
The clods of the *v* shall be . . . .Job 21:33
dwell in the cliffs of the *v* . . . . .Job 30:6
the *v* of the shadow of . . . . .Ps 23:4
mete out the *v* of Succoth . . . . .Ps 60:6
v also are covered over . . . . . . .Ps 65:13
through the *v* of Baca . . . . .Ps 84:6
the springs into the *v* . . . . .Ps 104:10
mete out the *v* of Succoth . . . . .Ps 108:7
ravens of the *v* shall pick . . . . . .Prov 30:17
and the lily of the *v* . . . . .Song 2:1
to see the fruits of the *v* . . . . . .Song 6:11
them in the desolate *v* . . . . .Is 7:19
ears in the *v* of Rephaim . . . . . .Is 17:5
of hosts in the *v* of vision . . . . .Is 22:5
head of the fat *v* of them . . . . .Is 28:1
wroth as in the *v* of Gibeon . . .Is 28:21
slaying..children in the *v* . . . . . .Is 57:5
beast goeth down into the *v* . . .Is 63:14
see thy way in the *v* . . . . .Jer 2:23
v of the son of Hinnom . . . . . . .Jer 7:32
but the *v* of slaughter: for . . . . .Jer 7:32
v of the son of Hinnom . . . . . . .Jer 19:6
but The *v* of slaughter . . . . .Jer 19:6
whole *v* of the dead bodies . . . .Jer 31:40
in the cities of the *v* . . . . .Jer 32:44
v also shall perish, and . . . . . . .Jer 48:8
gloriest thou in the *v* . . . . .Jer 49:4
to the rivers, and to the *v* . . . . .Ezek 6:3
in all the *v* his branches . . . . . . .Ezek 31:12
in thy hills, and in thy *v* . . . . . .Ezek 35:8
v of the passengers on the . . . . .Ezek 39:11
call it The *v* of Hamon-gog . . . .Ezek 39:11
Israel in the *v* of Jezreel . . . . . .Hos 1:5
into the *v* of Jehoshaphat . . . . .Joel 3:2
multitudes..*v* of decision . . . . . .Joel 3:14
Lord is near in the *v* of . . . . . . .Joel 3:14
v shall be cleft, as wax . . . . .Mic 1:4
stones thereof into the *v* . . . . . .Mic 1:6
in the *v* of Megiddon . . . . .Zech 12:11
to the *v* of the mountains . . . . .Zech 14:5
for the *v* of the mountains . . . .Zech 14:5

VALLEY GATE—*a gate in the northwestern area of Jerusalem*
Entrance into Jerusalem. .Neh 2:13

VALLEY OF DRY BONES—*the valley envisioned by Ezekiel in his dream*
Vision of Ezekiel . . . . .Ezek 37:1-14

VALOR—*bravery; heroism*
all the mighty men of *v* . . . . . . .Josh 1:14
thousand mighty men of *v* . . . . .Josh 8:3
all lusty, and all men of *v* . . . . .Judg 3:29
Jephthah..mighty man of *v* . . . .Judg 11:1
all these were men of *v* . . . . . . .Judg 20:44
was a mighty man of *v* 1Kin 11:28
was also a mighty man in *v* 2Kin 5:1
mighty men of *v*, famous 1Chr 5:24
fathers, mighty men of *v* 1Chr 7:9
Ulam were mighty men of *v* . . .1Chr 8:40
mighty men of *v* for the 1Chr 12:25
hundred, mighty men of *v* 1Chr 12:30
and his brethren, men of *v* 1Chr 26:30
his brethren, men of *v* 1Chr 26:32
being mighty men of *v* 2Chr 13:3
of war, mighty men of *v* 2Chr 17:13
thousand mighty men of *v* 2Chr 17:16
men of *v* out of Israel 2Chr 25:6
off all the mighty men of *v* 2Chr 32:21
mighty men of *v* . . . . .Neh 11:14

VALUE—*hold something in high regard; price; worth*

[*also* VALUED, VALUEST]
and the priest shall *v* him . . . . .Lev 27:8
And the priest shall *v* it . . . . . . .Lev 27:12
as thou *v* it, who art the . . . . . .Lev 27:12
barley seed shall be *v* at . . . . . .Lev 27:16
ye are..physicians of no *v* . . . . .Job 13:4
v with the gold of Ophir . . . . . .Job 28:16
neither shall it be *v* with . . . . . .Job 28:19
more *v* than many sparrows . . .Matt 10:31
price of him that was *v* . . . . . . .Matt 27:9
more *v* than many sparrows . . .Luke 12:7

VANIAH (vä-nī'ä)—*"praise, or nourishment, of Jehovah"*
Divorced his foreign wife .Ezra 10:36

VANISH—*to disappear*

[*also* VANISHED, VANISHETH]
they wax warm, they *v* . . . . .Job 6:17
cloud is consumed and *v* . . . . . .Job 7:9
heavens shall *v* away like . . . . . .Is 51:6
prudent? is their wisdom *v* . . . .Jer 49:7
and he *v* out of their sight . . . .Luke 24:31
knowledge, it shall *v* away 1Cor 13:8
old is ready to *v* away . . . . .Heb 8:13
little time, and then *v* away . . .James 4:14

VANITY—*emptiness; futility; conceit*

***Descriptive of*:**
Man's life . . . . .Ps 144:4
Sin's end . . . . .Prov 22:8
Man's thoughts . . . . .Ps 94:11
Idolatry . . . . .Acts 14:15

***Manifested in the wicked's*:**
Words . . . . .Ps 12:2
Thoughts . . . . .Ps 94:11
Trust . . . . .Is 59:4
Worship . . . . .Jer 51:17, 18

***Believer's attitude toward*:**
Request for removal from.Prov 30:8
"Turn away mine eyes" . .Ps 119:37
Should not walk in . . . . . .Eph 4:17

[*also* VANITIES]
me to anger with their *v* . . . . . .Deut 32:21
to anger with their *v* 1Kin 16:13
they followed *v*, and 2Kin 17:15
to possess months of *v* . . . . .Job 7:3
is deceived trust in *v* . . . . .Job 15:31
v shall be his recompense . . . . .Job 15:31
If I have walked with *v* . . . . . . .Job 31:5
how long will ye love *v* . . . . . . .Ps 4:2
tongue is mischief and *v* . . . . . .Ps 10:7
them that regard lying *v* . . . . . .Ps 31:6
to see me, he speaketh *v* . . . . . .Ps 41:6
men of low degree are *v* . . . . . .Ps 62:9
altogether lighter than *v* . . . . . .Ps 62:9
days did he consume in *v* . . . . .Ps 78:33
Whose mouth speaketh *v* . . . . . .Ps 144:8
whose mouth speaketh *v* . . . . . .Ps 144:11
Wealth gotten by *v* shall . . . . . .Prov 13:11
by a lying tongue is a *v* . . . . . . .Prov 21:6
V of *v*, saith the Preacher . . . . .Eccl 1:2
v of *v*; all is *v* . . . . .Eccl 1:2
all is *v* and vexation of spirit . .Eccl 1:14
and, behold, this also is *v* . . . . .Eccl 2:1
heart, that this also is *v* . . . . . .Eccl 2:15
the sun. This is also *v* . . . . .Eccl 2:19
rest in the night. This is also *v* .Eccl 2:23
above a beast: for all is *v* . . . . .Eccl 3:19
and I saw *v* under the sun . . . . .Eccl 4:7
also is *v* and vexation . . . . .Eccl 4:16
this is *v*, and it is an evil . . . . . .Eccl 6:2
is also *v* and vexation . . . . .Eccl 6:9
laughter..this also is *v* . . . . .Eccl 7:6
so done: this is also *v* . . . . .Eccl 8:10
There is a *v* which is . . . . .Eccl 8:14
I said that this also is *v* . . . . . . .Eccl 8:14
days of the life of thy *v* . . . . . . .Eccl 9:9
all the days of thy *v* . . . . .Eccl 9:9
childhood and youth are *v* . . . . .Eccl 11:10
V of *v*, saith the Preacher . . . . .Eccl 12:8
all is *v* . . . . .Eccl 12:8
less than nothing, and *v* . . . . . . .Is 40:17
they are all *v*; their . . . . .Is 41:29
away; *v* shall take them . . . . . . .Is 57:13
trust in *v*, and speak lies . . . . . .Is 59:4
and have walked after *v* . . . . . . .Jer 2:5
images and with strange *v*? . . . .Jer 8:19
the *v* of the Gentiles . . . . .Jer 14:22
fathers have inherited lies, *v* . . .Jer 16:19
have burned incense to *v* . . . . . .Jer 18:15
They have seen *v* and . . . . .Ezek 13:6
the prophets that see *v* . . . . .Ezek 13:9
they see *v* unto thee . . . . .Ezek 21:29
Gilead? surely they are *v* . . . . . .Hos 12:11
observe lying *v* forsake . . . . .Jon 2:8

weary themselves for..*v*? . . . . . .Hab 2:13
the idols have spoken *v* . . . . . . .Zech 10:2
was made subject to *v* . . . . .Rom 8:20
great swelling words of *v* 2Pet 2:18

VAPOR—*fog; smoke; something transitory*

[*also* VAPORS]
rain according to the *v* . . . . .Job 36:27
cattle also concerning the *v* . . . .Job 36:33
He causeth the *v* to ascend . . . .Ps 135:7
Fire and hail; snow and *v* . . . . .Ps 148:8
he causeth the *v* to ascend . . . .Jer 10:13
he causeth the *v* to ascend . . . .Jer 51:16
blood..fire, and *v* of smoke . . . .Acts 2:19
a *v*, that appeareth for a . . . . . .James 4:14

VARIABLENESS—*changeableness*
with whom is no *v* . . . . .James 1:17

VARIANCE—*disagreement; at odds with*
man at *v* against his father . . . .Matt 10:35
v, emulations, wrath . . . . .Gal 5:20

VASHNI (văsh'nī)—*"the second"*
Son of Samuel 1Chr 6:28

VASHTI (văsh'tī)—*"beautiful woman; best"*
Queen of Ahasuerus, deposed and divorced . .Esth 1:9-22

he remembered *V*, and . . . . .Esth 2:1
be queen instead of *V* . . . . .Esth 2:4
her queen instead of *V* . . . . .Esth 2:17

VATS—*holding pots*
the *v* shall overflow with . . . . . .Joel 2:24

VAU (vô)
Letter in the Hebrew alphabet . . . . .Ps 119:41-48

VAUNT—*to vainly display one's own worth or accomplishments*

[*also* VAUNTETH]
lest Israel *v* themselves . . . . .Judg 7:2
charity *v* not itself, is not 1Cor 13:4

VEAL—*the meat from a young calf*
Prepared for King Saul . .1Sam 28:21-25

VEGETABLES—*plants grown for the edible parts*
Part of God's creation . . .Gen 1:11, 12
Controversy regarding . . .Rom 14:1-23
Preferred by Daniel . . . . .Dan 1:12, 16

VEHEMENT—*marked by forceful energy; forcefully expressed*

[*also* VEHEMENTLY]
which hath a most *v* flame . . . .Song 8:6
God prepared a *v* east wind . . .Jon 4:8
But he spake the more *v* . . . . . .Mark 14:31
stream beat *v* upon that . . . . . . .Luke 6:48
the stream did beat *v* . . . . .Luke 6:49
Pharisees began to urge him *v* .Luke 11:53
stood and *v* accused him . . . . . .Luke 23:10
fear yea, what *v* desire 2Cor 7:11

VEIL—*piece of cloth worn over the face*
which put a *v* over his face 2Cor 3:13

VEIL—*the screen separating the Holy Place and the Holy of Holies in the tabernacle and temple*

Features regarding:
Made by divine command. Ex 26:31, 32
Used to separate the holy and most holy . . . . .Ex 26:33
Means of concealing the divine persion . . . . .Ex 40:3
In the Temple also 2Chr 3:14
Rent at Christ's death . . .Matt 27:51

Entrance through:
By the high priest alone .Heb 9:6, 7
On Day of Atonement only . . . . .Heb 9:7
Taking blood . . . . .Heb 9:7

Figurative of:
Old Testament dispensation . . . . .Heb 9:8
Christ's flesh . . . . .Heb 10:20
Access now into God's presence . . . . .Heb 10:19-22

set the table without the *v* . . . .Ex 26:35
congregation without the *v* . . . .Ex 27:21
the *v* that is by the ark . . . . . . .Ex 30:6
and the *v* of the covering . . . . .Ex 35:12
be made a *v* of blue, and . . . . .Ex 36:35
the sockets of the *v* . . . . .Ex 38:27
and the *v* of the covering . . . . .Ex 39:34
set up the *v* of the covering . . .Ex 40:21
northward, without the *v* . . . . . .Ex 40:22
congregation before the *v* . . . . .Ex 40:26
the *v* of the sanctuary . . . . .Lev 4:6
Lord, even before the *v* . . . . . . .Lev 4:17
holy place within the *v* . . . . .Lev 16:2
and bring it within the *v* . . . . . .Lev 16:12
his blood within the *v* . . . . .Lev 16:15
shall not go in unto the *v* . . . . .Lev 21:23
the *v* of the testimony . . . . .Lev 24:3
take down the covering *v* . . . . .Num 4:5
altar, and within the *v* . . . . .Num 18:7
v of the temple was rent . . . . . .Matt 27:51
v of the temple was rent . . . . . .Mark 15:38
v of the temple was rent . . . . . .Luke 23:45
entereth into that within the *v* .Heb 6:19
after the second *v*, the . . . . .Heb 9:3

VEIL, WOMAN'S—*a cloth worn by women as a covering of the face or head*

Literal uses of:
For modesty . . . . .Gen 24:65
For adornment . . . . .Is 3:23
To conceal identity . . . . . .Gen 38:14
To soften the divine glory of God . . . . .Ex 34:33-35

Figurative of:
Coming of the Lord . . . . .Is 25:7
Turning to the Lord 2Cor 3:14-16

laid by her *v* from her, and . . .Gen 38:19
Bring the *v* that thou hast . . . . .Ruth 3:15
keepers..took away my *v* . . . . . .Song 3:5
keepers..took away my *v* . . . . . .Song 5:7

VEIN—*mass of a specific mineral encased in rock*
there is a *v* for the silver . . . . . .Job 28:1

VENGEANCE—*retribution; punishment*

Belonging to God, as:
Judgment upon sin . . . . . .Jer 11:20-23
Right not to be taken by man . . . . .Ezek 25:12-17; Heb 10:30
Set time . . . . .Jer 46:9, 10

Visitation of, by God, at:
Nation's fall . . . . .Jer 51:6, 11, 36
Christ's first coming . . . . .Is 35:4-10
Jerusalem's destruction . . .Luke 21:22
Sodom's destruction . . . . .Jude 7
Christ's return 2Thess 1:8

See REVENGE

v shall be taken on him . . . . . . .Gen 4:15
To me belongeth *v*, and . . . . . . .Deut 32:35
render *v* to his adversaries . . . .Deut 32:43
the Lord hath taken *v* for . . . . .Judg 11:36
rejoice when he seeth the *v* . . .Ps 58:10
God, to whom *v* belongeth. . . .Ps 94:1
O God, to whom *v* belongeth. .Ps 94:1
thou tookest *v* of their . . . . .Ps 99:8
To execute *v* upon the . . . . .Ps 149:7
not spare in the day of *v* . . . . . .Prov 6:34
is the day of the Lord's *v* . . . . .Is 34:8
I will take *v*, and I will . . . . . . .Is 47:3
Lord, and the day of *v* of . . . . .Is 61:2
heart, let me see thy *v* on . . . . .Jer 20:12
for it is the *v* of the Lord . . . . .Jer 50:15
take *v* upon her; as she . . . . . .Jer 50:15
in Zion the *v* of the Lord . . . . .Jer 50:28
God, the *v* of his temple . . . . . .Jer 50:28
Thou hast seen all their *v* . . . . .Lam 3:60
fury to come up to take *v* . . . . .Ezek 24:8
execute *v* in anger and . . . . .Mic 5:15
take *v* on his adversaries . . . . . .Nah 1:2
the sea, yet *v* suffereth . . . . .Acts 28:4
V is mine; I will repay . . . . .Rom 12:19

VENISON—*the flesh of deer*
Isaac's favorite dish . . . . . .Gen 27:1-33

because he did eat of his *v* . . . .Gen 25:28

VENOM—*poison; poisonous*

[*also* VENOMOUS]
and the cruel *v* of asps . . . . .Deut 32:33
saw the *v* beast hang on . . . . . . .Acts 28:4

VENT—*a place for gases to escape; outlet*
as wine which hath no *v* . . . . . .Job 32:19

VENTURE—*random*
man drew a bow at a *v* 1Kin 22:34
man drew a bow at a *v* 2Chr 18:33

VERDICT—*a judicial decision*
Unjustly rendered . . . . . . .Luke 23:13-26
Pronounced by hypocrites. John 8:1-11

VERIFIED—*confirmed the truth*
so shall your words be *v* . . . . . .Gen 42:20
thy word, I pray thee be *v* 1Kin 8:26
of Israel, let thy word be *v* 2Chr 6:17

VERILY— *"truly"*—*a strong affirmation*

Concerning Christ's:
Glory . . . . .John 1:51
Eternity . . . . .John 8:58
Uniqueness . . . . .John 10:1, 7
Mission . . . . .John 6:32
Betrayal . . . . .John 13:21
Death . . . . .John 12:24

Concerning man's:
Spiritual bondage . . . . .John 8:34
Spiritual darkness . . . . . . .John 6:26
Need of regeneration . . . .John 3:3, 5
Need of salvation . . . . .John 5:24, 25
Means of salvation . . . . . .John 6:47, 53
Life eternal . . . . .John 8:51

Concerning the believer's:
Fickleness . . . . .John 13:38
Work . . . . .John 14:12
Mission . . . . .John 13:16, 20
Prayer . . . . .John 16:23
Life .John 21:18

We are *v* guilty concerning . . . .Gen 42:21
V my sabbaths ye shall . . . . .Ex 31:13
I *v* thought that thou . . . . .Judg 15:2
V our lord king David 1Kin 1:43
V she hath no child, and 2Kin 4:14
v buy it for the full price 1Chr 21:24
are *v* estranged . . . . .Job 19:13
and *v* thou shalt be fed . . . . . . .Ps 37:3
V there is a reward for the . . . .Ps 58:11
v he is a God that judgeth . . . .Ps 58:11
V thou art a God that . . . . .Is 45:15
V it shall be well with thy . . . . .Jer 15:11
v I will cause the enemy to . . . .Jer 15:11
For *v* I say unto you, Till . . . . .Matt 5:18
V I say unto thee, Thou . . . . . .Matt 5:26
V I say unto you, They have . .Matt 6:2
V I say unto you, I have . . . . . .Matt 8:10
V I say unto you, It shall . . . . .Matt 10:15
v I say unto you, he shall . . . . .Matt 10:42
V I say unto you, Among . . . . .Matt 11:11
For *v* I say unto you. That . . . .Matt 13:17
V I say unto you, There . . . . . .Matt 16:28
for *v* I say unto you, If ye . . . .Matt 17:20
V I say unto you, Except . . . . .Matt 18:3
v I say unto you, he . . . . .Matt 18:13
V I say unto you, That . . . . .Matt 19:23
V I say unto you, That . . . . .Matt 19:28
V I say unto you, If ye . . . . . . .Matt 21:21
V I say unto you, That . . . . .Matt 21:31
V I say unto you, All . . . . .Matt 23:36
v I say unto you, There . . . . . . .Matt 24:2
V I say unto you, This . . . . .Matt 24:34
V I say unto you, That . . . . .Matt 24:47
V I say unto you, I know . . . . .Matt 25:12
V I say unto you. Inasmuch . . .Matt 25:40
V I say unto you. Wheresoever. Matt 26:13
V I say unto you, that . . . . .Matt 26:21
V I say unto thee, That . . . . . . .Matt 26:34
V I say unto you, All . . . . .Mark 3:28
V I say unto you, It . . . . .Mark 6:11

v I say unto you, There .... Mark 8:12
V I say unto you, That .... Mark 9:1
Elijah *v* cometh first, and ..... Mark 9:12
v I say unto you, he shall ..... Mark 9:41
V I say unto you, Whosoever .. Mark 10:15
V I say unto you, There ...... Mark 10:29
v I say unto you, That .... Mark 11:23
V I say unto you, That .... Mark 12:43
V I say unto you, that .... Mark 13:30
V I say unto you, Wheresoever. Mark 14:9
V I say unto you, One of ..... Mark 14:18
V I say unto you, I will .... Mark 14:25
V I say unto thee, That .... Mark 14:30
V I say unto you, No .... Luke 4:24
v I say unto you, It shall ...... Luke 11:51
v I say unto you, that he ...... Luke 12:37
and *v* I say unto you, Ye ..... Luke 13:35
V I say unto you, Whosoever .. Luke 18:17
V I say unto you, This .... Luke 21:32
V I say unto thee, To day ..... Luke 23:43
V, *v*, I say unto thee, We ..... John 3:11
V, *v*, I say unto you, The ..... John 5:19
V, *v*, I say unto you .... John 6:32
nay *v*; but let them come ..... Acts 16:37
John *v* baptized with the ...... Acts 19:4
I am *v* a man which am a Jew . Acts 22:3
I *v* thought with myself .... Acts 26:9
circumcision *v* profiteth .... Rom 2:25
Yes *v*, their sound went .... Rom 10:18
It hath pleased them *v* .... Rom 15:27
For I *v*, as absent in body 1Cor 5:3
V that, when I preach the 1Cor 9:18
For thou *v* givest thanks 1Cor 14:17
v righteousness should .... Gal 3:21
For *v*, when we were with 1Thess 3:4
v he took not on him the ..... Heb 2:16
For men *v* swear by the .... Heb 6:16
there is *v* a disannulling .... Heb 7:18
For they *v* for a few days ..... Heb 12:10
Who *v* was foreordained 1Pet 1:20
v is the love of God 1John 2:5

VERITY—*trustworthy; truth*

works of his hands are *v* ...... Ps 111:7
Gentiles in faith and *v* 1Tim 2:7

VERMILION—*a brilliant red color*

Ceiling painted with ..... Jer 22:14

portrayed with *v* .... Ezek 23:14

VERY—*true; actual; particularly*

and, behold, it was *v* good .... Gen 1:31
woman that she was *v* fair ..... Gen 12:14
their sin is *v* grievous .... Gen 18:20
the damsel was *v* fair to .... Gen 24:16
thou be my *v* son Esau .... Gen 27:21
Isaac trembled *v* .... Gen 27:33
and *v* ill-favored and .... Gen 41:19
v much, until he left .... Gen 41:49
it was a *v* great company ...... Gen 50:9
and waxed *v* mighty .... Ex 1:20
be a *v* grievous murrain .... Ex 9:3
to rain a *v* grievous hail .... Ex 9:18
v grievous were they .... Ex 10:14
herds even *v* much cattle ...... Ex 12:38
any man die *v* suddenly .... Num 6:9
man Moses was *v* meek .... Num 12:3
Moses was *v* wroth, and ...... Num 16:15
had a *v* great multitude ...... Num 32:1
the Lord was *v* angry .... Deut 9:20
the cities which are *v* far ...... Deut 20:15
get up above thee *v* high ...... Deut 28:43
thou shalt come down *v* low ... Deut 28:43
tender..and *v* delicate .... Deut 28:54
a *v* froward generation .... Deut 32:20
strong and *v* courageous ...... Josh 1:7
go not *v* far from the city ..... Josh 8:4
of the *v* long journey .... Josh 9:13
with a *v* great slaughter .... Josh 10:20
horses and chariots *v* many .... Josh 11:4
and with *v* much cattle .... Josh 22:8
and with *v* much raiment ...... Josh 22:8
ye therefore *v* courageous ..... Josh 23:6
Eglon was a *v* fat man .... Judg 3:17
hast brought me *v* low .... Judg 11:35
land..behold, it is *v* good ...... Judg 18:9
dealt *v* bitterly with me .... Ruth 1:20
sin of the young men was *v* ... 1Sam 2:17
was a *v* great slaughter 1Sam 4:10
hand of God was *v* heavy 1Sam 5:11
a *v* great discomfiture 1Sam 14:20
And Saul was *v* wroth 1Sam 18:8
been to thee-ward *v* good 1Sam 19:4
that he dealeth *v* subtilly 1Sam 23:22
But the men were *v* good 1Sam 25:15
for he was *v* drunken 1Sam 25:36
v pleasant hast thou been 2Sam 1:26
Then was Abner *v* wroth 2Sam 3:8
David, and it was *v* sick 2Sam 12:15
things, he was *v* wroth 2Sam 13:21
a *v* great heap of stones 2Sam 18:17
Barzillai was a *v* aged 2Sam 19:32
for he was a *v* great man 2Sam 19:32
the damsel was *v* fair 1Kin 1:4
and the king was *v* old 1Kin 1:15
with a *v* great train 1Kin 10:2
v much gold, and 1Kin 10:2
I have been *v* jealous 1Kin 19:10
that it was *v* bitter 2Kin 14:26
innocent blood *v* much 2Kin 21:16
v able men for the work 1Chr 9:13
for I have done *v* foolishly 1Chr 21:8
sons of Rehabiah were *v* 1Chr 23:17
God in *v* deed dwell with 2Chr 6:18
with a *v* great company 2Chr 9:1
they carried away *v* much 2Chr 14:13
made a *v* great burning 2Chr 16:14
delivered a *v* great host 2Chr 24:24
him substance *v* much 2Chr 32:29
transgressed *v* much 2Chr 36:14
a *v* great congregation .... Ezra 10:1
for the people wept *v* sore .... Ezra 10:1
We have dealt *v* corruptly ..... Neh 1:7
then they were *v* wroth .... Neh 4:7
was *v* great gladness .... Neh 8:17
was the king *v* wroth .... Esth 1:12
and a *v* great household .... Job 1:3
grayheaded and *v* aged men ... Job 15:10
inward part is *v* wickedness .... Ps 5:9
a *v* present help in trouble .... Ps 46:1
O God, is *v* high .... Ps 71:19
establish in the *v* heavens ..... Ps 89:2
Thy testimonies are *v* sure .... Ps 93:5
few men in number; yea, *v* few. Ps 105:12
righteous and *v* faithful .... Ps 119:138
for I am brought *v* low .... Ps 142:6
separateth *v* friends .... Prov 17:9
unto us a *v* small remnant ..... Is 1:9
For yet a *v* little while .... Is 10:25
remnant shall be *v* small ...... Is 16:14
it not yet a *v* little while ...... Is 29:17
the land that is *v* far off .... Is 33:17
hast thou *v* heavily laid .... Is 47:6
extolled, and be *v* high .... Is 52:13
and afflict us *v* sore? .... Is 64:12
be ye *v* desolate, saith the ..... Jer 2:12
dealt *v* treacherously .... Jer 5:11
with a *v* grievous blow .... Jer 14:17
making him *v* glad .... Jer 20:15
basket had *v* good rigs .... Jer 24:2
basket had *v* naughty figs ..... Jer 24:2
Figs; the good figs, *v* good .... Jer 24:3
evil, *v* evil, that cannot ...... Jer 24:3
wine and summer fruits *v* ...... Jer 40:12
thou art *v* wroth against .... Lam 5:22
even unto this *v* day .... Ezek 2:3
made *v* glorious in the .... Ezek 27:25
were *v* many in the open ...... Ezek 37:2
and, lo, they were *v* dry ...... Ezek 37:2
were *v* many trees on the ..... Ezek 47:7
king was angry..*v* furious ...... Dan 2:12
the he goat waxed *v* great ..... Dan 8:8
for his camp is *v* great .... Joel 2:11
v dark, and no brightness ..... Amos 5:20
and he was *v* angry .... Jon 4:1
shall labor in the *v* fire .... Hab 2:13
weary..for *v* vanity? .... Hab 2:13
I am *v* sore displeased .... Zech 1:15
Zidon, though it be *v* wise .... Zech 9:2
the *v* hairs of your head .... Matt 10:30
cured from that *v* hour .... Matt 17:18
v great multitude spread ..... Matt 21:8
box of *v* precious ointment .... Matt 26:7
multitude being *v* great ...... Mark 8:1
and to be *v* heavy .... Mark 14:33
rolled away..was *v* great ...... Mark 16:4
all things from the *v* first ...... Luke 1:3
Even the *v* dust of your city ... Luke 10:11
hast paid the *v* last mite .... Luke 12:59
he was *v* sorrowful .... Luke 18:23
for he was *v* rich .... Luke 18:23
been faithful in a *v* little ...... Luke 19:17
v early in the morning .... Luke 24:1
that this is the *v* Christ? .... John 7:26
spikenard, *v* costly .... John 12:3
proving that this is *v* Christ ... Acts 9:22
as thou *v* well knowest .... Acts 25:10
Isaiah is *v* bold, and saith ..... Rom 10:20
is a *v* small thing that I 1Cor 4:3
zeal hath provoked *v* many 2Cor 9:2
the *v* chiefest apostles 2Cor 12:11
confident of this *v* thing .... Phil 1:6
to esteem them *v* highly 1Thess 5:13
sought me out *v* diligently 2Tim 1:17
and not the *v* image of the .... Heb 10:1
with a *v* small helm .... James 3:4

VESSEL—*hollow container*

Made of:

Wood or stone .... Ex 7:19
Gold and silver .... Dan 5:2
Clay .... Rom 9:21
Copper .... Ezra 8:27

Of the tabernacle:

Under care of Levites .... Num 3:31, 32
Carried away into Babylon 2Chr 36:18
Belshazzar uses in feast .. Dan 5:1-4
Returned to Jerusalem ... Ezra 1:7-11

Figurative of:

Mankind .... Rom 9:21-23
Human weakness 2Cor 4:7
Believers 2Tim 2:20, 21
Person's body or wife 1Thess 4:4
Chosen person .... Acts 9:15

[*also* VESSELS]

fruits in the land in your *v* .... Gen 43:11
he make it, with all these *v* ... Ex 25:39
All the *v* of the tabernacle .... Ex 27:19
And the table and all his *v* .... Ex 30:27
the candlestick and his *v* ...... Ex 30:27
his staves, and all his *v* .... Ex 35:13
he made the *v* which were .... Ex 37:16
made all the *v* of the altar .... Ex 38:3
all the *v* thereof made he ..... Ex 38:3
The table, and all the *v* .... Ex 39:36
his staves, and all his *v* .... Ex 39:39
hallow it, and all the *v* .... Ex 40:9
earthen *v* wherein it is .... Lev 6:28
the altar and all his *v* .... Lev 8:11
whether it be any *v* of wood ... Lev 11:32
whatsoever *v* it be, wherein ... Lev 11:32
such *v* shall be unclean .... Lev 11:34
an earthen *v* over running ..... Lev 14:50
the *v* of earth, that he .... Lev 15:12
every *v* of wood shall be ...... Lev 15:12
over all the *v* thereof .... Num 1:50
and all the *v* thereof .... Num 1:50
all the *v* thereof, and all ...... Num 3:36
put it and all the *v* thereof .... Num 4:10
shall put upon it all the *v* ..... Num 4:14
all the *v* of the altar .... Num 4:14
sanctuary, and in the *v* .... Num 4:16
holy water in an earthen *v* .... Num 5:17
shall be put thereto in a *v* .... Num 19:17
upon all the *v*, and upon ...... Num 19:18
shalt not put any in thy *v* ..... Deut 23:24
and *v* of brass and iron .... Josh 6:19
go unto the *v*, and drink ...... Ruth 2:9
bread is spent in our *v* 1Sam 9:7
sanctified this day in the *v* 1Sam 21:5
brought with him *v* of silver ... 2Sam 8:10
v of gold, and *v* of brass 2Sam 8:10
all these *v*, which Hiram 1Kin 7:45
Solomon made all the *v* 1Kin 7:48

V

holy *v* that were in the 1Kin 8:4
Solomon's drinking *v* were 1Kin 10:21
all the *v* of the house of 1Kin 10:21
silver, and gold, and *v* 1Kin 15:15
a little water in a *v* 1Kin 17:10
Go, borrow thee *v* abroad 2Kin 4:3
even empty *v*; borrow not 2Kin 4:3
who brought the *v* to her 2Kin 4:5
Bring me yet a *v* 2Kin 4:6
There is not a *v* more 2Kin 4:6
full of garments and *v* 2Kin 7:15
all the *v* that were found 2Kin 14:14
cut in pieces all the *v* of 2Kin 24:13
these *v* was without weight 2Kin 25:16
charge of the ministering *v* 1Chr 9:28
pillars, and the *v* of brass 1Chr 18:8
the holy *v* of God, unto the . . .1Chr 22:19
for all the *v* of service in 1Chr 28:13
Solomon made all these *v* 2Chr 4:18
holy *v* that were in the 2Chr 5:5
the drinking *v* of king 2Chr 9:20
all the *v* of the house of 2Chr 9:20
silver, and gold, and *v* 2Chr 15:18
even *v* to minister, and to 2Chr 24:14
and *v* of gold and silver 2Chr 24:14
the *v* of the house of God 2Chr 28:24
cut in pieces the *v* of the 2Chr 28:24
offering with all the *v* 2Chr 29:18
with all the *v* thereof 2Chr 29:18
also carried of the *v* of 2Chr 36:7
v of the house of the Lord 2Chr 36:10
their hands with *v* of silver . . . .Ezra 1:6
and other *v* a thousand . . . . . . .Ezra 1:10
v also of gold and silver . . . . . . .Ezra 5:14
golden and silver *v* of the . . . . .Ezra 6:5
and the gold, and the *v* . . . . . . .Ezra 8:25
v are holy also; and the . . . . . . .Ezra 8:28
and the gold, and the *v* . . . . . . .Ezra 8:30
the *v* of the sanctuary . . . . .Neh 10:39
v of the house of God . . . . .Neh 13:9
they gave them drink in *v* . . . . .Esth 1:7
v being diverse one from . . . . . .Esth 1:7
in pieces like a potter's *v* . . . . . .Ps 2:9
shall come forth a *v* for . . . . . . .Prov 25:4
v of bulrushes upon the . . . . . . .Is 18:2
all *v* of small quantity . . . . .Is 22:24
v of cups, even to all the *v* . . . .Is 22:24
breaking of the potters' *v* . . . . .Is 30:14
things is in their *v* . . . . .Is 65:4
returned with their *v* empty . . .Jer 14:3
v that he made of clay . . . . .Jer 18:4
he made it again another *v* . . . .Jer 18:4
a *v* wherein is no pleasure . . . . .Jer 22:28
v which are left in the . . . . .Jer 27:18
the *v* that remain in . . . . .Jer 27:21
put them in an earthen *v* . . . . . .Jer 32:14
and put them in your *v* . . . . . . .Jer 40:10
have broken Moab like a *v* . . . .Jer 48:38
their *v*, and their camels . . . . . .Jer 49:29
brass of all these *v* was . . . . . . .Jer 52:20
fitches, and put them in one *v* .Ezek 4:9
the persons of men and *v* . . . . .Ezek 27:13
the *v* of the house of God . . . . .Dan 1:2
he brought the *v* into the . . . . .Dan 1:2
brought the *v* of his house . . . .Dan 5:23
v of silver and of gold . . . . .Dan 11:8
a *v* wherein is no pleasure . . . . .Hos 8:8
treasure of all pleasant *v* . . . . . .Hos 13:15
to draw out fifty *v* out of . . . . .Hag 2:16
gathered the good into *v* . . . . . .Matt 13:48
and pots, brazen *v* . . . . .Mark 7:4
carry any *v* through the . . . . . . .Mark 11:16
covereth it with a *v* . . . . .Luke 8:16
set a *v* full of vinegar . . . . .John 19:29
a certain *v* descending . . . . .Acts 10:11
the *v* was received up . . . . .Acts 10:16
vision, A certain *v* descend . . . .Acts 11:5
all the *v* of the ministry . . . . . . .Heb 9:21
wife, as unto the weaker *v* 1Pet 3:7
v of a potter shall they be . . . . .Rev 2:27

VESTMENT—*clothing; garments*

[*also* VESTMENTS]
v for all the worshipers 2Kin 10:22
he brought them forth *v* 2Kin 10:22

VESTRY—*a room where clothing is stored*
him that was over the *v* 2Kin 10:22

VESTURE—*formal clothing*

[*also* VESTURES]
arrayed him in *v* of fine . . . . . . .Gen 41:42
four quarters of thy *v* . . . . .Deut 22:12
and cast lots upon my *v* . . . . . . .Ps 22:18
as a *v* shalt thou change . . . . . . .Ps 102:26
upon my *v* did they cast . . . . . . .Matt 27:35
for my *v* they did cast lots . . . .John 19:24
as a *v* shalt thou fold . . . . .Heb 1:12
with a *v* dipped in blood . . . . . .Rev 19:13
on his *v* and on his thigh . . . . . .Rev 19:16

VEX—*to irritate; agitate*

Caused by:
Nagging . . . . .Judg 16:16
Lust .2Sam 13:2
Evil environment 2Pet 2:7, 8
Temptations . . . . .Num 25:18
Evil men . . . . .Num 20:15
Demons . . . . .Matt 15:22

Agents of:
God .Ps 2:5
People . . . . .Ex 22:21
King . . . . .Acts 12:1
Enemies . . . . .Judg 10:8

Objects of:
Human soul . . . . .Job 19:2
Righteous soul 2Pet 2:8
Holy Spirit . . . . .Is 63:10

[*also* VEXED]
to her sister, to *v* her . . . . .Lev 18:18
ye shall not *v* him . . . . .Lev 19:33
V the Midianites . . . . .Num 25:17
shall *v* you in the land . . . . .Num 33:55
oppressed them and *v* . . . . .Judg 2:18
he turned himself, he *v* 1Sam 14:47
how will he then *v* 2Sam 12:18
her soul is *v* within her 2Kin 4:27
God did *v* them with all 2Chr 15:6
of their enemies, who *v* . . . . . . .Neh 9:27
who hath *v* my soul . . . . .Job 27:2
heal me; for my bones are *v* . . .Ps 6:2
be ashamed and sore *v* . . . . .Ps 6:10
against Judah, and *v* it . . . . .Is 7:6
Judah shall not *v* Ephraim . . . .Is 11:13
art infamous and much *v* . . . . . .Ezek 22:5
in thee have they *v* the . . . . . . .Ezek 22:7
v the poor and needy . . . . .Ezek 22:29
I will also *v* the hearts of . . . . .Ezek 32:9
awake that shall *v* thee . . . . .Hab 2:7
he is lunatic, and sore *v* . . . . . . .Matt 17:15
that were *v* with unclean . . . . . .Luke 6:18
v with unclean spirits . . . . .Acts 5:16

VEXATION—*trouble; affliction; irritation*

[*also* VEXATIONS]
send upon thee cursing, *v* . . . . .Deut 28:20
but great *v* were upon all 2Chr 15:5
vanity and *v* of spirit . . . . .Eccl 1:14
vanity and *v* of spirit . . . . .Eccl 2:11
and of the *v* of his heart . . . . . .Eccl 2:22
vanity and *v* of spirit . . . . .Eccl 4:4
vanity and *v* of spirit . . . . .Eccl 4:16
be such as was in her *v* . . . . . . .Is 9:1
shall howl for *v* of spirit . . . . . . .Is 65:14

VIAL—*a small flask or vessel*
Used for anointing 1Sam 10:1
Full of incense . . . . .Rev 5:8
Filled with God's wrath . .Rev 16:1-17

[*also* VIALS]
seven golden *v* full of the . . . . .Rev 15:7
which had the seven *v* . . . . .Rev 17:1
the seven *v* full of the . . . . .Rev 21:9

VICARIOUS SUFFERING OF CHRIST—*His suffering on behalf of humanity*

Expressed in Old Testament, by:
Types . . . . .Gen 22:7, 8, 13
Explicit prophecies . . . . . .Is 53:1-12
Acts 8:32-35

Expressed in the New Testament, by:
John the Baptist . . . . .John 1:29
Christ Himself . . . . .Mark 10:45
Peter 1Pet 1:18, 19
John 1John 3:16
Paul .Gal 2:20
Hebrews . . . . .Heb 2:9, 17

VICTORY—*winning the mastery in battle over odds or difficulties*

Of Christ
Promised . . . . .Ps 110:1-7
Accompanied by suffering.Is 53:10-12
By resurrection . . . . .Acts 2:29-36
By His return . . . . .Rev 19:11-21

Of Christians:
Through Christ . . . . .Phil 4:13
By the Holy Spirit . . . . . . .Gal 5:16, 17, 22, 25

Over:
Flesh . . . . .Gal 5:16-21
World 1John 5:4
Satan . . . . .James 4:7

the *v* that day was turned 2Sam 19:2
Lord wrought a great *v* 2Sam 23:10
Lord wrought a great *v* 2Sam 23:12
and the glory, and the *v* 1Chr 29:11
hath gotten him the *v* . . . . .Ps 98:1
swallow up death in *v* . . . . .Is 25:8
forth judgment unto *v* . . . . .Matt 12:20
Death is swallowed up in *v* 1Cor 15:54
O grave, where is thy *v*? 1Cor 15:55
v through our Lord Jesus 1Cor 15:57
the *v* over the beast . . . . .Rev 15:2

VICTUAL—*food; nourishment*

[*also* VICTUALS]
Gomorrah, and all their *v* . . . . .Gen 14:11
for themselves any *v* . . . . .Ex 12:39
nor lend him thy *v* for . . . . .Lev 25:37
usury of money, usury of *v* . . . .Deut 23:19
saying, Prepare you *v* . . . . .Josh 1:11
the men took up their *v* . . . . . . .Josh 9:14
the people took *v* in their . . . . .Judg 7:8
to fetch *v* for the people . . . . . .Judg 20:10
and gave him *v*, and gave 1Sam 22:10
provided *v* for the king 1Kin 4:7
those officers provided *v* 1Kin 4:27
in them, and store of *v* 2Chr 11:11
gave them *v* in abundance 2Chr 11:23
or any *v* on the sabbath . . . . . . .Neh 10:31
of the guard gave him *v* . . . . . . .Jer 40:5
and buy themselves *v* . . . . .Matt 14:15
about, and lodge, and get *v* . . .Luke 9:12

VIEW—*to look at*

[*also* VIEWED]
Go *v* the land, even Jericho . . .Josh 2:1
men went up and *v* Ai . . . . .Josh 7:2
and stood to *v* afar off 2Kin 2:7
and I *v* the people . . . . .Ezra 8:15
v the walls of Jerusalem . . . . . . .Neh 2:13

VIGILANT—*alert; watchful*
husband of one wife, *v* 1Tim 3:2
Be sober, be *v*; because 1Pet 5:8

VIGOR IN OLD AGE
Moses at 120 . . . . .Deut 34:7
Caleb at 85 . . . . .Josh 14:10-13
Jehoiada at 130 . . . . .2Chr 24:15, 16

VILE—*physically or morally corrupt*

Described as:
Worthless 1Sam 15:9
Dirty and filthy . . . . .James 2:2
Frail and weak . . . . .Phil 3:21
Something insignificant . . .Job 40:4

Caused by:
God's judgment . . . . .Jer 29:17
Human corruption . . . . . . .Judg 19:24

[*also* VILELY, VILER, VILEST]
thy brother should seem *v* . . . . .Deut 25:3
mighty is *v* cast away 2Sam 1:21
I will yet be more *v* than 2Sam 6:22
reputed *v* in your sight? . . . . . . .Job 18:3

were *v* than the earth ....Job 30:8
the *v* men are exalted ....Ps 12:8
a *v* person is contemned ......Ps 15:4
v person shall be no more .....Is 32:5
v person will speak villany ....Is 32:6
the precious from the *v* ....Jer 15:19
consider; for I am become *v*...Lam 1:11
thy grave; for thou art *v* ......Nah 1:14
upon thee, and make thee *v*...Nah 3:6
them up unto *v* affections .....Rom 1:26

VILLAGE—*a settlement*

[*also* VILLAGES]
out of the *v*, and out of ....Ex 8:13
houses of the *v* which have ....Lev 25:31
Heshbon, and in all the *v* .....Num 21:25
took Kenath, and the *v* ....Num 32:42
the cities and the *v* ....Josh 13:23
sixteen cities with their *v* ......Josh 15:41
with her towns and her *v*......Josh 15:45
with her towns and her *v*......Josh 15:47
with her towns and her *v*......Josh 15:47
nine cities with their *v* ....Josh 15:54
six cities with their *v*..........Josh 15:59
six cities with their *v*..........Josh 15:62
twelve cities with their *v* ......Josh 18:24
thirteen cities and their *v*......Josh 19:6
the cities and their *v*..........Josh 19:23
these cities with their *v* ....Josh 19:31
the cities and their *v*..........Josh 19:39
fields of the city, and the *v*....Josh 21:12
The inhabitants of the *v*.......Judg 5:7
cities, and of country *v*........1Sam 6:18
And their *v* were, Etam 1Chr 4:32
fields of the city and the *v* 1Chr 6:56
by their genealogy in their *v*...1Chr 9:22
the cities, and in the *v* 1Chr 27:25
and Shocho with the *v* 2Chr 28:18
and Timnah with the *v*........2Chr 28:18
Gimzo also and the *v* 2Chr 28:18
in some one of the *v*..........Neh 6:2
for the *v*, with their fields .....Neh 11:25
Kirjath-arba, and in the *v* .....Neh 11:25
at Dibon, and in the *v* ....Neh 11:25
at Jekabzeel, and in the *v* .....Neh 11:25
at Mekonah, and in the *v* .....Neh 11:28
and in their *v*, at Lachish .....Neh 11:30
at Azekah, and in the *v*........Neh 11:30
from the *v* of Netophathi......Neh 12:28
Therefore the Jews of the *v* ...Esth 9:19
lurking places of the *v* ....Ps 10:8
let us lodge in the *v* ....Song 7:11
v that Kedar doth inhabit .....Is 42:11
to the land of unwalled *v* ......Ezek 38:11
staves the head of his *v* ....Hab 3:14
about all the cities and *v* ......Matt 9:35
that they may go into the *v* ...Matt 14:15
Go into the *v* over against ....Matt 21:2
he went round about the *v* ....Mark 6:6
he entered into the *v* ....Mark 6:56
Go your way into the *v* ....Mark 11:2
throughout every city and *v* ...Luke 8:1
into a *v* of the Samaritans .....Luke 9:52
they went to another *v*.........Luke 9:56
he entered into a certain *v* ....Luke 10:38
through the cities and *v* ....Luke 13:22
he entered into a certain *v* ....Luke 17:12
Go ye into the *v* over..........Luke 19:30
to a *v* called Emmaus ....Luke 24:13
they drew nigh unto the *v*.....Luke 24:28
the gospel in many *v*...........Acts 8:25

VILLANY—*depravity; villainous conduct*
vile person will speak *v* ....Is 32:6
they have committed *v* ....Jer 29:23

VINE—*grapevine; a planting of grapevines*

Features regarding:
Grown by Noah ....Gen 9:20
Native of Palestine ......Deut 6:11
Reaping of, by poor 2Kin 25:12
Fruit of, God's gift ......Ps 107:37
Pruning of, necessary ....Lev 25:3, 4
Dead branches burned ...John 15:6

Enemies of:
Hail and frost ....Ps 78:47
Foxes ....Song 2:15
Boars ....Ps 80:13
Thieves ....Jer 49:9
Stones ....Is 5:2
Sloth ....Prov 24:30, 31

Laws concerning:
Care of, exempts from military service ....Deut 20:6
Diverse seed forbidden in. Deut 22:9
Neighbors may eat ......Deut 23:24
No cultivation of, during Sabbatical year ....Ex 23:11
Second gathering of, forbidden ....Lev 19:10
New, five years' waiting . .Lev 19:23-25
Nazirites forbidden to eat of ....Num 6:3, 4
Rechabites forbidden to plant ....Jer 35:7-9
Not to be mortgaged ....Neh 5:3, 4

Figurative of:
Jewish nation ....Is 5:1-7
Growth in grace ....Hos 14:7
Purifying afflictions ......John 15:2
Peacefulness 1Kin 4:25
Worthlessness ....John 15:2, 6
Fruitful wife ....Ps 128:3
God's kingdom ....Matt 20:1-16

[*also* VINES]
behold, a *v* was before me ....Gen 40:9
Binding his foal unto the *v* ....Gen 49:11
ass's colt unto the choice *v* ....Gen 49:11
grapes of thy *v* undressed .....Lev 25:5
seed, or of figs, or of *v* ....Num 20:5
wheat, and barley, and *v* ......Deut 8:8
For their *v* is of the *v* of ......Deut 32:32
said the trees unto the *v* ......Judg 9:12
that cometh of the *v* ....Judg 13:14
herbs, and found a wild *v* 2Kin 4:39
every man of his own *v* 2Kin 18:31
and *v* dressers in the..........2Chr 26:10
his unripe grape as the *v* ......Job 15:33
brought a *v* out of Egypt ......Ps 80:8
He smote their *v* also and .....Ps 105:33
v with the tender grape ....Song 2:13
see whether the *v* flourished ...Song 6:11
be as clusters of the *v*.........Song 7:8
were a thousand *v* at a........Is 7:23
and the *v* of Sibmah ....Is 16:8
the *v* languisheth ....Is 24:7
leaf falleth off from the *v* .....Is 34:4
I had planted thee a noble *v* ..Jer 2:21
plant of a strange *v* ....Jer 2:21
they shall eat up thy *v* and ....Jer 5:17
be no grapes on the *v*.........Jer 8:13
plant *v* upon the mountains ...Jer 31:5
What is the *v* tree more.......Ezek 15:2
a spreading *v* of low ....Ezek 17:6
so it became a *v*, and ....Ezek 17:6
that it might be a goodly *v* ....Ezek 17:8
destroy her *v* and her fig ......Hos 2:12
Israel is an empty *v*, he ....Hos 10:1
He hath laid my *v* waste ......Joel 1:7
v do yield their strength.......Joel 2:22
sit every man under his *v* .....Mic 4:4
marred their *v* branches ....Nah 2:2
shall fruit be in the *v* ....Hab 3:17
the *v*, and the fig tree ....Hag 2:19
his neighbor under the *v* ......Zech 3:10
neither shall your *v* cast.......Mal 3:11
of this fruit of the *v* ....Matt 26:29
more of the fruit of the *v* .....Mark 14:25
drink of the fruit of the *v* .....Luke 22:18
I am the true *v*, and my ......John 15:1
except it abide in the *v* ....John 15:4
I am the *v*, ye are the ....John 15:5
olive berries? either a *v* ....James 3:12
gather the clusters of the *v* ....Rev 14:18

VINEDRESSERS—*those who cultivate grape-vines*
poor of the land to be *v* 2King 25:12
your plowmen and your *v* .....Is 61:5
the land for *v* and for ....Jer 52:16
howl, O ye *v*, for the wheat ..Joel 1:11

VINEGAR—*wine; fermented strong drink*
Hard on teeth ....Prov 10:26
Forbidden to Nazarites ...Num 6:3
Offered to Christ in mockery ....Ps 69:21

dip thy morsel in the *v*........Ruth 2:14
they gave me *v* drink ....Ps 69:21
and as *v* upon nitre, so is .....Prov 25:20
v to drink mingled with ....Matt 27:34
sponge, and filled it with *v* ....Matt 27:48
filled a sponge full of *v* ....Mark 15:36
was set a vessel full of *v* ......John 19:29
filled a sponge with *v* ....John 19:29
had received the *v*............John 19:30

VINEYARD—*a planting of grapevines*

[*also* VINEYARDS]
a field or *v* to be eaten ....Ex 22:5
of the best of his own *v*.......Ex 22:5
inheritance of fields and *v* .....Num 16:14
the fields, or through the *v* ....Num 20:17
the fields, or into the *v* ....Num 21:22
stood in a path of the *v* ....Num 22:24
the grapes of thy *v* ....Deut 24:21
thou shalt plant a *v*, and ......Deut 28:30
Thou shalt plant *v* ....Deut 28:39
v and oliveyards which ye .....Josh 24:13
and gathered their *v* ....Judg 9:27
came to the *v* of Timnath .....Judg 14:5
lie in wait in the *v* ....Judg 21:20
your fields, and your *v* 1Sam 8:14
one of you fields and *v* 1Sam 22:7
the Jezreelite had a *v* 1Kin 21:1
Give me thy *v*, that I may 1Kin 21:2
give thee for it a better *v* 1Kin 21:2
Give me thy *v* for money 1Kin 21:6
I will give thee another *v* 1Kin 21:6
take possession of the *v*.......1Kin 21:15
he is in the *v* of Naboth.......1Kin 21:18
and oliveyards, and *v* 2Kin 5:26
and reap, and plant *v* 2Kin 19:29
the *v* was Shimei the..........1Chr 27:27
over the increase of the *v* 1Chr 27:27
men have our lands, and *v* ....Neh 5:5
this day, their lands, their *v* ...Neh 5:11
wells digged, *v*, and ....Neh 9:25
not the way of the *v* ....Job 24:18
the *v* which thy right hand ....Ps 80:15
her hands she planteth a *v* ....Prov 31:16
me houses; I planted me *v* ....Eccl 2:4
me the keeper of the *v*.........Song 1:6
own *v* have I not kept ....Song 1:6
Let us get up early to the *v* ...Song 7:12
Solomon had a *v* at...........Song 8:11
let out the *v* unto keepers .....Song 8:11
is left as a cottage in a *v* ......Is 1:8
ten acres of *v* shall yield ......Is 5:10
in the *v* there shall be no .....Is 16:10
unto her, A *v* of red wine .....Is 27:2
plant *v*, and eat the fruit ......Is 37:30
have destroyed my *v* ....Jer 12:10
build houses, and plant *v*......Ezek 28:26
I will give her her *v* from .....Hos 2:15
your gardens and your *v* ......Amos 4:9
in all *v* shall be waiting ....Amos 5:17
and as plantings of a *v*.........Mic 1:6
they shall plant *v*, but not .....Zeph 1:13
go work today in my *v*.........Matt 21:28
cast him out of the *v*, and.....Matt 21:39
and will let out his *v* unto .....Matt 21:41
A certain man planted a *v* ....Mark 12:1
and cast him out of the *v* .....Mark 12:8
the lord of the *v* do? ....Mark 12:9
will give the *v* unto others.....Mark 12:9
fig tree planted in his *v* ....Luke 13:6
unto the dresser of his *v* .....Luke 13:7
A certain man planted a *v* ....Luke 20:9
Then said the lord of the *v*....Luke 20:13
they cast him out of the *v*.....Luke 20:15
shall the lord of the *v* do......Luke 20:15
who planteth a *v*, and eateth ..1Cor 9:7

VINTAGE—*a season's yield of grapes or wine from a vineyard*
that the *v* of Abi-ezer?........Judg 8:2

they gather the *v* of the ....Job 24:6
I have made their *v* shouting ..Is 16:10
for the *v* shall fail ....Is 32:10
fruits and upon thy *v* ....Jer 48:32
grape gleanings of the *v* ....Mic 7:1
the forest of the *v* is come ....Zech 11:2

VIOL—*a stringed musical instrument*
Used in merrymaking ..Is 5:12
Destruction of.........Is 14:11

[*also* VIOLS]
hear the melody of thy *v* ......Amos 5:23
to the sound of the *v* ....Amos 6:5

VIOLATED—*broken; disregarded*
Her priests have *v* my law .....Ezek 22:26

VIOLENCE—*intense affliction of destruction or injury*

[*also* VIOLENT, VIOLENTLY]
earth was filled with *v* ....Gen 6:11
servants had *v* taken away .....Gen 21:25
a thing taken away by *v*.......Lev 6:2
that which he took *v*..........Lev 6:4
thine ass shall be *v* taken .....Deut 28:31
thou savest me from *v* 2Sam 22:3
delivered me from the *v* 2Sam 22:49
he hath *v* taken away a ....Job 20:19
they *v* take away flocks ....Job 24:2
v dealing shall come down ....Ps 7:16
him that loveth *v* his soul .....Ps 11:5
ye weigh the *v* of your ....Ps 58:2
v covereth them as a..........Ps 73:6
the assemblies of *v* men.......Ps 86:14
evil shall hunt the *v* man ......Ps 140:11
and drink the wine of *v* ....Prov 4:17
transgressors shall eat *v* ....Prov 13:2
A *v* man enticeth his ....Prov 16:29
v perverting of judgment ......Eccl 5:8
v turn and toss thee like ......Is 22:18
because he had done no *v*......Is 53:9
V shall no more be heard .....Is 60:18
v and spoil is heard in her ....Jer 6:7
do no *v* to the stranger ....Jer 22:3
The *v* done to me and to .....Jer 51:35
v taken away his tabernacle ...Lam 2:6
V is risen up into a rod of ....Ezek 7:11
have filled the land with *v*.....Ezek 8:17
hath spoiled none by *v*........Ezek 18:7
neither hath spoiled by *v*......Ezek 18:16
the midst of thee with *v*.......Ezek 28:16
v against the children of ......Joel 3:19
who store up *v* and robbery ...Amos 3:10
thy *v* against thy brother ......Obad 10
v that is in their hands ....Jon 3:8
and take them by *v*...........Mic 2:2
even cry out unto thee of *v* ...Hab 1:2
They shall come all for *v*......Hab 1:9
the *v* of Lebanon shall ....Hab 2:17
for the *v* of the land ....Hab 2:17
masters' houses with *v* ....Zeph 1:9
one covereth *v* with his ....Mal 2:16
of swine ran *v* down a ....Matt 8:32
of heaven suffereth *v* ....Matt 11:12
and the *v* take it by ....Matt 11:12
the herd ran *v* down a ....Mark 5:13
Do *v* to no man, neither ......Luke 3:14
the herd ran *v* down a ....Luke 8:33
brought them without *v* ....Acts 5:26
with great *v* took him ....Acts 24:7
Quenched the *v* of fire ....Heb 11:34
v shall that great city ....Rev 18:21

VIPER—*a deadly snake*
Figurative of spiritual transformation ....Is 11:8
Jewish leaders compared to ....Matt 3:7
Paul bit by ....Acts 28:3-5

[*also* VIPER'S, VIPERS]
asps; the *v* tongue shall ....Job 20:16
the *v* and fiery flying ....Is 30:6
breaketh out into a *v* ....Is 59:5
O generation of *v*, how ....Matt 12:34
ye generation of *v*, how ....Matt 23:33
O generation of *v*, who ....Luke 3:7

VIRGIN—*a woman untouched sexually*
Penalty for seduction of ..Deut 22:28, 29
Parable of ten ....Matt 25:1-13
Specifications regarding ..1Cor 7:28-38
Christ born of...........Luke 1:26-35
Figurative of Christians ..Rev 14:4

[*also* VIRGIN'S, VIRGINS]
very fair to look upon, a *v* ....Gen 24:16
v cometh forth to draw ....Gen 24:43
according to the dowry of *v* ...Ex 22:17
for his sister a *v*, that is.......Lev 21:3
an evil name upon a *v* of .....Deut 22:19
the young man and the *v*......Deut 32:25
four hundred young *v* that ....Judg 21:12
for she was a *v*, and Amnon ..2Sam 13:2
king's daughters that were *v* ...2Sam 13:18
lord the king a young *v* 1Kin 1:2
The *v* the daughter of Zion ...2Kin 19:21
Let there be fair young *v* .....Esth 2:2
sight more than all the *v* ......Esth 2:17
the *v* her companions that.....Ps 45:14
therefore do the *v* love thee ...Song 1:3
Behold, a *v* shall conceive .....Is 7:14
young men, nor bring up *v* ....Is 23:4
The *v*, the daughter of ....Is 37:22
a young man marrieth a *v* .....Is 62:5
v daughter of my people is ....Jer 14:17
thou shalt be built, O *v* ....Jer 31:4
O *v* of Israel, turn again ......Jer 31:21
Lord hath trodden the *v* ......Lam 1:15
Lament like a *v* girded ....Joel 1:8
The *v* of Israel is fallen ....Amos 5:2
the fair *v* and young men .....Amos 8:13
a *v* shall be with child ....Matt 1:23
be likened unto ten *v* ....Matt 25:1
came also the other *v* ....Matt 25:11
and the *v* name was Mary .....Luke 1:27
man had four daughters, *v* ....Acts 21:9
Now concerning *v* I have 1Cor 7:25
you as a chaste *v* to Christ ...2Cor 11:2
with women, for they are *v*....Rev 14:4

VIRGIN CONCEPTION—*conceiving without sexual intercourse*
Prophesied ....Is 7:14
Christ conceived of Holy Spirit ....Matt 1:18; Luke 1:26-35
Born of virgin ....Matt 1:19-25

VIRGINITY—*state of sexual inexperience*
shall take a wife in her *v* ......Lev 21:13
tokens of the damsel's *v* ....Deut 22:15
tokens of *v* be not found ......Deut 22:20
bewail my *v*, I and my ....Judg 11:37
the teats of their *v*............Ezek 23:3
Seven years from her *v* ....Luke 2:36

VIRTUE—*moral excellence*
that *v* had gone out of him ....Mark 5:30
for there went *v* out of him ...Luke 6:19
perceive that *v* has gone out ..Luke 8:46
there be any *v*, and if there ...Phil 4:8
and called us to glory and *v* ...2Pet 1:3
add to your faith *v* 2Pet 1:5
and to *v* knowledge 2Pet 1:5

VIRTUOUS WOMAN—*a woman with desirable qualities*
Graphically described ....Prov 31:10-31
Illustrated by Sarah 1Pet 3:1-7
Adornment of 1Tim 2:9, 10

know that thou art a *v w*......Ruth 3:11
A *v w* is a crown to her.......Prov 12:4

VIRTUOUSLY—*in a commendable manner*
daughters have done *v* ....Prov 31:29

VISAGE—*one's face*
his *v* was so marred more .....Is 52:14
v is blacker than a coal ....Lam 4:8
form of his *v* was changed.....Dan 3:19

VISIBLE—*able to be seen*
in earth, *v* and invisible ....Col 1:16

VISION—*divine revelation: often involves a supernatural appearance and/or prediction, direction, or instruction*

Characterics of:
Understandable ....Dan 7:15-19
Authenticated by divine glory ....Ezek 8:1-4
Personal and phenomenal.Dan 10:7-9
Prophetic ....Dan 9:23-27
Dated and localized .....Ezek 1:1-3
Causes trembling and dread.................Dan 10:7-17
Meaning of, interpreted ..Dan 9:21-24
Absence of, tragic ....Prov 29:18
Performances of, sure....Ezek 12:21-28
Proof of Messianic times .Joel 2:28; Acts 2:17
Imitated by false prophets.Jer 14:14

Productive of:
Guidance ....Gen 46:2-5
Direction ....Acts 16:9, 10
Encouragement..........Acts 18:9, 10
Warning ....Is 21:2-6
Judgment 1Sam 3:15-18
Action for the Lord .....Acts 26:19, 20

Objects of, revealed in:
Israel's future ....Gen 15:1-21
Succession of world empires...............Dan 7:1-8
Ram ....Dan 8:1-7, 20
Expanding river ....Ezek 47:1-12
Throne of God ....Rev 4:1-11

[*also* VISIONS]
known unto him in a *v*........Num 12:6
saw the *v* of the Almighty.....Num 24:4
days; there was no open *v*.....1Sam 3:1
according to all this *v* so 2Sam 7:17
according to all this *v* so 1Chr 17:15
v of Iddo the seer against 2Chr 9:29
in the *v* of God 2Chr 26:5
written in the *v* of Isaiah 2Chr 32:32
from the *v* of the night........Job 4:13
terrifiest me through *v* ....Job 7:14
chased away as a *v* of the .....Job 20:8
in a *v* of the night, when......Job 33:15
thou speakest in *v* to thy ......Ps 89:19
The *v* of Isaiah the son of.....Is 1:1
burden of the valley of *v* ......Is 22:1
they err in *v*, they stumble ....Is 28:7
the *v* of all is become unto ....Is 29:11
they speak a *v* of their ....Jer 23:16
find no *v* from the Lord.......Lam 2:9
v is touching the whole ....Ezek 7:13
seek a *v* of the prophet ....Ezek 7:26
in a *v* by the Spirit of.........Ezek 11:24
the *v* that I had seen went ....Ezek 11:24
Have ye not seen a vain *v*.....Ezek 13:7
see *v* of peace for her.........Ezek 13:16
In the *v* of God brought he ...Ezek 40:2
appearance of the *v* which ....Ezek 43:3
according to the *v* that I ......Ezek 43:3
the *v* were like the *v* that .....Ezek 43:3
understanding in all *v* and .....Dan 1:17
unto Daniel in a night *v*........Dan 2:19
the *v* of my head troubled.....Dan 4:5
Thus were the *v* of mine ......Dan 4:10
I saw in the *v* of my head .....Dan 4:13
I saw in the night *v*, and .....Dan 7:13
understanding of the *v* ....Dan 10:1
to establish the *v* ....Dan 11:14
I have multiplied *v*, and.......Hos 12:10
The *v* of Obadiah. Thus ......Obad 1
that ye shall not have a *v* .....Mic 3:6
book of the *v* of Nahum ......Nah 1:1
Write the *v*, and make it......Hab 2:2
the *v* is yet for an ....Hab 2:3
ashamed every one of his *v*....Zech 13:4
Tell the *v* to no man..........Matt 17:9
he had seen a *v* in the ....Luke 1:22
they had also seen a *v* of......Luke 24:23
him said the Lord in a *v* ......Acts 9:10
seen in a *v* a man named .....Acts 9:12
He saw in a *v* evidently ....Acts 10:3
what this *v* which he had......Acts 10:17
Peter thought on the *v* ....Acts 10:19
and in a trance I saw a *v*......Acts 11:5
but thought he saw a *v*........Acts 12:9

I will come to *v* and 2Cor 12:1
saw the horses in the *v*........Rev 9:17

VISIT—*to go see a person*
Descriptive of:
Going to a person ....Acts 15:36
God's care ....Ps 65:9
God's purposed time.....Luke 19:44

[*also* VISITED, VISITEST, VISITETH, VISITING]
the Lord *v* Sarah as he........Gen 21:1
I have surely *v* you ....Ex 3:16
Lord had *v* the children ....Ex 4:31
God will surely *v* you ....Ex 13:19
v the iniquity of the ....Ex 20:5
the day when I *v* I will *v*......Ex 32:34
v the iniquity of the ....Ex 34:7
I do *v* the iniquity thereof.....Lev 18:25
v the iniquity of the ....Num 14:18
if they be *v* after the..........Num 16:29
v the iniquity of the ....Deut 5:9
that Samson *v* his wife ....Judg 15:1
the Lord had *v* his people .....Ruth 1:6
And the Lord *v* Hannah 1Sam 2:21
and thou shalt *v* thy ....Job 5:24
when he *v*, what shall..........Job 31:14
he hath *v* in his anger.........Job 35:15
son of man, that thou *v*.......Ps 8:4
thou hast *v* me in the ....Ps 17:3
Israel, awake to *v* all the ......Ps 59:5
Then will I *v* their ....Ps 89:32
he shall not be *v* with evil.....Prov 19:23
that the Lord will *v* Tyre ......Is 23:17
many days shall they be *v*.....Is 24:22
hast thou *v* and destroyed .....Is 26:14
in trouble have they *v* thee ....Is 26:16
Thou shalt be *v* of the ....Is 29:6
neither shall they *v* it ....Jer 3:16
this is the city to be *v*.........Jer 6:6
time that I *v* them they ....Jer 6:15
iniquity and *v* their sins ....Jer 14:10
and have not *v* them............Jer 23:2
v upon you the evil of your ...Jer 23:2
shall he be until I *v* him ......Jer 32:5
the time that I will *v* him .....Jer 49:8
he will *v* thine iniquity, O .....Lam 4:22
many days thou shalt be *v*.....Ezek 38:8
will *v* upon her the days of....Hos 2:13
iniquity and *v* their sins ....Hos 8:13
he will *v* their sins ....Hos 9:9
the Lord their God shall *v* ....Zeph 2:7
the Lord of hosts hath *v* ......Zech 10:3
v those that be cut off ....Zech 11:16
from on high hath *v* us........Luke 1:78
God hath *v* his people ....Luke 7:16
to *v* his brethren the ....Acts 7:23

VISITATION—*arrival; judgment*
thy *v* hath preserved my ......Job 10:12
will ye do in the day of *v* .....Is 10:3
the time of their *v* they ....Jer 8:12
even the year of their *v*.......Jer 11:23
and the time of their *v*........Jer 46:21
come, the time of their *v*......Jer 50:27
The days of *v* are come ....Hos 9:7
watchmen and thy *v* cometh ...Mic 7:4
God in the day of *v* 1Pet 2:12

VISITORS—*those who call as guests*
Moses and Elijah ....Matt 17:3

VOCATION—*a calling*
We must walk worthy of .Eph 4:1

VOICE—*spoken sounds*

[*also* VOICES]
v of thy brother's blood ....Gen 4:10
hearkened unto the *v* of ......Gen 16:2
The *v* is Jacob's but the ....Gen 27:22
as I lifted up my *v*............Gen 39:18
of him, and obey his *v* ....Ex 23:21
people answered with one *v* ...Ex 24:3
hear the *v* of swearing ....Lev 5:1
Lord heard the *v* of ....Deut 1:34
ye heard the *v* of ....Deut 4:12
any noise with your *v* ....Josh 6:10
lifted up his *v*, and cried .....Judg 9:7
lifted up their *v*, and..........Judg 21:2
they lifted up their *v*..........Ruth 1:9
her *v* was not heard 1Sam 1:13
people lifted up their *v*........1Sam 11:4
king lifted up his *v* 2Sam 3:32
heard the *v* of Elijah 1Kin 17:22
there was neither *v* 2Kin 4:31
lifting up the *v* with joy 1Chr 15:16
wept with a loud *v* ....Ezra 3:12
cried with a loud *v* ....Neh 9:4
they lifted up their *v*.........Job 2:12
organ into the *v* of them ......Job 30:12
After it a *v* roareth he ....Job 37:4
the *v* of his excellency ....Job 37:4
not stay them when his *v*......Job 37:4
thou lift up thy *v* to the ....Job 38:34
unto the Lord with my *v* ......Ps 3:4
my *v* shalt thou hear in ....Ps 5:3
heard the *v* of my weeping ....Ps 6:8
the *v* of joy and praise ....Ps 42:4
she uttereth her *v* in ....Prov 1:20
my *v* is to the sons of man ....Prov 8:4
a fool's *v* is known by ....Eccl 5:3
The *v* of my beloved..........Song 2:8
moved at the *v* of him ....Is 6:4
thee at the *v* of thy cry ....Is 30:19
the *v* of weeping shall be......Is 65:19
nor the *v* of crying ....Is 65:19
When he uttered his *v* ....Jer 10:13
have heard a *v* of.............Jer 30:5
there fell a *v* from heaven .....Dan 4:31
and thou heardest my *v* ....Jon 2:2
as with the *v* of doves ....Nah 2:7
their *v* shall sing in the........Zeph 2:14
v of one crying in the ....Matt 3:3
v of one crying in the ....Mark 1:3
v of one crying in the ....Luke 3:4
And they lifted up their *v*.....Luke 17:13
were instant with loud *v* ......Luke 23:23
v of them and of the chief ....Luke 23:23
v of one crying in the ....John 1:23
him; for they know his *v* ......John 10:4
of the truth heareth my *v* .....John 18:37
is the *v* of a god, and not .....Acts 12:22
nor yet the *v* of the...........Acts 13:27
and then lifted up their *v* .....Acts 22:22
kinds of *v* in the world........1Cor 14:10
by my *v* I might teach 1Cor 14:19
if ye will hear his *v*...........Heb 3:7
v then shook the earth ....Heb 12:26
if any man hear my *v*.........Rev 3:20
and thunderings and *v* ....Rev 4:5
of the other *v* of the..........Rev 8:13
had uttered their *v* ....Rev 10:4
lightnings, and *v* and..........Rev 11:19

VOICE OF GOD—*a figure of speech to express God's communicating His will to people*
Importance of:
Must be obeyed ....Gen 3:1-19
Disobedience to, judged. .Jer 42:5-22
Obedience to, the essence of true religion 1Sam 15:19-24
Obedience to, rewarded . .Gen 22:6-18
Sign of the covenant .....Josh 24:24, 25
Heard by:
Adam ....Gen 3:9, 10
Moses ....Ex 19:19
Israel...................Deut 5:22-26
Samuel 1Sam 3:1-14
Elijah 1Kin 19:12, 13
Isaiah ....Is 6:8-10
Ezekiel ....Ezek 1:24, 25
Christ ....Mark 1:11
Peter, James and John ...Matt 17:1, 5
Paul....................Acts 9:4, 7
John ....Rev 1:10-15
v of God speaking out of the . .Deut 4:33
obey the *v* of the Lord thy ....Deut 27:10
unto the *v* of the Lord ....Deut 28:1
unto the *v* of the Lord ....Deut 28:2
not unto the *v* of the Lord ....Deut 28:45
not obey the *v* of the Lord ....Deut 28:62
obey the *v* of the Lord........Deut 30:8
hearken unto the *v* of the .....Deut 30:10
obeyed not the *v* of the Lord . .Josh 5:6
not obey the *v* of the Lord 1Sam 12:15
the *v* of the words of the......1Sam 15:1
obeyedst not the *v* of the 1Sam 28:18
not obeyed the *v* of the Lord . .1Kin 20:36
obeyed not the *v* of the Lord . .2Kin 18:12
v of the Lord is upon the .....Ps 29:3
v of the Lord is powerful .....Ps 29:4
v of the Lord breaketh the ....Ps 29:5
v of the Lord divideth the .....Ps 29:7
v of the Lord shaketh the .....Ps 29:8
v of the Lord maketh the hinds.Ps 29:9
Today if ye will hear his *v* ....Ps 95:7
not unto the *v* of the Lord ....Ps 106:25
the *v* of the Lord shall the ....Is 30:31
a *v* of the Lord that rendereth .Is 66:6
not obeyed the *v* of the Lord . .Jer 3:25
obeyeth not the *v* of the Lord .Jer 7:28
obey the *v* of the Lord your . . .Jer 26:13
the *v* of the Lord............Jer 38:20
will obey the *v* of the Lord....Jer 42:6
obey the *v* of the Lord your . . .Jer 42:13
obeyed not the *v* of the Lord . .Jer 43:4
not obeyed the *v* of the Lord . .Jer 44:23
as the *v* of the Almighty God. .Ezek 10:5
and his *v* was like a noise .....Ezek 43:2
The Lord's *v* crieth unto the. . .Mic 6:9
obeyed the *v* of the Lord .....Hag 1:12
diligently obey the *v* of the ....Zech 6:15

VOID—*containing nothing; having no use or effect; devoid*
earth was without form, and *v* .Gen 1:2
made them *v* on the day ......Num 30:12
husband hath made them *v*....Num 30:12
husband may make it *v* ....Num 30:13
For they are a nation *v* ....Deut 32:28
in a *v* place in the 1Kin 22:10
sat in a *v* place at the..........2Chr 18:9
made *v*..covenant of thy ......Ps 89:39
man *v* of understanding ....Prov 7:7
He that is *v* of wisdom........Prov 11:12
A man *v* of understanding.....Prov 17:18
shall not return unto me *v* ....Is 55:11
it was without form, and *v* ....Jer 4:23
She is empty, and *v*, and......Nah 2:10
conscience *v* of offense........Acts 24:16
make *v* the law through ....Rom 3:31
should make my glorying *v* 1Cor 9:15

VOLCANO—*eruption from the earth's interior*
Descriptive of God's presence ....Judg 5:4, 5

VOLUME—*scroll; roll*
in the *v* of the book it is ......Ps 40:7
(in the *v* of the book it is .....Heb 10:7

VOLUNTARILY—*by one's own choice*

[*also* VOLUNTARY]
offer it of his own *v* will ......Lev 1:3
shalt prepare a *v* burnt........Ezek 46:12
you of your reward in a *v*.....Col 2:18

VOLUNTEERS—*those who help without coercion or pay*
Christ calls for ....Matt 11:28-30

VOMIT—*to throw up*
Used literally of:
Dog ....Prov 26:11
One who eats in excess . .Prov 25:16
Drunken man ....Is 19:14
Great fish..............Jon 2:10
Used figuratively of:
False teaching 2Pet 2:22
Judgment ....Jer 48:25, 26
Riches ....Job 20:15

[*also* VOMITETH]
land itself *v* out her...........Lev 18:25
hath eaten shalt thou *v*.........Prov 23:8
For all tables are full of *v* .....Is 28:8

VOPHSI (vŏf'sī)—*"fragrant; rich"*
Naphtalite spy...........Num 13:14

V

VOW—*a pledge to fulfill an agreement; to make a pledge*
Objects of one's:
Life ....Num 6:1-21
Children 1Sam 1:11-28
Possessions.............Gen 28:22
Gifts ....Ps 76:11
Features concerning:
Must be voluntary ....Deut 23:21, 22
Must be uttered ....Deut 23:23
Once made, binding .....Eccl 5:4, 5
Benefits of, sometimes included ....Gen 28:20-22
Invalidity of, specified ...Num 30:1-16
Abuse of, condemned....Matt 15:4-6
Rashness in, condemned .Prov 20:25
Perfection in, required ...Lev 22:18-25
Wickedness of some .....Jer 44:25

[*also* VOWED, VOWEDST, VOWEST, VOWETH, VOWS]
where thou *v* a *v* unto me .....Gen 31:13
of his offering be a *v* ....Lev 7:16
his oblation for all his *v*.......Lev 22:18
shall make a singular *v*........Lev 27:2
to his ability that *v* ....Lev 27:8
sacrifice in performing a *v*.....Num 15:3
And Israel *v* a *v* unto the .....Num 21:2
beside your *v*, and your ....Num 29:39
If a man *v* a *v* unto the Lord ..Num 30:2
also *v* a *v* unto the Lord ......Num 30:3
your *v*, and your freewill ......Deut 12:6
v which ye *v* unto the Lord....Deut 12:11
any of thy *v* which thou *v* .....Deut 12:17
And Jephthah *v* a *v* unto......Judg 11:30
to his *v* which he had *v* ....Judg 11:39
let me go and pay my *v*.......2Sam 15:7
I have *v* unto the Lord.........2Sam 15:7
For thy servant *v* a *v* while I ..2Sam 15:8
and thou shall pay thy *v* ......Job 22:27
I will pay my *v* before ....Ps 22:25
Thy *v* are upon me, O God ...Ps 56:12
I may daily perform my *v* .....Ps 61:8
unto thee shall the *v* be ....Ps 65:1
I will pay my *v* unto ....Ps 116:14
v unto the mighty God of .....Ps 132:2
day have I paid my *v* ....Prov 7:14
what, the son of my *v*? ....Prov 31:2
When thou *v* a *v* unto God, ...Eccl 5:4
pay that which thou hast *v* ....Eccl 5:4
that thou shouldest not *v*......Eccl 5:5
that thou shouldest *v* and .....Eccl 5:5
they shall *v* a *v* unto ....Is 19:21
unto the Lord, and made *v*....Jon 1:16
pay that that I have *v*.........Jon 2:9
feasts, perform thy *v*..........Nah 1:15
and *v*, and sacrificeth ....Mal 1:14
Cenchrea; for he had a *v*......Acts 18:18

VOYAGE—*an extended journey by boat*
Paul's to Rome..........Acts 27:10

VULTURE—*a flesh-eating bird of prey*
Classed as unclean.......Lev 11:13, 14

[*also* VULTURE'S, VULTURES]
the kite, and the *v* after.......Deut 14:13
the *v* eye hath not seen ....Job 28:7
the *v* also be gathered ....Is 34:15

W

WAFER—*a thin cake made from flour*
Often made with honey ..Ez 16:31
Used in various offerings .Ex 29:2
Lev 2:4

[*also* WAFERS]
one *w* out of the basket ....Ex 29:23
unleavened *w* anointed ....Lev 7:12
of oiled bread, and one *w*.....Lev 8:26
w of unleavened bread ....Num 6:15
and one unleavened *w* ....Num 6:19

WAG—*to shake*

[*also* WAGGING]
astonished, and *w* his head ....Jer 18:16
w their head at the ....Lam 2:15
shall hiss, and *w* his hand ......Zeph 2:15
reviled him, *w* their heads .....Matt 27:39
on him, *w* their heads.........Mark 15:29

WAGES—*hire; payment for work performed*
Principles governing payment of:
Must be paid promptly...Deut 24:14, 15
Withholding of, forbidden.James 5:4
Laborer worthy of ....Matt 10:10
Paid to such classes as:
Soldiers.................2Sam 10:6
Fishermen ....Mark 1:20
Shepherds ....John 10:12, 13
Masons and carpenters ...2Chr 24:12
Farm laborers ....Matt 20:1-16
Male prostitutes ....Deut 23:18
Nurses..................Ex 2:9
Ministers 1Cor 9:4-14
Teachers................Gal 6:6-7
Figurative of:
Spiritual death ....Rom 6:23
Unrighteousness 2Pet 2:15

what shall thy *w* be? ....Gen 29:15
changed my *w* ten times ......Gen 31:7
changed my *w* ten times ......Gen 31:41
w of him that is hired.........Lev 19:13
service without *w* ....Jer 22:13
yet had he no *w*, nor his ......Ezek 29:18
and he that earneth *w* ....Hag 1:6
earneth *w* to put it into a .....Hag 1:6
the hireling in his *w* ....Mal 3:5
be content with your *w* ....Luke 3:14
that reapeth receiveth *w* ......John 4:36
other churches, taking *w* 2Cor 11:8

WAGON—*a vehicle, usually with four wheels*
Used to move Jacob to Egypt ....Gen 45:19, 21
Used in moving objects ..Num 7:3-9

[*also* WAGONS]
when he saw the *w* which .....Gen 45:27
in the *w* which Pharaoh ....Gen 46:5

WAIL—*to cry out; mourn*
Caused by:
King's decree ....Esth 4:3
City's destruction ....Ezek 27:31, 32
God's judgment ....Amos 5:16, 17
Girl's death ....Mark 5:38-42
Christ's return...........Rev 1:7
Hell's torments ....Matt 13:42, 50
Performed by:
Women..................Jer 9:17-20
Prophets ....Mic 1:8
Merchants ....Rev 18:15, 19
See MOURNING

[*also* WAILING]
I take up a weeping and *w* ....Jer 9:10
neither shall there be *w* ....Ezek 7:11
w for the multitude of ....Ezek 32:18

WAIT—*to delay; stay in anticipation of; to serve*

[*also* WAITED, WAITETH, WAITING]
if a man lie not in *w*..........Ex 21:13
shall *w* on their priest's ....Num 3:10
cease *w* upon the service ......Num 8:25
hurl at him by laying of *w*.....Num 35:20
and lie in *w* for him ....Deut 19:11
ye shall lie in *w* against ....Josh 8:4
set liers in *w* for him in ....Judg 9:25
and they laid *w* against........Judg 9:34
laid *w* in the field, and........Judg 9:43
there were men lying in *w*.....Judg 16:9
Israel set liers in *w* round .....Judg 20:29
trusted unto the liers in *w* .....Judg 20:36
liers in *w* hasted, and ....Judg 20:37
liers in *w* drew themselves.....Judg 20:37
Go and lie in *w* in the ....Judg 21:20
how he laid *w* for him in......1Sam 15:2
against me, to lie in *w* 1Sam 22:8
and *w* for the king by the 1Kin 20:38
she *w* on Naaman's wife 2Kin 5:2
I *w* for the Lord any longer ...2Kin 6:33
then they *w* on their office 1Chr 6:32
w in the king's gate...........1Chr 9:18
was to *w* on the sons of 1Chr 23:28
did not then *w* by course 2Chr 5:11
priests *w* on their offices 2Chr 7:6
the porters *w* at every 2Chr 35:15
of such as lay in *w* by.........Ezra 8:31
for the Levites that *w*..........Neh 12:44
the companies of Sheba *w*.....Job 6:19
appointed time will I *w* ....Job 14:14
the adulterer *w* for the ....Job 24:15
unto me men gave ear, and *w* .Job 29:21
when I *w* for light, there ......Job 30:26
if I have laid *w* at my.........Job 31:9
Behold, I *w* for your words ...Job 32:11
He lieth in *w* secretly as ......Ps 10:9
he lieth in *w* to catch the .....Ps 10:9
none that *w* on thee be ....Ps 25:3
me; for I *w* on thee ....Ps 25:21
Our soul *w* for the Lord:......Ps 33:20
and *w* patiently for him ....Ps 37:7
I will *w* on thy name ....Ps 52:9
when they *w* for my soul......Ps 56:6
they lie in *w* for my soul......Ps 59:3
strength will I *w* upon thee ....Ps 59:9
Praise *w* for thee, O God .....Ps 65:1
they that lay *w* for my soul....Ps 71:10
wicked have *w* for me to ......Ps 119:95
let us lay *w* for blood, let .....Prov 1:11
they lay *w* for their own ......Prov 1:18
lieth in *w* at every corner .....Prov 7:12
w at the posts of my doors ....Prov 8:34
the wicked are to lie in *w* .....Prov 12:6
w on the Lord, and he ....Prov 20:22
She also lieth in *w* as for.......Prov 23:28
Lay not *w*, O wicked man.....Prov 24:15
he that *w* on his master ....Prov 27:18
O Lord, have we *w* for thee ...Is 26:8
therefore will the Lord *w* ....Is 30:18
not be ashamed that *w* for ....Is 49:23
w for light, but behold ....Is 59:9
Surely the isles shall *w* ....Is 60:9
they lay *w*, as he that ....Jer 5:26
in heart he layeth his *w* ....Jer 9:8
we will *w* upon thee ....Jer 14:22
me as a bear lying in *w* ....Lam 3:10
laid *w* for us in the ....Lam 4:19
Blessed is he that *w*, and......Dan 12:12
as troops of robbers *w* ....Hos 6:9
oven, whiles they lie in *w* .....Hos 7:6
of Maroth *w* carefully for .....Mic 1:12
nor *w* for the sons of men......Mic 5:7
they all lie in *w* for blood .....Mic 7:2
w for the God of my ....Mic 7:7
though it tarry, *w* for it ....Hab 2:3
Therefore *w* ye upon me ......Zeph 3:8
poor of the flock that *w*.......Zech 11:11
people *w* for Zacharias.........Luke 1:21
they were all *w* for him ....Luke 8:40
w for the moving of the ....John 5:3
that *w* on him continually .....Acts 10:7
Paul *w* for them at Athens ....Acts 17:16
lying in *w* of the Jews..........Acts 20:19
heard of their lying in *w* ......Acts 23:16
for there lie in *w* for him .....Acts 23:21
Jews laid *w* for the man.......Acts 23:30
laying *w* in the way to kill.....Acts 25:3
do we with patience *w* ....Rom 8:25
let us *w* on our ministering ....Rom 12:7
they which *w* at the altar......1Cor 9:13
w for the hope of.............Gal 5:5
they lie in *w* to deceive ....Eph 4:14
the patient *w* for Christ 2Thess 3:5
husbandman *w* for the ....James 5:7

WAITING ON THE LORD—*anticipating the Lord's leading*
Agents of:
Creatures ....Ps 145:15
Creation ....Rom 8:19, 23

Gentiles ... Is 51:5
Christians ... 1Cor 1:7

Manner of:
With the soul ... Ps 62:1, 5
With quietness ... Lam 3:25, 26
With patience ... Ps 40:1
With courage ... Ps 27:14
All the day ... Ps 25:5
Continually ... Hos 12:6
With great hope ... Ps 130:5, 6
With crying ... Ps 69:3

Objects of God's:
Salvation ... Is 25:9
Law ... Is 42:4
Protection ... Ps 33:20
Pardon ... Ps 39:7, 8
Food ... Ps 104:27
Kingdom ... Mark 15:43
Holy Spirit ... Acts 1:4
Son ... 1Thess 1:10

Blessings attending, described as:
Spiritual renewal ... Is 40:31
Not be ashamed ... Ps 69:6
Inherit the land ... Ps 37:9, 34
Something unusual ... Is 64:4
Unusual blessing ... Luke 12:36, 37

WAKE—*to be (remain) awake; to alert*

[*also* WAKED, WAKENED, WAKENETH, WAKETH, WAKING]

Thou holdest mine eyes *w* ... Ps 77:4
I sleep, but my heart *w* ... Song 5:2
he *w* morning by morning ... Is 50:4
w mine ear to hear as the ... Is 50:4
perpetual sleep, and not *w* ... Jer 51:39
w up the mighty men ... Joel 3:9
Let the heathen be *w* ... Joel 3:12
came again, and *w* me ... Zech 4:1
a man that is *w* out of his ... Zech 4:1
whether we *w* or sleep ... 1Thess 5:10

WALK—*to move about; travel on foot; behave*

[*also* WALKED, WALKEDST, WALKEST, WALKETH, WALKING]

Lord God *w* in the garden ... Gen 3:8
Enoch *w* with God after he ... Gen 5:22
and Noah *w* with God ... Gen 6:9
Arise, *w* through the land ... Gen 13:17
The Lord, before whom I *w* ... Gen 24:40
man is this that *w* in the ... Gen 24:65
her maidens *w* along by ... Ex 2:5
they will *w* in my law, or ... Ex 16:4
w abroad upon his staff ... Ex 21:19
ye *w* in their ordinances ... Lev 18:3
not *w* in the manners of ... Lev 20:23
I will *w* among you, and ... Lev 26:12
will *w* contrary unto me ... Lev 26:23
but *w* contrary unto me ... Lev 26:27
they have *w* contrary unto ... Lev 26:40
he knoweth thy *w* through ... Deut 2:7
Ye shall *w* in all the ways ... Deut 5:33
when thou *w* by the way ... Deut 6:7
w after other gods, and ... Deut 8:19
to *w* in all his ways, and to ... Deut 11:22
God commanded thee to *w* ... Deut 13:5
Lord thy God *w* in the ... Deut 23:14
God, and to *w* in his ways ... Deut 26:17
I *w* in the imagination of ... Deut 29:19
w forty years in the ... Josh 5:6
Go and *w* through the land ... Josh 18:8
way which their fathers *w* ... Judg 2:17
the way of the Lord to *w* ... Judg 2:22
w through the wilderness ... Judg 11:16
w before me for ever ... 1Sam 2:30
his sons *w* not in his ways ... 1Sam 8:3
thy sons *w* not in thy ways ... 1Sam 8:5
the king *w* before you ... 1Sam 12:2
his men *w* all that night ... 2Sam 2:29
w all the children of ... 2Sam 7:7
to *w* in his ways, to keep ... 1Kin 2:3
w abroad any whither ... 1Kin 2:42
w in the statutes of David ... 1Kin 3:3
he *w* before thee in truth ... 1Kin 3:6
if thou wilt *w* in my ways ... 1Kin 3:14
as thy father David did *w* ... 1Kin 3:14
thou wilt *w* in my statutes ... 1Kin 6:12
my commandments to *w* in ... 1Kin 6:12
w before me as thou hast ... 1Kin 8:25
him, to *w* in all his ways ... 1Kin 8:58
wilt *w* before me, as David ... 1Kin 9:4
as David thy father *w*, in ... 1Kin 9:4
And he *w* in all the sins ... 1Kin 15:3
w in the way of Jeroboam ... 1Kin 15:34
he *w* in the way of ... 1Kin 16:26
a light thing for him to *w* ... 1Kin 16:31
w in the way of his father ... 1Kin 22:52
w in the house to and fro ... 2Kin 4:35
w in the way of the house ... 2Kin 8:27
no heed to *w* in the law ... 2Kin 10:31
made Israel sin: but he *w* ... 2Kin 13:11
w in the statutes of the ... 2Kin 17:8
children of Israel *w* in all ... 2Kin 17:22
And he *w* in all the way ... 2Kin 21:21
way that his father *w* in ... 2Kin 21:21
w in all the way of David ... 2Kin 22:2
I have *w* with all Israel ... 1Chr 17:6
that *w* before thee with all ... 2Chr 6:14
as thou hast *w* before me ... 2Chr 6:16
wherein they should *w* ... 2Chr 6:27
if thou wilt *w* before me ... 2Chr 7:17
they *w* in the way of David ... 2Chr 11:17
w in his commandments ... 2Chr 17:4
w in the way of the kings ... 2Chr 21:6
w in the way of the kings ... 2Chr 21:13
w also after their counsel ... 2Chr 22:5
w in the ways of David his ... 2Chr 34:2
w in the fear of our God ... Neh 5:9
Mordecai *w* every day before ... Esth 2:11
and from *w* up and down ... Job 1:7
and he *w* upon a snare ... Job 18:8
I *w* through darkness ... Job 29:3
and mine heart *w* after ... Job 31:7
the moon *w* in brightness ... Job 31:26
and *w* with wicked men ... Job 34:8
that *w* not in the counsel ... Ps 1:1
wicked *w* on every side ... Ps 12:8
I have *w* in mine integrity ... Ps 26:1
I will *w* in mine integrity ... Ps 26:11
every man *w* in a vain show ... Ps 39:6
w unto the house of God ... Ps 55:14
w before God in the light ... Ps 56:13
and Israel had *w* in my ... Ps 81:13
they *w* on in darkness ... Ps 82:5
I will *w* in thy truth ... Ps 86:11
w not in my judgments ... Ps 89:30
the pestilence that *w* in ... Ps 91:6
who *w* upon the wings of ... Ps 104:3
feet have they, but they *w* ... Ps 115:7
w in the law of the Lord ... Ps 119:1
w at liberty: for I seek ... Ps 119:45
way wherein I should *w* ... Ps 143:8
w not thou in the way with ... Prov 1:15
w in the ways of darkness ... Prov 2:13
thou *w* in thy way safely ... Prov 3:23
w with a froward mouth ... Prov 6:12
He that *w* with wise men ... Prov 13:20
understanding *w* uprightly ... Prov 15:21
just man *w* in his integrity ... Prov 20:7
w uprightly shall be saved ... Prov 28:18
but the fool *w* in darkness ... Eccl 2:14
the living which *w* under ... Eccl 4:15
and princes *w* as servants ... Eccl 10:7
and *w* in the ways of thine ... Eccl 11:9
and we will *w* in his paths ... Is 2:3
w with stretched forth ... Is 3:16
w and mincing as they go ... Is 3:16
people that *w* in darkness ... Is 9:2
w to go down into Egypt ... Is 30:2
He that *w* righteously ... Is 33:15
but the redeemed shall *w* ... Is 35:9
I have *w* before thee in ... Is 38:3
and spirit to them that *w* ... Is 42:5
thou *w* through the fire ... Is 43:2
w in the light of your fire ... Is 50:11
one *w* in his uprightness ... Is 57:2
w in a way that was not ... Is 65:2
and have *w* after vanity ... Jer 2:5
neither shall they *w* any ... Jer 3:17
is the good way, and *w* ... Jer 6:16
they said, We will not *w* ... Jer 6:16
revolters, *w* with slanders ... Jer 6:28
w after other gods to your ... Jer 7:6
w ye in all the ways that ... Jer 7:23
but *w* in the counsels and ... Jer 7:24
obeyed my voice, neither *w* ... Jer 9:13
that *w* to direct his steps ... Jer 10:23
w every one in the ... Jer 11:8
w in the imagination of ... Jer 13:10
and *w* after other gods, to ... Jer 13:10
w after our own devices ... Jer 18:12
commit adultery, and *w* in ... Jer 23:14
cause them to *w* by the ... Jer 31:9
voice, neither *w* in thy law ... Jer 32:23
Lord, nor *w* in his law ... Jer 44:23
is desolate, the foxes *w* ... Lam 5:18
statutes, they have not *w* ... Ezek 5:6
have not *w* in my statutes ... Ezek 11:12
they may *w* in my statutes ... Ezek 11:20
heart *w* after the heart of ... Ezek 11:21
Hath *w* in my statutes ... Ezek 18:9
they *w* not in my statutes ... Ezek 20:13
w in my statutes, and keep ... Ezek 20:19
they *w* not in my statutes ... Ezek 20:21
hast *w* up and down in the ... Ezek 28:14
I will cause men to *w* upon ... Ezek 36:12
also *w* in my judgments ... Ezek 37:24
w in the midst of the fire ... Dan 3:25
w in the palace of the ... Dan 4:29
those that *w* in pride he is ... Dan 4:37
w after the commandment ... Hos 5:11
shall *w* after the Lord: he ... Hos 11:10
w every one in his path ... Joel 2:8
which their fathers have *w* ... Amos 2:4
two *w* together, except ... Amos 3:3
do good to him that *w* ... Mic 2:7
man *w* in the spirit and ... Mic 2:11
and we will *w* in his paths ... Mic 4:2
w every one in the name of ... Mic 4:5
w in the name of the Lord ... Mic 4:5
and ye *w* in their counsels ... Mic 6:16
shall stumble in their *w* ... Nah 2:5
even the old lion, *w*, and ... Nah 2:11
didst *w* through the sea ... Hab 3:15
shall *w* like blind men ... Zeph 1:17
to *w* to and fro through ... Zech 1:10
We have *w* to and fro ... Zech 1:11
If thou wilt *w* in my ways ... Zech 3:7
w among these that stand ... Zech 3:7
w to and fro through the ... Zech 6:7
w to and fro through the ... Zech 6:7
he *w* with me in peace and ... Mal 2:6
Jesus, *w* by the sea of ... Matt 4:18
or to say, Arise and *w*? ... Matt 9:5
and the lame *w*, the lepers ... Matt 11:5
he *w* through dry places ... Matt 12:43
disciples saw him *w* on ... Matt 14:26
he *w* on the water, to go to ... Matt 14:29
lame to *w*, and the blind to ... Matt 15:31
he *w* by the sea of Galilee ... Mark 1:16
and take up thy bed, and *w*? ... Mark 2:9
unto them, *w* upon the sea ... Mark 6:48
said, I see men as trees, *w* ... Mark 8:24
two of them, as they *w* ... Mark 16:12
before God, *w* in all the ... Luke 1:6
or to say, Rise up and *w*? ... Luke 5:23
he *w* through dry places ... Luke 11:24
the men that *w* over them ... Luke 11:44
desire to *w* in long robes ... Luke 20:46
upon Jesus as he *w*, he ... John 1:36
take up thy bed, and *w* ... John 5:8
Take up thy bed, and *w* ... John 5:11
Take up thy bed, and *w*? ... John 5:12
see Jesus *w* on the sea ... John 6:19
and *w* no more with him ... John 6:66
he would not *w* in Jewry ... John 7:1
Jesus *w* in the temple in ... John 10:23
If any man *w* in the day ... John 11:9
if a man *w* in the night ... John 11:10
W while ye have the light ... John 12:35
he that *w* in darkness ... John 12:35
w whither thou wouldest ... John 21:18
of Nazareth rise up and *w* ... Acts 3:6
he leaping up stood, and *w* ... Acts 3:8

into the temple, *w*, and ....Acts 3:8
w in the fear of the Lord .....Acts 9:31
And he leaped and *w* ....Acts 14:10
nations to *w* in their own .....Acts 14:16
w orderly, and keepest the ....Acts 21:24
also *w* in the steps of that .....Rom 4:12
w in newness of life ....Rom 6:4
Let us *w* honestly, as in ....Rom 13:13
now *w* thou not charitably .....Rom 14:15
not carnal, and *w* as men? 1Cor 3:3
every one, so let him *w* 1Cor 7:17
dwell in them, and *w* in 2Cor 6:16
w according to the flesh 2Cor 10:2
though we *w* in the flesh 2Cor 10:3
w we not in the same spirit?...2Cor 12:18
w we not in the same steps?...2Cor 12:18
w not uprightly according .....Gal 2:14
w according to this rule ....Gal 6:16
time past ye *w* according ......Eph 2:2
that we should *w* in them .....Eph 2:10
let us *w* by the same rule .....Phil 3:16
mark them which *w* so as .....Phil 3:17
For many *w*, of whom I ......Phil 3:18
w honestly toward them 1Thess 4:12
w in lasciviousness, lusts 1Pet 4:3
w about, seeking whom he 1Pet 5:8
them that *w* after the flesh 2Pet 2:10
w after their own lusts 2Pet 3:3
him, and *w* in darkness 1John 1:6
w in darkness, and knoweth ...1John 2:11
found of thy children *w* in.....2John 4
w after their own lusts ....Jude 16
w after their own ungodly .....Jude 18
w in the midst of the seven....Rev 2:1
shall *w* with me in white ......Rev 3:4
can see, nor hear, nor *w* ......Rev 9:20
lest he *w* naked, and they see .Rev 16:15
saved shall *w* in the light......Rev 21:24

WALK OF BELIEVERS—*figurative description of the Christian life*

Stated negatively, not:
In darkness ....John 8:12
After the flesh ....Rom 8:1, 4
As Gentiles ....Eph 4:17
In craftiness............2Cor 4:2
In sin ....Col 3:5-7
In disorder.............2Thess 3:6, 11

Stated positively:
In the light 1John 1:7
In the truth 3John 3, 4
In Christ...............Col 2:6
In the Spirit ....Gal. 5:16, 25
In love ....Eph 5:2
As children of light ......Eph 5:8
As Christ walked 1John 2:6
After His commandments.2John 6
By faith 2Cor 5:7
In good works ....Eph 2:10
Worthy ....Eph 4:1
Worthy of the Lord .....Col 1:10
Worthy of God..........1Thess 2:12
Circumspectly ....Eph 5:15
In wisdom ....Col 4:5
Pleasing God...........1Thess 4:1

WALL—*a rampart or partition*

Used for:
Shooting arrows from 2Sam 11:24
Observation.............2Sam 18:24

Unusual events connected with:
Woman lives on ....Josh 2:15
Jericho's, falls by faith ..Josh 6:5, 20
Saul's body fastened to ..1Sam 31:10, 11
Woman throws stone from 2Sam 11:20, 21
27,000 killed by 1Kin 20:30
Son sacrificed on 2Kin 3:27
Warning inscribed on ....Dan 5:5, 25-28
Paul escapes through ....Acts 9:25

Figurative of:
Defense 1Sam 25:16
Protection ....Ezra 9:9
Great power ....Ps 18:29
Peacefulness ....Ps 122:7
Self-sufficiency ....Prov 18:11
Powerless ....Prov 25:28
Salvation ....Is 26:1
God's kingdom..........Is 56:5
Heaven.................Is 60:18-21
Spiritual leaders ....Is 62:6
God's messengers ....Jer 1:18, 19
Protection ....Zech 2:5
Hypocrisy..............Acts 23:3
Ceremonial law ....Eph 2:14
New Jerusalem ....Rev 21:12-19

Of Jerusalem:
Built by Solomon........1Kin 3:1
Broken down by Jehoash .2Kin 14:13
Destroyed by Babylonians 2Chr 36:19
Seen at night by Nehemiah ....Neh 2:12-18
Rebuilt by returnees .....Neh 6:1, 6, 15
Dedication of ....Neh 12:27-47

[*also* WALLS]
they digged down a *w*.........Gen 49:6
waters were a *w* unto them....Ex 14:22
plague be in the *w* of the .....Lev 14:37
sight are lower than the *w*.....Lev 14:37
plague be spread in the *w* .....Lev 14:39
a *w* being on this side.........Num 22:24
side, and a *w* on that side .....Num 22:24
thrust herself unto the *w* ......Num 22:25
Balaam's foot against the *w* ...Num 22:25
shall reach from the *w* ....Num 35:4
were fenced with high *w* ......Deut 3:5
high and fenced *w* come ......Deut 28:52
smite David even to the *w* 1Sam 18:11
smite David even to the *w* 1Sam 19:10
the javelin into the *w* 1Sam 19:10
even upon a seat by the *w* 1Sam 20:25
that pisseth against the *w* 1Sam 25:22
his sons from the *w*...........1Sam 31:12
with Joab battered the *w*......2Sam 20:15
God have I leaped over a *w*...2Sam 22:30
great cities with *w* and 1Kin 4:13
that springeth out of the *w*....1Kin 4:33
against the *w* of the house 1Kin 6:5
in the *w* of the house he 1Kin 6:6
he built the *w* of the house....1Kin 6:15
and the *w* of the ceiling 1Kin 6:15
the one touched the one *w* 1Kin 6:27
cherub touched the other *w* ...1Kin 6:27
he carved all the *w* of the 1Kin 6:29
tree, a fourth part of the *w*....1Kin 6:33
that pisseth against the *w* 1Kin 14:10
that pisseth against a *w* 1Kin 16:11
that pisseth against the *w* 1Kin 21:21
eat Jezebel by the *w* of 1Kin 21:23
I pray thee, on the *w* 2Kin 4:10
he passed by upon the *w* 2Kin 6:30
that pisseth against the *w* 2Kin 9:8
people that are on the *w* 2Kin 18:26
he turned his face to the *w*....2Kin 20:2
of the gate between two *w* 2Kin 25:4
to overlay the *w* of the........1Chr 29:4
w thereof, and the doors 2Chr 3:7
graved cherubim on the *w*.....2Chr 3:7
reaching to the *w* of the.......2Chr 3:11
about them *w*, and towers.....2Chr 14:7
brake down the *w* of Gath 2Chr 26:6
w of Jabneh, and the *w* of 2Chr 26:6
on the *w* of Ophel he built 2Chr 27:3
built up all the *w* that was 2Chr 32:5
the towers, and another *w*.....2Chr 32:5
built a *w* without the city 2Chr 33:14
and have set up the *w* ....Ezra 4:12
and the *w* thereof set up ......Ezra 4:16
and to make up this *w*? ....Ezra 5:3
and to make up these *w*? .....Ezra 5:9
w of Jerusalem also is........Neh 1:3
and for the *w* of the city ......Neh 2:8
Jerusalem unto the broad *w* ...Neh 3:8
w of the pool of Siloah by ....Neh 3:15
turning of the *w* unto the .....Neh 3:20
the turning of the *w* ....Neh 3:25
that we builded the *w*.........Neh 4:1
So built we the *w*; and all .....Neh 4:6
the *w* was joined together .....Neh 4:6
the *w* of Jerusalem were ......Neh 4:7
lower places behind the *w*.....Neh 4:13
which builded on the *w* ....Neh 4:17
in the work of this *w* ....Neh 5:16
when the *w* was built, and ....Neh 7:1
Why lodge ye about the *w*? ...Neh 13:21
make oil within their *w* ....Job 24:11
thou the *w* of Jerusalem ......Ps 51:18
go about it upon the *w*........Ps 55:10
as a bowing *w* shall ye be .....Ps 62:3
the stone *w* thereof was ....Prov 24:31
he standeth behind our *w* .....Song 2:9
keepers of the *w* took.........Song 5:7
I am a *w*, and my breasts .....Song 8:10
and upon every fenced *w*......Is 2:15
breaking down the *w*, and.....Is 22:5
down to fortify the *w* ....Is 22:10
of the high fort of thy *w* ......Is 25:12
swelling out in a high *w*.......Is 30:13
men that sit upon the *w*.......Is 36:12
w are continually before ......Is 49:16
We grope for the *w* like.......Is 59:10
shall build up thy *w* ....Is 60:10
all the *w* thereof round ....Jer 1:15
up upon her *w*, and destroy ...Jer 5:10
people a fenced brazen *w* .....Jer 15:20
besiege you without the *w*.....Jer 21:4
the gate betwixt the two *w* ....Jer 39:4
fallen, her *w* are thrown ......Jer 50:15
the *w* of Babylon shall fall ....Jer 51:44
broad *w* of Babylon shall.......Jer 51:58
brake down all the *w* of.......Jer 52:14
of the enemy the *w* of her ....Lam 2:7
to destroy the *w* of the........Lam 2:8
the rampart and the *w* ....Lam 2:8
it for a *w* of iron between .....Ezek 4:3
of man, dig now in the *w* .....Ezek 8:8
when I had digged in the *w* ...Ezek 8:8
Dig thou through the *w* in ....Ezek 12:5
shall dig through the *w*........Ezek 12:12
when the *w* is fallen ....Ezek 13:12
my wrath upon the *w* ....Ezek 13:15
The *w* is no more, neither.....Ezek 13:15
destroy the *w* of Tyrus ....Ezek 26:4
w shall shake at the noise .....Ezek 26:10
army were upon thy *w* ....Ezek 27:11
their shields upon thy *w*.......Ezek 27:11
them dwelling without *w* ......Ezek 38:11
w thereof, were of wood ......Ezek 41:22
be built again, and the *w*......Dan 9:25
make a *w*, that she shall ......Hos 2:6
climb the *w* like men of.......Joel 2:7
a fire on the *w* of Gaza ....Amos 1:7
a fire in the *w* of Rabbah .....Amos 1:14
a *w* made by a plumbline .....Amos 7:7
that thy *w* are to be built .....Mic 7:11
make haste to the *w* ....Nah 2:5
stone shall cry out of the *w* ...Hab 2:11
inhabited as towns without *w* ..Zech 2:4
was I let down by the *w* 2Cor 11:33
By faith the *w* of Jericho fell ..Heb 11:30

WALLED—*bordered or enclosed by a wall*
sell a dwelling house in a *w* ...Lev 25:29
w city shall be established .....Lev 25:30
and the cities are *w*, and very. .Num 13:28

WALLOW—*to roll about in an indolent or ungainly manner*

In:
Blood 2Sam 20:12
Vomit ....Jer 48:26
Ashes ....Jer 6:26
On the ground ....Mark 9:20
Mire 2Pet 2:22

w yourselves in the ashes......Jer 25:34
w themselves in the ashes .....Ezek 27:30

WANDER—*to roam about aimlessly or from place to place*

Descriptive of:
Hagar's travels ....Gen 21:14
Israel's wilderness travels .Num 32:13
God's pilgrims ....Heb 11:37, 38
Captivity................Hos 9:17
Joseph in the field ....Gen 37:15

Syrian ....Deut 26:5
Early Saints ....Heb 11:38

Figurative of:

Apostasy ....Ps 119:10
Dissatisfaction ....Prov 27:8
Hopelessness ....Jude 13

[*also* WANDERED, WANDEREST, WANDERETH, WANDERING, WANDERINGS]

w from my father's house .....Gen 20:13
he was *w* in the field ....Gen 37:15
shall *w* in the wilderness ......Num 14:33
maketh the blind to *w* out.....Deut 27:18
Israel *w* in the wilderness .....Josh 14:10
them to *w* in a wilderness .....Job 12:24
He *w* abroad for bread........Job 15:23
they *w* for lack of meat ....Job 38:41
then would I *w* far off, and ...Ps 55:7
Thou tellest my *w*: put ....Ps 56:8
They *w* in the wilderness ......Ps 107:4
to *w* in the wilderness.........Ps 107:40
bird by *w*, as the swallow .....Prov 26:2
than the *w* of the desire ....Eccl 6:9
as a *w* bird cast out of the ....Is 16:2
bewray not him that *w* ....Is 16:3
w through the wilderness ......Is 16:8
w every one to his quarter ....Is 47:15
every green tree thou *w* ....Jer 2:20
shall gather up him that *w* ....Jer 49:5
They have *w* as blind men ....Lam 4:14
My sheep *w* through all ....Ezek 34:6
shall *w* from sea to sea........Amos 8:12

WANDERER—*one who roams*

Curse on Cain ....Gen 4:12, 14
Curse on the wicked .....Ps 109:10
Professional exorcists called ....Acts 19:13

[*also* WANDERERS]

I will send unto him *w* ....Jer 48:12
shall be *w* among the nations ..Hos 9:17

WANT—*to desire; need*

Caused by:

Hastiness ....Prov 21:5
Greed ....Prov 22:16
Sloth ....Prov 24:30-34
Debauchery ....Dan 5:27
God's judgments ....Amos 4:6
Physical need 2Cor 8:14

Provision against, by:

Trusting the Lord ....Ps 23:1
God's plan ....Jer 33:17, 18

[*also* WANTED, WANTETH, WANTING, WANTS]

need, in that which he *w*......Deut 15:8
nakedness, and in *w* of all.....Deut 28:48
shall eat them for w of all.....Deut 28:57
there is no *w* of any thing .....Judg 19:19
let all thy *w* lie upon me ......Judg 19:20
his priests; let none be *w*......2Kin 10:19
whosoever shall be *w*, he......2Kin 10:19
rock for *w* of a shelter ....Job 24:8
For *w* and famine they ....Job 30:3
perish for *w* of clothing ....Job 31:19
is no *w* to them that fear......Ps 34:9
Lord shall not *w* any good ....Ps 34:10
and thy *w* as an armed........Prov 6:11
him that *w* understanding .....Prov 9:4
of words there *w* not sin ......Prov 10:19
is destroyed for *w* of..........Prov 13:23
but in the *w* of people is ......Prov 14:28
with words, yet they are *w* ....Prov 19:7
is *w* cannot be numbered......Eccl 1:15
he *w* nothing for his soul......Eccl 6:2
goblet, which *w* not liquor ....Song 7:2
fail, none shall *w* her mate ....Is 34:16
w a man to stand before ......Jer 35:19
we have *w* all things, and .....Jer 44:18
w of the fruits of the field.....Lam 4:9
may *w* bread and water ....Ezek 4:17
she of her *w* did cast in all ....Mark 12:44
when they *w* wine, the ....John 2:3
present with you, and *w* 2Cor 11:9
that ministered to my *w*.......Phil 2:25
nothing be *w* unto them.......Titus 3:13
be perfect and entire, *w*.......James 1:4

WANTON—*lustful or immoral*

In suggestive movements .Is 3:16
Characteristic of doctrinal laxity 2Pet 2:18
Unbecoming to a Christian ....Rom 13:13

[*also* WANTONNESS]

to wax *w* against Christ 1Tim 5:11
on the earth, and been *w* .....James 5:5

WAR—*armed conflict between nations; to battle*

Caused by:

Sin ....James 4:1, 2
God's judgments 2Sam 12:10
God's decree ....Ex 17:16

Regulations concerning:

Consultation of:
Urim 1Sam 28:6
Ephod 1Sam 30:7, 8
Prophets 1Kin 22:7-28
Troops mustered ......Judg 3:27
Some dismissed ....Deut 20:5-8
Spies dispatched ....Num 13:17
Ark brought in 1Sam 4:4-6
Sacrifice offered 1Sam 7:9
Speech delivered 2Chr 20:20-22
Demand made for surrender ....Deut 20:10
Trumpet sounded........Num 10:9

Methods of attack, by:

Ambush ....Josh 8:3-26
Surprise attack ....Judg 7:16-22
Personal combat of champions 1Sam 17:1-51
Divided tactics 2Sam 10:9-14
Massed formation 1Kin 22:31-33
Battle cry ....Jer 4:19

Captives of:

Sometimes eliminated ....Josh 6:21
Made servants...........2Sam 8:2
Ruled over.............2Sam 5:2
Deported 2Kin 17:6

See SIEGE

[*also* WARRED, WARRETH, WARRING, WARS]

made *w* with Bera king ....Gen 14:2
there falleth out any *w* ....Ex 1:10
The Lord is a man of *w*.......Ex 15:3
a noise of *w* in the camp ......Ex 32:17
to go forth to *w* in Israel......Num 1:3
to go forth to *w* in Israel......Num 1:45
if ye go to *w* in your land .....Num 10:9
book of the *w* of the Lord ....Num 21:14
able to go to *w* in Israel ......Num 26:2
of yourselves unto the *w* ......Num 31:3
twelve thousand armed for *w* ..Num 31:5
Moses sent them to the *w* .....Num 31:6
Eleazer the priest, to the *w* ...Num 31:6
w against the Midianites ......Num 31:7
them that took the *w* upon ....Num 31:27
the men of *w* had caught ....Num 31:32
men of *w* which are under ....Num 31:49
shall your brethren go to *w*....Num 32:6
over, every man armed for *w* ..Num 32:27
every man his weapons of *w*...Deut 1:41
generation of the men of *w*....Deut 2:14
all that are meet for the *w* ....Deut 3:18
will make *w* against thee ......Deut 20:12
the city that maketh *w* ....Deut 20:20
he shall not go out to *w*.......Deut 24:5
thousand prepared for *w* ......Josh 4:13
people that were men of *w* ....Josh 5:6
take all the people of *w*.......Josh 8:1
all the people of *w* with ....Josh 10:7
all the people of *w* with ....Josh 11:7
the land rested from *w*.........Josh 11:23
the land had rest from *w*......Josh 14:15
go up to *w* against them ....Josh 22:12
Moab, arose and *w* against ....Josh 24:9
had not known all the *w* ......Judg 3:1
know, to teach them *w*........Judg 3:2
Israel, and went out to *w* .....Judg 3:10
of Ammon made *w* against ....Judg 11:4
appointed with weapons of *w* ..Judg 18:11
appointed with weapons of *w* ..Judg 18:17
each man his wife in the *w* ....Judg 21:22
make his instruments of *w*.....1Sam 8:12
man of *w*, and prudent in 1Sam 16:18
set him over the men of *w* 1Sam 18:5
the people together to *w* 1Sam 23:8
weapons of *w* perished! 2Sam 1:27
was *w* between the house 2Sam 3:6
for Hadadezer had *w* with.....2Sam 8:10
things concerning the *w* 2Sam 11:18
thy father is a man of *w* 2Sam 17:8
He teacheth my hands to *w* ...2Sam 22:35
and shed the blood of *w* in....1Kin 2:5
the blood of *w* upon his.......1Kin 2:5
w which were about him 1Kin 5:3
of Jeroboam, how he *w* 1Kin 14:19
was *w* between Rehoboam 1Kin 14:30
was *w* between Abijam 1Kin 15:7
they be come out for *w* 1Kin 20:18
he showed, and how he *w*.....1Kin 22:45
king of Syria *w* against........2Kin 6:8
w against Hazael king of 2Kin 8:28
Selah by *w*, and called 2Kin 14:7
and strength for the *w* 2Kin 18:20
king of Assyria *w* against......2Kin 19:8
men of *w* fled by night by.....2Kin 25:4
days of Saul they made *w* 1Chr 5:10
with bow, and skillful in *w* 1Chr 5:18
that went out to the *w* 1Chr 5:18
because the *w* was of God 1Chr 5:22
to go out for *w* and battle 1Chr 7:11
men, helpers of the *w*.........1Chr 12:1
were ready armed to the *w* 1Chr 12:23
men of valor for the *w* 1Chr 12:25
forth to battle, expert in *w* 1Chr 12:33
with all instruments of *w* 1Chr 12:33
battle, expert in *w*, forty 1Chr 12:36
All these men of *w*, that 1Chr 12:38
there arose *w* at Gezer with ...1Chr 20:4
again there was *w* at Gath 1Chr 20:6
and hast made great *w* 1Chr 22:8
If thy people go out to *w* 2Chr 6:34
were *w* between Rehoboam ...2Chr 12:15
w between Abijah and 2Chr 13:2
he had no *w* in those years 2Chr 14:6
no *w* against Jehoshaphat 2Chr 17:10
ready prepared for the *w*......2Chr 17:18
Ahab king of Israel to *w* 2Chr 22:5
w against the Philistines 2Chr 26:6
men, that went out to *w* by ...2Chr 26:11
of Jotham, and all his *w* 2Chr 27:7
them that came from the *w*....2Chr 28:12
and put captains of *w* in all ...2Chr 33:14
in *w* from the power of the....Job 5:20
the day of battle and *w*? ......Job 38:23
He teacheth my hands to *w* ...Ps 18:34
maketh *w* to cease unto ....Ps 46:9
but *w* was in his heart ....Ps 55:21
I speak, they are for *w*........Ps 120:7
teacheth my hands to *w*.......Ps 144:1
with good advice make *w* .....Prov 20:18
of *w*, and a time of peace .....Eccl 3:8
is better than weapons of *w* ...Eccl 9:18
swords, being expert in *w* .....Song 3:8
neither shall they learn *w* .....Is 2:4
and thy mighty in the *w*.......Is 3:25
from the grievousness of *w* ....Is 21:15
king of Assyria *w* against......Is 37:8
come forth to make *w* with....Is 37:9
jealousy like a man of *w* ......Is 42:13
trumpet, the alarm of *w*.......Jer 4:19
Prepare ye *w* against her ......Jer 6:4
set in array as men for *w* .....Jer 6:23
turn back the weapons of *w* ..Jer 21:4
the hands of the men of *w* ....Jer 38:4
there, and the men of *w* ......Jer 41:3
where we shall see no *w* ......Jer 42:14
an alarm of *w* to be heard ....Jer 49:2
men of *w* shall be cut off ....Jer 50:30
men of *w* are affrighted ......Jer 51:32
charge of the men of *w* ....Jer 52:25
make for him in the *w* ....Ezek 17:17

thine army, thy men of w .....Ezek 27:10
with their weapons of w ....Ezek 32:27
made w with the saints ....Dan 7:21
the wall like men of w ....Joel 2:7
Prepare w, wake up the ....Joel 3:9
let all the men of w draw .....Joel 3:9
as men averse from w ....Mic 2:8
neither shall they learn w .....Mic 4:3
of w, and rumors of w ....Matt 24:6
of w, and rumors of w ....Mark 13:7
w against another king ....Luke 14:31
hear of w and commotions ....Luke 21:9
w against the law of my ....Rom 7:23
flesh, we do not w after the ...2Cor 10:3
mightest w a good warfare 1Tim 1:18
which w against the soul 1Pet 2:11
pit shall make w against ....Rev 11:7
make w with the remnant .....Rev 12:17
make w with the saints ....Rev 13:7
he doth judge and make w ....Rev 19:11

WARD—*custody; duty; post*

[*also* WARDS]
he put them in w in the ....Gen 40:3
him in the w of his lord's .....Gen 40:7
put them altogether into w ....Gen 42:17
they put him in w, that the ....Lev 24:12
they put him in w, because ....Num 15:34
them in w, and fed them 2Sam 20:3
of the tabernacle, by w 1Chr 9:23
the w of the house of Saul 1Chr 12:29
they cast lots, w against 1Chr 25:8
against w, as well the 1Chr 26:16
of God, w over against w .....Neh 12:24
porters kept the w of their ....Neh 12:45
the w of the purification ....Neh 12:45
the w of the priests and ....Neh 13:30
set in my w whole nights ......Is 21:8
a captain of the w was ....Jer 37:13
put him in w in chains ....Ezek 19:9
the first and the second w .....Acts 12:10

WARDROBE—*one's clothing; one who oversees apparel*
Woman's ....Is 3:18-23
Directions concerning 1Pet 3:3-5
Keeper of..............2Kin 22:14

of Harhas, keeper of the w 2Kin 22:14
of Hasrah, keeper of the w 2Chr 34:22

WARE—*merchandise*
Sold in Tyrus ....Ezek 27:1-27

[*also* WARES]
people of the land bring w ....Neh 10:31
sellers of all kind of w ....Neh 13:20
Gather up thy w out of the ....Jer 10:17
of the w of thy making........Ezek 27:16
thy w went forth out of the ...Ezek 27:33
the w that were in the ship ....Jon 1:5

WARE—*to be aware of*
Of whom be thou w also 2Tim 4:15

WARFARE—*active military conflict*
their armies together for w 1Sam 28:1
her w is accomplished ....Is 40:2
Who goeth a w any time at ...1Cor 9:7
weapons of our w are not 2Cor 10:4
mightest war a good w 1Tim 1:18

WARFARE, SPIRITUAL
Enemies combated:
World ....James 4:1-4
Flesh 1Pet 4:1-4
Devil 1Pet 5:8
Invisible foes............Eph 6:12
Conquest over, by:
God's Word ....Eph 6:17
God's armor ....Eph 6:10-17
Faith 1John 5:4, 5
Christ's promise ....John 16:33
Soldiers of, must:
Avoid worldly entanglements.........2Tim 2:4
Pray....................Eph 6:18
Deny self 1Cor 9:25-27
Endure hardness 2Tim 2:3, 10
Be self-controlled........1Thess 5:6
Be alert 1Cor 16:13
Wear armor.............Eph 6:11

WARM—*to give out heat; to heat*

[*also* WARMED, WARMETH, WARMING]
flesh of the child waxed w 2Kin 4:34
What time they wax w ....Job 6:17
were not w with the fleece ....Job 31:20
earth, and w them in dust .....Job 39:14
how can one be w alone? .....Eccl 4:11
will take thereof and w ....Is 44:15
w himself and saith, Aha ......Is 44:16
shall not be a coal to w at ....Is 47:14
but there is none w ....Hag 1:6
and w himself at the fire ......Mark 14:54
she saw Peter w himself ....Mark 14:67
and they w themselves ....John 18:18
stood with them, and w ....John 18:18
Simon Peter stood and w......John 18:25
peace, be ye w and filled......James 2:16

WARN—*to caution against*

[*also* WARNED]
of God told him and w him ...2Kin 6:10
w them that they trespass 2Chr 19:10
and the people be not w ......Ezek 33:6
not speak to w the wicked ....Ezek 33:8
if thou w the wicked of ....Ezek 33:9
being w of God in a dream....Matt 2:12
w you to flee from the ....Matt 3:7
w you to flee from the ....Luke 3:7
but as my beloved sons I w ...1Cor 4:14
w them that are unruly........1Thess 5:14

WARNING—*a caution; counsel; advise; admonish*
Means of, by:
God's Word ....Ps 19:9-11
Prophet.................Ezek 3:17-27
Messenger ....Acts 20:31
Dream ....Matt 2:12, 22
Angel ....Acts 10:22
God....................Heb 11:7
Reactions to:
Obeyed.................Jon 3:1-10
Accepted ....Heb 11:7
Ignored.................2Sam 2:20-23
Rejected................Gen 2:16, 17
Scoffed at..............Gen 19:14
Disobeyed ....Num 14:40-45
Disobedience to, brings:
Judgment ....Jude 6, 7
Torments ....Luke 16:23-28
Destruction ....Prov 29:1

shall I speak, and give w......Jer 6:10
trumpet, and taketh not w ....Ezek 33:4
trumpet, and took not w ......Ezek 33:5
w shall deliver his soul ....Ezek 33:5
w every man and teaching .....Col 1:28

WARP—*series of yarns extended lengthwise in a loom*
it be in the w or woof ....Lev 13:48
whether the w or woof, in.....Lev 13:52
the w, or out of the woof .....Lev 13:56
the garment, either w, or .....Lev 13:58

WARRED, WARRETH, WARRING—*See* WAR

WARRIOR—*one who fights in battle*

[*also* WARRIORS]
chosen men, which were w 1Kin 12:21
chosen men, which were w 2Chr 11:1
battle of the w is with ....Is 9:5

WAS—*See* INTRODUCTION

WASH—*to cleanse; remove by rubbing or drenching with liquid*
Kinds of:
Ceremonial ....Ex 30:18-20
Miraculous ....John 9:7, 11, 15
Demonstrative ....John 13:5-14
Symbolic...............Matt 27:24
Typical ....Ps 51:2, 7
Spiritual ....Acts 22:16
Regenerative ....Titus 3:5
Materials used:
Water ....Gen 24:32
Tears...................Luke 7:38, 44
Snow ....Job 9:30
Wine ....Gen 49:11
Blood ....Ps 58:10
Objects of:
Hands ....Matt 27:24
Face....................Gen 43:31
Feet....................Gen 18:4
Body 2Sam 11:2
Clothes 2Sam 19:24
See PURIFICATION

[*also* WASHED, WASHEST, WASHING, WASHINGS]
tarry all night and w your .....Gen 19:2
water, and they w their feet ...Gen 43:24
of Pharaoh came down to w ...Ex 2:5
and they w their clothes ....Ex 19:14
shalt w them with water.......Ex 29:4
they shall w their hands ....Ex 30:21
and w them with water.........Ex 40:12
near unto the altar, they w ....Ex 40:32
legs shall he w in water ....Lev 1:9
thou shalt w that whereon .....Lev 6:27
and washed them with w ......Lev 8:6
them shall w his clothes ....Lev 11:25
and he shall w his clothes .....Lev 13:6
plague, after that it is w.......Lev 13:55
somewhat dark after the w ....Lev 13:56
it be, which thou shalt w ......Lev 13:58
to be cleansed shall w his .....Lev 14:8
and w himself in water ....Lev 14:8
and he shall w his clothes .....Lev 14:9
also he shall w his flesh in ....Lev 14:9
house shall w his clothes ......Lev 14:47
issue shall w his clothes ....Lev 15:6
things shall w his clothes ......Lev 15:10
w his clothes and bathe ....Lev 15:13
shall be w with water, and ....Lev 15:17
her bed shall w his clothes ....Lev 15:21
and shall w his clothes ....Lev 15:27
w his flesh with water in ......Lev 16:24
burneth them shall w his ......Lev 16:28
he w them not, nor bathe .....Lev 17:16
let them w their clothes ....Num 8:7
and they w their clothes.......Num 8:21
burneth her shall w his........Num 19:8
himself and w his clothes ......Num 19:19
w your clothes on the ....Num 31:24
w their hands over the ....Deut 21:6
w their feet, and did eat ......Judg 19:21
W thyself therefore, and ......Ruth 3:3
w the feet of the servants 1Sam 25:41
roof he saw a woman w.......2Sam 11:2
down to thy house and w 2Sam 11:8
from the earth, and w 2Sam 12:20
w the chariot in the pool 1Kin 22:38
and they w his armor 1Kin 22:38
w in Jordan seven times.......2Kin 5:10
to thee, W and be clean? 2Kin 5:13
and five on the left to w 2Chr 4:6
burnt offering they w in 2Chr 4:6
one put them off for w........Neh 4:23
thou w away the things ....Job 14:19
I w my steps with butter ......Job 29:6
I will w mine hands in ....Ps 26:6
w my hands in innocency......Ps 73:13
w from their filthiness.........Prov 30:12
which came up from the w ....Song 4:2
I have w my feet; how ....Song 5:3
W you, make you clean ....Is 1:16
Lord shall have w away ....Is 4:4
thou w thee with nitre ....Jer 2:22
thou w in water to supple .....Ezek 16:4
Then w I thee with water .....Ezek 16:9
I throughly w away thy ....Ezek 16:9
for whom thou didst w........Ezek 23:40
anoint thine head, and w......Matt 6:17
except they w their hands .....Mark 7:3
received to hold, as the w.....Mark 7:4

and were *w* their nets ....Luke 5:2
not first *w* before dinner ......Luke 11:38
whom when they had *w* ....Acts 9:37
night, and *w* their stripes ......Acts 16:33
w, but ye are sanctified 1Cor 6:11
cleanse it with the *w* of ....Eph 5:26
she have *w* the saints' feet 1Tim 5:10
and drinks, and divers *w* ......Heb 9:10
sow that was *w* to her 2Pet 2:22
and have *w* their robes ....Rev 7:14

WASHPOT—*a kettle for washing*
Moab described as God's .Ps 60:6-8

WAST—*See* **Introduction**

WASTE—*ruin; destruction*

Objects of:
Cities ....Ezek 19:7
Nations ....Nah 3:7
Captives ....Ps 137:3
Possessions.............Luke 15:13
Temple ....Is 64:11
Church ....Gal 1:13
Parents ....Prov 19:26
Body ....Job 14:10

Caused by:
God's judgments ....Amos 7:9
Unbelief ....Num 14:33
Failure to serve God.....Is 60:12
God's hatred ....Mal 1:3
Squandering ....Luke 15:11-32

State of:
Lamented...............Neh 2:3, 17
To be corrected ....Is 61:4

[*also* **wasted, wasteness, wastes, wasteth, wasting**]
I will make your cities *w* ......Lev 26:31
we have laid them *w* even .....Num 21:30
the Kenite shall be *w* until ....Num 24:22
the men of war were *w* out....Deut 2:14
in the *w* howling wilderness ...Deut 32:10
barrel of meal shall not *w* 1Kin 17:14
And the barrel of meal *w* 1Kin 17:16
to lay *w* fenced cities into 2Kin 19:25
of wickedness *w* them any 1Chr 17:9
w the country of the 1Chr 20:1
former time desolate and *w* ...Job 30:3
laid *w* his dwelling place ......Ps 79:7
destruction that *w* at ....Ps 91:6
will lay it *w*, it shall not.......Is 5:6
be *w* without inhabitant ....Is 6:11
night Ar of Moab is laid *w* ....Is 15:1
night Kir of Moab is laid *w* ...Is 15:1
the river shall be *w* and ....Is 19:5
for your strength is laid *w* .....Is 23:14
The highways lie *w*, the ....Is 33:8
Assyria have laid *w* all the ....Is 37:18
I will make *w* mountains ......Is 42:15
w and thy desolate places .....Is 49:19
comfort all her *w* places.......Is 51:3
ye *w* places of Jerusalem ......Is 52:9
thee shall build the old *w* .....Is 58:12
w and destruction are in ......Is 59:7
w nor destruction within ......Is 60:18
and they made his land *w* .....Jer 2:15
should this city be laid *w*......Jer 27:17
they are *w* and desolate ....Jer 44:6
a reproach, a *w*, and a curse ..Jer 49:13
shall be perpetual *w* ....Jer 49:13
moreover, I will make thee *w* .Ezek 5:14
places..shall be laid *w*.........Ezek 6:6
your altars may be laid *w* .....Ezek 6:6
inhabited shall be laid *w* ......Ezek 12:20
of Egypt utterly *w* and ....Ezek 29:10
the cities that are *w* ....Ezek 30:7
I will make the land *w* ....Ezek 30:12
w of the land of Israel ....Ezek 33:24
to the desolate *w*, and to ......Ezek 36:4
cities, and the *w* shall be ......Ezek 36:33
w and desolate and ruined ....Ezek 36:35
which have been always *w*.....Ezek 38:8
He hath laid my vine *w* ....Joel 1:7
The field is *w*, the land ....Joel 1:10
mourneth, for the corn is *w* ...Joel 1:10
shall build the *w* cities ....Amos 9:14
shall *w* the land of Assyria ....Mic 5:6
is empty, and void, and *w* .....Nah 2:10
a day of *w* and desolation .....Zeph 1:15
I made their streets *w*.........Zeph 3:6
houses, and this house lie *w*? . .Hag 1:4
of mine house that is *w* ....Hag 1:9
To what purpose is this *w*? ....Matt 26:8
was this *w* of the ointment ....Mark 14:4
that he had *w* his goods ....Luke 16:1

WASTER—*one who ravages and plunders*
to him that is a great *w* ....Prov 18:9
created the *w* to destroy ......Is 54:16

WATCH—*attend to; guard; wait for*
The Lord ....Gen 31:49
As guards...............2Kin 11:4-7

[*also* **watched, watches, watcheth, watching, watchings**]
Lord *w* between me and thee . .Gen 31:49
in the morning *w* the Lord ....Ex 14:24
beginning of the middle *w*.....Judg 7:19
had but newly set the *w*.......Judg 7:19
a seat by the wayside *w* 1Sam 4:13
the host in the morning *w* 1Sam 11:11
young man that kept the *w* 2Sam 13:34
keepers of the *w* of the 2Kin 11:5
keep the *w* of the house 2Kin 11:7
Judah came toward the *w* 2Chr 20:24
W ye, and keep them, until ...Ezra 8:29
set a *w* against them day ......Neh 4:9
w of the inhabitants of ....Neh 7:3
over against them in the *w* ....Neh 12:9
thou settest a *w* over me? .....Job 7:12
The wicked *w* the righteous ...Ps 37:32
and they *w* the house to ......Ps 59:*title*
on thee in the night *w* ....Ps 63:6
and as *w* in the night ....Ps 90:4
eyes prevent the night *w* ......Ps 119:148
that *w* for the morning ....Ps 130:6
heareth me *w* daily at my .....Prov 8:34
all that *w* for iniquity ....Is 29:20
w in the watchtower ....Is 21:5
leopard shall *w* over their .....Jer 5:6
All my familiars *w* for my .....Jer 20:10
that like as I have *w* over .....Jer 31:28
I will *w* over them for evil ....Jer 44:27
beginning of the *w* pour.......Lam 2:19
in our *w* we have *w* for a .....Lam 4:17
the end is come: it *w* for ......Ezek 7:6
a *w* and an holy one came ....Dan 4:13
is by the decree of the *w*......Dan 4:17
the king saw a *w* and ....Dan 4:23
the Lord *w* upon the evil......Dan 9:14
w the way, make thy loins ....Nah 2:1
I will stand upon my *w* ....Hab 2:1
w to see what he will say .....Hab 2:1
w of the night Jesus went .....Matt 14:25
tarry ye here, and *w* with me . .Matt 26:38
W and pray, that ye enter .....Matt 26:41
sitting down they *w* him.......Matt 27:36
were with him *w* Jesus ....Matt 27:54
the stone, and setting a *w* .....Matt 27:66
they *w* him, whether he ....Mark 3:2
the fourth *w* of the night ......Mark 6:48
commanded the porter to *w* ...Mark 13:34
unto you I say unto all, *W* ....Mark 13:37
not thou *w* one hour?.........Mark 14:37
keeping *w* over their flock.....Luke 2:8
scribes and Pharisees *w* ....Luke 6:7
he cometh shall find *w*........Luke 12:37
shall come in the second *w* ....Luke 12:38
or come in the third *w* ....Luke 12:38
sabbath day, that they *w* ......Luke 14:1
they *w* the gates day and ......Acts 9:24
in tumults, in labors, in *w* 2Cor 6:5
painfulness, in *w* often 2Cor 11:27
w in the same with ....Col 4:2
but let us *w* and be sober 1Thess 5:6
But *w* thou in all things 2Tim 4:5
sober and *w* unto prayer 1Pet 4:7
therefore thou shalt not *w*......Rev 3:3
Blessed is he that *w*, and......Rev 16:15

WATCHER—*lookout; scout*

[*also* **watchers**]
w come from a far country ....Jer 4:16
a *w* and a holy one came .....Dan 4:13
the king saw a *w* and ....Dan 4:23

WATCHES OF DAY, NIGHT—*designated periods of time*
Jesus walks on water ....Matt 14:25
Time of coming ....Matt 24:43
Luke 12:37, 38

WATCHFUL—*spiritually alert*

Required in:
Prayer..................Eph 6:18
Daily living 1Cor 16:13
Time of testing..........Luke 21:34-36
Waiting Christ's return ...Matt 24:42-51
Matt 25:13

Against:
False teachers ....Acts 20:29-31
Our words ....Ps 141:3
Failure ....Heb 12:15
Temptation ....Mark 14:38

Be *w*, and strengthen the .....Rev 3:2

WATCHMAN—*one who keeps watch; a guard*

[*also* **watchman's, watchmen**]
w of Saul in Gibeah of........1Sam 14:16
the *w* went up to the roof 2Sam 18:24
the *w* saw another man 2Sam 18:26
w called unto the porter 2Sam 18:26
stood a *w* on the tower in 2Kin 9:17
And the *w* told, saying, He ...2Kin 9:20
from the tower of the *w*.......2Kin 17:9
The *w* that go about the ......Song 3:3
set a *w*, let him declare ....Is 21:6
Thy *w* shall lift up the ....Is 52:8
have set *w* upon thy walls .....Is 62:6
I set *w* over you, saying, ...Jer 6:17
watch strong, set up the *w* ....Jer 51:12
I require at the *w* hand ....Ezek 33:6
w of Ephraim was with my ....Hos 9:8
the day of thy *w* and thy......Mic 7:4

WATCHMEN, SPIRITUAL—*those who guard spiritual truths*
Set by God ....Is 62:6
Message to.............Is 21:11, 12
Responsibility of ....Ezek 33:1-9
Some are faithful........Ezek 3:17-21
Some are faithless ....Is 56:10
In vain without the Lord .Ps 127:1
Leaders in the church....Heb 13:17

WATCHTOWER—*a guard tower*
table, watch in the *w*, eat .....Is 21:5
continually upon the *w* in .....Is 21:8

WATER—*a colorless liquid; to moisten; sprinkle*

Described as:
Living ....Jer 2:13
Cold ....Jer 18:14
Still ....Ps 23:2
Deep ....Ps 69:2, 14
Standing ....Ps 107:35
Mighty ....Is 28:2

God's control over, He:
Creates ....Gen 1:2, 6, 7
Gives...................Ps 104:13
Blesses the earth with....Is 55:10
Withholds...............Is 50:2
Reveals His wonders in ..Ps 107:23-32
Sets bounds to ....Ps 104:5-9

Miracles connected with:
Changed into blood......Ex 7:17-25
Divided.................Ex 14:21-29
Bitter made sweet ....Ex 15:22-25
From a rock ....Ex 17:1-7
Jordan divided ....Josh 3:14-17
From a jawbone.........Judg 15:17-19
Consumed by fire 1Kin 18:38
Valley, full of 2Kin 3:16-24
Axe floats on 2Kin 6:5-7

Christ walks on ....Mark 6:49-52
Changed into wine ....John 2:1-11
Healing of 2Kin 2:19-22

Normal uses of, for:

Drinking ....Gen 24:43
Washing ....Gen 18:4
Animals ....Ps 42:1
Vegetation ....Deut 11:10, 11
Sea creatures ....Ps 104:25, 26

Special uses of, for:

Ordination ....Ex 30:18-20
Cleansing ....Ex 40:7-32
Purification ....Ex 19:10
Baptism ....Acts 8:36-39
Sanctification ....Eph 5:26
Business ....Ps 107:23

Figurative of:

Instability ....Gen 49:4
Cowardice ....Josh 7:5
Spiritual growth ....Ps 1:3
Peace ....Ps 23:2
Afflictions ....Is 43:2
Persecution ....Ps 124:4, 5
Adultery ....Prov 9:17
Universal Gospel ....Is 11:9
Salvation ....Is 55:1
Gospel age ....Is 41:17-20
Holy Spirit ....Ezek 47:1-12
Eternal life ....Rev 22:17
Christ ....John 4:10-15
Regeneration ....John 7:37, 38

Cure for:

Doubting captain 2Kin 5:1-15
Afflicted ....John 5:1-7
Blind man ....John 9:6-11

Used for a test:

By Gideon ....Judg 7:4-7

Conduit:

Hezekiah builds 2Kin 20:20

[*also* WATERS]

Let the *w* under the heaven ...Gen 1:9
of the *w* called he Seas ....Gen 1:10
w bring forth abundantly ....Gen 1:20
the *w* brought forth ....Gen 1:21
and fill the *w* in the seas ....Gen 1:22
flood of *w* upon the earth ....Gen 6:17
flood of *w* was upon the ....Gen 7:6
the *w* of the flood were ....Gen 7:10
w prevailed and were ....Gen 7:18
went upon the face of the *w* ...Gen 7:18
upward did the *w* prevail ....Gen 7:20
earth and the *w* assuaged ....Gen 8:1
w returned from off the ....Gen 8:3
days the *w* were abated ....Gen 8:3
until the *w* were dried up ....Gen 8:7
the *w* were on the face of ....Gen 8:9
w were dried up from off ....Gen 8:13
w shall no more become a ....Gen 9:15
her by a fountain of *w* in ....Gen 16:7
bread, and a bottle of *w* ....Gen 21:14
and she saw a well of *w* ....Gen 21:19
filled the bottle with *w* ....Gen 21:19
by a well of *w* at the time ....Gen 24:11
women go out to draw *w* ....Gen 24:11
stand here by the well of *w* ...Gen 24:13
city come out to draw *w* ....Gen 24:13
and *w* to wash his feet ....Gen 24:32
there a well of springing *w* ....Gen 26:19
unto him, We have found *w* ...Gen 26:32
that well they *w* the flocks ....Gen 29:2
gutters in the *w* troughs ....Gen 30:38
and gave them *w* and they ....Gen 43:24
I drew him out of the *w* ....Ex 2:10
and they came and drew *w* ....Ex 2:16
take of the *w* of the river ....Ex 4:9
the *w* which thou takest ....Ex 4:9
lo, he goeth out unto the *w* ...Ex 7:15
hand over the *w* of Egypt ....Ex 8:6
he cometh forth to the *w* ....Ex 8:20
nor sodden at all with *w* ....Ex 12:9
w were gathered together ....Ex 15:8
sank as lead in the mighty *w* ..Ex 15:10
again the *w* of the sea ....Ex 15:19
were twelve wells of *w* ....Ex 15:27
encamped there by the *w* ....Ex 15:27
in the *w* under the earth ....Ex 20:4
bless thy bread, and thy *w* ....Ex 23:25
shalt wash them with *w* ....Ex 29:4
and strawed it upon the *w* ....Ex 32:20
eat bread, nor drink *w* ....Ex 34:28
legs shall he wash in *w* ....Lev 1:9
scoured, and rinsed in *w* ....Lev 6:28
inwards and the legs in *w* ....Lev 8:21
eat of all that are in the *w* ....Lev 11:9
fins and scales in the *w* in ....Lev 11:9
of all that move in the *w* ....Lev 11:10
thing which is in the *w* ....Lev 11:10
on which such *w* cometh ....Lev 11:34
w be put upon the seed ....Lev 11:38
creature..moveth in the *w* ....Lev 11:46
killed over the running *w* ....Lev 14:6
he shall wash his flesh in *w* ....Lev 14:9
in the running *w* and ....Lev 14:51
with the running *w*, and ....Lev 14:52
not rinsed his hands in *w* ....Lev 15:11
and bathe himself in *w* ....Lev 15:11
his flesh in running *w* ....Lev 15:13
shall be washed with *w* ....Lev 15:17
both bathe themselves in *w* ....Lev 15:18
shall he wash his flesh in *w* ....Lev 16:4
and bathe his flesh in *w* ....Lev 16:26
he wash his flesh with *w* ....Lev 22:6
priest shall take holy *w* in ....Num 5:17
take, and put it into the *w* ....Num 5:17
free from this bitter *w* ....Num 5:19
them out with the bitter *w* ....Num 5:23
to drink the bitter *w* ....Num 5:24
w that causeth the curse ....Num 5:24
made her to drink the *w* ....Num 5:27
w that causeth the curse ....Num 5:27
shall bathe his flesh in *w* ....Num 19:7
shall wash his clothes in *w* ....Num 19:8
bathe his flesh in *w*, and ....Num 19:8
w of separation was not ....Num 19:13
hyssop and dip it in the *w* ....Num 19:18
the *w* of separation hath ....Num 19:20
that sprinkleth the *w* of ....Num 19:21
that toucheth the *w* of ....Num 19:21
is there any *w* to drink ....Num 20:5
it shall give forth his *w* ....Num 20:8
to them *w* out of the rock ....Num 20:8
w came out abundantly ....Num 20:11
drink of the *w* of the wells ....Num 20:17
word at the *w* of Meribah ....Num 20:24
and I will give them *w* ....Num 21:16
will not drink of the *w* of ....Num 21:22
as cedar trees beside the *w* ....Num 24:6
sanctify me at the *w* before ....Num 27:14
w of Meribah in Kadesh ....Num 27:14
purified with the *w* of ....Num 31:23
make go through the *w* ....Num 31:23
was no *w* for the people to ....Num 33:14
buy *w* of them for money ....Deut 2:6
in the *w* beneath the earth ....Deut 4:18
in the *w* beneath the earth ....Deut 5:8
a land of brooks and *w* ....Deut 8:7
where there was no *w* ....Deut 8:15
w out of the rock of flint ....Deut 8:15
did eat bread nor drink *w* ....Deut 9:9
a land of rivers of *w* ....Deut 10:7
made the *w* of the Red Sea ...Deut 11:4
eat of all that are in the *w* ....Deut 14:9
it upon the ground as *w* ....Deut 15:23
not with bread and with *w* ....Deut 23:4
shall wash himself with *w* ....Deut 23:11
the *w* of Meribah-Kadesh ....Deut 32:51
strive at the *w* of Meribah ....Deut 33:8
dried up the *w* of the Red ....Josh 2:10
brink of the *w* of Jordan ....Josh 3:8
rest in the *w* of the Jordan ....Josh 3:13
w of the Jordan shall be ....Josh 3:13
from the *w* that come down ...Josh 3:13
w of Jordan were cut off ....Josh 4:7
God dried up the *w* of ....Josh 4:23
Lord had dried up the *w* ....Josh 5:1
and drawers of *w* unto all ....Josh 9:21
of *w* for the congregation ....Josh 9:27
together at the *w* of Merom ...Josh 11:5
the well of *w* of En-shemesh ..Josh 15:7
give me also springs of *w* ....Josh 15:19
the well of *w* of Nephtoah ....Josh 18:15
give me also springs of *w* ....Judg 1:15
the clouds also dropped *w* ....Judg 5:4
by the *w* of Megiddo ....Judg 5:19
He asked *w*, and she gave ....Judg 5:25
the fleece, a bowl full of *w* ....Judg 6:38
the *w* unto Beth-barah ....Judg 7:24
drew *w*, and poured it out 1Sam 7:6
take my bread, and my *w* 1Sam 25:11
the cruse of *w* from Saul's 1Sam 26:12
they made him drink *w* 1Sam 30:11
me, as the breach of *w* 2Sam 5:20
have taken the city of *w* 2Sam 12:27
as *w* spilt on the ground 2Sam 14:14
pass quickly over the *w* 2Sam 17:21
dark *w*, and thick clouds 2Sam 22:12
of the *w* of the well of 2Sam 23:15
nor drink *w* in this place 1Kin 13:8
I eat bread nor drink *w* 1Kin 13:16
eat bread and drink *w* 1Kin 13:18
eaten bread and drunk *w* 1Kin 13:22
no bread, and drink no *w* 1Kin 13:22
I pray thee, a little *w* in 1Kin 17:10
unto all fountains of *w* 1Kin 18:5
Fill four barrels with *w* 1Kin 18:33
the *w* ran round about the 1Kin 18:35
the trench also with *w* 1Kin 18:35
a cruse of *w* at his head 1Kin 19:6
and with *w* of affliction 1Kin 22:27
smote the *w*, and they were ...2Kin 2:8
and smote the *w*, and said 2Kin 2:14
he also had smitten the *w* 2Kin 2:14
was no *w* for the host 2Kin 3:9
w on the hands of Elijah 2Kin 3:11
stopped all the wells of *w* 2Kin 3:25
set bread and *w* before 2Kin 6:22
cloth, and dipped it in *w* 2Kin 8:15
one the *w* of his cistern 2Kin 18:31
digged and drunk strange *w* ...2Kin 19:24
of the *w* of the well of 1Chr 11:17
the breaking forth of *w* 1Chr 14:11
and with *w* of affliction 2Chr 18:26
men to stop the *w* of the 2Chr 32:3
eat no bread, nor drink *w* ....Ezra 10:6
against the *w* gate toward ....Neh 3:26
that was before the *w* gate ....Neh 8:3
stone into the mighty *w* ....Neh 9:11
w for them out of the rock ....Neh 9:15
unto the *w* gate eastward ....Neh 12:37
are poured out like the *w* ....Job 3:24
the flag grow without *w*? ....Job 8:11
it as *w* that pass away ....Job 11:16
through the scent of *w* it ....Job 14:9
As the *w* fail from the sea ....Job 14:11
not given *w* to the weary to ...Job 22:7
and abundance of *w* cover ....Job 22:11
heat consume the snow *w* ....Job 24:19
He bindeth up the *w* in his ....Job 26:8
take hold on him as *w* ....Job 27:20
the *w* forgotten of the foot ....Job 28:4
was spread out by the *w* ....Job 29:19
as a wide breaking in of *w* ....Job 30:14
small the drops of *w* ....Job 36:27
of the *w* is straitened ....Job 37:10
by *w* he wearieth the thick ....Job 37:11
for the overflowing of *w* ....Job 38:25
abundance of *w* may cover ....Job 38:34
about him were dark *w* ....Ps 18:11
drew me out of many *w* ....Ps 18:16
I am poured out like *w* ....Ps 22:14
voice..is upon the *w* ....Ps 29:3
in the floods of great *w* ....Ps 32:6
He gathereth the *w* of ....Ps 33:7
Though the *w* thereof ....Ps 46:3
Let them melt away as *w* ....Ps 58:7
land, where no *w* is ....Ps 63:1
which is full of *w* ....Ps 65:9
through fire and through *w* ....Ps 66:12
the *w* are come in unto ....Ps 69:1
and out of the deep *w* ....Ps 69:14
of the dragons in the *w* ....Ps 74:13
The clouds poured out *w* ....Ps 77:17
thy path in the great *w* ....Ps 77:19

caused *w* to run down ... Ps 78:16
thee at the *w* of Meribah ... Ps 81:7
about me daily like *w* ... Ps 88:17
his chambers in the *w* ... Ps 104:3
He turned their *w* into ... Ps 105:29
w covered their enemies ... Ps 106:11
into his bowels like *w* ... Ps 109:18
flint into a fountain of *w* ... Ps 114:8
Rivers of *w* run down ... Ps 119:136
the earth above the *w* ... Ps 136:6
deliver me out of great *w* ... Ps 144:7
ye *w* that be above the ... Ps 148:4
Drink *w* out of thine own ... Prov 5:15
w out of thine own well ... Prov 5:15
fountains abounding with *w* ... Prov 8:24
the *w* should not pass ... Prov 8:29
mouth are as deep *w* ... Prov 18:4
of man is like deep *w* ... Prov 20:5
give him *w* to drink ... Prov 25:21
the *w* in a garment? ... Prov 30:4
earth..not filled with *w* ... Prov 30:16
I made me pools of *w* ... Eccl 2:6
Cast thy bread upon the *w* ... Eccl 11:1
a well of living *w* and ... Song 4:15
Many *w* cannot quench love ... Song 8:7
thy wine mixed with *w* ... Is 1:22
and the whole stay of *w* ... Is 3:1
the *w* of Shiloah that go ... Is 8:6
them the *w* of the river ... Is 8:7
draw *w* out of the wells of ... Is 12:3
bittern, and pools of *w* ... Is 14:23
the *w* of Nimrim shall be ... Is 15:6
the rushing of mighty *w* ... Is 17:12
bulrushes upon the *w* ... Is 18:2
spread nets upon the *w* ... Is 19:8
brought *w* to him that ... Is 21:14
And by great *w* the seed ... Is 23:3
w shall overflow the ... Is 28:17
and the *w* of affliction ... Is 30:20
ye that sow beside all *w* ... Is 32:20
wilderness shall *w* break ... Is 35:6
thirsty land springs of *w* ... Is 35:7
measured the *w* in the ... Is 40:12
a path in the mighty *w* ... Is 43:16
pour *w* upon him that is ... Is 44:3
he drinketh no *w*, and is ... Is 44:12
out of the *w* of Judah ... Is 48:1
Caused the *w* to flow out ... Is 48:21
rock also, and the *w* gushed ... Is 48:21
by the springs of *w* shall ... Is 49:10
this is as the *w* of Noah ... Is 54:9
the *w* of Noah should no ... Is 54:9
whose *w* cast up mire and ... Is 57:20
shalt be like a *w* garden ... Is 58:11
like a spring of *w*, whose *w* ... Is 58:11
fire causeth the *w* to boil ... Is 64:2
to drink the *w* of Sihor? ... Jer 2:18
drink the *w* of the river? ... Jer 2:18
us *w* of gall to drink ... Jer 8:14
Oh that my head were *w* ... Jer 9:1
is a multitude of *w* in the ... Jer 10:13
loins and put it not in *w* ... Jer 13:1
a liar, and as *w* that fail? ... Jer 15:18
the fountain of living *w* ... Jer 17:13
them drink the *w* of gall ... Jer 23:15
to walk by the rivers of *w* ... Jer 31:9
soul shall be as a *w* garden ... Jer 31:12
whose *w* are moved as the ... Jer 46:7
w rise up out of the north ... Jer 47:2
A drought is upon her *w* ... Jer 50:38
of *w* in the heavens ... Jer 51:16
eye runneth down with *w* ... Lam 1:16
down with rivers of *w* ... Lam 3:48
W flowed over mine head ... Lam 3:54
like the noise of great *w* ... Ezek 1:24
drink also *w* by measure ... Ezek 4:11
may want bread and *w* ... Ezek 4:17
drink thy *w* with trembling ... Ezek 12:18
wast thou washed in *w* to ... Ezek 16:4
in a good soil by great *w* ... Ezek 17:8
blood, planted by the *w* ... Ezek 19:10
by reason of many *w* ... Ezek 19:10
and also pour *w* into it ... Ezek 24:3
brought thee into great *w* ... Ezek 27:26
The *w* made him great ... Ezek 31:4
his root was by great *w* ... Ezek 31:7
height all that drink *w* ... Ezek 31:14
the great *w* were stayed ... Ezek 31:15
from beside the great *w* ... Ezek 32:13
have drunk of the deep *w* ... Ezek 34:18
like a noise of many *w* ... Ezek 43:2
their *w* they issued out ... Ezek 47:12
even to the *w* of strife in ... Ezek 47:19
unto the *w* of strife in ... Ezek 48:28
to eat and *w* to drink ... Dan 1:12
was upon the *w* of the ... Dan 12:6
me my bread and my *w* ... Hos 2:5
as the foam upon the *w* ... Hos 10:7
for the rivers of *w* are ... Joel 1:20
Judah shall flow with *w* ... Joel 3:18
unto one city, to drink *w* ... Amos 4:8
that calleth for the *w* ... Amos 5:8
judgment run down as *w* ... Amos 5:24
he that calleth for the *w* ... Amos 9:6
The *w* compassed me about ... Jon 2:5
not feed, nor drink *w* ... Jon 3:7
as the *w* that are poured ... Mic 1:4
is of old like a pool of *w* ... Nah 2:8
that had the *w* round it ... Nah 3:8
Draw thee *w* for the siege ... Nah 3:14
as the *w* cover the sea ... Hab 2:14
overflowing of the *w* ... Hab 3:10
the heap of great *w* ... Hab 3:15
the pit wherein is no *w* ... Zech 9:11
w shall go out from ... Zech 14:8
baptize you with *w* unto ... Matt 3:11
up straightway out of the *w* ... Matt 3:16
and perished in the *w* ... Matt 8:32
little ones a cup of cold *w* ... Matt 10:42
come unto thee on the *w* ... Matt 14:28
he walked on the *w* to go ... Matt 14:29
fire and oft into the *w* ... Matt 17:15
took *w*, and washed his ... Matt 27:24
have baptized you with *w* ... Mark 1:8
coming up out of the *w* ... Mark 1:10
the fire, and into the *w* ... Mark 9:22
a cup of *w* to drink in my ... Mark 9:41
bearing a pitcher of *w* ... Mark 14:13
I indeed baptize you with *w* ... Luke 3:16
thou gavest me no *w* for ... Luke 7:44
they were filled with *w* ... Luke 8:23
and the raging of the *w* ... Luke 8:24
even the winds and *w* ... Luke 8:25
and lead him away to *w*? ... Luke 13:15
the tip of his finger in *w* ... Luke 16:24
bearing a pitcher of *w* ... Luke 22:10
saying, I baptize with *w* ... John 1:26
sent me to baptize with *w* ... John 1:33
a man be born of *w* and ... John 3:5
there was much *w* there ... John 3:23
woman of Samaria to draw *w* ... John 4:7
where he made the *w* wine ... John 4:46
poureth *w* into a basin ... John 13:5
came there out blood and *w* ... John 19:34
John truly baptized with *w* ... Acts 1:5
Can any man forbid *w* ... Acts 10:47
John indeed baptized with *w* ... Acts 11:16
any thing neither he that *w* ... 1Cor 3:7
planteth and he that *w* ... 1Cor 3:8
perils of *w*, in perils of ... 2Cor 11:26
Drink no longer *w* but ... 1Tim 5:23
calves and of goats, with *w* ... Heb 9:19
bodies washed with pure *w* ... Heb 10:22
the same place sweet *w* ... James 3:11
yield salt *w* and fresh ... James 3:12
souls were saved by *w* ... 1Pet 3:20
These are wells without *w* ... 2Pet 2:17
standing out of the *w* and ... 2Pet 3:5
being overflowed with *w* ... 2Pet 3:6
that came by *w* and blood ... 1John 5:6
not by *w* only but by *w* ... 1John 5:6
the spirit and the *w* ... 1John 5:8
clouds they are without *w* ... Jude 12
as the sound of many *w* ... Rev 1:15
unto living fountains of *w* ... Rev 7:17
upon the fountains of *w* ... Rev 8:10
the third part of the *w* ... Rev 8:11
many men died of the *w* ... Rev 8:11
have power over *w* to turn ... Rev 11:6
his mouth *w* as a flood ... Rev 12:15
as the voice of many *w* ... Rev 14:2
and the fountains of *w* ... Rev 14:7
rivers and fountains of *w* ... Rev 16:4
heard the angel of the *w* ... Rev 16:5
w thereof was dried up ... Rev 16:12
that sitteth upon many *w* ... Rev 17:1
w which thou sawest, where ... Rev 17:15
as the voice of many *w* ... Rev 19:6
fountain of the *w* of life ... Rev 21:6
a pure river of *w* of life ... Rev 22:1

WATER—*to supply with water*

[*also* WATERED, WATEREST, WATERETH]
w the whole face of the ... Gen 2:6
of Eden to *w* the garden ... Gen 2:10
mouth; then we *w* the sheep ... Gen 29:8
w the flock of Laban his ... Gen 29:10
troughs to *w* their father's ... Ex 2:16
them, and *w* their flock ... Ex 2:17
I *w* my couch with my tears ... Ps 6:6
visitest the earth and *w* it ... Ps 65:9
Thou *w* the ridges thereof ... Ps 65:10
and he that *w* shall be *w* ... Prov 11:25
to *w* therewith the wood ... Eccl 2:6
w thee with my tears ... Is 16:9
I will *w* it every moment ... Is 27:3
he might *w* it by the ... Ezek 17:7
also *w* with thy blood the ... Ezek 32:6
w the valley of Shittim ... Joel 3:18
have planted, Apollos *w* ... 1Cor 3:6

WATER AND BLOOD
A mixture that flowed from the body of Christ ... John 19:34

WATER BASIN—*a bowl for carrying water*
Christ uses ... John 13:5

WATER CARRIERS—*those whose responsibility it was to provide water to a household or institution*
Task of young maidens ... 1Sam 9:11
And of older women ... John 4:7, 28

WATER GATE—*a gate of Jerusalem*
Law is read there ... Neh 8:1, 2

WATERCOURSE—*a channel through which water flows*
the upper *w* of Gihon ... 2Chr 32:30
w for the overflowing of ... Job 38:25

WATERFLOOD—*flood*
Let not the *w* overflow ... Ps 69:15

WATERPOT—*container for holding or transporting water*

[*also* WATERPOTS]
set there six *w* of stone ... John 2:6
Fill the *w* with water ... John 2:7
woman then left her *w* ... John 4:28

WATERPROOFING—*making vessels watertight*

By means of:
Pitch ... Gen 6:14
Slime and pitch ... Ex 2:3

WATERSPOUTS—*waterfalls; cataracts*
at the noise of thy *w* ... Ps 42:7

WATERSPRINGS—*natural springs*
the *w* into dry ground ... Ps 107:33

WAVE—*to move back and forth (applied to sacrifices); a moving ridge or swell on water*

[*also* WAVED, WAVES]
w them for a *w* offering ... Ex 29:24
w it for a *w* offering ... Ex 29:26
heave offering, which is *w* ... Ex 29:27
the breast may be *w* for ... Lev 7:30
for a *w* offering before ... Lev 7:30
for a *w* offering before ... Lev 8:27
w it for a *w* offering before ... Lev 8:29
w for a *w* offering before ... Lev 9:21
w breast shall they bring ... Lev 10:15
w it for a *w* offering ... Lev 10:15
w them for a *w* offering ... Lev 14:12
trespass offering to be *w* ... Lev 14:21

w them for a w offering before . Lev 14:24
w the sheaf before the . . . . Lev 23:11
the priest shall w it . . . . Lev 23:11
sheaf of the w offering . . . . Lev 23:15
w them with the bread . . . . Lev 23:20
for a w offering before . . . . Lev 23:20
w the offering before . . . . Num 5:25
w them for a w offering . . . . Num 6:20
the w offerings of the . . . . Num 18:11
the w of death compassed 2Sam 22:5
treadeth upon the w of . . . . Job 9:8
all thy w and thy billows . . . . . . Ps 42:7
afflicted me with all thy w . . . . . Ps 88:7
the floods lift up their w . . . . . . Ps 93:3
which lifteth up the w . . . . Ps 107:25
as the w of the sea . . . . Is 48:18
the w thereof toss themselves . . Jer 5:22
the multitude of the w . . . . Jer 51:42
the sea causeth his w to . . . . Ezek 26:3
billows and thy w passed . . . . . . Jon 2:3
smite the w in the sea . . . . Zech 10:11
was covered with the w . . . . Matt 8:24
the sea, tossed with w . . . . Matt 14:24
sea and the w roaring . . . . Luke 21:25
with the violence of the w . . . . . Acts 27:41
Raging w of the sea, foaming . . Jude 13

WAVERING—*vascillating irresolutely*

Between:

God and idols 1Ki 18:19-40
Faith and doubt . . . . Jas 1:5-8
Truth and error 1John 4:1-6
Gospel and rituals . . . . Gal 5:1-10

Admonition against:

"Be ye steadfast" 1Cor 15:58
"Be strong in the Lord" . Eph 6:10-17
"Hold fast" . . . . Heb 3:6, 14

of our faith without w . . . . Heb 10:23

WAX—*beeswax*

Figurative of persecution . . Ps 22:14
Of the wicked before God . . . . Ps 68:2
Of the mountains . . . . Ps 97:5

WAX—*to grow; increase*

Of material things:

Power 2Sam 3:1
Prestige . . . . Esth 9:4
Age . . . . Josh 23:1
Sound . . . . Ex 19:19

Of immaterial things:

Courage . . . . Heb 11:34
Spirituality . . . . Luke 2:40
God's hand . . . . Num 11:23
Old covenant . . . . Heb 8:13
God's kingdom . . . . Luke 13:18, 19

[*also* WAXED, WAXEN, WAXETH, WAXING]

After I am w old shall I . . . . Gen 18:12
cry of them is w great . . . . Gen 19:13
And the man w great, and . . . . Gen 26:13
the famine w sore in the . . . . . . Gen 41:56
multiplied and w exceeding . . . . Ex 1:7
when the sun w hot, it . . . . Ex 16:21
long and w louder and . . . . Ex 19:19
my wrath shall w hot . . . . Ex 22:24
why doth thy wrath w hot . . . . . Ex 32:11
Moses' anger w hot . . . . Ex 32:19
If thy brother be w poor . . . . . . Lev 25:25
by thee be w poor . . . . Lev 25:39
or stranger w rich . . . . Lev 25:47
dwelleth by him w poor . . . . Lev 25:47
Thy raiment w not old . . . . Deut 8:4
clothes are not w old . . . . Deut 29:5
thy shoe is not w old . . . . Deut 29:5
filled themselves, and w fat . . . . Deut 31:20
But Jeshurun w fat and . . . . Deut 32:15
thou art w fat, thou art . . . . Deut 32:15
of Israel were w strong . . . . Josh 17:13
children is w feeble 1Sam 2:5
his eyes began to w dim 1Sam 3:2
and David w faint 2Sam 21:15
flesh of the child w warm 2Kin 4:34
So David w greater and 1Chr 11:9
Abijah w mighty and 2Chr 13:21
And Jehoshaphat w great 2Chr 17:12
Jehoiada w old and was 2Chr 24:15
their clothes w not old . . . . Neh 9:21
What time they w warm . . . . . . Job 6:17
it w old because of all . . . . Ps 6:7
bones w old through my . . . . . . Ps 32:3
all of them shall w old . . . . Ps 102:26
of his flesh shall w lean . . . . . . Is 17:4
they all shall w old as a . . . . Is 50:9
become great and w rich . . . . . . Jer 5:27
our hands w feeble . . . . Jer 6:24
Damascus is w feeble . . . . Jer 49:24
increased and w great . . . . Ezek 16:7
the he goat w very great . . . . . . Dan 8:8
it w great, even to the . . . . Dan 8:10
as w before the fire . . . . Mic 1:4
people's heart is w gross . . . . . . Matt 13:15
love of many shall w cold . . . . . Matt 24:12
child grew, and w strong . . . . . . Luke 1:80
bags which w not old . . . . Luke 12:33
Paul and Barnabas w bold . . . . . Acts 13:46
of this people is w gross . . . . Acts 28:27
w confident by my bonds . . . . . . Phil 1:14
w wanton against Christ 1Tim 5:11
seducers shall w worse 2Tim 3:13
all shall w old as doth a . . . . Heb 1:11
of the earth are w rich . . . . Rev 18:3

WAY—*route; course of action*

[*also* WAYS]

up early, and go on your w . . . Gen 19:2
do any w hide their eyes . . . . . . Lev 20:4
if he shall any w make them . . . Num 30:15
flee before thee seven w . . . . . . Deut 28:7
and flee seven w before . . . . Deut 28:25
sons walked not in his w 1Sam 8:3
behaved..in all his w 1Sam 18:14
man according to his w 1Kin 8:39
he walked in all the w of 1Kin 22:43
Turn ye from your evil w 2Kin 17:13
according unto all his w 2Chr 6:30
turn from their wicked w 2Chr 7:14
first w of his father David 2Chr 17:3
walked in the w of 2Chr 21:12
nor in the w of Asa king 2Chr 21:12
prepared his w before the 2Chr 27:6
in the w of the kings of 2Chr 28:2
any w able to deliver their 2Chr 32:13
the uprightness of thy w . . . . . . Job 4:6
not the knowledge of thy w . . . Job 21:14
shall shine upon thy w . . . . Job 22:28
his eyes are upon their w . . . . . Job 24:23
the w of their destruction . . . . . Job 30:12
to find according to his w . . . . . Job 34:11
not consider any of his w . . . . . Job 34:27
His w are always grievous . . . . . Ps 10:5
heart are the w of them . . . . Ps 84:5
I thought on my w, and . . . . Ps 119:59
aside unto the crooked w . . . . . Ps 125:5
the w of every one that is . . . . . Prov 1:19
Whose w are crooked, and . . . . Prov 2:15
w are w of pleasantness . . . . Prov 3:17
all thy w be established . . . . . . Prov 4:26
the w of man are before the . . . Prov 5:21
heart decline to her w . . . . Prov 7:25
go right on their w . . . . Prov 9:15
that is perverse in his w . . . . Prov 14:2
be filled with his own w . . . . Prov 14:14
When a man's w please . . . . Prov 16:7
pervert the w of judgment . . . . . Prov 17:23
Lest thou learn his w, and . . . . Prov 22:25
that is perverse in his w . . . . Prov 28:6
nor thy w to that which . . . . Prov 31:3
and walk in the w of thine . . . . Eccl 11:9
in the broad w I will seek . . . . . Song 3:2
he will teach us of his w . . . . . . Is 2:3
and I will direct all his w . . . . . . Is 45:13
They shall feed in the w . . . . . . Is 49:9
I have seen his w, and will . . . . Is 57:18
not doing thine own w, nor . . . Is 58:13
dromedary traversing her w . . . Jer 2:23
in the w hast thou sat for . . . . . Jer 3:2
Stand ye in the w, and see . . . . Jer 6:16
amend your w and your . . . . Jer 7:5
diligently learn the w of . . . . Jer 12:16
eyes are upon all their w . . . . . . Jer 16:17
and make your w and your . . . . Jer 18:11
slippery w in the darkness . . . . . Jer 23:12
all the w of the sons of . . . . Jer 32:19
one according to his w . . . . Jer 32:19
The w of Zion do mourn . . . . . . Lam 1:4
He hath turned aside my w . . . . Lam 3:11
judge..according to thy w . . . . . Ezek 7:3
judge..according to thy w . . . . . Ezek 7:8
ye see their w and their . . . . Ezek 14:23
not walked after their w . . . . . . Ezek 16:47
than they in all thy w . . . . Ezek 16:47
should return from his w . . . . . . Ezek 18:23
are not your w unequal? . . . . . . Ezek 18:29
shall ye remember your w . . . . . Ezek 20:43
of man, appoint thee two w . . . Ezek 21:19
according to thy w, and . . . . Ezek 24:14
turn ye from your evil w . . . . . . Ezek 33:11
remember your own evil w . . . . . Ezek 36:31
confounded for your own w . . . Ezek 36:32
whose are all thy w, hast . . . . . . Dan 5:23
punish them for their w . . . . Hos 4:9
snare of a fowler in all his w . . Hos 9:8
march every one on his w . . . . . Joel 2:7
another in the broad w . . . . Nah 2:4
of hosts; Consider your w . . . . . Hag 1:5
Turn..from your evil w . . . . Zech 1:4
went their w into the city . . . . . Matt 8:33
in a place where two w met . . . Mark 11:4
the Lord to prepare his w . . . . . . Luke 1:76
Go your w: behold, I send . . . . Luke 10:3
them went their w to the . . . . . . John 11:46
known to me the w of life . . . . . Acts 2:28
to walk in their own w . . . . Acts 14:16
and misery are in their w . . . . . Rom 3:16
of my w which be in Christ 1Cor 4:17
is unstable in all his w . . . . James 1:8
man fade away in his w . . . . James 1:11
follow their pernicious w 2Pet 2:2
Go your w, and pour out . . . . . Rev 16:1
See HIGHWAY; PATH

WAY, CHRIST AS THE

Leading to Father . . . . John 14:6

WAY, GOD'S

Right . . . . Hos 14:9
Just . . . . Dan 4:37
True . . . . Rev 15:3
Higher than man's . . . . Is 55:8, 9
Unsearchable . . . . Rom 11:33

[*also* WAYS]

walk in all the w which the . . . . Deut 5:33
to walk in all his w, and to . . . . Deut 10:12
and to walk ever in his w . . . . . Deut 19:9
to walk in his w, and . . . . Deut 30:16
to walk in all his w, and . . . . . . Josh 22:5
For I have kept the w of 2Sam 22:22
to walk in his w, to keep 1Kin 2:3
have not walked in my w 1Kin 11:33
Show me thy w, O Lord . . . . . . Ps 25:4
teach transgressors thy w . . . . . . Ps 51:13
Israel had walked in my w . . . . . Ps 81:13
they have not known my w . . . . Ps 95:10
iniquity: they walk in his w . . . . Ps 119:3
have respect unto thy w . . . . Ps 119:15
shall sing in the w of the . . . . . . Ps 138:5
is righteous in all his w . . . . Ps 145:17
remember thee in thy w . . . . Is 64:5
Israel, are not my w equal? . . . Ezek 18:29
he will teach us of his w . . . . . . Mic 4:2
his w are everlasting . . . . Hab 3:6
If thou wilt walk in my w . . . . . Zech 3:7
as ye have not kept my w . . . . . Mal 2:9
they have not known my w . . . . Heb 3:10

WAY OF GOD'S PEOPLE

With reference to God's way, to:

Understand . . . . Ps 119:27
Pray for direction in . . . . . Ex 33:13
Walk in . . . . Deut 8:6
Remember . . . . Deut 8:2
Known . . . . Ps 67:2
Teach to transgressors . . . Ps 51:13
Rejoice in . . . . Ps 119:14

God's attitude toward, He:
Knows . . . . . Ps 1:6
Is acquainted with . . . . . Ps 139:3
Delights in . . . . . Ps 37:23
Leads us in . . . . . Ps 139:24
Teaches . . . . . Ps 25:9, 12
Makes known . . . . . Ps 103:7
Makes perfect . . . . . Ps 18:32
Blesses . . . . . Prov 8:32

With reference to our way:
Acknowledge Him in . . . . Prov 3:6
Commit to the Lord . . . . . Ps 37:5
Makes prosperous . . . . . Josh 1:8
All before God . . . . . Ps 119:168
Teach me . . . . . Ps 143:8

WAY OF MAN

Described as:
Perverse before God . . . . . Num 22:32
Hard . . . . . Prov 13:15
Abomination . . . . . Prov 15:9
Not good . . . . . Prov 16:29
Dark . . . . . Prov 2:13

WAYFARING—*traveling*
a *w* man in the street of . . . . . Judg 19:17
the *w* man that was come 2Sam 12:4
lie waste, the *w* man ceaseth . . Is 33:8
the *w* men, though fools . . . . . Is 35:8
a lodging place of *w* men . . . . . Jer 9:2
as a *w* man that turneth . . . . . Jer 14:8

WAYMARKS—*roadmarkings*
Give direction . . . . . Jer 31:21

WAYSIDE—*side of a road*
sat upon a seat by the *w* 1Sam 4:13
have spread a net by the *w* . . . . Ps 140:5

WE—*See* INTRODUCTION

WEAK—*feeble; vacillating; diluted*

Kinds of:
Political 2Sam 3:1
Physical . . . . . Judg 16:7, 17
2Cor 11:30
Spiritual . . . . . Is 35:3
Moral 2Sam 3:39

Caused by:
Fasting . . . . . Ps 109:24
Discouragement . . . . . Neh 6:9
Sin 1Cor 11:26-30
Discouraging preaching . . Jer 38:4
Conscientious doubts . . . . Rom 14:1-23

Victory over, by:
Christ 2Cor 13:3, 4
Grace 2Cor 12:9, 10
Faith . . . . . Heb 11:33, 34

Our duty toward, to:
Bear . . . . . Rom 15:1
Support . . . . . Acts 20:35
1Cor 9:22
Not become a stumbling block 1Cor 8:9

Our duties with reference to:
Pleasure in 2Cor 12:10
Help those afflicted with. . Rom 15:1

[*also* WEAKER, WEAKNESS]
whether they be strong or *w* . . . Num 13:18
and let not your hands be *w* . . . 2Chr 15:7
strengthened the *w* hands . . . . . Job 4:3
upon me, O Lord: for I am *w* . Ps 6:2
Art thou also become *w* as . . . . Is 14:10
knees shall be *w* as water . . . . . Ezek 7:17
How *w* is thine heart . . . . . Ezek 16:30
knees shall be *w* as water . . . . . Ezek 21:7
let the *w* say, I am strong . . . . . Joel 3:10
willing, but the flesh is *w* . . . . . Matt 26:41
ready, but the flesh is *w* . . . . . Mark 14:38
being not *w* in faith, he . . . . . Rom 4:19
it was *w* through the flesh . . . . . Rom 8:3
w of God is stronger than 1Cor 1:25
chosen the *w* things of the 1Cor 1:27
I was with you in *w*, and 1Cor 2:3
are *w*, but ye are strong 1Cor 4:10
their conscience being *w* 1Cor 8:7
conscience of him which is *w* . . 1Cor 8:10
shall the *w* brother perish 1Cor 8:11
wound their *w* conscience 1Cor 8:12
sown in *w*; it is raised in 1Cor 15:43
his bodily presence is *w* 2Cor 10:10
as though we had been *w* 2Cor 11:21
Who is *w*, and I am not *w*? . . . 2Cor 11:29
we are *w*, and ye are strong . . . 2Cor 13:9
to the *w* and beggarly . . . . . Gal 4:9
support the *w*, be patient 1Thess 5:14
the *w* and unprofitableness . . . . Heb 7:18
wife, as unto the *w* vessel 1Pet 3:7

WEAKEN—*to deplete strength*

[*also* WEAKENED, WEAKENETH]
w the hands of the people . . . . . Ezra 4:4
w the strength of the . . . . . Job 12:21
He *w* my strength in the way . . Ps 102:23
which didst *w* the nations . . . . . Is 14:12

WEAKHANDED—*discouraged*
he is weary and *w* 2Sam 17:2

WEALTH—*riches; abundance of possessions*

Descriptive of:
Material possessions . . . . . Gen 34:29

Advantages of:
Given by God . . . . . Deut 8:18, 19
Source of security . . . . . Prov 18:11
Adds friends . . . . . Prov 19:4

Disadvantages of:
Produces self-sufficiency . . Deut 8:17
Leads to conceit . . . . . Job 31:25
Subject to loss . . . . . Prov 13:11
Lost by dissipation . . . . . Prov 5:8-10
Cannot save . . . . . Ps 49:6, 7
Must be left to others . . . . Ps 49:10

See RICHES

[*also* WEALTHY]
a mighty man of *w*, of the . . . . Ruth 2:1
the *w* which God shall give 1Sam 2:32
all the mighty men of *w* 2Kin 15:20
not asked riches, *w*, or 2Chr 1:11
their peace or their *w* . . . . . Ezra 9:12
They spend their days in *w* . . . . Job 21:13
not increase thy *w* by their . . . . Ps 44:12
W and riches shall be in his . . . Ps 112:3
rich man's *w* is his strong . . . . . Prov 10:15
the *w* of the sinner is . . . . . Prov 13:22
W maketh many friends . . . . . Prov 19:4
hath given riches and *w* . . . . . Eccl 5:19
God hath given riches, *w* . . . . . Eccl 6:2
you up unto the *w* nation . . . . . Jer 49:31
w of all the heathen round . . . . Zech 14:14
this craft we have our *w* . . . . . Acts 19:25
but every man another's *w* 1Cor 10:24

WEAN—*to cause children to become independent of their mothers' milk supply*
Celebrated . . . . . Gen 21:8
Figurative of spiritual rest. Ps 131:2

[*also* WEANED]
the child grew, and was *w* . . . . . Gen 21:8
same day that Isaac was *w* . . . . Gen 21:8
go up until the child be *w* 1Sam 1:22
until thou have *w* him 1Sam 1:23
son suck until she *w* him 1Sam 1:23
Tahpenes *w* in Pharaoh's 1Kin 11:20
that is *w* of his mother . . . . . Ps 131:2
soul is even as a *w* child . . . . . Ps 131:2
w child shall put his . . . . . Is 11:8
that are *w* from the milk . . . . . Is 28:9
she had *w* Lo-ruhamah . . . . . Hos 1:8

WEAPON—*military arms*

[*also* WEAPONS]
take, I pray thee, thy *w* . . . . . Gen 27:3
smite him with a hand *w* . . . . . Num 35:18
girded on..his *w* of war . . . . . Deut 1:41
have a paddle upon thy *w* . . . . . Deut 23:13
men appointed with *w* . . . . . Judg 18:11
appointed with *w* of war . . . . . Judg 18:17
my sword nor my *w* with me . . 1Sam 21:8
and the *w* of war perished! 2Sam 1:27
every man with his *w* in his . . . 2Kin 11:8
every man with his *w* in his . . . 2Chr 23:7
having his *w* in his hand 2Chr 23:10
the other hand held a *w* . . . . . Neh 4:17
shall flee from the iron *w* . . . . . Job 20:24
Wisdom is better than *w* of . . . . Eccl 9:18
the *w* of his indignation . . . . . Is 13:5
No *w* that is formed against . . . Is 54:17
turn back the *w* of war . . . . . Jer 21:4
the *w* of his indignation . . . . . Jer 50:25
with his destroying *w* in . . . . . Ezek 9:1
to hell with their *w* of war . . . . Ezek 32:27
shall burn the *w* with fire . . . . . Ezek 39:10
lanterns and torches and *w* . . . . John 18:3
w of our warfare are not 2Cor 10:4

WEAPONS, SPIRITUAL—*provisions for doing spiritual warfare*

Against:
World—faith 1John 5:4
Satan—armor of God . . . . Eph 6:11-17
Flesh—the Spirit . . . . . Gal 5:16-25

WEAR—*to be clothed with; to diminish or decay*

[*also* WEARETH, WEARING]
Thou wilt surely *w* away . . . . . Ex 18:18
woman shall not *w* that . . . . . Deut 22:5
incense, to *w* an ephod 1Sam 2:28
priest in Shiloh, *w* an ephod . . . 1Sam 14:3
which the king useth to *w* . . . . . Esth 6:8
The waters *w* the stones . . . . . Job 14:19
and *w* our own apparel . . . . . Is 4:1
w out the saints of the . . . . . Dan 7:25
w a rough garment to . . . . . Zech 13:4
they that *w* soft clothing . . . . . Matt 11:8
the day began to *w* away . . . . . Luke 9:12
Jesus forth, *w* the crown of . . . . John 19:5
to him that *w* the gay . . . . . James 2:3
the hair, and of *w* of gold 1Pet 3:3

WEARY—*tired*

Caused by:
Journeys . . . . . John 4:6
Ritualism . . . . . Is 1:14
Study . . . . . Eccl 12:12
Anxiety . . . . . Gen 27:46
Words . . . . . Mal 2:17
Not speaking . . . . . Jer 20:9
Too frequent visits . . . . . Prov 25:17

Overcome by:
Waiting on the Lord . . . . . Is 40:30, 31
Appropriate word . . . . . Is 50:4
God's promise . . . . . Is 28:12
Persevering faith . . . . . Gal 6:9
Promised ruler . . . . . Is 32:1, 2
Looking to Jesus . . . . . Heb 12:2, 3

[*also* WEARIED, WEARIETH, WEARINESS, WEARISOME]
w themselves to find the . . . . . Gen 19:11
when thou wast faint and *w* . . . Deut 25:18
he was fast asleep and *w* . . . . . Judg 4:21
unto thy men that are *w*? . . . . . Judg 8:15
that were with him, came *w* . . . 2Sam 16:14
him while he is *w* and 2Sam 17:2
people is hungry, and *w* 2Sam 17:29
and there the *w* be at rest . . . . . Job 3:17
w nights are appointed to . . . . . Job 7:3
But now he hath made me *w* . Job 16:7
by watering he *w* the thick . . . . Job 37:11
I am *w* with my groaning . . . . . Ps 6:6
I am *w* of my crying: my . . . . . Ps 69:3
be *w* of his correction . . . . . Prov 3:11
the foolish *w* every one of . . . . . Eccl 10:15
much study is a *w* of the . . . . . Eccl 12:12
None shall be *w* nor . . . . . Is 5:27
thing for you to *w* men . . . . . Is 7:13
but will ye *w* my God also? . . . Is 7:13
that Moab is *w* on the high . . . . Is 16:12
fainteth not, neither is *w*? . . . . . Is 40:28
thou hast been *w* of me . . . . . Is 43:22
offering, nor *w* thee with . . . . . Is 43:23
a burden to the *w* beast . . . . . Is 46:1
art *w* in the multitude of . . . . . Is 47:13
that seek her will not *w* . . . . . Jer 2:24
soul is *w* because of . . . . . Jer 4:31

I am *w* with holding in........Jer 6:11
w themselves to commit.......Jer 9:5
and they have *w* thee, then....Jer 12:5
thou trustedst, they *w* thee ....Jer 12:5
I am *w* with repenting ....Jer 15:6
have satiated the *w* soul.......Jer 31:25
fire, and they shall be *w* ......Jer 51:58
She hath *w* herself with ....Ezek 24:12
wherein have I *w* thee? ....Mic 6:3
shall *w* themselves for.........Hab 2:13
Behold, what a *w* is it!........Mal 1:13
continual coming she *w* me ....Luke 18:5
In *w* and painfulness, in.......2Cor 11:27
be not *w* in well doing 2Thess 3:13

WEASEL—*a small carnivorous mammal that was unclean*
the *w*, and the mouse, and ....Lev 11:29

WEATHER—*state of the atmosphere*
Proverb concerning ......Job 37:9-11
Under divine control.....1Sam 12:16-19
Signs of ....Luke 12:54-57

away a garment in cold *w* .....Prov 25:20
ye say, It will be fair *w* ....Matt 16:2
It will be foul *w* today ....Matt 16:3

WEAVE—*to interlace threads*

[*also* WEAVEST, WOVE, WOVEN]
have a binding of *w* work .....Ex 28:32
fine linen of *w* work for.......Ex 39:27
If thou *w* the seven locks .....Judg 16:13
women *w* hangings for the 2Kin 23:7
they that *w* networks, shall ....Is 19:9
and *w* the spider's web........Is 59:5
seam, *w* from the top ....John 19:23

WEAVER—*one who weaves*

[*also* WEAVER'S]
his spear was like a *w* beam ...1Sam 17:7
spear was like a *w* beam 2Sam 21:19
was a spear like a *w* beam 1Chr 11:23
staff was like a *w* beam 1Chr 20:5
cut off like a *w* my life........Is 38:12

WEAVING—*interlacing threads to produce cloth*
Men endowed in art of ..Ex 35:35
Performed by worthy women ....Prov 31:13, 19
Figurative of life's shortness ....Job 7:6
See SPINNING

WEB—*cobweb; ensnarement*

[*also* WEBS]
locks of my head with the *w*...Judg 16:13
trust shall be a spider's *w* .....Job 8:14
and weave the spider's *w*......Is 59:5
w shall not become garments ..Is 59:6

WEDDING—*marriage ceremony with accompanying festivities*
that were bidden to the *w*.....Matt 22:3
w was furnished with guests ...Matt 22:10
not having a *w* garment? ......Matt 22:12
he will return from the *w* .....Luke 12:36
bidden of any man to a *w*.....Luke 14:8
See MARRIAGE

WEDGE—*gold item of uncertain identity, possibly serving as a means of identification in commerce*
Stolen by Achan ....Josh 7:20, 21

the *w* of gold, and his sons ....Josh 7:24
than the golden *w* of Ophir ...Is 13:12

WEDLOCK—*the state of being married*
as women that break *w* and ...Ezek 16:38

WEEDS—*plants of no value*
Wrapped around Jonah's head ....Jon 2:5

WEEK—*seven days*
Origin of, early ....Gen 2:1-3
Used in dating events....Gen 7:4, 10
One, length of mourning .Gen 50:10
Part of ceremonial Law ..Ex 13:6, 7
Seventy, prophecy of ....Dan 9:24
Christ arose on first day of ....Matt 28:1
Christians worship on first day of..........Acts 20:7; 1Cor 16:2
See PENTECOST

[*also* WEEKS]
Fulfill her *w*, and we will .....Gen 29:27
observe the feast of *w* ....Ex 34:22
she shall be unclean two *w*....Lev 12:5
after your *w* be out, ye ....Num 28:26
Seven *w* shalt thou number....Deut 16:9
to number the seven *w* from...Deut 16:9
keep the feast of *w* unto ......Deut 16:10
in the feast of *w*, and in 2Chr 8:13
appointed *w* of the harvest ....Jer 5:24
the Prince shall be seven *w*....Dan 9:25
and threescore and two *w* .....Dan 9:25
covenant with many for one *w* .Dan 9:27
in the midst of the *w* he ......Dan 9:27
was mourning three full *w*.....Dan 10:2
the first day of the *w* ....Matt 28:1
the first day of the *w* ....Mark 16:2
I fast twice in the *w*, I ....Luke 18:12
the first day of the *w* ....Luke 24:1
first day of the *w* cometh .....John 20:1
the first day of the *w* ....John 20:19

WEEP—*to cry intensely; mourn*

Kinds of:
Rebellious ....Num 11:4-20
Hypocritical.............Judg 14:16, 17
Sincere 1Sam 20:41
Exhausting..............1Sam 30:4
Secret ....Jer 13:17
Permanent ....Matt 8:12
Bitterly ....Matt 26:75
Divine...................John 11:35
Sympathetic.............Rom 12:15

Caused by:
Despair.................Gen 21:16
Death ....Gen 50:1
Loss of blessing ....Gen 27:34, 38
Love ....Gen 29:11
Joy of reunion ....Gen 33:4
Loss of child ....Gen 37:35
Restraint of joy ....Gen 42:24
Hearing God's Word ....Neh 8:9

Passing away of:
After a child's death 2Sam 12:21-23
In the morning ....Ps 30:5
In eternity ....Is 65:19
After seeing the Lord ....John 20:11-18

[*also* WEEPEST, WEEPETH, WEEPING, WEPT]
mourn..and to *w* for her ......Gen 23:2
his chamber, and *w* there .....Gen 43:30
And he *w* aloud ....Gen 45:2
Benjamin's neck, and *w*.......Gen 45:14
Benjamin *w* upon his neck ....Gen 45:14
and *w* on his neck a good .....Gen 46:29
Joseph *w* when they spake ....Gen 50:17
and, behold, the babe *w* ......Ex 2:6
people *w* throughout their .....Num 11:10
the people *w* that night ....Num 14:1
were *w* before the door of ....Num 25:6
and *w* before the Lord ....Deut 1:45
days of *w* and mourning for ...Deut 34:8
lifted up their voice, and *w*....Judg 2:4
she *w* before him the seven ...Judg 14:17
and *w* before the Lord until ...Judg 20:23
the house of God, and *w*......Judg 20:26
up their voice, and *w* ....Ruth 1:9
therefore she *w*, and did 1Sam 1:7
to her, Hannah, why *w* thou? .1Sam 1:8
up their voices, and *w* 1Sam 11:4
the people that they *w* 1Sam 11:5
lifted up his voice, and *w* 1Sam 24:16
they mourned, and *w*, and 2Sam 1:12
daughters of Israel, *w* over 2Sam 1:24
went with her along *w* 2Sam 3:16
w at the grave of Abner 2Sam 3:32
and all the people *w* 2Sam 3:32
yet alive, I fasted and *w* 2Sam 12:22
lifted up their voice and *w* 2Sam 13:36
his servants *w* very sore 2Sam 13:36
and *w* as he went up..........2Sam 15:30
w and mourneth for Absalom..2Sam 19:1
and the man of God *w*........2Kin 8:11
Hazael said, Why *w* my lord? .2Kin 8:12
And Hezekiah *w* sore 2Kin 20:3
clothes, and *w* before me 2Chr 34:27
eyes, *w* with a loud voice .....Ezra 3:12
the noise of the *w* of the ......Ezra 3:13
that I sat down and *w* ....Neh 1:4
fasting, and *w*, and wailing ....Esth 4:3
lifted up their voice, and *w*....Job 2:12
My face is foul with *w* ....Job 16:16
and his widows shall not *w* ....Job 27:15
Did not I *w* for him that ......Job 30:25
the voice of them that *w* ......Job 30:31
heard the voice of my *w* ......Ps 6:8
I *w*, and chastened my soul ....Ps 69:10
mingled my drink with *w*......Ps 102:9
He that goeth forth and *w* ....Ps 126:6
A time to *w*, and a time to....Eccl 3:4
the high places, to *w*..........Is 15:2
shall howl, *w* abundantly ......Is 15:3
bewail with the *w* of Jazer ....Is 16:9
God of hosts call to *w* ....Is 22:12
thou shalt *w* no more ....Is 30:19
And Hezekiah *w* sore..........Is 38:3
w and supplications of the.....Jer 3:21
I might *w* day and night for ...Jer 9:1
W ye not for the dead ....Jer 22:10
w sore for him that goeth .....Jer 22:10
They shall come with *w*........Jer 31:9
lamentation, and bitter *w* .....Jer 31:15
Rachel *w* for her children .....Jer 31:15
w all along as he went ....Jer 41:6
will *w* for thee with the *w*.....Jer 48:32
She *w* sore in the night ....Lam 1:2
For these things I *w* ....Lam 1:16
there sat women *w* for ....Ezek 8:14
shalt thou mourn nor *w* ....Ezek 24:16
shall *w* for thee with..........Ezek 27:31
he *w*, and made supplication ..Hos 12:4
Awake, ye drunkards, and *w* ..Joel 1:5
fasting, and with *w*, and ......Joel 2:12
at Gath, *w* ye not at all ....Mic 1:10
Should I *w* in the fifth ....Zech 7:3
with tears, with *w*, and........Mal 2:13
lamentation, and *w*, and ......Matt 2:18
Rachel *w* for her children .....Matt 2:18
shall be *w* and gnashing ....Matt 22:13
shall be *w* and gnashing ....Matt 25:30
them that *w* and wailed ....Mark 5:38
make ye this ado, and *w*? .....Mark 5:39
as they mourned and *w* ....Mark 16:10
Blessed are ye that *w* now ....Luke 6:21
and said unto her, *W* not .....Luke 7:13
to you, and ye have not *w* ....Luke 7:32
at his feet behind him *w* ......Luke 7:38
all *w*, and bewailed her ....Luke 8:52
Peter went out, and *w* ....Luke 22:62
Daughters..*w* not for me ......Luke 23:28
but *w* for yourselves, and .....Luke 23:28
goeth unto the grave to *w*.....John 11:31
Jesus therefore saw her *w*.....John 11:33
Jews also *w* which came.......John 11:33
her, Woman, why *w* thou? ....John 20:13
the widows stood by him *w*....Acts 9:39
they all *w* sore, and fell ....Acts 20:37
What mean ye to *w* and to ....Acts 21:13
and *w* with them that *w*.......Rom 12:5
that *w*, as though they *w* not ..1Cor 7:30
and now tell you even *w* ....Phil 3:18
afflicted, and mourn, and *w* ...James 4:9
w and howl for your ....James 5:1
And I *w* much, because no ....Rev 5:4
W not: behold, the Lion of....Rev 5:5
her torment, *w* and wailing ....Rev 18:15
w and wailing, saying, Alas....Rev 18:19

WEIGH—*to determine the heaviness; consider; evaluate*

[*also* WEIGHED, WEIGHETH, WEIGHING]
Abraham *w* to Ephron the ....Gen 23:16
chargers of silver *w* can ....Num 7:85
the silver vessels *w* two ....Num 7:85

of incense, *w* ten shekels ...... Num 7:86
and by him actions are *w* 1Sam 2:3
he *w* the hair of his head 2Sam 14:26
found it to *w* a talent 1Chr 20:2
w unto them the silver .... Ezra 8:25
ye *w* them before the chief .... Ezra 8:29
vessels *w* in the house .... Ezra 8:33
my grief were thoroughly *w* ... Job 6:2
he *w* the waters by measure ... Job 28:25
Let me be *w* in an even .... Job 31:6
ye *w* the violence of your ..... Ps 58:2
the Lord *w* the spirits .... Prov 16:2
dost *w* the path of the just .... Is 26:7
and *w* the mountains in .... Is 40:12
w silver in the balance .... Is 46:6
w him the money, even .... Jer 32:9
take thee balances to *w* .... Ezek 5:1
Thou art *w* in the balances .... Dan 5:27
they *w* for my price thirty ..... Zech 11:12

WEIGHT—*heaviness; pressure*

[*also* WEIGHTS]
earring of half a shekel *w* ..... Gen 24:22
of ten shekels *w* of gold .... Gen 24:22
shall there be a like *w* .... Ex 30:34
in meteyard, in *w*, or in .... Lev 19:35
Just balances, just *w* .... Lev 19:36
w whereof was a hundred ..... Num 7:13
w whereof was a hundred ..... Num 7:37
w whereof was a hundred ..... Num 7:49
w whereof was a hundred ..... Num 7:61
have in thy bags divers *w* ..... Deut 25:13
have a perfect and just *w* ..... Deut 25:15
gold of fifty shekels *w* .... Josh 7:21
w of the golden earrings ...... Judg 8:26
w of the coat was five 1Sam 17:5
w thereof was a talent 2Sam 12:30
w of whose spear weighed 2Sam 21:16
shekels of brass in *w* 2Sam 21:16
was the *w* of the brass 1Kin 7:47
vessels was without *w* 2Kin 25:16
shekels of gold by *w* 1Chr 21:25
brass in abundance without *w* .. 1Chr 22:3
of gold by *w* for things of 1Chr 28:14
instruments of silver by *w* 1Chr 28:14
w for the candlesticks of 1Chr 28:15
by *w* for every candlestick 1Chr 28:15
candlesticks of silver by *w* 1Chr 28:15
he gave gold by *w* for 1Chr 28:17
silver by *w* for every basin 1Chr 28:17
the *w* of the nails was 2Chr 3:9
Now the *w* of gold that 2Chr 9:13
Levites the *w* of the silver ..... Ezra 8:30
By number and by *w* of .... Ezra 8:34
all the *w* was written at .... Ezra 8:34
To make the *w* for the .... Job 28:25
a just *w* is his delight .... Prov 11:1
all the *w* of the bag are .... Prov 16:11
Divers *w* are an abomination .. Prob 20:23
vessels was without *w* .... Jer 52:20
shalt eat shall be by *w* .... Ezek 4:10
the bag of deceitful *w*? .... Mic 6:11
he cast the *w* of lead upon .... Zech 5:8
about a hundred pound *w* ..... John 19:39
and eternal *w* of glory 2Cor 4:17
let us lay aside every *w* .... Heb 12:1
about the *w* of a talent .... Rev 16:21

WEIGHTS AND MEASURES—*means of determining weight, volume, and size*

Monies:
Beka .... Ex 38:26
Gerahs .... Ex 30:13
Mite .... Mark 12:42
Pence .... Matt 18:28
Pieces of silver .... Matt 26:15
Shekel .... Ex 30:24
Shekels of Brass 2Sam 21:16
Shekels of gold 1Chr 21:25
Shekels of silver 2Sam 24:24
Silver 2Chr 21:3
Talents .... Matt 18:24
Talents of brass 1Chr 29:7
Talents of gold 1Chr 29:4
Talents of iron 1Chr 29:7
Talents of silver 1Chr 29:4

Distance or length measurements:
Acre 1Sam 14:14
Cubit .... Gen 6:15
Fathom .... Acts 27:28
Finger .... Jer 52:21
Furlong .... Luke 24:13
Handbreadth .... Ex 25:25
Measuring reed .... Ezek 40:3
Pace 2Sam 6:13
Span .... Ex 28:16
Sabbath day's journey ... Acts 1:12

Liquid measures:
Bath 1Kin 7:26
Cor .... Ezek 45:14
Firkin .... John 2:6
Hin .... Ex 29:40
Homer .... Ezek 45:11
Kab 2Kin 6:25
Log .... Lev 14:10

Dry measures:
Cab 2Kin 6:25
Ephah .... Ex 16:36
Homer .... Lev 27:16
Log .... Lev 14:10
Omer .... Ex 16:16
Gerah .... Ex 30:13
Pound 1Kin 10:17

Weight measures:
Bekah .... Ex 38:26
Shekel 2Sam 14:26
Talents .... Ex 38:27

WEIGHTY—*heavy; serious*

[*also* WEIGHTIER]
is heavy, and the sand *w* ...... Prov 27:3
the *w* matters of the law ...... Matt 23:23
letters, say they, are *w* 2Cor 10:10

WELCOME—*to receive with gladness*

Extended to:
Returning brother .... Gen 33:1-11
Father .... Gen 46:29-34
Hero 1Sam 18:6, 7
Prodigal son .... Luke 15:20-32
Messiah .... Matt 21:6-10

Circumstances attending:
Courtesies offered .... Gen 18:1-8
Discourtesies shown 2Sam 10:1-5
Fear expressed 1Sam 16:4, 5
Fellowship denied 2John 10, 11

WELFARE—*well-being; good fortune; one's condition*
he asked them of their *w* ...... Gen 43:27
asked each other of their *w* ... Ex 18:7
David, to inquire of his *w* 1Chr 18:10
the *w* of the children of .... Neh 2:10
w passeth away as a cloud ..... Job 30:15
have been for their *w* .... Ps 69:22
seeketh not the *w* of this ...... Jer 38:4

WELL—*issue of water from the earth; pits dug for water; a source*

Features concerning:
Women come to, for water .... Gen 24:13, 14; John 4:7
Surrounded by trees ..... Gen 49:22
Often very deep .... John 4:11
Covered with large stone . Gen 29:2, 3
Sometimes cause strife ... Gen 21:25

Names of:
Beer .... Num 21:16-18
Beer-lahai-roi .... Gen 16:14
Beer-sheba .... Gen 21:30, 31
Beeroth .... Deut 10:6
Esek .... Gen 26:20
Jacob .... John 4:6
Rehoboth .... Gen 26:22
Sitnah .... Gen 26:21

Figurative of:
Salvation .... Is 12:3
False teaching 2Pet 2:17
One's wife .... Prov 5:15
The Holy Spirit .... John 4:10

[*also* WELL'S, WELLS]
by a *w* of water at the time ... Gen 24:11
she went down to the *w* .... Gen 24:16
unto the man, unto the *w* ..... Gen 24:29
came this day unto the *w* ..... Gen 24:42
she went down unto the *w* .... Gen 24:45
Isaac dwelt by the *w* .... Gen 25:11
the *w* which his father's .... Gen 26:15
digged again the *w* of water ... Gen 26:18
there a *w* of springing .... Gen 26:19
Isaac's servants digged a *w* .... Gen 26:25
concerning the *w* which .... Gen 26:32
stone from the *w* mouth ...... Gen 29:8
stone from the *w* mouth ...... Gen 29:10
drink of the water of the *w* .... Num 20:17
of the waters of the *w* .... Num 21:22
pitched beside the *w* of .... Judg 7:1
a covering over the *w* 2Sam 17:19
they came up out of the *w* 2Sam 17:21
water out of the *w* of 2Sam 23:16
and stop all *w* of water 2Kin 3:19
stopped all the *w* of water 2Kin 3:25
the water of the *w* of 1Chr 11:17
even before the dragon *w* ..... Neh 2:13
w digged, vineyards, and ...... Neh 9:25
valley of Baca make it a *w* .... Ps 84:6
a *w* of living waters .... Song 4:15
Jacob, which gave us the *w* .... John 4:12

WELL—*in a good manner or state; satisfactory; thoroughly*
If thou doest *w*, shalt thou .... Gen 4:7
if thou doest not *w*, sin .... Gen 4:7
entreated Abram *w* for her .... Gen 12:16
that it was *w* watered .... Gen 13:10
were old and *w* stricken .... Gen 18:11
and *w* stricken in age .... Gen 24:1
he said unto them, Is he *w*? ... Gen 29:6
And they said, He is *w* .... Gen 29:6
I will deal *w* with thee .... Gen 32:9
see whether it be *w* with ...... Gen 37:14
w with the flocks; and .... Gen 37:14
on me when it shall be *w* ..... Gen 40:14
the seven *w* favored and fat ... Gen 41:4
Is your father *w*, the old ...... Gen 43:27
and it pleased Pharaoh *w* ..... Gen 45:16
God dealt *w* with the .... Ex 1:20
I know that he can speak *w* ... Ex 4:14
as *w* the stranger, as he .... Lev 24:16
w for the stranger, as for ...... Lev 24:22
for it was *w* with us in .... Num 11:18
we are *w* able to overcome .... Num 13:30
shall hear the small as *w* ...... Deut 1:17
brethren, as *w* as unto .... Deut 3:20
maidservant my rest as *w* as ... Deut 5:14
w said all that they have ...... Deut 5:28
that it may be *w* with you ..... Deut 5:33
shalt *w* remember what the .... Deut 7:18
because he is *w* with thee .... Deut 15:16
that it may go *w* with thee .... Deut 19:13
that it may be *w* with thee .... Deut 22:7
the Lord, as *w* the stranger .... Josh 8:33
for she pleaseth me *w* .... Judg 14:3
it may be *w* with thee? .... Ruth 3:1
Saul to his servant, *W* said 1Sam 9:10
now a that man can play *w* 1Sam 16:17
it pleased David *w* to be 1Sam 18:26
If he say thus, It is *w* 1Sam 20:7
will he let him go *w* away? 1Sam 24:19
have dealt *w* with my lord 1Sam 25:31
W; I will make a league 2Sam 3:13
as *w* to the women as men 2Sam 6:19
devoureth one as *w* as 2Sam 11:25
saying pleased Absalom *w* 2Sam 17:4
then it had pleased thee *w* 2Sam 19:6
W; I will speak for thee 1Kin 2:18
and said, It is *w* spoken 1Kin 18:24
she said, It shall be *w* 2Kin 4:23
her, Is it *w* with thee? 2Kin 4:26
is it *w* with thy husband? 2Kin 4:26
is it *w* with the child? 2Kin 4:26
And she answered, It is *w* 2Kin 4:26

he said, All is *w*. My master . .2Kin 5:22
said unto him, Is all *w*? 2Kin 9:11
it shall be *w* with you 2Kin 25:24
as *w* the small as the 1Chr 25:8
didst *w* in that it was in 2Chr 6:8
as *w* to the great as to 2Chr 31:15
understanding as *w* as you . . . . .Job 12:3
Mark ye *w* her bulwarks . . . . . .Ps 48:13
steps had *w* nigh slipped . . . . . .Ps 73:2
Thou hast dealt *w* with. . . . . . . .Ps 119:65
my soul knoweth right *w* . . . . . .Ps 139:14
When it goeth *w* with the . . . . .Prov 11:10
prudent man looketh *w* to . . . . .Prov 14:15
three things which go *w* . . . . . . .Prov 30:29
be *w* with them that fear . . . . . .Eccl 8:12
Learn to do *w*; seek . . . . .Is 1:17
instead of *w* set hair . . . . .Is 3:24
not *w* strengthen their mast . . .Is 33:23
unto me, Thou hast *w* seen . . . .Jer 1:12
Verily it shall be *w* with . . . . . . .Jer 15:11
to entreat thee *w* in the . . . . . . .Jer 15:11
and then it was *w* with him? . . .Jer 22:15
so it shall be *w* unto thee . . . . .Jer 38:20
I will look *w* unto thee . . . . .Jer 40:4
that it may be *w* with us . . . . . .Jer 42:6
under it, and make it boil *w* . . .Ezek 24:5
play *w* on an instrument . . . . . .Ezek 33:32
Son of man, mark *w*, and . . . . .Ezek 44:5
mark *w* the entering in of . . . . .Ezek 44:5
no blemish, but *w* favored . . . . .Dan 1:4
Doest thou *w* to be angry? . . . .Jon 4:4
thou *w* to be angry for . . . . .Jon 4:9
he said, I do *w* to be angry . . .Jon 4:9
I thought..to do *w* . . . . .Zech 8:15
Son, in whom I am *w* pleased .Matt 3:17
whom my soul is *w* pleased . . . .Matt 12:18
Son, in whom I am *w* pleased .Matt 17:5
W done, good and faithful . . . .Matt 25:23
Son, in whom I am *w* pleased .Mark 1:11
Full *w* ye reject the . . . . .Mark 7:9
he had answered them *w* . . . . . .Mark 12:28
now *w* stricken in years . . . . . . .Luke 1:7
in thee I am *w* pleased . . . . .Luke 3:22
W, thou good servant . . . . .Luke 19:17
when men have *w* drunk . . . . . .John 2:10
Thou hast *w* said, I have . . . . . .John 4:17
Say we not *w* that thou . . . . . . .John 8:48
and Lord; and ye say *w* . . . . .John 13:13
thou hast *w* done that . . . . .Acts 10:33
ye shall do *w*. Fare ye *w* . . . . . .Acts 15:29
as thou very *w* knowest . . . . . . .Acts 25:10
continuance in *w* doing . . . . .Rom 2:7
keep his virgin, doeth *w* 1Cor 7:37
as *w* as other apostles 1Cor 9:5
thou verily givest thanks *w* 1Cor 14:17
unknown, and yet *w* known . . .2Cor 6:9
affect you, but not *w* . . . . .Gal 4:17
not be weary in *w* doing . . . . . .Gal 6:9
That it may be *w* with thee . . . .Eph 6:3
ye have *w* done . . . . .Phil 4:14
is *w* pleasing unto the Lord . . .Col 3:20
be not weary in *w* doing 2Thess 3:13
ruleth *w* his own house 1Tim 3:4
the office of a deacon *w* 1Tim 3:13
the elders that rule *w* be 1Tim 5:17
thou knowest very *w* 2Tim 1:18
please them *w* in all things . . . .Titus 2:9
preached, as *w* as unto . . . . .Heb 4:2
as thyself, ye do *w* . . . . .James 2:8
praise of them that do *w* 1Pet 2:14
when ye do *w*, and suffer 1Pet 2:20
ye suffer for *w* doing 1Pet 3:17
Son, in whom I am *w* pleased .2Pet 1:17
godly sort, thou shalt do *w* 3John 6

WELL-BELOVED—*much-beloved person*
of myrrh is my *w* unto . . . . .Song 1:13
I sing to my *w* a song of . . . . . . .Is 5:1
My *w* hath a vineyard in . . . . . .Is 5:1
therefore one son, his *w*, he . . .Mark 12:6
Salute my *w* Epaenetus . . . . . . .Rom 16:5
The elder unto the *w* Gaius . . .3John 1

WELL-FAVORED—*good-looking*
whoredoms of the *w* harlot . . . .Nah 3:4

WELL-PLEASING—*giving pleasure to*
acceptable, *w* to God . . . . .Phil 4:18
which is *w* in his sight . . . . .Heb 13:21

WELLSPRING—*a gushing stream*
the *w* of wisdom as a . . . . .Prov 18:4

WEN—*a running sore*
Makes an animal unacceptable . . . . .Lev 22:22

WENCH—*a maid or female servant*
Informant 2Sam 17:17

WENT, WENTEST—*See* INTRODUCTION

WEPT—*See* WEEP

WERE, WERT—*See* INTRODUCTION

WEST—*the opposite direction from east*

[*also* WESTERN, WESTWARD]
having Beth-el on the *w* . . . . . . .Gen 12:8
and eastward, and *w* . . . . .Gen 13:14
a mighty strong *w* wind . . . . .Ex 10:19
sides of the tabernacle *w* . . . . . .Ex 26:22
sides of the tabernacle *w* . . . . . .Ex 36:27
the *w* side were hangings . . . . . .Ex 38:12
On the *w* side shall be the . . . .Num 2:18
behind the tabernacle *w* . . . . . . .Num 3:23
And as for the *w* border . . . . . .Num 34:6
on the *w* side two thousand . . .Num 35:5
and lift up thine eyes *w* . . . . . . .Deut 3:27
possess thou the *w* and . . . . .Deut 33:23
on the side of Jordan *w* . . . . . . .Josh 5:1
and Ai, on the *w* side of Ai . . .Josh 8:9
wait on the *w* of the city . . . . . .Josh 8:13
on the east and on the *w* . . . . . .Josh 11:3
Baalah *w* unto mount Seir . . . . .Josh 15:10
the *w* border was to the . . . . . . .Josh 15:12
Tappuah *w* unto the river . . . . .Josh 16:8
border went out on the *w* . . . . .Josh 18:15
reacheth to Carmel *w* . . . . .Josh 19:26
on this side Jordan *w* . . . . .Josh 22:7
three looking toward the *w* 1Kin 7:25
w Gezer, with the towns 1Chr 7:28
toward the east, *w*, north, and .1Chr 9:24
At Parbar *w*, four at the 1Chr 26:18
three looking toward the *w* 2Chr 4:4
on the *w* side of Gihon 2Chr 33:14
east, nor from the *w* . . . . .Ps 75:6
the east, and from the *w* . . . . . .Ps 107:3
Philistines toward the *w* . . . . . . .Is 11:14
from the *w*, that there is . . . . . .Is 45:6
of the Lord from the *w* . . . . . . .Is 59:19
end toward the *w* was . . . . .Ezek 41:12
the city, from the *w* side *w* . . . .Ezek 45:7
the *w* border unto the east . . . .Ezek 45:7
w side also shall be the . . . . . . .Ezek 47:20
Hamath. This is the *w* side . . . .Ezek 47:20
east side unto the *w* side . . . . . .Ezek 48:2
east side unto the *w* side . . . . . .Ezek 48:4
east side unto the *w* side . . . . . .Ezek 48:7
and toward the *w* ten . . . . .Ezek 48:10
toward the *w* two hundred . . . .Ezek 48:17
eastward, and ten thousand *w* .Ezek 48:18
east side unto the *w* . . . . .Ezek 48:23
I saw the ram pushing *w* . . . . . .Dan 8:4
he goat came from the *w* . . . . . .Dan 8:5
shall tremble from the *w* . . . . . .Hos 11:10
and from the *w* country . . . . . . .Zech 8:7
come from the east and *w* . . . . .Matt 8:11
cloud rise out of the *w* . . . . .Luke 12:54
the south *w* and north . . . . .Acts 27:12
the south..and north *w* . . . . .Acts 27:12
and on the *w* three gates . . . . . .Rev 21:13

WET—*covered or soaked with liquid*
They are *w* with the showers . .Job 24:8
be *w* with the dew of heaven . .Dan 4:15
his body was *w* with the dew . .Dan 4:33

WHALE—*a large, sea-dwelling mammal*
Jonah swallowed by . . . . .Matt 12:40
Created by God . . . . .Gen 1:21

Am I a sea, or a *w*, that . . . . . .Job 7:12
thou art as a *w* in the seas . . . .Ezek 32:2

WHAT—*See* INTRODUCTION

WHATSOEVER—*whatever*
w Adam called every living . . . .Gen 2:19
and *w* thou hast in the city . . . .Gen 19:12
w they did there, he was . . . . . .Gen 39:22
w openeth the womb . . . . .Ex 13:2
w toucheth the altar shall . . . . .Ex 29:37
w uncleanness it be that . . . . . . .Lev 5:3
W shall touch the flesh . . . . .Lev 6:27
W parteth the hoof, and . . . . . .Lev 11:3
W hath no fins nor scales . . . . .Lev 11:12
upon *w* any of them, when . . . .Lev 11:32
w vessel it be, wherein . . . . .Lev 11:32
W goeth upon the belly . . . . . . .Lev 11:42
w goeth upon all fours . . . . . . .Lev 11:42
or *w* hath more feet among . . .Lev 11:42
w she sitteth upon shall . . . . . . .Lev 15:26
w man there be of the . . . . .Lev 17:10
w man he be that hath . . . . .Lev 21:18
W he be of the house of . . . . . .Lev 22:18
w soul it be that shall not . . . . .Lev 23:29
w passeth under the rod . . . . . .Lev 27:32
w any man giveth the priest . . .Num 5:10
w the unclean person . . . . .Num 19:22
w he showeth me I will tell . . . .Num 23:3
w the Lord our God forbade . .Deut 2:37
w thy soul lusteth after . . . . .Deut 12:15
w thy soul lusteth after . . . . .Deut 12:21
for *w* thy soul lusteth . . . . .Deut 14:26
us *w* seemeth good unto thee . .Judg 10:15
Do *w* seemeth good unto thee .1Sam 14:36
w cometh to thine hand unto . .1Sam 25:8
w the king did pleased all 2Sam 3:36
w thou shalt require of me 2Sam 19:38
w plague, *w* sickness there 1Kin 8:37
w is pleasant in thine eyes 1Kin 20:6
w sore or *w* sickness there 2Chr 6:28
w shall seem good to thee . . . . .Ezra 7:18
w Ezra the priest, the . . . . .Ezra 7:21
w she desired was given . . . . . . .Esth 2:13
do *w* he commandeth them . . . .Job 37:12
w he doeth shall prosper . . . . . .Ps 1:3
hath done *w* he hath pleased . .Ps 115:3
w mine eyes desired I kept . . . .Eccl 2:10
he doeth *w* pleaseth him . . . . . .Eccl 8:3
w I command thee thou shalt . .Jer 1:7
w thing goeth forth out . . . . . . .Jer 44:17
w is more than these cometh . .Matt 5:37
w city or town ye..enter . . . . . . .Matt 10:11
by *w* thou mightest be . . . . .Matt 15:5
w thou shalt bind on earth . . . .Matt 16:19
w thou shalt loose on earth . . . .Matt 16:19
W ye shall bind on earth . . . . . .Matt 18:18
w is right I will give you . . . . . .Matt 20:4
w ye shall ask in prayer . . . . . . .Matt 21:22
things *w* I have commanded . . .Matt 28:20
Ask of me *w* thou wilt . . . . .Mark 6:22
by *w* thou mightest be . . . . .Mark 7:11
done unto him *w* they listed . . .Mark 9:13
do for us *w* we shall desire . . . .Mark 10:35
w shall be given you in . . . . . . .Mark 13:11
w we have heard done in . . . . .Luke 4:23
And into *w* house ye enter . . . .Luke 10:5
w thou spendest more, when . .Luke 10:35
W he saith unto you, do it . . . .John 2:5
w thou wilt ask of God . . . . . . .John 11:22
w ye shall ask in my name . . . .John 14:13
if ye do *w* I command . . . . .John 15:14
w he shall hear, that shall . . . . .John 16:13
w thou hast given me are . . . . .John 17:7
all things *w* he shall say . . . . . . .Acts 3:22
w is not of faith is sin . . . . .Rom 14:23
assist her in *w* business . . . . .Rom 16:2
W is sold in the shambles 1Cor 10:25
w ye do, do all to the glory . . .1Cor 10:31
w they were, it maketh no . . . .Gal 2:6
w doth make manifest is . . . . . .Eph 5:13
brethren, *w* things are true . . . .Phil 4:8
w things are honest . . . . .Phil 4:8
w things are just . . . . .Phil 4:8
w things are pure . . . . .Phil 4:8
w things are lovely . . . . .Phil 4:8
w things are of good report . . .Phil 4:8
w state I am, therewith to . . . . .Phil 4:11

w ye do in word or deed ......Col 3:17
w we ask, we receive of.......1John 3:22
w we ask, we know that we ...1John 5:15
w thou doest to the...........3John 5
of *w* craft he be, shall ....Rev 18:22
w worketh abomination, or ....Rev 21:27

WHEAT—*a cereal grass used for food*

Features concerning:
Grown in Egypt ....Ex 9:32
Grown in Palestine 1Kin 5:11
Made into bread ....Ex 29:2
Used in trade ....Ezek 27:17
Harvested...............Ruth 2:23
Threshed ....Judg 6:11
Gathered ....Matt 3:12
Harvesting of, celebrated .Ex 34:22

Figurative of:
Spiritual blessings ....Ps 81:16
Christians ....Matt 3:12
Christ's death ....John 12:24
Resurrection 1Cor 15:37

[*also* WHEATEN]
in the days of *w* harvest.......Gen 30:14
best..wine, and of the *w* ......Num 18:12
A land of *w*, and barley.......Deut 8:8
the fat of kidneys of *w*........Deut 32:14
in the time of *w* harvest.......Judg 15:1
reaping their *w* harvest in 1Sam 6:13
Is it not *w* harvest today? 1Sam 12:17
they would have fetched *w* 2Sam 4:6
vessels, and *w*, and barley.....2Sam 17:28
thousand measures of *w*........1Kin 5:11
Now Ornan was threshing *w*...1Chr 21:20
measures of beaten *w*..........2Chr 2:10
ten thousand measures of *w* ...2Chr 27:5
w, salt, wine, and oil ....Ezra 6:9
thistles grow instead of *w* .....Job 31:40
with the finest of the *w* ....Ps 147:14
fool in a mortar among *w*.....Pr 27:22
a heap of *w* set about.........Song 7:2
cast in the principal *w*........Is 28:25
They have sown *w*, but shall ..Jer 12:13
for *w*, and for wine, and ......Jer 31:12
in the field, of *w*, and of ......Jer 41:8
Take thou also unto thee *w* ...Ezek 4:9
an ephah of a homer of *w*.....Ezek 45:13
the *w* and for the barley ......Joel 1:11
take from him burdens of *w*...Amos 5:11
sell the refuse of the *w*?.......Amos 8:6
sowed tares among the *w* .....Matt 13:25
gather the *w* into my barn.....Matt 13:30
the *w* into his garner..........Luke 3:17
a hundred measures of *w*......Luke 16:7
that he may sift you as *w* .....Luke 22:31
cast out the *w* into the sea ....Acts 27:38
A measure of *w* for a penny...Rev 6:6
oil, and fine flour, and *w* .....Rev 18:13

WHEEL—*a circular item capable of turning on an axle*

Used on:
Carts ....Is 28:27, 28
Threshing instrument ....Prov 20:26
Chariots ....Nah 3:2
Jehovah's throne ....Ezek 10:1-22

Figurative of:
Future things............Ezek 1:15-28
Punishment ....Prov 20:26
Cycle of nature
("course") ....James 3:6
God's sovereignty ....Ezek 10:9-19

[*also* WHEELS]
took off their chariot *w* ....Ex 14:25
the *w* of his chariots? ....Judg 5:28
base had four brazen *w* 1Kin 7:30
the borders were four *w* 1Kin 7:32
axletrees of the *w* were 1Kin 7:32
height of a *w* was a cubit 1Kin 7:32
God, make them like a *w*.....Ps 83:13
w broken at the cistern ....Eccl 12:6
their *w* like a whirlwind ....Is 5:28
wrought a work on the *w* .....Jer 18:3
at the rumbling of his *w*.......Jer 47:3
noise of the *w* over ....Ezek 3:13
and the *w* beside them ....Ezek 11:22
chariots, wagons, and *w* ....Ezek 23:24
horsemen, and of the *w* ....Ezek 26:10
his *w* as burning fire ....Dan 7:9

WHELP—*offspring of certain animals*

Figurative of:
Judah ....Gen 49:9
Dan ....Deut 33:22
Babylonians ....Jer 51:38
Assyrians ....Nah 2:11, 12
Princes of Israel ....Ezek 19:2-9

[*also* WHELPS]
a bear robbed of her *w* 2Sam 17:8
lion's *w* are scattered ....Job 4:11
The lion's *w* have not ....Job 28:8
a bear robbed of her *w* ....Prov 17:12
bear..bereaved of her *w*.......Hos 13:8

WHEN—*See* INTRODUCTION

WHENCE—*from what place*
maid, *w* camest thou?.........Gen 16:8
unto them, *W* come ye?.......Gen 42:7
W should I have flesh to ......Num 11:13
land *w* thou broughtest........Deut 9:28
I wist not *w* they were ....Josh 2:4
the city from *w* he fled........Josh 20:6
I asked him not *w* he was .....Judg 13:6
and *w* comest thou? ....Judg 19:17
I know not *w* they be?........1Sam 25:11
him, From *w* comest thou? 2Sam 1:3
W comest thou, Gehazi? 2Kin 5:25
w came they unto thee?.......2Kin 20:14
Satan, *W* comest thou?........Job 1:7
I go *w* I shall not return ......Job 10:21
W then cometh wisdom? ......Job 28:20
from *w* cometh my help.......Ps 121:1
place from *w* the rivers ....Eccl 1:7
w come the young and ....Is 30:6
look unto the rock *w* ye.......Is 51:1
the hole of the pit *w* ye ....Is 51:1
w I caused you to be ....Jer 29:14
and *w* comest thou? ....Jon 1:8
w shall I seek comforters .....Nah 3:7
my house from *w* I came......Matt 12:44
W hath this man this..........Matt 13:54
W should we have so ....Matt 15:33
w hath this man these.........Mark 6:2
and *w* is he then his son? .....Mark 12:37
And *w* is this to me ....Luke 1:43
I know you not *w* ye are ......Luke 13:25
could not tell *w* it was ....Luke 20:7
W knowest thou me? ....John 1:48
not tell *w* it cometh...........John 3:8
W shall we buy bread ....John 6:5
know this man *w* he is ....John 7:27
no man knoweth *w* he is ......John 7:27
I know *w* I came, and ....John 8:14
ye cannot tell *w* I come ....John 8:14
ye know not from *w* he is .....John 9:30
Antioch, from *w* they had .....Acts 14:26
w also we look for the ....Phil 3:20
from *w* they came out ....Heb 11:15
w come wars and fightings ....James 4:1
from *w* thou art fallen ....Rev 2:5
robes? and *w* came they? .....Rev 7:13

WHENSOEVER—*whenever*
w the stronger cattle did ......Gen 30:41
w ye will ye may do them .....Mark 14:7
W I take my journey into .....Rom 15:24

WHERE—*place; location*
Havilah, *w* there is gold.......Gen 2:11
W is Abel thy brother? ....Gen 4:9
was well watered every *w* .....Gen 13:10
W are the men which ....Gen 19:5
thee: dwell *w* it pleaseth ......Gen 20:15
w is he that hath taken ....Gen 27:33
Beth-el, *w* thou anointedst ....Gen 31:13
w thou vowedst a vow ....Gen 31:13
in the place *w* he talked.......Gen 35:13
the place *w* God spake........Gen 35:15
I pray thee, *w* they feed ......Gen 37:16
w the king's prisoners.........Gen 39:20
he sought *w* to weep..........Gen 43:30
w is he? why is it that ye .....Ex 2:20
upon the houses *w* ye are .....Ex 12:13
w were twelve wells of ....Ex 15:27
thick darkness *w* God was.....Ex 20:21
w I will meet you, to ....Ex 29:42
w I will meet with thee ....Ex 30:36
w the ashes are poured ....Lev 4:12
w they kill the burnt ....Lev 4:33
place *w* they kill the ....Lev 7:2
w Ahiman, Sheshai, and ......Num 13:22
w was no way to turn ....Num 22:26
place *w* his lot falleth ....Num 33:54
w thou hast seen how ....Deut 1:31
w thou sowedst thy seed ......Deut 11:10
Israel, *w* he sojourned ....Deut 18:6
W are their gods, their ....Deut 32:37
place *w* the priests' feet ....Josh 4:3
place, *w* ye shall lodge ....Josh 4:3
in the place *w* the feet of .....Josh 4:9
w he bowed, there he fell .....Judg 5:27
W is now thy mouth ....Judg 9:38
to sojourn *w* I may find ....Judg 17:9
man's house *w* her lord ....Judg 19:26
out of the place *w* she ....Ruth 1:7
W thou diest, will I die ....Ruth 1:17
W hast thou gleaned ....Ruth 2:19
w wroughtest thou? ....Ruth 2:19
w the ark of God was.........1Sam 3:3
city *w* the man of God........1Sam 9:10
God, *w* is the garrison of 1Sam 10:5
of the holes *w* they had hid ...1Sam 14:11
W are Samuel and David?.....1Sam 19:22
his place *w* his haunt is 1Sam 23:22
the way, *w* was a cave 1Sam 24:3
w Saul had pitched 1Sam 26:5
beheld the place *w* Saul 1Sam 26:5
w those that were left.........1Sam 30:9
to the place *w* Asahel fell 2Sam 2:23
w he knew that valiant........2Sam 11:16
w is thy master's son?.........2Sam 16:3
W is Ahimaaz and Jonathan? ..2Sam 17:20
w the Philistines had 2Sam 21:12
w was a man of great 2Sam 21:20
place *w* the officers were 1Kin 4:28
house *w* he dwelt had.........1Kin 7:8
up into a loft *w* he abode 1Kin 17:19
W is the Lord God 2Kin 2:14
w we dwell with thee is 2Kin 6:1
of God said, *W* fell it? 2Kin 6:6
W are the gods of Hamath 2Kin 18:34
w are the gods of.............2Kin 18:34
w the women wove 2Kin 23:7
w the Jebusites were 1Chr 11:4
unto our brethren every *w* 1Chr 13:2
w the Lord appeared unto.....2Chr 3:1
w they were servants to 2Chr 36:20
place *w* he sojourneth..........Ezra 1:4
the place *w* they offered ......Ezra 6:3
w are the vessels of the ....Neh 10:39
W were white, green ....Esth 1:6
or *w* were the righteous ....Job 4:7
and *w* the light is as ....Job 10:22
bread, saying, *W* is it? ....Job 15:23
him shall say, *W* is he? ....Job 20:7
say, *W* is the house of ....Job 21:28
w are the dwelling places......Job 21:28
w he doth work, but I ....Job 23:9
But *w* shall wisdom be ....Job 28:12
And *w* is..understanding? .....Job 28:12
w the workers of iniquity......Job 34:22
broad place, *w* there is........Job 36:16
W is the way *w* light ....Job 38:19
w is the place thereof ....Job 38:19
w the slain are, there is ......Job 39:30
language *w* their voice ....Ps 19:3
unto me, *W* is thy God? ......Ps 42:3
great fear, *w* no fear was......Ps 53:5
deep mire, *w* there is no ......Ps 69:2
W is their God? let him ....Ps 79:10
w she may lay her young......Ps 84:3
W the birds make their ....Ps 104:17
say, *W* is now their God? .....Ps 115:2
W no counsel is, the ....Prov 11:14
dinner of herbs *w* love is ......Prov 15:17

W

W no wood is, the fire ....Prov 26:20
w there is no talebearer ....Prov 26:20
to his place *w* he arose........Eccl 1:5
city *w* they had so done ....Eccl 8:10
w thou feedest, *w* thou ....Song 1:7
w there were a thousand ......Is 7:23
W are they? *W* are thy wise ...Is 19:12
w the grounded staff ....Is 30:32
W is the scribe? *w* is ....Is 33:18
w is he that counted the ......Is 33:18
W are the gods of Hamath ....Is 36:19
w are the gods of Sepharvaim .Is 36:19
these, *w* had they been? ......Is 49:21
and *w* is the fury of the ....Is 51:13
W is he that brought..........Is 63:11
w is he that put his holy ......Is 63:11
house *w* our fathers...........Is 64:11
w is the house that ye ....Is 66:1
w is the place of my rest? .....Is 66:1
W is the Lord that............Jer 2:6
and *w* no man dwelt? ....Jer 2:6
said not, *W* is the Lord? ......Jer 2:8
see *w* thou hast not been......Jer 3:2
w I set my name at the ....Jer 7:12
w is the flock that was ....Jer 13:20
W is the word of the...........Jer 17:15
land *w* ye be strangers ....Jer 35:7
W are now your prophets .....Jer 37:19
w he gave judgment ....Jer 39:5
w he gave judgment ....Jer 52:9
W is corn and wine? ....Lam 2:12
and I sat *w* they sat ....Ezek 3:15
w was the seat of the ....Ezek 8:3
w ye have been scattered......Ezek 11:17
in the furrows *w* it grew.......Ezek 17:10
country *w* they sojourn.........Ezek 20:38
w they have been scattered....Ezek 34:12
w the priests that approach....Ezek 42:13
place *w* the priests shall ....Ezek 46:20
w they shall bake the meat ....Ezek 46:20
he came near *w* I stood ....Dan 8:17
the place *w* it was said ....Hos 1:10
people. *W* is their God? ......Joel 2:17
w no gin is for him? ....Amos 3:5
W is the Lord thy God?.......Mic 7:10
W is the dwelling of the.......Nah 2:11
w the lion, even the old.......Nah 2:11
land *w* they have been ....Zeph 3:19
Your fathers, *w* are they? .....Zech 1:5
w is mine honor?.............Mal 1:6
a master, *w* is my fear? ....Mal 1:6
W is he that is born King .....Matt 2:2
stood over *w* the young ....Matt 2:9
w moth and rust doth ....Matt 6:19
w thieves break through.......Matt 6:19
w neither moth nor rust.......Matt 6:20
w thieves do not break.........Matt 6:20
man hath not *w* to lay ....Matt 8:20
For *w* two or three are.........Matt 18:20
reaping *w* thou hast...........Matt 25:24
and gathering *w* thou ....Matt 25:24
that I reap *w* I sowed.........Matt 25:26
W wilt thou that we ....Matt 26:17
w the scribes and the ....Matt 26:57
w Jesus had appointed ....Matt 28:16
uncovered the roof *w* he ......Mark 2:4
side, *w* the word is sown ......Mark 4:15
w they heard he was ....Mark 6:55
W their worm dieth not ....Mark 9:48
standing *w* it ought not ....Mark 13:14
W is the guest chamber ....Mark 14:14
w I shall eat the passover .....Mark 14:14
the place *w* they laid him .....Mark 16:6
w he had been brought up ....Luke 4:16
them, *W* is your faith? ....Luke 8:25
not *w* to lay his head ....Luke 9:58
w to bestow my fruits?........Luke 12:17
w your treasure is, there ......Luke 12:34
said unto him, *W* Lord?.......Luke 17:37
house *w* he entereth in........Luke 22:10
W is the guest chamber ....Luke 22:11
w I shall eat the passover .....Luke 22:11
Master, *w* dwellest thou?......John 1:38
The wind bloweth *w* it ....John 3:8
w he made the water wine ....John 4:46
man ascend up *w* he was ......John 6:62
w I am, thither ye cannot .....John 7:34
Bethlehem *w* David was? .....John 7:42
him, *W* is thy Father?.........John 8:19
w John at first baptized ....John 10:40
place *w* Martha met him ......John 11:30
W have ye laid him?..........John 11:34
if any man knew *w* he ....John 11:57
w Lazarus was which ....John 12:1
that *w* I am, there ye ....John 14:3
w was a garden, into the ......John 18:1
w Jesus was crucified ....John 19:20
we know not *w* they have .....John 20:2
I know not *w* they have ....John 20:13
w the disciples were ....John 20:19
w abode both Peter, and ......Acts 1:13
w they were assembled........Acts 4:31
w thou standest is holy........Acts 7:33
unto the house *w* I was ....Acts 11:11
city *w* we have preached ......Acts 15:36
w was a synagogue of.........Acts 17:1
w we abode seven days ....Acts 20:6
men every *w* against the ......Acts 21:28
falling into a place *w* two ....Acts 27:41
that every *w* it is spoken ......Acts 28:22
W is boasting then?...........Rom 3:27
But *w* sin abounded ....Rom 5:20
not *w* Christ was named ....Rom 15:20
W is the wise? *w* is the........1Cor 1:20
w is the disputer of this 1Cor 1:20
eye, *w* were the hearing?......1Cor 12:17
w were the smelling? 1Cor 12:17
O death, *w* is thy sting?.......1Cor 15:55
w the Spirit of the Lord.......2Cor 3:17
W is then the blessedness .....Gal 4:15
every *w* and in all things ......Phil 4:12
w Christ sitteth on the ....Col 3:1
that men pray every *w* 1Tim 2:8
w a testament is, there ....Heb 9:16
w envying and strife is ....James 3:16
w shall the ungodly and 1Pet 4:18
W is the promise of his 2Pet 3:4
and *w* thou dwellest ....Rev 2:13
even *w* Satan's seat is ....Rev 2:13
you, *w* Satan dwelleth ....Rev 2:13
w she hath a place ....Rev 12:6
w the whore sitteth ....Rev 17:15

WHEREABOUT—*about which*
business *w* I send thee 1Sam 21:2

WHEREAS—*since; although*
W thou hast searched ....Gen 31:37
w he was not worthy of death .Deut 19:6
w I have rewarded thee 1Sam 24:17
W I have not dwelt in 2Sam 7:6
W it was in thine heart........1Kin 8:18
w now thou shalt smite 2Kin 13:19
w my father put a heavy 2Chr 10:11
W our substance is not.........Job 22:20
w also he that is born in ......Eccl 4:14
W thou hast prayed to ....Is 37:21
w the sword reacheth unto ....Jer 4:10
W ye say, The Lord ....Ezek 13:7
w none followeth thee to......Ezek 16:34
w it lay desolate in the........Ezek 36:34
w thou sawest the feet ....Dan 2:41
w the king saw a watcher .....Dan 4:23
w four stood up for it.........Dan 8:22
W Edom saith, We are........Mal 1:4
that, *w* I was blind, now ......John 9:25
w there is among you 1Cor 3:3
W ye know not what...........James 4:14
w they speak against 1Pet 2:12
W angels, which are 2Pet 2:11

WHEREBY—*by; through; by what*
w shall I know that I ....Gen 15:8
drinketh, and *w* indeed ....Gen 44:5
w he may be made unclean....Lev 22:5
w an atonement shall be ......Num 5:8
w the Lord thy God ....Deut 7:19
w Jonathan knew that it 1Sam 20:33
w the people fall under ....Ps 45:5
w thou didst confirm..........Ps 68:9
w backsliding Israel ....Jer 3:8
name *w* he shall be called ....Jer 23:6
w they have sinned ....Jer 33:8
w they have transgressed ......Jer 33:8
w ye have transgressed........Ezek 18:31
w they have trespassed ....Ezek 39:26
the way of the gate *w* he ......Ezek 46:9
w they have reproached ....Zeph 2:8
W shall I know this?..........Luke 1:18
w we must be saved ....Acts 4:12
w we may give an account ....Acts 19:40
w we cry, Abba, Father ....Rom 8:15
W, when ye read, ye may .....Eph 3:4
w he is able even to ....Phil 3:21
w we may serve God ....Heb 12:28
W are given unto us 2Pet 1:4
w we know that it is the 1John 2:8

WHEREFORE—*therefore; for what reason or purpose*
w it is said, Even as ....Gen 10:9
W did Sarah laugh ....Gen 18:13
them, *W* come ye to me ......Gen 26:27
W didst thou flee away........Gen 31:27
W is it that thou dost ask .....Gen 32:29
W look ye so sadly ....Gen 40:7
W have ye rewarded evil ......Gen 44:4
W shall we die before ....Gen 47:19
w the name of it was ....Gen 50:11
W smitest thou thy fellow? ....Ex 2:13
W have ye not fulfilled........Ex 5:14
w hast thou so evil ....Ex 5:22
w hast thou dealt with us .....Ex 14:11
W the people did chide ....Ex 17:2
w do ye tempt the Lord?......Ex 17:2
W is this that thou hast ....Ex 17:3
W the children of Israel.......Ex 31:16
W have ye not eaten the ......Lev 10:17
W ye shall do my statutes .....Lev 25:18
w are we kept back, that......Num 9:7
w then were ye not afraid .....Num 12:8
W now do ye transgress ....Num 14:41
w have ye made us to.........Num 20:5
W have ye brought us up .....Num 21:5
W they that speak in..........Num 21:27
w camest thou not unto ....Num 22:37
W, said they, if we have ......Num 32:5
W it shall come to pass ....Deut 7:12
W I command thee, saying ....Deut 19:7
W the name of the place ......Josh 5:9
w hast thou at all brought .....Josh 7:7
W the name of that place .....Josh 7:26
W have ye beguiled us ....Josh 9:22
W I also said, I will not ....Judg 2:3
W I have not sinned ....Judg 11:27
w then are ye come up.........Judg 12:3
W she went forth out of.......Ruth 1:7
W it came to pass, when 1Sam 1:20
W kick ye at my sacrifice 1Sam 2:29
W hath the Lord smitten 1Sam 4:3
W then do ye harden your 1Sam 6:6
W he put forth the end 1Sam 14:27
W Saul sent messengers 1Sam 16:19
W Saul said to David 1Sam 18:21
w then wilt thou sin 1Sam 19:5
W cometh not the son of......1Sam 20:27
W shall he be slain? 1Sam 20:32
w he came down into a 1Sam 23:25
W hearest thou men's 1Sam 24:9
W let the young men 1Sam 25:8
w then hast thou not..........1Sam 26:15
w Ziklag pertaineth unto 1Sam 27:6
W then dost thou ask of 1Sam 28:16
W now rise up early in........1Sam 29:10
w that place was called........2Sam 2:16
w Abner with the hinder 2Sam 2:23
W thou art great, O Lord 2Sam 7:22
W approached ye so nigh 2Sam 11:20
is dead, *w* should I fast? 2Sam 12:23
W have thy servants set 2Sam 14:31
W goest thou also with........2Sam 15:19
W wilt thou run, my son 2Sam 18:22
W wentest not thou with 2Sam 19:25
W, David said unto the 2Sam 21:3
W his servants said 1Kin 1:2
W is this noise of the city 1Kin 1:41
W he said unto the 1Kin 20:9

W wilt thou go to him 2Kin 4:23
w consider, I pray you 2Kin 5:7
w came this mad fellow 2Kin 9:11
W they spake to the king 2Kin 17:26
W Hanun took David's........1Chr 19:4
W David blessed the Lord.....1Chr 29:10
W now let the fear of the 2Chr 19:7
W he did evil in the sight 2Chr 22:4
W the anger of the Lord 2Chr 25:15
W the wrath of the Lord 2Chr 29:8
W the Lord brought upon 2Chr 33:11
W the king said unto me ......Neh 2:2
w Haman sought to destroy ...Esth 3:6
W is light given to him........Job 3:20
W then hast thou brought .....Job 10:18
W hidest thou thy face ....Job 13:24
W do the wicked live ....Job 21:7
W, Job, I pray thee, hear .....Job 33:1
W doth the wicked contemn ...Ps 10:13
W should I fear in the ....Ps 49:5
W hast thou made all ....Ps 89:47
W is there a price in the ......Prov 17:16
W I praised the dead ....Eccl 4:2
w, when I looked that it ......Is 5:4
W my bowels shall sound ......Is 16:11
W hear the word of the ....Is 28:14
W thus saith the Holy..........Is 30:12
W, when I came, was there ...Is 50:2
W have we fasted, say ....Is 58:3
w have we afflicted our ....Is 58:3
W I will yet plead with.........Jer 2:9
w say my people, We are ......Jer 2:31
W thus saith the Lord..........Jer 5:14
W doth the way of the ....Jer 12:1
w are all they happy that.......Jer 12:1
W hath the Lord pronounced ..Jer 16:10
W are they cast out, he ....Jer 22:28
w should this city be laid ......Jer 27:17
W dost thou prophesy...........Jer 32:3
w should he slay thee ....Jer 40:15
W commit ye this great ....Jer 44:7
W gloriest thou in the..........Jer 49:4
W doth a living man ....Lam 3:39
W, as I live, saith the ....Ezek 5:11
W thus saith the Lord..........Ezek 13:20
w turn yourselves, and ....Ezek 18:32
W I gave them also ....Ezek 20:25
W sighest thou? that ....Ezek 21:7
W thus saith the Lord ....Ezek 24:6
W I poured my fury upon ......Ezek 36:18
W at that time certain ....Dan 3:8
W king Darius signed ....Dan 6:9
Knowest thou *w* I come ....Dan 10:20
w should they say among.......Joel 2:17
W they cried unto the..........Jon 1:14
w lookest thou upon them.....Hab 1:13
Yet ye say, *W*? Because ....Mal 2:14
W, if God so clothe the ....Matt 6:30
W think ye evil in your ....Matt 9:4
W it is lawful to do well ......Matt 12:12
faith, *w* didst thou doubt?.....Matt 14:31
W they are no more twain ....Matt 19:6
W, behold, I send unto ....Matt 23:34
Friend, *w* art thou come? .....Matt 26:50
W neither thought I ....Luke 7:7
W then gavest not thou ....Luke 19:23
hear: *w* would ye hear it ....John 9:27
W of these men which ....Acts 1:21
cause *w* ye are come?..........Acts 10:21
W my sentence is, that ....Acts 15:19
W if Demetrius, and the ....Acts 19:38
w they cried so against.........Acts 22:24
the cause *w* they accused......Acts 23:28
W I have brought him ....Acts 25:26
W, sirs, be of good cheer .....Acts 27:25
W God also gave them..........Rom 1:24
W, my brethren, ye also ....Rom 7:4
W? Because they sought ....Rom 9:32
W ye must needs be ....Rom 13:5
W I beseech you, be ye 1Cor 4:16
W let him that thinketh 1Cor 10:12
W whosoever shall eat 1Cor 11:27
W I give you to understand ...1Cor 12:3
W tongues are for a sign 1Cor 14:22
W I beseech you that ye 2Cor 2:8
W henceforth know we........2Cor 5:16
W, though I wrote unto 2Cor 7:12
W? because I love you 2Cor 11:11
W then serveth the law? ......Gal 3:19
W thou art no more a ....Gal 4:7
W I also, after I heard ....Eph 1:15
W I desire that ye faint ....Eph 3:13
W putting away lying ....Eph 4:25
W be ye not unwise, but ....Eph 5:17
W God also hath highly ....Phil 2:9
W if ye be dead with ....Col 2:20
W we would have come 1Thess 2:18
W comfort one another 1Thess 4:18
W comfort yourselves 1Thess 5:11
W also we pray always 2Thess 1:11
W I put thee in 2Tim 1:6
W rebuke them sharply ....Titus 1:13
W, though I might be ....Philem 8
W in all things it behooved ....Heb 2:17
W (as the Holy Ghost ....Heb 3:7
W he is able also to ....Heb 7:25
W when he cometh into ....Heb 10:5
W seeing we also are ....Heb 12:1
W we receiving a kingdom ....Heb 12:28
W, my beloved brethren ......James 1:19
W he saith, God resisteth .....James 4:6
W gird up the loins of 1Pet 1:13
W also it is contained in 1Pet 2:6
W the rather, brethren 2Pet 1:10
W, beloved, seeing that 2Pet 3:14
w slew he him? Because 1John 3:12
W, if I come, I will 3John 10
W didst thou marvel? ....Rev 17:7

WHEREIN—*in which; in what way; how*
w there is life, I have ....Gen 1:30
w is the breath of life ....Gen 7:15
w thou hast sojourned ....Gen 21:23
w they were strangers ....Gen 36:7
w they made them serve ......Ex 1:14
houses, *w* they shall eat ....Ex 12:7
show them the way *w* ....Ex 18:20
w shall it be known here ......Ex 33:16
w he hath sinned, come ....Lev 4:23
vessel *w* it is sodden ....Lev 6:28
w there is plenty of water .....Lev 11:36
of skin, *w* the plague is ....Lev 13:52
burn that *w* the plague is......Lev 13:57
w we have done foolishly .....Num 12:11
and *w* we have sinned ....Num 12:11
burnt all their cities *w* ....Num 31:10
pollute the land *w* ye are......Num 35:33
A land *w* thou shalt eat ....Deut 8:9
w the nations which ye........Deut 12:2
or sheep, *w* is blemish ....Deut 17:1
wilderness *w* they chased ......Josh 8:24
w the Lord's tabernacle ....Josh 22:19
in all the way *w* we went......Josh 24:17
see *w* his great strength ....Judg 16:5
told me *w* thy great............Judg 16:15
w the jewels of gold were 1Sam 6:15
places *w* I have walked 2Sam 7:7
ark, *w* is the covenant of......1Kin 8:21
w they have transgressed 1Kin 8:50
w Jehoiada the priest 2Kin 12:2
their cities *w* they dwelt 2Kin 17:29
w this passover was holden 2Kin 23:23
w Solomon was instructed 2Chr 3:3
way, *w* they should walk 2Chr 6:27
w he built high places..........2Chr 33:19
him, *w* was written thus ....Ezra 5:7
W was written, It is............Neh 6:6
w the king had promoted ....Esth 5:11
days *w* the Jews rested ....Esth 9:22
day perish *w* I was born........Job 3:3
understand *w* I have erred .....Job 6:24
Zion, *w* thou hast dwelt........Ps 74:2
to the days *w* thou hast ....Ps 90:15
years *w* we have seen evil .....Ps 90:15
w are things creeping ....Ps 104:25
the way *w* I should walk ......Ps 143:8
labor *w* I have labored.........Eccl 2:19
w I have showed myself........Eccl 2:19
in that *w* he laboreth? ....Eccl 3:9
w is he to be accounted ....Is 2:22
w shall go no galley with ......Is 33:21
w thou hast labored ....Is 47:12
cities, *w* thou trustedst ....Jer 5:17
land..*w* thou trustedst..........Jer 12:5
be the day *w* I was born ......Jer 20:14
day *w* my mother bare ....Jer 20:14
w they shall not stumble ....Jer 31:9
pit *w* Ishmael had cast ....Jer 41:9
a vessel *w* is no pleasure ......Jer 48:38
w ye are scattered ....Ezek 20:34
w ye have been defiled.........Ezek 20:43
enter into a city *w* is...........Ezek 26:10
w they have sinned, and ......Ezek 37:23
w she burned incense to ......Hos 2:13
w are more than sixscore ......Jon 4:11
w I have wearied thee? ....Mic 6:3
w thou hast transgressed ......Zeph 3:11
out of the pit *w* is no ....Zech 9:11
W hast thou loved us? ....Mal 1:2
W have we polluted thee? .....Mal 1:7
said, *W* shall we return? ......Mal 3:7
w most of his mighty works ...Matt 11:20
w the sick of the palsy lay.....Mark 2:4
w thou hast been instructed ...Luke 1:4
his armor *w* he trusted ....Luke 11:22
w was never man yet laid .....John 19:41
tongue, *w* we were born? .....Acts 2:8
W were all manner of..........Acts 10:12
w thou judgest another........Rom 2:1
dead *w* we were held ....Rom 7:6
same calling *w* he was called ..1Cor 7:20
received, and *w* ye stand 1Cor 15:1
that *w* they glory, they 2Cor 11:12
w he hath made us ....Eph 1:6
W in time past ye walked .....Eph 2:2
w ye were also careful ....Phil 4:10
w also ye are risen with ....Col 2:12
W I suffer trouble, as 2Tim 2:9
W God, willing more ....Heb 6:17
w was the golden pot ....Heb 9:4
W ye greatly rejoice 1Pet 1:6
W they think it strange........1Pet 4:4
w the heavens being on 2Pet 3:12
days *w* Antipas was my ....Rev 2:13

WHEREINSOEVER—*wherever*
w any is bold, (I speak........2Cor 11:21

WHEREINTO—*into which*
w any of them falleth ....Lev 11:33
into the land *w* he went.......Num 14:24
one *w* his disciples ....John 6:22

WHEREOF—*of what; of which; with or by which*
w I commanded thee ....Gen 3:11
w any of the blood is ....Lev 6:30
w men bring an offering ......Lev 27:9
in the midst *w* I dwell ....Num 5:3
well *w* the Lord spake ....Num 21:16
to pass, *w* he spake unto ......Deut 13:2
by the way *w* I spake ....Deut 28:68
w I spake unto you by ....Josh 20:2
kingdom, *w* Samuel spake 1Sam 10:16
weight *w* was a talent of 2Sam 12:30
his sickness *w* he died..........2Kin 13:14
w was according to the........2Chr 3:8
w were made vessels for 2Chr 24:14
w one went on the right.......Neh 12:31
poison *w* drinketh up my......Job 6:4
w shall make glad the..........Ps 46:4
for us; *w* we are glad ....Ps 126:3
any thing *w* it may be..........Eccl 1:10
w every one bear twins ....Song 4:2
this city, *w* ye say ....Jer 32:36
famine, *w* ye were afraid ......Jer 42:16
of that *w* it was full...........Ezek 32:15
w the word of the Lord ....Dan 9:2
w she hath said, These ....Hos 2:12
things *w* ye accuse him.........Luke 23:14
raised up, *w* we all are ....Acts 2:32
new doctrine, *w* thou ....Acts 17:19
w they were informed ....Acts 21:24
things *w* they now accuse .....Acts 24:13
things *w* I am accused of......Acts 26:2

W

he hath *w* to glory; but ....Rom 4:2
w I may glory through Jesus...Rom 15:17
things *w* ye wrote unto me 1Cor 7:1
your bounty, *w* ye had 2Cor 9:5
W I was made a minister ......Eph 3:7
he hath *w* he might trust ......Phil 3:4
w ye heard before in the ......Col 1:5
W I am made a minister ......Col 1:25
say, nor *w* they affirm 1Tim 1:7
to come, *w* we speak ....Heb 2:5
w all are partakers............Heb 12:8
w ye have heard that it 1John 4:3

WHEREON—*on which*

[*also* WHEREUPON]
land *w* thou liest, to thee .....Gen 28:13
place *w* thou standest is ....Ex 3:5
that *w* it was sprinkled........Lev 6:27
w any part of their ....Lev 11:35
w is the seed of copulation ....Lev 15:17
any thing *w* she sitteth ....Lev 15:23
bed *w* she lieth all the ....Lev 15:26
w the soles of your feet ....Deut 11:24
place *w* thou standest is ....Josh 5:15
the pillars *w* the house ....Judg 16:26
Abel, *w* they set down 1Sam 6:18
of gold, *w* the showbread 1Kin 7:48
w the showbread was set 2Chr 4:19
W the princes of Israel........2Chr 12:6
in safety, *w* he resteth ....Job 24:23
W are the foundations ....Job 38:6
w there hang a thousand ......Song 4:4
w if a man lean, it will go .....Is 36:6
the cherub, *w* he was ....Ezek 9:3
w they set their minds ....Ezek 24:25
sticks *w* thou writest ....Ezek 37:20
w also they laid the............Ezek 40:42
the piece *w* it rained not ......Amos 4:7
W he promised with an ....Matt 14:7
a colt tied, *w* never man ......Mark 11:2
the hill *w* their city was ....Luke 4:29
a colt tied, *w* yet never man...Luke 19:30
to reap..*w* ye bestowed no ....John 4:38
W certain Jews from ....Acts 24:18
W as I went to Damascus .....Acts 26:12
W neither the first............Heb 9:18

WHERESOEVER—*wherever*
w the priest looketh ....Lev 13:12
w thou canst sojourn..........2Kin 8:1
W I have walked with all......1Chr 17:6
or go *w* it seemeth ....Jer 40:5
w the children of men ....Dan 2:38
w the carcase is, there ....Matt 24:28
w he taketh him, he ....Mark 9:18
w he shall go in, say ye ....Mark 14:14
W the body is, thither ....Luke 17:37

WHERETO—*to which; to what place*

[*also* WHEREUNTO]
tribe *w* they are received......Num 36:4
from off the land *w* ye go .....Deut 4:26
w the ark of the Lord.........2Chr 8:11
w the king advanced him ......Esth 10:2
w might the strength of ....Job 30:2
w I may continually resort.....Ps 71:3
in the thing *w* I sent it ....Is 55:11
w they desire to return........Jer 22:27
w I will not do any more......Ezek 5:9
w shall I liken this...........Matt 11:16
W shall we liken the ....Mark 4:30
W then shall I liken the ....Luke 7:31
W shall I liken the............Luke 13:20
them *w* this would grow.......Acts 5:24
nigh *w* was the city of ....Acts 27:8
w ye desire again to be in .....Gal 4:9
w we have already attained ....Phil 3:16
W I also labor, striving........Col 1:29
W he called you by our 2Thess 2:14
W I am ordained a preacher...1Tim 2:7
w thou art also called 1Tim 6:12
W I am appointed a 2Tim 1:11
w also they were appointed....1Pet 2:8
w ye do well that ye take 2Pet 1:19

WHEREUPON—*See* WHEREON

WHEREWITH—*with what; by means of*

[*also* WHEREWITHAL]
w his father blessed him ......Gen 27:41
w thou shalt do signs ....Ex 4:17
w thou smotest the river ......Ex 17:5
sanctuary *w* they minister .....Num 3:31
w they minister unto it ....Num 4:9
w they minister about it ....Num 4:14
w they have beguiled ....Num 25:18
her bond *w* she hath ....Num 30:4
bond *w* she hath bound ....Num 30:4
w she bound her soul ....Num 30:6
w she bound her soul ....Num 30:8
w she bound her soul ....Num 30:11
of wood, *w* he may die ....Num 35:18
w the Lord was wroth ....Deut 9:19
vesture, *w* thou coverest ......Deut 22:12
w thine enemies shall ....Deut 28:55
heart *w* thou shalt fear ....Deut 28:67
w he stretched out the ....Josh 8:26
w shall I save Israel? ....Judg 6:15
w by me they honor God .....Judg 9:9
w thou mightest be ....Judg 16:6
tell us *w* we shall send it 1Sam 6:2
for *w* should he reconcile 1Sam 29:4
hatred *w* he hated her 2Sam 13:15
than the love *w* he had 2Sam 13:15
and *w* shall I make the........2Sam 21:3
w I have made supplication....1Kin 8:59
w he made Israel to sin 1Kin 15:26
w he made Israel to sin 1Kin 15:34
w thou hast provoked..........1Kin 21:22
w he fought against...........2Kin 13:12
w his anger was kindled.......2Kin 23:26
w Solomon made the 1Chr 18:8
w David his father had........2Chr 2:17
Lord said unto him, *W*?.......2Chr 18:20
w thou didst testify ....Neh 9:34
speeches *w* he can do no ......Job 15:3
w they have reproached ....Ps 79:12
W thine enemies have.........Ps 89:51
w they have reproached ....Ps 89:51
girdle *w* he is girded ....Ps 109:19
W the mower filleth not.......Ps 129:7
w his mother crowned him ....Song 3:11
w ye may cause the weary.....Is 28:12
w I said I would benefit.......Jer 18:10
w ye fight against the king ....Jer 21:4
vessels of brass *w* they ....Jer 52:18
w the Lord hath afflicted......Lam 1:12
w ye there hunt the souls .....Ezek 13:20
labor *w* he served against .....Ezek 29:20
idols *w* they had polluted .....Ezek 36:18
w his spirit was troubled ......Dan 2:1
W shall I come before the .....Mic 6:6
w the Lord will smite all ......Zech 14:12
the fear *w* he feared me.......Mal 2:5
savor, *w* shall it be salted? ....Matt 5:13
or, *W* shall we be clothed? ....Matt 6:31
w soever they shall ....Mark 3:28
w shall it be seasoned?........Luke 14:34
the towel *w* he was girded.....John 13:5
w one may edify another ......Rom 14:19
w we ourselves are 2Cor 1:4
w I think to be bold 2Cor 10:2
w Christ hath made us free ....Gal 5:1
great love *w* he loved us ......Eph 2:4
w ye shall be able to...........Eph 6:16
joy *w* we joy for your sakes ...1Thess 3:9
w he was sanctified, an ....Heb 10:29

WHET—*to sharpen*
If I *w* my glittering sword .....Deut 32:41
he turn not, he will *w* his .....Ps 7:12
and he do not *w* the edge .....Eccl 10:10

WHETHER—*which of the two*
see *w* they have done ....Gen 18:21
w stolen by day, or stolen .....Gen 31:39
now *w* it be thy son's coat ....Gen 37:32
man *w* ye had yet a brother? ...Gen 43:6
and see *w* they be yet alive....Ex 4:18
w they will walk in my law ....Ex 16:4
W he have gored a son or.....Ex 21:31
see *w* he have put his hand....Ex 22:8
w ox or sheep, that is male....Ex 34:19
w it be a male or female ......Lev 3:1
w it be a carcase of an ....Lev 5:2
w it be any vessel of wood ....Lev 11:32
w it be a woolen garment .....Lev 13:47
W it be in the warp or ....Lev 13:48
w in a skin, or in anything ....Lev 13:48
w it be bare within or.........Lev 13:55
w it be one of your own ......Lev 16:29
w she be born at home, or ....Lev 18:9
estimate it, *w* it be good ......Lev 27:14
w of the seed of the land .....Lev 27:30
w it was by day or by night ...Num 9:21
w my word shall come to .....Num 11:23
they dwell in, *w* it be good ...Num 13:19
w in tents, or in strongholds ...Num 13:19
what the land is, *w* it be ......Num 13:20
w there be wood therein or ...Num 12:20
w it be of men or beasts ......Num 18:15
w there hath been any such ...Deut 4:32
to know *w* ye love the Lord ...Deut 13:3
w they be young ones or ......Deut 22:6
w the gods which your ....Josh 24:15
w they will keep the way......Judg 2:22
W is better for you, either ....Judg 9:2
not young men, *w* poor or ....Ruth 3:10
Who can tell *w* God will be ...2Sam 12:22
W they be come out for........1Kin 20:18
or *w* they be come out for 1Kin 20:18
w I shall recover of this 2Kin 1:2
w with many, or with them....2Chr 14:11
small or great, *w* man or 2Chr 15:13
seed, *w* they were of Israel....Ezra 2:59
w it be unto death or ....Ezra 7:26
seed, *w* they were of Israel....Neh 7:61
w Mordecai's matters would ...Esth 3:4
w thou art come to the ....Esth 4:14
w it be done against a ....Job 34:29
w for correction, or for his ....Job 37:13
w his work be pure, and *w* ....Prov 20:11
w he shall be a wise man or ...Eccl 2:19
knowest not *w* shall prosper ...Eccl 11:6
w they both shall be alike .....Eccl 11:6
w it be good, or *w* it be evil...Eccl 12:14
see *w* the vine flourished ......Song 6:11
w a man doth travail with .....Jer 30:6
w they will hear, or *w* they ....Ezek 2:5
w they will hear, or *w* they ....Ezek 3:11
w is easier, to say, Thy sins ...Matt 9:5
for *w* is greater, the gold......Matt 23:17
tell us *w* thou be the Christ ...Matt 26:63
w Elijah will come to save ....Matt 27:49
W is it easier to say to the ....Mark 2:9
w Elijah will come to save ....Mark 15:36
w he were the Christ, or ......Luke 3:15
w he would heal on the ....Luke 6:7
w he be able with ten..........Luke 14:31
asked *w* the man were a ....Luke 23:6
the doctrine, *w* it be of God...John 7:17
or *w* I speak of myself ....John 7:17
w of these two thou hast ......Acts 1:24
w ye sold the land for so ......Acts 5:8
asked *w* Simon, which was ....Acts 10:18
w there be any Holy Ghost....Acts 19:2
obey; *w* of sin unto death .....Rom 6:16
w we live, we live unto the....Rom 14:8
w we die, we die unto the.....Rom 14:8
w we live therefore or die .....Rom 14:8
I know not *w* I baptized any ..1Cor 1:16
w thou shalt save thy 1Cor 7:16
man, *w* thou shalt save thy 1Cor 7:16
W therefore ye eat, or 1Cor 10:31
w we be Jews or Gentiles 1Cor 12:13
w we be bond or free; and 1Cor 12:13
w there be prophecies, they ...1Cor 13:8
w there be tongues, they 1Cor 13:8
w there be knowledge, it 1Cor 13:8
w it were I or they, so 1Cor 15:11
w we be afflicted, it is for 2Cor 1:6
w we be comforted, it is for ...2Cor 1:6
w present or absent, we 2Cor 5:9
w we be beside ourselves, it ...2Cor 5:13
W any do inquire of Titus 2Cor 8:23
(*w* in the body, I cannot tell...2Cor 12:2

or *w* out of the body, I 2Cor 12:2
w ye be in the faith.............2Cor 13:5
Lord, *w* he be bond or free ...Eph 6:8
w in pretense, or in truth .....Phil 1:18
w I come and see you, or .....Phil 1:27
w they be thrones, or.........Col 1:16
w we wake or sleep, we.......1Thess 5:10
w by word or our epistle 2Thess 2:15
w it be to the king, as 1Pet 2:13
the spirits *w* they are of God . .1John 4:1

WHICH—*See* INTRODUCTION

WHILE—*during the time that*

[*also* WHILES, WHILST]
W the earth remaineth ....Gen 8:22
from Isaac his son, *w* he yet...Gen 25:6
w Joseph made himself........Gen 45:1
w my glory passeth by, that ...Ex 33:22
thee with my hand *w* I pass ...Ex 33:22
his face shone *w* he talked ....Ex 34:29
w he doeth somewhat.........Lev 4:27
w the flesh was yet between ...Num 11:33
w I meet the Lord yonder .....Num 23:15
the slayer *w* his heart is ....Deut 19:6
w the children of Israel ....Josh 14:10
And Ehud escaped *w* they ....Judg 3:26
death *w* it is yet morning......Judg 6:31
a *w* after, in the time of ......Judg 15:1
came *w* the flesh was in........1Sam 2:13
but stand thou still a *w* 1Sam 9:27
w yet I live show me the 1Sam 20:14
the *w* they were in Carmel 1Sam 25:7
the *w* he dwelleth in the 1Sam 27:11
w there was war between 2Sam 3:6
house for a great *w* to come...2Sam 7:19
weep for the child, *w* it was ...2Sam 12:21
w they were in the way 2Sam 13:30
from Giloh *w* he offered 2Sam 15:12
w he was yet alive in the......2Sam 18:14
thine enemies *w* they 2Sam 24:13
w thou yet talkest there 1Kin 1:14
w he yet spake, behold 1Kin 1:42
house, *w* it was in building 1Kin 6:7
a *w* that the brook dried 1Kin 17:7
w he yet talked with them.....2Kin 6:33
Ziklag, *w* he yet kept himself. .1Chr 12:1
his father *w* he yet lived 2Chr 10:6
Lord is with you, *w* ye be 2Chr 15:2
w he was yet young, he 2Chr 34:3
the work cease, *w* I leave .....Neh 6:3
w they stand by, let them .....Neh 7:3
w Mordecai sat in the king's...Esth 2:21
W he was yet speaking.........Job 1:16
exalted for a little *w*, but.....Job 24:24
w ye searched out what to ....Job 32:11
w there is none to deliver .....Ps 7:2
little *w* and the wicked.........Ps 37:10
w I was musing the fire ....Ps 39:3
w they say daily unto me......Ps 42:10
Thus will I bless thee *w* ....Ps 63:4
w their meat was yet in ....Ps 78:30
God *w* I have my being ....Ps 104:33
w that I withal escape.........Ps 141:10
W I live will I praise the ....Ps 146:2
unto my God *w* I have any....Ps 146:2
W as yet he had not made ....Prov 8:26
Chasten thy son *w* there is ....Prov 19:18
madness is in their heart *w* ....Eccl 9:3
W the sun or the light or......Eccl 12:2
W the king sitteth at his........Song 1:12
For yet a very little *w*, and ....Is 10:25
it not yet a very little *w*........Is 29:17
Seek ye the Lord *w* he may ...Is 55:6
call ye upon him *w* he is .....Is 55:6
w they are yet speaking, I ....Is 65:24
w ye look for light, he turn ...Jer 13:16
W their children remember ....Jer 17:2
w he was yet shut up in the ...Jer 33:1
now *w* he was not yet gone ...Jer 40:5
w they sought their meat to ...Lam 1:19
to pass *w* they were slaying....Ezek 9:8
W they see vanity unto........Ezek 21:29
w they divine a lie unto ....Ezek 21:29
W the word was in the ....Dan 4:31
Belshazzar, *w* he tasted the....Dan 5:2
Yea, *w* I was speaking in .....Dan 9:21
for yet a little *w*, and I ....Hos 1:4
an oven, *w* they lie in wait ....Hos 7:6
w they be folden together .....Nah 1:10
w they are drunken as ....Nah 1:10
little *w*, and I will shake ......Hag 2:6
away *w* they stand upon ......Zech 14:12
But *w* he thought on these .....Matt 1:20
w thou art in the way with ....Matt 5:25
W he yet talked to the people .Matt 12:46
w men slept his enemy came ..Matt 13:25
w he sent the multitudes ......Matt 14:22
w they abode in Galilee ....Matt 17:22
W the bridegroom tarried .....Matt 25:5
w I go and pray yonder ....Matt 26:36
after a *w* came unto him .....Matt 26:73
stole him away *w* we slept.....Matt 28:13
rising up a great *w* before .....Mark 1:35
W he yet spake, there came ...Mark 5:35
w he sent away the people ....Mark 6:45
Sit ye here *w* I shall pray .....Mark 14:32
whether he had been any *w* ...Mark 15:44
w he executed the priest's .....Luke 1:8
w the bridegroom is with......Luke 5:34
W he yet spake, there ....Luke 8:49
w they wondered every one ...Luke 9:43
w the other is yet a great .....Luke 14:32
w he yet spake, behold a......Luke 22:47
w he yet spake, the cock ......Luke 22:60
w he talked with us by.........Luke 24:32
w they yet believed not ....Luke 24:41
w I was yet with you, that ....Luke 24:44
Yet a little *w* am I with ....John 7:33
little *w* is the light with ....John 12:35
w ye have the light lest ....John 12:35
children, yet a little *w* I.......John 13:33
A little *w* and ye shall not .....John 16:16
a little *w* and ye shall see .....John 16:16
A little *w* and ye shall not .....John 16:17
a little *w* and ye shall see .....John 16:17
that he saith, A little *w*? ......John 16:18
A little *w* and ye shall not ....John 16:19
a little *w* and ye shall see .....John 16:19
W I was with them in the ......John 17:12
w they beheld, he was taken ..Acts 1:9
W it remained was it not ......Acts 5:4
Dorcas made, *w* she was ......Acts 9:39
w Peter doubted in himself ....Acts 10:17
W Peter yet spake these ......Acts 10:44
w Paul waited for them at.....Acts 17:16
w Apollos was at Corinth .....Acts 19:1
w I prayed in the temple ......Acts 22:17
W he answered for himself ....Acts 25:8
they had looked a great *w*.....Acts 28:6
thoughts the mean *w*..........Rom 2:15
So then if, *w* her husband .....Rom 7:3
w one saith, I am of Paul 1Cor 3:4
I trust to tarry a *w* with.......1Cor 16:7
W we look not at the things ...2Cor 4:18
w we are at home in the 2Cor 5:6
W by the experiment of 2Cor 9:13
w we seek to be justified......Gal 2:17
in pleasure is dead *w* she......1Tim 5:6
daily, *w* it is called Today ......Heb 3:13
w as the first tabernacle ....Heb 9:8
w ye were made a gazingstock .Heb 10:33
w ye became companions .....Heb 10:33
For yet a little *w* and he ......Heb 10:37
W they behold your chaste 1Pet 3:2
that ye have suffered a *w* 1Pet 5:10
deceivings *w* they feast 2Pet 2:13
W they promise them liberty ..2Pet 2:19

WHIP—*a lash used for flogging*

[*also* WHIPS]
hath chastised you with *w* 1Kin 12:11
father chastised you with *w*....2Chr 10:11
father chastised you with *w*....2Chr 10:14
A *w* for the horse, a bridle ....Prov 26:3
The noise of a *w* and the .....Nah 3:2

WHIRLETH—*rotate with force or speed*
it *w* about continually and.....Eccl 1:6

WHIRLWIND—*a great storm or tempest*
Used literally of:
Elijah's translation.......2Kin 2:1
Its fury ....Is 17:13
Used figuratively of:
Sudden destruction ......Prov 1:27
Suddenness ....Is 5:8
God's anger............Jer 23:19
God's might ....Nah 1:3

[*also* WHIRLWINDS]
Elijah went up by a *w* into 2Kin 2:11
answered Job out of the *w* ....Job 38:1
Lord unto Job out of the *w* ...Job 40:6
take them away as with a *w* ...Ps 58:9
As the *w* passeth so is the....Prov 10:25
As *w* in the south pass ....Is 21:1
w shall take them away as.....Is 40:24
the *w* shall scatter them ....Is 41:16
with his chariots like a *w*......Is 66:15
chariots shall be as a *w* ....Jer 4:13
great *w* shall be raised up .....Jer 25:32
come against him like a *w*.....Dan 11:40
that is driven with the *w* ......Hos 13:3
out as a *w* to scatter me ......Hab 3:14
I scattered them with a *w* .....Zech 7:14
go with *w* of the south ....Zech 9:14

WHISPER—*to speak very softly*

[*also* WHISPERED, WHISPERINGS]
saw that his servants *w*........2Sam 12:19
that hate me *w* together.......Ps 41:7
and thy speech shall *w* out ....Is 29:4
w, swellings, tumults 2Cor 12:20

WHISPERER—*a gossiper*
Separates chief friends ...Prov 16:28

[*also* WHISPERERS]
and a *w* separateth chief ......Prov 16:28
deceit, malignity, *w* ....Rom 1:29

WHIT—*the smallest part imaginable*
all the spoil thereof every *w* ...Deut 13:16
Samuel told him every *w*.......1Sam 3:18
I have made a man every *w* ...John 7:23
feet, but is clean every *w* .....John 13:10
not a *w* behind the very.......2Cor 11:5

WHITE—*the absence of color*

[*also* WHITED, WHITER]
every one that had some *w* ....Gen 30:35
pilled *w* strakes in them ....Gen 30:37
w appear which was in the ....Gen 30:37
and his teeth *w* with milk .....Gen 49:12
was like coriander seed, *w* ....Ex 16:31
in the plague is turned *w*.......Lev 13:3
bright spot be *w* in the skin ...Lev 13:4
hair thereof be not turned *w* ..Lev 13:4
the rising be *w* in the skin.....Lev 13:10
it have turned the hair *w*, and .Lev 13:10
again, and be changed unto *w* .Lev 13:16
boil there be a *w* rising ....Lev 13:19
or a bright spot, *w*, and ....Lev 13:19
there be no *w* hairs therein....Lev 13:21
that burneth have a *w* bright ..Lev 13:24
somewhat reddish, or *w* ....Lev 13:24
be no *w* hair in the bright .....Lev 13:26
of their flesh be darkish *w* ....Lev 13:39
of the sore be *w* reddish in....Lev 13:43
became leprous, *w* as snow ....Num 12:10
ye that ride on *w* asses ....Judg 5:10
his presence a leper as *w*.......2Kin 5:27
being arrayed in *w* linen 2Chr 5:12
Where were *w*, green and ....Esth 1:6
and *w*, and black, marble ....Esth 1:6
taste in the *w* of an egg? ......Job 6:6
me, and I shall be *w* than .....Ps 51:7
it was *w* as snow in Salmon ...Ps 68:14
thy garments be always *w* .....Eccl 9:8
My beloved is *w* and ruddy....Song 5:10
they shall be as *w* as snow ....Is 1:18
snow, they were *w* than milk ..Lam 4:7
the wine of Helbon and *w*.....Ezek 27:18
whose garment was *w* as snow .Dan 7:9
shall be purified and made *w* ..Dan 12:10
branches thereof are made *w* ..Joel 1:7

W

red horses, speckled and *w* ....Zech 1:8
the *w* go forth after them .....Zech 6:6
make one hair *w* or black .....Matt 5:36
are like unto *w* sepulchers.....Matt 23:27
and his raiment *w* as snow ....Matt 28:3
shining, exceeding *w* as snow ..Mark 9:3
no fuller on earth can *w* ......Mark 9:3
his raiment was *w* and ....Luke 9:29
for they are *w* already to ......John 4:35
men stood by them in *w* ......Acts 1:10
God shall smite thee, thou *w* ..Acts 23:3
and his hairs were *w* like ......Rev 1:14
as *w* as snow and his eyes .....Rev 1:14
shall walk with me in *w* ....Rev 3:4
w raiment, that thou mayest ...Rev 3:18
and behold a *w* horse ....Rev 6:2
w robes were given unto ....Rev 6:11
are arrayed in *w* robes? ....Rev 7:13
I looked and behold a *w* ......Rev 14:14
in fine linen, clean and *w* .....Rev 19:8
followed him upon *w* horses ...Rev 19:14
clothed in fine linen, *w* ....Rev 19:14
See COLORS

WHITHER—*to whatever place*

[*also* WHITHERSOEVER]
thou? and *w* wilt thou go? ....Gen 16:8
in all places *w* thou goest .....Gen 28:15
is not; and I, *w* shall I go? ....Gen 37:30
a place *w* he shall flee ....Ex 21:13
w I bring you, shall ye not ....Lev 18:3
the land *w* thou sentest us.....Num 13:27
of his refuge *w* he was fled ....Num 35:25
W shall we go up? our ....Deut 1:28
land *w* ye go to possess it .....Deut 4:5
w the Lord shall lead you .....Deut 4:27
w thou goest to possess ....Deut 7:1
w thou goest in to possess .....Deut 11:10
w thou goest to possess ....Deut 11:29
thou shalt let her go *w*........Deut 21:14
w thou goest to possess ....Deut 23:20
w thou goest to possess it .....Deut 28:21
w the Lord thy God hath .....Deut 30:1
w thou passest over Jordan ....Deut 30:18
w they go to be among ....Deut 31:16
in the mount *w* thou goest ....Deut 32:50
mayest prosper *w* thou ....Josh 1:7
w thou sendest us, we will ....Josh 1:16
w the men went I wot not.....Josh 2:5
W they went out, the hand ....Judg 2:15
W goest thou? and whence ....Judg 19:17
for *w* thou goest, I will go ....Ruth 1:16
and to his servant, *W* went 1Sam 10:14
w he turned himself, he 1Sam 14:47
Keilah, and went *w* they 1Sam 23:13
David said, *W* shall I go up? ..2Sam 2:1
with thee *w* thou wentest......2Sam 7:9
seeing I go *w* I may, return ...2Sam 15:20
w thou turnest thyself 1Kin 2:3
go not forth thence any *w* 1Kin 2:36
land *w* they were carried 1Kin 8:47
shall carry thee *w* I know 1Kin 18:12
said, Thy servant went no *w* ..2Kin 5:25
prospered *w* he went forth 2Kin 18:7
thee *w* thou hast walked 1Chr 17:8
the land *w* they are carried 2Chr 6:37
w he had fled from the 2Chr 10:2
And the rulers knew not *w* ....Neh 2:16
w the king's commandment ....Esth 4:3
W the tribes go up the ....Ps 122:4
W shall I go from thy Spirit ...Ps 139:7
or *w* shall I flee from thy .....Ps 139:7
w it turneth, it prospereth .....Prov 17:8
in the grave *w* thou goest .....Eccl 9:10
W is thy beloved gone, O .....Song 6:1
w is thy beloved turned ....Song 6:1
w we flee for help to be ......Is 20:6
places *w* I have driven them ...Jer 8:3
lands *w* he had driven them ...Jer 16:15
place *w* they have led him.....Jer 22:12
countries *w* I had driven ....Jer 23:8
city *w* I have caused you to ...Jer 29:7
nations *w* I have driven ....Jer 29:18
w I have driven them in.......Jer 32:37
in all places *w* thou goest .....Jer 45:5
nation *w* the outcasts of ....Jer 49:36
w the spirit was to go they ....Ezek 1:12
W the spirit was to go, they ...Ezek 1:20
w they shall be carried ....Ezek 6:9
among the heathen *w* they ....Ezek 12:16
the heathen, *w* they went .....Ezek 36:20
heathen, *w* they be gone ......Ezek 37:21
w the rivers shall come........Ezek 47:9
w thou hast driven them ....Dan 9:7
place *w* ye have sold them ....Joel 3:7
Then said I, *W* goest thou?....Zech 2:2
follow thee *w* thou goest ......Matt 8:19
And *w* he entered into ....Mark 6:56
follow thee *w* thou goest ......Luke 9:57
place *w* he himself would .....Luke 10:1
whence it cometh and *w* it ....John 3:8
W will he go, that we shall ....John 7:35
whence I came and *w* I go ....John 8:14
whence I come and *w* I go ....John 8:14
W I go, ye cannot come.......John 8:22
W I go, ye cannot come.......John 13:33
unto him, Lord *w* goest thou? .John 13:36
W I go, thou canst not ....John 13:36
we know not *w* thou goest ....John 14:5
w the Jews always resort ......John 18:20
walkedst *w* thou wouldest .....John 21:18
carry thee *w* thou wouldest....John 21:18
me on my journey *w* I go 1Cor 16:6
W the forerunner is...........Heb 6:20
w the governor listeth.........James 3:4
knoweth not *w* he goeth 1John 2:11
follow the Lamb *w* he goeth...Rev 14:4

WHO—*See* INTRODUCTION

WHOLE—*complete; free of wounds or injury; restored; sound*

Means of making, by:
Normal healing..........Josh 5:8
Touch ....Matt 9:21
Faith ....Mark 10:52
Risen Christ ....Acts 4:9, 10

Effects of, seen in:
Perfect restoration ....Matt 14:36
Instantaneous healing ....John 5:9
Complete obedience .....John 5:11-15

[*also* WHOLLY]
watered the *w* face of the .....Gen 2:6
the *w* land of Ethiopia ....Gen 2:13
on the face of the *w* earth.....Gen 8:9
the *w* earth was of one........Gen 11:1
Is not the *w* land before ......Gen 13:9
w assembly of the ....Ex 12:6
to kill this *w* assembly ....Ex 16:3
and the *w* mount quaked ......Ex 19:18
the fat thereof and the *w*......Lev 3:9
the *w* congregation of.........Lev 4:13
Lord it shall be *w* burnt........Lev 6:22
Moses burnt the *w* ram ....Lev 8:21
not *w* reap the corners of .....Lev 19:9
redeem it within a *w* year .....Lev 25:29
of the *w* congregation ....Num 3:7
they are *w* given unto him ....Num 3:9
For they are *w* given unto.....Num 8:16
w piece shalt thou make ....Num 10:2
they may eat a *w* month ......Num 11:21
according to your *w* number ...Num 14:29
w congregation journeyed .....Num 20:22
have *w* followed the Lord .....Num 32:12
hath *w* followed the Lord .....Deut 1:36
are under the *w* heaven ....Deut 2:25
Lord thy God of *w* stones.....Deut 27:6
w burnt sacrifice upon ....Deut 33:10
an altar of *w* stones, over .....Josh 8:31
So Joshua took the *w* land ....Josh 11:23
I *w* followed the Lord my .....Josh 14:8
he *w* followed the Lord God ..Josh 14:14
w congregation of the ....Josh 22:12
w congregation of Israel.......Josh 22:18
w dedicated the silver unto ....Judg 17:3
was there four *w* months ......Judg 19:2
offering *w* unto the Lord 1Sam 7:9
because my life is yet *w* in 2Sam 1:9
w multitude of Israel..........2Sam 6:19
w house be overlaid with......1Kin 6:22
w kingdom out of his hand 1Kin 11:34
the *w* house of Ahab shall 2Kin 9:8
w at thy commandment 1Chr 28:21
blessed the *w* congregation 2Chr 6:3
w number of the chief of the ..2Chr 26:12
according to the *w* law and....2Chr 33:8
w congregation together was...Ezra 2:64
w congregation together was ...Neh 7:66
the *w* kingdom of Ahasuerus ..Esth 3:6
and his hands make *w* ....Job 5:18
full strength being *w* at ....Job 21:23
who hath disposed the *w* ......Job 34:13
is under the *w* heaven ....Job 41:11
O Lord, with my *w* heart .....Ps 9:1
offering and *w* burnt offering ..Ps 51:19
of the Lord of the *w* earth ....Ps 97:5
praise the Lord with my *w* ....Ps 111:1
my *w* heart have I sought .....Ps 119:10
favor with my *w* heart ....Ps 119:58
I cried with my *w* heart ....Ps 119:145
w, as those that go down.......Prov 1:12
be showed before the *w*.......Prov 26:26
conclusion of the *w* matter ....Eccl 12:13
this is the *w* duty of man......Eccl 12:13
w head is sick, and the *w* .....Is 1:5
staff, the *w* stay of bread......Is 3:1
and the *w* stay of water ....Is 3:1
w work upon mount Zion .....Is 10:12
The *w* earth is at rest, and ....Is 14:7
Rejoice not thou, *w* Palestina..Is 14:29
set in my ward *w* nights ....Is 21:8
w gone up to the housetops? ..Is 22:1
God of the *w* earth shall he ...Is 54:5
walls against the *w* land ....Jer 1:18
a noble vine, *w* a right seed ...Jer 2:21
w land shall be desolate ....Jer 4:27
even the *w* seed of Ephraim ...Jer 7:15
w land is made desolate ....Jer 12:11
me the *w* house of Israel ......Jer 13:11
and the *w* house of Judah .....Jer 13:11
be *w* carried away captive .....Jer 13:19
cannot be made *w* again ......Jer 19:11
w land shall be a desolation ...Jer 25:11
my *w* heart and with my *w* ....Jer 32:41
had smitten the *w* army of ....Jer 37:10
leave thee *w* unpunished ......Jer 46:28
hammer of the *w* earth cut ....Jer 50:23
w land shall be confounded....Jer 51:47
of beauty, The joy of the *w* ...Lam 2:15
the *w* remnant of thee will ....Ezek 5:10
w body, and their backs, and ..Ezek 10:12
all the house of Israel *w* ......Ezek 11:15
of the *w* earth with thee ......Ezek 32:4
are the *w* house of Israel......Ezek 37:11
may keep the *w* form thereof..Ezek 43:11
be for the *w* house of Israel ...Ezek 45:6
mountain, and filled the *w* ....Dan 2:35
be over the *w* kingdom ....Dan 6:1
shall devour the *w* earth ......Dan 7:23
on the face of the *w* earth.....Dan 8:5
three *w* weeks were fulfilled ...Dan 10:3
captive the *w* captivity ....Amos 1:6
the *w* family which I ....Amos 3:1
shall rise up *w* as a flood......Amos 8:8
the Lord of the *w* earth ....Mic 4:13
w land shall be devoured ......Zeph 1:18
to and fro through the *w* ......Zech 4:10
forth over the face of the *w* ...Zech 5:3
robbed me, even this *w* ....Mal 3:9
thy *w* body should be cast .....Matt 5:29
thy *w* body should be cast.....Matt 5:30
w body shall be full of ....Matt 6:23
the *w* city came out to meet...Matt 8:34
be *w* need not a physician ....Matt 9:12
his garment, I shall be *w* ......Matt 9:21
thy faith hath made thee *w* ....Matt 9:22
woman was made *w* from .....Matt 9:22
w multitude stood on the......Matt 13:2
till the *w* was leavened ....Matt 13:33
was made *w* from that very....Matt 15:28
if he shall gain the *w* world ...Matt 16:26
him the *w* band of soldiers ...Matt 27:27
that are *w* have no need of....Mark 2:17
w multitude was by the sea ....Mark 4:1
thy faith hath made thee *w* ....Mark 5:34

and be *w* of thy plague ....Mark 5:34
ran through that *w* region .....Mark 6:55
if he shall gain the *w* world ...Mark 8:36
than all *w* burnt offerings ....Mark 12:33
scribes and the *w* council......Mark 15:1
darkness over the *w* land ......Mark 15:33
w multitude of the people .....Luke 1:10
hand was restored *w* as the ....Luke 6:10
servant *w* that had been.......Luke 7:10
published throughout the *w*....Luke 8:39
and she shall be made *w* ......Luke 8:50
w body also is full of light.....Luke 11:34
w body therefore be full of ....Luke 11:36
the *w* shall be full of light .....Luke 11:36
thy faith hath made thee *w* ....Luke 17:19
dwell on the face of the *w* ....Luke 21:35
believed and his *w* house ......John 4:53
him, Wilt thou be made *w*? ...John 5:6
whit *w* on the sabbath day? ...John 7:23
the *w* nation perish not ....John 11:50
pleased the *w* multitude ....Acts 6:5
a *w* year they assembled ......Acts 11:26
elders with the *w* church ......Acts 15:22
city *w* given to idolatry........Acts 17:16
w years in his own hired ......Acts 28:30
spoken of throughout the *w* ...Rom 1:8
of the *w* church saluteth ......Rom 16:23
leaven leaveneth the *w* lump? .1Cor 5:6
If the *w* body were an eye 1Cor 12:17
If the *w* were hearing 1Cor 12:17
is a debtor to do the *w* law....Gal 5:3
w family in heaven and ....Eph 3:15
Put on the *w* armor of God ...Eph 6:11
God of peace sanctify you *w* ..1Thess 5:23
your *w* spirit and soul and.....1Thess 5:23
thyself *w* to them; that........1Tim 4:15
who subvert *w* houses ....Titus 1:11
whosoever shall keep the *w* ...James 2:10
and we turn about their *w*.....James 3:3
for the sins of the *w* world 1John 2:2
deceiveth the *w* world.........Rev 12:9

WHOLESOME—*good; sound*
A *w* tongue is a tree of life ...Prov 15:4
and consent not to *w* words ...1Tim 6:3

WHOM—*See* INTRODUCTION

WHOMSOEVER—*whoever*
w thou findest thy gods ....Gen 31:32
w he toucheth that hath the ...Lev 15:11
w I say unto thee, This ....Judg 7:4
giveth it to *w* he will, and .....Dan 4:17
appointeth over it *w* he ....Dan 5:21
w the Son will reveal him .....Matt 11:27
W I shall kiss, that same is ....Matt 26:48
W I shall kiss, that same is ....Mark 14:44
and to *w* I will I give it ....Luke 4:6
w it shall fall, it will grind.....Luke 20:18
receiveth *w* I send ....John 13:20
on *w* I lay hands, he may .....Acts 8:19

WHORE—*a promiscuous woman; prostitute*
[*also* WHORE'S, WHORES]
to cause her to be a *w*........Lev 19:29
herself by playing the *w*.......Lev 21:9
to play the *w* in her father's ...Deut 22:21
not bring the hire of a *w*......Deut 23:18
concubine played the *w* ....Judg 19:2
For a *w* is a deep ditch ....Prov 23:27
the adulterer and the *w* ....Is 57:3
thou hadst a *w* forehead ......Jer 3:3
hast played the *w* also ....Ezek 16:28
They give gifts to all *w*........Ezek 16:33
are separated with *w*..........Hos 4:14
judgment of the great *w* ......Rev 17:1
these shall hate the *w*.........Rev 17:16
hath judged the great *w*.......Rev 19:2

WHOREDOM—*the practice of indiscriminate sexual activities*
she is with child by *w*.........Gen 38:24
lest the land fall to *w*, and ....Lev 19:29
and bear your *w*, until your ...Num 14:33
people began to commit *w* ....Num 25:1
w of thy mother Jezebel 2Kin 9:22
w of the house of Ahab 2Chr 21:13
the land with thy *w*..........Jer 3:2
the lightness of her *w*.........Jer 3:9
and didst commit *w* with ......Ezek 16:17
of thy *w* a small matter ....Ezek 16:20
and multiplied thy *w* ....Ezek 16:25
from other women in thy *w* ...Ezek 16:34
followeth thee to commit *w* ...Ezek 16:34
commit ye *w* after their ....Ezek 20:30
committed *w* in Egypt ....Ezek 23:3
committed *w* in their youth ....Ezek 23:3
left she her *w* brought from ...Ezek 23:8
her *w* more than her sister ....Ezek 23:11
defiled her with their *w* ....Ezek 23:17
So she discovered her *w* ....Ezek 23:18
of thy *w* shall be discovered ...Ezek 23:29
thy lewdness and thy *w* ....Ezek 23:29
Will they now commit *w* with..Ezek 23:43
their kings, by their *w* ....Ezek 43:7
w and children of *w* ....Hos 1:2
hath committed great *w* ....Hos 1:2
they be the children of *w* .....Hos 2:4
W and wine and new wine ....Hos 4:11
when they commit *w*..........Hos 4:14
thou committest *w*, and Israel. .Hos 5:3
spirit of *w* is in the midst .....Hos 5:4
the *w* of the well-favored......Nah 3:4
nations through her *w*.........Nah 3:4

WHOREMONGER—*one who consorts with whores*
[*also* WHOREMONGERS]
that no *w*, nor unclean ....Eph 5:5
For *w*, for them that defile 1Tim 1:10
w and adulterers God ....Heb 13:4
and *w*, and sorcerers..........Rev 21:8

WHORING—*practicing indiscriminate sexual activities*
go a *w* after their gods ....Ex 34:15
go a *w* after their gods ....Ex 34:16
go a *w* after their gods ....Ex 34:16
whom they have gone a *w*.....Lev 17:7
to go a *w* after them, I ....Lev 20:6
which ye use to go a *w* ....Num 15:39
and go a *w* after the gods .....Deut 31:16
they went a *w* after other .....Judg 2:17
went a *w* after Baalim ....Judg 8:33
went a *w* after the gods 1Chr 5:25
Jerusalem to go a *w* 2Chr 21:13
all them that go a *w* from .....Ps 73:27
go a *w* after their idols........Ezek 6:9
a *w* from under their God .....Hos 4:12

WHORISH—*whore-like*
by means of a *w* woman ......Prov 6:26
I am broken with their *w* .....Ezek 6:9

WHOSE—*of whom; that which belongs to whom*
w seed is in itself, upon ....Gen 1:11
in *w* nostrils was the ....Gen 7:22
Egyptian, *w* name was Hagar ..Gen 16:1
W daughter art thou? ....Gen 24:23
W art thou? and whither ......Gen 32:17
w are these before thee? ......Gen 32:17
Canaanite, *w* name was ....Gen 38:2
man, *w* these are, am I ....Gen 38:25
I pray thee, *w* are these......Gen 38:25
w branches run over the ......Gen 49:22
Lord, *w* name is Jealous ......Ex 34:14
the women *w* heart stirred ....Ex 35:26
in *w* heart the Lord had.......Ex 36:2
one *w* heart stirred him up ....Ex 36:2
w hair is fallen off his.........Lev 13:40
w seed goeth from him........Lev 15:32
w head the anointing oil ......Lev 21:10
w father was an Egyptian .....Lev 24:10
the man *w* eyes are open......Num 24:3
a land *w* stones are iron.......Deut 8:9
w hills thou mayest dig........Deut 8:9
a nation *w* tongue thou ....Deut 28:49
of the Amorites, in *w* land ....Josh 24:15
the captain of *w* host was .....Judg 4:2
son, *w* name he called ....Judg 8:31
w name was Delilah ....Judg 16:4
w sight I shall find grace ......Ruth 2:2
under *w* wings thou art ....Ruth 2:12
w name was Kish, the son.....1Sam 9:1
of men, *w* hearts God had 1Sam 10:26
w ox have I taken? 1Sam 12:3
or *w* ass have I taken? 1Sam 12:3
of *w* hand have I received.....1Sam 12:3
w height was six cubits........1Sam 17:4
w son is this youth? 1Sam 17:55
W son art thou, thou young ...1Sam 17:58
a concubine *w* name was 2Sam 3:7
w name is called by the 2Sam 6:2
had a young son, *w* name 2Sam 9:12
had a friend, *w* name was 2Sam 13:3
w name was Shimei, the son...2Sam 16:5
w heart is as the heart of 2Sam 17:10
w name was Sheba, the son ...2Sam 20:1
w spear was like a weaver's ...2Sam 21:19
woman *w* the living child......1Kin 3:26
servant, *w* mother's name 1Kin 11:26
a lord on *w* hand the king.....2Kin 7:2
w son he had restored 2Kin 8:1
is not that he, *w* high places...2Kin 18:22
and *w* altars Hezekiah hath....2Kin 18:22
W sisters were Zeruiah, and ...1Chr 2:16
an Egyptian, *w* name was 1Chr 2:34
w sister's name was Maachah ..1Chr 7:15
Axel had six sons, *w* names ...1Chr 8:38
Axel had six sons, *w* names ...1Chr 9:44
w spear staff was like a 1Chr 20:5
w brethren were strong men ...1Chr 26:7
ways, *w* heart thou knowest ...2Chr 6:30
Lord was there, *w* name was ..2Chr 28:9
all them *w* spirit God had .....Ezra 1:5
w habitation is in Jerusalem ...Ezra 7:15
a certain Jew, *w* name was ....Esth 2:5
the land of Uz, *w* name was ..Job 1:1
of clay, *w* foundation is in.....Job 4:19
W hope shall be cut off, and ..Job 8:14
and *w* trust shall be a.........Job 8:14
In *w* hand is the soul of.......Job 12:10
and *w* spirit came from thee? ..Job 26:4
Out of *w* womb came the ice? .Job 38:29
In *w* eyes a vile person is .....Ps 15:4
In *w* hands is mischief, and....Ps 26:10
is he *w* transgression is........Ps 32:1
is forgiven, *w* sin is covered ...Ps 32:1
w mouth must be held in......Ps 32:9
and in *w* mouth are no........Ps 38:14
w spirit was not steadfast......Ps 78:8
is the man *w* strength is in ....Ps 84:5
in *w* heart are the ways of ....Ps 84:5
W mouth speaketh vanity .....Ps 144:8
is that people, *w* God is the ...Ps 144:15
W ways are crooked, and .....Prov 2:15
a generation, *w* teeth are as ..Prov 30:14
w heart is snares and nets .....Eccl 7:26
shall be as an oak *w* leaf ......Is 1:30
W arrows are sharp, and ......Is 5:28
as an oak, *w* substance is .....Is 6:13
them captives, *w* captives .....Is 14:2
w land the rivers have ....Is 18:7
w antiquity is of ancient.......Is 23:7
w merchants are princes.......Is 23:8
w traffickers are the ....Is 23:8
w glorious beauty is a.........Is 28:1
w fire is in Zion, and his......Is 31:9
is it not he, *w* high places .....Is 36:7
and *w* altars Hezekiah ....Is 36:7
w right hand I have holden....Is 45:1
divided the sea, *w* waves ......Is 51:15
rest, *w* waters cast up ....Is 57:20
w language thou knowest......Jer 5:15
and *w* hope the Lord is ....Jer 17:7
them *w* face thou fearest ......Jer 22:25
w wickedness I have hid ......Jer 33:5
know *w* words shall stand .....Jer 44:28
king, *w* name is the Lord .....Jer 46:18
they *w* judgment was not......Jer 49:12
w words thou canst not ....Ezek 3:6
king, *w* oath he despised ......Ezek 17:16
and *w* covenant he brake, even. Ezek 17:16
in *w* sight I brought them .....Ezek 20:14
w day is come, when iniquity ..Ezek 21:25
w day is come, when their ....Ezek 21:29
w flesh is as the flesh of ......Ezek 23:20

W

w issue is like the issue of .....Ezek 23:20
the pot w scum is therein .....Ezek 24:6
w scum is not gone out ....Ezek 24:6
w appearance was like the .....Ezek 40:3
w prospect is toward the ......Ezek 40:46
gate w prospect is toward .....Ezek 43:4
w dwelling is not with ....Dan 2:11
image, w brightness was ....Dan 2:31
w bodies the fire had no ....Dan 3:27
w name was Belteshazzar .....Dan 4:19
W leaves were fair, and ....Dan 4:21
upon w branches the fowls .....Dan 4:21
God in w hand thy breath .....Dan 5:23
and w are all thy ways ....Dan 5:23
w teeth were of iron ....Dan 7:19
w kingdom is an everlasting ...Dan 7:27
w name was called ....Dan 10:1
w teeth are the teeth of ....Joel 1:6
w height was like the ....Amos 2:9
of the rock, w habitation ....Obad 3
w cause this evil is upon ....Jon 1:7
w goings forth have been ....Mic 5:2
w rampart was the sea ....Nah 3:8
w name is The Branch ....Zech 6:12
w shoes I am not worthy ....Matt 3:11
w surname was Thaddaeus .....Matt 10:3
W wife shall she be of the .....Matt 22:28
w shoes I am not worthy ....Mark 1:7
them, W is this image and .....Mark 12:16
man w name was Joseph ....Luke 1:27
w shoes I am not worthy ....Luke 3:16
w right hand was withered .....Luke 6:6
w blood Pilate had mingled .....Luke 13:1
W image and superscription ...Luke 20:24
w name was Cleopas ....Luke 24:18
from God, w name was ....John 1:6
nobleman w son was sick ......John 4:46
w own the sheep are not ......John 10:12
his kinsman w ear Peter ....John 18:26
young man's feet, w name .....Acts 7:58
w house is by the sea side .....Acts 10:6
Simon, w surname is Peter .....Acts 11:13
John, w surname was Mark ...Acts 12:25
John, w surname was Mark ...Acts 15:37
w house joined hard to the ....Acts 18:7
of the island, w name was .....Acts 28:7
w praise is not of men ....Rom 2:29
W mouth is full of cursing .....Rom 2:14
w iniquities are forgiven ....Rom 4:7
and w sins are covered ....Rom 4:7
w praise is in the gospel 2Cor 8:18
w eyes Jesus Christ hath ....Gal 3:1
W end is destruction, w ....Phil 3:19
w names are in the book ......Phil 4:3
w coming is after the 2Thess 2:9
W mouths must be stopped .....Titus 1:11
w house are we, if we hold .....Heb 3:6
w end is to be burned ....Heb 6:8
w builder and maker is ....Heb 11:10
w faith follow, considering .....Heb 13:7
w stripes ye were healed 1Pet 2:24
w daughters ye are, as long ...1Pet 3:6
w judgment now of a long 2Pet 2:3
trees w fruit withereth ....Jude 12
w names are not written ....Rev 13:8
w names were not written ......Rev 17:8

WHOSO—*whoever*

[*also* WHOSOEVER]

W slayeth Cain, vengeance .....Gen 4:15
W sheddeth man's blood ....Gen 9:6
w toucheth the mount shall .....Ex 19:12
W compoundeth any like it .....Ex 30:33
w putteth any of it upon ....Ex 30:33
w doeth any work therein ......Ex 31:14
W hath any gold, let them .....Ex 32:24
w doeth work therein shall .....Ex 35:2
For w eateth the fat of the .....Lev 7:25
w beareth ought of the ....Lev 11:25
w toucheth their carcase ....Lev 11:27
w toucheth his bed shall ....Lev 15:5
w toucheth her shall be ....Lev 15:19
w toucheth any thing that ......Lev 15:22
w eateth it shall be cut off .....Lev 17:14
w lieth carnally with ....Lev 19:20
W he be of thy seed in ....Lev 21:17
w toucheth any creeping ....Lev 22:5
W curseth his God shall ....Lev 24:15
w is defiled by the dead ....Num 5:2
W cometh any thing near .....Num 17:13
w toucheth one that is ....Num 19:16
w hath killed any person ......Num 31:19
w hath touched any slain .....Num 31:19
W killeth any person, the .....Num 35:30
w will not hearken unto ....Deut 18:19
W killeth his neighbor ....Deut 19:4
W he be that doth rebel ....Josh 1:18
w shall go out of the doors ....Josh 2:19
w shall be with thee in the ....Josh 2:19
W is fearful and afraid ....Judg 7:3
W cometh not forth after 1Sam 11:7
W getteth up to the gutter 2Sam 5:8
w heareth it will say 2Sam 17:9
w would, he consecrated 1Kin 13:33
w shall be wanting, he 2Kin 10:19
w smiteth the Jebusites 1Chr 11:6
w cometh to consecrate 2Chr 13:9
and w else cometh into the 2Chr 23:7
w followeth her, let him 2Chr 23:14
w remaineth in any place ....Ezra 1:4
w will not do the law of ....Ezra 7:26
w, whether man or woman ....Esth 4:11
W offereth praise glorifieth ....Ps 50:23
W is wise, and will observe ....Ps 107:43
w toucheth her shall not be ...Prov 6:29
But w committeth adultery ....Prov 6:32
W is simple, let him turn ....Prov 9:4
W despieth the word shall .....Prov 13:13
W mocketh the poor ....Prov 17:5
W provoketh him to anger .....Prov 20:2
W stoppeth his ears at the .....Prov 21:13
W boasteth himself of ....Prov 25:14
W hideth her hideth the ....Prov 27:16
W keepeth the fig tree ....Prov 27:18
W causeth the righteous ....Prov 28:10
W walketh uprightly shall .....Prov 28:18
w walketh wisely, he shall .....Prov 28:26
W is partner with a thief ......Prov 29:24
w pleaseth God shall escape ...Eccl 7:26
w breaketh an hedge, a ....Eccl 10:8
w shall gather together ....Is 54:15
which w heareth, his ears .....Jer 19:3
Then w heareth the sound .....Ezek 33:4
w falleth not down and ....Dan 3:6
W shall read this writing ....Dan 5:7
w shall call on the name ....Joel 2:32
that w will not come up ....Zech 14:17
W therefore shall break ....Matt 5:19
w shall do and teach them .....Matt 5:19
w shall kill shall be in ....Matt 5:21
w is angry with his brother ....Matt 5:22
w shall say to his brother .....Matt 5:22
but w shall say, Thou fool .....Matt 5:22
W shall put away his wife .....Matt 5:31
w shall put away his wife ......Matt 5:32
w shall marry her that is ....Matt 5:32
w shall compel thee to go .....Matt 5:41
w shall not receive you ....Matt 10:14
w shall deny me before ....Matt 10:33
w shall not be offended in .....Matt 11:6
w speaketh a word against .....Matt 12:32
w speaketh against the ....Matt 12:32
For w hath, to him shall ....Matt 13:12
w hath not, from him shall ....Matt 13:12
w will save his life shall ....Matt 16:25
W therefore shall humble ......Matt 18:4
w shall receive one such ....Matt 18:5
w marrieth her which is put ...Matt 19:9
w will be great among you .....Matt 20:26
w shall fall on this stone ....Matt 21:44
W shall swear by the temple ...Matt 23:16
w shall swear by the gold .....Matt 23:16
W shall swear by the altar .....Matt 23:18
w sweareth by the gift that ....Matt 23:18
w readeth, let him ....Matt 24:15
w shall do the will of God .....Mark 3:35
W curseth father or ....Mark 7:10
W will come after me, let .....Mark 8:34
w will save his life shall ....Mark 8:35
w shall lose his life for my ....Mark 8:35
W shall receive one of such ...Mark 9:37
w shall receive me, receiveth ..Mark 9:37
w shall offend one of these ....Mark 9:42
W shall not receive the ....Mark 10:15
w of you will be the chiefest ...Mark 10:44
W cometh to me, and ....Luke 6:47
w hath, to him shall be ....Luke 8:18
w hath not, from him shall ....Luke 8:18
For w will save his life ....Luke 9:24
w will lose his life for my .....Luke 9:24
W shall receive this child .....Luke 9:48
w shall receive me receiveth ...Luke 9:48
w shall speak a word against ..Luke 12:10
w doth not bear his cross .....Luke 14:27
W putteth away his wife ....Luke 16:18
w marrieth her that is put .....Luke 16:18
W shall seek to save his life ...Luke 17:33
w shall lose his life shall ......Luke 17:33
W shall fall upon that ....Luke 20:18
w believeth in him should .....John 3:15
w drinketh of the water ....John 4:14
W eateth my flesh, and ....John 6:54
W committeth sin is the ....John 8:34
w believeth on me should .....John 12:46
w maketh himself a king ....John 19:12
w sins ye remit, they ....John 20:23
w sins ye retain, they ....John 20:23
w shall call on the name ......Acts 2:21
w among you feareth God ......Acts 13:26
man, w thou art that judgest ..Rom 2:1
W believeth on him shall ......Rom 10:11
W therefore resisteth the ......Rom 13:2
w shall eat this bread, and 1Cor 11:27
w of you are justified ....Gal 5:4
w looketh into the perfect .....James 1:25
w shall keep the whole law ....James 2:10
w keepeth his word, in him 1John 2:5
W denied the Son, the 1John 2:23
W abideth in him sinneth 1John 3:6
w sinneth hath not seen 1John 3:6
w doeth not righteousness 1John 3:10
W shall confess that Jesus 1John 4:15
w is born of God sinneth 1John 5:18
w transgresseth, and 2John 9
w receiveth the mark of his ....Rev 14:11
w loveth and maketh a lie .....Rev 22:15

WHY—*for what reason; cause; purpose*

W art thou wroth? ....Gen 4:6
w is thy countenance fallen? ...Gen 4:6
W saidst thou, She is my ......Gen 12:19
w should I be deprived also ...Gen 27:45
w should we die in thy ....Gen 47:15
W have ye done this thing .....Ex 1:18
w the bush is not burnt ....Ex 3:3
W have we done this, that ....Ex 14:5
w sittest thou thyself alone ....Ex 18:14
W came we forth out of ....Num 11:20
W should the name of our .....Num 27:4
therefore w should we die? ....Deut 5:25
W hast thou troubled us? .....Josh 7:25
w have ye done this? ....Judg 2:2
w did Dan remain in ships ....Judg 5:17
W is his chariot so long in .....Judg 5:28
w tarry the wheels of his .....Judg 5:28
W hast thou served us thus .....Judg 8:1
w are ye come unto me now ..Judg 11:7
W askest thou thus after ......Judg 13:18
w is this come to pass ....Judg 21:3
w will ye go with me? ....Ruth 1:11
W have I found grace ....Ruth 2:10
w weepest thou? and w 1Sam 1:8
w is thy heart grieved? 1Sam 1:8
w his hand is not removed 1Sam 6:3
W camest thou down 1Sam 17:28
W hast thou deceived me 1Sam 19:17
w should I kill thee? 1Sam 19:17
w shouldest thou bring me 1Sam 20:8
W have ye conspired 1Sam 22:13
W hast thou deceived me? 1Sam 28:12
w is it that thou hast sent 2Sam 3:24
w then didst thou not go 2Sam 11:10
W art thou, being the king's ...2Sam 13:4
W should this dead dog 2Sam 16:9
w didst thou not smite him 2Sam 18:11

W are ye the last to bring 2Sam 19:11
w should the king recompense .2Sam 19:36
w then did ye despise us 2Sam 19:43
w wilt thou swallow up the 2Sam 20:19
w doth my lord the king 2Sam 24:3
W hast thou done so?.........1Kin 1:6
w dost thou ask Abishag 1Kin 2:22
W hath the Lord done this 1Kin 9:8
W is thy spirit so sad 1Kin 21:5
them, *W* are ye now turned ...2Kin 1:5
Hazael said, *W* weepeth.......2Kin 8:12
W have ye not built me an 1Chr 17:6
w then doth my lord require...1Chr 21:3
w will he be a cause of 1Chr 21:3
W hath the Lord done thus....2Chr 7:21
W transgress ye the 2Chr 24:20
w shouldest thou be 2Chr 25:16
W should the king of Assyria ..2Chr 32:4
w should damage grow to the..Ezra 4:22
W is thy countenance sad .....Neh 2:2
w should the work cease ......Neh 6:3
W lodge ye about the wall? ...Neh 13:21
W transgressest thou the ......Esth 3:3
W died I not from the ....Job 3:11
w did I not give up the ....Job 3:11
W did the knees prevent ......Job 3:12
w the breasts that I should ....Job 3:12
w hast thou set me as a mark .Job 7:20
be wicked, *w* then labor ......Job 9:29
W do ye persecute me as......Job 19:22
w should not my spirit be .....Job 21:4
w then are ye thus altogether ..Job 27:12
W dost thou strive against.....Job 33:13
W do the heathen rage........Ps 2:1
W standest thou afar off ......Ps 10:1
w hidest thou thyself in ....Ps 10:1
my God, *w* hast thou ....Ps 22:1
w art thou so far from ....Ps 22:1
W hast thou forgotten.........Ps 42:9
w go I mourning because......Ps 42:9
W art thou cast down..........Ps 42:11
w art thou disquieted ....Ps 42:11
w dost thou cast me off? ......Ps 43:2
w go I mourning because......Ps 43:2
W art thou cast down ....Ps 43:5
w art thou disquieted ....Ps 43:5
W boastest thou thyself in .....Ps 52:1
w hast thou cast us off ....Ps 74:1
w doth thine anger smoke .....Ps 74:1
W hast thou then broken ......Ps 80:12
w castest thou off my soul?....Ps 88:14
w hidest thou thy face ....Ps 88:14
w should he take away thy ....Prov 22:27
w was I then more wise? ......Eccl 2:15
w shouldest thou die ....Eccl 7:17
w should I be as one that .....Song 1:7
W should ye be stricken........Is 1:5
w hast thou made us to err....Is 63:17
slave? *w* is he spoiled? ....Jer 2:14
W gaddest thou about so ......Jer 2:36
W do we sit still? assemble ....Jer 8:14
w then is not the health ....Jer 8:22
W shouldest thou be as a .....Jer 14:9
W is my pain perpetual ....Jer 15:18
W will ye die, thou and thy ...Jer 27:13
W criest thou for thine ....Jer 30:15
W are thy valiant men ....Jer 46:15
W? doth not the son bear .....Ezek 18:19
w will ye die, O house ....Ezek 33:11
w should he see your faces ....Dan 1:10
W hast thou done this? ....Jon 1:10
w dost thou cry out aloud? ....Mic 4:9
W dost thou show me ....Hab 1:3
W? saith the Lord ....Hag 1:9
w do we deal treacherously ....Mal 2:10
w take ye thought for ....Matt 6:28
W are ye fearful, O ye ....Matt 8:26
W do we and the Pharisees ....Matt 9:14
W do thy disciples ....Matt 15:2
w reason ye among ....Matt 16:8
W could not we cast him ......Matt 17:19
W callest thou me good? ......Matt 19:17
W did ye not then believe .....Matt 21:25
W trouble ye the woman? .....Matt 26:10
God, *w* hast thou forsaken ....Matt 27:46
W doth this man thus ....Mark 2:7
W do the disciples of John ....Mark 2:18
W are ye so fearful? how is ....Mark 4:40
W make ye this ado, and......Mark 5:39
W doth this generation ....Mark 8:12
W say the scribes that Elijah ..Mark 9:11
W callest thou me good? ......Mark 10:18
W then did ye not believe .....Mark 11:31
W was this waste of the ....Mark 14:4
W, what evil hath he done? ...Mark 15:14
w hast thou thus dealt ....Luke 2:48
W do the disciples of John .....Luke 5:33
w beholdest thou the mote ....Luke 6:41
w take ye thought for the .....Luke 12:26
w cumbereth it the ground? ...Luke 13:7
W do ye loose him? ....Luke 19:31
ask you, *W* loose ye the colt? .Luke 19:33
unto them, *W* tempt ye me?...Luke 20:23
W, what evil hath he done? ...Luke 23:22
W are ye troubled? ....Luke 24:38
w do thoughts arise ....Luke 24:38
W baptizest thou them ....John 1:25
W go ye about to kill me? ....John 7:19
W do ye not understand ......John 8:43
W herein is a marvelous ......John 9:30
W was not this ointment ......John 12:5
W askest thou me? ask them ..John 18:21
Woman, *w* weepest thou? .....John 20:13
w stand ye gazing up into .....Acts 1:11
W did the heathen rage ......Acts 4:25
w hast thou conceived ....Acts 5:4
Saul, *w* persecutest thou ......Acts 9:4
Now therefore *w* tempt ye ....Acts 15:10
And now *w* tarriest thou? .....Acts 22:16
Saul, Saul, *w* persecutest ......Acts 26:14
w yet am I also judged........Rom 3:7
W doth he yet find fault? .....Rom 9:19
But *w* dost thou judge thy ....Rom 14:10
w dost thou set at nought .....Rom 14:10
w dost thou glory, as if 1Cor 4:7
W do ye not rather take 1Cor 6:7
w do ye not rather suffer......1Cor 6:7
w am I evil spoken of.........1Cor 10:30
w stand ye in jeopardy 1Cor 15:30
w compellest thou the.........Gal 2:14
w, as though living in the .....Col 2:20

WICKED—*evil; disposed to wrongdoing; vile*
the righteous with the *w*? .....Gen 18:23
the righteous with the *w* ......Gen 18:25
should be as the *w* ....Gen 18:25
w in the sight of the Lord .....Gen 38:7
thine hand with the *w*.........Ex 23:1
it is a *w* thing; and ....Lev 20:17
the tents of these *w* men ......Num 16:26
thought in thy *w* heart ....Deut 15:9
thee from every *w* thing.......Deut 23:9
w man be worthy to be ....Deut 25:2
the *w* shall be silent 1Sam 2:9
answered all the *w* men 1Sam 30:22
man falleth before *w* men 2Sam 3:34
servants, condemning the *w* ...1Kin 8:32
wrought *w* things to provoke ..2Kin 17:11
servants by requiting the *w*....2Chr 6:23
turn from their *w* ways........2Chr 7:14
turned..from their *w* works ....Neh 9:35
letters that his *w* device ....Esth 8:25
w cease from troubling ....Job 3:17
the perfect and the *w* ....Job 9:22
If I be *w*, why then labor .....Job 9:29
knowest that I am not *w* ......Job 10:7
eyes of the *w* shall fail ....Job 11:20
into the hands of the *w* ....Job 16:11
the dwellings of the *w* ....Job 18:21
hand of the *w* shall come .....Job 20:22
Wherefore do the *w* live ....Job 21:7
dwelling places of the *w*?......Job 21:28
w is reserved to the day.......Job 21:30
counsel of the *w* is far ....Job 22:18
gather the vintage of the *w*....Job 24:6
the portion of a *w* man ....Job 27:13
not destruction to the *w*.......Job 31:3
say to a king, Thou art *w* .....Job 34:18
his answers for *w* men ....Job 34:36
the judgment of the *w* ....Job 36:17
from the *w* their light ....Job 38:15
tread down the *w* in their .....Job 40:12
God is angry with the *w* ....Ps 7:11
the *w* is snared in the work ...Ps 9:16
w in his pride doth persecute ..Ps 10:2
The *w*, through the pride .....Ps 10:4
the arm of the *w* and ....Ps 10:15
lo, the *w* bend their bow......Ps 11:2
The *w* walk on every side .....Ps 12:8
deliver my soul from the *w*....Ps 17:13
of the *w* have inclosed ....Ps 22:16
the *w*, even mine enemies .....Ps 27:2
Draw me not away with the *w* .Ps 28:3
sorrows shall be to the *w*......Ps 32:10
transgression of the *w*.........Ps 36:1
not the hand of the *w*.........Ps 36:11
who bringeth *w* devices ....Ps 37:7
The *w* plotteth against ....Ps 37:12
than the riches of many *w*.....Ps 37:16
The *w* borroweth, and payeth .Ps 37:21
w watcheth the righteous ......Ps 37:32
when the *w* are cut off........Ps 37:34
deliver them from the *w* ......Ps 37:40
while the *w* is before me ......Ps 39:1
of the oppression of the *w* ....Ps 55:3
w are estranged from the......Ps 58:3
to any *w* transgressors ....Ps 59:5
w perish at the presence ......Ps 68:2
out of the hand of the *w* ......Ps 71:4
the multitude of the *w* ....Ps 74:19
the *w*, Lift not up the horn....Ps 75:4
the *w* also will I cut off ....Ps 75:10
the persons of the *w* ....Ps 82:2
see the reward of the *w* ....Ps 91:8
desire of the *w* that rise.......Ps 92:11
the pit be digged for the *w* ....Ps 94:13
set no *w* thing before mine ....Ps 101:3
destroy..the *w* of the land .....Ps 101:8
may cut off all the *w* doers ....Ps 101:8
the flame burned up the *w* ....Ps 106:18
Set thou a *w* man over him ...Ps 109:6
The *w* shall see it, and ....Ps 112:10
desire of the *w* shall ....Ps 112:10
the *w* have robbed me ....Ps 119:61
The *w* have laid a snare.......Ps 119:110
Salvation is far from the *w* ....Ps 119:155
asunder the cords of the *w* ....Ps 129:4
Surely thou wilt slay the *w* ....Ps 139:19
Lord, the desires of the *w*.....Ps 140:8
further not his *w* device ....Ps 140:8
Let the *w* fall into their ....Ps 141:10
way of the *w* he turneth.......Ps 146:9
the *w* down to the ground .....Ps 147:6
w shall be cut off from........Prov 2:22
is in the house of the *w*.......Prov 3:33
the way..the *w* is as darkness ..Prov 4:19
w man walketh with a ....Prov 6:12
he that rebuketh a *w* man .....Prov 9:7
covereth the mouth of the *w* ..Prov 10:6
covereth the mouth of the *w* ..Prov 10:11
heart of the *w* is little.........Prov 10:20
so is the *w* no more ....Prov 10:25
of the *w* shall perish ....Prov 10:28
w speaketh frowardness ....Prov 10:32
When a *w* man dieth, his .....Prov 11:7
the *w* perish, there is ....Prov 11:10
The *w* worketh a deceitful.....Prov 11:18
the expectation of the *w* ......Prov 11:23
man of *w* devices will ....Prov 12:2
words of the *w* are to lie ......Prov 12:6
w are overthrown, and are ....Prov 12:7
The *w* desireth the net of .....Prov 12:12
w shall be filled with..........Prov 12:21
a *w* man is loathsome, and ....Prov 13:5
w messenger falleth into ......Prov 13:17
The house of the *w* shall ......Prov 14:11
w at the gates of the ....Prov 14:19
in the revenues of the *w* ......Prov 15:6
the *w* is an abomination.......Prov 15:9
A *w* doer giveth heed to ......Prov 17:4
A *w* man taketh a gift out ....Prov 17:23
When the *w* cometh, then .....Prov 18:3
mouth of the *w* devoureth.....Prov 19:28
the plowing of the *w* is sin ....Prov 21:4
The *w* shall be a ransom ......Prov 21:18

W

WIDOW—*a woman whose husband has died*

Provision of, for:

Remarriage ... Rom 7:3
Food ... Deut 24:19-21
Protection ... Is 1:17, 23
Vows of ... Num 30:9
Raiment ... Deut 24:17

Mistreatment of, by:

Children ... 1Tim 5:4
Neglect ... Acts 6:1
Scribes ... Mark 12:40
Creditors ... 2Kin 4:1
Princes ... Is 1:23
Judges ... Is 10:1, 2

Protection of, by:

God ... Ex 22:22-24
Law ... Deut 24:17
Pure religion ... James 1:27
Honor ... 1Tim 5:3

Examples of:

Naomi ... Ruth 1:20, 21
Woman of Tekoa ... 2Sam 14:4, 5
Woman of Zarephath ... 1Kin 17:9, 10
Anna ... Luke 2:36, 37
"A certain poor widow" ... Luke 21:2, 3

[*also* WIDOW'S, WIDOWS, WIDOWS']

Remain a *w* at thy father's ... Gen 38:11
she put her *w* garments ... Gen 38:14
A *w*, or a divorced woman ... Lev 21:14
priest's daughter be a *w* ... Lev 22:13
of the fatherless and *w* ... Deut 10:18
fatherless, and the *w* ... Deut 16:11
the fatherless, and *w* ... Deut 27:19
was a *w* son of the tribe of ... 1Kin 7:14
name was Zeruah, a *w* ... 1Kin 11:26
evil upon the *w* with ... 1Kin 17:20
Thou hast sent *w* away ... Job 22:9
they take the *w* ox for a ... Job 24:3
doeth not good to the *w* ... Job 24:21
I caused the *w* heart to ... Job 29:13
and a judge of the *w* ... Ps 68:5
They slay the *w* and the ... Ps 94:6
the fatherless and *w* ... Ps 146:9
establish the border of the *w* ... Prov 15:25
on their fatherless and *w* ... Is 9:17
I shall not sit as a *w* ... Is 47:8
the fatherless, and the *w* ... Jer 7:6
Their *w* are increased to ... Jer 15:8
alive; and let thy *w* trust ... Jer 49:11
how is she become as a *w* ... Lam 1:1
our mothers are as *w* ... Lam 5:3
the fatherless and the *w* ... Ezek 22:7
made her many *w* in the ... Ezek 22:25
take for their wives a *w* ... Ezek 44:22
or a *w* that had a priest ... Ezek 44:22
And oppress not the *w* ... Zech 7:10
hireling in his wages, the *w* ... Mal 3:5
for ye devour *w* houses ... Matt 23:14
there came a certain poor *w* ... Mark 12:42
That this poor *w* hath cast ... Mark 12:43
many *w* were in Israel in ... Luke 4:25
unto a woman that was a *w* ... Luke 4:26
mother, and she was a *w* ... Luke 7:12
because this *w* troubleth ... Luke 18:5
Which devour *w* houses and ... Luke 20:47
all the *w* stood by him ... Acts 9:39
to the unmarried and *w* ... 1Cor 7:8
that is a *w* indeed, and ... 1Tim 5:5
not a *w* be taken into the ... 1Tim 5:9
But the younger *w* refuse ... 1Tim 5:11
that believeth have *w* ... 1Tim 5:16
relieve them that are *w* ... 1Tim 5:16
I sit a queen, and am no *w* ... Rev 18:7

WIDOWHOOD—*married status of a woman after her husband's death*

put on the garments of her *w* ... Gen 38:19
of their death, living in *w* ... 2Sam 20:3
loss of children, and *w* ... Is 47:9
the reproach of thy *w* ... Is 54:4

WIFE—*a married woman*

Described as:

"A helpmeet" ... Gen 2:18, 20
"A crown to her husband" ... Prov 12:4
"A good thing" ... Prov 18:22
"The weaker vessel" ... 1Pet 3:7
"The wife of his youth" ... Mal 2:14, 15
"Thy companion" ... Mal 2:14

Duties of, to:

Submit to husband ... 1Pet 3:5, 6
Reverence her husband ... Eph 5:33
Love her husband ... Titus 2:4
Learn from her husband ... 1Cor 14:34, 35
Be trustworthy ... Prov 31:11, 12
Love her children ... Titus 2:4
Be chaste ... Titus 2:5
Be keepers at home ... Titus 2:5

Duties of husband toward, to:

Love ... Eph 5:25, 28
Honor ... 1Pet 3:7
Provide for ... 1Tim 5:8
Instruct ... 1Cor 14:35
Protect ... 1Sam 30:1-19
Not divorce ... 1Cor 7:11

Relationship with her husband, to be:

Exclusive ... Prov 5:15-17, 20
Satisfying ... Prov 5:18, 19
Mutually agreeable ... 1Cor 7:1-5
Undefiled ... Heb 13:4

Special temptations of:

Disobedience ... Gen 3:1-19
Unfaithfulness ... John 4:17, 18
Contentiousness ... Prov 19:13
Assertion of authority ... 1Tim 2:11-15

Types of:

Disobedient—Eve ... Gen 3:1-8
Obedient—Sarah ... 1Pet 3:5, 6
Worldly—Lot's ... Gen 19:26
Humble—Manoah's ... Judg 13:22, 23
Prayerful—Hannah ... 1Sam 1:1-15
Prudent—Abigail ... 1Sam 25:3, 14-35
Criticizing—Michal ... 2Sam 6:15, 16
Unscrupulous—Jezebel ... 1Kin 21:5-15
Modest—Vashti ... Esth 1:11, 12
Foolish—Job's wife ... Job 2:7-10
Cruel—Herodias ... Matt 14:3-12
Righteous—Elisabeth ... Luke 1:5, 6
Lying—Sapphira ... Acts 5:1-10

[*also* WIFE'S, WIVES, WIVES']

shall cleave unto his *w* ... Gen 2:24
naked, the man and his *w* ... Gen 2:25
unto the voice of thy *w* ... Gen 3:17
And Adam called his *w* ... Gen 3:20
Adam knew Eve his *w* ... Gen 4:1
took unto him two *w* ... Gen 4:19
Lamech said unto his *w* ... Gen 4:23
ye *w* of Lamech, hearken ... Gen 4:23
Adam knew his *w* again ... Gen 4:25
thy *w*, and thy sons' *w* with ... Gen 6:18
his sons, and his *w* ... Gen 7:7
the three *w* of his sons ... Gen 7:13
ark, thou, and thy *w* ... Gen 8:16
his *w*, and his sons' *w* with ... Gen 8:18
the name of Abram's *w* ... Gen 11:29
law, his son Abram's *w* ... Gen 11:31
he said unto Sarai his *w* ... Gen 12:11
because of Sarai Abram's *w* ... Gen 12:17
taken her to me to *w* ... Gen 12:19
behold thy *w*, take her ... Gen 12:19
Egypt, he, and his *w* ... Gen 13:1
Abram's *w* took Hagar ... Gen 16:3
As for Sarai thy *w*, thou ... Gen 17:15
Where is Sarah thy *w*? ... Gen 18:9
take thy *w*, and thy two ... Gen 19:15
upon the hand of his *w* ... Gen 19:16
said of Sarah his *w* ... Gen 20:2
restore the man his *w* ... Gen 20:7
restored him Sarah his *w* ... Gen 20:14
of Sarah Abraham's *w* ... Gen 20:18
him a *w* out of the land ... Gen 21:21
buried Sarah his *w* ... Gen 23:19
thou shalt not take a *w* ... Gen 24:3
thou shalt take a *w* unto ... Gen 24:7
Sarah my master's *w* bare ... Gen 24:36
kindred, and take a *w* ... Gen 24:38
be thy master's son's *w* ... Gen 24:51
again Abraham took a *w* ... Gen 25:1
he took Rebekah to *w* ... Gen 25:20
entreated the Lord for his *w* ... Gen 25:21
and Rebekah his *w* conceived ... Gen 25:21
asked him of his *w* ... Gen 26:7
to say, She is my *w* ... Gen 26:7
of a surety she is thy *w* ... Gen 26:9
toucheth this man or his *w* ... Gen 26:11
if Jacob take a *w* of the ... Gen 27:46
shalt not take a *w* of the ... Gen 28:1
to take him a *w* from ... Gen 28:6
shalt not take a *w* of the ... Gen 28:6
and took unto the *w* which ... Gen 28:9
Give me my *w*, for my ... Gen 29:21
Bilhah her handmaid to *w* ... Gen 30:4
set his sons and his *w* ... Gen 31:17
and took his two *w* ... Gen 32:22
Get me this damsel to *w* ... Gen 34:4
give me the damsel to *w* ... Gen 34:12
ones, and their *w* took ... Gen 34:29
And Esau took his *w*, and ... Gen 36:6
the son of Adah the *w* ... Gen 36:10
son of Bashemath the *w* ... Gen 36:10
sons of Bashemath Esau's *w* ... Gen 36:13
sons of Aholibamah Esau's *w* ... Gen 36:18
daughter of Anah, Esau's *w* ... Gen 36:18
and his *w* name was ... Gen 36:39
go in unto thy brother's *w* ... Gen 38:8
daughter of Shuah Judah's *w* ... Gen 38:12
his master's *w* cast her ... Gen 39:7
because thou art his *w* ... Gen 39:9
gave him to *w* Asenath ... Gen 41:45
little ones, and for your *w* ... Gen 45:19
sons of Rachel Jacob's *w* ... Gen 46:19
besides Jacob's sons' *w* ... Gen 46:26
Abraham and Sarah his *w* ... Gen 49:31
Isaac and Rebekah his *w* ... Gen 49:31
And Moses took his *w* and ... Ex 4:20
sister of Naashon, to *w* ... Ex 6:23
took Zipporah, Moses' *w* ... Ex 18:2
and thy *w*, and her two ... Ex 18:6
come not at your *w* ... Ex 19:15
then his *w* shall go out ... Ex 21:3
master have given him a *w* ... Ex 21:4
the *w* and her children ... Ex 21:4
If he take him another *w* ... Ex 21:10
are in the ears of your *w* ... Ex 32:2
father's *w* shalt thou not ... Lev 18:8
nakedness of thy father's *w* ... Lev 18:11
she is thy son's *w*, thou ... Lev 18:15
take a *w* to her sister ... Lev 18:18
with another man's *w* ... Lev 20:10
with his neighbor's *w* ... Lev 20:10
if a man take a *w* and her ... Lev 20:14
shall take his brother's *w* ... Lev 20:21
he shall take a *w* in her ... Lev 21:13
If any man's *w* go aside ... Num 5:12
the man bring his *w* unto ... Num 5:15
he be jealous over his *w* ... Num 5:30
that our *w* and our ... Num 14:3
between a man and his *w* ... Num 30:16
Our little ones, our *w* ... Num 32:26
But your *w*, and your ... Deut 3:19
desire thy neighbor's *w* ... Deut 5:21
that hath betrothed a *w* ... Deut 20:7
and she shall be thy *w* ... Deut 21:13
If a man have two *w*, one ... Deut 21:15
unto this man to *w* ... Deut 22:16
humbled his neighbor's *w* ... Deut 22:24
not take his father's *w* ... Deut 22:30
and be another man's *w* ... Deut 24:2
her again to be his *w* ... Deut 24:4
man hath taken a new *w* ... Deut 24:5
shall cheer up his *w* ... Deut 24:5
the *w* of the dead shall ... Deut 25:5
take her to him to *w*, and ... Deut 25:5
to take his brother's *w* ... Deut 25:7
his brother's *w* go up to ... Deut 25:7
with his father's *w* ... Deut 27:20
and toward the *w* of his ... Deut 28:54
Your *w*, your little ones ... Josh 1:14
Achsah my daughter to *w* ... Josh 15:16

daughters to be their *w* .... Judg 3:6
a prophetess, the *w* of .... Judg 4:4
Then Jael Heber's *w* took ..... Judg 4:21
Gilead's *w* bare him sons...... Judg 11:2
and his *w* sons grew up .... Judg 11:2
and went after his *w* .... Judg 13:11
and Manoah and his *w* .... Judg 13:20
get her for me to *w*.......... Judg 14:2
they said unto Samson's *w* ..... Judg 14:15
But Samson's *w* was given..... Judg 14:20
Samson visited his *w* with ..... Judg 15:1
will go in to my *w* into the .... Judg 15:1
daughter unto Benjamin to *w*.. Judg 21:1
How shall we do for *w* for .... Judg 21:7
of our daughters to *w*? .... Judg 21:7
How shall we do for *w* for .... Judg 21:16
every man his *w* of the........ Judg 21:21
took them *w*, according .... Judg 21:23
of Moab, he and his *w*........ Ruth 1:1
them *w* of the women of ...... Ruth 1:4
the Moabitess, the *w* of .... Ruth 4:5
Ruth the Moabitess, the *w* .... Ruth 4:10
I purchased to be my *w*....... Ruth 4:10
Elkanah knew Hannah his *w* .. 1Sam 1:19
blessed Elkanah and his *w* ... 1Sam 2:20
the name of Saul's *w* was 1Sam 14:50
Adriel the Meholathite to *w*... 1Sam 18:19
Michal David's *w* told him 1Sam 19:11
his *w* had told him these 1Sam 25:37
to take her to him to *w* 1Sam 25:39
David, and became his *w* 1Sam 25:42
also both of them his *w* 1Sam 25:43
even David with his two *w* 1Sam 27:3
Carmelitess, Nabal's *w* 1Sam 27:3
save to every man his *w*....... 1Sam 30:22
up thither, and his two *w* 2Sam 2:2
Abigail Nabal's *w* the 2Sam 2:2
by Eglah David's *w* 2Sam 3:5
Eliam, the *w* of Uriah the 2Sam 11:3
when the *w* of Uriah.......... 2Sam 11:26
and thy master's *w* into 2Sam 12:8
taken his *w* to be thy *w* 2Sam 12:9
and hast taken the *w* 2Sam 12:10
Hittite to be thy *w* 2Sam 12:10
I will take thy *w* before 2Sam 12:11
he shall lie with thy *w* in 2Sam 12:11
comforted Bath-sheba his *w* ... 2Sam 12:24
Abishag the Shunammite to *w* . 1Kin 2:17
daughter of Solomon to *w*..... 1Kin 4:11
his daughter, Solomon's *w*..... 1Kin 9:16
he had seven hundred *w* 1Kin 11:3
and his *w* turned away 1Kin 11:3
for all his strange *w* 1Kin 11:8
Jeroboam said to his *w*........ 1Kin 14:2
not known to be the *w* of 1Kin 14:2
w of Jeroboam cometh 1Kin 14:5
Jeroboam's *w* arose, and 1Kin 14:17
he took to *w* Jezebel the 1Kin 16:31
gold, and thy *w*, and thy 1Kin 20:5
whom Jezebel his *w* stirred 1Kin 21:25
certain woman of the *w* of 2Kin 4:1
she waited on Naaman's *w* 2Kin 5:2
daughter to my son to *w* 2Kin 14:9
and his *w* name was 1Chr 1:50
children of Azubah his *w*...... 1Chr 2:18
had also another *w* 1Chr 2:26
Jarha his servant to *w*......... 1Chr 2:35
father of Tekoa had two *w* 1Chr 4:5
And his *w* Jehudijah bare 1Chr 4:18
And Machir took to *w* the 1Chr 7:15
when he went in to his *w* 1Chr 7:23
and Baara were his *w* 1Chr 8:8
whose *w* name was Maachah .. 1Chr 9:35
My *w* shall not dwell in 2Chr 8:11
Absalom above all his *w* 2Chr 11:21
for he took eighteen *w* 2Chr 11:21
And he desired many *w* 2Chr 11:23
their *w*, and their............. 2Chr 20:13
daughter of Ahab to *w*........ 2Chr 21:6
his sons also, and his *w* 2Chr 21:17
daughter to my son to *w* 2Chr 25:18
our *w* are in captivity 2Chr 29:9
a *w* of the daughters of .... Ezra 2:61
have taken strange *w* of....... Ezra 10:2
and have taken strange *w* ..... Ezra 10:10
have taken strange *w* in .... Ezra 10:14
that had taken strange *w* ...... Ezra 10:18
some of them had *w* by .... Ezra 10:44
daughters, your *w*, and........ Neh 4:14
the Gileadite to *w* .... Neh 7:63
their *w*, their sons .... Neh 10:28
Jews that had married *w* ...... Neh 13:23
w shall give to their .... Esth 1:20
friends, and Zeresh his *w* ..... Esth 5:10
Haman told Zeresh his *w* ..... Esth 6:13
wise men and Zeresh his *w*.... Esth 6:13
breath is strange to my *w* ..... Job 19:17
Then let my *w* grind unto ..... Job 31:10
be fatherless, and his *w* .... Ps 109:9
w shall be as a fruitful .... Ps 128:3
in to his neighbor's *w* .... Prov 6:29
and a prudent *w* is from ...... Prov 19:14
Live joyfully with the *w*....... Eccl 9:9
be spoiled, and their *w*........ Is 13:16
children of the married *w* ..... Is 54:1
If a man put away his *w* ...... Jer 3:1
after his neighbor's *w* .... Jer 5:8
with their fields and *w* .... Jer 6:12
to bury them, their *w* .... Jer 14:16
shalt not take thee a *w* .... Jer 16:2
let their *w* be bereaved of..... Jer 18:21
Take ye *w*, and beget .... Jer 29:6
take *w* for your sons, and ..... Jer 29:6
our *w*, our sons, nor our ...... Jer 35:8
the wickedness of their *w* ..... Jer 44:9
the wickedness of your *w* ..... Jer 44:9
Ye and your *w* have both ..... Jer 44:25
as a *w* that committeth........ Ezek 16:32
defiled his neighbor's *w* .... Ezek 18:11
at even my *w* died; and I ..... Ezek 24:18
every one his neighbor's *w* .... Ezek 33:26
shall they take for their *w* .... Ezek 44:22
his *w*, and his concubines ..... Dan 5:2
w, and thy concubines .... Dan 5:23
take unto thee a *w* of......... Hos 1:2
Israel served for a *w* .... Hos 12:12
for a *w* he kept sheep......... Hos 12:12
Thy *w* shall be a harlot .... Amos 7:17
David apart, and their *w* ...... Zech 12:12
Nathan apart, and their *w* ..... Zech 12:12
Levi apart, and their *w* .... Zech 12:13
Shimei apart, and their *w* ..... Zech 12:13
between thee and the *w* of .... Mal 2:14
her that had been the *w*....... Matt 1:6
and took unto him his *w* ...... Matt 1:24
shall put away his *w* .... Matt 5:32
house, he saw his *w* mother ... Matt 8:14
to be sold, and his *w*, and.... Matt 18:25
and shall cleave to his *w* ...... Matt 19:5
you to put away your *w*........ Matt 19:8
man be so with his *w* .... Matt 19:10
brother shall marry his *w*...... Matt 22:24
when he had married a *w* ...... Matt 22:25
issue, left his *w* unto his ...... Matt 22:25
seat, his *w* sent unto him...... Matt 27:19
Simon's *w* mother lay sick ..... Mark 1:30
his brother Philip's *w* .... Mark 6:17
a man to put away his *w*? ...... Mark 10:2
shall put away his *w* .... Mark 10:11
and leave his *w* behind .... Mark 12:19
brother should take his *w* ..... Mark 12:19
rise, whose *w* shall she be .... Mark 12:23
the seven had her to *w*........ Mark 12:23
w was of the daughters........ Luke 1:5
and my *w* well stricken........ Luke 1:18
with Mary his espoused *w* ...... Luke 2:5
And Simon's *w* mother was ... Luke 4:38
the *w* of Chuza Herod's .... Luke 8:3
father, and mother, and *w* .... Luke 14:26
they drank, they married *w*.... Luke 17:27
Remember Lot's *w* .... Luke 17:32
brother die, having a *w* .... Luke 20:28
brother should take his *w* ..... Luke 20:28
the second took her to *w*...... Luke 20:30
whose *w* of them is she? ...... Luke 20:33
for seven had her to *w* .... Luke 20:33
Mary the *w* of Cleophas ...... John 19:25
Italy, with his *w* Priscilla ...... Acts 18:2
on our way, with *w* and .... Acts 21:5
should have his father's *w* 1Cor 5:1
Let not the *w* depart from 1Cor 7:10
brother hath a *w* that 1Cor 7:12
is sanctified by the *w* 1Cor 7:14
w is sanctified by the 1Cor 7:14
what knowest thou, O *w* 1Cor 7:16
thou shalt save thy *w* 1Cor 7:16
Art thou bound unto a *w*? 1Cor 7:27
from a *w*? seek not a *w* 1Cor 7:27
have *w* be as though they 1Cor 7:29
difference also between a *w* ... 1Cor 7:34
The *w* is bound by the 1Cor 7:39
W, submit yourselves unto .... Eph 5:22
is the head of the *w* .... Eph 5:23
let the *w* be to their own...... Eph 5:24
shall be joined unto his *w* ..... Eph 5:31
W, submit yourselves unto .... Col 3:18
Husbands, love your *w*........ Col 3:19
the husband of one *w*......... 1Tim 3:2
Even so must their *w* be 1Tim 3:11
refuse profane and old *w*...... 1Tim 4:7
having been the *w* of one 1Tim 5:9
the husband of one *w*......... Titus 1:6
ye *w*, be in subjection to...... 1Pet 3:1
conversation of the *w* 1Pet 3:1
his *w* hath made herself .... Rev 19:7
the bride, the Lamb's *w*....... Rev 21:9

WILD—*untamed; uncivilized*

And he will be a *w* man ...... Gen 16:12
also send *w* beasts among ..... Lev 26:22
fallow deer, and the *w* goat ... Deut 14:5
the pygarg, and the *w* ox...... Deut 14:5
and to the *w* beasts of 1Sam 17:46
light of foot as a *w* roe 2Sam 2:18
herbs and found a *w* vine 2Kin 4:39
gathered thereof *w* gourds..... 2Kin 4:39
a *w* beast that was in 2Chr 25:18
w ass bray when he hath ...... Job 6:5
as *w* asses in the desert .... Job 24:5
Who hath sent out the *w* ass .. Job 39:5
the bands of the *w* ass .... Job 39:5
the *w* beasts of the field....... Ps 50:11
the *w* asses quench their ...... Ps 104:11
it brought forth *w* grapes...... Is 5:2
w beasts of the desert......... Is 13:21
a joy of *w* asses, a pasture .... Is 32:14
w beasts of the desert......... Is 34:14
also meet with the *w* beasts ... Is 34:14
A *w* ass used to the .... Jer 2:24
the *w* beasts of the desert ..... Jer 50:39
w beasts of the islands .... Jer 50:39
dwelling was with the *w*........ Dan 5:21
Assyria, a *w* ass alone by ..... Hos 8:9
meat was locusts and *w* honey . Matt 3:4
he did eat locusts and *w* ...... Mark 1:6
w beasts, and creeping .... Acts 10:12
being a *w* olive tree .... Rom 11:17

WILDERNESS—*a desolate, uncultivated region*

Descriptive of:
Israel's wanderings ...... Ex 16:1
Desolate place .... Matt 3:1, 3
Desolation .... Jer 22:6

Characterized by:
Wild creatures .... Deut 8:15
No water .... Deut 8:15
"Great and terrible" things .... Deut 1:19
Uninhabited .... Ps 107:4, 5

Israel's journey in, characterized by:
God's provisions......... Deut 2:7
God's guidance .... Ps 78:52
God's mighty acts .... Ps 78:15, 16
Israel's provoking God ... Ps 78:17-19, 40
Israel's sin .... Heb 3:7-19
Testings .... Deut 8:2

Significant events in:
Hagar's flight .... Gen 16:6-8
Israel's journeys .... Ps 136:16
John's preaching......... Matt 3:1-12
Jesus' temptation .... Matt 4:1
Jesus' miracle .... Matt 15:33-38
Moses' serpent .... John 3:14

which is by the *w* ... Gen 14:6
wandered in the *w* of ... Gen 21:14
And he dwelt in the *w* ... Gen 21:21
pit that is in the *w* ... Gen 37:22
days' journey into the *w* ... Ex 3:18
feast unto me in the *w* ... Ex 5:1
days' journey into the *w* ... Ex 8:27
the way of the *w* of the ... Ex 13:18
the land, the *w* hath shut ... Ex 14:3
we should die in the *w* ... Ex 14:12
they went out into the *w* ... Ex 15:22
three days in the *w* ... Ex 15:22
I have fed you in the *w* ... Ex 16:32
journeyed from the *w* ... Ex 17:1
unto Moses into the *w* ... Ex 18:5
came they into the *w* ... Ex 19:1
unto the Lord, in the *w* ... Lev 7:38
of a fit man into the *w* ... Lev 16:21
spake unto Moses in the *w* ... Num 1:1
before the Lord, in the *w* ... Num 3:4
unto Moses in the *w* ... Num 9:1
journeys out of the *w* ... Num 10:12
cloud rested in the *w* ... Num 10:12
and pitched in the *w* ... Num 12:16
from the *w* of Zin unto ... Num 13:21
we had died in this *w* ... Num 14:2
in Egypt and in the *w* ... Num 14:22
shall fall in this *w* ... Num 14:29
shall wander in the *w* ... Num 14:33
be wasted in the *w* ... Num 14:33
Israel were in the *w* ... Num 15:32
of the Lord into this *w* ... Num 20:4
in the *w* which is before ... Num 21:11
the *w* they went to ... Num 21:18
set his face toward the *w* ... Num 24:1
shall surely die in the *w* ... Num 26:65
in Kadesh in the *w* of Zin ... Num 27:14
yet leave them in the *w* ... Num 32:15
of the sea into the *w* ... Num 33:8
days' journey in the *w* ... Num 33:8
their journey out of the *w* ... Num 33:12
pitched in the *w* of Zin ... Num 33:36
this side Jordan in the *w* ... Deut 1:1
And in the *w*, where thou ... Deut 1:31
our journey into the *w* ... Deut 2:1
by the way of the *w* of ... Deut 2:8
Bezer in the *w*, in the ... Deut 4:43
Who fed thee in the *w* ... Deut 8:16
out to slay them in the *w* ... Deut 9:28
from the *w* and Lebanon ... Deut 11:24
in the waste howling *w* ... Deut 32:10
From the *w* and this ... Josh 1:4
that were born in the *w* ... Josh 5:5
fled by the way of the *w* ... Josh 8:15
in the *w* wherein they ... Josh 8:24
Israel, wandered in the *w* ... Josh 14:10
In the *w*, Beth-arabah ... Josh 15:61
at the *w* of Beth-aven ... Josh 18:12
ye dwelt in the *w* a long ... Josh 24:7
of Judah into the *w* of ... Judg 1:16
and thorns of the *w* and ... Judg 8:16
went along through the *w* ... Judg 11:18
the way of the *w* ... Judg 20:42
fled to the *w* unto the rock ... Judg 20:47
all the plagues in the *w* ... 1Sam 4:8
those few sheep in the *w*? ... 1Sam 17:28
David abode in the *w* in ... 1Sam 23:14
in a mountain in the *w* ... 1Sam 23:14
his men were in the *w* ... 1Sam 23:24
rock, and abode in the *w* ... 1Sam 23:25
after David in the *w* of ... 1Sam 23:25
David is in the *w* of ... 1Sam 24:1
and went down to the *w* ... 1Sam 25:1
messengers out of the *w* ... 1Sam 25:14
and went down to the *w* of ... 1Sam 26:2
to seek David in the *w* ... 1Sam 26:2
But David abode in the *w* ... 1Sam 26:3
Saul..after him into the *w* ... 1Sam 26:3
by the way of the *w* of ... 2Sam 2:24
tarry in the plain of the *w* ... 2Sam 15:28
in the plains of the *w* ... 2Sam 17:16
in his own house in the *w* ... 1Kin 2:34
a days' journey into the *w* ... 1Kin 19:4
The way through the *w* of ... 2Kin 3:8
the entering in of the *w* ... 1Chr 5:9
into the hold to the *w* ... 1Chr 12:8
Lord had made in the *w* ... 2Chr 1:3
the brook, before the *w* ... 2Chr 20:16
the watch tower in the *w* ... 2Chr 20:24
them not in the *w* ... Neh 9:19
sustain them in the *w* ... Neh 9:21
came great wind from the *w* ... Job 1:19
the *w* yieldeth food for ... Job 24:5
the *w*, wherein there is ... Job 38:26
of the Lord shaketh the *w* ... Ps 29:8
when he was in the *w* ... Ps 63:*title*
didst march through the *w* ... Ps 68:7
people inhabiting the *w* ... Ps 74:14
of temptation in the *w* ... Ps 95:8
depths as through the *w* ... Ps 106:9
overthrow them in the *w* ... Ps 106:26
turneth rivers into a *w* ... Ps 107:33
them to wander in the *w* ... Ps 107:40
better to dwell in the *w* ... Prov 21:19
that cometh out of the *w* ... Song 3:6
That made the world a *w* ... Is 14:17
they wandered through the *w* ... Is 16:8
and left like a *w* ... Is 27:10
shall dwell in the *w* ... Is 32:16
w and the solitary place ... Is 35:1
him that crieth in the *w* ... Is 40:3
I will plant in the *w* the ... Is 41:19
even make a way in the *w* ... Is 43:19
I make the rivers a *w* ... Is 50:2
as a horse in the *w* ... Is 63:13
Thy holy cities are a *w* ... Is 64:10
Zion is a *w*, Jerusalem a ... Is 64:10
wentest after me in the *w* ... Jer 2:2
A wild ass used to the *w* ... Jer 2:24
as the Arabian in the *w* ... Jer 3:2
fruitful place was a *w* ... Jer 4:26
the habitations of the *w* ... Jer 9:10
that dwell in the *w* ... Jer 9:26
places through the *w* ... Jer 12:12
parched places in the *w* ... Jer 17:6
places of the *w* are dried ... Jer 23:10
like the heath in the *w* ... Jer 48:6
the nations shall be a *w* ... Jer 50:12
the ostriches in the *w* ... Lam 4:3
of the sword of the *w* ... Lam 5:9
than the *w* toward Diblath ... Ezek 6:14
brought them into the *w* ... Ezek 20:10
against me in the *w* ... Ezek 20:13
upon them in the *w* ... Ezek 20:13
end of them in the *w* ... Ezek 20:17
against them in the *w* ... Ezek 20:21
bring you into the *w* of ... Ezek 20:35
brought Sabeans from the *w* ... Ezek 23:42
dwell safely in the *w* ... Ezek 34:25
and make her as a *w*, and ... Hos 2:3
Israel like grapes in the *w* ... Hos 9:10
shall come up from the *w* ... Hos 13:15
the pastures of the *w* ... Joel 1:19
behind them a desolate *w* ... Joel 2:3
shall be a desolate *w* ... Joel 3:19
forty years through the *w* ... Amos 2:10
unto the river of the *w* ... Amos 6:14
and dry like a *w* ... Zeph 2:13
for the dragons of the *w* ... Mal 1:3
went ye out into the *w* ... Matt 11:7
voice of one crying in the *w* ... Mark 1:3
driveth him into the *w* ... Mark 1:12
bread here in the *w*? ... Mark 8:4
son of Zacharias in the *w* ... Luke 3:2
the Spirit into the *w* ... Luke 4:1
went ye out into the *w* for ... Luke 7:24
ninety and nine in the *w* ... Luke 15:4
of one crying in the *w* ... John 1:23
did eat manna in the *w* ... John 6:49
in the *w* of mount Sinai ... Acts 7:30
was in the church in the *w* ... Acts 7:38
of witness in the *w* ... Acts 7:44
leddest out into the *w* ... Acts 21:38
were overthrown in the *w* ... 1Cor 10:5
city, in perils in the *w* ... 2Cor 11:26
woman fled into the *w* ... Rev 12:6
the spirit into the *w* ... Rev 17:3

WILDERNESS WANDERINGS—*the course Israel took during the Exodus*

Leave Egypt ... Ex 12:29-36
Cross Red Sea ... Ex 14:1-31
Bitter water sweetened ... Ex 15:22-26
Manna in wilderness ... Ex 16:1-36
Water from a rock ... Ex 17:1-7
Defeat of Amalek ... Ex 17:8-16
At Sinai ... Ex 19:1-25
Depart Sinai ... Num 10:33, 34
Lord sends quails ... Num 11:1-35
Twelve spies ... Num 13:1-33
Rebellion at Kadesh ... Num 14:1-45
Korah's rebellion ... Num 16:1-34
Aaron's rod ... Num 17:1-13
Moses' sin ... Num 20:2-13
Fiery serpents ... Num 21:4-9
Balak and Balaam ... Num 22:1—24:25
Midianites conquered ... Num 31:1-24
Death of Moses ... Deut 34:1-8
Accession of Joshua ... Deut 34:9

WILES—*trickery; guile*

[*also* WILILY]
vex you with their *w* ... Num 25:18
They did work *w*, and ... Josh 9:4

WILFULLY—*See* WILLFULLY

WILL—*to intend*

[*also* WILLETH, WILT]
if thou *w* take the left hand ... Gen 13:9
thou? and whither *w* thou go? ... Gen 16:8
w thou also destroy and not ... Gen 18:24
w thou slay also a righteous ... Gen 20:4
But if thou *w* give it, I pray ... Gen 23:13
if thou *w* do this thing for ... Gen 30:31
W thou give me a pledge ... Gen 38:17
But if thou *w* not send him ... Gen 43:5
hand of him whom thou *w* ... Ex 4:13
let them go, and *w* hold them ... Ex 9:2
long *w* thou refuse to humble ... Ex 10:3
w diligently hearken to the ... Ex 15:26
and *w* do that which is right ... Ex 15:26
Thou *w* surely wear away ... Ex 18:18
if thou *w* forgive their sin ... Ex 32:32
w thou put out the eyes ... Num 16:14
If thou *w* indeed deliver ... Num 21:2
so that thou *w* not hear ... Deut 30:17
what *w* thou do unto thy ... Josh 7:9
said unto her, What *w* thou? ... Judg 1:14
If thou *w* go with me ... Judg 4:8
but if thou *w* not go with ... Judg 4:8
thou *w* save Israel by mine ... Judg 6:37
and if thou *w* offer a burnt ... Judg 13:16
If thou *w* redeem it ... Ruth 4:4
but if thou *w* not redeem ... Ruth 4:4
thou *w* indeed look on the ... 1Sam 1:11
but *w* give unto thine ... 1Sam 1:11
w thou deliver them into the ... 1Sam 14:37
w thou sin against innocent ... 1Sam 19:5
thou *w* not cut off my seed ... 1Sam 24:21
that thou *w* not destroy my ... 1Sam 24:21
that thou *w* neither kill me ... 1Sam 30:15
w thou not tell me? And ... 2Sam 13:4
why *w* thou swallow up the ... 2Sam 20:19
thou *w* show thyself merciful ... 2Sam 22:26
thou *w* show thyself upright ... 2Sam 22:26
with the pure thou *w* show ... 2Sam 22:27
thou *w* show thyself unsavory ... 2Sam 22:27
or *w* thou flee three months ... 2Sam 24:13
if thou *w* walk in my ways ... 1Kin 3:14
And if thou *w* walk before me ... 1Kin 9:4
and *w* keep my statutes and ... 1Kin 9:4
w hearken unto all that I ... 1Kin 11:38
and *w* walk in my ways ... 1Kin 11:38
If thou *w* be a servant unto ... 1Kin 12:7
and *w* serve them, and ... 1Kin 12:7
W thou go with me to battle ... 1Kin 22:4
w thou go with me against ... 2Kin 3:7
the evil that thou *w* do ... 2Kin 8:12
their strongholds *w* thou ... 2Kin 8:12
men *w* thou slay with the ... 2Kin 8:12
w dash their children ... 2Kin 8:12
w thou deliver them into ... 1Chr 14:10
if thou *w* walk before me ... 2Chr 7:17

affliction, then thou *w* hear 2Chr 20:9
But if thou *w* go, do it 2Chr 25:8
and when thou *w* return? ..... Neh 2:6
unto her, What *w* thou .... Esth 5:3
with thee, *w* thou be .... Job 4:2
How long *w* thou not .... Job 7:19
that thou *w* not hold me ...... Job 9:28
and thou *w* not acquit .... Job 10:14
W thou break a leaf .... Job 13:25
and *w* thou pursue the .... Job 13:25
I know that thou *w* bring ..... Job 30:23
W thou hunt the prey for ..... Job 38:39
W thou trust him, because .... Job 39:11
or *w* thou leave thy labor ..... Job 39:11
W thou also disannul my .... Job 40:8
w thou condemn me, that ..... Job 40:8
W thou play with him .... Job 41:5
or *w* thou bind him for .... Job 41:5
Lord, *w* thou bless the .... Ps 5:12
with favor *w* thou compass .... Ps 5:12
w prepare..heart, thou *w* ...... Ps 10:17
How long *w* thou forget .... Ps 13:1
long *w* thou hide thy face ..... Ps 13:1
For thou *w* not leave my ...... Ps 16:10
w thou suffer thine Holy ...... Ps 16:10
thee, for thou *w* hear me ..... Ps 17:6
thou *w* show thyself .... Ps 18:25
man thou *w* show thyself .... Ps 18:25
the pure thou *w* show .... Ps 18:26
thou *w* show thyself .... Ps 18:26
For thou *w* save the .... Ps 18:27
but *w* bring down high .... Ps 18:27
Lord, how long *w* thou .... Ps 35:17
thou *w* not deliver him .... Ps 41:2
heart, O God, thou *w* not ..... Ps 51:17
W not thou, O God, which .... Ps 60:10
in righteousness *w* thou .... Ps 65:5
how long *w* thou be angry ..... Ps 80:4
W thou be angry with us ...... Ps 85:5
w thou draw out thine .... Ps 85:5
upon thee: for thou *w* .... Ps 86:7
Lord? *w* thou hide thyself ..... Ps 89:46
W not thou, O God, who .... Ps 108:11
w not thou, O God, go .... Ps 108:11
w thou execute judgment ...... Ps 119:84
Surely thou *w* slay the .... Ps 139:19
My son, if thou *w* receive ..... Prov 2:1
How long *w* thou sleep, O .... Prov 6:9
when *w* thou arise out of ...... Prov 6:9
Thou *w* keep him in .... Is 26:3
shooteth forth, thou *w* .... Is 27:8
w thou make an end .... Is 38:12
w thou call this a fast .... Is 58:5
W thou refrain thyself .... Is 64:12
w thou hold thy peace .... Is 64:12
W thou not from this .... Jer 3:4
If thou *w* return, O Israel ..... Jer 4:1
and if thou *w* put away .... Jer 4:1
w thou do in the swelling ..... Jer 12:5
w thou not be made clean? .... Jer 13:27
How long *w* thou go about .... Jer 31:22
w thou not surely put me ..... Jer 38:15
w thou not hearken unto ...... Jer 38:15
But if thou *w* not go forth .... Jer 38:18
thou *w* bring the day .... Lam 1:21
w thou destroy all the .... Ezek 9:8
W thou judge them, son ...... Ezek 20:4
w thou judge them? cause ..... Ezek 20:4
thou son of man, *w* thou ...... Ezek 22:2
w thou judge the bloody ...... Ezek 22:2
W thou not tell us what .... Ezek 24:19
W thou not show us what ..... Ezek 37:18
O Lord: what *w* thou give? .... Hos 9:14
w cast all their sins into .... Mic 7:19
shall I cry, and thou *w* .... Hab 1:2
violence, and thou *w* not ...... Hab 1:2
I said, Surely thou *w* fear ..... Zeph 3:7
thou *w* receive instruction ..... Zeph 3:7
how long *w* thou not have ..... Zech 1:12
If thou *w* walk in my .... Zech 3:7
and if thou *w* keep my .... Zech 3:7
if thou *w* fall down and .... Matt 4:9
I *w*, be thou clean .... Matt 8:3
W thou then that we go .... Matt 13:28
if thou *w*, let us make..three .. Matt 17:4
if thou *w* be perfect, go and ... Matt 19:21
Where *w* thou that we prepare . Matt 26:17
not as I *w*, but as thou *w* ..... Matt 26:39
if thou *w*, thou canst make .... Mark 1:40
What *w* thou that I should .... Mark 10:51
Where *w* thou that we go ..... Mark 14:12
If thou therefore *w* worship ... Luke 4:7
w thou that we command ..... Luke 9:54
and *w* thou rear it up in ...... John 2:20
whatsoever thou *w* ask of God . John 11:22
that thou *w* manifest thyself ... John 14:22
shall ask what ye *w* .... John 15:7
Father, I *w* that they also ..... John 17:24
w thou at this time restore .... Acts 1:6
thou *w* not leave my soul ..... Acts 2:27
neither *w* thou suffer thine .... Acts 2:27
Lord, what *w* thou have me to . Acts 9:6
W thou go up to Jerusalem .... Acts 25:9
for to *w* is present with me .... Rom 7:18
it is not of him that *w* .... Rom 9:16
mercy on whom He *w* have ... Rom 9:18
Thou *w* say then unto me ..... Rom 9:19
W thou then not be afraid ..... Rom 13:3
let him do what he *w* 1Cor 7:36
to be married to whom she *w* . 1Cor 7:39
to every man..as He *w* 1Cor 12:11
a readiness to *w*, so there 2Cor 8:11
both to *w* and to do of his .... Phil 2:13
I *w* therefore that men pray ... 1Tim 2:8
I *w* that thou affirm .... Titus 3:8
thou *w* also do more than I ... Philem 21
But *w* thou know, O vain ..... James 2:20
If the Lord *w*, we shall live ... James 4:15
plagues, as often as they *w* .... Rev 11:6
whosoever *w*, let him take .... Rev 22:17

WILL—*intention; volition*
in their self *w* they digged ..... Gen 49:6
of his own voluntary *w* .... Lev 1:3
offer it at your own *w* .... Lev 19:5
own *w* a male without blemish . Lev 22:19
offer (it) at your own *w* .... Lev 22:29
that do after the *w* of .... Ezra 7:18
not over unto the *w* of mine ... Ps 27:12
to do thy *w*, O my God .... Ps 40:8
not deliver him unto the *w* .... Ps 41:2
Teach me to do thy *w* .... Ps 143:10
delivered thee unto the *w* ..... Ezek 16:27
according to his *w* in the ...... Dan 4:35
he did according to his *w* ..... Dan 8:4
and do according to his *w* ..... Dan 11:3
do according to his own *w* .... Dan 11:16
shall do according to his *w* .... Dan 11:36
Thy *w* be done in earth .... Matt 6:10
doeth the *w* of my Father ..... Matt 7:21
whosoever shall do the *w* ..... Matt 12:50
not the *w* of your Father ...... Matt 18:14
of them twain did the *w* of .... Matt 21:31
except I drink it, thy *w* .... Matt 26:42
shall do the *w* of God .... Mark 3:35
Thy *w* be done, as in heaven .. Luke 11:2
which knew his lord's *w* .... Luke 12:47
did according to his *w* .... Luke 12:47
not my *w*, but thine .... Luke 22:42
delivered Jesus to their *w* ..... Luke 23:25
nor of the *w* of the flesh ...... John 1:13
meat is to do the *w* of him .... John 4:34
seek not mine own *w* .... John 5:30
not to do mine own *w* .... John 6:38
Father's *w* which hath sent .... John 6:39
the *w* of him that sent me ..... John 6:40
do his *w*, he shall know of .... John 7:17
of God, and doeth his *w* ...... John 9:31
which shall fulfil all my *w* ..... Acts 13:22
his own generation by the *w* ... Acts 13:36
saying, The *w* of the Lord ..... Acts 21:14
shouldest know his *w* .... Acts 22:14
prosperous journey by the *w* .. Rom 1:10
w, and approvest the things ... Rom 2:18
for who hath resisted his *w*? ... Rom 9:19
acceptable, and perfect *w* of ... Rom 12:2
to you with joy by the *w* .... Rom 15:32
Jesus Christ through the *w* 1Cor 1:1
power over his own *w* 1Cor 7:37
w was not at all to come at ... 1Cor 16:12
Jesus Christ by the *w* of God .. 2Cor 1:1
unto us by the *w* of God 2Cor 8:5
according to the *w* of God .... Gal 1:4
Jesus Christ by the *w* of God .. Eph 1:1
the good pleasure of his *w* .... Eph 1:5
the mystery of his *w* .... Eph 1:9
the counsel of his own *w* ...... Eph 1:11
understanding what the *w* of... Eph 5:17
servants of Christ, doing the *w* . Eph 6:6
Jesus Christ by the *w* of God .. Col 1:1
the knowledge of his *w* .... Col 1:9
For this is the *w* of God 1Thess 4:3
for this is the *w* of God 1Thess 5:18
Jesus Christ by the *w* of God .. 2Tim 1:1
captive by him at his *w* 2Tim 2:26
according to his own *w* .... Heb 2:4
Lo, I come..to do thy *w* ...... Heb 10:7
Lo, I come to do thy *w* .... Heb 10:9
which *w* we are sanctified ..... Heb 10:10
ye have done the *w* of God ... Heb 10:36
every good work to do his *w* .. Heb 13:21
For so is the *w* of God 1Pet 2:15
if the *w* of God be so 1Pet 3:17
lusts of men, but to the *w* 1Pet 4:2
suffer according to the *w* 1Pet 4:19
not in old time by the *w* 2Pet 1:21
the *w* of God abideth for 1John 2:17
anything according to his *w* 1John 5:14
their hearts to fulfill his *w* ..... Rev 17:17

WILL OF GOD—*God's desire*

Defined in terms of:
Salvation 2Pet 3:9
Salvation of children ..... Matt 18:14
Belief in Christ .... Matt 12:50
Everlasting life .... John 6:39, 40
Thanksgiving 1Thess 5:18
Sanctification 1Thess 4:3

Characteristics of:
Can be:
Known .... Rom 2:18
Proved .... Rom 12:2
Done .... Matt 6:10

Sovereign over:
Nations .... Dan 4:35
Individuals .... Acts 21:14

God's power in doing, seen in:
Predestination .... Rom 9:18-23
Sovereignty .... Dan 4:35
Man's salvation 1Tim 2:4
Believer's salvation ...... James 1:18
Redemption .... Gal 1:4

Believer's relationship to, seen in his:
Calling 1Cor 1:1
Regeneration .... James 1:18
Sanctification .... Heb 10:10
Transformation .... Rom 12:2
Instruction .... Ps 143:10
Prayers 1John 5:14
Submission .... Acts 21:14
Whole life 1Pet 4:2
Daily work .... Eph 6:6
Travels .... Rom 1:10
Plans .... James 4:13-15
Suffering 1Pet 3:17
Perfection .... Col 4:12

WILL OF MAN—*See* FREEDOM; LIBERTY, SPIRITUAL

WILLFULLY—*deliberately*
For if we sin *w* after that ..... Heb 10:26

WILLING—*favorably disposed in mind; prompt to act or respond*

On God's part, to:
Exercise mercy 2Kin 8:18, 19
Rule sovereignly .... Dan 4:17
Save men 1Tim 2:4
2Pet 3:9

On Christ's part, to:
Do God's will .... Heb 10:7, 9
Submit to the Father ..... John 8:28, 29
Reveal the Father .... Matt 11:27
Heal people .... Matt 8:2, 3
Die .... Mark 14:36

On man's part, to:
Do Satan's will ....John 8:44
Refuse salvation ....John 5:40
Pervert the truth 2Pet 3:5
Follow evil.............Mark 15:15
Persecute the righteous ..Matt 2:13

On the believer's part, to:
Be saved ....Rev 22:17
Follow Christ ....Matt 16:24
Live godly 2Tim 3:12
Give 2Cor 8:3-12
Die 2Cor 5:8

[*also* WILLINGLY]
the woman will not be *w*......Gen 24:5
will not be *w* to follow ....Gen 24:8
every man that giveth it *w* ....Ex 25:2
of Israel brought a *w* ....Ex 35:29
whose heart made them *w*.....Ex 35:29
the people *w* offered..........Judg 5:2
answered, We will *w* give .....Judg 8:25
heart and with a *w* mind 1Chr 28:9
who then is *w* to consecrate ...1Chr 29:5
king's work, offered *w* 1Chr 29:6
for that they offered *w* 1Chr 29:9
heart they offered *w* to the 1Chr 29:9
be able to offer so *w* 1Chr 29:14
I have *w* offered all these 1Chr 29:17
present here, to offer *w* 1Chr 29:17
w offered himself unto 2Chr 17:16
princes gave *w* unto the 2Chr 35:8
beside all that was *w* offered ..Ezra 1:6
offering *w* for the house ......Ezra 7:16
that *w* offered themselves .....Neh 11:2
Will the unicorn be *w* to ......Job 39:9
Thy people shall be *w* in ......Ps 110:3
and worketh *w* with her ....Prov 31:13
If ye be *w* and obedient.......Is 1:19
For he doth not afflict *w* ......Lam 3:33
because he *w* walked after ....Hos 5:11
not *w* to make her a public....Matt 1:19
the spirit indeed is *w* ....Matt 26:41
But he, *w* to justify himself ...Luke 10:29
Father, if thou be *w*, remove ..Luke 22:42
Pilate..*w* to release Jesus ......Luke 23:20
ye were *w* for a season to .....John 5:35
they *w* received him into ......John 6:21
w to show the Jews a pleasure .Acts 24:27
w to do the Jews a pleasure ...Acts 25:9
But the centurion, *w* to save ..Acts 27:43
subject to vanity, not *w* ....Rom 8:20
if God, *w* to show his.........Rom 9:22
For if I do this thing *w*, I 1Cor 9:17
distribute, *w* to communicate ..1Tim 6:18
it were of necessity, but *w* ....Philem 14
w more abundantly to show ...Heb 6:17
in all things *w* to live ....Heb 13:18
not by constraint, but *w*.......1Pet 5:2
For this they *w* are ignorant ...2Pet 3:5

WILLINGHEARTED—*generous*
whosoever is of a *w* ....Ex 35:5
many as were *w* ....Ex 35:22

WILLOW—*a tree*
Booths made of ....Lev 23:40, 42
Grows beside brooks ....Job 40:22
Harps hung on ....Ps 137:2
See POPLAR TREE

[*also* WILLOWS]
the *w* of the brook ....Job 40:22
to the brook of the *w*.........Is 15:7
and set it as a *w* tree ....Ezek 17:5

WILT—*See* WILL

WIMPLES—*shawls*
Worn by women ....Is 3:22

WIN—*to gain the victory*
[*also* WINNETH, WON]
Out of the spoils *w* in.........1Chr 26:27
thought to *w* them for 2Chr 32:1
life, and he that *w* souls.......Prov 11:30
is harder to be *w* than ....Prov 18:19
but dung, that I may *w* ....Phil 3:8
without the word be *w* 1Pet 3:1

WIND—*movement of the air*
Characteristics of:
Movement of, significant .Luke 12:54, 55
Cannot be seen ....John 3:8
Sometimes destructive ...Job 1:19
Dries the earth..........Gen 8:1
Often accompanies rain ..1Kin 18:44, 45
Makes sea rough ....Ps 107:25
Drives ships ....Acts 27:7, 13-18
Drives chaff away ....Ps 1:4
Possesses weight.........Job 28:25

God's relation to, He:
Creates ....Amos 4:13
Sends ....Ps 147:18
Brings out of His treasuries ....Ps 135:7
Gathers.................Prov 30:4
Controls ....Ps 107:25

Directions of, from:
East ....Jer 18:17
West ....Ex 10:19
North ....Prov 25:23
South ....Acts 27:13
All directions ....Ezek 37:9

Miracles connected with:
Flood subsided by ....Gen 8:1
Locust brought and taken by...................Ex 10:13, 19
Red Sea divided by.......Ex 14:21
Quail brought by ....Num 11:31
Rain brought by.........1Kin 18:44, 45
Mountains broken by 1Kin 19:11
Jonah's ship tossed by ...Jon 1:4
Christ calms ....Matt 8:26

Figurative of:
Empty speech ....Job 8:2
Empty boasting ....Prov 25:14
Vanity..................Eccl 5:16
Calamity................Is 32:2
God's discipline ....Hos 13:15
God's judgment ....Jer 22:22
Dispersion ....Ezek 5:10
Rain ....Hos 8:7
Holy Spirit..............Acts 2:2
False teaching ....Eph 4:14

[*also* WINDS, WINDY]
blasted with the east *w*........Gen 41:6
didst blow with thy *w* ....Ex 15:10
upon the wings of the *w* 2Sam 22:11
Ye shall not see *w*, neither 2Kin 3:17
desperate which are as *w*?.....Job 6:26
belly with the east *w*?.........Job 15:2
The east *w* carrieth him ....Job 27:21
liftest me up to the *w* ....Job 30:22
but the *w* passeth, and ....Job 37:21
scattereth the east *w* ....Job 38:24
upon the wings of the *w* ......Ps 18:10
as chaff before the *w* ....Ps 35:5
my escape from the *w* ....Ps 55:8
He caused an east *w* to ....Ps 78:26
a *w* that passeth away.........Ps 78:39
For the *w* passeth over it......Ps 103:16
stormy *w* fulfilling his ....Ps 148:8
house shall inherit the *w* ......Prov 11:29
hideth her hideth the *w* ....Prov 27:16
w goeth toward the south .....Eccl 1:6
the *w* returneth again ....Eccl 1:6
observeth the *w* shall not......Eccl 11:4
Awake, O north *w*; and.......Song 4:16
are moved with the *w*..........Is 7:2
mountains before the *w* ....Is 17:13
he stayeth his rough *w* ....Is 27:8
in the day of the east *w*.......Is 27:8
and the *w* shall carry ....Is 41:16
the *w* shall carry them ....Is 57:13
snuffeth up the *w* at her ......Jer 2:24
w from those places shall......Jer 4:12
forth the *w* out of his ....Jer 10:13
snuffed up the *w* like ....Jer 14:6
I will scatter into all *w* ....Jer 49:32
will I bring the four *w* ....Jer 49:36
them toward all those *w* .....Jer 49:36
me, a destroying *w* ....Jer 51:1
shalt scatter in the *w*..........Ezek 5:2
third part into all the *w* ....Ezek 5:12
fall; and a stormy *w* shall .....Ezek 13:11
when the east *w* toucheth .....Ezek 17:10
scattered toward all *w*.........Ezek 17:21
the east *w* hath broken........Ezek 27:26
and the *w* carried them ....Dan 2:35
the four *w* of the heaven ......Dan 7:2
toward the four *w* of..........Dan 11:4
The *w* hath bound her up .....Hos 4:19
Ephraim feedeth on *w* ....Hos 12:1
followeth after the east *w* .....Hos 12:1
shall sup up as the east *w* .....Hab 1:9
as the four *w* of the ....Zech 2:6
and the *w* was in their ....Zech 5:9
came, and the *w* blew..........Matt 7:25
even the *w* and the sea ....Matt 8:27
A reed shaken with the *w*?....Matt 11:7
But when he saw the *w* ....Matt 14:30
elect from the four *w* ....Matt 24:31
arose a great storm of *w* ....Mark 4:37
arose, and rebuked the *w* .....Mark 4:39
the *w* ceased, and there ....Mark 4:39
for the *w* was contrary ....Mark 6:48
elect from the four *w* ....Mark 13:27
A reed shaken with the *w*?....Luke 7:24
rebuked the *w* and the ....Luke 8:24
commandeth even the *w* ....Luke 8:25
by reason of a great *w* ....John 6:18
because the *w* were ....Acts 27:4
up the mainsail to the *w* ......Acts 27:40
one day the south *w* ....Acts 28:13
sea driven with the *w*..........James 1:6
are driven of fierce *w*, yet .....James 3:4
carried about of *w* ....Jude 12
shaken of a mighty *w* ....Rev 6:13
holding the four *w* of the .....Rev 7:1
the *w* should not blow ....Rev 7:1

WINDING—*wrapping*
[*also* WOUND]
and they went up with *w*......1Kin 6:8
a *w* about still upward to......Ezek 41:7
w about of the house ....Ezek 41:7
and *w* it in linen clothes.......John 19:40
the young men arose, *w*.......Acts 5:6

WINDOW—*an opening in a shelter for air or light*
[*also* WINDOWS]
A *w* shalt thou make to ....Gen 6:16
and the *w* of heaven were .....Gen 7:11
looked out at a *w* ....Gen 26:8
by a cord through the *w* ......Josh 2:15
scarlet line in the *w*...........Josh 2:21
Sisera looked out at a *w* ......Judg 5:28
David down through a *w*......1Sam 19:12
looked through a *w*...........2Sam 6:16
he made *w* of narrow 1Kin 6:4
And there were *w* in three 1Kin 7:4
and looked out at a *w* 2Kin 9:30
And he said, Open the *w* 2Kin 13:17
looking out at a *w* saw........1Chr 15:29
at the *w* of my house I........Prov 7:6
that look out of the *w* be .....Eccl 12:3
he looketh forth at the *w* .....Song 2:9
for the *w* from on high.......Is 24:18
I will make thy *w* of ....Is 54:12
is come up into our *w* ....Jer 9:21
and cutteth him out *w* ....Jer 22:14
narrow *w* to the little ....Ezek 40:16
and *w* were round about ....Ezek 40:16
were *w* in it and in the.......Ezek 40:25
round about, like those *w* .....Ezek 40:25
were *w* therein and in the .....Ezek 40:33
posts, and the narrow *w* ....Ezek 41:16
ground up to the *w* ....Ezek 41:16
and the *w* were covered ....Ezek 41:16
his *w* being open in his ....Dan 6:10
shall enter in at the *w* ....Joel 2:9
voice shall sing in the *w*.......Zeph 2:14
will not open you the *w*.......Mal 3:10
sat in a *w* a certain young .....Acts 20:9
through a *w* in a basket 2Cor 11:33

W

WINDOWS OF HEAVEN—*a figure of speech for a means through which God pours out his blessing or judgment*

Descriptive of:

Judgment rendered "opened" ....Gen 7:11
Unbelief 2Kin 7:2, 19
Blessings ....Mal 3:10

WINDY—*See* WIND

WINE—*fermented juice of grapes*

Kinds of:

New ....Luke 5:37-39
Old ....Luke 5:39
Fermented ....Num 6:3
Refined ....Is 25:6

Features concerning:

Made from grapes ....Gen 40:11
Mixed ....Prov 23:30
Kept in bottles ....Jer 13:12
Kept in wineskins ....Matt 9:17

Used by:

Noah ....Gen 9:20, 21
Melchizedek ....Gen 14:18
Isaac ....Gen 27:25
Esther ....Esth 5:6
Jesus ....John 2:1-11
Timothy 1Tim 5:23

Uses of, as:

Offering ....Lev 23:13
Drink ....Gen 27:25
Festive drink ....Esth 1:7
Disinfectant ....Luke 10:34
Drug ....Mark 15:23
Medicine 1Tim 5:23

Evil effects of:

Leads to violence ....Prov 4:17
Mocks a man ....Prov 20:1
Make poor ....Prov 23:20, 21
Bites like a serpent ......Prov 23:31, 32
Impairs the judgment ....Prov 31:4, 5
Inflames the passions ....Is 5:11
Takes away the heart ....Hos 4:11

Intoxication from, falsely charged to:

Hannah 1Sam 1:12-16
Jesus ....Matt 11:19
Apostles ....Acts 2:13

Used of, in:

Offering ....Num 15:4-10
Miracle ....John 2:1-9
Lord's Supper ....Matt 26:27-29

Figurative of:

God's wrath ....Ps 75:8
Wisdom's blessings ......Prov 9:2, 5
Gospel ....Is 55:1
Christ's blood ....Matt 26:27-29
Fornication ....Rev 17:2

See DRUNKENNESS; TEMPERANCE

Noah awoke from his *w* ....Gen 9:24
make our father drink *w* ......Gen 19:32
make him drink *w* this ....Gen 19:34
their father drink *w* ....Gen 19:35
plenty of corn and *w* ....Gen 27:28
washed his garments in *w* .....Gen 49:11
part of a hin of *w* ....Ex 29:40
Do not drink *w* nor strong ....Lev 10:9
Nazarite may drink *w* ....Num 6:20
all the best of the *w*, and .....Num 18:12
be half a hin of *w* ....Num 28:14
land, thy corn, and thy *w* .....Deut 7:13
of thy corn, or of thy *w* ....Deut 12:17
for sheep, or for *w*, or ....Deut 14:26
also of the corn, of thy *w* .....Deut 18:4
leave thee either corn, *w* ......Deut 28:51
Their *w* is the poison of ....Deut 32:33
a land of corn and *w* ....Deut 33:28
and *w* bottles, old, and ....Josh 9:4
Should I leave my *w* ....Judg 9:13
now drink no *w* nor ....Judg 13:7
there is bread and *w* also .....Judg 19:19
flour, and a bottle of *w* 1Sam 1:24
bread, and a bottle of *w* 1Sam 16:20
loaves, and two bottles of *w* ...1Sam 25:18
and a flagon of *w* 2Sam 6:19
fruits and a bottle of *w* 2Sam 16:1
a land of corn and *w* 2Kin 18:32
fine flour, and the *w* 1Chr 9:29
and a flagon of *w* 1Chr 16:3
thousand baths of *w* 2Chr 2:10
victual, and of oil and *w* 2Chr 11:11
increase of corn, and *w* 2Chr 32:28
heaven, wheat, salt, *w* ....Ezra 6:9
the king, that *w* was ....Neh 2:1
the *w*, and the oil, that ....Neh 5:11
store of all sorts of *w* ....Neh 5:18
the corn, of the new *w* ....Neh 10:39
the new *w* and the oil ....Neh 13:12
as also *w*, grapes, and ....Neh 13:15
king was merry with *w* ....Esth 1:10
at the banquet of *w* ....Esth 7:2
of the banquet of *w* ....Esth 7:8
and drinking *w* in their ....Job 1:13
belly is as *w* which hath ....Job 32:19
their corn and their *w* ....Ps 4:7
the *w* of astonishment ....Ps 60:3
shouteth by reason of *w* ....Ps 78:65
w that maketh glad the ....Ps 104:15
shall burst out with new *w* ....Prov 3:10
he that loveth *w* and oil ....Prov 21:17
and *w* unto those that be ......Prov 31:6
to give myself unto *w* ....Eccl 2:3
laughter, and *w* maketh merry .Eccl 10:19
love is better than *w* ....Song 1:2
is thy love than *w*! ....Song 4:10
like the best *w* for my ....Song 7:9
dross, thy *w* mixed with ....Is 1:22
pipe, and *w*, are in their ......Is 5:12
tread out no *w* in their ....Is 16:10
The new *w* mourneth, the .....Is 24:7
is a crying for *w* in the ....Is 24:11
are overcome with *w*! ....Is 28:1
have erred through *w* ....Is 28:7
are swallowed up of *w* ....Is 28:7
a land of corn and *w* ....Is 36:17
drunken, but not with *w* ......Is 51:21
say they, I will fetch *w* ....Is 56:12
new *w* is found in the ....Is 65:8
like a man whom *w* hath ......Jer 23:9
for wheat, and for *w*, and .....Jer 31:12
pots full of *w*, and cups ....Jer 35:5
unto them, Drink ye *w* ....Jer 35:5
We will drink no *w* ....Jer 35:6
Ye shall drink no *w* ....Jer 35:6
his sons not to drink *w* ....Jer 35:14
gathered *w* and summer ....Jer 40:12
have drunken of her *w* ....Jer 51:7
Where is corn and *w*? ....Lam 2:12
in the *w* of Helbon, and ......Ezek 27:18
meat, and of the *w* which .....Dan 1:5
and the *w* that they ....Dan 1:16
while he tasted the *w* ....Dan 5:2
concubines, have drunk *w* .....Dan 5:23
I gave her corn, and *w* ....Hos 2:8
the corn, and the *w* ....Hos 2:22
and love flagons of *w* ....Hos 3:1
sick with bottles of *w* ....Hos 7:5
and the new *w* shall fail ....Hos 9:2
shall be as the *w* of ....Hos 14:7
all ye drinkers of *w* ....Joel 1:5
because of the new *w* ....Joel 1:5
send you corn, and *w* ....Joel 2:19
sold a girl for *w*, that ....Joel 3:3
drink the *w* of the ....Amos 2:8
but ye shall not drink *w* ....Amos 5:11
shall drop sweet *w* ....Amos 9:13
prophesy unto thee of *w* ....Mic 2:11
with oil; and sweet *w* ....Mic 6:15
but shalt not drink *w* ....Mic 6:15
he transgresseth by *w* ....Hab 2:5
not drink the *w* thereof ....Zeph 1:13
upon the new *w*, and ....Hag 1:11
a noise as through *w* ....Zech 9:15
rejoice as through *w* ....Zech 10:7
putteth new *w* into old ....Mark 2:22
the new *w* doth burst the .....Mark 2:22
and the *w* is spilled, and ......Mark 2:22
but new *w* must be put ....Mark 2:22
drink neither *w* nor ....Luke 1:15
bread nor drinking *w* ....Luke 7:33
doth set forth good *w* ....John 2:10
hast kept the good *w* ....John 2:10
he made the water *w* ....John 4:46
eat flesh, nor to drink *w* ......Rom 14:21
And be not drunk with *w* .....Eph 5:18
Not given to *w*, no striker 1Tim 3:3
not given to much *w*, not 1Tim 3:8
not given to *w*, no striker .....Titus 1:7
lusts, excess of *w* 1Pet 4:3
not the oil and the *w* ....Rev 6:6
drink of the *w* of the ....Rev 14:10
the cup of the *w* of the ....Rev 16:19
have drunk of the *w* of ....Rev 18:3
and *w*, and oil, and fine ....Rev 18:13

WINE VAT—*a winepress*

treadeth in the *w v* ....Is 63:2
digged a place for the *w v* .....Mark 12:1

WINEBIBBER—*a drinker of wine*

[*also* WINEBIBBERS]

Be not among *w* ....Prov 23:20
a *w*, a friend of publicans .....Matt 11:19
a *w*, a friend of publicans .....Luke 7:34

WINEFAT—*See* WINE VAT

WINEPRESS—*vat from which grapejuice is extracted for wine*

[*also* WINEPRESSES]

as the fulness of the *w* ....Num 18:27
floor, and out of thy *w* ....Deut 15:14
threshed wheat by the *w* ......Judg 6:11
barnfloor, or out of the *w*? 2Kin 6:27
tread their *w*, and suffer ......Job 24:11
of it, and also made a *w* ....Is 5:2
wine to fail from the *w* ....Jer 48:33
of Judah, as in a *w* ....Lam 1:15
The floor and the *w* shall .....Hos 9:2
Hananeel unto the king's *w* ...Zech 14:10
and digged a *w* in it, and .....Matt 21:33
great *w* of the wrath of ....Rev 14:19
w was trodden without ....Rev 14:20
blood came out of the *w* ......Rev 14:20

WING—*appendage used by birds to fly*

Used literally of:

Flying creatures ....Gen 1:21
Cherubim ....Ex 25:20

Used figuratively of:

God's mercy ....Ps 57:1
Protection ....Luke 13:34

[*also* WINGED, WINGS]

and every *w* fowl after ....Gen 1:21
I bare you on eagles' *w* ....Ex 19:4
stretch forth their *w* ....Ex 25:20
mercy seat with their *w* ....Ex 25:20
spread out their *w* ....Ex 37:9
and covered with their *w* ....Ex 37:9
shall cleave it with the *w* ......Lev 1:17
likeness of any *w* fowl ....Deut 4:17
spreadeth abroad her *w* ....Deut 32:11
beareth them on her *w* ....Deut 32:11
under whose *w* thou art ....Ruth 2:12
was seen upon the *w* of 2Sam 22:11
was the one *w* of the 1Kin 6:24
cubits the other *w* of the 1Kin 6:24
part of the one *w* unto 1Kin 6:24
they stretched forth the *w* 1Kin 6:27
w of the one touched the 1Kin 6:27
w of the other cherub 1Kin 6:27
their *w* touched one 1Kin 6:27
spread forth their two *w* 1Kin 8:7
that spread out their *w* 1Chr 28:18
w of the cherubim were 2Chr 3:11
one *w* of the one cherub 2Chr 3:11
other *w* was likewise five 2Chr 3:11
reaching to the *w* of the 2Chr 3:11
one *w* of the other cherub 2Chr 3:12
and the other *w* was five 2Chr 3:12
w of the other cherub 2Chr 3:12
even under the *w* of the 2Chr 5:7
the goodly *w* unto the ....Job 39:13
or *w* and feathers unto ....Job 39:13
the shadow of thy *w* ....Ps 17:8

in the shadow of thy *w*........Ps 57:1
the shadow of thy *w* will......Ps 63:7
and under his *w* shall.........Ps 91:4
If I take the *w* of the.........Ps 139:9
make themselves *w*; they......Prov 23:5
which hath *w* shall tell........Eccl 10:20
each one had six *w*...........Is 6:2
none that moved the *w*.......Is 10:14
land shadowing with *w*........Is 18:1
Give *w* unto Moab, that it....Jer 48:9
and spread his *w* over.........Jer 49:22
every one had four *w*.........Ezek 1:6
hands of a man under their *w*.Ezek 1:8
their faces and their *w*........Ezek 1:8
their *w* were stretched........Ezek 1:11
two *w* of every one were......Ezek 1:11
the noise of their *w*...........Ezek 1:24
they let down their *w*.........Ezek 1:24
of the *w* of the living.........Ezek 3:13
hand under their *w*...........Ezek 10:8
lifted up their *w* to...........Ezek 10:16
and every one four *w*.........Ezek 10:21
hands..was under their *w*......Ezek 10:21
A great eagle with great *w*....Ezek 17:3
dwell all fowl of every *w*......Ezek 17:23
lion, and had eagle's *w*........Dan 7:4
till the *w* thereof were........Dan 7:4
bound her up in her *w*........Hos 4:19
the wind was in their *w*.......Zech 5:9
they had *w* like the *w* of......Zech 5:9
arise with healing in his *w*.....Mal 4:2
her chickens under her *w*.....Matt 23:37
her brood under her *w*.........Luke 13:34
had each of them six *w*.......Rev 4:8
given two *w* of a great........Rev 12:14

WINK—*to close and open one eye quickly*

[*also* WINKED, WINKETH]
what do thy eyes *w* at........Job 15:12
w with the eye that hate me...Ps 35:19
He *w* with his eyes...........Prov 6:13
He that *w* with the eye.......Prov 10:10
this ignorance God *w* at.......Acts 17:30

WINNETH—*See* WIN

WINNOW—*to remove chaff by a current of air; rid oneself of something unwanted*

Used literally of:
Fork for winnowing grain.Is 30:24

Used figuratively of judgments:
God's.................Is 30:24
Nation's................Jer 51:2
Christ's................Matt 3:12

[*also* WINNOWETH]
he *w* barley tonight in........Ruth 3:2

WINTER—*the cold season of the year; to lodge during the winter*
Made by God..........Ps 74:17
Continuance of, guaranteed...........Gen 8:22
Time of snow..........2Sam 23:20
Hazards of travel during.2Tim 4:21

[*also* WINTERED]
w is past, the rain is over.....Song 2:11
the beasts..shall *w* upon.......Is 18:6
I will smite the *w* house.......Amos 3:15
in summer and in *w* shall.....Zech 14:8
flight be not in the *w*.........Matt 24:20
flight be not in the *w*.........Mark 13:18
dedication, and it was *w*......John 10:22
not commodious to *w* in......Acts 27:12
Phoenix, and there to *w*......Acts 27:12
which had *w* in the isle.......Acts 28:11
abide, yea, and *w* with you....1Cor 16:6
determined there to *w*........Titus 3:12

WINTER HOUSE—*home inhabited during the winter months*
the king sat in the *w h* in.....Jer 36:22

WIPE—*clean or dry; expunge*

Used literally of:
Dust removal...........Luke 10:11
Feet dried.............John 13:5

Used figuratively of:
Jerusalem's destruction...2Kin 21:13
Tears removed..........Rev 7:17

[*also* WIPED, WIPETH]
reproach shall not be *w*.......Prov 6:33
eateth, and *w* her mouth......Prov 30:20
God will *w* away tears........Is 25:8
did *w* them with the hairs.....Luke 7:38
w them with the hairs of......Luke 7:44
we do *w* off against you.......Luke 10:11
w his feet with her hair.......John 11:2
w his feet with her hair.......John 12:3
God shall *w* away all tears....Rev 21:4

WIRES—*threads*
Used in ephod..........Ex 39:3

WISDOM—*knowledge guided by understanding*

Sources of, in:
Spirit..................Ex 31:3
Lord...................Ex 36:1, 2
God's Law.............Deut 4:6
Fear of the LORD.......Prov 9:10
Righteous..............Prov 10:31

Ascribed to:
Workmen...............Ex 36:2
Women.................Prov 31:26
Bezaleel...............Ex 31:2-5
Joseph.................Acts 7:9, 10
Moses.................Acts 7:22
Joshua.................Deut 34:9
Hiram.................1Kin 7:13, 14
Solomon...............1Kin 3:12, 16-28
Children of Issachar.....1Chr 12:32
Ezra...................Ezra 7:25
Daniel.................Dan 1:17
Magi..................Matt 2:1-12
Stephem...............Acts 6:3, 10
Paul...................2Pet 3:15

Described as:
Discreet...............Gen 41:33
Technical skill..........Ex 28:3
Common sense.........2Sam 20:14-22
Mechanical skill........1Kin 7:14
Understanding.........Prov 10:13, 23
Military ability..........Is 10:13
Commercial industry.....Ezek 28:3-5

Value of:
Gives happiness........Prov 3:13
Benefits of, many.......Prov 4:5-10
Keeps from evil.........Prov 5:1-6
Better than rubies.......Prov 8:11
Above gold in value.....Prov 16:16
Should be acquired......Prov 23:23
Excels folly............Eccl 2:13
Gives life..............Eccl 7:12
Makes strong...........Eccl 7:19
Better than weapons.....Eccl 9:18
Insures stability.........Is 33:6
Produces good fruit......James 3:17

Limitations of:
Cannot save us..........1Cor 1:19-21
Cause of self-glory.......Jer 9:23
Can pervert............Is 47:10
Nothing, without God...Jer 8:9
Can corrupt............Ezek 28:17
Of this world, foolishness.1Cor 3:19
Earthly, sensual.........James 3:15
Gospel not preached in..1Cor 2:1-5

Of believers:
Given by Christ.........Luke 21:15
Gift of the Spirit........1Cor 12:8
Given by God...........Eph 1:17
Prayed for.............Col 1:9
Means of instruction.....Col 1:28
Lack of, ask for.........James 1:5

[*also* WISE, WISELY, WISER]
be desired to make one *w*.....Gen 3:6
and all the *w* men thereof.....Gen 41:8
discreet and *w* as thou art.....Gen 41:39
let us deal *w* with them.......Ex 1:10
Pharaoh also called the *w*.....Ex 7:11
the gift blindeth the *w*........Ex 23:8
wisehearted I have put *w*......Ex 31:6
heart stirred them up in *w*....Ex 35:26
he filled with *w* of heart......Ex 35:35
And all the *w* men, that......Ex 36:4
Take you *w* men, and.........Deut 1:13
chief of your tribes, *w* men....Deut 1:15
blind the eyes of the *w*........Deut 16:19
O that they were *w*, that......Deut 32:29
Her *w* ladies answered her....Judg 5:29
and behaved himself *w*........1Sam 18:5
behaved himself very *w*.......1Sam 18:15
fetched thence a *w* woman....2Sam 14:2
my lord is *w*, according.......2Sam 14:20
to the *w* of an angel of.......2Sam 14:20
for thou art a *w* man, and.....1Kin 2:9
child, and in no *w* slay........1Kin 3:26
child, and in no *w* slay........1Kin 3:27
Saw that the *w* of God was....1Kin 3:28
Solomon's *w* excelled the *w*...1Kin 4:30
and all the *w* of Egypt........1Kin 4:30
For he was *w* than all men....1Kin 4:31
to hear the *w* of Solomon.....1Kin 4:34
which had heard of his *w*.....1Kin 4:34
given unto David a *w* son.....1Kin 5:7
the Lord gave Solomon *w*.....1Kin 5:12
with *w*, and understanding....1Kin 7:14
had seen all Solomon's *w*....1Kin 10:4
w and prosperity exceedeth....1Kin 10:7
earth for riches and for *w*.....1Kin 10:23
his *w*, are they not written....1Kin 11:41
Only the Lord give thee *w*....1Chr 22:12
Zechariah his son, a *w*........1Chr 26:14
a *w* man, and a scribe........1Chr 27:32
Give me now *w* and...........2Chr 1:10
W and knowledge is granted...2Chr 1:12
to David the king a *w* son.....2Chr 2:12
thine acts, and of thy *w*......2Chr 9:5
thee, and hear thy *w*..........2Chr 9:7
of Solomon, to hear his *w*.....2Chr 9:23
he dealt *w*, and dispersed.....2Chr 11:23
the king said to the *w* men....Esth 1:13
said his *w* men and Zeresh....Esth 6:13
they die, even without *w*.....Job 4:21
taketh the *w* in their own.....Job 5:13
thee the secrets of *w*.........Job 11:6
For vain man would be *w*.....Job 11:12
With the ancient is *w*........Job 12:12
With him is strength and *w*....Job 12:16
thou restrain *w* to thyself?.....Job 15:8
w men have told from........Job 15:18
is *w* may be profitable........Job 22:2
where shall *w* be found?......Job 28:12
Whence then cometh *w*?......Job 28:20
multitude of years..teach *w*....Job 32:7
and I shall teach thee *w*......Job 33:33
Hear my words, O ye *w*......Job 34:2
maketh us *w* than the fowls...Job 35:11
any that are *w* of heart.......Job 37:24
God hath deprived her of *w*...Job 39:17
Be *w* now therefore, O ye....Ps 2:10
he hath left off to be *w*.......Ps 36:3
the righteous speaketh *w*......Ps 37:30
he seeth that *w* men die.......Ps 49:10
shalt make me to know *w*.....Ps 51:6
charming never so *w*..........Ps 58:5
shall *w* consider of his........Ps 64:9
apply our hearts unto *w*.......Ps 90:12
behave myself *w* in a.........Ps 101:2
and teach his senators *w*......Ps 105:22
is *w*, and will observe.........Ps 107:43
hast made me *w* than.........Ps 119:98
by *w* made the heavens.......Ps 136:5
know *w* and instruction.......Prov 1:2
w man will hear, and will.....Prov 1:5
attain unto *w* counsels........Prov 1:5
fools despise *w* and..........Prov 1:7
incline thine ear unto *w*.......Prov 2:2
He layeth up sound *w* for.....Prov 2:7
not *w* in thine own eyes.......Prov 3:7
Lord by *w* hath founded......Prov 3:19
sound *w* and discretion........Prov 3:21
consider her ways, and be *w*...Prov 6:6
Say unto *w*, Thou art my.....Prov 7:4
Doth not *w* cry and..........Prov 8:1

W

O ye simple, understand w .... Prov 8:5
I w dwell with prudence ...... Prov 8:12
Counsel is mine, and sound w . Prov 8:14
Hear instruction, and be w .... Prov 8:33
W hath builded her house ..... Prov 9:1
rebuke a w man, and he ...... Prov 9:8
a w man, and he will be yet w . Prov 9:9
thou be w, thou shalt be w .... Prov 9:12
A w son maketh a glad .... Prov 10:1
w in heart will receive .... Prov 10:8
refraineth his lips is w .... Prov 10:19
fools die for want of w .... Prov 10:21
but with the lowly is w .... Prov 11:2
that is void of w despiseth ..... Prov 11:12
servant to the w of heart ...... Prov 11:29
according to his w .... Prov 12:8
hearkeneth unto counsel is w .. Prov 12:15
w son heareth his father's ..... Prov 13:1
with the well advised is w ..... Prov 13:10
that walketh with w men ...... Prov 13:20
Every w woman buildeth ...... Prov 14:1
A scorner seeketh w, and ..... Prov 14:6
w of the prudent is to .... Prov 14:8
A w man feareth, and .... Prov 14:16
W resteth in the heart of ...... Prov 14:33
is toward a w servant .... Prov 14:35
the w useth knowledge .... Prov 15:2
will he go unto the w .... Prov 15:12
him that is destitute of w ...... Prov 15:21
of life is above to the w ...... Prov 15:24
Lord is the instruction of w ... Prov 15:33
a w man will pacify it .... Prov 16:14
better is it to get w than ...... Prov 16:16
that handleth a matter w ...... Prov 16:20
heart of the w teacheth .... Prov 16:23
w servant shall have rule ...... Prov 17:2
hand of a fool to get w .... Prov 17:16
his peace, is counted w .... Prov 17:28
intermeddleth with all w ...... Prov 18:1
the ear of the w seeketh ...... Prov 18:15
getteth w loveth his own ...... Prov 19:8
thou mayest be w in thy ...... Prov 19:20
deceived thereby is not w ..... Prov 20:1
the simple is made w .... Prov 21:11
when the w is instructed ...... Prov 21:11
A w man scaleth the city ...... Prov 21:22
hear the words of the w .... Prov 22:17
cease from thine own w .... Prov 23:4
My son, if thine heart be w ... Prov 23:15
also w, and instruction .... Prov 23:23
that begetteth a w child .... Prov 23:24
Through w is a house .... Prov 24:3
A w man is strong; yea, a ..... Prov 24:5
W is too high for a fool .... Prov 24:7
things also belong to the w .... Prov 24:23
a w reprover upon an .... Prov 25:12
he be w in his own conceit .... Prov 26:5
be w, and make my heart ..... Prov 27:11
keepeth the law is a w son .... Prov 28:7
but whoso walketh w, he ...... Prov 28:26
Whoso loveth w rejoiceth ..... Prov 29:3
w men turn away wrath .... Prov 29:8
but a w man keepeth it in ..... Prov 29:11
I neither learned w, nor .... Prov 30:3
but they are exceeding w ...... Prov 30:24
seek and search out by w ..... Eccl 1:13
have gotten more w than ...... Eccl 1:16
had great experience of w ..... Eccl 1:16
in much w is much grief .... Eccl 1:18
my w remained with me ...... Eccl 2:9
w man's eyes are in his head .. Eccl 2:14
no remembrance of the w ..... Eccl 2:16
how dieth the w man? as ...... Eccl 2:16
shall be a w, man or a fool? .. Eccl 2:19
I have showed myself w .... Eccl 2:19
man whose labor is in w ...... Eccl 2:21
Better is a poor and a w ...... Eccl 4:13
the w more than the fool? ..... Eccl 6:8
heart of the w is in the .... Eccl 7:4
maketh a w man mad .... Eccl 7:7
thou dost not inquire w .... Eccl 7:10
W is good with an .... Eccl 7:11
W strengtheneth the w .... Eccl 7:19
this have I proved by w .... Eccl 7:23
seek out w, and the reason .... Eccl 7:25
Who is as the w man? and .... Eccl 8:1
man's w maketh his face ...... Eccl 8:1
a w man think to know .... Eccl 8:17
the righteous, and the w ..... Eccl 9:1
nor knowledge, nor w .... Eccl 9:10
found in it a poor w man ..... Eccl 9:15
his w delivered the city ...... Eccl 9:15
W is better than strength ..... Eccl 9:16
poor man's w is despised ..... Eccl 9:16
in reputation for w and .... Eccl 10:1
A w man's heart is at his ..... Eccl 10:2
w is profitable to direct .... Eccl 10:10
the preacher was w, he .... Eccl 12:9
unto them that are w in .... Is 5:21
w counselors of Pharaoh ...... Is 19:11
I am the son of the w, the .... Is 19:11
the w of their w men .... Is 29:14
turneth w men backward ...... Is 44:25
they are w to do evil, but .... Jer 4:22
w men are ashamed, they ..... Jer 8:9
w man glory in his w .... Jer 9:23
established..by his w .... Jer 10:12
nor counsel from the w .... Jer 18:18
Is w no more in Teman? ...... Jer 49:7
is their w vanished? .... Jer 49:7
established..by his w .... Jer 51:15
princes, and her w men .... Jer 51:57
thy w men, O Tyrus, that ..... Ezek 27:8
and skillful in all w, and ...... Dan 1:4
in all matters of w and .... Dan 1:20
destroy all the w men .... Dan 2:12
with counsel and w to .... Dan 2:14
slay the w men of Babylon .... Dan 2:14
he giveth w unto the w .... Dan 2:21
who hast given me w and ..... Dan 2:23
to destroy the w men of .... Dan 2:24
Destroy not the w men of ..... Dan 2:24
all the w men of Babylon ..... Dan 2:48
all the w men of Babylon ..... Dan 4:6
and said to the w men of ..... Dan 5:7
and understanding and w ...... Dan 5:11
like the w of the gods, was .... Dan 5:11
the w men, the astrologers .... Dan 5:15
the w shall understand .... Dan 12:10
Who is w, and he shall .... Hos 14:9
destroy the w men out of ..... Obad 8
the man of w shall see thy .... Mic 6:9
Zidon, though it be very w .... Zech 9:2
was mocked of the w men ..... Matt 2:16
inquired of the w men .... Matt 2:16
liken him unto a w man .... Matt 7:24
ye therefore w as serpents .... Matt 10:16
But w is justified of her .... Matt 11:19
these things from the w .... Matt 11:25
to hear the w of Solomon ..... Matt 12:42
you prophets, and w men ..... Matt 23:34
a faithful and w servant ...... Matt 24:45
And five of them were w ..... Matt 25:2
w took oil in their vessels ..... Matt 25:4
foolish said unto the w .... Matt 25:8
the w answered, saying .... Matt 25:9
w is this which is given .... Mark 6:2
to the w of the just .... Luke 1:17
strong in spirit, filled with w .. Luke 2:40
w is justified of all her .... Luke 7:35
these things from the w .... Luke 10:21
to hear the w of Solomon ..... Luke 11:31
Also said the w of God .... Luke 11:49
faithful and w steward .... Luke 12:42
because he had done w .... Luke 16:8
w than the children of .... Luke 16:8
the w, and to the unwise ..... Rom 1:14
Professing themselves to be w . Rom 1:22
be w in your own conceits ..... Rom 11:25
the riches both of the w .... Rom 11:33
w in your own conceits .... Rom 12:16
w unto that which is good ..... Rom 16:19
To God only w, be glory ...... Rom 16:27
not with w of words, lest 1Cor 1:17
the Greeks seek after w 1Cor 1:22
of God is w than men 1Cor 1:25
not many w men after the 1Cor 1:26
world to confound the w 1Cor 1:27
a w masterbuilder, I have 1Cor 3:10
you seemeth to be w in 1Cor 3:18
a fool, that he may be w 1Cor 3:18
He taketh the w in their 1Cor 3:19
the thoughts of the w 1Cor 3:20
but ye are w in Christ 1Cor 4:10
not a w man among you? 1Cor 6:5
I speak as to w men 1Cor 10:15
not with fleshly w, but 2Cor 1:12
themselves, are not w 2Cor 10:12
seeing ye yourselves are w 2Cor 11:19
not as fools, but as w .... Eph 5:15
indeed a show of w in will .... Col 2:23
in you richly in all w .... Col 3:16
the only w God, be honor 1Tim 1:17
thee w unto salvation 2Tim 3:15
the seventh day on this w ..... Heb 4:4
Who is a w man and endued .. James 3:13
works with meekness of w ..... James 3:13
only w God our Savior .... Jude 25
and w, and strength, and ...... Rev 5:12
Blessing and glory, and w ...... Rev 7:12
Here is w. Let him that .... Rev 13:18
is the mind which hath w ..... Rev 17:9
there shall in no w enter ...... Rev 21:27

WISDOM OF CHRIST

Predicted .... Is 11:1, 2
Incarnated 1Cor 1:24
Realized .... Luke 2:52
Displayed .... Matt 13:54
Perfected .... Col 2:3
Imputed 1Cor 1:30

WISDOM OF GOD

Described as:

Universal .... Dan 2:20
Infinite .... Ps 147:5
Unsearchable .... Is 40:28
Mighty .... Job 36:5
Perfect .... Job 37:16

Manifested in:

Creation .... Ps 104:24
Nature .... Job 38:34-41
Sovereignty .... Dan 2:20, 21
The Church .... Eph 3:10

WISE—*manner*

thou afflict them in any w ..... Ex 22:23
but ye shall in no w eat .... Lev 7:24
shalt in any w rebuke .... Lev 19:17
field will in any w redeem ..... Lev 27:19
On this w ye shall bless .... Num 6:23
shalt in any w bury him .... Deut 21:23
in any w keep yourselves ..... Josh 6:18
if ye do in any w go back ..... Josh 23:12
w return him a trespass 1Sam 6:3
Jesus Christ was on this w ..... Matt 1:18
tittle shall in no w pass .... Matt 5:18
he shall in no w lose his ...... Matt 10:42
not deny thee in any w .... Mark 14:31
in no w lift up herself .... Luke 13:11
child shall in no w enter ...... Luke 18:17
to me I will in no w cast ...... John 6:37
And God spake on this w ..... Acts 7:6
said on this w, I will give ..... Acts 13:34
ye shall in no w believe ..... Acts 13:41
No, in no w: for we have ..... Rom 3:9
faith speaketh on this w ...... Rom 10:6

WISEHEARTED—*characterized by wisdom*

unto all that are w .... Ex 28:3
hearts of all that are w .... Ex 31:6
w among you shall .... Ex 35:10
the women that were w .... Ex 35:25
every w man among them ..... Ex 36:8

WISH—*to have a desire for; want*

[*also* WISHED, WISHING]

to sin by w a curse to his ..... Job 31:30
I am according to thy w in .... Job 33:6
to shame that w me evil .... Ps 40:14
and w in himself to die .... Jon 4:8
stern, and w for the day ...... Acts 27:29
could w that myself were ...... Rom 9:3
and this also we w, even 2Cor 13:9
I w above all things that 3John 2

WIST—*to know; knew*
for they *w* not what it was ....Ex 16:15
w it not, yet is he guilty.......Lev 5:17
but I *w* not whence they ......Josh 2:4
w not that the Lord was ......Judg 16:20
For he *w* not what to say .....Mark 9:6
w they what to answer ....Mark 14:40
w ye not that I must be ....Luke 2:49
healed *w* not who it was ......John 5:13
w not that it was true ....Acts 12:9
Then said Paul, I *w* not ....Acts 23:5

WIT—*that is to say; know; knowingly*

[*also* WIT'S]
to *w* whether the Lord had ....Gen 24:21
w, for Machir the first-born ...Josh 17:1
w, Abner the son of Ner 1Kin 2:32
w, for the prophet whom......1Kin 13:23
to *w*, the golden calves........2Kin 10:29
their father's house, to *w*......1Chr 7:2
To *w*, the two pillars, and.....2Chr 4:12
to *w*, the army that was 2Chr 25:10
to *w* six months with oil.......Esth 2:12
and are at their *w* end ....Ps 107:27
To *w*, Jerusalem, and the .....Jer 25:18
w, the prophets of Israel ......Ezek 13:16
to *w*, the redemption of ....Rom 8:23
w, that God was in Christ 2Cor 5:19
to *w* of the grace of God......2Cor 8:1

WITCH—*one who practices sorcery*
Saul consults one 1Sam 28:7-25

not suffer a *w* to live ....Ex 22:18

WITCHCRAFT—*the practice of sorcery*
Forbidden in Israel ......Deut 18:9-14
Used by Jezebel 2Kin 9:22
Condemned by the prophets ....Mic 5:12
Practiced by Manasseh ...2Chr 33:6
Suppressed by Saul 1Sam 28:3, 9
Work of the flesh ....Gal 5:20
See DIVINATION; WIZARD

[*also* WITCHCRAFTS]
rebellion is as the sin of *w* 1Sam 15:23
mistress of *w*, that selleth .....Nah 3:4
families through her *w* ....Nah 3:4

WITH—*See* INTRODUCTION

WITHAL—*therewith*
bowls thereof, to cover *w* .....Ex 25:29
also of brass, to wash *w*.......Ex 30:18
to cover *w*, of pure gold ......Ex 37:16
water there, to wash *w*........Ex 40:30
a man shall be defiled *w* ....Lev 5:3
to leap *w* upon the earth ......Lev 11:21
and covers to cover *w*.........Num 4:7
right hands to blow *w*.........Judg 7:20
and *w* of a beautiful 1Sam 16:12
w how he had slain all the 1Kin 19:1
the walls of the houses *w* 1Chr 29:4
minister, and to offer *w* 2Chr 24:14
array the man *w* whom ....Esth 6:9
to scrape himself *w* ....Job 2:8
whilst that I *w* escape ....Ps 141:10
w be fitted in thy lips ....Prov 22:18
water *w* out of the pit ....Is 30:14
I am baptized *w* shall ye ......Mark 10:39
that ye mete *w* it shall be .....Luke 6:38
w to signify the crimes ....Acts 25:27
to every man to profit *w* 1Cor 12:7
W praying also for us ....Col 4:3
w they learn to be idle 1Tim 5:13
w prepare me also a lodging...Philem 22

WITHDRAW—*to take back or away; remove*

[*also* WITHDRAWEST, WITHDRAWETH, WITHDRAWN, WITHDREW]
w the inhabitants of their .....Deut 13:13
the priest, *W* thine hand 1Sam 14:19
and *w* the shoulder, and ......Neh 9:29
God will not *w* his anger ......Job 9:13
w man from his purpose ....Job 33:17
He *w* not his eyes from the ...Job 36:7
Why *w* thou thy hand ....Ps 74:11
W thy foot from thy ....Prov 25:17
this *w* not thine hand ....Eccl 7:18
my beloved had *w* himself.....Song 5:6
neither shall thy moon *w* ......Is 60:20
not *w* his hand from ....Lam 2:8
w his hand from iniquity ......Ezek 18:8
Nevertheless I *w* mine hand ...Ezek 20:22
hath *w* himself from them .....Hos 5:6
stars shall *w* their shining .....Joel 2:10
he *w* himself from thence .....Matt 12:15
Jesus *w* himself with his ....Mark 3:7
he *w* himself into the ....Luke 5:16
And he was *w* from them .....Luke 22:41
w and separated himself.......Gal 2:12
w yourselves from every 2Thess 3:6
godliness: from such *w* 1Tim 6:5

WITHER—*to dry up; shrivel*

Caused by:
God's judgment ....Is 40:7, 24
Christ's judgment........Matt 21:19, 20
No root ....Matt 13:6
Heat ....James 1:11

Applied literally to:
Ear of grain ....Gen 41:23
Gourd ....Jon 4:7
Man's hand ....Luke 6:6, 8

[*also* WITHERED, WITHERETH]
w before any other herb ......Job 8:12
his leaf also shall not *w* ....Ps 1:3
it is cut down, and *w* ....Ps 90:6
is smitten, and *w* like grass ....Ps 102:4
for the hay is *w* away, the.....Is 15:6
reeds and flags shall *w* ....Is 19:6
sown by the brooks, shall *w* ...Is 19:7
The grass *w*, the flower ....Is 40:7
herbs of every field *w*.........Jer 12:4
it is *w*, it is become like.......Lam 4:8
fruit thereof, that it *w*? ....Ezek 17:9
w in all the leaves of her......Ezek 17:9
shall it not utterly *w* ....Ezek 17:10
w in the furrows where it .....Ezek 17:10
rods were broken and *w* ......Ezek 19:12
trees of the field, are *w* ....Joel 1:12
joy is *w* away from the........Joel 1:12
top of Carmel shall *w*.........Amos 1:2
whereupon it rained not *w* ....Amos 4:7
man which had his hand *w* ....Matt 12:10
man there which had a *w* .....Mark 3:1
it had no root, it *w* away......Mark 4:6
it *w*..it lacked moisture........Luke 8:6
w, waiting for the moving .....John 5:3
grass *w*, and the flower 1Pet 1:24
trees whose fruit *w* ....Jude 12

WITHES—*a slender flexible branch or twig used as a band or line*
bind me with seven green *w* ...Judg 16:7
to her seven green *w* ....Judg 16:8
he brake the *w*, as a thread ...Judg 16:9

WITHHOLD—*to keep back; refrain from giving*

[*also* WITHHELD, WITHHELDEST, WITHHOLDEN, WITHHOLDETH]
I also *w* thee from sinning.....Gen 20:6
hast not *w* thy son, thine ......Gen 22:16
w from thee his sepulcher .....Gen 23:6
w thee from coming to shed ...1Sam 25:26
he will not *w* me from thee ...2Sam 13:13
w not thy manna from their ...Neh 9:20
w himself from speaking? .....Job 4:2
he *w* the waters, and they .....Job 12:15
w bread from the hungry......Job 22:7
If I have *w* the poor from .....Job 31:16
no thought can be *w* from.....Job 42:2
w the request of his lips.......Ps 21:2
W not thou thy tender ....Ps 40:11
W no good from them to......Prov 3:27
that *w* more than is meet .....Prov 11:24
I *w* not my heart from any ....Eccl 2:10
in the evening *w* not thine ....Eccl 11:6
W thy foot from being ....Jer 2:25
the showers have been *w*......Jer 3:3
hath not *w* the pledge.........Ezek 18:16
drink offering is *w* from.......Joel 1:13
I have *w* the rain from you....Amos 4:7
what *w* that he might be 2Thess 2:6

WITHIN—*inside*
pitch it *w* and without ....Gen 6:14
Sarah laughed *w* herself.......Gen 18:12
righteous *w* the city ....Gen 18:26
men of the house there *w* .....Gen 39:11
stranger that is *w* thy gates ....Ex 20:10
w the veil of the ark of ....Ex 26:33
not brought in *w* the holy .....Lev 10:18
the house to be scraped *w*.....Lev 14:41
bring it *w* the veil ....Lev 16:12
it *w* a whole year after ....Lev 25:29
w a full year may he..........Lev 25:29
together *w* your cities ....Lev 26:25
w a covering of badgers' skins .Num 4:10
stranger that is *w* thy gates ....Deut 5:14
Levite that is *w* thy gates .....Deut 12:18
shalt lay it up *w* thy gates .....Deut 14:28
brethren *w* any of thy gates ...Deut 15:7
passover *w* any of thy gates ...Deut 16:5
widow that are *w* thy gates ....Deut 16:14
controversy *w* thy gates ....Deut 17:8
in thy land *w* thy gates........Deut 24:14
stranger that is *w* thee ....Deut 28:43
without, and terror *w* ....Deut 32:25
w three days ye shall pass .....Josh 1:11
their inheritance *w* the ....Josh 19:9
and lamps *w* the pitchers ......Judg 7:16
not *w* the border of Moab.....Judg 11:18
declare it me *w* the seven .....Judg 14:12
camest not *w* the days 1Sam 13:11
Nabal's heart was merry *w* 1Sam 25:36
Saul lay sleeping *w* the........1Sam 26:7
ark of God dwelleth *w*.........2Sam 7:2
w with boards of cedar........1Kin 6:15
cedar of the house *w* was 1Kin 6:18
house *w* with pure gold 1Kin 6:21
cherubim *w* the inner house ...1Kin 6:27
overlaid with gold, *w* 1Kin 6:30
sawed with saws, *w* and 1Kin 7:9
for her soul is vexed *w*........2Kin 4:27
to the king's house *w* 2Kin 7:11
overlaid it *w* with pure gold ...2Chr 3:4
w the same of old time ....Ezra 4:15
servant lodge *w* Jerusalem .....Neh 4:22
of the Almighty are *w* me .....Job 6:4
reins be consumed *w* me ....Job 19:27
is the gall of asps *w* him ......Job 20:14
spirit *w* me constraineth ....Job 32:18
wicked saith *w* my heart ....Ps 36:1
yea, thy law is *w* my heart .....Ps 40:8
my soul is cast down *w* me ....Ps 42:6
art thou disquieted *w* me?.....Ps 43:5
renew a right spirit *w* me ......Ps 51:10
multitude of my thoughts *w* ...Ps 94:19
deceit shall not dwell *w* ....Ps 101:7
my heart is wounded *w* me ....Ps 109:22
Peace be *w* thy walls, and.....Ps 122:7
and prosperity *w* thy ....Ps 122:7
spirit was overwhelmed *w* .....Ps 142:3
spirit overwhelmed *w* me.......Ps 143:4
my heart *w* me is desolate.....Ps 143:4
if thou keep them *w* thee .....Prov 22:18
little city, and few men *w* .....Eccl 9:14
hast doves' eyes *w* thy locks ...Song 4:1
thy temples *w* thy locks ....Song 6:7
w threescore and five ....Is 7:8
W a year, according to ....Is 21:16
and *w* my walls a place ....Is 56:5
put his holy Spirit *w* him?.....Is 63:11
vain thoughts lodge *w* thee? ...Jer 4:14
W two full years will..........Jer 28:3
mine heart is turned *w* me ....Lam 1:20
of fire round about *w* it ....Ezek 1:27
shut thyself *w* thine house.....Ezek 3:24
will put a new spirit *w* you ....Ezek 11:19
new spirit will I put *w* you ....Ezek 36:26
porch of the gate *w* was.......Ezek 40:7
posts *w* the gate round ....Ezek 40:16
side chambers that were *w* ....Ezek 41:9
of the inner court, and *w* .....Ezek 44:17
God or man *w* thirty days .....Dan 6:12

W

mine heart is turned *w* me ....Hos 11:8
When my soul fainteth *w*......Jon 2:7
and as flesh *w* the caldron.....Mic 3:3
w her are roaring lions........Zeph 3:3
the spirit of man *w* him ....Zech 12:1
not to say *w* yourselves ....Matt 3:9
For she said *w* herself, If I ....Matt 9:21
that which is *w* the cup ....Matt 23:26
w ye are full of hypocrisy .....Matt 23:28
so reasoned *w* themselves .....Mark 2:8
indignation *w* themselves ......Mark 14:4
w three days I will build ......Mark 14:58
not to say *w* yourselves ....Luke 3:8
began to say *w* themselves ....Luke 7:49
that which is *w* also?..........Luke 11:40
steward said *w* himself ....Luke 16:3
but afterward he said *w* ....Luke 18:4
not our heart burn *w* us.......Luke 24:32
his disciples were *w*...........John 20:26
we found no man *w* ....Acts 5:23
we ourselves groan *w* ....Rom 8:23
ye judge them that are *w*? 1Cor 5:12
fightings, *w* were fears 2Cor 7:5
into that *w* the veil ....Heb 6:19
they were full of eyes *w*.......Rev 4:8
throne a book written *w* ......Rev 5:1

WITHOUT—*outside; lacking*
earth was *w* form, and void ...Gen 1:2
told his two brethren *w* ....Gen 9:22
camels to kneel down *w*.......Gen 24:11
Joseph is *w* doubt rent in .....Gen 37:33
for it was *w* number ....Gen 41:49
lamb shall be *w* blemish.......Ex 12:5
thou shalt set the table *w* .....Ex 26:35
congregation *w* the veil ....Ex 27:21
and two rams *w* blemish ....Ex 29:1
and pitched it *w* the camp .....Ex 33:7
which was *w* the camp ....Ex 33:7
northward, *w* the veil ....Ex 40:22
him offer a male *w* blemish ...Lev 1:3
he shall offer it *w* blemish .....Lev 3:1
a young bullock *w* blemish ....Lev 4:3
the bullock *w* the camp ....Lev 4:21
goats, a female *w* blemish .....Lev 4:28
a ram *w* blemish out of the....Lev 5:15
a ram *w* blemish out of the....Lev 6:6
burnt with fire *w* the camp ....Lev 8:17
the first year, *w* blemish ......Lev 9:3
eat it *w* leaven beside the .....Lev 10:12
it be bare within or *w*.........Lev 13:55
two he lambs *w* blemish.......Lev 14:10
of the first year *w* blemish ....Lev 14:10
w the city into an unclean .....Lev 14:41
own will a male *w* blemish .....Lev 22:19
seven lambs *w* blemish of .....Lev 23:18
hath cursed *w* the camp ....Lev 24:14
w the camp shall ye put.......Num 5:3
lamb of the first year *w* ....Num 6:14
one ram *w* blemish for ....Num 6:14
with stones *w* the camp ....Num 15:35
thee a red heifer *w* spot.......Num 19:2
her forth *w* the camp ....Num 19:3
w the camp in a clean ....Num 19:9
two lambs of the first year *w* ..Num 28:3
lambs of the first year *w* ......Num 28:11
be unto you *w* blemish) ....Num 28:31
lambs of the first year *w* ......Num 29:2
they shall be *w* blemish ....Num 29:13
lambs of the first year *w* ......Num 29:20
lambs of the first year *w* ......Num 29:26
to meet them *w* the camp .....Num 31:13
measure from *w* the city ......Num 35:5
thing *w* laying of wait ....Num 35:22
w the borders of the city ......Num 35:27
eat bread *w* scarceness ....Deut 8:9
marry *w* unto a stranger ......Deut 25:5
sword *w*, and terror ....Deut 32:25
will *w* fail drive out from......Josh 3:10
w driving them out hastily .....Judg 2:23
camels were *w* number ....Judg 7:12
left thee..*w* a kinsman ....Ruth 4:14
to slay David *w* a cause? 1Sam 19:5
even a morning *w* clouds 2Sam 23:4
w in the wall of the house 1Kin 6:6
with gold, within and *w* 1Kin 6:30
and they were not seen *w* 1Kin 8:8
appointed fourscore men *w* 2Kin 10:24
the king's entry *w*, turned 2Kin 16:18
burned them *w* Jerusalem 2Kin 23:4
these vessels was *w* weight 2Kin 25:16
but Seled died *w* children 1Chr 2:30
offer burnt offerings *w* cost....1Chr 21:24
but they were not seen *w* 2Chr 5:9
hath been *w* the true God 2Chr 15:3
w a teaching priest and *w* 2Chr 15:3
departed *w* being desired 2Chr 21:20
set it *w* at the gate of the 2Chr 24:8
and another wall *w* 2Chr 32:5
given them day by day *w* fail ..Ezra 6:9
we are not able to stand *w* ....Ezra 10:13
ware lodged *w* Jerusalem ......Neh 13:20
to destroy him *w* cause........Job 2:3
they die, even *w* wisdom ......Job 4:21
unsavory be eaten *w* salt? .....Job 6:6
the rush grow up *w* mire? .....Job 8:11
the flag grow *w* water?........Job 8:11
multiplieth my wounds *w*......Job 9:17
lift up thy face *w* spot ....Job 11:15
naked to lodge *w* clothing .....Job 24:7
helped him that is *w* power.....Job 26:2
or any poor *w* covering ....Job 31:19
am clean *w* transgression ......Job 33:9
shall be taken away *w* ....Job 34:20
hath spoken *w* knowledge .....Job 34:35
words *w* knowledge ....Job 35:16
by words *w* knowledge? ....Job 38:2
like, who is made *w* fear ......Job 41:33
w cause is mine enemy........Ps 7:4
did see me *w* fled from me ....Ps 31:11
w cause have they hid for .....Ps 35:7
w cause they have digged .....Ps 35:7
that hate me *w* a cause ....Ps 69:4
and fought against me *w* a ....Ps 109:3
persecuted me *w* a cause ......Ps 119:161
for the innocent *w* cause ......Prov 1:11
Strive not with a man *w*.......Prov 3:30
he be broken *w* remedy ....Prov 6:15
fair woman which is *w* ....Prov 11:22
great revenues *w* right ....Prov 16:8
There is a lion *w*, I shall ......Prov 22:13
Prepare thy work *w*, and ......Prov 24:27
clouds and wind *w* rain ....Prov 25:14
and that *w* remedy ....Prov 29:1
will bite *w* enchantment ....Eccl 10:11
and virgins *w* number ....Song 6:8
and fair, *w* inhabitant ....Is 5:9
be wasted *w* inhabitant........Is 6:11
and the houses *w* man ....Is 6:11
valiant ones shall cry *w* ....Is 33:7
confounded world *w* end ......Is 45:17
oppressed them *w* cause.......Is 52:4
are burned *w* inhabitant.......Jer 2:15
and, lo, it was *w* form ....Jer 4:23
desolate, *w* an inhabitant......Jer 9:11
besiege you *w* the walls ....Jer 21:4
desolate *w* an inhabitant? .....Jer 26:9
desolate *w* man and *w* beast ...Jer 33:10
that are desolate, *w* man ......Jer 33:10
w inhabitant, and *w* beast .....Jer 33:10
Judah a desolation *w* ....Jer 34:22
a curse, *w* an inhabitant.......Jer 44:22
desolate, *w* any to dwell ......Jer 48:9
desolation *w* an inhabitant.....Jer 51:29
vessels was *w* weight..........Jer 52:20
w strength before the ....Lam 1:6
sore, like a bird, *w* cause .....Lam 3:52
was written within and *w*......Ezek 2:10
w cause all that I have ....Ezek 14:23
w committing iniquity ....Ezek 33:15
of the inner court *w* ....Ezek 40:19
w the inner gate were the .....Ezek 40:44
the inner house, and *w*.........Ezek 41:17
round about within and *w* .....Ezek 41:17
wall that was *w* over ....Ezek 42:7
kid of the goats *w* blemish ....Ezek 43:22
young bullock *w* blemish ....Ezek 43:23
a ram out of the flock *w* ......Ezek 43:23
young bullock *w* blemish ......Ezek 45:18
the porch of that gate *w* ......Ezek 46:2
be six lambs *w* blemish........Ezek 46:4
and a ram *w* blemish ....Ezek 46:4
young bullock *w* blemish ......Ezek 46:6
they shall be *w* blemish ....Ezek 46:6
me about the way *w* unto .....Ezek 47:2
stone was cut out *w* hands ....Dan 2:34
shall be broken *w* hand ....Dan 8:25
w a king, and *w* a prince ......Hos 3:4
w a sacrifice, and *w* an image ..Hos 3:4
w an ephod, and *w* teraphim ..Hos 3:4
like a silly dove *w* heart.......Hos 7:11
land, strong, and *w* number ...Joel 1:6
inhabited as towns *w* walls ....Zech 2:4
angry with his brother *w* ......Matt 5:22
and his brethren stood *w* ......Matt 12:46
w a parable spake he not .....Matt 13:34
also yet *w* understanding? .....Matt 15:16
but was *w* in desert places.....Mark 1:45
brethren *w* seek for thee .....Mark 3:32
w a parable spake he not .....Mark 4:34
is nothing from *w* a man ......Mark 7:15
Are ye so *w* understanding ....Mark 7:18
w entereth into the man ......Mark 7:18
will build another made *w*.....Mark 14:58
praying *w* at the time of ......Luke 1:10
might serve him *w* fear........Luke 1:74
that *w* a foundation built......Luke 6:49
made that which is *w* ....Luke 11:40
and he die *w* children ....Luke 20:28
When I sent you *w* purse .....Luke 22:35
w him was not any thing ......John 1:3
w me ye can do nothing.......John 15:5
Peter stood at the door *w* .....John 18:16
stood *w* at the sepulcher ......John 20:11
the keepers standing *w*........Acts 5:23
he was three days *w* sight .....Acts 9:9
prayer was made *w* ceasing ....Acts 12:5
w any delay on the morrow ....Acts 25:17
w ceasing I make mention ....Rom 1:9
W understanding ....Rom 1:31
w natural affection............Rom 1:31
many as have sinned *w* law ....Rom 2:12
shall also perish *w* law ....Rom 2:12
righteousness of God *w* ....Rom 3:21
righteousness *w* works ....Rom 4:6
w the law sin was dead ....Rom 7:8
they hear *w* a preacher? ......Rom 10:14
love be *w* dissimulation ....Rom 12:9
have reigned as kings *w* 1Cor 4:8
a man doeth is *w* the body 1Cor 6:18
attend..Lord *w* distraction 1Cor 7:35
that are *w* law, as *w* law 1Cor 9:21
not *w* law to God, but 1Cor 9:21
gain them that are *w* law......1Cor 9:21
is the man *w* the woman 1Cor 11:11
the woman *w* the man, in 1Cor 11:11
none..is *w* signification 1Cor 14:10
w were fightings, within were ..2Cor 7:5
of things *w* our measure 2Cor 10:15
and *w* blame before him in ...Eph 1:4
that time ye were *w* Christ ....Eph 2:12
and *w* God in the world.......Eph 2:12
be holy and *w* blemish ....Eph 5:27
w offense till the day of.......Phil 1:10
Do all things *w* murmurings ...Phil 2:14
circumcison made *w* hands ....Col 2:11
Remembering *w* ceasing.......1Thess 1:3
toward them that are *w* 1Thess 4:12
w wrath and doubting.........1Tim 2:8
w controversy great is the 1Tim 3:16
keep this commandment *w* 1Tim 6:14
w ceasing I have remembrance .2Tim 1:3
w thy mind would I do........Philem 14
like as we are, yet *w* sin ......Heb 4:15
W father, *w* mother, *w* descent .Heb 7:3
not *w* an oath he was ....Heb 7:20
not *w* blood, which he ....Heb 9:7
was dedicated *w* blood ....Heb 9:18
time *w* sin unto salvation ......Heb 9:28
Moses law died *w* mercy ......Heb 10:28
w us should not be made......Heb 11:40
w which no man shall see .....Heb 12:14
are burned *w* the camp ....Heb 13:11
unto him *w* the camp ....Heb 13:13
have judgment *w* mercy ....James 2:13

me thy faith *w* thy works......James 2:18
faith *w* works is dead?........James 2:20
body *w* the spirit is dead......James 2:26
so faith *w* works is dead......James 2:26
who *w* respect of persons.....1Pet 1:17
may *w* the word be won......1Pet 3:1
These are wells *w* water.......2Pet 2:17
feeding themselves *w* fear.....Jude 12
clouds they are *w* water.......Jude 12
w fruit, twice dead, plucked...Jude 12
which is *w* the temple.........Rev 11:2
poured out *w* mixture into....Rev 14:10
w are dogs, and sorcerers.....Rev 22:15

WITHS—*See* WITHES

WITHSTAND—*to stand against; oppose; resist*

[*also* WITHSTOOD]
I went out to *w* thee..........Num 22:32
and could not *w* them.........2Chr 13:7
that none is able to *w* thee?...2Chr 20:6
they *w* Uzziah the king.......2Chr 26:18
and no man could *w* them.....Esth 9:2
against him, two shall *w*......Eccl 4:12
kingdom of Persia *w* me......Dan 10:13
the arms..shall not *w*.........Dan 11:15
there be any strength to *w*....Dan 11:15
was I, that I could *w* God.....Acts 11:17
w them, seeking to turn.......Acts 13:8
I *w* him to the face...........Gal 2:11
be able to *w* in the evil day...Eph 6:13
as Jannes and Jambres *w*......2Tim 3:8
hath greatly *w* our words......2Tim 4:15

WITNESS—*to testify; attest; one who gives testimony*

[*also* WITNESSED, WITNESSES, WITNESSETH]
they may be a *w* unto me.....Gen 21:30
bear false *w* against thy......Ex 20:16
to be an unrighteous *w*........Ex 23:1
there be no *w* against.........Num 5:13
into the tabernacle of *w*.......Num 17:8
death by the mouth of *w*......Num 35:30
but one *w* shall not testify.....Num 35:30
call heaven and earth to *w*....Deut 4:26
At the mouth of two *w*.......Deut 17:6
three *w*, shall he that is.......Deut 17:6
at the mouth of one *w* he.....Deut 17:6
at the mouth of two *w*.......Deut 19:15
or at the mouth of three *w*....Deut 19:15
a false *w* rise up against.......Deut 19:16
are *w* against yourselves.......Josh 24:22
And they said, we are *w*......Josh 24:22
this stone shall be a *w*........Josh 24:27
it shall be therefore a *w*.......Josh 24:27
The Lord be *w* between us....Judg 11:10
w against me before the Lord..1Sam 12:3
The Lord is *w* against you.....1Sam 12:5
his anointed is *w* this day.....1Sam 12:5
they answered, He is *w*........1Sam 12:5
to bear *w* against him.........1Kin 21:10
men of Belial *w* against him...1Kin 21:13
for the tabernacle of *w*?.......2Chr 24:6
renewest thy *w* against me....Job 10:17
which is a *w* against me.......Job 16:8
me beareth *w* to my face......Job 16:8
the eye saw me, it gave *w*.....Job 29:11
false *w* are risen up against....Ps 27:12
False *w* did rise up; they......Ps 35:11
as a faithful *w* in heaven......Ps 39:37
false *w* that speaketh lies......Prov 6:19
A faithful *w* will not lie.......Prov 14:5
a false *w* will utter lies.......Prov 14:5
A true *w* delivereth souls.....Prov 14:25
deceitful *w* speaketh lies......Prov 14:25
An ungodly *w* scorneth........Prov 19:28
A false *w* shall perish: but....Prov 21:28
beareth false *w* against his.....Prov 25:18
countenance doth *w* against...Is 3:9
took unto me faithful *w* to....Is 8:2
ye are my *w*, saith the Lord...Is 43:10
declared it? ye are even my *w*..Is 44:8
for a *w* to the people.........Is 55:4
and am a *w*, saith the Lord...Jer 29:23
field for money, and take *w*...Jer 32:25
take *w* in the land of.........Jer 32:44
Lord be a true and faithful *w*..Jer 42:5
shall I take to *w* for thee?.....Lam 2:13
Lord God be *w* against you...Mic 1:2
Lord hath been *w* between....Mal 2:14
w against the sorcerers........Mal 3:5
thefts, false *w*, blasphemies....Matt 15:19
mouth of two or three *w*......Matt 18:16
shalt not bare false *w*.........Matt 19:18
ye be *w* unto yourselves.......Matt 23:31
false *w* against Jesus.........Matt 26:59
though many false *w* came....Matt 26:60
At the last came two false *w*..Matt 26:60
these *w* against thee?.........Matt 26:62
things they *w* against thee?....Matt 27:13
Do not bear false *w*..........Mark 10:19
many bare false *w* against him.Mark 14:56
their *w* agreed not together....Mark 14:56
neither so did their *w* agree...Mark 14:59
need we any further *w*?........Mark 14:63
things they *w* against thee.....Mark 15:4
all bear him *w*, and...........Luke 4:22
Do not bear false *w*..........Luke 18:20
need we any further *w*?.......Luke 22:71
ye are *w* of these things.......Luke 24:48
and ye receive not our *w*......John 3:11
Ye yourselves bear me *w*......John 3:28
If I bear *w* of myself..........John 5:31
my *w* is not true..............John 5:31
is another that beareth *w*......John 5:32
I know that the *w* which......John 5:32
he bear *w* unto the truth......John 5:33
evil, bear *w* of the evil........John 18:23
bear *w* unto the truth.........John 18:37
dead; whereof we are *w*........Acts 3:15
And set up false *w*, which.....Acts 6:13
tabernacle of *w* in the.........Acts 7:44
w laid down their clothes......Acts 7:58
are *w* of all things which......Acts 10:39
are his *w* unto the people.....Acts 13:31
left not himself without *w*.....Acts 14:17
Holy Ghost *w* in every city....Acts 20:23
high priest doth bear me *w*....Acts 22:5
thou bear *w* also at Rome.....Acts 23:11
God is my *w*, whom I serve...Rom 1:9
being *w* by the law and the....Rom 3:21
conscience also bearing me *w*..Rom 9:1
shalt not bear false *w*.........Rom 13:9
are found false *w* of God.....1Cor 15:15
mouth of two or three *w*......2Cor 13:1
covetousness; God is *w*.......1Thess 2:5
Ye are *w*, and God also.......1Thess 2:10
profession before many *w*.....1Tim 6:12
Pontius Pilate *w* a good.......1Tim 6:13
heard of me among many *w*...2Tim 2:2
This *w* is true. Wherefore.....Tit 1:13
of whom it *w* that he liveth....Heb 7:8
the Holy Ghost also is a *w*....Heb 10:15
mercy under two or three *w*...Heb 10:28
w that he was righteous.......Heb 11:4
with so great a cloud of *w*.....Heb 12:1
rust of them shall be a *w*.......James 5:3
have seen it, and bear *w*......1John 1:2
three that bear *w* in earth.....1John 5:8
If we receive the *w* of men....1John 5:9
the *w* of God is greater........1John 5:9
the *w* of God which he hath...1John 5:9
have borne *w* of thy charity...3John 6
Christ, who is the faithful *w*...Rev 1:5
give power unto my two *w*....Rev 11:3
beheaded for the *w* of Jesus...Rev 20:4

WITNESSING—*bearing testimony to something*

Elements of, seen in:
Public transaction.......Ruth 4:1-11
Signing a document......Jer 32:10-12
Calling witnesses........Lev 5:1
Requiring two witnesses..1Tim 5:19
Rejection of false witnesses............Prov 24:28

Material means of, by:
Heap stones...........Gen 31:44-52
Song..................Deut 31:19-1
Altar..................Josh 22:26-34
Works.................John 10:25
Sign (miracles)..........Heb 2:4

Spiritual means of, by:
God's Law.............Deut 31:26
Gospel................Matt 24:14
Father................John 5:37
Conscience.............Rom 2:15
Holy Spirit.............Rom 8:16

To Christ as object, by:
John the Baptist.........John 1:7, 8, 15
His works..............John 5:36
Father.................John 8:18
Himself................John 8:18
Holy Spirit.............John 15:26, 27
His disciples...........John 15:27
Prophets...............Acts 10:43

Of Christians to Christ:
Chosen................Acts 10:41
Commissioned..........Acts 1:8
Empowered............Acts 4:33
Confirmed.............Heb 2:3, 4

Objects of Christ's:
Resurrection...........Acts 2:32
Saviorhood............Acts 5:31, 32
Life...................Acts 1:21, 22
Mission...............Acts 10:41-43
Sufferings.............1Pet 5:1
See TESTIMONY

w both to small and great.....Acts 26:22

WITTINGLY—*intentionally*
head, guiding his hands *w*.....Gen 48:14

WITTY—*archaic for "intelligent"*
Applied to inventions....Prov 8:12

WIVES, WIVES'—*See* WIFE

WIZARD—*one skilled in the practice of magic; a male witch*

[*also* WIZARDS]
neither seek after *w*, to be....Lev 19:31
w, to go a whoring after......Lev 20:6
is a *w*, shall surely be put.....Lev 20:27
or a *w*, or a necromancer.....Deut 18:11
and the *w*, out of the land....1Sam 28:3
and the *w*, out of the land....1Sam 28:9
with familiar spirits and *w*.....2Kin 21:6
familiar spirits and the *w*......2Kin 23:24
a familiar spirit, and with *w*...2Chr 33:6
unto *w* that peep, and that....Is 8:19
familiar spirits, and to the *w*..Is 19:3
See WITCHCRAFT

WOE—*an expression of grief or distress; condition of deep suffering*

[*also* WOES]
W to thee, Moab; thou art....Num 21:29
W unto us! for there hath.....1Sam 4:7
If I be wicked, *w* unto me....Job 10:15
W is me, that I sojourn in....Ps 120:5
Who hath *w*? who hath.......Prov 23:29
but *w* to him that is alone.....Eccl 4:10
W unto their soul! for they....Is 3:9
W unto them that join........Is 5:8
W unto them that draw.......Is 5:18
W unto them that are wise....Is 5:21
I, *W* is me! for I am undone..Is 6:5
W to the multitude of.........Is 17:12
my leanness, *w* unto me!......Is 24:16
W to Ariel, to Ariel, the city..Is 29:1
W to the rebellious children...Is 30:1
W to thee that spoilest, and...Is 33:1
W unto him that saith unto....Is 45:10
W unto us! for we are spoiled.Jer 4:13
W unto us! for the day........Jer 6:4
W unto thee, O Jerusalem....Jer 13:27
W unto him that buildeth.....Jer 22:13
Thou didst say, *W* is me......Jer 45:3
W be unto thee, O Moab!.....Jer 48:46
w unto us, that we have.......Lam 5:16
and mourning, and *w*.........Ezek 2:10
W to the women that sew.....Ezek 13:18
W to the bloody city, to the..Ezek 24:6
Howl ye, *W* worth the day!...Ezek 30:2

W

W unto them! for they have . . .Hos 7:13
W unto you that desire the . . . .Amos 5:18
W to them that devise . . . . .Mic 2:1
W to the bloody city! it is . . . . .Nah 3:1
W to him that increaseth . . . . . .Hab 2:6
W to him that buildeth a . . . . . .Hab 2:12
W unto him that saith to . . . . . .Hab 2:19
W unto the inhabitants of . . . . .Zeph 2:5
W to the idol shepherd that . . .Zech 11:17
W unto thee, Chorazin! . . . . . . .Matt 11:21
w unto thee, Bethsaida! for . . . .Matt 11:21
W unto the world because . . . .Matt 18:7
but *w* to that man by whom . . .Matt 18:7
W unto you, scribes and . . . . . .Matt 23:14
W unto you, ye blind . . . . .Matt 23:16
w unto them that are with . . . . .Matt 24:19
w to them that are with . . . . . . .Mark 13:17
w unto you that are rich! . . . . . .Luke 6:24
W unto you that are full! . . . . . .Luke 6:25
W into you that laugh . . . . .Luke 6:25
W unto thee, Chorazin! . . . . . . .Luke 10:13
w unto thee, Bethsaida! for . . .Luke 10:13
W unto you, Pharisees! for ye .Luke 11:43
W unto unto you also, ye . . . . .Luke 11:46
W unto you, lawyers! for . . . . . .Luke 11:52
w unto them that are with . . . . .Luke 21:23
w is unto me, if I preach 1Cor 9:16
W unto them! for they . . . . .Jude 11
W, *w*, *w*, to the inhabiters . . . . .Rev 8:13
come two *w* more hereafter . . .Rev 9:12
The second *w* is past; and . . . .Rev 11:14
the third *w* cometh quickly . . . .Rev 11:14
W to the inhabiters of the . . . . .Rev 12:12

WOEFUL—*overcome with woe*
neither have I desired the *w* . . .Jer 17:16

WOLF—*large, carnivorous animal, related to the dog*

Characteristics of:
Ravenous . . . . .Gen 49:27
Nocturnal . . . . .Jer 5:6
Sheep-eating . . . . .John 10:12

Figurative of:
False prophets . . . . .Matt 7:15
Gospel transformation . . .Is 11:6

[*also* WOLVES]
w and the lamb shall feed . . . . .Is 65:25
like *w* ravening the prey . . . . . .Ezek 22:27
fierce than the evening *w* . . . . .Hab 1:8
her judges are evening *w* . . . . . .Zeph 3:3
as sheep in the midst of *w* . . . .Matt 10:16
forth as lambs among *w* . . . . . . .Luke 10:3
grievous *w* enter in among . . . .Acts 20:29

WOMAN—*a member of the female sex*

Described as:
Beautiful 2Sam 11:2
Wise 2Sam 20:16
Widow 1Kin 17:9, 10
Evil .Prov 6:24
Foolish . . . . .Job 2:10
Gracious . . . . .Prov 11:16
Virtuous . . . . .Prov 12:4
Contentious . . . . .Prov 21:19
Adulterous . . . . .Prov 30:20
Honorable . . . . .Acts 17:12
Silly 2Tim 3:6
Holy 1Pet 3:5

Work of:
Kneading meal . . . . .Gen 18:6
Drawing water . . . . .Gen 24:11, 13, 15
Tending sheep . . . . .Gen 29:6
Making cloth . . . . .Prov 31:13, 19
Caring for the household .1Tim 5:14
Prov 31:27

Rights of, to:
Marry 1Cor 7:36
Hold property . . . . .Num 27:6-11
Make vows . . . . .Num 30:3-9

Position of, in relation to man:
Created from man . . . . . . .Gen 2:21-25
Made to help man . . . . . . .Gen 2:18, 20
Glory of man 1Cor 11:7-9
Becomes subject to man .Gen 3:16
Weaker than man 1Pet 3:7

Position of, in spiritual things:
Insight of, noted . . . . .Judg 13:23
Prayer of, answered 1Sam 1:9-28
Understanding of, rewarded 1Sam 25:3-42
Faith of, brings salvation .Luke 7:37-50
Made equal in Christ . . . .Gal 3:28
Labor of, commended . . .Phil 4:2, 3
Faith of, transmitted 2Tim 1:5

Good traits of:
Obedience 1Pet 3:5-7
Concern for children . . . . .Ex 2:2-10
Loyalty . . . . .Ruth 1:14-18
Desire for children 1Sam 1:9-28
Modesty . . . . .Esth 1:10-12
Industry . . . . .Prov 31:10-31
Complete devotion . . . . . .Luke 7:38-50
Tenderness . . . . .John 11:20-35

Bad traits of:
Inciting to evil . . . . .Gen 3:6, 7
Subtle . . . . .Prov 7:10
Fond of adornments . . . . .Is 3:16-24
Self-indulgent . . . . .Is 32:9, 11
Easily led into idolatry . . .Jer 7:18
Led away 2Tim 3:6

Prohibitions concerning, not to:
Wear man's clothing . . . . .Deut 22:5
Have head shaved 1Cor 11:5-15
Usurp authority 1Tim 2:11-15
Be unchaste 1Pet 3:1-7

[*also* WOMAN'S, WOMEN, WOMEN'S]
unto the *w*, yea, hath God . . . .Gen 3:1
w said unto the serpent . . . . . . .Gen 3:2
said unto the *w*, Ye shall . . . . . .Gen 3:4
w whom thou gavest to be . . . .Gen 3:12
Lord God said unto the *w* . . . . .Gen 3:13
w said, The serpent beguiled . .Gen 3:13
between thee and the *w* . . . . . . .Gen 3:15
art a fair *w* to look upon . . . . . .Gen 12:11
w was taken into Pharaoh's . . . .Gen 12:15
the *w* also, and the people . . . .Gen 14:16
Sarah after the manner of *w* . . .Gen 18:11
w will not be willing to . . . . . . .Gen 24:5
Peradventure the *w* will not . . .Gen 24:39
the custom of *w* is upon me . . .Gen 31:35
his pledge from the *w* hand . . .Gen 38:20
the son of a Canaanitish *w* . . . .Gen 46:10
a midwife to the Hebrew *w* . . .Ex 1:16
w are not as the Egyptian *w* . . .Ex 1:19
every *w* shall borrow of her . . .Ex 3:22
every *w* of her neighbor . . . . . . .Ex 11:2
all the *w* went out after her . . .Ex 15:20
according as the *w* husband . . .Ex 21:22
If an ox gore a man or a *w* . . .Ex 21:28
w that were wise-hearted . . . . . .Ex 35:25
man and *w*, whose heart . . . . . .Ex 35:29
looking glasses of the *w* . . . . . . .Ex 38:8
If a *w* have conceived seed . . . .Lev 12:2
a man also or a *w* have in . . . . .Lev 13:38
The *w* also with whom man . . . .Lev 15:18
If a *w* have an issue of her . . . .Lev 15:25
uncover the nakedness of a *w* .Lev 18:17
shall any *w* stand before a . . . . .Lev 18:23
as he lieth with a *w*, both . . . . .Lev 20:13
w approach unto any beast . . . .Lev 20:16
shalt kill the *w*, and the . . . . . . .Lev 20:16
or *w* that hath a familiar . . . . . .Lev 20:27
the son of an Israelitish *w* . . . . .Lev 24:10
Israelitish *w* son blasphemed . . .Lev 24:11
ten *w* shall bake your bread . . .Lev 26:26
man or *w* shall commit any . . . .Num 5:6
the *w* head, and put the . . . . . . .Num 5:18
the *w*, If no man have lain . . . .Num 5:19
charge the *w* with an oath of . .Num 5:21
priest shall say unto the *w* . . . . .Num 5:21
the *w* to drink the bitter . . . . . .Num 5:24
offering out of the *w* hand . . . .Num 5:25
w shall be a curse among . . . . .Num 5:27
set the *w* before the Lord . . . . .Num 5:30
man or *w* shall separate . . . . . . .Num 6:2
Ethiopian *w* whom he had . . . .Num 12:1
married an Ethiopian *w* . . . . . . .Num 12:1
the *w* through her belly . . . . . . .Num 25:8
took all the *w* of Midian . . . . . .Num 31:9
every *w* that hath known man .Num 31:17
w children, that have not . . . . . .Num 31:18
destroyed the men, and the *w* .Deut 2:34
Hebrew *w*, be sold unto thee . .Deut 15:12
forth that man or that *w* . . . . . .Deut 17:5
But the *w*, and the little . . . . . .Deut 20:14
the captives a beautiful *w* . . . . .Deut 21:11
a man put on a *w* garment . . . .Deut 22:5
this *w*, and when I came to . . .Deut 22:14
lying with a *w* married to . . . . .Deut 22:22
the man that lay with the *w* . . .Deut 22:22
the *w*: so shalt thou put away .Deut 22:22
be among you man, or *w* . . . . .Deut 29:18
w took the two men, and . . . . .Josh 2:4
and bring out thence the *w* . . .Josh 6:22
that day, both of men and *w* . .Josh 8:25
Sisera into the hand of a *w* . . .Judg 4:9
Blessed above *w* shall Jael . . . .Judg 5:24
blessed shall she be above *w* . .Judg 5:24
fled all the men and *w* . . . . .Judg 9:51
not of me, A *w* slew him . . . . .Judg 9:54
Lord appeared unto the *w* . . . . .Judg 13:3
of God came again unto the *w* .Judg 13:9
that spakest unto the *w*? . . . . . .Judg 13:11
w bare a son, and called . . . . . .Judg 13:24
seen a *w* in Timnath of the . . . .Judg 14:2
down, and talked with the *w* . .Judg 14:7
a *w* in the valley of Sorek . . . . .Judg 16:4
house was full of men and *w* . .Judg 16:27
three thousand men and *w* . . . .Judg 16:27
w his concubine was fallen . . . .Judg 19:27
and every *w* that hath lain . . . .Judg 21:11
of the *w* of Jabesh-gilead . . . . . .Judg 21:14
took them wives of the *w* . . . . .Ruth 1:4
w was left of her two sons . . . .Ruth 1:5
that thou art a virtuous *w* . . . . .Ruth 3:11
The Lord make the *w* that . . . .Ruth 4:11
the *w* her neighbors gave . . . . . .Ruth 4:17
give thee seed of this *w* 1Sam 2:20
how they lay with the *w* 1Sam 2:22
thy sword hath made *w* 1Sam 15:33
mother be childless among *w* . .1Sam 15:33
w answered one another as 1Sam 18:7
of the perverse rebellious *w* . . .1Sam 20:30
Of a truth *w* have been kept . .1Sam 21:5
neither man nor *w* alive 1Sam 27:9
a *w* that hath a familiar 1Sam 28:7
is a *w* that hath a familiar 1Sam 28:7
w said unto him, Behold 1Sam 28:9
when the *w* saw Samuel, she . .1Sam 28:12
the *w* said unto Saul, I saw 1Sam 28:13
with the *w*, compelled him 1Sam 28:23
had taken the *w* captives 1Sam 30:2
passing the love of *w* 2Sam 1:26
a fault concerning this *w* 2Sam 3:8
and inquired after the *w* 2Sam 11:3
the *w* conceived, and sent 2Sam 11:5
put now this *w* out from me . . .2Sam 13:17
and fetched thence a wise *w* . . .2Sam 14:2
the *w* of Tekoah spake to 2Sam 14:4
king said unto the *w*, Go 2Sam 14:8
w said, Let thine handmaid 2Sam 14:12
answered and said unto the *w* .2Sam 14:18
the *w* said, Let my lord the . . .2Sam 14:18
a *w* of a fair countenance 2Sam 14:27
the king left ten *w* which 2Sam 15:16
the *w* took and spread 2Sam 17:19
servants came to the *w* 2Sam 17:20
And the *w* said unto them 2Sam 17:20
the king took the ten *w* 2Sam 20:3
the *w* said, Art thou Joab 2Sam 20:17
w went unto all the people 2Sam 20:22
Then came there two *w* 1Kin 3:16
one *w* said, O my lord 1Kin 3:17
this *w* dwell in one house 1Kin 3:17
w child died in the night 1Kin 3:19
other *w* said, Nay; but the 1Kin 3:22
loved many strange *w* 1Kin 11:1
w of the Moabites 1Kin 11:1
name was Zeruah, a widow *w* .1Kin 11:26
son of the *w*, the mistress 1Kin 17:17
Now there cried a certain *w* . . .2Kin 4:1

w conceived, and bare a son . . . 2Kin 4:17
This *w* said unto me, Give 2Kin 6:28
spake Elisha unto the *w* 2Kin 8:1
the *w* returned out of the 2Kin 8:3
the *w*, whose son he had 2Kin 8:5
this is the *w*, and this is 2Kin 8:5
rip up their *w* with child 2Kin 8:12
See now this cursed *w*, and 2Kin 9:34
w wove hangings for the 2Kin 23:7
man and *w*, to every one 1Chr 16:3
son of a *w* of the daughters 2Chr 2:14
of Athaliah, that wicked *w* 2Chr 24:7
w, sons, and daughters 2Chr 28:8
singing men and singing *w* . . . . . Ezra 2:65
singing men and singing *w* . . . . . Neh 7:67
before the men and the *w* . . . . . Neh 8:3
queen made a feast for the *w* . . Esth 1:9
palace, to the house of the *w* . . Esth 2:3
chamberlain, keeper of the *w* . . Esth 2:3
of Hegai, keeper of the *w* . . . . . Esth 2:8
the court of the *w* house . . . . . . Esth 2:11
to the manner of the *w* . . . . Esth 2:12
for the purifying of the *w* . . . . . Esth 2:12
the second house of the *w* . . . . . Esth 2:14
loved Esther above all the *w* . . Esth 2:17
whether man or *w*, shall come . Esth 4:11
both little ones and *w*, and . . . . Esth 8:11
of the foolish *w* speaketh . . . . . . Job 2:10
that is born of a *w* is of few . . . Job 14:1
clean that is born of a *w*? . . . . . Job 25:4
were among thy honorable *w* . . Ps 45:9
pain, as of a *w* in travail . . . . . . Ps 48:6
maketh the barren *w* to keep . . Ps 113:9
thee from the strange *w* . . . . Prov 2:16
by means of a whorish *w* . . . . . . Prov 6:26
committeth adultery with a *w* . . Prov 6:32
thee from the strange *w* . . . . Prov 7:5
fair *w* which is without . . . . Prov 11:22
A virtuous *w* is a crown to . . . . Prov 12:4
pledge of him for a strange *w* . Prov 20:16
with a brawling *w* in a wide . . . Prov 21:9
of strange *w* is a deep pit . . . . . Prov 22:14
brawling *w* in a wide house . . . . Prov 25:24
contentious *w* are alike . . . . Prov 27:15
an odious *w* when she is . . . . . . Prov 30:23
not thy strength unto *w* . . . . Prov 31:3
a *w* that feareth the Lord . . . . . Prov 31:30
gat me men singers and *w* . . . . . Eccl 2:8
more bitter than death the *w* . . Eccl 7:26
O thou fairest among *w* . . . . Song 1:8
O thou fairest among *w*? . . . . . . Song 6:1
w shall take hold of one man . . Is 4:1
pain as a *w* that travaileth . . . . . Is 13:8
shall Egypt be like unto *w* . . . . Is 19:16
Like as a *w* with child, that . . . Is 26:17
w come, and set them on fire . . Is 27:11
be troubled, ye careless *w* . . . . Is 32:10
or to the *w*, What hast thou . . . Is 45:10
w forsaken and grieved in . . . . . Is 54:6
a voice as of a *w* in travail . . . . Jer 4:31
of us, and pain, as of a *w* in . . Jer 6:24
call for the mourning *w* . . . . Jer 9:17
cunning *w*, that they may . . . . . Jer 9:17
thee, the pain as of a *w* in . . . . Jer 22:23
the *w* with child and her . . . . . . Jer 31:8
w that are left in the king . . . . . Jer 38:22
and those *w* shall say, Thy . . . . Jer 38:22
and the *w*, and the children . . . Jer 41:16
cut off from you man and *w* . . . Jer 44:7
the *w* that stood by, a great . . . Jer 44:15
to the men, and to the *w* . . . . . Jer 44:20
to all the *w*, Hear the word . . . Jer 44:24
heart of a *w* in her pangs . . . . . Jer 49:22
him, and pangs as of a *w* . . . . . Jer 50:43
I break in pieces man and *w* . . Jer 51:22
failed; they became as *w* . . . . . . Jer 51:30
Jerusalem is as a menstrous *w* . Lam 1:17
Shall the *w* eat their fruit . . . . . Lam 2:20
They ravished the *w* in Zion . . . Lam 5:11
sat *w* weeping for Tammuz . . . . Ezek 8:14
to the *w* that sew pillows . . . . . . Ezek 13:18
of an imperious whorish *w* . . . . Ezek 16:30
as *w* that break wedlock . . . . Ezek 16:38
were two *w*, the daughters . . . . Ezek 23:2
w that playeth the harlot . . . . . . Ezek 23:44
unto Aholibah, the lewd *w* . . . . Ezek 23:44
all *w* may be taught not . . . . Ezek 23:48
uncleanness of a removed *w* . . . Ezek 36:17
give him the daughter of *w* . . . . Dan 11:17
a *w* beloved of her friend . . . . . Hos 3:1
their *w* with child shall be . . . . . Hos 13:16
they have ripped up the *w* . . . . Amos 1:13
w of my people have ye cast . . Mic 2:9
have taken thee as a *w* in . . . . . Mic 4:9
in the midst of thee are *w* . . . . . Nah 3:13
this is a *w* that sitteth in . . . . . . Zech 5:7
behold, there came out two *w* . Zech 5:9
rifled, and the *w* ravished . . . . . Zech 14:2
whosoever looketh on a *w* . . . . . Matt 5:28
w was made whole from that . . Matt 9:22
them that are born of *w* . . . . Matt 11:11
a *w* of Canaan came out of . . . . Matt 15:22
thousand men, beside *w* and . . . Matt 15:38
last of all the *w* died also . . . . . Matt 22:27
Why trouble ye the *w*? . . . . Matt 26:10
many *w* were there beholding . . Matt 27:55
certain *w*, which had an . . . . Mark 5:25
a certain *w*, whose young . . . . . Mark 7:25
if a *w* shall put away her . . . . . . Mark 10:12
a *w* having an alabaster box . . . Mark 14:3
also *w* looking on afar off . . . . . Mark 15:40
blessed art thou among *w* . . . . . Luke 1:28
unto a *w* that was a widow . . . . Luke 4:26
those that are born of *w* . . . . . . Luke 7:28
w having an issue of blood . . . . Luke 8:43
a certain *w* named Martha . . . . Luke 10:38
was a *w* which had a spirit . . . . Luke 13:11
ought not this *w*, being a . . . . . . Luke 13:16
what *w* having ten pieces of . . . Luke 15:8
Two *w* shall be grinding . . . . Luke 17:35
saying *W*, I know him not . . . . . . Luke 22:57
w that followed him from . . . . . Luke 23:49
and other *w* that were with . . . . Luke 24:10
even so as the *w* had said . . . . . Luke 24:24
W, what have I to do with . . . . John 2:4
the *w* of Samaria unto him . . . . John 4:9
which am a *w* of Samaria? . . . . John 4:9
The *w* saith unto him, Sir . . . . . John 4:15
The *w* saith unto him, Sir . . . . . John 4:19
The *w* saith unto him, I . . . . John 4:25
w then left her waterpot . . . . . . John 4:28
said unto the *w*, Now we . . . . . . John 4:42
w was taken in adultery . . . . John 8:4
saw none but the *w*, he said . . . John 8:10
W, where are..thine accusers . . John 8:10
his mother, *W*, behold thy . . . . John 19:26
and supplication, with the *w* . . . Acts 1:14
haling men and *w* committed . . Acts 8:3
whether they were men or *w* . . Acts 9:2
w was full of good works . . . . . . Acts 9:36
spake unto the *w* which . . . . Acts 16:13
a certain *w* named Lydia . . . . . . Acts 16:14
and of the chief *w* not a few . . Acts 17:4
w did change the natural . . . . . . Rom 1:26
the natural use of the *w* . . . . Rom 1:27
for a man not to touch a *w* 1Cor 7:1
w which hath an husband 1Cor 7:13
head of the *w* is the man 1Cor 11:3
is the man without the *w* 1Cor 11:11
is the *w* without the man 1Cor 11:11
For as the *w* is of the man 1Cor 11:12
so is the man also by the *w* . . . 1Cor 11:12
if a *w* have long hair, it is 1Cor 11:15
w keep silence in the 1Cor 14:34
w to speak in the church 1Cor 14:35
forth his Son, made of a *w* . . . . Gal 4:4
as travail upon a *w* with 1Thess 5:3
w adorn themselves in 1Tim 2:9
becometh *w* professing 1Tim 2:10
The elder *w* as mothers 1Tim 5:2
man or *w* that believeth 1Tim 5:16
The aged *w* likewise, that . . . . . Titus 2:3
may teach the young *w* to . . . . . Titus 2:4
W received their dead . . . . Heb 11:35
sufferest that *w* Jezebel . . . . Rev 2:20
had hair as the hair of *w* . . . . . . Rev 9:8
a *w* clothed with the sun . . . . . . Rev 12:1
w fled into the wilderness . . . . . Rev 12:6
the *w* were given two wings . . . Rev 12:14
the earth helped the *w*, and . . . Rev 12:16
were not defiled with *w* . . . . Rev 14:4
w sit upon a scarlet-colored . . . Rev 17:3
I saw the *w* drunken with . . . . . Rev 17:6
on which the *w* sitteth . . . . Rev 17:9

WOMANKIND—*all women*
lie with mankind, as with *w* . . . Lev 18:22

WOMB—*the uterus*

God's control over, to:
Close . . . . Gen 20:18
Open . . . . Gen 29:31
Fashion us in . . . . Job 31:15
Separate and call . . . . Gal 1:15
Cause to conceive . . . . Luke 1:31
Make alive . . . . Rom 4:19-21

Babe inside:
Grows mysteriously . . . . Eccl 11:5
Known by God . . . . Ps 139:13-16
Deformed . . . . Acts 3:2
Leaps . . . . Luke 1:41, 44

Man coming from:
Different . . . . Gen 25:23, 24
Consecrated . . . . Judg 13:5, 7
Naked . . . . Job 1:21
Helpless . . . . Ps 22:9, 10
Sustained . . . . Ps 71:6
Estranged . . . . Ps 58:3

[*also* WOMBS]
from thee the fruit of the *w* . . . Gen 30:2
to her, and opened her *w* . . . . . Gen 30:22
behold, twins were in her *w* . . . Gen 38:27
of the beasts, and of the *w* . . . . Gen 49:25
whatsoever openeth the *w* . . . . . Ex 13:2
of such as open every *w* . . . . Num 8:16
cometh out of his mother's *w* . . Num 12:12
also bless the fruit of thy *w* . . . Deut 7:13
God from my mother's *w* . . . . . Judg 16:17
yet any more sons in my *w* . . . . Ruth 1:11
the doors of my mother's *w* . . . Job 3:10
me forth out of the *w* . . . . Job 10:18
carried from the *w* to the . . . . . Job 10:19
The *w* shall forget him; the . . . . Job 24:20
her from my mother's *w* . . . . . . Job 31:18
it had issued out of the *w*? . . . . Job 38:8
of whose *w* came the ice? . . . . . Job 38:29
that took me out of the *w* . . . . . Ps 22:9
from the *w* of the morning . . . . Ps 110:3
fruit of the *w* is his reward . . . . Ps 127:3
grave; and the barren *w* . . . . Prov 30:16
and what, the son of my *w*? . . . Prov 31:2
came forth of his mother's *w* . . Eccl 5:15
no pity on the fruit of the *w* . . . Is 13:18
that formed thee from the *w* . . . Is 44:24
a transgressor from the *w* . . . . . Is 48:8
me from the *w* to be his . . . . . . Is 49:5
bring forth, and shut the *w*? . . . Is 66:9
camest forth out of the *w* . . . . . Jer 1:5
he slew me not from the *w* . . . . Jer 20:17
her *w* to be always great . . . . . . Jer 20:17
fire all that openeth the *w* . . . . . Ezek 20:26
the birth, and from the *w* . . . . . Hos 9:11
give them a miscarrying *w* . . . . . Hos 9:14
beloved fruit of their *w* . . . . Hos 9:16
brother by the heel in the *w* . . . Hos 12:3
born from their mother's *w* . . . . Matt 19:12
even from his mother's *w* . . . . . Luke 1:15
blessed is the fruit of thy *w* . . . Luke 1:42
he was conceived in the *w* . . . . . Luke 2:21
Blessed is the *w* that bare . . . . . Luke 11:27
the *w* that never bare . . . . Luke 23:29
time into his mother's *w* . . . . . . John 3:4
cripple from mother's *w* . . . . Acts 14:8

WOMEN—*See* WOMAN

WOMEN OF THE BIBLE
Abi, wife of Ahaz 2Kin 18:1, 2
Abiah, wife of Hezron . . . 1Chr 2:24
Abigail
1. Wife of Nabal 1Sam 25:3
2. Sister of David 1Chr 2:15, 16
Abihail, wife of Abishur . 1Chr 2:29
Abishag, nurse of David . 1Kin 1:1-3
Abital, David's wife 2Sam 3:1, 4

W

Achsah, daughter of Caleb .... Josh 15:16
Adah
1. A wife of Lamech .. Gen 4:19
2. Canaanite wife of Esau .... Gen 36:2
Ahinoam
1. Wife of Saul 1Sam 14:50
2. A Jezreelitess 1Sam 25:43
Aholah .... Ezek 23:4
Aholibah .... Ezek 23:4
Aholibamah .... Gen 36:2
Anah, daughter of Zibeon .... Gen 36:2
Anna, an aged widow .... Luke 2:36, 37
Apphia, a Christian of Colossae .... Philem 2
Asenath, wife of Joseph . Gen 41:45
Atarah, wife of Jerahmeel 1Chr 2:26
Athaliah, mother of Ahaziah 2Kin 8:6
Azubah
1. First wife of Caleb .. 1Chr 2:18
2. Daughter of Shilhi .. 1Kin 22:42
Baara, wife of Shaharaim . 1Chr 8:8
Basemath
1. Daughter of Elon ... Gen 26:34
2. A third wife of Esau. Gen 36:2-3
Bath-sheba, wife of David 2Sam 11:3, 27
Bernice, sister of Agrippa. Acts 25:13
Bilhah, Rachel's handmaid .... Gen 29:29
Bithiah, daughter of a Pharaoh 1Chr 4:17
Candace, a queen .... Acts 8:27
Chloe, woman of Corinth. 1Cor 1:11
Claudia, Christian of Rome 2Tim 4:21
Cozbi, Midianite slain .... Num 25:15-18
Damaris, woman of Athens .... Acts 17:34
Deborah
1. Rebekah's nurse .... Gen 35:8
2. Judge .... Judg 4:4
Delilah, Philistine woman. Judg 16:4, 5
Dinah, daughter of Jacob . Gen 30:19, 21
Dorcas, called Tabitha ... Acts 9:36
Drusilla, wife of Felix .... Acts 24:24
Eglah one of David's wives 2Sam 3:5
Elisabeth, mother of John the Baptist .... Luke 1:5, 13
Elisheba, wife of Aaron .. Ex 6:23
Ephah, concubine of Caleb 1Chr 2:46
Ephrath, mother of Hur . 1Chr 2:19
Esther, a Jewess who became queen of Persia. Esth 2:16, 17
Eunice, mother of Timothy 2Tim 1:5
Euodias, a deaconess .... Phil 4:2
Eve, first woman .... Gen 3:20
Gomer, wife of Hosea .... Hos 1:2, 3
Hagar, Sarai's maid ...... Gen 16:1
Haggith, wife of David ... 2Sam 3:2, 4
Hammoleketh, mother of Ishod 1Chr 7:18
Hamutal, daughter of Jeremiah 2Kin 23:31
Hannah, mother of Samuel 1Sam 1:20
Hazelelponi, in genealogies of Judah ... 1Chr 4:1-3
Helah, one of the wives of Ashur 1Chr 4:5
Hephzibah, mother of Manasseh 2Kin 21:1
Herodias, sister-in-law of Herod .... Matt 14:3-6
Hodesh, wife of Shaharaim 1Chr 8:8, 9
Hoglah, a daughter of Zelophehad .... Num 26:33
Huldah, a prophetess 2Kin 22:14
Hushim, a Moabitess 1Chr 8:8-11

Iscah, daughter of Haran . Gen 11:29
Jael, wife of Heber ...... Judg 4:17
Jecholiah, wife of Amaziah 2Kin 15:1, 2
Jedidah, mother of Josiah. 2Kin 22:1
Jehoaddin, wife of Joash . 2Kin 14:1, 2
Jehosheba, daughter of Joram 2Kin 11:2
Jemima, Job's daughter .. Job 42:12, 14
Jerioth, wife of Caleb 1Chr 2:18
Jerusha, daughter of Zadok 2Kin 15:33
Jezebel, wife of Ahab 1Kin 16:30, 31
Joanna, wife of Chuza ... Luke 8:3
Jochebed, mother of Moses .... Ex 6:20
Judith, daughter of Beeri . Gen 26:34
Julia, Christian woman of Rome .... Rom 16:15
Keren-happuch, Job's daughter .... Job 42:14
Keturah, second wife of Abraham .... Gen 25:1
Kezia, daughter of Job .. Job 42:14
Leah, wife of Jacob ..... Gen 29:21-25
Lois, grandmother of Timothy 2Tim 1:5
Lo-ruhamah, daughter of Gomer .... Hos 1:3-6
Lydia, first Christian convert in Europe ..... Acts 16:14
Maachah
1. Daughter of Nahor . Gen 22:23, 24
2. Daughter of Talmai . 2Sam 3:3
3. Daughter of Abishalom 1Kin 15:2
4. Mother of Asa 1Kin 15:9, 10
5. Concubine of Caleb . 1Chr 2:48
6. Wife of Machir 1Chr 7:16
7. Wife of Jehiel 1Chr 8:29
Mahalath
1. Wife of Esau .... Gen 28:9
2. Granddaughter of David 2Chr 11:18
Mahlah, daughter of Zelophehad .... Num 26:33
Mara, another name for Naomi .... Ruth 1:20
Martha, friend of Christ . Luke 10:38-41
Mary
1. Mother of Jesus .... Matt 1:16
2. Mary Magdalene .... Matt 27:56-61
3. Mary, sister of Martha .... Luke 10:38, 39
4. Mary, wife of Cleophas .... John 19:25
5. Mary, mother of Mark .... Acts 12:12
6. A Christian at Rome .... Rom 16:6
Matred, mother-in-law of Hadar .... Gen 36:39
Mechetabeel, daughter of Matred .... Gen 36:39
Merab, King Saul's eldest daughter 1Sam 14:49
Meshullemeth, wife of Manasseh 2Kin 21:18, 19
Michal, daughter of King Saul 1Sam 14:49
Milcah
1. Daughter of Haran . Gen 11:29
2. Daughter of Zelophehad ...... Num 26:33
Miriam
1. Sister of Moses ..... Ex 15:20
2. Disputed daughter of Ezra 1Chr 4:17
Naamah
1. Daughter of Lamech. Gen 4:19-22
2. Wife of Solomon ... 1Kin 14:21
Naarah, one of the wives of Ashur 1Chr 4:5
Naomi, wife of Elimelech. Ruth 1:2

Nehushta, daughter of Elnathan 2Kin 24:8
Noadiah, a false prophetess .... Neh 6:14
Noah, daughter of Zelophehad .... Num 26:33
Orpah, sister-in-law of Ruth .... Ruth 1:4
Peninnah, one of the wives of Elkanah 1Sam 1:1, 2
Persis, convert of early Church .... Rom 16:12
Phebe, a deaconess ...... Rom 16:1-2
Priscilla, wife of Aquila .. Acts 18:2
Puah, a midwife .... Ex 1:15
Rachel, wife of Jacob .... Gen 29:28
Rahab, aid to Israel's spies .... Josh 2:1-3
Reumah, mother of Tebah .... Gen 22:24
Rhoda, a damsel .... Acts 12:13
Rizpah, concubine of Saul 2Sam 3:7
Ruth, daughter-in-law of Naomi .... Ruth 1:3, 4
Salome, wife of Zebedee . Matt 27:56
Mark 15:40
Sapphira, wife of Ananias. Acts 5:1
Sarah, (Sarai) wife of Abraham (Abram) .... Gen 11:29
Serah, daughter of Asher . Gen 46:17
Shelomith
1. Daughter of Dibri .. Lev 24:11
2. Daughter of Zerubbabel 1Chr 3:19
Sherah, daughter of Beriah 1Chr 7:23, 24
Shimeath, mother of Zabad 2Chr 24:26
Shimrith, mother of Jehozabad 2Chr 24:26
Shiphrah, a midwife ..... Ex 1:15
Shua, daughter of Heber . 1Chr 7:32
Susanna, ministered to Jesus .... Luke 8:3
Syntyche, convert of Church at Philippi ..... Phil 4:2
Tabitha, same as Dorcas . Acts 9:36
Tahpenes, queen of Egypt 1Kin 11:19
Tamar
1. Daughter-in-law of Judah .... Gen 38:6
2. A daughter of David 2Sam 13:1
3. Daughter of Absalom 2Sam 14:27
Taphath, one of Solomon's daughters ... 1Kin 4:11
Timna, concubine of Eliphaz .... Gen 36:12
Tirzah, one of daughters of Zelophehad .... Num 26:33
Tryphaena, convert at Rome .... Rom 16:12
Tryphosa, convert at Rome .... Rom 16:12
Vashti, wife of Ahasuerus. Esth 1:9
Zebudah, mother of Jehoiakim 2Kin 23:36
Zeresh, wife of Haman .. Esth 5:10
Zeruah, a widow 1Kin 11:26
Zeruiah, mother of Joab . 2Sam 17:25
Zibiah, mother of Jehoash 2Kin 12:1
Zillah, wife of Lamech ... Gen 4:19
Zilpah, Leah's handmaid . Gen 29:24
Zipporah, wife of Moses . Ex 2:21

WOMENSERVANTS— *female servants*
and *w*, and gave them unto ... Gen 20:14
and menservants, and *w* ..... Gen 32:5
two *w*, and his eleven sons .... Gen 32:22

WON— *See* WIN

WONDER—*a miraculous work*

Performed by:
God ....Heb 2:4
Moses and Aaron ....Ex 11:10
Christ ....Acts 2:22
Apostles ....Acts 2:43
Jesus' name ....Acts 4:30
Stephen ....Acts 6:8
Paul and Barnabas ......Acts 14:3
Paul 2Cor 12:12

Places of:
Egypt ....Acts 7:36
Land of Ham ....Ps 105:27
Canaan ....Josh 3:5
Deeps ....Ps 107:24
Heaven ....Dan 6:27
Among the peoples ......Ps 77:14

Described as:
Numerous ....Ex 11:9
Great ....Acts 6:8
Mighty ....Dan 4:3

Man's reactions to:
Did not remember.......Neh 9:17
Forgetful of ....Ps 78:11, 12
Not understanding ....Ps 106:7
Not believing ....Ps 78:32
Inquiring about..........Jer 21:2

Believer's attitude toward, to:
Remember 1Chr 16:9, 12
Declare ....Ps 71:17
Give thanks for ....Ps 136:1, 4
Consider ....Job 37:14

[*also* WONDERS]
smite Egypt with all my *w*.....Ex 3:20
all those *w* before Pharaoh ....Ex 4:21
my *w* in the land of Egypt ....Ex 7:3
fearful in praises, doing *w*? ....Ex 15:11
by signs, and by *w* and by.....Deut 4:34
and the *w*, and the mighty ....Deut 7:19
giveth thee a sign or a *w* ......Deut 13:1
thee for a sign and for a *w* ....Deut 28:46
the *w*, which the Lord sent ....Deut 34:11
inquire of the *w* that was......2Chr 32:31
signs and *w* upon Pharaoh.....Neh 9:10
yea, and *w* without number ...Job 9:10
I will remember thy *w* of old ..Ps 77:11
his *w* in the field of Zoan .....Ps 78:43
thy *w* be known in the dark? ..Ps 88:12
his *w* among all people........Ps 96:3
his *w*, and the judgments......Ps 105:5
Who sent tokens and *w* into ...Ps 135:9
w in Israel from the Lord .....Is 8:18
a sign and *w* upon Egypt......Is 20:3
a marvelous work and a *w* ....Is 29:14
and *w* in the land of Egypt....Jer 32:20
w that the high God hath .....Dan 4:2
it be to the end of these *w* ....Dan 12:6
And I will show *w* in the......Joel 2:30
shall show great signs and *w*...Matt 24:24
and shall show signs and *w* ....Mark 13:22
Except ye see signs and *w*.....John 4:48
will show *w* in heaven above ..Acts 2:19
and many *w* and signs were ...Acts 2:43
many signs and *w* wrought ....Acts 5:12
what miracles and *w* God .....Acts 15:12
Through mighty signs and *w*...Rom 15:19
power and signs and lying *w*...2Thess 2:9
both with signs and *w*.........Heb 2:4
appeared a great *w* in heaven..Rev 12:1
appeared another *w* in heaven .Rev 12:3
And he doeth great *w*, so......Rev 13:13

WONDER—*to express curiosity, doubt or surprise*

[*also* WONDERED, WONDERING]
the man *w* at her held his .....Gen 24:21
as a *w* unto many: but ....Ps 71:7
w that there was no ....Is 59:16
and the prophets shall *w* ......Jer 4:9
regard, and *w* marvelously ....Hab 1:5
for they are men *w* at.........Zech 3:8
Insomuch that the multitude *w*.Matt 15:31
beyond measure, and *w* ....Mark 6:51
heard it *w* at those things .....Luke 2:18
they being afraid *w*, saying ....Luke 8:25
spake; and the people *w* ......Luke 11:14
w in himself at that which.....Luke 24:12
and they were filled with *w*....Acts 3:10
called Solomon's, greatly *w*....Acts 3:11
Moses saw it, he *w* at the .....Acts 7:31
Behold, ye despisers, and *w*...Acts 13:41
the world *w* after the beast ....Rev 13:3
dwell on the earth shall *w*.....Rev 17:8

WONDERFUL—*unusually good; admirable; astonishing; marvelous*

Ascribed to:
Human love 2Sam 1:26
Lord's works ....Ps 78:4
Mysterious things ....Prov 30:18
Lord's Law ....Ps 119:18
Lord's testimonies ....Ps 119:129
Lord's knowledge ....Ps 139:6
Our being ....Ps 139:14
Messiah's name ....Is 9:6

Descriptive of the Lord's work, as:
Numerous ....Ps 40:5
Transmitted ....Ps 78:4
Remembered............Ps 111:4
Praised ....Is 25:1

[*also* WONDERFULLY]
will make thy plagues *w*.......Deut 28:59
he had wrought *w* among 1Sam 6:6
am about to build shall be *w* ..2Chr 2:9
too *w* for me, which I knew ...Job 42:3
which is *w* in counsel, and ....Is 28:29
w and horrible thing is ....Jer 5:30
therefore she came down *w* ...Lam 1:9
and he shall destroy *w*, and ...Dan 8:24
name done many *w* works?....Matt 7:22
saw the *w* things that he did...Matt 21:15
tongues the *w* works of God...Acts 2:11

WONDROUS—*amazing; amazingly*

[*also* WONDEROUSLY, WONDROUSLY]
angel did *w*; and Manoah .....Judg 13:19
w works of him which is ......Job 37:16
name is near thy *w* works .....Ps 75:1
thou art great, and doest *w*....Ps 86:10
talk ye of all his *w* works .....Ps 105:2
W works in the land of Ham ..Ps 106:22
shall I talk of thy *w* works ...Ps 119:27
of thy majesty, and of thy *w* ..Ps 145:5
God, that hath dealt *w*........Joel 2:26

WONT—*accustomed*
ox were *w* to push with his ....Ex 21:29
ever *w* to do so unto thee? ....Num 22:30
and his men were *w* to haunt ..1Sam 30:31
They were *w* to speak in old ..2Sam 20:18
times more than it was *w* .....Dan 3:19
governor was *w* to release .....Matt 27:15
and, as he was *w*, he taught ...Mark 10:1
and went, as he was *w*, to.....Luke 22:39
where prayer was *w* to be .....Acts 16:13

WOOD—*the hard fibrous substance of trees*

Descriptive of:
Part of a tree ....Num 19:6
Forest ....Josh 17:15, 18

Place of:
Animals 2Kin 2:24
Fortresses 2Chr 27:4

Used for:
Fire 1Kin 18:23-38
Carts 1Sam 6:14
Weapons ....Num 35:18
Ships ....Gen 6:14
Chariots ....Song 3:9
Musical instruments......1Kin 10:12
Buildings 1Kin 6:15-33
Tabernacle furniture .....Ex 25:9-28
Pulpit ....Neh 8:4
Gods ....Is 37:19

[*also* WOODS]
the *w* for the burnt offering ...Gen 22:3
Behold the fire and the *w*.....Gen 22:7
and laid the *w* in order, and...Gen 22:9
him on the altar upon the *w*...Gen 22:9
both in vessels of *w*, and in ...Ex 7:19
make the staves of shittim *w* ..Ex 25:28
the tabernacle of shittim *w* ....Ex 26:15
four pillars of shittim *w* ....Ex 26:32
staves of shittim *w*, and ....Ex 27:6
make the staves of shittim *w* ..Ex 30:5
whom was found shittim *w* ....Ex 35:24
the tabernacle of shittim *w* ....Ex 36:20
four pillars of shittim *w* ....Ex 36:36
made staves of shittim *w* ......Ex 37:4
made the staves of shittim *w* ..Ex 37:15
made the staves of shittim *w* ..Ex 37:28
made the staves of shittim *w* ..Ex 38:6
w in order upon the fire ......Lev 1:7
on the *w* that is on the fire....Lev 1:12
the *w* that is on the fire.......Lev 3:5
priest shall burn *w* on it.......Lev 6:12
and cedar *w*, and scarlet ......Lev 14:4
and cedar *w*, and scarlet ......Lev 14:49
with the cedar *w*, and with ....Lev 14:52
whether there be *w* therein ....Num 13:20
and all things made of *w* ......Num 31:20
work of men's hands, *w* and...Deut 4:28
I made an ark of shittim *w*....Deut 10:3
a man goeth into the *w* ....Deut 19:5
with his neighbor to hew *w*....Deut 19:5
known, even *w* and stone .....Deut 28:64
and their idols, *w* and stone ..Deut 29:17
sacrifice with the *w* of the .....Judg 6:26
they of the land came to a *w* ..1Sam 14:25
people were come into the *w* ..1Sam 14:26
wilderness of Ziph in a *w*.....1Sam 23:15
and David abode in the *w*.....1Sam 23:18
instruments made of fir *w* 2Sam 6:5
w devoured more people 2Sam 18:8
instruments of the oxen for *w* .2Sam 24:22
to Jordan, they cut down *w* ...2Kin 6:4
the trees of the *w* sing out 1Chr 16:33
brought much cedar *w* to......1Chr 22:4
will cut *w* out of Lebanon 2Chr 2:16
people, for the *w* offering .....Neh 10:34
the *w* offering, at times ....Neh 13:31
straw, and brass as rotten *w*...Job 41:27
boar out of the *w* doth........Ps 80:13
the trees of the *w* rejoice .....Ps 96:12
it in the fields of the *w* ....Ps 132:6
Where no *w* is there the ......Prov 26:20
the *w* that bringeth forth ......Eccl 2:6
among the trees of the *w*......Song 2:3
as the trees of the *w* are ......Is 7:2
thereof is fire and much *w* ....Is 30:33
the *w* of their graven image ...Is 45:20
fire, and this people *w* ....Jer 5:14
hast broken the yokes of *w*....Jer 28:13
for money; our *w* is sold ......Lam 5:4
w be taken thereof to do......Ezek 15:3
Heap on *w*, kindle the fire ....Ezek 24:10
wilderness and sleep in the *w* ..Ezek 34:25
ceiled with *w* round about.....Ezek 41:16
of *w* was three cubits high.....Ezek 41:22
walls thereof, were of *w* ......Ezek 41:22
of iron, of *w*, and of stone ....Dan 5:4
dwell solitarily in the *w* ....Mic 7:14
him that saith to the *w*........Hab 2:19
the mountain, and bring *w* ....Hag 1:8
hearth of fire amoung the *w*...Zech 12:6
stones, *w*, hay, stubble 1Cor 3:12
but also of *w* and of earth.....2Tim 2:20
brass, and stone, and of *w* ....Rev 9:20
scarlet, and all thyine *w*.......Rev 18:12
vessels of most precious *w*.....Rev 18:12

WOOD, HEWERS OF—*woodcutters*
Gibeonites made, because of deception ....Josh 9:21-27

WOODSMEN—*those skilled in woodcraft*
Provided with food 2Chr 2:3, 10

WOOF—*the threads crossing the warp of a woven fabric*
Inspection of, for leprosy .Lev 13:48-59

WOOL—*the soft hair of sheep*
Inspection of, for leprosy .Lev 13:47-59
Mixture of, forbidden ....Deut 22:11

W

Used as a test . . . . .Judg 6:37
Valuable article of trade .Ezek 27:18
Figurative of whiteness . . .Is 1:18

thousand rams, with the *w* 2Kin 3:4
He giveth snow like *w*; he . . . . .Ps 147:16
She seeketh *w*, and flax . . . . . . .Prov 31:13
worm shall eat them like *w* . . . .Is 51:8
ye clothe you with the *w* . . . . . .Ezek 34:3
of his head like the pure *w* . . . .Dan 7:9
my *w* and my flax, mine oil . . .Hos 2:5
and scarlet *w* and hyssop . . . . . .Heb 9:19
his hairs were white like *w* . . . .Rev 1:14

WOOLLEN—*made of wool*
whether it be a *w* garment . . . .Lev 13:47
woof; of linen, or of *w* . . . . .Lev 13:48
leprosy in a garment of *w* . . . . .Lev 13:59
mingled of linen and *w* . . . . .Lev 19:19
as of *w* and linen together . . . . .Deut 22:11

WORD—*utterance; message*
Described as:
Acceptable . . . . .Eccl 2:10
Lying and corrupt . . . . . . .Dan 2:9
Enticing 1Cor 2:4
Easy 1Cor 14:9, 19
Unspeakable 2Cor 12:4
Vain . . . . .Eph 5:6
Flattering 1Thess 2:5
Wholesome 1Tim 6:3
Power of, to:
Stir up wrath . . . . .Prov 15:1
Wound . . . . .Prov 26:22
Sustain . . . . .Is 50:4
Determine destiny . . . . . . .Matt 12:36, 37

[*also* WORD'S, WORDS]
w of the Lord came unto . . . . . .Gen 15:1
he heard the *w* of Rebekah . . .Gen 24:30
their *w* pleased Hamor . . . . .Gen 34:18
so shall your *w* be verified . . . .Gen 42:20
w that Joseph had spoken . . . . .Gen 44:2
told him the *w* of my lord . . . . .Gen 44:24
spake all the *w* which . . . . .Ex 4:30
feared the *w* of the Lord . . . . . .Ex 9:20
Moses told the *w* of the . . . . . . .Ex 19:9
all the *w* of the Lord . . . . .Ex 24:4
the *w* of the covenant . . . . .Ex 34:28
according to the *w* of Moses . . .Lev 10:7
pardoned according to thy *w* . .Num 14:20
unto him the *w* of Balak . . . . . .Num 22:7
the *w* which I shall say . . . . .Num 22:20
Lord: at his *w* shall they go . . .Num 27:21
and brought us *w* again . . . . . . .Deut 1:25
will make them hear my *w* . . . .Deut 4:10
of the *w* of this people . . . . .Deut 5:28
these *w* which I command . . . .Deut 12:28
w which he shall speak in . . . . .Deut 18:19
to speak a *w* in my name . . . . .Deut 18:20
w of this law that are . . . . .Deut 28:58
these *w* unto all Israel . . . . .Deut 31:1
shall receive of thy *w* . . . . .Deut 33:3
according to the *w* of the Lord .Deut 34:5
I brought him *w* again . . . . .Josh 14:7
the *w* that the children of . . . . .Josh 22:30
city heard the *w* of Gaal . . . . . .Judg 9:30
pressed him daily with her *w* . .Judg 16:16
the Lord establish his *w* 1Sam 1:23
of the Lord, and thy *w* 1Sam 15:24
servants told David these *w* . . .1Sam 18:26
according to all those *w* 1Sam 25:9
for the *w* of Ish-bosheth 2Sam 3:8
spake I a *w* with any of the . . .2Sam 7:7
speak ye not a *w* of bringing . .2Sam 19:10
w of the men of Judah 2Sam 19:43
w of the Lord came unto 2Sam 24:11
after thee, and confirm thy *w* . .1Kin 1:14
w that I have heard is good . . .1Kin 2:42
not failed one *w* of all 1Kin 8:56
speak good *w* to them 1Kin 12:7
given by the *w* of the Lord 1Kin 13:5
disobedient unto the *w* of the . .1Kin 13:26
w of the Lord against Baasha . .1Kin 16:7
w of the Lord came unto him . .1Kin 17:8
whom the *w* of the Lord 1Kin 18:31
w which Naboth the Jazreelite .1Kin 21:4

therefore the *w* of the Lord . . .1Kin 22:19
according to the *w* of the Lord .2Kin 4:44
the *w* that thou speakest 2Kin 6:12
This is the *w* of the Lord 2Kin 9:36
answered him not a *w* 2Kin 18:36
all the *w* of Rab-shakeh 2Kin 19:4
brought the king *w* again 2Kin 22:9
the *w* of this book that is 2Kin 22:13
the *w* of this covenant 2Kin 23:2
according to the *w* of the Lord .1Chr 11:3
w prevailed against Joab 1Chr 21:4
Israel, let thy *w* be verified 2Chr 6:17
the *w* of the prophets declare . .2Chr 18:12
let thy *w* therefore, I pray 2Chr 18:12
heard the *w* of the law 2Chr 34:19
So they brought the king *w* 2Chr 34:28
the *w* of the covenant 2Chr 34:31
whosoever shall alter this *w* . . .Ezra 6:11
w of Nehemiah the son of . . . . .Neh 1:1
according to these *w* . . . . .Neh 6:7
and hast performed thy *w* . . . . .Neh 9:8
none spake a *w* unto him . . . . .Job 2:13
Thy *w* have upholden him . . . . .Job 4:4
w of thy mouth be like . . . . .Job 8:2
w go out of thy mouth? . . . . . . .Job 15:13
that my *w* were now written! . .Job 19:23
After my *w* they spake not . . . .Job 29:22
and hearken to all my *w* . . . . . .Job 33:1
For the ear trieth *w*, as the . . . .Job 34:3
my *w* shall not be false . . . . . . .Job 36:4
concerning the *w* of Cush . . . . .Ps 7:*title*
the *w* of my roaring? . . . . .Ps 22:1
w of his mouth were . . . . .Ps 55:21
In God I will praise his *w* . . . . .Ps 56:4
to the *w* of my mouth . . . . .Ps 78:1
He sent his *w* . . . . .Ps 107:20
me according to thy *w* . . . . .Ps 119:25
take not the *w* of truth . . . . .Ps 119:43
but now have I kept thy *w* . . . . .Ps 119:67
thy *w* is settled in heaven . . . . .Ps 119:89
are thy *w* unto my taste! . . . . . .Ps 119:103
according unto thy *w* . . . . .Ps 119:116
I might meditate in thy *w* . . . . .Ps 119:148
I rejoice at thy *w* as one . . . . . .Ps 119:162
hast magnified thy *w* above . . . .Ps 138:2
stormy wind fulfilling his *w* . . . .Ps 148:8
the *w* of understanding . . . . .Prov 1:2
flattereth with her *w* . . . . .Prov 2:16
with the *w* of thy mouth . . . . . .Prov 6:2
All the *w* of my mouth . . . . . . .Prov 8:8
Pleasant *w* are as an . . . . .Prov 16:24
from the *w* of knowledge . . . . . .Prov 19:27
and lose thy sweet *w* . . . . .Prov 23:8
A *w* fitly spoken is like . . . . . . .Prov 25:11
man that is hasty in his *w*? . . . .Prov 29:20
therefore let thy *w* be few . . . . .Eccl 5:2
w of wise men are heard . . . . . .Eccl 9:17
upright, even *w* of truth . . . . . . .Eccl 12:10
despised the *w* of the Holy . . . .Is 5:24
Lord hath spoken this *w* . . . . . .Is 24:3
ears shall hear a *w* behind . . . . .Is 30:21
the poor with lying *w* . . . . .Is 32:7
hear the *w* of Rabshakeh . . . . . .Is 37:4
Good is the *w* of the Lord . . . .Is 39:8
put my *w* in thy mouth . . . . . . .Is 51:16
So shall my *w* be that goeth . . .Is 55:11
the *w* of the Lord came unto . .Jer 1:4
put my *w* in thy mouth . . . . . . .Jer 1:9
see ye the *w* of the Lord . . . . . .Jer 2:31
and proclaim there this *w* . . . . .Jer 7:2
ye trust in lying *w* . . . . .Jer 7:8
Hear ye the *w* which the Lord .Jer 10:1
ye the *w* of this covenant . . . . .Jer 11:6
speak unto them this *w* . . . . . . .Jer 13:12
Thy *w* were found, and I did . .Jer 15:16
Where is the *w* of the Lord? . .Jer 17:15
Hear ye the *w* of the Lord . . . .Jer 19:3
they might not hear my *w* . . . . .Jer 19:15
and speak there this *w* . . . . .Jer 22:1
and he that hath my *w* . . . . .Jer 23:28
steal my *w* every one from . . . .Jer 23:30
w of the Lord came unto me . .Jer 24:4
w that I command thee to . . . . .Jer 26:2
to all the *w* of Jeremiah . . . . . . .Jer 26:2
w unto Jeremiah from the . . . . .Jer 27:1

perform thy *w* which thou . . . . .Jer 28:6
perform my good *w* toward . . . .Jer 29:10
are the *w* that the Lord . . . . . . .Jer 30:4
w that came to Jeremiah . . . . . .Jer 32:1
the *w* of the Lord came unto . .Jer 33:1
w that came unto Jeremiah . . . .Jer 34:8
all the *w* that I have spoken . . .Jer 36:2
book all the *w* of the Lord . . . .Jer 36:11
pronounced all these *w* . . . . .Jer 36:18
the *w* of the Lord came to . . . . .Jer 36:27
w of the book which Jehoiakim .Jer 36:32
no man know of these *w* . . . . . .Jer 38:24
w that came to Jeremiah . . . . . .Jer 40:1
to them, even all these *w* . . . . .Jer 43:1
w that thou hast spoken . . . . . . .Jer 44:16
w that the Lord spake to . . . . . .Jer 46:13
shalt read all these *w* . . . . .Jer 51:61
he hath fulfilled his *w* . . . . .Lam 2:17
with my *w* unto them . . . . .Ezek 3:4
hear the *w* of the Lord God . . .Ezek 6:3
w of the Lord came to me . . . .Ezek 12:17
w which I have spoken . . . . .Ezek 12:28
w of the Lord came unto me . .Ezek 14:12
w of the Lord came unto me . .Ezek 18:1
w of the Lord came unto me . .Ezek 21:1
drop thy *w* toward the holy . . .Ezek 21:2
w of the Lord came unto me . .Ezek 26:1
w of the Lord came again . . . . .Ezek 30:1
hear the *w* at my mouth . . . . . .Ezek 33:7
for they hear thy *w* . . . . .Ezek 33:32
w of the Lord came unto me . .Ezek 35:1
w of the Lord came again . . . . .Ezek 37:15
great *w* which the horn spake . .Dan 7:11
w of the Lord came to . . . . .Dan 9:2
I heard the voice of his *w* . . . . .Dan 10:9
shut up the *w*, and seal . . . . . . .Dan 12:4
w of the Lord that came to . . . .Joel 1:1
The *w* of Amos, who was . . . . .Amos 1:1
hear thou the *w* of the Lord . . .Amos 7:16
according to the *w* of the Lord .Jon 3:3
w of the Lord which came . . . .Zeph 1:1
came the *w* of the Lord by . . . .Hag 2:10
But my *w* and my statutes . . . . .Zech 1:6
w of the Lord came unto me . .Zech 6:9
w by the mouth of the . . . . .Zech 8:9
burden of the *w* of the Lord . . .Zech 9:1
there until I bring thee *w* . . . . .Matt 2:13
idle *w* that men shall speak . . . .Matt 12:36
the *w*, and he becometh . . . . . . .Matt 13:22
they had heard these *w* . . . . . . .Matt 22:22
remembered the *w* of Jesus . . . .Matt 26:75
where the *w* is sown . . . . .Mark 4:15
such as hear the *w*, and . . . . . . .Mark 4:20
wondered at the gracious *w* . . .Luke 4:22
at thy *w* I will let down . . . . . . .Luke 5:5
Jesus' feet, and heard his *w* . . .Luke 10:39
with him in many *w* . . . . .Luke 23:9
and the *W* was with God . . . . . .John 1:1
believed the *w* that Jesus . . . . . .John 4:50
how shall ye believe my *w*? . . . .John 5:47
As he spake these *w* . . . . .John 8:30
because ye cannot hear my *w* . .John 8:37
if any man hear my *w* . . . . .John 12:47
the *w* might be fulfilled that . . .John 15:25
them the *w* which thou . . . . .John 17:8
received his *w* were baptized . .Acts 2:41
hearing these *w* fell down . . . . .Acts 5:5
preached the *w* of the Lord . . .Acts 8:25
and to hear *w* of thee . . . . .Acts 10:22
preaching the *w* to none . . . . . .Acts 11:19
gave testimony unto the *w* . . . .Acts 14:3
have troubled you with *w* . . . . .Acts 15:24
Holy Ghost to preach the *w* . . .Acts 16:6
for the *w* which he spake . . . . .Acts 20:38
him audience unto this *w* . . . . . .Acts 22:22
obedient, by *w* and deed . . . . . .Rom 15:18
good *w* and fair speeches . . . . . .Rom 16:18
five *w* with my understanding . .1Cor 14:19
us the *w* of reconciliation 2Cor 5:19
him that is taught in the *w* . . . .Gal 6:6
ye heard the *w* of truth . . . . . . .Eph 1:13
man deceive you with vain *w* . .Eph 5:6
heard before in the *w* of the . . .Col 1:5
sounded out the *w* of the Lord .1Thess 1:8
stablish you in every good *w* . .2Thess 2:17

dividing the *w* of truth 2Tim 2:15
hath greatly withstood our *w* ..2Tim 4:15
by the *w* of his power.........Heb 1:3
For if the *w* spoken by........Heb 2:2
suffer the *w* of exhortation ....Heb 13:22
any man offend not in *w* ......James 3:2
if any obey not the *w* 1Pet 3:1
and his *w* is not in us 1John 1:10
against us with malicious *w* 3John 10
and hast kept my *w*, and ......Rev 3:8
for these *w* are true ....Rev 21:5

WORD OF GOD—*communication from God to man, especially that which was given in Jesus Christ and in the Scriptures*

Called:
Book of the Law ....Neh 8:3
Law of the Lord ....Ps 1:2
Scriptures ....John 5:39
Holy Scriptures..........Rom 1:2
Word of God ....Heb 4:12
Word...................James 1:21-23
Word of life ....Phil 2:16
Book ....Rev 22:19

Descriptive of:
Old Testament Law .....Mark 7:13
God's revealed plan .....Rom 9:6
God's completed revelation.............Col 1:25-27
Christ's message ....Luke 5:1
Christian Gospel ....Acts 4:31

Described as:
Pure....................Ps 19:8
Restraining ....Ps 119:11
Perfect ....Ps 19:7
Sure....................Ps 111:7, 8
Truth...................Ps 119:142, 151, 160
Enduring ....Is 40:8
Effectual...............Is 55:11
Sanctifying ....Eph 5:26
Harmonious.............Acts 15:15
Inspired 2Pet 1:21
Living and active ....Heb 4:12

Compared to:
Lamp ....Ps 119:105
Fire ....Jer 5:14
Hammer.................Jer 23:29
Seed ....Matt 13:18-23
Sword ....Eph 6:17

Agency of, to:
Heal ....Ps 107:20
Make free ....John 8:32
Illuminate...............Ps 119:130
Bear witness ....John 20:31
Produce faith ....Rom 10:17
Make wise 2Tim 3:15-17
Exhort 2Tim 4:2
Rejoice the heart ....Jer 15:16
Create the world ....Heb 11:3
Regenerate ....James 1:18
Destroy the world 2Pet 3:5-7

Proper attitude toward, to:
Stand in awe of ....Ps 119:161
Tremble at..............Is 66:2, 5
Speak faithfully ....Jer 23:28
Search..................Acts 17:11
Speak boldly ....Acts 4:29, 31
Preach..................Acts 8:25
Receive.................Acts 11:1
Glorify ....Acts 13:48
Teach ....Acts 18:11
Obey 1Pet 3:1
Handle accurately 2Tim 2:15
Do ....James 1:22, 23
Suffer for ....Rev 1:9

In the believer's life, as:
Restraint ....Ps 119:9, 11
Guide ....Ps 119:133
Source of joy ....Ps 119:47, 97, 162
Standard of conduct .....Titus 2:5
Source of new life 1Pet 1:23
Spiritual food 1Pet 2:2

Prohibitions concerning, not to be:
Preached in man's wisdom 1Cor 2:4, 13
Used deceitfully 2Cor 4:2
Altered.................Rev 22:18, 19

the *w* of *G* came unto.........1Kin 12:22
the *w* of *G* came to Nathan ...1Chr 17:3
Every *w* of *G* is pure ....Prov 30:5
the *w* of *G* came unto John ...Luke 3:2
but by every *w* of *G* ....Luke 4:4
The seed is the *w* of *G*........Luke 8:11
which hear the *w* of *G* ....Luke 8:21
that hear the *w* of *G* ....Luke 11:28
unto whom the *w* of *G* came ..John 10:35
we should leave the *w* of *G* ...Acts 6:2
And the *w* of *G* increased .....Acts 6:7
had received the *w* of *G*.......Acts 8:14
the *w* of *G* grew and..........Acts 12:24
they preached the *w* of *G* .....Acts 13:5
together to hear the *w* of *G* ...Acts 13:44
necessary that the *w* of *G* .....Acts 13:46
w of *G* was preached of.......Acts 17:13
mightily grew the *w* of *G*......Acts 19:20
came the *w* of *G* out from.....1Cor 14:36
which corrupt the *w* of *G* 2Cor 2:17
w of *G* which ye heard........1Thess 2:13
is in truth, the *w* of *G* 1Thess 2:13
the *w* of *G* is not bound.......2Tim 2:9
tasted the good *w* of *G*........Heb 6:5
unto you the *w* of *G* ....Heb 13:7
the *w* of *G* abideth in you 1John 2:14
record of the *w* of *G*..........Rev 1:2
slain for the *w* of *G*...........Rev 6:9
name is called The *W* of *G* ....Rev 19:13
and for the *w* of *G*, and.......Rev 20:4

WORK—*deeds; industry; to do*

[*also* WORKETH, WORKING, WORK'S, WORKS, WORKS']
us concerning our *w* ....Gen 5:29
the people from their *w*? ......Ex 5:4
your *w* shall be diminished ....Ex 5:11
Go therefore now, and *w* .....Ex 5:18
no manner of *w* shall be ......Ex 12:16
saw that great *w* which the ....Ex 14:31
the *w* that they must do........Ex 18:20
labor, and do all thy *w*........Ex 20:9
it thou shalt not do any *w*.....Ex 20:10
days thou shalt do thy *w* ......Ex 23:12
them, nor do after their *w* ....Ex 23:24
a paved *w* of a sapphire.......Ex 24:10
of beaten *w* shall the ....Ex 25:31
cherubim of cunning *w*........Ex 26:1
linen, with cunning *w* ....Ex 28:6
w of an engraver in stone .....Ex 28:11
of judgment with cunning *w* ...Ex 28:15
after the *w* of the ephod ......Ex 28:15
binding of woven *w* round.....Ex 28:32
w in all manner of............Ex 31:5
Six days may *w* be done ......Ex 31:15
doeth any *w* in the sabbath ....Ex 31:15
shall see the *w* of the Lord ....Ex 34:10
Six days shall *w* be done ......Ex 35:2
whosoever doeth *w* therein ....Ex 35:2
for any *w* of the service ....Ex 35:24
to *w* in gold, and in silver ......Ex 35:32
And to devise curious *w* ......Ex 35:32
manner of *w*, of the ....Ex 35:35
even of them that do any *w* ...Ex 35:35
those that devise cunning *w* ...Ex 35:35
to know how to *w* ....Ex 36:1
all manner of *w* for the ....Ex 36:1
for the *w* of the service ....Ex 36:3
all the *w* of the sanctuary .....Ex 36:4
came every man from his *w* ...Ex 36:4
woman make any more *w* .....Ex 36:6
the *w* of the tabernacle ....Ex 36:8
cherubim of cunning *w*........Ex 36:8
beaten *w* made he the ....Ex 37:17
to the *w* of the apothecary ....Ex 37:29
engraver, and a cunning *w* ....Ex 38:23
that was occupied for the *w* ...Ex 38:24
all the *w* of the holy place ....Ex 38:24
w it in the blue, and in the....Ex 39:3
fine linen, with cunning *w*.....Ex 39:3
breastplate of cunning *w* ......Ex 39:8
the *w* of the ephod; of gold ...Ex 39:8
of the ephod of woven *w*......Ex 39:22
all the *w* of the tabernacle ....Ex 39:32
did look upon all the *w* ....Ex 39:43
any *w* is done, it must be .....Lev 11:32
do no *w* at all, whether ....Lev 16:29
Six days shall *w* be done ......Lev 23:3
ye shall do no *w* therein ......Lev 23:3
ye shall do no servile *w* ....Lev 23:21
ye shall do no *w* in that.......Lev 23:28
Ye shall do no manner of *w*...Lev 23:31
do the *w* in the tabernacle ....Num 4:3
do the *w* of the tabernacle ....Num 4:30
this *w* of the candlestick ......Num 8:4
thereof, was beaten *w*.........Num 8:4
ye shall do no servile *w* ....Num 28:25
and all *w* of goats' hair ....Num 31:20
in all the *w* of thy hand ....Deut 2:7
gods, the *w* of men's hands....Deut 4:28
it thou shalt not do any *w*.....Deut 5:14
shall bless thee in all thy *w*....Deut 15:10
do no *w* with the firstling .....Deut 15:19
in all the *w* of thine hands ....Deut 16:15
in all the *w* of thine hands ....Deut 24:19
to bless all the *w* of thine .....Deut 28:12
through the *w* of your hands ..Deut 31:29
accept the *w* of his hands .....Deut 33:11
They did *w* wilily, and ....Josh 9:4
had known all the *w* of the....Josh 24:31
all the great *w* of the Lord ....Judg 2:7
came an old man from his *w* ..Judg 19:16
The Lord recompense thy *w*...Ruth 2:12
the *w* which they have done ...1Sam 8:8
and put them to his *w* 1Sam 8:16
which were over the *w* 1Kin 5:16
that wrought in the *w*.........1Kin 5:16
fitted upon the carved *w* 1Kin 6:35
cunning to *w* all *w* in brass 1Kin 7:14
and wrought all his *w* 1Kin 7:14
And nets of checker *w* 1Kin 7:17
and wreaths of chain *w* 1Kin 7:17
of the pillars was lily *w* 1Kin 7:22
was the *w* of the pillars 1Kin 7:22
additions made of thin *w*.......1Kin 7:29
w of the wheels was like 1Kin 7:33
was like the *w* of a chariot 1Kin 7:33
the *w* that king Solomon 1Kin 7:51
that were over Solomon's *w* ...1Kin 9:23
that wrought in the *w*.........1Kin 9:23
w evil in the sight of the 1Kin 21:20
of them that did the *w* 2Kin 12:11
hand of the doers of the *w* 2Kin 22:5
give it to the doers of the *w*...2Kin 22:5
all the *w* of their hands 2Kin 22:17
and the wreathen *w*, and 2Kin 25:17
pillar with wreathen *w* 2Kin 25:17
with the king for his *w*........1Chr 4:23
able men for the *w* of the 1Chr 9:13
employed in that *w* day and ...1Chr 9:33
ye of all his wondrous *w* 1Chr 16:9
Remember his marvelous *w* ...1Chr 16:12
men for every manner of *w* ...1Chr 22:15
the *w* for the service of 1Chr 23:24
number of the *w* according 1Chr 25:1
did the *w* of the field for 1Chr 27:26
all the *w* of this pattern 1Chr 28:19
the *w* for the service of the....1Chr 28:20
w to be made by the hands....1Chr 29:5
man cunning to *w* in gold 2Chr 2:7
to set the people a *w* 2Chr 2:18
the *w* of the brim of a cup 2Chr 4:5
all the *w* that Solomon made ..2Chr 5:1
w of Solomon was prepared ...2Chr 8:16
Ramah, and let his *w* cease ...2Chr 16:5
the Lord hath broken thy *w* ...2Chr 20:37
and the *w* was perfected by ...2Chr 24:13
in every *w* that he began 2Chr 31:21
men did the *w* faithfully.......2Chr 34:12
all the *w* of their hands 2Chr 34:25
unto the treasure of the *w*.....Ezra 2:69
the *w* of the house of God ....Ezra 4:24
the *w* of this house of God ....Ezra 6:7
this a *w* of one day or two ....Ezra 10:13

W

to the rest that did the *w* .....Neh 2:16
necks to the *w* of their Lord...Neh 3:5
and cause the *w* to cease......Neh 4:11
servants wrought in the *w*......Neh 4:16
The *w* is great and large......Neh 4:19
continued in the *w* of this.....Neh 5:16
gathered thither unto the *w*...Neh 5:16
be weakened from the *w*.......Neh 6:9
according to these their *w*.....Neh 6:14
the fathers gave unto the *w*...Neh 7:70
w of the house of our God....Neh 10:33
the singers, that did the *w*.....Neh 13:10
sentence against an evil *w*.....Esth 8:11
according to the *w* of the.....Esth 8:14
blessed the *w* of his hands.....Job 1:10
despise the *w* of thine hands...Job 10:3
left hand, where he doth *w*....Job 23:9
things *w* God oftentimes......Job 33:29
w of a man shall he render....Job 34:11
he showeth them their *w*......Job 36:9
all men may know his *w*......Job 37:7
wondrous *w* of him which.....Job 37:16
dominion over the *w* of thy...Ps 8:6
snared in the *w* of his own....Ps 9:16
Concerning the *w* of men.....Ps 17:4
tell of all thy wondrous *w*.....Ps 26:7
and all his *w* are done in......Ps 33:4
wonderful *w* which thou.......Ps 40:5
what *w* thou didst in their.....Ps 44:1
sharp razor, *w* deceitfully.....Ps 52:2
Come and see the *w* of God...Ps 66:5
I may declare all thy *w*.......Ps 73:28
break down the carved *w*.....Ps 74:6
thy wondrous *w* declare.......Ps 75:1
wonderful *w* that he hath.....Ps 78:4
not for his wondrous *w*.....Ps 78:32
thy *w* appear unto thy........Ps 90:16
establish thou the *w* of our....Ps 90:17
w of our hands establish......Ps 90:17
Lord, how great are thy *w*!....Ps 92:5
proved me, and saw my *w*....Ps 95:9
He that *w* deceit shall not.....Ps 101:7
heavens are the *w* of thy......Ps 102:25
his *w* in all places of his.......Ps 103:22
with the fruit of thy *w*.......Ps 104:13
Man goeth forth unto his *w*...Ps 104:23
ye of all his wondrous *w*......Ps 105:2
heathen, and learned their *w*..Ps 106:35
The *w* of his hands are........Ps 111:7
gold, the *w* of men's hands.....Ps 115:4
declare the *w* of the Lord.....Ps 118:17
the *w* of thine own hands.....Ps 138:8
wicked *w* with men that.......Ps 141:4
with men that *w* iniquity......Ps 141:4
carved *w*, with fine linen......Prov 7:16
weights of the bag are his *w*...Prov 16:11
doings, whether his *w* be......Prov 20:11
Prepare thy *w* without........Prov 24:27
a flattering mouth *w* ruin.......Prov 26:28
her own *w* praise her in the...Prov 31:31
have seen all the *w* that are...Eccl 1:14
w that my hands had wrought .Eccl 2:11
w that is wrought under.......Eccl 2:17
What profit hath he that *w*....Eccl 3:9
their *w*, are in the hand of....Eccl 9:1
bring every *w* into judgment...Eccl 12:14
w of the hands of a cunning *w* .Song 7:1
worship the *w* of their own....Is 2:8
speed, and hasten his *w*.......Is 5:19
altars, the *w* of his hands.....Is 17:8
Egypt to err in every *w*.......Is 19:14
Assyria the *w* of my hands....Is 19:25
his children, the *w* of mine....Is 29:23
his heart will *w* iniquity......Is 32:6
the *w* of men's hands, wood...Is 37:19
and your *w* of nought.........Is 41:24
all vanity; their *w* are.........Is 41:29
tongs both *w* in the coals......Is 44:12
themselves with their *w*.......Is 59:6
their *w* are *w* of iniquity......Is 59:6
I measure their former *w*......Is 65:7
the *w* of their own hands.......Jer 1:16
w of the hands of the.........Jer 10:3
the *w* of the *w* and...........Jer 10:9
all the *w* of cunning men......Jer 10:9
neither do ye any *w*, but......Jer 17:22
he wrought a *w* on the........Jer 18:3
with the *w* of your hands......Jer 25:7
with the *w* of their hands.....Jer 32:30
with the *w* of your hands......Jer 44:8
according to the *w* of their....Lam 3:64
w was like unto the color.....Ezek 1:16
and their *w* was as it were....Ezek 1:16
your *w* may be abolished.......Ezek 6:6
Is it meet for any *w*?.........Ezek 15:4
and silk, and embroidered *w*..Ezek 16:13
linen with embroidered *w*.....Ezek 27:7
clothes, and embroidered *w*...Ezek 27:24
shall be shut the six *w* days...Ezek 46:1
him he shall *w* deceitfully.....Dan 11:23
of them that *w* iniquity........Hos 6:8
more to the *w* of our hands...Hos 14:3
and *w* evil upon their beds...Mic 2:1
the *w* of the house of Ahab...Mic 6:16
shall uncover the cedar *w*.....Zeph 2:14
w in the house of the Lord....Hag 1:14
is every *w* of their hands......Hag 2:14
that *w* wickedness are set.....Mal 3:15
me, ye that *w* iniquity........Matt 7:23
but do not ye after their *w*....Matt 23:3
could there do no mighty *w*...Mark 6:5
in which men ought to *w*......Luke 13:14
believe me for the very *w*.....John 14:11
the *w* of their own hands......Acts 7:41
we had much *w* to come by...Acts 27:16
w that which is unseemly......Rom 1:27
to every man that *w* good.....Rom 2:10
show the *w* of the law........Rom 2:15
By what law? of *w*? Nay......Rom 3:27
Because the law *w* wrath......Rom 4:15
did *w* in our members to......Rom 7:5
not of *w*, but of him that.....Rom 9:11
then is it no more of *w*.......Rom 11:6
But if it be of *w*, then is it....Rom 11:6
are not a terror to good *w*....Rom 13:3
man's *w* shall be made........1Cor 3:13
fire shall try every man's *w*....1Cor 3:13
man's *w* shall be burned......1Cor 3:15
labor, *w* with our own hands..1Cor 4:12
another the *w* of miracles.....1Cor 12:10
may abound to every good *w*..2Cor 9:8
be according to their *w*......2Cor 11:15
not justified by the *w* of......Gal 2:16
not by the *w* of the law.......Gal 2:16
by the *w* of the law shall......Gal 2:16
Christ Jesus unto good *w*......Eph 2:10
for the *w* of the ministry......Eph 4:12
to *w* all uncleanness with......Eph 4:19
w out your own salvation.....Phil 2:12
for the *w* of Christ he was....Phil 2:30
fruitful in every good *w*.......Col 1:10
ceasing your *w* of faith........1Thess 1:3
in love for their *w* sake.......1Thess 5:13
the *w* of faith with power.....2Thess 1:11
of iniquity doth already *w*.....2Thess 2:7
is after the *w* of Satan.......2Thess 2:9
godliness with good *w*.........1Tim 2:10
he desireth a good *w*.........1Tim 3:1
followed every good *w*........1Tim 5:10
the good *w* of some are.......1Tim 5:25
not according to our *w*........2Tim 1:9
prepared unto every good *w*...2Tim 2:21
do the *w* of an evangelist.....2Tim 4:5
but in *w* they deny him.......Titus 1:16
every good *w* reprobate.......Titus 1:16
people, zealous of good *w*.....Titus 2:14
be ready to every good *w*.....Titus 3:1
hath ceased from his own *w*...Heb 4:10
your conscience from dead *w*..Heb 9:14
unto love and to good *w*......Heb 10:24
but a doer of the *w*, this......James 1:25
hath faith, and have not *w*?...James 2:14
hast faith, and I have *w*......James 2:18
me thy faith without thy *w*....James 2:18
show thee my faith by my *w*...James 2:18
faith without *w* is dead?.......James 2:20
faith wrought with his *w*......James 2:22
w was faith made perfect?.....James 2:22
by *w* a man is justified.......James 2:24
so faith without *w* is dead....James 2:26
confusion and every evil *w*....James 3:16
they may by your good *w*.....1Pet 2:12
w that are therein shall be....2Pet 3:10
might destroy the *w* of the....1John 3:8
I know thy *w*, and thy........Rev 2:2
thy *w*, and tribulation, and....Rev 2:9
I know thy *w*, and charity.....Rev 2:19
thy patience, and thy *w*.......Rev 2:19
keepeth my *w* unto the end...Rev 2:26
for I have not found thy *w*....Rev 3:2
know thy *w*, that thou art.....Rev 3:15
yet repented not of the *w*.....Rev 9:20
the spirits of devils, *w*........Rev 16:14
double according to her *w*.....Rev 18:6
whatsoever *w* abomination....Rev 21:27

WORK, CHRIST'S

Defined as:
Doing God's will........John 4:34
Limited in time.........John 9:4
Incomparable...........John 15:24
Initiated by God........John 14:10
Finished in the cross.....John 17:4

Design of, to:
Attest His mission.......John 5:36
Encourage faith.........John 14:11, 12
Judge men..............John 15:24

WORK, THE CHRISTIAN'S

Agency of, by:
God....................Phil 2:13
Spirit...................1Cor 12:11
God's Word............1Thess 2:13
Faith...................Gal 5:6

Characteristics of:
Designed for God's glory .Matt 5:16
Divinely called.........Acts 13:2
Produces eventual glory..2Cor 4:17
Subject to examination...Gal 6:4
Final perfection in.......Heb 13:21

God's regard for, will:
Reward.................Jer 31:16
Perfect.................Phil 1:6
Not forget..............Heb 6:10

See LABOR, SPIRITUAL

WORK, PHYSICAL
Part of the curse........Gen 3:19
Required of Christians...2Thess 3:7-14
Nehemiah's zeal.........Neh 6:1-4
Paul's example..........Acts 18:1-3

See LABOR, PHYSICAL

WORKER—*doer; laborer*

[*also* WORKERS]
and of the cunning *w*.........Ex 35:35
her right hand to the *w*.......Judg 5:26
man of Tyre, a *w* in brass.....1Kin 7:14
But they gave that to the *w*...2Kin 12:14
money to be bestowed on *w*...2Kin 12:15
Moreover the *w* with.........2Kin 23:24
and *w* of stone and timber....1Chr 22:15
w with thee in abundance.....1Chr 22:15
So the *w* wrought, and the....2Chr 24:13
w that had the oversight......2Chr 34:10
w that wrought in the house...2Chr 34:10
the *w* in the house of God....Ezra 3:9
punishment to the *w* of.......Job 31:3
in company with the *w* of.....Job 34:8
hatest all *w* of iniquity.......Ps 5:5
the *w* of iniquity no..........Ps 14:4
with the *w* of iniquity.........Ps 28:3
against the *w* of iniquity.....Ps 37:1
Deliver me from the *w* of.....Ps 59:2
all the *w* of iniquity do........Ps 92:7
w of iniquity boast............Ps 94:4
them forth with the *w* of......Ps 125:5
be to the *w* of iniquity........Prov 10:29
w melteth a graven image.....Is 40:19
and the *w*, they are of men...Is 44:11
w of the hands of.............Jer 10:3
the *w* made it; therefore......Hos 8:6
for the *w* is worthy of his.....Matt 10:10
me, all ye *w* of iniquity.......Luke 13:27
the *w* of like occupation......Acts 19:25

are all *w* of miracles? ... 1Cor 12:29
as *w* together with him ... 2Cor 6:1
of dogs, beware of evil *w* ... Phil 3:2

WORKFELLOW—*a companion in a task*
Timothy my *w*, and Lucius ... Rom 16:21

WORKMAN—*skilled craftsman*

[*also* WORKMEN, WORKMEN'S]
and of the cunning *w* ... Ex 35:35
engraver, and a cunning *w* ... Ex 38:23
her right hand to the *w* ... Judg 5:26
But they gave that to the *w* ... 2Kin 12:14
money to be bestowed on *w* ... 2Kin 12:15
w with thee in abundance ... 1Chr 22:15
number of the *w* according ... 1Chr 25:1
So the *w* wrought, and the ... 2Chr 24:13
w that had the oversight ... 2Chr 34:10
w that wrought in the house ... 2Chr 34:10
the *w* in the house of God ... Ezra 3:9
the hands of a cunning *w* ... Song 7:1
w melteth a graven image ... Is 40:19
unto him a cunning *w* to ... Is 40:20
and the *w*, they are of men ... Is 44:11
work of the hands of the *w* ... Jer 10:3
the *w* made it; therefore ... Hos 8:6
for the *w* is worthy of his ... Matt 10:10
the *w* of like occupation ... Acts 19:25
a *w* that needeth not to be ... 2Tim 2:15

WORKMANSHIP—*art or skill of a workman; something produced*
and in all manner of *w* ... Ex 31:3
according to all the *w* ... 2Kin 16:10
thee for all manner of *w* ... 1Chr 28:21
w of thy tabrets and of ... Ezek 28:13
For we are his *w*, created ... Eph 2:10

WORKS, GOD'S—*God's acts of creation and salvation*

Described as:
Perfect ... Deut 32:4
Terrible ... Ps 66:3
Incomparable ... Ps 86:8
Honorable and glorious ... Ps 111:3
Marvelous ... Ps 139:14
Holy ... Ps 145:17
Strange ... Is 28:21
Great and marvelous ... Rev 15:3

Manifested in:
Creation ... Gen 1:1-3
Heavens ... Ps 8:3
Deeps ... Ps 107:24
Regenerate people ... Is 19:25

God's attitude toward:
Rejoice in ... Ps 104:31
Made known to His people ... Ps 111:6
His mercies over ... Ps 145:9
Glorified in ... Is 60:21

Believer's attitude toward, to:
Consider ... Ps 8:3
Behold ... Ps 46:8
Meditate ... Ps 77:12
Meditate upon ... Ps 143:5
Triumph in ... Ps 92:4
Declare ... Ps 107:22
Praise God for ... Ps 145:4, 10
Pray for revival of ... Hab 3:2

Unbeliever's attitude toward:
Not regarding ... Ps 28:5
Forgetting ... Ps 78:11
Not believed ... Acts 13:41

WORKS, GOOD—*beneficial deeds*

Considered negatively, they cannot:
Justify ... Rom 4:2-6
Determine God's election ... Rom 9:11
Secure righteousness ... Rom 9:31, 32
Substitute for grace ... Rom 11:6

Considered positively:
Reward for ... 1Cor 3:13-15
Created for ... Eph 2:10
Prepared for ... 2Tim 2:21
Furnished for ... 2Tim 3:17

WORKS, SATAN'S—*See* SATAN

WORKS, THE UNBELIEVER'S—*sinful deeds*

Described as:
Wicked ... Col 1:21
Done in darkness ... Is 29:15
Abominable ... Ps 14:1
Deceitful ... Prov 11:18
Evil ... John 7:7
Unfruitful ... Eph 5:11

God's attitude toward, will:
Never forget ... Amos 8:7
Reward ... Prov 24:12
Bring to judgment ... Rev 20:12, 13

Believer's relation to:
Cast off ... Rom 13:12
Have no fellowship with ... Eph 5:11
Be delivered from ... 2Tim 4:18

WORLD—*our planet; also refers to that which is temporal rather than eternal*

God's relation to, as:
Maker ... Jer 10:12
Possessor ... Ps 24:1
Redeemer ... John 3:16
Judge ... Ps 96:13

Christ's relation to, as:
Maker ... John 1:10
Sin-bearer ... John 1:29
Savior ... John 12:47
Life ... John 6:33, 51
Light ... John 8:12
Judge ... Acts 17:31
Overcomer ... John 16:33
Reconciler ... 2Cor 5:19

Christian's relation to:
Light of ... Matt 5:14
Not of ... John 17:14, 16
Chosen out of ... John 15:19
Tribulation in ... John 16:33
Sent into by Christ ... John 17:18
Not conformed to ... Rom 12:2
Crucified to ... Gal 6:14
To live soberly ... Titus 2:12
Unspotted from ... James 1:27
Overcomers of ... 1John 5:4, 5
Denying desires of ... Titus 2:12

Dangers of, arising from:
Wisdom ... 1Cor 3:19
Love of ... 2Tim 4:10
Friendship ... James 4:4
Corruptions ... 2Pet 1:4
Lusts ... 1John 2:15-17
False prophets ... 1John 4:1
Deceivers ... 2John 7

In the plan of redemption:
Elect chosen before ... Eph 1:4
Revelation made before ... Matt 13:35
Sin's entrance into ... Rom 5:12
Its guilt before God ... Rom 3:19
Original revelation to ... Rom 1:20
God's love for ... John 3:16
Christ's mission to ... John 12:47
Spirit's conviction of ... John 16:8
Gospel preached in ... Matt 24:14
Reconciliation of ... 2Cor 5:19
Destruction of ... 2Pet 3:7
Final judgment of ... Acts 17:31
Satan deceives ... Rev 12:9

[*also* WORLD'S, WORLDS]
hath set the *w* upon them ... 1Sam 2:8
foundations of the *w* were ... 2Sam 22:16
the *w* also shall be stable ... 1Chr 16:30
and chased out of the *w* ... Job 18:18
face of the *w* in the earth ... Job 37:12
shall judge the *w* in ... Ps 9:8
the foundations of the *w* ... Ps 18:15
of the *w* shall remember ... Ps 22:27
inhabitants of the *w* stand ... Ps 33:8
for the *w* is mine, and the ... Ps 50:12
lightnings lightened the *w* ... Ps 77:18
formed the earth and the *w* ... Ps 90:2
w also shall be established ... Ps 96:10
His..enlightened the *w* ... Ps 97:4
shall he judge the *w* ... Ps 98:9
part of the dust of the *w* ... Prov 8:26
set the *w* in their heart ... Eccl 3:11
punish the *w* for their evil ... Is 13:11
fill the face of the *w* with ... Is 14:21
all the kingdoms of the *w* ... Is 23:17
w will learn righteousness ... Is 26:9
the face of the *w* with fruit ... Is 27:6
the inhabitants of the *w* ... Is 38:11
unto the end of the *w* ... Is 62:11
all the kingdoms of the *w* ... Jer 25:26
all the inhabitants of the *w* ... Lam 4:12
the *w*, and all that dwell ... Nah 1:5
all the kingdoms of the *w* ... Matt 4:8
him, neither in this *w* ... Matt 12:32
neither in the *w* to come ... Matt 12:32
and the care of this *w* ... Matt 13:22
field is the *w*; the good ... Matt 13:38
it be in the end of this *w* ... Matt 13:40
if he shall gain the whole *w* ... Matt 16:26
and of the end of the *w*? ... Matt 24:3
the beginning of the *w* ... Matt 24:21
be preached in the whole *w* ... Matt 26:13
And the cares of this *w* ... Mark 4:19
in the *w* to come eternal ... Mark 10:30
Go ye into all the *w*, and ... Mark 16:15
been since the *w* began ... Luke 1:70
all the kingdoms of the *w* ... Luke 4:5
the foundation of the *w* ... Luke 11:50
the children of this *w* are ... Luke 16:8
children of this *w* marry ... Luke 20:34
man that cometh into the *w* ... John 1:9
the *w* to condemn the *w* ... John 3:17
the *w* through him might be ... John 3:17
Christ, the Savior of the *w* ... John 4:42
show thyself to the *w* ... John 7:4
The *w* cannot hate you ... John 7:7
above: ye are of this *w* ... John 8:23
I am not of this *w* ... John 8:23
As long as I am in the *w* ... John 9:5
I am the light of the *w* ... John 9:5
I am come into this *w* ... John 9:39
seeth the light of this *w* ... John 11:9
the *w* is gone after him ... John 12:19
is the judgment of this *w* ... John 12:31
prince of this *w* be cast ... John 12:31
depart out of this *w* unto ... John 13:1
own which were in the *w* ... John 13:1
while, and the *w* seeth me ... John 14:19
not as the *w* giveth, give I ... John 14:27
w may know that I love ... John 14:31
If the *w* hate you, ye know ... John 15:18
prince of this *w* is judged ... John 16:11
a man is born into the *w* ... John 16:21
and am come into the *w* ... John 16:28
I leave the *w*, and go to the ... John 16:28
with thee before the *w* was ... John 17:5
I pray not for the *w*, but ... John 17:9
I am no more in the *w* ... John 17:11
but these are in the *w*, and ... John 17:11
things I speak in the *w* ... John 17:13
take them out of the *w* ... John 17:15
w may know that thou hast ... John 17:23
the *w* hath not known thee ... John 17:25
kingdom is not of this *w* ... John 18:36
this cause came I into the *w* ... John 18:37
holy prophets since the *w* ... Acts 3:21
dearth throughout all the *w* ... Acts 11:28
turned the *w* upside down ... Acts 17:6
God that made the *w* and ... Acts 17:24
all Asia and the *w* ... Acts 19:27
of throughout the whole *w* ... Rom 1:8
how shall God judge the *w*? ... Rom 3:6
should be the heir of the *w* ... Rom 4:13
the law sin was in the *w* ... Rom 5:13
them be the riches of the *w* ... Rom 11:12
be the reconciling of the *w* ... Rom 11:15
is the disputer of this *w*? ... 1Cor 1:20
the wisdom of this *w*? ... 1Cor 1:20
w by wisdom knew not God ... 1Cor 1:21
the foolish things of the *w* ... 1Cor 1:27
the weak things of the *w* ... 1Cor 1:27
And base things of the *w* ... 1Cor 1:28
not the wisdom of this *w* ... 1Cor 2:6
nor of the princes of this *w* ... 1Cor 2:6

the princes of this *w* knew 1Cor 2:8
to be wise in this *w*..........1Cor 3:18
or the *w*, or life, or death 1Cor 3:22
made as the filth of the *w*.....1Cor 4:13
the fornicators of this *w*......1Cor 5:10
ye needs go out of the *w*......1Cor 5:10
saints shall judge the *w*? 1Cor 6:2
w shall be judged by you......1Cor 6:2
And they that use this *w*......1Cor 7:31
fashion of this *w* passeth 1Cor 7:31
for the things of the *w*........1Cor 7:34
flesh while the *w* standeth.....1Cor 8:13
ends of the *w* are come 1Cor 10:11
kinds of voices in the *w*.......1Cor 14:10
our conversation in the *w* 2Cor 1:12
god of this *w* hath blinded 2Cor 4:4
sorrow of the *w* worketh 2Cor 7:10
us from this present evil *w* ....Gal 1:4
under the elements of the *w*...Gal 4:3
named, not only in this *w* .....Eph 1:21
to the course of this *w*........Eph 2:2
and without God in the *w*.....Eph 2:12
beginning of the *w* hath.......Eph 3:9
of the darkness of this *w*......Eph 6:12
ye shine as lights in the *w*......Phil 2:15
you, as it is in all the *w*.......Col 1:6
the rudiments of the *w*........Col 2:20
as though living in the *w*......Col 2:20
into the *w* to save sinners 1Tim 1:15
brought nothing into this *w*....1Tim 6:7
them that are rich in this *w* ...1Tim 6:17
Christ Jesus before the *w* 2Tim 1:9
promised before the *w* began ..Titus 1:2
whom also he made the *w*.....Heb 1:2
first begotten into the *w* ......Heb 1:6
the foundation of the *w*.......Heb 4:3
the foundation of the *w*.......Heb 9:26
once in the end of the *w*......Heb 9:26
the *w* were framed by the .....Heb 11:3
which he condemned the *w*....Heb 11:7
whom the *w* was not worthy...Heb 11:38
the poor of this *w* rich in .....James 2:5
is a fire, a *w* of iniquity ....James 3:6
the foundation of the *w*.......1Pet 1:20
brethren that are in the *w*......1Pet 5:9
And spared not the old *w*.....2Pet 2:5
upon the *w* of the ungodly 2Pet 2:5
the pollutions of the *w*........2Pet 2:20
for the sins of the whole *w*.....1John 2:2
therefore the *w* knoweth us ...1John 3:1
my brethren, if the *w* hate 1John 3:13
But whoso hath this *w* good ...1John 3:17
now already is it in the *w*.....1John 4:3
than he that is in the *w*.......1John 4:4
They are of the *w*............1John 4:5
speak they of the *w*...........1John 4:5
and the *w* heareth them.......1John 4:5
to be the Savior of the *w*......1John 4:14
the whole *w* lieth in 1John 5:19
shall come upon all the *w*.....Rev 3:10
kingdoms of this *w* are........Rev 11:15
deceiveth the whole *w*.........Rev 12:9
the *w* wondered after the .....Rev 13:3
the foundation of the *w*.......Rev 13:8
earth and of the whole *w* .....Rev 16:14
the foundation of the *w*.......Rev 17:8

WORLDLY—*temporal; earthly*
ungodliness and *w* lusts ....Tit 2:12
service and a *w* sanctuary .....Heb 9:1

WORM—*a destructive insect larva, as a grub or maggot; a wretched person*

Ravages of:
On bread ....Ex 16:15, 20
On plants ....Jon 4:7
On the body ....Acts 12:23
In the grave ....Job 24:19, 20
In hell.................Mark 9:44-48

Figurative of:
Insignificance ....Job 25:6
Messiah ....Ps 22:6

[*also* WORMS]
was there any *w* therein ....Ex 16:24
for the *w* shall eat them.......Deut 28:39
My flesh is clothed with *w* ....Job 7:5
to the *w*, Thou art my ....Job 17:14
after my skin *w* destroy ....Job 19:26
the *w* is spread under thee ....Is 14:11
and the *w* cover thee ....Is 14:11
Fear not, thou *w* Jacob ....Is 41:14
for their *w* shall not die ....Is 66:24
holes like *w* of the earth ......Mic 7:17
he was eaten of *w*, and gave ..Acts 12:23

WORMWOOD—*a bitter-tasting plant; something bitter or grievous*
Figurative of idolatry ....Deut 29:18
Of adultery ....Prov 5:4
Of God's judgments .....Jer 9:15
Symbol of doom.........Rev 8:11

I will feed them with *w* ....Jer 23:15
hath made me drunken with *w*.Lam 3:15
my misery, the *w* and the .....Lam 3:19
Ye who turn judgment to *w*...Amos 5:7

WORRY—*See* CARES, WORLDLY

WORSE—*more inferior; more faulty; more incorrect*

[*also* WORST]
will we deal *w* with thee ......Gen 19:9
that will be *w* unto thee.......2Sam 19:7
did *w* than all that were.......1Kin 16:25
Judah was put to the *w* 2Kin 14:12
put to the *w* before Israel 1Chr 19:16
Israel be put to the *w*.........2Chr 6:24
to do *w* than the heathen 2Chr 33:9
did *w* than their fathers ....Jer 7:26
bring the *w* of the heathen ....Ezek 7:24
w liking than the children .....Dan 1:10
and the rent is made *w*.......Matt 9:16
last error shall be *w* than......Matt 27:64
and the rent is made *w* ....Mark 2:21
man is *w* than the first........Luke 11:26
then that which is *w* ....John 2:10
if we eat not, are we the *w*....1Cor 8:8
and is *w* than an infidel 1Tim 5:8
seducers shall wax *w* and *w*....2Tim 3:13
the latter end is *w* with 2Pet 2:20

WORSHIP—*expression of the relationship between believers and God; involves reverence and adoration of God; devotion to false gods*

Of God:
Defined ....John 4:20-24
Commanded 1Chr 16:29
Corrupted ....Rom 1:25
Perverted 2Kin 21:3, 21
Debated 1Kin 18:21-39

Of Christ, by:
Angels ....Heb 1:6
Magi ....Matt 2:1-2, 11
Men...................John 9:30-38
Women................Matt 15:25
Disciples...............Matt 28:17
Heavenly choir ....Rev 4:10, 11

Of wrong objects; such as:
Heavenly host..........Deut 17:3
Other gods.............Ex 34:14
Demons ....Deut 32:17
Creatures ....Rom 1:25
Images ....Dan 3:5-18
Man..................Acts 10:25, 26
Antichrist ....Rev 13:4-13

Of wrong objects, by:
Israel.................2Kin 21:3, 21
Pagans ....Rom 1:25
Professing Christians.....Col 2:18
World 2Thess 2:3-12

[*also* WORSHIPED, WORSHIPETH, WORSHIPING]
lad will go yonder and *w*......Gen 22:5
his head, and *w* the Lord .....Gen 24:26
my head, and *w* the Lord .....Gen 24:48
their words, he *w* the Lord.....Gen 24:52
bowed their heads and *w*......Ex 4:31
of Israel; and *w* ye afar off....Ex 24:1
a molten calf, and have *w* it...Ex 32:8
head toward the earth, and *w* .Ex 34:8
shouldest be driven to *w* ......Deut 4:19
serve other gods, and *w*.......Deut 11:16
other gods, and *w* them ....Deut 29:26
w other gods, and serve ....Deut 30:17
face to the earth, and did *w*...Josh 5:14
thereof, that he *w* ....Judg 7:15
out of his city yearly to *w*.....1Sam 1:3
w before the Lord, and 1Sam 1:19
I may *w* the Lord thy God 1Sam 15:30
Saul; and Saul *w* the Lord 1Sam 15:31
house of the Lord, and *w* 2Sam 12:20
other gods, and *w* them 1Kin 9:6
other gods, and have *w* them ..1Kin 9:9
served Baal, and *w* him 1Kin 16:31
the house of Rimmon to *w*....2Kin 5:18
w all the host of heaven.......2Kin 17:16
w before the altar in..........2Kin 18:22
w in the house of Nisroch 2Kin 19:37
down their heads, and *w* 1Chr 29:20
w, and praised the Lord 2Chr 7:3
serve other gods, and *w* them .2Chr 7:19
before the Lord, *w* the Lord ..2Chr 20:18
And all the congregation *w*....2Chr 29:28
bowed their heads and *w*......2Chr 29:30
and *w* the Lord with their.....Neh 8:6
the host of heaven *w* thee .....Neh 9:6
down upon the ground, and *w* .Job 1:20
I *w* toward thy holy temple....Ps 5:7
the nations shall *w* before .....Ps 22:27
upon earth shall eat and *w*....Ps 22:29
w the Lord in the beauty of ...Ps 29:2
thy Lord; and *w* thou him.....Ps 45:11
All the earth shall *w* thee .....Ps 66:4
thou *w* any strange god ....Ps 81:9
shall come and *w* before ......Ps 86:9
let us *w* and bow down ....Ps 95:6
w the Lord in the beauty of ...Ps 96:9
of idols: *w* him, all ye gods....Ps 97:7
our God, and *w* at his ....Ps 99:5
our God, and *w* at his holy....Ps 99:9
Horeb, and *w* the molten .....Ps 106:19
we will *w* at his footstool......Ps 132:7
I will *w* toward thy holy.......Ps 138:2
w the work of their own ....Is 2:8
shall *w* the Lord in the........Is 27:13
w in the house of Nisroch .....Is 37:38
he maketh a god, and *w* it ....Is 44:15
down unto it, and *w* it ....Is 44:17
they fall down, yea, they *w*....Is 46:6
all flesh come to *w* before.....Is 66:23
w the works of their own .....Jer 1:16
these gates to *w* the Lord .....Jer 7:2
served them, and have *w*......Jer 16:11
serve them, and to *w* them ....Jer 25:6
did we make her cakes to *w*...Jer 44:19
w the sun toward the east.....Ezek 8:16
w at the threshold of the ......Ezek 46:2
way of the north gate to *w*....Ezek 46:9
w Daniel, and commanded ....Dan 2:46
might not serve nor *w* any ....Dan 3:28
more *w* the work of thine .....Mic 5:13
that *w* the host of heaven .....Zeph 1:5
w and that swear by the.......Zeph 1:5
year to year to *w* the King ....Zech 14:16
that I may come and *w* him ...Matt 2:8
if thou wilt fall down and *w*...Matt 4:9
there came a leper and *w* .....Matt 8:2
the ship came and *w* him......Matt 14:33
But in vain do they *w* me .....Matt 15:9
fell down, and *w* him ....Matt 18:26
w him, and desiring a ....Matt 20:20
by the feet, and *w* him........Matt 28:9
afar off, he ran and *w* him ....Mark 5:6
Howbeit in vain do they *w* me .Mark 7:7
and bowing their knees *w* .....Mark 15:19
thou therefore wilt *w* me ......Luke 4:7
shalt *w* the Lord thy God .....Luke 4:8
w in the presence of them .....Luke 14:10
they *w* him, and returned to...Luke 24:52
Lord, I believe. And he *w* .....John 9:38
came up to *w* at the feast .....John 12:20
them up to *w* the host of......Acts 7:42
come to Jerusalem for to *w* ...Acts 8:27
Thyatira, which *w* God, heard .Acts 16:14

Neither is *w* with men's ....Acts 17:25
named Justus, one that *w* .....Acts 18:7
persuadeth men to *w* God .....Acts 18:13
all Asia and the world *w* ......Acts 19:27
a *w* of the great goddess ......Acts 19:35
w I the God of my fathers ....Acts 24:14
on his face he will *w* God 1Cor 14:25
which *w* God in the spirit .....Phil 3:3
a show of wisdom in will *w*....Col 2:23
is called God, or that is *w*.....2Thess 2:4
to come and *w* before thy .....Rev 3:9
w him that liveth for ever .....Rev 5:14
on their faces, and *w* God.....Rev 7:11
they should not *w* devils ......Rev 9:20
and them that *w* therein ......Rev 11:1
their faces, and *w* God.......Rev 11:16
w the image of the beast ....Rev 13:15
If any man *w* the beast ....Rev 14:9
shall come and *w* before ......Rev 15:4
and upon them which *w* his ...Rev 16:2
beasts fell down and *w* God ...Rev 19:4
I fell at his feet to *w* him .....Rev 19:10
w God: for the testimony .....Rev 19:10
which had not *w* the beast ....Rev 20:4
sayings of this book; *w* God ...Rev 22:9

WORSHIPER—*one who takes part in worship*

[*also* WORSHIPERS]
he might destroy the *w* of 2Kin 10:19
vestments for all the *w* of 2Kin 10:22
said unto the *w* of Baal 2Kin 10:23
but the *w* of Baal only 2Kin 10:23
true *w* shall worship the ....John 4:23
any man be a *w* of God, and ..John 9:31
the *w* once purged should .....Heb 10:2

WORTH—*having value; estimable; prominent or wealthy people*
money as it is *w* he shall ......Gen 23:9
the *w* of thy estimation ......Lev 27:23
w a double hired servant ......Deut 15:18
thou art *w* ten thousand of 2Sam 18:3
thee the *w* of it in money 1Kin 21:2
make my speech nothing *w*? ...Job 24:25
of the wicked is little *w* ....Prov 10:20
Howl ye, Woe *w* the day! .....Ezek 30:2

WORTHIES—*worthy or prominent people*
He shall recount his *w* ....Nah 2:5

WORTHILY—*having worth or value*
do thou *w* in Ephratah ....Ruth 4:11

WORTHLESS—*of no value; useless; despicable*
Applied to Job's friends..Job 13:4
Sacrifice ....Is 1:13
Faith 1Cor 15:17
Religion ....James 1:26
Worship ....Jer 51:17, 18

WORTHY—*of value; honor; merit*
Of Christ:
For more glory ....Heb 3:3
To open the book ....Rev 5:2, 4
To receive worship ......Rev 5:9-14
Of believers, for:
Provisions..............Matt 10:10
Discipleship ....Matt 10:37
Their calling ....Eph 4:1
Suffering...............Acts 5:41
Their walk ....Col 1:10
Honor 1Tim 6:1
Kingdom 2Thess 1:5

I am not *w* of the least of .....Gen 32:10
is *w* of death be put to........Deut 17:6
have committed a sin *w* of ....Deut 21:22
wicked man be *w* to be ....Deut 25:2
unto Hannah he gave a *w* 1Sam 1:5
the Lord, who is *w* to be......2Sam 22:4
will show himself a *w* man 1Kin 1:52
the Lord, who is *w* to be......Ps 18:3
This man is *w* to die ....Jer 26:11
whose shoes I am not *w* to ....Matt 3:11
I am not *w* that thou ....Matt 8:8
inquire who in it is *w* ....Matt 10:11
if the house be *w*, let your ....Matt 10:13
if it be not *w*, let your ....Matt 10:13
followeth after me, is not *w* ...Matt 10:38
I am not *w* to stoop down.....Mark 1:7
fruits *w* of repentance ....Luke 3:8
w for whom he should do ......Luke 7:4
thought I myself *w* to come ...Luke 7:7
laborer is *w* of his hire ....Luke 10:7
did commit things *w* of........Luke 12:48
am no more *w* to be called ....Luke 15:21
accounted *w* to obtain that ....Luke 20:35
nothing *w* of death is done ....Luke 23:15
I am not *w* to unloose ....John 1:27
of his feet I am not *w* to ......Acts 13:25
very *w* deeds are done unto ...Acts 24:2
had committed nothing *w* of ...Acts 25:25
such things are *w* of death ....Rom 1:32
are not *w* to be compared .....Rom 8:18
ye would walk *w* of God 1Thess 2:12
count you *w* of this calling 2Thess 1:11
and *w* of all acceptation.......1Tim 1:15
be counted *w* of double 1Tim 5:17
shall he be thought *w*, who ....Heb 10:29
whom the world was not *w* ....Heb 11:38
they blaspheme that *w* name ..James 2:7
in white: for they are *w* ....Rev 3:4
Thou art *w*, O Lord, to ....Rev 4:11
to drink; for they are *w* ....Rev 16:6

WOT—*to know*

[*also* WOTTETH]
I *w* not who hath done this....Gen 21:26
my master *w* not what is ......Gen 39:8
w not what is become ....Ex 32:1
I *w* that he whom thou ....Num 22:6
whither the men went I *w* .....Josh 2:5
I *w* that through ignorance ....Acts 3:17
W ye not..scripture saith ......Rom 11:2
what I shall choose I *w* not....Phil 1:22

WOULD—*wish; want; intention; preference*

[*also* WOULDEST]
Adam to see what he *w* call ...Gen 2:19
and *w* thou take away my .....Gen 30:15
I *w* that it might be...........Gen 30:34
thou *w* take by force thy ......Gen 31:31
ye *w* not hear? therefore ......Gen 42:22
his father, his father *w* die ....Gen 44:22
afar off, to wit what *w* be .....Ex 2:4
behold, hitherto thou *w* ....Ex 7:16
w he let the children of ....Ex 9:35
he *w* not let the children of ...Ex 10:20
he *w* not let the children of ...Ex 11:10
W to God we had died by.....Ex 16:3
w God that all the Lord's .....Num 11:29
Lord *w* put his spirit upon ....Num 11:29
W God that we had died in the.Num 14:2
w God we had died in this ....Num 14:2
Sihon *w* not suffer Israel .....Num 21:23
w there were a sword in mine .Num 22:29
in mine hand for now I *w* kill .Num 22:29
Notwithstanding ye *w* not .....Deut 1:26
Lord *w* not hearken to your ...Deut 1:45
sakes and *w* not hear me ......Deut 3:26
he *w* keep the oath which .....Deut 7:8
w keep his commandments ....Deut 8:2
the Lord had said he *w* ....Deut 9:25
God *w* not hearken unto ......Deut 23:5
w not adventure to set ....Deut 28:56
w not obey the voice of ....Deut 28:62
say, *W* God it were even ......Deut 28:67
W God it were morning ....Deut 28:67
I said, I *w* scatter them ....Deut 32:26
I *w* make the remembrance ...Deut 32:26
that he *w* not show them .....Josh 5:6
fathers that he *w* give ....Josh 5:6
w to God we had been.........Josh 7:7
unto her, What *w* thou? ......Josh 15:18
But I *w* not hearken unto .....Josh 24:10
Canaanites *w* dwell in that ....Judg 1:27
w dwell in mount Heres.......Judg 1:35
to know whether they *w* ....Judg 3:4
them, I *w* desire a request ....Judg 8:24
w give me every man the .....Judg 8:24
w to God this people were ....Judg 9:29
w I remove Abimelech ....Judg 9:29
the king of Edom *w* not.......Judg 11:17
king of Moab; but he *w* ....Judg 11:17
he *w* not have received a......Judg 13:23
neither *w* he have showed .....Judg 13:23
nor *w* as at this time have .....Judg 13:23
her father *w* not suffer him....Judg 15:1
the men *w* not hearken to .....Judg 19:25
of Benjamin *w* not hearken ...Judg 20:13
W ye tarry for them till ....Ruth 1:13
w ye stay for them from ......Ruth 1:13
he *w* answer him, Nay 1Sam 2:16
for now *w* the Lord have 1Sam 13:13
and *w* let him go no more......1Sam 18:2
servants of the king *w* not 1Sam 22:17
I *w* not stretch forth mine 1Sam 26:23
Asahel *w* not turn aside 2Sam 2:21
that I *w* have given him a 2Sam 4:10
knew ye not that they *w* 2Sam 11:20
but he *w* not, neither did 2Sam 12:17
he *w* not hearken unto her 2Sam 13:14
howbeit he *w* not go, but 2Sam 13:25
w not suffer the revengers 2Sam 14:11
king; but he *w* not come 2Sam 14:29
and I *w* do him justice! 2Sam 15:4
yet *w* I not put forth mine 2Sam 18:12
that one *w* give me drink 2Sam 23:15
therefore he *w* not drink 2Sam 23:17
the king said, What *w* 1Kin 1:16
he *w* dwell in the thick........1Kin 8:12
as great as *w* contain two 1Kin 18:32
away his face and *w* eat 1Kin 21:4
But Jehoshaphat *w* not........1Kin 22:49
when the Lord *w* take up 2Kin 2:1
w thou be spoken for to 2Kin 4:13
W God my lord were with 2Kin 5:3
he *w* recover him of his 2Kin 5:3
w thou smite those whom 2Kin 6:22
Lord *w* make windows in 2Kin 7:2
Lord *w* not destroy Judah 2Kin 8:19
But Amaziah *w* not hear 2Kin 14:11
Notwithstanding they *w* 2Kin 17:14
the Lord *w* not pardon 2Kin 24:4
Oh that thou *w* bless me 1Chr 4:10
thou *w* keep me from evil 1Chr 4:10
his armorbearer *w* not 1Chr 10:4
David *w* not drink of it 1Chr 11:18
said that they *w* do 1Chr 13:4
he *w* increase Israel like 1Chr 27:23
he *w* dwell in the thick........2Chr 6:1
that thou *w* put thy name 2Chr 6:20
that he *w* not destroy him 2Chr 12:12
he *w* not prophesy good 2Chr 18:17
but they *w* not give ear 2Chr 24:19
but they *w* not hearken 2Chr 33:10
w not thou be angry with .....Ezra 9:14
w not come within three ......Ezra 10:8
that thou *w* send me unto .....Neh 2:5
w go into the temple to ....Neh 6:11
do with them as they *w* ....Neh 9:24
yet *w* they not give ear ....Neh 9:30
w not buy it of them on the ...Neh 10:31
w leave the seventh year ......Neh 10:31
Mordecai's matters *w* ....Esth 3:4
that *w* assault them ....Esth 8:11
w keep these two days ....Esth 9:27
I *w* seek unto God ....Job 5:8
unto God *w* I commit my .....Job 5:8
that God *w* grant me the......Job 6:8
w please God to destroy me ...Job 6:9
he *w* let loose his hand ....Job 6:9
I loathe it, I *w* not live ....Job 7:16
If thou *w* seek unto God ......Job 8:5
righteous, yet *w* I not ....Job 9:15
I *w* make supplication to ......Job 9:15
yet *w* I not know my soul .....Job 9:21
I *w* despise my life ....Job 9:21
But oh that God *w* speak .....Job 11:5
For vain man *w* be wise.......Job 11:12
ye *w* altogether hold your .....Job 13:5
Oh that thou *w* hide me in ....Job 14:13
thou *w* keep me secret ....Job 14:13
that thou *w* appoint me ....Job 14:13
I *w* order my cause before ....Job 23:4
I *w* know the words which ....Job 23:5

he *w* answer me, and ....Job 23:5
understand what he *w* say .....Job 23:5
he *w* fain flee out of his.......Job 27:22
and *w* root out all mine ....Job 31:12
Oh that one *w* hear me! ......Job 31:35
the Almighty *w* answer me ....Job 31:35
I *w* declare unto him the ......Job 31:37
as a prince *w* I go near ....Job 31:37
w not consider any of his .....Job 34:27
one *w* think the deep to be....Job 41:32
on the Lord that he *w* ....Ps 22:8
if I *w* declare and speak.......Ps 40:5
not sacrifice; else *w* I give .....Ps 51:16
Lo, then *w* I wander far off ...Ps 55:7
then I *w* have hid myself......Ps 55:12
Mine enemies *w* daily ....Ps 56:2
w destroy me, being mine .....Ps 69:4
people *w* not hearken to ......Ps 81:11
and Israel *w* none of me ......Ps 81:11
men *w* praise the Lord ....Ps 107:8
there was no man that *w* ......Ps 142:4
and *w* none of my reproof ....Prov 1:25
him and *w* not let him go .....Song 3:4
I *w* lead thee, and bring ......Song 8:2
house, who *w* instruct.........Song 8:2
w cause thee to drink of ......Song 8:2
if a man *w* give all the ....Song 8:7
for love, it *w* utterly be ....Song 8:7
who *w* set the briers and ......Is 27:4
I *w* go through them...........Is 27:4
I *w* burn them together ....Is 27:4
be your strength and ye *w*.....Is 30:15
that thou *w* deal very ....Is 48:8
I *w* not be wroth with thee....Is 54:9
thou *w* rend the heavens ......Is 64:1
that thou *w* come down ....Is 64:1
I *w* comfort myself against ....Jer 8:18
glory; but they *w* not hear ....Jer 13:11
yet *w* I pluck thee hence ......Jer 22:24
king that he *w* not burn.......Jer 36:25
but he *w* not hear them ....Jer 36:25
w they not leave some ....Jer 49:9
w not have believed that ......Lam 4:12
they *w* have hearkened unto...Ezek 3:6
hope that they *w* confirm .....Ezek 13:6
I *w* pour out my fury upon ....Ezek 20:13
I *w* pour out my fury upon ....Ezek 20:21
that I *w* bring thee against ....Ezek 38:17
that he *w* not defile himself ...Dan 1:8
of the king that he *w* give .....Dan 2:16
w show the king the ....Dan 2:16
whom he *w* he slew...........Dan 5:19
whom he *w* he kept alive ......Dan 5:19
and whom he *w* he set up ......Dan 5:19
whom he *w* he put down ....Dan 5:19
he *w* accomplish seventy ....Dan 9:2
I *w* have healed Israel ....Hos 7:1
w they not have stolen till.....Obad 5
he had said that he *w* do ......Jon 3:10
cried, and they *w* not hear ....Zech 7:13
that *w* shut the doors for......Mal 1:10
and *w* not be comforted.......Matt 2:18
ye *w* that men should do.......Matt 7:12
they *w* have repented long ....Matt 11:21
ye *w* not have condemned.....Matt 12:7
w have put him to death ......Matt 14:5
w show them a sign from .....Matt 16:1
he *w* not; but went and ....Matt 18:30
we *w* not have been ....Matt 23:30
w I have gathered thy.........Matt 23:37
her wings and ye *w* not!.......Matt 23:37
in what watch the thief *w* ......Matt 24:43
come he *w* have watched ......Matt 24:43
w not have suffered his ....Matt 24:43
thereof, he *w* not drink ....Matt 27:34
he *w* heal him on the sabbath .Mark 3:2
w not send them away out .....Mark 5:10
sat with him, he *w* not ....Mark 6:26
w have no man know it ....Mark 7:24
he *w* not that any man ....Mark 9:30
we *w* that thou shouldest ......Mark 10:35
how he *w* have him called .....Luke 1:62
w thrust out a little from ......Luke 5:3
w that men should do to ......Luke 6:31
desired him that he *w* eat .....Luke 7:36
he *w* not command them ......Luke 8:31
him that he *w* come into ......Luke 8:41
whither he himself *w*..........Luke 10:1
hour the thief *w* come ....Luke 12:39
he *w* have watched and not ...Luke 12:39
w I have gathered thy.........Luke 13:34
her wings and ye *w* not!.......Luke 13:34
angry, and *w* not go in........Luke 15:28
which *w* pass from hence ....Luke 16:26
that *w* come from thence ......Luke 16:26
w send him to my father's.....Luke 16:27
And he *w* not for a while .....Luke 18:4
that he *w* touch them ....Luke 18:15
the stones *w* immediately......Luke 19:40
as though he *w* have gone.....Luke 24:28
Jesus *w* go forth into ....John 1:43
w have asked of him...........John 4:10
w have given thee living ....John 4:10
that he *w* tarry with them .....John 4:40
Moses, ye *w* have believed ....John 5:46
fishes as much as they *w* ......John 6:11
he *w* not walk in Jewry ....John 7:1
ye *w* do the works of ....John 8:39
wherefore *w* ye hear it ....John 9:27
not so, I *w* have told you .....John 14:2
the world *w* love his ....John 15:19
then *w* my servants fight ......John 18:36
walkedst whither thou *w* ....John 21:18
carry thee whither thou *w* .....John 21:18
w raise up Christ to sit........Acts 2:30
he *w* give it to him for a ......Acts 7:5
w have understood how ....Acts 7:25
that God by his hand *w* ....Acts 7:25
our fathers *w* not obey ....Acts 7:39
he *w* not delay to come to ....Acts 9:38
w cleave unto the Lord ....Acts 11:23
w have done sacrifice with ....Acts 14:13
and *w* have killed himself .....Acts 16:27
reason *w* that I should ....Acts 18:14
that he *w* not adventure.......Acts 19:31
he *w* not spend the time in....Acts 20:16
he *w* have known the ....Acts 22:30
ye *w* inquire something ....Acts 23:15
that thou *w* bring down ....Acts 23:20
when I *w* have known the .....Acts 23:28
he *w* send for him to ....Acts 25:3
he *w* go to Jerusalem ....Acts 25:20
the beginning, if they *w* ....Acts 26:5
they *w* have cast anchors.......Acts 27:30
Now I *w* not have you ....Rom 1:13
for what I *w* that do I not.....Rom 7:15
the good that I *w* I do not ....Rom 7:19
the evil which I *w* not ....Rom 7:19
when I *w* do good, evil is .....Rom 7:21
yet I *w* have you wise.........Rom 16:19
they *w* not have crucified 1Cor 2:8
as though I *w* not come 1Cor 4:18
I *w* have you without 1Cor 7:32
and I *w* not that ye should 1Cor 10:20
if we *w* judge ourselves 1Cor 11:31
I *w* that ye all spake with 1Cor 14:5
For we *w* not, brethren 2Cor 1:8
you that ye *w* confirm 2Cor 2:8
that we *w* receive the gift 2Cor 8:4
that they *w* go before 2Cor 9:5
W to God ye could bear 2Cor 11:1
not find you such as I *w* 2Cor 12:20
unto you such as ye *w* not ...2Cor 12:20
w pervert the gospel ....Gal 1:7
This only *w* I learn of you ....Gal 3:2
they *w* exclude you, that ye ...Gal 4:17
do the things that ye *w* ....Gal 5:17
That he *w* grant you ....Eph 3:16
I *w* ye should understand .....Phil 1:12
To whom God *w* make ....Col 1:27
God *w* open unto us a door ...Col 4:3
we *w* not be chargeable 1Thess 2:9
we *w* have come unto you.....1Thess 2:18
I *w* not have you to be 1Thess 4:13
our God *w* count you 2Thess 1:11
Whom I *w* have retained ......Philem 13
w he not afterward have ......Heb 4:8
and offering thou *w* not ....Heb 10:5
w fail me to tell of Gideon ....Heb 11:32
w no doubt have continued....1John 2:19
I *w* thou wert cold or hot .....Rev 3:15
as many as *w* not worship .....Rev 13:15

WOUND—*an injury; to injure*

Of physical injury, by:

God ....Deut 32:39
Battle 1Sam 31:3
Adultery ....Prov 6:32, 33
Robbers ....Luke 10:30, 34
Evil spirit ....Acts 19:16

Of spiritual injury, by:

Discouragement ....Prov 18:14
God's punishment ....Jer 30:14
Drunkenness ....Prov 23:29, 30
Adultery ....Prov 6:32, 33
Sin ....Is 1:6

[*also* WOUNDED, WOUNDEDST, WOUNDETH, WOUNDING, WOUNDS]

I have slain a man to my *w* ...Gen 4:23
burning *w* for *w*, stripe for ....Ex 21:25
were overthrown and *w* ....Judg 9:40
the *w* of the Philistines........1Sam 17:52
consumed them and *w* them ...2Sam 22:39
that in smiting he *w* him 1Kin 20:37
the blood ran out of the *w* 1Kin 22:35
and the Syrians *w* Joram 2Kin 8:28
healed in Jezreel of the *w* 2Kin 8:29
he was *w* of the archers 1Chr 10:3
the host; for I am *w* 2Chr 18:33
in Jezreel because of the *w* 2Chr 22:6
he *w*, and his hands make .....Job 5:18
multiplieth my *w* without ......Job 9:17
soul of the *w* crieth out ....Job 24:12
my *w* is incurable without .....Job 34:6
w them that they were not ....Ps 18:38
My *w* stink and are corrupt ...Ps 38:5
But God shall *w* the head .....Ps 68:21
of those whom thou hast *w*.....Ps 69:26
and bindeth up their *w*.........Ps 147:3
blueness of a *w* cleanseth .....Prov 20:30
of a talebearer are as *w* ....Prov 26:22
Faithful are the *w* of a ....Prov 27:6
me, they smote me, they *w*....Song 5:7
the stroke of their *w* ....Is 30:26
Rahab and *w* the dragon? .....Is 51:9
continually is grief and *w*......Jer 6:7
my hurt! my *w* is grievous .....Jer 10:19
and thy *w* is grievous ....Jer 30:12
I will heal thee of thy *w* ......Jer 30:17
there remained but *w* men ....Jer 37:10
her land the *w* shall groan.....Jer 51:52
swooned as the *w* in the ......Lam 2:12
thy fall, when the *w* cry ....Ezek 26:15
groanings of a deadly *w* ....Ezek 30:24
and Judah saw his *w* ....Hos 5:13
sword, they shall not be *w* ....Joel 2:8
bread have laid a *w* under.....Obad 7
her *w* is incurable; for it ......Mic 1:9
bruise; thy *w* is grievous ......Nah 3:19
thou *w* the head out of the ....Hab 3:13
What are these *w* in thine .....Zech 13:6
was *w* in the house of my .....Zech 13:6
and *w* him in the head ....Mark 12:4
they *w* him also, and cast .....Luke 20:12
w their weak conscience.......1Cor 8:12
his heads as it were *w* to ......Rev 13:3
his deadly *w* was healed........Rev 13:3
had the *w* by a sword ....Rev 13:14

WOUND—*See* WINDING

WOVE, WOVEN—*See* WEAVING

WRAP—*to cover; enfold; embrace*

[*also* WRAPPED]

with a veil and *w* herself ......Gen 38:14
w in a cloth behind the 1Sam 21:9
that he *w* his face in his.......1Kin 19:13
mantle and *w* it together 2Kin 2:8
His roots are *w* about the .....Job 8:17
than that he can *w* himself ....Is 28:20
is *w* up for the slaughter .....Ezek 21:15
the weeds were *w* about my ...Jon 2:5
desire so they *w* it up ....Mic 7:3
w it in a clean linen cloth .....Matt 27:59
and *w* him in the linen ....Mark 15:46

w him in swaddling clothes . . . . Luke 2:7
it down, and *w* it in linen . . . . . Luke 23:53
but *w* together in a place . . . . . . John 20:7

WRAPPING—*clothes for the dead*
Lazarus attired in . . . . John 11:43, 44
Jesus lays His aside . . . . . . Luke 24:12

WRATH—*strong anger or indignation*

[*also* WRATHFUL, WRATHS, WROTH]
Cain was very *w* and his . . . . . . Gen 4:5
unto Cain, Why art thou *w*? . . . Gen 4:6
that his *w* was kindled . . . . Gen 39:19
Pharaoh was *w* against two . . . . Gen 40:2
Pharaoh was *w* with his . . . . Gen 41:10
Moses was *w* with them . . . . Ex 16:20
my *w* shall wax hot and I . . . . . Ex 22:24
my *w* may wax hot against . . . . Ex 32:10
thy *w* wax hot against thy . . . . . Ex 32:11
Turn from thy fierce *w* and . . . . Ex 32:12
w upon the congregation . . . . . . Num 1:53
And Moses was very *w* and . . . Num 16:15
w with all the congregation . . . . Num 16:22
no *w* any more upon the . . . . . . Num 18:5
w away from the children . . . . . Num 25:11
words, and was *w* and sware . . Deut 1:34
I feared the *w* of the enemy . . . Deut 32:27
he be very *w*, then be sure 1Sam 20:7
was Abner very *w* for the 2Sam 3:8
be that the king's *w* arise 2Sam 11:20
shook, because he was *w* 2Sam 22:8
man of God was *w* with him . . 2Kin 13:19
fell *w* for it against Israel 1Chr 27:24
Asa was *w* with the seer 2Chr 16:10
of your fathers was *w* with 2Chr 28:9
builded the wall, he was *w* . . . . Neh 4:1
then they were very *w* . . . . Neh 4:7
too much contempt and *w* . . . . . . Esth 1:18
w of king Ahasuerus was . . . . . . Esth 2:1
his *w* went into the palace . . . . . Esth 7:7
kindled the *w* of Elihu the . . . . Job 32:2
against Job was his *w* . . . . Job 32:2
friends was his *w* kindled . . . . . . Job 32:3
hypocrites in heart heap up *w* . Job 36:13
abroad the rage of thy *w* . . . . . . Job 40:11
from anger, and forsake *w* . . . . Ps 37:8
me and in *w* they hate me . . . . Ps 55:3
both living and in his *w* . . . . Ps 58:9
w of man shall praise thee . . . . Ps 76:10
of *w* shalt thou restrain . . . . Ps 76:10
w was kindled against us . . . . . . Ps 124:3
the *w* of mine enemies . . . . Ps 138:7
profit not in the day of *w* . . . . . Prov 11:4
fool's *w* is presently known . . . . Prov 12:16
He that is slow to *w* is of . . . . . Prov 14:29
A *w* man stirreth up strife . . . . . Prov 15:18
The *w* of a king is as . . . . Prov 16:14
kings *w* is as the roaring . . . . . . Prov 19:12
reward in the bosom strong *w* . Prov 21:14
a fool's *w* is heavier than . . . . . . Prov 27:3
but wise men turn away *w* . . . . Prov 29:8
forcing of *w* bringeth forth . . . . Prov 30:33
he hath much sorrow and *w* . . . Eccl 5:17
and his pride, and his *w* . . . . Is 16:6
princes were *w* with Jeremiah . Jer 37:15
I know his *w*, saith the Lord . . Jer 48:30
and he kept his *w* for ever . . . . Amos 1:11
was exceeding *w* and sent . . . . . Matt 2:16
king heard thereof, he was *w* . . Matt 22:7
things were filled with *w* . . . . . . Luke 4:28
rather give place unto *w* . . . . . . Rom 12:19
to execute *w* upon him that . . . Rom 13:4
be subject not only for *w* . . . . . Rom 13:5
debates, envyings, *w*, strifes . . . 2Cor 12:20
by nature the children of *w* . . . . Eph 2:3
sun go down upon your *w* . . . . . Eph 4:26
w, and anger, and clamor . . . . . Eph 4:31
not your children to *w* . . . . Eph 6:4
anger, *w*, malice, blasphemy . . . Col 3:8
without *w* and doubting 1Tim 2:8
So I sware in my *w*, They . . . . . Heb 3:11
As I have sworn in my *w* . . . . . Heb 4:3
fearing the *w* of the king . . . . . . Heb 11:27
slow to speak, slow to *w* . . . . . . James 1:19
For the *w* of man worketh . . . . James 1:20
angry and thy *w* is come . . . . . . Rev 11:18
having great *w* because he . . . . . Rev 12:12
dragon was *w* with the woman . Rev 12:17
of the *w* of her fornication . . . . Rev 14:8
of the *w* of her fornication . . . . Rev 18:3

WRATH OF GOD—*God's strong anger directed against sin*

Described as:
Anger . . . . Num 32:10-13
Fury . . . . Ps 90:9
Great . . . . Zech 7:12
Willing . . . . Rom 9:22
Revealed . . . . Rom 1:18
Stored up . . . . Rom 2:5-8
Abiding . . . . John 3:36
Accomplished . . . . Rev 6:16, 17

Caused by:
Apostasy 2Chr 34:24, 25
Sympathy with evil . . . . . . Lev 10:1-6
Unfaithfulness . . . . Josh 22:20
Provocations 2Kin 23:26
Fellowship with evil 2Chr 19:2
Mockery 2Chr 36:16
Idolatry . . . . Ps 78:58, 59
Intermarriage . . . . Ezra 10:10-14
Profaning the Sabbath . . . Neh 13:18
Speaking against God . . . . Ps 78:19-21

Effects of, seen in:
Egypt's destruction . . . . . . Ex 15:4, 7
Great plague . . . . Num 11:33
Israel's wanderings . . . . . . Num 32:10-13
Withholding of rain . . . . . . Deut 11:17
Destruction of a people . . 1Sam 28:18
Trouble . . . . Ps 90:7
Man's death . . . . Ps 90:9
Jerusalem's destruction . . . Luke 21:23, 24
Punishments of hell . . . . . . Rev 14:10
Final judgments . . . . Rev 19:15
Israel's captivity 2Chr 36:16, 17

Deliverance from, by:
Atonement . . . . Num 16:46
Keeping an oath . . . . Josh 9:19, 20
Humbling oneself 2Chr 32:26
Intercession . . . . Ps 106:23
Christ . . . . Rom 5:8, 9
God's appointment 1Thess 5:9

[*also* WRATH, WRATHFUL, WROTH]
the Lord was *w* with me for . . . Deut 3:26
the Lord thy God to *w* . . . . Deut 9:7
ye provoked the Lord to *w* . . . . Deut 9:8
Lord was *w* against you to . . . . Deut 9:19
ye provoked the Lord to *w* . . . . Deut 9:22
in his anger and in his *w* . . . . . Deut 29:23
w, and in great indignation . . . . Deut 29:28
he will be *w* with the whole . . . Josh 22:18
w shall not be poured out 2Chr 12:7
and so *w* come upon you, and . 2Chr 19:10
fierce *w* of the Lord is upon . . . 2Chr 28:11
w of the Lord was upon 2Chr 29:8
of his *w* may turn away 2Chr 30:8
there was *w* upon him 2Chr 32:25
the God of heaven unto *w* . . . . Ezra 5:12
his power and his *w* is . . . . Ezra 8:22
me secret, until thy *w* be . . . . . . Job 14:13
hath also kindled his *w* . . . . Job 19:11
the fury of his *w* upon him . . . . Job 20:23
of the *w* of the Almighty . . . . . . Job 21:20
he speak unto them in his *w* . . . Ps 2:5
shaken, because he was *w* . . . . . Ps 18:7
swallow them up in his *w* . . . . . Ps 21:9
rebuke me not in thy *w* . . . . Ps 38:1
Consume them in *w* . . . . Ps 59:13
w anger take hold of them . . . . Ps 69:24
w of God came upon them . . . . Ps 78:31
fierceness of his anger, *w* . . . . . Ps 78:49
w with his inheritance . . . . Ps 78:62
Pour out thy *w* upon the . . . . . . Ps 79:6
hast taken away all thy *w* . . . . . Ps 85:3
Thy *w* lieth hard upon me . . . . . Ps 88:7
been *w* with thine anointed . . . . Ps 89:38
shall thy *w* burn like fire? . . . . . Ps 89:46
Unto whom I sware in my *w* . . Ps 95:11
thine indignation and thy *w* . . . Ps 102:10
kings in the day of his *w* . . . . . . Ps 110:5
turn away his *w* from him . . . . . Prov 24:18
Through the *w* of the Lord . . . . Is 9:19
against the people of my *w* . . . . Is 10:6
both with *w* and fierce anger . . Is 13:9
who smote the people in *w* . . . . Is 14:6
shall be *w* as in the valley . . . . . Is 28:21
In a little *w* I hid my face . . . . . Is 54:8
I would not be *w* with thee . . . . . Is 54:9
his covetousness was I *w* . . . . . . Is 57:17
I hid me, and was *w*, and . . . . . Is 57:17
in my *w* I smote thee, but . . . . . Is 60:10
Be not *w* very sore, O Lord . . . Is 64:9
the generation of his *w* . . . . Jer 7:29
w the earth shall tremble . . . . . . Jer 10:10
turn away thy *w* from them . . . Jer 18:20
and in fury and in great *w* . . . . Jer 21:5
in my fury, and in great *w* . . . . Jer 32:37
me unto *w* with the works . . . . . Jer 44:8
Because of the *w* of the Lord . . Jer 50:13
in his *w* the strongholds . . . . Lam 2:2
thou art very *w* against us . . . . . Lam 5:22
w is upon all the multitude . . . . Ezek 7:12
accomplish my *w* upon the . . . . Ezek 13:15
you in the fire of my *w* . . . . Ezek 22:21
in the fire of my *w* have I . . . . . Ezek 38:19
I will pour out my *w* upon . . . . Hos 5:10
and he reserveth *w* for his . . . . . Nah 1:2
in *w* remember mercy . . . . Hab 3:2
day is a day of *w*, a day of . . . . Zeph 1:15
fathers provoked me to *w* . . . . . Zech 8:14
to flee from the *w* to come? . . . Matt 3:7
to flee from the *w* to come? . . . Luke 3:7
Because the law worketh *w* . . . . Rom 4:15
things cometh the *w* of God . . . Eph 5:6
things' sake the *w* of God . . . . . Col 3:6
delivered us from the *w* to 1Thess 1:10
for the *w* is come upon them . . 1Thess 2:16
winepress of the *w* of God . . . . Rev 14:19
is filled up the *w* of God . . . . . . Rev 15:1
vials full of the *w* of God . . . . . Rev 15:7
the vials of the *w* of God . . . . . Rev 16:1
of the fierceness of his *w* . . . . . . Rev 16:19

WREATH—*something intertwined into a circular shape*

[*also* WREATHED, WREATHEN, WREATHS]
of *w* work shalt thou make . . . . Ex 28:14
fasten the *w* chains to the . . . . . Ex 28:14
shalt put the two *w* chains . . . . . Ex 28:24
the ends, of *w* work of pure . . . Ex 39:15
two *w* chains they fastened . . . . Ex 39:18
w of chain work, for the 1Kin 7:17
w work, and pomegranates 2Kin 25:17
had the second pillar with *w* . . 2Kin 25:17
w to cover the two pommels . . . 2Chr 4:12
of pomegranates on each *w* 2Chr 4:13
are *w*, and come up upon . . . . . Lam 1:14

WREST—*to pervert; twist; distort*
after many to *w* judgment . . . . . Ex 23:2
Thou shalt not *w* judgment . . . . Deut 16:19
Every day they *w* my words . . . Ps 56:5
unlearned and unstable *w* 2Pet 3:16

WRESTLING—*to contend with an opponent by grappling*
Sisters . . . . Gen 30:8
Jacob . . . . Gen 32:24-30
Christians . . . . Eph 6:12

WRETCHED—*distressed; miserable*

[*also* WRETCHEDNESS]
and let me not see my *w* . . . . . . Num 11:15
O *w* man that I am! who . . . . . . Rom 7:24
knowest not that thou art *w* . . . Rev 3:17

WRING—*to squeeze or twist*

[*also* WRINGED, WRINGING, WRUNG]
w off his head and burn it . . . . . Lev 1:15
blood thereof shall be *w* . . . . . . Lev 1:15
and *w* off his head from his . . . Lev 5:8
w the dew out of the fleece . . . Judg 6:38
full cup are *w* out to them . . . . Ps 73:10
of the earth shall *w* them . . . . . Ps 75:8

the *w* of the nose bringeth ....Prov 30:33
cup of trembling and *w* them ..Is 51:17

WRINKLE—*a crease*

[*also* WRINKLES]
thou hast filled me with *w*.....Job 16:8
or *w*, or any such thing ....Eph 5:27

WRITE—*to form characters or words with a pen, pencil or other device; compose*

Purposes of, to:
Record God's Word .....Ex 24:4, 12
Record history ....Luke 1:3
Record dictation.........Jer 36:2, 27, 28
Make legal...............Deut 24:1-4
Issue orders.............Esth 8:5, 8, 10
Insure a covenant ....Neh 9:38
Indicate name ....Luke 1:63
Indicate the saved ....Rev 20:15
Establish inspiration .....Rev 22:18, 19

Unusual:
By God's finger ....Ex 31:18
Destroyed and restored ..Jer 36:21-32
On a wall...............Dan 5:5-29
On the sand ....John 8:6, 8
On the cross ....John 19:19-22
In hearts................Rom 2:15

Of the Bible as written, involving its:
Authority ....Acts 24:14
Determination of events .Heb 10:7
Fulfillment ....Luke 21:22
Messianic character ......Luke 24:44, 46
Saving purpose ....John 20:31
Harmony ....Acts 15:15
Spiritual aim ....Rom 15:4
Finality ....Rev 22:18, 19

Figurative of:
God's real people ....Rev 20:12, 15
Indelible character 2Cor 3:2, 3
Innate knowledge ....Rom 2:15

[*also* WRITEST, WRITETH, WRITING, WRITINGS, WRITTEN, WROTE]
W this for a memorial in a ....Ex 17:14
were *w* on both their sides ....Ex 32:15
on the other were they *w* .....Ex 32:15
the *w* was the *w* of God.......Ex 32:16
unto Moses, *W* thou these.....Ex 34:27
he *w* upon the tables the ......Ex 34:28
pure gold, and *w* upon it......Ex 39:30
priest shall *w* these curses .....Num 5:23
were of them that were *w* ......Num 11:26
w Aaron's name upon the rod .Num 17:3
And Moses *w* their goings out .Num 33:2
w them upon two tables of ....Deut 4:13
thou shalt *w* them upon the ...Deut 6:9
w with the finger of God......Deut 9:10
was *w* according to all the.....Deut 9:10
he *w* on the tables, according..Deut 10:4
according to the first *w* ....Deut 10:4
shalt *w* them upon the door ...Deut 11:20
he shall *w* him a copy of ......Deut 17:18
w upon them all the words .....Deut 27:3
is not *w* in the book of this ...Deut 28:61
covenant that are *w* in this ....Deut 29:21
statutes which are *w* in this....Deut 30:10
w ye this song for you ....Deut 31:19
Moses therefore *w* this song ...Deut 31:22
according to all that is *w* ......Josh 1:8
he *w* there upon the stones....Josh 8:32
is *w* in the book of the law....Josh 8:34
is *w* in the book of the law....Josh 23:6
w these words in the book ....Josh 24:26
and *w* it in a book, and laid ...1Sam 10:25
David *w* a letter to Joab, and .2Sam 11:14
it is *w* in the law of Moses 1Kin 2:3
w in the book of the acts of ...1Kin 11:41
w in the book of the chronicles.1Kin 14:19
So she *w* letters in Ahab's......1Kin 21:8
w in the book of the chronicles.1Kin 22:39
not *w* in the book of the 2Kin 1:18
Jehu *w* letters, and sent to 2Kin 10:1
not *w* in the book of the.......2Kin 12:19
is *w* in the book of the law....2Kin 14:6
not *w* in the book of the 2Kin 16:19
commandment, which he *w*....2Kin 17:37
not *w* in the book of the 2Kin 20:20
which is *w* concerning us 2Kin 22:13
w in the book of this 2Kin 23:21
not *w* in the book of the 2Kin 23:28
w by name came in the days ..1Chr 4:41
is *w* in the law of the Lord 1Chr 16:40
w them before the king 1Chr 24:6
made me understand in *w* 1Chr 28:19
king of Tyre answered in *w* ...2Chr 2:11
w in the book of Nathan 2Chr 9:29
w in the story of the prophet ..2Chr 13:22
are *w* in the book of Jehu 2Chr 20:34
w in the story of the book 2Chr 24:27
w in the book of the kings 2Chr 25:26
prophet, the son of Amoz, *w* ..2Chr 26:22
w in the book of the kings 2Chr 28:26
w letters also to Ephraim 2Chr 30:1
otherwise than it was *w* 2Chr 30:18
w also letters to rail on the....2Chr 32:17
they are *w* in the vision of 2Chr 32:32
w among the sayings of the....2Chr 33:19
the curses that are *w* in the ...2Chr 34:24
w of David king of Israel 2Chr 35:4
to the *w* of Solomon his son...2Chr 35:4
is *w* in the book of Moses.....2Chr 35:12
w in the law of the Lord 2Chr 35:26
w in the book of the kings 2Chr 36:8
kingdom, and put it also in *w*. .Ezra 1:1
is *w* in the law of Moses ......Ezra 3:2
w they unto him an accusation .Ezra 4:6
was *w* in the Syrian tongue ....Ezra 4:7
Shimshai the scribe *w* a letter..Ezra 4:8
we might *w* the names of the ..Ezra 5:10
and therein was a record..*w* ...Ezra 6:2
weight was *w* at that time .....Ezra 8:34
wherein was *w*, It is reported ..Neh 6:6
w in the law which the Lord...Neh 8:14
Lord our God, as it is *w* in....Neh 10:34
w in the book of the..........Neh 12:23
w among the laws of the ......Esth 1:19
province according to the *w* ...Esth 1:22
it be *w* that they may be ......Esth 3:9
w according to all that ....Esth 3:12
king Ahasuerus was it *w* ......Esth 3:12
the *w* for a commandment ......Esth 3:14
copy of the *w* of the decree ...Esth 4:8
found *w*, that Mordecai had ...Esth 6:2
province according to the *w* ...Esth 8:9
Jews according to their *w* ......Esth 8:9
Mordecai *w* these things ....Esth 9:20
Mordecai had *w* unto them ....Esth 9:23
days according to their *w*......Esth 9:27
Mordecai..*w* with all authority .Esth 9:29
not *w* in the book of the ......Esth 10:2
w bitter things against me .....Job 13:26
that my words were now *w* ....Job 19:23
volume of the book it is *w* ....Ps 40:7
when he *w* up the people .....Ps 87:6
be *w* for the generation to ....Ps 102:18
upon them the judgment *w* ....Ps 149:9
w them upon the table of .....Prov 3:3
not I *w* to thee excellent ......Prov 22:20
which was *w* was upright ......Eccl 12:10
that is *w* among the living .....Is 4:3
w in it with a man's pen ......Is 8:1
be few that a child may *w* .....Is 10:19
w of Hezekiah king of Judah ..Is 38:9
Judah is *w* with a pen of ......Jer 17:1
W ye this man childless, a .....Jer 22:30
all that is *w* in this book ......Jer 25:13
and *w* it in their hearts........Jer 31:33
w therein all the words.........Jer 36:2
w from the mouth of ....Jer 36:4
he had *w* these words in a ....Jer 45:1
Jeremiah *w* in a book all ......Jer 51:60
that are *w* against Babylon ....Jer 51:60
was *w* within and without .....Ezek 2:10
was *w* therein lamentations ....Ezek 2:10
neither shall they be *w* in .....Ezek 13:9
w of the house of Israel.......Ezek 13:9
one stick, and *w* upon it ......Ezek 37:16
take another stick, and *w* .....Ezek 37:16
sticks whereon thou *w* shall ...Ezek 37:20
the decree, and sign the *w* ....Dan 6:8
Daniel knew that the *w* was ...Dan 6:10
Darius *w* unto all people ......Dan 6:25
he *w* the dream, and told .....Dan 7:1
is *w* in the law of Moses ......Dan 9:11
shall be found *w* in the book ..Dan 12:1
w to him the great things .....Hos 8:12
W the vision, and make it......Hab 2:2
book of remembrance was *w* ..Mal 3:16
thus it is *w* by the prophet ...Matt 2:5
w, He shall give his angels ....Matt 4:6
w, Thou shalt worship the.....Matt 4:10
give her a *w* of divorcement ...Matt 5:31
this is he, of whom it is *w*.....Matt 11:10
Son of man goeth as it is *w* ...Matt 26:24
his head his accusation *w*......Matt 27:37
As it is *w* in the prophets .....Mark 1:2
how it is *w* of the Son of......Mark 9:12
to *w* a bill of divorcement.....Mark 10:4
heart he *w* you this precept ...Mark 10:5
it not *w*, My house shall be ...Mark 11:17
Master, Moses *w* unto us......Mark 12:19
w, I will smite the shepherd ...Mark 14:27
is *w* in the law of the Lord ....Luke 2:23
It is *w*, That man shall not ....Luke 4:4
it is *w*, He shall give his ......Luke 4:10
This is he, of whom it is *w* ....Luke 7:27
What is *w* in the law? how ....Luke 10:26
and sit down quickly, and *w* ...Luke 16:6
w, My house is the house .....Luke 19:46
Moses *w* unto us, If any ......Luke 20:28
that is *w* must yet be ....Luke 22:37
a superscription also was *w*....Luke 23:38
law, and the prophets, did *w* ..John 1:45
remembered that it was *w*.....John 2:17
have believed me: for he *w*.....John 5:46
if ye believe not his *w*, how ...John 5:47
It is *w* in the prophets, And ...John 6:45
Is it not *w* in your law, I ......John 10:34
these things were *w* of him ....John 12:16
be fulfilled that is *w* in ....John 15:25
are not *w* in this book ....John 20:30
things, and *w* these things .....John 21:24
if they should be *w* every ......John 21:25
is *w* in the book of Psalms ....Acts 1:20
had fulfilled all that was *w* ....Acts 13:29
of the prophets; as it is *w* ....Acts 15:15
But that we *w* unto them ......Acts 15:20
w letters by them after this ....Acts 15:23
the brethren *w*, exhorting ......Acts 18:27
for it is *w*, Thou shalt not .....Acts 23:5
he *w* a letter after this ....Acts 23:25
I have no certain thing to *w* ...Acts 25:26
I might have somewhat to *w*...Acts 25:26
is *w*, The just shall live by ....Rom 1:17
through you, as it is *w* ....Rom 2:24
w, There is none righteous ....Rom 3:10
It was not *w* for his sake ......Rom 4:23
As it is *w*, Jacob have I loved .Rom 9:13
it is *w*, How beautiful are .....Rom 10:15
as it is *w*, There shall come ...Rom 11:26
For it is *w*, As I live, saith ....Rom 14:11
is *w*, For this cause I will .....Rom 15:9
as it is *w*, To whom he was ...Rom 15:21
Tertius, who *w* this epistle ....Rom 16:22
it is *w*, I will destroy the 1Cor 1:19
it is *w*, Eye hath not seen 1Cor 2:9
men above that which is *w* 1Cor 4:6
I *w* not these things to 1Cor 4:14
I *w* unto you in an epistle 1Cor 5:9
it is *w* in the law of Moses 1Cor 9:9
have I *w* these things 1Cor 9:15
are *w* for our admonition 1Cor 10:11
is *w*, The first man Adam was .1Cor 15:45
we *w* none other things 2Cor 1:13
And I *w* this same unto you ...2Cor 2:3
w and engraven in stones 2Cor 3:7
I *w* unto you, I did it not 2Cor 7:12
is *w*, He that had gathered 2Cor 8:15
is superfluous for me to *w*.....2Cor 9:1
I *w* these things being absent ..2Cor 13:10
things which I *w* unto you.....Gal 1:20
it is *w*, Cursed is every one ...Gal 3:10
which are *w* in the book of....Gal 3:10
w, that Abraham had two .....Gal 4:22

large a letter I have *w* unto ...Gal 6:11
as I *w* afore in few words .....Eph 3:3
w the same things to you ......Phil 3:1
need not that I *w* unto you 1Thess 4:9
in every epistle; so I *w*........2Thess 3:17
These things *w* I unto thee 1Tim 3:14
I Paul have *w* it with mine ....Philem 19
in thy obedience I *w* unto .....Philem 21
which are *w* in heaven ....Heb 12:23
w a letter unto you in few.....Heb 13:22
Because it is *w*, Be ye holy....1Pet 1:16
I have *w* briefly, exhorting 1Pet 5:12
beloved, I now *w* unto you 2Pet 3:1
unto him hath *w* unto you.....2Pet 3:15
these things *w* we unto you....1John 1:4
I *w* no new commandment 1John 2:7
I *w* unto you, little children ...1John 2:12
I *w* unto you, fathers 1John 2:13
I *w* unto you, young men 1John 2:13
I *w* unto you, little children 1John 2:13
I have *w* unto you, fathers 1John 2:14
I have not *w* unto you because.1John 2:21
These things I have *w*.........1John 2:26
These things have I *w*.........1John 5:13
I *w* a new commandment 2John 5
many things to *w* unto you 2John 12
I would not *w* with paper 2John 12
I *w* unto the church: but 3John 9
things to *w*, but I will.........3John 13
not with ink and pen *w* 3John 13
w unto you of the common ....Jude 3
those things which are *w* ......Rev 1:3
thou seest, *w* in a book ....Rev 1:11
of the church of Ephesus *w* ...Rev 2:1
the church in Pergamos *w* .....Rev 2:12
in the stone a new name *w* ....Rev 2:17
of the church in Sardis *w* ......Rev 3:1
w upon him the name of my ..Rev 3:12
w upon him my new name .....Rev 3:12
book *w* within and on the .....Rev 5:1
voices, I was about to *w* ......Rev 10:4
thunders uttered, and *w* ....Rev 10:4
not *w* in the book of life ......Rev 13:8
Father's name *w* in their ......Rev 14:1
not *w* in the book of life ......Rev 17:8
W, Blessed are they which ....Rev 19:9
and on his thigh a name *w* ....Rev 19:16
and names *w* thereon ....Rev 21:12
are *w* in the Lamb's book .....Rev 21:27

WRITER—*a scribe*

[*also* WRITER'S]
handle the pen of the *w*.......Judg 5:14
is a pen of a ready *w* ....Ps 45:1
a *w* inkhorn by his side ....Ezek 9:2

WRONG—*to injure; incorrect; to injure*

[*also* WRONGED, WRONGETH, WRONGFULLY]
Abram, My *w* be upon thee ...Gen 16:5
said to him that did the *w*.....Ex 2:13
against him that which is *w*....Deut 19:16
doest me *w* to war against.....Judg 11:27
there is no *w* in mine hands ...1Chr 12:17
I cry out of *w*, but I am ......Job 19:7
ye *w* imagine against me ......Job 21:27
enemies *w* rejoice over me ....Ps 35:19
being mine enemies *w*, are ....Ps 69:4
suffered no man to do them *w* .Ps 105:14
against me *w* his own soul.....Prov 8:36
and do no *w*, do no violence ..Jer 22:3
Lord, thou hast seen my *w* ....Lam 3:59
oppressed the stranger *w* ......Ezek 22:29
w judgment proceedeth ....Hab 1:4
I do thee no *w*: didst not ......Matt 20:13
seeing one of them suffer *w* ...Acts 7:24
he that did his neighbor *w* ....Acts 7:27
the Jews have I done no *w* ....Acts 25:10
do ye not rather take *w*? 1Cor 6:7
have *w* no man, we have 2Cor 7:2
cause that had done the *w* 2Cor 7:12
his cause that suffered *w* 2Cor 7:12
But he that doeth *w* shall .....Col 3:25
If he hath *w* thee, or oweth ...Philem 18
endure grief, suffering *w* 1Pet 2:19

WROTE—*See* WRITE

WROTH—*See* WRATH

WROUGHT—*worked*

[*also* WROUGHTEST]
he had *w* folly in Israel ....Gen 34:7
things I have *w* in Egypt ......Ex 10:2
w Bezaleel and Aholiab ....Ex 36:1
w the work of the tabernacle ..Ex 36:8
they have *w* confusion ....Lev 20:12
of Israel, What hath God *w* ...Num 23:23
abomination is *w* among ......Deut 13:14
w wickedness in the sight .....Deut 17:2
which hath not been *w* with ...Deut 21:3
which they shall have *w* ....Deut 31:18
he hath *w* folly in Israel.......Josh 7:15
that they have *w* in Israel .....Judg 20:10
today? and where *w* thou? ....Ruth 2:19
law with whom she had *w*.....Ruth 2:19
whom I *w* today is Boaz ......Ruth 2:19
w wonderfully among them 1Sam 6:6
w this great salvation in 1Sam 14:45
hath *w* with God this day 1Sam 14:45
I should have *w* falsehood 2Sam 18:13
Lord *w* a great victory 2Sam 23:12
over the people that *w* in 1Kin 5:16
w like the brim of a cup 1Kin 7:26
his treason that he *w*, are 1Kin 16:20
he *w* evil in the sight of the ...2Kin 3:2
w wicked things to provoke ...2Kin 17:11
of them that *w* fine linen......1Chr 4:21
linen, and *w* cherubim 2Chr 3:14
as *w* iron and brass to mend...2Chr 24:12
w that which was good and 2Chr 31:20
that *w* in the house of 2Chr 34:10
half of my servants *w* in the ...Neh 4:16
this work was *w* of our God ...Neh 6:16
they *w* great provocations .....Neh 9:26
the hand of the Lord hath *w* ..Job 12:9
thou hast *w* for them that .....Ps 31:19
that which thou hast *w* for ....Ps 68:28
curiously *w* in the lowest ......Ps 139:15
works that my hands had *w* ...Eccl 2:11
hast *w* all our works in us .....Is 26:12
Who hath *w* and done it ......Is 41:4
she hath *w* lewdness with .....Jer 11:15
w for my name's sake ....Ezek 20:9
because they *w* for me ....Ezek 29:20
high God hath *w* toward me ...Dan 4:2
unto us, for the sea *w*, and....Jon 1:11
which have *w* his judgment ....Zeph 2:3
last have *w* but one hour ......Matt 20:12
works are *w* by his hands .....Mark 6:2
she hath *w* a good work on ...Mark 14:6
and wonders *w* among the.....Acts 5:12
God had *w* among the Gentiles.Acts 15:12
God had *w* among the Gentiles.Acts 21:19
w in me all manner of ....Rom 7:8
hath *w* us for the selfsame 2Cor 5:5
signs of an apostle were *w* 2Cor 12:12
For he that *w* effectually in....Gal 2:8
Which he *w* in Christ, when ...Eph 1:20
w with labor and travail........2Thess 3:8
w righteousness, obtained .....Heb 11:33
how faith *w* with his works ....James 2:22
w the will of the Gentiles 1Pet 4:3
things which we have *w* 2John 8
the false prophet that *w*.......Rev 19:20

WRUNG—*See* WRING

Y

YARN—*thread used in weaving*

out of Egypt, and linen *y* 1Kin 10:28
received the linen *y* at a 1Kin 10:28
out of Egypt, and linen *y* 2Chr 1:16
received the linen *y* at a 2Chr 1:16

YE—*See* INTRODUCTION

YEA—*See* INTRODUCTION

YEAR—*365 ¼ solar days; era; period of time*

[*also* YEARLY, YEAR'S, YEARS, YEARS']
six hundredth *y* of Noah's .....Gen 7:11
thirteenth *y* they rebelled .....Gen 14:4
him that is a hundred *y* old ...Gen 17:17
that is ninety *y* old bear?......Gen 17:17
this set time in the next *y* .....Gen 17:21
with him yet seven other *y* ....Gen 29:30
for all their cattle for that *y* ...Gen 47:17
When that *y* was ended, they ..Gen 47:18
came unto him the second *y* ...Gen 47:18
be the first month of the *y* ....Ex 12:2
in his season from *y* to *y* .....Ex 13:10
a feast unto me in the *y*.......Ex 23:14
times in the *y* all thy males....Ex 23:17
two lambs of the first *y* day ...Ex 29:38
the horns of it once in a *y* ....Ex 30:10
once in the *y* shall he make ...Ex 30:10
of ingathering at the *y* ....Ex 34:22
Lord thy God thrice in the *y* ..Ex 34:24
a lamb, both of the first *y*.....Lev 9:3
one ewe lamb of the first *y*....Lev 14:10
in the fourth *y* all the fruit ....Lev 19:24
blemish of the first *y*..........Lev 23:12
two lambs of the first *y* for ....Lev 23:19
the seventh *y* shall be a ....Lev 25:4
shall hallow the fiftieth *y* ....Lev 25:10
y of this jubilee ye shall.......Lev 25:13
upon you in the sixth *y* ....Lev 25:21
old fruit until the ninth *y*......Lev 25:22
a whole *y* after it is sold ....Lev 25:29
a full *y* may he redeem it .....Lev 25:29
within the space of a full *y* ....Lev 25:30
serve thee unto the *y* of.......Lev 25:40
that bought him from the *y*....Lev 25:50
him unto the *y* of jubilee ......Lev 25:50
as a *y* hired servant shall he ...Lev 25:53
go out in the *y* of jubilee .....Lev 25:54
unto the *y* of the jubilee ......Lev 27:18
the *y* of the jubilee the field...Lev 27:24
in the second *y* after they .....Num 1:1
one he lamb of the first *y* .....Num 6:14
one ewe lamb of the first *y*....Num 6:14
five lambs of the first *y* ....Num 7:17
five lambs of the first *y* ....Num 7:23
five lambs of the first *y* ....Num 7:29
five lambs of the first *y* ....Num 7:35
five lambs of the first *y* ....Num 7:41
five lambs of the first *y* ....Num 7:47
five lambs of the first *y* ....Num 7:53
five lambs of the first *y* ....Num 7:59
five lambs of the first *y* ....Num 7:65
five lambs of the first *y* ....Num 7:71
five lambs of the first *y* ....Num 7:77
five lambs of the first *y* ....Num 7:83
the lambs of the first *y* sixty ...Num 7:88
or a *y*, that the cloud ....Num 9:22
each day for a *y*, shall ye .....Num 14:34
lambs of the first *y* without ....Num 28:3
lambs of the first *y* without ....Num 28:11
seven lambs of the first *y* .....Num 28:19
seven lambs of the first *y* .....Num 29:2
fourteen lambs of the first *y* ...Num 29:13
seven lambs of the first *y* .....Num 29:36
came to pass in the fortieth *y*..Deut 1:3
thy God led thee these forty *y* .Deut 8:2
from the beginning of the *y* ...Deut 11:12
even unto the end of the *y* ...Deut 11:12
of thine increase the same *y* ...Deut 14:28
seventh *y* thou shalt let him ...Deut 15:12
Three times in a *y* shall all ....Deut 16:16
of thine increase the third *y* ...Deut 26:12
which is the *y* of tithing ....Deut 26:12
of the land of Canaan that *y* ..Josh 5:12
y they vexed and oppressed ...Judg 10:8
of Israel went *y* to lament .....Judg 11:40
shekels of silver by the *y*......Judg 17:10
out of his city *y* to worship.....1Sam 1:3
And as he did so *y* by *y*.....1Sam 1:7
to offer the *y* sacrifice 1Sam 2:19
from *y* to *y* in circuit to 1Sam 7:16

Y

the Philistines was a full *y* 1Sam 27:7
after the *y* was expired, at 2Sam 11:1
every *y* end that he polled 2Sam 14:26
each man his month in a *y* 1Kin 4:7
and eightieth *y* after the 1Kin 6:1
fourth *y* of Solomon's reign ...1Kin 6:1
in the eleventh *y*, in the.......1Kin 6:38
came to Solomon in one *y* 1Kin 10:14
fifth *y* of king Rehoboam 1Kin 14:25
twentieth *y* of Jeroboam 1Kin 15:9
the third *y* of Asa king of 1Kin 15:28
twenty and seventh *y* of Asa ..1Kin 16:10
thirty and eighth *y* of Asa 1Kin 16:29
the return of the *y* the king ...1Kin 20:22
came to pass in the third *y* 1Kin 22:2
seventeenth *y* of Jehoshaphat ..1Kin 22:51
in the second *y* of Jehoram 2Kin 1:17
came to pass at the seven *y* ...2Kin 8:3
fifth *y* of Joram the son of 2Kin 8:16
reigned one *y* in Jerusalem 2Kin 8:26
the seventh *y* Jehoiada sent ...2Kin 11:4
three and twentieth *y* of 2Kin 12:6
and seventh *y* of Joash king ...2Kin 13:10
second *y* of Joash son of 2Kin 14:1
and seventh *y* of Jeroboam 2Kin 15:1
and thirtieth *y* of Uzziah 2Kin 15:13
fiftieth *y* of Azariah king of ...2Kin 15:23
twentieth *y* of Jotham the 2Kin 15:30
seventeeth *y* of Pekah the 2Kin 16:1
as he had done *y* by *y* 2Kin 17:4
in the third *y* of Hoshea 2Kin 18:1
fourth *y* of king Hezekiah 2Kin 18:9
was the seventh *y* of Hoshea ..2Kin 18:9
in the sixth *y* of Hezekiah 2Kin 18:10
the ninth *y* of Hoshea king 2Kin 18:10
this *y* such things as grow 2Kin 19:29
y that which springeth 2Kin 19:29
the third *y* sow ye, and reap...2Kin 19:29
in the eighteenth *y* of king 2Kin 23:23
in the ninth *y* of his reign 2Kin 25:1
is the nineteenth *y* of king 2Kin 25:8
thirtieth *y* of the capivity 2Kin 25:27
y that he began to reign.......2Kin 25:27
pass, that after the *y* was......1Chr 20:1
fortieth *y* of the reign of 1Chr 26:31
month, in the fourth *y* of his ..2Chr 3:2
came to Solomon in one *y* 2Chr 9:13
fifth *y* of king Rehoboam 2Chr 12:2
the fifteenth *y* of the reign 2Chr 15:10
and thirtieth *y* of the reign 2Chr 16:1
the one and fortieth *y* of his...2Chr 16:13
reigned one *y* in Jerusalem 2Chr 22:2
house of your God from *y* 2Chr 24:5
y a hundred talents of 2Chr 27:5
him, both the second *y*........2Chr 27:5
in the eighth *y* of his reign 2Chr 34:3
twelfth *y* he began to purge ...2Chr 34:3
eighteenth *y* of the reign of ...2Chr 35:19
the first *y* of Cyrus king of 2Chr 36:22
the first *y* of Cyrus king of ....Ezra 1:1
the second *y* of the reign......Ezra 4:24
In the first *y* of Cyrus the .....Ezra 6:3
the seventh *y* of Artaxerxes ...Ezra 7:7
Chisleu, in the twentieth *y* ....Neh 1:1
the twentieth *y* even unto .....Neh 5:14
thirtieth *y* of Artaxerxes ......Neh 5:14
ourselves *y* with the third .....Neh 10:32
at times appointed *y* by *y* .....Neh 10:34
and thirtieth *y* of Artaxerxes ..Neh 13:6
In the third *y* of his reign .....Esth 1:3
twelfth *y* of king Ahasuerus ...Esth 3:7
fifteenth day of the same, *y* ...Esth 9:21
unto the days of the *y* ....Job 3:6
crownest the *y* with thy ....Ps 65:11
For a thousand *y* in thy sight ..Ps 90:4
y that king Uzziah died I......Is 6:1
y that Tartan came unto ......Is 20:1
add ye *y* to *y*; let them kill ....Is 29:1
the fourteenth *y* of king.......Is 36:1
eat this *y* such as groweth .....Is 37:30
the second *y* that which ....Is 37:30
the third *y* sow ye, and reap...Is 37:30
y of my redeemed is come ....Is 63:4
thirteenth *y* of his reign ....Jer 1:2
the *y* of their visitation........Jer 11:23
the *y* of their visitation........Jer 23:12
fourth *y* of Jehoiakim the .....Jer 25:1
first *y* of Nebuchadrezzar......Jer 25:1
thirteenth *y* of Josiah the......Jer 25:3
came to pass the same *y* ......Jer 28:1
fourth *y*, and in the fifth ......Jer 28:1
prophet died the same *y* ....Jer 28:17
tenth *y* of Zedekiah king of ...Jer 32:1
eighteenth *y* of Nebuchadrezzar.Jer 32:1
in the fifth *y* of Jehoiakim.....Jer 36:9
the eleventh *y* of Zedekiah ....Jer 39:2
the fourth *y* of Jehoiakim .....Jer 46:2
shall both come one *y* ....Jer 51:46
in another *y* shall come a .....Jer 51:46
in the fourth *y* of his reign ....Jer 51:59
eleventh *y* of king Zedekiah ...Jer 52:5
seventh *y* three thousand ......Jer 52:28
twentieth *y* of Nebuchadrezzar .Jer 52:30
thirtieth *y* of the captivity .....Jer 52:31
first *y* of his reign lifted up ....Jer 52:31
to pass in the thirtieth *y*.......Ezek 1:1
thee each day for a *y* ....Ezek 4:6
to pass in the seventh *y* ....Ezek 20:1
to pass in the eleventh *y* ......Ezek 26:1
to pass in the eleventh *y* ......Ezek 30:20
to pass in the twelfth *y*........Ezek 32:1
twelfth *y* of our captivity ......Ezek 33:21
twentieth *y* of our captivity ....Ezek 40:1
in the beginning of the *y*, in ...Ezek 40:1
fourteenth *y* after that the .....Ezek 40:1
be his to the *y* of liberty ......Ezek 46:17
y of the reign of Jehoiakim....Dan 1:1
the second *y* of the reign of ...Dan 2:1
third *y* of the reign of king ....Dan 8:1
first *y* of his reign I Daniel ....Dan 9:2
first *y* of Darius the Mede .....Dan 11:1
with calves of a *y* old? ....Mic 6:6
second *y* of Darius the king ...Hag 1:1
in the second *y* of Darius .....Hag 2:10
in the second *y* of Darius .....Zech 1:1
even go up from *y* to *y* to .....Zech 14:16
went to Jerusalem every *y*.....Luke 2:41
began to be about thirty *y*.....Luke 3:23
acceptable *y* of the Lord ......Luke 4:19
the high priest that same *y* ....John 11:49
the high priest that same *y* ....John 18:13
in the wilderness forty *y* ......Acts 7:36
a whole *y* they assembled .....Acts 11:26
also to be forward a *y* ago 2Cor 8:10
priest alone once every *y*......Heb 9:7
offered *y* by *y* continually .....Heb 10:1
continue there a *y*, and buy ...James 4:13
day, and a month, and a *y* ....Rev 9:15

YEARN—*to long for*

[*also* YEARNED]
bowels did *y* upon his brother .Gen 43:30
her bowels *y* upon her son 1Kin 3:26

YEARS, THOUSAND
In God's sight, one day ..2Pet 3:8
Time of Satan's bondage .Rev 20:2-7

YELL—*to cry loudly; roar*

[*also* YELLED]
lions roared upon him, and *y* ..Jer 2:15
shall *y* as lions' whelps ....Jer 51:38

YELLOW—*sallow; the color of dandelions*
there be in it a *y* thin hair ....Lev 13:30
and there be in it no *y* hair ...Lev 13:32
the priest shall not seek for *y*..Lev 13:36
and her feathers with *y* gold...Ps 68:13

YES—*an expression of agreement*
He saith, *Y*, And when he was .Matt 17:25
said unto him *Y*, Lord ....Mark 7:28
Gentiles? *Y*, of the Gentiles ...Rom 3:29
Y, verily, their sound went into.Rom 10:18

YESTERDAY—*the last day past; a short time ago*
task in making brick both *y* ...Ex 5:14
meat, neither *y*, nor today? ...1Sam 20:27
Whereas thou camest but *y*....2Sam 15:20
seen *y* the blood of Naboth ...2Kin 9:26
For we are but of *y*; and ......Job 8:9
in thy sight are but as *y* ....Ps 90:4
Y at the seventh hour the .....John 4:52
thou didst the Egyptian *y*? ....Acts 7:28
Jesus Christ the same *y*, and ..Heb 13:8

YESTERNIGHT—*last night*
I lay *y* with my father.........Gen 19:34
hands, and rebuked thee *y* ....Gen 31:42

YET—*See* INTRODUCTION

YIELD—*to produce; surrender*

Used literally of:
Plants ....Gen 1:11-29
Earth...................Ps 67:6
Standing grain...........Hos 8:7
Death ....Acts 5:10
Fountain ....James 3:12
God's servants ....Dan 3:28

Used figuratively of:
Discipline ....Heb 12:11
Spiritual fruit ....Mark 4:8
Surrender ....Rom 6:13, 16

[*also* YIELDED, YIELDETH, YIELDING]
not henceforth *y* unto thee ....Gen 4:12
y up the ghost, and was ....Gen 49:33
it may *y* unto you the increase .Lev 19:25
land shall *y* her increase ......Lev 26:4
the field shall *y* their fruit .....Lev 26:4
shall not *y* her increase ....Lev 26:20
the trees of the land *y* their ...Lev 26:20
blossoms, and *y* almonds ......Num 17:8
the land *y* not her fruit ....Deut 11:17
y yourselves unto the Lord 2Chr 30:8
it *y* much increase unto the....Neh 9:37
wilderness *y* food for them ....Job 24:5
the earth *y* her increase ....Ps 67:6
may *y* fruits of increase ....Ps 107:37
speech she caused him to *y*....Prov 7:21
the root of the righteous *y* ....Prov 12:12
y pacifieth great offenses ......Eccl 10:4
vineyard shall *y* one bath......Is 5:10
seed of a homer shall *y* an ....Is 5:10
neither shall cease from *y* .....Jer 17:8
tree of the field shall *y* her ....Ezek 34:27
earth shall *y* her increase ......Ezek 34:27
king's word, and *y* their ....Dan 3:28
the bud shall *y* no meal ....Hos 8:7
if so be it *y*, the strangers .....Hos 8:7
vine do *y* their strength ....Joel 2:22
and the fields shall *y* no meat .Hab 3:17
loud voice, *y* up the ghost.....Matt 27:50
and choked it, and it *y* no.....Mark 4:7
do not thou *y* unto them ......Acts 23:21
no fountain both *y* salt water ..James 3:12
y her fruit every month ....Rev 22:2

YOKE—*frame by which animals are joined for working together*

Used literally on:
Animals ....Deut 21:3
Captives ....Jer 28:10-14
Slaves 1Tim 6:1

Used figuratively of:
Oppression..............Deut 28:48
Hard service 1Kin 12:4-14
Submission..............Jer 27:8
Bondage to sin ....Lam 1:14
Discipleship ....Matt 11:29, 30
Legalistic ordinances .....Gal 5:1
Marriage................2Cor 6:14

[*also* YOKES]
break his *y* from off thy.......Gen 27:40
broken the bands of your *y*....Lev 26:13
upon which never came *y* .....Num 19:2
which there hath come no *y* ...1Sam 6:7
And he took a *y* of oxen 1Sam 11:7
a *y* of oxen might plow 1Sam 14:14
plowing with twelve *y* of 1Kin 19:19
took a *y* of oxen, and slew 1Kin 19:21
Thy father made our *y* 2Chr 10:4
his heavy *y* that he put upon ..2Chr 10:4
father made our *y* heavy 2Chr 10:10
my father put a heavy *y*.......2Chr 10:11
will put more to your *y*; my ...2Chr 10:11

and five hundred *y* of oxen ....Job 1:3
broken the *y* of his burden ....Is 9:4
and his *y* from off thy neck ...Is 10:27
the *y* shall be destroyed ....Is 10:27
thou very heavily laid thy *y* ...Is 47:6
from the midst of thee the *y*...Is 58:9
time I have broken thy *y*......Jer 2:20
altogether broken the *y* ....Jer 5:5
Make thee bonds and *y* ....Jer 27:2
y of the king of Babylon ......Jer 28:2
y of the king of Babylon ......Jer 28:4
the *y* of Nebuchadnezzar ......Jer 28:11
prophet had broken the *y* .....Jer 28:12
hast broken the *y* of wood ....Jer 28:13
shalt make for them *y* of ......Jer 28:13
his *y* from off thy neck........Jer 30:8
unaccustomed to the *y* ....Jer 31:18
husbandman and his *y* of......Jer 51:23
he bear the *y* in his youth .....Lam 3:27
break there the *y* of Egypt ....Ezek 30:18
broken the bands of their *y* ...Ezek 34:27
take off the *y* on their jaws ...Hos 11:4
I break his *y* from off thee ....Nah 1:13
have bought five *y* of oxen ....Luke 14:19
y upon the neck of the........Acts 15:10

YOKEFELLOW—*compatriot*
entreat thee also, true *y*.......Phil 4:3

YONDER—*an indicated distant place*
lad will go *y* and worship .....Gen 22:5
and scatter thou the fire *y*.....Num 16:37
while I meet the Lord *y*.......Num 23:15
with them on *y* side Jordan....Num 32:19
y is that Shunammite 2Kin 4:25
Remove hence to *y* place .....Matt 17:20
here, while I go and pray *y* ...Matt 26:36

YOU—*See* INTRODUCTION

YOUNG—*youthful; new*

[*also* YOUNGER, YOUNGEST]
and a *y* man to my hurt.......Gen 4:23
what his *y* son had done ......Gen 9:24
turtledove and a *y* pigeon .....Gen 15:9
house round, both old and *y* ..Gen 19:4
y arose and lay with him ......Gen 19:35
Abraham said unto his *y* ......Gen 22:5
the elder shall serve the *y* .....Gen 25:23
and called Jacob her *y* son ....Gen 27:42
for Rachel thy *y* daughter .....Gen 29:18
goats have not cast their *y* ....Gen 31:38
y man deferred not to do .....Gen 34:19
the *y* is this day with our......Gen 42:13
bring your *y* brother unto .....Gen 42:20
bring your *y* brother unto .....Gen 42:34
is this your *y* brother, of ......Gen 43:29
the sack's mouth of the *y* .....Gen 44:2
your *y* brother come down ....Gen 44:23
if our *y* brother be with us ....Gen 44:26
except our *y* brother be ....Gen 44:26
y brother shall be greater .....Gen 48:19
our *y* and with our old ....Ex 10:9
y men of the children of ......Ex 24:5
the son of Nun, a *y* man ......Ex 33:11
turtledoves or of *y* pigeons ....Lev 1:14
offer a *y* bullock for the sin ...Lev 4:14
two *y* pigeons, then he that ...Lev 5:11
a *y* pigeon, or a turtledove ....Lev 12:6
two *y* pigeons, such as he is ...Lev 14:22
or two *y* pigeons, and come ...Lev 15:14
y bullock for a sin offering ....Lev 16:3
y bullock and two rams ....Lev 23:18
two *y* pigeons, to the priest ...Num 6:10
One *y* bullock, one ram ....Num 7:81
let them take a *y* bullock......Num 8:8
y bullock shalt thou take ......Num 8:8
one of his *y* men answered ....Num 11:28
lift up himself as a *y* lion......Num 23:24
one *y* bullock, one ram ....Num 29:2
offer twelve *y* bullocks ....Num 29:17
whether they be *y* ones ....Deut 22:6
dam sitting upon the *y* ....Deut 22:6
not take the dam with the *y* ...Deut 22:6
nor show favor to the *y* ....Deut 28:50
fluttereth over her *y*, spreadeth.Deut 32:11
both man and woman *y* and ...Josh 6:21
his *y* son shall he set up.......Josh 6:26
Kenaz, Caleb's *y* brother ......Judg 1:13
Take thy father's *y* bullock ....Judg 6:25
the *y* son of Jerubbaal was ....Judg 9:5
y man his armorbearer ....Judg 9:54
y man thrust him through .....Judg 9:54
and *y* lion roared against him..Judg 14:5
her *y* sister fairer than she? ...Judg 15:2
y man out of Beth-lehem.......Judg 17:7
y man became his priest ......Judg 17:12
the house of the *y* man the....Judg 18:15
have I not charged the *y* ......Ruth 2:9
that which the *y* men have ....Ruth 2:9
shalt keep fast by my *y* ....Ruth 2:21
give thee of this *y* woman .....Ruth 4:12
Shiloh, and the child was *y*....1Sam 1:24
your goodliest *y* man and 1Sam 8:16
y maidens going out to........1Sam 9:11
Jonathan said to the *y* man....1Sam 14:6
the name of the *y* Michal 1Sam 14:49
There remaineth yet the *y*.....1Sam 16:11
if I say thus unto the *y* man ...1Sam 20:22
vessels of the *y* men are.......1Sam 21:5
David sent out ten *y* men 1Sam 25:5
David said unto the *y* men 1Sam 25:5
Ask thy *y* men and they will ..1Sam 25:8
let the *y* men find favor 1Sam 25:8
So David's *y* men turned 1Sam 25:12
handmaid saw not the *y* men ..1Sam 25:25
let one of the *y* men come 1Sam 26:22
save four hundred *y* men......1Sam 30:17
David said unto the *y* man 2Sam 1:5
David said unto the *y* man 2Sam 1:13
Let the *y* men now arise 2Sam 2:14
David commanded his *y* men ..2Sam 4:12
the *y* men the king's sons 2Sam 13:32
bring the *y* man Absalom 2Sam 14:21
for my sake with the *y* man ...2Sam 18:5
y men that bare Joab's armor..2Sam 18:15
Is the *y* man Absalom safe? ...2Sam 18:32
do thee hurt, be as that *y* 2Sam 18:32
my lord the king a *y* virgin 1Kin 1:2
Solomon seeing the *y* man 1Kin 11:28
thereof in his *y* son Segub 1Kin 16:34
against their *y* brethren 1Chr 24:31
hath chosen, is yet *y* and......1Chr 29:1
himself with a *y* bullock 2Chr 13:9
save Jehoahaz the *y* of his.....2Chr 21:17
both *y* bullocks, and rams .....Ezra 6:9
be fair *y* virgins sought........Esth 2:2
all Jews, both *y* and old.......Esth 3:13
fell upon the *y* men, and ......Job 1:19
y children despised me ....Job 19:18
y than I have me in derision...Job 30:1
I am *y*, and ye are very old ...Job 32:6
his *y* ones cry unto God.......Job 38:41
y ones are in good liking ......Job 39:4
y ones also suck up blood .....Job 39:30
a *y* lion lurking in secret ......Ps 17:12
y lions do lack, and suffer.....Ps 34:10
out the great teeth of the *y*....Ps 58:6
the ewes great with *y* ....Ps 78:71
where she may lay her *y* ......Ps 84:3
the *y* lions roar after their .....Ps 104:21
to the *y* ravens which cry .....Ps 147:9
Both *y* men, and maidens .....Ps 148:12
out, and the *y* eagles shall.....Prov 30:17
beloved is like a roe or a *y*....Song 2:9
two *y* roes that are twins ......Song 4:5
like to a roe or to a *y* hart ....Song 8:14
they shall roar like *y* lions .....Is 5:29
have no joy in their *y* men ....Is 9:17
y ones shall lie down ....Is 11:7
Ethiopians captives, *y* and.....Is 20:4
come the *y* and old lion ....Is 30:6
upon the shoulders of *y* ....Is 30:6
y lion roaring on his prey .....Is 31:4
lead those that are with *y* .....Is 40:11
For as a *y* man marrieth a ....Is 62:5
the *y* lions roared upon him ...Jer 2:15
the *y* men from the streets ....Jer 9:21
against the mother of the *y*....Jer 15:8
the *y* of the flock and of the ..Jer 31:12
his chosen *y* men are gone ....Jer 48:15
shall her *y* men fall in the .....Jer 50:30
I break in pieces old and *y*....Jer 51:22
the *y* man and the maid.......Jer 51:22
against me to crush my *y*......Lam 1:15
the life of thy *y* children ......Lam 2:19
y and the old lie on the ....Lam 2:21
virgins and my *y* men are .....Lam 2:21
gate, the *y* men from their ....Lam 5:14
Slay utterly old and *y*, both ...Ezek 9:6
thy *y* sister that dwelleth ......Ezek 16:46
thine elder and thy *y* ....Ezek 16:61
from the top of his *y* twigs ....Ezek 17:22
it became a *y* lion, and it .....Ezek 19:3
he became a *y* lion, and.......Ezek 19:6
all of them desirable *y* men ...Ezek 23:12
like a *y* lion of the nations ....Ezek 32:2
face of a *y* lion toward the ....Ezek 41:19
y bullock without blemish .....Ezek 43:23
y bullock without blemish .....Ezek 45:18
as a *y* lion to the house of ....Hos 5:14
y men shall see visions ....Joel 2:28
and of your *y* men for ....Amos 2:11
your *y* men have I slain ....Amos 4:10
y lion among the flocks of.....Mic 5:8
her *y* children also were.......Nah 2:10
feedingplace of the *y* lions.....Nah 3:11
Run, speak to this *y* man .....Zech 2:4
of the roaring of *y* lions ....Zech 11:3
search diligently for the *y* .....Matt 2:8
the *y* child with Mary his......Matt 2:11
the *y* child and his mother ....Matt 2:13
seek the *y* child to destroy ....Matt 2:13
the *y* child and his mother ....Matt 2:20
sought the *y* child's life ....Matt 2:20
the *y* child and his mother ....Matt 2:21
y daughter had an unclean ....Mark 7:25
followed him a certain *y* ......Mark 14:51
and the *y* men laid hold on....Mark 14:51
of turtledoves, or two *y* ....Luke 2:24
you, let him be as the *y*.......Luke 22:26
when he had found a *y* ass ....John 12:14
y men shall see visions ....Acts 2:17
y men came in, and found her .Acts 5:10
their clothes at a *y* man's .....Acts 7:58
they brought the *y* man alive ..Acts 20:12
prayed me to bring this *y* .....Acts 23:18
The elder shall serve the *y* ....Rom 9:12
and the *y* men as brethren 1Tim 5:1
But the *y* widows refuse 1Tim 5:11
teach the *y* women to be sober.Titus 2:4
ye *y*, submit yourselves unto...1Pet 5:5

YOUNG MEN

Characteristics of, seen in:
Unwise counsel..........1Kin 12:8-14
Godly fervor 1John 2:13, 14
Passion ....Prov 7:7-23
Strength ....Prov 20:29
Impatience ....Luke 15:12, 13

Special needs of:
God's Word ....Ps 119:9
Knowledge and discretion.Prov 1:4
Encouragement..........Is 40:30, 31
Full surrender ....Matt 19:20-22
Soberness ....Titus 2:6
Counsel 1John 2:13, 14

YOUR—*See* INTRODUCTION

YOURS—*that which belongs to you*
of all the land of Egypt is *y* ...Gen 45:20
feet shall tread shall be *y* .....Deut 11:24
Our life for *y*, if ye utter not ..Josh 2:14
battle is not *y*, but God's 2Chr 20:15
in a land that is not *y*........Jer 5:19
for *y* is the kingdom of God...Luke 6:20
my saying, they will keep *y*....John 15:20
in men; for all things are *y* 1Cor 3:21
this liberty of *y* become a 1Cor 8:9

YOURSELVES—*those who are you*
your feet, and rest *y* under ....Gen 18:4
Gather *y* together that I may ...Gen 49:1
heed to *y*, that ye go not up...Ex 19:12
Consecrate *y* today to the .....Ex 32:29
neither shall ye make *y* unclean Lev 11:43

Y

ye shall therefore sanctify *y* . . .Lev 11:44
neither shall ye defile *y* . . . . . .Lev 11:44
and that ye defile not *y* . . . . . . .Lev 18:30
Sanctify *y* therefore, and be . . .Lev 20:7
Sanctify *y* against tomorrow . . .Num 11:18
lift ye up *y* above the . . . . .Num 16:3
Arm some of *y* unto the war . .Num 31:3
purify both *y* and your . . . . . . .Num 31:19
take ye good heed unto *y* . . . . .Deut 2:4
Lest ye corrupt *y*, and make . . . .Deut 4:16
corrupt *y*, and make a graven .Deut 4:25
nations and mightier than *y* . . .Deut 11:23
present *y* in the tabernacle . . . .Deut 31:14
and hide *y* there three days . . .Josh 2:16
keep *y* from the accursed . . . . .Josh 6:18
say, Sanctify *y* against . . . . .Josh 7:13
serve them, nor bow *y* unto . . .Josh 23:7
Ye are witnesses against *y* . . . . .Josh 24:22
ye will not fall upon me *y* . . . . .Judg 15:12
y fat with the chiefest of 1Sam 2:29
strong, and quit *y* like men 1Sam 4:9
quit *y* like men, and fight 1Sam 4:9
said, Disperse *y* among the 1Sam 14:34
Choose you one bullock for *y* .1Kin 18:25
y to them, nor serve them 2Kin 17:35
sanctify *y*, both ye and your . . .1Chr 15:12
set *y*, stand ye still, and see . . .2Chr 20:17
consecrated *y* unto the Lord . . .2Cor 29:31
give over *y* to die by famine . . .2Chr 32:11
the passover, and sanctify *y* . . .2Chr 35:6
separate *y* from the people . . . .Ezra 10:11
unto your sons, or for *y* . . . . . . .Neh 13:25
that ye make *y* strange to . . . . .Job 19:3
Behold, all ye *y* have seen it . .Job 27:12
Associate *y*, O ye people . . . . . .Is 8:9
Stay *y*, and wonder; cry ye . . . .Is 29:9
Remember this, and show *y* . . .Is 46:8
that are in darkness. Show *y* . .Is 49:9
that compass *y* about with . . . . .Is 50:11
Against whom do ye sport *y* . . .Is 57:4
their glory shall ye boast *y* . . . .Is 61:6
Circumcise *y* to the Lord . . . . . .Jer 4:4
gather *y* to flee out of the . . . . .Jer 6:1
Humble *y*, sit down . . . . .Jer 13:18
and wallow *y* in the ashes . . . . .Jer 25:34
Deceive not *y*, saying, The . . . .Jer 37:9
Put *y* in array against . . . . .Jer 50:14
and turn *y* from your idols . . . .Ezek 14:6
wherefore turn *y*, and live ye . .Ezek 18:32
nor defile *y* with their idols . . . .Ezek 20:18
ye shall loathe *y* in your own . .Ezek 20:43
field. Assemble *y*, and come . . .Ezek 39:17
gather *y* on every side to . . . . . .Ezek 39:17
to *y* in righteousness, reap . . . .Hos 10:12
Gird *y* and lament, ye priests . .Joel 1:13
Assemble *y*, and come, all . . . .Joel 3:11
and gather *y* together round . . .Joel 3:11
Assemble *y* upon the . . . . .Amos 3:9
Gather *y* together, yea . . . . .Zeph 2:1
ye eat for *y*, and drink for *y*? . .Zech 7:6
think not to say within *y* . . . . . .Matt 3:9
lay up for *y* treasures in . . . . . . .Matt 6:20
for ye neither go in *y* . . . . .Matt 23:13
ye be witnesses unto *y* . . . . .Matt 23:31
ye *y* apart into a desert . . . . . . .Mark 6:31
Have salt in *y* and have . . . . . . .Mark 9:50
within *y*, We have Abraham . . .Luke 3:8
ye entered not in *y*, and . . . . . .Luke 11:52
And ye *y* like unto men that . .Luke 12:36
God, and you *y* thrust out . . . .Luke 13:28
they which justify *y* before . . . .Luke 16:15
them, Go show *y* unto the . . . .Luke 17:14
this and divide it among *y* . . . . .Luke 22:17
Ye *y* bear me witness, that I . .John 3:28
inquire among *y* of that . . . . . . .John 16:19
midst of you, as ye *y* also . . . . .Acts 2:22
take heed to *y* what ye . . . . .Acts 5:35
from which if ye keep *y*, ye . . .Acts 15:29
Take heed therefore unto *y* . . .Acts 20:28
also *y* to be dead indeed . . . . . .Rom 6:11
whom ye yield *y* servants to . . .Rom 6:16
from among *y* that wicked 1Cor 5:13
may give *y* to fasting and 1Cor 7:5
That ye submit *y* unto such 1Cor 16:16
you, yea, what clearing of *y* . . .2Cor 7:11
fools gladly, seeing ye *y* are . . .2Cor 11:19
and that not of *y*; it is the . . . . .Eph 2:8
Submitting *y* one to another . . .Eph 5:21
submit *y* unto your own . . . . . . .Col 3:18
For *y*, brethren, know our 1Thess 2:1
for ye *y* are taught of God 1Thess 4:9
wherefore comfort *y* together . .1Thess 5:11
which is good, both among *y* . .1Thess 5:15
ye withdraw *y* from every 2Thess 3:6
knowing in *y* that ye have . . . . .Heb 10:34
rule over you, and submit *y* . . . .Heb 13:17
Are ye not then partial in *y* . . .James 2:4
Humble *y* in the sight of . . . . . .James 4:10
not fashioning *y* according 1Pet 1:14
arm *y* likewise with the 1Pet 4:1
ye younger, submit *y* unto 1Pet 5:5
Humble *y* therefore under 1Pet 5:6
Little children, keep *y* from . . .1John 5:21
look to *y*, that we lose not 2John 8
building up *y* on your most . . . .Jude 20
gather *y* together unto the . . . . .Rev 19:17

YOUTH—*the early years of one's life*

Evils of, seen in:
Sin . . . . .Ps 25:7
Lusts 2Tim 2:22
Enticement . . . . .Prov 1:10-16
Self-will . . . . .Luke 15:12, 13

Good of, seen in:
Enthusiasm 1Sam 17:26-51
Children . . . . .Ps 127:3, 4
Hardships . . . . .Lam 3:27
Godly example 1Tim 4:12

[*also* YOUTHS]
heart is evil from his *y* . . . . .Gen 8:21
cattle from our *y* even until . . .Gen 46:34
father's house, as in her *y* . . . . .Lev 22:13
her father's house in her *y* . . . .Num 30:3
the *y* drew not his sword . . . . . .Judg 8:20
because he was yet a *y* . . . . .Judg 8:20
Abner, whose son is this *y*? . . .1Sam 17:55
that befell thee from thy *y* 2Sam 19:7
fear the Lord from my *y* 1Kin 18:12
possess the iniquities of my *y* . .Job 13:26
I was in the days of my *y* . . . . .Job 29:4
my *y* he was brought up . . . . . .Job 31:18
They die in *y*, and their life . . .Job 36:14
ready to die from my *y* up . . . .Ps 68:15
thy *y* is renewed like the . . . . . .Ps 103:5
thou hast the dew of thy *y* . . . .Ps 110:3
they afflicted me from my *y* . . .Ps 129:1
plants grown up in their *y* . . . . .Ps 144:12
forsaketh the guide of her *y* . . .Prov 2:17
I discerned among the *y*, a . . . .Prov 7:7
Rejoice, O young man in thy *y*.Eccl 11:9
thee in the days of thy *y* . . . . . .Eccl 11:9
childhood and *y* are vanity . . . .Eccl 11:10
y shall faint and be weary . . . . .Is 40:30
hast labored from thy *y* . . . . . . .Is 47:12
forget the shame of thy *y* . . . . .Is 54:4
kindness of thy *y*, the love . . . .Jer 2:2
of our fathers from our *y* . . . . .Jer 3:24
been thy manner from thy *y* . . .Jer 22:21
evil before me from their *y* . . . .Jer 32:30
been at ease from his *y* . . . . . . .Jer 48:11
from my *y* up even till now . . .Ezek 4:14
thee in the days of thy *y* . . . . . .Ezek 16:60
in her *y* they lay with her . . . . .Ezek 23:8
the lewdness of thy *y* . . . . .Ezek 23:21
as in the days of her *y* . . . . .Hos 2:15
for the husband of her *y* . . . . . .Joel 1:8
me to keep cattle from my *y* . .Zech 13:5
have I kept from my *y* up . . . . .Matt 19:20
have I observed from my *y* . . . .Mark 10:20
have I kept from my *y* up . . . . .Luke 18:21
manner of life from my *y* . . . . .Acts 26:4

YOUTHFUL—*typical of young people*
Flee also *y* lusts 2Tim 2:22

YOU-WARD—*you; in your direction*
and more abundantly to *y* 2Cor 1:12
which to *y* is not weak, but is .2Cor 13:3
grace which is given me to *y* . .Eph 3:2

Z

ZAANAIM—*See* ZAANANNIM

ZAANAN (zā'ä-năn)—*"pointed"*
Town in west Judah . . . . .Mic 1:11

ZAANANNIM (zā-ä-năn'ĭm)
Border point of Naphtali .Josh 19:32
Same as Zaanaim . . . . .Judg 4:11

ZAAVAN (zā'ä-văn)—*"causing fear"*
Son of Ezer . . . . .Gen 36:27

ZABAD (zā'băd)—*"endower"*
1. Descendant of Judah 1Chr 2:3, 36
2. Ephraimite 1Chr 7:20, 21
3. One of Joash's murderers 2Chr 24:26
Called Jozacar 2Kin 12:21
4. Son of Zattu . . . . .Ezra 10:27
5. Son of Hashum . . . . .Ezra 10:33
6. Son of Nebo . . . . .Ezra 10:43

And *Z* begat Ephlal, and 1Chr 2:37
Hittite, *Z* the son of Ahlai 1Chr 11:41

ZABBAI (zăb'ā-ī)—*"roving about; pure"*
1. Man who divorced his foreign wife . . . . .Ezra 10:28
2. Father of Baruch . . . . . . .Neh 3:20

ZABBUD (zăb'ŭd)—*"endowed"*
Postexilic returnee . . . . . .Ezra 8:14

ZABDI (zăb'dī)—*"Jehovah is endower"*
1. Achan's grandfather . . . . .Josh 7:1, 17
See ZIMRI 1
2. Benjamite 1Chr 8:1, 19
3. One of David's officers . .1Chr 27:27

ZABDIEL (zăb'dĭ-ĕl)—*"my gift is God"*
1. Father of Jashobeam 1Chr 27:2
2. Postexilic official . . . . .Neh 11:14

ZABUD (zā'bŭd)—*"bestowed"*
Son of Nathan 1Kin 4:5

ZABULON—*See* ZEBULUN

ZACCAI (zăk'ā-ī)—*"pure"*
Head of a postexilic family . . . . .Ezra 2:9

ZACCHEUS (ză-kē'ŭs)—*"pure"*
Wealthy tax-gatherer converted to Christ . . . .Luke 19:1-10

ZACCUR, ZACCHUR (zăk'ûr)—*"well-remembered"*
1. Father of the Reubenite spy . . . . .Num 13:2, 4
2. Simeonite 1Chr 4:24, 26
3. Merarite Levite 1Chr 24:27
4. Asaphite Levite 1Chr 25:2, 10
5. Signer of the covenant . .Neh 10:1, 12
6. A treasurer . . . . .Neh 13:13

ZACHARIAH (zăk-ä-rī'ä)—*"memory of the Lord"*
1. Son and successor of King Jeroboam II . . . 2Kin 14:29; 2Kin 15:8-10
2. Grandfather of Hezekiah.2Kin 18:1, 2
See ZECHARIAH

ZACHARIAS—*See* ZECHARIAH

ZACHER (zā'ker)—*"fame"*
Benjamite 1Chr 8:31

ZADOK, SADOC (zā'dŏk, sā'dŏk)—*"righteous"*
1. Descendant of Aaron . . .1Chr 24:1-3
Co-priest with Abiathar .2Sam 20:25
Loyal to David 2Sam 15:24-29
Gently rebuked by David.2Sam 19:11-14
Remained aloof from Adonijah's usurpation .1Kin 1:8-26
Commanded by David to anoint Solomon 1Kin 1:32-45
Replaces Abiathar 1Kin 2:35
Sons of, faithful . . . . .Ezek 48:11
2. Priest, the son or grandson of Ahitub . . .1Chr 6:12

3. Jotham's maternal grandfather 2Kin 15:33
4. Postexilic workman, son of Baana ....Neh 3:4
5. Postexilic workman, son of Immer............Neh 3:29
6. Ancestor of Christ ......Matt 1:14

[*also* ZADOK'S]
thou not there with thee **Z** 2Sam 15:35
thou shalt tell it to **Z** and 2Sam 15:35
Ahimaaz **Z** son, and Jonathan .2Sam 15:36
Then said Hushai unto **Z**......2Sam 17:15
said Ahimaaz the son of **Z** 2Sam 18:19
said Ahimaaz the son of **Z** 2Sam 18:22
of Ahimaaz the son of **Z** 2Sam 18:27
Z and Abiathar were the 2Sam 20:25
Azariah the son of **Z** the 1Kin 4:2
Z and Abiathar were the 1Kin 4:4
Ahitub begat **Z**, and **Z** 1Chr 6:8
Z his son, Ahimaaz his son....1Chr 6:53
of Meshullam, the son of **Z** ...1Chr 9:11
Z, a young man mighty of.....1Chr 12:28
called for **Z** and Abiathar 1Chr 15:11
And **Z** the priest, and his 1Chr 16:39
And **Z** the son of Ahitub 1Chr 18:16
of David the king, and **Z**......1Chr 24:31
Kemuel; of the Aaronites, **Z** ..1Chr 27:17
chief governor, and **Z** to be ...1Chr 29:22
Jerushah, the daughter of **Z** ...2Chr 27:1
priest of the house of **Z**.......2Chr 31:10
son of Shallum, the son of **Z** ..Ezra 7:2
Meshezabeel, **Z**, Jaddus ....Neh 10:21
of Meshullam the son of **Z** ....Neh 11:11
the priest, and **Z** the scribe ....Neh 13:13
are the sons of **Z** among the...Ezek 40:46
that be of the seed of **Z**.......Ezek 43:19
the sons of **Z**, that kept the ...Ezek 44:15

ZAHAM (zā'hăm)—*"fatness"*
Son of Rehoboam 2Chr 11:18, 19

ZAIN (zä'ĭn)
Letter of the Hebrew alphabet ....Ps 119:49-56

ZAIR (zā'ĭr)—*"small"*
Battle camp in Edom 2Kin 8:21

ZALAPH (zā'lăf)—*"purification"*
Father of Hanum ....Neh 3:30

ZALMON (zăl'mŏn)—*"terrace; accent"*
1. One of David's mighty men 2Sam 23:28
2. Mount near Shechem....Judg 9:48
Called Salmon ....Ps 68:14

ZALMONAH (zăl-mō'nä)—*"shade"*
Israelite camp ....Num 33:41, 42

ZALMUNNA (zăl-mŭn'ä)—*"withdrawn from protection"*
Midianite king ....Judg 8:4-21

princes as Zebah and as **Z** ....Ps 83:11

ZAMZUMMIM (zăm-zŭm'ĭm)—*"murmurers"*
Race of giants...........Deut 2:20, 21
Same as the Zuzim ......Gen 14:5

ZANOAH (zä-nō'ä)—*"marsh"*
1. Town in south Judah ....Josh 15:1, 34
2. Town of Judah ....Josh 15:56

Jekuthiel the father of **Z** 1Chr 4:18
and the inhabitants of **Z** ......Neh 3:13
Z, Adullam, and in their ......Neh 11:30

ZAPHNATH-PAANEAH (zăf-năth-pā-ä-nē'ä)—*"revealer of secrets"*
Name given to Joseph by Pharaoh ....Gen 41:45

ZAPHON (zā'fŏn)—*"north"*
Town of Gad east of the Jordan...............Josh 13:24, 27

ZARA, ZARAH—*See* ZERAH

ZAREAH—*See* ZORAH

ZAREATHITES—*See* ZORATHITE

ZARED (zā'rĕd)—*"brook"*
Brook and valley crossed by Israel.............Num 21:12

[*also* ZERED]
get you over the brook **Z** .....Deut 2:13
we went over the brook **Z**.....Deut 2:13
were come over the brook **Z** ..Deut 2:14

ZAREPHATH (zăr'ĕ-făth)—*"smelting pot"*
Town of Sidon where Elijah restores widow's son.................1Kin 17:8-24; Luke 4:26
Called Sarepta ....Luke 4:26

ZARETAN, ZARTANAH, ZARTHAN (zăr'ĕ-tăn, zär'tā-nä, zär'than)—*"cooling"*
Town near Jezreel ....Josh 3:16; 1Kin 4:12
Hiram worked near 1Kin 7:46

ZARETH-SHAHAR (zā-rĕth-shā'här)—*"beauty of the dawn"*
City of Reuben..........Josh 13:19

ZARHITES (zär'hīts)—*descendants of the family of Zerah*
Zerah, the family of the **Z** ....Num 26:13
Zerah, the family of the **Z** ....Num 26:20
the Hushathite of the **Z**.......1Chr 27:11
the Netophathite of the **Z**.....1Chr 27:13

ZARTANAH, ZARTHAN—*See* ZARETAN

ZATTU, ZATTHU (zăt'ū; zăt'thū)—*"lovely; pleasant"*
Founder of a postexilic family ....Ezra 2:2, 8
Members of, divorced foreign wives........Ezra 10:18, 19, 27
Signs covenant ....Neh 10:1, 14

ZAVAN—*See* ZAAVAN

ZAZA (zā'zä)—*"projection"*
Jerahmeelite 1Chr 2:33

ZEAL—*ardent interest or desire in pursuit of something*

Kinds of:
Divine....................Is 9:7
Glorious ....Is 63:15
Wrathful.................Ezek 5:13
Stirring 2Cor 9:2
Intense 2Cor 7:11
Boastful ....Phil 3:4, 6
Ignorant ....Rom 10:2, 3
Righteous................John 2:15-17
Sinful 2Sam 21:1, 2

Manifested in concern for:
Lord's sake ....Num 25:11, 13
Others' salvation ....Rom 10:1
Missionary work..........Rom 15:18-25
Reformation of character .2Cor 7:11
Desire for spiritual gifts ..1Cor 14:12
Doing good works ....Titus 2:14

Illustrated in Paul's life by his:
Desire to reach the Jews .Rom 9:1-3; Rom 10:1
Determination to evangelize all 1Cor 9:19-23
Willingness to lose all things for Christ.......Phil 3:4-16
Place to minister to unreached places ......Rom 1:14, 15
Support of himself 2Cor 11:7-12

Examples of:
Moses ....Ex 32:19-32
Phinehas.................Num 25:7-13
Joshua...................Josh 24:14-16
Gideon ....Judg 6:11-32
David 1Sam 17:26-51
Elijah 1Kin 19:10
Jehu.....................2Kin 9:1-37
Josiah 2Kin 22:1-20
Ezra.....................Ezra 7:10
Nehemiah................Neh 4:1-23
Peter and John ....Acts 4:8-20
Timothy ....Phil 2:19-22
Epaphroditus............Phil 2:25-30
Epaphras ....Col 4:12, 13

slay them in his *z*............2Sam 21:2
and see my *z* for the Lord 2Kin 10:16
z of the Lord of hosts shall....2Kin 19:31
z of thine house hath eaten....Ps 69:9
My *z* hath consumed me ......Ps 119:139
z of the Lord of hosts shall .....Is 37:32
was clad with *z* as a cloak .....Is 59:17
is thy *z* and thy strength ......Is 63:15
Lord have spoken it in my *z*...Ezek 5:13
z of thine house hath eaten....John 2:17

ZEALOT, ZEALOTES—*"zealous one"—a party of the Jews violently opposed to the Romans*
Applied to Simon, the Canaanite; a party of fanatical Jews ....Luke 6:15

ZEALOUS—*ardently interested*

[*also* ZEALOUSLY]
and they are all *z* of the law...Acts 21:20
was *z* toward God, as ye all ...Acts 22:3
z of the traditions of my ......Gal 1:14
They *z* affect you, but ....Gal 4:17
good to be *z* affected ....Gal 4:18

ZEBADIAH (zĕb-ä-dī'ä)—*"Jehovah is endower"*
1. 2. Two Benjamites 1Chr 8:1, 15, 17
3. Benjamite warrior among David's mighty men ...1Chr 12:1-7
4. One of David's commanders 1Chr 27:7
5. Korahite Levite 1Chr 26:1, 2
6. Levite teacher under Jehoshaphat 2Chr 17:8
7. Officer of Jehoshaphat ..2Chr 19:11
8. Postexilic returnee ......Ezra 8:8
9. Priest who put away his foreign wife ....Ezra 10:20

ZEBAH (zē'bä)—*"victim"*
King of Midian killed by Gideon ....Judg 8:4-28

ZEBAIM (zĕ-bā'ĭm)—*"gazelles"*
Native place of Solomon's slaves ....Ezra 2:55, 57

ZEBEDEE (zĕb'ĕ-dē)—*"the gift of Jehovah"*
Galilean fisherman; father of James and John ....Matt 4:21, 22

the son of **Z** and John his .....Matt 10:2
Peter and the two sons of **Z** ...Matt 26:37
he saw James the son of **Z** ....Mark 1:19
left their father **Z** in the.......Mark 1:20
And James the son of **Z** ......Mark 3:17
and John, the sons of **Z**.......Mark 10:35
and John, the sons of **Z**.......Luke 5:10
and the sons of **Z**, and two ....John 21:2

ZEBINA (zĕ-bē'nä)—*"bought"*
Priest who put away his foreign wife ....Ezra 10:43

ZEBOIM (zĕ-bō'ĭm)—*"gazelles"*
1. One of five cities destroyed with Sodom and Gomorrah........Gen 10:19
2. Valley in Benjamin 1Sam 13:16-18
3. City of Judah ....Neh 11:34

[*also* ZEBOIIM]
Shemember king of **Z**, and the .Gen 14:2
king of **Z** and the king of .....Gen 14:8
Gomorrah, Admah, and **Z** ....Deut 29:23
how shall I set thee as **Z**? .....Hos 11:8

ZEBUDAH (zĕ-bū'dä)—*"endowed"*
Mother of Jehoiakim 2Kin 23:36

ZEBUL (zē'bŭl)—*"dwelling"*
Ruler of Shechem; exposes Gaal's revolt ..Judg 9:26-41

ZEBULUN (zĕb'ū-lŭn)—*"dwelling"*
1. Sixth son of Leah and Jacob ....Gen 30:19, 20
2. Descendants of 1; a tribe of Israel ....Num 2:7
Predictions concerning ...Gen 49:13
First numbering of ......Num 1:30, 31
Second numbering of ....Num 26:27
Representatives of ......Num 1:9
Territory of ....Josh 19:10-16
Warriors of, fight with Deborah ....Judg 5:14, 18
Warriors of, aid Gideon .Judg 6:34, 35
Judge Elon, member of .Judg 12:11, 12
Warriors of, in David's army 1Chr 12:33, 40
Some of, respond to Hezekiah's reforms 2Chr 30:10-18
Christ visits land of .....Is 9:1; Matt 4:13-15
Those sealed of ....Rev 7:8

[*also* ZABULON]
Judah, and Issachar, and **Z** ....Gen 35:23
sons of **Z**, Sered and Elon ....Gen 46:14
Issachar, **Z**, and Benjamin ....Ex 1:3
prince of the children of **Z** ....Num 7:24
the children of **Z** was Eliab ....Num 10:16
the tribe of **Z**, Gaddiel the ....Num 13:10
of **Z** after their families ....Num 26:26
tribe of the children of **Z** ....Num 34:25
Gad, and Asher, and **Z**, Dan ..Deut 27:13
of **Z** he said, Rejoice, **Z**, in ...Deut 33:18
reacheth to **Z**, and to the .....Josh 19:27
reacheth to **Z** on the south ....Josh 19:34
the tribe of **Z**, twelve cities ....Josh 21:7
the tribe of **Z**, Jokneam ....Josh 21:34
Z drive out the inhabitants ....Judg 1:30
and of the children of **Z**? .....Judg 4:6
called **Z** and Naphtali to ......Judg 4:10
and Judah, Issachar, and **Z** 1Chr 2:1
the tribe of **Z**, twelve cities 1Chr 6:63
given out of the tribe of **Z** 1Chr 6:77
of **Z**, Ishmaiah the son of 1Chr 27:19
of **Z**, and the princes of ....Ps 68:27
the west side, **Z** a portion .....Ezek 48:26
And by the border of **Z** ....Ezek 48:27
of Issachar, one gate of **Z** .....Ezek 48:33

ZEBULUNITES (zĕb'ū-lŭ-nīts)—*natives of Zebulun*
Descendants of Jacob's son ....Num 26:27
Elon thus called ....Judg 12:11, 12

ZECHARIAH (zĕk-ä-rī'ä)—*"Jehovah is renowned"*
1. Benjamite 1Chr 9:35, 37
2. Levite porter and counselor 1Chr 9:21, 22
3. Levite musician in David's reign 1Chr 15:18, 20
4. Priestly trumpeter 1Chr 15:24
5. Kohathite Levite 1Chr 24:25
6. Merarite Levite in David's reign 1Chr 26:10, 11
7. Manassite 1Chr 27:21
8. Teaching prince under Jehoshaphat 2Chr 17:7
9. Asaphite Levite 2Chr 20:14
10. Son of King Jehoshaphat 2Chr 21:2-4
11. Son of Jehoiada killed in the Temple .....2Chr 24:20-22; Matt 23:35
12. Prophet in Uzziah's reign 2Chr 26:5
13. King of Israel; last ruler of Jehu's dynasty 2Kin 15:8-12
14. Reubenite chief 1Chr 5:7
15. Faithful man in Isaiah's time ....Is 8:2
16. Hezekiah's maternal grandfather 2Chr 29:1
17. Levite during Hezekiah's reign 2Chr 29:13
18. Kohathite Levite employed as overseer .2Chr 34:12
19. Temple ruler during Josiah's reign 2Chr 35:8
20. Postexilic returnee .....Ezra 8:3
21. Son of Bebai ....Ezra 8:11
22. Man sent by Ezra to secure Levites ....Ezra 8:15, 16
23. One of Ezra's assistants .Neh 8:4
24. Jew who divorced his foreign wife ....Ezra 10:26
25. Levite trumpeter ....Neh 12:35, 36
26. Priest in dedication ceremony ....Neh 12:41
27. Man of Judah, family of Perez ....Neh 11:4
28. Man of Judah, son of a Shilonite ....Neh 11:5
29. Postexilic priest ....Neh 11:2
30. Postexilic prophet and priest ....Ezra 5:1; Zech 1:1, 7
31. Father of John the Baptist ....Luke 1:5-17

[*also* ZACHARIAH, ZACHARIAS]
the chief and next to him **Z** ...1Chr 16:5
Z, the first-born, Jediael the ...1Chr 26:2
Z his son, a wise counseler 1Chr 26:14
prophet and **Z** the son of .....Ezra 6:14
Of Iddo, **Z**; of Ginnethon .....Neh 12:16
of the Lord came unto **Z** ......Zech 7:1
of the Lord came unto **Z** ......Zech 7:8
And when **Z** saw him, he was .Luke 1:12
came unto John the son of **Z** ..Luke 3:2
of Abel unto the blood of **Z** ...Luke 11:51

ZECHARIAH, THE BOOK OF—*a book of the Old Testament*
Call to repentance ....Zech 1:2-6
The visions ....Zech 1:7—6:15
Against insincerity and disobedience ....Zech 7:1-14
Restoration of Jerusalem .Zech 8:1-23
Against nations ....Zech 9:1-8
The King comes ....Zech 9:9-17
Parable of shepherds .....Zech 11:4-17
Jerusalem spoiled ....Zech 14:1-6
Jerusalem restored ....Zech 14:7-21

ZEDAD (zē'dăd)—*"mountainside"*
Place on Palestine's north boundary ....Num 34:8; Ezek 47:15

ZEDEKIAH, ZIDKIJAH (zĕd-ĕ-kī'ä; zĭd-kī'jä)—*"Jehovah is righteousness"*
1. False prophet who counsels Ahab unwisely 1Kin 22:6-24
2. Immoral prophet killed by Nebuchadnezzar ...Jer 29:21-23
3. Prince under King Jehoiakim ....Jer 36:12
4. Son of Jeconiah 1Chr 3:16
5. Last king of Judah; uncle and successor of Jehoiachin 2Kin 24:17, 18
Reigns wickedly for 11 years 2Chr 36:11-13
Rebels against Jeremiah .2Chr 36:12
Rebels against Nebuchadnezzar ......Jer 52:3
Makes alliance with Egypt ....Ezek 17:11-21
Rebellion of, denounced by Jeremiah ....Jer 34:1-22
Consults with Jeremiah . .Jer 37:15-21; Jer 38:14-28
Imprisons Jeremiah .....Jer 38:1-13
Captured, blinded, taken to Babylon ....Jer 39:1-14; 2Kin 25:1-7
See MATTANIAH 1
6. High official who signs the covenant ....Neh 10:1

[*also* ZEDEKIAH'S]
Z the son of Chenaanah 1Kin 22:24
Z rebelled against the king 2Kin 24:20
Jehoiakim, the third **Z** 1Chr 3:15
Z the son of Chenaanah 2Chr 18:10
Z the son of Chenaanah 2Chr 18:23
made **Z** his brother king 2Chr 36:10
eleventh year of **Z** the son ....Jer 1:3
Z sent unto him Pashur ....Jer 21:1
them, Thus shall ye say to **Z** ..Jer 21:3
I will deliver **Z** king of........Jer 21:7
will I give **Z** the king of.......Jer 24:8
come to Jerusalem unto **Z** .....Jer 27:3
I spake also to **Z** king of ......Jer 27:12
beginning of the reign of **Z** ....Jer 28:1
whom **Z** king of Judah ....Jer 29:3
Lord in the tenth year of **Z** ...Jer 32:1
For **Z** king of Judah had ......Jer 32:3
Z king of Judah shall not .....Jer 32:4
he shall lead **Z** to Babylon ....Jer 32:5
Z the son of Josiah reigned....Jer 37:1
Z the king sent Jehucal ....Jer 37:3
I gave **Z** king of Judah ....Jer 44:30
beginning of the reign of **Z** ....Jer 49:34
with **Z** the king of Judah ......Jer 51:59
Z was one and twenty ....Jer 52:1
the eleventh year of king **Z** ....Jer 52:5
overtook **Z** in the plains of ....Jer 52:8
slew the sons of **Z** before .....Jer 52:10
he put out the eyes of **Z** ......Jer 52:11

ZEEB (zē'ĕb)—*"wolf"*
Midianite prince slain by Gideon's men ....Judg 7:25

of Midian, Oreb and **Z** ....Judg 8:3
nobles like Oreb and like **Z** ...Ps 83:11

ZELAH (zē'lä)—*"rib"*
Towns assigned to Benjamin ....Josh 18:28
Burial place of Kish, Saul, and Jonathan 2Sam 21:14

ZELEK (zē'lĕk)—*"split"*
One of David's mighty men 2Sam 23:37

ZELOPHEHAD (zĕ-lō'fĕ-hăd)—*"firstborn"*
Manassite whose five daughters secure female rights ....Num 27:1-7

came the daughters of **Z** ......Num 27:1
The daughters of **Z** speak ......Num 27:7
the inheritance of **Z** our ....Num 36:2
concerning the daughters of **Z** .Num 36:6
so did the daughters of **Z** .....Num 36:10
the daughters of **Z** were ....Num 36:11
Z, the son of Hepher, the .....Josh 17:3
Z; and **Z** had daughters 1Chr 7:15

ZELOTES—*See* ZEALOT

ZELZAH (zĕl'zä)—*"noontide"*
Town in south Benjamin near Rachel's tomb ....Gen 48:7

the border of Benjamin at **Z** ..1Sam 10:2

ZEMARAIM (zĕm-ä-rā'ĭm)—*"wool"*
1. Town of Benjamin near Jericho ....Josh 18:22
2. Mountain in Ephraim ...2Chr 13:4

ZEMARITE (zĕm'ä-rīt)
Tribe of Canaanites......Gen 10:18

ZEMIRA (zĕ-mī'rä)—*"song"*
Grandson of Benjamin ...1Chr 7:6, 8

ZENAN (zē'năn)—*"coldness"*
Town in Judah ....Josh 15:21, 37

ZENAS (zē'näs)—*"living"*
Christian lawyer ....Titus 3:13

ZEPHANIAH (zĕf-ä-nī'ä)—*"Jehovah is darkness; Jehovah has treasured"*
1. Ancestor of Samuel 1Chr 6:33, 36
2. Author of Zephaniah ....Zeph 1:1
3. Priest and friend of Jeremiah during Zedekiah's reign .....Jer 21:1
4. Father of a certain Josiah in Zechariah's time ...Zech 6:10

and **Z** the second priest 2Kin 25:18
to **Z** the son of Maaseiah .....Jer 29:25

And **Z** the priest read this.....Jer 29:29
Z the son of Maaseiah the ....Jer 37:3
and **Z** the second priest ....Jer 52:24

ZEPHANIAH, THE BOOK OF—*a book of the Old Testament*
Coming judgment ....Zeph 1:2-18
Call to repentance ....Zeph 2:1-3
The nations judged ......Zeph 2:4-15
Jerusalem is blessed .....Zeph 3:9-20

ZEPHATH (zē'făth)—*"which beholds"*
Canaanite town destroyed by Simeon and Judah . .Judg 1:17
See Hormah

ZEPHATHAH (zĕf'ä-thä)—*"watchtower"*
Valley near Mareshah....2Chr 14:10

ZEPHO, ZEPHI (zē'fō, zē'phī)—*"watch"*
Grandson of Esau and a duke of Edom ...... Gen 36:15,19; 1Chr 1:36

ZEPHON (zē'fŏn)—*"dark; wintry"*
Son of Gad and tribal head ....Num 26:15
Called Ziphion ....Gen 46:16

ZEPHONITES (zē'fŏn-īts)—*descendants of Zepho*
of Zephon, the family of the **Z**.Num 26:15

ZER (zûr)—*"perplexity"*
City assigned to Naphtali .Josh 19:32, 35

ZERAH, ZARA, ZARAH (zē'rä, zā'rä)—*"sprout"*
1. Son of Reuel and duke of Edom .... Gen 36:17,19; 1Chr 1:44
2. Son of Judah ....Num 26:20
Ancestor of Achan ......Josh 7:1-18
Ancestor of Christ ......Matt 1:3
3. Son of Simeon and tribal head ....Num 26:12, 13
Called Zohar ....Gen 46:10
4. Gershomite Levite 1Chr 6:20, 21, 41
5. Ethiopian general defeated by King Asa .2Chr 14:8-15

and Jobab the son of **Z** of.....Gen 36:33
took Achan the son of **Z**......Josh 7:24
Did not Achan the son of **Z**...Josh 22:20
of Reuel; Nahath, **Z**..........1Chr 1:37
law bare him Pharez and **Z**....1Chr 2:4
of **Z**, Zimri, and Ethan 1Chr 2:6
Jamin, Jarib, **Z** and Shaul 1Chr 4:24
sons of **Z**; Jeuel and their 1Chr 9:6
children of **Z** the son of.......Neh 11:24

ZERAHIAH (zĕr-ä-hī'ä)—*"Jehovah has come forth"*
1. Ancestor of Ezra ....Ezra 7:1, 4, 5
2. Son of Pahath-moab ...Ezra 8:4

Uzzi begat **Z** and **Z** begat 1Chr 6:6
son, Uzzi his son, **Z** his son ...1Chr 6:51

ZERED—*See* Zared

ZEREDA, ZEREDATHAH (zĕr'ĕ-dä, zĕr-ĕ-dā'thä)—*"ambush; cool"*
1. City of Ephraim; birthplace of Jeroboam.1Kin 11:26
2. City in the Jordan valley .2Chr 4:17
Same as Zarthan in 1Kin 7:46

ZERERATH (zĕr'ĕ-răth)
Town in the Jordan valley.Judg 7:22
Same as Zarthan 1Kin 7:46

ZERESH (zē'rĕsh)—*"gold"*
Wife of Haman ....Esth 5:10, 14

Haman told **Z** his wife and ....Esth 6:13
wise men and **Z** his wife ......Esth 6:13

ZERETH (zē'rĕth)—*"brightness"*
Judahite 1Chr 4:5-7

ZERETH-SHAHAR (zē-rĕth-shā'här)—*"the splendor of dawn"*
City of Reuben..........Josh 13:19

ZERI (zē'rī)—*"balm"*
Jeduthun; Gedaliah, and **Z**....1Chr 25:3

ZEROR (zē'rôr)—*"bundle"*
Benjamite 1Sam 9:1

ZERUAH (zĕ-rōō'ä)—*"full-breasted"—mother of Jereboam I*
name was **Z**, a widow woman .1Kin 11:26

ZERUBBABEL, ZOROBABEL (zĕ-rŭb'ä-bĕl, zō-rŏb'ä-bĕl)—*"seed of Babylon"*
Descendant of David 1Chr 3:19
Leader of Jewish exiles ..Neh 7:6, 7
Restores worship in Jerusalem ....Ezra 3:1-8
Rebuilds the Temple.....Zech 4:1-14
Prophecy concerning .....Hag 2:23
Ancestor of Christ ....Matt 1:12, 13; Luke 3:27

Which came with **Z**...........Ezra 2:2
Then they came to **Z**, and.....Ezra 4:2
But **Z**, and Jeshua and the ....Ezra 4:3
up **Z** the son of Shealtiel......Ezra 5:2
Levites that went up with **Z**...Neh 12:1
all Israel in the days of **Z**.....Neh 12:47
the prophet unto **Z** the........Hag 1:1
The **Z** the son of Shealtiel.....Hag 1:12
stirred up the spirit of **Z**......Hag 1:14
Speak now to **Z** the son of ....Hag 2:2
Yet now be strong, O **Z**......Hag 2:4
Speak to **Z**, governor of ......Hag 2:21
take thee, O **Z**, my servant....Hag 2:23

ZERUIAH (zĕr-ōō-ī'ä)—*"balm"—mother of Joab*
the son of **Z**, brother to.......1Sam 26:6
Joab the son of **Z**, and the 2Sam 2:13
three sons of **Z** there, Joab 2Sam 2:18
sons of **Z** be too hard for me ..2Sam 3:39
son of **Z** was over the host ...2Sam 8:16
son of **Z** perceived that the 2Sam 14:1
said Abishai the son of **Z**.....2Sam 16:9
to do with you, ye sons of **Z**? .2Sam 16:10
to **Z** Joab's mother 2Sam 17:25
hand of Abishai the son of **Z**..2Sam 18:2
the son of **Z** answered 2Sam 19:21
ye sons of **Z** that ye should....2Sam 19:22
the son of **Z** succored him.....2Sam 21:17
Z, was chief among three 2Sam 23:18
to Joab the son of **Z**..........2Sam 23:37
Joab the son of **Z**............1Kin 1:7
also what Joab the son of **Z**...1Kin 2:5
and for Joab the son of **Z**.....1Kin 2:22
Whose sisters were **Z** and 1Chr 2:16
Z; Abishai and Joab, and 1Chr 2:16
Joab the son of **Z** went first ...1Chr 11:6
of Joab the son of **Z**..........1Chr 11:39
of **Z** slew of the Edomites.....1Chr 18:12
son of **Z** was over the host ...1Chr 18:15
Joab the son of **Z**, had........1Chr 26:28
son of **Z** began to number.....1Chr 27:24

ZETHAM (zē-thăm)—*"shining"*
Gershonite Levite 1Chr 23:7, 8

ZETHAN (zē'thăn)—*"olive tree"*
Benjamite 1Chr 7:6, 10

ZETHAR (zē'thär)—*"conquerer"*
One of the seven chamberlains of King Ahasuerus ....Esth 1:10

ZIA (zī'ä)—*"terrified"*
Gadite..................1Chr 5:11, 13

ZIBA (zī'bä)—*"plantation"*
Saul's servant 2Sam 9:9
Befriends David 2Sam 16:1-4
Accused of deception by Mephibosheth 2Sam 19:17-30

servant whose name was **Z**....2Sam 9:2
said unto him, Art thou **Z**?....2Sam 9:2
Z said unto the king 2Sam 9:3
Z said unto the king, Behold ..2Sam 9:4
Then the king called to **Z**.....2Sam 9:9
Then said **Z** unto the king.....2Sam 9:11
that dwelt in the house of **Z**...2Sam 9:12

ZIBEON (zĭb'ĕ-ŭn)—*"wild robber"—son of Seir*
daughter of **Z**, Esau's wife ....Gen 36:14
Lotan; and Shobal, and **Z**.....Gen 36:20
Shobal, duke **Z**, duke Anah ...Gen 36:29
Shobal, and **Z**, and Anah 1Chr 1:38
sons of **Z**; Aiah, and Anah 1Chr 1:40

ZIBIA (zĭb'ĭ-ä)—*"gazelle"*
Benjamite and household head 1Chr 8:8, 9

ZIBIAH (zĭb'ĭ-ä)—*"gazelle"*
Mother of King Jehoash. .2Kin 12:1

ZICHRI (zĭk-rī)—*"renowned"*
1. Kohathite Levite ....Ex 6:21
2, 3, 4. Three Benjamites .1Chr 8:19, 23, 27
5. Son of Asaph..........1Chr 9:15
6. Descendant of Moses...1Chr 26:25
7. Reubenite 1Chr 27:16
8. Judahite...............2Chr 17:16
9. Mighty man in Pekah's army................2Chr 28:7
10. Benjamite ....Neh 11:9
11. Postexilic priest ....Neh 12:17

ZIDDIM (zĭd-ĭm)—*"huntings"*
City of Naphtali ....Josh 19:35

ZIDKIJAH—*See* Zedekiah

ZIDON (zī'dŏn)—*"hunting"—ancient city of Caanan*
his border shall be unto **Z**.....Gen 49:13
chased them unto great **Z**.....Josh 11:8
of Syria and the gods of **Z**.....Judg 10:6
because it was far from **Z**.....Judg 18:28
which belongeth to **Z**.........1Kin 17:9
begat **Z** his first-born 1Chr 1:13
and oil, unto them of **Z**.......Ezra 3:7
whom the merchants of **Z**.....Is 23:2
Be thou ashamed, O **Z**; for ...Is 23:4
virgin, daughter of **Z**.........Is 23:12
Tyrus, and all the kings of **Z**..Jer 25:22
the king of **Z**, by the hand ....Jer 27:3
off from Tyrus and **Z** every ...Jer 47:4
inhabitants of **Z** and Arvad....Ezek 27:8
man, set thy face against **Z**....Ezek 28:21
I am against thee, O **Z**........Ezek 28:22
Tyrus, and **Z**, though it be ....Zech 9:2
See Sidon

ZIDONIANS (zī-dō'nĭ-ăns)—*"hunting"—residents of Zidon*
The **Z** also and the Amalekites.Judg 10:12
after the manner of the **Z**.....Judg 18:7
they were far from the **Z**......Judg 18:7
Ammonites, Edomites, **Z**......1Kin 11:1
Ethbaal king of the **Z**.........1Kin 16:31
the abomination of the **Z**......2Kin 23:13
all of them and all the **Z**......Ezek 32:30

ZIF (zĭf)—*"splendor; bloom"*
Second month of the Jewish year 1Kin 6:1

ZIHA (zī'hä)—*"dried"*
Head of a Nethinim family ....Ezra 2:43

children of **Z**, the children ....Neh 7:46
Z and Gispa were over the ....Neh 11:21

ZIKLAG (zĭk'lăg)—*"measure pressed down"*
City on the border of Judah ....Josh 15:1, 31
Assigned to Simeon .....Josh 19:1, 5
Held by David 1Sam 27:6
Overthrown by Amalekites 1Sam 30:1-31
Occupied by returnees ...Neh 11:28

had abode two days in **Z**......2Sam 1:1
and at Hormah and at **Z**......1Chr 4:30
they that came to David to **Z**. .1Chr 12:1
As he went to **Z**, there fell 1Chr 12:20

ZILLAH (zĭl'ä)—*"protection; screen"*
One of Lamech's wives ..Gen 4:19-23

ZILPAH (zĭl'pä)—*"myrrh dropping"*
Leah's maid.............Gen 29:24
Mother of Gad and
Asher ....Gen 30:9-13

of Z, Leah's handmaid ....Gen 35:26
with sons of Z, his father's ....Gen 37:2
These are the sons of Z.......Gen 46:18

ZILTHAI (zĭl'thī)—*"shadow"*
1. Benjamite 1Chr 8:20
2. Manassite captain 1Chr 12:20

ZIMMAH (zĭm'ä)—*"counsel"*
Gershonite Levite 1Chr 6:20, 42, 43

ZIMRAN (zĭm'răn)—*"celebrated"*
Son of Abraham and
Keturah ....Gen 25:1, 2

ZIMRI (zĭm'rī)—*"celebrated"*
1. Grandson of Judah......1Chr 2:3-6
Called Zabdi ....Josh 7:1-18
2. Simeonite prince slain by
Phinehas ....Num 25:6-14
3. Benjamite 1Chr 8:1, 36
4. King of Israel for seven
days 1Kin 16:8-20
5. Place or people
otherwise unknown ...Jer 25:25

ZIN (zĭn)—*"swelling"*
Wilderness through which
the Israelites passed ...Num 20:1
Border of Judah and
Edom ....Josh 15:1-3

wilderness of Z unto Rehob ...Num 13:21
in the desert of Z............Num 27:14
in the wilderness of Z.........Num 27:14
in the wilderness of Z.........Num 33:36
from the wilderness of Z ......Num 34:3
Akrabbim and pass on to Z ...Num 34:4
in the wilderness of Z.........Deut 32:51

ZINA (zī'nä)—*"fruitful"*
Son of Shimei 1Chr 23:10
Same as Zizah 1Chr 23:11

ZION, SION (zī'ŭn, sī'ŭn)—*"monument; fortress; set up"—one of the hills on which Jerusalem was built*

Used literally of:
Jebusite fortress captured
by David 2Sam 5:6-9
Place from which
Solomon brings the ark.2Chr 5:2
Area occupied by the
Temple ....Is 8:18

Used figuratively of:
Israel as a people of God.2Kin 19:21
God's spiritual kingdom..Ps 125:1
Eternal city ....Heb 12:22, 28
Heaven ....Rev 14:1

[*also* ZION'S]
that escape out of mount Z....2Kin 19:31
David took the castle of Z 1Chr 11:5
King upon my holy hill of Z...Ps 2:6
Lord, which dwelleth in Z.....Ps 9:11
gates of the daughter of Z.....Ps 9:14
of Israel were come out of Z..Ps 14:7
strengthen thee out of Z ......Ps 20:2
the whole earth is mount Z....Ps 48:2
Let mount Z rejoice, let ......Ps 48:11
Walk about Z, and go round ..Ps 48:12
Z the perfection of beauty.....Ps 50:2
in thy good pleasure unto Z...Ps 51:18
Israel were come out of Z! ....Ps 53:6
for thee, O God, in Z ....Ps 65:1
For God will save Z, and .....Ps 69:35
this mount Z, wherein thou ...Ps 74:2
and his dwelling place in Z....Ps 76:2
mount Z which he loved ......Ps 78:68
every one of them in Z ....Ps 84:7
Lord loveth the gates of Z ....Ps 87:2
And of Z it shall be said ......Ps 87:5
Z heard, and was glad; and ...Ps 97:8
The Lord is great in Z; and ...Ps 99:2
and have mercy upon Z.......Ps 102:13
the Lord shall build up Z .....Ps 102:16
the name of the Lord in Z ....Ps 102:21
rod of thy strength out of Z...Ps 110:2
again the captivity of Z ....Ps 126:1
and turned back that hate Z...Ps 129:5
For the Lord hath chosen Z...Ps 132:13
upon the mountains of Z......Ps 133:3
earth bless thee out of Z......Ps 134:3
Blessed be the Lord out of Z..Ps 135:21
when we remembered Z ......Ps 137:1
us one of the songs of Z ......Ps 137:3
for ever, even thy God, O Z..Ps 146:10
praise thy God, O Z..........Ps 147:12
children of Z be joyful in .....Ps 149:2
Z shall be redeemed with .....Is 1:27
for out of Z shall go forth.....Is 2:3
daughters of Z are haughty....Is 3:16
head of the daughters of Z.....Is 3:17
pass, that he that is left in Z..Is 4:3
filth of the daughters of Z.....Is 4:4
dwelling place of mount Z.....Is 4:5
whole work upon mount Z....Is 10:12
my people that dwellest in Z..Is 10:24
mount of the daughter of Z...Is 10:32
shout, thou inhabitant of Z....Is 12:6
the Lord hath founded Z......Is 14:32
mount of the daughter of Z...Is 16:1
Lord of hosts, the mount Z...Is 18:7
hosts shall reign in mount Z...Is 24:23
lay in Z for a foundation......Is 28:16
that fight against mount Z.....Is 29:8
dwell in Z at Jerusalem ....Is 30:19
down to fight for mount Z ....Is 31:4
the Lord, whose fire is in Z...Is 31:9
filled Z with judgment ....Is 33:5
The sinners in Z are afraid....Is 33:14
Look upon Z, the city of......Is 33:20
for the controversy of Z.......Is 34:8
and come to Z with songs .....Is 35:10
of Z, hath despised thee ......Is 37:22
that escape out of mount Z....Is 37:32
O Z that bringest good........Is 40:9
The first shall say to Z........Is 41:27
place salvation in Z for ......Is 46:13
Z said, The Lord hath ....Is 49:14
the Lord shall comfort Z......Is 51:3
come with singing unto Z .....Is 51:11
say unto Z, Thou art my......Is 51:16
put on thy strength, O Z.....Is 52:1
O captive daughter of Z ......Is 52:2
unto Z, Thy God reigneth! ....Is 52:7
Lord shall bring again Z ......Is 52:8
Redeemer shall come to Z ....Is 59:20
Z of the Holy One of Israel...Is 60:14
unto them that mourn in Z....Is 61:3
For Z sake will I not hold.....Is 62:1
Say ye to the daughter of Z...Is 62:11
Z is a wilderness, Jerusalem...Is 64:10
for as soon as Z travailed .....Is 66:8
and I will bring you to Z......Jer 3:14
up the standard toward Z .....Jer 4:6
voice of the daughter of Z ....Jer 4:31
likened the daughter of Z to...Jer 6:2
thee, O daughter of Z ....Jer 6:23
Is not the Lord in Z? is not ...Jer 8:19
of wailing is heard out of Z ..Jer 9:19
hath thy soul lothed Z? ....Jer 14:19
Z shall be plowed like a.......Jer 26:18
This is Z, whom no man ......Jer 30:17
go up to Z unto the Lord .....Jer 31:6
and sing in the height of Z ....Jer 31:12
They shall ask the way to Z...Jer 50:5
declare in Z the vengeance ....Jer 50:28
in Z the work of the Lord.....Jer 51:10
that they have done in Z.......Jer 51:24
shall the inhabitant of Z ......Jer 51:35
The ways of Z do mourn......Lam 1:4
from the daughter of Z all ....Lam 1:6
Z spreadeth forth her ....Lam 1:17
covered the daughter of Z......Lam 2:1
of the daughter of Z..........Lam 2:4
sabbaths to be forgotten in Z..Lam 2:6
wall of the daughter of Z .....Lam 2:8
elders of the daughter of Z....Lam 2:10
O virgin daughter of Z?........Lam 2:13
O wall of the daughter of Z...Lam 2:18
The precious sons of Z........Lam 4:2
and hath kindled a fire in Z...Lam 4:11
O daughter of Z; he will ......Lam 4:22
ravished the women in Z......Lam 5:11
of the mountain of Z ....Lam 5:18
Blow the trumpet in Z ....Joel 2:15
glad then, ye children of Z ....Joel 2:23
for in mount Z and in ....Joel 2:32
also shall roar out of Z ....Joel 3:16
Lord your God dwelling in Z..Joel 3:17
for the Lord dwelleth in Z ....Joel 3:21
The Lord will roar from Z ....Amos 1:2
them that are at ease in Z.....Amos 6:1
upon mount Z shall be........Obad 17
come up on mount Z to........Obad 21
the sin to the daughter of Z...Mic 1:13
They build up Z with blood ...Mic 3:10
Z for your sake be plowed ....Mic 3:12
the law shall go forth of Z ....Mic 4:2
reign over them in mount Z...Mic 4:7
hold of the daughter of Z .....Mic 4:8
bring forth, O daughter of Z..Mic 4:10
and let our eye look upon Z...Mic 4:11
and thresh, O daughter of Z...Mic 4:13
O daughter of Z; shout ....Zeph 3:14
Z, let not thine hands be......Zeph 3:16
for Jerusalem and for Z.......Zech 1:14
Lord shall yet comfort Z ......Zech 1:17
Deliver thyself, O Z that ......Zech 2:7
rejoice, O daughter of Z ......Zech 2:10
jealous for Z with great ....Zech 8:2
I am returned unto Z and .....Zech 8:3
greatly O daughter of Z.......Zech 9:9
raised up thy sons, O Z.......Zech 9:13
Tell ye the daughter of Z .....Matt 21:5
Fear not, daughter of Z ....John 12:15
I lay in Z a stumbling stone ...Rom 9:33
shall come out of Z the ....Rom 11:26
ye are come unto mount Z ....Heb 12:22
lay in Z a chief corner 1Pet 2:6
Lamb stood on the mount Z...Rev 14:1

ZIOR (zī'ôr)—*"smallness"*
Town of Judah ....Josh 15:54

ZIPH (zĭf)—*"refining place"*
1. Town in south Judah ....Josh 15:24
2. City in the hill country
of Judah ....Josh 5:55
David hides from Saul in
wilderness here 1Sam 23:14, 15
3. Son of Jehaleleel.........1Chr 4:16

and went to Z before Saul 1Sam 23:24
down to the wilderness of Z...1Sam 26:2
David in the wilderness of Z ..1Sam 26:2
which was the father of Z 1Chr 2:42
Gath, and Mareshah, and Z ...2Chr 11:8

ZIPHAH (zī'fä) —*"lent"*
Son of Jehaleleel 1Chr 4:16

ZIPHIM—*See* ZIPHITES

ZIPHION—*See* ZEPHON

ZIPHITES (zĭf'īts)—*inhabitants of Ziph*
Betray David 1Sam 23:19-24

when the Z came and ....Ps 54:*title*

ZIPHRON (zĭf'rŏn)—*"rejoicing"*
Place in north Palestine ..Num 34:9

ZIPPOR (zĭp'ôr)—*"bird"*
Father of Balak ....Num 22:4, 10

saith Balak the son of Z ......Num 22:16
unto me, thou son of Z ....Num 23:18
Balak the son of Z, king of ...Josh 24:9
Balak the son of Z, king of ...Judg 11:25

ZIPPORAH (zĭ-pō'rä)—*"little bird"*
Daughter of Jethro; wife
of Moses ....Ex 18:1, 2

Then Z took a sharp stone ....Ex 4:25
father-in-law, took Z, Moses'..Ex 18:2

ZITHRI (zĭth'rī)—*"Jehovah is protection"*
Grandson of Kohath .....Ex 6:18, 22

ZIZ (zĭz)—*"flower"*
Pass leading from Dead Sea to Jerusalem 2Chr 20:16

ZIZA (zī'zä)—*"shining; brightness"*
1. Simeonite leader 1Chr 4:24, 37, 38
2. Son of Rehoboam 2Chr 11:18-20

ZIZAH (zī'zä)—*"shining; brightness"*
Gershonite Levite 1Chr 23:7, 10, 11

ZOAN (zō'ăn)—*"motion"*
City in Lower Egypt .....Num 13:22
Places of God's miracles. .Ps 78:12, 43
Princes resided at........Is 30:2, 4
Object of God's wrath ...Ezek 30:14

the princes of **Z** are fools .....Is 19:11
princes of **Z** are become ......Is 19:13

ZOAR (zō'er)—*"small"*
Ancient city of Canaan originally named Bela . .Gen 14:2, 8
Spared destruction at Lot's request ....Gen 19:20-23
Seen by Moses from Mt. Pisgah ....Deut 34:1-3
Object of prophetic doom. Is 15:5

Egypt, as thou comest unto **Z** .Gen 13:10
of the city was called **Z** ....Gen 19:22
Lot went up out of **Z** and .....Gen 19:30
for he feared to dwell in **Z** ....Gen 19:30
from **Z** even unto Horonaim ...Jer 48:34

ZOBAH, ZOBA (zō'bäh)—*"station"*
Syrian kingdom; wars against Saul .... { 1Sam 14:47, 2Sam 10:6, 8 }

the son of Rehob, king of **Z**...2Sam 8:3
succor Hadadezer king of **Z** ...2Sam 8:5
son of Rehob, king of **Z** 2Sam 8:12
Igal the son of Nathan of **Z** ...2Sam 23:36
lord Hadadezer king of **Z** 1Kin 11:23
when David slew them of **Z** ...1Kin 11:24
smote Hadarezer king of **Z** 1Chr 18:3
help Hadarezer king of **Z** 1Chr 18:5
host of Hadarezer king of **Z** ...1Chr 18:9
Syria-maachah and out of **Z** ...1Chr 19:6

ZOBEBAH (zō–bē'bä)—*"the affable"*
Judahite 1Chr 4:1, 8

ZOHAR (zō'här)—*"nobility; distinction"*
1. Father of Ephron the Hittite ....Gen 23:8
2. Son of Simeon ....Gen 46:10
See Zerah 3

field of Ephron the son of **Z** . .Gen 25:9
Ohad, and Jachin, and **Z** ......Ex 6:15

ZOHELETH (zō'hĕ-lĕth)—*"that creeps; serpent"*
Stone near En-rogel 1Kin 1:9

ZOHETH (zō'hĕth)—*"strong"*
Descendant of Judah 1Chr 4:1, 20

ZOPHAH (zō'fä)—*"watch"*
Asherite 1Chr 7:30, 35, 36

ZOPHAI (zō'fī)—*"watcher"—a brother of Samuel*
sons of Elkanah; **Z** his son 1Chr 6:26
See Zuph

ZOPHAR (zō'fer)—*"hairy; rough"*
Naamathite and friend of Job...................Job 2:11

answered **Z** the Naamathite . . .Job 11:1
answered **Z** the Naamathite . . .Job 20:1
Z the Naamathite went.........Job 42:9

ZOPHIM (zō'fĭm)—*"place for a watchman"*
Field on the top of Mt. Pisgah ....Num 23:14

ZORAH, ZOREAH, ZAREAH (zō'rä, zō-rē'ä, zā-rē'ä)—*"leprosy; wasp, hornet"*
Town of Judah ....Josh 15:1, 33
Inhabited by Danites ....Josh 19:40, 41
Place of Samson's birth and burial .... { Judg 13:24, 25, Judg 16:30, 31 }
Inhabited by returnees . . .Neh 11:25, 29

the valley, Eshtaol, and **Z**.....Josh 15:33
there was a certain man of **Z** . .Judg 13:2
and buried him between **Z** ....Judg 16:31
men of valor, from **Z** and .....Judg 18:2
unto their brethren to **Z** ......Judg 18:8
of the Danites out of **Z** ....Judg 18:11
And **Z**, and Aijalon, and......2Chr 11:10
at En-rimmon, and at **Z**.......Nah 11:29

ZORATHITE, ZORATHITES (zôr'ä-thīt, zôr'ä-thīts)
Native of Zorah 1Chr 4:2
Descendants of Caleb 1Chr 2:50, 53

ZORITE (zôr'īt)
Same as Zorathite 1Chr 2:54

ZOROBABEL—*See* Zerubabbel

ZUAR (zū'er)—*"little"*
Father of Nethaneel .....Num 1:8

Nethaneel the son of **Z** ....Num 2:5
day Nethaneel the son of **Z** . . .Num 7:18
of Nethaneel the son of **Z**.....Num 7:23
was Nethaneel the son of **Z** . . .Num 10:15

ZUPH (zŭf)—*"watcher"*
1. Ancestor of Samuel 1Chr 6:33, 35
Same as Zophai 1Chr 6:26
2. Region in Judah 1Sam 9:4-6

ZUR (zûr)—*"rock"*
1. A Midianite leader......Num 25:15, 18
2. Son of Jehiel 1Chr 8:30

Evi, and Rekem and **Z**........Num 31:8
Evi, and Rekem and **Z**........Josh 13:21
first-born son Abdon, then **Z** . .1Chr 9:36

ZURIEL (zū'rĭ-ĕl)—*"God is my rock"*
Merarite Levite ....Num 3:35

ZURISHADDAI (zū-rĭ-shăd'ī)—*"the Almighty is a rock"*
Father of Shelumiel......Num 7:36, 41

Shelumiel the son of **Z**........Num 1:6
be Shelumiel the son of **Z**.....Num 2:12
was Shelumiel the son of **Z**....Num 10:19

ZUZIM (zū'zĭm)—*"prominent; giant"*
Tribe east of the Jordan. .Gen 14:5
Probably same as Zamzummim ....Deut 2:20